W9-BXB-873

WHO'S WHO IN AMERICAN ART

The 20th edition of WHO'S WHO IN AMERICAN ART
was prepared by R.R. Bowker's Data Base Publishing Group.

Senior Staff of the Data Base Publishing Group includes:
Dean Hollister, Director, Data Base Planning; Andrew Grabois, Editorial Director;
Elizabeth A. Onaran, Managing Editor; Kimberly A. Willard, Senior Editor;
Judy Redel, Director, Research; Tanya Hurst, Senior Editor, Research.

Peter Simon, Vice President, Data Base Publishing Group.

WHO'S WHO IN AMERICAN ART

1993-94

20TH EDITION

R.R. BOWKER

Published by R.R. Bowker, a Reed Reference Publishing Company

Copyright © 1993 by Reed Publishing (USA) Inc. All rights reserved.

No part of this publication may be reproduced or transmitted in any form or by any means stored in any information storage and retrieval system, without prior written permission of R.R. Bowker, 121 Chanlon Road, New Providence, NJ 07974.

International Standard Book Number: 0-8352-3274-3
International Standard Serial Number: 0000-0191
Library of Congress Catalog Card Number: 36-27014
Printed and bound in the United States of America

R.R. Bowker has used its best efforts in collecting and preparing material for inclusion in *Who's Who in American Art 1993-94* but does not warrant that the information herein is complete or accurate, and does not assume, and hereby disclaims, any liability to any person for any loss or damage caused by errors or omissions in *Who's Who in American Art 1993-94* whether such errors or omissions result from negligence, accident or any other cause.

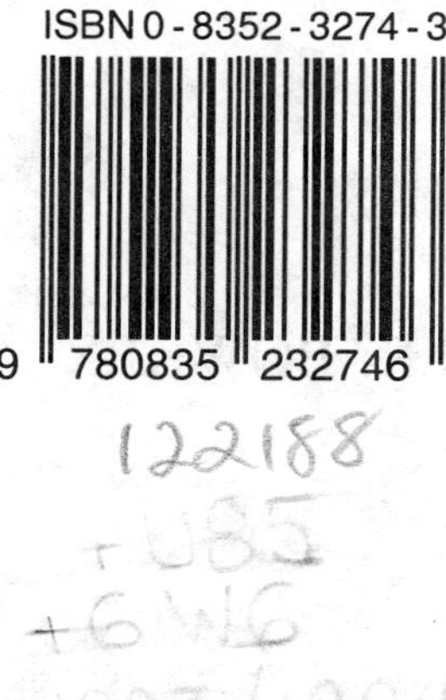

Contents

Preface vii

Abbreviations ix

Biographies 1

Geographic Index 1307

Professional Classification Index 1393

Necrology 1455

Preface

The 20th edition of *Who's Who in American Art* profiles 11,824 contributors to the visual arts in the United States, Canada and Mexico. These representatives from all segments of the art world include artists, administrators, historians, educators, collectors, librarians, critics, curators and dealers. The biographies are arranged alphabetically and are also indexed by geographic location and professional classification. In addition, a necrology is provided, cumulative from 1953.

Listing proofs were sent to all those listed in the 19th edition. Every effort was made to update listings for individuals who did not return a proof through direct calls and secondary sources.

More than 700 new entries appear in the 20th edition. The names of the these individuals were obtained from nominations provided by current entrants, art associations, galleries and museums, or from citations in professional publications. Each nominee received a questionnaire, and selection for inclusion was based upon the information submitted by each nominee. For artists, consideration was given to work in public collections, commissioned works, and exhibitions of an international, national and wide regional scope in noncommercial galleries and museums. Inclusion of entrants other than artists was based on position and experience in the art world. Among those represented are art administrators and curators of major museums, scholars and librarians of prominent institutions, and widely published art writers and critics.

Individual entries can be composed of many different elements depending upon the activity of the entrant. These elements can include: vital statistics, *professional classifications, education and training, *works in public collections, *commissions, *exhibitions, *publications, positions held with schools, museums or organizations, *memberships in art societies, *honors and awards, interest or research statement, media, dealer, and mailing address. Elements preceded by an asterisk are limited as to the number of items included. If the entrant exceeded these limitations, the editors selected the most current and/or most notable information.

All material submitted was included as completely as possible within limits set by format restrictions. While all precautions have been taken to avoid errors, the publishers do not assume and hereby disclaim any liability to any party for any loss or damage caused by errors or omissions, whether such errors or omissions result from negligence, accident or any other cause. In any event, the sole responsibility of the publisher will be the entry of correct data in succeeding editions.

The editors would like to thank the many individuals and associations who sent information and nominations. The editors also thank Nana Rizinashvili for her expert programming contributions; and Bruce Glaunert, Bonnie Walton, Lori Mercurio and Val Lowman of International Computaprint Corporation for their dedicated efforts in helping to produce this edition.

Though strenuous efforts were made to achieve the highest inclusivity, omissions will inevitably occur and the editors welcome the submission of artist nominations, suggestions and comments for future editions.

Elizabeth A. Onaran
Managing Editor

March, 1993

Abbreviations

abstr—abstract(s)
acad—academia, academic, academica, academie, academique, academy
accad—accademia
acoust—acoustic(s), acoustical
actg—acting
addn—addition, additional
adj—adjunct
Adm—Admiral
admin—administration, administrative
adminr—administrator
admis(s)—admission
adv—adviser(s), advisory
advan—advance(d), advancement
advert—advertisement, advertising
aesthet—aesthetics
affil—affiliate, affiliation
agr—agricultural, agriculture
akad—akedemi, akademia
Ala—Alabama
Alta—Alberta
Am—America, American
anal—analysis, analytic, analytical
analog—analogue
anat—anatomic, anatomical, anatomy
ann—annual
anthrop—anthropological, anthropology
antiq—antiquary, antiquities, antiquity
antiqn—antiquarian
app—appoint, appointed
appl—applied
approx—approximate, approximately
Apr—April
apt—apartment(s)
arch—archiv, archiva, achives, archivio, archivo
archeol—archeological, archeologie, archeologique, archeology
archit—architectural, architecture
Arg—Argentina
Ariz—Arizona
Ark—Arkansas
asn—association
asoc—asociacion
assoc(s)—associate(s), associated
asst(s)—assistant(s)
atty—attorney
Aug—August
auth—author
AV—audiovisual
Ave—Avenue

b—born
BC—British Columbia
bd—board
Belg—Belgian, Belgium
bibliog—bibliografia, bibliographic, bibliographical, bibliography(ies)
bibliot—biblioteca, bibliotek, bibliotheca, bibliothek, bibliotheque
biog—biographical, biography
bk(s)—book(s)
Bldg—Building(s)
Blvd—Boulevard
br—branch(es)
Brit—Britain, British
bull—bulletin
bur—bureau
bus—business
BWI—British West Indies

Calif—California
Can—Canada, Canadian, Canadien, Canadienne
Capt—Captain
Cath—Catholic
CBS—Columbia Broadcasting System
cent—central
Cent Am—Central America
cert—certificate(s), certification, certified
chap—chapter
chmn—chairman
c/o—care of
co—companies, company
Co—County
coauth—coauthor
co-dir—co-director
co-ed—co-editor
co-educ—co-educational
CofC—Chamber of Commerce
Col—Colonel
col(s)—college(s), collegiate
collab—collaboration, collaborative
collabr—collaborator
Colo—Colorado
com—commerce, commercial
comdr—commander
commun—communication(s)
comn(s)—commission(s), commissioned
comnr—commissioner
compos—composition
comt(s)—committee(s)
conf—conference
Cong—Congress, Congressional
Conn—Connecticut
conserv—conservacion, conservation, conservatiore, conservatory
construct—construction
consult—consult, consultant, consultantship, consultation, consulting
contemp—contemporary
contrib—contribute, contributing, contribution
contribr—contributor
conv—convention
coop—cooperating, cooperation, cooperative
coord—coordinate, coordinating, coordination
coordr—coordinator
corp—corporate, corporation
corresp—correspondent, corresponding
coun—council, counsel, counseling
counr—councilor, counselor
Ct—Court
ctr—center
cult—cultural, culture
cur—curator
curric—curriculum
Czech—Czechoslovakia

DC—District of Columbia
Dec—December
Del—Delaware
deleg—delegate, delegation
demonstr—demonstrator
dept—department, departmental
develop—development, developmental
dict—dictionaries, dictionary
dig—digest
dipl—diplom, diploma, diplomate, diplome
dir(s)—director(s), directory
dist—district
distribr—distributor
div—division, divisional, divorced
doc—document(s), documentary, documentation
Dom—Dominion
Dr—Doctor, Drive

E—East
econ—economic(s), economical, economist, economy
ed—edicion, edit, edited, editing, edition, editor(s), editorial, edizione
educ—educate, educated, educating, education, educational
elec—electric, electrical, electricity
elem—elementary
emer—emeritus, emeriti
encyl—encyclopedia
eng—engineering
Eng—England, English
environ—environment(s), environmental
equip—equipment
estab—established, establishment
estud—estudante, estudas, estudiante, estudio, estudo
Europ—European
exec(s)—executive(s)

exhib(s)—exhibit(s), exhibition
exped(s)—expedition(s)
explor—exploration(s), exploratory
expos—exposition
exten—extension

fac—faculty
Feb—February
fed—federal
fedn—federation
fel(s)—fellow(s), fellowship(s)
Fla—Florida
for—foreign
found—foundation
Fr—French
Ft—Fort
ft—feet, foot

Ga—Georgia
gen—general, generale
Ger—German, Germany
Ges—Gesellschaft
gov—governing, governor
govt—government, governmental
grad—graduate, graduated
Gt Brit—Great Britain
gym—gymnasium

handbk(s)—handbook(s)
hist—historia, historic, historica, historical, historique, historisch(e), history
HM—Her Majesty
hochsch—hochschule
hon(s)—honor(s), honorable, honorary
hosp(s)—hospital(s), hospitalization
hq—headquarters
Hwy—Highway

Ill—Illinois
illum—illuminating, illumination
illus—illustrate, illustrated, illustration
illusr—illustrator
Inc—Incorporated
incl—include, included, includes, including
Ind—Indiana
indust(s)—industrial, industries, industry
info—information
inst—institut, instituto
inst(s)—institute(s), institution(s)
instnl—institutional,institutionalized
instr(s)—instruct, instruction, instructors
instrnl—instructional
int—internacional, international, internazionale
introd—introduction
ist—istituto
Ital—Italia, Italian, Italiana, Italiano, Italica, Italien, Italienisch, Italienne(s)

J—Journal (title)
Jan—January
jour—journal (descriptive)
jr—junior
juv—juvenile(s)

Kans—Kansas
Ky—Kentucky

La—Louisiana
lab(s)—laboratories, laboratory
lang—language(s)
lect—lecture(s)
lectr—lecturer(s)
lett—letter(s)
lib—liberal
libr—libraries, library, librerio
librn—librarian
lit—literary, literaure, literatura, literature, littera, litterature
Lt—Lieutenant
ltd—limited

mag—magazine
maj—major
Man—Manitoba
Mar—March
Mass—Massachusetts
mat—material(s)
Md—Maryland
med—medical, medicine, medicinal
mem—member(s), membership(s), memoirs
Mem—Memorial
metrop—metropolitan
Mex—Mexican, Mexicano, Mexico
mgr—manager
mgt—management
Mich—Michigan
Minn—Minnesota
Miss—Mississippi
Mo—Missouri
mo—month
mod—modern, moderna, moderne, moderno
monogr—monograph
Mont—Montana
Mt—Mount
munic—municipal, municipalities
mus—musee, museo, museum(s)

N—North
nac—nacional
nat—nationaal, national, nationale, nationalis
naz—nazionale
NB—New Brunswick
NC—North Carolina
NDak—North Dakota
Nebr—Nebraska
Neth—Netherlands
Nev—Nevada
New Eng—New England
Nfld—Newfoundland
NH—New Hampshire
NJ—New Jersey
NMex—New Mexico
Norweg—Norwegian
Nov—November
NS—Nova Scotia
NSW—New South Wales
NY—New York
NZ—New Zealand

Oct—October
off—office, official
Okla—Oklahoma
Ont—Ontario
oper(s)—operation(s), operational, operative
Ore—Oregon
orgn—organization, organizational

Pa—Pennsylvania
Pac—Pacific
Pan-Am—Pan-American
partic—participant, participating
PEI—Prince Edward Island
philos—philosophic, philosophical, philosophy
photog—photographic, photography
photogr—photographer(s)
Pkwy—Parkway
Pl—Place
PO Box—Post Office Box
polytech—polytechnic, polytechnical
Port—Portugal, Portuguese
PQ—Province of Quebec
PR—Puerto Rico
prehist—prehistoric, prehistory
pres—president
Presby—Presbyterian
preserv—preservation
prof—profession, professional, professor, professorial
prog(s)—program(s), programmed, programming
proj(s)—project(s), projection(s), projectional, projective
prom—promotion
prov—province, provincial
pub—public
publ—publication(s), published, publisher(s), publishing
pvt—private

Quart—Quarterly
Que—Quebec

Rd—Road
RD—Rural Delivery
rec—record(s), recording
regist—register, registered, registration
registr—registrar
relig—religion, religious
rep—represent, representative
Repub—Republic
res—research
rev—review, revised, revision
RFD—Rural Free Delivery
RI—Rhode Island

RM—Room
RR—Rural Route
Rte—Route
Russ—Russian

S—South
S Africa—South Africa
S Am—South America, South American
Sask—Saskatchewan
SC—South Carolina
Scand—Scandinavia, Scandinavian
sch(s)—school(s)
scholar—scholarship
sci—science(s), scientific
SDak—South Dakota
sec—secondary
sect—section
secy—secretary
sem—seminar, seminary
Sen—Senator, Senatorial
Sept—September
ser—series
serv—service(s), serving
soc(s)—sociedad, societa, societas, societate, societe, societet, societies, society
Span—Spanish
spec—special
Sq—Square
sr—senior
St—Saint, Street
sta(s)—station(s)
Ste—Sainte
struct—structural, structure(s)
super—superieur, superior, superiore
suppl—supplement, supplemental, supplementary
supt—superintendent
supv—supervising, supervision
Swed—Swedish
Switz—Switzerland
symp—symposium(s)

tech—technical, technique
technol—technologic, technological, technology
tel—telegraph(y), telephone
Tenn—Tennessee
Terr—Terrace
Tex—Texas
transl—translation(s)
translr—translator
treas—treasurer, treasury
Twp—Township

UN—United Nations
undergrad—undergraduate
UNESCO—United Nations Educational, Scientific & Cultural Organization
univ(s)—universidad, universite, universities, university
US—United States
USA—United States Army
USAF—United States Air Force
USMC—United States Marine Corps
USN—United States Navy

Va—Virginia
var—various
vchmn—vice chairman
Vet—Veteran(s)
VI—Virgin Island
vis—visiting
vol(s)—volume(s)
vpres—vice president
Vt—Vermont

W—West
Wash—Washington
Wis—Wisconsin
wk—week
WVa—West Virginia
Wyo—Wyoming

yearbk—yearbook
YMCA—Young Men's Christian Association
YMHA—Young Men's Hebrew Association
yr(s)—year(s)
YWCA—Young Women's Christian Association
YWHA—Young Women's Hebrew Association

Who's Who in American Art

A

AALUND, SUZY
PAINTER
b Amityville, NY, Apr 28, 32. *Study:* Extensive independent studies. *Exhib:* One-woman shows, Robert Brooks Gallery, Hyannis, Mass, 72 & 74 & Garden City Galleries, NY, 72 & 74; Am Soc Marine Artists Ann, 78, 79 & 86; Int Maritime Art Awards Show, 80-84; Contemp Am Marine Art, Peabody Mus, Salem, 81; Gallery 31, Greenwich, Conn, 83; and many others. *Awards:* Second Prize Oils, Long Beach Art Asn, 72; First Prize Oils, Nat Miniature Art Show, Miniature Art Soc NJ, 73. *Bibliog:* Article, La Rev Mod, 74. *Mem:* Charter mem Am Soc Marine Artists; Mystic Art Asn. *Media:* Egg Tempera, Watercolor. *Dealer:* Tuesday's World PO Box 45 Mystic CT 06355. *Mailing Add:* 8 Maple St Stonington CT 06378

AARON, EVALYN (WILHELMINA) KEISLER
PAINTER
b New York, NY. *Study:* Art Students League; pvt study with Mario Cooper, Motoi Oi, Prof Kawai & Betty Holiday. *Work:* Skirbull Mus, Calif. *Exhib:* Sumi-e Soc, Nippon Club, 72 & Japan House, 73, New York; Art Fac Show, Great Neck House, NY, 74; Great Neck Pub Libr, 75; one-person shows, Gallery 7 Soho Ltd, Great Neck, 75 & Mirage Gallery, New York, 78. *Pos:* Gov-Int Platform Asn Chmn Hanging Comt-art show. *Teaching:* Instr sumi-e brush painting, Great Neck Continuing Educ, 64- 74 & 88-; pres & teacher painting, Workshop for Art, Port Washington, NY, 67-73; lectr & demonstr, Int Platform Asn, 73, 74 & 77 & Art League Nassau Co, 78. *Awards:* Sumi-e Soc Award, Sumi-e Soc Am, 64 & Cup of Consul Gen of Japan, 66; Popular Award, Int Platform Asn, 74. *Bibliog:* Rhoda Amon (auth), article in Newsday, 11/74; Elizabeth Moore (auth), article in Talent, 5/75; Malcolm Preston (auth), review in Newsday, 8/75. *Mem:* Art League of Nassau Co; Sumi-e Soc Am (secy, 62-67, pres, 72-74, bd mem, 86-); Int Platform Asn (gov, 83-); Salmagundi Club. *Media:* Watercolor, Acrylic. *Publ:* Auth & illusr, Sumi painting, Am Artist Mag, 9/78. *Dealer:* Caryl Shorin 320 E Shore Rd Great Neck NY 11023. *Mailing Add:* 270-20K Grand Central Parkway Floral Park NY 11005

ABAD, PACITA
PAINTER
b Batanes, Philippines, 1946. *Study:* Univ Philippines, BA, 68; Univ San Francisco, MA, 72; Corcoran Sch Art, Washington, DC, 75-77; Art Students League, 78. *Work:* Mus Nat Ctr Afro-Am Artists, Boston, Mass; Museo Nacional de Bellas Artes, Havana, Cuba; Museo de Arte Moderno, Santo Domingo, Dom Repub; Nat Mus Contemp Art, Seoul, Korea; Nat Mus, Manila, Philippines; Jane Voorhees Zimmerli Art Mus, New Brunswick, NJ; Embassy Philippines, Washington, DC. *Exhib:* Solo exhibs, Mus Nat Ctr Afro-Am Artists, Boston, Mass, 82, Mus Philippine Art, 84, Cult Ctr Philippines, 85, Underwater Paradise (installation show), Ayala Mus, Manila, Philippines, 86, Hong Kong Arts Ctr, 86, Philippines Ctr, New York, 87, 90 & 92, Int Monetary Fund, Washington, DC, 87, Martin Luther King Libr, Washington, DC, 88 & 89, Astraea Gallery, Washington, DC, 90 & Ayala Mus, Makati, Philippines, 91; Musee des Arts Africains et Oceaniens, Paris, France, 88; Olympiad of Art in conjunction with 24th Olympics, Seoul, Korea, 88; Art for Africa, traveling, Oslo, Cologne, Algiers, London & Rome, 88-89; WPA At the Hemicycle, Corcoran Gallery, 92; Crossing Over/Changing Places, travelling in US & throughout Europe, 92-95; D C Comn on Arts & Humanities Visual Arts Grantees, Willow St Gallery, 92. *Pos:* Bd mem, Arlington Arts Ctr, Va, 89-92; bd mem, Cult Alliance Greater Wash, 91-93. *Awards:* Washington, DC, Commission Arts, GIA grant, 88-92; Gwendolyn Caffritz Award, Pyramid Atlantic, 91; Residency Fel, Va Ctr Creative Arts, 92. *Bibliog:* In Duck Kim (auth), Feature Artist: Pacita Abad-a very nice combination, Better Homes & Garden, Seoul, Korea, 3/91; Paul Clements (auth), Eight paths to a journey, cultural identity & the immigration experience, Wash Rev, 3/92; JoAnn Lewis (auth), Local artists' modest show at hemicycle, Wash Post, 6/22/92. *Mem:* Philippine Arts, Lett & Media, Washington, DC; Wash Proj Arts; Coalition Wash Artists; Women's Caucus Art; Asian Am Arts & Media, Washington, DC. *Dealer:* Franz Bader Gallery 1500 K St NW Washington DC 20005. *Mailing Add:* 5315 16th St NW Washington DC 20011

ABADI, FRITZIE
PAINTER, SCULPTOR
b Aleppo, Syria; US citizen. *Study:* Art Students League, New York; with Nahum Tschacbasov, New York. *Work:* Butler Inst Am Art, Youngstown, Ohio; Evansville Mus Arts & Sci, Ind; Slater Mem Mus, Norwich, Conn; Ga Mus Art, Athens. *Exhib:* Watercolor, Brooklyn Mus, NY; Ann Invitational, Whitney Mus Am Art, New York; Ann Invitational, Carnegie Inst, Pa; Ann Print Invitational, Libr Cong, DC; Acquisitional, Butler Inst Am Art, Youngstown, Ohio; ten solo shows in New York. *Awards:* Acrylic Painting Award, Nat Asn Women Artists, 74; Box Assemblage Award, Am Soc Contemp Artists, 78 & Oil Painting Award, 79. *Mem:* Nat Asn Women Artists (bd mem, 70); Am Soc Contemp Artists (pres, 70-72); New York Soc Women Artists (bd mem, 80); Women in the Arts; Hudson River Contemp Artists. *Media:* Box Assemblage. *Publ:* Contribr, Collage and Small Environment, 74 & Assemblage and Construction, 75, Crown Inc. *Mailing Add:* 201 W 70th St Apt 30E New York NY 10023

ABANY, ALBERT CHARLES
PAINTER, PRINTMAKER
b Boston, Mass, Mar 30, 21. *Study:* Sch Mus Fine Arts, Boston, M O H Longstreth scholar, 42, dipl, 48; Tufts Univ, BS(educ), 49. *Exhib:* One-man shows, Carl Siembab Gallery, Boston, 56; Clark Univ, 63; Northeastern Univ, 67; Wessell Libr, Tufts Univ, 71; Art Inst Boston, 72. *Teaching:* Art teacher drawing & painting, Boston Ctr Adult Educ, 49-51; art teacher drawing, painting, printmaking & art hist, Art Inst Boston, 65-73; art teacher oil & acrylic painting, Brockton Art Mus, Mass, 75-77; art teacher drawing & painting, Danforth Mus Sch, Framingham, 75-77; teacher drawing, painting & hist art, Quincy Jr Col, 75-76; teacher drawing & painting, S Shore Art Ctr, Cohasset, Mass, 83- *Media:* Oil, Graphics, Mixed Media. *Mailing Add:* 42 MacArthur Rd Natick MA 01760

ABBE, ELFRIEDE MARTHA
SCULPTOR, PRINTMAKER
b Washington, DC. *Study:* Col Archit, Cornell Univ, BFA, 40. *Work:* Rosenwald Collection, Nat Gallery Art; Mus Fine Arts, Boston; Houghton Libr, Harvard Univ; Sloniker Collection, Cincinnati Art Mus; Mus Fine Arts, Venice, Italy. *Comn:* The Hunter (large statue), New York World's Fair, 39; oak frieze, Mann Libr, Cornell Univ, 55 & bronze sculptures, Clive McCay Mem, 67; Napoleon (bronze head), McGill Univ Libr; The Illuminator (walnut carving), Sterling Mem Hunt Libr, Carnegie-Mellon Univ, 69. *Exhib:* Nat Acad Design, New York; San Diego Fine Arts Gallery, 60; Printing in the USA & United Kingdom, London Chappel Exhib, Eng, 63; Int Botanical Artists, Hunt Libr, Carnegie-Mellon Univ, 68; Nat Arts Club, New York, 69 & 70. *Awards:* Gold Medal, Nat Arts Club, 70 & Acad Artists Asn, Springfield, Mass, 76; Elliot Liskin Cash Award, Salmagundi Club, 79. *Bibliog:* Norman Kent (auth), The Book Art of Elfriede Abbe, Am Artist Mag, 60. *Mem:* Nat Arts Club; fel Nat Sculpture Soc; Nat Soc Mural Painters. *Media:* Wood; Woodcut. *Publ:* Designed, illus & printed, Garden Spice & Wild Pot-Herbs, Cornell Univ, 55, The American Scholar, 56, Seven Irish Tales, 57 & Significance of the Frontier, 58. *Mailing Add:* Box 571 Manchester Center VT 05255

ABBETT, ROBERT KENNEDY
PAINTER
b Hammond, Ind, Jan 5, 26. *Study:* Purdue Univ, BSc, 46; Univ Mo, BA(art), 48; Chicago Acad Fine Art, 48-50; Am Acad Art, Chicago, 49. *Work:* Cowboy Hall of Fame & Western Heritage Ctr, Oklahoma City; Diamond M Mus, Snyder, Tex; Genesee Country Mus, Rochester, NY. *Comn:* Portrait of Mrs Roy Larsen, Audubon Soc, Fairfield, Conn, 73; portrait of Jimmy Stewart, Cowboy Hall of Fame, Oklahoma City, 75; portrait of Luther Burbank, Burbank Ctr Arts, Santa Rosa, Calif, 75; portrait of Silver comn by Ann Cox Chambers, US Embassy, Brussels, Belgium, 77; Gens Jackson and Lee, Am Military Collection, 84. *Exhib:* Easton Waterfowl Festival, Md, 81 & 86; Artists Am, Denver 82-85 & 90-92; Leigh Yawkey Woodson Mus, Wassau, Wis, 84-87; Thomas Gilcrease Mus, Tulsa, 84 & 85; and many others. *Teaching:* Instr media, Silvermine Col, New Canaan, Conn, 59-61; instr drawing, Sisters of Notre Dame, Wilton, Conn, 70 & Washington Art Asn, Conn, 77. *Awards:* Outstanding Work, Artists & Books, Soc Illusr, 65; First Prize, Salmagundi Club, New York, 73; Artist Year, Nat Wildlife Art Collectors Soc, Minneapolis, 84. *Bibliog:* Nick Meglin (auth), Robert Abbett, Am Artist, 7/77; Michael McIntosh (auth), Robert Abbett, Southwest Art,

11/88; Tom Davis (auth), The Magic Show of Robert Abbett, Wildlife Art News, 9-10/88. *Mem:* Soc Illusr; Westport Artists (pres, 67); Soc Animal Artists. *Media:* Oil. *Publ:* Contrib, Great American Shooting Prints, Knopf, 72; Western Art Today, Watson-Guptill, 75; coauth, Outdoor Paintings of Robert K Abbett, Peacock/Bantam, 76; coauth with Michael McIntosh, Abbett Briar Patch Pubs, 89; auth, From behind the easel, column, Wildlife Art News, 85- *Dealer:* Russell Fink Box 250 Lorton VA 22199. *Mailing Add:* Oakdale Farm Bridgewater CT 06752

ABBRESCIA, JOESEPH LEONARD
PAINTER, INSTRUCTOR
b Oct 1, 36; US citizen. *Study:* Am Acad Art, Chicago, cert, 56. *Comn:* Dr Raymond Carhart portrait, Northwestern Univ, Evanston, Ill, 73; Nicholas Santucci portrait, comn by Santucci family, Skokie, Ill, 75. *Exhib:* Classic American Art Show, Beverly Hills, Calif, 85-89; solo exhib, Mus SW, Midland, Tex, 86; Annual Plein Art Show, Catalina Island, Calif, 87-89; Northwest Rendezvous, Holter Mus, Helena, Mont, 88 & 92; Four American Impressionists, Cincinnati, 91; Am Collectors Invitational, Scottsdale, Ariz, 92; and others. *Pos:* Dir (founder), Village Art Sch, 66-76, consultant, 76- *Awards:* Best of Show, Eighth Ann NW Art Show, 78; Artist of Yr, Am Royal Asn, 84. *Bibliog:* Scott E Dial (auth), Montana's special light, SW Art Mag, 1/77; Susan Hallsten McGarry (auth), Joe Abbrescia, SW Art Mag, 9/86. *Media:* Oil. *Mailing Add:* 5110 N 73rd St Scottsdale AZ 85253

ABDELL, DOUGLAS
SCULPTOR, PAINTER
b Boston, Mass, Mar 16, 47. *Study:* Syracuse Univ, BFA(sculpture, hons), 70. *Work:* Corcoran Gallery Art, Washington, DC; H H Thyssen Bornemisza Collection, Lugano, Switz; Univ Notre Dame, Ind; Wichita Art Mus, Kans; Davenport Munic Art Gallery, Iowa; and many others. *Comn:* Edwin Ulrich Mus Art, Wichita, Kans. *Exhib:* One-man exhibs, Andrew Crispo Gallery, New York, 75, 78 & 79-82, Miami-Dade Community Col, 79-80, Sweet Briar Col, 80, Washington & Lee Univ, 80, Davenport Munic Art Gallery, Iowa, 80 & Dartmouth Col, NH, 80; and many others. *Awards:* Artists & Writers Revolving Fund, Nat Inst Arts & Lett, 71 & 72; Silvermine Award, New Canaan, Conn, 73; Artist Fel, Vt Coun on Arts, 73. *Bibliog:* John Canaday (auth), article, 72 & Grace Gluek (auth), article, 77, NY Times; Heinz Ohff (auth), rev, Der Tagesspeigel, Berlin, 81; and others. *Media:* Cast Bronze, Welded Steel. *Publ:* Auth, Kryad Poems, Chelsea Press Inc, 78; coauth, Mirror Magnetic Interval, Begonia Korta-Zaharra Inst-Intervalist-Itute, New York, 84. *Mailing Add:* 458 Broadway 2nd Floor New York NY 10013

ABEL, RAY
ILLUSTRATOR, PRINTMAKER
b Chicago, Ill, Sept 19, 14. *Study:* Univ Chicago, AB; Art Inst Chicago; NY Univ, MA; Art Students League, with Kenneth Hayes Miller, George Grosz, Alexander Brook & Ernest Fiene. *Comn:* Aviation (mural frieze), US Army Air Corps Cafeteria, Mitchel Field, NY, 44-45; bk illustrations, McKay, Prentice-Hall, Grolier, Knopf, Lippincott, Viking & others, 50-; bk jackets, Harper & Row, Putnam, Dodd, Mead, Dutton & others, 50- *Exhib:* Artists of Chicago & Vicinity, Art Inst Chicago, 43; Nat Acad Design Ann Am Exhib, 42; Ann Exhib Am Art, Mint Mus, 44. *Pos:* Ed publ, Art Students League, The League Mag, 41-43; art dir, Ray Abel Assoc, 51- *Teaching:* Instr, Packer Inst, 51-52, Newark Acad Art, 48-51 & Am Art Sch, 55-58. *Awards:* Hon Mentions, Ill State Mus Ann; Mint Mus Ann, 73; Cert Excellence, Am Observed, Soc Illusr, New York, 72. *Mem:* Soc Illusr; life mem Art Students League NY (mem bd control, 41-49); Artist in Res, Kala Inst. *Media:* Pen and Ink. *Publ:* Coal: Energy and Crisis, Harvey House, 74; Wylie Sypher (auth), 4 children's novels, Atheneum, 76; Bret Harte (auth), The Outcasts of Poker Flat, Listening Libr, 77; co-illusr, The Complete Illustrated Shakespeare, Crown, 79; illusr, The Seven Ages of Man, Shakespeare, State Univ NY, Purchase, 86. *Mailing Add:* 2550 Dana St Berkeley CA 94704

ABELES, KIM VICTORIA
PAINTER, SCULPTOR
b Richmond Heights, Mo, Aug 28, 52. *Study:* Ohio Univ, BFA(painting), 74; Univ Calif, Irvine, MFA(studio art), 80. *Work:* Washington & Jefferson Col, Washington, Pa; Fashion Inst, Los Angeles, Calif; Cal State Univ; Long Beach Art Mus, Long Beach, Calif; City of Santa Monica, Calif. *Comn:* Artistic enhancements for the new Secretary of State/State Archives Building, Sacramento, Calif, 90. *Exhib:* Munic Art Gallery, 81, Karl Bornstein Gallery, 81-83, 85 & 87, Los Angeles City Hall, 82; Phyllis Kind Gallery, Chicago & New York, 83; AIR Gallery, New York, 86; Mt St Mary's Col, Los Angeles, 87; Calif Mus Sci & Indust, Los Angeles, 90; Atlanta Pavilion, Atlanta, GA, 90. *Teaching:* Distinguished vis artist, Calif State Univ, Fullerton, 85-87; vis artist, Claremont Grad Sch, 86, 87 & 90 & Univ Calif, Irvine, 87-89. *Awards:* Handhollow Found Fel, East Chatham, NY, 84; Purchase Award, Am Acad & Inst Art & Lett, 87; Grant, Pollock-Krasner Found, 90. *Bibliog:* Linda Burnham (auth), Image of St Bernadette, High Performance, No 37, 87; Patterson Sims (essayist), Kim Abeles, ART Press, 89; Andrea Liss (auth), The Insistent Voice, After Image, 3/90. *Mem:* Los Angeles Contemp Exhibs; Int Sculpture Ctr. *Media:* Acrylic; Miscellaneous. *Publ:* Auth, Crafts, Cookery and Country Living, Van Nostrand Reinhold, 76; contribr, Artery, William Patterson Col, 79; Fiction International, San Diego State Univ, 85; The Image of St Bernadette, private publ, 87; contribr, High Performance, spring/summer, 88. *Mailing Add:* 2401 Santa Fe No 100 Los Angeles CA 90058

ABELES, SIGMUND
PRINTMAKER, PAINTER
b New York, NY, Nov 6, 34. *Study:* Pratt Inst; Univ SC, BA, 55; Art Student League; Skowhegan Sch Painting & Sculpture; Brooklyn Mus Sch; Columbia Univ, MFA, 57. *Work:* Mus Mod Art, New York; Mus Arte, Ponce, PR; Philadelphia Mus Art; Boston Mus Fine Arts; Brit Mus; Albert & Victoria Mus, London, Gt Brit; Smithsonian Inst, Washington, DC; Metrop Mus Art, New York; Nat Acad Design, New York. *Exhib:* One-man exhibs, Isis Gallery, Notre Dame Univ, South Bend, Ind, 88, Brattleboro Mus, Vt, 88, Yeshiva Univ Mus, New York, 88-89, Shaare Zedek Med Ctr, Jerusalem, Israel, 89, Univ WVa Art Galleries, Charlottesville, Starr Gallery, Leventhal-Sidman Jewish Community Ctr, Newton Ctr, 89, Barridoff Galleries, Portland, Maine, 90; As They See Themselves Self-Portraits, John Szoke Gallery, New York, 89; To Save & To Share, Selected Acquisitions 1984-89, Judah L Magnes Mus, Berkeley, Calif, 89; With Nothing On, New Orleans Mus Art, La, 90; American Drawing Invitational, Hastings Col, Nebr, 90. *Teaching:* Instr, Swain Sch Design, New Bedford, Mass, 61-64, Wellesley Col, 64-69, Boston Univ, 69-70, Univ NH, 70-; Wellesley Col, 64-69; Boston Univ, 69-70; Univ NH, 70-87; prof emer, Univ NH, 87- *Awards:* Grant for Graphics, Louis Comfort Tiffany Found, 67; Academic Seminar to Israel, Am Jewish Comt, 81; Summer Sr Fac Fel, Univ NH, 84. *Bibliog:* J Barry Mathes (auth) Temptations (review), Press Herald, Portland, Maine, 3/14; Philip Isaacson (auth), Fine Artists Turn Talented Hands to Applied Art (review), Maine Sunday Telegram, 3/25; Louise Dunn Yochim (auth), Michael Weinberg (ed), The Harvest Freedom, Jewish Artists in America, 1930-80's, Am References, Chicago, IL, 90. *Mem:* Soc Am Graphic Artists; Assoc Nat Acad Design; Pastel Soc Am; NH Art Asn. *Media:* Etching, Lithography; Oil. *Publ:* Illusr, Maggie, A Girl of the Streets, Limited Ed Press, 75; The Max Drawings, Tom Bolt (auth), Am Artist Mag, 11/87. *Dealer:* U'Farrell Gallery Brunswich ME; Portfolio Gallery Columbia SC. *Mailing Add:* RFD 3 Huckins Rd Dover NH 03820

ABER, ITA
CURATOR, TAPESTRY ARTIST
b Montreal, Can, Mar 27, 32; US citizen. *Study:* Empire State Col, BA; Valentine Mus, Richmond, Va, cert hons; Jewish Theological Sem, NY grad courses. *Work:* Jewish Mus, Cooper-Hewitt Mus & Jewish Theological Sem, New York; Valentine Mus, Richmond, Va; Smithsonian Inst, Washington, DC; Skirball Mus, Los Angeles; Israel Mus, Jerusalem; and others. *Comn:* Wall hangings, holy scroll covers & ark curtains throughout US, Can & Israel, 74- *Exhib:* NY Univ Small Works Show, 85; NY Feminist Art Inst Invitational, 85 & 86; Joods Hist Mus, Amsterdam, 86; solo exhib, Seltz Gallery, 88, Empire State Col, 89, Soho, NY; Berliner Festspiele, 91-92; and others. *Pos:* Cur hist, Hudson River Mus, Yonkers, formerly; cur collection, Park Ave Synagogue, New York, 87-; cur, Hebrew Home for Aged, Riverdale, NY, 89-; bd mem, Hudson River Contemp Artists Asn, 90-; comnr, Yonkers Landmarks Comn, 91- *Teaching:* Lecturer at many museums & institutions. *Bibliog:* Russell Barber (auth), program on WNBC TV, 77; Video, Tarbuth Found, 84; Cassandra Langer (auth), article Women Artists News, 88. *Mem:* Nat Asn Corp Art Mgrs; NY Artists Equity; Am Inst Conservation; Women's Caucus Arts; New Eng Appraisers Asn; and others. *Media:* Paint, Thread. *Res:* 15th Century carpets from Spain; ancient synagogue architecture and Jewish crafts. *Publ:* The Art of Judaic Needlework, Charles Scribner's Sons, NY, 79; Textile Study Guide, Ind Univ, 85; Woman's Art J, 87; Jewish Art, 87; Jewish Art, Sepharad, 92; and others. *Mailing Add:* One Fanshaw Ave Yonkers NY 10705-3714

ABERNETHY-BALDWIN, JUDITH ANN
PAINTER
b Cincinnati, Ohio, May 15, 42. *Study:* With Philip Pearlstein, Dan'l Greene & Robert Natkin; Cincinnati Art Acad, 70-74; Univ Cincinnati, 75-78. *Work:* Sun Bank NA & Orlando Regional Med Ctr, Orlando, Fla; Scripps-Howard Newspapers, Cincinnati, Ohio; Feldman Group Inc, West Chester, NY; Kennedy Capital Management Inc, St Louis, Mo; Keep Fla Beautiful Inc. *Exhib:* 34th Ann Knickerbocker and Grand Nat Exib, Salmagundi Club, New York, 84; 48th Ann Nat Midyear, Butler Inst Am Art, Youngstown, Ohio, 84; Invitational Exhib, High Mus, Atlanta, Ga, 88; Abernethy At-Large, Brest Mus, Jacksonville Univ, 86; 37th Ann All Fla, Boca Raton Mus, 88; Places Revisited, Brevard Art Mus, Melbourne, Fla, 88; Atlantic Ctr Arts, New Smyrna, Fla, 88; Judith Abernethy, Boca Raton Mus Art, 91. *Teaching:* Seminole Community Col, 87. *Awards:* Second Prize, 83 & 88, Judges Award, 84, Ridge Art Asn. *Bibliog:* Chris Schneider (auth), Judith Abernathy, Ctr Stage Mag, 6/86; Jim Runnels (auth), Artist depicts, Lake Sentinal, 11/88; Sally Henderson (auth), Light taking possession, Zelo Mag, 2/89; Keep Fla Beautiful Mag, Cover Spring, 91. *Mem:* Nat Asn Women Artists; Int Women Artists Archive; Women's Caucus Art; Women Artists of West. *Media:* Acrylic. *Dealer:* Albertson-Peterson 329 Park Ave S Winter Park FL 32789. *Mailing Add:* PO Box 4061 Enterprise FL 32725

ABID, ANN B
LIBRARIAN
b St Louis, Mo, Mar 17, 42. *Pos:* Asst librn, St Louis Art Mus, 63-68, librn, 68-85; head librn, Cleveland Mus Art, 85- *Mem:* Mus, Arts, & Humanities Div, Spec Libr Asn; Art Libr Soc NAm; Soc Am Archivists. *Publ:* Contribr, Museum column, Vol 7, No 4-5, 79 & Archives in art museums, Vol 8, No 2, 80, Art Libr Soc NAm Newsletter. *Mailing Add:* Cleveland Mus Art 11150 East Blvd Cleveland OH 44106

ABISH, CECILE
SCULPTOR, INSTRUCTOR
b New York, NY. *Study:* Brooklyn Col, BFA. *Comn:* Boxed Monuments-3, Multiples, Inc, New York, 69, Field Quartering, Lakeview Ctr Arts, Peoria, Ill, 72; Renaissance Fix, Independent Curators, Inc, New York, 79; Atlanta Arts Festival, Piedmont Park, Ga, 80; Land Marks, Bard Col, 84. *Exhib:* Wright State Univ, Ohio, 78; Carpenter Ctr, Cambridge, 79; New Mus, New

York, 80; Anderson Gallery, Richmond, Va, 81; Kunstgebaude, Stuttgart, Ger, 81; Fine Art Ctr, State Univ NY, Stony Brook, 84; Long Beach Mus, Calif, 83; Ctr Creative Photography, Tucson, Ariz, 84; Mus Mod Kunst, Vienna, Austria, 85. *Teaching:* Instr art, Queens Col, NY, Univ Mass, Amherst, Cooper Union, NY & Harvard Univ. *Awards:* Creative Artists Pub Service Fel, 75; Nat Endowment for Arts Fel, 77 & 80; Deutscher Akademischer Austavschdienst, Berlin, 87. *Bibliog:* Lawrence Alloway (auth), article, Arts Mag, 2/77; Jeffrey Keeffe (auth), article, Artforum, 10/78; Donald B Kuspit (auth), article, Art in Am, 1/82. *Mem:* Col Art Asn. *Publ:* Firsthand, Photo/work, Wright State Univ, Dayton, Ohio, 78; Situation esthetics, Artforum, 1/80; Greek Gifts, LAICA J, winter 86; Chinese Crossing Photo/work, Conjunctions 9, 86; 99: The New Meaning, Photo/work, Burning Deck, 90. *Mailing Add:* PO Box 485 Cooper Sta New York NY 10276

ABLOW, JOSEPH
PAINTER, WRITER
b Salem, Mass, Aug 16, 28. *Study:* Sch Mus Fine Arts, Boston, Paige Traveling Fel, dipl with highest hons, 51; Bennington Col, BA, 54; Harvard Univ, MA, 55; Fulbright Grant, Paris, 58; advan study in painting with Oskar Kokoschka & in design with Gyorgy Kepes. *Work:* De Cordova Mus, Lincoln, Mass; Univ Mass, Boston; Amherst Col; Middlebury Col, Vt; Rose Art Mus, Brandeis Univ, Maine. *Exhib:* 62nd Am Exhib, Art Inst Chicago, 57; retrospectives, Bard Col, 72, Simmons Col, 83 & Fitchburg Art Mus, 87; A Selection of American Art: The Skowhegan School, 1946-76, Inst Contemp Art, Boston; one-man shows, Mirski Gallery, 61, 66 & 69, Princeton Gallery & 71, Pucker-Safrai Gallery, 79, 81, 83, 87 & 89; and others. *Pos:* Contrib ed, Bostonia Mag, 86- *Teaching:* Instr, Middlebury Col, 55-58; asst prof, Bard Col, 59-61 & Wellesley Col, 62-63; chmn div art, Boston Univ, 64-67, prof art, 72-; vis prof, Mass Inst Technol, 73-75; vis artist, Amherst Col, 75-76, 81. *Media:* Multimedia. *Publ:* Auth, Two cheers for realism, 9/78 & Boston expressionism, 2-3/79, New Boston Rev; Gombrich's art and-or illusion, Boston Univ J, Vol XXXV, No 3, 78; Phillip Guston, the last paintings, 4-5/86, Inter Stella Space, 2-3/87 & The musée d'Orsay's other 19th century, 4-5/87, Bostonia Mag. *Dealer:* Pucker Gallery 171 Newbury St Boston MA 02116. *Mailing Add:* 16 Monmouth Ct Brookline MA 02146

ABLOW, ROSELYN KAROL
PAINTER, CURATOR
b Allentown, Pa. *Study:* Bennington Col, BA, 54; Boston Univ Sch Arts, with Walter Murch, 59-61; studied in Europe, 59-60 & 68-69. *Work:* Mobil Corp, Chemical Bank, New York; New England Mutual Life Insurance Co, Boston; Conn Gen Life, Hartford; Sears, Roebuck & Co, Chicago. *Comn:* Diptych mixed media on paper, Broadway Crown Plaza Hotel, New York, 89. *Exhib:* New American Monotypes, Smithsonian Inst Traveling Exhib, 78-80; Contemporary American Monotypes, Smith Anderson Gallery, Palo Alto, Calif, 79; solo exhibs, Impressions Gallery, Boston, 79, Clark Gallery, Lincoln, 84, David Brown Gallery, Provincetown, 87 & Pine Manor Col, Brookline, Mass, 91; Nine Alumni, Boston Univ, 81; Monotypes, Philadelphia Print Club, 82; Three Artists: Works on Paper, Newton Arts Ctr, Mass, 87; New England Impressions: The Art of the Print, Fitchburg Art Mus, 88; Three Grant Recipients, The Bunting Inst, Radcliffe Col, 88; David Brown Gallery, Provincetown, Mass, 88. *Collections Arranged:* Four Sculptors: Public Commisions-Private Works, 85, Watercolor in the 1980s, 86, & Volume and Plane, Wall Sculpture, 91, Newton Arts Ctr. *Teaching:* Monotype workshops, Bunting Inst, 88, Newton Arts Ctr, 89-92. *Awards:* Fel, Bunting Inst, Radcliffe Col, 88; Mass Arts Lottery Coun Grant, 90-91. *Bibliog:* Robert Taylor (auth), article, Boston Sunday Globe, 6/10/79; Kenneth Baker (auth), Lasting impressions, Boston Phoenix, 2/9/81; Christine Temin (auth), The Work of the Superiors, Boston Globe, 4/24/91. *Media:* Mixed. *Mailing Add:* 16 Monmouth Ct Brookline MA 02146

ABRAHAM, CAROL JEANNE
ASSEMBLAGE ARTIST, CERAMIST
b Philadelphia, Pa, 1949. *Study:* Tyler Sch Art, Philadelphia, 64-67; Boston Mus Sch Fine Arts, 67-71; Tufts Univ, Medford, Mass, BS, 67-71; Rochester Inst Technol, Sch Am Craftsmen, MFA, 73; Penland Sch Crafts, NC, 75, Brooks Inst Photog, dipl, 88. *Work:* Rochester Inst Technol, NY; Mus Ceramics, Bassano Del Grappa, Italy; Renwick Gallery, Smithsonian Inst, Washington, DC; Brigham Young Univ, Provo, Utah; Int Acad Ceramics, Canada; Brooks Inst Photog. *Comn:* Mural, sculpture, Romerbad Hotel, Ger, 84. *Exhib:* Renwick Gallery, Smithsonian Inst, Washington, DC, 75; Tweed Mus Art, Duluth, Minn, 81; Celebration 81, Spokane, Wash; Interfaith Forum Relig, Art & Archit, 81; State Univ Mus Art, University Park, Pa, 81; Fletcher Brownbuilt Pottery Exhib, Auckland, NZ, 81; and many others. *Pos:* Cur, Western States Mus Photog, Santa Barbara, Calif, 85-89. *Teaching:* Silk screening, Boston Pub Sch System (Pilot Sch), 70; instr ceramics, Rochester Inst Technology, NY, 72-73; asst prof ceramics & sculpture, Southern Utah State Col, Cedar City, 75-77; ceramics, El Camino Col, Torrance, Calif, 80-81; ceramics, Ventura Community Col, 82-84; design, Brooks Inst Photog, 89- *Awards:* Third Prize, Ceramics International 1973, Canada; Grant, Burbank Fine Arts Fedn, 81; Purchase Award, Second Crossing Gallery, 81. *Bibliog:* Hildegard Storr-Britz (auth), Contemp Int Ceramics, 80; Jan Axel & Karen McCready (coauths), Porcelain: Traditions and New Visions, 81; Glen C Nelson (auth), Ceramics, A Potters Handbook, 4th & 5th eds, 78-84. *Media:* Photography, Fiber; Porcelain, Thixotropic Porcelain. *Publ:* Auth, The Mirror Book, Jay & Lee Newman, 78; Crafts Horizons, 8/73, 12/73, 2/76; Ceramics Monthly, 9/73, 5/75, 5/76, 10/76; Decorazione - Ceramica, Nino Caruso, Italy, 88; Egypt: Land of Adventures, 89. *Mailing Add:* 932 Cheltenham Rd Santa Barbara CA 93105-2234

ABRAMOWICZ, JANET
PAINTER, PRINTMAKER
b New York, NY. *Study:* Art Students League, with Morris Kantor; Columbia Univ, Accad delle Belle Arti, Bologna, Italy, BFA & MFA, with Giorgio Morandi. *Work:* Mus Mod Art, Kyoto; Dept of Prints, New York Pub Libr & Metrop Mus Art, New York; Ohara Mus, Kurashiki; Contemporary Art, Mus d'Arte Mod, Bologna; Mus d'Arte Mod, La Spezia, Italy. *Exhib:* Twenty-third Nat Exhib Prints, Libr Cong-Nat Collection Fine Arts, 73; Works on Paper, Harvard Sch Design, 74; Abstract Art (sculpture), Boston City Hall, 75; solo exhib, Susan Caldwell Gallery, New York, 80, Nantenshi Gallery, Tokyo, 81 & Galleria del Milione, Milano, Italy, 81; Prints Recently Acquired, RI Sch Design & Metrop Mus Art, New York, 85; 24th Nat Print Exhib, Brooklyn Mus, 86; British 11th Int Print Biennale (invitational), 90-91. *Collections Arranged:* Giorgio Morandi (with catalog), Busch-Reisinger Mus, Harvard Univ, 68. *Pos:* Critic, Asahi Evening News, Tokyo & Print Collector's Newsletter; vis artist, Am Acad Rome, 84-85. *Teaching:* Instr, Radcliffe Col, Worcester Art Mus, Accad delle Belle Arti & Univ Ill; lectr art hist, Div Educ, Boston Mus Fine Arts, 58-70; sr lectr painting, printmaking & drawing, Fine Arts Dept, Fogg Art Mus, Harvard Univ, 71-91. *Awards:* Rockefeller Found, Bellagrio, 89; Am Coun Learned Soc Fel, 90-91; Guggenheim Fel, 92. *Mem:* Fel Am Acad Rome; hon mem Accademia Clementina, Bologna, Italy. *Publ:* Auth, Vision and Technique, The Etchings of Giorgio Morandi, 9/10/82 & A European Sensibility: The Photographs of Andre Kertesz, 9/10/83, Print Collector's Newsletter; Milan: The Liberation of the Object, Art Am, 83; auth, Technique of the Graphic Works of Giorgio Morandi; In memoriam: Kasuo Shimizu, Ahsahi Evening News, Tokyo; La tecnia dell 'arte incisonia di Giorgio Morandi, exhib catalog, Rome, 90. *Dealer:* Tokyo Nanten Shi Gallery Kyo-Bashi Tokyo. *Mailing Add:* 30 W 15th St 8 North New York NY 10011

ABRAMS, EDITH LILLIAN
SCULPTOR, INSTRUCTOR
b New York, NY. *Study:* Brooklyn Col, BA, 74; Pratt Inst, MFA, 78. *Work:* Evansville Mus Arts & Science, Ind; Brookdale Hosp, NY. *Comn:* Many pvt portrait sculpture comn. *Exhib:* Int Sculpture Fair, Sheraton Hotel, New York, 79; 4th & 6th Ann Exhib Painting & Sculpture; Brooklyn Mus, 79-81; Catharine Lorillard Wolfe Art Club, Nat Arts Club, New York, 79-88; Audubon Artists 38th Ann Exhib, New York, 80; ArtExpo, New York Coliseum, New York, 80; Providence Art Club Centennial Exhib Sculpture, RI, 80; Brooklyn Mem Am Soc Contemp Artists, 15th Ann Exhib, 84, Brooklyn Mus; Nat Acad Design, 86-88. *Teaching:* Instr sculpture & ceramics, Sephardic Community Ctr, New York, 82-85. *Awards:* Purchase Award, 1st Prize, Schulman Rehabilitation Inst, Brookdale Hosp, NY, 76; Margaret Hirsch Levine Mem Prize, Audubon Artists 38th Ann, 80; Ann Hyatt Huntington Bronze Medal, Catharine Lorillard Wolfe Art Club 84th Ann, 80 & 89th Ann, Helen McCahill Slottman Mem Award, 85; Charles D Murphy Award, Nat Asn Women Artists, 82. *Mem:* Metrop Painters & Sculptors; New York Artists Equity Asn; Am Soc Contemp Artists (pres, 83-85); Nat Asn Women Artists; Catharine Lorillard Wolf Art Club. *Media:* All. *Mailing Add:* 2820 Ave J Brooklyn NY 11210

ABRAMS, HERBERT E
PAINTER, LECTURER
b Greenfield, Mass, Mar 20, 21. *Study:* Norwich Art Sch, Conn; Pratt Inst, hon grad in illus; Art Students League, with Frank Vincent Du Mond. *Work:* The White House, Washington, DC; US House of Rep, Washington, DC; US Senate, Washington, DC; Conn State Libr Mus, Hartford. *Comn:* Portraits, Pres Jimmy Carter, The White House, Washington, DC; six portraits, Johns Hopkins Med Ctr, Baltimore, Md; Alan S Boyd, Chmn, Nat Trust Hist Preserv, Washington, DC; Clement Conger, Cur Art, US State Dept, Washington, DC; Sen Howard Baker, US Senate, Washington, DC; and others. *Exhib:* Okla Mus Art, 69; West Point Libr, 73 & 74; SC Mus, Beaufort, 75; New Brit Mus Am Art, Conn; S Vt Art Ctr, Manchester; and others. *Teaching:* TV lectr & demonstr, 67-80; guest lectr cadets, West Point Military Acad, 73-74. *Awards:* Best Still Life, Dr Byron Kenyon Award, Hudson Valley Art Asn, 68; Best Portrait, 70; Dines Carlsen Award, Hudson Valley Art Asn, 77. *Bibliog:* Herbert Abrams: Portrait Artist, Conn Northwest, 7/29/83; Putting the VIP's on Canvas, New York Times, 4/7/86; Washington's Master of Official Portraits, Int Herald Tribune, 4/18/86. *Mem:* Art Students League; Artists Equity Asn. *Media:* Oil. *Publ:* Auth, The Teachings of Frank Vincent DuMond: Penetrating Light, Vol 38, 36-67, Am Artist, 3/74. *Mailing Add:* 178 Kent Rd Warren CT 06754

ABRAMS, JANE ELDORA
PAINTER
b Eau Claire, Wis, Jan 2, 40. *Study:* Univ Wis-Stout, Menomonie, BS, 62, MS, 67; Ind Univ, Bloomington, with Pozzath & Lowe, MFA(with distinction), 71. *Work:* Ind Univ Mus Fine Arts; Univ Dallas, Tex; Tex Tech Univ; Tamarind Inst; Mus NMex; and others. *Exhib:* Works on Paper traveling exhib, Univ Utah, Salt Lake City, Univ Tex, Houston & Los Angeles Co Mus of Art, Calif, 77; Works on Paper: Southwest 1978, Dallas Mus Fine Arts, 78; Art Inst Chicago, 81; New Mexico Impressions, Mus Fine Arts, Santa Fe; Modes of Expression, State Univ Mus, Potsdam; Common Ground-New Acquisitions, Albuquerque Mus; Retrospective, Fine Arts Gallery, Ind Unv; and many others. *Teaching:* Instr art, Univ Wis-Stout, Menomonie, 67-69; from asst prof to regents prof art, painting, drawing & grad studies, Univ NMex, 71-; guest artist, Ind Univ, Bloomington, 76 & Univ Tex, Austin, 83; and others. *Awards:* Artist-in-Res Grant, Roswell Mus, 85-86; Distinguished Alumni Award, Ind Univ, Bloomington, 91 & Univ Wisc, 92; and others. *Mem:* Col Art Asn Am; Women's Caucus Art; Los Angeles Print Soc; Soc Am Graphic Artists. *Media:* All Media. *Publ:* Contribr, Colorprints, USA (slide series), 71-72; Two

Decades of Change (exhib catalog), Ind Univ, 91; contribr, Clinton Adams, Printmaking in New Mexico. *Dealer:* Robischon Gallery Denver CO; Richard Levy Gallery Albuquerque NM. *Mailing Add:* Dept Art Univ NMex Albuquerque NM 87131

ABRAMS, JOYCE DIANA
PAINTER, SCULPTOR
b New York, NY, Dec 8, 45. *Study:* Cooper Union, New York, BFA, 66; Columbia Univ, MFA, 72. *Work:* Gannett Ctr Media Studies, New York, NY; Atlantic Richfield Co, Anchorage, Alaska; Burlington Northern, Inc, Seattle, Wash; Anaconda Co, Denver, Colo; Alberta Gas Trunk Line, Ltd, Calgary, Alta, Can. *Exhib:* 5 and Japan, The Nippon Club Gallery, NY, 82; Newscapes Land & City-States of Mind, One Penn Plaza, New York, 84; Painted Constructions-Constructed Paintings, Rockland Ctr Arts, Nyack, NY, 85; Mid Am Biennial, Owensboro Mus Fine Art, Ky, 88; one-person show, Edward Williams Gallery, Fairleigh Dickinson Univ, Hackensack, NJ, 88; Works on Paper, Knoxville Mus Fine Art, Tenn, 89; Spirit of the Object, Humphrey Fine Art, New York, 92. *Pos:* Art consult, Neville Lewis & Assoc, New York, NY, 80-82 & Tokyo Cent Mus, 83, 89-; cur, Orgn Int Artists, New York, 82; cur, Rockland Ctr Arts, West Nyack, New York, 91. *Teaching:* Instr painting, City Univ New York, 78-81; Univ South Maine, 87; Parsons Sch Design, 89- *Awards:* MacDowell Colony Fel, 85 & 87; Fel, Corp Yaddo, 88. *Bibliog:* Diana Morris (auth), Summer group show, Arts Mag, 10/83; Steve Bush (auth), See here, now-back to the present, Artspeak, 2/16/86. *Mem:* New York Artists Equity Asn. *Media:* Paint; Wood. *Publ:* Auth, A personal view of the MacDowell experience, Artist's Proof, 4/88; Discarded, Rockland Ctr Arts. *Mailing Add:* 100 W 94th St New York NY 10025

ABRAMS, VIVIEN (JOY)
PAINTER
b Cleveland, Ohio, July 26, 46. *Study:* Carnegie-Mellon Univ, BFA, 68; Inst Allende, San Miguel Allende, Mex, MFA, 71. *Work:* Cleveland Mus Art; Aldrich Mus Contemp Art; Columbus Mus Arts & Sci, Ga; Currier Gallery Art, NH; Nat City Bank Cleveland. *Comn:* Memory Structures (constructed painting), AT&T Longlines. *Exhib:* Solo exhibs, Akron Art Inst, Ohio, 76, New Gallery Contemp Art, Cleveland, Ohio, 77 & 80, Luise Ross Gallery, New York, 84, Manhattanville Col, Purchase, NY, 86 & Coup de Grace Gallery, New York, 92; Butler Inst Am Art, 76 & 77; Cleveland Mus Art, 76, 77, 79, 81 & 84; Drawing as Process, Akron Art Inst traveling show, 77; New York Now, Phoenix Mus Art, 79; two-artist show, Soho Ctr Visual Artists, New York, 79; Little Rock Art Mus, Ark, 82; Sculpture Ctr, New York, 83; Aldrich Mus Contemp Art, Ridgefield, Conn, 84 & 86; Cleveland Ctr Contemp Art, 87; Geometric Abstraction: A Cleveland Tradition, Cleveland Inst Art, 88; Squibb Gallery, Princeton, NJ, 88; OIA Salon, New York, 91. *Teaching:* Vis artist, State Univ NY, Purchase, 83; instr design, Manhattanville Col, Purchase, NY, 85-86. *Awards:* MacDowell Colony Fels, 79, 81 & 85; Yaddo Fels, 79 & 82; First Prize Painting, 62nd May Show, Cleveland Mus Art, 81; Athena Found Grant, 84. *Bibliog:* Helen Cullinan (auth), Art: A matter of math and logic, Sunday Plain Dealer Mag, 9/25/77; Stephen Westfall (auth), Arts reviews, Arts Mag, 10/82 & 11/84. *Dealer:* Luise Ross 50 W 57th St New York NY 10019. *Mailing Add:* 11 Worth St New York NY 10013

ABRAMSON, ELAINE SANDRA
CARTOONIST, GRAPHIC ARTIST
b Cleveland, Ohio, Aug 27, 42. *Study:* NY Univ, Cert; Kent State Univ, Ohio, BS(art); Cleveland Inst Art, Ohio; Hayim Greenberg Inst, Scholar, Jerusalem, Israel. *Work:* State Capitol, Austin, Tex; Cleveland Mus Art, Ohio; Maryland Pub Television, Baltimore; Kent State, traveling exhibs, Ohio; Times Newspapers, Baltimore, Md. *Exhib:* Invitational Maryland Artists, Baltimore Harbor, 71-75; PCM Hall of Fame, PCM Exhibit, Dallas, Tex, 85; Texas State Artist, 88-90 & Tex Woman's Hall of Fame, 89, State Capitol, Austin; Int Platform Asn Invitational, Washington, DC, 91-92; Composers, Authors & Artists of Am, New York & FTW, 91-92. *Pos:* Syndicated columnist, Appraisals by Abramson, currently. *Teaching:* Art, Cleveland Pub Sch, 65-67. *Bibliog:* B J Hennersdorph, article, Tex Woman, fall 89; Campaigning characters, Greetings Mag, winter/spring 90. *Mem:* Metrop Mus Art; Soc Craft Designers; Nat Enamelists Guild; Am Crafts Coun; Md Art League; Graphic Artists Guild; Cartoonists Guild. *Media:* Pen and Ink, Mixed Media Painting. *Dealer:* Cache 9830 S 51st Street Suite A-128 Phoenix Ariz 85044. *Mailing Add:* Create-A-Craft PO Box 330008 Ft Worth TX 76163

ABRIL, BEN (BENJAMIN)
PAINTER
b Los Angeles, Calif, Apr 11, 23. *Study:* Sch Allied Arts, 45-46; Glendale Col, 46-47; Los Angeles Art Ctr, 47. *Work:* Los Angeles Co Mus Hist, Los Angeles; Charles & Emma Frye Art Mus, Seattle; US Navy Combat Art Collection, DC; Laguna Beach Art Mus, Calif; Glendale Fed Savings, Calif Art Collection; Vatican City Collection, Rome, Italy. *Comn:* Rec Am Occupation in Japan, Secy Navy, Washington, DC, 65; Transportation of Water to Los Angeles, Dept Water & Power, Los Angeles, 65; Ann Los Angeles Times Christmas Cards, 76-79. *Exhib:* Calif Watercolor Soc, Mus Fine Arts, Richmond, Va, 57; Watercolor USA, Springfield Art Mus, Mo, 59; US Navy Collection, Frank Lloyd Wright-Barnsdal Park Mus, Los Angeles, 66; Calif Watercolor Soc, US Embassy Belles Art Mus, Mexico City, 68; Ben Abril's Bunker Hill, Los Angeles Co Mus Hist, Los Angeles, 69; American Masters, Nat Mus, Taiwan. *Pos:* Archit coordr, Los Angeles Co, 66-77. *Teaching:* Instr oil painting, Laguna Beach Art Sch, 66; instr oil painting, Glendale, Calif, 74. *Awards:* Dagmar-Haggstrom-Tribble, Am Watercolor Soc, New York, 59; First Prize, Calif Mus Sci, Los Angeles Trade Union, 76; Purchase Award, Santa Paula Calif Ann, 79. *Bibliog:* Stephany Edwards (auth), Ben Abril's Los Angeles, Ralph Story TV Prog, 68; William Pugsley (auth), Bunker Hill-Last of the Lofty Mansions, Trans-Anglo Bks, 77; Images of a Golden Era, 87. *Mem:* Am Watercolor Soc; Nat Watercolor Soc; San Gabriel Art Asn; Glendale Art Asn. *Media:* Oil, Watercolor. *Publ:* Illusr, How Engines Talk, 61, Piggy Back, 62 & Shoofly, 62, Follet, Chicago. *Dealer:* Biltmore Galleries 515 S Olive Los Angeles CA 90013. *Mailing Add:* 2137 Via Venado La Canada CA 91011

ABT, JEFFREY
PAINTER, WRITER
b Kansas City, Mo, Feb 27, 49. *Study:* Drake Univ, Des Moines, BFA, 71; MFA, 77; Biblical & Archaeol Inst, Hebrew Union Col, Jerusalem, Fel, 71-72. *Work:* Des Moines Art Ctr, Iowa; Minn Mus Art, St Paul; Nelson-Atkins, Mus Art, Kansas City, Mo; Washington & Jefferson Col, Pa; Wichita Art Mus, Kans. *Comn:* Bas relief, Iowa Jewish Guild, Des Moines, 74; sculpture, Waldinger Found, Des Moines, 75. *Exhib:* Celebration 76, Northern Ill Univ Gallery, Dekalb, 76; 23rd Nat Drawing Show, Ball State Univ, Muncie, Ind, 77, Dobrick Gallery, Ltd, Chicago, 82; Art/Work, Art Inst Chicago Gallery, 87; Egg Tempera, Contemp Art Workshop, Chicago, 88; Drawings, Detroit Artists Market, 91; Exquisite Visions, Meadowbrook Gallery, Oakland Univ, Rochester, Mich, 92; and others. *Pos:* Exhibs coordr, Dept Spec Collections, Univ Chicago Libr, 80-86; asst dir, Smart Mus Art, Univ Chicago, 86-87, acting dir, 87-89. *Teaching:* Assoc prof painting & criticism, Dept Art & Art Hist, Wayne State Univ, Detroit, 89- *Awards:* Various awards, Nat Endowment Humanities, Nat Endowment Arts & Inst Mus Servs. *Bibliog:* Andy Argy (auth), Art/Work, New Art Examiner, 87. *Mem:* Col Art Asn, 74-; Ragdale Found, Artists Colony (trustee, 85-); Nat Asn Schs Art & Design, 89-; Asn Art Hist, 89-; Detroit Inst Arts, Libr Adv Comt, 90- *Media:* Miscellaneous. *Publ:* Auth, The Printers Craft, 82 & The Book Made Art, 86, Univ Chicago Libr; article, Library trends, 87; contribr, Guide to the Collections, Smart Mus Art, 90; Dictionary of Art, MacMillan (in prep). *Mailing Add:* 26881 York Rd Huntington Woods MI 48070

ABULARACH, RODOLFO MARCO
PAINTER, PRINTMAKER
b Guatemala City, Guatemala, Jan 7, 33. *Study:* Nat Sch Plastic Arts, Guatemala City; Art Students League; Pratt Graphic Art Ctr, New York. *Work:* Mus Mod Art, New York Pub Libr & Metrop Mus Art, New York; World Print Council, San Francisco; Philadelphia Mus Art, Pa; and others. *Comn:* Print-engraving-etching, Hommage Aux Prix Nobel, Malmo, Sweden, 77; print edition, etching & engraving, World Print Coun, San Francisco, 80. *Exhib:* Mus Mod Art, New York, 60, 63, 64, 69 & 70; 100 Contemporary Graphics, Pratt Graphic Art Ctr at Jewish Mus, New York, 64; 17th Nat Exhib Graphics, Brooklyn Mus, New York, 70; 12 Latin-Am Artists, Ringling Mus, Fla, 71; Biennial PanAmerican Graphic Arts, Mus Mod Art, La Tertulia, Columbia, 73; Biennial, Firence, Italy, 74; Biennal Prints, Mus Mod Art, Tokyo, Japan, 79; and others. *Teaching:* Instr graphic workshop, Univ Costa Rica, 76; taller nove arte, Bogota, Columbia, 82 & 83. *Awards:* First Prize in Drawing, Panamerican Exhib Graphic Arts, Columbia, 70; Special Ed Prize & Award of Merit. World Print Council, San Francisco, 80; Silver Medal, Buenos Aires, Arg, 87. *Bibliog:* Stuart Preston (auth), 20th century sense & sensibility, New York Times, 5/7/61; John Canaday (auth), New talent in printmaking, New York Times, 5/27/67; Elisabeth Perez Luna (auth), The eyes of Abularach, Hombre Mag, 7/79. *Media:* Oil; Pen & Ink. *Publ:* Tamarind: Homage to Lithography, Mus Mod Art, New York, 69; Biblioteca Luis Angel, Mus Plastic Arts, Bogota, Columbia, 79; The Council House, The Art Collection by Lee Nordness, Perimeter Press Inc, 80; Modern Masters, Galerie Borjeson, Malmo, Sweden, 80; Artists of Am, Rafeal Squirru, Art Editions, Gaglione, 84; Mus Mod Art Latin Am, selections from the permanent collection, Orgn Am States, Washington, DC, 85; Mus Mod Art, La Tertulia, Carvajal, Colombia, 86; The Latin Am Spirit, 1920-1970, Bronx Mus, N Abrams Inc, 88. *Mailing Add:* 14 W 17th St New York NY 10011

ACCETTA, SUZANNE RUSCONI
PAINTER, INSTRUCTOR
b Cincinnati, Ohio, June 26, 53. *Study:* Univ Cincinnati, BA, 75, and with Everet Raymond Kinstler, 87, 88 & 89. *Work:* Vanderbilt Univ Hosp & Northern Telcom Inc, Nashville, Tenn; Cincinnati Bell Tel, Scioto Mem Hosp, Ohio; Franklin Park Conserv, Columbus, Ohio. *Comn:* Portrait of Reggie Williams, NFL Man of the Year, Van Levnans Co, Cincinnati, Ohio. *Exhib:* Midwest Watercolor Soc, Madison, Wis, 89; Ohio Realist Group, Springfield Art Ctr, 90; Elyria Ohio Art Ctr, 90; Middletown Ohio Art Ctr, 91; Great Southern Hotel, 92; and many others. *Pos:* Chmn bd, Okla Artist Guild, Oklahoma City, Okla, 83-84; dir, Ohio Realist Group, Columbus, Ohio, 87-90; show dir, Ohio Realist Group, 87-; pres, Bexley Art Guild, 90-91. *Teaching:* Instr drawing, Cheekwood Fine Art Ctr, Nashville, Tenn, 81-82, North Light Art Sch, Cincinnati, Ohio, 86-87; Delaware Art Ctr, Oh, 89-91, Westerville Art League, 89-92 & Dublin Art League, 91. *Awards:* Jurors Merit Award, Tenn All State Exhib, 81; Best of Show, Oklahoma City Artist Guild, 84; Best of Show, 86-88 & Awards, 89-91, Central Ohio Watercolor Soc. *Bibliog:* Clara Hieronymus (auth), Fine Drawings, Watercolors, Tennessean, 3/83; Patty Hillis Carol (auth), You ought to be in pictures, Columbus Monthly, 10/88; Calvin J Goodman (auth), Supplementing Gallery Sales, Am Artist, 6/89. *Mem:* Bexley Area Artist Guild (vpres); Ohio Realist Group (dir, 87-); Cent Ohio Watercolor Soc; Ohio Watercolor Soc Signature; The Artists Fel. *Media:* Watercolor, Oil. *Publ:* Auth, Capturing emotion, Gallery J Ohio Realist Group, 87; Capturing emotion, Am Artist, 1/91. *Dealer:* Madison Rd Gallery 1991 Madison Rd Cincinnati OH 45208; Columbia Portraits 291 S Columbia Ave Columbus OH 43209. *Mailing Add:* 4787 Rustic Bridge Dr Columbus OH 43214

ACCONCI, VITO
SCULPTOR
b New York, NY, Jan 24, 40. *Study:* Holy Cross Col, AB; Univ Iowa, MFA. *Work:* Mus Mod Art, Paris; Mus Mod Art, Whitney Mus Am Art, New York; Los Angeles Co Mus; Williams Col Mus Art, Williamstown, Mass. *Comn:* Coca Cola Co, Atlanta. *Exhib:* Sonnabend Gallery, New York, 72, 73, 76, 77, 79 & 80; Eight Contemporary Artists, Mus Mod Art, New York, 74; Venice Biennale, 76, 78 & 80; Whitney Biennial, 77, 81 & 91; Stedelijk Mus, Amsterdam, 78; Kunstmuseum Luzern, 78; Mus Contemp Art, Chicago, 80; Kunstverein Koln, 81; Brooklyn Mus, 85; Vienna Festival, 86; LaJolla Mus, Calif, 87; one-man shows, Mus Mod Art, San Francisco, 78, Williams Col Mus Art, Mass, 83, Brooklyn Mus, NY, 85 & 88, Galeria Il Ponte Rome, Italy, Rhona Hoffman Gallery Chicago, Ill, Galerie Eric Franck, Geneva, Switzerland, 88, Photographic Works 1969-70, Cirrus, Los Angeles (also traveling US & abroad), 88, James Corcoran Gallery, Los Angeles, 90, Museo D'Arte Contemp Prato, Italy, 92; Committed to Print, Mus Mod Art, New York 88; 15th Ann Exhib, Rhona Hoffman Gallery, Chicago, Ill, 92. *Teaching:* Instr art, Sch Visual Arts, New York, 68-71, Nova Scotia Col Art, 71 & 78, Calif Inst Art, 76, Cooper Union, New York, 82 & 86, Chicago Art Inst, 83 & Minn Col Art, 84. *Awards:* Nat Endowment Arts Fel, 76, 80 & 83; Guggenheim Fel, 79. *Bibliog:* R Pincus-Witten (auth), Vito Acconci & the conceptual performance, Artforum, 4/72; Alan Sondheim (auth), Vito Acconci: Work 1973-4, Arts, 3/75; Mario Diacono (auth), Vito Acconci: Dal Testo-Azione Al Corpo Come Testo, Out-of-London Press, 76; G Celant (auth), Dirty Acconci, Artforum, 11/80; S Platt (auth), Vito Acconci: The sheltering city, Artweek, 9/83; P Phillips (auth), Vito Acconci at Nature Morte, Artforum, 2/85. *Media:* All. *Publ:* Contribr, Conceptual Art, Dutton, 72; Vito Acconci Issue, Avalanche Mag, 72; auth, Pulse: From my mother, Multiplicata, 72; Ten-Point Plan for Video, Video Art, Harcourt-Brace, 76; Think-Leap-Rethink-Fall, Wright State Univ Press, 77; Television, Furniture and Sculpture: The Room with an American View, Stedelijk Mus, Amsterdam, 84; Notes on Vienna, Wienfluss, Austria, 86. *Dealer:* Sonnabend Gallery 420 W Broadway New York NY; Crown Point Press 545 Broadway New York NY 10012. *Mailing Add:* 39 Pearl St Brooklyn NY 11201

ACHEPOHL, KEITH ANDEN
PRINTMAKER, PAINTER
b Chicago, Ill, Apr 11, 34. *Study:* Knox Col, BA; Univ Iowa, MFA; Pac Lutheran Univ, DFA, 89. *Work:* Nat Gallery Art & Pennell Collection, Libr Cong, Washington, DC; Los Angeles Co Mus, Calif; Art Inst Chicago; Bibliot Nac, Madrid, Spain; and many others. *Comn:* Garden of Stone & Light, paintings, Atrium Durhan Ctr, Iowa State Univ, 89. *Exhib:* Nat Print Exhib, Libr Cong, 60, 61, 63 & 69; Brooklyn Mus, 68-74; Intaglio Invitational, Biella, Italy; First Int Print Exhib, Segovia, Spain; Des Moines Art Ctr, 79; Utah Mus Fine Arts, 80; Masters Am Watercolor, Mid Am Arts Alliance Travel Exhib, 80; Art Inst, Chicago, 81; Nat Mus Am Art, Washington, DC, 82; Joslyn Mus, Omaha, Nebr, 83; Philadelphia Print Club Int, 86; Honolulu Acad Art Exhib, Japan, 90; Nat Mus Arts, Cairo, Egypt, 90. *Teaching:* Instr printmaking, Univ Iowa, 64-67; vis artist printmaking, Univ Wash, summer 67; assoc prof, Pac Lutheran Univ, 69-72; vis artist printmaking, Univ Iowa, 72-73, assoc prof, 73-78, prof, 78- *Awards:* Tiffany Found Award, 66; Fulbright Sr Lectureship Award, Cairo, Egypt, 79-80 & Ankara, Turkey, 84; Gold Medal Printmaking, Mediterranean Biennale, Alexandria, Egypt, 82; Edmondson Award, Des Moines Art Ctr, 90. *Dealer:* Struve Gallery 309 W Superior Chicago IL 60610; Carega Foxley Leach Gallery Washington DC. *Mailing Add:* 650 Kirkwood Ave Iowa City IA 52240

ACKERMAN, GERALD MARTIN
HISTORIAN, EDUCATOR
b Alameda, Calif, Aug 21, 28. *Study:* Univ Calif, BA, 52; Munich Univ, 56-58, with Prof Sedlmayr; Princeton Univ, MFA, 60, PhD, 64, with Prof Lee & Panofsky. *Collections Arranged:* Thiebaud Figures, Stanford Univ Mus, 65; Gerome, Dayton Art Inst, Minneapolis Art Inst, Walters Art Gallery, Baltimore, 72-73. *Teaching:* Instr art hist, Bryn Mawr Col, 60-64; asst prof, Stanford Univ, 65-70; assoc prof, Pomona Col, 71-76, prof, 76-89, emer prof, 89- chmn art dept, 72-81; Fulbright prof, Univ Leningrad, USSR, 79. *Res:* American & British orientalist painters, in particular academic realists such as Jean Leon Gerome and Thomas Eakins; art theory. *Publ:* Lomazzo's treatise on painting, Art Bull, 59; Thomas Eakins and His Parisian Masters, Gerome and Bonnat, Gazette des Beaux Arts, 72; The Life and Works of J L Gerome, New York, 86; Les Orientalistes de l'Ecole Britannique, Paris, 91; Les Orientalistes de l'Ecole américaine, Paris, 93. *Mailing Add:* Art Dept Pomona Col Claremont CA 91711

ACKERMAN, JAMES S
HISTORIAN, EDUCATOR
b San Francisco, Calif, Nov 8, 19. *Study:* Yale Univ, BA, 41; NY Univ, MA, 47, PhD, 52; Kenyon Col, LHD, 61; Md Inst Art, Hon DFA, 72; Univ Md, Baltimore Co, LHD, 76; Univ Venice, DArch, 84. *Pos:* Ed-in-chief, Art Bulletin, 56-60; ed, Annalidi Architettura, 92- *Teaching:* Lectr, Yale Univ, 46 & 49; asst prof hist art & archit, Univ Calif, 52-56, assoc prof, 56-60; fel, Coun Humanities, Princeton Univ, 60-61; prof fine arts, Harvard Univ, 61-90, chmn dept, 63-8 & 82- 84, Arthur Kingsley Porter prof, emer, 90-; Mellon lectr, Nat Gallery Art, 85; SMeyer Schapiro vis prof art hist, Columbia Univ, 88, vis prof, 91; vis prof fine arts, NY Univ, 92. *Awards:* Centennial Award, Univ Calif, 70; Gold Medal, Istituto di Storia dell 'Arte Lombarda, 87; Institute Honors, Am Inst Archs, 87. *Mem:* Am Acad Arts & Sci; corresp Accademia Olimpica Vicenza; corresp Brit Acad; corresp Royal Acad Uppsala; corresp Ateneo Veneto. *Res:* History of architecture; critical and historical theory; interaction of art and science in the period of 1200-1700. *Publ:* Auth, Palladio, Penguin, Eng, 66; coauth, Looking for Renaissance Rome (film), 77; auth, Palladio the Architect and his Influence in America (film), 80; The Villa: Form & Ideology of Country Houses, Princeton Univ Press, Thames & Hudson, London; Distance Points: Studies in Theory and Renaissance Art and Architecture, Cambridge, Mass, 91 & American Inst of Archits Award in History & Theory, 92; and others. *Mailing Add:* Dept Fine Arts Fogg Art Mus Harvard Univ Cambridge MA 02138

ACKERMAN, RUDY SCHLEGEL
PAINTER, EDUCATOR
b Allentown, Pa, Mar 30, 33. *Study:* Kutztown State Col, BS(art educ), 58; Temple Univ, MS(educ), 63; Pa State Univ EdD, 67. *Work:* Allentown Art Mus, Pa; Pa State Col; Lehigh Univ; Moravian Col, Pa. *Comn:* 14 ft metal sculpture, Pa Power & Light Co, Allentown, 67; tunnel mural, Allentown-Bethlehem-Easton Airport, Pa, 76; murals, The Marketplace, Bethlehem Mall, 78, Civic Ctr, Bethlehem, Pa, 84. *Exhib:* The Circle, Allentown Art Mus, 74; Works on Paper, Studio Proposte, Florence, Italy, 79; one-man show, Gallery Doshi, Harrisburg, 79, Lehigh Univ, 80 & Monotypes 81, Alain Bilham Gallery, New York, 81; Allenton Art Mus, 83; Moravian Col, 85; Muhlenberg Col, 88. *Pos:* Chmn art dept, Moravian Col, 63-; exec dir, Baum Sch Art, Allentown, 65- *Teaching:* Prof studio art & art hist, Moravian Col, 63- *Media:* Oil Paint. *Mailing Add:* 2708 W Washington Allentown PA 18104

ACOSTA, MANUEL GREGORIO
PAINTER, SCULPTOR
b Villa Aldama, Mex, May 9, 21; US citizen. *Study:* Univ Tex, El Paso; Chouinard Art Inst, Los Angeles; also with Urbici Soler, sculptor. *Work:* El Paso Mus, Tex; WTex Mus, Lubbock; Time Inc Collection, New York; Harmsen's Western Collection, Colo; Nat Portrait Gallery, Washington, DC. *Comn:* Pioneer murals (with Peter Hurd), WTex Mus, 52; Southwest History (aluminum mural), Casa Blanca Motel, Logan, NMex, 56; fresco mural, First Nat Bank, Las Cruces, NMex, 57; aluminum fresco mural & hist panels, Bank of Tex, Houston. *Exhib:* Art USA, Mo, 58; Tex Watercolor Soc, Austin, 60; one-man show, Chase Gallery, New York, 62; Am Watercolor Soc, New York, 65; Nat Tour of Watercolor Show, Burlington Indust, 84. *Media:* Oil, Watercolor. *Publ:* Illusr, Cesar Chavez (cover), Time Mag, 69; Canto y Grito mi Liberacion, Doubleday, 72. *Mailing Add:* 336 Buena Vista St El Paso TX 79905

ACTON, ARLO C
SCULPTOR
b Knoxville, Iowa, May 11, 33. *Study:* Wash State Univ, BA, 58; Calif Inst Arts, MFA, 59. *Work:* San Francisco Mus Art. *Exhib:* Some Points of View for '62, Stanford Univ, 62; The Artist's Environment: The West Coast, Ft Worth, Tex, 62; Fifty California Artists, Whitney Mus Am Art, New York, 62-63; California Sculpture, Kaiser Ctr, Oakland, Calif, 63; 3rd Paris Biennial, 63; and many others. *Teaching:* Univ Calif, Berkeley, 63. *Awards:* Edgar Walter Mem Prize, San Francisco Mus Art, 61; Second Prize, Richmond Art Asn Ann, 61; Award, San Francisco Art Asn, 64; plus others. *Bibliog:* Peter Selz (auth), Funk, Univ Calif, Berkeley, 67; Maurice Tuchman (auth), American Sculpture of the Sixties, Los Angeles Co Mus Art, 67. *Mailing Add:* PO Box 75 North San Juan CA 95960

ADAMS, ALICE
SCULPTOR
b New York, NY, Nov 16, 30. *Study:* Columbia Univ, BFA, 53; Fulbright travel grant, 53-54; French govt fel, 53-54; L'Ecole Nat d'Art Decoratif, Aubusson, France. *Work:* Haags Gemeentemuseum, The Hague, Neth; Univ Nebr, Lincoln; Hertz Corp, New York; Univ NC; Chase Manhattan Bank, New York; Stamford Mus & Nature Ctr, Conn; Weatherspoon Gallery, Univ NC, Greensboro. *Comn:* Small Park with Arches, Crosby Gardens, Toledo, 84; Downtown Seattle Transit Project, Wash, 85-; Glider Park, Bronx, NY, 90; The Roundabout, Philadelphia, Pa, 92. *Exhib:* Contemp Am Sculpture, Whitney Mus Am Art, 70-71 & 73; Penthouse Gallery Exhib, Mus Mod Art, New York, 71; Am Women Artists, Kunsthaus, Hamburg, Ger, 72; 55 Mercer, NY, 70, 72, 73 & 75; Hal Bromm Gallery, 79; Neuberger Mus, Purchase, NY, 79-80; An International Survey of Painting and Sculpture, Mus Mod Art, New York, 84; Builtwork-Installation, Sarah Lawrence Col Gallery, Bronxville, NY, 85. *Teaching:* Instr sculpture, Manhattanville Col, 61-79; asst prof, Pratt Inst, 79-80; instr, Sch Visual Arts, 80-85. *Awards:* MacDowell Colony, MacDowell Found, 67; Nat Endowment Arts Grant, 79 & 84-85; Princeton Univ Fel, 80; Fel, Guggenheim Found, 81-82; Award Sculpture, Am Acad & Inst Arts & Letts, 84; Prizewinning entry, Westside Competition, Munic Art Soc, New York. *Bibliog:* Barbara Kafka (auth), The woven structures of Alice Adams, Craft Horizons, 3/67; Lucy Lippard (auth), The Abstract Realism of Alice Adams, Art Am, 9/79. *Mem:* Am Abstr Artists (secy, 67). *Media:* Wood, Metal. *Mailing Add:* 3370 Ft Independence St Bronx NY 10463

ADAMS, BOBBI
PAINTER
b Plainfield, NJ, July 30, 39. *Study:* Wheaton Col, Ill, BS(high honors), 61; Art Students League, with R Brackman, R Philipp, M Cooper & V Vytlacil, 70-74; Nat Acad Design, New York, 73-74. *Work:* SC State Collection & Nat Bank SC, Columbia. *Comn:* Two murals, William S Hall Psychiatric Inst, 88; mural, Manning High Sch, 89; mural, Redcliffe Elem, Aiken, 90. *Exhib:* 43rd & 44th Ann Mid-year, Butler Inst Am Art, Youngstown, Ohio, 79 & 80; Guild of SC Artists, Gibbes Gallery, Charleston, 80; Joint Guilds Exhib, Columbia Mus, SC, 81; Chautauqua Nat, 82; Guild SC Artists, Columbia Mus Art, 82. *Pos:* SC artist in res, 84- *Awards:* Purchase Award, State SC, 80; Westvaco Award, Gibbes Gallery, 80; Certificate Merit, Columbia Mus, 81. *Bibliog:* The Adams Papers, NJ Music-Arts, 75. *Mem:* Artists Equity Asn Inc; life mem Art Students League; assoc Allied Artists Am; Guild of SC Artists. *Media:* Oil, Pastel. *Mailing Add:* 215 S Heyward St Bishopville SC 29010

ADAMS, CELESTE MARIE
CURATOR, WRITER
b Cleveland, Ohio, July 4, 47. *Study:* Univ Mich, Ann Arbor, BA, 69; Univ Pa, Philadelphia, AM(art hist), 70; Harvard Univ, AM, 78. *Work:* Cleveland Mus Art, Ohio; Mus Fine Arts, Houston, Tex. *Collections Arranged:* In the Way of the Master: Chinese & Japanese painting & calligraphy (auth, catalog), 81, Sunlight on Leaves: The Impressionist Tradition (auth, catalog), 81, The Diaghilev Tradition: Selections from the Robert Tobin Collection (auth, catalog), 81, Japanese Landscape and Figure Painting (auth, catalog), 83 & Visions of the American West (auth, catalog), 86, Mus Fine Arts, Houston. *Pos:* Asst dir & cur, Mus Fine Arts, Houston, Tex, 80- *Mailing Add:* c/o Mus Fine Arts 1001 Bissonnet Houston TX 77005

ADAMS, CLINTON
PAINTER, HISTORIAN
b Glendale, Calif, Dec 11, 18. *Study:* Univ Calif, Los Angeles, BEd, 40; MA, 42. *Work:* Mus Mod Art, New York; Chicago Art Inst, Ill; Amon Carter Mus Western Art, Ft Worth, Tex; Achenbach Found Graphic Arts, San Francisco, Calif; Grunwald Ctr Graphic Arts, Univ Calif, Los Angeles; Nat Acad Design, New York. *Exhib:* Lithographs, Univ NMex Art Mus, 48-72; Tamarind: Homage to Lithography, Mus Mod Art, New York, 69; Retrospective Exhib: Paintings, 61-71, Roswell Mus & Art Ctr, NMex, 72; Retrospective Exhib: Paintings & Watercolors, 45-87; Tamarind: From Los Angeles to Albuquerque, Grunwald Ctr Graphic Arts, Univ Calif, Los Angeles, 84-85; Univ NMex Art Mus, 87; and others. *Pos:* Assoc dir, Tamarind Lithography Workshop, Los Angeles, 60-61; dir, Tamarind Inst, Albuquerque, 70-85; ed, Tamarind Papers, 74-90. *Teaching:* Asst prof painting & lithography, Univ Calif, Los Angeles, 46-54; chmn dept art, Univ Ky, 54-57; chmn dept art, Univ Fla, 57-60; dean col fine arts, Univ NMex, 61-76, prof art, 61- *Awards:* Gov Award for Outstanding Contribr to the Arts NMex, 85. *Bibliog:* Van Deren Coke (auth), Clinton Adams, Univ NMex Art Mus, 73; Peter Walch (auth), Clinton Adams: Paintings & Watercolors, Univ NMex Art Mus, 87; David Acton (auth), A Spectrum of Innovation: Color in American Printmaking, 1890-1960, Worcester Art Mus & Norton, 90. *Mem:* Nat Acad Design (assoc 91, acad 92). *Publ:* Co-auth, Tamarind Book of Lithography: Art and Techniques, Abrams, 71; auth, Fritz Scholder: Lithographs, NY Graphic Soc, 75; The Woodstock Ambience, Univ NMex Art Mus, 81; American Lithographers, 1900-1960: The Artists and Their Printers, Univ NMex, 83; Printmaking in New Mexico: 1880-1990, Univ NMex, 91. *Dealer:* Tobey C Moss Gallery 7321 Beverly Blvd Los Angeles CA 90036; Janus Gallery 225 Canyon Rd Santa Fe NM 87501. *Mailing Add:* 1917 Morningside Dr NE Albuquerque NM 87110

ADAMS, DENNIS PAUL
SCULPTOR, CONCEPTUAL ARTIST
b Des Moines, Iowa, Nov 15, 48. *Study:* Drake Univ, BFA, 69; Tyler Sch Art, Philadelphia, Pa, MFA, 71. *Work:* Etablissement Public pour L'Amanagement de la Defense & Centre Nat d'Art Contemporain, Paris, France; Mus Mod Art, New York; Gemäldegalerie Staatliche Museen Preussischer Kulturbesitz, Ger; Israel Mus, Jerusalem; Lenbachhaus Städtische Galerie, Munich; Whitney Mus Am Art, New York. *Comn:* Bus Shelter IV, Skulptur Projekte Münster, WGer, 87; Fallen Angels, Steirischer Herbst, Graz, Austria, 88; Pedestrian Tunnels, Villa Merkel, Esslingen, Ger, 89; Terminus II, de Achterstraat, Hoorn, Holland, 90; Seige, TSWA Four Cities Proj, Derry, Northern Ireland, 90; Emancipation, Boston, 91; Arcadian Blind, Floriadepark, Holland, 92; Réservoir, Musée d'Art Contemporain de Montreal, 92; Port View, Marseille, France, 92. *Exhib:* Solo exhib, Alternative Mus, New York, 87; Images Critiques, Musee d'Art Mod de La Ville de Paris, 89 & Passages de L'Image, 90, Magiciens de la Terre, 89, Musee Nat d'Art Mod, Centre Pompidou, Paris, France; Image World: Art & Media Culture, Whitney Mus, New York, 89; Photography of Invention, Nat Mus Am Art, Smithsonian Inst, 89 & Works: The Archive, Hirschhorn Mus, 90, Washington, DC; Images in Transition, Nat Mus Mod Art, Kyoto, Japan, 90; Mus Mod Art, New York, 91; Sala Montcado de la Fundacío "la caixa", Barcelona, 92. *Pos:* Bd govs, NY Found for Arts, 89-92. *Teaching:* Vis artist sculpture, Tyler Sch Art, Philadelphia, Pa, 87, Cooper Union Sch Art, 88, Parsons Sch, 90, New York, Ecole Nationale Superieure des Beaux-Arts, Paris, 92 & Rijkakademi, Amsterdam, 92. *Awards:* Nat Endowment Arts Fel, 84 & 88; Deutscher Akademischer Austauschdienst, WGer, 89. *Bibliog:* Eleanor Heartney (auth), Dennis Adams, Flash Art, summer 89; Daniella Goldmann (auth), Interview with Dennis Adams, Noema Art J, 10-11/91; Lynne Cooke (auth), Dennis Adams, Galeries Mag, 2-3/91. *Media:* All Media. *Publ:* Coauth, Dennis Adams: Building Against Image 1979-1987, Alternative Mus, 87; Public Difference--Dennis Adams, Christine Burgin Gallery, 89; Works--Hirshhorn Mus--Dennis Adams, Hirshhorn Mus, 90; Architecture of Amnesia--Dennis Adams, Kent Fine Art, 90; Dennis Adams: El Pavelló de l'Est, Sala Montcado de la Fundacio "la Caixa", Barcelona, 92. *Dealer:* Kent Gallery 47 E 63rd New York NY 10021. *Mailing Add:* 42 Walker St New York NY 10013

ADAMS, HANK M
CRAFTSMAN
b Philadelphia, Pa, 1956. *Study:* RI Sch Design, BFA, 78; Penland Sch, Spruce Pine, NC, 80; Pilchuck Sch, Stanwood, Wash, 81; Tenn Technol Univ, Cookeville, Tenn. *Work:* Detroit Inst Art, Mich; Brooks Mus Memphis, Tenn; Oberglas Mus, Barnbach, Austria; Corning Mus Glass, NY; Contemp Arts Ctr, Honolulu, Hawaii. *Exhib:* Solo exhibs, Traver Sutton Gallery, Seattle, Wash, 86, Mich Gallery, Detroit, Mich, 87, Great Am Gallery, Atlanta, Ga, 87, Dorothy Weiss Gallery, San Francisco, Calif, 87, 89 & 92, Kohler Arts Ctr, Sheboygan, Wis, 88, Heller Gallery, New York, 88 & 90; May 1991, New Art Forms, Betsy Rosenfield Gallery, Chicago, Ill, 91; World Class Now, Hokkaido Mus Mod Art, Sapporo, Japan, 91; New Sculpture, Dorothy Weiss Gallery, San Francisco, Calif, 91; Studio Glass: Selections from the David Jacobs Chodorkoff Collection, Detroit Inst Art, Mich, 91; National Object Invitational, Ark Arts Ctr Decorative Arts Mus, Little Rock, Ark, 91. *Pos:* Designer, Benko Glass Co, Milton, WVa, 88-91. *Teaching:* Appalachian Ctr, Smithville, Tenn, 81-85; Ctr Creative Studies, Detroit, Mich, 87; vis artist, Cranbrook Educ Community, Bloomfield Hills, Mich, 91. *Mailing Add:* Fort Orange St Box 6933 Albany NY 12206

ADAMS, HENRY
CURATOR, EDUCATOR
b Boston, Mass, May 12, 49. *Study:* Harvard Univ, BA, 71; Yale Univ, MA, 77, PhD, 80. *Pos:* Cur fine arts, Carnegie Inst Mus Art, Pittsburgh, Pa, 82-85; Samuel Sosland cur Am art, Nelson-Atkins Mus Art, Kansas City, 85- *Teaching:* Asst prof art hist, Univ Ill, 81-82; adj prof, Univ Pittsburgh, 83- & Univ Kansas, currently. *Awards:* Frances Blanshard Prize, Yale Univ; Arthur Kingsley Porter Prize, Col Art Asn; Distinguished Serv Medallion, William Jewell Col. *Publ:* Auth, A Fish by John LaFarge, Art Bulletin, 80; Mortal themes: Winslow Homer, Art Am, 83; The Development of William Morris Hunt's the Flight of Night, Am Art J, 83; New books on Japonisme, 83 A new interpretation of Bingham's Fur Traders Descending the Missouri, 83, Art Bull; contribr (essay), John La Farge, Abbeville Press, 87; Thomas Hart Benton: An American Original, Alfred Knopf, 89; Thomas Hart Benton: Drawing from Life, Abbeville Press, 90. *Mailing Add:* Nelson-Atkins Mus Art 4525 Oak St Kansas City MO 64111-1873

ADAMS, JAY H
JEWELER, MEDALIST
b Clinton, Iowa, Sept 11, 37. *Study:* Lincoln Col, Ill, 58; Ill Wesleyan Univ, BFA, 62; Ill State Univ, MS, 68. *Work:* St Charles Art Ctr, Ill; Park Forest Art Ctr, Ill; Brooks Mem Art Gallery, Memphis, Tenn; Western Ill Univ Art Gallery. *Comn:* Candelabra, Lincoln Col, Ill, 71. *Exhib:* Goldsmith NAm Exhib, Renwick Gallery, Smithsonian Inst, Washington, DC, 74; Prof Jewelry Exhib, Univ Mo Fine Arts Gallery, Columbia, 76; NAm Goldsmith Exhib, Phoenix Art Mus, Ariz, 77; Am Goldsmiths Now, Washington Univ Gallery Art, St Louis, Mo, 78; Pewter Exhib, Tulsa Jr Col, Okla, 79; and others. *Teaching:* Instr jewelry-metals, Ill State Univ, 68-69; assoc prof jewelry-metals, Southwest Mo State Univ, 69- *Awards:* Best of Show, Mo Crafts Coun Ann Show, 76. *Bibliog:* Edgar A Albin (auth), The Arts, 11/28/71 & View Mag, 10/22/77, Springfield News-Leader & Jay Adams, Art Craft Mag, 12/79-1/80. *Mem:* Am Crafts Coun; Soc NAm Goldsmiths; Mo Crafts Coun. *Media:* Gold; Pewter. *Publ:* Auth, Goldsmiths J, Soc NAm Goldsmiths, 10/79. *Mailing Add:* 910 S Kickapoo Ave Springfield MO 65804

ADAMS, JOHN MICHAEL
EDUCATION, ADMINISTRATOR
b Peoria, Ill, Oct 22, 47. *Study:* Ill State Univ, BS, 69; Univ Ill, MS, 72; Southern Ill Univ, PhD, 76. *Pos:* Dean, Nesbitt Col Design, Drexel Univ, 84- *Teaching:* Prof graphic arts, State Univ NY, 72-84. *Awards:* Chancellor's Award Teaching Excellence, State Univ NY, 78; Soc Fels, Graphic Arts Tech Found, 90; Edwin Wise Award, Graphic Arts Sales Found, 92. *Mem:* Int Graphic Arts Educ Asn (pres, 80); Graphic Arts Sales Found (bd dirs); Nat Asn Schs Art & Design. *Res:* Inter-cultural issues of creativity. *Publ:* Ed, What is Graphic Arts Education?, Graphic Arts Asn, 80; coauth, Photography for the Graphic Arts, 83 & Painting Technology, rev ed 88, Delmar; auth, Publication Gravure, Gravure Assoc, 83; Career Change, McGraw-Hill, 83. *Mailing Add:* 4161 Apalogen Rd Philadelphia PA 19144

ADAMS, LISA KAY
PAINTER, PRINTMAKER
b Bristol, Pa, Aug 3, 55. *Study:* Univ Heidelberg, Ger, 75; Scripps Col, BA, 77; Claremont Grad Sch, MFA, 80. *Work:* Edward Albee Found, Montauk, NY; Aratex Corp, San Francisco, Calif; Laguna Mus Art, Laguna Beach, Calif; Nippon Steel, USA Inc, Los Angeles; Tajima Corp, Los Angeles. *Exhib:* Solo exhib, Physical Curiosities, New Space Gallery, Los Angeles, 92; Instincts of Intuition, New Space Gallery, Los Angeles, 92; Symbology, Security Pac Bank Space, Los Angeles, 92; New Los Angeles Abstraction, Col Mainland, Texas City, Tex, 92; Painterly Gesture, Armory Ctr Arts, Pasadena, Calif, 92. *Teaching:* Instr drawing, Univ Calif Los Angeles Extension, 88-92; instr painting, Santa Monica Col Design, Art & Archit, 90-92; instr watercolors, Pepperdine Univ, Malibu, Calif, 92. *Awards:* Blessing Semler Award Printmaking, 91; Brody Arts Fund Fel, 92. *Bibliog:* David diMichele (auth), Back to Abstraction, Art Week & Conceptualism's Ironic Legacy, Visions, 92. *Mem:* Los Angeles Contemp Exhib; Los Angeles Downtown Arts Partnership (artist adv). *Media:* Miscellanous. *Mailing Add:* 2118 E Seventh Place Los Angeles CA 90021

ADAMS, MAC
SCULPTOR, PHOTOGRAPHER
b South Wales, Gt Brit, 43. *Study:* Cardiff Col Art (nat dipl design), 61-66, ATD, 66-67; Rutgers Univ, MFA, 67-69. *Work:* Brooklyn Mus, Guggenheim Mus, NY; Wallraf Richartz Mus, Cologne, Ger; Univ Iowa Mus; Victoria & Albert Mus, London, Eng; Musee De Toulon, France; Los Angeles Co Mus, Calif; Ga Mus Art, Athens; La Jolla Mus Contemp Art, Calif; and many others. *Comn:* Sweptaway, N Princeton Develop Ctr, NJ State Coun Arts, Skillmen, 83; Serpent Bearer, Montclair State Col, NJ Governer's Challenge for Excellence Grant, 87; NY Korean War Mem, Battery Park, New York, 91; and many others. *Exhib:* One-man shows, Hammerskjold Plaza Sculpture Garden, New York, 84, Galerie Maier-Hahn, Dusseldorf, Ger, 87, Montclair State Col, NJ, 88, La Jolla Mus Contemp Art, Calif, 88-89, Gracie Mansion Gallery, New York, 90; New York Diary: Almost 25 Different Things, PS 1

Mus, Inst Contemp Art, 91; The Seventies, John Gibson Gallery, New York, 92; The Order of Things: Toward a Politic of Still Life, Widner Gallery, Trinity Col & Real Art Ways, Conn, 92; Quotations, The Second History of Art, Aldrich Mus Contemp Art & Mus Contemp Art, Wright State Univ, 92; and many others. *Pos:* Chmn, State Univ NY, 88- *Teaching:* Asst prof photog, State Univ NY Col, Old Wesbury, 88- *Awards:* Nat Endowment Fel Arts, 76, 80, 82; Berlin Artist in Residence Prog, 81; NY State Fel Arts (sculpture), 88. *Bibliog:* Shoichiro Higuchi (auth), Water as Environmental Art, p 148, Kashiwashobo Publ Co, 91; Julia Ballerini (auth), The Surrogate Figure: Intercepted Identities in Contemporary Photography, Ctr Photog, 91; Charles Hagen (auth), NY Times Reviews, 3/92; and many others. *Media:* All. *Dealer:* John Gibson Broadway New York NY 10012. *Mailing Add:* 311 Church St New York NY 10013

ADAMS, MARK
TAPESTRY ARTIST, PAINTER
b Fort Plain, NY, Oct 27, 25. *Study:* Syracuse Univ; with Hans Hofmann & Jean Lurcat, France. *Work:* Dallas Mus Fine Arts; San Francisco Pub Libr; Santa Rosa-Sonoma Pub Libr, Calif; Hall Justice, San Francisco. *Comn:* Baptistry, All Saints' Episcopal Church, Carmel, Calif, 68; Man Flying (tapestry), Bank Calif, San Francisco, 68; tapestry, Weyerhaeuser Co, Tacoma, Wash, 71; stained glass, Temple Emanuel, 72 & St Thomas More Cath Church, San Francisco, 74. *Exhib:* Int Biennial of Tapestry, Lausanne, Switz, 62 & 65; Collector: Object/Environment, Mus Contemp Crafts, New York, 65; San Francisco Art Inst Ann, San Francisco Mus Art, 65; 400 Years of Tapestry, Norfolk Mus Arts & Sci, 66; one-man retrospective, Calif Palace Legion Honor, San Francisco, 70. *Media:* Watercolor, Stained Glass. *Mailing Add:* 4627 Briarcliff Rd Baltimore MD 21229

ADAMS, PAT
PAINTER, EDUCATOR
b Stockton, Calif, July 8, 28. *Study:* Univ Calif, Berkeley, BA, 49; Brooklyn Mus Art Sch, with Max Beckmann & John Ferren; Fulbright fel, France, 56-57. *Work:* Whitney Mus; Joseph Hirshhorn Mus; Yale Gallery Art; Brooklyn Mus; Berkshire Mus; Montclair Mus, NJ; New Brit Mus Am Art. *Comn:* TRW Hq, Lyndhurst, Ohio. *Exhib:* Yale Painting Faculty 1950-1990, Marilyn Pearl, New York, 90; Transformations: Adams, Gillespie, Hermansader, Brattleboro Art Mus, Vt, 91; Bennington Col Collects, Williams Col Mus Art, 91; Traditional Sources: Contemporary Visions, Webb & Parsons Gallery, Burlington in collaboration with Shelburne Mus, Vt, 91; one-person, Biennial, Zabriskie, New York, 92; and many others. *Teaching:* Art fac painting, Bennington Col, 64-; vis critic painting, Yale Univ, 71-72, vis prof, 90-; grad sem, Queens Col, 72, RI Sch Design, 81; vis prof, Grad Sch Art, Yale Univ, 83; vis artist, Univ Iowa, Univ NMex, Western Ky Univ, Columbia Univ, Kent State Univ & Cornell Univ, Mills Col; lectr & critic, RI Sch Design, 89, Univ Mass, Amherst, 89 & Skidmore Col, summer 92; lectr, The Not as Yet, Nat Asn Women Artists, New York. *Awards:* Painting Award, Nat Coun Arts, 68; Nat Endowment Arts Grant, 76; Childe Hassam Purchase, Am Acad Arts & Letters, 80, 84 & 89; Distinguished Teaching of Art Award, Col Art Asn, 84; Achievement Award, Stockton Arts Comn, Calif, 85; Painting Award, Am Acad Inst Arts & Lett, 86; Grant, Nat Endowment Arts, 87. *Bibliog:* Emmy Donadio (auth), Nightflight to Byzantium: Pat Adams' new work, Arts, summer 86; Debra Bricker Blaken (auth), Pat Adams, Paintings, 68-88, Berkshire Mus Pittsfield, Mass, 88; Sherrye Cohn (auth), Circles, Spheres & Other Correspondances, New York Acad Sci, 88; Jed Perl (auth), Religion, Reality and Relativity in Scientific Tradition in Art, Gallery Going, 91. *Mem:* Williamstown Regional Art Conserv Lab (bd dirs, 85-86); Vt Acad Arts & Sci (elections fel, 90); Nat Acad Design (assoc mem painting, 92). *Media:* Oil-Isobutyl Methacrylate, Acrylic. *Publ:* Auth, Art Now, 6/72; On working, Quadrille, fall 77; Subject and being, Art J (Col Art Asn Am), 82; The Making of Art & the Making of Artists Colloquium, Atlanta Col Art, 87. *Dealer:* Virginia Zabriskie Gallery 29 W 57th St New York NY 10019. *Mailing Add:* Bennington Col Bennington VT 05201

ADAMS, PHOEBE
SCULPTOR
b Greenwich, Conn, 53. *Study:* Philadelphia Col Art, Pa, BFA, 76; Skowhegan Sch Painting & Sculpture, Maine, 77; State Univ NY, Albany, MFA, 78. *Work:* Solomon R Guggenheim, Metrop Mus Art, New York; Brooklyn Mus, NY; AT&T, Chicago, Ill; Pa Acad Fine Arts, Philadelphia; Philadelphia Mus Art, Pa; Prudential Insurance Co; Walker Art Ctr, Minneapolis, Minn; and others. *Exhib:* Solo shows, Lawrence Oliver Eds, Philadelphia, Pa, 90, Curt Marcus Gallery, NY, 90, Pence Gallery, Santa Monica, Calif, 91 & Locks Gallery, Philadelphia, Pa, 93; Curt Marcus Gallery, New York, 92; Philadelphia Art Alliance, Pa, 92; Locks Gallery, Philadelphia, 92; and others. *Awards:* Pa Coun Arts, 82 & 84; Guggenheim Sculptor in Residence, Chesterwood, Stockbridge, Mass, 86; Nat Endowment Arts Fel Grant, 86. *Bibliog:* Joe Jarrell (auth), Art: eight women out, Village View, 31, 9/20/91; Embracing the ridiculous, LA Times, calendar sect, F5, 9/26/91; Peter Frank (auth), Art picks of the week: Phoebe Adams, Lynda Benglis, Eric Johnson, LA Weekly, C61, 9/27/91. *Mailing Add:* Locks Gallery 600 Washington Sq S Philadelphia PA 19106

ADAMS, ROBERT HICKMAN
PHOTOGRAPHER
b Orange, NJ, May 8, 37. *Work:* Mus Mod Art, New York; Mus Fine Arts, Houston; Metrop Mus Art, New York; Philadelphia Mus Art; Int Mus Photog, George Eastman House, Rochester, NY; and others. *Exhib:* One-man shows, Prairie, Mus Mod Art, New York, 79, The New West: Photographs, Philadelphia Mus Art, 81, Milwaukee Art Mus, 83, Summer Nights, Denver Art Mus, 86, Portland Art Mus, Ore, Perfect Times, Perfect Places, Fraenkel Gallery, San Francisco, Calif, To Make It Home: Photographs of the American West 1965-1986, Philadelphia Mus Art; Fourteen Am Photogrs, Baltimore Mus Art, 75; Mirrors & Windows, American Photography Since 1960 (catalog), Mus Mod Art, New York, 78; American Landscapes (catalog), Mus Mod Art, 81; Three Americans, Mus Mod Art, New York, 84; American Images: Photography 1945-1980 (catalog), Barbican Art Gallery, 85; Artists in Mid-Career (catalog), San Francisco Mus Mod Art, 86; On the Art of Fixing a Shadow (catalog), Nat Gallery Art, 89. *Awards:* Guggenheim Found Fel, 73 & 81; Peer Award, Friends of Photog, 83; Charles Pratt Mem Award, 87. *Bibliog:* John Szarkowski (auth), Foreward to, The New West, 74; Lewis Baltz (auth), The New West, Art in Am, 3-4/75; Barry Lopez (auth), Faith in the Light, Northwest Review, Vol 29, No 2, 33-36. *Publ:* Auth & illusr, The New West: Landscapes Along the Colorado Front Range, Colo Assoc Univ, 74; Denver: A Photographic Survey of the Metropolitan Area, Colo Assoc Univ Press, 77; From the Missouri West, Aperture, New York, 80; Summer nights, Aperture, 85; Los Angeles spring, Aperture, New York, 86; To make it home: Photographs of the American West, Aperture, New York, 89. *Mailing Add:* 326 Lincoln St Longmont CO 80501

ADAMS, ROBERT MCCORMICK
ADMINISTRATOR, WRITER
b Chicago, Ill, July 23, 26. *Study:* Univ Chicago, PhB, 47 AM, 52, PhD, 56; Univ Pittsburgh, Dr Sci, 85; Hunter Col, City Univ New York, LHD, 86; Ill Univ, Edwardsville, LHD, Col William and Mary, LHD, 89; Dartmouth Col, Dr Sci, 89. *Pos:* Trustee, Nat Opinion Res Ctr, 70-, Russell Sage Found, 78-, Santa Fe Inst, 84- & George Washington Univ, 86-; auth, column, Smithsonian Horizons, Smithsonian Mag, 84-; chief exec, Smithsonian Inst, currently. *Teaching:* Instr, Univ Chicago, 55-63, dir Oriental Inst, 62-68 & 81-83, prof, 64-84, dean Social Sci, 70-74 & 79-80, Harold Swift Distinguished Serv Prof, 75-84, provost, 83-84, res assoc dept anthropology, 84-; adj prof, dept anthropology & Near Eastern studies, John Hopkins Univ, 84- *Mem:* Am Oriental Soc; assoc mem Iraqi Acad; fel Am Acad Arts & Sci; Soc Antiquaries London. *Publ:* Auth, Heartland of Cities: Surveys of Ancient Settlement and Land Use on the Central Floodplain of the Euphrates, Univ Chicago Press, 81; co-ed, Behavioral and Social Science Research: A National Resource, Vol 1 & 2, Nat Acad Press, 82; auth, Change and continuity in faculty, student body and research support: A decade-long perspcetive, Chicago Chronicle, 5/10/84; approx 100 articles & reviews. *Mailing Add:* Smithsonian Inst 1000 Jefferson Dr SW Washington DC 20560

ADAMSON, JEROME D, JR
ART DEALER, CONSULTANT
b Glendale, Calif, July 14, 44. *Study:* Whittier Col, BA, 67. *Pos:* Dir, Adamson-Duvannes Galleries, 80- *Mem:* Am Art Coun; Art Dealers Asn Calif. *Specialty:* 19th and 20th Century American and European painting, emphasizing California Plein Air through Modernism; representing the work of Charles Zlatkoff. *Publ:* Auth, With an Eye Toward Collecting California Painting (exhib catalog), 85; American Art 1830-1940: A Century Observed (exhib catalog), 89; The California Vision: Watercolors in the California Style (exhib catalog), 90. *Mailing Add:* Adamson/Duvannes Galleries 484 S San Vicente Blvd Los Angeles CA 90048

ADAMSON, LINNY J
CURATOR, WEAVER
b Portland, Ore, Jan 4, 52. *Study:* Ore State Univ, 70-73; Portland State Univ, 74; special studies with Britt Warsinki, Norway & Peter Collingwood, Eng. *Work:* Timberline Lodge, Nat Hist Landmark, Ore. *Comn:* Wall hanging (woven), Rankin, McMurry & Osborn Attys, Portland, Ore, 76; office dividers (woven), Wilamette Dental Group, Portland, 77; International Kings Table (wall woven pieces), Eugene, Ore, 78; (wall piece), Clatskanie Ore Savings & Loan, 78. *Exhib:* Ore Artists Under 35, Portland Art Mus, Ore, 74. *Collections Arranged:* LACE Collection, Portland Art Mus, 81; Mountain High IV-Glass, 83; Mountain High V-Metal, Northwest Blacksmiths, 85; Timberline Textiles, Ore Hist Soc, 86; Rachael Griffin Hist Exhib Ctr, 86. *Pos:* Dir, Fibres Gallery, Portland, Ore, 75-77; weaver, Friends of Timberline, 75-78; dir, Timberline Textile Wkshp, 78-80 & 40 volunteer rug hookers, 83-86; cur, Timberline Lodge, 78-86; bd mem, Ore Sch Arts & Crafts, 84-86. *Teaching:* Instr sales & weaving, Wildflowers Fibres, Portland, Ore, 73-76; instr weaving, Portland Parks Bureau, 74-79. *Awards:* First Place, Valley Invitational, Corvallis Art Ctr, 74. *Bibliog:* Portraits in Art, Linda Adamson, Handweaver, Curator (film), Rogers Cable Systems, 84. *Media:* Textiles. *Res:* 1930's Works Progress Administration arts and crafts. *Mailing Add:* c/o Timberline Lodge Timberline OR 97028

ADAMY, GEORGE E
EDUCATOR, SCULPTOR
b Manchester, Conn, Apr 19, 32. *Study:* Univ Conn, BS, 52; NY Univ, MBA, 54, PhD credits, 55; New Sch Social Res, with M Borne, 63; Mus Mod Art, with R Carpentier & S Weiner, 63-64; Scarsdale studio workshop with F Dzubas & Knox Martin, 63-65. *Work:* Aldrich Mus of Contemp Art, Ridgefield, Conn; Vatican Art Collection, Vatican City; White Plains Hosp, NY; Mayo Clinic, Minn. *Comn:* Outdoor sculpture environment containing five 5 ft laminated acrylic discs in an 800 sq ft area, 77 Water St, New York, 69-70; Designer & fabricator, Hutchinson Art Garden, Pelhan, NY, 87- *Exhib:* Aldrich Mus of Contemp Art, 65; Neuberger Mus, State Univ NY, Purchase, 75; Hudson River Mus, Yonkers, NY. *Pos:* Owner, art materials innovator and consult to industs & artists, GEA Co, 62-; owner, Adamy's Concrete & Paper Workshops, 79-; founder & pres, Life Reproductions Ltd, 81; sr partner, Impressions, 83. *Teaching:* Instr pvt workshops, 68-; lectr plastics, State Univ NY Col, Purchase, 73-84; vis adj prof, Univ Bridgeport,

Conn, 75; lectr, Elizabeth Seton Col, 74, Sarah Lawrence Col, 77; lectr, Parsons Sch Design, 82, Moorhead State Univ, 89, Carleton Col, 90. *Awards:* Numerous awards for sculpture & collage in plastics. *Bibliog:* Luisa Kriesberg & Kathie Beals (auths), articles in Westchester-Rockland newspapers, 63-; and others. *Mem:* Hudson River Contemp Artists. *Media:* Cement, Paper Pulp. *Publ:* Auth, The POLYADAM Concrete System: State of the Art Construction and Casting & The ADAMATE System of Molding Humans and Delicate Objects, 86. *Mailing Add:* 11-1 Woods Brooke Circle Ossining NY 10562

ADAN, SUZANNE RAE
PAINTER
b Woodland, Calif, Feb 12, 46. *Study:* Calif State Univ, Sacramento, BA, 69, MA, 71. *Work:* Crocker Art Mus, Sacramento; Continental Bank, Houston, Tex; Lexecon, Inc, Chicago, Ill; Impact Commun, Bloomington, Ill. *Exhib:* San Francisco Art Institute Centennial Exhibition, San Francisco Mus Mod Art, 71; Extraordinary Realities, Whitney Mus Art, New York, 73-74; one-person exhib, Womanspace, Los Angeles, 74, Betsy Rosenfield Gallery, Chicago, 83 & 85, Himovitz-Salomon Gallery, Sacramento, 84 & 86 & John Berggruen Gallery, San Francisco, 87; three-person show, Richard Nelson Gallery, Univ Calif, Davis, 79; two-person show, Crocker Art Mus, Sacramento, 80 & Betsy Rosenfield Gallery, Chicago, 82; Welcome to the Candy Store, Crocker Art Mus, Sacramento, 81; The Finals in Painting & Sculpture & Small Wonder, Jan Baum Gallery, Los Angeles, 84; two person show, NMex State Univ, Las Cruces, 85; and others. *Teaching:* Instr drawing, Am River Col, Sacramento, Calif, 75-76. *Awards:* Ayling Watercolor Award, 68 & Purchase Award, 73, Crocker Art Mus; Hardison, Komatsu, Ivelich & Tucker Award, Richmond Art Ctr, 80. *Mem:* Col Art Asn. *Media:* Oil on Canvas. *Dealer:* Betsy Rosenfield Gallery Inc 212 W Superior St Chicago IL 60610. *Mailing Add:* c/o Michael Himovitz Gallery 1020 Tenth St Sacramento CA 95814

ADDISON, BYRON KENT
PAINTER, EDUCATOR
b St Louis, Mo, July 12, 37. *Study:* Washington Univ, St Louis, Mo, BFA, 59; Univ Notre Dame, South Bend, Ind, MA, 60. *Work:* Univ Tulsa Libr, Okla; Maryville Col Libr, St Louis, Mo; Springfield Art Mus, Springfield, Mo; Neville Pub Mus, Green Bay, Wis. *Comn:* Forest Park sculpture, St Louis Award Comt, Mo, 65; entrance wall sculpture, Continental Tel Co, Wentzville, Mo, 67; wall sculpture, Westinghouse Elec Corp, Abington, Va, 71; fountain & sculpture, United Methodist Church, Sun City, Ariz, 74; religious sculpture, St Joseph Church, Manchester, Mo, 80. *Exhib:* Nat Competition, Nat Watercolor Soc, Muckenthaler Cultural Ctr, Fullerton, Calif, 92; Nat Exhib Transparent Watercolors, Midwest Watercolor Soc, Neville Pub Mus, Green Bay, Wis, 92; Five State Exhib, Wichita Art Mus, Kans, 92; Rocky Mountain Nat Watermedia Exhib, Foothills Art Ctr, Colo, 92; Watercolor USA, Springfield Art Mus, MO, 92. *Teaching:* Prof drawing & sculpture, Maryville Col, St Louis, Mo, 61-, chmn, Art Dept, 65-79. *Awards:* Springfield Art Mus Cash Award, 92; Purchase, Neville Pub Mus, 92; Winsor & Newton Art Award, Adirondack Exhib, 92. *Bibliog:* Herbert Gralnick (auth), Alone with his God, St Louis Mag, 3/84; Betsy Schein Goldman (auth), Kent Addison, Am Artist Mag, 12/84. *Mem:* Watercolor USA Honor Soc; Midwest Watercolor Soc; Ga Watercolor Soc; Nat Watercolor Soc, Rocky Mountain Nat Watermedia Soc. *Media:* Welded Steel, Watercolor. *Mailing Add:* 616 Spring Meadows Dr Ballwin MO 63011

ADDISON, CHAUNCEY See Day, Chon

ADELMAN, BUNNY
SCULPTOR
b New York, NY, May 7, 35. *Study:* Mt Holyoke Col, Columbia Univ, BA, 56; Nat Acad Sch Fine Arts, with Stephen Csoka & Evangelos Frudakis, scholar, 76. *Comn:* Figure, comn by A Petaccio, Clifton, NJ, 77; B'Nai Brith Medal, comn by Roger Williams Mint, 78; presidential relief, M H Lamston Inc, New York, 78; Manager of Year Award, M H Lamston Inc, New York, 79; mem relief, W R Thomas Co, Warsaw, Ind, 80. *Exhib:* Allied Artists Am, Nat Acad Design, New York, 74-79 & 81; Nat Acad Ann, Nat Acad Design, New York, 76-78; Salmagundi Club Ann, New York, 78; one-woman show, Bergen Community Mus, Paramus, NJ, 79; Pen & Brush Soc, New York, 81. *Awards:* Gold Medal, Catherine Lorillard Wolfe Ann Show, 74; Coun Am Artists Soc Award, Nat Sculpture Soc, 75; Bronze Casting Award, Pen & Brush Ann, Joel Meisner Foundry, 81. *Mem:* Nat Sculpture Soc; Catherine Lorillard Wolfe Club; Sculptors Asn NJ (vpres, 79-81). *Media:* Bronze. *Mailing Add:* 68 Homestead Rd Tenafly NJ 07670

ADELMAN, DOROTHY (LEE) MCCLINTOCK
PRINTMAKER, INSTRUCTOR
b New York, NY. *Study:* Art Students League, with Roberto Delamonico & Michael Ponce de Leon; Westchester Art Workshop, White Plains, NY, with Ruth Bamberger, also in Paris & Jerusalem; Silvermine Guild Artists, Inc, New Canaan, Conn. *Work:* Hudson River Mus; Westchester Art Workshop; Beneficial Life Insurance Co; Sears Roebuck; Int Bus Machines; MCI Corp. *Exhib:* Katonah Gallery, NY, 71-72, 78-80, 85 & 86-87; 2nd NH Int Graphic Ann; Greenwich Art Barn, Conn, 72 & 75; Nat Arts Club, New York; Manhattanville Col, Purchase, NY, 74; Lever House, New York; Knickerbocker Artist Juried Exhib, New York. *Teaching:* Instr painting, Am Red Cross, White Plains, 71 & Westchester Art Workshop, 71-82; instr, Elizabeth Seton Col, Yonkers, NY; E Seton Col, Yonkers, NY, 76. *Awards:* Purchase Award, Westchester Art Workshop, 69 & Hudson River Mus, 71; First & Third Award, Mamaroneck Artist Guild, 72; First Award, Westchester Art Soc, 73 & 75. *Mem:* Art Students League; Mamaroneck Artists Guild; Abraxas Art Group; Coun Mem Katonah Mus Katonah, NY. *Media:* Intaglio, Printing. *Publ:* Illusr, Spot Lite Mag, 5/86. *Dealer:* Sound Shore Gallery Inc Port Chester NY; Art Search New York Hastings-On-Hudson NY 10106. *Mailing Add:* 36-A E Hill Dr Somers NY 10589

ADICKES, DAVID (PRYOR)
PAINTER, SCULPTOR
b Huntsville, Tex, Jan 19, 27. *Study:* Kansas City Art Inst, 48; Sam Houston Univ, Huntsville, Tex, BS, 48; Atelier Fernand Leger, Paris, 48-50. *Work:* Houston Mus Fine Art, Tex; Pa Acad Fine Art, Philadelphia; James A Michener Found Mus, Univ Tex, Austin; Witte Mus Art, San Antonio; World Bank, New York. *Comn:* Permian Basin (tapestry), Petroleum Club, Houston, 61; Spring Trees (tapestry), Hyatt Regency Hotel, Houston, 69; Virtuoso (sculpture monument), Lyric Ctr Bldg, Houston, 83. *Exhib:* One-man shows, Mus Fine Art, Houston, 51, New Works, Witte Mus Art, San Antonio, 57 & Laguna Gloria Art Mus, Austin, 57; retrospective, Ft Worth Art Ctr, 66. *Teaching:* Instr painting, Univ Tex, Austin, 55-57. *Awards:* First Purchase Prize, Houston Artists, Contemp Arts Asn, 54; First Purchase Prize, Houston Artists Ann, Mus Fine Arts, Houston, 55; Purchase Prize, Texas Art, D D Feldman, Dallas, 57. *Bibliog:* Campbell Geeslin (auth), Adickes (monograph), James Bute Co, 57; A Cantey (auth), Adickes (monograph), 62 & James A Michener (auth), Adickes, 68, Seix y Barral, Barcelona. *Media:* Oil, Bronze. *Publ:* Illusr, El Centauro, Seix Barral, 67 & illusr, Ingenioso Caballero Don Quixote de la Mancha: Cervantes, 68. *Dealer:* Carter Art Gallery 4130 N Marshall Way Scottsdale AZ 85251. *Mailing Add:* 2409 Kingston St Houston TX 77019

ADKINS, TERRY R
SCULPTOR
b Washington, DC, May 9, 53. *Study:* Fisk Univ, BS, 75; Ill State Univ, MS (printmaking), 77 & Univ Ky, MFA (sculpture), 79. *Work:* Bank Julius Bär, Zurich, Switz; Hig Mus Art, Atlanta; Prudential Insurance Am, Newark, NJ; Washington Post Collection, Washington, DC; TimeBased Media (video archives), Amsterdam, Neth. *Exhib:* Portfolio, Va Mus Fine Arts, Richmond, 80; Experiments in Paper, Va Mus Fine Arts, Richmond, 83; Solo exhibs, Projekt Binz 39, Zurich, Switz, 86, Galerie Emmerich-Baumann, Zurich, Switz, 87, Liz Harris Gallery, Boston, Mass, 88, Galerie Andy Jilien, Zurich, Switz, 89, Miami-Dade Community Col, Fla, 90, Valencia Community Col, Orlando, Fla, 90, Anderson Gallery, Va Commonwealth Univ, Richmond, 90; Object Makers, Southeastern Ctr Contemp Art, Winston-Salem NC, 89; The Blues Aesthetic, Wash Project for Arts, DC, 89; Selections, Williams Col Mus Art, Williamstown, Mass, 89; Taking Shape, Memorial Arch, Brooklyn, NY, 90; Cadences: Icon & Abstraction in Context, New Mus Contemp Art, New York, 91. *Pos:* Artist-in-residence, Kenkeleba House, New York, 88-89, Koprod, Zurich, Switz, 89. *Awards:* Artists Fel, Sculpture, Nat Endowment Arts, 86; Künstler-Austauschs Stipendium, Binz 39, Zurich, Switz, 86. *Bibliog:* Peggy Cyphers (auth), New York in review, Arts Mag, 1/90. *Media:* Wood, Metal. *Publ:* Auth, Eagle Eyed: The Ethereal Vision of Joseph Egan (catalog), Kunstraum Muchen, Munich, Ger. *Mailing Add:* 433 W 24th St New York NY 10011

ADKISON, KATHLEEN (GEMBERLING)
PAINTER
b Beatrice, Nebr. *Study:* With Mark Tobey. *Work:* Seattle Art Mus; Seattle First Nat Bank; Bank Wash, Tacoma & Spokane; Butler Inst Am Art, Youngstown, Ohio; Cheney Cowles Mus, Spokane; Northwest Bell & Boeing, Seattle. *Exhib:* Butler Inst Am Art Ann, 61-69; World's Fair Northwest Artists, Seattle, 62 & 74; Pa Acad Fine Arts 159th Ann, 64; one-person shows, Univ Wash Mus Art, Pullman, 76, Univ Ore Mus Art, Eugene, 77 & Wash State Art Mus, Olympia, 77; Spokane World's Fair Expo 74 Northwest Art, Wash; and others. *Teaching:* Instr painting, Wash State Univ Exten, 55-67. *Awards:* Sun Carnival First Prize, El Paso Mus, 61; Dr Fuller Purchase Award, Northwest Ann, 61; Prize for Winter Retreat, Friends Am Art, 69. *Bibliog:* Twenty five years painting, Bellevue Art Mus, Wash, 81. *Media:* Oil. *Dealer:* Gordon Woodside Gallery 1101 Howell Seattle WA 98101. *Mailing Add:* 1203 Overbluff Blvd Spokane WA 99203

ADLER, LEE
PAINTER, PRINTMAKER
b New York, NY, May 22, 34. *Study:* Art Students League, 62-64; Brooklyn Mus Art Sch, 64-65; Pratt Graphics Ctr, New York, 69. *Work:* Metrop Mus Art, New York; Brit Mus, London; Whitney Mus Am Art, New York; Art Inst Chicago; Corcoran Gallery Art, Washington, DC. *Comn:* Graham Gallery, New York, 70; Book-of-the-Month Club, 73; New York Times-Quadrangle Books, 73; Hagley Mus, Wilmington, Del, 74. *Exhib:* Butler Inst Am Art, Youngstown, Ohio, 67, 68 & 77; Nat Acad Design, New York, 69; 17th Nat Print Biennial, Brooklyn Mus, 70; Print Acquisitions, Whitney Mus Art, 70; Mint Mus Art, Charlotte, NC, 78; Weatherspoon Art Gallery, Univ NC, Greensboro, 78; Aldrich Mus Contemporary Art, Ridgefield, Conn, 79; Edwin A Ulrich Mus Art, Wichita, Kans, 80; Nat Mus Art, New Delhi, 82; Mus Mod Art, Mexico City, 83; and others. *Awards:* Grumbacher Award, Jersey City Mus, 68; Purchase Award, Childe Hassam Fund Competition, 69; Federico Castellon Purchase Award, Soc Am Graphic Artists, 79. *Bibliog:* Juan Acha (auth), Lee Adler, Mexico City Mus Mod Art, 76; Jeffrey Hoffeld (auth), Lee Adler, New York, 78; Carlus Dyer (auth), Lee Adler, Arts, 10/78. *Mem:* Soc Am Graphic Artists; Audubon Artists; Allied Artists Am; Painters & Sculptors Soc NJ. *Media:* Oil, Silk Screen Printing. *Dealer:* Allan Stone Gallery 48 E 86th St New York NY 10028. *Mailing Add:* 168 Clinton St Brooklyn NY 11201

ADLER, MYRIL
PAINTER, PRINTMAKER
b Vilebsk, Byeforuss, Sept 22, 20; US citizen. *Study:* Brooklyn Mus Art Sch; Art Students League; Theatre Arts Workshop, NY, with Moi Solotaroff; Pratt Graphics Ctr. *Work:* New York Pub Libr, NY, Hudson River Mus, Yonkers, NY; Mus Mod Art, Caracas, Venezuela; Univ Calif, Berkeley; Univ RI, Providence; and others. *Comn:* 50 Years/50 Faces: 50 Year Portrait Retrospective (painting, drawing, printmaking), Fine Art Gallery, 91. *Exhib:* One-person shows, Westbroadway Gallery, New York, 72, 74 & 76, Hudson River Mus, Yonkers, 72 & 74, Katonah Mus Art Gallery, NY, 72, 76 & 80, Ossining Pub Libr, Ossining, NY, 90, & Royal Athena Gallery, New York; Contemp North American Prints, Mus Mod Art, Caracas, Venezuela, 84; Nat Juried Printmaking Exhib, Silvermine, Conn, 84; High Tech/High Touch: Computer Graphics Printmaking, Pratt Manhattan Gallery, New York, 87; Rubelle & Norman Schafer Gallery, Pratt Inst, Brooklyn, 89; Javitz Ctr, New York, 90; and others. *Pos:* Dir, Myril Adler Arts Workshop, Briarcliff Manor, New York, 56-; artist-in-residence, Pratt Graphics Ctr, New York, 82-86. *Awards:* Purchase Award, Hudson River Mus, Yonkers, NY; 100th Ann Award, Nat Asn Women Artists; Abel Silvan Mem Award for Printmaking, 83; Hortense Ferne Mem Award, 89. *Bibliog:* Norman Lalibert & Alex Mogelon (coauths), The Reinhold Book of Art Ideas, Van Nostrand Reinhold, 77; coauth, The Complete Printmaker, Ross, Romand & Ross, Free Press-Macmillan, 90; Jules Heller (auth), Encyclopedia of American Woman Artists. *Mem:* Artists Equity, New York; Nat Asn Women Artists; Abraxas Artists Group (secy, treas). *Media:* Oil; Mixed media; Intaglio etching, Monoprinting. *Publ:* Illusr, Dances of Palestine, B'Nai B'Rith Hillel Foundations, New York, 47. *Dealer:* Images Art Gallery Inc 1157 Pleasantville Rd Briarcliff Manor NY 10510. *Mailing Add:* 266 Dalmeny Rd Briarcliff Manor NY 10510

ADRIAN, BARBARA (MRS FRANKLIN TRAMUTOLA)
PAINTER, COLLECTOR
b New York, NY, July 25, 31. *Study:* Art Students League, with Reginald Marsh, 47-54; Hunter Col, 51; Columbia Univ, 52-54. *Work:* Butler Inst Am Art, Youngstown, Ohio; Univ Southern Ill, Carbondale; City Hall, San Juan, PR. *Exhib:* Butler Inst Am Art, 70; Suffolk Mus, Stony Brook, NY, 71; Whitney Mus, 75; Ranger Fund Exhib, Nat Acad Design, 81; Women in the Making of Art History, Art Students League, New York, 82; Seventh Ann Nat Invitational Drawing Exhib, Norman Eprink Gallery, Emporia State Univ, & Univ Kans; Art and the Law, five locations, 86; Nat Acad Design, 90. *Pos:* Art consult, R H Macy, New York, 60-61; Saks Fifth Ave, New York, 60; Doyle Dane & Bernbach, New York, 60. *Teaching:* Art instr painting & drawing, Art Student League, 68- *Awards:* Benjamin Altman Prize, Nat Acad Design, 68; Dorothy Haphman Ferriss Award, Pen & Brush, 83, & Walker Award, 85; Forbes Award, 1990. *Bibliog:* Lucia Salemme (auth), Painting Techniques, Comprehensive Treatise, 81; Am Artists, 9/90; Maine Bar J Cover, 9/90. *Mem:* Life mem Art Students League; Pen & Brush; Nat Acad Design, 92. *Media:* Oil. *Collection:* Reginald Marsh, John Sloan, Will Barnet, Henry Pearson, Rouault, Versalius, Goya, Martin Lewis. *Dealer:* Grete Meilman Fine Art Ltd 42 E 76th St New York NY 10021; Capricorn Galleries Washington DC 20014. *Mailing Add:* 420 E 64th St New York NY 10021

AEBI, ERNST WALTER
ILLUSTRATOR, PAINTER
b Zurich, Switz, Mar 25, 38; US citizen. *Study:* Zurich Univ, lic oec publ, 65. *Work:* Montclair Mus & Kasser Found, Montclair, NJ; Adriance Mus, Westchester, NY; Klimastation, Gais, Switz. *Comn:* Roosevelt Raceway (mural in lobby), NY Racing Comn, Long Island, 70; sculpture, Swiss Am Soc, New York, 70; sculpture, Sandoz Inc, Hanover NJ, 74. *Exhib:* New York Artists, Southampton Parrish Mus, 66; Community Art, Brooklyn Mus, 68; Contemporary Swiss Art, Prague State Mus, Czech, 69; Biennale Europeenne, Berheim-Jeune, Paris, 69; one-man show, NY Univ, 76. *Collections Arranged:* One Trillion People Falling Off the Edge of the Earth, James Yu, New York, 77. *Bibliog:* Henry J Seldis (auth), Phantasmagoria, Los Angeles Times, 66; Malcolm Preston (auth), The world of Ernst Aebi, Newsday, 70; Stuart Murray (auth), The restless artist, New York Times, 74. *Media:* Pen and Ink; Concrete. *Publ:* Illusr, New York Times & Harpers Mag, 76-79, Harvard Bus Rev & Time Mag, 77. *Dealer:* James Yu 393 W Broadway New York NY 10012. *Mailing Add:* 460 W Broadway New York NY 10012

AFSARY, CYRUS
PAINTER
b Middle East, Oct 18, 40; US citizen. *Study:* Liberal Arts Col, BA(fine arts) & BA(interior design), 70. *Comn:* Murals & portraits, MGM Grand Hotel, Las Vegas, Nev, 81. *Exhib:* C M Russell Show & Auction, C M Russell Mus, Great Falls, Mont, 84-86; Gilcrease Mus Show, Tulsa, Okla, 85; Southwest Fine Art Competition, Mus Fine Arts, Santa Fe, NMex, 85; Northwest Rendevous Show, Helena, Mont, 85-88; Nat Acad Western Art, Cowboy Hall Fame, Oklahoma City, Okla, 86-88. *Awards:* Best of Show, C M Russell Show, 85; Nat Arts Club Award Exceptional Merit, Pastel Soc Am, 86; Gold Medal in Oil, 87 & Robert Lougheed Mem Award, 88; Silver Medal in Drawing, Nat Acad Western Art; and others. *Mem:* Nat Acad Western Art Northwest Rendezvous. *Media:* Oil, Pastel. *Publ:* Southwest Art, 1/87; Art of the West, 11-12/88; Int Fine Arts Collectors Mag, 3/92. *Mailing Add:* PO Box 3217 Scottsdale AZ 85271

AGAR, EUNICE JANE
PAINTER, WRITER
b Great Barrington, Mass, May 14, 34. *Study:* Wellesley Col Mass, BA(art hist), 56; Art Students League, 57-60 & 69, study under Jean Liberte, 57-63. *Work:* Columbia-Greene Community Col, Hudson, NY. *Exhib:* One-woman shows, Le Moyne Art Ctr, Tallahassee, Fla, 66 & 91, Albany Inst Hist & Art, NY, 67, Ainilian Gallery, Washington, DC 85, 87, & 90, Windham Gallery, NY, 86 & Columbia-Greene Community Col, Hudson, NY, 88. *Collections Arranged:* Monotypes, The Painterly Print, Catskill Gallery, Catskill, NY, NY State Coun Arts, 86. *Pos:* Asst ed, Am Artist, New York, 58-60, managing ed, 60-63, writer, 80-, contrib ed, 83- *Teaching:* Instr painting, drawing & printmaking, Simon's Rock Early Col, 69-78, chmn studio arts, 74-78, chmn arts div & studio arts, 75-78. *Bibliog:* Article, Am Artist, 2/84. *Mem:* Life mem, Art Students League New York. *Media:* Oil, Casein. *Publ:* Interview articles, Am Artist. *Dealer:* Agnes Ainilian 232 7th St SE Washington DC 20003; Yvonne Rapp 2007 Frankfort Ave Louisville KY 40206. *Mailing Add:* RD 1 Box 18 Egremont Plain Rd Great Barrington MA 01230

AGEE, WILLIAM C
EDUCATOR, HISTORIAN
b New York, NY, Sept 26, 36. *Study:* Princeton Univ, AB, 60; Yale Univ, MA, 63. *Collections Arranged:* Synchromism and American Painting (auth, catalog), 65; Donald Judd (auth, catalog), 68; Modern American Painting: Toward a New Perspective (auth, catalog), 77; Patrick Henry Bruce (auth, catalog), 79; Morton Livingston Schamberg (auth, catalog), 82. *Pos:* Dir, Mus Fine Arts, Houston, 74-82; sr vis scholar, Arch Am Art, Smithsonian Inst, 83-85; ed, Stuart Davis Catalogue Raisonné, 85-; prof art hist, Hunter Col, 90- *Teaching:* Am Modernism, Hurto Col, 87 & 89. *Mem:* Am Asn Mus; Col Art Asn. *Res:* Modern American and European art. *Publ:* Auth, Ralston Crawford, Twelve Trees Press, 83; Herbert Ferber, Mus Fine Arts, Houston, 83; The Advent of Modernism, High Mus, Atlanta, 86. *Mailing Add:* 5 Dusenberry Rd Bronxville NY 10708

AGNEW, ELLEN SCHALL
MUSEUM DIRECTOR
b Pensacola, Fla, Feb 19, 58. *Study:* Randolph-Macon Woman's Col, BA(cum laude), 80; State Univ NY, Binghamton, MA(art hist), 83. *Collections Arranged:* A Celebration of Contemporary American Craft, 85; Artists on Our Wish List, 86; Prints by Our Painters, 88; Focus on Photography, 91; Jennifer Bartlett, 92. *Pos:* Asst registrar, The Chrysler Mus, Norfolk, VA, 81; Cur, Maier Mus Art, Lynchburg, VA, 84-88, dir 88- *Mem:* Southeastern Mus Conf; Am Asn Mus; Va Comn Arts (adv panel 89-90); Va Asn Mus (sec exec coun 89-90 & dir-at-large 91-92). *Publ:* Ed, Maier Mus of Art Newsletter, 84-; The Creative Spirit: A Celebration of Contemporary American Craft (exhib catalog), 85; 75 Years of American Art at Randolph-Macon Woman's College (exhib catalog), 86; The Art Collection on Tour, Randolph-Macon Woman's Col Alumnae Bull, 90; American Art: American Vision, Maier Mus Art, 90. *Mailing Add:* Randolph-Macon Woman's College Maier Museum of Art One Quinlan St Lynchburg VA 24503

AGOSTINI, PETER
SCULPTOR
b New York, NY, Feb 16, 13. *Study:* Leonardo da Vinci Sch Art, NY. *Work:* Mass Inst Technol; Univ Calif; Wadsworth Atheneum; Weatherspoon Mus, Greensboro, NC; Whitney Mus Am Art, Mus Mod Art, Geggenheim Mus & Metrop Mus Art, New York; Walker Art Ctr, Minneapolis, Minn; Hirshhorn Mus & Sculpture Garden, Washington, DC. *Comn:* World's Fair, NY State Exhib, 64-65. *Exhib:* Whitney Mus Am Art, 64, 70 & 72; Sculpture of the 60's, Los Angeles Co Mus, 67; Int Sculpture, Guggenheim Mus, 67 & Toronto, Ont, 68; Am Acad Arts & Lett Exhib, 72; Sculpture in the 70's: The Figure, Pratt Manhattan Ctr Gallery, New York, 80; Art on Paper, Weatherspoon Art Gallery, Univ NC, Greensboro, 81; Animals! Tradition and Fantasy in Animal Sculpture, Washington Sq, Washington, DC, 84; Third Biennial of Yugoslav Art, Equitable Gallery, NY, 84; one-man exhibs, New York Studio Sch, 81 & 83, Recent Sculpture, 85, Horses Make a Landscape Look More Beautiful, 86, Bernice Steinbaum Gallery, New York; Elders of the Tribe, Bernice Steinbaum Gallery & travelling (with catalog), 86-89; Old Apollo's, Bernice Steinbaum, New York, 88. *Teaching:* Lectr & summer courses, Columbia Univ, 61-66; prof art, Univ NC, Greensboro, 66-; mem staff, Wagner Col, 68. *Awards:* Longview Found Purchase Awards, 60-62; Brandeis Univ Creative Arts Award, 64; Guggenheim Fel, 66; Nat Arts Coun Award, 69. *Bibliog:* Carl Goldstein (auth), Peter Agostini's heads, Art Int, Vol 18, 1/74; Patricia Bailey (auth), Peter Agostini, Art World, Vol 7, 4/83; Grace Glueck (auth), Art: Sculptured figures of the 70s at Pratt Gallery, New York Times, 11-7-80; Lisa Phillips (auth), The Third Dimension: Sculpture of the New York School (exhib catalog), Whitney Mus Am Art, New York, 84; Michael Brenson (auth), Six sculptors of the 60s at Zabriskie, New York Times, 6/22/84. *Dealer:* Olaf Clasen Broome & Greene Sts New York NY 10012. *Mailing Add:* 47-49 Greene St New York NY 10012

AHEARN, JOHN
SCULPTOR
b Binghamton, NY, 51. *Study:* Cornell Univ, Ithaca, NY, BFA, 73. *Work:* Australian Nat Gallery, Canberra; Metrop Mus, New York; Wallrat-Richartz Mus, Mus Ludwig, Cologne; Lannan Found, Lake Worth, Fla; Eli Broad Family Found, Los Angeles; Greenville County Art Mus. *Exhib:* One-man exhibs, South Bronx Hall of Fame, Fashion Moda, New York, 79, Galerie Rudolf Zwirner, Cologne, 83, Brooke Alexander Inc, New York, 84, 85, 86 & 88, Portraits from the Bronx: Life Casts from 1979 to Present, Bronx Mus, NY, 85 & The Nelson-Atkins Mus Art, Kansas City, MO, 90; After Street Art, Boca Raton Mus Art, 88; The Future Now, Bass Mus Art, Miami, 89; Personae: Contemporary Portraiture & Self-Portraiture, Islip Art Mus, NY, 89; The Blues Aesthetic: Black Culture-Modernism, Traveling, 89. *Awards:* Sculpture Fel, 80 & Art in Pub Places, 82, Nat Endowment Arts; Block Grant, Housing & Urban Development, 81. *Bibliog:* Brigitte Engler (auth), Behind

the Mask, Paper, 11/89; Jonathan Phillips (auth), Ahearn at Alexander, Art World, 89; Robert C Morgan (auth), John Ahearn, Arts, 1/89; Suzanne Muchnic (auth), Family Puts Art on a Firm Foundation, Los Angeles Times, 12/5/89. *Mailing Add:* c/o Brook Alexander Inc 59 Wooster St New York NY 10012

AHL, HENRY C
PAINTER, WRITER
b Springfield, Mass. *Study:* Harvard Col, with Arthur Pope & Martin Mower, AB; also with Henry Hammond Ahl. *Work:* Walker Gallery, Bowdoin Col; Farnsworth Mus, Rockland, Maine; Mus Art, Hickory, NC; Ga State Mus, Athens; Vanderpoel Art Collection, Beverly Hills-Chicago, Ill; plus others. *Mem:* Tommaso Camponella Int Acad Arts & Sci; NShore Arts Asn. *Media:* Oil. *Publ:* Auth & illusr, Dunes & Beaches of Essex County, Some Common Insects of Massachusetts, A Visit to Orchard House, A Visit to the Old Manse, Edgar Allan Poe; and others. *Mailing Add:* 24 Batchelder Seabrook NH 03874

AHLANDER, LESLIE JUDD
CRITIC, CONSULTANT
b New York, NY. *Study:* Acad Mod, Paris, with Fernand Leger; Pa Acad Fine Arts, with Henry MacCarter, dipl. *Collections Arranged:* Contemporary Religious Imagery (with catalog), 74; Syd Solomon (with catalog), 75; Doris Leeper (with catalog), 75; Continuing Surrealism (with catalog), 76; Latin Am Horizons (with catalog), 76; The Circus in Art (with catalog), 77; Haitian Art (with catalog), 86. *Pos:* Asst to dir, Mus Mod Art, New York, 41-43; dir exhibs, US Off Educ, Washington, DC, 43-44; chief div visual arts, Pan-Am Union, Washington, DC, 44-45; art critic, Washington Post, Washington, DC, 50-63; cur educ, Corcoran Gallery, Washington, DC, 69-70; from dir educ to cur contemp art, John & Mabel Ringling Mus Art, Sarasota, Fla, 71-78; art coordr, Dade Co, Miami, Fla, 78-83; art critic, Miami News, 83-88; Arte en Colombia, Art Nexus, Art News, 88- *Awards:* Cresson Traveling Scholar, Pa Acad Fine Arts, Philadelphia, 38; Art Critics Award, Col Art Asn Am, 52 & 53. *Publ:* Auth, Lynn Gelfman, 85, Trevor Bell, 86 & Hal Kaye, 86; Six Cuban painters, 85; Connie Lloveras (auth), Cuba-USA - The First Generation, 90. *Mailing Add:* 1111 N Gulfstream Ave No F8 Sarasota FL 34236

AHLGREN, ROY B
PAINTER, PRINTMAKER
b Erie, Pa, July 6, 27. *Study:* Erie Tech Sch; Univ Pittsburgh, BS Ed. *Work:* US Info Agency, Washington, DC; Minn Mus Art, St Paul; Gornoslaskie Mus, Krakow, Poland; Kanagawa Prefectural Gallery, Yokahama, Japan; Butler Art Inst, Youngstown, Ohio; Mus Wroclaw & Silesia, Poland, 86; Mus Contemp Art, Fredrikstad, Norway; and others. *Comn:* Ed of serigraphs, Assoc Am Artists, New York, 70; Int Art Guild, Santa Barvara, 74; serigraphs (54), WQLN, public TV stations, 79. *Exhib:* 21st Nat Exhib Prints, Libr Cong, Washington, DC, 69; 7th, 8th, 10th, 11th & 12th Int Print Biennale, Krakow, Poland; Intergrafia, Katowice, Poland, 78, 80, 84, 86 & 88; Int Exhib Graphic Art, Frechen, Ger, 80; Tokyo Met Mus Art, 85; Norwegian Int Print Biennale, 86; and others. *Pos:* Assoc, Galerie 8, Erie, 67-75; bd mem, Erie Art Ctr, 70-72. *Teaching:* Instr art, Tech Mem High Sch, Erie, 70-90; asst prof printmaking, Edinboro State Col, 74; artist-in-residence, Hope Col, Holland, Mich, 78; Seventh Ann Spring Conf Southern Graphics Coun, Univ Auburn, Ala, 80. *Awards:* Purchase Award, Drawings, USA, Minn Mus Art, St Paul, 70 & 73; Merit Award, 4th Miami Int Graphic, Biennial, Miami, Fla, 80; Prize Winner, Norwegian Int Print Biennale, 86; and others. *Bibliog:* Jane Abrams (auth), Educational slide collection, Univ NMex, 71; Lynwood Kreneck (auth), Colorprint USA filmstrip, Tex Tech Univ, 71; Joseph Cain (auth), Corpus Christi, Tex, Iman show, 73. *Mem:* Boston Printmakers; Northwest Pa Artists Asn; Erie Art Ctr; The Pa Soc; Albright-Knox, Buffalo, NY. *Media:* Acrylic; Serigraphy. *Dealer:* Benjaman Gallerie Buffalo NY 14222; Concept Art Gallery Pittsburgh PA. *Mailing Add:* 1012 Boyer Rd Erie PA 16511

AHLSTED, DAVID R
PAINTER, EDUCATOR
b Minneapolis, Minn, 43. *Study:* Minneapolis Col Art, BFA, 65; Indiana Univ, MFA, 68. *Work:* Whitney Mus Am Art, Mus Mod Art, New York; Aldrich Mus Contemp Art, Ridgefield, Conn; Pepsico Inc, Purchase, NY; State Univ NY, Cortland, NY. *Exhib:* Solo Exhibs, Hawthorn Gallery, Skidmore Col, Saratoga, NY, 71, Art Gallery, State Univ NY, Cortland, 75, SoHo Ctr Visual Arts, New York, 76, Art Gallery, Stockton State Col, Pomona, NJ, 84, Marian Locks Gallery, Philadelphia, Pa, 86 & 89 & Perlow Gallery, New York, 92; David Ahlsted, Art Gallery, State Univ Cortland, NY, 75; Contemporary Reflections, Aldrich Mus Art, Ridgefield, Conn, 76; David Ahlsted, SoHo Ctr Visual Arts, New York, 76; David Ahlsted, Art Gallery, Stockton State Col, Pomona, NJ, 84; Nature Morte, Southern Alleghenies Mus Art, Loretto, Pa, 86; David Ahlsted, Marian Locks Gallery, Philadelphia, PA, 86, 89; Fel Exhib, Morris Mus, Morristown, NJ, 87; Philadelphia Mus Art, Pa, 90. *Teaching:* Asst prof painting, Skidmore Col, 69-75; assoc prof painting, State Univ NY, Cortland, 75-76; prof painting, Stockton State Col, 76- *Awards:* Painting Fel, NJ State Coun Arts, 81 & 85. *Bibliog:* Corinna Smith (auth), David Ahlsted, SoHo Weekly News, 76; Anne Fabbri (auth), Celebration of NJ Artists The NOYES Mus Art, 83; Anne d'Harnoncourt (auth), Contemp Philadelphia Artists, Philadelphia Mus Art. *Media:* Oil on Linen, Pastel on Paper. *Dealer:* Katharina Rich Perlow Gallery 560 Broadway New York NY 10012. *Mailing Add:* 842 Clarks Landing Rd Egg Harbor NJ 08215

AHLSTROM, RONALD GUSTIN
COLLAGE ARTIST, PAINTER
b Chicago, Ill, Jan 17, 22. *Study:* Art Inst Chicago, BFA, with Paul Weighart; Univ Chicago; DePaul Univ. *Work:* Art Inst Chicago, Blue Cross Collection & Ill Bell Telephone, Chicago; Tacoma Art Mus, Wash; Philbrook Art Ctr, Tulsa. *Exhib:* 27th Corcoran Biennial, Washington, DC, 61; Chicago & Vicinity Exhib, Art Inst Chicago, 62; 12 Chicago Artists, McCormick Pl Gallery, 62; 50th Northwest Ann, Seattle Art Mus, 64; 6 American Artists, Touchstone Gallery, New York, 73; Zriny-Hayes Gallery, Chicago, 78; Collection Container Corp, Smithsonian Inst, Washington, DC, 88. *Pos:* Asst Dir, McCormick Place Art Gallery, Chicago; dir, Tacoma Art Mus, Wash. *Awards:* Clyde Carr Prize, 55 & William H Bartels Prize, 58, Art Inst Chicago; Purchase Prize, 50th Northwest Ann, Ford Found, 64. *Bibliog:* Meilach & Ten Hoor (auth), Collage and Found Art, 64 & Collage, Trends and Technique, 73, Reinholt Publ; Gerald F Brommer (auth), The Art of Collage, Davis Publ, 78. *Media:* Collage & Acrylic; Mixed Media. *Mailing Add:* 121 W Park St Lombard IL 60148

AHN, DON C
PAINTER, ART DEALER
b Seoul, Korea, Jan 9, 37. *Study:* Art Students League; Miami Univ; Seoul Univ, BFA; Pratt Inst, MFA; NY Univ. *Work:* Mus Mod Art, New York; Dayton Mus Art, Ohio; Evansville Mus, Ind; C W Post Col, Long Island Univ. *Exhib:* Ohio Regional Show, Dayton, 63; one-man shows, Dayton Mus, 63 & Downey Mus, Los Angeles, 69; Int Print Biennale, Grenchen, Switz, 67 & Mus Mod Art, Tokyo, 71. *Pos:* Art dir, Korea Today, 61; dir, Ahn Tai Chi Studio, New York, 70-; adj instr, Dance Dept, Hunter Col, 74; dir, Lotus Gallery, New York, 74-87; dir, Don Ahn Gallery, 87- *Teaching:* Instr print, C W Post Col, Long Island Univ, 64-68; asst prof painting, NY Inst Technol, 65-77; instr painting, Cooper Union, 66-71. *Awards:* First Prize for Painting, Ohio Regional Show, 63; McDowell Asn Fel, 64; First Prize for Print, E Coast Printer, Village Art Ctr, 64. *Bibliog:* John Canaday (auth), Drawings, New York Times, 12/11/71; Barbara Schwarts (auth), article, Art News, 12/71; Alvin Smith (auth), article, Art Int, 12/72. *Mem:* Col Art Asn Am. *Specialty:* Contemporary art done by minority Asian artists in the US. *Interests:* Promote arts which synthesize Western visual formality with Eastern spirituality. *Collection:* Indian; Far Eastern religious sculpture and painting; Chinese; Japanese; Korean; Tibetan; contemporary Asian artists in New York. *Mailing Add:* 81 Spring St New York NY 10012

AHRENDT, CHRISTINE
PAINTER
b Dayton, Ohio. *Study:* Fla State Univ; Ohio Univ; Provincetown Workshop, with Ben Shahn, Will Barnet, Victor Candell & Leo Manso. *Exhib:* Columbus Gallery Fine Arts, Ohio, 61-65, 69 & 70; Provincetown Art Asn Summer Shows, 62-72; Pa Acad Fine Arts, Philadelphia, 64; Butler Inst Am Art Midyear Show, Youngstown, Ohio, 65 & 74; one-man show, E Coast Gallery, Provincetown, 69; Salute the Women, Butler Inst Am Art, 75. *Awards:* Huntington Galleries Awards, WVa, 62-66; MacDowell Colony Fel, 65, 66 & 71; S M Levy Mem Award, Columbus Art League, 69. *Media:* Mixed. *Dealer:* Gallery 200 200 W Mound Columbus OH 43215. *Mailing Add:* 5 Old Peach Ridge Rd Athens OH 45701

AHRENDT, MARY E
CONCEPTUAL ARTIST
b Chicago, Ill, Oct 19, 40. *Study:* Univ Ill, Chicago, BA(scuplture hons), 78; Art Inst Chicago, Ill, MFA(painting & performance), 80. *Work:* Mus Contemp Art, Chicago, Ill. *Exhib:* Seven Artists, 81 & Alternative Spaces, 84, Mus Contemp Art, Chicago, Ill; Sculpture Today, 1982, Indianapolis Mus Art, Ind; Recent Color, San Francisco Mus Mod Art, Calif, 82; Construction Works, Inst Contemp Art, Va Mus, Richmond, 84; Drawings, Chicago & Vicinity, Art Inst Chicago, Ill, 85; Self-Portraits by Women Artists, Collage Arts Asn, Los Angeles, Calif, 85; Nude, Naked Stripped, Albert & Vera List Visual Ctr, Mass Inst Technol, Boston, 86; Images for Human Conduct (catalog), Mus Contemp Art, Chicago, 86, First Person Singular: Self-Portrait Photography (catalog), High Mus Art, Atlanta, 88, Toward the Future: Contemporary Art in Context (catalog), Mus Contemp Art, Chicago, 90. *Pos:* Bd mem, Artemisia Gallery, 78-79 & NAME Gallery, 81-86, Chicago, Ill. *Teaching:* Vis artist painting, Univ Ind, Terre Haute, 83 & Univ Ill, Champaign, 85; vis artist painting & photogr, Minneapolis Col Art & Design, Minn, 83. *Awards:* Ill Artists Grant, 83-87. *Bibliog:* David Elliott (auth), Chicago enjoys it's own eclecticism, Art News, 5/82; Catherine Reeve (auth), The New Photography, Prentice-Hall, 83; Alan G Artner (auth), Arts, Chicago Tribune, 6/15/84. *Media:* Photography, Film. *Dealer:* Ehlers Caudill Gallery Ltd 750 N Orleans Chicago IL 60610. *Mailing Add:* 5424 Main St Skokie IL 60076

AHRENS, HANNO D
SCULPTOR
b Ft Worth, Tex, 54. *Exhib:* One-man shows, Santa Cruz Art Ctr, 77, Dan McHenrey Libr, Santa Cruz, 79 & Deborah Sharpe Gallery, New York 87 & 88; Univ Art Gallery, Albany, 89; Farnesworth Mus, Rockport, Maine, 90; David Beitzel Gallery, New York, 90; two-person show, Frumkin/Adams Gallery, New York, 91. *Awards:* Pollock-Krasner Found Grant, 86 & 91; Nat Endowment Arts Grant, 86 & 90; New York Found Arts Grant, 89. *Bibliog:* Corrine Robbins (auth), Hanno Ahrens, Sculpture, 7-8/88; Dan Rubey, Hanno Ahrens, Studio, 2/89; AFC, Mass appeal, Vanity Fair, 1/90. *Dealer:* Frumkin/Adams Gallery 50 W 57th St New York NY 10019. *Mailing Add:* 285 Hudson St New York NY 10013

AHRENS, KENT
MUSEUM DIRECTOR, HISTORIAN
b Martinsburg, WVa. *Study:* Dartmouth Col, AB, 61; Univ Md, MA, 66; Univ Del, PhD, 72. *Collections Arranged:* Paintings from the Netherlands and German Speaking Countries, Wadsworth Atheneum, 78; The Drawings and Watercolors by Truman Seymour (1824-1891) (auth, catalog), Everhart, 86; Frederic C Knight (1898-1979), Everhart, 87; Edward D Boit (auth, catalog), Oil & Watercolors, Everhart, 90. *Pos:* Assoc cur paintings, Wadsworth Atheneum, 77-78; dir, Everhart Mus, 82-90 & Rockwell Mus, 90- *Teaching:* Fac mem, Fla State Univ, 71-74 & Georgetown Univ, 79-82; fac mem & cur, Randolph-Macon Womans Col, 74-77. *Awards:* Kress Fel, 68 & Dale Fel, 70, Nat Gallery Art. *Mem:* Mus Asn Pa (chmn, 84-90); Williamstown Regional Art Conserv Lab Inc (trustee, 84-92); Mus West (bd dirs, 90-). *Res:* American art. *Publ:* Auth, The portraits by Robert W Weir, 74 & Henry R Newman (1843-1917), 76, Am Art J; Constantino Brumidi's Apotheosis of Washington, 76 & Nineteenth Century History Painting in the United States Capitol, 80, Rec Columbia Hist Soc; American paintings before 1900 at the Wadsworth Atheneum, Antiques, 78; Jennie Brownscombe, 81 & Priscilla Longshore Garrett, 85, Womans Art J; Peter F Rothermel, Pa Heritage, 92. *Mailing Add:* Rockwell Mus Cedar St at Denison Pkwy Corning NY 14830

AHYSEN, HARRY JOSEPH
PAINTER, MURALIST
b Port Arthur, Tex, Sept 6, 28. *Study:* Tulane Univ; Univ Houston, BFA, 55; Univ Tex, Austin, MFA, 62. *Work:* Gulf Oil Corp, Dallas; M Grumbacher, New York; Jacques Costeau Mus, Monte Carlo, Monaco; Univ Houston; over 150 pvt collections; City of Hunstville mural, Texaco Inc, New York; Brownsville Mus; Beaumont Mus; Galveston Mus; Tex Artists Mus; West Palm Beach Mus; Zanesville Mus, Ohio. *Comn:* Fifteen paintings & watercolors, Banker's Land Co. West Palm Beach, Fla, 83; sculpture, Boca Raton, Fla, 84; Pelican, Point Jupiter, Fla, 84; four murals, Casa Thomas, Tex, 85-86; ten paintings, Methodist Hosp Houston; mural 16' x 30', Washington Court House, Ohio, 92. *Exhib:* First Nat Bank, Huntsville, 82; Odessa Oil Field Show, 82; All State Artists Show, Senate Chambers, Austin, 82; Tex Artists Mus Soc, Port Arthur, 82; Brazos Valley Art League Show, Bryan, 83; one-man shows, The Drawing Room, Houston, Hearnwood Gallery, Hearne, Honorarium, Texas A & M at Galveston & Allen Acad, Bryan, 85, Tex; Zanesville Mus, Ohio, 88; and 104 others. *Pos:* Bd dirs, Tex Artist Mus. *Teaching:* From asst prof to prof oil painting & watercolor, Sam Houston State Univ, 63-; lectr, Univ Houston, 65 & Univ Tex, 85. *Awards:* State Artist of Tex, State Legislature, 80-81; First Place Watercolor, 11th Int Show Brownsville Art League Mus, 82; Hon Mention, Brazos Valley Art Asn Show, Bryan, 83; Italian "Oscar" of Italia, Accade Mia Italia, Italy, 85; and others. *Mem:* Nat Soc Marine Painters, 92; Leesberg Art Guild. *Media:* Oil, Watercolor. *Publ:* Auth, Sketch Workbook: Landscape and Seascape Devices, Kendall Hunt Publ, 78; auth, article, Palette Talk, No 52. *Mailing Add:* Dept of Art Sam Houston State Univ Huntsville TX 77340

AIGNER, LUCIEN
PHOTOGRAPHER, LECTURER
b Nove Zamky, Czech, Sept 14, 01; US citizen. *Study:* Univ Berlin, 20; Univ Budapest, 23; Sorbonne, 30; Columbia Univ; Winona Sch Photog, cert, 56; NY Univ, dipl(movie making), 68; Prof Photogr Am, MA(photog), 71. *Work:* Metrop Mus Art & Mus Mod Art, New York; Int Mus Photog, Rochester, NY; Libr Cong; Bibliot Nat, Paris; Mus Mod Art, Stockholm; Kunsthaus, Zurich. *Comn:* Einstein Mural, Smithsonian Inst, 79. *Exhib:* Solo exhibs, Forty Years of Candid Camera, Prof Photogr Am Convention, Denver, 79 & Mus Mod Art, Stockholm, 82; Paris des annees 30s, Carnavalet, Paris, 81; Glimpses of History from Two Worlds, Addison Gallery Am Art, 82; Glimpses of History, Nagase Photo Salon, Tokyo, 82; retrospective, Nat Gallery, Budapest, 82; and many others. *Teaching:* Instr photo wkshp, Brandeis Univ, 73. *Awards:* Leica Award, Third Ann Leica Show, 36; New York Art Directors Award, 41; First Prizes & Courts Hon, Prof Photog Asns New England & Conn, 58-76; Chevalier, Fr Order Arts & Letts; Master Photog, Prof Photog Am. *Bibliog:* C R Wasserman (auth), Aigner's 100,000 photos, Boston Globe, 4/16/72; Al Coleman (auth), Master of the picture story, 3/25/73 & Gene Thorton (auth), Remembrance of Paris Past, 80, New York Times. *Mem:* Life mem Prof Photogr Am. *Publ:* Coauth, Are We to Disarm, Art Suisse, 32; illusr, What Prayers Can Do, Doubleday, 53; photo commentator, Windows of Heaven, Harper Brothers, 54. *Mailing Add:* 15 Dresser Ave Great Barrington MA 01230

AIKEN, WILLIAM A
PAINTER
b Pittsburgh, Pa, May 26, 34. *Study:* Carnegie-Mellon Univ, BFA, 55. *Work:* City of San Francisco & Embarcadero Ctr, Calif; Carnegie Mellon Univ; ABC, Washington, DC; Univ Santa Clara, Calif; Delaware Mus of Art, Wilmington, Del. *Comn:* Oil painting, Shaklee Corp, Emeryville, Calif, 74. *Exhib:* Paintings, USA, Mus Mod Art, New York, 61; Allied Artists Am, Nat Acad, New York, 74, 80 & 82; 39th Ann Midyear Show, Butler Inst Am Art, Youngstown, Ohio, 75; Sun Carnival Nat Art Exhib, El Paso Mus Art, Tex, 77; one-man show, San Francisco Art Comn Gallery, 78; The New Realists, Mongerson Gallery, Chicago, 82; Nature Interpreted, Cincinnati Mus Nat Hist, 82; and others. *Awards:* Purchase Awards, City of San Francisco, 61, 63 & 78 & Univ Santa Clara, 67; One-Man Show Award, San Francisco Art Comn, 78; Charles F Romans Award for Oil Painting, Allied Artists Am Ann Exhib, 80. *Bibliog:* Paul Perry (auth), View from the rorshach canvas, Southwest Art, 12/77. *Mem:* Allied Artists of Am; Artists Equity. *Media:* Oil Paint; Oil Glaze. *Dealer:* Alma Gilbert Gallery 1419 Burlingame Ave Burlingame CA 94010; Water Street Gallery Saugatuck Michigan. *Mailing Add:* 1587 35th Ave San Francisco CA 94122

AISTARS, JOHN
PAINTER, EDUCATOR
b Riga, Latvia, Jun 9, 38; US citizen. *Study:* Sch Art Inst Chicago, BFA, 61; Syracuse Univ, MFA, 65. *Work:* Syracuse Univ, Marine Midland Bank & Crouse-Irving Hosp, Syracuse, NY; Ohio Dominican Col, Columbus; First City Nat Bank, Binghamton, NY. *Exhib:* Sch Art Inst Chicago, Ill, 57, 59, 60 & 61; Everson Regional Exhib, Everson Mus, Syracuse, 66; Regional Exhib, Mem Art Gallery, Rochester, NY, Munson-Williams-Proctor Inst, Utica, NY, Robeson Ctr Arts & Sci, Binghamton, NY; Cooperstown Nat, Cooperstown Art Asn, NY. *Collections Arranged:* Various exhibs for Chapman Art Ctr Gallery, Cazenovia Col. *Pos:* Dir, Chapman Art Ctr Gallery, Cazenovia Col. *Teaching:* Grad asst color & lettering, Syracuse Univ, 64-65; prof painting & drawing, Cazenovia Col, NY, 65-90. *Awards:* First City National Award, Susquehanna Regional, 75; First Prize, Central NY Regional Exhib, 89; M Bevier Prize, Cooperstown National, 89. *Bibliog:* Articles in numerous publications. *Mem:* Cooperstown Art Asn. *Media:* Oil. *Publ:* Auth & illusr of 40 articles, Laiks, Brooklyn, 81-90. *Dealer:* Steuben Park Gallery 25 Hopper St Utica NY 13501. *Mailing Add:* Oran Delphi Rd Manlius NY 13104

AJAY, ABE
PAINTER, SCULPTOR
b Altoona, Pa, Mar 24, 19. *Study:* Art Students League; Am Artists Sch. *Work:* Solomon R Guggenheim Mus, New York; Hirshhorn Mus, Washington, DC; Roy R Neuberger Mus, State Univ NY, Purchase; Pa Acad of the Fine Arts, Philadelphia; Johnson Mus Art, Cornell Univ. *Exhib:* White on White, De Cordova Mus, Lincoln, Mass, 65; Pa Acad of Fine Arts Ann, Philadelphia, 68; Flint Inst of Art, 69; A Plastic Presence, Jewish Mus, New York, Milwaukee Art Ctr & San Francisco Mus of Art, 69; Storm King Art Ctr, Mountainville, NY, 72; Roy R Neuberger Mus, 74; Elaine Benson Gallery, Bridgehampton, NY, 78; Aldrich Mus Contemp Art, Ridgefield, Conn, 90. *Teaching:* Vis artist painting, Univ Minn, Duluth, 69-70; prof visual arts, State Univ NY, Purchase, 73- *Bibliog:* Irving Sandler (auth), The Poetic Constructivism of Abe Ajay, Arts Mag, 77; Burt Chernow (auth), Abe Ajay, Arts Mag, 12/78; Cathy Silver (auth), Abe Ajay, Arts Mag, 5/82; Lee Hall (auth), Abe Ajay, Illustrated Biography, U of Wash Press, 90. *Media:* Acrylic; Plaster, Wood. *Publ:* Auth, The prize, 71, Working for the WPA, 72 & Rev of the New Deal art projects & Art for the millions, by Francis V O'Connor, 72, Art Am. *Mailing Add:* Walnut Hill Rd Bethel CT 06801

AKAMU, NINA
SCULPTOR
b Midwest City, Okla, July 11, 55. *Study:* Md Inst Col Art, BFA, 76. *Work:* Jane Voorhess Zimmerli Mus, Rutgers Univ, NJ. *Comn:* Bas relief (bronze), Soc Prevention of Cruelty to Animals, Washington DC, 80. *Exhib:* Game Conserv Int, San Antonio, Tex, 80; Soc Animal Artists, New York, 81-86; Allied Artists Am, 82, 84 & 86; Nat Acad, New York, 82 & 86; Nat Sculpture Soc Ann, New York, 82-86. *Awards:* Nat Sculpture Soc Award, 82-84 & 86; Allied Artists Award, 82 & 85; Pen & Brush Awards, 83 & 84; Joyce & Elliot Liskin Purchase Award, Nat Sculpture Soc, 83; Mint Award, Soc Animal Artists, 85. *Mem:* Soc Animal Artists; Nat Sculpture Soc; Allied Artists Am; Pen & Brush Artists. *Media:* Bronze, Marble. *Dealer:* Grand Central Art Galleries 24 W 57th St New York NY 10019; King Gallery 136 E 74th St New York NY 10021. *Mailing Add:* c/o Venable Neslage Galleries 1803 Connecticut Ave NW Washington DC 20009

AKAWIE, THOMAS FRANK
EDUCATOR, PAINTER
b New York, NY, Feb 22, 35. *Study:* Los Angeles City Col, 53-56; Univ Calif, Berkeley, BA(art hist), 59, MA(painting), 63. *Work:* Milwaukee Art Ctr, Wis; Ithaca Col Art Mus, NY; Oakland Mus, Calif; Williams Col Mus, Williamstown, Mass. *Exhib:* One-man shows, La Jolla Mus Art, Calif, 67, Calif Palace Legion Hon, San Francisco, 72 & San Jose Mus Art, Calif, 77; Ann Exhib, Whitney Mus Am Art, New York, 69; Painting & Sculpture in Calif, San Francisco Mus Mod Art, 76 & Nat Collection Fine Arts, Smithsonian Inst, Washington, DC, 77; 4th Triennale-India 78 Inc, Thailand & Iran, 78; Calif Visionary Painting, Japan, 78; and others. *Teaching:* Asst prof painting & drawing, Univ Calif, Los Angeles, 65-66; lectr painting & drawing, Univ Calif, Berkeley, 72-73; instr spray-painting & drawing, San Francisco Art Inst, 66- *Awards:* Los Angeles All-City Exhib Award, City of Los Angeles, Calif, 65; First Prize, Ann Downey Mus Invitational, Calif, 66; First Prize, Jack London Art Exhib, Oakland, Calif, 69. *Bibliog:* Charles Shere & John Coney (auths), Art of Tom Akawie, KQED-TV, 71. *Media:* Acrylic. *Publ:* Contribr, Visions, Pomegranate Publ, 77. *Dealer:* Gallery K 2032 P St NW Washington DC 20036. *Mailing Add:* 1740 University Ave Berkeley CA 94703

AKE, JOHN
SCULPTOR
b Akron, Ohio. *Study:* Kenyon Col; Pa Military Col, BA, 43. *Work:* pvt and corporate collections. *Exhib:* Whirlpool Found Nat Tour, 87-88; Art Expo, Los Angeles, 89; Allied Artists of Am, New York, 90; Art Expo, New York, 90; Sculpture in the Park Ann, Loveland, Colo, 91; Nat Sculpture Soc Ann, New York, 92. *Bibliog:* Art News, 12/87 & 3/88; Art Business News, 3/90 & 4/90; The Art of Ballet, Ft Lauderdale Mag, 1/92. *Mem:* Natl Sculpture Soc. *Media:* Bronze. *Dealer:* DeLigney Gallery 709 Las Olas Blvd Ft Lauderdale FL 33316. *Mailing Add:* 1700 SE 15th St, #105 Ft Lauderdale FL 33316

AKERS, ADELA
WEAVER, CRAFTSMAN
b Santiago de Compostela, Spain, 1933. *Study:* Univ Havana, 55; Sch Art Inst Chicago, 57-60; Cranbrook Acad Art, 60,-61 & 62-63. *Work:* W B Saunders Publs, Philadelphia, Pa; Sumitono Bank, New York; Manchester Community Col, Conn; Olympia-York, Toronto, Ont; Chase Manhattan Bank, New York. *Exhib:* Solo exhibs, Bloomsburg State Col, Pa, 77, Fiberworks Gallery, Berkeley, Calif, 80, Triangle Gallery, San Francisco, 81, Mandell Gallery, Los Angeles, 81, Modern Master Tapestries, New York, 84, Pa Acad Fine Arts, Philadelphia, 86 & Patrick King Contemp Art, Indianapolis, Ind, 87; Multiplicity in Clay-Metal-Fiber, Skidmore Col, Saratoga Springs, NY, 84; Inaugural Exhib, Am Crafts Mus, New York, 86; Fiber: The Next Generation, Ill State Univ, Normal, 87; Maple Hill Gallery, Portland, Maine, 88. *Pos:* Lectr, Ctr for Textile Arts, Berkeley, Calif, 84, NC Weaver's Guild, Charlotte, 86, Philadelphis Textile Soc, Pa, 86, Philadelphia Weaver's Guild, Pa, 88; designer for Oaxaca Loom, cottage industry in Diaz Ordas, Oaxaca, Mex, 87; Seminar leader, Nat Conference Handweaver's Guild of Am, Chicago, 88. *Teaching:* Inst, crafts prog, City of Chicago, 65-67; Penland Sch Crafts, NC, summers 68, 69, & 70; New Sch Social Res, 70-71; Cooper Square Art Ctr, New York, 71; San Francisco State Univ, 81; prof, Tyler Sch Art, Temple Univ, Philadelphia, Pa, 72- *Awards:* Artist in Residence Penland Sch, 69 & 71, Craftsman's Fel, 74 & 80, Nat Endowment Arts; NJ State Coun Arts Grants, 71; Research Grants, Temple Univ, 75, 79, 84 & 88; Pa Coun Arts Grants, 83. *Bibliog:* Articles in Crafts Horizons Mag, 2/77 & Fiberarts Mag, 3/4/81. *Mailing Add:* c/o Helen Drutt Gallery 1721 Walnut St Philadelphia PA 19103

AKERS, GARY
PAINTER
b Pikeville, Ky, Feb 22, 51. *Study:* Morehead State Univ, BA, 72, MA, 74; 1 yr grant from Greenshields Found, Montreal, Can. *Work:* Boone Co Pub Libr & Art Gallery & St Luke Hosp, Florence, Ky; Mus Art Ogunquit, Maine; Ky Fried Chicken Corp, Louisville,Ky; Coca Cola Bottling Co, Zaring Nat Corp, Cincinnati Financial Corp & Proctor & Gamble Corp, Cincinnati, Ohio; USF&G Co, Baltimore, Md; Morehead State Univ, Ky. *Comn:* Seltman Home, Florence, Ky, 78; Boone Co Exten Agent 4-H, Burlington, Ky, 80; Betsy Layne Boosters Club, Ky, 81; White Elephant Gallery, Flemingsburg, Ky, 82. *Exhib:* Ky Watercolor Soc, 78, 81, 83, & 85; Southern Watercolor Soc, 79, 83, & 84; Am Watercolor Soc, New York, 79, 82, 84-86; Allied Artists Am, Nat Arts Club, New York, 81 & 82; Ky Watercolor Invitational, Owensboro Mus Fine Art, 85; Gary Akers: Country Life, Asheville Art Mus, NC, 86; Ky Art Exhib, J B Speed Art Mus, Louisville, Ky, 86. *Awards:* Friends Ky Watercolor Soc Award, 78; Dale Meyers Cooper Medal Honor, Southern Watercolor Soc Award, 83, Lee Printing Co Award, 84; Top Merit Award, Aqueous, Ky Watercolor Soc, 83, Ky Artist Award, Ky WC Soc, 85; Mario Cooper Award, Am Watercolor Soc, 84. *Bibliog:* Bill R Booth (auth), Painting: border brothers farm, Am Artist, 82 & Pages from a passing scene, Southwest Art, 82; The Artist's Mag, 10/84 & 2/88; US Art, July-Aug, 89. *Mem:* Ky Watercolor Soc; Am Watercolor Soc; Southern Watercolor Soc. *Media:* Egg Tempera, Watercolor. *Publ:* Auth, Building clear images in egg tempera, cover story, The Artist's Mag, 84; A New Spirit of Watercolor, N Light Bks, 89; Watercolor 90, An Am Artist Publ; The Creative Artist, N Light Bks, 90; Being an Artist, N Light Bks, 92. *Dealer:* Gary-Lynn Galleries 10100 Meiman Dr Union Ky 41091. *Mailing Add:* PO Box 100 Union KY 41091

AKIN, GWEN
PHOTOGRAPHER
b New York, NY, July 26, 50. *Study:* Boston Mus Sch; Tufts Univ. *Work:* San Francisco Mus Mod Art; Mus Photogr Arts, San Diego; Ctr Creative Photog, Tuscon, Ariz; Shadai Gallery, Tokyo Inst Tech; Los Angeles Co Mus Art; Mus Fine Arts, Houston, Tex; Espace Photographique de Paris. *Exhib:* Solo exhibs, Shaidai Gallery, Tokyo, Japan, 87, Faridert Cadot Gallery, New York, 88, XYZ Gallery, Ghent Belg, 89 & Northern Light Gallery, Ariz State Univ, Tempe, 90; Natural History & Formaldehyde Photog, Musee Zoologique de l'Univ Louis Pasteur, Strasbourg, France, 90; Photog: 1980's: Discovery & Invention, Art 21-90, Basel, Switz, 90; Insect Politics, Hallwalls, Buffalo, NY, 90; Natural Hist & Formaldehyde Photog, Natur Mus Senckenberg Forschungsinstitut, Frankfort, Ger, 91; Pamela Auchin Closs Gallery, New York, 92; and others. *Awards:* Materials grant, Polaroid Corp, 86 & 87; Materials grant, Agfa Corp, 90; Nat Endowment Arts, 91; and others. *Bibliog:* Newspaper article in De Cenbenaar, Ghent, Belg, 5/5/89; Kate McQuaid (auth), Photo surrealism, South End News, Boston, 2/15/90; articles in numerous other newspapers, mags & J's. *Media:* Photography. *Publ:* Article, Cliche, Brussels, Belg, 5/89; contribr, Photography 150 Years: Its Light and Shadow, Dept Photog, Col Art, Nihon Univ, Tokyo Inst Technol, 89; The Photography of Invention: American Pictures of the 1980's, Mass Inst Technol Press, 89; The Interruped Life, New Mus, New York, 91; Megalopolis: Contemporary Cultural Sensibilities, Celeste Olalquiaga, 92; and others. *Dealer:* Pamela Auchin Closs Gallery 558 Broadway New York NY 10012; Galerie Farideh Cadot 77 Rue Des Archives 75003 Paris France. *Mailing Add:* 55 Prince St New York NY 10012

AKINS, FUTURE RENÉE
PRINTMAKER, SCULPTOR
b Hampton, Va, Feb 5, 50. *Study:* Tex Tech Univ, Lubbock, BA(art hist), 72, MFA(printmaking), 77. *Work:* Sch of Art Inst Chicago, Ill; World Bank Am, San Francisco; Red River Mus, Moorhead, Minn; Valley Nat Bank, Phoenix, Ariz; Mus Southwest, Midland, Tex. *Comn:* Print ed, Tex Fine Arts Asn, Austin, 81 & The Mus, Tex Tech Univ, Lubbock, 83. *Exhib:* World Print Competition III, Smithsonian Inst, Washington, DC, 76-78; Breaking the Bindings: American Book Art Now, Univ Wis, Madison, 83; Artists Books, San Antonio Art Inst, Tex, 83; Women Artists of Tex, Nat Mus for Women in the Arts, Washington, DC. *Collections Arranged:* Nothin Else to Do (auth, catalog), Music Heritage W Tex, 84; Con Dios, Retabloes, 85; Peter Hurd in Lubbock, Drawings Mural, 86; Honky Tonk Visions (auth, catalog), Art & Music W Tex, 86. *Pos:* Asst to dir, The Museum, Tex Tech Univ, 83-85, cur art, 85-88. *Awards:* Cash Awards, Los Angeles Printmaking Soc, 77 & Brand Gallery, 78; Jurors Award, Objects in Transition, Temari-Book Art, Honolulu, Hawaii, 84. *Mem:* Nat Orgn Women; World Print Coun; Tex Asn Museums. *Dealer:* Charles Adams Gallery 2109 Broadway Lubbock TX 79401. *Mailing Add:* 4715 27th St Lubbock TX 79410

ALAUPOVIC, ALEXANDRA V
SCULPTOR, EDUCATOR
b Slatina, Yugoslavia, Dec 21, 21; US citizen. *Study:* Acad Visual Arts, Univ Zagreb, cert(sculpture & teaching), 48; Acad Visual Arts, Prague, 49; Univ Ill, Urbana-Champaign, 59-60; Univ Okla, MFA, 66. *Work:* Univ Okla Mus Art, Norman; Okla State Art Col; Continental Fed Savings & Loan, Okla Art Ctr, Okla Aviation & Space Mus, Okla City; Okla City Art Mus, Okla City, Okla. *Comn:* Okla Med Res Found, 64 & First Unitarian Church, Okla city, 64; busts & pub sculpture, Mercy Health Ctr, Okla City, 74; sculpture, Okla Univ, Sam Viersen Gym Ctr, Norman, 82; Univ Okla, Col Med, Okla City, 88. *Exhib:* Exposition Asn Peintres, Graveurs et Sculpteurs de Croatie, Dubrovnik, Yugoslavia, 56; 35th Ann Springfield Art Mus, Mo, 65; On Music, Univ Okla Mus Art, 68; Salon des Nations, Paris, 83; Gallery II, Charlottesville, Va, 83; 50 yr retrospective, Okla Art Ctr, Okla City, 87. *Teaching:* Instr drawing, basic form & sculpture, Univ Okla, 64-66; instr sculpture, Okla Sci & Arts Found, Okla City, 69-75; assoc prof, Okla City Univ, 72-77. *Awards:* Jacobson Award, Univ Okla, 64; Philbrook Art Ctr, Tulsa, 70; Sculpture Award, Okla City Arts Coun, 86. *Bibliog:* Virginia Watson Jones (auth), Contemporary American Women Sculptors, 86. *Mem:* Int Sculpture Ctr; New York Artists Equity Asn. *Media:* Marble, Metals. *Mailing Add:* 11908 N Bryant Oklahoma City OK 73131

ALBANO, PATRICK LOUIS
ART DEALER
b St Louis, Mo, June 19, 47. *Study:* Univ Miss, BA, 69; Univ Iowa, MA, 71. *Pos:* Dir, Aaron Galleries, Chicago, Ill, currently. *Mem:* Int Fine Print Dealers; Am Hist Print Collectors Soc. *Specialty:* American masters of the 19th and 20th centuries. *Publ:* Auth, articles in: Antique Market Report, Bales Publ, 1/86 & 9/86. *Mailing Add:* Suite 1225 620 N Michigan Ave Chicago IL 60611

ALBERGA, ALTA W
ETCHER, PAINTER
b Tuscaloosa, Ala. *Study:* Univ Wichita (Wichita State), Kans, AB, AM; Wash Univ, St Louis, BFA; Univ Ill, Urbana-Champaign, MFA; Art Students League, with Morris Kantor & Robert Beverly Hale. *Work:* Little Gallery, Wichita State Univ; Univ Ill, Champaign; SC Arts Commission. *Comn:* Print, Columbia Mus Art, SC, 73; painting, Daniel Int (Construct) Inc, Greenville, SC, 75; American Spinning, Greenville, SC, 78. *Exhib:* One-man shows, Falls Cottage, Metrop Arts Coun, 82, 84 & 85, Presbyterian Col, Clinton, 84, Tryon Fine Arts Ctr, NC, 87-88, Greenville City Mus Art, 89 & SC State Univ, Orangeburg, 92; Greenville Artists Guild, Greenville Mus Art, SC, 75, 79, 81, 82, 84, 86 & 88; Interart, Washington, DC, 81-83; Gurmukh Gallery, Aspen Hill & Silver Springs, Md, 84; Univ NC invitational, Charlotte, 88; Furman Univ invitational, Womans Show, 89; and others. *Teaching:* Instr art hist & drawing, Wichita State Univ, 54-55; instr design, Webster Col, St Louis, 55-61; head visual arts, Presby Col, Clinton, SC, 69-75; lectr, Tri-county Tech Col, Pendleton, SC, 75-; instr, drawing & oil painting, Duke Street Gallery, Pendleton, SC & Greenville Co Mus Art, formerly. *Awards:* Richard K Weil Award, City Mus of St Louis, 57; St Louis Artists' Ann Guild, 60; Purchase Prize, print, Columbia Mus, SC, 71; Merit Award, Greenville Artists Guild, 85. *Mem:* Artists Equity Asn (pres, St Louis Chap, 61); life mem, Art Students League; Southeastern Graphics Coun; Guild SC Artists; Greenville Artists Guild (pres, 84-85). *Media:* Oil, Acrylic; Intaglio. *Res:* Modern art history. *Publ:* Auth, Book reviews for Southeastern Col Art Conf publ, 73. *Dealer:* Duke St Gallery Pendelton SC; Second St Gallery Philadelphia PA. *Mailing Add:* 11 Overton Dr Greenville SC 29609

ALBERS, ANNI
DESIGNER, GRAPHIC ARTIST
b Berlin, Ger, June 12, 1899; US citizen. *Study:* Bauhaus, Weimar & Dessau, Ger, dipl; Md Col Art, Hon Dr, 72; York Univ, Toronto, Hon Dr, 73; Philadelphia Col Art, Hon Dr, 76; Univ Hartford, Hon Dr, 79; RI Sch Design, 90; Royal Col, London, Eng, 90. *Work:* Jewish Mus, Metrop Mus Art & Mus Mod Art, New York; Bauhaus Archives, Berlin; Art Inst Chicago; Baltimore Mus Art, Md; Busch Reisinger-Harvard Univ, Cambridge, Mass; Wadsworth Atheneum, Hartford, Conn; Yale Univ Art Gallery, New Haven, Conn. *Comn:* Mem to Nazi victims, comn by List Family for Jewish Mus; Ark Curtain, Dallas & Woonsocket, RI. *Exhib:* Mus Mod Art, New York; Brooklyn Mus; Katonah Gallery, NY; Univ Hartford Art Sch; Queens Col Libr, NY; Monmouth Mus, NJ; Univ Calif, Riverside; Retrospectives, Renwick Gallery, Nat Mus Art, Smithsonian Inst, Washington, DC, 85, Yale Univ Art Gallery, New Haven, Conn, 86, Ackland Art Mus, Chapel Hill, NC, 86, Fredrick Wight Gallery Univ Calif, Los Angeles, 86, Portland Mus Art, Ore, 86, Villa Stuck, Munich, 89 & Mus Modern Art, NY, 90. *Teaching:* Asst prof art, Black Mountain Col, 33-49; lectr, leading univs & mus. *Awards:* Award, Decorative Arts Bk, 65; Gold Medal, Am Craft Coun, 80; Award, Women's Caucus Art, 80; and others. *Bibliog:* Gene Baro & Nicholas Fox Weber (auths), Anni Albers, Brooklyn Mus, 77; Nicholas Fox Weber (auth),

The Woven and Graphic Art of Anni Albers, Smithsonian Inst Press, 85. *Media:* Textile. *Publ:* Auth, Anni Albers: On Designing, Wesleyan Univ Press, 62 & 71; Anni Albers: On Weaving, Wesleyan Univ Press, 65 & 72; Anni Albers: Pre-Columbian Mexican Miniatures, Praeger, 70. *Mailing Add:* 808 Birchwood Dr Orange CT 06477

ALBERT, CALVIN
SCULPTOR, EDUCATOR
b Grand Rapids, Mich, Nov 19, 18. *Study:* Grand Rapids Art Gallery, with Otto Karl Bach; Art Inst Chicago; Inst Design, with Moholy-Nagy & Gyorgy Kepes; Archipenko Sch Sculpture. *Work:* Metrop Mus, Whitney Mus Am Art & Jewish Mus, New York; Art Inst Chicago; Detroit Inst Arts. *Comn:* Ark Doors & Candelabra, Steinberg House, Park Ave Synagogue, New York, 54; Outdoor Candelabra, Temple Israel, Tulsa, Okla, 55; Crucifix, Tabernacle & Candlesticks, St Paul's Church, Peoria, Ill, 59; Facade Relief, Congregation Emanuel, Grand Rapids, 74. *Exhib:* Unknown Political Prisoner Prizewinners, Mus Mod Art, New York & Tate Gallery, London, 53; le Dessin Contemporains aux Etats Unis, Musee Nat d'Arte Moderne, Paris, 54; Whitney Ann Am Artists, 54-68; Univ Ill Contemp Painting & Sculpture, 57 & 65; 20th Century Masters of Drawing, Mus Mod Art, New York, 64; Benton Gallery, 86; Vered Gallery, 88 & 89; Boca Raton Mus Art, 90. *Teaching:* Instr sculpture & design, Inst Design, Chicago, 42-46; instr color & drawing, Brooklyn Col, 47-49; prof art & head grad sculpture prog, Pratt Inst, 49-85, prof emer. *Awards:* Guggenheim Fel 66; Nat Inst Arts & Lett Award, 75; Nat Acad Design Award, 81. *Media:* Bronze, Terra Cotta. *Publ:* Coauth, Figure drawing comes to life, 57. *Mailing Add:* 624 95th St Surfside FL 33154

ALBERTI, DONALD WESLEY
PAINTER
b Fort Eustis, Va, Dec 25, 50. *Study:* Col William & Mary, BA, 71. *Exhib:* Die Gegenwart Der Farbe, Kunsthalle Bielefeld, Ger, 86; La Couleur Seule; L'Experience De Monochrome, Musee St Pierre, Lyon, France, 88; Mediterranean Abstraction, French Inst Naples, Italy, 92. *Awards:* Fel, NY Found Arts, 87; Fel, Igor Found, 90. *Bibliog:* Clio Mitchell (auth), Instant myth, Art Int, winter 88. *Mem:* Nat Artists Equity Asn. *Media:* All Media. *Mailing Add:* 93 Crosby St New York NY 10012

ALBRECHT, MARY DICKSON
SCULPTOR, DESIGNER
b Dothan, Ala, June 4, 30. *Study:* Univ Houston; Tex Woman's Univ, BS(sculpture, with hons), 70. *Work:* Okla Art Ctr Mus, Oklahoma City; City Dallas Park & Recreation Dept, Tex; Univ Tex at Arlington. *Comn:* Sculpture, Allied Tower at Fountain Place, comn by Sharon Criswell, Criswell Development Co, 86; The Kim, Dallas Commun Coun, 88. *Exhib:* 13th Nat Exhib Prints & Drawings, Okla Art Ctr, 71; 15th Tex Crafts Exhib, Dallas Mus Fine Arts, 71; Tex Fine Arts Asn State Citation Show, 72, 75 & 76 & 61st Ann Nat Exhib, 72, Laguna Gloria Mus, Austin; 14th Midwest Biennial, Joslyn Art Mus, Omaha, Nebr, 76; Tenth Nat Drawing & Small Sculpture Show, Del Mar Col, Corpus Christi, Tex, 76. *Awards:* Juror's Choice & Circuit Merit Awards, Tex Fine Arts Asn State Citation Show, 71, 72 & 76; Purchase Award, Univ Tex, Arlington, 72. *Mem:* Soc NAm Goldsmiths; Am Craft Coun; Smithsonian Inst. *Media:* Steel, Bronze. *Mailing Add:* PO Box 163536 Austin TX 78716-3536

ALBRIGHT, MALVIN MARR
PAINTER, SCULPTOR
b Chicago, Ill, Feb 20, 1897. *Study:* Univ Ill; Art Inst Chicago; Pa Acad Fine Arts. *Work:* Corcoran Gallery Art; Toledo Mus Art; Butler Inst Am Art; Libr Cong; Pa Acad Fine Arts; and others. *Exhib:* Nat Acad Design; Whitney Mus Am Art; Mus Mod Art; Pa Acad Fine Arts; Carnegie Inst; plus others. *Awards:* Altman Prize, Nat Acad Design, 42 & 62, Palmer Mem Prize; Corcoran Silver Medal, Washington, DC; Dana Medal, Pa Acad Fine Arts, 65; and others. *Mem:* Nat Acad Design; fel Royal Soc Arts; Int Inst Arts & Lett; Nat Sculpture Soc; fel Pa Acad Fine Arts; and others. *Mailing Add:* 1500 N Lake Shore Dr Chicago IL 60610

ALBUQUERQUE, LITA
PAINTER
b Santa Monica, Calif, Jan 3, 46. *Study:* Univ Calif, Los Angeles, BFA, 68; Otis Art Inst, 71. *Work:* Newport Harbor Art Mus, Newport Beach, Calif; Assoc Tel & Tel, Chicago; Los Angeles Co Mus Art, Security Pac Bank, Arco Corp, Los Angeles. *Exhib:* Mus Mod Art, New York, 76; Aesthetics of Graffiti, San Francisco Mus of Mod Art, 78; Change West, Los Angeles Co Mus Art, 78; Marianne Jism Gallery, Chicago, Ill, 80; Diane Brown Gallery, Washington, DC, 80; Int Sculpture Conf, Washington, DC, 80; Directions, Hirshhorn Mus, Washington, DC, 81; Robin Cronin Inc, Houston, Tex, 82; and many other group & one-man shows. *Pos:* Gallery dir, Gallery 707, Los Angeles, Calif, 73-75; cur, Cedars-Sinai Med Ctr Exhib Comt, Los Angeles, 76-77. *Teaching:* Lectr painting & drawing, Calif State Univ, Los Angeles, 75-77; vis artist painting & drawing, Univ Calif, Santa Barbara, 77-78, Art Ctr Col Design, 79-80, Claremont Grad Sch, 80 & Univ Calif, Irvine, 80. *Awards:* Individual Artist Fel Grant, Nat Endowment Arts, 75. *Bibliog:* Carrie Rickey (auth), Curatorial conceptions, the Hirshhorn: Danger curves ahead, Artforum, 4/81; Grace Glueck (auth), How emerging artists really emerge: Putting the biennials together, Art News, 5/81; Jo Ann Lewis (auth), The new of the best, but the best of the new?, Art News, 5/81. *Dealer:* Janus Gallery 8000 Melrose Ave Los Angeles CA. *Mailing Add:* c/o The Worlus Gallery 106 W Third St Long Beach CA 90802

ALCALAY, ALBERT S
PAINTER, LECTURER
b Paris, France, Aug 11, 17; US citizen. *Study:* Studied in Paris, France & Rome, Italy; Belgrade, Yugoslavia. *Work:* Fogg Mus, Harvard Univ; De Cordova & Dana Mus; Mus Mod Art; Boston Mus Fine Arts; Rome Mus Mod Art; Boston Pub Libr. *Exhib:* Mus Mod Art, 55; Whitney Mus Am Art, 56, 58 & 60; Inst Contemp Art, Boston, 60; Pa Acad Fine Arts, 60; 44 one-man shows, De Cordova Mus, Lincoln, Mass; retrospective, Carpenter Ctr, Harvard Univ, 82; and others incl 42 one-man shows. *Teaching:* Lectr design, Carpenter Ctr, Harvard Univ, 59- *Awards:* Guggenheim Fel, 59-60; prize, Boston Art Festival, 60. *Media:* Oil; Gouache and Pen & Ink on Rice Paper. *Publ:* Auth, forwards in numerous exhib catalogs. *Mailing Add:* c/o Eliza Spencer Gallery 168 Newbury St Boston MA 02116

ALDANA, CARL
FILMMAKER, PAINTER
b Guatemala City, Guatemala, Sept 26, 36; US citizen. *Study:* Self taught. *Work:* US Air Force, Wash, DC; City of Hockaichi Collection, Japan; US Embassy, El Salvador; Auto Club of Calif, Los Angeles; Long Beach Mus Art, Calif. *Comn:* Portrait of Margret Mead, 69, portrait Dr Jan Mayer, 68, portrait B F Skinner, 73, Psychology Today, San Diego, Calif; portrait Richard Nixon, Los Angeles Times, Calif, 72; painting, CRM Books, San Diego, Calif, 68. *Exhib:* Abercrombie & Fitch, NY, 66; 70 Years of Westway Covers, Mus Sci & Industry, Los Angeles, 74; one-man show, Compton Col, Calif, 77, Arco Ctr for Visual Arts, Los Angeles, 77, Rio Hondo Col, Whittier, 88; Rhode Island Mus Art, 78; Los Angeles As Seen By Los Angeles Artists, Municipal Gallery, 81. *Pos:* Art dir print, Calif State Univ, Long Beach, 67-68; prod illusr and art dir for numerous motion pictures, 77- *Teaching:* Instr drawing, Calif State Univ, Long Beach, 67-68, 80-81; instr drawing & painting, Fullerton Col, Calif, 72-77, Santa Monica, 75-78. *Awards:* Gold Medel & Award of Merit, Soc of Illusr, NY, 67. *Mem:* Movie Illusr Union (bd dir); Pub Corp for the Arts, Long Beach; Acad Motion Pictures Arts & Sciences. *Media:* Oil. *Dealer:* Mary Sullivan 315 W Third No 307 Long Beach CA 90802. *Mailing Add:* 386 Ultimo Long Beach CA 90814

ALDEN, GARY WADE
ART CONSERVATOR, CONSULTANT
b Somerville, NJ, May 18, 51. *Study:* Univ Chicago, BA, 73; Intermuseum Conserv Asn Training Prog, Oberlin Col, with Richard D Buck, cert(conserv), 76. *Collections Arranged:* Preserving Our Cultural Heritage: Conservation in the San Diego Museum of Art, 79; What Is Conservation and Why Is Conservation Necessary, Casa de Balboa, 85. *Pos:* Conservator, Intermuseum Conserv Asn Lab, Oberlin, 76-77; chief conservator, Balboa Art Conserv Ctr, San Diego, Calif, 77-78; dir, Balboa Art Conserv Ctr, San Diego, 78-88; panel reviewer, Nat Endowment Arts; int team conservator, Retablo de Fernando Gallego, San Lorenzo, Toro, Spain, 85; field reviewer, 84 & 88, review panelist, 88 & 90, Inst Mus Servs. *Teaching:* Instr, Am Asn State & Local Hist, 88. *Mem:* Assoc mem Am Inst Conserv Hist & Artistic Works (chmn, bd examiners cert, 84-86); Western Asn Art Conserv (secy/treas, 79-81); assoc mem Int Inst Conserv; Asn Regional Conserv Ctrs (chmn, 86-88). *Mailing Add:* 7818 Camino Raposa San Diego CA 92122

ALDEN, RICHARD
PAINTER
US citizen. *Study:* Pratt Inst, Brooklyn, BA(archit), 66, MA(archit), 68; Archit Asn, Fulbright Grant, 67. *Work:* Milford Fine Arts Coun, Conn; Trenton State Col, NJ. *Exhib:* Salmagundi Club 3rd Ann, New York, 80; Audubon Artists 38th Ann Nat, New York, 80; Springfield Art League 61st Nat, Mass, 80; Nat Print Exhib, Holman Art Gallery, Trenton, NJ, 80; Mamaroneck Artists Guild, Larchmont, NY, 81; and others. *Teaching:* Asst prof design, Pa State Univ, 68- *Awards:* Third Prizes, 8th Ann, York Art Asn, 78 & Cent Pa Festival Arts, 78; First Prize, 21st Three Rivers Arts Festival, 80. *Media:* Colored Pencil. *Publ:* Fragments of a Total Picture: Beyond Style & Fashion, Alden Publ, 86. *Dealer:* Capricorn Gallery 4849 Rugby Ave Bethesda MD 20014. *Mailing Add:* Penn State Univ/Dept Archit State College PA 16827

ALDEN, TODD
CRITIC, CONCEPTUAL ARTIST
b Oct 7, 63. *Study:* Grad Ctr, City Univ New York, MA(art hist), 91. *Mem:* Col Art Asn; Conceptual Clearinghouse Ltd (dir, 92-). *Publ:* Ed & auth, The Library of Babel (exhib catalog), Hallwalls Cont Arts Ctr, Buffalo, NY, 91; auth, Sophie Calle & the Aesthetics of the Uncanny Arts, 91, Louise Lawler: Love for Sale, 91 & coauth, Total Metal, 91, Arts; auth, Marcel Broodthaers: on the tautology of art & merchandise, Print Collector's Newsletter, 92. *Mailing Add:* 225 W 14th St Apt 3E New York NY 10011

ALDRICH, LARRY
ART COLLECTOR
b New York, NY, June, 1906. *Pos:* Chmn & founder, Larry Aldrich Mus Contemp Art, Ridgefield, Conn; founder & pres, Soho Ctr Visual Arts, New York, currently. *Collection:* Contemporary painting and sculpture. *Mailing Add:* Larry Aldrich Assocs 40 Central Park S Rm 6 New York NY 10019

ALEXANDER, ANTHONY K
SCULPTOR, JEWELER
b Granite City, Ill, May 21, 51. *Comn:* Tribal Totem Pole, 88 & Tribal Symbols, 89, Greater Albany Sch Dist, Ore; Caduceus Sculptor, com by Dr Roger P Setera, Portland, Ore, 90; Northwest Coast Art, Larry Day Assoc, Portland, Ore, 90. *Exhib:* Wildlife & Western Wildlife Exhib, Minneapolis, 90; Roughrider Art Show, Williston, NDak, 91; Jazzed About Art, Newberg, Ore, 91-92. *Media:* Bronze, Wood. *Mailing Add:* 1981 Lockwood Place SE Albany OR 97321

ALEXANDER, EDMUND BROOKE
ART DEALER, PUBLISHER
b Los Angeles, Calif, Apr 26, 37. *Study:* Yale Univ, BA, 60. *Pos:* Dir Editions Alecto, New York, 67 & Brooke Alexander, Inc, 68-; owner, Brooke Alexander Gallery & Brook Alexander Editions Inc, 75-; partner, Galeria Weber, Alexander Wa, Madrid, 90; mem gov bd, Yale Univ Art Gallery; bd mem, Lower Manhattan Cult Coun. *Mem:* Art Dealers Asn Am. *Specialty:* Contemporary American prints; contemporary paintings, drawings and sculpture. *Publ:* Ed, Robert Motherwell-Selected Prints 1961-1974, 74, Jasper Johns-Screenprints, 77 & Sam Francis--The Litho Shop 1970-1979, 79, pvt publ. *Mailing Add:* c/o Brooke Alexander Gallery 59 Wooster St New York NY 10012

ALEXANDER, JOHN E
PAINTER
b Beaumont, Tex, Oct 26, 45. *Study:* Lamar Univ, BA; Southern Methodist Univ, MFA. *Work:* Contemp Arts Mus, Houston; Mus Fine Art, Amarillo, Tex; Am Tel Collection, Chicago; Mus Fine Art, Beaumont; Southern Methodist Univ, Dallas. *Comn:* Poster (lithograph), Am Civil Liberties Union, 74; poster, comn by Dir James Harithas, Contemp Arts Mus, 75. *Exhib:* Drawings USA, Springfield, Ill, 70-71; Dallas Mus Art, 72; Artist of the Southwest, Atlanta, Ga, 72; one-man show, Contemp Arts Mus, Houston, 75. *Teaching:* Asst prof art, Univ Houston, 71- *Media:* Oil. *Mailing Add:* c/o Marlborough Gallery 40 W 57th St New York NY 10019

ALEXANDER, JUDITH
ART DEALER, COLLECTOR
b Atlanta, Ga, Mar 31, 32. *Study:* Univ NC, Chapel Hill, BA, 52; Acad Fine Art & Barnes Found, Philadelphia, 53-54; Hans Hoffman Sch Art, Provincetown, 55. *Pos:* Art dealer, New Arts Gallery, 57-65 & Alexander Gallery, 65-89. *Specialty:* Nationally known and local artists, specializing in abstract expressionism and Georgia folk art. *Mailing Add:* 3060 Pharr Ct North NW Atlanta GA 30305

ALEXANDER, KENNETH LEWIS
CARTOONIST
b Gridley, Calif, June 16, 24. *Study:* Univ Calif, Berkeley, 42-43; Rutgers Univ, 43-44; Calif Col Arts & Crafts, 46-47. *Pos:* Freelance com artist, 47-58; ed, Pictorial Living Mag, San Francisco Examnr, 58-63, Sunday art dir, 63-66, ed cartoonist, 66-; TV ed cartoonist, KGO-TV, 68-69. *Mem:* Soc Am Ed Cartoonist; Nat Cartoonists Soc; Am Newspaper Guild; Am Fedn TV Radio Artists. *Mailing Add:* 1182 Glen Rd Lafayette CA 94549

ALEXANDER, MARGARET AMES
HISTORIAN, EDUCATOR
b Sharon, Mass, May 21, 16. *Study:* Wheaton Col, AB, 38; Inst Fine Arts, NY Univ, MA, 41, PhD, 58. *Pos:* Co-dir, Corpus des Mosaiques de Tunisie, Tunis, 68- *Teaching:* Prof art, Univ Iowa, 62-86. *Mem:* Archaeol Inst Am; Asn Int Study Antique Mosaics; Col Art Asn; Int Comn Conserv Mosaics. *Res:* Roman and Early Christian mosaics. *Publ:* Auth of articles on NAfrica, Archaeol, 49-51, Apollo, 83, Dumbarton Oaks Papers, 87 & Acts of Aiema; coauth, Quelques Precisions a propos de la Chronologie des Mosaiques d'Utique, La Mosaique Greco-Romaine, Vol II; coauth, Utique et ses Environs, Fasc 1, 73 & Fasc 3, 76 & ed, Fasc 2, 74, Corpus des Mosaiques de Tunisie, Vol I; coauth & ed, Thuburbo Majus, Fasc 1, 80 & Fasc 2, 85 & Fasc 3, 87. *Mailing Add:* 9 Forest Glen Iowa City IA 52245

ALEXANDER, PETER
SCULPTOR
b Los Angeles, Calif, Feb 27, 39. *Study:* Univ Pa, University Park, 57-60; Univ London, Eng, 60-62; Univ Calif, Berkeley, 62-63; Univ Southern Calif, Los Angeles, 63-64; Univ Calif, Los Angeles, BA, 65, MFA, 68. *Work:* Walker Art Ctr, Minneapolis, Minn; Mus Mod Art, Brooklyn Mus, Guggenheim Mus, Metrop Mus Art, New York; Corcoran Gallery Art, Washington, DC; Los Angeles Co Mus Art; San Francisco Mus Mod Art, Calif; Fogg Mus, Harvard Univ, Cambridge, Mass; and others. *Exhib:* Whitney Mus Am Art Ann, 69; Highlights: 1968-1969, Aldrich Mus Contemp Art; Am Exhibs, Art Inst Chicago, 69 & 72; Painting & Sculpture in Calif: The Modern Era, San Francisco Mus Mod Art, 76; one-man exhibs, James Corcoran Gallery, Los Angeles, Calif, 81, 85-90, Charles Cowles Gallery, New York, 82 & 84-85, Stephen Wirtz Gallery, San Francisco, Calif, 84, Van Straaten Gallery, Chicago, Ill, 84, Fuller Goldeen Gallery, San Francisco, Calif, 84, Gallery 454 North, West Hollywood, Calif, 88 & Work Gallery, Costa Mesa, Calif, 91; Brooklyn Mus, 83; Mus Mod Art, New York, 84; and others. *Pos:* Artist-in-residence, Calif Inst Technol, Pasadena, 70-71, Calif State Univ, Long Beach, 76, Fullerton Col, Calif, 76, Univ Colo, Boulder, 81, Centrum Found, Wash, 82 & Cirrus Publ, Los Angeles, 83. *Awards:* Nat Endowment Arts Fel, 80. *Bibliog:* Elizabeth Perlmulter (auth), Clear, cloudy, smoggy, 1/75 & Dizzy in the Ganzfeld, summer 76, Artnews; Nancy Marmer (auth), Sky Show, Artforum, 2/76; Henry Seldis (auth), article, Los Angeles Times, 8/7/77; Merle Schipper (auth), Sunsets and velvets: a ten year survey, Images and Issues, 7-8/83; William Wilson (auth), California ceramics, shape of things to come, Los Angeles Times, 8/9/84. *Mailing Add:* PO Box 1124 8233 Tuna Canyon Rd Malibu CA 90265

ALEXANDER, ROBERT SEYMOUR
EDUCATOR, DESIGNER
b Pittsburgh, Pa, Feb 1, 23. *Study:* Ad-Art Studio Sch, 41-42; Shrivenham Am Univ, Eng, 45; Carnegie Inst Technol, 47; Univ Ill, BFA, 51; Cranbrook Acad Art, MFA, 52. *Comn:* Indust designs for FMC Corp, Mich Dept Agr, Recordio Corp, Planet Corp & others. *Exhib:* Kresge Art Mus, Mich State Univ, 78, 82, 84 & 91; Ann Painting, Lansing Art Gallery, Mich, 81, 83 & 87; Partners Gallery, Okemos, Mich, 83; Vintage Artists of Michigan, Nat Coun on Ageing Gallery, Washington, DC, travels to nine Michigan cities, 87 & 88; and others. *Pos:* Artist-designer, James H Matthews Co, Pittsburgh, 46-47; training aids designer, USA, Ft Eustis, Va, 48; automotive designer, Ford Motor Co, Dearborn, Mich, 52-53; independent designer, 55-; group leader, design for educ proj, Princeton Univ, 66. *Teaching:* Prof art, Mich State Univ, 54-87, chair, 84, prof emeritus (active), 87-; Int Acad Merz Design, 91; Lansing CC, 90 & 91. *Awards:* First Prize, Int furniture design competition, Nat Cotton Coun, 59; Second Prize, 7th Photographic Art Competition, Saginaw Mus, 77. *Bibliog:* J Fisher (auth), Education for design, Format Mag; Tom LaBelle (auth), Creeping up on Dudley & other Leland art objects, Grand Rapids (Mich) Press Sunday Mag, 9/8/74; T Gasdik (auth), Art Prof honored for dance works, State News, 4/3/87. *Media:* Art Furniture, Mixed Media. *Publ:* Auth, Industrial design, the alumni show, Kresge Art Ctr Bulletin, 4/75. *Mailing Add:* 5040 Alqonquin Okemos MI 48864

ALEXANDER, VIKKY M
CONCEPTUAL ARTIST
b Jan 30, 59. *Study:* NS Col Art & Design, BFA, 79. *Work:* Edmonton Art Gallery; Winnipeg Art Gallery; Household Finance Corp; Prudential Insurance Co; Progressive Corp. *Exhib:* Window installation, New Mus Contemp Art, New York, 85; The Castle, Documenta, Kassel, WGer, 87; Art of the Real, De Appel, Amsterdam, Holland, 87; New Territories in Art: Europe-America, Fondabione Michetti, Rome, Italy, 87; Past/Future/Tense, Winnipeg Art Gallery, Winnipeg & Vancouver Art Gallery, British Columbia, 90-91; James Welling & Vikky Alexander, Kunsthalle Bern, Switz, 90. *Teaching:* Assoc prof photog, New York Univ, 89- *Awards:* Visual Arts Grants, Can Coun, 83, 85 & 87. *Bibliog:* Nancy Tousley (auth), Vikky Alexander, Canadian Arts, 88; Brian Wallis (auth), Vikky Alexander (catalog), Stride Gallery, 89; Bruce Ferguson (auth), GLAS (NOT) Sculpture (catalog), 900. *Media:* Mixed Media. *Publ:* Contribr, Tropical codes, Kunstforum, 86; Thought Objects, JAA, 87; Contemporary photography, Art & Auction, 87; Fabrications, Abbeville Press, 88. *Dealer:* Ace Contemp Exhibitions 5514 Wilshire Blvd Los Angeles CA 90036; Galerie Brenda Wallace 372 Suite Catherine St West Montreal Quebec. *Mailing Add:* 135 Grand St New York NY 10013

ALEXANDER, WICK
PAINTER
Study: San Diego State Univ, 73-75; Univ Calif, San Diego, BA, 77- 79, MFA, 80-83. *Exhib:* Solo exhibs, Patty Aande Gallery, San Diego, 85, San Diego Inst Arts Educ, Jungle Life, 80 ft store front, Pacific Beach, Calif, 87, New Paintings, 88 & Paintings, 89, Dietrich Jenny Gallery & Games, Java Art Space, 92; The Biennial, Insatallation Gallery, San Diego, Calif, 87; Dietrich Jenny Gallery, 88; retrospective, Installation Gallery, 91; La Calle, Tijuana River Estuary, 91; Orange Co Ctr Contemp Art, 92; Transcending Borders, Centro Cultural Tijuana, 92. *Teaching:* Instr, Metrop Correctional Ctr, US Dept Justice, San Diego, 83-87 & San Diego State Univ, 89; Artist in Residence, Young at Art, San Diego City Sch, 91-92. *Awards:* Ford Found Grant, 82; Nat Endowment Arts Fel, 89; CAC Artist Fel Painting, 90. *Mailing Add:* 3327 Nile St 660 Ninth Ave San Diego CA 92104

ALEXANDER-GREENE, GRACE GEORGE
EDUCATOR, MUSEUM DIRECTOR
b Cleveland, Ohio, Sept 18, 18. *Study:* NJ State Teachers Col, with Sybil Browne, BS, 40; Hunter Col; NY Univ; Queens Col; Univ PR; Columbia Univ. *Exhib:* Lever House, 86. *Pos:* TV producer-broadcaster art, New York City Bd Educ, 65-73, supervisor art, 73-77, dir art, 77-79; bd mem, Inst Study Art in Educ, 78 & 79; freelance TV producer art, 79-; consult, Am Mus Moving Image, 85. *Teaching:* Instr visual literacy, Am Festival in Britain, 73; instr art educ, Queens Col, 71-72; instr art educ, Sch Visual Arts, New York, 79- *Awards:* Ohio State Award, 63 & 73; Outstanding Alumni Award, Kean Col, 80; Monitor Award, Video Production Asn, 84. *Bibliog:* Barbara Y Newsom (auth), The Art Museum as Educator, Univ Calif, Press, 78; Potell Herbert (ed), Rationale for Art Education in the Eighties, High Points, 80. *Mem:* Nat Art Educ Asn; Univ Coun Art Educ; Am Women Radio & TV; New York City Art Teachers Asn. *Publ:* Auth, Artists in New York, 66 & The Moving Image, 70, New York City Bd Educ; From the Teachers Corner, Am Educ US Dept Health Educ & Welfare, 78. *Mailing Add:* 12 W 72nd St New York NY 10023

ALEXENBERG, MEL
PAINTER, EDUCATOR
b Brooklyn, NY, Feb 24, 37. *Study:* Queens College, City Univ New York, BS, 58; Yeshiva Univ, MS, 59; Art Students League; NY Univ, EdD, 69. *Work:* Metro Mus Art, New York; Baltimore Mus Art, Md; Israel Mus, Jerusalem; Haags Gemeente Mus, The Hague, Netherlands; Victoria & Albert Mus, London, Eng. *Comn:* Skyart Sukkah, BMW Mus, Munich, Germany, 83; Mem to Six Million, Dachau Death Camp, Germany, 83; Torah Spectrogram, Ramat Hanegev College, Yeroham, Israel, 84; Pinim/Panim: Biofeedback-computer graphics interactive system, Yeshiva Univ Mus, New York, 87; Faxart Homage to Rembrandt, AT&T, New York, 89. *Exhib:* Imagining Antarctica, State Mus, Linz, Austria, 86; The Artist and the Computer, Bronx Mus Arts, NY, 87; Solo show, Angels of Peace, Fine Arts Mus Long Island, Hempstead, NY, 87; Crash: Computer Assisted Hardcopy, Wright Mus Art, Beliot, Wis, 88; Golem, Jewish Mus, New York, 88; Lights/Orot, Yeshiva Univ Mus, New York, 88; Faxart Mem, Mus Het Rembrandthuis, Amsterdam, Netherlands, 89; High Tech/High Touch, Miami Univ Art Mus, Oxford, Ohio, 90; Imagenes Norteamericanas, Instituto Chileno Nortamericano de Cultura, Santiego, Chile, 92. *Pos:* Research fel,

MIT Ctr Advanced Vis Studies, 84-88; Dean, vis arts, New World Sch Arts, Miami, Fla, 90- *Teaching:* Senior lectr, Tel Aviv Univ, Israel, 69-73; assoc prof art, Columbia Univ, New York, 73-77; assoc prof & aesthetic educ, Bar-Ilan Univ, Ramat Gan, Israel, 77-84; prof & chmn fine arts, Pratt Inst, Brooklyn, NY, 85-90. *Awards:* Founder's Day Award, NY Univ, 69; MIT/CAVS Fel, 84-85; NY State Coun on Arts, 87-88. *Bibliog:* Barbara Dalatiner (auth), Artist's Angel to Fly by Computer, NY Times, 8-16/87; Elizabeth Hayt-Atkins (auth), Lights Orot, Art News, 9/88; John Ross, Clare Romano & Tim Ross (auths), The Complete Printmaker, Macmillan, 90. *Mem:* Int Soc Educ Through Art; Nat Art Educ Asn; Israel Soc Painters and Sculptors. *Media:* Acrylic, Electronic Media. *Publ:* Auth, Light and Sight, Prentice-Hall, 69; Aesthetic experience in creative process, Bar-Ilan Univ Press, 81; coauth, Lights Orot, MIT/CAVS, 88; ed, The Visual Computer, Springer, 88; auth, Aesthetics in Judaism, Wellsprings, 90. *Dealer:* Klarfeld Perry Gallery 472 Broome St New York NY 10012. *Mailing Add:* 300 NW Second Ave Miami FL 33132-3649

ALEXICK, DAVID FRANCIS
EDUCATOR, PAINTER
b Philadelphia, Pa, Jan 25, 42. *Study:* Richmond Prof Inst, BFA, 64; Va Commonwealth Univ, MFA, 66; Pa State Univ, PhD, 76. *Exhib:* Va Artists Biennial, Va Mus Fine Arts, Richmond, 64; one-man show, Robinson House, Va Mus Fine Arts, Richmond, 65; Longwood Col Fac Show, Bedford Gallery, Farmville, Va, 71-78; James River Show, Mariners Mus, Newport News, Va, 73. *Teaching:* Instr art, York Col Pa, 66-68; asst prof art, Longwood Col, Farmville, Va, 71-78; instr art educ, Col William & Mary, Williamsburg, Va, 79-80; asst prof art, Christopher Newport Col, VA, 79-82, dir art, Dept Arts & Communications, 82-88, assoc prof, 82- *Awards:* Cert Distinction, Va Mus Fine Arts, 64; 1st Prize, South Eastern Regional, Lynchburg Fine Arts Ctr, 67; Patron Arts Award, Lynchburg Art Festival, 78. *Mem:* Col Art Asn; Nat Art Educ Asn; Va Art Educ Asn. *Media:* Oil, Acrylic. *Res:* Programs of art and perceptual awareness for institutionalized retarded children. *Mailing Add:* 6436 Centerville Rd Williamsburg VA 23188

ALF, MARTHA JOANNE
PAINTER, WRITER
b Berkeley, Calif, Aug 13, 30. *Study:* San Diego State Univ, with Everett Gee Jackson, BA, MA(painting), 63; Univ Calif, Los Angeles, with James Weeks, William Brice & Richard Diebenkorn, MFA(pictorial arts), 70. *Work:* Los Angeles Co Mus Art; San Diego Mus Art; Santa Barbara Mus Art; Newport Harbor Art Mus, Newport Beach, Calif; Israel Mus Art, Jerusalem; Chemical Bank, New York. *Exhib:* Whitney Biennial Contemp Art, Whitney Mus Am Art, 75; Ft Worth Art Mus, Tex, 80; Decade: Los Angeles Painting in the Seventies, Art Ctr Col Design, 81; Southern Calif Artists 1940-1980, Laguna Beach Mus Art, Calif, 81; The Michael and Dorothy Blankfort Collection, Los Angeles Mus Art, Calif, 82; Drawings by Painters, Long Beach Mus Art, 82 & Oakland Mus, Calif, 83; one-person retrospective, Los Angeles Munic Art Gallery & San Francisco Art Inst, 84; Contemp Am Luminism, Henry Gallery, Univ Wash, 85; Martha Alf-Helen Ludenberg: Two Views: 1970-1987, Palos Verdes Art Ctr, Calif, 87; and many other group and one-person shows. *Pos:* Guest cur, Painting: Color Form & Surface (17 Los Angeles Painters), Lang Art Gallery, Scripps Col, Claremont, Calif. *Teaching:* Instr drawing & painting, Los Angeles Harbor Col, Wilmington, Calif, 71-75; instr, current art in Los Angeles, Univ Calif Extn, Los Angeles, 71-78. *Awards:* Nat Endowment Arts Visual Artist Grant for Drawing, 89; Nat Endowment Arts Grant, 79; Kay Nielsen Mem Purchase Award, Los Angeles Co Mus Art, 79; and others. *Bibliog:* Susanne Muchnic (auth), Martha Alf, Retrospective catalog essay, 84; Merle Schipper (auth), Martha Alf (Tortue Gallery), Art News, pp 24, 27, 2/87; Wendy Beckett (auth), Martha Alf, pp 18, 19, Contemporary Woman Artists, Phaidon, Oxford, 88. *Media:* Multimedia. *Publ:* Auth, My interest in women artists of the past, Womanspace J, Vol 1, No 2; The psychological world of Joyce Treiman, 3/76, The structural language of Claire Falkenstein, 4/76 & Women artists throughout history, 1/77, Artweek. *Dealer:* Newspace Gallery 5241 Melrose Ave Los Angeles CA 90038. *Mailing Add:* c/o Newspace Gallery 5241 Melrose Ave Los Angeles CA 90038

ALFANO, ANGEL
PAINTER
b Cosenza, Italy, Oct 6, 40. *Study:* Liceo Artistico, Rome, Italy. *Work:* Garibaldi-Meucci Mus, New York; Current Art Boston; W Broadway Gallery, New York; Alternate Space Gallery, New York. *Exhib:* Salon Int De L'Art Libre, Paris, France, 68; 10th Art Exhib, New York, 75; Contemp Art Show, Santa Fe, NMex, 78; Fine Art Gallery, Westchester Community Col, Valhalla, NY, 86; Garibaldi-Meucci Mus, New York, 91; and others. *Awards:* Gold Medal Award, Miami, Fla, 65; Prize Special Au Salon Int De L'Art Libre, Paris, France, 65; First Place, Nat Art Show, Naples, Italy, 70. *Media:* Oil, Watercolor. *Publ:* Illusr, Concoa de Armor, Kim Sam Young, 88; Poesie, Teresinka Pereira, 89. *Mailing Add:* 44 Merritt Ave Eastchester NY 10709

ALFORD, GLORIA K
PAINTER, SCULPTOR
b Chicago, Ill, Oct 3, 28. *Study:* Univ Calif, Berkeley, AB; Art Inst Chicago; Penland Sch Crafts, NC; Columbia Univ; Pratt Graphics Ctr. *Work:* Elvehjem Mus, Univ Wis-Madison; CUNA Art Collection, Madison, Wis; Prudential Art Collection, Monterey Mus Art, Calif; Paper construction, Silicon Graphics, Mountain View, Calif. *Comn:* Four paper sculptures, Ask Computer Systems, Inc, 88. *Exhib:* Environ-Vision, Nat Competitive Exhib, Everson Mus, Syracuse, 72; In Her Own Image, Philadelphia Mus Art, 74; 19th Ann Print Exhib, Brooklyn Mus, 74; Wis Directions, Milwaukee Art Ctr, 75; Glass Backwards, Kohler Arts Ctr, Sheboygan, Wis, 79; solo shows, Monterey Peninsula Mus Art, 80, Netherlands Inst Advan Study, Wassenar, 82 & Djurovich Gallery, Sacramento, Calif, 86; Placement-Displacement Sculpture Show, Cabrillo Col, 83; Content Contemporary Issues, Euphrat Gallery, 86; The Chaminade Artists Series, Santa Cruz, Calif, 90; Computer Technology in the Arts, Sesnon Art Galley, Univ Calif, 90, Galerie Reve, Los Angeles, Calif, 90. *Pos:* Vis artist, Cult Exchange Prog, France, 76. *Teaching:* Guest lectr, Printmaking, Univ Calif Santa Cruz, summer 92. *Awards:* Top Honors, Univ Wis Art Show, Richland Ctr, 72. *Bibliog:* Donna Maurillo (auth), Gloria Alford of Santa Cruz, Monterey Life Mag, 11/84. *Mem:* Santa Cruz Art League (bd mem). *Media:* Miscellaneous Media. *Mailing Add:* 435 Meder St Santa Cruz CA 95060

ALHILALI, NEDA
ENVIRONMENTAL ARTIST, PAINTER
b Cheb, Czech, Nov 26, 38. *Study:* St Martin's Sch Art, London, Eng; Kunst Akademie, Munich, WGer; Univ Calif, Los Angeles, BA, 65, MA, 68. *Work:* Banff Art Ctr, Canada; Crocker Art Mus, Sacramento, Calif; Albright Col, Pa; ARAMCO, Houston; Central Mus Textiles, Lodz, Poland; and others. *Comn:* Blue Cross Hq, Los Angeles, 77; Hyatt Regency Hotels, Chicago, 77, also Los Angeles, Columbus, Maui & Palm Beach; Tishman Corp, Los Angeles, 78; Prince Kuhio Hotel, Hawaii, 80; Sheraton Hotel, Crystal City, Va; and others. *Exhib:* Mus of Contemp Art, Chicago, Pac Design Ctr, Los Angeles & Mus of Sci & Indust, Los Angeles, 76; Fiberworks, Cleveland Mus of Art, Ohio, 77; The Americas & Japan--Fiberworks, Nat Mus Mod Art, Tokyo & Kyoto, Japan, 77; one-woman shows, Allrich Gallery, San Francisco, Vanguard Gallery, Los Angeles, 77, Hunsaker Gallery, Los Angeles, Calif, 80 & 82 & Renwick Gallery, Washington, DC; Art Fabric: Mainstream, Am Fedn Arts: Mus Mod Art, San Francisco, Calif. *Collections Arranged:* Fiberworks (auth, catalog), Lang Art Gallery, Scripps Col, Claremont, Calif, 73; Inaugural Exhib, Mano Gallery, Chicago, 76; Paper Art (coauth, catalog), Galleries of the Claremont Cols, 77. *Teaching:* Asst prof art, Univ Calif, Los Angeles Exten, 70-77; from asst prof to assoc prof, Scripps Col & Claremont Grad Sch, 71-, chmn dept art, Scripps Coi, 82- *Awards:* Nat Endowment for the Arts Grants, 74 & 79; First Scripps Col Fac Recognition Award, 81. *Bibliog:* Betty Pawk (auth), Interview with N Al-Hilali, Fiberarts Mag, 7/8/79; Scott Miller (auth), Cassiopeia's Court, Images & Issues, Vol 3, No 1; Nan Hackett (auth), Opposites, Seattle Post Intelligencer, 7/2/82. *Mem:* Artists Equity Asn; Am Crafts Coun; World Crafts Coun. *Media:* Mixed. *Res:* Historic textiles. *Dealer:* Allrich Gallery San Francisco CA; Joyce Munsaker Gallery 812 N La Cienega Blvd Los Angeles CA 90069. *Mailing Add:* c/o Munsaker-Schlesinger Gallery 812 N La Cienega Blvd Los Angeles CA 90069

ALICEA, JOSE
PRINTMAKER
b Ponce, PR, Jan 12, 28. *Study:* Acad Pov, Ponce; Inst PR Cult, with Lorenzo Homar. *Work:* Philadelphia Mus Art; Mus Mod Art, New York; Libr of Cong, Washington, DC; Boston Pub Libr; Mus Arte Ponce. *Comn:* Woodcut mural, Inst PR Cult for Guayanilla High Sch, 70. *Exhib:* 4th Int Exhib of Drawing, Yugoslavia; 10th & 11th Biennalle Int d'Art, Menton, France; 12th Bienal de Sao Paulo, Brazil; 2nd & 3rd Bienal Int de Grafica, Frechen, Ger; and others. *Pos:* Asst to dir, Inst PR Cult Workshop, 58-62, instr, currently. *Teaching:* Instr printmaking, Escuela Artes Plasticas, San Juan, 67- *Awards:* Prize for Graphic, Ateneo Puertorriqueno, 65; Mildred Boerike Prize, Print Club Philadelphia, 67; Travel Grant, Casa Del Arte, San Juan, 68. *Bibliog:* E Ruiz de la Mata (auth), The art of Jose R Alicea, San Juan Rev Mag, 7/66 & Graphics by Alicea, San Juan Star, 8/9/70; Gloria Borras (auth), El grabado en la vida de Jose R Alicea, El Mundo, 69. *Media:* Miscellaneous. *Publ:* Illusr, Trovas larenas, 68; auth, Rio grande de Loiza (portfolio of prints), 68; Cancion de Baquine (portfolio of prints), 70; En las manos del pueblo, 72; Calambrenas. *Dealer:* Galeria Palomas 207 Cristo St Old San Juan, PR 00901. *Mailing Add:* c/o Galeria Palomas 207 Cristo St Old San Juan PR 00901

ALIKI
ILLUSTRATOR, WRITER
b Philadelphia, Pa. *Study:* Philadelphia Mus Col Art, grad. *Work:* Kerlan Collection, Walter Libr, Univ Minn, Minneapolis; de Grummond Collection, Univ Southern Miss, Hattiesburg; Seattle Pub Libr, Wash; Falvey Mem Libr, Villanova Univ, Pa; Rutgers Univ Children's Literature Collection, New Brunswick. *Exhib:* Children's Bk Coun Showcase Exhib; Biennale of Illus, Bratislava, Czech, 75; Soc Illusr Exhib, New York; Am Inst Graphic Arts Bk Exhib. *Awards:* First Prize of NY Acad Science's Children's Bk Award, 76; Drexel Univ Free Libr Philadelphia Citation, 91; Pa Sch Librns Asn Award, 91. *Bibliog:* Grace Hogarth (auth), Illustrators of Children's Books, Horn Bk Inc, 78; Iris M Tiedt (auth), Exploring Books with Children, Houghton Mifflin, 79; Monson & Sutherlan (auths), Children & Books, Scott, Foresman, 81. *Media:* Gouache, Crayon. *Publ:* A Medieval Feast, 83, How a Book is Made, 86 & Digging Up Dinosaurs, 88, Harper/Collins; Feelings, Greenwillow, 84; Manners, Greenwillow, 90. *Mailing Add:* 17 Regent's Park Terr London NW 1 7ED England United Kingdom

ALINDER, JAMES GILBERT
GALLERY OWNER, PHOTOGRAPHER
b Glendale, Calif, Mar 31, 41. *Study:* Macalester Col, BA, 62; Univ Minn, 62-64; Univ NMex, MFA, 68. *Work:* Mus Mod Art, New York; Bibliot Nat, Paris; Art Inst Chicago; Int Mus Photog, George Eastman House, Rochester, NY; Nat Gallery Can, Ottawa; San Francisco Mus Mod Art; Victoria & Albert Mus, London, Eng. *Exhib:* Light, Hayden Gallery, Mass Inst Technol, 68; solo exhibs, Sheldon Gallery, Univ Nebr, 69, Camerawork Gallery, San Francisco, 79 & Spiva Art Ctr, Joplin, Mo, 80; Be-Ing Without Clothes, Hayden Art Gallery, Mass Inst Technol, 70; The Great West: Real-Ideal, Univ Colo Art Mus & traveling, 77; The Extended Frame, Visual Studies

Workshop, Rochester, New York, 77; 20th Century Photography, Centre Pompidou, Paris, 77; The Diana Show, Wynn Bullock Gallery, Carmel, Calif, 80; Am Photog Today: Univ Colo, 82; Exposed & Developed, Nat Mus Am Art, Washington, DC, 84; Family Portraits, Wright State Univ, 87; Photographic Truth: Bruce Mus, 88; retrospective, Int Photog Hall of Fame, 92. *Collections Arranged:* Wright Morris: Structures & Artifacts, Sheldon Mem Art Gallery, Lincoln, Nebr, 75; Crying for a Vision, 76; Twelve Photographers: A Mid-America Contemporary Document, 78; Jerome Liebling: Retrospective, 78; New Color Work: Divola, Fitch, North, Ollman & Pfahl, 78; Ruth Bernhard Retrospective (with catalog), 79; The Contact Print (with catalog), 82; Ansel Adams Classic Images (with catalog), 86; Light Years, 87. *Pos:* Exec dir, Friends of Photog, Carmel, Calif, 77-87, bd trustees, 87; bd trustees, Monterey Pen Mus Art, 86-, vpres, 87, pres, 88; actg exec dir, Friends Photog, San Francisco, Calif, 88-89. *Teaching:* Assoc prof photog & photog hist, Univ Nebr, Lincoln, 68-77; instr, Ansel Adams Yosemite Workshop, 79-81. *Awards:* Nat Endowment Arts Fel, 73 & 80; Woods Found Fel, 74. *Bibliog:* N Geske (ed), Photographs, Univ Nebr Press, 77; J Enyeart (ed), Kansas Album, Kans Bankers Asn, 77; J Green (auth), Am Photog, Abrams, 84. *Mem:* Soc Photog Educ (ed Exposure, 73-77, secy, 73-75, vchmn, 75-77, chmn, 77-79); Photog Arts & Sci Found (pres, 85); Monterey Co Cult Coun (chmn, 81-82); Am Asn Mus. *Media:* Photography. *Publ:* Auth, Ansel Adams: Photographs of the American West, 80; Wright Morris: Photographs and Words, 82; Picture America, 82; Harry Callahan: Eleanor, 84; coauth, Ansel Adams: Classic Images, 85; and others. *Mailing Add:* Alinder Gallery PO Box 1146 Gualala CA 95445

ALINDER, MARY STREET
WRITER, CURATOR
b Bowling Green, Ohio, Sept 23, 46. *Study:* Univ Mich; Univ NMex; Univ Nebr, BA, 76. *Comn:* Authentication of the work of Ansel Adams for mus, auction houses, insurance co and pvt individuals. *Collections Arranged:* Ansel Adams: 80th Birthday Retrospective - 150 Prints (auth, catalog), Monterey Mus Art & Calif Acad Sci, 82; Ansel Adams - 200 prints (auth, catalog), Denver Mus Natural Hist, 83; Ansel Adams - A 125 Print Exhib, Nat Mus Art, Beijing & People's Cultural Palace, Shanghai, People's Repub China; One with Beauty - A 168 print Exhib retrospective of Ansel Adams, The M H deYoung Mem Mus, San Francisco, 87; Ansel Adams: American Artist, The Ansel Adams Ctr, San Francisco, 89. *Pos:* Mgr, Weston Gallery, Carmel, Calif, 78-79; exec asst to Ansel Adams, Carmel, Calif, 79-84; exec ed & bus mgr, Ansel Adams Publ Rights Trust, 84-87; freelance, & co-owner Alinder Gallery, Gualala, Calif, currently. *Teaching:* Lectr & instr workshops in US, France, Eng and People's Rep China, 82-86; Nat Gallery Art, Washington, DC, 85; Los Angeles Co Mus, M H De Young Mus, Univ Calif, Berkeley, Univ Mich, Univ Cincinnati, Cleveland Mus Natural Hist, Stanford Univ, High Mus Art, Calif Wilderness Collection. *Mem:* Friends of Photog. *Res:* Work and life of Ansel Adams; Group f/64; creative photography. *Publ:* Auth, Ansel Adams: 1902-1984, Ansel's Last Day, the Friends of Photog, 84; coauth, Ansel Adams: An Autobiography, 85 & coed, Ansel Adams: Letters & Images, 1916-1984, 88, Little, Brown; auth, Ansel Adams' Polaroid Connection, Parts I & 2, The Polaroid Newsletter for Photographic Educ, spring & summer, 87, Ansel Adams: A Man of Our World, Skinner, Inc, Boston, 89; auth, Picturing Yosemite, Places, New York, 90. *Mailing Add:* c/o Alinder Gallery 39165 S Coastal Hwy Gualala CA 95445

ALLAIN, RENÉ PIERRE
PAINTER, SCULPTOR
b Montreal, Can, Dec 28, 51. *Study:* Loyola Montreal, Que, CEGEP, 71; Univ Ottawa, Ont, BA(fine arts), 81; Hunter Col, City Univ New York, MFA, 86. *Work:* Brooklyn Mus, NY; Nat Gallery Can, Ottawa, Ont; London Regional Art & Historical Mus, Ont; Can Coun Art Bank, Ottawa, Ont. *Comn:* Pub sculpture, City of Ottawa, 82. *Exhib:* Solo Show, The Core Island Complex, London Regional Art & Historical Mus, Ont, 84; Présent Antérieur, Mus Contemp Art, Montreal, Que, 84; Building of Architectural Vision, City Gallery New York, 86 & Princeton Univ Sch Architecture, Princeton, 87; selected New York Found Arts Artists, Univ Art Gallery, State Univ NY, Albany, 90; Open Mind: The Lewitt Collection, Wadsworth Atheneum, Hartford, Conn, 91-92; Slow Art: Painting in New York Now, PS 1 Mus, 92. *Teaching:* Instr drawing, Sch Visual Arts, New York, 90- *Awards:* B Grants, Can Coun, 84 & 88; New York Found Arts Fel, 90; Nat Endowment Arts Fel, 91. *Bibliog:* Eleanor Heartney (auth), review, Art in Am, 9/90; Dena Shottenkirk (auth), review, Art Forum, 10/91; Ihor Holubizky (auth), The Necessity of Impassioned Arguments, ETC Montreal, 2/92. *Media:* Plaster, Pigments; Steel. *Publ:* Coauth, The Core Island Complex (exhib cat), London Regional Art & Historical Mus, 84. *Dealer:* Julian Pretto 103 Sullivan St New York NY 10012. *Mailing Add:* 139 N 10 St Brooklyn NY 11211

ALLAN, WILLIAM GEORGE
PAINTER, EDUCATOR
b Everett, Wash, Mar 28, 36. *Study:* San Francisco Art Inst, BFA. *Work:* Dallas Mus Art; San Francisco Mus Art; Philadelphia Mus Art; Whitney Mus Am Art, Mus Mod Art, New York. *Exhib:* Carnegie Int Exhib, Pittsburgh, 57; Continuing Surrealism, La Jolla Mus Art, Calif, 71; Whitney Painting Ann, New York, 72; 70th Am Exhib, Art Inst Chicago, 72; Indianapolis Mus Art Exhib, 72; Whitney Mus Am Art, New York, 73-74; Painting & Sculpture in California: The Mod Era, San Francisco Mus Mod Art, 76; Chicago Arts Club, 78. *Teaching:* Instr painting, Univ Calif, Davis, 65-67; instr painting, Univ Calif, Berkeley, 69; prof art, Calif State Univ, Sacramento, 68- *Media:* Acrylic, Watercolor. *Dealer:* Hansen-Fuller Gallery 228 Grant Ave San Francisco CA 94108. *Mailing Add:* c/o Gallery Paul Anglim 14 Geary St San Francisco CA 94108

ALLARA, PAMELA EDWARDS
EDUCATOR, ADMINISTRATOR
b Scarsdale, NY, Sept 11, 43. *Study:* Brown Univ, BA, 65; Johns Hopkins Univ, PhD, 71. *Teaching:* Assoc Dean, Mus Sch progs & sr lectr art hist, Fine Arts Dept, Tufts Univ, 73-90; asst prof, Fine Art Dept, Brandeis Univ, Waltham, Mass, 90- *Res:* Contemporary art; modern art in Boston; history of photography. *Publ:* Coauth (with S Prokopoff), Christo's Urban Projects: A Survey, Inst Contemp Art, Boston, 79; auth, Nicholas Nixon's anonymous immortals, Art New England, 1/80; The broad scope of Boston arts, Art News, 11/81; A Boston School: Four Artists, Tufts Univ Gallery II, 82; Herb Jackson: Drawings, Mint Mus Art, 83; A loud song, Views, fall 86; Expressionism in Boston, de Cordova Mus, 86; Cross Currents/Cross Country, Photog Resource Ctr, Boston, 88. *Mailing Add:* Dept Fine Arts Brandeis Univ Waltham MA 02254

ALLEN, BRUCE WAYNE
EDUCATOR, SCULPTOR
b Columbia, Mo, Feb 27, 53. *Study:* Centenary Col, La, with Willard Cooper, BA, 75, BS, 77; Acad Der Bildenden Kunst, Stuttgart, WGer, 80-81; Univ Wyo, with David Reif & John van Alstein, MFA, 81. *Work:* Wyo State Mus, Cheyenne; Horizons Gallery, Ft Collins, Colo. *Comn:* Sculpture, Glory Bound, Univ Wyo, Laramie, 82; sculpture, Building Blocks, Red Devil Corp, Cincinatti, Ohio, 86. *Exhib:* Solo Exhib, Wyo State Mus, Cheyenne, 81. *Pos:* Acting cur, Meadows Mus Art; dir, Turner Art Ctr Gallery & Magale Libr Gallery, currently. *Teaching:* Assoc prof studio & art history, Centenary Col La, 83-90. *Mem:* Art in Action (co-founder, 86); La Artists Inc, (pres, 88-90); Int Sculpture Conf; Col Art Asn; Women's Caucus for Arts. *Media:* All Media. *Mailing Add:* 305 Linden St Shreveport LA 71104

ALLEN, CATHERINE MACDONALD
PAINTER
b Virginia, Aug 8, 49. *Study:* Am Univ, BA, 71; Boston Univ, with Philip Guston, MFA, 76. *Work:* Zale Corp, Dallas, Tex; New York City Health & Hospitals Corp; Chemical Bank, New York; Boston Univ, Mass. *Exhib:* Solo, Sotto 20 Gallery, NY, 85, 86, 89 & Rutgers Univ, New Brunswick, NJ, 87; group shows, American Drawings III, Smithsonian Inst, Washington, DC, 81, Everson Mus, Syracuse, NY, 84, Albright Knox Members Gallery, Buffalo, NY, 88, Wade Gallery, Los Angeles, Calif, 90. *Pos:* Bd dirs, New York Feminist Art Inst, NY, 80-88. *Teaching:* instr painting & drawing, Mt Wachusett Community Col, 77-79; instr, NY Feminist Art Inst, New York, 80-88; lectr, Calif State Univ, Long Beach, 91. *Awards:* Fel Nat Endowment Arts, 89-90; Yaddo Fel, 82. *Bibliog:* Palm Latitudes, Los Angeles Times Mag, 4/28/91; A Natural Indulgence, Martin, Victoria, Artweek, 1/23/92. *Mem:* Women's Caucus Arts; Col Art Asn. *Media:* Oil. *Dealer:* Wade Gallery 308 N Sycamore No 208 Los Angeles CA 90036; Soho 20 Gallery New York NY. *Mailing Add:* c/o Soho 20 469 Broome St New York NY 10013

ALLEN, CONSTANCE OLLEEN WEBB
PAINTER, JEWELRY DESIGNER
b Camphill, Ala, June 10, 23. *Study:* George Washington Univ; Inst Allende, San Miguel de Allende, Mex; also with Richard Goetz, Oklahoma City & Roy Swanson, Green Valley, Ariz. *Work:* Jane Brooks Sch Deaf; Chickasha Pub Libr. *Comn:* 20 Indian Portraits, A C Leftwich, Duncan, Okla, 72; Landscapes of Southwest Okla, comn by Susan Johnston, Oklahoma City, 78. *Exhib:* 39th & 41st Ann Miniature Painters, Sculptors & Gravers Soc of Washington, DC, Art Club of Washington, 72 & 74; Ann Festival of the Arts, Tubac, Ariz, 85, 87, 88, 89, 90 & 92; Ariz State Exhib, Nat League Am Pen Women, Sedona, 87, Phoenix, 89, Ariz; Mont Miniature Art Soc Ninth Ann Int Show, Billings, Mont, 87. *Teaching:* Instr drawing & painting, Univ Sci & Arts of Okla, Chickasha, 74-76. *Awards:* First Place for Pastel, Chickasha Art Guild, Okla, 73; Merit Award Graphic, Fla Nat Miniature Art Show, Okla, 76; First Place Watercolor, Santa Rita Art League Show, Nogales, Ariz, 87; hon Mention, Santa Cruz Valley Art Asn, Tubac, Ariz, 86; and others. *Bibliog:* A C Leftwich (auth), Indian Hall of Fame, painted by Mrs Webb, 72 & Mrs N H Welch (auth), Mrs Webb has exhib, 74 Chickasha Daily Express; Dale Parish (auth), Artist paints favorite subjects, Green Valley News, 84. *Mem:* Santa Rita Art League, Ariz (pres, 83-84); Nat League Am Pen Women (pres, Sonora Desert Br, 88-90); Arts & Crafts Asn, Green Valley, Ariz, (vpres, 86-87); Santa Cruz Vallery Art Asn, Tubac, Ariz. *Media:* Multimedia; Precious Metals, Gemstones. *Mailing Add:* 2791 S Calle Morena Green Valley AZ 85614

ALLEN, EDDA LYNNE
PAINTER, ART DEALER
b Big Spring, Tex, July 29, 32. *Study:* With Randall Davey, Will Schuster & William Longley, 57-62; Southern Methodist Univ; Tex Tech Univ; Univ NMex; Col Santa Fe, BA(summa cum laude), 68. *Work:* Santa Fe Co Munic Ct, NMex State Capitol, Mayors Off, Santa Fe; NMex State Police Off. *Exhib:* Joslyn Art Mus, Omaha, Nebr, 72; Artist Alpine Holiday, Ouray Arts Asn, Colo, 72; Arts Festival, NMex Art League, Albuquerque, 72-74; Roswell Mus & Art Ctr, NMex, 73; one-man show, NMex State Fair, 75. *Teaching:* Instr tech, Col of Santa Fe, 67-68; lectr Alla Prima tech, Univ NMex, 70-71. *Awards:* Award of Merit, Am Arthritis Found, 75; First in Show, Rio Grande Arts & Crafts, 77-78. *Mem:* Santa Fe Soc Art. *Media:* Oil, Watercolor. *Mailing Add:* 1456 Diolinda St Santa Fe NM 87501

ALLEN, (HARVEY) HAROLD
PHOTOGRAPHER, ART HISTORIAN
b Portland, Ore, June 29, 12. *Study:* Art Inst Chicago, 37-41, Sch Design, Chicago, 40-41, Univ Chicago, 48-54. *Work:* Art Inst Chicago; Metrop Mus Art; Columbia Col, Chicago; Libr of Cong; Ill State Mus. *Exhib:* The Photographer and the City, Mus Contemp Art, Chicago, 77; Harold Allen's

Egypt, Evanston Art Ctr, Ill, 77; Tut-Tut: A Survey of Egyptomania, Stanford Univ Mus Art, 79; Father Ravalli's Missions, Mont His Soc, Helena, 84; Harold Allen: Photographer & Teacher, Art Inst Chicago, 84-85; Egypt (American style), Northern Ill Univ, Dekalb, 88. *Teaching:* Instr photog, Art Inst Chicago, 48-60 & 66-77, Frederick Latimer Wells Prof, 71, retired, 77; instr beginning & documentary photog, Columbia Col, Chicago, 71 & 72. *Awards:* Chicago Art Awards, 78; Hon DFA, Art Inst Chicago, 79. *Bibliog:* Michael Starenko (auth), In search of Harold Allen's Egypt, New Art Examiner, 81. *Mem:* Soc Photog Educ. *Res:* Egyptian Revival art and architecture in Europe and America. *Publ:* Auth & illusr, Egyptian influences in Wedgwood designs, Seventh Wedgwood Int Sem, 62; Father Ravalli's Missions, The Good Lion, Art Inst Chicago, 72; Egyptian Wedgwood, twenty-sixth Wedgwood Int, Sem, 81. *Mailing Add:* 1725 S Des Plaines St Chicago IL 60616

ALLEN, JANE ADDAMS
EDITOR, CRITIC
b Chicago, Ill. *Study:* Univ Chicago, with Joshua Taylor and Harold Rosenberg, BA & MFA; San Francisco Sch Fine Arts, with Richard Diebenkorn. *Collections Arranged:* Chicago Like It Is and Was, Centennial Photog Exhib, Chicago State Univ, Chicago Civic Ctr, 69. *Pos:* Art & photog critic, Chicago Tribune, 71-73; ed, New Art Examiner, 73-82; art critic, Washington Times, 82-, Insight Mag, 85- & Washington Post, currently. *Awards:* Critics Fel, Nat Endowment Arts, 75 & 80; Art World Award for Distinquished Art Criticism, Manufacturers Hanover, 84 & 89. *Bibliog:* Sophy Burnham (auth), The Critics, Mus and Arts Washington, Vol III, No 6, 11-12/87. *Mem:* Chicago New Art Asn (pres, 70-82); Col Art Asn. *Publ:* Auth, Letting go, Art Am, 1/86; Art for profit's sake, Insight Mag, 3/31/86; Awards in the Visual Arts (catalog, essay), 89; The Sacred and the Profane, New Art Examiner, summer 90. *Mailing Add:* 2718 Ontario Rd NW Washington DC 20009

ALLEN, JERE HARDY
PAINTER, EDUCATOR
b Selma, Ala, Aug 15, 44. *Study:* Ringling Sch Art, Sarasota, Fla, four yr cert, 69, BFA, 70; Univ Tenn, Knoxville, MFA, 72. *Work:* Mobile Art Gallery, Ala; Coos Art Mus, Ore; Liberty Corp, Greenville, SC; R I Kahn Gallery, Houston; Meridian Mus Art, Miss; City of Hameln, WGer. *Exhib:* West 79 and 80/The Law, Minn Mus Art, 79 & 80; Der Kunstkreis Hameln, 89; Oldenburger Kunstuerein, 89; Stadtische Galerie, Paderborn, WGer, 90; Brenau Col, Gainsville, Ga, 92; Carol Robinson Gallery, New Orleans, La, 92; and others. *Teaching:* Instr drawing, Carson-Newman Col, 71-72; prof painting, Univ Miss, 72- *Awards:* Tenn Art League Purchase Award, The Parthenon, 74; Award of Distinction, Mainstreams of Marietta Col, 75; Award, Shreveport Nat, Barnwell Art Ctr, La, 75. *Mem:* Southeastern Col Arts Conf. *Media:* Oil, Mixed Media. *Mailing Add:* 1103 S 14th St Oxford MS 38655

ALLEN, JESSE
PRINTMAKER, PAINTER
b Nairobi, Kenya, Mar 11, 36; US citizen. *Study:* Oxford Univ, BA, 58, MA, 60. *Work:* Stanford Univ Mus Art, Palo Alto, Calif; Ft Wayne Mus Art, Ind; Palm Springs Desert Mus, Calif; Mus Asn North Orange Co, Fullerton, Calif; Allen Mem Gallery, Oberlin, Ohio. *Exhib:* Cult Found Fed Dist Brasilla, Brazila, 86; Mitsukoshi Gallery, Chiba City, Japan, 87; solo exhib, Vorpal Gallery, San Francisco, Calif, 88 & New York, 89; Gallery Floresta, Tokyo, Japan, 90; Yokohama Art Gallery, Japan, 90. *Bibliog:* Muldoon Elder (producer), Bright Tempest: The Art of Jesse Allen (film); Thelma Newman (auth), Innovative Printmaking, Crown Publ, 77; Marsha Semmel (auth), Jesse Allen (catalog), Taft Mus. *Media:* Acrylic; Graphics. *Mailing Add:* c/o Vorpal Gallery 393 Grove St San Francisco CA 94102

ALLEN, JUDITH S
PHOTOGRAPHER
b New York, NY, Jan 21, 56. *Study:* Oberlin Col, BA, 77; Mills Col, MFA, 90. *Exhib:* Richmond Art Ctr, Calif, 91; San Francisco Arts Comn Gallery, 91; Berkeley Art Ctr, Calif, 91. *Teaching:* Lectr photog, San Francisco State Univ, 91-92; instr art, Cornish Col Arts, 92- *Awards:* Trefethen Award, Mills Col, 89; Visual Artist Fel, Nat Endowment Arts, 90-91. *Mem:* Col Art Asn. *Mailing Add:* 222-A 11th Ave E Seattle WA 98102

ALLEN, KAOLA
COLLAGE ARTIST, PAINTER
b Cincinnati, Ohio, June 16, 52. *Study:* Univ NC, Chapel Hill, BA(art), 74. *Work:* R J Reynolds, Winston-Salem, NC; NCNB, Charlotte, NC; Duke Med Ctr, Durham, NC; Chapel Hill Children's Clinic, Chapel Hill, NC. *Exhib:* Forty-eighth Southeastern Competition for Drawing, Photog & Printmaking, Southeastern Ctr Contemp Art, 80; Charlotte Juried Exhib, Spirit Sq Galleries, NC, 81; Ensemble: Collage & Assemblage, Green Hill Art Ctr, Greensboro, NC, 82; Southeastern Graphics, Mint Mus Art, 82; Collage: Southeast, Southeastern Ctr Contemp Art & traveling with Southern Arts Fedn, 82-83; Xerox Show, Southeastern Ctr Contemp Art, 84; Women Printmakers of the Southeast, McKissick Mus, Columbia, SC, 84; The Artist's Self, Southeastern Ctr Contemp Art & traveling with Southern Arts Fedn, 85-86. *Awards:* Juror's Merit Award, Charlotte Exhib, 81; Best in Show Purchase Award, Southeastern Graphics Invitational, NC Nat Bank, 82; Grant, funded by Nat Endowment Asn & Feminist Am Art Inst, Visual Artists' Exchange in collaboration, 83. *Bibliog:* Allen, Irwin, Holsenbeck & Foster (producers), Birth Days: A Collaborative Room Installation (videotape), 82. *Media:* Miscellaneous. *Mailing Add:* 103 Longwood Dr Chapel Hill NC 27514

ALLEN, LORETTA B
PAINTER, DESIGNER
b Caney, Kans. *Study:* Fed Arts Schs, Minneapolis; Famous Artists Sch; also with Grace Chadwick & Marshall Lakey, Oklahoma City, Molly Guion & Dimitri Romanofsky, New York. *Exhib:* Oklahoma City Art Ctr; Tulsa Studio Group, 61 & 62; Osage Co Hist Mus, 69; Pastel Ballerinas, Birkbeck Designs Gallery, Tulsa, Okla, 91 & 92; plus others. *Pos:* Illusr, children's bks; fashion designer; fashion illusr, local publ. *Mem:* Am Artists Prof League. *Media:* Pen & Ink; Pastel, Acrylic. *Mailing Add:* 1645 E 17th Pl Tulsa OK 74120

ALLEN, NANCY SCHUSTER
LIBRARIAN, EDUCATOR
b Buffalo, NY, Jan 10, 48. *Study:* Univ Rochester, BA(fine arts), 71, MA(fine arts), 73; Rutgers Univ, MLS, 73. *Pos:* Reference librn, Mus Fine Arts, Boston, 75-77, head librn, 77- *Teaching:* Lectr, art librarianship, Simmons Col Grad Sch Libr & Info Sci, 84- *Mem:* Art Libr Soc NAm (exec bd, 82-85, chair, 83-84); Mus Computer Network (chair, Art & Arch Prog Comt, Res Libr Group, 84-87); Int Fedn Art Libr (financial officer, Art Sect, 86-); Fenway Libr Online Inc (vpres, 87-89, pres, 89-91); Comm Preservation & Access, Scholarly Advisory Comt on Art History, 90 & Joint Task Force on Text & Image, 89-92. *Res:* Computer applications to accessing art object information, visual resources & bibliographic citations for museum objects, conservation & preservation of art library collections. *Publ:* Auth, Art libr, 1984 American Library Association Yearbook of Library & Information Services, Am Libr Asn, Chicago, 85; The History of Western Language Sources for the Study of Japanese Art, Art Libr J, Vol 11, No 4, 86; Bibliographic systems & their object catalog system counterparts, In: Procedural Guide to Automating an Art Library (ARLIS/NA Occasional Papers, No 7), 87; The museum prototype project of the J Paul Getty Art History & Information Program: A view from the library, In: Linking Art Objects & Art Information (Library Trends, Vol 37, No 2), 88; The Art & Architectural Program of the Research Libraries Group, Vol 13, No 4, Art Libr J, 88, 5-10 & Vol 23, No 3, Inspel, 89, 141-154. *Mailing Add:* 465 Huntington Ave Boston MA 02115

ALLEN, RALPH
PAINTER, EDUCATOR
b Eng, 1926. *Study:* Sir John Cass Sch Art & Slade Sch Fine Arts, London. *Work:* Nat Gallery Can; Art Gallery Toronto; Queen's Univ, Ont; Queen's Park, Toronto; also in pvt collections. *Teaching:* Assoc prof art hist & dir, Agnes Etherington Art Ctr, Queen's Univ, Ont, formerly; retired. *Awards:* Jessie Dow Award, Montreal, 59; Can Coun Scholar, 59 & Sr Fel, 68; Baxter Award, Toronto, 60. *Mem:* Ont Soc Artists; Royal Can Acad Arts. *Mailing Add:* 199 Albert St Kingston ON K7L 3V4 Canada

ALLEN, ROBERTA
CONCEPTUAL ARTIST, PAINTER
b New York, NY, Oct 6, 45. *Work:* Mus Mod Art, New York; Metrop Mus Art, New York; Cooper-Hewitt Mus, New York; Cincinnati Art Mus; Univ Wis-Milwaukee; Stadtische Galerie im Lenbachhaus, Munich. *Exhib:* Solo exhibs, John Weber Gallery, New York, 74, 75, 77 & 79, Kunstforum, Staadtische Gallerie im Lanbachhaus, Munich, 81, Galerie Walter Storms, Munich, 81 & Galeria Primo Piano, Rome, 81, Perth Inst Contemp Arts, Australia, 89; Contemp Abstract Art: Works on Paper, Baltimore Mus of Art, 76; Abstract Drawings, Albright-Knox Art Gallery, Buffalo, NY, 76; MTL Galerie, Brussels, Belg, 78; and others. *Awards:* Creative Artist Pub Serv Grant, 78-79; LINE grant, 85; Artist-in-Residence Fel, Art Gallery of Western Australia, Perth Australia, 89. *Bibliog:* Jeff Deitch (auth), Roberta Allen, Arts Mag, 6/77; Judith Lopez Cardozo (auth), Roberta Allen, Artforum, 2/78; Margaret Ann Escher (auth), Women Artists News, 9/88. *Media:* Drawing; Acrylic. *Publ:* Auth, Pointless Arrows, pvt publ, 76; Pointless Acts, Collation Ctr, 77; Possibilities, John Weber Gallery & Parasol Press, 77; Everything in the World There is to Know by Somebody, But Not by the Same knower, Ottenhausen Verlag, Munich, 81; The Traveling Woman, Vehicle Ed, 86. *Mailing Add:* 5 W 16th St New York NY 10011

ALLEN, TERRY
VIDEO ARTIST
b Wichita, Kan, May 7, 43. *Study:* Chouinard Art Inst, Los Angeles, BFA, 66. *Work:* Metrop Mus Art, New York; Mus Mod Art, New York; Detroit Inst Arts, Mich; La Jolla Mus Contemp Art, Calif; Mus Contemp Art, Los Angeles, Calif. *Exhib:* Solo exhibs, Big Witness, San Francisco Art Inst, 89, The Artists Eye: Terry Allen, Kimbell Art Mus, Ft Worth & Terry Allen: New Work, Los Angeles Louver, Venice, 91, Gallery Paule Anglim, San Francisco, Betty Moddy Gallery, Houston, Tex, Wexner Ctr Visual Arts, Columbus, Ohio & Youth in Asia, Southeastern Ctr Contemp Art, Winston-Salem, NC, 92; Critical Reactions, Rena Branston Gallery, San Francisco, Calif, 91; Text Context, San Jose Inst Contemp Art, San Jose, Calif, 91; The Political Arm, John Weber Gallery, New York & Wash Univ, St Louis, Mo, 91; Positions in the Desert, Gallery Paule Anglim, San Francisco, Calif, 91; Profiles II: On Paper, Adair Margo Gallery, El Paso, Tex, traveling to Weber State Univ, Ogden, Utah & Arlington Mus, Tex, 92. *Pos:* Faculty, Calif State Univ, Fresno, 71-79. *Teaching:* Instr drawing, Chouinard Art Inst, Los Angeles, 68-69. *Awards:* Bessie Award, New York, 86; Nat Endowment Arts, Guggenheim Fel, 86; Adaline Kent Award, San Francisco, 89. *Bibliog:* Jody Zellen (auth), Terry Allen, Arts Mag, 10/91; Joan Smith (auth), He'll take it and make art, San Francisco Examiner, 10/91; Benjamin Weissman (auth), Terry Allen, Artforum, 11/91. *Mailing Add:* c/o Wanda Hansen 615 Main St Sausalito CA 94965

ALLEN, TOM, JR
SCULPTOR, DESIGNER
b Havana, Cuba, Jan 23, 27; US citizen. *Study:* Univ Havana, cert(archit); Univ Madrid, cert(lit); Royal Acad Fine Arts San Fernando, Spain; Corcoran Sch Art; George Washington Univ, AA. *Work:* Am Numismatic Soc, New York; Carnegie Mus Natural Hist, Pittsburgh; Metrop Mus Art, New York; Muzeum Sztuki Medalierkiej, Crakow, Poland; World Heritage Mus, Champaign, Ill. *Comn:* Heroic frieze, Poor Richard Club, Philadelphia, 52; statuary, John Wanamaker, Inc, Philadelphia, 53-55; insignia & medal, Dept Recreation, City Philadelphia, 58; monument, Zoological Garden Philadelphia, 74; plus many busts of numerous personalities. *Exhib:* Nat Sculpture Soc Ann Exhib, 57 & 72; Fidem Int Exhib; Cologne, Ger, 58; Artists Equity Exhib, Philadelphia Mus Art, Philadelphia Civic Ctr, 71 & 74; one-man show, Rutgers Univ, 72; Ten Crucial Days, NJ State Mus, Trenton, 76-77; and others. *Pos:* Scenic designer, Valley Forge Music Fair, Pa, 55; art dir, Burroughs Corp, Philadelphia, 56-57; dir advert & promotion, Johnson & Johnson Int, New Brunswick, NJ, 59-62. *Teaching:* Instr art, 20th Army Air Force, Guam, 46; instr arts & crafts, Moyamensing Prison, Philadelphia, 58-59; artisan-instr sculpture, Johnson Atelier, Princeton, 74-77; fac, Arts Inst, Rutgers Univ, summer 81 & 82. *Awards:* First Prize Drawing, Buenos Aires Herald, Arg, 39; Winner Nat Open Competition, Soc Medalists, 70. *Media:* Multimedia. *Publ:* Auth & contribr, numerous how-to articles. *Mailing Add:* Dept Art Univ Kans Lawrence KS 66045

ALLEN, WILLIAM J
HISTORIAN, EDUCATOR
b Tuscaloosa, Ala, Nov 8, 45. *Study:* Univ Ala, BA, 68; Johns Hopkins Univ, MA, 73, PhD(Kress Fel, Am Res Inst Turkey Fel), 81. *Teaching:* Vis asst prof, Okla State Univ, 77-79; assoc prof art hist, Ark State Univ, Jonesboro, 79-, chmn art dept, 83-87, dean Col Fine Arts, 87-91, prof art hist, 91- *Mem:* Col Art Asn Am; Hist Photog Group (nat coordr 87-). *Publ:* Auth, The Spirit of fact in court: Southworth's testimony in Marcy vs Barnes, In: History of Photography, 83 & The Abdul Hamid II collection, 83, Legal Tests of Photography-as-Art: Sarony and Others, 86, History of Photography; Sixty-Nine Istanbul Photographers in Shadow and Substance: Essays on the History of Photography in Honor of Heinz K Henisch, 90. *Mailing Add:* Dept Art Ark State Univ Main Campus State University AR 72467

ALLENTUCK, MARCIA EPSTEIN
HISTORIAN, EDUCATOR
b New York, NY, June 8, 28. *Study:* New York Univ, BA; Columbia Univ, PhD, 64. *Teaching:* Prof hist art, Graduate Ctr, City Univ NY, 72-88, prof emer, 88- *Awards:* Sr Res Fel, Dumbarton Oaks, 72-73 & Nat Endowment Humanities, 73-74; Vis Fel, Wolfson Col, Oxford Univ, Eng, 74; Res Fel Brit Acad, 80; Inst Advan Studies, Univ Edinburgh, 83-84; vis scholar, Burnall Art Collection, Glasgow, Scotland, 87- 88; Swann Found Fel, 89-90; vis scholor, Wolfson Col, Oxford, 90- *Mem:* Col Art Asn; Soc Archit Historians Gt Brit; Soc Archit Historians; fel Royal Soc Arts; PEN, Soc of Authors. *Res:* British, American & Canadian art & architectural history. *Publ:* Auth, The work of Henry Needler, Clark Libr, Univ Calif Press, 60; Henry Fuseli: The artist as man of letters & critic, Univ Microfilm Am, 64; The achievement of Isaac Bashevis Singer, Southern Ill Univ Press, 69; Rosettis Burd-Alane, Burlington Mag, 12/70; John Graham's System & Dialects of Art, Johns Hopkins Univ Press, 71; Mark Gertler, Apollo, 10/74; Fuseli & Macklin, J of the Warburg & Courtauld Inst, 76. *Mailing Add:* 5 W 86th St Apt 12B New York NY 10024

ALLGOOD, CHARLES HENRY
ART HISTORIAN, PAINTER
b Augusta, Ga, Apr 24, 23. *Study:* Univ Ga, with Lamar Dodd, Carl Holty, Yasuo Kunyoshi, BFA, MFA; Ecole du Louvre, Paris. *Exhib:* Painting of the Year, Atlanta, Ga, 63 & 65; Southeastern Art Exhib, Atlanta, 65; Miss Nat Exhib, Jackson, 66; Mid-South Exhib, Memphis, Tenn, 71. *Collections Arranged:* African Art & Artifacts, 74; Egyptian Art & Artifacts, 75. *Pos:* Dir, E H Little Gallery, Memphis State Univ; illusr children's bks, 89. *Teaching:* Prof painting, Judson Col, Marion, Ala, 51-55; prof painting, Memphis State Univ, 55-89. *Media:* Oil, Transparent Watercolor. *Mailing Add:* 3886 Healy Rd Memphis TN 38111

ALLING, CLARENCE (EDGAR)
MUSEUM DIRECTOR, CERAMIST
b Dawson Co, Nebr, Jan 28, 33. *Study:* Washburn Univ, BFA; Ohio State Univ, with Edgar Littlefield; Univ Kans, with Sheldon Carey, MFA. *Work:* Excelsior Ins Co, New York. *Exhib:* One-man shows, Mulvane Art Ctr, Topeka, Kans, 63 & Sioux City Art Ctr, Iowa, 63; Area Artists, Sioux City, 63 & 65 & Des Moines, Iowa, 64; two-man show, L'Atelier, Cedar Falls, Iowa, 65; and others. *Pos:* Dir, Waterloo Mus Art, currently. *Awards:* Prizes, Designer-Craftsman Show, Lawrence, Kans, 59-61; Purchase award, Ceramic Nat, Everson Mus, Syracuse, NY, 60; Merit award, Sioux City, 65. *Mailing Add:* c/o Waterloo Museum Art 225 Commercial St Waterloo IA 50701

ALLING, JANET D
PAINTER
b New York, NY Dec 19, 39. *Study:* Skidmore Col, 57-60; Yale Univ Sch Art, MFA, 64; Studied with Alex Katz, Neil Welliver, Philip Pearlstein. *Work:* Univ Va Art Mus, Charlottesville; Bellevue Hosp, New York; City Univ NY--York Col & NY City Tech Col, NY; Florists Transworld Deliveries Art Collection, Mich; Secuirty Pacific Nat Bank, Los Angeles, Calif. *Comn:* Cape Primrose (painting), comn by Hugh Hardy, New York, 81; Garvins Restaurant, comn by Richard Garvin, New York, 82; Lobelia, comn by Virginia Stein, Somerville, NJ, 88. *Exhib:* Ann Exhib, Berkshire Art Mus, 64-64; Painterly Realists, Art Sch, Art Inst Chicago, 72; Komblee Gallery, 74 & 79; Color Light Image Exhib for United Nations, New York, 75; one person exhibs, St Mary's Col Md, 90, Vassar Col, Poughkeepsie, NY, 90. *Pos:* CETA Artist, Cult Coun Found Artists Proj, 79-80; Artist in Residence, Millay Colony, Austerlitz, NY, 90- *Teaching:* Art instr art appreciation, Univ Seven Seas, 64-65; art instr painting, Brooklyn Mus Art Sch, NY, 73-77 & Bronxville Adult Sch, NY, 89-92. *Awards:* CAPS Award, NY State Coun Arts, 73; Support Grant, Adolph Gottlieb Found, 88; Fel grant, Nat Endowment Arts, 89. *Bibliog:* Cindy Nemser (auth), The Close Up Vision-Representative Art, Arts Mag, 72. *Mem:* Col Art Asn. *Media:* Oil, Watercolor. *Mailing Add:* 652 Broadway New York NY 10012

ALLMAN, MARGO
SCULPTOR, PAINTER
b New York, NY, Feb 23, 33. *Study:* Smith Col; Moore Col Art; Univ Pa; Univ Del; with Reginald Marsh & Hans Hofmann. *Work:* Del Art Mus, Wilmington; Philadelphia Mus Art. *Comn:* Travertine sculpture, comn by Mrs Werner Hutz & family, Kennett Square, Pa, 73; cor-ten steel sculpture, comn by Richard Vanderbilt, Chadds Ford, Pa, 74; ferro-cement sculpture, Tidewater Publ Co, Centerville, Md, 75; bronze sculpture, comn by Wesley & Harriet Memeger Jr, Wilmington, Del, 90. *Exhib:* Del Art Mus, 56-81; Nat Woodcut & Wood Engraving Show, Print Club, Philadelphia, 56, 59 & 60; Univ Del, 65-72 & 76; one-person shows, Haas Gallery Art, Bloomsburg State Col, Pa, 76 & 77, Moore Col Art, 79 & Del State Art Coun, 81; and others. *Teaching:* Instr, Del Inst Arts Educ, 84-85. *Awards:* Mildred Boericke Prize, 32nd Ann Nat Exhib Woodcuts & Wood Engravings, Print Club Philadelphia, 58; Drawing Prize, 51st Ann Show, Del Art Mus, 65; Best Landscape, Wilmington Trust Bank Prize, Del Art Mus, 69. *Mem:* Del Ctr Contemp Arts; Del Art Mus; Nat Mus Women Arts. *Media:* Carved Concrete, Wood; All Media. *Mailing Add:* 202 E State Rd West Grove PA 19390

ALLMOND, CHARLES (M)
SCULPTOR
b Wilmington, Del, Apr 25, 31. *Study:* Univ Del, BS, 53, MS, 57; Sch Law, Temple Univ, JD, 63. *Work:* St Hubert's Giralda, Madison, NJ; Del State Bar Asn, Wilmington; DuPont-Mitsui Polychemicals, Tokyo; Wilmington Trust Co, Wilmington; Summit Associates, Edison, NJ. *Comn:* Madonna and Child, Christ in Christmas Committee, Wilmington, 89. *Exhib:* Nat Acad of Design Ann, New York, 88; Soc of Animal Artists Ann, 87-92; Art and the Animal Touring, 90-92; Soho Int Art Competition Winners Show, New York, 90; Central Park Zoo Gallery, New York, 91; Salmagundi Club Ann, New York, 89-92; Salmagundi Club Graphics and Sculpture, New York, 1990. *Awards:* Award of Excellence, Soc Animal Artists, 87; Elliott Liskin Memorial Award, Soc Animal Artists, 88; Ogden Pleissner Memorial Award, Salmagundi Club, 91. *Bibliog:* Sculpting Adds Third Dimension, News Journal Papers, 3/19/87; Charles Allmond: Hands Recreate Nature, The Whale, 6/30/90. *Mem:* Soc Animal Artists (exec bd, 90-); Salmagundi Club; Rehoboth Art League. *Media:* Stone, Wood. *Publ:* Contribr, Del Mag Today, 7/91. *Dealer:* Shidoni Galleries Bishops Lodge Rd Tesuque NMex 87574. *Mailing Add:* 104 Rowland Park Blvd Wilmington DE 19803

ALLNER, WALTER H
PAINTER, DESIGNER
b Dessau, Ger, Jan 2, 09; US citizen. *Study:* Bauhaus-Dessau, with J Albers, V Kandinsky, Paul Klee & Joost Schmidt. *Work:* Salon des Surindépendants & Salon des Réalités Nouvelles, Paris, France. *Exhib:* Galeria Bonino, Soho, New York, 76; Bauhaus-Archiv, Berlin, Ger, 76; Toledo Art Mus, Ohio, 77; Kunstbibliothek, Staatliche Museen, Berlin, Ger, 80; Univ Del, Newark, 80; Lahti Art Mus, Finland, 81; Cooper-Hewitt Mus, New York, 81; Place Ville-Marie, Montreal, Can, 82; Salon des Surindépendants & Salon des Réalités Nouvelles, Paris, France; retrospective of editorial & graphic designs, Bauhaus Dessau, Weimer, Ger, 89. *Pos:* Design consult, Johnson & Johnson, New Brunswick, NJ, 54-55; art dir, Fortune Mag, 63-74; design consult, RCA, 65-67; asst typographer, Piet Zwart, Holland, formerly; chmn jury, International Poster Exhib, Colorado State Univ, Fort Collins, 79 & 81; partner, ONMIUM Graphique, formerly; art dir, Formes, & Editions d'Art Graphique et Photographique, formerly; ed, Swiss Art Mag, Grahiis, formerly; founder & ed, Int Poster Ann; co-ed, Editions Paralléles, Paris, 79-; correspondent, Signes Mag, Paris, 90-; contrib ed, Design J, Seoul, Korea, 90- *Teaching:* Mem fac, Parsons Sch Design, New York, 74-86; vis critic, Yale Univ Sch Art, 76, Ecole Superieure d'Art Graphique, Paris, 79-; lectr, Swinburne Inst Technol, Melbourne, 83. *Awards:* Medal Bauhau-Dessau, Ger Acad Archit, 79. *Mem:* Alliance Graphique Int (pres US Section, 72-74, int pres, 74-); Am Inst Graphic Arts; Art Dirs Club; hon mem, Associazione Italiana Creativi Comunicazione Visiva. *Publ:* Compiler & ed, A M Cassandre, Peintre d'Affiches; Posters, Reinhold Publ Corp, NY, 52. *Mailing Add:* 110 Riverside Dr New York NY 10024

ALLRICH, M LOUISE BARCO
ART DEALER
b Ft Monroe, Va, Feb 16, 47. *Study:* Univ Calif, Davis, BA, 68; Univ Calif, Berkeley, post-grad work art hist & theory. *Pos:* Pres, Allrich Gallery, San Francisco, 71-; trustee, Fiberworks Ctr for Textile Arts, Berkeley, 72-81. *Teaching:* Lectr, Alta Col Art, 73, Wash State Univ, Pullman, 78, Los Angeles Co Mus, 79, Oakland Mus, 82, Art Inst Chicago, 82 & Portland Art Mus, 83. *Mem:* Soc Encouragement Contemp Art. *Specialty:* Contemporary textile art, painting and sculpture. *Publ:* Auth, Center for the Arts, pvt publ, 74; contribr, A look at fiber, Currant Mag, 76. *Mailing Add:* Allrich Gallery 251 Post St San Francisco CA 94108

ALLUMBAUGH, JAMES
SCULPTOR, EDUCATOR
b Dallas, Tex, Jan 27, 41. *Study:* ETex State Univ, BS, 63 & MS, 65; NTex State Univ, EdD, 68. *Work:* Richardson Pub Libr, Tex; Beaumont Art Mus, Tex; Houston Ctr 2, Tex; Tyler Art Mus, Tex; Seaman Collection, Corpus Christi, Tex. *Exhib:* Island Introductions, Galveston Art Ctr, 90; Greater Midwest Int, Cent Mo State Univ, 90; Matrix Gallery Int, Sacramento, 90; solo shows, Colo State Univ, Ft Collins, 83, Frontroom Gallery, Dallas, Tex, 85, D'Art Gallery, Dallas, 85, Rockhouse Gallery, Arlington, Tex, 86, Eastfield Col, Dallas, 87 & E Tex State Univ, Commerce, 87; and many others. *Pos:* Dir, Tex Col Sculpture Symposium, Dallas, 77-; photogr and consult, Central Time Zone Sculpture Symposium, Firmilab, Batavia, Ill, 91; photographic liaison, Tex Sculpture Asn, Dallas, 90, 91 & 92. *Teaching:* Fel design, NTex State Univ, 66-68; assoc prof 3-D design, ETex State Univ, 68-81, prof, 81- *Awards:* Award, BACA Exhib, Berkeley Art Ctr, 89; Award, Louisiana Festival Arts, Masur Mus Art, 88; Nat Arts Prog, Dallas City Hall, Tex, 90. *Bibliog:* Dennis Kowal & Donna Meilach (auth), Sculpture Casting, Crown, 72; Jan Butterfield (auth), The young Texans, Arts Mag, 72; Jeanne Sturdevant (auth), Texas Designer/Craftsmen, Vol 31, 87. *Mem:* Int Sculpture Ctr; Tex Sculpture Asn; Artists Equity (vpres, Dallas chap, 77); Tex Designer Craftsmen. *Media:* Metal, Photography. *Publ:* Illusr (cover illus), 16th Ann Invitational Exhib, Longview Arts Ctr, 74 & 45th Ann Exhib, Springfield Art Mus, 75; auth, Cubes Space and Light, Spiral Enterprises, 77; Basic Techniques for Photographing Sculpture, Tex Sculpture Asn, fall journal 92. *Dealer:* Rockhouse Gallery 1311 W Abram Arlington TX. *Mailing Add:* 2009 St Francis Dallas TX 75228

ALLYN, JERRI
CONCEPTUAL PERFORMANCE ARTIST
b Patterson, NJ, Feb 2, 52. *Study:* Goddard Col, VT, MA(art & society), 78. *Work:* Mus Mod Art, New York. *Exhib:* A Decade of Feminist Performance Art, Continental Arts Mus, New Orleans, 80; Atomic Salon, Ronald Feldman Gallery, New York, 82; At Home, Long Beach Mus Art, Calif, 83; Rape, Univ Gallery, Ohio State Univ, Columbus & Nat Tour, 85-87; Committed to Print, Mus Mod Art, New York, Nat Tour, 88-90; Ageless, Woman's Building Gallery, Los Angeles, 90; Art in the Anchorage, Creative Time, New York, 90; Am Dining: A Working Woman's Moment, New Mus Contemp Art, New York, Nat Tour, 86-88; Angels Have Been Sent to Me, Creative Time, 91-92. *Pos:* Panelist, NY Coun Arts, Visual Arts Prog, 85; consult, Develop Performance Art Prog, Syracuse Univ, 86; panelist, Yellow Springs Inst, Chester Springs, Pa, 88; policy & guideline development, NEA Interarts, Washington, DC, 88; Seattle Arts Comn, 89; NY Found Arts, 90. *Teaching:* Prof conceptual-performance art, New School for Social Research, New York, 87-; prof, Western Wash Univ, Bellingham, 87-90; artist-in-residence, Univ Ill, Champagne/Urbana, 88 & Cal Col Arts & Crafts, Oakland. *Awards:* Nat Endowment for the Arts, 81, 85, 87, 89 & 90; Media/Radio Grant & Individual Artist Proj Award, NY State Coun Arts, 91. *Bibliog:* Art on a raft, politics to go, Village Voice, 12/8/87; A show on issues, New York Times, 6/27/90; Angels have been sent to me, High Performance, 9/91; Hidden reserves of the handicapped, NY Times, 12/22/91; Exposures: women & their art, New Sage Press, Ca, 89. *Media:* Interdisciplinary. *Mailing Add:* 118 Forsyth St No 1 New York NY 10002-5126

ALMOND, PAUL
FILMMAKER, WRITER
b Montreal, Can, Apr 26, 31. *Study:* Bishop's Col Sch, 44-48; McGill Univ; Balliol Col, Oxford, BA & MA. *Exhib:* Dimensions in Art, Int Design Ctr, Montreal, 88; Armenians of the Holy Land, Manougian Cult Ctr, Detroit, 89; Visual Concepts, Art at the Platt, 90 & 91; Univ Judaism, Los Angeles, 90; Celebrating Children, Jacob Javits Conv Ctr, New York, 92; Jerusalem, The Gathering of Nations, Soc Contemp Photog, Kans City, 92; Egyptian Village Life, Ministry Cult, Nile Gallery, Cairo, Egypt, 92. *Pos:* Dir & producer, Can Broadcasting Corp, 53-65. *Awards:* Special Award of Merit for Documentary Film, Prague, 63; Canadian Film Awards, Best Motion Picture Director, 70; Best Television Drama Dir, 79. *Bibliog:* Janet Edsforth (auth), The Flame Within (a study of Paul Almond's Films), Can Film Inst, 71. *Mem:* Dir Guild Am; Dir Guild Can (hon, life); Acad Can Cinema & TV, Royal Can Acad Art. *Publ:* Auth, The Hill (TV play); co-auth, The Broken Sky (TV play); writer, producer & dir, Isabel (film), 68, Act of the Heart (film), 70 & Journey (film), 72; Ups & Downs (film), 82; And the Dance Goes On, (film), 91. *Mailing Add:* PO Box 954 Malibu CA 90265

ALMY, MAX (MARILYNN IRENE)
VIDEO ARTIST, DIRECTOR
b Omaha, Nebr, Sept 9, 48. *Study:* Univ Nebr, BFA, 70; Univ Minn, 71; Calif Col Arts & Crafts, MFA, 78. *Work:* Mus Mod Art, New York; Long Beach Mus Art; San Francisco Mus Mod Art; Va Mus Fine Arts; Stedilijk Mus, Amsterdam. *Comn:* Deadline (video installation), Mus Contemp Art, Chicago. *Exhib:* Electronic Art, Mus Contemp Art, Chicago, 80; Biennale Paris, Mus Art Mod, Paris, 80; California Video, Long Beach Mus Art, 80; Exchange Show, Arsenal, Berlin, 81; Performance Art, Mus Mod Art, New York, 82; Video Festivals, Ithaca, 82 & Athens, 83; Nat Video Festival, Am Film Inst, Los Angeles, 83; Video Art: A History Part II, Mus Mod Art, New York, 83. *Pos:* Mgr productions, One Pass Film & Video, 78-83; creative dir, Group One, 84- *Teaching:* Instr, Calif Col Arts & Crafts, 77-78; vis artist video, Art Inst Chicago, 84. *Awards:* Nat Endowment Arts Fel, 82; US Film & Video Festival Award, 82; Western States Regional Media Arts Fel, 83. *Bibliog:* Steve Seid (auth), Deadline for the future, Networks, 82; MOMA-TV: The push to artsify video, Village Voice, 83. *Mem:* Bay Area Video Coalition; Am Film Inst; Northern Calif Women Film & Video. *Media:* Video, Computer Animation. *Dealer:* Electronic Arts Intermix 84 Fifth Ave New York NY 10011. *Mailing Add:* 3454 Standish Dr Encino CA 91436

ALPEN-WHITESIDE, DALE
PAINTER, PRINTMAKER
b St Boniface, Man, Can, Nov 22, 42. *Study:* Univ BC, BA, 62; Vancouver Sch Art, with Jack Shadbolt, 62; Parson Sch Art & Design, individual study with Shaio Ping Liao; also with Bruno Bobac & Alex Millar. *Work:* Day, Wilson Campbell, Toronto, Ont; Bio-Research, Ste Anne De Belleville, Que; Diplomatic Mission, Austria & Switz; The Right Honourable Pierre Elliot Trudeau, Former Prime Minister Can, Montreal, Que. *Comn:* Bio Research, Senneville Quebec. *Exhib:* Solo exhibs, Night Flight, Dorval Cult Ctr, Que, 83, Night Journeys, Ottawa City Hall, Ont, 84 & Rock, River, Reflection, Chateau Versailles, Montreal, Que, 85; Ann Juried Exhib, Burlington Mus, Ont, 83-85; Agnes Etherington Fall Exhib, Kingston, Ont, 85; Gallery 89, Ste Anne De Belleville, Que, 90. *Teaching:* Technician printmaking, John Abbott Col, Ste Anne De Belleville, Que, 79- *Media:* Acrylic, Watercolor; Etching. *Publ:* Coauth, Stones to Harvest, Poetry Art Book. *Dealer:* E Monaghan 214 Owl Dr Ottawa Ont K1V 9P6. *Mailing Add:* 44 Home Ave Van Kleek Hill ON K0B 1R0 Canada

ALPERN, MERRY B
PHOTOGRAPHER
Study: Grinnel Col, Iowa, 73-77. *Work:* Mus Mod Art, New York. *Pos:* Photo lab technician, Exposure/Effects, New York, 77-78; staff photog & studio mgr, LGI Photo Agency, 78-80; asst photog ed, Rolling Stone Mag, 80-81; freelance photogr, 81- *Teaching:* Guest instr, Int Ctr Photog, New York, 89; guest lectr, New Sch, New York, 90. *Awards:* Second Place, Pictures Yr, Mag Picture Story, 88; Leica Medal Excellence Photojournalism Award, 88; Nat Endowment Arts, Visual Artists Fel Grant, 90. *Bibliog:* A D Coleman (auth), Letter From: New York #3, Photo Metro, San Francisco, 21, 5/89; Vince Aletti (auth), Desparate living, Village Voice, New York, 51, 5/2/89; A D Coleman (auth), article, New York Observer, New York, 14, 5/8/89. *Publ:* Many credits in var newspapers & mags. *Mailing Add:* 149 W 12th St, Studio B2 New York NY 10011

ALPERT, BILL (WILLIAM H)
PAINTER, SCULPTOR
b Bronx, NY, Dec 21, 34. *Study:* Univ Calif Los Angeles, BA, 63, grad sch, 63-65. *Work:* Power Gallery Contemp Art, Sydney, Australia. *Exhib:* Constructs Orgn Independent Artists, Bleecker Renaissance, New York, 78; Orgn Independent Artists Postcard Show, Bologna Art Fair, Italy, 78; Painting & Sculpture Today, Indianapolis Mus Art, 78; Albright-Knox Mus, 78 & 79; Current New York, Joe & Emily Lowe Art Gallery, Syracuse Univ, 80; Color on Structure, W Paterson Collection of NJ Wayne, 81; Col Charleston, SC, 86 & 89; and others. *Collections Arranged:* Orgn of Independent Artists: Group Show, US Courthouse, 77 & Art in Public Places, 26 Fed Plaza, New York, 77; Six Artists View Development, NY Acad Sci, 78. *Teaching:* Adj prof painting, Cooper Union Sch Art, New York, 79-82; adj instr drawing, Parsons Sch Design, New York, 81-82; Sch Visual Art, New York, 89-92. *Awards:* Creative Artist Pub Serv Prog Finalist, 77-78, 80-81 & 81-82. *Bibliog:* Peter Frank (auth), New York Reviews, Art News, 11/77 & Ellen Lubell (auth), Arts Mag, 11/77; JoAnn Lewis (auth), Sculpture room, Washington Post, 5/27/78; Gregory Battcock (auth), Art Information, 5/81; Nancy S Smith (auth), articles, The News & Courier/The Evening Post, Charleston SC, 2/23/86. *Mem:* NY Artists Equity Asn; Orgn Independent Artists (mem exhib comt, 77-78). *Media:* Watercolor, Oil; Miscellaneous Media. *Publ:* Contribr, New York Art Yearbook, 75-76; Re-View, Vol I, Issue 1, Vered Lieb, 77; The Whitney Counterweight Catalog, 77; Sciences, New York Acad Sci, 3/78; contribr, NY Art Rev, 88. *Mailing Add:* 64 Grand St New York NY 10013

ALPERT, GEORGE
PHOTOGRAPHER, PAINTER
b New York, NY, Apr 3, 22. *Study:* NY Univ; NC State Col; Stanford Univ; Univ Calif, Berkeley; Inst Seven Arts, NY. *Work:* Il Diaframma, Milan, Italy; Miller-Plummer Collection, Philadelphia. *Exhib:* One-man shows, Alfred Stieglitz Gallery, Neikrug Gallery, Light Gallery, New York, Period Gallery West, Scottsdale, Ariz, Everson Mus, Heard Mus, Udinotti Gallery & O'Brien Art Emporium, Ariz, C G Rein. *Pos:* Chmn, pres & dir gallery, Sohophoto Found, 70- *Teaching:* Mem fac creative photog, New Sch Social Res, New York, 74-79. *Bibliog:* George Alpert: paintings, sculpture. *Media:* Acrylic. *Specialty:* Photography, paintings, sculpture. *Publ:* Auth, The Queens, 75 & coauth, Second Chance to Live: The Suicide Syndrome, 75, Da Capo Press; auth, Taos Pueblo, Paradise House, 83. *Mailing Add:* 5702 N 55 Pl Paradise Valley AZ 85253

ALPERT, RICHARD HENRY
VIDEO ARTIST
b Apr 11, 47. *Study:* Univ Pittsburgh, BA, 70; San Francisco Art Inst, MFA(sculpture), 73. *Work:* Mus Conceptual Art, San Francisco; J H Cohn & Co, New York; Va Mus Fine Art, Richmond. *Exhib:* Projekt '74, Kolnischer Kunstverein, Koln, Ger, 74; solo exhibs, La Mamelle Art Ctr, San Francisco, 76 & 80, Los Angeles Inst Contemp Art, 79 & Washington Proj Arts, Washington, DC, 81; Space Time Sound 1970's: A Decade in the Bay Area, San Francisco Mus Mod Art, 79; California Performance Now and Then, Mus Contemp Art, Chicago, 81. *Teaching:* Instr, San Francisco Art Inst, 72-73 & 77 & Calif Col Arts & Crafts, Oakland, 78-79. *Awards:* Artist's Fel Grant, Nat Endowment Arts, 79-80. *Mailing Add:* 2123 Castro St San Francisco CA 94131

ALPS, GLEN EARL
EDUCATOR, PRINTMAKER
b Loveland, Colo, June 20, 14. *Study:* Univ Northern Colo, BA; Univ Wash, MFA; Univ Iowa, advanced study with Mauricio Lasansky. *Work:* Mus Mod Art, New York; Philadelphia Art Mus; Chicago Art Inst; Los Angeles Co Mus Art, Calif; Libr Cong, Washington, DC; Seattle Art Mus, Wash; Tacoma Art Mus, Wash. *Comn:* Sculptural panel, Seattle Pub Libr, 60; fountain, Munic Bldg, City of Seattle, 61; wall sculpture, Magnolia Br, Seattle Pub Libr, 64; ed of prints, Wash State Arts Comn, 71; bronze fountain, First Christian Church, Greeley, Colo, 72. *Exhib:* 1st Editions traveling exhib, Ore & Wash Arts Comn, 78; The Collagraph: A New Print Medium, nat traveling exhib, Pratt Graphics, 78; Eight Pioneers in Collagraph Printmaking, Wenninger Gallery, Boston, 79; A Glen Alps Retrospective Exhib: The Collagraph Idea 1956-1980, Bellevue Art Mus, Wash, 79; solo exhibs, James Michener Arch Libr, Univ NColo, 85, NCent Wash State Mus, 89; Soviet Union Exchange Exhib, 89; Gov's Invitational, In Retrospect, 25 Years, Wash State Capitol Mus, 89. *Pos:* Treas, Northwest Printmakers, 49-51, pres, 51-53 & 62-64. *Teaching:* Prof art, Univ Wash, 45-84, chmn div printmaking, formerly, prof emer, currently. *Awards:* Gov Award, 72 & 78; Alumnus Trailblazer Award, Univ NColo, 85; Artist-in-Residence, Pilchuck Glass Sch, Wash, 87; Hall of Fame Award, Univ NColo Centennial, 89. *Bibliog:* Jules Heller (auth), Printmaking Today, Holt Rinehart & Winston, 72; articles, The Complete Collagraph & The Art of the Print, 80. *Mem:* Soc Am Graphic Artists; Northwest Print Coun. *Mailing Add:* 6523 40th Ave NE Seattle WA 98115

ALQUILAR, MARIA
PAINTER, SCULPTOR
b Brooklyn, NY, May 25, 35. *Study:* Hunter Col, New York, AB, 55. *Work:* Chase Manhattan Bank, New York & Phoenix; Nat Gallery Art, Washington, DC; Sacramento Metrop Arts Comn; San Francisco Arts Comn; Downey Mus, Calif; and others. *Comn:* Light Rail Sta, Sacramento, 84; ceramic and metal altar, US Border Sta, San Luis, Ariz, 85; ceramic mural, fountain & waterfall, Water & Sewer Admin Bldg, Sacramento, 86; ceramic mural, Los Viajeros Vienen a San Jose, San Jose Int Airport, Calif, 90; 16th St Viaduet Mod Proj, Denver, Colo, 92; Fairbairn Water Treatment Plant, Sacto, Calif, 93. *Exhib:* Inedible Renwick Birthday Cake, Smithsonian Inst, 82; Downey Mus Art, Calif, 82 & 83; Crocker Art Mus, Sacramento, Calif, 83 & 84; one-person exhib, Gorman Mus, Univ Calif, Davis, 83; Raku and Smoke, Newport Art Mus, RI, 84; New Faces, New Works, II, Triton Mus Art, Santa Clara, Calif, 86; Artist and the Myth, Monterey Peninsula Mus Art, Monterey, Calif; Los Animales Del Sol, Art Corridor, Menlo Park, Calif, 88; Mermaids & Myths of the Sea, Melveny & Myers Asn, Los Angeles, 89; Sacramento, San Francisco Mus of Art Rental Gallery, 90; retrospective exhib, Redding Mus Art, Redding, Calif, 92; Works in Cast Iron & Brass, John M Kohler Art Ctr, Sheboygan, Wis, 90. *Pos:* Dir, Jennifer Pauls Gallery, Sacramento, Calif, 70-. *Awards:* Residency, John Michael Kohler Art Ctr, Sheboygan, Wis. *Bibliog:* Ellen Schlesinger (auth), Sunday woman-artist in residence, Sacramento Bee, 8/83; article, Ceramics Monthly, 5/88. *Media:* Clay; Acrylic, Pastel. *Specialty:* Narrative art. *Publ:* Contribr, Taxi "Mosaics", 5/89; auth, Artsearch Int Catalog, 89. *Dealer:* Jennifer Pauls Gallery 1020 Tenth St Sacremento CA 95814. *Mailing Add:* 703 Darwin St Santa Cruz CA 95062

ALQUIST, LEWIS
SCULPTOR
b Glen Cove, NY, Sept 27, 46. *Study:* Cranbrook Acad Art, MFA, 72. *Work:* The Exploratorium, San Francisco. *Exhib:* Eccentric Machine, Kohler Art Ctr, Sheboygan, Wis, 87; Movers & Shakers, Hope Col, Holland, Mich, 88; Sleeping Mutations-Anxious Situations, Univ Tex, El Paso, 89; Gifts & Facsimilies, Weber State Univ, Ogden, Utah, 90; Domestic Disorders, Diverse Works Art Space, Houston, Tex, 90. *Teaching:* Assoc prof sculpture, Ariz State Univ, 84-. *Awards:* Nat Endowment Arts Grant, 87; Visual Artists Fel, 3-D Media, Ariz Comm Arts, 88. *Mailing Add:* Sch Art Sculpture Dept Ariz State Univ Tempe AZ 85287-1505

ALTEN, JERRY
DIRECTOR, DESIGNER
b Philadelphia, Pa. *Study:* Philadelphia Col Art; Temple Univ, BA(fine arts). *Pos:* Owner, Shirt Sleeve Studio, Philadelphia, 59-62; sr designer, Container Corp Am, Oaks, Pa, 62-67; art dir, TV Guide Mag, 67-; mem staff, Triangle Publ Inc, Radnor, Pa, currently. *Teaching:* Lectr, cols in US & Europe. *Awards:* Awards of Excellence & Gold & Silver Medals, NY Art Dirs Club, Soc Publ Designers & Soc Illusr. *Mem:* Soc Publ Designers; Art Alliance Philadelphia; NY Art Dirs Club; Philadelphia Art Dirs; Philadelphia Col Art Alumni Asn. *Mailing Add:* 10 Wynnedale Circle Narberth PA 19072

ALTERMANN, TONY
ART DEALER
b Dallas, Tex, Aug 10, 40. *Study:* NTex State Univ, BA & MS. *Pos:* Dir publicity & pub relations, MGM, Dallas, Tex, 70-72; vpres, Tex Art Gallery, Dallas, 72-78; owner & pres, Altermann Art Gallery, Dallas, Tex, 78- & Altermann & Morris Galleries, Houston & Dallas, 83. *Mem:* Dallas Art Dealers Asn; Dallas Visual Arts Ctr (bd dirs, currently). *Specialty:* Western, wildlife and Americana subjects in all media. *Mailing Add:* c/o Altermann Art Gallery 2504 Cedar Springs Dallas TX 75201

ALTFELD, MERWIN RICHARD
PAINTER, EDUCATOR
b Elyria, Ohio, Sept 19, 13. *Study:* Case Western Reserve, BA, 34; Univ Calif, Los Angeles, Art Teaching Credential, 68. *Work:* Queen Mary Ship & Senior Eye Gallery, Long Beach, Calif; Brugger Art Collection, Los Angeles, Calif; Hollywood Press Club, Calif; Univ Calif, Los Angeles. *Exhib:* San Diego Art Guild, San Diego Art Mus, 63; Nat Watercolor (traveling exhib), 66-82; Calif Group, Old Bergen Art Guild, 76-88; Artist Influenced by the Circle Traveling Exhib, 78-80; American Artists Invitational, Swedish Mus, Stockholm, Sweden, 72; Watercolor USA, Springfield, Art Mus, 72-88, 90-92. *Pos:* Pres Los Angeles Art Asn, 91-92. *Teaching:* instr drawing & painting, Los Angeles Adults Schs, 68-73; bd dirs, So Calif Contemporary Gallery Los Angeles, 87-88; instr creative painting, Univ Judaism, 88. *Awards:* Cash Award for Drawing, Southern Calif Expos, 64; Cash Award, Nat Watercolor Soc, Laguna Beach Mus, 74; Cash Award, San Diego Watercolor Soc Int Exhib, 85. *Bibliog:* David Fessenden (dir), Merwin Altfeld, Malibu (film, 78; Robert Perine (auth), Calif Romantics (art catalogue), 85. *Mem:* Nat Watercolor Soc (pres, 72); Artists for Educ Action (bd dirs, 78-82); Los Angeles Art Asn, (pres, 90). *Media:* Acrylic, Watercolor; Mixed. *Publ:* Auth, Canon Laser Creative Ideas, Copyspot Inc, Santa Monica, Calif, 10/90. *Mailing Add:* 18426 Wakecrest Dr Malibu CA 90265

ALTMAN, EDITH
SCULPTOR, CONCEPTUAL ARTIST
b Altenberg, Ger, May 5, 31; US citizen. *Study:* Wayne State Univ, Detroit, Mich, 49; Marygrove Col, with Paul Weigardt (from the Bauhaus), 56-57. *Work:* Standard Oil Co, Chicago; State of Ill; Ball State Univ, Chicago; Mus Contemp Art, Chicago; Spertus Mus, Chicago. *Exhib:* Mus Contemp Art, Chicago, 81 & 83; Adrogyne, Akadamie der Kuntz, Berlin, 85; Art Inst Chicago Vicinity Exhib, 85; Rebuilding the Temple, Spertus Mus, Chicago, 88; Edith Altman, Rock Art Mus, Rockford, Ill, 89; Jewish Esp in the Art of the 20th Century, Barbican Ctr, London, 90; Reclaiming the Symbol, State of Ill Mus Gallery, Chicago, 92. *Pos:* Asst prof art, Univ Chicago, currently; asst prof art, Art Inst Sch Art, Chicago, currently. *Teaching:* vis artists & print proj, Univ Omaha, Neb, 84; Asst prof art, Univ Chicago, 84-85; vis prof painting, Sch Art Inst Chicago, 85-86. *Awards:* GAAP Grant, 88; Ill Arts Coun Fel for Sculpture, 89; Nat Endowment Arts for Sculpture, 90 & 91. *Bibliog:* Allemaines Lexikon Der Builder, Theme/Baecker, Germany, 86; Contemporary American Women Sculptures VW, Jones Oryk Press, 87; Gloria Orenstiein (auth), The Reflowering of the Goddess, Pergamon Press, 89. *Mem:* Womans Caucas Art; Chicago Artist Coalition; founding mem, Comt Artists Rights, 88; hon mem, State of Ill, 92. *Publ:* Auth, articles in Art in Am, 79 & 87, Artforum, 83, Chicago Tribune, Chicago Sun-Times & New Art Examiner, 92. *Mailing Add:* 811 W 16 St Chicago IL 60608

ALTMAN, HAROLD
PRINTMAKER, EDUCATOR
b New York, NY, Apr 20, 24. *Study:* Art Students League, 41-42; Cooper Union, 41-47; New Sch Social Res, 47-49; Acad Grande Chaumiere, Paris, 49-52; Black Mountain Col, NC. *Work:* Mus Mod Art, Metrop Mus Art & Whitney Mus Art, New York; Art Inst Chicago; Nat Gallery Art, Washington, DC; and others. *Comn:* Entire print ed, Mus Mod Art, 60, Soc Am Graphic Artists, 62, Hilton Rockefeller Hotel, 63 & Jewish Mus, NY, 64. *Exhib:* One-man shows, Martha Jackson Gallery, New York, 58, Art Inst Chicago, 60, San Francisco Mus Art, 61, Sagot Le Garrec Gallery, Paris, 68 & 74 & State Gallery Fine Arts, Istanbul, Turkey, 75; and others. *Teaching:* Asst prof art, NY State Col Ceramics, Alfred Univ, 52-54, Univ NC, Greensboro, 54-56 & Univ Wis-Milwaukee, 56-62; prof art, Pa State Univ, 62-76. *Awards:* Two Guggenheim Fels, 60-62; Nat Inst Arts & Lett Award, 63; Fulbright Hays Sr Res Fel, 64-65. *Bibliog:* Articles, New York Times, Los Angeles Times, Vie Des Arts, and numerous others. *Mem:* Societé des Peintres, Graveurs, Francais; Nat Acad Design. *Publ:* Illusr, The Four Seasons, Pa State Univ, 65. *Dealer:* Multiple Impressions 128 Spring St New York NY 10012. *Mailing Add:* c/o Multiple Impressions 128 Spring St New York NY 10012

ALTMANN, HENRY S
PAINTER, EDUCATOR
b New York, NY, Dec 4, 46. *Study:* Pratt Inst, Brooklyn, BFA(art educ), 68; Queens Col, Flushing, NY, MFA(painting), 70; Fulbright fel painting, 70-71, Fine Arts Acad, Munich, Ger. *Work:* First Nat Bank New York; Skowhegan Sch Painting & Sculpture, New York; Shawmut Bank of Boston, Mass. *Comn:* Three stained glass windows & paintings for rear portal (with Maxine Ann Sorokin), Kehillath Jakob Synagogue, Newton, Mass, 73. *Exhib:* One-man shows, First St Gallery, New York & Meetinghouse Gallery, Boston, 73; Young Realist Show, Harbor Gallery, Cold Spring Harbor, Long Island, NY, 72; two-person exhib, Goethe Inst, Boston, 80, Young Adult Ctr, Boston, 84 & Univ Cinncinati, Rose Warner Gallery, 86; Jewish Community Ctr, Southern NJ Gallery, Cherry Hill, 80; plus many others. *Pos:* Exhib chmn, West Roxbury Art Asn, 77-; res comt arch, West Roxbury Hist Soc, 77-, dir visual arts, Jewish Community Ctr, Newton, Mass, 83- *Teaching:* Instr art, Boston Univ, 71-75; adj assoc prof, Art Inst Boston, 75-; Framingham State Col, Mass, 72-80; Mass Bay Community Col, 90- *Awards:* Finalist, Mass Found Arts Fel Competition, 83. *Bibliog:* W Rox (auth), Boston Globe article, 5/81; Norman Keyes (auth), Transcript Newspaper article, 81. *Mem:* Boston Vis Artists Union. *Media:* Oil, Pastel. *Dealer:* Crieger Art Assoc 35 Newbury St Boston MA 02116; Boston Fine Arts Boylston St Boston MA. *Mailing Add:* 61 Perham St West Roxbury MA 02132

ALTMAYER, JAY P
COLLECTOR
b Mobile, Ala, Mar 1, 15. *Study:* Tulane Univ La, BA & LLB; Mobile Col, LHD, 92. *Pos:* Mem, Fine Arts Comt, State Dept. *Collection:* American paintings many dealing with plantation life and workers and marine paintings; paintings by William Aiken Walker, Sully, Rembrandt Peale, Gilbert Stuart, Severn Rosen and others. *Publ:* American Presentation Swords. *Mailing Add:* 75 St Michael Mobile AL 36602

ALTSCHUL, ARTHUR G
COLLECTOR, PATRON
b New York, NY, Apr 6, 20. *Pos:* Former mem trustees coun, Nat Gallery Art; former mem nat bd, Smithsonian Assoc, Smithsonian Inst; vice-chmn gov bd, Yale Art Gallery, New Haven, Conn; chmn bd, Int Found Art Res. *Mem:* Fel perpetuity, benefactor, Metrop Mus Art, New York. *Collection:* American Impressionists and The Eight; Cubists and lesser known members of the Neo-Impressionist, Nabis and Pont-Aven schools. *Mailing Add:* 85 Broad St New York NY 10004

ALTWERGER, LIBBY
PAINTER, GRAPHIC ARTIST
b Toronto, Ont, July 13, 21. *Study:* Ont Col Art. *Exhib:* One-man shows, Pascell Gallery, Toronto, 64, Sonneck Gallery, Kitchener, Ont, 68, Gallery, Shedeke & Holy Blossom Gallery; Sarnia Gallery, Sarnia; Mississauga Gallery, Mississauga; McLaughlin Gallery, Oshawa; London Art Gallery, Ont; Hamilton Art Gallery, Ont; and others. *Pos:* Can exchange artist with Am Watercolor Soc. *Teaching:* Former instr drawing, Ryerson Polytech Inst. *Awards:* Sterling Trust Award for Lithograph, 65; Royal Bank of Can Purchase Award, Ont Soc Artists Show, 79; Purchase Award, Watercolor Soc, 81. *Mem:* Ont Soc Artists; Printing & Drawing Coun of Can; Can Soc Painters in Water Colour. *Media:* Watercolor. *Mailing Add:* 105 Red Robin Way Willowdale ON M2R 3K6 Canada

ALVAREZ, CANDIDA
PAINTER
b Brooklyn, NY, Feb 2, 55. *Study:* Fordham Univ, BA, 77, Skowhegan Sch Painting and Sculpture, 81. *Work:* Studio Mus Harlem, New York; Univ Del, Newark, Del; Brandywine Workshop; Am Tel & Tel, New York City; The Readers Digest, New York; El Museo Del Barrio, New York. *Comn:* Selected Works by Langston Hughes (mural), CETA Artists proj, New York, 79; drawings, Children's Psychiatric Div, Bellevue Hosp, New York, 84; stained percent for art, New York, Glass Windows for IS 206A South Bronx. *Exhib:* Recollections, Brooklyn Mus, NY, 79; Books Alive, Met Mus Art, New York, 83; Surfacing Images: A Selection of Works on Paper, Bronx Mus Art, NY, 85; Treasures from the Permanent Collection 1970-1987, The Studio Mus, Harlem, New York, 88; Working on Paper: Contemporary American Drawing, High Mus Art, Atlanta, Ga, 90; Lines of Vision: Drawings by Contemporary Women, Hillwood Art Gallery, Long Island Univ & Blum Helman Gallery, 89; one-man shows; Paintings and Drawings, June Kelly Gallery, NY, 89, John Street Series, Galerie Schniderei, Cologne, Ger, 90, Paintings and Works on Paper, Queens, Mus, Flushing, NY, 91 & Recent Paintings, Bronx Mus Art, NY, 92; The Blues Aesthetic: Black Culture and Modernism, Wash Proj Arts, Washington, DC, 87; Third International Bienal of Painting, Chenca, Ecuador, 91. *Awards:* MacDowell Colony Resident Painting Fel, Peterboro, NH, 86; NY Found Arts Fel, 86; Mid-Atlantic Nat Endowment Arts Reg Fel, 88; Artist Fel, Art Matters, New York, 89. *Bibliog:* Michael Brenson (auth), New Visions, New York Times, 1/9/87; Coco Fusco (auth), Hispanic artist and other slurs, Village Voice, NY, 8/9/88; Peggy Cyphers (auth), ARTS, New York in Review, 2/90; Pactrick Pacheco (auth), The New Faith in Painting, Art & Antiques, 61-62, 5/91; Art Feature review, Latin Am Lit & Arts, 30-33, 7/12/91. *Dealer:* June Kelly Gallery 591 Broadway New York NY 10012. *Mailing Add:* 155 Foster St No 4 New Haven CT 06511

ALVAREZ-CERVELA, JOSE MARIA
EDUCATOR, HISTORIAN
b La Guardia, Spain, Sept 21, 22. *Study:* Univ Santiago, Spain, BA, 48, Lic en Derecho, 56, PhD(law & artistic works), 68; Middlebury Col, Vt, MA, 65. *Pos:* Dir, Fine Arts Mus, Univ PR, Mayaguez, 58-64. *Teaching:* Prof art & humanities, Univ PR, Mayaguez, 57- *Awards:* 1983 Citizen of the Year in Mayaguez in Education, 84. *Mem:* PR Acad Arts, Hist & Archaeol. *Res:* Woodcarving of saints in Puerto Rico; mural paintings on ceilings and vaults; funerary art in Puerto Rico. *Publ:* Auth, Signos y Firmas Reales, La Comercial, Santiago, Spain, 57; A Pintura Mitologica e Alegorica nos Tectos e Abobadas do Escorial e do Palacio Real, Ed Imperio, Lisbon, 68; Los Contratos de Obra Artistica de la Catedral de Santiago de Compostela en Siglo XVII, Industrias Graficas Noroeste, Spain, 68; La Arquitectura Clasica Actual en Mayaguez, Antillian Col Press, Mayaguez, 83; El Portico Federico Degetau en UPR Mayaguez, Universidad de Puerto Rico en Mayaguez, 88. *Mailing Add:* c/o Univ Puerto Rico Art Dept PO Box 5000 Mayaguez PR 00381

AMADO, JESSE V
SCULPTOR
b San Antonio, Tex, 51. *Study:* Univ Tex, Austin BA(Eng), 76; Univ Tex, San Antonio, BFA(studio art), 87, MFA(studio art), 90. *Work:* Michael Tracy, pvt collection, San Ygnacio, Tex; Ken Bentley, AIA, pvt collection, San Antonio, Tex; Matthews & Branscomb, Attorneys, corp collection, San Antonio, Tex; Sunbelt Corp, corp collection, San Antonio, Tex. *Exhib:* Solo shows, Koehler Cult Art Ctr, San Antonio, Tex, 89, Southwest Craft Ctr, San Antonio, Philadelphia Fabric Workshop, Pa & San Antonio Mus Art, Tex, 91 & Jansen-Perez Gallery, San Antonio & Galveston Art Ctr, Tex, 92; Sangre de Cristo Art Ctr, Pueblo, Colo, 91; San Antonio Mus Art, Tex, 91; Blue Star Art Space, San Antonio, Tex, 92; and others. *Awards:* Touring Citation, Laguna Gloria Art Mus, Austin, Tex, 89; Visual Arts Orgn Grant Artist-in-residence, 90 & Visual Artists Fel Grant (sculpture), 90, Nat Endowment Arts; Visual Arts Fel Grant, Art Matters Inc, New York, 92. *Mailing Add:* 621 1/2 E Woodlawn Ave San Antonio TX 78212

AMALTITANO, LELIA
CURATOR, GALLERY DIRECTOR
b New York, NY. *Study:* Calif Inst Arts, Valencia, BFA, 74; Sch Art Inst Chicago, MFA, 78. *Collections Arranged:* Undercurrent, exhib of work by Joseph Beuys, Louise Bourgeois, Robert Morris, (ed & preface, catalog), 87, Mixed Meaning, exhib of work by Gretchen Bender, Mary Kelly, Roberta Friedman & Graham Weinbren, (essay, catalog), 88, Heroics Recast, exhib of work by Terry Allen, Francesco Clemente & Mia Westerlund-Roosen, (ed, catalog), 89, Changing Context, exhib of work by Richard Artschwager & John Baldessari, (catalog), 89 & New Territory: Art from East Germany, travelling exhib of work by seventeen contemp artists from East Germany (ed), 90, Grossman Gallery, Boston. *Pos:* Vis artist, Art Resources Open to Women, Schenectady, NY, 78; dir & cur, Rathbone Gallery, Russell Sage Jr Col Albany, NY, 83-86; cur, Stux Gallery, Boston & New York, 86-87; dir, Exhibs & Vis Artists Progs, Grossman Gallery, Sch Mus Fine Arts, Boston, 86- *Teaching:* Instr, Women in Art, an art hist survey, Albany Inst Hist & Art, NY, 79; instr, Coun Int Educ, Italy, 84. *Bibliog:* Reviews in many publ including, Art New England, Boston Globe, Art Am, Boston Phoenix & Albany Times Union. *Mailing Add:* School of the Museum of Fine Arts/ Barbara & Steven Grossman Gallery 230 The Fenway Boston MA 02115

AMANO, TAKA
PAINTER
b Toyama, Japan, Apr 24, 50. *Study:* Ikvei Col, Tokyo, BA, 71; Sch Visual Arts, New York, BFA, 77. *Work:* Solomon R Guggenheim Mus, New York; NY State Univ, Albany; Bronx Mus Arts, Bronx, NY. *Exhib:* Five-person show, Artists Space, New York, 84; Curators Choice, Bronx Mus Arts, 85; Selections 30, Drawing Ctr, New York, 85; Ten from the Drawing Ctr, New York, 85; Four-person show, Soho Ctr Visual Artists, New York, 87; New Acquisitions, Guggenheim Mus, New York, 87; Group Show, Jilian Pretto Gallery, New York, 89; Solo Shows, Jilian Pretto Gallery, New York, 89 & 90. *Awards:* Working Space Prog PS 1, Inst for Art & Urban Resources, 77-79; Nat Endowment Arts Regional Fel, Mid-Atlantic Arts Found, 88; Individual Artist Fel, Nat Endowment Arts, 89. *Bibliog:* Kay Larson (auth), article, New York Mag, 10/20/86; Marc Furstenberg (auth), article, Downtown Mag, 4/8/87. *Media:* Watercolor. *Mailing Add:* 6 Greene St New York NY 10013

AMASON, ALVIN ELI
PAINTER
b McKenny, Tex, Apr 6, 48. *Study:* Cent Wash Univ, BA, 73, MA, 74; Ariz State Univ, MFA, 76. *Work:* Nat Collection Fine Arts, Smithsonian Inst, Washington, DC; Nordjyllands Kunstmuseum, Aalborg, Denmark; Alaska State Mus, Juneau; Anchorage Hist & Fine Arts Mus, Alaska; Am Embassy, Brasilia, Brazil. *Comn:* Painting (with Robert Hudson, Sam Francis & Dan Flavin), Govt Serv Admin, Anchorage, 79. *Exhib:* Nat Collection Fine Arts, Washington, DC, 80. *Awards:* Jurors Award, Phoenix Mus Art, 75; Purchase Award, Alaska State Coun Arts, 80. *Bibliog:* Jamake Highwater (auth), The Sweet Grass Lives On, Harper & Row, 80; Sculpture out in the open, Newsweek, 8/18/80; Sandra B Betz (auth), Alvin Eli Amason, Arts & Cult N, 81. *Mem:* Alaska State Coun Arts (councilman, 79-80). *Media:* Oil, Mixed. *Mailing Add:* c/o Stonington Gallery 415 F St Anchorage AK 99501

AMATEAU, MICAELA See Amato, Michele

AMATNIEK, SARA
PRINTMAKER, GRAPHIC ARTIST
b New York, NY, Feb 6, 22. *Study:* Brooklyn Col, BA, 42; Columbia Univ, MA, 52; Pratt Graphic Ctr, 64. *Work:* Rembrant Graphic Arts, Rosemont, NJ; Joseph P Kennedy Enterprises, New York, NY; Red Devil Found, Mt Vernon, NY. *Exhib:* Paper Works 80, Hudson River Mus, Yonkers, NY; Solo show, Printmaker, The Katonah Gallery, NY, 82 & Etching & Monoprints, Garrison Art Ctr, NY, 90; 68th Ann, 83, 69th Ann, 84 & 75th Ann Exhib, 90, Hudson River Mus, Yonkers, NY, 83; Somerstown International Print Show, Somerstown Gallery, Somers, NY, 86; Nat Asn Women Artist, Monmouth Mus, NJ, 87; Adelphi Univ, Manhattan Ctr, New York, 91. *Awards:* Barbara Egan Award for Graphics, Nat Miniature Art, Nutley, NJ, 76; House of Heyendryk Jr Award, Nat Asn Women Artists Ann, 80 & 90; Dr & Mrs James McGarvey Award, 7th Int Miniature Art Soc Fla, 82. *Bibliog:* Malcolm Preston (auth), Different styles of prints, Newsday, 78; William A Titus (auth), Photographing Works of Art, Watson Guptill, 81; Kathie Beals (auth), Works on paper, Gannett Westchester Newspaper, 85. *Mem:* Nat Asn Women Artists (vpres, 80-84); New York Artists Equity; Women's Caucus Art; Hudson River Contemp Artists (bd dir, 88-92). *Mailing Add:* 4797 Boston Post Rd Pelham Manor NY 10803

AMATO, MICHELE
PAINTER
b New York, NY, July 29, 45. *Study:* Boston Univ, BFA, 68; Univ Colo, Boulder, MFA, 73. *Work:* Chase Manhattan Bank, New York; Subaru Inc & Amoco Productions, Denver, Colo; Harte Hanks Inc Investments, San Antonio, Tex; Denver Art Mus, Colo; Rose Art Mus, Brandeis Univ. *Exhib:* Kornblee Gallery, New York, 75, 77, 78 & 85; Painting Invitational, 78 & Print Invitational, 82-88, Denver Art Mus; Cleveland Art Mus, 79; one person exhibs, Sheldon Art Mus, Univ Nebr, Lincoln, 79, Minneapolis Col Art & Design, Minn, 80 & Marianne Deson Gallery, Chicago, 82-84; Laguna Gloria Art Mus, Austin, Tex; Bernice Steinbaum Gallery, New York, 85; Tampa Art Mus, 86; San Antonio Art Inst, 86; Caroline Lee Gallery, Houston, 87-88; Mus Contemp Hispanic Art, New York, 88; RS Levy Gallery, Austin, 88 & 89; Lehigh Univ Gallery, Bethlehem, Pa, 89; More Gallery, Philadelphia, Pa, 90. *Pos:* Interviewer & reviewer art & dance, Straight Creek J, Denver, 73-75 & Boulder Daily Camera, Colo, 76-77, Ocular Mag 76-79 & Pa State Univ,

88- *Teaching:* Grad painting & drawing dept head, Wichita State Univ, Kans, 77-78; vis artist, Minneapolis Col Art & Design, 79-80, Univ Tex, San Antonio, 81-82, Univ Tex, Austin, 84, Univ Colo, 84-85 & E Carolina Univ, NC, 86, Penn State Univ, 88- *Awards:* Painting Award, Nat Endowment Art, 87, 88 & 92; Res & travel grants, Inst Arts & Humanistic Studies, Penn State Univ, 90 & 91. *Bibliog:* article in Los Angeles Times, 9/80; Vivien Raynor (auth), article in New York Times, 85; Ricardo Pau Llosa, Magical Realism (catalog), Lehigh Univ Press. *Mem:* Nat Orgn Women Artists; Women's Caucus Art; founding mem Front Range Women, Colo; Col Art Asn. *Media:* All. *Publ:* Auth, In Praise of Paradox & Contradiction, Westminster Col, Pa. *Dealer:* More Gallery 1630 Walnut Philadelphia PA 19103; Lyons Matrix Gallery 1712 Lavaca Austin TX 78701. *Mailing Add:* 1721 Linden Hall Rd Boalsburg PA 16827

AMAYA, ARMANDO
SCULPTOR
b Puebla, Pue, Mex, Nov 29, 35. *Study:* Escuela Nac Pintura & Escultura La Esmeralda, with Francisco Zuniga. *Work:* Mex Mus, San Francisco, Calif. *Comn:* Benito Juarez (bronze mask), Mex Govt, Santa Ursula, 69. *Exhib:* Pasquale Iannetti Gallery, San Francisco Mus; Mus Contemp Art, Israel; Museo de Arte Latino Americano, Chile; Galeria Tasende, Mex. *Teaching:* Prof art, Escuela Nac Pintura & Escultura La Esmeralda, 69- *Bibliog:* Mexican Studies, Univ Calif Press, Vol 3, No 2, 87; Diccionario de escultura mexicana del siglo XX, Universidad Nacional Autonoma de Mex, 83. *Media:* Bronze. *Mailing Add:* c/o Pasquale Iannetti Art Gallery 522 Sutter San Francisco CA 94102

AMBROSE, CHARLES EDWARD
PAINTER, EDUCATOR
b Memphis, Tenn, Jan 6, 22. *Study:* Univ Ala, BFA, 49, MA, 50. *Work:* Univ Southern Miss; Carey Col; Biloxi Art Asn; First Nat Bank, Hattiesburg, Miss. *Comn:* Portrait reliefs, 58 & portraits, 60, Univ Southern Miss; Pat Harrison Waterways Bldg, 65; Carey Col; Miss Archives Bldg, 72. *Exhib:* Mid-Continent Exhib, Mo, 71; Watercolor USA, Springfield, Mo, 73; 1st Ann Bi-State, Meridian, Miss, 73; Central South, Nashville, Tenn, 75; 17th Dixie Ann, Montgomery, Ala, 75. *Teaching:* Assoc prof drawing & painting, Univ Southern Miss, 50-70; head art dept, Miss Univ for Women, 70-82. *Awards:* First Place Watercolor, Miss Art Asn, 68; First Place Drawing, Edgewater Ann, 70; Purchase Award/Drawing, 1st Ann Bi-State, 73. *Mem:* Southeastern Col Arts Conf; Nat Coun Art Adminr; Southern Asn Sculptors; Col Art Asn; Miss Art Asn. *Media:* Watercolor, Oil. *Mailing Add:* 1125 N Seventh St Columbus MS 39701

AMEN, IRVING
PAINTER, PRINTMAKER
b New York, NY, July 25, 18. *Study:* Pratt Inst, scholar, 32-39; study in Paris, 50 & Italy, 53. *Work:* Mus Mod Art & Metrop Mus, New York; Butler Inst Am Art; Victoria & Albert Mus, London; Bibliot Nat, Paris; Albertina Mus, Vienna; and others; Bezalel, Jerusalem; Smithsonian Inst, Washington, DC. *Comn:* Peace Medal (commemorating end of Viet Nam War); Twelve Tribes of Israel (12 stained glass windows 16ft high), comn by Agudas Achim Synagogue, Columbus, Ohio. *Exhib:* Master Prints, Mus Mod Art, New York; Int Ausstellung Von Holzschnitten, Zurich, Switz; I Mednarodna Graficna Razstava, Ljubljana, Yugoslavia; L V Biannale di Pittura Americana, Bordighera, Italy; Dessins Americains Contemporains, US Info Serv; Collection of the Butler Inst Am Art, Youngstown, Ohio. *Teaching:* Instr art, Pratt Inst & Univ Notre Dame. *Awards:* Directors Prize, Audubon Artists, NY. *Mem:* Int Inst Arts & Lett; Int Soc Wood Engravers; Accad Fiorentina delle Arti Disegno; Soc Am Graphic Artists; Am Color Print Soc; Audubon Artists; Asca; Artist Fel; Artists Equity, NY. *Media:* Oil, Etching, Woodcut. *Publ:* Print ed, Irving Amen woodcuts 1948-1960, Irving Amen: 1964, Amen: 1964-1968 & Amen: 1968-1970; illusr, Gilgamesh, Ltd Ed Club. *Mailing Add:* 90 SW 12th Terrace Boca Raton FL 33486

AMEND, EUGENE MICHAEL
HISTORIAN, ADVISOR
b Jefferson City, Mo, Oct 31, 50. *Study:* Univ Mo-Columbia, BA, 75, MA, 77; studied with Dr Saul Weinberg, Dr Edzard Baumann, Dr Osmond Overby & Dr Vera Townsend. *Collections Arranged:* Nathan Jones: Works on Paper, Univ Tex-Dallas, 79; Arie Van Selm: Recent Works, Tex Woman's Univ, Denton, 79; Charles Campbell: Retrospective, Longview Mus & Art Ctr, Tex, 79; Auguste Ravier, 1814-1895, Univ Tex, Dallas, 81. *Pos:* Cur & art historian, Stewart Gallery, Dallas, 78-80; art adv & free lance cur, E M Amend & Assoc, Dallas, 80-; Dir, Omni Art, Dallas, 84-; consult, Texas Instruments, Inc, 87-89, Achievement Video Network Inc, 88- *Teaching:* Instr art hist & humanities, Univ Mo-Columbia, 75-76; instr art hist, Richland Col, 80-85. *Mem:* Col Art Asn; Artist Coalition Tex (pres, 79-80). *Res:* American artists and current art patrons and patronage in regional localities; Australian artist, Norman Lloyd (1895-1983). *Mailing Add:* 3130 Chatsworth Farmers Branch TX 75234

AMENOFF, GREGORY
PAINTER
b St Charles, Ill, 48. *Study:* Beloit Col, BA. *Work:* Albright-Knox Art Gallery, Buffalo, NY; Art Inst of Chicago; Metrop Mus Art, New York; Mus Mod Art, New York; Whitney Mus Am Art. *Exhib:* Works on Paper, Hayden Corridor, Mass Inst Technol, 76; Stephen Wirtz Gallery, San Francisco, 83; Texas Gallery, Houston, 84; The Monotypes, Butler Inst Am Art, Columbus, Ohio, 89; Hirschl & Adler Modern, New York, 90; over 65 group exhibs, 74-90. *Teaching:* Prof grad painting, Sch Visual Arts, 87 & Yale Univ Sch Art, 91. *Awards:* Mass Bicentennial Painting Award, 76; Nat Endowment Arts, 80, 81 & 89; Tiffany, 80. *Bibliog:* Ed Hallahan (auth), Gregory Amenoff: The Monotypes, Dialogue, 3/4/89; A painter's images of Southwest myths, Philadelphia Inquirer, 10/26/89. *Publ:* Notes on identity a look at the landscape in American painting, Napa Contemp Arts Found J, Vol 1, 92. *Mailing Add:* c/o Hirschl & Adler Modern 851 Madison Ave New York NY 10021

AMES, LEE JUDAH
ILLUSTRATOR, WRITER
b New York, NY, Jan 8, 21. *Study:* Columbia Univ, with Carnahan. *Work:* Many pieces, layouts & finished illus in Univ Ore & Univ Southern Miss permanent collections. *Pos:* Art dir, Weber Assocs, New York, 47-52; pres, Ames Advert, New York, 53-54; artist-in-residence, Doubleday Publ Co, New York, 55-60; pres, Lee Ames & Zak Ltd, 75- & Lee J Ames Enterprises Inc. *Teaching:* Instr comic art, Sch Visual Arts, New York, 48-49; lectr advert art, Dowling Col, 70-72. *Awards:* Garden State Children's Book Award, 86. *Mem:* Nat Cartoonists Soc; Berndt Toast Gang. *Media:* Mixed Media. *Publ:* Auth & illusr, Draw 50 Ser (23 titles), Make 25 Crayon Drawings of the West, Make 25 Felt Tipped Drawings of the Circus & The Dot, Line and Shape Connection, Doubleday; plus illusr for over 100 addn bks. *Mailing Add:* 87 Heartside Dr Mt Sinai NY 11766

AMES, POLLY SCRIBNER
PAINTER
b Chicago, Ill, Feb 16, 08. *Study:* Art Inst Chicago, 29; Hans Schwiegerle, Munich, Ger, 32; Chicago Sch Sculpture 33; with Jose de Creft, New York, 34 & Hans Hofmann, New York, 35 & 36. *Work:* Young Satyr and friend, 61; Col Jerusalem. *Comn:* portrait, Povla Frijsh; portrait, Sigurd Rasher, New York. *Exhib:* One-man show, Cultur Centrum, Willemstad, Curacao, 47, Chardin Galerie, Paris, 49, Esher-Surrey, the Hague, 50, Int Music Festival, Pavillon Boisy Aix-En-Provence, 50, 1020, Mus Adlai Stevenson's Gallery, Chicago. *Pos:* gen secy, British Art Ctr, 41-43. *Publ:* Auth, Chances of My Working, Marsden Hartley in Maine, Univ Maine. *Mailing Add:* 5834 S Stony Island Ave Chicago IL 60637

AMFT, ROBERT
PAINTER, PHOTOGRAPHER
b Chicago, Ill, Dec 7, 16. *Study:* Art Inst Sch, grad; Oxbow Sch, Saugatuck, Mich. *Work:* Butler Inst Am Art, Youngstown, Ohio; Brown Foreman, Louisville, Ky. *Exhib:* Pa Acad Ann, 58; Butler Inst Art, 58; one-man shows, Art Inst Chicago Sales Gallery, 78, Hammer Gallery, Chicago, 81 & Watercolors, Kans State Univ, 84; Midwestern Sculpture, South Bend Art Ctr, 90; Photography of Folk Art Environments, Houston, 91; Amalgamations, Gallery 2, Chicago, 92; Re-Creations, 1800 Clybourn Gallery, 92; New Horizons Ann, Chicago, 92; Pointillism, Color Photos, Rotunda Gallery, Highland Park, Ill, 92. *Awards:* First Prize Painting, 72 & Spec Award, 75, New Horizons; Renaissance Prize, 75th Artists of Chicago, 74; Painting Award, Beverly Art Ctr, 85; Art Inst Curator's Choice, Art Rental Gallery, 86. *Bibliog:* Great treasures from the Art Institute of Chicago, Chicago Mag, 4/77; Udo Kultermann (auth), Van Gogh in Contemporary Art, Art Voices South, 11-12/78; Alan Artner (auth), rev, Chicago Tribune, 7/24/81. *Mem:* Arts Club Chicago. *Publ:* Illusr, Photographs of sculptor Fred Smith, Life Mag, 11/69; SPOT, Publications of the Houston Ctr for Photography, 91; Reproduction of Amft's Peacock in Chicago, Sun Times, 1/10/92. *Dealer:* Joy Horwich 333 E Ontario Chicago IL 60611. *Mailing Add:* 7340 N Ridge Chicago IL 60645

AMICO, DAVID MICHAEL
PAINTER, INSTRUCTOR
b Rochester, NY, Sept 24, 51. *Study:* Calif State Univ, Fullerton, BA, 74; Hunter Col, New York, 75. *Exhib:* New Figuration in America, Milwaukee Art Mus, Wis, 82; Circus Boy, 87 & Profound Visions, 88, Ace Contemp Exhibs, Los Angeles; Ace Gallery, Los Angeles, 89 & 90; Los Angeles Munic Gallery, Sociedade Cult Arte Brazil, 90; solo show, Marc Jancou Galerie, Zurich, Switz, 91; Physical Abstraction in Los Angeles, Ace Gallery, Los Angeles, 92; and others. *Teaching:* Guest lectr studio painting, Clairmont Grad Sch, 85 & 88 & Art Ctr Design, Pasadena, Calif, 86 & 87; guest instr painting & drawing & guest lectr drawing, Calif State Univ Fullerton, 92; guest instr painting & drawing, Spring Semester Univ Calif, Los Angeles, 92-93. *Awards:* Guest of Honorarium Cartier Found, Juey es Josas France, 90. *Bibliog:* Christopher Knight (auth), Amico's paintings portray private mystery, Los Angeles Herald Examiner, 81; Ralph Rugoff (auth), Hottest new artists, Los Angeles Mag, 85; Lee Wohlfert-Wihldorg (auth), LA's electric, eclectic artists, Town & Country, 86; Margaret Lazzari (auth), Parameters of Meaning, Artweek, 6/90. *Media:* Oil, Drawing Graphite. *Dealer:* Douglas Chrismas 5514 Wilshire Blvd 90036. *Mailing Add:* 443 S San Pedro No 503 Los Angeles CA 90013

AMINOFF, JUDITH
WRITER, EDITOR
b San Diego, Calif, July 9, 47. *Study:* Univ Calif, Berkeley, BA, 70; McGill Univ, Montreal, 72-75. *Pos:* New York corresp, Flash Art, Milan, 79; contrib ed, Umbrella Mag, Calif, 79; ed, Cover Mag, 79-83; translr, Mus Mod Art, Paris, 82-; collabr, Editions Territories, 82-; ed, BHD Buchloh, Abigail Solomon-Godeau, 86- *Res:* Magazine of art presenting new works; artists in their own words and in dialogue with each other, critics, dealers. *Mailing Add:* Moulin de Torcay Ste Ange et Torcay 28170 France

AMORY, CLAUDIA
PAINTER
b Hampton, VA. *Study:* Va Commonwealth Univ, BFA, 76; Md Inst Col of Art, MFA, 85. *Comn:* Painting, Steuart Hughes, Williamsburg, Va, 86. *Exhib:* Art in the Bell Tower, Bell Tower Commons, Baltimore, Md, 85; Univ Md, Baltimore Co, 88; Excavations, Arlington Art Ctr, Va, 89; 1989 McDonogh Ann Exhib, Tuttle Gallery, Md, 89. *Pos:* Admin asst, off grad studies, Md Inst, Col Art, 83-85; gallery selection panel mem, Sch 33 Art Ctr, Baltimore, 88-90, dir, 90- *Teaching:* Art inst, pub sch system, York Co, 76-82; grad inst asst, Mt Royal Grad Sch Art, Md Inst, Col Art, 83-85. *Awards:* Jurors Merit Award, Area Wide Juried Painting Exhib, Arlington Arts Ctr, 85; Fel, Nat Endowment Arts, 87. *Mem:* Arlington Arts Ctr. *Mailing Add:* 1427 Light St Baltimore MD 21218

AMOS, EMMA
PAINTER, PRINTMAKER
b Atlanta, Ga, Mar 16, 38. *Study:* Antioch Col, Yellow Springs, Ohio, BA, 58; London Central Sch Art, Eng, BFA, 59; New York Univ, MA, 66. *Work:* Mus Mod Art, New York; Schomburg Collection, New York; Newark Mus, NJ; NJ State Mus, Trenton; Minn Mus Art, Minn. *Comn:* Mosaic Ceiling, New York Bd Educ, 94. *Exhib:* Committed to Print, Mus Mod Art, New York, 88-90; Selections, 6 Contemporary African/American Artists, Williams Col Mus, Williamstown, Mass, 89; New Acquisitions, NJ State Mus, Trenton, 90; The Wild Blue Yonder Series, Newark Mus, NJ, 90; The Decade Show, Mus Contemp Hispanic Art, New York, 90; Bronx Mus, McIntosh Gallery, Ga; and others. *Teaching:* Prof fine art, Mason Gross Sch Arts, Rutgers Univ, NJ, 80; gov, Skowhegan Sch Painting & Sculpture, 87. *Awards:* Nat Endowment Fel-Drawing, 83; NY Found Fel--Painting, 89. *Bibliog:* Claudia Rowe (auth), article, Cover Mag, summer 89; Lucy Lippard (auth), Mixed Blessings, Pantheon Books, 90; Arlene Raven (auth), article, Village Voice, NY, 5/91. *Mem:* Printmaking Workshop, New York, 65; Col Art Asn; Am Craft Coun. *Media:* Acrylic, oil; All. *Publ:* Coauth, Racism is the issue, Issue 15, 82, & The Art of Education, Issue 25, 90, Heresies Collective; illusr, IKON--Creativity and Change, No 5/6, Ikon Inc, 86; auth & co-host, Show of Hands (ser), WGBH Educ TV, Boston, Mass, 87-88; coauth, M/E/A/N/I/N/G Magazine, Mira Schor & Susan Bee, 90. *Dealer:* McIntosh Gallery 587 Virginia Ave Atlanta GA 30306. *Mailing Add:* 21 Bond St New York NY 10012

AMOSS, BERTHE
ILLUSTRATOR, PAINTER
b New Orleans, La, Sept 26, 25. *Study:* Newcomb Col, BA; Univ Hawaii; Kunsthalle Bremen, Ger, three yrs; Acad des Beaux Arts, Antwerp, Belg, one yr; Tulane Univ, MA(literature & art). *Work:* La State Libr; De Grummond Collection, Univ Southern Miss, Kerlan; Town of Kerlan, Minn; Tulane Univ. *Exhib:* One person show, Exhib of Illustrators, Howard Tilton Libr, Tulane Univ, 82. *Pos:* Children's bk rev ed, New Orleans Times Picayune, currently; pres, More Than a Card, Inc, currently. *Teaching:* Instr, writing & illustrating children's books, Tulane Univ, 76-82, children's literature & folklore, 82- *Bibliog:* Selma Lanes (auth), Down the Rabbit Hole, Children's Literature, Stewig. *Media:* Watercolor. *Publ:* Auth & illusr, The Marvelous Catch of Old Hannibal, 70, Old Hasdrubal and the Pirates, 71, Parents Publ; Secret Lives, Atlantic-Little-Brown, 79; The Loup Garou, Pelican, 79; auth, Mockingbird Song, Tom in the Middle, What did you lose Santa, Harper & Row, 87 & 88; auth, More Than a Card, private publ, 88. *Mailing Add:* 3723 Carondelet St New Orleans LA 70115

AMYX, LEON KIRKMAN
PAINTER, EDUCATOR
b Visalia, Calif, Dec 20, 08. *Study:* San Jose State Col, AB, 31; Claremont Grad Sch, MA, 42; Univ Calif, Berkeley; Mills Col; Calif Col Arts & Crafts, with McFee, Kroll, Sheets, Hinkle & Chapin. *Work:* Chaffey Found, Ont, Can; Buck Collection, Laguna Hills, Calif. *Comn:* Textile designs, Seneca Textile Corp, New York, 54; paintings, Granite Construction Co, Watsonville, Calif, 73; paintings, Bud Antle Inc, Salinas, Calif, 79. *Exhib:* San Francisco Mus Art, 35; Golden Gate Expos, Treasure Island, San Francisco, 39; Am Watercolor Soc, Nat Acad Galleries, New York, 42; Traveling Exhib Through Latin Am, San Francisco Mus Art, 44; Nat Watercolor Soc, Riverside Mus, New York, 46; Calif Artists Invitational, San Jose State Univ, 58; Regionalism: The California View, Santa Barbara Mus Art, 88. *Teaching:* Prof painting & hist art, Hartnell Col, Salinas, Calif, 36-72; prof painting, Sacramento State Univ, summers 49-52, San Jose State Univ, summers 55 & 56 & Univ Pac, Stockton, summer 59. *Awards:* Silver Medal, Oakland Calif Art Mus, 44; First Award, Monterey Calif Dist Fair, 49. *Bibliog:* Mary M Riddle (auth), Amyx's show demonstrates that it takes a complication of knowledge to be simple in art, Carmel Pine Cone, 11/19/48; Victoria Dalkey (auth), Visions of Vanished Landscapes, Watercolors of Leon Amyx capture a way of Life, Sacramento Bee, 3/12/89. *Mem:* Nat Watercolor Soc; Carmel Art Asn (bd dirs, 48-49, 73-74, 80); hon mem Laguna Beach Art Asn; Assoc Am Watercolor Soc. *Media:* Watercolor, Oil, Acrylic. *Publ:* Auth, The California Style, Calif Watercolor Artist, 1925-1955, Hillcrest Press Inc. *Dealer:* Ackeley Galleries 2456 Edna St Sacramento CA 95821; Arlington Gallery 819 Anacopa Santa Barbara CA 93101. *Mailing Add:* PO Box 363 Georgetown CA 95634

ANACKER, JOHN WILLIAM
GALLERY DIRECTOR, PAINTER
b Bozeman, Mont, June 22, 60. *Study:* Mont State Univ, BAA, 83; Univ NC, Chapel Hill, MFA, 86. *Exhib:* 29th Ann Nat Exhib Am Art, Chautauqua Art Asn Galleries, NY, 86; Celebrating Paper, Yellowstone Art Ctr, Billings, Mont, 88. *Pos:* Gallery dir, Haynes Fine Arts Gallery, Bozeman, Mont, 86- *Teaching:* Instr painting, Mont State Univ Sch Art, 86- *Mem:* Mont Art Gallery Dirs Asn (treas, 89-90 & pres, 90-). *Media:* Watercolor. *Mailing Add:* c/o Western Montana Col Gallery & Mus 710 S Atlantic Dillon MT 59725

ANARGYROS, SPERO
SCULPTOR
b New York, NY, Jan 23, 15. *Study:* With William Zorack, New York, 34-35; asst to Mahonri Sharp Young, This is the Place Monument, Salt Lake City, Utah, 44-47. *Comn:* Bronze portrait of Father Terry, pres, Santa Clara Univ, 77; Jubail commemorative plague, Saudi Arabia, 77; bronze portrait of John Daley, pres, World Airways, 79; bronze portrait, Capt John A Sutter, Sutter Hosp, Sacramento, 87; Ancient Coffee Drinker (9' tall polychomed bronze statue), Hills Bros Coffee Co Hq, San Francisco, 92; and others. *Exhib:* Nat Acad Design, 38-40, 53-56, 59 & 77; M H De Young Mem Mus, 53 & 62-63; one-man shows, Houston & Corpus Christi, Tex, 68, San Francisco, Calif, 69 & Egyptian Mus, San Jose, Calif, 69; Nat Sculpture Soc Ann, 77; plus many others. *Awards:* First Award Sculpture, Tenth Ann Nat Exhib, Acad Artists Asn, 59; John Spring Art Founder Award, 42nd Ann Exhib, 75 & Coun Am Soc Award, 45th Ann Exhib, 78, Nat Sculpture Soc. *Bibliog:* Terence Busch (auth), Spero Anargyros and his 23 ton rock, San Francisco Mag, 11/65; Frederick Whitaker (auth), Spero Anargyros, sculptor, Am Artist, 2/67; Valerie Shields (auth), Man with a masterful thumb, Spectator, 2/57. *Mem:* Life mem Art Students League; fel Nat Sculpture Soc; fel Int Inst Arts & Lett; Nat Soc Lit & Arts. *Media:* Bronze, Marble. *Mailing Add:* PO Box 522 541A Tunnel Ave Brisbane CA 94005

ANASTASI, WILLIAM (JOSEPH)
PAINTER, SCULPTOR
b Philadelphia, Pa, Aug 11, 33. *Study:* Univ Pa, 53-58. *Work:* Metrop Mus Art & Brooklyn Mus, New York; Walker Art Inst, Minneapolis; Phoenix Mus Art, Ariz; Ga Mus Art, Athens; Univ NC, Greensboro; Des Moines Art Inst; Philadelphia Mus Art; Mus Contemp Art, Los Angeles, Calif; Chicago Art Inst, Ill; Mus Mod Art, New York; Moderna Museet, Stockholm, Sweden. *Comn:* Viewing a Film of the Period (film), 78, Collapse (photo installation), 81 & Terminus II (photo installation), 81, Whitney Mus Am Art; Photo installation, Kunstmus, Dusseldorf, Ger, 79; Terminus I (photo installation), Hudson River Mus, New York, 79. *Exhib:* Revisions, Perspectives and Proposals in Film and Video, Whitney Mus Am Art, 79; Für Augen und Ohren, Akad Kunste, West Berlin, Ger, 80; Ecouter par les Yeux, Mus D'Art de la Ville de Paris, France, 80; Coincidents, Whitney Mus Am Art, New York, 81; American Awards Exhib, Am Acad Arts & Lett, New York, 82; Exhib in Hon of John Cage, Am Ctr, Paris, France, 82; Ball State Univ, Muncie, Ind, 91; Joyce, Cage, Fats & Crazy, Art Inst Chicago, 91; and others. *Pos:* Artistic co-adv, Merce Cunningham Dance Co, New York, 84- *Teaching:* Sch Visual Arts, New York, 68-87; lectr, Art After Duchamp, Chicago Art Fair, 88, Yale Univ, 91. *Bibliog:* Gregory Battcock (auth), Minimal Art (Introduction), Dutton, 68; Lucy R Lippard (auth), Six Years: The Dematerialization of the Art Object, Praeger, 73; Brian O'Doharty, Inside the white cube: Notes on the Gallery Space, Artforum, 3/76. *Media:* All Media. *Publ:* Duchamp on the Jarry Road, Artforum, 9/91; Me Innerman Monophone & Even Haha, Notes on Jarry & Duchamp with Joyce, Anders Tornberg Gallery, Lund, Sweden, 5/92. *Dealer:* Anders Tornberg Gallery Lund Sweden; Sandra Gering Gallery New York. *Mailing Add:* 924 West End Ave New York NY 10025

ANBINDER, PAUL
ART PUBLISHER, COLLECTOR
b Brooklyn, NY, Apr 19, 40. *Study:* Cornell Univ, AB, 60; Columbia Univ, grad work, 60-61. *Collections Arranged:* Cornell Collects (co-organizer), Hudson River Mus, Yonkers, NY, 76-77. *Pos:* Ed in chief, Shorewood Publ Inc, 64-69; exec ed & vpres, Harry N Abrams Inc, New York, NY, 69-74 & pres, 74-75; dir spec projs, Alfred A Knopf, Random House & ed/vpres, Ballantine Bks, New York, 75-78; pres, Hudson Hills Press, Inc, New York, 78- *Mem:* Col Art Asn; Friends of Johnson Mus, Cornell Univ (mem exec coun); Century Asn. *Collection:* Contemporary American prints and drawings. *Publ:* Auth, Editing the Illustrated Book, Editors on Editing, Harper & Row, New York, 85. *Mailing Add:* c/o Hudson Hills Press Inc 230 Fifth Ave Suite 1308 New York NY 10001-7704

ANDELL, NANCY
PAINTER, PRINTMAKER
b Boston, Mass, Nov 14, 53. *Study:* Sch Mus Fine Arts, Boston, Mass, dipl, 74, 5th yr certif, 76; Tufts Univ, Medford, Mass, 75. *Work:* Metrop Mus Art, New Mus Contemp Art, New York; Brooklyn Mus, NY; Worcester Art Mus, Mass; Mobil Corp, New York. *Exhib:* Solo exhibs, New York, Flag Gallery, 78, Pastels, Gouaches, Monotypes & Drypoints, 79, Nancy Andell, Recent Works on Paper, Impressions Gallery, Boston, Mass, 80, Art on Main Street, Studio Installation, Chatham, 89, Monotype Installation, Amtrack Sta Hudson, 90, Pondorowth: Painting, Drawings & Prints, Shaker Mus & Libr, Old Chatham, NY, 91; The Boston Printmakers, Brocton Art Ctr, Mass, 80; Contemp Monotypes, Smith Anderson Gallery, Palo Alto, Calif & Impressions Gallery, Boston, Mass, 80; Images in Landscape, The Past Decade, Univ NH, Durham, 80; Monotypes, 81, New York's Salong Hanging, 83, Nancy Andell & Barbara Andrus, New Impressions Gallery, 88, Experimental Etching Studio 20th Anniversary Exhibit, Boston Pub Libr, Boston, Mass, 92; Landscape, Int Monetary Fund Gallery, Washington, DC, 81; Scapism, Boston Col Gallery, Newton, Mass, 81; Prints from Impressions Gallery, Philadelphia Print Club, 82, Printed by Women, A Nat Exhibit of Photog & Prints, Port His Mus Penn's Landing, Philadelphia, Pa, 83; Small Paitings, 83, A Sense of Place, Victoria Munroe Gallery, 84, Pandora's Box, New Mus Contemp Art, New York, NY, 85; Works on Paper, Hamilton Gallery, Elmira Col, NY, 84; Queens Artists' Salon, Flushing Gallery, NY, 86; Five Points Gallery, E Chatham, NY, 88; Doldrums, 89, On the Verge: Visions of the 90's, 90, Working Arts, Albany Inst Hist & Art, Harmanus Bleecker Ctr, Albany, NY, 91; Faculty/Student Exhibit, Rensselaer Co Coun

Arts Gallery, Troy, NY, 91; Eight Artists Respond to War, Brickbottom Gallery, Somerville, Mass, 91; Water/Clay/Stone, Smithy-Pioneer Gallery, Cooperstown, NY, 92. *Teaching:* Fac, Renssaeler Co Coun for the Arts, Troy, NY, 89-92. *Awards:* Spec Opportunity Stipend: NY Found Arts & Rennselaer Co Coun Arts, 91; Face to Face with the Arts, Columbia Co Initiative Prog, 91; Skidmore Col Fel, Saratoga Springs, NY, 91. *Bibliog:* Martin Moynihan (auth), This Art Show Comes With Instructions, Albany Times Union, 9/17/89; Lois Tarlow (auth), Profile: Ten Years Later, Art New Eng, 12/89; Lael Locke (auth), Idealized Landscapes, The Paper, 10/91. *Media:* Oil, Mixed Media. *Mailing Add:* PO Box 46 Chatham NY 12037

ANDERSEN, DAVID R L
PAINTER, CURATOR
b Logan, Utah, Sept 30, 57. *Study:* Brigham Young Univ, Provo, Utah, MFA, 88. *Work:* Darthmouth Col, Hanover, NH; Ohio Univ; Utah State Collection; Mauritian Embassy, Washington, DC. *Exhib:* Solo exhibs, Calculations for Future Events, Darthmouth Col, Hanover, NH, 90 & Spiritus Mundi, Grossmont Col, San Diego, Calif, 91; two-person shows, Midland Col, Tex, 90 & Diverse Works Gallery, Houston, Tex, 90; Nat Draw Exhib, Brigham Young Univ, Provo, Utah, 89; Nat Juried Exhib, Natsoulas/Novelozo Gallery, Davis, Calif, 90; Animals, Centennial Mus, El Paso, Tex, 90. *Collections Arranged:* Robert Colescott (paintings), 89; Sera Siempre Asi? (prints; catalog); Sleeping Mutations (sculpture), 89; Cont Graphic Design, 90; Prints From Life, 90. *Pos:* Preparator, Brigham Young Univ, Provo, Utah, 85-88; dir galleries, Univ Tex at El Paso, 88-91; Instr painting/drawing, Brigham Young Univ, Provo, Utah, 85- 88; drawing/design, Univ Tex, El Paso, 88-91. *Awards:* URI Grant, Tex Comn on the Arts. *Media:* Mixed media. *Mailing Add:* University of Texas El Paso Main Gallery Fox Fine Art Center El Paso TX 79968

ANDERSEN, LEIF (WERNER)
PAINTER
b Baltimore, Md, Mar 6, 25. *Study:* Art Students League, with Reginald Marsh & Louis Bouche, 46-48. *Work:* Bordighera Mus, Italy. *Exhib:* Am Group Show, Venice, Italy, 52; Nat Acad Design Ann, New York, 57 & 62; Allied Artist Am Ann, Nat Acad Design, 58 & 61; and numerous one-man shows. *Awards:* S J Wallace Truman Award, Nat Acad Design Ann, 57; Margaret Cooper Prize, Allied Artist Am, Nat Acad Design, 61. *Media:* Oil, Acrylic. *Mailing Add:* 246 E 51st St New York NY 10022

ANDERSEN, WAYNE VESTI
ART HISTORIAN, EDUCATOR
b July 7, 30; US citizen. *Study:* Univ Calif, BA, 59; Columbia Univ, MA, 61 & PhD, 66; Boston Art Inst, hon MFA. *Pos:* Sr cur, Walker Art Ctr, Minneapolis, Minn, formerly; dir, Hayden Gallery, Mass Inst Technol, 65-77; pres, Vesti Corp, Boston, Mass, 78-88. *Teaching:* Prof art hist, Mass Inst Technol, 64-88; vis prof, Yale Univ, New Haven, Conn, 69; prof visual studies, Harvard Univ, 77-79. *Awards:* William Bayard Cutting fel, 61-62; Belg-Am Found CRB Fel, 62; Am Coun Learned Soc Fel; Ford Found Grant Humanities, 62-63. *Mem:* Col Art Asn Am; New York Acad Sci. *Res:* Late nineteenth century painting; twentieth century art; art theory. *Publ:* Auth, Gauguin's paradise lost, 71; American sculpture in process, 75; Scenario for an artist's apocalypse, 90; My Self, 90; Phobic Raptures, 91; and numerous articles in scholarly mags. *Mailing Add:* 4, Ave de Versailles Rue-Malmaison 92500 France

ANDERSON, BILL (WILLIAM MAXWELL)
PAINTER, PRINTMAKER
b Mankato, Minn, July 31, 41. *Study:* Mankato State Univ, BS, 59-63; grad studies, 74; Calif State Univ Long Beach, grad studies, 64-68. *Work:* Carnegie Mus Art, Oxnard, Calif; Mex Consulate, Los Angeles; Conejo Valley Mus, Thousand Oaks, Calif; Bergstrom Art Ctr, Neenah, Wis; Mankato State Univ, Minn. *Comn:* Murals, Mankato State Univ, 90. *Exhib:* Solo shows, Galeria Coyoacan, Mexico City, 80, Geometry & Line, Carnegie Art Mus, Oxnard, Calif, 88, Europe, Univ Calif, Los Angeles, 90 & Homecoming, Mankato State Univ, 90; The Olympic Exchange-Calif & Mex, Huntington Beach City Gallery, Calif, 84; An Evening with the Stars, Mex & Am Round Found, San Diego, 87; The Year of the Horse, Conejo Valley Art Mus, Thousand Oaks, Calif, 90; The Figure and the Horse, Calif State Univ, Los Angeles, 91. *Pos:* Art curric chmn, Los Alamitos Unified Sch Dist, 84-88; gallery dir, Los Alamitos Unified Sch Dist Gallery, 84-92. *Teaching:* Art teacher, gen visual art, Long Beach Unified Sch Dist, Calif, 63-69 & Anaheim & Los Alamitos Sch Dist, Calif, 72-92; art teacher printmaking, drawing & painting, Appleton Unified Sch Dist, Wis, 69-72. *Awards:* Huntington Beach, The First Outstanding Artist of the Year, 86; Teacher of the Year, Anaheim Union HS Dist, 78-79; Art Mentor, Los Alamitos Unified Sch Dist, 87-88. *Bibliog:* Luis Bruno Ruiz (auth), Estampas Romanticas Caballos en la Pintora Bill Anderson, Excelsior, Mexico City, 80; auth, Anderson, George Zada Publishing, 85; Elaine Craft, The Art of Bill Anderson, cable channel 3, Huntington Beach, 92. *Mem:* Arts Comn Huntington Beach (pres 81-87); Arts Assocs Huntington Beach; Studio Artists Huntington Beach (founder, 83, pres, 83-87). *Media:* Oils, Watercolor. *Publ:* Illus, Creative Experience, Kendall/Hunt Pub, 89; Raul Anguiano's 75th Anniversary, Excelsior, 90; illus, El Completo de Circe, Eda Mex Pub, 91. *Dealer:* Lodi Art Gallery, 230 Lake St, Pasadena, CA 91101. *Mailing Add:* 17831 San Leandro Ln Huntington Beach CA 92647

ANDERSON, BRAD J
CARTOONIST
b Jamestown, NY, May 14, 24. *Study:* Syracuse Univ, BFA, 51. *Work:* Albert T Reid Col; William Allen White Found, Univ Kans; Complete Collection Grandpa's Boy Original Comic Strips, Syracuse Univ Manuscripts Libr; Birchfield Mus, Buffalo, NY. *Exhib:* San Diego Fair Fine Arts & Cartoon Exhib; Punch, Brit-Am Exhib, 54; Cartoon Exhib, The Selected Cartoons of 14 Saturday Evening Post Cartoonists; Cartoon Americana, overseas exhib; Birchfield Mus, Buffalo, NY, 76; Albright-Knox Mus, Buffalo, NY, 76; San Francisco Mus Fine Arts, 77. *Pos:* Art dir, Graphic Art Dept, Syracuse Univ, 50-52; free-lance cartoonist, 50-; int syndicated cartoonist, Marmaduke, 54- & Grandpa's Boy, 54- *Mem:* Nat Cartoonists Soc; Newspaper Comics Coun. *Publ:* Illusr, Marmaduke Treasury, Sheed Andrews & McMeel, 78; Meet Marmaduke, Signet, 83; Marmaduke Mystery Puzzles, Scholastic, 83; Marmaduke Super Dog, Andrews & McMeel, 83; Marmaduke Large and Lovable, Tor, 83; and many others. *Mailing Add:* 422 Santa Marina Court Escondido CA 92029

ANDERSON, BRUCE A
GOLDSMITH, SCULPTOR
b Spokane, Wash, Sept 14, 48. *Study:* Western Wash State Univ, BA, 73; Syracuse Univ, with Michael Jerry, MFA(metalsmithing), 79. *Exhib:* Young Americans Exhib, Am Craft Mus, New York, 77; German-American Blacksmithing Exhib, Goethe The Inst, Atlanta, Ga, 81-82; The First Int Shoebox Sculpture Exhib, Univ Hawaii, Manoa, 82; Jewelry USA, 84 & American Jewelry, 85, Am Craft Mus, New York. *Mem:* Soc NAm Goldsmiths. *Media:* Metal. *Dealer:* Quadrum Gallery The Mall at Chestnut Hill Chestnut Hill MA. *Mailing Add:* RR 1 Box 308 Bulls Head Rd Stanfordville NY 12581

ANDERSON, BRUCE JAMES
STAINED GLASS ARTIST, ART DEALER
b Denver, Colo, Nov 18, 40. *Study:* Ottawa Univ, Kans, BA, 63; Univ Manchester, Eng, 64; Univ Colo, Boulder, MA, 72. *Work:* Agate Community Church, Colo; Holy Mother of God Byzantine Church, Denver; St Stephen Protomartyr Episcopal Church. *Comn:* Dutchman Restaurant, Denver, 73; Continental Broker, Denver, 76; six panels, Rik Fulcher, Denver, 79; Blackhawk Hotel, Davenport, Iowa, 79; Lunt Ave Marble Club, Scottsdale, Ariz, 79; Brown Palace Hotel, 85; and others. *Exhib:* Colo Glass Art, Boulder, 76-78. *Pos:* Owner, dir & designer, Wild Rose Studio & Gallery, 72- *Bibliog:* Joy Overbeck (auth), article, Leisure Living, fall 74; Marjorie Barrett (auth), Home living section, Rocky Mountain News, 10/23/76; Grant Tyson (auth), Gifts worth waiting for, Denver, 11/78. *Specialty:* Glass by Gary Feltner, Miles Thompson. *Mailing Add:* 1066 Pennsylvania Ave 400 First Ave N Denver CO 80203

ANDERSON, DANIEL J
CERAMIST, EDUCATOR
b Nov 2, 45. *Study:* Univ Wis-River Falls, BS(ceramics), 63-68; Cranbrook Acad Art, Bloomfield Hills, Mich, MFA(ceramics), 68-70. *Work:* Philadelphia Mus Art, Pa; Ill State Mus, Springfield; Cranbrook Mus Art, Bloomfield Hills, Mich; Eastern Mich Univ, Ypsilanti, Mich; Univ Wis, River Falls. *Exhib:* One person shows, Pro Art, St Louis, Mo, 88, Isis Gallery, Notre Dame Univ, Ind, 91, Schneider-Bluhm-Loeb Gallery, Chicago, Ill & Nora Eccles Harrison Mus Art, Utah State Univ, Logan, 92; Teapot Invitational Southeastern La Univ, Clark Gallery, Hammond, 92; Cups: 100 Nationally and Internationally Recognized Ceramic Artists, Pro Art, St Louis, Mo, 92; Graduation: MFA Candidates and Their Instructors, Farrell Collection, Washington, DC, 92; Woodfire, Ferrin Gallery, Northampton, Mass, 92; Midwest Potters, Work's Gallery, Philadelphia, Pa, 92; and many others. *Teaching:* Prof & area head ceramic dept, Southern Ill Univ, Edwardsville, 70- *Awards:* Artist Fel, Nat Endowment Arts, 90; Individual Artist Fel, Ill Arts Coun, 91; and many others. *Mailing Add:* 5519 Old Poag Rd Edwardsville IL 62025

ANDERSON, DAVID
ART DEALER, COLLECTOR
b Buffalo, NY, June 26, 35. *Pos:* Pres & owner, Anderson Gallery Inc, currently. *Specialty:* Art of 20th century since 1945. *Mailing Add:* Anderson Gallery Inc Martha Jackson Pl Buffalo NY 14214

ANDERSON, DAVID C
SCULPTOR, PHOTOGRAPHER
b Jamestown, NY, Mar 10, 31. *Study:* Univ Tulsa, with Alexandre Hogue & Dwayne Hatchett, BA, 64. *Work:* Tulsa S Regional Libr; Univ Tulsa; Okla Educ TV Authority. *Comn:* Sculpture, Price Waterhouse & Co, Houston, 79, Univ Tulsa, 81, Western Nat Bank, Tulsa, 82, Excelsior Hotel, Tulsa, 82 & Royal Bank Can, Dallas, 83. *Exhib:* Oklahoma Sculpture Today, Okla Mus Art, 80; Sculpture in Wood, Wichita Art Mus, 81; Shidoni Ann, Santa Fe, 81 & 82; Art Ann IV, 83 & Okla Sculpture Exhib, 83, Okla Mus Art. *Teaching:* Private lessons sculpture, 78-; adj prof art, Univ Tulsa, 82. *Awards:* Best of Show & First Place Photog, Bartlesville, Okla, 79. *Bibliog:* Clive Cussler (auth), King Dave--from pinstriping to sculpture, Tulsa Mag, 6/78 & David Anderson--Oklahoma Art Gallery, Wall & Wall Publ, 80. *Mem:* Charter mem Okla Sculpture Soc; Int Sculpture Ctr. *Dealer:* 26 East Art Ctr Tulsa OK; Adelle M Fine Arts Dallas TX. *Mailing Add:* 4985 E 26th St Tulsa OK 74114

ANDERSON, DAVID PAUL
SCULPTOR
b Los Angeles, Calif, Feb 3, 46. *Study:* San Francisco Art Inst, 67-71; asst to Peter Voulkos, 72-73. *Work:* Mus Mod Art, San Francisco; Mus Fine Arts, Santa Fe; Sheldon Mem Art Mus, Lincoln, Nebr; San Antonio Mus Art, Tex. *Comn:* City of Albuquerque. *Exhib:* One-person shows, San Francisco Art Inst, 79, Braunstein Gallery, San Francisco, 75, 78, 80, 83, 85, 87 & 90, Linda Durham Gallery, Santa Fe, 79, 81, 83, 85, 87 & 89, Christopher Grimes Gallery, Santa Monica, Calif, 91, Hokin/Kaufman Gallery, Chicago, 91, San

Antonio Mus Art, 93 & Allene Lapides Gallery, Santa Fe, 93; Public Sculpture/Urban Environment, Oakland Mus, Calif, 74; 1975 Biennial Exhib Contemp Art, Whitney Mus, New York, 75; and other one-man shows. *Teaching:* Sculpture, San Francisco Art Inst, 76-79, Calif Col Arts & Crafts, Oakland, 79 & Univ NMex, 84-92. *Awards:* Grant, Soc for Encouragement of Contemp Art, San Francisco Mus, 73; Nat Endowment Arts Fel Grant, 74, 81 & 88; Pollock-Krasner Found Grant, 86. *Bibliog:* Art Am, 5-6/78; Art News, 3/86; Artspace, 3-4/90. *Media:* Bronze, Steel. *Dealer:* Braunstein Quay Gallery San Francisco; Christopher Grimes Gallery Santa Monica CA. *Mailing Add:* Rte 14 Box 204 Santa Fe NM 87505

ANDERSON, DONALD MYERS
ART WRITER, CALLIGRAPHER
b Bridgewater, SDak. *Study:* Univ Iowa, MA, study with Phillip Guston & H W Janson; Mexico City Col, Mex; Univ Wis, 47. *Teaching:* Prof watercolor & calligraphy, Univ Wis, 47-82; retired. *Awards:* Typographical Excellence Award, Type Dir Club, New York, 71; Cert of Award, Chicago Bk Clinic, 73; Selected for Exhib, Am Inst Graphic Arts, 77. *Res:* History of writing. *Publ:* Auth & illusr, Elements of Design, 61 & The Art of Written Forms, 69, Holt, Rinehart & Winston, New York; All, Calligraphy--Encyclopedia of Library and Information Science, Marcel Dekker, 70; A Renaissance Alphabet, Univ Wis Press, 71; Part, Calligraphy--Current Encyclopedia of Britain, W Benton, 74. *Mailing Add:* Rte 1 7822 Hwy 19 Dane WI 53529

ANDERSON, DOUG
PAINTER
b Syracuse, NY, 1954. *Study:* Sch Mus Fine Arts, Tufts Univ, Medford, Mass, MA, 79. *Exhib:* One-man shows, Stux Gallery, Boston, 82, 84, 86 & 88, New York, 88 & Kicken Pauseback, Koln, 90; group exhibs, Stux Gallery, New York & Boston, 88 & 89, Galerie Arteunido, Barcelona, Spain, 89, Karl Bornstein Gallery, Santa Monico, Calif, 89, Mayor Rowan Gallery, 90; The Re-Invention of Painting, Rastovski Gallery, N Y, 89; Pre-Pop Post-Appropriation, Stux Gallery, NY, 89; Miniatures, Stux Gallery, Boston, 87; On and Off the Wall, Stux Gallery, Boston, 87; Triennial, Brockton Art Mus, Mass, 87. *Awards:* Mass Coun Arts Fel, 82; Engelhard Award, 86; Fel, Nat Endowment Arts, 87. *Bibliog:* Pamela Allara (auth), Veiled images, Artnews, 11/81; Henry Gerrit (auth), Doug Anderson, Artnews, 3/87; Thomas Frick (auth), Doug Anderson at Stux, Art in Am, 7/87; Roberta Smith (auth), A penchant for the past, NY Times, 9/16/88; Robert Pincus-Witten (auth), Entries: Concentrated Juice & Kitschy Kitschy Koons, Arts Mag, 2/89; Christine Temin (auth), Romance is in the galleries, Boston Globe, 3/23/89. *Mailing Add:* c/o STUX Gallery 155 Spring St New York NY 10012

ANDERSON, GUNNAR DONALD
PAINTER, ILLUSTRATOR
b Berkeley, Calif, Mar 3, 27. *Study:* Calif Sch Fine Arts, with Clyfford Still; Art Ctr Col Design, BFA, with Lorser Feitelson. *Work:* Brown-Forman Distillers, Louisville, Ky. *Comn:* Gov Lamar Alexander, Tenn; Mr & Mrs Meredith Long, Houston, Tex, 71; Mr & Mrs George Weyerhauser, Tacoma, Wash, 72; Mr & Mrs Charlie Rich, Memphis, Tenn; Mr & Mrs Charles Schulz, Calif. *Exhib:* 5th Winter Invitational, Calif Palace of Legion of Honor, San Francisco, 64; M H de Young Mem Mus, San Francisco, 25th Ann, Soc of Western Artists, 68; Charles & Emma Frye Mus, Seattle, 71; Calif State Fair, Sacramento, 71; Mainstream 72, Grover M Hermann Fine Arts Ctr, Marietta Col, Ohio, 72. *Pos:* Bd Trustees, Soc Western Artists. *Awards:* Best figure or portrait, 29th Ann, Soc Western Artists, 71 & first place, Ann, 85, 90 & 91; Best in Fine Art, Exhib One, Soc Art Ctr, Alumni, 72; Grumbacher Gold Medallion, 86. *Bibliog:* Mrs Linda Hardwick (auth), Collage, educational TV, Memphis Community TV Found, 71-72; TV interview, Memphis, Tenn, 71; Don J Anderson (auth), Paintings of children, Chicago Today, 72. *Mem:* Soc Western Artists; Soc Art Ctr Alumni; Nat Soc Lit & Arts; Bohemian Club. *Media:* Oil. *Publ:* Illusr, Oscar Lincoln Busby Stokes, Harcourt, Brace & World Inc, 70. *Dealer:* Phillips Galleries Dallas TX; El Presidio Galleries Tucson AZ. *Mailing Add:* 4583 Belmont Ct Sonoma CA 95476

ANDERSON, GUY IRVING
PAINTER
b Edmonds, Wash, Nov 20, 06. *Study:* Pvt classes; Tiffany Found Fel. *Work:* Seattle Art Mus, Wash; Brooklyn Mus; Munson-Williams-Proctor Inst, Utica, NY; Metrop Mus Art, New York; Smithsonian Inst Nat Collection. *Comn:* Mural (oil on wood), Seattle Opera House, 62; cement & metal panels, Hilton Inn, Seattle; panel, workers, Edmonds Pub Libr; stone inlay, terrace, Seattle First Nat Bank; mural (oil on canvas), Bank of Calif, Seattle, 74. *Exhib:* Fine Arts Pavilion, Seattle World's Fair, 62; solo exhibs, Otto Seligman Gallery, Seattle, 63 & 65 & Francine Seders Gallery, Seattle, 71, 73, 75 & 77; A University Collects: Oregon, 67-68 & The Drawing Soc Nat Exhib, 70-72, Am Fedn Arts; 73rd Western Ann, Denver Art Mus, 72; Art of the Pacific NW, Smithsonian Inst Nat Collection; retrospective, Seattle Art Mus, Mod Pavilion, 77 & Henry Gallery, Univ Wash, 77. *Awards:* First Prize, Anacortes Art Festival, Wash, 64; Award Merit, Am Inst Archit, Seattle, 65; Guggenheim Fel, 75-76. *Bibliog:* Article, Holiday Mag, 59; article, Art in Am, 62; Guy Anderson, Gear Press, Seattle, 65. *Media:* Oil, Watercolor. *Mailing Add:* c/o Clark College Index Gallery 1800 E McLaughlin Blvd Vancouver WA 98663

ANDERSON, JAMES P
SCULPTOR, EDUCATOR
b Tulsa, Okla, Mar 30, 29. *Study:* Eastern NMex Univ, BA, 54; Hardin-Simmons Univ, MA, 60; George Peabody Col, EdD, 64. *Work:* Franklin Co Hall of Justice, Columbus, Ohio. *Comn:* Sculpture (silver, plexiglas, wood), Morehead State Univ, 61; Urschlein XIV (bronze), Muskingum Col, 70; Benjamin Franklin (bronze), Columbus Found, Ohio, 72; Bone Form VI (bronze), Mus Arte Mod, Milan, Italy, 74; Benjamin Franklin (bronze), Columbus, Ohio, 74. *Exhib:* X Mostro Int di Sculpture all Aperto, Mus Arte Mod, 74; Gallerie Pagani, Milan, Italy, 76; Ianuzzi Gallery, 78; Husberg Gallery, 78; Davenport Gallery of Art, 79. *Teaching:* Assoc prof art educ, Tex Tech Univ, 64-65; prof & chmn dept art, Muskingum Col, 66-74; prof & chmn dept art, Northern Ariz Univ, 74-78; prof art, St Ambrose Col, Davenport, Iowa, 79- *Bibliog:* M McGarey (auth), The shaping of a statue, Columbus Dispatch Mag, 5/74. *Publ:* Contribr, Franz Cizek, art education's man for all seasons, 10/69 & Humanism, art educational philosophy in transition, 10/75, Art Educ; Who shall teach children art, 11/69 & It's nice to be a pioneer, 12/70, Sch Arts. *Dealer:* Maxwell Gallery Ltd 551 Sutter St San Francisco CA 94102; Ianuzzi Gallery 7340 E Shoeman Lane Scottsdale AZ 85251. *Mailing Add:* 132 Oklahoma St Portales NM 88130

ANDERSON, JOHN S
SCULPTOR
b Seattle, Wash, Apr 29, 28. *Study:* Los Angeles Art Ctr, Pratt Inst. *Work:* Mus Mod Art & Whitney Mus Am Art, New York. *Exhib:* Int Arts Festival, Providence, RI, 65; Albert A List Show, New Sch Social Res, 65; Cummer Gallery Art, Jacksonville, Fla, 66; eight one-man shows, Allan Stone Gallery, New York, 65-74, 77 & 81. *Teaching:* Instr sculpture, Pratt Inst, 59-62; instr sculpture, Sch Visual Arts, 68-70; instr sculpture, Cooper Union, 70-76; vis sculptor, Univ NMex, 69-70 & Univ Conn, 77-78. *Awards:* Guggenheim Found Grant, 65-66; Mini Grant, NJ State Coun Arts, 72. *Mailing Add:* PO Box 59 Asbury NJ 08802

ANDERSON, KENNETH EDMUND
SCULPTOR, EDUCATOR
b Alameda, Calif, Sept 22, 50. *Study:* Univ Nebr, Omaha, BGS, 77, BFA, 80; Univ Nebr, Lincoln, MFA, 83. *Work:* Sheldon Mem Art Gallery, Lincoln, Nebr. *Exhib:* Great Plains Sculpture Exhib, Sheldon Mem Art Gallery, Lincoln, Nebr, 81; First Int Shoebox Sculpture Exhib, Univ Hawaii, Honolulu, 82; two-person exhib, Joslyn Art Mus, Omaha, 82; 42nd Sioux City Exhib, Sioux City Art Mus, Iowa, 82; Biennial exhib, Joslyn Art Mus, Omaha, 84. *Teaching:* Asst prof art, Peru State Col, Peru, Nebr, currently. *Awards:* Second Place, Master's Touch Exhib, Col St Mary's, 80; Merit Award, Great Plains Sculpture Exhib, Nebr Arts Coun, 81. *Bibliog:* Dr Donald Doe (auth), article, Art Express, 9-10/81. *Mem:* Col Art Asn. *Media:* Steel, Wood. *Mailing Add:* c/o Locus 710 N Tucker No 315 St Louis MO 63101

ANDERSON, LAURIE
CONCEPTUAL ARTIST
b Chicago, Ill, 1947. *Study:* Columbia Univ, MFA, 72. *Pos:* Art Critic, Art Forum, Art News, Art in Am. *Teaching:* Instr art hist, City Col New York, 73-75. *Awards:* Grants, NY State Coun, 75 & 77 & Nat Endowment Arts, 77 & 79; Fel, Guggenheim Found, 83. *Dealer:* Original Artists 129 W 69th St New York NY 10023. *Mailing Add:* 530 Canal St New York NY 10013

ANDERSON, LENNART
PAINTER, INSTRUCTOR
b Detroit, Mich, Aug 22, 28. *Study:* Art Inst Chicago, BFA, 46-50; Cranbrook Acad Art, MFA, 50-52; Art Students League, studied with Edwin Dickinson, 54. *Work:* Hirshhorn Mus; Whitney Mus Am Art; Brooklyn Mus, NY; Pa Acad Fine Arts, Philadelphia; Mus Fine Arts, Boston; Weatherspoon Gallery, Univ NC, Greensboro; Minneapolis Inst Arts, Min; Cleveland Mus Art, Ohio; and others. *Exhib:* Carnegie Inst Mus Art, 64 & 67; Contemp Art USA, Norfolk, Va, 66; Whitney Mus Am Art Ann, 67; Vassar Col, 68; Ravinia Festival, High Park, Ill, 68; solo exhibs, Meredith Long & Co, Houston, 74, Davis & Long Co, New York, 76 Delaware Art Mus, Wilmington, 92 & Davis & Langdale Co, New York, 92; Figurative-Realist Art, Artist's Chice Mus, New York, 79; Reallegory, Chrysler Mus Art, Norfolk, Va, 83; Drawings by Contemporary artists, Md Inst Col Art, 84; Recent American Portraiture, Robert Schoelkopf Gallery, New York, 85; Form or Formula: Drawing and Drawings, Hudson River Mus, Yonkers, NY, 86; Direct Response: Contemporary Landscape Painting, Mem Art Gallery, Univ Rochester, NY, 89; Art with a View, Oglethorpe Univ Art Gallery, Atlanta, Ga, 90. *Teaching:* Instr, Chatham Col, 61-62, Pratt Inst, 62-64, Swain Sch, New Bedford, Mass, summer 63 & 64, Art Students League, Yale Univ, 67 & Skowhegan Sch, 68; prof painting & drawing, Brooklyn Col, 74- *Awards:* Nat Coun Arts Award, 66; Guggenheim Fel, 83; Emil and Dines Carlsen Award, Nat Acad Design, 88. *Bibliog:* Alan Gussow (auth), A Sense of Place, 72; William Gerdts (auth), The Great American Nude, 74; Frank H Goodyear (auth), Contemporary American Realism, 81; Mark Strand (auth), Art of the Real: Nine American Figurative Painters, 83. *Mem:* Nat Inst Arts & Lett; Nat Acad Design; Am Acad & Inst Arts & Lett; Assoc Nat Acad Design. *Publ:* Auth, William Gerdts, The Great American Nude, 74; Frank H Goodyear, Jr, Contemporary American Realism, 81; ed, Mark Strand, Art of the Real: Nine American Figurative Painters, 83; auth, Charles Jencks, Post Modernism: The New Classicism in Art and Architecture, 87; Ronald Pisano, Long Island Landscape Painting Vol II: The Twentieth Century, 90. *Dealer:* Davis & Langdale 746 Madison Ave New York NY 10021. *Mailing Add:* 877 Union St Brooklyn NY 11215

ANDERSON, MARGARET POMEROY
WRITER, CONSULTANT
b San Francisco, Calif, Mar 26, 43. *Study:* Univ Calif, Berkeley, BA, 65. *Pos:* Researcher, Pomeroy Galleries, San Francisco, 65-69; archivist, Hoover Gallery, San Francisco, 69-81, consult, 78-; owner, Pomeroy-Anderson, 82-, Accredited Senior Appraiser, 81-; regist contractor, Resolution Trust Corp & Fed Deposit Insurance Corp, 91- *Teaching:* Lectr art, Westport Arts Ctr, 85-,

Fairfield Univ, Conn, 86- & Wadsworth Atheneum, Hartford, 91. *Awards:* Conn Press Club, 89-91. *Mem:* Arch Am Art; West Coast Area Support Comt (chmn, 78-80); Am Soc Appraisers (accredited senior appraiser, 81-); Archives Am Art (NY Area Comt, 83-); Fairfield Hist Soc (pres, 89-). *Res:* Life of Marie Laurencin; nineteenth and twentieth century American and European provenance searches; Paul Manship. *Publ:* Contribr, Antiques & the Arts Weekly; Maine Antique Digest; Antiques West Newspaper, New York Correspondent; Antique Monthly; Art & Auction. *Mailing Add:* PO Box 787 Southport CT 06490

ANDERSON, MARK ROBERT
STAINED GLASS ARTIST, SCULPTOR
b Iola, Kans, Aug 14, 48. *Study:* Am Craft Coun, 75-79; Art League Sch, Alexandria, Va, 79-82; Pilchuck Glass Sch, Stanwood, Wash, 79 & 85. *Comn:* Solar Collectors with Stained glass, Brandon Residence, Cabin John, Md, 81-83; Spiral Staircase (sculpture), Torpedo Factory Art Ctr, Alexandria, Va, 84; Stained Glass Window, Bolling Air Force Base Officers Club, Washington, DC, 85; Stained Glass Window, Montgomery Co Pub Schs, Woodlin-Silver Spring, 86; Glass & Neon wall panels, May Ctrs Inc, Ballston Common Ctr, Arlington, Va, 86. *Exhib:* Virginia Craftsmen, Va Mus Fine Arts, Richmond, 80; Studio Glass-Contemp Am Survey, Redding Mus, Calif, 85; Spotlight: Southeast Crafts, Longwood Col, Farmville, Va, 85; Spotlight: Southeast Crafts, Univ Gainesville, Fla, 86; one-man show, Jackie Chalkley Fine Crafts, Washington, DC, 86; New Art Forms I & II: Virginia, Hand Workshop, Richmond Va, 88 & 89; Beyond Function: New Directions in Decorative Arts, Wash Sq Bldg, Washington, DC, 88; Breaking Boundaries: Craft Now, Va Mus Fine Arts, Richmond, 88-91; Creative Craft Coun Winners, Renwick Gallery, Smithsonian, Washington, DC, 89; Rhapsody in Neon, Zenith Gallery, Washington, DC, 89. *Collections Arranged:* High Style, Tomlinson Craft Collection, 83. *Pos:* Exec dir, Friends of Torpedo Factory Art Ctr, Alexandria, Va, 82-84. *Teaching:* Instr stained glass, Art League Sch, Alexandria, Va, 80- *Awards:* First Prize for Glass, Arlington Arts Ctr, Va, 78; Schwarzschild Award, Schwarzschild Jewelers, 85; First Prize for Glass, Creative Craft Coun, Washington, DC, 86. *Bibliog:* Karen M E Alexis (auth), Washington's fragile world of glass art, Washington Post, 81; Clare Fiore (auth), Which Are Jewels?, Reston Connection, 85; Joseph Porcelli (auth), Profile, Prof Stained Glass, 87; Patricia Dane Rogers (coauth with Cristina Del Sesto), The Move From Down Home to Uptown, Wash Post, 88. *Mem:* Torpedo Factory Artists Asn (vpres, 82-83); Coalition Wash Artists, (steering comt, 86-87); Am Craft Coun. *Media:* Glass. *Dealer:* Glass Arts Collaborative 31 Norfolk Rd Arlington MA 02174. *Mailing Add:* 105 N Union St Studio 316 Alexandria VA 22314

ANDERSON, MAXWELL L
MUSEUM DIRECTOR, EDUCATOR
b New York, NY, May 1, 56. *Study:* Dartmouth Col, AB, 77; Harvard Univ, AM 78, PhD, 81. *Collections Arranged:* The Vatican Collections: The Papacy and Art, 82; Treasures of the Holy Land, 86; Roman Portraits in Context, 88; Radiance in Stone, 89. *Pos:* Asst cur, Metrop Mus Art, 82-87; dir, Emory Univ Mus, Atlanta, 87- *Teaching:* Lectr Roman art, Princeton Univ, 85; vis prof, Univ di Roma, 87; adj assoc prof, Emory Univ, 89- *Mem:* Am Asn Mus; Col Art Asn; Archeol Inst Am; Asn Int d'Archeol Classique. *Publ:* Coauth, Greece and Rome, Metrop Mus, 87; Pompeian Frescoes in the Metropolitan Museum of Art, Metrop Mus, 87; Roman Portraits in Context, De Luca, 88; Radiance in Stone, De Luca, 89. *Mailing Add:* Michael C Carlos Mus, Emory Univ 571 S Kilgo St Atlanta GA 30322

ANDERSON, ROBERT ALEXANDER
PAINTER, ILLUSTRATOR
b Wyandotte, Mich, Jan 26, 46. *Study:* Yale Univ, BA, 64-68, drawing with Bernard Chaet, portrait painting with Deane Keller; Wayne State Univ, 66; Sch of Mus Fine Arts, Boston, dipl, 72-75, with Henry Schwartz & John Clift. *Work:* Boston Pub Libr, Mass; Phillips Exeter Acad, Exeter, NH; Mass Gen Hosp, Boston; Mass Med Soc, Walton; Univ Pa, Philadelphia. *Comn:* Portrait, Sidney Farber, Md, Dana Farber Cancer Inst, Boston, Mass, 84; Eleven drawings & portraits, US Postage Stamps, US Postal Serv, Washington, DC, 84-86; portraits, Andrew G DeRocco, Pres Denison Univ, Granville, Ohio & Hon Edward J King, Gov of Massachesetts, Boston, MA, 90 & Rev William Sloane Coffin, Yale Univ, New Haven, Conn, 90. *Exhib:* Boston Symphony, John F Kennedy Pres Libr & Mus, Dorchester, 81 & Symphony Hall, Boston, 82, Mass; Soc Illustrators, New York, 87; Francesca Anderson Gallery, Boston, Mass, 84-88; Soc Illusr, New York, 87; St Botolph Club, Boston, Mass, 88; Boston Atheneum, Mass, 89. *Awards:* First Prize, 81 & Grand Prize for best of show, 82, Nat Portrait Seminar Nat Competition, 82. *Bibliog:* Crumpled, But Unruffled; The Breck Girl, Advertising Techniques, 10/78; Laura White (auth), A Letter Will Take Two of These, Boston Globe, 2/10/85; John D Beeler (auth), Artist Puts His Stamp on US Mail, Lexington Minute-Man, 2/21/85. *Mem:* Arts-Lexington (bd dirs, 83-); Schwamb Mill Preserv Trust (trustee, 85-); St Botolph Club. *Media:* Oil, Pastel. *Publ:* Illusr advertising, (TV & print), Breck Shampoo, 76- & Coca Cola USA, 80; Heath Sci Textbks, D C Heath, 79 & 81; album cover, Karen Kayen; You Don't Have to Take What You Get, Rooster Records, 81. *Dealer:* Portraits Inc 985 Park Ave New York NY 10028. *Mailing Add:* 17 Carley Rd Lexington MA 02173

ANDERSON, ROBERT RAYMOND
PAINTER, CONSULTANT
b Orange, NJ, Nov 9, 45. *Study:* NJ Inst of Technol, 64-66; State Univ NY, Brockport, BS, 69; Pratt Inst, MFA, 72. *Work:* Univ Mass, Amherst; Public Serv Electric & Gas Co, NJ; Morris Mus of Arts & Sci, Morristown, NJ; State Univ NY, Brockport; Bloomfield Col, NJ; and others. *Comn:* Bicentennial painting of Nat Hist Site, 76; poster, Nat Coun Jewish Women. *Exhib:* Pratt Printers, Brooklyn Mus, 72; one-artist shows, Newark Mus, NJ, 75 & NJ State Mus, Trenton, 78; About Face, Squibb Gallery, 78; The Artist and the Airbrush, San Jose State Univ, 82; Littlejohn-Smith Gallery, New York, 88; OK Harris South Gallery, Miami, Fl, 89; Wethermolt Gallery, Washington, DC, 92. *Collections Arranged:* Traveling exhib, NJ State Coun on the Arts, 71; 16 Contemp Artists, Hartwick Col, Oneonta, NY, 75; Presence & Absence in Realism, State Univ NY, Potsdam, 76; Viewpoint 76, Morris Mus of Arts & Sci, Morristown, NJ, 76; Contemp Portraits, E R Squibb Gallery, Princeton, NJ, 78; Sequential Imagery, Pyramid Art Ctr, Rochester, NY, 88; Electronic Media, Eastern Wash Univ, Cheney, 88. *Pos:* Treas, Artists Educ & Welfare Fund, 76-80; art materials consult, Binney & Smith, 90- *Teaching:* Instr painting, Summit Art Ctr, NJ, 74-79 & Newark Mus, 76-79; asst prof art, County Col, Morris, NJ, 78-90, Learnshops, 83-90. *Awards:* Grand Prize, New Eng Exhib, Silvermine Guild of Artists, 72; fel grant, NJ State Coun Arts, 76 & 84; fel Nat Endowment Arts, 85. *Bibliog:* Ruthann Williams (auth), Bob Anderson: an artist evolving, NJ Music & Arts Mag, 74; David Shirey (auth), Exhibit in Newark a tribute to Jersey artist, NY Times, 75, New realism on view at the Morris Museum, NY Times, 76 & At the Squibb-anthology of faces, 78. *Mem:* NJ Volunteer Lawyers Arts (steering comt); Assoc Artists of NJ; and others. *Media:* Acrylic, Computer Graphics. *Publ:* Coauth, Advanced Airbrush Techniques--The Art of the Dot, Van Nostrand Reinhold, 85; Striking Appropriations, Airbrush Action Mag, 86. *Dealer:* Wethermolt Gallery Washington DC; Robin Hutchins Gallery Maplewood NJ. *Mailing Add:* 37 Glenfield Rd Bloomfield NJ 07003

ANDERSON, ROSS CORNELIUS
MUSEUM DIRECTOR, HISTORIAN
b Washington, DC, May 2, 51. *Study:* Princeton Univ, AB, 73; Harvard Univ, MA, 77. *Pos:* Chief cur, Everson Mus Art, Syracuse, NY, 79-83; dir, Montgomery Mus Fine Arts, Ala, 83-87; Riverside Art Mus, Calif, 87-90, art consult, 91- *Teaching:* Instr, Syracuse Univ, 81-83. *Res:* 19th and 20th century American painting and sculpture. *Publ:* Contribr, Grueby Pottery, 81, Abbott Handerson Thayer, 82 & American Clay Sculpture 1925-1950, 83, Everson Mus Art; Maurice and Charles Prendergast Raisonne (exhib catalog), Williams Col Mus Art, Prestel, 90. *Mailing Add:* 4640 Rubidoux Riverside CA 92506

ANDERSON, SALLY J
PAINTER, PRINTMAKER
b Rockford, Ill, Feb 5, 42. *Study:* Inst Allende, San Miguel Allende, Mex, 62; Beloit Col, BA, 64; Univ Wis, 67. *Work:* Fed Bldg, Vickers Corp, Oklahoma City; Sunwest Bank, Albuquerque; Saks Fifth Ave, New York; Marriott Hotel Corp, Washington, DC; Product design, Swan/Dolphin Hotel, Orlando, Fla, Connie Chung set, CBS Network, New York, 90. *Exhib:* Solo exhib, Roswell Art Mus, NMex, 70; Southwest Fine Arts Biennial, Mus NMex, Santa Fe, 75 & 79; Convergence 76, Carnegie Inst Mus Art, Pittsburgh, Pa, 76; Ariz Biennial, Phoenix Art Mus, 79; One Space, Three Visions, Albuquerque Mus, 80; and others. *Awards:* First Prize, NMex Crafts Biennial, Mus NMex, Santa Fe, 75; Nat Endowment Arts Grants, 76 & 77. *Bibliog:* Donald Locke (auth), article, Arts Mag, 9/83. *Media:* Acrylic, Oil; Lithography, Product Design. *Dealer:* C G Rein Galleries Edina MN; C G Rein Galleries Scottsdale AZ. *Mailing Add:* 7522 Bear Canyon Albuquerque NM 87109

ANDERSON, TROY
PAINTER, SCULPTOR
b Siloam Springs, Ark, Aug 23, 48. *Study:* WTex State Univ, Canyon, BS(art), 70. *Work:* Ark State Bank, Siloam Springs; Bur Indian Affairs, Washington, DC; Five Civilized Tribes Mus, Muskogee, Okla; Capital, State of Ark, Little Rock, Ark. *Comn:* Cherokee Sesquicentennial Trail of Tears Commemorative Gold Medallion, 89. *Exhib:* Denver Mus Natural Hist, 80; Am Indian & Cowboy Artists, San Dimas, Calif, 80-83; Five Civilized Tribes Mus, Muskogee, Okla, 81; Cherokee National History Museum; and others. *Pos:* Formerly pres, Am Indian & Cowboy Artist, Inc. *Awards:* Ambassor of the Year Award, Ctr Am Indian, Kirkpatrick Ctr, Okco; Grand Award Master Artists, Five Civilized Tribes Mus, 82-88; First Place Painting, Cherokee Nat Hist Mus, Tahlequah, Okla, 83-90; Heritage Grand Award, 89; Am Indian & Cowboy Artist Indian Heritage Award, 90. *Bibliog:* Southwest Art, 2/90. *Mem:* Am Indian & Cowboy Artists Inc (vpres, 84-85, pres, 86-87). *Media:* Acrylic, Oil; Mixed Media. *Publ:* Contrib, Southwest Art, 2/90. *Dealer:* Studio of Troy Anderson RR 5 Box 171TA Siloam Springs AR 72761; Indian Territory Gallery 1030 Taft Sapalpa OK 74066. *Mailing Add:* Rte 5 Box 171 TA Siloam Springs AR 72761

ANDERSON, WARREN HAROLD
GRAPHIC ARTIST, PAINTER
b Moline, Ill, Sept 27, 25. *Study:* Western Ill Univ, BS, 50; Univ Iowa, MA, 51; Stanford Univ, PhD, 61. *Work:* Joseph H Hirshhorn Collection, Washington, DC; Phoenix Art Mus; Tucson Mus Art; Valley Nat Bank, Ariz; Univ Ariz Mus Art. *Exhib:* Highway Drawings/Video, Phoenix Art Mus, Ariz, 79; US 80, Drawings, El Paso Mus Art, Tex, 79; one-man show, Vanishing Roadside America (prismacolor drawings), Tucson Mus Art, 82 & Elaine Horwitch Galleries, Scottsdale, Ariz, 82; 30 year retrospective, Univ Ariz Mus Art, 86; Tohono Chul Gallery, Tucson, Ariz, 89; Univ NMex, A E Gallery, 91. *Teaching:* Prof art, Univ Ariz, Tucson, 56-86, prof emer, currently. *Awards:* Several state and Southwest regional awards, 58-90; Creative Teaching Award in Art, Ariz Found, 82. *Bibliog:* John Perreault (auth), Impressions of Arizona, Art in Am, 4/81; Art on the highway, Americana, 4/82; Vanishing roadside America, Mod Maturity, 9/84; Art for arts sake, Recreation Life, 86. *Media:* Prismatic Pencil; Oil. *Res:* Environmental aesthetics; vernacular roadside art forms; cartifacts--artifacts that exist because of cars. *Publ:* Vanishing Roadside America, Univ Ariz Press, 81. *Dealer:* Automobilia Art 6802 N Longfellow Tucson AZ 85718. *Mailing Add:* 6802 N Longfellow Dr Tucson AZ 85718

ANDERSON, WILLIAM THOMAS
PAINTER, PRINTMAKER
b Minneapolis, Minn, Dec 13, 36. *Study:* Calif State Univ, Los Angeles, with Leonard Edmondson, Bob Fiedler & Walter Askin; Chaffey Col; El Camino Col, with Charles Blusk. *Work:* Downey Mus Art; Civil Air Patrol, Calif Wing; Humboldt Cult Ctr; Humboldt State Univ; and others. *Comn:* Mural, CAP, Calif Wing; drawing, Kinnebrew Mem. *Exhib:* 18th Ann Nat Printmaking Show, Brooklyn Mus, NY, 73; World Print Competition, San Francisco Mus of Mod Art, 77; Invitational, Univ Puget Sound, 79; Stages/ Four Printmakers, Mt St Mary's Col, Los Angeles, 79; Works on a Transparent Support, John Kohler Arts Ctr, Sheboygan, Wis, 79; Invitational, C N Gorman Mus, Univ Calif, Davis, 81; Nat Screenprint Show, Old Dominion Univ, Norfolk, Va, 85-86; and many others. *Pos:* Chief reader, ETS, AP Studio Art; chmn, Art Dept, Humboldt State Univ. *Teaching:* Prof art, Humboldt State Univ, 67- *Media:* Miscellaneous; Silkscreen. *Mailing Add:* Dept Art Humboldt State Univ Arcata CA 95521

ANDERSON, WINSLOW
DESIGNER, PAINTER
b Plymouth, Mass, May 17, 17. *Study:* State Univ NY Col Ceramics, Alfred Univ, BFA; Plymouth Pottery, Mass; Hans Hofmann Sch Art, Provincetown, Mass; Pa Acad Fine Arts, Philadelphia; Pratt Graphics Ctr, New York. *Comn:* Triptych mural, Church of St Mary the Virgin Concert Hall, New York. *Exhib:* 5th & 11th Ceramic Exhibs, Syracuse Mus Fine Arts, NY, 40 & 46; Guggenheim Mus Ann, NY, 43-46; Kanawha Artists Asn, Charleston, WVa, 50. *Pos:* Glass designer, Blenko Glass Co, Milton, Va, 46-53; design dir, Lenox China Inc, Trenton, NJ, 53-64, dir dimensional design, 64-80. *Awards:* First Prize for African Mask (sculpture), Nat USA Contest, 44; First Prize for Fish (stained glass), Stained Glass Soc Washington, DC, 53. *Bibliog:* Don Wallace (auth), Shaping America's Products, Reinhold Publ Co, 56. *Media:* Clay, Glass; Pastel, Oil. *Collection:* Haitian primitives. *Publ:* Auth, Offhand design for offhand glass, Am Ceramic Soc J, 4/49. *Mailing Add:* 1245 Washington Ave Milton WV 25541

ANDRADE, BRUNO
PAINTER
b San Antonio, Tex, Nov 3, 47. *Study:* Tex A & I Univ, BS, 70; Univ Mich, MFA, 77. *Work:* Mus Contemp Hispanic Art, NY; Art Mus South Tex, Corpus Christi; Sondra & Charles Gilman Jr Found, NY; McAllen Int Mus, Tex; Mexican Mus, San Francisco, Calif. *Exhib:* Solo Exhibs, Bruno Andrade, Lynn Goode Gallery, Houston, Tex, 89 & Edith Baker Gallery, Dallas, Tex, 90; group exhib, Abstract Visions, Mus Contemp Hispanic Art, NY, 87. *Teaching:* Instr painting, Stephens Col, Columbia, Mo, 77-80; prof art painting, Corpus Christi State Univ, Tex, 81- *Awards:* Artist Fel Grant, Nat Endowment Arts, 80 & 89. *Media:* Oil on Canvas. *Dealer:* Lynn Goode Gallery 2719 Colquitt Houston TX 77098. *Mailing Add:* 1933 Ramfield Rd Corpus Christi TX 78418

ANDRADE, EDNA WRIGHT
PAINTER, EDUCATOR
b Portsmouth, Va, Jan 25, 17. *Study:* Pa Acad Fine Arts, 33-38; Univ Pa Sch Fine Arts, BFA, 37. *Work:* Philadelphia Mus Art; Pa Acad Fine Arts, Philadelphia; Yale Art Gallery, New Haven; Montclair Art Mus, NJ; Marian Koogler McNay Art Inst, San Antonio, Tex. *Comn:* Mosiac mural, Columbia Br, Free Libr Philadelphia, 62; marble intarsia mural, Welsh Rd Br, Free Libr Philadelphia, 68; granite paving, Salvation Army Div Hq, Philadelphia, 72; poster, Please Touch Mus, Philadelphia, 85; poster, Art Now, Philadelphia, 88. *Exhib:* One-person shows, Pa Acad Fine Arts, Philadelphia, 67, Marian Locks Gallery, Philadelphia, 71, 74, 77, 83 & 89 & Hollins Col, Va, 85; two-person show, Rutgers Univ Art Gallery, New Brunswick, NJ, 71; Woman's Work, American Art 1974, Philadelphia Civic Ctr, 74; Philadelphia: 300 Yrs of Am Art, 76, Philadelphia Mus Art; In This Acad, Pa Acad of Fine Arts, 76; 20th Century Prints, Philadelphia Mus of Art, 77; Women's Caucus Art, Port Hist Mus, Philadelphia, 83; Philadelphia Artists: A Juried Exhibition, Philadelphia Mus Art, 90; and others. *Teaching:* Prof art, Philadelphia Col Art, 57-72, 73-82, prof emer, 82-; prof art, Temple Univ, 72-73; artist-in-residence, Ariz State Univ, 81, adj prof art, 86-; vis critic, Pa Acad Fine Arts, 88- *Awards:* Mary Smith Prize, Pa Acad Fine Arts, 68; Gov Pa Hazlett Award, 80; Honor Award, Nat Women's Caucus Art, 83; Hunt Award, Women's Way, Philadelphia, 84; Roland Gallimore Award, Interior Design Coun, Philadelphia, Pa, 90; Mayor's Arts & Culture Award, Philadelphia, 91. *Bibliog:* A Vision Transformed, Blue Ridge Pub Television, Roanoke, Va, 86; Archives of Am Art, Smithsonian Inst. *Mem:* Pa Acad Fellowship; Print Club (mem bd, 72); Col Art Asn. *Dealer:* Marian Locks Gallery 600 Washington Sq S Philadelphia PA 19106. *Mailing Add:* 415 S Carlisle St Philadelphia PA 19146

ANDRE, CARL
SCULPTOR
b Quincy, Mass, Sept 16, 35. *Study:* With Patrick & Maud Morgan, Hollis Frampton; Michael Chapman, Frank Stella. *Work:* Nat Gallery Can, Ottawa; Tate Gallery, London; Mus Mod Art, New York; Albright-Knox Art Gallery, Buffalo; Art Inst Chicago; and others. *Comn:* Found Pub Giving, Hartford, Conn. *Exhib:* One-man shows, Stadtisches Mus, Monchengladbach, 68, Haags Gemeentemuseum, Den Haag, 69, Guggenheim Mus, 70, St Louis Art Mus, 71, Mus Mod Art, New York, 73, Kunsthalle Bern, Switz, 75 & Palacio de Cristal, Madrid, 88; and others. *Media:* All. *Publ:* 12 Dialogues 1962-1963, with Hollis Frampton, New York Univ Press, 80. *Mailing Add:* c/o Paula Cooper Gallery 155 Wooster St New York NY 10012

ANDRES, GLENN MERLE
HISTORIAN, EDUCATOR
b Chicago, Ill, July 15, 41. *Study:* Cornell Univ, BArch, 64; Princeton Univ, MFA, 67, PhD, 71; Am Acad Rome, fel, 67-69. *Collections Arranged:* Builders and Humanists, Univ St Thomas, Houston, 66; Hardy Holzman Pfeiffer Associates: Twenty-Five Years, Middlebury Col, Vt, 93. *Pos:* Assoc dir, Johnson Gallery, Middlebury Col, 76-78. *Teaching:* Asst prof art hist, Middlebury Col, Vt, 70-78, assoc prof, 78-83, prof, 83-, Christian A Johnson prof art, 84-87; Fulbright lectr in Am visual cult, Univ Exeter, United Kingdom, 87-88. *Mem:* Sheldon Mus, Middlebury, Vt (trustee, 75-84 & vpres, 78-82); Vermont Adv Council for Hist Preservation, 86- *Res:* 16th century Italian architecture; 19th century American architecture. *Publ:* Auth, A Walking History of Middlebury, Vermont, Addison Press, 75; auth, The Villa Medici in Rome, Garland Press, 76; contribr, New England Meeting House and Church: 1630-1850, Dublin Sem, 80; coauth (with J M Hunisak & A R Turner), The Art of Florence, Abbeville Press, 88; contribr La Villa Medicis, Ecole Francaise de Rome, 91. *Mailing Add:* Art Dept Middlebury Col Middlebury VT 05753

ANDRESON, LAURA F
CERAMIST, EDUCATOR
b San Bernardino, Calif, Oct 7, 02. *Study:* Univ Calif, Los Angeles, BA, 32; Columbia Univ, MA, 37. *Work:* Walker Art Ctr, Minneapolis; Baltimore Mus Art; Boston Mus Fine Arts; Acad Art, Honolulu. *Exhib:* One-man show, Calif Palace Legion Hon, 74; Calif Ceramics & Glass, Oakland Mus Art, 74; Everson Mus Art, 75; Craft Exhib, Philadelphia Mus Art, 77; Calif Ceramics 1898-1952, Oakland Mus Art, 78; A Century of Ceramics in US, Everson Mus Art, 79; Porcelain Exhib: 20 Ceramic Artists in USA, 80, Renwick Gallery, Smithsonian Inst. *Teaching:* Prof ceramics, Univ Calif, Los Angeles, 33-70, emer prof, 70- *Awards:* First Prize, Los Angeles Co Fair, Pomona; Purchase Prize, Oakland Mus Art, Calif; First Prize, Crocker Art Gallery, Sacramento, Calif. *Bibliog:* Elaine Levin (auth), Laura Andreson and Erwin and Mary Scheier, Ceramic Mo, 5/76; Hildegard Storr-Britz (auth), Ornaments and surfaces on ceramics, Kunst & Handwerk Verlagsanstalt, Dortmund, Ger, 77; Garth Clark & Margie Hughto (coauths), A Century of Ceramics, E P Dutton, 79. *Mem:* Am Ceramic Soc Southern Calif; fel Am Craft Coun; Calif Design; Southern Calif Designer Craftsmen (pres, 40-41); Contemp Craft Coun Los Angeles. *Media:* Porcelain. *Mailing Add:* 1950 N Edgemont St Los Angeles CA 90027

ANDREW, DAVID NEVILLE
PAINTER, EDUCATOR
b Redruth, Eng, Apr 19, 34; Can citizen. *Study:* Falmouth Sch of Art, 54; Slade Sch of Fine Art, London, 58; influenced by Patrick Heron & Ben Nicholson. *Work:* Kettles Yard Mus, Cambridge Univ, Eng; Art Gallery of Ont, Toronto. *Exhib:* Imprint, Can Nat Exhib (touring), 76; Brit Int Print Biennale, 76 & 78; Premio Int Biella por Incisione, Italy, 76; Int Grafik Biennale, Grenchen, WGer, 76; 9th Burnaby Biennial Print Show, BC, 77; and others. *Pos:* External assessor, Croydon Col of Art, Eng, 73; dir, Falmouth Summer Sch, Cornwall, Eng, 74-77. *Teaching:* Vis artist painting, Portsmouth Col of Art, Eng, 61-70; vis artist painting & print, Bournemouth Col of Art, Eng, 62-69; assoc prof painting & printmaking, Queen's Univ, 71- *Awards:* Purchase Award, Can Cult Exchange to Hawaii, US Comn on Cult & Arts, 74; Horniansky Award, Imprint, Print & Drawing Coun of Can, 76; Purchase Award, 9th Burnaby Biennial Print Show, Burnaby Art Gallery, 77. *Mem:* Ont Soc Artists; Soc Can Artists; Print & Drawing Coun of Can. *Media:* Collage, Silkscreen. *Dealer:* Mira Godard Gallery 22 Hazleton Ave Toronto ON Can. *Mailing Add:* Dept of Art Queens Univ Kingston ON K7L 3N6 Canada

ANDREWS, BENNY
PAINTER, LECTURER
b Madison, Ga, Nov 13, 30. *Study:* Ft Valley State Col, 48-50; Univ Chicago, 56-58; Chicago Art Inst, BFA, 58. *Work:* Mus Mod Art, New York; Detroit Inst Art, Mich; Mus African Art, Washington, DC; High Mus, Atlanta; Butler Inst Am Art, Youngstown, Ohio; O'Hara Mus, Tokyo, Japan; Joslyn Mus Art, Nebr; Hirshhorn Mus, Washington, DC; Metropolitan Mus Art, New York; Brooks Mus, Memphis, Tennta, Ga. *Comn:* Atlanta Int Airport, 80. *Exhib:* Thirty Contemporary Black Americans, Minneapolis Inst Arts, Minn, 68; Martin Luther King Memorial, Mus Mod Art, 69; Afro-Americans: Boston and New York, Mus Fine Arts, Boston, 70; Symbols, Studio Mus Harlem, New York, 71; Artists as Adversary, Mus Mod Art, 71; NJ State Mus, Trenton, 80; Mus Afro-Am Culture, Philadelphia, Pa, 80; Everson Mus, Syracuse, NY, 81; Albright-Knox Gallery, Buffalo, NY, 82; Newark Mus, NJ, 82; one-man shows, Armstrong Gallery, New York, 84-85, Hyde Mus, 87 & Studio Mus, New York, 88-89; Birmingham Mus, Al, 88; Work on Paper, Wentell St Gallery, Cambridge, Mass, 89; Southland, Deutch Gallery, New York, 90; Recent Works, Gross McCleaf Gallery, 90; Thirty Years of Painting, Ratner Gallery, Chicago, Ill, 90; Folk Art of Benny & George Andrews, Brook Mus, Memphis, Tenn, 90; Recent Works, Sherry Washington Gallery, Detroit, Mich, 90. *Pos:* Co-chmn, Black Emergency Cult Coalition, New York, 69-; dir, Visual Arts Prog, Nat Endowment Arts, 82-84 & Nat Arts Productions, 84-86. *Teaching:* Instr art, New Sch Social Res, 67-70; lectr art, Queens Col, 68-72; Dorne vis prof, Univ Bridgeport, 70; prof art, CUNY Queens Col, New York, currently. *Awards:* John Hay Whitney Fel, 65-66; NY State Creative Arts Prog Serv Grant, 71; Nat Endowment Arts, 74 & 86; Elizabeth Cattlett Mora Award for Excellence, 75. *Bibliog:* Samella Lewis & Ruth Waddy (auth), Black artists on art, Contemp Crafts, 71; Elton Fax (auth), 17 Black Artists, Dodd, 71; Barry Schwartz (auth), The New Humanism, Praeger, 74; S Lewis (auth), Art: African American, Harcourt, Brace & Jovanovich, 77; E L Smith (auth), Art of the

Seventies, Cornell Univ Press, 80. *Mem:* MacDowell Colony (bd dirs, 87-); Creativedrama Soc; Sculpture Ctr. *Media:* Oil & Collage, Ink. *Publ:* Auth, A wonderful potpourri of styles and sources, Art J, summer 80; Benny Andrews: An artist's journal, Atlanta Art Papers, 9-10/80; Is there a Black Esthetic?, Art Papers, 12/85; Decentralization: The Greening of America, Art Papers, 4/86; The Mule Is About Keeping On Keeping On, Am Visions, 4/88. *Mailing Add:* 130 W 26th St New York NY 10001

ANDREWS, CHARLEEN KOHL
SCULPTOR
b New York, NY, July 27, 25. *Study:* Univ Southern Calif, BA, 54; Scottsdale Artist Sch with Bruno Luchesi & Ken Bunn, 87 & 89. *Work:* Descanso Gardens, La Canada, Calif; Carnegie Cult Arts Mus, Oxnard, Calif; Los Angeles Arboretum; Whittier City Hall, Calif; Brand Art Gallery. *Comn:* Pelicans, wood sculpture, State Farm Insurance, Los Angeles, 87; Bronze Indian, McDonalds Franchises, Glendora, Calif, 89. *Exhib:* Artists Soc Int, San Francisco, 86; Burbank City Art Competition, Burbank Libr, 87; Anniversary Show, Los Angeles Arboretum, 87; Glendale Arts Coun, Glendale Galleria, 88; Winners Circle, Alhambra City Hall, 88; and others. *Bibliog:* Mary Forgione (auth), For arts sake, Glendale Star, 86; Art highlights, W Art, 89; Bill Youngs (auth), Sculpture in wood, Star/News Herald, 89. *Mem:* Pasadena Soc Artists; Burbank Art Asn; San Gabriel Fine Arts; Int Sculptors Asn & Calif Sculptors Asn. *Media:* Wood. *Mailing Add:* 1278 Upton Place Eagle Rock CA 90041

ANDREWS, EDWIN C
SCULPTOR
b Emporia, Kans, Dec 16, 56. *Study:* Kans City Art Inst, BFA, 79; Ind Univ, MFA, 82. *Work:* Essex Inst, Salem, Mass; Allegheny Col, Meadville, Pa; Moneta Group Inc, St Louis Sci Ctr, Mark Twain Banks, Patience & Al Jung, St Louis, Mo. *Comn:* Sculpture, Le Frack Commission, Washington, DC; Fed Reserve Bank Plaza, Cincinnati, Ohio; Art Link, Arts in Transit, Light Rail Proj, St Louis, Mo. *Exhib:* No Mans Land, Socrates Sculpture Park, New York, 90; Critical Mass, Decker Gallery, Md Inst, Col Art, Baltimore, Md, 91; Site, Space, Object, Megahan Gallery, Allegheny Col, Meadville, Pa, 91; Art of the Mask Exhibit, Artists' Found Gallery, Boston, Mass, 91; Fear of Freedom of Fear, Solo Installation, Dodge Gallery, Northeastern Univ, Boston, Mass, 92. *Teaching:* Ass prof, Univ Ky, Lexington, 82-86, Wash Univ, Sch Fine Arts, St Louis, Mo, 86-90, Northeastern Univ, Boston, Mass, 90-; lectures at numerous universities and institutions 1985-1991. *Awards:* Nat Grant in Sculpture, Nat Endowment Arts Visual Artists Fel, 90; Finalist Award in Sculpture, 91; Mass Artists Fel, 91. *Bibliog:* John Dorsey (auth), Critical Mass, Baltimore Sun, 1/29/91; Michael Brenson (auth), Sculpture Borne by the Earth and Lighted by the Sky, NY Times, 3/8/91; Christine Temin (auth), A Haunting Last Show at NU's Art Gallery, Boston Globe, 6/92. *Mailing Add:* 123 Grove St N Attleboro MA 02760

ANDREWS, KIM
PAINTER
b Aug 4, 39. *Study:* Univ Alberta, Dipl Art, 61, BFA, 63, Brooklyn Col, City Univ NY, MFA, 68. *Work:* Canada Coun Art Bank; Owens Art Gallery, Sackville, NB; Westburne Industries, Montreal. *Exhib:* Solo exhibs, The Gallery, Scarborough Col, Univ Toronto, 81, Gallery Wack, Ger, 87, Galerie Dr Luise Krohn, Ger, 89; Rational Alternatives, Harbourfront Gallery, Toronto, 83; Cologne Int Art Fair, Ger, 86 & 87; 49th Parallel, New York, 89. *Pos:* Course dir, drawing, York Univ, Toronto, 73-74 & 76-77; spec lectr, Univ Toronto, 75-80, asst prof, drawing & painting, 80-82, assoc prof, 82- *Mailing Add:* c/o Olga Korper Gallery 17 Morrow Ave Toronto ON M6R 2H9 Canada

ANDREWS, LAWRENCE
VIDEO ARTIST, SCULPTOR
b May 7, 64. *Study:* San Francisco Art Inst, Sobel Scholar, 85. *Exhib:* Solo exhibs, Western Adition Cult Ctr, San Francisco, 87, Rene Coelho Gallery Monte Video, Amsterdam, 90, Whitney Biennial, 91, The Kitchen, 92 & Washington Project for Arts, 92; Am Film Inst, Los Angeles, 89; The Blue Aesthetic, Washington Project for Arts, Washington, DC, 89; The Kitchen, New York, 89; Open Channels, Long Beach Mus Art, Calif, 90. *Pos:* Freelance ed, Bay Area Video Coalition, Video Free Am; bd dirs, New Am Makers & New Langton Arts. *Teaching:* Asst prof film & video, Univ Calif, Santa Cruz. *Awards:* SECA Video Award, San Francisco Mus Mod Art, 88; Western States Regional Media Arts Fel, 90; Film Arts Found, personal works, 91. *Bibliog:* Articles in San Francisco Mag, 1/89, Artweek, 7/1/89, Los Angeles Times, 7/29/89 & High Performance Mag, summer 89. *Publ:* Shift Mag, Vol 2, No 4, 40-41; Art Week, 2/22/90 & 11/8/90. *Mailing Add:* 942 60th St Oakland CA 94608

ANDREWS, MARI
PAINTER
b Feb 12, 55. *Study:* Santa Monica Col; Tucson Mus Art Sch; Univ Ariz; Univ Dayton, BFA, 77; Otis Art Inst of Parsons Sch Design, MFA, 82. *Work:* De Saisset Mus, Santa Clara, Calif. *Exhib:* Black Lines, Gwydion Gallery, La Jolla, Calif, 87; Loyola Law Sch Gallery, Los Angeles, 88; Art Space Gallery, Woodland Hills, Calif, 88; Art & Soul Exhib, Pence Gallery, Santa Monica, Calif, 89; Venice Art Walk, Calif, 89; solo exhib, Shoshana Wayne Gallery, Santa Monica, Calif, 88 & 89; group exhib, Without Walls, Newark, NJ, 90. *Pos:* Printmaker, curator, archivist. *Awards:* Nat Endowment of Arts Grant, 89. *Media:* Oil, Mixed Media. *Mailing Add:* c/o Shoshana Wayne Gallery 1454 Fifth St Santa Monica CA 90401

ANDREWS, MICHAEL FRANK
EDUCATOR, SCULPTOR
b Cairnbrook, Pa, Mar 4, 16. *Study:* Univ Kans, BFA, MS; Ohio State Univ, PhD. *Work:* Wichita Mus Art, Kans; Univ Kans, Lawrence; Ohio State Univ; Univ Wis-Madison. *Exhib:* 3rd Int Sculpture Exhib, Philadelphia, 50; Finger Lakes Exhib, Rochester Mem Art Gallery, NY, 69; Sculptors Exhib, Elmira Col, 72; Everson Mus Art, Syracuse, NY, 72; William Rockhill Nelson Art Gallery, Kansas City, Mo, 73. *Pos:* Ed, Synaesthetic Educ, 71. *Teaching:* Instr sculpture, Univ Kans, Lawrence, 45-48; prof art educ, Univ Southern Calif, 50-52; prof sculpture, Univ Wis-Madison, 52-55; chmn dept synaesthetic educ, Syracuse Univ, 55-82, emer prof, 82- *Awards:* Award, NY State Art Teachers Asn, 78; Sculptor Award, Finger Lakes Exhib, Rochester, NY, 80; Kans Univ Athletic 50th Yr Ring Distinction, 89; and others. *Bibliog:* James Schinneller (auth), Art, Search & Self-Discovery; Richard Lowe (auth), Problems in Paradise. *Mem:* Eastern Arts Asn (pres, 60-64); Nat Art Educ Asn (pres, Eastern Region, 60-64); Int Soc Educ Through Art; Creative Leadership Coun, Creative Educ Found. *Media:* Metal, Wood. *Publ:* Auth, Creative Printmaking, 64 & Sculpture & Ideas, 65, Prentice-Hall; auth, Creative Education: The Liberation of Man, Syracuse Univ, 65; Creative Education: The Liberation of Man, Syracuse Univ, 65; Synaesthetic Education, 71 & Sensory Learning at Syracuse University, 81, Syracuse Univ Press. *Mailing Add:* 101 Trinity Lakes Dr Po Box 223 Sun City Center FL 33573-5736

ANDREWS, SYBIL (SYBIL ANDREWS MORGAN)
PAINTER, PRINTMAKER
b Bury St Edmunds, Eng, 1898. *Study:* Heatherley Sch Fine Art, London, with Henry G Massey; also with Boris Heroys, London. *Work:* Victoria & Albert Mus, London; Nat Gallery South Australia; Dublin Mus, Ireland; Los Angeles Co Mus Art; Leeds Mus, Eng; Metrop Mus Art; Boston Mus Fine Arts; Art Inst Chicago; Cleveland Mus Art; Brit Mus; Brit Ctr, Yale Univ; Toledo Mus Art. *Exhib:* Sybil Andrews Exhib Colour Linocut Prints, Vancouver Art Gallery, 48; Primera Expos Arte Sacro Moderno, Buenos Aires, Arg, 54; Print Makers Soc Calif; Art Gallery of Greater Victoria, BC, 76; de Vooght Galleries, Vancouver, 78; Mary Ryan Gallery, New York, 84 & 87; and others. *Teaching:* Pvt classes. *Awards:* G A Reid Award, Soc Can Painters, Etchers & Engravers, 51. *Mem:* Soc Can Painter, Etchers & Engravers; Print & Drawing Coun Can. *Media:* Oil, Watercolor. *Mailing Add:* c/o Mary Ryan Gallery 24 W 57th St New York NY 10019

ANDRIULLI, ROBERT
PAINTER, EDUCATOR
b Paterson, NJ, Jan 18, 48. *Study:* William Paterson Col, BA, 75; Penn State Univ, MFA, 78. *Exhib:* Solo exhib, Caldwell Col, NJ, 84, David Olenick Fine Art, New York, 84, Broadway Gallery, Paterson, NJ, 86, Gianetta Gallery, Philadelphia, Pa, 87 & 89, St Univ NY, Fredonia, 87, Hudson Walker Gallery, Provincetown, Mass, 88, Westmoreland Mus Art, Greensburg, Pa, 88; Two-person exhib, Gianetta Gallery, Pa, 85, Wyckoff Gallery, Wyckoff, NJ, 89, Icon Gallery, Brunswick, Maine, 90; Fifty-Second Annual Cooperstown Art Asn, Juried, 97; Fine Arts Work Ctr Gallery, Provincetown, Mass, 87-88; Wyckoff Gallery, Wyckoff, NJ, 89. *Pos:* Dir, Zoller Gallery, Pennsylvania State Univ, 79-80. *Teaching:* Instr art, Pennsylvania State Univ, 78-82; prof art, Bowdoin Col, Brunswick, Maine, 88-90, Millersville Univ, Millersville, Pa, 90. *Awards:* NJ State Coun Arts Fel, 79 & 85; Visual Artist Fel, Nat Endowment Arts, 87; Artist-in-Residence Fel, Yaddo Found, NY, 87, Millay Colonie Arts, NY, 87, Fine Arts Ctr, Mass, 87 & Va Ctr Creative Arts, Va, 88. *Dealer:* Wyckoff Gallery Wyckoff NJ 07481. *Mailing Add:* 533 W Chestnut No 6 Lancaster PA 17603

ANDRUS, JAMES ROMAN
PRINTMAKER, PAINTER
b St George, Utah, July 11, 07. *Study:* Otis Art Inst, Los Angeles; Colorado Springs Fine Arts Ctr; Art Students League; Brigham Young Univ, BA & MA; Columbia Univ; Univ Colo, EdD. *Work:* Utah State Capitol Collection, Salt Lake City; Brigham Young Univ; Dixie Col Collection, St George; Provo City Schs Collections; Granite Sch Dist Collection, Salt Lake City. *Comn:* Mural, St George Temple, Utah, 43; oil painting, Cent Utah Ment Health Ctr, 72; portraits of Charles E Maw, Joseph K Nicoles & Charles Redd, Brigham Young Univ & J C Moffitt, Provo Sch Dist. *Exhib:* Calif State Fair Exhib, 39; Utah State Inst Fine Arts Exhibs; Boston Mus Ann, Mass; Wichita Print Asn, Kans; Univ Utah Ann, Salt Lake City. *Pos:* Mem, Utah State Fair Art Comt, Salt Lake City; chmn visual arts div, Utah State Inst Fine Arts; mem, Utah State Bd Educ Elem Art Curric. *Teaching:* Spec instr painting, Brigham Young Univ, 40-43, asst prof painting & printmaking, 50-53, prof art, 58-74, emer prof art & educ, 75- *Awards:* Fac Award of Merit, Otis Art Inst, 38; Univ Colo Art Fel, 52; Purchase Prizes, Utah State Inst Fine Arts, 45, 50 & 54. *Mem:* Nat & Western Art Educ Asns; Utah Acad Sci, Arts & Lett; Cent Utah Art Bd. *Media:* Oil. *Mailing Add:* 1765 N 651 E Provo UT 84601

ANDRY, KEITH ANTHONY
PAINTER, INSTRUCTOR
b Thibodaux, La, June 28, 60. *Study:* Special instruction with Ed Whitney, Robert E Wood, Millard Sheets & Milford Zornes, 73-84; Calif Sch of Art, with Rex Brandt, 86; Nicholls State Univ, AB, 86. *Work:* Fine Arts Mus S, Mobile, Ala; Zigler Mus Art, Jennings, La; Baton Rouge Waterworks, Baton Rouge, La; George's Inc, Springdale, Ark; Andry Interior's, Thibodaux, La. *Comn:* Three paintings, Disney World Dixie Landings Resort, 92. *Exhib:* Georgia Watercolor Soc 3rd Ann, Mus Arts & Sci, Macon, Ga, 82; Georgia Watercolor Soc 6th Ann, Madison-Morgan Cult Ctr, Madison Ga, 85; Rocky Mountain Nat Watermedia Exhib, Foothills Art Ctr, Golden, Colo, 86-87; Nat Watercolor Soc 66th Ann Muckenthaler Cult Ctr, Fullerton, Calif, 87;

and othrs. *Pos:* Chmn Arts, 1984 World's Fair, New Orleans, La, 84. *Awards:* Grumbacher Art Award, Grumbacher, 80; Foothills Art Ctr Award, Foothills Art Ctr, 86; Muckenthaler Cult Found, Muckenthaler Cult Ctr, 87. *Bibliog:* Trent Angers (auth), Keith Andry: Watercolorist on a winning streak, Anger's Publ Corp, 83; Sheila Elliot (auth), Keith Andry: Rocky Mountain Watermedia Asn, F & W Publ Corp, 87; Stephen Doherty (auth), Painting on Location - Special Feature, Am Artist Mag, 89. *Mem:* Nat Watercolor Soc signature mem; Ky Watercolor Soc; La Watercolor Soc life mem; Midwest Watercolor Soc life mem; Ga Watercolor Soc signature mem. *Media:* Watercolor. *Publ:* Illusr, The Longest Street, 82; Keith Andry: Watercolorist on a Winning Streak, Anger's Publ Corp, 83; contrib, Louisiana Men are Dinamight, Elm Publ, 84; illusr, Keith Andry: Rocky Mountain National Watermedia Exhibition, F & W Publ Inc, 87; Painting on Location, Stephen Doherty, 89. *Mailing Add:* 10860 Weiner Creek Dr Baton Rouge LA 70816

ANGELINI, JOHN MICHAEL
PAINTER, WRITER
b New York, NY, Nov 18, 21. *Study:* Newark Sch Fine & Indust Art; spec studies in Europe, 61. *Work:* David L Yunich Collection, Bambergers, NJ; Morris Mus of Art, Morristown, NJ; Paterson Main Libr, NJ; Longlines Div, Am Tel & Tel; Morgan Guarantee Trust Co, New York. *Exhib:* Nat Arts Club Watercolor Ann, New York, 64; NJ Pavillion, New York World's Fair, 65; Watercolor USA, Nat Ann & Traveling Exhib, Springfield Mus, Mo, 66; NJ Watercolor Soc Ann, Newark, 74-80; Int Exhib, Nabisco World Hq; plus many one-man shows in NY & NJ. *Pos:* Art dir, Berles Carton Co, Inc, Paterson, NJ, 50-79; adv bd, NJ Music & Arts, Chatham, 72-78. *Awards:* Silver Medal for Watercolor, NJ Watercolor Soc, 63; Medal of Honor for Watercolor, Audubon Artists, Nat Acad, 63 & Nat Arts Club, 64; Artist of the Year, Hudson Artists, Inc, NJ, 74. *Bibliog:* L Pessolano (auth), John Angelini--a profile, 70 & R Williams (auth), John Angelini--A W S, 71, NJ Music & Arts; interview & watercolor demonstration, cable TV networks, NY & NJ. *Mem:* Am Watercolor Soc; Audubon Artists; Fla & NJ Miniature Art Soc; Miniature Artists of Am. *Media:* Watercolor, Pencil Rendering. *Publ:* Contrib, NJ Music & Arts, 70-77; auth, articles in Am Artist, 72; The North Light Art Competition Handbook, North Light Books, 86; Watercolor 86, Am Artist, 86; contribr, 59 More Studio Secrets, North Light Bks, 90. *Dealer:* Gallery Nine 215 Main St Chatham NJ 07928. *Mailing Add:* 18211 Autumn Lake Blvd Hudson FL 34667-6494

ANGELL, TONY
SCULPTOR, PAINTER
b Los Angeles, Calif, Nov 15, 40. *Study:* Univ Wash, BA, 62. *Work:* Rainier Bank, Safeco Plaza, Seattle; Tacoma Art Mus, Wash; Gilcrease Mus, Tulsa, Okla; Frye Art Mus, Seattle, Wash; Lywam Art Mus, Wausau, Wis. *Comn:* Raven into Flight (sculpture) J S West Comm, Seattle, 81; Family of Otters (sculpture), Olympia Pub Libr, Wash; Artic Visitor, Safeco Plaza Bldg, 82; Ascending Eagles, Bellevue, Wash; Trumpeter Swans, Lywam Art Mus, Wausau, Wis. *Exhib:* Animals in Art, Royal Ont Mus, Toronto, 75-76; Tony Angell Retrospective, T Gilcrease Mus, Tulsa, Okla, 86; Animals in Art, Leigh Yawkey Woodson Art Mus, Wasau, Wis, 86-88; Nat Acad Western Art, Oklahoma City, 81-88; Artists of Am Show, Denver, 81-90. *Collections Arranged:* Northwest Collection (with catalog), Rainier Bldg, Seattle, 78; Gilcrease Mus, Tulsa, Okla, 86; Artist of America, Denver, 88. *Pos:* Comnr & chair, Visual Arts Comt, King Co Arts Comn, 78-82. *Teaching:* Guest lectr, City of Seattle, 83 & Artists of Am, Denver, 83-88. *Awards:* Wash State Gov Awards, 76, 79 & 86; 50 Best Books Design Award, 86; Golden Acorn, 90. *Bibliog:* Rebecca Kelly (auth), PM Northwest: Tony Angell (film), TV Station KOMO, 80; Ivan Doig (auth), Stone Spirits (Tony Angell), Wash Mag, 86; Evening Edition (T Angell), KCTS TV, Seattle, Wash, 87; New York Art Rev, 89. *Mem:* Nat Acad Western Artists; Nat Sculpture Soc. *Media:* Marble, Bronze; Oils, Ink. *Publ:* Auth-illusr, Birds of Prey, Pac Search, 72; auth-illusr, Owls, 74 & Ravens, Crows, Magpies and Jays, 78, Univ Wash; co-auth-illusr, Marine Birds and Mammals of Puget Sound, Nat Oceanic & Atmospheric Admin, 82; illusr, Blackbirds of the Americas, Univ Wash Press, 84; illusr, Sea Brothers, Univ Pa Press, 88. *Mailing Add:* c/o Foster-White Gallery 311 1/2 S Occidental Ave Seattle WA 98104

ANGELOCH, ROBERT
PAINTER, PRINTMAKER
b Richmond Hill, NY, Apr 8, 22. *Study:* Art Student League; Acad Fine Arts, Florence, Italy; also with Fiske Boyd, Martin Lewis & Y Kuniyoshi. *Work:* Art Student League; Munson-Williams-Proctor Inst, Utica, NY; Russell Sage Col; Western Ky Univ. *Comn:* Murals, New York Bd Educ, Kellogg Corp, Brunswick, NJ & Queensboro Pub Libr. *Exhib:* Metrop Mus; Nat Acad; Libr Congress. *Pos:* Supvr, Woodstock Summer Sch, Art Students League, 60-68; artist-in-residence, Western Ky Univ, 74; dir, Woodstock Sch Art Inc, 80-86. *Teaching:* Instr, Art Students League, Woodstock Summer Sch, 64-79; instr, Woodstock Sch Art, 68-; instr, Russell Sage Col, 71-72. *Awards:* Purchase award, Woodstock Art Asn, 64; Jane Peterson Prize, Allied Artists Am, 64; First Prize, Springfield Mus Fine Arts, 68; plus others. *Bibliog:* S R Day (auth), Creative Woodstock, Mead Mt Press, 66; Fridolf Johnson (auth), Robert Angeloch, Am Artists Mag, 85. *Mem:* Art Student League; Woodstock Artists Asn. *Media:* Oil; Etching. *Publ:* Auth, Basic Oil Painting Techniques, Pitman, 70; Outdoor sketching, Am Artist Mag, 70; contribr, Angeloch: Color Prints, 80. *Dealer:* Paradox Gallery Woodstock NY 12498. *Mailing Add:* PO Box 95 Woodstock NY 12498

ANGLIN, BETTY LOCKHART
EDUCATOR, PAINTER
b Greenwood, SC, Apr 23, 37. *Study:* Univ Ga, 58, with Lamar Dodd; Col of William & Mary, Williamsburg, Va, BA, 72; additional study with Barclay Sheaks, Leone Cooper, Ferdinand Warren & Earnest Johnson. *Work:* Hampton Sch Syst, Va; Va Nat Bank Collection; Va Fair Collection; Ft Eustis Collection; Cecil Rawls Mus, Courtland, Va; and others. *Comn:* Painting, Newport News Shipyard, 72; hist paintings, Hampton City Calendar, 77; four hist paintings, City of Stoney Creek, Va, 78. *Exhib:* Peninsula Fine Arts Show, 90; Chrysler Hermitage Miniature Show, 90; Four-State Irene Leache Show, Chrysler Mus, 90; Faculty Show, Christopher Newport Col, 90; and others. *Teaching:* Guest prof, Va Wesleyan Col, 72 & 74; prof fine arts, Christopher Newport Col, 77-; instr, Peninsula Fine Arts Ctr. *Awards:* Award, Parthenon, Nashville, Tenn, 76; Life Bravissimo Award, Life Fed Savings & Loan Asn & WGH Radio, 80; Grant, Va Comn for the Arts, 92; and others. *Mem:* Pa Art Asn; Va Beach Art Asn; Va Watercolor Asn. *Media:* All Media. *Publ:* Illusr, Painting with Acrylic from Start to Finish, 74 & Landscape Painting, 74, Davis Publ; illusr, Christmas Tugboat, 83; Addition in Work (Paintings printed in B Sheaks Books). *Mailing Add:* 213 Parkway Dr Newport News VA 23606

ANGUIANO, RAUL
MURALIST, PAINTER
b Guadalajara, Mexico, Feb 26, 15. *Study:* Studies with prominent art teachers in Guadalajara; Art Students League. *Work:* Mus Mod Art, Mex; Mus Mod Art, New York; San Francisco Mus Art, Calif; Royal Mus Art & Hist, Brussels; Arch Monumental Art Mus, Lund, Sweden. *Comn:* Three murals, Centro Escolar Revolucion, Ministry of Educ, Mexico City, 37; Birth in the Jungle (mural), Laboratorios Hormona, Mexico City, 62; three murals, Mus Anthorp, Sect of Educ, Mexico City, 63; The Baptism of Christ (mural), Church of San Marcos, Jalisco, Mex, 65; mural, Nat Ballet of Jamaica, Olympia Hotel, Kingston, 70. *Exhib:* San Francisco Mus Mod Art, 53; Salon de la Plastica Mex, Mexico City, 69; one-man shows, Mus de Arte Mod, Mex, 71, Instituto-Italo-Latin-Americano, Rome, Italy, 75, Ctr Cult Mex, Paris, 80 & Palace Fine Arts, Mexico City, 82; and others. *Pos:* Gen secy, Art Teachers Union, Mexico City, 36-38; vpres, Mex Asn Plastic Arts, UNESCO Br, 70-. *Teaching:* Art supvr adult educ, Esmeralda Art Sch, Mex, 42-64; teacher life drawing, Univ Mexico City, 42-69. *Awards:* Dipl Honor, Comt Int Exhib Bk Art, Leipzig, Ger, 60; Commendatore decoration, Pres of Italy, 75; Diploma Honor, City Los Angeles, 82; Premio Jalisco, 88. *Bibliog:* Justino Fernandez (auth), Raul Anguiano, Ediciones de Arte, SAm, 48; Margarita Nelken (auth), Raul Anguiano, Editorial Estaciones, Mex, 58; Jorge Juan Crespo de la Serna (auth), En torno al arte y personalidad de Raul Anguiano, Cuadernos de Bellas Artes, 62. *Mem:* Soc Europeenne Cult; Acad Arts, Mex, 82. *Media:* Oil, Drawing. *Publ:* Auth, Expedicion a Bonampak, travel diary, Univ Mex, 59; auth, Adventura en Bonampak, Ediciones Novaro, Mex, 68; auth & illusr, Mawarirra, Ediciones Estaciones, Mex, 72. *Dealer:* Lodi Art Gallery 2557 Colorado Blvd Los Angeles CA 90041. *Mailing Add:* Francisco Sosa 114 Coyancan Mexico 21 DF Mexico

ANGULO, CHAPPIE
PAINTER, ILLUSTRATOR
b Mar 3, 28; US citizen. *Study:* Los Angeles City Col; Univ Calif, Los Angeles; Kahn Art Sch; Esmeralda, Inst Nac Bellas Artes, Mexico City; London Art Ctr, Fort Mason, San Francisco, 90. *Work:* Mus Cult, Mexico City; Univ Mus Sci & Art, Mexico, DF. *Comn:* Reproduction murals, Bonampak, 57, Chichen Itza & Tomb 7 Oaxaca, 58, Nat Mus Anthrop, Moneda; reproduction mural, Teotihuacan, Ballet Nac, Mex, 59. *Exhib:* One-man shows, Olympic Cult Prog, 69, Mus Fronterizo, Juarez, Mex, 71, Age Aquarius, Univ Las Americas, Cholula, 73, La Ciudadela, Monterrey, 74 & Gentes y Lugares Mus de las Cult, Mexico; retrospective, Museo Las Culturas, Mex, 76; La Mujer en la Plastica Bellas Artes, Mexico, Anglo Mexicano, 81; La Muerte-UNAM-Bienal, Mex, 86-87; 3 decades of Plastic Art-UNAM, Mex, DF, 90. *Teaching:* Pvt instr, currently. *Bibliog:* M Vazquez (auth), Museo de las Culturas, Inst Nat Antropologia, 65; A Pastrana (auth), El concreto, Arquitectura Arte & Urbanism Mag, 68. *Mem:* Consejo Mundial de Artes Plasticas. *Media:* Paper, Acrylic; Monotype. *Publ:* Illusr, Systema Hidraulicos El'l, Chalcatzingo, 88; The Cuauhnahuac Museum-A Historic Recopilation; A Guide to Coatetelco; Iconographic Analysis of Ancient Chalcatzingo, 87; El Axayotl--Un sistema de drenaje aljibe--,Agricultura Indigena, Ciesas, Mex, 90; Aspects of a Culture thru its Pictoric Expression--Section Teotihuacan--Prehispanic Mural Painting in Mexico, Int Esthetic Investigation, UNAM, Mex, 92. *Mailing Add:* A P Postal 21-609 Mexico, DF 04000 Mexico

ANKER, SUZANNE C
SCULPTOR, PAINTER
b Brooklyn, NY, Aug 6, 46. *Study:* Brooklyn Col, BA; Univ Colo, MFA. *Work:* St Louis Art Mus, Mo; Denver Art Mus, Colo; Williams Col Mus Art. *Comn:* Cleveland Art Mus. *Exhib:* New Ways With Paper, Nat Collection Fine Arts, Smithsonian Inst, Washington, DC, 77 & Paper as Medium, 78; Walker Art Ctr, Minneapolis, 79; Richard Gray Gallery, Chicago, 79; Greenberg Wilson Gallery, New York, 88 & 90. *Teaching:* Asst prof experimental printmaking, Washington Univ, St Louis, 76-78. *Awards:* NY Found Grant in Sculpture, 89. *Bibliog:* Meyer Raphael Rubinstein (auth), Suzanne Anker, Arts, 12/88; Carter Ratcliff (auth), Swamp things, Vogue, 4/89; rev, Howard Risatti, Artforum, summer 90. *Mem:* Col Art Asn. *Media:* Paper, Stone. *Mailing Add:* 101 Wooster St New York NY 10012

ANKRUM, JOAN
ART DEALER
b Los Angeles, Calif. *Collections Arranged:* Of Time & the Image, Calif Artists, Phoenix Mus Art, Ariz, 64; People to People, exhib honoring People's Repub China, 72; The Art of African Peoples, private Black Collections, Ankrum Gallery, 73; Calif Artists Exhib, State Capitol Bldg, Sacramento, 75; Morris Broderson Retrospectives, Univ Ariz Mus Art, 75; Ankrum Gallery,

Rochester Nat Tech Inst for the Deaf, 86. *Pos:* Dir, Ankrum Gallery, Los Angeles. *Bibliog:* H Wurdeman (auth), Los Angeles Galleries, Art in Am, 62; Camilla Snyder (auth), A language without sound, Los Angeles Herald Examr, 5/10/70; Curtis (auth), A woman's place, New York Times, 11/26/71. *Mem:* Art Dealers Asn Southern Calif (bd mem, 70); Am Fedn Arts. *Specialty:* West Coast contemporary artists, primarily Californian, ethnic, including Black, Mexican-Indian (Huichol). *Publ:* Auth & ed, Drawings & Haiku, Janet Lessing, Commun Sci, 65. *Mailing Add:* Ankrum Gallery 327 N Orange Dr Los Angeles CA 90069

ANNIS, NORMAN L
EDUCATOR, SCULPTOR
b Des Moines, Iowa, May 26, 31. *Study:* Univ Northern Iowa, BA, 53; Drake Univ; Univ Iowa, MFA, 59. *Work:* Central Col, Pella, Iowa; Corcoran Gallery Art, DC; Washington & Lee Univ, Lexington, Va. *Comn:* Life-size bronze figure, Gettysburg Col, Pa, 70; life-size welded steel figure, Frey Village, Middletown, 76; life-size cor-ten steel figure, Gettysburg Sr High Sch, 77. *Exhib:* Fourth Dulin Nat Prints, Dulin Gallery, Knoxville, 61; 4th Nat Drawing Exhib, Okla Art Ctr, Oklahoma City, 61; Drawings USA, St Paul Art Ctr, Minn, 61 & 63; 4th Nat Ultimate Concerns, Ohio Univ, Athens, 65; Washington Area Artists Series, Corcoran Gallery Art, DC, 65; Living Am Artists & Human Figure, Pa State Univ Mus Art, State College, 74. *Teaching:* Instr sculpture, Univ Ill, Champaign, 59-60; prof sculpture, Gettysburg Col, 60-78; prof & head dept art, Southwest Mo State Univ, Springfield, 78- *Awards:* First Sculpture Award, Fifth Ann Pennational, 62; Purchase Award, St Paul Art Ctr, 63; Anna Hyatt Huntington Award, Corcoran Gallery Art, 63. *Media:* Bronze, Welded Steel. *Dealer:* Michelson Gallery 707 G St NE Washington DC 20002. *Mailing Add:* 42 W Keller St Mechanicsburg PA 17055-6339

ANNUS, JOHN AUGUSTUS
PAINTER, PHOTOGRAPHER
b Riga, Latvia, Oct 25, 35; US citizen. *Study:* Pratt Inst, with Richard Lindner & Enrico Catellon, BFA, 58; Nat Acad Design, with Louis Bouche, 58-59; Prix de Rome, Am Acad Rome, 59; Acad Belli Arti Liceo Artistico, Rome, 62-64. *Work:* Baltimore Mus Fine Art, Md; Ohio Dominican Col, Columbus; Nat Acad Design, New York. *Exhib:* Nat Acad Design Annuals, New York, 62, 64, 65, 67, 75, 77, 78, 80, 87 & 88; one-man shows, Contract Design, Odessa, Tex, 79, MaGee Gallery, Scottsdale, Ariz, 80, Clasing Gallery, Munster, Ger, 81, Julia Black Gallery, Taos, NMex, 82, 83 & 84, Toronto Art Gallery, 84, Labyrinth of Light, Int Latvian Music & Arts Festival, Munster, Ger, 87, Gallery Southwest, Hensley Gallery, Taos, NMex, 89 & Labyrinth of Light, Reitern Gallery, Riga, Latvia, 92; First Riga Int, Latvia, 89; Marble & Granite Gallery, 91; 166th Ann Academicians and--Assoc, Nat Acad Design, 91; and others. *Awards:* H W Ranger Fund Purchase Prize, Nat Acad Ann, 65 & 75; S J Wallace Truman Prize, Nat Acad Design, New York, 67; Italian Govt Purchase Prize, Mostra Int de Arti Figurativi, 62. *Bibliog:* Carlo Battaglia (auth), Mostra del pittore John Annus, Giornale de Sicilia, 63; Giuseppe Sicaari (auth), Annus, un pittore lettone innamorato dell'Italia, Arte Sintesi, 64; Raffaele Carrieri (auth), Preferiscono il colosseo, Epoca, 68; and others. *Mem:* Nat Acad Design; Soc Fel Am Acad in Rome; Nat Soc Mural Painters. *Media:* Oils, Multi-media. *Mailing Add:* Ostmarkstrasse 4400 Munster West Falen Germany

ANSELL, JOSEPH PAUL
EDUCATOR, HISTORIAN
b Bethesda Md, Jul 19, 49. *Study:* Knox Col, BA, 71; George Washington Univ, MFA, 75. *Work:* Poster Collection, Libr Cong, Washington, DC; Poster Collection, Mus de la Publicite, Paris, France; Kresge Art Mus, Mich State Univ, E Lansing, Mich; Md Artists Collection, Univ Col Md, College Park; Tyrone Guthrie Ctr Annaghmakerrig, Co Monaghan, Ireland. *Exhib:* Window Room Furniture, Houghton Gallery, Cooper Union, NY, 82; Window Room Furniture, Axis Gallery, Tokyo, Japan, 83; 50th Ann Miniature Soc Washington DC, Art Club, Washington, 83; Haifa, Israel, 84; group shows, Danville Mus Fine Art, Danville, Va, 87, Maier Mus, Lynchburg, Va, 87 & Sawtooth Ctr Visual Design, Winston-Salem, NC, 88. *Collections Arranged:* Contemporary Am Posters, Union Gallery Univ Md, 88. *Teaching:* Vis asst prof painting drawing, Sweet Briar Col, 78-79; lectr graphic design, Univ Md, 79-84 & asst prof graphic design, 84-91; vis tutor, Leicester Polytech, Eng, 90 & 91; assoc prof & dept chair, Otterbein Col, 91- *Awards:* Grant-in-Aid, Swann Found, 84; Creative Arts Award, Grad Sch Univ Md, 87; Gen Res Board & Int Travel, Univ Md, 85 & 87. *Bibliog:* Exhibition des Miniatures, La Revue Modern des Arts, 72; Jill Wechsler (auth), Vistas on a Small Scale, Am Artist, 83. *Mem:* Col Art Asn (panel co-chmn, 83, prog chmn, 91, treas-, Gay & Lesbian Caucus; Design Forum Col Art Asn (sessions chmn, 87); Univ & Col Designers Asn (conf co-chmn, 88); Illusr Club, Washington DC. *Media:* Gouache. *Res:* History of design and illustration, specifically the history of posters as well as a book on the illustrator Arthur Szyk, research on political cartoons and book illustration. *Publ:* Auth, Contemporary American Posters, Union Gallery, Univ Md, 88; Auth, Why I Teach Where I Teach, Fullbleed, Art Dir, DC, 88; coauth, Arthur Szyk, The book illustrations, Novum, 7/88; auth, Art against prejudice: Arthur Szyk's Statue of Kalish, J Decorative & Propaganda Arts, fall 89; Polish American Connections in the Art of Arthur Szyk, Polish Am Studies, spring 92. *Dealer:* David Adamson Gallery 406 Seventh St NW Washington DC; Kerlin Gallery Dublin Ireland. *Mailing Add:* 247 E Blenkner St Columbus OH 43206-1254

ANSON, LESIA
SCULPTOR
b Kassel, Ger, Jan 14, 46; US citizen. *Study:* Westchester Community Col, AAS, 63; Art Students League, 75; sculpture with Cleo Hartwig. *Exhib:* Allied Artists, 78 & Audubon Artists, 79, Nat Acad Design, New York; Nat Asn Women Artists, Equitable Gallery, New York, 80; Wildlife, Pub Libr Mus Gallery, White Plains, NY, 81; Soc Animal Artists, Philadelphia Acad Sci, 81. *Awards:* Bronze Medal, Catherine Lorillard Wolfe Art Club, 77; Award of Merit for Sculpture, Soc Animal Artists, 80; Excalibur Award, Knickerbocker Artists, 80. *Mem:* Soc Animal Artists; Nat Asn Women Artists; Catherine Lorillard Wolfe Art Club; Artists Equity Asn, New York. *Media:* Stone, Marble. *Mailing Add:* 60 E 83rd St New York NY 10028

ANSPACH, ERNST
COLLECTOR
b Glogau, Ger, Feb 4, 13; US citizen. *Study:* Univ Munich; Breslau Univ, PhD, 35. *Work:* Metrop Mus, New York; Nat Mus Art, Washington, DC; Brooklyn Mus, NY. *Mem:* Fel in perpetuity Metrop Mus Art, New York. *Collection:* African tribal sculpture. *Mailing Add:* 118 W 79th St New York NY 10024

ANTHONISEN, GEORGE RIOCH
SCULPTOR, PAINTER
b Boston, Mass, July 31, 36. *Study:* Univ Vt, BA, 61; Nat Acad Design, with Douglas Gorsline, 61-62; Art Students League, with Jose De Creeft & John Hovannes, 62-64. *Work:* Carnegie Hall, New York; US Capitol Bldg, Washington, DC; Atlanta Univ, Ga; World Health Orgn, Geneva, Switz; James A Michener Art Mus, Doylestown, Pa. *Comn:* Sculpture, Dartmouth Med Sch, Dartmouth-Hitchcock Med Ctr, Lebanon, NH, 69; sculpture, Washington Sch Psychiat, Washington, DC, 75; fresco, Rittenhouse Hotel, Philadelphia, Pa, 89; medallion, J Henry Schroder Bank & Trust Co, New York, 82; sculpture, Noble Lowndes Johnson, Newtown, Pa, 84. *Exhib:* Celebration of the Figure, Port of Hist Mus, Philadelphia, 87; Rotunda, Cannon House Off Bldg, US Capitol, Washington, DC; Inaugural Exhib, James A Michener Art Mus, 88; one man shows, Joy Berman Galleries, Philadelphia, 89; Woodmere Art Mus, 92; and others. *Awards:* Alaska State Coun Arts, 76; Sculptor in Residence, Augustus St Gaudens Nat Hist Site, US Dept Interior, 71; Exemplary Achievement in Arts Award, Bucks Co C of C, 85. *Bibliog:* Acceptance of the Statue of Senator Ernest Gruening, US Govt Printing Off, 78; Artists Three (TV prog), Home Vue Cable TV, 85; I Set Before You This Day (sculpture), James A Michener Art Mus, 90. *Mem:* Nat Sculpture Soc; Allied Art Am; Audubon Artists. *Media:* Miscellaneous Media; Miscellaneous Media. *Mailing Add:* Box 147 Solebury PA 18963

ANTHONY, AMY ELLEN
CRAFTSMAN, JEWELER
b Concord, Mass, May 11, 55. *Study:* Syracuse Univ, New York, BFA, 77; Sch Am Craftsmen, Rochester Inst Technol, NY, MFA, 85. *Work:* Temple Emmanuel, Woodcliff, NJ. *Exhib:* Table Top, 80, Young Americans, 80 & Approaches to Collecting, 82, Am Craft Mus, New York, NY; Containers 80, Ft Wayne Mus Art, Ind, 81; Four Jewelry Artists from the States, V & V Gallery, Vienna, Austria, 83; Contemporary Metals II, Downey Mus Art, Calif, 87; SNAG 88 Earring Competition, Jean Michilin Collection, New York, 88. *Teaching:* Lectr, Sch Am Craftsmen, Rochester, NY, 88. *Mem:* Am Crafts Coun. *Media:* Metals. *Publ:* Contribr, Amy Anthony: Studies in aluminum, J Soc NAm Goldsmiths, 85. *Mailing Add:* 36 Saint Paul St Rm 102 Rochester NY 14604

ANTHONY, LAWRENCE KENNETH
SCULPTOR, EDUCATOR
b Hartsville, SC, May 27, 34. *Study:* Washington & Lee Univ, BA; Univ Ga, MFA; study with Lamar Dodd & Howard Thomas. *Work:* Memphis Brooks Mus, Tenn; Vanderbilt Univ Art Dept, Nashville, Tenn; Ark State Univ, Jonesboro; Gibbes Art Gallery, Charleston, SC; SC Art Comn, Columbia; Audubon Park, Memphis. *Comn:* Menorah sculpture, Jewish Community Ctr, Memphis, 67; sculpture, Corinthian Broadcasting Co, New York, 71; wall sculpture, CBS-TV, Sacramento, Calif, 72; Audubon Park, Memphis; Vanderbilt Univ, Nashville. *Exhib:* One-man shows, Columbia Mus Art, 66, Memphis Brooks Mus, 68, Vanderbilt Univ, 72, 74 & Terre Des Hommes, Pavilion, Montreal, 79. *Teaching:* Prof sculpture & drawing, Rhodes Col, Memphis, 61- *Media:* Metal, Wood. *Mailing Add:* Dept Art Rhodes Col 2000 N Parkway Memphis TN 38112

ANTHONY, PETER
SCULPTOR
b Long Island, NY, July 8, 58. *Study:* Sch Visual Arts, New York. *Exhib:* Triangle Workshop Ann Exhib, Pine Plains, 86; Solo exhib, Delphine Gallery, Santa Barbara, Calif, 87. *Awards:* Nat Endowment Arts Fel, 86. *Mailing Add:* 170 E 90th St New York NY 10128

ANTHONY, WILLIAM GRAHAM
PAINTER, DRAFTSMAN
b Ft Monmouth, NJ, Sept 25, 34. *Study:* Yale Univ, BA, 58, with Josef Albers; San Francisco Art Inst, 59-60; Art Student League. *Work:* Whitney Mus Am Art, New York; Ludwig Mus, Cologne, Ger; Art Inst Chicago; Metrop Mus Art, NY; Corcoran Gallery Art, Washington, DC; plus others. *Exhib:* One man shows, Calif Palace Legion Hon, San Francisco, 62, Frank Marino Gallery, New York, 81, Herlin Gallery, New York, 85, Jane Baum Gallery, NY, 86, Berland-Hall Gallery, NY, 91 & Stuart Katz Gallery, Laguna Beach, Calif, 92. *Teaching:* Instr figure drawing, San Francisco Acad Art, 62-63. *Media:* Pencil, Oil. *Publ:* Auth, A New Approach to Figure Drawing, Crown Publ, 65, Odhams, Ltd, Eng, 67 & Bonanza Publ; auth & illusr, Bible Stories, 78 & Bill Anthony's Greatest Hits, Jargon Soc, 88. *Dealer:* Stuart Katz Gallery 1914 Upper Rim Rock Canyon Rd Laguna Beach CA 19651. *Mailing Add:* 903 Westbeth 463 West St New York NY 10014

ANTIN, DAVID A
ART CRITIC, WRITER
b New York, NY, Feb 1, 32. *Study:* Col City New York, BA, 55; NY Univ, MA, 66. *Teaching:* Prof visual arts, Univ Calif, San Diego, 68-, chmn dept, 70-72, 80-81, 87-89. *Awards:* Guggenheim Fel, 76-77; Nat Endowment Humanities Fel, 82-83. *Bibliog:* Barry Alpert (ed), Antin/Rothenberg, VORT 7, Eng Dept, Ind Univ, Bloomington, spring 75; Marjorie Perloff (auth), The Poetics of Indeterminacy, Princeton Univ Press, 81; Sherman Paul (auth), In Search of the Primitive, L S Univ Press, 86. *Mem:* Col Art Asn; Int Asn Art Critics. *Res:* Studies in modernism and post modernism; history of art criticism and theory; sociology of art; interpretation & meaning in cult & language. *Publ:* Auth, Talking at the Boundaries, New Directions, 76; Biography: Representations 16, fall 86; The Stranger at the Door, Genre, Vol XX, No 3-4, fall, winter 87; Selected Poems 1963-1973, Sun & Moon, 89; The real thing, Art Am, 5/81; Tuning, New Directions, 84. *Mailing Add:* PO Box 1147 Del Mar CA 92014

ANTIN, ELEANOR
CONCEPTUAL & PERFORMANCE ARTIST
b New York, NY, Feb 27, 35. *Study:* City Col NY, BA; Tamara Daykarhanove Sch for the Stage. *Work:* Wadsworth Atheneum, Hartford, Conn; Long Beach Mus Art, Calif; San Francisco Mus Modern Art; Mus Mod Art, New York. *Exhib:* One-woman exhibs, Mus Mod Art, New York, 73, Everson Mus, Syracuse, NY, 74, Clocktower, New York, 76, M L D'Arc Gallery, New York, 77, Wadsworth Atheneum, Hartford, Conn, 77, Whitney Mus Am Art, New York, 78 & Long Beach Mus Art, Calif, 79; Nurse & the Hijackers, 77, Before the Revolution, 79, Recollections of My Life with Diaghilev, 80, El Desdichado, 83 & Loves of a Ballerina, 86, Ronald Feldman Fine Arts Gallery, New York; Venice Biennale, Contemp Art Mus, Calif, 76; Last Night of Rasputin, Whitney Mus Biennial, 89 & Hirsihhorn Mus, Washington, DC, 89. *Teaching:* Prof visual arts, Univ Calif, San Diego, 75- *Awards:* Pushcart Prize XI, Best of the Small Presses, Sun & Moon, 81-82; Vesta Award, Women's Bldg, 85; Dorothy Arzner Spec Reception Award, 16th Ann Crystal Awards, Women in Film, 91; and others. *Bibliog:* Eleanor Munro (auth), Originals: American Women Artists, Simon & Schuster, 79; Frantisck Deak (auth), Eleanor Antin: Before the revolution: Acting as an art paradigm, Images & Issues, 1-2/84; Kim Levin (auth), Beyond Modernism, Harper & Row, 88; Henry Sayre (auth), The Object of Performance: The American Avante Garde Since 1970, Univ Chicago Press, 89; J Hoberman (auth), It's Deja Vu All Over Again, Premiere, 92; and others. *Media:* Performance; Video & Film. *Publ:* Auth, Autobiography of the artist as an autobiographer, J Los Angeles Inst Contemp Art, 10/74; Some thoughts on autobiography & Olga Feodorova's story, winter 78-79 & A romantic interlude from: Recollections of My Life with Diaghilev, summer 80, Sun & Moon; Being Antinova, Astro Artz Press, 83; Before the revolution, women & performance, J Feminist Theory, Vol 5, No 1, 90; The man without a world (film), 91. *Dealer:* Ronald Feldman Fine Arts New York NY; Milestone Film & Video New York NY. *Mailing Add:* PO Box 1147 Del Mar CA 92014

ANTOKAL, GALE
PAINTER
b New York, NY, June 5, 51. *Study:* Long Island Univ, BA, 72; Calif Col Arts & Crafts, BFA, 80, MFA, 84. *Work:* McDonald's Corp, San Jose, Calif; Brobeck, Thlager & Harrington, San Francisco, Calif; Stephen Oliver Collection, Orinda, Calif. *Exhib:* Faculty Draw, San Jose State Univ, Calif, 87; 110 Pots, Untitled, San Francisco, Calif, 91; Free Hand: Drawings Loosely Defined, DeAnza Col, Euphrat Gallery, Cupertino, Calif, 91. *Teaching:* Instr art, San Jose State Univ, 86-92. *Awards:* Visual Art Fel, Nat Endowment Arts, 91-92. *Dealer:* Untitled 49 Geary St San Francisco CA 94108. *Mailing Add:* 1054 Spruce St Berkeley CA 94707

ANTOL, JOSEPH JAMES (JAY)
SCULPTOR, CONCEPTUAL ARTIST
b Rexis, Pa, May 2, 47. *Study:* Old Dominion Univ, BFA, 78, MFA, 84; Tamarind Inst, 81. *Work:* Old Dominion Univ, Norfolk, Va. *Exhib:* Still Alive in 85, LAS, Modesto, Calif, 85; Now That We're Home, Art Consortium, Art Ctr, Cincinnati, Ohio, 86; Bookworks, WPA, Washington, DC, 86; Les Hommes, TAG Gallery, D'art Ctr, 87, Va Artists, 88, Peninsula Fine Arts Ctr, 88, Va Comn Arts, 1708 Gallery, 88 & Irene Leach Mem, Chrysler Mus, Virgina, 88; Visual Arts Home, Ctr UNICEF, Atlanta, Ga, 88. *Teaching:* instr printing drawing, Old Dominion Univ, 81-84; instr lithography, Hampton Univ, 86; instr drawing, Governor's Sch Arts, 88-89. *Awards:* Old Dominion Univ fel, 84; D'art Ctr Fel, 86-87; Va Commission/Arts, State Va, 88. *Bibliog:* Joseph Perrin (auth), Visual Arts for the Home, Southern Homes, 88. *Mem:* Peninsula Fine Art Ctr; Artist Against Hunger; Va Beach Arts Ctr. *Media:* Installation, All Media. *Mailing Add:* 2565 Shore Dr Virginia Beach VA 23456

ANTONAKOS, STEPHEN
SCULPTOR
b Greece, Nov 1, 26; US citizen. *Work:* Whitney Mus Am Art, Mus Mod Art, Guggenheim Mus, New York; Milwaukee Art Ctr, Wis; La Jolla Mus, Calif. *Comn:* Neons for Back Bay/South End Station, Orange Line, Boston, 90; Neon for 59th St Marine Transfer Station, New York; Neons for Buttonwood, Philadelphia, Pa, 90; Neons for Pershing Sq, Art in Transit Prog, Los Angeles, Calif; Neons for Momochi, Eukuoka City, Japan. *Exhib:* Neon, Fischbach Gallery, New York, 67-70 & 72, Ileana Tounta Contemp Art Ctr, Athens, Greece, 92; Contemp Am Sculpture Ann, Whitney Mus Am Art, 70; Works in Spaces, San Francisco Mus Art, 73; Ten Outdoor Neons, Ft Worth Art Mus, Tex, 74; John Weber Gallery, New York, 74 & 75; A Shade of Light, San Francisco Mus Art, Downtown Ctr, 78; Site Sculpture Proj, Joslyn Art Mus, Omaha, 78; Minimal Tradition, Aldrich Mus Contemp Art, Ridgefield, Conn, 79; Drawings, Bali Miller Gallery, New York, 88; Neons & Collages, Ileana Tounta Contemp Art Ctr, Athens, 89; Architectural Art, Am Crafts Mus, 88. *Teaching:* Vis artist, Yale Univ, fall 68; artist-in-residence, sculpture, Univ Wis-Madison, spring 71 & Fresno State Col, fall 71. *Awards:* NY State Creative Artists Pub Serv Prog Grant; Individual Artist's Grant, Nat Endowment Arts, 73. *Media:* Neon. *Mailing Add:* 435 W Broadway New York NY 10012

ANTONOVICI, CONSTANTIN
SCULPTOR, LECTURER
b Neamt, Romania, Feb 18, 11; US citizen. *Study:* Fine Arts Acad, Romania, MA; Fine Arts Acad, Vienna, Austria, with Prof Fritz Behn, 42-45; study with Constantin Brancusi, Paris, 47-51. *Work:* Le Salon des Artistes Independants, Paris; Vatican, Roma, Italy; Mus Fine Arts, Montreal. *Comn:* Monuments of St George, Fine Arts Comt, Vienna, 43 & St Joseph, 47; General De Gaulle, French Army Commandment, Tyrol, Austria, 46; Gen Dwight D Eisenhower, Pres Nixon Collection; Bishop Manning, Cathedral St John the Divine, 54; St Luke, St Luke's Hosp, New York, 55; Hacklei Art Mus, Muskegon, Mich, 76. *Exhib:* Asn Federative L'Art Libre, Paris, 51; Silver Anniversary, Can Artists Asn, 53; Art Alliance Gallery Am, Philadelphia, 62; NJ Mus Art Ann, 64; Nat Sculpture Soc Ann Exhib, New York, 71-81, 88 & 90; Va Mus, Richmond, 77. *Awards:* Pro Mundi Beneficio Medal, Brazilian Acad, 76; Mrs Louis Bennett Prize for Sculpture Exhib, Nat Sculpture Soc, 83. *Bibliog:* Ralph Fabri (auth), Sculpture, Today's Art, 3/70; Constantin Antonovici, Sculptor of Owls, Educ Res Coun Am, 75; Susan E Harrison (auth), article, Chronicle, Muskegon, Mich, 76; and others. *Mem:* Nat Soc Lit & Arts; fel Nat Sculpture Soc; Int Platform Assoc. *Media:* Marble, Bronze, Wood. *Mailing Add:* 310 W 106th St New York NY 10025

ANTREASIAN, GARO ZAREH
PAINTER, EDUCATOR
b Indianapolis, Ind, Feb 16, 22. *Study:* Herron Sch Art, BFA; studied with Stanley William Hayter & Will Barnet; Indiana/Purdue Univ, Indianapolis, Hon DFA, 72. *Work:* Metrop Mus Art, Mus Mod Art & Guggenheim Mus, New York; Art Inst Chicago; Los Angeles Co Mus Art, Calif. *Comn:* History of Indiana University, Bloomington, Ind, 54; Lincoln in Indiana (with Ralph Peck), Ind State Off Bldg, Indianapolis, 63. *Exhib:* Tamarind: Homage to Lithography, Mus Mod Art, New York, 69; Robischon Gallery, Denver, 84, 86 & 90; Pace Gallery, NY, 91; Albuquerque Mus, 91; Worcester Art Mus, 91; Rettig/Martinez Gallery, 81, 91 & 92; and others. *Collections Arranged:* John F Kensett: An American Master, Worcester Art Mus, 85. *Pos:* Tech dir lithography, Tamarind Lithography Workshop, Inc, Los Angeles, 60-61, Tamarind Inst, Univ NMex, 70-72. *Teaching:* Instr, Herron Sch Art, 48-64; prof art, Univ NMex, 64-87, chmn, Dept Art, 81-84. *Awards:* Purchase Awards, Nat Print Exhib, Northern Ill Univ, 68, State Univ NY Albany, 68 & 1st Hawaii Int, Honolulu Acad Arts, 71; Visual Artists Grant, Nat Endowment Arts, 82-83; Fulbright lectr, Brazil, 85. *Media:* Acrylic. *Publ:* Auth, The Tamarind Book of Lithography: Art & Techniques, 71. *Dealer:* Rettig/Martinez Gallery 901 W San Mateo Santa Fe NM 87501; Robischon Gallery 1340 Wazee Denver CO 80202. *Mailing Add:* 7711 Hermanson Place NE Albuquerque NM 87110

ANTRIM, CRAIG KEITH
PAINTER, DRAFTSMAN
b Pasadena, Calif, Sept 6, 42. *Study:* Univ Calif, Santa Barbara, BA, 65; Claremont Grad Sch, MFA, 70. *Work:* Mus Mod Art, New York; San Francisco Mus Mod Art; Corcoran Gallery Art, Washington, DC; Los Angeles County Mus Art, Calif. *Comn:* Float Light (canvas), Los Angeles County/Univ Southern Calif Med Credit Union, Los Angeles, 77; Painting, Fairmont Hotel, San Jose, Calif; Painting, Emerald Schaffer Ctr, San Diego, Calif; Los Angeles County Univ S Calif Med Credit Union, Los Angeles, Calif. *Exhib:* Solo exhibs, Calif State Univ, Bakersfield, 80, Monterey Peninsula Mus Art, Calif, 80, Laguna Beach Sch Art, Calif, 81, Saddleback Col, Mission Viejo, Calif, 81, Stella Polaris Gallery, Los Angeles, Calif, 83, 385 North, Los Angeles, Calif, 85, Ruth Bachofner Gallery, Santa Monica, Calif, 88 & Works Gallery, Costa Mesa, Calif, 92; California Artists, Art Space Newz, Tokyo, Japan, 84; Five Artists from Los Angeles, Dongsanbang Gallery, Seoul, Korea, 84; Pan Pacific Art Exhib, Fine Art Ctr, Seoul, Korea, 85; New Directions/Calif Painting 1985, Vis Arts Ctr Alaska, Anchorage, Fairbanks, Juneau; Concerning the Spiritual in Art: The Eighties, San Francisco Art Inst, 85; Spiritual in Art/Abstract Painting 1890-1985, Los Angeles County Mus Art, Calif, Mus Contemp Art, Chicago & Haags Gemeentemuseum, The Hague, Holland, 87; Sacred Symbols/New Visions, Riverside Art Mus, Calif, 89; John Thomas Gallery, Santa Monica, Calif, 91; Sanctuaries: Recovering the Holy in Contemporary Art, Mus Contemp Relig Art, St Louis Univ, Mo, 92. *Pos:* Studio Asst, Dockum Mobil-Color Proj System, Altadena, Calif, 68-70. *Teaching:* Instr, Univ Fla, Gainesville, 70-72; asst prof color & design, Scripps Col, Claremont, Calif, 74-76; instr painting & drawing, Univ S Cal, Los Angeles, 89-90, instr painting, 91; Instr painting & drawing, Harbor Col, Wilmington, Calif, 75-92; instr painting, drawing, design & art apprec, El Camino Col, Torrance, Calif, 74-92; instr adv painting workshop, Otis/Parsons Sch Art, Los Angeles, Calif, 86-92; vis artist/grad supv, Claremont Grad Sch, Claremont, Calif, 75-76, 88 & 92; vis asst prof painting & drawing, Loyola Marymount Univ, Los Angeles, Calif, 92-93. *Bibliog:* Edward Lucie-Smith (auth), American Art Now, Morrow Press, New York, 85; John Dillenberger (auth), The Visual Arts and Christianity in America, Crossroads, New York, 88; Edward Lucie-Smith (auth), Art in the Eighties, Phaidon, Oxford, Eng, 90; Nancy Ann Jones (auth), Eating the angels portion/Craig Antrim at Works, Artweek, Vol 21, No 4, p13, 90; Kinney Littlefield (auth), Meaningful mystery in spiritual objects, Long Beach

Press Telegram, 8/25/91; Mario Cutajar (auth), The slow growth alternative, Artweek, Vol 22, No 32, p17, 91. *Media:* Acrylic, Oil. *Publ:* Auth, Color Consciousness: Seven Los Angeles Artists (catalog), Lang Art Galleries, 78. *Dealer:* Ruth Bachofner Gallery 804 N La Cienega Blvd Los Angeles CA 90069. *Mailing Add:* 1129 N LaBrea Ave Inglewood CA 90302

ANUSZKIEWICZ, RICHARD JOSEPH
PAINTER
b Erie, Pa, May 23, 30. *Study:* Cleveland Inst Art, BFA, 53; Yale Univ, MFA, 55; Kent State Univ, BSEd, 56. *Work:* Corcoran Gallery Art, Washington, DC; Fogg Art Mus; Mus Mod Art, Guggenheim Mus, Metrop Mus Art & Whitney Mus Am Art, New York; Philadelphia Mus Art; Art Inst, Chicago; Albright Knox Gallery, Buffalo, NY; Smithsonian Inst Washington, DC. *Comn:* Mural, comn Univ Medicine & Dentistry, NJ, 85; Astral Squares, comn Neward Int Airport, NJ, 88; Chroma Avenue, NJ State Dept Transportation Bldg, Trenton, NJ, 89. *Exhib:* The Structure of Color, Whitney Mus Am Art, New York, 70; Whitney Mus Am Art, New York, 71; Richard Anuszkiewicz-Recent Paintings, Andrew Crispo Gallery, New York, 74 & 75; Hirshhorn Mus, Washington, DC, 74; Corcoran Biennial, Washington, DC, 75; Two Decades of Printmaking, Mus Mod Art, New York, 79; one-man exhibs, Brooklyn Mus, 80, Carnegie Inst, 80, Mus Fine Arts, St Petersburg, Fla, 81, Butler Inst Am Art, Youngstown, Ohio, 84, Graham Modern, New York, 84, Hokin-Kaufman Gallery, Chicago, 85 & 89, Richard Green Gallery, New York, 88, Newark Mus, NJ, 90 & ACA Gallery, NY, 90; 50th Anniversary Exhib, Guggenheim Mus, New York, 87; Vital Signs-Organic Abstraction, Whitney Mus Am Art, 88; Olympiad of Art, Seoul Olympics, Korea, 88; Made in Fla, Univ SFla Mus Col Fine Arts, Univ SFla, 89; Color in Art: American Expressions from Mid-Twentieth Century to the Present, Samuel P Harn Mus Art, Univ Fla, Gainesville, 90. *Teaching:* Artist-in-residence, Dartmouth Col, 67; instr, Univ Wis, 68, Cornell Univ, 68 & Kent State Univ, 68; instr grad painting, Sch Visual Arts, 83- *Awards:* Philosopher's Stone Prize, 63 & First Prize, 64, Silvermine Guild. *Bibliog:* Karl Lunde (auth), Anuskiewicz, Abrams, 77. *Mem:* Am Abstract Artists; Century Club. *Media:* All. *Mailing Add:* 76 Chestnut St Englewood NJ 07631

AOKI, CAROLE I
CERAMIST
Study: Univ Utah, Salt Lake City, 69-71; Calif Col Arts & Crafts, Oakland, BFA, 77. *Work:* Munic Anchorage Capital Projs, Performing Arts Ctr, Alaska; Everson Mus, Syracuse, NY; Upjohn, Kalamazoo, Mich; IBM, Raleigh, NC; Franklin Mint, Pa; numerous pvt & corp collections. *Exhib:* Solo shows, Joyce Petter Gallery, Sangatuck, Minn, 87, Andrea Schwartz Gallery, San Francisco, Calif, 89, Works Gallery, Philadelphia, Pa, 90 & Worth Gallery, Taos, NMex, 92; Schneider-Bluhm-Loeb, Chicago, Ill, 92; Cheltenham Ctr Arts, Pa, 92; Sybaris Gallery, Royal Oak, Mich, 92. *Pos:* Dir ceramic dept, Berkeley Parks & Recreation & Ctr Blind, Oakland, Calif, 72-74. *Teaching:* Lect/workshop, var art ctrs, art coun, univ & col, 85-89; instr ceramics, 92nd St Y, 90 & 91; guest lectr, Teacher's Col, Columbia Univ, 91. *Awards:* Ceramic Art Award, Calif Mus Art, Luther Burbank Ctr Arts, Santa Rosa, 89; Artist-in-residence, Lakeside Studio, Lakeside Group, Mich; Visual Arts Fel, Nat Endowment Arts, 90-91. *Bibliog:* Am Ceramics, Vol 9, No 1, spring 91; American Craft, Gallery, Vol 52, No 4, 8-9/92; Judy Rowland (auth), The Craftperson Speaks, Greenwood Press, 92. *Mailing Add:* 2231 Broadway New York NY 10024

APEL, BARBARA JEAN
PAINTER, EDUCATOR
b Falls City, Nebr, June 16, 35. *Study:* Kansas City Art Inst, BFA, 65; Univ Ill, MFA, 67. *Work:* Worcester Art Mus, Mass; Hood Mus Art, Dartmouth Col; Boston Pub Libr, Mass; Chemical Bank, New York; Mus Fine Arts, Boston. *Exhib:* Boston Printmakers' Ann Exhib, 68 & 74; NW Printmaker's Int Exhib, Seattle Art Mus, Wash, 68; Nat Print Exhib, State Univ NY Col at Potsdam, 68; New Am Monotypes Traveling Exhib, Smithsonian Inst, Washington, DC, 78-80; Contemp Am Monotypes, Impressions Gallery, Boston, 81; Bridgewater Col Invitational, 81; Art State, Decordova & Dana Mus, Lincoln, Mass. *Teaching:* Art Inst Boston, 67-81. *Awards:* Print Prizes, Boston Printmakers, 68 & 74; Semi-Finalist, Mass Artists Found, 77; MacDowell Fel, 79; Finalist, Mass Artists Found, 83. *Publ:* Contribr, Women Artists in America II, Univ Tenn, 75; The Art of Responsive Drawing, 3rd ed, Prentice-Hall, 83. *Dealer:* Impressions Gallery 415 W Broadway New York NY. *Mailing Add:* 235 Rawson Rd Brookline MA 02146

APGAR, JEAN E
PRINTMAKER
b Rockford, Ill, May 19, 49. *Study:* Northern Ill Univ, BA, 71, MA, 78. *Work:* Swed Am Hosp, Rockford, Ill. *Comn:* Rose Day (serigraph), Rockford Breakfast Lions, Ill, 80 & 92. *Exhib:* Images/4, Freeport Art Mus, Ill, 80; Rockford Int, Rockford Col, Ill, 81; All on Paper Nat, Columbia Green Col, Palenville, NY, 82; Nat Asn Women Artists Traveling Print Exhib, USA, 84-86; Nat Drawing Exhib, Bergen Community Mus, Paramus, NJ, 84; Naturally, Earth, Sea & Sky, Adelphi Univ, New York, 91. *Pos:* Chmn, special events, Beattie Is Festival, Rockford, Ill, 79-80; pres, Images/4, Rockford, Ill, 80-84; partner/publicist, Gallery Ten, Rockford, Ill, 90- *Teaching:* Instr drawing painting, Rock Valley Col, Rockford, Ill, 72- 79. *Mem:* Nat Asn Women Artists; Chicago Artists Coalition; Rockford Area Arts Coun; Wis Women Arts. *Media:* Serigraphy, Silkscreen. *Publ:* Art Calendar, 4/92. *Mailing Add:* 2513 Knight Ave Rockford IL 61101

APGAR, NICOLAS ADAM
PAINTER, EDUCATOR
b Gaillon, France, Dec 8, 18; US citizen. *Study:* Syracuse Univ, BFA, 58, MFA, 60; Univ Va, cert, 64; also with Louis Bouche, Fletcher Martin, Louis Bosa, Josef Albers & Jean Charlot. *Work:* Syracuse Univ, NY; Albany Inst Hist & Art, NY; Hyde Collection, Glens Falls, NY; Suksdorf Mem Collection, Hartwick Col, Oneonta, NY; also in private collections. *Exhib:* One-man shows, Skidmore Col, Saratoga Springs, 45, Albany Inst Hist & Art, NY, 50 & Randolph-Macon Woman's Col, Lynchburg, Va, 69; State Teachers Col, Albany, 58; Everson Mus Regional, Syracuse, 60. *Teaching:* Lectr anat, Syracuse Univ, 58-61; asst prof design & drawing, Richmond Prof Inst, 62-67; assoc prof design & drawing, Va Commonwealth Univ, 67-77, prof, 77- *Media:* Oil. *Publ:* Contribr, Interaction of color, 63; Search vs research, 71. *Mailing Add:* 2207 Buford Rd Richmond VA 23284

APP, TIMOTHY
PAINTER, EDUCATOR
b Akron, Ohio, July 5, 47. *Study:* Kent State Univ, BFA, 70; Tyler Sch Art, MFA, 74. *Work:* Univ NMex Art Mus, Albuquerque; Mus Albuquerque, NMex; Roswell Mus & Art Ctr, NMex; Mus Fine Arts, Santa Fe, NMex; Archer M Huntington Gallery, Univ Tex, Austin. *Exhib:* Geometric Formalism in Am Art, Univ NMex, 82; Phoenix Biennial, Phoenix Art Mus, 83; Linda Durham Gallery, 83, 85, 87 & 88 & 20-Year Survey, 89, Santa Fe, NMex; Roswell Mus, NMex, 85; Uncommon Spaces, Mus Albuquerque, NMex, 87; Residential Competition, Mus Fine Arts, Santa Fe, 88; Anthony Ralph Gallery, 88, 89 & 90; Archer M Huntington Gallery, Univ Tex, Austin, 88; Five New Painters, John Davis Gallery, New York, 88. *Teaching:* Asst prof painting, Pomona Col, 74-78; assoc prof, Univ NMex, Albuquerque, 78-; vis artist, Md Inst Col Art, 90-91. *Awards:* Mellon Grant, Pomona Col, 78; Univ NMex Res Grant, 82, 83, 87; Nat Endowment Arts Fel, 87-88. *Bibliog:* William Peterson (auth), Timothy App, Artspace, 82; Malin Wilson (auth), Two Views of Night, Artlines, 83; Peter Frank (auth), Reconstructive painting: Neo-modern abstraction in the United States, Artspace, 90. *Media:* Acrylic. *Dealer:* Jan Turner Gallery, Los Angeles. *Mailing Add:* c/o Anthony Ralph Gallery 43 E 78th St New York NY 10021

APPEL, ERIC A
SCULPTOR, PAINTER
b Brooklyn, NY, Dec 26, 45. *Study:* Pratt Inst, 63-67, BID, 67; Tyler Sch Art, Rome, 67-68; Tyler Sch Art, Temple Univ, Philadelphia, Pa, MFA(painting), 70. *Exhib:* Garden of Delight, Cooper-Hewitt Mus, New York, 81; Spring Garden, Yves Arman Gallery, New York, 81; solo exhibs, Winter Garden, Queens Mus, NY, 81, Joy Horwich Gallery, Chicago, Ill, 83, Field Mus Nat Hist & Chicago Sculpture Int Navy Pier, 83-84 & Windows on Broadway, NY Univ, 85, OK Harris, New York, 91. *Bibliog:* Beth Fallow (auth), Make yourself at home in the mansion gardens, Daily News, 7/24/81; Robin Brentano & Mark Savitt (auth), 112 Workshop, 112 Green St, NY Univ Press, 81. *Media:* Mixed. *Mailing Add:* 102 Christopher St New York NY 10014

APPEL, KAREL
PAINTER, SCULPTOR
b Amsterdam, Holland, Apr 25, 21. *Study:* Royal Acad Fine Arts, Amsterdam, 40-43. *Work:* Tate Gallery, London, Eng; Mus Mod Art, New York, NY; Stedelijk Mus, Amsterdam; Mus Fine Arts, Boston, Mass; Mus Nat Art Mod, Paris. *Comn:* Four relief murals (painted wood), State Bldg, Brabant, Neth, 71; tapestry, Rotterdam Trade Ctr, 71 & polycrome statue, 73; aluminum polychrome sculpture, City Univ Dijon, France, 76; silk tapestry, Student Ctr, State Univ NC, Raleigh, 78. *Exhib:* One-man exhibs, Palais des Beaux-Arts, Brussels, 53, Stedelijk Mus, Amsterdam, 55, 56 & 65, Inst Contemp Art, London, 57, travelling exhibs at mus in Calif, 61, Can & US, 72-73, Brasil, Colombia & Mex, 78-81, Palazzo di Medici, Florence, 85, Japan, 89 & Europe, 90-92; Works from the Peggy Guggenheim Foundation, Guggenheim Mus, New York, 69; Bonn Mus, Ger, 80; State Univ NY, Binghamton, 80; Bede Gallery, Jarrow, England, 80; FAME Gallery, Houston, Tex, 81; London Arts Gallery, Detroit, 81; also several retrospectives. *Awards:* Int Painting Prize, 5th Sao Paulo Biennale, 59; First Prize for Painting, Guggenheim Int Exhib, New York, 60; Guggenheim Int Prize, 61. *Bibliog:* Sir Herbert Read, W Sandberg & Hugo Claus (auth), Karel Appel: Painter, Abrams, 62; Michel Tapie (auth), Karel Appel, Le Grandi Monografie, Fratelli Fabbri Editori, Milano, 68; Simon Vinkenoog (auth), Appel's Oogappels & Het Verhaal van Karel Appel, Brunz & Zoon, Altrecht-Antwerpen, 70. *Media:* Oil, Acrylic; Wood. *Publ:* Illusr, Appel: A Beast-Drawn Man, 62; auth, Karel Appel over Karel Appel, Triton Press, Amsterdam, 71; Works on Paper, 80 & Street Art, 85, Abbeville; Karel Appel: The Early Years 1937-1957, Galilee, 88; Dupe of Being, 89 & Complete Sculptures 1936-1990, 90, Ed Lafayette. *Dealer:* Rodi Karkazis Gallery 168 N Michigan Suite 300 Chicago IL 60601. *Mailing Add:* 154 W 18 St Apt 5C New York NY 10011

APPEL, KEITH KENNETH
PAINTER, SCULPTOR
b Bricelyn, Minn, May 21, 34. *Study:* Mankato State Col, BA, BS & MS; Ohio State Univ. *Comn:* Sculpture, Alaska Art in Public Places, 81; sculpture, Anchorage C of C, 81; sculpture, Anchorage Art in Public Places; sculpture, Fairbanks Art in Public Places. *Exhib:* All Alaska Exhib, 64-80; Alaska Centennial, 67; one-man shows, 64, 65, 70, 74-81; Alaskan Smithsonian Exhib, 78. *Pos:* Chmn art dept, Univ Alaska, Anchorage, 78-81. *Teaching:* Assoc prof art, Univ Alaska, Anchorage, 70-78; retired. *Awards:* Alaska Centennial, 67; All Alaska Juried Exhibition Awards, var times, 67-77. *Mem:* Alaska Artists Guild; Alaska State Arts Coun (mem bd); Nat Art Educ Asn. *Media:* Miscellaneous. *Mailing Add:* 4705 Malibu Dr Anchorage AK 99517

APPEL, THELMA
PAINTER, INSTRUCTOR
b Tel Aviv, Israel, Jan 6, 40; US citizen. *Study:* St Martins Sch Art, London, dipl art & design, 61; Hornsey Col Art, London, art teacher's dipl, 62. *Work:* Milwaukee Arts Ctr, Wis; Am Tel & Tel Co, New York & Summit, NJ; Chase-Manhattan Bank & Metrop Life Co, New York; Vt State Legislature, Montpelier; Port Authority, NY; IBM Corp, Lawrence, NJ; Bank of Toyko, New York, NY; Xerox Corp, New York, NY; Cabot Corp, Boston, Mass; Hale & Dore Assocs, Boston; Prudential Collection, New York. *Comn:* Five paintings, Western Corp Bldg, Dallas, Tex, 80; two paintings, Hospital Insurance Co, Grand Prairie, Tex, 85; two paintings, Farm Credit Bank, Austin, Tex, 85. *Exhib:* solo shows Adelle M Gallery Fine Art, Dallas, Tex, Fischbach Gallery, New York, 79, 82 & Weschester Co Ctr, White Plains, NY, 92; Realism Today, Clary Miner Gallery, Buffalo, NY, 87; Int Art Competition, Pyramid Gallery, New York, 90; Current River View, Hastings Creative Arts Coun, NY, 91; Neighbors, Krasdale Foods Art Gallery in conjunction with Lehman Col Art Gallery, 92; and others. *Teaching:* Instr, Southern Vermont Col, 75-76; instr, Parsons Sch Art, 76-77; Summer Painting Workshop, Bennington Col, 76-83; Northern Westchester Ctr Arts, 89-; Putnam Arts Coun, 90- *Awards:* Vt Coun Arts Award, 73; Yaddo Residency fel, 74; State of Vt Purchase Award, Vt Coun Arts & Nat Endowment Arts, 78. *Bibliog:* M Andre (auth), Art In America, 11/75; E Lubell (auth), Arts Mag, 75; Gabrielle V Arnhem (auth), American Romantic Painting, Art Ger, 80; Sunday Times (Westchester Sect), 10/4/92. *Mem:* Women's Caucus Arts; NY Artists Equity Asn. *Media:* Oil, Acrylic. *Mailing Add:* 3586 Gomer St Yorktown Heights NY 10598

APPELHOF, DR RUTH A
CURATOR, HISTORIAN
b Washington, DC, Feb 14, 45. *Study:* Syracuse Univ, BFA (painting & art hist), 65, MFA (art hist), 75; PhD, 88. *Collections Arranged:* Outside New York City: From Drawing to Sculpture (auth, catalog), 82; Margaret Bourke-White: The Humanitarian Vision (auth, catalog), Syracuse Univ, 83; The New Figure, Birmingham Mus, 85; The Expressionist Landscape, Birmingham Mus, Ala, 87 & Looking South, 88; The Common Wealth: Twentieth Century American Masterpieces, Va Collections, 90; and others. *Pos:* Lectr, Whitney Mus Am Art, 80-; cur exhib, Syracuse Univ, 81-85; cur paintings & sculpture, Birmingham Mus, 84-89; exec dir, Art Mus Western, Va, 89- *Teaching:* Assoc prof art, Cayuga Co Community Col, 74-79, gallery dir, 78-79; asst prof museology, Syracuse Univ, 81-85; adj prof, Univ Ala, Birmingham, 85. *Mem:* Col Art Asn; Women's Caucus Art; Nat Women's Studies Asn; Women in the Arts; Asn Am Mus. *Res:* Modern and contemporary women in art; iconography and historical context. *Publ:* Auth, Beth Ames Schwartz: Israel Revisted, Whitney Mus, 81; auth, Recent Developments in Landscape Painting, Whitney Mus, 81; auth, Nature as Image and Metaphor, Women's Caucus Arts, 82; The Expressionist Landscape, 87 & Looking South, 88. *Mailing Add:* 4952 Hunting Hills Circle Roanoke VA 24014

APPELSON, HERBERT J
EDUCATOR, PRINTMAKER
b Brooklyn, NY, Dec, 31, 37. *Study:* Brooklyn Col, NY, BA, 59; Univ Wis, Madison, MS, 60, MFA, 61; Columbia Univ, New York, EDD, 72. *Work:* Noyes Mus, Oceanville, NJ; Auburn Univ, Ala; Kans State Univ, Manhattan; Columbia Univ, New York; Fairmount Inst, Philadelphia, Pa. *Exhib:* Celebration of NJ Artists, Noyes Mus, Oceanville, 83; solo exhib, ETS Conant Gallery, Princeton, 85; New Jersey Arts Ann, Noyes Mus, 86; Art Ann, Woodmere Art Mus, Philadelphia, Pa, 86; Abstraction in Art, Philadelphia Sketch Club, Pa, 87; Philadelphia Watercolor Club, Port Hist Mus, Pa, 88; Ellarslie Open, Trenton City Mus, NJ, 88; Am Color Print Soc Members' Exhib, Port of Hist Mus, Philadelphia, 88. *Collections Arranged:* Images of Southern New Jersey from the Heartland to the Seashore (with catalog), Hollybush Invitation Art Exhib, 86; American Artists/Russian Roots (with catalog), Hollybush Arts Festival, 87; Light-Chemistry and a Creative Vision (with catalog), Hollybush Arts Festival, 88; Forms to Figure (with catalog), Hollybush Arts Festival, 89; Abstract Art, Intuition-Invention-Expressionism (with catalog), Hollybush Arts Festival, 90. *Teaching:* Prof printmaking & drawing, Glassboro State Col, NJ, 67- *Awards:* Thornton Oakley Mem Prize, Philadelphia Water Color Club, 89; Pres Prize Excellence, Southern NJ Advocates for the Arts Ann Exhib. *Bibliog:* Burton Wasserman (auth), Exploring the visual arts, Davis, Worchester, Mass, 76. *Mem:* Philadelphia Watercolor Club; Am Color Print Soc; Cheltenham Graphics Guild; Am Color Print Soc. *Mailing Add:* 17 Highgate Lane Cherry Hill NJ 08003

APPLE, JACKI (JACQUELINE B)
MEDIA AND PERFORMANCE ARTIST, WRITER
b New York, NY. *Study:* Syracuse Univ; Parsons Sch Design. *Comn:* Last Rites After Angkor Wat (radio play), Mus Contemp Art, Los Angeles, 84; Urban Suite (soundtrack), Rudy Perez Performance Ensemble, Los Angeles, 84; Swan Lake (a film noir "ballet" for radio), New Am Radio, 88-89; Palisade 1987, Fluctuations of the Field (performance), Santa Monica Arts Comn, 89; Redefining Democracy in America, Parts 1-5 (radio art), New Am Radio, New York, 91, 92. *Exhib:* Story Art: Recent American Narrative Traveling Exhib, Contemp Arts Mus, Houston, 77-78; Mus Mod Art, New York, 78; Schemes: A Decade of Installation Drawings Traveling Exhib, Elise Meyer Gallery, New York, 81-82; Sydney Biennale, Australia, 82; Live to Air, Tate Gallery, London, 82; Sonorita Prospettiche Traveling Exhib, Contemp Art Gallery, Rimini, Italy, 82-83; Whitney Mus Philip Morris, New York, 90. *Collections Arranged:* Visual and Sculptural Bookworks, Montclair Mus, NJ & Seibu Mus, Tokyo, 79; Artists Bookworks: Alterations and Transformations, Nelson Gallery, Kansas City, Mo, 80; Alternatives in Retrospect: An Historical Overview 1969-1975, New Mus, New York, 81; Art Lobby, Lower Manhattan Cult Coun, New York, 82. *Pos:* Cur exhibs & performances, Franklin Furnace, 77-80; guest cur, New Mus, New York, 81; producer/host, KPFK-FM, Pacifica Radio, Los Angeles, 82-; freelance writer, 82-; contrib ed, Artweek, 83-90; contribr ed, Los Angeles Wkly, 85-89, High Performance Mag, 84- & Media Arts, 83-90; producer/writer, US EAR, 87-88. *Teaching:* Instr, Concordia Univ, Montreal, fall 80, Calif State Univ, Long Beach, spring 83, Art Ctr Col Design, Pasadena, 83- & Otis Art Inst, Los Angeles, 84-85, 90. *Awards:* Individual Artist Fel, Nat Endowment Arts, 79 & 81, Inter Arts Prog Grant, 84, 91; NY State Coun Arts Grant, Creative Artists Pub Serv, 81; Individual Artist Grant, Dept of Cult Affairs, Los Angeles, 90; Vesta Award, Los Angeles, 90. *Bibliog:* Steven Durland (auth), Sound Philosophies: The audio art of Jacki Apple, High Performance, 84; Douglas Sadownick (auth), Palisade: exploring love as a high art form, Los Angeles Times, 7/28/87; Colin Gardner (auth), Colonialism and postmodernism, Artweek, 9/7/85; and others. *Mem:* Int Asn Art Critics; Nat Writers Union; Cactus Found. *Media:* Audio, Radio; Performance Installation. *Publ:* Auth, Performance in the 80's: the TV generation, High Performance Mag, No 26, 84; Commerce on the edge: the convergence of art and entertainment, High Performance Mag, No 34, 86; Doing It Right in LA-Self-Producing for the Performing Artist, Astro Artz/Fringe Festival, Los Angeles, 90; The Life & Times of Lin Hixson: The LA Years, Drama Rev, winter 91; Voices in the Dark (CD) Aerial, 92; and others. *Dealer:* New American Radio 284 Eastern Parkway Brooklyn NY 11225. *Mailing Add:* 3827 Mentone Ave Culver City CA 90232

APPLEBROOG, IDA
PAINTER
b Bronx, NY, Nov 11, 29. *Study:* NY State Inst Appl Arts & Sci, 48-50; Art Inst Chicago, 65-68. *Work:* Metrop Mus Art, Mus Mod Art, New Mus Contemp Art, Guggenheim Mus, New York; Denver Mus Art; Sol Lewitt Collection, Wadsworth Atheneum, Hartford, Conn. *Exhib:* Solo exhibs, Whitney Mus Am Art, New York, 78, Chrysler Mus, Norfolk, Va, Ronald Feldman Gallery, New York, 87, 89 & 91, Contemp Arts Mus, Houston, Tex, 90, Kunsthallen Brandts Klaedefabrik, Odense, Denmark, 92 & Realistmus Studio, Berlin, Ger, 92; Directions '83, Hirshhorn Mus, Washington, DC, 83; 23 Nat Print Exhib, Brooklyn, 83; Mus Mod Art, New York, 84; Documenta 8, Kassel, Ger, 87; Los Angeles Co Mus Art, Calif, 92; Jersey City Mus, NJ, 92; PS 1 Mus, Long Island City, NY, 92. *Teaching:* Asst painting, Art Inst Chicago, 62-66; instr painting & sculpture, Univ Calif, San Diego, 73-74. *Awards:* Nat Endowment Arts Grants, 80 & 85; Grant, NY Found Arts, 86 & 90; Guggenheim Fel, 90. *Bibliog:* John Ashbery (auth), article, Newsweek, 4/18/83; Elizabeth Hess (auth), article, Village Voice, 11/7/89; Ruth Bass (auth), article, Art News, 5/88; Mira Schor (auth), article, Artforum, 3/90; Robert Storr, Ida Applebroog, Ulmer Mus, Ger, 91; Gertrud Astrom & Yvonne Nirdman (auths), Kontraks Ikris, Carlssons, P 201-213, 92. *Media:* Oil on Canvas. *Publ:* Auth, The I am Heathcliffe, says Catherine, syndrome: Women's humor, Heresies, 5/77. *Dealer:* Ronald Feldman Fine Arts New York NY 10012. *Mailing Add:* 491 Broadway New York NY 10012

APPLEBY, DANIEL BART
FILMMAKER
b St Paul, Minn, Oct 28, 54. *Study:* Simpson Col, Indianoloa, Iowa, 72-74; Minneapolis Col Art & Design, BFA(Magna Cum Laude), 77; studied with Tim McBride, 88. *Exhib:* The Antennae Project, Ordway Theater, St Paul, Minn, 82; Conversations, High Hope Media Festival, Seattle, Wash, 84, San Francisco Poetry Film Festival, 84, New York Film Festival, New York, 84 & Athens Int Film & Video Festival, 85; The Larger Picture, Smithsonian Inst, Washington, DC, 86 & The Other Theater, New York, 86; 20th Ann Filmmaker's Expos, Metrop Mus Art, New York, 86. *Awards:* Nat Endowment Arts Fel, 84, 86 & 87; Promising New Dir Award, Am Film Inst, Los Angeles, 87. *Publ:* Coauth, co-produced (with Bruce Carlson) & directed, Ryman, 79, Ability to Kill, 82 & Some Girls, 89; coauth, directed & co-produced, Conversations, 84; coauth & directed, The Larger Picture, 86; auth, dir & coproduced, meantime a feature length Black comedy, 90-92. *Mailing Add:* 13 1/2 NE Fifth St Minneapolis MN 55413

APPLEMAN, DAVID EARL
DESIGNER, PAINTER
b Mansfield, Ohio, May 9, 43. *Study:* Bob Jones Univ, BA & MA. *Work:* Bernhardt Industs; Westinghouse Corp; Pee Dee SC State Bank; SC State Art Comn Collection; Sunoco Oil Corp. *Comn:* Polymer painting, First Fed Bank, Greenville, SC, 73. *Exhib:* Massilon Mus Art, Ohio, 70; Hunter Mus Art Ann, Chattanooga, Tenn, 74; Guild SC Artists, Gibbes Gallery, Charleston, 74; State Col Ark, Conway, 75; Mid-S, Parthenon Mus, Nashville, Tenn, 75; Piedmont Painting & Sculpture Exhib, Mint Mus, Charlotte, NC, 77; Greenville Artists Guild, Greenville Mus, SC, 77; Hampton III Gallery, Greenville, SC. *Pos:* Art dir, Bob Jones Univ Media Mgt, 68- *Teaching:* Prof commun art, Bob Jones Univ, Greenville, SC, 68- *Awards:* Top Award, Mansfield Guild, Mansfield Mus, 69; Purchase Awards, 16th Guild of SC Artists, Gibbes, Greenville & Florence Mus, 72 & Appalachian Corridors, Charleston Gallery of Sunrise, 74. *Mem:* Guild SC Artists (mem bd adv, 75, treas, 81); Greenville Artists Guild; Greenville Art Asn. *Media:* Polymer; Collograph. *Mailing Add:* 111Carmel St Greenville SC 29614

APT, CHARLES
PAINTER
b New York, NY, Dec 10, 33. *Study:* Pratt Inst, BFA, 56. *Work:* Chem Bank; Bowery Bank; Celanese Corp; Paine, Webber, Jackson & Curtis, New York; Principality of Monaco, France. *Comn:* Painting, Am Stock Exchange, 68. *Exhib:* Allied Artists Am, New York, 64, 65, 67 & 69; Am Watercolor Soc,

New York, 65, 66, 68 & 69; Nat Acad Design, New York, 65, 68, 73-81, 83, 85 & 87; Exposition Intercontinentale, Monaco, France, 66 & 68; Nat Mus Racing Ann, Saratoga, NY, 67; One-man shows, Loring Gallery, Cederhurst, NY, 85, 87 & 92; and many others. *Teaching:* Instr painting & drawing, Nat Acad Design, 77-81 & Art Students League. *Awards:* Best in Show, Saratoga Mus Racing, 67; 2nd Benjamin Altman Award, Nat Acad Design, 68; Le Prix Prince Souverain, Prince Rainier, Monaco, 68. *Bibliog:* Joan Hess Michael (auth), Charles Apt in Portugal, Am Artist Mag, 4/70; Leonard Kriegel (auth), Charles Apt, Arts Mag, 10/78. *Mem:* Nat Acad Design (academician); Artists Equity Asn New York. *Media:* Oil, Pastel, Watercolor. *Publ:* Auth, article, House Beautiful, Hearst Publ, 2/85. *Dealer:* Talisman Gallery Bartlesville OK; Loring Art Gallery Cedarhurst NY. *Mailing Add:* No 19 St Raphael Laguna Niguel CA 92677

APTEKAR, KEN
PAINTER
b Detroit, Mich, May 13, 50. *Study:* Univ Mich, BFA, 73, Pratt Inst, MFA, 75. *Work:* Niagara Univ, Buffalo, NY; Denver Mus Art; Progressive Corp; Jewish Mus, NY; Bell Atlantic Corp, Philadelphia. *Comn:* Conrad Hilton, Hong Kong. *Exhib:* The Other Man, New Mus, New York, 87; Gender Fictions, Binghamton Art Mus, 89; Serious Fun, Truthful Lies, Randolph St Gallery, Chicago, 89; Critical Revisions, Bess Cutler Gallery, New York, 90; Post-Boys & Girls: Nine Painters, Artists Space, New York, 90; New Generation: New York, Carnegie-Mellon Univ Mus, Pittsburg, Pa, 91. *Awards:* Fel, Nat Endowment Arts, 87; Pollock-Krasner, 89; Rockefeller Found, Bellagio Residency, 92. *Bibliog:* Gerrit Henry (auth), Art in Am, 6/90; Robert Atkins (auth), Seven Days, 12/90; James Saslow (auth), The Advocate, 5/90. *Mailing Add:* 201 W 85th St No 7E New York NY 10024

AQUINO, EDMUNDO
PAINTER, PRINTMAKER
b Zimatlan Oaxaca, Mex, June 30, 39. *Study:* Nat Sch Plastics Art, Nat Univ Mex, cert(teacher fine arts), 62; Ecole Nat Superieure Beaux-Arts, Paris, Fr Govt Scholar, 67-69; Slade Sch Fine Arts, London, Brit Coun Scholar, 69. *Work:* Nat Libr Paris; Univ Mass Collection; Mus Mod Art Latin Am, Washington, DC; Nat Inst Fine Arts, Mexico City, Mex; AGPA (Panamerican Graphic Art), Mus Mod Art, New York; and others. *Exhib:* Mus Mod Art, Mexico City, 77-78; Biennial of Sao Paulo, Brazil, 79; Picasso Mus, Antibes, France, 80; Mex Mus, San Francisco, Calif, 80; Contemporary Latin American Art and Japan, Nat Mus Art, Osaka, 81; and others. *Teaching:* Instr drawing & painting & head plastic arts sect, Sch Fine Arts, Oaxaca, Mex, 64-67. *Awards:* First Prize Painting & Drawing, Hotel Monnaie, Paris, 69; Nat Prize, 6th Int Festival Painting, Cagnes-Sur-Mer, France, 74; Third Prize, First Iberoamerican Biennial of Painting, Mexico City, 78; DAAD Fel, Artists in Berlin Prog, West Berlin, 86. *Bibliog:* Jorge J Crespo de la Serna (auth), article in Noredades, Mexico City, 3/75; Mariana Frenk-Westheim (auth), article in Unomasuno, Mexico City, 11/83; Antonio Rodriguez (auth), article in Excelsior, Mexico City, 7/88. *Media:* All. *Mailing Add:* Calle Ave Maria 60-1 Coyoacan 04000 Mexico DF Mexico

AQUINO, HUMBERTO
PAINTER
b Lima, Peru, Oct 20, 47. *Study:* Nat Sch Fine Arts Lima, Peru, with Alberto Davila, 70; Cardiff Col Art, Wales, Great Britain, 73; Pratt Inst, Brooklyn, NY, 78. *Work:* Smithsonian Inst, Washington, DC; Art Inst Chicago, Ill; Univ Tex Art Mus, Austin; Mus Mod Art Latin Am, Washington, DC; Biblioteca Lvis Angel Arango, Bogota, Columbia. *Exhib:* Latin Am Drawings, Indianapolis Mus Art, 76; Drawings of the 70's, Art Inst Chicago, 77; one-man show, Mus Mod Art Latin Am, Washington, DC, 78; Latin Am Artists in NY Since 1970, Univ Tex Art Mus, 87; Latin American Drawings Today, San Diego Mus Art, Calif, 4/91. *Pos:* Lectr, Soc of the Americas, NY, 85, Mus of the City of NY, 86. *Awards:* Fulbright Fel, 77; Artist's Fel, NY Found Arts, 85; Mid-Atlantic Regional, Nat Endowment Arts, 88. *Bibliog:* Sebastian Dominguez (auth), Six Artists Working in New York, Visiones - NBC Television, Channel 4, 5/87; Jacqueline Barnitz (auth), Latin Am Artists in New York, Archer M Huntington Art Gallery, 9/87; Framing the Past: essays on art education, Nat Art Educ Asn, 90. *Media:* Oils, Mixed Media. *Dealer:* Odon Wagner 194 Daveport Rd Toronto ON M5R 1J2. *Mailing Add:* 335 E 58th St 4F New York NY 10022

ARAKAWA, (SHUSAKU)
PAINTER
b Japan, July 6, 36. *Work:* Mus Mod Art, New York; Basel Mus, Switz; Walker Art Ctr, Minneapolis; Japan Nat Mus, Tokyo; Metrop Mus Art, New York; Solomon R Guggenheim Mus, New York; Seibu Mus, Tokyo. *Exhib:* One-person shows, Henie Onstad Mus, Oslo, Norway, 75, Stadisch Kunsthalle, Dusseldorf, Ger, 77, Minneapolis Inst Arts, Minn, 79, Wadsworth Atheneum, Hartford, Conn, 83, Aldrich Mus Contemp Art, Ridgefield, Conn, 84, Seibu Mus, Tokyo, 87 & Process in Question, Williams Col Mus, Touko Mus Contemp Art, Joseloff Gallery, Univ Hartford, Conn, 89 & 90; Painting & Sculpture Today, Indianapolis Mus Art, Ind & Cincinnati Contemp Arts Ctr, Ohio, 74; Wallraf-Richartz Mus, Cologne, WGer, 74; Kennedy Ctr for Performing Arts, Washington, DC, 74; Nat Mus Mod Art, Tokyo, 91; Nat Mus Kyoto, 92; and others. *Awards:* DAAD Fel, WBerlin, 72; Fel, John Simon Guggenheim, 87-88. *Bibliog:* L Alloway (auth), Introduction to the mechanism of meaning, Bruckman Verlag, 71; N & E Calas (auth), Images & Icons, Dutton, 71; Italo Calvino (auth), The arrow in the mind, Artforum, 9/85 & Blank Arakawa, reprint & interview with Madeline Gins, El Paseante, No 7, 88; Jean Francoise Lyotard (auth), Quebeindre, Paris, Editions de la Difference, 88. *Publ:* Coauth, The Mechanism of Meaning, 71; Coauth (with Madeline Gins), To Not To Die, Editions de la Différence, 87; Persons as Site in Respect to a Tentative Constructed Plan, Anywhere J, fall 92. *Dealer:* Ronald Feldman Fine Arts Inc 31 Mercer St New York NY 10013. *Mailing Add:* 124 W Houston St New York NY 10012

ARBITMAN, KAHREN J
CURATOR, HISTORIAN
b Pittsburgh, Pa, May 16, 48. *Study:* Penn State Univ, BA, 69; Univ Pittsburgh, MA, 71; PhD, 80. *Collections Arranged:* Rembrandt Etchings from the Charles J Rosenbloom Collection, 83; Pre-Rembrandt Etchers from the Boymans-van Beuningen Mus, 85; An Englishman Abroad: Watercolors of Edward Lear, 86; Gardens of Earthly Delight: 16th and 17th Century Netherlandish Gardens, 86; At Home in Pittsburgh: Art and Furnishings of Henry Clay Frick, 88. *Pos:* Cur, Frick Art Mus, 85- *Teaching:* Asst prof art history, West Va Univ, Morgantown, 84-5; adjunct assoc prof art history, Univ Pittsburgh, 85-; vis prof art history, Carnegie Mellon Univ, Pittsburgh, 89- *Mem:* Historians of Netherlandish Art (board of dir, 85-88); Am Assoc Netherlandish Studies; Am Assoc Mus; Col Art Assoc. *Res:* 16th and 17th century Netherlandish Art and Iconography. *Publ:* auth, From These Slopes & Flats: The Paintings of Lee Dittley, PA Council on Humanities, 76; contribr, Landscape Painting in Rome, 1595-1675, Richard Feigen & Co, 85; co-auth, Pre-Rembrandt Etchers (illustrated Bartsch Vol 53) Abaris Books, 85; auth, Gardens of Earthly Delight; co-auth, Clayton, The Pittsburgh Home of Henry Clay Frick, Univ Pittsburgh Press, 88. *Mailing Add:* c/o Pennsylvania State University Palmer Museum of Art University Park PA 16802-2507

ARCHAMBAULT, LOUIS
SCULPTOR
b Montreal, Que, Can, Apr 4, 15. *Study:* Univ Montreal, BA; Ecole des Beaux-Arts de Montreal, dipl ceramics. *Work:* Nat Gallery Can, Ottawa; Art Gallery Ont, Toronto; Mus Prov Quebec; Mus Int Della Ceramica, Faenza, Italy; Can Imperial Bank Com, Montreal; and others. *Comn:* Mural sculpture, Place de Arts, Montreal, 63; aluminum sculpture, Toronto Airport, 64; 12 steel sculptures, Can Pavilion, Montreal's Expos, 67; bronze sculpture, Queens's Park, Toronto, 70; aluminum structural sculpture, Palais Justice Quebec, 83; and others. *Exhib:* 28th Venice Biennale, 56; Pittsburgh Int, 58; Int Exhib Contemp Sculpture, Expo 67, Montreal, 67; 11th Middelheim Biennale, 71; 10th Int Sculpture Conf, Toronto, 78; and others. *Awards:* Can Gov & Can Coun Fels, 53, 59, 62 & 69; Serv Medal, Order Can, 68; Awards, Ministere de l'Education, Que, 70-72; Diplome d'honneur, Can Conf of the Arts. *Bibliog:* Bill Stephenson (auth), Louis Archambault's wonderful wall, MacLean's, Can, 1/18/58; Guy Robert (auth), Archambault, Vie des Arts, summer 72; Luc Epivent (auth), Vie Arts, Montreal, spring 81. *Mem:* Academician Royal Can Acad Arts. *Media:* Multimedia. *Mailing Add:* 278 Sanford Ave St Lambert PQ J4P 2X6 Canada

ARCHER, CYNTHIA
PRINTMAKER, PAINTER
b New Martinsville, WVa, Mar 28, 53. *Study:* Goucher Col, BA, 75; WVa Univ, MFA, 78. *Work:* Nat Art Gallery, Wellington, New Zealand; Portland Art Mus, Ore; Ill State Mus, Springfield; MacDonald's Corp Hq, Oakbrook, Ill; Danforth Mus, Framingham, Mass. *Comn:* Foyer installation, Pepsi-Cola Corp, Itasca, Ill; Chicago Pub Libr, Westlawn Br; Color Lithograph Editions, Lakeside Studio, Lakeside, Mich; edition of hand-painted ceramic plates, Jane Meyer Fine Art, Eiburn, Ill, 92. *Exhib:* Chicago Int Art Expo, 87-88; solo exhibs, Malton Gallery, Cincinnati, Ohio, 87 & 90 & Marcus Gordon Gallery, Pittsburgh, 91; Provenance Inc, Chicago & Kenilworth, Ill, 91-92; New Acquisitions, Col Lake Co, Grayslake, Ill, 92; Open Spectrum, David Adler Cult Ctr, Libertyville, Ill, 92; and others. *Pos:* Workshop S, Lakeside Studios, Mich, 77-79; Master lithographer, Plucked Chicken Press, Chicago, 78-; workshops, Shepherd Col, Shepherdstow, WV, 78; vis artist, Southern Ill Univ, Edwardsville, Ill, 84 & Univ Nevada, Reno, 87. *Teaching:* Forum in printmaking, Bradley Univ, Peoria, Ill, 87. *Awards:* Purchase Award, Huntington Art Galleries, Huntington, WVa, 77; Governor's Award, WVa Exhib, Charleston, 79; Merit Award, 6th Baer Art Competition, Beverly Art Ctr, Chicago, 82. *Bibliog:* Contemporary Chicago Lithography, Exhib Catalog Reproduction, Ill State Mus, 83; Bruce Ingram (auth), Diversions: College Gallery Reaps Donation Bonanza, Pioneer Press, 92. *Media:* Lithography; Acrylic. *Dealer:* Provenance Inc 1225 Greenwood Evanston IL 60201; Jane Meyer Fine Arts 3 N 692 Highpoint Elburn IL 60119. *Mailing Add:* 1604 Greenleaf Evanston IL 60202

ARCILESI, VINCENT J
PAINTER, DRAFTSMAN
b St Louis, Mo, May 5, 32. *Study:* Furman Univ, 49-50; Univ Okla, BFA(design), 53; Art Inst Chicago, BFA(painting), 56, MFA, 61. *Work:* Art Inst Chicago Mus; Ill State Mus, Springfield; Fashion Inst of Technol, New York; Hirshhorn Collection; Kemper Ins, Long Grove, Ill; plus pvt collections. *Exhib:* 70th Ann, Art Inst Chicago, 67; Visions/Painting & Sculpture, Distinguished Alumni 1945-Present, Art Inst Chicago Gallery, 76; one-man shows, Westbroadway Gallery, 73-75 & 77, Noho Gallery, New York, 81, 85 & 88 & Z Gallery, New York, 91; America 1976 Traveling Exhib, Corcoran Gallery, 76-78; The First Eight Years, Artists Choice Mus, New York, 84; Contemporary Nudes, One Penn Plaza, New York, 88; New Art, F I T Galleries, New York, 90; Vincent Arcilesi & Don Perlis, Garrison Art Ctr, New York, 91; Contemporary Realism, Farrington-Keith Creative Arts Ctr, Dexter, Mich, 92; and others. *Teaching:* Asst prof art, Fash Inst Tech, New York, 74- *Awards:* American 1976 Grant, US Dept Interior, Washington, DC, 74-75; Creative Artists Pub Serv Prog Fel, 81-82; Nat Endowment Arts Grant, 82. *Bibliog:* Hilton Kramer (auth), Art: five gallery realist show, New York Times, 9/12/80; Frank H Goodyear Jr (auth), Contemporary American Realism Since 1960, New York Graphic Soc, 81; Pat Van Gelder (auth), Vincent Arcilesi, Am Artist, 10/83; John Arthur (auth), Spirit of Place, Contemporary Landscape Painting & the American Tradition, Bulfinch Press, Little Brown & Co, 89. *Mem:* NY Artists' Equity, (bd dirs, 86-90); Orgn Independent Artists. *Media:* Oil, Pastel. *Mailing Add:* 116 Duane St New York NY 10007

ARCOMANO, CATHRYN
PAINTER
US citizen. *Study:* New Sch Art Workshops. *Work:* Brooklyn Mus, New York; Everson Mus Art, Syracuse, NY; Heckscher Mus, Huntington, NY; Newark Mus, NJ; Snite Mus Art, Univ Notre Dame. *Exhib:* Contemporary Reflections 1977-78, Aldrich Mus Contemp Art, Ridgefield, Conn, 78; Mid-America Exhib, Owensboro Mus Fine Art, Owensboro, Ky, 80; New Eng Exhib Painting, Drawing & Sculpture, Silvermine, Conn, 81; Mod Drawings from Permanent Col, Snite Mus Art, Univ Notre Dame, Ind, 83; solo exhibs, Arnot Art Mus, Elmira, NY, 83 & Chastein Gallery, Atlanta, Ga, 84; 21st Biennial Art Exhib, Univ Gallery/Mus Studies, Univ Delaware, Newark, Del, 84; Everson Biennial, Everson Mus Art, Syracuse, NY, 86; two-person exhib, Alvin Gallery & Gallery Ninety-Seven, Hong Kong, 88. *Awards:* Gertrude Romm Levy Award, New Sch Soc Res, 74; First Award, Painters & Sculptors Soc NJ Ann Exhib, 78; Olaf Oloffson Mem Award, Painters & Sculptors Soc NJ Ann Exhib, 83. *Dealer:* David Adamson Gallery 406 Seventh St NW Washington DC 20004. *Mailing Add:* 160 Riverside Dr New York NY 10024

ARD, SARADELL (SARADELL ARD FREDERICK)
EDUCATOR, PAINTER
b Macon, Ga, Mar 22, 20. *Study:* Asbury Col, AB(art), 42; Univ Mich, MA, 43; Columbia Univ Teachers Col, DEd(art), 70. *Work:* Univ Ill, Edwardsville; Alaska State Mus, Juneau; Alaska Methodist Univ Collection Alaskan Artists, Univ Alaska & Anchorage Mus Hist & Art, Anchorage. *Exhib:* Solo exhibs, Teachers Col Galleries, Columbia Univ, New York, 68 & 70, Alaska State Mus, Juneau, 72 & Anchorage Mus Hist & Art, 76 & 84; Contemporary Alaskan Art, Smithsonian Inst, Washington, DC, 78; Univ Alaska Campus Ctr Gallery, Anchorage, 78-83; Alaskaland Gallery, Fairbanks, 83; and others. *Collections Arranged:* 20th Century Alaska Eskimo Art (with catalog), Smithsonian Inst, 82. *Pos:* Dir arts & crafts prog, European Theatre, US Army, 60-62; vchmn bd dirs, Visual Arts Ctr, Anchorage, 73-76; mem bd dirs, Mayor's Comt, Fine Arts Mus, Anchorage, 73-82. *Teaching:* Prof art, Alaska Methodist Univ, 62-73; prof art, Univ Alaska, Anchorage, 73-85, actg dean, 76-77, prof art emer, 85- *Awards:* Juror's Choice, Ann All Alaska Art Exhib, 66 & 1st Award Drawing, 67; Gov's Award, 80. *Mem:* Nat Art Educ Asn; Col Art Asn; Anchorage Mus Asn (pres, 81-82). *Media:* Oil, Acrylic. *Res:* Eskimo art of the Arctic Circle. *Publ:* Auth, Alaskan Eskimo Art Today, 72 & Inuit Sculpture, summer 80, Alaska J; Native Alaskan Art Today, Am Illus, 76; Roots in the past, Smithsonian Inst Press, 82; Schitz-und gravierkunst der Alaska-Eskimo in geschichte und gegenwart, In: Inuitkunst, Linden Mus, Stuttgart, Ger, 83; and others. *Mailing Add:* 12400 Toilsome Hill Rd Anchorage AK 99516

ARELLANES, AUDREY SPENCER
EDITOR, ART HISTORIAN
b Lance Creek, Wyo, Feb 23, 20. *Study:* Univ Calif, Los Angeles, 44. *Collections Arranged:* Bookplates-Miniature Works of Art, Altadena Pub Libr, Calif, 71, Friends of Mobile, Ala, 74 & Univ of Connecticut, Storrs, 74; Evolution of a Bookplate, from Idea to Print, Pasadena Pub Libr, Calif, 71; Prints in Miniature-Bookplates, Santa Barbara Pub Libr, Calif, 73. *Pos:* Proprieter, Bookworm Press, 65-; ed & founder, Bookplates in the News, 70-; dir, Am Soc Bookplate Collectors & Designers, 70- *Awards:* Award Distinction, Manuscript Soc, 81. *Bibliog:* James L Weygand (auth), Bookworm Press-Audrey Arellanes, Am Bk Collector, 11-12/69; Lois Rather (auth), Women as printers, Rather Press, 70; Clare D Kinsman (ed), Contemporary Authors, vols 33-36, Gale Research, 73. *Mem:* Manuscript Soc (Nat exec sec, 75-80, local treas, 70-90); Rounce & Coffin Club; Miniature Book Soc. *Res:* Bookplates, the artists who design them, the owners who commission and/or collect them, the literature (books and periodicals) which record the history of the bookplate through many centuries and countries. *Publ:* Auth, Bookplates: A Selective, Annotated Bibliography of the Periodical Literature, Gale Research, 71; ed, Bookplates in the News: 1970-1985, Gale Research, 85. *Mailing Add:* 605 N Stoneman Ave Suite F Alhambra CA 91801

ARENDS, STUART
PAINTER
b Waterloo, Iowa, 1950. *Study:* Western State Col, Gunnison, Colo, BA, 74; Banff Sch Fine Arts, Alberta, Can, 76-77; Otis Art Inst, Los Angeles, MFA, 81. *Exhib:* Mus Art, Birmingham, Ala, 77; solo exhibs, Roswell Mus & Art Ctr, Roswell, NMex, 84 (catalog), Craig Cornelius Gallery, New York, 87, Asher/Faure, Los Angeles, 88 & 90 & S Bitter-Larkin, New York, 92; Christ Church Hall, Nailsworth, Gloucestershire, Eng, 85; Hirschl & Adler Mod, New York, 87; Ctr Contemp Arts, Santa Fe, NMex, 88; Bistborno Gallery, Malmo, Sweden, 89; Nohra Haine Gallery, New York, 90; Univ NMex Art Mus, Albuquerque, 91; Lugano, Switzerland, 92. *Awards:* Artist-in-Residence Grant, Roswell Mus & Art Ctr, 83; Nat Endowment Arts, 89. *Bibliog:* Kathleen Shields (auth), Stuart Arends, Objects of context, Artspace, Vol 14, No 5, 47-48, 7-8/90; William Wilson (auth), Arends Whispers, Los Angeles Times, 9/28/90. *Mailing Add:* c/o Craig Cornelius Gallery 170 Fifth Ave 10th fl New York NY 10012

ARGUE, DOUGLAS
PAINTER
Study: Bemidji State Univ, Minn, 80-82; Univ Minn, 83. *Work:* Walker Art Ctr, Minneapolis; First Banks Minneapolis; Gen Mills, Minneapolis. *Exhib:* Solo exhibs, Bemidji Art Ctr, 82, B Square One Gallery, 84, Talley Gallery, 85, McGalley, 86, Rochester Art Ctr, 86, Bockley Gallery, 87, 88, 89 & 90; Five Jerome Artist, New Mus Contemp Art, New York, 85; Eight McKnight Artists, Minneapolis Col Art & Design, 86; Viewpoints: Doug Argue & Jim Lutes, Walker Art Ctr, Minneapolis, 85-86; Figurative Paintings, Rochester Art Ctr, Rochester, Minn, 86; Art and the Law, Plaza Gallery (travelling show), San Francisco, Calif, 87; Food/Art/USA, Edith C Blum Art Inst, Bard Col, NY, 89; Katherine Nash Gallery, Univ Minn, 92. *Awards:* Visual Artist Fel, Nat Endowment Art, 87; Minn State Arts Bd Fel, 91; McKnight Found Fel, 92. *Bibliog:* Liz Armstrong (auth), Viewpoint: Doug Argue, Walker Art Ctr, 12/85; Melissa Stang (auth), Doug Argue at Bockley Artpaper, 7/88. *Media:* All. *Mailing Add:* c/o Bockley Gallery 400 First Ave N Minneapolis MN 55401

ARIAS-MISSON, ALAIN
VISUAL POET, GRAPHIC ARTIST
b Brussels, Belg, Dec 11, 39; US citizen. *Study:* Harvard Univ, BA(Greek lit; magna cum laude), 59. *Work:* State Mus (Stedelijk), Amsterdam, Holland; Archive H Sohm, State Gallery, Stuttgart, Ger; Galleria Schwarz, Milan; Cabinet d'Estampes, Bibliotheque Nat, Paris; Dresden Mus; Mus Casabianca, Vicenza; Mus de Senigallia; Liublin Mus, Poland; Jean Brown Collection, Getty Mus, Calif. *Comn:* Public Poem-Beethoven Bicentennial, Bonn, W Ger; Public Art, City of Bielefeld, 91. *Exhib:* Galerie Donguy, Paris, 88; Poesia Viviva & Group Art-Documents 8 Mus Santos Rocha, Portugal, 88; Le Mois de La photographie, Paris, Oct 88; Visual Poetry, Otis Art Inst, Los Angeles, 90; Domus Jani, Int Inst Total Art, Verona, 92, The Lyon Biennale, 93; and others. *Teaching:* Creative writing, Columbia Univ, 81-82. *Awards:* NJ State Coun Arts, 85-86; Artists Liaison, 88. *Bibliog:* S H Anderson (auth), When Reality becomes Superfiction, Int Herald Tribune, 5/75; M Dachy (auth), New York art, Critique, 81, & L'espace Amerique, Change, Paris; and others in Art Vivant, Flashart & Artpress; Orange County Regist, Los Angeles, Jan 88. *Mem:* Poets & Writers. *Publ:* Co-ed, 5 anthologies in Europe & America, 74, Poesia Visiva, Chicago Rev, 76 & Visual poetry, Paris Rev; auth, Confessions of a Murderer, Bomber, Fascist, Rapist, Thief, Chicago Rev Press & Swallow, 75; The Public Poem Book, Arias-Misson, Factotum Press, Italy, 78-79; Verbo-visual Sins of a Literary Saint, Rara Bks, Italy, 92; The Parabolic Pilgrimage of August Saint, amateur detective. *Mailing Add:* PO Box 24 Clarksburg NJ 08510

ARIAS-MISSON, NELA
PAINTER
b Havana, Cuba, Sept 8, 25; US citizen. *Study:* Art Students League, 55; Hans Hoffman Sch, Provincetown, 56-58. *Work:* State Mus Lindenau, Altenburg, EGer; Circulo de Arte, Cordoba, Spain; Archivo Denza, Brescia, Italy. *Exhib:* Nat Asn Woman Artists Exhib, Argent Gallery, 59; solo exhib, Charlottenborg Gallery-Acad Fine Arts, Copenhagen, Denmark, 62; Galleria Brescia-Artists, Dusseldorf Art Fair, Ger, 72; Kunstmesse-Brescia Gallery, Basel Art Fair, Switz, 73; Phantomas, Mod Mus, Ixelles-Brussels, Belg, 75; Segel der Zeit, State Mus of Lindenau, Altenburg, EGer, 85-86; Ruth Wiseman Gallery, Dallas, 88; St Lifer Art Exchange, 88. *Awards:* First Prize, Nat Asn Women Artists, 60. *Bibliog:* Paul de Vree (auth), Nela Arias-Misson, De Periscoop, Belg, 11/68; Adolfo Castaño, Nela Arias-Misson, Estafeta Literaria, Madrid, Spain, 70; Jacques Halber, Artistes Américainà Bruxelles, Annuaire des Beaux-Arts, 72. *Media:* Oil on Canvas. *Publ:* Illusr, The Umbrella, 9/67 & The Tree of Life, 75, Chicago Rev; Table with Bott & Lamp, L'VII (Brussels), No 33, 72. *Dealer:* Int Inst for Total Art Verona 37031 Italy. *Mailing Add:* PO Box 24 Clarksburg NJ 08510

ARISS, HERBERT JOSHUA
PAINTER, ILLUSTRATOR
b Guelph, Ont, Can, Sept 19, 18. *Study:* Ont Col Art. *Work:* Nat Gallery Can; Art Gallery Ont; Winnipeg Art Gallery; Vancouver Art Gallery; London Art Gallery, Ont. *Comn:* Casein, Huron & Erie Co, Chatham, 58; ceramic, John Labatt Brewery, London, 59; multimedia, Sir Adam Beck Sec Sch, London, 67; multimedia, Ont Govt Bldg, Toronto, 68; mural, Sch Med, Univ Western Ont, London. *Exhib:* 2nd & 3rd Can Biennial, Ottawa, 64-66; Can Soc Graphic Arts, 70; Can Printmakers, Nat Gallery, Can Int Show, 71; Can Soc Painters in Watercolour, London & New York, 72. *Pos:* Pres, Western Art League, 57-60; mem, London Art Gallery Bd, 68-71; dir, London Art Gallery Asn, 69-72; chmn acquisition comt, London Pub Libr & Art Mus, 70-71. *Teaching:* Instr drawing & painting, Doon Sch Fine Arts, 55-58; head dept art, H B Beal Art Sch, London, Ont, 65- *Awards:* Can Coun Senior Fel, 60-61; Can Soc Painters in Watercolor Hon Award, 65; Mayor's Hon Award, London, 80. *Bibliog:* Bright lights of London, Time, 68; Barry Lord (auth), How Beal has made London an art centre, Toronto Star, 70; J Bryce (auth), Herb Ariss retrospective, Arts Can, 71. *Mem:* Royal Can Acad Arts; Can Soc Painters in Watercolor. *Publ:* Illusr, Lectures variees, 58; La double mort de Frederic Belot, 58; Contes d'Aujour d'hui, 63; War, 71; auth, Encounters, London Regional Art Gallery, 82. *Mailing Add:* 770 Leroy Ave London ON N5Y 4G7 Canada

ARISS, MARGOT (JOAN PHILLIPS)
PAINTER
b Belleville, Ont, Can, Sept 14, 29. *Study:* London Cent Col, Ont; H B Beal Sec Sch, London, Ont. *Work:* Can Coun Art Bank, Ottawa; London Regional Art Gallery, Ont; London Free Press Newspaper, Ont; Vancouver Art Gallery, BC; McIntosh Art Gallery, London, Ont. *Comn:* Ceramic mural, City of London, Ont; ceramic & fibre mural, City of Kingston, Ont; and many other pvt commissions. *Exhib:* Ceramic Objects, Art Gallery Ontario, 73, Ariss-Hogbin-Hunt, York Univ, 78, Toronto; McIntosh Gallery, Univ Western Ont, 75; Words & Images, Trent Univ, McKenzie Art Gallery, 76; London & Area Artists Part I, 80, Clay & Fibre Show, 86, 40th Ann Western Ontario Exhib, 87, London Regional Art Gallery; Univ Western Ont Collection, Art Gallery, Windsor, 82; one-person show, Univ Waterloo, Ont, 83; Ten Years After, Spectrum Art Gallery, London, Ont, 85; Yellow Show, 87, Box Art (touring) 87, Durham Art Gallery; retrospective, Zen Song,

London Regional art Gallery, 89. *Bibliog:* Articles, Arts Can, 8/69 & Craft Horizons, 10/73 & 6/74; cover & article, Craftsman, 8/78. *Mem:* Royal Can Acad. *Media:* Mixed Media. *Mailing Add:* 770 Leroy Crescent London ON N5Y 4G7 Canada

ARKUS, LEON A
CONSULTANT, MUSEUM DIRECTOR
b NJ, May 6, 15. *Study:* City Col New York, with Townsend Harris Prep. *Collections Arranged:* 1970 Pittsburgh Int, 70-71; Fresh Air Sch, 72; Art in Residence, 73; Twelve Years of Collecting, 74; Celebration, 74-75; Pittsburgh Corporations Collection, 75-76; Pittsburgh Int Series, Pierre Alechinsky, 77, Eduardo Chillida/Willem de Koonig, 79. *Pos:* Asst dir, Mus Art, Carnegie Inst, Pittsburgh, 54-62, assoc dir, 62-68, dir, 68-80, consult & dir emer, 80- *Awards:* Knight Cross of the Order of Dannebrog, Queen Margrethe II of Denmark, 74; and others. *Mem:* Am Asn Mus; hon mem Assoc Artists Pittsburgh; Asn Art Mus Dirs; Pittsburgh Plan for Art (gov, 58-80); Century Club; and others. *Publ:* Auth, Three Self-Taught Pennsylvania Artists: Hicks, Kane, Pippin, 66; Carl-Henning Pedersen: Paintings, Watercolors, Drawings, 68; The Art of Black Africa, 69; John Kane, Painter (catalogue raisonne), Univ Pittsburgh Press, 71. *Mailing Add:* 213 S Craig St Pittsburgh PA 15213

ARMAJANI, SIAH
SCULPTOR
b Teheran, Iran, 1939. *Study:* Macalester Col, St Paul, Minn, BA, 63. *Comn:* St Rose of Lima Park, Sacramento, Calif; Waiting Room, St Joseph Med Ctr, Brainerd, Minn; Irene Hixon Whitney Bridge, Minneapolis; Yerba Buena Tower (Building Top), San Francisco (collab with Cesar Pelli & Assoc); bandstand, Hitchcock Park, Mitchell, SDak, 89; covered walkway, General Mills Inc, Minneapolis, Minn, 89; reading garden, Lannan Found, Los Angeles, Calif, 90; Gazebo for two architects, Gabriella & Arberto Antolini, Storm King Art Park, Mountainville, NY, 92. *Exhib:* Solo exhibs, New Gallery Contemp Art, Cleveland, 79, Max Protetch Gallery, NY, 81, 83-85, 89 & 91, Bridges-Houses-Communal Spaces, Inst Contemp Art, Univ Pa, Philadelphia, 85, Kunsthalle Basel, Switz & Stedelijk Mus, Amsterdam, Holland, 87, List Visual Arts Ctr, Mass Inst Technol, Cambridge, 88; Postminimalism (with catalog), Aldrich Mus Contemp Art, Ridgefield, Conn, 82; New Art (with catalog), Tate Gallery, London, Eng, 83; Content: A Contemporary Focus: 1974-84, Hirshhorn Mus & Sculpture Garden, Washington, DC, 84; Spring Loan Exhib, Weatherspoon Art Gallery, Univ NC, Greensboro, 85; Sonsbeek Int Sculpture Exhib, Arnhem, Holland, 86; Documenta 8, Kassel, WGer, 87; Avant-Garde in the Eighties, Los Angeles, 87; View Points: Post-war Painting & Sculpture, Solomon R Guggenheim Mus, New York, 88; Carnegie Int, Carnegie Mus Art, Pittsburgh, Pa, 88; Culture and Commentary: An Eighties Perspective, Hirshhorn Mus & Sculpture Garden, Smithsonian Inst, Washington, DC, 90; 20th Century Art, Mus Mod Art, Frankfurt, 91; The Open Work, John Good Gallery, New York, 92. *Bibliog:* Ken Johnson (auth), Poetry and Public Service, Art in Am, 3/90; Christopher Knight (auth), A metaphor grows in 'The poetry garden', Los Angeles Times, 3/23/92; Ann Jarmusch (auth), Art and architecture/ urban oasis, San Diego-Union Tribune, 4/12/92. *Mailing Add:* c/o Max Protech Gallery 560 Broadway New York NY 10012-3412

ARMAN
SCULPTOR
b Nice, France, 1928; US citizen. *Study:* Ecole Nat Art Decoratif, BPh; Ecole Louvre. *Work:* Hirshhorn Mus & Sculpture Garden, Washington, DC; Metrop Mus Art, New York; Mus Mod Art, New York; Mus Georges Pompidou, Paris; Nationale Gallery, Berlin. *Comn:* A ma Jolie, Pablo Picasso Mus, Antibes, France, 81; Long Term Parking, Le Montcel, France, 82; pvt collection, Pablo Casal's Obelisk, 83; La Republic, Paris, 83; Accumulation of Marine Anchors, Palma de Mallorica, Spain, 84; The Centrum Project, Dallas, Tex, 86; Venus des Arts, St Germain, Paris, 88. *Exhib:* Selected Works 1958-1974 (solo exhib), La Jolla Mus Contemp Art, Calif (and US tour), 74; Objets Armes 1971-1974 (solo exhib), Mus d'Art Mod de la Ville, Paris, France, 75; solo exhibs, Veraneman Found, Gand, Belg, 78, Found de Jau, Perpignan, France, 79, Art in Progress Gallery, Munich, Ger, 80 & Mus d'Arte Mod, Parma, Italy, 84; Parade der Objekte Retrospective 1955 bis 1982 (solo exhib) Kunstmus Hannover, Ger (and Europ tour), 82; Pinceaux Pieges (solo exhib), Mus Beaux Arts, Nimes, France, 88; solo retrospective, Pavillion Werd, Zurich, Switz, 88; many other solo exhibs throughout US & Europe. *Teaching:* Instr, Univ Calif, Los Angeles, 67-68. *Awards:* Tokyo Biennel Second Prize, 64; Grand Marzotto Prize, 66; Commander Arts & Lett, 84. *Bibliog:* Otto Hahn (auth), Arman, Hatzan, 72; Henry Martin (auth), Arman, Abrams, 73; Bernard LeMarche-Vadel (auth), Arman, La Difference Publ, 88; plus others. *Media:* Bronze, Metal. *Mailing Add:* 430 Washington St New York NY 10013

ARMSTRONG, BILL HOWARD
PAINTER, EDUCATOR
b Horton, Kans, Dec 13, 26. *Study:* Bradley Univ, Peoria, Ill, BFA(cum laude), 49; Univ Ill, Urbana, MFA, 55, with Abraham Rattner. *Work:* Brooklyn Mus, NY; San Francisco Mus of Art, Calif; Springfield Art Mus, Mo; Albrecht Gallery, St Joseph, Mo; Art and the Law, West Publ Co, St Paul, Minn. *Comn:* Hist mural, Am Bank, Irving, Tex, 75. *Exhib:* Am Fedn Arts Int Traveling Exhib, 56; 20th & 24th Print Exhib, San Francisco Mus Art, 56 & 59; Butler Inst Am Art, Youngstown, Ohio, 56-67; Pa Acad Fine Art, Philadelphia, 56-67; 10th Ann Print Exhib, Brooklyn Mus, 59; Soc Am Graphic Artist Int Traveling Exhib, 60; Watercolor USA Nat Exhib, Springfield, Mo, 65-76; Calif Nat Watercolor Soc, Los Angeles, 69-71; Art and the Law, 82-83. *Collections Arranged:* Watercolor USA Nat Invitational Exhib, 76. *Pos:* Art adv, Burma Transl Soc, Rangoon, Ford Found, 57-58; co-founder & chmn, Watercolor USA Hon Soc, 85-86. *Teaching:* Asst prof painting, Univ Wis, Madison, 56-63; prof watercolor & graphic design, Southwest Mo State Univ, 63- *Awards:* Purchase Awards, Watercolor USA, 62-71 & Calif Nat Watercolor Soc, 69 & 70; Purchase Awards, West Publ Co Art & the Law Exhib, 82 & 83; and others. *Media:* Watercolor. *Mailing Add:* 1711 E Walnut St No E Springfield MO 65804

ARMSTRONG, CAROL
PAINTER
Study: Cent State Univ, Edmond, Okla, BA, 78. *Exhib:* Okla Art Guild Juried Exhib, 82, 85, 86 & 87; Lawton Jr Serv League 15th, 17th & 18th Ann Exhibs, 84, 85 & 87; Nat Watercolor Okla, 86; Tex and Neighbors Art Competition, 86; Art in the Woods, Fifth Juried Exhib, 88. *Teaching:* Painting instr, Norman Woodward's Art & Crafts, Oklahoma City Tabco Hobbies, 80-88 & Firee House Art Ctr, 89-90. *Bibliog:* Best of Show, Lawton Jr Serv League 18th Ann Exhib, 86. *Mem:* Okla Watercolor Asn; Okla Art Guild. *Mailing Add:* 1808 Lakeview Circle Norman OK 73071

ARMSTRONG, GEOFFREY
PAINTER, ARCHITECT
b Toronto, Ont, Can, May 27, 28. *Study:* Univ Toronto, BArch, 52. *Work:* Art Gallery Windsor, Ont; Univ Nebr, Fredericton; City North Bay, Ont; Esso Resources, Calgary, Alta; Royal Bank, Toronto. *Exhib:* Art Gallery Hamilton; Montreal Mus Fine Arts; Art Gallery Ont; Trent Univ; Queens Univ, Kingston; Ont Soc Artists Traveling Exhib; Soc Can Artists Traveling Exhib. *Mem:* Royal Archit Inst Can; Soc Can Artists; Ont Soc Artists; Royal Can Acad. *Media:* Acrylic. *Publ:* Contribr, Art Mag, 68-70. *Dealer:* Roberts Gallery 641 Yonge St Toronto ON M4Y 1Z9. *Mailing Add:* 188 Davenport Rd Toronto ON M5R 1J2 Canada

ARMSTRONG, JANE BOTSFORD
SCULPTOR
b Buffalo, NY, Feb 17, 21. *Study:* Middlebury Col; Pratt Inst; Art Students League, with Jose De Creeft. *Work:* Burchfield Arts Ctr, Buffalo, NY; Wichita Art Mus, Kans; Brookgreen Gardens, SC; Northern Telecom, Research Triangle Park, NC; Gift Gardens Botanical/Fine Art Park, Palm City, Fla; and others. *Comn:* Tex Gulf Chemical Hq Bldg, Raleigh, NC; Wichita Art Mus, Kans; Tex Gulf Chemicals, Raleigh, NC; Southern Life Insurance Co, Greensboro, NC. *Exhib:* One-man shows, Columbia Mus Art, SC, 75, Spec Children's Exhib, Dallas Fine Arts Mus, Tex, 78, Wichita Art Mus, Kans, 78 & 82, Wadsworth Atheneum, Hartford, Conn, 79, Southeastern Ctr Contemp Art, 80, The Sculpture Ctr, New York, 81 & 86, Burchfield Ctr, Buffalo, NY, 85, New Sculptures, Schiller-Wappner Gallery, New York, 87, Journey Into Stone, Saint-Gardens Nat Hist site, Cornish, NH, 88 & Grand Cent Art Galleries, New York, 89; Artists Am Exhib, Colo State Mus, Denver, 81-92. *Awards:* Nat Sculpture Soc, Bronze Medal, 76 & 89; Maurice B Hexter Prize, 81; Percival Dietsch Prize, 86; Gold Medal of Honor for Distinguished Achievement in Sculpture, Knickerbocker Artists, 86; US Art Mag Award Excellence, Artists Am Exhib, Denver, Colo, 90. *Bibliog:* Max Wyckes-Joyce (auth), Int Herald Tribune, London, 5/15/76; Diana Loercher (auth), Jane Armstrong--late blooming sculptor, Christian Sci Monitor, 12/19/77; Jane B Armstrong, sculpture to touch, Florida Style, mid-winter, 85; Romance of stone, Buffalo News Art Rev, 4/19/85. *Mem:* Sculptors Guild; fel Nat Sculpture Soc; Allied Artists Am; Audubon Artists; Nat Asn Women Artists. *Media:* Stone. *Publ:* Auth, Discovery in Stone, Eastwoods Press, 74; From the mountains of Vermont, Nat Sculpture Rev, 74; The gallery paradox, Int Sculpture, 3-4/86. *Dealer:* Gerald Peters Galleries Dallas TX; Foster Harmon Galleries of American Art Sarasota FL. *Mailing Add:* RR Box 684 Dorset Hill Rd East Dorset VT 05253

ARMSTRONG, MARTHA (ALLEN)
PAINTER, PHOTOGRAPHER
b Brunswick, Ga, 1935. *Study:* Converse Col, under August Cook, 53-56; Heatherly Sch Fine Art, London, Eng, advan painting, 67-69. *Work:* C G Jung Educ Ctr, Rovi Tex Corp, Rapada Corp & Apple Computers, Dallas, Tex; United Energy Resources, Dresdner Bank, Texaco USA, Houston, Tex; Smithsonian Inst, Washington, DC; Lowell Early Childhood Ctr, Fresh Meadows, NY; Enpro Int, Jeddah, Saudi Arabia. *Comn:* Cover art, Performing Arts Mag, 81; cover art, spring brochure, C G Jung Educ Ctr, Houston, 84; cover art, inaugural brochure, Tex Inst Arts Educ, 84; cover art, Houston on Stage Mag, 85. *Exhib:* Houston Mus Fine Arts, Glassell Sch, 78; solo shows, La Gallery, Houston, 81, McMurtrey Gallery, Houston, 81, 82, 90 & 92, Univ Houston, Clear Lake, 83, NY Pub Libr, Donnell Libr Ctr, New York, 84, Univ St Thomas, 85 & Graham Gallery, 86; Houston Ctr Photog, 83 & 84; Diverse Works, Houston, Tex, 84 & 85; Fed Reserve Bank, Philadelphia, Pa, 85; Univ Houston, Lowndale Annex, Houston, 85; Houston Foto Fest, 86. *Collections Arranged:* 34 Houston Artists Working in their Studios, 77. *Pos:* Visual arts panelist, La State Coun for the Arts, Baton Rouge, 86. *Bibliog:* Donna Tennant (auth), Light & movement dominate paintings of Martha Armstrong, Houston Chronicle, 81 & Houston Exhib, Artspace, summer, 86; Patricia Johnson (auth), Martha Armstrong's photography is softly personal, Houston Chronicle, 82; Carol Everingham (auth), New York exhibit features Armstrong photos, Art News, Houston Post, 84. *Mem:* Cult Arts Coun Houston (bd dir 79-85, vpres, 81, pres, 82, chmn bd, 83); Houston Ctr Photography (trustee, 83-85); Contemp Arts Mus (trustee, 78-80); Fellows of Contemp Art, Los Angeles. *Media:* Acrylic, Oil. *Dealer:* McMurtrey Gallery 3508 Lake St Houston TX 77006. *Mailing Add:* 1527 Kirby Dr Houston TX 77019-3301

ARMSTRONG, ROGER JOSEPH
PAINTER, CARTOONIST
b Los Angeles, Calif, Oct 12, 17. *Study:* Pasadena City Col; Chouinard Art Inst; Sueo Serisawa Workshop; Art Inst S Calif, Laguna Beach, hon PhD, 90. *Work:* City of Santa Fe Springs, Calif; City of Pico Rivera; Banking House of Rothschild, San Francisco; Laguna Beach Art Mus, Calif. *Exhib:* International Masters of Watercolor, Dalzell-Hatfield Galleries, Los Angeles, 67; one-man shows, Muckenthaler Cult Ctr, 69, Newport Beach Munic Gallery, 70 & Ettinger Gallery, Laguna Beach Sch of Art, 78; Griswold Gallery, Claremont, Calif, 74; Calif 100 Exhib, Laguna Beach Mus Art, 77; Dana Point Marine Inst, 81; Nat Watercolor Soc Exhib, Brea Civic Cultural Ctr, Calif, 84 & 85; Stary Sheets Gallery, Irvine, Calif, 92. *Collections Arranged:* Three-man exhib, Keith Finch, Edgar Ewing & Robert Frame, 63; West Coast Figurative, 64; First Ann West Coast Sculpture Exhib, 64; plus others. *Pos:* Bk illusr & cartoonist, Walt Disney Co, 78-88. *Teaching:* Instr cartooning & watercolor painting, Laguna Beach Sch Art, 65-; instr watercolor, Pasadena City Col, 74-78; instr oil painting, Saddlebrook Community Col, Mission Viejo, 78; instr cartooning, Orange Coast Col, Costa Mesa, Calif, 81-91; So Calif Art Inst, 88- *Awards:* First Purchase Award, First Ann Pio Pico Art Festival, 68; Honorable Mention, East Meets West Exhib, Calif Nat Watercolor Soc, 72; Motion Picture Screen Cartoonists (MPSC) Golden Award, 92. *Bibliog:* Raymond Fisher & John Barnard (auths), Roger Armstrong, triple threat artist, World of Comic Art, winter 66-67; Shel Dorf (auth), Comic Interviews, Roger Armstrong, 86; R C Harvey (auth), Cartoonist Profiles, comics by Roger Armstrong, 91. *Mem:* Laguna Beach Art Asn; Los Angeles Art Asn; Nat Cartoonists Soc; Comic Artists Professional Soc; Southern Calif Cartoonist Soc. *Media:* Watercolor, Ink. *Publ:* Coauth & illusr, Ella Cinders comic strip, United Features Syndicate, 50-61 & Napoleon & Uncle Elby, Los Angeles Times Syndicate, 50-60; auth & illusr, Flintstones, Little Lulu & others, Western Publ, 60-72; comic strip illusr, Scamp, Walt Disney Productions; artist, auth, How to Draw Comic Strips, Walter Foster Publ Co, 90. *Mailing Add:* 34202 Del Obispo No 24 Dana Point CA 92629

ARMSTRONG, THOMAS NEWTON, III
MUSEUM DIRECTOR
b Portsmouth, Va, July 30, 32. *Study:* Art Students League, summer 53; Cornell Univ Col Arch, Art & Planning, BFA, 54; Inst Fine Arts, NY Univ, 65-67. *Pos:* From cur to assoc dir, Abby Aldrich Rockefeller Folk Art Col, Williamsburg, Va, 67-71; dir, Pa Acad Fine Arts, Philadelphia, 71-73; assoc dir, Whitney Mus Am Art, New York, 73-74, dir, 74-90, dir emer, 90- *Mailing Add:* 765 Park Ave New York NY 10021

ARNESON, WENDELL H
PAINTER
b Madison, Wis, Sept 10, 46. *Study:* Luther Col, BA, 68; Bowling Green State Univ, MA, 77, MFA, 78. *Work:* Miller Mus Art, Sturgeon Bay, Wis. *Comn:* Univ Wis Hosp, Madison, 82; watercolor triptych, Prudential Life Insurance Corp, Minneapolis, 83; watercolor triptych, Benson Optical Corp, 84; watercolor triptych, 3M Corp, 84; watercolor triptych, IBM Corp, 85. *Exhib:* Minn State Competition Exhib, Rochester Art Ctr, 79; Nat Watercolor Invitational, Clarks Art Ctr, Rockford, Ill, 84. *Teaching:* Prof painting & drawing, St Olaf Col, Northfield, Minn, 78-, chmn dept, 84-91. *Awards:* Drawing Award, Toledo Mus Art, 78; Painting Award, Watercolor USA, Springfield Art Mus, 84. *Mem:* Col Art Asn. *Media:* Watercolor, Oil Painting. *Mailing Add:* Dept Art St Olaf Col Northfield MN 55057

ARNHEIM, RUDOLF
EDUCATOR, WRITER
b Berlin, Ger, July 15, 04; US citizen. *Study:* Univ Berlin, PhD, 28; Guggenheim fel, 42-43; RI Sch Design, Hon DFA, 76. *Teaching:* Mem fac psychol art, Sarah Lawrence Col, 43-68; prof, Harvard Univ, 68-74; vis prof, Univ Mich, 74-84. *Awards:* Distinguished Serv Award, Nat Art Educ Asn; Resident, Am Acad Rome, 78. *Mem:* Am Soc Aesthet (pres & trustee); Am Psychol Asn (pres, div arts, 70-72); Col Art Asn. *Publ:* Auth, The dynamics of architectural form, 77; The power of the center, 82 & rev ed, 88; New essays on the psychology of art, 86; Parables of Sun Light, 89; To the Rescue of Art, 92. *Mailing Add:* 1200 Earhart Rd #537 Ann Arbor MI 48105

ARNHOLM, RONALD FISHER
DESIGNER, EDUCATOR
b Barre, Vt, Jan 4, 39. *Study:* RI Sch Design, BFA(graphic design), 61; Yale Univ, MFA(graphic design), 63. *Work:* Ga Comn Arts Traveling Exhib. *Comn:* Corp design prog (with Jack MacDonald), Am Tube & Controls, West Warwick, RI, 62; typeface: Jenson Roman, Mergenthaler Linotype Co, Plainview, NY, 64; wall mural, Mead Corp, Atlanta, Ga, 65; typefaces: Aquarius series, 70-74, Fovea series, 77-79, Visual Graphics Corp, Tamarac, Fla, Veritas series, 89, World Typeface Ctr, New York, Headline series, 80, Financial & Classified Types, 88, Los Angeles Times, Legacy Series, Int Typeface Corp, NY, 92. *Exhib:* Composing Rm Award Typography Exhib, Gallery 303, New York, 63; one-man show, Ga Mus Art, Athens, 65; 45th Ann Art Dir Club New York Ann Exhib, 66; Southeastern Ann, High Mus Art, Atlanta, 67; Typomundus 20/2 Int Typography Exhib, Stuttgart, Ger, 70. *Pos:* Art dir, The Moderator Mag, New Haven, Conn, 62-63. *Teaching:* From instr to asst prof art, Univ Ga, 63-71, assoc prof, 71-82, prof, 82- *Awards:* Composing Room Award for Excellence in Typography, New York, 63; Award of Distinctive Merit, Art Dir Club, New York, 66; Cert of Merit, Typomundus 20/2, 70. *Bibliog:* Eugene Ettenberg (auth), The Word Paintings of Ronald Arnholm, Am Artist, 11/70; Edward M Gottschall (auth), The Word Paintings of Ronald Arnholm, Typographic, Vol 3, No 3. *Mailing Add:* Dept Art Univ Ga Athens GA 30602

ARNING, BILL A
CURATOR, ADMINISTRATOR
b New York, NY, Sept 16, 60. *Study:* New York Univ, BA, 84. *Exhib:* Stux Boston, Stux Gallery, New York; The Second Second at Althea Viafora Gallery; The Anti-Masculine, Kimlight Gallery, Los Angeles, 92. *Pos:* Asst dir, Kathryn Markel, 84; asst dir, White Columns, 84-85, exec dir, 85-; art ed, Bomb Mag, 91- *Teaching:* Guest lectr, Pace Univ, 85, Art Inst Chicago, 88, Sch Visual Arts, New York Univ, 90, Snug Harbor, 92, Toronto Col Art, 91, Tyler Sch Art, Philadelphia, 92 & Tama Art Univ, Japan, 91. *Publ:* Auth, Update 86, Update 87, Update 88, Update 89, Update 90 & Update 91 & 92 (catalogs), White Columns; Tom Brazelton's fickle abstractions, In: USA Pavilion Catalog, 87; Glittering Prize, 87, Ecuadorian Bienial, 88 & Russel Floersche, 88, Stux Gallery; auth, catalog, Peter Scott, Riverside Studios, London; Jeffrey Jenkins (catalog), Stux Gallery, 89. *Mailing Add:* c/o White Columns 142 Christopher St New York NY 10014

ARNITZ, RICK
PAINTER
b St Louis, Mo, 49. *Study:* Univ Calif, Berkeley, BA, 75, MA, 80, MFA, 82. *Work:* Saks Fifth Avenue, New York; San Francisco, Bank Am, Achenbach Found, Palace Legion Hon, San Francisco, Calif; Principal Finance Group, Des Moines, Iowa; Continental Securities, Bentall Centre, Vancouver, BC; San Francisco Mus Mod Art; Park Hyatt Hotel, San Francisco. *Exhib:* Solo exhibs, Margins 2, Univ Art Mus, Santa Barbara, 90, Stephen Wirtz Gallery, San Francisco, Calif, 91; Oakland's Artists, Oakland Mus, Calif, 90; White Out, Thomas Babeor Gallery, La Jolla, Calif, 90; Framed, Stephen Wirtz Gallery, 91, Recent Acquisitions of the Achenbach Foundation for Graphic Arts; Part Two: 1950-1991, Calif Palace Legion Hon, San Francisco, Calif, 91; Bay Area and Beyond, Elizabeth Leach Gallery, Portland, Ore, 91; Abstraction: Recent Prints, Betsy Senior Contemp Prints, New York, 91; Susan Cummins Gallery, Mill Valley, Calif, 92. *Awards:* Roslyn Schneider Eisner Award, Univ Calif, Berkeley, 80; Art Space, Support Grant, San Francisco, Calif, 90; Nat Endowment Arts Award, 92. *Bibliog:* David Bonetti (auth), Whose community? What standards?, San Francisco Chronicle, 6/29/90; Mark Levy (auth), Four bay area abstract painters, Artspace, Jan/Feb 91; Jennifer Crohn (auth), The tricky business: a talk with East Bay painter Rick Arnitz, East Bay Guardian, 5/91. *Mailing Add:* c/o Stephen Wirtz Gallery 49 Geary 3rd flr San Francisco CA 94108

ARNOLD, FLORENCE M
PAINTER
b Prescott, Ariz, Sept 16, 1900. *Study:* Mills Col, degree in music; Univ Southern Calif, BA; Claremont Grad Sch. *Work:* Long Beach Mus Art; Laguna Mus Art, Calif State Univ, Fullerton; Media Art Gallery, Santa Ana, Calif; Newport Harbor Art Mus, Mills Col Print Collection, City of Fullerton. *Exhib:* Gallerias Numero, Florence, Rome, Milan & Prato Venice, 63; Calif Hard-edge Painting, Newport Beach, 64; one-man shows, Long Beach Mus Art, 62-69 & Fresno Art Ctr, 69; Retrospective, Muckenthaler Cult Ctr, 75; retrospective, North Orange County Mus honoring 80th birthday. *Awards:* First Prize, Muckenthaler Cult Ctr, 67 & 69; First Prize, Orange Co Art Asn, 68; La Mirada Festival Arts Purchase Award, 68. *Bibliog:* Monogr, Calif State Univ, Fullerton, 69; Nat Archives of Am Art, Smithsonian Inst, Washington, DC; Oral Hist Prog (interview) Fullerton Col. *Mem:* Los Angeles Art Asn; Muckenthaler Cult Ctr (bd mem, 60-77); Fullerton Cult & Fine Arts Comn; Los Angeles Mus Art (charter mem). *Media:* Oil on Canvas. *Mailing Add:* 1136 Valencia Mesa Dr Fullerton CA 92633

ARNOLD, JACK
ART DEALER, PUBLISHER
b New York, NY. *Study:* Syracuse Univ, BS, 50. *Pos:* Pres, Collector's Workshop, New York, 76-78; vpres, Gallery Hawaii, Honolulu, 78-80; pres, Falcon Fine Art, New York, 80-82; pres, Arnold Fine Arts, New York, 83- *Teaching:* Dir lithography, Shorewood Atelier, New York, 72-75. *Specialty:* Contemp paintings, drawings, watercolors & graphics. *Publ:* Contribr, The Contemporary Lithographic Workshop Around the World, Van Nostrand Reinhold Co, 74. *Mailing Add:* 5 East 67th St New York NY 10021

ARNOLD, PAUL BEAVER
EDUCATOR, PRINTMAKER
b Taiyuanfu, China, Nov 24, 18; US citizen. *Study:* Oberlin Col, AB, 40, MA, 41; Cleveland Inst Art; Univ Minn, MFA, 55. *Work:* Libr Cong, Washington, DC; Seattle Art Mus, Wash; Baltimore Mus, Md; Dayton Art Inst, Ohio. *Comn:* Pheasant (color intaglio), Int Graphic Arts Soc, New York, 56; White Peacock (color woodcut), Int Graphic Arts Soc, New York, 57; mural, Gilford Instrument Co, Oberlin, Ohio, 71; Martin Luther King Monument, Oberlin, Ohio, 87. *Exhib:* May Show, Cleveland Mus, 61, 63, 66, 74 & 76; one-man shows, Jersey City State Col, NJ, 66, 78 & 86, Miami Univ, Oxford, Ohio, 68, Univ Kans, Manhattan, 70; Contemporary Prints for Collectors, Columbus Gallery Art, Ohio, 75; two-man show, US Info Serv, US Embassy, Ankara, Turkey, 75; one-man shows, Firelands Asn Visual Arts, Oberlin, 85 & Allen Art Mus, Oberlin, 85; Jane Haslem Gallery, Washington, DC, 90. *Teaching:* From instr to prof art & chmn dept, Oberlin Col, 41-86, Young-Hunter prof, 82-86; guest prof, Tunghai Univ, Taiwan, 72, Sarah Lawrence Col, Lacoste, France, 79 & 80 & Lacoste Cleveland Inst Art, 85. *Awards:* Ford Found Fac Fel Prog, 51-52; Audubon Artists Medal of Honor, 57; Great Lakes Cols Asn Res Grant, 65-66. *Mem:* Nat Asn Schs Art (bd dir, 70-81, vpres, 72-75, pres, 75-78); Col Art Asn (bd dir, 79-, secy, 82-, vpres, 84-86, pres, 86-88); Mid-Am Col Art Asn (bd dir, 89-91). *Media:* Woodcut, Intaglio. *Publ:* Illusr, General chemistry & laboratory experiments in general chemistry, Campbell & Steiner, 55; coauth, The Humanities at Oberlin, 57; auth, Printmaking today, 4/70 & Silkscreen printing, 12/74, Lalit Kala Contemp, New Delhi, India; contribr, Terra cotta army of Quin Shihuangdi, Ceramics Monthly, 11/80. *Mailing Add:* 396 Morgan St Oberlin OH 44074

ARNOLD, RALPH MOFFETT
PAINTER, EDUCATOR
b Chicago, Ill, Dec 5, 28. *Study:* Roosevelt Univ, BA; Art Inst Chicago, with Vera Berdich. *Work:* Whitney Mus Am Art, New York; Fisk Univ, Nashville, Tenn; Rockford Col, Ill; Commonwealth Pa; Ill Bell Tel Co, Chicago. *Comn:* Wall murals, James House, Arthur Rubloff Realty Co, 71. *Exhib:* Violence in American Art, Mus Contemp Art, Chicago, 69; American Prints Today, Mus Art, Utica, NY, 70; Afro-American Arts 1800-1969, Mus Philadelphia Civic Ctr, 70; Contemporary Black Artists in America, Whitney Mus Am Art, 71; Cornell Univ, 75. *Pos:* Adv bd, Arts & Sales & Rental Gallery, Art Inst Chicago; artist adv bd, Ill Arts Coun. *Teaching:* Instr painting, Rockford Col, 69-70; asst prof, Barat Col, Lake Forest, 70-; prof fine arts, Loyola Univ Chicago, 70-, chmn dept, currently. *Awards:* Artists-in-residence to help underprivileged children, Ill Art Coun, 69. *Mem:* Arts Club Chicago. *Mailing Add:* 1858 N Fedgwich Chicago IL 60614

ARNOLD, RICHARD R
DESIGNER, ADMINISTRATOR
b Detroit, Mich, July 14, 23. *Study:* Southwestern Univ; Wayne State Univ, BFA; Cranbrook Acad Art, MFA, with Zoltan Sepeshy; Tulane Univ; Univ Mich. *Work:* Cranbrook Mus Art; Northwestern Nat Life Insurance Collection; Gen Mills Collections; Grey Found; Wayne State Univ. *Comn:* Mural, Essex Bldg, Minneapolis; designs, Chrysler Corp, Am Motors Corp, Gen Mills Co, Gen Elec Co & others. *Teaching:* Instr, Univ Wis, 48-51; asst prof, Cornell Univ, 53-56; asst prof, San Jose State Col, 58-60; assoc prof, Rochester Inst Technol, 60-64; prof & head design div, Minneapolis Sch Art, 64-71; vis prof, Univ Victoria, summer 68; prof & chmn art dept, State Univ NY Col Brockport, 71-77; prof art & dir, Sch Art, Univ Wash, 77- *Mailing Add:* Sch of Art Univ of Wash Seattle WA 98195

ARNOLD, ROBERT LLOYD
PAINTER, EDUCATOR
b Buffalo, NY, June 28, 40. *Study:* NY State Univ Col, Buffalo, BS, 66; Fla State Univ, MS, 68; Ind Univ, EdD, 72. *Work:* NY Col Ceramics, Alfred; Nat Art Gallery NZ, Wellington; Fla State Univ, Tallahassee; Ind Univ. *Exhib:* Sign/Symbol, Nat Art Gallery NZ, 77; Artwords & Bookworks, Los Angeles Inst Contemp Art, 78; one-man shows, Ind Univ, Bloomington, 78, Ohio State Univ, 78, Ashland Col, Ohio, 79, Bowling Green State Univ, 80 & Ohio State Univ, Newark, 82; Spangler Cummings Gallery, 86. *Teaching:* Assoc Provost, Ohio State Univ, 90-; prof art & art educ, Ohio State Univ, 70- *Awards:* Mem Award, Lester C Bush, 74; Battelle Exhib Award, Dollar Savings, 76; Columbus Mus Award, 79. *Bibliog:* Gina Franz (auth), Six in Ohio, New Art Examiner, 78; Robert Pincus-Witten (auth) Six in Ohio, Ohio State Univ/Ohio Arts Coun, 78; Donald Kuspit (auth), Columbus, Art in Am, 79. *Mem:* Ohio Art Educ Asn; Nat Art Educ Asn; Columbus Art League (pres, 79 & 80). *Media:* Acrylic Paint; Canvas. *Res:* Contemporary art; art education. *Publ:* Auth, An analysis of selected teacher preparation programs: 1975, Art Educ, 76; The spoken retrospective: Chris Burden at 30, Midwest Art, 76; The development of a pluralistic avant-garde, Art Educ, 76; An interview with Lawrence Alloway, Midwest Art, 77; A new look at the teacher-critic, Ohio Art Educ Asn J, 78. *Mailing Add:* 289 Odessa Lane Dublin OH 43017

ARNOLDI, CHARLES ARTHUR
SCULPTOR, PAINTER
b Dayton, Ohio, April 10, 46. *Study:* Chouinard Art Inst, Los Angeles, 68. *Work:* Los Angeles Co Mus Art; Mus Mod Art, New York; Chicago Art Inst; Metrop Mus Art, New York; San Francisco Mus Mod Art. *Comn:* Wood relief paintings, Continental Nat Bank, Ft Worth, 81 & First Int Bank, Houston, 82; Hughes Corp, Los Angeles, 85; State of Calif, State Office Bldg, San Francisco, 88. *Exhib:* solo exhibs, Tex Gallery, Houston, 72, 77, 79, 81, 83 & 87, Nicholas Wilder Gallery, 74-75, 77-78 & 79, Seattle Art Mus, 76, Robert Elkon Gallery, New York, 78 & 79, James Corcoran Gallery, Los Angeles, 80, 85, Charles Arnoldi: Unique Prints, Los Angeles Co Mus Art, 84, Fuller Goldeen Gallery, San Francisco, 85 & 87, Charles Cowles Gallery, New York, 85-87, Arts Club Chicago, 86, Univ Mo-Kansas City Gallery Art, Univ Art Mus, Calif State Univ, Long Beach, 87 & Museo Italo Am, San Francisco, 88; Whitney Bienniel, 81; Am: The Landscape, Contemp Arts Mus, Houston, 81; 38th Bienniel, Corcoran Gallery Art, Washington, DC, 83; Am Prints Today, Brooklyn Mus, 86; 70's in 80's: Printmaking Now, Mus Fine Arts, Boston, 86; Cast in Bronze, Univ Mo-Kansas City Gallery Art, 87; New Works, Charles Cowles Gallery, New York, 87; Prints by Los Angeles Artists, Asahi Shimbun Gallery, Tokyo, 87; Recent Works: Charles Arnoldi, Ron Cooper, Laddie John Dill, Sena Galleries West, Santa Fe, 87; The 1980's: A New Generation, Metrop Mus Art, New York, 88. *Awards:* Wittkowsky Award, Art Inst Chicago, 72; Fels, Nat Endowment Arts, 74 & 82 & John Simon Guggenheim Found, 75; Maestro Fel, Calif Arts Coun, 82. *Bibliog:* Jane Livingston (auth), Four Los Angeles artists, Art in Am, 9-10/70; Jan Butterfield (auth), Charles Arnoldi, Laddie John Dill, Calif State Univ, Fullerton, 83; Jane Livingston (auth), Charles Arnoldi/A Survey: 1971-1986, Arts Club of Chicago, 1986; Nicholas Wilder (auth), The Recent Paintings of Charles Arnoldi, Univ Mo, Kansas City, 86. *Media:* Wood, Bronze. *Dealer:* Fred Hoffman Gallery 912 Colorado Ave Santa Monica CA 90401; Charles Cowles Gallery 420 W Broadway New York NY 10012. *Mailing Add:* c/o Fred Hoffman Gallery 912 Colorado Ave Santa Monica CA 90401

ARONSON, DAVID
PAINTER, SCULPTOR
b Shilova, Lithuania, Oct 28, 23; US citizen. *Study:* Boston Mus Fine Arts Sch, with Karl Zerbe, cert, 45; Nat Soc Arts & Lett grant, 58; Guggenheim fel, 60. *Work:* Smithsonian Inst, Washington, DC; Art Inst Chicago; Va Mus Fine Arts, Richmond; Boston Mus Fine Arts; Whitney Mus Am Art, New York. *Comn:* Great Ideas of Western Man, Container Corp Am, 63; Brandeis Univ Libr. *Exhib:* Fourteen Americans, Mus Mod Art, 45; Va Mus Fine Arts Biennial, 45; Nat Collection Fine Arts Opening Exhib, Smithsonian Inst, 65; retrospective exhibs, Brandeis Univ, 79, Jewish Mus, New York, 79 & Mus Am Jewish Hist, Philadelphia, 79; Bronfman Ctr, Montreal, 82; Southeastern Mass Univ, 83. *Teaching:* Instr painting, Boston Mus Fine Arts Sch, 43-55; chmn div art, Boston Univ, 55-63, prof art, 62-89, chmn painting dept, 63-89, emer prof art, 89- *Awards:* Grand Prize, Boston Arts Festival, 52-54; Nat Acad Design, 73, 74 & 75. *Bibliog:* Article in Time Mag, 11/63; Newman (auth), Wax as art form, 66 & Grossman (auth), Art & tradition, 67, Yosellof. *Mem:* Academician Nat Acad Design. *Media:* Pastel; Encaustic, Bronze. *Publ:* Auth, Encaustic, Artist Mag, 62; Real & Unreal: The Double Nature of Art, Boston Univ, 67. *Dealer:* Pucker Gallery 171 Newbury St Boston MA 02116; Louis Newman Galleries 322 N Beverly Dr Beverly Hills CA 90210. *Mailing Add:* 137 Brimstone Lane Sudbury MA 01776

ARONSON, GEORGIANNA B See Nyman, Georgianna Beatrice

ARONSON, SANDA
ASSEMBLAGE ARTIST
b New York, NY, Feb 29, 40. *Study:* Oswego State Col, BS, 60; study with J De Creeft & Paul Pollaro at New Sch for Social Res, New York; Tulane Univ, New Orleans; Art Students League. *Work:* NC Print & Drawing Soc. *Comn:* Handprint Harper's Woodcut's, comn by Dr Marvin Oleshanky, 82. *Exhib:* Solo exhibts, Bloomingdale Regional Branch, New York Pub Libr, 74 & 75, Barnard Col, New York, McIntosh Ctr, 85 & Assembled Object, Atlanta Col, Art Gallery, 89; Artists' Soc Int Exhib, ASI Galleries, San Francisco, 87; Tenth Am NDak, Nat Exhib, Minot Art Gallery, 87; Tenth Ann US Print & Drawing Exhib, NC Print & Drawing Soc, 87; Nat Small Works Exhib, Guggenheim Mus, New York, 87; Winter Soltice Invitational, Ceres Gallery, New York, 87; Am Hist, Atlanta Col Art Gallery, 88-90; Third Am Int Juried Exhib of Minis, Del Bello Gallery, Toronto; Three Artists, Matrix Gallery, Sacramento, Calif, 88. *Teaching:* Founder Sch Project Studio, 77-79; Artist-in-residence, NY Found Arts. *Awards:* Purchase Award, NC Print & Drawing Soc, 87; Pollock-Krasner Found Grant, 86-88; First Place, Sculpture, Emerald City Classic VI, Nepthe Nundi Soc Int Competition, 87; Hon Mention, Emerald City Classic V, 86; Hon Mention, Bodyparts Contest, McDonalds Inc, 88. *Bibliog:* J L Collins (ed), Women Artists in America, Vol II, Univ Tenn at Chattanooga Press, 75; Eleanor Tufts (auth), American Women Artists, Vol II, 89. *Mem:* Founder Disabled Artists' Network; New York Artists Equity Asn; Women Arts Found (bd-mem-at-large, 75-76). *Media:* Collage, Handmade Paper. *Publ:* Contribr frontpiece, John Beecher (auth), Hear the Wind Blow, Int Press, 68. *Mailing Add:* PO Box 20781 New York NY 10025

ARSENAULT, KATE WHITMAN
PAINTER
b Camden, NJ, Oct 25, 22. *Study:* Wellesley Col, BA, 44; Univ Bridgeport, MS, 77; Silvermine Sch Art, Conn, studied with Dom Stone, Charles Reid, Herb Olsen & Ed Whitney. *Work:* Union Trust Co, Darien, Conn; Darien Libr, Conn. *Comn:* Long Island Sound House, comn by Eliz Lucas, Darien, Conn, 78; Vt pitcher & bowl, St Lukes Church, Darien Conn, 79; Cape Cod House, comn by Barbara Moyes, Vero Beach, Fla, 81; Wellfleet House, comn by Stephen Ambler, Peterborough, Ont, 83; shells, comn by Jeanne Rich, Dallas, Tex, 87. *Exhib:* Wellesley Col-Jewett M Wellesley, Mass, 70; one-woman shows, Salmagundi Club, New York, 80, Copley Soc, Boston, Mass, 85-86, New England Gallery Art & Cape Cod Art Asn; Boston Univ Art Gallery, Mass, 80; Cape Cod Conserv, Barnstable, Mass, 87; Monotype Guild New Eng Inc, Clyde Gallery, Mosman Park, Boston, Mass, 88; two-woman show, Creations of Cap Artists, Osterville, Mass, 90; Cahoon Mus Am Art, Cutuit, Mass; Gallery of Creations, Nokomis, Fla. *Pos:* News ed, Darien News, 70-80. *Teaching:* instr, Darien Art Gallery, Conn, 74-76; instr, Darien Adult Educ, 76-77; art therapist, Darien Convalescent Ctr, 77-80; art therapist, Pocasset Mental Health Ctr, 87- *Bibliog:* Peter Konig (auth), Dir Duxbury, Mass Art Asn, 87. *Mem:* Salmagundi Club; Am Watercolor Soc; Copley Soc; Guild of Boston Artists; Cape Cod Art Asn; assoc mem New Eng Watercolor Soc. *Media:* Watercolor, Oil. *Publ:* illusr, Print-Nantucket, Globe Press, 87; L and Art, Cape Cod Life, Nantucket, Cape Cod Life, 88. *Mailing Add:* 9 Red Brook Pond Dr Box 710 Cataumet MA 02534

ARTEMIS, MARIA (MARIA ARTEMIS PAPAGEORGE SAWYER)
SCULPTOR, EDUCATOR
b Greensboro, NC, Apr, 21, 45. *Study:* Agnes Scott Col, Decatur, Ga, BA, 69; Univ Ga, Athens, MFA, 77; Ga Inst Technol, Col Archit, MS, 91. *Work:* Columbia Mus Art & Sci, SC; High Mus Art, Atlanta, Ga; Huntsville Mus Art, Ala; City of Atlanta, Ga; CGR Advisors, Atlanta, Ga; and others. *Comn:* Open Axis (permanent Site work), City of Atlanta, 87. *Exhib:* Mostra, Cortona, Italy, 79; Avant-Garde/12 in Atlanta, High Mus Art, Ga, 79; Earth Art: Sand & Clay Southeastern Ctr Contemp Art, Winston-Salem, NC, 80; solo exhibs, Nexus Inc 3rd floor Gallery, Atlanta, Ga, 80, Fine Art Gallery, Univ Tenn, Chattanooga, Upstairs Gallery, Tryon, NC, 84 & Works on Paper, Univ Central Fla Gallery, Orlando, 87; Atlanta Women's Art Collective, AIR Gallery, New York, 80; Origins and Evolutions, Part II, Atlanta Col Art Gallery, Mem Art Ctr, Ga, 84; First Atlanta Bienniale, Nexus Gallery, Ga, 84; Avant Garde/12 in Atlanta-Five Years Later, Heath Gallery, Ga, 84; Analemma, On Site Work, Atlanta Arts Fest, Piedmont Park, Ga, 85; Contemp Artists in Ga, High Mus Art, Atlanta, 88; New South Group: Installations and Drawings, 112 Greene St, New York, 89. *Pos:* Vis artist slides, Univ Wis, Superior, 79; artist-in-residence, Cortona, Italy, 79 & Southeastern Ctr Contemp Art, Winston-Salem, NC, 80; artist fel, Va Ctr Creative Arts, 84 & 91; bd dir, treas, artists initiated projs, New South Group,

89; panel moderator, S Arts Fedn NEA Regional Fel in Sculpture, 90. *Teaching:* Fac mem sculpture foundation design, Atlanta Col Art, 79-81; lectr, Atlanta Col Art, spring 83; guest lectr, Ga Inst Technol, Col Archit, Atlanta, Ga, 84; vis prof, Dept Art, Agnes Scott Col, Decatur, Ga, 87-90; adj prof, Atlanta Col Art, 92-93. *Awards:* Exhib Grant, 80 & Individual Fel Grant, 88, Nat Endowment Arts; Regional on Site Work Grant, Atlanta Arts Fest, Piedmont Park, Atlanta, Ga, 85; Honorable Mention, Int Design Competition, Redesign Peachtree St, 91; and others. *Bibliog:* City on a Hill, Twenty Years of Artists at Corona (catalog), 89; Ann Glenn Crowe (auth), New South Group, Art Papers, 89; Donna Young (auth), ARS NATURA (J), Working Maps of Reality: Three Artists, vol III, No 1, 2/90. *Mem:* Int Sculpture Ctr. *Media:* Mixed. *Publ:* Andy Nasisse: Works off the Wall, Craft Horizon, 78; Art and the sacred, Art Papers, 11-12/86; auth, Rethinking the Sacred Image, Artpapers, vol IV & V, 90. *Mailing Add:* 2854 N Hills Dr Atlanta CA 30305

ARTINIAN, ARTINE
COLLECTOR, PATRON
b Bulgaria, Dec 8, 07; US citizen. *Study:* Bowdoin Col, BA, 31; Harvard Univ, MA, 33; Columbia Univ, PhD, 41; Bowdoin Col, Hon LittD, 66. *Exhib:* Drawings by French Writers & Illustrators, var Am col & univs, 68-74, Art Gallery, Auckland City, NZ, 77 & Fr Embassy-sponsored tour in US, 79-84; Music in Art, traveling, 71-73, Hats by French Artists, 80 & Florida Self-Portraits, 81, Henry Morrison Flagler Mus, Palm Beach, Fla; Artists' Letters with Drawings, Seton Hall Univ Libr, So Orange, NJ, 78; Norton Gallery of Art, West Palm Beach, Fla, 89; Self-portraits, NC artists, Appalachian Cult Mus, Boone, NC; Fla artists, Ritter Gallery, Fla Atlantic Univ, Boca Raton, Fla; French Costume designs, Hewey Morrison Flagler Mus, Palm Beach, Fla; Guy de Maupassant Collection, Humanities Research Ctr, Univ Tex, Austin, Tex. *Teaching:* Bard Col, 35-64; dir, Jr Yr in France, Sweet Briar Col, Va, 53-55 & US House, Cite Universitaire, Paris, summer 55, 56 & 58. *Awards:* Officier d'Academie, France, 48; Fulbright Res Scholar, France, 49-50; Am Philos Soc Res Grant, Paris, 60. *Mem:* Fel Am Coun Learned Soc, 43; Expressions, Paris (hon pres, 83-); Am Asn Univ Prof (pres, 51-52). *Collection:* Exhibited: Drawings and Paintings by French Writers; French Illustrators; The French Visage, A Century and a Half of French Portraits; Music in Art; Florida Self-portraits; Carolina Self-portraits; Miguel Covarubias Drawings of 1930. *Publ:* Auth numerous publ incl eight bks. *Mailing Add:* Winthrop House 100 Worth Ave PH6 Palm Beach FL 33480

ARTSCHWAGER, RICHARD ERNST
SCULPTOR, PAINTER
b Washington, DC, Dec 26, 23. *Study:* Cornell Univ, AB; studio study with Amedee Ozenfant. *Work:* Whitney Mus Am Art; Tate Gallery; Chicago Art Inst; Mus Mod Art & Metrop Mus Art; Hirsehhorn Mus; and others. *Comn:* Battery Park City, NY, 88; General Mills Corp, Minneapolis, 88; Elvehjen Mus Art, Madison, Wis, 91. *Exhib:* Cool Art-67, Larry Aldrich Mus, Ridgefield, Conn, 67; Documenta 4, 5, 7, 8 & 9, Kassel, Ger, 68; Radical Realism, Mus Contemp Art, Chicago, 70; Sonsbeek '71, Arnhem/Utrecht, Holland, 71; Documenta, Kassel, Ger, 68 & 72; Venice Biennale, 76; Two Hundred Years of Am Sculpture, Whitney Mus Mod Art, 76; solo exhib, Kunstuerein, Hamburg, 78, Albright-Knox Art Gallery, Buffalo, Inst Contemp Art, Univ Pa, 79, La Jolla Mus Contemp Art, Calif, 80 & Contemp Mus, Houston, Tex, 80; The Destroyed Print, Pratt Manhattan Ctr Gallery, New York, 82; Actual Size, Larry Gagosian Gallery, Los Angeles, 85; An American Renaissance: Painting and Sculpture Since 1940, Mus Art, Ft Lauderdale, Fla, 85, Retrospective Whitney Mus; Mary Boone Gallery, 90; Kunstnernes Hus, Oslo, 92; Mus Fine Arts, Boston, 92. *Awards:* Nat Endowment Arts, 71; Archit League New York. *Bibliog:* John Russell (auth), article, NY Times, 79; Roberta Smith (auth), article, Art in Am, 80; Coosje van Bruggen (auth), Richard Artschwajer, Artforum, 9/83. *Publ:* Auth, The hydraulic door check, Arts Mag, 11/67; contribr, Art and Reason, Parkette, No 23, 90. *Dealer:* Mary Boone Gallery 417 W Broadway New York NY 10012. *Mailing Add:* 158 S Oxford St Brooklyn NY 11217-1604

ARUM, BARBARA
SCULPTOR
b Des Moines, Iowa, Oct 9, 37. *Study:* With Raymond Rocklin, Vincent Leggiadro, Chaim Gross & Philip Listengart. *Work:* Alan Towers, Inc. *Exhib:* Hudson River Mus, 82-90; Andre Zarre Gallery, 86; Elaine Benson Gallery, 87; Monmouth Mus Fine Arts, 87; Hammond Mus, 92; and others. *Awards:* Bus Community Award, North Am Sculpture Exhib, Golden, Colo, 87; Dir max Ellenberg Mem Award, 89 & Gretchen Richardson Freelander Mem Award, 90 & 91, Nat Asn Women Artists, New York; Salvatore Maida Mem Award, Am Soc Contemp Artists, New York, 91. *Bibliog:* Reporters Dispatch, 11/12/82; articles, New York Times, 83, 85 & 87; article, Art World, 10/15/83. *Mem:* Nat Asn Women Artists (sculptor juror, 86-88); NY Artists Equity Asn; Allied Artists (treas, 86); NY Soc Women Artists (pres 90-93); Am Soc Contemp Artists (treas, 92-94); and others. *Media:* Steel, Bronze. *Mailing Add:* 138 W 17th New York NY 10011

ARVIN, IRMGARD PINCKERNELL
PAINTER, INSTRUCTOR
b Berlin, Ger, Jan 5, 23; Nat US. *Study:* Md Inst Art, 39-41; studied with Jacque Maroger & Frank Rodelius. *Work:* Danville Mus Art & Hist, Va. *Comn:* large triptych, comn by Mr & Mrs Earle MacAusland, NY, 77; paint Easter eggs, White House, Washington, DC, 87. *Exhib:* Corcoran Gallery, Washington, DC, 56; Acad Artists Mus, Springfield, Mass, 60; Knickerbocker Artists, New York, 65; Catherine Lorillard Wolfe, New York, 78; Danville Mus Fine Arts, Va, 83. *Teaching:* Instr still life, Baltimore City Col, Md, 56-58 & Va Ctr Creative Arts, Charlottesville, 71-72, Nantucket, Mass. *Awards:* James Hunt Barker Award, Artists Asn, Nantucket, 81. *Bibliog:* Rosette Lamont (auth), Still life, Inquirer Mirror, Nantucket, Mass, 69; Ruth Latter (auth), The Southern artist, Southern Accents, 86. *Mem:* Artists Equity; Nantucket Artists Asn; Silvermine Guild Artists; Women in Arts; Va Mus Art. *Publ:* Contribr, House & Garden Mag, 67 & 79; Palm Beach Life Mag, 70; Palm Beach Illus Mag, 70; Gourmet Mag, 80; auth, article in Southern Accents Mag, 86. *Dealer:* Robert Wilson Gallery Main St Nantucket MA 02554; Gooley Gallery Olde Lyme CT. *Mailing Add:* 35 Georgetown Green Charlottesville VA 22901

ARYE, LEONORA E
SCULPTOR
b New York, NY, May 22, 31. *Study:* Art Students League, 64-66; with Hana Geber, 65-70; with Lorrie Goulet, 70-72; Univ Mex. *Work:* Albany Inst Hist & Art, NY; Galeria Moderna, Mex; Mus Art, Bogota, Colombia. *Comn:* L'Chaim (stone), Jewish Community Ctr, Harrison, NY, 76; Justice (stone), Judge Jacob Fuchsberg, New York, 77; Mermaid (wood), Mamaroneck Beach Club, NY, 85. *Exhib:* Silvermine Guild Artists, New Canaan, Conn, 80; Nat Asn Women Artists, City Gallery, New York, 81; Bergen Mus, Paramus, NJ; Couturier Gallery, Los Angeles, 91; Nadeau Gallery, Philadelphia, 92; Roz Sailor Gallery, Margate, NJ, 92; and others. *Awards:* Paul Manship Memorial Award, Catherine Lorillard Wolfe Art Club, 88; ASCA Contemp Art Award for Sculpture, 89; Top Award (Margaret Sussman), Pen & Brush Club, New York, 90. *Bibliog:* A Williams (auth), Sculpture-Technique, Form & Content, Davis Publications, 89; J Klausner (auth), Enjoying the arts/sculpture, Richard Rosen Press, 81; Art Quest '88, Jonette Slabney, 88. *Mem:* Nat Asn Women Artists (publ comt, 80-81); Am Soc Contemp Artists; Silvermine Guild Artists; Knickerbocker Artists; Allied Artists of Am. *Media:* Stone, Wood. *Dealer:* Mari Galleries East Prospect Mamaroneck NY 10543; Couturier Gallery 1814 Newfield Ave Stamford CT 06903. *Mailing Add:* Cove Island Mamaroneck NY 10543

ASCIAN
PRINTMAKER, PAINTER
b Aug 29, 43; US citizen. *Work:* Whitney Mus Am Art, Metrop Mus Art, New York; Corcoran Gallery Art, Nat Collection Fine Art, Hirshhorn Mus, Washington, DC; and others. *Comn:* Serigraphs, Off Equal Employment Opportunity, 73; lithographs, Washington Printmakers' Workshop Proj, 74; serigraph, Washington Print Club, 75. *Exhib:* One-person shows, Corcoran Gallery Art, Dupont Ctr, 69, Green Panther Gallery, Frankfurt, Ger, 82, Fla Southern Col, 82; Seven Young Artists, Corcoran Gallery Art, Washington DC, 72; Baltimore Mus, 72; Illumination, San Francisco, Calif, 80; Sylvia Ullman Gallery, Cleveland, Ohio, 80; Zenith Gallery, Washington, DC, 80; House of Artists, Moscow, USSR, 89; and many others. *Awards:* Stern Family grant, 70; Washington Printmaker's Proj, 74; Printmakers Grant, Nat Endowment Arts, 74. *Bibliog:* Dreamtime, The Washingtonian, 4/75; Paul Richard (auth), Making it as an artist, The Washington Post, 10/77. *Media:* Mixed. *Collection:* Fantasy and surrealism: Klinger, Milton. *Publ:* Auth, The Unicorn, Viking Press, 80; illusr, The Unicorn Calendar, Pomegranite Press, 80 & 82. *Mailing Add:* PO Box 97 Mill Valley CA 94942-0097

ASHBAUGH, DENNIS JOHN
PAINTER
b Red Oak, Iowa, Oct 25, 46. *Study:* Orange Coast Col, Costa Mesa, Calif, AA, 66; Calif State Univ, Fullerton, BA, 68, MA, 69. *Work:* Rolls Royce Inc, New York; Miami Art Ctr, Fla; Toledo Art Mus, Ohio; Seattle Art Mus, Wash; Owens Corning Inc, New York; Met Mus Art, Mus Mod Art, New York. *Exhib:* One-man shows, Whitney Mus Am Art, 75, Charles Cowles Gallery, New York, 82, Calif State Univ, Fullerton, Calif, 84, Kasmin Gallery, 89 & 90, Margulies-Taplin, Miami, Fla, 91 and many others; The Painter & His Occasion, Marta Cervera Gallery, New York, 90; Abstraction, Margulies-Taplan Gallery, Boca Raton, Fla, 91; Invisible Body, Rempire Fine Art Gallery, New York, 91; Abstract Painting the '90's, Andre Emmerich, New York; Behind Bars, Thread Waxing Space, New York, 92. *Awards:* Creative Artists Pub Serv Grant, NY Coun Arts, 75; Guggenheim Found Fel, 76. *Bibliog:* Guy Martin (auth), Read it Once, Esquire, 5/92; Garvin Edwards (auth), Details, 6/92; Rhonda Lieberman, Artforum, 6/92; and others. *Media:* Oil. *Mailing Add:* 67 Greene St New York NY 10012

ASHBERY, JOHN LAWRENCE
CRITIC
b Rochester, NY, July 28, 27. *Study:* Harvard Col, BA(Eng lit), 49; Columbia Univ, MA(Eng lit), 51; grad study, French lit, New York Univ, 57-58. *Pos:* Art critic Europ ed, New York Herald-Tribune, Paris, 60-65; Paris corresp, Art News, 64-65; art critic, Art Int, Lugano, Switz, 61-64; ed, Locus Solus, France, 60-62; ed, Art & Lit, Paris, 63-66; exec ed, Art News, 66-72; art critic, New York Mag, 78-80; poetry ed, Partisan Review, New York, 76-80; art critic, Newsweek, New York, 80-85. *Teaching:* Prof, Brooklyn Col, NY, 74-90, distinguished prof, 80-90; Charles Eliot Norton Prof Poetry, Harvard Univ, 89-90; Charles P Stevenson Jr Prof Lang & Lit, Bard Col, Annandale-on-Hudson, NY, 90- *Awards:* Creative Arts Award Poetry, Brandeis Univ, 89; Ruth Lilly Poetry Prize, Poetry Mag, Mod Poetry Asn & Am Coun Arts, 92; Antonio Feltrinelli Int Prize Poetry (Accademia Nazionale dei Lincei, Rome), 92; and others. *Bibliog:* David K Kermani (auth), John Ashbery: A Comprehensive Bibliography, Garland, 76. *Mem:* Am Acad & Inst Arts & Lett; Am Acad Arts & Sci. *Res:* Life & Work of Raymond Roussel. *Publ:* Art criticism in anthologies & periodicals; texts for numerous exhib catalogs; Reported Sightings: Art Chronicles 1957-87, Knopf, 89 & Carcanet, Manchester, England, 89; auth, April Galleons, Viking, 87, Penguin, 88 & Carcanet, 88; Flow Chart, 91 & Hotel Lautréamont, 92, Knopf & Careanet. *Mailing Add:* c/o George Borchardt Inc 136 E 57th St New York NY 10022

ASHBY, CARL
PAINTER, INSTRUCTOR
b San Rita, NMex, Mar 2, 14. *Study:* Univ Utah, BS; NY Univ, MA; Art Students League, NY; Grand Cent Sch Art, Atelier 17; also with Morris Kantor; New Sch Art Work Shop, Etching & Block Printing. *Work:* Purdue Univ. *Exhib:* Pa Ann; Corcoran Gallery, Washington, DC; Whitney Mus Ann, 47 & 49; Libr Cong Print Show; Tirca Karlis Gallery, 64-75; New Sch Social Res, 76, 77, 79 & 90; Nat Acad Art Ann, 77, 79, 80 & 91. *Pos:* Owner, Ashby Gallery, 45-48 & 80- *Teaching:* Instr painting, New Sch Social Res, 71-92. *Awards:* First Prize Landscape, Nat Acad Altman, 86; Silver Medal, Audubon Artists, 87. *Mem:* Artists Equity Asn; Art Students League (rec secy, Bd Control, 46); Audubon Artist. *Media:* Oil, Watercolor. *Mailing Add:* 18 Cornelia St New York NY 10014

ASHCRAFT, EVE
PAINTER
b Pontiac, Mich, Mar 1, 63. *Study:* RI Sch Design, BFA, 85. *Awards:* Nat Endowment Arts Fel, 87. *Mailing Add:* 172 E Fourth St Apt 10-G Apt 101 New York NY 10009

ASHER, ELISE
PAINTER, POET
b Chicago, Ill. *Study:* Art Inst Chicago; Bradford Jr Col; Simmons Col, BS. *Work:* Nat Acad Sci, Washington, DC; Univ Calif Art Mus, Berkeley; John Michael Kohler Arts Ctr, Sheboygan, Wis; Corcoran Gallery, Washington, DC; Provinceton Art Asn Mus, Mass; William Benton Mus, Storrs, Conn; Poets' House, New York. *Comn:* Oil on Plexiglas window, comn by Dr John P Spiegel, Cambridge; cover for Poetry Northwest, autumn-winter 64-65; cover for The Chelsea, No 27, 70; jacket for Stanley Kunitz, The Testing-Tree (poems), Little, Brown, 71. *Exhib:* Lettering Traveling Show, Mus Mod Art, New York, 67; solo exhibs, Bertha Schaefer Gallery, New York, 73, Univ Richmond, Va, 75 & Ingber Gallery, New York, 79, 81 83, 85 & 87, William Benton Mus, 88, June Kelly Gallery (with catalog), New York, 91, Princeton Art Asn & Mus, NJ, 92; Nat Collection Fine Arts, 76 & Nat Acad Sci, 83, Smithsonian Inst; Fine Arts Mus Long Island, 83; group exhibs, Am Acad Arts & Letters, New York, 80 & 89, Pompidou Ctr, France, Anita Shapolsky Gallery, New York. *Bibliog:* Brian O'Doherty (auth), articles, Art in Am & Art World, 79, 81 & 83; P Carlson (auth), Asher at the Ingber, Art In Am, 10/79; Eleanor Munro (auth), Originals: American Women Artists, Simon & Schuster, 79 & Avon Press, 82; Rose Slivka (auth), article, Art News, 6/85; Carl Little (auth), Asher at the Ingber, Art Am, 6/87; David Sutton (auth), When Art Becomes Poetry & Poetry Art, Reporter, spring 91; Christopher Busa (auth), Princeton Arts, 92. *Media:* Oil, Pencil & Ink. *Publ:* Auth, The Meandering Absolute, Morris Gallery Press, NY, 55; illus, This Book is a movie, 71; contribr, Acrylic for Sculpture & Design, Van Nostrand, 72; Art: A woman's Sensibility, Calif Inst Arts, 75. *Dealer:* June Kelly & June Kelly Gallery 591 Broadway New York NY 10012. *Mailing Add:* 37 W 12th St New York NY 10011

ASHER, FREDERICK M
HISTORIAN, EDUCATOR
b Chicago, Ill, May 25, 41. *Study:* Dartmouth Col, BA; Univ Chicago, MA & PhD. *Pos:* Actg dir, Univ Gallery, Univ Minn, 71-72, chair, dept art hist, 78-81; assoc dean, Col Lib Arts, 85-91, chair, dept art hist, 91- *Teaching:* Instr art hist, Lake Forest Col, 67-70; assoc prof art hist, Univ Minn, Minneapolis, 70-81, prof, 81. *Mem:* Am Comt SAsian Art (treas, 72-74); Am Inst Indian Studies (treas, 87-). *Res:* South Asian art. *Publ:* Various publications pertaining to the art of India. *Mailing Add:* Dept Art Univ Minn Minneapolis MN 55455

ASHER, LILA OLIVER
PRINTMAKER, PAINTER
b Philadelphia, Pa. *Study:* With Gonippo Raggi, Joseph Grossman & Frank B A Linton; Philadelphia Col Art, grad. *Work:* Corcoran Gallery Art, Georgetown Univ, Howard Univ & Nat Mus Am Art, Washington, DC; Fisk Univ, Nashville; Univ Va, Charlottesville; Nat Mus Women Arts. *Comn:* Oil paintings, two panels, Congregation Rodeph Shalom, Philadelphia, 40; murals, two rooms, Indian Spring Country Club, Glenmont, Md. *Exhib:* Retrospective Exhib, Howard Univ, 78 & 91; one-woman shows in US, Japan, India, Taiwan, Denmark, Iran & Pakistan, var times, 51-85; Univ Calif Los Angeles; Rockville Art Mansion, Md; Cosmos Club, Washington, DC; and others. *Teaching:* Instr art, Howard Univ, 47-51; instr art, Wilson Teachers Col, 53-54; from lectr to prof art, Howard Univ, 61- *Awards:* Printmaker of the Year, High School Graphics Program, Nat Mus Am Art, 81. *Bibliog:* American Prints from Wood, Smithsonian Inst; Catalogues, Kastrugardsamlingen Kunst Mus Denmark Howard Univ, Washington, DC. *Mem:* Am Asn Univ Prof; Soc Washington Artists; Soc Washington Printmakers (rec secy, 68-75); Artist Equity Asn (treas, DC Chap, 71-74); Washington Watercolor Asn; Cosmos Club Washington, DC. *Media:* Wood & Linoleum Block; Oil. *Mailing Add:* 4100 Thornapple St Chevy Chase MD 20815

ASHER, MICHAEL
SCULPTOR
b Los Angeles, Calif, July 15, 43. *Study:* Orange Coast Col, Costa Mesa, Calif, 61-63; Univ NMex, Albuquerque, 63-64; New York Studio Sch, 64-65; Univ Calif, Irvine, BA(fine arts), 66, 66-67. *Exhib:* I am Alive, Los Angeles Co Mus of Art, Calif, 67; Anit-Illusion: Procedures: Materials, Whitney Mus, New York, 69; solo exhibs, La Jolla Mus Art, 69 & Gladys K Montgomery Art Ctr, Pomona Col, Claremont, Calif, 70; 24 Young Los Angeles Artists, Los Angeles Co Mus Art, 71; Galleria Toselli, Milano, Italy, 73; Lisson Gallery, London, Eng, 73; Otis Art Inst Gallery, Los Angeles, 75; Abbe Mus, Eindhogen, Holland, 77; A Pierre Etr Marie, Paris, 83; Hofhour Gallery, Albuquerque, NM, 84 & 86; In Contact, Mus Contemp Art, Los Angeles, 85. *Teaching:* Asst instr sculpture, Univ Calif, Irvine, 66-67, painting instr, 67-68; instr industrial arts, Anaheim Union High Sch District & Garden Grove Sch District, Calif; vis artist, Univ Calif, 73, Calif Inst Arts, Valencia, 73 & 76, NS Col Art & Design, 74 & Otis Art Inst, Los Angeles, 75; Instr, Calif Inst Arts, 75- *Awards:* Art Purchase Award, Contemp Art Coun, Los Angeles Co Mus, 67; John Simon Guggenheim Mem Fel, 74; Artist Fel Grant, Nat Endowment Arts, 75. *Publ:* Writings 1973-1983, On Works, 1969-1979, NS Col Art & Design, 83. *Mailing Add:* 2262 Carmelina Ave Los Angeles CA 90064

ASHTON, DORE
ART CRITIC, WRITER
b Newark, NJ. *Study:* Univ Wis, BA; Harvard Univ, MA; Moore Col Art, hon degree; Hamline Univ, hon degree. *Pos:* Assoc ed, Art Digest, New York, 52-54; art critic, New York Times, 55-60; contrib ed, Opus Int, Paris, 65-75 & Arts Mag, 74- *Teaching:* Prof art hist, Cooper Union, 69- *Awards:* Mather Award Art Criticism, Col Art Asn, 63; Guggenheim Fels, 64 & 69; Ford Found Award, 65; and others. *Mem:* Int Asn Art Critics (gov bd mem, 60-); Pen Club (mem exec bd); Col Art Asn. *Res:* Modern art. *Publ:* Ed, 20th Century Artists on Art, 85; Out of the Whirlwind, 87; Fragonard in the Universe of Painting, 88; Noguchi East and West, 92; Terence La Noue, 92; and others. *Mailing Add:* 217 E 11th St New York NY 10003

ASIHENE, EMMANUEL V
EDUCATOR, PAINTER
b Asamankese, Ghana, Dec 1, 37. *Study:* Ohio State Univ, PhD (Art Educ), 73. *Work:* Ohio Pub Libr & Ohio Mus Art, Columbus; Ohio State Univ, Columbus. *Exhib:* One-man show, Afro-Ganza Art Exhib, Mus Fine Art, Columbus, Ohio, 72; Grad Student Show, Ohio State Univ, Columbus, Ohio, 73; Art Fac Show, Atlanta Univ Ctr, Ga, 74; Artists USA, New York, 76; Black Artists South, Huntsville Mus Art, Ala, 79. *Pos:* Prof, Clark Atlanta Univ, Ga, 73-86. *Teaching:* Art Appreciation & African Art, Clark Atlanta Univ, Ga, 73- *Awards:* Aggrey & Hazen Found Fel. *Mem:* Nat Art Educ Asn; Ga Alliance Arts Educ; Nat Coun Art Adminr; Dekalb Coun Arts; Am Asn Univ Prof. *Media:* Oil, Watercolor. *Publ:* Auth, Understanding the Traditional Art of Ghana, Assoc Univ Press, 78; Apoo Festival, Ghana Publ Co, 80. *Mailing Add:* 2562 Farley St East Point GA 30344

ASKEVOLD, DAVID
CONCEPTUAL ARTIST, INSTRUCTOR
b Conrad, Mont, Mar 30, 40. *Study:* Univ Mont; Brooklyn Mus Sch Art, painting cert; Kansas City Art Inst, BFA(sculpture). *Work:* Van Abbe Mus, Eindhoven, Holland; Can Coun Art Bank & Nat Gallery Can, Ottawa; Vancouver Art Gallery, BC; Art Metropole, Toronto, Can; Art Gallery of Nova Scotia, Can. *Exhib:* Mus Mod Art, New York, 70 & 71; one-man shows, Found Art Resources, Los Angeles, 79 & Jancar/Kuhlenschmidt Gallery, 81, Coburg Gallery, Vancouver, BC, 84, Anna Leonowens Gallery, Halifax, 85; Text Visual, Commune di Milano, Italy, 79; Artist & Camera, Arts Coun Gt Brit, 80; Head Hunters, Los Angeles Contemporary Exhibitions, 83; Lucarno Switz Int Video Festival, 84; Curt Myers Gallery, Broadway New York, 91; New Canadian Embassy, Tokyo, Japan, 91; Brian Butler Gallery, Santa Monica, Calif, 92; and others. *Pos:* Vis artist video & special topics, Minneapolis Col Art & Design, 84-85. *Teaching:* Asst prof art, NS Col Art & Design, 68-73; vis lectr studio art, Univ Calif, Irvine, 76-77; spec appt photog & post studio art, Calif Inst Arts, Valencia, 77-78; lectr, Art Ctr, Col Design, Pasadena, Calif, 80-81 & Visual Art Dept, York Univ, Downsview, Ont, Can, 81-82; vis artist, Minn Col Art & Design, 84-85; adj prof, Nova Scotia Col Art & Design, 85-88 & 91. *Awards:* Sr Photog Production Grant, 83 & Video Production Grant, 84, Ont Art Coun; Proj Cost Grant exhib, 84, Photo Production Grant, Can Coun, 84; A Grant, 86-87, 89-90 & Visual Arts Production Grant, 90, Can Coun. *Bibliog:* Alan Sondheim (auth), Individuals, Dutton, 77; Howard Singerman (auth), article, Artforum, 5/81; Fredric Dolan (auth), essay, Vanguard, 3/88; Red Rider, Ctr for Art Tapes, Halifax, NS, 8/92. *Media:* Film, Audio, Video. *Publ:* auth, article, Drulwerk De Zaak, Groningen, 9/85. *Dealer:* Enzo Cannaviello Piazza Beccaria 10 20122 Milan Italy; Paul Maenz 23 Lindenstrasse Koln D-500 WGer. *Mailing Add:* 6305 North St #1 Halifax NS P3L 1P4 Canada

ASKEW, PAMELA
EDUCATOR, WRITER
b Poughkeepsie, NY. *Study:* Vassar Col, AB, 46; Inst Fine Arts, NY Univ, MA, 51; Courtauld Inst, Univ London, PhD, 54. *Teaching:* Instr art hist, Vassar Col, 56-57, asst prof, 57-62, assoc prof, 62-69, prof, 69-85, chmn dept art, 71-74. *Awards:* Fulbright Fel Art Hist, 65-66; Fel Inst Advan Studies, Princeton, 76 & 77; Distinguished Teaching Award, Col Art Asn, 88. *Mem:* Col Art Asn; Am Soc 18th Century Studies; Renaissance Soc. *Res:* Sixteenth to Eighteenth Century painting. *Publ:* The angelic consolation of St Francis of Assisi in post-tridentine Italian painting, J Warburg & Courtauld Insts, 69; Domenico Fetti'setti's portrait of an actor reconsidered, Burlington Mag, 2/78; Ferdinando Gonzaga's patronage of the pictorial arts: The villa favorita, Art Bulletin, 6/78; ed & auth intro, Claude Lorrain 1600-1682: A Symposium, Studies in Hist of Art, No 14, 84; auth, Caravaggios Death of the Virgin, Princeton, Univ Press, 90; plus others. *Mailing Add:* Valley Farm Rd Millbrook NY 12601

ASKIN, WALTER MILLER
PAINTER, PRINTMAKER
b Pasadena, Calif, Sept 12, 29. *Study:* Univ Calif, Berkeley, BA & MA; Ruskin Sch Drawing & Fine Art, Oxford Univ. *Work:* Mus Contemp Art, Chicago;

Oxford Mus Mod Art, Eng; San Francisco Mus Art; Kunstlerhaus, Vienna; Albright-Knox Gallery, Buffalo. *Exhib:* One-man shows, La Jolla Mus Art, Calif, 67, Abraxas Gallery, Calif, 79, 80 & 81, Univ Southern Calif, 80 & Kunstlerhaus, Vienna, Austria, 81; Prints by Seven, Whitney Mus Am Art, 70; Int Biennial Graphic Art, Mus Mod Art, Ljubljana, Yugoslavia, 83; Lizardi/Harp Gallery, Pasadena, 88 & 90. *Pos:* Bd trustees, Pasadena Art Mus, 63-68; bd dir, Los Angeles Inst of Contemp Art, Los Angeles, 77-81; bd gov, Baxter Art Gallery, Calif Inst Technol, 80-; artist rep, Graphic Arts Council, Los Angeles Co Mus Art, 80-; chmn visual arts panel, Nat Art Awards, 81-82; advan placement, studio art exam comt, The Coll Bd, 85-, chmn arts advi comt, 86- *Teaching:* Prof art, Calif State Univ, Los Angeles, 56-; vis prof art, Univ Calif, Berkeley, 68-69, Calif State Univ, Long Beach, 74-75 & Univ Hawaii, 83; vis artist, Kelpra Studio, London, 69 & 73, Tamarind Inst, Univ NMex, 72, Athens Sch Fine Arts, 73, Cranbrook Acad Art, 79, Ariz State Univ, 80 & 83, Ossabaw Island Found, Ga, 82, Va Ctr Creative Arts, 83, 86 & Vt Studio Colony, 88. *Awards:* Senator James Phelan Award, San Francisco Mus Art, 69; Artist Award, Pasadena Arts Coun, 70; Outstanding Prof Award, Calif State Univ, Los Angeles, 73. *Bibliog:* Violante (auth), American Printmakers '74, Graphics Group, 74; Newman (auth), Innovative Printmaking, Crown, 77; Walter Askin 1970-1980, Univ Southern Calif, 80. *Mem:* Col Art Asn Am; Los Angeles Printmaking Soc. *Media:* Oil, Acrylic; Mixed Media. *Mailing Add:* PO Box 50381 Pasadena CA 91115-0381

ASKMAN, TOM K
PAINTER, EDUCATOR
b Leadville, Colo, Oct 27, 41. *Study:* Univ Colo, MFA; Calif Col Arts & Crafts, BFA. *Work:* City Seattle, Wash; Cheney Cowles Art Mus, Spokane, Wash; Ft Worth Art Mus, Tex; Mus Art, Univ Okla, Norman; Mus Art, Univ Colo, Boulder. *Comn:* City Hall, Laguna Beach, Calif, 92; Plaza Area Nutrition Ctr Complex, Iowa State Univ, Ames, 92. *Exhib:* New Orleans Mus Art, La, 71; Addison Gallery Am Art, Andover, Mass, 71; Minneapolis Art Inst, Minn, 71; Va Mus Fine Arts, Richmond, 72; Extraordinary Realities, Whitney Mus Am Art, New York, 73; Springfield Art Mus, Mo, 73-74; Contemp Arts Ctr, Cincinnati, Ohio, 74; Seattle Art Mus, Wash, 74; Private Views, Henry Gallery, Univ Wash, 80. *Teaching:* Instr, Univ Minn, Minneapolis, 68-70; assoc prof, Nicholls State Univ, Thibodaux, La, 70-72 & Eastern Wash Univ, Cheney, 72- *Awards:* Cheney Cowles Art Mus, Spokane, 74, 76, 80 & 81; Painting Award, 60th Ann NW Artists, Seattle Art Mus, Wash, 74; State Wash Commissions, 79. *Mailing Add:* Eastern Washington Univ Cheney WA 99004

ASMAR, ALICE
PAINTER, PRINTMAKER
b Flint, Mich. *Study:* Lewis & Clark Col, BA(magna cum laude); with Edward Melcarth & Archipenko, Univ Wash, MFA; Woolley fel, Ecole Nat Superieure des Beaux-Arts, Paris, with M Souverbie; Huntington Hartford Found residence fels, 61-64. *Work:* Gene Autry Hotel, Palm Springs; Franklin Mint, Pa; Smithsonian Inst; Pub Int Mus, Gabrova, Bulgaria; Huntington Beach Cultural Ctr; Kaiser Permanente, Panorama City; Smith & Assocs, Boise, Idaho; and others. *Comn:* Series ltd ed Lumigraphs, Dreamscape Productions, Burnaby, BC, 91; painting of doves, Bangs Manufacturing Co, Burbank, 92; paintings of Calif quail, Maples, San Marino, 92; paintings of Indian dancers, Navarros, Hillsboro, Ore, 92; 45 ink drawings for educational brochures & posters, Small Wilderness Area Preserv, 92. *Exhib:* Seattle Art Mus, 52; Drawings USA, Minn Mus Art Nat Travel Show, 71-73; West 79/The Law, Minn Mus Art, 79-80; one-woman shows, Sedona Art Ctr, Ariz, 79, Mus of Sci & Indust, Los Angeles, 81, Sr Eye Art Gallery, Long Beach, 77 & 82, Circle Gallery Ltd, Houston, 83, Hilton Hotel, 91 & Abbott Hall Gallery, William Temple House, Portland, Ore, 92; Art Expo, LA Convention Ctr, 89; City of Hope Art Auction, 90; and others. *Pos:* Eng draftsman, Boeing Aircraft, 52-54; engraver, Nambe Mills, Santa Fe, NMex, 66-; free-lance illusr, Los Angeles Times, 77-81; free-lance illus for publs, 83-87; art consult, art judging, lectr & demos, var art groups, 88-92. *Teaching:* Asst prof painting & drawing, Lewis & Clark Col, 55-58; instr painting, Lennox Adult Educ, Calif, 63-65; part-time, Woodbury Col & Santa Monica City Col, 65-66; watercolor, Descanso Gardens, 88; art instr with admin duties, McGroathy Arts Ctr, Los Angeles Cult Affairs, 88-90; pvt teaching, 90-92. *Awards:* Sale Century Purchase Award, NBC, 88; 2000 Notable Am Women, 89; hon mem Nat League Am Pen Women, Washington, DC, 91. *Bibliog:* Larry Johnson & Paul Currier (dirs), All About Burbank (video), City Burbank, 89; David Howard (dir), Alice Asmar Documentary (video), Visual Studies, San Francisco, 91; Le-Ann Jolakian (interviewer), Creating World Peach (video), United Artists Production, 91. *Mem:* Artists Equity; League of the Americas; Art Pub Places, Burbank City Coun, 91-; and others. *Media:* Casein, Oil; India Ink, Lithographs. *Publ:* Contribr, Ariz Highways Mag, 6/73; Southwest Arts Mag, 11/78; LA Times Home Mag, 3/26/78 & 12/3/78; Lewis & Clark J, fall 86; Tolucan, 1/15/92. *Dealer:* Sachs Gallery Pacific Design Ctr 8687 Melrose Ave Los Angeles CA 90069; Dukow Gallery 10999 Riverside Dr Toluca Lake CA 91602. *Mailing Add:* Asmar Studios PO Box 1963 Burbank CA 91507

ASO, KAJI
PAINTER, EDUCATOR
b Tokyo, Japan. *Study:* Tokyo Univ Art, MFA. *Work:* Mus Fine Arts, Boston; Mus Mod Art, New York; Rockefeller Collection, Chase Manhattan Bank; Xerox Corp; Mus Mod Art Tokyo. *Exhib:* Int Invitation, Tokyo Mod Art Mus, 63; Int Invitation, Wagner Festival, Bayreuth, Ger, 64; Nature and Temptation, Alumni Gallery, Sch MFA, Boston, 69; Selected American Artists, Inst Contemp Art, Boston, 71; Selected American Artists, Worcester Art Mus, Mass, 73-75; one-man exhibs, Mall Galleries, London, Eng, 81, Fed Reserve Bank, Boston, 85 & 89 & Fuller Mus Art, Brockton, Mass, 92. *Pos:* Exec Dir, Kaji Aso Studio, Inst Arts, Boston, 73- *Teaching:* Art prof painting, Sch Mus Fine Arts, 67- *Awards:* Distinguished Bostonian, City Boston, 80; Honorary Citizen of New Orleans, 82; Works Registered as Nat Property, Nat Mus Mod Art, Tokyo, Japan, 87; Inscribed Paul Revere Bowl, Cult Contributions, Mayor Raymond Flynn, Boston, 89. *Bibliog:* Reviews & articles, Sansai Japanese Art Mag, 87, 89 & 92 & Asashi, Nat Japanese Mag, 8/9/89; Meeting with Remarkable Men and Women, East West Health Bks, 89; Etching in Moonlight, East West J, 80. *Media:* Watercolor, Acrylic. *Publ:* Auth, Proteaus (vol of original poetry), Nature & Temptation, 77; ed & contibr, Substance and Phenomenon (philosophical treatise), 77 & auth, Thoughts Passing by (translation of Kenko), 77, Kaji Aso Studio; What is the source of art, Boston Univ J Educ, 84. *Mailing Add:* Kaji Aso Studio 40 St Stephen St Boston MA 02115

ASOMA, TADASHI
PAINTER
b Iwatsuki, Japan, Apr 28, 23. *Study:* Saitama Teachers Col, Urawa, MS; Bijitsu Gakko, Tokyo, govt scholar; Grande Chaumiere, Paris, govt scholar; Art Students League. *Work:* Nelson Gallery, Kansas City; Am Express Co, New York; 3M Co, St Paul; Andrew Dickson White Mus, Ithaca, NY; San Diego Mus Art. *Exhib:* One-man shows, David Findlay Galleries, NY, biennially 65-85, Dubins Gallery, Los Angeles, 79 & 85, Foundry Sch Mus NY, 79 & Steckler-Haller Galleries, Scottsdale, Ariz; Tokyo Central Mus, 81 & 84. *Teaching:* Instr art educ, Iwatsuki Jr High Sch, 50-64. *Awards:* Second Prize, Saitama Bijitsu Ten, 55; Second Prize, Nat Exhib Prof Art, 68; People's Westchester Savings Bank Award Best in Show, 20th Ann Fine Art Show, Putnam Art Coun, Mahopac, NY, 82. *Bibliog:* Articles in Art News, New York Times & New York Post, 65, 67, 69, 79 & 83; and others. *Media:* Oil. *Dealer:* David Findlay Galleries 984 Madison Ave New York NY 10021. *Mailing Add:* c/o David Findlay Galleries 984 Madison Ave New York NY 10021

ASPELL, AMY SUZANNE
DIRECTOR, WEAVER
b Chicago, Ill, June 28, 42. *Study:* Knox Col, Galesburg, Ill, BA(art), 63, Univ SFla, Tampa, MA(art educ), 76. *Comn:* Woven relief wall hanging, Caspers Inc, Tampa, Fla, 80. *Pos:* Dir, Tampa Community Design Ctr, 79-81, Ark Arts Coun, 84-87 & Irvine Fine Arts Ctr, 87- *Media:* Fiber Art. *Publ:* Auth, Cookbook Weaving I, Craft Publications Inc, 77. *Mailing Add:* 32772 Via Malaga San Juan Capistrano CA 92675

ASTLEY-BELL, RITA DUIS See Duis, Rita

ASTMAN, BARBARA ANN
PHOTOGRAPHER, PAINTER
b Rochester, NY, July 12, 50. *Study:* Rochester Inst Technol, AA, 70; Ont Col Art, Toronto, Assoc, 73. *Work:* Victoria & Albert Mus, London, Eng; Art Gallery Ont, Toronto; Winnipeg Art Gallery; Nat Film Bd Can, Ottawa; Bibliot Nat, Paris, France. *Comn:* CIL Corp, Toronto, Can; Calgary Winter Olympics, 88; C N Real Estate, Toronto, 90; City of Ottawa, Art in Public Places Programme. *Exhib:* Xerography, Art Gallery Ont, Toronto, 77; New Images, Nat Film Bd, Ottawa, 78; Contemp Can Photog Portrait, Edmonton Art Gallery, Alta, 78; Winnepeg Perspectives, Winnipeg Art Gallery, 79; Alternative Imageing Systems, Everson Mus, Syracuse, NY, 79; Electroworks, George Eastman House, Rochester, NY, 79-80; one-woman show, Centre Culturel, Paris, France, 82; Generation Polaroid, Forum des Halles, Paris, France, 85; Visual Facts, Third Eye Ctr, Glasglow, Scotland & Musee du Quebec, Quebec City, 86; Porkkanna Collection, Pro Mus Contemp Art, Helsinki, Finland, 89; Thunder Bay Art Gallery, Ont, 92. *Pos:* Coordr, Color Xerox Prog, Visual Arts Ont, 77-83; mem, Pub Art Comn, Toronto, currently; bd dirs, Toronto Arts Awards Found, 92. *Teaching:* Fac, camera art, Ont Col Art, 75- *Awards:* Can Coun Arts Awards Grants, 76, 77, 80, 81, 83, 84, 86 & 88; Prov Ont Coun Arts Grants, 74-82, 84 & 92. *Bibliog:* Articles in Arts Can, 3/75 & Prints Rev, No 7, Pratt Graphics, 77; Barbara Astman (catalog), Centre Cult Can, Paris, 82; Astman Places, Nickle Arts Mus, Univ Calgary, Can, 83. *Media:* Multi Media, Camera Art. *Dealer:* Sable Castelli Gallery Ltd 33 Hazelton Ave Toronto ON M5R 2E3 Can. *Mailing Add:* 23 Alcina Ave Toronto ON M6G 2E7 Canada

ASTON, MIRIAM
SCULPTOR, PAINTER
b New York, NY. *Study:* Soc Arts & Crafts, Detroit, with Sarkis Sarkisian, 54-58; Wayne State Univ, BA & MA; Univ Mich, with Gerald Damrowski; Claremont Grad Sch, Calif. *Work:* Nat Mus Women, Washington, DC. *Comn:* Pvt, nat & int comns. *Exhib:* Detroit Inst Art Ann, 50-72; Calif Mus Science & Industry; Univ Ohio, Athens; Mich Acad Arts, Letters & Sci, Ann Arbor; Riverside Mus Art, New York; Invitational exhib, Women's Conf UN, Nairobi, Kenya, 85; solo exhibs, Wayne State Univ, Detroit, Mich, Los Angeles, Ontario & Calif. *Pos:* Dir develop, Mus Hist & Art, Ontario, Calif. *Teaching:* Instr painting & sculpture, Univ Mich, Dearborn, 68-73; instr sculpture, Calif Polytech Univ, Pomona, 75-; instr drawing, Chaffey Col, Calif; instr painting, Ontario & Claremont, Calif. *Awards:* Gold Medal, 65 & Best Sculpture, Scarab Club; Best Sculpture, Scarab Club; Best Painting, Mich Acad Arts, Lett & Sci. *Mem:* Artists Equity Asn; Women's Caucus Art; hon mem Scarab Club, Detroit, Mich; Sculpture Ctr, Washington, DC. *Media:* Mixed. *Mailing Add:* PO Box 241 Claremont CA 91711

ATAIE, MARY LEE
SCULPTOR
b Lakewood, NJ, Nov 30, 36. *Study:* Vanderbilt Univ, BA, 58; Chelsea Col Art, London, BA, 75. *Work:* Boca Raton Mus, Fla. *Exhib:* '29 & '30, Hortt,

Mus Art, Ft Lauderdale, 87 & 88; Abstraction, Frances Wolfson Gallery, Miami, Fla, 89; Steel, Boca Raton Mus, Fla, 90. *Awards:* Sculpture Fel, Nat Endowment Arts, 90 & 91. *Dealer:* Jaffe Baker Gallery 608 Banyon Trail Boca Raton FL 33431. *Mailing Add:* 4395 Ingraham Hwy Coral Gables FL 33133

ATKINS, BILL (BILLY WAYNE ATKINS)
MUSEUM DIRECTOR, CURATOR
b Puryear, Tenn, Sep 07, 43. *Study:* Murray St Univ, BS, 67; Sangamon St Univ, MA 73; Univ Ill, MA, 76. *Collections Arranged:* Duveneck: Lost Paintings Found, 87 & Thomas Walsh Retrospective, 87, Triton Mus Art, Santa Clara, Calif. *Pos:* Dir, Arts Ctr on the Strand, Galveston, Tex, 76-78; exec dir, Del Rio Coun for Arts, Tex, 78-80; asst dir, Ark Arts Ctr, Little Rock, 80-86; exec dir, Triton Mus Art, Santa Clara, Calif, 86- *Teaching:* Instr painting, MacMurray Col, 69-75; instr aesthetic educ, Univ Houston, Clear Lake City, 77; instr mus studies, Univ Ark, Little Rock, 80-86. *Mem:* Am Asn Mus; Calif Asn Mus. *Mailing Add:* Triton Mus Art 1505 Warburton Ave Santa Clara CA 95050

ATKINS, GORDON LEE
DESIGNER, ARCHITECT
b Calgary, Alta, Mar 5, 37. *Study:* Col Archit & Urban Planning, Univ Wash, BArch. *Work:* Royal Can Acad Art; Nat Gallery Can; Massey Found. *Comn:* Studio, comn by Ed Drahanchuk, Bragg Creek, Alta, 68; Mayland Heights Sch, Calgary Pub Sch Bd, 68; Pinebrook Golf & Winter Club, comn by Wilbur Griffith, West of Calgary, 74-75; Stoney Indian Band Admin Bldg, comn by Chief John Snow. *Exhib:* Royal Can Acad Art, Ottawa; Environment '69 & '70, Edmonton & Calgary. *Teaching:* Archit technol, Southern Alta Inst Technol, 61-63; design, Dept Environmental Design, Univ Calgary, 63; interior design, Mount Royal Col, Calgary, 64-66. *Awards:* City Calgary Urban Design Award, 79 & 80; Practice Profile Award, Alberta Asn Architects 75th Anniv, 81; Gov Gen Medal, 82. *Bibliog:* Gordon Atkins/Architect, Cult Develop Br, Dept Prov Cult & South Alta, 70. *Mem:* Alta Asn Archit (pres Calgary chap, 64); Royal Archit Inst Can; academician Royal Can Acad Art. *Publ:* Contribr, Canadian Architecture 1960-1970, 70; auth, Plywood World, 70; Investigation North, Arctic Housing Research for Fed Govt, 75. *Mailing Add:* 1909 17th Ave SW Calgary AB T2T 0E9 Canada

ATKINS, ROBERT
CRITIC, CURATOR
b Cleveland, Ohio. *Study:* Univ Calif, Berkeley, MA(art hist), 76; Univ Calif, Riverside, BA 72, Hon Dr, Phi Beta Kappa, 72. *Collections Arranged:* David Ireland (auth, catalog), New Mus Contemp Art, 84; Between Science & Fiction (auth, catalog), Sao Paulo Biennial, 85; Decoding Gender (auth, catalog), 92; From Media to Metaphor: Art About AIDS (auth, catalog), traveling, 92-94. *Pos:* Art columnist, Village Voice, New York, 88-; Founder, Visual AIDS, New York, 89; Founder, Artists' Survival Workshop, New York, 84. *Teaching:* San Francisco State Univ, summers, 84- *Awards:* Manufacturers Hanover Art/World Award Distinguished Art Criticism, 85; Art Critics Fel, 81 & Summer Seminar Col Teachers, 81, Nat Endowment Arts. *Mem:* Col Art Asn; Visual AIDS. *Publ:* Auth, Artspeak: A Guide To Contemporary Ideas, Movements and Buzzwords, 1945-Present, 90 & Artspoke: A Guide to Modern Ideas, Movements and Buzzwords, 1848-1944 93, Abbeville. *Mailing Add:* 603 W 111th St Apt 6W New York NY 10025

ATKINS, ROSALIE MARKS
PAINTER
b Charleston, WVa, July 21, 21. *Study:* Mason Col Music & Fine Arts, Charleston, WVa; Morris Harvey Col, Charleston; workshops with Leo Manso & Victor Candell, Provincetown, Mass; also with Bud Hopkins, Truro, Mass. *Work:* WVa Arts & Humanities Permanent Collection. *Exhib:* Nat League Am Pen Women Ann Show, Washington, DC, 72; Provincetown Art Asn Nat Show, Mass, 72-78; Am Drawing Show, Portsmouth, Va, 76; 39th Ann Exhib Contemp Am Paintings, Four Arts, Palm Beach, Fla, 77; Lighthouse Gallery, Tequesta, Fla, 78-79; Nat League Am Pen Women, Wash, 87. *Awards:* Selected for traveling show, Art in the Embassies Prog, 70 & Nat League Am Pen Women, 72 & 77; Purchase Awards, WVa Arts & Humanities, 72; Purchase Award, Celebration Arts Show, Lighthouse Gallery, Tequesta, Fla. *Bibliog:* Dorothy Seckler (auth), article in Provincetown Painters; article in Artists/USA, 79-80; article, Focus, 5/83. *Mem:* Allied Artists of WVa (vpres, 67); Am Pen Women (pres, Charleston Br, 73-74); Sunrise, Inc; Provincetown Art Asn. *Media:* Acrylic, Oil. *Mailing Add:* 2015 Kanawha Ave Charleston WV 25304

ATKINSON, CONRAD
SCULPTOR, PAINTER
b Cumbria, Eng, June 15, 40. *Study:* Liverpool Col Art, NDD, ATD, 61; Royal Acad Sch, London, Cert, RAS, Hons, 65; Manchester Col Art, AFD, 67. *Work:* Tate Gallery, Victoria & Albert Mus & Brit Mus, London; Mus Mod Art, New York; Australian Nat Gallery, Canberra; Power Inst, Sydney. *Comn:* Arts Coun Northern Ireland/Irish Trades Union, Belfast, 75; banners, Gen & Munic Workers Union, Newcastle, Eng, 77; record/sound, comn by Geoff Gordon/Ronald Feldman, New York, 83; painting, Lewisham Borough Coun, London, 85. *Exhib:* Royal Academy Bicentenary, London, 68; Bienale de Paris, Mus d'Art Mod, 75; Art for Whom?, Serpentine Gallery, London, 78; Un Certain Art Anglais, Mus d'Art Mod, Paris, 79; Directions, Hirshhorn Mus, Washington, DC, 80; At the Heart of the Matter, Inst Contemp Art, London, 81; solo exhib, Power Gallery, Sydney, Australia, 83; 1984, Art Inst Chicago, 85; For Emily, Henry Moore Sculpture Trust Studio Dean Clough, Haufax, Eng, 92. *Pos:* Vis arts adv, Greater London Coun, 81-86 & Inner London Educ Authority, 86-; chair art & art hist, Univ Calif, Davis. *Teaching:* Lectr fine art, Slade Sch Fine Art, 75-78. *Awards:* Churchill Fel, 72; Artist-in-residence, Lewisham, Eng, 84-85 & Edinburgh Univ, 86. *Bibliog:* Richard Cork (auth), interview, Studio Int, 76; Carrie Rickey (auth), One stings, the other doesn't, Village Voice, 79; Lucy Lippard, Sandy Nairns & Caroline Tisdall (auths), Picturing the System, Pluto Press, Inst Contemp Art, London, 81. *Mem:* Arts Coun Gt Brit; Percent for Art, Nat Steering Comt. *Media:* Multi. *Publ:* Illusr text, Artforum Mag, New York, 80. *Dealer:* Ronald Feldman Fine Arts Inc 31 Mercer St New York NY 10013. *Mailing Add:* 172 Erlanger Rd London SE 14 England United Kingdom

ATKINSON, ERIC NEWTON
PAINTER, EDUCATOR
b Hartlepool, Durham, Eng, July, 23, 28, UK & Can. *Study:* Hartlepool Col Art, UK, NDD(hons), 52; Royal Acad Sch, London, UK, 55. *Work:* Contemporary Art Soc; Leeds City Art Gallery; Arts Coun, Gt Brit, London; Univ Marburg, Ger; London Regional Art Gallery, Ont. *Exhib:* Figures in their Settings, Tate Gallery, London, Eng, 53; Four Northern Artists, Hatton Gallery, Newcastle, 59; Art from Yorkshire, Stadhausgalerie Mus, Dortmund Ger, 65; Edinburgh 100, Demarco Gallery, Edinburgh, Scotland, 67; British Painting, Corcoran Gallery, Washington, DC, 70; retrospective, Mendel Art Gallery, Saskatoon, Saskatchewan, 80; Lewis Collection, Carnegie Mus Art, Pittsburgh, 80; Associations, London Regional Art Gallery, Ont, 84. *Teaching:* Lectr fine arts, Leeds Col Art, Yorkshire, 56-65, dept head, fine arts, 65-69; dean fac fine arts, Fanshawe Col, London, Ont, 73-82. *Awards:* David Murray Travel Scholar, Royal Acad, London, 52-54; J M Turner, Landscape Bursary, Royal Acad, London, 54. *Bibliog:* Atkinson-Pollock (auth), Artists proof (film), 82; Univ Western Ont, Canadian Art Collection, 84. *Mem:* Royal Canadian Acad Arts. *Media:* Mixed. *Publ:* Auth, Alfred Wallis Cornish Primitive, Accent, Leeds, 64; coauth, Art Education at Leeds, Studio Int, 69; auth, Art Education, MASH, Chicago Art Inst, 70; exhib rev, Arts, Can, 76; Forum: Imaginative Use of Space for Arts, London, Ont, 81; Visual education on the back burner, Bulletin Mag, 86. *Dealer:* Concept Gallery 1031 S Braddock Ave Pittsburgh PA 15218; Thielsen Galleries Inc 1038 Adelaide St London ON. *Mailing Add:* Fanshawe Col A A & Tech PO Box 4005 London ON N5W 5H1 Canada

ATKINSON, LESLIE JANE
PAINTER, SCULPTOR
b Oklahoma City, Okla, July 11, 51. *Study:* Oklahoma City Univ, BS(ed & art), 72; grad work, Central State Univ, 72-73. *Work:* Monumental Work, Mus Outdoor Art, Englewood, Colo; Denver Pub Libr Permanent Collection, Western Hist Dept, Denver, Colo; Eight sculptures, one painting, Founders Corp, New York; sculptures & painting, Serrano Corp, Mexico City; also pvt collections of Dr Patricia Ellison, Denver Colo & Denny LeRoux, New York; Midwest Pub Libr, Permanent Collection, Midwest City, Okla. *Comn:* Nude Female, marble statute, Mus Outdoor Art, Englewood, Colo; Mother & Child, bronze statute, Consortium for Community Centered Comprehensive Child Care, Tanzania, Africa; Bronze Portrait, Child, Dr David Clausen, Denver, Colo, 85; Bronze Portrait, Pres, Founders Corp, New York, 88; Bronze Portrait, Camille Cosby, Bill Cosby, Greenfield, Mass, 88. *Exhib:* NAm Sculpture Exhib, Golden, Colo, 82, 83 & 84; Greely Invitational, Greely, Colo, 83; High Plains Sculpture Exhib, Loveland, 84, 86, 87 & 88; Catherine Lorillard Wolfe, 92nd Ann, Nat Arts Club, New York, 88; Am Artists Prof League, 60th Grand Nat Exhib, Salmagundi Club, New York, 88. *Pos:* Pres, CEO/CFO, SLA Arch/Couture Inc-An Environmental Enrichment Design Co, 90-; SLA Concrete Construction Inc-An Environmental Enrichment Design Co, 90-; Advisory Comt, Colo Dept Transportation; advisor, Native Am, Denver Indian Ctr, 83-; bd dirs for Construction Women Owners & Executives, 92-93. *Teaching:* Art, Oklahoma City Fin Arts Mus, 71-72; art & art hist, Our Lady of Lourdes Sch, Denver, 85-87. *Awards:* Drawing I, Best of Show, Greely Invitational, 83; Hon Mention, Sculpture, Nat Jewish Community Ctr, 86. *Bibliog:* American Artists, An illustrated Survey of Leading Contemp, 90; Sculptor's Resistance Mirrors Her Withdrawal, The Sunday Oklahoman, 7/8/84; The Mus Outdoor Arts(bk & film), Englewood, Colo. *Mem:* Denver Art Students League (82-92). *Publ:* Coauth, with George Carlson, The Tarahumara, private publ, 76; auth, A Body of Work, private publ, 82; documentary film, Art in Process, produced by Mus of Outdoor Art, copyright, 90. *Mailing Add:* 2088 S Pennsylvania Denver CO 80210

ATKINSON, TRACY
CONSULTANT, MUSEOLOGIST
b Middletown, Ohio, Aug 10, 28. *Study:* Ohio State Univ, BFA(summa cum laude), 50; Mexico City Col, 50; Univ Pa, MA, 51; Bryn Mawr Col, 53. *Collections Arranged:* Pop Art and the American Tradition, 65, The Inner Circle, 66, Botero, 67, Options & The Bradley Collection, 68, Seymour Lipton & A Plastic Presence, 69, Aspects of a New Realism, 70, Portraits Exhibition, 71, Six Painters, 72 & The Urban River, 73, Milwaukee Art Mus; Tremaine Collection, Sol Lewitt Wall Drawings, JP Morgan Collector, The Great River, David Bermant Collection, Hartford, Conn. *Pos:* Curatorial asst, Albright-Knox Art Gallery, 55-59; asst dir, Columbus Gallery Fine Arts, 59-61, actg dir, 61-62; dir, Milwaukee Art Ctr, 62-76; dir, Wadsworth Atheneum, 77-88, emer dir, 88-; Pvt consultant, 88; vpres art market opers, Atkinsons & Bibou Inc, 90- *Publ:* articles in prof journals, nat art news mags & newspapers. *Mailing Add:* 117 Ciderbrook Rd Avon CT 06001

ATLAS, NAVA
WRITER, DESIGNER
b Jaffa, Israel, Apr 29, 55; US citizen. *Study:* Univ Mich, BFA, 77. *Work:* Wichita Art Mus, Kans; New York Pub Libr Print Collection; Col Art Gallery, State Univ NY, New Paltz. *Exhib:* The Radwaste & Stonehenge Series, traveling exhib, collab with Chaim Tabak, 85-89; Humor, Wit &

Whimsy, Bowie State Col, MD, 86; Painted Surfaces, Albany Inst Hist & Art, NY, 86. *Bibliog:* Howard Dalee Spencer (auth), A Collaborative Exhibition: The Radwaste & Stonehenge Series, Wichita Art Mus, 85. *Publ:* Auth & illusr, American Harvest, Ballantine, 87; Vegetarian Celebrations, 90 & vegetarian, 93, Little, Brown. *Mailing Add:* 65 Prospect St New Paltz NY 12561

ATLEE, EMILIE DES
PAINTER, INSTRUCTOR
b Bethlehem, Pa, July 6, 15. *Study:* Spring Garden Inst, Philadelphia; also with Roswell Weidner & Joseph & Gertrude Capolino. *Work:* United Airlines, Philadelphia Airport; Palasaides High Sch, Bucks Co, Pa; La Salle Col & Franklin Inst, Philadelphia; Cult Arts Ctr Ocean City, NJ. *Comn:* Portraits, Libr Univ Del & Berks Co Ct House, Pa. *Exhib:* One-woman shows, Little Gallery, 63 & Newmans Gallery, Philadelphia, 70; Knickerbocker Artists Ann, New York, 64; Philadelphia Art Teachers Asn, 69-71; Harrisburg Mus, Pa, 71. *Pos:* Critic, 78- *Teaching:* Instr, 53-69; instr, Main Line Ctr Arts, Bryn Mawr, Pa, 69-77. *Awards:* Hon mention, Nat, Ogunquit Art Ctr, 59 & Nat Benedictine Art Awards, 69; First Prize, Main Line Ctr Arts Members Show, 85. *Bibliog:* Dorothy Grafly (ed), The changing moods of art, Art in Focus, 71. *Mem:* Artists Equity Asn; Pa Acad Fine Arts; Main Line Ctr Arts. *Media:* Oil, Pastel. *Dealer:* Newman Galleries 1624 Walnut St Philadelphia PA 19103. *Mailing Add:* 2117 Chestnut Ave Ardmore PA 19003

ATTIE, DOTTY
DRAFTSMAN
b Pennsauken, NJ, Mar 20, 38. *Study:* Philadelphia Col Art, BFA, 59; Brooklyn Mus Art Sch, Beckmann fel, 60; Art Students League, 67. *Work:* Allen Mem Art Mus; Univ Mass, Amherst; Fairleigh Dickinson Univ; Smith Col Art Mus; Spencer Art Mus; and others. *Exhib:* One-man shows, Air Gallery, New York, 76, O K Harris Gallery, New York, 77, Univ RI, 78, Contemporary Arts Mus, Tex, 79, Wadsworth Atheneum, Conn, 80, Pennsylvania Acad Fine Arts, Pa, 81; New Dimensions in Drawing, Aldrich Mus, Ridgefield, Conn, 81; Words as Images, Renaissance Soc, Chicago, 81; and other. *Teaching:* Adjunct prof, New York Univ & Manhattanville Col, 77. *Awards:* Creative Artists Pub Serv Grant, NY State Coun Arts, 76-77; Nat Endowment Arts Grants, 76-77 & 83-84. *Bibliog:* Corinne Robins (auth), Dotty Attie, Arts, 11/78; Susan Putterman (auth), Dotty Attie, Arts, 12/80; Maurice Berger (auth), The Empty Frame, Arts, 9/81; and others. *Media:* Pencil. *Dealer:* PPO W 532 Broadway New York NY 10012. *Mailing Add:* 334 E 22nd St New York NY 10010

ATWELL, ALLEN
EDUCATOR, PAINTER
b Pittsburgh, Pa, Oct 19, 25. *Study:* Cornell Univ, BA, 49 & MFA, 51. *Work:* Herbert F Johnson Mus Art, Cornell Univ, Ithaca, NY. *Exhib:* Everson Mus Art, Syracuse, NY, 74; Contemp Reflections, Aldrich Mus Contemp Art, Ridgefield, Conn, 75; Artists of Cent NY, Munson-Williams-Proctor Inst, Utica, NY, 74 & 75, The Abstract Tradition in Cent NY, 79; Herbert F Johnson Mus Art, Cornell Univ, Ithaca, NY, 74, 77 & 79; Art & Frame House, Ithaca, NY 81-88; Kahala Hilton, HI, 89; and others. *Teaching:* From instr art to assoc prof art, 51-64, Cornell Univ, assoc prof art, New York Exten Prog, 64-65; lectr art, NY Univ, 65-66, Manhattan Community Col, 66 & Ithaca Col, NY, 71-77; teaching fel art, Inst Allende, Univ Guanajuato, Mex, 73. *Awards:* Ford Found Fel, India, 53-54; Fulbright Fel, India & Nepal, 61-62; Rockefeller Found Fel, Southeast Asia, Indonesia & Japan, 62-63. *Mem:* Col Art Asn. *Publ:* Auth & illusr, Kuo Hsi's Clearing Autumn Skies Over Mountains & Valleys and Indian Miniature Paintings & The Yama Tanka, 72, Aspen; auth & illusr, Indian art: From multiplicity to unity, Fulbright Newsletter, spring, 74. *Mailing Add:* 2101 Nuvanu Ave Apt 2107 Honolulu HI 96817

ATWOOD PINARDI, BRENDA
PAINTER, EDUCATOR
b Hyannis, Mass, Mar 14, 41. *Study:* Mass Col Art, BSE(art educ), 63; Acad Belle Arte, Rome, 63-64; RI Sch Design, MFA(painting), 67. *Work:* Coop Belle Arte, Verona, Italy; New World Bank, Lowell, Mass; De Cordova Mus, Lincoln, Mass. *Exhib:* One-person show, Le Fantasme di Venezia, Clark Gallery, Lincoln, Mass, 86; Fuller Mus Triennial, 87 & 90; New Work, Clark Gallery, 88; Recent Acquisitions, De Cordova Mus, 90; Triennial, Fuller Mus Art, Brockton, Mass. *Teaching:* Prof painting & drawing, Univ Lowell, Mass, 67-, coordr, Gallery 410, 75-80, chairperson art dept, 76-80. *Awards:* Best of Show, Northeast Art Competition, Univ Mass, Amherst, 81; Purchase Award, Appalachian Nat, Appalachian State Univ, 82; Best of Show, Germanow Gallery, Rochester, NY, 86; Best of Show, Current visions, Rochester, NY, 86. *Bibliog:* Ann Schecter (auth), Artist's anigma, Lowell Sun, 83, 85 & 88; Christine Temin (auth) article, Boston Globe, 86, 88 & 90; article, Art New England, 86. *Mem:* Artists for Survival; Boston Visual Artists Union. *Media:* Oil. *Dealer:* Clark Gallery Lincoln Mass. *Mailing Add:* 87 Child St Hyde Park MA 02136

AUBIN, BARBARA
PAINTER, ASSEMBLAGE ARTIST
b Chicago, Ill, Jan 12, 28. *Study:* Carleton Col, BA, 49; Art Inst Chicago, BAE, 54, MAE, 55, George D Brown foreign travel fel, France & Italy, 55-56; Buenos Aires Conv Act grant, Haiti, 58-60. *Work:* Ill State Mus; Art Inst Chicago; Ball State Univ; Centre d'Art, Port-au-Prince, Haiti. *Comn:* Collage, 100th Anniversary of the First Exhib of Seurat's Sunday Afternoon on the Island of Grand Jatte, Roy Boyd Gallery, Chicago, 86. *Exhib:* Mid-Year Shows, Butler Inst Am Art, Ohio, 61 & 62; 10th Ann Nat Prints & Drawings Exhib, Okla Art Ctr, 68; Fairweather-Hardin Gallery, Chicago, 75, 78, 81, 85 & 90; Ill Union Gallery, Univ Ill at Champaign-Urbana, 86; Clocktower, New York, 86; Am Herstory: Women & the US Constitution, Atlanta, Ga & travelling, 88; Survey of Contemporary Illinois Watercolor, Springfield Art Asn, 91; and others. *Pos:* Reporter, Women Artists News, 77-78 & 83-90; critic for var publ; cur, Send a Postcard to Barbara, Loyola Univ & traveling, 79-80. *Teaching:* Asst prof painting, drawing & watercolor, Art Inst Chicago, 60-68; asst prof painting, drawing & design, Loyola Univ (Chicago), 68-71; lectr painting, drawing & design, St Joseph's Col, 71-74; prof painting, drawing & visual fundamentals, Chicago State Univ, 71- *Awards:* Hon Mention for Dana Medal, Pa Acad Fine Arts, 53; Mich Watercolor Soc Award, 65 & 70; Ill Arts Coun Proj Completion grant, 77 & 78. *Mem:* Col Art Asn Am; Chicago Artists Coalition; Women's Caucus Art (vpres, midwest, 82-85). *Media:* Watercolor, Mixed Media. *Mailing Add:* 939 W Belden Chicago IL 60614-3239

AUDETTE, ANNA HELD
PAINTER, EDUCATOR
b New York, NY. *Study:* Smith Col, BA, 60; Sch Art, Yale Univ, BFA, 62 & MFA, 64. *Work:* Fitzwilliam Mus, Cambridge, Eng; Rijksprentenkabinett, Rijksmuseum, Amsterdam, Holland; Metrop Mus Art, New York; Nat Gallery Art & Nat Libr Sci, Washington, DC. *Comn:* Print ed, Barnard Col, New York, 79 & Barbara Gladstone Gallery, New York, 79, 80 & 83; NASA, 90. *Exhib:* Silvermine Print Show, Silvermine Gallery, Conn, 66, 72 & 76; Two Women Artists, Smith Col, 76; Mt Holyoke Col Mus, Mass, 76; solo shows, Gallery Fikrun Wa Fann, Alexandria, Egypt, 77, Clark Art Inst, Williamstown, Mass, 78, Wesleyan Univ, 82 & Munson Gallery, New Haven, 85, 87 & 90; Fitzwilliam Mus, Cambridge, Eng, 86. *Collections Arranged:* In Their Own Image?, Southern Conn State Univ, New Haven, 75, 76 & 78. *Teaching:* Prof art, Southern Conn State Univ, 64- *Bibliog:* Articles, Print Collectors Newslett, 7-8/79 & Art News, 9/80. *Mem:* Conn Acad Arts & Scis; Col Art Asn. *Media:* Painting, Photography. *Publ:* Auth & illusr, The Impress of Anatomy, Pratt Graphic Art Ctr, 65; illusr, Past & Present, The Continuity of Classical Myths, Hakkert, Ltd, Toronto, 72; Song in Stone, 83 & Click, Rumble, Roar, 87, T Y Crowell. *Mailing Add:* 24 Everit St New Haven CT 06511

AUER, JAMES MATTHEW
ART CRITIC, FILM MAKER
b Neenah, Wis, Dec 2, 28. *Study:* Writers Inst, Univ Wis-Madison, 49; Lawrence Col, BA, 50. *Work:* Milwaukee Art Mus; Carroll Col, Waukesha, Wis. *Comn:* An Artist's Vision: Born on the Stone, 87. *Pos:* Asst Sunday ed, The Post-Crescent, Appleton, Wis, 60-65, Sunday ed & arts reviewer, 65-72; art critic, Milwaukee Journal, 72- *Awards:* Award of Merit, State Hist Soc Wis; A Brush with History Award, 62; President's Award, Wis Heart Asn, 66. *Mem:* Am Asn Sunday & Feature Ed (pres, 71-72); Friends Bergstrom Art Ctr, Neenah (pres, 67-68); City Neenah Munic Found. *Publ:* The City of Light (play), 61 & Tell It to Angela (play), 70, Attic Theatre, Lawrence Univ; art reviews to various mags including Craft Horizons Antique World, Glass Mag & Wis Mag Hist. *Mailing Add:* 1849 N 72nd St Milwaukee WI 53213

AUERBACH, FRANK
PAINTER
b Apr 29, 31; Brit citizen. *Study:* St Martin's Sch Art, London, 48-52; Royal Col Art, London, 52-55. *Work:* Arts Coun Gr Brit, London; Brit Coun, London; Tate Gallery, London; Metrop Mus, Mus Mod Art, New York. *Exhib:* One-man exhibs, Hayward Gallery, London, 78, Brit Pavilion XLII Venice Biennale, 86 & Rijksmuseum Vincent van Gogh, Amsterdam, 89. *Awards:* Golden Lion Prize, Venice Biennale, 86. *Bibliog:* Robert Hughes (auth), Frank Auerbach, Thames & Hudson, 90. *Media:* Oil, Acrylic. *Mailing Add:* c/o Marlborough Fine Art (London) Ltd Six Albemarle St London W1X 4BY England United Kingdom

AUPING, MICHAEL GRAHAM
CURATOR, HISTORIAN
b Portland, Ore, Oct 17, 49. *Study:* Santa Ana Col, AA, 69; Calif State Univ, Fullerton, BA(art hist), 71; Calif State Univ, Long Beach, MA(art hist), 75. *Exhib:* Matrix: A Changing Exhib Contemp Art, Univ Art Mus, Berkeley, Calif, 78-80; Francesco Clemente, Walker Art Ctr, Minneapolis, Minn, Dallas Mus Art, Albright-Knox Art Gallery, Buffalo, NY; Susan Rothenberg: Paiantings and Drawings 1973-1993, Seattle Art Mus, travelling; Jenny Holzer: The Venice Installation, Albright-Knox Art Gallery, Buffalo, NY, Walker Art Ctr, Minneapolis, Minn, travelling; Hamish Fulton: Selected Walks 1969-1989, Nat Gallery Can, Ottawa, travelling; Selected Geometric Abstract Painting in America since 1945, Milwaukee Art Mus, Wis, travelling; Abstract Expressionism: The Critical Developments; Structure to Resemblance: Work by Eight American Sculptors; and others. *Collections Arranged:* Richard Serra Collection; Robert Irwin Collection; John Chamberlain Collection; Francesco Clemente Collection. *Pos:* Ed, Los Angeles Inst Contemp Art J, 76-78; assoc cur, Univ Art Mus, Berkeley, 78-80; cur 20th century art, John & Mable Ringling Mus Art, Sarasota, Fla, 80-84; prof adv comt, Art Pub Places, Metro-Dade Area, Miami, 84-; chief cur, Albright-Knox Art Gallery, Buffalo, NY, 84-; var consults, 73-90. *Teaching:* Instr art hist, Citrus Col, Azusa, Calif, summer 77 & San Francisco Art Inst, spring 78; adj lectr art hist, Univ Calif, Santa Barbara, fall 77 & Univ Buffalo, 88-89; lectr, Inst Contemp Art, Boston, Baltimore Mus Art, St Louis Art Mus, Nelson-Atkins Mus Art, Kansas City, Milwaukee Art Mus, 89-91 & Int Conf, Univ York, Toronto, Can, 91. *Awards:* Comnr, American Pavilion 1990 Venice Biennale, Italy. *Res:* Post-War American and European Art. *Publ:* Auth, John Chamberlain Wall Reliefs: 1960-1983, 83; Francesco Clemente, Harry N Abrams Inc, 85; Abstract Expressionism: The Critical Developments, Harry V Abrams Inc, 87; Jenny Holzer, Universe Bks, New York, 92; Clyfford Still in New York: The Buffalo Project, Clyfford Still, Munich: Prestel Verlag, 92; and others. *Mailing Add:* c/o Albright-Knox Art Gallery 1285 Elmwood Ave Buffalo NY 14222

AUSBY, ELLSWORTH AUGUSTUS
PAINTER, INSTRUCTOR
b Portsmouth, Va, Apr 5, 42. *Study:* Sch Visual Arts, BFA, 75; Pratt Inst. *Work:* Aldrich Mus Contemp Art, Ridgefield, Conn; Cinque Gallery, New York; Rice Univ, Houston; Atlanta Airport. *Comn:* Three pastel paintings, comn by Jean de Mevil, Houston, 71; Space Odyssey (enamel on steel), Howard Johnsons Co, New York, 79-80; Rock Paper Scissor (silkscreen), Path Train Station, New York; Space Odyssey (stainless steel sculpture), New York Technical Col, City Univ New York, 81. *Exhib:* New Black Artist, Brooklyn Mus Fine Arts, 69; Lamp Black, Boston Mus Fine Arts, 70; Black Artist, Whitney Mus Am Art, New York, 71; one-man show, Pa Acad Fine Arts, Philadelphia, 72; Millenium, Mus Philadelphia Civic Ctr, 73; Herbert F Johnson Mus Art, Cornell Univ, Ithaca, NY, 74; Contemp Reflections, Aldrich Mus Contemp Art, 75; Afro-American Abstractions, Public Sch 1, Long Island City, 80; Everson Mus, Syracuse, New York, 81. *Collections Arranged:* Some American History (auth, catalog), Rice Univ, 71; Contemporary Reflections (auth, catalog), Am Fedn Art, 75. *Teaching:* Instr painting, Sch Visual Arts, 75- *Awards:* Comprehensive Employment & Training Act artist grant, 78; Creative Artists Pub Serv Prog painting grant, NY State Coun Arts, 80. *Bibliog:* Barbara Rose (auth), Black artist, 9/70 & Henri Ghent (auth), Quo Vadis black art, 11/74, Art in Am; April Kingsley (auth), Ausby at the Soho Center, Soho Weekly News, 12/75. *Mem:* Cult Coun Found New York; Harlem Cult Coun Found. *Media:* Acrylic, Enamel. *Publ:* Illusr, Slavery (film), Silvermine Productions, 71; illusr, Tuesdays and Every Other Sunday Off, Doubleday, 72; illusr, Black Review Number Two, William Morrow & Co, 72; contribr, Encore Mag, 72; illusr, The Crossroads, Reed, Cannon, Johnson, 75. *Mailing Add:* c/o Fine Arts Dept Sch Visual Arts 209 E 23rd St New York NY 10010

AUSTIN, BARBARA JEAN See Adams, Bobbi

AUSTIN, DARREL
PAINTER
b Raymond, Wash, June 25, 07. *Study:* Univ Notre Dame; Univ Ore; European Sch Art, with Emil Jaques. *Work:* Metrop Mus Art & Mus Mod Art, New York; Mus Fine Arts, Boston; Nelson Gallery Art, Kansas City, Mo; Phillips Mem Gallery, Washington, DC. *Comn:* Four oil panels, Med Col, Univ Ore, 36. *Exhib:* Whitney Mus, New York; Carnegie Inst, Pittsburgh; City Art Mus, St Louis; Contemp Painting in the US, toured in Latin Am countries; Inst Contemp Art, Boston; retrospective, McNay Art Inst, San Antonio, 82; and others. *Awards:* Lippincot Award for Figure Oil, Pa Acad Art, 53. *Bibliog:* Miller (auth), Americans 1942, Mus Mod Art, 42; Bird (auth), Darrel Austin, Art in Am, 43; Darrel Austin, Life Mag, 45. *Media:* Oil. *Dealer:* Perls Gallery 1016 Madison Ave New York NY 10021; Harmon Meek Gallery 386 Broad Ave S Naples FL 33940. *Mailing Add:* c/o Harmon Meek Gallery 386 Broad Ave S Naples FL 33940

AUSTIN, PAT
PAINTER, PRINTMAKER
b Detroit, Mich, Mar 17, 37. *Study:* Univ Mich, AB, 59; Univ Alaska with Alex Duffs Combs, Jr, 65, MFA, 76; Univ Wash, BFA(art), 71; Univ Alaska, Anchorage, MFA, 77. *Work:* Evergreen State Col, Olympia; Anchorage Hist & Fine Arts Mus, Alaska; Alaska State Coun Arts, Printmakers Alaska Permanent Collection, Anchorage; Anchorage Borough Sch Dist Permanent Print Collection; Visual Arts Ctr, Permanent Print Collection. *Comn:* Providence Hospital Print Project, 86; mural, Family Resource Ctr, 87. *Exhib:* All Alaska Juried Exhib, Anchorage, 66-69 & 72-86; 20 Printmakers Touring Invitational, Wash State Artmobile, 71-72; one-man shows, Anchorage Hist & Fine Arts Mus, 75 & 83 & Stoningtor Gallery, Anchorage, 86; Northwest Print Coun, group exhib, 84-86. *Teaching:* Instr art & Eng, Anchorage Borough Sch Dist, 65-69; instr printmaking & painting, Univ Alaska, 71-87. *Awards:* Printmaking Award, All Alaska Juried Exhib, 69 & 74; Mel Kohler Painting Award, 75; Artist Fel, Alaska State Coun Arts, 85. *Bibliog:* Connie Godwin (auth), Pat's art is exploring world, Anchorage Daily Times, 11/3/75; Virginia McKinney (auth), Pat Austin: Printmaker and more, Alaska J, winter 83. *Mem:* Anchorage Hist & Fine Arts Mus Asn; Anchorage Arts Coun; Visual Arts Ctr; Northwest Print Coun (bd mem); Col Art Asn. *Media:* Watermedia, Etching. *Publ:* Auth, National Collection of Fine Arts (catalog), Washington, DC, 78; Passing off reproductions as real art, Alaska J, winter 80. *Mailing Add:* 1309 Ninth Ave Port Townsend WA 98368

AUSTIN, PHIL
PAINTER, LECTURER
b Waukegan, Ill, Jan 27, 10. *Study:* Univ Mich, AB, 33. *Work:* Ill State Libr, Lincoln Collection, Ill State Mus, Springfield; Wheaton Col Art Collection, Ill; and others. *Exhib:* Five shows, Am Watercolor Soc Ann, New York, NY, 61-69; Watercolor USA, Springfield, Mo, 72 & 74; Nat Acad Design, New York; Am Artists Prof League Grand Nat, New York, 79 & 81; Ky Aqueous, 81 & 85; plus others. *Pos:* Mem staff, Kling Studios, Chicago, 45-50. *Teaching:* Guest instr watercolor, Wheaton Col, 63-70. *Awards:* Fox Purchase Award, Watercolor USA 74, Springfield, Mo, 74; President's Award, Am Artists Prof League, 79; Grumbacher Gold Medal, Okla Christian Col Watercolor Gala, 84; Eldridge Award, Adirondacks Nat, 85. *Bibliog:* Phil Austin, Watercolorist, Am Artist, 10/71. *Mem:* Am Watercolor Soc; Nat Watercolor Soc; Midwest Watercolor Soc (bd dirs); Am Artists Prof League. *Media:* Watercolor. *Publ:* Auth, Capturing Mood in Watercolor, North Light Publ, 84. *Dealer:* Jack Anderson Art Gallery Sister Bay WI 54234. *Mailing Add:* 772 Wisconsin Bay Dr Ellison Bay WI 54210

AUSTIN-NUHFER, OLIVE H
PAINTER, SCULPTOR
Study: Okla Univ, MA, 33. *Comn:* Okla Univ Art Dept, Norman, 31; Carnegie Inst, Pittsburgh, Pa, 41; Conley's Corp, Monroeville, 43 & 50. *Exhib:* Pittsburgh Assoc Artists, Pittsburgh Ctr Arts, 37-88; Pittsburgh Garden Market, Ann Mellon Park, 40-70. *Teaching:* Instr theory of color design, Okla Univ, 31-33; instr, Pittsburgh Ctr for Arts, 52-54. *Publ:* Illusr, Dancing Bear, 87 & Tough of Happiness, 88 (both by Genevieve Jones), Innovations. *Dealer:* 1214 Toman Ave Clairton PA 15025. *Mailing Add:* 216 Falconhurst Dr N Pittsburgh PA 15238-2628

AUTH, ROBERT R
PRINTMAKER, PAINTER
b Bloomington, Ill, Oct 27, 26. *Study:* Ill Wesleyan Univ, BFA; Wash State Univ, MFA. *Work:* Salt Lake Art Ctr, Utah; Col Southern Idaho, Twin Falls; Ricks Col, Rexburg, Idaho; Boise Gallery Art, Idaho; Wash State Univ. *Comn:* Five works, Dept Interior-Big Hole Nat Battlefield, Wisdom, Mont; one work, Nat Governor's Conf, 85. *Exhib:* Intermountain Painting & Sculpture 4th Biennial, Salt Lake Art Ctr, 69; Fedn Rocky Mountain States Traveling Exhib, 71-72; Inaugural Exhib, Denver Art Mus, Colo, 71; one-man retrospective, Boise Gallery Art, 80; Sawtooths & Other Ranges of Imagination, Contemp Art from Idaho, Smithsonian Inst, Washington, DC, 83. *Pos:* Bd dir, Boise Gallery Art, 69-; exec bd dirs, Idaho Alliance for the Arts in Educ, 82-; appointment to Mayor's Comn on the Arts, Boise City, 84- *Teaching:* Instr art, Burley High Sch, Idaho, 60-61; instr art & humanities, Boise High Sch, 61-81; supervisor art, Boise Independent Sch District, 81-87. *Awards:* Allied Arts Coun Artist of Year Award, 72; Governor of Idaho's Medal for Excellence in Arts, 84; Distinguished Citizen Award, The Idaho Statesman, 89. *Mem:* Idaho Art Asn (vpres, 70-72); Boise Art Asn (trustee, 69-). *Media:* All; Acrylic, Oil. *Dealer:* Brown's Gallery 711 S Latah St Boise ID 83705. *Mailing Add:* 530 Hillview Dr Boise ID 83702

AUTH, SUSAN HANDLER
CURATOR, EDUCATOR
b New York, NY, June 25, 39. *Study:* Swarthmore Col, BA; Univ London; Univ Mich, MA; Am Sch Classical Studies, Athens, Fulbright Scholar, 64-65; Bryn Mawr Col, PhD, 68. *Work:* Toledo Mus of Art, Ohio; Newark Mus, NJ. *Collections Arranged:* Myth & Gospel: Art of Coptic Egypt, Newark Mus, 77, Ancient Greece: Life and Art, 80; The Classical Collection, 81 & 89; Coptic Art of Ancient Egypt, Nadler Collection & Newark Mus, NJ, 86; Stepping Into Ancient Egypt: House of the Artist Pashed, 91. *Pos:* Curatorial asst, Toledo Mus Art, Ohio, 67; cur classical collection, Newark Mus, 71- *Teaching:* Asst prof ancient art & archaeol, Dept Art, Rutgers Univ, Newark, 68-71. *Awards:* Am Numismatic Soc Summer Fel, 63; Travel Grants, Smithsonian Inst, Washington, DC, summer 71, Ford Found Publ, 75, Nat Endowment Arts, Mellow, 90. *Mem:* Archaeol Inst Am; Int Asn Hist Glass; Am Research Ctr, Egypt; Int Asn Egyptologists. *Res:* Ancient glass; Greek, Roman and Egyptian art and archaeology. *Publ:* Auth, Ancient Glass at the Newark Museum, from the Eugene Schaefer Collection of Ancient Glass, Newark Mus, 76; var articles, Am J Archaeol, J Glass Studies, Archaeol & Annales Int d'Etude Hist du Verre; Coptic Glass, The Coptic Encyclopedia, 91; Pottery & Glass, Beyond the Pharaohs, 89. *Mailing Add:* Newark Mus 43-49 Washington St Newark NJ 07101

AUTH, TONY (WILLIAM ANTHONY), JR
EDITORIAL CARTOONIST
b Akron, Ohio, May 7, 42. *Study:* Univ Calif, Los Angeles, BA(biological illus). *Pos:* Syndicated ed cartoonist, Philadelphia Inquirer, 71- & Universal Press Syndicate. *Awards:* Sigma Delta Chi Award, Soc of Prof Journalists, 76; Pulitzer Prize, Columbia Univ Trustees, 76. *Bibliog:* Stephen Hess & Milton Kaplan (co-auth), The Ungentlemanly Art: A History of American Political Cartoons, MacMillan, 75. *Mem:* Soc Illustrators. *Media:* Pen and ink. *Publ:* Auth, Behind the Lines, Houghton-Mifflin, 77; Lost in Space-The Reagan Years, Andrews & McMeel, 88. *Dealer:* Rosenfeld Gallery 113 Arch St Philadelphia PA 19104. *Mailing Add:* 400 N Broad St Philadelphia PA 19101

AUTIO, (A) RUDY
CERAMIST, EDUCATOR
b Butte, Mont, Oct 8, 26. *Study:* Mont State Univ, BS, 50; Wash State Univ, MFA, 52; Md Inst, Col Art, Baltimore, DFA, 86. *Work:* Renwick Gallery, Smithsonian Mus; Everson Mus, Syracuse, NY; Victoria & Albert Mus, London; Nat Nus, Stockholm; Taideteollisusmuseo, Helsinki. *Comn:* Carved brick relief, First Methodist Church, Great Falls, Mont, 54; ceramic tile relief, Union Bank & Trust Co, Helena, 59-60; metal sculpture, Farm Credit Banks, Spokane, 71; mural, State Security Bank, Polson, Mont, 71; RYA wallhanging, Performing Arts Bldg, Univ Mont, Missoula, 86. *Exhib:* One-man shows, Henry Gallery, Univ Wash, Seattle, 63, Toledo Art Mus, 65, Retrospectives, Am Crafts Mus, New York, 83, John Michael Kohler Art Mus, Sheboygan, Wis, 83, Bellevue Art Mus, Wash, 83 & Montana Horses, Ryijy Tapestry, Taideteollisuusmuseo, Helsinki, Finland, 85; Everson Mus, Syracuse, 64; two-man show, Chicago Art Mus, 68; Am Studio Potters & Victoria & Albert Mus, London, 72; San Francisco Mus Mod Art, 72; Mus Contemp Crafts, New York, 74; Seattle Art Mus, 79; retrospective (with catalog), Am Crafts Mus, New York & Bellevue Mus, Seattle, 84; Western States Arts Found 3rd Ann Exhib, Brooklyn Mus, 86; Contemporary American Ceramics, Nat Mus Mod Art, Seoul, Korea, 87; American Ceramics Now: 27th Ceramics Nat, Everson Mus, Syracuse, NY, 87; Clay as Art, Gummerson's Konstgalleri, Stockholm, Sweden, 87. *Pos:* Resident artist-dir, Archie Bray Found, 52-56; asst cur, Mont Mus Hist Soc, 56. *Teaching:* Prof ceramics & sculpture, Univ Mont, 57-84. *Awards:* Tiffany Found Award, 63; Purchase Award, Everson Mus, 64; Ceramic Art Award, Am Ceramic

Soc, 78; Nat Endowment Award, 80; First Governor's Award in Visual Arts' Most Outstanding Artist, 80; Distinguished Scholar Award, Univ Mont, 84. *Bibliog:* Julie Hall (auth), Tradition and Change, 77 & Clark & Hughto (coauths), A Century of Ceramics in the United States, 79, E P Dutton; Lamar Harrington (auth), Ceramics in the Pacific Northwest: A History, Univ Wash Press, 79; Garth Clark (auth), American Potters, Watson-Guptill Publ, New York, 81; Peter Lane (auth), Studio Ceramics, Chilton Book Co, Radnor, Pa, 83. *Mem:* hon mem Nat Coun Educ Ceramic Arts; fel Am Craftsmen Coun; Archie Bray Found (trustee, 74); Int Ceramic Soc, Geneva; hon mem ORNADO (Finland designers), Helsinki. *Publ:* Auth, About drawing, 12/85 & Figure drawing on clay and other surfaces, 12/87, The Studio Potter. *Dealer:* Dorothy Weiss Gallery 256 Sutter St San Francisco CA 94108. *Mailing Add:* c/o Dorothy Weiss Gallery 256 Sutter St San Francisco CA 94108

AUTRY, CAROLYN
PRINTMAKER, EDUCATOR
b Dubuque, Iowa, Dec 12, 40. *Study:* Yale-Norfolk Summer Sch, 62; Univ Iowa, Iowa City, BA, 63, MFA, 65; artist resident, Sch of Arts in France, Lacoste, fall semesters, 84, 87. *Work:* Libr of Cong, Washington, DC; Philadelphia Mus Art; Worcester Art Mus; Portland Art Mus, Boulder; Elvewjem Mus Art, Univ Wis at Madison; and others. *Exhib:* Solo exhib, Am Embassy Cult Ctr, Belgrade & other Yugoslav Ctr, 83-84 & Drake Univ, Des Moines, 85; Int Invitational Exchange Exhib Prints, 89, Gallery Fine Arts Ctr, Seoul; Contemp am Printmaking, Ringling Sch Art & Design, Sarasota, Fla, 90; Int Impact Art Festival, Kyoto City Mus, Japan, 90 & 92; Found Mona Bismarck, Paris, 91; Exchanged Impressioins, Fine Arts Asn Gallery, Hanoi, Vietnam; and others. *Teaching:* Instr art & art hist, Baldwin-Wallace Col, Berea, Ohio, 65-66; adj assoc prof art hist, Univ Toledo, Toledo Mus Art, 66-; assoc instr, printmaking, Sch of Arts in France, Lacoste, fall semester, 87. *Awards:* Boston Printmakers Awards, 71, 81 & 87; Philadelphia Print Club Awards, 72, 75 & 79; Ohio Arts Coun grant to individual artist, 80 & 89; Award, Soc Am Graphic Artists, 85 & 86. *Mem:* Soc Am Graphic Artists; Calif Soc Printmakers; Boston Printmakers; Los Angeles Printmakers Soc; Women's Caucus for Art. *Media:* Etching, Aquatint. *Mailing Add:* 26114 West River Rd Perrysburg OH 43551-9786

AUVIL, KENNETH WILLIAM
EDUCATOR, PRINTMAKER
b Ryderwood, Wash, Dec 18, 25. *Study:* Univ Wash, BA, 50, MFA, 53. *Work:* Achenbach Found, Palace Legion Honor, San Francisco; Seattle Art Mus, Wash; US Embassy, Bonn, Ger; Wichita Art Asn, Kans; Victoria & Albert Mus, London, Eng. *Comn:* Ed of 170 screen prints, Hilton Collection, New York, 62. *Exhib:* Northwest Printmakers Int Exhibs, Seattle Art Mus, 53-67 & 70; 4th Biennial di Pittura Americana, Bordighera, Italy, 57; Libr Cong Nat Exhibs, 59, 63 & 66; New Impressions for the Decade, Oakland Art Mus, Calif, 70; Int Print Exhib, Richmond Art Ctr, Calif, 72. *Teaching:* Prof art & printmaking, Calif State Univ, San Jose, 56-88. *Mem:* Northwest Printmakers (pres, 55-56); Calif Soc Printmakers. *Media:* Serigraphy, Silkscreen. *Publ:* Auth, Serigraphy-Silk Screen Techniques for the Artist, Prentice-Hall, 65; Perspective Drawing, Mayfield, 90. *Mailing Add:* 605 Olson Rd Soquel CA 95073

AVAKIAN, JOHN
PAINTER, INSTRUCTOR
b Worcester, Mass. *Study:* Yale Univ Sch Art & Archit, BFA & MFA. *Work:* Kans State Univ; Western Mich Univ; Bucknell Univ; Tulsa Civic Ctr, Okla; White, Weld & Co, Inc, Boston. *Exhib:* 20th Nat Exhib Prints, Libr Cong, Washington, DC; 38th Int Printmakers Exhib, Seattle Art Mus; one-man show, Higgins Wing, Worcester Art Mus, Mass; 21st Ann Int Exhib, Beaumont Art Mus, Tex, 72. *Teaching:* Instr color & design, Northeastern Univ, Mass, 89 & Mt Ida Jr Col, 69-, chmn art dept, 69-83. *Awards:* Blanche E Colman Found Award, 70; Art Patrons League of Mobile Award, 72. *Mem:* Col Art Asn Am. *Media:* Acrylic, Collage. *Mailing Add:* 43 Morse St Sharon MA 02067

AVEDISIAN, EDWARD
PAINTER, SCULPTOR
b Lowell, Mass, 1936. *Study:* Boston Mus Sch Art. *Work:* Guggenheim Mus, Whitney Mus Am Art & Metrop Mus Art, New York; Los Angeles Co Mus Art; Wadsworth Atheneum; Chicago Art Inst; Cleveland Mus, Ohio. *Comn:* Greens, San Francisco; Desert Cafe, Santa Fe. *Exhib:* John Powers Collection, Larry Aldrich Mus, 66; Robert Rowan Collection, San Francisco Mus Art, 67; Boston Inst Contemp Art, 67-68; Painters Under 40, Whitney Mus Am Art, 68; Six Painters, Albright-Knox Art Gallery, Buffalo, 71; solo exhibs, Gallery Moos, Toronto, 71, Janie C Lee Gallery, Houston, 74, Carriage House Gallery, Buffalo, 75, NY Univ, 77, Nina Freudenheim Gallery, Buffalo, 78, Jason McCoy, New York, 84 & Baghoomian Gallery, 89. *Teaching:* Artist in residence, Univ Kans, 69; instr, Sch Visual Arts, New York, 69-70, Univ Calif, Irvine, 72 & Univ La, 73. *Awards:* Guggenheim Found Fel, 67; Nat Coun Arts Award, 68; Paula Krasner Found Grant, 92. *Media:* Acrylic, Oil; All Media. *Dealer:* Vreg Baghoomian 611 Broadway New York NY 10012. *Mailing Add:* 26 Warren Hudson NY 12534

AVEDON, BARRY
PAINTER, EDUCATOR
b Brooklyn, NY, Jan 2, 41. *Study:* Rochester Inst Technol Sch Art, BFA, 62, MFA, 64. *Work:* Eastern Mich Univ, Ypsilanti; Rochester Inst Technol, NY; Bank of Com, Hamtramck, Mich. *Exhib:* Ann Exhib, Albright-Knox Mus Art, 64; Butler Inst Am Art Mid-Year Show, 66; Michigan Biennial, Detroit Inst Art, 71; Midland Ann, Midland Ctr Arts, Mich, 78; Ball State Nat Drawing Ann, Ball State Univ Gallery, 79; Mich Artists 80/81, Flint Inst Arts, Mich, 81; The Corporation Collects Art, Muskegon Mus Art, Mich, 83; Focus Gallery, Detroit, 85; Battle Creek Art Ctr, 86. *Teaching:* Prof painting & drawing, Eastern Mich Univ, 66- *Awards:* 26th Regional of Ossining Ann Award, Westchester Arts Coun, 61; Julius Hallgarten Award, Nat Acad Design Ann, 64; Purchase Award, Ethno-Art '81, Bank of Commerce, Hamtramck, Mich, 81. *Bibliog:* A Scaglione & B Parker (auth), Detroit Summer III, Park West Galleries, Inc, 82; Robert Iglehart (auth), article, Ann Arbor News, 83. *Mem:* Artists Equity Asn, Mich. *Media:* Oil; Pencil. *Mailing Add:* Dept Art 114 Ford Hall Eastern Mich Univ Ypsilanti MI 48197

AVEDON, RICHARD
PHOTOGRAPHER
b New York, NY, May 15, 23. *Study:* Columbia Univ, Royal Col Art, JD, London, 89; Kenyon Col, Gambier, Ohio, Hon Degree, 93. *Work:* Smithsonian Inst, Washington, DC; Metrop Mus Art, Mus Mod Art, New York; High Mus, Atlanta GA; Mus Fine Arts, Houston; Minneapolis Inst Arts, Minn; San Francisco Mus Mod Art, Calif; Amon Carter Mus, Ft Worth, Tex; Victoria & Albert Mus, London, Gt Brit. *Exhib:* Family of Man, Mus Mod Art, New York, 55; Metrop Mus Art, 59, 60, 63 & 67; Musee Reattu, Arles, France, 65; NY World's Fair, 65-66; Fogg Art Mus, Cambridge, Mass, 67; Rhodes Nat Gallery, Salisbury, Rhodesia, 68; Expo 70, Osaka, Japan; one-man shows, Smithsonian Inst, 62, Minneapolis Inst Arts, 70, Mus Mod Art, 74, Whitney Mus Am Art, New York, 74, Marlborough Gallery, New York, 75, Metrop Mus Art, New York 78 & Aron Carter Mus, Ft Worth, Tex, 84, Corcoran Gallery, Washington DC, 85 & Nat Gallery Art, Washington DC, 89. *Pos:* Staff photogr, Harper's Bazaar, 45-65; photogr, French collections in Paris, 47-84; staff photogr, Vogue Mag, 66-; contribr photogr, Life, Look, Graphis Mag, US Camera Ann; visual consult, Paramount film Funny Face; television consult, dir & advert photogr. *Awards:* Photographer of the Year, Am Soc Mag Photogr, 85; Lifetime Achievement Award, Fashion Designers of Am, 89; Erna & Victor Hasselblad Found Int Photog Prize, 91; and others. *Bibliog:* Roland Barthes (auth), Avedon, Photo, 1/77; Janet Malcolm (auth), A series of proposals, The New Yorker, 10/23/78; Charles Michener (auth), The Avedon look, Newsweek, 10/16/78; Dore Ashton (auth), This silent theatre: The portrait photographs of Richard Avedon's in the American West, Arts Mag, 9/85; plus numerous articles & essays by Susan Sontag, Harold Brodkey, Hiton Kramer, Barbara Rose and others. *Mem:* Am Soc Mag Photogr. *Publ:* Photogr, Observations text by Truman Capote, 59; Nothing Personal, text by James Baldwin; ed, Diary of a Century, 70; photogrs, Alice in Wonderland: The Forming of A Company, the Making of a Play, text by Doon Arbus, 73; auth & photogr, Portraits, 76; Avedon: Photographs 1947-1977, 78; In the American West, 85. *Dealer:* Norma Stevens 418 E 59th St New York NY 10022. *Mailing Add:* 407 E 75th St New York NY 10021

AVERBUCH, ILAN
SCULPTOR
b Tel Aviv, Israel, 1953. *Study:* Wimbledon Sch Art, London, Eng, 77-78, Sch Visual Arts, BFA, 79-81, Hunter Col, NY, MFA, 83-84. *Work:* Israel Mus, Jerusalem; Martin Margulies, Coconut Grove, Fla; Vera List, Bryam, Conn; Michael Haas, Toytlof, Berlin, Ger; Ashley D Hoffman, Kings Point, NY. *Exhib:* Solo exhibs, Kunstlerhaus Bethanien, Berlin, Ger, 85, Daadgalerie, Berlin, Ger, 86, Mabat Gallery, Tel Aviv, Israel, 86, Jewish Mus, New York, 86, O K Harris Works of Art, New York, 87, Nancy Hoffman, New York, 89; Peace Biennale, Hamburg, WGer, 85; Sculpture in the Square, Lincoln Ctr, New York, 85-86; Mythos Berlin Concept Show (with catalog), 86; 49th Parallel, New York, 89; International Contemporary Art, Art Gallery Ont, Toronto, 89. *Pos:* Steel instr & coordr sculpture dept, Sch Visual Arts, New York, 80-82; lectr, Brown Univ, Providence, RI, 83, Berlin Technical Univ, 86. *Awards:* DAAD Award, Berlin, WGER. *Bibliog:* Gil Goldfine (auth), Averbuch Sculpture, Jerusalem Post, 10/11/86; Thomas Wulfen (auth), Donald Judd, Carlm Andre, Ilan Averbuch, Tages Spiegel, 6/87; Beatrice V Bismark (auth), Reviews: Ilan Averbuch, Daad Galene, Berlin, Flash Art, winter 86, 87. *Mailing Add:* c/o Olga Korper Gallery 17 Morrow Ave Toronto ON M6R 2H9 Canada

AVERY, FRANCES
PAINTER, PHOTOGRAPHER
b Kitchener, Ont, Can, Aug 23, 10; US citizen. *Study:* John Wickers Art Sch, Detroit; Art Students League, 31-34; Beaux Arts Sch Design; Columbia Univ with Meyer Shapiro; New Sch Social Research with Berenice Abbott, 39. *Comn:* Three easel paintings: Public Sch Noll, Fordham Hosp & New York Public Libr, Public Works Art Proj, New York, 34-35; mural, Lincoln Hosp, Bronx, NY, 36-39. *Exhib:* Solo exhibs, Eighth St Playhouse, New York, 35, Adelphi Univ, Garden City, 61, 63 & 75, Panoras Gallery, New York, 71; group exhibs, Corcoran Gallery, Washington, DC, 40; Nat Acad Design, 41; Mus Mod Art, New York, 42; Whitney Mus Am Art, New York, 54; Educ Alliance Exhib, portraits of well-known artists, 88; Invitational shows, No Ho Gallery, Winston Unity Ctr Libr, 88-91 & Westbeth Fall Exhib, 89; Open House, Union Sq Studio, 89-92; New York Soc Women Artists, Cork Gallery, Lincoln Ctr, 90; Nat Asn Women Artists Ann, 90; group exhib, Dialogue with Nature, Adelphi Univ, 92. *Teaching:* Pvt art class, 46-70; instr painting & drawing, Bergen Sch, NJ, & YWCA, schools in Bronx, Brooklyn, New York, Bergen & Jersey City, NJ, 50-59; asst prof drawing & painting, anatomy, color & media, Adelphi Univ, 59-79; teacher, mural artist, Educ Alliance, 92. *Awards:* Louis Comfort Tiffany Fel, 33; Purchase Award, Mus Mod Art, New York, 41; Yolens Ineriors Award Contemp Oil, Silvermine Guild, 56; Res & Travel Grant, Adelphi Univ, 73 & 77; Ziuta & Joseph Akston Found Prize, Nat Asn Women Artists, 81. *Bibliog:* Lucia A Salemme (auth), The Complete Book of Painting Techniques, 82; Interview, WNYC (radio prog), Works Proj Admin Murals, lost or destroyed, 84. *Mem:* Artists Equity; life mem, Art

Students League; Nat Soc Mural Artists; Nat Asn Women Artists, 40-92; New York Soc Women painters in sculptors, 39-92. *Media:* All. *Publ:* Contribr, photographs in Parade, US Camera & other mags. *Mailing Add:* 14 Horatio St Apt 4H New York NY 10014

AVISON, DAVID
PHOTOGRAPHER
b Harrisonburg, Va, July 13, 37. *Study:* Mass Inst Technol, ScB, 59; Brown Univ, PhD, 67; Inst Design, Ill Inst Technol, MS, 74. *Work:* Dallas Mus Fine Art; Int Mus Photog, George Eastman House, Rochester, NY; Mus Mod Art, New York; Mus Fine Arts, Boston, Mass; Art Inst Chicago; Mesa Southwest Mus, Ariz. *Comn:* The Architectural City, comn by City of Chicago, Chicago Art Inst; As We See It, comn by IBM for 75th anniversary, 89. *Exhib:* One-man shows, Recent Acquisitions, 77, 78 & 84, American Photography in the 70's, 79 & Chicago Architecture, 83, The City Inside and Out, Art Inst Chicago, 89; The Wider Show, Photog Archs, Univ Louisville, Ky, 88; Public Rituals and Diversions, Chicago Hist Soc, Ill, 89; Behold, Photographs from the Permanent Collection, Mus Contemp Photog, Chicago, 89; Partners in Purchase: Selected Works 1976-87, State of Ill Gallery, 89 & Lakeview Mus, 90; Three Decades of Midwestern Photography: The 1960's, 1970's and 1980's (exhib catalog), Davenport Mus. *Teaching:* Prof photog, Columbia Col, Chicago, 70-86. *Awards:* Nat Endowment Arts Photogr Award, 77; Ill Arts Coun Permanent Collection Grant, 84; Focus/Infinity Fund, Chicago, 87-88. *Bibliog:* Gretchen Garner (auth), Organic landscapes, Afterimage, 4/75; David Elliott (auth), Wide view of Chicago, Chicago Daily News, 4/77; Lynne Warren (auth), David Avison, Midwest Art Quart, 4/77. *Publ:* The New Vision: Forty Years of Photography at the Institute of Design, Traub & Grimes, 82; Twentieth Century Masters of Photography 1900-1985, Hallmark Collections, 86; Changing Chicago, a Photodocumentary, Rosenblum, Univ Ill Press, 89. *Dealer:* Baker Gallery Kansas City MO; Afterimage Gallery Dallas TX. *Mailing Add:* 421 W Melros Chicago IL 60614

AVLON-DAPHNIS, HELEN BASILEA
PAINTER, SCULPTOR
b New York, NY, June 18, 32. *Study:* Hunter Col, New York, BA, 59, MA, 72; Aspen Mus Sch, 70; Provincetown Sch Fine Arts, Mass, 70-75. *Work:* Gallery I, Westbeth, New York; Cook Gallery, New York. *Comn:* Mural, 250 W 57th Street, New York; The Sea, Provincetown Art Asn Mus. *Exhib:* Solo exhib, Gallery I Mus, Westbeth, New York, 84; Bertha Schaeffer Gallery, New York, 60-65; Provincetown Art Mus, Show of the 60's, 82; Forum Gallery, New York; Baltimore Art Mus. *Bibliog:* Articles in New York Daily News, Art News, Art Digest, Art Speaks and others. *Mem:* Westbeth Workshop Graphics Int. *Media:* Watercolor, Acrylic. *Mailing Add:* 463 West St New York NY 10014

AWALT, ELIZABETH GRACE
PAINTER
b Baltimore, Md, 56. *Study:* Skowhegan Sch Painting, ME, 77; Boston Col, BA, 78; Univ Pa, MA(painting), MFA, 81. *Work:* Bank Boston; Boston Co; Prudential Ins Co; Rose Mus; AT&T. *Exhib:* Brave New Works, Mus Fine Arts, Boston, 84; solo exhibs, Thomas Segal Gallery, Boston, 85 & G W Einstein Co, New York, 88, 90; Southeastern Mass Univ, North Dartmouth, Mass, 86; Nature observed, Danforth Mus Art, Framingham, Mass, 89; Fort Point Artists, Fed Reserve, Boston; Ten Artists-Ten Visions, DeCordova Mus Art, Lincoln, Mass, 89; The 80's: A Post Pop Generation, S Alleghenies Mus Art, 90; Beyond the Picturesque: Landscape on Paper, G W Einstein Gallery, New York, 91; The University of Notre Dame Friends & Alumni Collection (with catalog), Snite Mus Art, Ind. *Teaching:* Instr painting, drawing, ceramics, Wyncote Acad, Pa, 81; instr art, Boston Col, Newton, Mass, 84-87; instr painting, Waltham Sr Citizen Ctr, Mass, 85-86; instr painting, watercolor, drawing, Danforth Mus Sch, Framingham, Mass, 85-86; instr beginning painting, DeCordova Mus Sch Art, Lincoln, Mass, 86; asst prof, painting & drawing, Boston Col. *Awards:* Mass Artist Fel, Painting, 83; Nat Endowment Arts Grant, Painting, 87; Finalist, Mass Artist Found, 90. *Media:* Oil, Pastel. *Publ:* Contribr, Oil Pastel: Watson Guptill, 90; Pilgrims & Pioneers: New England Women in the Arts, Faxon & Moore, 87. *Dealer:* G W Einstein 591 Broadway New York NY 10012. *Mailing Add:* Box 481 18 Ridge St Millis MA 02054

AXELROD, MIRIAM
SCULPTOR
b Russia; US citizen. *Study:* Art Students League, 35, studied with Yasuo Kunyoshi, Robert Cronbach & Jason Seeley; Pratt Inst, cert, 40; Brooklyn Mus Art Sch, 45. *Work:* C W Post Col; Brooklyn Col; Nassau Community Col, NY; Sun Oil Chemical Corp, New York; IBM Corp, Long Island, NY. *Exhib:* Brooklyn Mus, NY, 45; Audubon Artists, New York, 63, 66 & 70; Fordham Univ, NY, 73; solo shows, C W Post Col, Long Island, NY, 76 & Adelphi Univ, Garden City, NY, 82; New York Inst Technol, Long Island, 76; and others. *Teaching:* Instr sculpture, Mepham High Sch, 63-78; adult educ prog, Calhoun High Sch, 63-78. *Awards:* Intra-Am Award, Ceceile Gallery, New York, 62; First Prize, Emily Lowe Gallery Ann, 64. *Bibliog:* Jean Paris (auth), reviews, Long Island Press, 65, 66, 69 & 74; Malcolm Preston (auth), Art, Newsday, 69, 70, 74 & 76. *Media:* Mixed. *Mailing Add:* 18 Tower Lane New Haven CT 06519

AYASO, MANUEL
PAINTER, SCULPTOR
b Riviera, Spain, Jan 1, 34; US citizen. *Study:* Newark Sch Fine & Indust Arts, cert. *Work:* Whitney Mus Am Art, New York; Worcester Mus, Mass; Pa Acad Fine Arts, Philadelphia; NJ State Mus, Trenton; Newark Mus, NJ. *Exhib:* 22nd Int Watercolor Biennial, Brooklyn Mus, NY, 63; El Neo-Humanismo en el Dibujo de USA, Italia y Mexico, Univ Mex, 63; American Painting & Sculpture, Pa Acad Fine Arts, 67; Contemporary American Artists, Nat Inst Arts & Lett, 71; Contemp Am Spiritual Art, Mus Contemp Art, Vatican, Rome, 76; The Fine Line: Drawing with Silver in America, circulating exhib, 85 & 86; Objects & Drawings, circulatory exhib, Sanford M & Diane Besser Collection, 92-93; and others. *Awards:* Tiffany Found Scholar in Painting, 62; Ford Found Purchase Award, 64; Childe Hassam Fund Purchase Award, 71. *Bibliog:* Brian O'Doherty (auth), NY Times, 5/31/61; John Canaday (auth), NY Times, 12/8/63; Barry Schwartz (auth), The New Humanism, Praeger Publ, 74. *Mem:* Am Fedn Arts. *Media:* Goldpoint, Mixed Media. *Dealer:* Jean Frank 25 E 83rd St New York NY 10021. *Mailing Add:* 12 Vincent Pl Verona NJ 07044

AYCOCK, ALICE
SCULPTOR
b Harrisburg, Pa, Nov 20, 46. *Study:* Douglass Col, New Brunswick, NJ, 64-68, BA; Hunter Col, New York, 68-71, MA, study with Robert Morris. *Work:* Mus Mod Art, Metrop Mus Art & Guggenheim Mus, Whitney Mus Am Art, New York; Mus Ludwig, Koln, Germany; Kunstmuseum, Basel, Switzerland; Walker Art Ctr, Minneapolis, Minn. *Comn:* Humanic Corp, Graz, Austria; Roanoke Col, Roanoke, Va; and others. *Exhib:* One-woman shows, Three-Fold Manifestation II, Storm King Art Ctr, Mountainville, NY, 87, The Six of Pentacles: To Know All Manner of Things, Kunstforum, Munich, WGer, 90, The Island of the Rose Apple Tree Surrounded by the Oceans of the World for You, My Darling, Western Wash Univ, Bellingham, 90, Universe Wheel, State Univ, Buffalo, NY, 88, Impossibilism, City Gallery Contemp Art, Raleigh, NC, 89, The Islands of the Moon and Suns, Sculpture Garden, La Jolla, Calif, 89, Univ Mich, Ann Arbor, 92; Enclosures & Encounters: Architectural Aspects of Recent Sculpture, Storm King Art Ctr, Mountainville, NY, 91; Photons, Phonons, Electrons, Jacksonville Art Mus, Fla, 91; Schwerlos, Mus Fur Moderen Kunst (auth, catalog), Berlin, Ger, 92; Cross Section, World Financial Ctr, New York, 92. *Pos:* Vol asst, Conserv Dept, Guggenheim Mus, New York, 67; cur, Art Hist Slide Libr, Hunter Col, New York, 69-72. *Teaching:* Instr, Found Sculpture & Advanced Sculpture Courses, Sch Vis Arts, New York, 77-78; vis sculptor & teacher, Princeton Univ, Princeton, NJ, spring semester, 79; vis sculptor & teacher, San Francisco Art Inst, Calif, spring semester, 79; asst prof, Hunter Col, New York, 82-85; teaching res, Kansas City Art Inst, 87; sr critic, Yale Univ, New Haven, Conn, 88-90; teaching res, Atlantic Ctr Arts, New Smyrna Beach, Fla, 89; teaching res, Ecole Nat Superieure des Beaux-Arts, Paris, France, 91; dir grad sculpture studies, Yale Univ, New Haven, Conn, 91-92; undergrad sculpture, Sch Visual Arts, New York, 92. *Awards:* Nat Endowment Arts Grant, 75, 76 & 80; Creative Artist Public Serv Grant, 76; City Univ NY Research Grant, 83; Fel, Nat Endowment Arts, 86. *Bibliog:* Howard Fox (auth), Hoodo, Mag Los Angeles Co Mus Art, 14, 7-8/91; Robert Hobbes (auth), Fattoria Celle, Site Specificity in Tuscany, Sculpture, 48-53, 3-4/91; Timothy Porges (auth), Letters/Chicago, Contemporanea, No 24, 25, 1/91. *Media:* Mixed. *Publ:* Five Semi-Architectural Projects, c 7500, Valencia, Calif, 73; New York City orientations, Triquarterly, Evanston, winter 75; The Beginnings of a Complex: Notes, Drawings, Photographs, Lapp Princess, Press Ltd, 77; Work 1972-1974, In: Individuals: Post-Movement Art in America, E P Dutton & Co, Inc, New York, 76; Auth, Making Their Mark, Women Artists Move Into the Mainstream 1970-85, Abbeville Press, 89. *Mailing Add:* 142 Greene Street New York NY 10012

AYERS, CAROL LEE
PAINTER, GALLERY DIRECTOR
b Newark, NJ, Dec 25, 29. *Study:* Basically self-taught; studied with David Kwo & Allan Eldredge, 75-76. *Work:* Bicentennial Expos, Everson Mus, Syracuse, NY; Am Telephone & Telegraph Corp Hq, Bedminster, NJ; Westinghouse Corp, Bath, NY; Sterling Drug Corp, New York & Athens, Greece; Trenton Mus; Corning Glass, Corning, NY; and others. *Comn:* acrylic wall panel, Archdiocese of Rochester, Geneva, NY, 70; mural, comn by B Burley, vpres Sterling Drug Corp, New York, 75; Highland Telephone Corp, Warwick, NY, 86; Mr & Mrs George Plimpton Collection, Southampton, NY, 86-88. *Exhib:* Silvermine Guild Artists, New Canaan, Conn, 75; Northeast Watercolor Soc, Hall Fame Trotter, Goshen, NY, 84-90; West Point Acad, 85; Connoisseur Gallery, Rhinebeck, NY 87-90; Springhouse Gallery, Philadelphia, Pa, 90; Dutot Mus, Del Water Gap, Pa, 92. *Pos:* Dir, Esperanza Gallery, Yates Co, NY, 68-73; dir, Erincourt Gallery, Penn Yan, NY, 73-79; dir, Gallery-in-the-Gap, Delaware Water Gap, Pa, 80-83; dir, Sunflower Studio, 83- *Teaching:* Demonstr acrylic painting, Rotring-Koh-I-Noor, Inc. *Awards:* First Awards, Monroe Co Mus, 83, Chester Art Asn, NJ, 83 & Suburban Art League, 83 & Kevka Lake Art Asn, 70, 73-74, 79 & 84-85; Ringwood Manor an Landscape Award, Ridgewood AA Awards. *Bibliog:* Articles in NJ Music & Art Mag, Ridgewood, NJ, 6/77; T Noverro (auth), Save the gallery, Easton Publ Co, Pa, 9/81; articles in NY Art Review, 88 & Am Artist Mag, 89, Watercolor '92 Spring & Fall Issues, The Artist's Mag, 3/92. *Mem:* Signature mem, Northeast Watercolor Soc; Pocono Mt Art Group; Hunterdon Co Art Ctr, Clinton, NJ. *Media:* Watercolor, Mixed Media. *Specialty:* Original contemporary paintings. *Publ:* Auth, Manuscript on liquid acrylic, Am Artist Mag, 90-91. *Dealer:* Dorothy Espinola 11 Edgemere Terr Washington NJ 07882; The Connoisseur Gallery Rhinebeck NY. *Mailing Add:* Sunflower Studio 70 Mt Hermon Rd Blairstown NJ 07825

AYLON, HELENE
PAINTER, CONCEPTUAL ARTIST
b New York, NY. *Study:* Brooklyn Col, BA(cum laude); with Ad Reinhardt. *Work:* Whitney Mus Am Art, New York; Mass Inst Technol, Cambridge.

Comn: Wall painting, Chapel, John F Kennedy Airport, NY, 66; lobby mural, NY Univ Med Ctr, New York, 67. *Exhib:* Lyrical Abstraction, Whitney Mus Am Art, Aldrich Mus Contemp Art & traveling, 69; one-woman shows, Max Hutchinson Gallery, New York, 70-72, Betty Parsons Gallery, New York, 75, Susan Caldwell Gallery, New York, 75, Grapestake Gallery, San Francisco, 76 & 78 & Mass Inst Technol, Cambridge, 76, Sand Carrying, Women's Bldg, San Francisco, 81 & Two Sacs en Route, Japan, 85; Season's Highlights, Aldrich Mus Am Art, Ridgefield, Conn, 71; Four Painters, Skidmore Col, Saratoga, NY, 71; Cleveland Ctr Contemp Art, 89; Creative Time: Art n the Anchorage, 92. *Teaching:* Instr painting, Brooklyn Mus & Hunter Col, 72-73; instr, San Francisco State Univ, 73-76. *Awards:* Nat Endowment Arts Fel, 73, 74 & 80; NY State Coun Arts Grant, 79 & 85. *Bibliog:* Grace Glueck (auth), Art: Highlights of downtown scene, New York Times, 12/11/70; Gregoire Muller (auth), Materiality and painterliness, Arts Mag, 9-10/71; Carter Ratcliff (auth), New York letter, Art Int, 6/73. *Media:* Installation, Environmental Land Art. *Publ:* Video productions, Sand Sounds, Sand Carrying, Calif, 81; Its Own Sac, 83; Postscript, Japan, 85. *Dealer:* Sondra Gering Gallery 376 Broome St New York NY 10012; Thread Waxing Space 476 Broadway New York NY 10012. *Mailing Add:* 463 West St 808A New York NY 10014

AYRES, JULIA SPENCER
PAINTER, WRITER
b Havana, Cuba, Aug 16, 31; US citizen. *Study:* Boston Mus Fine Art Sch, Mass Col Art, 48-49; Art Inst Chicago, 50-52; pvt study with William Maynard, Frederic Taubes & Ralph Love. *Work:* Home Savings Am; Marriott Corp; Unocal Corp, Calif; First Interstate Bank, San Diego; Hilton Corp, Daytona Beach, Fla; Toyota Corp, Calif. *Comn:* Landscapes, seascapes, monotypes & suite of 18 watercolors, Marriott Corp, var locations. *Exhib:* Nat Arts Club Watercolor Ann, New York, 85; Am Artist Prof League Grand Nationals, New York, 85 & 86; Nat Watercolor Soc 64th Ann, Calif; Nat Watercolor Okla, Okla Art Ctr Mus, Oklahoma City, 87; Los Angeles Audubon Nat Art Exhib, Beverly Hills, Calif, 87. *Awards:* Winsor & Newton Award, Nat Watercolor Soc 64th Ann. *Bibliog:* Art Marketing Handbook, Gee Tee Bee, 86; Dorothy Hoyal (auth), Taking oneself seriously as an artist, Am Artist, 6/88. *Mem:* Am Artists Prof League; Okla Watercolor Asn. *Media:* Watercolor, Monotypes. *Publ:* Auth, Brushes, the critical tools, In: Watercolor 86, Am Artist Publ, 86; Paper, the critical support, In: Watercolor 87, Am Artist Publ, 87; Making watercolor monotypes, In: Watercolor 88, Am Artist Publ, 88; Fracoise Gilot's Monotypes, Am Arts Mag, 1/90; Monotype, Medius and Methods of Painterly Printmaking, 91 & Printmaking (in press), Watson Guptill Pub. *Dealer:* Riggs Galleries La Jolla CA 92037. *Mailing Add:* PO Box 489 Chouteau OK 74337

AYRES, LARRY MARSHALL
HISTORIAN
b Nov 15, 39. *Study:* Dartmouth Col, AB, 64; Univ Oxford, BLitt, 66; Harvard Univ, PhD, 70. *Pos:* Bd dirs, Int Ctr Medieval Art, 77-80. *Teaching:* Asst prof art hist, Univ Calif, Santa Barbara, 70-74, assoc prof, 74-79, chmn, 76-88, prof, 79- *Awards:* Alexander von Humboldt Stiftung Res Fel, 79-80 & 86 & 93; Am Philos Soc Grants, 81 & 82; Prix Rome Res Fel, Am Acad Rome, 83-84. *Mem:* Col Art Asn Am; Mediaeval Acad Am; Southern Calif Art Historians. *Res:* Medieval art; history of the book. *Publ:* Auth, Sources of the lyre drawings, Speculum, 74; English painting and the Continent, Eleanor of Aquitaine: Patron and Politician, 76; Salzburg affliations of a Bible fragment in Vienna, Zeitschrift Kunstgeschichte, 82; Parisian Bibles in Berlin Staatsbibliotek, Pantheon, 82; in Dumbartou Oaks Papers, 87; in Studi Gregoriani, 92; Romanesque Manuscript illumination, Braziller (in prep). *Mailing Add:* Dept Art History Univ Calif Santa Barbara Santa Barbara CA 93106

AYRES, LINDA L
ADMINISTRATOR, CURATOR
b Berlin, Md, May 25, 47. *Study:* Wash Col, Chestertown, Md, BA(cum laude), 69; Tufts Univ, MA, 73. *Pos:* Asst to dir, Fogg Mus Art, Harvard Univ, 75-76; asst cur Am art, Nat Gallery Art, Washington, 78-84; cur paintings & sculpture, Amon Carter Mus, Ft Worth, Tex, 84-89; assoc dir exhib & prog, Wadsworth Atheneum, 89-90, deputy dir, 90- *Mem:* Am Asn Mus; Asn Historians Am Art. *Res:* 19th and 20th century American art. *Publ:* George Bellows: Artist & Lithographs, 16-24; coauth, An American Perspective: Nineteeth Century Art From the Collection of JoAnn & Julian Ganz Jr, 81; American Paintings, Watercolors and Drawings from the Collection of Rita & Daniel Fraad, Amon Carter Mus, 85 & 88; John Singer Sargent, Abrams, 86; Am Frontier Life: Early Western Painting & Parents, Abbeville, 87. *Mailing Add:* Wadworth Atheneum 600 Main St Hartford CT 06103

AZACETA, LUIS CRUZ
PAINTER
b Marianao, Cuba, Apr 5, 42; US citizen. *Study:* Sch Visual Arts, New York, with Leon Golub, Frank Roth & Michael Loew, cert, 69. *Work:* Metrop Mus Art, Mus of Mod Art, New York; Va Mus Fine Arts, Richmond; RI Sch Design Mus; Del Art Mus. *Exhib:* Crimes of Compassion, The Chrysler Mus, Norfolk, Va, 81; The Age of Anxiety: 20th Century Art in the Lila Acheson Wing, Metrop Mus Art, New York, 87; Committed to Print, Mus Mod Art, New York, 88; Large Works New York New York, Kunst Station, Sankt Peter, Cologne, WGer, 88; and many others. *Teaching:* Vis artist, Univ Calif, Davis, La State Univ, Baton Rouge, Univ Calif, Berkeley & Cooper Union, New York. *Awards:* Nat Endowment Arts, 80-81, 85-86; Guggenheim Mem Found Grant, NY, 85-86; NY Found Arts Grant, 85-86. *Bibliog:* Grace Glueck (auth), article, New York Times, 1/27/84; Ellen Schlesinger (auth), No room for apathy, Artweek, 84; Linda McGreevy (auth), Painting his heart out, Arts Mag, 6/85; Jose Gomez Sicre (auth), Cuban Artist in Exile, 86. *Media:* Acrylic, Watercolor. *Dealer:* Frumkin/Adams Gallery 50 W 57th St New York NY 10019. *Mailing Add:* c/o Frumkin/Adams Gallery 50 W 57th St New York NY 10019

AZARA, NANCY J
SCULPTOR, PAINTER
b New York, NY, Oct 13, 39. *Study:* Finch Col, AAS, 59; Art Students League, sculpture with John Hovannes, painting & drawing with Edwin Dickinson, 64-67; Empire State Col, BS(sculpture), 74. *Work:* Sculptors, sound film strip, Harcourt, Brace, Jovanovich; Everson Mus, Syracuse, NY; Univ Southern Ill, Edwardsville; Franklin Furnance, New York. *Comn:* About the Goddess KALI (wood sculpture), Pamela Oline, S France, 77. *Exhib:* One-woman shows, Soho Gallery, New York, 84 & 87, Artemisa Gallery, Chicago, 85, Women Art Register Minn Gallery, Minneapolis, 86, WARM Gallery, Minneapolis, 86, Inskirts Gallery, Women's Studio Workshop, Rodendale, NY, 86, AIR Gallery, New York, 89 & 92 & Lannon Gallery, Chicago, 90; In Homage to Ana Mendieta, Zeus-Trabia Gallery, New York, 86; Contemporary Primitivism, Gallery Contemp Art, Univ Colo, Colorado Springs, 86; Art as a Healing Force, Bolinas Mus, Calif, 91; The Awakened Goddess, MUSE Gallery, Philadelphia, 91; Hail Columbia! Arch, Grand Army Plaza, Brooklyn, NY, 91; and others. *Teaching:* Lectr art, Sch Contemp Studies, Brooklyn Col, 73-75, lectr sculpture, 75-76; instr sculpture, Brooklyn Mus Sch, 74-77; instr, Col New Rochelle, NY, 79-82; instr, founding mem & mem bd dirs, New York Feminist Art Inst, currently. *Awards:* Adolph & Esther Gottlieb Found Grant, 85. *Bibliog:* Robin Rice (auth), My goddess, Philadelphia City Paper, 9/13-20/91; Carol Roland (auth), Found Objects, Delaware Ctr Contemp Arts, Art Matters, 11/91; Ronnie Cohen (auth), Nancy Azara, AIR Gallery, Art Forum, 5/92; and others. *Mem:* Art Students League; Womens Caucus Art (adv bd, 80-83); Col Art Asn. *Media:* Wood, Oil; Paper, Paint. *Publ:* Auth, Artists in their own image, Ms Mag, 73; The Group, Anandala, Heresies Mag, spring 79; and others. *Dealer:* AIR Gallery 63 Crosby St New York NY 10012. *Mailing Add:* 91 Franklin St New York NY 10013

AZUMA, NORIO
PRINTMAKER, PAINTER
b Kii-Nagashima-cho, Japan, Nov 23, 28. *Study:* Kanazawa Art Col, Japan, BFA; Chouinard Art Inst, Los Angeles; Art Students League. *Work:* Nat Collection Fine Arts, Smithsonian Inst, Washington, DC; Whitney Mus Am Art, New York; Philadelphia Mus Art; Brooklyn Mus Art; Art Inst Chicago. *Comn:* 1500 serigraph prints, IBM Corp, NY, 66. *Exhib:* Corcoran Biennial, Washington, DC, 63; 3rd Int Triennial Original Graphic, Grenchen, Switz, 64; Mus Mod Art, Tokyo Exhib, 65; Sculpture & Prints, Whitney Mus Am Art, 66; Silkscreen, History of a Medium, Philadelphia Mus Art, 72. *Awards:* Int Print Show, Seattle Mus Art, 60; Print Exhib, Soc Am Graphic Artists, 68; Print Exhib, Boston Printmakers, 70. *Media:* Serigraphy; Oil. *Dealer:* AAA Gallery 663 Fifth Ave New York NY 10022; Azuma Gallery 50 Walker St New York NY 10013. *Mailing Add:* 276 Riverside Dr New York NY 10025

AZUZ, DAVID
PAINTER, PRINTMAKER
b Tel Aviv, Isreal, Jan 11, 42. *Study:* Schawartzamn Acad, Tel Aviv, 55; Avni Acad, 58; Acad des Beaux Arts, Paris, 63. *Work:* Leo Beck Temple, Cedars Art Gallery, Skirhall Mus, Los Angeles; Newport Harbor Art Mus, Calif; Haifa Art Mus; Tel Aviv Art Mus; plus many others in various Univs. *Exhib:* Solo exhibs, Ltd Ed Gallery, Los Angeles, 75 & 76, Galerie Cardo Matignon, Paris, 78, Galerie Daniel Binn, Metz, 79, Rosenbaum Gallery, Palm Beach, Fla, 79, Soufer Gallery, New York, 80, 81, 82, 84, 86 & 89, Galerie Rene Drouet, Paris, 83, plus many others; Mus Mod Arts, Haifa, 58, 59, & 60 Gallery Jean Tiroche, Jaffa, 61, Givon Art Gallery, Hadassa Klaskin Art Gallery, Tel Aviv, Israel, 74; Gallery Dagmar Wirth, Berlin, Ger, 63, 64, 65, 66; Galerie du Fleuve, 65, Galerie Carpentier, 66, Galerie St-Peres, 67, Expos, Hotel Royal-Monceau, 70, Galerie Abel Rambert, 71, 72, 73, Expo Artistes Independants, 77, Galerie Haik, 88, Galerie Francis Barlier, Paris, France, 89; Skirall Mus, Los Angeles, 78, 81; Art Expo, New York, 80, 81, 82 & 83; Forum-Expo, Licra, 82, Galerie Turenne, Troyes, France, 89. *Mem:* Soc Auteurs dan les Arts; Graphiques Plastiques, France; Int Asn Art. *Media:* Oil, Watercolor. *Mailing Add:* 150 E 69 St New York NY 10021

B

B(ECK), ROSEMARIE
PAINTER, EDUCATOR
US citizen. *Study:* Oberlin Col; Columbia Univ; NY Univ. *Work:* Whitney Mus Am Art; Vassar Col Mus; State Univ NY, New Paltz; Trenton Mus, NJ; Nebr Art Mus; Corcoran Gallery Art & Hirshhorn Mus, Washington, DC. *Comn:* Mural painting, Rotron Mfg Co, 58. *Exhib:* Pa Acad Fine Arts; Nat Inst Arts & Lett; Whitney Mus Am Art; Art Inst Chicago; solo exhibs, eleven at Peridot Gallery, two at Poindexter Gallery, two at Ingber Gallery, New York. *Teaching:* Lectr painting, Vassar Col, 57-58, 61-64 & Middlebury Col, 58-60 & 63; prof painting, Queens Col, 68- *Awards:* Ingram-Merrill Grant, 67 & 79; Nat Endowment Arts Grant, 86. *Media:* Oil. *Dealer:* Ingber Art Gallery 3 E 78th New York NY 10021. *Mailing Add:* 6 E 12th St New York NY 10003

BAAS, JACQUELYNN
MUSEUM DIRECTOR, HISTORIAN
b Grand Rapids, Mich, Feb 14, 48. *Study:* Mich State Univ, with Elizabeth G Holt, BA, 71; Univ Mich, MA, 73, PhD, 82. *Collections Arranged:* The Artistic Revival of the Woodcut in France 1850-1900 (coauth, catalog), Univ Mich, Ann Arbor 83-84; The Dartmouth Collection (coauth, catalog), 85, Encounter in Space: Double Images in the Graphic Art of Edward Munch (auth, catalog), 86, Toys from the Collection of Charles W Moore, 86-87, The Second Stage of Modernism, 87 & Mills and Factories of New England, 88, Hood Mus Art, Dartmouth Col, Hanover, NH. *Pos:* Registr, Univ Mich Mus Art, Ann Arbor, 74-78, asst dir, 78- 82; chief cur, Hood Mus Art, Dartmouth Col, Hanover, NH, 82-83, acting dir, 84, dir, 85-89; dir, Univ Art Mus, Berkeley, Calif, 89- *Teaching:* Prof hist print media, Univ Mich, 81. *Awards:* Nat Endowment Arts Fel, 88-89. *Mem:* Col Art Asn Am; Am Asn Mus; Print Coun Am; Asn Art Mus Dirs. *Res:* Nineteenth-century French art, the history of the print media,(work of the Mexican muralists). *Publ:* Coauth, The Artistic Revival of the Woodcut in France, 1850- 1900, Univ Mich, 83; Auth, Treasures of the Hood Museum of Art, Dartmouth College, Hudson Hills Press, 85; Edouard Manet and Civil War, Art J, 85; Encounter in Space: The Graphic Art of Eduard Munch, Hood Mus, 86; Reconsidering Walter Benjamin, In: The Documented Image, Syracuse Univ Press, 87. *Mailing Add:* Univ Art Mus Univ Calif-Berkeley Berkeley CA 94720

BABCOCK, JO (JOSEPH WARREN BABCOCK)
PHOTOGRAPHER, SCULPTOR
b Saint Louis, Mo, Feb 24, 54. *Study:* Univ Calif Los Angeles, with Robert Heinicken, Todd Walker, Bea Nettles, 75; San Francisco Art Inst with, Pirkle Jones, BFA, 76; with Linda Conner, MFA, 79. *Work:* Brooklyn Mus; San Francisco Mod Art; George Eastman House, Rochester, NY; Newport Harbor Art Mus, Newport Beach, Calif; La Biblioteque, Avignon, France. *Comn:* Photo installation (site specific), Levi Strauss Mus, San Francisco, 90; hist display, Levi Strauss & Co, San Francisco, 91; photos in bus shelters, Arts Comn, San Francisco, 92. *Exhib:* Art Inst Student & Friends Photo, Carmel, Calif, 76; Sao Paulo Bienale, Auditorium, Brazil, 85; Group Material, DIA Found, New York, 88; California Color, San Francisco Mus Mod Art, 89; Constructing Images, Lieberman & Saul, New York, 91, Tampa Mus Art, Fla, 92, Ctr Creative Photog, Tucson, Ariz, 92, & San Jose Mus Art, Calif, 92. *Teaching:* Assoc prof new genres in photog, San Francisco Art Inst, 9/89 - 12/89 & 7/90 - 12/90; vis prof pinhole photog, Visual Studies Workshop, Rochester, NY, 6/90. *Awards:* NY State Coun Arts, 88; Art in Transit, Market St Bus Shelter, San Francisco Arts Comn, 92; Fel, Nat Endowment Arts, 90. *Mem:* San Francisco Camerawork (bd mem & exhibs); San Francisco Mus Mod Art. *Media:* Alternative Photography. *Publ:* Illusr, Low Tech - Camera and Photographs (catalog), San Francisco, 89. *Dealer:* Visual Studies Workshop 31 Prince St Rochester NY 14607. *Mailing Add:* 375 Day St No 3 San Francisco CA 94131

BABIOR, DANIEL
PHOTOGRAPHER
b Brooklyn, NY, Dec 23, 53. *Study:* State Univ NY, Buffalo, BA, 74; RI Sch Design, MFA, 78. *Work:* Brooklyn Mus, NY; Israel Mus, Jerusalem. *Exhib:* Aldrich Art Mus, Ridgefield, Conn, 91; Crocker Art Mus, Sacramento, Calif, 92. *Teaching:* Photog, Marin Acad, 88- *Awards:* Photog Fel, Nat Endowment Art, 90 & 91. *Dealer:* Dean Moniz Gallery 1825 Q St Sacramento CA 95814. *Mailing Add:* 918 Louisiana St Vallejo CA 94590

BACARELLA, FLAVIA
PAINTER
b Brooklyn, NY. *Study:* New School Soc Res, MA, 75; New York Studi Sch Drawing/Painting/Sculpting, 77-80; Brooklyn Col, NY, MFA, 83. *Work:* Arthur Andersen, Minneapolis; Va Ctr Creative Arts, Sweet Briar. *Exhib:* 4th Annual Miniatures, Brooklyn, NY, 86; The Landscape, New Haven, Conn, 88; Col New Rochelle, 88; Prince St Gallery, 85 & 88. *Teaching:* Lectr painting, Herbert H Lehman Col, 85-; instr drawing, Port Jervis Arts Ctr, 90. *Awards:* Painting Fel, NY Found Arts, 86; Grant, City Univ NY Res Found, 88. *Mem:* Women's Caucus Art; Col Art Asn. *Media:* Oils. *Mailing Add:* c/o Prince Street Gallery 121 Wooster St New York NY 10012

BACH, DIRK
PAINTER, EDUCATOR
b Grand Rapids, Mich, Nov 27, 39. *Study:* Univ Denver, BFA(painting), 61, MA(painting), 62; Univ Mich, Ann Arbor, MA(Orient art hist), 64. *Work:* Denver Art Mus, Colo; Hopkins Ctr Art Galleries, Dartmouth Col, Hanover, NH; Lamont Gallery, Phillips Exeter Acad, NH; Loretto-Hilton Gallery, Webster Col, St Louis, Mo; Mus Art, RI Sch Design, Providence. *Comn:* Wall reliefs, Denver Art Mus, 62, NH Comn Arts NH Voc Inst, Berlin, 68 & Grad & Music Schs, Univ NH, 68; St Gaudens Nat Hist Site, Cornish, NH, 72. *Exhib:* New Eng Drawing Exhib, Addison Gallery, Andover, Mass, 70; New England Drawing Competition, DeCordova Mus, Lincoln, Mass, 74; Phillips-Exeter Acad, 67, 74 & 79; Newport Art Asn, RI, 76, 77-81; RI Sch Design Mus of Art, Providence, 69-83; Seasons Gallery, Den Haag, Netherlands, 80-81; Susan Cumming Gallery, Mill Valley, Calif, 90; and many others. *Collections Arranged:* One Hundred Years of American Art, 66 & The Rose Art Museum Collection at New Hampshire (with catalog), 69, Scudder Gallery, Durham, NH. *Pos:* Dir, Scudder Gallery, Univ NH, 65-69; adv & contribr, Newport Rev, 79-; coun mem, Art Asn Newport, 80-83. *Teaching:* Asst prof painting, Univ NH, 65-69; assoc prof art hist, RI Sch Design, 69-90, prof, 90- , chmn art hist dept, 78-; assoc & lectr, Asian Studies, Brown Univ, 70-; dir, RI Sch Design, European Honors Program, Rome, 74-75. *Awards:* Univ NH Cent Univ Res Grant Commemorative Stamp Paintings, 68; Nat Endowment Humanities Travel & Res Grant, Japan, 71; Mellon Fel, Egypt, 84. *Mem:* Col Art Asn Am; Artists Equity Asn; Newport Art Asn; NH Art Asn. *Media:* Graphite, Paper. *Res:* Development of Ch'an painting in China; production of cosmic diagrams in the Far East. *Publ:* Contribr, The Painting of Tao Chi, Univ Mich Mus Art, 67; auth, The stamp collection of Dirk Bach, Ramparts, 11/68; auth, Selections From the Oriental Collections, RI Sch Design, 72. *Mailing Add:* 506 Carolina Back Rd Charlestown RI 02813

BACH, LAURENCE
PHOTOGRAPHER, EDUCATOR
b Philadelphia, Pa, Jan 2, 47. *Study:* Philadephia Col Art, BFA, 68; Allgemeine Gewerbeschule, Basel, Switz, grad, 70. *Work:* Philadelphia Mus Art; Mus Fine Arts, St Petersburg, Fla. *Exhib:* Three Centuries Am Art, Philadelphia Mus Art, 76; solo exhibs, Modernism Gallery, San Francisco, 79, Robert Samuel Gallery, New York, 81, Photo Ctr Athens, Greece, 82 & Wesleyan Univ, Conn, 83; Group Photographs, Inst Contemp Art, Philadelphia, 80; and others. *Teaching:* Asst prof photog & design, Moore Col Art, 70-72, Philadelphia Col Art, 72-74 & State Univ NY, Purchase, 74- *Awards:* Photog Grant, Nat Endowment Arts, 80; Photog Study Grant, Polaroid Corp, 81; NY State Coun Arts Grant, Visual Studies Workshop, 82. *Bibliog:* William Stapp (auth), Three Centuries of American Art (exhib catalog), Philadelphia Mus, 76; Don Ernst (auth), Laurence Bach: Paros shards, Aperture, No 82, 2/79; Owen Edwards (auth), Laurence Bach portfolio, Am Photog, 9/81. *Publ:* Auth, The Paros Dream Book, Visual Studies Workshop Press, 83. *Mailing Add:* 2115 Fitzwater St Philadelphia PA 19146

BACHARDY, DON
PAINTER, DRAFTSMAN
b Los Angeles, Calif, May 18, 34. *Study:* Chouinard Art Inst, 56-60; Slade Sch Art, London Univ, 61. *Work:* Metrop Mus Art, New York; Nat Portrait Gallery England, London; Princeton Univ; Fogg Art Mus; Univ Tex, Austin. *Comn:* Official portrait Calif State Capitol Bldg, Former Gov G Edmund Brown Jr. *Exhib:* Solo exhib, De Young Mem Mus, 64, Los Angeles Munic Art Gallery, 73 & 83 & New York Cult Ctr, 74; Inside-Out: Self Beyond Likeness, Newport Harbor Art Mus, 81; Portland Art Mus, 81; James Corcoran Gallery, Santa Monica, Calif, 87 & 91. *Bibliog:* One Hundred Drawings, 83 & Drawings of the male nude, 85, Twelvetrees Press; 70XI, Drawings of Seventy Artists, Illuminati Press, 83; Last Drawings of Christopher Isherwood, Faber & Faber, 91. *Media:* Ink, Acrylic. *Publ:* Illusr, Michigan Quart Rev, Univ Mich, winter 80; Paris Rev, Vol 23, No 79, 81; Paris Rev, Vol 25, No 89, 83. *Dealer:* James Cocoran Gallery 1327 Fifth St Santa Monica CA 90401. *Mailing Add:* 145 Adelaide Dr Santa Monica CA 90402

BACHERT, HILDEGARD GINA
ART DEALER
b Mannheim, Ger, Apr 3, 21; US citizen. *Study:* Hunter Col, BA(summa cum laude), 54. *Collections Arranged:* Grandma Moses (contribr, catalog), Nat Gallery Art, Washington, DC, 79; Alfred Kubin, 83; Paula Modersohn-Becker, 83; Kollwitz/Modersohn-Becker traveling exhibition, 84-86; Grandma Moses traveling exhib, Japan, 90. *Pos:* Secy & asst, Nierendorf Gallery, New York, 39-40; exec secy, Galerie St Etienne, New York, 40-78, co-dir, 78- *Mem:* Art Dealers Asn Am. *Specialty:* Early 20th century Austrian and German art: Schiele, Klimt, Kokoschka, Kollwitz & Corinth; 19th and 20th century naive art. *Publ:* Contribr, Otto Kallir's Egon Schiele: Oeuvre Catalog of the Paintings, 66 & contribr, Otto Kallir's Egon Schiele: The Graphic Work, 70, Zsolnay, Vienna & Crown; Otto Kallir's Grandma Moses, Crown & Harry N Abrams, 73, Ger transl, DuMont, Cologne, Ger, 79, Jane Kallir's Egon Schiele: The Complete Works, Harry N Abrams, 90; auth, Collecting the Art of Käthe Kollwitz, Käthe Kollwitz by Elizabeth Prelinger, Nat Gallery Art & Yale Univ Press, 92. *Mailing Add:* 290 West End Ave New York NY 10023

BACHINSKI, WALTER JOSEPH
PAINTER, DRAFTSMAN
b Ottawa, Ont, Aug 6, 39; Can citizen. *Study:* Ont Col Art, AOCA, 65; printmaking with Frederick Hagen; Univ Iowa, with Mauricio Lasansky, MA(printmaking), 67. *Work:* Montreal Mus Fine Arts, Que; Uffizi Gallery, Florence, Italy; Can Coun Art Bank, Ottawa, Ont; Civic Mus, Lugano, Switz; Kitchener-Waterloo Art Gallery, Kitchener, Ont. *Comn:* Three bas-reliefs on a humanitarian theme, Univ Waterloo, Ont, 75; The Sculptor's Studio (bas-relief), MacLean-Hunter Bldg, College Park, Toronto; Mother and Child (bronze relief), Donald Forster Sculpture Park, MacDonald Stewart Art Gallery, Guelph, Ont, 85; Pastoral (pastel), Cineplex-Odean Theatre, Kiochener, Ont; The Four Seasons (pastel), Mine & Minerals Res Ctr, Laurentian Univ, Sudbury, Ont. *Exhib:* One-man travelling exhibs, Mt St Vincent Univ, 73, Walter Bachinski: Sculpture & Drawing, Art Gallery, Hamilton, 81; Bachinski, A Decade (travelling exhib), Kitchener-Waterloo Art Gallery, 76-77; Approaching Classicism, Selected Works, 1979-89, Kiochener-Waterloo Art Gallery, 91; Still-life, 10 Years, McLaren Art Ctr, Barrie, 92. *Teaching:* Prof drawing & printmaking, Dept Fine Arts, Univ Guelph, 67- *Awards:* Can Coun Arts Grants, 69, 78, 79 & 82; Arts Coun Ont Grants, 78 & 79; Premio dell Instituto Bancario Si Paolo di Torino, 4th Int Biennale of Graphic Art, Florence, Italy, 74; Can Coun Materials Grant, 78-79; and others. *Bibliog:* Bachinski: A Decade, Kitchener-Waterloo Art Gallery, 76; Walter Bachinski: Sculpture and Drawing, Art Gallery of Hamilton, 81; Walter Bachinski: Approaching Classicism, Kiochener-Waterloo Art Gallery, 91. *Media:* Pastels, Oil Paint. *Dealer:* Heffel Gallery Vancouver BC Can; Drabinsky Gallery Toronto ON Can. *Mailing Add:* 65 Mont St Guelph ON N1H 2A5 Canada

BACIGALUPA, ANDREA
SCULPTOR, PAINTER
b Baltimore, Md, May 26, 23. *Study:* Art Students League, painting with Arnold Blanch, summer 49; Md Inst Fine Arts, BFA, 50, painting with Jacques Maroger; Accad de Belli Arti, Florence, Italy, PG, painting with Ottone Rosai, 50-51. *Work:* City of Santa Fe, NMex; Basilica Santa Maria del Lauro, Meta di Sorrento, Italy. *Comn:* Conceptual design, Bishop De Falco Retreat Ctr, Amarillo, Tex, 82; 14 panels etched glass, St Francis Cathedral, Santa Fe, NMex, 85; Our Lady of Guadalupe (mural), St Johns, Borger, Tex, 88; stained glass, St Thomas More Church, Manhattan, Kans, 90; interior design, Holy Rosary Church, Aalbuquerque, NMex, 92. *Exhib:* One-man show, Mus of NMex, 59; Am House, New York, 60; US Church Archit Guild, Pittsburgh, 61; Gov's Gallery, Sante Fe, NMex, 78; Cooper-Hewitt Mus, New York, 81. *Pos:* Designer & consult, St Lawrence Cathedral, Amarillo, Tex, 75 & St Thomas More, Manhattan, Kans, 88-90; columnist, Santa Fe Reporter, currently. *Awards:* Bronze Medallion Fine Arts, Md Inst, 50; 1st Prize, Santa Fe Competition, Art in Pub Places, 79. *Bibliog:* Maurice Lavanoux (auth), Liturgy & art, Liturgical Arts, 73; Clifford Stevens (auth), Sacred arts, Out Sunday Visitor, 74; Denise Kusel (auth), Mem in Old Country, Santa Fe NMex, 10/10/85; Cathy Flores (auth), Dream Realized, Las Cruces, Sun-News, 3/30/86. *Media:* Bronze; Oil. *Publ:* Auth, Santos & Saints Days, Sunstone Press, 72; The coffeebreak journal (Sunday column), Santa Fe New Mexican, 72-75; Journal of an itinerant artist, Our Sunday Visitor, 77; A Good and Perfect Gift, OSV, 78; The Song of Guadalupana, OSV, 79; Franco and Pirata, Pickwick Press, 85. *Mailing Add:* 626 Canyon Rd Santa Fe NM 87501

BACOT, HENRY PARROTT
MUSEUM DIRECTOR, CURATOR
b Shreveport, La, Dec 13, 41. *Study:* Baylor Univ, Waco, Tex, BA, 63; La State Univ, Baton Rouge, 64-65; Attingham Park Summer Sch Study Great English Country Houses, Shropshire, fel, 66; State Univ NY Cooperstown, MA(Scriven Found Fel, Cooperstown Grad Progs), 67. *Collections Arranged:* American Folk Art 1730-1968, 68; Southern Furniture & Silver: The Federal Period 1788-1830, 68; Louisiana Landscape 1800-1969, 69; Natchez-Made Silver of the 19th Century, 70; Sail & Steam in Louisiana Waters, 71; Louisiana Folk Art, 72; Crescent City Silver, 80; Rhoda Stokes: A Retrospective (with catalog), 84; Louisiana Art from the Roger M Ruton Ogden Collection, 92. *Pos:* Dir, Anglo-Am Art Mus, Baton Rouge, 67-; hist interiors consult, Kings' Tavern, Natchez, Miss, 71-, Kent Plantation House, Alexandria, La, 71- & Magnolia Mound Plantation House, Baton Rouge, 72-; sponsor, Am Friends of Attingham Summer Sch, 77-; exec dir, La State Univ Mus Complex, 82. *Teaching:* Asst prof art hist, La State Univ, 67-84, asst prof hist of interior design, 73, prof art hist, 84- *Mem:* Soc Archit Historians; Am Victorian Soc; Found Hist La (bd mem, 72-74); Old State Capitol Adv Comt. *Res:* Fine arts, architecture and decorative arts of the Deep South. *Publ:* Coauth, Nineteenth century Natchez-made Silver, 71, Crescent City silver, Historic New Orleans collection, 80; articles, Antiques, 72-91; contribr, Soc Archit Historians J, 74; auth, Nineteenth Century Lighting: Candle-Powered Devices: 1783-1883, Schiffer Pub Ltd, 87. *Mailing Add:* PO Box 20249 La State Univ Baton Rouge LA 70803

BACZEK, PETER GERARD
PAINTER, PRINTMAKER
b Webster, Mass, June 6, 45. *Study:* San Jose State Univ, BA(art), 70. *Work:* Achenbach Found Graphic Arts, Calif Palace Legion Hon, San Francisco; Brooklyn Mus; Philadelphia Mus Art; Metrop Mus Art Ctr, Coral Gables, Fla; Cooper-Hewitt Mus, New York. *Exhib:* 21st Nat Print Exhib, Brooklyn Mus, 79; Eighth Int Print Biennial, Crakow, Poland, 80; Subjective Realities (with catalog), Calif Palace Legion Hon, San Francisco, 82; Urban Documents: 20th Century American Prints, Cooper-Hewitt Mus, New York, 83; Rockford Int, Rockford Col, 83; Boston Printmakers 37th Nat Exhib Art Mus, Brandeis Univ, 85; Crocker-Kingsley Ann, Crocker Mus Art, Sacramento, Calif; Ninth British Int Print Biennale, Bradford, Eng, 86. *Awards:* Patron Award, Print Club, Pa, 82; Jurors Spec Mention, Cabo Frio Int Print Biennial, Brazil, 83; Monotype Award, Northern Calif Print Competition, 86. *Bibliog:* Roberta Loach (auth), Book of Hours: A Portfolio of 21 Prints, Visual Dialog, 79; Julie van der Ryn (auth), Shadows and Patterns in the Everyday, City Arts Monthly Mag, 81. *Mem:* Calif Soc Printmakers; The Print Club Philadelphia, Pa; Boston Printmakers, MA. *Media:* Oil; Etchings. *Dealer:* Suzy R Locke & Assocs 201 Estates Dr Piedmont CA 94611. *Mailing Add:* 2433 Scenic Ave Oakland CA 94602

BADALAMENTI, FRED
PAINTER, EDUCATOR
b Long Island, NY, June 25, 35. *Study:* Pratt Inst, 53-55; State Univ NY Col, New Paltz, BS, 60; Brooklyn Col, MFA(fel), 67; studied with Philip Pearlstein, Carl Holty & Burgoyne Diller. *Work:* Brooklyn Col, NY; State Univ NY, Stony Brook. *Comn:* Bellevue Hosp, New York. *Exhib:* One-person exhibs, First St Gallery, New York, 76, 80 & 89; two-person exhib, First St Gallery, 73; Brooklyn College Art Department Past & Present, Robert Schoelkopf Gallery, NY, 77; Leopold Hoesch Mus, Duren, Ger, 80; Gallery North, Long Island, 85, 86 & 91; Nassau County Mus Fine Arts, 87; St Joseph's Col, 87; Cuny Research Found, 89; Contemp Realist Gallery, San Francisco, Calif, 90. *Pos:* Dir, First St Gallery, 78-79. *Teaching:* Full prof drawing & painting, Brooklyn Col, 67-, deputy chmn grad art, 72-89, dep chmn undergrad art, 89-; vis assoc prof drawing & painting, State Univ NY, Stony Brook, 77-78 & summers 80, 81 & 83. *Awards:* Fel, Brooklyn Col, 65-67. *Mem:* Col Art Asn; Am Asn Univ Prof. *Media:* Oil, Drawing. *Dealer:* First Street Gallery 560 Broadway New York NY 10012. *Mailing Add:* 182 Lower Sheep Pasture Rd Setauket NY 11733

BADEN, MOWRY T
SCULPTOR
b Los Angeles, Calif, 1936. *Study:* Pomona Col, BA, 58; Stanford, MA, 65. *Comn:* Univ Calif, Irvine; Art Park, Lewiston, NY; Exploratorium, San Francisco; Wash Proj for the Arts; Am Psychological Asn. *Exhib:* One-man shows, Mercer Union, Toronto, 87, Contemp Art Gallery, Vancouver, BC, 88, Drawing Room, Tucson, Ariz, 88, Alta Col Art Gallery, Calgary, Alta, 89, Capp St Proj, San Francisco, 91, San Diego Mus, La Jolla, Calif, 91; Surrey Art Gallery, BC, 90; World Trade Ctr, New York, 90; Un-Natural Traces, Barbican Gallery, London, Eng, 91. *Teaching:* Univ Victoria, 75- *Awards:* Can Coun Proj Cost Grant, 76-77, 80-81, 81-82, 87, 88 & 89; Nat Endowment Arts Grant, 77-78, 80-81, 84 & 90. *Bibliog:* The True North & Unnatural Traces, What's On, Barbican Art Gallery, London, Eng, 5/1/91; Peter Hackett (auth), The True North: Canadian Landscape Painting 1896-1939 and Unnatural Traces: Contemporary Art from Canada, The Month, London, Eng, 5/91; Kim Masters (auth), Artists Want Out of Exhibit, Washington Post, 7/13/91. *Mailing Add:* 5450 W Saanich Rd R R 5 Victoria BC V8X 4M6 Canada

BADER, FRANZ
PHOTOGRAPHER
b Vienna, Austria, Sept 19, 03; US citizen. *Study:* Univ Vienna; George Washington Univ, DC, DFA(hon), 84; Corcoran Sch Art, Docter Humane Letters(hon), 84. *Work:* Air & Space Mus, Washington, DC; Phillips Collection, Washington, DC; Cheekwood, Nashville, Tenn; Watkins Gallery, Am Univ, Washington, DC; Corcoran Gallery Art; Mus Am Hist, Smithsonian Inst; Libr Cong. *Exhib:* Corcoran Gallery Art, Washington, DC, 73; Nat Acad Sci, 75; one-man shows, Phillips Collection, 77, Cheekwood, Nashville, Tenn, 80, Watkins Gallery, Am Univ, Washington, DC, 81, Brody Gallery, Washington, DC, 88 & Susan Conway Gallery, Washington, DC, 91. *Pos:* Owner, Wallishaussersche Bookshop, Vienna, 39; vpres & gen mgr, Whyte Gallery, Washington, DC, 39-52; pres, Franz Bader Gallery, Washington, DC, 52-; retired. *Awards:* Goldene Ehrenzeichen Verdienste, Austria; Verdienstkreuz Erster Klasse, Germany; Mayor's Art Award, Washington, DC, 81. *Specialty:* Contemporary American art; Washington artists; original graphics; Can Eskimo Art. *Collection:* Original graphics; contemporary artists and sculpture. *Mailing Add:* 2244 48th St NW Washington DC 20007

BAECHLER, DONALD
PAINTER
b Hartford, Conn, 1956. *Study:* Maryland Inst Col Art Baltimore, 74-77; Cooper Union, New York, 77-78; Staatliche Hochschule fuer bildende Kuenste, Frankfurt, Ger, 78-79. *Work:* Mus Mod Art, New York; Metrop Mus Art, New York; Philadelphia Mus Art; Centre Pompidou, Paris, France; William Alan Mus, Oberlin, Ohio. *Exhib:* 1989 Whitney Biennal, Whitney Mus Art, New York. *Mailing Add:* c/o Tony Shafrazi Gallery 163 Mercer St New York NY 10012

BAEDER, JOHN
PAINTER
b South Bend, Ind, Dec 24, 38. *Study:* Auburn Univ, Ala, AB, 60. *Work:* Denver Art Mus; Whitney Mus of Am Art; Mus Mod Art Lending Serv; Cooper-Hewitt Mus; High Mus, Atlanta; and others. *Exhib:* Place, Product, Package, Cooper-Hewitt Mus, Smithsonian Inst, New York, 78; Kunstgewerbemuseum, Zurich, Switzerland, 79; Danforth Mus, Framington, Mass, 80; Philbrook Art Ctr, Tulsa, Okla, 80; Real, Really Real, Super Real, San Antonio Mus, 81; Contemp American Realism Since 1960, Pa Acad Fine Arts, 81; Painting New York, Mus City New York, 83-84; and others. *Bibliog:* Gregory Battcock (auth), Super Realism, Dutton, 75; D Filipacchi (auth), Les Hyper Realists Americans. *Media:* Lithography, Oil. *Publ:* Auth, Diners, Harry N Abrams, Inc, New York, 78; auth, Gas, Food and Lodging, Abbeville Press, 82. *Dealer:* O K Harris 383 W Broadway New York NY 10012. *Mailing Add:* 1025 Overton Lea Rd Nashville TN 37220

BAER, JO
PAINTER, WRITER
b Seattle, Wash, Aug 7, 29. *Study:* Univ Wash; Grad Fac, New Sch Social Res. *Work:* Mus Mod Art & Guggenheim Mus, New York; Kolnischer Kunstverein, Koln, WGer; Albright-Knox Art Gallery, Buffalo, NY; Nat Mus, Canberra, Australia; Whitney Mus Am Art; Tate Gallery, London, England; Norton Simon Mus, Pasadena, Calif; and others. *Exhib:* Systematic Paintings, Guggenheim Mus, 66; Whitney Mus Am Art Biennial, New York, 67, 69, 73 & 75 & solo show, 75; Documenta IV, Mus Friedericianum, Kassel, Ger, 68; 31st Biennial, Corcoran Gallery Art, Washington, DC, 69; Options and Alternatives, Yale Univ, 73; one-person shows, MOMA, Oxford, 77, Scottish Arts Coun Gallery, Edinbugh, The Douglas Hyde Gallery, Trinity Col, Dublin, Stedelijk Vanabbe Mus, Eindhoven, Holland, 78 & 86, Galerie Ricke, Cologne, 78, Lisson Gallery, London, 80; Ft Worth Mus, Tex, 77; Indianapolis Mus, Ind, 77; Chicago Art Inst, 77; Städtische Kunsthelle, Dusseldorf, 82; The Window in 20th Century Art, Neuberger Mus, State Univ NY, Purchase, 86-87; La Couleur Seule, Musce St Pierre, Lyon, France, 88; and many others. *Teaching:* Instr painting, Sch Visual Arts, New York, 69-70; guest instr painting, Brighton Tech, England, 82 & Rijksakedemie, Amsterdam, 87-88. *Awards:* Nat Coun Arts Award, 68-69. *Bibliog:* P Schjeldahl (auth), Jo Baer: Playing on the senses, New York Times, 5/14/72; C Ratcliff (auth), Jo Baer: Notes on 5 recent paintings, Artforum, 5/72; L R Lippard (auth), Color at the edge, Art News, 5/72; Paintings 1962-1974 (exhib catalog), Mus Mod Art, Oxford, Eng, 77;; Barbara Rose (auth), Vogue Upfront, Vogue, 6/75;; Kenneth Baker (auth), Less is Less, The Boston Phoenix, Mar 27, 79;; Richard Pacheco (auth), Boston Institute Gives

Showcase to Minimalism, Std Times, 4/15/79; Viven Raynor (auth), At Ridgefield, Definition of Minimalism, New York Times, 5/13/79. *Media:* Oil. *Publ:* Auth, Edward Kienholz: A sentimental journeyman, Art Int, 4/68; auth, Mach bands: Art & vision & Xerography & edge-effects (collateral essay), Aspen Mag, fall-winter 70; contribr, Symposium on art & politics, Artforum, 9/70; auth, Fluorescent light culture, Am Orchid Soc Bull, 9-10/71; auth, I am no longer an abstract artist, Art in Am, 10/83. *Mailing Add:* Rozengracht 207 Amsterdam, 1016 LZ Netherlands

BAER, MORLEY
PHOTOGRAPHER
b Toledo, Ohio, Apr 5, 16. *Study:* Univ Mich, MA, 37. *Work:* San Francisco Mus Art & DeYoung Mus, Calif; Amon Carter Mus, Ft Worth, Tex; Monterey Peninsula Mus Art, Calif. *Teaching:* Instr photog, Ansel Adams June Workshop, 70- & Univ Calif Exten, 72- *Awards:* Medal Photog, Am Inst Architects, 65; Fel, Am Acad, Rome, Italy, 80. *Mem:* Friends of Photog, Carmel, Calif (trustee, 72-); Am Soc of Mag Photogs, 66. *Publ:* Contribr, Room and Time Enough, Northland Press, 79; The Wilder Shore, Sierra Club Books, 84; Light Years, Photo West Graphics, 88. *Dealer:* Photography West Box 4829 Carmel CA 93921. *Mailing Add:* PO Box 222537 Carmel CA 93922

BAER, NORBERT SEBASTIAN
EDUCATOR
b Brooklyn, NY, June 6, 38. *Study:* Brooklyn Col, BSc(physical chemistry), 59; Univ Wis, MSc(chemistry), 62; NY Univ, PhD(physical chemistry), 69. *Pos:* Ed adv & assoc ed, Studies in Conservation, J Int Inst for Conserv, 71-; co-chmn, Conserv Ctr, Inst Fine Arts, NY Univ, 75-83, actg dir admin, 78-79; assoc ed, Restaurator, 75-; US exec ed, Conservation in the Arts, Archeol & Archit, Butterworths, 79-; chmn, Adv Comt on Preserv, Nat Archives & Rec Serv, 80-; chmn, Comt Conserv Historic Store Bldgs & Monuments, Nat Mat Adv Bd, Nat Acad Sci, 80-82; mem, Vis Comt Dept Objects Conserv, Metrop Mus Art, 80- *Teaching:* Prof conserv, Inst Fine Arts, NY Univ, 69- *Awards:* Guggenheim Fel, 83-84. *Mem:* Fel Int Inst Conserv; fel Am Inst Conserv (bd dir, 73-76); fel Am Inst Chemists; Am Chemical Soc; Sigma Xi. *Res:* Application of physico-chemical techniques to the preservation and examination of artistic and historic works. *Publ:* Coauth, Chemical Investigations on Ancient Near Eastern Archaeological Ivory Artifacts: III, Fluorine & Nitrogen Composition & Chemical Aspects of the Conservation of Archaeological Materials, Archeological Chemistry II, Advances in Chemistry, 78; coauth, Synthetic Blue Pigments: IX-XVI Centuries, I, Literature, Studies in Conservation, 80; coauth, Mechanisms of air pollution-induced damage to stone, Sixth World Congress Air Quality, Paris, Vol 3, 83; and others. *Mailing Add:* 25 Columbus Sq Amsterdam NY 12010

BAER, ROD
SCULPTOR
b Los Angeles, Calif. *Study:* San Diego State Univ, BA; Claremont Grad Sch, MFA. *Work:* Skirball Mus, Los Angeles; Munic Collection, Pasadena, Calif; Del Mar Col, Corpus Christi, Tex; Tri-City Centre, San Bernardino, Calif; Calif State Univ, Bakersfield. *Comn:* Fictions, Art Coun, Los Angeles Co Mus Art, Calif, 89; Award Excellence, Mus Found, Calif Mus Sci, Los Angeles, 91; Endless Columns, Carnation Co, Los Angeles, 91; Pocketwatch and Others, Metro-link Train Depot/City Claremont, Calif, 92; Surf n' Set, downtown & beachwalk, ID sites, City of Manhattan Beach, Calif, 92. *Exhib:* Personal Evolution: 3 Sculptors, Security Pac Downtown Plaza, Los Angeles, 87; Tableaux: Vivante/Morte, Installation Gallery, San Diego, 88; Art and Architecture, Santa Monica Heritage Mus, 88; On Site, Calif State Univ, San Bernardino, 89; Solo exhit, The Cost of Implosion, Meyers/Bloom Gallery, Santa Monica, 89; Three Sculptors/Three Coasts, Blue Star Art Space, San Antonio, Tex, 90; 2-man show, Pima Col, Tucson, Ariz, 92; Permanent display, Skirball Mus, Los Angeles, Calif, 92. *Teaching:* Instr sculpture, Otis Parsons Art Inst, 90-91. *Bibliog:* Howard Fox (auth), Carnation Company Art Collection (cat), 90; Kim Levin (auth), Choices: The book as art, Village Voice, New York, 8/90; Martin Miller (auth), Is this the wave of the future?, LA Times, 6/92. *Mem:* Int Sculpture Ctr. *Media:* Mixed, Concrete. *Mailing Add:* 3803 San Rafael Ave Los Angeles CA 90065

BAGERIS, JOHN
PAINTER, EDUCATOR
b Fremont, Ohio, May 11, 24. *Study:* Art Inst Chicago, BFA, 50, MFA, 52. *Work:* Mus Mod Art & Whitney Mus Am Art, New York; Brooklyn Mus, NY; Wadsworth Atheneum, Hartford, Conn; Newark Art Mus, NJ. *Teaching:* Instr painting, Sch Visual Arts, New York, 61-72; instr painting, Art Inst Boston, Mass, 73- *Awards:* Fulbright Traveling Fel, Munich, Ger, 53-54. *Mailing Add:* 2 Mount Auburn St Cambridge MA 02138

BAGGETT, WILLIAM CARTER, JR
PAINTER, EDUCATOR
b Montgomery, Ala, Jan 12, 46. *Study:* Auburn Univ, BFA, 68, MFA, 73. *Work:* US Info Agency Embassy Collections, (worldwide); Auburn Univ; Montgomery Mus Fine Arts, Ala; Univ Miss Mus, Oxford; Vision Nouvelle, Paris, France; Grapholith Atelier, Paris, France; Mokpo Nat Col, Seoul, Korea. *Comn:* Portraits, William Faulkner, Univ Miss, Oxford, 77, T K Mattingly & H M Hartsfield, Auburn Univ, 82; multicolor lithographs, Vision Nouvelle, Paris, 80 & Nahan Ed, New Orleans, 81. *Exhib:* New Orleans Biennial, New Orleans Mus Art, 73; 107th Ann Exhib Am Watercolor Soc, Nat Acad Design, New York, 74; Rocky Mountain Nat Watermedia Exhib, Foothills Art Ctr, Golden, Colo, 74. *Teaching:* Asst prof design, Univ Miss, 73-76; assoc prof & coordr visual commun, Auburn Univ, 76-83; prof & chmn dept art, Univ Southern Miss, 83-86, actg dean, 86-87, prof, 87- *Awards:* Jurors Best in Show, Tenth Dixie Ann Exhib, Montgomery Mus Art, 69; Endowed Chair Alumni Prof, Auburn Univ, 82. *Media:* Egg Tempera, Watercolor. *Dealer:* Nahan Galleries 381 W Broadway New York NY 10012. *Mailing Add:* Univ of Southern Miss Box 5033 Southern Station Hattiesburg MS 39406

BAHC, MO
PAINTER
b Busan, Korea, June 23, 57. *Study:* Hong-ik Univ, Seoul, Korea, BFA, 81; Pratt Inst, New York, MFA, 85. *Work:* Parson Sch Design, New York. *Exhib:* Speak American, Bronx Mus, New York, 90; Official Language, San Francisco Art Inst, Calif, 90; Public Mirror, Clocktower Gallery, New York, 90; Points of View, Rockland Ctr Arts, West Nyack, NY, 91; In Plural America, Hudson River Mus, Yonkers, NY, 92; and others. *Awards:* Fel Painting, NY Found Arts, 89; Macdowell Residency, 91; Fel Painting, Nat Endowment Arts, 91. *Bibliog:* Holly Block (auth), Mo Bahc, Village Voice, 5/16/88; Lucy Lippard (auth), Mixed Blessing, Pantheon, 90; Esther Iverem (auth), American Culture, Refracted, NY Newsday, 1/8/91. *Media:* Mixed Media. *Mailing Add:* 1205 Manhattan Ave 5th fl Brooklyn NY 11222

BAILEY, BARBARA ANN
PAINTER, INSTRUCTOR
b Kokomo, Ind, Mar 20, 28. *Study:* Art Inst Pittsburgh; Univ Hawaii; Univ Pittsburgh, BA(cum laude); Seton Hill Col, with Frank Webb & Foster Caddell. *Work:* Air Force Mus Art Collection, Dayton, Ohio; Hoyt Inst Fine Art, New Castle, Pa. *Exhib:* Three Rivers Art Festival, 72, 75 & 83; Hoosier Salon Indianapolis, 72; Am Artists Prof League Exhib, New York, 74 & 75; Washington & Jefferson Nat Painting Exhib, Washington, Pa, 75 & 81; one-person show, Clarion State Col, Pa, 75 & Pa State Univ, 83; Mus Show Assoc Artists, Butler Inst Am Art, Youngstown, Ohio, 79; Aqueous Open Nat Show, 80 & 82-83; Hoyt Inst Fine Art, 84. *Teaching:* Instr oil painting, Boyce Community Col. *Awards:* Best of Show Award, Indiana Co Fair Art Exhib, Pa, 73; Mus Award, Greensburg Art Asn, Pa, 73; Painting Grant, Monroville Arts Coun, Pa. *Mem:* Pittsburgh Watercolor Soc; E Suburban Artists League, Pittsburgh; Assoc Artists Pittsburgh. *Media:* Oil, Pastel. *Publ:* Auth, Create glowing florals in watercolor, Artist's Mag, 8/90. *Mailing Add:* 111 Marion Ave Pittsburgh PA 15221

BAILEY, BARRY STONE
SCULPTOR, PAINTER
b High Point, NC, Oct 21, 52. *Study:* ECarolina Univ, BS(art educ), 75, studies with Norman Keller, MFA(sculpture), 79; studies at Univ Ga, Cortona, Italy prog, 77. *Work:* New Orleans Mus Art; R J Reynolds World Trade Ctr, Winston-Salem, NC; Westminster Corp. *Comn:* Welded steel kiosk, Pan Am Life, New Orleans, 82; New Orleans Palms, eight paintings on paper, Hotel Intercontinental, New Orleans, 82; Palm Shrine, Pontchartrain Beach, Contemp Arts Ctr, New Orleans, 83; Rain Pavilion, 2 kinetic bronze sculptures, Hist New Orleans collection, 84; 8' wall sculpture, Saratoga Bldg, Westminster Corp, New Orleans, 85. *Exhib:* Solo exhibs, Arthur Roger Gallery, New Orleans, La, 84, & Louisiana World Expo, New Orleans, 84; Perspectives, Cross Creek Gallery, Malibu, Calif, 87; Palazzo Vagnotti, Cortona, Italy, 77; Seven Sculptors, Alternative Mus, New York, 81; Contemporary Arts Ctr, New Orleans, 87; 112 Greene Street, New York, 85; Chicago International, Navy Pier, 87. *Collections Arranged:* First Louisiana Sculpture Biennial, 81 & The New Louisiana Landscape, 81, Contemp Arts Ctr, New Orleans. *Pos:* asst cur & supvr exhib artworks, La World Expo, 84. *Teaching:* Teaching fel art appreciation & 3D design, ECarolina Univ, Greenville, NC, 75-77; teaching asst sculpture, Univ Ga abroad, Cortona, Italy, 77; instr sculpture, La State Univ, Baton Rouge, 85; Instr, Newcomb Sculpture Dept, Tulane Univ, currently. *Awards:* Ford Found Fel, 77; Best in Show, Durham Arts Coun, 25th Ann, NC, 79. *Bibliog:* Roger Green (auth), Environmental influence on shape, Times-Picayune, 7/11/82; Marion Orr (auth), article, in: Gambit, Vol 5, No 37, 9/15/84; Roger Green (auth), Barry Bailey, Randy Ernst at Arthur Roger Gallery, Artnews, 12/86. *Mem:* Young Artists' Movement; South Eastern Col Art asn; Contemp Arts Ctr. *Media:* Miscellaneous Media. *Dealer:* Arthur Roger Gallery 3005 Magazine St New Orleans LA 70115. *Mailing Add:* c/o Arthur Roger Gallery 432 Julia St New Orleans LA 70130

BAILEY, CLAYTON GEORGE
SCULPTOR, EDUCATOR
b Antigo, Wis, Mar 9, 39. *Study:* Univ Wis-Madison, BS, 61, MS, 62. *Work:* Oakland Mus, Calif; Mus Contemp Crafts, New York; Addison Gallery Am Art, Andover, Mass; Milwaukee Art Ctr; San Francisco Mus Mod Art. *Comn:* Exec Teapot, Kohler Co, Kohler, Wis, 79; Sacramento Metrop Light Rail, 86. *Exhib:* Solo exhibs, Milwaukee Art Ctr, 61, Mus Contemp Crafts, New York, 63, M H DeYoung Mus, San Francisco, 75, Triton Mus, Santa Clara, Calif, 81, Monterey Mus Art, Calif, 84 & Henry Gallery, Seattle; Objects USA, Smithsonian traveling exhib, 69; A Decade of American Ceramics, San Francisco Mus Mod Art, 73; A Century of Ceramics, Syracuse Mus, 79; American Porcelain, Renwick Gallery, 80; Humor in Art, Los Angeles Co Mus, 81; and others. *Teaching:* Prof ceramics, Wis State Univ, Whitewater, 63-66; prof ceramics, Calif State Univ, Hayward, 68-, chmn art dept, 79-81. *Awards:* Artists Grants, Louis Comfort Tiffany Found, 63, Am Craftsmen Coun, 63 & Nat Endowment Arts, 79 & 90; Nominated for Nobel Prize, 76; and others. *Bibliog:* Julie Hall (auth), Tradition and Change, Dutton, 79; Jan Axel (auth), American Porcelain, 81; Tom Albright (auth), California Art, 86; Donhauser (auth), Am Ceramics, 78. *Mem:* Hon fel Nat Coun for Educ in Ceramic Arts (dir at large, 78-80). *Media:* Ceramic, Metal. *Publ:* Coauth, My father is a sculptor, Jack & Jill Mag, 70; auth, Wonders of the World Catalog of Kaolithic Curiosities, Artist, 75. *Mailing Add:* Wonders of the World PO Box 69 Port Costa CA 94569

BAILEY, JANN L M
EDUCATOR, CURATOR
b Hamilton, Ont, Mar 12, 52. *Study:* Ont Col Art, AOCA, 76; Sarah Lawrence Col; Emily Carr Col Art & Design; Banff Sch Mgt. *Collections Arranged:* Photographic Sequences (auth, catalog), Art Gallery Peterborough, 82; Richard Prince (auth, catalog), Spencer I Harrison (auth, catalog), Harvey Volaine (auth, catalog), Exploration Est/Ouest (catalog), Centre du Exposition, St Jerome, Quebec, Kamloops Art Gallery. *Pos:* Educ coordr, Art Gallery Hamilton, Ont, 77-80; educ officer, Art Gallery Peterborough, Ont, 81-84. *Teaching:* Program coordr arts admin, Sir Sandford Fleming Col, 84-87; Dir/Cur, Kamloops Art Gallery 87- *Awards:* Design Awards, Ont Asn Art Galleries, 77-79; Photographic Award, Ont Arts Coun, 78; Western Can Art Asn, 87-89. *Mem:* Can Asn Art Admin Educators (vpres, 86); Asn Cult Execs; Can Mus Asn; Ont Asn Art Galleries; BC Mus Asn; Western Can Art Asn (pres, 90); Can Art Mus Dirs. *Publ:* Ontario Association of Art Galleries Handbook II, Can Art, Spencer J Harrison. *Mailing Add:* Kamloops Art Gallery 207 Seymour St Kamloops BC V2C 2E7 Canada

BAILEY, MARCIA MEAD
PAINTER
b Hartford, Conn, Jan 10, 47. *Study:* Self-taught. *Exhib:* Henry Ward Ranger Ann Exhib, Nat Acad Design, New York, 80; 39th-45th Ann, Audubon Artists, New York, 81-87 & at Lever House, 86; 68th-74th Ann, Allied Artists Am, New York, 81-87; Dr Maury Leibovitz Exhib, New York, 86. *Awards:* S J Wallace Truman Prize, Nat Acad Design, New York, 80; Binney and Smith Liquitex Award, Audubon Artists, New York, 81; Gold Medal Honor, Allied Artists Am, 81. *Mem:* Audubon Artists; Allied Artists Am. *Media:* Oil. *Dealer:* Arts Exclusive Inc 690 Hupmeadow St Simsbury CT 06070. *Mailing Add:* 189 Wickham Rd Glastonbury CT 06033

BAILEY, OSCAR
PHOTOGRAPHER, EDUCATOR
b Barnesville, Ohio, July 23, 25. *Study:* Wilmington Col, Ohio, BA; Ohio Univ, Athens, MFA. *Work:* Int Mus Photog, George Eastman House, Rochester, NY; Hist of Photog Collection, Smithsonian Inst, Washington, DC; New Orleans Mus Art, La; Mus Fine Arts, St Petersburg, Fla; Boston Mus Fine Arts. *Exhib:* The Sense of Abstraction in Contemp Photog, Mus Mod Art, New York, 60; Photog USA, De Cordova Mus, Lincoln, Mass & George Eastman House, Rochester, NY, 62; Photog in Fine Arts, Metrop Mus Art, New York, 63 & 76; Four Directions in Photog, Albright-Knox Art Gallery, Buffalo, NY, 64; Photog in the 20th Century, Nat Gallery of Can, Ottawa, 67; Wider View, Int Mus Photog, George Eastman House, 72; Light & Lens, Hudson River Mus, Yonkers, NY, 73; Time & Transformation, Lowe Art Mus, Univ Miami, Fla, 75; Photo/Synthesis, Cornell Univ, Ithaca, NY, 76; The Contemporary American South Traveling Exhib, US Info Agency, SE Asia & Europe, 77; Extended Frame Traveling Exhib, Visual Studies Workshop, Rochester, 78. *Pos:* Artist-in-residence, Artpark, Lewiston, NY, summer 77. *Teaching:* Prof photog, State Univ NY, Buffalo, 58-69 & Univ SFla, Tampa, 69-85. *Awards:* Photog Fel Grant, Nat Endowment Arts, 76. *Bibliog:* John Canaday (auth), New Talent--1960, Art in Am, 60; J Kirk T Varneodoe (ed), Modern Portraits--The Self & Others, Columbia Univ, 76. *Mem:* Founding mem Soc Photog Educ. *Publ:* Coauth, Found Objects, State Univ NY, Buffalo, 65; ed, Silver Bullets, Dept Photog, Univ SFla, 72; contribr, Marcel DuChamp, Mus Mod Art, 73. *Mailing Add:* Rte 2 Box 1007 Burnsville NC 28714-9231

BAILEY, RICHARD H
SCULPTOR
b Dover, Del, June 24, 40. *Study:* Del Art Ctr, Wilmington; Art Students League; New Sch Soc Res, New York City; study in Carrara, Italy, Barre, Vt, Goddard Col, Plainfield, Vt; also with Jose DeCreeft, Lorrie Goulet & Leroy Smith. *Work:* Am Mus Natural Hist, New York; Univ Del; Newark Pub Libr; Blue Cross Blue Shield; Bell Tel, Del. *Comn:* Sculpture, comn by Reverend C Jones, 67; sculpture, comn by John Gilbert, 69; sculpture, St Polycarp's Roman Cath Church, 73; medallian, De Trust Co, 76; sculpture, 2nd Baptist Church, 84. *Exhib:* Int Exhib Sculpture, Carrara, Italy; one-man show, Springfield Mus Art, 67, Del Art Mus, 74 & 85 & Baltimore Art Mus, 78; Randall Galleries, New York; Nelson Rockefeller Collections; Peel Gallery Fine Art; Annapolis Marina Art Gallery. *Teaching:* Monitor, New Sch for Soc Res, 68; Rehoboth Art League, 72; YWCA, Newark, 73. *Awards:* Founders Award, Rehoboth Art League, Del, 71 & 75-80 & 86-87; Silvermine Guild Award Sculpture, 72 & 73. *Bibliog:* Del Today Mag, 77; VCR, Day with Bailey, 87; Television special, 10/86. *Mem:* Del Art Mus; Rehoboth Art League. *Media:* Stone; Miscellaneous Media. *Dealer:* Annapolis Marina Gallery Annapolis MD; Carspecken-Scott Gallery Wilmington DE. *Mailing Add:* Woodland Beach Rd Smyrna DE 19977

BAILEY, VIRGINIA ELLEN
PAINTER, COLLECTOR
b Luray, Va. *Study:* Cornell Univ, BS, 38; graduate work Catholic Univ, Washington, DC, 42; Inst Mod Art, Mus Mod Art, NY, 60-64. *Work:* Univ Iowa Mus, Iowa City; Drew Univ Collection, Madison, NJ. *Exhib:* Bertram Russell, Triton Mus, San Jose, Calif, 67; Int Art Exhib, Rotunda Gallery, London, Eng, 72-73. *Bibliog:* Bert & Rene Williams (auth), Some slightly crude creations, Los Angeles Times, 6/16/68; David L Shirey (auth), Animal rhythm caged, New York Times, 9/10/79; Sign, symbol & script, Roslyn News, 11/1/84. *Mem:* Metrop Mus Art; Am Sch Oriental Res; Archeol Inst Am. *Media:* Oil; Mixed. *Collection:* Near Eastern stamp and cylinder seals. *Mailing Add:* Cyrus Gallery 11 E 57 St New York NY 10022

BAILEY, WILLIAM
PAINTER, EDUCATOR
b Council Bluffs, Iowa, Nov 17, 30. *Study:* Univ Kans, Sch Fine Arts, 51; Yale Univ, BFA(Alice Kimball English Traveling Fel), 55, MFA, 57; with Josef Albers; Univ Utah, LHD, 87. *Work:* St Louis Mus Art; Whitney Mus Am Art, New York; Pa Acad of Fine Arts, Philadelphia; Joseph Hirshhorn Mus; Mus Mod Art, New York; plus others. *Exhib:* One-man shows, RI Sch Design Mus, Providence, 88, Robert Schoelkopf Gallery, New York, 68, 71, 74, 79, 86 & 91, Donald Morris Gallery, Birmingham, Mich, 91, André Emmerich Gallery, New York, 92; Twenty-two Realists, Whitney Mus Am Art, New York, 70; Galleria Il Gabbiano, Rome, 80 & 85; John Berggruen Gallery, San Francisco, Calif, 88. *Teaching:* Prof fine arts, Ind Univ, 62-69; prof art, Yale Univ, 69-78, Kingman Brewster Prof, 78-, dean sch art, 74-75. *Awards:* Yale Arts Medal for Distinguished Contrib in Painting, 85; Accademico di Merito, Accademia di Belle Arti Pietro Vanucci, Perugia. *Bibliog:* Mark Stephens (auth), cover story, Art imitates life: The Revival of realism, Newsweek, 6/7/82; Andrew Forge (auth), DisegnieTempere Di William Bailey, Olivetti, Milano, 88; John Hollander & Guiliano Brigante (coauths), Bailey, Fabbri Editore, Turino 90 & Rizzoli, New York, 90; Richard Kalina (auth), William Bailey, Arts Mag, 5/91. *Mem:* Elected Am Acad & Inst Arts & Letters, 86. *Media:* Oil. *Dealer:* Robert Schoelkopf 825 Madison Ave New York NY 10021. *Mailing Add:* Dept Painting & Printmaking Yale Univ New Haven CT 06520

BAILIN, DAVID
PAINTER
b SDak, July 3, 54. *Study:* Univ Colo, Boulder, BFA; Hunter Col, New York, MA. *Work:* Goldman Sachs & Co, New York; Ark Arts Ctr Found Collection, Systematics Inc, Stephens Inc, Mitchell Law Firm, Rose Law Firm, Little Rock, Ark. *Exhib:* One-man shows, Broomfield Gallery Backspace, Boston, 86, Urbi et Orbi Gallery, Little Rock, 87, Alice Bingham Gallery, Memphis, 88, Territorial Restoration, Little Rock, 89, Snow Fine Arts Gallery, Univ Cent Ark, Conway, 89, Chroma Gallery, Little Rock, 92; Ark Exhib, Hot Springs Art Ctr, Hot Springs, Ark, 87 & 91; Mind's Eye Gallery, State Univ, Dickinson, NDak, 88; Nelson-Atkins Mus Art, Kansas City, Mo, 89; Six Ark Artists, Alice Bingham Gallery, Memphis, Tenn, 89; La Festival Art, Masure Mus Art, Monroe, La, 89; Larson Biennial Drawing Competition, Austin Peay State Univ, Clarksville, Tenn, 89; Biennial Prints, Drawings & Photog Show, Ark Arts Ctr, 89, 91 & 92, URBI ET ORBI Gallery, 89, Ark Arts Coun Fel Winners Exhib, Repertory Theater Gallery, 89, 91, Ark Collects, Univ Gallery, Univ Ark, Little Rock, 91; Artitudes 7th Int Art Competition, New York, 89; The First Hendrix Col Painting & Drawing Invitational Exhib, Trieschmann Fine Arts Bldg, Conway, Ark, 89; 52nd Ann Competition, Butler Inst Am Art, Youngstown, Ohio, 90; Tornados Invitational, Sarratt Art Gallery, Vanderbilt Univ, Nashville, Tenn, 90. *Pos:* Dir, Ark Arts Ctr Mus Sch, Little Rock, 90- *Teaching:* Studio & theory classes in painting, drawing, figure drawing & painting, art history & art appreciation. *Awards:* Nat Endowment Arts, 88 & 89; Ark Arts Coun Fel, 89. *Bibliog:* John W Linn (auth), 15th Arkansas Exhibition, Art Papers, Nov/Dec, 91; Favorite Artist, Spectrum Weekly, 3/92. *Mem:* Nat Art Educ Asn; Asn for Supv & Curric Develop; Ark Art Educ Asn. *Media:* Oil, Charcoal. *Publ:* Designer & auth, The Studio Project, Jonsson Found, Dallas, Tex, 91; A Spectrum Reader, Aug House Publ, Little Rock, Ark, 91. *Dealer:* Chroma Gallery 5701 Kavanaugh Blvd Little Rock AR 72207. *Mailing Add:* c/o The Ark Arts Ctr MacArthur Park Nineth & Commerce Little Rock AR 72202

BAILIN, HELLA
PAINTER
b Dusseldorf, Ger, Oct 17, 15; US citizen. *Study:* Berlin Acad, 34, Reimann Sch, Berlin, 36, Newark Sch Fine & Indust Arts, 47 & 52-56. *Work:* Washington Sch Psychiatry, Washington, DC; Temple Beth Ahm, Springfield, NJ; Morgan Guaranty Trust, New York; and others. *Comn:* Painting & mural, Marshall Sch, South Orange, NJ, 63; murals, Mennen Prod, Morristown, NJ, 63 & Consol Gas Co, Metuchen, NJ, 63. *Exhib:* Nat Acad Design; Trenton Mus; Newark Mus; Jersey City Mus. *Pos:* Pvt instr & demonstr watercolor, portraits & figure painting. *Teaching:* Instr, NJ Ctr Visual Arts, Summit; adult education, Union, NJ; instr, Union County Col, Cranford, NJ, 90. *Awards:* Ted Kautzky Award, Am Watercolor Soc, 70; David Wuject-Key Mem Prize, Allied Artists Am, 72; Marion de Sola Mendes Award, Nat Soc Painters in Casein & Acrylic, 73, Nat Asn of Women Arts, 90. *Mem:* Am Watercolor Soc; Allied Artists Am; Assoc Artists NJ; Audubon Artists, Inc; NJ Watercolor Soc; Nat Asn Women Artists; and others. *Media:* All. *Mailing Add:* 829 Bishop St Union NJ 07083

BAIRD, JOSEPH ARMSTRONG, JR
WRITER, CONSULTANT
b Pittsburgh, Pa, Nov 22, 22. *Study:* Oberlin Col, BA(magna cum laude), 44; Harvard Univ, MA, 47, PhD, 51. *Collections Arranged:* Numerous exhib, Calif Hist Soc, San Francisco, 62-63, 67-70 & Univ Calif, Davis, 53- *Pos:* Cur, Calif Hist Soc, 62-63; art consult, 67-70; cataloguer, Robert B Honeyman, Jr Collection, Bancroft Libr, Univ Calif, Berkeley, 64-65; owner, North Point Gallery, San Francisco, formerly. *Teaching:* Instr art hist, Univ Toronto, 49-53; from instr to prof, Univ Calif, Davis, 53-85; retired. *Awards:* Calif Hist Soc Merit Award, 62. *Mem:* Nat Trust Hist Preserv; Soc Archit Historians. *Res:* Latin American architecture; California architecture, painting and graphic arts. *Collection:* Urban art and life in the 19th and 20th centuries. *Publ:* Auth, Historic Lithographs of San Francisco, 72; The West Remembered, Calif Hist, 73; Wine and the Artist, Dover, 79; Sacred Places, Presidio Press, 85; Los retablos del Siglo, XVIII, UNAM, 87. *Mailing Add:* 1830 Mountain View Dr Tiburon CA 94920

BAKANOWSKY, LOUIS J
SCULPTOR, ARCHITECT
b Norwich, Conn, Oct 8, 30. *Study:* Yale Univ with Joseph Albers, 56; Syracuse Univ, BFA, 57; Harvard Univ, M Arch, 61. *Work:* Harvard Univ; Syracuse Univ; Trinity Col. *Comn:* Mem structure, Brunswick, Maine, 73. *Exhib:* View, 60 & Selection, 61, Inst Contemp Art, Boston, Mass; one-man show, Siembab Gallery, Boston, 60; Sculpture, DeCordova Mus, Lincoln, Mass, 64; New England Art Today, Boston, 65; Immanent Domains, Boston, New York & Philadelphia, 77; Decordova Mus, 87. *Pos:* Archit, Cambridge Seven Assocs, Inc, 62- *Teaching:* Asst prof design, Cornell Univ, 61-62; prof design, Grad Sch Design, Harvard Univ, 63-81, prof & chmn, Dept Visual & Environ Studies, 72-85; dir, Carpenter Ctr Visual Arts, Harvard Univ, 83-90. *Awards:* Sculpture Prizes, Boston Arts Festival, 58 & Providence Art Festival, 59. *Bibliog:* Sculpture of Louis J Bakanowsky, Connection Mag, 61; article, Kenchiku Bunka Mag, 71. *Mem:* Fel Am Inst Archit. *Media:* Mixed. *Mailing Add:* 19 Loring Rd Lexington MA 02173

BAKATY, MIKE
PAINTER, SCULPTOR
b Trenton, NJ, Aug 19, 36. *Study:* Miami-Dade Jr Col, Fla, AA, 64; Fla Atlantic Univ, BA, 65; Univ Ore, MFA, 69. *Work:* Colo State Univ, Ft Collins; Miami-Dade Community Col. *Comn:* Outdoor monument, Colo State Univ, 75. *Exhib:* Mike Bakaty, Paley & Lowe Inc, New York, 71-72; Painting & Sculpture Today, 1972, Indianapolis Mus Art, 72; NY Artists, Baltimore Mus Art, Md, 72; Here Comes Tomorrow, Owen Corning Fiberglass Bldg, New York, 73; Mellon Art Ctr, Wallingford, Conn, 74; Am Inst Archit, 74 & Henri Gallery, 74, Washington, DC; and many others. *Teaching:* Adj asst prof art, NY Univ, 71-74; asst prof painting, Fla Int Univ, Miami, 73; adj lectr sculpture, Fiorello LaGuardia Community Col, City Univ New York, 73-78, asst prof, 78-82. *Awards:* State-wide Touring Exhib, State of Fla, 66; Award for Sculpture, Ft Lauderdale Mus Arts, 66. *Bibliog:* Julia Busch (auth), A Decade of Sculpture, Assoc Univ Press, 74; Thelma Newman (auth), Plastics as Sculpture, Chilton Bks, 74; Marcia Tucker (auth), Tatoo, state of the art, Artforum, 5/81. *Media:* Fiberglass; Graphite. *Mailing Add:* 295 Bowery New York NY 10003

BAKER, CORNELIA DRAVES
PRINTMAKER, PAINTER
b Woodbury, NJ, Mar 2, 29. *Study:* Ohio Wesleyan Univ, 47-50; Kunst Stadel Inst, Ger, 50. *Work:* Bergen Mus Art & Sci, Paramus. *Comn:* Oil painting, comn by Paul Nelson, Wyckoff, NJ, 86; gouache work, comn by Jane Gut, Wayne, NJ, 87; monoprint, Stratton Travel Inc, Franklin Lakes, 90. *Exhib:* Solo exhibs, Ramapo Col Gallery, Mahwah, NJ, 86, Sekaikan Gallery, Tokyo, 90, Shimada Mus, Kumamoto, Japan, 90, Presbyterian Church Gallery, Franklin Lakes, NJ, 92 & Bergen Mus Art & Sci, Paramus, NJ, 93; Bergen Mus Art & Sci, Paramus, NJ, 88 & 90; Nat Asn Women Artists, traveling exhib, India, 89; 100 Years/100 Works, Nat Asn Women Artists, traveling exhib, USA, 89-90; 14th Ann Small Works, S Washington Sq E Gallery, New York, 90; Barn Gallery, Ringwood State Park, NJ, 92. *Awards:* Emeriti Award for Excellence, NJ Ctr Visual Arts, Summit, 89; Judges Award, Bergen Mus Art Exhib. *Bibliog:* A clearer picture at Bergen Museum, Bergen Record, 1/3/88; At the Bergen Museum Art Show--less is more, Bergen Record, 12/7/89; Monoprints, Nishinippon Simbum, 6/5/90. *Mem:* Nat Asn Women Artists (nominating vice chmn, 90-91, chair, printmaking jury, 92-94); Salute to Women in Arts Inc (pres, 89-90); Ringwood Manor Asn of Arts (dir, Ann exhib, 88 & 89); Community Arts Asn (prog chmn, 87); Printmaking Coun of NJ. *Dealer:* Wyckoff Gallery 210 Everett Ave Wyckoff NJ 07481; Jain Marunouchi Gallery 560 Broadway New York NY 10012. *Mailing Add:* 293 Green Ridge Rd Franklin Lakes NJ 07417

BAKER, DINA GUSTIN
PAINTER
b Philadelphia, Pa. *Study:* Philadelphia Col Mus Sch Fine Art; Barnes Found, Merion, Pa, with Dr Albert C Barnes & Violet DeMazia; Temple Univ Tyler Sch Fine Art, Philadelphia; Art Students League; Atelier 17, New York. *Work:* NY Univ; Barnes Found; Philadelphia Art Mus; Butler Mus Am Art, Youngstown, Ohio; Bergen Mus Arts & Sci, Paramus, NJ; Gannet Found, Columbia Univ, New York. *Exhib:* One man shows, Roko Gallery, NY, 60-63, Angeleski Gallery, NY, 65, Southampton East Gallery, Long Island & New York, 68, Amerika House, Hamburg, Munich & Regensburg, Ger, 74 & Ingber Gallery (with catalog), NY, 76, 78, 80, 84 & 87; Utah State Univ, Logan, 83; and many others. *Teaching:* Instr, Henry St Settlement, 54-55; dir pvt art classes, New York, 60-63. *Awards:* Barnes Found Award, 42-45; Art Students League Award, 46-47; Edward MacDowell Fel, 59. *Bibliog:* Allen Ellenzweig (auth), article, Arts Mag, 79; Laurel Bradley (auth), article, Arts Mag, 1/79; Grace Glueck (auth), article, NY Times, 3/84; Claude Lesver (auth), article in Artspeak, 9/87. *Mem:* Women in the Arts. *Media:* Oil, Acrylic. *Dealer:* Ingber Gallery 3 E 78th St New York NY 11004. *Mailing Add:* 88 Eisenhower Dr Cresskill NJ 07626

BAKER, ELIZABETH C
ART EDITOR, CRITIC
b Boston, Mass. *Study:* Bryn Mawr Col, BA; Radcliffe Col, MA. *Pos:* From assoc ed to managing ed, Art News, 63-73; ed, Art in Am, 73- *Teaching:* Instr art hist, Boston Univ, 58-59, Wheaton Col, Norton, Mass, 60-61 & Sch of Visual Arts, New York, 68-74. *Mailing Add:* 575 Broadway New York NY 10012

BAKER, GEORGE P
EDUCATOR, KINETIC ARTIST
b Corsicana, Tex, Jan 23, 31. *Study:* Col Wooster; Occidental Col, BA; Univ Southern Calif, MFA. *Work:* Mus Mod Art & Mus Am Art, New York; Mus 20th Century Art, Vienna, Austria; Forest of Sculptures, Hakone, Japan; San Diego State Col, Calif. *Comn:* Kinetic sculpture, Nebr Bicentennial Sculpture Proj; kinetic wall sculpture, German Opera, Berlin, comn by Am CofC for 75th Anniversary, Ger, 78; hanging kinetic sculpture, Cruise Ship Star Princess, 88; kinetic fountain, World Trade Ctr, Long Beach, Calif, 90; kinetic fountain, Calif Inst Technol, Pasadena, 91; and others. *Exhib:* Occidental Col, Los Angeles; Mus Mod Art, New York, 68; Whitney Mus Am Art, 68 & 70; Studio Marconi, Milan, Italy, 70; Springer Gallery, Berlin, 75; Wenger Gallery, Los Angeles, 91. *Teaching:* Instr sculpture, Univ Southern Calif, 60-64, Sun Valley Ctr Arts & Humanities, Sun Valley, Idaho, 91; prof sculpture, Occidental Col, 64-; artist-in-residence, WTex State Univ, 78. *Bibliog:* Articles in Art & Artists, London, 66, Art in Am, 66 & 67 & Leonardo, fall 75. *Mailing Add:* Occidental Col Dept Art 1600 Campus Rd Los Angeles CA 90041

BAKER, JILL WITHROW
PAINTER, ILLUSTRATOR
b Ilion, NY, Oct 12, 42. *Study:* Baylor Univ, BA, 64; Fla State Univ, with Karl Zerbe; Acad di Belle Arti, Florence, Italy, with Silvio Lofreddo; Pratt Inst, MFA, 81. *Work:* Merton Collection, Bellarmine Col, Louisville, Ky; Am Nat Bank, St Thomas Aquinas Chapel, Col Educ Collection, Western Ky Univ, Bowling Green; Goethe House, New York. *Exhib:* Solo shows, US Info Serv, Seoul, Korea, 77, Ward-Nasse Gallery, New York, 80, Long Island Univ, Brooklyn, 81 & Baylor Univ, Waco, Tex, 81; Pratt Alumni Invitational, 85; SOHO/20, New York, 86; L A Installations One, 91; Artists Space, 92. *Collections Arranged:* Target LA, Pasadena, Calif, 83; Thinking Eye Gallery, Calif, 85; Student Art Show, Calif State Univ, Northridge, 86; SPARC Gallery, Venice, Calif, 86. *Pos:* Mem bd dirs, Ward-Nasse Gallery, 76-81; western corresp ed, Women Artists News, 84-88; mem, Graphic Arts Coun, LA Co, Mus Art, 85-89; regional vpres, Artists Equity (nat). *Teaching:* Instr, adult painting community educ prog, Bowling Green, Ky, 76-81; teaching asst, Pratt Inst, Brooklyn, NY, 78-79; instr, Pierce Col, Woodland Hills, Calif, 84-85. *Awards:* Achievement Award, Bank Am, State Calif, 60; Achievement Trophy, 60; scholar, Southern Women's Club, 63; Awards, Coca Cola Art Show, Elizabethtown, NJ, 78, LA'84, Brand Galleries, 84 & Window to the Future, Scottsdale, Ariz, 84 & Pratt Alumni Invitational, 85. *Bibliog:* article, Courier-J, Louisville, Ky, 8/17/80; article, Artspeak, New York, 2/4/82. *Mem:* Artists Equity Asn (regional vpres, 89-); founding mem Southern Ky Guild Artists & Craftsmen; Kappa Pi (Baylor chap vpres, 60-63); founding mem Northern Fla Guild Artists & Craftsmen; Women Arts; Los Angeles Artists Equity (pres, 84-86 & bd mem, 88); Los Angeles Visual Artists Guild (mem bd dirs, 84-). *Media:* All. *Publ:* Illusr, The More Things Change, Whippoorwill Press, 71; Songs of Bloody Harlan, Westburg Asn Press, 75; Spring of Violets, 76, Under the Sign of the Waterbearer, 76 & I Knew A Woman, 77, Love St Bks. *Mailing Add:* 552 Broadway No 48 New York NY 10012-3922

BAKER, JOE
PAINTER
b Bartlesville, Okla, Jan 14, 46. *Study:* Univ Tulsa, BFA, 68, MFA, 78. *Work:* Atlantic Richfield Corp, Los Angeles, Calif; Metrop Mus Mod Art, New York; Indianapolis Mus Art, Ind; Smithsonian Inst, Washington, DC; Fine Arts Mus NMex, Santa Fe; Phoenix Art Mus, Ariz; Colorado Springs Fine Arrts Ctr; Chase Manhattan Bank. *Exhib:* Arizona Invitational, Tucson Mus Art, Ariz & Centro de Arte Moderno de Guadalajara, Mex, 82; 38th Biennial of American Painting, Corcoran Gallery Art, Washington, DC, 83; Eight, Laguna Beach Art Mus, Calif, 84; 2nd Western State Biennial, San Francisco, San Francisco Mus Mod Art, Calif, 84; Signal, Hartje Gallery, Frankfurt, Ger, 85; Eight Contemporary Artists, Southwest Mus, Los Angeles, Calif, 85; New West, Colorado Springs Fine Art Ctr, 86; I-40 Connections: Contemporary Art of the Southwest, Oklahoma Art Ctr, Oklahoma City, 88; Animals, Casa Grande Art Mus, Ariz, 89; solo exhib, Elain Horwitch Gallery, Santa Fe, NMex, 89. *Pos:* Vis artist, Marie Walsh Sharpe Found, Colo Col, Colorado Springs, summers, 88, 89 & 90. *Bibliog:* Barbara H Perlman (auth), Phoenix: A sun palace in the land of government, Art News, 81; Lissa August (auth), Picks & pans, People Mag, 83; Elizabeth Skidmore Sasser (auth), Joe Baker, Arts Mag, 85; Susanna Nicholson (auth), Sr Gallery-Joe Baker, Saturday Rev Mag, 86. *Media:* Oil. *Publ:* Illusr, The Complete Book of Country Swing and Western Dance and A Bit About Cowboys, Doubleday Publ, 81; coauth, American West: The Modern Vision, NY Graphics Soc, 84; illusr, Louise Erdich-Love Medicine, Rowoholt Publ Co, Ger, 86. *Dealer:* Elaine Horwitch Galleries 4211 N Marshall Way Scottsdale AZ 85251. *Mailing Add:* c/o Elaine Horwitch Galleries 4211 N Marshall Way Scottsdale AZ 85251

BAKER, KENNETH
CRITIC, WRITER
b Weymouth, Mass, May 3, 46. *Study:* Bucknell Univ, BA, 68. *Pos:* Art critic, Boston Phoenix, Mass, 72-85; sr art critic, San Francisco Chronicle, Calif, 85- *Teaching:* Adj fac art hist, RI Sch Design, Providence, 79-81 & Boston Col, Chestnut Hill, Mass, 79-85. *Awards:* Distinguished Newspaper Art Criticism Award, Manufacturers Hanover Trust & Art-World, 85; Nominated for Non-fiction Award by Bay Area Book Reviewers Assoc, 90. *Mem:* Int Asn Art Critics; Nat Book Critics Circle. *Res:* Studies in aesthetics, history & criticism of Minimal art. *Publ:* Auth, Giorgio Morandi: Redemption through painting, Des Moines Art Ctr, 81; Julian Opie, Kölnische Kunstverein, 84; Second generation: Mannerism or momentum & Report from London: The Saatchi museum opens, 85, Art Am; Flashes of understatement: Elmer Bischoff, Artforum, 86; auth, Minimalism, Abbeville Press, 89. *Mailing Add:* c/o San Francisco Chronicle San Francisco CA 94119

BAKER, RICHARD BROWN
COLLECTOR
b Providence, RI, Nov 5, 12. *Study:* Yale Univ, BA, 35; Oxford Univ, BA & MA(Rhodes Scholar), 38; Art Students League; Hans Hofmann Sch Fine Arts; RI Sch Design, Hon DFA, 78. *Exhib:* Collection exhibited: RI Sch Design Mus Art, 59, 64, 73 & 85; Eighty Works from the Richard Brown Baker Collection, Walker Art Ctr, Minneapolis, 61; Yale Univ Art Gallery, 63, 75 & 85; Oakland Univ Art Gallery, Rochester, Mich, 67, 74 & 79; Mus Mod Art, Mexico City, 68; Newark Mus, 74; Squibb Gallery, Princeton, NJ, 79; San Diego Mus Art, Calif, 85; plus others. *Pos:* Mem comt on art gallery of univ coun, Yale Univ, 62-66 & 71-76, mem governing bd, 74-, acquisition comt, 79-; mem mus comt, RI Sch Design, 66-75, mem fine arts comt, 75-; mayoral app, Art Comn of New York, 77-80; mem drawings comt, Whitney Mus, 77- *Bibliog:* Kenneth B Sawyer (auth), Richard Brown Baker, US collector of modern art, Studio Int, London, 1/65; Paul Gardner (auth), Richard Baker's amazing mini-museum, Art News, 1/78; Nelson W Aldrich Jr (auth), Mr Baker takes a sabbatical, Art/World, 10/79; Brooks Peters (auth), Baker's Dozens, Quest, 3/92. *Mem:* Mus Mod Art; life fel Metrop Mus Art; Whitney Circle, Whitney Mus Am Art; fel Pierpont Morgan Libr; Friends of Amer Arts at Yale. *Collection:* Recent art in all media (earliest 1944), international in origin, although preponderantly by US artists. *Publ:* Auth, Notes on the formation of my collection, Art Int, 9/20/61. *Mailing Add:* 1185 Park Ave New York NY 10128

BAKKE, KAREN LEE
ASSEMBLAGE ARTIST, CALLIGRAPHER
b Everett, Wash, Nov 21, 42. *Study:* Univ Wash; Syracuse Univ, NY, BFA(design), 67, MFA(design), 69. *Work:* Everson Mus, Syracuse. *Comn:* Extensive calligraphy, Syracuse Univ. *Exhib:* Two-person show, Fabric Forms, Kirkland Art Ctr, Clinton, NY, 76; Rubberstamp Invitational, Lightworks Gallery, Syracuse, 81; Calligraphy & Rubberstamps, Everson Mus, 82; Clothing, The Put-On and the Poor Man's Art, Am Home Econ Asn NY State Convention, 82; Suspended in Media, You Are What You See, Cornell Univ, 82; International Calligraphy Today, Women in Design, 83. *Pos:* Asst cur, Syracuse Univ Art Collection, 67-69; vis artist soft sculpture, NY State Summer Sch of Arts, Fredonia & Chautauqua Inst. *Teaching:* Assoc prof & chairperson dept environ arts, Syracuse Univ, 69- *Awards:* Hancock Purchase Prize & One-Person Show Award, Cent NY Regional, Everson Mus, 71. *Mem:* Am Crafts Coun; Soc Scribes; Handweavers Guild Am; Women in Design. *Media:* Fabric, Metal. *Publ:* Auth, Sewing Machine as a Creative Tool, Prentice-Hall, 76. *Mailing Add:* 1136 Cumberland Syracuse NY 13210

BAKKE, LARRY HUBERT
EDUCATOR, PAINTER
b Vancouver, BC, Can, Jan 16, 32. *Study:* Univ Wash, BA & MFA; Syracuse Univ, PhD, art hist with Laurence Schmeckebier. *Exhib:* Figure Painting, Univ BC Fine Arts Gallery, Vancouver, 63; Nat Exhib Small Paintings, Purdue Univ Art Gallery, Ind, 54; The Painter & the Photograph, Univ NMex Art Gallery, Albuquerque, 64-65; 97th Ann, Am Watercolor Soc, New York, 64; Seven Syracuse Artists, Cortland Fine Arts Gallery, NY, 70; One-man shows, Rockefeller Art Ctr Gallery, State Univ NY, Fredonia, 82, 83 & 85. *Pos:* Guest critic, RI Sch Design, 81; consult, Honeywell Inc, Edina, Minn, 81; guest artist, Alfred Univ, 83. *Teaching:* Vis prof, Univ Victoria, summers, 58-71; instr art hist, drawing & painting, Everett Col, 59-63; prof aesthetics, painting & art history, Syracuse Univ, 63-; vis prof, Villa Giglucci, Florence, Italy, summer 68; guest artist, NY Summer Sch Visual Arts, State Univ Col Fredonia & Chautauqua Inst, summers 76, 77, 79 & 81-86. *Awards:* First Prize, Northwest Watercolor, Seattle Art Mus, 62; Northwest Painters Award, Puget Sound Group Northwest Painters, 63; First Prize for Painting, Spokane-Northwest Painters, 63. *Bibliog:* Margaret Harold (auth), Prize-Winning Watercolors, Allied Publ, 63; Van Deren Coke (auth), Painter & the Photograph, Univ NMex, 64; Laurence Schmeckebier (auth), Larry Bakke, Drawings & Paintings, 1957-1969, Syracuse Univ, 69. *Media:* Oil, Collage. *Publ:* Auth intro, The Golden Age of Comics (catalog), Soc Illusr Mus Am Illus, 7/83. *Mailing Add:* 1136 Cumberland Ave Syracuse NY 13210

BAKKEN, HAAKON
ADMINISTRATOR, CRAFTSMAN
b Madison, Wis, Nov 28, 32. *Study:* Univ Wis, BSc, 58; Univ Oslo(Fulbright Fel), 59; Sch for Am Craftsmen, Rochester Inst Technol, MFA, 62. *Work:* Chalmers Collections, Ont Crafts Coun, Toronto; Sheridan Col Study Collection, Mississauga, Ont. *Comn:* Bronze door pull, Ont Crafts Coun, 76; sterling cigar box, Law Soc of Upper Can, Toronto, 74. *Pos:* Dir, Sch of Crafts & Design, Sheridan Col, 77-81; assoc dean, Sch of Visual Arts and Sch of Crafts & Design, Sheridan Col, 81- *Teaching:* Inst master metal & jewelry , Sch of Crafts & Design, Sheridan Col, 67-77. *Mailing Add:* Sch of Crafts & Design Sheridan Col Trafalgar Rd Oakville ON L5H 1Z7 Canada

BALABAN, DIANE
PAINTER
b Ogden, Utah, Nov 29, 35. *Study:* With Robert E Wood, Charles Reid, Randal Lake & Valoy Eaton. *Comn:* Painting, St Mary Catholic Church, Park City, Utah, 83; Painting ser, Stein Erikson Lodge, Deer Valley, Utah, 84. *Exhib:* San Diego Art Inst, Calif, 75; Sun Valley Western Art, Idaho, 79; Utah Watercolor Soc, Salt Lake City, 80; one-woman show, Kimball Art Ctr, Park City, Utah; Eccles Art Ctr Invitational, Ogden, Utah. *Pos:* Pres, Park City Artist Asn, 81-83; dir, Kimball Art Ctr, 83-; lectr & judge various art groups. *Teaching:* Instr watercolor workshops, Kimball Art Ctr, Park City, currently. *Awards:* First Place Watercolor, Kimball Art Centennial Exhib, Park City Gallery Asn, 84. *Mem:* Utah Watercolor Soc; Park City Artist's Asn. *Media:* Watercolor, Oil. *Mailing Add:* 3 Bonanza Ct Park City UT 84060

BALAHUTRAK, LYDIA BODNAR
PAINTER, EDUCATOR
b Cleveland, Ohio, May 6, 51. *Study:* Kent State Univ, BS (art educ), 73; Corcoran Sch Art, 76-77; George Washington Univ, MFA (painting), 77. *Work:* George Washington Univ, Washington, DC; Univ Houston, Transco Energy Co & Baylor Col Med, Houston; Hoyt Inst Fine Arts, New Castle, Pa. *Exhib:* Nat Small Painting & Drawing Competition, Col of Mainland, Texas City, Tex, 83; Solo shows, Univ Houston, 83 & 85, Graham Gallery, Houston, Tex, 88 & Galveston Arts Ctr, 93; Sept Int Competition, Alexandria Mus, La, 84; Hoyt Nat Drawing & Painting Show, Hoyt Inst Fine Arts, 84; 47th Ann Nat Midyear Show, Butler Inst Am Art, 84; Tex Visions Juried travelling show, Transco Art Gallery, Abilene Fine Arts Mus & McAllen Int Mus, 86; Frivolity & Mortality, traveling exhib, 87-89; Int Travelling Show, The Barrett Collection, 93-94. *Pos:* Art exhibs coordr, Univ Houston, Clear Lake City, 81-82. *Teaching:* Instr drawing & painting, San Jacinto Col, North City, 77-79; lectr drawing 2-D design, Univ Houston, Clear Lake City, 79- 82, 86-87 & 93; guest lectr art, Univ Pittsburgh, 83; vis guest artist, Inst Art, Lviv, Ukraine, 91. *Awards:* First Prize Award, Nat Small Drawing & Painting Competition, Col of the Mainland, 83; La Napoule Art Found Grant, 85; Irex Grant International Research & Exchange, 90. *Bibliog:* Donna Tennant (auth), art rev, Houston Chronicle, 12/14/79; Jill Kyle (auth), Lydia Bodnar-Balahutrak: Portrait of a Figure Painter, In Art, 6/85; Robin Longman (auth), Emerging Artists, Am Artist, 8/85; Susan Chadwick (auth), rev, Houston Post, 6/88; Michael Crespo (auth), Watercolor Day By Day, Watson-Guptill, 87. *Media:* Oil, Paint; Pencil. *Dealer:* Edith Baker Gallery 2404 Cedar Springs Dallas TX 75201. *Mailing Add:* 2528 Dryden Houston TX 77030

BALANCE, JERRALD CLARK
PAINTER
b Ogden, Utah, July 20, 44. *Study:* Univ Utah, Salt Lake City; mainly self-taught. *Work:* Chrysler Mus at Norfolk, Va; Atlantic City Fine Arts Ctr & Atlantic City Munic Bldg Collection, NJ; Coopers & Lybrand Corp, Washington, DC; US State Dept, Washington, DC; Sperry Corp, Reston, Va. *Exhib:* 19th Area Exhib, Corcoran Gallery Art, Washington, DC, 74; 14th Md Biennial, Baltimore Mus Art, 74; Five Am Abstract Painters, Northeastern Univ Gallery, Boston, 77; Best of NY--A Survey, Root Art Ctr, Hamilton Col, Clinton, 77; one-man shows, Genesis Gallery, New York, 78-79 & US State Dept, Washington, DC; Art in the Embassies Prog, Madrid, Spain & Bangkok, Thailand, 78-80. *Awards:* Nat Endowment Grant, Va Commission Arts & Humanities & Emerson Gallery, 76; Washington Cherry Blossom Festival Nat Art Competition Award in Sculpture, 72. *Bibliog:* Joe Mayer (producer), Beyond Abstract Expressionism: Balance & Chelimsky, Prince Georges Community Col. *Media:* Oil, Enamel; Plastic. *Publ:* Contribr, Washington artists, Artists Equity, 72. *Dealer:* Harriet Lebish Gallery 41 E 57th St New York NY 10022; Jane Hasley Gallery 406 Seventh St Washington DC. *Mailing Add:* 30 Steven Ct Gaithersburg MD 20877

BALAS, IRENE
PAINTER
b Budapest, Hungary, Feb 28, 28; US citizen. *Study:* Acad Fine Arts, Vienna, Austria, MA, 48; studied art, therapy with Hans Hoffman & psychiatry with Karl Kaufman. *Work:* Mus Luis Angel Arango, Bogota, Columbia; Mus Vatican, Rome, Italy; Rockefeller Collection, Henry Ford Collection, New York. *Comn:* portrait of the Pres, comn by Victor Paz Estenssoro, La Paz, Bolivia, 55; Bolivia Pintoresca, comn by Ger Embassador, La Paz, Bolivia, 55; religious abstracts, Mus el Minuto de Dios, Bogota, Columbia, 67; Birth of Emerald, Banco de Colombia, Bogota, Colombia, 72; Expedition Hungary-USA, Hungarian Air Force, 90; and others. *Exhib:* En Honor del Presidente, Mus Victor Paz, La Paz, Bolivia, 55; solo show, Luis Angel Arango, Bogota, Columbia, 60; South America, Ed Nacional, Madrid, Spain, 65; The Beauty of America, Casements, Ormond Beach, Fla, 82; Space, Mus Hist & Art, Palm Beach, Fla, 89; Wings of Ambitions, Art Mus, Budapest, Hungary, 90; and others. *Teaching:* Instr bellas artes, Santiago de Chile, 53-54; Universidad La Javeriana, Bogota, Colombia, 69-71. *Awards:* Nat Prize, Austrian Painters, Künstlerhaus, 48; Bronze Medal, Salon Oficial, Museum de Bellas Artes, 51; Gold Medal, Concepcion, Univ Medicin, 56. *Bibliog:* Gladys Ostrom (auth), Irene Balas Painter of Presidents, Ann Fabe Isaacs, 77; Tom Elliot (auth), Petit Museum of Irene Balas (film), Fla, 77-78; Lizette Alvarez (auth), Little museum, Miami Herald, 88. *Media:* Oil, Acrylic. *Publ:* Auth, Exposicion del mes, El Correo; auth, Notas de arte, Aramen Dia, 67; auth, The best exhibition; Irene Balas, Andean Times, 69; auth, Irene Balas communicates through her art, Morning J, 82; Artist profile, Directions, 88. *Mailing Add:* 1621 Collins Ave Apt 907 Miami Beach FL 33139

BALAY, FELICIE
ART DEALER
b New York, NY, June 14, 40. *Study:* New York Univ. *Pos:* Pres, Felicie Inc, New York, 65- & FKH Editions, New York, 74-75. *Specialty:* Works by Joseph Correale, Ralph Fasanella, Oliver Johnson and others. *Mailing Add:* 141 E 56th St New York NY 10022

BALCIAR, GERALD GEORGE
SCULPTOR
b Medford, Wis, Aug 28, 42. *Work:* Wildlife World Art Mus, Monument, Colo; Cowboy Hall of Fame, Oklahoma City; Lutheran Med Ctr, Denver, Colo. *Comn:* Challenge (bronze elk monument), Wildlife World Art Mus, Monument, Colo, 81; Centennial (bronze moose monument), Loyal Order of Moose, Mooseheart, Ill. *Exhib:* Nat Acad Design, New York, 77, 86, 90 & 92; Nat Sculpture Soc, New York, 77-92; Allied Artists Am, New York, 77-90; Nat Acad Western Art, Cowboy Hall Fame,Oklahoma City, 78 & 84-92; Artists of America, Denver, 85-92. *Awards:* Prix de West & Gold

Medal, Nat Acad Western Art, 85; Ellin Speyer Prize, Nat Acad Design, 86; Hubbard Art Award for Excellence, 90; People's Choice Award, Silver Medal, Nat Acad Western Art, 90. *Mem:* Nat Sculpture Soc; Soc Animal Artists; Nat Acad Western Art; Allied Artist Am; Northwest Rendezvous. *Media:* Marble, Bronze. *Mailing Add:* 5307 Jellison St Arvada CO 80002

BALDERACCHI, ARTHUR EUGENE
SCULPTOR, ADMINISTRATOR
b New York, NY, Mar 25, 37. *Study:* Duke Univ, BA, 60; Univ Ga, MFA, 65. *Work:* Duke Univ, Durham; St Lawrence Univ; State Univ NY Potsdam; Univ Ga, Athens. *Comn:* Seven ft high mem to Dr Martin Luther King, Roland Gibson Art Found, Potsdam, NY. *Exhib:* Numerous solo & group exhibs in the Northeast. *Pos:* Chmn dept arts, Univ NH, 74-80. *Teaching:* Prof art, Univ NH, Durham, 65- *Mem:* Col Art Asn Am; NH Art Asn. *Media:* Welded Metals, Cast Metals. *Publ:* Coauth (with C Pratt), In the Orchard, Tidal Press, 86; Drawings, 1948, Univ Va Press, 90. *Mailing Add:* 321 Sagamore Ave Portsmouth NH 03801

BALDESSARI, JOHN ANTHONY
CONCEPTUAL ARTIST
b National City, Calif, June 17, 31. *Study:* San Diego State Col, BA, 53, MA, 57; Univ Calif, Berkeley, 54-55; Univ Calif, Los Angeles, 55; Otis Art Inst, Los Angeles, 57-59. *Work:* Mus Mod Art, New York; Basel Mus, Switz; Los Angeles Co Mus Art; Chicago Art Inst; Whitney Mus, New York. *Exhib:* Konzeption-Conception, Stadtischen Mus, Leverkusen, Ger, 69; Information, Mus Mod Art, New York, 70; Prosepect, Statischen Kunsthalle, Dusseldorf, Ger, 71; Documenta 5 & 7, Kassel, Ger, 72 & 83; Contemporanea, Rome, 73; Carnegie Inst, Pittsburgh, Pa, 86; John Baldessari: Oeuvres Recentes, Palais des Beaux Arts, Brussels, Belgium, 88, Photoarbeiten, Kestner-Gesellschaft (auth, catalog), Hanover WGer, 88-89, Ni Por Esas/Not Even So (auth, catalog), Ctr de Arte Reina Sofia, Madrid, 89; Bilderstiet, Mus Ludwig in den Rheinhallen der KolnerMesse, Cologne, West Germany, 89; Magiciens de la Terre, Ctr Georges Pompidou; and Grande Halle-La Villette, Paris, 89; John Baldessari Retrospective, Mus Contemp Art, Los Angeles, San Francisco Mus Mod Art, Hirshhorn Mus and Sculpture Garden, Walker Art Ctr, Whitney Mus Am Art, Mus d'Art Contemp de Montreal, 90. *Teaching:* Asst prof art, Univ Calif, San Diego, 68-70; prof art, Calif Inst Arts, Valencia, 70-87. *Awards:* Nat Endowment Arts Grants, 73-75; Guggenheim Grant, 86-; Skowhegan Medal, 88. *Bibliog:* James Collins (auth), John Baldessari, Artforum, 10/73; Coosje von Bruggen (auth), John Baldessari, Rizzoli, NY, 90. *Media:* Photography, Printmaking. *Publ:* Auth, Ingres & Other Parables, 72; Choosing: Green Beans, 72; Throwing Three Balls in the Air to Get a Straight Line (Best of 36 Attempts), 73; Close Cropped Tales, 81; The Telephone Book (with Pearls), 88. *Dealer:* Sonnabend Gallery 420 W Broadway New York NY 10012. *Mailing Add:* 2001 1/2 Main St Santa Monica CA 90405-1021

BALDRIDGE, MARK S
GOLDSMITH, EDITOR
b Lyons, NY, Dec 7, 46. *Study:* State Univ NY Col, Buffalo, BS(art educ), 68; Cranbrook Acad Art, Bloomfield Hills, Mich, MFA(metalsmithing), 70. *Exhib:* 10th Piedmont Crafts Exhib, Mint Mus Art, Charlotte, NC, 73; Profiles in US Jewelry, 73, Lubbock, Tex, 73; Va Artists 1973, Va Mus Fine Arts, Richmond, 73; 11th Ann Southern Tier Art & Crafts Show, Corning Glass Ctr, NY, 74; Reprise, Cranbrook Acad Art Mus, Bloomfield Hills, Mich, 75; Objects 75 Designer/Craftsman Show, Grand Junction, Colo, 75; Craft Art & Relig, Vatican Mus, Rome, 76; Marietta Col Crafts Nat, Ohio, 77; Va Craftsmen Biennial, Va Mus Fine Arts, Richmond, 80; SE Metalsmiths, Mint Mus Art; Metalsmith 81, Univ Kans, Lawrence, 81. *Pos:* Ed & creator, Goldsmiths J, 74-; co-ed, Metalsmith Mag, 86. *Teaching:* Instr metal-jewelry, Univ Evansville, 70-72; from asst to prof metal-jewelry, Longwood Col, 72-; chmn art dept, 89- *Awards:* First Prize-Metal, 40th Nat Cooperstown, NY, 75; First Prize, Lake Superior Int, 75; Merit Award, Goldsmiths 77, Soc NAm Goldsmiths, Phoenix Art Mus, 77. *Mem:* Va Crafts Coun (bd mem, 78-80); Soc NAm Goldsmiths (bd mem, 79-87); SE Am Craft Coun (Va rep, 82-). *Media:* Gold. *Res:* American metalsmithing in the 1940's and 1950's. *Publ:* Auth, Bi-metal casting to titanium, Metalsmith, Vol 6, No 2, spring 86; Kenneth Bates: Dean of American Enameling, Metalsmith, Vol 8, No 2, spring 88. *Mailing Add:* 1600 Otterdale Midlothian VA 23113

BALDWIN, HAROLD FLETCHER
SCULPTOR, PAINTER
b Lebanon, NH, May 24, 23. *Study:* Self-taught. *Comn:* Carved map of Northeastern Seaboard, 200 Mormon Missionaries, Cambridge, Mass, 71; The Good Samaritan McKerley Med Care Ctr, Concord, NH, 76. *Exhib:* One-man shows, Concord Pub Libr, NH, 71 & Springfield Art & Hist Soc, Vt, 73; Burlington Mall, Mass, 73; NH Art Gallery, Concord; New Eng Woodcarvers' Asn, Concord Gallery, Mass, 73. *Awards:* Springfield Bicentennial Medallion, Springfield Pub Libr, Vt, 77-78. *Mailing Add:* Baldwin Studios 11 Woodland Dr Springfield VT 05156

BALDWIN, RICHARD WOOD
ILLUSTRATOR, SCULPTOR
b Needham, Mass, June 8, 20. *Study:* Pa Acad Fine Arts, with George Harding; also with Harold Von Schmidt. *Work:* Smithsonian Inst, Washington, DC; Whitney Gallery Western Art. *Comn:* Murals, comn by USA, 42-45, now in Smithsonian Inst. *Pos:* Sr master sculptor, Franklin Mint, 70- *Awards:* Cresson Fel, Pa Acad Fine Arts, 41. *Media:* Oil, Watercolor; Clay, Plaster. *Publ:* Illusr books & periodicals, 46-65. *Mailing Add:* 944 Dutton Mill Rd West Chester PA 19380

BALDWIN, ROGER N
CRITIC, CURATOR
b Norristown, Pa, Jan 28, 50. *Study:* Ursinus Col, BA, 72; Univ Mass, Amherst, MA, 75; Brown Univ, 75-77. *Exhib:* Solo exhibs, Recent Photographs, Art Gallery, Univ Mass, 75; Architectural Works: Pope-Riddle, Theodore Roosevelt House, New York, 79; At Home: Recent Photographs, Albertus Magnus Col, New Haven, Conn, 84; Eye & Hand, Klein Gallery, Brookfield, Conn, 84; Drive-in-Demise & Legacy, Carlson Gallery, Univ Bridgeport, 84; Connecticut Circumscribed Invitational Show, Erector Square, New Haven, 85. *Collections Arranged:* New England's Teaching Photographs (auth, catalog), 81; Contemporary Figural Photography, 83; Alchemies: Contemporary Handcoated Photography (auth, catalog), 84; Palladium Print Today, 84; The New New England Landscape (auth, catalog), 86. *Pos:* Assoc ed, Art New England, Brighton, Mass, 83-85; dir, Carlson Gallery, Univ Bridgeport, 84- *Teaching:* Instr photog hist, Univ Bridgeport, 80-; instr photog, Fairfield Univ, Conn, 81-84; instr art hist, Southern Conn State Univ, 86- *Mem:* Soc Photog Educ; Col Art Asn; Bridgeport Arts Coun (bd dirs, 84-). *Publ:* Coauth, Kertesz' Chez Mondrian (with Mark Roskill), Arts Mag, 77; Jack Sal: Mark Making, Combinations Press, 81; The Invented Black-Photography's Racial Stereotypes, Catskill Ctr Photog Quart, 83; Current Palladium Photography, Lumen, 84. *Mailing Add:* Univ of Bridgeport Carlson Gallery, 84 Iranistan Ave Bridgeport CT 06601

BALDWIN, RUSSELL W
EDUCATOR, GALLERY DIRECTOR
b San Diego, Calif, May 26, 33. *Study:* San Diego State Univ, BA, 58, MA, 63. *Work:* Joseph Hirshhorn Collection, Washington, DC; La Jolla Mus Contemp Art, Calif; Santa Barbara Mus Art; San Francisco Mus Mod Art; Newport Harbor Mus, Calif. *Exhib:* One-man shows, Santa Barbara Mus Art, 64, La Jolla Mus Contemp Art, 64, 73 & 81, Jewish Community Ctr, San Diego, 74 & Casat Gallery, La Jolla, 78; San Francisco Mus Mod Art, 81; Space Gallery, 82. *Collections Arranged:* Paintings by John Baldessari, 72; Robert Irwin (installation piece), 75; Photog as a Means, 76; James Collins, 77; Wayne Thiebaud, 78; William Wiley, 78; Masami Tenaoka, 80; Roland Reiss, 81. *Pos:* Dir, Dwight Boehm Gallery. *Teaching:* Assoc prof sculpture & printmaking, Palomar Col, San Marcos, Calif, 65- *Awards:* First Painting Award, La Jolla Mus Contemp Art, 60; Sculpture Award, Long Beach Mus Art, 63; First Award, Calif-Hawaii Regional, Fine Arts Mus San Diego, 74. *Mem:* La Jolla Mus Contemp Art. *Specialty:* Information art. *Mailing Add:* 675 S Sierra Ave No 33 Solana Beach CA 92075

BALES, J (JEAN ELAINE)
PAINTER, SCULPTOR
b Pawnee, Okla, Dec 25, 46. *Study:* Okla Col Liberal Arts, BA(art), 69, Univ Sci & Art, BA; prof study, Inst San Miguel de Allende, Mex. *Work:* Southern Plains Indian Mus, Anadarko, Okla; Denver Mus Natural Hist, Colo; US Dept Interior, Washington, DC; Mus Northern Ariz, Flagstaff; Univ Calif at San Diego Med Sch; Lincoln Plaza Ctr; Mus of Western Prairie. *Exhib:* Nat Indian Art Exhib, Heard Mus, Phoenix, 73-79; Am Indian Art Ann, Okla Art Ctr, Oklahoma City, 79-81; Images 80, Denver Mus Natural Hist, Colo, 80; Trail of Tears, Cherokee Nat Mus, Talequah, Okla, 80; Native Am Invitational, Santa Fe Festival Arts, NMex, 81; Circles of the World, Calif Acad Sci, 85; Eye of Man Exhib, San Diego Mus of Man, 85; Fruitland Mus, Harvard, Mass, 87; Kirkpatrick Ctr, Oklahoma City, Okla, 88. *Pos:* Bd dir, Indian Arts & Crafts Asn, 78-79. *Awards:* First in Watercolor, Indian Art Exhib, Heard Mus, 77 & 79; Div Award, Trail of Tears Show, Cherokee Nat Mus, 80; Mountain Bell Award, Gallup Int Tribal Ceremonial Exhib, Mountain Bell, 81; Merit Award, Cherokee Nat Mus, 85, 86, 87 & 88; O'Odham Tash, First & Second Prize, Graphics & Watercolor, Third Prize, Watercolor, 88; Second Prize Prints, Little Classic Art Show. *Bibliog:* Tricia Hurst (auth), Nine major Indian artists, 80 & Crossing bridges, 81, Southwest Art. *Publ:* Illusr, Indian Cultures of Oklahoma, Okla State Dept Educ, 78; Preserving heritage, Lefthander Mag, 10/88; articles in High Plain Lit Rev, spring & fall 88. *Mailing Add:* One Plaza, Suite 102 South Tahlequah OK 74464

BALES, JEWEL
PAINTER
b Purcell, Okla, Aug 28, 11. *Study:* With William B Schimmel, Douglas Greenbowe & others. *Work:* Alhambra High Sch, Phoenix, Ariz; Mesa City Libr, Ariz; Baptist Hosp, Phoenix. *Exhib:* Tucson Regional, Art Ctr, Ariz, 63, 66 & 68; Ann, Ariz State Fair, Phoenix; Ann Traveling Exhib, Ariz Watercolor Asn; Open Watercolor Show, Phoenix Art Mus; Am Southwestern, Taipei, Taiwan, 74; and others. *Awards:* First Award for Tree Study, Mesa Art League, 61; People's Choice for Winter Fun, Ariz State Fair, 69; Purchase Award for Winter Fun, Ariz Bank, 69. *Mem:* Ariz Watercolor Asn (pres, 69-71, treas, 72-78); Ariz Artist Guild (vpres, 64-66); Nat League Am Pen Women (treas, 73-76). *Media:* Watercolor, Acrylic. *Mailing Add:* 3030 W Altadena Phoenix AZ 85029

BALKIND, ALVIN LOUIS
CURATOR
b Baltimore, Md, Mar 28, 21; Can citizen. *Study:* Johns Hopkins Univ, BA; study at the Sorbonne. *Pos:* Dir fine arts gallery, Univ BC, 62-73; cur contemp art, Art Gallery Ont, 73-75; chief cur, Vancouver Art Gallery, 75-78; Can comnr, Biennale de Paris, 80; head, Visual Art Studio, Banff Ctr, Banff, 85-87. *Teaching:* Assoc prof, Univ BC, 62-73. *Awards:* Hon Dipl, Emily Carr Col, Vancouver, 91; $50,000 Award, Vancouver Inst Visual Arts, 92. *Bibliog:* Contribr, Visions, Douglas & McIntyre Publ, 83 & Vancouver Forum I, 92. *Mailing Add:* 4416 W 11th Ave Vancouver BC V6R 2M3 Canada

BALL, EDWARD R
CRITIC, WRITER
Pos: Archit critic, Village Voice, New York, 90-; contrib ed, J Art, New York, 90-; assoc ed, Lusitania Mag, New York, 91- *Res:* Art, architecture and motion pictures. *Publ:* Contribr, Village Voice; Artforum; NY Times; Yale French Studies; Am Film. *Mailing Add:* c/o Village Voice 36 Cooper Sq New York NY 10003

BALL, LILLIAN
SCULPTOR
b Augusta, Maine, Jan 6, 55. *Study:* Nordenfjords Verdens Univ, Copenhagen, BA, 72; Harvard Univ, Cambridge, 76-77; Columbia Univ, NY, 85-86. *Work:* Nynex Corp, White Plains, NY; Oppenheimer & Co, New York; Bingham, Dana & Gould, Boston, Mass; Best Products, Ashland, Va. *Comn:* Outdoor sculpture, Artpark, Lewiston, NY, 79; Wall sculpture, Cone Mills, New York, 80. *Exhib:* Solo exhibs, Hudson River Mus, Yonkers, NY, 90 & Rubin Spangle Gallery, 4/92; Lick of the Eye, Soshona Wayne, Santa Monica, 91; Tabloid, Hawkins, New York, 92; Ecstasy, Dooley le Cappelain Gallery, New York, 92; An Esemplastic Shift, A C Proj Rm, New York, 92; and others. *Teaching:* NY Feminist Art Inst, 88-91; Vis Artist RISD, 87, NY Univ, 92 & Sch Visual Arts, 92. *Awards:* Nat Heritage Trust Grant, Artpark, 79; Sculpture Fel, Nat Endowment Arts, 86-87; NY Found Arts Grant, 91. *Bibliog:* Susan Kandel (auth), LA in Review Arts Mag, 11/91; Terry Myers (auth), Lillian Ball's Sculptures and the Real World, Ger Juni Mag, 92; David Carner (auth), Lillian Ball at Rubin Spangle Tena Celeste, 9/92. *Mem:* NY Artists Equity; Orgn Independent Artists. *Media:* Miscellaneous Media. *Mailing Add:* Seven Harrison St New York NY 10013

BALL, LYLE V
PAINTER, ILLUSTRATOR
b Reno, Nev, Dec 24, 09. *Study:* Am Watercolor Soc, with Edgar Whitney, New York & with Jack Pellow, Conn; Col of Pacific Union, St Helena, Calif, with Vernon Nye. *Work:* Nev Legis Bldgs, Carson City; Sparks Fire Dept, Nev; Reno City Hall; Las Vegas Art League; Senate Off Bldg, Washington, DC. *Comn:* Oil landscapes, comn by Security Nat Bank, Reno, Nev, 65, Settlemeyer Family, Gardnerville, 72, George Mason, 73 & Marvin Humphreys, Reno, 74; Watercolor wildlife, Edward LeBaron Las Vegas, 74. *Exhib:* Soc Western Artists Ann, DeYoung Mus, San Francisco, 67-70; Death Valley 49ers' Ann Encampment Show, 68-81; Artists Prof League, New York, 71- *Pos:* Gov Appt, Nev State Coun Arts, 71-76. *Awards:* Silver Medal/Watercolor, Am Indian & Cowboy Artists Show, San Dimas, Calif, 77; First Prize/Mixed Media & Second Prize/Watercolor, Death Valley 49ers Show, 77; and others. *Mem:* Soc Western Artists, San Francisco; Am Indian & Cowboy Artists; Am Artists Prof League, New York; life mem Nev Art Gallery, Reno (dir, 70-71); charter mem Artists Co-op, Reno. *Publ:* Illusr, Ponderosa Country, Stanley W Paher, 72 & Int Turquoise Ann, Int Turquoise Asn, 75. *Mailing Add:* 181 Bret Harte Ave Reno NV 89509

BALL, SUSAN L
ADMINISTRATOR, HISTORIAN
b Altadena, Calif, May 25, 47. *Study:* Scripps Col, BA, 69; Univ Calif, Riverside, MA, 74; Yale Univ, PhD, 78. *Collections Arranged:* The Impressionists & the Salon (contribr), Univ Calif, Riverside & LACMA, 74; Richard Brown Baker Collects (contribr), Yale Univ, 75; Rossetti & the Double Work of Art (contribr), Yale Univ, 76. *Pos:* Dir govt & found affairs, Art Inst Chicago, Ill, 85-86; exec dir, Col Art Asn NY, pres, 86- *Teaching:* Asst prof art hist, Univ Delaware, Newark, 78-81. *Mem:* Am Asn Mus; Art Table; bd mem, Nat Cult Alliance & Nat Humanities Alliance; exec comt mem, Conference Admin Officers Am Coun of Learned Soc. *Res:* Late nineteenth and early twentieth century European painting and architecture. *Publ:* Auth, The impressionists and the salon Los Angeles County Mus, 74; auth, Richard Brown Baker collects! (essays), Yale, 75; auth, Works before 1962, Dante Gabriel Rossetti, 76; auth, The early figural paintings of Andre Derain, 1905- 1910, Zeitschrift für Kunstgeschichte, 80; auth, Ozenfant and Purism: The evolution of a style 1915-1930, UMI Press, 81. *Mailing Add:* 314 State St Brooklyn NY 11201

BALL, WALTER N
PAINTER, EDUCATOR
b Pratt, Kans, Dec 14, 30. *Study:* Baker Univ, Baldwin City, Kans, BA, 55; Wichita State Univ, Kans, MFA, 57; Ohio State Univ, Columbus, PhD(painting), 68. *Work:* Evansville Mus Arts & Sci, Ind; NE Mo State Univ, Kirksville; Univ Mont, Dillon; Wichita State Univ. *Exhib:* Mid-Am Exhib, Nelson-Atkins Gallery, Kansas City, Mo, 58 & 62; one-man shows, Oshkosh Pub Mus, Wis, 68, Northeast Mo State Univ Gallery, 77 & Noho Gallery, New York, 88; Mid-States Art Exhib, Evansville Mus Arts & Sci, Ind, 77; Artists of Chicago & Vicinity, Art Inst Chicago, 77; Ann Exhib Contemp Am Painting, Soc Four Arts, Palm Beach, Fla, 80, 84 & 91; The Legacy of Hoyt Sherman, Colo Inst of Art, Denver & Univ Gallery of Fine Art, Ohio State Univ, Columbus, Ohio, 82; Mid-Am Biennial Nat Art Exhib, Owensboro Mus Fine Arts, Ky, 84 & 86; Fifty-Sixth Ann Art Exhib, Cooperstown Art Asn, NY, 91; and others. *Teaching:* Instr painting & drawing, Sacramento State Col, 63-65; asst prof painting & drawing, Wis State Univ, Oshkosh, 65-68; prof painting & drawing, Northern Ill Univ, DeKalb, 68- *Awards:* Juror's First Award, Washington & Jefferson Col, Washington, Pa, 77; Mus Guild Purchase Award, Evansville Mus Arts & Sci, 77. *Media:* Acrylic, Oil. *Dealer:* Noho Gallery in Soho Inc 168 Mercer St New York NY 10012; Helander Gallery 125 Worth Ave Palm Beach FL 33480. *Mailing Add:* 821 Normal Rd De Kalb IL 60115

BALLANTYNE, CATHERINE TURK
PAINTER
b Wilmington, Del, Nov 2, 12. *Study:* Wilson Col, AB, 34; Columbia Univ, 35-36; studied under Herb Olsen (10 yrs) & Diana Kan (21 yrs). *Work:* Elliott Mus, Stuart, Fla. *Exhib:* Am Watercolor Soc, 72; Nat Arts Club, New York, 76-81, 83, 85, 86 & 87; Salmagundi Club, New York, 78-80; Am Inst Arts & Lett, New York, 80; Elliott Mus, Stuart, Fla, 84; solo exhibs, Hurlbutt Gallery, Greenwich, Conn, Pen & Brush Club, 80-88; Nat Acad Design, Open Exhib, 88. *Awards:* President's Award (solo show), Nat Arts Club, 80; Ralph Fabri Award 81, Creative Watercolor 87, Allied Artists Am; Kuhn Fine Paper Award 82, Chang d'ai Chien Mem Award 84, William Shaffer Award 86, Sumie Soc Am; Grumbacher Art Award, 82, 85 & 87, Emily Morse Genius Award, 84, Pen & Brush Club; Creative Hands Award, Catherine Lorillard Wolfe, 86; and others. *Bibliog:* Articles, Greenwich Times, The Nutmegger, Greenwich, Conn & Focus, Stuart, Fla. *Mem:* Allied Artists Am (chmn pub relations, 79-88); Am Artists Prof League; Nat Arts Club (artist mem); Am Pen Women; Pen & Brush Club, Sumei Soc Am, Catherine Lorillard Wolfe, 88. *Media:* Watercolor; Fusion Techniques. *Publ:* Contribr, Flowers in Watercolor--Ethel Todd George, Northlight, 80. *Dealer:* Orchard Knoll Gallery 825 LongTree Rd Elm Groves WI 53122. *Mailing Add:* 29 West Way Old Greenwich CT 06870

BALLARD, LOCKETT FORD, JR
MUSEUM DIRECTOR, ADMINISTRATOR
b Cold Springs, NY, Aug 1, 46. *Study:* Hamilton Col, Clinton, NY, BA, 68; Cooperstown Grad Prog, NY, MA, 79. *Collections Arranged:* Pewter in America (auth, catalog), 75; Lost Litchfield (auth, catalog), 81. *Pos:* Dir, Litchfield Hist Soc, Conn, 85-87; exec dir, Historic Southwest Ohio Inc, Cincinnati, 87-88; gen mgr & mus consult, Woodburne Assoc, Madison, Ind, 88; free-lance consult, currently; dir, Rockford Mus, Lancaster, Pa, 91- *Mem:* Am Asn Mus; Am Asn State & Local Hist; Nat Trust Hist Presv; Victorian Soc Am. *Collection:* 1893 Victorian House Museum; 1904 Civic Museum collection of world art & ethnographic materials; 1800-1875 re-created village of American architecture & decorative art. *Mailing Add:* 414 1/2 E Orange St Lancaster PA 17603

BALLINGER, JAMES K
MUSEUM DIRECTOR, HISTORIAN
b Kansas City, Mo, July 7, 49. *Study:* Univ Kans, BA, 72, MA(art hist), 74. *Collections Arranged:* Painter in Taos, Eiteljorg Collection, 80; Visitors to Arizona: 1846-80 (auth, catalog), Phoenix Art Mus, 80; Charles M Russell (auth, catalog), The Renner Collection, 81; Dale Eldred: Phoenix Project, 81; Beyond the Endless River Western Am Drawings & Watercolors (auth, catalog), Phoenix Art Mus, 79; Americans in Brittany and Normandy: 1810-1910, 82; Peter Hurd: Insight to a Painter (auth, catalog), 83; Diego Rivera: The Cubist Years, 84; Frank Lloyd Wright Drawings, Frank Lloyd Found, 90. *Pos:* Registrar, Univ Kans Mus Art, Lawrence, 73-74; cur collections, Phoenix Art Mus, Ariz, 74-81, asst dir & chief cur, 81-82, dir, 82-; bd mem, Balboa Art Conservation Ctr, San Diego, 81-89. *Mem:* Western Asn Art Mus; Central Ariz Mus Asn; Am Asn Mus; Am Art Mus Dirs. *Publ:* Auth, American Painting from the Whitney Mus, Phoenix Art Mus, 76; Biennial 1979, Phoenix Art Mus, 79; Frederic Remington, Abrams, 89. *Mailing Add:* 1625 N Central Ave Phoenix AZ 85004

BALLOU, ANNE MACDOUGALL See MacDougall, Anne

BALMACEDA, MARGARITA S
EDUCATOR, VIDEO ARTIST
b Ponce, PR, Dec 30, 33; US citizen. *Study:* Manhattanville Col, Purchase, NY, BFA; Immaculate Heart Col, Hollywood, Calif, teaching cert; Cath Univ of PR, Ponce, MA. *Pos:* Asst dir, Ponce Art Mus, 67-74. *Teaching:* Assoc prof art appreciation & art hist, Colegio Regional de Ponce, 73-, dir, humanities dept, currently. *Mem:* Sociedad de Autores Puertorriquenos. *Res:* Expressionism; Puerto Rican art. *Publ:* Auth, poems, Tierra y Alma, Ed Ponce de Leon, Spain, 68; auth, El Uso del Museo de Art de Ponce en la Ensenanza del Barroco, Ceiba, 77; Oller Artista (video), 85; Campeche de Ayer, de Hoy y de Siempre (video), 89; auth, poems, Un inmenso suspiro imprenta Fortuno, Ponce, PR. *Mailing Add:* Dept of Art Univ of PR Ponce Regional Col Ponce PR 00731

BALOSSI, JOHN
SCULPTOR, PAINTER
b Staten Island, NY, May 28, 31. *Study:* Columbia Univ, BFA & MA. *Work:* Mus Mod Art, Finch Col Mus & Chase Manhattan, New York; Ponce Mus, PR; Mus Art, Ft Lauderdale, Fla. *Comn:* Mural, Student Union Bldg, Univ PR, 69; aluminum wall relief, Inst Puerto Rican Cult, 71; mural, CRUV Pub Housing, Manati, PR, 72; mural, Pan Am Games, San Juan, 79. *Exhib:* Sculpture in Clay from Puerto Rico, Mus Fine Arts, Springfield, Mass, 80; Art Mus STex, Corpus Christi, 80; Newark Mus, 81; Bacardi Gallery, Miami, Fla, 81; 39th & 40th Int Competition of Artistic Ceramics, Faenza, Italy, 81 & 82. *Teaching:* Assoc prof fine arts, Univ PR, Rio Piedras. *Awards:* Ateneo Puertorriqueno Award, San Juan, 67; UNESCO Salon Award, San Juan, 74 & 79; R J Reynolds Tobacco Co Award, San Juan, 79. *Bibliog:* Gottfried Borrmann (auth), Keramik der Welt, Kunst & Handwerk, Vertagsanstalt, Dusseldorf, 81; Myrna Rodrigues (auth), Balossi: A Selection of His Work from 1960-1982, 82; Charlotte F Speight (auth), Images in Clay Sculpture, Harper & Row, 83. *Media:* Clay (fired); Acrylic on Canvas & Paper. *Dealer:* Studio B 865 49 St SE Reparto Metro Rio Piedras PR 00921. *Mailing Add:* c/o The Studio 453 Hostos Ave Hato Rey PR 00919

BALSLEY, JOHN GERALD
PAINTER, SCULPTOR
b Cleveland, Ohio, Apr 15, 44. *Study:* Univ Americas, 65; Ohio Northern Univ, BA, 67; Northern Ill Univ, MFA, 69. *Work:* St Louis Mus Art, Mo; Nelson-Atkins Gallery, Kansas City, Mo; Des Moines Art Ctr, Iowa; Joslyn Mus Art, Omaha, Nebr; Univ Iowa Art Mus, Iowa City. *Exhib:* Solo exhibs, Madison Art Ctr, Wis, 79, Univ Del, 79, Frumpkin-Struve Gallery, Chicago, Ill, 79 & 80, New Gallery of Contemp Art, Cleveland, 80, Rahr-West Mus, Manitowoc, Wis, 82; Sheldon Mem Art Gallery, Univ Nebr, Lincoln, 82; Univ Wis, Eau Clair, 83; Kansas City Art Inst, 83; Yarres Gallery, Scottsdale, Ariz, 83; Birmingham Art Mus, 83, 87 & 88; Painting & Sculpture Today, Indianapolis Mus Art, Ind, 76; Realisms, Ulrich Mus, Wichita State Univ, 76; Chicago Vicinity Show, Art Inst Chicago, 77; and others. *Teaching:* Asst prof sculpture, Univ Wis-Milwaukee, 76- *Awards:* Louis Comfort Tiffany Found Grant, 72; Nat Endowment Arts Grant, 72 & 80; Univ Wis-Milwaukee Grant, 78; Milwaukee Artists Found Grants, 82 & 87. *Bibliog:* Lou Dunkak (auth), Balsley sculptures explore man and machines, Arts, 12/76; Josh Kind (auth), Model art: The intimate enviroment, New Art Examr, 1/78; Betty Kaufman (auth), John Balsley at Allan Stone, Art World, 1/78. *Mem:* Col Art Asn Am. *Dealer:* Perimeter Gallery Chicago IL; Carrega Foxley Leach Gallery Washington DC. *Mailing Add:* 8325 N Cedarburg Rd Milwaukee WI 53209

BALTZ, LEWIS
PHOTOGRAPHER
b Newport Beach, Calif, Sept 12, 45. *Study:* San Francisco Art Inst, BFA, 69; Claremont Grad Sch, MFA, 71. *Work:* Mus Mod Art, Metrop Mus Art, New York; Art Inst Chicago; Los Angeles Mus Contemp Art; Victoria & Albert Mus, London; Nat Gallery Australia, Moderna Museet, Stockholm; Palazzo Fortuny, Venice, Italy; Nat Mus Mod Art, Kyoto; and 60 other collections in US, Canada, Australia, Europe & Japan. *Comn:* Courthouse, The Joseph E Seagrams Co, 76; American Images, Am Tel & Telgr Co, 78; Nev State Arts Comn, 86; La Mission photographique, Datar, France, 86; Toshiba Project, Japan, 89; Linea di Confine, Reggio Emilia, Italy, 91. *Exhib:* One-man shows: Newport Harbor Art Mus, 86, City Mus, Higashikawa-Ku, Japan, 88, NY Inst Contemp Art, 90, Univ Md, Baltimore, 91, Des Moines Art Ctr, 92, Seibu Contemp Art, Tokyo, 92, Germans Van Eck, New York, 92; Corcoran Gallery Art, 74-76; Philadelphia Col Art, 75; Mus Fine Arts, Houston, 76; San Francisco Mus Mod Art, 81; RI Sch Design, 83; Univ Art Mus, Univ Calif, Berkeley, 84; Victoria and Albert Mus, London, 85; Ringling Mus, Sarasota, Fla, 91; Des Moines Art Ctr, Iowa, 91; Los Angeles City Mus Art, Calif, 92. *Teaching:* Vis prof, Univ Calif, Riverside, 90; vis art, Calif Inst Arts, 92; vis artist, Yale Univ, 92; vis artist, Ecole des Beaux Arts, Paris, 92. *Awards:* Guggenheim Mem Found fel in photography; US-UK Bicentennial Exchange Fel, 80; Charles Pratt Mem Award, 91. *Bibliog:* Paul Hill (auth), Approaching Photography, Focal Press, London & Boston, 82; Dr Naomi Rosenblum (auth), The World History of Photography, Abbeville Press, New York, 85; Estelle Jussim (coauth Elizabeth Lindquist-Coci), Landscape As Photograph: Reflections on Nature, 85; Ideology, Yale Univ Press, New Haven, 85; Arthur Rothstein (auth), Documentary Photography, p 131, Stoweham, Mass, 86. *Publ:* Auth, Candlestick Point, 89; Giocchi di Simulazione, 91; Rule Without Exception, 91; Ronde de Nuit, 92; Lewis Baltz: 5 Projects, Stedelijk Mus. *Dealer:* Janet Borden Inc 560 Broadway New York NY 10012; Stephen Wirtz Gallery 49 Geary Blvd San Francisco CA 94102. *Mailing Add:* PO Box 42 Sausalito CA 94966

BAMBER, JUDIE
PAINTER
b Detroit, Mich, 61. *Study:* Calif Inst Arts, Valencia, 83. *Exhib:* Solo exhibs, Laurie Rubin Gallery, New York, 89, Ray Boyd Gallery, Santa Monica, 90 & 91; Thick and Thin, Fahey/Klein Gallery, Los Angeles, 89; Faces, Marc Richards Gallery, Los Angeles, 90; Not So Simple Pleasures, MIT List Visual Arts Ctr, Cambridge, Mass, 90; LA Times, Boise Art Mus, 91; Uprooted, NAME, Chicago, Ill, 91. *Bibliog:* Amy Gerstler (auth), rev, Art Issues, 9-10/90; Susan Kandel (auth), rev, Arts, 10/90; Lawrence Gipe (auth), The aesthetics of containment, Artspace, 11-12/90. *Mailing Add:* c/o Laurie Rubin Gallery Inc 155 Spring St New York NY 10012

BANANA, ANNA
PUBLISHER, CONCEPTUAL ARTIST
b Victoria, BC, Feb 24, 40. *Study:* Univ BC, Vancouver, BEd, 67. *Work:* Smithsonian Inst Libr, Nat Gallery of Art Serials Libr, Washington, DC; Mus Mod Art Libr, New York; G Pompidou Libr, Paris, France; Art Bank, Can Coun, Ottawa; Jean Brown Collection, Getty Mus, Los Angeles; Getty Mus, Jean Brown Collection. *Exhib:* Can tour, 15 performances, 14 cities, 80; Univ Calif, Irvine, 80; San Diego State Univ, 80; Inter-Dada Festival, Ukiah, San Francisco, Calif, 80 & 84; Can/USA Tour, 15 performances in 15 cities, including Vancouver, Edmonton, Toronto, Montreal, Columbia, SC, Dallas & San Jose, Calif, 82; European tour, Copenhagen performance & installation, 86; European Tour (Copenhagen, Umea, Rosenheim, Ghent, Den Hague & London), 86, 89 & 91; Ltd edition artist stamp sheets, Davidson Galleries, Seattle, Wash, 89 & 91, Bombershoot Arts Festival, Seattle, 90 & Gallery 56, Vancouver, BC, 92; and many others. *Pos:* dir, ed & publ, Banana Productions, 72-88; vis artist & lectr, Can cols & univs, 80-; cur, Artropolis Show, Vancouver, 87. *Awards:* Coord Coun of Lit Mag Assistance Awards, 75, 77 & 79; Can Coun Grants, 80-83, 86, 87 & 88. *Bibliog:* Elizabeth Godly (auth), Artist Banana puts stamp on a ripping good time, Vancouver Sun, 12/88; Whimsy VI/International Humor, Eng dept, Ariz State Univ, 88; John Held Jr (auth), A World Bibliography of Mail Art, Dallas Pub Libr, 89; Peat O'Neil (auth), Art is in the mail, Washington Post, 9/5/89; Freya Zabitsky (auth), Still a Banana after all these years, Rubber Stamp Madness, 5-6/90. *Mem:* Cent Visual Artists Asn; Vancouver Community Arts Coun. *Media:* Performance. *Res:* Collection of information on a given topic via the mail-art network on an international basis; grass-roots level of art activity not represented in the art media or establishment; performance and organization of participatory public art events. *Interests:* Recycling Imagery from mass media; artist stamps. *Publ:* Contribr, The transformation of Anne Long, Maclean's Mag, Toronto, 72; ed & publ, Vile Mag, No 1, 2, 3 & 5, 74-77, contrib & ed, No 4 & 6, 76-78, Banana Productions; contribr, The Rubber Stamp Album, Workman Publ, 78; ed & publ, About Vile, Vancouver, 83; ed & publ, International Art Post, Vol 1, No 1, 2/88, Vol 1, No 2, 12/88, Vol 2, No 1, 5/89, Vol 2, No 2, 8/89, Vol 2, No 3, 12/89, Vol 3, No 1, 5/90, Vol 3, No 2, 8/90, Vol 3, No 3, 12/90, Vol 4, No 1, 12/91 & Vol 5, No 1, 7/92; 20 Years of Fooling Around with A Banana, Banana Productions, 2/90; Encyclopedia Bananica, Vol 1, No 1, 6/90; Artistamp News, Vol 1, No 1, 1/91, Vol 1, No 2, 12/91 & Vol 2, No 1, 8/92. *Mailing Add:* PO Box 3655 Vancouver BC V6B 3Y8 Canada

BANAS, ANNE
PAINTER, EDUCATOR
b Long Beach, Calif, Dec 9, 48. *Study:* Orange Coast Col, 67-69; Calif State Univ, Fullerton, BA, 71; Claremont Grad Sch, MFA, 74. *Work:* Security Pac Bank, Santa Barbara, Beverly Hills & La Jolla, Calif; Eastern NMex Univ, Roswell; Daytona Beach Int Airport, Barnett Bank, Accordia Corp, Fla. *Comn:* Profiler's (mural), Daytona Beach Int Airport, Jacksonville, Fla. *Exhib:* One woman shows, Grandview Gallery, Los Angeles, 75, Art Rental Gallery, Santa Barbara Mus Art, 78, Alice Benjamin Gallery, Santa Barbara, 80 & Hills Gallery, Santa Fe, 81; Contemporary Idioms: Los Angeles, Univ Calif, Santa Barbara, 74 & E Lambert Gallery, Santa Fe, 87 & 88; Selections from Roswell, Albuquerque Downtown Ctr Arts, 81; Southwest Invitational, Midland Col, Tex, 84; Gallery 88, Jacksonville, Fla, 90; Fla Community Col, Jacksonville, 91; Contemporania Gallery, Jacksonville, Fla, 91 & 93; Orlando Mus Art, 92. *Collections Arranged:* Sensibilities, McCullock Oil Bldg, Westwood, Calif, 75 & Eastern NMex Univ, Roswell, 85-86. *Pos:* Founding mem, steering comt, Grandview Gallery, Los Angeles, 73-75; founding mem, Double X, educational art orgn, Los Angeles, 75; dir, art in the community, Santa Barbara Mus, Calif, 77-78. *Teaching:* Instr painting & drawing, West Los Angeles City Col, 75-77; instr painting, drawing, art hist & printmaking, Eastern NMex Univ, Roswell, 82-89; prof art, Fla Community Col, Jacksonville, Fla, 89- *Bibliog:* Kalliope, Vol XIV, No 2, 5/92. *Media:* Oil. *Dealer:* Contemporania Sally Ann Freeman Owner Jacksonville FL. *Mailing Add:* 1775 Forest Blvd Jacksonville FL 32216

BAND, DAVID MOSHE
PAINTER, ART DEALER
b Portland, Maine, Oct 16, 47. *Study:* Self taught. *Work:* US Air Force Collection, Washington, DC; First Texas Savings, Dallas, Tex; and other corporate and pvt collections in the US, Germany, Israel, Turkey, Spain and Australia. *Pos:* Mem bd dirs, N Tex Artists Guild, 84-; dir, Eden Gallery, Wichita Falls, Tex, currently. *Teaching:* Instr, Wichita Falls Mus & Art Ctr, 73-74 & N Tex Artists Guild, 84- *Mem:* Am Watercolor Soc; Allied Artists Am. *Media:* Watercolor, Acrylic. *Specialty:* American prints 1900-1950. *Publ:* Splash II, Americas Best Contemporary Watercolors, North Light & Writer's Dig Bks, 92. *Dealer:* Baker Gallery 1301 13th St Lubbock TX 79408; Ft Meigs Gallery San Patricio NM 88348. *Mailing Add:* 1903 Eden Lane Wichita Falls TX 76306

BANDEL, LENNON RAYMOND
PAINTER
b Kansas City, Mo, Dec 10, 06. *Study:* Kansas City Art Inst, with Thomas H Benton & Ross Braught; Dayton Art Inst, with John King & Burroughs; John Huntington Polytech Inst, Cleveland, with Rolf Stoll & F Wilcox. *Work:* Luxemburg Mus, Europe. *Comn:* Six portraits of pres, Reorganized Church of Jesus Christ of Latter-Day Saints, 60; six portraits, Hillyard Chem Co, St Joseph, Mo, 70-71; portrait of Joseph Boley & Dr Frank Mantz, Univ Kans Med Ctr, 71; mural of River Jordan, First Christian Church, Iowa, Kans, 72; Trader's Nat Bank, Kansas City, Mo. *Exhib:* May Art Show, Cleveland Mus Art, 44-46; Plaza Art Fair, Kansas City, Mo, 56-74; Kansas City Art Inst Alumni Show, 73; Heritage Show, Kansas City Mus Natural Hist, 74. *Pos:* Designer-artist, Hallmark Cards Inc, Kansas City, 27-37; designer-artist, Stanley Mfg Co, Dayton, Ohio, 37-42; artist-art dir, Am Greeting Corp, Cleveland, 42-57. *Teaching:* Instr portrait, Kansas City Art Inst, 65-71; instr painting & drawing, Jewish Community Ctr, Kansas City, 65-71. *Awards:* Cleveland Mus Art Award, 44; Kansas City Mus Natural Hist Award, 61 & 64; Cowboy Hall of Fame. *Media:* Oil, Pastel. *Mailing Add:* 5327 Rosewood Kansas City MO 64118

BANDES, SUSAN JANE
MUSEUM DIRECTOR, EDUCATOR
b New York, NY, Oct 18, 51. *Study:* New York Univ, BA, 71; Bryn Mawr Col, MA, 73, PhD, 78; Mus Mgmt Inst, Berkeley, Calif, 90. *Pos:* Asst prof, Sweet Briar Col, Va, 78-83; proj dir, Am Asn Mus, Wash, 83-84; prog officer, J Paul Getty Trust Grant Prog, Los Angeles, 84-86; assoc prof & dir, Kresge Art Mus, Mich State Univ, E Lansing, 86- *Awards:* Whiting Fel, 76-77; Am Philos Soc, 81; Publ Award AIA, 90. *Mem:* Nat Inst for Conserv (treas, 86-90); Mich Alliance for Conserv; Mich Mus Asn (bd dirs, 87-); Mich Coun for Humanities (coun, 88-). *Publ:* Auth & ed, Caring for Collections, 84; Affordable Dreams: The Goetsch-Winckler House and Frank Lloyd Wright, 91; contrib articles to prof jour. *Mailing Add:* 13294 Peacock Rd Laingsburg MI 48848-9257

BANDY, GARY
PAINTER, EDUCATOR
b Pontiac, Mich, May 10, 44. *Study:* Oakland Univ, BA, 65; Columbia Univ, MFA, 68. *Work:* Norton Simon Inc & Muriel Siebert, New York, New Sch Social Res, New York; St Peter's Col, Jersey City, NJ. *Exhib:* Artists Market, Detroit, Mich, 64; Aldrich Mus Contemp Art, Ridgefield, Conn, 74; solo shows, Herbert H Lehman Col Gallery, Bronx, NY, 79 & F Marino Gallery, New York, 82; Large Drawings, Independent Curators Inc traveling, 85-86; and others. *Teaching:* Adj instr art hist, St Peter's Col, Jersey City, NJ, 68-72; lectr & workshop instr, Mus Mod Art, New York, 77- *Awards:* Artist's Fel, Nat Endowment Arts, 83. *Bibliog:* Review, Art News, 9/74; Palmer Poroner (auth), review, Art Speak, 4/80; Susan Filen Yeh (auth), Gary Bandy, Arts Mag, 4/82. *Media:* Acrylic. *Dealer:* Fawbush Gallery New York NY. *Mailing Add:* 118 W 29th St New York NY 10001

BANDY, MARY LEA
EDITOR, ADMINISTRATOR
b Evanston, Ill, June 16, 43. *Study:* Stanford Univ, BA, 65. *Pos:* Asst ed, Harry N Abrams, New York, 67-73; assoc coordr exhibs, Mus Mod Art, New York, 76-78, dir film dept, 80- *Publ:* Ed, Rediscovering French film (catalog), Mus Mod Art, 83; Michael Balcon (catalog), Mus Mod Art, 84. *Mailing Add:* Museum Modern Art 11 W 53rd St New York NY 10019

BANDY, RON F
PAINTER, EDUCATOR
b Dayton, Ohio, Feb 18, 36. *Study:* Ohio Univ, Athens, BFA, 62; Univ Fla, Gainesville, MFA, 64; also with Hiram Williams & Enrique Montenegro. *Work:* Weatherhead Found; Ft Wayne Mus, Ind; Owens-Corning Corp, Toledo, Ohio; Hope Colgate Sloane, Bowling Green, Ohio. *Exhib:* Solo exhib, Ft Wayne Mus, Ind, 74; Owens-Corning Collection Show, 76 & Toledo May Show, 81, Toledo Mus, Ohio; Ft Wayne Mus Exhib, Ind, 82; Lady Poverty, Mem Mus, Lima, Ohio, 83. *Teaching:* Prof art, Bowling Green State Univ, 68- *Bibliog:* Lynn Stevenson (auth), Art from a can, Sunday Mag, Blade, 4/22/73. *Media:* Mixed. *Mailing Add:* 10271 Napolean Rd Bowling Green OH 43402

BANERJEE, (BIMAL)
PAINTER, SCULPTOR
b Calcutta, India, Sept 4, 39; US citizen. *Study:* Indian Col Art, Calcutta, grad(first class hon), 55-60; Col Art, New Delhi, Indian Govt Nat Cult Scholar, 65-67; Atelier 17, Paris, Fr Govt Grant, 67-69; École des Beaux Arts, Paris, Fr Govt Grant, 67-70; Pratt Inst Exten, New York, inst grants, 69 & 70-72; NY Univ, with H Jensen, 76; Columbia Univ MA, 78, EdM, 78, EdD, 88. *Work:* Mus Mod Art, Paris, France; Mus Fine Arts, Boston; Brooklyn Mus; Nat Gallery Mod Art, New Delhi; plus many others. *Comn:* Mural with five panels, comn by Mario Manto, Levanto, Italy, 68; mural with three panels, Proj Find Clinton Sr Citizens Ctr, New York, 79; Silk Screen Proj, NY & NJ Port Authority, CCF/CETA Artists Proj, New York, 79; plus others. *Exhib:* Brooklyn Mus Biennial, 72-73 & 81; World Print Competition, San Francisco Mus Mod Art, 77-79; Inter-Grafik Triennale, Berlin, 84; Ibizagraphic, Mus Contemp Art, Ibiza, 86; 39 one-man shows, including Galerie Haut Pave, Paris, 68, Columbia Univ, 78, 79 & 84, Art Heritage Gallery, New Delhi, Chitrakoot Art Gallery, Calcutta, 90 & Bertha Urdang Gallery, New York, 91; Ljubljana Biennial, Mus Mod Art, Ljubljana, Yugoslavia, 87; Kanagawa Biennial, Knagawa, Japan, 90, 92; and others. *Pos:* Therapist, art & educ, St John's Episcopal Hosp, Far Rockaway, NY, 81-83; art consult, New York City Bd Educ, 83-84. *Teaching:* Vis asst teacher graphics, Nat Acad Fine Arts, New York, 69; guest lectr, Parsons Sch Design, New York, 79; lectr philos educ, Bloomfield Col, NJ, 80-81, New Sch Social Res, Parsons Sch Design, NY, 83-88, New York City Bd Educ, 83-; Columbia Univ, Teachers' Col, 88. *Awards:* Ctr Cult Int Award, City Univ, Paris, 68; Grant Award, Adolph and Esther Gottueb Found, New York, 89- 90; World Cultural Prize, Statue of Victory for Arts, Letters & Sciences, Nat Ctr Study & Res, Salsomaggiore, Italy, 84; and others. *Bibliog:* Ajit K Dutta (auth), Bimal Banerjee, Nat Art Acad J, 9/74; Ajit K Dutta (auth), Fumage: Works on Paper, catalog for the one-person show of Banerjee, 80-90, Banerjee's Fumages: Behind the Smoke Screen, Art Heritage Gallery, New Delhi, 90. *Mem:* Col Art Asn Am, New York; World Print Coun, San Francisco; Found Community Artists, NY; Print Club, Philadelphia; Ancient Art, Paris. *Media:* Fumage, Mascara; Eyeliner, Latex House Paint. *Publ:* Coauth, Mine, 64; contribr, Revolutionist Master-Artist Henri Matisse, 70, Painter Sonia Delaunay, 70, Metaphysical Master-Artist de Chirico, 72 & Picasso, 82; Painter Sonia Delaunay, 70; Picasso, 82; and many others. *Dealer:* Bertha Urdang Gallery 23 E 74th St New York NY 10021. *Mailing Add:* Loft 2C 106 Ridge St New York NY 10002

BANEY, RALPH RAMOUTAR
SCULPTOR
b Trinidad, West Indies, Sept 22, 29. *Study:* Brighton Col Art, Eng, 57-62; Univ Md, MFA, 73, PhD, 80; also with Kenneth Campbell & Arthur J Ayres. *Work:* Nat Mus Art Gallery, Trinidad; Cent Bank, Trinidad; Washington Co Mus, Hagerstown, Md; Univ West Indies; Van Leer Found, Amsterdam, Holland. *Comn:* relief sculpture, Norweg Seamen's Mission, Trinidad, 69; nat coat of arms, Cent Bank Trinidad, 70; mosaic mural (with Vera Baney), Bishop's High Sch, Trinidad, 71; monumental marble sculpture, City Hall, Valjevo, Yugoslavia, 84; mural for Scotiabank Hq, Trinidad. *Exhib:* Sao Paulo Biennial, Brazil, 67 & 69; one-man shows, Sculpture House Gallery, New York 73, Pan Am Union, Washington, DC, 74 & Washington Co Mus, Hagerstown, Md, 84; Sculptors Guild Mem Ann, Lever House, New York, 74-89. *Teaching:* Supvr art, Ministry Educ & Cult, Trinidad, 63-71; instr art, Univ Md, 72-75; instr art, Smithsonian Inst, 74-79; prof, Dundalk Community Col, 76- *Awards:* Gold Medal Merit, Govt Trinidad & Tobago, 73; First Prize Sculpture, Ten & 22nd Md Juried Exhib, Easton Acad Md, 74 & 86; First Prize Sculpture, Spanish Am Art Exhib, 74. *Bibliog:* Rod Naylor (auth), Woodcarving Techniques, Batsford, 79; Nicholas Roukes (auth), Masters of Wood Sculpture, Watson Guptill, 80; Anthony Padovano (auth), Sculpture Processes, Doubleday, 81. *Mem:* Royal Soc Brit Sculptors; Sculptors Guild; Sculptors' Inc Baltimore; Wash Sculptors Group. *Media:* Wood, Bronze. *Mailing Add:* Dept Art Dundalk Community Col 7200 Sollers Pt Rd Baltimore MD 21222

BANEY, VERA
SCULPTOR, CERAMIST
b Trinidad, West Indies, June 6, 30. *Study:* Brighton Col Art, Eng, 59-62; State Univ NY Col Ceramics, Alfred Univ, 68; Univ Md, BA, 80. *Work:* Nat Mus & Art Gallery, Trinidad; Cent Bank, Trinidad; Hilton Hotel, Trinidad; Mika Simic V'tric, Arangelovac, Yugoslavia; Scotia Centre, Trinidad. *Comn:* Ceramic cross, Norweg Seamen's Mission, Trinidad, 69; ceramic relief, Alston's Ltd, Trinidad, 70; mosaic mural (with Ralph Baney), Bishop's High Sch, Trinidad, 71; wall sculpture, Scotia Bank, 85; ceramic sculpture, Cent Bank Trinidad. *Exhib:* Expo 67, Montreal, 67; one-man shows, Trinidad, 67 & 69, Clay Sculpture, Washington Co Mus Fine Arts, Md, 85; Commonwealth Inst, London, 74; Sao Paulo Biennial, Brazil, 75; 3 Artists from Trinidad, Pan Am Union, Washington, DC, 76. *Teaching:* Instr ceramics, Dundalk Community Col, currently. *Awards:* Outstanding Young Potter, Creative Crafts Coun 11 Biennial, 74; First Place Ceramics, 2nd Int Art Exhib, Washington, DC, 74; Humming Bird Gold Medal Nat Award, Trinidad, 82. *Mem:* Nat Mus Women in Arts; Sculpture Inc; Smithsonian Assocs. *Mailing Add:* 5203 Talbots Landing Ellicott City MD 21043

BANGERT, COLETTE STUEBE
PAINTER
b Columbus, Ohio, July 7, 34. *Study:* John Herron Art Inst, BFA, 57; Boston Univ, MFA, 58; Ind Univ; Kans Univ. *Work:* Mulane Art Ctr, Topeka, Kans; Mus Mod Art, New York, NY; Univ Okla Mus Art, Norman; Springfield Art Mus, Mo; Sheldon Mem Art Gallery, Lincoln, Nebr. *Comn:* Grassland Garden, Topeka Pub Libr, 69 & Landlace: Greening III, Townsite Eatery, 77, Topeka, Kans. *Exhib:* Computer Genesis, Lowe Art Gallery, Syracuse, NY, 77; solo exhib, Sheldon Mem Art Gallery, Lincoln, Nebr, 78 & Albrecht Art Mus, Mo, 84; High Arts Technology, Libr Cong, Washington, DC, 80; Computer Art, Ben Shahn Galleries, Wayne, NJ, 85; ACM Siggraph 86 Art Show: A Twenty Year Retrospective Computer Art, Dallas, Tex; Computers and Art, Everson Mus Art & IBM Gallery, Syracuse, New York; Second Emerging Expression Biennial: The Artist and the Computer, Bronx Mus Art, 87; Computer and Video Art, Southern Alleghenies Mus Art, 88; At the Speed of Thought: Two Dimensional Algorithmic Art, Print Club, Philadelphia, Pa, 89. *Bibliog:* Allan Millstein (auth), Artist abstracts Kansas terrain, Topeka Capital J, 7/14/79; Patrick White (auth), Colette Bangert, New Art Examiner, 5/83; Carolyn McMaster (auth), Personal Visions, Lawrence J World, 9/14/86. *Mem:* Kansas City Artists Coalition (pres, 77-78). *Media:* Mixed, Computer Drawing. *Publ:* Coauth, Experiences in making drawings by computer and by hand, Leonardo, 74; illusr, Appreciating Poetry (ed, R P Sugg), Houghton Mifflin, 75; coauth, Computer grass is natural grass, In: Artist and Computer (ed, Ruth Leavitt), Harmony Bks, 76. *Dealer:* Kellas Gallery Lawrence KS 66044. *Mailing Add:* 721 Tennessee Lawrence KS 66044

BANKS, ALLAN R
PAINTER
b Dearborn, Mich, Feb 15, 48. *Study:* Sch Fine Arts, Detroit, Mich, 66-68; Atelier of Richard F Lack, Minneapolis, 70-73; R H Ives Gammell Studios, Boston, 76. *Work:* Wadsworth Atheneum, Hartford; Springville Mus Art, Utah; Vixseboxse Galleries, Cleveland Heights, Ohio. *Comn:* Dr James McBride (portrait), Friends of Bowling Green State Univ, Huron, Ohio; two portraits, Hamilton Fish Found, Garrison, NY, 81; five portraits of corporate chairmen, Brush-Wellman Corp, Cleveland, 84; Dr Algalee Adams (portrait), Friends of Bowling Green State Univ, Huron, Ohio, 85. *Exhib:* Butler Inst Am Art, Youngstown, Ohio, 77; Grand Central Art Founders Show, Grand Central Galleries, New York, 81; Art Expo, Nat Coun Jewish Women, Teaneck, NJ, 82; Classical Realism, Amarillo Art Ctr, Tex, 82. *Pos:* Dir, Atelier of Plein Air Studies, 91- *Awards:* E T Greenshields Award, Greenshields Found, Montreal, 72 & 73; Stacey Award, Stacey Found, NMex, 74; Gold Medal, April Salon, Springville Mus Art, Utah, 82. *Bibliog:* Helen Cullinan (auth) Current day Sargent, Cleveland Plain Dealer, 82; Richard Lack (auth), article, in: Realism in Revolution, Taylor, Dallas, 85; artist subject of film profile, Bowling Green State Univ, Ohio, 85. *Mem:* New Am Acad Art, New York (exec dir); full mem, Soc Classical Realism, Minn. *Media:* Oil. *Dealer:* Vixseboxse Art Galleries 12413 Cedar Rd Cleveland Heights OH 44106. *Mailing Add:* PO Box 145 Safety Harbor FL 34695-0145

BANKS, ANNE JOHNSON
COLLAGE ARTIST, EDUCATOR
b New London, Conn, Aug 10, 24. *Study:* Wellesley Col, BA, 46; Honolulu Sch Art, with Willson Stamper, 48-50; George Washington Univ, with Thomas Downing, MFA, 68. *Work:* Lyman Allyn Mus, New London; George Washington Univ; Va Ctr Creative Arts, Sweetbriar; Nat Mus Women Arts, Washington, DC. *Exhib:* Northern Va Fine Arts Asn Area Exhib, 72-74; one-person shows, Alexandria Art League, 73, Foundry Gallery, Washington, DC, 78, 81, 83 & 86 & Gallery 10 Ltd, Washington, DC, 93; Hyatt Regency Competition, 81; Va Mus, Richmond, 83; Chrysler Mus, Norfolk, Va, 88. *Teaching:* Lectr art, George Washington Univ, summer 68; instr art, George Mason Univ, 68-69; instr art, Northern Va Community Col, 71-72, asst prof, 73-80, chmn dept, 73-89, assoc prof, 80-89, prof emer, 90. *Awards:* Six Merit

Awards, Art League, Alexandria, Va, 71-74; Merit Award, Northern Va Fine Arts Asn, 72; Va Ctr Creative Arts Fel, Sweetbriar, 82, 85 & 92. *Mem:* Womens Caucus Art; Alexandria Art League; Col Art Asn Am; Design Forum; Design Hist Soc. *Media:* Drawing, Mixed Media. *Publ:* Articles, Northern Va Rev, 81 & 87; articles, NY Art Rev, 88. *Mailing Add:* Dept Art No Va Community Col Alexandria 3001 N Beauregard St Alexandria VA 22311

BANKS, ELLEN
PAINTER
Work: Addison Gallery Am Art, Andover, Mass; Atlanta Pub Libr, Ga; Boston Pub Libr; Citicorp, New York; Chicago Art Inst. *Exhib:* One-person exhibs, Hampden Gallery, Univ Mass at Amherst, 89, McIntosh Gallery, Atlanta, Ga, 89, Soho 20, New York, 90, Akin Gallery, Boston, Mass, 90, Amerika Haus, Berlin, 91, Fine Arts Ctr, Neubrandenburg, Ger, 92; Newport Art Mus, RI, 90; Espace Riquet, 90, Centre de Documentation, 90, CC Gallery, Paris, France, 92; Kennesaw State Col, Marietta, Ga, 91; Stephen Rosenberg Gallery, New York, 91. *Awards:* Nat Endowment Arts, Visual Artist Grant, 87; Nexus Press Bk Grant, 88; Mass Artists Fel, 91. *Bibliog:* Addison Parks (auth), The Christian Science Monitor, 1/91; Alicia Faxon (auth), Women Artists News, winter 91; Renee Schipp (auth), Berliner Morgenpost, 92. *Mailing Add:* 30 Ipswich Boston MA 02215

BANNARD, WALTER DARBY
PAINTER, ART WRITER
b New Haven, Conn, Sept 23, 34. *Study:* Phillips Exeter Acad; Princeton Univ. *Work:* Whitney Mus Am Art, Guggenheim Mus, Metrop Mus Art, New York; Albright-Knox Art Gallery, Buffalo, NY; NJ State Mus; Boston Mus Fine Arts; Houston Mus Fine Arts; Honolulu Mus; plus many others. *Exhib:* Whitney Mus Ann, New York, 72; Abstract Painting in the 70's, Mus Fine Arts, Boston, 72; maj retrospective, Baltimore Mus Art, 73; The Great Decade of American Abstraction, Mus Fine Arts, Houston; Art in America after World War II, Guggenheim Mus, 79; New Works in Clay, Syracuse Univ, 81; Definitive Statements: American Art 1964-66, Brown Univ, 86; one-man shows, Brush Art Gallery, St Lawrence Univ, 87, Richard Love Gallery, Chicago, Ill, 88, Greenberg Wilson Gallery, New York, 89, Rider Col Art Gallery, Lawrenceville, NJ, 89, Greenberg/Wilson Gallery, New York, 90, Jaffe Baker Gallery, Boca Raton, Fla, 92; retrospectives, Montclair Mus Art (with catalog), 91 & Knoedler Gallery, London, Eng, 91; Stars in Florida, Ft Lauderdale Art Mus, 92. *Pos:* Contrib ed, Artforum Mag, 73-74; deleg, Europ-Am Assembly Art Mus, England, 75; cur, Hans Hofmann, Hirshhorn Mus, Washington, DC, 76; mem, Int Exhib Comt, 78-79; co-chmn, Nat Endowment Arts Int Comt Visual Arts, 79-81. *Teaching:* Lectr at numerous universities; symposium & sem, Princeton Univ, New York Univ, Mus Fine Arts, Boston & others, 66-; grad fac, Sch Visual Arts, New York, NY, 84-89; chmn dept art & art history, Univ Miami, 89- *Awards:* Nat Found Arts Award, 68-69; Guggenheim Fel, 68-69; Francis J Greenberger Found Award, 86. *Bibliog:* W Zimmer (auth), Paintings that Reveal the Alchemy of Creation, NY Times 3/3/91; C Wilkinson (auth), Putting the Paint into 'Painterly Abstraction', Trenton Times, 10/91. *Publ:* Auth, Touch and scale, Artforum, 6/71; The Art Museum and the Living Artist, Prentice-Hall, 75; Hans Hofmann, Hirshhorn Mus, 76; auth, The emperor's old clothes, Arts Mag, 9/82; Painting of the 50s, Duke Univ, 83; What It's Like to Be An Artist, Miami Mag, Vol 3, No 2, winter 92; and others. *Dealer:* Greenberg-Wilson Gallery 560 Broadway New York NY 10012. *Mailing Add:* 25 Morningside Dr Coral Gables FL 33133

BANNING, JACK (JOHN PECK), JR
ART DEALER, LECTURER
b Mt Vernon, NY, June 12, 39. *Study:* Brown Univ, AB, 61. *Pos:* Owner, Banning & Assocs Ltd, 74- *Mem:* Poster Soc, Inc (founder, treas & bd mem); New Amsterdam Symphony Orchestra (treas & bd mem); Guggenheim Mus Int Asn. *Specialty:* American & European poster art, 1890-1950; original graphic design & vintage modernist photography. *Mailing Add:* 138 W 18th St New York NY 10011

BANNISTER, PATI (PATRICIA BROWN BANNISTER)
PAINTER, SCULPTOR
b London, Eng, Oct 29, 29; US citizen. *Study:* Slade Acad, London; Studied with father Harold Brown. *Work:* Daytona Beach Mus Arts & Sci, Fla. *Comn:* portraits, Del Mar Race Track, Turf Paradise Ariz Downs; portrait, Comm by Cambrell Jone. *Exhib:* One-woman show, Daytona Beach Mus, Fla, 79, Southwest Arts Found, Houston, Tex, 83, Rotary Club Art Exhib, Amarillo, Tex; portrait, Comn by, Robert Unsell, 87. *Awards:* Nat Publishing Inst, Award Gold Medal for Color Printing; E Emerson Albright Award. *Bibliog:* Dr Gary Libby (dir), Pati Bannister, SW Art Mag, 4/82; Peggy Samuels (coauth) with Harold Samuels, Pati Bannister, Contemp Western Artists, 82; Dr Gary Libby (dir), Romantic Pati Bannister, Daytona Beach Mus Mag, fall, 84. *Media:* Oil, Acrylic; Bronze. *Publ:* Equestrian illustrations, Riding, London; Various children's books, England. *Dealer:* The Bannister Collection 2301 14th St Gulfport MS 39501. *Mailing Add:* 24368 Oaklawn Plantation Rd Pass Christian MS 39571

BANNISTER, PATRICIA BROWN See Bannister, Pati (Patricia Brown Bannister)

BANSEMER, ROGER L
PAINTER, WRITER
b Brockton, Mass, July 25, 48. *Study:* Ringling Sch Art, Sarasota, Fla, BA, 69. *Work:* Sperry Rand Corp, New York; Clearwater Oaks Bank & Barnett Bank, Clearwater,Fla; Rutgers Univ, New Brunswick, NJ; Pioneer Bank, Fla; Forbes, Chateau Balleroy, France. *Comn:* Wall Mural, Spyglass Hotel, Clearwater, 79; etching for Pres Carter, City of Clearwater, 79; mural, City Clearwater, 8; The Rocks (mural), Sydney, Australia, 82; painting for poster, City of Clearwater, 83; mural (20 ft x 30 ft), Home Shopping Network, St Petersburg, Fla, 88; and others. *Exhib:* Infinite Space & Kinetic Color, Adelphi Univ, 77; 15th Ann Maj Fla Artists, Harmon Gallery, Naples, Fla, 77; Pan-Am Bldg, DC, 79; Adelphi Univ, New York, 80; Byways Gallery, Sarasota, Fla, 81; St Petersburg Mus Fine Arts, Fla, 85 & 86; Voorhees Gallery Sarasota, Fla, 88; Upham Gallery, St Petersburg, Fla, 88 & 90; Mystic Seaport Gallery, Conn, 90. *Pos:* Artist-in-residence, City of Clearwater, 78. *Awards:* Int Award of Excellence, Mystic Mus, Conn, 91. *Bibliog:* Review by Gene Shalit Today Show, 89; review, Forbes Mag, 89 & Playboy Mag, 90; feature story, Artist Mag, 89. *Media:* Acrylics; Etching. *Publ:* Auth, Smithsonian, Air & Space Mag, 88, Am Artist Mag, 88, Tampa Tribune, 88, Tampa Bay Life Mag, 88, Homes Mag, 88; The Art of HotAir Ballooning; Southern Shores; Rachael's Splendifilous Adventure; Art Water's Edge, The Birds of Florida. *Mailing Add:* 2352 Alligator Creek Road Clearwater FL 34625

BANTEL, LINDA
MUSEUM DIRECTOR
b King City, Calif, May 30, 43. *Study:* Inst Fine Arts, New York Univ, MA, 71; Wharton Advand Mgt Prog, Univ Pa, cert, 92. *Pos:* Res assoc, Metrop Mus Art, New York 78-80; assoc to chief cur, Pa Acad Fine Arts, 80-85, dir mus, 85- *Mem:* Am Asn Mus; Asn Art Mus Dirs; Cosmopolitan Club, Philadelphia. *Publ:* Auth, William Rush, American Sculptor, 82 & introduction, Searching Out the Best, 88, Pa Acad Fine Arts, Philadelphia; coauth, American Paintings in the Metropolitan Museum of Art, Vol II: A Catalog of Works by Artists Born Between 1816-1845, Princeton Univ Press, 85; Raphaelle Peale in Philadelphia, Nat Gallery Art & Pa Acad Fine Arts, 88; The Potamkin collection of American art, Mag Antiques, 8/89; and others. *Mailing Add:* 255 S 44th St Philadelphia PA 19104

BANZ, GEORGE
WRITER, ARCHITECT
b Lucerne, Switz, Dec 21, 28; Can citizen. *Study:* Swiss Fed Inst Technol, Zurich, with S Giedion, dipl archit; Okla State Univ, Stillwater, exchange fel, MS(archit eng). *Exhib:* Ontario Architecture: the Past, the Present, the Future, Art Gallery of Ont, Toronto, 63; Royal Can Acad of Arts Traveling Exhib, 68; Academicians Collection, 90. *Pos:* Spec consult, Ministry State Urban Affairs, Ottawa, 72-74; delegate, RAIC Mission, China, 83; delegate, OCA Mission to Brazil, 87. *Teaching:* Part-time fac mem, Dept of Archit, Univ of Toronto, 59-63 & 70-75; sessional lectr computers archit, 78-85, adj prof, 86-87; sch archit, Univ Waterloo, 80; part-time fac mem, Dept Indust Des, Ontario Col Art, 80- *Awards:* Massey Award for Archit, V Massey Found & Can Govt, 61 & 67. *Mem:* Royal Archit Inst of Can; Royal Can Acad of Arts. *Res:* Systems aspects of form, particularly with regard to problems of design automation. *Publ:* Auth, Elements of Urban Form, 70; Computer Aids in Building Design, 83; Design Automation (in prep). *Mailing Add:* Ontario Col Art 100 McCaul St Toronto ON M5T 1W1 Canada

BAPST, SARAH
CONCEPTUAL ARTIST
b Chicago, Ill, May 21, 50. *Study:* Ind Univ, Bloomington, with Mary Ellen Solt, BA 73; Cranbrook Acad Art, studied with Richard DeVore, MFA, 77. *Exhib:* 67th Hudson River Ann, Hudson River Mus, 82; Last Nat Sculpture Show, Art Dept Gallery, Univ Ga, Athens, 82; 37th Art Northeast USA, Silvermine Galleries, New Canaan, Conn, 86; Tenth Ann Boston Drawing Show, Boston Ctr Arts, Mass, 89; Eleventh Ann Boston Drawing Show, Boston Ctr Arts, Mass, 90. *Teaching:* Assoc Prof Studio Foundations, Mass Col Art, Boston, Mass, 84- *Awards:* Last Nat Sculpture Show, Univ of Ga, Athens, 82; NJ Ctr for the Arts, 88; Fel Works on Paper, Nat Endowment Arts, 91. *Bibliog:* Ron Jones (auth), The last national sculpture show, Art Papers, 1-2/83; Mary Sherman (auth), Tenth annual Boston drawing show, Art New Eng, 9/89. *Mailing Add:* Five Linnaean St No 35 Cambridge MA 02138

BARANIK, RUDOLF
PAINTER
b Lithuania, Sept 10, 20; US citizen. *Study:* Art Inst Chicago, 46; Art Students League, 47; Acad Julian, Paris, France, 48; and with Fernand Leger, 49-50. *Work:* Whitney Mus Am Art & Mus Mod Art, New York; Nat Mus, Stockholm, Sweden; Hirshhorn Mus & Sculpture Garden; New Mus Contemp Art, New York. *Exhib:* Whitney Mus Am Art Ann, 58 & 61; Art of Conscience: The Last Decade Traveling Exhib, 81-82; War Games, Ronald Feldman Gallery, New York, 82; Four Manifestos, Lenner-Heller Gallery, New York, 82; The End of the World: Contemporary Visions of the Apocalypse, New Mus, New York, 83; Committed to Print, Mus Mod Art, New York, 88; Concrete Utopia, Int Exhib, Kunsthalle, Dusseldorf, 90; solo exhib, Exit Art Gallery, New York, 93. *Teaching:* prof, Pratt Inst, 66-76, adj prof art, 77-; instr painting, Art Students League, 68- *Awards:* Am Acad Arts & Lett Award in Art, 73; NY State Creative Artists Pub Serv Award in Painting, 75; Guggenheim Grant, 81. *Bibliog:* Edward Lucie-Smith (auth), Art in the Seventies, Phaidon Press Ltd, London, 80; Dane Ashton (auth), American Art Since 1945, Oxford Univ Press, 82; Lucy Lippard (auth), Get the Message?, Dutton, 84; and many others. *Media:* Oil, Acrylic. *Publ:* Coauth, The Attica Book, 72; Baranik's Dictionary from the 24th Century, Bee-sting Press, 90. *Dealer:* Exit Art Gallery New York NY. *Mailing Add:* 97 Wooster St New York NY 10012

BARAZANI, MORRIS
EDUCATOR, PAINTER
b Highland Park, Mich, June 24, 24. *Study:* Inst Design, Cranbrook Acad Art, Bloomfield Hills, Mich. *Work:* Gutenberg Mus, Ger; Blue Cross Blue Shield, Chicago, Ill; Gov's State Univ, Ill. *Exhib:* Art Inst Chicago, 59; Ill State Mus, 71; Pamlemousse, Chicago, 75; Chicago Gallery, Ill, 76; Zriny-Hayes Gallery, Chicago, 77 & 79-81; Gilman Galleries, 83-88; one-man show, Gilman Galleries, 85, 87, 90. *Teaching:* Prof painting, Univ Ill, Chicago, 69- *Media:* Oil, Collage. *Mailing Add:* 5340 N Magnolia Ave Chicago IL 60640

BARBEAU, MARCEL (CHRISTIAN), ARC
PAINTER, SCULPTOR
b Montreal, Que, Feb 18, 25. *Study:* Ecole Meuble, dipl, 47; with Paul-Emile Borduas. *Work:* Nat Gallery, Can & Washington; Stedelijk Mus, Amsterdam; Chrysler Mus, Norfolk, Va; Rose Art Mus, Brandeis Univ; Art Gallery Ont. *Comn:* Pipes' Dreams (tube sculptures), Confederation Ctr Art Gallery & Mus, Charlottetown, PEI, 74; aluminum sculpture, Lavallin, Boucherville, Que, 76; Don Quichotte (aluminum sculpture), Cojo, Montreal, Joliette, Que, 76; Liberté, liberté chérie (painted welded steel), Lachine-Marina, Qué, 86; Laurentians (acrylic on aluminium mural), Via Rail intercontinental train, 89; Les portes du regard (painted welded steel), City Hall Parc, Montreal-Est, 90; Nadia or Le saut du tremplin (painted welded aluminum sculpture), '76, Musée d'art contemporain de Montréal, from SNC-Lavalin, Boucherville-Montréal, Que, 92; Window on Future (painted welded steel sculpture), McLennan Libr Terr, McGill Univ, 92. *Exhib:* Pen House Show, Mus Mod Art, New York, 65; Nine Canadians, Inst Contemp Art, Boston, 69; retrospectives, Winnipeg Art Gallery & Mus Art Contemp, Montreal, 69; solo exhibs, Mus Que & Mus Contemp, Montreal, 74-75 & Mus Beaux Arts Montreal, 77; Modern Painting in Canada, 78 & The Contemporary Art Society: Montreal 1939-1947, 80, Edmonton Art Gallery; Montreal Fine Art Mus, 91; Opening exhib, Musée d'art contemporain de Montréal, 92; Quebec Painting in the Fifties, Nat Gallery Can, 92; Canadian Abstract Painting & Design in Fifties, Winnipeg Art Gallery, 92; Mod Sculpture in Quebec: 1947-1960, Muse du Quebec, 92. *Teaching:* Artist-in-residence painting, Bishop Univ, Que, 78-80. *Awards:* Zacks Prize, Royal Can Acad, 64; Lynch-Staunton Award, Can Art Coun, 73; First Prize, McDonalds Sculpture Restaurants, 85; Cert of Excellence, Int Art Competition, NY, 88. *Bibliog:* Don Thompson (producer), A Passionate Harmony (TV film), Vision Ser, TV Ont, 83; Carolle Gagnon & Ninon Gauthier, introd by Charles Delloye, Marcel Barbeau: Fugato, CECA Publ, Montreal, 90. *Mem:* Conseil artistes peintres (vpres, 78-79); Fedn artistes arts visuels Que (pres, 78-79); Artist for Peace. *Media:* Acrylic; Welded Metal, Wood. *Publ:* Auth, Grande probite intellectuelle, Devoir, Que, 60; L'artiste devant son oeuvre, Cahiers, Que, 79. *Dealer:* Galerie Michel-Ange 450 Bonsecours Montreal H2Y 3C4; Galerie Donguy 57 rue de la Roquette 75011 Paris. *Mailing Add:* 1635 Amherst Montreal PQ H2L 3L4 Canada

BARBEE, ROB
PAINTER
b Memphis, Tenn, March 26, 40. *Study:* Covenant Col, BA, 63; Memphis State Univ, BS, 73. *Exhib:* Ky Watercolor Soc Nat Exhib, Louisville, 82; Am Watercolor Soc Ann, New York, 83; Allied Artists Am Ann, New York, 83; Nat Arts Club Ann Watercolor Exhib, New York, 83; Southern Watercolor Soc Ann, Asheville, NC, 83. *Awards:* Second Merit Award, Caroliniana Watercolor Exhib, 81; Fifth Merit Award, 81 & Ninth Merit Award, 83, SC Watercolor Soc Ann Exhib. *Mem:* Artists Guild, Greenville, SC; Guild SC Artists; Southern Watercolor Soc. *Media:* Watercolor. *Dealer:* Tempo Gallery 125 W Stone Ave Greenville SC 29609. *Mailing Add:* 205 Cardinal Dr Greenville SC 29609

BARBEE, ROBERT THOMAS
PAINTER, GRAPHIC ARTIST
b Detroit, Mich, Sept 25, 21. *Study:* Cranbrook Acad Art, BA & MFA; Centenary Col; also in Mex. *Work:* Butler Inst Am Art, Youngstown, Ohio; Cranbrook Acad Art, Bloomfield Hills, Mich. *Exhib:* Five shows, Va Mus Fine Arts, Richmond, 53-65 & Traveling Exhibs, 58 & 62; Birmingham Mus Art, 59; Norfolk Mus Art & Sci, 60; Mus Art of Ogunquit, Maine, 62 & 63; Am Fedn Arts, New York, 65; and others. *Teaching:* Instr painting & drawing, Univ Va, assoc prof art, 70- *Awards:* Prizes, Irene Leach Mem Exhib, Norfolk Mus Arts & Sci, 62 & 64 & Thalheimer's Exhib, Richmond, 63. *Mailing Add:* 1521 Rugbe Rd Charlottesville VA 22903

BARBER, BRUCE ALISTAIR
SCULPTOR, CRITIC
b Auckland, NZ, Dec 11, 50; Can & NZ citizen. *Study:* Auckland Univ Sch Fine Arts, BFA, 73, MFA, 74; NS Col Col Art & Design, Halifax, NS, MFA, 78. *Exhib:* The Art of Memory-The Loss of History (with catalog), New Mus, New York, 85-86; A Different War: Vietnam in Art (catalog), W Latcom Mus, Bellingham De Cordova Travelling, 89-92; Interscop Festival (catalog), Warsaw, Poland, 90; Memory Works (catalog), London Regional Art Gallery, travelling, 90-91; Story Telling/Real Time (catalog), Gdansk, Poland, 91; and others. *Pos:* ECoast ed, FUSE Mag, Toronto, 84-; bd mem, Univ Art Asn Can, 89- *Teaching:* Jr lectr sculpture, Auckland Univ, NZ, 74-75; asst prof fine art, Simon Fraser Univ, 79-81; asst prof intermedia-studio, NS Col Art & Design, 81-89, assoc prof, 90- *Awards:* Queen Elizabeth II Arts Coun, 77 & 79; Can Coun B Grant (proj grants), Criticism & Visual Arts, 84, 88 & 90; Ont Critics Grant, 85; SSHRC Res Awards, 82, 83, 89, 91 & 92. *Bibliog:* L Lippard (auth), article, Village Voice, 2/29/85; L Lippard (auth), Vietnam in Art, Real Comet Press, San Francisco, 90; M Cheetham (auth), Remembering Postmodernism, Oxford Univ Press, Can. *Mem:* Univ Art Asn Can; Can Artists Representation; Popular Cult Asn Am. *Res:* Popular culture, theory & politics. *Publ:* Auth, C Pontbriand (ed), Performance Texts & Documents, Parachute Publ, 81; ed, essays on Performance & Cultural Politicization, Open Letter 5: 5 & 6, 83; D Lander, M Lexier, Sound by Artists, Art Metropole Publ, Toronto, 90; auth, Reading Rooms, Halifax, Eyelevel Pub, 92. *Mailing Add:* Studio Div NS Col Art & Design 5163 Duke St Halifax NS B3J 3J6 Canada

BARBER, CYNTHIA
SCULPTOR, PRINTMAKER
b Boston, Mass, Dec 12, 39. *Study:* Barnard Col, BA, 61; Brandeis Univ, MA, 63; Richmond Col, Eng, 71-73. *Work:* George Meany Ctr Labor Studies, Silver Spring, Md; Grants Mining Mus, NMex; Beth Ami Synagogue, Rockville, Md; Duke Univ, Durham, NC. *Comn:* Holocaust Memorial, Gaithersburg Hebrew Congregation, Md, 81; outdoor sculpture for office complex, Bakersfield, Calif, Carver Develop Co, 86; outdoor sculpture, Harbor Park Assoc, Stamford, Conn, 88; wall sculpture, Landmark Systems, Vienna, Va, 88; outdoor sculpture, Hacienda Towers, Los Angeles, Calif, 90. *Exhib:* Association Internationale de Defense des Artistes, Amsterdam, 81, traveling throughout Europe, 81-82; Nat Coun Art Jewish Life Judaic Art Exhib, Lever House, New York, 83; Festival Arts: Sculpture for Public Spaces, Albuquerque, NMex, 85; North Am Sculpture Exhib, Golden, Colo, 86; Art of Albuquerque, Albuquerque Mus, 90. *Pos:* Founding mem & bd dir, Touchstone Gallery, Washington, DC, 76-77 & Association Internationale de Defense des Artistes, US, 81-85. *Teaching:* Instr humanities, Howard Univ, Washington, DC, 66-70. *Awards:* NMex Art in Pub Places Purchase Awards, Harriet B Samons State Office Bldg, Farmington, NMex, 86; Grants, Mus Mining, NMex, 86. *Bibliog:* Joe D Stevenson (auth), Sculpture adds final touch to tower, Bakersfield Californian, 1/23/87; Henry Allen (auth), Inside the art circle: 18 dupont studios celebrate new talent, Washington Post, 6/27/87; Commisions,Sculpture Mag, 11-12/87. *Media:* All; Woodcut. *Mailing Add:* PO Box 2507 Corrales NM 87048

BARBER, PHILIP JUDD
PAINTER, PRINTMAKER
b Cleveland, Ohio, Sept 27, 51. *Study:* Ohio Univ, BS, 73, BFA, 77. *Work:* Minneapolis Inst Arts; Purdue Univ, Ind; First Banks Systs, Minneapolis; Chemical Bank, New York; Frans Masereel Centrum, Kasterlee, Belg. *Exhib:* Boston Printmakers, DeCordova Mus, Boston, 78; Chautauqua Nat Exhib of Am Art, Chautauqua Art Mus, NY, 83; May Show, Cleveland Mus Art, 83; Small Print Exhib, Purdue Art Mus, Ind, 84; Minn Artists Exhib Prog - 10th Anniversary Exhib, Minneapolis Inst Arts, 86. *Pos:* Studio mgr, Vermillion Ed Ltd, Minn, 78- *Awards:* First Place, Art Ctr Minn, 85. *Media:* Tempra, Oil; Stick. *Dealer:* Vermillion Ed Ltd 2919 Como Ave SE Minneapolis MN 55414. *Mailing Add:* 2904 Buchanan St NE Minneapolis MN 55418-2209

BARBER, RONALD
ADMINISTRATOR
Study: Union Col, Schenectady, NY; Goddard Col, Plainfield, Vt; Univ Without Walls, Skidmore Col, Saratoga, NY. *Collections Arranged:* Norman Rockwell Retrospective, 73; Pa Acad Fine Arts Fel Exhib, 74; Woman's Work, 74. *Pos:* Dir, Mus Philadelphia Civic Ctr, currently. *Teaching:* Adj fac painting & photog, Empire State Col, Albany, NY, 70-71. *Mailing Add:* Port of Hist Mus Penn's Landing Delaware Ave at Walnut St Philadelphia PA 19106

BARBER, SAM
PAINTER, SCULPTOR
b Naples, Italy, April 9, 43. *Study:* Art Students League, Nat Acad Fine Art, New York, Cape Sch Art, Provincetown, Mass. *Work:* Miss Mus Art, Jackson; New Orleans Mus Art, La; Midwest Mus Am Art, Elkhart, Ind; Hickory Mus Art, NC; Memphis Brooks Mus Art, Tenn. *Exhib:* eleven one-man exhibs, 83-90. *Awards:* Purchase Prize, La Grange Col, Ga, 74; Philip Eisenberg Award, Salmagundi Club, New York, 81. *Media:* Oil. *Mailing Add:* 10 Hyannis Ave Hyannis Port MA 02647

BARBERA, JOE
CARTOONIST
b New York, NY. *Study:* Am Inst Banking. *Pos:* Freelance mag cartoonist; story man, MGM, 37; co-producer with Bill Hanna, Tom & Jerry Cartoon Series; partner, Hanna & Barbera Prod, New York, 57-, producers of Ruff & Reddy, Huckleberry Hound, Quick Draw McGraw, The Flintstones, Yogi Bear, The Jetsons & many others. *Awards:* Numerous awards for animated cartoons. *Mailing Add:* Hanna-Barbera Productions, Inc 3400 Cahuenga Blvd Hollywood CA 90068

BARBERA, ROSS WILLIAM
PAINTER
b Brooklyn, NY, Dec 11, 50. *Study:* St John's Univ, Jamaica, NY, BFA, 73; Pratt Inst, Brooklyn, NY, MFA, 75. *Work:* Harley Sch, Wilson Arts Ctr, Rochester, NY; Univ Wis, Milwaukee; La Grange Col, Ga; Chautauqua Arts Ctr, NY. *Comn:* Landscape painting (oil on canvas), Univ Wis, Milwaukee, 85. *Exhib:* One-man shows, Jean Lumbard Gallery, New York, 83 & Clark Whitney Gallery, Lenox, Mass, 89; And the Living is Easy, Visual Arts Mus, New York, 84; The Razor Show, Jayne Baum & Hudson Ctr Galleries, New York, 85; Six Long Island Artists, Islip Art Mus, NY, 85; The Landscape, Columbus Mus Ohio, 87; and others. *Teaching:* Asst prof fine art, St John's Univ, Jamaica, NY, 80-; adj asst prof fine art, Nassau Community Col, Garden City, NY, 87- *Awards:* Creative Artist Pub Serv Painting Fel, NY State, 76; Nat Endowment Arts Painting Fel, 85-86. *Bibliog:* Ellen Lubell (auth), Rev, Arts Mag, 10/75; Laurie Hurwitz (auth), Airbrush techniques for landscape painters, Am Artist, 10/87; Helen A Harrison (auth), Visual puns at Islip juried show, NY Times, 2/89. *Media:* Acrylic, Oil. *Dealer:* Clark Whitney Gallery 25 Church St Lenox MA 01240. *Mailing Add:* 340 Croaton St Ronkonkoma NY 11779

BARBERIS, DOROTHY WATKEYS
PAINTER
b Newport, Va, Sept 20, 18. *Study:* Syracuse Univ, 37 & 38; many private studies and workshops. *Exhib:* Int Soc Art, Nat Arts Club, New York, 78; Allied Artists, Am Acad & Inst Arts & Lett, New York, 80; Church Women United Womens Art Exhib, Purdue Univ, West Lafayette, Ind, 84; Midwest Watercolor Soc, Neville Pub Mus Brown Co, Green Bay, Wis, 86 & 91; Springfield Art League, George Walter Vincent Smith Art Mus, Mo, 87 & 91; and others. *Pos:* Designer (linens), Sherwin Brothers, New York, 38-39; designer (fabrics), Wynborough Studio, New York, 43-44; draftsman, Johnson Cushing & Neville, 44-45. *Teaching:* Watercolor, pvt studio, 77-80; Saddlebrook High Sch (adult educ), 80-83; pvt studio, 92- *Awards:* Best in Show, Ocean County Col, 85; Best in Show, Clara & Ida Stroud Mem, 90; Mary Hill Award, Catherine Lorillard Wolfe Art Club, Nat Arts Club, 91. *Bibliog:* World Who's Who of Women, 90; Int Leaders Achievement, 91; First Five Hundred, 91. *Mem:* Catherine Lorillard Wolfe Art Club (bd, 80-89 & 90, 2nd vpres, 80-83 & 90-, asst treas, 82-89, mem, 82-89); Salmagundi; Nat Asn Women Artists; NJ Watercolor Soc; Nat Soc Painters Casein & Acrylic (corresp secy, 89-); and others. *Media:* Watercolor, Acrylic. *Mailing Add:* 217 Lincoln Ave Elmwood Park NJ 07407

BARBOUR, ARTHUR J
PAINTER, WRITER
b Paterson, NJ, Aug 23, 26. *Study:* Newark Sch Fine & Indust Art; and with Avery Johnson, Syd Brown & James Carlin. *Work:* US Navy Dept; Marietta Col; Norfolk Mus Arts & Sci; Prudential Life Ins Co; & many pvt collections. *Comn:* Watercolors, Woman's Day Mag, Ford Motor Co & Essex Chem Corp; mural, Am Artists Christmas Card Group. *Exhib:* Nat Acad Design, New York; Am Watercolor Soc, New York; Am Artists Prof League; one-man show, Beaumont Mus Art, Tex, 65; Wolf Gallery, Franklin, NJ, 73; Fritchman Galleries, Boise, Idaho, 74; and others. *Awards:* Plainfield Art Asn Awards, 64; Grumbacher Award, NJ Watercolor Soc & Silver Medal, 75; Allied Artists Am, 72. *Mem:* Am & NJ Watercolor Socs; Painters & Sculptors Soc NJ; Allied Artists; Nat Soc Painters Casein & Acrylic. *Media:* Watercolor. *Publ:* Auth, Painting Building in Watercolor 73, Painting the Seasons in Watercolor, 75 & Watercolor: The Wet Technique, Watson-Guptill; and others. *Mailing Add:* 29 Voorhis Pl Ringwood NJ 07456

BARBOZA, ANTHONY
PHOTOGRAPHER, PAINTER
b New Bedford, Mass, May 10, 44. *Study:* Self taught. *Work:* Mus Mod Art & Studio Mus Harlem, New York; Oberlin Col, Ohio; Newark Art Mus, NJ; Howard Univ, Washington, DC. *Exhib:* Solo exhibs, Light Gallery, 74 & Studio Mus Harlem (with monograph), New York; Kamoinge Workshop, Int Ctr Photog, New York, 75; Mirrors & Windows, Mus Mod Art, New York, 78; Nine Contemporary Photographers, Witkin Gallery, New York, 79; Polaroids, Photokina, Cologne Ger, 82 & 84; Nude in Photography, Munchner Stadtmuseum, Munich, WGer, 85; LA Expression, Los Angeles Co Mus Art, 90. *Teaching:* Lectr, Int Ctr Photog, New York, 75 & 83, Columbia Col, Chicago, 84 & Rochester Inst Technol, 91. *Awards:* Photog Grants NY State Coun Arts, 74 & 76; Nat Endowment Arts Photog Grant, 80. *Bibliog:* Allen Porter (auth), Portraits, Camera Mag, Switz, 6/80. *Media:* Oil. *Publ:* Contribr, Creative Camera, Cov Press Ltd, London, Eng, 5/75; Exposure: Ten Photog, Creative Artists Pub Serv, 76; Fashion Theory, Lustum Press, 80; auth, Black Borders, private, publ, 80. *Dealer:* Harold Simon 31 The Crescent Suite 32 Montclair NJ 07042. *Mailing Add:* 853 Broadway #1208 New York NY 10003-4703

BARD, GAYLE
ENVIRONMENTAL ARTIST, PAINTER
b Kansas City, Kans. *Study:* DePauw Univ, Univ Chicago, Univ Wis, Milwaukee, Yale Univ, Cornish Col Arts. *Work:* City of Seattle, various collections; Key Corp, Albany, NY; Howard Hughes Corp, Las Vegas, Nevada; Microsoft Corp & Federal Home Loan Bank, Seattle, Wash. *Comn:* Univ Hosp, Univ Wash; Seattle Arts Comn; Wash State Arts Comn; Virginia Mason Hosp. *Exhib:* Artquest 87, Sculpture, Art Inst Boston, 87; paintings, Davidson Galleries, Seattle, 88 & 91; New Art Forms, Chicago Expos, 88; Whatcom Mus Hist & Art, 89; Northwest Monotypes, Documents Northwest, Seattle Art Mus, 89; Bellevue Art Mus, Seattle, Wash, 91; Art Expo, Los Angeles, Calif, 91; Security Pac, Seattle, Wash, 91. *Teaching:* Fac, Cornish Inst Arts, Seattle, Wash, 88-90. *Awards:* Fel, Nat Endowment Arts, 87; Fel printmaking, Centrum Found, 88. *Bibliog:* Ron Glowen (auth), Four directions, Artweek, 5/21/86; Deloris Tarzan (auth), Artists Exhibition offers 'double' vision, Seattle Times, 4/27/86; Christopher Schnoor (auth), Contemporary art, citation & the past, Vision Mag, summer, 86; Helen Mershon (auth), Step inside, The Oregonian, 3/9/87. *Dealer:* Davidson Gallery Seattle WA; Peyton/Wright Gallery Sante Fe NM. *Mailing Add:* c/o Davidson Galleries 313 Occidental Ave S Seattle WA 98104

BARD, JOELLEN
PAINTER, SCULPTOR
b Brooklyn, NY, June 19, 42. *Study:* Syracuse Univ Art Sch, 59-62; Brooklyn Col, painting with Philip Pearlstein, MA, 67, adv cert, 87; Brooklyn Mus Art Sch, Max Beckman, scholar class, 70-73; Pratt Inst, Hon BFA. *Work:* Many pvt & corp collections. *Exhib:* Brooklyn Mus, 73 & 74; one-man shows, Brooklyn Mus Little Gallery, 73, Gallery 91, Brooklyn, 74-76 & Pleiades Gallery, New York, 75, 77, 79 & 82; Windows of Bergdorf Goodman NYC 89, Brooklyn Botanic Garden, 89. *Collections Arranged:* Tenth St Days--The Co-ops of the 50s. *Pos:* Dir, Asn Artist Run Galleries, 77- *Teaching:* Art teacher, New York Bd Educ, 64-69 & 78-, Kingsborough Community Col, 79-83 & 86- *Bibliog:* Eileen Blair (auth), Mindscapes, Phoenix, 3/21/75; David Shirey (auth), Artists forming sobro, NY Times, 3/75; Helen Thomas (auth), article in Arts Mag, 3/79. *Mem:* Asn Artist Run Galleries; Women in the Arts; Col Art Asn; Found for Community of Artists. *Media:* Acrylic on canvas; Plexiglas. *Dealer:* Pleiades Gallery 164 Mercer St New York NY 10012. *Mailing Add:* 1430 E 24th St Brooklyn NY 11210

BARDAZZI, PETER
PAINTER
b New York, NY, Mar 5, 43. *Study:* Pratt Inst, BFA, 67; Yale Univ, MFA, 69; also study art & archit, Asia. *Work:* Mus Mod Art, New York; Purchase Mus, NY; Corcoran Gallery, Washington, DC; Rockefeller Univ. *Exhib:* One-man shows, Cordier & Ekstrom Gallery, 71, 72, 74, 76 & 78 & St Mary's Col, Md, 75; Whitney Mus Am Art Painting Ann, 72; Indianapolis Mus Art Painting & Sculpture Today, 72; Am Acad Arts & Lett, 73; Cordier & Ekstrom, 76; Corcoran Gallery, 76; Univ Tex, Austin, 76. *Pos:* Guest lectr & artist in residence, St Mary's Col, Md, 75. *Awards:* Fed Work Study Prog Award, 68; Painting Award, New Britain Mus, Conn, 69. *Bibliog:* Hilton Kramer (auth), 10/74 & Vivian Raynor (auth), 5/78, articles, New York Times; Peter Frank (auth), article, Art News Mag, 10/78; and others. *Mailing Add:* 611 Broadway PO Box 60 Canal St Sta New York NY 10013

BARDIN, JESSE REDWIN
PAINTER
b Elloree, SC, Mar 27, 23. *Study:* Univ SC, AB & cert(painting); Art Students League, with Will Barnet & Harry Sternberg, Bernay Merit Scholar for advan study with Byron Browne & Vyclav Vytlaci. *Work:* Mint Mus, Charlotte, NC; Williams Col Art Mus, Williamstown, Mass; La State Univ, Baton Rouge, La; SC State Art Collection, Columbia Mus Art. *Comn:* Paintings in bus collections throughout the US. *Exhib:* Pa Acad Fine Arts Ann, Philadelphia; 50 Artists-50 States (with catalog), Am Fedn Arts, Burpee Mus, Ill & traveling; Art Patron Art, Southeastern Ctr Contemp Art, Winston-Salem, NC, 81; retrospective, Columbia Mus Art, 82 & Atlanta Arts Festival, 82; Portrait of the South Exhib, Venice Palace Mus, Rome, Italy, 84; Ctr Int D'Art Contemp, Paris, France, 85; plus numerous other int, nat & regional exhibs. *Awards:* First Prize, Springs Mill Art Exhib for NC & SC, 3 consecutive years, 61, 62 & 63; First Purchase Prize, Winners Then & Now, York Co Mus, SC, 90; 40th Anniversary SC Artists, State Mus, 90. *Bibliog:* Nina Parris, PhD (auth), Retrospective, 82; New York Art Review, 88. *Mem:* Life mem Art Students League, NY. *Media:* Acrylic, Oil; Mixed Media. *Mailing Add:* 1723 Devine St Columbia SC 29201

BAREISS, PHILIP C
ART DEALER, COLLECTOR
b New York, NY, Oct 5, 49. *Study:* Yale Univ Grad Sch, MA, 73. *Collections Arranged:* Hermann Nitsch: Das Orgies Mysteries Theatre. *Pos:* Owner, Phillip Bareiss Contemp Exhibs. *Specialty:* Contemporary Artists; photography, painting, sculpture. *Collection:* Contemporary graphics, paintings and southwest art. *Mailing Add:* Philip Bareiss Contemporary Exhibitions Ski Valley Rd Box 2739 Taos NM 87571

BAREISS, WALTER
PATRON
b Tubingen, Ger, May 24, 19. *Study:* Yale Univ, BS; Columbia Law Sch. *Work:* Yale; Mus Mod Art; Metrop, New York; Toledo, Ohio Mus Fine Arts; Bavarian State Mus; 20th century art, Yale. *Exhib:* Greek vases, Getty Mus; Greek vases, Metrop Mus. *Pos:* Chmn gov bd, Art Gallery, Yale Univ; comt for prints & illus bks, Mus Mod Art; vis comt 20th century art, Metrop Mus, New York. *Mem:* Bavarian State Asn Contemp Art. *Collection:* Twentieth century art; Greek vases, fifth & sixth centuries, BC; African art 19th & 20th century; contemporary Japanese ceramics; Italian 15th & 16th century ceramics. *Mailing Add:* 60 E 42nd St New York NY 10165

BARKER, AL C
PAINTER, PRINTMAKER
b West Patterson, NJ, June 19, 41. *Study:* WVa Univ, BS, 64; Univ RI, MS, 67; Rutgers Univ, 69-70. *Work:* Sportman's Edge Ltd, New York; Easton Waterfowl, Md; Chesapeake Maritime Mus, Md; NJ Bell Tel; Coun Arts, Easton, Md. *Comn:* NH Ducks Unlimited, 79 & 80; Theodore Gordon Flyfishers, New York, 81-83, 90 & 92; Am Hotel, Freehold, NJ, 81; First Nat State Bank, Newark, NJ, 81; NJ State Ducks Unlimited, Monmouth, 81-92. *Exhib:* Easton Waterfowl Festival, Md, 70-91; Philadelphia Waterfowl Expos, Mem Hall, 79-81 & 83; Safari Club Int, Am Fac Dallas-Ft Worth Airport, Tex, 80; Tulsa Wildlife Expos, Okla, 80 & 84; Southeastern Wildlife Expos, Charleston, SC, 82-86. *Pos:* Instr painting, Montclair Art Mus, NJ, 91. *Teaching:* Instr forestry, wildlife, Essec Agr Inst, Danvers, Mass, 67-69; instr, Univ RI, Kingston, 67 & NJ State Conserv Sch, Branchville, 69; instr biology, Hightstown High Sch, NJ, 71-78. *Awards:* Whisky Painters Am, Akron, Ohio, 86; Best in Show, Fels Point Nat, Md, 91; SCNY Award & Greata Kempton, Salmagundi Club, New York, 92. *Mem:* Salmagundi Club, New York (bd dir 78-81); Miniature Artists Am; Whisky Painters Am; Miniature Art Socs, NJ, Fla, Wash, DC; Artist Fel. *Media:* Watercolor, Oil; Graphics. *Publ:* Illusr, Deer Hunting, 82, The Grizzly Book, 82, The Bear Book, 83, Trout Book, 84 & North Light, 85. *Mailing Add:* 224 Prince St PO Box 703 Bordentown NJ 08505

BARKER, WALTER WILLIAM, JR
PAINTER, WRITER
b Coblenz, Ger, Aug 8, 21; US citizen. *Study:* Washington Univ, BFA, 48, with Horst Janson, Phillip Guston & Max Beckmann; Iowa Univ, with Mauricio Lassansky; Univ Ind, with Alton Pickens & Henry Hope, MFA, 50. *Work:* Mus Mod Art & Brooklyn Mus, New York; Hirshhorn Collection,

Washington, DC; Boston Mus Fine Arts; James Michener Collection, Univ Tex, Austin; and others. *Exhib:* Int Exhib Mod Graphic Art, Mus Mod Art, New York, 52; American Painting, Va Mus Fine Art, Richmond, 62; Painting & Sculpture Today, Herron Inst Art, Indianapolis, Ind, 67; Univ Tex, Austin; Weatherspoon Gallery; James A Michener Collection, Univ Tex, Austin, 75; Univ NC, Greensboro, 77; Joseph Pulitzer Jr Collection. *Pos:* Spec corresp, St Louis Post-Dispatch, 62-78. *Teaching:* Lectr art hist, Salem Col, 49-50; instr painting, Washington Univ, 50-62; instr basic found, Brooklyn Mus Sch, 63-66; assoc prof painting, Univ NC, 66-85; prof painting, Univ NC, 85-92, prof emer, 92. *Awards:* New Talent USA Award, 56; Spec Citation Art Rev, Col Art Asn Am, 66; Distinguished Alumnus, Washington Univ, 72. *Bibliog:* Ernest Smith (auth), Walter Barker, 1958-1968, Webster Col, 68; Joseph Pulitzer, Jr (auth), Walter Barker, Fogg Mus Art, Harvard Univ, 71; Patricia Krebs (auth), On the making of an artist, Greensboro Daily News, 77. *Mem:* Max Beckmann Gesellschaft, Munich, Ger; and others. *Media:* All. *Res:* Max Beckmann's last years in the US. *Publ:* Auth introd, Max Beckmann in America (catalog), Viviano Gallery, 69; auth, Lucian Krokowski & Max Beckmann, Joseph Pulitzer Collection, Vol 3, 71; auth, Max Beckmann's advice to his students, Weatherspoon Gallery Asn Bulletin, Univ NC, 79; auth, Max Beckmann as a Teacher (exhib catalog), Prestel-Verlag, Munich, 84. *Dealer:* Peter Wallach Gallery St Louis MO. *Mailing Add:* Dept Art Univ NC Greensboro NC 27412

BARKUS, MARIONA MARCIA
PAINTER
b Harvey, Ill, Mar 26, 48. *Study:* Art Inst Chicago, Ill, 66; Northwestern Univ, Evanston, Ill, BA, 70; Univ Calif, Los Angeles, 72; Pepperdine Univ, 74. *Work:* Freeport Art Mus, Ill; KKBR, Radio, Los Angeles, Calif; Calif Inst Arts Libr; Mus Mod Art Libr, NY; Newport Harbor Art Mus. *Exhib:* Solo exhibs, Founders Gallery, Knox Col, Ill, 79, Freeport Art Mus, Ill, 80, Eastern Wash Univ, 86, Southern Oregon State Col, 89, Univ Calif Berkeley Extension, San Francisco, 91 & SUSHI, San Diego, 91; Wichita Art Asn, 90; Arvada Ctr for Art & Humanities, Colo, 90; Color & Spirit Pierce Col, Los Angeles, 91; Themes: Social & Political, Mount St Mary's Col, Los Angeles, 91; Sazama Gallery, Chicago, 92; and many others. *Pos:* Coordr, Open Wall Gallery, Woman's Bldg, Los Angeles, 79-80. *Awards:* Inserts, New York State Coun Arts, Woodstock Times, 90; Earth Banner, Fullerton Mus, Fullerton Cultural & Fine Arts Div, Calif, 91; Individual Artist's Grant, Los Angeles Cult Affairs Dept, 91. *Bibliog:* Paul Von Blum (auth), Women political artists in Los Angeles: Kim Abeles, Barbara Carrasco & Mariona Barkus, Z Mag, 2/92; Nancy Kapitanoff (auth), Students communicate in English, art, Los Angeles Times, 2/2/92; Victoria Martin (auth), Where humans tread, Artweek, 2/28/92, and others. *Mem:* Womens Caucus Art; Artists Equity. *Media:* Acrylic; Color Xerox, Collage. *Publ:* Auth, Illustrated History-1982, 83, 84, 85, 86, 87 & 88, Litkus Press; Visual Satire (catalog), Fla State Univ; Of Nature & Nation (catalog), Security Pacific, Los Angeles, 90; Multiples (catalog), Chastain Gallery & Nexus Ctr Contemp Art, Atlanta, 90. *Mailing Add:* 11944 Culver Dr Culver City CA 90230

BARLOW, DEBORAH LYNN
LIBRARIAN
b Cooperstown, NY, Dec 14, 58. *Study:* Univ San Diego, BA, 81; Simmons Col Grad Sch Libr & Info Sci, MS, 84; Boston Univ Grad Sch Arts Sci, MA, 85. *Pos:* Visual resources librn, Cooper Union Libr, 85-87; art librn, asst prof & cur, Queens Col, 87-90; reference librn, Univ S Calif, Archit Fine Arts Libr, 90- *Mem:* Art Libraries Soc NA. *Interests:* Seventeenth-twentieth century western art, general western art & American art. *Publ:* Hendrick Goltzius and the Classical Tradition, Univ SCalif, Fisher Gallery, 92. *Mailing Add:* Univ Southern Calif Archit & Fine Arts Libr Univ Park CA 90089

BARNARD, ROB(ERT E)
CERAMIST, CRITIC
b Lexington, Ky, Dec 16, 49. *Study:* Univ Ky, Lexington, 71-74; Kyoto Univ Fine Arts, Japan, 74-77. *Work:* Renwick Gallery, Washington, DC; Everson Mus, Syracuse, NY; Dickerson Col, Carlisle, Pa; Millersville Univ, Pa. *Exhib:* New Faces/Japan, British Embassy, Tokyo, Japan, 78; Continuity Exchange, Southern Alleghenie Mus Art, Loretto, Pa, 82; Fragile Blossoms, Enduring Earth, Everson Mus, Syracuse, NY, 89; Spirit Material, McLean Project Arts, McLean, Va, 90; Revolving Techniques, James Michner Mus, Doylestown, Pa, 92. *Pos:* ceramics ed, New Art Examiner, 86- *Awards:* Craftsmen's Fel, 78 & Visual Arts Fel, 90, Nat Endowments Arts. *Bibliog:* Jane Adams Allen (auth), Master potter, Washington Times, 87; Michael Welzenbach (auth), Rob Barnard, potter, American Ceramics, 87; Janet Koplos (auth), Rob Barnard, Ichi no Ichi/Mainichi Daily News, Tokyo, 92. *Media:* Clay. *Dealer:* Gail Enns-Anton Gallery 2108 "R" St NW Washington DC 20016. *Mailing Add:* Rte 2, Box 362 Timberville VA 22853

BARNES, CAROLE D
PAINTER
b Bellefonte, Pa, Nov 12, 35. *Study:* Pa State Univ, BA(art ed), 57; also with Edward Betts, Glenn Bradshaw & Alex Nepote. *Work:* IBM, Austin, Tex; Utah State Univ, Logan; United Banks & Midland Savings, Colo. *Exhib:* Rocky Mountain Nat Watermedia Soc, Golden, Colo, 78, 80, 82-84, 86, 87, 89-92; Am Watercolor Soc, New York, 75-78, 83, 86, 89 & 91; Nat Acad Design Ann, New York, 76, 78, 81, 82, 84, 86 & 92; Allied Artists Ann, New York, 76, 77, 81, 83, 85 & 87; Nat Watercolor Soc, Los Angeles, 77, 78, 80, 82, 84 & 87. *Teaching:* Instr, Watercolor Workshops, numerous cities across the US; juror, Nat Watercolor Soc & Am Watercolor Soc. *Awards:* Over 30 Nat Award incl: Ralph Fabri Medal Honor, Nat Soc Painters Casein & Acrylic, 80; Gold Medal, San Diego Nat, Calif, 82; Ford Times Award, Am Watercolor Soc, New York, 83. *Bibliog:* Maxine Masterfield (auth), Painting Spirit of Nature; Marilyn Hughey Phillis (auth), Watercolor Techniques for Releasing the Creative Spirit; Greg Albert (auth), Splash; and others. *Mem:* Am Watercolor Soc; Allied Artists; Nat Watercolor Soc; Nat Soc Painters Casein & Acrylic; Rocky Mountain Nat Watermedia Soc; Audubon Artists. *Media:* Watercolor, Acrylic. *Mailing Add:* 3772 Lakebriar Dr Boulder CO 80304

BARNES, CLIFF (CLIFFORD V)
PAINTER, ILLUSTRATOR
b Bell, Calif, Mar 19, 40. *Study:* Art Ctr Sch Design, Los Angeles, BFA, 62. *Work:* San Bernardino County Govt Ctr, Redlands, Calif, 84-88; Gilcrease Mus, Tulsa, Okla, 85; Crosbyton Co Mus, Tex, 88; Pomona Fairgrounds, Calif, 88; Festival Western Art, San Dimas, Calif, 92. *Comn:* Two paintings, San Bernardino Co Govt Ctr, 84; Protrait of Frederic Renner, City of San Dimas, 85. *Exhib:* San Bernardino Co Mus, Redlands, Calif, 88 & 92; Wildlife West Show, San Bernardino Co Mus, Redlands, 86-88; American Indian & Cowboy Artists, San Dimas Mus, Calif, 80-92; Nat Western Artists, Lubbock, Tex, 86-88; Watercolor West, Riverside, Calif, 86-92; Cliff Barnes, Western Am Art, Los Angeles Co Fair, Pamona, Calif, 87. *Pos:* Cur, juror & demonstr, San Bernardino County Mus, Redlands, Calif, 86-88 & 92. *Teaching:* Sem & workshop, Rocky Mountain Nat Park, 90. *Awards:* City of Paramount Best of Show, 85; Nat Western Artists Golden Spur in Drawing, 88; Eagle Feather Aeard, 86; Two gold medals, Am Indian & Cowboy Aritsts, 88. *Bibliog:* Profiling Cliff Barnes, Inland Empire Mag, 10/84. *Mem:* Am Indian & Cowboy Artists (pres, 81-82, bd mem, 82-91); Nat Western Artists, 85-86; Fine Arts Inst (vpres, 87-91); Watercolor West, 86-88; Am Indian & Cowboy Artists, 81-92; Watercolor West, 87-92; Fine Arts, 85-92. *Media:* Oil, Watercolor; Charcoal. *Publ:* Illusr, Palette Pleasers Cookbook, City of San Dimas, 84; Contemporary Western Artists, 81. *Mailing Add:* PO Box 741 Lake Arrowhead CA 92352

BARNES, CURT (CURTIS EDWARD)
PAINTER, INSTRUCTOR
b Taft, Calif, Jan 17, 43. *Study:* Univ Calif, Berkeley, BA, 64; Pratt Inst, MFA, 66. *Work:* Mus Contemp Art, Bogota, Columbia; Prudential Insurance Corp Am, Newark, NJ; Franklin Furnace Arch, New York. *Exhib:* Chicago Ann, Art Inst of Chicago, 67; Salon Exhib, O K Harris Gallery, New York, 70, 72, 79, 85 & 88; Contemporary Reflections, Aldrich Mus Contemp Art, Ridgefield, Conn, 75; one-man show, Allesandra Gallery, New York, 76; Whanki Found Exhib, Centre Nat Des Arts Plastiques, Paris, 87; Terry Dintenfass Gallery, New York, 89; Gray Gallery, East Carolina Univ, Greenville, NC, 90; Physicality Hunter Col Art Gallery, New York, 91. *Pos:* Guest ed, Col Art Asn, Art Journal, spring 91. *Teaching:* Instr painting & drawing, Univ Wis, Stevens Point, 66-67; instr drawing, Parsons Sch Design, New York, 67-71; assoc prof painting, drawing & 20th century art hist, Fordham Univ, 69-84; vis assoc prof, Hampshire Col, 79-80 & 84-86; vis adj prof, Pratt Institute, 81; lect art, Princeton Univ, 91. *Awards:* Yaddo Fel, summer 76 & 88. *Bibliog:* John Perreault (auth), Catching up, Soho Weekly News, 3/76; Nancy Grove (auth), Curt Barnes (rev), Arts Mag, 4/76; Joseph Wiltsee (auth), Investing in young artists, Bus Wk, 5/76. *Mem:* Col Art Asn, 90. *Media:* Acrylic, Oil. *Publ:* Auth, Table of Contents Allesandra Publ, 76. *Mailing Add:* 114 W Houston St New York NY 10012

BARNES, EDWARD LARRABEE
ARCHITECT
b Chicago, Ill, Apr 22, 15. *Study:* Harvard Univ, BS(cum laude), 38; Harvard Grad Sch Design, MArchit, 42, RI Sch Design, Hon Dr Fine Arts, 83. *Comn:* Walker Art Ctr, T B Walker Found, Minneapolis, 71; Sarah M Scaife Gallery, Carnegie Inst, Pittsburgh, 74; Asia Soc, New York, 81; Dallas Mus Art, City of Dallas, Tex, 83; Mus Art, Ft Lauderdale, Fla, 86. *Exhib:* Archit for Arts: State Univ NY Purchase Master Plan, Mus Mod Art, New York, 71; retrospective, Scaife Gallery, Carnegie Inst Mus Art, Pittsburgh, 74; New Am, Mus Archit, Whitney Mus, 82. *Pos:* Hon trustee, Haystack Mountain Sch Arts & Crafts, 80-, NY Studio Sch Painting & Sculpture, 76-; trustee, Mus Mod Art, 76- *Teaching:* Vis critic archit design, Yale Univ, New Haven, Conn, 57-64; vis critic archit design, Harvard Grad Sch Design, 79-80; vis comt, 78-; prof archit, Thomas Jefferson, Univ Va, 80. *Awards:* Fel, 66 & Honor Awards, 72, 77 & 86, Firm Award 80, Am Inst Archit; Award Hon for Art & Cult, Mayor of the City of New York, 82; Harvard Univ 350th Anniversary Medal, 86; and others. *Bibliog:* Hilton Kramer (auth), Grace, flexibility, esthetic tact, 7/71 & John Russell (auth), An American success story, 1/23/84 & Dallas christens its exemplary home grown museum, 1/29/84, New York Times; Helen Searing (auth) New American Art Museums, Whitney Mus Art Press, NY, 82. *Mem:* Academician Nat Acad Design; fel Am Acad Arts & Sci; Am Acad & Inst Arts & Letts. *Mailing Add:* 320 W 13th St New York NY 10014

BARNES, KITT
PAINTER
b Wilson, NC, June 24, 46. *Study:* Univ NC, Chapel Hill, BFA, 73, MFA, 75. *Work:* Ackland Mus; Sovereign Am Arts Corp; Fayetteville Arts Coun. *Exhib:* 37th Ann NC Artists Exhib, NC Mus Art, Raleigh, 74; Thesis Show, Ackland Mus, 75; Drawing Presentation of MFA Candidates, Corcoran Gallery, 75; The Glass Door: Artists Immigrant of Washington, Washington Proj Arts, 76; Biennial Exhib Piedmont Painting & Sculpture, Mint Mus, 79; solo exhib, PS1, Long Island City, NY, 79; Art on Paper, Weatherspoon Art Gallery, Greensboro, NC, 82; Chinese Chance 4th Ann Exhib, 1 Univ Pl, New York, 82-83; Born in North Carolina, Jerald Melberg Gallery, Charlotte, 86. *Bibliog:* Valentin Tatransky (auth), Group show, Arts Mag, 3/83. *Media:* Oil on Canvas and Paper. *Mailing Add:* PO Box 1244 Madison Sq Sta New York NY 10159

BARNES, MARGO
PAINTER
b New York, NY, Sept 3, 47. *Study:* Brooklyn Mus Art Sch, with Isaac Soyer; Boston Univ Sch Fine Arts, BFA, 69. *Exhib:* Solo exhibs, Benson Gallery, Bridgehampton, NY, 76, Meredith Long Contemp Gallery, New York, 78-79, A M Sachs Gallery, New York, 83, Capricorn Galleries, Washington, DC, 84 & Watermill Mus, NY, 85; Waterworks, Heckscher Mus, Huntington, NY, 85; Views of Reality, Starr Gallery, Newton, Mass, 85; 10 Year Retrospective (with catalog), Guild Hall Mus, East Hampton, NY, 86. *Teaching:* Pvt instruction in studio, New York, 75- *Awards:* Fulbright Grant, 72; Best in show, Guild Hall Mus Artists Mem Show, East Hampton, NY, 85. *Bibliog:* Gerrit Henry (auth), rev, Art News, 11/79; Nina French-Frazier (auth), rev, Art Int, 12/79; Amei Wallach (auth), Water, water everywhere, Newsday, 10/6/85. *Media:* Oil. *Mailing Add:* 346 East 78th Street New York NY 10021

BARNES, MOLLY
ART DEALER, WRITER
b London, Eng, May 18, 36; US citizen. *Study:* Univ Calif, Berkeley, BA, 57. *Pos:* Art critic, KFWB Radio, Los Angeles, 74-78; owner & dir, Anhalt-Barnes Gallery, 74-79; asst, Frank Perls Gallery, 78; writer, Hollywood Reporter, 78-; owner & dir, Molly Barnes Gallery, 79- *Specialty:* Contemporary Californians, Robert Cottingham, Don Eddy, John Baldessari & Jack Reilly. *Mailing Add:* Molly Barnes Gallery 474 S Rodeo Dr Beverly Hills CA 90212-4220

BARNES, ROBERT M
PAINTER, EDUCATOR
b Washington, DC, Sept 24, 34. *Study:* Art Inst Chicago, BFA, 56; Univ Chicago, BFA, 56; Columbia Univ, 56; Hunter Col, 57-61; Univ London Slade Sch, Fulbright Grant, 61-63. *Work:* Mus Mod Art, Whitney Mus Am Art, New York; Art Inst Chicago; Pasadena Art Mus, Calif. *Comn:* Ed lithographs, New York Hilton Hotel, 62. *Exhib:* Mus Civico, Bologna, 65; Galerie Dragon, Paris, 67; Univ Ill, 67; Kansas City Art Inst, 72; Galeria Fanta Spade, Rome, 72; and others. *Teaching:* Instr grad painting, Ind Univ, 60-61; vis artist, Kansas City Art Inst, 63-64; asst prof painting & drawing, Ind Univ, Bloomington, 65-70, prof, Dept Fine Arts, 70- *Awards:* Copley Found Award, 61. *Dealer:* Allan Frumkin Gallery 620 N Michigan Ave Chicago IL 60603. *Mailing Add:* 731 E University St Bloomington IN 47401

BARNES, WILLIAM DAVID
PAINTER, PRINTMAKER
b Chicago, Ill, Apr 13, 46. *Study:* Drake Univ, Des Moines, Iowa, BFA, 69; Univ Ariz, Tucson, MFA, 74. *Work:* Bowery Gallery, New York; Montgomery Mus, Ala; Lamar Dodd Art Ctr, Labrange, Ga; Portsmouth Art Ctr, Va; CSX Corp. *Exhib:* 30th Irene Leache Mem, Chrysler Mus Norfolk, Va, 90; Gabriel Laderman Selects, First St Gallery, New York, 91; Faculty Show, Muscarelle Mus, Williamsburg, Va, 91; solo show, Monotypes, Peninsula Fine Arts Ctr, Newport News, Va, 92; Paintings and Monotypes, Bowery Gallery, New York, 92; and others. *Teaching:* Instr painting, Univ Ariz, Tucson, 74-75; assoc prof painting, Col William & Mary, Williamsburg, 75- *Awards:* Best in Show, 17th Dixie Ann, Montgomery Mus, 76; Cert Distinction, Va Artists, Va Mus, 79; Best in Show, LaGrange Nat, Lamar Dodd Art Ctr, 86. *Mem:* Bowery Gallery, New York. *Media:* Oil Paint. *Mailing Add:* 716 Jamestown Rd Williamsburg VA 23185

BARNET, WILL
PAINTER, PRINTMAKER
b Beverly, Mass, May 25, 11. *Study:* Boston Mus Fine Arts Sch, with Phillip Hale, 27-30; Art Students League, with Charles Locke, 30-33. *Work:* Boston Mus Fine Arts; Whitney Mus Am Art; Metrop Mus Art; Guggenheim Mus; Cincinnati Art Mus; and others. *Exhib:* Inst Contemp Art, Boston; Mus Mod Art; Pa Acad Fine Arts, 70; retrospective, Assoc Am Artists, 72 & Portraits, Terry Dintenfass Gallery, New York, 82; one-man show, Hirschl & Adler Galleries Inc, 76 & 81; Will Barnet, 20 Years of Painting & Drawing, Neuberger Mus, Purchase, 79-80; Ringling Mus, Sarasota, Fla, 80; Wichita Art Mus, 83; Traveling Mus Retrospective, Currier Gallery Art, NH, 84, Huntsville Mus Art, Ala, 84, Minn Mus Art, St Paul, 84-85, Art Gallery Hamilton, Ont, 85 & Farnsworth Libr & Art Mus, Miami, 85. *Teaching:* Instr, Art Students League, 36-; Cooper Union Art Sch, 45-65, prof, 65-; Mont State Col, summer 51; vis critic, Yale Univ, 52 & 53; instr, Univ Ohio, Univ Minn, Duluth, 58 & Univ Wash, 63; Des Moines Art Ctr, Iowa, 65; distinguished vis prof, Pa State Univ, 65-66; instr, Pa Acad Fine Arts, 67-; vis prof, Cornell Univ, 68-69. *Awards:* Walter Lippincott Prize, Pa Acad Fine Arts, 68; Benjamin Altman Prize, 77, Proctor Portrait, 84 & Gladys Emerson Cooh Prize, 86, Nat Acad Design; Childe Hassam Award, Arts & Letters, 82. *Bibliog:* James T Farrell (auth), Paintings of Will Barnet, Press Eight, New York, 50; Robert Beverly Hale (auth), Will Barnet--27 Paintings Completed 1960-1968, New York, 68; Will Barnet Paintings, Abrams Publ, 84. *Mem:* Am Abstr Artists; Nat Acad Design; Century Asn; Royal Soc Arts, London; Am Acad & Inst Arts & Lett. *Publ:* Illusr, The World in a Frame, Brazilles Pub. *Dealer:* Terry Dutenfass Gallery 50 W 57 St New York NY. *Mailing Add:* 15 Gramercy Park New York NY 10003

BARNETT, DAVID J
ART DEALER, COLLECTOR
b Milwaukee, Wis, Feb 22, 46. *Study:* Lincoln Col; Univ Wis-Milwaukee. *Pos:* Owner, David Barnett Gallery, currently; pres, Van Go Frame & Art America's Gallery to You, currently. *Teaching:* Lecturer on art acquisition to professional organizations, private individuals and corporations. *Mem:* Milwaukee Art Mus; Chicago Art Inst; Milwaukee Pub Mus; Appraisers Asn Am; Prof Picture Framers Assoc. *Specialty:* Nineteenth and twentieth century European and American masters; leading Wisconsin artists; contemporary American artists; American historical prints; African & Indonesian Art. *Publ:* Art experts can save money and reputation for the wary dealer, Art Business News, 2/84. *Mailing Add:* David Barnett Gallery 1024 E State St Milwaukee WI 53202

BARNETT, EARL D
PAINTER, PORTRAITIST
b Trenton, Tenn. *Study:* Cleveland Sch Art, with Henry G Keller, Viktor Schreckengost, Willard Combes, Kenneth Bates & Frank Wilcox. *Work:* Butler Inst Am Art; Grover M Hermann Fine Arts Ctr, Marietta, Ohio; Dickinson State Univ, NDak. *Comn:* Six past pres portraits, Bd Dir Room, Benefit Trust Life Ins Co, Chicago, Ill, 64-70; portrait, Hon Robert Downing, Glenview, Ill, 67; 58 past pres portraits, Contracting Plasterers' & Lathers' Int Asn Union Hall, 67-88; portrait, Adm James Ross, Naval Armory, Chicago, 70; Robert Snediker, Chicago Printing, 86; Sam Davidson, pres of Dacor Corp, Northbrook, Ill, 87. *Exhib:* Cooperstown Art Asn, NY, 62-72; Allied Artists, New York, 64-73; Butler Inst Am Art, 65-82; Union League Club Ann, Chicago, 67, 68 & 72; Mainstreams, Marietta, 72, 73, 76 & 78; Tex Fine Arts Asn Ann, 73 & 79; Alamo Kiawanas Western Art Show, San Antonio, Tex, 82-85; Dakota 100/88, Montana Water Media, 88; Arts for the Parks Top 100/90, 200/91. *Pos:* Art dir, W L Stensgaard & Assocs, Chicago, 45-47; asst art dir & designer, Kling Studios, Chicago, 48-61; vpres & creative dir, J M Callan Co, Chicago, 61-67; vpres & creative dir, Conway Displays, Inc, Niles, Ill, 67-74; merchandise mgr, NCM Int, Arlington Heights, Ill, 74-79; creative dir, Chicago Show Print, Morton Grove, Ill, 79-88. *Awards:* First Place W/C, Tex Fine Arts Asn Ann, 79; Spec Mention, Butler Inst Am Art, 82; Purchase Award, Dakota 100/88, Dickson, NDak. *Mem:* Cowboy Hall of Fame, Oklahoma City, OK. *Media:* Oil, Watercolor. *Mailing Add:* 4150 Central Rd Glenview IL 60025

BARNETT, EMILY
PAINTER, INSTRUCTOR
b Brooklyn, NY, Oct 23, 47. *Study:* Queens Col, NY, BFA, 69, Louisiana State Univ, MFA, 76. *Work:* Nassau Community Col, NY; Fine Arts Mus Long Island, NY. *Exhib:* 33rd New England Exhib, Silvermine Ctr Arts, Conn, 82; Ann Long Island Exhib, Heckscher Mus, Huntington, NY, 81, 82, & 85; Nat Acad Design Ann Juried Exhib, NY, 81, 82 & 90; Ann juried exhib, Fine Arts Mus of Long Island, 88. *Pos:* Dir, Noho Gallery, NY, 86-87. *Teaching:* Instr, drawing color theory, Parsons Sch Design, New York, 80-; adj prof design, Dowling Col, Oakdale, NY, 87; instr drawing painting, Nassau Co Mus Art, 87-; adj prof, Suffolk Community Col, 92- *Awards:* Richardson-Vicks, Silvermine, New England Exhib, 82; Mem Award, Nat Asn Women Artists, 85; First Prize, Contemp Portraiture From Northeast, 87; Thomas B Clarke Prize, Nat Acad Design, 90. *Bibliog:* The Originals, WLIW-TV, 8-88; Emily Barnett's painting, Life and Art in the Studio (monogr), 88. *Mem:* Nat Asn Women Artists; Inter-Soc Color Coun. *Media:* Oil. *Dealer:* Portraits Inc 985 Park Ave New York NY 10028. *Mailing Add:* C/O NOHO 222 Carle Pl New York NY 11514

BARNETT, HELMUT
PAINTER, PRINTMAKER
b Stuttgart, Ger, Feb, 16, 46; US citizen. *Study:* Univ Tex, Austin, BFA(studio art) & BA, 73. *Comn:* Mixed media paintings on canvas, Shefelman & Nix, & IBM, Austin, Tex, 84, Am Security Life Insurance Co, San Antonio, 85, Houston Showroom, Hayworth Inc, 85 & Clann, Bell & Murphy, Houston, 85. *Exhib:* Soc Photogrs & Artist Reps National, Shreveport, La, 76; Western Asn Art Mus Traveling Exhib, 79; one-man show, Amdur Gallery, Austin, Tex, 84 & 86; II Ann Exhib, Art Mus S Tex, Corpus Christi, 83; Soho Invitational Show, Works on Paper, Austin, 85; 11th Int Independents Exhib of Prints, Kanagawa Prefectural Gallery, Japan, 85; New American Talent, Tex Fine Arts Asn, Laguna Gloria Art Mus, Austin, 86. *Media:* Acrylic, Pastel. *Dealer:* Martin/Rathburn Gallery The Blue Star San Antonio TX. *Mailing Add:* 908 Congress Ave Austin TX 78701

BARNETT, VIVIAN ENDICOTT
CURATOR, HISTORIAN
b Putnam, Conn, July 8, 44. *Study:* Vassar Col, AB, 65; Inst Fine Arts, NY Univ, MA, 71; Grad Ctr, City Univ New York. *Collections Arranged:* Kandinsky Watercolors from Solomon R Guggenheim Collection (auth, catalog), 81-82; Vasily Kandinsky (auth, catalog), Art Gallery NSW, 82; Kandinsky in Munich, 82, Kandinsky: Russian and Bauhaus Years, 83, Kandinsky in Paris, 85, Hans Reichel, 88, Guggenheim Mus Kandinsky Och Sverige, 89 (auth Oakly); Kandinsky Kleine Freuden (auth, catalog), 92. *Pos:* Res asst, Solomon R Guggenheim Mus, 73-77, curatorial asst, 78-79, assoc cur, 80-81, res cur, 81-82, cur, 82-91; dir, Roethel-Benjamin Archive, 91- *Awards:* John Simon Guggenheim Fel, 90. *Mem:* Col Art Asn Am; Am Asn Mus; Int Coun Mus. *Res:* Kandinsky; German Expressionism; Drawings. *Publ:* Jenseits des Bildes: Werke von Robert Barry, Sol LeWitt, Robert Mangold, Richard Tuttle aus der Sammlung Dorothy und Herbert Vogel, Kunsthalle Bielefeld, 5-7/87; Kandinsky and Sweden, 89; New Perspectives on Kandinsky, 90; Kandinsky Watercolors: Catalogue Raisonne, Vol I 1900-1921, 92; The Russian Presence in the 1924 Venice Biennale, Russian Avant-Garde Art 1915-1932, 92; and others. *Mailing Add:* Solomon R Guggenheim Mus 1071 Fifth Ave New York NY 10128

BARNHILL, GEORGIA BRADY
CURATOR, HISTORIAN
b Mt Kisco, NY, Dec 8, 44. *Study:* Wellesley Col, BA(art hist), 66. *Pos:* Cur graphic arts, Am Antiqn Soc, Worcester, Mass, 69- *Awards:* Fel, First Pub

Humanities Inst, Mass Found Humanities & Pub Policy, 82; Bibliog Soc Am Fel, 86; Am Philos Soc Fel, 86, Huntington Lib, Fel 91; Maurice Rickards Award, Ephemera Soc Am, 87; Fel, Huntington Libr, 91; and others. *Mem:* Fitchburg Art Mus (pres, bd trustees, 91-); Am Hist Print Collectors Soc (vpres, currently); Archives Am Art; Colonial Soc Mass; New Eng Mus Asn; and others. *Res:* Eighteenth & nineteenth century American prints; American literary illustration. *Publ:* Coauth, Massachusetts Broadsides of the American Revolution, Univ Mass, 76; auth, Graphic arts: seventeenth-nineteenth century, Arts Am, 79; Aspects of American book illustration: technology, natural science and literature, Imprint, Vol 5, No 2, autumn 80; Vignettes of the Past: American historical broadsides through the war of 1812, Printing Hist, Vol IV, No 7-8; ed, Prints of New England, Am Antiqn Soc, 91; and others. *Mailing Add:* Am Antiqn Soc 185 Salisbury St Worcester MA 01609

BARNWELL, JOHN L
PAINTER
b Los Angeles, Calif, Mar 17, 22. *Study:* Univ Calif, Berkeley, BA; Newark Sch Fine & Indust Art, NJ; Art Students League, with Frank Reilly; watercolor with Ed Whilney & Ferdinand Petrie. *Work:* Blue Cross, Blue Shield, Rochester, NY. *Exhib:* Am Artists Prof League Grand Nat Show, New York, 72-75 & 86; Jersey City Mus, NJ, 77; Bergen Community Mus, NJ, 77; NJ Watercolor Soc Show, 84, 87, 88 & 89; one-man show, Hamilton, Mass, 87, Bloomfield, NJ 90. *Awards:* Purchase Award, Hudson Artists State Show, 79; Best Watercolor, 83, Winsor & Newton Award, 90, Miniature Art Soc, NJ; Best Still Life, Am Artist Professional League, 83; Merit Award, NJ Watercolor Soc, 84; NJ Watercolor Soc Award, 88; Windsor & Newton Award, 90. *Mem:* Assoc NJ Watercolor Soc; fel Am Artists Prof League; Miniature Art Soc NJ (pres, 75-80); Art Students League. *Media:* Oil, Watercolor. *Dealer:* Essex Fine Art Gallery 13 S Fullerton St Montclair NJ; Art-on-the-Ave Verona NJ. *Mailing Add:* 11 Kingsland Rd Boonton NJ 07005

BARONS, RICHARD IRWIN
MUSEUM DIRECTOR, HISTORIAN
b Bergen, NY, Apr 25, 46. *Study:* State Univ NY Col, New Paltz, BA, 70. *Collections Arranged:* Eighteenth and Nineteenth Century American Folk Pottery (auth, catalog), State Univ NY Col, New Paltz, 68; The American Cooking Hearth: Colonial and Post-Colonial Cooking Tools (auth, catalog), Broome Co Hist Soc, 76; The Folk Arts and Crafts of the Susquehanna and Chenango River Valleys, Roberson Ctr Arts & Sci, 78; Multiples: American Printmaking of the Last Ten Years, 79; Emil Holzhauer: Seventy-Five Years of an Artist's Life (auth, catalog), 80. *Pos:* Cur, Genesee Co Mus, 70-74; cur hist, Roberson Ctr Arts & Sci, 74-79; Preservation dir, Bement-Billings House, Newark Valley NY, 83-89; dir, Preservation Asn of the Southern Tier, 86. *Teaching:* Instr art hist & archit, Broome Community Col, Binghamton, NY, 79- *Mem:* Am Asn Mus; Asn State & Local Hist; Soc Preserv Technol; Mus Am Folk Art; Nantucket Hist Soc. *Res:* Eighteenth and nineteenth century American arts, crafts and architecture. *Publ:* Coauth, Franck Taylor Bowers 1875-1932, 77 & auth, The Folk Tradition: The Early Arts and Crafts of the Susquehanna River Valley, 81, Roberson Ctr Arts & Sci; Our Homes, Our Shops: The Early 19th Century Architecture of the Susquehanna Region of New York, Bowers Corners Press, 86. *Mailing Add:* Ransom House Maine NY 13802

BAROOSHIAN, MARTIN
PAINTER, PRINTMAKER
b Chelsea, Mass, Dec 18, 29. *Study:* Boston Mus Fine Arts Sch, full tuition scholars, dipls with highest hons, 52 & 55; Albert H Whitin Traveling Fel, Europe, 52; Tufts Univ, BSEd, 53; Boston Univ, MA(art hist), 58; and with Gaston Dorfinant & S W Hayter, Paris. *Work:* Mus Mod Art & Metrop Mus Art, New York; Libr Cong, Washington, DC; Mus Mod Art, Yerevan, USSR; Montreal Art Mus; and others. *Exhib:* Boston Printmakers Traveling Exhibs; Soc Am Graphic Artists, New York; First Int Can Graphic Art Exhib, Montreal Mus Fine Art, 71; 1st & 2nd NH Int, 73 & 74; Retrospective, Art Complex Mus, Duxbury, Mass, 83; and others. *Pos:* Consult, Works on Paper, Swann Galleries, NY, 88-; fine arts consult, prints & drawings. *Teaching:* Instr printmaking workshops, Pratt Inst, New York, 60-69. *Awards:* Asian Studies Grant, US Dept Educ, 70; Print Prize, Nat Acad Design, 76; USSR Studies Grant, US Dept Educ, 79; and others. *Bibliog:* Helen Terzian (auth), Martin Barooshian, the changing face of art, Ararat, No 21, winter 65. *Mem:* Soc Am Graphic Artists (pres, 72-74); Long Island Printmakers Soc. *Dealer:* Martin Sumers Gallery 50 W 57th St New York NY 10019; Robert Royal Gallery 300 E 74th St New York NY 10021. *Mailing Add:* 17 West Dr Kings Park NY 11754-3814

BAROWITZ, ELLIOTT
PAINTER
b Westwood, NJ, Aug 22, 36. *Study:* Carnegie-Mellon Univ; RI Sch of Design, BFA; San Francisco Art Inst; Univ Cincinnati; Cincinnati Art Acad, MFA. *Work:* NJ State Mus, Trenton; Rose Mus, Brandeis Univ; Cincinnati Art Mus; Paterson Mus, NJ. *Exhib:* San Francisco Art Asn Mus, 61; Counterweight 3, 81, Blue Mountain Gallery, 83 & Ingber Gallery, 83 & 88, New York; Art Against Apartheid, New York, 84-85; Masters of War, AMMO, Brooklyn, NY, 85; NOPO, Portland, Maine, 86; South Bronx Fantasies, Fashion Moda, Bronx, NY, 87; Mayday Maidez, Tallahassee Gallery, Fla, 90; one-man retrospective, Patterson, NJ, 90; and others. *Pos:* Exec ed, Art & Artist, 80-,. *Teaching:* Prof painting & art theory, Drexel Univ, Philadelphia, 66-; instr painting & design, Portland Sch Art, Maine, summers 76-; adv in art & art hist, NY Univ. *Awards:* Grant, NY State Coun Arts. *Bibliog:* Articles, Arts Mag, 69, 80 & 84, Art in Am, 64, Art News 69 & Art in America, 88. *Mem:* Artists Tenants Asn; Found Community Artists (pres bd dirs, 78-79); US Comt-Int Asn of Art, Inc (vpres). *Media:* Oil, Photocopy Prints. *Publ:* Auth, The arts world: Who needs training, 79, auth & ed, The education of artists, 80, coauth, The critics' choice, 80 & auth, The polemics of realism, 82, Artworkers News; The bear and the eagle, 83 & The appropriateness of art to modern times, 86, Art and Artists; The Menace to Lofty Ideal, About Culture, NY Newsday, 86; rev, Leon Golub: Existential/Activist Painter by Donald Kuspit, Art & Artists, 86; and others. *Mailing Add:* 330 Lafayette St New York NY 10012

BARR, BURT
VIDEO ARTIST
b Lewiston, Maine, Nov 12, 38. *Study:* Boson Univ, BA; San Francisco Art Inst, MFA. *Exhib:* Solo show, Anthology Film Archives, New York. *Awards:* Nat Endowment Arts Award, 89; NY State Coun for Arts Award, 89; Contemp Art Television Award. *Publ:* Festivals (film), PBS, Toronto, Ont; The Women Next Door, 84; Trisha and Carmen, 88; The Dogs, 89; Aeros, 90. *Dealer:* Electronic Arts Intermix 536 Broadway New York NY 10012. *Mailing Add:* 541 Broadway New York NY 10012

BARR, DAVID JOHN
SCULPTOR, CONCEPTUAL ARTIST
b Detroit, Mich, Oct 10, 39. *Study:* Wayne State Univ, BFA & MA. *Work:* Detroit Inst Arts; Wayne State Univ Alumni Bldg; John Hancock Bldg; Portland Art Mus; AT&T; and others. *Comn:* nine-part outdoor sculpture, Macomb Col, Warren, Mich, 76; five wall reliefs, Detroit Renaissance Ctr, 77; Sunset Cube, Oakland Univ, Rochester, Mich, 81; Lakeview Square, Battle Creek, Mich, 83; Polaris Ring, Lansing, Mich, 88. *Exhib:* Evanston Art Ctr, 69; Chicago Contemporary, Herron Mus, Atlanta High Mus & Cranbrook Art Mus, 69; one-man shows, San Jose Mus, Calif, 78; and others. *Teaching:* Prof sculpture, Macomb Co Col, 64- *Awards:* Arts Found Mich, 77; Mich Found of the Arts Award, 77; Concerned Citizens Arts Award, 88. *Bibliog:* Time is No Object, Grace Productions, 85; Realities and Impressions, Brady Production, 88; Arctic Arc, Grace Productions, 88. *Media:* Masonite, Steel. *Publ:* Auth, Notes, 70; Notes III, 72; Structurist, 76; Notes on Celebration, 80; article, CoEvolution Quart, fall 81. *Dealer:* Richard Gray Gallery 620 N Michigan Ave Chicago IL 60611; Donald Morris Gallery Birmingham MI 48009. *Mailing Add:* 22600 Napier Novi MI 48374

BARR, NORMAN
PAINTER
b Melitopol, Russia, Mar 9, 08; US citizen. *Study:* Nat Acad Design. *Work:* Provincetown Heritage Mus, Mass; Mus City New York. *Comn:* Portraits. *Exhib:* Pepsi-Cola Nat Traveling Exhib, US, 43; Conn Acad Fine Arts, 53; Tupperware Nat Traveling Exhib, US, 56; Eastern States Expos & Mus Fine Arts, Springfield, Mass, 57; Art: USA, New York, 58; solo exhibs, Shore Studio Gallery, Boston, Mass, 54, Alexander Gallery, New York, 67, Stable Gallery, Scottsdale, Ariz, 71, Karlis Gallery, Provincetown, Mass, 79 & Susan Teller Gallery, New York, 89. *Pos:* Exec vpres NY chap, Artists Equity Asn, 46-50, mem nat exec comt, 48-50 & regional dir, 49-50; pres, New York Wash Proj for the Arts Artists, Inc, 77- *Teaching:* Parsons Sch Design, New York, 81-85. *Awards:* Honorable Mention, ACA Gallery & Artists Cong, 42; Grumbacher Award, Am Soc Contemp Artists, 57; Bocour Award, Am Soc Contemp Artists, 64. *Mem:* Am Soc Contemp Artists. *Media:* Oil on canvas, Acrylic on board. *Dealer:* Susan Teller Gallery, New York, NY. *Mailing Add:* 775 Riverside Dr New York NY 10032

BARR, ROGER
COLLAGE ARTIST, SCULPTOR
b Milwaukee, Wis, Sept 17, 21. *Study:* Pomona Col, BA, 47; Claremont Grad Sch, MFA, 49; Jepson Art Inst, 49-50; Catherwood Found Travel Fel, 56-57. *Work:* Hirshhorn Mus & Sculpture Garden, Washington, DC; Mus Fine Arts, Boston; Nat Mus of Art, Goteborg, Sweden; Nat Acad Design, New York; San Francisco Mus of Mod Art. *Comn:* Arch/Flight One, State Bldg, Redding, Calif, 85; sculpture, Calif First Bank, San Ramon, 86; Kaiser-Permanente Med Ctr, Calif, 89; Cent Corp Ctr, Riverside, Calif, 90; Catellus Develop Corp, Santa Fe Springs, Calif, 91. *Exhib:* Solo exhibs, Palo Alto Cultural Ctr, 81 & Victor Fischer Galleries, Oakland, Calif, 84; Fischer Galleries, San Francisco, Calif, 88; Gallery 30, Burlingame, Calif; and others. *Pos:* Founder & dir, Col Art Study Abroad, Paris, 57-69. *Teaching:* Instr, Univ Calif, Los Angeles, 50-52 & San Francisco Art Inst, 54-56; prof, Am Col, Paris, 61-68; prof art, Calif State Univ, Hayward, 69-70. *Awards:* Fel, Djerassi Found, 84; Finalist, Sculpture Competition, Loussac Mem Libr, Anchorage, Alaska, 85. *Bibliog:* Noel Barber (auth), 30,000 Painters of Paris, Holiday, 60; Why Paris, Design, 60; Abstract Painting From Kandinsky to the Present, M Seuphor Abrams, 61. *Mem:* Int Sculpture Ctr; Artists Equity Asn. *Media:* Stainless Steel, Bronze. *Mailing Add:* 920 McDonald Ave Santa Rosa CA 95404

BARRELL, BILL
PAINTER, COLLECTOR
b London, England, Dec 4, 32. *Work:* Crysler Mus, Norfolk, Va; Walker Art Inst; Dayton Mus Fine Art; Housatonic Mus Fine Art, Conn; Columbia Univ. *Exhib:* One-man shows, Dorsky Gallery, New York; Ingber Gallery, NY; Jupiter Gallery, NJ; Art Banque, Minniapolis, Minn; Jersey City Mus. *Pos:* Owner, Sun Gallery, Provincetown, 59-61. *Teaching:* Vis artist, La State Univ, fall 82. *Awards:* Harry Devlin Award, NJ State Coun Arts. *Bibliog:* Barry Barrell (dir), Fruits and Vegetables (film), Barrell Productions, 12/6/67; Peter Schjeldahl (auth), Bill Barrell hits the streets & George Preston (auth), The urbanscape as ideal still life, Potholes, 1/3/78. *Mem:* Orgn Independent Artists. *Media:* Oil-Base Paints; Mixed Media. *Collection:* Red Groom's wood sculpture, Oldenburg's paper collage, Bob Beauchamp's drawings, Mimi Gross Groom's watercolors, Bob Thompson's paintings and drawings and Gandy Brody's gouache. *Publ:* Potholes, Custombook Inc, 78. *Dealer:* Ingber Gallery 415 W Broadway New York NY 10012. *Mailing Add:* 71 Sussex St Jersey City NJ 07302

BARRERES, DOMINGO
PAINTER, EDUCATOR
b Oliva, Valencia, Spain, Feb 23, 41; US citizen. *Study:* Sch Mus Fine Arts, Boston. *Work:* Worcester Mus, Mass; Addison Gallery Am Art, Andover, Mass; Minneapolis Inst Fine Arts, Minn; Brockton Mus, Mass. *Exhib:* Whitney Biennial, Whitney Mus Am Art, New York, 75; solo exhib, Victoria Munroe Gallery, New York, 86; Abstract Visions, Mus Contemp Hispanic Art, New York, 87. *Teaching:* Instr painting, Sch Mus Fine Arts, Boston, 67- *Awards:* Clarissa Barlett Traveling Grant, Sch of the Mus of Fine Arts, Boston, 65; Mass Artists Fel Award, Artists Found 84 & 88. *Bibliog:* Kay Larson (auth), Art: Domingo Barreres, New York Mag, 10/86; Nancy Grimes (auth), Domingo Barreres at Victoria Monroe, Art News, 1/87. *Media:* Oil, Acrylic. *Dealer:* Victoria Munroe Gallery 115 W Broadway New York NY 10012. *Mailing Add:* 249 A St Boston MA 02210

BARRETT, BILL
SCULPTOR
b Los Angeles, Calif, Dec 21, 34. *Study:* Univ Mich, Ann Arbor, BS(design), 58, MS(design), 59, MFA, 60. *Work:* Cleveland Mus Art, Ohio; Aldrich Mus Contemp Art; Norfolk Mus Art, Va; Hakone Open Air Mus, Tokyo; Va Mus Fine Arts, Richmond, Va. *Comn:* Welded aluminum sculpture, Class of 42 for Univ Mich Dent Sch, 71; sculpture, Scottsdale Ctr for the Arts, Ariz, 79; sculpture, New Dorp Sch, New York, 82; 81 Main St, Schulman Realty Corp, White Plains, NY, 84; Charles B Goddard Ctr Arts, Ardmore, Okla, 86; sculpture, John Portman Corp, San Francisco, Calif. *Exhib:* Nat Art Inst Show, San Francisco Mus Art, 64; Whitney Mus Am Art Sculpture Ann, New York, 70; Storm King Art Ctr, NY, 75; Shidoni, Santa Fe, NMex, 82-83; Outdoor Sculpture Exhib, Bronx Psychiatric Ctr, NY, 82-83; Phoenix Botanical Gardens, Ariz, 82-83; Sid Deutsch Gallery, New York, 83; one-man show, Sculpture Ctr, New York, 83, Kouros Gallery, New York, 85, Bellvue Sculpture Garden, 85-86 & Roswitha Benkert Gallery, Zurich, Switz, 86 & 90, De Graaf Gallery, Chicago, 89, Shidoni, Santa Fe, NMex, 90. *Teaching:* Assoc prof sculpture, Eastern Mich Univ, 60-68; instr, Cleveland Art Inst, 63-64; asst prof, City Col New York, 69-76; lectr, Columbia Univ, 79-; vis artist, Univ Pa, Columbia Univ, & Vt Studio Sch. *Awards:* R S Reynolds Mem Award For Sculpture, 86; Hakone Open Air Mus Award, Japan. *Bibliog:* Michael Bronson (auth), articles, NY Times, 7/19/85 & 5/24/88; Mac McCloud (auth), The Santa Fean, New Mexican, 10/19/90. *Mem:* Sculptors Guild New York (pres, formerly); Audubon Artists, NY; Int Sculpture Ctr, Washington, DC. *Media:* Bronze. *Mailing Add:* 11 Worth St New York NY 10013

BARRETT, LENI MANCUSO See Mancuso, Leni

BARRETT, THOMAS R
PAINTER, INSTRUCTOR
b Woodhaven, NY, Feb 17, 27. *Study:* Wesleyan Univ, BA; Brooklyn Mus Art Sch; Univ NH, MA. *Work:* DeCordova & Dana Mus, Lincoln, Mass; Portland Art Mus, Maine; Phillips Exeter Acad, Exeter, NH; Farnsworth Mus, Rockland, Maine; Kresge Collection, Detroit; NH State Art Bank. *Comn:* Chamber Commerce, Manchester, NH, 88. *Exhib:* Currier Gallery Art, 74-87; Univ Maine, Orono, 77; Maine Coast Artists, Rockport, 78-79; Lamont Gallery, Exeter, NH, 79; Deer Isle Art Asn, Maine; Manchester Inst Art & Sci, NH, 86; Art Ctr in Hargate, St Paul's Sch, 86, 87; and others. *Pos:* Pres, NH Visual Arts Coalition, 79-81; pres, Independent Sch Art Inst Asn, 77-80; adv bd visual arts, New England Found Arts, 82-85; dir, Art Ctr-Hargate, St Pauls Sch, Concord, 69-89. *Teaching:* Instr painting & art hist & head art dept, St Paul's Sch, Concord, NH; retired. *Awards:* Currier Gallery Art Award, 60 & 62; City of Manchester Award, NH, 65; DeKalb Award, 72. *Bibliog:* Thomas Barrett at Manchester Inst, Art/New England, 4/86. *Mem:* NH Art Asn (pres, 68-69); Asn Am Mus; Col Art Asn; Deer Isle Artists Asn; Union Maine Visual Artists. *Media:* All. *Publ:* Masterworks of New England Artists, Art/New England, 5/82; William Maxwell at Lamont Gallery, Art/New England, 3/87; Cabot Lyford Retrospective, Art/New England, 4/88. *Dealer:* Arnold Klein Gallery 4520 N Woodward Royal Oak MI 48072; Gallery Le Va-Tout Waldoboro, ME. *Mailing Add:* PO Box 303 Castine ME 04421-0303

BARRETT, WILLIAM O
ADMINISTRATOR
b Hartford, Conn, Sept 1, 45. *Study:* RI Sch Design, BFA, 67; New York Univ, MA, 78. *Pos:* Asst Dean, Parsons Sch Design, 79-81; dean, Corcoran Sch Art, Washington, DC, 81-87; pres, San Francisco Art Inst, 87- *Mem:* Asn Independent Col Art & Design (bd dir); Nat Asn Schs Art & Design (pres). *Mailing Add:* San Francisco Art Inst 800 Chestnut St San Francisco CA 94133

BARRIE, DENNIS RAY
MUSEUM DIRECTOR, HISTORIAN
b Cleveland, Ohio, July 9, 47. *Study:* Oberlin Col, MA, 70; Wayne State Univ, PhD, 83. *Exhib:* Body & Soul: Recent Figurative Sculpture, 85; Jenny Holzer & Cindy Sherman: Personae, 86; New Art of Italy: Chia, Clemente, Cucchi, Paladino, 86; The Ties That Bind: Folk Art in Contemp Am Cult, 87; Standing Ground: Sculpture by Am Women, 87. *Collections Arranged:* The New British Painting, 88; Drawings Jim Dine, 1973-87, 88; Mike & Doug Starn: The Starn Twins, 90; The Continuous Presence of Organic Archit, 91; Mechanika, New Kinetic Sculpture, 91. *Pos:* Midwest regional dir & contrib ed Jour, Arch Am Art, Smithsonian Inst, Detroit, 72-83; dir, Contemp Arts Ctr, Cincinnati, 83-92. *Bibliog:* Peter Plagens (auth), Mixed signals on obscenity, Newsweek, 10/15/90; Jayne Merkel (auth), Art on Trial, Art in Am, 12/90; James R Petersen (auth), Showdown in Cincinnati, Playboy, 3/91. *Mem:* Col Art Asn; Am Asn Mus; Asn Art Mus Dir. *Res:* American 20th century art. *Publ:* Auth, The school years 1926-1976, In: Arts and Crafts in Detroit 1906-1970, The Movement, The Society, The School, Detroit Inst Arts, 76; auth & producer TV docs, Artists in Residence--Portraits of Five Ohio Artists, 80, Artists in America--Portraits of Roger Brown, Richard Hunt, John Hegarty and Marshall Fredericks, 83 & Celebration: The Four Corners--Project of David Barr, 83, Smithsonian Inst; auth, Artists in Michigan in the 20th Century, Wayne State Univ Press, 88. *Mailing Add:* Contemp Arts Ctr 115 E Fifth St Cincinnati OH 45202

BARRIO, RAYMOND
WRITER, PRINTMAKER
b West Orange, NJ, 1921. *Study:* Univ Calif, Berkeley, BA, 47; Art Ctr Col Design, Calif, BPA, 52. *Work:* Boston Printmakers; Philadelphia Color Print Soc. *Comn:* Print ed, Collectors Am Art, New York, 59 & 60. *Exhib:* Oakland Art Mus, Calif, 55-60; San Francisco Mus Art, 56-58; Am Color Print Soc, Philadelphia, 56-60; Boston Printmakers, 56-60; Los Angeles Co Mus, 56-60; plus over 60 nat exhibs. *Teaching:* Instr painting & drawing, var Calif cols, 61-75; instr Chicano art & literature, Sonoma State Univ, 85- *Awards:* Philadelphia Color Print Soc, 57; Boston Printmakers, 59; San Francisco Mus Art, 66. *Bibliog:* Zev Pressman (dir), Wet paint (film), 70; Graphics Group, Calif graphics-1974, Arcadia, Calif, 74; Biog essay, Contemp Authors, Gale/Detroit, 92. *Media:* Acrylic. *Publ:* Auth, Prism, 68, Art: Seen, 68, Selections from Walden, 69, Mexico's Art, 75 & Devil's Apple Corps, 76, Ventura Press. *Mailing Add:* Ventura Press PO Box 1076 Guerneville CA 95446

BARRIO-GARAY, JOSE LUIS
ART ADMINISTRATOR, ART HISTORIAN
b Zaragoza, Spain, Mar 17, 32. *Study:* Univ Madrid, Professorship(design); Columbia Univ, PhD(art hist); studied with Enrique Lafuente Ferrari, George Collins, Theodore Reff & Meyer Schapiro. *Pos:* Consult, Choice, 68-; foreign corresp in US & Can, Goya, Madrid, 72-; ed-in-chief, Newsletter, Am Soc Hispanic Art Hist Studies, 78-80, gen secy, 80-82. *Teaching:* Asst prof art hist & design, Univ Southern Miss, Hattiesburg, 62-65; preceptor art hist, Columbia Univ, 66-67; asst prof art hist, Univ Wis-Milwaukee, 67-73; dir & assoc prof art hist & criticism, Sch Art, Ohio Univ, Athens, 73-76; prof art hist & criticism & chmn, Dept Visual Arts, Univ Western Ont, London, 76- *Awards:* Var Fels & Grants. *Mem:* Col Art Asn Am; Univs Art Asn of Can; Am Asn Univ Prof; Can Asn of Univ Teachers; corresp mem Hispanic Soc Am; bd mem, Containers of Mind Found, New York. *Res:* Nineteenth and twentieth century European and American art history and criticism; history of Spanish art and architecture. *Publ:* Auth, Newton Harrison's fourth lagoon: Strategy against entropy, Arts, 11/74; Jose Gutierrez Solana: Paintings and Writings, 75; George Segal: Environments, New Lugano Rev, No 10, 76; Intention, object and signification in the work of Tapies, In: Antoni Tapies: Thirty-Three Years of His Work (exhib catalogue), Albright-Knox Art Gallery, 77; Antropofagia y hematofagia en la iconografica de Goya In: Nuevas Visiones, Madrid, 87. *Mailing Add:* Dept Visual Arts Univ Western Ont London ON N6A 5B9 Canada

BARRIOS, BENNY PEREZ
PAINTER, ART DEALER
b Bisbee, Ariz, Mar 20, 25. *Study:* Sacramento City Col, AA, 48; Chouinard Art Inst, 53; Calif State Univ, Sacramento, BA, 74. *Work:* Crocker Art Gallery, Sacramento; Oakland Art Mus, Calif; Smithsonian Inst, Washington, DC. *Exhib:* One-man shows, Los Angeles Co Mus, 52, San Francisco Mus, 52, De Young Mus, 52, Oakland Mus, 52 & Crocker Art Gallery, 53 & 63; 1st, 2nd & 3rd Invitational, Calif Palace Legion Hon, San Francisco, 56-58; Butler Inst Am Art, Youngstown, Ohio, 58; Gov Brown Invitational Chicano Art Exhib, Sacramento, 75. *Pos:* Owner, Barrios Gallery, Sacramento, 59- *Teaching:* Instr oils & acrylics, San Juan Unified Sch Dist, Sacramento, 62-77, Sacramento Unified Sch Dist, 68-77 & Sacramento City Col, 77-82. *Awards:* Second in Watercolor, Laguna Art Festival, 56; First in Oil, Northern Calif Arts, 58; Second in Oil, Auburn Art Festival, 62. *Bibliog:* Alfred Frankenstein (auth), Wetbacks, San Francisco Chronicle, 54; Charles Johnson (auth), Farm workers plight inspires artist, Sacramento Bee, 75; Peter Moore (auth), Lynton Kistler: The happy printer, Art News, 78. *Media:* Acrylic, Watercolor. *Specialty:* All medias; contemporary artists. *Mailing Add:* 4220 Watkins Dr Fair Oaks CA 95628

BARRON, ROS
PAINTER, VIDEO ARTIST
b Boston, Mass, July 4, 33. *Study:* Mass Col Art, BFA; and with Carl Nelson; Bunting Inst, Harvard Univ, fel, 66-68. *Work:* Addison Gallery Am Art, Andover, Mass; Worcester Art Mus; Dartmouth Col Collection; Harvard Univ; Boston Mus Fine Arts; and others. *Comn:* Seasons (wall painting), YMCA, Roxbury, Mass, 65; Rainbow, Rocket, Road (wall painting), Lawrence Sch, Brookline, Mass, 67; polarized light painting, comn by SDI, San Francisco, 69; ser wall paintings for Community Ctr, Wilmington, Del, 70; and others. *Exhib:* Whitney Ann Am Painting, Salon, 71-72; Surreal Image, De Cordova Mus; UNESCO Art in Architecture, Rotterdam, Holland; American Painting & Sculpture, US Info Agency Exhib, Europe; Montevideo Gallery, Holland, 78; Carnegie Inst, 78; Mus Mod Art, New York, 80; and many others. *Pos:* Dir, Zone, Visual Theater, currently. *Teaching:* Assoc prof, Univ Mass, Boston, formerly; vis artist, Univ Colo, Boulder, 83, and others. *Awards:* Guggenheim Found Award for Zone's Yellow Sound, 72; Rockefeller Found Grants, 77-79; Nat Endowment Arts Individual Fel, 75-76; Mass Coun Individual Art Fel in Video, 80-81; and others. *Bibliog:* Frames of reference: Ros Barron (film), co-produced by WGBH Educ Found, 80. *Mailing Add:* 30 Webster Pl Brookline MA 02146

BARRON, THOMAS
PAINTER
b Newton, Mass, Dec 14, 49. *Study:* Harvard Univ, 67-70, study painting with Marilyn Powers & Jason Berger, 71-73. *Work:* Boston Mus Fine Arts, Bank of Boston; Rose Art Mus, Brandeis Univ, Waltham, Mass; Duxbury Art Complex Mus, Mass; Mills Col Art Gallery, Oakland, Calif. *Comn:* Portrait, Ms Kevin Kling, Paris, France, 77; Ms Catherine Ventura, New York, 80. *Exhib:* The Direct Vision, Fitchburg Art Mus, Mass, 73, Acad Arts, Easton, Md, 76 & Rose Art Mus, Waltham, Mass, 88; invitational show, Boston Painters & Sculptors, Southshore Arts Festival, Cohasett, Mass, 84; Panorama Symposium, Centre d'Arte, Baie St Paul, Quebec, Can, 89. *Pos:* Instr painting & drawing, pvt classes, 75- *Awards:* Grant, Mass Coun Arts & Humanities, 73 & 75. *Bibliog:* Edgar Driscoll (auth), A nice feeling, Art News, Vol 73, 74; Kenworth Moffett (auth), Abstraction offers most exciting possibilities, Vol 6, Art New Eng, 9/85; Claire Gravel (auth), L'Art Contemporain Descend dans L'Arene, Le Devoir, Montreal, Can. *Media:* All. *Publ:* Contribr, drawings, An empty glass house, New Renaissance Mag, spring 86. *Dealer:* Andrea Marquit Fine Arts 207 Newbury St Boston MA 02116; Sound Shore Gallery Six Landmark Sq Stamford CT 06901. *Mailing Add:* 25 Parkman St Brookline MA 02146

BARROW, THOMAS FRANCIS
PHOTOGRAPHER, EDUCATOR
b Kansas City, Mo, Sept 24, 38. *Study:* Kansas City Art Inst, BFA(graphic design), 63; Northwestern Univ, film courses with Jack Ellis, 65; Inst Design, Ill Inst Technol, photog with Aaron Siskind, MS, 67. *Work:* Nat Gallery Can, Ottawa; Mus Mod Art, New York; San Francisco Mus Mod Art, Calif; Philadelphia Mus Fine Arts; Fogg Art Mus, Cambridge, Mass. *Exhib:* Sharp Focus Realism: A New Perspective, Pace Gallery, New York, 73; Light & Lens: Methods of Photography, Hudson River Mus, Yonkers, NY, 73; one-man show, Light Gallery, New York, 74, 76 & 79; The Extended Document, Int Mus Photog, Rochester, NY, 75; Am Photog: Past & Present, Seattle Art Mus, 76; Contemp American Photog Works, Mus Fine Arts, Houston, 77; one-man retrospective, San Francisco Mus Mod Art, 86, Los Angeles Co Mus Art, 87. *Collections Arranged:* Light and substance (with Van Deren Coke), 73 & Self as Subject, 83, Univ NM Art Mus. *Pos:* Asst dir, George Eastman House, Rochester, NY, 71-72; assoc dir, Univ NMex Art Mus, 73-76, actg dir, 85. *Teaching:* Assoc prof, Univ NMex, 73-81, prof art, 81-85, Presidential Prof, 85-90. *Awards:* Nat Endowment Arts Grant, 73 & 78. *Bibliog:* The Art of Photography, Time-Life Bks, 71; William Jenkins (auth), The Extended Document, Int Mus Photog, George Eastman House, 74; Inventories and Transformations: The Photographs of Thomas Barrow, Los Angeles Co Mus Art-Univ NM Press, 86. *Media:* Photography, Lithography. *Publ:* Auth, 600 faces by Benton, Aperture, Vol 15, No 2; The camera fiend, Image, Vol 14, No 4; contribr, Britannica Encycl Am Art, 73; auth, Three photographers and their books, In: A Hundred Years of Photographic History: Essays in Honor of Beaumont Newhall, 75; ed, Reading Into Photography, Univ NMex Press, 82; Perspectives on Photography: Essays in Honor of Beaumont Newhall, 86. *Dealer:* Andrew Smith 76 E San Francisco St Santa Fe NM 87501. *Mailing Add:* Dept Art Univ NMex Albuquerque NM 87131

BARR-SHARRAR, BERYL
ART HISTORIAN, PAINTER
b Norfolk, Va. *Study:* Mt Holyoke Col Mus, BA; Univ Calif, Berkeley, MA; Inst Fine Arts, NY Univ, MA, PhD. *Work:* Mt Holyoke Col Mus; Los Angeles Saving & Loan Asn. *Exhib:* Galerie LeFranc, 65 & Galerie Lucien Durand, Paris, 67; Maisons Cult Amiens, Bourges, Mus Avignon, Besancon Montpellier, Nancy & Ste-Etienne, 67; Mus Bordeux, Menton & le Havre, 68; Sachs Gallery, 73, Livingstone-Learmonth Gallery, 75, New York & Art Galaxy Gallery, New York, 81. *Pos:* Co-founder, Col Art Study Abroad, Paris, 61, co-dir, 61-68. *Teaching:* Vis lectr painting, Mt Holyoke Col, 68-69; vis lectr art hist, Pratt Inst, 78-79; adj asst prof art hist, Fordham Univ, 81-82; vis prof art hist, Vassar Col, 82-83. *Awards:* Prix le Franc pour le jeune peinture, Paris, 64; Am Philos Soc Grants, 80 & 82; Am Coun Learned Socs Grant, 81; Fel, Ctr Advan Study Visual Arts, Nat Gallery, Wash, DC, 85. *Mem:* Am Inst Archaeology; Col Art Asn; Asn Ancient Historians. *Media:* Acrylic on canvas, Paper. *Publ:* Ed, Macedonia & Greece in Late Classical & Early Hellenistic Times, Studies in the History of Art, Vol 10, Nat Gallery Art, 82; The Hellenistic House in From Alexander to Cleopatra: Greek Art of the Hellenistic Age, The Walters Art Gallery, 89; Coroplast, Potter & Metalsmith in the Coroplastis Art: Greek Terracottas of the Ancient World, New Rochelle, 91; The Antikythera Fulcrum attachment: A portrait of Arsinöe III, vol 89, No 4, Am J Archaeology, 10/85; How Important is Protenance? Archaeological & Stylistic Questions in the Attribution of Ancient Bronzes in Small Bronze Sculpture from the Ancient World, Los Angeles, 91; Vergina Tomb II: Dating the Objects in Alexander the Great, VII, The Ancient World, Vol 22, No 2, 91. *Mailing Add:* 30 West Ninth St New York NY 10011

BARRY, ANNE MEREDITH
PRINTMAKER, INSTRUCTOR
b Toronto, Ont, Aug 31, 32. *Study:* Ont Col of Art, 49-54, with Carl Schaefer & Eric Friefield; also printmaking with N Hornyansky, 63. *Work:* St Mary's Univ Art Gallery, Halifax, NS; Toronto Dominion Can Collection; Inco Can Collection, Toronto; Arts & Cult Centre, St John's, Nfld; Norcen Can Collection, Toronto; and many others. *Comn:* Ltd ed seriographs, Dow Chemical Co, Can Ltd, 72, Can Soc Crippled Children, 73 & Gallery Fore, Winnipeg, 75; ltd ed collagraphs, Arts Coun, Brantford Art Gallery, 74; Ont Assoc Art Galleries, 78-79; Toronto Dominion Bank, 82; and others. *Exhib:* One-person shows, Arts & Cult Centre, St John's, Nfld, 75 & 79, travelling exhibs; Int Miniature Print Exhib, Pratt Graphic Gallery, New York, 75 & 77; Biennial Am De Artes Graficas, Mus la Tertulia, Cali, SAm, 76; Japan-Can Print Exhib, Japanese Cult Centre, Toronto, 77; Printmaking Experience, traveling pub art galleries, 78-80 & Graphex VII, 79 & 80; Art Gallery Ont, 80, 82 & 83; and others. *Teaching:* Printmaking serigraphy, Mt St Vincent Univ, NS, 74 & 76; Instr workshops, Emily Carr Col Art & Design, 79-84. *Awards:* Merit Award, Art Gallery of Brant, 74. *Bibliog:* Barry and Henry Dunsmore (dirs), Shoreslines (film), 82; Kay Kritzwiser (auth), article, Arts Atlantic, spring 83; John Flood (auth), article, Northward J 28, 83. *Mem:* Print & Drawing Coun of Can; Visual Arts Ont (chmn bd, 76-78); Print & Drawing Coun Can (bd dirs, 79-80). *Media:* Woodcut, Collograph; Mixed Media. *Publ:* Auth, Dateline: Newfoundland, 72 & The Collage Print, Art Mag, 73; co-auth, An Introduction to the Collagraph Print, Ont Ministry of Cult & Recreation, 77; illusr, The Private Eye, pvt publ, 77. *Dealer:* Buschlen/Mowatt Gallery 1445 W Georgia St Vancouver BC V6G 2T3. *Mailing Add:* c/o Buschlen Mowatt Gallery 111 1445 W Georgia St Vancouver BC V6G 2T3 Canada

BARRY, ROBERT E
ILLUSTRATOR, EDUCATOR
b Newport, RI, Oct 7, 31. *Study:* Kunstgewerbeschule, Zurich, Switz; RI Sch Design, BFA & MAT. *Work:* Kerlan Collection of Children's Literature & Illus, Univ Minn; Klingspor Mus, Frankfurt, Ger; Mus of the Book, San Juan, PR; Mus of the Virgin Islands, St Thomas. *Pos:* Dir, Art Gallery Southeastern Mass Univ, 77-78; originator & owner, Sportcards, 79- *Teaching:* Instr art, Averett Col, Danville, Va, 67-68; asst prof art, Tex Woman's Univ, Denton, 68-69; assoc prof art-design, Univ Mass Dartmouth, North Dartmouth, 69-81, prof, 81- *Awards:* Am Inst Graphic Arts 50 Books of the Year, 61; Award of Merit, NY Soc Illusrs, 65; New York Times Ten Best Illus Books of the Year, 65. *Mem:* Guild Natural Sci Illusrs. *Publ:* Auth & illusr, Faint George, Houghton Mifflin Co, 63; The Musical Palm Tree, 71 & The Riddle of Castle Hill, 72, McGraw Hill; auth, Snowman's Secret, MacMillan, 75; Mr Willowby's Christmas Tree, Dell, 92. *Mailing Add:* Driftwood Cliff Ave Newport RI 02840

BARRY, ROBERT THOMAS
CONCEPTUAL ARTIST
b New York, NY, Mar 9, 36. *Study:* Hunter Col, BFA, 57, MA, 63. *Work:* Stedelijk Mus, Amsterdam, Holland; Mus Mod Art, New York; Wadsworth Atheneum, Hartford, Conn; Wallraf-Richartz Mus, Cologne, Ger; Ctr George Pompidou, Paris; and others. *Exhib:* Informations, Mus Mod Art, New York, 70; solo shows, Van Abbe Mus, Eindhoven, Holland, 77 & Folkwang Mus, Essen, WGer, 78; Documenta 6, Kassel, 77 & Cologne, 81, WGer; Joslyn Art Mus, 80; Documenta 7, Kassel, WGer, 82; Ulmer Mus, Ulm, WGer, 82; and others. *Pos:* Guest artist, Calif Inst of Art, 71 & 76, RI Sch of Design, Providence, 74 & Herron Sch Art, Indianapolis, 81. *Teaching:* Asst prof, Hunter Col, 69-79. *Awards:* Nat Endowment Arts Fel Grant, 76. *Bibliog:* Lucy Lippard (auth), Six Years: The De-Materialization of Art, Praeger, 73; Caolla Gottlieb (auth), Beyond Modern Art, Dutton, 76; Nikos Stangos (ed), Concepts of Modern Art, Harper & Row, 81; Robert Morgan (auth) & Erich Franz (ed), Robert Barry, Karl Kerber, 86; and others. *Media:* Projections, Mixed. *Dealer:* Leo Castelli 420 W Broadway New York NY 10013; Holly Soloman Gallery New York NY. *Mailing Add:* 1091 Emerson Ave Teaneck NJ 07666

BARRY, STEVE
SCULPTOR
b Jersey City, NJ, June 22, 56. *Study:* Sch Visual Arts, New York, NY, BFA, 80; Hunter Col, MFA, City Univ New York, 84. *Work:* Albuquerque Mus Art. *Exhib:* Improbable Machines, Santa Barbara Mus Art, 90; Mechanika, Contemp Arts Ctr, Cinnat, 91; one-person show, Contemp Arts Mus, Houston, 92. *Teaching:* Adj instr sculpture, Hunter Col, New York, 84-; asst prof, Univ NMex, 89- *Awards:* Fel Nat Endowment Arts, 86 & 90; Awards in the Visual Arts, 90; Visual Arts Awards, X Hirshorn Mus & Sculpture Garden, Washington, DC, 91. *Bibliog:* Motion, Motion, Kinetic Art, Perrigrine Press, 89. *Media:* Steel, Film. *Mailing Add:* PO Box 1046 Corrales NM 87048

BARSANO, RON (RONALD JAMES)
PAINTER, SCULPTOR
b Chicago, Ill, Jan 13, 45. *Study:* Am Acad Fine Art, William Mosby Scholar, 62-67. *Work:* Harwood Found Mus, Taos, NMex; US Army Hq, Wash, DC. *Exhib:* Allied Artists Am, New York, 72; Meadowbrook Hall, Mich, 75; Maxwell Gallery, San Francisco, Calif, 75; The Taos 6, Philbrook Mus, Tulsa, Okla, 77; Western Art, Grand Central Art Galleries, New York, 78; Am Western Art, Beijing Exhib Palace, China, 81; Pioneer Mus, Colorado Springs, Colo, 85. *Bibliog:* Steve Parks (auth), articles, Profile Mag, 7/78 & Art Lines, 9/81; Brand Shelton (auth), article, SW Profile Mag, 10/83; Tricia Hurst (auth), article, SW Art Mag, 2/85. *Mem:* Fechin Inst, Taos, NMex; Taos Art Asn, NMex. *Media:* Oil, Conte Crayon; Clay. *Publ:* Contribr, Taos Mag, 10/88, NMex Mag, 2/82, Artists of the Rockies Mag, spring 82, Am Artist, 6/82 & Art Gallery Mag, 12/83. *Dealer:* Collins-Pettit Gallery 1 Ledoux St Taos NM 87571. *Mailing Add:* Drawer 00 Taos NM 87571

BARSCH, WULF ERICH
PAINTER, PRINTMAKER
b Reudnitz, Ger, Aug 27, 43; US citizen. *Study:* Staatliche Hochschule für Bildende Künste, Hamburg, 63; Studienatelier K Kaschak, Hamburg, 62; Werkkunstschule, BFA, 68; Brigham Young Univ, MA, 70, MFA, 71. *Work:* Utah Mus of Fine Arts; Utah State Div of Fine Arts; San Francisco Mus of Art; Calif Col of Arts & Crafts, Oakland; States Senate, Hamburg, Ger. *Exhib:* Calif Col Arts & Crafts World Print Competition, San Francisco Mus, 73-76;

Mus of Art, Monterey, Calif, 74; Am Acad in Rome, Italy, 76; Smithsonian Inst Travelling Exhib, 77; Corcoran Biennial, 83; Tamarind, Twenty-five Years, 85 & 86; The New West, Colorado Springs Mus Art, 86; solo exhibs, Kimbal Art Ctr, Park City, Utah, 79, Utah Mus Fine Arts, 84, Okla Art Ctr, Scottsdale Ctr Arts, 85, Gremillion Fine Arts, Houston, 86, 87 & 88, Mus Church Hist & Art, Salt Lake City, 86 & River Ctr Gallery, Memphis, Tenn, 88, Dolores Chase Fine Arts, Salt Lake City, 89; 4x4 Western State Printmakers, Nora Eccles Harrison Mus Art, Logan, Utah, 88. *Teaching:* Utah Tech Col, 72, Prof printmaking & painting, Brigham Young Univ, 72- *Awards:* World Culture Prize-Centro Studie Ricerecke Belle Nazioni, Salromaggiore, Italy, 83; Karl Maeser Res & Creative Arts Award, Karl G Maeser Found, 83; Cliff Lodge Inaugural Exhib, Purchase Award, Utah, 87; Springville Mus of the Arts, Purchase Award, Utah, 86. *Media:* Lithography; Oil. *Publ:* Auth, articles, This People, fall 80, Art Space, fall 84, Art News, June 86, Corporate Art News, 87; In the Desert (exhib catalog), 85; Looking Toward Home (exhib catalog), 86. *Mailing Add:* PO Box 1359 Boulder UT 84716-1359

BARSCHEL, HANS J
DESIGNER, PHOTOGRAPHER
b Berlin-Charlottenburg, Ger, Feb 22, 12; US citizen. *Study:* Munic Art Sch; Acad Fine & Appl Art, Berlin, MA, 35. *Work:* Mus Mod Art; New York Pub Libr; Libr Cong, Washington, DC. *Comn:* Graphic arts prog brochure, 54, photo art catalog of new campus art, 75, Rochester Inst Technol. *Exhib:* Am Inst Graphic Arts; Art Dir Club, 38, 39 & 50; A-D Gallery, 46; one-man shows, Bevier Gallery, Rochester Inst Technol, 54 & 65; Fac Art Exhibs, 57-76. *Pos:* Free-lance designer, Berlin, Ger & New York, 35-50; art dir, Bur Pub Health Educ Dept, Health City, NY, 50-52; exp designer for two printing co, Rochester, NY, 52-54. *Teaching:* Prof graphic commun & instr advan design for reproduction, Col Fine & Applied Arts, Rochester Inst Technol, 53-76, prof emer design, 76- *Awards:* Prize, Am Inst Graphic Arts, 38; Statue of Victory, Accademia Italia, 83; Man of Achievement Award, Int Biog Ctr, Cambridge, Eng, 84. *Mem:* Nat Wildlife Fedn; Wilderness Soc; Am Inst Graphic Arts; Art Dirs Club New York. *Media:* Graphics. *Publ:* Auth, A plea for substantialism & Personal reflections on my era, 64; Exploits into the Neo-Cosmos: A Search for Man's Creative Sources, 74; Personal Recollections: Companion in Hell; Personal Philosophy: Neo-Realism; article in NOVUM Mag, Munich, Ger, 2/76. *Mailing Add:* 37 Hartfeld Dr Rochester NY 14625-1707

BARTA, DOROTHY ELAINE
PAINTER, LECTURER
b Toledo, Ohio, June 23, 24. *Study:* Tex Women's Univ, Denton, 41; Dallas Mus Fine Arts, with Ed Bearden, Chapman Kelley, Stephen Wilder & Roger Winter, 45-49; Art Students League, with Gustav Rehberger, Ray Goodbred, Thomas Fogarty, Ray Froman, Robert E Wood, Ed Whitney, Joseph Magniani & Jan Herring, 78-80. *Work:* Russell Daniel Trust, El Paso, 83; John Herring Newcomb Hall, Univ Va, 85. *Comn:* Record cover, comn by Maestro Tino Comini, 78; pvt comns by Dr & Mrs Richard M Vadala, Houston, 84, Cathy Keener Brown, Dallas, 85, Mr & Mrs John Lilly, Dallas, 85 & 86, James Babcock, Dallas, 87 & Harriet Ragland, Dallas, 88, Hilary Nichols, Dallas, 92. *Exhib:* Dallas Mus Fine Arts Co Ann, 56; Southwestern Watercolor Soc, 78, 82 & 83-85; Tex Fine Arts Citation, Dallas, 80 & 83; Pastel Soc Am, 80, 82-84, 88 & 91; Pastel Soc Southwest, 81-85, 87-88 & 90-91; Knickerbocker 28th Ann, 81; Copley Pastel Exhib, 81; solo exhibs, Artisan's Studio-Gallery, 81-85, Watercolors, Univ Va, 85 & Images of the Ballet, Sheraton Hotel Gallery, Dallas, 88; Okla Art Ann, 82; El Paso Mus Show, 84; Presenting Nine Dallas Women Artists, 85; Artists & Craftsmen, 86-90; Tex Watercolor Soc, 87; Irving Art Asn, 87; Western Fedn Watercolor Socs, 87 & 90; La Watercolor Soc, 87 & 90. *Teaching:* Instr portrait painting, Brookhaven Col, Dallas, Tex; instr life drawing & portrait figure painting, Artisan's Studio-Gallery, Dallas, 81-86; instr, painting workshops nationwide, also international. *Awards:* McMurray Grant, 85; Senior Hall of Fame Award for Creative Endeavors, 90; Am Artist Achievement Award for pastel artist, 92. *Bibliog:* Article in, Am Artist Mag, 11/85; article in, Tex Womens News, 85; Am Artist Mag, 6/92. *Mem:* Pastel Soc Am, New York; Pastel Soc Southwest, Dallas (founder & pres, 79-83); Tex Fine Arts Asn, Dallas; Southwestern Watercolor Soc, Dallas; Tex Watercolor Soc. *Media:* Various and Mixed, Pastel. *Dealer:* Artisan's Studio-Gallery Dallas TX; Barta Originals 5952 Royal Lane Suite 109 Dallas TX 75230. *Mailing Add:* 3151 Chapel Downs Dr Dallas TX 75229

BARTEK, TOM
PAINTER
b Omaha, Nebr, July 25, 32. *Study:* Creighton Univ, Omaha, 50-53; Cooper Union Art Sch, New York, with Robert Gwathmey, 55-56; and studied with Arnold Blanch, 65 & 68. *Work:* Joslyn Art Mus, Omaha; Inst Mex-NAm Relaciones Cult, Mexico City; State Bldgs Iowa; Neville Pub Mus, Green Bay, Wis; Wichita Art Mus, Kans. *Comn:* World Insurance Co, Omaha; 10 murals, executed in glass mosaic by Scuola Mosaici, Murano, Italy. *Exhib:* Midwest Biennial, Joslyn Art Mus, Omaha, 62, 64, 66, 70 & 86; one-man shows, Inst Mex-NAm Relaciones Cult, Mexico City, 65, Sheldon Gallery, Univ Nebr, Lincoln, 74, Joslyn Art Mus, Omaha, 78, Weselyan Univ, Nebr, 81, Hastings Col, 82 & Kearney Col, Peter H Davidson Gallery, New York, 88; A Sense of Place, traveling, 73-74; Nebraska Seen, Sheldon Art Gallery, Univ Nebr, Lincoln & traveling, 78; Mid-Four, William Rockhill Nelson Gallery Art, Atkins Mus Fine Arts, Kansas City, Mo, 78. *Pos:* Exhib mgr, Joslyn Art Mus, Omaha, 63-66. *Teaching:* Instr, Col St Mary, Omaha, 64-66; assoc prof, Creighton Univ, Omaha, 66-74. *Awards:* Honorable Mentions, Midwest Biennial, Joslyn Art Mus, 62, 64 & 66 & Mid-Four, Atkins Mus Fine Arts, Kansas City, Mo, 78; Purchase Award, Anderson Winter Show, Anderson Fine Arts Ctr, Ind, 85. *Media:* Acrylic, Assemblage. *Mailing Add:* 1314 S 9th St Omaha NE 68108

BARTELS, PHYLLIS ELAINE
PAINTER
b Joliet, Ill, Mar 8, 30. *Study:* Ray Sch Design, Chicago, 48-49; Gerald Merfeld, 70-92. *Exhib:* Alaskan Wild Life Exhib, Fine Arts Mus, Anchorage, 88-91; Park Forest Art Ctr Show, Ill 80-92; Brookwood Gallery Teachers, New Lenox, Ill, 88-91; Ray Col Design Invitational, Schaumburg, Ill, 90; Akron Soc Artists Grand Exhib, Sheraton Inn, Cuyahoga Falls, Ohio, 91-92; and others. *Teaching:* Pastel painting, Brookwood Gallery, 89-92. *Awards:* Merit Award, Pastel Soc Am, 82; Town Gallery Award, Acad Artists Asn, 84; Julia Lucille Award, Salmagundi Club, 84. *Mem:* Pastel Soc Am; Midwest Pastel Soc. *Media:* Pastel. *Publ:* Today's Art, Erwin Feldman, Vol 27, 79. *Mailing Add:* 19555 Noel Rd Elwood IL 60421

BARTER, JUDITH A
CURATOR, HISTORIAN
b Chicago, Ill, May 21, 51. *Study:* Ind Univ, Bloomington, BA, 73; Univ Ill, Urbana, MA, 75; Univ Calif, Berkeley, studied museum management, 83; PhD, Univ Mass Amherst, 91. *Collections Arranged:* Currents of Expansion (auth, catalog), St Louis Mus Art, 77; Women Artists 1600-1980: Five College Selections (auth, catalog), 80 & Ideas in Contemporary Papers, 84, Amherst Col; Traveling Exhibs, Invention and Tradition in Russian Modermist Art (auth, catalog), 81-82 & American Watercolors & Drawings (auth, catalog), 85-86. *Pos:* Curatorial asst, St Louis Art Mus, 75-77; cur collections, Amherst Col, 77-86, assoc dir, 87-; cur Am art, Marshall Field III, Art Inst Chicago. *Teaching:* Decorative arts, Worcester Art Mus, 80; hist of paints, Amherst Col, 89. *Awards:* Nat Endowment of Humanities Grant. *Mem:* Am Asn Mus; Col Art Asn; Victorian Soc; Decorative Arts Soc. *Res:* 18th-20th Century American art; decorative arts, prints, drawings & watercolors, particularly 20th Century; corporate support of art. *Publ:* Auth, Currents of Expansion, St Louis Art Mus, 77; auth, American paintings at Amherst College, Mag Antiques, 82; coauth, Rules of the Game: Culture Defining Gender & American Watercolors & Drawings, Amherst Col, 86; auth, American Watercolors & Drawings, Wadsworth Atheneum, Hartford, Conn, 1987. *Mailing Add:* Amherst Col Mead Art Mus Amherst MA 01002

BARTH, CHARLES JOHN
EDUCATOR, PRINTMAKER
b Chicago, Ill, Nov 27, 42. *Study:* Chicago State Univ, BEduc; Inst Design, Ill Inst Technol, MS(art educ); Ill State Univ, EdD. *Work:* Art Inst Chicago; Philadelphia Mus Art; Okla Art Ctr, Oklahoma City; Cedar Rapids Mus Art, Iowa; Ma Bolom, San Cristobal, Chiapas, Mex. *Comn:* Two prints & plates, Okla Christian Col, Oklahoma City, 71. *Exhib:* Ann Mid-Western Graphics Competition & Exhib, Tulsa City-County Libr, Okla, 74, 78 & 79; Ann Int Open Exhib, The Print Club, Philadelphia, 79, 84 & 88; Kans Nat Small Painting, Drawing & Print Exhib, Fort Hays State Univ, 80-83, 86, 88 & 90. *Teaching:* Instr art, Lincoln Univ, Jefferson City, Mo, 69-72; from assoc prof art to prof, Mt Mercy Col, Iowa, 72- *Awards:* Benton Spruance Mem Purchase Award, Black & White Exhib, The Print Club, Philadelphia, 69; Purchase Award, 16th Exhib Print Club, Albany, NY, 89; Catherine E Eatman Purchase Award, Nat Works Paper, Univ Miss, 90. *Mem:* The Print Club, Philadelphia; Am Color Print Soc, Philadelphia; Boston Printmakers, Mass; Soc Am Graphic Artists, New York; The Print Consortium, St Joseph, Mo. *Media:* Etching, Collagraph. *Mailing Add:* 1307 Elmhurst Dr NE Cedar Rapids IA 52402

BARTH, FRANCES
PAINTER
b New York, NY, July 31, 46. *Study:* Hunter Col, BFA & MA. *Work:* Whitney Mus, Mus Mod Art, Metrop Mus Art, New York; Albright-Knox Art Gallery, Buffalo; Dallas Mus Fine Art, Tex. *Comn:* Louisville Ballet, Ky; Atlanta Ballet, Ga. *Exhib:* Whitney Biennial Painting, New York, 72 & 73; Three NY Artists, Corcoran Gallery Art, Washington, DC, 73; Susan Caldwell Gallery, New York, 74-76, 78-83; American Painting of the 1970's, Albright-Knox Art Gallery, Buffalo; American Painting: The Eighties, Grey Art Gallery; Seven American Artists, Cleveland Mus Art; Jan Cicero, Chicago, 81-92. *Pos:* Sr critic, Yale Univ, New Haven. *Teaching:* Instr, Sarah Lawrence Col, Bennington Col, Princeton Univ, Yale Univ, New Haven. *Awards:* Creative Artists Publ Serv Grant, NY, 73; Nat Endowment Arts Grant, 74 & 82; Guggenheim Found Grant, 77; NJ State Council on the Arts Grant, 87. *Bibliog:* C Robins (auth), article, Art in Am, 9-10/74; Hayden Herrera (auth), article, Art in Am, 7-8/78; C Robins (auth), The Pluralist Era, American Art 1968-1981, Harper & Row, 84; W Thompson (auth), Art in Am, 9/89. *Mem:* Col Art Asn. *Media:* Acrylics, Oils. *Publ:* Auth, Art and the Science of Botany 1840-1985 (cataloge), Sarah Lawrence Col, 85. *Mailing Add:* 99 Vandam St New York NY 10013

BARTH, JACK ALEXANDER
PAINTER
b Los Angeles, Calif, Sept 25, 46. *Study:* Calif State Univ, Northridge, BA, 69; Univ Calif, Irvine, MFA, 71. *Work:* Los Angeles Co Mus Art; San Francisco Mus Art; Oakland Mus Art, Calif; Brown Univ; Newport Harbor Mus Art, Calif; and others. *Exhib:* One-man shows, Karen Jaen Bernier Gallery, Athens, 83, Peder Bonnier Gallery, New York, 84, Blum Helman Gallery, New York, 89; Points of View: Contemp Landscapes, Univ Gallery, Univ Mass, Amherst, 88; Summer Group Show: Works on Paper, Blum Helman Gallery, New York, 89; The Observatory, Thomas Soloman's Garage, Los Angeles, Calif, 89; Nocturnal Landscapes in Contemporary Painting, Whitney Mus Am Art at Equitable Ctr, New York, 89; Harmony & Discord: American Landscape Today, VA Mus, Richmond, 90. *Teaching:* Instr art, Cooper Union, 83- & New York Univ, 85- *Bibliog:* Susan Lubowsky (auth), Nocturnal Visions (exhib pamphlet), Whitney Mus Am Art, New

York, 89; Frederick R Brandt (auth), Harmony & Discord: American Landscape Painting Today (exhib catalog), VA Mus Fine Arts, Richmond, 90; Saul Ostrow (auth), Jack Barth, Arts Mag, 2/90. *Media:* Miscellaneous. *Dealer:* Blum Helman Gallery 20 W 57th St New York NY 10019. *Mailing Add:* 472 Broome St New York NY 10013

BARTH, UTA
CONCEPTUAL ARTIST, PHOTOGRAPHER
b Berlin, Ger, Jan 29, 58. *Study:* Univ Calif, Davis, BA, 82; Univ Calif, Los Angeles, MFA, 85. *Work:* Norton Family Found, Santa Monica, Calif. *Exhib:* 4 Artists Show, Werkstadt fur Photographie, Berlin, Ger, 84; Deliverate Investigations (with catalog), Los Angeles Co Mus Art, Calif, 89; Proof & Perjury, Los Angeles Inst Contemp Art, Calif, 85; Spirit of Our Time, Contemp Arts Forum, Santa Barbara, Calif, 90; one-woman show (auth, catalog), Addison Gallery Am Art, Andover, Mass, Howard Yezersky Gallery, Boston, Mass, 90; LA Times (auth, catalog), Boise Art Mus, Idaho, 91-92; Conceptual Impulse (auth, catalog), Security Pac Gallery, Costa Mesa, Calif, 90; and others. *Teaching:* Lectr & adj grad fac fine arts, Art Ctr Col Design, Pasadena, Calif, 88-; asst prof art, Univ Calif, Riverside, 90- *Awards:* Grant, Nat Arts Asn, 83; Fel, Nat Endowment Arts, 90-91. *Bibliog:* K Gauss & C Conkleton (coauths), Deliberate Investigations, Los Angeles Co Mus Art, 89; Ralph Rugoff (auth), Remembering the present: advertisements against our own amnesia, Los Angeles Weekly, 11/89; Colin Gardner (auth), Uta Barth: Los Angeles County Museum of Art, Artforum, 11/89. *Mem:* Found Art Resources (bd dirs). *Media:* Mixed. *Dealer:* Wooster Gardens 40 Wooster St New York NY 10013; Irit Krygier 925 Gayley Ave #12 Los Angeles CA 90024. *Mailing Add:* 245 Ruth Ave Venice CA 90291

BARTHOLET, ELIZABETH IVES
ART DEALER, ART CONSULTANT
b New York, NY. *Study:* Bryn Mawr Col, BA; Grenoble Summer Sch, cert; Harvard Summer Sch, cert. *Pos:* Art columnist, Cambridge Tribune, Mass, 25-27 & Fortune, 29-31; owner/dir, Bartholet Gallery, New York, 57- *Mem:* Cosmopolitan Club, New York; Appraisers Asn Am, New York. *Specialty:* Nineteenth and twentieth century American paintings, with emphasis on impressionistic American paintings and The Eight. *Publ:* Auth, Solving the problems of art by x-ray, Am Art Mag, 26. *Mailing Add:* 55 E 76th St New York NY 10021

BARTLE, DOROTHY BUDD
CURATOR, LECTURER
b Caldwell, NJ, May 17, 24. *Study:* Randolph-Macon Women's Col, BA(art), 45; Columbia Univ, MA(fine arts), 50. *Pos:* Staff mem jr mus, Newark Mus, 51-54, staff mem exhibs dept, 54-63, cur classical, crosses & coin collections, 63-71, cur coin collection, 71- *Teaching:* Instr art, Upsala Col, East Orange, NJ, 48-49; docent art hist, Newark Mus, 51- *Mem:* Am Asn Mus; Am Numismatic Soc; Mid-Atlantic Asn Mus. *Publ:* Co-auth, Crosses in the collection, 60, co-auth, Fires & firefighters of Newark, 68 & auth, Black heroes in history, 71, Newark Mus Quart; ed, New Jersey's Money, Kenny Press, 76. *Mailing Add:* 80 Forest Ave Colwell NJ 07006

BARTLETT, BARRY THOMAS
SCULPTOR
b Detroit, Mich, Dec 15, 52. *Study:* RI Sch Design, Providence (sculpture), 71-73; Kansas City Art Inst, Mo, BFA, 73-75; NY State Col Ceramics, Alfred, MFA, 75-77. *Exhib:* Kansas City Art Inst, Nelson Atkins Mus Art, Mo, 85. *Teaching:* Vis artist ceramics, Camberwell Sch Arts & Crafts, London, Eng, 78 & Arco Sch, Ctr Arts, Lisbon Port, 90; art fac ceramics, Bennington Col, Vt, 87- *Awards:* Visual Arts Fel, Nat Endowment Arts, 82 & 90. *Media:* Ceramics. *Mailing Add:* 508 E Sixth St New York NY 10009

BARTLETT, CHRISTOPHER E
GALLERY DIRECTOR, ILLUSTRATOR
b Stratford-on-Avon, Eng, Dec 11, 44. *Study:* St Paul's Col, Eng, cert educ, 70; Bristol Univ, hon BEd, 71; Syracuse Univ, with James McMullan, Robert Weaver, Tom Allen & Isadore Seltzer, MFA, 78. *Work:* Towson State Univ. *Comn:* Illus & design, Van Sant Dugdale Advert, 79, General Electric, 80, Soc Security Admin, Baltimore Sunpapers, Johnson & Higgins, 89. *Exhib:* Nat Paper & Clay, Memphis State Univ Art Mus, 78; Mus Am Illustration, New York, 81; American Clay, Baltimore, 81; Art Direction Awards Exhib, New York, 82; Maryland Ann, Annapolis, 83; Am Soc, Marine Artists Ninth Ann Juried, Md Hist Soc Mus, 89; New Species in Illustration Exhib, Art Dir Club, New York, London, 90; Marine Artists Exhib, Mystic Seaport Mus, 92. *Collections Arranged:* Illustrators Invitational, Holtzman Gallery, Towson State Univ, 75, Technol Art Exhib, 76, New Directions in Fabric Design, 77, Function-non-Function, 79 & Low-Fire Clay Sculpture, 81; Clay in the East III, 86. *Pos:* Dean, Md Col Art & Design, 72-74, pres, 73-74; dir, Holtzman Gallery, Towson State Univ, 74- *Teaching:* Assoc prof illus, Md Col Art & Design, 71-74; from asst prof illus & ceramics to assoc prof, Towson State Univ, Baltimore, 74- *Awards:* Cert Distinction, Creativity, 82; Cert Merit, Soc Am Illusr, 82 & 86; Silver Medal and 4 Merit Awards, Three Dimensional Illus, The Best in 3-D Advert and Publ Worldwide, 91. *Bibliog:* Barbara Tipton (auth), article in Ceramics Mo, 77; Dr D Blum (auth), article, Chesapeake Bay Mag, 85; Inda Schaenen (auth), Watercolors-The Art, Baltimore Messenger, 89. *Mem:* Am Craft Coun; Artists Equity Asn; Am Soc Marine Artists. *Media:* Watercolor. *Publ:* Illusr, Baltimore Mag; The marvels of animal behaviour, Nat Geographic, 73; auth, Remains to be seen, Ceramics Monthly, 80; article, Royal Col Art, 11/81; Mixed media, Graphics World, London, 2/83. *Dealer:* Eucalyptus Tree Studio 2220 N Charles St Baltimore MD 21218. *Mailing Add:* 2211 Woodbox Lane Apt B Baltimore MD 21209-1670

BARTLETT, JENNIFER LOSCH
PAINTER, WRITER
b Long Beach, Calif, Mar 14, 41. *Study:* Mills Col, BA, 63; Yale Univ, BFA, 64 & MFA, 65, with Jack Tworkov, James Rosenquist, Al Held & Jim Dine. *Work:* Walker Art Ctr, Minneapolis; Mus Mod Art, Metrop Mus Art, Whitney Mus Am Art, New York; Philadelphia Mus Art. *Comn:* 9-painting series, oil-painted canvas & baked enamel steel plates, Gen Serv Admin, 79. *Exhib:* Seven Walls, Mus Mod Art, New York, 71; Painting Ann, Whitney Mus Am Art, New York, 72; New York Now, Phoenix Art Mus, 79; solo exhibs, Brandeis Univ, Waltham, Mass, 84, Knight Gallery, Charlotte, NC, 85, Cleveland Mus Art, Ohio, 86, Greg Kucera Gallery, Seattle, Wash, 86-, Richard Grey, Chicago, 91 & Mair Mus, Randolph-Macon Woman's Col, Lynchburg, Va, 92; Block Prints, Whitney Mus Am Art, New York, 82; Valentines, Multiples, Marian Goodman Gallery, New York, 83; New Vistas: Contemporary American Landscapes, Hudson River Mus, Yonkers, NY & Tucson Mus Art, Ariz, 84; In Tandem, Whitechapel Art Gallery, London, Eng, 86; Selections from the Permanent Collection: Part II, La Jolla Mus Contemp Art & Three Decades: The Oliver Hoffman Collection, 88-89; New Art on Paper, Philadelphia Mus Art, 88; Earthly Delights: Garden Imagery In Contemporary Art, Fort Wayne Mus Art, 88; Influenced by the Victorians?, Galerie Saqqavah, Gstaad, Switz, 92; Marking the Decades Prints 1960-1990, Baltimore Mus Art, Md, 92. *Teaching:* Instr painting, Univ Conn, 68-72; vis artist, Chicago Art Inst, fall 72; instr painting, Sch Visual Arts, New York, 72-77. *Awards:* Fel, Creative Artists Pub Servs, 74; Harris Prize, Art Inst Chicago, 76 & Harris Prize & M V Kohnstamm Award, Art Inst Chicago, 86; Lucas Vis Lect Award, Carleton Col, 79; Brandeis Univ Creative Arts Award, 83; Am Acad Arts & Letters Award, 83; Am Inst Architects Award, 87. *Bibliog:* Many articles & reviews in Am & Europ publ, incl Eric Gibson (auth), New York reviews, Rhapsody, Art Int, 3/79; Thomas B Hess (auth), Les nouvelle images de la peinture americane, Art Press Int, 5/79; Roberta Smith (auth), Bartlett's Summers, Art in Am, 11/79 and others. *Mem:* NY Inst Humanities. *Publ:* Auth, Cleopatra I-IV, Adventures in Poetry Press, 71. *Dealer:* Paula Cooper Gallery 155 Wooster St New York 10012. *Mailing Add:* c/o Paula Cooper Gallery 155 Wooster St New York NY 10012

BARTNICK, HARRY WILLIAM
PAINTER, EDUCATOR
b Newark, NJ, July 30, 50. *Study:* Tyler Sch Art, Temple Univ, BFA, 72; Syracuse Univ, MFA, 74. *Work:* Hyde Collection, Glens Falls, NY; DeCordova Mus, Lincoln, Mass. *Exhib:* New Directions in Realism, Danforth Mus, Framingham, Mass, 80; DeCordova Mus, Lincoln, Mass, 80; State Mus, Albany, NY 81; Fashion Inst of Tech, NY, 81; Univ Mass, Amherst, 82; Mass Inst Technol, Cambridge, 90; Univ Baltimore, College Park, Md, 90. *Collections Arranged:* Contemporary Drawing Invitational, Ctr for Music, Drama & Art, Lake Placid, NY, 76-77. *Teaching:* Instr painting & drawing, Lake Placid Sch Art, 74-78; New England Sch Art & Design, 78- *Awards:* Trustee's Prize, Everson Regional, 74; Creative Artists Pub Serv Grant, 77; Mass Artists Found Grant, 81; Nat Endowment Arts Fel, New England Found Arts, 92. *Bibliog:* Article, Boston Globe, 10/16/80; The Boston art party, Art News, 11/80. *Media:* Oil, Acrylic on Canvas. *Mailing Add:* 14 Prospect St Beverly MA 01915

BARTON, GEORGIE READ
PAINTER, SCULPTOR
b Summerside, PEI; US citizen. *Study:* Mt Allison Sch Fine Arts, cert(fine arts), 24-27; Art Students League, with Frank Vincent Dumond, Edward McCartan & Arthur Lee, 29-34; Univ PEI, LLD, 83. *Work:* Art of the Western Hemisphere, IBM Corp Collection; Bruckner Mus, Albion, Mich; Confederation Art Gallery, Charlottetown, PEI; Owen Mus, Sackville, NB. *Exhib:* Am Artists Prof League, New York; Hudson Valley Art Asn, White Plains, NY; Allied Artists Am, New York, 71-; Confederation Art Gallery, Charlottetown, PEI; Univ PEI, 83. *Teaching:* Art dir, Ottawa Ladies Col, Ont, 34-40; art dir, St Agnes Sch, Albany, NY, 40-44; pvt classes, 44- *Awards:* DuMond Award, Hudson Valley Art Asn, 81; Academician Ital Acad Fine Art, 81 & Gold Centaur Award, 82; Statue of Victory, World Culture Prize, Italy, 85. *Bibliog:* Articles, Atlantic Advocate, 1/83 & Atlantic Insight, 12/83. *Mem:* Hudson Valley Art Asn (secy, 58-65, pres, 65-69, first vpres, 69-); Coun Am Artists Socs (dir bd, 66-); Salmagundi Club; fel Royal Soc of Arts; fel Am Artists Prof League (dir nat bd, 64-). *Media:* Oil. *Publ:* Contribr, Am Artists Prof League Bulletin, 71. *Mailing Add:* Three Hillside Ave Summerside East PE C1N 4H3 Canada

BARTON, JOHN MURRAY
PAINTER, PRINTMAKER
b New York, NY, Feb 8, 21. *Study:* Art Students League; Tschacbasov Sch Art, New York. *Work:* Metrop Mus Art, New York; Mus Mod Art, Haifa, Israel; Butler Inst Am Art, Youngstown, Ohio; Philadelphia Mus Art, Pa; Bibliotheque Nationale, Paris; plus others. *Comn:* Murals (with Lumin Martin Winter), New York Bd Educ; History of Money (oil, with Louise August), SC State Bank, Columbia; oil & lacquer mural, Polyclinic Hosp, New York; acrylic on concrete (with Louise August), Gilbert's Hotel, Fallsburgh, NY. *Exhib:* Numerous nat & regional exhibs. *Teaching:* Pvt classes at studio on creative expression, 60-65; lectr, creative expression, univ art depts, throughout the East Coast, 60-65. *Mem:* Artists Equity Asn. *Media:* Oil; Woodcut. *Publ:* Illusr, Space aeronautics, Print Mag & Printers Ink. *Mailing Add:* 45 Christopher New York NY 10014

BARTON, PHYLLIS SETTECASE
ART HISTORIAN, WRITER
b Dubuque, Iowa, Nov 5, 34. *Study:* Mount St Mary's Col, Los Angeles; Calif State Univ, Long Beach, BA(art hist), 78, MA(art hist), 82. *Pos:* Art ed & columnist, Santa Ana Register, Calif, 68-69; antique dealer & appraiser, Artistique, 68-; lectr, Am children's book illus; owner, Pictus Orbis Collectible Children's Books, Old Town, Temecula, Calif, currently. *Awards:* Awards for Excellence of Book Design, Cecil C Bell, 1906-1970 (monogr), 77 & Alexander Dzigurski (monogr), 79, Printing Indust Asn Am. *Mem:* Nat League Am Pen Women; Am Soc Appraisers; Am Illusr Res Group. *Res:* Designing and writing the first definitive monograph on Am painter, Julian Ritter; Cataloging of selected childrens book illustrators. *Interests:* Development of 20th century American art; Oriental arts; American children's book illustration (1900-1950). *Collection:* Picasso, Roualt, Moti, Kuniysohi, Dali, Kathe Kollwitz, Harold Frank, Marco Sassone, Cecil C Bell, Cecil Aldin, Ira Moskowitz, Peter Max, Will Foster & childrens illustrated books, 5,000 titles. *Publ:* Sassone-California, Il Torchio, Italy, 73; Cecil C Bell 1906-1970, McGrew Color Graphics, 76; The Art of Alexander Dzigurski, McGrew Color Graphics, 79; Sassone Serigraphs (catalogue raisonne), Il Torchio, 84; William Frederick Foster, Portrait of a Painter, Richlaine Publ, 89; Eulalie Banks, Children's Book Illustrator, An Annotated Bibliography, 92. *Mailing Add:* 2601 E Victoria Apt 191 Dominguez Hills CA 90220

BARTSCHERER, JOSEPH
CONCEPTUAL ARTIST, PHOTOGRAPHER
b New York, NY, Aug 30, 54. *Study:* Harvard Univ, BA, 76; Nova Scotia Col Art & Design, MFA, 79. *Work:* Mus Mod Art, New York; State Libr Archives, Seattle; State of Nevada, Carson City. *Exhib:* Mus Mod Art, New York, 87; Mus Contemp Photography, Chicago, 88; The Human Presence, Yale Univ, New Haven, Conn, 89. *Teaching:* Instr, Cornish Col Arts, Seattle, Wash, currently. *Awards:* Visual Artist Fel Grants, Nat Endowment Arts, 84 & 88; John Simon Guggenheim Fel Grant, 87-88. *Mailing Add:* 4010 Woodlawn N Seattle WA 98103

BARTZ, JAMES ROSS
PAINTER
b Blufton, Ohio, Feb 20, 42. *Study:* Ohio State Univ, BS, 64, MA(art educ), 70. *Work:* Wichita Art Asn, Wichita Art Mus; First Nat Bank, Topeka, Kans. *Comn:* The Baptism of Christ, Messiah Lutheran Church, Cleveland, Ohio. *Exhib:* Winter Art, Strecker Gallery, Manhattan, Kans, 83; Third Ann Small Oil Painting, Wichita Art Asn, 83; Mid-Four, Nelson-Atkins Mus Art, Kansas City, Mo, 83; Smoky Hill Art Exhib, Hays Libr, Kans, 83; Art Ann IV, Okla Art Ctr, Oklahoma City, 83; Fifth Salina Ann, Salina Art Ctr, Kans, 83; Lenox Hill Artists Forum, New York, NY; and others. *Teaching:* Asst prof art educ, Wichita State Univ, Kans, 70-78; painting instr figure, Wichita Art Asn, 80-83. *Awards:* Best Show, Second Ann Small Oil Painting, Wichita Art Asn, 82; Best Show, Fifth Salina Ann, Salina Art Ctr, Kans, 83; Best of Show, Smoky Hill Art Exhib, Hays, Kans Art Ctr, 85. *Media:* Acrylic, Oil. *Mailing Add:* 7618 Woodmore Terrace Apt 705 Indianapolis IN 46260

BARUCH, ANNE
ART DEALER, LECTURER
b Chicago, Ill. *Study:* Art Inst Chicago, jr scholar, study with George Beuhr & Dudley Crafts Watson; Gonzaga Univ, Spokane, Wash, LHD. *Collections Arranged:* Contemporary Czechoslovakian Printmakers, Smithsonian Inst Traveling Exhib Serv, 79-; Jan Saudek, Photographs, Camden Arts Centre, London, Eng, 80; Images from Czechoslovakia: Jan Saudek and Josef Sudek, Univ Iowa Mus Art, Iowa City, 83; Passages in Time: The Prints of Jiri Anderle 1962-1983, Pratt Inst traveling exhib, 84-85; Greek Myths Undated: Four Eastern European Printmakers, Carleton Col, Northfield, Minn, 85; Contemporary Tapestries, Silvermine Galleries, Stamford, Conn, 88; Jan Saudek, Walker Hill Art Ctr, Seoul, Korea, 89. *Pos:* Pres & dir, Jacques Baruch Gallery Ltd, Chicago, 67- *Awards:* Medal of the Order of Cultural Merit, Minister Cult & Fine Arts of Peoples Repub of Poland, 87; Silver Medal of Merit, Ministry of Foreign Affairs, Soc Int Relations, Czechoslovakia, 88; Medal of National Artist Karel Plicka, Minister of Cult, Czechoslovakia, 89. *Bibliog:* Kathy Brainard Cook (auth), Gallery owner mixes art with compassion, Spokesman-Review Spokane Chronical, 5/10/87; Cornelia Tuite (auth), Ann Baruch, Today's Chicago Woman, 9/87; Romancing Art, Chicago Tribune, 10/1/89; Marcia Pally (auth), Women, Penthouse, 12/89. *Mem:* Chicago Art Dealers Asn; Asn Int Photog Art Dealers; Int Fine Print Dealers Asn; Col Art Asn; Am Asn of Mus; Nat Mus of Women in Arts Ill (comt bd mem). *Specialty:* Contemporary art from Czechoslovakia, Poland, Hungary, Yugoslavia, United States and Europe; prints, drawings, photography, tapestry, fiber art; paintings and sculpture. *Collection:* Outstanding prints, drawings, tapestries, photographs and paintings. *Publ:* Auth, Jiri Balcar--The Archives of an Artist, 79; The World of Jan Saudek--Photographs, 79; Jiri Anderle--Master Graphics, 80; Josef Ehm--A Retrospective Exhibition, 90; Twenty Years of Czechoslovak Art: 1968-1988 A Tribute to Jacques Baruch, 90. *Mailing Add:* c/o Jacques Baruch Gallery Ltd 40 E Delaware Pl Suite 1702 Chicago IL 60611

BARUCH, RUTH-MARION EVELYN
PHOTOGRAPHER, WRITER
b Berlin, Ger, June 15, 22; US citizen. *Study:* Univ Mo, Columbia, BA & BJ, 44; Ohio Univ, MFA(photog), 46; Calif Sch Fine Arts, with Ansel Adams & Minor White, 46-47. *Work:* George Eastman House Mus Photog, Rochester, NY; Oakland Mus Art, Oakland, Calif; San Francisco Mus Mod Art; Polaroid Corp, Cambridge, Mass; Ctr Creative Photog, Univ Ariz, Tucson; Ariz State Univ, Sch Art, Temple. *Exhib:* I Hear America Singing, Kongresshalle, Berlin, Ger & Poland, 57; Photography USA, De Cordova Mus, Lincoln, Mass, 62 & 67-68; Photography of the Twentieth Century, Nat Gallery Can, 67; solo exhibs, Illusion for Sale, San Francisco Mus Mod Art, 66, Haight-Ashbury 1967, De Young Mem Mus, San Francisco, 68, Amon Carter Mus Western Art, Ft Worth, 68, The Shado Gallery, Oregon City, 73 & The Shape of Birth, Focus Gallery, San Francisco, 76; The Theo Jung Collection, 79 & Faces, 84, San Francisco Mus Mod Art; Monterey Peninsula Tradition: The Weston Years, Monterey Peninsula Mus Art, 86. *Teaching:* Grad asst photog, Ohio Univ, 44-46; instr, home studio workshops, Mill Valley, Calif, 69-71; guest artist, San Francisco Art Inst, 70-85. *Bibliog:* Margery Mann (auth), Walnut Grove: Portrait of a town, Art Forum, 64; Arthur Ollman (dir), Life and Work of Ruth-Marion Baruch and Pirkle Jones (video), 75. *Publ:* Contribr, Photography in the Twentieth Century, Horizon Press, 67; coauth (with Pirkle Jones), The Vanguard: A Photographic Essay on the Black Panthers, Beacon Press, 70. *Mailing Add:* 663 Lovell Ave Mill Valley CA 94941

BARZUN, JACQUES
WRITER, ART CRITIC
b Creteil, France, Nov 30, 07; US citizen. *Study:* Columbia Col, BA, 27; Columbia Univ, MA, 28 & PhD, 32. *Pos:* Lit consult, Charles Scribner's Sons, New York, currently. *Teaching:* Instr hist, Columbia Col, 29-38; asst prof hist, Columbia Univ, 38-42, assoc prof hist, 42-45, prof hist, 45-75, retired. *Res:* Intellectual history and culture. *Publ:* Auth, reviews and articles in Mag of Art, 43-53; articles in Am Scholar, Art Digest & Harper's, 56-; Art--by act of Congress, The Public Interest, fall 65; Museum piece, 1967, Mus News, 4/68; The arts to-day; consolidation or confrontation?, J of Royal Soc Arts, 3/72; The Use & Abuse of Art, Mellon Lectures, Nat Gallery, 73 & Princeton Press, 74. *Mailing Add:* 1170 Fifth Ave New York NY 10029

BASCOM, EARL W
SCULPTOR, PRINTMAKER
b Vernal, Utah, June 19, 06. *Study:* Brigham Young Univ, Provo Ut, BS, 40, 65-66; Univ Calif, 69; with B F Larsen, E H Eastmond and Torleif Knaphus. *Work:* Frederic Remington Art Mus, Ogdensburg, NY; Old West Mus, Cheyenne, Wyo; Nat Cowboy Hall of Fame, Oklahoma City; Can Rodeo Hall of Fame, Alberta; Utah Mus Fine Art, Salt Lake City, Ut; Gene Autry Western Heritage Mus, Los Angeles, Calif; and many others. *Comn:* Equestrian bronze sculpture, Santa Anita Horse Show, Arcadia, Calif, 82; Cheyenne Frontier Days, Wyo, 83; Viking Ranch, 83 & Double M Ranch, Apple Valley, Calif, 85; 3M Group, New Orleans, 85. *Exhib:* Santa Anita Nat Horse Show, Arcadia, Calif, 82; Nat Salon, Springville Mus Art, Utah, 83-87; Weighorst/Bascom, Alpine, Calif, 84; Old Time Athlete Asn, Salt Lake City, 85; Tex Classic, Ft Worth, 92; and others. *Pos:* Dir, Bascom Fine Arts Foundry, 70- *Teaching:* Instr art, Barstow High Sch & J F Kennedy High Sch, Barstow, Calif; Pvt sculpture instr. *Bibliog:* Jon Scott (dir), Midnight's Last Ride: 1933, KBTV, Denver, 83; Cowboy Cousins, Frederic Remington and Earl Bascom: Masters in Art, KVVT-64, Victorville, Calif, 90; Earl Bascom: An American hero, Congressional Record, Washington, DC, 85; Take Willy with You, 89; and others. *Mem:* High Desert Artists (pres, 64-65); Buckaroo Artists Am (pres, 78); Assoc Latter-Day Media Artists. *Media:* Bronze; Etching. *Publ:* Illusr, Memories I Could Do Without and Other Short Stories, Lyle Lybbert, 83; auth and illustr, The History of bareback bronc riding, Western Horseman, 7/90. *Mailing Add:* Diamond B Ranch 15669 Stoddard Wells Rd Victorville CA 92392

BASHOR, JOHN W
EDUCATOR, PAINTER
b Newton, Kans, Mar 11, 26. *Study:* Washburn Univ, BA, 49; Univ Iowa, MFA, 53. *Work:* Nelson/Atkins Mus, Kansas City, Mo; Washburn Univ, Topeka, Kans; Springfield Art Mus, Mo; Sandzen Mem Mus, Lindsborg, Kans; Kans State Univ, Manhattan. *Comn:* Murals, Kaw Valley State Bank, Topeka, 64, Bethany Col, Lindsborg, 65 & First Nat Bank, Grand Island, Nebr, 65. *Exhib:* Mid-Am Ann, Nelson/Atkins Mus, 56; Nebr Invitational, Univ Nebr, Lincoln, 62; solo traveling exhib, State Pa, 62-63; Kansas' Artist, Nat Gov Traveling Exhib, 66; Fedn Rocky Mountain States Traveling Exhib, 68. *Teaching:* Assoc prof painting & prints, Bethany Col, 54-66; prof painting, Mont State Univ, 66-, dir sch art, 66-77. *Mem:* Mid-Am Col Art Asn; Col Art Asn Am; Mont Art Educ Asn. *Media:* Acrylic. *Mailing Add:* 10680 Bridger Cyn Rd Bozeman MT 59715

BASKERVILLE, CHARLES
PAINTER, MURALIST
b Raleigh, NC, Apr 16, 1896. *Study:* Cornell Univ; Art Students League; Acad Julien, Paris. *Work:* Nat Fine Arts Collection & Nat Portrait Gallery, Washington, DC; 65 off portraits for USAAF, Pentagon, Washington, DC; Metrop Mus Art, New York; Nat Mus Racing, Saratoga Springs, NY. *Comn:* Mural in relief lacquer, Main Lounge of SS America, 40; mural, Joint Comt Mil Affairs, US Capitol, Washington, DC, 47; Two Tigers (mural), Princeton Univ, 59; Mexican Pavilion (mural), comn by Cornelius Vanderbilt Whitney; portrait of Nehru, Nehru Mem Libr & Mus, New Delhi, 86. *Exhib:* Carnegie Int, Pittsburgh, Pa, 40; Army Air Force Portraits, Nat Gallery Art, Washington, DC, 45 & Metrop Mus Art, New York, 47; Significant War Scenes, Chrysler Corp Collection, Corcoran Gallery Art, Washington, DC, 49; 17 one-man shows in New York & Palm Beach; retrospective 1918-1979, Johnson Mus, Cornell Univ, 79; Portrait of Nehru, Nehru Mem Libr & Mus, New Delhi, 86. *Bibliog:* Articles in Town & Country, 29, 32, 34 & 37, NY Times, 31, 32, 36 & 83, Arts, 37, Life, 41, Art Digest, 49 & The New Yorker, 49 & 59; Brendan Gill (auth), Here at the New Yorker, Random, 75; Janet Adams (auth), Decorative Folding Screens, Viking, 82; Joe Singer (auth), Painting Women's Portraits & Painting Men's Portraits, Watson-Guptill, 77. *Mem:* Nat Soc Mural Painters (pres, 56-59, hon pres 85-86); Artists Equity, Century; Am Artists Prof League. *Media:* Oil, Acrylic; Watercolor, Lacquer. *Mailing Add:* 220 E 72nd St Apt 25E New York NY 10021

BASKIN, LEONARD
SCULPTOR, GRAPHIC ARTIST
b New Brunswick, NJ, Aug 15, 22. *Study:* NY Univ, 39-41; Yale Sch Fine Arts, 41-43; New Sch Social Res, AB(Tiffany Found Fel), 49, DFA, 66; Acad Grande Chaumiere, 50; Acad Fine Arts, Florence, Italy, 51; Clark Univ, LHD, 66; Univ Mass, DFA, 68; Rutgers Univ; Univ Mass. *Work:* Mus Mod Art; Metrop Mus Art; Brooklyn Mus; Nat Gallery Art, Washington, DC; Fogg Mus Art; plus others. *Exhib:* Peale House, Pa Acad Fine Arts, Philadelphia, 66; West 79 - The Law, Minnesota Mus Art, 79; A Penthouse Aviary, Mus Mod Art, NY, 80; New York Gallery Showcase, Okla Art Ctr, Oklahoma City, 81; Leonard Boskin; Sculptures, Drawings, Graphics, Leinster Fine Art, London, 81; Four American Sculptors Working in Britain, Sainsbury Centre, Norfolk, 81; Leonard Boskin: Sculpture and Watercolors, Kennedy Galleries, NY, 82; Homage to Leonard Boskin for his 60th Birthday, Reading Mus & Art Gallery, 82, Ulster Mus, Belfast, 82 & Leinster Fine Art, London, 83; 120 Drawings and Graphics by Leonard Boskin, Albertina, Vienna, 84. *Teaching:* Instr printmaking, Worcester Art Mus, Mass, 52; prof art, Smith Col, North Ampton, Mass, 53-74; vis prof art, Hamshire Col, Amherst, Mass, 84. *Awards:* Gold Medal Graphic Arts, Nat Inst & Acad Arts & Letters, 69; Gold Medal Graphics, Skowhegan Sch, ME, 73; Gold Medal, Nat Acad Design, 89. *Bibliog:* Raphael Soyer (auth), article, In: Homage to Thomas Eakins, etc, 65; Wayne Craven (auth), article, In: Sculpture in America, 68; Jaffe (auth), The Sculpture of Leonard Baskin, Viking Press, New York, 80; and others. *Mem:* Royal Acad, Belgium, 85; Nat Inst & Acad Arts & Letters, 85; Accademia del Designo, Florence, Italy, 85. *Dealer:* Bowles-Sorokko 314 N Rodeo Dr Beverly Hills CA 90210. *Mailing Add:* Leeds MA 01053

BASQUIN, KIT (MARY SMYTH)
CURATOR, EDUCATOR
b New York, NY, July 3, 41. *Study:* Goucher Col, BA, 63; Ind Univ, Bloomington, MA(art hist), 70; Bread Loaf Writers Conf, Middlebury Col, 83 & 85: Yale Summer Sch, 85. *Pos:* Owner & dir, Washington Gallery, Indianapolis, 77-79 & Kit Basquin Gallery, Milwaukee, 81-83; Wis ed, New Art Examiner, 80; Interim cur, Haggerty Mus Art, Milwaukee, 88-89; asst dir collections & pub progs, Haggerty Mus, Marquette Univ, Milwaukee, 89-90, cur ed, 90- *Teaching:* Instr art hist, Fine Arts Sch, Addis Ababa, Ethiopia, 67-68; instr art hist, Concordia Univ Meghon, 92; teacher adult ed, Marquette Univ, 92. *Bibliog:* Holly Day (auth), Indianapolis, Cincinnati, Dayton, Art in Am, 7-8/79; Dean Jensen (auth), Basquin Gallery has different air, Milwaukee Sentinel, 10/2/81. *Mem:* Arts Club Chicago; Contemp Art Soc (pres, 86-87); Univ Club Milwaukee; Re-Univ Club, NY. *Res:* Contemporary art in the Midwest. *Publ:* Paintings and push pins, In: Art & the World, 83; Was art erotic or pornographic, Milwaukee Sentinel, 9/3/84; Windy Tuesday nights (bk rev), Cream City Rev, 1/88; review, New Art Examiner, 12/89; Images of Death in Contemporary Art, calalog, 90; auth, Dale Chihuly: Reflections in Glass, Sch Arts, 3/92; Francesco Spicuzza: Wisconsin Impressionist, catalog, 92. *Mailing Add:* 7019 N Barnett Lane Milwaukee WI 53217

BASS, DAVID LOREN
PAINTER
b Conway, Ark, July 19, 43. *Study:* Univ NC, Greensboro, MFA; Univ NC, Chapel Hill; Aspen Sch of Contemp Art; Univ Cent Ark, BSE; study with Peter Agostini, Walter Barker, Andrew Martin & Larry Day. *Work:* Mint Mus, Charlotte, NC; Dillard Collection, Weatherspoon Art Gallery, Greensboro, NC; Fayetteville Mus Art, NC; Duke Univ, Durham, NC; US Dept State, Washington, DC; Washington & Lee Univ, Lexington, Va. *Exhib:* Biennial Exhib of Piedmont Painting & Sculpture, Mint Mus, Charlotte, 79 & 81; one man shows, Asheville Art Mus, 80 & Weymouth Ctr, Southern Pines, NC, 86; Summer Leisure: Mountains to the Sea, Mint Mus, Charlotte, 82; Key West, 1989-90, Jennifer Moore Gallery, Greensboro, NC, 90; David Loren Bass: Selected Works, 1983-1989, Theater Art Galleries, High Point, NC, 90; 19th Ann Competition NC Artists, Fayetteville Mus Art, 91; Third Ann Exhib, Corrales Hist Soc, NMex, 91; NC Invitational, Hickory Mus Art, 91; and many others. *Collections Arranged:* Drawings & Sculpture by Peter Agostini, Du Pont Art Gallery, 76 & Prints, Dept of Fine Arts, 76, Du Pont Art Gallery, Washington & Lee Univ. *Teaching:* Instr painting, Washington & Lee Univ, Lexington, Va, 76. *Awards:* Yaddo Residency, Saratoga Springs, NY, 78, 81 & 84. *Bibliog:* Tom Dewey (auth), Southern realism, Miss Mus Art, 79. *Media:* Oil, Watercolor. *Mailing Add:* PO Box 1482 Corrales NM 87048

BASS, JOEL
PAINTER
b Los Angeles, Calif, Dec 23, 42. *Study:* Art Ctr Col Design, BA, 65-67. *Work:* Ft Worth Art Ctr; Mus Mod Art, Whitney Mus Am Art, New York; Albright-Knox Mus Art, Buffalo; San Francisco Mus Art; Metrop Mus Art, New York. *Exhib:* The Structure of Color, Whitney Mus Am Art, New York, 71; Color & Scale: Eight Contemp Calif Painters, Oakland Mus, 71; The State of Calif Painting, Govett-Brewster Art Gallery, New Plymouth, NZ, 72-73; Southern Calif Attitudes, Pasadena Art Mus, Calif, 72; 1973 Biennial Exhib: Contemp Am Art, 73 & Recent Acquisitions Exhib, 73, Whitney Mus, New York; Printsequence, Mus Mod Art, New York, 75; Recent Am Etching, Davison Art Ctr, Wesleyan Univ, Middletown, Conn, 75; solo exhib, Kathryn Markel Fine Arts, New York, 77, Janus Gallery, Los Angeles, 77 & 81 & Burnett Miller Gallery, Los Angeles, 86; and others. *Teaching:* Instr art, Art Ctr Col Design, 76-86 & Otis Art Inst, 86- *Bibliog:* Jerome Tarshis (auth), article, Artforum, 4/71; Peter Plagens (auth), From school painting to a school of painting in Los Angeles, Art in Am, 3-4/73 & Just another rectangle painter, Artforum, 5/74. *Mailing Add:* PO Box 218 Sagaponack NY 11962

BASS, JUDY
PAINTER
b Baltimore, Md, Mar 17, 46. *Study:* Univ Md, College Park, BA, 67; George Washington Univ, MFA, 74. *Work:* The Phillips Collection, Washington, DC; George Washington Univ, Washington, DC; Dept of Health & Human Servs, Washington, DC; Univ NMex, Alberquerque, NMex. *Exhib:* Emerging Artists, Wash Proj for the Arts, 79; one-woman shows, Phillips Collection (with catalog), 81, Cath Univ of Am Art Gallery, Washington, 81 & Univ NMex Teaching Gallery, 81, Marsha Mateyka Gallery, Washington, DC, 84, 86 & 88; Color as Light, Washington County Mus, Hagerstown, Md, 86. *Teaching:* Instr art, Mt Vernon Col, Washington, 79-85 & Maryland Inst Col Art, Baltimore, 83-84; Vis asst prof painting, Univ NMex, 81-82; assoc prof fine arts, Marymount Col Va, Arlington, 84. *Awards:* Cecile R Hunt Memorial Prize for Painting, Alumni Show, George Washington Univ, Washington, DC, 86. *Bibliog:* Benjamin Forgery (auth), The uptown downtown insider world of Washington Art, Art News, 9/79; Lee Fleming (auth), Washington Iconoclassicism, 8 Washington Women (catalog), 5/82. *Mem:* Col Art Asn; Smithsonian Assoc Prog. *Media:* Acrylic Paint; Color Pencils. *Mailing Add:* c/o Marsha Mateyka Gallery 2012 R St NW Washington DC 20009

BASS, RUTH
EDUCATOR, CRITIC
b Boston, Mass, 38. *Study:* Radcliffe Col, BA(magna cum laude), 60; study with Irving Marantz, Victor Candell, Gabriel Laderman & Maurice Golubov, 60-64; Art Students League, 61-74; NY Univ, MA, 62, PhD, 78. *Exhib:* One-person show, Brata Gallery, New York, 73, Portraits of Women, Rotunda Hall of Fame for Great Americans, Bronx, NY, 87; Works on Paper--Women Artists, Brooklyn Mus, NY & Fairleigh Dickinson Univ, 75-76; Shreveport Parks & Recreation Dept Nat, Shreveport, La, 76; Artists Choice Traveling Exhib, 76-77; Women in Definition, First Women's Bank, New York, NY, 83. *Collections Arranged:* Portraits: Form and Content, First Women's Bank, New York, 84; Contemporary Images and Universal Images, 86, John Gundel Finger Paintings, 20 Broad Street, New York, 86. *Pos:* Guest cur, First Women's Bank, New York, 84, The Mendik Co, 86. *Teaching:* Lectr, Univ Bridgeport, Conn, 63-64 & Queens Col, NY, 65-66; from instr to assoc prof art, Bronx Community Col, City Univ New York, 65-81, prof, 81-; instr, New York Univ, 80-81. *Awards:* Women's Res and Develop Fund Award, City Univ New York, 86- 88; Fel, Arts & Soc, funded by Andrew W Mellon Found, Community Col Proj, 82, Humanities, Fel, 90; Borchard Found Grant, 92; and others. *Bibliog:* Lawrence Campbell (auth), review, Art News, 3/73; Michael Brenson (auth), review, NY Times, 6/29/84; Don Gray (auth), article, Art World, 5/87. *Mem:* Col Art Asn; Am Asn of Univ Prof; Int Asn Art Critics; Art Students League; Int Soc Humor Studies. *Media:* Oil, Charcoal. *Res:* Comedy in Contemporary Art, Contemporary American realist painting, including painterly realism; phenomenological criticism and aesthetics. *Publ:* Auth, The illusion of reality, 12/81 & Bland power, 4/86, Artnews; Minimalism Made Human on Joel Shapiro, Art News, 3/87 & Ordinary People on Ida Applebroog, Art News, 5/88; contribr, Macmillan London Dictionary Art, Vol 30, 94. *Mailing Add:* 125 E 87th St New York NY 10028

BASSET, GENE
POLITICAL CARTOONIST
b Brooklyn, NY, July 24, 27. *Study:* Univ Mo; Brooklyn Col, BA(design); Cooper Union; Art Students League; Pratt Inst. *Work:* Syracuse Univ Libr, NY; Wichita State Univ; Univ Mo; Univ Southern Miss. *Pos:* Polit cartoonist, Honolulu-Star Bull, 61-62, Scripps-Howard Newspapers, Washington, DC, 62- & United Features Syndicate, 72-; ed cartoonist, Atlanta J, 82- *Teaching:* Instr seminar, Gustavus Adolphus Col, Famous Artist Sch. *Awards:* Best Ed Cartoon, Population Inst, 74. *Mem:* Asn Am Ed Cartoonists (pres, 73-74); Nat Cartoonist Soc. *Media:* Ink. *Mailing Add:* 3210 Beechwood Dr Marietta GA 30067

BASSIN, JOAN
HISTORIAN, EDUCATOR
b St Louis, Mo, Oct 29, 38. *Study:* Swarthmore Col, BA; Ind Univ, MA & PhD; fel in residence for col teachers, Nat Endowment for Humanities, 78-79; Andrew W Mellon sr fel in humanities, 81. *Pos:* Art columnist, City Mag, 78-79; art reviewer, Austin American-Statesman, 82-83; asst to dean, Sch of Archit, New York Inst of Technol, 86-89; exec Dir, Nat Inst Arch Educ. *Teaching:* Lectr mod archit, Dartmouth Col, Hanover, NH, 70; instr mod archit & mod sculpture, Kansas City Art Inst, 72-74, asst prof, 74-78, assoc prof, 78-83; assoc prof archit, New York Inst of Technol, 85- *Mem:* Northeast Victorian Studies Asn; William Morris Soc; Roslyn Landmarks Soc. *Res:* Nineteenth and twentieth century architecture; Frank Lloyd Wright. *Publ:* Auth, The English landscape garden in the eighteenth century: The cultural importance of an English Institution, Albion, Spring 79; Architectural Competitions in 19th Century England, UMI Res Press, 84. *Mailing Add:* 25 Center Dr Roslyn NY 11576

BASTIAN, LINDA
PAINTER, EDUCATOR
b Ayer, Mass, Nov 7, 40. *Study:* Antioch Col, BA, 63; Tufts Univ, Boston Mus Sch, MEd, 65; New York Univ, PhD, 72. *Work:* Art in Embassies Prog, US Dept State; Port Authority NY & NJ; Hosp Corp, Bellevue, New York; Temple Univ, Pa. *Exhib:* Works on Paper, Brooklyn Mus, New York, 75 & Weatherspoon Mus, Univ NC, Greensboro, 79; one-woman shows, Soho 20 Gallery, 78, 80, 83, 84, & 86 & Birds, Fish & Flowers, Bronx Mus Arts, 85; Animals in Art, Dept Cult Affairs, New York, 81; Home Work, Women Make Art for the Home, Henry St, Syracuse Univ, 81; Translucency/Transparency,

Fordham Univ & Col Art Asn, New York, 82; Artists of Merit, Hudson River Mus, 85. *Teaching:* Chairperson art educ, Sch Visual Arts, New York, 79- *Awards:* Salamagundi Third Ann Drawing Prize, 80. *Bibliog:* Articles in Arts Mag, 78, Diversion Mag, 82 & House Beautiful, 82. *Media:* Oil, Watercolor. *Dealer:* Soho 20 Gallery 99 Spring St New York NY 10012. *Mailing Add:* 325 Church St New York NY 10013

BATCHELOR, ANTHONY JOHN
PRINTMAKER, DRAFTSMAN
b Hull, Eng, Sept 3, 44. *Study:* Brighton Col Art, Eng, dipl(art & design), 67-69; Brit Prix Rome, Italy, 72-74. *Work:* S London Gallery, Eng; Glasgow Art Gallery, Scotland; Bradford City Art Gallery, Eng; Ind State Univ; Cincinnati Art Mus, Ohio. *Comn:* Screen printed ceramic mural, Dept of Music, Ohio Univ, 71. *Exhib:* First & Third Brit Int Print Biennale, Bradford, 68 & 72; 8th Tyler Nat, Tyler Mus Art, Tex, 71; Mostra 73 & 74, Brit Acad, Rome, Italy, 73 & 74; one-man show, Cincinnati Art Mus, 75; Cincinnati Comn Arts Gallery, 83; and others. *Teaching:* Lectr, Sunderland Polytechnic, Eng, 69-70; vis asst prof printmaking & basic design, Ohio Univ, Athens, 70-72; instr printmaking & drawing, Art Acad Cincinnati, 75-, chmn found dept, 83- *Awards:* All-Ohio Graphics Biennale, Ohio Arts Coun, 71; Research Award, Assoc Independent Col & Univ Ohio, 89; Award for excellence in teaching, Greater Cincinnati Consortium Col & Univ, 88. *Bibliog:* Articles in Screen Printing Mag, 6/83, 9/83 & 10/87. *Mem:* Col Art Asn; Soc of Rome Scholars; Found Art theory & Education. *Media:* Water-based Screen Printing. *Publ:* Auth, Water-based screen printing, Art Acad of Cincinnati, 83; Water-based ink in education, Screen Printing, 10/84; Foundation studies in art: reaching the high school audience, FATE in Review, spring, 87; Creativity in the first semester - what's possible? FATE Newsletter, fall, 88. *Mailing Add:* 1159 Herschel Ave Cincinnati OH 45208

BATCHELOR, BETSEY ANN
PAINTER, EDUCATOR
b Wilmington, Del, Dec 12, 52. *Study:* Philadelphia Col Art, BFA, 75; RI Sch Design, MFA, 77. *Work:* Continental Ill Bank & Trust, Chicago; Leif Johnson; CIGNA Corp. *Exhib:* Marietta Col Nat, 78; Young Artists Show, Provincetown Art Asn & Mus, Mass, 80; Ann Exhib, Attleboro Mus, Mass, 80; Small Works, NY Univ, 80; Affect, Effect, Philadelphia, Col Art, 83; Goldey Paley Gallery, Philadelphia, Pa, 89; Woodmere Art Mus, Philadelphia, Pa, 90; solo exhib, Matthews Hamilton Gallery, Philadelphia, Pa, 84, Florence Wilcox Gallery, Swarthmore, Pa, 85, Munson-Williams-Proctor Inst, Utica, NY, 85 & Jessica Berwind Gallery, 89. *Teaching:* Instr painting, drawing & design, RI Sch Design, 76-80 & Community Col RI, 77-80; asst prof painting & design, Millersville Univ, 83-; asst prof, Munson-Williams-Proctor Inst, 84-85 & Swarthmore Col, 86, Moore Col Art & Design, 86-89, Swarthmore Col, 89-90, Beaver Col, 90- *Awards:* RI State Coun Arts, 80; Pa State Coun Arts, 84; MacDowell Colony Fel. *Bibliog:* Ronald J Onorato (auth), Gallery, Art Express, 3/82; Sid Sachs (auth), Does Philadelphia have an imagist tradition too?, New Art Examiner, 2/83; Edward Sozanski (auth), Philadelphia Inquirer, 6/85, 10/89. *Mem:* Col Art Asn. *Dealer:* Jessica Berwind Gallery 301 Cherry St Philadelphia PA. *Mailing Add:* 709 W Carpenter Lane Philadelphia PA 19119

BATEMAN, ROBERT MCLELLAN
PAINTER
b Toronto, Ont, May 24, 30. *Study:* Univ of Toronto, BA(hon); pvt lessons at Toronto Arts & Lett Club from Gordon Payne; five yrs with Carl Schaeffer; Carlton Univ, Ottawa, DSc, 82; Brock Univ, St Catherines, LLD, 82; McMaster Univ, Hamilton, Ont, LHD, Guelph Univ, Ont, DDL, 85. *Work:* Art Gallery of Hamilton, Ont; Dominion Foundaries & Steel Corp Collection, Hamilton, Ont; Devonian Found, Calgary, Alta; Toronto Board of Trade; Prince of Wales; Am Artist Col, New York; (The Late) Serene Highness, Princess Grace of Monaco. *Comn:* Polar Bear (silver bowl commemorating endangered species), World Wildlife Fund, 76; Sugar Maple & Blue Jay, Toronto Bd Trade, 77; Endangered Species Stamps: Eastern Cougar, 77, Peregrine Falcon, 78, Bowhead Whale, 79 & Prairie Chicken, 80, Can Post Off; Polar Bear, World Wildlife Fund, 85; Mallard Pair--Early Winter, Wildlife Habitat Can, 85; Snowy Blizzard--Red Tailed Hawk, Art Gallery of Hamilton, 86; Royal Can Mint-Platinum Polar Bear Ser,90. *Exhib:* Birds of Prey, Glenbow Inst, Calgary, Alta, 77; Bird Art Exhib, Leigh Yawkey Woodson Art Mus, Wausau, Wis, 77-80 & 86; Queen Elizabeth Jubilee Show, Tryon Gallery, London, 77; one-man shows, Endangered Species Show, Tryon Gallery, 75 & 79 & Beckett Gallery, Hamilton, Ont, 78 & 87; Smithsonian Inst, Washington, DC, 80 & 87; Images of the Wild, Nat Mus Natural Sci, Ottawa & traveling, Can, USA and Europ, 81-84; Beckett Gallery, Hamilton, Ont, 85; Gilcrease Art Mus, Tulsa, Okla, 86; and others. *Pos:* Art consult, Halton Co Bd of Educ, 68-70; art teacher, Lord Elgin High Sch, Burlington, Ont, 70-76; self-employed artist, 77- *Teaching:* Head dept art, Nelson High Sch, 59-68 & Lord Elgin High Sch, 70-76, Burlington. *Awards:* Merit Award, Soc Animal Artists, 79, 80 & 81; Merit Award, NW Rendezvous Show, 81; Master Artist, Leigh Yawkey Art Mus, Wausau, Wis, 82. *Bibliog:* Manuel Escott (auth), Creatures of the snow, Int Wildlife Mag, 3-4/78; Norman Lightfoot (dir), Images of the Wild (film), Nat Film Bd of Can, 78; Ramsay Derry (auth), The Art of Robert Baleman, Penguin-Viking Publ, Madison Press, 81; Ramsay Derry (auth), The World of Robert Bateman, Random House, 85; Charles Kuralt (prod), A Day in the Life of Robert Bateman, Can Broadcasting Syst, 85. *Mem:* Soc Animal Artists; Royal Can Acad Arts; hon life mem Fedn Can Artists; hon life mem Fedn Ont Artists; Brit Soc Wildlife Artists; and others. *Media:* Acrylic and Oils. *Publ:* Illusr, The Nature of Birds, Natural Hist of Can Series, 74. *Dealer:* Mill Pond Press Inc 310 Center Court Venice FL 33595. *Mailing Add:* c/o Mill Pond Press 310 Center Court Venice FL 34292-3505

BATEMAN, RONALD C
PAINTER
b Caerphilly, Glamorgan, Wales, July 26, 47. *Study:* Cardiff Col of Art, predipl, study with Tom Hudson; Swansea Col of Art, study with William Price; Tyler Sch of Art, Temple Univ, study with David Pease & J Moore, MFA. *Work:* Philadelphia Mus of Art; AT&T, Basking Ridge, NJ; Museo de Ayuntaimento De Pego, Alicante, Spain. *Comn:* Three murals, Wistar Inst, Univ of Pa, Philadelphia, 77; Creative Walls, Inc, Univ Pa. *Exhib:* Pego Ayuntamiento Mus Group Exhib, Alicante Province, Spain, 76; Contemp Artists in Philadelphia, 77; one-man show, Marian Locks Gallery, 77, 82 & 87; About Face, Squibb Gallery, Princeton, NJ; What's Real, Marian Locks Gallery, 81. *Awards:* Elizabeth Greenshields Mem Found Grant, Can, 73; Primero Primio, Certimen de Pintura, Pascual Hermanos, Spain, 76; Mus Purchase, Cheltenham Art Ann, Philadelphia Mus of Art, 76. *Media:* Oil over Acrylic Underpainting on Canvas. *Mailing Add:* c/o Marian Locks Gallery 600 Washington Square S Philadelphia PA 19106

BATES, DAVID
PAINTER
b Dallas, Tex, 1952. *Study:* Southern Methodist Univ, Dallas, BFA, 76 MFA, 77. *Work:* Archer M Huntington Art Gallery, Univ Tex, Austin, Dallas Mus Art, Fort Worth Mus, Tex; Contemp Art Ctr, Honolulu, Hawaii; Metrop Mus Art, New York; New Orleans Mus Art, La; San Francisco Mus Mod Art. *Exhib:* One-person exhib, Charles Cowles Gallery, New York, 84, 85, 86 & 87, Tex Gallery, Houston, 84 & 86, traveling exhib, Fort Worth Mus Art, Tex, 88; The Innovative Still Life, Holly Solomon Gallery, New York, 85; 50th Anniversary Acquistitions, San Francisco Mus Mod Art, 85; The Figure in the Landscape, Art Mus, Fla Int Univ, Miami, 86; Contemporary Still Life, Rathbone Gallery, Junior Col Albany, 86; Texas Landscape 1900-1986, Mus Fine Arts, Houston, 86; Sculpture and Works in relief, John Berggruen Gallery, San Francisco, 86; Biennial Exhibition, Whitney Mus Am Art, New York, 87. *Awards:* Artist Grant, Dallas Mus Fine Arts, 82; Hassam & Speicher Fund Purchase, Acad & Inst Arts & Letters, 84. *Media:* Oil. *Mailing Add:* 34 Horatio Street No 4B New York NY 10014

BATES, GLADYS EDGERLY
SCULPTOR
b Hopewell, NJ, July 15, 1896. *Study:* Corcoran Gallery Sch Art, Washington, DC, 10-16; Pa Acad Fine Arts, 16-21, Cresson European scholar, 20. *Work:* Pa Acad Fine Arts, Philadelphia; NJ State Mus, Trenton. *Exhib:* A Century of Progress, Art Inst Chicago, 34; Tex Centennial, Dallas, 36; Am Sculpture Exhib, Carnegie Inst, Pittsburgh, 38; Artists for Victory, Metrop Mus Art, New York, 42; Third Sculpture Int, Philadelphia Mus, 49. *Awards:* George D Widener Gold Medal, Pa Acad Fine Arts, 31; Third Purchase Prize, Artists for Victory, Metrop Mus Art, New York, 42; Nat Asn Women Artists Prize, 48. *Mem:* Fel Nat Sculpture Soc; Nat Asn Women Artists; Pen & Brush Club; Conn Acad Fine Arts; Mystic Art Asn. *Media:* Wood, Stone. *Dealer:* Stone Ledge Studio Art Galleries Noank CT 06340. *Mailing Add:* Stonecroft 15 Grove Ave Mystic CT 06355

BATES, KENNETH FRANCIS
ENAMELIST, CRAFTSMAN
b North Scituate, Mass, May 24, 04. *Study:* Mass Sch Art, BSEduc; also study abroad. *Work:* Cleveland Mus Art, Ohio; Butler Inst Am Art, Youngstown, Ohio; Arch Am Art, Smithsonian Inst. *Comn:* Murals, Campus Sweater Co, Cleveland & Lakewood Pub Libr; ecclesiastical enamels, Univ Notre Dame. *Exhib:* Cleveland Mus Art, 28-79; Smithsonian Inst Traveling Exhib; Nat Syracuse Traveling Exhib; one-man shows, Brooklyn Mus & Art Inst Chicago, 61; plus others. *Teaching:* Instr & lectr, Cleveland Inst Art, 27-71, emer instr, 71- *Awards:* Silver Medal, Cleveland Mus Art, 49, 57 & 66; Fine Arts Award of Cleveland, 63; Fac Grant Study Abroad, Cleveland Inst Art, 65; Gold Medal, Cleveland Inst Art, 92. *Mem:* Fel Int Inst Arts & Lett. *Publ:* Auth, Enameling, Principles & Practice, 51, Principles & Practice, 60, The Enamelist, 67 & Basic Design, 70, World Publ; Salome's Heritage, Vantage, 77; articles on enameling in Design Mag, Ceramics Mo, Encycl Arts; and others. *Mailing Add:* 7 E 194th St Euclid OH 44119

BATES, LEO JAMES
PAINTER, FILMMAKER
b Pittsburgh, Pa, Apr 12, 44. *Study:* Yale Univ Summer Sch, 65; Carnegie Mellon Univ, BFA, 66. *Work:* Albright-Knox Art Gallery; Brooklyn Mus; Carnegie Mus Art, Pittsburgh; Columbia Mus Art, SC; NJ State Mus, Trenton. *Exhib:* One-person shows, Whitney Mus Art Resources Ctr, New York, 73, Albright-Knox Art Gallery, 75, Picker Art Gallery, Dana Arts Ctr, Colgate Univ, 75 & Harriman Col, 78; All in Line, Joe & Emily Lowe Art Gallery, Syracuse Univ, 80 & Terry Dintenfass Inc, New York, 81; CAPS Grantees in Brooklyn, Brooklyn Mus, 81. *Awards:* Creative Artists Pub Serv Grant, 74. *Bibliog:* Rosemary Mayer (auth), article, Arts Mag, 11/73; Jean Reeves (auth), Bates pastel drawings visual challenge, Buffalo Evening News, 2/3/75; Robyn Brentano (auth), 112 Workshop, NY Univ Press, 81. *Media:* Casein & Rhoplex on Canvas; Film & Computer Animation. *Mailing Add:* 499 11th St Brooklyn NY 11215

BATISTA, KENNETH
PAINTER, EDUCATOR
b Pittsburgh, Pa, Oct 1, 52. *Study:* Columbus Col Art & Design, BFA, 75, Tyler Sch Art, Temple Univ, MFA, 77. *Work:* Westmoreland Co Mus Art, Greensburg, Pa; Grand Rapids Mus Art, Mich; Curtis Inst, Philadelphia, Pa; Hoyt Inst Fine Arts, New Castle, Pa; Erie Art Ctr, Pa. *Exhib:* Pensacola Nat Watermedia Exhib, Pensacola Jr Col, Fla, 82; Nat Watermedia Biennial, Zauer Gallery, Rochester, NY, 82; Am Drawings IV, (traveling exhib)

Smithsonian Inst, 83-84; Tyler Sch Art Alumni Exhib, Tyler Sch Art, Philadelphia, Pa, 87; Perspectives from Pennsylvania, Carnegie Mellon Art Gallery, Pittsburgh, Pa, 88. *Pos:* Chmn admin, Univ Pittsburgh, Pa, 87- *Teaching:* Instr drawing, Kendall Sch Design, Grand Rapids, Mich, 77-78; assoc prof drawing, Univ Pittsburgh, Pa, 78- *Awards:* Jurors Award, Assoc Artists Pittsburgh, 71st Ann US Steel, 80; Purchase Award, Hoyt Nat Painting Show, 82; Jurors Award, Nat Watermedia Biennial, 82. *Mem:* Col Art Asn; Nat Asn Sch Art & Design. *Media:* Watermedia; Drawing. *Dealer:* Rosenfeld Gallery 113 Arch St Philadelphia Pa 19106; Concept Gallery, 1031 S Braddock Ave, Pittsburg, PA 15218. *Mailing Add:* 701 E End Ave Pittsburgh PA 15221

BATKO, BLAISE JOSEPH
SCULPTOR
b New Brunswick, NJ, Feb 3, 61. *Study:* DuCret Sch Arts, Plainfield, NJ, 79-81; Sch Visual Arts, NY, 81-83. *Work:* Del Art Mus, Wilmington; Newark Mus, NJ; AT&T, Hopewell, NJ; Exxon, Linden, NJ; Nat Aeronautics & Space Admin, Cape Kennedy, Fla. *Exhib:* Just Desserts, Del Art Mus, Wilmington, 82; 47th Biennial, State Mus NJ, Trenton, 83; Sweet Stuff, Newark Mus, NJ, 84; Young US Artists, Christies Contemp Art, London, 85; Rock Candy, Columbia Univ, NY, 88. *Teaching:* Instr Sculpture, Adult Enrichment Woodbridge High Sch & Arts Work Shop Newark Mus, 85-86; instr 3D design, Kean Col NJ, 88. *Bibliog:* Vivien Raynor (auth), article, New York Times, 83; William Zimmer (auth), article, New York Times, 83; Eilee Watkins (auth), article, Star Ledger, 88. *Mem:* Assoc Artists NJ; Sculptors Asn NJ. *Media:* Stone. *Mailing Add:* 2 Marks Pl South River NJ 08882

BATT, MILES GIRARD
PAINTER, INSTRUCTOR
b Nazareth, Pa, Oct 12, 33. *Work:* Purdue Univ, Calumet, Ind; Ft Lauderdale Mus Arts; Home Savings & Loan Banking Group, Los Angeles; Southeast Banking Group, Miami, Fla; Art & the Law, West Publ, St Paul; plus many others. *Comn:* Posters & stage settings, Theatre Wing, Nat Endowment for the Arts, Hollywood, Fla, 75; five paintings, Dade Co Art in Pub Bldg, Miami, Fla; two paintings, Fla State House of Rep, Tallahassee; seven paintings, Hollywood/Ft Lauderdale Int Airport, Broward Co Art in Pub Places; and others. *Exhib:* Nat Exhib of Contemporary Painting, Soc of the Four Arts, Palm Beach, Fla, 67-82; Miami Metrop Mus Art Ann, 68-74; Watercolor USA, Springfield, Mo, 68-81; Abstract Real-Real Abstract, Louis K Meisel Gallery, NY, 74; A Change of View, Aldrich Mus, Conn, 75; '77 Photo Realists, Hollywood Cult Ctr, Fla & St Petersburg Mus Fine Arts, Fla, 78; plus others. *Teaching:* Instr watercolor, oil & acrylic, Ft Lauderdale Mus Arts, 69-78; instr watercolor, Norton Gallery & Sch Art, West Palm Beach, 70-73, Miami Art Inst, 74-79 & Hewitt Int Painting Workshops, 79-84; instr, Broward Community Col, 80, 82, 92; vis artist, Ill State Univ, 92. *Awards:* Atwater Kent Award, Soc Four Arts Nat Exhib Contemp Am Painting, 73-81; Purchase Award, Nat Watercolor Soc, 85; Cash & Purchase Award, Watercolor USA, Springfield Mus, 81; and many others. *Bibliog:* Jeanne Wolf (dir), Miles Batt, in Portrait (film), WPBT-2, Miami, 73; Howard Whitman (auth), Palm Beach has always had the cash-now it gets the culture, Art News, 2/74; Griffin Smith (auth), Why shouldn't a pro win four times in a row, Miami Herald Newspapers, 4/74. *Mem:* Nat Watercolor Soc (Los Angeles area rep, 71-86); Am Watercolor Soc; charter mem Fla Watercolor Soc; Rocky Mountain Nat Water Media Soc; Watercolor West, Redlands. *Media:* Acrylic; Watercolor. *Publ:* Contribr, Transparent Watercolor, Davis Publ, 73; auth, Watercolor Workshop, slide-cassette, Exploring Watercolor, 78; contribr, Creative Seascape, Watson Guptil, 80; The Expressive Watercolor, Davis Publ, 81; auth, The Complete Guide to Creative Watercolor, Creative Art Publ, 88. *Dealer:* Zwickler Gallery 233 N Fed Hwy #51 Dania FL 33004. *Mailing Add:* 2120 Hammock Ln Ft Lauderdale FL 33312

BATTENFIELD, JACKIE
PAINTER, EDUCATOR
b Pittsburgh, Pa, May 13, 50. *Study:* Pa State Univ, BS, 71; Syracuse Univ, MFA, 78. *Work:* Dow Jones & Co, Inc, Princeton, NJ; Davis, Polk & Wardwell, New York; Sasaki Collection, Tokyo, Japan; Citibank, NA, NY; Marsh Corp, Indianapolis, Ind. *Comn:* The United States Pharmacopeial Convention, Inc, Rockville, Md. *Exhib:* 42nd Ann Nat Art Competition & Exhib, Cooperstown Mus Art, NY, 77; Del Mus Art, Wilmington, 78; solo exhib, Zoller Gallery, Pa State Univ Mus, 80, Dreams and Schemes, DTW Gallery, NY; Selections from the Sasaki Collection, Gallerie Saison, Tokyo, 82; Multiple Choice, Art in General, New York, 86; Abstraction, Soho Ctr Vis Artists, New York, 87. *Pos:* Cur & dir, Rotunda Gallery, Brooklyn, 81-89; Proj Coord, Artist in the Marketplace Seminar (AIM), Bronx Mus Arts, 92-93. *Teaching:* vis artist fiber arts, Syracuse Univ Col Visual & Performing Arts, 80; adj prof textile design, RI Sch Design, 80-81; adj asst prof, Laguardia Community Col, 87-93; Empire State Col, 89-92. *Awards:* Pollock-Krasner Found; First Prize Sculpture, Cooperstown Arts Asn 42nd Nat Art Competition & Exhib, 77; Judges Award, Marietta Col Nat Exhib, 78. *Mem:* Nat Asn Artists Orgns. *Media:* All Media. *Publ:* Auth, Ikat Technique, Van Nostrand Reinhold, 78. *Dealer:* Schaeffer Fine Art 500 E 77th St New York NY; Goldberg & Feldman Fine Arts 12800 Shelborne Road Carmel IN. *Mailing Add:* 158 Franklin St New York NY 10013

BAUER, RUTH KRUSE
PAINTER
b Dallas, Tex, July 26, 56. *Study:* RI Sch Design, BFA, 78. *Work:* Mass Inst Technol; Graham Gund Found, Boston; Chase Manhattan Bank, New York; Equitable Life, New York; Chemical Bank, New York; DeCordova Mus, Lincoln, Mass. *Exhib:* Solo exhib, Kathryn Markel Gallery, New York, 84; Art of the State, Rose Art Mus, Waltham, 82; Selections 18, Drawing Ctr, New York, 82; Brave New Works, Boston Mus Fine Arts, 83; New Vistas: Contemporary American Landscapes (with catalog), Hudson River Mus & Tuscon Mus Art, 84; Landscape of the Spirit, Bruce Mus, Greenwich, Conn & Maxwell Davidson Gallery, New York, 89. *Pos:* Artist-in-residence, City Arts Prog, Dallas, 79-80. *Bibliog:* In a Quiet Way, Art & Antiques, 9/84; Christine Temin (auth), Bauer's landscapes pull in viewer, Boston Globe, 5/86. *Mem:* Women's Caucus Art. *Media:* Oil, Watercolor. *Dealer:* Clark Gallery PO Box 339 Lincoln MA 01773; Hokin-Kaufman 210 W Superior Chicago IL 60610. *Mailing Add:* c/o Clark Gallery PO Box 339 Lincoln Sta Lincoln MA 01773

BAUM, DON
SCULPTOR, CURATOR
b Escanaba, Mich, June 2, 22. *Study:* Univ Chicago, BA, 46; Art Inst Chicago, Hon Dr Fine Arts, 84. *Work:* Arthur Anderson & Co, Chicago, Ill; First Nat Bank Chicago; Ill State Mus, Springfield; Krannert Mus, Univ Ill, Champaign; Milwaukee Art Mus, Wis. *Exhib:* Solo Exhibs, Galerie Darthea Speyer, Paris, France, 85, Betsy Rosenfield Gallery, Chicago, Ill, 87, 89 & 92 & traveling exhib, Madison Art Ctr, 88-89, Art Ctr, Battlecreek, Mich, 89, Rockford Col Art Gallery, Ill 89 & Siena Art Gallery, Adrian, Mich, 90; Face to Face: Self Portraits by Chicago Artists, Chicago Cult Ctr, 92; Assemblage, Southeastern Ctr Contemp Art, Winston-Salem, NC, 92; The Home Show: Objects for and About the Home, Ctr Creative Studies, Detroit, Mich, 92; May 1992, Betsy Rosenfield Gallery, Chicago Int Art Expo, Ill, 92; and others. *Collections Arranged:* Don Baum Says Chicago Needs Famous Artists, 69 & Made in Chicago: Some Resources, 75, Mus Contemp Art, Chicago; Urgent Messages, Chicago Cult Ctr, 88. *Pos:* Bd mem & dir exhibs, Hyde Park Ctr, 56-72; Am comnr US entry Sao Paulo Biennale, Brazil, 73; chmn exhibs, Mus Contemp Art, Chicago, Ill, 74-79, mem bd trustees, 74-86; mem int exhibs comt, Washington, DC, 77-79. *Teaching:* Fac mem art dept, Roosevelt Univ Chicago, 48-84; instr painting, Hyde Park Art Ctr, Chicago, 55-65; grad adv, Art Inst Chicago, 88-92. *Awards:* Pauline Palmer Prize, 80th Exhib Chicago & Vicinity Artists, 84; Visual Arts Fel Award, Nat Endowment Arts, 84; Sidney Yates Arts Advocacy Award, Ill Arts Alliance, 89. *Bibliog:* Barbara Kirshenblatt-Gimblett (auth), Who's bad? accounting for taste, Vol XXX, No 3, 10/91 & James Yood (auth), Don Baum, Vol XXX, No 11, 9/92, Artforum; Sue Taylor (auth), Introductory essay, Don Baum: Domus, Madison Art Ctr, pg 10-23, 9/92. *Media:* Assembled Found Objects. *Mailing Add:* c/o Betsy Rosenfield Gallery 212 W Superior St Chicago IL 60610

BAUM, HANK
ART DEALER, LECTURER
b New York, NY. *Study:* Los Angeles City Col, AA; Univ Southern Calif, BA; New York Sch Printing, printing & related graphic arts degree; Univ Calif, Los Angeles, with Lester Longman & E Maurice Bloch; Calif State Col, Los Angeles, with H Glicksman. *Pos:* Assoc dir, Tamarind Lithography Workshop, Los Angeles, formerly; exec dir, Atelier Mourlot, New York, formerly; assoc dir, Collectors Press, San Francisco, formerly; dir, Hank Baum Gallery, San Francisco, currently; ed, Calif Art Rev, currently. *Teaching:* Lectr contemp graphics art & artists, Univ Calif, Berkeley, triann & Univ Calif, Los Angeles, biann. *Specialty:* Contemporary art; painting, drawings, fine original limited edition prints, works on paper. *Collection:* Contemporary art. *Mailing Add:* Hank Baum Gallery PO Box 26689 San Francisco CA 94126

BAUM, JAYNE H
ART DEALER
b Newark, NJ, Dec 3, 54. *Study:* Clark Univ, Mass; NY Univ, BS(fine arts). *Pos:* Assoc & cur, Margo Feiden Galleries, New York, 75-77; dir & consult, Dan Greenblat Assoc, New York, 77-82; owner, Jayne Baum Gallery, New York, currently. *Bibliog:* Gallery exhibs reviewed in Arts Mag, Artnews, Artscribe & Village Voice. *Specialty:* Contemporary photography, paintings, drawings, limited edition prints and sculpture. *Publ:* Auth, Interior design, Whitney Comn Mag Div, 83; auth, Facilities Design and Management, Gralla Publ, 83. *Mailing Add:* 588 Broadway Second Floor New York NY 10012

BAUM, MARILYN RUTH
PAINTER, PRINTMAKER
b Pittsburgh, Pa, May 24, 39. *Study:* Univ Calif, Los Angeles, BFA, 62, 63-65. *Work:* Mus Mod Art, New York; Nat Mus Am Art; Achenbach Found Graphic Arts, Fine Arts Mus San Francisco; San Jose Mus, Calif; Jacksonville Art Mus, Fla. *Exhib:* Solo exhib, San Jose Mus, 81; California Artists, Oakland Mus, Calif, 81; Recent Acquisitions Part II, Achenbach Found, San Francisco, 83. *Bibliog:* Elise Miller (auth), Marilyn Baum--new paintings, Art Express, 3/82; Jeffrey Weiss (auth), article, Arts, 6/82; Frank Cebulski (auth), The selfish eye, Artweek, 1/83. *Dealer:* Olga Dollar Gallery 126 Post St San Francisco CA 94108. *Mailing Add:* c/o Allport Gallery 210 Post St Second Fl San Francisco CA 94108

BAUMBACH, HAROLD
PAINTER, PRINTMAKER
b New York, NY, 05. *Study:* Pratt Inst; Educ Alliance. *Work:* Hirshhorn Mus, Washington, DC; Fleischer Art Mem; Chrysler Mus; NY Univ; Univ Ga Mus; Whitney Mus; and others. *Comn:* Five lithographs ed in color, Bank St Atelier, New York, 72; 4 lithographs comn by Duke Univ; painting comn by Vermont Univ. *Exhib:* Carnegie Int, 47; Ariz Mus Purchase Exhib, Metrop Mus Art, New York, 47; Second Ann Summer Show, Park-Bernet Galleries, New York, 64; one-man show, Univ Iowa Mus, 67; Free Form Exhib, Whitney Mus Am Art, 72; Am Acad & Inst Arts & Lett Ann, 77. *Teaching:* Spec lectr art appreciation, Brooklyn Col, 60-66; adj asst prof art appreciation, Long Island Univ, 66-67; vis prof painting, Univ Iowa, 67, vis artist, 72-73. *Awards:* Hon Mention, Pepsi Cola Artists for Victory Competition, 46. *Mem:* Fedn Mod Painters & Sculptors; Am Acad & Inst Arts & Lett. *Media:* Oil; Etching. *Mailing Add:* 278 Henry St Brooklyn NY 11201

BAVINGER, EUGENE ALLEN
PAINTER, EDUCATOR
b Sapulpa, Okla, Dec 21, 19. *Study:* Univ Okla, BFA; Inst Allende, Mex, MFA. *Work:* Addison Gallery Am Art, Andover, Mass; Nelson Gallery, Atkins Mus, Kansas City, Mo; Joslyn Art Mus, Omaha, Nebr; Masur Mus, Monroe, La; Mulvane Art Ctr, Topeka, Kans. *Comn:* Mural, Exxon Oil, Chemical Technol Ctr, Baytown, Tex, 82; mural, Westin Hotel Lobby, Denver, Colo, 86. *Exhib:* American Painting Today, Metrop Mus Art, New York, 50; 70th Western Ann Invitational-19 artists, Denver Art Mus, Colo, 64; Fifty Artists from Fifty States, Am Fedn Arts Traveling Exhib, 66; one-man shows, Sheldon Art Gallery, Lincoln, Nebr, 67 & retrospective (with catalog), Mus Art, Univ Okla, 86; Razor Gallery, New York, 78; Kauffman Gallery, Houston, 88; Dubins Galllery, Los Angeles, Calif, 88. *Teaching:* Prof art, Univ Okla, 47-; retired. *Awards:* First Award, 22nd Ann Exhib, Ft Smith Art Ctr, Ark, 72; First Award, 22nd Ann Exhib, Ft Smith Art Ctr, Ark, 72; Purchase Award, 19th Ann, Ark Art Ctr, Little Rock, 76; Grand Award, Art Ann I, Tulsa, Okla, 80. *Bibliog:* Les Krantz (ed), American Artists, 85. *Publ:* Review, Arts Mag, 5/78; Review, Art Voices/South, Susan Caldwell, 9/79. *Mailing Add:* 730 NE 60th Ave Norman OK 73071

BAXTER, BONNIE JEAN
PRINTMAKER, PAINTER
b Texarkana, Tex, July 30, 46. *Study:* Monticello Col, AS, 64-66; Kans Univ, 66-67; Cranbrook Art Acad, BFA, 67-69. *Work:* Mus Mod Art, Montreal; Monticello Col, Godfrey, Ill; Maison de la Cult, Montreal; Galleria Fenwick, Forano, Italy; Maison des Metiers, Rennes, France. *Comn:* Mural, Mich High Sch, Bloomfield Hills, 69; mural for tomb, comn by Gen Paciantiani, Forano, Italy, 73. *Exhib:* Que-Boston Exchange, Experimental Etching Studio, Boston, 82; 171 Artistes Quebecoise, Maison de la Cult, Montreal, 82; Quebec Artists, Maison des Metiers, Rennes, France, 83; Artists Book L'lle, Mus Mod Art, Montreal, 83; l'Atelier de L'lle, Delegation du Que, New York, 83; and others. *Pos:* Owner & dir, Le Scarabee Printing Studio, Val-David, Que, 82-; printer in residence, l'Atelier de L'lle Asn, 80-82, master printer, 82- *Teaching:* Instr wood-cut, Les Createurs Assoc, Que, 82-83. *Bibliog:* Jacques Gireldeau (dir), Etoile de Aurainegiea (film), Can Nat Film Bd, 78. *Mem:* Conseil Gravare Que; Am Graphics Soc; Les Createur Assoc Val-David (pres, 82-); Conseil Regional Cult Laurentides (exec dir, 83-87). *Media:* All. *Publ:* Auth, Atelier d l'lle a Boston, 81 & Atelier d l'lle a New York, 82, Skis-Dite; illusr, L'Ille, Iconia Ed, 82; auth, Bonnie Baxter: Printmaker--fine arts director, Skis-Dite, 82; contribr, Quebec Artists 1970-1983, Iconia Ed, 83. *Mailing Add:* 3224 Ave du Pins CP 375 Val-David PQ J0T 2N0 Canada

BAXTER, DOUGLAS W
ART DEALER
b Ohio, Nov 8, 49. *Study:* Oberlin Col, with Ellen Johnson, BA(art hist), 72. *Exhib:* Cy Twombly: Works on Paper 1957-87, 88; Barnett Newman: Paintings, 88. *Pos:* Art dealer, Fischbach Gallery, 73-74; art dealer, Paula Cooper Gallery, New York, 74-87; vpres, Pace Gallery, 87-; pres, 87- *Mem:* Co-chmn, Art Against AIDS, 87; international organizing comt, ARCO Art Fair, Madrid, 86-; auction comt chmn, Contemp Art Auction, 88. *Specialty:* Contemporary art. *Publ:* Auth, catalogs for Twombly and Newman exhibs, Pace Gallery, New York, 88. *Mailing Add:* Pace Gallery 32 E 57th St New York NY 10022

BAXTER, IAIN
PAINTER
b Middlesborough, Eng, 36. *Study:* Univ Idaho, BS, 59, MA(educ), 62; Wash State Univ, MFA, 64. *Work:* Mus Mod Art, New York; Sol LeWitt Collection, Wadsworth Atheneum, Hartford, Conn. *Exhib:* Art by Telephone, Chicago Mus Contemp Art, 70; Information, Mus Mod Art, New York, 70; 49th Parallels, Chicago Mus Contemp Art, 70; Collecting Art of the 70's, Seattle Art Mus, 72; Soft Ware Show, Guggenheim Mus, New York, 72. *Mailing Add:* c/o Crown Point Press 568 Broadway New York NY 10012

BAXTER, PAULA ADELL
LIBRARIAN, WRITER
b Hackensack, NJ, Sept 21, 54. *Study:* State Univ MY, Binghamton, BA(art hist), 75, MA, 77; Columbia Univ, MSLS, 79. *Collections Arranged:* Victorian Ornament: Excerpts in Design History, Edna Barnes Salomon Gallery, New York Pub Libr, 89-90. *Pos:* Visual arts libr, State Univ NY, Purchase, 81-83; assoc librn reference, Mus Mod Art, NY, 83-87; cur art & archit collection, New York Pub Libr, 87- *Mem:* Art Librs Soc NAm (exec bd, 87-); Col Art Asn. *Res:* Literature and bibliography of art history. *Interests:* British and Native American art; history of decorative arts and design. *Publ:* Contribr (book reviews), Libr, R RBowker, 84-; International Bibliography of Art Librarianship, K G Saur, 87; auth, A Tangled Web: Reconsidering Victorian Ornamental Design, Design & Sign, 1/1/90; Thirty Years Growth in the Literature of Interior, Design, J Design Hist, winter 91. *Mailing Add:* New York Pub Libr 42nd St & 5th Ave Rm 313 New York NY 10018

BAXTER, VIOLET
PAINTER, CALLIGRAPHER
b New York, NY. *Study:* Cooper Union Sch Art, New York, with Morris Kantor, Paul Standard, Robert Gwathmey, Adya Yunkers, dipl, 60; Columbia Univ, New York, with Ralph Mayer, 60-61; Pratt Graphic Art Ctr, New York, 81; Hunter Col, New York. *Work:* Hon Shunichi Suzuki, Gov Tokyo; Cooper-Hewit Mus; Bacardi Rum Co, San Juan, PR; Guy Carpenter Co, Insurance, World Trade Ctr, Consolidated Edison Co, & World Trade Inst, New York. *Comn:* Calligraphy for mural, Bacardi Rum Co, San Juan, PR. *Exhib:* Solo exhibs, Manhattan Borough Pres Gallery, New York, 85, Images of Union Sq, Peconic Gallery, Suffolk Co Community Col, Riverhead, NY, 86, Recent Works, Pleiades Gallery, New York, 87, 89 & 91, Cornerstone Gallery, Falls Village, Conn, 90; Haenah-Kent Gallery, New York, 91; Bowery Gallery, New York, 91; Smithtown Township Arts Coun, NY, 92; and many others. *Pos:* Mentor, Integrative Studies (calligraphy), Pratt Inst, New York, 74-75; guest lectr, Parsons Sch Design, New York, 91 & slide talk, Educ Alliance, New York, 92. *Bibliog:* Jed Perl (auth), Gallery Going, Four Seasons in the Art World: Harcourt Brace Jovanovitch, 91; John Gabriel Hunt (auht), Violet Baxter, Omnibus Mag, 6/91; Jed Perl (auth), Real Worlds, Art & Antiques, 1/92; and others. *Mem:* Pastel Soc Am, 84-; New York Artists Equity Asn (bd dirs, 88-, vpres, 91-); Am Soc Contemp Artists (bd dirs, 89-). *Media:* Pastel, Watercolors. *Mailing Add:* 333 E 30th St # 18L New York NY 10016

BAYEFSKY, ABA
PAINTER, PRINTMAKER
b Toronto, Ont, Apr 7, 23. *Study:* Cent Tech Sch, Toronto. *Work:* Nat Gallery Can, Ottawa; Nat Gallery Victoria, Melbourne, Australia; Art Gallery Ont; Libr Cong, Washington, DC; Hebrew Univ, Jerusalem; and others. *Comn:* Mural, Northview Colliate, Toronto; tapestry, Synagogue Ont; mural, Ont Govt Bldg. *Exhib:* Major Can Art Soc Exhibs & 27 one-man shows. *Teaching:* Instr, Ont Col Art, formerly. *Awards:* Can Coun Grant to India, 58; Centennial Citation, Toronto, 67; Order of Canada, 79; and others. *Mem:* Academician Royal Can Acad Art; Can Soc Graphic Art; Can Soc Painters in Water Colour; Can Group Painters. *Media:* Graphics; Watercolor, Oil. *Mailing Add:* Seven Paperbirch Dr 100 McCaul St Don Mills ON M3C 2E6 Canada

BAYER, ARLYNE
PAINTER, PRINTMAKER
b Washington, DC. *Study:* State Univ NY, Buffalo, BFA; Hunter Col, with Tony Smith, John McCracken & Rosalind Krauss, MA(fine arts). *Work:* Herbert F Johnson Mus Art, Ithaca, NY; Chase Manhattan Bank, Equitable Life Assurance, New York; Prudential Insurance Co, Newark, NJ; Housatonic Mus Art, Bridgeport, Conn. *Comn:* Shearman & Sterling, New York. *Exhib:* Contemporary Reflections, Aldrich Mus Contemp Art, 75; Drawings, Jersey City Mus, NJ, 77; 15 New Talents, Aldrich Mus Contemp Art, 79; Young Painters: 1980, Bronx Mus Arts, 80; Solo exhib, Hudson Gallery, New York, 86; Four Corners of Abstraction/White Columns, New York, 87; Pastel Anthology II, Grace Borgenicht Gallery, New York, 87; Invitational, Richard Green Gallery, Santa Monica, Calif, 91; group show, Michael Walls Gallery, New York, 92. *Awards:* Creative Artists Pub Serv Grant, 76-77; MacDowell Colony Fel, 77. *Bibliog:* Jacqueline Moss (auth), article, in: Arts Mag, 2/80. *Mailing Add:* 116 W Houston St New York NY 10012

BAYLESS, RAYMOND
PAINTER
b Los Angeles, Feb 13, 20. *Study:* Self-taught. *Work:* US Dept of the Navy Art Collection, Washington, DC; US Dept of the Air Force Art Collection, Washington, DC; Nat Air & Space Mus, Smithsonian Inst, Washington, DC; Int Aerospace Hall of Fame, San Diego, Calif; United States Dept of State, Art in Embassies Program. *Exhib:* One-man shows, O'Thompson Gallery, Phoenix, Ariz, 74-87; Smoke Tree Ranch, Otis Art Inst, Parsons Sch Design, Palm Springs, Calif, 80. *Media:* Oil. *Publ:* Auth, Excursion into the past, Southwest Art, 74. *Mailing Add:* 11348 Cashmere St Los Angeles CA 90049

BAYLISS, GEORGE
PAINTER, EDUCATOR
b Washington, DC, Oct 14, 31. *Study:* Univ Va; Univ Md, with Herman Maril, BA, 55; Cranbrook Acad Art, with Zoltan Sepeshy, MFA, 56; Corcoran Sch Art. *Work:* Akron Art Inst, Ohio; State Univ NY; Corcoran Gallery Art; Univ Mich; Ford Motor Co. *Comn:* Mural, Rural Elect Transmission, Mus Hist & Technol, Smithsonian Inst, 56-57. *Exhib:* Corcoran Biennial Contemp Am Painters, 55 & 59; New Accessions USA, Colorado Springs Fine Arts Ctr, 58; 12 Washington Painters, Univ Ky, 60; Four Washington Artists, Corcoran Gallery Art, 61; Drawings USA, circulated by Smithsonian Inst, 62. *Pos:* Dean, Parsons Sch Design, New York, 63-67. *Teaching:* Instr painting & drawing, Sch Akron Art Inst, Ohio, 57-59; instr painting & drawing, Flint Jr Col, Mich, 59-62; asst prof painting & drawing, State Univ NY Col Potsdam, 62-63; chmn dept art, State Univ NY Col, Fredonia, 67-72; chmn dept art, Univ Mich, 72-74, dean, Sch Art, 74-84; dean, Tyler Sch Art, 84-89, prof painting, 89- *Awards:* Principal Purchase Prize, Corcoran Gallery Art, 55; Award of Merit, South Bend Art Asn, Ind, 56; Bundy Co Prize, Bloomfield Hills Art Asn, 56. *Mem:* Col Art Asn; Nat Asn Schs Art & Design (bd dirs & pres). *Media:* Oil, Watercolor. *Mailing Add:* Temple Univ Tyler Sch Art Philadelphia PA 19126

BAYNARD, ED
PAINTER, PRINTMAKER
b Washington, DC, Sept 5, 40. *Work:* Chase Manhattan Bank, New York; Wadsworth Atheneum, Hartford, Conn; Whitney Mus, New York; Inst Contemp Art, Univ Pa, Philadelphia; Mus Mod Art, New York; Walker Art Ctr, Minneapolis, Minn; High Mus Atlanta, Ga; San Francisco Mus Fine Art, Calif; Ameranda Hess Oil, Woodbridge, NJ; Metrop Mus Art, New York; Norton Mus, Palm Beach, FL. *Exhib:* Landscape, Mus Mod Art, New York, 72; Am Drawing 1963-1973, Whitney Mus, New York, 73; Am Drawing, Fine Arts Gallery of San Diego, 77; Drawing Show, Cleveland Mus of Art, 78; A Collection of Contemporary Paintings and Sculpture, Nabisco, Inc World Hq, East Hanover, NJ, 79; Walker Art Ctr, Minneapolis, 80; American Still Life 45-83, Contemp Art Mus, Houston, 83; solo exhibs, Bernice Steinbaum Gallery, New York, 85-86, Elaine Horwitch Galleries, Scottsdale,

Ariz, 87, Barbara Green, Miami, Fla, 89, Erika Meyerovich Gallery, San Francisco, Calif, 89, Kleinert Found, Woodstock, NY, 89, Marcuse Pfeifer Gallery, New York, 90 & Assoc Am Artists, New York, 90; Mus Choice Exhib, Loch Haven Art Ctr, Orlando, Fla, 85; Contemporary Still Life, Associated Am Artists, New York, 88; 1988 Masters of the 20th Century, Democratic Nat Conv, Atlanta, Ga. *Bibliog:* Kenneth Wahl (auth), Ed Baynard, Arts Mag, 77; David Bourdon (auth), Contemporary still life, Portfolio, 11-12/80; Randy McAusland (auth), Ed Baynard's still lifes, Am Artist, 12/81; Baynard's bouquets, Woodstock Times, 85. *Media:* Oil, Watercolor. *Publ:* Illusr, Somewhere in Ho, Buffalo Press, 72; illusr (cover & frontispiece), Paris Rev, 74; illusr (cover), Miami, Donnes, 75; auth (interview), Arlene Slavin & Ed Baynard, NY Arts J, 76. *Mailing Add:* 90 E 10th New York NY 10003

BEACH, WARREN
PAINTER, MUSEUM DIRECTOR
b Minneapolis, Minn, May 21, 14. *Study:* Phillips Acad, Andover, Mass; Yale Univ, BFA, 39; Univ Iowa, MA, 40; Harvard Univ, MA, 47. *Exhib:* Art & Artists Along the Mississippi, 41; one-man shows, Minn State Fair, 41, Harriet Hanley Gallery, Minneapolis, 44 & 45, & Grace Horne Gallery, Boston, Mass, 45; one-man retrospective, Telfair Acad Arts & Sci, Savannah, Ga, 75; Trend House Gallery, Tampa, Fla, 75. *Pos:* Dir exten serv, Walker Art Ctr, Minneapolis, 40-41; asst art mus, Addison Gallery Am Art, 46-47; asst dir, Columbus Gallery Fine Arts, 47-55; dir, Fine Arts Gallery San Diego, 55-69. *Teaching:* Dean, Columbus Art Sch, 47-49. *Mem:* Am Asn Mus; Fine Arts Soc San Diego. *Media:* Oil, Watercolor. *Mailing Add:* 3740 Pio Pico St San Diego CA 92106

BEACHUM, SHARON GARRISON
PHOTOGRAPHER, GRAPHIC ARTIST
b Oklahoma City, Okla, Dec 1, 53. *Study:* Univ Okla, BFA, 75; Old Dominion Univ & Norfolk State Univ, coop prog, MFA, 86. *Work:* Chrylser Mus, Norfolk, Va; Franklin Furnace, New York. *Exhib:* Why Do Girls Have to Act Like That?, Va Beach Art Ctr, 86; Chromatic Abberations, Washington Ctr Photog, Washington, DC, 88; The Portrait in America, Chyrsler Mus, Norfolk, Va, 90; solo exhib, Mich State Univ, East Lansing, 90; Light Aberations, Univ Tex, San Antonio, 90; Mid-Atlantic State Photog, James Madison Univ, Harrisonburg, Va, 91. *Pos:* Owner, Swift Graphics, Okla & Va, 77-; tech illusr, Telemedia, Norfolk, Va, 80-82; graphic designer, Off PR, E Va Med Sch, Norfolk, 82-83. *Teaching:* Asst prof graphic designs & photog, Hampton Univ, Va, 88- , chmn art dept, 90- *Awards:* Mat & Equip Grant, Four Sharp Artists, Copy Data Group, 87; Communs Excellence, Donor Recruitment, 88 & First Place in Nation, Donor Recruitment Campaign, 90, Nat Red Cross. *Bibliog:* Stephen Perloff (auth), Photo Review, Pa Coun Arts, 87; Brooks Johnson (auth), The Portrait in America, Chrysler Mus, 90. *Mem:* Graphic Design Educators Asn; Va Soc Photog Art; Tidewater Artists Asn (bd & publicity, 86-87); Washington, DC Ctr Photog; Col Art Asn. *Mailing Add:* Hampton University Dept of Art Box 6205 Hampton VA 22668

BEADLESTON, WILLIAM L
ART DEALER
b 1938; US citizen. *Pos:* Dir, William L Beadleston Inc, currently. *Specialty:* European and American impressionist and 20th century masters. *Mailing Add:* 60 E 91st St New York NY 10028

BEAL, GRAHAM WILLIAM JOHN
DIRECTOR, CURATOR
b Stratford-on-Avon, Eng, Apr 22, 47. *Study:* Manchester Univ, BA, 69; Courtauld Inst, London Univ, MA, 72. *Collections Arranged:* Wiley Territory (with catalog), 79; Jim Dine: Five Themes (coauth, catalog), 84; Giacometti: The Last Two Decades (with catalog), 84; Second Sight (with catalog), 86; Recent British Sculpture (with catalog), 87 Sainsbury Ctr, UK, 83-84. *Pos:* Dir, Washington Univ Art Gallery, 74-77; chief cur, Walker Art Ctr, Minneapolis, 77-83; dir, Sainsbury Ctr, UK, 83-84; chief cur, San Francisco Mus Mod Art, 84-89; dir, Joslyn Art Mus, Omaha, currently. *Mem:* Asn Art Mus Dirs. *Res:* Contemporary art and the surrealist tradition. *Mailing Add:* c/o Joslyn Art Museum 2200 Dodge St Omaha NE 68102

BEAL, JACK
PAINTER
b Richmond, Va, June 25, 31. *Study:* Norfolk Div, Col William & Mary - Va Polytech Inst, 50-53; Art Inst Chicago, with Briggs Dyer, Isobel MacKinnon & Kathleen Blackshear, 53-56; Art Inst Boston, Hon Doctorate Fine Arts, 92. *Work:* Whitney Mus Am Art, New York; Va Mus Fine Arts, Richmond; Art Inst Chicago; Nat Gallery, Washington, DC; Metrop Mus, New York. *Comn:* Washington & Lee Univ, 74-75; US Dept Interior, 75-76; The Hist of Labor in Am (murals), US Labor Bldg, Washington, DC, 75-77. *Exhib:* 14 One-man shows Allan Frumkin Gallery, New York & Chicago, 65-; Galerie Claude Bernard, Paris, 73 & 81; Ten-Yr Retrospective, Boston Univ, Va Mus & Mus Contemp Art, Chicago, 73-74; Print Retrospective, Madison Art Ctr & Art Inst Chicago, 77-78; Contemporary American Realism since 1960, Pa Acad Fine Arts, Va Mus Fine Arts, Oakland Mus, Gulbenkian Found, Lisbon, Sala des Esposiciones-Madrid & Kunsthalle-Nurenberg, 81-82; Focus on the Figure: Twenty Years, Whitney Mus Am Art, 82; American Realism: Twentieth Century Drawings and Watercolors, San Francisco Mus Mod Art, 85-87; American Realism and Figurative Art: 1952-1990, traveling exhib touring 5 mus in Japan, 91-92. *Teaching:* Vis lectr at over 100 schools, universities & museums; occupant-endowed chair, Col William & Mary, Va, 92- *Awards:* Nat Endowment Arts Grant. *Bibliog:* Mark Strand (auth), Art of The Real, Potter, 83; John Arthur (auth), Realists at Work, Watson Guptill, 83; Eric Shanes (auth), Jack Beal (monogr), Hudson Hills Press, 93. *Mem:* NY Acad Art; Nat Acad Design. *Media:* Oil, Pastel. *Dealer:* Frumkin/Adams Gallery 50 W 57th St New York NY 10019. *Mailing Add:* 83A Delhi Stage HC64 Oneonta NY 13820-9117

BEAL, MACK
SCULPTOR
b Boston, Mass, Apr 20, 24. *Study:* Harvard Univ, BS, 46; grad study, Dept of Art, Univ NH, Durham; apprentice to master blacksmith Joe Tucker, Milford, NH. *Work:* Addison Gallery Am Art, Phillips Acad, Andover, Mass; New Eng Ctr, Univ NH, Durham; Worcester Art Mus, Mass; Permanent Exhib, Symp Lindabruun, Bad Voslau, Austria. *Exhib:* Inst Contemp Art, Boston, 70-73; Addison Gallery Am Art, Phillips Acad, Andover, Mass, 74; Norfolk Art Ctr, Nebr, 79; Nat Ornamental Metal Mus, Memphis, 79; Rowe Gallery, Univ NC, 80; Int Conf Exhib, Hereford, Eng, 80; NH Comn Arts, 81; and many others. *Pos:* Dir, The Sculptors Workshop, Somerville, Mass, 70-80, New Eng blacksmith Asn, NH League Craftsmen's Scholar Awards, NH Coun on The Arts Awards Comt. *Teaching:* Pvt classes at MB's Studio in blacksmithing & sculpture in wood & stone. *Awards:* Silver Medals, Int Teaching Ctr for Metal Design, Aachen, Ger, 86 & 91; FIFI Exhib, Cardiff, Wales, 89; HEFAISTON 90, Int Blacksmiths Prerov, Czech, 90. *Mem:* NH League Craftsmen; Boston Visual Artists Union; Ogunquit Art Asn; Artist Blacksmith Asn NAm (dir, 76-80); and others. *Media:* Wrought iron & stainless steel, wood. *Dealer:* NH Art Asn West Bridge St Manchester NH 03105. *Mailing Add:* PO Box One Jackson NH 03846

BEALE, ARTHUR C
ADMINISTRATOR, CONSERVATOR
b Needham, Mass, Apr 12, 40. *Study:* Brandeis Univ, BA, 62; Boston Univ Sch Fine & Appl Arts, 62-64; Harvard Univ Fogg Art Mus, apprentice conservator, 66-68. *Pos:* Conservator, Joint Am Exped Idalion, Cyprus, 71; assoc conservator, Fogg Art Mus, Harvard Univ, 71-74, head conserv, Ctr Conserv & Tech Studies, 75-81, dir, 81-86; conservator, Kress Collection Renaissance Bronzes & Medals, Nat Gallery Art, 72-75; dir res, Mus Fine Arts, Boston, 86-; vis comt, J Paul Getty Conserv Inst, 87-; Nat Mus Serv Bd, 88- *Teaching:* Asst appl arts, Boston Univ, 62-64; lectr fine arts, Harvard Univ, 74-77 & 87-, sr lectr, 77-86. *Mem:* Fel Int Inst Conserv; fel Am Inst Conserv; Nat Inst Conserv (pres, 81-82, chmn, 82-85). *Publ:* Contribr, Daumier sculpture: a critical and comparative study, In: Materials and Techniques, 69 & Metamorphoses in Nineteenth Century Sculpture, 75, Fogg Art Mus, Harvard Univ; auth, The Varying Role of the Conservator in the Care of Outdoor Monuments, Ethical Dilemmas in Sculptural Monuments in an Outdoor Environment, Pa Acad Fine Arts, 85; Technical perspectives on Italian medals, surface characteristics and their interpretation, Studies Hist Art, 87; Scientific Approaches to the Question of Authenticity, small bronze sculpture from the Ancient World, J Paul Getty Mus, 90. *Mailing Add:* Boston Mus Fine Arts Dir Res Boston MA 02115

BEALL, DENNIS RAY
PRINTMAKER, EDUCATOR
b Chickasha, Okla, Mar 13, 29. *Study:* Oklahoma City Univ; San Francisco State Univ. *Work:* Achenbach Found for Graphic Arts, San Francisco; San Francisco Mus Mod Art; Mus Mod Art, New York; Libr Cong, Washington, DC; Philadelphia Mus. *Comn:* Lone Star (ed 20, collagraph), C Troup Gallery-Codex Press, Inc, Dallas, 66; Emblem V (ed 75, relief & etching), Univ Calif, Berkeley Mus, 67; Emblem VI (ed 50, collagraph), San Francisco Mus Mod Art, 67; Miz Am (ed 20, etching), Hansen-Fuller Gallery, 68; Ars Medicus (ed 20, etching & screen print), San Francisco Art Comn, 71. *Exhib:* San Francisco Mus Mod Art, 60-65 & 67; 14th & 15th Nat, Brooklyn Mus, 64 & 65; Original Prints, Calif Palace of Legion of Honor, San Francisco, 64; Art in the Embassies Prog, US Dept State, Oakland Art Mus, Calif, 66; NY Ann, Whitney Mus Am Art, 66-67; one-man show, Achenbach Found Graphic Arts, 68-69; Cincinnati Art Mus, 73; 1st Bienal Int, Segovia, Spain, 73; 11th Biennial Graphic Art, Ljubljana, Yugoslavia, 75; Collagraph, Univ Mont, touring, 87-93. *Teaching:* Prof art, San Francisco State Univ, 65- *Awards:* Purchase Awards, Ultimate Concerns, Ohio Univ, Athens, 63, 25th & 26th San Francisco Art Festivals, 71 & 72 & 5th Ann Graphics Competition, De Anza Col, Cupertino, Calif, 76. *Bibliog:* Leonard Edmondson (auth), Etching, Van Nostrand, Reinhold, 73; Ross & Romano (coauth), The Complete Collagraph, MacMillian; Una Johnson (auth), American Printmakers, Doubleday. *Mem:* Calif Soc Printmakers (past chmn). *Media:* Intaglio, Collagraph. *Mailing Add:* One Appian Way 705-7 San Francisco CA 94080

BEALL, JOANNA
PAINTER, SCULPTOR
b Chicago, Ill, Aug 17, 35. *Study:* Yale Sch Fine Art, with Josef Albers, 53-57; Art Inst Chicago, 57. *Comn:* Sculpture (wood), comn by B H Freidman, New York, 63. *Exhib:* Extraordinary Realities, Whitney Mus Am Art, New York, 73; Wadsworth Atheneum Group Exhib, Hartford, Conn, 73; Univ Calif Riverside Group Exhib, 73; Visions, Art Inst Chicago, 76; one-woman shows, James Corcoran Gallery, Los Angeles, 74 & Rebecca Cooper Gallery, Washington, DC, 75; Reality of Illusion, Denver Art Mus, 79, Univ Southern Calif Art Galleries, 79 & Xavier Fourcade, Inc, New York, 79 & 85; plus others. *Pos:* Practicing prof artist. *Teaching:* Vis artist, Univ Colo, Boulder, 79 & 84; Vis artist, Ogden, Utah, 84. *Bibliog:* New Talent USA, Art in Am, New York, 64; Melinda Wortz (auth), The World of Joanna Beall, Art Week, Los Angeles, 74; Dennis Adrian (auth), Visions, Art Inst Chicago, 76. *Mem:* Artists Equity. *Media:* Oil, Watercolor; Wood. *Dealer:* James Corcoran Gallery 8223 Santa Monica Blvd Los Angeles CA 90046. *Mailing Add:* Box 28 Brookfield Center CT 06805

BEALL, KAREN FRIEDMANN
CURATOR, WRITER
b Washington, DC. *Study:* Am Univ, BA, 59, grad work, 61-62; Johns Hopkins Univ, grad work, 65-66. *Collections Arranged:* Graphic Landscape,

Libr Cong, 70, Prints from Europe, 71 & The Pennell Legacy, 82-83, Libr Cong; Eloquence of the Simple: Shaker & Japanese Craft & The Day of the Dead: A Living Tradition in Mexican Folk Art, Carleton Col, 91. *Pos:* Cur fine prints, Libr Cong, Washington, DC, 68-82; Res assoc, art hist, Carleton Col, Northfield, Minn, 82- *Mem:* Print Coun Am; Col Art Asn; Am Asn Mus; Nat Coun Educ Ceramic Arts; Minn Independent Scholars Forum. *Res:* Specialist in American graphic arts, 20th century prints of Czechoslovakia, Poland, Yugoslavia and research in folk crafts of Japan, Greece and Mexico. *Publ:* Auth, American Prints in the Library of Congress, John Hopkins Univ, 70; Cries and Itinerant Trades, Hauswedell Verlag, 75; coauth, Viewpoints, Libr Cong, 75; Spectrum of Innovation: Color In American Printmaking, Worcester Art Mus, 90; Graphic Excursions: American Prints in Black & White, Am Fed Arts, 91. *Mailing Add:* Dept Art & History, Carleton College One N College St Northfield MN 55057-4025

BEALLOR, FRAN
PAINTER, PRINTMAKER
b New York, NY, Sept 27, 57. *Study:* Pvt study with August Mosca, 71-76; Antioch Col, 74-75; Brooklyn Mus Art Sch, 75-76; also with Charles Pfahl, 76-78. *Work:* Antioch Col, Yellow Springs, Ohio; PPG Corp, Pittsburgh, Pa; Bellevue Hosp, New York. *Exhib:* Solo exhibs, Hudson River Mus Ann, Yonkers, NY, 82 & 91, Light in the Air, Nicholas Roerich Mus, New York, 88, Tranquility of the East, Grand Cent Art Galleries, New York, 90, Clark-Whitney Gallery, Lenox, Mass, 91 & 92 & Get Real-Survey of Contemporary Realism, N Miami Ctr Contemp Art, Fla, 91; Artist Choice Mus, 83 & Six Are Selected, 85, Sherry French Gallery, NY; American Artist Competition Winners Exhib, Grand Cent Gallery, NY, 85; Springville Mus Art, Springville, Utah, 88. *Pos:* Painting, MFA Prog, Norwich Univ, Montpelier, Vt, 90- *Teaching:* Instr painting, MFA Prog, Norwich Univ, Montpelier, Vt, 90- *Awards:* Artists Space Grant, New York, NY, 89; First place, Salmon River Arts Guild, Riggins, Idaho, 90; Cover, Art Calendar, 5/91. *Bibliog:* Article, Winners of the American Artists Annual Competition, Am Artist Mag, 78; Stephen Parks (auth), Top of the line, Art Lines, Taos, NMex, 80; articles, Newsday, NY, 6-8/78, Santa Fe Reporter, 10/80, Houston Post, 7/15/84 & Miami Herald, 12/7/91. *Mem:* Artists Equity. *Media:* Oil; Serigraphy, All Media. *Publ:* illusr, Contemporary Women Artists (calendar), Bo Tree Publ, 85; cover illus, Happy All the Time, Penguin, 85; illustr, Notes of a Madman, poetry, Winston-Derek publ, 89. *Dealer:* Grand Cent Art Galleries 24 W 57 St New York NY 10019. *Mailing Add:* 839 West End Ave New York NY 10025

BEALMER, WILLIAM
CONSULTANT, EDUCATOR
b Atlanta, Mo, Sept 9, 19. *Study:* Northeast Mo State Teachers Col, BSc; Univ Colo, MFA; Chicago Inst Design; Des Moines Art Ctr; Univ Iowa. *Exhib:* Univ Colo Art Ctr; Des Moines Art Ctr; Sioux City Art Ctr; Joslyn Art Mus, Omaha, Nebr; Art Dept, Grinnell Col & Iowa State Col. *Pos:* Special consultant to many universities, schools, filmmakers, televisions, art conferences and other organizations and institutions; asst supt & state supvr art educ, Springfield, Ill; dir educ, Springfield Art Asn, formerly; retired, currently. *Teaching:* Assoc prof art, Northern Ill Univ, 70- *Awards:* Nat Art Educ Asn Distinguished Fel, 83. *Mem:* Nat Art Educ Asn (pres, 69-71); Int Soc Educ Through Art; Ill Educ Asn; Nat Educ Asn; Am Craftsmen's Coun; and others. *Publ:* Ed, The Arts: A basic component of general education, State Ill, 83. *Mailing Add:* 2106 Cardinal Dr Springfield IL 62704

BEAM, MARY TODD
PAINTER
b Dayton, Ohio, Feb 12, 31. *Study:* Cent State Univ, 61-65; Univ Dayton, 62-63; studied with Edward Betts, Maxine Masterfield, Homer Hacker, Edgar Whitney & John Pike. *Work:* Zanesville Art Ctr, Ohio; Bank One & Bank Ohio, Cambridge; Goodyear Corp, Akron, Ohio; Dow Chemical Corp; Fishel Corp, Columbus, Ohio. *Exhib:* San Diego Watercolor Soc Int Exhib, Hyde Gallery, Grossmont Col, 88; Nat Watercolor Soc Ann, Desert Mus, Muckenthaler Cultural Ctr, 88; Am Watercolor Soc 125th Ann, New York, 88; Keynote Exhib, Shrines & Sacred Places, Albuquerque NMex, 88; Ohio Watercolor Soc Ann, 89, 90, 91 & 92. *Teaching:* Instr art, Zanesville Art Ctr, 79-, experimental workshops, nat. *Awards:* Ann Experimental Award, Nat Watercolor Soc, Fullerton, Calif, 88; First Award, WVa Watercolor Soc, Regional, Moundsville, WVa, 88; Silver Medal, Ohio Watercolor Soc, 90. *Bibliog:* Jacqueline Hall (auth), Exuberant paintings show both versatility, dynamics, Columbus Dispatch, 10/81; Mary Carroll Nelson (auth), Shrines & Sacred Spaces, 88; Betsy Schein Goldman (auth), Watercolor Workshops, Am Artist Mag, 90. *Mem:* Nat Watercolor Soc; Nat Soc Painters Casein & Acrylic; Am Watercolor Soc; Soc Layerists Multi-Media; Ohio Watercolor Soc. *Media:* Watercolor, Acrylic. *Publ:* Maxine Masterfieldl (auth), Painting the Spirit of Nature, Marilyn Phillis, Drawing Out the Artist Within, 92, Watson-Guptill, 84; Michael Ward (auth), The New Spirit of Painting, 89 & Nita Leland (auth), The Creative Artist, North Light Publ, 90. *Dealer:* Windon Gallery 1644 W Fifth St Columbus OH 43215. *Mailing Add:* 400 N Seventh St Cambridge OH 43725

BEAM, PHILIP CONWAY
ART ADMINISTRATOR, EDUCATOR
b Dallas, Tex, Oct 7, 10. *Study:* Harvard Col, AB, 33; Courtauld Inst, Univ London, cert, 36; Harvard Univ, MA, 43, PhD, 44. *Pos:* Dir, Bowdoin Col Mus Art, 39-64, cur, Winslow Homer Collection, 67-83; consult, World of Winslow Homer, Time-Life Bks, 66, consult, World of John Singleton Copley, currently. *Teaching:* Asst prof art, Bowdoin Col, 39-46, assoc prof, 46-49, prof, 49-82, chmn dept, 49-82, Henry Johnson prof art & archaeol, 58-82, emer prof, 82-; vis prof, Wesleyan Univ, summers 60 & 69; lectr, Shelburne Mus, summers 67 & 70; vis prof art, Univ Vt. *Mem:* Am Asn Univ Prof; Am Asn Mus; Maine Art Comn (chmn, 54-55); Col Art Asn Am. *Publ:* Auth, The Language of Art, Ronald, 58; The Art of John Sloan, 62 & Winslow Homer at Prouts Neck, 66, Little; contrib ed, A Dictionary of the Visual Arts, NY Graphic Soc, 73; auth, Winslow Homer, McGraw-Hill, 75; Winslow Homer's Magazine Engravings, Harper, 79. *Mailing Add:* c/o Bowdoin Col Art Dept Visual Art Center Brunswick ME 04011

BEAMENT, TIB (THOMAS HAROLD)
PAINTER
b Montreal, PQ, Can, Feb 17, 41. *Study:* Fettes Col, Edinburgh, Scotland, O level cert; Ecole Beaux-Arts, Montreal, dipl; Acad Belle Arti, Rome, Italian Govt grant; Ecole Beaux-Arts, Montreal, postgrad studies & teaching cert; Sir George Williams Univ, MA(art educ); also in graphic studios of Shirly Wales, France; Richard Lacroix, Albert Dumouchel & Atelier 838, Montreal. *Work:* Tate Gallery, London; Mus Mod Art, New York; Mus Rio de Janeiro; Nat Gallery Can, Ottawa; Art Inst Chicago. *Exhib:* 4th Biennial Paris, France, 65; Int Exhib Northwest Printmakers, Seattle, Wash, 65; 1st Biennial Graphics, Crakov, Poland, 66; Int Art Fair, Basel, Switz, 74; one-man show, Switzerland Union Bank, Zurich, 81. *Pos:* Mem, Executive Comt & Bd Dirs, Greenshields Foundation. *Teaching:* Dir art dept, Edgars & Cramps Sch, Montreal, 67-79; lectr drawing, McGill Univ, 74-82; lectr design & drawing, Concordia Univ, 76-83. *Awards:* Can Coun Grant, 66; Spec Mention, Price Fine Arts Awards, 70; Elizabeth T Greenshields Found Grant, 71 & 75. *Mem:* Royal Can Acad Arts; Print & Drawing Coun Can. *Media:* Acrylic, Lithography. *Dealer:* Walter Klinkhoff Gallery 1200 Sherbrooke St W Montreal PQ Can; Roberts Gallery 641 Yonge St Toronto ON Can. *Mailing Add:* RR #1 Ayers Cliff PQ J0B 1C0 Canada

BEAN, BENNETT
CERAMIST
b Cincinnati, Ohio, Mar 25, 41. *Study:* Grinnell Col, 59-61; Univ Iowa, BA, 63; Claremont Grad Sch, MFA, 66. *Work:* Whitney Mus Am Art, New York; Newark Mus, NJ; Royal Ont Mus, Toronto; St Louis Mus Art, Mo; NJ State Mus, Trenton. *Exhib:* Musee Des Arts Decoratifs de la Ville de Lausanne, Switz, 82; Raku and Smoke NAm, Newport Art Mus, 85 & Am Craft Mus, NY, 85; 40th Ceramic Ann Invitational, Scripps Col, Claremont, Calif, 85; Craft Today: Poetry of the Physical, Am Craft Mus,New York, 86; Firing the Imagination, New York, 88; Fired with Enthusiasm, The Campbell Mus, NJ, 88-; and over 50 one-man shows over the years in ceramics & sculpture. *Pos:* Artist-in-residence, Sun Valley Ctr, Idaho, 80 & ArtPark, Lewiston, NY, 80. *Teaching:* Asst prof art, Wagner Col, Staten Island, 66-79. *Awards:* Research Grant, Wagner Col, 68, 70, 77 & 78; NJ State Coun Arts Fel, 78 & 88; Nat Endowment Art Fel, 80. *Bibliog:* Elaine Levin (auth), History of American Ceramics, Harry N Abrams, Inc, 88; Akiro Busch (auth), article, Am Craft, 4/5/88; article, Ceramistas americanos, Ceramica, Madrid, No 32, 88. *Mem:* Am Craft Coun (trustee, 80-84); Am Craft Enterprises (bd trustee, 82-85); Peters Valley Craftsmen (chmn bd, 79, 81-82, bd dir, 77-82). *Media:* Clay. *Publ:* Auth, At Eye Level, Studio Potter, 85. *Mailing Add:* RD 3 Box 212 Blairstown NJ 07825

BEAR, MARCELLE L
PRINTMAKER, PAINTER
b Chicago, Ill, Jan 13, 17. *Study:* Chicago Acad & Am Acad, Chicago; Ecole des Arts Decoratifs, Paris, France; Art Inst Chicago, with Elliot O'Hara, John Caceres, Peterdi, W M Parker, M Ponce De Leon, A Daschaes, K Kerslake. *Work:* Jacksonville Art Mus, Fla; Wright State Univ, Dayton, Ohio; Ira Koger Corp Collection; Leonard Bocour Collection; Glidden Organics Corp Collection. *Comn:* Mural, comn by Mrs Ruth Ullrick, Mandarin, Fla, 56; painting, comn by Ben Jones, Universal Marion Corp, Jacksonville, 62; carved doors, Temple Ahavath Chesed, Jacksonville, 64 & 66; painting, comn by Duckett, Hubbard, Mason & Dow, 69; painting, comn by George Dickerson, Sutton Place, Jacksonville, 72. *Exhib:* Tenth Ann Drawing & Print, San Francisco Mus Art, 46; 14th New Yrs Show, Butler Art Inst, Youngstown, Ohio, 46; Mint Mus, Charlotte, NC, 64, 66 & 68; Hunterdon Co, Clinton, NJ, 63; Hunter Gallery, Charlotte, NC, 64 & 65; Metrop Mus & Art Ctr, Miami, Fla, 77; Nat, Panama City, Fla, 77, 78 & 79; Jacksonville Univ, 83; Jacksonville Art Mus, 83-84; and others. *Teaching:* Instr painting, Santa Maria Jr Col, Calif, 45; instr painting, Southside Womans Club, Jacksonville & Jacksonville Art Mus. *Awards:* Best in Show, 48-49 & First Painting, 61, 66 & 78, Jacksonville Art Mus; Seas Grand Award, 78. *Mem:* Fla Artists Group (treas, 75-80, vpres, 80-81). *Media:* Oil, Acrylic. *Mailing Add:* 6000 San Jose Blvd #1001 Jacksonville FL 32217

BEARCE, JEANA DALE
PAINTER, PRINTMAKER
b St Louis, Mo, Oct 3, 29. *Study:* St Louis Sch Fine Arts, Washington Univ, with Fred Conway, Fred Becker, Paul Burlin & George Lockwood, BFA, 51; NMex Highlands Univ, MA, 54; Independent study, Italy, France, India. *Work:* St Louis City Art Mus, Mo; Brooklyn Mus Art; Sarasota Art Asn, Fla; Calif Col Arts & Crafts, Oakland; Cornell Univ; and others. *Comn:* Indian Sand Paint (mural), NMex Highlands Univ, Las Vegas, 54; Seven Gifts (cross), Good Shepherd Church, Brunswick, Maine, 62; Search for Truth (mural), Bowdoin Col Libr, Brunswick, Maine, 65; 14 Stations to the Cross, St Charles Borromeo, Brunswick, Maine, 75; Monumental Mary and Bartholomew, St Bartholomew's, Cape Elizabeth, Maine, 77; and others. *Exhib:* Solo exhibs, Univ Maine, 57, 65, 80 & 85; The Boston Show, Boston Mus Fine Arts, Mass, 57; Print Show, Philadelphia Print Club, 58; St Peter's Church Gallery, New York, 74; India Revisited, Ctr Arts, Bath, 88; and others. *Teaching:* Instr, drawing, painting & printmaking, Univ Maine, Portland, 65-66, asst prof, 66-70, assoc prof, 70-81; prof, Univ Southern

Maine, 81- *Awards:* Purchase Prize, Sarasota Art Asn, 58; Eight Maine Artists, State of Maine, 64; Sabbatical & Research Awards, India, 80-81, 85, 88 & 93; and others. *Bibliog:* Pat Boyd Wilson (auth), Paintings of the Taj, Christian Sci Monitor, 68; Milldred Burrage (auth), Five Women Artists, Maine Art Gallery, 75. *Media:* Oil, Encaustic; Intaglio. *Dealer:* Benbow Gallery 515 Thane St Newport RI. *Mailing Add:* 327 Maine St Brunswick ME 04011

BEARD, RICHARD ELLIOTT
PAINTER, EDUCATOR
b Kenosha, Wis, June 13, 28. *Study:* Univ Wis-Madison, BS & MA; Ohio State Univ, PhD. *Work:* Ohio State Univ; Univ Ky; Defiance Col; Kankakee Comm Col; Northern Ill Univ. *Exhib:* Purdue Univ, 74; Chicago Artists & Vicinity, Chicago Art Inst, 77;; Beverly Art Ctr, Chicago, 78;; New Horizons Show, Chicago, Ill, 80;; West 80, Art and The Law, Minn Mus Art, St Paul, 80;; Open Spectrum, Libertyville, Ill, 87; Anderson Winter Show, Anderson, Ind, 88; Municipal Art League Show, Chicago, 88; one-man show, Woodstock Opera Gallery, Woodstock, Ill, 88; and others. *Teaching:* Asst prof art, Maryville Col, 52-61; asst instr art, Ohio State Univ, 61-63; vis prof art, Univ Ky, 63-64; assoc prof art, Wis State Univ, Stevens Point, 64-66; prof art, Northern Ill Univ, 66- *Awards:* Catalog Prize, Cincinnati Artists & Vicinity Show, 63; Best Painting in Show, Kenosha Art Asn, 66; Rockefeller Residency Grant, Bellagio, Italy, 83. *Mem:* Col Art Asn; Mid Am Col Art Asn. *Media:* Oil, Acrylic, Chalk. *Publ:* Collabr, Bells of Lombardy (paintings by artist, poetry by Lucien Stryck), Northern Ill Univ Press. *Dealer:* Am Print & Drawing De Kalb IL 60115; Neville-Sargent Gallery Chicago IL. *Mailing Add:* 730 W Taylor De Kalb IL 60115

BEARDSLEY, BARBARA H
CONSERVATOR
b New York, NY, Mar 30, 45. *Study:* Elmira Col, BA; Europ Study Prog, Univ Wis, cert; Univ NMex; State Univ NY, Cooperstown, study with Kecks, MA(conserv), cert(advan standing); study with Louis Pomerantz; McCrone Res Inst. *Comn:* Cleveland Mus Art; I Tatti, Harvard Univ, Florence, Italy; Currier Gallery, Manchester, NH; William Hayes Fogg Art Mus, Cambridge, Mass. *Collections Arranged:* Mary Lester Field Collection of Santos, Albuquerque, NMex, 70; Harwood Collection, Span Colonial Art, Taos, NMex, 71. *Pos:* Conservator, Intermuseum Conserv Assoc Lab, Oberlin, Ohio, 73-75; conserv intern, Newberry Libr, Chicago, 74-75; guest lectr conserv methods, State Univ NY, Cooperstown, 75-77; conservator, New England Coun, Am Asn Mus, six locations, 75-76; chief conservator, Art Conserv Lab Inc, 75- *Bibliog:* K Schaal (auth), New life for old masters, NH Profiles, 10/77; J Dueland (auth), Barbara Beardsley's barn, Christian Sci Monitor, 1/78; S Goss (auth), The Art Conservation Laboratory, NH Times, 2/82. *Mem:* Int Coun Mus; fel Am Inst Conserv Hist & Artistic Works; Nat Conserv Adv Coun; Am Inst Conserv (dir, 76-79); Festival of Arts, Waterville Valley, NH (mem, exec bd, 84); Center for Art (co-chmn, 88-). *Res:* Polarizing pigment analysis, material studies, art history research, Spanish Colonial Santos. *Publ:* Auth, The field collection of Santos, Univ NMex Art Mus Bulletin, 70; The adaptation of an examination microscope, Am Inst Conserv Bulletin, 72; Basic Guide to a Healthy Collection, Art Conserv Lab, rev ed 76; A Flexible Back for the Stabilization of a Botticelli Panel Painting, Oxford Wood Conference, Int Inst Conserv, 78. *Mailing Add:* Dudley Homestead Raymond NH 03077

BEASLEY, BRUCE
SCULPTOR
b Los Angeles, Calif, May 20, 39. *Study:* Dartmouth Col; Univ Calif, Berkeley, BA. *Work:* Mus Mod Art & Solomon R Guggenheim Mus, New York; Los Angeles Co Mus Art; Musee d'Art Moderne, Paris, France; Nat Mus Am Art, Washington, DC; Oakland Mus, Calif. *Comn:* Apolymen (cast acrylic sculpture), State Calif, 70; cast acrylic sculptures, US Govt-GSA Art in Pub Places, San Diego, Calif, 76 & City of San Francisco, Calif, 77; metal sculptures, City of Eugene, Ore, 74, San Francisco Int Airport, 79; metal sculpture, Fed Home Loan Bank, San Francisco, Calif, 92. *Exhib:* Art of Assemblage, 61 & painting & sculpture acquisitions, 64, Mus Mod Art, New York; Biennale de Paris, 63 & Salon de la Jeune Sculpture, 73, Musee d'Art Moderne, Paris; Soloman R Guggenheim Mus, New York, 66; one-man retrospective, M H DeYoung Mem Mus, San Francisco, Santa Barbara Mus Art & San Diego Mus Art, 72-73; Across the Nation, Nat Mus Am Art, Washington, DC, 80; Calif Sculpture, Mus Contemp Art, Bordeaux, France, 87; Monumenta, 19th Sculpture Biennale, Middleheim Sculpture Park, Antwerp, Belg, 87; Triennial Int Sculpture Exhib, Budapest, Hungary, 88; Forty Am Sculptors, XII Int Sculpture Conference, Washington DC, 80; and many others. *Awards:* Andre Malraux Purchase Award, Biennale de Paris, 63; Frank Lloyd Wright Mem Purchase Award, Marin Mus Asn, 65; Purchase Prize, San Francisco Arts Festival, 67. *Bibliog:* Bruce Beasley--Sculptor, Research & Architecture, 5/73 of Architecture, Chelsea Press, 80; Thomas Albright (auth), The Art of the San Francisco Bay Area: 1945 to 1980, Berkeley Univ Calif Press, 85. *Media:* Metal, Stone. *Mailing Add:* 322 Lewis St Oakland CA 94607

BEASON, DONALD RAY
EDUCATOR, SCULPTOR
b Camden, Ark, Oct 22, 43. *Study:* Kilgore Col, 63; Stephen F Austin State Univ, BA, 65; Mich State Univ, MFA, 67. *Work:* Cult Exchange Between Italy & US, Rome; Centro Int Ceramica, Rome; Cameron Univ. *Exhib:* Drawing USA, Minn Mus Art, 71; solo exhib, San Antonio Sun Shine, San Antonio Art Inst, 82, Amarillo Sun Set, Amarillo Art Mus, 83 & Midnight Air, Tyler Mus Art, 83; East Texas Show, Tyler Mus Art, 82; Triennial 1983, New Orleans Mus, 83. *Pos:* Mem, fine arts panel, Tex Comn on the Arts, 85- *Teaching:* Prof art, Stephen F Austin State Univ, 67-, Regents prof, 83- *Awards:* Fulbright-Hays Fel, 72; Nat Endowment Arts Fel, 82. *Mailing Add:* Art Dept Stephen F Austin Univ Nacogdoches TX 75962

BEATTIE, GEORGE
PAINTER, ART ADMINISTRATOR
b Cleveland, Ohio, Aug 2, 19. *Study:* Cleveland Inst Art, 38-41. *Work:* Whitney Mus Am Art, New York; Montclair Mus, NJ; High Mus, Atlanta; Mead Corp; Larry Aldrich Collection, Conn. *Comn:* Murals, History of Agriculture in State of Georgia, State Agr Bldg, Atlanta, 56 & History of Middle Georgia, Fed Post Off Bldg, Macon, Ga, 68. *Exhib:* Mead Painting of the Year, 55 & 61; Int Drawing Ann, Uffizi Loggia, Florence, Italy, 57; Fulbright Exhib, Rome, Italy, 57; Smithsonian Traveling Exhib, 58-59; Art USA, 59; Italy Revisited, Swan Coach House Gallery, Atlanta, 85, Venice, 89. *Pos:* Artist, Link Archeol Exped to Israel, 60 & Sicily, 62; exec dir, Ga Coun Arts, 67-75; dir pub serv in art, Ga State Univ, 75-81; adv bd, Northside High Sch Performing Arts, currently. *Teaching:* Head creative drawing, Ga Inst Technol Sch Archit, 57-67. *Awards:* Nat Inst Arts & Lett Grant, 55; Fulbright Grant to Italy, 56-57; Governor's Award Visual Arts, State Ga, 78. *Bibliog:* Nina Kaiden & Bartlett Hayes (auth), Artist & advocate, Renaissance Ed, 67. *Mem:* Atlanta Woodruff Arts Ctr; hon life mem bd trustees Arts Festival Atlanta, Inc; bd dir, High Mus. *Media:* All Media. *Mailing Add:* 857 Woodley Dr NW Atlanta GA 30318

BEATTY, FRANCES FIELDING LEWIS
HISTORIAN, CRITIC
b New York, NY, Nov 23, 48. *Study:* Vassar Col, BA; Columbia Univ, with Meyer Schapiro & Theodore Reff, MA(art hist; Noble Found Fel), PhD(Vassar Col Fel, Grant). *Pos:* Sr ed, Art-World, 76-84; vpres, Richard L Feigen & Co, currently. *Teaching:* Instr surrealism, Renaissance & 19th & 20th century art hist & lit, Ramapo Col, NJ, 74; instr art hist, Columbia Col, 74-76. *Res:* Work of Andre Masson in the 1920s and its relation to surrealist poetry and prose. *Publ:* Coauth, Louise Nevelson (catalog), Centre Nat d'Art Contemporain, Paris, 74; contribr, Andre Masson (catalog), Mus Mod Art, New York, 76. *Mailing Add:* c/o Richard L Feigen & Co 49 E 68th St New York NY 10021

BEAUCHAMP, GEORGE
COLLAGE ARTIST, PAINTER
b Detroit, Mich, July 23, 33. *Study:* Univ Mich, Ann Arbor, BS(design), 56, MS(design), 58. *Exhib:* Pa Acad Fine Arts Ann Exhib Watercolors, Prints & Drawings, 63; Davidson Col Nat Print & Drawing Competition, 74; Butler Inst Ann Mid-Year Show, 78; Small Works, NY Univ, 80, 85 & 90; Exhib Small Works, Key Gallery, New York, 81 & 83; Audubon Artists Ann Exhib, 88; one person exhib, Kendall Gallery, New York, NY, 89. *Media:* Photo Collage, Oil. *Mailing Add:* 151 Coles St Jersey City NJ 07302

BEAUCHAMP, ROBERT
INSTRUCTOR, PAINTER
b Denver, Colo, Nov 19, 23. *Study:* Colorado Springs Fine Arts Ctr; Cranbrook Acad of Art, Bloomfield Hills, Mich, BFA, 49; Hans Hofmann Sch Art. *Work:* Mus Mod Art, New York, Whitney Mus Am Art, Metrop Mus Art, New York; Carnegie Inst, Pittsburgh; Hirshhorn Mus & Sculpture Garden, Washington, DC; Denver Art Mus; Brooklyn Mus, NY; Aldrich Mus Contemp Art, Ridgefield, Conn; and pvt collections. *Exhib:* Walker Art Ctr, Minneapolis, 53; Carnegie Int, Carnegie Inst Technol Mus Art, Pittsburgh, 58 & 61; Whitney Mus Am Art, 61-63, 65, 67 & 69; Mus Mod Art, New York, 62; Artists Abroad, Inst of Int Educ, New York, 69; Ten Independents, Solomon R Guggenheim Mus, New York, 72; solo exhibs, Dain Gallery, New York, 72 & 73, Univ South Fla, Tampa, 74, Terry Dintenfass Gallery, New York, 76, Monique Knowlton Gallery, New York, 78-81, Landmark Gallery, 82, Berta Walker Gallery, New York, 91, Long Point Gallery, 92; M-13 Gallery, New York, 86 & 88-89; Locus Gallery, New York, 86 & 89; Gruenebaum Gallery, New York, 87; "Figurative Fifties", Nat Group Show, (traveling exhib), 88-89; Vanderwoude Tanabaum Gallery, New York, 89; Berta Walker Gallery, 90 & 91. *Pos:* Prof, Lamar Dodd chair, Univ Ga, 81-84. *Teaching:* Instr painting, Brooklyn Col, 73 & Sch of Visual Arts, 74-76; instr, Art Students League, currently. *Awards:* Fulbright Grant, 59; Nat Found of Arts Grant, 66; Guggenheim Found Fel, 74; Nat Endowment Arts, 85. *Bibliog:* Scott Burton (auth), Paint the devil, Art News, 66; Kay Larson (auth) article, Village Voice, 10/79; Grace Glueck (auth), article, NY Times, 10/79. *Mem:* Artists Equity. *Media:* Oil, Graphite. *Dealer:* Berta Walker Gallery 208 Bradford St Provincetown MA 02657. *Mailing Add:* 463 West St, #346 New York NY 10014

BEAUDOIN, ANDRE EUGENE
PRESS MANUFACTURER, PHOTOGRAPHER
b Calais, France, Apr 11, 20; US citizen. *Study:* Ecole des Arts de Metiers, Paris, France, machine design & metallurgy; Brown Univ, photog. *Pos:* Owner, designer & constructor of etching & lithographic presses for artist printmakers, Am-French Tool Co, 69- *Mailing Add:* PO Box 227 Coventry RI 02816

BEAUMONT, MONA
PAINTER, PRINTMAKER
b Paris, France; US citizen. *Study:* Univ Calif, Berkeley, BA & MA; grad study, Fogg Mus, Harvard Univ, Cambridge, Mass; spec study with Hans Hoffman, New York. *Work:* Oakland Mus Art, Calif; City & Co San Francisco; Hoover Found; Bulart Found, San Francisco. *Exhib:* San Francisco Art Inst, 58, 62-66 & 74, traveling exhib, 64 & 65; Calif Painters & Sculptors, Univ Calif, Los Angeles, 59; Regional Painters, De Young Mem Mus Art, San Francisco, 62; San Francisco Gallery Artists, Stanford Univ Art Mus, 66; Print & Drawing Ann, Richmond Art Ctr, Va, 68; Bell Tel Print-Drawing, Chicago, 69; one-person shows, Calif Palace of Legion of Honor, San Francisco, 64, San Francisco Mus Art, 68 & Palo Alto Cult Ctr, Calif, 77;

L'Armetiere Gallery, Rouen, France, 72; Honolulu Acad Art, Hawaii, 80; and others. *Awards:* Purchase Award, US Artists Tour of Asia, Grey Found, 63; Purchase & One-Person Show Awards, San Francisco Art Festival Ann, 66 & 75; Ackerman Award, San Francisco Woman Artists Ann, 68. *Bibliog:* Thomas Albright (auth), Art in the San Francisco Bay Area, 85; Andrew De Shong (auth), Works on Paper--San Francisco Art Inst, Art Week Mag, 11/74. *Mem:* Arch Am Art; Soc Encouragement Contemp Art. *Media:* Acrylic, Mixed. *Publ:* Contribr, articles in Artforum, 5/64 & 12/64; Frankenstein, San Francisco Chronicle, 66 & 67. *Mailing Add:* 1087 Upper Happy Valley Rd Lafayette CA 94549

BECHTLE, C RONALD
PAINTER, DRAFTSMAN
b Philadelphia, Pa, Nov 14, 24. *Study:* ETenn Univ; Tyler Sch Fine Arts, Temple Univ; Fleisher Mem, Sch Indust Art; also with Benton Spruance, 52-53. *Work:* Munson-Williams-Proctor Inst, Utica, NY; Carnegie Inst Mus Art; Santa Barbara Mus Art, Calif; Columbus Gallery Fine Art, Ohio; Nat Mus Am Art, Washington, DC; and many others. *Exhib:* Pa Acad Fine Arts Regional, 65 & 69; one-man shows, Panoras Gallery, New York, 66, Santa Barbara Mus Art, 67, Miami Mus Mod Art, Fla, 68 & Philadelphia Art Alliance, 73, Storelli Gallery, 74 & E Tenn Univ, 77. *Pos:* Pres, Group 55, 56-57; pres, Philadelphia Abstract Artists, 57-63. *Mem:* Am Fedn Arts; Col Art Asn Am. *Media:* Watercolor, Gouache; Crayon, Pencil. *Publ:* Auth, Information theory of art, Mensa J, 61. *Mailing Add:* 26 Strawberry Hill Ave Apt 12B Stamford CT 06902

BECHTLE, ROBERT ALAN
PAINTER
b San Francisco, Calif, May 14, 32. *Study:* Calif Col Arts & Crafts, BA & MFA; Univ Calif, Berkeley. *Work:* Whitney Mus Am Art, Mus Mod Art & Guggenheim Mus, New York; San Francisco Mus Art; Univ Calif Art Mus, Berkeley. *Exhib:* Image, Form & Color: Recent Paintings by 11 Americans, Toledo Mus of Art, Ohio, 75; Painting & Sculpture in Calif: The Mod Era, San Francisco Mus of Mod Art, 76; Am 1976, Corcoran Gallery of Art, Washington, DC, 76; Aspects of Realism-Du Realisme, Rothmans of Can Ltd, Montreal, 76-77; Illusion & Reality, Australian Gallery Dirs Coun, 77-78; Representations of Am, Pushkin Fine Arts Mus, Moscow, USSR, 78; Contemporary American realism since 1960, Pa Acad Fine Arts, Philadelphia, 81; Realism, Photorealism, Philbrook Art Ctr, Tulsa, Okla, 81; and many others. *Teaching:* Prof printmaking, Calif Col Arts & Crafts, 57-; guest artist, Univ Calif, Davis, 66-68; prof art, San Francisco State Univ, 68-. *Awards:* James D Phelan Award in Painting, 65; Nat Endowment Arts Grant, 77 & 82. *Bibliog:* W Seitz (auth), The real and the artificial: painting of the new environment, Art in Am, 11-12/72; G Battcock (auth), Super Realism, A Critical Anthology, Dutton, 75; C Lindey (auth), Superrealist Painting and Sculpture, William Morrow & Co, 80; and others. *Dealer:* O K Harris Gallery 383 W Broadway New York NY 10012. *Mailing Add:* c/o Gallery Paule Anglim 14 Geary St San Francisco CA 94108

BECK, DOREEN
WRITER, AV PRODUCER
b Medomsley, Durham, Eng, Mar 12, 35; US & UK citizen. *Study:* Leicester Univ Col, Univ London, BA(hons in French), 57; NY Univ, film prod; NY Sch Visual Arts, screen writing with Andrew Sarris. *Comn:* The Sound (quilted, applique wall hanging), Pvt collector, 86. *Pos:* Writer & producer AV mat, UN; researcher & writer, Med Newsmag; research, ed & writing, BBC, World Bk Enc (int ed), The Observer, Thames & Hudson, Julian Press, Ved Mehta & New Yorker. *Publ:* Auth, Britain: An Enduring Heritage (script), 69; Book of Bottle Collecting, 73; Book of American Furniture, 73; Country & Western Americana, 75; Photo book, Disarmament, NOW! Investment in Living NOW!, 85; auth & producer, exhibs on visitors Tour Route at UN hq, New York. *Mailing Add:* 100 W 57th St New York NY 10019

BECK, JAMES
HISTORIAN, CRITIC
b New Rochelle, NY, May 14, 30. *Study:* Oberlin Col, BA, 52; NY Univ, MA, 54; Columbia Univ, PhD, 63. *Teaching:* From asst prof to assoc prof, Columbia Univ, 64-72, prof art hist, 72-, chmn dept art hist & archeol, 84-90. *Awards:* Commendatore of the Ital Repub. *Mem:* Col Art Asn; Renaissance Soc Am. *Publ:* Auth, The Doors of the Florentine Baptistry, 85; ed, Raphael Before Rome, 86; auth, The Sepulchral Monument for Ilaria del Carretto by Jacopo della Quercia, 89; The Tyranny of the Detail, Willis Locker, 92; Jacopo Della Quercia, Columbia Univ Press, 92. *Mailing Add:* Dept Art Hist & Archeol Columbia Univ New York NY 10027

BECK, LONNIE LEE
PAINTER, EDUCATOR
b Marion, Ind, Jan 6, 42. *Study:* Herron Sch Art, Ind Univ, BFA(advan design), 65, BFA(painting), 67; Miami Univ, MFA(painting), 69. *Work:* Herron Sch Art, Ind Univ, Indianapolis. *Exhib:* Indianapolis Mus Art, 68 & 69; Owensboro Mus Fine Arts, Ky, 80; Evansville Mus Art & Sci, Ind, 80; Appalachian State Univ, Boone, NC, 80; Okla Art Ctr, Oklahoma City, 81; Ball State Univ, Muncie, Ind, 82; and many others. *Collections Arranged:* Robert Berkshire Paintings, 75, Rockwell Kent (coauth, catalog), 79, Dean Howell Sculpture, 80, Terrance LaNoue, Jim Sullivan & Frank Owens Paintings, 81 & Dennis Puhalla Paintings, 82, Hiestand Gallery, Miami Univ. *Awards:* Best Show Painting, 500 Festival Arts Comn, 67; Purchase Award, Del Mar Col, 75; Purchase Award, Ball State Univ, 82. *Media:* Oil, Charcoal. *Mailing Add:* 125 E Central Ave Oxford OH 45056

BECK, MARGIT
PAINTER, EDUCATOR
b Tokay, Hungary. *Study:* Inst Fine Arts, Oradea Mare, Roumania; Art Students League; McDowell Resident Fels, 56, 57, 59, 60 & 75. *Work:* Whitney Mus Am Art, New York; J B Speed Mus, Louisville, Ky; Edwin A Ulrich Mus Art, Wichita, Kans; Lyman Allyn Mus, New London, Conn; Norfolk Mus Arts & Sci, Va; plus others. *Comn:* Traveling Drawing Exhib, Southern Mus. *Exhib:* Corcoran Gallery Art Biennial, 65; four shows, Pa Acad Fine Arts Ann, 57-68; Whitney Mus Am Art Ann, 58-61; four shows, Brooklyn Mus Int Watercolor Biennial, 59-67; Art Inst Chicago, 60-61; Childe Hassam Fund Exhib, Am Acad of Arts & Lett, 60, 62 & 66-71; Ann Exhib of Candidates for Grants, Nat Inst of Arts & Lett, New York, 60, 66-68; 22 one-woman exhibs. *Teaching:* Lectr art, Hofstra Univ, 66-67; adj asst prof art, New York Univ, 67-; adv & tutor art hist, Empire State Col, 74- *Awards:* Childe Hassam Purchase Award, Am Acad Arts & Lett, 68, 70 & 71; Medal of Hon, 68 & 72 & Stephen Hirsh Mem Award, Audubon Artists; plus others. *Bibliog:* Sharon Theobold (auth), Homes of distinguished Nassau artists, Mag Nassau, 6/74; John Gruen (auth), Margit Beck (monogr), Soho News, 3/3/75; Jeanne Paris (auth), Margit Beck (monogr), Long Island Press, 3/30/75; plus others. *Mem:* Artists Equity (exec bd mem, 65-70); Audubon Artists; academician Nat Acad Design; Col Art Asn Am. *Media:* Oil, Ink. *Publ:* contribr, Women Artists: 25 Best Investments, Working Woman, 7/80. *Dealer:* ACA Gallery 21 E 67th St New York NY 10021. *Mailing Add:* 35 Knightsbridge Rd S Great Neck NY 11021

BECK, MARTHA ANN
MUSEUM DIRECTOR, CURATOR
b Cleveland, Ohio, June 16, 38. *Study:* Vassar Col, BA, 60; NY Univ Inst Fine Arts, studied under Erwin Panofsky, 63-67. *Collections Arranged:* The Drawings of Antonio Gaudi, 77, The Travel Sketches of Louis I Kahn, 78, Musical Manuscripts, 78-79, Visionary Drawings of Architecture and Planning, 79, Sculptors' Drawings over Six Centuries, 81, Reading Drawings, A Selection from the Victoria and Albert Mus, 84, Great Drawings from the Royal Institute of British Architects, 83, Drawings from Venice, Masterworks from the Museo Correr, 85, The Northern Landscape: Flemish, Dutch and British Drawings from the Courtauld Collections, 86. *Pos:* Curatorial asst, Mus Mod Art, New York, 68-75; dir, The Drawing Ctr, 75-90, dir emeritus & cur special exhib, 90-; dir, Ctr Int Exhibs Inc, New York, 91- *Publ:* Auth, New Drawing in America, The Drawing Ctr, 82. *Mailing Add:* 9 Gramercy Park S New York NY 10003

BECK, THERESA
PAINTER
b Norfolk, Va, Dec 1, 53. *Study:* Old Dominion Univ, BFA, 75, Northern Ill Univ, MA (painting), 79. *Work:* St Joseph's Hosp & Holland & Knight, Attys, Tampa, Fla; IDS, Chaska, Minn. *Comn:* First Fla Bank, 11/89. *Exhib:* One-woman shows, Fla Gulf Coast Art Ctr Teaching Gallery, Bellair, Fla, 86, Tampa Elec Co, Tampa, Fla, 87, Osceola Ctr Arts, Kissimmee, Fla, 90; First Fla Bank, Tampa, 89; Beck-Taylor-Edelson-Lurie, Polk Community Col, Winter Haven, Fla, 89; Beck-Hott-Rensel-Smith, Thompson Land Group Property, Ybor City, Tampa, Fla, 92. *Teaching:* Instr drawing, Renton Parks & Recreation Dept, Wash, 80-81; instr airbrush painting, Cape Coral Art Studio, Fla 84-85, Fla Gulf Coast Art Ctr, Belleair, 86-87 & Old Hyde Park Art Ctr, Tampa, Fla, 89-90. *Awards:* Fel, Nat Endowment Arts, 87. *Mem:* Woman's Caucus Art, Fla West Coast Chap (vpres & treas, 87-89); Fla Ctr Contemp Art (exhib comt, 90-91). *Publ:* Art Papers, Photog Installation, Vol 12, No 6, Atlanta, Ga, 11/88; NAAO Directory, Photog Installation, Nat Asn Arts Orgns, 90; Arts News, Illus, Newsletter Arts Coun Hillsborough Co, summer 90; Organica Quarterly, Illus, Vol 11, No 39, spring 92. *Mailing Add:* 5322 Russell St Tampa FL 33611

BECKER, BETTIE (BETTIE GERALDINE WATHALL)
PAINTER, GRAPHIC ARTIST
b Peoria, Ill, Sept 22, 18. *Study:* Univ Ill, BFA; Art Students League, with John Carroll; Art Inst Chicago, with Lewis Ritman; Inst Design, Ill Inst Technol, with Hans Weber. *Work:* Witte Mem Mus, San Antonio, Tex; Union League Club, Chicago, Ill; Bank Sturgeon Bay, Wis; Standard Oil Collection, Chicago; State Medical Soc, Madison Wis; Miller Art Ctr, Sturgeon Bay, Wis. *Comn:* Mural (with Frank Wiater), Talbot Materials Testing Lab, Univ Ill, Urbana, 40. *Exhib:* One-woman show, Crossroad's Gallery, Art Inst Chicago, 73; Print & Drawing Exhib, Artist's Guild, Chicago, 76; 36th NE Wis Art Ann, Neville Mus, Green Bay Wis, 45th Art Ann, 87, 48th & 49th Art Ann, 90 & 91, Expressions & Commentary, Wis Women Arts, 91; Women in Art, Appleton Gallery Art, Wis, 82; Chicago Soc Artists Retro Exhib, Mus Sci & Industry, 83; Update Wisconsin, Milwaukee Art Mus, 86; and others. *Pos:* Instr creative drawing, Clearing in winter, 79, 80, summer, 81-, Ellison Bay, Wis; instr art appreciation, Peninsula Art Sch, Fish Creek, Wis, 82-87. *Awards:* Newcomb Prize, Univ Ill Col Fine & Appl Arts, 40; First Prize for Print, Chicago Soc Artists, 67, 71 & 74; Award for mural, Dept Engineering, Univ Ill, 88; plus others. *Bibliog:* Article, La Revue Moderne, Paris, 73; Louise Dunn Yochim (auth), Role & Impact, Chicago Soc Artists; Marina Neri (auth), monograph, Accad Italia, 85. *Mem:* Chicago Soc Artists (rec secy, 68-77); Alumni Asn Art Inst Chicago; Northeastern Wis Arts Coun; Peninsula Arts Asn; Door County Art League, Sister Bay, Wis; Wis Women Arts. *Media:* Enamel, Acrylic. *Publ:* Auth, Life with Liberty, 43; illusr, Sat Rev Lit, 48, New York Times, 48, Chicago Tribune, 48 & 49 & Evanston Rev, 68; A child of autumn, Insight Mag, Milwaukee J, 79; auth, Mural History, Technique, Layout, Univ Ill, 86. *Dealer:* Valperine Gallery 1719 Monroe St Madison WI 53711; Wis Arts Gallery 1780 E Allouez Green Bay WI 54311. *Mailing Add:* 3992 Juddville Rd Fish Creek WI 54212

BECKER, DAVID
PRINTMAKER, EDUCATOR
b Milwaukee, Wis, Aug 16, 37. *Study:* Univ Wis-Milwaukee, BS, 61; Univ Ill, Urbana, MFA, 65. *Work:* Libr Cong, Washington, DC; Brooklyn Mus, NY; Mus de Arte Mod, Cali, Colombia; Art Inst Chicago; Detroit Inst Arts, Mich; Nat Mus Am Art, Washington, DC; Portland Art Mus, Ore. *Comn:* Print, Detroit Inst Art Drawing & Print Club, 83. *Exhib:* 30 Yrs of Am Printmaking, Brooklyn Mus, NY, 76; New American Graphics 3, US Info Serv Agency, 83; Boston Printmakers Nat Print Exhib, 34th, 36th, 38th & 42nd, 82, 84, 86 & 90; Intergrafik 84, East Berlin, GDR, 84 & 87; Ninth British Int Print Biennale, Bradford, Eng, 86; 162nd, 165th , 166th & 167th Ann, Nat Acad Design, 87 & 90- 92; solo exhib, Jane Haslem Gallery, Washington, DC, 90. *Teaching:* Prof art, Wayne State Univ, Detroit, Mich, 65-85; vis prof printmaking, Univ Wis-Madison, 78-79; vis artist, Utah State Univ, Logan, summer 81; prof art, Univ Wis-Madison, 85- *Awards:* Hunterdon Art Ctr Purchase Award, 30th Nat Print Exhib, 86; Nat Acad Design Loggie Prize, 162nd & 166th Ann, 87 & 91; Cannon Prize, 165th Ann, 90. *Bibliog:* Gene Baro (auth), 30 Years of American Printmaking, Brooklyn Mus, 77; James Watrous (auth), A Century of American Printmaking, Univ Wis Press, 84; John Ross, Clare Romano & Tim Ross (coauths), The Complete Printmaker, Free Press, 89. *Mem:* Soc Am Graphic Artists; Nat Acad Design; Fel, MacDowell Colony. *Dealer:* Jane Haslem 2025 Hillyer Pl NW Washington DC 20009. *Mailing Add:* 2512 Lunde Lane Mt Horeb WI 53572

BECKER, JOHANNA LUCILLE
EDUCATOR, HISTORIAN
b Denver, Colo, Dec 17, 21. *Study:* Univ Colo, BFA, 43; Ohio State Univ, MA, 45; Univ Mich, MA, 67, PhD, 74. *Pos:* Cur, permanent collection, Col St Benedict, 81-84. *Teaching:* Chmn dept art, Mayville Col, St Louis, Mo, 45-46; instr studio art & hist, Ill State Univ, Bloomington, 47-48; chmn & prof studio art & hist, Col St Benedict, St Joseph, & St John's Univ, Collegeville, Minn, 57-, chmn art dept, 83-85, 87-90. *Awards:* Fulbright Fel, (res India), US Govt, 63; Am Asn Univ Women Fel (res Japan), 69; Metrop Ctr Far Eastern Studies, Kyoto, Japan, 84. *Mem:* Minneapolis Inst Art, Asian Art (bd dirs & acquisitions). *Res:* Ceramics; prehistoric through the 17th century Asian ceramics; 17th & 18th century Japanese ceramics. *Publ:* Auth, Karatsu Ceramics of Japan: Origins, Fabrication and Types, Vol 1 & II, Microfilms, 74; Chinese art under the Mongols: Ceramics and Yuan aesthetics, J Asiatic Soc Japan, 75; Der Karatsu stil und Koreanishe einflusse, Keramos, Rasch Druckerei & Co, Bramsche, 79; Japanese export porcelain at the Princessesdorf, Oriental Art Mag Ltd, London, 82; Karatsu Ware, Kodansha Int, New York & Tokyo, 86. *Mailing Add:* Convent of St Benedict St Joseph MN 56374-0277

BECKER, NATALIE ROSE
PAINTER, INSTRUCTOR
b Philadelphia, Pa. *Study:* Fleisher Art Mem, Philadelphia; Temple Univ, AA; Pa Acad Fine Arts; Art Students League, with Robert Phillip & Henry Gasser. *Work:* Fine Arts Galleries, Carnegie Inst; Bloomfield Col. *Exhib:* Allied Artists Am, Nat Acad Design, New York, 74-86; Audubon Artists Am, 73-86; Nat Arts Club Invitational, 78; Bergen Mus Invitational, 80. *Teaching:* Instr drawing & painting, Union Col, Cranford, NJ. *Awards:* Grumbacher Award of Merit, Catharine Lorillard Wolfe Art Club, 72, 82 & 87; Grumbacher Award, Nat Arts Club, 75; First Prize & Medal of Honor, Audubon Artists Ann Exhib, 80. *Mem:* Audubon Artists (bd mem); Allied Artist Am; Pen & Brush Club; Catharine Lorillard Wolfe Art Club; Nat Asn Women Artists. *Media:* Oil, Pen & Ink. *Mailing Add:* 97 Barchester Way Westfield NJ 07090

BECKERMAN, NANCY GREYSON
PAINTER, CRAFTSMAN
b New York, NY. *Study:* Cornell Univ, 60-62; Hunter Col, BA(magna cum laude & phi beta kappa), 62-64; NY Univ, 65; Boston Univ, 65. *Work:* ABC Collection, New York. *Exhib:* Hudson River Open, Hudson River Mus, Yonkers, NY, 76 & 77; New England Open, Silvermine Gallery, Conn, 81; Bergen Community Mus, Paramus, NJ, 83; Women's Art Invitational, Ecumen Assembly, Purdue Univ, WLaffayette, Ind, 84; Four in 64, Johnson Mus Art, Cornell Univ, Ithaca, NY, 84; Color Reflections, Cork Gallery, Lincoln Ctr, New York, 86; Painted Surfaces, Albany Inst Hist & Art, NY, 86; Innovative Traditions, The Museums, Stonybrook, NY. *Awards:* Marion deSola Mendes Mem Award, 79; Juror's Prize, Washington & Jefferson Painting Exhib, 81. *Bibliog:* Rev, La Revue Moderne, Paris, 80; Robin Bergstrom (dir), Meet the VIP's: Nancy Beckerman, WVIP(radio, cable-tv), 83; Lauren Otis (auth), A powerful presence of women, Artspeak, 86. *Mem:* Nat Asn Women Artists; Artists Equity NY; Women in the Arts. *Media:* Acrylic on Canvas; Fabric. *Mailing Add:* Rte 1 Box 351 Pound Ridge NY 10576

BECKHARD, ELLIE (ELEANOR)
PAINTER, PHOTOGRAPHER
b Brooklyn, NY. *Study:* Brooklyn Col, 47-51; studied Hans Hoffman Technique with Shirley Gorelick (student of Hoffman) & studied with Leo Manso & Jerry Okimoto, 78. *Exhib:* Silvermine juried show, Silvermine Mus, New Canaan, Conn, 78; 157th Ann, Nat Acad Design, New York, 82; Long Island Invitational, 83 & juried show, 83 & 89, Islip Mus, New York; Fine Arts juried shows, Fine Arts Mus Long Island, Hempstead, NY, 83, 85, 88, 89 & 91; The Expert Eye, Coun Arts N Shore, Glen Cove, NY, 84; Showcase of Excellence III Invitational, Midge Karr Art Ctr, Brookville, NY, 89. *Awards:* Award, Parsons: Leland Bell & Jane Freilicker, 81 & Award Merit, G McCarthy & Irving Sandler, 87 Huntington Township Art League at Heckscher Mus; Ziuta & Joseph Akston Found Award, Nat Asn Women Artists, 86. *Bibliog:* Helen Harrison (auth), Debut of a museum series, 10/83 & Unusual energy mark juried show, 4/87, NY Times; Karin Lipson (auth), Showcase 100 artists, 4/87 & Four gallery exhibition, 6/87, News Day. *Mem:* Nat Asn Women Artists; Huntington Township Art League. *Media:* Acrylic, Pastel. *Publ:* Contribr, Contract Interiors (cover), Donald J Carroll, 9/77; Process Architecture: The Legacy of Marcel Breuer, no 32, p 5, Bunji Murotani, 82; NY Times: Home, section C1, 7/23/81. *Mailing Add:* Red Spring Lane Glen Cove NY 11542

BECKLEY, BILL
POST-CONCEPTUAL ARTIST
b Hamburg, Pa, Feb 11, 46. *Study:* Kutztown State Col, Pa, BFA; Tyler Sch Art, Temple Univ, with Steven Greene & Italo Scanga, MFA. *Work:* Mus Mod Art, New York; Basel Kunst Mus, Switz; Guggenheim Mus; Monchengladbach Mus; Boston Mus Art; Whitney Mus Art; and others. *Exhib:* 7, Mus Mod Art, New York, 73; Sequenced Photographs, Univ Art Mus, Austin, Tex, San Francisco Art Mus, Calif & Broxtan Art Gallery, Los Angeles, 76; Whitney Bienniel Exhib, New York, 79; Morton Neuman Collection, Chicago Art Inst & Los Angeles Co Mus, 79; Image & Text, Chicago Art Inst, 79; Photographic Art, Mus Mod Art, Paris, 80; This is Not a Photograph, John & Mable Ringling Mus Art, Sarasota, Fla, 88 & Akron Art Mus, Ohio, 88 & travelled; Large Scale Photography, Los Angeles Co Mus, Calif, 88; Ten Years of Collecting, 1976-86, Edward Downe Collection, Wellesley Col Mus, Mass, 88; Image World Art & Media Culture, Whitney Mus, New York, 89; one-man shows, G-7, Bologna, 89, Galerie Milano, 89, Daniel Templeton, Paris, 90, John Gibson, New York, 91, Drawings, Ace Contemp Exhibs, Los Angeles, 91, Pasquale Trisorio Gallery, Naples, 92 & Hans Mayer, Dusseldorf, 93; Words, Tony Shafrazi Gallery, New York, 90; The Seventies, John Gibson Gallery, 92. *Teaching:* Instr, Sch Visual Arts, 71- *Awards:* Nat Endowment, 79. *Bibliog:* Image World, Art and Media Culture (exhib catalog), Whitney Mus Am Art, 89; Alan Jones (auth), Books in artists' lives, Art Mag, 1/91; Lisa Phillips (auth), Image World, Art and Media Culture, New Art, Rizzoli, 92; and others. *Dealer:* Hans Mayer Grabbeplatz 2 4000 Dusseldorf Ger; Ace Gallery 5541 Wilshire Blvd Los Angeles CA 40036 & New York NY. *Mailing Add:* Sch Vis Arts Humanities & Sci 209 E 23rd St New York NY 10010

BECKMAN, ERICKA
FILMMAKER, PHOTOGRAPHER
b Hempstead, NY, July 7, 51. *Study:* Wash Univ, BFA, 74; Whitney Independent Study Prog, 75; Calif Inst Arts, MFA, 76. *Work:* Inst Contemp Art, London; Am Fedn Arts, New York. *Exhib:* Pictures Today, Padligione D'Artes Contemp, Milan, Italy, 80; Preview: Out of Hand, Kitchen, New York, 80; Super-8 Series, Bleeker St Cinema, New York, 81; Film as Play, WNET-Channel 13, New York, 83; You the Better, New York Film Festival & ICA, London, 83; Whitney Mus Biennial, 83; The Forge, New Mus, New York, 86; Film Screening Cindrella, Walker Art Inst, Minneapolis, Minn, 86; Coeur du Malstrom, Palais Des Beaux Arts, Brussels, 86; Boss Cutler Gallery, 88; Hirshhorn Mus, 89; MOCA, 89. *Teaching:* Asst prof art, Fordham Univ, 80-83; asst prof film, New Sch Social Res, 80-83 & Mass Col Art, 83- *Awards:* Grants, NY State Coun Arts, 88, Jerome Found, 81 & 83 & Nat Endowment Arts, 83; CAPS Film Grant, The Jerome Found Grant, 83; Artist Fel Prog Film Award, New York Found Arts, 87. *Bibliog:* J Hoberman (auth), article, 81 & Carrie Rickey (auth), article, 83, Art Forum; Sally Banes (auth), Films by Ericka Beckman, Millenium Film J, 83; J Hoberman (auth), Avant to Live, Village Voice, 6/18/87, Bernice Reynaud (auth), Erika Beckman-Independent America New Film (catalog essay), Am Mus Moving Image, Astoria, Queens, 88. *Publ:* Coauth, The spot syndrome, New Observations Mag, 83; auth, Chances territory, Effects Mag, 83; auth, The turn-about, Wedge Mag, 83; Illusr, The Journal, LAICA, Los Angeles, Calif, 1/85; Auth, Polities, Desire & Everyday Life, New Observations, No 45, 87; Auth & photogr, The Beanstalk and Jack, Hallwalls Books, Buffalo, New York, 88. *Mailing Add:* 358 Broadway New York NY 10013

BECKMANN, JOHN
DESIGNER
b Mt Kisco, New York, Sept 3, 60. *Study:* Parsons Sch Design, New York, BFA (environ design), 82. *Exhib:* Fine Art of Industrial Design, Nat Arts Club, New York, 88; Young Americans 88, Am Crafts Mus, New York, NY, 88; Interior Objects 1991, Design Gallery, New York, 91; International Furniture Design for the 90's, Fullscale Gallery, New York, 91; Inaugural Exhib, Entree Libre, New York, 92. *Bibliog:* Alberto Alessi (auth), Paisaje Domestico-Seleccion Internationale de Objectos, ARDI, 11-12/91; The Graphic Life, Vogue Decoration, No 34, 11-12/91; 20 best sellers of 1991, NY Times, 1/2/92. *Mem:* Indust Design Soc Am. *Dealer:* Galerie Gastou-Yves Gastou 12 rue Bonaparte Paris France 75002. *Mailing Add:* 361 W 36th St New York NY 10018

BEEBE, MARY LIVINGSTONE
ART ADMINISTRATOR
b Portland, Ore, Nov 5, 40. *Study:* Bryn Mawr Col, Pa, BA, 62. *Pos:* Mus apprentice, Portland Art Mus, 63-64; asst to registr & secy, Mus Fine Arts, Boston, 65-66; secy & curatorial asst, Fogg Art Mus, Harvard Univ, 66-68; producer, Am Theater Co, Portland, 68-71; dir, Portland Ctr Visual Arts, 72-81; dir, Stuart Collection Sculpture, Univ Calif, San Diego, 81- *Awards:* Nat Endowment Arts Fel, 79; AIA Allied Profession Award, 92. *Mem:* Art Matters Inc, New York (bd mem); Russell Found, La Jolla (bd mem); Arts Advisory Comt, Univ Wash, Seattle, 89-; Art Table. *Mailing Add:* B-027, 230 Mandeville Ctr Univ Calif San Diego La Jolla CA 92093

BEELER, JOE (NEIL)
PAINTER, SCULPTOR
b Joplin, Mo, Dec 25, 31. *Study:* Univ Tulsa; Kans State Univ, BFA; Art Ctr Sch, Los Angeles. *Work:* Gilcrease Mus, Tulsa, Okla; Nat Cowboy Hall of Fame, Oklahoma City; Mont Hist Soc, Helena; Phoenix Art Mus; Five Civilized Tribes Mus, Muskogee, Okla. *Exhib:* One-man shows, Gilcrease Mus, 61 & 80, Nat Cowboy Hall of Fame, 63, Heard Mus, Phoenix, 68 & C M Russell Mus, Great Falls, Mont, 70; Cowboy Artist of Am Ann Show, 66-79; and others. *Awards:* Best of Sculpture, Cowboy Artist Show, 67, Silver Medal Sculpture, 69-74, Colt Award for Best Over All of Show, 71 & Silver Medal Drawing, 74. *Bibliog:* Jeff Dykes (auth), 50 Great Western Illustrators, Northland Press, 75; Don Hedgepeth (auth), The Joe Beeler Story, Northland Press, 78. *Mem:* Founding mem Cowboy Artist Am (pres, 70-71). *Media:* Oil, Watercolor; Bronze. *Publ:* Auth, Cowboys and Indians, Univ Okla, 67; illusr, Ben Green, Last Trail Drive through Downtown Dallas, 72; contribr, Abrams & Pat Broder, Bronzes of the American West, 74; auth, Joe Beeler Sketch Book, Northland Press, 75; illusr, Cowboy in Art, World Pub, 69. *Mailing Add:* PO Box 989 Sedona AZ 86336

BEEMAN, MALINDA
PAINTER, PRINTMAKER
b Pomona, Calif, Jan 23, 49. *Study:* Calif State Univ, BA, 71; San Francisco Art Inst, MFA, 73. *Work:* IBM Corp, Houston, Tex; Menil Collection, Houston, Tex; Chattahoochee Valley Art Asn, La Grange, Ga; Crystal Energies, Houston; Apple Corp, Dallas, Tex. *Comn:* USS Houston (painting), Houston, TX. *Exhib:* Solo exhibs, Harris Gallery, Houston, 86 & 87; Fac Exhib, Blaffer Gallery, Univ Houston, 86; Houston Printmakers, Goethe Inst, Ger Cult Ctr, 86; Printmaking '86, Galveston Guild, Tex, 86; Prisoners of Conscience, Diverse Works, Houston; Plates by Houston Artists, Perception Gallery, Houston, 86; Texas Art Celebration, Assistance League, Two Houston Ctr, Houston, 87; Flower & Garden Show, D W Gallery, Dallas, 87; Koplin Gallery, Los Angeles, Calif, 89; Fed Reserve Board Bldg, Washington, DC; NY State Mus, Albany, 89. *Pos:* Prog Dir painting, Anderson Ranch Arts Ctr, Snowmass Village, Colo, currently. *Awards:* Visual Artist Fel Grant, Nat Endowment Arts, 87; Res Initiation Grant, Univ Houston, 87. *Bibliog:* Grace Glueck (auth), Art: A Houston school emerges, New York Times, 5/24/85; Reine Hauser (auth), Hometown bravura, Art News, summer, 85; Edward Lucie Smith (auth), American Art Now, Morrow, 85. *Mailing Add:* PO Box 5923 Snowmass Village CO 81615

BEENEN, RICHARD
PHOTOGRAPHER
b Los Angeles, Calif, Nov 23, 53. *Study:* Calif State Univ, Fullerton, MA. *Work:* Holtzman, Wise, Shepard Inc, Phall & Plomkin Inc, Timothy A Geaney Inc, New York; Phylis Lutjeans, Newport Beach, Calif; Cunningham & Assocs, Orange, Calif; Josetta Speglia, Los Angeles, Calif; Lynn Garnier Found, Richard Plumgren Inc, Laguna Beach, Calif. *Exhib:* Newport Harbor Art Mus, Newport Beach, Calif, 79 & 84; Irvine Fine Arts Gallery, Univ Calif, Irvine, 85; Series, Gallery Artists, Los Angeles Co Mus, 86; White Columns, New York, NY, 89; Retro Future, Richard/Bennett Gallery, Los Angeles, 89; Ihara Ludens Gallery, New York, 90; Parsons Sch Design, 91; and others. *Pos:* Ed illusr, Orange Coast Mag, 78-80; prop & advert designer, JC Penny, Macy's, Bloomingdales, Lee Jeans & Self Mag, 86-88; prop designer, David Spagnolo Studios Inc, 89- *Teaching:* Instr, Parsons Sch Design, New York, NY, 86- *Awards:* Nat Endowment Arts Grant, 89; NY Found Arts Fel, 89; Pollock-Krasner Found, 90. *Publ:* Conde Nast Publ; Hearst Publ. *Mailing Add:* 167 W 21st St New York NY 10011

BEER, KENNETH JOHN
EDUCATOR, SCULPTOR
b Ferndale, Mich, May 4, 32. *Study:* Wayne State Univ, BA & MA. *Work:* Detroit Inst of Art; Thalhimers & First Merchants Bank, Richmond & Va Beach Art Ctr, Va. *Comn:* Campus libr relief, Eastern Mennonite Col, Harrisonburg, Va, 69; James Madison Mem (cast bronze), James Madison Univ, Harrisonburg, 77; Arboretum Gates, James Madison Univ, Harrisonburg, 88. *Exhib:* Ann Mich Artists, Detroit Inst of Art, 55-62; Va Artists Biennial, Va Mus, Richmond, 65, 67 & 73; Southern Sculpture, Mint Mus, Charlotte, NC, 65 & Birmingham Mus, Ala & Columbus Mus, Ga, 66; solo exhib, Columbia Mus, SC, 69 & Va Mus, 73; Drawing & Sculpture Ann, Ball State Univ Art Gallery, 74 & 76. *Teaching:* Assoc prof sculpture, James Madison Univ, Harrisonburg, 61- *Awards:* Whitcomb Prize, Mich Artists Ann, Detroit Inst of the Arts, 61; Best in Show, Thalhimers Invitational, 66; Distinction Award, Va Artists Biennial, Va Mus, 73. *Media:* Bronze, Steel. *Publ:* Auth, Sanctum, The Emergence of a Form, Studies & Res Bull of Madison Col, 64. *Mailing Add:* Rt 1 Box 343 Bridgewater VA 22812

BEERMAN, HERBERT
PAINTER, EDUCATOR
b Newark, NJ, Nov 8, 26. *Study:* Rutgers Univ, 47-59 & 52-54; Univ Miami, BA, 52; Yale Univ Sch Design, with Josef Albers and Bernard Chaet, BFA, 56. *Comn:* US Air Force Permanent Collection. *Exhib:* Solo exhibs, Gloria Gallery, Nocosia, Cyprus, Rutgers Univ, NJ, Yaddo, Morristown Unitarian Fellowship & Mercer Art Theater, New York; Artist's Gallery, New York; Ball State Univ, Muncie, Ind; Mus Mod Art, New York, Montclair Univ; Coliseum, New York; Pentagon & Smithsonian Inst, Washington, DC. *Teaching:* Pro art, Pratt Inst, Brooklyn, NY, 61-; vis prof, Werkkunstschuler, Offenbach, Ger, Rutgers Univ, Hochschuler for Music & Drama, Stuttgart, Ger, Seton Hall Univ, S Orange, NJ, Cornell Univ, Ithaca, NY & Newark Mus Art Workshops, NJ. *Awards:* McDowell Fel (3); Yaddo Fel (3); Award in drawing, 64 & Grand Prize, 66, Saratoga Arts Festival. *Mailing Add:* c/o Pratt Institute 200 Willoughby Dr Brooklyn NY 11205

BEERMAN, MIRIAM (MIRIAM BEERMAN-JAFFE)
PAINTER
b Providence, RI. *Study:* RI Sch Design, BFA; Art Students League, with Yasuo Kuniyoshi; New Sch Social Res, with Adja Yunkers; Atelier 17, Paris, with Stanley Hayter. *Work:* Whitney Mus Am Art, New York; Brooklyn Mus; Newark Mus, NJ; New Sch Social Res, New York; Univ Ore, Eugene. *Exhib:* One-woman exhibs, Long Island Univ, Brooklyn, 65 & 80, The Enduring Beast, Brooklyn Mus, 71-72, Graham Gallery, New York, 72 & 78, Montclair Art Mus, NJ, 74 & 87, Cathedral Mus at Cathedral of St John the Divine, 77, Montclair State Col, NJ, 78, 87, & Camargo Found, Cassis, France; 40 Year Restrospective State Mus New Jersey, 1/91-3/91; Decade Show - Studio Mus Harlem, New York; Retrospective Exhib, NJ State Mus, 91. *Pos:* Guest artist, Burston Graphic Center, Jerusalem, Israel, 80; guest artist, Rutgers Univ, New Brunswick, NJ, 87. *Teaching:* Adj prof, Queensborough Community Col, City Univ New York, 72-92; vis artist, Montclair Mus Art Sch, 74-89 & Montclair State Col, 79-89. *Awards:* Fulbright Fel, 51-53; Creative Artists Pub Serv Grant, 71; Childe Hassam Purchase Award, Am Acad Arts & Lett, 77; Ossabaw Island Proj Award, Ga, 78; Camargo Found Award, France, 80; NJ State Coun Arts Grant, 84; women's Research and Development Fund, CUNY grant, 86; Distinguished Artist grant, NJ State Coun, 87. *Bibliog:* The new grotesques, Time Mag, 6/13/69; Barry Schwartz (auth), The New Humanism, Art in a Time of Change, Praeger; Gert Schiff (auth), Images of Horror and Fantasy, Abrams, 79. *Media:* Oil, Intaglio. *Publ:* Ed & illusr, The Enduring Beast, Doubleday, 72. *Mailing Add:* 6 Macopin Ave Montclair NJ 07043

BEERY, ART (ARTHUR O)
PAINTER
b Marion, Ohio, Mar 4, 30. *Study:* Self taught. *Work:* Butler Inst Am Art, Youngstown, Ohio; Lessco Data, New York; J M Katz Collection, Pa; Johnson Art Mus, Cornell Univ; Sweet Briar Mus, Sweet Briar Univ; and others. *Comn:* Murals on canvas of Athens, Greece, Monte Carlo, Stromboli, Rock of Gibralter & Charleston, SC for US Navy Minecraft Base, Charleston, 54. *Exhib:* Pa Acad Fine Arts, Philadelphia, 68; Butler Inst Am Art, 68, 70, 72, 73, 79 & 81; one-man shows, Galerie Cernuschi, New York, 77 & 80; Nat Exhib, Butler Inst Am Art, Youngstown, Ohio, 79; 28th Ann Chautauga Nat Exhib Am Art, 85; Le Salon De Nations, Paris, France, 83; Watercolor USA Hon Soc Biennial Exhib, 87, 89, 91 & 93; Watercolor USA Hon Soc Exhib, Osnabruck, Ger, 93; plus many others. *Awards:* Butler Inst Am Art Award, 68 & 74; Richard P Stahl Award, Watercolor USA, 71; Oscar D'Italia Award, Accademia Italia, 85; and others. *Mem:* Mansfield Fine Arts Guild, Ohio; Columbus Art League, Ohio; Watercolor USA Hon Soc. *Media:* Oils, Watercolor. *Dealer:* Art's Gallery 452 E Church St Marion OH 43302. *Mailing Add:* 452 E Church St Marion OH 43302

BEGININ, IGOR
PAINTER, EDUCATOR
b Susak, Croatia, Aug 31, 31; US citizen. *Study:* Wayne State Univ, AB, 63, MA, 66. *Work:* Fisher New Ctr, Chrysler Corp, Ford Motor Co, Detroit; Gen Motors, New York; Tung-Hai Univ, Taichong, Taiwan. *Comn:* Detroit Free Press, Mich Med Mag. *Exhib:* Cranbrook Acad Art, 64; Mid-Year Show, Butler Inst Am Art, 67-69; Nat Exhib Drawing & Small Sculpture, Ball State Univ Art Gallery, 68; Winter Show, Anderson Fine Arts Ctr, Ind, 71, 78, 79, 81, 82 & 92; Kentucky Aqueous, Louisville, 86; Flint Inst Art, 86; Int Watercolor, San Diego, Calif, 88; Krasl Art Ctr, Mich, 89; and others. *Teaching:* Asst prof watercolor, Eastern Mich Univ, 70-77, assoc prof, 77-83, prof, 83- *Awards:* Soc Illusr Award, 68; Mich Watercolor Soc Ann Award, 67, 71, 83, 89 & 91; Int Exhib, San Diego Watercolor Soc, 88. *Bibliog:* The Daily Sentinel, 70; Ann Arbor News, 73; Associated Newspapers, 87. *Mem:* Mich Watercolor Soc (bd mem, 66-70 & 82-91, chmn, 74-77); Detroit Inst Arts Founders Soc. *Media:* All Media. *Publ:* Illusr, Detroit, Detroit Free Press, 65-69 & Michigan Medicine, 69. *Mailing Add:* 43524 Bannockburn Dr Canton MI 48187

BEGLEY, J (JOHN PHILLIP)
MUSEUM DIRECTOR
b Akron, Ohio, Mar 21, 47. *Study:* Univ NMex, BFA (hons), 69; Ind Univ, MFA, 75; Mus Management Inst, Getty Trust, AFA, 89. *Collections Arranged:* Traveling Exhibs, Making it in Crafts (auth, catalog), 78, Fiber: State of the Art, 81, Making it in Paper: Twinrocker, 83, Individual Talent (auth, catalog), 84, Kentucky Guild 25th Anniversary Ceremony (auth, catalog), 86 & Contemporary Directions in Fiber (assembled & arranged), 88; Ladies Lunch (producer), 92. *Pos:* Dir, New Harmony Gallery Contemp Art, 75-83; exec dir, Louisville Visual Art Asn, 83- *Teaching:* Lectr art, Univ Evansville, 76-83 & Univ Louisville, 88-89. *Awards:* Louis Comfort Tiffany Fel, 78. *Media:* All Media Contemporary. *Mailing Add:* Louisville Visual Art Asn 3005 Upper River Rd Louisville KY 40207

BEGLEY, WAYNE E
HISTORIAN, PAINTER
b Kenvir, Ky, Dec 29, 37. *Study:* Univ Louisville, BA, 58; Univ Iowa, MFA, 62; Harvard Univ, 62-63; Univ Pa, PhD, 66. *Work:* Butler Inst Am Art, Ohio; Rose Art Mus, Mass; Albright-Knox Art Gallery, Buffalo, NY; Des Moines Art Ctr, Iowa. *Exhib:* Louisville Art Ctr Ann, J B Speed Art Mus, 56-63; one-man shows, Am Acad, Rome, 60, Louisville Art Ctr, 61 & Univ Ky Art Gallery, Lexington, 62; Mid-Am Ann, William Rockhill Nelson Gallery Art, 62. *Collections Arranged:* Indian Buddhist Sculpture (auth, catalog), J B Speed Art Mus, 68; Pala Art (auth, catalog), Univ Iowa Mus Art, 69; The Hindu Pantheon (auth, catalog), Rice Mus, Houston, 75. *Teaching:* From asst prof to prof Indian & Islamic art, Univ Iowa, 66-; vis prof Indian & Islamic art, Univ Ill, Urbana, 67; A W Mellon prof Indian & Islamic art, Rice Univ,

74-75; Maude Kerns prof Indian & Islamic art, Univ Ore, 78. *Awards:* Rome Prize Fel, Am Acad in Rome, 59-61; Research Fel, Am Inst Indian Studies, 67-68 & 70-71; Guggenheim Fel, 75-76. *Bibliog:* In the abstract, Courier-Journal Mag, 10/61. *Res:* Indian and Islamic art. *Publ:* Auth, Indian Buddhist Sculpture in American Collections, J B Speed Art Mus, 68; Identification of Ajanta Fragment in Boston Mus, Oriental Art, 68; Visnu's Flaming Wheel: Iconography of Sudarsana-cakra, NY Univ Press, 73; The myth of Taj Mahal and new theory of symbolic meaning, Art Bulletin, 79; Amanat Khan and Calligraphy on Taj Mahal, Kunst des Orients, 80. *Mailing Add:* Dept Art & Art Hist Univ Iowa Iowa City IA 52242

BEHL, WOLFGANG
SCULPTOR, EDUCATOR
b Berlin, Ger, Apr 13, 18; US citizen. *Study:* Acad Fine Art, Berlin; RI Sch Design. *Work:* Pa Acad Fine Arts, Philadelphia; Addison Gallery Am Art; Conn Gen Ins Co; New Britain Mus Am Art; Cornell Univ. *Comn:* Welded menorah & eternal light, Temple Beth Sholom, Manchester, Conn, 64; bronze tabernacle & processional cross, Church of the Resurrection, Wallingford, Conn, 66; Reredos, Immanuel Lutheran Church, Attleboro, Mass, 69; woodcarving monument, Elemer Nagy Millard Auditorium, Univ Hartford, 75; welded sculpture, Town Bloomfield, Conn, 76; large bronze group, Univ Conn Health Ctr, 86. *Exhib:* Plastics USA, Soviet Union, 60; Carnegie Inst Int, Pittsburgh, 64; Fogg Art Mus, Harvard Univ, Cambridge, 66; Hemisfair 68, San Antonio, Tex, 68; Retrospectives, New Britain Mus, 68; Sculpture Ctr, New York, 80; Univ Hartford, Bloomfield, Conn, 83; and others. *Teaching:* Asst prof sculpture & drawing, William & Mary Col, 45-53; prof sculpture, Univ Hartford, 55-83, prof emer. *Awards:* Sculpture Awards, Conn Acad Fine Arts, 61, 63 & 64; Nat Inst Arts & Lett Grant, 63; Ford Found Purchase Award, 64. *Bibliog:* Eye to Eye (film), WGBH TV, Boston, 71. *Mem:* Nat Sculpture Ctr (chmn adv bd, 68-); Sculptors Guild (dir, 72). *Media:* Wood, Bronze, Stone. *Publ:* Contribr, Masters of Wood Sculpture, 80; The Process of Sculpture, 81; Woodworking--The New Wave, 81; Adonis and Aphrodite, Viernheim Verlag, Ger, 61. *Dealer:* Arts Exclusive Gallery Simsbury CT; Rosenfeld Gallery 113 Arch St Philadelphia PA 19106. *Mailing Add:* 179 Kenyon St Hartford CT 06105

BEHNKE, LEIGH
PAINTER
b Hartford, Conn, Dec 22, 46. *Study:* Pratt Inst, BFA, 69; New York Univ, MA, 76. *Work:* H J Heinz Corp, Pittsburgh, Pa; Deloitte, Haskins, Sells, Marsh & McClennan Co & Xerox Corp, New York; Southeast Banking Corp, Miami, Fla; Currier Mus, Manchester, NH; and others. *Exhib:* Urban Landscape, Wave Hill, New York, 79; New Am Still Life, Westmoreland Mus, Pa; On Paper, Inst Contemp Art, Va Mus, Richmond, 80; Real, Really Real, Super Real, San Antonio Mus, Tex, 81, Carnegie Inst, Pittsburgh, 81 & Indianapolis Mus, Ind, 81; Contemp Am Realist, Univ Art Gallery, Pittsburgh, Pa, 81; Lower Manhattan from Street to Sky, Whitney Mus, 82; Fischbach Gallery, 91; Flint Inst Arts, 91; Nassau Co Mus, 92; Nat Acad Sci, 92. *Pos:* Master teacher & panelist, Nat Foun Adv Arts, 89- *Teaching:* Lectr fine art, drawing and painting, Sch Visual Arts, New York, 79- *Bibliog:* New Editions: Leigh Behnke, Art News, 4/82; Christopher Finch (auth), Twentieth Century Watercolors, 88; Roni Cohen (auth), Artforum Mag (rev), 91. *Mem:* Col Art Asn. *Media:* Watercolor, Oil; Silkscreen. *Dealer:* Fischbach Gallery 29 W 57th St New York NY 10019. *Mailing Add:* Dept Fine Arts, School of Visual Arts 543 Broadway #3 New York NY 10012

BEHRENS, MARY SNYDER
CRAFTSMAN, PAINTER
b Milwaukee, Wis, Oct 26, 57. *Study:* Mt Mary Col, Milwaukee, 75-77; Minneapolis Col Art & Design, 78-80; Univ Wis, Milwaukee, BFA, 82. *Work:* pvt collections of Cinncinnati Bell Info Systems, IBM & Thriftway, Cincinnati, Ohio. *Comn:* Rivertown Trading Corp, St Paul, Minn. *Exhib:* Wis Focus, Milwaukee Art Mus, 83-84; Women Artists, Appalachian State Univ, Boone, NC, 89; Crafts Nat: 24, Penn State Univ, State College, 90; Needlework Expo 90, Textile Arts Int, Minneapolis, 90; Celebrating the Stitch, Textile Arts Ctr, Chicago, 91; Newton Arts Ctr, Boston, 92; and others. *Awards:* Individual Artists Grant, Ohio Artists Coun, 88 & 90; Merit Award, Crafts Nat: 24, Penn State Univ, 90. *Bibliog:* Kate Mattews (auth), Fiberarts Design Book III, Larkbooks, 87; Anon (auth), Gallery: Fiber, Am Craft Mag 87 & 89; Barbara L Smith (auth), Celebrating the Stitch, Taunton Press, 91. *Mem:* Northeast Iowa Weavers & Spinners Guild; Midwest Weavers Asn. *Media:* Miscellaneous Media. *Dealer:* Textile Arts Int Inc 400 First Ave N Minneapolis MN 55401; Malton Gallery 2709 Observatory Cincinnati OH 45208. *Mailing Add:* 2022 X Ave Dysart IA 52224-9767

BEHRENS, ROY R
EDITOR, DESIGNER
b Independence, Iowa, June 27, 46. *Study:* Pond Farm Sch, with Bauhaus Potter, M Wildenhain, 64; Univ Northern Iowa, BA, 68; RI Sch Design, MA(art educ), 72. *Exhib:* 8th Ann Ed Design, New York, 73; Commun Arts Ann, Palo Alto, 90; Print Regional, New York, 90; Soc Am Illusrs, New York, 90. *Pos:* Design ed, NAm Rev, 72-92; ed, Ballast Quart Rev, 85-; Chmn, Commun Design, Art Acad Cincinnati, 87-90; contrib ed, Print Mag, 92- *Teaching:* Assoc prof art design, Univ Northern Iowa, 72-77 & Univ Wis, Milwaukee, 77-87; prof art design, Art Acad Cincinnati, 87-90; prof art design, Univ Northern Iowa, 90- *Awards:* Res grants, Univ Wis, Milwaukee, 78, 80, 85; Res grant, Univ Northern Iowa, 91; Prof Develop Leave, Univ Northern Iowa, 92. *Bibliog:* The 85 most interesting people in Milwaukee, Milwaukee Mag, 1/86; Ballast, Whole Earth Rev, summer 88; Stealth program on Nova, PBS science series, spring 89; Steve Heller & Anne Fink (auths), Low Budget High Quality Design, Watson Guptill, 90. *Mem:* Art Dirs Asn Iowa. *Res:* History and theory of camouflage; relation of visual arts to perceptual psychology, creativity and humor; life of psychologist Adelbert Ames, Jr; design theory. *Publ:* Auth, Art and camouflage: Concealment and deception in nature, art and war, 81, NAm Rev; Design in the Visual Arts, 84 & Illustration as an Art, 86, Prentice-Hall; The life and unusual ideas of Adelbert Ames, Jr, 87 & The theories of Abbott H Thayer: Father of camouflage, 88, Leonardo; The art of dazzle camouflage, Defense Analysis, 88; Drawing in the Dark (print), 92. *Mailing Add:* Dept of Art Univ Northern Iowa Cedar Falls IA 50614

BEILIN, HOWARD
ART DEALER
Pos: Owner & dir, Howard Beilin Inc, currently. *Specialty:* Nineteenth and 20th century American art with a special emphasis on Norman Rockwell; European impressionists and post-impressionists. *Mailing Add:* 1360 York Ave New York NY 10021

BEIRNE, BILL
VIDEO ARTIST
b Brooklyn, NY, Oct 25, 41. *Study:* Pratt Inst, with Louise Bourgeois BFA, 68; Hunter Col, with Robert Morris, MA, 74. *Exhib:* Rooms, PS 1 Mus, New York, 76; Alternatives in Retrospect, The New Mus, New York, 81; Video as Attitude, Mus Fine Arts Sante Fe, NMex, 83; The Commuter, Fashion Moda, New York, 89; You Connect the Dots, Whitney Mus Am Art, New York, 91; Grief in an Age of Scientific Advance, Int Ctr of Photog, New York, 92. *Teaching:* video, NY Univ, 89- *Awards:* Nat Endowment Arts Grant, 80; NY State Coun Arts Fell (video), 79. *Bibliog:* Ann Sargent-Wooster (auth), Formerly formalists, High Performance 14, 91; John G Hanhardt (auth), Understanding television, TV Mag, 80; Elizabeth Hayt-Atkins (auth), megaloculus, 11/92. *Media:* Video Installation & Performance. *Publ:* Auth, A Pedestrian Blockade, Collation Ctr & Wittenbourn Bks, 76. *Mailing Add:* 157 E 72nd St New York NY 10021

BEKER, GISELA
PAINTER
b Zoppott, Ger; US citizen. *Study:* Kunstinstitut, Rostock, Ger, 48-50; with Rudolf Kroll (of Bauhaus Sch), Dusseldorf, Ger. *Work:* Everson Mus, Syracuse, NY; Palm Springs Mus, Calif; Arts & Sci Ctr, Baton Rouge, La; Aldrich Mus, Ridgefield, Conn; Herbert Johnson Mus Art, Ithaca, NY; Fine Art Ctr, Nashville; and others. *Exhib:* Solo exhibs, Art & Sci Ctr, Baton Rouge, La, 75, NY Univ, 76, Tower Gallery, Southampton, NY, 76 & 79, Int Festival de Peinture, Paris, 79 & Sander Fine Art, Daytona Beach, Fla, 84; Mus Mod Art, Paris, France, 74; Chrysler Mus, Norfolk, Va; New Orleans Mus Art, La; Phoenix Art Mus, Ariz; Acad Italia Delle Arte, Salsomaggiore, Terme, 82 & 83; and others. *Awards:* Gold Medal, Int Exhib Painters & Sculptors, Paris, 74; Silver Medal (watercolor), Grand Prix Humanitaire de France, Paris, 75; Gold Medal, Acad Italia Delle Arte, Salsomaggiore, 80 & 82. *Bibliog:* The feminist movement in art, Southwest Art, 7/74; Gisela Beker's art at Arts & Science Center, Arts Mag, 2/75; Gregory Battcock (auth), Why Art, Dutton, 77. *Mailing Add:* One Oceans West Blvd 7 B5 Daytona Beach Shores FL 32118

BELAG, ANDREA
PAINTER, GRAPHIC ARTIST
b New York, NY, Nov 21, 51. *Study:* New York Studio Sch with Guston, McNeil, Cajori, Matter, 71-74, Hunter Col, 79, Bard Col, 68-69, Boston Univ, 70. *Work:* Newark Mus, NJ; Morris Mus Arts & Sci, Morristown, NJ; Jersey City Mus, NJ; Quaker Oats Corp, Chicago; Florence Loughheim Found, New York. *Exhib:* Recent Paintings: Andrea Belag, NJ State Mus, Trenton, 84; Tenth Anniversary Exhib, Jersey City Mus, NJ, 86; The Potent Image, Morris Mus, Morristown, NJ, 86; Realism & Abstraction: 20th Century Art in the Newark Mus, NJ, 87; one man shows, David Beitzel Gallery, New York, 91 & Richard Anderson Gallery, New York, 92. *Teaching:* Adj lectr arts, State Univ NY, 90- *Awards:* Fel, NJ Coun Arts, 84; Individual Fel, Nat Endowment Arts, 87; Triangle Artists Workshop Award, 91. *Bibliog:* Steven Henry Madoff (auth), Andrea Belag: An Appreciation, NJ State Mus, 84; Ronny Cohen (auth), Andrea Belag/John Davis Gallery, Artforum, 4/87; Stephen Westfall (auth), Andrea Belag at John Davis, Art in Am, 9/87. *Publ:* Auth, Eight Painters, Jersey City Mus, 80; Selected Drawings, Jersey City Mus, 83. *Dealer:* Richard Anderson Gallery New York NY. *Mailing Add:* 7 Harrison St New York NY 10013

BELCHER, GEORGE
ART DEALER
b Raymondville, Tex, Oct 21, 41. *Study:* Pan Am Univ, Edinburg, Tex, BA, 64. *Pos:* Owner, George Belcher Gallery, San Francisco, currently. *Specialty:* Nineteenth and twentieth century Mexican and Latin American paintings. *Mailing Add:* George Belcher Gallery 340 Townsend Suite 407 San Francisco CA 94107

BELFORT-CHALAT, JACQUELINE
SCULPTOR, PAINTER
b Mt Vernon, NY, Feb 23, 30. *Study:* With Frederick V Guinzburg, 43, Ruth Nickerson, 44, Columbia Univ, sculpture with Oronzio Maldarelli & casting with Ettore Salvatore, 47; Art Students League, life drawing with Klonis, 48; Univ Chicago, AB, 48; Fashion Inst Technol, 48-50; Royal Acad Fine Arts, Copenhagen, Denmark, 60-62. *Work:* Smithsonian Inst, Washington, DC; Govt of Nigeria; Our Lady of Victory, New York; Everson Mus, Syracuse, NY. *Comn:* Dr Eugene J Fisher, Washington, DC, 83; Holy Family (terra cotta relief), St Michael's Church, NY, 83; Mary (life-size mixed media), Cathedral Immaculate Conception, Syracuse, NY, 86; Heroic Size Christ,

Mixed Media, Most Holy Rosary Church, NY, 92; Dolphin, life-size, Lemoyne Athletic Ctr, Syracuse, 93; and others. *Exhib:* Nat Collection of Fine Arts, Washington, DC, 63; Washington Gallery Art, 66; Everson Mus, Syracuse, NY, 72; one-man shows, Everson Mus, 79, City Hall, 81 & Wilson Gallery, Le Moyne Col, 83, Syracuse; and others. *Teaching:* Prof & chair fine arts, Lemoyne Col, Syracuse, NY, 69- *Bibliog:* P Scala (auth), Begotten not made (film), ABC-TV, Syracuse, NY, 74; Idea to Image (video), R Smith, 89. *Mem:* Int Sculpture Ctr; Am Aesthetic Soc; Soc for Art, Relig & Cult; Col Art Asn Am; Int Womens Writers Guild. *Media:* All. *Publ:* Open Sesame, City New York Bus J, 92. *Mailing Add:* 321 Hurlburt Rd Syracuse NY 13224

BELIAN, GARABED
DEALER, HISTORIAN
b Jerusalem. *Study:* Detroit Inst Musical Art, BM, 68; Wayne State Univ, MA, 75. *Pos:* Pres, Art Ctr Chamber Music Players, 66-68; Dir, Wayne County Community Col Found, 85-; mem, Mich Coun for Arts, 87-; owner & dir, Belian Art Ctr, Troy, Mich, currently. *Specialty:* Twentieth century American and European sculpture, paintings and graphics, ancient art, African sculpture. *Mailing Add:* Belian Art Ctr 5980 Rochester Rd Troy MI 48098

BELIAN, ISABELLE
ADMINISTRATOR
B Addis Ababa, Ethiopia. *Study:* Beirut Univ Col, BA. *Pos:* Man dir, Belian Art Ctr, Troy, Mich, currently. *Mailing Add:* Belian Art Ctr 5980 Rochester Rd Troy MI 48098

BELING, HELEN
SCULPTOR, INSTRUCTOR
b New York, NY, Jan 1, 14. *Study:* Nat Acad Design, with Paul Manship & Lee Lawrie, 30-37; Art Students League, with William Zorach, 44-45. *Work:* Butler Inst Am Art, Youngstown, Ohio; Hirshhorn Mus, Washington, DC; Norfolk Mus Arts & Sci, Va; St Lawrence Univ, Canton, NY; Syracuse Univ Mus; and others. *Comn:* Menorah (bronze), Temple Israel, Waterbury, Conn, 59; Eternal Light (bronze), Temple B'nai Jacob, Woodbridge, Conn, 61; Eternal Light (bronze), Temple Beth Am Shalom, White Plains; Candelabra Room (ceramic), Pleasant Valley Home, West Orange, NJ, 62; Exodus (wall relief), Temple Emanu-el, Yonkers, NY, 66. *Exhib:* Nine one-man shows, Pa Acad Fine Arts, 50-66; Metrop Mus Art Sculpture Exhib, 51; Sculptors Guild Ann, 54-83; St Louis Mus, Mo; Everson Mus, Syracuse, NY; Whitney Mus Am Art, 55; Univ Ill, 57; Am Acad & Inst Arts & Lett, 81; Sculpture Exhib, Sculpture Ctr, Pa Acad Fine Arts, 84. *Teaching:* Instr sculpture, Westchester Art Workshop, White Plains, 50-66 & 77-82, NY Univ, 61-62 & Col New Rochelle, 70-71. *Awards:* Medal Honor, Audubon Artists, 65, 80 & 86; Medal Merit, Audubon Artists, 80-86. *Mem:* Nat Asn Women Artists; Sculptors Guild (pres, 72-74); Fine Arts Fedn (vpres, 74-83, dir, 78-79). *Media:* Reinforced Fiberglass, Welded Stainless Steel. *Dealer:* Sculpture Ctr 167 E 69th St New York NY 10021. *Mailing Add:* Oceanview 2790 Beach Loop Rd Bandon OR 97411

BELINOFF, DEANNE
PAINTER
Study: Univ Iowa, BA(cum laude), 62; Calif State Univ, Long Beach, MA(cum laude), 74. *Work:* Los Angeles Co Mus Art, Security Pac Bank, Los Angeles; AT&T, Los Angeles; Bank of Am, San Francisco. *Exhib:* Solo exhibs, Long Beach Mus Art, Calif, 87, Karl Bornstein Gallery, Santa Monica, Calif, 89 & 90, Calif State Univ, Dominguez Hills, 90, Pima Col, Tucson, 91, Bentley/Tomlinson Gallery, Scottsdale, 92, Radix Gallery, Phoenix, Ariz, 92; The Works Gallery, Long Beach, Calif, 90, 91 & 92; Selections from the Norton Collection, Rand Corp, Santa Monica, Calif, 91; Maquettes, Sharon Truax Fine Art, Venice, Calif, 91; Collaborative Desert Project, Joshua Tree Nat Monument, Calif, 92; Transamerica Bldg (with catalog), San Francisco, Calif, 92. *Teaching:* Numerous lectures at various universities and galleries. *Awards:* Calif Arts Coun Grant, 79-80; Artist-in-Residence, Blue Mountain Ctr, New York, 90; Nat Endowment Arts Fel Grant, 91-92. *Bibliog:* Dinah Berland (auth), Works Themselves, Press Telegram, 7/90; Jusith Samuel (auth), Light, Gesture, Surface, Artweek, 7/5/90; Kathy Zimmerer (auth), Deanne Belinoff, Artspace, 9/90. *Mailing Add:* 12629 Caswell Ave Los Angeles CA 90066

BELL, ALISTAIR MACREADY
PRINTMAKER, PAINTER
b Darlington, Eng, Oct 21, 13; Can citizen. *Work:* Nat Gallery Can, Ottawa, Ont; Mus Mod Art, New York; Victoria & Albert Mus, London, Eng; Mus Ugo Carpi, Italy; Vancouver Art Gallery, BC. *Exhib:* First Int Biennial Graphics, Tokyo & Osaka, Japan, 57; 3rd Int Exhib Graphics, Lubljana, Yugoslavia, 59; 6th Bianco e Nero, Lugano, Switz, 60; Recent Prints, Canada, Mus Mod Art, 67; 1st Int Triennial of Contemp Xylography, Carpi, 69; and others. *Awards:* Can Coun Sr Arts Fel, 59, Sr Arts Award, 67. *Mem:* Royal Can Acad Art. *Media:* Woodcut, Etching; Watercolor. *Dealer:* Bau-Xi Gallery 3045 Granville St Vancouver BC V6H 3J9 Can. *Mailing Add:* 2566 Marine Dr West Vancouver BC V7V 1L4 Canada

BELL, CHARLES S
PAINTER
b Tulsa, Okla, Feb 2, 35. *Study:* Univ Okla, Norman, BBA. *Work:* Phoenix Art Mus, Ariz; Solomon R Guggenheim, NY; Metrop Mus Art, NY; Hiroshima City Mus Contemp Art, Japan. *Comn:* Spieser Collection, 74. *Exhib:* New Realism, Wadsworth Atheneum, 74; Butler Inst Am Art, 75; Sewall Gallery, Rice Univ, Houston, 77; Solomon R Guggenheim Mus, New York, 77 & 81; Tulane Univ, La, 78; Indianapolis Mus, 78; Phoenix Art Mus, 79; Mus Art, Ft Lauderdale, Fla, 91-92. *Bibliog:* Articles, Illus London News, 1/75, Chicago Tribune, 76 & Jacksonville J, 2/77; Louis K Meisel (auth), Photorealism, Harry N Abrams Inc, NY, 80 & Photorealism 1980-1990, 93; Henry Geldzahler (auth), Charles Bell - The Complete Works 1970-1990, Abrams, 91; Toys Transformed by Wit and Whimsy, NY Times, 8/23/92. *Media:* Oil. *Mailing Add:* c/o Louis K Meisel 141 Prince St New York NY 10012

BELL, COCA (MARY CATLETT)
PAINTER
b Weleetka, Okla, Sept 26, 24. *Study:* Univ Okla, BA; painting with Milford Zornes, Edith & Richard Goetz & Charles Reid; drawing with Don Coen & Robert Kaupelis. *Comn:* Oil painting, Gov Mansion, Oklahoma City, 70; three comns, Kerr Conf Ctr, 83; poster, Arts Coun Oklahoma City, 84; watercolor, Omniplex Sci & Arts Ctr, Oklahoma City, 84; Oklahoma City Tree Bank Found, 88; White House, 88. *Exhib:* 14th Ann Eight State Exhib, Okla Art Ctr, 72; 18th Ann Eight State Exhib, 76, four-man show, 77 & two-man shows, 78, 79 & 81, Okla Art Ctr, Oklahoma City; Distinguished Artists of Okla Exhib, Midwestern Gov's Conf, 77; Living Women, Living Art, Gov Gallery, 81; Nat Gov Asn Conf, Okla, 82; Diamond Jubilee Arts Festival, Okla State Capitol, 82; Smithsonian Inst, 88; and others. *Awards:* Fourth Award, 10th Ann Southwestern Watercolor Soc Regional Exhib, 73; Second Award, Watercolor 74, Okla Watercolor Asn, 74. *Bibliog:* Interview, Okla Educ TV, 79. *Mem:* Okla Arts Ctr; Okla Watercolor Asn. *Media:* Watercolor, Oil. *Mailing Add:* 2 Colony Lane Oklahoma City OK 73116

BELL, DONALD ALLEN
ART DEALER, CONSULTANT
b Chicago, Ill, Sept 1, 38. *Study:* Univ Colo, BFA, 59. *Mem:* Accredited Sr Appraiser Am Soc Appraisers. *Specialty:* 19th and 20th century American painting. *Publ:* Contribr, Am Art Antiques Mag, Billboard, 3/4/79; Western Art Digest, spring 84. *Mailing Add:* 2201 N Central Ave Phoenix AZ 85004

BELL, DOZIER
PAINTER
b Lewiston, Maine, 1957. *Study:* Smith Col, BA, 81; Skowhegan Sch Painting & Sculpture, 85; Univ Pa, MFA, 86. *Work:* Portland Mus Art, Maine; A T & T, New York; Farnsworth Mus, Rockland, Maine; Arthur Andersen & Co, Minneapolis, Minn; Prudential Insurance Co, Newark, NJ. *Exhib:* Maine Artists Invitational, Farnsworth Mus, Rockland, 89; Curator's Invitational, Maine Coast Artists, Rockport, 89; Landscape of the spirit, Bruce Mus, Greenwich, Conn, 89; Portland Mus Art, 90; one-person show, Ogunquit Mus Art, Maine, 91. *Awards:* Visual Artist Fel Grant, Nat Endowment Arts Grant, 87; Millay Colony for the Arts Resident, 90; Bellagio Study & Conf Ctr Residency, Rockefeller Found, 93. *Dealer:* Schmidt-Bingham Gallery 41 W 57th St New York NY 10019. *Mailing Add:* 2 Springer St Richmond ME 04357

BELL, JAMES M
ART ADMINISTRATOR
Study: NTex State Univ, BA; Stephen F Austin Univ, MA. *Pos:* All level art supvr, Pub Sch Syst, Texarkana, Ark, 66-68; asst educ cur, Wichita Art Mus, Kans, 68-70; dir, Abilene Fine Arts Mus, Tex, 70-73; dir, Tampa Bay Art Ctr, 73-78; dir, Ft Wayne Mus Art, Ind, 78-82; develop dir, Oklahoma Art Ctr, Oklahoma City, formerly. *Mailing Add:* 2708 Cashion Pl Oklahoma City OK 73112

BELL, KATHRYN LEISE
CALLIGRAPHER, EDUCATOR
b Chicago Ill, Mar 9, 42. *Study:* Bob Jones Univ, BS, 65, MA, 67; with Peter Thornton & Michael Hughey, 81. *Work:* Lloyd J Reynolds Mem Collection Calligraphy, Portland Art Mus, Ore; Off of Congressman Carroll A Campbell, DC. *Comn:* Manuscripts, Hebrews 3:4, Northway Construct, Greenville, SC, 78 & Ezekiel 36:34-36, Jack E Shaw Builders, Greenville, SC, 79. *Exhib:* Guild SC Artists' Ann, Columbia Art Mus, 77; Calligraphy--the Art of Letterforms, Presby Col, Clinton, SC & Silver Eye Studio, Greenville, SC; Greenville Artists Guild, Falls Cottage, 81; Pickens Co Art Mus, 81; Teasler Libr, Wafford Col, 82; and others. *Teaching:* Instr calligraphy & hist art, Bob Jones Univ, 67- *Bibliog:* Michael Ginsberg (auth), World of art thumbs nose at calligraphers, Greenville News, 9/77; Jim Barnhill (producer), Calligraphy, radio presentation, WEPR, 10/79. *Mem:* Greenville Co Art Asn; Greenville Artists' Guild; Carolina Lettering Arts Soc (vpres, 79-80); Soc Scribes. *Media:* Mixed. *Publ:* Contribr, 1978 Calligrapher's Calendar, Soc of Scribes, 78; Soc Scribes Calendar, 81; Ligature, 83. *Mailing Add:* 102 Buena Vista Ave Greenville SC 29607

BELL, LARRY STUART
SCULPTOR
b Chicago, Ill, Dec 6, 39. *Study:* Chouinard Art Inst, Los Angeles, with Robert Irwin, Richards Ruben, Robert Chuey & Emerson Woelfer, 57-59. *Work:* Nat Collection Fine Arts, Washington, DC; Mus Mod Art, Whitney Mus Am Art, Solomon R Guggenheim Mus, New York; Whitney Mus Am Art, New York; Tate Gallery, London, Eng; Menil Collection, Houston, Tex. *Comn:* Gen Elec Corp, Gen Hg Fairfield, Conn; City of Abilene, Abilene Zoological Gardens, Tex. *Exhib:* Mus Mod Art, New York, 65; Contemp Am Sculpture & Prints Ann Exhib, Whitney Mus Am Art, 66; Guggenheim Mus, New York, 67 & 89; Walker Art Ctr, Minneapolis, 68; USA WCoast, Kunstverein, Hamburg, Ger, 72; Sculpture: American Directions 1945-1975, Nat Collection Fine Arts, Smithsonian Inst, Washington, DC, 75; Painting & Sculpture in California: The Mod Era, San Francisco Mus Mod Art, 76 & Smithsonian Inst, 77; Fullerton Art Gallery, Calif State Univ, 80; Fruitmarket Gallery,

Edinburgh, Scotland, 80; Chairs in Space: How the Game Evolved, Colorado Springs Fine Art Ctr, Colo, 84; The Game, Works Gallery, Long Beach, Calif, 85; Contained Space and Trapped Light: Sculpture Environment, Boise Gallery Art, Idaho, 86; Chairs in Space, Braustein Gallery, San Francisco, 86; Kiyo Higashi Gallery, Los Angeles, Calif, 87-89; Phoenix Art Mus, Ariz, 87; Laguna Art Mus, Calif, 88; Galerie Juan Prats, Barcelona, Spain, 89; Galerie Rolf Ricke, Koln, Ger, 90; Braunstein/Quay Gallery, San Francisco, 91; Whitney Mus Am Art Equitable Ctr, New York, 91; Retrospective and Prospective: The Art Rental & Sales Gallery Salutes the 25th Anniversary of the Los Angeles County Museum of Art, Los Angeles Co Mus Art, Los Angeles, 91; solo exhibs, Kiyo Higashi Gallery, Los Angeles, 91, Dartmouth St Gallery, Albuquerque, NMex, 91, Kiyo Higashi Gallery, Los Angeles, 92, New Gallery, Houston, Tex, 92, Tampa Mus Art, Fla, 92 & Galerie Rolf Ricke, Cologne, Ger, 93. *Teaching:* Instr sculpture, Univ SFla, Tampa, Univ Calif, Berkeley & Univ Calif, Irvine, 70-73, Southern Calif Inst Archit, Santa Monica, 88 & Taos Inst Arts, NMex, 89-90. *Awards:* Guggenheim Mus Fel, 70; Nat Endowment for the Arts Grant, 75; Gov Award for Excellence & Achievement in the Arts, Visual Arts, State of NMex, 90. *Bibliog:* Shirle Gottlieb (auth), Chairs in Space Take Front Seat at Opening of New Gallery, Weekend Plus, Long Beach Calif, 1/85; Jody Jacobs (auth), Art Vapor Made, The Los Angeles Weekend Guide, 11/15/85; Kenneth Baker (auth), Larry Bell's Lights, San Francisco Chronicle, At the Galleries, 6/14/86; Albert Hall (auth), Glass Art, Southwest Art, 2/87. *Media:* Light. *Mailing Add:* c/o Sena Galleries West 116-118 W San Francisco, Plaza Mercado Sante Fe NM 87501

BELL, LILIAN A
SCULPTOR, ASSEMBLAGE ARTIST
b London, Eng, Nov 5, 43; US citizen. *Study:* William Morris Tech Sch, London; Linfield Col, McMinnville, Ore, 69-70. *Work:* Portland Art Mus; Visual Art Ctr, Beer Sheva, Israel; Univ Ore Mus Art; Seattle City Light, Wash; State of Ore Pub Art Collection. *Exhib:* One-man shows, Blackfish Gallery, Portland, Ore, 90 & Nat Mus, San Jose, Costa Rica, 91; Book as Art IV, Nat Mus Women Arts, Washington, DC, 91; Cross Currents, Calif State Univ, Hayward, 91; Book Objects, Leopold Hoesch Mus, Duren, Ger, 92; Medium Paper, Budapest Mus Fine Arts, Hungary, 92; Omame Project, Nat Theater, Brasilia, Brazil, 92. *Pos:* Guest lectr, US & abroad, 73-; guest cur, Univ Ore Traveling Exhib, 80-82; abstr writer, Art & Archeology, Getty Conserv Inst, 81- *Awards:* Western States Arts Found Visual Arts Fel, 77; Ore Arts Comn Individual Artist Fel, 89. *Bibliog:* Mike E Walsh (auth), Symbolic images from four artists, Artweek, 4/29/78; Marlene Kerrigan (auth), Lilian Bell, vol XV, no 1, Fiberarts, 88; Juan Carlos Flores (auth), The death of the icon: The post modern paper sculpture of Lilian A Bell, vol 4 no 2, Reflex, 90. *Mem:* Artists Equity Asn (bd mem Ore chap, 78-79); Int Soc Arts, Sci & Technol, Berkeley, Calif; Int Asn Paper Artists, Siegen, Ger. *Media:* Cast Paper, Mixed Media. *Publ:* Contribr, Collage and Assemblage, Crown, 73; The Art of Papermaking, Davis, 83; auth, Papyrus, Tapa, Amate & Rice Paper, Liliaceae Press, 83; Contemporary American Women Sculptors, Virginia Watson-Jones, Oryx Press, 86; contribr, Sculpture: Technique, Form/Content, Davis, 89. *Dealer:* Oregon Art Inst Rental Sales Gallery 1219 SW Park Ave Portland OR. *Mailing Add:* PO Box 1235 McMinnville OR 97128-1235

BELL, MARY CATHERINE
ART DEALER
b Richmond, Va, Jan 1, 46. *Study:* Wayne State Univ, Detroit, BA(art hist), 71. *Pos:* Asst sales dir, Samuel Stein Fine Arts, Chicago, 73-76; owner, Mary Bell Galleries, Chicago, 76- *Bibliog:* Gladys Riskind (auth), Corporate art up and coming, Avenue M Mag, 6/81. *Specialty:* Contemporary American art; Unique paper paintings, sculpture and graphics; Corporate art collections. *Publ:* Auth, Art in the corporate suite, Commerce Mag, 82. *Mailing Add:* 215 W Superior Chicago IL 60610

BELL, MICHAEL STEVEN
CURATOR, ADMINISTRATOR
b Joplin, Mo, July 4, 46. *Study:* Calif Inst Arts, with Emmett Williams, BFA(scholar), 70; Univ Ky, with Wendell Berry, MFA, 72; Mus Mgt Inst, Univ Calif, Berkeley, cert(scholar), 79. *Work:* Mills Col Art Gallery. *Comn:* Mills Col Art Gallery. *Collections Arranged:* William Hahn: Genre Painter, 76, Gordon Onslow-Ford Retrospective, 78 & George Inness: Signature Years, 79, Oakland Mus; 20 American Artists: 1982, San Francisco Mus Mod Art, 82; deFORMATION transFORMATION, Capp St Proj, 92. *Pos:* Registrar, Oakland Mus, 76-80; dir, Midland Art Coun, Mich, 80-81; curatorial asst, San Francisco Mus Mod Art, 82-84; asst dir, SF Arts Comm, 84-87; cur, Visual Art Access, 87- *Teaching:* UC Davis, 89-90. *Awards:* Nat Endowment Arts Scholar, 80; G Murphy Award Promotional Lit, 83; Mayor's Award Outstanding Pub Serv, 86. *Mem:* Proj Sculpture, Pub Sites (treas, 83); Am Asn Mus. *Res:* Contemporary American Art. *Publ:* Contribr, Visual dialog, Roberta Loach, 76; Fine Arts Insurance Handbook, Asn Art Mus Dirs, 80; auth, CCAC: 75 Years, San Francisco Mus Mod Art, 83; contribr, Artweek, 83 & Leonardo, 84; ZYZZYVA 87, Visions Art Quart, 91; and others. *Mailing Add:* 3235 20th St San Francisco CA 94110

BELL, PHILIP MICHAEL
ADMINISTRATOR, HISTORIAN
b Toronto, Ont, Dec 31, 42. *Study:* Univ Toronto, BA & MA(fine art). *Collections Arranged:* W H Coverdale Collection of Canadiana, 73, Western Odyssey, Drawings by S P Hall, 74, Ouebec and Its Environs, Drawings by J P Cockburn (with catalog), 75; Goodridge Roberts: Drawings, 76; William Sawyer: Portrait Painter, 79; Life Forces: Photographs by Carol Marino, Agnes Etherington Art Ctr, 87; Pictorial Incidents: Photographs by William Gordon Shields, Agnes Etherington Art Ctr, 89. *Pos:* Cur paintings, drawings & prints, Public Archives Can, Ottawa, Ont, 68-73; dir, Agnes Etherington Art Ctr, Queen's Univ, 73-78; visual arts officer, Ont Arts Coun, 78-79; asst dir, Public Programs, Nat Gallery Can, 79-81, actg dir, 81; dir & chief exec officer, McMichael Can Collection, 81-86; assoc cur, Agnes Etherington Art Ctr, 86-92; dir, Carleton Univ Art Gallery, Ottawa, Ont, 92- *Teaching:* Instr Can art hist, Queen's Univ, Kingston, Ont, 75-76. *Awards:* Governor-General's Award for Non-Fiction for Painters in a New Land, Can Coun, 74. *Mem:* Coun Can Mus Asn. *Res:* Nineteenth century Canadian art. *Publ:* Auth, Painters in a New Land, 73; ed, Braves and Buffalo, Paintings by A J Miller, 73; auth, William Goodridge Roberts 1904-1974: Drawings, 76; The Last Lion , Rambles in Quebec with J P Cockburn, 78; William Sawyer: Portrait Painter, 79. *Mailing Add:* RR 1 Roblin ON L0J 1C0 Canada

BELL, R MURRAY
COLLECTOR
Study: Univ Alta; Osgoode Hall Law Sch, Toronto. *Collection:* Chinese ceramics, with special interest in blue and white Chinese porcelain. *Mailing Add:* 134 Forest Hill Rd Toronto ON M4V 2L9 Canada

BELL, TEMMA
PAINTER
b New York, NY, June 29, 45. *Study:* Boston Univ, Ind Univ, Philadelphia Col Art, BFA, 67; studied in Europe. *Work:* Canton Art Inst, Ohio. *Exhib:* Family of Painters, Canton Art Inst, Ohio, 73. *Media:* Oil. *Publ:* Contribr, Jed Perl (auth), Goings on in Art. *Mailing Add:* 45 Belcher Rd Warwick NJ 10990

BELL, TREVOR
PAINTER, EDUCATOR
b Leeds, Eng, Oct 18, 30. *Study:* Leeds Col Art, NDD, 49, ATD, 50. *Work:* Tate Gallery, London; Victoria and Albert Mus, London; IBM, Atlanta, New York; Rouse Company, Ohio; Shearson, Lehman, Hutton, New York; Cummer Mus, Fla; Coca-Cola, Atlanta; Arts Coun Great Britain; Contemp Art Soc, London; Balliol, Stannes, St Catherines & Trinity Col, Oxford, Eng; Am Express, Fla. *Comn:* (painting) The Art of Fugue, Phillips Collection, Holland, 64; Southern Light (painting), Lewis State Bank, Fla, 75; Fla Queen (painting), Orlando Aviation Authority, Fla, 81; painting, Tallahassee Civic Ctr, Fla, 82; I B M, New York, 85; Miami Center, Fla, 88. *Exhib:* Retrospective, Demarco, Edinburgh Arts Coun N Ireland, Sheffield, England, 70; New Work, Corcoran Gallery, Washington, DC, 73; Print Exhib, Tate Gallery, London, 77; Spoleto Festival, SC, 78; New Works, Nat Acad Sci, Washington, DC, 82; Metrop Mus & Gloria Luria Gallery, Miami, 85, 89 & 91; Eves Mannes Gallery, atlanta, 86 & 90; Cummer Mus, Jacksonville, Fla, 86; New Art Centre, London, 89; Fort Lauderdale Mus, Fla, 89; Lydon Fine Arts, Chicago, 90-92; Gillian Jason Gallery, London, 90; Ctr Arts, Vero Beach, Fla, 90. *Pos:* Fla Fine Arts Coun Grants Review Panel, 79 & 80. *Teaching:* Head of painting, Winchester Col Art, United Kingdom, 66-70; chairperson art, Fanshawe Col, Ontario, 70-71; prof graduate painting, Fla State Univ, Tallahassee, 72- *Awards:* Int Painting Prize, Paris Biennale, 59; Gregory Fel, Univ Leeds, United Kingdom, 60-64; Fla Fine Arts Coun Individual Fel, State Fla, 81. *Bibliog:* Jon Meyer (auth), catalog essay, Fort Lauderdale Mus, 89; Cris Hassold (auth), art papers, 90; Kevin Dean (auth), New Art Examiner, 90. *Media:* Acrylic. *Dealer:* Lydon Fine Art 203 W Superior St Chicago IL 60610; Jaffe Baker Gallery Boca Raton FL. *Mailing Add:* Dept Art Fla State Univ Tallahassee FL 32306

BELLAMY, RICHARD
ART DEALER
b Cincinnati, Ohio, Dec 3, 27. *Pos:* Pres, HEGD Co; dealer, Oil & Steel Gallery Inc, 80- *Mailing Add:* PO Box 2218 Long Island City NY 11102

BELLE, ANNA (ANNA BELLE BIRCKETT)
PAINTER
b Crescent, Okla. *Study:* Cent State Univ, Edmond, Okla; also with John Pike, Robert E Wood, Mel Crawford, Merlin Enabnit, John Pellew, Edgar Whitney, Gene Dougherty, Jack Vallee, Ray Vanilla & Ellwood Smith. *Work:* Dr Lloyd Owens, Oklahoma City; Oklahoma City Chamber Com; Gene Green Printing Co, Oklahoma City; City Market, Raton, NMex; Dr Norwood, Otar, Oklahoma City; Presbyterian Hosp, Oklahoma City; Great Plains, Woodward Mus, Okla; Raton, NMexico Mus. *Exhib:* Eight Okla Mus Art Ann; Southwestern Watercolor Soc, Dallas; one-man shows, Haven Collectable Gallery, Raton, NMex, 74, Ponca City, Okla, Owens Gallery & Wilson Gallery, Oklahoma City, 74 & 75; 8th Ann Watercolor Okla; Platt Nat Park, Sulphur, Okla. *Pos:* Dir, Okla Mus Art, 67-75. *Teaching:* Instr watercolor, Okla Mus Art, 73-74. *Awards:* Purchase Awards, Watercolor Okla. *Mem:* Okla Mus Art; Southwestern Watercolor Soc (vpres, 69, pres, 70); Watercolor Okla Soc (secy, 74-75). *Media:* Watercolor, oils. *Dealer:* Eloise Taos NM; House Gallery 5536 N Western Oklahoma City OK 73118. *Mailing Add:* 417 NW 41st Oklahoma City OK 73118

BELLIN, MILTON R
PAINTER, MURALIST
b New Haven, Conn. *Study:* Yale Univ, BFA, 36; Grad Sch, New York Univ; study with Yasuo Kuniyoshi & Eugene Francis Savage. *Work:* Slater Mem Mus, Norwich, Conn; Marine Hosp, Washington, DC; Fairfield State Hosp, Conn. *Comn:* Fairfield Court (mural), Fed Arts Proj, Stamford, Conn, 37; mural, 40 & restored murals comn by students, Cent Conn State Univ, New Britain, 84. *Exhib:* Artist as Reporter, Mus Mod Art, 40, Metrop Mus Art, 52, Audubon Artists, Nat Arts Club, 81, NY; Pastel Soc Am, Hermitage Mus, Norfolk, Va, 83; Nature Interpreted, Mus Natural Hist, Cincinnati, Ohio, 84; American Artist National Competition, Grand Central Galleries, New York,

85; Mus Fine Arts, Springfield, Mass, 86; Hudson Valley Art Asn, Westchester County Ctr, White Plains, NY, 86 & 88; Knickerbocker Artist, New York, NY, 88; Nat Open Print Exhib, Albany, NY, 92; Oil Painters Am, Chicago, Ill, 92. *Pos:* Art dir, Repub Aviation Corp, Farmingdale, NY, 58-64; coordr, Air France-French Am student competition, 75-76. *Teaching:* Artist-in-residence mural painting, New Britain Teachers Col, Conn, 37-40; asst principal art, High Sch Art & Design, NY, 66-78. *Awards:* Graphic Award, Mus Mod Art, 40; First Prize Still Life, Ridgewood Inst Art, NJ, 86 & 88; First Prize pastel, Harrisburg Art Asn, Pa, 89. *Bibliog:* Stephanie Della Cagna (auth), Lost Murals, Hartford Courant, 4/16/84; M Stephen Doherty (auth), Milton R Bellin, Am Artist, 7/85; Nancy Hall (auth), Famed Arts, Works Given to Slater Memorial Museum (feature story), Norwich, Conn, 12/27/91. *Mem:* Pastel Soc Am (bd dirs, 81-86); Oil Painters Am; Allied Artists; Conn Watercolor Soc; Am Artist Prof League. *Media:* Watercolor, Oil; Pastel. *Mailing Add:* 303 E 37th St New York NY 10016

BELTRÁN, FÉLIX
PAINTER, PRINTMAKER
b Havana, Cuba, June 23, 38; Mex citizen. *Study:* Sch Visual Arts, New York, NY, 60; New Sch, New York, 61; Am Art Sch, 62. *Work:* Stedelijk Mus, Amsterdam; Kunstgewerbemuseum, Zurich; Moderna Musset, Stockholm; Victoria & Albert Mus, Paris; Ermitage Mus, Leningrad. *Comn:* Murals, Cuban Pavilion, Osaka, 69. *Exhib:* The Art of the Book, Mus der Bilden Kunste, Leipzig, 65; The Art in Cuba, Kunstgewerbemuseum, Zurich, 65; The Art in Cuba, Lunds Konsthall, Lunds, 68; New Prints, Nat Mus, Stockholm, 68; The Art of Cuba, Museo de Arte, Chile, 71; The Art of Cuba, Stedelijk Mus, Amsterdam, 71; New Prints, Ermitage Mus, Leningrad, 73; The Art of Cuba, Altes Mus, Berlin-East, 75. *Pos:* Pres, Unión de Artistas de Cuba, Havana, 77-81 & Nat Comt Int Asn Art, Havana, 79-82. *Teaching:* Titular prof fine art, Inst Superior de Arte, Havana, 75-81, Univ Autónoma Metrop, 82- & Univ Iberoamericana, 85- *Awards:* Excellence Award, Am Inst Graphic Art, New York, 61. *Mem:* Alliance Graphic Int (nat pres, 76); Am Inst Graphic Art; Print Club, Philadelphia. *Media:* All. *Dealer:* Marcela Sotelo-Galería Trazo-Montañas Rocallosas 508 Lomas de Virreyes México 11000 DF. *Mailing Add:* Apartado De Correos M 10733 Mexico 06000 Mexico

BELVILLE, SCOTT ROBERT
PAINTER, EDUCATOR
b Jan 8, 52; US citizen. *Study:* Ohio Univ, Athens, MFA, 77. *Work:* Hirshhorn Mus, Washington, DC; Ga Mus Art, Athens; Greenville County Mus Art, SC; Chase Manhattan Bank & Walker Art Ctr, Minneapolis, Minn; First Bank Systems, Minneapolis, Minn. *Exhib:* Solo exhibs, Monique Knowlton Gallery, New York, 77, High Mus Art, Atlanta, 78, Del Art Mus, Wilmington, 79, PS 1, New York, 79, Nexus Gallery, Atlanta, 83, Southeastern Ctr Contemp Art, Winston-Salem, NC, 84, Jus de Pomme Gallery, New York, 86, Greenville County Mus Art, SC, 86; Thomas Barry Fine Arts, Minneapolis, Minn, 88 & 90; Sandler/Hudson Gallery, Atlanta, Ga, 89 & 91. *Teaching:* Artist-in-residence, Univ Ga, Athens, 77-78, instr painting, 80-81, asst prof, 84-86; instr painting, Converse Col, Spartanburg, SC, 82-84 & 86-88; assoc prof painting, Univ Ga, Athens, 89. *Awards:* Ford Found Fel, Univ Ga, Athens, 77-78; MacDowell Colony Fel; Nat Endowment Arts Grant, 83-84; South Carolina Individual Artist Grant in Painting, 88-89. *Mem:* Col Art Asn. *Media:* Oil. *Dealer:* Thomas Barry Fine Art Minneapolis MN; Sandler/ Hudson Gallery Atlanta GA. *Mailing Add:* 230 Milledge Circle Athens GA 30606

BELZ, CARL IRVIN
MUSEUM DIRECTOR
b Camden, NJ, Sept 13, 37. *Study:* Princeton Univ, BA, 59, MFA, 62, PhD, 63. *Pos:* Dir, Mills Col Art Gallery, 65-68; dir, Rose Art Mus, Brandeis Univ, 74- *Teaching:* Asst prof mod art, Mills Col, Oakland, Calif, 65-68; asst prof mod art, Brandeis Univ, 68-74, lectr mus studies, 74- *Mem:* Rose Art Mus, 88. *Publ:* Auth, Painted in Boston, Inst Contemp Art, Boston, 75; Mitchell Siporin: A Retrospective, 76, Frank Stella: Metallic Reliefs, 79, Frankenthaler: The 1950's, 81, Charles Grabedian: Twenty Years of Work, 83, William Beckman-Gregory Gillespie, 84, Katherine Porter: Paintings, 1969-1984, 85 & Stephen Antonakos: Neons and Drawings, 86, Brandeis Univ; Jake Berthot: Paintings, 1969-1988; Todd Mickie-Judy Kensley McKie, 90; Robert Hudson Sculptures/William Wiley Paintings, 91; Stanley Boxer: 45 Years, 92. *Mailing Add:* Rose Art Mus Brandeis Univ Waltham MA 02254

BEMAN, LYNN SUSAN
ART HISTORIAN, CURATOR
b Buffalo, New York, Dec, 23, 42. *Study:* Goucher Col, 60-62; Briarcliff Col, BA, 75. *Collections Arranged:* American Watercolors: 1860-1940, Trisdonn Gallery, 82; 19th Century Painters & Paintings of Rockland Co Hopper House, 84; Julian O Davidson: Am Marine Artist, Hist Soc Rockland Co, 86; Elmer Stanley Hader: The GrandView Years, Hopper House, 88. *Pos:* Cur, ADC Fine Art Inc, 73-78; dir, Trisdonn Gallery Ltd, 80-84, Beman Galleries, Inc, 84-89; Cur, Hudson River Maritime Mus, 90, actg dir, 90-91, exec dir, 91- *Awards:* Distinguised Historian, Tappantown Hist Soc, 85; Historical Serv, Lower Hudson Conf, Award for Excellence Hist Agencies & Mus, 87. *Mem:* Appraiser's Asn Am; Decorative Arts Found; Hudson River Maritime Ctr (bd Dir, 88-90). *Res:* 19th and early 20th-century American art with emphasis on the rediscovery of artists and their work; American marine art. *Specialty:* 19th and 20th century American paintings. *Publ:* Auth George Merritt Clark: A Buffalo Bohemian, NY-PA Collector, 83; auth, 19th-Century Painters & Paintings of Rockland Co, NY, Ed Hopper Found, 84; auth, Julian O Davidson (1853-1894): American Marine Artist, Hist Soc Rockland Co, 86; auth, Julian O Davidson A Rediscovery in American Marine Art, Sea Hist Mag, 87; auth, Elmer Stanley Hader (1889-1973): Rediscoveed American Impressionist, Nyack Publ, 89. *Mailing Add:* 1 Roundout Landing Kingston NY 12401

BENDELL, MARILYN
PAINTER, INSTRUCTOR
b Grand Ledge, Mich, Sept 19, 21. *Study:* Am Acad Art; and with Arnold E Turtle & Pierre Nuyttens. *Work:* Principia Col, St Louis; Saginaw Mus, Mich; Hadley Sch for Blind, Winnetka, Ill; Huntington Mus Fine Arts, WVa. *Comn:* Juggler of Notre Dame, comn by Sen Schuch, Saginaw Mus, 50; portrait of founder Principia Col, comn by William E Morgan, St Louis, 58; portrait of Helen Keller, Hadley Sch for Blind, 58; portrait of Mrs Paul Schulze, comn by Paul Schulze, Chicago, Ill, 60; David & Kim, Huntington Mus Fine Arts, 65. *Exhib:* Chicago Galleries, Ill, 55; Ill State Fair, Springfield, 58; 16th Ann Mem Exhib, Acad Artists Asn, Springfield, Mass, 64; Famous Florida Artists, Frank Oehlschlaeger Galleries, Sarasota, 64 & 65; Acad Artists Asn Nat Show, Springfield, 72; solo show, Joe Wade Fine Arts, Santa Fe, NMex, 88; Aikens Fine Art, Scottsdale, Ariz, 90; Huntsman Gallery Fine Art, Aspen, Colo, 91; Aidan Flores Gallery Fine Arts, Scottsdale, Ariz, 91. *Teaching:* Instr portrait, figure & still life, Longboat Key Art Ctr, Fla, 52-68; instr still life, Oak Park-River Forest Art League, Ill, 57-59; instr portrait, figure & still life, Cortez Art Sch, Fla, 68-74; pvt art classes, 74-; instr, Bendell Galleries & Art Sch, Fla, 74-82 & Scottsdale Artists Sch, 87-92. *Awards:* Popular Award for Bus Stop, Ill State Fair, 61; First in Portrait for Jeri, 64 & First in Portrait & Figure, Portrait of a Young Woman, 70, Springfield Mus Fine Arts. *Bibliog:* Edith Weigle (auth), Wonderful world of art, Chicago Tribune 8/17/58; W C Burnett (auth), Two art shows reviewed, Sarasota Herald Tribune, 64; Charles Benbow (auth), She reflects her colorful oil paintings, St Petersburg Times, 11/13/71; Don Jones (auth), 5/82 & Ann Katherine (auth), 5/85, Art Mag; Joy Murphy (auth), Southwest Art Mag, 4/88; Shirley Behrens (auth), Art of the West, 7/90; Vicki Stauig (auth), Art of the West, The Studio, 92; Cecelia Logan (auth), The Artistic Majic of Marilyn Bendell, Int Fine Art Collection, 92. *Mem:* Brown Co Art Gallery Asn; fel Royal Soc Arts; Am Artists Prof League; Acad Artists Asn, Springfield; Sarasota Art Asn. *Media:* Oil. *Mailing Add:* Route 1 Box 92MN Santa Fe NM 87501

BENDER, BEVERLY STERL
SCULPTOR, ENVIRONMENTAL ARTIST
b Washington, DC, Jan 14, 18. *Study:* Knox Col, BA; Art Students League; Sculpture Ctr, New York; Mus Natural Hist, New York. *Work:* James Ford Bell Mus Natural Hist, Minneapolis; Schmidgall Fine Art Gallery, New York; Shellborn Mus, Norwich, Conn. *Comn:* Mem, Mrs Disco, Mystic Seaport, Conn, 69; and private collectors. *Exhib:* St Hubert's Giralda, Madison, NJ, 88 & 90; Cummings Nature Ctr, Rochester, NY, 88; Cleveland Mus Natural Sci, 89; Mus Sci, Boston, Mass, 90; Roger Tory Peterson Inst Natural Sci, Jamestown, NY, 92; and others. *Pos:* Artist & designer, Johns-Manville, New York, 43-72. *Teaching:* Instr sculpture, The Uncommon Chislers, currently. *Awards:* Knox Col Alumni Achievement Award in Field of Fine Art, 79; Award of Excellance, Soc Animal Artists, 81, 89; Anna Hyatt Hutington Award, 83; AAPL Grand Nat Exhib, 87. *Mem:* Soc Animal Artists (bd dir, 74-); Southern Vt Art Ctr; Catharine Lorillard Wolfe Art Club (mem bd dirs, 76-80 & 83-88); Knickerbocker Artists; Am Artists Prof League; Pen & Brush NY. *Media:* Stone, Wood. *Mailing Add:* RR 4 Box 58A Westchester Ave Pound Ridge NY 10576-9648

BENDER, BILL
PAINTER
b El Segundo, Calif, Jan 5, 19. *Work:* US Air Force Acad, Colorado Springs, Colo; US Navy, Pensacola, Fla; Pentagon, Washington, DC; Living Desert Asn, Palm Desert, Calif; Visitors Ctr, Death Valley, Calif. *Exhib:* Mountain Oyster Contemp Western Art Show, Tucson, Ariz, 72-90; High Plains Heritage Ctr, Spearfish, SDak. *Awards:* Hon Deputy Sheriff, San Bernardino Co. *Bibliog:* Ed Ainsworth (auth), Painters of the desert, Desert Mag, 60; Ed Ainsworth (auth), The Cowboy in Art, World Publ, 69; Peggy & Harold Samuels (auths), Contemporary Western Artists, 83. *Mem:* Life mem Cowboy Hall of Fame, Okla; hon life mem, Mountain Oyster Club, Tucson; Death Valley 49ers Inc (hon dir); life mem, Westerners, San Dimas, Calif. *Media:* Oil, Watercolor. *Publ:* Illusr, Christmas cards, stationery & calendars, Leanin' Tree Publ, 60-88; Beakoning Desert, Prentice-Hall, 62; auth & illusr, My Friend John, Los Angeles Westerners, 70; Day I Clumb Down from the Horse, Brand Bk 3m, San Diego Westerners, 73; illusr, Paul Bailey (auth), An Unnatural History of Death Valley, 78. *Mailing Add:* 24887 Nat Trails Hwy Oro Grande CA 92368

BENDER, MAY
PAINTER
b Newark, NJ, Feb 8, 21. *Study:* Art Students League, New York, 45-50, 68-74 & 88-90. *Exhib:* Ellarslie Show, Trenton City Mus, NJ, 91; one-woman show, Image Gallery, Princeton, NJ, 91; Image Gallery, Princeton, NJ, 91; Carrier Found Show, Belle Mead, NJ, 92. *Pos:* Creative dir & pres, May Bender Design Assocs, NY & NJ, 68-91. *Teaching:* Instr marketing & package design, Parsons, New York, 80; lectr packaging seminars, Rutgers Univ, Pratt Inst, Long Island Univ & others. *Awards:* Clio Award for packaging, Ann Awards, 77, 78 & 79. *Mem:* Artists League, NJ; Artists League of Central NJ, 92. *Media:* Oil, Ink. *Publ:* Auth, Package Design & Social Change, Am Mgt Asn, 75; Package Design in New York, Japanese Publ; numerous articles on package design. *Dealer:* Image Gallery 7 Deer Park Dr Suite D South Brunswick NJ 08852. *Mailing Add:* 16 Woodland Ave East Brunswick NJ 08816

BENEDICT-JONES, LINDA
PHOTOGRAPHER, CURATOR
b Beloit, Wis, Oct 21, 47. *Study:* Univ Wis-LaCrosse, BS, 69, Univ Lisboa, Portugal, dipl, 72, Mass Inst Tech, MS(visual studies, Arts Coun Gr Brit Grant), 82. *Work:* Bibliotheque Nat, Paris; Mus Cantini, Marseilles, France;

Mus Art Hist Fribourg, Switz; Dept Environ, London; Polaroid Collection, Cambridge, Mass. *Exhib:* Imagens de Portugal, Ctr Cult Am, Lisboa, Portugal, 73; solo exhib, Madison Art Gallery, Wis, 76; Serpentine Gallery, London, 78; Quiet Places, Graves Art Gallery, Sheffield, Eng, 79; Les Autoportraits, Ctr Georges Pompidou, Paris, 81; Contemporary Self Portraiture, Hayden Gallery, Mass Inst Technol, 83; Latvian Photo Soc, 91. *Pos:* Dir, Clarence Kennedy Gallery, Polaroid Corp, Cambridge, Mass, 84-90, cur, Polaroid Collection, 90- *Teaching:* Lectr photog, London Col Printing, Eng, 77-79; instr, Mass Inst Technol Creative Photo Lab, 81, DeCordova Mus Sch, Lincoln, Mass, 82-83 & Northeastern Univ, Mass, 83; lectr hist photog, Harvard, 87- *Bibliog:* Au Coeur d'Elle Meme, Le Nouveau Photo-Cinema, Paris, 76; Roberto Salbitani (auth), Linda Benedict-Jones Progresso Fotografico, Milan, 78; Women on Women, Aurum Press, London, 78. *Mem:* Soc Photog Educ. *Publ:* Auth, biography, Print Letter 24, Switz, 79; Minor White: Contributions & Controversy, Positive, Mass Inst Technol, 81; Lee Friedlander, Positive, Mass Inst Technol, 82; Whither documentary? Ten contemporary British photographers, Positive, Mass Inst Technol, 82; Black British Photographers, Spot, 92. *Dealer:* Galerie Viviane Esders, Paris, France; Photogr Gallery 8-12 Gt Newport St London England. *Mailing Add:* Polaroid Corp The Kennedy Gallery 770 Main St Cambridge MA 02139

BENEDIKT, MICHAEL
WRITER, CONSULTANT
b New York, NY, May 26, 35. *Study:* NY Univ, BA; Columbia Univ, MA. *Pos:* New York corresp, Art Int Zurich, Switz, 65-67; ed assoc, Art News, New York, 63-72; mem mixed media panels, NY State Coun Arts, 77; consult mem, NY Art Critics Circle, 79-; designated panelist, Nat Endowment Humanities, 82. *Teaching:* Vis prof writing, Sarah Lawrence Col, Bronxville, NY, 69-73; assoc prof, Hampshire Col, Amherst, Mass, 73-75; vis prof writing, Vassar Col, 76-77 & Boston Univ, 77-79. *Awards:* Guggenheim Fel, 68; Creative Artist Pub Serv Prog, NY State Coun Arts Grant, 74; Nat Endowment Arts Fel, 79. *Bibliog:* Benedikt: A Profile (monogr), Logbridge Rhodes, 78. *Mem:* PEN Am Ctr; Am Film Inst. *Res:* 19th century French painting; preparation of revised edition of Modern Theatre: The Avant Garde, Dada & Surrealism, anthology originally issued by Dutton, 1964; realist tradition in American art, historical and contemporary; links of recent US painting to still photography, film and especially video. *Publ:* Auth, The continuities of Pierre Bonnard, Art News, 64; ed, Theatre Experiment: An Anthology of American Plays from Gertrude Stein to "Happenings", L Doubleday, 68; auth, New York Letter on Sculpture as Architecture in Minimal Art (anthology), Dutton, 68; auth, The visionary French Symbolist painters in the Grand Eccentrics (anthology), 71; Notes on Yoko Ono, Art & Artists, 72; The Poetry of Surrealism (anthology), Little Brown, 75; Poetry & Videotape in New Artists Video, Dutton, 78; and others. *Mailing Add:* 315 West 98th St New York NY 10025

BENENSON, EDWARD HARTLEY
COLLECTOR, PATRON
b New York, NY, Mar 27, 14. *Study:* Duke Univ, BA, 34. *Mem:* Friends Duke Univ Mus Art. *Collection:* Highly diversified, quality pieces only, ranging from Courbet to present-day artists. *Mailing Add:* 510 Park Ave New York NY 10022

BENES, BARTON LIDICE
COLLAGE ARTIST, SCULPTOR
b NJ, Nov 16, 42. *Study:* Pratt Inst, painting with Walter Murch, 60-61; Beaux Arts, Avignon, France, graphics, 68; Atelier Jean D'Orcier, Le Barroux, France, batik, 68. *Work:* Univ Iowa Mus Art; Princeton Univ Rare Bks Collection; Bibliot Nat, Paris; Nat Gallery, Australia; Art Inst Chicago; Albequerque Mus Art, Fed Reserve Bd, Washington, DC. *Comn:* Fed Reserve System, Washington, DC; Am Express; Artes and Leiloes, Lisbon, Portugal; NDak Mus Art, Grand Forks. *Exhib:* Artists Books, Albright-Knox Gallery, Buffalo, 77; The Object as Poet, Renwick-Gallery, Nat Collection Fine Arts, 77; The Open and Closed Book, Victoria & Albert Mus, London, Eng, 79; Patterns Plus, Dayton Art Inst, Ohio, 79; Galleriet-Lund, Sweden; 7 Artists, 7 Visions, Queens Mus, NY; The State Mus, Albany, NY; and others. *Collections Arranged:* The Book as Art, Fendrick Gallery, 76; The Animal Image, Renwick Gallery, Nat Collection Fine Arts, Washington, DC; Remains to Be Seen, Kohler Arts Ctr, Sheboygan, Wis; Decorative Fabricators, Inst Contemp Art Va Mus, Richmond; Ikons-Logos, Word As Image, Alternative Mus, New York. *Awards:* Creative Artists Pub Serv Prog grant, 77; Ariana Found Arts Grant, 82; Grant for Graphics, Rutgers Univ, 83; Pollock Krasner Found Grant, 88. *Bibliog:* Lowry Thompson & Joni Miller (auth), Prince of Rubberstamps, Workman Publ Co, 78; Jacqueline Brody (auth), On and off the wall with Benes, Print Collectors Newslett, 79; Meg Cox (auth), It Does Take Money to Make Money, Wall Street Journal, 8/6/84; Cover-Art News, 11/88. *Media:* Rubberstamps; Mixed. *Publ:* Illusr, Excerpts from the Diaries of the Late God, Harper & Row, 68; auth, The Dog Bite, Plainwrapper Press, 70; The Mugging (A Primer of Urban Living), Winterhouse Ltd, 70; I Have Found a Cockroach in Your Product, Wedgepress & Cheese, 82; illusr, Money Matters, Solo Press, 83. *Dealer:* Barbara Fendrick Gallery 568 Broadway New York NY 10012; Fendrick Gallery 3059 M St NW Washington DC 20007. *Mailing Add:* 463 West St Apt 956H New York NY 10014

BENGLIS, LYNDA
SCULPTOR, PAINTER
b Lake Charles, La, Oct 25, 41. *Study:* Yale Norfolk Summer Fel, 63; Newcomb Col, Tulane Univ, with Ida Kohlmeyer, Pat Trivigno, Zolton Buki & Halrold Carney, BFA, 64; Brooklyn Mus Art Sch, with Rubin Tam, Max Beckman Scholar, 65. *Work:* Whitney Mus Am Art; Solomon R Guggenheim Mus; Am Mus Mod Art, New York; Hokkaido Mus Mod Art, Sapporo, Japan; Gihon Found, Dallas; and others. *Comn:* Adhesive products, Walker Art Ctr, Minneapolis, 71; Hartsfield Int Airport, Atlanta, 80; Leo W O'Brien Fed Bldg, Albany, 81; Fairmont Hotel, Denver, 82; Prudential Life Insurance Co, Parsippanny, NJ, 82; Cadillac Fairview, Dallas, Tex, 84; Crocker Bldg, Crocker Properties, San Francisco, 85. *Exhib:* Directions 3: 8 Artists, Milwaukee Art Ctr, 71; one-person exhibs, Hayden Gallery, Mass Inst Technol, Cambridge, 71, Univ SFla Tampa, 80 Lowe Art Mus, Miami, Fla, 80, Margo Leavin Gallery, Los Angeles, 80, 82 & 87, Paula Cooper Gallery, New York, 80, 82, 84-85 & 87, Suzanne Hilberry Gallery, Birmingham, Mich, 80 & 83, Galerie Albert Baronian, Brusels, 80 & 81, Dart Gallery, Chicago, 81, 83 & 85, Margo Leavin Gallery, 80, 82 &87; 32nd Ann Exhib, Soc Contemp Art, Art Inst Chicago, 72; 1973 Biennial Exhib Am Painting & Sculpture, 73 & Art at Work: Recent Art From Corporate Collections, 78, Whitney Mus Am Art; 14 Artists, Baltimore Mus Art, 75; Recent Acquistions, Guggenheim Mus, 77; Pittura Ambiente, Palazzo Reale, Milan, 79; Developments in Recent Sculpture, Whitney Mus Am Art, 81; Galerie Albert Baronian, Brussels, 81; 74th Am Exhib, Art Inst Chicago, 82; Postminimalism, Aldrich Mus Contemp Art, Ridgefield Conn; 20th Century Sculpture: Process & Presence, Whitney Mus Am Art, New York , 83; Am Art Since 1970; Painting , Sculpture, & Decorative Arts, From the Collection of the Whitney Mus of Am Art, Whitney Mus Am Art, New York, 84; Hirschhorn Mus & Sculpture Garden, Washington, DC, 84; Selections from the William J Hokin Collection, Mus Contemp Art, Chicago, 85; 20th Anniversary of the National Endowment for the Arts, Mus Mod Art, New York, 86; Philadelphia Collects: European & Am Art Since 1940, Philadelphia Mus Art, Pa, 86; Contemp Painting & Sculpture Galleries, Mus Mod Art, New York, 86-87; Structure to Resemblance: Work by Eight Am Sculptors, Albright-Knox Art Gallery, Buffalo, NY, 87; one-woman retrospectives, Dual Natures, High Mus of Art, Atlanta, Contemp Arts Ctr in conjunction with The New Orleans Mus of Art, San Jose Mus of Art, 91; Art in Europe and America: The 1960s and 1970s, Wexner Ctr Visual Arts, Ohio State Univ, Columbus, 90; The New Sculpture 1965-1975: Between Geometry and Gesture, Whitney Mus Am Art, 90; and many others. *Teaching:* Asst prof, Hunter Col, 72-73, prof, 80-81; vis prof, Calif Inst Arts, 74 & 76, Princeton Univ, 75; vis artist, Kent State Univ, 77 & Skowhegan Sch Painting & Sculpture, 79; vis prof, Univ Ariz, 81 & 82; vis artist, Sch Visual Arts, New York, 82-83, vis prof, Fine Arts Workshop, 85-87 & autumn 91. *Awards:* Guggenheim Fel, 75; Australian Art Coun Award, 76; Nat Endowment Arts Grant, 79; Award of Distinction, Nat Coun Art Adminstr, 89. *Bibliog:* Robert Pincus-Witten (auth), The Frozen Gesture & Benglis, Video Medium to Media, In: Post Minimalism, 77; Doug Davis (auth), article, Art Cult, 77; Lynda Benglis (auth), interview in Ocular, summer 79; Michael Brenson (auth), Art, New York Times, 8/3/86; Lisbet Nelson (auth), Chicago's Art Explosion, Artnews, 5/87; Suzanne Muchnic (auth), Lynda Benglisat Margo Leavin, Los Angeles Times 5/22/87; Holland Cotter (auth), Lynda Benglis at Paula Cooper, Art in Am, 7/87; Phyllis Braff (auth), Faculty Show: Range of Ideas, The New York Times, 9/6/87; Robert C Morgan (auth), American Sculpture & the Search for a Referant, Arts Mag, 11/87; and many others. *Dealer:* Paula Cooper Gallery 155 Wooster St New York NY 10012. *Mailing Add:* 222 Bowery St New York NY 10012

BENGSTON, BILLY AL
PAINTER
b Dodge City, Kans, June 7, 34. *Work:* Mus Mod Art, New York; Art Inst Chicago; Los Angeles Co Mus Art; Whitney Mus Am Art, New York; Centre Georges Pompidou, Paris, France. *Comn:* Calif State Off Bldg, Calif Arts Coun, Los Angeles. *Exhib:* Chicago Biennial Painting Exhib, Art Inst Chicago, 63 & 72; Eighth Biennial, Sao Paulo, Brazil, also shown Smithsonian Inst, 65; Whitney Ann Painting Exhib, Whitney Mus Am Art, 67, 69 & 79; retrospective, Los Angeles Co Mus Art, 68; Kompas IV, Stekelijk van Abbemuseum, Eindhoven, Holland, 69; solo exhibs, Honolulu Acad Arts, Hawaii, 80, Corcoran Gallery Art, Washington, DC, 80, San Diego State Univ, Calif, 81; Billy II, Paintings of Three Decades, Contemp Arts Mus, Houston, Oakland Mus, Los Angeles Co Mus Art, Contemp Arts Crt, Honolulu, 88. *Pos:* Founder, Artist Studio, Venice, Calif, 60; pres, Westside Strokers, Los Angeles, 78-79 & Pelican Publ, Ltd. *Awards:* Nat Found Arts Grant, 67; Tamarind Fel, Tamarind Lithography Workshop through Ford Found, 68 & 82; Guggenheim Found Fel, 75. *Bibliog:* Fidel Danieli (auth), Billy Al Bengston's Dentos, 5/67 & Peter Plagens (auth), Billy Al Bengston's new paintings, 3/75, Artforum. *Mem:* Outrigger Canoe Club. *Media:* Mixed. *Publ:* Coauth, Business cards, Heavy Indust Publ, 68; auth, Late fifties at the Ferus, Artforum, 1/69; Los Angeles artists' studios, Art in Am, 11-12/70; Paintings of Three Decades, Billy II, Chronicle Books. *Mailing Add:* 811 Hampton Dr Venice CA 90291

BEN-HAIM, TSIPI
CRITIC, ART ADMINISTRATOR
b Mar 6, 51. *Study:* Tel-Aviv Univ, BA, 79; NY Univ, MA, 83; Columbia Univ, 87. *Collections Arranged:* Back to Earth (sculpture; catalog), 87; Creative Process (catalog), 87; MozArt (catalog), 91. *Pos:* Art critic & NY corresp, Sculpture Mag, 82-; exec dir, City Arts Inc, 89- *Awards:* Am Israel Cult Found, 84; NY Univ, 82-83. *Mem:* Int Sculpture Ctr; Int Art Critics Asn Am; Art Table. *Publ:* Auth, Cartier Foundation/France/Sculpture Park, 86, Isamu Noguchi - The Cullen Sculpture Park, 86 & Awakening the Brooklyn, 90, Sculpture Mag; The Creative Process (catalog) City Arts, 89 & Charlotto Kotik, Sculpture Mag, 90. *Mailing Add:* Cityarts Workshop 625 Broadway New York NY 10012

BEN-HAIM, ZIGI
SCULPTOR, PAINTER
b Bagdad, Iraq, Nov 28, 45; US citizen. *Study:* Avni Inst Fine Arts, Tel Aviv, Israel, 66-70; Calif Col Arts & Crafts, Oakland, 71; Calif State Univ, San Francisco, MFA, 74. *Work:* Guggenheim Mus, Jewish Mus & Brooklyn Mus, New York; Israel Mus, Jerusalem; Ghent Mus, Belg; Ursinus Col, Pa; Weisman Found. *Comn:* Groovy Groove (sculpture), AREA, New York, 83; Legion of Titans, (sculpture), Tel-Hai Art Col, Israel, 83; Wind Hunter (sculpture), Israel Mus, Jerusalem, 84; Blooming Stone (sculpture), Frederick Weisman Found, Los Angeles, 86; Rising Path (sculpture), Snug Harbor, Staten Island, New York, 86; Univ Md (sculpture), College Park, 88. *Exhib:* Solo exhibs, Art Gallery Hamilton, Ont, 82 & Israel Mus, Jerusalem, 84, Jewish Mus Sculpture Court, 87; With Paper about Paper, Albright-Knox Gallery, Buffalo, NY, 80; Wallpaper-Roompaper, Inst Contemp Art, Los Angeles, 81; The New Explosion, Fine Arts Mus Long Island, Hempstead, NY, 82; Brooklyn Mus, New York, 85; Walking Field, PS 1, Long Island City, New York, 86; American Experience, Bass Mus, Miami Beach, Fla, 86. *Awards:* Nat Endowment Arts Sculpture Grant, 84. *Bibliog:* Joan Marter (auth), Contradictory worlds: The art of Zigi Ben-Haim, Arts Mag, 11/85; Michael Brenson (auth), Critics' Choice, NY Times, May 3, 87; Henry Scarupa (auth), Outdoor Sculpture, 11/13/87. *Mem:* Int Sculpture Ctr, Washington, DC. *Media:* Concrete, Steel Wire Mesh, Stainless Steel; Oil, Lead. *Mailing Add:* 94 Mercer St New York NY 10012

BENHAM, PAMELA J
PAINTER
b Hollywood, Calif, Sep 25, 47. *Study:* Art Students League New York, with N B Hale & Bruce Dorfman, 68-71; Cooper Union, New York, with Leland Bell, Paul Resika & Cusamano, BFA, 72; Skowhegan Sch Painting & Sculpture, Maine, scholar, 73; Ecole des Beaux-Arts, Paris, Ateliere Caron, 73-75. *Exhib:* Mus Mod Art, Paris, 75; Mus de Luxembourg, Paris, 76; Wood Gallery, Montpelier, Vt, 84; Governor Cuomo Group Show, New York, 85; John Christian Gallery, New York, 85; Am Acad Arts & Sci Exhib, Washington, DC, 86; Am Asn Advan Sci, 88; May Arts Festival, RAPP Art Ctr, New York, 90; Altos de Chavon, Dominican Republic, 90; Solo exhibs, Condon Gallery, New York, 82, Wood Gallery, Montpelier, Vt, 84, Open Studios/RAPP Art Ctr, New York, 89, Tompkins Sq Gallery, New York, 90, Taller Latinoamericano Cult Ctr, New York, 90, Nicholas Roerich Mus, New York, 91. *Awards:* Fel, Altos de Chavon, Dominican Republic, 90. *Media:* Acrylic, Oil. *Dealer:* Grenville Collins of Breyberry Ltd Oxford England. *Mailing Add:* 361 E Tenth St Apt A New York NY 10009

BENHAM, ROBERT CHARLES
PAINTER
b Gloucester, Mass, June 29, 13. *Study:* Bucksport Acad, Maine; also with Paul Strisik. *Exhib:* Allied Artist, Nat Acad, New York; Salmagundi Club, New York; Rockport Art Asn; Springfield Mus Fine Arts; Butler Mus, Ohio. *Teaching:* Instr in pvt classes. *Awards:* Curtis News Award, 69; Aldro Hibbard Award, 74; Harriet Preston Award, 74; and others. *Bibliog:* Herb Rugoff (auth), Some notions on oceans, 69, Painting fog, 75, Surf & rocks, 80, Palette Talk. *Mem:* Rockport Art Asn; North Shore Art Asn; Allied Artist of Am; Acad Artists, Springfield; Am Artists Prof League. *Media:* Oil. *Mailing Add:* 4 Harbor Rd Bass Rocks Gloucester MA 01930

BENINI
PAINTER, SCULPTOR
b Imola, Bologna, Italy, April, 17, 41. *Study:* Liceo Classico, Cento & Bologna, Italy, 54-57; Enalc, Assisi, Italy, 57-59; also with Morandi, 61-63; Jan Hus Univ (fine art), Hon PhD, 84. *Work:* Pensacola Art Ctr & Mus, Fla; Jacksonville Univ, Fla; Brevard Art Ctr & Mus, Melbourne, Fla; Empire Am, Deland, Fla; Thomas Ctr Arts, Gainesville, Fla. *Exhib:* 100 solo exhibs mus, pub insts & univ, Fla State Capitol, 84; Thomas Ctr for the Arts, Fla, 84; Ormond Beach Mus, 84; Brevard Art Ctr & Mus, Fla, 84; Brainwell Art Ctr Shreveport, La 84; Bottega di Cimbue, Florence, Italy, 84; Univ Nev, Reno, 84; Galleria Cairoli, Ravenna, Italy, 85; City Las Vegas' Charleston Heights Arts Ctr & Reed Whipple Cult Ctr, Nev, 85; Jacksonville Univ, Fla, 85; City Orlando/Landmark Ctr, Fla, 85; Daytona Beach Community Col, Fla, 85; Osceola Ctr Arts, Fla, 86; Nat Count Art Adminr Art Gallery, Ohio, 86; Fort Smith Art Ctr, Ark, 87; Portland State Univ, Ore, 87; Univ Ill, Champaign, 87; Koehnling Community Col, Ill, 87; Bridgewater State Col, Mass, 88; Duke Univ, NC, 88; Univ SC, 88; Northern Ind Art Asn, Muncie, 89; Ark State Univ, 89; Beverly Art Ctr, Chicago, 90; WVa Univ, 90; Goddard Ctr, Performing & Visual Arts, Okla, 90; Coker Col, 90; Mid-Am Mus, Ark, 91; Ind State Univ, 91. *Media:* Acrylics. *Mailing Add:* 520 Central Ave Hot Springs National Park AR 71901

BENJAMIN, ALICE (ALICE BENJAMIN BOUDREAU)
PAINTER, EDUCATOR
b Minneapolis, Minn, May 2, 36. *Study:* Wellesley Col, Mass, 54-56; Univ Minn, Minneapolis, Minn, BA, 58, BS, 63; San Francisco Art Inst, Calif, BFA, 61; State Univ NY, New Paltz, MS, 67; Instituto Allende, San Miguel d'Allende, Mex, 71; Frederic Munoz Workshop, 88. *Work:* 3M Co, St Paul, Minn; Univ Art Mus, Northrop Auditorium, Minneapolis, Minn; East Cent Reg Libr & Cambridge Ctr Anoka-Ramsey Community Col, Cambridge, Minn. *Exhib:* Life in Rural Minnesota, State Capitol, St Paul, 85; Six Painters, Katherine E Nash Gallery, Minneapolis, 86; Minn State Fair, 90 & 92; Five Points of View, Plymouth Church, 90; En Plein Air-Landscapes, Wilensky Arts Gallery, Minn, 92; Our Bodies Ourselves, Figure Show, Banfill Locke Art Ctr, Fridley, Minn, 92. *Pos:* Illusr zoology dept, Univ Minn, Minneapolis, 58-60. *Teaching:* Instr elem art, Onteora Pub Schs, Boiceville, NY, 63-66; Northrop & Blake Schs, Minneapolis, Minn, 69-75; instr art, drawing, painting & design, Cambridge Ctr, Anoka-Ramsey Community Col, Cambridge, Minn, 78-92. *Awards:* First Place Painting, Images, East Cent Reg Artists Coun, 75, 84, 85, 88 & 89, Purchase Award, 88; Best of Show, Liberty Studios, White Bear, Minn. *Bibliog:* Joanne Frank (auth), Alice Benjamin Boudreau, Minn Rural Artists Asn, 6/86. *Mem:* Women's Art Registry Minn (assoc mem); Minn Rural Artists Asn; Isanti Co Arts Guild (pres, 84-92); and others. *Media:* Acrylic. *Dealer:* Brush in Hand Gallery White Bear Lake MN 55110. *Mailing Add:* Rte 4 Box 128 Isanti MN 55040

BENJAMIN, KARL STANLEY
PAINTER, EDUCATOR
b Chicago, Ill, Dec 29, 25. *Study:* Northwestern Univ; Univ Redlands, BA, 49; Claremont Grad Sch, MA, 60. *Work:* Whitney Mus Am Art, New York; Los Angeles Co Mus Art; San Francisco Mus Art; Wadsworth Atheneum, Hartford, Conn; Nat Collection Fine Arts, Smithsonian Inst, Washington, DC. *Exhib:* Painting & Sculpture in Calif: The Modern Era, San Francisco Mus of Mod Art & Nat Collection of Fine Arts, Smithsonian Inst, Washington, DC, 76-77; Los Angeles Hard Edge: The Fifties & the Seventies, Los Angeles Co Mus Art, 77; Am Art from Corp Collections, Corcoran Gallery, Washington, DC & Ala, Indianapolis & San Diego Mus, 79; Color in Contemporary Painting, Henry Gallery, Univ Wash, 82; The Twentieth Century: San Francisco Mus Art Collection, San Francisco Mus Mod Art, 84; Ten California Colorists, Pomona Col, Univ NMex, and others, 85-86; Selected Works 1979-1986, Los Angeles Munic Art Gallery, 86; A Retrospective 1955-1987, Redding Mus, Shasta Col, Univ Pacific, & Calif State Univ, Northridge, 89-90; Santa Barbara Mus, Oakland Mus, 90-92. *Teaching:* Prof art & artist-in-residence, Pomona Col & Claremont Grad Sch. *Awards:* Nat Endowment Arts Grant, 83-84 & 89-90. *Bibliog:* Archives Am Art (interview), Smithsonian, Calif Oral History Project. *Media:* Oil. *Dealer:* Ruth Bachofner Gallery 926 Colorado Ave Santa Monica CA 90401; Francine Seders Gallery 6701 Greenwood Ave N Seattle WA 98103. *Mailing Add:* 675 W Eighth St Claremont CA 91711

BENJAMIN, LLOYD WILLIAM, III
HISTORIAN, ADMINISTRATOR
b Painesville, Ohio, Sept 2, 44. *Study:* Emory Univ, BA, 66; Univ NC, Chapel Hill, PhD, 73. *Collections Arranged:* The Art of Designed Environments in the Netherlands (auth, catalog), 83-85. *Pos:* Chmn, Southeastern Col Art Conf, 74-76 & 80-83, dean, 83- & vpres, 91- *Teaching:* Asst prof art hist, ECarolina Univ, 70-76, chmn dept, 74-76; from asst to assoc prof, Univ Ark, Little Rock, 76-82, chmn dept art, 80-, prof, 83-, dean, Col Fine Arts, 83-88, dean, Col Arts, Humanities & Soc Sci, 88- *Mem:* Ark Endowment Humanities (bd mem & treas, 77-83); Southeastern Col Art Conf (bd mem, 78-83); Col Art Asn Am; Medieval Acad Am. *Res:* Twentieth century Dutch art and environmental design. *Publ:* Auth, The art of designed environments in the Netherlands, Livability, 82 & Stichting Kunst Bedrijf, 83; coauth, Drawings from the Collection of Herbert and Dorothy Vogel, Univ Ark at Little Rock & Pa State Univ, 86; contribr, Nederlandse opdrachtgebonden kunst in de Verenigde Staten-een primeur: Harmonius Wedding of Art and Technology, Kwartaalblad Kunst en Bedrijf, 87; Public Art in the Netherlands, Dutch Heights: Art and Culture in the Netherlands, 4/88; Painting for the Delectation of the Inner Eye in Sammy Peters: Baser Matter (exhib catalog), 89; and others. *Mailing Add:* Dept Art Univ Ark 2801 S University Ave Little Rock AR 72204

BENNETT, DON BEMCO
PAINTER, PRINTMAKER
b McGlaughlin, SDak, Jan 8, 16. *Study:* Univ Wash; Edison Voc Sch, Seattle; also with the late Eliot O'Hara. *Work:* Cheney-Cowles Fine Arts Mus, Spokane, Wash; Ford Motor Co Collection of Am Art, Dearborn, Mich; Boise Cascade Corp, Boise, Idaho; Valley Nat Bank, Phoenix, Ariz; ITT Sheraton Corp, Boston, Mass. *Exhib:* Fourth Ann Art Exhib, Merchant Seamen UN, Corcoran Gallery, 46; US Info Agency Exhib Contemp Am Artists Worldwide Traveling Exhib, 60; Craftsman Competition, Pac Northwest Painters, Fry Mus, Seattle, 68; 15th Ann Exhib, Acad Artists Asn, Mus Fine Arts, Springfield, Mass, 64; Am Natural Hist Art Show, James Ford Bell Mus, Univ Minn, Minneapolis, 71. *Awards:* First Place in graphics, Acad Artists Asn, 64; Top Twenty Award, Craftsman Press, Seattle, 68; Second Place Award, Representational Watercolor, 28th Ann Exhib Idaho Artists, Boise Art Asn. *Media:* Watercolor, Oil; Lithography. *Publ:* Auth & illusr, Ford Times Mag, 58- *Mailing Add:* PO Box 105 Sun Valley ID 83353

BENNETT, JAMIE
ENAMELIST, SCULPTOR
b Philadelphia, Pa, Oct 6, 48. *Study:* Univ Ga, BBA & BFA, 70; State Univ NY New Paltz, MFA, 74. *Work:* Univ Ga; Ark Art Ctr; Kunst Industr, Trondheim, Norway; Mus App Arts, Oslow, Finland; Brockton Art Mus, Mass; Renwick Gallery, Smithsonian Inst, Wash, DC. *Exhib:* Annual Show, Clark Gallery, 87, 88 & 89; solo exhibs, Fergus-Jean Gallery, Cleveland, Ohio, 88 & CDK Gallery, New York, 89; Seven Views, Univ Gallery, El Paso, Tex, 89; American Metal, Walker Mus, Seoul, Korea, 89; Craft Today, Musee'de Decoratifs, Paris, France, 89; Color and Image, GANYS, NY State Traveling Exhib, 89; Six plus Six, Carver Etc Arts, San Antonio, Tex, 89; New Work, Clark Gallery, Lincoln, Mass, 89; and others. *Collections Arranged:* Six at Univ Tex, Arlington, group exhib & symp, 77; Enamelists, Established & Emerging, Chastain Arts Ctr, 77. *Pos:* Artist-in-residence, Kohler Art Ctr, Sheboygan, Wis, 74; vis artist, Penland Sch Crafts, 74, 76, 77 & 80, Fla Int Univ, 77 & Colo Mountain Col, 77 & 78, Boston Univ, 79-80, Carnegie-Mellon Univ, 80 & Haystack, Deer Isle, Maine, 80. *Teaching:* Instr metal, Bradley Univ, Peoria, Ill, 74-76; asst prof metal & drawing, Memphis Acad Art, Tenn, 76-; assoc prof art, SUNY, New Paltz, 85-87, prof, 88- *Awards:*

Nat Endowment Arts, Craftsmen's fel, 75 & 79; First Place, Nat Enamels Exhib, Alexandria, Va, 79; First Place, Nat Prints, Drawings & Crafts Exhib, Ark Art Ctr, Little Rock, 79; Craftsmen's Fel, Nat Endowment Arts, 88. *Bibliog:* Sandy Ballatore (auth), Jewelers USA, 3/76 & Enamelists, 11/76, Art News; Lisa Hammel (auth), Enameling, New York Times, 12/76. *Mem:* Soc NAm Goldsmiths. *Media:* Precious Metals; Acrylic, Oil. *Publ:* Contribr, Jewelry Making, Prentice Hall, 74; The Box Book & The Mirror Book, Crown, 76. *Dealer:* Clark Gallery Lincoln Station Lincoln MA 01773. *Mailing Add:* PO Box 128 New Paltz NY 12561

BENNETT, JOHN M
WRITER, GRAPHIC ARTIST
b Chicago, Ill, Oct 12, 42. *Study:* Wash Univ, St Louis, BA(cum laude), 64, MS, 66; Univ Calif, Los Angeles, PhD, 70. *Exhib:* Solo exhibs, Hopkins Gallery, Ohio State Univ, 74 & 75 & Ten Window on 8th Avenue, New York, 80; Columbus Art League; Ft Hayes Gallery, Columbus, 88; Cultural Arts Ctr, Columbus Sch Fine Arts, Willoughby, 90; Art Gallery, Dayton, Ohio, 91; and others. *Awards:* Film & Publ Grants, 79-85, Artist Fels, 80, 82, 88, 89, 90 & 91, Ohio Arts Coun. *Bibliog:* Edward Lense (auth), Floating in My Voice: The Word Art of John M Bennett, Columbus Art, 11/79; John McClintock (producer), Mail Art Romance (film), 82; Leonard Trawick (auth), John Bennett's Poetry of Beauty and Disgust, The Gamut, 85. *Publ:* Auth, Somation, Pneumatic Press, Ventura, Calif, 92; Neuf Poëmes, Les Editions Jeta Garenne, Lyon, France, 92; Bleached, BGS Press, Racine, Wis, 92; Bag Talk, Music You Can Almost See, Denver, 92; Pod King, Luna Bisonte Prods, Columbus, Ohio, 92. *Mailing Add:* c/o Luna Bisonte Prods 137 Leland Ave Columbus OH 43214

BENNETT, PHILOMENE DOSEK
PAINTER, CERAMIST
b Lincoln, Nebr, Jan 2, 35. *Study:* Univ Nebr, BFA, 56. *Work:* Albrecht Art Mus, St Joseph, Mo; Mushkin Art Mus, Atcheson, Kans; Nelson-Atkins Mus Art, Kansas City, Mo; Mulvane Mus, Washburn Univ, Topeka, Kans; Nat Women's Mus, Washington, DC; Hallmark Collection, Kansas City, Mo; United Mo Bank, Kansas City; Prudential Ins, New York. *Comn:* Paintings, Crown Ctr Hotel, Kansas City, Mo, 74 & Rockhurst Col Libr, Kansas City, Mo, 75; stained glass windows, St Charles Church, North Kansas City, Mo, 74; 14 Stations of the Cross, Conway Chapel, Rockhurst Col, Kansas City, Mo, 75. *Exhib:* 7 Mo Painters, Mo State Coun on Arts Presentation, 71; Selected Painters' Invitational, Mulvane Mus, Topeka, Kans, 77; Biennial, Joslyn Art Mus, Omaha, Nebr, 78; Summer Show, Atkins Mus Fine Arts, William Rockhill Nelson Gallery Art, Kansas City, Mo, 79; Artists Choose Artists, Univ Mo-Kansas City, 79; Porcelains, Sheldon Gallery, Univ Nebr, 81. *Pos:* Mem prof bd, Mo Arts Coun, Kansas City, 79-82; art ed, Helicon Nine, 79-; mem bd, Kansas City Arts Council, 82-83. *Teaching:* Artist-in-residence painting, Rockhurst Col, 69-70, Kans City Art Inst, 83, 84-85 & 90, Univ Ark, 89-; pvt instr painting, Bennett-Marak Studio, Kansas City, Mo, 73-86. *Awards:* Purchase Award, William Rockhill Nelson Gallery Art, Kansas City, Mo, 62; Award Winner, Univ Mo-Kansas City Women's Caucus for Arts, 77; Eller Outdoor Advert & Kansas City Arts Comn Billboard Award, 79. *Bibliog:* Film-interview, Johnson Co Community Col, 74; Patrick White (auth), article, New Art Examiner, 82; Don Lambert (auth), Images from heaven, Saturday Rev, 1-2/86. *Mem:* Kansas City Artists Coalition (co-founder, vpres, 75, pres, 76, prog chmn, 77); Women's Nat Caucus for Arts; Soc Contemporary Photog, Kansas City, Mo; Kansas City Arts Coun (bd mem). *Media:* Acrylic, Oil; Porcelain. *Dealer:* Jayne Gallery Co Club Plaza Kansas City MO; Studio Cerrillos NM. *Mailing Add:* 1776 Fort Union Dr Santa Fe NM 87501

BENNETT, RAINEY
PAINTER, ILLUSTRATOR
b Marion, Ind, July 26, 07. *Study:* Univ Chicago, PhD, 30; Art Inst Chicago; Am Acad Art; Art Students League; George Grosz-Maurice Sterne Sch. *Work:* Metrop Mus Art, Mus Mod Art, New York; Cranbrook Mus; Art Inst Chicago; many pvt collections. *Comn:* Mural, Post Off, Dearborn, Mich, 37, Rushville, Ill, 38 & Naperville, Ill, 41; 13 panel mural, Neil House, Columbus, Ohio, 39; watercolors, comn by Nelson Rockefeller, Standard Oil Co, SAm, 39 & 41; oil painting, Chicago and NWestern Railroad Exec Off, 62. *Exhib:* Downtown Gallery, New York; Art Inst Chicago; Cleveland Mus; Toledo Mus; Whitney Mus; Fairweather Hardin Gallery, Chicago. *Pos:* Supvr, Fed Art Proj, Chicago, 35-38. *Awards:* Oppenheimer Purchase Prize, Chicago, 60. *Mailing Add:* 2412 N Burling Chicago IL 60614

BENNEY, ROBERT
PAINTER, ILLUSTRATOR
b New York, NY. *Study:* Cooper Union; Nat Acad Design; Grand Cent Art Sch; Art Students League. *Work:* Corcoran Gallery Art, Washington, DC; USN, USA, USAF & USMC Art Collections, Washington, DC; De Young Mus Art, San Francisco; Mariners Mus Art, Newport News, Va; Chrysler Collection, Detroit Mus, Mich; and others. *Comn:* Accredited war corresp US Army, USN, WW II; Paintings, Am Sugar Refining Co, New York, 52-55; hist illust, Vietnam combat art, Reader's Digest, USMC, 68- 70; and many portraits. *Exhib:* Nat Gallery Art, Washington, DC; Metrop Mus Art, New York; De Young Mus; Brooklyn Mus; Corcoran Gallery Art; Fine Arts Gallery, San Diego; Portland Art Mus, Ore; Norfolk Mus Arts & Sci; Dallas Mus Fine Arts, Tex; one-man shows, Mus City New York, Lincoln Ctr Libr-Mus, Archit League, New York, New York Public Libr, Pratt Inst & Soc Illustr; Carnegie Inst; Brooklyn Mus; Art Inst Chicago; and others. *Teaching:* Instr painting, drawing & compos, Sch Visual Arts; instr illus, Pratt Inst, 49-52; assoc prof art, Dutchess Co Col, 63-73. *Awards:* First Award, Philadelphia Mus Art, Pa; Gold Medal, Chicago Art Dirs Club; Cert Commendation Fine Arts, USN, 74; 1st Place Award, Philadelphia Mus; Gold Medal Award, Chicago; Certificate of Commendation, Dept of Navy; Art Achievement Award, Centennial Comt 7th Regiment Armory Vets. *Mem:* Soc Illusr; Artists Equity Asn; life mem Art Students League; Artists & Writers Asn; Appraisers Asn Am. *Media:* Oil, Acrylic; Etching, Aquatint. *Publ:* Illusr, Reader's Digest, True, Argosy, Time, Life & Fortune; contribr, Life's Picture History of World War II, Our Flying Navy--James Jones' WWII, Men without Guns, Life of Joshua; The Illustrator in Am, 1880-1980, Winston Churchill Memoirs, 69, WWII James Jones, 75; Images of War, Orion Books, 90; and others. *Mailing Add:* 50 W 96th St New York NY 10025

BENNION, JOSEPH W
CERAMIST
b Sept 4, 52; US citizen. *Study:* Tuscarora Pottery Sch, 80; Brigham Young Univ, MFA, 86. *Work:* Pushkin Mus, Moscow, Russ; State Mus Fine Arts, Riga, Latvia; Detroit Inst Art, Mich; Mus Ceramic Art Alfred, NY; Nora Eccles Harrision Mus Art, Logan, Utah. *Exhib:* solo exhib, Useful Pottery, Dartmouth Col, Hanover, NH; 28th Ceramic Nat, Everson Mus Art, Syracuse, NY; Clay Nat, Erie Mus, Pa; NCELA Mem Exhib, Taft Mus, Cincinnati; Works in Clay VII, Wichita Falls Mus, Tex; American Woodfire, Univ Iowa Mus. *Teaching:* Pottery, various workshops & seminars. *Awards:* Nat Endowment Arts Fel Grant, 91. *Bibliog:* Gerry Williams (auth), Utah Potters, Studio Potter, 88; Steven Olpin (dir), The Potter's Meal (film), 92. *Mem:* Nat Coun Educ Ceramic Arts (mem 82-92). *Media:* Clay. *Publ:* Auth, social, ethical and environmental responsibilities of ceramic artists, 86 & emerging talent, 91, nat coun educ for the ceramic arts; An integration of pots and life, 91 & eloquent irony, 92, ceramics: art & perception. *Mailing Add:* PO Box 186 Spring City UT 84662

BENNY, SANDRA
GRAPHIC ARTIST
b Cleveland, Ohio, June 14, 44. *Study:* Ohio Univ, Athens, BFA, 66; Northern Ill Univ, De kalb, MA, 70. *Work:* Aramco Corp, Saudi Arabia; Arthur Anderson & Co, Huntington, NY; Washington Co Mus Fine Art, Haggerstown, Md. *Exhib:* Juried Painting Competition, Hudson River Mus, Yonkers, NY, 77; Silvermine Art Competition, Conn, 82; Invitational, Heckscher Mus, Huntington, NY, 83; May Show Competition, Cleveland Mus Art, Ohio, 85; Washington Co Mus Fine Arts, Haggerstown, Md, 86. *Teaching:* Adj prof art, C W Post Col, Long Island Univ, 76- *Mem:* Huntington Township Art League; Nat Drawing Asn. *Media:* Colored Pencil, Paint. *Publ:* New York Art Review, 91. *Mailing Add:* 4 Lloyd Lane Lloyd Neck NY 11743

BENSIGNOR, PAULETTE
PAINTER, PRINTMAKER
b Philadelphia, Pa, Dec 4, 48. *Study:* Univ Pa, BFA, 71; Temple Univ, Tyler Sch Fine Arts, MEd, 73. *Work:* Bell Atlantic, Dupont Inc, Colonial Penn Insurance, Fidelity Bank, Green Tree Insurance. *Exhib:* 31st Ann Award Exhib, Cheltenham Art Ctr, Pa, 78; Woodmere Mus, 70-72 & 83-86; Fel of Pa Acad Fine Arts Travelling Exhib, 84; Women Artists, Pa Art Mus, 85; regional juried show, Artists Equity, 88; solo shows, The Craft Store, Philadelphia, 77, Gloucester Co Col, NJ, 78 & 84, Suzanne Gross Gallery, Philadelphia, 88, Gross McCleaf Gallery, Philadelphia, 88-, Slater-Price, New York, 89-, Helio Gallery, New York, 90, Noyes Mus, NJ, 90, Hanson Galleries, New York, 90- *Teaching:* Instr fine art, Pa Sch Dist, 72-88, Gratz Col, 89-; instr, Philadelphia Acad Fine Arts, 91. *Awards:* Pacard Prize, Pa Acad Fine Arts, 70; First Prize, 82 & Edith Emerson Prize, 85, Woodmere Art Mus; Harry Rockower Mem Award, Cheltenham Ctr, Pa, 91. *Mem:* Fel of Pa Acad Fine Arts (exec bd mem, 79-81); Pa Watercolor Club; Artist Equity; Nat Drawing Soc. *Media:* Oil. *Publ:* Auth, Cosmopolitan, Japan Edition, 4/92; An Illustrated Survey of Leading Contemporaries, Am Artist, 91. *Mailing Add:* 124 Rockland Ave Bala Cynwyd PA 19004

BENSON, ELAINE K G
ART DEALER, WRITER
b Philadelphia, Pa, Apr 30, 24. *Study:* Univ Pa, BA, 44; Long Island Univ, Hon Dr Fine Arts, 87. *Pos:* Dir pub rels, Philadelphia Col Art, 57-64; dir, Elaine Benson Gallery, 65-; co-dir summer art prog, Southampton Col, 67-69; ed, Hamptons Mag, 83- & Our Hampton Heritage, 83-84. *Teaching:* Coordr fashion fields, Philadelphia Col Art, 63-64. *Mem:* Am Fedn Art. *Specialty:* Contemporary European, Southeast Asian, and American paintings, sculpture and fine crafts. *Publ:* Criticism & articles on art & artists in many publications. *Mailing Add:* Elaine Benson Gallery Montauk Hwy Bridgehampton NY 11932

BENSON, ELIZABETH POLK
HISTORIAN, WRITER
b Washington, DC, May 13, 24. *Study:* Wellesley Col, BA, 45; Cath Univ Am, MA, 56. *Pos:* Cur & aide, Nat Gallery Art, Washington, DC, 47-61; cur, Dumbarton Oaks, Washington, DC, 62-79; dir, Ctr Pre-Columbian Studies, 71-78; res assoc, Inst Andean Studies, Berkeley, Calif, 80- *Teaching:* Lectr, Catholic Univ, Washington, DC, 68-69; adj prof, Columbia Univ, New York, 73, Univ Tex, Austin, 85; Am Univ, Washington, DC, 87. *Mem:* Soc Women Geographers. *Res:* Pre-Columbian art of the Moche (Peru), Maya and Olmec. *Publ:* Auth, The Maya World, Thomas Y Crowell, 67, 72 & 77; The Mochica: A Culture of Peru, Praeger Publ, 72; ed, The Olmec and their neighbors, Dumbarton Oaks, 81; coauth, Museums of the Andes, Newsweek Books, 81; Coauth, Atlas of Ancient America, Facts on File, 86. *Mailing Add:* 8314 Seven Locks Rd Bethesda MD 20817

BENSON, MARTHA J
JEWELER, ASSEMBLAGE ARTIST
b Kansas City, Mo, July 30, 28. *Study:* Univ Kansas City; Baker Univ, BA; spec study Kans Univ, Iowa State Univ, Utrecht, Holland, London, England, Glasgow & Scotland. *Comn:* Five wood-assemblage panels, St David's Episcopal Church, Ames, 75; six wood-assemblage panels, Chapel, Mary Greeley Hosp, Ames, 77; wall assemblages for pvt homes, Ames, Iowa & Fairmont, Minn; restoration of village oratonio, Bilek, Czech. *Exhib:* One-person shows, Iowa State Univ Mem Union, 82 & Unitarian Fellowship, Ames, Iowa, 84; Group-shows, Ann Exhib, womens Art Registry of Minn, 90, 91, Homer in Craft, Vista Gallery, Middleburg, Va, 89. *Collections Arranged:* Twelve Dutch Potters,; Three Chilean Printmakers, 73; Technol & the Artist-Craftsman-A Nat Crafts Exhib, 73-75; The Artists of San Miguel, 74-75; British Ceramics Today, US Tour (auth, catalog), 79; Hand, Mind & Spirit: Crafts Today (auth, catalog), 83; Women in Clay: The Ongoing Tradition (auth, catalog), 84; Legends in Fiber, 86, Textiles of Indian: A Living History; and over 200 other exhibs. *Pos:* found & dir, The Octagon Art Ctr, Ames, 68-91; bd dirs, British Am Art Asn, Am Asn Mus, Iowa Designers Crafts Asn. *Teaching:* Prof oil painting, Iowa State Univ, 69, basic design, 72. *Awards:* Recognition Award: One of Five Outstanding Women Art Dir, Iowa Women's Caucus, 76; Nat Endowment Arts Fel, 78-79; Christian Peterson Award, Iowa State Univ Col Design, 84; Outstanding Achivement Award, Iowa Arts Coun, 84. *Bibliog:* Annabelle Liu (auth), Martha Benson-A Profile, Craft Connection, 75. *Mem:* Am Craft Coun; Am Asn Mus; Art Mus Asn; Iowa Mus Asn. *Media:* Wood, Metal. *Dealer:* Lightside Gallery Sante Fe NM. *Mailing Add:* 928 Garfield Ames IA 50010

BENTLEY, CLAUDE
PAINTER, MURALIST
b New York, NY, June 9, 15. *Study:* Northwestern Univ; Art Inst Chicago. *Work:* Krannert Mus, Univ Ill; Denver Art Mus; Art Inst Chicago; Ill State Mus; plus others. *Comn:* Murals, 3600 Lake Shore Dr Bldg, Chicago, Ill; comn as design consult, Plaza del Lago Shopping Ctr, Winnetka, Ill. *Exhib:* Corcoran Gallery Art; San Francisco Mus Art; Whitney Mus Am Art; Art Inst Chicago; Denver Art Mus; plus others. *Teaching:* Artist-in-residence, Layton Sch Art, Milwaukee, 55-58, Claude Bentley Workshop, Chicago, 58-59 & Art Inst Chicago, 59-60. *Awards:* John G Curtis Jr Award, 63; Old Orchard Art Fair Award, 63; Purchase Award, Ill State Mus, 63; and others. *Bibliog:* Literary Times, 4/65; Creating art from anything, Meilach, 68; The Collage Handbook, Digby, 84. *Media:* Multi, Collage. *Collection:* African, oceanic, pre-Columbian art & Spanish colonial art of Mexico and New Mexico. *Dealer:* Boritzer/Gray Gallery 3110 Main St #100 Santa Monica CA 90405. *Mailing Add:* 310 Otero St Santa Fe NM 87501

BENTLEY-SCHECK, GRACE MARY
PRINTMAKER
b Troy, NY, Apr 20, 37. *Study:* NY State Col Ceramics Alfred Univ, BFA, 59, MFA, 60. *Work:* Knoxville Mus Art, Tenn; Portland Art Mus; Silvermine Guild Artists, New Canaan, Conn; Hunterdon Art Asn, Clinton, NJ; Univ NDak, Grand Forks. *Comn:* Theme: the Celebrated Worker (2 prints), State of RI, 92. *Exhib:* Los Angeles Printing Soc 11th Nat Exhib, Calif, 90; The Prints and the Paper, San Diego Art Inst, Calif, 91; Boston Printmakers 43rd NAm Print Exhib, DeCordova Mus, Lincoln, Mass, 91; 1992 Stockton Nat VI, Haggin Mus, Calif; Pac States Biennial, Univ Hawaii, Hilo, 92; Prints Int 1992, Silvermine Guild Galleries, New Canaan, Conn, 92. *Pos:* Vis artist, Univ SDak, Vermillion, 90- *Awards:* Arjomari/Arches/Rives Award, 11th Nat LAPS Exhib, Arjomari/Arches/Rives Paper Co, 90; Louis Lozowick Award, 50th Nat Exhib Audubon Artists, 92; Juror's Award, NDak Print & Drawing Ann, 92. *Bibliog:* The History of Hera: A Women's Art Cooperative, Hera Gallery, 90; Buildings cycle reflect our own (rev), Boston Globe, 90; Ordinary is spectacular in art show (rev), Wichita Eagle, 90; and others. *Mem:* Boston Printmakers; Los Angeles Printmaking Soc; Soc Am Graphic Artist; Print Club Philadelphia. *Media:* Collagraph. *Dealer:* Wenniger Graphics 174 Newbury St Boston MA. *Mailing Add:* 63 Sassafrass Trail Narragansett RI 02882

BENTON, FLETCHER
SCULPTOR
b Jackson, Ohio, Feb 25, 31. *Study:* Miami Univ, BFA, 56. *Work:* Whitney Mus Am Art, New York; Hirshhorn Mus, Washington, DC; San Francisco Mus Mod Art, Calif; Univ Calif, Los Angeles; Rockefeller Collection, New York; and others. *Comn:* IBM Corp, Morgan Hill, Calif; Thruman Arnold Bldg, Washington, DC; Univ Calif, Los Angeles; Davies Symphony Hall, San Francisco; public sculpture, City of Offend Bach, WGermany; and others. *Exhib:* Solo exhibs, Harcus Gallery, Boston Mass, 87, Haasner Gallery, Weisbaden, WGer, 87, Dorothy Goldeen Gallery, Santa Monica, Calif, 88 & John Berggruen Gallery, Monadnock Bldg, San Francisco, Calif, 89; Summer Selections, Thomas Babeor Gallery, La Jolla, Calif, 88; Sculpture, John Berggruen Gallery, Monadnock Gallery, San Francisco, Calif, 89; American Pop Culture Today III, Laforet Mus, Jarajuku, Japan, 89; 5X5, The Conly Gallery Art, Calif State Univ, Fresno, 89; Albright-Knox Art Gallery, Buffalo, NY, 69 & 71; San Francisco Mus Art, 70, 76, 82 & 83; Int Mus Fine Arts, Osaka, Japan, 70; Stanford Univ Mus, Calif, 70-72; Hirshhorn Mus, Washington, DC; John Berggruen Gallery, San Francisco, 77, 79, 81, 84 & 86; and many others. *Teaching:* Instr, Calif Col Arts & Crafts, 59 & San Francisco Art Inst, 64-67; prof art, Calif State Univ, San Jose, 67-; prof art, San Jose State Univ, 68- *Awards:* Award in Sculpture for Work of Distinction, Am Acad & Inst Arts & Letters, 79; President's Scholar Award, San Jose State Univ, Calif; Award of Hon for Outstanding Achievement in Sculpture, San Francisco Art Comn, 82. *Bibliog:* Peter Selz (auth), article in Directions in Kinetic Sculpture, Univ Calif, Berkeley, 66; George Rickey (auth), Constructivist Tendencies, 71; J Butterfield (auth), Interview with Fletcher Benton, Art Int, 80. *Dealer:* John Berggruen Gallery 228 Grant Ave San Francisco CA 94108. *Mailing Add:* 250 Dore St San Francisco CA 94103

BENTON, SUZANNE E
SCULPTOR, ART WRITER
b New York, NY, Jan 21, 36. *Study:* Queens Col, New York, BA(fine arts), 56; studies in New York at Art Students League, Columbia Univ, NY Univ, Brooklyn Col, Brooklyn Mus Art Sch & Mus Mod Art; Silvermine Col Art, Conn. *Work:* Oakton Community Col, Ill; Nat Mus Mod Art, New Delhi, India; Birla Acad, Calcutta, India; Tokyo Sch Fine Arts, Japan; Deree Pierce Col, Athens, Greece; Temple Beth-El, Houston; Cent Conn State Univ; and others. *Comn:* Sculptured theatre sets, Viveca Lindfor's I Am A Woman Theatre Co, 73; The Sun Queen, large-scale bronze sculpture & Throne of the Sun Queen, bronze & corten steel, Art Park, Lewiston, NY, 75; Constellation (steel & bronze), comn by Wardlaw, 83-84; Ravage: Sun (sheet bronze), 85; Secret Future Work #1, Vivien Leone Collection, 90. *Exhib:* Expo 74, Spokane, Wash, 74; one-person shows, Touching Ritual, Wadsworth Atheneum, Hartford, Conn, 75, Art Park, Lewiston, NY, 75, Hellenic Am Union, Athens, Greece, 76, AB Condon Gallery, New York, 81 & Korean Cult Ctr, NY, 83; Amerika Haus, Koln, 83 & 89, Stuttgart, 86, Hanover, 88 & C G Jung Ctr, 88, WGer; Asia Soc, 85; Interchurch Ctr, 89; On the Wall, New York, 89; Studio exhib of New Direction, 90; Cathedral of St John The Devine, 91; Hurlbutt Gallery, Greenwich, Conn, 92. *Pos:* Convener-coordr, Arts Festival-Metamorphosis I, New Haven, Conn, 69-70 & Conn Feminists in the Arts, 69-72; performance artist, Mask Ritual Tales, 69-; producer-dir, Four Chosen Women, New York, 72; art consult, Xerox, 73-76; Boeringer Ingelheim Ltd, 80-83. *Teaching:* Instr welded sculpture, Brookfield Craft Ctr, Brookfield, Conn, 72-73, Norwalk Community Col, fall 80 & various art appreciation workshops, mask & all performances & workshops at cols throughout USA, 71-, and 19 countries world-wide; Fulbright lectr India, 92-93. *Awards:* Susan B Anthony Award, Eastern Regional Conf, Nat Orgn Women, 72; An Outstanding Conn Woman for the Undecade of Women (sculpture), 88. *Bibliog:* Phyllis Rosser (auth), Suzanne Benton: Sculptured in Power, Pain and Herstory, In Arts, New Directions for Women, 7-8/91; Jan Howari (auth), Storyteller helps children see into their past, Weekly Star, 10/26/91; Beth Liebenson (auth), An artist's masks reveal and conceal, New York Times, 4/12/92. *Mem:* Artists Equity; Silvermine Guild Artists (mem bd, 88-90); hon mem Nat Korean Sculptress Asn; Nat Asn Women Artists; Archit Adv Comt, Ridgefield, Conn, 81- *Media:* Welded Metal, Monoprints; Performance art. *Publ:* Contribr, Masks, Face Coverings and Headgear, Van Nostrand Reinhold, 73; contribr, Woman in the Year 2000, Arbor House, 74; auth, The Art of Welded Sculpture, Van Nostrand Reinhold, 75; illusr, Women Artists in America, Collins, 75; auth, Köln: An artist's reflection, Art & Artists, 12/84; Masks: Past & Present, Anima, 6/87; contribr, The Once Future Goddess, Harper & Row, 89. *Mailing Add:* 22 Donnelly Dr Ridgefield CT 06877

BENTOV, MIRTALA See Mirtala

BEN TRE, HOWARD B
SCULPTOR, DRAFTSMAN
b Brooklyn, NY, May 13, 49. *Study:* Portland State Univ, BSA, 78; RI Sch Design, MFA, 80. *Work:* Metrop Mus Art, New York; Nat Mus Mod Art, Tokyo, Japan; Nat Mus Am Hist, Smithsonian Inst; Leigh Yawkey Woodson Art Mus, Wausau, Wis; Mus Art, RI Sch Design; Fed Reserve Bd, Washington, DC; Philadelphia Mus Art, Pa. *Comn:* Outdoor installation, Vernal House, Los Angeles, 83; fountains, Post Office Sq Park Redevelop, 91; sculpture, Toledo Mus Art, 92. *Exhib:* New Glass Touring Exhib, Corning Mus Glass, Metrop Mus Art & Renwick Gallery, Nat Collection Art, 78-82; Contemp Glass, Nat Mus Mod Art, Kyoto & Tokyo, Japan; Art Gallery Western Australia, Perth, 82; World Glass Now 82, Hokaido Mus Mod Art, Sapporo, Japan, 82; Four Sculptors, Jesse Besser Mus, Alpena, Mich, 82; Columns, Ornament & Sculpture, Cooper Hewitt Mus, New York, 82; solo exhibs, Hadler Rodriguez Galleries, Houston, Tex, 81, 83 & 85; Habatat Galleries, Detroit, 81, 83, 84, 85 & 92; Foster/White Gallery, Seattle, Wash, 81 & 83; Clarke Gallery, Lincoln, Mass, 83 & 91; Charles Cowles Gallery, New York, 85, 86, 88, 89 & 91; John Berggruen Gallery, San Francisco, 86; solo exhibs, Fay Gold Gallery, Atlanta, Ga, 87, Dorothy Goldeen Gallery, Santa Monica, Calif, 89 & 91, The Phillips Collection, Washington, DC, 89-90, Carnegie-Mellon Art Gallery, Pittsburgh, Pa, 90, Toledo Mus Art, 92. *Awards:* Grant, RI State Coun Arts, 79, 84 & 90; Nat Endowment Arts Fel, 80, 84 & 90; The Rakow Award, 88. *Bibliog:* N Stapen (auth), An Elegant, Handsome, Hybrid, Boston Globe, 12/5/90; J Koplos (auth), Howard Ben Tre at Charles Cowles, Art Am, 12/91; L Morgenroth (auth), City of Fountains, Boston Globe, 9/10/92. *Media:* Cast Glass, Metal. *Dealer:* Habatat Galleries Lathrup Village MI & Bay Harbor Islands, FL. *Mailing Add:* c/o Charles Cowles Gallery 420 W Broadway New York NY 10012

BENTZ, HARRY DONALD
EDUCATOR, PAINTER
b Robesonia, Pa, Dec 2, 31. *Study:* Kutztown State Col, 53; Pa State Univ, with Hobson Pittman, 58; Lehigh Univ, 68; watercolor portraiture with Lester Stone. *Work:* Bank of Pa, Reading. *Comn:* Two murals, Spec Educ Ctr, Reading Sch Dist, 62; 15 display units, Daniel Boone Homestead, Birdsboro, Pa, 63. *Exhib:* Pa Art Educ Exhib, William Penn Mem Mus, 54; Washington Co Mus of Fine Arts Exhib, 65-67; Second Ann Watercolor Exhib, Millersville State Col, 76. *Teaching:* Art, Columbia High Sch, 55-60; art supervisor, Reading Sch Dist, 60-71; prof painting, Shippensburg State Col, 70-, chmn dept art, 71- *Awards:* Hayes Art Materials Award, 43rd Ann Cumberland Valley Exhib, 75; Purchase Award, 43rd Ann Cumberland Valley Exhib, Farmers & Merchants Bank, 75; First Prize, Huntingdon Co Arts Festival, Huntingdon Co Arts Coun, 76. *Mem:* Nat Art Educ Asn; Pa Art Educ Asn; Cumberland Valley Arts Coun; Pa Soc Watercolor Painters. *Media:* Watercolor, Oil. *Mailing Add:* 1429 Union St Reading PA 19604

BENVENUTO, ELIO
SCULPTOR
b Pietrasanta, Lucca, Italy, Jan 7, 14; US citizen. *Study:* San Marco Lyceum, Florence, Italy, BFA, 38; Univ San Francisco-San Francisco Art Inst, 64. *Work:* San Francisco City Collection; Univ Utah; Richmond Art Ctr, Calif; Univ Calif Med Ctr; Gallery Mod Art, Rome. *Comn:* Monument to Engineers, Legnao, Italy, 41; sculpture, Corpus Christi Church, San Francisco, 50; bronze fountain, Harbor City, Calif, 59; bronze fountain, San Jose, Calif, 60; St Luke's Church (all appurtenances), Stockton, Calif, 65. *Exhib:* Parterre San Gallo National, Florence, Italy, 37; 69th Annual, San Francisco Art Asn, Mus Mod Art, San Francisco, 50; Religious Art, DeYoung Mus, San Francisco, 52; American Federation Exhib, traveling, 58-59; Awards show, Palace Legion Honor, San Francisco, 60; San Francisco Art Inst, 61-66; 50-Year retrospective, Mus Italo Am, Richmond Art Ctr, Calif, 82; one-man show, Italian Mus, April 18-July 5, 88. *Collections Arranged:* San Francisco Annuals, City Art Comn, 67-81; Capricorn Asunder Gallery Shows, San Francisco, 70-73; San Francisco Sculpture, Osaka Expo. *Pos:* Dir, arts progs, San Francisco City Art Comn, 67-81; bd dirs, Calif Expo, Sacramento, Calif, 77-81. *Teaching:* Instr sculpture, San Francisco Community Col, 60-85. *Awards:* Award, Calif State Fair, 52; Award of Honor, Corpus Christi Church, Am Inst Archit, 57; Award, 18th Ann Art Festival, San Francisco, 64. *Bibliog:* Alfred Frankenstein (auth), essay, in: San Francisco Chronicle, 10/26/52; E M Polley (auth), Tradition-Invention, Artforum Mag, 62; Thomas Albright (auth), Art in the San Francisco Bay Area 1945-1980, Univ Calif Press, 85. *Media:* All. *Mailing Add:* 870 45th Ave San Francisco CA 94121

BENZLE, CURTIS MUNHALL
CERAMIST, EDUCATOR
b Lakewood, Ohio, Apr 20, 49. *Study:* Ohio State Univ, BFA, 72; Sch Am Craftmen/RIT, 73; Northern Ill Univ, MA, 78. *Work:* Nat Collection Am Art/Smithsonian Inst, Washington, DC; Int Mus Ceramics, Faenza, Italy; Cleveland Mus Art, Ohio; Los Angeles Co Mus Art, Calif; Everson Mus, Syracuse, NY. *Comn:* Governor's Art Award, State Ohio, Columbus, 82. *Exhib:* Ann, Cleveland Mus Art, Ohio, 71 & 73; Int Competition Artist Ceramics, Faenza, Italy, 81 & 82; Featured Artists, Renwick Gallery/ Smithsonian Inst, Washington, DC, 83; American Porcelain, Suntory Art Mus, Tokyo, Japan, 84; solo exhib, Indianapolis Mus Art, Indiana, 84 & Akaska Green Gallery, Tokyo, Japan, 87 & 90; Ceramic National, Everson Mus Art, Syracuse, NY, 87; Limoges Creative Porcelain Invitational, Limoges, France, 88. *Pos:* Pres, Ohio Designer Craftsman, 84-86; pres, Japan/ USA Exchange Exhib, 87-91; bd dir, Am Craft Retailer Asn, 90-92; vice chair, Am Craft Asn/Am Craft Coun, 92- *Teaching:* Instr ceramics, Univ SC, 78-79; Savannah Col Art, 79-80; assoc prof ceramics, CCAD, Columbus, 82- *Awards:* Fel Grant, Nat Endowment Art Craftsmen, 80; Individual Fel Grant, Ohio Arts Coun, 81, 83, 84 & 88; Individual Fel Grant, Greater Columbus Arts Coun, 87. *Bibliog:* Hideto Satonaka (auth), Patterns & Styles, Honoho Geijutsu, 87; Engracia Schuster (auth), Curtis & Suzan Benzle, Ceramica, 1/88; MJ VanDeventer (auth), Benzle Porcelains, Art Gallery Int, 3/88. *Mem:* Ohio Designer Craftsmen; Japan/USA Exchange Exhib (pres, 87); Ohio Citizens Com Arts; Nat Coun Educ Ceramic Arts; Am Crafts Coun. *Media:* Ceramic. *Publ:* Auth, Edible Art, Sch Arts, 80; The Craft Aesthetic, Dialogue, 81; David Leach, Dialogue, 82; Earning Your Worth, Ceramics Monthly, 88. *Dealer:* Martha Schneider Gallery Inc 2055 Green Bay Rd Highland Park IL 60035. *Mailing Add:* c/o Benzle Porcelain Co 6100 Hayden Run Rd Hilliard OH 43026

BERD, MORRIS
PAINTER, EDUCATOR
b Philadelphia, Pa, Mar 12, 14. *Study:* Philadelphia Col Art; Univ per Strangeri, Perugia, Italy, cert. *Work:* Philadelphia Mus Art; Pa Acad Fine Arts, Philadelphia; Philadelphia Col Art; Arco Collection, Los Angeles; Barnes Found, Merion, Pa. *Comn:* History of Oil (mural), Sun Oil Co, Franklin Inst; History of Architecture (mural), Gimbel Bros, Philadelphia. *Exhib:* Many Pa Acad Fine Arts Ann & Philadelphia Mus Art Regionals; also over 18 one-man shows, including Wilcox Gallery, Swarthmore Col, 73 & The Four Season, Marian Locks Gallery, 80; Am Col Bryn Mawr, Pa, 88; Ross-Constantine, New York, 90. *Teaching:* Prof painting, Philadelphia Col Art, 36-76, co-chmn dept, 50-71, prof emer, 82. *Awards:* Silver Medal, YMHA Jubilee show; Katzman Prize, Philadelphia Print Club, 62; Philadelphia Col Art Alumni Award, 65. *Bibliog:* Alan Gussow (auth), A Sense of Place, Vol II, 74; William Scott (auth), Four seasons, Am Artist, 2/80; Elizabeth Leonard (auth), Painting the Landscape, 84. *Media:* Oil, Watercolor. *Mailing Add:* 350 Howarth Rd Media PA 19063

BEREN, STANLEY O
PATRON
b Parkersburg, WVa, Feb 1, 20. *Study:* Harvard Col, AB, 41, Harvard Univ, MBA, 43. *Pos:* Pres, Wichita Art Mus Endowment Asn Inc, 68, chmn bd, 86-88, Wichita Art Mus, 70-72, mem bd, 72-; mem adv bd, JFK Ctr, 70- *Mem:* Am Asn Mus; Int Coun Mem. *Interests:* Special interest in raising funds for accessions for Wichita Art Mus. *Collection:* Modern painting and pre-Columbian artifacts. *Mailing Add:* 9123 Autumn Chase St Wichita KS 67206

BERG, MONA LEA
MUSEUM DIRECTOR
b Los Angeles, Calif, Nov 9, 35. *Study:* Univ Minn, studied with Cameron Booth, BA(art hist & studio), 60; Univ Kans, 69; Univ Okla, MLS(mus studies), 86. *Collections Arranged:* Old Students & Old Masters: The School of Rembrandt, 80, The Geometric Vision: Arts of the Zulu, 83, Renaissance & Baroque Prints, 83, L'Estampe Française, 85, Japanese Packages, 86, Italian Baroque Paintings, 87 & David & Bonnie Ross Collection of Precolumbian Art, 88, Purdue Univ Galleries, Ind. *Pos:* Gallery coordr, Purdue Univ Galleries, Ind, 78-80, dir galleries, 80- *Mem:* Am Asn Mus; Asn Ind Mus; Asn Col & Univ Mus & Galleries; Midwest Mus Conf. *Res:* 19th & 20th century American art. *Mailing Add:* Creative Arts Bldg No 1 Purdue Univ West Lafayette IN 47907

BERG, SIRI
PAINTER, INSTRUCTOR
b Stockholm, Sweden; US citizen. *Study:* Inst Art & Archit, Univ Brussels; Pratt Graphics Ctr, New York. *Work:* Chase Manhattan Bank, New York; Pace Univ Col, New York; IBM, AT&T, Revlon, Wang Indust, Chemical Bank, GCI Int; Herbert F Johnson Mus, Cornell Univ; Guggenheim Mus; Gloria Vanderbilt for Murjani; Coca Cola Co, Atlanta Hq(s); and others. *Comn:* Kreab-Ann Report Cover, 89-93. *Exhib:* solo exhib, The Am Swed Mus, Philadelphia, Pa, 86, Paula Allen Gallery, 86-87, Carol Hasto Fine Arts, 88, Alena Adlung Gallery, 89, Yeshiva Univ Mus, New York, 91 & Galerie Konstruktiv Tendens, Stockholm, Sweden, 92; Galerie Jamileh Weber, Galerie I, Zurich, Switz, 86; Fay Gold Gallery, Archit Images in Art, Atlanta, Ga, 86; Biennale Int Quebec-France, Can, 88; Galerie Fontainas, Richesse du Papier, Brussels, Belgium, 88; Galerie Konstruktiv Tendens, Geometric Abstration, Stockholm, Sweden, 91; and many others. *Pos:* Mem fac, New Sch/Parsons Sch Design 77- *Teaching:* Instr, Col New Rochelle, 74-82; color theory workshop, New Sch-Parsons Sch Design, 77- *Awards:* Arts Grant, NY State Coun, Artist in Residence, 78; Top Award 8th Ann Works on Paper, Art Gallery City Univ New York, 90. *Bibliog:* Katarina Cerny (introduction) catalog, Black & White, Am Swed Mus, 76, 81, 86; Monica Geran (auth), mag, Post Perfect Vol VIII, Interior Design, State of the Art, 8/88; article in IBM News, spec issue, 3/89. *Mem:* Am Scand Found; Am Scand Soc; Jewish Mus, Stockholm, Sweden. *Media:* Collage, Oil. *Publ:* Contrib, Contemp Graphic Artists, Vol III, 88; Uses of art in educational day treatment center, Am J Art Ther, 70. *Mailing Add:* 93 Mercer Apt 6F New York NY 10012

BERG, TOM
PAINTER
b Aberdeen, SD, Feb 10, 43. *Study:* Univ Wyo, BA, 66, MA, 68, MFA, 72; Univ Ore, 69. *Work:* Amoco Corp, Champlin Oil, Getty Oil & Exeter Corp, Denver; Standard Oil, Chicago; Okla Arts Inst, Oklahoma City; Univ Okla Mus Art, Norman; Univ Wyo Mus Art, Laramie; Mus of NMex, Santa Fe; Western Athletic Clubs, San Francisco, Calif; Chemical Bank, New York; Whitney Mus of Am Art, New York; Phillip Morris Collection, New York. *Exhib:* Ten Artists, Western States Arts Found Touring Show, Mus in Idaho, NDak, NMex, Wis, Utah, Wash & Ariz, 77-79; one-person shows, Heydt Bair Gallery, Santa Fe, 80-82, Eason Gallery, Santa Fe, 82-83, Davis-McClain Gallery, Houston, 84, Linda Durham Gallery, Santa Fe, 85, 87 & 89, Robischon Gallery, Denver, 86, Wade Gallery, Los Angeles & Mus Art, Univ Okla, Norman, 89; Rosalind Constable Invites Santa Fe Art Festival, 81; Southwest '85, Mus NMex, Santa Fe; and others. *Collections Arranged:* US Mail (mail art), Univ Maine, Augusta, 73. *Pos:* Vis lectr, Univ Rochester, 71, NMex State Univ, Las Cruces, 89, Univ Okla, Norman, 89 & Okla Arts Inst, Oklahoma City, 89 & 91; artist-in-residence, Univ Maine, Augusta, 72-73 & 87, Wyo Artists in Schs Prog, 73-76 & Delta State Univ, Cleveland, Miss, 76. *Teaching:* Instr art, Point Park Col, Pittsburgh, Pa, 69-71; vis lectr painting, Univ Wyo, Laramie, summer 77. *Awards:* Visual Arts Fel Wyo, Western States Arts Found, Denver, 76-77. *Bibliog:* Bruno Gilberti (auth), Furniture al Fresco, Art & Archit, Vol 2 No 2, 83; Wade Wilson (auth), chairs, Art Gallery Int, Vol 6, 8-9/85; David Bell (auth), Report from Santa Fe, Art in Am, Vol 73, No 9, 9/85. *Media:* Oil. *Dealer:* Janus Gallery 225 Canyon Rd Santa Fe NM 87501; Mill Street Gallery 112 S Mill St Aspen CO 81611. *Mailing Add:* Rt 1 Box 171A Santa Fe NM 87501

BERGE, DOROTHY ALPHENA
SCULPTOR, INSTRUCTOR
b Ottawa, Ill, May 8, 23. *Study:* St Olaf Col, Northfield, Minn, BA, 45; Minneapolis Sch Art, BFA, 50; Ga State Univ, Atlanta, MVA, 76. *Work:* Minneapolis Inst Art, Walker Art Ctr & Univ Minn Gallery, Minneapolis; High Mus Art, Atlanta, Ga. *Comn:* Copper wall sculpture, Mead Packaging Corp, Atlanta, Ga, 66; corten steel sculptures, Great Southwest Indust Park, Atlanta, 68 & 100 Colony Sq, 69; corten steel sculpture, St Olaf Col, comn by Mrs John Oslund, Northfield, Minn, 75; aluminum wall sculpture, Metrop Atlanta Rapid Transit Authority, 80. *Exhib:* Minn Biennial, Minneapolis Inst Art, 54; Recent Sculpture USA, Mus Mod Art, New York, 57; 16 Younger Minn Artists, Walker Art Ctr, Minneapolis, 58; one-person shows, Walker Art Ctr, 59 & High Mus Art, Atlanta, 68; Ga Artists 1, 2 & 6, High Mus Art, Atlanta, 71, 72 & 79. *Pos:* Registr, Walker Art Ctr, Minneapolis, 54-60; coordr circulating exhibs, Mus Mod Art, New York, 60-63. *Teaching:* Instr sculpture, drawing & ceramics, St Olaf Col, Northfield, Minn, 46-48; artist-in-residence sculpture, Nat Endowment Arts, Ga, 71-72. *Awards:* Purchase Award, Ford Found Prog Humanities & Arts, 60. *Media:* Welded Metal. *Dealer:* Heath Gallery 416 E Paces Ferry Rd NE Atlanta GA 30309. *Mailing Add:* 1311 S Everett St Stillwater MN 55082

BERGE, HENRY
SCULPTOR
b Baltimore, Md, May 29, 08. *Study:* Md Inst Fine Arts; Rhinehart Sch Sculpture with J Maxwell Miller. *Work:* Hagerstown Mus Fine Arts; approx 300 portrait heads for figures in 15 waxworks mus in US & Can. *Comn:* Portrait reliefs, Henrietta & Jacob Blaustein, Oheb Shalom Temple, Baltimore, 63; over life-size bust, Gov Millard Tawes, State Off Bldg, Baltimore; sea urchin figure, Mt Vernon place, Baltimore; and others. *Exhib:* Baltimore Mus Art, 40; Nat Acad Design, New York, NY; Pa Acad Fine Arts;

Nat Sculpture Soc Ann, Lever House, New York, 68-75; Rhinehart Sch Sculpture 75th Anniversary, Baltimore, 71. *Mem:* Fel Nat Sculpture Soc; Charcoal Club, Baltimore. *Media:* Plastic, Bronze. *Mailing Add:* 5 Merrymount Rd Baltimore MD 21210

BERGEN, D THOMAS
COLLECTOR
b Albert Lea, Minn, June 16, 30. *Study:* Harvard Col, AB, 52, Harvard Bus Sch, MBA, 54. *Collection:* Works on paper by late nineteenth to early twentieth century Germanic artists, notably focusing on Die Brucke; expressionism and German art to circa 1930. *Mailing Add:* PO Box 1666 FDR Sta New York NY 10150

BERGEN, JOHN AXEL VON
SCULPTOR
b Stockholm, Sweden, Apr 27, 39, US citizen. *Study:* Hamilton Col, with James Penney, BA(hons), 63; Art Student's League, with Jose deCreeft, 64-65; Pratt Inst, with Calvin Albert, MFA, 67. *Work:* Munson-Williams-Proctor Inst, Utica, NY; Lake George Arts Proj, Lake George, NY. *Comn:* Cast bronze sculpture, Wellspring, Camden Heritage Comt, NY, 93. *Exhib:* Prospect Mountain Show: Homage to David Smith, Lake George Arts Proj, Lake George, NY, 79; New Work, Munson-Williams-Proctor Inst, Utica, NY, 81; Sculpture/Penn's Landing, Port of Hist Mus, Philadelphia, 83; Sculpture Space-Recent Trends, Munson-Williams-Proctor Inst, Utica, NY, 84; New York Artists V, Herbert F Johnson Mus, Cornell Univ, Ithaca, NY, 86; solo exhib, Art Mus, Colby Col, Waterville, Maine, 87. *Pos:* Dir, Kirkland Art Ctr, Clinton, NY, 68-71. *Teaching:* Instr sculpture, Sch Art, Munson-Williams-Proctor Inst, Utica, NY, 72-85; adj prof sculpture, Hamilton Col, Clinton, NY, 73-84; asst prof sculpture, Colgate Univ, Hamilton, NY, 85-89. *Awards:* Fel, Hand Hollow Found, 83; New York Found Arts Fel, 90; Yaddo Fel, 85. *Bibliog:* April Kingsley (auth), Essay: Major Albany Sculpture Sites, Col St Rose, 82; Edward J Sozanski (auth), Penn's Landing sculpture show, Philadelphia Inquirer, 8/7/83; Sarah Clark-Langager (auth), Sculpture Space-Recent Trends, Munson-Williams-Proctor Inst, 84. *Mem:* Sculpture Space (co-founder & mem bd, 75 & pres). *Media:* Bronze, Wood. *Mailing Add:* Box 1028 RD 2 Post St Clinton NY 13323

BERGEN, SIDNEY L
ART DEALER, GALLERY DIRECTOR
b New York, NY, Sept 27, 22. *Study:* Alfred Univ. *Pos:* Owner & dir, ACA Galleries, New York, currently. *Mem:* Art Dealers Asn Am. *Specialty:* Early 20th century and contemporary American and European art. *Mailing Add:* c/o ACA Galleries 41 E 57th St New York NY 10022-1909

BERGER, GUSTAV A
CONSERVATOR
b Vienna, Austria, July 28, 20; US citizen. *Work:* Hirshhorn Mus & Sculpture Garden, DC; Metrop Mus Art, New York; Boyman-van Beuningen Mus, Rotterdam, Holland; High Mus Art, Atlanta, Ga; Nat Gallery Australia, Canberra. *Comn:* Paxson Murals, Bd Co Comnr, Missoula, Mont, 78-79; Atlanta Cyclorama, City of Atlanta, Ga, 79-81; Vanderlyn Panorama, Metrop Mus, New York, 82. *Teaching:* Vienna Acad Fine Art, Sch Restoration & Conserv, 90-91; Laboratory of the Valencia Mus Fine Arts, 92. *Awards:* Samuel H Kress Found Res Grants, 67, 68, 72, 83, 87 & 90; Nat Endowment Arts Res Grant, 73; Austrian Cross of Honor for Art & Sci First Class, 90. *Bibliog:* Adam Raft (auth), Beva 371, Ein neues Klebemittel fuer Restauratoren, Maltechnik/Restauro, 72; R B Renshaw-Beauchamp (auth), Another use of Beva 371, 74 & Pat Reeves (auth), Use of Beva in the conservation of a Nazca textile, 79, Bull of Am Inst Conserv. *Mem:* Fel Int Inst Conserv Hist & Artistic Works; fel Am Inst Conserv Hist & Artistic Works; Appraisers Asn Am; Int Coun on Mus. *Publ:* Auth, The Testing of Adhesives for the Consolidation of Paintings, Int Inst Conserv-Am Group, 70; Formulating Adhesives for the Conservation of Painting In: Conservation & Restoration of Pictorial Art, Butterworth, London, 76; Unconventional Treatments for Unconventional Paintings, Studies in Conserv, 76; Preventive Conservation of Painted Objects, Int Coun on Mus, 78; coauth, The Behavoir of Canvas as a Structural Support for Painting, Int Inst Conserv, 82; and others. *Mailing Add:* 115 W 73rd St New York NY 10023

BERGER, JASON
PAINTER, PRINTMAKER
b Malden, Mass, Jan 22, 24. *Study:* Boston Mus Fine Arts Sch, 42-43 & 46-49; Univ Ala, 43-44; Ossip Zadkine Sch Sculpture, Paris, 50-52. *Work:* Guggenheim Mus Art, Mus Mod Art, Chase Manhattan Bank, New York; Smith Col Mus Art; Brandeis Univ; and others. *Exhib:* Carnegie Inst Mus, 54 & 55; Recent Drawings USA, Mus Mod Art, New York, 56; Pa Acad Fine Arts, 62; Silvermine Guild; Providence Art Festival, RI, 69; and others. *Teaching:* Instr painting, Boston Mus Fine Arts Sch, 55-69; vis prof, State Univ NY, Buffalo, 69-70; instr painting, Art Inst Boston, 73-88. *Awards:* Grand Prize, 55 & First Prize, 61, Boston Art Festival; Boston Mus Fine Arts Sch Traveling Fel; Purchase Prize, Sheraton-Boston Hotel, 65; and others. *Media:* Oil, Watercolor; Woodcut. *Publ:* Illusr, Foundation Course in French, 56. *Dealer:* Alon Gallery Modern Art Brookline MA. *Mailing Add:* 1665 A Beacon St Brookline MA 02146

BERGER, JERRY ALLEN
DIRECTOR, CURATOR
b Buffalo, Wyo, Oct 8, 43. *Study:* Univ Wyo, BA, 65, BA(art), 71, MA(art hist), 72. *Pos:* Cur collections, Univ Wyo Art Mus, Laramie, 72-88, actg dir, 84-86, asst dir, 80-83 & 87-88; dir, Springfield Art Mus, Springfield, Mo, 88- *Mailing Add:* Springfield Art Museum 1111 E Brookside Dr Springfield MO 65807

BERGER, MAURICE
CRITIC, HISTORIAN
b New York, NY, May 22, 56. *Study:* Hunter Col, City Univ New York, BA(Thomas Hunter Scholar), 78; City Univ New York Grad Ctr, PhD, 88. *Pos:* Asst to dir exhibs, City Univ New York Grad Ctr, 81-; cur, Hunter Col Art Gallery, 83-85, cur, special projects, 85-; jr fel, New York Inst Humanities, 83-85. *Teaching:* Adj lectr art hist, Hunter Col, New York, 80-84; vis lectr, Queens Col, City Univ New York, 81; vis asst prof, Hunter Col, City Univ, New York, 85-91; lectr, Parsons Sch Design, 86; vis lectr, Yale Univ, 87; vis lectr, State Univ NY, Stony Brook, 89 & Rutgers Univ, 90. *Mem:* Int Asn Art Critics. *Res:* History and theory of contemporary modern art; history of performance art; critical theory; American Cultural History. *Publ:* Auth, Labyrinths: Robert Morris, Minimalism, and the 1960's Harper & Row, 89, Remaking Anti-form, In: Robert Morris: Felt Pieces, Grey Art Gallery, New York, 89; Are Museums Racist?, Art in Am, 90; How Art Becomes History, Harper Collins, 92; Objects of Liberation: The Sculptor of Eva Hesse, in Eva Hesse: A Retrospective, Yale Univ Art Gallery, 92,. *Mailing Add:* 740 West End Ave New York NY 10025

BERGER, OSCAR
GRAPHIC ARTIST
b Presov, Eperjes, Czechoslovakia, May 12, 01; US citizen. *Work:* Libr of Cong & Nat Portrait Gallery, Washington, DC; Metrop Mus Art, New York; also pvt collections & mus. *Comn:* Design, League of Nations, Geneva, 26; posters, Brit Transport & Gen Post Off, London, 38; curtain design, Palladium, London; mag pages (San Francisco Conf of UN), New York Times, London Daily Telegraph, King Features Syndicate, 45; logo design, United Nations World Assembly Aging, New York, 82. *Exhib:* One-man show, Gallery of Mod Art, New York Cult Ctr, 68. *Bibliog:* Geoffrey Holme (auth), Caricature of today, The Studio, London, 28; Oscar Berger, France Dimanche, Paris, 48; Norman Kent (auth), Famous faces by Oscar Berger, Am Artist, 63. *Mem:* Nat Press Club, Washington, DC. *Media:* Pencil, Ink. *Publ:* Auth, Aesop's Foibles, 49; Famous Faces, 50; My Victims, 52; I Love You, 60 & The Presidents, 68. *Mailing Add:* 120 Central Park S Apt 6C New York NY 10019

BERGER, PAT (PATRICIA EVE)
PAINTER
b New York, NY. *Study:* Art Ctr Col Design, 48; Univ Calif, Los Angeles, 50-55; studied with Sam Amato, Richard Boyce & John Altoon. *Work:* Long Beach Mus Art; San Diego Mus Art; Palm Springs Desert Mus, Calif; Springfield Art Mus, Mo; Sodertalje Konsthall, Jarnagatan, Sweden; Skirball Mus, Calif; and others. *Comn:* Olympic mural, Cent Adult High Sch, Los Angeles, 84; Pacific Bell, Exec Floor, Los Angeles, Calif, 89. *Exhib:* Solo exhib, Palm Springs Desert Mus, 70, Mus N Orange Co, Fullerton, Calif, 81, Light, Illusion & Reality, Riverside Art Ctr & Mus, 83, Paintings of the Homeless, Capitol Bldg, Sacramento & Bridge Gallery, City Hall, 86, Int Contemp Art Fair, Los Angeles, Calif, 86, Jewish Fedn Galleries, Los Angeles, Calif, 88 & Univ Judaism, Los Angeles, Calif, 91; Flower Imagery in Art, Downey Mus Art, Calif, 84; Am Watercolors, Chateau de Tours, France, 87; Jewish Mus, San Francisco, Calif, 87; travel exhibs, Nat Women Artists Centennial, India, 89, Hunger 1990's, Not by Bread Alone, Carson Sq House Mus, Panhandle, Tex, 90; and others. *Pos:* Muralist, Millard Sheets, Claremont, 75-77. *Teaching:* Instr painting & drawing, Los Angeles Community Adult Schs, 71-; instr murals, Cent Adult High Sch, Los Angeles, 82-85. *Awards:* Purchase Awards, Pa Acad Fine Arts, Ford Found, 64, Los Angeles All City Exhib, Ahmanson Collection, 69 & 76 & Art & the Law, West Publ Co, 91; Fel, Brody Arts Fund, Calif Community Found, 88. *Bibliog:* Laurel Erickson (dir), Tent City & the Homeless, NBC-TV Channel 4, 1/2/86; Marge Bulmer (auth), Fallen Angel, Artweek, 6/14/86; Carole Katchen (auth), Generating Energy in Acrylics, The Artist's Mag, 8/91. *Mem:* Hon life mem Nat Watercolor Soc (pres, 73-74); Calif Art Educ Asn; Nat Asn Women Artists; Watercolor USA Honor Soc (secy, 94). *Media:* Acrylic, Watercolor. *Publ:* Contribr, Museum Opening Exhibit, Desert Sun, Palm Springs, 70; illusr, Coalescence, 73 & Socrates Jones, 75, Almark Publ Co; contribr, West '84 Art & the Law, West Publ Co, 83 & 84; auth, California Romantics, Harbingers of Watercolorism, Perine, 86. *Dealer:* Valerie Miller Gallery 72-785 Hwy 111 Palm Desert CA 92260; Adelle M Fine Art 3317 McKinney Ave Dallas TX 75204. *Mailing Add:* 2648 Anchor Ave Los Angeles CA 90064

BERGER, PAUL ERIC
COLLAGE ARTIST, PHOTOGRAPHER
b The Dalles, Ore, Jan 20, 48. *Study:* Art Ctr Col of Design, Los Angeles, with Tod Walker, 67-69; Univ of Calif, Los Angeles, with Robert Heinecken & Robert Fichter, BA, 69-70; Visual Studies Workshop, State Univ NY, Buffalo, with Nathan Lyons, MFA, 70-73. *Work:* Int Mus of Photog/George Eastman House, Rochester, NY; Bibliot Nationale, Paris, France; Art Inst Chicago; San Francisco Mus Mod Art; Los Angeles County Mus Art, CA. *Exhib:* One-man shows, Photographs, 75-90, Opened Bk, Art Inst Chicago, 75 Mathemaics Series, 77, Seattle Subtext, 82, Light Gallery, New York & Cards, USC Altier Gallery, Santa Monica, Calif; Works 1976-1989, Seattle Art Mus, Wash. *Teaching:* Lectr photog, Univ Ill, Champaign, 74-78; from asst to assoc prof photog, Univ Wash, Seattle, 78- *Awards:* Young Photogr Award, Int Meeting Photog, Arles, France, 75; Nat Endowment for Arts photogr fel, 79; Nat Endowment Arts, Visual Artsts Fel, 86. *Bibliog:* Leroy Searle (auth), Paul Berger's mathematics photographs, Afterimage, Rochester, 78; Jim Burns (auth), From Old Images to New, Argus Publ, Seattle, Wash, 79; Rod Slemmons (auth), Paul Berger: Marco Polo in the Land of the Computer, Photo Education (Polaroid Newsletter), 90; Rod Slemmons (auth), Paul Berger: The Machine in the Window, Seattle Art Mus, Wash, 90. *Mem:* Soc Photog Educ (bd dirs, 80-84). *Media:* Photography. *Publ:* Auth, Seattle Subtext, USW and Real Comet Press, 84. *Mailing Add:* Dept Art Univ Wash Seattle WA 98195

BERGER, SANDRA CHRISTINE Q
DESIGNER, STAINED GLASS ARTIST
b San Francisco, Calif, May 18, 48. *Study:* Univ Calif, Santa Barbara, BA, 70; Annenberg Sch, Univ Southern Calif, MA(summa cum laude), 78, studied glass design with Narcissus Quagliata, 79-80; Pilchuck Glass Ctr, Washington; studied archit glass design with Jochim Poensgen, Dusseldorf, WGer & Ed Carpenter, Portland, Ore. *Work:* Cancer Research Ctr, Honolulu, Hawaii; Minot Symphony & Concert Theatre, NDak. *Comn:* Minot Ctr Theatre entrance & Dakota Northwestern Univ Alumni Found, NDak; Tanforam Prof Ctr, Raiser Archit Group, San Mateo, Calif, 85; grand entrance, Patrick Sulliban & Assocs, Palo Alto, Calif, 86; neon glass scultpure, comn by George Omen, Palo Alto, Calif, 89. *Exhib:* Art & the Child, VI Int Women Archit Cong, Paris, France, 83; Design Calloborations, Int Design Conf, San Francisco, Calif, 84; Silver Jubilee - Glass Art, Honolulu Int Airport, Hawaii, 84-85; Design Showcase, Galleiea Design Ctr, San Francisco, Calif, 87-88. *Pos:* Exec bd/workshop dir, Stained Glass Asn, Hawaii, 79-82; dir, Design Int, San Francisco, Calif, 81-85. *Teaching:* Dir & lectr, Adv Glass Workshop, Stained Glass, Hawaii, 80; guest lectr, Glass Comm, San Jose Univ, Calif, 83; master artist, glass art & design, Apprentice Alliance, San Francisco, Calif, 85- *Awards:* First place award, San Francisco Comt, 82; Honor & Excellence Awards, Berlin Cong, 84. *Bibliog:* Larry Frakes (auth), Contemporary Glass Art, PBS-TV News feature, 82; Hardy Lieberg (auth), Stained Glass for University, Minot Daily News, 85; H W Moss (auth), Learning from a Master, Bay Nites Art Rev, 87. *Mem:* Glass Art Soc; Am Crafts Coun; Aprentice Alliance; San Francisco Arts Coun; Design Int (bd dirs, 84-85, treas, 82-83). *Media:* Glass, Two Dimensional Sculptures. *Publ:* Auth, Glass of the West, Glass Mag, 81; ed, Facets, Stained Glass Asn Hawaii, 79-80; auth, International Design Comperdium, Women in Desing Int, 82; contribr, International Review of Glass Artists, Glass Art Soc, 83-84; The Guild, Kraus-Sikes, 86-90. *Mailing Add:* c/o Quintal Unlimited 100 El Camino Real, No 202 Burlingame CA 94010

BERGGRUEN, JOHN HENRY
ART DEALER
b San Francisco, Calif, June 18, 43. *Study:* San Francisco State Col, AB, 67. *Pos:* Pres & owner, John Berggruen Gallery, San Francisco, 70-; mem bd trustees, San Francisco Art Inst. *Mem:* Soc Encouragement Contemp Art; Art Dealers Asn Am. *Specialty:* Paintings, drawings and original prints of the 20th century. *Mailing Add:* 228 Grant Ave 3rd Floor San Francisco CA 94108

BERGHASH, MARK W
PHOTOGRAPHER, PAINTER
b Buffalo, NY, Mar 8, 35. *Study:* Univ Buffalo, 52-55; Univ Vienna, Austria, 55-56; Art Students League, with George Grosz, 57-60; with George Tice & Philippe Halsman, 76-78. *Work:* Metrop Mus Art, Jewish Mus & Franklin Furnace Archive, New York; Calif Mus Photography, Riverside; Dayton Art Inst, Ohio; Cameraworks, San Francisco, Calif; Int Ctr Photog, New York. *Exhib:* The Portrait Extended, Mus Contemp Art, Chicago, Ill, 80; Counterparts and Affinities, Metrop Mus Art, New York, 82; Indelible Images, The Jewish Mus, New York, 82; Holocaust Survivors Remembered, Jewish Ctr, Buffalo, NY; one-man shows, Nudes in Parts, Gallery Photographic Art, Tel Aviv, 84, Segmented Photographs, Marcuse Pfeifer Gallery, New York, 84, 87 & 89, San Francisco Cameraworks, Calif, 88, CEPA, Buffalo, NY, 88, Trienrak Int de la Photographis, Fribourg, Switz, 88, Art Inst, Chicago, 89, Hilton Hotel, New York, 89 & Port Washington Libr, NY, 89; Jews and Germans: Aspects of the True Self (with catalog), Calif Mus Photog, Riverside, 85; Two to Tango, Int Ctr Photog, New York; Golem, Danger, Deliverance & Art (with catalog), Jewish Mus, New York, 88; The Photographer of Invention (with catalog), Mus Am Art, Washington, DC, Mus Contemp Art, Chicago & Walker Art Ctr, Minneapolis, 89-90; Laurence Miller Gallery, New York, 89; Phyllis Rothman Gallery, Farleigh Dickenson Univ, Madison, NJ, 89; Portraits of Me Rooted and Uprooted, SF Camerawork, San Francisco, Calif, 92. *Pos:* Pres, Twenty-Twenty Serv, Inc. *Bibliog:* Any Grundberg (auth), Why the holocaust defies pictorialization, NY Times, 5/2/82; Zan Dubin (auth), Jews & Germans, Los Angeles Times, 12/2/85; Carol Stevens (auth), Still performances, Print Mag, 3/88; Richard Woodard (auth), Serving up the Poor as Exotic Fare for Voyeurs?, NY Times, 6/89; Catherine Calhoun (auth), Just How Life Is, New York Press, 6/89. *Mem:* Art Students League. *Media:* Silver Emulsion, Color Coupler Print. *Publ:* Coauth, Jews & Germans, CMP, 85. *Mailing Add:* 7 E 20th St Apt 8R New York NY 10003

BERGMAN, ROBERT P
MUSEUM DIRECTOR, HISTORIAN
b Bayonne, NJ, May 17, 45. *Study:* Rutgers Univ, BA, 66; Princeton Univ, MFA(Fulbright Fel), 69, PhD, 72. *Pos:* Dir, Walters Art Gallery, 81- *Teaching:* Prof, Princeton Univ, 72-76, Harvard Univ, 76-81 & Johns Hopkins Univ, 81- *Awards:* Guggenheim Fel; Nat Endowment Humanities Fel; Am Acad Rome Fel. *Mem:* Asn Art Mus Dirs; Col Art Asn; Int Ctr Medieval Art (mem bd, 86); Am Asn Univ Profs; Soc Archit Historians; Am Arts Alliance (mem bd, 89-). *Res:* Medieval art and architecture. *Publ:* Auth, The Salerno Ivories Ars Sacra from Medieval Amalfi, Harvard Univ Press, 80. *Mailing Add:* Walters Art Gallery 600 N Charles St Baltimore MD 21201

BERGNER, LANNY MICHAEL
SCULPTOR
b Anacortes, Wash, Dec 4, 52. *Study:* Univ Wash, Seattle, BFA(sculpture), 81; Tyler Sch Art, Philadelphia, Pa, MFA(sculpture), 83. *Work:* Philadelphia Mus Art, Pa; Delaware Art Mus, Wilmington; Walker Hill Art Ctr, Seoul, Korea. *Comn:* Wall Sculpture, Philadelphia Int Airport, Pa, 93. *Exhib:* Four Contemp Artists, Allentown Art Mus, Pa, 87; one man shows, Locks Gallery, Philadelphia, Pa, 87, 90, 92 & Gallery K, Washington, DC, 89 & 91; Biennial 89 & 91, Del Art Mus, Wilmington, 89 & 91; Contemp Philadelphia Artists, Philadelphia Mus Art, Pa, 90; Artists Choose Artists, Inst Contemp Art, Philadelphia, Pa, 91. *Awards:* Mildred Bougher Prize, Works on Paper, Beaver Col Art Gallery, 89; Best Show, Biennial 89, Del Art Mus, 89; Sculpture Prize, Contemp Philadelphia artists, Philadelphia Mus Art, 90. *Bibliog:* Jennifer Crohn (auth), A Sculptor Crosses Gender Lines, 4/6/90 & Kenneth Baker (auth), The Philadelphia Scene, Philadelphia Inquirer, 7/15/90; Miriam Seidel (auth), Lanny Bergner at Marian Locks, New Art Examiner, 9/90. *Media:* Mixed. *Dealer:* Locks Gallery 600 Washington Sq S Philadelphia PA 19106. *Mailing Add:* 1231 N 6th St Philadelphia PA 19122

BERGSTROM, EDITH HARROD
PAINTER
b Denver, Colo. *Study:* Pomona Col, BA, 63; Stanford Univ, MA, 64; Study with Richard Diebenkorn. *Work:* Palm Springs Desert Mus, Calif; San Jose Mus Art, Calif; Utah State Univ, Logan; Achenbach Found for Graphic Arts, Calif, Palace of the Legion of Hon, San Francisco; Claremont Graduate Sch, Calif; Springfield Art Mus, Springfield, Mo; and others. *Comn:* Ten paintings, Hyatt Corp, Houston, Tex. *Exhib:* Am Watercolor Soc, 75, 76, 82, 83 & 85; Rocky Mountain Nat Watermedia Exhib, 76, 77, 78, 81-83, 86, 87; Nat Watercolor Soc, 76, 79, 80, 81, 83-85; Watercolor USA, 79-81, 83-86, 87; Butler Inst Am Art 45th Nat, Youngstown, Ohio, 81 & 86; one-woman shows, Capricorn Galleries, Bethesda, Md, 86, A Gallery, Palm Desert, Calif, 89; group show, Palm Springs Desert Mus, 80, Tropical Topics, Monterey Peninsula Mus Art, 88. *Pos:* jury chmn, Nat Watercolor Soc, 87. *Awards:* The Foothill Art Ctr Award, Rocky Mountain Nat Watermedia Exhib, 87; Southwest Mo Mus Assoc Purchase Award, Springfield Art Mus, 87; Calif State Fair Award, 87; and others. *Bibliog:* Mary Carhartt (auth), Watercolor: See for Yourself, Grumbacher, 84; Gerald Brommer (auth), Exploring the Art of Painting, Davis Publ, 87; Michael Ward (auth), The New Spirit of Watercolor, N Light Publ, 89. *Mem:* Rocky Mountain Nat Watermedia Soc; Nat Watercolor Soc; Am Watercolor Soc; W Coast Watercolor Soc (past-pres); Watercolor USA Hon Soc. *Media:* Oil, Watercolor. *Publ:* Auth, article, Am Artist, 1/82; auth, article, Artist's Mag, 7/87. *Dealer:* View Point Gallery The Crossroads Carmel CA 93923; A Gallery El Paseo Dr Palm Desert CA 92261. *Mailing Add:* 149 Hawthorn Dr Atherton CA 94027

BERGUSON, ROBERT JENKINS
PAINTER, EDUCATOR
b Blossburg, Pa, Dec 6, 44. *Study:* Corning Community Col, NY, AA, 64; Univ Iowa, Iowa City, BA, 67, MA, 68, MFA, 70. *Work:* Norfolk Mus Arts & Sci, Va; Univ NDak Art Gallery, Grand Forks; Univ Iowa Sch Art Gallery, Iowa City; Hunter Mus Art, Bluff View, Chattanooga, Tenn; Miss Mus Art, Jackson; La State Univ, Alexandria. *Exhib:* XXIII Am Drawing Biennial, Smithsonian Traveling Exhib Serv, Norfolk Mus Arts & Sci, Va, 69; Washington Sq East Galleries, 80; 7th Ann Small Works Show, NY Univ, 83; Louisiana: Major Works 1984, La World Expo, Inc, New Orleans, 84; Louisiana Competition, Baton Rouge, 87 & 90; Fifth Ann Fla Nat, Fla State Univ, Tallahassee, 90; 23 one-man painting & drawing exhibs; and others. *Teaching:* Asst prof painting & drawing, La Tech Univ, Ruston, 70-76, assoc prof, 77-83, prof, 83- *Awards:* Purchase Award, XXIII Am Drawing Biennial, Norfolk Art Mus, 69 & 13th NDak Exhib Prints & Drawings, Univ NDak, 70; Merit Award, 16th Hunter Mus Art, Lincoln-Davies, Inc, Bluff View, Chattanooga, Tenn, 77; Honorable Mention, SPAR Nat Art Exhib, Shreveport, La, 82; Cash Award, 80. *Mem:* Col Art Asn; Mus Mod Art, New York, NY; Contemp Art Ctr, New Orleans. *Media:* Graphite, Acrylic. *Publ:* Auth, article, Art Voices-South, 7-8/79; illusr, Upper & lower case, Int J Typographics, 79. *Mailing Add:* 1211 Robinette Dr Ruston LA 71270

BERHANG, MATTIE
SCULPTOR, LECTURER
b New York, NY. *Study:* Tyler Sch Art, BFA; Art Students League, with R B Hale & J DeCreeft; New York Studio Sch, with G Spaventa, R Nakian & M Matter. *Work:* Lannan Found Mus, Los Angeles, Calif; Reich & Tang Inc, Leukemia Soc Am, New York; Sigal Construction Corp, Washington, DC; Albert & Vera List Gallery, Brown Univ, Providence, RI; David Bermant Found, Harrison, NY. *Comn:* Construct, comn by Ann M Hatch, San Francisco, Calif, 84; mobile construct, comn by Cermak Plaza Assocs, Berwyn, Ill, 87; construct, comn by Eldon & Sally Mayer, Mount Kisco, NY, 87; mobile construct, comn by Jane Abrams, Palm Beach, Fla, 89; mobile construct, comn by Dr Joseph & Helene Chazan, Providence, RI, 90. *Exhib:* Los Angeles Visual Arts Group Exhib, Stella Polaris Gallery, Los Angeles, 85; The Trash Project, New York, 85; The Best of Ann Juried (with catalog), Queens Mus, NY, 89; Discarded (with catalog), Rockland Ctr Arts, West Nyack, NY, 91; The Big Picture (with catalog), O K Harris Works Art, New York, 92; and many others. *Teaching:* Guest lectr, Syracuse Univ, 81 & 85, New Sch Social Res, New York, 81, Univ Wis, Eau Claire, 83 & Univ Cincinnati, 84. *Awards:* 1987-88 Artists' Space Individual Artist Grant, Artists' Space, INC, New York; 1989 Artists' Space Individual Artist Grant, Artists Space, Inc, New York. *Bibliog:* The artist framed, Esquire, 4/86; Harvey Stein (auth), Artists Observed, Harry N Abrams, New York, 86; Majory E Bevlin (auth), Design Through Discovery, Holt, Rinehart and Winston, Inc, New York, 89. *Media:* Miscellaneous Media, Mixed Materials. *Mailing Add:* PO Box 486 Spring Glen NY 12483

BERKMAN, LILLIAN
COLLECTOR
Pos: Pres, Rojtman Found Inc; fel, Morgan Libr; fel in perpetuity, Metrop Mus Art, New York; overseer, Univ Pa Mus; trustee, Telfair Mus, Savannah, Ga; mem exec bd adv, Inst Fine Arts, NY Univ; trustee Nat Coun, Mem

Acquisition Comt Fine Arts Mus, San Francisco. *Awards:* Pere Marquett Award; Presidential Award for Cult Interchange, Costa Rica; Doctor of Humanities, Univ Philippines; Kyros Award, Marquette Univ. *Mem:* Asia Soc (president's coun); Drawing Soc; Japan Soc, founding mem; Lotos Club, New York. *Collection:* Paintings, prints, drawings, sculpture, porcelains; 18th century French furniture; 18th century Chinese jades, archaic Chinese bronzes. *Mailing Add:* 22 E 64th St New York NY 10021

BERKO, FERENC
PHOTOGRAPHER
b Nagyvárad, Hungary, Jan 28, 16; US citizen. *Study:* London Univ Exten, 38. *Work:* Mus Mod Art, Metrop Mus Art, New York; San Francisco Mus Art; Ctr Creative Photog, Tucson; Gernsheim Collection, Austin, Tex; Mus Ludwig, Koeln, Ger; Kunsthaus, Zuerich, Switz; Kunstmuseum, Muenchen; Bibliotheque Nationale, Paris, France. *Comn:* Time Capsule (film), World's Fair, Westinghouse, 50. *Exhib:* Bronzes of Southern India, Victoria & Albert Mus, 47; Photography USA, De Cordova Mus, Lincoln, Mass, 68; solo exhib, Amon Carter Mus, Ft Worth, 72 & New Gallery Contemp Photog, Cleveland, 81; Color Photography 30 Years Ago, Photokina, Koeln, Ger, 78; two-person exhib, Ctr Creative Photog, Tucson, 80; Portrait Exhib, Aspen, Colo & New York, NY, 85; Color print show, Aspen Institute; Vintage print show, Fotoforum, Frankfurt, Germany, 88. *Pos:* Staff Captain, Directorate of Kinematography, Brit-Indian Army, 44-47. *Teaching:* Instr film & photog, Inst Design, Chicago, 47-48. *Bibliog:* Karl Steinorth (auth), Ferenc Berko--a master of muted color, Format, Ger, 78; James Enyeart (auth), Ferenc Berko, Am Photogr, 80; Helmut Gernsheim (auth), Ferenc Berko, In: The World's Ten Greatest, Foto Mag, Ger, 83; Leica Fotografie, 84 & 86; Photo Technik International, 86 & 87. *Mem:* Asn Cinematography, Television & Allied Technicians, Eng, 64; Am Soc Mag Photogr, 49. *Publ:* Contribr, Creative Camera, Maco Corp, 60; The Aspen Idea, Univ Okla Press, 75; Camera, Switz, 10/76; Histoire Mondiale de la Photographie en Couleurs, Hachette, France, 81-82; Lexikon der Fotografen, Rowohlt, Ger, 81; Photographers International, Auer & Auer, Hermance, Switz, 85; contribr to many other mags, 38-; auth, Das Aktfoto, Köln, 85; auth, 50 Years of Modern Color Photography, Heiting, Photokina, Koln, 86; auth, The Naked & the Nude, Levinski, London, 87. *Mailing Add:* Box 360 Aspen CO 81612

BERKON, MARTIN
PAINTER
b Brooklyn, NY, Jan 30, 32. *Study:* Brooklyn Col, BA; New York Univ, MA; Pratt Inst. *Work:* Aldrich Mus Contemp Art; Texaco Inc, White Plains, NY; NASA Gallery of Art, Kennedy Space Ctr, Cape Canaveral, Fla; Pepsico Inc, Somers, NY. *Comn:* Painting, NASA, 84 & 87. *Exhib:* One-man shows, Genesis Gallery, New York, 78 & Adelphi Univ, 83; Brooklyn Mus, 58; Butler Inst Am Art Ann Midyear Show, 65, 67 & 69; Contemporary Reflections, 74, A Change of View, 75, A Look Back A Look Forward, 82, Aldrich Mus Contemp Art, Ridgefield, Conn; New Britain Mus Am Art, Conn, 74; Oakland Univ, Rochester, Mich, 75; Am Fedn Arts Traveling Exhib, 75-76; Kennedy Space Center, Cape Canaveral, Fla, 84 & 87; Visions of Flight: Retrospective From NASA Art Collection, Smithsonian Inst Traveling Exhib World Tour, 1988-91. *Teaching:* Instr elements of design, Fairleigh Dickinson Univ, 66-67; instr drawing & painting, City Col New York, 68-69; guest lectr, Middlebury Col, 77 & Nassau Community Col, 82. *Bibliog:* Grace Glueck (auth), Art notes, New York Times, 12/1/74; Evalyn E Milman (auth), article, in: Birdgeport Sunday Post, 1/24/82; Merle English (auth), article, in: Newsday, 10/5/84; Shirley Romaine (interviewer), Long Island Artscene, Cox Cable TV, 9/86; Robert Schulman & Lori Dempsey (auth), Visions of Flight: A Retrospective from the NASA Art Collection, catalogue, 88. *Media:* Oil, Acrylic. *Mailing Add:* 51-25 Van Kleek St Elmhurst NY 11373

BERKOWITZ, HENRY
PAINTER, DESIGNER
b Brooklyn, NY, Feb 5, 33. *Study:* Brooklyn Mus Art Sch, with Sidney Simon; Workshop Sch Advert & Ed Art; Sch Visual Arts, New York. *Work:* Gutenberg Mus, Main, Ger. *Exhib:* Berkshire Mus, Pittsfield, Mass, 71; Galeries Raymond Duncan, Paris, 74; Art Festival Thours, France, 74; Parrish Art Mus, 75; Surindependants, Paris, 75; plus others. *Pos:* Art dir, Pyramid Publ, New York, 63-77. *Awards:* Award of Merit, New York Coliseum, 70; Am Vet Soc for Artists Award for an Abstract Work of Art, 72; Palmas de Oro, Int Art Festival, Paris, 74; plus others. *Mem:* Am Vet Soc Artists; Huntington Art League; Berkshire Art Asn; Awixa Pond Art Asn; Shore Arts Asn. *Media:* Oil, Mixed Media. *Publ:* Auth & illusr, Fish, Facts and Fancies, 81 & Amphibians & Reptiles, 85, Banyan Books; Dinosaurs, 87 & Sharks, 88, Henart Books. *Dealer:* Ligoa Duncan Gallery 1045 Madison Ave New York NY 10021. *Mailing Add:* 4711 NW 24th Ct Lauderdale Lakes FL 33308

BERKOWITZ, ROGER M
CURATOR, ADMINISTRATOR
b Denver, Colo, May 30, 44. *Study:* Western Reserve Univ, AB, 66; Univ Mich, MMP, 70, PhD, 77. *Collections Arranged:* Reinstallation permanent collection, Toledo Mus Art, 83 & 91; Impressionism: Selections from Five Am Mus, 90. *Pos:* Cur, Decorative Arts, Toledo Mus Art, 77- & deputy dir, 86-. *Teaching:* Vis lectr art hist, Univ Mich, 73 & 79- *Awards:* Chester Dale Fel, Nat Gallery Art, 72-73. *Mem:* Decorative Arts Chap, Soc Archit Historians; Am Asn Mus; Fr Porcelain Soc. *Res:* Eighteenth and nineteenth century English silver. *Publ:* Contribr, Toledo Mus Art: European Paintings, 76 & The Museum Collects: Treasures by Sculptors and Craftsmen, 80, Toledo Mus Art; auth, The patriotic fund vases, regency awards to the navy, Apollo, 81. *Mailing Add:* Toledo Mus Art 2445 Monroe St Toledo OH 43620

BERKOWITZ, TERRY
INSTALLATION ARTIST
b Brooklyn, NY. *Study:* Sch Visual Arts, New York, cert, 71, Art Inst, Chicago, MFA, 73. *Work:* Alternative Mus, New York. *Exhib:* Solo exhibs, People Who Live In Glass Houses, Alternative Mus, New York, 80, Contemp Art Mus, Houston, Tex, 90 & Whitney Mus Am Art, 92; Group Exhib Schemes, Herbert F Johnson Mus Art, Ithaca, NY, 81; Film as Installation, The Clocktower, New York, 83; El Sueño Imperativo, Circulo De Bellas Artes, Madrid, Spain, 91. *Pos:* Artists adv bd, Alternative Mus, New York, 83-86. *Teaching:* Assoc Prof, Graphic Communications, Baruch Col, Cuny, New York, 88- *Awards:* Fel, Nat Endowment Arts, 74; fel, Creative Artists in Pub Serv, 74; Macdowell Art Colony Fel, Summer, 89; Jerome Found Film/Video Prod Grant, 90. *Bibliog:* John Paoletti (auth), At the edge where art becomes media and message becomes polemic: Disinformation at the Alternative Museum, Arts Magazine, 5/85; Sue Cramer (auth), Report from Poland: Back to the Future, Art in Am, 3/91; Judy Cantor (auth), El SueñO Imperativo, Art News, 5/91. *Mem:* Parabola Art Found; Media Alliance. *Media:* Multi-media. *Publ:* Auth, Report from behind the scenes, Art Criticism, Vol 2, No 3, 86; Bloodstone, Contemp Arts Mus, Houston, 91. *Mailing Add:* 38 N Moore St New York NY 10013

BERKSON, BILL
CRITIC, POET
b New York, NY, Aug 30, 39. *Study:* Brown Univ, 57-59; New Sch, NY, 59-60; Columbia Univ, 59-60. *Pos:* Ed assoc, Artnews, 60-63; film ed, Kulchur, 62-63; managing ed, Location, 64-65; assoc prod, Art-New York, WNDT-TV, 64-65; guest ed, Mus Mod Art, 64-69; ed & publ, Big Sky, 71-78; coordr, Bay Area Consortium for the Visual Arts, 85-87; corresp ed, Art in Am, 89-; interim dean, San Francisco Art Inst, 92. *Teaching:* Assoc prof art hist, Calif Col Arts & Crafts, 83-84; prof art history, San Francisco Art Inst, 84- *Awards:* Artspace art criticism award, 90. *Bibliog:* Irving Sandler (coauth), Alex Katz, 71; Joe LeSueur (coauth), Homage to Frank O'Hara, 78; Rackstraw Downes (coauth), Arts J, DeKooning issue, 89. *Mem:* Int Art Critics Asn. *Res:* Contemporary art. *Publ:* Auth, The Ambassador of Light, Art Am, 89; Five Bay Area Painters, Art Int, 89; The Dark Pictures, Philip Guston, McKee, 90; Invocations of the Surge Protector, Art Forum, 90; Critical Reflections, Art Forum, 90; Ronald Bladen: Early & Late (catalog), San Francisco Moma, 91; A Moment of the Psyche, Artspace, 92; and others. *Mailing Add:* 230 Fern Rd PO Box 389 Bolinas CA 94924

BERLANT, TONY
SCULPTOR, COLLAGE ARTIST
b New York, NY, Aug 7, 41. *Study:* Univ Calif, Los Angeles, BA, MA(painting) & MFA(sculpture). *Work:* Whitney Mus Am Art, New York; Art Inst Chicago; Los Angeles Co Mus Art & Mus Contemp Art, Los Angeles; Philadelphia Mus Art; Wichita Mus Art, Kans. *Comn:* Permanent gallery door, Xavier Fourcade Inc, New York, 86; double entry doors, Rebecca's Restaurant, Venice, Calif, 86; murals, San Francisco Int Airport, San Francisco Arts Comn, 87, Davis Dept Motor Vehicles, Calif Arts Comn, 87 & Home Savings & Loan Asn, Los Angeles, 88. *Exhib:* Newport Harbor Art Mus, 78 & 84; Tex Gallery, Houston, 79; Xavier Fourcade, Inc, New York, 81, 82, 84 & 86; Los Angeles Louver Gallery, 82, 84, 85, 86 & 88; Los Angeles Mus Art, 82 & 87; John Berggruen Gallery, San Francisco, 83 & 87; Anders Tornberg Gallery, Lund, Sweeden, 88; Centro Cult Arte Contemporaneo, Mexico City, 88; one-man shows, Louver Gallery, New York, 90, Binder Gallery, Cologne, WGer, 90, LA Louver Gallery, Venice, Calif, 90, John Berggruen Gallery, San Francisco, Calif, 91; LA Pop in the Sixties, Newport Harbor Art Mus, Calif, 89; Forty Years of California Assemblage, Wight Art Gallery, Univ Calif, Los Angeles, Calif, 89; Miniature Environments, Whitney Mus Am Art, New York, 89. *Teaching:* Instr, Univ Calif, Los Angeles, 65-69. *Awards:* Ann Exhib Award, San Francisco, Calif, 63; Ford Found Purchase Award, Houston, Tex, 63; New Talent, Los Angeles Co Mus Art, 63. *Bibliog:* Jan Butterfleld (auth), On place & space, Arts & Archit, Vol 3, No 3, 1/85; Dan Cameron (auth), Tony Berlant, Arts, 1/85; William Zimmer (auth), Enigmatic Interiors at Noyes, NY Times, 8/25/85. *Media:* Tin. *Publ:* Auth, The Navajo Blanket, Praeger Publ Inc, 72; Walk in Beauty, NY Graphic Soc-Little Brown & Co, 77; Mimbres Pottery, Hudson Hills Press, NY, 83. *Dealer:* John Berggruen Gallery 228 Grant Ave San Francisco CA 94108; L A Louver 55 N Venice Blvd Venice CA 90291. *Mailing Add:* c/o L A Louver Gallery 55 N Venice Blvd Venice CA 90291

BERLIN, BEATRICE WINN
PRINTMAKER, PAINTER
b Philadelphia, Pa, May 27, 22. *Study:* Fleisher Art Mem, Philadelphia; Moore Col Art; Philadelphia Col Art; printmaking with Sam Maitin & Victor Lasuchin. *Work:* Philadelphia Mus Art; Brooklyn Mus Art; Lessing J Rosenwald, Jenkintown, Pa; Grunwald Col, Univ Calif; New York Pub Libr Print Collection; Achenbach Col; San Francisco Art Mus. *Exhib:* Nat Acad Design Ann, New York, 65 & 66; Pa Acad Fine Arts Ann (watercolor & prints), 65, 67 & 69; Libr of Cong 21st Nat Print Show, 69; Print Club Philadelphia Ann Int, 69, 73 & 75; one-woman show, Philadelphia Print Club, 70. *Awards:* First Prize, Cheltenham Art Ctr Print Show, 70; Purchase Prize, Lebanon Valley Col, 73; Best in Show, Ocean City Boardwalk, NJ, 73. *Bibliog:* Wenniger (auth), Collograph-Printmaking, Watson-Guptill, 75; Frym (auth), Second Stories, Chronicle Books, 79; Am Artist Mag, 5/89. *Mem:* Artists Equity Asn; Calif Soc Printmakers; Philadelphia Print Club. *Media:* Miscellaneous media; Watercolor. *Mailing Add:* 1333 Warren St Martinez CA 94553

BERLIND, ROBERT
PAINTER, EDUCATOR
b New York, NY, Aug 20, 38. *Study:* Columbia Col, BA, 60; Sch Art & Archit, Yale Univ, BFA, 62, MFA, 63. *Work:* J B Speed Art Mus, Louisville, Ky. *Exhib:* Solo shows, Alexander Milliken Gallery, New York, 81 & 82, Ruth Siegel Gallery, New York, 84, 86, 88 & 90, Gallery One, Toronto, 85 & Del Valley Arts Asn, 92; group shows, Bronx Mus Arts, NY, 87, Three River Arts Festival, Pittsburg, Pa, 89, Art Mus Fla Int Univ, Miami, Fla, 89, Mem Art Gallery Univ Rochester, NY, 89, Md Inst, Col Art, Baltimore, Md, 89, Foundation Mona Bismarck, Paris, France, 91. *Teaching:* Asst prof, Minneapolis Sch Art, 64-66 & 69-70; asst prof art hist & humanities, Haarlem, Neth, 66-68; assoc prof & dir grad studies, NS Col Art & Design, 74-76; assoc prof, State Univ NY at Purchase, full prof, currently & coordr grad prog. *Awards:* Am Acad Inst Arts & Lett, 92. *Bibliog:* Robert Storr (auth), Art in Am, 3/85; Stephen Westfall (auth), Art in Am, 11/88; Karen Wilkin, Partisan Review, summer, 90. *Media:* Oil. *Mailing Add:* 215 W 20th St New York NY 10011

BERLYN, SHELDON
PAINTER, PRINTMAKER
b Worcester, Mass, Sept 6, 29. *Study:* Yale Norfolk Summer Art Sch, 49; Worcester Art Mus Sch, cert, 50; Art Acad Cincinnati with Herbert Barnett, 54-55. *Work:* Worcester Art Mus, Mass; E B Crocker Art Gallery, The Art Mus City Sacramento, Calif; Albright-Knox Art Gallery, Buffalo, NY; State Univ NY Brockport Gallery Collection; and numerous pvt & corp collections. *Exhib:* One-man shows, Dana & Decordova Mus, Lincoln, Mass, 55 & Schuman Gallery, Rochester, NY, 65-66 & 70; Western NY Exhib, Albright-Knox Art Gallery, Buffalo, NY, 58-66 & 77 & one-man show, 76; Drawings Above the Pa Line, Roberson Ctr Arts, Binghamton, NY, 68; American Drawings, Moore Col Art, Philadelphia, 68; Begegnung-Mass Inst Technol, Auslands Inst, Dortmund, WGer, 76. *Teaching:* Assoc prof painting & drawing, State Univ NY Buffalo, 58- *Awards:* Stephen Wilder Traveling Fel, Cincinnati Mus Asn, 55-56; State Univ NY Res Found Fel, 66-68; Sattler Award Painting, Western NY Exhib, Albright-Knox Art Gallery, 60 & Reeb Award Drawing, 64. *Media:* Acrylic, Oil; Serigraphy. *Mailing Add:* Dept Art Rm 303 Bethune Hall Buffalo NY 14214

BERMAN, AARON
ART DEALER, COLLECTOR
b New York, NY, Nov 21, 22. *Study:* Brooklyn Col, BA; Columbia Univ, MA; Bezalel Acad, Jerusalem, dipl painting & sculpture, with Itzhak Danziger. *Pos:* Art dir mod & contemp art, Spencer Enterprises, New York, 57- & Aaron Berman Gallery, 76-; art consult & appraiser, Am Friends Haifa Univ, Israel, 73-; art appraiser, GAB Serv Inc, Interval Video Prog, Chan 13, Sotheby's, IRS & Art Inst. *Teaching:* Lectr contemp art, New Sch for Social Res, New York, 76-, United Jewish Appeal, New York, 88 & Minskoff Ctr, New York. *Bibliog:* Robin Landa (auth), Introduction to Design, Prentice Hall, 83; Les Krsntz (auth), Am Art Galleries. *Mem:* Am Fedn Arts; Brooklyn Mus Art Sch (bd trustee, 73); fel Whitney Mus Art; assoc mem Guggenheim Mus; contrib mem MOMA & Metrop Mus Art. *Specialty:* Modern and contemporary art: American, Israeli and European. *Collection:* Flemish period to modern and contemporary American, Israeli and European art, 19th and 20th centuries. *Publ:* Auth, 13 Mini Retros-Pictures on Exhibit, 4/79; Grace Knowlton, Arts, 9/81; Women's Art-Miles Apart, Valencia Col, 2/82. *Mailing Add:* Aaron Berman Gallery 660 E 19th St Brooklyn NY 11230

BERMAN, ARIANE R
PAINTER, PRINTMAKER
b Freeport Danzig, Mar 27, 37; US citizen. *Study:* Hunter Col, BFA, 59; Yale Univ, MFA(scholar), 62; Ecole Beaux Artes, Am Asn Univ Women & Fondation Etats-Unis Grants, 62-63; and with Stanley William Hayter & Jacques Desjobert. *Work:* Metrop Mus Art; Philadelphia Mus Art & Philadelphia Art Alliance; Wustum Mus Fine Arts, Duke Univ; Litton Indust; Hearst Corp. *Comn:* Painting, Seventeen Mag, 71; painting, Shipley Sch, Bryn Mawr & Charles E Ellis, Newton Sq, Pa, 71; UNICEF, Philadelphia Child Guidance. *Exhib:* Butler Inst Am Art 36th Ann, 72; Philadelphia Art Alliance, 80; one-man shows, Kornblee Gallery, 82, Phoenix Gallery, New York, 85-87, Concordia Col, Bronxville, NY, 89 & Gallery 84 Inc, New York, 92; Fairleigh Dickinson Univ; Allentown Art Mus; and many others. *Awards:* Artists Equity Award; Purchase Award & Gold Medal, Am Color Print Soc; D L Ferriss Award, Pen & Brush Inc. *Bibliog:* Cover story, Host Mag, 73. *Mem:* Am Color Print Soc; Nat Asn Women Artists; Silvermine Guild Artists; Philadelphia Art Alliance; Artists Equity Asn. *Media:* Acrylic; Serigraphy. *Dealer:* Gallery 84 50 W 57th St New York NY 10017. *Mailing Add:* 161 W 54th St New York NY 10019

BERMAN, BERNARD
COLLECTOR
b Pennsburg, Pa, Aug 28, 20. *Mem:* Am Asn Mus, Washington, DC (trustee); Allentown Art Mus, Pa (pres bd trustees, 71-). *Collection:* German Expressionist, Italian sculpture, American artists. *Mailing Add:* 2830 Gordon St Allentown PA 18104

BERMAN, ELEANORE (ELEANORE B LAZAROF)
PAINTER, PRINTMAKER
b New York, NY, Sept 2, 28. *Study:* Black Mountain Col, with Albers & Zadkine, 45; Univ Calif Los Angeles, BA, 50; spec study with Manfred Schwartz, New York & Fernand Leger, Paris, 50-51. *Work:* Grunwald Ctr Graphic Arts, Los Angeles; Exxon Corp Original Print Collection, Darien, Conn; Brooklyn Mus, NY; Los Angeles Co Mus Art; Nippon Tel & Tel, Tokyo, Japan. *Comn:* Crescent Court Hotel, Dallas, Tex; Compri Hotel, Santa Ana, Calif; Doubletree Hotel, Atlanta, Ga; L'Hotel Sofitel, Toledo, Ohio; Hyatt Regency Hotel, Birmingham, Eng. *Exhib:* one-woman shows, Amerika Haus, Berlin, 72, Paintings, Pastels, Prints, Riverside Mus Art, Calif, 78, Stuhr Mus, Grand Island, Nebr, 78 & Tweed Mus, Univ Minn, 79; Los Angeles City Mus Art, 80; Kirk de Gooyer Gallery, Los Angeles, 81; Cult Ctr, Amstelveen, Holland, 85; Downey Mus Art, 88; Kurts Gallery, Memphis, Tenn, 89; Silvermine, Int Graphics Exhib, 89. *Collections Arranged:* Graphic Arts Coun Mem Exhib, Calif Palace Legion Honor, 78. *Awards:* Purchase Prize, Los Angeles All City Exhib, Home Savings & Loan, 69; Purchase Award, Brand VI Graphics Exhib, 76. *Bibliog:* Article, Archit Digest, 6/83; article, Libre Belgique, 1/85; article, Kunstbeeld, 4/85. *Mem:* Los Angeles Printmaking Soc; Nat Watercolor Soc; Artists Equity Asn; Womens Caucus for the Arts; Nat Asn Women Artists. *Media:* Oil, Acrylic. *Dealer:* Gloria Delson Los Angeles CA. *Mailing Add:* 718 N Maple Dr Beverly Hills CA 90210

BERMAN, ELLEN MERCIL TREW
PAINTER
b Paris, Tex, Dec 5, 46. *Study:* Univ Tex, Austin, BA(cum laude), 69; Univ Houston, Univ Park, MA, 77; Glassell Sch Art, Mus Fine Arts, Houston, 81-84. *Work:* Tex Commerce Bank, Houston; M Bank, Houston. *Exhib:* one-person show, McMurtrey Gallery, Houston, 86; group show, Pindar Gallery, New York, 87; Texas Realism, Laguna Gloria Art Mus, Austin, 87; Tex State Exhib, Nat Mus Women Arts, Washington, DC, 88; Mid-Am Biennial, Nelson-Atkins Mus Art, Kansas City, Mo, 89; Recent Paintings, Goethe Inst, Houston, 88; Paintings, Art Mus Southeast Tex, Beaumont, 89; Swimmers' Progress, Col Mainland Art Gallery, Texas City, 89; Recent Paintings, Mexic-Arte Mus, Austin, Tex, 90. *Pos:* Vpres & adv bd, Women's Caucus for Art, 85-90; artists adv bd, Lawndale Art & Performance Ctr, Houston, 88-89. *Awards:* First Place, Houston Jewish Comn Ctr, 87; Best of Show, San Antonio Women's Caucus Art, 88; Mid Am Arts Alliance, Regional Fel, Nat Endowment Arts, 88-89. *Bibliog:* Betty Ann Brown & Arlene Raven (coauths), Exposures: Women and their Art, NewSage Press, 89. *Mem:* Tex Watercolor Soc; Tex Fine Arts Asn. *Media:* Oil, Watercolor. *Mailing Add:* c/o McMurtrey Gallery 3508 Lake St Houston TX 77098

BERMAN, FRED J
PAINTER, PHOTOGRAPHER
b Milwaukee, Wis, Nov 3, 26. *Study:* Milwaukee State Teachers Col, BS; Univ Wis-Madison, MS. *Work:* Elvejhem Art Ctr, Madison, Wis; Milwaukee Art Mus; Brown Univ, Providence, RI; Haggerty Mus Art, Marquette Univ, Milwaukee; Nelson Atkins Mus Art, Kansas City, Mo. *Exhib:* Sixth Biennial Contemp Am Paintings, Va Mus Fine Arts, Richmond, 48; Pa Acad Fine Arts Ann, Philadelphia, 51-53; Corcoran Biennials, Corcoran Gallery Art, Washington, DC, 53, 55 & 59; American Artists Paint the City: Venice Biennale, Italy, 56; Annual, 59 & Young America (with catalog), 60, Whitney Mus Am Art, New York; San Francisco Mus Art, 60 & 65; Summer Exhib, Royal Acad Arts, London, 67; one-man exhibs, Bradley Galleries, Milwaukee, 76, Collectors Gallery, Milwaukee, 81, Kresge Art Gallery, Mich State Univ, 82, Reading Univ, Eng, 83, Camden Arts Ctr, London, 83, Crescent Art Ctr, Scarborough, Eng, 84, Haggerty Mus Art, Milwaukee, 88 & Charles Allis Art Mus, Milwaukee, 90; two-man exhib, Bradley Galleries, Milwaukee, 83; Some Photographic Uses of Color, Brown Univ, Providence, RI, 84; 100 Years of Wisconsin Art, Milwaukee Art Mus, 88; Boite Alert, Boxes by 20th Century Artists, Renee Fotouhi Fine Art, New York 89; Wisconsin Acad Art, Madison, Wis, 91. *Collections Arranged:* Guest cur exhib, Steichen/109, Univ Wis Art Mus, Milwaukee, 88. *Teaching:* Instr painting & printmaking, Layton Sch Art, Milwaukee, Wis, 49-60; prof design & drawing, Univ Wis-Milwaukee, 60-; exchange lectr, Reading Univ, Eng, 66-67. *Awards:* Milwaukee Art Inst Award, Milwaukee Art Ctr, 47 & 52-56; Joseph Eisendrath Award, Chicago & vicinity, Art Inst Chicago, 50; Wis Union Top Purchase Award, Wis Salon Art, Univ Wis-Madison, 67; Amoco Award for Distinguished Teaching, Univ of Wis-Milwaukee, 85. *Bibliog:* Article in Art in Am, 2/56; article in Saturday Review, 5-6/85. *Media:* Oil, Charcoal. *Mailing Add:* 3133 N Marietta Ave Milwaukee WI 53211

BERMAN, GRETA W
HISTORIAN, CURATOR
b New York, NY. *Study:* Antioch Univ, BA, 65; Univ Stockholm, MA, 68; Columbia Univ, with Theodore Reff & Barbara Novak, PhD, 75. *Collections Arranged:* Amerika: Traum und Depression 1920-1940 (contribr, catalog), West Berlin & Hamburg, 80-81; Realism & Realities: The Other Side of American Painting 1940-1960 (co-auth, catalog), Rutgers Univ, 82; Relations, Lehman Col Art Gallery, 84-85; Ethel Schwabacher (co-auth, catalog), Zimmerli Mus, Rutgers Univ, 87. *Teaching:* Instr art hist, State Univ NY, Stony Brook, 70-79; prof art hist, Juilliard Sch, 79-, Parsons Sch Design, 81 & Manhattan Sch Music, 84-85; vis asst prof mus studies, New York Univ, 87-88; prof art hist, Westminster Choir Col, Princeton, NJ, 88-89. *Awards:* Dissertation Research Grant, Smithsonian Inst, 74; State Univ NY Fac Fel, 77; Chester Dale Fel, Metrop Mus Art, 79-80. *Mem:* Col Art Asn Am; Asn Historians Am Art. *Res:* 19th and 20th century American and European painting, especially American 1930-60; French 19th century symbolism interrelationship between art & music. *Publ:* Auth, The Paradox of Odilon Redon, Konsthistorisk Tidskrift, 70; Strindberg, Painter, Critic, Modernist, Gazette des Beaux Arts, 75; The Lost Years: Mural Painting in New York Under the WPA-FAP 1935-1943, Garland Press, 78. *Mailing Add:* 45 Woodside Lane Princeton NJ 08540

BERMAN, MURIEL MALLIN
COLLECTOR, PATRON
b Pittsburgh, Pa, June 21, 24. *Study:* Univ Pittsburgh; Carnegie-Mellon Univ; Pa Col Optom; Cedar Crest Col; Muhlenberg Col. *Exhib:* Albert Jean

Adolphe (with catalog); Art from Behind the Iron Curtain, Eastern Europ (with catalog); Art in Israel (with catalog); The Eight and Their Contemp Ams foremost Impressionists (with catalog); French Impressionists (with catalog); Roualt, The Misere Series; Chagall, Drawings from the Bible Series (with catalog); African Art Sculptures; these & other exhibs compiled from pvt collection currently circulating cols & mus in the East. *Pos:* Mem, Pa Coun Arts; hon chmn, Bucks Co Collectors Art Show, New Hope, Pa, 66; co-chmn, Episcopal Diocese Bicentennial Art Comn, 71; numerous other govt, civic & educ positions. *Teaching:* Lectr on African art and its origins, American, French, Picasso, Wyeth, fakes, forgeries and reproductions. *Awards:* Mt Scopus Award, State Israel Bonds, 84; Women of the Year, Am Friends Hebrew Univ, 84; George Washington Hon Medal, 85. *Mem:* Art Collectors Club Am; Am Fedn Arts; Friends Whitney Mus Am Art; Arch Am Art, Detroit; plus many others. *Interests:* Collection on loan, Art in the Embassies Programs founder and donor, Carnegie-Berman College Art Slide Library Exchange; Berman Circulating Art Exhibitions, in colleges and museums in the East. *Collection:* Early 20th century American modern, pop and op art; Eskimo, Japanese, Aboriginal Australian, French and African. *Mailing Add:* 20 Hundred Nottingham Rd Allentown PA 18103

BERMAN, PHILIP I
COLLECTOR, PATRON
b Pennsburg, Pa, June 28, 15. *Study:* Ursinus Col, LLD, 68; Lehigh Univ, LHD, 69; Hebrew Univ, DrPhil, 79. *Work:* Ursinus Col; Lehigh Univ; Allentown City Parks Sculpture Garden. *Comn:* Prints, Calder, Chadwick, Liberman, Kadishman & Tumarkin. *Exhib:* Nat Gallery; Gauguin-Philadelphia Mus; Miro-Metrop Mus; Degas-Baltimore Mus; B West Nat Gallery; Degas-Ottowa. *Pos:* Pres, Philip & Muriel Berman Found, 55-; founding mem bd, 64 & pres, 73-77, Lehigh Valley Educ TV, Channel 39; chmn, Pa State Pub Television Network Comn, 70-; art comt mem, Metrop Opera Asn; chmn, Trexler Trust, Allentown, Pa. *Awards:* Am Acad Achievement Golden Plate Award, 73; The Newcomen Soc Award, Sci Mus, London, Eng, 74; Golden Deeds Award, Allentown Exchange Club, 82; Hazlett mem Award Excellence arts, Governor Richard Thornburgh, 82; George Washington Honor Medal, Freedoms Found at Valley Forge, 84. *Bibliog:* Television interview, Channel 12, Philadelphia. *Mem:* Life fel Metrop Mus Art, New York; Aspen Ctr; Am Fedn Arts; Art Collectors Club Am; Arch Am Art; life fel, Pa Acad Fine Arts, Philadelphia, 73- *Interests:* Collections on traveling exhibitions and temporary loan in the US; many paintings on permanent loan to civic and educational institutions in Lehigh Valley area; participant in Art in the Embassies Program. *Collection:* American, French and Japanese art; Eng, Fr & Am sculpture. *Mailing Add:* 2200 Hamilton St Suite 312 Allentown PA 18104

BERMAN, VIVIAN
PRINTMAKER
b New York, NY, Aug 28, 28. *Study:* Cooper Union, BFA; Art Students League; Brandeis Univ. *Work:* Libr Cong; Wiggin Collection, Boston Pub Libr, Mass; Pa Acad Art; De Cordova Mus, Lincoln, Mass; Hopkins Art Ctr, Dartmouth Col; United States Information Agency. *Exhib:* Boston Printmakers Ann, 68-92; Libr Cong Nat Print Exhib, 70; 18th Nat Print Exhib, Brooklyn Mus, 73; Nat Exhib Collagraphs, Pratt Graphic Ctr, New York, 75; British Biennale 1979, Bradford, England; The Making of a Print, Delaware Ctr Comtemp Art, 90. *Teaching:* Instr, DeCordova Mus Sch, Lincoln, Mass. *Awards:* Purchase Award, Libr Cong Pennel Fund, 70 & Nat Print Show, Western NMex Univ, 71; MacDowell Colony Fel, 81; and others. *Bibliog:* Ross & Ramano (auth), The Complete Collagraph, Free Press, 80; Wenniger (auth), Collagraph Printmaking, Macmillan, 78. *Mem:* Philadelphia Print Club; Boston Visual Artists Union; Boston Printmakers. *Media:* Miscellaneous Media. *Dealer:* Spectrom Gallery of Art Brewster Mass; Gallery on the Green 1837 Massachusetts Ave Lexington MA 02173. *Mailing Add:* 11 Barberry Rd Lexington MA 02173

BERMAN, ZEKE
PHOTOGRAPHER
Study: Philadelphia Col Art, BFA, 72. *Work:* Mus Mod Art, Metrop Mus Art, New York; San Francisco Mus Mod Art; Mus Fine Art, Boston, Mass. *Exhib:* Solo exhibs, Everson Mus, Syracuse, NY, 80, Mus Mod Art, Bern, Switz, 84, Art Inst Chicago, 86 & Calif Mus Photog, Riverside, 88; Counterparts: Form & Emotion in Photographs, Metrop Mus Art, New York, NY, 82; Mus Mod Art, New York, 82, 84 & 85; Nat Mus Am Art, Washington, DC, 89. *Teaching:* Instr, Fordham Univ at Lincoln Ctr, New York, 83- & Sch Visual Arts, New York, 86- *Awards:* Guggenheim Fel, 84 & 85; NY Found Arts Fel, 88; Nat Endowment Arts, 88; McDowell Colony Residency, 88. *Mailing Add:* c/o Lieberman & Saul Gallery 155 Spring St New York NY 10012

BERMANT, DAVID W
COLLECTOR, DIRECTOR
b New York, NY, July 16, 19. *Study:* Yale Univ, BA, 40. *Pos:* Pres, Nat Shopping Ctr, Inc, 65-; Dir art for Public Space, Inc. *Mem:* Life fel Metrop Mus Art, New York; assoc Guggenheim Mus, New York; Whitney Mus (directors circle). *Collection:* Art based on technology and science plus its placement in the work-a-day world. *Mailing Add:* 1104 La Vista Rd Santa Barbara CA 93110

BERMINGHAM, ANN
EDUCATOR, HISTORIAN
b Warton, NJ, May 22, 48. *Study:* Manhattanville Col, BA, 70; Univ Mass, Amherst, MA, 72; Harvard Univ, PhD, 82. *Pos:* Assoc Dean, Sch Fine Arts, Univ Calif, Irvine, 88-90; Editorial bd, Eighteenth-Century Studies, 89; Editorial bd rural hist, 90- *Teaching:* Assoc prof art hist, Univ Calif, Irvine, 83-; Clark prof, Univ Calif, Los Angeles, 90-91. *Awards:* J Paul Getty Postdoctoral Fel, 87-88; Huntington-Exxon Grant, 86. *Bibliog:* Art Bulletin, Vol 64, 3/88. *Mem:* Col Art Asn. *Publ:* Auth, Landscape and Ideology: The English Rustic Tradition, 1740-1860, Univ Calif Press, 86; Reading Constable, Art History, Vol 10, 3/87. *Mailing Add:* 146 Granada Ave Long Beach CA 90803

BERMINGHAM, DEBRA PANDELL
PAINTER
Northhampton, Mass, Sept 18, 53. *Study:* Cornell Univ, Ithaca, NY, BFA, 76; Univ Wash, Seattle, MFA, 79. *Work:* Smith Col Mus; Kalamazoo Inst of Arts, Mich. *Exhib:* Meticulous Realist Drawing, Squibb Gallery, Princeton, NJ, 89; 165th Ann Exhib, Nat Acad Design, 90; New Viewpoints: Contemporary Paintings by Distinguished American Women Artists, organized by Nat Mus Women in the Arts for US pavilion, World's Fair, Seville, Spin, 91-92; Against the Grain: Images in American Art 1960-1990, Southern Alleghenies Mus Art, Loretto, Pa; solo exhib, Debra Bermingham: Still Interiors, Midtown Payson Galleries, New York, 91; Illumination and Radiance: Epiphanies in Contemporary Painting, Sherry French Gallery, New York, Kalamazoo Inst rts, Mich, Riverside Art Mus, Calif, Mus Southwest, Midland, Tex & Rahr-West Art Mus, Manitowoc, Wis, 90-92; and others. *Awards:* Millay Colony for the Arts Fel, Austerlitz, NY, 80; Visual Arts Fel Grant, Nat Endowment Arts, 85-88; Am Scand Found, Artist Travel Grant, 91. *Bibliog:* John Baur & Betsy Carpenter (auths), Realism Today-Drawings from the Rita Rich Collection, Nat Acad Design, 87; An Ill Survey of Leading Contemporaries, Am Artists, 90; Debra Bermingham, Still Interiors, 91 (catalogue essay by Carl Little). *Media:* Oil, Graphite. *Dealer:* Midtown Payson Galleries 745 Fifth Ave New York NY 10151. *Mailing Add:* 2700 Vineyard Rd Romulus NY 14541

BERMINGHAM, JOHN C
PAINTER
b Wharton, NJ, Jan 12, 20. *Study:* Univ Notre Dame, Ind, BFA, 42. *Exhib:* Audubon Artists Ann Exhib, Nat Acad Galleries, New York, 73-77 & 81; Allied Artists Ann Exhib, Nat Acad Galleries/Salmagundi Club Galleries, New York, 73-79, 81, 83-87 & 91; Ann Exhib Am Watercolor Soc, Nat Acad Galleries/Salmagundi Club, New York, 73, 74, 76-78, 81, 89 & 91; Am Watercolor Soc Traveling Exhib, 74, 78, 81 & 89; Acad Artists Nat Exhib, Springfield Mus, Mass, 75-82; Ann Exhib Nat Acad Design, Nat Acad Galleries, New York, 76, 80, 82, 84, 88 & 92; Adirondacks Nat Exhib Am Watercolors, 85-87 & 92. *Awards:* Medal of Honor, NJ Watercolor Soc, 88; CFS Medal, Am Watercolor Soc, 89; Nat Exhib Am Watercolors, 92; and others. *Mem:* Allied Artists Am; Am Watercolor Soc; NJ Watercolor Soc (pres, 77-78); Acad Artists; Hudson Valley Art Asn. *Media:* Watercolor. *Mailing Add:* 245 S Main St Wharton NJ 07885

BERMINGHAM, PETER
MUSEUM DIRECTOR, CURATOR
b Buffalo, NY, Nov 6, 37. *Study:* Univ Md, BA(Nat Endowment Humanities Mus Training Fel), 64, MA(art hist), 68; Univ Mich, PhD(Smithsonian Doctoral Fel), 72. *Collections Arranged:* Jasper Cropsey: Retrospective View of America's Painter of Autumn (auth, catalog), Univ Md, 68; American Art in the Barbizon Mood (auth, catalog), 74, The Art of Poetry (auth, catalog), 77 & Alan Sonfist/Trees (auth, catalog), 78, Nat Collection Fine Arts, Smithsonian Inst; New Deal in the Southwest: Arizona and New Mexico (auth, catalog), Univ Ariz Mus Art, 80. *Pos:* Cur educ, Nat Collection Fine Arts, Smithsonian Inst, 73-78; dir/chief cur, Univ Ariz Mus Art, 78- *Teaching:* Asst prof art, Univ Cincinnati, 72-73. *Awards:* Smithsonian Res Fel, 82 & 88; Scholars Travel Award, Nat Endowment Arts, 88; Partners in The Americas Fel, 88. *Mem:* Western Asn Art Mus; Col Art Asn. *Res:* Primarily in 19th century American landscape painting; early 20th century American painting. *Publ:* American Art in The Barbizon Mood, Nat Collection of Fine Arts, 76; The New Deal in The Southwest: Arizona and New Mexico, 80; Ed, Paintings and Sculpture in the University of Arizona Museum of Art (exhib catalog), Univ Ariz Mus Art, 83; Looking Around with Horatio Walker, Musee de Quebec, 86. *Mailing Add:* Univ Ariz Mus of Art Olive & Speedway Tucson AZ 85721

BERMUDEZ, EUGENIA M See Dignac, Geny

BERMUDEZ, JOSE YGNACIO
SCULPTOR, PAINTER
b Havana, Cuba, Aug 6, 22; US citizen. *Study:* With Roberto Diago, Havana, Cuba, 52-53; Bell Voc Sch, Washington, DC, 61. *Work:* Mus Mod Art, New York; Corcoran Gallery Art, Washington, DC; Phoenix Art Mus, Ariz; Philadelphia Mus Art; Mus Mod Art, Cali, Colombia. *Comn:* Metal Relief 1961, First Americana Ann Mural Competition, 61; Galaxy (mural), Module 3, Phoenix Airport, 79. *Exhib:* New Media-New Form I & II, Martha Jackson Gallery, New York, 60; Corcoran Gallery Art, Washington, DC, 61; Mus Bellas Artes, Caracas, 67; Sculptures & Drawings, Pyramid Galleries, Washington, DC, 70; 3rd Biennial Art Coltejer, Medellin, Colombia, 72; Fountain at Scottsdale Civic Ctr Mall, Ariz, 76. *Pos:* Asst visual arts, Cult Dept, Orgn Am States, Washington, DC, 53-58, chief graphic serv div, 58-71. *Teaching:* Instr, Univ Costa Rica, San Jose, 76, 81. *Awards:* Fourth Prize for Painting, 6th Ann Art Exhib, Havana, 53; Second Prize, 9th Festival Art, Cali, 69. *Bibliog:* L J Ahlander (auth), article in Washington Post, 7/29/62; T Alvarengo (auth), Imagen, Arte y Technologia, 71. *Media:* Metal. *Mailing Add:* 4109 E Via Estrella Phoenix AZ 85028

BERMUDEZ, LUIS A
SCULPTOR, EDUCATOR
b Los Angeles, Calif, July 12, 53. *Study:* Calif State Univ, Northridge, BA, 76, MA, 78; Univ Calif, Los Angeles, MFA, 80. *Work:* Los Angeles Co Mus Art; E B Crocker Art Gallery, Sacramento, Calif; Long Beach Mus Art. *Exhib:* Ceramic Conjunction 1976, Long Beach Mus Art, 76; Mandell Gallery, Los Angeles, 80; Elaine Potter Gallery, San Francisco, 84; Tacoma Art Mus, Wash, 86; one-man show, Garth Clark Gallery, Los Angeles, 86; Twentieth Century Ceramics, Los Angeles Co Mus Art, 89; Couturier Gallery, Los Angeles, 91. *Teaching:* Asst prof, Calif State Univ, Nothridge, 80 & 84; instr, Palos Verdes Art Ctr, Calif, 80; lectr, Univ Calif, Los Angeles, 85-91, vis asst prof, 91- *Awards:* Chancellor's Patent Fund Grant, UCLA, 80; Nat Endowment Arts, 88. *Bibliog:* At The Galleries, Los Angeles Times, 4/25/86. *Mem:* Nat Coun Educ Ceramic Arts. *Media:* Clay, All Media. *Mailing Add:* c/o Joanne Warfield Gallery 508 N San Vincente Blvd Los Angeles CA 90048

BERNAL, LOUIS CARLOS
PHOTOGRAPHER
b Douglas, Ariz, Aug 18, 41. *Study:* Ariz State Univ, BA, 56; MFA, 72. *Work:* Ctr Creative Photog, Tucson, Ariz; Mus Mod Art, San Francisco. *Exhib:* Mus Fine Arts, Lubbock, Tex; Portraits of Women, Etherton Stern Gallery, Tucson, Ariz, 88; Eastman House, Rochester, NY. *Teaching:* Instr art, Pima Community Col, 72- *Awards:* Nat Endowment Arts Grant, 80; Am Visual Arts Grant, 88; Tucson Comm Found Award, 88. *Mailing Add:* 412 S Elias Tucson AZ 85701

BERNARD, DAVID EDWIN
PRINTMAKER, EDUCATOR
b Sandwich, Ill, Aug 8, 13. *Study:* Univ Ill, BFA; Univ Iowa, MFA; and with Mauricio Lasansky & Humbert Albrizio. *Work:* Wichita Art Mus, Kans; Otis Art Inst, Los Angeles, Calif; Free Pub Libr, Philadelphia, Pa; Joslyn Mus, Omaha, Nebr. *Comn:* Mural (steel & wood), Duerksen Fine Art Ctr, Wichita State Univ, 57; free standing tree symbol (steel), Camp Fire Girls Orgn, Wichita Art Mus, Kans, 60; sculpture (steel, wood & brass), Irene Vickers Baker Children's Theatre, Wichita; pair of standing tree shapes, Art Asn Wichita, 71-72. *Exhib:* God and Man in Art, Am Fedn Arts Traveling Exhib, 57; First Ann, Otis Art Inst, 61; Univ Nebr Print Exhib, Sheldon Art Gallery, Lincoln, 67; one-man exhib prints, Philbrook Art Ctr, Tulsa, Okla, 67; retrospective, Wichita Art Mus, Kans, 83. *Teaching:* Instr art prog, Maryville Col, 46-48; prof printmaking, Wichita State Univ, 49-83, prof emer, 83. *Awards:* Purchase Award for Hombre y Toro (intaglio), Pennell Collection, Libr Cong, 53; Purchase Award for Calvary (colored intaglio), Mid-Am Ann, Nelson Gallery, 55; Kans Gov's Artist's Award, Kans Arts Comn, Topeka, 82. *Bibliog:* Howard E Wooden (auth), David Bernard: Prints and Sculpture, A Retrospective, 1947-1982, Wichita Art Mus, 83. *Mem:* Soc Am Graphic Artists; Artists Guild Wichita (pres, 56); Wichita Art Mus Mem. *Media:* Intaglio, Collagraph. *Publ:* Auth, The collagraph print, Artists Proof, 62; illusr, A West Wind Rises, 62 & Sun City, 64, Univ Nebr Press; artist & auth, Ten Mayan Gods, (hand made book, original print; Artists: A Kansas Collection, Artists Registry Inc, 89. *Mailing Add:* 2243 N Yale Ave Wichita KS 67220

BERNAY, BETTI
PAINTER
b New York, NY. *Study:* Pratt Inst; Nat Acad Design, New York, with Louis Bouche; Art Students League, with Frank Mason; also with Robert Brackman. *Work:* Circulo Amistad, Cordoba, Spain; Columbus Mus Arts & Crafts, Ga; Columbia Mus Art, SC; Andre Weil Collection, Paris. *Comn:* Painting, pres of Renault, Madrid, Spain, 64; painting, Children Have No Barriers, IOS Found, Geneva, 69; paintings, Macaws, Seacost E Bldg, Miami Beach, Fla, 69 & mural, Sandy Cove, S Bldg, 70. *Exhib:* Mus Mod Art, Paris, 63; Salon Populiste, Mus Mod Art, Paris, 63; Bacardi Gallery, Miami, Fla, 67; Metrop Mus & Art Ctr, Miami, 75; Rosenbaum Gallery, Palm Beach, Fla, 77; and many other group & one-man shows; one-man shows - Columbus Mus, GA; Columbia Mus, SC. *Awards:* Artistic Merit Medal, City of New York, 42; Prix de Paris, 58; Medal of Honor, Mus Bellas Artes, Malaga, 65. *Mem:* Artists Equity Asn; Am Artists Prof League; Nat Asn Painters & Sculptors Spain; Soc Artistes Francais; Prof Artists Guild; and others. *Media:* Oil, Pastel. *Mailing Add:* 10155 Collins Ave Apt 1705 Bal Harbour FL 33154

BERNDT, JERRY W
PHOTOGRAPHER
b Milwaukee, Wis, Nov 11, 43. *Study:* Univ Wis, 64-67. *Work:* Mus Mod Art, New York; Mus Fine Arts, Boston, Mass; Addison Gallery Am Art, Andover, Mass; Mus Fine Art, Houston, Tex; San Diego Mus, Photog Arts. *Exhib:* The Homeless, Brockton Art Mus, Mass, 86; Mass Artist Fels, Polaroid Gallery, Cambridge, 86; Recent Aquisitions, Mus Mod Art, New York, 87; The Dream, Phillips Exeter, NH, 88; Cross Currents, Photog Resource Ctr, Boston, Mass, 88 & San Francisco, Camerawork, 88; The Homeless, St Anselms Col, 89 & Groton Acad, Manchester, NH, 89. *Teaching:* Prof, photog & art, Univ Mass, Boston, 86-88. *Awards:* Mass Productions, Mass Arts & Humanities, 86, 89; Artist Fel, Mass Artists Found, 86-89; Nat Endowment Art Fel, Fed Govt, 87. *Bibliog:* Russell Hart (auth), Invisible in America, Views/PRC, Boston, summer 86; Kelly Wise (auth), Haiti in Turmoil, Boston Globe, 4/15/87; Jan Grover (auth), Inadequacy of systems, San Francisco Mag, 1/87. *Mem:* Am Soc Mag Photogr. *Publ:* Auth, Missing Persons-The Homeless, Many Voices, 86. *Mailing Add:* 41 Magnolia Ave Cambridge MA 02138

BERNECHE, JERRY DOUGLAS
EDUCATOR, PAINTER
b Greentown, Ind, July 24, 32. *Study:* John Herron Art Sch, BFA, 56, studies painting and printmaking with Garo Antreasian; Ohio Univ, MFA, 59, study with Robert Friemark. *Work:* Butler Mus Am Art, Youngstown, Ohio; Springfield Art Mus, Mo; Canton Art Mus & Massillon Mus, Ohio; Mo State Hist Soc, Columbia. *Exhib:* Drawing USA Nat, Walker Art Mus, 62; Mid-Am Nat Exhib, Butler Mus Art, 62-64; Chautauqua Exhib Art, NY, 65-67; Springfield Regional Exhib, 66-75; Watercolor USA Nat, Springfield, 73-74. *Teaching:* Instr art, Cooper Art Sch, Cleveland, Ohio, 62-65 & Mont State Univ, Bozeman, 65-66; assoc prof drawing & painting, Univ Mo, Columbia, 66-81, prof, 81- *Awards:* Mrs E J Bellinger Award, Chautauqua Nat Exhib, 65 & 67; Watercolor Purchase Award, Watercolor USA, 73; Purchase Award, Mo State Fair, 83. *Media:* Acrylic, Watercolor. *Mailing Add:* 3708 Oakland Rd Columbia MO 65202

BERNHARD, RUTH
PHOTOGRAPHER
b Berlin, Ger, Oct 14, 05; US citizen. *Study:* Acad Art, Berlin, 25-27. *Work:* San Francisco Mus Mod Art; Mus Mod Art, New York; Ctr Creative Photog; Bibliot Nat, Paris; George Eastman House, Rochester. *Comn:* Photographs for book, Machine Art, Mus Mod Art, New York, 34. *Exhib:* Inst Cult Relations, Mexico City, 58; Oakland Art Mus, 58; Mus Mod Art, New York, 62; Photog in the Fine Arts, Metrop Mus Art, New York, 67; Friends of Photog, Carmel, Calif, 75; Recollections: Ten Women of Photog, Int Ctr Photog (traveling exhib), 79; Photographers' Gallery, London, Eng, 83; Recontres Int Phtotg, Arles, France, 83; 101 Photographs: Selections from the Steinman Collection, Santa Barbara Mus Art, 84; Das Aktfoto, Mus Art & Culture, Dortmund, WGer, (traveling exhib), 85-86; and many others. *Teaching:* Instr workshops, Univ Calif Exten, San Francisco, 66-74. *Awards:* Dorothea Lange Award, Oakland Mus, 76; Outstanding Achievement Visual Arts, Womens Caucus Art, 81; Honoree, Rencontres Int Photog, Arles, France, 83; Outstanding Achievement Photog, San Francisco Art Comn, 84. *Bibliog:* Margaretta Mitchell (auth), Recollections: Ten Women of Photography, Viking Press, 79; Collecting Light-The Photographs of Ruth Bernhard (monogr), Friends of Photog, 79; Ruth Bernhard, A Retrospective Exhibition (monogr), Friends of Photog, 79. *Mem:* Friends Photog, Carmel, Calif; Mus Soc, San Francisco. *Publ:* Auth, Growth of a photographer, Contact Mag, 64. *Mailing Add:* 2982 Clay St San Francisco CA 94115

BERNHEIM, STEPHANIE HAMMERSCHLAG
PAINTER, PRINTMAKER
b New York, NY. *Study:* Sarah Lawrence Col, BA, 62; NY Univ, MA, 67. *Work:* IBM, Sommers, NY; Jerry I Speyer, Cinema 5 Ltd, Hans Bertram-DeBevois Plimpton & John B Elliot, New York; Estée Lauder Corp; Franklin Furnace, NY; Michael Kritchman, San Diego, Calif. *Exhib:* Exchanges I, Henry St Settlement, Louise Abrons Art for Living Ctr, 79; PS1 Mus, Long Island, NY, 81; Barbara Mathes Gallery, 86, 87 & 88; Primal Forces, Cooper Union, New York, 90; Burning in Hell, Franklin Furnace, 91; Experimental Paintmaking & Photography, Contemp Artists Ctr, North Adams, Mass, 92. *Pos:* Created & organized art events/community panels at Air Gallery, New York, 11/91 & Sarah Lawrence Col, Bronxville, NY, 4/92. *Bibliog:* Kay Larson (auth), Talkin bout my generation, Voice, 80; Mary Delahoyd, Material Message (catalog), 89; Joseph Ruzicka, Stephanie Bernheim at AIR Gallery, Art in Am, 90. *Mem:* Women's Caucus for Arts; AIR Gallery (exec comt 89-92); Women in Arts Found; Women's Action Coalition; Col Art Asn. *Media:* Acrylic; Mixed Media. *Dealer:* AIR Gallery 63 Crosby St New York NY 10013. *Mailing Add:* 50 Walker St Apt 4A New York NY 10013

BERNS, PAMELA KARI
PAINTER, ADMINISTRATOR
b Sturgeon Bay, Wis, Sept 4, 47. *Study:* Lawrence Univ, Appleton, Wis, BA, 69; Univ Wis, Madison, MFA(painting), 71. *Work:* Bergstrom Art Ctr, Neenah, Wis; Kemper Insurance Co's, Inc, Long Grove, Ill; Miller Art Ctr, Sturgeon Bay, Wis; Andersen Window Corp, Bayport, Minn. *Exhib:* One-person show, Bergstrom Art Ctr, Neenah, Wis, 70; Watercolor Wis, Wustum Mus Art, Racine, 72-79 & 81-82; New Horizons, Chicago, 75; Women in the Arts, West Bend Mus Art, Wis, 76; Art Inst Chicago, 83. *Pos:* Coordr educ programs, Chicago Artists' Coalition, 80-83; publ, Chicago Life Mag, 84- *Awards:* Second Prizes, Artists Guild Chicago, 76 & Watercolor Wis, 81; Best of Show in Painting, Idea Corp, 79. *Bibliog:* M Tourtelot (auth), Resume--A Selective Guide, The Studios, 75; R Dozer (auth), Recording Door County's singularity, Chicago Tribune, 75; Door County Creations, Strom Channel 10, 77. *Mem:* Chicago Artists' Coalition (int dir, 79); Wis Watercolor Soc; Wis Painters & Sculptors Asn; Peninsula Arts Asn, Fish Creek, Wis. *Media:* Watercolor, Acrylic. *Dealer:* Edgewood Orchard Gallery Peninsula Players Rd Fish Creek WI 54212. *Mailing Add:* 447 Oakdale Chicago IL 60657

BERNSTEIN, BENJAMIN D
COLLECTOR
b New York, NY, June 24, 07. *Study:* LaSalle Univ, Dr, 84; Univ London, 85 & 86; also studied at Oxford, 86. *Work:* Philadelphia Art Mus; LaSalle Univ Art Mus; Metrop Mus Art; Carnegie Art Mus; Villanova Univ Mus; Tel Aviv Mus Art; Dusseldorf Mus Art. *Pos:* Patron, Whitney Mus; mem bd trustees, Pa Acad Fine Arts. *Mem:* Life mem Am Fedn Arts; fel Philadelphia Mus Art; Mus Mod Art, New York; Buten Mus of Wedgewood; Philadelphia Art Alliance. *Collection:* Large collection of contemporary oils, gouache, drawings, prints and sculpture including a great many Cobra works; large collections of art from New Guinea, Africa, and American Indian art. *Mailing Add:* 1824 Delancey Pl Philadelphia PA 19103

BERNSTEIN, EDWARD I
COLLECTOR
b Philadelphia, Pa, Nov 15, 17. *Work:* Located at Philadelphia Mus Art, Pa Acad Fine Arts, La Salle Col Art Gallery & Dept Art & Hist, Villanova Univ, Pa. *Mem:* Wilson Peale Soc; Pa Acad Fine Art; Haviland Soc; Royal Acad Fine Arts, London, Eng; Philadelphia Mus Art (assoc mem). *Collection:* Contemporary art includes oils, gouche, drawings, prints and sculpture; African paintings and sculpture; Elizabeth Frink. *Mailing Add:* 1810 Rittenhouse Sq Philadelphia PA 19103

BERNSTEIN, GERALD
PAINTER, RESTORER
b Indianapolis, Ind, Aug 25, 17. *Study:* John Herron Art Inst; Art Students League, with George Bridgman & Yasuo Kuniyoshi; NY Univ, BA, Inst Fine Arts, MA. *Work:* Staten Island Inst Arts & Sci. *Exhib:* Staten Island Inst Arts & Sci Ann, 50-81; Pietrantonio Gallery, New York, 59-62; one-man show, Kade Gallery, Wagner Col, 73; Metrop Mus, 75; Avery Fisher Hall, Lincoln Ctr, 75; one-man exhib, West Indian Themes, La Galerie. *Collections Arranged:* Artist Look at Nature, Surveys of American Painting & one-man & group exhibs, Staten Island Mus, 50-56. *Pos:* Cur art, Staten Island Mus, 50-56; owner & dir, Island Art Ctr, Staten Island, 58-83. *Teaching:* Artist in residence, Staten Island Community Col, 70-71. *Awards:* Dennen Award, 77; Staten Island Savings Bank Award, 79; Islander Award, 82; NY Telephone Award, 83. *Media:* Oil, Watercolor. *Mailing Add:* 45 Gardenia Dr Maple Shade NJ 08052

BERNSTEIN, GERDA MEYER
SCULPTOR, PAINTER
b Westphalia, Ger; US citizen. *Study:* Art Inst Chicago, MFA, 77. *Work:* Karl Ernst Osthaus Mus, Hagen, WGer. *Exhib:* One-person exhibit, Art Inst Chicago, 81-82 & 89, Ministerio de Cultura, Madrid, Spain, 87, Badischer Kunstrerein, Karlsruhe, 87, Bochum Mus, Ger, 87, Northern Ill Univ Art Mus, De Kalb, 90; travelling exhib, Nat Mus Am Art, Smithsonian Inst, Washington, DC, Nat Acad Design, New York, Ill State Mus, Springfield, 81-82; Karl Ernst Osthaus Mus, Hagen, Ger, 81-82; A Chicago Hist, Northern Ill Univ, Swen Parson Gallery, DeKalb, Ill, 84; Mus Contemp Art, 84, Chicago Off Fine Arts, Cult Ctr, Chicago, 89; Neur Berliner Kunstverein, Berlin, Ger, 84 & 87; Am Women in Art, AIR Gallery, 85, 89, Franklin Furnace Gallery, New York, 91; UN Conf on Women, Nairobi, Kenya, 85; Politica Cult, Vanderbilt Univ, Nashville, Tenn, 86; Burning in Hell, Rockford Col, Ill, 91. *Pos:* Founder, Women's Co-operative, ARC Gallery Chicago, 73-77; cur, Univ Mo, St Louis, 77 & Chicago Pub Libr Cult Ctr, 81. *Awards:* Ill Arts Coun Fel, 91-92. *Bibliog:* Dr Johann Muller (auth), Gerda Meyer Bernstein, Karl Ernst Osthaus Mus, Hagen, Ger, 9/82; Dr Lucie Schauer (auth), Political Visions, Neuer Berliner Kunsstverein, Berlin, Ger, 2/87; Sue Taylor & Gergor Knight (auths), Present at the Creation, Chicago Cult Ctr, 10/89. *Mem:* Artists Equity; Womens Caucus Art; Chicago Aritsts Coalition. *Media:* All. *Publ:* Numerous articles from 82-91. *Dealer:* AIR Gallery 63 Crosby St New York NY 10012. *Mailing Add:* Artspace 954 W Wash St Chicago IL 60607

BERNSTEIN, JUDITH
PAINTER, PRINTMAKER
b Newark, NJ, Oct 14, 42. *Study:* Pa State Univ, BS & MS, 64; Yale Univ Sch Art, BFA & MFA, 67. *Work:* Mus Mod Art, Brooklyn Mus, New York; Univ Colo Mus, Boulder; Yale Art Gallery, New Haven, Conn; Kronhausen, Lund, Sweden; Colgate Univ Mus, Hamilton, NY. *Comn:* Two on Site Wall Installation, William N Copley, 77. *Exhib:* One-person shows, AIR Gallery, 73 & 84, State Univ New York, Stony Brook, 77, Brooks Jackson Iolas Gallery, New York, 78, Univ Ark, Fayetteville, 87; Year of the Women, Bronx Mus Arts, NY, 75; Contemporary Women: Consciousness & Content, Brooklyn Mus, NY, 77; Venerezia-Revenice, Palazzo Grassi, Venice, Italy, 78; Feministische Kunst Int, Haags Gemeentemuseum, Noordbrants Mus & Niimeegs Mus, Holland, 79-81; Impact Art Festival, Kyoto Int Art Ctr, Japan, 82; Facets, Ackland Art Mus, Chapel Hill, NC, 85; Drawing in Situ (with catalog), C W Post Campus, NY, 86; 100 Drawings by Women: European USIA, Hillwood Art Mus, Greenvale, NY, Traveling Exhib, 89-90; Man Revealed, Graham Mod Gallery, New York, 92; Centered in the USA, Visual Arts Ctr, Anchorage, Alaska, 92. *Teaching:* Pratt Inst; Rutgers Univ; asst prof fine arts, State Univ NY, Stony Brook, 74-78; assoc prof fine arts, State Univ NY, Purchase, 78- *Awards:* Elizabeth Canfield Hicks Mem Scholar, Yale Univ Sch Art & Archit, 64-67; Nat Endowment Arts Grant, 74-75 & 85-86; New York Found for the Arts, 88. *Bibliog:* John Russell (auth), Judith Berstein, NY Times, 4/27/84; Karin Lipson (auth), Drawing on the Wall, Newsday, 3/21/86; Elinor Gadon (auth), The Once and Future Goddess, Phantasmasmagoria: The Sexual Metaphors of Judith Bernstein, Harper and Row, 89; Judy K Collischan Van Wagner, Lines of Vision, Hudson Hill Press, 89; Steven Dubin (auth), Arresting Images, Routeledge, 92. *Mem:* Col Art Asn Am; Nat Soc Lit & Arts; Women's Caucus Art. *Media:* Charcoal, Oil. *Publ:* Guggenheim Panel Discussion Drawings, Soho Weekly News, Centerfold, 3/12-18/80. *Mailing Add:* PO Box 1045, Knickerbocker Sta New York NY 10002-0145

BERNSTEIN, SARALINDA
ART DEALER, HISTORIAN
b New York, NY, Jan 7, 51. *Study:* Ecole Pratique des Hautes Etudes, Sorbonne, Paris, 70-71; Swarthmore Col, Pa, BA(magna cum laude), 72; NY Univ Sch Arts, 72; New Sch Social Res, New York, 74. *Collections Arranged:* Edvard Munch: Paradox of Woman (auth, catalog), Aldis Browne Fine Arts, New York, 81; Prints about Prints, 81-82; Nineteenth and Twentieth Century Works on Paper (auth, catalog), 82 & Edgar Chahine: Images of Venice and The Belle Epoque (auth, catalog), 83, Aldis Browne Fine Arts. *Pos:* Asst to dir, Asn Am Artists, New York, 72-78; exec vpres & dir, Int Exhibs, Aldis Browne Fine Arts, New York, 78- *Teaching:* Lectr, Soc Ethical Cult, New York, 81. *Res:* Form and function of original prints in society; the concept and definition of form in visual arts, particularly in late 19th through early 20th century European works. *Publ:* Contribr, 10 Jahre Galerie Kühl, Galerie Kühl, 77. *Mailing Add:* 265 Massachusetts Ave Haworth NJ 07641

BERNSTEIN, THERESA
PAINTER, PRINTMAKER
b Philadelphia, Pa. *Study:* Pa Acad Fine Arts; Art Students League; Philadelphia Sch Design. *Work:* Metrop Mus Art, New York; Brooklyn Mus; Harvard Univ; Phillips Art Gallery, Washington, DC; Nat Mus, Smithsonian Inst. *Comn:* First Orchestra in America, Treas Dept for Mannhein, Pa, 40; portrait of David Lyons, Harvard Univ Biblical Mus Fac, 54; portrait Robert Pheiffer, Harvard Univ, 56; portrait Henrietta Szold, Hadassan, 59. *Exhib:* Exhib Am Painters, Metrop Mus Art, New York, 50; Carnegie Inst, Pittsburgh; Biennial Am Art, Corcoran Gallery Art, Washington, DC; Nat Mus, Smithsonian Inst, Washington, DC, 56; New York Ann, Nat Acad Design; one-woman show, Summit Gallery, New York, 78; New York Hist Soc Exhib, 83-84; Mus city of New York 90-91. *Awards:* Jeanne d'Arc Medal, Fr Inst Arts & Lett, 29; John A Johnson Award, North Shore Arts Asn, 71; Matson Mem Award, Rockport Art Asn, 79. *Bibliog:* E A Jenell (auth), articles, New York Times, 45 & Menorah J, 48; article, Am Artist, 80. *Mem:* Nat Asn Women Artists; Audubon Artists; Soc Am Graphic Artists; Allied Artists Am; New York Soc Women Artists (dir, 28-). *Media:* Oil, Aquarelle; Graphics. *Res:* Graphic art; American art. *Publ:* Auth, William Meyerowitz, 58 & History of Jewish Artists, 58, Zukenft; History-American artists, Gloucester Times, 70; History North Shore Arts Association, 72; History New York Society of Women Artists, 72. *Mailing Add:* c/o Strawgow Gallery 73 Spring St New York NY 10012

BERNSTEIN, WILLIAM JOSEPH
DESIGNER, GLASSBLOWER
b Newark, NJ, Dec 3, 45. *Study:* Philadelphia Col Art, BFA, 68; Penland Sch, NC, 68-70. *Work:* International Glasmuseum, Ebeltoft, Denmark; Australian Coun Arts, Sidney; Corning Mus Glass, NY; Renwick Gallery, Nat Mus Am Art, Smithsonian Inst, Washington, DC; Glasmuseum Frauenau, Bavaria, WGer; Yamaha Corp, Japan; Chrysler Mus, Norfolk, Va; Mint Mus Art, Charlotte, NC. *Exhib:* Baroque '74, Mus Contemp Crafts, New York, 74; In Praise of Hands, 1st World Crafts Exhib, Toronto, Can, 74; Craft Multiples, Renwick Gallery, Smithsonian Inst, Washington, DC, 75; Philadelphia Mus of Art, 77; Am Crafts in the White House, White House, Washington, DC, 77; Victoria & Albert Mus, Eng; USA: Portrait of the South, Palazzo Venezia, Rome, Italy; Am Studio Glass, Isetan Galleries, Japan; Glass from the Corning Collection, Spaso House, Moscow, USSR; one-man exhib, Somerhill Gallery, Chapel Hill, NC, Grohē Glass Gallery, 91, Marx Gallery, Chicago, Ill, 91; Vessels: From Use to Symbol, Am Craft Mus, New York. *Teaching:* Penland Sch Crafts, NC, Univ Southern Calif, Los Angeles, Pilchuck Glass Ctr, Stanwood, Wash & Naples Mill Sch, NY; Summervail Workshop, Vail, Colo. *Awards:* Nat Endowment Arts Fel, 74 & Grant, 76; Louis Comfort Tiffany Found Grant, 75; NC Arts Coun Fel, 83; Masterworks Fellowship, Creative Glass Ctr Am, 90. *Bibliog:* R L Grover (auth), Contemporary Art Glass, Crown Publ, 75; F Kulasiewicz (auth), Glassblowing, Watson-Guptill, 75; Design in Modern Interiors, Studio Vista, 75; Dan Klein (auth), Glass, A Contemporary Art, Rizzoli. *Publ:* NY Mag, NY Times; Atlanta Constitution Sunday Mag; State Mag NC; Am Craft (portfolio sect); Crafts Report. *Mailing Add:* 469 Hannah Branch Rd Burnsville NC 28714

BERRESFORD, VIRGINIA
PAINTER
b New Rochelle, NY, Oct 11, 02. *Study:* Teachers Col, Columbia Univ, 23-24, Art Students League. *Work:* Whitney Mus Am Art, Mus Mod Art, New York; Columbus Mus Art, Ohio; Univ Maine, Orono. *Comn:* Mural, comn by Katherine Cornell, Vineyard Haven, Mass. *Exhib:* Carnegie Int, Carnegie Inst, Pittsburgh, 38; Am Art, Worlds Fair, New York, 39; many one-man shows. *Media:* Oil, Watercolor. *Publ:* Auth, Virginia's Journal, autobiography, 89. *Mailing Add:* RFD Vineyard Haven MA 02568

BERRY, CAROLYN
PAINTER, BOOK DEALER
b Sweet Springs, Mo, June 27, 30. *Study:* Univ Mo, BA, 53; Humboldt Univ, 71; Univ Calif, 85-87. *Work:* Sackner Collection, Miami Beach, Fla; Monterey Peninsula Mus Art, Calif; Nat Mus Women Art; Mus Mod Art Libr; Art Inst Chicago; Museo Internacional De Electrografia, Cuenca, Spain. *Exhib:* Pac Grove Art Ctr, 73-92; Bookworks, Washington, DC, 82 & 85; Univ Calif, Los Angeles, 85; Rutgers Univ, 88; Anchorage Mus Hist & Art, Alaska, 90-91; Royal Photographic Soc, Bath, UK, 90; Pacific Rim Exhib, 90-93. *Pos:* Artist-in-residence, Calif Arts Coun. *Teaching:* Instr bk art, Monterey Peninsula Col, 87. *Awards:* First Graphic Award, 74 & 3rd Award, 85 Monterey Peninsula Mus Art. *Bibliog:* Irene Leon Masteller (auth), Literary Assemblages, Coast Weekly, 86; Artists & Their Cats, Midmarch, New York, 90. *Mem:* Women's Caucus for Art; Artists Equity Asn; Ctr Book Arts; Int Soc Copier Artists. *Media:* Watercolor, Mixed. *Publ:* Contribr, Zoom Mag, France, 89. *Dealer:* Winfield Gallery 224 Crossroads Blvd Carmel CA; Clay Poole-Freese Gallery 216 Grand Ave Pacific Grove CA 93950. *Mailing Add:* 78 Cuesta Vista Monterey CA 93940

BERRY, GLENN
PAINTER, EDUCATOR
b Glendale, Calif, Feb 27, 29. *Study:* Pomona Col, BA(magna cum laude); Art Inst Chicago, BFA & MFA. *Work:* Storm King Art Ctr, Mountainville, NY; Joseph H Hirshhorn Collection, Washington, DC; Kaiser Aluminum & Chem Corp, Oakland, Calif; Palm Springs Desert Mus, Calif; Calif State Univ, Humboldt. *Exhib:* Phelan Awards Exhib & Artists Behind Artists, Calif Palace Legion Hon, San Francisco, 67; one-man shows, Ankrum Gallery, Los Angeles, 70, Esther Bear Gallery, Santa Barbara, Calif, 71 & Humboldt State Univ, 75; Six Northern Calif Artists, Henry Gallery, Univ Wash, 75; two-man show, Humboldt Cult Ctr, Eureka, Calif, 77; and others. *Teaching:* Prof painting, Humboldt State Univ, 56-81, prof emer, 81- *Media:* Acrylic, Oil. *Mailing Add:* PO Box 2241 McKinleyville CA 95521

BERRY, WILLIAM AUGUSTUS
EDUCATOR, GRAPHIC ARTIST
b Jacksonville, Tex, Sept 29, 33. *Study:* Univ Tex, Austin, BFA(summa cum laude), 55; Circolo Artistico, Rome, 56; Univ Southern Calif, MFA, 57. *Work:* Hoyt Inst Fine Arts, New Castle, Pa; Univ NDak, Grand Forks; Univ Mo, Columbia; Harwell Mus, Poplar Bluff, Mo; Stedman Art Gallery, Rutgers Univ, Camden, NJ. *Exhib:* Solo Shows, Muscarelle Mus Art, Williamsburg, Va, 84, Galleria Scheider, Rome, Italy, 85, Campbell Gallery, San Francisco, Calif, 87, Brunnier Mus, Ames, Iowa, 88 & Harwell Mus, Poplar Bluff, 88, Traveling exhib sponsored by Mid Am Alliance & NEA, 90-93; more than 200 national juried exhib (group), 79-90. *Pos:* Freelance illusr, The Reporter, Newsweek, Esquire, Opera News Mag, New York, 60-68; art dir & designer, Tex Mo Mag, 72-73. *Teaching:* Asst prof art, Univ Tex, Austin, 68-74; assoc prof art & chmn graphic design area, Sch Visual Art, Boston Univ, 74-78; vis assoc prof, Grad Summer Sch Teachers, Wesleyan Univ, 76; prof art, dir grad studies in visual art & head graphic design area, Univ Mo-Columbia, 78- *Awards:* Artist-in-residence, Rockefeller Found, Bellagio, Italy, 88; Artist-in-residence, MacDowell Colony, 84; Artist-in-residence, Camargo Found, Cassis, France, 89. *Bibliog:* Susan E Meyer (auth), William A Berry, illustrator-painter, Am Artist, 3/70; Ruth Seidler (auth), Drawing the Human Form, Libr J, 11/01/77; Betsy Goldman (auth), William A Berry, Am Artist, 2/87. *Mem:* Am Inst Graphic Art; Col Art Asn Am. *Media:* Multimedia, Color Pencils. *Res:* Drawing, technique and theory. *Publ:* Coauth, Paper Construction for Children, Van Nostrand Reinhold, 66; illusr, Carter Wilson's on Firm Ice, Crowell, 69; auth, Visual puns, Print Mag, 9/71; Drawing the Human Form, Simon & Schuster, NY, 77. *Mailing Add:* Dept Art Univ Mo Columbia Columbia MO 65211

BERSENTES, NAFSIKA J
PAINTER
b Peloponnesus, Greece, Sept 9, 31; US citizen. *Study:* Syracuse Univ, 76-79. *Exhib:* Solo exhib, Everson Mus, Syracuse, NY, 82 & Metrop Sch Arts, Syracuse, NY, 89; Regional Show, Everson Mus, Syracuse, NY, 75; Colgate Univ, Hamilton, NY, 80; Pre-Postmodern, St Lawrence Univ, Canton, NY, 85; Six from Syracuse, Skidmore Col, Saratoga Springs, NY, 85; Greek Cult Festival, Syracuse, NY, 86; Artstruck, Metrop Sch Arts, Syracuse, NY, 89; Canal Town Mus & Canastota Pub Libr, 90. *Media:* Acrylic. *Mailing Add:* 120 Harrington Rd Syracuse NY 13224

BERSHAD, DAVID L
HISTORIAN, EDUCATOR
b San Francisco, Calif, Mar 11, 42. *Study:* Stanford Univ, AB, 62; Univ Calif, Los Angeles, PhD(with distinction), 70. *Teaching:* Asst prof art hist, Ariz State Univ, 70-72; assoc prof art hist, Univ Calgary, 75-85, prof, 85- *Awards:* Fulbright Fel, 68; Kress Fel, 69; Distinguished Scholar, Univ Lethbridge, 80. *Mem:* Univ Art Asn Can. *Res:* Seventeenth and 18th century Italian painting and sculpture, with specific emphasis on Roman art. *Publ:* Auth, A series of papal busts by Domenico Guidi, 70, Domenico Guidi and Nicolas Poussin, 71, The cardinal Marco Bragadino tomb in the church of San Marco in Rome, 77 & auth, New documents concerning Michelangelo's deposition in Florence, 78, Burlington Mag; The tapestries of Raphael and their re-acquisition in 1808, 78 & P E Monnot: Newly discovered sculpture and documents, 84, Antologia di Belle Arti. *Mailing Add:* c/o University Calgary Dept Art, 2500 University Dr NW Calgary AB T2N 1N4 Canada

BERTHOT, JAKE
PAINTER
b Niagara Falls, NY, Mar 30, 39. *Study:* New Sch for Social Res, 60-61; Pratt Inst, Brooklyn, NY, 60-62. *Work:* Baltimore Mus Art, MD; Va Mus Fine Arts, Richmond; Whitney Mus Am Art & Mus Mod Art, New York; Dallas Mus Fine Art, Tx; Fogg Art Mus, Cambridge, Mass; Philadelphia Mus Art, Pa; Solomon R Guggenheim Mus, New York. *Exhib:* Ann, 69 & 73, Recent Acquisitions, 71 & Continuing Abstraction in Am Art, 74, Whitney Mus Am Art; Contemp Drawings, Chicago Art Inst, 71; Eight New York Painters, Univ Calif Art Mus, Berkeley, 72; Paris Biennale, France, 73; Pratt Inst, Brooklyn, NY, 74, 88; Corcoran Biennial, Corcoran Gallery, Washington, DC, 75; Fundamental Painting, Stedelijk Mus, Amsterdam, 75; Venice Biennale, US Pavilion, 76; From Women's Eyes, Rose Art Mus, Brandeis Univ, Mass, 77; Mus Mod Art, New York, 77, 83, 84 & 85; Eight Abstract Painters, Inst Contemp Art, Univ Pa, 78; New Painting--New York, Hayward Gallery, London, 79; one-man exhibs, Nigel Greenwood Gallery, London, 79, Nina Nielsen Gallery, Boston, 79, 84 & 88, David McKee Gallery, 76, 78, 82, 83, 86-89 & 91, Galleri Olsson, Stockholm, Sweden, 87 & 90, Rose Art Mus, Waltham, Mass, 88; Nat Gallery Art, Washington, DC, 89; Ruggerio Gallery, New York, 90; Nielsen Gallery, Boston, Mass, 90; Works on Paper, Nigel Greenwood Gallery, London, 91; Painting, Galerie Lelong, 91, Drawings Only, Galerie Denise Cade, Art Prospect Inc, 91, Drawings 1991, Cork Gallery, Lincoln Ctr, New York, 91. *Teaching:* Instr, Yale Univ, New Haven, Conn, 82. *Awards:* Guggenheim Fel, 81; Nat Endowment Arts Grant, 83. *Bibliog:* David Reisman (auth), Jake Berthot, Artscribe, 3-4/90; Kenneth Wahl (auth), Jake Berthot, Arts mag, 3/90; William Heller (auth), Without You, We're Nothing, Ave Mag, 2/91. *Mailing Add:* c/o David McKee Gallery 745 Fifth Ave New York NY 10151

BERTMAN, STEPHEN
HISTORIAN, WRITER
b New York, NY, July 20, 37. *Study:* New York Univ, BA, 59; Brandeis Univ, MA, 60; Am Sch Classical Studies, Athens, 62; Columbia Univ, PhD, 65. *Teaching:* Asst prof classics, Fla State Univ, Tallahassee, 63-67; prof classics, Univ Windsor, Ont, 67- *Mem:* Archaeol Inst Am; Col Art Asn Am *Res:* Archeology and ancient art. *Publ:* Auth, Art and the Romans, Coronado, 75; ed, The Conflict of Generations in Ancient Greece & Rome, Grüner, 76; auth, Doorways through Time, Jeremy Tarcher-St Martin's Press, 87. *Mailing Add:* 5959 Piccadilly Circle N West Bloomfield MI 48322

BERTOIA, (MR) VAL (BERTOIA STUDIO)
DESIGNER, SCULPTOR
b Santa Monica, Calif, June 27, 49. *Study:* Ind Inst Technol, grad, 71; studied with Dr Harry Bertoia, 72-78; Elizabethtown Col, 86. *Work:* James Allen Ctr, Northwestern Univ, Evanstown, Ill; R Greenberg Assoc, New York; Call Chronicle, Allentown, Pa; J Haight of Allentown Art Mus; Cleveland Pub Lib, Ohio; and others. *Comn:* wooden playground, Palm Schwenkfelder Church, Palm, Pa, 85; Bronze Tortoise in Action, 87, Cement People in the Park, 88, Mayfair, Allentown, Pa; bronze mosaic, cubic frame, 88, Seven Spheres of Bronze Pebbles, 89, comn by Ross & Wendy Born, Allentown, Pa; Sounding-Forest 92, Stein-Bartlow Gallery, Chicago, 92; John Smith Memorial, Unitarian Universalists, Pottstown, Pa. *Exhib:* two-person show, Wyomissing Inst Fine Art, Pa, 87; Juries Show at Nittany Lion, Penn State Univ, 90; Mayfair Juried Show, Muhlenberg Col, 90; 3 Generations of Bertoia, Reading Mus, 90; Wooden 5-Seasons' Gallery, Penn State Univ, 90. *Teaching:* Instr, stone sculpture & sculpture jewelry, Wyomissing Inst Fine Arts, 87-88. *Awards:* Fourth place sculpture, Festival Arts, Cornerstone, 84; Speaker of the Year, Ind Inst of Tech, 69. *Bibliog:* Marilyn Fox (auth), V Bertoia Sounds Off, Reading Eagle, 87. *Media:* Bronze, Copper; Nickle, Silver. *Publ:* Auth, James with the Invisible Neck, Boyertown Publ, 85; Optimum Wind-Driven Alternator, Bertoia Studio Ltd, 85; coauth, Bertoia Catalogue, Boyertown Publ, 86; Sonambient (R) CDS, 92. *Mailing Add:* PO Box 383 644 Main St Bally PA 19503

BERTOLLI, EUGENE EMIL
SCULPTOR, DESIGNER
b Boston, Mass, Feb 19, 23. *Study:* Boston Col, AB, 43; Hartford Col Grad Sch, cert art educ, 49; private study with E G Chandler, 78-83. *Comn:* Stained glass windows, Madigan Convalescent Hosp, Ft Lewis, Wash, 45; sculptured gold pectoral cross, Bishop McGurkin, Tanganyika, Africa, 56; commemorative medal, City of Meriden, Conn, 85; also numerous pvt commissions in sculpture and precious jewelry. *Exhib:* One-man shows, Conn Town & County Asn, Hartford, 80 & Rockport Art Asn, Mass, 85; Nat Exhib, Hudson Valley Arts Asn, Hudson Valley, NY, 83-88; Ann Nat Exhib, Acad Artists Asn, Springfield, Mass, 84-90; Ann Awards Exhib, Guild Boston Artists, Mass, 85. *Pos:* Dir art & educ, Madigan Convent Hosp, Ft Lewis, Wash, 45-47; sr vpres & chief designer, Napier Co, New York, 47-85. *Awards:* Paul Manship Sculpture Award, Rockport Art Asn, 86; Coun Am Artists Soc Award, Acad Artists Asn Nat Exhib, 92; Paul Manship Mem Award Excellence Sculpture, North Shore Arts Asn, 92; and others. *Bibliog:* Linda Fridy (auth), kBertolli: Dean of American jewelry designers, Accent Mag, 86. *Mem:* Am Artists Prof League; Guild of Boston Artist; Acad Artists Asn (mem, exec comt, Springfield, Mass, 83); Hudson Valley Art Asn; Am Medallic Sculpture Asn; Salmagundi Club; New England Sculptors Asn. *Media:* Metals. *Publ:* Auth & illusr, Continuity through change: A history of jewelry design, Conn Mag, 60. *Mailing Add:* Bertolli Studios 73 Reynolds Dr Meriden CT 06450

BERTONI, CHRISTINA
CERAMIST, PAINTER
b Ann Arbor, Mich, Jan 15, 45. *Study:* Univ Mich, BFA (painting), 67; Cranbrook Acad Art, MFA (ceramics), 76. *Work:* Brooklyn Mus, Brooklyn, NY; Victoria & Albert Mus, London; Crocker Art Mus, Sacramento, Calif; Mus Fine Arts, Boston, Mass. *Exhib:* Victoria Munroe Gallery, New York, 86 & solo exhib, 87; American Potters Today (with catalog), Victoria & Albert Mus, London, Eng, 86; Material as Metaphor (with catalog), Chicago Pub Libr Cult Ctr, Ill, 86; Pewabic Pottery, Detroit, Mich, 86; The Works Gallery, Philadelphia, Pa, 87; The Eloquent Object (with catalog), Philbrook Mus, Tulsa, Okla, 87-88. *Pos:* Assoc prof art, RI Sch Design, Providence, RI, 77- *Awards:* Purchase Prize, Crocker Art Mus, Calif, 77; Nat Endowment Arts Craftsman Fel, 79 & 86; Craftsman Grant, RI State Coun Arts, 83. *Bibliog:* Lois Tarlow (auth), Christina Bertoni, Art New Eng, 4/84; James Cobb (auth), article, Am Ceramics, 88; On the spititual art, Agni Rev, fall, 88. *Media:* Clay; Paint. *Dealer:* Victoria Munroe Gallery 130 Prince St New York NY. *Mailing Add:* 152 Laurel Hill Ave Pascoag RI 02859

BERTONI, DANTE H
PAINTER, ILLUSTRATOR
b New York, NY, Nov 13, 26. *Study:* Parsons Sch Design, New York, Advert Design Cert, 51; Art Students League, with Bernard Klonis, 52-54; NY Univ, 60. *Work:* US Navy Combat Art Collection, Wash Naval Yard; Forbes Mag Collection & Mutual Benefit Life Ins Co Collection, New York; Hotel DuPont Collection, Wilmington, Del; Cent Intel Agency off, White House,

Washington, DC. *Comn:* Sea Mule (illus), Lederle Labs, Am Cyanamid Co, Wayne, NJ, 71; Atomic Submarine Base, New London, Conn, Rear Adm L R Geis, US Navy, 70, Exotic Dancer (exercise), Rear Adm William Thompson, 71, Oper Homecoming & Endsweep, Capt D M Cooney, 73; Proceedings (cover illus), US Naval Inst, Annapolis, Md, 72; Oper Cuba-Sealift, Adm John B Hayes US Coast Guard, Washington, DC. *Exhib:* Am Watercolor Soc, NY, 55-; Nat Acad Fine Arts, 56-; Nat Arts Club, 60-; Salmagundi Sketch Club, 55-; US Navy Combat Art Exhibit Travel Show, Washington Navy Yard, 70- *Pos:* Asst art dir, J Walter Thompson, New York, 51-57; graphics designer, Lippencott & Margulies Co, 62-63; package designer, Reigel Paper Co, 64-66; artist, Equitable Bag Co, 72- *Awards:* NACAL Gold Medal, Louis E Seley, 72; Grand Prize Washington Sq Outdoor Art Exhib, Lufthansa Air Lines, 73; First US Coast Guard Art Program Medal, 83. *Bibliog:* Mary O'Flaherty (auth), Artist pictures way through Navy activity, New York News, 11/14/71. *Mem:* Am Watercolor Soc, New York; Salmagundi Sketch Club (vchmn NACAL, 70); US Naval Inst, Annapolis, Md; Long Beach Art Asn, NY. *Media:* Watercolor, Ink. *Publ:* Auth, Painting in contrasts, Palette Talk, Vol 41, 80. *Dealer:* Chadd's Ford Gallery Inc Rte 1 & 100 Chadd's Ford PA 19317. *Mailing Add:* 52-02 Eighth Ave Brooklyn NY 11220

BESANT, DEREK MICHAEL
PAINTER, INSTRUCTOR
b Ft MacLeod, Alta, July15, 50. *Study:* Univ Calgary, Alberta Can, BFA, 73. *Work:* De Cordova Mus, Boston, Mass; Metrop Mus, Miami, Fla; Can Coun Art Bank, Ottawa, Ont; Cineplex Odeon Corp, New York; Royal Bank Can. *Comn:* Flatiron mural, A E LePage, Royal Insurance Lavalin Inc, Toronto, Ont, 80; Eau Claire Peel, Bourgeau Developments Sturgets Architects, Calgary, Alta, 82; cardboard windows installation proj, Liberty of London, Eng, 87; paintings, Amoco, Mt Royal Col, Calgary & Bank of Nova Scotia, Toronto. *Exhib:* Boston Printmakers, Boston Ctr Arts, Mass, 78; 8th Int Triennial Color Prints, Grenchen Arts Mus, Switzerland, 79; Other Realities, Can House London England, Paris, France, 79; Royal Canadian Soc Arts, Mickle Arts Mus, Calgary, Alta, 80; Canadian Prints, Asn Print Workshops Great Britain, Edinborough, Scotland, 80; Ten Canadian Print Artists, Nat Mus Can Japanese Print Coun, Tour Japan Nat Mus, 80-81; Int Print Exhibs Repub China, Taipei, 84; 6th Int Impact Art Festival, Kyoto City Mus, 85; Diagrams, Mira Godard Gallery, Toronto, 86; Asian-Pacific, Univ New Delhi, India, 86; Solo exhib, Woltjen Udell Gallery, Vancouver & Mira Godard Gallery, Toronto, 89, Art Gallery of Hamilton, 90; San Antonio Mus Art, Tex, 92; São Paulo, Brazil, 92; Centre de Langues, Brussels, Belg, 92; and others. *Pos:* Exhibs designer, Glenbow Mus, Calgary, 73-77; Alta ed, Artmagazine, Toronto, 74-; drawing chmn, Alta Col Art, 77-; comt mem, Alta Legislature Art Acquisition Comt, 81-82. *Teaching:* Guest artist collaborations, Univ Arts Asn, Univ Alta, 76; guest artist printmaking, Mem Univ, Newfoundland, 77; lectr public art, Univ Regina, Sask, 81; lectr murals, Red Deer Col, 82 & Southwest Tex State Univ, 89. *Awards:* Canada Coun Grant, 77, 85 & 92; Second Prize, Miami Biennale, Mus Mod Art, 77; Award Winner, Andrew Nelson Wheehead Co, 78; World Cult Prize for Lett, Arts & Sci, 84; Alberta Achievement Award, 84. *Bibliog:* Nancy Tousley (auth), Falls transplanted to Toronto, Calgary Herald, 5/89; Christopher Hume (auth), Huge waterfall graces Scotia Plaza, The Sunday Star, Toronto, 5/89; Patrick McHugh (auth), Toronto Architecture, McClelland & Stewart, Can, 89. *Mem:* Royal Can Acad Arts; Print & Drawing Coun Can (vchmn, 76-78); Can Artists Representation; Visual Arts Ont; World Print Coun. *Media:* Watercolor, Ink. *Res:* Contemporary Canadian. *Publ:* Illusr, The Back Room, Oberon, 80; A Culinary Palette, Merritt, 81; contribr, Artmagazine, 81; Artviews, Visual Arts Ont, 82; Macleans, Maclean Hunter, 82. *Mailing Add:* Dept Art Alta Col Art 1407 14th Ave NW Calgary AB Canada

BESNER, J JACQUES
MURALIST, KINETIC ARTIST
b Vaudreuil, Que, Sept 28, 19. *Study:* Teachers' Col, Univ Montreal, Que, 42; study of archit, Int Corresp Sch, Chicago, Ill, three yrs. *Work:* Phoenix Art Mus, Ariz; Bhirla Mus, Calcutta, India; Mus d'Art Contemporain, Thomas More Inst & Mus Fine Arts, Montreal, Que; Winston Collection, Dearborn, Mich. *Comn:* Alcan, Montreal, 81; Gatineau Hosp, Que, 83; Nat Harbors Bd, 84; Indalex, Toronto, 89; Montreal N, 90. *Exhib:* Montreal Mus Fine Arts, Can, 64; Mus d'Art Contemporain, Montreal, Que, 65-68; Pagani Found, Milan, Italy, 68; Rose Fried Gallery, New York, 68; Nat Cult Ctr, Ottawa, Ont, 70; Que Pavilion, Expo 70, Osaka, Japan, 70; Int Arts Fair, Basel, Switz, 73; and others. *Collections Arranged:* Stratford Festival, Ont, Can, 76; Salon de l'Acier, Brussels, Belg, 68; Pagani Found, Milan, Italy, 68; 20 Years of Que Sculpture, Mus Rodin, Paris, 70. *Pos:* Dir visual arts (Man the Creator), Expo 67, Montreal, Que, 64-67; dir, Maison des Arts la Sauvegarde, Montreal, 67-69. *Teaching:* Part-time prof, Visual Arts Ctr, Montreal, 69-71 & Saydie Bronfman Ctr, Montreal, 71-73; prof sculpture, Dawson Col, Montreal, 73-75; chmn dept visual arts, Univ Que, Trois Rivieres, 75-; instr, Univ Que, Hull, 82- *Awards:* Rothman's Award, Rothman's of Pall Mall, Stratford, Ont, 65; Que Competition Award, Mus Art Contemporain, Montreal, Cult Affairs, Que, 66; Thomas More Award, Thomas More Inst, Montreal, 69. *Bibliog:* F Sigouin (auth), Critique, Le Figaro, Paris, 66; Nicolas Calas (auth), article, in: Arts Mag, New York, 69; L Levesque (auth), pictorial article, Vie des Arts Mag, Montreal, 71. *Mem:* Arts Club, Montreal; Prof Artists Asn Que. *Media:* Metal; Stained Glass. *Dealer:* Galerie Daniel McKay St Montreal Que. *Mailing Add:* 404 St Henri St Montreal PQ H3C 2P5 Canada

BESSER, ARNE CHARLES
PAINTER
b Hinsdale, Ill, May 11, 35. *Study:* Univ NMex; Art Ctr Sch, Los Angeles, with John Audobon Tyler and Lorser Feidelsson. *Comn:* Portrait of Mr Aldrich, Chmn Bd, Chemical Bank, 68; painting, Stuart M Speiser, 73; painting, Gen Chas Spofford, 76; painting, Dr S Grossman, 77. *Exhib:* Lowe Art Mus, Coral Gables, Fla, 74; Pa State Mus Art, University Park, 74; Butler Inst Am Art, Youngstown, Ohio, 75; Louis K Meisel Gallery, New York, 75; Baltimore Mus Art, 75; Smithsonian Inst, 81; Terra Mus Am Art, Evanston, Ill, 83. *Awards:* Butler Inst of Am Art Medal of Merit, Today's Art Mag, 75. *Media:* Oil on Canvas, Watercolor. *Mailing Add:* c/o Louis K Meisel Gallery 141 Prince St New York NY 10012

BETENSKY, ROSE HART
PAINTER, ART ADMINISTRATOR
b New York, NY. *Study:* Painting with Josef Presser. *Exhib:* Nat Acad Galleries, New York, 60-77; Royal Acad, Edinburgh, Scotland, 63; Norfolk Mus of Arts & Sci, Va, 64; Cult Inst of Tolsa, Guadalajara, Mex, 65; Palazzo Vecchio, Florence, Italy, 72. *Pos:* Pres, New York Soc of Women Artists, 69-70, Nat Asn of Women Artists, 70-72 & Am Soc of Contemp Artists, 77-79. *Awards:* Marion de Sola Mendel Award, Nat Asn Women Artists, 78; Award of Merit, Am Soc Comtemp Artists, 81; Dr Samuel Gelband Prize, Nat Asn Women Artists, 83, Adele M Sciff Award, 85; Grumbacher Gold Medal, Nat Asn Women Artists, 87. *Mem:* Audubon Artists; Nat Asn of Women Artists; New York Asn of Women Artists; Am Soc of Contemp Artists. *Media:* Acrylic. *Mailing Add:* 66 Hayloft Lane Roslyn Heights NY 11577

BETTERIDGE, LOIS ETHERINGTON
SILVER & GOLDSMITH, LECTURER
b Drummonville, Que, Nov 6, 28. *Study:* Ont Col Art, 47-48; Univ Kans, BFA, 51; Cranbrook Acad Art, MFA, 57. *Work:* Nat Mus Natural Sci & Nat Mus Man, Ottawa; Seagrams Mus, Kitchener; Cranbrook Acad Art, Mich; Scottish Mus, Edinburgh. *Comn:* Communion set, Christ Church Cathedral, Vancouver, 74; bronze sculptures, IBM Can, 75; desk sets, Can Pac Railways; bronze sculptures, Imperial Oil Can; medals, McLuhan Teleglobe Can Award, Int Commun, UNESCO. *Exhib:* Contemp Ont Crafts, Agnes Etherington Gallery, Kingston, Ont, 77; Metalsmiths, Soc NAm Goldsmiths, Phoenix Art Mus, Ariz, 77; Artisans Touring Exhib, Can, 78; Reflections in Silver and Gold Traveling Exhib (solo), Mus Natural Sci, Ottawa & seven others, 81-83; Remains To Be Seen, John Michael Kohler Arts Ctr, Sheboygan, Wis, 82; Silversmithing--Three and a Half Decades, Cranbrook Acad Art, Mich, 82; The Michigan Influence, Eastern Mich Univ, Ypsilanti, 82; Masters of Am Metalsmithing, Nat Ornamental Metal Mus, Memphis, 88; Recent Works, traveling exhib, Art Gallery of Hamilton, Ont, 88. *Teaching:* Lectr design, metal & weaving, Univ Guelph, Ont, 57-61; vis lectr & workshop leader, worldwide, 69-; vis prof, NS Col Art & Design, summer 81. *Awards:* Two Commendations, De Beers Int Diamond Ring Competition, London, 66; Citation Distinguished Prof Achievement, Univ Kans, 75; Saidye Bronfman Award for Excellence in Crafts, 78. *Mem:* Ont Crafts Coun (mem bd, 72-73); distinguished mem Soc NAm Goldsmiths (mem bd, 85-); Can Crafts Coun; Visual Arts Ottawa Region (crafts chmn & vpres, 74-77); fel Royal Can Acad Arts. *Media:* Silver, Gold. *Publ:* Auth, The function of the artist in Canada, Ont Crafts Coun Rev, 58; The techniques of chasing and repousse, Crafts Can, 75. *Mailing Add:* 142 Oxford Street Guelph ON N1H 2M7 Canada

BETTINSON, BRENDA
PAINTER, PRINTMAKER
b King's Lynn, Eng, Aug 17, 29; US citizen. *Study:* St Martins Sch Art, London, 46-48; Cent Sch Arts & Crafts, London, 48-50, Nat Dipl in Design, 50; Acad de la Grande Chaumiere, Paris, 51; Ecole Pratique des Hautes Etudes, Sorbonne, 51-53, Eleve Titulaire, 52. *Comn:* St Anselm's Abbey, Washington, DC; St Mary's Benedictine Abbey, Morristown, NJ; Dominican House of Studies, Washington, DC; murals, Calvary Hosp, Bronx, 78; and others. *Exhib:* numerous one-person and group shows in Europe and USA. *Pos:* Art ed, Riverside Radio WRVR-FM, New York, 61-65; consult, Soc for Renewal of Christian Art, 69- *Teaching:* Prof art, Pace Univ, New York, 63-90, chairperson Art & Design, 79-85; lectr art, Katonah Gallery, NY, 72-75, instr Docents' Prog, 88 & 89; prof emer, Pace Univ, 90. *Awards:* Gold Medal, Nat Arts Club, New York, 66. *Bibliog:* The Beginning (film), Columbia Univ Press, 62; Rosemary Gordon (auth), Dying and Creating, Soc Anal Psychology, London, 78. *Media:* Acrylic, Woodcut. *Publ:* Auth, Maurice Lavanoux, Crusader Extraordinary, Sign Mag, 75; illusr, Gates of Heaven & Gates of Joy, C Stern, 79. *Dealer:* Mathias Fine Art Trevett ME 04571. *Mailing Add:* RR#1, Box 61 Trevett ME 04571

BETTISON, JAMES
PAINTER
Study: Mich State Univ, 77; Columbia Col, 80. *Work:* Shell Oil Co, Houston, Tex; Southwestern Bell Corp & Texas Instruments, Dallas, Tex. *Exhib:* Pearl Harbor Invitational, On Waugh, Houston, Tex, 85; Expressionism, Goethe Inst, Houston, Tex, 85; Contemp Art Ctr, New Orleans, La, 87; Paint Movers, New Gallery, Houston, Tex, 87; Black & White, Air Gallery, Austin, Tex, 88; solo shows, New Gallery, Houston, Tex, 88 & 89; Another Reality, Hooks-Epstein Galleries, Houston, Tex, 89; and others. *Awards:* Nat Endowment Arts, 89. *Mailing Add:* c/o New Gallery 2639 Colquitt Houston TX 77098

BETTMANN, OTTO LUDWIG
ART HISTORIAN
b Leipzig, Ger, Oct 15, 03; US citizen. *Study:* Univ Leipzig, PhD, 27, MSLS, 32; Fla Atlantic Univ, LHD, 79. *Exhib:* Bettmann Panopticon Exhib, New York, 63. *Pos:* Assoc ed, C F Peters Co, Leipzig, 27-28; ed, Axel Juncker Publ, Berlin, 28-30; cur rare bks, State Art Libr, Berlin, 30-33; founder, Bettmann Archive, Inc, 36-78; cur rare books, Fla Atlantic Univ Libr, 89- *Teaching:* Adj prof Am studies, Fla Atlantic Univ, 74-81; scholar-in-residence, Fla Atlantic Univ Libr, 88. *Awards:* Award of Merit, Inst Graphic Arts, 67, 68 & 71.

Bibliog: John F Baker (auth), Living in the past with Dr Otto Bettmann, Publ Weekly, 11/25/74; Helen Markel (auth), The Bettmann behind the archives, NY Times, 10/81; article, From Freud to bicyling monks, Time Mag, 3/21/81. *Res:* Pictorial documentation of all aspects of cultural history. *Publ:* Co-auth, Pictorial history of music, 60; auth, The good old days-they were terrible, 74; The Bettmann Portable Archive, 67, A Word From the Wise, 77 & The Bettmann Archive Picture History of the World, 78; The Delights of Reading, 87; Bettmann the Picture Man, 92; and others. *Mailing Add:* 3001 Deer Creek Blvd, Suite 563 Deerfield Beach FL 33442

BETTS, EDWARD HOWARD
PAINTER
b Yonkers, NY, Aug 4, 20. *Study:* Art Students League; Yale Univ, BA, 42; Univ Ill, MFA, 52. *Work:* Fogg Mus Art, Cambridge, Mass; Butler Inst Am Art, Youngstown, Ohio; Va Mus Fine Arts, Richmond, Va; Univ Rochster Mem Art Gallery, NY; Indianapolis Art Mus, Ind; and others. *Exhib:* Five Corcoran Biennials, Washington, DC, 47-59; American Painting Today-1950, Metrop Mus Art, New York, 50; Am Watercolor Soc, NY, 50-91; Int Watercolor Exhibs, Brooklyn Mus, NY, 53, 55 & 61; Nat Acad of Design 53-; Watercolor USA, Springfield Art Mus, Mo, 63-71 & 74-75. *Teaching:* Prof painting, Univ Ill, Champaign, 49-84; retired. *Awards:* First Altman Landscape Prize, Nat Acad Design, 57, 59 & 66; Purchase Award, Childe Hassam Purchase Fund Exhib, 66; M Cooper Award, Am Watercolor, Soc, NY, 77; and others. *Bibliog:* A S Weller (auth), Edward Betts, Art in Am New Talent Issue, 2/55. *Mem:* Nat Acad Design; Am Watercolor Soc; life mem Art Students League. *Media:* Acrylic, Watercolor. *Publ:* Auth, Master Class in Watercolor and Acrylics, Watson-Guptill, 75; Creative Landscape Painting, Watson-Guptill, 78; Creative Seascape Painting, Watson-Guptill, 81. *Mailing Add:* Two Wonderbrook Dr Kennebunk ME 04043

BEVERIDGE, KARL J
PHOTOGRAPHER
b Ottawa, Ont, Nov 7, 45. *Study:* Ont Col Art, 65-66; New Sch, Toronto, Ont, 66-67. *Work:* Nat Gallery Can & Can Coun Art Bank, Ottawa, Ont; Art Gallery Ont, Toronto; Owens Art Gallery, Sackville, NB; Stedelijk Mus, Amsterdam; National Photography Collection, Pub Archives of Can. *Exhib:* Social Criticism & Art Practice, San Francisco Art Inst, Calif, 77; one-man shows, ICA, London, 83, Cepa Gallery, Buffalo, NY, MIA Gallery, Stockholm, 88, Mus Folkswang, Essen, WGer, 88, Hippolyte Gallery, Helsinki, 89, Neue Gesellschaft fur Bildenda Kunst, WBerlin, 89, Perspekteif Gallery, Rotterdam; group exhibs, Lettering in Photography, Centre Nat de la Photographie, Polais de Tokyo, Paris, 89 4eme Triennale Internationale de la Photographie a Charleroi, Musee de la Photographie, Centre d'Art Contemporain, Charleroi, Belg, 90, Fotobiennal 1990 Vigo, Spain, 90 & Fotografie Biennale Rotterdam, Wilhelminakade, Rotterdam, 90; Centre Culturel Triangle Rennes, France, 91; Museet For Fotokunst Odense, Denmark, 92; and others. *Pos:* Ed, Fox Mag, New York, 76; ed, Red Herring Mag, New York, 77-78; ed, Centerfold/Fuse Mag, Toronto, 79-80. *Teaching:* instr, NS Col Art & Design, Halifax, 75-76. *Awards:* Can Coun grants, 68-71, 76, 79, 81, 82, 86 & 87. *Bibliog:* Josephine van Bennekom (auth), Carole Conde & Karl Beveridge - Staged Political Photography, Perspektief, #35, Rotterdam, 89; Irene Berggren (auth), New Documentary, Bildtidningen, #41, Stockholm, 89; David Evans & Sylvia Gohl (auths), Photomontage: A Political Weapon, Gordon Fraser, London, 86. *Mem:* Can Artists Representation (chmn, 79-80). *Publ:* Auth, A forum on Art Forum, The Fox, 75; Oshawa, A History of Local 222, United Autoworkers, Toronto, 84; Standing Up, Toronto, 86; First Contract, Between the Lines Press, Toronto, 86; Class Work, Communications and Electrical Workers of Canada, Toronto, 90. *Mailing Add:* 131 Bathurst St Toronto ON M5V 2R2 Canada

BEVLIN, MARJORIE ELLIOTT
PAINTER, WRITER
b The Dalles, Ore, May 9, 17. *Study:* Univ Colo, BFA; Univ Wash, Col Archit; NY Univ, MS; studied with Jimmy Ernst, 56. *Comn:* Two murals, Otero Jr Col, La Junta, Colo, 55. *Exhib:* Brit Women's Exhib, Liverpool, 64; 8th Ann Prix de Deauville, France, 72; Prix de Rome, 72; one-man shows, Colo, 75, Orcas Island, 81 & 86. *Pos:* Founding chmn fine arts, Otero Jr Col, 55-75; dir & founder, Ark Valley Sch Arts Festival, 56-75. *Awards:* Selectionée de Jury, Prix de Deauville, 72. *Mem:* Nat Asn Women Artists; Delta Phi Delta (vpres Rho Chap, 38). *Media:* Mixed Watercolor, Acrylic. *Res:* All areas of design; drawings at Cabinet des Dessins, The Louvre, Albertina Gallery, Vienna. *Publ:* Auth, Design Through Discovery, Harcourt Brace Jovanovich, 6th ed, 93; Design Through Discovery: The Elements and Principles, Holt, Rinehart & Winston Inc, 84; contribr numerous prof journals. *Mailing Add:* Star Rte 95 Eastsound WA 98245

BEYER, STEVEN J
SCULPTOR, EDUCATOR
b Minneapolis, Minn, Aug 27, 51. *Study:* Macalester Col, St Paul, Minn, BA, 73. *Work:* Whitney Mus Am Art, New York; Walker Art Ctr & Minneapolis Inst Art, Minn; Newport Harbor Art Mus, Newport Beach, Calif; Madison Art Ctr, Wis. *Comn:* Sculpture, City St Paul, Park Bd, Minn, 75; sculpture, Spring Hill Conference Ctr, Wayzata, Minn, 77; sculpture, General Mills Corp, Minneapolis, Minn, 78; sculpture, Northern Ill Univ, DeKalb, 81; Pacific Enterprises, Los Angeles, Calif. *Exhib:* Recent Acquisitions, Walker Art Ctr, Minneapolis, Minn, 79; Artists and Printer, Walker Art Ctr, Minneapolis, Minn, 80; Words as Images, Univ Chicago, Ill, 81; Comparaisons, Grand Palais, Paris, France, 84; Mile 4, Chicago Sculpture Int, Chicago, Il, 85; Atlantic Sculpture, Art Ctr, Pasadena, Calif, 87; A Matter of Time, Pa Acad Fine Arts, Philadelphia, 88; solo & group exhibs, Diane Brown Gallery, 86, 88, 89 & 90; Rope, Christian Leigh, Barcelona, Spain, 91; The Fabric Workshop, Philadelphia, 91; Lawrence Oliver, Philadelphia, 91; Kunsthall Gallery, New York, 92. *Collections Arranged:* Sexuality; The play of the World, an Evening of Performance, C A A Ann Conference, New York, 86; Atlantic Sculpture, Art Ctr, Pasadena, Calif, 87. *Teaching:* Vis artist sculpture, Kansas City Art Inst, Mo, 79; vis assoc prof sculpture, Univ Iowa, Iowa City, 79-81; instr sculpture, Minneapolis Col Art & Design, 81-82; assoc prof sculpture, Tyler Sch Art, Philadelphia, Pa, 84-90 & head sculpture dept, 86-90. *Awards:* Guggenheim Fel, 78; Nat Endowment Arts Fel, 81 & 88; Bush Found Fel, 82; Pew Fels Arts Grant, 91. *Bibliog:* Articles, Midwest Art & Art Am, 79; Bob Arnold (dir), Family Systems (film), 81. *Mem:* Col Art Asn Am. *Res:* Kitsch as it relates to the Great Sadness with continuing interest in Language, Commerce, & Sexuality. *Publ:* You Must Bend in Order to Go Through the World, (exhib catalog), Diane Brown Gallery, New York, 86; Atlantic Sculpture, Art Ctr, Pasadena, Calif, 87; Angels of Language, (exhib catalog), Crow Wing Press, Philadelphia, Pa, 88. *Mailing Add:* 312 Righter's Mill Rd Gladwyne PA 19035

BHAVSAR, NATVAR PRAHLADJI
PAINTER
b Gothava, India, Apr 7, 34. *Study:* Bombay State Higher Art Exam, India, AM, 58, Govt Dipl Art, 59; Gujarat Univ, India, BA, 60; Univ Pa, MFA, 65. *Work:* Whitney Mus Am Art, Metrop Mus Art, New York; Mass Inst Technol, Cambridge; Guggenheim Mus, New York; Australian Nat Gallery, Canberra; Wichita Mus Art; and others. *Exhib:* Whitney Mus Am Art Painting Ann, 70-71; Two Generations of Color Painting, Inst Contemp Art, Univ Pa, Philadelphia, 70; Beautiful Paintings & Sculpture, Jewish Mus, New York, 70; one-man shows, Max Hutchinson Gallery, New York, 71, 72, 77 & 78 & Gloria Luria Gallery, Miami, 78 & 92; Natvar Bhavsar-Color Experiences, 79, Twenty Years of Works on Paper (catalog), Wichita Art Mus, Kans, 85. *Teaching:* Art instr, Univ RI, spring semesters 67-69. *Awards:* John D Rockefeller III Fund Fel, 65-66; Guggenheim Fel, 75-76; Vishva Gurjari, Gvjarat, India, 88. *Bibliog:* Carter Ratcliff (auth), article, Art Int, 10/72; Elwyn Linn (auth), article, Art Int, 4/77. *Media:* Dry Pigment, Acrylic. *Mailing Add:* 131 Greene St New York NY 10012

BIALA, JANICE
PAINTER
b Biala, Poland, Oct 18, 03; US citizen. *Study:* Nat Acad Art, New York; Art Students League. *Work:* Whitney Mus, New York; Centre Contemp Art, Paris, France; Duncan Phillips Collection, Washington, DC; Mus Cantonal de Lausanne, Switz; Corcoran Gallery; Musee de Grenoble, France; Musee Ingres; and others. *Exhib:* Bignou Gallery, New York, 42; Jeanne Bucher Gallery, Paris, 46; Stable Gallery, New York & Le Point Cardinale, Paris, 61; Rina Gallery, Jerusalem, 63; Greenbaum Gallery, 78-85, 87; exposition, La Famille in Portrait, Mus Arts Decorative, Louvre Mus, 79; The Portrait, Mus Mod Art; Galerie Jocob, Paris, 87-88; Kouros Gallery, New York, 90. *Awards:* Chevaliér officies des Arts et Lettres, Paris; Medal, Jean Louis Wuerller. *Bibliog:* Biala paints a picture, Art News, 56; Chefs--d'oeuvre de l'art, Hachette, 65; Dora Vallier (auth), Biala, Pour l'Art, 60 & Rep-res la Peinture en France: 1870-1970, Alferi & Lacroix. *Mailing Add:* 8 Rue du General Bertrand Paris France

BIALOBRODA, ANNA
PAINTER
b Lodz, Poland, 1946. *Study:* Otis Art Inst, BFA, 71, MFA, 73; Whitney Mus Am Art Independent Study Prog, 73. *Work:* Albright-Knox Art Gallery; Chemical Bank, DeBevoise & Plimpton, E F Hutton Corp, Michael Blackwood Productions, Capitol Holding Group, Neuberger Berman & Atlantic Bell, New York, NY; European Fine Art Found, Geneva; Galerie Fahlbusch, Ludwigshafen, Ger; Arthur Andersen & Co, Chicago, ILL; and others. *Comn:* Zacheta Mus, Warsaw,Poland, 91; Jason McCoy Gallery, New York, 91; Simon Watson Gallery, New York, 91. *Exhib:* Galeria Krytyków Pokaz, Warsaw, Poland, 91; Shea & Bornstein Gallery, Santa Monica, Calif, 91; Contemp Arts Forum, Santa Barbara, Calif, 91; Simon Watson's Living Room, New York, NY, 92; White Columns, New York, NY, 92; and others. *Awards:* Nat Endowment Arts Grant, 74 & 75; NY Found Arts Grant, 91. *Bibliog:* Peggy Cyphers (auth), New York in Review, Arts Mag, summer 91; Rhonda Lieberman (auth), Anna Bialobroda, Artforum, summer 91; Eileen Myles (auth), Anna Bialobroda at Jason McCoy, Art in America, 12/91. *Media:* Miscellaneous. *Mailing Add:* P O Box 20237 New York NY 10009

BICKFORD, GEORGE
COLLECTOR
b Berlin, NH, Nov 28, 01. *Study:* Harvard Col, AB, 22, Harvard Law Sch, LLB, 26. *Pos:* Trustee & vpres, Cleveland Inst Art, Ohio, 55-; trustee, Cleveland Mus Art, 57-; trustee, Am Comt S Asian art; vis comt, Dept Fine Arts, Harvard Univ. *Teaching:* Lectr Indian hist & cult, Cleveland Col, 48-50. *Mem:* Am Asn Mus; Am Oriental Soc; Am Asn Asian Studies. *Collection:* East Indian antiquities. *Mailing Add:* 13415 Shaker Blvd Cleveland OH 44120

BICKLEY, GARY STEVEN
EDUCATOR, SCULPTOR
b Lebanon, Va, Apr 25, 53. *Study:* E Carolina Univ, BFA, 76; Univ Ga, MFA, 78. *Work:* Southeastern Ctr Contemp Art, Winston-Salem, NC; Portsmouth Community Arts Ctr, Va; City of Rockville, Md; First Nat Bank, Roanoke, Va. *Exhib:* Painting and Sculpture Today, Indianapolis Mus Art, 78; solo exhibs, Southeastern Ctr Contemp Art, Winston-Salem, NC, 78, 80 & 82; American Drawing III, Portsmouth Fac & Smithsonian Inst, traveling, 80; Rutgers Nat Works on Paper, Stedman Art Gallery, Camden, NJ, 81; Virginia Painting and Sculpture, Va Mus Fine Arts, Richmond, 81; Clayworks, New

York; Exhib 280, Huntington Galleries, WVa; 20 Sculptors Outdoor Exhib, Va Mus Fine Arts. *Teaching:* Asst prof, Va Polytech Inst & State Univ, Blacksburg, 78-; vis prof, Univ Ga, Cortona, Italy, 81. *Awards:* Ford Found Scholar, Univ Ga, 77-78; Summer Stipend, Nat Endowment Humanities, Va Polytech Inst & State Univ, 81; Work Stipend for Clayworks Workshop, Nat Endowment Arts. *Media:* Welded & Cast Metals. *Mailing Add:* Dept Art Virginia Polytechnic Inst 201 Draper Rd Blacksburg VA 24061

BIDDLE, JAMES
ADMINISTRATOR, COLLECTOR
b Philadelphia, Pa, July 8, 29. *Study:* Princeton Univ, BA, 51. *Pos:* Cur, Am Wing, Metrop Mus Art, 63-67; pres, Nat Trust Hist Preservation, Washington, DC, 67-80; chmn, Nat Preservation Inst & Preservation Coalition of Greater Philadelphia. *Mem:* Drawing Soc. *Mailing Add:* Box 158 Andalusia PA 19020

BIDDLE, LIVINGSTON LUDLOW, JR
ART ADMINISTRATOR
b Bryn Mawr, Pa, May 26, 18. *Study:* Princeton Univ, AB, 40; Mt St Mary Col, LHD, 78; Univ Cincinnati, Hon DFA, 79; Catholic Univ Am, Hon DL, 79; Long Island Univ, Hon DFA, 79; Providence Col, RI, Hon DFA, 80; Drexel Univ, Pa, Hon DLett, 80; Notre Dame Univ, Hon DFA, 80. *Pos:* Dep chmn, Nat Endowment Arts, 65-67, liaison dir, 74-76, chmn, 77-81; chmn div arts, Liberal Arts Col, Fordham Univ, 67-70; dir, Subcommittee, Educ Arts & Humanities, US Senate, 76-77; co-chmn, Fed Coun Arts & Humanities, 77-81. *Awards:* Distinguished Service Award, Asn Am Univ Presses, 79; Bronze Medallion for Outstanding Public Service, The Chapel of Four Chaplains, 80; Medal of Achievement, Philadelphia Arts Alliance, 80. *Mem:* Int Coun Fine Arts Deans. *Publ:* Author of works of fiction & non-fiction. *Mailing Add:* 3050 P Street NW Washington DC 20007

BIDLO, MIKE
PAINTER, CONCEPTUAL ARTIST
b Chicago, Ill, Oct 20, 53. *Study:* Univ Ill, Chicago, BA, 73; Southern Ill Univ, MFA, 75; Teachers Col, Columbia Univ, MA, 78. *Work:* Chase Manhattan Bank & New York Stock Exchange, New York; Omaha Nat Bank, Nebr; Mod Mus Stockholm; Fashion Inst Technol, Univ Colo, Boulder. *Exhib:* Grey Art Gallery, NY Univ, 89; Daniel Templon, Paris, 90; Sezon Mus, Japan, 91; Saatchi Collection, London, 91; Bruno Bischofberger Gallery, Zurich, Switz, 92; and others. *Teaching:* Guest lects, Art Ctr, Pasadena, 78, Pratt Inst, New York, 84, Univ Colo, Boulder, 85, Univ Calif, Los Angeles, 88, Otis Art Inst, Los Angeles, 88, Bard Col, 89 & State Univ Calif, Fullerton, 91. *Awards:* Fel Nat Endowment Arts. *Bibliog:* Peter Scheldal & Joe Masheck (auths), Bidlo's Pablo, Art in Am, spring 88; Robert Rosenblum (auth), Masterpieces (catalogue essay), Bischofberger Gallery, 89; Oliveier Zahm & Joe Mascheck (auths), Not Dechirico (catalog essays), Daniel Templon Gallery, 90; and others. *Mem:* Am Art Therapy Asn. *Media:* All. *Dealer:* Bruno Bischofberger Gallerie Zurich Switzerland. *Mailing Add:* 432 W 38th St New York NY 10018

BIEBER, ELINORE MARIA KOROW
PAINTER, INSTRUCTOR
b Akron, Ohio, July 31, 34. *Study:* Cleveland Inst Art, with Rolf Stoll, Paul Riba & John Teyral; Sienna Heights Womens Col; Sawyer Col Bus. *Work:* Hebrew Acad, Cleveland Heights, Ohio; Berkowitz Kumin Mem Chapel; Cleveland Play House Gallery; Bd Rm, Blue Cross/Blue Shield, Cleveland, Ohio. *Comn:* Portraits of Richard Oberlin, Dir, Playhouse Gallery, Collection, Cleveland; Rabbi Boruch Sorotzkin, Pres of Rabbinical Col Telshe, Wickliffe, Ohio; George Hilden, Pres of Osco Drugs, Chicago; Jerome Weinberger, Pres Gary Drugs, Cleveland; Charles Walgreen, Pres Walgreen Drugs, Chicago; and others. *Exhib:* Butler Inst Am Art, Youngstown, Ohio, 68-70; Nat Acad Design, New York, 73; World Trade Ctr, Am Artists Prof League, New York, 80; one-woman show, Chagrin Valley Little Theatre, Ohio, 80, Nat Acad Design, New York, 73; Miniature Painting Show, Bath, Ohio, 81; All Ohio-Canton Art Inst, 88; Boston Mills Nat Show, Peninsula, Ohio, 88; Mansfield Art Mus, 88; and many others. *Pos:* Staff artist & designer, Am Greeting Corp, Cleveland, 57-58 & 71-73. *Teaching:* Instr painting, drawing & portraiture, Eastern Campus Elders Prog, Cuyahoga Community Col, 79- *Awards:* Hon Mention, Valley Art Ctr, 17th Ann Exhib, 89; Hon Mention, Orange Arts Coun, 16th Ann Artists & Craftsman's Show, 89; Third Place, Drawing, Gallery East, Cuyahoga Community Col, 91; and many others. *Mem:* Charter mem Ohio Watercolor Soc; Women's Art Club Cleveland, 71-72; New Orgn Visual Arts; Am Portrait Soc; Am Artists Prof League; and others. *Media:* All. *Mailing Add:* 19201 Van Aken Blvd Apt 404 Shaker Heights OH 44122

BIEDERMAN, CHARLES (KAREL JOSEPH)
SCULPTOR
b Cleveland, Ohio, Aug 23, 06. *Study:* Art Inst Chicago, 26-29; Minneapolis Col Art & Design, Hon DFA, 73. *Work:* Tate Gallery, London; Walker Art Gallery; Albright-Knox Art Gallery, Buffalo; Dallas Mus Fine Arts, Tex; Milwaukee Art Ctr; Weisman Art Found; Minneapolis Inst Arts; Metrop Mus, Whitney Mus, New York; Philadelphia Mus; Carnegie Mus, Pittsburgh; Kroller-Muller Mus, Otterlo. *Comn:* Three constructionist pieces, Interstate Med Clin, Red Wing, Minn, 40; work in pub plaza, Nat Endowment Arts, Red Wing, 71. *Exhib:* One-man show, Gallery 12, Minneapolis, 71; retrospectives, Walker Art Ctr, Minneapolis, 65, Hayward Gallery, London, 69, Minneapolis Inst Arts, 76 & Grace Borgenicht Gallery, New York, 80 & 82; De Stijl 1917-1931, Walker Art Ctr, Minneapolis, Minn, 82; Abstract Painting and Sculpture in America 1927-1944, Mus Art, Carnegie Inst, Pittsburgh, Pa, 83-84; Hirshorn Sculpture Garden, Smithsonian Inst, Washington, DC; Stedelijk Mus, Amsterdam & Kroller-Muller Mus, Otterloo, Netherland; Beyond the Plane, American Constructions 1930-1965, NJ State Mus, 83; The Art Gallery, Univ Md, 84; San Francisco Mus Mod Art, Calif; Minneapolis Inst Arts, Minn & Whitney Mus Am Art, NY, 84. *Awards:* Ford Found Purchase Award, 64; Nat Coun Arts Grant, 66; Nat Endowment Arts Award, 73. *Bibliog:* Jan van der Marck (auth), Charles Biederman & the structurist direction in art, Feistbundel F vanderMeer, 66; Leif Sjoberg (auth), London ahead of New York?, Studies in the 20th Century, 71; Alastair Grieve (auth), Charles Biederman and the English Constructionists, 1, Biederman and Victor Pasmore, Burlington Mag, 9/82; Alastair Grieve (auth), Charles Biederman and the English Constructionists, 2, an exchange of theories about abstact art during the 1950's, Burlington Mag, 2/84. *Media:* Aluminum. *Publ:* Auth, Letters on the New Art, 51; The New Cezanne, 58; Dialogue II, Creative or Conditioned Vision, Faber, 68; A Note on New Arts, Studio Int, 70; Art-Science-Reality, 88. *Dealer:* Grace Borgenicht Gallery 724 Fifth Ave New York NY. *Mailing Add:* Rte 2 Red Wing MN 55066

BIEDERMAN, JAMES MARK
PAINTER, SCULPTOR
b New York, NY, Nov 8, 47. *Study:* Whitney Mus Independent Study prog; Yale Univ, MFA, 73. *Work:* Kroller-Muller Riks Mus, Otterlo, Netherlands; Pompidou Ctr, Paris; Mus Mod Art & Metrop Mus Art, New York; Mus Contemp Art, Chicago; Hirshorn Mus, Washington, DC. *Comn:* Wall sculpture, Home Box Off, New York, 85. *Exhib:* Sculpture, Clocktower Gallery, New York, 81; 2nd International Jugend, Kunsthalle, Nuremberg, WGer, 82; Choix Pour Aujourd'hui, Ctr Pompidou, Paris, 82; Documenta 7, Kassel, WGer, 82; Kunstmuseum Aalborg & Rander, Denmark, 83; Mus Mod Art, New York; Triennale, Musee Cantonal des Beaux Arts, Lausanne, Switz; Geometric Abstraction, Bronx Mus, New York, 85. *Teaching:* Vis artist sculpture, Boston Mus Sch, 83 & Yale Univ, formerly; painting, New York Univ, 84-86. *Awards:* Nat Endowment Arts Drawing Award, 79 & Sculpture Award, 82; Painting Award, New York Found Arts, 86. *Bibliog:* Ronnie Cohn (auth), rev, Art Forum, 4/83; Himmel Freeman (auth), New Art, Harry Abrams, 84; Curt Barnes (ed), Contructed PTH, Art J, spring 91; and others. *Media:* Oil on Linen, Oil on Wood. *Dealer:* John Weber Gallery 142 Greene St New York 10012; Galerie Winkelman Neubrückstabe 12 Düsseldorf Fed Repub Ger. *Mailing Add:* Jaycox Rd Rd 2 Box 392 Cold Springs NY 10516

BIELER, TED ANDRE
EDUCATOR, SCULPTOR
b Kingston, Ont, July 23, 38. *Study:* Sculpture with Ossip Zadkine, Paris, 53; tapestry with Jean Lurcat, St Cere, France, 54; Slade Sch Art, London, 54; Cranbrook Acad Art, BFA, 61. *Work:* Montreal Mus Fine Arts; Can Coun, Ottawa; Univ Toronto; Agnes Etherington Art Centre, Queen's Univ, Kingston; McMaster Univ; York Univ. *Comn:* Star-Cross'd (sculpture ballet set), comn by Brian MacDonald, Ottawa, 73; stainless steel sculpture, Forensic Sci Bldg, Govt Ont, 75; aluminum tetrahedra sculpture, Portsmouth Harbour, Kingston, Govt Can, 75; sculpture for Govt of Can Bldg, comn by Macy Dubois & Shore Tilbe Henschel Irwin, Architects, Toronto, 77; cast aluminum relief sculpture for Wilson Sta, comn by Spadina Subway Line, Toronto, 78; and others. *Exhib:* Signs & Symbols, Art Gallery Ont Traveling Show, 71; Rehearsal, Harbourfront Art Gallery, Toronto, 77; one-man shows, York Univ, 77 & Univ Rochester, 77; Performance, Harbourfront Art Gallery, Toronto, Ont, 78; Monumental Sculpture, Toronto Dominion Ctr, 78. *Teaching:* Prof sculpture, York Univ, 70- *Awards:* Allied Arts Medal, Royal Archit Asn Can, 69. *Bibliog:* L Sabbath (auth), Sculpture in Canada, 62 & H McPherson (auth), Scope of Sculpture in '64, 64, Can Art; William Withrow (auth), Canadian Sculpture, Graph, Montreal, 67; R Burnett & M Schiff (coauths), Contemporary Canadian Art, Hurtig Publ, 83. *Mem:* Royal Can Acad Arts (mem coun, 75-77); Int Sculpture Ctr, Lawrence, Kans. *Mailing Add:* Visual Arts Dept York Univ 4700 Keele St Downsview ON M3J 1P3 Canada

BIERLY, EDWARD J
PAINTER, ILLUSTRATOR
b Buffalo, NY, Apr 23, 20. *Study:* Univ Buffalo, NY, BFA, 49. *Work:* Mar de Plata Lace, Int Mus Horse, Lexington, Ky. *Comn:* Mohini & Cub (print), Smithsonian Save the Tiger Fund, 71; Snow Leopard (print), NY Zoological Soc, Buffalo, 75; Bluebirds of America (prints), Campfire Inc, 83. *Exhib:* One-man shows, Abercrombie & Fitch, New York, 68, Nat Zoo, Washington, DC, 73, Nat Wildlife Fedn, Washington, 74, 83 & 91 & Broadway Gallery, Fairfax, Va, 88; Am Natural Hist Art Show, James Ford Bell Mus, Minneapolis, Minn, 71; Animals in Art, Royal Ontario Mus, Toronto, Can, 75; Soc Animal Artists, Acad Natural Sci, Philadelphia, 81. *Pos:* Free-lance illusr, 49-56; mus exhibs designer, Nat Park Service, Washington, DC, 56-70; free-lance artist, 70- *Awards:* Winner Migratory Waterfowl Hunting Stamp Competition, 56-57, 63-64 & 70-71. *Bibliog:* Prints Mag, fall 80; Wildlife Art News, 11-12/92. *Mem:* Soc Animal Artists. *Media:* Oil, Acrylic. *Publ:* Illusr, Mammals of the Southwest Mountains & Mesas, Southwest Monuments Asn, 61; Mammals Rhodesia, Zambia & Malawi, Collins, London, 66; Grzimeks Tierleben, Kindler, Munchen, 72; auth & illusr, Nat Wildlife & International Wildlife Mag, Nat Wildlife Fedn, 72-84; illusr, The History of Wildlife in America, Nat Wildlife Fedn, 75. *Dealer:* Broadway Gallery 11213-J Lee Hwy Fairfax VA 22030; McBride Gallery 215 Main St Annapolis MD 21401. *Mailing Add:* c/o EJB Editions 8833 Lake Hill Dr Lorton VA 22079

BIERMAN, IRENE A
EDUCATOR
b Bogota, NJ. *Study:* Harvard Univ, MA, 66; Univ Chicago, PhD, 80. *Collections Arranged:* The Warp & Weft of Islam (auth catalog), Seattle, Portland & Tocoma, Reno, 79; The Common Cord, Seattle Art Mus, 86;

Permanent Near East Collection, Seattle Art Mus. *Teaching:* Vis lectr Islamic art hist, Univ Wash, Seattle, 76-80; assoc prof Islamic art hist, Univ Calif, Los Angeles, 82- *Awards:* Fel, Ctr for Advanced Study in the Visual Arts, 81-83; Fel, Am Res Ctr Egypt, 80-81; Fulbright-Hays Fel to Egypt & Turkey, 81-82. *Mem:* Col Art Asn; Middle East Studies Asn; Am Oriental Soc; Am Res Ctr Egypt; NAm Hist Islamic Art. *Res:* Public arts in the Islamic world with emphasis on the Mediterranean areas. *Publ:* Coauth, The Warp & Weft of Islam, Univ Washington, 78; auth, The message of Urban Space: The Case of Crete, Espace et Sociétée; Oriental Carpets, In: Decorative Arts & Household Furnishings Used in Am, Winterthur Mus, 86; co-auth, Symbols of Islam, Univ Wash Int Studies, 86; auth, The fatimid public text, In: Actes, Congres International de l'Histoire de l'arte XXVI, 86; co-ed, Urban Structure and Social Order: The Ottoman City and its Parts, Caratzas Bros, New York, 91. *Mailing Add:* Dept Art Design & Art Hist Univ Calif 405 Hilgard Ave Los Angeles CA 90024

BIFERIE, DAN (DANIEL ANTHONY), JR
PHOTOGRAPHER, EDUCATOR
b Miami, Fla, Dec 17, 50. *Study:* Daytona Beach Community Col, AS(with honors), 71; Ohio Univ, BFA(summa cum laude), 72, MFA, 74. *Work:* High Mus; New Orleans Mus Art; Baltimore Mus Art; Santa Barbara Mus Art; Bibliotheque Nationale, Paris; Nat Mus Am Art. *Exhib:* One-man show, Albany Mus Art, 86, Lakeland's Unique Architectural Heritage, Polk Mus Art, Fla, 87; Four Photographers, Mass Inst Technol, Boston, 76; Fla Light Invitational, Orlando Mus Art, Fla, 79; Four Southeastern Photographers, Contemp Arts Ctr, New Orleans, La, 81; Contemporary Photography as Phantasy (with catalog), Santa Barbara Mus Art, 82-83; Fact & Fiction: The State of Florida Photography (traveling exhib), Norton Gallery Art, West Palm Beach, Fla, 90. *Pos:* Found, Gallery Fine Arts, Daytona Beach Community Col, Fla, 78-90, chmn visual arts dept, 85-88. *Teaching:* Instr photog, Daytona Beach Community Col, Fla, 75- *Awards:* Our Children to the South Photo-documentary project Grant, Fla, Int Alliance, 85; Lakelands Architectural Heritage, Photo-documentary Grant, Polk Mus Art; Fla Endowment for the Humantities. *Bibliog:* Lakeland's Unique Architectural Heritage (exhib catalog) Polk Mus Art, 87; The New Movement, Focal Point Press, 87; Churchscapes in Black & White (studio photog), 88. *Mem:* Soc Photog Educ (pres 77-84); Daytona Beach Community Col Photog Soc (founder & pres 79-81); Fla Art Mus Dirs Asn; Am Asn Mus; Arts Coun Volusia Co (pres, 91-). *Media:* Silver Print. *Res:* History and criticism of photography, photographic aesthetics. *Publ:* Contribr, Photographic Annual, Middle Tenn State Univ, 75; Florida Light, Loch Haven Art Ctr, 79; Photographers Forum, Darkroom Section, 81; Photography in Florida, Catskill Ctr for Photog Quart Mag, 85; Churchscapes, Studio Photog, 88. *Mailing Add:* Daytona Beach Community Col PO Box 2811 Daytona Beach FL 32115

BIGELOW, ANITA (ANNE EDWIGE LOURIE)
GRAPHIC ARTIST, PRINTMAKER
b Los Angeles, Calif, Mar 3, 46. *Study:* Reed Col, with Llyod Reynolds & Willard Midgette, BA, 67; San Francisco Art Inst, with Jack Stauffacher & Gerry Gooch: Portland State Univ, MA, 75; Portland Community Col, AA, 85. *Work:* Lloyd Reynolds Collection, Portland Mus Art, Ore. *Comn:* Bookplates (set of 4), comn by Mary Barnard, Vancouver, Wash, 79-81; bookplates (set of 10), Reed Col Libr, Portland, Ore, 81; bookplates (set of 2), Boston Atheneum, Mass, 82. *Exhib:* Contemporary Ex-Libris 1980-1982, XIX Int Ex-Libris Cong, Oxford, Eng, 82. *Media:* Woodcut, Linoleum Cut; Pastel, Pencil. *Publ:* Illusr, Mississippi Mud and various articles-items, Joel Weinstein, 82-86; Time and the White Tigress, B Breitenbush Books, 86. *Mailing Add:* 2922 SE Salmon Portland OR 97214

BIGELOW, ROBERT CLAYTON
EDUCATOR, PAINTER
b Los Angeles, Calif, July 31, 40. *Study:* Chouinard Art Inst, BFA, 67. *Work:* Gruenwald Graphic Arts Found, Univ Calif, Los Angeles; Mus Mod Art, New York; Nat Gallery Can, Ottawa; Can Coun Art Bank, Ottawa; Bank of Montreal, Can. *Exhib:* Two-man show, Univ Calgary, Alta, 69; Contemp Am Prints, Krannert Art Mus, Univ Ill, 70; Contemp Prints & Drawings, Hartnell Col Art, Salinas, Calif, 71; Otis Art Inst Gallery, Los Angeles, 74; Prints & Drawings from The West Coast, traveling, Can, 75. *Pos:* Printer, Gemini Gel, Los Angeles, Calif, 66-67 & 74-75; asst mgr & printer, Tyler Workshop, 75-76; studio mgr, Robert Motherwell, Greenwich, Conn, 76-78. *Teaching:* Instr painting, Vancouver Sch Art, BC, 60-70; sr lectr lithography, Nottingham Col Art, UK, 72-73; MFA dir studio arts, Concordia Univ, 78 & 83. *Awards:* Tamarind Fel, Ford Found, 66; Canada Coun Grants, Can Govt, 69 & 70. *Media:* Oil, Acrylic; Lithography. *Publ:* Coauth, Reconciliation Elergy, Rizzoli Int Publ, 80; contribr, The Painter and the Printer, Am Fedn Art, 80. *Dealer:* Don Stewart Gallery 1460 Ouest Rue Sherbrooke Montreal PQ Canada H3G 1K4. *Mailing Add:* Facility of Fine Arts Concordia Univ 1455 Demaisonneuve Blvd W U-G Williams Montreal PQ H3G 1M8 Canada

BIGGER, MICHAEL D
SCULPTOR
b Waukegan, Ill, Oct 10, 37. *Study:* Miami Univ, Oxford, Ohio, BA(archit), 66; RI Sch Design, MFA(sculpture), 68. *Work:* Oakland Mus Art, Calif; Evansville Mus Arts & Sci, Ind; Atlantic Richfield Collection, Los Angeles; Embarcadero Ctr, San Francisco; Vassar Col. *Comn:* Monumental sculpture, Provincial Govt Man, Thompson, 77; large-scale sculpture, First Nat Bank, Erie, Pa, 80; monumental sculpture, Cincinnati Zoological Soc; Univ Maine, Augusta. *Exhib:* Annual Contemporary Sculpture, Whitney Mus Am Art, 68; Structured Art, DeCordova Mus, Lincoln, Mass, 69; Sculpture on the Prairies, Winnipeg Art Gallery, Man, 77; 25th Ann, Longview Mus, Tex, 83; Int Art Expos, Navy Pier, Chicago, 83; Fifth Tex Sculpture Symp, Dallas, 85; Melnychenko Gallery, Winnipeg, 90; Minneapolis Col Art & Design Fac Exhib, 91; Adelle M Gallery, Dallas, 91; Gallery Artists, Flanders Contemp Art, Minneapolis, 92. *Teaching:* Instr 3-D design, Atlanta Sch Art, 70-71; chmn sculpture dept, Univ Man, Winnipeg, 75-79; asst prof, Univ Tex, San Antonio, 81-88; assoc prof, Minneapolis Col Art & Design, 88-; vis artist bronze casting, Univ Maine, Augusta, summer 90. *Awards:* Olivetti Award Sculpture, 23rd Ann New England Exhib, 72; Judge's Award, Drawing & Small Sculpture, Galveston Art Ctr, 81; First Prize, Expos Plaza Sculpture Competition, 4-M Properties, 81. *Media:* Multi-Media. *Mailing Add:* 237 SE Arthur Ave Minneapolis MN 55414

BIGGERS, JOHN THOMAS
EDUCATOR, PAINTER
b Gastonia, NC, Apr 13, 24. *Study:* Hampton Inst, 41-46; Pa State Univ, BS & MS(art educ), 48, DEduc, 54. *Work:* Houston Mus Fine Arts; Dallas Mus Fine Arts; Reader's Digest Collection; Tex Southern Univ; Golden State Mutual Life Ins Co. *Exhib:* Tex Contemp Artist, M Knoedler & Co, New York, 52; Regional & Nat Drawing Soc Exhib, Houston & New York, 65; one-man show, Houston Mus Fine Arts, 68; Tex Painting & Sculpture, the 20th century, six Tex mus & galleries, 71-72; Reflections: The Afro-Am Artist, Benton Conv Ctr, Winston-Salem, NC, 72. *Pos:* Mem, Houston Fine Arts Comn, 68-72 & Tex Fine Arts Comn, Houston, 70-73. *Teaching:* Distinguished prof painting, drawing & art hist, Tex Southern Univ, Houston, 49-, head art dept, currently. *Awards:* Art Fel in Africa, UNESCO, 57. *Bibliog:* Cedric Dover (auth), American Negro Art, New York Graphic Soc, 60; Ralph E Shikes (auth), The Indignant eye, Beacon Press, 69; Elton Fax (auth), 17 Black Artists, Dodd, Mead, 71. *Mem:* Fel Int Inst Arts & Lett; Tex Col Art Asn; Tex Fine Arts Soc; Nat Soc Mural Painters; Pa State Grad Club in Art Educ. *Media:* Conte Crayon; Oil & Tempera. *Res:* African art and culture. *Publ:* Auth, Ananse, Web of Life in Africa, 69; illusr, Good earth, Readers' Digest Series, 66; illusr, I Momolu, Crowell Co, 66; illusr, Cross timbers, Univ Tex, 66; contribr, Afro-American Art, Van Nostrand Reinhold Co, 72. *Mailing Add:* 3338 Prospect St Houston TX 77004

BIGGERSTAFF, MYRA
PAINTER, DESIGNER
b Logansport, Ind, Feb 6, 05. *Study:* Bethany Col, Lindsborg, Kans, BFA, 32; Swedish Royal Acad, 40-42; Columbia Univ, New York, MFA, 53. *Work:* Mus Nebr Art, Kearney; John F Kennedy Mem Mus, Dorchester, Mass; The Sheldon Mem Galleries, Lincoln, Nebr. *Exhib:* Solo exhibs, Alebys Art Gallery, Grand Hotel Royal, Stockholm, Sweden, Joslyn Mus, Omaha, Nebr, 47, White Mus, San Antonio, 49, Mus Art Kearney, Nebr, 88 & Agora Gallery, New York, 92; participated in nat exhibs in New York for over 30 years. *Pos:* Chair, Textile Design Dept, Fashion Inst, 69-72. *Teaching:* Assoc prof fine arts, Trinity Univ, San Antonio, Tex, 48-50; assoc prof design, Fashion Inst Technol, New York, 60-72. *Awards:* Bainbridge Watercolor Award Nat Acad, 60; Watercolor Award, Nat Arts Club, 77; Ethel Lerer Keller Award, Nat Asn Women Artists, 79 & 80; over 20 other awards from nat exhibs. *Bibliog:* Watercolorist of the month, Am Artist, 4/53; Les Krantz (auth), article, New York Art Rev, 88, article, Am Artists, 90; Articles in Manhattan Arts Mag, 2/92, Art Speak, 4/92. *Mem:* Nat Asn Women Artists; Audubon Artists Inc; Pastel Soc Am. *Media:* Watercolor, Oil. *Mailing Add:* 1609 14th St Auburn NE 68305

BIGGS, JANET
PAINTER
b Harrisburg, Pa, Jan 12, 59. *Study:* Moore Col Art, BFA, 81; RI Sch Design, 83. *Exhib:* Made in Philadelphia (catalog), Inst Contemp Art, Pa, 87; Membership Has Its Privileges, Lang & O'Hara Gallery, New York, 90; Shared Skin: Sub-Social Identifiers (catalog), Dooley Le Cappellaine Gallery, New York, 91; Josh Baer Gallery, New York, 92; Kunsthall, New York, 92. *Awards:* Painting Fel, Nat Endowment Arts, 89-90; Project Grant, Art Matters, 90. *Bibliog:* Roberta Smith (auth), The group show as crystal ball, NY Times, 7/6/90; Gretchen Faust (auth), New York reviews, review of Shared Skin: Sub-Social Identifiers, Arts Mag, 1/92; Kim Levin (auth), Village Voice, 7/21/92 & 8/11/92. *Mailing Add:* 121 Essex St New York NY 10002

BILLECI, ANDRE GEORGE
SCULPTOR, EDUCATOR
b New York, NY, Dec 2, 33. *Study:* State Univ NY Col of Ceramics, Alfred, BFA(ceramics; cum laude), 60, MFA(ceramic art), 61. *Work:* Corning Mus of Glass, NY; Toledo Mus Art; Australian Nat Gallery, Canberra; Galleries Nat de Prague, Czech; Mus für Kunsthandwerk, Frankfurt, Ger. *Comn:* Glass sculptures, Penn Mutual Life Insurance, 84 & E I Du Pont de Nemours, 85. *Exhib:* One-man shows, Mus Contemp Crafts, New York, 70, Corning Mus Glass, 72 & NY State Col Ceramics, Alfred Univ, 80; Reflection, Long Beach Mus Art, Calif, 71; Int Glass Sculpture, Huntington Galleries, WVa, 76; Glassmaking & Purchase Exhib, Corning Mus Glass, 76; and others. *Pos:* Artist-in-residence, Blenko Art Glass Co, Milton, WVa, 71 & Steuben Glass Co, Corning, NY, 72; consult, Corning Mus Glass, India Proj, 86 & 87 & Mary McFadden Inc, New York, 80. *Teaching:* Prof sculpture & glass, State Univ NY Col, Alfred, 61-88 & Summer Sch, Sheridan Col of Applied Arts & Technol, Toronto, Ont, 7; lectr, Cleveland Art Inst, 78, Carnegie-Mellon Univ, 78, Univ Ill, Champaign-Urbana, 79 & Univ Wis, 81; lectr, Fundacion Centro del Vidrio, La Granja, Spain & Centre del Vidre de Barcelona, Spain, 90; Glass Seminar, Glass Technol for Artists, State Univ New York, Col Ceramics, Alfred, 91, lectr, Elderhostel Program on Ceramic Arts, 92; retired, currently. *Awards:* Nat Sci Found Res Travel Grant, Indian Hand Glass Mfgr; Corning Glass Found Grant, 76. *Mem:* Int Sculpture Ctr; Am Ceramic Soc;

Comt XVII Int Cong Glass, Delhi, India. *Media:* Glass; Mixed. *Publ:* Auth, Electric Melting Unit for Covered Melting, Corning Mus of Glass, 76; Annealing Glasses & Understanding Glass Calculations, Glass Studio Mag Publ Develop Corp, 78 & 79. *Mailing Add:* Thurston Studio RD 1 Box 408 Campbell NY 14821

BILLIAN, CATHEY R
SCULPTOR, EDUCATOR
b Chicago, Ill. *Study:* Art Inst Chicago, Univ Ariz, BFA, 71; Pratt Inst, fel, MFA, 77. *Work:* Philadelphia Mus Art; New York Pub Libr Print Collection; Morris Mus; Norton Simon Inc & Chem Bank, New York; Brooklyn Mus; Nat Park Serv; City of Phoenix, Ariz; US Forest Serv; and others. *Comn:* sculpture, Creative Time, Battery Park, New York, 81; light, sculpture & dance environment, Whitney Mus, 84; sculpture, Prospect Park, New York, 85; archit sculpture, United States Forest Service: Southwest Region, 90- & City of Phoenix, 92. *Exhib:* Recent Trends in Light, Morris Mus, 83 & Hofstra Univ (with catalog), 83; Stopped Time, Four Projected Environments, Sculpture Ctr, New York & Rockland Ctr Arts (with catalog), 84; Recent Acquisitions/Louis Comfort Tiffany Foundation Purchase, Brooklyn Mus, NY; Cathey Billian, Michael Graves, Charles Simonds at Liberty State Park, Jersey City Mus, (with catalog); New York Experimental Glass, Soc Art Craft, Pittsburgh, Pa (with catalog); Luminous Visions, FIT Gallery, New York (with catalog); Four Sculptors from the NY Experimental Glassworks, Nina Owen Ltd, Chicago, Ill; one-man shows, Cross-Cut Piedra Lumbre, Pratt Inst Gallery, New York, Ctr Contemp Art, Santa Fe, NMex, Frozen Moments, Gallery of NY Experimental Glassworks & Future Antiquities, Whitney Mus Sculpture Court, NY. *Pos:* Consult, Artpark, NY; NY & NJ State Coun Arts, 82-; artist in residence, NY Experimental Glassworks; Bob Blackburn's Printmaking Workshop, NY, Nat Park Serv, Utah, Dept of Interior, NMex & Del Water Gap, NJ; corresp, Pub Art Review. *Teaching:* Lectr current art topics, Columbia Univ, Brown Univ & NY State Coun on the Humanities; instr, Parsons Sch, 80-81, Pratt Inst Grad Dept, 80, Rutgers Univ, 80-82; vis asst prof, Pratt Inst, 84- *Awards:* Sculpture Fel, Nat Endowment for the Arts, 84; Proj Grant, NY Coun Art, Whitney Mus, 85. *Bibliog:* Lucy Lippard (auth), Overlay: Contemporary Art and the Art of Prehistory, 83; Cathey Billian/Frozen Moments, Craft Int, 6/88; Lynn Miller (auth), Lives and Works - 14 Women Artists, 92. *Mem:* Nat Ed Bd, Pub Art Rev; Int Sculpture Ctr; Col Art Asn; fel, Hirsch Farm Proj Environ Art. *Media:* Mixed; Light Environments & Objects. *Dealer:* Elise Meyer Gallery 477 Broome St New York NY 10013. *Mailing Add:* 456 Broome St New York NY 10013

BILLMYER, JOHN EDWARD
DRAFTSMAN, EDUCATOR
b Denver, Colo, Aug 17, 12. *Study:* Univ Denver; Kirkland Sch Art; Case Western Reserve Univ, BA & MA; also study abroad. *Work:* Cleveland Mus Art; Denver Art Mus. *Exhib:* Cleveland Mus Art; Denver Art Mus, 47-68 & Metrop Show, 52-67; five shows, Syracuse Mus Fine Art, 48-56; Wichita Mus Art, 51, 55 & 57; Colorado Springs Fine Arts Ctr, 60; and others. *Mem:* Denver Art Mus (trustee, 62-71); Col Art Asn Am. *Mailing Add:* 7301 E Placita Sinaloa Tucson AZ 85710

BILLS, LINDA
SCULPTOR, CRAFTSPERSON
b New York, NY, July 22, 43. *Study:* Beaver Col, BFA, 65. *Work:* Am Craft Mus, New York; Erie Art Mus, Pa. *Exhib:* American Baskets: The Eighties, Chicago Pub Libr, 88; The Tactile Vessel (with catalog), Erie Art Mus, Pa, 88 & Am Craft Mus, New York, 89; Md Invitational 1989, Baltimore Mus Art; Meeting Ground: Basket Traditions & Sculptural Forms, The Forum, St Louis, Mo, 90 & Art Mus, Ariz State Univ, 90; Recent Acquisitions, Am Craft Mus, New York, 92. *Awards:* Swan Prize, Philadelphia Craft Show, Swan Gallery, 87; Visual Artist Fel Grant, Nat Endowment Arts, 88, 90 & 92; Grant-In-Aid, Md State Arts Coun, 89. *Bibliog:* Jack Lenor Larsen curator, The Tactile Vessel, Erie Art Mus, 89; Margo Shermeta (auth), Linda Bills: a balance between strength & delicacy, 9-10/91 & Patricia Malarche (auth), The vessel form, summer 92, Fiber Arts Mag. *Media:* Miscellaneous. *Mailing Add:* 3000 Chestnut Ave No 343C Baltimore MD 21211

BILLS, MITCHELL
DESIGNER, VIDEO ARTIST
b Auburn, NY, Dec 23, 50. *Study:* Tyler Sch Art Temple Univ with Joe Scorsone & Peter D'Agostino, MFA, 84. *Work:* Tyler Sch Art Libr, Elkins Park, Pa; Intermedia Arts Minn; Pa State Univ Libr, University Park; Experimental Television Ctr, Owego, NY, 91; UCLA Film & Television Arch, Los Angeles, 92. *Exhib:* Univ & the Arts, Wayne State Univ, Detroit, Mich, 89; 48th Ann Juried Show, Sioux City Fine Arts Ctr, Iowa, 89; Siggraph 92: 19th Int Conf on Computer Graphics & Interactive Techniques, Chicago, 92. *Pos:* Design assoc, Home Viewer Publ, Philadelphia, 85-88. *Teaching:* Asst prof graphic design, SDak State Univ, Brookings, 88-90 & Southern Conn State Univ, 90- *Awards:* Second Place Award, Prof/Experimental Video, Video 12 regional juried competition, 92. *Mem:* Arts Coun of Greater New Haven/Media Arts Ctr; Col Art Asn. *Media:* Computer, Video. *Publ:* Auth & illusr, Zero Through One; Poems & Drawings, Moonlight Express, 84; auth, Dog star man, Home Viewer, 88. *Mailing Add:* 75A Fairview Ave Hamden CT 06514

BILOUS, PRISCILLA HALEY See Haley, Priscilla J

BIMROSE, ARTHUR SYLVANUS, JR
CARTOONIST
b Spokane, Wash, Mar 18, 12. *Study:* San Francisco Art Inst Col, 31; Univ Ore, 33. *Work:* State Hist Soc, Mo; Wayne State Univ; Libr Cong; Lyndon Johnson Libr; John F Kennedy Libr. *Exhib:* Pavilion of Humor: Man and his World, Montreal, Can; Festival of Cartoon Art, Ohio State Univ; Ore Hist Soc, Portland, 89. *Pos:* Free-lance commercial artist, 34-37; staff artists, Oregonian, Portland, 37-39, ed cartoonist, 49-83; retired. *Awards:* Freedoms Found Award, 52, 61 & 65; Bronze Smokey Award, US Forest Serv, 81. *Mailing Add:* 1632 SW Westwood Ct Portland OR 97201

BINAI, PAUL FREYE
PAINTER, ART CURATOR
b Lancaster, Pa, July 3, 32. *Study:* Ind Univ, with Alton Pickens & Leo Steppat, AB & MFA; Yale Univ; Ecole Fontainebleau, Paris, France, Walter Damrosch Fel for Study Painting, 62. *Work:* Purdue Univ Art Ctr; Carnegie Mellon Univ; Westinghouse Corp, Pittsburgh, Pa; Univ Pittsburgh. *Exhib:* Am Fedn Arts, 64-65; one-man shows, Miami Mus Mod Art, Ligoa Duncan Gallery, New York & Raymond Duncan Gallery, Paris, 64; Univ of Pittsburgh, 85; Joy Horwich Gallery, Chicago, 88-91; Katharina Rich Parlow Gallery, NY, 92. *Pos:* Asst cur graphic arts, Detroit Inst Art, 71-75; cur, Mus Art, Carnegie Inst, Pittsburgh, PA, 73-80; cur Fine Arts, Southern Alleghenies Mus Art, Loretto, PA, 89- *Teaching:* Instr art & design, Purdue Univ, 60-64; instr art, Akron Art Inst, 64-68; instr, Chatham Col, Pittsburgh, Pa, 77-78 & Univ Pittsburgh, Informal Prog, 82-; vis artist-lithography, Carnegie Mellon Univ, 87. *Awards:* Purdue Univ Res Found Grant, 61; Visual Arts Grants, Pa Coun on Arts, 86-87; Pa Coun Arts, grants 86-87. *Mem:* Col Art Asn Am; Del Ctr Contemp Arts; Pa Coun Arts (mus adv panel, 90-). *Publ:* The Eighties: A Post Pop Generation, 90; Against the Grain: Image in American Art, 91; auth, Beyond Realism: Image and Enigma, 92. *Mailing Add:* 616 Walnut St Hollidaysburg PA 16648

BINDER, ERWIN
SCULPTOR
b Philadelphia, Pa, Jan 24, 34. *Study:* Otis Art Inst, 62, Gemological Inst Am, 64. *Work:* Palm Springs Desert Mus, Calif; Hebrew Univ Jerusalem; Butler Inst Am Art, Youngstown, Ohio; Univ Judaism, Los Angeles. *Comn:* Marilyn & Monty Hall Statesman Award, Home of the Aged; Solitude, United ChemiCon, Inc, Brea, Calif, 88; Faceless Crowd, Louis & Co, Brea, Calif; Int Soc of the Benefactors, comn by Tel Aviv Univ, Beverly Hills, Calif; First Experience, Paul Amir & Co, Beverly Hills, Calif. *Exhib:* 20th Century Mexican Masters, Palm Springs Desert Mus, Palm Springs, Calif, 79; Oklahoma Art Ctr, Oklahoma City, 80; solo exhib, Otis Parsons Inst, Los Angeles, 84; Solitude, When Sculpture & Music Are One, Calif Inst Arts, Los Angeles, 85; 75th Diamond Jubilee, Cushman Art Ctr, Burbank, Calif, 86; The Art of Love, Riverside Art Mus, Calif; and others. *Awards:* Beautification Award for outstanding public art work for 1990, City of Brea, Calif. *Bibliog:* Gerald Schiller (dir), Sculptures of Binder (film), S & L Producions, 81; Claude Lesuer, New talent is coming from new areas, Art Speaks, 83; Greg Baxton, Dedication of a war shrine, Los Angeles Times, 88. *Mem:* Intl Sculpture Ctr (prof level, 88); Bilingual Found Arts (trustee, 88). *Media:* Bronze, Marble. *Mailing Add:* Topaz Universal Inc 4632 W Magnolia Blvd Burbank CA 91505

BINGHAM, ALICE
ART DEALER, CONSULTANT
b Memphis, Tenn, Dec 9, 36. *Study:* Bennett Col, AA, 56; Univ Florence, Italy; Memphis State Univ; Memphis Col Art. *Collections Arranged:* First Tennessee Heritage Collection Traveling Exhibit (auth, catalog), 83; Dulin Gallery Art, Knoxville, 83; Hunter Mus Art, Chattanooga, 83; Fine Arts Ctr-Cheekwood, Nashville, 83-84; Holiday Corp Art Collection, 85-86. *Pos:* Cur, First Tenn Bank Collection, 79-92; pres, Alice Bingham Gallery, 79-90; bd dir, Art Today, Memphis Brooks Mus Art, 84-92; trustee, Memphis Col Art, 85-; partner, Schmidt-Bingham Gallery, New York, currently; partner, Bingham Kurts Gallery, Memphis, Tenn, 91-92. *Specialty:* Original works by regional artists; works on paper by regional and international artists. *Mailing Add:* 766 S White Station Rd Memphis TN 38117

BINGHAM, LOIS A
ART ADMINISTRATOR, LECTURER
b Iowa Falls, Iowa, July 8, 13. *Study:* Oberlin Col, BA & MA(scholar); Sch Fine Arts, Yale Univ(scholar); Inst d'Art & Archeol, Univ Paris, Carnegie Grant. *Collections Arranged:* More than 200 exhibs arranged & supervised incl Nation of Nations, to inaugurate Berlin Cong Hall, 54, Modern Painting & Sculpture, Moscow, 59 & biennial exhibs at Sao Paulo, Venice, Santiago, New Delhi & Paris, 61- *Pos:* Staff, Nat Gallery Art, 43-48, assoc cur educ, 48-54; chief fine arts div, exhib br, US Info Agency, 54-65; chief, Int Art Prog, Smithsonian Inst, Nat Mus Am Art, Washington, DC, 65-72, chief, Off of Exhibs Abroad, 72-76, chief, Off of Prog Support, 76-81; retired, 81. *Teaching:* Lects, Medici: Patrons of Art, Index of Am Design, Dutch Painting, Manuscripts of the Middle Ages & Duccio's Maestra, Nat Gallery Art. *Publ:* Auth, How to look at works of art, Nat Gallery Art; Highlights of American painting, Care, NY; contribr, Favorite paintings from The National Gallery of Art. *Mailing Add:* 374 North St SW Washington DC 20024

BINGHAM, MRS HARRY PAYNE
COLLECTOR
Collection: Paintings. *Mailing Add:* 475 Park Ave New York NY 10022

BINKS, RONALD C
PHOTOGRAPHER, PAINTER
b Oak Park, Ill, Oct 20, 34. *Study:* George Eastman House, with Minor White, 54; RI Sch Design, BFA, 56; Berlin Art Acad, cert, 58; Yale Univ, MFA, 60. *Work:* Southwest Art Mus, Lubbock, Tex; San Antonio Mus Art, Tex; Ammon Carter Mus, Ft Worth, Tex; Del Mar Col, Corpus Christi, Tex; Springfield Art Mus, Mo; and others. *Exhib:* Fulbright Aritsts, Whitney Mus Am Art, New York, 58; 20th Century Photog, George Eastman House, Rochester, 60; Abilene Mus Fine Arts, 83. *Pos:* Ed adv, Photographer's Forum, 79- *Teaching:* Assoc prof art, RI Sch Design, 62-76, chmn film dept, 68-72; prof, Div Art & Archit, Univ Tex, San Antonio, 76- *Awards:* Fulbright Fel, 58-60; Prix de Rome, Am Acad Rome, 60-62. *Bibliog:* Beaumont Newhall (auth), Young photographers, Art in Am, 60. *Mem:* Soc Photog Educ; Nat Asn Sch Art; Tex Asn Schs Art (bd dir, 80-82); Col Art Asn Am; Nat Coun Art Adminr (chmn, 82-83). *Publ:* Aperture, spring 61. *Mailing Add:* Dept Art Univ Tex San Antonio 6700 N Rm 1604 W San Antonio TX 78285

BIOLCHINI, GREGORY PHILLIP
PAINTER
b Peoria, Ill, Mar 24, 48. *Study:* Famous Artist Course, Westport, Conn, 70; Edison Community Col, Ft Myers, Fla, printmaking, 80 & 88; Ringling Art Inst, Sarasota, Fla, figure sculpture, ceramics, workshops in watercolor, pastel & oil, 90. *Work:* State Fla, Capitol Bldg, Tallahassee; Ft Myers Hist Mus, Barbara B Mann Performing Arts Hall, Univ SFla Campus, Harborside Conv Ctr, Ft Myers, Fla; Embry Riddle Aeronautical Univ, Daytona, Fla. *Comn:* Oil portrait, Mayor Zee Butler, comn by Brent Scheneman, LaBelle Gallery, Sanibel, Fla, 81; oil portraits, J Paul Riddle, 86, T H Embry, 87, Embry-Riddle Univ, Daytona, Fla; oil portrait, Barbara B Mann, comn by Sen Frank Mann, Ft Myers, Fla, 88; bronze portrait, Chief Billy Bowlegs, comn by D J Wilkins, Ft Myers, Fla, 90. *Exhib:* Pastels Only, Nat Arts Club Gallery, New York, 81-92; solo exhib, Florida Cowboy, Ft Myers Hist Mus, 84; Societee des Pastellistes de France, Paris, 87; Degas Pastel Soc Second Biennial, Nat Exhib, New Orleans, La, 88; Three Notable Pastelists, Fla Southern Univ, Lakeland, 90; Nat Pastel Soc Master Pastelists, Harmon-Meek Gallery, Naples, Fla, 92; and others. *Pos:* Co-founder & vpres, Co-operative Gallery, Bell Tower, Ft Myers, Fla, 83-86. *Awards:* Seacape Award, Pastels Only, Nat Arts Club, Flora Baldini Giffuni, 81; Award for Nude, Pastels Only, Nat Arts Club, Vincent Giffuni, 83; Award for Nude, Pastels Only, Nat Arts Club, Hon & Mrs DiGiovanna, 88. *Mem:* Pastel Soc Am (master pastelist status, 88); Degas Pastel Soc; Fla Artists Group. *Media:* Pastel. *Dealer:* Harmon-Meek Gallery 386 Broad Ave S Naples FL 33940. *Mailing Add:* 1617 Hendry St Studio 412 Ft Myers FL 33901

BIRCH, WILLIE M
SCULPTOR, PAINTER
b New Orleans, La, Nov 26, 42. *Study:* Southern Univ, BA(painting), 69; Md Inst, Col Art, MFA, 73. *Work:* Pa Acad Fine Arts, Philadelphia; New Orleans Mus Art, La; Health Public Hospital, New York; Dade Public Library, Miami, Fla; Wilfredo Lamb Ctr, Havana, Cuba; Metrop Mus Art, New York. *Exhib:* One-man shows, Miami Dade Libr, Fla, 84, State Univ NY, Old Westbury, 88, Voices from the Field, Gallery 1199, New York, 90 & Duel Consciousness-African & American, Pa Art Alliance, Philadelphia, 90, Exit Art, New York, 92. *Awards:* Nat Endowment Arts Scholarship Grant, 84 & Visual Artist Grant, 89-90; NY Found Arts Fel for Painting, 86; NY State Coun Arts Visual Arts Prog Grant, 89-90. *Bibliog:* Roberta Smith (auth), Social Commentary in Works by Willie Birch, NY Times, 4/10/92; Robert Taplin (auth), Review of Exhibitions, Willie Birch at the Sulpture Center, 122-123, 7/91. *Mem:* NY ArtistsEquity Asn. *Media:* All Media. *Publ:* Auth, Knowing Our History, Teaching Our Culture, New Soc Publ, 90. *Dealer:* Arthur Roger 136 Prince St New York NY 10012. *Mailing Add:* 346 S Third St Cadman Plaza W & Orange St Brooklyn NY 11211

BIRCKETT, ANNA BELLE See Belle, Anna (Anna Belle Birckett)

BIRDSALL, BYRON
PAINTER
b Buckeye, Ariz, Dec 18, 37. *Study:* Seattle Pacific Col, BA; Stanford Univ, MA. *Work:* Anchorage Hist & Fine Arts Mus; Jean Haydon Territorial Mus, Pago Pago, Am Samoa. *Comn:* Painting, Alaska Bank of Com, Anchorage, 76; Alyeska Pipeline Co, Anchorage, 77; RCA, Anchorage, 77; stone lithos, Anchorage Opera Soc, 85; painting, Anchorage Olympic Organizing Comt, 85; King County Libr System, 86; and others. *Exhib:* All Alaska Watercolor Exhib, Alaska Watercolor Soc, 75-77; Anchorage Hist & Fine Arts Mus, 76 & All Alaska Exhib, 78; also many one-man shows. *Teaching:* Instr, Makerere Univ, Kampala, Uganda, 66-70; feature prog, art dir, KVZK Television, Pago Pago, Am Samoa, 72-73 & Graphix West Advertising Agency, Anchorage, Alaska, 75-76. *Awards:* Alaska Arts & Crafts League First Prize in Watercolor; Alaska Watercolor Soc First Prize, 76 & Second Prize, 77, Alaska Watercolor Show; Third Prize, All Alaska Art Exhib, 82. *Bibliog:* Lana Johnson (auth), Watercolorist forsakes his palm trees, Anchorage Times, 11/77; Barbara Whipple (auth), Byron Birdsall paints Alaska, Am Artist, 4/81; Janet O'Hara (auth), Byron Birdsall, artist of the world, Wien Air Alaska Flight Time, 9/83. *Mem:* Alaska Watercolor Soc (pres, 76); Alaska Artists Guild. *Media:* Watercolor, Stone. *Publ:* Auth, Letters from Africa, Anchorage Times, 6/81. *Dealer:* Artique Gallery 314 G St Anchorage AK 99501; Kirsten Gallery 5320 Roosevelt Way NE Seattle WA 98105. *Mailing Add:* c/o Artique Ltd 314 G St Anchorage AK 99501

BIRELINE, GEORGE LEE
PAINTER, EDUCATOR
b Peoria, Ill, Aug 12, 23. *Study:* Bradley Univ, BFA, 49; Univ NC, MACA, 52. *Work:* Everson Mus, Syracuse, NY; NC Mus Art, Raleigh; Mint Mus Art; Sydney & Francis Lewis Collection; Hirshhorn Mus & Sculpture Garden; Va Mus Fine Art. *Comn:* Wall mural relief, Mecklenberg Co Off Complex, 61; decorative solar screen, bank bldg, SC, 63 & NCNB Bldg, Charlotte, 65; outdoor environ sculpture cast concrete, Mecklenburg Co Libr, Albemarle, 71. *Exhib:* Post Painterly Abstraction, Los Angeles Co Mus Art, 64; retrospective, NC Mus Art, Raleigh, 76; Late 20th Century Art, Francis & Sydney Lewis Found, 79; NC Artists, Squibb Int Hq Gallery, Princeton, NJ, 81; Realist Invitational, SECCA, Winston-Salem, 81; Painting in the South, Va Mus, Richmond, 83. *Teaching:* Vis lectr design & painting, Univ NC, Chapel Hill, 65-66; prof design, Sch Design, NC State Univ, 57-86, emer prof, 86- *Awards:* First Purchase Awards, NC Mus Art, Artists Ann, 56, 57 & 64; Nat Coun on Arts Grant, 67-68; Guggenheim Found Grant for painting, 68-69. *Bibliog:* L Lippard (auth), rev in Art Forum, 67; D Kuspit (auth), Southern Realism, rev in Art in Am, 12/80; Frederic R Brant (auth catalog), Late 20th century Art. *Media:* Oil, Watercolor. *Mailing Add:* 228 East Park Dr Raleigh NC 27605

BIRENBAUM, CYNTHIA See Barber, Cynthia

BIRMELIN, A ROBERT
PAINTER, DRAFTSMAN
b Newark, NJ, Nov 7, 33. *Study:* Cooper Union Art Sch; Yale Univ, BFA, 56, MFA, 60. *Work:* Metrop Mus Art & Mus Mod Art, New York; Nat Mus Am Art, Smithsonian Inst & Hirshhorn Mus, Washington, DC; Mus Contemp Art, Nagaoka, Japan; plus others. *Comn:* Two panoramic highwayscapes, NJ Dept of Transportation Headquarters; Paterson (mural painting), Federal Building, Paterson, NJ, 91. *Exhib:* Claude Bernard Gallerie, Paris, 81; one-man shows, Montclair Art Mus, NJ, 84, Sherry French Gallery, New York, 84 & 86, Claude Bernard Gallerie, New York, 88 & 90, Morris Mus, Morristown, NJ, 91; States of War, New Galerie Mara, Buenos Aires, Argentina, 89; American Imagist and Abstract Painting, Moscow, USSR, 89. *Teaching:* Prof art, Queens Col, New York, 64- *Awards:* Am Acad Fel, Rome, 61-64; Nat Endowment Arts, 82 & 90; NJ Coun Arts, 88. *Bibliog:* Donald Kuspit (auth), Robert Birmelin, Art Forum, 6/86; Laurie Hurwitz (auth), Contemporary Masters: Robert Birmelin, Am Artist, 4/90; Robert Berlind (auth), From the corner of the minds eye: the paintings of Robert Birmelin, Art in America, 3/91. *Mem:* Assoc, Nat Acad Design. *Media:* Acrylic, Oil. *Dealer:* Claude Bernard Gallery 33 E 74th St New York NY 10021. *Mailing Add:* 176 Highwood Ave Leonia NJ 07605

BIRNBAUM, DARA
PAINTER, VIDEO ARTIST
b New York, NY. *Study:* Carnegie Mellon Univ, Pittsburg, Pa, BA(archit), 69; San Francisco Art Inst, BFA(painting), 73; Video Study Ctr Global Village, New Sch Social Res, New York, 76. *Exhib:* Solo shows, Rhona Hoffman Gallery, Chicago, Ill, 91 & 92, John Baer Gallery, New York, 90, Hamburger Kunstverein, Hamburg, 92, Klnischer Kunstverein, Cologne, 92; Kunsthalle Basel, 92; Documenta IX, Kassel, 92; Mus Contemp Art, Chicago, Ill, 92. *Teaching:* Vis artist's sem, Nova Scotia Col Art & Design, Halifax, 78; coadj appointment, Mason Gross Sch Arts, Rutgers Univ, New Brunswick, NJ, 80; instr video & post-studio, Calif Inst Arts, Valencia, 82; experimental video instr, Sch Visual Arts, New York, 83-86; Perkins jr fel, Prog Vis Arts, Princeton Univ, 87-88 & vis jr fel Coun Humanities, 87-88; adj fac mem dept art, Grad Sch, Hunter Col City Univ New York, 91. *Awards:* Certif Merit Experimental Video, 27th Chicago Int Film Festival, 91; Visual Arts Fel, Nat Endowment Arts, 91; Spec Jury Prize, Deutscher Videokunstpreis, Sudwestfunk, Baden-Baden & Zentrum fur Kunst und Medientechnologie, Karlsruhe, 92. *Mem:* Found Independent Video & Film, New York (bd dirs, 83-85); Creative Time (bd dirs, 88-). *Mailing Add:* 140 Thomson St Apt 3A New York NY 10012

BISGYER, BARBARA G (COHN)
SCULPTOR
b New York, NY, June 7, 33. *Study:* Sarah Lawrence Col; Sculptors & Ceramic Workshop, New York; also indust design with R R Kostellow. *Work:* US Consular Small Sculpture Collection, Smithsonian Inst; Larry Aldrich Mus Contemp Art; Savin Bus Machines Corp. *Comn:* Sculpture, pvt residence, Delray, Fla, 84. *Exhib:* Union Carbide; Aldrich Mus; Avery Fisher Hall, Lincoln Ctr; Hudson River Mus; Pratt Sch Design; Sarah Lawrence Col; and others. *Awards:* Merit Award for Outstanding Design & Craftsmanship in Sculpture, Artist Craftsmen New York; President's Award, Mamaroneck Artists Guild, Westchester Art Soc. *Bibliog:* Articles in Art News & Today's Art. *Mem:* Artists Craftsmen, New York; Mamaroneck Artists Guild; Artists Equity Asn, NY; Am Soc Contemp Artists; Abraxas. *Media:* Miscellaneous. *Dealer:* Judy Wasserman Agent 30 Whippoorwill Rd Armonk NY 10504. *Mailing Add:* 50 Lake Rd Rye NY 10580

BISHOP, BEN
PAINTER, SCULPTOR
b New York, NY, Feb 10, 23. *Study:* Art Students League, 45-47; Univ Nebr, BFA; NY Univ Inst Fine Arts, 50-51; Columbia Univ; Univ Calif, Berkeley, MA, 65. *Work:* Norfolk Mus Art & Sci, Va; State Univ NY Col Potsdam; Univ Mass, Amherst; Syracuse Univ Mus; State Univ NY Binghamton. *Exhib:* Retrospective, SUNY, New Paltz, 80, Monoprints, Vassar Col, 81 & People, Places & Things, Barrett House, Poughkeepsie, New York, 84; Small Paintings, Found Landscapes, Summergroup Gallery, Mid- Hudson Art & Sci Ctr, 86; A Rock in the Sea, Cathedral of St John the Devine, NY, 87;

Watermark, Cargo Gallery, Kingston, 92. *Teaching:* Instr art, Memphis Acad Art, Tenn, 47-48, Vassar Col, 51, Univ Mo, Columbia, 52-54 & Santa Catalina Sch Girls, Monterey, Calif, 64-65; prof art, State Univ NY Col New Paltz, 65-85; prof emer. *Awards:* Delta Pi Delta Award, Joslyn Art Mus, 48; First Prize for Drawing, Monterey Co Fair, Calif, 65; Childe Hassam Fund Purchase Award, Am Acad Arts & Lett, 68. *Media:* Watercolor, All Media. *Mailing Add:* Rte 1 Box 450B High Falls NY 12440

BISHOP, BUDD HARRIS
MUSEUM DIRECTOR
b Canton, Ga, Nov 1, 36. *Study:* Shorter Col, Ga, AB, 58; Univ Ga, MFA, 60, with Lamar Dodd & Howard Thomas; Arts Admin Inst, Harvard Univ, 70. *Collections Arranged:* Tenn State Collection of Sculpture; The First American Collections of Hunter Mus of Art; Sculpture Collection, Columbus, Mus; Ogilvy Collection Chinese & Japanese Art. *Pos:* Dir creative serv, Transit Advert Asn, New York, 64-66; dir, Hunter Mus Art, 66-76 & Columbus Mus Art, Ohio, 76-87; dir, Harn Mus Art, Gainesville, Fla, 87- *Teaching:* Lectr art hist, Vanderbilt Univ, 61-62; art dir children's prog, Ensworth Sch, Nashville, Tenn, 61-64; lectr art, Univ Chattanooga, 67-68. *Awards:* Tenn Arts Comt Award, 71; Shorter Col Alumni Award, 79. *Mem:* Am Asn Mus; Tenn Asn Mus (pres, 71-); Asn Art Mus Dirs. *Res:* Early Tennessee artists; early Southern American painting; George Bellows. *Mailing Add:* Samuel P Harn Mus Univ Fla Gainesville FL 32601

BISHOP, JACQUELINE K
PAINTER
b Corona, Calif, Oct 1, 55. *Study:* Univ Kansas, Lawrence, 73-75; Univ New Orleans, BA, 76-78; Tulane Univ, MFA, 80-82. *Work:* New Orleans Mus Art, La; Alabama Power Co, Birmingham, Ala; City New Orleans - Arts Coun, New Orleans, La; Albrecht Art Mus, St Joseph, Mo; Tulane Univ, New Orleans, La. *Exhib:* Contemp Art, Winston-Salem, NC, 84; For the Birds: Artists Examine Aviary Abodes, Wustum Art Mus, Racine, Wisc, 90; Visionary Imagists, Contemp Arts Ctr, New Orleans, La, 90; System of Nature, Gasperi Gallery, New Orleans, 90; Exhibitions- Sistema da Natureza, Mus Southeastern Tex, 91- 92; Visionary Imagists, Ga Mus Art, 91; and others. *Teaching:* Instr drawing & painting, Newcomb Col, Tulane Univ, New Orleans, 82-84; asst prof advan painting, Loyola Univ, New Orleans, La, 90. *Bibliog:* Pamela Kessler (auth), Menagerie A Deux, Washington Post, 87; Amy Jinker Lloyd (auth), The Real, The Unreal, The Surreal, Atlanta Constitution, 88; Mary Warner Marien (auth), Art Evoking Particular Places, Christian Science Monitor, 6/25/90. *Media:* Oil, Mixed Media. *Publ:* D Eric Bookhardt (auth), Visionary Imagists, 90; Lew Thomas (auth), Louisiana Artists Pages, Love in the Ruins, 89. *Dealer:* Richard Gasperi Gallery 320 Julia St New Orleans LA 70130. *Mailing Add:* 1217 Philip St New Orleans LA 70130

BISHOP, JAMES
PAINTER
b Neosho, Mo, Oct 7, 27. *Study:* Syracuse Univ, New York, BA, 46-50; Wash Univ Sch Fine Arts, 51-54; Black Mountain Col, study with Esteban Vicente, 53; Columbia Univ, 55-56. *Work:* San Francisco Mus of Art; Mus Mod Art, NY; Chase Manhattan, Paris, France; Gillman Paper Co, NY. *Exhib:* One-man shows, Galerie Jean Fournier, Paris, France, 76, Frank Kolbert Gallery, New York, 80, Anne Marie Verna Gallery, Zurich, Switz, 81, Daniel Weinberg Gallery, San Francisco, Calif, 81 & Simon/Neuman Gallery, New York, 87; L'Art Moderne Dans les Musees Francaises, Grand Palais, Paris, 78; Dessin et Couleur, Beaubourg, Paris, 79; Three Paintings, Annemarie Verna Gallery, Zurich, Switz, 86; Counterpoint, Simon/Neuman Gallery, New York, 86 & On View, 86; On View, Simon/Neuman Gallery, New York, 86; PS1, Inst Art and Urban Resources. *Pos:* Ed assoc, Art News, 69-72. *Teaching:* Instr, Cooper Union, 69-70, Univ Calif, Irvine, 70, Carnegie-Mellon Inst, 71 & Sch of Visual Arts, New York, 72. *Awards:* Guggenheim Found Fel, 70; Grant, Nat Endowment Arts, 76. *Bibliog:* Abstract Painting 1960-69 (catalog), PS1, NY, 83; The Sixites in Abstract (interview), Art in America, 10/83; Carter Ratcliff (auth), Remembering How to See, Artforum, 5/88, 127. *Dealer:* Matthew Marks Gallery 1018 Madison Ave New York NY 10021. *Mailing Add:* 5 Lispenard St New York NY 10013

BISHOP, JEFFREY BRITTON
PAINTER, EDUCATOR
b Berkeley, Calif, Feb 18, 49. *Study:* Boston Mus Sch, Dipl(with honors), 73; Tufts Univ, BFA, 74; Univ Wash, MFA, 77. *Work:* Seattle Art Mus, Wash. *Comn:* Large wall installation, City Seattle, Wash, 80. *Exhib:* New Ideas, Seattle Art Mus, Wash, 78; Wash Open, Seattle Art Mus, Wash, 79; one-man shows, Linda Farris Gallery, Seattle, Wash, 80 & 82, Mirage Gallery, Los Angeles, Calif, 81 & Seattle Art Mus, 83; Eight Seattle Artists: Installations, Los Angeles Inst Contemp Art, 80; Wash Year, Henry Gallery, Univ Wash, Seattle, 81; Collage & Assemblage, Miss Mus Art, Jackson & traveling, 81-83. *Teaching:* Lectr mod art, Univ Wash, Seattle, 78; program dir, Henry Gallery Lecture Series, Seattle, Wash, 78-82; lectr & instr mod art, drawing & painting, Cornish Inst, Seattle, Wash, 79-82. *Awards:* 66th James William Paige Traveling Fel, Boston Mus Fine Arts, 74; Betty Bowen Award, Seattle Art Mus, 82. *Bibliog:* Mathew Kangas (auth), Seattle, Artforum, 5/79 & Art in Am, 81; Barbara Taylor (auth), Eight Seattle Artists, Los Angeles Inst Contemp Art, 80. *Mem:* Allied Arts of Seattle; founding mem Ctr Contemp Art. *Media:* Water Media, Charcoal. *Publ:* Auth, interview with Susan Sontag, Insight, 82. *Mailing Add:* 6032 31st NE Seattle WA 98115

BISHOP, JEROLD
EDUCATOR, PAINTER
b Salt Lake City, Utah, Apr 14, 36. *Study:* Southern Utah State Col, Cedar City, AB, 56; Utah State Univ, Logan, BS, 60, MFA, 66. *Work:* Valley Nat Bank, Phoenix; Glendale Community Col, Ariz; Starr Commonwealth Boys, Albion, Mich; Court House Collection, Douglas, Ariz. *Comn:* Ariz Hwy Mag, Phoenix, Ariz, 84, 85 & 86; Collector Plate Series, Fine Arts Mktg, 85. *Exhib:* Mormon Festival Arts, Brigham Young Univ Art Ctr, Provo, Utah, 77-79; Watercolor USA, Springfield Art Mus, Mo, 77 & 80; Univ Ariz Fac Shows, Mus Art, Tucson, 77-85; Watercolor Biennial, Scottsdale Ctr Arts, Ariz, 80; and others. *Pos:* Art dir, Thiokol Chemical Corp, Brigham City, Utah, 63-64 & 66-67; production artist & art dir, Utah State Univ, Logan, 64-66. *Teaching:* Asst prof art, Univ Ariz, Tucson, 67-72, assoc prof, 72- *Awards:* Masters Meed Medallion, Tubac Festival Arts, Santa Cruz Valley Art Asn, 76; Special Award, 4th Ann Western Fedn Watercolor Socs Exhib, 79; Silver Medal, 57th Ann Nat, Springville Mus Art, Utah, 81; Merit Award, Ariz Watercolor Asn, Scottsdale, 84; Phippen Family Award, Prescott, Ariz, 85. *Mem:* Western Fedn Watercolor Socs; Southern Ariz Watercolor Guild; Ariz Watercolor Asn. *Media:* Watercolor, Mixed. *Mailing Add:* 9133 E Speedway Blvd Tucson AZ 85710

BISHOP, MARJORIE CUTLER
PAINTER
b Melrose, Mass. *Study:* Art Students League; New Sch Social Res; and with Guy Pene du Bois, Moses Soyer, Sol Wilson & Valero, Paris, France. *Work:* Walker Art Ctr, Minneapolis, Minn; Photo Researchers, Inc, New York. *Exhib:* Carnegie Inst, Pittsburgh, Pa, 45; Pa Acad Fine Arts, Philadelphia, 45; Audubon Artists, New York, 47, 52 & 54; Heckscher Mus, Huntington, NY & Guild Hall, Easthampton, NY, 65; State Univ NY Col, Stony Brook, 78; Gallery North, Setauket, NY, 80 & 83; Stony Brook Mus, 92; and many one-man shows in New York & Long Island. *Pos:* Art Coun, Suffolk Mus, Stony Brook, NY, 61-65; vpres, Gallery North, Setauket, NY, 65-92. *Teaching:* Instr creative painting & art hist, Bishop Art Studio, Oldfield, NY, 56-92. *Awards:* Purchase Prize, Walker Art Ctr, 45; Exhib Award, St Paul-de-Vence, France, 53. *Mem:* Nat Mus Women Art, Washington, DC. *Media:* Oil, Sand. *Publ:* Women Artists in America: 18th Century to the Present. *Mailing Add:* 23 Flax Pond Woods Setauket NY 11733

BISSELL, CHARLES OVERMAN
CARTOONIST
b Nashville, Tenn, June 29, 08. *Pos:* Lithographic artist, 24-45; ed cartoonist & mem staff, Nashville Tennessean, 43-; art dir, Sunday Mag, 45-70. *Awards:* Cartoon Award, Nat Headliners Club, 63; Distinguished Serv Award, Sigma Delta Chi, 64; Pub Serv Award, Nat Safety Coun, 66. *Mem:* Asn Am Ed Cartoonists; Nat Cartoonist Soc. *Publ:* Creater cartoon feature Bissell's Brave New World, 62. *Mailing Add:* 4221 Farrar Ave Nashville TN 37215

BISSELL, PHIL
CARTOONIST, ILLUSTRATOR
b Worcester, Mass, Feb 1, 26. *Study:* Sch Practical Art, Boston; Art Instr Inc, Minneapolis, grad. *Work:* Baseball Hall Fame, Cooperstown, NY; Basketball Hall Fame, Springfield, Mass; Football Hall Fame, Canton, Ohio; Hockey Hall Fame, Toronto; Swimming Hall of Fame, Ft Lauderdale; and others. *Comn:* New Eng Patriots (Nat Football League) insignia; Rourke Bridge Plaques, Lowell, Mass. *Exhib:* Southern Calif Expo, 64; Nat Cartoonists Soc, New York, 71 & Washington, DC, 72-79; Man & His World, Ninth Int Salon Cartoons, Montreal, annually. *Pos:* Cartoon Corner, Rockport, Mass. *Teaching:* Cartooning A-Z, Rockport Art Asn, summer sessions. *Awards:* Best Ed Cartoons, 74-88; Scarlet Quill Award for Outstanding Coverage of Intercollegiate Athletics, 76. *Media:* Ink, Tempera. *Publ:* The World Encyclopedia of Cartoons, Horn, Chelsea House, 80. *Mailing Add:* 5 Shetland Rd Rockport MA 01966

BISSETTE, SAMUEL DELK
PAINTER, PHOTOGRAPHER
b Wilson, NC, Aug 10, 21. *Study:* Student of John Pike, Woodstock, NY, 72 & 75. *Work:* Gov's Mansion, Raleigh, NC; Wachovia Bank, Winston-Salem, NC; Fed Reserve Bank, Richmond, Va; Duke Univ Med Ctr, Durham, NC; NC Mus Hist, Raleigh. *Comn:* Paintings, Planters Bank, Wilmington, NC & Rocky Mount, NC, 75; Portrait of North Carolina (40 paintings), Wachovia Bank, Winston-Salem, NC, 76; Boykin/Bissette Coll of Old Wilson, Wilson, NC, 87; murals, Belk Beery Co, Wilmington, NC, 78-79; Paintings, First Union Nat Bank, Charlotte, NC, 82. *Exhib:* Solo exhib, St John's Mus Art, Wilmington, NC, 74 & 84; Univ NC Weatherspoon Gallery, Greensboro, NC, 74 & 76; Asheville Mus Art, NC, 75; NC Mus Art, Raleigh, 77; 82nd US Open Watercolor Exhib, Nat Arts Club, New York, 82; and others. *Pos:* Pres, St John's Mus Art Inc, Wilmington, NC, 72-74; corp dir, NC Art Soc, Raleigh, 75-82; trustee, NC Mus Art, 80-85. *Awards:* First Place, NC Watercolor Soc, 75; Purchase Award, Hunt Manufacturing Co, Philadelphia, 75; First Place Awards, Southern Star Astronomical Conv, 91; and others. *Bibliog:* W B Wright (auth), North Carolina - Circa 1900, State Mag, Raleigh, 84; interview, Univ NC Pub Television, 8/85; Kent Day Coes (auth), Vignettes of AWS People, Am Watercolor Soc Mewslett, 85; article, Am Artist, 3/84. *Mem:* Assoc Am Watercolor Soc New York; NC Watercolor Soc (vpres, 80). *Media:* Watercolor, Astrophotography. *Publ:* Auth, Watercolor page, Am Artist, 3/84. *Dealer:* St John's Mus Art Inc 120 Orange St Wilmington NC 28401. *Mailing Add:* 1939 South Live Oak Parkway Wilmington NC 28403

BITTLEMAN, DOLORES DEMBUS
WEAVER, CONSERVATOR
b New York, NY, Jan 3, 31. *Study:* Columbia Univ, BS(cum laude), 52; Fulbright Fel, Paris, 54-55; Univ Calcutta, 55-56. *Work:* Mus Mod Art, New York; Yale Univ, New Haven, Conn; Silvermine Col Art, New Canaan, Conn; Columbia Univ, New York. *Exhib:* New Weavings to Look At, Silvermine Col Art, New Canaan, Conn, 67; Wall Hangings, Mus Mod Art, New York, 69, 70 & 72; Biennale Int de la Tapisserie, Mus des Beaux Arts, Lausanne, Switz, 71; Warszawskiej Ekspozycji V Miedzynarodowego Biennale Tkaniny Artystycjej W Lozannie, Zacheta Gallery, Poland, 71; Artists & Craftsmen of Cent NY, Munson-Williams-Procter Inst, Utica, 73; Collaborations in Art, Science & Technology, Everson Mus Art, 75. *Collections Arranged:* Five Process Sculptors, Schenectady Mus, NY (auth, catalog), 76-77. *Pos:* Instr textile, Creative Arts Workshop, New Haven, Conn, 62; instr weaving, Troy Arts Workshop, NY, 66; proprietor & founder, Cambridge Textiles, NY, 79- *Teaching:* Instr art, Union Col, Schenectady, NY, 69-74. *Awards:* Purchase Prize, Columbia Univ, 52; Nat Endowment Arts Master Craftsman & Apprentice Grant, 75-76. *Bibliog:* Jack Lenor Larsen (auth), Two views of the fifth tapestry biennale, Craft Horizons Mag, 10/71. *Mem:* Centre Int D'Etude Textiles Anciens; Am Inst Conserv of Hist & Artistic Works. *Media:* Silk, Natural Fibers. *Mailing Add:* Turnpike Rd Cambridge NY 12816

BITTNER, HANS OSKAR
PAINTER, ILLUSTRATOR
b Breslau, Ger, Jan 25, 05; US citizen. *Study:* Breslau Kunstschule; Munich Acad. *Work:* Crown Prince William of Ger; Breslau Kunst Mus; Breslau Art Galleries; also in pvt collections. *Exhib:* Ill Festival Art, Chicago, 64; Three Main Libr, Chicago; Chicago Chap Artists Equity Asn; Rockford Col, Kenosha Col & Univ Wis-Stevens Point; work also exhibited on ABC & NBC. *Pos:* Glass & display designer, Goldblatt Stores, Chicago, 30-35; commercial artist, Vogue Wright, 35-45; artist & designer, Wilding Picture Studio, 52-68. *Awards:* Several Second Place Awards, Palette & Chisel Acad & Munic Art League, Chicago; Col Frank Chesrow Gold Medal, Chicago, 72. *Mem:* Palette & Chisel Acad; Munic Art League; Artist Guild Chicago. *Mailing Add:* 10357 W Loma Blanca Dr Sun City AZ 85351

BJORKLUND, LEE
PAINTER, EDUCATOR
b Wadena, Minn, June 20, 40. *Study:* Univ Minn, Minneapolis, BA, 69 & MFA, 73. *Work:* Walker Art Ctr, Minneapolis Inst Art, Fed Reserve Bank, Norwest Nat Bank & First Nat Bank, Minneapolis; Amerada Hess Corp, New York. *Comn:* Norwest Bank, Minneapolis, Minn, 78; RAUTI, Rochester, Minn, 87; Mayo Clinic, Scottesdale, Ariz, 87. *Exhib:* Walker Art Ctr, 66, 72 & 75; Univ Gallery, 67, 71 & 81; Minn Inst Arts, 75, 81, 86 & 90; Peter M David Gallery, 80-82 & 85; Kuopio Mus, Kuopio, Finland, 81. *Pos:* Visual art coordr, Minn State Arts Bd, Minneapolis, 74-75, co-founder, Minn Artists Exhib Prog, 75, chmn, Visual Studies Div, 75-78, acad adv, 82 & acting dean students, 85-86. *Teaching:* Instr, Univ Minn, 70-72, Art Ctr Minn, 71-72, Minn Mus Art Sch, St Paul, 72-73, Winona State Univ, 72, Minneapolis Col Art & Design, 73-90, assoc prof. *Awards:* Minn State Arts Bd Grant, 72 & 79; Ford Found Grant, 77; Mellon Found Grant, 82-84; and others. *Bibliog:* Mike Steele (auth), Practitioners explore the modern art mystique, Minneapolis Tribune, 5/18/75; Eleanor Heartney (auth), article, New Art Examiner, summer 81; William Hegeman (auth), article, Art News, 11/81; Margot Kriel Galt (auth), The artists who came in from the cold, Minn Monthly, 1/86. *Mem:* Minneapolis Soc Fine Arts. *Media:* Mixed. *Dealer:* Peter M David Gallery 400 First Ave N Minneapolis, Minn. *Mailing Add:* 2742 Bryant Ave S Minneapolis MN 55408

BJURMAN, JOHAN PAUL
MURALIST, PAINTER
b Providence, RI, July 21, 47. *Work:* Providence Pub Libr, RI. *Comn:* Trompe L'oeile (8 stories bldg), Providence Land Co, RI, 86; 80' Civil War Mural (with Mark Dunkleman, Historian), Gettysburg, Pa, 88; 4 story bldg trompe, Loedy & Loedy Architects, Poughkeepsie, NY 90; L'oeile (18 x 75 mural), Nat Lumber Co, Newton, Mass, 91. *Awards:* Providence Preservation Soc, Trompe L'oeile Bldg, 87; RI State Coun Arts, Individual Artist Community, 92; Town of North Providence Recognition Archievment, RI, 92. *Mem:* Pastel Soc Am; Providence Art Club. *Media:* Oil, Paint. *Mailing Add:* Five Merritt Ave North Providence RI 02911

BLACK, DAVID EVANS
SCULPTOR
b Gloucester, Mass, May 29, 28. *Study:* Skowhegan Sch, Maine, summer 49; Wesleyan Univ, AB, 50; Ind Univ, Bloomington, MFA, 54. *Work:* Neue Nat Galerie, West Berlin, Ger; Dayton Art Inst; Utsukushi-Ga-Hara Mus, Japan; Kalamazoo Col, Mich; Ft Wayne Mus Art, Ind; Cent Mich Univ Mt Pleasant, Clarkson Univ, Potsdam, NY. *Comn:* Neue Nat Galerie Sculpture Ct, West Berlin, 72,; Int Airport, Columbus, Ohio, 81; Ohio State Univ, 82; Island Park, Belmont, Calif, 90; Main Libr Plaza, Tucson, Ariz, 91; and others. *Exhib:* One-man show, Amerika-Haus, West Berlin, 71; Neue Nat Gallerie, WBerlin, Ger, 77 & Lehmbruck Mus, Duisberg, Ger, 77; Taft Mus, Cincinnati, Ohio, 85; Indianapolis Mus Art, 85; Kalamazoo Art Inst, Mich, 87. *Pos:* Mem, DAAD Artists Prog, Berlin & WGer Govt, 70-72. *Teaching:* Prof sculpture, Ohio State Univ, 54- *Awards:* Berlin Artists' Prog, DAAD, 70-72; Int Sculpture Prize, Hakone Mus, Japan, 85; Ohio Spec Recognition, 91. *Bibliog:* Donald Kuspit (auth), Sculpture as proto-architecture (catalog essay), Kalamazoo Art Inst, Mich, 87; World Sculptors, Japan Art & Cult Soc, 92; Stanley Collyer (auth), cover, Competitions Mag, spring 91. *Media:* Metals, Environments. *Dealer:* David Black Studio 1066 Lincoln Rd Columbus OH 43212. *Mailing Add:* Dept Art 128 N Oval Mall Ohio State Univ Columbus OH 43210

BLACK, LISA
PAINTER, PHOTOGRAPHER
b Lansing, Mich, June 19, 34. *Study:* Univ Paris, Sorbonne, dipl, 55; Univ Mich, BA, 56. *Comn:* Mural, Easter Seal Rehabilitation Ctr, 89. *Exhib:* New Haven Paint & Clay Club Art Exhib, Conn, 71, 72 & 83; Springfield Art League 53rd Nat Exhib, Mass, 72; 32nd Ann Art Exhib, Cedar City, Utah, 72; 15th Nat Exhib Am Art, Chautauqua, NY, 72; Milford Fine Arts Art Exhib, 83; Stamford Mus Conn Art, 89, 90 & 92. *Teaching:* Children's art lessons, pvt studio, 78-79. *Awards:* First Award Graphics, Conn Painters, Sculptors & Printmakers Exhib, 75; First Prize, Rowayton Arts Ctr, 89 & 91; Fred Kraus Mem Award, Stamford Mus Conn Art, 92. *Mem:* Rowayton Arts Ctr; Stamford Art Asn; New Haven Paint & Clay Club; Greenwich Art Soc; Old Greenwich Art Soc; Westport Arts Ctr. *Media:* All Media. *Dealer:* Noroton Gallery 1977 Post Rd Darien CT 06820. *Mailing Add:* 17 Brushy Hill Rd Darien CT 06820

BLACK, MARY MCCUNE
CURATOR, PAINTER
b Broadwell, Ohio, Feb 14, 15. *Study:* Ohio Univ, BS(educ), 37, MFA, 58; Amagansett Sch Art, Sarasota, Fla; workshop study with Charles Burchfield, William Thon, Aaron Bohrod, Paul Sample, Eliot O'Hara & Hilton Leech. *Work:* FMC Corp; McJunkin Corp; Kanawha Co Pub Libr; WVa State Col, Permanent Collection; Lutheran Church, Parkersburg, WVa. *Exhib:* Smithsonian Inst, 63; Exhib WVa Artists, 77; Nat Exhib, Sacramento, 78; WVa Juried Exhib, 79 & 83; Allied Artists WVa, 82; Duo exhib, WVa State Col, 86; and others. *Collections Arranged:* Permanent collection exhibition; Fiber & Fabrics; Collectors Exhibition of Kanawha Valley. *Pos:* Dir, Charleston Art Gallery Sunrise, 63-75, cur fine arts of Sunrise, 75-77; art juror, Fine Arts Exhib at Art & Craft Fair, Cedar Lakes, WVa, 79-88; retired; mem adv bd, Fine Arts Dept, West State Col. *Teaching:* Instr art, Sandusky Jr High Sch, 37-39; instr painting, adult prog, Kanawha Co Bd Educ, 58-64; instr art, Valley Day Sch, 60-63; instr painting, YMCA & Charleston Art Gallery, 63-68. *Awards:* Pat Buster Award, Venice Area Art League, 90; Purchase Award, Tri-State Asn, Huntington, WVa, 90; Merit Award, WVa Watercolor Soc Juried Exhib, 92. *Mem:* Allied Artists WVa; Nat League Am Pen Women; Southern Watercolor Soc; Venice Area Art League, Fla; charter mem WVa Watercolor Soc. *Media:* Watercolor, Acrylic. *Dealer:* Gallery Eleven 1033 Quarrier St Charleston WV 25301; Burke Findley Gallery 1460 S McCall Rd Englewood FL 34223. *Mailing Add:* 954 Ridgemont Rd Charleston WV 25314

BLACK, RICHARD R
EDUCATOR, PRINTMAKER
b Farnhamville, Iowa, July 18, 32. *Study:* Drake Univ, BFA, 57; Univ Wis, Madison, 58. *Work:* Bankside Gallery, London, Eng; The Kemper Group Art Collection, Long Grove, Ill; Des Moines Art Ctr, Iowa; Milwaukee Art Ctr, Wis; Indianapolis Mus Art, Ind. *Comn:* Lithograph, Univ of Iowa Patrons' Print (ed of 200), 88; lithograph, Des Moines Art Ctr Print Club 11th Yr Print (ed of 50), 91. *Exhib:* Bankside Gallery, London, Eng; Dome Gallery, New York; Graham Horstman Gallery, Denton, Tex; Des Moines Art Ctr, Iowa; 1988 Open Print Exhib, Bankside Gallery, London, Eng; Boston Printmakers Exhib, Mus Fine Arts, Mass; Color Print USA, Tex Tech Univ; Prints International, Silvermine Galleries, Conn; Iowa/Venice Print Exhib, Scuala Internazionale Di Graphica, Di Veniza, 89. *Pos:* Dir, David Strawn Art Gallery, Jacksonville, Ill, 59-60. *Teaching:* Instr art, Ill Col, Jacksonville, 59-60; prof art, Drake Univ, Des Moines, Iowa, 60- *Awards:* First Friends of Drake Arts Awards in Teaching & Artistic Achievement, 87; Greater Des Moines Chamber of Commerce Fedn First Ann Artist Recognition Award, 87; Francis Witherspoon Printmakers Award, 91. *Bibliog:* Douglas Warner (auth), Workshop-Lakeside Studio, Graphics Mag, 1-2/79; Charles Roberts (auth), The prints the thing, Iowan, 80; Joseph Winkelman (auth), Talks about the Drake Symposium in Iowa, The Printmakers Jour, London, 92. *Mem:* Royal Soc Painter-Etchers & Engravers, London, Eng; Col Art Asn Am; Mid-Am Print Coun; Southern Graphics Coun. *Media:* Intaglio, Lithography. *Mailing Add:* Dept Art Drake Univ 25th St Univ Des Moines IA 50311

BLACKBURN, ED M
PAINTER
b Amarillo, Tex, June 15, 40. *Study:* Univ Tex, BFA, 62; Brooklyn Mus, Beckman Scholar, 63; Univ Calif, Berkeley, MA, 65. *Work:* Ft Worth Art Mus; Dallas Mus Fine Art. *Comn:* Mural on canvas, USAA, San Antonio, 75; Larger Canvas II (billboard), Houston Nat Bank, 78. *Exhib:* Off the Wall, San Antonio Mus Art, 81; solo exhib, Ft Worth Art Mus, 82; American Still Life 1945-1983, Contemp Arts Mus, Houston, 83; Texas Images and Vision, Univ Tex Huntington Gallery, Austin & Amarillo Art Ctr, 83; 38th Corcoran Biennial & Second Western States, 83-84. *Awards:* Painting Grant, Nat Endowment Arts, 77 & 89-90. *Bibliog:* Ken Harrison (dir), Ed Blackburn (film), PBS, 75. *Media:* Acrylic, Oil. *Dealer:* Barry Whistler Gallery 2909A Canton St Dallas TX 75226; Moody Gallery 2815 Colquit Houston TX 77098. *Mailing Add:* 3901 Bilglade 2909A Canton Ft Worth TX 76109

BLACKBURN, LENORA WHITMIRE
COLLECTOR
b Midland, Tex, Aug 21, 04. *Study:* Univ Tex, Austin, BA, 27; also grad study. *Mem:* Mobile Art Asn; Art Patrons League Mobile. *Interests:* Exhibiting collection for groups and giving lectures on artists. *Collection:* Old Masters including Titian, Ghirlandaio, Rubens, Van der Helst, Bol, Franz van Mieris, Van Dyck, Constable, Turner, Watteau, Ingres, John F Herring Sr, Daubigny, Theodore Rousseau, Gainsborough, Monet, Roualt and many others; Americans including Charles Wilson Peale, Inness, Sully, Easkins, William Marshall, Bierstadt, Blakelock, Robert Henri, Peter Hurd, John Sloan, Childe Hassam, Guy Wiggins, Thomas Moran, George Lukas, Potthast, John Carroll, Grandma Moses, Endre Szabo, Melvin Warren and many others. *Mailing Add:* 4505 N Sunset Dr Mobile AL 36608

BLACKBURN, LINDA Z
PAINTER
b Baltimore, Md, July 5, 41. *Study:* Univ Tex, Austin, BFA, 62; Univ Calif, Berkeley, MA, 65. *Work:* Mod Mus Ft Worth, Tex; Longview Mus, Tex; Crescent Collection, Dallas; ARCO, Dallas; Zales, Chicago. *Exhib:* Four Texas Painters, Univ Ill, Chicago, 84; Women of the American West, Bruce Mus, Greenwich, Conn, 85; solo exhib, Tyler Mus Art, Tex, 89; Texas Women, Nat Mus Women Arts, Washington, DC, 89; Mid American Biennial, Nelson-Adkins, Kansas City, 89; and others. *Awards:* Grant, Mid-Am Nat Endowment Arts, 88; Grant, Nat Endowment Arts, 89. *Bibliog:* Susan Freudenheim (auth), A survey of Texas art, Arts & Archit Mag, winter 81; Susan Freudenheim (auth), Linda Blackburn at Mattingly-Baker, Art Am, 1/84; Mark Thistlethwaite (auth), article, Artspace Mag, summer 84. *Media:* All Media. *Dealer:* James Gallery 2930 Revere Suite 200 Houston TX 77098. *Mailing Add:* 3901 Bilglade Ft Worth TX 76109

BLACKBURN, LOREN HAYNER
PAINTER, ILLUSTRATOR
b South Glens Falls, NY, Mar 5, 29. *Study:* Self-taught. *Work:* Coopers Cave Collection Lake George; Summer Youth Theater Group, Lake George, NY; US Air Force Permanent Collection. *Comn:* First Nat Bank, Glen Falls; NAm Med Instrument Corp; Champlain Stone Ltd; Garwood Boat Manufacturing; Albany Int. *Exhib:* Solo exhibs, Crandall Libr Mus, Glens Falls, NY, 79, Saratoga Golf & Polo Club, NY, 81, Appleland Gallery, Burnt Hills, NY, 83, Aqueduct Race Track, Jamaica, NY, 83, Smith Opera House, Geneva, NY, 84, Saratoga City Ctr, NY, 84 & 85 & Gallery of Arts Guild, Old Forge, NY, 85; Fine Arts Pavilion, Worlds Fair, Knoxville, Tenn, 82; Nat Am Watercolor Exhib, Old Forge, NY, 84 & 85; Sarasota Racing Series Paintings, 87 & 88; Saratoga Series, Chapman Hist Mus, 89. *Awards:* Blue Ribbon, 32nd Ann Glens Falls Regional Art Exhib, 79; Second Place & Artists Choice, 12th Ann Old Saratoga Hist Asn Exhib, 80; Best of Watercolors, Lower Adirondack Regional Art Coun Outdoor Show, 80; Todah Moshe Award, Nat Am Exhib, Old Forge, NY, 84. *Bibliog:* Jeffrey Wilkin (auth), Artist spotlights local themes, Glens Falls Post Star, 5/17/80; Tina Lincer (auth), A man of the times, Sunday Albany Times Union, 12/20/81; Peg Churchill Wright (auth), Area artist gets national attention, Schenectady Gazette, 2/23/83; Renown North Country Artist (film), Spotlight Channel 10, Albany, NY. *Mem:* Lower Adirondack Regional Art Coun (mem exec bd, 80-85, pres, 81-82). *Media:* Watercolor, Pastels; Oil. *Publ:* Auth, Watercolor page, Am Artist Mag, 3/83. *Dealer:* Blackburn Gallery 261 Bay Rd Glens Falls NY 12801; Primrose Press New Hope PA. *Mailing Add:* 261 Bay Rd Glens Falls NY 12801

BLACKETER, JAMES RICHARD
PAINTER, ART DEALER
b Laguna Beach, Calif, Sept 23, 31. *Study:* Santa Ana Col; also with Bennett Bradbury. *Exhib:* Laguna Beach Invitational Marine Show, Calif, 59; Los Angeles Co Fair Invitational Exhib, Pomona, Calif, 60; Hunt-Wesson Foods Show, Fullerton, Calif, 72. *Pos:* Art dir, Fed Sign & Signal Corp, Los Angeles, 58-60, Santa Ana, 60-72; owner, The Studio (art gallery), Laguna Beach. *Teaching:* Pvt classes oil painting, 60- *Awards:* Laguna Beach Art Asn Awards, 51, 58, 59 & 60; Festival of Arts Award, 58; Ebell Club Los Angeles Award, 60. *Mem:* Laguna Beach Art Asn (secy, 60); Am Inst Fine Arts; Laguna Beach Festival Arts, Showcase 21. *Media:* Oil. *Specialty:* Marine oil paintings. *Mailing Add:* 266 Canyon Acers Dr Laguna Beach CA 92651

BLACKEY, MARY MADLYN
PAINTER, PRINTMAKER
b Glen Cove, NY. *Study:* Albright Art Sch, NY, cert, 52; State Univ NY, Buffalo, BS(art educ), 53; Art Students League, 54-55 & 61-63; Ruth Leaf Etching Studio, 71-73; Donn Steward Etching Workshop, 77-79. *Work:* Columbia Broadcasting Studio, NY; Col Eastern Utah; Int Bus Machines; Conoco Oil; Nassau Community Col; and others. *Exhib:* Am Watercolor Soc Travel Show, Butler Inst Am Art, 66; one-man shows, Nassau Co Ctr Fine Arts, NY, 75 & New Eng Ctr/Univ NH, 77; Project Diomede, Inst Contemp Art, The Clocktower, 89; Positive Actions: Visual Aids, billboard design, Inst Contemp Art, New York, 90; Selected Works on Paper, Widener Univ Mus, Pa, 91; Philadelphia Watercolor Club Ann, Noyes Mus, NJ, 92; Aqueous Open 92, Westmoreland Mus Art, Pa, 92; Bucks Biennial 1, The James Michner Art Mus, Pa, 92; and others. *Teaching:* Instr watercolor, Jackson Heights Art Club, 71-72, Five Towns Music & Art Found, 77-79, Great Neck Adult Prog, 81-83 & Islip Art Mus, 86. *Awards:* The Pennel Memorial Award, Philadelphia Watercolor Club Ann, Pa, 91; Fourth Prize, Arches Nat Watercolor Competition, 91; Patron Purchase Award, Watercolor, USA, Springfield Art Mus, Mo, 92; and others. *Bibliog:* Barbara Nechis (auth), Watercolor--A Creative Experience, Von Nostrand Reinhold, 79; Malcolm Preston (auth), Vision in space and form, Newsday, 90. *Mem:* Am Watercolor Soc; Nat Soc Painters Casein & Acrylic (bd dir, 82-84); Philadelphia Art Alliance; Found for Archit, 90-; Philadelphia Watercolor Club, 90- *Media:* Watercolor, Acrylic; Etching. *Publ:* Who's Who in the East, Marquis Publs; The Foole, print collection, Philadelphia Print Club, 92. *Dealer:* Art Resource Consultants Denver Co. *Mailing Add:* 1032 Radcliffe St C-15 Bristol PA 19007

BLACKMAN, THOMAS PATRICK
DIRECTOR, PRINTMAKER
b Des Moines, Iowa, May 15, 51. *Study:* Univ Iowa, Iowa City, BFA, 76. *Collections Arranged:* Chicago Sculpture Int-Mile 1, 2, 3, 82-84. *Pos:* Sponger & shop asst, Landfall Press, Chicago, 78-80; intaglio printer, Metropress, Chicago, 80-81; dir, Chicago Int Art Exposition, 81-, Chicago Int Antique Show, 84-91. *Mailing Add:* Chicago Int Art Expo 600 N McClurg Ct Suite 1302A Chicago IL 60611

BLACKMUN, BARBARA WINSTON
EDUCATOR, ART HISTORIAN
b Merced, Calif, June 29, 28. *Study:* Univ Calif, Los Angeles, BA(fine arts; hons), 49 & PhD(art hist), 84; Ariz State Univ, MA(art hist), 71. *Pos:* Founding dir, Univ Arts Workshop, Malawi, Africa, 68-69; co-founder & chmn, Pub Arts Adv Coun, Co of San Diego, 76-78. *Teaching:* Lectr art hist & chmn art subject bd, Univ Malawi, Limbe, Malawi, Africa, 67-69; prof art hist, San Diego Mesa Col, Calif, 71-, chmn dept visual arts, 76-78 & 83-85; adj asst prof, Univ Calif, San Diego, 87; adj assoc prof, Univ Calif, Los Angeles, 88. *Awards:* Dickson Travel Grant, Univ Calif, Los Angeles, 80; Fulbright Hays Doctoral Res Fel, Nat Endowment Humanities Fel for College Teachers & Independent Scholars, 92. *Mem:* Col Art Asn; Archaeol Inst Am; African Studies Asn; Art Historians Southern Calif. *Res:* The Nyau masks of the Maravi and their significance in African art; the bronze and terracotta sculpture of Ife, Nigeria, a classification through style analysis; the iconography of carved figural altar tusks from Benin Kingdom, Nigeria; African Ivories. *Publ:* Coauth, Masks of Malawi, African Arts, 72; The Art of Power: The Power of Art, UCLA Mus Cult Hist, 83; From Trader to Priest in 200 Years: Art Journal, Col Art Asn, summer 88; Obas Portraits in Benin, African Arts, Vol XXIII, No 4, 61-69, 102-104, 7/90; Who Commissioned the Queen Mother Tusks? A Problem in the Chronology of Benin Ivories, African Arts, Vol XXIV, No 2, 54-65, 90-91, 4/91; Ivory and the Trunk Hand in Benin in The Elephant and its Ivory, Mus Cul Hist, UCLA, 92. *Mailing Add:* 9850 Ogram Dr La Mesa CA 92041

BLACKWELL, TOM (THOMAS LEO)
PAINTER
b Chicago, Ill, Mar 9, 38. *Work:* Guggenheim Mus, Mus Mod Art, Metrop Mus Art, New York; Elveh Jem Mus Art, Madison, Wis; Nat Air & Space Mus, Smithsonian Inst; Ball State Univ Art Gallery, Muncie, Ind. *Exhib:* Human Concern-Personal Torment, Whitney Mus Am Art, New York, 69; Whitney Mus Am Art Painting Ann, 72; Prospectus, Art in the Seventies, Aldrich Mus Contemp Art, Ridgefield, Conn, 79; National Air & Space Mus, Smithsonian Inst, Washington, DC, 77-78 & 80; Seven Photorealists from New York Collections, Solomon R Guggenheim Mus, New York, 81; Contemp Am Realism since 1960, Pa Acad Fine Art, Philadelphia, Pa, 81-82; American Realism-The Precise Image, Isetan Mus Art, Japan, 85; Second Inaugural Exhib, Carlo Lamagna Gallery, New York, 86; solo exhibs, Selected works 1970-1980, Dartmouth Col, Hanover, NH, 80, Univ Ariz Mus Art, Tuscon, 81; Louis K Meisel Gallery, New York, 77, 80, 82 & 91, Currier Gallery Art, Manchester, NH, 85, Carlo Lamagna Gallery, New York, 86. *Teaching:* Artist in residence, Dartmouth Col, Hanover, NH, 80; Univ Ariz, Tuscon, 81; instr, Sch Visual Arts, New York, 85- *Awards:* Grant, New Hampshire Comn Arts, 85. *Bibliog:* John Russell (auth), Painters from Brussels, New York Times, 5/21/82; Terence Mullaly (auth), Icy reflections of life, London Daily Telegraph, 83; Vivien Raynor (auth), Tom Blackwell, New York Times, 5/2/86. *Media:* Oil. *Mailing Add:* c/o Louis K Meisel Gallery 141 Prince St New York NY 10012

BLACKWOOD, DAVID (LLOYD)
PAINTER, PRINTMAKER
b Wesleyville, Nfld, Can, Nov 7, 41. *Study:* Ont Col Art, Toronto, 59-64. *Work:* Nat Gallery Can; Nat Gallery Australia; Art Gallery Ont; Montreal Mus Fine Arts; NB Mus. *Exhib:* Int Graphics, Montreal Mus Fine Arts, 71; 1st Norweg Biennial, Frederickstad, 72; Biennial Int de l'Estampe, Paris, France, 73. *Pos:* Artist-in-residence, Univ Toronto, 69-75. *Teaching:* Art master, Trinity Col Sch, Port Hope, Ont, 63-75. *Awards:* Ingres Medal, Govt France, 63; Purchase Award Can Biennial, Nat Gallery Can, 64; Hornansky Award Int Graphics, Montreal Mus Fine Arts, 71. *Bibliog:* Rex Bromfield (auth), David Blackwood (film), CBC, 72; Farley Mowat (auth), Survivor, Wake of the Great Sealers, McClelland & Little Brown, 73; Blackwood (film), NFB, 75. *Mem:* Royal Can Acad Art (vpres, 79). *Dealer:* Gallery Quan 112 Scollard St Toronto ON M5R 1G2 Can. *Mailing Add:* 22 King St Port Hope ON L1A 2R5 Canada

BLAEDEL, JOAN STUART ROSS
PAINTER, PRINTMAKER
b Boston, Mass, Sept 21, 42. *Study:* Conn Col, with R Lukosius & W McCloy BA, 64; Yale Univ, with J Albers, G Peterdi & Stillman, 65; Univ Iowa, with M Lasansky & E Ludins, MA, 67, MFA, 68. *Work:* Seattle City Light Collection; Ore Arts Found, Salem; Seattle Art Mus; Sea First Bank; Security Pacific Bank. *Comn:* Environ sculpture, Seattle Arts Comn & Nat Endowment Arts, Seattle, 76; five woodcut prints, King Co Arts Comn, 78-79; 7 mixed-media panels, King Co Architecture Division, 80; painting, Seafirst Bank, Seattle, 86. *Exhib:* Original Ed, traveling exhib, Ore Arts Found, 78; 31st Spokane Ann Exhib, Cheney-Cowles Mem Mus, 79; Rutgers Nat Drawing, Rutgers Univ Mus, 79; New Ideas IV, Seattle Art Mus, 81; Northwest Now, Tacoma Art Mus, 86; Focus: Seattle, San Jose Art Mus, 86; NW Monotypes, Seattle Art Mus. *Pos:* Mem, Seattle Arts Comn, 81-85; chair, Art in Pub Places Comn, 83-85; Bumbershoot Festival Comn, 85-91. *Teaching:* Instr printmaking & drawing, Seattle Pac Univ, 70-90; instr printmaking, Factory Visual Art, 74-76; instr drawing, Green River Community Col, 78; instr drawing, Univ Wash, 88; instr drawing, Monotype & paintig, Edmonds Community Col, 92. *Awards:* Original Editions Award, Ore Arts Found, 78; Gaiser Award, Cheney-Cowles Mem Mus, 79; Betty Bowen Award, Seattle Art Mus, 81. *Bibliog:* Ruth Hayes (auth), Seattle Artists, film doc, Seattle Arts Comn, 79; R Glowen (auth), Gesture and control, Artweek, 81. *Mem:* Northwest Print Coun (charter mem). *Media:* Miscellaneous Media; Miscellaneous Media. *Publ:* Illusr, The Lamp in the Spine, Moore & Hampl, 71; Backbone: Seven Northwest Poets, 77 & Talk and Contact, 78, Seal Press; Fifty Northwest Artists, Chronicle Books, 83; two covers, Copper Canyon Press, 86-89; Bumbershoot Arts Festival, poster, 92. *Dealer:* Grover/Thurston Gallery 532 First Ave S Seattle WA 98104. *Mailing Add:* 4102 Second Ave NW Seattle WA 98107

BLAGDEN, ALLEN
PAINTER, PRINTMAKER
b New York, NY, Feb 21, 38. *Study:* Hotchkiss Sch; Yale Univ Summer Art Sch; Cornell Univ, BFA. *Work:* Berkshire Mus, Pittsfield, Mass; Garvan Collection, Peabody Mus, New Haven, Conn; New Britain Mus Am Art, Conn; Adirondack Mus, Blue Mountain Lake, NY; Leigh Yawkey Woodson Mus, Wausau, Wis. *Comn:* Many private portrait commissions. *Exhib:* Father and Son Show, Mongerson Wunderlich Gallery, Chicago, 89; one-man shows, Rehn Gallery & Kennedy Galleries, New York, Indian Images, Mongerson Wunderlich Gallery, Chicago, 90; Birds in Art, Leigh Yawkey Woodson Art Mus, Wausau, Wis, 90; Artists of America, Denver, Colo, 90; and others. *Pos:* Illusr dept ornithology, Smithsonian Inst, Washington, DC, 62-63. *Teaching:* Instr painting, Hotchkiss Sch, 68-69; artist in residence, Cornell Univ, 82. *Awards:* Allied Artist Award, 63; Century Club Art Prize, 71. *Mem:* Century Asn, New York; Artists' Fel, New York. *Media:* Watercolor, Oil; Etching, Lithography. *Publ:* Wildlife Painters at Work, Watson-Gupthill. *Dealer:* Mongerson-Wunderlich 704 N Wells St Chicago IL 60610. *Mailing Add:* Box 248 Salisbury CT 06068

BLAGDEN, THOMAS P
PAINTER
b Chester, Pa, Mar 29, 11. *Study:* Yale Univ, BA, 33; Pa Acad Fine Arts, 33-35; spec study with Henry Hensche & George Demetrios. *Work:* Addison Gallery Am Art, Andover, Mass; Wadsworth Atheneum, Hartford, Conn; Berkshire Mus, Pittsfield, Mass; New Britain Mus Am Art, New Britain, Conn; Neuberger Mus, Purchase, NY; Currier Gallery, Manchester, NH. *Exhib:* Pa Acad Fine Arts, Philadelphia, 38; Corcoran Gallery Art, Washington, DC, 41; Metrop Mus Art, New York, 50; Am Acad Arts & Lett, NY, 61; Loeb Drama Ctr, Harvard Univ, Cambridge, Mass, 71; one-man show, Keene State Col, NH, 79 & 21 other one-man exhibs, incl nine in New York (Milch Galleries & others), St Gaudens Mus, New Britain Mus, Americanart. *Teaching:* Instr art, Hotchkiss Sch, Lakeville, Conn, 35-56. *Awards:* Purchase Prize, Wadsworth Atheneum & Berkshire Mus. *Mem:* Century Club, New York; Conn Watercolor Soc. *Media:* Oil, Watercolor. *Mailing Add:* 26 Town Hill Rd Lakeville CT 06039

BLAHOVE, MARCOS
PAINTER
b Ukraine, Apr 22, 28; US citizen. *Study:* Acad Vicente Puig, Buenos Aires, Arg; Nat Acad Design, New York. *Work:* Nat Collection Fine Arts, Nat Portrait Gallery, Smithsonian Inst, Washington, DC; Duke Univ, NC; NC State Univ, Raleigh; Salmagundi Club, New York. *Comn:* Portrait of Aaron Copland, Mrs F Copland, New York, 72; Lt Barbara A Allen, Naval Art Coop & Liaison Comt, 74; Bill Koghlerr, Salmagundi Club, New York, 74; Senator Sam J Ervin, Jr, NC State Univ, Humanities Found, 81; Terry Sanford, Pres of Duke Univ, NC, 85; Mr Smith Richardson, Pres of Smith Richardson Found, Col Ctr Creative Leadership, Greensboro, NC. *Exhib:* Fine Arts Festival, Parrish Art Mus, Southampton, NY, 71; Artists Exhib, Southampton Col, NY, 71; Art on Paper, Weatherspoon Art Gallery, Univ NC, Greensboro, 74; Contemporary Portraits by American Painters, Lowe Art Mus, Coral Gables, Fla, 74. *Awards:* Purchase Prize, Artists Exhib, Southampton Col, NY, 71; Eliot Liskin Award, Salmagundi Club, 72; Fine Arts Comn Purchase Award, Am Drawings 76, Portsmouth Mus, 76. *Bibliog:* Lois Miller (auth), Marcos Blahove at the heart of his subject, Am Artist, 7/73; Susan E Meyer (auth), 20 Figure Painters and How They Work, Watson-Guptill, 79. *Mem:* Salmagundi Club. *Publ:* Coauth, (with Joe Singer), Painting Children in Oil, Watson-Guptill, 78. *Dealer:* Art Gallery Originals 120 Reynolda Village Winston-Salem NC 27106. *Mailing Add:* 4908 Manning Dr Greensboro NC 27410

BLAI, BERTHA
CERAMIST, CRAFTSMAN
b Baltimore, Md. *Study:* Tyler Sch Art, Temple Univ, BFA; with Rudy Staffel, Raymond Gallucci, Toshieko Takieuzi & Karen Karns. *Exhib:* Philadelphia Civic Ctr, 70; Paley Libr, Temple Univ, 71; DuCret Sch Art, North Plainfield, NJ, 71; Widener Col, Chester, Pa, 72; Glassboro State Col, NJ, 74; Camp Scatico, Elizaville, NY. *Teaching:* Instr, Ocean Co Col, 68-69; DuCret Sch Art, 69-72; artist-in-residence ceramics, Glassboro State Col, 72-75; dir ceramic, Camp Scatico, Elizaville, NY, 89-90. *Mem:* Hon mem Pa Guild Craftsmen; Am Craftsmen Asn; Artists Equity Asn; life mem Long Beach Island Found of Arts & Sci, NJ. *Media:* Pottery Clay, Glazes. *Mailing Add:* 1500 Locust St Apt P 313 Philadelphia PA 19102

BLAINE, MATTHEW FREDERICK
SCULPTOR, EDUCATOR
b Baltimore, Md, May 24, 47. *Study:* Univ Miss, BA, 70. *Work:* Metrop Mus Art, The Tate, The Getty, Mus Mod Art, The Australia Nat Gallery. *Exhib:* 24th, 25th & 26th Ann Nat Show, Acad Arts, Easton, Md, 88; 47th Ann Nat Competition, Lakeworth, Fla, 88; Artist's Equity 3rd & 4th Ann Awards Exhib, Washington, DC, 88; one-man show, DCCA Gallery, Wilmington, Del, 89; Biannual Show Del Art Mus, 89. *Pos:* bd trustees, Rehoboth Art League, 88- *Teaching:* Instr art-sec, Seaford Sch Dist, 69-; asst prof ceramics & sculpture, Salisbury State Univ, 83-, lectr art, 84- *Awards:* Jury of Selection Awards, Mont Miniature Internat, (show), 88; First Place Sculpture, RAL 50th Ann Member Show, 88. *Mem:* Int Artist Equity; Del Ctr Contemp Art; Del Art Educ Asn; Int Sculpture Ctr. *Media:* All. *Publ:* contribr, Sculpture: Technique, Form, Content, Davis Publ, 88. *Mailing Add:* 908 W St Laurel DE 19956

BLAINE, NELL
PAINTER, PRINTMAKER
b Richmond, Va, July 10, 22. *Study:* Richmond Prof Inst, 39-42; Hans Hofmann Sch Fine Arts, 42-44; Atelier 17, etching & engraving with William S Hayter, 45; New Sch Social Res, 52-53; Moore Col Art, Hon Dr, 80; Va Commonwealth Univ, Hon Dr, 85. *Work:* Mus Mod Art, Whitney Mus Am Art, Metrop Mus Art, New York; Brooklyn Mus, NY; Va Mus Fine Arts, Richmond; Hirschhorn Carnegie Inst; plus many others. *Comn:* Two murals, landscapes & cityscapes of Paris, Revlon, Inc, New York, 58. *Exhib:* Solo exhibs, Jane St Gallery, NY, 45 & 48, Poindexter Gallery, New York, 8 shows 56-76, Fischbach Gallery, New York, 79, 81, 83, 85, 87, 89 & 91, Va Mus Fine Art, 73 & 79 & Hull Gallery, Washington, DC, 79; Nat Acad Design Ann, 78; The New American Still Life, Westmoreland Co Mus Art, 78; Hans Hofmann as Teacher: Drawings by His Students, Mus Mod Art, 79; The Fifties: Aspects of Painting in New York, Hirshhorn Mus, Washington, DC, 80. *Pos:* Designer, Village Voice, 55. *Teaching:* Instr, Great Neck Pub Sch Adult Prog, 56. *Awards:* Guggenheim, 74; Nat Endowment Arts Grant, 75; Louise Nevelson Award, Am Acad & Inst Arts & Letters, 90; Guggenheim Fel, 75; Nat Endowment Arts Award, 76; Gov Award Art, Va, 79. *Bibliog:* Homage to Nell Blaine, Art News Mag, 12/59; James R Mellow (auth), The flowering summer of Nell Blaine, NY Times, 10/11/70; Eleanor Munro (auth), article, In: Originals: American Women Artists, Simon & Schuster, 79. *Mem:* Artists Equity Asn; Women's Caucus Art; Nat Acad Design. *Media:* Oil, Watercolor; Etching, Serigraphy. *Publ:* Coauth, Prints/Nell Blaine-Poems/Kenneth Koch, 53; illusr, In Memory of My Feelings, Mus Mod Art, 68; auth, Getting with Lester & Mondrian in the forties, Jazz & Painting, 72; contribr, A Sense of Place-the Artist & the American Landscape, 72; illusr, Loves Aspects, 75; coauth, The Earth Shines Secretly a Book of Days, 90; Nell Blaine Sketchbook, The Arts Publ, NY, 86. *Dealer:* Fischbach Gallery 24 W 57th St New York NY 10019. *Mailing Add:* 210 Riverside Dr Apt 8A New York NY 10025

BLAIR, CARL RAYMOND
PAINTER, ART DEALER
b Atchison, Kans, Nov 28, 32. *Study:* Univ Kans, BFA, 56; Kansas City Art Inst; Sch Design, MFA, 57. *Work:* Mint Mus Art, Charlotte, NC; Greenville Co Mus Art, SC; Greenville Col, Ill; SC Arts Comn, Columbia; Clemson Univ, SC. *Comn:* IBM; McDonalds Inc. *Exhib:* 33rd Butler Ann Painting Exhib, Youngstown, Ohio; Soc Four Arts, Palm Beach, Fla; Piedmont Painting & Sculpture Exhib, Charlotte, 65; Appalachian Corridors I, Charleston, WVa, 68; Int Platform Asn, Washington, DC, 71; Palazzo Venezia, Rome, Italy, 84. *Pos:* Co-founder & pres, Hampton III Gallery, Taylors, SC. *Teaching:* Prof drawing & painting, Bob Jones Univ, 57-; summer sch, Kansas City Art Inst & Greenville Co Mus Art. *Awards:* Appalachian Corridors I, SC Arts Comn, 68; Int Platform Asn, 68; SC Arts Commission, 88. *Bibliog:* La Revue Moderne, Paris, France, 65-68; Jack A Morris, Jr (auth), Contemporary artists of South Carolina, 70. *Mem:* SC Artists Guild (adv bd, 57-); Upstate Visual Artists. *Media:* Oil. *Dealer:* Hampton III Gallery Ltd Gallery Ctr Taylors SC 29687; Gerald L Melberg Gallery Charlotte NC. *Mailing Add:* No 2 Oakleaf Rd Greenville SC 29609

BLAIR, DIKE
PAINTER
b New Castle, Pa, Aug 2, 52. *Study:* Univ Colo, 71-75; Skowhegan Sch Painting & Sculpture, 74; Whitney Mus Independent Study Prog, 76; Sch Art Inst Chicago, MFA, 77. *Comn:* Construction (7ft x 30ft), Hosp Corp Am, Nashville, 82; photo glass mural (7 ft x 1/2 ft), Murray Hill Cinema, New York, 90. *Exhib:* I-80 Series, Joslyn Art Mus, Omaha, 81; Energy New York, Center D'Echanges, Lyon, France, 82; Activated Walls, Queens Mus, New York, 84; Painting & Sculpture Today, Ind Mus Art, 86; Landscape in the Age of Anxiety, Lehman Col Art Gallery, 86; The New Romantic Landscape, Whitney Mus, Fairfield County, 87; Image World, Whitney Mus Am Art, New York, 89; Bellevue, Mus Mod Art, Vienna, Austria, 89. *Awards:* Fel, Mid-Atlantic Regional, Nat Endowment Arts, 88-89. *Bibliog:* Jeffrey Rian (auth), Reviews, Art in America, 4/87; Mary Ellen Haus (auth), The Unnatural Landscape, Art News, 1/88; Robert Mahoney (auth), Reviews, Arts Mag, 1/92. *Media:* Paint & Photo on Glass. *Publ:* Auth, GFWFQ recalled, Issue No 6, summer 86. *Mailing Add:* 235 E 11th St New York NY 10003

BLAIR, HELEN
SCULPTOR, ILLUSTRATOR
b Hibbing, Minn, Dec 29, 10. *Study:* Mass Sch Art, with Cyrus Dallin; Boston Mus Sch; Archipenko Sch Art, with Archipenko. *Comn:* Plaques of Dr Waring, Colo Med Sch, 69 & of Dr Porter, Porter Mem Hosp, Denver, 70; Robert Ledbettor, Rome, Ga; bust of Peter Dominick, Colo State Capitol, Denver; bas-relief of Ed Sinu, Glendale, Ariz. *Exhib:* One-man shows, Ardan Studios, New York, 38, Portraits, Inc, New York, 41-42, Vose Galleries, Boston, 44, St Paul Art Ctr, Minn, 62 & Martin Gallery, Phoenix, 73-74; C G Rein Gallery, Palm Beach, 79; O'Meara Galleries, Scottsdale, Ariz, 89. *Teaching:* Instr art educ, Boston Univ, 37-40; St Paul Art Sch, 70-72. *Awards:* Nat Soc Arts & Letts Medallion of Merit, 86. *Bibliog:* K S Thompson (auth), Figurines step into a new role, Boston Transcript, 34; Peter Martin (auth), Moulder of youth, Am Mag, 46; Marjorie Barrett (auth), Helen Blair's little people, Denver Post, 70. *Mem:* Artists Equity Asn; Nat Arts & Lett Soc; Ariz Artists Guild. *Media:* Cast Metal. *Publ:* Illusr, Jeanne-Marie, 34, Great Day in the Morning, 46, Assorted Sisters, 47, House Under the Hill, 49 & Hetly & the Grand Deluxe, 51, Houghton Mifflin; auth, Visual Thinking Patterns, 86. *Dealer:* Ratliff-Williams Gallery 556 Hwy 79 Sedona AZ 86336. *Mailing Add:* 1919 E Claremont St Phoenix AZ 85016

BLAIR, LEE EVERETT
PAINTER, FILMMAKER
b Los Angeles, Calif, Oct 1, 11. *Study:* Chouinard Sch Art, Los Angeles, 33; Art Students League, New York, 47-50. *Work:* Calif Palace Legion Hon, San Francisco; Los Angeles Co Mus Art, Los Angeles; Am Watercolor Soc, William Church Osborn Collection, New York; Art Inst Chicago. *Exhib:* Int Olympic Art Competition, Los Angeles, 32 & Berlin, Ger, 36; Calif Watercolor Soc, Los Angeles Co Mus, 35-49; Los Angeles Co Fair, Pomona, Calif, 35-58; Am Watercolor Soc, Nat Acad Art, New York, 35-; Soc Illusr, New York, 58-67; Santa Cruz Art League Statewide, Calif, 78-80; Santa Barbara Art Mus, 88. *Teaching:* Instr landscape painting, Chouinard Sch Art, Los Angeles, 38-42; instr film animation art, Cabrillo Col, Aptos, Calif, 75-79 & Univ Calif, Santa Cruz, 77-80. *Awards:* Silver Medal, 47 & William Church Osborn Purchase Award, 53; Watercolors Award, Santa Cruz Art League, 79. *Bibliog:* Dale Pollock (auth), Animating fantasia, Santa Cruz Sentinel, 75; Gordon T McClelland (auth), The California Style-Watercolor Artists 1925-1955, Hillcrest Press. *Mem:* Calif Watercolor Soc (pres, 38-42); New York Film Producers Asn (pres, 68-70); life mem Am Watercolor Soc; Soc Western Artists (exhib mem); Calif Inst Arts. *Media:* Watercolor, Oil. *Mailing Add:* 3465 Crestline Way Soquel CA 95073

BLAIR, ROBERT NOEL
PAINTER, SCULPTOR
b Buffalo, NY, Aug 12, 12. *Study:* Sch Mus Fine Arts, Boston, Mass. *Work:* Metrop Mus Art, New York; Butler Inst Am Art, Youngstown, Ohio; Munson-Williams-Proctor Inst, Utica, NY; Twain Mus Hist Art; Ford Motor Co Collection, Dearborn, Mich; and others. *Comn:* Sermon on the Mount (oil, tempera), US Army Chapel, Ft McClellan, Ala, 43; Open Hearth (oil), Bethlehem Steel Plant, Lackawanna, NY, 47. *Exhib:* Corcoran Biennial, Corcoran Gallery Art, Washington, DC, 47; Watercolor Int, Art Inst Chicago, Ill, 48; Pa Acad Fine Arts Nat, Philadelphia, 48; Butler Art Inst Nat & Metrop Mus Art Watercolor Nat, 53; one-man retrospective, Community Tribute Exhibition, State Univ NY Col Buffalo, 66, 100 paintings & drawings of World War II - Entitled: A Solpiers Portfolio Burchfield Art Ctr, Buffalo, New York, 85; and others. *Pos:* Dir, Art Inst Buffalo, 46-49; illusr, Ford Times Mag, 58-61. *Teaching:* Instr painting, Art Inst Buffalo, 38-55, Albright Art Sch, 55 & State Univ NY Col Buffalo, 71. *Awards:* Guggenheim Fels, 46 & 51; Watowsky Prize, Art Inst Chicago, 48; First Watercolor Prize, Butler Inst Am Art, 53. *Mem:* Buffalo Soc Artists. *Media:* Watercolor, Oil. *Res:* Expansion of technical possibilities in painting. *Publ:* Illusr, St Lawrence Seaway, 57; illusr, Am Artist Mag, 66; illusr, Jeannie's world, 66; illusr & auth, Watercolorists at work, 71. *Mailing Add:* c/o Burchfield Art Center 1300 Elmwood Ave Buffalo NY 14222

BLAKE, JANE
PAINTER, SCULPTOR
b Burgaw, NC, Oct 12, 33. *Study:* Cent Wesleyan Col, SC, AB, 55; Studied with Marilyn Bendell, 71-72 & Bede Zel Angle, 74. *Work:* Govs Mansion, SC; State Senate & Govs Mansion, Tallahassee, Fla. *Comn:* Portraits, Families of Hospital Founders, Burgaw, NC, 80-90; Seven miniatures of Fla First Ladies, Govs Mansion Found, Tallahassee, 83-90; Bronze Sculpture comn by Herbert Shevins, Indian Rocks Beach, Fla, 89; Three miniature portraits comn by June Baumgartner Gelbart, Fla & Australia, 90-92. *Exhib:* Ulster Soc Miniaturist, Northern Ireland, 92; Miniature Painters, Sculptors & Gravers, Washington, DC, 92; Miniature Art Soc NJ, Nutley, 89 & 92; Miniature Art Soc Ga, Atlanta, 92; Int Miniature Art Show, St Petersburg Mus Fine Arts, Fla, 90; and others. *Awards:* Gold Mem Bowl Award, Royal Soc Miniature Painters, Sculptors & Gravers, 87; First Place Portraiture & Permanent Collection Award, Int Exhib Miniature Art Soc Fla, 89. *Bibliog:* Maymie Eschwey (auth), Portraits in Miniature, Alpha Eds, 88. *Mem:* Royal Soc Miniature Sculptors, Painters & Gravers; Miniature Art Soc Fla (awards chmn, 86-90); Miniature Art Soc NJ; Ulster Soc Miniaturist, Northern Ireland; Miniature Painters, Sculptors & Gravers Soc, Washington, DC. *Media:* Oil; Clay, bronze. *Mailing Add:* 11148 Freedom Way Seminole FL 34642

BLAKE, JANE SALLEY
PUBLISHER, EDITOR
b Tallahassee, Fla, Sept 3, 37. *Study:* Fla State Univ, Tallahassee, BA(fine arts & journalism), 58. *Pos:* Founder, pres & chmn bd, Arts Forum Inc, Louisville, Ky, 78-84; publ, exec ed, Beaux Arts mag, 80-84; pres, Blake Publ Inc, Louisville, Ky, 83-86; pres, principal, J S Blake Commun Group, Louisville, Ky, 86-; pres, principal, Ctr Mag, Inc, 86. *Awards:* 13 Louie Awards, Advert Club, Louisville, Ky, 81-84; 4 Landmarks Excellence Awards, PRSA & IABC, Louisville, Ky; Gov's Arts Award for Media Excellence, 89; Above & Beyond the Call of Duty Award, 90. *Mem:* Advert Club Louisville; Bus Advocates; Sigma Delta Chi Prof Journalism Soc; Pub Relations Soc Am; Women in Commun; Entrepreneur Soc (bd dir, 88-90). *Publ:* Ctr Mag Ky Ctr Arts, 83; Publ, Practical Pub Relations for Non-professionals, 85; Kentucky Marquee, 86. *Dealer:* The Center Magazine Inc 118 Bauer Ave Louisville KY 40207. *Mailing Add:* 118 Bauer Ave Louisville KY 40207

BLAKE, PETER JOST
ARCHITECT, CRITIC
b Berlin, Ger, Sept 20, 20; US citizen. *Study:* Univ London, 38; Regent St Polytech, Sch Archit, London, 39; Univ Pa, 41; Sch of Archit, Pratt Inst, BArch, 49. *Comn:* Experimental Theaters in New York, Nashville, TN, 63-81; Apartment Building for IBA, St Lukes Church, West Berlin, 87-88; Projects for nat & int competition. *Pos:* Writer, Archit Forum, New York, 42-43, assoc ed, 50-54 & 58-61, managing ed, 61-64, ed, 64-72; cur archit & design, Mus Mod Art, New York, 48-50; partner, Peter Blake & Julian Neski, 58-61; partner, James Baker & Peter Blake, Architects, New York, 64-72; ed-in-chief, Archit Plus, New York, 72-75; chmn, Sch Archit, Boston Archit Ctr, Mass, 75-79; chmn dept archit & planning, Catholic Univ Am, Washington, DC, 79-86; US Delegate for Archit at Helsinki Conf, Budapest, Hungary, 85. *Teaching:* Vis critic/lectr, var US & foreign cols & univs; prof archit, Catholic Univ Am, Wash, DC, 79- *Awards:* Archit Critic's Medal, Am Inst Archit, 75; Hon Mention, Vietnam Veterans' Mem Compt, 81; Distinguished Designer Fel, Nat Endowment Arts, 84. *Mem:* Fel Am Inst Architects; Archit League New York (vpres archit, pres, 71-72); Int Design Conf, Aspen, Colo (bd dirs, 65-70); Regional Plan Asn. *Publ:* Auth, Master Builders, Knopf, 60; God's Own Junkyard, Holt, Rinehart & Winston, 64; Form Follows Fiasco, Why Modern Architecture Hasn't Worked, Atlantic Monthly Press & Little, Brown & Co, 77; contribr, articles in pop mags & newspapers. *Mailing Add:* Dept Archit Catholic Univ Am Washington DC 20064

BLAKE, PRISCILLA ANN
MURALIST, CERAMIST
b Fall River, Mass, Oct 14, 52. *Study:* Moore Col Art, Philadelphia, Pa, 72; Univ Wis, Madison, BS(textile design), 75. *Work:* Tile Dicarlo Showroom, Chicago, Ill. *Comn:* Jungle design mural, Kwang Herline, Bayside, NY, 86; Trellis mural with leaves, Minchell Residence, Dix Hills, NY, 87; Peacock subject matter, Horvat Residence, Providence, RI, 87; Ocean scene, Padden Residence, Warwick, RI, 88. *Pos:* Textile designer & colorist, Ametex, New York, 77-80; owner, Priscilla Ceramic Tiles, West Yarmouth, Mass, 80- *Mem:* Am Craft Coun. *Media:* Ceramic Tiles. *Publ:* Darlyn Brewer (auth), Home Section (Art), New York Times, 10/17/85; Kraus Sikes (coauth), The Guild, Kraus & Sikes, 87 & 88. *Dealer:* Karen Joy Miller Interiors 5 Broadview Dr Huntington NY 11743. *Mailing Add:* 20 Deep Brook Rd West Yarmouth MA 02673

BLAKE, WENDON See Holden, Donald

BLAKELY, GEORGE C
PHOTOGRAPHY, SCULPTOR
b Long Beach, Calif, Apr 7, 1951. *Study:* Calif State Univ, Fullerton, MA, 76; Tyler Sch Art, MFA, 78. *Exhib:* Solo exhib, San Francisco Mus Mod Art, Calif, 81; Southern Expressions, High Mus Art, Atlanta, Ga, 89; over 200 group exhibitions. *Teaching:* Assoc prof art, Fla State Univ, Tallahassee, currently. *Awards:* Grants, Nat Endowment Arts, 81 & 88. *Mem:* Soc Photog Educ. *Mailing Add:* 304 Bradford Rd Tallahassee FL 32303

BLAKENEY, RAE
HISTORIAN
US citizen. *Study:* Wright State Univ, with Dr Eugene Cantelupe, BA, 76; Union Grad Sch, with Dr Barbara Novak, PhD, 87. *Pos:* Guest cur, Tex Humanities Resource Ctr, Austin, 85. *Teaching:* Adj prof urban esthetics, Inst Urban Studies, Univ Tex, Arlington, currently. *Mem:* Col Art Asn; Midwest Art Hist Soc; C G Jung Found. *Res:* Psychological basis for meaning of visual form and visual language. *Publ:* Coauth & ed, Rudolf Baranik: Napalm Elegy and Other Works, Wright State Univ Fine Art Galleries, 77; coauth, Alpha, Trans, Chung, A Photographic Model: Semiotics, Film & Interpretation, NFS Press, 78; coauth & ed, Roland Reiss, Psycho-Social Environments, Santa Barbara Mus Art, 81; auth, Image and individuation: Archetypes in the Vervschka Trans-Figurations, SPE Journal, 87. *Mailing Add:* 4701 Chapel Springs Court Arlington TX 76017

BLAKESLEE, SARAH
PAINTER
b Evanston, Ill, Jan 13, 12. *Study:* Corcoran Sch Art; Pa Acad Fine Arts, Cresson Europ Traveling Scholar; Barnes Found; also with Catherine Critcher, Washington, DC. *Work:* Pa Acad Fine Arts; Nat Acad Design; NC Mus Art; Muskegon Mus, Mich; Greenville Mus Art, NC; St John's Mus, Wilmington, NC. *Comn:* Portraits, ECarolina Univ, Greenville & St Mary's Col, Raleigh. *Exhib:* Art Inst Chicago Ann, 39 & 40; Corcoran Gallery Art Biennial, 40; Pa Acad Fine Arts Ann, Philadelphia; Nat Acad Design Ann; NC Mus Art Collectors Exhib, 68; solo exhibs, Hines Gallery, Rocky Mt & Greenville Art Ctr. *Teaching:* Instr art, Lankenau Sch, Philadelphia, 52-61; instr art, var art ctrs, NC, 61- *Awards:* Mary Smith Prize, Pa Acad Fine Arts, 41; First Prize, Woodmere Art Gallery, Philadelphia, 56; First Prize & Gold Medal, Penn-Nat-Ligonier Pa, 61. *Media:* Oil. *Mailing Add:* c/o Marita Gilliam Gallery 126 Glenwood Ave Raleigh NC 27603

BLANC, (WILLIAM) PETER
SCULPTOR, PAINTER
b New York, NY, June 29, 12. *Study:* Harvard Univ, BA; St John's Univ, LLB; Corcoran Sch Art; Am Univ, MA. *Work:* Va Mus Fine Arts, Richmond; Ft Worth Art Mus, Tex; Old Jail Art Ctr, Albany, Tex; Tweed Mus, Duluth, Minn; Guild Hall, East Hampton, NY. *Exhib:* Ashawagh Hall, Springs, NY, 71-78, 80, 83-87, 89-92; Hudson River Mus, Yonkers, NY; Guild Hall Mus, East Hampton, NY, 81; Goat Alley Gallery, Sag Harbor, NY, 84 & 86, 87-92; Baltimore Mus of Art, Md; Brooklyn Mus, NY; Corcoran Gallery, Washington, DC; Fogg Art Mus, Cambridge, Mass; Mus of Santa Fe, NMex; Nat Collection of Arts, Washington, DC; Va Mus of Fine Arts, Richmond, Va; Whitney Mus of Am Art, New York; Westbeth Gallery, New York, 88-90; and others. *Teaching:* Pvt classes in painting & drawing, 47-54; instr painting & drawing, Am Univ, 50-53. *Awards:* First Prize for Drawing, Corcoran Gallery Art, 49; Special Award, Washington Watercolor Club, 49 & 52; Hon Mention, Soc Washington Artists, 51 & 53. *Mem:* Artists Equity Asn New York (bd dir, 63-71); Am Soc Contemp Artists. *Media:* Wood; Oil, Charcoal. *Publ:* Auth, Artist & the atom, Mag of Art, 51, reprinted, Smithsonian Report, 51, Hudson River Mus, 63 & Long Island Univ, 70. *Dealer:* Goat Alley Gallery Division St Sag Harbor NY 11963. *Mailing Add:* 161 W 75th St New York NY 00023

BLANCO, SYLVIA
CERAMIST
b Santurce, PR, Nov 29, 43. *Study:* Univ PR, BBA, 64; Inst Cult Puertorriquena, 74; studied with John Balossi, 77; Liga Arte, 77. *Work:* Inst Cult Puertorriquena, San Juan; Ponce Art Mus, PR; Performing Arts Ctr, Ateneo Puertorriqueno, Santurce, PR; Mus Ceramica, Faenze, Italy. *Comn:* Sculptures (clay), Copan & Art Students League, Santurce, PR, 79. *Exhib:* Peter Valley Craftsmen, NJ, 76; Livingston Art Gallery, Rutgers Univ, 77; Concorso Int Ceramica, Faenza, Italy, 78-82; Sculpture in Clay From Puerto Rico, Mus Fine Arts, Springfield, Mass, Art Mus STex, Corpus Christi, Newark Mus & Bacardi Gallery, Miami, 80-81; Women Artists From Puerto Rico, Cayman Gallery, New York, 83. *Teaching:* Instr ceramics, Art Students League, 79-; prof, Interamerican Univ, 82- *Awards:* Purchase Prize, Concorso Ceramica, Faenza, Italy, 83; Purchase Prize & First Prize Sculpture, Ateneo Puertorriqueno, 83. *Media:* Ceramics. *Mailing Add:* c/o Galeria Botello II Plaza Las Americas No 143 Hato Rey PR 00919

BLATTNER, ROBERT HENRY
PAINTER, ILLUSTRATOR
b Lynn, Mass, Dec 8, 06. *Study:* Mass Col Art, BS(educ & design). *Work:* Painting: Soc Illusr Mus. *Pos:* Illusr, Christian Sci Monitor, 34-42; art dir, Marschalk & Pratt Advert Agency, 43-45; art dir, Reader's Digest, 45-72, consult art dir, 77-78; retired 78. *Teaching:* Instr design, Boston Univ, 37-38; instr design, Col New Rochelle, 39-41. *Awards:* Soc Illustrators Award of Merit & Gold Medal, 71; Hon Mention & Gold Medal, Am Watercolor Soc; Silver Medal, Art Dirs Club. *Mem:* Soc Illustrators; Art Dirs Club (pres, 60-61); Am Inst Graphic Arts (dir, 58-59); hon mem Am Watercolor Soc; Dutch Treat Club, New York; Artists' Fel. *Media:* Watercolor. *Publ:* Illusr, Reader's Digest & 25 covers. *Mailing Add:* 7 Loch Lane Rye Brook NY 10573

BLAU, DOUGLAS
CRITIC, CURATOR
b Los Angeles, Calif, Oct 11, 55. *Study:* Washington Univ, St Louis, BA & BFA, 77. *Collections Arranged:* Fictions: A selection of Pictures from the 18th, 19th & 20th Centuries, Kent Fine Art & Curt Marcus Gallery, New York, 87; The Observatory, Thomas Solomon's Garage, Los Angeles, 89; The Times, The Chronicle & the Observer, Kent Fine Art, New York, 91; The Library, Josh Baer Gallery, New York, 91; The Naturalist Gathers, Thomas Solomon's Garage, Los Angeles, 92. *Bibliog:* Roberta Smith (auth), Fictions: Views of the Futures & the Past, NY Times, 12/11/87; Robert Harbison (auth), Douglas Blau's Fictions, C Mag, summer 88; Peter Schjeldahl (auth), Past Perfect, Village Voice, 1/22/91. *Publ:* Auth & Ed, Pictures, Fictions, Kent Fine Art & Curt Marcus, 87; The Observer, The Times, The Chronicle & The Observer, Kent Fine Art, 91; Consider The Sphere, The Library, Josh Baer, 91; contribr, Solid Air, Vija Celmins, Inst Contemp Art, Philadelphia, 92; auth, Index, Alexis Rockman, Jay Gorney & Thomas Solomon, 92. *Mailing Add:* 200 E 16th St New York NY 10003

BLAUSTEIN, AL
PAINTER, PRINTMAKER
b Bronx, NY, Jan 23, 24. *Study:* Cooper Union Art Sch, grad fine arts. *Work:* Whitney Mus Am Art, Metrop Mus Art, New York; Chicago Art Inst; Libr Cong, Washington, DC; Pa Acad Fine Arts, Philadelphia. *Comn:* Drawing assignment, Life & Brit Overseas Food Corp, Tanzania, EAfrica, 48-49; fresco mural, S Solon Meeting House, Maine, 53; painting assignment, Fortune Mag, 70. *Exhib:* Four shows, Pa Acad Fine Arts, 51-67; Metrop Mus Art, 50 & 66; Whitney Mus Am Art Ann, 53 & 57; six shows, Brooklyn Mus Print Ann, 57-70; one-man shows, Nordness Gallery, New York, Terry Dintenfass Gallery, Philadelphia Art Alliance, Albany Art Inst & Laeubli Gallery, Zurich, Switz; and others. *Teaching:* Lectr fine arts, Yale Univ, 59-62; prof fine arts, Pratt Inst, 59-; instr printmaking, Pratt Graphic Ctr, 64-69. *Awards:* Prix de Rome Fel, 54-57; Am Acad Arts & Lett Grant, 58; Guggenheim Fel, 58 & 61. *Media:* Acrylic, Oil; Etching. *Mailing Add:* 141 E 17th St New York NY 10003

BLAYTON, BETTY (BETTY BLAYTON-TAYLOR)
PAINTER, ADMINISTRATOR
b Williamsburg, Va, July 10, 37. *Study:* Syracuse Univ, BFA, 59; Art Students League, 61; studied with Arnold Prince & Munoru Niizuma. *Work:* Studio Mus Harlem, Metrop Mus Art, New York; Fisk Univ; Philip Morris Corp; Chase Manhattan Bank. *Exhib:* Thirty Contemporary Black Artists, Minneapolis & traveling, 68; Professional Artist for Young Artists, Metrop Mus Art, New York; Black American Contemporary Artist, Zamoia, Africa, 75; solo exhib, Caravan House Gallery, New York, 75 & Fisk Univ, 80; Eight Women, Harvard Univ Gallery, 76; San Francisco Mus Art; Boston Mus Art; High Mus Art; Minneapolis Inst Art; Everson Mus Art; Milwaukee Art Ctr. *Pos:* Supv artist graphics & plastics, Harlem Youth Unlimited, 64-67; pres & artistic dir, Children's Art Carnival, New York, 68- *Teaching:* Consult, New York City Bd Educ, 72-; prof art educ, City Col New York, 78- *Awards:* Award Empire State Woman of the Year, 84; Black Women in the Arts Award, 88. *Bibliog:* Five (film), Silvermine Films, 72; Forever Free, Univ Ill Press, 81; Muriel Silverstein (auth), Doing Art Together, 81. *Mem:* Studio Mus Harlem (founding mem, 68); Printmaking workshop, NY, (bd mem, 79-). *Media:* Oil Collage. *Publ:* Auth, People who make things happen, Art Gallery Guide, 69; auth, Making Thoughts Become, 78. *Mailing Add:* 2001 Creston Ave Bronx NY 10453

BLAZEJE, ZBIGNIEW (ZIGGY BLAZESE)
SCULPTOR, PAINTER
b Barnaul, USSR, June 2, 42; Can citizen. *Study:* Royal Conserv Music, Toronto; Ont Col Art. *Work:* Art Gallery Ont, Toronto; Norman McKenzie Art Gallery, Regina, Sask; Confedn Art Gallery, Charlettetown, PEI; Hart House, Univ Toronto; Sir George William Univ, Montreal, PQ. *Comn:* Structrual sculpture, Libr-Ross Bldg, York Univ, 72; and others. *Exhib:* Canadian Art, Art Gallery Can Pavillion Expo 67, Montreal; Sculpture 67, City Hall Toronto; Electric Art, Univ Calif, Los Angeles Art Gallery & Phoenix, Ariz, 69; Sensory Perceptions Traveling Exhib, Art Gallery Ont, 70-71; Electronic Paintings, Cybernetic Environment, Hart House Art Gallery, Univ Toronto, 81; and others. *Pos:* Pres & dir, Arts Sake Inc, Inst Visual Art, 79- *Teaching:* Instr environ, Ont Col Art, 70-81; instr environ, New Sch Art, Toronto, 71-72. *Awards:* Can Coun Jr Grants, 66, 67 & 69; Ont Art Coun Grants, 79 & 81. *Bibliog:* H Malcomson (auth), Sculpture in Canada, Artforum, 10/67; G M Dault (auth), In the galleries Toronto, Artscanada, 6/71; Electric Gallery plus 3, McCurdy-Bursell Films, Toronto, 4/72. *Mem:* Royal Can Acad Arts. *Mailing Add:* c/o Art Research Ctr PO Box 30098 Kansas City MO 64112

BLAZEY, LAWRENCE EDWIN
DESIGNER, PAINTER
b Cleveland, Ohio, Apr 6, 02. *Study:* Cleveland Inst Art, grad(scholar), 24; Slade Sch, Univ London, with Prof Tonks, 26; Cranbrook Acad, Bloomfield Hills, Mich, with Mia Grotell, 51. *Work:* Cleveland Mus Art; Butler Inst Am Art, Youngstown, Ohio; City of Cleveland Munic Art Collection; Goodyear Tire; Elwell Parker Electric. *Comn:* Chapel Furniture & Holocaust Plaque, 12 Tribes Panel, Lorain, Aguduth B'nai Israel Synagogue, Ohio. *Exhib:* Everson Mus Nat Ceramic, Syracuse, NY, 50-54; Ann Nat Watercolor Show, Butler Inst Am Art, 72-73; Ann Ceramic Show, Butler Inst; Bratenahl Ann Invited Exhib, Cleveland, OH, 79-91. *Pos:* Vpres & dir design, Designers for Indust Inc, Cleveland, 42-52; vpres & chief eng, Tapco Products, 63-68. *Teaching:* Instr ceramics, John Huntington, Commercial Art, Cleveland Sch Art, 41-43; instr painting, Beck Ctr, Lakewood, Ohio, 78-88. *Awards:* Prize for the only contemp house design in all steel welded panels, Lincoln Electric Co, Cleveland, 42; Butler Inst Am Arts Ceramic Prizes, 69-70; Ohio Watercolor Soc Award, 86 & 90. *Mem:* Ohio Watercolor Soc; Indust Designers Soc Am; Cleveland Artists Found; Ohio Designer Craftsmen; New Orgns Visual Artists (Nova). *Media:* Ceramics; All Media. *Mailing Add:* 537 Juneway Dr Bay Village OH 44140

BLEACH, BRUCE R
PRINTMAKER, PAINTER
b Monticello, NY, Mar 23, 50. *Study:* Orange County Community Col, AA, 70; Hartford Art Sch, Univ Hartford, BFA, 72; State Univ NY, New Paltz, MFA, 74. *Work:* IBM, Merrill Lynch Pierce Fenner Smith Inc & Nat Westminster Bank, New York; Provincial Mus, Taiwan; Southeast Banking Corp, Fla; plus others. *Comn:* Triptych, RCA Americom, Princeton, NJ, 80; embossed aluminum, Shulte Inc, New York, 84; monoprint series on handmade paper, Gallery Sho, Tokyo, Japan, 85; cast paper with multi-media, Fred Dorfman Inc, New York, 86; metal tryptech, comn by Skoke-Koo Gallery for ADP Corp, Calif. *Exhib:* Contemporary Prints, Nat Prov Mus, Taiwan, 77; Works on Paper, Hudson River Mus, Yonkers, NY, 78; Artists Who Make Prints, Fordham Univ at Linclon Ctr, New York, 81; Invitational, Cayman Gallery, New York, 83; one-man exhibs, Contemp Ltd Eds, Fla, 85, Hersh Gallery, Long Island, 86, Fred Dorfman Inc, New York, 87, Syd Entel Gallery, Tampa, Fla, 88, Art Forms Gallery, Redbank, NJ, 89, Inner Visions of Georgetown, Washington, DC, 89; Faculty Exhib, Parsons Sch Design, Lake Placid, NY, 84-85; Five Printmakers, Castle Gallery, Col New Rochelle, NY, 85; Zola Fine Art, Los Angeles, 86; Alumni Art, State Univ NY, New Paltz, 87; Los Angeles Expo, 88; NY Expo, 88, 89 & 90; Save Our Shores, Art Forms Gallery, 88; C S Schulte Gallery, New York, 89. *Awards:* Best of Show, Sullivan County Art Asn, 73; Directors Award Graphics, Knickerbocker Artists, 75; Drawing Award, Paperworks Exhib, Hastings Gallery, 80. *Bibliog:* Robert Smallman (dir), Printmaking (film), 78. *Media:* Etchings, Monoprints; Mixed Media on Wood & Aluminum. *Dealer:* Fred Dorfman Inc 831 Broadway New York NY 10003. *Mailing Add:* c/o Art Forms 16 Monmouth St Red Bank NJ 07701

BLECHMAN, R O
ILLUSTRATOR, FILMMAKER
b Brooklyn, NY, Oct 1, 30. *Study:* Oberlin Col, BA, 52. *Work:* Mus Mod Art, New York; Libr Cong, Washington, DC; Chase Manhattan Bank, New York. *Comn:* Three murals for US Pavilion, Expo '67, Montreal, 67; illusr for Candide, comn by Olivetti, Milan, Italy, 75; three murals for The Hall of Man, Am Mus Nat Hist, New York, 77; poster based on New Yorker cover, Munic Art Soc, New York, 80; poster, Museum Mile, New York, 82. *Exhib:* One-man shows, Galerie Delpire, Paris, France, 67, Graham Gallery, New York, 78 & Galerie Bartsch & Chariau, Munich, WGer, 82 & 92. *Awards:* Gold Medal, NY Art Dir Club, 68; Gold Medal, Cannes Film Festival, France, 77; Emmy, Outstanding Individual Achievement in Animation Programming, 84. *Bibliog:* Interview, In: Graphic Designers in the USA, Vol 2, Universe Bks, 71; Maurice Sendak (auth), Introduction to R O Blechman: Behind the Lines, Hudson Hills Press, 80. *Mem:* Alliance Graphique Int; Cartoonist Guild; Am Inst Graphic Arts. *Media:* Watercolor. *Publ:* Auth & illusr, The Juggler of Our Lady, Henry Holt, 52; Onion Soup, Odyssey Press, 63; No Room at the Inn, Milano Libri, 70. *Mailing Add:* 2 W 47th St, 16th Floor New York NY 10036

BLECKNER, ROSS
PAINTER
b New York, NY, 1949. *Study:* NY Univ, BA, 71; Calif Inst Arts, MFA, 73. *Work:* Joslyn Art Mus; J B Speed Art Mus. *Exhib:* 10 Plus 10: Contemporary Soviet and American Painters, Milwaukee Art Mus, Wis, The Corcoran Gallery Art, Washington, Artists' Union Hall of the Tretyakov Embankment, Moscow, USSR & Tsentralnyi Zal Khudozhnikov, Tbilisi, USSR, 90; The Last Decade: American Artists of the 80's, Tony Shafrazi Gallery, NY, 90; Weitersehen, Mus Haus Esters & Mus Haus Lange, Krefeld, Ger, 90; solo exhibs, Art Gallery, Ontario, Toronto, Can, 90, Galeria Soledad Lorenzo, Madrid, Spain, 90, Heland Wetterling Gallery, Stockholm, Sweden, 90, Kunsthalle, Zurich, Switz, 90, Kolnscher Kunstverein, Koln, WGer, 91, Moderna Museet, Stockholm, Sweden, 91; Pintura de los Ochenta en las Americas, Museo de arte contemporaneo de Monterrey, Mex, 91; Carnegie Inst, Mus Art, Pittsburgh, Pa, 88; The Binational/Die Binationale, Kunsthalle Dusseldorf, W Ger, 88; The Image Of Abstraction, Mus Contemp Art, Los Angeles, Calif, 88; solo exhibs, Milwaukee Art Mus, Wis, 89 & Contemp Art Mus, Houston, Tex, 89; and others. *Bibliog:* Roberta Smith (auth), article, Art in Am, 1/81; Peter Halley (auth), article, 5/82 & Robert Pincus-Witten (auth), Defenestrations, 11/82, Arts Mag; Elizabeth Hess (auth), Celestial Navigations, Village Voice, 88; Kay Larson (auth), article, New York Mag, 11/88; Michael Brenson (auth), article, New York Times, 10/88. *Media:* Oil on Canvas. *Mailing Add:* c/o Mary Boone Gallery 417 W Broadway New York NY 10012

BLEDSOE, JANE KATHRYN
HISTORIAN, ADMINISTRATOR
b Independence, Mo, Sept 9, 37. *Study:* Calif State Univ, Long Beach, BA, MA(art hist) & cert mus studies; Western Asn Art Mus, Mus Mgt Inst, 81. *Collections Arranged:* Maria Poveka, American Potter (with catalog), 74; Anna A Hills, American Impressionist, 76; Brian Hunt, Monumental Sculpture Commission, 82; Anders Zorn Rediscovered, (cur/ed exhib & catalog, 84), 84; Figurative Sculpture, 84. *Pos:* Admin dir, Art Mus & Galleries, Calif State Univ, Long Beach, 74-88; dir, Ga Mus Art, Univ Ga, Athens, 88-92. *Mem:* Asn Art Mus Dirs; Am Asn Mus; Col Art Asn; ArtTable, Inc; Athens Area C of C. *Res:* Southwestern American Indian ceramics, 19th and 20th centuries; western art & photog. *Mailing Add:* 12534 Valley View No 162 Garden Grove CA 92645

BLEIBERG, GERTRUDE TIEFENBRUN
PAINTER, PRINTMAKER
b New York, NY. *Study:* Univ Calif Los Angeles, BEd, 41; Univ Southern Calif Grad Sch Bus Admin, 42; San Francisco Art Inst, BFA, 75; MFA, 77. *Work:* San Francisco Mus Mod Art, Calif; Brooklyn Mus, NY; San Jose, Mus Art, Calif; Jane Voorhees Zimmerle Mus, Rutgers Univ, New Brunswick, NJ; Bank Am, San Francisco, Calif; Palo Alto Cult Ctr, Calif; Raychem Corp, Menlo Park, Calif. *Exhib:* Solo exhib, Plumas Co Mus, Quincy, Calif, 75, Monterey Peninsula Mus Art, Calif, 82, San Jose Mus Art, Calif, 83, Elizabeth S Fine Mus, Temple Emanuel, San Francisco, Calif, 88; Monterey Peninsula Mus Art, Calif, 82; Let Us Savor This Moment, San Jose Mus Art, Calif, 83; Printed by Women: Nat Exhib, Port Hist Mus, Philadelphia, 83; Wedding Series, Quincy Series, Print Club Invitational, Philadelphia, 86; Eccentric Imagery, Galerie Ek y Mose Contemp, Bordeaux, France, 86-88; Northern Calif Artist Photog & Prints, Judah Magnes Mus, Berkeley, Calif, 87; Los Angeles Foot Show, Community Arts Publ, Calif, 88; Works on Paper, Sch Art, Univ Mich, 90; Directions in Bay Area Printmaking: Three Decades (catalog), Palo Alto Invitational, Palo Alto Cult Ctr, 92. *Awards:* Lifetime Achievement Award, Women's Caucus Art, South Bay Peninsula Chap (Western Region), 92. *Bibliog:* Charles Shere (auth), Two visions of life in San Jose, Oakland Tribune, 83; Andre Workman-Phil Limhares (coauths), Eccentric Imagery, Galerie Ek y Mose Contemp, Bordeaux, France, 87; Sheila Braufman, Northern Calif Artists: Jewish Themes-Judah Magnes Mus, 87; Leigh Ann Clifton (auth), Catching up with the Women's Caucus, Artweek, 8/92. *Mem:* Women's Caucus Art; Calif Soc Printmakers; Artists Equity. *Dealer:* Jennifer Pauls Gallery 1825 Q Street Sacramento CA 95814. *Mailing Add:* 275 Southwood Dr Palo Alto CA 94301

BLEIFELD, STANLEY
SCULPTOR, MEDALIST
b Brooklyn, NY, Aug 28, 24. *Study:* Albert C Barnes Found, Merion, Pa, 42-43; Tyler Sch Art, Temple Univ, BFA, 49, BS(educ), 49, MFA, 50. *Work:* Temple Univ, Philadelphia, Pa; Westmoreland Mus Art, Pa; Pa State Mus, Philadelphia; New Britain Mus of Am Art, Conn; Univ Edinburgh, Great Britain. *Comn:* Vatican Pavilion, New York Worlds Fair, 64-65; Kokomo Pub Libr, Ind, 69; Alberta Family, Calgary, Can, 81; Knights of Columbus Plaza, New Haven, Conn, 82; US Navy Memorial, Washington, DC, 82; Navy Mem, Jacksonville, Fla. *Exhib:* Am Fedn Arts, 66-67; IFA Galleries, Washington, DC, 68 & 71; FAR Gallery, New York, 71, 73 & 77; New Britain Mus Am Art, 74; Reflections, Images of Am, US Info Agency Traveling Exhib, 76-77; and others. *Pos:* Nat Sculpture Soc Council. *Teaching:* Asst prof art, Southern Conn State Col & Western Conn State Col, 53-63; dir sculpture, Bleifeld Studio, Westport, Conn, 66- *Awards:* Tiffany Found Fel, 65 & 67; Shikler Award, Nat Acad Design, 77; Proskauer Prize, 83; Bennett Prize, 85; Tallix Prize, 86. *Bibliog:* A sculptor hails the Bible, Life Mag, 6/28/63; article, Am Artist Mag, 72; Artists of the Rockies, 81. *Mem:* Fel Nat Sculptor Soc; Artists Equity. *Dealer:* Jones Gallery La Jolla Ca 92037; Stremmel Gallery Reno NV. *Mailing Add:* 27 Spring Valley Rd Weston CT 06883

BLESER, KATHERINE ALICE
PAINTER
b Los Angeles, Calif, Apr 3, 42. *Study:* Northwestern Univ, Evanston, Ill, BA, 73; Ga State Univ, Atlanta, MA, 75. *Work:* Ga Inst Technol & Fed Reserve Bank, Atlanta; Chattahoochee Valley Art Mus, LaGrange, Ga; State of Ga, Atlanta. *Comn:* Six oil paintings, S Trust Bank, Birmingham, Ala, 87; Two oil paintings, Ga Inst Technol, 88; One oil painting, Johnson & Higgins, Inc, Atlanta, 91. *Exhib:* Am Artists Mag Nat Art Competition, Grand Cent Gallery, New York, 85; Allied Artists Am, Nat Arts Club, New York, 87 & 91; Knickerbocker Artists, Salmagundi Club, New York, 87, Fine Arts Inst Ann Exhib, San Bernardino Co Mus, Redlands, Calif, 87 & 92; Springfield Art League Ann Exhib, George Walter Vincent Smith Mus, Mass, 88 & 90; Nat Asn Women Artists Exhib to India, Sansker Kendra Mus, Ahmedebad, India, 89-90; Arts for the Parks Ann Competition, Lakeview Mus Arts & Sci, Peoria, Ill & Cincinnati Mus Nat Hist, Ohio, 89-90. *Awards:* Honorable Mention, Artists Mag Landscape Painting Competition, 87; Catharine Lorillard Wolfe Art Club Medal of Honor, Oil, 90; Merit Award, Springfield Art League Ann Exhib, 88. *Bibliog:* Valerie Rivers, (auth), Entering art competition, Am Artists, 9/86; Bebe Raupe, (auth), the 1987 landscape painting competition winners, Artist's Mag, 12/87. *Mem:* Catharine Lorillard Wolfe Art Club; Nat Asn Women Artists; Am Artists Prof League; Academic Artists; Oil Painters Am. *Media:* Oil. *Dealer:* Capricorn Galleries 4849 Rugby Ave Bethesda MD 20814; Lagerquist Gallery 3235 Paces Ferry Pl NW Atlanta GA. *Mailing Add:* 1935 Ponce De Leon Ave NE Atlanta GA 30307

BLEVINS, JAMES RICHARD
ART ADMINISTRATOR, EDUCATOR
b Feb 1, 34; US citizen. *Study:* David Lipscomb Col, BA, 56; George Peabody Col, MA, 60, PhD, 70; Univ Calif, Los Angeles, 75. *Pos:* Chmn, Div Humanities, Univ Southern Ind, 69-; mem bd dirs, Evansville Mus, 70-, chmn, Fine Arts Comt, 76-; chmn, Ohio River Arts Festival, 72; prod, New Harmony Theatre, 88-; prod, Young Abe Lincoln, 89- *Mem:* Evansville Arts & Educ Coun (vpres, 73); Int Comt Humanities, 80-86 (chmn, 83-84); Nat Fedn State Humanities Couns, 83-85. *Mailing Add:* Univ Southern Ind 8600 Univ Blvd Evansville IN 47712

BLINDER, MARTIN S
ART DEALER, PUBLISHER
b Brooklyn, NY, Nov 18, 46. *Study:* Adelphi Univ, BBA, 68. *Work:* Hirshhorn Mus, DC; Chicago Inst Fine Art; Los Co Mus Art; Guggenheim Mus & Mus Mod Art, New York; Newport Art Mus; and others. *Pos:* Publ, Martin Lawrence Ltd Ed, 75; project orgn, American Bicentennial Comt Manned Space Flight, 76. *Teaching:* Lectr, art & bus symposia. *Awards:* Los Angeles City Resolution Award, 84; RI State Resolution for Contrib to the Arts. *Specialty:* Publisher of Limited Edition graphics by Andy Warhol, Sam Frances, Doug Webb, Folon, Joan Miro, Hiro Yamagata, Charles Bragg, Fritz Scholder, Susan Rios, Yaacov Agam. *Mailing Add:* Martin Lawrence Ltd Eds 16250 Stagg St Van Nuys CA 91406

BLINDERMAN, BARRY ROBERT
CURATOR, DIRECTOR
b Bethlehem, Pa, June 11, 52. *Study:* Boston Univ, BA(art hist), 75; Univ Pa, MA(art hist), 78. *Pos:* Free-lance writer, Arts Mag & Arts Exchange Mag, 78-82; dir, Semaphore Gallery, New York, 80-87; dir, Univ Galleries, Ill State Univ, Normal, 87- *Teaching:* Guest lectr, Tyler Sch Art, Univ Pa, Boston Mus Fine Art, Name Gallery, 79-, Chrysler Mus, Norfolk, Rice Univ, Houston & Univ Ill, Champaign, Ill; lectr art hist & contemp art, Ill State Univ, Normal. *Awards:* Panelist, Ill Arts Coun, Mus Prog Grants, 90. *Res:* Contemporary American Art. *Specialty:* Paintings, drawings, sculpture, and video by contemp artists. *Publ:* Auth, Steve Reich's minimal music, Arts Exchange, 79; Robert Longo's Men in the Cities: Quotes and commentary, 81, Keith Haring's Subterranean Signatures, 81, Modern myths: An interview with Andy Warhol, 81 & Ed Paschke: Reflections and digressions on The Body Electric, 82, Arts Mag; The Veil of the Soul (essay), Mark Innerst: Landscape and Beyond, Exhib & catalogs, 88-89; David Wojnarowicz: The Compression of Time (interview), David Wojnarowicz: Tongues of Flame, catalog, 89. *Mailing Add:* 509 E Grove St Bloomington IL 61701

BLIZZARD, ALAN
PAINTER, EDUCATOR
b Boston, Mass, Mar 25, 39. *Study:* Mass Sch Art, Boston, with Lawrence Kupferman; Univ Ariz, with Andreas Andersen; Univ Iowa, with Stuart Edie, James Lechay & Byron Burford. *Work:* Brooklyn Mus, NY; Metrop Mus Art, New York; Art Inst Chicago; Denver Art Mus, Colo; La Jolla Mus Art, Calif; and others. *Exhib:* Many exhibs in leading mus, col & univs. *Teaching:* Chmn & prof painting, Scripps Col & Claremont Grad Sch, currently; chmn art dept, Scripps Col. *Mailing Add:* 2349 S Santa Fe Ave Studio #B Los Angeles CA 90058

BLOCH, MILTON JOSEPH
ART ADMINISTRATOR, MUSEUM DIRECTOR
b Bronx, NY, Apr 4, 37. *Study:* Pratt Inst, Brooklyn, NY, BID, 58; Univ Fla, Gainesville, MFA, 61. *Exhib:* Romare Bearden 1920-1980, 80; Three Centuries of Art in New Jersey, 71; NJ Arts & Crafts; The Colonial Expression, 73; Romare Bearden, 79; Landon Col Am Art, 80; Ed Budnagurio Paintings, 82; Herb Jackson Paintings, 83; Ida Kohl Meyer, 30 Years, 85; American Masterpieces, 85; Ramesses the Great, 89; Splendors of the New World, 92. *Pos:* Dir, Pensacola Art Ctr, Fla, 64-66; dir, Mus Sci & Natural Hist, Little Rock, Ark, 66-68; dir, Monmouth Mus, Lincroft, NJ, 69-76; dir, Mint Mus, 76-91 & Munson Williams Proctor Inst, 91- *Teaching:* Instr art & chmn dept, Lake Sumter Col, Fla, 61-63; instr art, Belmont Abbey Col, NC,

79-80. *Mem:* Am Asn Mus; Int Conf Mus; NC Arts Coun; Asn of Art Mus Dirs. *Publ:* Series of six articles on improvised exhibition design, Mus News, 66-68; Articles for Southeastern Mus Conf J, 80-81 & Mus News, 85. *Mailing Add:* Mint Mus 2730 Randolph Rd Charlotte NC 28207

BLOCK, AMANDA ROTH
PAINTER, PRINTMAKER
b Louisville, Ky, Feb 20, 12. *Study:* Smith Col; Univ Cincinnati; Art Acad Cincinnati; Art Students League; Herron Sch Art, Ind Univ-Purdue Univ, Indianapolis, BFA; and with Garo Antreasian. *Work:* J B Speed Mus, Louisville, Ky; Cincinnati Art Mus, Ohio; Brooklyn Mus, NY; Tucson Mus of Art, Ariz; Philadelphia Mus Art, Pa. *Exhib:* American Sculpture Show, Chicago Art Inst, Ill, 41; Soc Am Graphic Artists Show, 67-; Philadelphia Print Club; Watercolor, Drawing & Print Biennial, Pa Acad Fine Arts, Philadelphia, 69; Butler Inst Am Art, Youngstown, Ohio; Bus & Corp Collect, Indianapolis Mus of Art, Ind, 77; Retrospective, Indianapolis Art League, Ind, 92. *Teaching:* Lectr lithography & drawing, Herron Sch Art, 69-72; Indianapolis Art League, 72-82. *Awards:* Katherine Mattison Watercolor Award, Indianapolis Mus Art, 63; Watercolor Award, Indiana Artists Exhib, Sheldon Swope Art Gallery, 64; Ben & Beatrice Goldstein Award, Soc Am Graphic Artists Exhib, Kennedy Gallery, New York, 71. *Mem:* Soc Am Graphic Artists. *Media:* Acrylic, Oil; Serigraph, Lithograph. *Dealer:* Editions Limited Gallery 919 Westfield Blvd Indianapolis IN 46220; Editions Limited West San Francisco CA. *Mailing Add:* 6000 Spring Mill Rd Indianapolis IN 46208

BLOCK, GAY (S)
PHOTOGRAPHER
b Houston, Tex, Mar 5, 42. *Study:* Sophie Newcomb, 59-61; Univ Houston, 71-72 & 76; with Geoff Winningham, Garry Winogrand & Anne Tucker, 74-76. *Work:* Mus Fine Arts, Houston, Tex; Ft Worth Art Mus, Tex; Portland Mus Art, Maine; Ctr Creative Photog, Tucson, Ariz; Amon Carter Mus, Ft Worth, Tex; Univ of Tex, Humanities Res, Austin, Tex; Mus Mod Art, New York. *Comn:* Diptychs of Employees at Work and Home, HEB Grocery Co, 85; Ethnics of Houston, Foley's Dept Store: 85-86; Fifty Texas Artists, comn by Chronicle Books, 86. *Exhib:* SECA, San Francisco Mus Mod Art, Calif, 80; Triennial, New Orleans Mus Art, La, 80; Tex Photo Sampler, Washington Project Arts, Washington, DC, 81; Inside-Out: The Self Beyond Likeness, Newport Harbor Art Mus, Calif, 81; One-woman shows, Contemp Art Mus, Houston, Tex, 82; Northlight, Univ of Ariz, 85; Film in the Cities, St Paul, Minn, 86; Western States Biennial, Brooklyn Mus, NY, 86; Visual Studies Workshop, Rochester, NY, 87. *Teaching:* Vis artist photog, Univ Houston, 79-80 & 82-83; instr, Calif Inst Arts, 87. *Awards:* Nat Endowment Arts Photogr Fel Grant, 78; Nat Endowment Arts Survey Grant to Women & Their Work, 81; Tex Hist Found Photogr Survey Grant Tex Sesquicentennial. *Bibliog:* Jon Holmes (auth), Deep in the heart of Texas, Camera Mag, 8/77; Susie Kalil (auth), Portrait of a community, Artweek, 6/16/79; Demetra Bowles (auth), Lone-star tapestry, Artweek, 11/7/81; Margaret Berry (auth), American assignments, Views, Winter, 85. *Mem:* Women's Caucus Art; Houston Arts Coun; Rice Design Alliance; Houston Ctr Photog; Friends of Photog. *Media:* Black & White, Color. *Publ:* Contribr, Self-Portrayal, Friends of Photog, 78; illusr, My Body is Something Special, Union Am Hebrew Congregations, 81. *Mailing Add:* 2341 Sunset Blvd Houston TX 77005

BLOCK, VIRGINIA SCHAFFER
PAINTER, COLLAGE ARTIST
b Newark, NJ, Apr 24, 46. *Study:* Study with Tom Vincent, 74-78; William Paterson Col, Wayne, NJ, BA, 68, MA(visual arts), 69; Rutgers State Univ (serigraphy, advan printmaking), 89. *Work:* Hoesct Celanese, NJ; Mead Data Central, Cincinnati, Ohio; Nabisco Brands USA, Hanover, NJ; Berlex Laboratories, Wayne, NJ; Warner Lambert, NJ. *Comn:* Canvas, Kimmelman, Wolff & Samson, Roseland, NJ, 86; canvas, Mandelbaum, Salsburg, Gold, West Orange, NJ, 87; canvas/acrylic, Sandoz Pharmaceuticals, Hanover, NJ, 90. *Exhib:* Nat Touring Exhib, Ohio Found Arts, 82-83; Adirondacks Nat Exhib Am Watercolors, Arnot Mus, Elmira, NY, 82 & 86; Bergen Mus Arts & Sciences, Paramus, NJ, 83, 84 & 85; one-woman shows, Korby Gallery, Cedar Grove, NJ, 90; Retrospective, 15 Years From Figurative to Abstract Landscape, Berlex Laboratories Corp Hq, Wayne, NJ, 90-91; and others. *Pos:* Advert artist, 69; freelance artist, 74-80. *Teaching:* Grad asst fine arts, Wm Paterson Col, Wayne, NJ, 68-69; art teacher, Hanover Twp Pub Sch System, 70-73. *Awards:* Four top awards, Nature Interpreted, Cincinnati Mus Natural Hist, 82; Award, Adirondacks Nat Exhib Am Watercolor, 82; Lillian Cotton Award, Nat Asn Women Artists Inc, 83. *Mem:* Allied Artists Am; Audubon Artists Inc; Nat Asn Women Artists Inc (chmn, traveling painting exhib, USA, 83-85 & for exhibs, 84-85, exec bd, 83-89, newsletter ed, 86-89); Artists Equity, New York; Painters & Sculptors Soc NJ Inc. *Media:* All. *Dealer:* Susan Cloninger 189 Speedwell Ave Morris Plains NJ 07950; Summa Gallery 527 Amsterdam Ave New York NY. *Mailing Add:* 300 Highland Ave Upper Montclair NJ 07043

BLODGETT, ANNE WASHINGTON
PAINTER
b New York, NY, Apr 17, 40. *Study:* Smith Col, BA, 61; Boston Mus Sch Fine Arts, 61-62; with George Demetrios, Boston, 63; Sch of Fine Arts, Cambridge, Eng, 64. *Work:* Berkshire Mus, Pittsfield, Mass; Fitzwilliam Col Collection, Cambridge; Corp collections: Wilson Learning Co, Minneapolis; Charles River Partnership II, Boston; Quixote Co, Chicago; InnerAsia Co, San Francisco; Heublein Co, Hartford, Conn. *Comn:* Davis, Polk & Wardwell Co, New York, 81. *Exhib:* One-woman shows, Berkshire Mus, 71, Caravan House Gallery, New York, 71 & 74 & Medici Gallery, London, 73; New Grafton Gallery, London, 72; Bodley Gallery, New York, 80 & 82; Marbella Gallery, New York, 85 & 88; Millbrook Gallery, NY, 88; Saxon Gallery, Southampton, NY, 89. *Bibliog:* Les Krantz (auth), The New York Art Review, 88. *Media:* Oil. *Publ:* Auth, article in Artspeak, 85; Pictures on Exhibit, 89. *Mailing Add:* 55 E 72nd St New York NY 10021

BLOES, RICHARD K
VIDEO ARTIST
b Waterloo, Iowa, Sept 8, 51. *Study:* Univ Iowa Sch Art, BFA, 73, MA, 76, MFA, 77. *Work:* Donnell Media Libr, New York; Port Wash Media Libr, NY. *Comn:* Video production, Jerome Found, Minneapolis, 83; Video production, NY Found Art, 85; Video production, Nat Endowment Art, New Genres, Washington, DC, 87; Video production, NYSCA Media Grant, NY, 88 & 90. *Exhib:* Four Videotapes, New Mus Contemp Art, New York, 84; So There Orwell 1984, Lafort Mus, Tokyo, Japan, 85; The Kitchen, New York, 85; World Wide Video Fest, den Haag, Neth, 86; 21st Ann NY Film & Video, Metrop & Brooklyn Mus, NY, 87; Dissolved Light, Am Mus Moving Image, 89; Time Spans, Feature Gallery, New York, 90; 3rd Emerging Expression Biennial, Bronx Mus Arts, 91; Performance, Video, & Film, Ronald Feldman Gallery, 92. *Pos:* Video techniction & installer, Whitney Mus, 79- *Awards:* Special Distinction, Sixth Tokyo Video Fest, 83; Juror's Award, Three Rivers Arts Fest, Video, 87. *Bibliog:* Helan A Harrison (auth), Sunday New York Times, 90; Brooks Adams (auth), Art in Am, 90; David Reisman (auth), Artscribe, 90. *Mem:* Media Alliance, New York. *Media:* Video. *Mailing Add:* 60-38 Putnam Ave Ridgewood NY 11385

BLOMDAHL, SONJA
GLASS BLOWER
b Waltham, Mass, Sept 8, 52. *Study:* Mass Col Art, BFA, 74; Orrefors Glass Skolan, Sweden, 76. *Work:* Art in Public Places, Washington State Arts Comn, Olympia; Mathews Collection, Ariz State Univ, Tempee; Mus Decorative Art, Prague, Czechoslovakia; Corning Mus, NY; Am Craft Mus, NY. *Comn:* Blown Glass window, Everett Pub Libr, Wash. *Exhib:* Solo exhibs, William Traver Gallery, Seattle, Wash, 81-92; Crafts Today: Poetry of the Physical, Am Crafts Mus, New York, NY, 86; Design in America, traveling exhib to Eastern Europe, US Cult Exchange, 86-88; History of American Glass, from Corning Mus Glass, at Leningrad & Moscow, USSR, 89-90; Washington to Washington, Women in Art Today, Nat Mus of Women Arts. *Pos:* Partner, Berkshire Blown Glass Works, Stockbridge, Mass, 74- 76 & Glass Eye Studios, Seattle, Wash, 79-83; owner & operator, glass blowing studio, Seattle, Wash, 83- *Teaching:* Teaching asst, Pilchuck Sch, Stanwood, Wash, 78-81; instr glass blowing, Pratt Fine Arts Ctr, Seattle, Wash, 80- 84; summer instr, Summervail Workshop, Vail, Colo, 83-84, Pilchuck Sch, Stanwood, Wash, 85, Appalachian Ctr, Smithville, Tenn, 86 & Haystack Mountain Sch, Deer Isle, Maine, 88 & 92. *Awards:* Visual Artists Fel Grant, Nat Endowment Arts, 86; Artist's Trust Fel Grant, 87. *Bibliog:* Portfolio, Am Craft Mag, 8-9/83; New Glass Rev 4, 83 & Rev 6, 85, Corning Mus Glass, 85; Gallery glass, Seattle Times, 8/19/85. *Publ:* Contribr, Vogue Mag, 1/89; auth, Artists at Work: 25 Northwest Glassmakers, Ceramist, and Jewelers, 90; Out of the Fire: Contemporary Glass Artists & Their Work; International Crafts, 91. *Dealer:* William Traver Gallery 110 Union St Seattle WA 98101. *Mailing Add:* 1211 Aloha Seattle WA 98109

BLOOM, BARBARA
PHOTOGRAPHER
b Los Angeles, Calif, 1951. *Work:* Mus Contemp Art, Los Angeles, Calif; Mus Mod Art, New York, NY; Stedelijk Mus, Amsterdam, Gemeentemuseum, Arnhem, Groniger Mus, Gronigen, Neth. *Exhib:* Solo exhibs, Lost & Found, travelling Ger, Neth & Austria, 87-88, Esprit de l'Escalier (auth, book), travelling US, 88-89, The Reign of Narcissism (auth, book), travelling US, Ger, Switz & Eng, 89-90, The Tip of the Iceberg, Jay Gorney Mod Art, New York, 91, Echo, Galerie Sylvana Lorenz, Paris, France, 92, Never Odd or Even, Carnegie Mus Art, Pittsburgh, Pa, 92 & The Gaze, S L Simpson Gallery, Toronto, Can, 92; Cleveland Ctr Contemp Art, Ohio, 90; Selections from the Permanent Collection, installation: The Reign of Narcissism, Mus Contemp Art (The Temporary Contemp), Los Angeles, 91; Jay Gorney Mod Art, New York, 92. *Awards:* Louis Comfort Tiffany Found Award, 89; Nat Endowment Arts, 90; Frederick Weisman Found Award, 91. *Bibliog:* Barbara Bloom, Juliet Art Mag, 12/91 & 1/92; Rosa Olivares (auth), Art at the end of minimalism, Lapiz, 2/92; George Melrod (auth), The culture of consumerism, Atelier, 5/92. *Publ:* Auth, Esprit de l'Escalier, 88; auth, Ghost Writer, 88; auth, The Reign of Narcissism, 90; auth, Never Odd or Even, Verlag Silke Schreiber, Munich, Ger & Carnegie Mus Art, Pittsburgh, Pa, 92. *Mailing Add:* c/o Jay Gorney Modern Art 100 Greene St New York NY 10012

BLOOM, DONALD S
PAINTER, CARTOONIST
b Roxbury, Mass, Sept 3, 32. *Study:* Mass Col Art, BFA, 53; Art Students League, 53-55, with Barnet, Levi & Trafton; Inst Allende, San Miguel Allende, Mex, MFA, 57. *Work:* New Brunswick Pub Libr, NJ; NJ Food Coun; Fairleigh Dickinson Univ, Madison, NJ; Montclair State Col, NJ; Rutgers Univ. *Exhib:* Whitney Ann Am Painting, Whitney Mus Am Art, New York, 60; Silvermine Guild Ann, New Canaan, Conn, 63; Audubon Artists Ann, Nat Acad Galleries, New York, 63; NJ Pavilion, New York World's Fair, 65; Springfield Watercolor Asn Traveling Show, Mo, 65; NJ State Mus Ann, 66 & 73. *Pos:* Staff cartoonist, Sentinel (newspapers), 78-90. *Teaching:* Art instr, Piscatawny Schs, 58-92; instr painting & collage, Morris Co Art Asn, NJ, 60-68; instr painting, Bloomfield Col, 65-66; dist chmn art dept, Piscataway Schs, NJ, 66-84; instr watercolor, Summit Art Ctr, 74; instr art, Trenton State Col, 83. *Awards:* Guggenheim Fel Creative Painting, 61; Silvermine Guild Award, 63; Huntington Hartford Found Fel, 64; Second Award Ed

Cartooning, 85 & Third Award, 88. *Bibliog:* E Genauer (auth), rev in New York Herald Tribune, 9/61; J Beck (auth), rev in Art News, 10/61; V Raynor (auth), rev in Arts, 10/61. *Mem:* Nat Cartoonists Soc. *Media:* Acrylic, Oil. *Publ:* Auth, We learned about color & design, Sch Arts Mag, 58; illusr, Seventeen Mag, 61; Country & Western Issue, Billboard Mag, 63; auth, Batik in the classroom & Woodcuts by children, 72 & Two for one, 75, Instructor. *Mailing Add:* 31 Dexter Rd East Brunswick NJ 08816

BLOOM, EDITH SALVIN
ART DEALER, PAINTER
b Boston, Mass, April 26, 17. *Study:* Mass Col Art, 36-38; Boston Mus Sch Art, 39-45; Harvard Univ, 62, fine arts & 82-92, photog; DeCordova Mus Art Sch, 45-74; also with D Hall, Marian Steele, J Chetcuti & Emile Gruppe; Boston Univ Sch Fine & Applied Arts, Hon Degree. *Comn:* Wall murals (vitrified enamel), private comns, Mass & Maine, 65-92. *Exhib:* Islesboro Inn Exhib, Dark Harbor, Maine, 63-78; Camden Nat Bank, Maine, 63-92; Copley Soc Boston, 80; Shawmut Bank Boston, 81-83; Boston City Hall Exhib, 82. *Pos:* Art dir, Collector's Gallery, Chestnut Hill, Mass & Camden, Maine, 63-92. *Teaching:* Instr vitrified enamel, privately, 65-89. *Awards:* First Prize Landscape, DeCordova Mus, 60; First Prize Watercolors, TI Group Exhibs, 68-75; Juror's Choice Photog, Copley Soc, 82. *Bibliog:* Ivy Dodd (auth), Art along the shore, Courier-Gazette, Rockland, Maine, 7/29/82 & 10/89; Photo essay at Camden bank, Camden Herald, 5/26/83; article, Bangor Daily News, 6/3/83 & 91; Portland Press Sunday Telegram, 63-91. *Mem:* Copley Soc Boston (bd mem, 65-88). *Media:* Oil, Vitrified Enamel. *Specialty:* Paintings and photographs. *Publ:* Auth, Still There, Manuscript in 10 Chapters of Photography, Prose & Poetry. *Mailing Add:* Box 155 Chestnut Hill MA 02167

BLOOM, HYMAN
PAINTER
b Latvia, Mar 29, 13. *Study:* West End Community Ctr, Boston, Mass, study with Harold Zimmerman. *Work:* Harvard Univ; Hirshhorn Mus & Sculpture Garden, Smithsonian Inst, Washington, DC; Kalamazoo Inst Arts, Mich; Mus Mod Art, New York; Whitney Mus Am Art, New York; Univ Conn, Storrs. *Exhib:* Americans 1942, Mus Mod Art, New York; Mus Fine Arts, Boston; Whitney Mus Am Art, New York; two-man show, Univ Calif Los Angeles; one-man shows, Stuart Gallery, Boston, 45, Inst Contemp Art, Boston, Whitney Mus Am Art, 68, Univ Conn, 69 & Terry Dintenfass Inc, 72 & 75; Retrospective, Albright-Knox Art Gallery, Buffalo, NY, 54. *Teaching:* Instr, Wellesley Col, 49-51 & Harvard Univ, 51-53. *Media:* Acrylic, Oil. *Mailing Add:* 80 Hills Ferry Rd Nashua NH 03060

BLOOM, MARTHA
COLLAGE ARTIST, PRINTMAKER
b Paterson, NJ, Aug 5, 51. *Study:* Green Mountain Col (art maj), 69-70; Art Inst Boston, 70-71, Art Students League, 71-80. *Work:* Assoc Am Artists, New York; Sylvan Cole Gallery, New York; Art Students League; Columbia Mus, Columbia, SC; McNay Mus, San Antonio, Tex; Permanent installation, Art student league children's class etchings, D'Arcy-Massive-Benton-Bowles, New York, 90; Metrop Mus, New York, 91. *Comn:* Union Settlement Asn, New York City, 92. *Exhib:* Audubon Soc, Nat Acad Gallery, New York, 74; one-person show, MacDowell Sch, Art Students League, New York, 77; McNay Ann Collector's Show, McNay Mus, San Antonio, Tex, 84- 87; Assoc Am Artists, theme shows, 80-85; Midtown-Payson Gallery, New York, 89; Book Arts Gallery, New York, 91; Westport Hist Soc, Ct, 92; and others. *Teaching:* Lectr, printmaking, Cooper-Hewitt Mus, New York, 80-81; art instr, Art Students League, 85-; Silvermine Sch Art, Ct, 92-; Westport Arts Ctr, Ct, 92- *Awards:* MacDowell Traveling Scholarship, Art Student League, 74-77. *Mem:* Artists Equity Asn; life mem Art Students League (bd control, 3 yrs); Artists Fel Inc. *Media:* Multi-Media. *Dealer:* Sylvan Cole Gallery 200 W 57th St New York NY 10019. *Mailing Add:* 1023 Hulls Hwy Southport CT 06490

BLOOMFIELD, LISA DIANE
PHOTOGRAPHER, CONCEPTUAL ARTIST
b Los Angeles, Calif, Aug 9, 51. *Study:* Univ Calif, Berkeley, BA, 73; Calif Inst Arts, MFA(art & design; scholar), 80. *Work:* J Paul Getty Mus, Malibu, Calif. *Exhib:* Phantasy, Santa Barbara Mus Art, 82; solo show, Arco Ctr Visual Art, 83, Visual Studies Workshop, Rochester, NY, 89; Franklin Furnace, New York; two-person show, Lightwork, Syracuse, NY, 88; Biennial I, Calif Mus Photo, Riverside, 90; Systems, Los Angeles Munic Art Gallery, 90. *Collections Arranged:* Photographs: Griffith Observatory: 1935-1978, Los Angeles, 78; The Theater of Gesture, Los Angeles Ctr Photog Studies, 83. *Teaching:* Instr Otis Art Inst, 81-; lectr, Univ Washington; lectr, Univ Calif Los Angeles, 89; lectr, Univ Calif Riverside & Santa Barbara, 90. *Awards:* Purchase Award, Six State Exhib, Univ NMex, Albuquerque, 82; Calif Arts Coun Grant, 83; Visual Arts Fel, Nat Endowment Arts, 86; Fac Develop Fund, New Sch Soc Res, NY, 89. *Bibliog:* J Hugunin (auth), Mocking objects, Afterimage, 12/80; D Berland (auth), On photography, Los Angeles Times, 5/15/83; J Brumfield (auth), Loaded implications, Art Week, 5/28/83. *Mem:* Friends Photog; Los Angeles Ctr Photog Studies; Soc Photog Educ. *Publ:* Contribr, Impulse Mag, vol 10 #1, 82; Top stories #28, 89; CAA J, 90. *Mailing Add:* Dept Photog Otis Parsons Sch Design 2401 Wilshire Blvd Los Angeles CA 90057

BLOOMFIELD, SUZANNE
PAINTER
b Cleveland, Ohio, June 23, 34. *Study:* Ohio Univ, BS, 55; Univ Ariz, MA, 75. *Work:* Jewish Community Found & Peter Howell Sch, Tucson, Ariz; Interlochen Ctr Arts, Mich. *Comn:* Mural, Coun & Guidance Prog, Col Educ, Tucson, Ariz, 54. *Exhib:* UN World Conf on Women, Nairobi, Kenya, 86; Nat Asn Women Artists Centennial Year Foreign Exhib (touring India), 89-90; American Album & Permanent Collections Res Archives, Nat Mus Women in Arts, Washington, DC, 90. *Bibliog:* Calif Art Review, 89; Arizina Illus, KUAT Tv, Tucson, Ariz, 90. *Media:* Encaustics, Oil. *Mailing Add:* 4270 E Holmes Tucson AZ 87111

BLOOMGARDEN, JUDITH MARY
ART LIBRARIAN
b Brooklyn, NY, Jan 29, 42. *Study:* Univ London, 61-62; Elmira Col, BA, 63; Boston Univ, 63-64; Columbia Univ, 64-66; Pratt Inst, MLS, 69. *Pos:* Libr asst, Elmira Col Libr, 62-63, Sch Educ Libr, Boston Univ, 64 & Fine Arts Libr, Columbia Univ, 65; sr cataloguer, Mus of Mod Art Libr, New York, 66-70; libr consult, NY State Coun Arts, 69-71; head of tech servs, Art & Archit Libr, Yale Univ, 71-80; consult, Comt for the Preservation of Archit Records, NY, 77- *Mem:* Art Libr Soc NAm; Conn Archit Rec & Drawings Survey; Nat Arts Club; Nat Trust Hist Preserv; Soc Archit Historians. *Mailing Add:* 2708 Whitney Ave Baltimore MD 21215

BLOSSER, NICHOLAS
PAINTER
b Columbiana, Ohio, Nov 1, 58. *Study:* Ohio State Univ, BFA, 80, MFA, 82. *Work:* Contemp Art Workshop, Chicago. *Exhib:* One-person shows, Hopkins Hall Gallery, Ohio State Univ, 80, United Christian Ctr Gallery, Columbus, Ohio, 87, Olin Gallery, Kenyon Col, Gambier, Ohio, 87, Contemp Art Workshop, Chicago, Ill, 87, Bowling Green State Univ Art Gallery, Ohio, 89, Spaces Gallery, Cleveland, Ohio, 89; Drawing Our Own Conclusions, Fort Hayes Sch Arts Gallery, Columbus, Ohio, 88; Contemp Art Workshop, Figurative Painting, 88; Emily Davis Gallery, Univ Akron, Ohio, 89; Jamison-Thomas Gallery, Portland, Ore, 91 & 92; Montgomery Mus Art, Ala, 92. *Teaching:* Instr art, Mt Vernon Nazarene Col, 85-91, Mich Col, 91- *Awards:* Ohio Arts Coun Individual Fel, painting, 83; Rome Prize Fel, Am Acad Rome, 84-87; Nat Endowment Arts Fel, 87 & 91. *Dealer:* Jamison-Thomas Gallery Portland OR. *Mailing Add:* 402 Holly St Johnson City TN 37604

BLOVITS, LARRY JOHN
PAINTER, EDUCATOR
b Detroit, Mich, Oct 19, 36. *Study:* Wayne State Univ, Detroit, BFA, 64, MFA, 66; study with Daniel Greene, summers 83-86. *Work:* Muskegon Mus Art, Mich; Battle Creek Art Ctr, Mich; Beta Rho Delta Zeta Nat Sorority Mus, Oxford, Ohio; Mich Supreme Court Chambers, Lansing. *Comn:* Mich Supreme Court Justice Otis Smith, Lansing, 78; Hope Col Pres Gordon Van Wylen, Holland, Mich, 86; Pres Martin Essenberg, Covenant Col, Lookout Moutain, Tenn, 88; Pres John Bernhard, Western Mich Univ, Kalamazoo, 90; G W Haworth, Chmn, Haworth Corp, Holland, Mich, 91. *Exhib:* Soc Des Pastellistes de France Int, Palais Rameau, Lille, France, 87; OPA 5th Int, Ky Highlands Mus, Ashland, 88; Salmagundi Members Exhib, New York, 88; one-man show, Muskegon Mus Art, Mich, 88; 20th Ann Pastel Soc Ann Nat, Nat Arts Club, New York, 92; and others. *Pos:* Visual arts adv, Mich Coun Arts, Detroit, 76-81; apprentice master teacher, Nat Endowment Arts, Washington, DC, 83; vis artist, Mich Tech Univ, Houghton, 89. *Teaching:* adj instr drawing, Wayne State Univ, Detroit, 66-67; instr drawing & painting, Northern Mich Univ, Marquette, 67; prof art, drawing & painting, Aquinas Col, Grand Rapids, Mich 67- *Awards:* Member's Award, 9th Ann Nat, Pastel Soc Am, 81; 9th Ann Salmagundi nat, Metrop Portrait Soc, 86; Outstanding Achievement Portraiture, Nat Portrait Seminar, 91. *Bibliog:* Stephen Doherty (auth), Artist in residence, Am Artist Mag, 6/90; Who's Who Midwest, Marquis, 23rd ed, 91; Madelyn Woolwich (auth), Pastel Interpretation, Northern Light, 9/93. *Mem:* Am Soc Portrait Artists; Pastel Soc Am; Am Portrait Soc (co-chmn educ comt); Midwest Pastel Soc; Salmagundi Club, New York. *Media:* Oil, Pastel. *Publ:* Contribr, Photographing your art, Profile Mag, 84 & Directory of American Portrait Artists, 85, Am Portrait Soc; contribr & coauth, Artist in residence, Larry Blovits multipurpose studio, Am Artists Mag, 90; auth, Pastel Landscape, Technique & Procedure, video, pvt publ, 91. *Dealer:* Arnold Klein Gallery 4520 N Woodward Royal Oak MI 48072. *Mailing Add:* 0-1835 Luce SW Grand Rapids MI 49504-9503

BLUE, PATT
PHOTOGRAPHER, EDUCATOR
b Apr 27, 45; US citizen. *Study:* State Univ NY, Stony Brook, BA, 74; Art Inst Chicago, MFA, 87. *Work:* City Mus New York; John F Kennedy Libr, Boston; Pola; David C Ruttenberg, Chicago, Ill; Robert & Francis Kohler, Philadelphia, Pa; Lyons Inst, France; Brooklyn Mus, NY. *Exhib:* Light Work Retrospective, Everson Mus, Syracuse, NY, 85; Heart of Man, Nexus Contemp Art Ctr, Atlanta, Ga, 86 & Art Inst Chicago, 87; Le Corto, Figure, Fonds Regional d'Art Contemporain, Lyons, France, 87; Photo Active, Ronald Feldman Gallery, New York, 88; Photo Preceptions, Phyllis Rosman Gallery, Farley Dickenson Univ, Madison, Wis, 89; A selection of SELECTIONS, Parsons Sch Design, New York, 90; and others. *Collections Arranged:* New Spirit of Photography, FIT, New York, 85; Contemp European Photography Series, Art Inst, Chicago, 86-87. *Pos:* Asst prof photog, Kean Col, Union, NJ, 88- *Teaching:* Instr photog, Int Ctr Photog, 76- & NY Univ, 83-; asst prof, Moore Col Art, 84-; asst prof photog, Keane Col, Union, NJ, 88- *Awards:* New York Foun Arts Fel, 89-90; Nat Endowment Arts, Visual Arts Fel, 89-90; Kean Col Research Award, 89-90; and others. *Bibliog:* Threshold issue: the disturbing image, Cameraworks, Spring, 86. *Publ:* Contribr, Close-up, Polaroid, 83; auth, Babies having babies, Life Mag, 83; John Loengard, Classic Photog, 88; ed, D Friend, The Meaning of Life, Little Brown & Co, 91; Flesh and Blood, George/Heyman/Hoffman, The Picture Project, 92; and others. *Mailing Add:* 201 W 77th St 2E New York NY 10024

BLUE MAN GROUP, See Goldman, Matt

BLUE MAN GROUP, See Stanton, Phil

BLUE MAN GROUP, See Wink, Chris

BLUHM, NORMAN
PAINTER
b Chicago, Ill, Mar 28, 21. *Study:* Ill Inst Technol; and with Mies Van der Rohe. *Work:* Dallas Mus Art, Tex; Dayton Art Inst, Ohio; Mus Mod Art, Whitney MusAm Art, Met Mus Art, New York; Corcoran Gallery & Nat Mus Am Art, Washington, DC; Albright Knox Gallery, Buffalo; plus many others. *Exhib:* One-man shows, Corcoran Gallery Art, 69, 78, Everson Mus, 73, Vassar Coll, 74, Contemp Arts Mus, Houston, Tex, 76, Galerie Stadler, Paris, 82 & 88, Portland Art Mus, 86 & Washburn Gallery, New York, 86, 89 & 90, Ball State Univ, Muncie, 88, Univ Ariz Mus Art, Tucson, 89, Washburn Gallery, New York, 90 & 91; Large Scale Am Painting, Jewish Mus, 67; Ann Exhib Contemp Painting, Whitney Mus Am Art, 72; Color in Language, travelling exhib to S Am & Mus Mod Art, New York, 75; Recent Trends in Collecting 20th Century Painting & Sculpture, Nat Mus Am Art, Washington, 82; Action/Precision, Washburn Gallery, New York, 85; East Hampton Avant-Garade: A Salute to the Segna Gallery, Guild Hall Mus, East Hampton, NY, 90; and others. *Bibliog:* Lawrence Alloway (auth), Art, Chicago, 11/86; Holland Cotter (auth), Norman Bluhm at Washburn, Art in Am, 10/89; Richard Huntington (auth), The Courage to Explore a Drama in Paint, Buffalo News, 12/31/89; and many others. *Media:* Oil. *Mailing Add:* c/o Washburn Gallery 20 W 57th St New York NY 10019

BLUM, ANDREA
SCULPTOR
b New York, NY, Apr 6, 50. *Study:* Univ Denver; Boston Mus Sch Fine Arts, BFA, 73; Sch Art Inst Chicago, MFA, 76. *Work:* Art Inst Chicago; AT&T, Chicago; Marina Bank, Chicago; Univ Iowa Mus Art, Iowa City; Nat Collection Fine Arts, Washington, DC. *Exhib:* Boston Mus Sch, 73; Fel Exhib, Art Inst Chicago, 76, Drawings of '70's, 77 & Works on Paper, 78; 3 Sculptors, Northern Iowa Univ Gallery Art, Cedar Falls, 79; Art from Chicago, Koffler Found Collection, Nat Collection Fine Arts, Washington, DC; one-woman show, Marianne Deson Gallery, Chicago, 78 & 80; Beyond Object, Aspen Ctr for Visual Arts, Colo, 80; Creative Time, New York, 81; Installation, Hudson River Mus, New York, 81; DeCordova Mus, Mass, 81; and others. *Teaching:* Vis artist & lectr, Univ Iowa, Iowa City, 77, Kalamazoo Inst Art, Mich, 77, Univ Ill, Chicago Circle, 77, Univ Hartford, Conn, 78, Univ Northern Iowa, Cedar Falls, 79 & Univ Chicago, 79; vis artist, Art Inst Chicago, 81. *Awards:* Nat Endowment for Arts individual grants, 76 & 78. *Bibliog:* Franz Schulze (auth), Nothing but abstract, summer 76 & Kay Larson (auth), Rooms with a point of view, 10/77, Art News; C L Morrison (auth), rev in Artforum, 10/76. *Mem:* Col Art Asn Am. *Mailing Add:* 322 Seventh Ave 2nd Floor New York NY 10001

BLUM, HELAINE DOROTHY
SCULPTOR, PAINTER
b Cleveland, Ohio. *Study:* Cleveland Art Inst; Western Reserve Univ; Art Students League; Columbia Univ. *Work:* Detroit Inst Art; Israel Mus Art, Jerusalem; Skirball Mus, Los Angeles. *Comn:* Portrait Samuel Golter, City Hope Med Ctr, Duarte, Calif, 72; portrait Marcel Marceau, Friends Marcel Marceau, Paris, 76. *Exhib:* May Show, Cleveland Mus Art, 45-60s; American Sculpture, Metrop Mus Art, New York, 51; Max Weber Exhib, Jewish Mus, New York, 56; Jewish Art, Smithsonian Inst, 60s; Sculpture, Corcoran Mus, 65; Acad Med, New York, 68; American Art, Calif Palace Legion Hon, 68; Sculpture, O'Hara Gallery, London, 69. *Awards:* L'Esprit, Silvermine Guild Artists, 59 & 65; Nat Coun Jewish Women Award, 67-82; Nat Asn Women Artists Award, 68. *Bibliog:* Articles, New Yorker, 60, New York Times, 66 & Art News, 71. *Mem:* Artists Equity Asn; Nat Asn Women Artists; Silvermine Guild. *Media:* Bronze. *Mailing Add:* PO Box 93 Santa Monica CA 90406

BLUM, JUNE
PAINTER, SCULPTOR
b Maspeth, NY, Dec 10, 39. *Study:* Brooklyn Col, MA, 59; Brooklyn Mus Art Sch, with Reuben Tam & Tom Doyle, 59-67; New Sch, New York, with Laurie Goulet, 65. *Work:* Brooklyn Col, NY; Okla Art Ctr Mus; Cocoa Beach Libr, Fla. *Comn:* Light Environments (Time-Space), Suffolk Mus, Stony Brook, NY, 70, Okla Art Ctr Mus, Oklahoma City, 72, Hudson River Mus, Yonkers, NY, 73 & Nassau Co Mus Fine Arts, Roslyn, NY, 80. *Exhib:* Works on Paper/Women Artists, Brooklyn Mus, 75; Sons & Others, Queens Mus, Flushing, NY, 76; one-woman shows, Paintings, Bronx Mus, NY, 76, Brevard Community Col, Cocoa & Melbourne, Fla, 84; 3 Contemp Am Women Realists, Miami-Dade Community Col, 78; The Opposite Sex, Univ Mo-Kansas City, 79; A Woman's Space, Nassau Co Mus Fine Arts, Roslyn, NY, 80; Art to Wear, Barbara Gillman Gallery, Miami, Fla, 81; Brevard Performing Arts Ctr, Melbourne, Fla, 88. *Collections Arranged:* The Artists Use of Paper, Watercolors, Contemporary Outdoor Sculpture, 74, Suffolk Mus; Works on Paper-Women Artists (with catalog), Brooklyn Mus, 75; The Opposite Sex, A Realistic Viewpoint (with catalog), Univ Mo, Kansas City, 79; The Figure of 5 (with catalog), Miami-Dade Community Col, North Campus, 79; Women's Art, Miles Apart, (with catalog), Valencia Col, Orlando, Fla & Aaron Berman Gallery (with catalog), New York, 82; and others. *Pos:* Cur contemp art, Suffolk Mus, Stony Brook, NY, 71-76; dir, Women for Art, 76- *Awards:* Anne Eisner Putnam Mem Prize, Nat Acad, Nat Asn Women Artists, 68; Hon Mention, White Mountain Festival Arts, Jefferson, NH, 77. *Bibliog:* Judith A Hoffberg (auth), Letters, Umbrella Assocs, 9/78; Joan Gabriel (auth), Artists in the sunshine, Today, 2/81; Benita Budd (auth), June Blum: Enviromental images, Women Artists News, 84. *Mem:* Women's Caucus for Art (nat chap); Col Art Asn Am; Artists' Equity Asn. *Media:* Oil, Fabric. *Publ:* Auth, Metamorphosis of June Blum, 76, Betty Friedan ser, 76, Female connection, 78 & A woman's space, 80, Women for Art; Women's Art, Miles Apart (catalog intro), Valencia Community Col, Fla, 82; June Blum, Fiberarts, 3/86. *Dealer:* NN Gallery Seattle WA. *Mailing Add:* 120 Boca Ciega Rd Cocoa Beach FL 32931

BLUMBERG, BARBARA GRIFFITHS
PAINTER, INSTRUCTOR
b Wheelersburg, Ohio, Dec 30, 20. *Study:* Stratford Col, Danville, Va; Marshall Univ; also with Fletcher Martin, Elliott O'Hara, Leo Manso & Victor Caudall. *Work:* Charleston Art Gallery, WVa; WVa Col Grad Studies; WVa State Capitol Bldg; FMC Corp, New York; Kanawaha Co Libr, Charleston. *Comn:* Mural, Marshall Univ, 57; tapestry, WVa State House, 70; painting, comn by Gov Hulette Smith, 71; tapestry, T F Goldthorpe Collection, Fla, 73. *Exhib:* Two Hundred Eighty, Huntington, WVa, 54-74; Int Fabric Exhib, Asher Gallery, London, Eng, 68; Fabric Structures (one-man nat touring exhib), 69; Appalachian Corridors, Fabric Sculpture, 70; Norfolk Biennial Drawing & Graphics, Va, 70- *Pos:* Guest artist, Maine, 68-69 & Bowling Green, Ohio, 70-71; consult, State WVa, 72-75. *Teaching:* Instr creative expression, WVa Col Grad Studies, Institute, WVa, formerly, art therapist in pediatrics, currently; instr painting & drawing, Charleston Art Gallery, 70-; instr painting & drawing, Univ Hawaii, Honolulu, 70-71. *Awards:* Purchase Award, Huntington, WVa, 70, Ala Moana Art Festival, Honolulu, 72 & Allied Artists WVa, 74-75. *Bibliog:* Bill Bellinger (auth), Art with a purpose, WVa Illus, 70; Connie Shearer (auth), Full page life style, Charleston Gazette, 71. *Mem:* Nat Asn Am Pen Women (pres, 69); Allied Artists WVa (vpres, 70); Provincetown Art Asn, Mass; East Coast Gallery, Mass. *Media:* Watercolor, Oil. *Res:* Art therapy; art for mentally retarded and physically handicapped. *Publ:* Auth, Creative approach to mental retardation, WVa Sch J, 61; illusr & contribr, Inklings, Nat Asn Am Pen Women, 72-; illusr & contribr, Art & Develop Disabilities J, 74. *Mailing Add:* 1422 Wilkie Dr Charleston WV 25314

BLUMBERG, RON
PAINTER
b Reading, Pa. *Study:* Nat Acad Design; Art Students League, New York; Acad Grande Chaumiere, Paris, France. *Work:* Joseph Hirshorn Mus, Washington, DC; LA County Mus Art, Los Angeles; Exec Mansion, State of Calif, Sacramento; Bonita Granville; Mrs Mel Blanc. *Exhib:* Dallas Mus Fine Arts, Dallas, Tex, 35-36; Los Angeles County Mus Art, Los Angeles, 55-58; H de Young Mem Mus, San Francisco, 67; Art LA 88 & 89, Feingarten Galleries, Los Angeles, 88 & 89; Armory show, New York, NY, 89 & 90. *Media:* Oil. *Dealer:* Feingarten Galleries Box 5383 Beverly Hills CA 90209. *Mailing Add:* 974 Teakwood Rd Los Angeles CA 90049

BLUMENTHAL, FRITZ
PAINTER, PRINTMAKER
b Mainz, Ger, June 16, 13; US citizen. *Study:* Univ Wuerzburg, Frankfurt, Freiburg, Berne. *Work:* Metrop Mus Art, Mus Mod Art & Brooklyn Mus, New York; Nat Gallery Art & Nat Mus Am Art, Washington, DC; Boston Mus Fine Arts; Victoria & Albert Mus, London; Yale Univ Art Gallery, New Haven, Conn; Bibliot Nat, Paris; Stedelijk Mus, Amsterdam; Museu de Les Arts Grafiques, Museu Nacional d'Art de Catalunya, Barcelona, Spain; St Louis Art Mus, Mo; and others. *Comn:* Prog cover designs, Gtr Middletown Arts Coun, NY State Coun Arts in collection of Mus Performing Arts at Lincoln Ctr, New York Pub Libr. *Exhib:* Solo exhibs, Albany Inst Hist & Art, Albany, NY, 52, Kenneth Taylor Gallery, Nantucket, Mass, 61 & 65, Gutenberg Mus, Mainz, Ger, 64, Kunstverein Ulm, Ger, 65; Weintraub Gallery, New York, 84; Nat Mus Am Art, Washington, DC, 88; Marion Koogler McNay Art Inst, San Antonio, Tex, 88; Thermonotype: Degas to Picasso, Mus Fine Arts, Boston, 90; De Bonnard á Baselitz, Bibliothéque Nat, Paris, 92; and others. *Bibliog:* Dr Werner Spanner (auth), Fritz Blumenthal, Das Neue Mainz, 64 & Mainz, 83; La Liberte & Mogelon (coauths), The Art of Monoprint, Van Nostrand, 74; Dr D A W Koning (auth), article, De pharmacie en de Kunst, Vol IV, 76; and others. *Media:* Oil Casein; Monotypes. *Dealer:* Associated American Artists 20 W 57th St New York. *Mailing Add:* 422 Silver Lake Scotchtown Rd Middletown NY 10940

BLUMENTHAL, MARGARET M
DESIGNER
b Latvia, Sept 7, 05. *Study:* Berlin, Ger, with B Scherz & Bruno Paul. *Exhib:* Monza, Italy; Metrop Mus Art, New York; Pratt Inst Gallery. *Pos:* Indust & textile designer, 43-; freelance designer & stylist, Libbey-Owens Co, Fallani & Cohn Co, Drulane Co, Toscony Fabrics, Franco Mfg Co, Colortex Co & Astorloid Soc. *Media:* Textiles. *Mailing Add:* 689 Columbus Ave New York NY 10025

BLUMRICH, STEPHEN
DESIGNER
b Gotha, Ger, June 9, 41; US citizen. *Study:* Kunstgewerbeschule Dept Fabric Design, BFA, 58. *Work:* Nat Collection Fine Arts; Thomson Activities Coun, Thomson, Ga. *Comn:* S Cent Bell, Nashville, Tenn. *Exhib:* Ann Southern Tier Art Show, Corning Mus Glass, NY, 70-74; Lake Superior Int Craft Exhib, Tweed Art Mus, Duluth, Minn, 74; The New Fabric Surface, Renwick Gallery, 78; Surface Design Invitational, Purdue Univ, West Lafayette, Ind, 78; Games & Crafts, Philadelphia Art Alliance, 79; Show Biz, Fashion Inst Technol, New York, 80; Opening Exhib, Greenwood Gallery, 80. *Pos:* Ed, Surface Design J, 76-88; designer, Pea Ridge Purties, 84- *Awards:* Craft/Art S, Thomson, Ga, 81; Golden Isles Art Festival, St Simons Island, Ga, 81. *Bibliog:* Dona Z Meilach (auth), The Great Batik Revival, Sphere Mag, 73; Mike O'Brien (auth), A special craftsman, Regist Guard, Eugene, Ore, 75. *Mem:* Am Crafts Coun; World Crafts Coun; Surface Design Asn. *Media:* Fabrics, Quilts. *Dealer:* Zona New York Tokyo & Florence; Mus Am Folk Art Shops New York NY. *Mailing Add:* 323 Marks Ave Tullahoma TN 37388

BOARDMAN, DEBORAH
PAINTER
Study: Mt Holyoke Col, BA, 80; studied with Atelier Lucio Loubet, Paris, 81; Mass Col Art, BFA, 84; Tufts Univ, Sch Mus Fine Arts, MFA, 87. *Comn:* Some Fixed (E)Motions, 86, Brattle Theatre, Cambridge, Mass. *Exhib:* Solo exhibs: Good Luck (Lame Horse), Armstrong Gallery, Cornelle Col, Mt Vernon, Iowa, Stations of Mary, Gallery Eleven, Tufts Univ, Medford, Mass, 87, Mobius Performance Space, Boston, 88, Crane Gallery, Chicago, 89 Memento Mori, McAuley Gallery, Mt Mercy Col, Cedar Rapids, Iowa, 92; Memory & Influence, North Dakota Mus Art, 91; 1991 Iowa Artists Show, Des Moines Art Ctr, Iowa, 91; Positive/Negative, Slocumb Gallery, East Tenn Univ, 92; Anonymus Mus, Chicago, 92; Masters as Motif, N Lakeside Cult Ctr, Chicago, 92. *Pos:* Educ comt, NAME Gallery, Chicago, Ill, 91- *Teaching:* Vis painting, Univ Iowa, 88-89, asst prof 89-; vis artist, Moorhead State Univ, Minn, 91. *Awards:* Communit Arts Assistance Prog, City Chicago, Dept Cult Affairs, 92; Ill Arts Counc Access Prog. *Bibliog:* Mitchell Stevens (auth), Stations of Mary, New Art Examiner, 6/89; Eliot Nusbau (auth), Des Moines Register, 1/28/90; Elizabeth Condon (auth), The Mussell Secretes the Shell Which Shapes It, New Art Examiner, 9/90. *Media:* Oil. *Mailing Add:* 1839 N Leavitt Chicago IL 60647

BOARDMAN, SEYMOUR
PAINTER
b Brooklyn, NY, Dec 29, 21. *Study:* City Col New York, BSS, 42; Art Students League; Ecole Beaux Arts, Paris, France; Acad Grande Chaumiere, Paris; Atelier Fernand Leger, Paris, 46-52. *Work:* Whitney Mus Am Art, Guggenheim Mus & New York Univ, New York; Walker Art Ctr, Minneapolis, Minn; Santa Barbara Mus Art; plus others. *Exhib:* Whitney Mus Am Art, 55, 61 & 67; Kunsthalle, Basel, Switz, 64; Albright-Knox Gallery, Buffalo, NY, 67; Andrew Dickson White Mus of Art, Cornell Univ, 71; one-man shows, Galerie Mai, Paris, 51, Martha Jackson Gallery, NY, 55 & 56 & Dorsky Gallery, New York, 72; Anita Shapolsky Gallery, New York, 86; plus others. *Teaching:* Instr painting & drawing, Wagner Col, Staten Island, NY, 57-58. *Awards:* Longview Found Award, 63; Guggenheim Fel, 72; Gottlieb Found Award, 79 & 83; Krasner-Pollock Found Award, 85 & 91. *Bibliog:* Arts Digest, 4/55; Art News, 3/68; Arts, 1/80 & 3/92. *Mem:* New York Artists Equity Asn. *Media:* Acrylic, Oil. *Mailing Add:* 234 W 27th St New York NY 10001

BOBAK, BRUNO JOSEPH
PAINTER, PRINTMAKER
b Wawelowka, Poland, Dec 28, 23; Can citizen. *Study:* Art Gallery, Toronto, studied with A Lismer, D Medhurst, A Taylor, G Webber, 36, Cent Tech Sch, Ont, studied with C Goldhamer, R Ross, C Schaefer, E W Wood, dipl, 38-42, Cent Sch Art & Crafts, London, 44-45, City & Guilds Art Sch, London, 60. *Work:* Nat Gallery Can & Can Coun Art Bank, Ottawa, Ont; Oslo Kunstforening, Norway; S London Art Gallery, Eng; Seattle Art Gallery; Alberta Col Art, Calgary; Art Gallery, Greater Victoria, BC; Art Gallery, Hamilton, Ont; and many others. *Comn:* Murals, Expo, Montreal, 67, Univ NB & Dept Pub Works, Fredericton, 70. *Exhib:* One-man exhibs, City Art Gallery Leeds, 62, South London Art Gallery, 63, Oslo Kunstforening, Oslo & Stavanger Kunstforening, Stavanger, Norway, 63, Owens Art Gallery, Mt Allison Univ, Sackville, NB, 70-71; 1st Biennial Exhib, Mus Mod Art, Tokyo, 57; Brussels Int, Can Pavilion, Brussels, 58; 20th Biennial Int, Brooklyn Mus Art, 58; Contemp Can Art, Mex, 60; 19 Can Painters '62, Speed Mus, Louisville, 62; 4 Can Printmakers (traveling), Cent Wash State Col, 76; and others. *Pos:* Designer, concrete mural for facade, Vancouver Sch Art, 52-53; fine art coordinr & supevr, commissioner, sculpture & display, Atlantic artist for Expo, 67; resident artist, Univ New Brunswick. *Teaching:* Instr, head design, Vancouver Sch Art, BC, 47-57; dir, Space Art Ctr, Univ New Brunswick, Fredericton, NB, 62. *Awards:* First Prize Can Army Art Exhib, Nat Art Gallery Can, 44; Jessie Dow Prize, 71st Annual Spring, Exhib, Montreal Mus Fine Arts Montreal for Watercolor Eclipse, 54; C W Jefferys Award, Can Soc Graphic Art, Lugano, Switz, 55; K B Baker Memorial Purchase Award, Seattle Art Mus, Washington, DC, 55; Monsanto Art Compt Prize, Montreal, 57; Royal Soc Can Govt, Overseas Fel, 55; First Prize, Exhib of Contemp Art, Vancouver Art Gallery, 60; Can Coun Sr Fel, 72; Silver Jubilee Medal, 78; Chosen for reproduction of Can 30-cent postage stamp, 82. *Bibliog:* R H Hubbard (auth), Development of Can Art, Nat Gallery, Ottawa, 63; J R Harper (auth), Painting in Canada, Univ Toronto Press, 66; S Pickins (auth), History of Canadian Society of Painters in Watercolour, Art Mag, winter, 70; S Raphael (auth), In Review-Montreal Art Scene, Art Mag, winter, 72; C Mungal (auth), Fredericton, Could You Live There?, Chatelaine, 77; J Morris (auth), 100 Years of Canadian Drawings, Toronto, 80. *Media:* Oil; Woodcuts. *Dealer:* Walter Klinkoff Gallery 1200 Quest Rue Sherbrooke Montreal PQ H3A 1H9 Can. *Mailing Add:* c/o Walter Klinkoff Gallery 1200 Quest Rue Sherbrooke Montreal PQ H3A 1H9 Canada

BOB & BOB
PERFORMANCE ARTISTS
F Shishim, b Santa Monica, Calif, May 8, 53 & P Velick, b Detroit, Mich, Feb 8, 52. *Study:* P Velick, Art Ctr Col, Antioch Col, BFA, 75; F Shishim, Art Ctr Col, BFA, 75; both with Tom Wudl, Llyn Foulkes & Lorser Feitelson. *Work:* Ace Gallery, Toronto, Can. *Exhib:* Sex is Stupid, Los Angeles Inst Contemp Art, 79; Nature Is Perfect, Animals Are Perfect, What Are Humans?, Washington Hall Performance Gallery, Seattle, 80; Bob to Bob, Marianne Deson Gallery, Chicago, 82; We're All Lucky, Mus Contemp Art, Los Angeles, Calif, 85; retrospective (with catalog), Otis/Parson, 86. *Awards:* Golden Turkey Award, Young Turks, DTLA Administration. *Bibliog:* L F Burnham (auth), BOB & BOB: The First Five Years, Astro Artz, 80; Joan Hugo (auth), Bob & Bob again, Artweek Mag, 2/81; Alyson Pov (auth), Across america, Art Papers, 1/81; Alyson Pov (auth), Retrospective review, Los Angeles Times, 86; California Stories, KCET PBS-TV, Los Angeles. *Mem:* The Young Turks, Los Angeles. *Publ:* Contribr, High Performance/ Public Spirit, Astro Arts, 79; contribr, Performance Anthology, Carl Loeffler, 80; Across America (record), MITB Records, Beverly Hills, 81; The Least I Can Do (record), MITB Records, Beverly Hills, 82; We Know You're Alone (record), Polydor Records, 83; and many other forms of technological reproduction. *Mailing Add:* 2262 31st Santa Monica CA 90405

BOBICK, BRUCE
PAINTER, EDUCATOR
b Clymer, Pa, Oct 25, 41. *Study:* Indiana Univ Pa, BS, 63, MS, 67; Univ Notre Dame, MFA, 68. *Work:* Mt Mercy Col, Cedar Rapids, Iowa; Western Ill Univ, Macomb; Springfield Art Mus, Mo; Ill State Mus, Springfield; Krannert Art Mus, Univ Ill, Champaign-Urbana. *Comn:* three wall-hung quilts, Hilton Inn, Columbus, Ga, 82; watercolor painting & stained glass windows, Grace Lutheran Church, Carrollton, Ga, 83; stainless-steel kinetic sculptures, Carrollton Parks, Recreation & Cult Arts Dept, 88, Pinnacle Insurance Co, Carrollton, Ga, 89; wall-hung quilt, Omni Int Hotel, St Louis, Mo; two paintings for use as bedspread designs, All Star Sports & All Star Music; Disney World, Orlando, Fla, 92. *Exhib:* Watercolor USA, Springfield Art Mus, Mo 68, 69, 71, 73, 75, 77, 89 & 90; Nat Exhib Watercolor Soc of Ala, Birmingham Mus Art, 69-82; 164th Ann Am Watercolors, Prints & Drawings, Pa Acad Fine Arts, Philadelphia, 69; 145th & 146th Ann, Nat Acad Design, New York, 70 & 71; Oakland Art Mus, Kaiser Ctr, Oakland, Calif, 70; Laguna Beach Mus Art, Calif, 70, 71 & 79; 12th & 14th Midwest Biennial Exhib, Joslyn Art Mus, Omaha, Nebr, 72 & 76; 17th Hunter Ann Exhib Paintings & Drawings, Hunter Mus Art, Chattanooga, Tenn, 78; 1st Ann Ga Watercolor Soc Exhib, Mem Arts Ctr, Atlanta, 79; Mus Arts & Sci, Macon, Ga, 82, 85, 86 & 90; Am Cult Ctr, US Embassy, Brussels, Belg, 84; Palazzo Casali, Cortona, 89, Chiesadi San Stae, Venice, Italy, 89; Snite Mus Art, Univ Notre Dame, 90; Southern Quilts, A New View, 90-92; Ga Mus Art, 89, Mus Art, Columbus, 91. *Teaching:* Assoc prof art, Western Ill Univ, 68-76; from assoc prof to prof & chmn dept art, WGa Col, 76-; vis prof painting, Univ Ga Studies Abroad, Cortona, Italy, 80; Vis prof painting, Arrowmant Sch Arts & Crafts, Gatlinburg, Tenn, 84, 85, 86, 87 & 88. *Awards:* Purchase Award, Ill State Mus, 71, Watercolor USA, 75; Ga Watercolor Soc Award, 86 & 91. *Bibliog:* Dorothy M Joiner (auth), Bruce Bobick: Images upon the subconscious, Art Papers, 1/85; Laura Stewart Dishman (auth), A patchwork of memory, imagination, Orlando Sentinel, 2/20/86; Carlotta M Eike (auth), Artifacts from imaginary culture explore archeological implications, Mus News, 11/88. *Mem:* Watercolor Soc, Nat & Pittsburgh, Ga, Midwest & Ala. *Media:* Watercolor. *Res:* Communication between artist and viewer. *Publ:* Auth, Images upon the subconscious, The Flying Needle, 5/86. *Dealer:* Art Space 50 Hurt Plaza Suite 150 Atlanta GA 30303. *Mailing Add:* 40 Forrest Dr Carrollton GA 30117

BOBROWICZ, YVONNE PACANOVSKY
INSTRUCTOR, WEAVER
b Maplewood, NJ, Feb 17, 28. *Study:* Cranbrook Acad Art; study with Anni Albers; with Paolo Soleri at Haystack Mountain. *Work:* Philadelphia Mus Art, 90. *Comn:* Woven wall, comn by Louis I Kahn, Kimball Mus, Ft Worth Tex, 72; woven wall hanging, Savings & Loan Bank, Pittsburgh, Pa, 77; Dupont Corp, Wilmington, Del. *Exhib:* Walker Art Ctr, Minneapolis, Minn, 53; Mus Contemp Crafts, New York, 60; Philadelphia Mus Art, 63 & 300 yrs of Philadelphia Art, 76; Civic Ctr Mus Philadelphia, 67-73; Univ Pa Mus, Philadelphia, 75; Lousanne 14th Biennial of Tapestry, 89; group show, Tilburg Textile Mus, Holland, 89; and others. *Teaching:* Lectr textiles & weaving, Drexel Univ, Philadelphia, 66-; instr weaving, Peters Valley, Leyton NY, summers 72 & 76. *Awards:* First Prize, Los Angeles County Fair, 51. *Mem:* Am Craft Coun; World Craft Coun; Philadelphia Guild Handweavers. *Media:* Thread, fiber or metal. *Publ:* Contribr, Rugmaking, Golden Bks, 72; contribr, Hooked and Rya Rugs, Van Nostrand Reinhold, 74; contribr, Am Rugs and Carpets, William Morrow, 78. *Dealer:* Helen Drutt 1625 Spruce St Philadelphia PA 19103. *Mailing Add:* 2312 Spruce St Philadelphia PA 19103

BOCCIA, EDWARD EUGENE
PAINTER
b Newark, NJ, June 22, 21. *Study:* Pratt Inst Art Sch, NY; Art Students League; Columbia Univ, BS & MA. *Work:* City Art Mus St Louis; Denver Art Mus; Univ Mass; St Louis Univ; State Hist Soc Mo; Mus of Art, Fort Lauderdale, Fla; Nat Picture Gallery, Athens, Greece. *Comn:* Stained glass, Clayton Inn, Mo; four wall paintings, First Nat Bank, St Louis; mural, Stations of the Cross & stained glass windows, Newman Chapel, Washington Univ, St Louis; religious drawings & 14 mural paintings, Temple Brith Sholom Kneseth Israel, St Louis; and others. *Exhib:* Elliot Smith Gallery, St Louis, 88; Elaine Benson Gallery, Bridgehampton, NY, 89; Bell Gallery, Seattle, Wash, 90 & 92; Gallery of the Masters, St Louis, Mo, 90 & 92; Am Gallery, St Louis, Mo, 92; and many others. *Teaching:* Dean, Columbus Art Sch, Ohio, 48-51; guest instr, Univ Sask, summer 60; guest instr, Webster Groves Col, summer 65 & Univ Minn, 86; prof fine arts, Washington Univ, emer, currently. *Awards:* Bronze Medal, Temple Israel, St Louis, 62; Knighted to Cavaliere, Pres Ital Repub, 79; Order of the Crown of King St Louis IX of France, St Louis Univ, 90. *Bibliog:* Interview, Newsbeat Program, KSD-TV, St Louis & St Louis Skyline, KETC-TV; An Artist Who's Gone His Own Way, St Louis Post Dispatch, 85; Who's Who: Artist Edward Boccia, Dan's Papers Inc, Bridgehampton, NY, 92. *Publ:* Contribr, St Louis Post-Dispatch & Washington Univ Mags; Blue Unicorn-Poetry Journal, 88; CSS Publ, Poetry Anthology, 88; Poet Mag, 91. *Dealer:* American Gallery 4736 McPherson St Louis MO. *Mailing Add:* 600 Harper Ave Webster Groves MO 63119

BOCHNER, MEL
CONCEPTUAL ARTIST, ART WRITER
b Pittsburgh, Pa, 40. *Study:* Carnegie Inst Technol, Pittsburgh, BFA(painting), 62. *Work:* Los Angeles Co Mus Art, Calif; Mus Nat d'Art Mod, Paris, France; Whitney Mus Am Art. *Exhib:* One-man exhibs, David Nolan Gallery, NY, 90, Galleria Primo Piano, Rome, 90, Butler Inst Am Art, 91, Fontana's Light: Hommage to Lucio Fontana, Studio Casoli, Milan, 91, Stein Gladstone Gallery, NY, 91, Thomas Segal Gallery, Boston, 92 & Galerie Vega, Leige, Belg, 92; Drawings, Lorence Monk Gallery, NY, 91; Mel Bochner, Sol Lewitt & Chung Eun Mo, Primo Piano, Rome, Italy, 92; On certainty, Sonnanbend Gallery, New York, 92; Marking the Decades: Prints 1960-1990, Baltimore Mus Art, 92; American Art: 1930-1970, Lingotto, Torino, Italy; and many other one-man & group exhibs. *Teaching:* Instr, Sch Visual Arts, New York, 65. *Bibliog:* John Caldwell (auth), American Drawings and Watercolors in the Collection of the Museum of Art, Carnegie Institute, Univ Pittsburgh Press, 85; An american renaissance: Painting and Sculpture since 1940 (catalog), Mus Art, Ft Lauderdale, Fla, 86; Reconnecting: Recent Works by Jennifer Bartlett, Mel Bochner, Nancy Graves , Patrick Ireland, Lucio Pozzi, Detroit Inst Arts, 6/87. *Publ:* Auth, Background is not the margin, Art in Process, 69; Ten Misunderstandings: A Theory of Photography, New York, 70; No thought exists, Arts Mag, 4/70; Excerpts from speculation, Artforum, 5/70; Mental exercise: No 1 counting, Data, 2/72. *Mailing Add:* c/o Sonnabend Gallery 420 W Broadway New York NY 10012

BOCK, WILLIAM SAUTS-NETAMUX'WE
ILLUSTRATOR, PAINTER
b Sellersville, Pa, Sept 18, 39. *Study:* Philadelphia Col of Art, BFA(illus), spec study with Robert Riggs; Lutheran Sem, Philadelphia, MA. *Work:* US State Dept. *Comn:* Watercolor series of Am cities, comn by Marriott Corp for reproduction in many cities, 3-dimensional art (Indian Mex) & murals, Marriott Camelback Inn, Phoenix, Ariz, 69-70; watercolor for Christmas card, Book of the Month Club, New York, 71 & 74; Olympic designs for Plexiglas etching, McDonalds, Willow Grove, Pa, 75. *Awards:* Honored by Exhib for Illustrations for Crusader King, Am Inst of Graphic Arts, New York, 74; Monthly Choice Award for Illustrations for Malcolm Yucca Seed, Philadelphia Children's Reading Round Table, 78. *Bibliog:* Mr & Mrs Philip Berman (interview), Berman Collection, Pub TV, Allentown, Pa, 69; B A Bergman (auth), The First Aristocrats, Sunday Bulletin, Philadelphia, 2/75; Gerry Wallerstein (auth), William Sauts-Netamux'we Bock, Wolf-Clan Chief of the Lenape, Bucks Co Panorama Mag, 1/76. *Mem:* Philadelphia Children's Reading Round Table. *Media:* Pen & Ink; Watercolor, Acrylic. *Publ:* Illusr, Wolf Hunt, Little Brown, 70; illusr & auth, Coloring Book of the First Americans, Lenape Indian Drawings, Middle Atlantic Press, 74; illusr, Tom Sawyer, Field Enterprizes, World Bk, 75; Of Whales & Wolves, Lothrop, Lee, 78; White Fang (film strip), Spoken Arts, 78. *Mailing Add:* 252 E Summit St Souderton PA 18964

BOCOUR, LEONARD
PAINTER, LECTURER
b New York, NY, March 18, 10. *Study:* Jr Col Albany, NY, hon degree. *Teaching:* Instr, Brooklyn Mus Art Sch & The Skowhegan Sch of Painting & Sculpture, Skowhegan, Maine. *Awards:* Hall of Fame Art Materials Trade Asn, 74. *Mem:* Acrylic, Oil. *Interests:* Contemporary American Art. *Mailing Add:* 173 Riverside Dr New York NY 10024

BODE, ROBERT WILLIAM
DESIGNER, PAINTER
b New York, NY, Nov 20, 12. *Study:* Sch Fine & Appl Arts, Pratt Inst; also with Ogden Pleissner. *Comn:* Designs for US postal stamps, Johnny Appleseed, Davy Crockett & Energy Conservation. *Pos:* Exec art dir, Kudner Agency, 51-57; creative art supvr, J Walter Thompson, 57-67. *Awards:* Art Dirs Awards; Am Watercolor Soc; Hudson River Valley Awards. *Mem:* Am Watercolor Soc; Soc Illusr; Art Dirs Club. *Mailing Add:* PO Box 917 239 Chatham Rd Harwich MA 02645

BODEM, DENNIS RICHARD
MUSEUM DIRECTOR
b Milwaukee, Wis, July 27, 37. *Study:* Wabash Col, BA, 59; Grad Sch, Univ Wis-Madison, 59-61. *Pos:* Dir, Jesse Besser Mus, 74- *Mem:* Thunder Bay Arts Coun; Mich Coun Arts; Mich Mus Asn; Mich Asn Community Arts Agency. *Interests:* Representative works of outstanding US, Midwest and Michigan artists of the late 19th and 20th centuries for museum collection. *Mailing Add:* 121 E White Alpena MI 49707

BODIN, PAUL
PAINTER
b New York, NY, Oct 30, 10. *Study:* Nat Acad Design, 28; Art Students League, 29. *Work:* Albright Knox Art Gallery; Univ WVa. *Exhib:* One-man exhibs, Artist Gallery, 42, Laurel Gallery, 48 & 50 New Gallery, 52, Betty Parsons Gallery, 59 & 61, New York, Retrospective, Wilburton Art Gallery, Manchester, Vt, 88; Santa Barbara Mus, 49; Brooklyn Mus, 49 & 59; Metrop Mus, New York, 52; Springfield Mus, 52; Hudson River Mus, 60; one-man show retrospective, Wilburton Art Gallery, Manchester, Vt, 88; and others. *Awards:* USA Art Award, 58; Longview Found Award, 59. *Mem:* New York Artists Equity Asn. *Media:* Oil, Watercolor. *Dealer:* Mary Ryan Gallery 24 W 57th St New York NY 10019. *Mailing Add:* 207 W 86th St New York NY 10024

BODNAR, PETER
PAINTER, EDUCATOR
b Andrejova, Czech, Nov 27, 28; US citizen. *Study:* Flint Inst Arts, Mich, 41-44; Western Mich Univ, BS, 51; Mich State Univ, MA, 56. *Work:* Dallas Mus; Isaac Delgado Mus, New Orleans; Ft Worth Art Mus; Lakeview Ctr for Arts, Peoria, Ill; De Waters Art Ctr, Flint. *Exhib:* One-man retrospectives, Isaac Delgado Mus, 66, Ill Art Coun Galleries, Chicago, 71 & Newport Harbor Art Mus, Newport Beach, Calif, 74; Spirit of the Comics, Inst Contemp Art, Univ Pa, 69; one-man show, Lakeview Ctr for Arts, Peoria, 72. *Pos:* Vis artist, Bradley Univ, spring 70; vis artist, Southern Methodist Univ, Dallas, 72, artist in residence, summer workshop, Taos, NMex, 72; vis artist, Univ Southern Calif, 74. *Teaching:* Asst prof art, State Univ NY Col Plattsburgh, 56-58; asst prof art, Univ Fla, 60-62; prof painting, Univ Ill, Urbana-Champaign, 62- *Awards:* Tamarind Lithography Workshop Inc Grant, 64; Univ Ill Fel, Ctr for Advan Study, 67-68; Nat Endowment Arts Fel, 75- *Bibliog:* Hiram Williams (auth), Notes for a Young Painter, Prentice-Hall, 65; Franz Schulze (auth), article, Art Int, summer 67; Daniel Wells (auth), article, Chicago Tribune, summer 71. *Media:* Oil, Acrylic. *Publ:* Contribr, Strung Out with Elgar on a Hill, 70; contribr, Portrait: Converse, 75. *Mailing Add:* 2504 E Perkins Rd Urbana IL 61801

BODO, SANDOR
PAINTER, SCULPTOR
b Szamosszeg, Hungary, Feb 13, 20; US citizen. *Study:* Col Fine & Appl Art, Budapest, Hungary. *Work:* Tenn State Mus; First Tenn Bank, Nashville, Tenn; Pulaski Co Ct House, Little Rock, Ark; The Soc of the Cincinati, Wash, DC; Vatican Mus, Rome; Hist Mus, Budapest; Musée de l'armée, Paris. *Comn:* The Founding Fathers of Nashville, First Tenn Bank, Tenn; portrait of Andrew Jackson, Royal Palace, Copenhagen, Denmark, 71. *Exhib:* Nat Housing Ctr, Washington, DC; Butler Inst Am Art, Youngstown, Ohio; Nat Acad Galleries, New York; Smithsonian Inst, Washington, DC; Brooks Mem Art Gallery, Memphis, Tenn; Citadel Mus, Charleston, SC; Parthenon, Nashville, Tenn; Civic Ctr, Atlanta, Ga. *Pos:* Bodo's Art Studio, Nashville, Tenn, 73- *Awards:* Gold Medal Honor Watercolor, Am Art Week Exhib, 61; Gold Medal Honor Sculpture, 63 & Gold Medal Honor Oil Painting, 66, Nat Arts Club, New York; 200 Bicentennial Medal. *Mem:* Fel Am Artists Prof League; Nat Arts Club; Allied Artists Am; Am Medallic Sculpture Asn. *Mailing Add:* Bodo's Art Studio 6513 Hwy 100 Nashville TN 37305

BOEVE, EDGAR GENE
EDUCATOR, PAINTER
b Marshalltown, Iowa, Sept 27, 29. *Study:* J Franklin Sch of Prof Arts, Inc, New York, cert; Calvin Col, Grand Rapids, Mich, AB; Univ Mich, Ann Arbor, MSD. *Work:* Calvin Theological Seminary Grand Rapids, Mich; Dordt Col, Sioux Center, Iowa; Catholic Info Ctr, Lansing, Mich. *Comn:* Sculpture, Painting, Pine Rest Hosp, Cutlerville, Mich, 74, 77 & 87; banners, Woodland Church, Grand Rapids, Mich, 75; mural, Bethany, Holland, Mich, 76; sculpture, Faith, Prayer, Tract League, 83; logo, North Hills Church, Troy, Mich, 83 & 90; PLP Corp, Grand Rapids, Mich, 89; Polamar Hosp, San Diego, Calif, 90; Hope Lutheran Church, Park Forest, Ill, 90. *Exhib:* Detroit Art Inst, Mich, 65; Kresge Art Ctr, East Lansing, Mich, 68; Kalamazoo Art Ctr, Mich, 72; Grand Rapids Art Mus, Mich, 75. *Teaching:* Prof art hist, Calvin Col, Grand Rapids, Mich, 58-, chmn art dept. *Awards:* First Prize, 63 & 70 & Second Prize, 73 & 81, Christian Art Show, Peace Lutheran. *Mem:* Christians In the Visual Arts (pres, 79-83); Midwest Col Art Conf; Col Art Asn. *Media:* Oil, Acrylic. *Res:* Art educ, art hist. *Publ:* Auth, Childrens Art and the Christian Teacher, Nat Union Christian Sch, Concordia, Mo, 67, 2nd ed, 77; illusr, Youth Hymnal, Eerdmans, 68; illusr, The Touch of His Hand, World Home Bible, 76; illusr, The Gifted Church, Home Mission, Can Relig Conf, 77. *Mailing Add:* Dept Art Calvin Col 3233 Burton St Grand Rapids MI 49506

BOGARIN, RAFAEL
SERIGRAPHER, PAINTER
b El Tigre, Venezuela, Jan 20, 46. *Study:* Cristobal Rojas, Caracas, Venezuela, BA, 66; Pratt Graphics Ctr, New York, 70-71, study with Michael Ponce de Leon; Blackburn Workshop, New York, 71-73. *Work:* Mus of Fine Arts, Caracas; White House, Caracas; Corcoran Gallery of Art, Washington, DC; Chase Manhattan Bank, New York; Mus of Mod Art, New York. *Comn:* Three-floor-high mural, comn by Venezuelan Govt, Venezuelan Consulate, New York, 74. *Exhib:* Solo shows, Galeria Siete-Siete, Caracas, Venezuela, 82, Acquavella Gallery, Caracas, 84, Cult Ctr, Santa Fe, Bolivia, 85 & Complejo Cult, El Tigre, 87; Semana Cult, Miami Libr, Fla, 73; Young Artists, Union Carbide Bldg, New York, 74; one-man shows, Frank Fedele, Gallery, New York, 80, Galeria El Tunel, Guatemala City, 80, Galeria Garces Velasquez, Bogota, Colombia, 81; Rafael Bogarin Hwy Mus, El Tigre, Venezuela, 82; Hwy Mus, Roldanillo, Colombia, 83; Bicentennial Hwy, Cucuta, Colombia, 84. *Teaching:* Prof plastic arts, Sch of Plastic Arts, 67-70; prof plastic arts, Sch of Arts & Sci, Caracas, 69-70; asst etching & intaglio, Pratt Graphic Ctr, New York, 71-; instr serigraph workshop, Univ San Jose, Costa Rica. *Awards:* Roma Prize, Salon de Arte Venezoland, Italian Govt, 68; First Prize, Salon Aragua, Maracay, Venezuela. *Bibliog:* Calvin J Goodman (auth), Master Printers and Print Workshops, Am Artists, 10/76. *Mailing Add:* 14 W 17th St 5th Floor New York NY 10011

BOGART, GEORGE A
PAINTER
b Duluth, Minn, Oct 30, 33. *Study:* Univ Minn, Duluth, BA; Univ Wash, MFA; also with Fletcher Martin, Philip Evergood & Dong Kingman. *Work:* Delgado Mus Art, New Orleans, La; Ill State Univ; Washburn Univ, Topeka, Kans; Okla State Collection; Univ Okla. *Exhib:* Delgado Mus Art, 61 & 64;

Dallas Mus Fine Arts, 64 & 65; Okla Art Ctr, 75 & 78; Gruenbaum Gallery, New York, 83; Univ Kanas, 84; Ark Art Ctr, Little Rock, 90; and others. *Teaching:* Instr, Univ Wash, formerly; prof art, Univ Tex, Austin & Pa State Univ, State College, formerly; prof art, Univ artist, Univ Calif, Berkeley, 78-79; prof art, Univ Okla, 70- *Awards:* Prize, Washburn Univ, 71 & Amarillo Art Mus, 75; Visions '80-'81, Midwest Art Asn. *Media:* Oil. *Publ:* Contribr, Southwestern Art; illusr, George Bogart drawings and paintings, 67. *Mailing Add:* Dept Art Okla Univ Main Campus Norman OK 73019

BOGART, MICHELE HELENE
HISTORIAN, CURATOR
b New York, NY, Oct 5, 52. *Study:* Art Students League; Smith Col, BA, 79; Univ Chicago, MA, 75, PhD, 79. *Exhib:* The Seelye Years, Smith Col Mus Art, Northampton, Mass, 74; Am Art Quest for Unity, Detroit Inst Art, Mich, 82-83; Fauns and Fountains, Parrish Art Mus, Southampton, NY, 85. *Pos:* Guest cur, Parrish Art Mus, 82-84; guest cur sculpture, Detroit Inst Art, Mich, 80-83. *Teaching:* Instr art, Am Sch, Chicago, Ill, 76-77; asst prof art hist, Univ Ga, Athens, 79-82; assoc prof, State Univ NY, Stony Brook, currently. *Awards:* Fel, Smithsonian Inst, 77-78; Joint Award, Res Found State Univ NY, 83; Nat Endowment Humanities-Winterthur Res Fel; Provost Fac Travel Grant, 85 & 87; Am Coun Learned Socs Grant-in-Aid, 87; Benno M Forman Fel, Winterthur Mus, 88; Nuala McGann Drescher Leave Fund Award, 88; Smithsonian Sr Postdoctoral Fel, 90. *Mem:* Col Art Asn; Am Studies Asn; Asn Am Art Historians. *Res:* Nineteenth and twentieth century sculpture; architectural sculpture; reproductions and copies; illustration, photography, posters and commercial art. *Publ:* Auth, In art the ends don't always justify the means, Smithsonian, 6/79; auth, Photosculpture, Art Hist, winter 80; auth, On women and art, Ga Review, winter 80; auth, Development of a popular market for sculputre, J Am Culture, spring 81; auth, Four sculpture sketches for the New York Public Library, Bulletin Ga Mus, winter, 82; The Importance of Believing in Purity, Archives Am Art J, 84; Barking Architecture: the Sculpture of Coney Island, Smithsonian Studies Am Art, winter 88; Public Sculpture and the Civic Ideal in New York City 1890- 1930, Univ Chicago Press, 89; Artistic Ideals and Commercial Practices: The Problem of Status for the American Illustrator, Prospects 15, 90. *Mailing Add:* Dept Art State Univ NY Stony Brook NY 11794

BOGART, RICHARD JEROME
PAINTER
b Highland Park, Mich, Oct 30, 29. *Study:* Art Inst Chicago, dipl, 52; Univ Ill, 54; Black Mountain Col, NC, 56. *Work:* Brooklyn Mus; Yellowstone Art Ctr, Billings, Mont. *Exhib:* The American Landscape, A Living Tradition, circulated by Am Fedn Arts, Peridot Gallery, New York, 68; Conn Painting, Drawing & Sculpture Exhib, 78; Artist Showcase, Conn Comn on the Arts, 84; State of the Artists, Aldrich Mus, Ridgefield, Conn, 87; one-man shows, Poindexter Gallery, New York, 68-83, Meredith Long & Co, Houston, Tex, 77 & JPNatkin Gallery, 85,86,87 & 88. *Bibliog:* Alan Gussow (auth), A sense of place--the artist & the American land, Sat Rev Press; Les Krant (auth), American Artist: An Illustrated Survey & NY Art Review; other reviews in Art News, Arts, Art in Am & Time Mag. *Media:* Oil, Pastel. *Publ:* Auth, Richard Bogart: The Reflected Landscape (exhib catalog), 87. *Dealer:* J P Natkin 395 Broadway Suite 9E New York NY 10013. *Mailing Add:* 378 Judd Rd Easton CT 06612

BOGDANOVIC, BOGOMIR
PAINTER
b Senje, Yugoslavia, Aug 20, 23. *Study:* Belgrade Univ, with Prof S Strala, Prof A Samojlov. *Work:* Over 3,000 in private collections; Mus Anchorage, Alaska; Presidential Palace, Indonesia; New York Times. *Exhib:* One-man shows, Scarborough Gallery, New York & Quadrangle Gallery, Dallas, 67-80; Pa Acad Fine Arts, Philadelphia; Nat Acad Fine Art, New York; Am Watercolor Soc, New York; Kennedy Galleries, New York. *Pos:* Guest artist & demonstr for various art asns. *Awards:* Charles Dana Medal, Pa Acad Fine Arts, 63; Silver Medal, Am Watercolor Soc, 71; Gold Medal, Franklin Mint, 73. *Bibliog:* Article, Am Artist Mag, 12/71. *Mem:* The Dolphin Fel-Am Watercolor Soc; Audubon Artists; Allied Artists Am; Knickerbocker Artist; hon mem Southwestern Watercolor Soc. *Media:* Oil, Pastel Watercolor. *Mailing Add:* c/o Southwest Gallery 737 Preston Forest Center Dallas TX 75230

BOGGS, FRANKLIN
MURALIST, SCULPTOR
b Warsaw, Ind, July 25, 14. *Study:* Ft Wayne Art Sch, Ind; Pa Acad Fine Arts. *Work:* Univ Wis, Madison; Tulane Univ, New Orleans, La; US War Dept, Washington, DC; Univ Wis, Milwaukee; Am Telephone and Telegraph, NJ; and others. *Comn:* Post office mural, Federal Works Agency, Washington, DC, 46; mural, New Mayo Clinic, Rochester, Minn, 53; mural, Crippled Children's Sch, Helsinki, Finland, 59; sculpture relief mem wall, Cumberland Gap, Tenn, US Dept Interior, 73; bronze relief wall, Beloit Corp, Wis, 81; and many others. *Exhib:* Pa Acad Fine Arts. *Pos:* Illusr, Tenn Valley Auth, 40-44. *Teaching:* Prof & artist in residence, Beloit Col, 45-82, chmn art dept, 55-78; lectr Am Indian Exhib, Finland & Sweden, 58-59. *Awards:* Gimbels Wis Exhib Prize, 52; Fulbright Res Grant to Finland, 58; Award of Merit for Precast Concrete Sculpture, 63. *Publ:* Army med paintings reproduced in art mags. *Mailing Add:* 2542 Hawthorne Dr Beloit WI 53511

BOGGS, JEAN SUTHERLAND
MUSEUM DIRECTOR, ART HISTORIAN
b Negritos, Peru, June 11, 22; Can citizen. *Pos:* Dir, Nat Gallery Can, 66-76; dir, Philadelphia Mus Art, 79-82; chmn Sci Comt Degas Exhib, Nat Gallery Can, 84-88; sr adv, Andrew W Mellon Found, New York, 91- *Teaching:* Asst prof art, Skidmore Col, 48-49; asst prof art, Mt Holyoke Col, 49-52; assoc prof art, Univ Calif, 54-62; Steinberg prof hist art, Washington Univ, 64-66; prof fine arts, Harvard Univ, 76-79. *Awards:* Officer of the Order of Can. *Mem:* Am Asn Mus; Asn Art Mus Dirs; fel Royal Soc Can; Col Art Asn (bd mem, 78-); and others. *Publ:* Auth, Portraits by Degas, 62, Drawings by Degas, 66, The National Gallery of Canada, 71 & The Last Thirty Years, Picasso 1881-1973, 73. *Mailing Add:* 71 Somerset W Apt 202 Ottawa ON K2P 2G2 Canada

BOGGS, MAYO MAC
SCULPTOR, EDUCATOR
b Ashland, Ky, Mar 22, 42. *Study:* Univ Ky, with Mike Hall, BA(art); Univ NC, Chapel Hill, with Robert Howard, MFA(sculpture). *Work:* Gerald R Ford Libr; NC Govs Mansion; SC Govs Mansion; Huntington Galleries, WVa; NC Nat Bank, Charlotte; Jimmy Carter Libr. *Comn:* 12' welded brass & copper wall sculpture, comn by Dolmite Estate, Gaffney, SC, 86; painting & sculpture, comn by Dr & Mrs P A Higginbotham, 87; sculpture, comn by Ms Barbara Plott, Tryon, NC, 89; sculpture, comn by Mr & Mrs Marshall Chapman, Spartanburg, SC, 90; large scale computer graphics (3' x 6'), offices of Rudisill & Harris Law Firm, Spartanburg, SC, 92. *Exhib:* Spartanburg Co travelling exhib of twelve paintings, 91; Invitational Sculpture Exhib, Stone Hedge, Tryon, NC, 91; Invitational Group Exhib, Carolina Editions Gallery, Artista Vista, Columbia, SC, 91; Invitational exhib Art of the Upstate Gallery, Spartanburg/Greenville Airport, 91; Fourth Ann NCNB Art Exhib, Spartanburg, SC, 92; and others. *Teaching:* Assoc prof sculpture, Converse Col, Spartanburg, SC, 70-; guest artist, Penland Sch Crafts, NC. *Awards:* John W Oswald Res & Creativity Award, Univ Ky, 69; Kathryne Amelia Brown Fac Award, Converse Col, 72; Named Hon Artist of Spartanburg by proclamation of the Mayor of Spartanbug, 91; Best in Show Award, Fourth Ann NCNB Art Exhib, Spartanburg, SC, 92. *Mem:* Spartanburg Artists Guild; Am Asn Univ Profs. *Media:* Steel Construction, Bronze and Aluminum Casts. *Mailing Add:* Dept Art Converse Col Spartanburg SC 29301

BOGHOSIAN, VARUJAN
SCULPTOR, EDUCATOR
b New Britain, Conn, June 26, 26. *Study:* Vesper George Sch Art, Boston; Yale Univ Sch Art & Archit, BFA & MFA; Brown Univ, MA(hon), 59. *Work:* Mus Mod Art & Whitney Mus Am Art, New York; Addison Gallery Am Art, Andover, Mass; Worcester Mus, Mass; Currier Gallery Art, Manchester, NH. *Exhib:* One-man shows, Stable Gallery, 63-66 & Cordier & Ekstrom, 69, 71, 73, 75 & 77-80, New York. *Teaching:* Assoc prof art, Yale Univ, 62-64; assoc prof art, Brown Univ, 64-68; prof sculpture, Dartmouth Col, 68-, George Frederick Jewett art prof, 83- *Awards:* Fulbright Grant, 53; sculptor-in-residence, Am Acad Rome, 67; Nat Inst Arts & Lett Award, 72; Guggenheim Fel, 85. *Bibliog:* Dore Ashton (auth), article, Studio Int, 4/65; article, Time Mag, 2/9/70; article, Art Int, 3/81. *Mem:* Am Acad & Inst Arts & Letters, 85. *Media:* Constructions, Collage. *Dealer:* Cordier & Ekstrom Inc 417 E 75th St New York NY 10021. *Mailing Add:* One Read Rd Hanover NH 03755

BOGLE, JON
SCULPTOR
b Philadelphia, Pa, Jan 18, 40. *Study:* Tyler Sch Art, Temple Univ, BFA, 62, BS, 63, MFA, 68. *Work:* Philadelphia Mus Art. *Comn:* Modular steel, Temple Univ, Philadelphia, 63; fountain sculpture, 72 & weather vane sculpture, 85, Redevelopment Authority, Philadelphia, Pa; Reliance Insurance. *Exhib:* Solo show, Sculpture, Doshi Ctr Contemp Art, Harrisburg, Pa, 80, Lycoming Col, Williamsport, Pa, 86 & Lock Haven Univ, Lock Haven, Pa, 88; Juried Regional Awards, Civic Ctr Mus, Philadelphia, 80; New York Sculptor's Guild, Sculptor's Ctr, 80; NY Botanical Gardens, New York, 81, Univ Mall, Philadelpia, 82; Sculpture Juried Regional, Penn's Landing Mus, Philadelphia, 83; Union St, Minneapolis, Minn, 85; Invited-Regional, Cheltenham Art Ctr, Philadelphia, Pa, 87; Bi-Coastal exhib, San Francisco & Santa Fe, 89; Nat Invitational Sculpture Exhib, West Hartford, Conn, 89. *Teaching:* Instr sculpture, Tyler Sch Art, 68-70; prof art (sculpture), Lycoming Col, 76-, coordr BFA, 81- *Mem:* New York Sculptor's Guild; Col Art Asn. *Media:* Terra CottA. *Publ:* Auth, article on press formed sculpture, Sculptor's Int, 85. *Mailing Add:* Box 244 RD 1 Hughesville PA 17737

BOHAN, RUTH L
EDUCATOR, HISTORIAN
b Galesburg, Ill, Dec 27, 46. *Study:* Univ Ill, BA, 69; Univ Md, MA, 72, PhD, 80. *Pos:* Res assoc, Yale Univ Art Gallery, 79-80. *Teaching:* Assoc prof art hist, Univ Mo, St Louis, 81- *Awards:* Smithsonian Fel-Nat Collection Fine Arts, 75-76; Mellon Fel, Washington Univ, 80-81; J Paul Getty Fel, 85-86. *Mem:* Am Studies Asn; Col Art Asn; Mid-America Am Studies Asn; Midwest Art Hist Soc; Modern Language Asn. *Res:* Early twentieth-century American modernism; rural cemeteries; Walt Whitman and the visual arts. *Publ:* Auth, The Sociéte Anonyme's Brooklyn Exhibition: Katherine Dreier and Modernism in America, UMI Res Press, 82; contrib ed, The Societé Anonyme Collection and the Dreier Bequest at Yale University: A Catalogue Raisonne, Yale Univ Press, 84; American drawings and watercolors, 1900-1945, The St Louis Art Mus Bull, summer 89. *Mailing Add:* Dept Art Univ Missouri 8001 Natural Bridge St Louis MO 63121

BOHEN, BARBARA E
HISTORIAN, MUSEUM DIRECTOR
b Bradford, Wiltshire, Eng, Apr 24, 41; US citizen. *Study:* Queens Col, City Univ NY, BA, 69; NY Univ Inst Fine Arts, MA (fine arts), 73, PhD(classical art), 79. *Work:* Kerameikos Mus, Athens, Greece; World Heritage Mus, Urbana, Ill. *Collections Arranged:* In Search of the Ancient Egyptians, 88, Kings Crusaders & Craftsmen, 89, Beyond the Himalayas, 90; and others. *Pos:*

Dir, World Heritage Mus, Urbana, Ill, 81-; coauth & ed, Heritage (biannual), Newsletter of the World, Heritage Mus, 81- *Teaching:* Lectr art hist, Queens Col, City Univ NY, spring & summer, 73, Univ Ill, Urbana, fall 82. *Awards:* Fulbright Fel, Greek Archaeology (vases), 73; Danforth Fel, Greek vase painting studies, 74-76; Deutscheforschunggemeinschaft Fel, 79-81. *Mem:* Am Asn Mus; Archeological Inst Am. *Res:* Greek vase classification, Apulian vase studies, Egyptian mummies. *Publ:* Auth, Origins of Greek Civilization, 75 & Greece, the Foundations of Greatness, 87, (audio visual progs), Reading Lab Inc; Geometrischen Pyxiden, Walter de Gruyter, Berlin, 88; The role of the Dipylon Master in the Development of Greek art, J Aesthetic Educ, fall 90; The Boeotian Origin of an Unusual Geometric Vase, J Paul Getty J, Vol 20, 92; Collaborative Investigation of the UI Egyptian Mummy, ACTA Cong Int Mummy Studies, 93. *Mailing Add:* 2108 Georgetown Circle Champaign IL 68121

BOHLEN, NINA (CELESTINE EUSTIS BOHLEN)
PAINTER, DRAFTSMAN
b Boston, Mass, Mar 5, 31. *Study:* Radcliffe Col, drawing & painting with Hyman Bloom, BA, 53. *Work:* Fogg Mus Art; Boston Pub Libr; Brockton Mus. *Exhib:* Harvard Mus Comparative Zoology, 82; Van Buren Brazelton Cutling Gallery, 84; solo exhibs, Works on Paper, retrospective, Boston Pub Libr, 87 & Monotypes, retrospective, Pine Manor Col, 88 & 91; Drawings from Boston (with catalog), De Cordova Mus, Lincoln, Mass; Martin Sumers Gallery, New York, 91; and others. *Teaching:* Pvt instr drawing & painting, 73-77, Newton Arts Ctr, 84-89, Pine Manor Col, 85-92. *Awards:* Am Acad Arts & Lett Award in Art, 77; Camargo Found, Cassis, France. *Media:* All. *Publ:* Illusr, Baboon Orphan, E P Dutton, 81. *Mailing Add:* 56 Fuller St Waltham MA 02154-5053

BOHLER, JOSEPH STEPHEN
PAINTER
b Great Falls, Mont, June 12, 38. *Study:* With Robert Lougheed, Wilson Hurley, John Pike, Robert Wood, Bill Reese & others; Art Instruction Sch, Minneapolis, Minn, 60. *Work:* Coca Cola Bottling Co, Kansas City, Mo; Johnson Co Bank, Kansas City, Kans; Phoenix Bank & Trust, Ariz; Smithsonian Inst, Washington, DC. *Exhib:* Watercolor USA, Springfield Art Mus, Mo, 71; one-man show, C M Russell Mus, Great Falls, Mont, 72; Pastel Soc Am, New York, 80; Am Watercolor Soc, New York, 81; Allied Artists Am, Nat Arts Club, New York, 81-82. *Pos:* Bd dirs, Stuart Anderson Black Angus Enterprises, 80-81. *Teaching:* Jade Fon Watercolor Workshops, Pacific Grove, Calif, 84-86. *Awards:* Arjomari/Arches/Rives Award, Am Watercolor Soc, 90. *Mem:* Rocky Mountain Nat Watermedia Soc; Allied Artists Am; Am Soc; Nat Acad Western Art. *Media:* Watercolor, Pastel. *Publ:* Peggy & Harold Samuels, Contemp Western Artists, 82. *Dealer:* Grapevine Gallery Box 132 Oklahoma City OK 73101. *Mailing Add:* Box 387 Monument CO 80132

BOHNEN, BLYTHE
CONCEPTUAL ARTIST, PAINTER
b Evanston, Ill, July 26, 40. *Study:* Smith Col, BA(art), 62; Boston Univ, BFA, 67; Hunter Col, MA(painting), 72. *Work:* Dallas, Mus Fine Arts, Tex; McCrory Corp, New York; Whitney Mus Am Art, Mus Mod Art & Metrop Mus Art, New York; Fogg Art Mus, Harvard Univ, Cambridge, Mass; Brooklyn Mus Art, NY; Art Inst Chicago; Albright-Knox Art Gallery, Buffalo, NY; Philadelphia Mus Fine Art, Pa; Wadworth Atheneum, Hartford, Conn; Minneapolis Art Inst; Aldrich Mus Contemp Art, Ridgefield, Conn; Allen Art Mus, Oberlin Col, Ohio; Art Mus, Univ Calif, Berkeley; Heubelin Inc, West Hartford, Conn; and others. *Comn:* Ceramic tile relief, wall mural (15' x 30'), Libr Blind, Record Storage Ctr, Trenton, NJ, 80-82. *Exhib:* Annual Survey of American Painting (with catalog), Whitney Mus, 71-72; Penthouse, Mus Mod Art, New York, 72; Reflections 1971-72, Aldrich Mus Contemp Art, Conn, 71-72; Wadsworth Atheneum, Hartford, Conn, 75; Extraordinary Women, Mus Mod Art, New York, 77; Drawings of the 70's, Chicago Art Inst, 77; Permanent Collection of 20th Century Drawings, Metrop Mus Art; one-man exhibs, Int Cult Ctr (with catalog), Antwerp, Belg, 78, Galerie Camomille, Brussels, Belg, 78, Artline Gallery (with catalog), Hague, Holland, 79, Contemp Art Ctr (with catalog), New Orleans, La, 80, PSl, New York, 81, Light Gallery, New York, 84 & Galerie Mukai, Tokyo, Japan, 84; Self Portraits (with catalog), Gallery Plaza, Security Pac Nat Bank, Los Angeles, 85; Artists' Self-Portraits, Acad Arts, Honolulu, Hawaii, 85; New Portraiture, Light Gallery, New York, 86; First Person Singular, Self-Portrait Photography, 1840-1987 (with catalog), High Mus, Atlanta, Ga, 88; and others. *Teaching:* Lectr, Metrop Mus Art, 67-72; guest lectr mod mathematics & mod art, Metrop Mus Art, 78; FID; instr, Parsons Sch Design, 79-88. *Awards:* Artist-in-Residence Grant, 76 & Fel, 78, Nat Endowment Arts. *Bibliog:* Who's Who in American Art, 76-91; Victoria Thorson & Wendy Shore (auths), Great Drawings of all Time: The Twentieth Century, Vol 2, Shorewood/Talisman Press, 81; and others. *Media:* Acrylic, Graphite. *Publ:* Contribr, Old masters-new apprentices, Metrop Mus Art Bull. *Mailing Add:* 205 Mulberry St New York NY 10012

BOHNENKAMP, LESLIE GEORGE
SCULPTOR, INSTRUCTOR
b West Point, Iowa, Mar 28, 43. *Study:* St Ambrose Col, Davenport, Iowa, 64-66; Univ Iowa, Iowa City, BA, 66, MA, 71. *Work:* Portland Mus Art, Maine; Columbus Mus Fine Arts, Ohio; Univ Iowa, Iowa City. *Exhib:* New York: A Selection from the Last Ten Years, The Otis Inst Parsons Sch Design, Los Angeles, Calif, 79; Betty Parsons Gallery, New York, 79; Columbus Invitational, Columbus Mus Fine Arts, Ohio, 81; PS1, Richmond, Va, 82. *Pos:* Gallery asst, Betty Parsons Gallery, 78-80. *Teaching:* Vis artist sculpture, Worcester Art Mus Sch, 80- *Awards:* Individual Grant Sculpture, Nat Endowment Arts, 73; Fel, Fine Arts Work Ctr, Provincetown, Mass, 73-75; Individual Sculpture Grant, Nat Endowment Arts, 80. *Bibliog:* Michael Florescu (auth), Les Bohnenkamp, Arts Mag, 2/79; Lila Zeiger (auth), Les Bohnenkamp: Constructing Horizons, Arts Mag, 6/80. *Dealer:* Gimpel & Weitzenhoffer Gallery 724 Fifth Ave New York NY. *Mailing Add:* 184 Second Ave New York NY 10003

BOHNERT, THOM (THOMAS ROBERT)
CERAMIST, EDUCATOR
b St Louis, Mo, Jan 3, 48. *Study:* Southern Ill Univ, Edwardsville, BA, 69; Cranbrook Acad Art, Bloomfield Hills, Mich, MFA, 71. *Work:* Flint Inst Art, Mich; Minneapolis Art Inst, Minn; Univ Iowa Mus, Iowa City; Cranbrook Acad Art, Bloomfield Hills, Mich; Boyman Mus, Rotterdam, Holland. *Exhib:* Young Americans/Clay Glass, Tucson Mus Art, Ariz, 78; Century Ceramics in the US 1878-1978, Everson Mus, Syracuse, NY, Renwick Gallery, Smithsonian Inst, Washington, DC & Cooper-Hewitt, New York, 79; one-person show, Exhibit A Gallery, Chicago, Ill, 79 & 81; A Response to Wedgewood, 2 Yr Traveling Exhib, Mus Philadelphia Civic Ctr, Pa, 80; Basket-Works, John M Kohler Arts Ctr, Sheboygan, Wis, 81; Painting and Sculpture Today: 1982, Indianapolis Mus Art, 82; American Clay Artists: Philadelphia 83, Marian Locks Gallery East, 83; plus many others. *Teaching:* Instr ceramic & drawing, Southern Ill Univ, 71; instr ceramics & drawing, C S Mott Community Col, 71-; vis artist ceramics, Univ Mich, 77-78. *Awards:* Award, Detroit Inst Art, 76; Nat Endowment Arts Craftsmen Fel, 78-79; Creative Artists Grant, Mich Coun Arts, 83-84; John Simon Guggenheim Fel, 86-87. *Bibliog:* Helen Williams Drutt (auth), Contemporary Ceramics: A Response to Wedgewood, 81; Christopher Young (auth), Six Experiments in Sculpture: Thom Bohnert, Flint Inst Arts, 86; Gottfried Borrmann (auth), Ceramics of the world, Kunst & Handwerk, Dusseldorf, WGer, 84; Alice Westphal (auth), Putting Pottery in Perspective, Rockford Col, 90. *Media:* Ceramic, Metal. *Mailing Add:* 6337 Flushing Rd Flushing MI 48433-2548

BOIGON, BRIAN JOSEPH
CONCEPTUAL ARTIST, WRITER
Toronto, Ont, Aug 14, 55; Can citizen. *Study:* Ont Col Art, 73-76; Univ Toronto Sch Archit, BA, 76-80. *Work:* Art Gallery Ont, Toronto; Can Coun Art Bank, Ottawa, Ont. *Exhib:* Rauman und Installation, Wurttembergischer Kunstverein, Stuggart, WGer, 84; Mapping the Surface, Mendell Art Gallery, Saskatoon, Sask, 86; Logic Display, PS1, New York, 88; Speed Neutralization and the Spectacle of Sleep, 49th Parallel (with catalog), New York, 88. *Pos:* Ed, Impulse Mag, Toronto, 84-90. *Teaching:* Asst prof, Univ Toronto, Dept Fine Art & Archit, 86-90. *Bibliog:* Gordon Lebredt (auth), Staging Mondrian, C Mag, 84; Rick Rhodes (auth), Review, Art Forum, 88. *Media:* Mixed Media, Photography. *Publ:* Auth, Downtown, Impulse, 87; Kiss sugar good bye, Impulse Mag, 88; Victorian Spacing and the internationl style, New Observations, 88; Inboard/Outboard, Fifth Collumn, 89; auth, Speed Reading Tokyo, P3 Mus, Tokyo, 90. *Dealer:* S L Simpson Gallery 515 Queen St W Toronto ON Canada M5V 2B4. *Mailing Add:* 119 Cowan Ave Toronto ON M6K 2N1 Canada

BOLAS, GERALD DOUGLAS
MUSEUM DIRECTOR, EDUCATOR
b Los Angeles, Calif, Nov 1, 49. *Study:* Univ Calif, Santa Barbara, BA, 72, MA(art hist), 75; City Univ NY 84- *Collections Arranged:* Gyorgy Kepes, 78, Richard Hunt: Three Places, 79, Old and Modern Master Drawings, 80, Greek Vases and Roman Glass, 80 & Arthur Osver: The University Years, 81, Washington Univ Gallery Art; Paris in Japan: The Japanese Encounter with European Painting, 87 and many other exhib. *Pos:* Asst to dir, Yale Univ Art Gallery, 75-77; dir, Washington Univ Gallery Art, 77-88, Portland Art Mus, Ore, 88-92. *Teaching:* Asst, Univ Calif, Santa Barbara, 73-74; adj asst prof, Washington Univ, 77-88. *Awards:* NEH Mus Training Internship, Yale Univ Art Gallery, 75. *Mem:* Col Art Asn; Am Asn Mus. *Res:* Nineteenth century American art; history of taste, patronage and connoisseurship; medieval manuscript illumination. *Publ:* Auth, Illustrated Checklist of the Washington University Collection, 81; American Responses to Western-Style Japanese Painting, In Paris in Japan: The Japanese Encounter with European Painting, Tokyo & St Louis, 87; numerous other articles and catalog forewords. *Mailing Add:* 1219 SW Park Ave Portland OR 97205

BOLEN, JOHN E
ART DEALER, COLLECTOR
b Ft Gordon, Ga, Aug 27, 53. *Study:* Univ Calif, Los Angeles, AB, 75. *Collections Arranged:* Painting into Bronze: The Polychromed Bronze of Harry Jackson, Southwest Mus, Highland Park, Calif, 79; The Cowboy, San Diego Mus Art, 81. *Pos:* Co-dir, Bolen Gallery, Inc, Santa Monica & Los Angeles, Calif, 78-84, Bolen Publ, Playa del Rey, Calif, 79-84; co-owner, John & Lynne Bolen Fine Arts, Huntington Beach, Calif, 84- *Teaching:* Lectr art collecting, privately, 76-78; pvt art marketing consult, 76-78. *Mem:* Art Dealers Asn Calif (bd dirs, 80-83, vpres, 82-83). *Specialty:* Nineteenth and twentieth century American paintings, sculptures and original prints. *Publ:* Ed, Arthur Secunda, Monograph, 80, co-ed, Six Decades of American Prints, 1900-1960, 82, Grant Wood: Paintings, Drawings & Lithographs, 83 & The American Landscape: Current Visions, 83, Bolen Gallery, Inc. *Mailing Add:* PO Box 5654 Huntington Beach CA 92615-5654

BOLEN, LYNNE N
ART DEALER, COLLECTOR
b San Diego, Calif, Feb 19, 54. *Study:* Univ Calif, Los Angeles, BS, 76, post grad, 76-78. *Pos:* Co-dir, Bolen Gallery, Inc, Santa Monica & Los Angeles, Calif, 78-84, Bolen Publ, Playa del Rey, Calif, 79-84; co-owner, John & Lynne Bolen Fine Arts, Huntington Beach, Calif, 84- *Bibliog:* Critical reviews in

Santa Monica Evening Outlook, 78-; var issues, Art Voices, 80- *Mem:* Art Dealers Asn Calif (secy & mem bd dirs, 82-83). *Specialty:* Nineteenth and twentieth century American paintings, sculptures and original prints. *Publ:* Co-ed, Six Decades of American Prints 1900-1960, 82, Grant Wood: Paintings, Drawings & Lithographs, 83, The American Landscape: Current Visions, 83, Bolen Gallery, Inc. *Mailing Add:* PO Box 5654 Huntington Beach CA 92615-5654

BOLER, JOHN ALFRED
ART DEALER, COLLECTOR
b Minneapolis, Minn, Aug 26, 42. *Study:* Univ Minn, BA, 65; Univ Iowa, MA, 70. *Pos:* Dir & owner, Avanyu Gallery, Minneapolis, Minn, 82-87; pres & founder, Art Dealers Asn Twin Cities (Minneapolis & St Paul), 83-86; Private Dealer, John A Boler Indian and Western Art, Minneapolis, Minn, 87- *Teaching:* Arts Law Conf, Walker Art Ctr, 85; Panelist, Dakota Arts Congress, 92. *Mem:* Adv bd, Indian Arts Am; Partnership Comt, Minneapolis Mus Art; Minneapolis Inst Arts; Walker Art Ctr, Minneapolis, Minn; Judge, Twin Cities Indian Market, 5/91. *Specialty:* Classic and contemporary American Indian and southwestern art. *Publ:* Understanding American Indian Art, Parts I & II, Art Business News, 7 & 8/87; Anatomy of an Art Dealers' Association, Art Business News, 9/87; Indian Artists Are on Warpath, Art Business News, 9/88. *Mailing Add:* Indian And Western Art 4317 Third Ave S Minneapolis MN 55409

BOLGE, GEORGE S
MUSEUM DIRECTOR
Study: State Univ NJ, Rutgers, BA & BS; Inst Fine Arts, New York Univ, MA; Nova Univ, Ft Lauderdale, Fla, PhD, 87. *Pos:* Grad res asst & asst cur, Ancient Art dept, Brooklyn Mus Art, NY; exec dir, Mus Art, Ft Lauderdale, Fla, 70-; regional rep, div cultural affairs, Fla Dept State; dir, Meredith Ft Lauderdale Art Mus, 88-89; exec dir, NJ Ctr Vis Arts, Summit, NJ, 91- *Mem:* Am Asn Mus; Col Art Mus; Fla League Arts (bd trustees); Fine Art Mus Dir Asn, Fla (exec comt, pres, 86-). *Mailing Add:* c/o New Jersey Ctr for Visual Arts 68 Elm St Summit NJ 07901

BOLINSKY, JOSEPH ABRAHAM
SCULPTOR, EDUCATOR
b New York, NY, Jan 17, 17. *Study:* Columbia Univ, MA; Stourbridge Col Art, Eng; Skowhegan Sch Painting & Sculpture, with Jose de Creeft; Iowa Univ, MFA. *Work:* Newark Mus Art, NJ; Tel Aviv Mus Art, Israel; State Univ NY Col Buffalo; Waterloo Recreation Ctr, Iowa; Ashford Hollow Sculpture Park, NY, 90. *Comn:* Carved ark doors & welded menorah, Sons Jacob Synagogue, Waterloo, Iowa, 52; cast bronze group of six figures, Jewish Community Fedn Bldg, Cleveland, Ohio, 66; carved ark doors, Temple Shaarey Zedek, Amhurst, NY, 71; two wood carvings, Holocaust, Temple Sinai, Amherst, NY, 76; Carved cherry bas-relief, Kenmore Presbyterian Church, NY, 85. *Exhib:* Western NY Regional, Albright-Knox Gallery, Buffalo, NY, 59; Art on Paper, Skowhegan Sch Painting & Sculpture, 69; Our Legacy of Art in Western New York, Charles Birchfield Ctr, 72; retrospective 1948-78, Brock Univ, Can, 78; Sensation Art through Feeling, Senses, and Perception Traveling Exhib, Burchfield Ctr, Buffalo, NY, 82; Bridgestone Gallery, Toronto, Canada, 84. *Teaching:* Instr sculpture, Univ Northern Iowa, 49-53; prof sculpture, State Univ, NY Col Buffalo, 54-84; vis sculptor, Stanislaus State Univ, summer 71. *Awards:* First Prize for Stone Carving, Des Moines Art Ctr, 52; First Prize for Stone Carving, Albright-Knox Gallery, 59; Award for Bronze Casting, Rochester Festival of Religious Art, 70; State Univ NY Sculpture Scholarship, 66, 74 & 75. *Mem:* Patteran Art Asn, Buffalo. *Media:* Wood, Stone. *Publ:* Contribr, Jewish form symbolism, Ethos Mag, 58; demonstr, Carved Sculpture (film), US Info Serv, 68. *Mailing Add:* 10 Ames Ave Tonawanda NY 14150

BOLOMEY, ROGER HENRY
SCULPTOR
b Torrington, Conn, Oct 19, 18; US & Swiss citizen. *Study:* Acad Bella Arte, Florence, Italy, 47; Univ Lausanne, 47-48; Calif Col Arts & Crafts, Oakland, 48-50. *Work:* Mus Mod Art, Whitney Mus Am Art, New York; Univ Calif Mus Art, Berkeley; San Francisco Mus Mod Art, Calif; Stadtische Kunst, Mannheim, Ger. *Comn:* Aluminum sculpture, Southridge Mall, Milwaukee, Wis, 70; two reliefs, Mutual of NY, Syracuse, 71; two bronze sculptures, S Mall Proj, Albany, 71; cor-ten steel sculpture, Lehman High Sch, Bronx, 71-72; stainless steel sculpture, NY State Off Bldg, Hauppauge, 73. *Exhib:* Carnegie Inst Int, Pittsburgh, 64; Whitney Mus Am Art Sculpture Ann, 64; Quatriene Exposition Suisse Sculpture, Bienne, Switz, 66; Contemporary American Paintings & Sculpture, Univ Ill, Urbana, 67; American Sculpture, Univ Nebr, Lincoln, 70. *Collections Arranged:* Forgotten Dimension: A Survey of Small Sculpture in California Now Traveling Exhib, 82-84. *Teaching:* Assoc prof art, Herbert H Lehman Col, 68-75; prof & chmn dept art, Calif State Univ, Fresno, 75-83. *Awards:* First Prize & Purchase Award, Bundy Art Mus Sculpture Int, Waitsfield, Vt, 63; Sculpture Prize, San Francisco Art Inst 84th Ann, 65; Res Found Award, City Univ NY, 70. *Mem:* San Francisco Art Inst; Am Fedn Arts; hon fel Acad Fine Arts, The Hague, Netherlands. *Media:* Steel, Aluminum. *Mailing Add:* Route 113 North Fryeburg ME 04058

BOLT, RON
ENVIRONMENTAL ARTIST, PAINTER
b Toronto, Ont, Oct 13, 38. *Study:* Ont Art Col; Ryerson Polytechnic Sch. *Work:* Sir George Williams Univ, Montreal; Univ Guelph; Univ Western Ont; Xerox Corp; Shell Can Ltd. *Comn:* Stamp design, Can Post, 79; Newmarket Courthouse (mural), Govt Ont, 80; tapestry designs, Indo-Asian Tapestries Ltd, Toronto, 82; waterworks, Sheraton Hotels Int, Halifax, NS, 85; waterworks, Adaron, Hq Park, Res Triangle, Raleigh, NC, 86; Manpower Temp Services, Toronto, Ont, 87. *Exhib:* solo exhibs, Art Gallery Alcoma, Ont, 84, Galerie Mihalis, Montreal, 85, Goethe Inst, Toronto, 85 & Art Gallery of Peterborough, 85; 3rd Biennial Exhib Prints, Wakayama, Japan, 89; Gallery Moos, Toronto, 83, 84, 87, 88 & 90; Robertson Gallery, Ottawa, 84-87, 89 & 90; Solo exhibs, Art Gallery Algoma, 84, Galerie Michalis, Montreal, 85, Goethe Inst, Toronto, 85, Art Gallery of Peterborough, 88. *Pos:* Assoc, Royal Conservatory Music, Toronto. *Teaching:* Instr art, Northern Tech Sch, 71-74, Learning Resources Ctr, Toronto, 72-73 & Hibbs Cove Art & Music Ctr, Nfld, 72-73. *Awards:* Award Distinctive Merit, Graphica, Montreal, 70 & Hadassah, Montreal, 75; Purchase Award, Univ Guelph, Ont, 79. *Bibliog:* Barbara Young (dir, The Inner Ocean, CBC Nat News, 81. *Mem:* Visual Arts Ont (dir, 75-81); Can Artists Rep; Royal Can Acad Art (mem exec coun, 86-87). *Publ:* Contribr, Art Mag, 68-70; auth, High north, Beaver Mag, 81; coauth with Norman Levine, The Beat and the Still, 90. *Mailing Add:* RR 1 Baltimore ON K0K 1C0 Canada

BOLTON, RICHARD
PHOTOGRAPHER
b Omaha, Nebr, Mar 7, 56. *Study:* Art Acad Cincinnati, cert, 79; Cranbrook Acad Art, MFA (photog), 81; St John's Col, Annapolis, Md, MA, 85. *Exhib:* One-man shows, Wayne State Univ, Gallery 680, Detroit, Mich, 82, Photogallery, Detroit Pub Libr, 83, Sch Art Inst Chicago, Photog Gallery, 84, Fullerton Mus Ctr, Calif, 90, Calif Mus Photog, Calif, 90, List Visual Arts Ctr, Cambridge, Mass, 91, Capp St Proj, San Francisco, Calif, 92, Cranbrook Acad Art Mus, Bloomfield Hills, Mich, 92, Bellevue Art Mus, Seattle, Wash, 92 & Cambridge Arts Coun, Mass, 92; Andrea Ruggieri Gallery, Washington, DC, 90; The Charade of Mastery, Whitney Mus Am Art, Downtown at Fed Reserve Plaza, New York, 90; The Emperor's New Clothes, Calif Mus Photog, Calif, 90; Green Acres: Neo-Colonialism in the United States, Wash Univ Gallery Art, St Louis, Mo, 92. *Pos:* Dir pubs, Educators for Social Responsibility, Cambridge, Mass, 87-89; gen ed, Media & Society Ser, Univ Minn Press, 87-92; bd dirs, Ctr Ecology & Soc Justice, Washington, DC, 92-; assoc ed, Visual Sociology, 92-; ser adv, Manchester Univ Press, 92-; contrib ed, New Art Examiner, 92- *Teaching:* Instr, Lawrence Inst Technol, Sch Archit, 80-83; instr, Wayne State Univ, Dept Art & Art Hist, 83; asst prof cinema & photog, Southern Ill Univ, 83-86; instr, Visible Lang Workshop, Mass Inst Technol, 86-88, Visual Arts Prog, 89-91; assoc prof & chairperson, dept art studio, Univ Calif, Santa Barbara, 91-; vis artist, photog dept, Sch Mus Fine Arts, Boston, Mass, 91-92. *Awards:* Cambridge Arts Coun, Mass, 90-92; Nat Endowment Arts, 91-92; Capp St Found, San Francisco, 92. *Bibliog:* Patricia Johnston (auth), An interview with Richard Bolton, Views, fall 90 & winter 91; New Art Examiner, summer 91; Diane Douglas (auth), Interview with Richard Bolton, NCECA J 12, 91-92. *Publ:* Ed, Studies in Photographic Criticism, Southern Ill Univ, 86; ed, The Contest of Meaning: Critical Histories of Photography, MIT Press, Cambridge, 89; ed, Culture Wars: Documents from the Recent Controversies in the Arts, New Press, New York, 92. *Mailing Add:* 585 Las Palmas Rd Santa Barbara CA 93110

BOLTON, ROBIN JEAN
PAINTER
b Americus, Ga, Sept 13, 43. *Study:* Univ Ga, BFA(graphic design), 65. *Work:* Liverpool NY Pub Libr; Cobb Co Bd Educ, Marietta, Ga; Liverpool United Methodist Church, NY; Bridgeport United Methodist Church, NY. *Comn:* 12 paintings, IBM Collection, Binghamton, NY, 81-85; 3' x 6' paintings, Cannon Corp, Rochester, NY, 84; two 4' x 5' paintings, CitiBank, Nat Landmark Bldg, Albany, NY, 84-85; 4' x 5' painting, comn by Lee Iacocca, New York, 87-88. *Exhib:* 100 Years-100 Works, Kirpatrick Art Ctr, Oklahoma City, Conguien Mus Art, Longview, Tex, Chatanooga Regional Hist Mus, Tenn, Fine Arts Mus South, Mobile, Ala, Islip Art Mus, NY, 89. *Awards:* First Prize, Cooperstown Nat Juried, Cooperstown NY Art Asn, 76; First Prize, Arena Nat, Binghamton, NY, 76; Henry Mallory Mem Award, Cooperstown Art Asn, 78. *Bibliog:* Robin Bolton (film), WCNY Pub Television, 84; Colors of her life, Preview Mag, 84. *Mem:* Nat Asn Women Artists, NY; Liverpool Arts & Crafts Guild, NY (lifetime hon mem). *Publ:* Ann Hartranft (auth), Syracuse Herald J, 76; Jennie Paris (auth), Long Island Newsday, 77; Gordon Muck (auth), Syracuse Post Standard, 79; Gail Mountain (auth), Gloucester Daily Times, 92; Sharon Carson (auth), Boston Sunday Globe, 92. *Dealer:* Nan Miller Gallery 3450 Winton Pl Rochester NY 14623. *Mailing Add:* Box 336 Bridgeport NY 13030

BOLTON-SMITH, ROBIN LEE
CURATOR, HISTORIAN
b Washington, DC, Oct 30, 41. *Study:* Smith Col, Northampton, Mass, BA, 63; Inst Fine Arts, NY Univ, MA, 75. *Collections Arranged:* Lilly Martin Spencer: The Joys of Sentiment (co-auth, catalog), Smithsonian Inst, 73; Portrait Miniatures in Private Collections, Smithsonian Inst, 76; Miniature Collection (auth, catalog), Cincinnati Mus, 85; Tokens of Affection: The Miniature in America, Met Mus, 90 & 91, Nat Mus Am Art, Smithsonian Inst, 91 & Art Inst Chicago, 91. *Pos:* Cur res asst, Nat Collection Fine Arts, Smithsonian Inst, 63-67, asst cur, 71-76, assoc cur, 76-; cur res asst, Metrop Mus Art, New York, 67-69. *Res:* History of the American portrait miniature. *Publ:* Auth, Portrait Miniatures in Private Collections, Smithsonian Inst, 76; Five miniature collections, Col Art J, summer 79; Fraser's place in the evolution of miniature portrait, In: Charles Fraser of Charleston (exhib catalog), Gibbes Art Gallery, Charleston, SC, 83; Intro to Anson Dickinson, The Celebrated Miniature Painter 1779-1852 (exhib catalog), Conn Hist Soc, 83; The Miniature in America, Vol CXXXVIII, No 5, Antiques Mag, 11/90. *Mailing Add:* c/o Nat Mus Am Art Eighth & G St NW Washington DC 20007

BONAR, ALBERT J See Jalapeeno, Jimmy (Albert J Bonar)

BOND, ORIEL EDMUND
ILLUSTRATOR, PAINTER
b Altus, Okla, July 18, 11. *Study:* Rockford Col, exten courses with Marquis E Reitzel, Einar Lundquist & Alice McCurry. *Work:* Works in private collections only. *Exhib:* Six shows, Rockford Art Asn, Ill, 56-63; Ill State Fair, Springfield, 59-61; Sovereign Exhibs Ltd, Winston-Salem, NC & Williamsburg, Va, 70; Am Artists Prof League, New York, 71 & 72. *Pos:* Chief artist, J L Clark Mfg Co, Rockford, 38-77. *Awards:* Popular Award, Ill State Fair, 59; First Place Display Award, Trading Post Days, Rockton, 72; First Place & Popular Award, Colonial Village Mall, 72. *Mem:* Fel Am Artists Prof League; Nat Soc Lit & Arts. *Media:* Oil and Polymer. *Publ:* Illusr, Artists of America Calendar, 76-93. *Mailing Add:* 7816 Bond Dr The Ledges Roscoe IL 61073

BONEVARDI, MARCELO
PAINTER, SCULPTOR
b Buenos Aires, Arg, May 13, 29. *Study:* Univ Cordoba, 48-51. *Work:* Mus Mod Art, United Nations, Guggenheim Mus, Brooklyn Mus, New York; Mus d'Art Contemporain de Montreal, Can. *Exhib:* One-man exhibs, Galeria Pecanins, Mexico City, 74, Galeria Ponce, Mex, 78, Galeria Sandiego, Bogota, Colombia, 79, Art Contact Gallery, 79 & Galeria del Retiro, Buenos Aires, 79. *Teaching:* Instr, Nat Univ Cordoba, 56. *Awards:* Int Award, 10th Bienal de Sao Paulo, Brazil, 69. *Media:* Mixed. *Mailing Add:* 799 Greenwich St New York NY 10014

BONINO, FERNANDA
ART DEALER
b Torino, Italy, Jan 5, 27. *Pos:* Pres & dir, Galeria Bonino, Ltd, New York, 63-86, Buenos Aires, 74-81. *Mem:* Art Dealer Asn Am. *Specialty:* Contemporary paintings and sculptures; American; European; South American. *Mailing Add:* 48 Great Jones St New York NY 10012

BONNER, JONATHAN G
CRAFTSMAN
Study: Philadelphia Col Art, BFA, 71; RI Sch Design, 73. *Work:* Am Craft Mus, New York; Ariz State Univ Art Mus, Tempe; Marshall Fields, Chicago; Rhode Island Sch Design Mus Art; Mus Fine Arts, Boston, Mass. *Exhib:* Lily Iselin Gallery, Providence, 84; Dawson Gallery, Rochester, NY, 85; Joanne Rapp Gallry, Scottsdale, Ariz, 84 & 86; B Z Wagman Gallery, St Louis; Helander Gallery, Palm Beach, 90; solo exhibs, Joanne Rapp Gallery, Scottsdale, Ariz, 84, 86, 90, Helander Gallery, Palm Beach, Fla, 90, Brendan Walter Gallery, Santa Monica, Calif, 90, Clark Gallery, Lincoln, Mass, 91, Virginia Lynch Gallery, Tiverton, RI, 91, Holkin Kaufman Gallery, Chicago, Ill, 91, Peter Joseph Gallery, New York, 92; Neilson Gallery, Boston, Mass, 90; The New Bronze Age, Soc Contemp Craft, Pittsburgh, Pa, 91; Chicago Int New Art Forms, Chicago, Ill, 91; Masterworks, Peter Joseph Gallery, New York, 91; American Works in Metal, Pritam & Eames, E Hampton, NY, 90-92. *Awards:* Nat Endowment Arts, 76 & 88; Rhode Island State Coun Arts Fel, 87 & 90. *Bibliog:* RI Artists Exhibiting Art Work in the Big Apple, Providence J Bull; RI State Coun Arts, 3/27/92; 3 Bottles, RISD Views, 4/92; NAGA and Clark Galleries Spotlighting Studio Furniture, Boston Globe, 5/20/92. *Mailing Add:* c/o Works Gallery 319 South St Philadelphia PA 19147

BONY, JEAN VICTOR
ART HISTORIAN, EDUCATOR
b Le Mans, France, Nov 1, 08. *Study:* Univ Paris, licence & agregation, 33; studied hist art with Henri Focillon, 29-33. *Teaching:* Lectr art hist, French Inst, London, 46-61; Slade Prof Fine Art, Cambridge Univ, Eng, 58-61; prof art hist, Univ Calif, Berkeley, 62-80, prof emer, 80-; Kress prof, Nat Gallery Art, Washington, DC, 82; vis Andrew W Mellon prof fine arts, Univ Pittsburg, fall 83; Algur H Meadows prof art hist, Southern Methodist Univ, Dallas, 84-87; Getty Lectr art, Univ Southern Calif, Los Angeles, 88. *Awards:* John Simon Guggenheim Mem Fel, 81; Haskins Medal Medieval Acad Am, 83. *Mem:* Soc Francaise Archeol; Royal Archaeol Inst (vpres, 55-61); Col Art Asn; Medieval Acad Am; hon fel Soc Antiquaries, London. *Res:* Romanesque and Gothic architecture, particularly in France and England. *Publ:* Coauth, French Cathedrals, Thames & Hudson, 51; ed, H Focillon's The Art of the West in the Middle Ages, Phaidon Press, 63; auth, The English Decorated Style, Phaidon & Cornell Univ Press, 79; auth, French Gothic Architecture of the 12th & 13th Centuries, Univ Calif Press, 83. *Mailing Add:* 2550 Dana St Apt 4-H Berkeley CA 94704-2878

BOODMAN, H CITRON
PAINTER, PRINTMAKER
b Pittsburgh, Pa, July 17, 27. *Study:* Carnegie-Mellon Univ, BFA, 48; DeCordova Mus, Lincoln, Mass with Donald Stoltenberg. *Work:* Free Libr Philadelphia, Pa; Univ Wyo; DeCordova Mus, Lincoln, Mass; Atlantic Richfield Oil Company, New York; IBM Corporate Collection; and others. *Comn:* 50 prints, Cambridge Art Asn, Mass, 68. *Exhib:* Minot Print & Drawing Nat Exhib, NDak, 74; Okla Nat Print Exhib, 74 & 76; 8th & 10th Nat Print Exhib, Silvermine Guild Artists, Conn, 74 & 76; DeCordova Mus, Lincoln, Mass, 75, 78, 79 & 80; one-person show, Cummings Art Ctr, Conn Col, New London, 76, Piper Gallery, Lexington, Mass,80, 82, 85 & 89; Mus Fine Arts, Boston, Mass, 76; In Celebration of Prints, Philadelphia Print Club Invitational, Pa, 80; Bird in the Hand Gallery, Sewickley, Pa, 84. *Pos:* Designer, Architectural Design Dept, Pittsburgh Plate Glass, Pa, 48-50; illustrative draftsman, State Dept, Washington, DC, 50-53. *Teaching:* Instr printmaking, pvt classes. *Awards:* First Prize, Corcoran Gallery, Washington, DC, 50; Purchase Prize, Strathmore Paper Company Award, Springfield, Mass, 76; Purchase Prize, 6th Ann Art Festival, NH, 76. *Bibliog:* C R Wasserman (auth), Ms Boodman Traces Stages of Printmakers' Art, Boston Globe, 72; Peter P Donker (auth), Helen Citron Boodman, collographs filled with imaginary architectural images, luscious in their subdued colorations, Worcester Telegram, 2/17/82. *Mem:* Cambridge Art Asn; Boston Visual Artists' Union; Women Exhibiting Boston; Boston Printmakers (pres, 82-83, treas, 83-85). *Media:* Crayon, Pastels; Ink. *Dealer:* The Garret Galleries 340 Huron Ave Cambridge MA 02138. *Mailing Add:* 4 Linmoor Terrace Lexington MA 02173

BOOKATZ, SAMUEL
PAINTER, SCULPTOR
b Philadelphia, Pa, Oct 3, 10. *Study:* Cleveland Inst Art; Boston Mus Sch Art; Harvard Univ; Acad Grande Chaumiere & Colarossi, Paris; Am Acad Rome; also with Oskar Kokoschka Chaim Soutine & Ivan Mestrovic. *Work:* Corcoran Gallery Art, Phillips Gallery & Smithsonian Inst, Washington, DC; Cleveland Mus Art, Ohio; Norfolk Mus Art & Sci, Va. *Comn:* Portraits of Pres & Mrs F D Roosevelt, 41; murals, comn by US Govt, US Naval Hosp, Norfolk, Va & San Diego, Calif, 42-45; murals, Govt Turn Key Housing for Aged, Prince George's Co, Md & Della Ratta Off Bldg, Bethesda, Md, 71; portrait, Gov David L Lawrence, Pa, 65; portrait of Joseph H Hirshhorn, Hirshhorn Mus & Sculpture Garden, Washington, DC, 78. *Exhib:* One-man shows, Cleveland Mus Art, 40 & Corcoran Gallery Art, 46; Pa Acad Fine Arts, Philadelphia, 52; Va Mus Art, Richmond, 55; Baltimore Mus Art, Md, 60. *Pos:* Govt artist & White House artist, 41-43. *Teaching:* Dir art, Samuel Bookatz Sch Art, Washington, DC, 45- *Awards:* William Page Award & Prix de Rome Award in the Arts, Boston Mus, 37; Inst Allende Fel, 54; Ford Found Grant, 62. *Mailing Add:* 2700 Que St NW Washington DC 20007

BOONE, MARY
ART DEALER
b Pa, Oct 29, 51. *Collections Arranged:* New Work/New York, Los Angeles, Calif, 77; Painting 75/76/77, Sarah Lawrence Col, Bronxville, NY, 77; Painting, Hal Bromm Gallery, New York, 77. *Pos:* Asst dir, Bykert Gallery, formerly; dir, Mary Boone Gallery, 78- *Specialty:* Contemporary art. *Mailing Add:* 417 W Broadway New York NY 10012

BOOTH, BILL
EDUCATOR
b Wallins Creek, Ky, June 20, 35. *Study:* Cumberland Jr Col, Williamsburg, Ky, 55; Eastern Ky State Univ, Richmond, AB, 60; George Peabody Col, Nashville, Tenn, MA, 64, EdS, 65; Univ Ga, Athens, PhD, 70. *Pos:* Head dept, Morehead State Univ, Ky, 70- *Teaching:* Instr art appreciation, George Peabody Col, 63-65; asst prof art hist, Wis State Univ, Oshkosh, 65-68; prof art hist, Morehead State Univ, Ky, 70- *Bibliog:* A friendship renewed, J Oomoto Found, 10-12/81. *Mem:* Col Art Asn; Am Fedn Arts. *Res:* Frank Duveneck, 1848-1919. *Publ:* Auth, Oriental motifs in 19th century European and American art, Asian Cult Quart, autumn 81 & Bulletin Nat Mus Hist, 12/81. *Mailing Add:* Big Perry Rd Morehead KY 40351

BOOTH, DOT
PAINTER, PRINTMAKER
b Chicago, Ill. *Study:* Univ Ala, Birmingham, 63-64; Univ South Fla, Tampa, 68-70. *Work:* Miss Mus Art, Jackson; Macon Mus Arts & Sci, Ga; City Miami, Fla; Columbus Mus, Ga; Pensacola Art Ctr, Fla. *Comn:* Orlando Exec Airport, Fla. *Exhib:* 40th & 43rd Ann Contemp Am Paintings, Soc Four Arts, Palm Beach, Fla, 69, 78, 81 & 87; Best of Fla, Pensacola Art Ctr, 70; Invitational, Mus Arts & Sci, Daytona Beach, Fla, 72; Selections from Permanent Collection, Miss Mus Art, Jackson, 78; Artists in Ga, High Mus Art, Atlanta, 78-79; Loch Haven Art Ctr Show, Orlando, Fla, 83. *Pos:* Scenic artist, EPCOT, 82. *Teaching:* Vis instr, Ringling Sch Art, 89. *Awards:* Philip Hulitar Award, 49th Ann Soc Four Arts, Palm Beach, Fla, 87; Purchase Award, Frontal Images, Jackson, Miss, 70; Best of Show, Gasparilla, Tampa, Fla, 78. *Bibliog:* Dot Booth--Hard Edge Realism, Orange Co Public TV, Fla, 73. *Media:* Oil, Acrylic; Serigraphy. *Mailing Add:* Booth Davis Studios 1939 Taylor Ave Winter Park FL 32792

BOOTH, GEORGE WARREN
PAINTER, DESIGNER
b Omaha, Nebr, July 6, 17. *Study:* Ohio Univ, with L C Mitchell, AB, MA; Chouinard Sch Art, with Pruett Carter; John Huntington Polytech, with Rolf Stoll. *Comn:* Equine Prints, Philip Morris, Inc, 78. *Exhib:* San Francisco Mus Art; Neiman-Marcus, Dallas; Abercrombie & Fitch, New York; Petersen Galleries, Beverly Hills, Calif; Gateway Art Galleries, Palm Beach; Foster Harmon Galleries Am Art. *Pos:* Art dir, J Walter Thompson Co, New York, 48-59; Ted Bates Inc, New York, 60-64. *Teaching:* Instr photog, Ohio Univ, 41-42. *Awards:* Gold Medal & Kerwin H Fulton Medal, Art Dirs Club New York, 54; Grand Award, 100 Best Posters of Yr, Outdoor Advert Asn Am, 54. *Bibliog:* Linette Albert (auth), George Warren Booth: The thoroughbred scene, Am Artist, 7/75; Alyse Lounsberry (auth), Art over easy, Ocala Star-Banner, 4/12/81 & Equine artist George Warren Booth, Fla Horse, 9/81; Bill Giauque (auth), The Florida Horse, 11/85; Norm Froscher (auth), Gainesville Sun, 11/87. *Mem:* Art Dirs Club New York; Soc Illusr; Artists Equity, New York. *Media:* Acrylic, Oil. *Dealer:* Sporting Gallery Middleburg Va 22117; Crossroads of Sport New York NY 10036. *Mailing Add:* 1771 Southwest 55th St Rd Ocala FL 34474

BOOTH, LAURENCE OGDEN
SCULPTOR, ARCHITECT
b Chicago, Ill, July 5, 36. *Study:* Stanford Univ, BA, 58; Mass Inst Technol, BArch, 60. *Work:* Art Inst Chicago. *Exhib:* Richard Gray Gallery, 76; Chicago 7 Architects, Walter Kelly Gallery & Richard Gray Gallery, 77;

Frumkin Struve Gallery, Chicago, 80-81; New Chicago Architecture, Verone, Italy, 81; Harvard Grad Sch Design, 81; and many other group & one-man shows. *Pos:* Vis critic, Harvard Univ, 81-82; bd dirs, Mus Contemp Art, Chicago. *Teaching:* Instr archit, Univ Ill, Chicago Circle, 69-71; vis prof, Univ Ill, 82. *Bibliog:* Amy Goldin (auth), Vitality vs greasy kid stuff, Art Gallery Mag, 72; article, Chicago Archit J, 81; article, New Chicago Archit, 81; and others. *Media:* Multimedia. *Publ:* Auth, Spiritual content of order, Arc Mag, 68; auth, Review of Stanley Tigerman sculpture, Art Scene Mag, 69. *Mailing Add:* 553 W Fullerton Chicago IL 60614

BOOTH, ROBERT ALAN
SCULPTOR
b Mt Kisco, NY, 1952. *Study:* Art Inst Boston, 71-73; Mass Col Art, BFA, 76; Syracuse Univ, MFA, 78. *Comn:* Site sculpture, comn by Ted Stetler, Syracuse, NY, 77; sculpture, TRW Bearings Corp, Jamestown, NY, 81; site sculpture, Artpark, Lewiston, NY, 83. *Exhib:* Syracuse Show, Everson Mus Art, 78; solo exhibs, Henri Gallery, Washington, DC, 81 & Bruce Gallery, Edinboro Univ, 83; Outside New York City: From Drawing to Sculpture, Lowe Art Gallery, Syracuse Univ, 82; In Western New York, Albright-Knox Art Gallery, 83; Contemporary Art Acquisitions: 1980-1983, Equitable Gallery, 84; 1983 Artpark Proj Artists, Artculture Resource Ctr, Toronto, Can, 84; Henri Gallery, Washington, DC, 85 & 88; Barbara Gillman Gallery, Miami, Fla, 87-88; Stein Gallery, Tampa, Fla, 87-89; Psychotronic & Neopunkedelic Art, Bruce Gallery, Edinboro Univ, Pa, 87; Wet Paint, Gillman Baker Gallery, Boca Raton, Fla, 89; 43 Western NY Exhibs, Albright-Knox Art Gallery, Buffalo, NY, 90; The Chair Show, Oxford Gallery, Rochester, NY, 90; X Sightings, Anderson Gallery, Buffalo, NY. *Pos:* Pres, Council Art Dept Chairs, State Univ New York. *Teaching:* Assoc prof sculpture, State Univ NY Col, Fredonia, 78-, chmn, dept art; chmn & assoc prof, Art Dept, SUNY Col Fredonia, New York. *Awards:* State Univ NY Fac Res Fel, 82 & 83. *Mem:* Int Sculpture Ctr; Artists Equity Asn. *Media:* Mixed. *Dealer:* Jaffe Baker Gallery Boca Raton FL; Henri Gallery Washington DC. *Mailing Add:* 1450 Burns Rd RD 1 Angola NY 14006

BOOTH CABOT, M(ARY ANN)
PAINTER, PRINTMAKER
b Winston-Salem, NC, Sept 28, 42. *Study:* Univ Tenn, 66-67; Ga State Univ, 68-70. *Work:* Arthur Anderson & Co, Coca-Cola Inc, Kilpatrick & Cody Attorneys, Delta Airlines, Atlanta, Ga; Simon & Schuster Doubleday Publ, New York; Shamrock Hilton, Houston, Tex; and others. *Comn:* Four art deco murals, Noelles Restaurant, Atlanta, Ga,; Delta Air Lines Crown Room, Hartsfield Int Airport, Atlanta, Ga; Park Seed Co, Greenwood, SC; Atlanta Flower Show. *Exhib:* Harvard Univ, Boston, Mass, 85 & 88; Atlanta Flower Show, 89-93; New Eng Flower Show, 90-93; St Louis Flower Show, 91-93; Philadelphia Flower Show, 91-93; and others. *Bibliog:* Inside Cobb Mag, spring 84; American Artists: an illustrated survey of leading contemporary Americans, Les Krantz (auth), 85; article, Southern Homes Mag, 84, 86 & 88; Female Artists in the United States 1900-1985: a Research and Resource Guide, Rutgers Univ Press, 86; Artists of Georgia, Vol I, 89 & Artists of the South II, 92, Mountain Productions Inc, Albuquerque; and others. *Mem:* Southern Watercolor Soc; Ga Watercolor Soc; Ky Watercolor Soc. *Media:* Watercolor. *Dealer:* Booth-Owen Arts 3961 Loch Highland Pass Roswell GA 30075. *Mailing Add:* 3961 Loch Highland Pass Roswell GA 30075

BOOTHE, POWER
PAINTER, EDUCATOR
b Mar 12, 45; US citizen. *Study:* Colo Col, BA, 67; Whitney Mus, independent study prog, 67-68; Colo Col, Hon DA, 89. *Work:* Guggenheim Mus; Chase Manhattan Bank; New York Bank for Savings; Lehman Brothers; NJ State Mus; Stanford Univ Art Mus; and others. *Exhib:* Theodoron Award Show, 71, Art of this Decade, 74 & Recent Acquisitions, 75, Guggenheim Mus, New York; Painting Endures, Inst of Contemp Art, Boston, 75; one-man exhibs, A M Sachs Gallery, 73, 74, 76, 77, 81, 82 & 85, Pvt Images, Los Angeles Co Mus Art, Calif, 77, Painting Show, PS1 Gallery, Brooklyn, NY, 77, Art & Dance, Inst Contemp Art, Boston, 82, Souyun Yi Gallery, 87 & 89, Harrison Gallery, 90, Time-Life Bldg, New York, 90, Thenkmann Gallery, 91 & Robert Morrison Gallery, 92; Book-Objects by Contemp Artists, Albright-Knox Art Gallery, Buffalo, NY, 77; Transitions: American Abstract Artists, Summit Art Ctr, NJ, 81. *Teaching:* Instr painting, Sch Visual Arts, New York, 79-88; Princeton Univ, 89-93. *Awards:* NEA-iver Arts Grant, 86; NY State Coun Grant, 87 & 89; Guggenheim Fel, 85. *Bibliog:* Dore Ashton (auth), American Art Since 1945, Oxford Univ Press, 82; Vivian Raynor (auth), Works by Power Boothe in Stamford and Greenwich, New York Times, 88; Joan Acocella (auth), Power Boothe on Two Edges, Village Voice, 91; and others. *Media:* Oil, Acrylic. *Publ:* When the Fourth Soldier Falls, A Study of Pielo Della Francesca's Resurrection, issue, Reflex Horizons, 86. *Mailing Add:* 49 Crosby St New York NY 10012

BOOTZ, ANTOINE H
PHOTOGRAPHER
b Paris, France, Feb 27, 56; French citizen. *Study:* Sciences-Politiques, Paris, 74-75, Sorbonne, Paris, 76-77, Univ St Charles, Marseille, France, 77-78. *Work:* Fonds Nat d'Art Contemporain, Paris; Galerie Baudoin Lebon, Paris. *Exhib:* Des Photographies dans le Paysage, Galerie de France, Paris, 81; Une Autre Photographie, Mus Andre Malraux, Creteil, France, 82; Saus Titre, Galerie Baudoin Lebon, Paris, 83-85; Saus Titre, Contemp Photog & Video from France, travelling US, 85-87. *Awards:* Fel, Nat Endowment Arts, 86-87. *Mailing Add:* 133 W 22nd St New York NY 10011

BOPP, EMERY
PAINTER, EDUCATOR
b Corry, Pa, May 13, 24. *Study:* Pratt Inst Art Sch, NY; Yale Sch Painting & Design, with Josef Albers & William de Kooning, BFA; NY Univ; Rochester Inst Technol, MFA. *Work:* Addison Gallery Am Art, Andover, Mass; Greenville Co Mus Art, SC; SC Arts Comn Collection; Hunter Gallery, Chattanooga, Tenn. *Exhib:* Bob Jones Univ, 62-64; Butler Inst Am Art Exhib, 66; Birmingham Mus Art, 66; Southeastern Exhib, Atlanta, Ga, 67; Greenville Co Mus Art, 68; plus others. *Teaching:* Chmn div art, Bob Jones Univ, 55- *Awards:* Purchase Award, Hunter Gallery Art, Chattanooga, Tenn, 65; Merit Award, Southeastern Exhib, Atlanta, 67; Purchase Award, Greenville Co Mus Art, 68. *Mem:* Southeastern Col Art Conf; Guild SC Artists; Col Art Asn Am; Cooperstown Art Asn, NY. *Mailing Add:* Div of Art Bob Jones Univ Greenville SC 29614

BORAX, BENJAMIN
COLLAGE ARTIST, PAINTER
b New York, NY, July 10, 09. *Study:* Art Students League, studied with Leo Manso, Jerry Samuels, Jerry Okimoto & Phil Reisman, 60-80. *Work:* Nassau Community Col, Garden City, NY. *Exhib:* Art of Northeast, Silvermine Guild, New Canaan, Conn; Hecksher Mus, Huntington, NY; Ann, Am Watercolor Soc, NY; works on paper, Nassau Community Col, Garden City, NY; Audubon Artists, NY. *Mem:* Artists Equity Asn; Knickerbocker Artists; Am Soc Contemp Artists; Long Beach, NY Artists Asn (publicity chmn, 80). *Media:* Collage; Acrylic, Oil. *Dealer:* Northport/B J Spoke Gallery 302 New York Ave Huntington NY 11743. *Mailing Add:* 271-25 N Grand Central Pkwy Floral Park NY 11005

BORCOMAN, JAMES
CURATOR
b Ontario, Can, Jan 17, 26. *Study:* Univ NB, BA; Univ BC, Vancouver; State Univ NY, Buffalo, MFA; hist photog with Beaumont Newhall & Nathan Lyons. *Collections Arranged:* Goodridge Roberts Retrospective, 69, Four 19th Century Canadian Photographers, 70 & Photographs from the Collection, 75, Nat Gallery Can; The Photograph as Object Traveling Exhib (with catalog), 69; Nathan Lyons: Notations in Passing Traveling Exhib (with catalog), 72; Charles Negre (with catalog), Ottawa, 76; Brit Photographs from the Collection, 1844-1914, 76; Recent Acquisitions, 77; The Painter as Photogr: D O Hill, Charles Negre, Auguste Salzmann (with monograph), 78; The Magical Eye: Definitions of Photography, 80; Eugene Atget and his Precursors (with catalog), Ottawa, 82; Intimate Images (with catalog), Ottawa, 88; Karsh: The Art of the Portrait (with catalog), 89; The Cherished Image: The portrait in Photography, 89; Roger Mertin: O Tannenbaum, 91; Atget, Evans, Friedlander, 91. *Pos:* Educ officer, Nat Gallery Can, 60-66, dir educ dept, 66-69 & cur photographs, 67-83. *Teaching:* Part time lectr hist photog & photog workshop, Univ Ottawa, Ont, 71-75; hon adj prof, Ariz State Univ, Tempe. *Awards:* Prize for Distinguished Achievement in Photog Hist, Photog Hist Soc of NY; Seal of City of Arles, France; Bronze Medal, Leipzig Bk Fair. *Bibliog:* Peter Bunnell (auth), The National Gallery photographic collection: An inquiry into the aesthetics of photography (series), Artscanada, 75. *Mem:* Soc Photog Educ. *Res:* Canadian art; history of photography. *Publ:* Auth, Notes on the early use of combination printing, In: 100 Years of Photographic History, 75; David Heath: A Dialogue with Solitude, 75 & Eugene Atget 1857-1927, 84, Nat Gallery Can; Karsh: The Art of the Portrait, Nat Gallery, 89. *Mailing Add:* Nat Gallery Can 380 Sussex Dr Ottawa ON K1N 9N4 Canada

BORDEAUX, JEAN LUC
ART HISTORIAN, CURATOR
b Laval, France, Feb 13, 37. *Study:* Univ Paris, Fac Sci, PCB, 59; Mus Nat d'Art Mod, Paris, study of museology with Jean Cassou, 58-60; Iowa State Univ, BS(journalism), 64; Ariz State Univ, MA(art hist), 66; Univ Calif, Los Angeles, PhD(art hist), 70. *Pos:* Art critic & writer, Connaissance des Arts, 55-; lectr, J Paul Getty Mus, Malibu, Calif, 67-68, asst cur paintings, 69-72; dir, Fine Arts Gallery, Calif State Univ, Northridge, 72-81; guest cur, Calif Palace of the Legion of Honor, San Francisco, 75; charge de mission, Musee du Louvre, France, 79; organized and curated numerous exhibitions since 1972. *Teaching:* Instr art hist, Univ Calif, Los Angeles, 69-72; prof art hist, Calif State Univ, Northridge, 69- *Awards:* Kress Fel, Louvre, Hermitage & Pushkin Mus (France & Soviet Union), 70-71; Calif Arts Coun Exhib Grants, 74-75; J Paul Getty Trust Publ Award, 84; Found Paribas Publ Award, 84. *Mem:* Fr Soc Hist Art; Col Art Asn; Les Amis du Louvre; Los Angeles County Mus Art. *Res:* French painting from 17th to early 19th centuries; Twentieth Century Art Criticism. *Interests:* Contemporary art in New York and Los Angeles. *Publ:* Auth, articles, Burlington Mag, Am Art Rev, Art Int, Art in Am, Jour J Paul Getty Mus, Gaz des Beaux Arts, and others; François Le Moyne and His Generation 1688-1737, (catalog raisonné), Arthena, 84-85. *Mailing Add:* 6 rue Paul Baudry Paris 75008 France

BORDES, ADRIENNE
PAINTER, INSTRUCTOR
b New York, NY. *Study:* NY Univ, with Philip Guston, BA, 57; Hunter Col, New York, with Tony Smith & Vincent Longo. *Exhib:* One-person shows, Capricorn Gallery, New York, 67 & 68 & Wilkes Col, Pa, 78; Six Artists, NY Univ, 68; Some New Beginnings, Brooklyn Mus, 68; Women in the Arts, Univ Wis, 72; Transitions, Wallace Gallery, State Univ NY, 79; Four Artists & A Writer, Fed Hall, New York, 82. *Teaching:* Adj instr painting, Hunter Col, New York, 78-80 & Adelphi Univ, 79-80; tenured asst prof hist archit & interior design, Fashion Inst Technol, 80- *Awards:* Painting Grant, Millay Colony Arts, Austerlitz, NY, 75. *Bibliog:* Julia Ballerini (auth), Four Artists and a Writer, catalog, Fed Hall, NY, 82. *Mem:* Interior Design Educators Coun. *Media:* Acrylic. *Mailing Add:* 369 Seventh Ave New York NY 10001

BORETZ, NAOMI
PAINTER, EDUCATOR
b New York, NY. *Study:* Art Students League; Boston Mus Sch; Rutgers Univ; City Col New York, MA(fine arts), 71. *Work:* Joslyn Art Mus, Omaha, Nebr; Nat Mus Am Art, Washington, DC; Brit Mus London, Eng; Glasgow Mus, Scotland; Guggenheim Mus, New York; Walker Art Ctr, Minneapolis, Minn; Yale Univ Art Gallery, New Haven, Ct; and many others. *Exhib:* Awards Exhib, Brooklyn Mus Art, 72; solo exhib, Hudson River Mus, 75; Crawford Muni Art Gallery, Cork, Ireland, 88; Katonah Gallery, NY, 78; Middlesex Co Mus, NJ, 81; Condeso Lawler Gallery, New York, 87; Ulrich Mus Wichita State Univ, KS, 92; and many others. *Teaching:* Instr, City Col New York, 68-71 & Princeton Art Asn, 72-73; asst prof art & dir art prog, Rider Col, Lawrenceville, NJ, 73-80; assoc prof, Fine Arts, Wilson Col, Chambersburg, Pa, 85. *Awards:* Watercolor Award, Brooklyn Mus Art, 71; Va Ctr Creative Arts Fel, 86; Ossabaw Arts Found Fel, 75; Artist Fel, NJ State Coun Arts, 85-86; Tyrone Guthrie Art Ctr Fel, Ireland, 87; Writers-Artists Guild, Can, 88. *Bibliog:* Ian Woodcock (auth), article, Arts Mag, 7/72; interview, Brit Broadcasting Co Radio, 72-73; article, New York Times, 3/81. *Mem:* Am Abstract Artists. *Media:* All Media. *Publ:* Auth, The reality underlying abstraction, In: Perception and Pictorial Representation, Praeger, 79; auth, Watercolours with acetate, Leonardo, 78. *Mailing Add:* 15 Southern Way Princeton NJ 08540

BORGATTA, ISABEL CASE
SCULPTOR, EDUCATOR
b Madison, Wis, Nov 21, 22. *Study:* Smith Col, 39-40; Yale Univ Sch Fine Arts, BFA, 44; Studio of Jose de Creeft, 44-45; Art Students League, 46. *Work:* Benton Mus, Univ Conn; Hudson River Mus, Col New Rochelle Mus; 4 pieces NYNEX Hqs, New York & Grand Hyatt Hotel, New York; Smith Col Mus; Okla Art Ctr. *Comn:* Mem sculpture, New Rochelle, New York, 72; Grand Hyatt Hotel, New York; plus others. *Exhib:* Pa Acad Fine Arts Ann, Philadelphia, 49-55; Whitney Mus Am Art, 51-52; one-woman shows, Galerie St Etienne, 54 & 56 & Frank Rehn Gallery, 68, 71, 74 & 77; retrospective, Briarcliff Col Mus, 71; Hartford Atheneum, Nat Acad Ann Sculptors Guild, 71-88; Brooklyn Mus, 75; Sid Deutsch Gallery, 84 & 87; Sweet Briar Col Mus, 86; Oklahoma Art Ctr, 87. *Pos:* Deleg, Fedn Fine Arts, currently. *Teaching:* Lectr sculpture, City Col New York, 60-71; assoc prof, Col New Rochelle, 73-78, prof, 78- *Awards:* Edward Mac Dowell Fels, 68, 73 & 74; Yaddo Fel, 71, 72 & 73; Va Ctr Creative Arts Fel, 85, 86, 87, 88, 89, 90, 91 & 92; Sculpture residency, Govt Greece, Delphi, 92. *Bibliog:* Mark van Doren (auth), The sculptures of Isabel Case Borgatta, Galerie St Etienne, 54; William D Allen (auth), Borgatta's marbles, Arts Mag, 68; James R Mellow (auth), article in New York Times, 74; Virginia Watson-Jones (auth), American Women Sculptors, Oryx Press, 86; Isabel Case Borgatta: The Persistence of the Figure, Cincinnati Univ, 87. *Mem:* Col Art Asn; Women's Caucus Art; Artists Equity; Sculptors Guild (exec bd). *Media:* Stone, Wood. *Publ:* Auth, A Sculptor Changes, Women Artists Newsletter, 77; Casting landscapes in paper, Artists Mag, 86. *Mailing Add:* 463 West St Apt 1105 New York NY 10014

BORGATTA, ROBERT EDWARD
PAINTER, SCULPTOR
b Havana, Cuba, Jan 11, 21; US citizen. *Study:* Nat Acad Design, 34-37; NY Univ, Sch Archit & Allied Arts, BFA, 40, Inst Fine Arts, 46-53; Yale Univ Sch Fine Arts, MFA, 42. *Work:* Norfolk Mus, Va; Ford Found. *Comn:* Mural & sculpture, Gutman Assocs, New York; stained glass design, Temple Emanu-el, Yonkers, NY, 60. *Exhib:* Audubon Artists Ann, 53-72; Whitney Mus Am Art Prizewinners Show, 54; Schettini Gallery, Milan, Italy, 57; Corcoran Gallery Art, 68; one-man shows, Babcock Galleries, 64 & 68 & Southern Vt Art Ctr, 77. *Teaching:* Prof painting & drawing, City Col New York, 47-80. *Awards:* Tiffany Fel, 42; Emily Lowe Found Award, 57; Newman Medal, Nat Soc Painters Casein, 69. *Bibliog:* American artists in Italian exhibit, Valligia Diplomatica, 10/57; An artist in his studio, House Beautiful, 3/60; John Canaday (auth), article, New York Times, 3/15/69. *Mem:* Audubon Artists; Am Watercolor Soc; Nat Soc Painters Casein. *Media:* Oil, Marble. *Dealer:* Babcock Galleries 20 East 67th St New York NY 10021. *Mailing Add:* 366 Broadway New York NY 10013

BORGENICHT, GRACE
ART DEALER, COLLECTOR
b New York, NY, Jan 25, 15. *Study:* Columbia Univ, MA, 37; also with Andre Lhote, Paris, 34. *Pos:* Dir & owner, Grace Borgenicht Gallery, 51- *Specialty:* Contemporary American painting and sculpture. *Collection:* Matisse, Picasso, de Kooning, Bonnard, Mondrian, Degas, Vuillard, Avery, de Rivera. *Mailing Add:* 724 Fifth Ave New York NY 10019

BORGIA-ABERLE, NINA
CERAMIST
b New York, NY, 1955. *Study:* Mass Col Art, Boston, 73-75; Syracuser Univ, NY, 75; State Univ New York, New Paltz, BFA, 79; Ohio State Univ, Columbus, MFA, 86. *Exhib:* Solo exhibs, Columbus Cult Art Ctr, Ohio, 86, Licking Co Art Asn, Neward, 87, Sara Squeri Gallery, Cincinnati, 90, Swidler Gallery, Royal Oak, Mich & Leedy Voulkous Gallery, Kansas City, Mo, 91; 27th Ann Nat Ceramic Exhib, 87 & 28th, 90, Everson Mus Art, Syracuse, NY; Contiguous Elements: Contemporary Ohio Ceramics and Prints, Ft Hayes Metrop Educ Ctr, Columbus, Ohio, 90; Ohio Selections, Cleveland Ctr Contemp Art, 90; Making a Difference, Riffe Ctr Gallery, Columbus, Ohio, 91; Collaborations 91, John Michael Kohler Art Ctr, Sheboygan, Wis. *Teaching:* Instr ceramics, NY State Summer Sch Arts, Fredonia, 82, Ohio State Univ, 85-86; vis lectr drawing, Denison Univ, 87 & ceramics, Calif State Univ, Long Beach, 90; guest lectr, Ceramics Int Seminar, Calgary, Can, 91; sculptor in residence at numerous Ohio schools. *Awards:* Edith Fergus Gillmore Grant, 86; Nat Endowment Arts Individual Fel, 88 & 90; Ohio Arts Coun Individual Artist Fel, 89 & 91. *Mailing Add:* 11018 Jug St Johnstown OH 43031

BORIS, BESSIE
PAINTER
b Johnstown, Pa. *Study:* Art Students League, 40-42; study with George Grosz & Vaclav Vytlacil. *Work:* Smith Col Mus Art, Northhampton, Mass; Chase Manhattan Bank, New York; NJ Mus, Newark; Montclair Mus, NJ; Berkshire Mus, Pittsfield, Mass; Denver Mus, Colo. *Exhib:* Corcoran Gallery Art, Washington, DC, 49; Pa Acad Fine Arts Ann Drawing Show, 63 & 69; Babcock Gallery, New York, 76; Touchstone Gallery, New York, 76; Zone Gallery, Springfield, Mass, 86; Berkshire Mus, Pittsfield, Mass, 87; Katherina Rich Perlow Gallery, New York, 90 & 92; and others. *Bibliog:* Debra Bricker Balken (auth), Berkshire Mus Catalog, 87; Frederick Wights (auth), Six American painters, Chrysalis, Vol 4, No 3-451; Debra Balken (auth), Berkshire Mus Catalogue, 87. *Media:* Miscellaneous Media. *Mailing Add:* Box 813 Stockbridge MA 01262

BORN, JAMES E
SCULPTOR
b Toledo, Ohio, Nov 16, 34. *Study:* Toledo Mus Sch, cert; Univ Toledo, BA; Univ Iowa, Iowa City, MFA. *Work:* Univ Iowa, Iowa City; Art Ctr Mus, Pine Bluff, Ark. *Exhib:* San Diego Art Mus Ann Exhib, 68; Sculpture & Ceramics, Butler Inst Am Art, Youngstown, Ohio, 68, 74, 75 & 77; one-man shows, Cent Mich Univ, 69, 77 & 84, Muskegon Community Col, 79 & Ferris State Univ, 85; Biennial, Grand Rapids Art Mus, Mich, 70-72; 24th Drawing & Sculpture Show, Ball State Univ, 78; 19th Ann Mich Exhib, Midland Art Ctr; Eight State Ann, Speed Mus, Louisville, KY, 79; Mich Open, Saginaw Art Mus, 86. *Teaching:* Asst prof sculpture, painting, design & drawing, Univ Calif at Humboldt, Arcata, 62-64 & Calif Western Univ, San Diego, 64-65; asst prof sculpture, design & painting, Univ Calif at Stanislaus, Turlock, 65-68; assoc prof sculpture, Cent Mich Univ, Mt Pleasant, 68-76, acting chmn, 72-74, prof sculpture, 76- *Awards:* Sculpture Award, 28th Ann Exhib, Ball State Univ, 82; Grand Purchase Award, 15th Nat Exhib, Pine Bluff Art Mus, Ark, 82; Second Prize Award, Mich Fine Arts Competition, Birmingham-Bloomfield Art Ctr, 86. *Mem:* Col Art Asn; Mid-Am Art Asn. *Media:* Bronze. *Mailing Add:* 502 S Univ Mt Pleasant MI 48858

BORNSTEIN, ELI
PAINTER, SCULPTOR
b Milwaukee, Wis, Dec 28, 22. *Study:* Univ Wis, BS, 45 & MS, 54; Art Inst Chicago; Univ Chicago, 43; Acad Montmartre of Fernand Leger, Paris, 51; Acad Julian, Paris, 52, Univ Saskatchewan, D Litt, 90. *Work:* Walker Art Ctr, Minneapolis, Minn; Nat Gallery Can, Ottawa; Univ at Calgary, Alberta; Univ Sask & Mendel Art Gallery, Saskatoon; Saskatchewan Arts Board, Regina; and others. *Comn:* Aluminum construction, Sask Teacher's Fedn, Saskatoon, 56; structurist relief, Univ Sask, Saskatoon, 58; structurist relief, Int Air Terminal, Winnipeg, 62; structurist construction, Wascana Ctr Authority, Regina, 83. *Exhib:* Retrospectives, Mendel Art Gallery, Saskatoon, 64 & 83; Nat Gallery Can Biennial, Ottawa, 67; 2nd Int Biennial, Medellin, Colombia, 70; Can Cult Centre, Paris, France, 76; Glenbow-Alta Inst, Calgary, 76; York Univ Art Gallery, Toronto, 83; Fine Arts Gallery, Univ Wis, Milwaukee; and others. *Pos:* Ed, The Structurist, 60- *Teaching:* Instr drawing, painting & sculpture, Milwaukee Art Inst, 43-47; instr design, Univ Wis, 49; prof art, Univ Sask, 50-, head dept art, 63-71, prof emer, 90. *Awards:* Allied Arts Medal, Royal Archit Inst Can, 68; Hon mention, 2nd Int Biennial Exhib, Medellin, Colombia, 70; Gov Gen's Queen Elizabeth Silver Jubilee Medal, 77. *Bibliog:* Eli Bornstein: Selected Works/Oeuvres Choisies, 1957-1982, Mendel Art Gallery, 82. *Media:* Constructed Relief. *Publ:* Auth of numerous articles and essays in the Structurist since 1960- *Mailing Add:* Box 378 Univ Sask Saskatoon SK S7N 0W0 Canada

BOROCHOFF, (IDA) SLOAN
PAINTER, PRINTMAKER
US citizen. *Study:* High Mus Art, 39; Univ Ga, 39-40; Ga State Univ, 40; Chicago Sch Interior Decorating, dipl, 66; Atlanta Art Inst, 68. *Work:* Ga Inst Technol, Vet Admin & Lovett Sch, Atlanta; The Temple, Tucson, Ariz; Nat Acad Eng, Washington, DC. *Comn:* Noah's Ark (print), Atlanta Jewish Welfare Fedn, 71; painting, Am Ort Campaign, Atlanta, 72. *Exhib:* One-woman shows, Ga Inst Technol Student Ctr & Lovett Sch Show, 71 & 75; 3rd Nat Art Competition, B'nai B'rith Woman, 65 & Int Platform Asn Art Exhib, 71, Washington, DC; Atlanta Merchandise Mart; Corcoran Mus, Washington, DC; Athens Mus, Ga; Montgomery Mus, La; Kottler Gallery, New York; Rizzoli Gallery, New York. *Pos:* Vpres, Designs Unlimited Inc, Atlanta, 64-; pres, Sloan Borochoff Gallery; artist-auth, Atlanta Playhouse Theatre Ltd, 75-; artistic dir, Int Dogwood Festival Art Shows, Atlanta, 79-; producer/host weekly series Community TV, Atlanta Prime Cable. *Teaching:* Lectr, schs & workshops, 70-; dir, Int Jr Cult Exchange Art Shows. *Awards:* TV Caber Award, 84; Oscar d'Italia, Accademia Italia Premio, 85; Invitation to White House Coffee, 89. *Mem:* Women in Film; Acad Cable Programming; Women's C of C; Int Platform Asn; Mat Mus Women. *Media:* Oil, Prints. *Publ:* Artist-Auth, Images of Women, WGTV & Atlanta Playhouse Theatre. *Mailing Add:* 3450 Old Plantation Rd NW Atlanta GA 30327

BOROFSKY, JON
PAINTER
b Boston, Mass, 42. *Study:* Carnegie Mellon Univ, BFA, 64; Ecole de Fontainbleau, summer 64; Yale Sch Art & Archit, MFA, 66. *Exhib:* one-man exhibs, Paula Cooper Gallery, New York, 75, 76, 79, 80, 82, 88 & 90,

Contemporary Arts Mus, Houston, Tex, 81, Philadelphia Mus Art, Pa, 84, Cathedral St John the Divine, New York, 87, Tokyo Metrop Art Mus, Japan, 87, Galerie Yvon Lambert, Paris, France, 90, Glenn-Dash Gallery, Los Angeles, 90 & Gemini G E L, Los Angeles, 91; 10th Anniversary Group Show, Paula Cooper Gallery, New York, 78; Whitney Biennial, Whitney Mus of Am Art, New York, 79; Born in Boston, De Cordova Mus, Lincoln, Mass, 79; Int Austellung, Westkunst, Cologne, WGermany, 81; Baroques 81, Musee de la Ville de Paris, 81; Committed to Print, Mus Modern Art, New York, 88; 1988: The World of Art Today, Milwaukee Art Mus, 88; and many others. *Teaching:* Instr, Sch Visual Arts, New York, 69-77; instr, Calif Inst Arts, Los Angeles, 77-80. *Bibliog:* Mark Rosenthal (auth), Jon Borofsky, Matrix 18, Wadsworth Atheneum, 4-5/76; Phillip Smith, Jon Borofsky, Arts Mag, 3/78; John Russell (auth), Art: transformations of Jonathan Borofsky, New York Times, 10/24/80. *Mailing Add:* c/o Paula Cooper Gallery 155 Wooster St New York NY 10012

BORSTEIN, ELENA
PAINTER, EDUCATOR
b Hartford, Conn, Feb 5, 46. *Study:* Skidmore Col, BS; Univ Pa, BFA & MFA. *Work:* Mus Mod Art; Mass Inst Technol; Everson Mus; Newark Mus; Phoenix Mus; and others. *Comn:* Ottawa Silica Corp, Ill; Whitco Chemical Co, New York. *Exhib:* Contemporary Reflections, Aldrich Mus Art, Ridgefield, Conn, 74; 14 Am Artists, Corcoran Gallery/Aarhus Kunstmuseum Traveling Exhib, 77; Gifts of Drawing, Mus Mod Art, New York, 79; Herbert Johnson Mus Art, Ithaca, NY, 81; Rochester Inst Technol, 81; Everson Mus, 81; Skidmore Col, Saratoga Springs, NY, 82; Kathryn Markel Gallery, New York, 83; and others. *Pos:* Art consult, Aarhus Kunstmuseum, Denmark, 74-75; vis artist, St Marys Col, Ind, Md Art Inst & Sch Visual Arts, 81. *Teaching:* Asst prof painting & photog, York Col, City Univ New York, 70- *Awards:* Childe Hassam Purchase Award, Am Acad Arts & Lett, 75; Nat Endowment Arts Grant, 80; Creative Artists Pub Serv Prog Grant, 80. *Bibliog:* David Shirey (auth), article, Arts Mag, 9/78; articles, Art Int, 1/80 & New York Times, 3/16/80. *Mem:* Col Art Asn (mem, Women's Caucus). *Mailing Add:* Fine Arts Dept York Col 9420 Guy Brewer Blvd Jamaica NY 11451

BOSMAN, RICHARD
PAINTER, PRINTMAKER
b Madras, India, 44. *Study:* Byam Shaw Sch Painting & Drawing, London, 64-69; New York Studio Sch, NY, 69-71; Skowhegan Sch Painting & Sculpture, Maine, 70. *Work:* Albright-Knox Art Gallery, Buffalo, NY; Australian Nat Gallery, Canberra; Brooklyn Mus, NY; Fogg Art Mus, Harvard Univ, Cambridge; Nat Mus Am Art, Washington, DC; Weatherspoon Art Gallery, Greensboro. *Exhib:* One-man exhibs, Galerie Lucien Bilinelli, Brussels, 88, Mandeville Gallery, Univ Calif, San Diego, 89, Brooke Alexander, New York, 89 & 90, The Contemp Art Gallery, Seibu, Tokyo, 89, John Berggven Gallery, San Francisco, 90; Works on Paper, Curt Marrus Gallery, New York, 88; Sounding the Depths: 150 Years of American Seascape, Am Fedn Arts, New York, 89; First Impressions, Walker Art Ctr, Traveling from Minneapolis to Baltimore, 89; Monoprints/Monotypes-Images by Twenty Contemporary Artists, Univ Maine Mus Art, Orono, 89; Group show, Galeria La Maquina Espanola, Madrid, 89; Images of Death in Contemporary Art, Patrick & Beatrice Haggerty Mus Art, Milwaukee, 90; Selected Paintings, Drawings and Sculpture, John Berggruen Gallery, San Francisco, 90 718. *Teaching:* Instr, New York Studio Sch, 72, Skowhegan Sch Painting & Sculpture, Maine, 82 & Sch Visual Arts, New York, 82-84. *Bibliog:* Jole de Sanna (auth), Milan: Richard Bosman, Toselli Gallery, Artforum, 12/86; Chavarri Ardujar (auth), La Pintura con sangre entra, Las Priovincias, 7/87; Joy Hakanson Colby (auth), Richard Bosman, The Detroit News, 11/1/88. *Publ:* Coauth, Exit the Face, Mus Mod Art, New York, 82; illusr, Grasping at Emptiness, Kulchur Found, 85; The Captivity Narrative of Hannah Duston, Arion Press, San Francisco, 87; Nat Mus Am Art & Library of Congress, Washington, DC; Dannhoiser Found, Metrop Mus Art, Mus Mod Art, Whitney Mus Mod Arts Public Library, New York. *Dealer:* Brooke Alexander Inc 59 Wooster St New York NY 10012. *Mailing Add:* 285 Hudson St New York NY 10013

BOSSE, JANET C
PAINTER, CERAMIST
b Detroit, Mich. *Study:* Coronado Sch Fine Art, Calif, 53-54; Univ Mich, 55-56; Pratt Graphic Art Ctr, 63-70, Greenwich House Pottery, 86-90, Alfred Univ, NY, 86. *Work:* US Info Serv; Pace Univ, Am Express Int, IBM Corp & Chase Manhattan Bank, New York. *Exhib:* Dore Ashton Selects, Judy Caden Gallery & Marymount Manhattan Col Gallery, New York, 82; Connections: Painting and Poetry, Pace Univ, New York, 83; Color: Harmonious and Discordant, Marymount Manhattan Col Gallery, New York, 83; Critics Choice, Arsenal Gallery, New York, 83; Gathering of the Avant Garde, Kenkeleba Gallery, New York, 85; Art and the Spiritual Quest, WCA, The Open Center, New York, 86; Women's Visions: Themes from Nature, Nabisco Brands Gallery, E Hanover, NJ, 89; Kendall Gallery Show: 16 Artists, Kyosendo Gallery, Kobe, Japan, 89; solo-show, Kendall Gallery, 90; and others. *Pos:* Pres & found mem, Noho Gallery, 75- *Teaching:* Instr, Hofstra Univ, 72-73. *Bibliog:* Lawrence Albway (auth), Critics Choice Exhib (catalog), The Arsenal Gallery, New York, 10/83; Barnaby Ruhe (auth), Janet Bosse, Art World, 2/80; James T McCartin (auth), Janet Bosse, Arts Mag, 5/81. *Mem:* Womens Caucus for Art; Women in the Arts; Artists Equity. *Media:* Acrylic, Pastels. *Dealer:* Noho Gallery 168 Mercer St New York NY 10012. *Mailing Add:* 40 Perry St New York NY 10014

BOSSERT, EDYTHE H
PAINTER
b Jacksonville, Pa, July 18, 08. *Study:* Lock Haven Univ, 28; Yetter of Car Mellon, Pa, 32;. *Work:* Pa Mus, Harrisburg; Lock Haven Univ, Pa; Ross Libr, Lock Haven, Pa. *Comn:* Oil painting, Mill Hall Sch Libr, Pa, 68; Ross Libr, Lock Haven, 70; portrait, Judge Dale, Centre Co Court House, Bellefonte, Pa, 86; portrait, A Akeley, Akeley Bldg, Lock Haven Univ, Pa. *Exhib:* Nat Asn Women Artists Ann, Nat Acad Gallery, 45-76; Millbrook Art Gallery, Mill Hall, Pa, 60; three-man show, Britts Gallery, Williamsport, Pa, 67; one-man shows, Lock Haven Univ, 68, Ross Libr, 68-89; North Shore Arts Asn, Glouster, Mass; and others. *Pos:* Teacher & art supervisor, Keystone Ctr Sch Dis, Lock Haven, Pa, 61-70. *Teaching:* Greensburg, Pa, 28-32. *Awards:* Best of Show, Lock Haven, Fallon Hotel, 50. *Mem:* Nat Asn Women Artists. *Media:* Oil. *Mailing Add:* RD Box 36 Beech Creek Rd Beech Creek PA 16822

BOSSON, JACK (JOHN EDWIN), JR
PAINTER, MURALIST
b Charleroi, Pa, Sept 18, 37. *Study:* Cooper Union, with Victor Candell, Charles Cajori & John Kacere, cert(Fulbright fel), 63; Univ Paris, with Marcel Brion, 64; Cornell Univ, MFA, 66. *Work:* New York Port Authority Collection; Herbert F Johnson Mus Art, Ithaca, NY; Smithsonian Inst Space Mus Collection, DC; State Univ NY Albany. *Comn:* Painting of solar eclipse, Nat Aeronautics & Space Admin, Houston, 67; mural, Stephen Bochco Productions, Los Angeles, 90; two murals, Meisei Co Ltd (Meisei Moore), Osaka, Japan, 91. *Exhib:* Arts & Univ/Trends in the Sixties, Albright-Knox Art Gallery, Buffalo, NY, 67; 7th Ann Contemp Reflections, Aldrich Mus, Ridgefield, Conn, 78; At Work, Paintings & Working Drawings, Castle Gallery, New Rochelle, NY, 86; Drawings, group show, Les Ateliers, Paris, France, 86; Director's Invitational, Provincetown Group Gallery, Mass, 86; Paintings & drawings, Les Ateliers, Paris, France, 87; Layering/Connecting, Zanesville Art Ctr, Ohio & Wheeling Mus Art, WVa, 87; and others. *Collections Arranged:* The Ithaca Paintings, 1970-1976 (cataloged), Rathbone Gallery, Albany, NY, 77. *Pos:* Pres, 55 Mercer Gallery, New York, 79-80. *Teaching:* Asst prof drawing & painting, Cornell Univ, 69-75; assoc prof, Col New Rochelle, NY, 75-87, adj lectr, 89- *Awards:* Purchase Award, Albright-Knox Art Gallery, NY State Univ Comt Arts, 67; Artists Fel, Nat Endowment Arts, 80; and others. *Bibliog:* Fred Mangones & Philip Jones (auth), Tides (film), 72; Mary C Nelson (auth), Layering: an art of time and space (essay & catalog), Albuquerque Mus Fine Arts, 85; William Zimmer (auth), rev, NY Times, 12/85; and others. *Mem:* Col Art Asn. *Media:* Acrylic, Oil; Silkscreen, Lithography. *Mailing Add:* 11939 Gorham Ave Los Angeles CA 90049

BOSTELLE, THOMAS (THEODORE)
PAINTER, SCULPTOR
b West Chester, Pa, Nov 16, 21. *Work:* Del Art Mus; West Chester Univ, Pa; Butler Inst Am Art, Youngstown, Ohio; Phillips Collection, Washington, DC; Nat Portrait Gallery, Washington, DC; Tatnall Sch & Tower Hill Sch, Wilmington, Del. *Exhib:* Over 50 one-man shows; retrospectives, George Washington Univ, 69, Del Art Mus, 73, Woodmere Art Gallery, Philadelphia, 77 & 80 & Shippensburg State Col, 81, Pasadena City Col, Calif, 86, Brand Mus & Art Libr, 86, Del Art Mus, 89, West Chester Univ, Pa, 92. *Pos:* Aesthetic adv, One world or none & Stuff for stuff (documentaries), Phillip Ragan Assocs, 47-49. *Teaching:* Instr drawing & painting, Fleisher Art Mem, 52-55; instr, Wilmington Soc Fine Arts, 56-77 & Chester Co Art Asn, West Chester, Pa, 77-80; pvt classes & lectures, 60- *Awards:* Four Christian Brinton First Prize Awards & three NC Wyeth First Prize Awards, 46-72; Invited 147 Ann Exhib, Am Painting, PAFA, Philadelphia, Pa; First Prize, Philadelphia Trust Co, 56; Purchase Prize, Delaware Art Mus, 56; Delaware Art Mus, 57; Invited Mus Mod Art, Paris, 59; First Prize, drawing, Brecks Mill, 59. *Bibliog:* Jill Gollatz (auth), On Bostelle's Portrait of Horace Pippin, Daily Local News, 1/31/80; Edmund Morris (auth), A World of Suggestion, Quest, 6/81; Tania Boucher (auth), Bostelle: Seated Self, Aeolian Palace Press, 80; Penelope Bass Cope (auth), Mankind in the shadows, News J, 4/21/87; Erica Mears (auth), Artist Has Cast Haunting Shadows (Sunday local news), 2/1/87; John Chambless (auth), A Lifetime of Shadow & Light, Daily Local News, West Chester, Pa, 5/16/92; The Bridge May Be Icy, Daily Local News, West Chester, Pa, 92; Crowd, APP, 92. *Media:* Oil; Bronze. *Publ:* Auth, Hob House, Aeolian Palace Press, 83. *Mailing Add:* c/o Aeolian Palace Gallery Box 8 Pocopson PA 19366

BOSTICK, WILLIAM ALLISON
PAINTER, CALLIGRAPHER
b Marengo, Ill, Feb 21, 13. *Study:* Carnegie Inst Technol, BS; Cranbrook Acad Art, with Zoltan Sepeshy & Maija Grotel; Detroit Soc Arts & Crafts, with John Foster; Wayne State Univ, MA(art hist). *Work:* Detroit Inst Arts, Cranbrook Acad Art Mus, Detroit Pub Libr & Wayne State Univ, Detroit; Evansville Mus Arts & Sci, Ind. *Comn:* 32 calligraphic panels on wood, 11 calligraphic lecterns & 1 large calligraphic quotation (with Christopher Bostick), Cath Cemeteries of Chicago for Resurrection Mausoleum, Justice, Ill, 71; 6 large acrylic paintings on architectural roots of Mich Nat Corp Hq Bldg, 90. *Exhib:* Exhib Mich Artists, Detroit Inst Arts, 36-63; Pepsi-Cola Exhib, 45; Scarab Club Gold Medal Exhib, 47-90; Mich Watercolor Soc, 48-90; one-man exhib, Arwin Galleries, 67 & 75. *Pos:* Typographer & graphic designer, Evans-Winter-Hebb, Detroit, 36-37; exec secy, Founders Soc, Detroit Inst Arts, 46-60, adminr & secy, 46-76; ed, Midwest Mus Quart, 59-60. *Teaching:* Instr drawing, Wayne State Univ, 46-47; instr calligraphy, Detroit Soc Arts & Crafts Art Sch, 61-63; instr hist of the book, Wayne State Univ Grad Sch, 62-67; instr calligraphy & art hist, Grosse Pointe War Mem & Edison Inst, 73-86 & Ctr Creative Studies, Detroit, 86-90. *Awards:* Scarab Gold Medal, Scarab Club Detroit, 62, 68 & 79; Knight, Order of Italy

Solidarity; Chevalier, French Order of Arts & Lett. *Mem:* Scarab Club Detroit; Mich Watercolor Soc (cofounder); Soc Scribes; Am Asn Mus; Mich Asn Calligraphers. *Media:* Watercolor, Acrylic. *Publ:* Illusr, Many a Watchful Night, 45; auth & illusr, England Under GI's Reign, 46; illusr, The Mysteries of Blair House, 48; auth, A Guide to the Guarding of Cultural Property, UNESCO, 77; auth & publ, A Manual on the Acquiring of a Beautiful and Legible Handwriting, 77, rev ed, 80 & Calligraphy for Kids, 91, La Stampa Calligrafica. *Mailing Add:* 23350 Old Orchard Trail Bingham Farms MI 48025

BOSZIN, ANDREW
PAINTER, SCULPTOR
b Pilis, Hungary, May 5, 23; Can & UK citizen. *Study:* House Creation, Independent Sch Art; Col Art. *Work:* Musee des Beaux Arts, Budapest, Hungary; Scottish Camp Asn, Edinburgh, Scotland; Sculptors Soc Can, Toronto; Pa State Univ, Fayette Campus, Uniontown; British Mus, London; and others. *Exhib:* One-man shows, Old Nat Gallery, Budapest, Hungary, 48, J B Aird Gallery, Toronto, 90; Hungarian Graphics, Nat Mus Art, Stockholm, 48; London Group, British Royal Soc Art, London, 64; Hungarian Art Fedn, House Congress, Washington, DC, 70-75; Canadian Medal Exhib, Public Archive, Ottawa, 72; Sculpture Biennale, Budapest, 84; Homage to Dante, Dante Mus, Verona, Italy, 86-88; Contemp Canadian Art, Ernst Mus, Budapest; Challenge & Tradition, Sculp Soc Show, John B Aird Gallery, Toronto, 88. *Awards:* Grand Prix De Penture, Prix De Nat, 64; Honor Award, Spanish Medalist Asn, 68; Best Watercolor, Cosmopoliton Club, 81; Sculptors' Soc Can Medal Award, 85. *Bibliog:* Mikos Rajnai (auth), Endre Boszin, Woodstock Gallery, London, 59; Ian Ferguston (auth), Endre Boszin, Douglass Foulis, Edinburgh, 64; Tamas Tuz (auth), Endre Boszin, Kronika, Toronto, 79. *Mem:* Sculptors Soc Can (pres, 71-73, 79-83). *Media:* Cast Aluminum; Oil, Watercolor. *Publ:* Auth, A I Botar, Studio All, Toronto, Can, 92. *Mailing Add:* 39 Gilgorm Rd Toronto ON M5N 2M4 Canada

BOTERF, CHECK (CHESTER ARTHUR)
PAINTER, LECTURER
b Ft Scott, Kans, Apr 27, 34. *Study:* Univ Kans, BA, 59; Art Student League; Hunter Col, 63-64; Columbia Univ, MFA, 65. *Work:* Mus Mod Art, Chase Manhattan Bank, Columbia Univ, Fordham Univ, Rockefeller Univ & AT&T Corp, New York; Larry Aldrich Mus, Ridgefield, Conn; Des Moines Art Ctr, Iowa; and others. *Exhib:* Solo exhibs, Tibor De Nagy Gallery, New York, 67, 68 & 70, Rice Univ, 74 & John Bernard Myers Gallery, New York, 71, 73 & 74; Indianapolis Mus Art, Inc, 68-69; Finch Col, 71; Recent Acquisitions, Mus Mod Art, New York, 71; Sewall Art Gallery, Houston, Tex, 86 & 88. *Teaching:* Lectr design & drawing, Hunter Col, 65-71; Brooklyn Mus Art Sch, 73; vis assoc prof fine arts, Rice Univ, Houston, 73-75, assoc prof art, 76-, chmn art & art hist, 79-82. *Media:* Acrylic. *Mailing Add:* 46 MacDougal St New York NY 10012

BOTERO, FERNANDO
SCULPTOR
b Medellin, Colombia, 1932. *Study:* Acad San Fernando, Spain, 53; Prado Mus, Madrid, 54; Univ Florence, Italy, art hist with Roberto Longhi. *Work:* Mus d'Arte Mod del Vaticano, Rome; Mus de Arte Contemp, Madrid; Mus de Arte Mod, Bogota, Colombia; Mus Mod Art, Metrop Mus Art, New York; Guggenheim Mus, New York; Smithsonian Inst, Washington, DC; Ateneumin Taidemuseo, Helsinki, Finland; Museo de Bellas Artes, Caracas; Milwaukee Art Mus, Wis. *Exhib:* Solo Exhibs, Botero: Antologica 1949-1991, Palazzo delle Fesposizioni, Rome, Italy, Sculpture and Drawing, Marlborough Fine Art Ltd, Tokyo, 91, Fernando Botero in Monte Carlo, Marisa del Re Gallery, Monaco, Botero, Seville, Spain, Malerei, Zeichnungen und Skulpturen, Kunst Haus Wien, Vienna, Austria, Botero Sculpture, Champs-Elysées, Paris & Botero: La Corrida, Galeries Nationales du Grand Palais, Paris, 92; Latinoamerica España, Quintana Fine Art, New York at Salon de Mars, Paris, 90; Dibujos, Galeria Alfred Wild, Bogota, Colombia, 90; Marlborough en Pelaires, Centre Cultural Contemporani Pelaires, Palma de Mallorca, 90; Long Island Collects: The Figure & Landscape 1870's-1980's, Nassau Co Mus Art, Roslyn Harbor, NY, 90; Maestros Colombianos, Colombian Ctr, New York, 91. *Bibliog:* Giorgio Soavi (auth), Botero, Milan: Fabbri Editori, 88; José Manuel Caballero Bonald (auth), Botero: The Bullfight, Rizzoli, New York, 90; Mario Vargas Llosa (auth), Botero: Dessins et Aquarelles, Editions de la Difference. *Publ:* Auth, Esta Noche Con Usted, Interview by Maria Elvira Salazar, Telemundo TV, USA, 7/27/88 & 9/24/88. *Mailing Add:* c/o Marlborough Gallery 40 W 57th St New York NY 10019

BOTHMER, BERNARD V
HISTORIAN, INSTRUCTOR
b Ger, Oct 13, 12; US citizen. *Collections Arranged:* Egyptian Sculpture of the Late Period, 700 BC to AD 100 (auth, catalog),60; Akhenaten and Nefertiti, 73; Africa in Antiquity: The Arts of Ancient Nubia and the Sudan, 78. *Pos:* From asst to asst cur, Dept Egyptian Art, Mus Fine Arts, Boston, 46-56; assoc cur ancient art, Brooklyn Mus, 56-64, cur ancient art, 64-72, cur Egyptian & class art, 73-77, chmn dept Egyptian & class art, 78-82. *Teaching:* Adj prof fine arts, Grad Sch Arts & Sci, NY Univ, 60-78; prof fine arts, Inst Fine Arts, 79-82; Lila Acheson Wallace Prof Ancient Egyptian Art, 82- *Mem:* Am Res Ctr in Egypt; Egypt Explor Soc; Archaeol Inst Am; Col Art Asn Am; Int Coun Mus; Int Asn Egyptologists; Am Asn Mus. *Res:* Ancient Egyptian portraiture, Egyptian sculpture of the late period. *Publ:* Coauth, The Pomerance Collection of Ancient Art, 66; ed, Wibour monographs, Vol I-VIII, 68-83; coauth, Brief guide, Dept Ancient Art, Brooklyn Mus, 70 & 74; The Luxor Museum of Ancient Egyptian Art (catalog), 79, Ger ed, 81, Fr ed, 85 & Arabic ed, 87. *Mailing Add:* c/o NY Univ Inst Fine Arts One E 78th St New York NY 10021

BOTHMER, DIETRICH FELIX VON
CURATOR, EDUCATOR
b Eisenach, Ger, Oct 26, 18; US citizen. *Study:* Friedrich Wilhelm Univ, Berlin, Ger; Oxford Univ, dipl(class archaeol); Univ Chicago; Univ Calif, PhD. *Pos:* Asst cur, Dept Greek & Roman Art, Metrop Mus Art, 46-51, assoc cur, 51-59, cur, 59-73, chmn, 73-90, dist res cur, 90- *Teaching:* Adj prof Greek art, Inst Fine Arts, NY Univ, 65- *Awards:* Guggenheim Fel, 67. *Mem:* Archaeol Inst Am; Soc Promotion Hellenic Studies; Vereinigung der Freunde antiker Kunst; Deutsches Archaeol Inst; Acad Inscriptions & Belle-Lettres. *Res:* Greek and Roman art and archaeology. *Publ:* Auth, Ancient Art from New York Private Collections, 60; coauth, An Inquiry into the Forgery of the Etruscan Terracotta Warriors, 61; auth, Corpus Vasorum Antiquorum USA, Fascicule 12, 63, Fascicule 16, 76; Greek Vase Painting, 72; Greek Art of the Aegean Islands, 79; and others. *Mailing Add:* 401 Centre Island Oyster Bay NY 11771

BOTT, H(ARVEY) J(OHN)
SCULPTOR, PAINTER
b Greeley, Colo, Dec 28, 33. *Study:* Art Ctr Sch Los Angeles; Inst Fine Arts, NY Univ; Art Students League; Kunstakademie-Dusseldorf & Bamberg, Ger, MBK, 55. *Work:* Rice Univ; New Orleans Mus Art; San Antonio Art Mus; Denver Art Mus; Bekersfield Art Mus, Calif; and others. *Exhib:* Solo exhibs, Works, San Jose, Calif, 77, Contemp Arts Ctr, New Orleans, La, 85, Ga Southern Univ, Statesboro, 89; The Robot Exhibit, Contemp Arts Mus, Houston, Tex, 85; Madison Art Ctr, Wis, 85; Crocker Art Mus, Sacramento, Calif, 86; group exhibs, Texas Art Celebration, Houston, Tex, 89, Condeso-Lawler Gallery, New York, 90 & Galerie Muhlenbusch-Winklemann, Dusseldorf, Ger, 90-92; and many others. *Pos:* Artist in residence, Loft-on-Strand, Galveston, Tex, 69-78. *Awards:* Plastik Reisestipeduim, Museen der Stadt Koln, Ger, 56; Premier Les Plus Sculpture, Prix de Paris, France, 65; and many others. *Bibliog:* Robert M Murdock & Richard Van Buren (coauths), The Drawings & Sculpture of H J Bott, pvt publ, 2/77; Charlotte Mosher (auth), Squaring off, Art News, 4/77; Joe Cain (auth), H J Bott monochromes at Charlton, Art Voices, 12/78. *Media:* All. *Publ:* Auth, ROBOTT Opera: A Time-warp Newscast, Univ St Thomas, Houston, 83. *Dealer:* Margaret Deats 719 Leverkuhn St Houston TX 77007. *Mailing Add:* 4006 Barnes St Houston TX 77007-5706

BOTT, JOHN
PAINTER, CRITIC
b Gassaway, WVa, Sept 12, 36. *Study:* Troy State Univ, BS, 61; Univ NC, Chapel Hill, MFA, 69. *Work:* Witherspoon Gallery, Univ NC, Greensboro; NH Comn Arts, Concord; New Harmony Gallery Contemp Art, Ind; Bank NH, Concord; Chrystler Mus, Norfork, Va. *Comn:* Mural, Thoren Mus, Petersburg, Ind, 76-77; paintings, Highwood Building, Tewskbury, Mass. *Exhib:* Solo exhibs, Davidson Col, NC, 70 & Vanderbilt Univ, Nashville, 74; New Eng Contemp Artist, Center Arts, Nashua, NH, 87-88; New Harmony Gallery Contemp Art, Ind, 88; McGowan Fine Art, Concord, NH, 91; Diana Levine Fine Art, Boston, Mass, 92; and others. *Pos:* NH revs ed, Art New England, Boston, 84-86. *Teaching:* Prof painting, Greensboro Col, NC, 69-72 & Univ Evansville, Ind, 72-76; prof & chmn dept, Colby-Sawyer Col, New London, NH, 77- *Awards:* Burlington Industs Award, Guilford Co Exhib, 71; Excellence Award, 30th Wabash Valley, 74 & Hoffman Award, 33rd Wabash Valley, 77, Sheldon Swope Gallery. *Bibliog:* Margo Clark (auth), New England contemporary art, Art New Eng, 12-1/88. *Publ:* Paul Pollaro (exhib catalog), Phillips Exeter Sch & Lamont Gallery, 88. *Dealer:* New Harmony Gallery Contemp Art New Harmony IN; Mary McGowan Fine Arts Concord NH. *Mailing Add:* Dept Art Colby-Sawyer Col New London NH 03257

BOTT, MARGARET DEATS See Deats, Margaret

BOTT, PATRICIA ALLEN
PAINTER, ART CRITIC
b Old Lyme, Conn. *Study:* With George Burr & Malcolm Fraser; Art Students League, with Ivan Olinsky & Harry Sternberg. *Work:* Greenville Mus Art, SC; Hickory Mus Art, NC; Bronx Zoo Galleries, New York; Riveredge Found, Calgary; EAfrican Wildlife Soc, Nairobi, Africa. *Exhib:* Soc Animal Artists Travel & Ann Shows, New York, 55-; Grand Cent Art Galleries, New York, 65-; one-man shows, African Wildlife, Hilton Galleries, Nairobi, 70, EAfrican Wildlife Galleries, Nairobi, 71-72; Adler Fine Arts, Inc, New York, 78. *Pos:* Dir, Burr Galleries, New York, 50-61; art reviewer, Host, 56-, Villager, 56-70 & Pendulum, 59-; secy & sales, Salmagundi Club, 62-66; sales, Grand Cent Art Galleries, New York, 66-77; rep, Adler Fine Arts Inc, New York, currently. *Awards:* Am Vet Soc Artists Award; Best Show Medal, 69 & Medal, 70, Gotham Painters. *Bibliog:* Articles, The Standard, 71 & Christian Sci Monitor, 71. *Mem:* Hon mem Soc Animal Artists; Am Artists Prof League; Nat Asn Women Artists; Salmagundi Club; Catharine Lorillard Wolfe Club (bd, 79). *Media:* Oil, Watercolor. *Dealer:* Adler Gallery of Fine Arts 21 E 67th St New York NY 10021. *Mailing Add:* 151 Carroll St Bronx NY 10464

BOTTINI, DAVID M
SCULPTOR
b Santa Clara, Calif, June 1, 45. *Study:* Calif State Univ, San Jose, BA, 69, MA, 70. *Work:* De Saisset Mus, Univ Santa Clara; Oakland Mus; Calif State Univ, San Jose; San Jose City Col Permanent Collection. *Comn:* Sculptures, M & M Robert Bernard, Lafayette, Calif, 70, Oakland Mus, 74 & IBM, San Jose, Calif, 86. *Exhib:* One-man shows, Oakland Mus, 76, Reed Col Art Gallery, 77, Walnut Creek Civic Arts Ctr, 82, Fresno Art Ctr, 83, Triton Mus, 83 & Gallery Paule Anglim, 83, 84, & 86; Roy Boyd Gallery, Los Angeles, 84; Museo Italo-Americano, San Francisco, Calif, 86. *Teaching:* Instr, Calif

State, San Jose, 77-78, State, Fresno, 83-86. *Awards:* Contemp Art Comt Ann Artist Award, Oakland, Mus, 75; KQED Channel 9 Special Art Award, 75; James Phelan Award Sculpture, San Francisco Found, 82; and others. *Bibliog:* Alfred Frankenstein (auth), article, 77 & Allan Temko (auth), article, 82, San Francisco Chronicle; Frank Cebulski (auth), Artweek, 81. *Media:* Steel, Bronze. *Mailing Add:* Dept Art Calif State Univ Fresno CA 93740

BOTWINICK, MICHAEL
ADMINISTRATOR, PUBLISHER
b New York, NY, Nov 14, 43. *Study:* Rutgers Col, BA, 64; Columbia Univ, MA, 67. *Collections Arranged:* Coordr exhib, The Year 1200, Metrop Art Mus, NY, 69-70 & Masterpieces of 50 Centuries, 71. *Pos:* Asst cur, Medieval Art & the Cloisters, Metrop Mus Art, New York, 69, assoc cur, 70, asst cur in chief, 70-71; asst dir art, Philadelphia Mus Art, 71-74; dir, Brooklyn Mus, 74-82; dir, Corcoran Gallery Art, 82-86; sr vpres, Kroenier Monnaco, 86-88; pres, Fine Art Group, 88- *Teaching:* Instr, Columbia Univ, New York, 68-69 & City Univ New York, 69. *Awards:* Order of Leopold II, Belgian Govt, 80; Royal Order of Polar Star, Swedish Govt, 83. *Mem:* Am Asn Mus; Int Coun Mus; Col Art Asn; Asn Art Mus Dirs. *Mailing Add:* Newport Harbor Art Mus 850 San Clemente Dr Newport Beach CA 92660

BOUCHARD, PAUL E
PAINTER
b Providence, RI, Sept 26, 46. *Study:* Calif State Univ, Long Beach, BFA, 78. *Work:* Munic Collection, Beverly Hills, Calif; Art Mus, Calif State Univ, Long Beach; Coos Art Mus, Coos Bay, Ore; Viet Nam Vet Mus Art, Dural, NSW, Australia; US State Dept, Washington, DC. *Exhib:* Artists You Should Know, Los Angeles Art Asn, Calif, 87; Healing the Wounds, Chapman Col, Orange, Calif, 88; Mixing It Up, Coos Art Mus, Ore, 88; one-man shows, Dreams of Ancient Answers, Franklin Furnace, New York, 89, Univ SDak, Vermillion, 91, Calif Brand Munic Gallery, Glendale, 92, Chabot Col, Hayward, Calif, Human Condition, Eastern Wash Univ, Cheney, Wash, 92, Viet Nam Vets, Carriage House Art Ctr, Sydney, Australia, 92. *Awards:* Contribs to the Arts, Torrance, Calif, 85. *Bibliog:* Laurel Darrow (auth), Oh Say Can You See, Grants Pass Daily Courier 4/3/87; Russ Leadbrand (auth), Art Matters, The Cambrian, 10/21/87; Keith Dilis (auth), Art, San Louis Obispo Telegram Tribune, 10/31/87. *Media:* Miscellaneous Media, Watercolor. *Dealer:* Aquarious Gallery Cambria CA. *Mailing Add:* 31712-2A Suite 2 Casino Drive Lake Elsinore CA 92330

BOUCHER, TANIA KUNSKY
PAINTER, SCULPTOR
b Vilno, Russia, Feb 17, 27; US citizen. *Study:* City Col New York, BS; Univ Pa, MS; Univ Del, BA; study with Tom Bostelle. *Exhib:* Aeolian Palace Gallery, 78, 81, 90; Balto Art Mus, 88-89; Station Gallery, 89 & 92; Univ Del, Newark, 92; Hotel Dupont Gallery, Wilmington, 92; and others. *Pos:* Dir, Aeolian Palace Gallery, Pocopson, Pa, 75-85; ed, Aeolian Palace Press, 76- *Teaching:* Art instr, Westtown Friends Sch, Pa, 64-69; art teacher, West Chester Adult Night Sch, 70-72. *Awards:* First Drawing Award, Chester Co Art Asn, 67; First Painting Award, Del Art Mus, 68; Judges Award, Old York Rd Art Guild, 69. *Bibliog:* Warren Hope (auth), article in Wilmington News J, 4/23/78; Gordon Roehrs (auth), Daily Local News, West Chester, Pa, 4/29/78; Clint Collins (auth), biographical article, Delaware Today Mag, 9/81; Kerin Magill (auth), An exhibit of masks which reveal not conceal, Daily Local News, West Chester, Pa, 10/87; James G Blaine (auth), Boucher's mask's, The Kennett Paper, Pa 3/89. *Media:* Oil, Bronze. *Specialty:* Contemporary painting & sculpture. *Mailing Add:* Box 188 Mendenhall PA 19357

BOUCKAERT, HARM J G
ART DEALER
b Maastricht, Neth, June 7, 34; US citizen. *Study:* Neth Col Representation Abroad, BBA, 53. *Pos:* Owner, Harm Bouckaert Gallery Corp, 87. *Bibliog:* Articles, Venture Mag, 12/82 & Art Economist 5/31/82. *Specialty:* Contemporary American art. *Mailing Add:* 90 Fulton St New York NY 10038

BOUDREAU, ANNE MARIE
COLLAGE ARTIST, ADMINISTRATOR
b New Orleans, La, Oct 29, 59. *Study:* Univ Southwestern La, BFA, 84. *Exhib:* Solo exhib, La Art & Sci Ctr, Baton Rouge, 92. *Pos:* Asst to the dir, Univ Art Mus, Lafayette, La, 88-90; dir, Baton Rouge Gallery Inc, La, 90- *Media:* Collage. *Mailing Add:* 361 Ogden Dr Baton Rouge LA 70806

BOULDIN, MARSHALL JONES, III
PAINTER
b Dundee, Miss, Sept 6, 23. *Study:* Art Inst Chicago, 41-43; Belhaven Col, Jackson, Miss, Hon PhD Fine Arts, 72. *Work:* US House of Representatives, Washington; Fla State Capitol, Tallahassee; Sam J Ervin Mus, Morgantown, NC; Am Univ, Washington, DC; Mississippi State Capitol, Jackson. *Comn:* Portrait, children of Pres Richard Nixon, Republican Women, Washington, DC, 70; Sen Sam Ervin, NC Bar Assn, Charlotte, 74; Sen John Stennis, Miss State Univ Libr, Starkville, 77; Rep Claude Pepper, US House of Representatives, Washington, DC, 85. *Exhib:* One-man shows, Brooks Mus Art, Memphis, Tenn, 68, Lauren rodgers Mus, Laurel, Miss, 72, Fine Arts Mus of South, Mobile, Ala, 74, Mary Buie Mus Univ Miss, Oxford, 89, Miss Educ & Dev Ctr, Jackson, 89; Royal Soc British Artists, The Mall Galleries, London, England, 87, 88 & 89; Royal Soc of Portrait Painters, The Mall Galleries, London, England, 88, 89 & 90. *Bibliog:* Robert Thomas Jr (auth), His Portraits have Cachet in the South, The New York Times, 70; Jane Mortimer (auth), Protrait of a New Master, Miss Mag, 85; Stacy Doolittle (dir), Marshall Bouldin: A Delta Portrait (film), Miss Educ Television, 89. *Mem:* Nat Arts Club; Copley Soc Boston; Miss Inst Arts & Letters. *Media:* Oil. *Dealer:* Portraits Inc 985 Park Avenue New York NY 10028; Portrait Brokers of America 36B Church St Birmingham AL 35213. *Mailing Add:* 2500 Friars Point Rd Clarksdale MS 38614

BOURDEAU, ROBERT CHARLES
PHOTOGRAPHER
b Kingston, Ont, Nov 14, 31. *Study:* Univ Toronto; Queens Univ, Kingston, Ont. *Work:* Nat Gallery Can; Nat Film Board Can, Pub Arch Can, Ottawa; Smithsonian Inst; Mus d'art Contemp, Montreal. *Exhib:* Light 7, Hayden Gallery, 68; two-man exhib, New England Sch Photog, Cambridge, Mass, 75; Nat Gallery Can, 75; one-man exhib, Int Ctr Photog, New York, 80, Vancouver Art Gallery, 80, Art Gallery Ont, 81 & Aferimage Gallery, Dallas, 83. *Teaching:* Instr large format photog, Univ Ottawa, Ont, 80- *Bibliog:* P Cousineau (auth), The Banff Purchase, John Wiley Publ, 79; monograph, Mintmark Press, 80. *Mem:* Royal Can Acad Arts. *Dealer:* Jane Corkin Gallery 179 John St Toronto M5T 1X4 Ont. *Mailing Add:* 1462 Chomley Crescent Ottawa ON K1G 0V1 Canada

BOURDON, DAVID
ART CRITIC, WRITER
b Glendale, Calif, Oct 15, 34. *Study:* Columbia Univ, BS, 61. *Exhib:* Seoul Int Art Festival, Nat Mus Contemp Art, Korea, 90. *Pos:* Art critic, Village Voice, New York, 64-66 & 74-77; asst ed, Life Mag, New York, 66-71; assoc ed, Smithsonian Mag, Washington, DC, 72-74; art critic, Vogue, 78-81 & 83-86, sr features ed, 83-86; sr ed, Geo Mag, New York, 81-83. *Mem:* Am Sect Int Asn Art Critics (pres US section, 82-83). *Publ:* Auth, Christo, 72; Carl Andre Sculpture 1959-1977, 78; Calder: Mobilist, Ringmaster, Innovator, 80; Warhol (Abrams), 89. *Mailing Add:* 315 W 23rd St, Suite 3C New York NY 10011

BOURDON, ROBERT SLAYTON
SCULPTOR, EDUCATOR
b West Chester, Pa, Nov 13, 47. *Study:* Dartmouth Col, AB, 70; Univ Calif, Berkeley, with Harold Paris, Peter Voulkos & Robert Hudson, MA, 72. *Work:* Carnegie Inst Mus, Pittsburgh, Pa; Del Art Mus, Wilmington; Weatherspoon Art Mus, Greensboro, NC; Dartmouth Col Art Mus, Hanover, NH; Ariz State Univ Art Mus, Tempe. *Comn:* Dartmouth Col, Hanover, NH, 76; Miller Tabak Hirsch, New York, 84; Runnymeade Sculpture Farm, Woodside, Calif, 89; Mecom Sculpture Garden (50' x 50' x 9' steel & granite), Houston, Tex, 90; Univ Houston, Downtown Campus (entryway, oak & steel, 11' x 27' x 20'), Tex. *Exhib:* Trompe L'oeuil and Illusion, Boise Art Gallery, Idaho & touring, 83-85; Sculpture on The Wall, San Antonio Inst Art, Tex, 83; one-man shows, Moody Gallery, Houston, Tex, 86, 88 & 91, Roger Ramsey Gallery, Chicago, Ill, 87, Locus Gallery, St Louis, Mo, 87 & 90; Carsinart, Pennsacola Mus Art, Fla, 90; Twenty Years Later, Jaffe-Friede Gallery, Dartmouth Col, Hanover, NH, 91; Creative Partners, Sewall Art Gallery, Rice Univ, Houston, Tex, 91. *Collections Arranged:* Soul Series--Harold Paris, Dartmouth Col, 72; Drawings from New England Private Collections, Dartmouth Col, 73; Art of Caneroons, Dartmouth Col, 73; Wood Works (auth, catalog), touring exhib, 73-74. *Pos:* Head art sch, Wanganui, NZ, 93. *Teaching:* Asst prof sculpture, Univ Ky, Lexington, 79-80; vis lectr sculpture & art hist, Univ Calif, Santa Barbara, 81-82; asst prof, Univ Houston, 82-88, assoc prof, 88- *Awards:* Wyo Council Arts Fel, State Wyo, 78; Nat Endowment Arts Fel, 79 & 86; Faculty Development Leave, Univ Houston. *Bibliog:* John R Lane (auth), article, Arts, 6/80; Charles Stuckey (contrib ed), article, Art In Am, 9/80; Harold Oleijarz (auth), article, Arts, 9/80; Dennis Adrian (auth), Wood into the 80's, 3-5, 82. *Mem:* Col Art Asn; Brooklyn Waterfront Artist Asn; Santa Barbara Arts Forum. *Media:* Wood. *Dealer:* Allan Stone Gallery New York NY. *Mailing Add:* Dept Art Univ Houston Univ Park 4800 Calhoun Houston TX 77204-4893

BOURGEOIS, DOUGLAS
PAINTER
b Gonzales, La, Aug 31, 51. *Study:* La State Univ, Baton Rouge, BFA, 74. *Work:* Southeastern Ctr for Contemp Art, Winston-Salem, NC; Nat Mus Am Art, Washington, DC; Virlane Found, New Orleans, La; Life Equitable, New York; Morris Mus Art, Augusta, Ga. *Exhib:* A New Quarter--Contemporary New Orleans Artists, Lauren Rogers Libr & Mus Art, Laurel, Miss, 83; Gallery Review: New Orleans, Pensacola Mus Art, Pensacola, Fla, 86; Fine Arts Mus of the South, Mobile, Ala, 84; Boxes, Southeastern Ctr Contemp Art, Winston Salem, NC, 85, Elvis, 87, SECCA 7 Eleven, 88; 1986 New Orleans Triennial, New Orleans Mus Art, La, 86; Visionary Imagists, Contemp Arts Ctr, New Orleans, La, 90. *Awards:* Visual Arts Fel; SECCA/RJR Indiv Arts Fel, Southeast 7, 87; La Div Arts Fel, 92. *Bibliog:* Roger Green (auth), Ten for the 90's, Art News, 90. *Media:* Oil. *Dealer:* Arthur Roger Gallery 136 Prince St New York NY 10012. *Mailing Add:* c/o Arthur Roger Gallery 432 Julia St New Orleans LA 70130

BOURGEOIS, LOUISE
SCULPTOR
b Paris, France, Dec 25, 11; US citizen. *Study:* Lycee Fenelon, Paris, Baccalaureate, 32; Sorbonne, 32-35; Ecole du Louvre, 36-37; Acad Beaux-Arts, 36-38; Acad Grande Chaumiere, 37-38; Atelier Fernand Leger, 38, Vaclav Vytlacil, 39-40; numerous hon degrees from US univs, 77-87. *Work:* Mus Mod Art, Whitney Mus Am Art, Metrop Mus Art, New York; NY Univ; Albright-Knox Art Gallery, Buffalo, NY; Denver Art Mus, Colo; Musee d'Art Moderne, Paris; Storm King Art Ctr, Mountainville, NY. *Exhib:* The New American Painting & Sculpture, The First Generation, Mus Mod Art, 69; Whitney Biennial, 73; one-man exhibs, Hamilton Gallery Contemp Art,

New York, 78, Xavier Fourcade Inc, New York, 78-79, Univ Calif, 79, Laguna Gloria Art Mus, Austin, Tex, 88, Kroller-Muller Mus, Otterlo, The Netherlands, 89, Robert Miller Gallery, New York, 91 & Parrish Art Mus, Southampton, NY, 92; Perspective 78, Albright Col, 78; Hidden Desires, State Univ NY, Purchase, 80; Casting: A Survey of Cast Metal Sculpture in the 80's, Fuller Goldeen Gallery, San Francisco, 82; Correspondences: New York Choice 84, Laforet Mus Tokyo, 84; Individual: A Selected History of Contemporary Art 1945-1986, Los Angeles Mus Contemp Art, 86-; Carl Schlosberg Fine Arts, Sherman Oaks, Calif, 88; Whitney Mus Art, New York, 89; Museum Ludwig, Cologne, WGer, 89; Milwaukee Art Mus, Wis, 90; Mus Fine Arts, Boston, Mass, 90; Mus Mod Art, New York, 90-92; Solomon R Guggenheim Mus, New York, 92; other shows. *Teaching:* Instr sculpture, Pratt Inst, 64-65; instr sculpture, Brooklyn Col, 63 & 68; field fac sculpture, Goddard Col, 71; instr, Cooper Union, New York, 78-79. *Awards:* Award for Distinction in Sculpture, Sculpture Ctr, New York, 90; Lifetime Achievement Award (first recipient), Int Sculpture Ctr, Washington, DC, 91; Grand Prix National de Sculpture, French Ministry of Culture, 91. *Bibliog:* Brigid Grauman (auth), Hoots for Mr Hoet's huge festival of art that's hot, Wall Street Journal, 7/14/92; Michael Kimmelman (auth), After many a summer, a sculptor comes of age, New York Times, sect 2, p 1, 27, 8/30/92, reprinted International Herald Tribune, p16, 9/1/92; Keith Steward (auth), Psycho: Kunst Hall, Art forum, 9/92. *Mem:* Am Abstract Artists; fel Am Acad Art & Sci, Boston; Am Acad & Inst Arts & Letts, New York. *Media:* Mixed. *Publ:* Auth, Sculpture of the 80's (video), Business Arts Inc, 91. *Mailing Add:* 347 W 20th St New York NY 10011

BOUTIS, TOM
PAINTER, PRINTMAKER
b New York, NY, Aug 25, 22. *Study:* Cooper Union, New York, BFA, 48; Skowhegan Sch Painting & Sculpture, summer 51; Cooper Union, hon BS. *Work:* Art Inst Chicago: CIBA-Geigy Collection, Ardsley, NY; Canton Art Inst, Ohio; Colby Col; Everson Mus, Syracuse, NY; Russell Sage Col, Albany NY; St Michaels Hosp, Newark, NJ; Atlanta Univ, New Orleans, La; Billard Univ, New Orleans, La. *Comn:* Drawings, New York Hilton Collection Am Art, 62. *Exhib:* One-man shows, Landmark Gallery, New York, 73, 75 & 77; Drawings Exhib, Uffizzi Mus, Florence, Italy, 57; Selected Painters of Soho, Lehigh Univ Mus, 74; CIBA-Geigy Collection, Summit Art Mus, NJ, 74; Gathering of the Avant Garde, Kenkeleba, New York, 88; and others. *Teaching:* Artist in residence painting, Summer Art Prog, Cooper Union, 69. *Awards:* Mark Rothko Found, 76; Nat Endowment for the Arts, 76; Adolphe Esther Gotleib Found Grant, 83; Am Acad Art Inst, 88-90; Rockefeller Found, Bellagio, Italy, 89. *Media:* Monoprints, Oils; Collage. *Mailing Add:* 162 E 82nd St New York NY 10028

BOVA, JOE
SCULPTOR, CERAMIST
b Houston, Tex, June 1, 41. *Study:* Univ Houston, BFA, 67; Univ NMex, MA, 69. *Work:* Greenville Co Mus, SC; State of Tenn, Tenn Art Comn, Nashville; State of La, Old State Capitol Galleries, Baton Rouge; Miami Univ Gallerie, Oxford, Ohio; McAllen Mus, Tex. *Exhib:* Young Americans, 69 & The Great American Foot, 78, Mus of Contemp Crafts, New York; 7th-10th Ann Piedmont Crafts, Mint Mus, Charlotte, NC, 69-72; 12th Midwest Biennial, Joslyn Mus of Art, Omaha, 71; Artists of the Southeast & Tex, New Orleans Mus of Art, 72; 35 Artists of the Southeast, High Mus of Art, Atlanta, 77; Objects of Play, Pa State Univ, 78; 36th Ann Scripps Invitational, Claremont, Calif, 80. *Teaching:* Asst prof design & ceramics, Nicholls State Univ, Thibodaux, 69-71; assoc prof ceramics & sculpture, La State Univ, Baton Rouge, 71; instr ceramics, Penland Sch of Crafts, 74 & 77. *Bibliog:* Jacob Eleasari (auth), Clay artists, Eleasari & Hahn Films, Nashville, 75; Paul Donhauser (auth), History of American Ceramics, Kendall/Hunt, Dubuque, Iowa, 78. *Mem:* Am Crafts Coun; Nat Coun Educ Ceramic Arts; La Crafts Coun. *Dealer:* Bienville Gallery 1800 Hastings Pl New Orleans LA 70130. *Mailing Add:* Sch Art Rm 528 Ohio Univ Athens OH 45701

BOVE, RICHARD
PAINTER, EDUCATOR
b Brooklyn, NY, Oct 21, 20. *Study:* Pratt Inst, BFA; Art Students League; Brera Acad, Milan, Italy. *Exhib:* Am Acad Design, New York; Philadelphia Mus Art; Corcoran Gallery Art, Washington, DC; Whitney Mus Art & Metrop Mus Art, New York. *Teaching:* Instr painting, Art Students League, 55-65; chmn dept painting, Pratt Inst, 70-74, prof painting, Grad Sch, 73- *Awards:* Nat Acad Design Award; Louis Comfort Tiffany Found Award; Fulbright Fel, Italy. *Media:* Concrete, Plastics. *Mailing Add:* Dept Art Pratt Inst Brooklyn NY 11205

BOWATER, MARIAN
ART DEALER, COLLECTOR
b Emmons, Minn, Sept 5, 24. *Study:* Gustavous Adolphus Col. *Pos:* Owner, Bowater Gallery. *Specialty:* Late 19th & 20th century American paintings, Calif. *Collection:* American impressionists and English Old Masters, Calif. *Mailing Add:* 1168 Wales Place Cardiff-by-the-Sea CA 92007

BOWEN, CONSTANCE LEE
ART DEALER, CONSULTANT
b Ann Arbor, Mich, July 12, 52. *Study:* Northern Ill Univ, BA(art hist), 74; Univ Ill, MA(art hist), 78 & cert mus studies, 79; Ind Univ, MBA, 84. *Collections Arranged:* Henry Holmes Smith: Non-Camera Photographer (auth, catalog), Ind Univ Art Mus, 82; Dedication Exhibition: Selections from the Permanent Collection, 85 & Contemporary Virginia Woman Artists, 85, Sweet Briar Col Art Gallery; A Tribute to Alma Eikerman, Master Craftsman (auth, catalog), Ind Univ Art Mus, 85. *Pos:* Cur 19th & 20th century art, Ind Univ Art Mus, Bloomington, 79-83; dir, Sweet Briar Col Art Gallery, 84-86 & Francis Chapin estate collection, 90-; assoc dir art, Josyln Art Mus, Omaha, Nebr, 86-87; pvt art dealer, Chicago, 88- *Mem:* Am Asn Mus. *Res:* 19th and 20th century European and American art. *Publ:* Auth, Henry Holmes Smith: Non Camera Photographer, Ind Univ Art Mus dedication exhib, 82; A Tribute to Alma Eikerman: Master Craftsman, 85, Ind Univ Art Mus, Bloomington. *Mailing Add:* 813 Meadow Lane Barrington IL 60010

BOWEN, PAUL
SCULPTOR
b Wales, Brit, July 12, 51. *Study:* Chester Sch Art, 68-69; Newport Col Art, Wales, diploma, 69-72; Md Inst Col Art, Baltimore, MFA, 72-74. *Work:* Solomon R Guggenheim Mus, New York; Welsh Arts Coun, Cardiff, Wales; Provincetown Art Asn & Mus, Mass. *Exhib:* Innovations in Contemporary Sculpture, Aldrich Mus, Ridgefield, Conn, 88; one man shows, Mus Contemp Art, Ghent, Belgium, 89, Saidye Bronfman Ctr, Montreal, Can, 90. *Awards:* Welsh Arts Coun Award to Artists, 78; Mass Artists Found Fel, 81; Pollock-Krasner Found Grant, 87. *Bibliog:* Ann Wilson Lloyd (auth), Artifacts Reborn, Contemporanea, 10/89; Eleanor Heartney (auth), Paul Bowen, Kunst Nu, 10/89; Alfred MacAdam (auth), The Never Ending Chain - Paul Bowen, Tema Celeste, spring 90. *Media:* Mixed. *Dealer:* Jack Shainman Gallery 560 Broadway New York NY 10012. *Mailing Add:* Box 301 Provincetown MA 02657

BOWEN-FORBES, JORGE C
PAINTER
b Georgetown, Guyana, May 16, 37. *Work:* Nat Collection, Georgetown, Guyana; El Paso Mus Art, Tex; Kindercare Corp & Sellers Investment Corp, Montgomery, Ala; McCreary Cummings Fine Art Collection, Washington, Iowa. *Exhib:* Nat Sun Carnival, El Paso Mus, Tex, 74; Am Watercolor Soc, 74, 75, 77 & 84; Allied Artists of Am, Nat Acad, 75; African/American Art of 80's, Mus African Arts, Buffalo, NY, 82. *Pos:* Art dir, Bridgetown, Barbados. *Teaching:* Burrowes Sch Art, Guyana. *Awards:* Gold Medal of Honor, Allied Artists of Am, 75; High Winds Medal, Am Watercolor Soc; Gold Medal of Honor, Knickerbocker Artists, 78. *Mem:* Nat Watercolor Soc; Am Watercolor Soc; Nat Soc Painters in Casein & Acrylics; Audobon Artists Am; Knickerbocker Artists. *Media:* Watercolor. *Publ:* Am Artist Mag, 85; Splash 2, Am Contemp Watercolors, 92. *Dealer:* Leon Loard Gallery 2781 Zelda Rd Montgomery Al 36106. *Mailing Add:* PO Box 1821 Oakland CA 94612

BOWER, GARY DAVID
PAINTER
b Dayton, Ohio, May 10, 40. *Study:* Ohio State Univ, BA(philos), 62 & MFA(painting), 65. *Work:* Whitney Mus Am Art, New York; Allen Art Mus, Oberlin, Ohio; Akron Art Inst; Dayton Art Inst; Walker Art Ctr, Minneapolis; Cincinnati Art Mus, Ohio. *Exhib:* Four Painters, Leo Castelli Warehouse Gallery, New York, 69; Whitney Mus Ann, 70; one-man shows, O K Harris Gallery, New York, 69 & 72, Univ Ky, 71, Akron Art Inst, 72 & Edward Thorp Gallery, New York, 84, Cleveland Ctr Contemp Art, 88. *Teaching:* Staff critic painting, Dept Educ, Whitney Mus Am Art, 68-74; lectr painting, State Univ NY, 85- *Awards:* James Broadus Award, Chicago Art Inst, 67; Achievement in Painting, Ohio State Fair, 70; Grant, Nat Endowment Arts, 82. *Bibliog:* Carter Ratcliff (auth), Gary Bower at the New Gallery, Art Am, 5-6/78; Robert Berlind (auth), Gary Bower at Max Protech, Art Am, 1/81; Michael Klein (auth), Gary Bower, Arts, 5/82; and others. *Media:* Oil & Acrylic on Canvas. *Mailing Add:* 709 Xenia Ave Yellow Springs NY 45387

BOWES, BETTY MILLER
PAINTER, CONSULTANT
b Philadelphia, Pa. *Study:* Moore Col Art; Univ Pa; George W Elkins Europ Fel. *Work:* Philadelphia Mus Art, Pa Acad Fine Arts, Philadelphia; Reading Mus, Pa; Nat Acad Design, New York; Univ Southern Calif, Los Angeles. *Comn:* Maquette for tapestry, Sun Oil Co Inc, Radnor, Pa, 76 & comn by Mr & Mrs Harvey Stack, New York, 78. *Exhib:* Am Watercolor Soc, Nat Acad, New York, 58-79; Philadelphia Art Festival, Philadelphia Mus, 65; one-man shows, Reading Mus, Pa, 69 & Lehigh Mem Gallery, Bethlehem, 70; Nat Acad Ann, New York, 70-; Del Mus Ann, Wilmington Soc Fine Arts, 71; Pa Acad Fine Arts Ann, Philadelphia. *Pos:* Art consult, Sun Oil Co Inc, Radnor, 75- *Awards:* Bronze Medal, 75 & 77, Silver Medal, 79 & Gold Medal of Honor, 85, Am Watercolor Soc. *Bibliog:* Norman Kent (auth), 100 Watercolor Techniques, 68, Wendon Blake (auth), Complete Guide to Acrylic Painting, 71 & Edward Betts (auth), Creative Landscape Painting, 78, Watson-Guptill. *Mem:* Am Watercolor Soc; Nat Acad Design; Philadelphia Art Alliance; Philadelphia Watercolor Club; Audubon Artists. *Media:* Acrylic. *Dealer:* Newman & Saunders Gallieres Wayne PA. *Mailing Add:* 301 McClenaghan Mill Rd Wynnewood PA 19096

BOWIE, EFFIE BELLE
PAINTER, PRINTMAKER
b Chattanooga, Tenn, Jul 1, 09. *Study:* Univ Chattanooga, Tenn; Tex State Univ, Denton, BA, 30; TC Columbia Univ, New York, MA, 33. *Work:* 1980 US Air Force Art Collection, Washington, DC. *Comn:* Painting & 2 stained glass windows, Methodist Church, Hixson, Tenn, 54. *Exhib:* Art Students League Gallery, New York, 76; Burr Artists Group, Metrop Mus Art, New York, 77; Nat Arts Club, Gregg Gallery, 77; US Air Force Exhib, Soc Illusr, New York, 80; Nat Arts Club, New York, 82; UNICEF, United Nations Mus, New York, 87, 88, 89. *Teaching:* Supervisor art, 5 public schs, Norfolk, Va, 31-33, East Tex State, Commerce, 38-39 & West Tex State, Canyon, Tex. *Awards:* Photography Awards, Chattanooga, Tenn, 43. *Mem:* Art Students League (life mem); Burr Artist (mem bd); Composers, Authors & Artists of America (corresp bd secy); Soc of Illustrs; The Pen Woman, Nat League of Am Pen Women (vpres). *Media:* Oil. *Mailing Add:* 152 E 94th St 12A New York NY 10128

BOWIE, WILLIAM
SCULPTOR
b Youngstown, Ohio, Feb 15, 26. *Study:* Youngstown Univ; Bethany Col. *Work:* New York Bank Savings; Globe-Wernicke Showroom, New York; Hertz Skyctr Airport, Huntsville, Ala; Brown & Williamson Tobacco Corp, Louisville, Ky; Glass Container Div, Owens-Ill, Scarsdale, NY. *Comn:* Exec off, Am Brands, Inc, New York; Brooklyn Col Student Ctr; Honeywell, Inc, Framingham, Mass; Irving Trust Co, Caracas, Venezuela, Frankel Rare Book Room, Univ Houston Libr. *Exhib:* Meltzer Gallery; George Jensen's; Am House; Sculpture Exhib, Butler Inst Am Art, 65; For Your Home, Krannert Art Mus, Univ Ill; Symposium 66, Purdue Univ, 66; plus many others. *Pos:* Judge Sculpture Exhib, Butler Inst Am Art, 66. *Awards:* Purchase Award, Sculpture Exhib, Butler Inst Am Art, 65; Good Design Award, Purdue Univ, 66; spec award outstanding merit in craftsmanship, Artist-Craftsmen New York. *Media:* Metal. *Mailing Add:* 441 Lafayette St New York NY 10003

BOWLER, JOSEPH, JR
PAINTER, ILLUSTRATOR
b Forest Hills, NY, Sept 4, 28. *Study:* Charles E Cooper Studios, New York; Art Students League. *Work:* Sanford Low, Hartford Mus; Soc of Illusrs, Mus Am Illus; US Air Force. *Comn:* Portraits, Rose Kennedy, Rose Kennedy Wing, Albert Einstein Hosp, 71, Gen DeGaulle, Time cover, Julie & David Eisenhower, Saturday Evening Post cover, Dr Peter LaMotte, Hilton Head Hosp, 75, Mr & Mrs Frank E Fowler, Lookout Mountain, Tenn, 76, 80 & 84, Dwight Holder, 76 & 86 & Jack Nicklaus, Melrose Club, 87. *Exhib:* Ann Exhib of Published Work for 1977, Soc Illusr, 78. *Teaching:* Instr painting, Parsons Sch Design, New York, 68-72; instr, MFA Independent Study Degree Prog, Syracuse Univ, 80- *Awards:* Artist of Yr, Artists' Guild New York, 67; Elected to the Illustr Hall of Fame, 92. *Bibliog:* Cory SerVaas (auth), Artist in the White House, Saturday Evening Post, summer 72; Joe Bowler--Artist Illustrator (film), & Arts the Thing Joe Bowler--Portraits (film), SCE-TV; Artist Joe Bowler, Southern Accents, winter 82. *Mem:* Soc Illusr. *Media:* Oil. *Publ:* Portraits, The Artists Mag, 9/88. *Mailing Add:* Nine Baynard Cove Rd Hilton Head Island SC 29928

BOWLES, MARIANNE VON RECKLINGHAUSEN See Recklinghausen, Marianne von

BOWLING, FRANK
PAINTER
b Bartica, Guyana, Feb 29, 36; US & Guyanese citizen. *Study:* Slade Sch Fine Art, Univ London; ARCA. *Work:* Contemp Art Soc, Tate Gallery, London; NJ State Mus, Trenton; Mus Mod Art, Whitney Mus, New York; Mus Fine Arts, Boston; and others. *Exhib:* Whitney Ann, 69-72; Artist Immigrants to Am 1876-1976, Hirshhorn Mus, Washington, DC; solo exhibs, Whitney Mus Am Art, 71 & Tibor de Nagy Gallery, New York, 75, 76, 79, 80 & 82; Currier Gallery Art, Manchester, NH, 82; Art Ctr Hargate, St Pauls Sch, Concord, NH, 82; Heckscher Mus, Huntington, NY, 82; Kresge Art Ctr Gallery, Mich State Univ, 82. *Awards:* Guggenheim Fel, 67 & 73; Creative Artists Pub Serv Award, 75; Arts Coun Gt Brit Award, 77. *Media:* Acrylic, Oil. *Dealer:* Tibor de Nagy Gallery 29 W 57th St New York NY 10019. *Mailing Add:* c/o Tibor de Nagy Gallery 41 W 57th St New York NY 10019

BOWLING, GARY ROBERT
PAINTER
b Lamar, Mo, Feb 1, 48. *Study:* Mo Southern State Col, BS(art educ), 70, Univ Ark, Fayetteville, MFA, 74. *Work:* Sheldon Mem Art Gallery, Lincoln, Nebr; Mitchell Art Mus, Mt Vernon, Ill; Sioux City Art Ctr, Iowa; Johnson Co Community Col, Kans; Iowa State Univ, Ames; Univ Mo, Columbia; Univ Iowa, Iowa City. *Comn:* Paintings, Northwestern Life Insurance, Minneapolis, Minn, Iowa State Gateway Ctr, Ames, Norwest Bank, Hopkins, Minn, Fairview-Southdale Hosp, Minneapolis; McDonald's Hamb Univ, Chicago; N Lake Shore Hyatt, Chicago; Farm Bureau Hdq, Des Moines, Iowa. *Exhib:* Am Art: The Challenge of the Land, Pillsbury, Minneapolis, 81; Air, Earth & In-between, Sioux City Art Ctr, Iowa, 83; Prairie Vistas, Joslin Art Mus, Omaha, Nebr, 86; Of Vapor & Denser Surfaces, Mitchell Art Mus, Mt Vernon, Ill, 87; Contemp Landscape, Inst Creative Arts, Fairfield, Iowa, 87; Brunnier Art Mus, Ames, Iowa, 88; Mid Am Landscape, SW Minn, St Univ, Marshall, 89; New Masters, Huntington Mus Art, WVA, 92. *Teaching:* Instr painting & drawing, Univ Ark, Fayetteville, 74; chmn art dept, Westmar Col, Le Mars, Iowa, 74-83. *Bibliog:* John Couper (auth), A sense of place, Joplin Mag, 86; C Butler et al (auths), Of Vapor & Denser Surfaces, (exhib catalog), Mitchell Mus, 87; Mark Stegmaier, Gary Bowling, Am Artist Mag, 88. *Mem:* Yaddo Fel. *Media:* Oil, Watercolor. *Dealer:* Groveland Gallery 25 Groveland Terr Minneapolis MN 55403; Olson-Larson Gallery 203 5th St W Des Moines IA 50265. *Mailing Add:* PO Box 207 Lamar MO 64759

BOWLING, KATHERINE
PAINTER
b Washington, DC, 1955. *Study:* Va Commonwealth Univ, BFA, 78. *Work:* Metrop Mus Art, New York. *Exhib:* One-woman shows, Rosa Eastman Gallery, New York, 87 & 89, Albright-Knox Mem Gallery, Buffalo, NY, 88, Blum Helman, Los Angeles, 90 & New York, 90 & 92; Paula Cooper Gallery, New York, 90; Blum Helman, New York, 91 & 92; Hood Mus Art, Hanover, Mass, 92; Transamerica Pyramid Lobby Gallery, San Francisco, 92. *Awards:* Grant, Nat Endowment Arts, 91. *Bibliog:* Nancy Grimes (auth), Artnews, 151, 1/91; Gerrit Henry (auth), Katherine Bowling at Blum Helman, Art in Am, 134-135, 3/91; Edith Newhall (auth), Galleries, New York, 73-74, 9/92. *Dealer:* Blum Helman Gallery Inc 20 W 57th St New York NY 10019. *Mailing Add:* 529 E Sixth St Apt 1-C New York NY 10009

BOWLT, JOHN
ART HISTORIAN, EDUCATOR
b London, Eng, Dec 6, 43. *Study:* Univ Birmingham, Eng, BA, 65 & MA, 66; Moscow Univ, USSR, 66-68; Univ St Andrews, Scotland, PhD, 71. *Pos:* Dir, Inst of Modern Russian Cult, 79- *Teaching:* Lectr Russian, Univ St Andrews, Scotland, 68-69; asst prof Russian, Univ Kans, Lawrence, 70-71; prof Russian art & lang, Univ Tex, Austin, 71-88 & Univ Southern Calif, Los Angeles, 88-; prof Russian art & lang, Univ Southern Calif, Los Angeles, Calif. *Awards:* Brit Coun Scholar for Moscow Univ, USSR, 66-68; Woodrow Wilson Nat Fel, 71; Fel Nat Humanities Inst, Yale Univ, 77-78; Fulbright-Hays Award to France, 81; Internat Res & Exchanges Bd, 86, 88, 90. *Mem:* Am Asn Advan Slavic Studies. *Res:* Russian art and architecture of 18th, 19th and 20th centuries. *Publ:* Auth, The Russian Avant-garde, Theory & Criticism 1902-34, Viking, 76; translr, Benedikt Livshits: The One-and a Half-Eyed Archer, 77; auth, The Silver Age, 79; auth, Scenic Innovation-Russian Stage Design 1900-1930, 82; coauth, Pvel Filonov: A Hero and His Fate, 83; coauth, Ciurlionis, 86. *Mailing Add:* Dept of Slavic Lang Univ Southern Calif Los Angeles CA 90081-4353

BOWMAN, BRUCE
PAINTER, ART WRITER
b Dayton, Ohio, Nov 23, 38. *Study:* San Diego City Col, Calif, AA; Calif State Univ, Los Angeles, BA & MA; Univ Calif, Los Angeles. *Exhib:* Cypress Col, Calif, 77; Designs Recycled Gallery, Fullerton, Calif, 77; Pierce Col, Los Angeles, 78; Pepperdine Univ, Malibu, 78; Leopold-Gold Gallery, Santa Monica, 80-81. *Teaching:* Instr art, West Los Angeles Col, Culver City, 69-83, chmn art dept, 75-76, 83; instr art, Cypress Col, 76-77. *Media:* Acrylic. *Res:* Contemporary art forms and techniques. *Publ:* Auth, articles in Arts & Activities Mag, Design Mag & Sch Arts Mag; Shaped Canvas, 76 & Toothpick Sculpture & Ice Cream Stick Art, 76, Sterling; Ideas: How to Get Them, R & E Publ, 85. *Dealer:* The Options Gallery 2665 Shell Beach Rd Shell Beach CA 93449. *Mailing Add:* 28322 Rey De Copas Malibu CA 90265

BOWMAN, GEORGE LEO
PAINTER
b Newburyport, Mass, Dec 25, 35. *Study:* Boston Sch Mus Fine Arts, 60; Tufts Univ, Medford, Mass, BS, 60. *Work:* Harvard Univ, Brookline, Mass; Va Mortgage Co, Norfolk; Honeywell Corp, Minn. *Exhib:* Adelson Gallery, 70-72, Copley Soc, 70-73, Boston, Mass; Grand Cent Gallery, New York, 73-76; Rockport Art Asn, Mass, 74-82; Joseph Kilbridge Gallery, Groton, Mass, 89. *Pos:* Asst art dir, DC Heath Publ Co, Boston, Mass, 63-67; illusr & designer, ASEC, Burlington, Mass, 78-92. *Teaching:* Instr design & drawing, Boston Sch Mus Fine Arts, 63-70. *Awards:* Nat Casein Show Painting Award, New York; Aldro Hibbard Painting Award, Rockport Art Asn, Mass; Copley Soc Painting Award, Boston, Mass. *Media:* Oil. *Publ:* New York Life Calender, 80-81. *Mailing Add:* 3 Old Homestead Rd Westford MA 01886

BOWMAN, JEFF RAY
EDUCATOR, ADMINISTRATOR
b Oneida, Ky, Sept 5, 43. *Study:* Eastern Ky Univ, AB, 65; Ball State Univ, MA, 69, EdD(art, admin, coun psychol), 71; Yale Univ, 77. *Teaching:* Art instr, Jackson Co Sch Syst, McKee, Ky, 65-66; asst & doctoral fel, Dept Art & Teachers Col, Ball State Univ, 68-71; prog chmn art educ, Univ Houston, 71-74; guest lectr, Art & Pub Sch Groups, Tex & Miss, 73-75; prof art, Univ Southern Miss, 74-, chmn dept, 74-82. *Awards:* Nat Endowment for Humanities Award, 77. *Mem:* Nat Art Educ Asn; Ky Guild Artists & Craftsmen; Hattiesburg Civic Asn; Tex Art Educ Asn; Miss Alliance for Arts Educ. *Publ:* Coauth, Parochial Education Within the Diocese of Fort Wayne-South Bend, Ind, Phase I, Educ Serv Assocs, Muncie, 70; auth, Meeting the needs, Art Teacher, fall 74; auth, The spirit of the mountains, Southern Quart, 1/78; plus many others. *Mailing Add:* Dept Art Univ Southern Miss Hattiesburg MS 39406

BOWMAN, JOHN
PAINTER
b Sayre, Pa, 1953. *Study:* Rutgers Univ, BFA, 76. *Exhib:* Solo exhibs, Nine Gallery, New York, 83, White Columns & Virtual Garrison Gallery, New York, 84, Holly Solomon Gallery, New York, 85, 86, 87 & 89 & Jon Oulman Gallery, Minneapolis, Minn, 88; Petits Tableaux, Galerie Charles Cartwright, Paris, France, 86; Interiors, Proctor Art Ctr, Bard Col, Annandale-on-Hudson, 88; The Silent Baroque (with catalog), Galerie Thaddaeus Ropac, Salzburg, Austria, 89; Romance & Irony (traveling exhib), Mus Western Australia, Perth, Sydney, Australia, Auckland, NZ & Tampa, Fla, 90; Fernando Alcolea, Barcelona, Spain, 90. *Bibliog:* Richard Martin (auth), Fictions, Arts, 2/88; Eleanor Heartney (auth), Review: Fictions, Artnews, 2/88; Kim Levin (auth), Choices: Dwelling, Village Voice, 1/3/89. *Mailing Add:* c/o Johnathan O'Hara Fine Art 41 E 57th St 13th floor New York NY 10022

BOWMAN, KEN
PAINTER
b Denver, Colo, Mar 28, 37. *Study:* Univ Colo; Art Inst Chicago, BFA, 63. *Work:* Utah Mus Fine Arts, Salt Lake City; Univ Art Mus, Berkeley, Calif; Denver Art Mus. *Exhib:* One-man exhibs, Tibor de Nagy Gallery, Inc, New York, 70-71, 73 & 79; Art on Paper, Weatherspoon Gallery, Univ NC, 71; 3rd Biennial Art, Medellin, Colombia, SAm, 72; Painting and Sculpture Today 1972, Indianapolis Mus Art, Ind, 72; 100 Artists 100 Yrs, Art Inst Chicago, 80. *Teaching:* Instr painting, Black Hawk Sch Art, Colo, summers. *Media:* Acrylic Polymer, Collage. *Mailing Add:* 3115 W 25th Ave Denver CO 80211

BOWMAN, RICHARD
PAINTER
b Rockford, Ill, Mar 15, 18. *Study:* Art Inst Chicago, Ryerson Traveling Fel, 38-42; Univ Iowa, MFA, 49. *Work:* San Francisco Mus Art; Oakland Mus; Stanford Univ; Univ Tex Mus; Santa Barbara Art Mus; Recent Acquisitions, Mus Am Art, New Britain, Conn; plus others. *Exhib:* Retrospectives, Stanford Univ, 56 & San Francisco Mus Art, 61; Whitney Mus Am Art, 62; solo exhib, San Francisco Mus Art, 70; Roswell Mus & Art Ctr, NMex, 72; Gerard Schriener Gallery, Basel, Switz, 79; Retrospective Exhib, Harcourts Gallery, San Francisco, Calif, 86; Inner Visions (17 Am painters) UCLA Wight Gallery, 86; Mus Contemp Art, New Delhi, India, 87; and others. *Awards:* Prizes, Montreal, 52 & Winnipeg Art Gallery, 53; Artist in Residence Grant Painting, Roswell Mus & Art Ctr, 72; plus others. *Media:* Acrylic, Fluorescent Oil. *Dealer:* Harcourts Gallery 460 Bush St San Francisco CA 94108. *Mailing Add:* 178 Springdale Way Redwood City CA 94062

BOWMAN, RUTH
ART HISTORIAN, CRITIC
b Denver, Colo, June 14, 23. *Study:* Bryn Mawr Col, AB, 44; NY Univ Inst Fine Arts, MA, 71; Rockefeller Found Sr Fel, Metrop Mus Art, 76. *Collections Arranged:* The New York Painter, A Century of Teaching: From Morse to Hofmann, Marlborough-Gerson Gallery, 67; A University Collects (tour with Am Fedn Arts), 65-68; Murals Without Walls, Newark Airport Murals of Arshile Gorky, Newark Mus, 78-79; Am Fedn Arts tour six mus, 79-80. *Pos:* Asst cur, Jewish Mus, 62-63; cur & dir, NY Univ Art Collection, 63-74; dir educ, Los Angeles Co Mus Art, 74-75 79-82; art commentator, KUSC/fm, Los Angeles, 79-84. *Teaching:* Adj asst prof art hist, Sch Continuing Educ, NY Univ, 65-70 & Sch Educ, 68-73; lectr art, Mus Mod Art, New York, 64-71, Washington Sq Col, 72-73 (Sunrise Semester-CBS); mus training, art hist courses, lectrs radio & TV, New York & Los Angeles; visiting lectr, Univ Cal, Santa Barbara, spring 86. *Mem:* Am Asn Mus (vpres, 76-79); Am Fedn Arts (bd trustees); Col Art Asn; Asn Int des Critiques d'Art (AICA). *Res:* 19th and 20th century American and European art and architecture. *Mailing Add:* 200 E 66th St Apt B2101 New York NY 10021

BOWNE, JAMES DEHART
MUSEUM DIRECTOR, ART HISTORIAN
b Philadelphia, Pa, Mar 5, 40. *Study:* George Washington Univ; Corcoran Sch Art; Sandhills Community Col, Southern Pines, NC, AA, 68; ECarolina Univ, Greenville, NC, AB, 70; Univ NC, Chapel Hill, MA, 72. *Collections Arranged:* Reflections of Our Heritage--The Art of the American Indian, 76, 20th Century German Expressionist Prints, 76, Collectors Choice Exhibition, 76 & Annual Wabash Valley Exhib, 77, Sheldon Swope Art Gallery, Terre Haute, Ind; and many others. *Pos:* Dir & cur, Lauren Rogers Libr & Mus Art, 73-75; dir, Sheldon Swope Art Gallery, 75-78; dir, Everhart Mus, 78-81; exec dir, Greenville Co Mus Art, 81- *Teaching:* Instr drawing/painting, Lauren Rogers Libr & Mus of Art, Laurel, Miss, 73-75. *Mem:* Am Asn Mus; Col Art Asn; Assoc Coun Arts; Southeast Mus Conf; SC Fedn Mus; and others. *Res:* Reception of German expressionism in America between the World Wars. *Publ:* Contribr, A Medieval Treasury From Southeastern Collections, Univ NC, Chapel Hill, 71. *Mailing Add:* 726 Wynsom Dr SE Huntsville AL 35803-2049

BOWRON, EDGAR PETERS
ADMINISTRATOR, HISTORIAN
b Birmingham, Ala, May 27, 43. *Study:* Colgate Univ, AB, 65; Inst Fine Arts, NY Univ, MA, 69, PhD, 79. *Exhib:* A Scholar Collects: Selections from the Anthony Morris Clark Bequest, Philadelphia Mus Art, 80-81; Pompeo Batoni (1708-87), Colnaghi, New York, 82; Pompeo Batoni and His British Patrons, The Iveagh Bequest, Kenwood, London, 82; Modern Art from the Pulitzer Collection: 50 Years of Connoisseurship, Fogg Art Mus, Cambridge & The St Louis Art Mus, 88; A Prosperous Past: The Sumptuous Still Life in the Netherlands, 1600-1700, Fogg Art Mus, 88; The Maurice Wertheim Collection and Other Impressionist and Post-Impressionist Paintings and Drawings from the Fogg Art Mus, Tokyo & Yamaguchi, 90. *Pos:* Educ lectr, Metrop Mus Art, 68-70; registr, Minneapolis Inst Arts, 70-73; cur Renaissance & baroque art, Walters Art Gallery, 73-78; cur Renaissance & baroque art & admin asst to dir, Nelson Gallery-Atkins Mus, Kansas City, Mo, 78-81; dir, NC Mus Art, 81-85; Elizabeth and John Moors Cabot dir & prof fine arts, Harvard Univ Art Mus, 85-90; trustee, Asn Art Mus Dirs, 87-90 & Mus Fine Arts, Boston, 88-90; Andrew W Mellon Senior Consultative Cur, Nat Gallery Art, Washington, DC, 91- *Awards:* Nat Endowment Arts Fel, 75-76; Am Acad Rome Grant, 79-85; Award for Pompeo Batoni monogr, Col Art Asn, 84. *Mem:* Col Art Asn Am; Am Soc Eighteenth Century Studies; Master Drawings Asn (bd dir, 87-). *Res:* Italian painting, 16th, 17th and 18th centuries. *Publ:* Auth, Pompeo Batoni, (1708-1787), 82; Pompeo Batoni and His British Patrons, 82; ed, The North Carolina Museum of Art: Introduction to the Collections, 83; Pompeo Batoni, A Complete Catalogue of His Works, Anthony M Clark (auth), 85; auth, European Paintings before 1900 in the Fogg Art Mus, A Summary Illustrated Catalog, Cambridge, 90; and others. *Mailing Add:* 114 W 29th St New York NY 10001

BOXER, STANLEY (ROBERT)
PAINTER, SCULPTOR
b New York, NY, June 26, 26. *Study:* Brooklyn Col; Art Student League. *Work:* Whitney Mus, Guggenheim Mus, Mus Mod Art, New York; Boston Mus Fine Arts; Corcoran Gallery Art; Houston Mus Fine Arts, Tex; Walker Art Mus, Minneapolis, Minn; Santa Barbara Mus Art, Calif; Albright-Knox Mus, Buffalo; Metrop Mus Art. *Exhib:* Pa Acad Fine Arts, Philadelphia, 76, Boston Mus Fine Arts & Edmonton Art Gallery, 77, Monotypes 1980's, Smith Anderson Gallery, Palo Alto, Calif & Hokin Kaufman Gallery, Chicago, Ill, 92; retrospectives, Mint Mus Art, Charlotte, NC, 78, Hunter Mus Art, Chattanooga, Tenn, 79, Dorsky Gallery, New York, 91, Rose Art Mus, Brandeis Univ, Waltham, Mass, 92; One Over One, Riverside Art Mus, Calif, 91; Table Sculpture, Andre Emmerich Gallery, New York, 91; Academy-Institute Invitational Exhibition of Painting and Sculpture, Am Acad & Inst Arts & Letters, New York, 91. *Teaching:* Instr, Vt Art Sch, 86. *Awards:* John S Guggenheim Mem Found Fel, 75; Visual Artists Fel Grant, Nat Endowment Arts, 89. *Bibliog:* Jeanette Ross (auth), rev, Art week, 5/90; James Poel (auth), rev, The Milwaukee J, 7/15/90; Donald Kuspit (auth), Stanley Boxer at Andre Emmerich Gallery, Artforum, p 102, 3/92. *Publ:* Auth, articles, Tyler Graphics, Smith Anderson Ed, and others. *Dealer:* Andre Emmerich Gallery 41 E 57 St New York NY 10022; Meredith Long & Co 2323 San Felipe Rd Houston TX 77019. *Mailing Add:* 46 Foxhill Rd Ancramdale NY 12503

BOYCE, GERALD G
EDUCATOR, PAINTER
b Embarrass, Wis, Dec 29, 25. *Study:* Univ Wis, Milwaukee, BS; Milwaukee Art Inst; Am Guatemalan Inst, Guatemala City; Univ Iowa, MFA; Univ Ill; study & res, Brit Mus & Courtauld Inst, London; Worcester Col, Oxford Univ, Eng, 79. *Work:* DePauw Univ; Ball State Univ; Univ Iowa; Swope Art Mus; Univ Indianapolis; and others. *Exhib:* Los Angeles Co Mus; San Francisco Mus Art; Art Inst Chicago, 54; Mus Mod Art, New York, 56; Corcoran Gallery Art, Washington, DC, 71; Mus Contemp Crafts, New York. *Pos:* Consult, Ind Bell Tel Co, 67-70; consult, US Post Off Dept, 72 & Smithsonian Inst; mem, Gov Comn on the Arts, Ind. *Teaching:* Prof art hist & studio, Univ Indianapolis, 50-; lectr art hist, DePauw Univ, 68-, Wabash Col & St John's Univ, 89; prof emer, Univ Indianapolis, 88. *Awards:* First Prizes, Ind Artists Club, St John's Univ Nat & Minot Col Show, 71; Purchase Award, Clayfest, 91. *Mem:* Nat Col Art Conf; Am Crafts Coun; Nat Conf Art Adminr. *Media:* Mixed Media. *Mailing Add:* RR1 Box 230 Morgantown IN 46160

BOYD, JAMES HENDERSON
PRINTMAKER, SCULPTOR
b Ottawa, Ont, Dec 16, 28. *Study:* Art Students League, with Will Barnet; Nat Acad Design; Contemporaries Graphic Workshop, with M Ponce de Leon. *Work:* Nat Gallery Can, Ottawa; Mus Mod Art, New York; Victoria & Albert Mus, London; Lugano Art Mus; Sorsbie Art Gallery, Nairobi, SAfrica; Mus Contemp Art, Skopje, Yugoslavia. *Comn:* Carved doors, Centennial Libr, Campbellton, NB, 67 & 72; carved doors, Pub Serv Alliance Bldg, Ottawa, 69; entrance sculpture, Can Pavilion, Osaka World's Fair, 70; mural, MacDonald Bldg, Univ Ottawa, 73. *Exhib:* Cincinnati Biennial Prints, 62; 1st Biennial Prints, Santiago, Chile, 63; 8th Int Black & White Exhib, 64; Tokyo Biennial Prints, 64; Centennial Art Exhib, Toronto, 67; 18th Int Biennial Graphicart, Ljublijana, Yoguslavia, 89; Biennial of Humour & Satire, Gabrovo, Bulgaria, 89. *Pos:* Hon cur, Univ Western Ont, 67-69; adv, Visual Arts Ottawa, 74-; exec part-time prof union, Univ Ohio, 92. *Teaching:* Resident artist, Univ Western Ont, 67-69; prof printmaking, Ont Col Art, 71-, head dept, 70-71; prof painting, Munic Art Ctr, Ottawa, 70-72; prof visual arts dept, Univ Ottawa, 73- *Awards:* Purchase Award, 8th Int Black & White Exhib, 64; First Prize, 1st Nat Print Exhib, Burnaby, BC; Venezuela Prize, Best Foreign Artist, 2nd Biennial Prints, Santiago, Chile, 65. *Mem:* Fel & life mem Int Inst Arts & Lett; Royal Canadian Acad. *Mailing Add:* Box 2400 Station D Ottawa ON K1P 5W5 Canada

BOYD, JOHN DAVID
EDUCATOR, PRINTMAKER
b London, Ark, Jan 22, 39. *Study:* Calif State Univ, Long Beach, with Richard Swift, BA; Cranbrook Acad Art, with Lawrence Barker, MFA. *Work:* Tex Tech Univ; Ga State Univ; Univ NC, Chapel Hill; State Univ NY Col Potsdam; Springfield Art Mus, Mo. *Exhib:* 22nd Bradley Nat Print & Drawing Exhib, Bradley Univ, Peoria, Ill, 89; The Boston Printmaker 41st NAm Print Exhib, Emanuel Col, Boston, 89; Scratching the Surface, Nat Print Invitational, Visual Arts Ctr, Anchorage, Alaska, 89; Hunterdon Art Ctr 34th Nat, Payne Gallery, Morivian Col, Bethlehem, Pa, 90; Cimmaron Nat Works on Paper, Okla State Univ, Stillwater, 91; 23rd Bradley Nat Print & Drawing Exhib, Bradley Univ, Peoria, Ill, 91. *Teaching:* Prof printmaking & drawing, Wichita State Univ, 72- *Awards:* Purchase Award, Okla State Univ, Stillwater, 89; Honorable Mention, Hunterdon Art Ctr 34th Nat Morivian Col, Bethlehem, Pa, 90; Juror Award, Kans Watercolor Soc, 91. *Media:* Intaglio, Lithography. *Mailing Add:* 421 S Glenn Wichita KS 67213

BOYD, KAREN WHITE
EDUCATOR, FIBER ARTIST
b Akron, Ohio, Sept 8, 36. *Study:* Kent State Univ, BA(art educ), 58 & MA(studio art), 64; Tyler Sch Art, Temple Univ, MFA(weaving), 75. *Exhib:* Regional Craft Biennial, J B Speed Mus, Louisville, Ky, 70; Mid-States Craft Exhib, Evansville Mus, Ind, 73; Nat Fiber Design Show, Calif Polytech State Univ, San Luis Obispo, 75; 3rd Int Exhib Miniature Textiles, Brit Crafts Centre, London, 78. *Teaching:* Assoc prof weaving & textiles, Murray State Univ, 67-81, prof, 81- *Awards:* Juror's Award, Ted Hallman, Nat Fiber Design Show, 75; Honorable Mention, Southeast 80 Craft Exhib, Tallahassee, Fla. *Mem:* Ky Guild Artists & Craftsmen; Handweaver's Guild Am; Asn British Craftsmen. *Dealer:* Am Art Inc Atlanta GA. *Mailing Add:* Dept Art Murray State Univ Murray KY 42071

BOYD, LAKIN
EDUCATOR, PRINTMAKER
b Athens, Ala, Aug 27, 46. *Study:* Univ Ala, BFA, 68 & MA, 70; Pratt Graphic Ctr, 70-71, intaglio with Michael Ponce de Leon. *Work:* Oscar Wells Mem Mus, Birmingham, Ala; Univ Ala, Tuscaloosa; Ala Arts Comn; Univ

South; Pratt Graphic Ctr Print Collection, New York. *Exhib:* Nat Student Printmakers Travel Exhib, 68; 13th Dixie Ann, 72; one-man shows, Univ Ala & Judson Col, 73; 14th Ann Reece Regional, 74. *Teaching:* Asst prof graphics & art hist, Ala A&M Univ, Huntsville, 71-82. *Awards:* Purchase Award, Birmingham Art Asn, 67; Fulbright Grant to Belg & Neth, 75. *Mem:* Southeastern Col Art Conf; Am Asn Univ Prof; Nat Art Educ Asn; Am Crafts Coun; Ala Art Educ Asn. *Media:* Intaglio, Lithography. *Mailing Add:* 426 Eustis Ave SE Huntsville AL 35801

BOYD, MICHAEL
PAINTER, GRAPHIC ARTIST
b Waterloo, Iowa, Nov 27, 36. *Study:* With Philip Evergood, 57; Univ Northern Iowa, BA, 59. *Work:* Baltimore Mus Art; Albright-Knox Art Gallery, Buffalo, NY; Chrysler Mus Art, Norfolk, Va; Mint Mus Art, Charlotte, NC; Knoxville Mus Art, Knoxville, Tenn; Waterloo Mus Art, Iowa; Univ Ky Art Mus, Lexington; Robert Wood Johnson Univ Hosp, New Brunswick, NJ. *Comn:* Mural, E F MacDonald Co, Dayton, 82. *Exhib:* Art From New York, Mattingly-Baker Gallery, Dallas, 81; 101 Recent Acquisitions, Everson Mus Art, 81; Recent Acquisitions, Albright-Knox Art Gallery, 81; Recent Acquisitions, Baltimore Mus Art, 82; Ana Sklar Gallery, Miami, Fla, 84; Geometric Abstraction: Selections from a Decade, 1975-1985, Bronx Mus Art, NY, 85; J J Brookings Gallery, San Jose, Calif, 87; solo exhibs, Michael Boyd: Paintings from the 1980's, Davenport Mus Art, Iowa, Charles H MacNider Mus, Mason City, Iowa, Waterloo Munic Galleries, Iowa, 89, 90, Andre Zarre Gallery, New York, 90, Paintings by Michael Boyd: The Cathedral Series, Herbert F Johnson Mus Art, Ithaca, NY, Clinton, NY & Univ Ky Art Mus, Lexington, 91-92. *Teaching:* Prof design, Cornell Univ, 68- *Awards:* Purchase Award, Everson Mus Art, 71; Yaddo Fel, 74; NY Found Arts, 88. *Bibliog:* Pat Sloan (auth), article, Arts Mag, 79; Lawrence Campbell (auth), Michael Boyd, Art in Am, 84. *Media:* Acrylic on Canvas and Paper. *Dealer:* Andre Zarre Gallery 41 E 57th St New York NY 10022. *Mailing Add:* 78 Greene St New York NY 10012

BOYER, MARIETTA P
LIBRARIAN
b Vienna, Austria, July 26, 32; US citizen. *Study:* Wheaton Col, Norton, Mass, BA(art hist); Drexel Univ, Philadelphia, MLS. *Pos:* Photograph librn, Mus of Fine Arts, Boston, 56-61; asst, Slide Dept, Mus of Art, Philadelphia, 68-72; librn, Pa Acad of Fine Arts, 75- *Mem:* Art Librn Soc NAm; Special Librs Asn; Pa Libr Asn. *Mailing Add:* 242 Broughton Lane Villanova PA 19085

BOYLAN, JOHN LEWIS
PAINTER, PRINTMAKER
b Cleveland, Ohio, Oct 8, 21. *Study:* Oberlin Col, 39-42; Cleveland Inst Art, 42; Univ NMex, BFA, 47; Art Students League, 47-50; study with Vaclav Vytlacil, Morris Kantor, Harry Sternberg & Will Barnet. *Work:* Metrop Mus Art, New York; New York Pub Libr; Roswell Mus, NMex; Univ Pa Art Mus. *Exhib:* Soc Am Graphic Artists, 50 & 71; Royal Soc Painter-Etchers & Engravers, London, 54 & 56; solo exhib, Roswell Mus, 59 & 66; Japan Print Soc, Tokyo, 67. *Teaching:* Dir painting & design, Roswell Mus Art Sch, 50-51; instr painting & design, Inst Am Indian Art, Santa Fe, NMex, 66-, actg head fine arts, 74-75. *Awards:* Award of Merit, Am Asn State & Local Hist, 60. *Mem:* Soc Am Graphic Artists; Artists Co-op Gallery (co-dir, 75). *Media:* Oil, Acrylic; Woodcut, Metal Plate Lithograph. *Mailing Add:* 250 E Alameda Santa Fe NM 87501

BOYLE, KEITH
PAINTER, EDUCATOR
b Defiance, Ohio, Feb 15, 30. *Study:* Ringling Sch Art, Sarasota, Fla; Univ Iowa, BFA. *Work:* San Francisco Mus Art & Stanford Univ Mus, Calif; Mead Paper Corp, Atlanta, Ga; Nat Fine Arts Collection, Washington, DC; Oakland Mus, Calif; Continental Bank, Chicago. *Exhib:* Current Bay Area Art, Stanford Univ Mus, 64; The Colorists, San Francisco Mus Art, 65; Drawings by 100 American Artists, Ann Arbor, Mich, 65; A Century of California Painting, 1870-1970, 70; Looking Westward, Joslyn Art Mus, Omaha, Nebr, 70; Retrospective Exhib of Paintings: 1965-1977, San Jose Mus Art, Calif, 78; Paintings: 1983-1984, Stanford Art Gallery. *Teaching:* Prof painting & drawing, Stanford Univ, 62-88, chmn grad studio prog, 83-88. *Awards:* National Endowment Arts Grant, 81-82; Philosophy East & West Mem Trust Grant, 86. *Mailing Add:* 6285 Thompson Creek Rd Applegate OR 97530

BOYLE, (JAMES) NEIL
ILLUSTRATOR, PAINTER
b Granum, Alta, Can, Apr 5, 31. *Study:* Banff Sch Fine Art, 50; Art Ctr Col Design, BPA, 51-54; Chouinand Art Inst, 54-56. *Work:* US Air Force Hist Art Collection, Smithsonian Inst & Pentagon, Washington, DC; NASA, Cape Canaveral, Fla; Sheriff's Permanent Collection, Los Angeles, Calif. *Comn:* Heritage Garden (mosaic), Mt Sinai Cemetery, Los Angeles, Calif, 80. *Exhib:* Pepper Tree Fine Art, Pepper Tree Ranch, Santa Inez, Calif, 81-88; solo exhibs, Vancouver Jockey Club, BC, 82 & Calgary Inn, Alta, 83; AICA Show, San Dimas, Calif, 85 & 88; Western Art in the Grand Tradition, Fallbrook, Calif, 86 & 88. *Teaching:* Instr painting & sculpture, Inst Art, Calif, 86-88. *Awards:* Gold Medal, Art Dirs Club Los Angeles, 63; Best in Show, Illustration West, 75 & Life Achievement Award, 85, Soc Illusrs Los Angeles. *Bibliog:* Kay Kawolski (auth), Southwest Art, 80; John Manson (auth), Artist of the Rockies, 85; Vickie Stabik (auth), Art of the West, 88. *Mem:* Soc Illusrs Los Angeles (pres, 73, Air Force Chmn, 76); Am Indian Cowboy & Indian Artists. *Media:* Oil, Clay. *Mailing Add:* 5832 Hilltop Rd Calabasas CA 91302

BOYLE, RICHARD J
HISTORIAN, WRITER
b New York, NY, June 3, 32. *Study:* Adelphi Univ, BA; Oxford Univ, with Edgar Wind & John Pope-Hennessy; Art Student League, with Will Barnet. *Collections Arranged:* John Twachtman Retrospective, 66, Laser Light: A New Visual Art, 69, The Early Work of Paul Gauguin, 71 & Robert S Duncanson: A Centennial Exhibition, 72, Cincinnati Art Mus; American Paintings from Newport, Wichita Art Mus, 69. *Pos:* Cur, Int Art Found, Newport, RI, summer 62; dir, Middletown Fine Arts Ctr, Ohio, 63-65; cur painting, Cincinnati Art Mus, 65-73; dir, Pa Acad Fine Arts, 73-82; art comn chmn, Redevelop Authority, Philadelphia, 75-83; consult, continuing educ prog, Philadelphia Col Art, 85-86. *Teaching:* Visiting scholar, Moore Col Art, Philadelphia, 83-84; instr, Philadelphia Col Art, 84-; instr Art Hist, Tyler Sch Art, Temple Univ, 87. *Awards:* Benjamin Franklin Fel, Royal Soc of Art, London, Eng. *Mem:* Am Asn of Mus. *Res:* Late nineteenth and twentieth century painting, especially late nineteenth century American painting. *Publ:* Co-auth, Rediscovery: Thomas Cole's voyage of life, Art in Am, 67; auth, From Hiram Powers to laser light, Apollo, 71; contribr, French impressionists influence American impressionists, Lowe Art Mus, Fla, 71; contribr, Genius of American painting, Weidenfeld & Nicolson, 73; auth, American Impressionism, New York Graphic Soc, 74; John Twachtman, Watson & Guptill, 79; Auth, Philadelphia: Art Past, Art Prologue, TV doc on hist art in Philadelphia, CBS (90 min), 80; auth, John Twachtman's Gloucester Years, Twachtman in Gloucester: His Last Years, 1900-1902 (exhib catalog), IRA Spanierman Art, 87; auth, Lewis Henry Meakin: An American Landscape Painter Rediscovered, Cincinnati Art Galleries, 87; co-auth, Sunlight & Shadow: Life & Art of Willard Metcalf, 88. *Mailing Add:* 2121 Delancey Pl Philadelphia PA 19103

BOYLEN, MICHAEL EDWARD
CRAFTSMAN, ART WRITER
b Stoughton, Wis, Dec 12, 35. *Study:* Yale Univ, with Josef Albers, AB, 58; Sch Am Craftsmen, pottery with Frans Wildenhain; Univ Wis, with Harvey K Littleton, MS, MFA. *Work:* Corning Mus Glass, NY; Cleveland Mus Art, Ohio; Mus Kunst & Gewerbe, Hamburg, Ger; Victoria & Albert Mus, London; Chrysler Mus at Norfolk, Va. *Exhib:* New Am Glass, Dallas Mus Fine Arts, Tex, 67; Del Art Mus, Wilmington, 71 & 75; one-man shows, Fleming Mus, Univ Vt, Burlington, 75; Bergstrom Mus, Neenah, Wis, 76; Corning Mus Glass, NY; Mickelson Gallery, Washington, DC, 78; and others. *Teaching:* Instr ceramics, Cleveland Inst Art, Ohio, 66; lectr design & ceramics, Lyndon State Col, Lyndonville, Vt, 67-76; prof art, Marlboro Col, Vt, 80- *Awards:* L C Tiffany Found Grant, 65. *Bibliog:* Clemens Kalischer (auth), Glass--Michael Boylen, Vt Life Mag, 72; R & L Grover (auths), Contemporary Art Glass, Crown, 75; Paul Hollister (auth), Hollister on glass, Acquire, 12/76. *Mem:* Glass Art Soc; Vt Coun Arts (pres, 74-76). *Media:* Clay; Glass. *Publ:* Auth, Studio glass in perspective, Studio Potter, 73 & In: 74 Crafts Annual, NY State Craftsmen, 74; Glass of Joel Phillip Myers, 10-11/80, Malcolm Wright (ceramics), 10-11/85 & Joel Phillip Myers at Holsten Galleries, 10-11/88, Am Craft; Frans Wildenhain: master of form, Studio Potter, 6/91. *Dealer:* Azuma Gallery 50 Walker St New York NY 10013. *Mailing Add:* Dept Pottery Marlboro Col Marlboro VT 05344

BOYNTON, JACK (JAMES) W
PAINTER, PRINTMAKER
b Ft Worth, Tex, Jan 12, 28. *Study:* Tex Christian Univ, BFA & MFA. *Work:* Mus Mod Art, Solomon R Guggenheim Mus & Whitney Mus, New York; Mus Fine Arts, Houston; Los Angeles Co Mus, Calif; and others. *Comn:* Go Freedom, 2nd Liberty Gala, Houston ACLU, Equal Justice, 6th Liberty Gala & Law and Order, 7th Liberty Gala, Tex; Amarillo Art Ctr; Houston Festival 79, City of Houston. *Exhib:* Whitney Mus Am Art, 57-58 & 67-68; Los Angeles Mus Art, 69; Collections of Mus of Southwest, Washington, DC, 78; Wood in Art, Mus Fine Arts, Houston, 79; one-man show, Univ Houston, Clear Lake City, Tex, 79; retrospective, Amarillo Art Ctr, 80; and others. *Teaching:* Instr, Univ NMex, summer 63; instr, Houston Mus Sch, 68-69; instr art, Mus Fine Arts, Houston, 68-69; instr art, Univ St Thomas, Houston, formerly; Univ St Thomas, Tex, 69-70. *Awards:* Tamarind Workshop Fel, 67. *Bibliog:* Douglas MacAgy (auth), James Boynton (monogr), Barone Gallery Inc, 59. *Media:* Mixed. *Mailing Add:* 3723 Albans St Houston TX 77005

BRACH, PAUL HENRY
PAINTER
b New York, NY, Mar 13, 24. *Study:* State Univ Iowa, BFA, 48, MFA, 50. *Work:* Mus Mod Art & Whitney Mus Mod Am Art, New York; St Louis Mus; Los Angeles Co Mus of Art, Los Angeles; Phoenix Art Mus; Albuquerque Mus Fine Arts. *Exhib:* Solo retrospective, Mulvane Art Ctr, Topeka, Kans;

Leo Castelli, NY, 57 & 59; Dawn Gallery, Los Angeles, 60; Cordier, Ekstrom Gallery, NY, 62 & 64; Benson Gallery, Bridgehampton, NY, 75; Lerner Heller Gallery, NY, 78 & 80; Yares Gallery, Los Angeles, Calif, 79; Janus Gallery, Venice, Calif, 80; Yares Gallery, Scottsdale, Ariz, 80-81; Bernice Steinbaum Gallery, New York, 83, 85, 87, 90 & 92; solo exhib, Rancho Linda Vista, Anticah, Az, 92. *Pos:* Fel, Tamarind Lithog Workshop, Los Angeles, 64, Tamarina, NMex, 80 & 82; artist-in-residence, Am Fedn Arts, Albuquerque, 65. *Teaching:* Mem fac, Univ Mo, 50-51, New Sch Social Res, 52-55, NY Univ, 54-67 & 86-89, Parsons Sch Design, 56-67, Cooper Union, 60-62 & 79-82 & Cornell Univ, 65-67; chmn dept Visual Arts, Univ Calif, San Diego, 67-69; dean sch art, Calif Inst Art, 69-75; chmn div arts, Lincoln Ctr Campus, Fordham Univ, 75-79; Empire State Col, New York, 79- *Awards:* D Jerassi Grant, 89 & 91. *Bibliog:* Carol Kotrozo Donnel (auth), Art Int, 5-6/82; Susan Hellsten McGarry (auth), Southwest Art, 1/86; Vivien Raynor (auth), article, New York Times, 11/87, 7/90 & 11/90. *Publ:* Auth, John Mandel, Arts, 9/75; rev in Artforum, 10/76 & 12/78, Art in Am, 3-4/78, 1/79 & 1/84 & Art News, 1/79 & 12/85. *Dealer:* Bernice Steinbaum Gallery 132 Greene St New York NY 10012. *Mailing Add:* 393 W Broadway New York NY 10012

BRADBURY, ELLEN A
ADMINISTRATOR, EDUCATOR
b Louisville, Ky, Feb 26, 40. *Study:* Yale Univ; Univ Vienna, Austria, 60; Univ NMex, BA & MA, 66. *Collections Arranged:* African Oceanic Art, American Indians, North and South; American 20th Century, Regis Collection. *Pos:* Res asst, Minneapolis Inst Art, 69-70, asst registr, 70-72, registr, 72-75 & cur primitive art, 75-79; dir, Mus Fine Arts, Mus NMex, 79, Santa Fe Festival Arts, 82; founded, Recursos Santa Fe, 84- *Teaching:* Inst, Univ NMex, 67. *Mem:* Col Art Asn; Am Asn Mus; NMex Asn Mus; Maxwell Mus of Anthro; Nat Trust for Hist Preserv. *Res:* American Indian Ghost Dance. *Publ:* Co-auth, Moi Kavakava, Minneapolis Inst Arts Bull, Vol LX, 76-81; auth, Black Kingdoms, African Arts, 75; I Wear the Morning Star (catalog), American Indian Ghost Dance, 79; Art in Santa Fe and elsewhere, Artspace, fall 83, co-ed, Georgia O'Keeffe. *Mailing Add:* 510 Alto Santa Fe NM 87501

BRADFORD, HOWARD
PRINTMAKER, PAINTER
b Toronto, Ont, July 14, 19; US citizen. *Study:* Chouinard Art Inst, Los Angeles; Jepson Art Inst, Los Angeles; Calif Sch Fine Arts, San Francisco. *Work:* Philadelphia Mus Fine Arts; Boston Mus Fine Arts; Bibliotheque Nat France; Los Angeles Co Mus; New York Pub Libr. *Comn:* Print editions (100), Dallas Mus Fine Arts, 53, Hilton Hotel, New York, 64 & Asn Am Artists, New York, 67-69; Brentanos: Print Editions 1977-78. *Exhib:* Libr Cong Nat Print & Drawing Exhib, 51; Brooklyn Mus Print Ann, 52; Dallas Mus Fine Arts Nat Print Exhib, 53; 60 American Printmakers, US Info Serv, Europe, 56; Carmel Art Asn, Calif, 72 & 76, 80-89. *Teaching:* Instr, Jerson Art Inst, Los Angeles, 49-51; guest instr, Univ Wis, 57 & Univ Salt Lake City, 59. *Awards:* Birds by Beach (serigraph), Libr Cong, 51 & Dallas Mus Fine Arts, 53; Guggenheim Fel Creative Printmaking, 60. *Bibliog:* Who's Who in America, 88- *Mem:* Carmel Art Asn. *Media:* Silk Screen; Acrylic. *Publ:* Coauth (J Ross & C Romano), The Complete Printmaker, Free Press, NY, 72; coauth (C Zigorosser), Prints and Their Creators, Crown, 74. *Mailing Add:* 684 Alice St Monterey CA 93940

BRADLEY, DAVID P(AUL)
PAINTER, SCULPTOR
b Eureka, Calif, Mar 8, 54. *Study:* Inst Am Indian Arts, AFA, 79; Col Santa Fe, BFA, 80. *Work:* Atlantic Richfield Corp, Tucson; Inst Am Indian Arts Mus, NMex Fine Arts Mus, Santa Fe; Albuquerque Mus; Ann Maytag Found, Tesuque, NMex. *Comn:* State Arch Bldg, Santa Fe, 80. *Exhib:* Univ Minn Mus, Minneapolis, 80; Heard Mus, Phoenix, 80; Nat Mus Inst Art Am Indians, Lima, Peru, 81; Univ Calif Mus, Davis, 81; Mus SW, Midland, Tex, 81; and others. *Pos:* Bd regents, Native Am Coun Regents Inst Am Indian Arts, Santa Fe, 78-79; guest artist, Artists in Schs Program, 81-82. *Awards:* Award Merit, Minn Chippewa Tribe, 79; Fel, Southwestern Asn Indian Affairs, 80; Artist of Yr, Santa Fean Mag, 82. *Bibliog:* Jim Lenfestey (auth), American Indian artists with roots in Minnesota, Minneapolis-St Paul Mag, 7/81; Don H Jones (auth), David Bradley, artist, 8/81 & Betty Bauer (auth), Artists of the year, 1/82, Santa Fean Mag. *Media:* Acrylic; Stone, Bronze. *Dealer:* Elaine Horwitch Galleries 129 West Palace Ave Santa Fe NM 87501. *Mailing Add:* 129 W Palace Ave Santa Fe NM 87501

BRADLEY, DOROTHY
ART DEALER, PAINTER
b Wild Rose, Wis, Oct 21, 20. *Study:* Milwaukee State Teachers Col; Oshkosh State Teachers Col, cert; Layton Art Sch, Milwaukee, with Gerrit Sinclair. *Work:* Milwaukee Pub Libr, Wis. *Exhib:* Wis Painters & Sculptors, Milwaukee, 65; one-woman shows, Rahr-West Mus, Manitowoc, Wis, 71, Allis Art Libr, Milwaukee, 71, Oshkosh Pub Mus, Wis, 72 & Wustum Mus, Racine, Wis, 72. *Pos:* Dir, Bradley Galleries, Milwaukee, 60- *Media:* Watercolor. *Specialty:* Wisconsin artists and art of Haiti. *Mailing Add:* c/o Bradley Galleries 2639 N Downer Ave Milwaukee WI 53211

BRADLEY, LAUREL E
EDUCATOR, GALLERY DIRECTOR
b Santa Monica, Calif, July 6, 52. *Study:* Univ Ore, Eugene, BA, 75; Inst Fine Arts, New York Univ, MA, 78, PhD, 86. *Work:* Gallery 400, Univ Ill, Chicago. *Collections Arranged:* Bruce Charlesworth (auth, catalog), 84, The Idea of Big, 85, Ingenious Fabrications: Recent Projects From the Fabric Workshop, 85, Roland Ginzel: A Retrospective (auth, catalog), 86 & Tragic and Timeless Today: Contemporary History Painting, 87, Gallery 400, Univ Ill, Chicago. *Pos:* Dir, Gallery 400, Univ Ill, Chicago, 83-87. *Teaching:* Asst prof theory & criticism, Sch Art Inst, Chicago, 87- *Mem:* Col Art Asn. *Res:* Trends in contemporary art and architecture; Victorian art and culture. *Publ:* From Eden to Empire: John Everett Millaiss' Cherry Ripe, 179-204, winter 91; Humor in Art: Occasional Papers Ser, Mus Beloit Col, Vol 1, 49-53, 91; Millaiss' Bubbles & the Problem of Artistic Advertising, Assoc Univ Presses, forthcoming; Drawn into the Pre Raphaelite Circle: D G Rossetti's drawing of Elizabeth Siddali, forthcoming. *Mailing Add:* 304 S Taylor Ave Oak Park IL 60302

BRADLEY, WILLIAM STEVEN
MUSEUM DIRECTOR, CURATOR
b Salina, Kans, Aug 20, 49. *Study:* Univ Colo, BA, 71; Friedrich-Alexander Univ, 72; Northwestern Univ, MA, 74, PhD, 81. *Collections Arranged:* Gene Kloss: Six Decades of Printmaking, 84; Frank Reaugh: Scenes from the Texas Range, 84; Honky Tonk Visions, 86; Nine Texas Printmakers, 86; The Blue Star Exhibition: Contemporary Art in San Antonio, 86; Lin Emery/Emery Clark, 89; Kazuo Kadonaga, 90; Richard Johnson/John Scott, 91; Contemporary Art from the K & B Corp Collection, 91; Elmore Morgan Photographs, 92. *Pos:* Cur art, Tex Tech Univ Mus, 83-85; chief cur, San Antonio Mus Art, 85-86; dir, Alexandria Mus Art, 87-92 & Davenport Mus Art, 92- *Teaching:* Instr mod art, Wells Col, 79-81; lect mod art, Cornell Univ, 80-81, Univ Tex, 86-87. *Mem:* Col Art Asn; Am Asn Mus; Tex Art 150 (secy, 84-87); La Asn Mus (vpres, 88-89). *Res:* Modern European art; contemporary American art. *Publ:* Auth, Gene Kloss: Six Decades of Prints, Tex Tech Univ, 84; Emil Nolde and German Expressionism, UMI Res Press, 86; Contemporary Art in San Antonio, CASA, 86; contribr, Lynda Benglis/Keith Sonnier: A Decade of Sculpture, Alex Mus Art, 87; Ed, Emery Clark: Recent Work, Alexandria Mus Art, 89; and others. *Mailing Add:* 1737 W Twelfth St Davenport IN 52804

BRADSHAW, DOVE
PAINTER, SCULPTOR
b New York, NY, Sept 24, 49. *Study:* Boston Mus Sch Fine Arts, BFA, 73. *Work:* Metrop Mus Art, Mus Mod Art & Whitney Mus Am Art, New York; Brooklyn Mus, NY; Philadelphia Mus Art; Muestra Int de Arte Grafico, Bilbao, Spain; Piccolo Mus Novoli, Italy; Kunstmuseum, Dusseldorf, WGer; Art Inst Chicago; Le Centre Georges Pompidon, Paris; Moderna Museet, Stockholm; and others. *Comn:* Break to Activate (wall piece), PS1, Inst Art & Urban Resources, New York, 77; Dazzle Camouflage Set Design, Time and Space Theatre, New York, 83; Merce Cunningham Dance Co, 84; Native Green, Arcade, 85; Points in Space, costumes & lighting, 86, Brit Broadcasting Co, 86, Carousel, costumes & lighting, 87, Fabrications, decor & lighting, 87, The Paris Opera Ballet, 90; Cargo X, decor & lighting, 89; The Mattress Factory, Pittsburgh, Pa, 90; plain air, P S 1 Mus, Long Island Ctr, New York. *Exhib:* Couples, 78 & Sound, 79, PS1, Inst Art & Urban Resources, New York; Arteder '82, Muestra Int de Arte Grafico, 82; Awards Exhib, Am; Exhib in Honor of John Cage, Am Ctr Paris, France, 82; Wave Hill, New York; Syracuse Univ, 84 & 88; Koran-Sha Exhib, Tokyo, 85; Drawings of the 80's (from the permanent collection), Mus Mod Art, 90; The Drawing Ctr, New York; Carnegie Int, Pittsburgh, Pa; Drawings of the '90's, Katonah Mus, NY. *Pos:* Artistic adviser, Merce Cunningham Dance Co, 84- *Teaching:* Glass sculpture, Sch Visual Arts, New York, 75-81. *Awards:* Nat Endowment of the Arts, 75; Pollock-Krasner Award, 85. *Bibliog:* A piece of the Met, New York Mag, 79; Gene Moore (auth), Windows at Tiffany's: The Art of Gene Moore, Harry N Abrams, 80; Judith Collishan Van Wagner (auth), Lines of Vision, Hudson Hills Press, New York, 89; Thomas McEvilley (auth), New York reviews, Art Forum, 1/90. *Mem:* Whitney Mus Art, Paris; Art Inst Chicago; Kunsh Mus, Dusseldorf. *Media:* All. *Publ:* Fire Hose Postcard 1976-1992, Metrop Mus Art, NY. *Dealer:* Sandra Gering 476 Broome St New York NY. *Mailing Add:* 924 West End Ave New York NY 10025

BRADSHAW, GLENN RAYMOND
PAINTER, EDUCATOR
b Peoria, Ill, Mar 3, 22. *Study:* Ill State Univ, BS, 47; Univ Ill, MFA, 50. *Work:* Butler Inst Am Art, Youngstown, Ohio; Springfield Art Mus, Mo; Hollister, Inc, Libertyville, Ill; Landmark Systems Corp, Washington, DC; San Diego Mus, Calif; and others. *Exhib:* 200 Years of Watercolor Painting in America, Metrop Mus Art, New York, 66-67; Watermedia '70, Univ Colo, Boulder, 70; Watercolor USA Bicentennial, Springfield Mus Art, Mo, 76; Univ San Diego, 81; Univ Ill Fac Exhib, Nihon Univ, Tokyo, 83; Am Watercolor Soc invitational, Museo de la Acurela Mexicana, Mexico City, 89. *Teaching:* Prof art, Univ Ill, 52-86, emer prof, 86- *Awards:* Ed Whitney Prize, Am Watercolor Soc, 74; First Prize, Nat Watercolor Soc, 77; Barse Miller Mem Prize, 83; William A Paten Prize, Nat Acad Design, New York, 87. *Bibliog:* Lawrence Goldsmith (auth), Watercolor Bold & Free, Watson-Guptill, 80; Nita Leland (auth), Exploring Color, North Light, 85; Val Thelin (auth), Let the Medium Do It, Watson Guptill, 88. *Mem:* Am Watercolor Soc; Nat Watercolor Soc; Nat Soc Painters in Casein & Acrylic; Rocky Mountain Nat Watermedia Soc; assoc Nat Acad Design. *Media:* Watercolor, Collage. *Dealer:* Neville-Sargent Gallery 708 N Wells St Chicago IL 60610. *Mailing Add:* 906 Sunnycrest St Urbana IL 61801

BRADSHAW, LAWRENCE JAMES
EDUCATOR, PAINTER
b St Paul, Kans, Sept 21, 45. *Study:* Pittsburg State Univ, Kans, BFA, with Reed Schmickle, Bert Keeney, Alex Barde, Robert Blunk, Robert Russell, MA; Ohio Univ, MFA, with William Kortlander, Dana Loomis, Gary Pettigrew. *Work:* Mercantile Libr, New York; Sioux City Art Ctr, Iowa; Joslyn Art Mus, Omaha; Sheldon Art Mus, Univ Nebr, Lincoln; Bailey Lewis and Assocs, Lincoln, Nebr. *Comn:* Logo, Telesystems Inc, Omaha, 81;

Riverfront Forum, Assoc Artists Omaha, 77; Metrop Arts Coun, Omaha, 76; Omaha Symphony Assoc, 86; Reviewer of Manuscript, West Publ, Newburyport, Mass, 86. *Exhib:* Fifth Salon Des Nations a Paris, Centre Int D'Art Contemp D'Paris, France; two-person exhib, Joslyn Art Mus, 81, Esta Robinson Gallery, New York, 82; Invitational Group Exhibition, Sheldon Art Gallery, Lincoln, Nebr, 82; IV Permanent Exhibition, Museo Nazionale dell' Accademia Italia, Terme, Italy, 83; and many others. *Pos:* Production mgr, Writers' Serv, Hollywood, 68-69; dir, Art Gallery, 74-76. *Teaching:* Instr life-drawing, painting & silkscreen, Akron Art Inst, Ohio, summer 73; assoc prof drawing, design & painting, Univ Nebr at Omaha, 73- *Awards:* Best of Show, Col St Mary, Omaha, 78; Academic Italy with Gold Medal, Accademia Italia delle Arti e del Lavoro, Parma, 80. *Media:* Mixed. *Publ:* Illusr, Painting with Acrylics, Van Nostrand-Reinhold, 74; Painting with Acrylics, Van Nostrand-Reinhold, 74; August Fires, Glover Davies, Abattoir Press, 78; Folk and Progressive Art, Ancient and New Values in Contemporary Art, Accademia Italia, 84; InterGallery, Great Guide to Contemporary Art, Les Ed & Publ, Geneva, Switzerland, 85. *Mailing Add:* Dept Art Univ Nebr at Omaha Omaha NE 68182

BRADSHAW, ROBERT GEORGE
PAINTER, EDUCATOR
b Trenton, NJ, Mar 13, 15. *Study:* Princeton Univ, AB; Columbia Univ, MA. *Exhib:* NJ State Mus; Am Watercolor Soc; Boston Mus Fine Art; Cape Ann Soc Mod Art; New York World's Fair, 65; plus others. *Teaching:* Lectr art appreciation & hist; prof art, Douglass Col, Rutgers Univ, New Brunswick, 46-79, actg chmn dept art, 64-65, emer prof, 79- *Awards:* Prize, NJ Watercolor Soc, 59 & Montclair Art Mus, NJ, 63. *Mem:* NJ Watercolor Soc; Hunterdon Co Art Ctr. *Media:* Watercolor, Acrylic. *Mailing Add:* 48 Hilltop Blvd East Brunswick NJ 08816

BRADY, CAROLYN
PAINTER, PRINTMAKER
b Chickasha, Okla, May 22, 37. *Study:* Okla State Univ, 55-58; Univ Okla, BFA, 59, MFA, 61. *Work:* Del Art Mus, Wilmington; Metrop Mus Art, New York; Mint Mus, Charlotte; St Louis Art Mus; Worcester Art Mus, Mass. *Exhib:* Two Photo Realists, San Jose Mus Art, 78; Contemporary Naturalism, Nassau Coun Mus, Roslyn, NY 80; Realism Photo Realism, Philbrook Art Ctr, Tulsa, 80; Real Really Real Super Real, San Antonio Mus Art, 81; Contemporary American Realism Since 1960, Pa Acad Fine Art, 81; Women & Still Life, New Brittain Mus Am Art, Conn, 83; Focus on Realism, San Francisco Mus Mod Art, 85. *Bibliog:* Nina French-Frazier (auth), Carolyn Brady, Art Int, 9-10/80; Charles LeClair (auth), Carolyn Brady, Arts Mag, 5/85; Alvin Martin (auth), American Realism, Harry N Abrams, 85. *Media:* Watercolor. *Dealer:* Nancy Hoffman 429 W Broadway New York NY 10012. *Mailing Add:* c/o Nancy Hoffman Gallery 429 W Broadway New York NY 10012

BRADY, CHARLES
PAINTER, SCULPTOR
b New York, NY, July 27, 26. *Study:* Art Student League, 48-51, with John Groth & Morris Kantor; with Marjorie Fitzgibbon, Ireland. *Work:* Seven works in Irish Arts Coun Collection, Dublin; Northern Ireland Arts Coun; NW Trust; Northern Bank Finance Corp; Bank of Ireland Collection; Art Students League. *Exhib:* Pa Acad Fine Arts, Philadelphia, 67; one-man show, Keys Gallery, Derry, Northern Ireland, 77; John Taylor Gallery, Dublin, 79, 81, 86, 88, 89 & 90; Delighted Eye, London, 80; Keys Gallery, Derry, Northern Ireland, 80; and others. *Teaching:* Artist-instr graphics, dept archit, Col Technol, Dublin, 70-71; lectr, Nat Col Art, Dublin, 75-83. *Awards:* P J Carroll Award, Living Art Exhib, Trinity Col, Dublin, 78; Appointment to the Institution of Honor for Creative Artists, Irish Arts Coun, Aosdána, 81; Landscape Prize, Oireachtas Exhib, 9/89. *Mem:* Life mem Art Student League; United Arts Club (hon chmn artist group, 71), Dublin; Figurative Image Group, Dublin (chmn, 85); L&P Financial Trustees of Ireland Ltd. *Media:* Oil; Lost-Wax into Bronze. *Dealer:* John Taylor 34 Kildare St Dublin 2 Ireland; Charles Cambell Gallery 647 Chestnut St San Francisco CA 94133. *Mailing Add:* One Royal Terr W Dun Laoghaire Ireland

BRADY, LUTHER W
COLLECTOR, PATRON
b Rocky Mount, NC, Oct 20, 25. *Study:* George Washington Univ, Washington, DC, AB, 46, MD, 48; Colgate Univ, Hon DFA, Lehigh Univ, Hon DSc. *Work:* Philadelphia Mus Art; Picker Gallery, Colgate Univ. *Pos:* Chmn, Friends Philadelphia Mus Art, 67-70; bd dirs, Settlement Music Sch, Philadelphia, 75-; bd trustees, Philadelphia Mus Art, 75-; bd dirs, Art Alliance Philadelphia, 78-80; bd dirs, Santa Fe Opera, 79-; trustee, Curtis Inst Music, 90- *Teaching:* Prof & chmn, Hahnemann Univ, 59- *Collection:* American contemporary art; Asian and Far Eastern porcelains and stone carvings; English sculpture. *Mailing Add:* 230 N Broad St Philadelphia PA 19102

BRADY, ROBERT D
SCULPTOR
b Reno, Nev, 1946. *Study:* Calif Col Arts & Crafts, BFA, 75; Univ Calif, Davis, MFA, 78. *Work:* San Francisco Mus Mod Art; Oakland Mus; Crocker Mus, Sacramento, Calif. *Exhib:* California Design Ten, Pasadena Mus Art, 68; Crocker Art Gallery, Sacramento, Calif, 75; one-man shows, Newport Harbor Art Mus, Newport Beach, Calif, 79, Braunstein Gallery, San Francisco, 80, 81, 83, 86 & 89, Impressions Gallery, Boston, 82, Struve Gallery, Chicago, 86, Crocker Mus Art, Sacramento, 89, Lewellayn Gallery, Santa Fe, NMex, 89-91; Modern Masks, Whitney Mus Am Art, New York, 84; First International Crafts Triennial, The Art Gallery of Western Australia, Perth, 89. *Pos:* Prof art, Sacramento State Univ. *Mem:* ENSECA. *Media:* Ceramic, Wood. *Publ:* Robert Brady (auth), Ceramic Sculpture (catalog). *Mailing Add:* c/o Braunstein-Quay Gallery 250 Sutter St San Francisco CA 94108

BRAGAR, PHILIP FRANK
PAINTER, PRINTMAKER
b New York, NY, May 10, 25. *Study:* Esmeralda Sch Painting & Sculpture, Mex City, with Raul Anguiano, Carlos Orozco Romero, Alfonso Ayala & Ignacio Aguirre, 54-59. *Work:* New York Pub Libr; Pasadena Art Mus, Calif; NJ State Mus, Trenton; Los Angeles Co Mus Art; Libr Cong, Washington, DC; Mus Mod Art, Mex City; Jose Luis Cuevas Mus, Mexico City, Mex. *Exhib:* One-man shows, Galeria Antonio Souza, Mex City, 68, Galeria Pecanins, 69 & 73, Lynn Kottler Gallery, New York, 81 & Prehispanic Man/Contemporary Man, Place of Fine Arts, Mexico City, Mex, 92; Nineteen Years of Woodcut Prints, 78, & Kafka by Bragar, 85, Galeria Pecanins, Mex City; Biennial of Graphics, Mus Fine Arts, Mex City, 79; Mus Mod Art, Mex City, 87, Florencia Riestra Gallery, Mex City, 88 & Nat Print Mus, Mex City, 90. *Teaching:* Instr drawing, painting, design & printmaking & dir art dept, US Int Univ, Mex City, 70-75. *Awards:* 1 yr grant paintings, Prehispanic Man/Contemp Man, Nat Fund for Cult & Art, 90. *Bibliog:* Graciela Kartofel (auth), Bragar and Drawing, Excelsior, 4/28/83; Juan Garcia Ponce (auth & critic), Philip F Bragar and the World of Kafka, Novedades, 3/24/90; Roberto Vallarina (auth), Philip Bragar-Painting That Avoids Classification, Uno Mas Uno, Mex City, 90; Luis Carlos Emerich (auth & critic), Philip F Bragar The Persistence of the Image, Novedades-Mexico City, 3/92; Antonio Espinoza (auth), The Savage Expressionism of Philip F Bragar, El Nacional-Mexico City, 4/92; Lorna Scott Fox (reporter), Inseperable Man-Philip F Bragar, Poliester and Cotten-Mexico City, no 2, summer 92. *Media:* Oil, Woodcuts. *Publ:* Illusr poem, In: Armando Zarate's El Corazon Cae Fuera del Camino, 63; illusr, Dr Oswaldo Schon's Americans Under Mexican Law, 71. *Dealer:* Galeria Pecanins Durango 186 Mexico DF Mex; Galeria Oscar Roman Anatole France 26 Polanco Mexico DF. *Mailing Add:* Iztaccihuatl No 21 Depto 3 Col Hipodromo Condesa Mexico DF 06100 Mexico

BRAGDON, CATHERINE CREAMER
WEAVER, DESIGNER
b White Plains, NY, Dec 5, 57. *Study:* Gudbransdal Husflidskole, Lillehammer, Norway, 80, Rochester Inst Technol, AAS, BFA, 81. *Exhib:* Jayne Baum Gallery, New York, 82; Objects '83, Hand & the Spirit Gallery, Scottsdale, Ariz, 83; High Tech Meets High Touch, West Gallery, Univ Del, 86; Empire State Crafts Alliance Benefit Auction, Steuben Glass, 86 & 88; Am Crafts Coun Benefit Auction, Sotheby's, NY, 87. *Pos:* Handweaver, Charles Samelson, Inc, 83; weave technician, Boris Kroll Fabrics, 83-85; owner & designer, Creamer Textile Design, 85-; coordr, Textile Dept & mem bd govs, Parsons Sch Design, New York, 86-89; textile prog mgr, Herman Miller Inc, Zeeland, Mich, 89- *Teaching:* Fac mem, New Sch Soc Res, New York, 84-89, Parsons Sch Design, 85-89, textile prog coordinator, 87-89. *Bibliog:* Articles, Fiberarts, 9-10/81 & 9-10/86; Architecture, Am Inst Architects Jour, 7/83; Newsday, 10/17/86; Wall Works, 87. *Mem:* Empire State Crafts Alliance; Am Crafts Coun; Textile Study Group, NY. *Media:* Woven Textile. *Mailing Add:* 312 Hoffman St Saugatuck MI 49453-0678

BRAGG, E ANN (ANN BRAGG)
PAINTER
b Liberty, NY, Mar 8, 35. *Study:* State Univ Col, Buffalo, NY, BS, 58; study with Edgar A Whitney, 75-80 & Paul Wood, 80-85. *Work:* American Bond Inc. *Exhib:* Am Standard Gallery, New York, 85; Firehouse Gallery, Nassau Community Col, 86; Women's Art Show, Purdue Univ, Ind, 86; Autotech Show, Long Island Coliseum, Nassau Co, 86; Nat Asn Women Artists, Tweed Mus Art, Univ Minn, 87; Nassau Mus Fine Arts, Roslyn, NY, 89; and others. *Pos:* Guest inst, Valley Stream High Sch & Celebration of Drawing, Workshop, Nassau Community Col; Judge & Demonstrator for Art Leagues, New York & Long Island. *Teaching:* Pvt lessons for problem children in elementary sch, 76-81; instr, abstract experiment watercolor, 5 Towns Mus & Art Found, 81-92; guest instr, drawing, Nassau Community Col, 86. *Awards:* Mario Cooper Award, Am Watercolor Soc, 81; Elizabeth Morse Genius Found Award, Nat Asn Women Artists, 88; Heckshire Mus Award, 90. *Bibliog:* Malcolm Preston (auth), Showing a bit of abstraction, News Day, 4/20/85; Helen A Harrison (auth), Heart of the matter figures as motif, 1/22/89 & From exuberant abstraction to detailed realism, 6/10/90, NY Times. *Mem:* Nat Asn Women Artists; Nat Art League. *Media:* All. *Mailing Add:* 2921 Cleveland Ave Oceanside NY 11572

BRAIDEN, ROSE MARGARET J
PAINTER, ILLUSTRATOR
b Los Angeles, Calif, Nov 25, 23. *Study:* Mt St Mary's Col, Los Angeles, BFA; Calif Col Arts & Crafts, Oakland, MFA; Long Beach State, studied printmaking with Dick Swift; Univ Southern Calif; Univ Calif, Los Angeles. *Work:* Mt St Mary's Col, Libr & Gallery, Los Angeles. *Comn:* Stained glass windows, St Bernard's Church, Glendale; Design for wall mural, St Lawrence Church, 65; stained glass work, Roger Darricarrere Studios, 69; portraits, Univ Calif, Northridge, 76; bk illus, comn by Steve Pouliot, Banner & Assoc, 78; and others. *Exhib:* Etchings, Long Beach State Gallery, 68; Cody Gallery, Los Olivos, Calif; Paintings & Icons, Faulkner Gallery, Santa Barbara, Calif, 77. *Teaching:* Prof art hist, Mt St Mary's Col, 68-70; prof, Santa Barbara City Col, 70- & Cate Sch, Carpinteria, 82-88. *Bibliog:* Ann Vail Van Horn (auth), Iconography & icons of the spirit, News & Rev, 78. *Mem:* Los Padre Watercolor Soc (founder). *Media:* Egg Tempera, Watercolor; Ink, Pencil. *Publ:* Illusr, Choices, 82; A Mother's Diary, 91. *Dealer:* Yellow Dog Graphics Santa Barbara CA; Cody Gallery Los Olivos. *Mailing Add:* 2929 Paseo Tranquillo Santa Barbara CA 93105

BRAIG, BETTY LOU
PAINTER, GALLERY DIRECTOR
b Naylor, Mo, Apr 21, 31. *Study:* Phoenix Col, AA, 64; Ariz State Univ, BA, 70, MA, 73. *Work:* Valley Nat Bank, United Bank, Empire Machinery & Am Express, Phoenix, Ariz; Glendale Star, Ariz. *Comn:* Free Hanging Cross, Am Evangelical Lutheran Church, Phoenix, 72; Maryvale High Sch, Phoenix, 83; Heavenly Valley Resort, Lake Tahoe, Calif, 83. *Exhib:* Nat Soc Painters Casein & Acrylic, New York, 80; Am Watercolor Soc Traveling Exhib, 80, 82 & 83; San Diego Int Watercolor Exhib, San Diego Art Mus, 82; Nat Energy Art Exhib, Denver, 82; Ariz Biennial, Tucson Mus Art, 82; Western Fedn Watercolor, Rocky Mountain Nat. *Pos:* Phoenix Col, Ariz, Corrizo Sch Art, Ruiodoso, NMex; gallery dir, Phoenix Union High Sch Dist. *Teaching:* Instr art, Phoenix Union High Sch District, 70- *Awards:* Grumbacher Art Award, Ariz Watercolor Asn, 81; David Gayle Found Award, Western Fedn Watercolor, 82. *Mem:* Assoc mem Am Watercolor Soc; Ariz Watercolor Asn; Ariz Artist Guild; 22-30 Watercolorist Ariz. *Media:* Watercolor, Acrylic; Mixed. *Publ:* Ariz Arts & Travel, Scottsdale Mag, 85; Southwest Art, Southwest Profile, 85. *Dealer:* May Galleries 6166 N Scottsdale AZ 85254; Orlosky Gallery 671 Hwy 169 Box 2109 Hillside Sedona AZ 86336. *Mailing Add:* 5271 S Desert Willow Dr Gold Canyon AZ 85219

BRAINARD, JOE
GRAPHIC ARTIST, PAINTER
b Salem, Ark, Mar 11, 42. *Work:* Colorado Springs Fine Arts Ctr, Colo; Harvard Univ; Whitney Mus Am Art; Mus Mod Art, New York; Utah Mus Fine Arts, Salt Lake City. *Exhib:* In Memory of My Feelings: Frank O'Hara, Mus Mod Art, New York, 67; Va Mus Fine Arts, 68; White on White, Contemp Mus Art, Chicago, 72; Seven Young Artists, Corcoran, 72; solo exhibs, Suzette Schochett Gallery, Newport, RI, 76, Coventry Gallery, Paddington, NSW, 76, Hamilton Col, NY, 77, Benson Gallery, Bridgehampton, NY, 77 & Art 3 Assoc, Savannah, Ga, 78; Retrospective Show, Univ Calif, San Diego, 87; and others. *Teaching:* Instr, Cooper Union, 67-68; painting, Art Dept, Sch Vis Arts, 74-76. *Awards:* Copley Found Grant. *Mailing Add:* 8 Greene St New York NY 10013

BRAINARD, OWEN
PAINTER, EDUCATOR
b Kingston, NY, Sept 6, 24. *Study:* Columbia Univ, 46, with Dong Kingman; Syracuse Univ, BFA, 48, with Stephen Peck; State Univ NY Albany, 51; Syracuse Univ, with Fred Haucke, MFA, 52. *Work:* Ford Collection Am Art; Chicago Pub Libr; Univ Ryukyus, Okinawa; Mich State Univ; Oldsmobile Collection. *Comn:* Mosaic wall mural, Everett High Sch, Lansing, Mich, 59; Mixed media wall mural, Kellogg Ctr, Mich State Univ, 86. *Exhib:* Walker Art Ctr Biennial, Minneapolis, 53; Regional Art Today, Joslyn Mus, Omaha, 57; Art: USA, Madison Sq Garden, NY, 58; 16th Nat Print Exhib, Libr Cong, 58; 3rd Nat Print Exhib, New Canaan, Conn, 60; Drawing Exhib, Buenos Aires, Arg, 78; plus many others. *Teaching:* Asst prof design & painting, Drake Univ, 52-57; prof painting & serigraphy, Mich State Univ, 57-; retired. *Awards:* Purchase Award, Iowa Art Salon, 57; Western Mich Ann Award, Friends of Art, 60; Midland Art Asn Ann Award, 62; Lansing Arts Coun. *Mem:* Col Art Asn; Nat Soc Arts & Lit; Screen Printing Asn Int. *Media:* Acrylic. *Dealer:* Rubiner Gallery Royal Oak MI. *Mailing Add:* 321 Kresge Art Ctr Mich State Univ East Lansing MI 48824-1046

BRAITSTEIN, MARCEL
SCULPTOR, EDUCATOR
b Charleroi, Belg, July 11, 35; Can citizen. *Study:* École Beaux-Arts Montreal, dipl; Inst Allende, San Miguel Allende, Mex. *Work:* Montreal Mus Fine Arts, PQ; Art Gallery Ont, Toronto; Winnipeg Art Gallery, Man; Confederation Ctr, PEI; Can Coun Art Bank, Ottawa. *Comn:* monument, Right Hon A Meighen, Dept Pub Works, Can Govt, 69; wall sculpture & fireplace, Ministry of Social Affairs, Québec, 85; relief mural, Alcan House, Montreal, 89. *Exhib:* Spring Show, Montreal Mus Fine Arts, 61; Vermont USA, Bundy Art Gallery, 66; Panorama of Québec Sculpture, Mus Rodin, Paris, France, 70; First Int Biennial Small Sculpture, Budapest, Hungary, 71; Musée du Québec, 92. *Pos:* Dir, Dept Fine Arts, Univ Québec, Montreal, 86-91. *Teaching:* Prof sculpture, École Beaux-Arts Montreal, 65-69 & Univ Québec, Montreal, 69-73 & 75; prof, Mt Allison Univ, 73-75. *Awards:* Sculpture Prizes, Québec Govt, 59 & Montreal Mus Fine Arts, 61; Sculpture Prize, Montreal Mus Fine Arts, 61. *Bibliog:* Guy Robert (auth), Marcel Braitstein, Vie des Arts, Montreal, 62; E H Turner (auth), Sculpture in Canada, Can Art, 62; Jean Simard (auth), Marcel Braitstein, Sculpteur (monogr), Québec Sculptors Asn, 69. *Mem:* Québec Sculptors Asn (vpres, 69-71); Royal Can Acad Arts. *Media:* Welded Steel, Miscellaneous Media. *Mailing Add:* PO Box 385 Hudson Heights PQ J0P 1J0 Canada

BRAKHAGE, JAMES STANLEY
FILMMAKER, LECTURER
b Kansas City, Mo, Jan 14, 33. *Study:* San Francisco Art Inst, Hon Dr, 81. *Work:* Pacific Film Archives, Berkeley; Cinematheque Royale, Brussels; Mus Mod Art, New York; Centre Georges Pompidou, Paris; Osterreichishes Filmmuseum, Vienna. *Exhib:* Telluride & Denver Film Festivals, Colo, 88, 89; Mus Mod Art, 87, 90; San Francisco Cinematheque, 87, 88 & 89; LA Film Forum, 87; Public Theater, New York, 88; Am Mus of the Moving Image, Anthology Film Archives, Can, 89 & 90. *Pos:* Lectr film, US & Europe, 55-; lectr film hist, Art Inst Chicago, 69-81; prof, film studies, Univ Colo, Boulder, 81- *Teaching:* Prof film, Univ Colo, Boulder, 81- *Awards:* Nat Endowment Arts Grants, 74, 75, 77, 78, 80, 84, 86, & 88; Telluride Film Festival Medallion, 81; Univ Colo Coun Research & Creative Work, 83 & 88; Denver Int Film Festival Outstanding Achievement Award, 88; McDowell medal, 89. *Bibliog:* Eisenstein/Brakhage issue, Artforum Mag, 1/73; Barrett/Brabner (auths), Stan Brakhage: A Guide to References & Resources, G K Hall, 83. *Mem:* Film-Makers Co-op, New York; Canyon Cinema Co-op San Francisco; London Film-Makers Co-op; Canadian Film-Makers Distribution Centre. *Media:* Film. *Publ:* Auth, Metaphors on Vision, 63; A Moving Picture Giving & Taking Book, 71; The Brakhage Lectures, 72; Seen, 75; Film Biographies, 77; Brakhage Scrapbook, 82; I Sleeping, Being a Dream Journal & Parenthetical Explication, 89; Film at Wit's End, 89; The Domain Aura (in prep). *Mailing Add:* 2142 Canyon Blvd No 203 Boulder CO 80302

BRAKKE, P(ERRY) MICHAEL
PAINTER, EDUCATOR
b Douglas, Ariz, Apr 16, 43. *Study:* Univ Minn, BA, 66; Yale Univ Sch Art & Archit, BFA, 68, MFA, 68. *Work:* Solomon R Guggenheim Mus, New York; Joslyn Art Mus, Omaha; Mus Contemp Art, Chicago; Indianapolis Mus Art. *Exhib:* Solo exhib, Joslyn Art Mus, Omaha, 80 & High Mus Art, Atlanta, Ga, 87; Exxon Nat Exhib, Solomon R Guggenheim Mus, New York, 81; Art Inst Chicago, 81; Indianapolis Mus Art, 82 & 86; Mus Contemp Art, Chicago, 84; Bronx Mus Arts, New York, 87. *Teaching:* Prof painting, Oakland Univ, Rochester, 68-76, Univ Ill, Chicago Circle, 76-81 & Univ Tenn, Knoxville, 81- *Awards:* Proj Completion Grant, 80 & Artists' Fel, 81, Ill Arts Coun; Nat Endowment Arts Fel, 85-86. *Bibliog:* Jack Burnham (auth), Icons of the prairies: Mike Brakke's photo-paintings, New Art Examiner, Chicago, 80; Judith Russi Kirshner (auth), Michael Brakke, Artforum, summer 82; Paul Krainak (auth), Michael Brakke/sight specific, Atlanta Art Papers, 5-6/87. *Media:* Paint, Photographs. *Publ:* Co-ed, Artbook 2, 80 & auth, illusr, Anima Hostility, the Painting, Waiting, 80, NAME Gallery, Chicago & Nat Endowment Arts. *Dealer:* Marianne Deson Gallery 340 W Huron Chicago IL 60610. *Mailing Add:* Univ Tenn Knoxville TN 37996

BRALEY, JEAN
PRINTMAKER, PAINTER
b Wilkesboro, NC. *Study:* Univ Calif, San Diego BA; Pratt Graphics Ctr, New York; Art Students League; La Reparata Graphic, Florence, Italy; Sch Prof Art, New York; Atelier 17, Paris; NY Univ. *Work:* Nat Biblioteque, Paris; Libr Cong, Washington, DC; NZ Embassy, Washington, DC; Imperial Savings & Loan, Westwood, Calif; Pratt Graphics Ctr, New York; and others. *Comn:* Wall paintings, Glendale Fed Bank, San Diego, 75; five color intaglio ed, Orr's Graphic Ctr, San Diego, 76-77; wall paintings, Calif First Bank, San Diego, 77. *Exhib:* Calif-Hawaii Biennial, San Diego, 76; Palace Fine Arts, Mexico City, 76; 50 Calif Printmakers Nat Tour, 76 & 77; Soc Am Graphic Artists, New York, 77; Yokohoma Citizens Mus, Japan, 79; and many others. *Pos:* Prof illusr, publ & advert agencies, New York & Washington, DC, 50-68; vchmn docents, Fine Arts Gallery Mus, San Diego, 74-75. *Teaching:* Instr design & drawing, Luther Rice Col, Franconia, Va, 70-71; instr advan oil, San Diego Community Col, 71-78; instr, Mira Costa Col, 79- *Awards:* San Diego Top Woman Artist, 80; Purchase Awards, Southern Calif Expo, 81 & Pratt Graphics Ctr, 82; Awards, SW Ann Regional, Washington, DC, 68-70; and others. *Mem:* Artists Equity Asn San Diego (founder, 72, pres, 73 & 74); Calif Art Comn; Printmaker's Atelier (dir, 82-83); and others. *Media:* Intaglio, Oil. *Publ:* Contribr, M Petersen (auth), On view, Jean Braley, Applause, 11/80. *Dealer:* Tarbox Gallery 1202 Kettner Blvd San Diego CA 92101. *Mailing Add:* 12245 Carmel Vista #193 San Diego CA 92130

BRAMHALL, KIB
PAINTER
b Morristown, NJ, June 12, 33. *Study:* Princeton Univ, AB(art & archeol), 55. *Work:* First Nat Bank of Boston, John Hancock Mutual Life Insurance Co & New England Life, Boston; Russell Reynolds Assoc, New York; Smart Fabrics, Ltd, Montreal. *Comn:* Painting for Cox Cancer Ctr, comn by Henry Guild, Boston, 75. *Exhib:* Fourteen one-man shows, New York, Boston, Santa Fe, Cincinnati, Palm Beach, New Haven, Martha's Vineyard, Cape Cod and Nantucket, 60-86; 24 New England Realists, Munson Gallery, Santa Fe, 78; 300 Years of Northeast Art, Copley Soc, Boston, 80; American Realists, Coe Kerr Gallery, New York, 82, 83, 86 & 89. *Mem:* Copley Soc of Boston. *Media:* Oil. *Dealer:* Bramhall & Dunn Tisbury MA 02568. *Mailing Add:* Seven Gates Farm RFD Vineyard Haven MA 02568

BRAMLETT, BETTY JANE
ART ADMINISTRATOR, PAINTER
b Augusta, Ga. *Study:* Converse Col, Spartanburg, SC, BA; Univ NC, Chapel Hill; Columbia Univ, MA; Univ SC, Columbia, EdD, 83. *Work:* SC State Collection, Columbia; Spartanburg Arts Ctr Gallery, SC; Springs Mills Res & Develop Bldg, SC; C S Nat Bank Collection, Columbia, SC; Greenville City Hall Collection, SC. *Exhib:* C&S Nat Bank Statewide Art Competition, Florence Mus Art, SC, 87; 38th Ann Guild SC Artists, Juried Art Exhib, 88; 52nd Ann Exhib, Greenville Artists Guild, SC, 88; Joyce Dickinson Dowis Mem Art Exhib, Florence Mus Art, SC, 88; Invitational Women's Exhib, Roe Art Gallery, Furman Univ, Greenville, SC, 88; and others. *Pos:* Art Supvr, Spartanburg Co Sch Dist 7, 59-; arts comnr, SC Arts Comn, 77-80. *Teaching:* Instr art hist & art educ, Univ SC, Columbia, 69-73. *Awards:* SC Art Educator of the Yr, 88, Southeastern Supervisor of the Yr, 89; SC O'Neill Verner Award Art Educ, 89; Best in Show, Festival of Flowers, Greenwood, SC, 92; and others. *Bibliog:* Jack Bass (auth), Porgy Comes Home, World Publ, 70; Seth Vining (ed), article, Tryon Daily Bulletin, NC, 70; Bramlett's Art Goes on Display, Spartanburg Herald-J, 70. *Mem:* Greenville Artists Guild; SC Watercolor Soc; SC Artists Guild (pres 77); Nat Art Educ Asn (dir-elect, Southern Regional chap, formerly). *Media:* Watercolor, Acrylic. *Publ:* Auth, Glass on Glass, Sch Arts, 4/63; auth, Spartanburg's Adventure in Art, 4/67 & A Federal Program Can Be Successful, spring 73, SC State Dept; auth, Elementary Art Media, 73 & co-auth, Elementary Art Aids, 73, Spartanburg Co Sch Dist 7. *Mailing Add:* 502 Perrin Dr Spartanburg SC 29302

BRAMS, JOAN
PAINTER, SCULPTOR
b Montreal, PQ,. *Study:* Ont Col Art. *Comn:* Walter Heller Corp, NY; U P Corp Environ, Stockholm, Sweden; Russell, Gibson, Van D Ohlen, Inc, Conn; The Rowland Co, NY; Robert Lennox Asn, Minn; and others. *Exhib:* Columbia Mus Art, SC; Birmingham Mus Art, Ala; John Herron Mus Art, Indianapolis, Ind; Worcester Art Mus, Mass; Mountain View Col, Ind; Palm Beach Col, Fla; plus others. *Awards:* Award Merit, Ft Lauderdale Mus, Fla, 65 & 78; 2nd Prize, St Petersburg Art Ctr, Fla, 74; 1st Prize, Palm Beach Art Inst, Fla, 75; and others. *Bibliog:* Articles in La Revue Mod des Arts, France, 71, Art News, 74 & 1/78 & Arts Mag, 10/77. *Media:* Bronze; acrylic with aggregates on wood or fibre. *Dealer:* David Findlay Galleries 984 Madison Ave New York 10021; Gallery 99 1135 Kane Concourse Bal Harbour FL 33154. *Mailing Add:* c/o Joan Hodgell Gallery 46 S Palm Ave Sarasota FL 34236

BRAMSON, PHYLLIS HALPERIN
PAINTER, EDUCATOR
b Madison, Wis, Feb 20, 41. *Study:* Yale Summer Art Sch, Norfolk, Conn, 62; Univ Ill, Champaign, BFA, 63; Univ Wis, Madison, MA(Vilas Fel), 64; Art Inst Chicago, MFA, 73. *Work:* Hirshhorn Mus; Mus Contemp Art, Chicago; Art Inst Chicago; Mus de Toulon, France; Ill State Mus. *Exhib:* Chicago & Vicinity Show, Art Inst Chicago, 74; Smithsonian Inst, Washington, DC, 76; one-person show, Monique Knowlton Gallery, New York, 77, 79, 81, 82, 84 & 86; Works on Paper, Art Inst Chicago, 78; Marilyn Butler Gallery, Scottsdale, Ariz, 83; Seattle Art Mus, 85; Renaissance Soc, Chicago, Ill, 86; Ill State Mus, 90; Printworks, Chicago, Ill, 92; and others. *Pos:* Assoc Prof Studio Arts, Univ Ill, Chicago. *Teaching:* Instr drawing & painting, Columbia Col, Chicago, 72-82; vis artist, Univ Ill, 75, Univ Iowa, 79, Univ Chicago, 80, Art Inst Chicago, 81, Ind State Univ, 81, Univ Wis, 83 & Northwestern Univ, 83; assoc prof, Univ Ill, Chicago, 85-; vis artist & lectr, Univ Colo & Univ Nebr, 86 & Univ NMex, 90. *Awards:* Ill Arts Coun Fel, 81, 88; Nat Endowment Arts Fel Grant, 76, 83; Sr Fulbright Scholar, Australia, 88. *Bibliog:* John Russell (auth), article, NY Times, 3/12; Lisa Peters (auth), article, Arts Mag, 3/82; Cody Westerbeck (auth), Phyllis Bramson, Art Forum, Summer, 86. *Mem:* Col Art Asn (bd dir, 89-92). *Media:* Oil, Mixed Media. *Dealer:* GW Einstein 591 Broadway New York NY 10012; Dart Gallery 212 W Superior St Chicago IL 60610. *Mailing Add:* 1423 Blackthorn Dr Glenview IL 60025-2009

BRANDENBERG, ALIKI LIACOURAS See Aliki,

BRANDT, FREDERICK ROBERT
CURATOR
b Paterson, NJ, June 7, 36. *Study:* Pa State Univ, BA, 60, MA, 63. *Collections Arranged:* Art Nouveau (contribr, catalog), 71; American Pewter (with catalog), 76; American Marine Painting (with catalog), 76; Allan D'Arcangelo, 79; David True: Paintings 1977-84 (catalog), 84; Spiritual Impact: the Paintings of Edward Knippers (with catalog), 86; German Expressionist Art: The Ludwig & Rosy Fischer collection (with catalog), 87; Good Design Collection, Va Mus Fine Arts (with catalog); Harmony & Discord: American Landscape Painting Today (with catalog), 90; Uncommon Grounds: Virginia Artists (with catalog), 90; Louis Comfort Tiffany: An Empire in Glass (with catalog), 91. *Pos:* Interpretation asst, gallery div, Va Mus Fine Arts, 60-61; teaching asst, Pa State Univ, 61-63; asst prog dir, Va Mus Fine Arts, 63-77, assoc cur, 77-79, cur 20th century art, 83-; cur, Sydney & Frances Lewis Collection, 72-; dir, The Sydney & Frances Lewis Found, 80-; mem adv panel, Va Comn for Arts, 88-90; adv bd mem, Longwood Col Fine Arts, Farmville, Va, 90; bd ed adv, Studies in the Decorative Arts, 92. *Awards:* Distinguished Alumni Award, Col Arts Pa State Univ, 89. *Mem:* Am Asn Mus. *Publ:* Auth various articles in antique periodicals, 71-92; auth, Late 19th & Early 20th Century Decorative Arts: The Sydney and Frances Lewis Collection, 85; Late twentieth century art, 85; Twentieth Century Visions, Mag Antiques, 90; The Sydney and Frances Lewis Decorative Arts Collection: Art Nouveau and Art Deco, ca 1895-1935, Collections Mag, 91. *Mailing Add:* 3207 Monument Ave Richmond VA 23221

BRANDT, GRACE BORGENICHT See Borgenicht, Grace

BRANDT, KATHLEEN WEIL-GARRIS
EDUCATOR, ART HISTORIAN
b Cheam, Surrey, Eng. *Study:* Vassar Col, AB, 56; Univ Bonn, 57; Harvard Univ, AM, 58, PhD, 65. *Pos:* Ed-in-chief, Art Bull, 77-81; art historian in residence, Am Acad Rome, 75 & 81; consult Renaissance art, Vatican Mus, 87- *Teaching:* Prof Renaissance art, NY Univ, 65-, Inst Fine Arts, 66-; Harvard Univ, 80-81. *Awards:* Lindback Found Award for Distinguished Teaching, 67; Research Prize, Alexander von Humboldt Found, 85. *Mem:* Col Art Asn; Renaissance Soc Am; Soc Archit Hist; NY Acad Sci. *Res:* painting, sculpture & architecture of the 15th and 16th centuries in Italy. *Publ:* Auth, Leonardo and Central Italian Art, NY Univ Press, 74; The Santa Casa di Loreto, Garland Press, 77; coauth (with J D'Amico), The Renaissance Cardinal's Ideal Palace, Elefante Press, Rome, 82; auth, On Pedestals, Roemisches Jahrbuch fuer Kunstgeschicte, 84; Twenty-Five Questions About Michelangelo's Sistine Ceiling, Apollo, 87; Michelangelo's Pieta, Studies for Andre Chester, 87. *Mailing Add:* 37 Washington Sq W No 16C New York NY 10011

BRANDT, REX (REXFORD ELSON)
PAINTER, PRINTMAKER
b San Diego, Calif, Sept 12, 14. *Study:* Univ Calif, Berkeley, AB(art), 36; Stanford Univ, 38. *Work:* San Diego Fine Arts Gallery, San Francisco Mus Mod Art & Los Angeles Co Mus Art, Calif; Currier Gallery Am Art, Andover, NH; Nat Acad Design Galleries, New York. *Comn:* Metropolitan Aqueduct, portfolio for Fortune Mag, 37; scraffiti tile murals, Corona del Mar State Beach Park, 65; San Diego County, Calif, portfolio for Copley Found, La Jolla, Calif, 68; carved wall relief, Irvine Coast Country Club, 68; murals, Southern Calif First Nat Bank, Newport, 69. *Exhib:* Int Watercolor Exhib, Chicago Art Inst, 36, 37, 39 & 40; one-man shows, Los Angeles Co Mus of Art, 39 & 41, Calif Palace of the Legion of Honor, San Francisco, Crocker Gallery of Art, Sacramento, 40 & 60, Santa Barbara Art Mus, Major Retrospective, Laguna Beach Art Mus, 67, San Diego Fine Arts Gallery, Faulkner Gallery of Art, Santa Barbara & Southern Methodist Univ, Dallas, Tex; Nat Gallery Art, Washington, DC, 41; Royal Soc Painters in Watercolour, London, 62; Am Watercolor Soc Ann, 60-75; Nat Acad Design Ann, 62-75; plus many others. *Teaching:* Dir, Riverside Col Art Ctr, 38-43; dir, Brandt Painting Workshops, Corona del Mar, Calif, also in Europe & Mexico, 46-85. *Awards:* First Prize, Calif Watercolor Soc, 38 & 70; Samuel F B Morse Medal, Nat Acad Design Ann, 68 & 70; Bronze Medal, Am Watercolor Soc, 70. *Bibliog:* Jerome K Muller (auth), Rex Brandt, pvt publ, 72; Janis Lovoos (auth), Two From California, Riverside Art Mus, 84; Ruth Westphal (auth), American Scene Painting California 1930s & 1940s, 91. *Mem:* Am Watercolor Soc; Nat Acad Design; plus many regional soc. *Media:* Watercolor, Block Print. *Publ:* Auth, Watercolor Landscape, 63, The Artists' Sketchbook and its Uses, 66, San Diego, Land of the Sundown Sea, 69, Watercolor Technique and Methods, 77, West Coast Sketchbook, 78, Seeing with a Painter's Eye, 81 & About Landscape Painting, 88. *Mailing Add:* 405 Goldenrod Corona Del Mar CA 92625

BRANDT, WARREN
PAINTER
b Greensboro, NC, 18. *Study:* Pratt Inst, 35-38; Wash Univ, BFA(hons); with Philip Guston & Max Beckmann; John J Milliken traveling fel; Univ NC, Greensboro, MFA. *Work:* Metrop Mus Art, New York; Currier Gallery, NH; Nat Collection Fine Arts, Smithsonian Inst; Rochester Mus, NY; Carnegie Inst; and many other public & pvt collections. *Exhib:* Metrop Mus Watercolor Exhib; Am Fedn Arts; Whitney Mus Am Art; Artists by Artists, New Sch Social Res, 67 & Drawings of the Sixties, 69; one-man retrospectives, Allentown Art Mus, 69 & Beaumont Tex, 76; Weatherspoon Art Gallery, Greensboro, NC, 92. *Teaching:* Head dept art, Salem Col, 49-50; instr art, Pratt Inst, 50-51; instr art, Guilford Col, Greensboro, 52-54; chmn dept art, Univ Miss, 57-59; chmn dept art, Southern Ill Univ, 59-61; dir, New York Studio Sch, 67- *Mem:* Academician, Nat Acad Design, NY. *Media:* Oil. *Publ:* Auth, Painting With Oils, Van Nostrand Reinhold, 71; Nicholas Fox Weber, Warren Brandt, 88. *Mailing Add:* 870 United Nations Plaza New York NY 10017

BRANFMAN, STEVEN
CERAMIST, EDUCATOR
b Los Angeles, Calif, Mar 5, 53. *Study:* Cortland State Univ, BA, 74, RI Sch Design, MAT, 75, studied with Gerald DiGusto, Norm Shulman, Jun Kaneko. *Work:* Brockton Art Mus, Mass; Thayer Acad, Braintree, Mass. *Exhib:* RI Sch Design Alumni Invitational, Brockton Art Mus, 89; Artful Crafts, Fitchburg Art Mus, 89; The Artfull Goblet, Signature Galleries, 90; Great American Crafts, Starr Gallery, Mass, 90; Guilford Handcrafts Ctr, 91; and others. *Pos:* Pres-dir, The Potters Shop, Needham, Mass, 77-; pres, RI Sch design, Boston Alumni Asn; mem, RI Sch Design Alumni Coun, 86; vpres & bd trustees, Studio Potter Organization, 90- *Teaching:* Instr ceramics, Thayer Acad, Braintree, Mass, 78-; Artist-in-residence ceramics, Lasell Jr Col, Newton, Mass, 85-88. *Awards:* RI Sch Design Alumni Serv Award, 85; First-Prize Crafts, Concord Art Asn, 86. *Bibliog:* Pat Foley (auth), Service and solvency at the Potters Shop, Crafts Report, 1/83; Brigit Truex (auth), Steven Branfman: Raku Potter, Folio, 4/85; Lynda Morgenroth (auth), Japanese influence in America, Boston Globe, 86. *Mem:* Am Crafts Coun; Mass Asn Crafts. *Media:* Clay-Raku technique. *Publ:* Creative Identity: The Potter Shop, Ceramics Mo, 9/89; Raku: A Practical Approach, Chilton Bk Co, 91. *Dealer:* Signature Galleries Boston MA; Baak Gallery Cambridge MA. *Mailing Add:* 31 Thorpe Rd Needham MA 02194

BRANSBY, ERIC JAMES
MURALIST, EDUCATOR
b Auburn, NY, Oct 25, 16. *Study:* Kansas City Art Inst, Mo, with Thomas Hart Benton & Fletcher Martin, cert(painting & printmaking); Colorado Springs Fine Arts Ctr & Colo Col, with Boardman Robinson & Jean Charlot, BA & MA(mural painting); Yale Univ, with Josef Albers & Carol Meeks, MFA(painting). *Work:* Colorado Springs Fine Arts Ctr; Mo State Hist Soc Collection, Columbia; Brigham Young Univ Gallery; Nelson Gallery, Kansas City; Princeton Univ. *Comn:* mural, Munic Bldg, Liberty, Mo; Academic Achievement (20 paneled mural), Nichols Hall, Kansas State Univ, 85; Colo Springs Fine Arts Ctr (5 panel mural), 86; Loveland Mus (8 panel mural), Colo, 88; fresco mural, Parker Col Libr, Mo, 91; and many others. *Exhib:* Nat Soc Mural Painters Traveling Exhib, New York Archit League & Moscow, Russia, 63; one-man show, Colorado Springs Fine Arts Ctr, 67; Joslyn Mus Biennial, Omaha, 72 & 78; Nat Ctr Fine Arts, Washington, DC, 73-75; Housing & Urban Develop Nat Community Art Competition; and many others. *Teaching:* Instr drawing, Univ Ill, Urbana, 50-52 & Colorado Springs Fine Arts Ctr, 58-63; asst prof drawing & painting, Western Ill Univ, 63-65; assoc prof drawing, painting & printmaking, Univ Mo-Kansas City, 65-70, prof, 70- *Awards:* Edwin Austen Abbey Found Fel for Mural Painting, 52; Kansas City Asn Trusts & Founds, 70; Veatch Award, Univ Mo, 78. *Bibliog:* Brolin & Richards (auths), Sourcebook of Exterior Architectural Ornament, Nostrand & Reinhold; National Community Art Program, US Govt Printing Off (HUD), 73. *Mem:* Col Art Asn; Nat Soc Mural Painters; and others.

Media: Multimedia. *Res:* Design analysis of Piero della Francesca's mural cycle in the Church of San Francesco at Arezzo, Italy; development of lightweight portable presco panels. *Publ:* The Buon Fresco Process (video), Univ Mo Video Network. *Mailing Add:* 9080 Hwy 115 Colorado Springs CO 80926

BRANSTETTER, GWENDOLYN H
PAINTER
b Beeville, Bee Co, Tex. *Study:* Tex Technol Univ, 49-50; private instruction with Minnie Miller Simpson, 57-61. *Work:* Nat Cowgirl Hall Fame & Western Heritage, Hereford, Tex; Refugio Co Hist Mus, Refugio, Tex; Com State Bank, Beeville, Tex; Woodsboro Indepent Sch Dist, Tex; First Nat Bank, Refugio, Tex; Dr Pepper Mus, Waco, Tex. *Comn:* oils, comn by James W Witherspoon, Hereford, Tex, 87; Landscape in oil, comn by Jame Armour, Dallas, Tex, 88; Western in oil, comn by William L Leach, Houston, Tex, 88; Western, comn by, Mr & Mrs Jimmy Craft, Refugio, Tex, 88; Texas Bluebonnets, comn by Watson, Waco, 88. *Exhib:* Int Cultural Exchange, Tour Art Europe, Rome, Italy, 68; Western Heritage Art Show, Nat Cowgirl Hall Fame, Hereford, Tex, 77, 78 & 79; Texas Realism 1985, Tex Fine Arts Asn, Austin, Tex, 85; one-person Show, Refugio Co Mus, Refugio, Tex, 88; Invitational Western Art Show, Western Art Barn, San Antonio, Tex,. *Teaching:* Instr oils for adults, Refugio Co Mus, 86-, oil for children, 87- *Awards:* First Over-All in Show, Grumbacher, 58; First Over-All in Show, Winsor-Newton, 59; Selected to show from 1114, Tex Fine Arts Asn, 85; Nominated as honoree to be inducted into Nat Cowgirl Hall Fame, Hereford, Tex, 92. *Bibliog:* Adrian Shapiro (auth), Two Paths To Western Painting, Art Happenings Houston, summer 82; Joe Cavanaugh (auth), Branstetter Paintings, Refugio Co Press, 7/20/83; Mel McCombie (auth), Tex Realism, Austin Am-Statesman, 12/27/85. *Media:* Oil, Watercolor. *Dealer:* CMR Art Gallery 313 N Chaparral Corpus Christi TX 78401; Cuero Art Gallery 608 Clinton Cuero TX 77954. *Mailing Add:* PO Box 143 1004 Douglas St Refugio TX 78377

BRASELMAN, LIN EMERY See Emery, Lin

BRASETH, JOHN E
ART DEALER, CONSULTANT
b Seattle, Wash, May 23, 59. *Pos:* Dir, Gordon Woodside-John Braseth Galleries. *Specialty:* Northwest masters: Morris Graves, William Ivey, Mark Tobey, Paul Horiuchi, Hilda Morris; plus others. *Mailing Add:* Gordon Woodside-John Braseth Galleries 1533 Ninth Ave Seattle WA 98101

BRATCHER, DALE
PAINTER
b Rockport, Ky, Jan 10, 32. *Study:* Univ Louisville, BCE, MCE. *Work:* Citizens Bank, Evansville, Ind; Evansville Mus Arts & Sci, Ind; Morehead State Univ, Ky; Coca Cola Co, Elizabethtown, Ky; Household Int Corp, Prospect Heights, Ill; Lucille Parker Markey Cancer Ctr, Lexington, KY; Lilly Interprise Coatings, Indianapolis, Ind; Doncaster Mus Art, Eng; Hillard & Lyons Ctr, Louisville, Ky. *Comn:* Paintings, Lewisport Sch & Lewisport City Hall, Ky, 77; Pate House, Hancock Co, Ky, 77; 3 paintings, Hancock City, Ky; painting, Liberty Nat Bank & Trust, Louisville, Ky. *Exhib:* Watercolor USA, Springfield, Mo, 74, 83 & 88; Midwest Watercolor Soc Ann, 78-79 & 83; Rocky Mountain Nat Watermedia, Golden, Colo, 80-82; Nat Arts Club Open Watercolor Exhib, New York, 81-82; One-man shows, Grand Canyon Nat Park, Ariz, 81 & 83, Morehead State Univ, Ky, 83 & Doncaster Mus, South Yorkshire, Eng, 86 & 90; Headley-Whitley Mus Art, Lexington, Ky, 87; Evansville Mus Arts & Sci, Indiana, 91; Liberty Gallery, Louisville, Ky, 92. *Awards:* First Place, Art Works Show, Frankfort, KY, 81; Best of Show, Woman's Club Louisville, Ky, 82; Purchase Award, Reflections '83, Covington, Ky, 83. *Bibliog:* Articles, North Light, 3/83, Southwest Art, 9/84 & Am Artist, 3/85. *Mem:* Watercolor Soc Ala; Ky Watercolor Soc; Southern Watercolor Soc; Midwest Watercolor Soc; Ga Watercolor Soc. *Media:* Watercolor, Egg Tempera. *Dealer:* Owensboro Mus Fine Art 901 Frederica St Owensboro KY 42301; Indianapolis Mus Art 1200 W 38 St Indianapolis IN 46208. *Mailing Add:* 655 Upland Rd Louisville KY 40206-2826

BRATT, BYRON H
PRINTMAKER
b Everett, Wash, Dec 12, 52. *Study:* Western Wash Univ, BA(fine arts), 75. *Work:* Libr Cong, Washington, DC; Brooklyn Mus; Am Mus, Bath, England; New York Pub Libr; Addison Gallery Am Art, Phillips Acad, Andover, Mass. *Exhib:* American Prints Today & 22nd Ann Print Exhib, Brooklyn Mus, New York; Am Color Print Soc, Philadelphia; 24th Nat Print Exhib, Smithsonian Inst, Washington, DC; RI Sch Design, Providence; Carnegie Inst, Pittsburgh; Int Print Co, Tokyo, Japan & Philadelphia. *Bibliog:* Andrew Stasik (auth), Am Prints & Print Marlow, 56-81, Print Rev, 82; Van Deventer (auth), Six Masters of Mezzotint, 87; Carol Wax (auth), The Mezzotint, Abrams, 90. *Media:* Mezzotint. *Mailing Add:* 2907 Hewett Everett WA 98201

BRATTON, CHRISTOPHER
SCULPTOR, VIDEO ARTIST
b Akron, Ohio, July 3, 59. *Study:* Birmingham - Southern Col, 77-79; Atlanta Col Art, 80-82; Whitney Mus Independent Study Prog, 84-86. *Exhib:* The Public Art Fund, New York, 87; Literacy on the Table, Longwood Gallery, Bronx, New York, Franklin Furnace, New York, Hallwalls, Buffalo, 89; Counterterror: The North of Ireland, PBS/WNET, Channel 13 & Eng Film Festival, Boston, 90; Framing the Panthers in Black & White, Intercom, PBS/WNET Channel 13, 90; Video Viewpoints, Mus Mod Art, New York, 90. *Teaching:* Guest lectr video production, SUNY Westbury, New York, 86; asst prof video, Sch Visual Arts, New York, 90- *Awards:* Nat Endowment Arts, 82, 88 & 90. *Mailing Add:* 1723 N Winchester Chicago IL 60622

BRAUDY, DOROTHY
PAINTER, EDUCATOR
b Los Angeles, Calif. *Study:* Univ, Ky, BA; NY Univ, MA(art educ); pvt study with Richard Pousette-Dart; Art Students' League, with Stamos, Kantor & Glasier; Columbia Univ Teachers Col. *Work:* Fed Reserve Bank, Richmond, Va; Mason Co Mus, Maysville, Ky. *Comn:* Portrait comn by Richard Poirier, New York, 75; George Davis family, Calistoga, Calif, 79; John Irwin family, Baltimore, Md, 80; William Chamness family, Aberdeen, Ohio; Ira Brind family, Philadelphia, 85; Dorothy Lyman-Vincent Malle, Los Angeles, 86. *Exhib:* One-person shows, Philos Hall, Columbia Univ, 76, Viridian Gallery, New York, 77-78, B R Kornblatt Gallery, Baltimore, 79, Washington, DC, 81, Goucher Col, 82, UPB Gallery, Berkeley, Calif, 84 & Orlando Gallery, Los Angeles, 86. *Teaching:* Prof art educ, Pratt Inst, New York, 71-77; prof art hist & drawing, Towson State Univ, Md, 78-79; prof visual arts, Goucher Col, Towson, Md, 79-83. *Bibliog:* Article in New York J Arts, 9-10/78; articles in Baltimore Sun, 9/81 & 9/83; article in New Art Examiner, 10/81. *Media:* Oils, Watercolor. *Dealer:* Orlando Gallery 14553 Ventura Blvd Sherman Oaks CA 91403. *Mailing Add:* c/o Orlando Gallery 14553 Ventura Blvd Sherman Oaks CA 91403

BRAUER, CONNIE ANN
DESIGNER, GOLDSMITH
b Denver, Colo, May 4, 49. *Study:* Colo State Univ, BFA, 71; Inst of Europ Studies, Vienna, Austria, 71; Rochester Inst of Technol, 72-73. *Exhib:* All-Colo Show, Denver Art Mus, 74; Flux, Fusion & Fireworks, Contemp Crafts Gallery, Portland, Ore, 80; Young Americans/Metal, New York, 81; Metalsmith 81, Univ Kans; Concepts Gallery, Carmel, 82; Hanson Gallery, Houston, 83; and others. *Teaching:* Instr jewelery, Metrop State Col, 83. *Awards:* Cash Award, Copper, Brass & Bronze Exhib, Univ Ariz, Tucson, 77; Cash Award, Colo Artist Craftsman Ann Show, 80; Cash Award, Inamori Jewelry Design Competition, 83. *Bibliog:* Fashion swirls into spring, 2/82, Fall fashion forecast, 8/83 & Fashion forecast, 8/83, Jewelers Circular Keystone. *Mem:* Am Craft Coun; Soc N Am Goldsmiths; and others. *Media:* Precious metals, Enamel. *Publ:* Contribr cover photograph, Small Sculptures Nat Catalogue, Cypress Col, 76. *Mailing Add:* 3710 S Huron St Englewood CO 80110-3428

BRAUNSTEIN, H TERRY (MALIKIN)
PHOTOGRAPHER, EDUCATOR
b Washington, DC, Sept 18, 42. *Study:* l'Ecole des Beaux Arts, Aixen-en-Provence, France, 62; Univ Mich, Ann Arbor, BFA, 64; Md Inst Art, Baltimore, MFA, 68. *Work:* Mus Mod Art, New York; Bruce Peel Special Collections Libr, Univ Alta, Can; Libr Congress; Bibliotheque Nationale, Paris; and others. *Exhib:* Livres d'Artistes: Collection Semaphore, Int Artists Book Exhib (with catalog), Ctr George Pompidou, Paris, 85; Undercover, Fresno Mus, 87; Centric 28, Calif State Univ, Long Beach, 87; solo exhib, Marcuse Pfeifer, New York, 87, Orange Coast Col, Costa Mesa, Calif, 88, Calif State Univ, Long Beach, 89, Univ Mich, Ann Arbor, 89, Hampshire Col, Amherst, Mass, 90 & Almediterranea 92, Almeria, Spain, 90; Media Talk (with catalog), Security Pac Gallery, Costa Mesa, 89; Photomontage/Photocollage: The Changing Picture 1920-1989, Jan Turner Gallery, Los Angeles, 89; Biennial 1 (with catalog), Calif Mus Photog, Riverside, 90; Primavera Fotografica (with catalog), Sala Arcs Gallery, Barcelona, Spain, 90; and many others. *Pos:* Vis artist, Smithsonian Inst, 78; guest cur Bookworks, Washington Project Arts, Washington, DC, 80; artist mem, Advisory Comt Pub Art, Long Beach Percent-for- Art-Program, 90. *Teaching:* Instr, Prince Georges Community Col, Largo, Md, 71-74; instr, Washington Women's Art Ctr, 76- & Northern Va Community Col, Annandale, 76-78; instr printmaking, Corcoran Sch Art, Washington, DC, 78-79, assoc prof & coordr 3rd yr Fine Arts Prog, 79-; guest artist, Univ Wis, 81 & Chicago Art Inst, 84; prof painting & mixed media, advanced students, Calif State Univ, 89- *Awards:* Visual Arts Fel, Nat Endowment Arts, 85; Panel, Nat Endowment Arts, 88; Distinguished vis prof, Calif State Univ, 89. *Bibliog:* Coleen Creamer (auth), Terry Braunstein, the cutting edge of collage, Darkroom Photog, Vol 12, No 3, 3/90; Joan Fontcuberta (auth), Un nuevo reparto de atribuciones, La vanguardia, 4/24/90; La Primavera fotografica se abre con imagenes historicas y las ultimas tendencias del fotomontaje, El Pais, 4/25/90. *Mem:* Adhibit Comt, Washington, DC (mem bd dirs, currently); The List, Independent Curators Inc, New York; Washington Proj Arts, DC (mem bd dirs). *Media:* Book Artist. *Publ:* Auth, Windows, Vis Studies Workshop Press, 82; Theater for Life? (exhib catalog), Charlotte Salomon exhib, Judaic Mus, Washington, DC, 83; Station identification, Kalliope Mag, 85. *Dealer:* Tartt Gallery 2017 Q St NW Washington DC 20009. *Mailing Add:* 262 Belmont Ave Long Beach CA 90803

BRAUNSTEIN, MARK MATHEW
WRITER, PHOTOGRAPHER
b New York, NY, Aug 6, 51. *Study:* Carnegie-Mellon Univ, 72; Pratt Inst, 73, MS, 78; State Univ NY, Binghamton, BA, 74. *Exhib:* Solo show, Conn Col, 91, Mystic Nature Ctr, 92. *Pos:* Ed & researcher, Rosenthal Art Slides, Chicago, 78-80; asst ed, Art Index, 80-83; head, Slide & Photog Collection, RI Sch Design, Providence, 83-87; slide cur, Art Hist Dept, Conn Col, New London, 87- *Awards:* Fac Develop Grants, RI Sch Design, 84-86. *Bibliog:* Contemporary Authors, Vol 113; Who's Who in The East, 93. *Publ:* Auth, Vegetarianism in art (cover story), Vegetarian Times, 80; Rembrandt's Cologne Self-Portrait, Iris: Notes in the Hist of Art, 83; ed, Slide Buyers' Guide: International Directory of Slide Sources for Art & Architecture, Libr Unlimited, 86. *Mailing Add:* PO Box 456 Quaker Hill CT 06375-0474

BRAUNSTEIN, RUTH
ART DEALER
b Minneapolis, Minn. *Collections Arranged:* California Era, Update, Huntsville Art Mus, Ala; Richard Shaw: Illusionism in Clay (auth, catalog), 71-85. *Pos:* Dir, Braunstein/Quay Gallery, San Francisco, 61- *Mem:* San Francisco Art Dealers Asn (pres, 75-77); Hadassah; Art Table Inc. *Specialty:* Contemporary art: sculpture, painting and drawing; ceramic sculpture, mostly American artists. *Publ:* David Jones (auth), 1971 early work (catalog), 71; Peter Voulkos (auth), Anagama works (catalog), 91. *Mailing Add:* 250 Sutter St San Francisco CA 94108

BRAUNTUCH, TROY
PAINTER, PRINTMAKER
b Jersey City, NJ, 1954. *Study:* Calif Inst Arts, Valencia, BFA, 75. *Work:* Lannan Found, Los Angeles, Calif; Metrop Mus Art, Mus Mod Art, New York. *Exhib:* Solo exhibs, The Kitchen, New York, NY, 79, Mary Boone Gallery, New York, 82, 83 & 85 & Akira Ueda Gallery, Tokyo, Japan, 84; New Talent/New York, Gallery Contemp Art, Cleveland, Ohio, 80; US Art Now, Konsthallen, Goteborg, Sweden, 81; Venice Biennale, Venice, Italy, 82; Nat Mus Art, Osaka, Japan, 83; Mus Mod Art, 84; Mus & Sculpture Garden, Washington, DC, 84; Whitney Mus Am Art, New York, 89-90. *Mailing Add:* c/o Kent Gallery 47 E 63rd St New York NY 10021

BRAVERMAN, DONNA (DONNA BRAVERMAN KNOPF)
TAPESTRY ARTIST, SCULPTOR
b Chicago, Ill, Apr 4, 47. *Study:* Univ Mo, 65-68; Chicago Acad Fine Arts, BFA, 70. *Comn:* Sohio Petroleum, Dallas, Tex, 82; Phillips Petroleum, Houston, Tex 83; Reichold Chemical, White Plains, NY, 84; Rolm Telecommunications, Colo Springs, Colo, 85; Dictaphone World Hq, Stratford, Conn, 89. *Exhib:* Young Americans, Mus Contemp Art, New York, 77-79; Marietta Crafts Nat, Grover M Herman Fine Arts Ctr, Ga, 82; Ariz Archit Crafts, traveling exhib, 83-85; Ariz Biennial, Tucson Mus Art, 84; Paper Fiber VIII, Arts Ctr, Iowa City, Iowa, 85; Primavera, Tucson Mus Art, Ariz, 86; Wichita Nat, Kans, 86; Artist's Liason, Elaine Potter Galley, San Fracisco, Calif, 86. *Pos:* Interior designer, Perkins & Will Architects, Chicago, Ill, 70-77; Fiber artist, Scottsdale, Ariz, 77- *Awards:* Best of show, Crafts Elegant 80's, Cary-Windsor Gallery, Richmond, Va, 81; Award Winner, Catalog Mountain Plains Craft Art, Craft Range, 82; Best of show, Second Ariz Women's Fine Art Competition, Verde Valley Art Asn, Jerome, Ariz, 82. *Media:* Miscellaneous. *Publ:* Coauth, Fiber Arts Design Book II, Lark Books, 83; The Guild, Krause Sikes, 87 & 88; Fiber Arts Design Book III, Lark Books, 88; Design Source, Aztec Designs, 89. *Mailing Add:* 1041 E Glenrosa Phoenix AZ 85014

BRAVMANN, RENE A
ART HISTORIAN, EDUCATOR
b Marseilles, France, Dec 10, 39; US citizen. *Study:* Cleveland Mus Art, 57-61; Western Reserve Univ, BA, 61; Univ Wis, 61-63; Ind Univ, MA(fine arts), 65, PhD, 71. *Teaching:* Asst prof art hist, Univ Wash, Seattle, 68-72, assoc prof, 72-76, prof, 77-, chmn African studies, 69-75. *Awards:* Ford Found Fel, Am Coun Learned Socs, 66-68; Post-doctoral Res Grant, Soc Sci Res Coun, 72-73; Am Philos Soc Grant, 74. *Publ:* Auth, West African Sculpture, 70 & auth, Open Frontiers: The Dynamics of Art in Black Africa, 73, Univ Wash; auth, The diffusion of Ashanti political art, In: African Art & Leadership, 72; auth, Islam & Tribal Art in West Africa, Cambridge Univ, 74; auth, An urban way of death, African Arts, Vol 8, No 3. *Mailing Add:* Dept of Art History Univ of Wash Seattle WA 98195

BRAWLEY, ROBERT JULIUS
PAINTER, EDUCATOR
b Brainerd, Minn, April 24, 37. *Study:* Cent Wash Univ, 56-57; Frye Art Mus Sch, 58-61; San Francisco Art Inst, BFA, MFA, 64. *Work:* Art Inst Chicago; San Francisco Art Inst; Moore Col Art; Hoyt Inst Fine Arts, Lancaster, Pa; Nat Mus Am Art, Washington, DC. *Exhib:* Beyond the Actual--California New Realism, Haggin Galleries, Pioneer Mus, Stockton, Calif, 71; San Francisco New Realism--Through the Photograph to Painting, San Francisco Mus Art, 71; The New Realists, Mongerson Galleries, Chicago, 82; Small Works, New York Univ, 82; Hoyt Nat Painting Show, Hoyt Inst Fine Arts, Lancaster, Pa, 82; Mid-Year Nat Exhib, Butler Inst Am Art, Ohio, 82 & 83; Four American Realists, Mongerson Galleries, Chicago, 83; solo exhibs, Capricorn Galleries, Bethesda, Md, 84 & Mongerson-Wunderlich, Chicago, Ill, 85; Chicago Int Art Exhib, Chicago, Ill, 86. *Teaching:* Dir & instr drawing & painting, Acad Art Col, San Francisco, 69-71; assoc prof art hist & studio art, dir grad art studies & chmn art dept, Lone Mountain Col, 71-78; lectr, St Marys Col, Moraga, Calif, 81-; chmn art dept & prof studio art, Univ Kans, Lawrence, currently. *Awards:* Fulbright Fel, 66-67; Painting Awards, Mid-Year Painting Exhib, Butler Inst Am Art, 82 & 84 & Hoyt Nat Painting Show, Hoyt Inst Fine Arts, 82. *Bibliog:* Robin Longman (auth), article, Am Artist Mag, 8/83; Joann Lewis (auth), rev, Washington Post, 11/8/84; Margaret Hawkins (auth), rev, Chicago Sun-Times, 5/22/87. *Media:* Alkyd; Graphite. *Dealer:* Mongerson-Wunderlich Galleries 620 N Michigan Ave Chicago IL 60611; Capricorn Galleries 4849 Rugby Ave Bethesda MD. *Mailing Add:* 624 Louisiana St Lawrence KS 66044

BRECHT, GEORGE
CONCEPTUAL ARTIST, ASSEMBLAGE ARTIST
b New York, NY, 1926. *Study:* Philadelphia Col Pharmacy & Sci, Pa, BSc, 50; New Sch Social Res, New York, with John Cage, 58-59. *Work:* Mus Mod Art, New York; Stadtisches Mus, Monchengladbach, Ger, Arch Sohm, Margroningen, Ger; Musee Nat d'Art Moderne, Ctr Georges Pompidou, Paris; Nat Gallerie, Berlin; Mus Moderne Kunst, Vienna. *Comn:* Music and sets, James Waring Dance Co, New York. *Exhib:* One-man shows, Toward Events, Reuben Gallery, New York, 59, & Los Angeles Co Mus Art, Calif, 69; The Art of Assemblage, Mus Mod Art, New York, 61; Mixed-Media & Pop Art, Albright-Knox Art Gallery, Buffalo, NY, 63; Black, White & Gray, Wadsworth Atheneum, Hartford, Conn, 64; Eleven from the Reuben Gallery, Guggenheim Mus, New York, 65; Art by Tel, Mus Contemp Art, Chicago, 69; and many other one man shows and group exhibitions. *Teaching:* Res fel, Leeds Col Art, Eng, 68-69. *Awards:* Will-Grohmann Prize, Berlin, Ger, 83. *Bibliog:* Allan Kaprow (auth), Assemblage, Environments & Happenings, New York, 66; Jan van der Marck (auth), George Brecht: an art of multiple implications, Art in Am, 7-8/74; Henry Martin (auth), An Introduction to George Brecht's book of the Tumbler on Fire, Multhipla Edizioni, Milan. *Publ:* Auth, Chance imagery, Collage, Palermo, Italy, 12/64; Dances, events & other poems, Something, Vol 1, 65; coauth, Vicious Circles & Infinity, New York, 75; translr, Seng Ts'an, Hsin-hsin-ming, Editions Hossmann-Lebeer, Brussels, 80. *Dealer:* Arturo Schwarz via Gesu 17 Milan 20121 Italy. *Mailing Add:* Wildenburgstrabe 9 500 Koln 41 Cologne-Sulz Germany

BRECKENRIDGE, BRUCE M
CERAMIST, EDUCATOR
b Chicago, Ill, Oct 29, 29. *Study:* Wis State Col-Milwaukee, BS, 52; Cranbrook Acad Art, Bloomfield Hills, Mich, MFA, 53; Acad Grande Chaumier, Paris, 56. *Work:* Elvehjem Art Ctr, Univ Wis-Madison; Westum Mus, Racine, Wis. *Exhib:* Objects as Objects, Mus Contemp Crafts, New York, 68 & Coffee Tea and Other Cups, 71; Nat Ceramics Invitational Exhib, Nelson Gallery Atkins Mus, Kansas City, 69; Nat Ceramics Invitational, Scripps Col, 71; The Plastic Earth, John Michael Kohler Arts Ctr, Shebogan, Wis, 73. *Collections Arranged:* Richmond Art Ctr, Calif, 59-61; Mus Contemp Crafts, New York, 65-66. *Pos:* Asst dir, Richmond Art Ctr, 59-61; installation asst, Mus Mod Art, New York, 64-65; asst dir, Mus Contemp Crafts, New York, 65-66. *Teaching:* Instr ceramics, Brooklyn Mus Art Sch, 65-68; prof art-ceramics, Univ Wis-Madison, 68- *Media:* Ceramics. *Publ:* Auth, New ceramic forms, 65, Wisconsin designer-craftsman, 69, Don Reitz exhibition, 70 & National invitational exhibition II, glass, 71, Craft Horizons. *Mailing Add:* 1715 Regent St Madison WI 53705

BREDER, HANS DIETER
SCULPTOR, VIDEO ARTIST
b Herford, Ger, Oct 20, 35; US citizen. *Study:* Hochschule fuer Bildende Kunste, Hamburg, Ger, with Willem Grimm, asst to sculptor, George Rickey. *Work:* Cleveland Mus, Ohio; Joseph H Hirshhorn Collection, Washington, DC; Whitney Mus of Am Art, New York; Mus of Art, State Univ NY Col, Purchase; Mus of Art, Iowa City; Am Asn Advan Sci, Washington, DC; Prudential Ins Co NAm, Newark, NJ; Mus Mod Art, New York. *Comn:* Three outdoor sculptures, City of Hanover, Ger, 71. *Exhib:* Mus Contemp Art, Chicago, Ill, 68; Jewish Mus, 69, Exhibit Recent Acquisitions, Mus Mod Art, 84, Whitney Mus Am Art, New York, 87, 89 & 91; one-artist exhibs, Richard Feigen Gallery, Chicago, 67, 70, 72, New York, 67, 70, The Kitchen, Ctr Video & Music, New York, 75, Wolfgang Foerster Galerie, Munster, Ger, 79, 81, 82, 88 & 91, Schreiber/Cutler Inc, New York, 87, 88 & 89, Ruth Siegel Gallery, New York, 90; 2nd Videonale, Bonn, Ger, 86; 3rd Fukui Int Video Biennale, Japan, 89; Painting Beyond the Death of Painting, Kuznetzky Most Exhib Hall, Moscow, 89. *Pos:* Co-dir, Corroboree: Gallery of New Concepts, Univ Iowa, Iowa City, 77- *Teaching:* Prof multimedia, Univ Iowa, Iowa City, 77- *Bibliog:* Stephen Foster, Estera Milman (auths), The Media as Medium: Hans Breder's Berlin Work, Kans Quart, Vol 17, No 3, 85; Herman Rapaport (auth), Hans Breder and the Auras of Video, Art Criticism, Vol 4, No 1, 88; Donald Kuspit (auth), New York Reviews, Artforum, 5/89. *Publ:* Coauth, Speculum, Ctr for New Performing Arts, 73; coauth, Participatory Art and Body Sculpture with Mirrors, Leonardo: Art, Sci & Technol, 74. *Mailing Add:* Dept of Art & Art History Univ Iowa Iowa City IA 52242

BREDLOW, TOM
DESIGNER, BLACKSMITH
b Pontiac, Mich, Oct 18, 38. *Study:* Tex A&M Col, BA(math). *Comn:* Grilles, door hardware, fireplace accessories, weathervanes, gates, railings, tables & chandeliers, pvt residences in US & Mex, 64-; gates, railings, candlestick & flower stands, Washington Cathedral, 68-; Barrio-Historico (grilles, gates, doors, railings, downspouts), comn by H Kelley Rollings, Tucson, 70-; hand rails, comn by Harriet Hubbell, Hubbell House (SW Span Craftsmen), Santa Fe, NMex, 71; Peopleplay (public sculpture), Steven Nanini, Tucson, 80; and others. *Exhib:* One-man show, Boyer Gallery, Tucson, 68 & 70; Ann Western Art Show, Mountain Oyster Club, Tucson, 72-; Iron-Solid Wrought, Mus Southern Ill Univ, Mus Contemp Crafts, New York & Smithsonian Inst, Washington, DC, 76-77. *Pos:* Owner & sole craftsman, Bredlow's Blacksmith Shop, Tucson, 64- *Teaching:* Guest lectr hist archaeol, Univ Ariz, speaker-demonstr, Ironworking Conv,. *Awards:* Biennial Prize, Quinnell Biennial, Surrey, England, 76. *Bibliog:* Ty Harrington (auth), Last Cathedral, Prentice-Hall, 79; R T Feller (auth), For Thy Great Glory, Community, 79. *Mem:* hon artist Mountain Oyster Club, Tucson, 78. *Media:* Metals. *Publ:* Auth, Stagecoach, Frontier Times, summer 60; Anvils and coal smoke, Old West, winter 66; Crown Sculptural and Decorative Ironwork, Meilach, 77. *Mailing Add:* 3524 N Olive Road Tucson AZ 85719

BREED, CHARLES AYARS
SCULPTOR, DESIGNER
b Paw Paw, Mich, Jan 31, 27. *Study:* Western Mich Univ, BS; Univ Wis, MA. *Work:* Midland Ctr Arts, Mich; Dow Chemical, Mich. *Comn:* Cross (glass & brass), Mem Presby Church, Midland, Mich, 57; Eternal Flame (Plexiglas), Temple Beth El, Spring Valley, NY, 66; Icon Screen (polyester), Hellenic Orthodox Church, Bloomfield Hills, Mich, 68; sculptural panels, Richard

Howell, 81; sculpture, Alden D Dow Ctr Arts, Midland, 82; and others. *Exhib:* Craftsman USA 66, Mus Contemp Crafts, New York, 66, Plastic as Plastic Nat Invitational, 68; Made of Plastic Nat Invitational, Flint Inst Art, Mich, 68; Exhib 70, Columbus Art Gallery, Ohio, 70; First Biennial Int Small Sculpture Exhib, Budapest, Hungary, 71. *Pos:* Bd dirs, Awareness Inc, Lansing, Mich, 62-64; bd dirs, Midland Art Coun, Mich, 65-68; bd dirs, Midland Ctr Arts, 67-72. *Teaching:* Dir art, Nat Music Acad, 58-62; prof art & chmn dept, Delta Col, 62-83. *Awards:* Nat Merit Award, Mus Contemp Crafts, New York, 66; Outstanding Teacher Year, Bergstein Found, 67; Mich Coun Arts Artist Grant, 81. *Bibliog:* Jack Brickhouse (auth), Everything is Double in Paw Paw, Paramount Films, 48; Curtis Bessinger (auth), Where does the design of a house begin, House Beautiful, 1/62; Rite of Spring--Detroit (videotape), PM Mag, 81-83. *Media:* Plastic. *Publ:* Auth, Plastic as a new art form, House Beautiful, 2/62; co-auth, Plastic-the visual arts in crafts, Crafts & Craftsmen, 67; auth, Unite equal opposites, Symposium, 80; auth, Conceptual Art, Art in Am, 2/84. *Dealer:* Northwood Galleries 144 E Main Midland MI 48640. *Mailing Add:* Equiline Design 1320 W Main Midland MI 48640

BREEN, HARRY FREDERICK, JR
PAINTER, SCULPTOR
b Chicago, Ill, Mar 4, 30. *Study:* Art Inst Chicago, with John Rogers Cox & Paul Wiegarht, BA, 53; Univ Ill, Urbana-Champaign, MA, 59. *Work:* Ill State Mus, Springfield; Butler Mus Am Art, Youngstown, Ohio; Krannert Art Mus, Champaign, Ill; Union League Club, Chicago; Lakeview Ctr Arts & Sci, Peoria, Ill. *Comn:* chapel murals, Holy Cross Church, Champaign, Ill, 83; murals, St Mary's Cathedral, Peoria, Ill, 88; sculpture, Immaculate Conception Church, St Mary of Woods, Ind, 89; paintings & sculpture, Bishop's Chapel, St Mary's Cathedral Rectory, Peoria, Ill, 91; stained glass windows, St Philomena's Church, Monticello, Ill, 92. *Exhib:* Mid-Yr Ann, Butler Mus Am Art, Youngstown, Ohio, 62, 63 & 65; Pa Acad Fine Art, 63 traveling in Europe, 64; Realism Revisited, Flint Art Inst, Mich, 66; 5th Biennial Relig Art, Cranbrook Acad, Detroit, Mich, 66; Ill Arts Coun Traveling Exhib, 67; retrospective, Lakeview Ctr Arts & Sci, Peoria, Ill, 77; Univ Ill Painting Fac, Univ Tokyo & Nat Hist Mus Taipei, 81; and others. *Teaching:* Instr art, Pub Schs, Gary, Ind, 54-57; instr art, Univ High Sch, Univ Ill, 57-59; vis prof art, Univ Wis, Madison, 68-69; prof art, Sch Art & Design, Univ Ill, Champaign, 59-85. *Awards:* Second Purchase Prize, Fourth Union League Exhib, Chicago, 61; Fourth Purchase Prize Oils, Mid-Yr Ann, Butler Mus Am Art, 63; Second Prize Sculpture, Ann Exhib, Hoosier Salon, Indianapolis, 63. *Media:* All; Clay. *Mailing Add:* 1107 W Church St Champaign IL 61820

BREER, ROBERT C
SCULPTOR, FILMMAKER
b Detroit, Mich, Sept 30, 26. *Study:* Stanford Univ, BA. *Work:* Mus Mod Art, New York; Mod Mus, Stockholm, Sweden; Anthology Film Archives, New York; Mod Art Mus, Krefeld, Ger; Centre Beaubourg, Paris, France. *Comn:* Design Pepsi Cola Pavilion, Expo '70, Japan; kinetic sculpture, IBM Plaza, Pittsburgh Arts Fete, 74; Mural, Film Forum, New York, 81. *Exhib:* The Machine as Seen at the End of the Mechanical Age, Mus Mod Art, New York, 68; Albright-Knox Art Gallery, Buffalo, NY, 71; solo exhibs, Mus Mod Art, New York, Albright-Knox Art Gallery, 76, Collective Living Cinema, New York, 77, Walker Art Ctr, 79 & Millenium, New York, 79; retrospective, Whitney Mus Am Art, New York, 77 & 80; Drawings for Animated Film, Drawing Ctr, New York, 78; Film as Film, Hayward Gallery, London, 79; New York Film Festival, 79; Whitney Biennial, 79, 81, 83, 85, British Art Coun traveling Exhib, 83; 1900-2000 Gallery, Paris, 90. *Pos:* Mem bd dirs, Filmmakers Coop, New York, 67-72 & 75-88. *Teaching:* Prof kinetics, Cooper Union, 71-; instr, Hampshire Col, 74-79 & New York Univ, 77. *Awards:* Nat Endowment Arts Grant, 76; Am Film Inst Grant, 77; Guggenheim Found Fel, 78-79; Am Film Inst: Maya Deven Award 86. *Bibliog:* Adrienne Mancia & William Van Dyke (auth), Four artists as film makers, Art in Am, 1/67; Calvin Tompkins (auth), Onwards and upwards with the arts, New Yorker, 10/70; Lois Mendelson (auth), Robert Breer, UMI Res Press, 81; Robert Breer 5 & Dime Animator, Channel 4 England, 84. *Mailing Add:* Cooper-Union Cooper Sq New York NY 10003

BREIGER, ELAINE
PRINTMAKER, PAINTER
b Springfield, Mass. *Study:* Art Students League; Cooper Union, cert fine arts; spec master printing with Krishna Reddy. *Work:* Brooklyn Mus, NY; Libr Cong, Washington, DC; Honolulu Acad Art, Hawaii; Chase Manhattan Bank, New York; De Cordova Mus, Lincoln, Mass. *Comn:* Print, Container Corp Am, 70. *Exhib:* Glaser Gallery, La Jolla, Calif; Contemp Gallery, Dallas; Leslie Rankow Gallery, New York; Martha Jackson Gallery, New York, 74; Pace Gallery, New York, 76; Source Gallery, San Francisco, Calif, 77. *Pos:* Mgr, Printmaking Workshop, 68-70; chmn dept art, 92nd St YMCA, 72-76. *Teaching:* Instr techniques etching & intaglio printing, 92nd St YMHA, New York, 71-76; color etching, Sch of Visual Arts, New York, 77- *Awards:* Creative Arts Pub Serv Fel, 74; Nat Endowment Arts Grant, 75. *Bibliog:* Una Johnson (auth), American Prints & Printmakers, Doubleday, 80. *Mem:* Visual Artists & Galleries Asn. *Media:* Etching; Acrylic, Oil. *Mailing Add:* 112 Greene St New York NY 10012

BREININ, RAYMOND
PAINTER, SCULPTOR
b Vitebsk, Russia, Nov 30, 10. *Study:* Chicago Acad Fine Arts, Vitebsk Acad-Artist Uri Pen. *Work:* Metrop Mus Art; Mus Mod Art; Brooklyn Mus; Art Inst Chicago; Phillips Collection, Washington, DC; Boston Mus Fine Arts; San Francisco Mus; Am Acad Arts & Letters; Pa Acad Fine Arts; San Diego Fine Arts Soc. *Comn:* Costumes & settings, Ballet Theatre's Undertow; murals, Winnetka High Sch, Ill, State Hosp, Elgin, Ill, US Post Off, Wilmette, Ill & Ambassador E Hotel, Chicago; and others. *Teaching:* Artist-in-residence, Univ Southern Ill; instr art, Univ Minn; instr, Breinin Sch Art, Chicago; instr painting & drawing, Art Students League; instr, Nat Acad Design, New York. *Awards:* Prizes, Art USA, 58, Art Inst Chicago (seven) & Pa Acad Fine Arts (two); plus others. *Bibliog:* Rosamond Frost (auth), included in: Contemporary Art: The March of Art from Cezanne Until Now, Crown, 42; Emily Genauer (auth), included in: Best of Art, Doubleday, 48; and others. *Mem:* Nat Acad Design; Artists Equity Asn New York. *Mailing Add:* 121 Inwood Rd Scarsdale NY 10583

BREITENBACH, WILLIAM JOHN
SCULPTOR, EDUCATOR
b Milwaukee, Wis, Jan 21, 36. *Study:* Univ Wis, Milwaukee, BS, 62 & MS, 65; Stephen F Austin State Univ, MFA, 71. *Work:* Brentwood Col, NY; Del Mar Col, Corpus Christi, Tex; Stephen F Austin State Univ, Tex; Houston Baptist Univ, Tex; Sam Houston State Univ, Tex. *Comn:* Sculptural fountain, William Robert Murfin, Houston, 72; plywood wall sculpture, Performing Arts Ctr, Sam Houston State Univ, Huntsville, Tex, 76; Cent Tex Col, Killeen, 83. *Exhib:* Creative Collab, Rice Univ, Houston, 72; 9th Monroe Ann, Masur Mus Art, Monroe, La, 72; Southwest Graphics Invitational, Mex-Am Cult Exchange Inst, San Antonio, Tex, 72; Inst Visual Arts, Puebla, Mex, 81; Cultural Activities Ctr, Temple, Tex, 84; and others. *Pos:* Chmn, Houston Area Art Curric Develop Comt, 82-86. *Teaching:* Supvr elem art, South Door Co Sch Dist 1, Brussels, Wis, 62-65; full prof art educ, design & drawing, Sam Houston State Univ, 65- *Awards:* First Prize in sculpture, 5th Ann Exhib, Del Mar Col, 71; Merit Award for creative collab, Rice Univ, 71; Third Place Award, Assistance League Houston, 73. *Mem:* Tex Art Educ Asn; Nat Art Educ Asn. *Media:* Paper Mache, Fabricated Plywood; Ark. *Publ:* Auth, Art education and the modern age, Tex Trends in Art Educ, 68. *Dealer:* Umbrella Arts 2615 Old Houston Rd Huntsville TX 77340. *Mailing Add:* Box 2023 Sam Houston State Univ Huntsville TX 77341

BREITHAUPT, ERWIN M
PAINTER, HISTORIAN
b Columbus, Ohio, Nov 12, 20. *Study:* Miami Univ, BFA; Ohio State Univ, MA & PhD; Oak Ridge Inst Nuclear Studies. *Work:* Minn Mus Art. *Exhib:* Design of the Future, Mus Mod Art, New York, 54 & Merchandise Mart, Chicago, 55. *Collections Arranged:* F L Wright Centennial Exhib, 66. *Teaching:* Assoc prof art hist & design, Univ Ga, 47-62; prof art & chmn dept art hist & design, Ripon Col, 62-82, prof emer, 83-; adj prof art, NMex State Univ, 84- *Awards:* Gen Educ Bd Fel, Rockefeller Found, 51; Severy Award, 65 & Uhrig Award, 69, Ripon Col. *Mem:* Col Art Asn. *Res:* Area of the art institution and creativity. *Publ:* Auth, A New Approach to Art Education, 56; auth, The Basic Art Course at Georgia, 57; coauth, An Institutional Approach to Aesthetics, 59; contribr, The Creative Life of Man, 70. *Mailing Add:* 2230 Cimmarron Dr Las Cruces NM 88001

BREJCHA, VERNON LEE
GLASSBLOWER, EDUCATOR
b Ellsworth, Kans, Jan 30, 42. *Study:* Ft Hays State Univ, BA & MS; Univ Wis-Madison, MFA with Harvey K Littleton. *Work:* Corning Mus of Glass, NY; Mus of Contemp Crafts, New York; Kunstmuseum, Dusseldorf, WGer; Mus of Decorative Arts, Praque, Czech; Smithsonian Inst, Washington, DC; Mod Int Glaskunst Mus, Ebeltoft, Denmark; and others. *Exhib:* Three-man show, Departure Gallery, New York, 82; A Gather of Glass, Mindscape, Chicago, Ill, 85; Great Am Gallery, Atlanta, Ga, 86; Two Man Glass Gallery, Bethesda, Md, 87; one-man shows, Marx Gallery, Chicago, Ill, 90, Hall Fame, Bonner Springs, Kans, 91 & Cent Col, Pella, Iowa, 92; and others. *Teaching:* Asst prof glass, ceramics & sculpture, Tusculum Col, Greenville, Tenn, 72-76; asst prof design glass, Univ Kans, 77-81, assoc prof, 81- *Awards:* First Place Purchase, Ceramics Northwest, C M Russell Mus, Great Falls, Mont, 70; Purchase Award, Tenn Bicentennial Art Exhib, State of Tenn, 76; Artist Fel, Nat Endowment Arts, 84; Kans Governor's Artist, 85. *Bibliog:* Frank Kulasiewicz (auth), Glassblowing, Watson-Guptill, 74; Polly Rothenberg (auth), The Complete Book of Creative Glass Art, Crown, 74; Elizabeth Campbell (auth), Kansas-Theme of glass artist Vernon Brejcha, Neues Glas, Dusseldorf, 82. *Mem:* Am Crafts Coun; Nat Coun on Educ for the Ceramic Arts (glass panel chmn, 77); Glass Art Soc; Kans Artist-Craftsmen Asn. *Publ:* Auth, Throw the Lid First, Ceramics Monthly, 70; contribr, The Complete Book of Creative Glass Art, Crown, 74; contribr, Crafts & Craftsmen of the Tennessee Mountains, Summit Press; auth, British hot glass, Glass Studio, 82. *Dealer:* Glass Gallery 4931 Elm St Bethesda MD 20814; Marx Gallery 208 W Kinzie St Chicago IL 60610. *Mailing Add:* 3805 W 24th Lawrence KS 66047

BREMER, MARLENE S
PAINTER, SCULPTOR
b Coburg, WGer; US citizen. *Study:* Fairleigh Dickinson Univ, NJ, BA, 79; William Paterson Col, NJ, MA, 81; New York Univ, NY, cert(fine art appraisal), 89. *Work:* Pvt collections USA & Europe. *Exhib:* Solo exhibs, William Paterson Col, NJ, 83, Fairleigh Dickinson Col, NJ, 83, Jacob Javits Fed Bldg, New York, 85, Vereinigle Coburger Sparkassen, Coburg, WGer, 86, Salon des Artistes, New York, 88 & John Harms Ctr for Arts, Englewood, NJ, 89; 36th Art of the Northeast, Silvermine Guild Ctr, New Canaan, Conn, 85; 8th Ann Exhib--The New Romanticism, Pleiades Gallery, Soho, NY, 90; Ben Shahn Galleries, William Patterson Col, Wayne, NJ, 91; City Without Walls, 92; Jon Tanner Gallery, Westwood, NJ, 92; and others. *Pos:* Appraiser fine art, Athena Art Servs, New York, currently. *Teaching:* Instr sculpture, Ridgewood Community Sch, NJ, 84-85; adj prof art hist, Bergen Community

Col, NJ, 85- *Awards:* 2nd & 3rd Awards, NJ Fedn Women's Clubs, 74 & 76; First Place, Bicentennial Show, Bergen Community Col, NJ, 76; First in show, New York-Paris Show, Inst Audio-Visual, Paris, 82; Salute Award, Jacob Javits Bldg, NY, 88. *Bibliog:* Waku (auth), Natur Eindruecke in Farben umgesetzt, Neue Presse, Coburg, WGer, 86; Ron Stein (auth), Saluting Women at Lever House, Art Speak, 1/89; Marie Beth Zeman (auth), William Paterson Alumni; and others. *Mem:* Nat Asn Women Artists, (asst chair-nominating, New York Chap; Artists Equity Asn; Salute to Women in the Arts, NJ. *Mailing Add:* 440 Egan Pl Englewood NJ 07631

BRENDEL, BETTINA
PAINTER, LECTURER
b Luneburg, Ger; US citizen. *Study:* Hamburg, Ger, BA, 40; Kunstschule Schmilinsky, Hamburg, 41-42; Landes Hochschule Bildende Künste, Hamburg, 45-47, with Erich Hartmann; Univ Southern Calif, 55-58; New Sch Social Res, 68-69. *Work:* Grunwald Graphic Arts Ctr & Int Student Ctr, Univ Calif & Los Angeles Co Mus; Univ Southern Calif; San Francisco Mus Art; Long Beach Mus Art; La Jolla Art Mus; and others. *Exhib:* Los Angeles Co Mus Ann, 55, 57, 59 & 61; 58th Ann, San Francisco Mus Art, 66; On Mass and Energy, Santa Barbara Mus Art, 66; Spectrum Gallery, New York, 67; Women Artists, Santa Monica Col Art Gallery, Calif, 77; Los Angeles Artcore Gallery, 84; A Digital View, Art Store Gallery, Pasadena, 90; Digitals & Modules, Glendale, Calif, 90; and others. *Pos:* Computer artist, Calif Mus Sci & Indust, Los Angeles, currently. *Teaching:* Instr, The Emergence of Mod Painting, Univ Calif, Los Angeles, 58-61, lectr art, Exten, spring 76; lectr, Thematic Option Prog, Univ Southern Calif, 80, Gulbenkian Found, Paris, 85, Lisbon, Port, 87 & Max Planck Inst, Munich, Ger, 91. *Awards:* Award, La Jolla Art Mus, 58 & 59; Long Beach Mus Art, 60; First Purchase Award, San Francisco Mus Art, 66. *Bibliog:* Michel Tapie (auth), Musee manifeste, Fratelli Pozzo Editori, Torino, 62; Constance Perkins (auth), article, Art Forum, 4/62; H Von Breton (auth), article, Santa Barbara News Press, 2/66; Dr John Marburger (auth), Bettina Brendel, Paintings 70-82, 84. *Mem:* Am Coun Arts; Univ Calif Los Angeles Art Coun; Am Physical Soc. *Media:* Acrylic, Collage; Computer Art. *Res:* Theoretical physics and its relation to the arts. *Publ:* Auth, The painter and the new physics, Art J, fall 71; The influence of atomic physics, Leonardo Mag, 73; Whenever in the World (poems), Stockton Press, 77. *Mailing Add:* 1061 N Kenter Ave Los Angeles CA 90049

BRENER, ROLAND
SCULPTOR, EDUCATOR
b South Africa, 1942. *Study:* St Martin's Sch Art, London, Eng. *Work:* Art Gallery, Greater Victoria; Art Gallery Ont, Toronto; Can Coun Art Bank & Nat Gallery Can, Ottawa; Kasmin Gallery, London, Eng; Musee d'Art Contemporain de Montreal. *Exhib:* Solo exhibs, Edmonton Art Gallery, 83, Mercer Union Toronto, 84, Venice Biennale, 88, Mississauga Civic Centre Art Gallery, 89; Making History & Art in Victoria, Victoria Art Gallery, 86; 'Robots' History--Fantasy and Reality, Madison Art Ctr, Wis, 86; Sao Paolo Biennale, Brazil, 87; Art Cologne, Kandische Kunst, Ger, 87; 49th Parallel for Contemporary Canadian Art, New York, 89. *Teaching:* Lectr, St Martin's Sch Art, London, Eng, 66-69; guest lectr, Univ Calif, Santa Barbara, 70-71; asst prof, Univ Iowa, 71-72; prof, Univ Victoria, 72- *Bibliog:* Bruce Ferguson (auth), Nomad is an Island; Roland Brener, Vol 17, No 3, Vanguard, summer 88, 24-27; John Bentley Mays (auth), Engaging dialogues on art, 6/24/88, Caught between industry and art, 6/28/88, The Globe & Mail, Toronto; Linda Genereux (auth), Fast Forward, Vol 6, No 4, winter 89. *Mailing Add:* c/o Olga Korper Gallery 17 Morrow Ave Toronto ON M6R 2H9 Canada

BRENNAN, FANNY (FRANCES M)
PAINTER
b Paris, France. *Study:* Spence Sch, New York, grad, 38; Atelier Art et Jeunesse, Paris, 38-39. *Comn:* Time, Inc. *Exhib:* Parsons-Dreyfuss Gallery, 78; Betty Parsons Gallery, 78; Albright-Knox Mus Members Gallery, 78; Artist Postcard Series II & III, Cooper Hewitt Mus, 79; Country Art Gallery, Locust Valley, New York, 83; contemp & mod paintings, Coe Kerr Gallery, New York, 84; poster, Get It Straight, Mus Mod Art, Graphic Design Study Collection; and others. *Awards:* 58th Ann Exhib Distinctive Merit Award, Art Dirs Club, 79. *Publ:* Auth, Skyshades, Crown Panache Publ Press, 9/90. *Mailing Add:* Hampton House 123-35 82nd Rd Kew Gardens NY 11415

BRENNAN, FRANCIS EDWIN
EDITORIAL CARTOONIST, DESIGNER
b Maywood, Ill, July 14, 10. *Study:* Univ Wis; Art Inst Chicago. *Work:* New York Pub Libr; Libr Cong. *Exhib:* Barbara Nicholls Gallery, 77. *Pos:* Chief of graphics & exhib, OWI, 42-45; assoc art dir, Life Mag; art ed, Fortune Mag; picture ed, Life Picture Hist World War II; art adv to ed-in-chief, Time Inc; ed consult & cartoonist syndicated by Newsweek Int Ed Serv; retired. *Awards:* Order Merite Commercial, France, 50; Legion Honor, France, 60. *Bibliog:* Marshall Davidson (auth), The Drawing of America, Abrams, 83. *Mem:* Century Asn. *Publ:* Designer & picture ed, Sara & Gerald, NY Times Bks, 82. *Mailing Add:* Hampton House 123-35 82nd Rd Kew Gardens NY 11415

BRENNAN, NIZETTE
SCULPTOR, DESIGNER
b Washington, DC, July 6, 50. *Study:* Univ Md, studio art, 68-71; Pietrasanta, Italy, 76-79; Isamu Noguchi Studio, New York, 77. *Work:* Rockville (sculpture environment), Monument Park, City Rockville, Md, 88; Solar Farm (sundial sculpture), Maryland Nat Park & Planning Comn, 88. *Comn:* Zen Zag (plaza sculpture with fountain), comn by Noxell Corp, Cockeysville, Md, 82; The Bathers (pool sculpture), Gallery II, comn by Rouse Co, City of Philadelphia, Pa, 83; Rockledge Center Sculpture Gardens, comn by IBM & Spaulding & Slye, North Bethesda, Md, 84-86. *Exhib:* The Wash Show (with catalog), Corcoran Gallery Art, 85; one-man show, Franz Bader Gallery (table sculpture), 89, 90. *Teaching:* Adv drawing, Md Col Art & Design, Silver Spring, 87. *Awards:* Art Award, Am Acad Inst Arts & Lett, 82. *Bibliog:* Benjamin Forgey (auth), The uptown-downtown insider-outsider world of Washington art, Art News, New York, 9/79; Herbert Mitgang (auth), Arts and Letters group gives award to Knopf, NY Times, 5/20/82; article, Noxell puts on a new face, Corp Design, 5/6/83; Denise Arnot & Nizette Brennan (auth), Wallace went North Gallery, New Art Examiners. *Mem:* Coalition Washington Artists; Int Sculpture Ctr; Wash Sculptor's Group; founding mem. *Media:* Stone, Masonry. *Mailing Add:* c/o Franz Bader Gallery 1500 K St NW Washington DC 20006

BRENNO, VONNIE MEI-LIN
PAINTER
b Tokyo, Japan, July 2, 50; US citizen. *Study:* Univ Hawaii, 68-70; Univ Southern Calif, 70-71; Art Ctr Col Design, 71. *Exhib:* New York Street Life, Ogunquit, Maine, 82 & 83 & Recent Paintings, Dallas, Tex, 83, PS Galleries; Mid-Year Exhib, Butler Inst, Youngstown, Ohio, 82-85; Street Life Paintings, Hobe Sound Galleries, Fla, 84; Contemporary Realism, Leslie Levy Gallery, Scottsdale, Ariz, 84; Enthios Galleries, Palm Springs, Calif, 85-86; Public Portraits, Capricorn Galleries, Bethesda, Md, 86; Dassin Galleries, Los Angeles, Calif, 87-88. *Pos:* Art dir, Ogilvy & Mather Advert, Inc, 71-78; creative dir, Ad Marketing, 78-79. *Media:* Oil on Canvas. *Mailing Add:* 2835 Colorada Ave Santa Monica CA 90404-3613

BRESCHI, KAREN LEE
SCULPTOR
b Oakland, Calif, Oct 29, 41. *Study:* Calif Col Arts & Crafts, BFA, 63; Sacramento State Univ, 60-61; San Francisco State Univ, MA, 65; San Francisco Art Inst, 68-71; Calif Inst Integral Studies, San Francisco, PhD, 87. *Work:* Oakland Mus, Calif; Crocker Art Gallery, Sacramento; San Francisco Mus Art; Univ Art Mus (Berkeley); St Mary's Col Art Gallery (Moraga); Univ Ariz Art Mus. *Exhib:* Fac Show Sculpture, 73 & Ceramic Sculpture, 74, San Francisco Art Inst; solo shows, Braunstein/Quay Gallery, 73, 75, 78, 81 & 84; Clay, Whitney Mus, New York, 74; Exchange DFW/SFO, San Francisco Mus Art, 76; Illusionistic-Realism Defined in Contemp Ceramic Sculpture, Laguna Beach Mus, Calif, 77; The Great Am Foot, Mus Contemp Crafts, New York, 78; West Coast Sculptors, 78 & A Century of Clay, 79, Everson Mus; Clayworks, Univ Santa Barbara Mus, 79; A Century of Ceramics in the US 1878-1978, Renwick Gallery, Smithsonian Inst, 79-80; solo show, Braunstein/Quay Gallery, 81; and many others. *Teaching:* Instr sculpture, San Francisco Art Inst, 71-77; instr sculpture, San Francisco State Univ, 74-79; instr, Univ Calif, Davis, 80-81. *Awards:* First Place for Painted Flower, Oakland Art Mus, 62; Women's Archit League Award, Crocker Art Mus, 63; Award, Calif State Fair, 63. *Mem:* West/East Bag. *Media:* Clay, Mixed. *Mailing Add:* c/o Braunstein Quay Gallery 250 Sutter St San Francisco CA 94108

BRESLIN, WYNN
PAINTER, SCULPTOR
b Hackensack, NJ, Nov 6, 32. *Study:* Syracuse Univ, 50; Ohio Wesleyan Univ, BFA, 54; Univ Del, MFA, 60. *Work:* Univ Del Fine Arts Collection, Newark; Syracuse Univ Fine Arts Collection; Maine Collection, Haystack Sch Art, Deer Isle; Del Trust Co, Wilmington; Fine Arts Collection, Del Blue Cross & Blue Shield; and others. *Comn:* Teacher & Child (sculpture), Immanuel Episcopal Church, Wilmington, Del, 70; landscape painting, First Fed Savings & Loan, Wilmington, 73. *Exhib:* Del Art Mus Regional Shows, 56-75; Benedictine Art Awards, Am Fedn Arts, 67; Woodmere Art Gallery, Philadelphia, 73-75; Philadelphia Art Alliance, 74; Catharine Lorillard Wolfe Art Club, Nat Arts Club, 74; Four State Regional show, Univ Del, 88. *Teaching:* Art instr, Del Pub Schs, 54-63, Del Art Mus, 56-76 & Tatnall Sch, 64; instr adult pvt classes, 63-90; Artist-in-Educ Series, 83-90. *Awards:* First Prize Watercolor, Nat Orgn Women Art Exhib, Wilmington, 73; Ethel M Schnader Art Prize, Woodmere Art Gallery, Philadelphia, 74; First Prize Acrylic Painting, Univ Del, 88. *Bibliog:* From an artistic viewpoint, Univ News, Univ Del, 67. *Mem:* Nat League Am Pen Women (treas, Diamond State Br, 72-74); Wilmington Soc Fine Arts; Del Ctr Contemp Art; Chester Co Art Asn; and others. *Media:* Oil, Watercolor. *Mailing Add:* 470 Terrapin Ln Newark DE 19711

BRESSI, BETTY
PAINTER, GRAPHIC ARTIST
b Brooklyn, NY. *Study:* Calif Sch Fine Arts, San Francisco, with Clyfford Still & David Park, 48; Brooklyn Mus Art Sch, with Rueben Tam, 54-60; Columbia Univ, with Federico Castellon, MA, 65, EdD, 70. *Exhib:* Ann Exhib, Staten Island Mus, 85; New Liberty Monuments Invitational, Newhouse Gallery, 86; Invitational, Mauro Graphics, 86; solo show, Staten Island Mus, 87; Juried Exhib, State Island Mus, 92; and others. *Pos:* Ed, Glassworks Press, 75-78 & 90. *Teaching:* Instr fine arts, Queens Col, City Univ New York, 55-68, asst prof, Richmond Col, 68-74. *Awards:* First Award, Weissglas Fund, 72; Milnes-Dennen Award, 76. *Mem:* Univ Coun Art Educ (chmn exhib comt, 75-76). *Media:* Acrylic; Paper Weaving. *Publ:* Auth, article in Artview, Fed Staten Island Artists, Craftsmen, 77 & Women Artists News, 82. *Mailing Add:* 74 Claradon Lane Staten Island NY 10305

BRETT, NANCY
PAINTER
b Jackson, Mich. *Study:* Wayne State Univ, BFA, 69; Cranbrook Acad Art, MFA, 72. *Work:* Cranbrook Acad Art Mus, Bloomfield Hills, Mich; Herbert

Johnson Mus Art, Cornell Univ, Ithaca, NY; Kidder Peabody, New York; Prudential, IBM, JP Morgan, Chemical Bank, New York. *Exhib:* Michigan Focus, Detroit Inst Arts, Mich, 79; Celebrating Cranbrook, Cranbrook Acad Art Mus, Bloomfield Hills, Mich, 89; Painting Up Front, Johnson Mus, Cornell Univ, Ithaca, NY, 82; Kindred Spirits, Hillwood Art Mus, CW Post, Long Island Univ, NY, 86; three-person show, Distant Vision: Contemporary Landscape, Janice Charach Epstein Mus, West Bloomfield, Mich, 92. *Awards:* Yaddo Residency, 83-88; Nat Endowment Arts, Visual Arts Fel, 91-92. *Bibliog:* Judy Collischan (auth), Something Other, Catalog, 82; Judy Collischan (auth), Kindred Spirits, Catalog essay, 86; Judy Collischan (auth), Nancy Brett, ARTS Mag, 91. *Mem:* Artists Space. *Media:* Oil. *Dealer:* Victoria Monroe 9 E 84th St New York NY. *Mailing Add:* 457 Broome St New York NY 10013

BRETTELL, RICHARD ROBSON
DIRECTOR
b Rochester, NY, Jan 17, 49. *Study:* Yale Univ, BA, MA, PhD, 76. *Collections Arranged:* Four Directions in Modern Photography (auth, catalog), Yale Art Gallery, 73; The Drawings of Camille Pissarro (coauth, catalog), Ashmolean Mus, Oxford, England, 79; Camille Pissarro, Mus Fine Arts, Boston, 80-81; Paper and Light: The Calotype in France & Great Britain (coauth, catalog), Mus Fine Arts, Houston, 82-83; The Golden Age of Naples: Art & Civilization Under the Bourbons, 82, Mauristshuis: Dutch Painting of the Golden Age, 83-84, Degas in the Art Institute of Chicago (with Suzanne Folds, McCullagh, coauth catalog) 84 & The Art of the Edge: European Frames 1300-1900(coauth catalog), 86, Art Inst Chicago; Permanent Galleries, European Painting & Sculpture 1300-1900 (installation designer), Art Inst Chicago, 87-; The Art of Paul Gauguin, Nat Gallery Art, Washington, DC, Art Inst Chicago & Mus d'Orsay, Paris, 88-89; and many others. *Pos:* Cur, European Painting & Sculpture, Art Inst Chicago, 80-88; dir, Dallas Mus Art, Tex. *Teaching:* Asst prof hist art, Univ Tex, Austin, 75-80. *Mem:* Col Art Asn; Soc Archit Hist. *Res:* French drawing, printmaking & painting, 1800-1914; American architecture of the 19th century; landscape painting; history of photography 1839-1900. *Publ:* Coauth, The Drawings of Camille Pissarro in the Ashmolean Mus (with Christopher Lloyd), Oxford Univ Press, 80; auth, An Impressionist Legacy: The Collection of Sara Lee Corporation, Abbeville Press, 86; French Paintings of the 19th Century: The Art Institute of Chicago, 3 vols, Abrams, New York/Art Inst Chicago, Ill, 87; and many other books, catalogs and articles. *Mailing Add:* c/o Dallas Museum of Art 1717 N Harwood Dallas TX 75201

BREVERMAN, HARVEY
PAINTER, PRINTMAKER
b Pittsburgh, Pa, Jan 7, 34. *Study:* Carnegie-Mellon Univ, BFA; Ohio Univ, MFA. *Work:* Whitney Mus Am Art, New York; Albright-Knox Art Gallery, Buffalo; Baltimore Mus, Md; Jewish Mus, New York; Mus of Mod Art, New York. *Comn:* Print ed, Assoc Am Artists, 67; bronze ed, NY State Soc Pathologists, 73; print ed, Rochester Print Club, 80; print ed, Boston Pub Libr, 81; mural, Niagara Frontier Transportation Authority, Buffalo, 84. *Exhib:* Corcoran Biennial, Washington, DC, 63; Brooklyn Mus Biennial, New York, 64; 35 Yrs in Retrospect, Butler Inst Am Art, Youngstown, Ohio, 71; Three Artists, Mod Mus Art, Oxford, Eng, 74; 8th Int Art Fair, Basel, Switz, 77; Arte Fiera, 78, Int, Bologna, Italy, 78; Art Gallery Ont, Toronto, 79; Works on Paper: Recent Acquistions, Albright-Knox Art Gallery, Buffalo, 79; Hassam Fund Exhib, Am Acad & Inst Arts & lett, 80 & 81; Minn Mus Art, 82 & 86; Jewish Themes/Contemporary American Artists, Jewish Mus, New York, 82; Rose Art Mus, Brandeis Univ, 85; Art Gallery Hamilton, Can, 85; Va Mus Fine Arts, Richmond, 86; 2nd & 3rd Brit Int Print Biennale, Bradford Art Mus, Eng, 70 & 72; 2nd Norweg Int Print Biennale, 74; Contemp Arts Ctr, Cincinnati, 88; Mus Fine Arts, Houston, 88; Rochester Mem Art Gallery, 88; 4th Int Print Exhib, Taipei Fine Arts Mus, Taiwan, 89; 10th, 11th, 12th Print Int, Barcelona & Cadaques, Spain, 90-92; Grand Palais, Paris, Saga, 90; Yurakucho Art Forum, Tokyo, 91. *Teaching:* Prof art, State Univ NY Buffalo, 61-; artist-in-residence, State Acad Fine Arts, Amsterdam, Neth, 65-66; vis artist, Oxford Univ Ruskin Sch Fine Arts, Eng, summer 74 & 77. *Awards:* Tiffany Found Grant, 62; Creative Artists Pub Serv Grant, 72; Nat Endowment Arts Fels, 74-75 & 80-81. *Mem:* Nat Acad Design; Soc Am Graphic Artists. *Dealer:* Gadatsy Gallery 93 Prospect St Port Dover Ontario N0A 1N0; Wenniger Graphics Gallery 174 Newbury St Boston MA 02116. *Mailing Add:* 76 Smallwood Dr Buffalo NY 14226

BREWSTER, MICHAEL
SCULPTOR, EDUCATOR
b Eugene, Ore, Aug 15, 46. *Study:* Pomona Col, Claremont, Calif, studied with John Mason, David Gray, BA, 68; Claremont Grad Sch, with David Gray & Mowry Baden, MFA, 70. *Work:* La Jolla Mus Contemp Art, Calif; Corps de Garde, Neth; Fine Art Gallery, Univ Mass, Amherst; Mus RI Sch Design; Panza Collection, Milano, Italy. *Comn:* Sonic installations for pvt parties in NY, 77, San Francisco, 78, Los Angeles, 80 & Hollywood, 84. *Exhib:* Newport Harbor Art Mus, 72 & 75; Artists Space, New York, 77 & 84; Ft Worth Mus Art, 77; Baxter Art Gallery, Calif, 77; Joslyn Mus Art, Nebr, 79; Galleria del Cavallino, Venice, Italy, 79; Whitney Mus Am Art, New York, 81; Los Angeles Co Mus Art, Calif, 81; Commune di Rimini, Italy, 82; Mus Contemp Art, Los Angeles, 85. *Teaching:* Instr sculpture, drawing & painting, Pomona Col, 71-73; asst prof, Dept Fine Arts, Claremont Grad Sch, 73-81, acting chmn dept, 75, 79, 83 & 87 & assoc prof art, 81- *Awards:* Nat Endowment Arts Fel, 76, 78, 84 & 90; Fel, Guggenheim Found, 88. *Bibliog:* Richard Armstrong (auth), review, Artforum, 11/79; Kay Larson (auth), reviews, New York Mag, 3/2/81 & 6/25/84; Suzanne Muchnic (auth), review, 8/25/81 & Robert Pincus (auth), review, 1/31/85, Los Angeles Times. *Mem:* Int Sculpture Ctr; Los Angeles Inst Contemp Art; Los Angeles Contemp Exhib; Am Asn Univ Prof. *Media:* Sound, Light. *Publ:* Auth, Inside, Outside, Down & Soliloquies, Baxter Art Gallery, 77; Michael Brewster, Galleria de Cavallino, Italy, 79; Happen-Stance, Herron Sch Art, 79; Touch and Go, Fine Arts Gallery, Calif State Univ, 85; Gone to Touch, Words & Spaces, Smith & Delio, Univ Press Am, 89. *Mailing Add:* 1165 Palms Blvd Venice CA 90291-3524

BREZZO, STEVEN LOUIS
MUSEUM DIRECTOR
b Woodbury, NJ. *Study:* Clarion State Col, BA, 69; Univ Conn, MFA, 73. *Pos:* Chief cur, La Jolla Mus Contemp Art, 74-76; asst dir, San Diego Mus Art, 76-78, dir, 78- *Mem:* Am Coun Arts Educ; Am Asn Mus (nat planning comt, 82-83, nat chmn prog, 83); Advocates Arts. *Mailing Add:* 6190 Terryhill Dr La Jolla CA 92037

BRIANSKY, RITA PREZAMENT
PAINTER, INSTRUCTOR
b Grajewa, Poland, July 25, 25; Can citizen. *Study:* Montreal Mus Fine Arts, with Jacques de Tonnancour; also with Alexandre Bercovitch & Anne Savage, Montreal; Ecole Beaux-Arts Montreal; Art Students League. *Work:* Musée des Beaux Arts, Que; Nat Art Gallery, Ottawa, Ont; Montreal Mus Fine Arts, Que; Can Dept External Affairs, Ottawa, Ont; Dofasco, Hamilton, Ont; and others. *Exhib:* Second Int Biennial Exhib of Prints, Tokyo & Osaka, Japan, 60-61; Salon Int Femme Vichy, France, 60-61; UNICEF Int, UN, New York, 65; La Soc des Artistes Prof du Que, Edinburgh, Scotland & London, Eng; 28 solo shows since 1957. *Teaching:* Instr, Saidye Bronfman Ctr, Montreal, currently. *Awards:* Third Prize, 1st & 2nd Nat Exhib Prints, Burnaby, BC, 60 & 63; Can Coun Grant, 62 & Arts Award, 67; Purchase Award, Dawson Col, Montreal, 82. *Bibliog:* E Kilbourn (auth), 18 print-makers, Can Art, 61; and others. *Media:* Oil, Pastel. *Publ:* Illusr, Rubaboo Reader, 68; Grandmother Came From Dworitz, Tundra Bks, Montreal, 69; Ten Etchings from Wm Shakespeare's Sonnets, 72; On Stage Please, McClelland & Stewart, Toronto, 77 & Holt, Rinehart & Winston, New York, 79; Le Nu dams l'art au Quebec, Marcel-Broquet Publ, 82; Le Paysage dans la Peinture au Quebec, Marcel Broquet, Publ, 84. *Dealer:* Galerie de Bellefeuille 1212 Greene Ave Montreal Que H3Z2A3; Galerie Jean Pierre Valentin 1434 Sherbrooke St W Montreal PQ Can H3G1K4. *Mailing Add:* 2284 Regent Ave Montreal PQ H4A 2R1 Canada

BRICE, WILLIAM
PAINTER, PRINTMAKER
b New York, NY, Apr 23, 21. *Study:* Chouinard Art Inst; Art Students League. *Work:* Metrop Mus Art; Whitney Mus Am Art; Mus Mod Art; Los Angeles Mus Art; Santa Barbara Mus Art. *Exhib:* Va Mus Fine Arts, 66; Des Moines, 67; one-man shows, Univ Calif, San Diego, Dallas Mus Fine Arts, San Francisco Mus Art, 67, Mus Contemp Art, Los Angeles, 86, Grey Art Gallery & Study Ctr, New York, 86 & Los Angeles Co Mus Art, 90; Los Angeles Inst Contemp Art, 78; and others. *Teaching:* Prof art, Univ Calif, Los Angeles, 53-91, prof emer, 91- *Awards:* Award, Los Angeles, 47; Award, Los Angeles City Exhib, 51. *Bibliog:* Nathaniel Pousette-Dart (auth), Paintings, Watercolors, Lithographs, Clayton Spicer Press, 46. *Mem:* Artists Equity Asn. *Media:* Acrylic, Oil; Etching. *Mailing Add:* 427 Beloit St Los Angeles CA 90049

BRIER, HELENE
PAINTER, PRINTMAKER
b Bronx, NY, May 16, 24. *Study:* Art Students League, 42-45; Nat Acad Design, with Robert Philipp, 45-47; New York Univ, with Don Eddy, BS(fine art), 74, Magna Cum Laude, New York Univ, Founders Day Award, 74. *Work:* Andrew Dickson White Mus Art, Cornell Univ, New York; Univ Notre Dame Art Gallery, Ind; New York Univ Art Collection; Housatonic Mus & Univ Bridgeport, Conn; Slater Mem Mus, Norwich, Conn; Nat Mus Women Arts Archive, Libr & Res Ctr, Washington, DC. *Exhib:* Silvermine Ann, 70-80; Collection '83, Silvermine Ctr Arts, Richardson-Vicks Inc, Wilton, Conn, 83; solo exhibs, Silvermine Ctr Arts, 84, Slade Mem Mus, Norwich, 84, Mattatuck Mus, Waterbury, 84, Lyman Allyn Gus, New London, 85, Conn, Artist's Mus, New York, 91 & Munson Gallery, 92; Munson Gallery, New Haven, Conn, 88; Hermitage Mus, Norfolk, Va, 89; Neighbors-Artists of Westchester & Southern Conn, Lehman Col Art Gallery, White Plains, NY, 92; Variations on the Landscape, Silvermine Guild Libr, Curtis Pelham Gallery, New Caanan, Conn, 92; Seven Printmakers, Darien Libr, Conn, 92; Silvermine 70th Anniversary Jubilee, 92; and others. *Teaching:* Instr drawing & design, Univ Bridgeport, Conn, 75-79. *Awards:* First Prize, Lloyd Goodrich, 68; First Prize, Lawrence Alloway, 69; Silvermine Ann New Eng Exhib, Thomas Hess, 78. *Bibliog:* Bernard Hanson (auth), The Hartford Courant, 87 & The Middletown Press, 88; Eleanor Charles (auth), NY Times, 88; William Zimmer (auth), NY Times, 88 & 92; and others. *Mem:* Conn Acad Art; life mem Art Students League; New Haven Paint & Clay Club; Silvermine Ctr Arts; Nat Drawing Asn, New York. *Media:* Oil, Watercolor. *Publ:* Ed, Judy Chapman, Fairfield Citizen News, 78; contribr, Mia Brech, Fair Press, 79; Eliz O'Neil, Fairfield Co Mag, 79; Martha Scott, Bridgeport Post, 79; 6 Days on the Shoreline (cover), New Haven Advocate Mag, 7/2-8/92. *Dealer:* Munson Gallery New Haven CT; Silvermine Centre for the Arts New Canaan CT. *Mailing Add:* 58 Random Rd Fairfield CT 06432

BRIGGS, LAMAR A
PAINTER
b Lafayette, La, Nov 13, 35. *Study:* Univ Houston, 58; Art Ctr Los Angeles, 58; Colorado Inst Art, 60. *Work:* Chicago Art Inst, Ill; Mint Mus Art, Charlotte, NC; Mus Fine Arts, Houston; Denver Art Mus, Colo; Rutgers

Univ Arch, NJ. *Comn:* Pair of large canvases, Phoenician Hotel, Phoenix, Ariz, 88; large wall piece, Bd Room Miami Conv & Tourist Bur, Fla, 89; interior walls, 757 pvt plane, Geneva, Switz, 90. *Exhib:* Art for Public Places, Saginaw Art Mus, Mich, 79; Large Scale Contemporary Paintings, Mint Mus, 81; Acrylic on Paper, Amarillo Art Ctr, Tex, 82; Prints-USA 1982, Pratt Graphics Ctr, New York, 82 & Lockhaven Art Ctr, Orlando, Fla, 82; 50/50 Monotyped-Prints, Montgomery Col, Rockville, Md, 85; Then-Now-and-Then, Univ Houston Lavondale Annex, Tex, 85; Contemp Gallery Exhib, Mint Mus, Charlotte, 85; Small Wonders, Aspen Art Mus, Colo, 86; Intaglio Painting in the 1980's, Zimmerli Art Mus, New Brunswick, NJ, 90. *Pos:* Guest artist, Anderson Ranch Art Ctr, Snowmass, Colo, 90-92. *Bibliog:* Avis Berman (auth), Lamar Briggs: Paintings & Works on Paper, 80; Una Johnson (auth), Lamar Briggs Monotypes, Moody Gallery, 82; Amei Wallach (auth), Lamar Briggs Monotypes, Books & Co, 81. *Media:* Monotype, Acrylic on Canvas. *Dealer:* Moody Gallery 2815 Colquitt Houston TX 77098. *Mailing Add:* 325 Chilean Ave Palm Beach FL 33480

BRIGGS, PETER S
CURATOR, HISTORIAN
b Oak Park, Ill, Nov 6, 46. *Study:* Northern Ill Univ, BA, 72; Univ Ky, MA, 75; Univ NMex, PhD, 86. *Collections Arranged:* Pre-Columbian Costa Rica, Maxwell Mus Anthrop, 78; El Legado de la China Milenara, Museo del Hombre Panameno, 78; Artes Graficas de Mejico: Bks, Broadsides & Prints of the 17th through 20th Century, Mus NMex, 1982; Latin Am Art Univ Collections, 82; Landscape Art, Univ NMex Art Mus, 83; 100 Years of French Prints, Chronicles: Historical References in Contemp Clay & From 2 to 3 Dimensions: Richard Santiago's Sculpture & Drawings, 85; New Western Directions: Mark Klett & Rick Dingus, 86; 4x4: Sixteen Printmakers from the Four Corner States & The Brian Ranson Ceramic Ensemble, 87; Life & Land: The FSA Photographers in Utah, 1936-1941, Harrison Mus Art, 88; Human Components, Univ Ariz Mus Art, 92. *Pos:* Asst cur of collections, Maxwell Mus Anthrop, 76-78; registr, Univ NMex Art Mus, 79-82, cur collections, 82-84; dir & chief cur, Nora Eccles Harrison Mus Art, 84-89; chief cur, Tucson Mus Art, 89-90; cur of collections, Univ of Ariz Mus Art, 90- *Teaching:* Instr, Univ Ky, 73-74, Univ NMex, 76-77 & 81; asst prof Utah State Univ, 85-89. *Awards:* Res Fel, Orgn; Tinker Found Res Grant, 80; Bainbridge Bunting Fel, 80-81; Nat Endowment Art research grant, 83-84; Nat Endowment Art Prof Fel, 83 & 92; Fac Res Grant, Utah State Univ, 88. *Mem:* Col Art Asn; Am Asn Mus; Soc Am Archeol; Latin Am Studies Asn. *Res:* Precolumbian art history especially lower Cent America; 20th Cent American & Latin American Art History; Social Art History; Village planning and architecture. *Publ:* George Elbert Burr, Mitchell-Brown Gallery, 90; Moishe Smith: Printmaker, Utah Arts Coun, 90; Chris Terry, Utah Arts Coun, 92; A Portion of Space, Larry Elsner Found, 92; Fatal Attractions: Central American Mortuary Arts and Social Organization in The Central Americas and Their Neighbors, Univ Colo, 92. *Mailing Add:* 2785 W St Tropaz Tucson AZ 85713

BRIGHT, AL(FRED LEE)
PAINTER
b Youngstown, Ohio, Jan 9, 40. *Study:* Youngstown Univ, Ohio, BS(art educ), 64; Kent State Univ, Ohio, MA(painting), 65. *Work:* Canton Art Inst, Ohio; Roanoke Mus Fine Art, Va; Butler Inst Am Art, Youngstown, Ohio; Kent State Univ Gallery, Ohio; Trumbull Art Guild Mus, Warren, Ohio. *Comn:* Painting to live music of Art Blakey and the Jazz Messengers, Ohio Arts Coun, Columbus, 80; oil mural, IBM, Youngstown, Ohio, 83; oil paintings, Trumbull Mem Hosp, Warren, Ohio, 85; oil murals, First Fed Savings, Youngstown, Ohio, 85; performance art, Roanoke Mus Fine Arts, Va, 85; oil murals, Ohio Heart Inst, Youngstown, Ohio, 85. *Exhib:* Solo exhibs, Stanford Univ, Palo Alto, Calif, 71, Improvisations, Akron Art Mus, Ohio, 77, Canton Inst Art, Ohio, 78, Butler Inst Am Art, Youngstown, Ohio, 85, Roanoke Mus Fine Art, Va, 86, Harmon Meek Gallery, Naples, Fla, 86; May Show, Cleveland Mus Art, Ohio, 76; National Midyear Exhibition, Butler Inst Am Art, Youngstown, Ohio, 81-86. *Pos:* Bd dirs, Ohio Arts Coun, Columbus, Ohio, 73-78; pres, Youngstown Area Arts Coun, 80-81. *Teaching:* Prof art, Youngstown State Univ, 65- & Nat Humanities Fac, Atlanta, Ga, 74- *Awards:* Purchase Award, All-Ohio Show, Canton Inst Art, Ohio, 78; Individual Artists Award, Ohio Arts Coun, 80; Best of Show, 47th Area Artists Ann Show, 85, First Place, 48th Area Artists Ann Show, 86, Butler Inst Am Art, Youngstown, Ohio. *Media:* Oil on canvas. *Publ:* Coauth, An Interdisciplinary Introduction to Black Studies, Kendall-Hunt, 78. *Dealer:* Harmon-Meek Gallery 1258 3rd St South Naples FL 33940. *Mailing Add:* 257 1/2 Federal Plaza W Youngstown OH 44503

BRIGHT, BARNEY
SCULPTOR
b Shelbyville, Ky, July 8, 27. *Study:* Davidson Col; Univ Louisville; Art Ctr, Louisville, Ky. *Work:* J B Speed Art Mus, Louisville; Milwaukee Art Ctr, Wis; Childrens Art Gallery, Louisville; Univ Ky, Lexington; Libr Bldg, Jeffersonville, Ind; represented in more than 1200 pvt collections, more than 40 pub collections. *Comn:* Marble bust of Col Harlan Sanders-State Capital, Frankfort, Ky, 65; The Louisville Clock, Louisville, Ky; sculpture at WAVE Garden, WAVE Inc, Louisville; sculpture of Dean A C Russell, Univ Louisville Law Sch; The Search, Clark Co Pub Libr, New Albany, Ind; Julius Erving, Philadelphia, Pa; plus many others. *Exhib:* Friendship Exhib, France, 58; Sculpture Today, John Herron Art Inst, Indianapolis, 61; Tri-State Exhib, Evansville Mus Arts & Sci, Ind, 62; Parrish Art Mus, Southampton, NY, 70; Suffolk Co Mus, Stony Brook, NY, 71. *Teaching:* Instr sculpture, Univ Louisville, 55-58. *Awards:* Governor's Award, Lifetime Artist, Ky, 89. *Bibliog:* Two films, The Louisville Clock & The Search. *Media:* Cast Bronze, All. *Mailing Add:* 2031 Frankfort Ave 416 W Jefferson Ave Louisville KY 40206

BRIGHTWELL, WALTER
PAINTER
b Del Rio, Tex, July 14, 19. *Study:* Art Students League, with Frank Dumond. *Work:* US Navy Combat Art Collection, Washington, DC; Elliot Mus, Stuart, Fla. *Comn:* Mural, West Side Savings Bank, New York, 57. *Exhib:* Mus Marine, Paris, 63; Allied Artists Am, nat Acad Design, 66, Coun Am Artists Soc, 66 & Am Watercolor Soc, 69; Ft Lauderdale Mus Arts, Fla, 69; Elliot Mus, Stuart, Fla, 82. *Awards:* George Burr Gold Medal, Nat Arts Club, New York, 59; Gwynne Lennon Award, Salmagundi Club, New York, 63; Purchase Award, Am Watercolor Soc, 66. *Mem:* Allied Artists Am; Salmagundi Club (art chmn, 63-67); Artists Fel (corresp secy, 63-69); Am Watercolor Soc (dir, 69-71); Grand Cent Art Galleries. *Media:* Oil, Watercolor. *Dealer:* Annapolis Marine Art Gallery 110 Dock St Annapolis MD 21401. *Mailing Add:* 946 Reef Lane Vero Beach FL 32960

BRILL, GLENN
PAINTER, PRINTMAKER
b New York, NY, 1949. *Study:* Moravian Col, BA, 70; Calif Col Arts & Crafts, Oakland, BFA(printing), 73; Tamarind Inst, Albuquerque, NMex, 76; Cranbrook Acad Art, MFA(printmaking), 79. *Work:* Brooklyn Mus, NY; Phoenix Art Mus, Ariz; San Jose Mus Art, Calif; Tamarind Inst, NMex; Stanford Univ, Calif. *Comn:* US News World Report 2400 Collection, Washington, DC, 85; painting, Hyatt Regency, Long Beach, Calif, 86; painting, IBM Corp, Boca Raton, Fla, 88; painting, AT&T Educ Ctr, Atlanta, Ga, 88; painting, Apple Computer, Cupertinao, Calif, 90; Discovery Channel, Washington, DC, 92; PG & E, San Francisco, Calif, 92. *Exhib:* Solo exhib, San Jose Mus Art, Calif, 85; Between Painting & Sculpture, Palo Alto Cult Ctr, Calif; Paper Now, Cleveland Mus Art, Ohio, 86; Craft Today: Poetry of the Physical, Am Craft Mus, NY, 86; Aha Hana Lima, Honolulu Acad Art, Hawaii, 88; Fun & Games, Bruce Mus, Greenwich, Conn, 89; Beyond Words: The Book as a Metaphor for Art, Calif Craft Mus/San Francisco Craft Mus, 90; Pyramid Atlantic, A Decade of Paper, Montpelier Cult Ctr, Laurel, Md, 91; West Coast Monotypes, Sewell Art Gallery, Rice Univ, Houston, Tex, 91; James Renwick Alliance Auction, Renwick Gallery, Washington, DC, 92. *Pos:* Artist lectr acrylic paint educ prog, Binney & Smith, 92. *Teaching:* Instr, San Francisco State Univ, 83-90. *Awards:* Fel, Nat Endowment Arts, 84 & 86. *Bibliog:* Jessica Scarborough (auth), The seduction of pattern, Artweek Mag, 12/7/85; Victoria Geibel (auth), Beyond surface: paper objects, Metropolis Mag, 6/87; Cheryl White (auth), Glenn Brill/Allrich Gallery, Am Craft Mag, 6-7/89. *Media:* Painting, Printmaking. *Mailing Add:* 567 Forest St Oakland CA 94618

BRILLIANT, RICHARD
EDUCATOR, WRITER
b Boston, Mass, Nov 20, 29. *Study:* Yale Univ, BA, 51, MA, 56, PhD, 60; Harvard Univ, LLB, 54. *Comn:* The Fayum Portraits, Prog for Art on Film, New York, 88. *Pos:* Ed-designate, Art Bull, 90-91, ed-in-chief, 91-94. *Teaching:* From asst prof to prof art hist, Univ Penn, 62-70; prof, Columbia Univ, 70-; vis Mellon Prof fine arts, Univ Pittsburgh, 71; vis prof, Scuola Normale Superiore, Pisa, 74, 80 & 88, Princeton, 86. *Awards:* Fulbright Grant, 57-59; Am Acad Rome, 60-62; Guggenheim Found Fel, 67-68; Nat Endowment Humanities Sr Fel, 72-73. *Mem:* Col Art Asn; Ger Archaeol Inst; Am Numismatic Soc. *Res:* Greek and Roman art and archaeology; theory and method in art history. *Publ:* Auth, Arts of the Ancient Greeks, McGraw-Hill, 73; Roman Art, Phaidon, 74; Pompeii, AD 79: the Treasure of Rediscovery, Volair, 79; Visual Narratives, Cornell, 84; Portraiture, Reaktion & Harvard, 91; and others. *Mailing Add:* 10 Wayside Lane Scarsdale NY 10583

BRINKERHOFF, DERICKSEN MORGAN
HISTORIAN, EDUCATOR
b Philadelphia, Pa, Oct 4, 21. *Study:* Taft Sch, dipl, 39; Williams Col, BA(art), 43; Yale Univ, MA(art hist), 47; Univ Zurich, 48-49; Harvard Univ, PhD(fine arts), 58. *Teaching:* Instr art hist, Brown Univ, Providence, 52-55; from instr to assoc prof art hist, RI Sch Design, Providence, 52-59; assoc prof art hist, Pa State Univ, University Park, 61-62, Tyler Sch Art, Temple Univ, 62-65 & Univ Calif Riverside, 65-67, prof art hist, 67-92 (retired). *Awards:* Cash Prize, Am Numismatic Soc, New York, 52; Sr Fel Classical Studies, Am Acad Rome, 59-61. *Mem:* Col Art Asn Am; Riverside Art Asn (trustee, 68-72, mem exhib comt, 71-). *Publ:* Auth, New examples of the Hellenistic statue group, The Invitation to the Dance, and their significance, Am J Archaeol, 65; A Collection of Sculpture in Classical & Early Christian Antioch, 70; contribr, Studies Presented to G M A Hanfmann, 71; auth, Hellenistic Statues of Aphrodite, Outstanding Dissertations in the Fine Arts, 78. *Mailing Add:* Dept of Art Hist Univ of Calif Riverside CA 92521

BRISTOW, WILLIAM ARTHUR
PAINTER, EDUCATOR
b San Antonio, Tex, Feb 1, 37. *Study:* Univ Tex, BFA, 58; Univ Fla, MFA, 60; also with Clinton Adams, Ernest Briggs & George Lockwood. *Work:* Dallas Mus Art; Houston Mus Fine Art; San Antonio Art League; WTex Mus, Lubbock; Longview Jr League, Tex. *Comn:* Migration (aluminum fountain sculpture), US Govt, HemisFair, San Antonio, 68; steel sculpture fountain, Turbine Support Co, San Antonio, 69; two tapestry murals, La Mansion Hotels, San Antonio, 80 & 81; tapestry mural & tapestry, Frost Nat Bank, San Antonio. *Exhib:* Southwest Print & Drawing Soc, Dallas Mus Fine Art, 60, Tex Ann, 60-63; Painting in the Southwest, Okla Art Ctr, Oklahoma City, 62; Artist of the Year, San Antonio Art League, Witte Mus, 65; Nat Art Competition, Am Artist Mag, Circle Gallery, New York, 78; 14th Ann Prints & Drawings & 24th Ann Delta Competition, Ark Arts Ctr, Little Rock, 81. *Teaching:* Instr painting & drawing, Univ Fla, Gainesville, 58-60; assoc prof painting & drawing, Trinity Univ, San Antonio, 60-79, prof, 79-, chmn dept

design & drawing, 65-78. *Awards:* Purchase Prize, Tex Ann, Houston Mus Fine Art, 62; First Prize Southwest Print & Drawing, Mrs Edwin B Hopkins Fund, Dallas Mus, 64; Mus STex Prize for Sculpture, Coca Cola Bottling Co, 66. *Bibliog:* An artist & teacher, born of the space & light of Texas, Chronicle Higher Ed, 12/2/87. *Mem:* Col Art Asn Am. *Media:* Acrylic, Oil. *Publ:* Auth, True Gesso--and other truths, Art & Academe, Visual Arts Press, Ltd, fall 88; The fresh glories of the Sistine Chapel, Houston Chronicle Mag, 4/30/89; Sublime vision: Color, light and the fourth dimension, Art & Academe, Visual Arts Press, Ltd, fall 89. *Dealer:* Dorothy Katz Sol del Rio Gallery 1020 Townsend Ave San Antonio TX 78209. *Mailing Add:* 344 Wildrose Ave San Antonio TX 78209

BRITE, JANE FASSETT
CURATOR, DIRECTOR
b Chicago, Ill, July 11. *Study:* Marjorie Webster Col, BS, 57; Univ Wis, Milwaukee. *Collections Arranged:* Wisconsin Directions Three (auth, catalog), 84 & Wisconsin Directions Four (auth, catalog), 85; Schomer Lictner Retrospective (auth, catalog), 84; Emerging Imagist (auth, catalog), 85; Fiber R/Evolution, History of Fiber 50's-80's (auth, catalog), 86; The Force, Brian Richie & Dennis Nechtavel (performance/site installation curator), 87; Triangulation, Jill Sebastian, Debra Loewen, Jon Erickson, (performance/site installation curator); Women of Substance, Joyce Scott & Kay Lawal (performance/site installation curator); Diverse Works, Maryland Art Place (bd trustees). *Pos:* Bd mem, Wis Arts, Madison, 82-85 & Art Reach, Milwaukee, 82-86; rev, Inst Mus Serv, Washington, DC, 83-84; ed bd, Acad Sci, Arts & Letts, 85-86; Art Reach, 82-85 & 88; bd trustees, Dance Circus, 86- *Mem:* Tempo-Prof Women (sem comn, 85-86); Wis Painters & Sculptors; Wis Designer Craftsmen; Tal-N-Art Consortium Inc (adv, 86). *Res:* Development of fiber arts of the last thirty years; history of Wisconsin art of the 30's & 40's. *Publ:* Coauth, The new directions-old pleasures in ceramic art, 85 & The evolution of art in Milwaukee, 86, Wis Acad Rev (Wis Acad Sci, Arts & Letts); auth, The Milwaukee J Gallery of Wisconsin Art, exhib catalogue. *Mailing Add:* Walkers Point Ctr for Arts 911 W Nat Ave Milwaukee WI 53204

BRITO, MARIA
SCULPTOR, PAINTER
b Havana, Cuba, Oct 10, 47; US citizen. *Work:* Olympic Sculpture Park, Seoul, Korea; Archer M Huntington Mus, Austin, Tex; Univ Fla, Tallahassee; Art in Public Places, Metro-Dade Ctr, Miami; Miami-Dade Community Col, Miami. *Comn:* Sculpture, Seoul Olympic Organizing Comt, Seoul, Korea, 88. *Exhib:* Contemporary Sculpture from Florida Collections, Univ Gallery, Univ Fla, Gainesville, 89; From Narrative to Magic Realism: 34th Annual Contemporary American Art Exhibit, Wilson Gallery, Leghigh Univ, Bethlehem, Pa, 89; The Ceremony of Memory, Lannan Mus, Fort Worth, Fla, 89; Sculpture, Mus Contemp Hispanic Art, New York, 89; The Decade Show, Studio Mus Harlem, New Mus Contemp Art & Mocha, Mus Contemp Hispanic Art, New York, 90. *Awards:* Visual Artists Fel, Nat Endowment for Arts, 84 & 88; Pollock-Krasner Found Grant, Pollock-Krasner Found, 90. *Bibliog:* Virginia Watson Jones (auth), Directory of American Women Sculptors, Oryx Press, 86; Ricardo Pau-LLosa (auth), The Dreamt Objectivities of Maria Brito-Avellana, Dreamworks, Human Sci Press Inc, 86; John Stringer (auth), Maria Brito-Avellana: Recent Sculpture (catalog), Interamerican Art Gallery & Mus of Contemp Hispanic Art, 89. *Media:* Mixed. *Dealer:* Anne Jaffe Gallery 1088 Kane Concourse Bay Harbor FL 33154. *Mailing Add:* 8995 SW 75th St Miami FL 33173

BRITSKY, NICHOLAS
PAINTER, EDUCATOR
b Weldirz, Western Ukraine, Dec 11, 13; US citizen. *Study:* Yale Univ, BFA; Syracuse Univ; Cranbrook Acad Art. *Work:* Evansville Mus, Ind; Ford Motor Co Collection, Dearborn, Mich; Univ Ill, Chicago; Prudential Life Ins Co, New York; Springville Mus, Utah; and many others. *Comn:* Mosaic tile mural, Allen Park High Sch, Galesburg, Ill, 54; wood crucifix & mural decoration, St Boniface Church, Seymour, Ill, 78; fiberglass & stainless steel crucifix, St Patricks Church, Urbana, Ill, 80; plexiglas window, Chapel Mercy Hosp,, Urbana, Ill, 83; stained plexiglass window & ten foot wood sculpture, St Patrick's Church, Urbana, Ill, 91. *Exhib:* Denver Mus, Colo, 51, 53 & 55; Butler Inst Am Art, Youngstown, Ohio, 52-54; Nat Acad Design, New York, 60; Evansville Mus, 61, 67 & 68; Mainstreams USA, Marietta Col, Ohio, 69-72. *Teaching:* Prof art, Univ Ill, formerly, prof emer, currently. *Awards:* First Prize Oil-Casein, Evansville Ind Mus Art, 61; First Prize, Springville Mus Art, Utah, 74; Gov Award Outstanding Contrib Arts, Ill, 81; and others. *Media:* Multimedia. *Publ:* Contribr, Encycl Slavonica, Philos Press, 49; illusr, Ford Times Mag, 64. *Mailing Add:* 1410 S Vine Urbana IL 61801

BRITT, NELSON CLARK
MUSEUM DIRECTOR, PAINTER
b Rochester, NY, Nov 13, 44. *Study:* Yale Univ, 66; State Univ NY Col, Buffalo, BA, 67; RI Sch Design, MFA, 73. *Work:* RI Sch Design; Tishman Corp, Sperry Hutchinson Bldg, New York; Internal Revenue Bldg, State Ill; Caterpillar Corp. *Comn:* Sangomo Club, Springfield, Ill. *Exhib:* Newport Art Asn Nat, Newport, RI, 73; Silvermine Artist Guild, 75; one-man show, Winfisky Gallery, Salem State Col, 81; Springfield Art Asn Gallery, Ill, 82; 59th Ann, Burpee Art Mus, Rockford, Ill, 83; Midwest States Exhib, Evansville Mus Art & Sci, Ind, 83; Western NY Open, Albright-Knox Art Gallery; Southern Ill Univ Sch Med. *Pos:* Exec dir, Southeast Ark Arts & Sci Ctr, Pine Bluff, currently; mus dir, Kansas State Univ, Manhattan, NJ. *Teaching:* Instr painting, Newport Art Asn, RI, 71-73; teaching fel, RI Sch Design, 71-73; adj prof art educ, Boston Univ, 72 & Univ Ark, Pine Bluff, currently. *Awards:* First Prize Acrylic, Albright-Knox Art Gallery, 68; Best of Show, Westchester Open Competition, Pleasantville, NY, 70; Award Painting, Silvermine Artist Club, 75. *Mem:* Am Asn Mus; Nat Art Educ Asn. *Media:* Acrylic. *Mailing Add:* Greenville Museum of Art 802 S Evans St Greenville NC 27834

BRITT, SAM GLENN
EDUCATOR, PAINTER
b Ruleville, Miss, Sept 26, 40. *Study:* Memphis Acad Art, BFA; Univ Miss, MFA; Cape Cod Sch Painting, Provincetown, Mass, with Henry Hensche; Frudakais Acad Sculpture, Philadelphia, with Angelous Frudakais. *Work:* Union Bldg, Delta State Univ, Munic Art Gallery, Jackson, Miss; First Nat Bank, Cleveland, Miss. *Comn:* Drawing depicting the life style of ancient Indians, Winterville Mounds Mus, Miss, 67; painting, Union Planters Nat Bank, Memphis, Tenn; painting, Mrs Pat Kerr, Memphis, Tenn. *Exhib:* One-man show, Gov's Mansion, Jackson, Miss; Bryant Galleries, Jackson, Miss & New Orleans, La, 83; Nat Bank Com, Memphis, Tenn, 83; Symphony Ball, Peabody Hotel, Memphis, Tenn, 83; 7 American Impressionists, Gallery 3, Roanoke, Va, 85; and others. *Teaching:* Instr drawing & painting, Delta State Univ, 66-73, asst prof, 73-78, assoc prof art, 78-; pvt instr, Clarksdale, Miss, 73-; instr, Painting City Park, New Orleans, summer 85, Painting Workshops Unlimited, Jackson, Miss, 85 & 86 & Drawing Studio One, Gray, La, 85 & 86. *Awards:* Second Prize, Nat Painting Exhib, 64; Most Outstanding Work, Nat Small Painting Exhib, Hadley, 74; Best in Show, Crosstie Festival, 79. *Bibliog:* Ed Phillips (auth), Finding God's beauty in a simple world, Delta Scene Mag, 75; Featured on Miss Educ TV as a Miss Artist, spring 80. *Media:* Oil, Pastel. *Mailing Add:* Dept Art Delta State Univ Cleveland MS 38733

BRITTON, DANIEL ROBERT
PRINTMAKER, EDUCATOR
b Colorado Springs, Colo, Apr 1, 49. *Study:* Univ Colo, BFA, 74, MFA, 76. *Work:* Univ Colo, Boulder; Ariz State Univ, Tempe; Haggin Art Mus, Stockton, Calif; Brigham Young Univ, Provo, Utah. *Comn:* McDonalds Corp, Chicago & Denver, 88. *Exhib:* Tenth Nat Print Competition, Univ Art Gallery, Minot, NDak, 81; DeKalb 81 Nat Print Competition, Swen Parsons Gallery, Ill, 81; Moravian Print Nat, Church Street Gallery, Bethlehem, Pa, 81; American Drawing IV, Portsmouth Mus, 83; Haggin Art Mus, Stockton, Calif, 88; Albrecht Art Mus, St Joseph, Mo, 91; Bradley Univ Nat Print Exhib, Peoria, Ill, 91; North Dakota Nat Print & Drawing Competion, 92. *Teaching:* Assoc prof printmaking, Ariz State Univ, 83-; vis prof lithography, Univ Utah, Salt Lake City, 91. *Awards:* Award of Merit, DeKalb Print Nat, 81; Stockton Nat Print Competition, Haggin Art Mus, Stockton, Calif, 88; Nat Honor Soc, Ariz State Univ, 91; Heitland Found Grant, Ger, 91. *Bibliog:* Roberta Loach (auth), Printmakers, Visual Dialogue Mag, 79; Art in the Sun Belt, Art News, 80; Carol Kotrozo (auth), Drawing and Printmaking, Art Week, 81. *Media:* Lithography, Oil. *Publ:* Tamarind Technical Papers, 79 & 80. *Mailing Add:* Dept of Art Arizona State Univ Tempe AZ 85287

BROAD, ELI
COLLECTOR
b New York, NY, June 6, 33. *Study:* Mich State Univ, BA(cum laude), 54. *Pos:* Founding chmn & bd trustees, Mus Contemp Art, Los Angeles, Calif, 80-; Nat trustee, Baltimore Mus Art, Md, 85-91; bd trustees, Archives of Am Art, Smithsonian Inst, Washington, DC, 85-; painting & sculpture comt, Whitney Mus, New York, 87-89; chmn adv bd, Art/89, Los Angeles, Calif, 89. *Awards:* Honors Award in Visual Arts, Los Angeles Arts Coun, 89. *Collection:* Museum quality works from approximately 1913 to present with a concentration on American art of the 70's, 80's & 90's. *Mailing Add:* 11601 Wilshire Blvd Los Angeles CA 90025-1748

BROADLEY, HUGH T
HISTORIAN, ADMINISTRATOR
b Sacramento, Calif, June 5, 22. *Study:* Park Col, AB; Yale Univ, AM; NY Univ, PhD. *Pos:* Mus cur, Nat Gallery Art, 54-61; cur art collections, Ariz State Univ, 65-67; dir, Phoenix Art Mus, 67-69. *Teaching:* Prof art hist, Bowling Green State Univ, 61-65; prof art hist, Ariz State Univ, 69- *Mem:* Western Asn Art Mus (pres, 68); Col Art Asn Am; Am Asn Mus; Friends Mex Art; Int Coun Mus. *Res:* Flemish painting of the fifteenth and sixteenth centuries. *Mailing Add:* 4102 N 50th Pl Phoenix AZ 85018

BROCK, ROBERT W
SCULPTOR, EDUCATOR
b Tacoma, Ohio, June 27, 36. *Study:* Sch of Dayton Art Inst, 54-60, dipl, with Robert C Koepnick; Univ Dayton, BFA, 60; Ohio Univ, MFA, 62, with David Hostetler. *Work:* Dayton Art Inst; State Univ NY Col, Fredonia. *Exhib:* Artists of Southern Ohio, Dayton Art Inst, 60 & 61; Ohio Sculpture & Ceramic Show, Butler Inst Am Art, Youngstown, 62; Western NY Show, Albright-Knox Art Gallery, Buffalo, 65-67, 69 & 75 & Outdoor Sculpture Exhib, 68; Unordinary Realities, Xerox Ctr, Rochester, 75. *Pos:* Mem adv comt, Burchfield Ctr, 70-84; chmn fine arts dept, State Univ Col, Buffalo, 70-73 & 81-85; pres, Patteran Artists Inc, Buffalo, 77-78; mem adv comt, Art in Subway, Buffalo, 81-85. *Teaching:* Prof sculpture, State Univ NY Col, Buffalo, 62- *Mem:* Int Sculpture Ctr. *Media:* All Media. *Mailing Add:* 104 Fordham Dr Buffalo NY 14216

BROD, STANFORD
DESIGNER, EDUCATOR
b Cincinnati, Ohio, Sept 29, 32. *Study:* Col of Design, Archit, Art & Planning, Univ Cincinnati, BS(design), 55. *Work:* Nat Collection of Fine Arts, Washington, DC; Mus Mod Art, New York; Hebrew Union Col, Jewish Inst Relig Mus, Los Angeles; Contemp Art Ctr & Cincinnati Art Mus, Ohio.

Comn: Urban Walls: Cincinnati (ten story bldg wall mural), Solway Gallery for Cincinnati Community, 72; Six Urban Banners, Contemp Art Ctr, 75. *Exhib:* Greetings, Mus Mod Art, New York, 66; Int Calligraphy Today; Urban Banner Designs Cincinnati Downtown Commercial Districts, 81; Tel Aviv Mus, 82; Int Art Exhib DRUPA, Dusseldorf, Ger, 82; traveling show, Calligraphia USA/USSR, Russia & USA, 90-92; and others. *Pos:* Designer, Rhoades Studio, Cincinnati, 55-62; designer, Lipson, Alport & Glass Inc, Cincinnati, 62- *Teaching:* Exp typography, Art Acad Cincinnati, 60-75, illus, 91-92, packaging design, 91-92 & corporate design, 92-93; adj prof graphic design, Col Design, Archit, Art & Planning, Univ Cincinnati, 62- *Awards:* Communication Arts Award, Commun Arts J, 59, 64, 66 & 70; Typomundus 20/2 Int Award, 70; Int Typographic Composition Award, 70-72 & 75. *Publ:* Auth, International Calligraphy Today, Watson-Guptill, 82; Trademarks & Symbols of the World, 87; Letterheads 2; A Collection of Letterheads from Around the World, 89; Greeting Cards: A Collection from Around the World, 89; Expressive Typography, The Word As Image, 90. *Mailing Add:* 2349 Victory Pkwy Cincinnati OH 45206

BRODER, PATRICIA JANIS
HISTORIAN, WRITER
b New York, NY, Nov 22, 35. *Study:* Smith Col, 53-54; Barnard Col, Columbia Univ, BA, 57; Rutgers Univ Grad Sch, 62-63. *Pos:* Stock brokerage trainee, A M Kidder & Co, New York, 58; regist rep, Thomas & McKinnon, New York, 59-61; regist investment adv, 62-64; writer & lectr Am art hist, art appraisal & authentication & brokerage. *Awards:* Herbert Adams Mem Medal for serv to Am sculpture, Nat Sculpture Soc, New York, 75; Western Heritage Wrangler Award for best article on the Am West, Nat Cowboy Hall of Fame & Western Heritage Ctr, Oklahoma City, 76; Western Heritage Award for Best Book, Nat Cowboy Hall Fame, 81; and others. *Publ:* Auth, Hopi, Painting: The World of the Hopis, Brandywine Press/E P Dutton, 78; Great Paintings of Old American West, 79 & American Indian Painting and Sculpture, 80, Abbeville Press/Crown; Taos: A Painter's Dream, New York Graphic Soc, 80; The American West: The Modern vision, New York Graphic Soc, 84; Shadows on Glass: The Indian World of Ben Wittick, Rowman & Littlefield, 90. *Mailing Add:* 488 Long Hill Dr Short Hills NJ 07078

BRODERICK, HERBERT REGINALD, III
EDUCATOR
b Bethesda, Md, July 16, 45. *Study:* Columbia Col, AB, 67; Columbia Univ, MA, 68, MPhil, 75, PhD, 78. *Teaching:* Instr art hist, Columbia Univ, 74-77, asst prof, 78; asst prof, Herbert H Lehman Col, City Univ New York, 78-84, assoc prof, 85- *Awards:* Mrs Giles Whiting Found Fel, 74-75; Nat Endowment Humanities Fel, 81-82; PSC/City Univ New York Fac Res Awards, 81-82 & 88-89. *Mem:* Col Art Asn Am; Int Ctr Medieval Art. *Res:* Iconography of the Old Testament in medieval art; Anglo-Saxon manuscript illumination. *Publ:* Auth, Some attitudes toward the frame in Anglo-Saxon manuscripts of the 10th and 11th centuries, Artibus & Historiae, Vol V, 82; Observations on the method of illustration in manuscript Junius II, Scriptorium, Vol XXXVII, 83; Observations on the creation cycle of the Sarajevo Haggadah, Zeitschrift, für Kunstgechichte, XLVII, 84; A Note on the Garments of Paradise, Byzantion, LV, 250-254, 85; Early Medieval Aspects of the American Renaissance, Medievalism in Am Culture, Vol I, Binghampton, pg 89-114, 87; and others. *Mailing Add:* 530 West End Ave New York NY 10024

BRODERICK, JAMES ALLEN
ADMINISTRATOR, GRAPHIC ARTIST
b Chicago, Ill, July 25, 39. *Study:* St Ambrose Col, BA, 62; Univ Iowa, MA, 66. *Exhib:* States of Texas, Ctr Visual Commun, Dallas, 81; Photographs from the Permanent Collection, Mus Tex Tech Univ, Lubbock, 82; SAMA-Open, 86, San Antonio Mus Art, 86; Recent Photography, Blue Collar Gallery, San Antonio, 86; Heat & Light, Univ Tex San Antonio, 87; Close-Up, San Antonio Mus Art, 87; and others. *Teaching:* Prof prints & photog, Northwest Mo State Univ, Maryville, 66-76, chmn, Dept Art, 71-76; prof & chairperson, Dept Art, Tex Tech Univ, Lubbock, 76-83; prof & dir, Div Art & Design, Univ Tex, San Antonio, currently. *Mem:* Tex Asn Schs Art (bd dirs); Nat Coun Art Adminr; Nat Asn Schs Art & Design (bd dirs); Col Art Asn. *Media:* Miscellaneous Media. *Mailing Add:* Dept Art & Design Univ Texas San Antonio TX 78285

BRODERSON, MORRIS
PAINTER
b Los Angeles, Calif, Nov 4, 28. *Study:* Pasadena Mus, life drawing classes with De Erdeley; Univ Southern Calif, spec studies in art, four yrs. *Work:* Whitney Mus Am Art, New York; Mus Fine Arts, Houston; Joseph H Hirshhorn Collection & Nat Collection Fine Arts, Washington, DC; Guggenheim Mus, New York. *Exhib:* One-man shows, M H De Young Mem Mus, San Francisco, 61, Staempli Gallery, New York, 79, Gallaudet Col, Washington, DC, 81, San Diego Mus, 82 & Ankrum Gallery, Los Angeles, 83, 86 & 90; Am Watercolors, Mitchell Mus, Mt Vernon, Ill, 79. *Awards:* New Talent, USA, Art in Am, 60; Excellence in Art, Art Dirs Club Philadelphia, 63; Great Ideas of Western Man, Container Corp Am, 63. *Bibliog:* John Canaday (auth), The special world of Broderson, NY Times, 11/13/71; Diane Hines (auth), Speaking thru his art, Am Artist, 5/10/80; Arden Neisser (auth), The Other Side of Silence, 83. *Mailing Add:* 329 N Orange Dr Los Angeles CA 90036

BRODERSON, ROBERT
PAINTER
b West Haven, Conn, July 6, 20. *Study:* Duke Univ, AB, 50; State Univ Iowa, with Mauricio Lasansky, James Lechay & Stuart Edie, MFA, 52. *Work:* Nat Inst Arts & Lett, NY; Whitney Mus Am Art; Wadsworth Atheneum, Hartford, Conn; Colorado Springs Fine Arts Ctr; Princeton Univ Art Mus. *Exhib:* Four shows, Pa Acad Fine Arts, 51-67; Denver Art Mus, 63; Univ Ill, 63 & 65; Nebr Art Asn, 64; Carnegie Inst, 64; plus others. *Teaching:* Instr, Duke Univ, 57-64. *Awards:* Duke Univ Summer Res Fel, 63; Guggenheim Fel, 64; Childe Hassam Purchase Award, 68; plus others. *Dealer:* Terry Dintenfass Inc 18 E 67th St New York NY 10021. *Mailing Add:* c/o Art Placement 101 E Drewry Lane Raleigh NC 27609

BRODEUR, CATHERINE R
PAINTER
b Los Angeles, Calif. *Study:* Art Students League, New York, with Daniel Greene, 75; Jack Callahan, Rockport, Mass, 77-79; John Howard Sanden, New York, 79-80. *Work:* Permanent Naval Art Collection, Sheet Metal Worker's Union, Washington, DC; First Nat Bank Boston, Mass; Hamden Co Med Asn, Bay Bank Valley, Springfield, Mass. *Comn:* Nuclear Age Physicians (painting), Springfield Med Asn, Mass, 84; St Dominic (painting), Dominican Monastery, West Springfield, Mass, 85; The Last Supper (painting), St Alphonsus Col, Suffield, Conn, 87; portrait of Selectman, West Springfield Arts Coun, Mass, 88; series of 7 Saints, The Redemptorists Order, Washington, DC, 91. *Exhib:* Am Artists Prof League, Nat Arts Club, New York, 84; Coast Guard Artists, New England Air Mus, Windsor Locks, Conn, 84; two-person show, Western New England Col, Springfield, Mass, 87; Through Women's Eyes, Holyoke Mus, Mass, 88; Realists Today, Am Artists Mag, Denver, Colo, 89; Springfield Art League Invitational, Western New England Col, Mass, 89; The Realists, Mus Fine Art, Springfield, Mass, 90; 4 Women Artists, Wistariahurst Mus, Holyoke, Mass, 92. *Teaching:* Instr gen art, Holyoke Home Info Ctr, 79-81; instr portraits, Wistariahurst Mus, 88-90. *Awards:* Margaret Fernald Dole Award, Hudson Valley Arts Asn, In Trust, 82; Merit Award, Springfield Art League Nat, 86; Wilkins Award, Academic Artists Assoc, Wilkins Art Consults, 90. *Bibliog:* Herb Rogoff (auth), Getting the Feel for People, Palette Talk No 66, 86; Angela Carbone (auth), Voices-Profile, Transcript Telegram, 1/14/89; Ruth Reininghaus (auth), The Salmagundian, spring 89. *Mem:* Hudson Valley Art Asn; Copley Soc Boston; Acad Artists Asn (vice-pres, 90-); Pastel Soc Am; North Shore Artists Asn. *Media:* Oil, Pastel. *Mailing Add:* 63 Cherry Hill Holyoke MA 01040

BRODHEAD, QUITA
PAINTER
b Wilmington, Del. *Study:* Pa Acad Fine Arts; Grande Chaumiere & Julienne's, Paris; with Arthur Carles & Alexander Archipenko; Fel Pa Acad Fine Arts. *Work:* Westerdahl Collection, Spain; Widener Col Mus, Pa; Pa Acad Fine Arts, Philadelphia Mus Art, Philadelphia; Bryn Mawr Col; Del Art Mus; and many others. *Comn:* Mural, St Johns Episcopal Church, Bala Cynwyd, Pa, 30; mural, comn by E Ennalls Berl, Wilmington, Del, 33; portrait, comn by Mrs Graham Cummin, Paoli, Pa, 53; crucifixion, St Anthony's Cath Church, Wilmington. *Exhib:* Pa Acad Fine Arts; Phila Art Alliance; Civic Ctr Mus; Art Club; Sketch Club; one person exhibs, Bryn Mawr Col, 76, Kling Col, 77, Thomas Jefferson Gallery, 81, Chez Barbier, Paris, 82, Am Col Gallery, Philadelphia, 83, Carspecken-Scott Gallery, Wilmington, Del, 92 & Rosemont Col, PA, 92; one-man retrospective, Pa Acad Fine Arts; & many other one-man & group exhibs. *Pos:* Mem bd dirs, Fel Acad Fine Arts, Pa, 40-50; Chmn comt Nat Exhib Blind Artists. *Teaching:* Instr, Main Line Forum Arts. *Awards:* Gold Medal Award, 53 & Caroline Gibbons Grange Mem Award, 55, Fel Acad Fine Arts, Pa; and others. *Bibliog:* Edourdo Westerdahl (auth), The Painting of Quita Brodhead, El Dia, 61; Barbara Wolanin (auth), Quita Brodhead, Art Am, 92. *Mem:* Artists Equity; Philadelphis Mus Art; Mus Mod Art, NY; Fel Pa Acad Fine Arts; Woodmere Art Mus; and others. *Media:* Oil, Acrylic. *Publ:* auth, article, Arts Mag. *Mailing Add:* 211 Atlee Rd Wayne PA 19087

BRODIE, REGIS CONRAD
SCULPTOR
b Pittsburgh, Pa, Nov 19, 42. *Study:* Ind Univ Pa, BSc(art educ) & MEd; Temple Univ, MFA. *Work:* Univ Utah Art Mus, Salt Lake City; Del Art Mus, Wilmington; Everson Mus of Art, Syracuse, NY; Tyler Sch of Art, Temple Univ, Philadelphia; Schenectady Mus, New York; Mus de Ceramica, Barcelona, Spain; NYNEX Corp, White Plains, NY; The Albany Inst Hist Art, Albany, NY. *Exhib:* Nat Invitational Art 81, Nabisco World Hq, E Hanover, NJ; Echoes & Visions Inaugural Exhib, Carlyn Gallery, New York, 85; Teapots & Tea Bowls Nat Invitational, Crafts Gallery, Louisville, Ky, 87; Nat Exhib, Teapots, Arrowmont Sch Arts & Crafts, Gatlinburg, Tenn, 88; Nat Invitational Exhib, Tyler Sch Art, Philadelphia, Pa, 92; and others. *Pos:* Cur, Nat Invitational Exhib Multiplicity in Clay, Fiber, & Metal, Skidmore Coll, Saratoga, NY, 84. *Teaching:* Prof studio art, Skidmore Col, 69-, dir, Six summer art prog, 72- *Awards:* First Prize/Ceramics, Ann Nat Art Exhib, Cooperstown, NY, 74, 77 & 82; The Edwin M Moseley Fac Res Lect, The Creative Process: An Artist's Point of View, Skidmore Col, Saratoga, NY, 88; Smithsonian Inst Lecture/Demonstration, Washington, DC, 91. *Mem:* Nat Coun on Educ for Ceramic Arts; Am Crafts Coun; World Craft Coun. *Media:* Clay, Porcelain. *Publ:* Auth, The Energy-Efficient Potter, Watson-Guptill Publ, 82; Insulating existing kilns, Ceramics Monthly, 9/83; Ceramic Fiber 1984, The Studio Potter, 84; Close Encounters with the Third Dimension: Making College Resources Available, The Studio Potter, 6/88. *Mailing Add:* 27 Wedgewood Dr Saratoga Springs NY 12866

BRODSKY, EUGENE V
PAINTER
b New York, NY, 1946. *Study:* George Washington Univ, 63-64. *Work:* Metrop Mus Art, New York; Power Art Gallery, Sydney, Australia; Vassar Art Gallery, Poughkeepsie, NY; Picker Art Gallery, Colgate Univ, Hamilton,

NY. *Exhib:* Mus Mod Art, New York, 72; New Dimensions in Drawing, Aldrich Mus, Ridgefield, Conn, 81; Selected Drawings, Jersey City Mus, Jersey City, NJ, 83; New Britain Mus Am Art Invitational, Conn, 88. *Awards:* John Simon Guggenheim Fel, 79 & 87; Nat Endowment Arts, 85. *Bibliog:* Alan G Artner (auth), Brodsky paintings save exhibition, Chicago Tribune, 82; Peter Frank (auth), Catalogue essay, Arts Mag, 83; Dore Ashston (auth), An art of process, Arts Mag, 85. *Media:* Mixed Media. *Dealer:* Ivan Karp 383 W Broadway New York NY 10012; OK Harris Works of Art 430 N Woodward Ave Birmingham MI 48009. *Mailing Add:* 121 Prince St Apt 4W New York NY 10012

BRODSKY, HARRY
PRINTMAKER, PAINTER
b Newark, NJ, July 20, 08. *Study:* Philadelphia Col Art, 28-31; Univ Pa, 37-39. *Work:* Hirshhorn Mus & Sculpture Garden & Nat Mus Am Art, Washington, DC; Brooklyn Mus; Victoria & Albert Mus & Brit Mus, London; Princeton Univ; Springfield Mus; Cleveland Mus; Philadelphia Mus; Portland Mus; Philadelphia Print Club; and others. *Exhib:* Paintings & Prints, Philadelphia Artists, Whitney Mus, 34; Ann Exhib, Pa Acad Fine Arts, Philadelphia, 39, 49 & 62; Nat Exhib Prints, Libr Cong, 45-; American Watercolors, Drawings & Prints, Metrop Mus Art, 52; Les Peintres Gravers Actuels Aux Etats Unis, Bibliotheque Nat, Paris, 53; American Prints Around the World Travelling Exhib, S Am, US Info Agency, 63; Mary Ryan Gallery, New York, 85; Philadelphia Print Club, 88; Hahn Gallery, 90; and others. *Pos:* Art dir & mgr, Wescutt & Thomson Gallery, Philadelphia, 56-58; art dir, Campbell Soup Co, 70-72. *Teaching:* Instr vocational art & design, Dobbins Vocational Sch, Philadelphia, 37-43 & Mastbaum Vocational Sch, Philadelphia, 50-52. *Awards:* Purchase Award, First Nat Print Show, Brooklyn Mus, 47; Prize, Ann Print Show, Philadelphia Print Club, 48; Audubon Artists Prize, New York, 86. *Mem:* Audubon Artists; Artists Equity. *Media:* Lithography. *Dealer:* Miriam Fortunoff New York NY; Sylvan Cole Gallery New York NY. *Mailing Add:* 6633 N Eighth St Philadelphia PA 19126

BRODSKY, JUDITH KAPSTEIN
PRINTMAKER, EDUCATOR
b Providence, RI, July 14, 33. *Study:* Radcliffe Col, BA(art hist); Tyler Sch Art, Temple Univ, MFA. *Work:* Libr Cong, Washington, DC; Fogg Art Mus, Cambridge; NJ State Mus, Trenton; Princeton Univ, NJ; Newark Mus. *Comn:* The Magic Muse, traveling art environ (with Ilse Johnson, M K Johnson & Jane Teller), Asn Arts NJ State Mus, 72; Bicentennial Portfolio, Princeton, NJ, 75. *Exhib:* one-person shows, Brown Univ, 73, NY State Mus, 75, Douglas Col, 78 & Assoc Artists, Philadelphia, 79; many group shows, US & abroad. *Pos:* Assoc dir, Princeton Graphic Workshop, Inc, 66-68; owner, Castle Howard Press; nat pres, Women's Caucus Art, 76-78; assoc dean, Rutgers Univ, 81-82, assoc provost, 82- *Teaching:* Lectr art hist, Tyler Sch Art, 66-71; asst prof printmaking, Beaver Col, 72-77, assoc prof, 77, actg chmn art dept, 77; assoc prof & chmn art dept, Rutgers Univ, 78-81. *Awards:* Purchase Prizes, NJ State Mus, 70 & 71 & Boston Printmakers, 71; Stella C Drabkin Mem Award, Am Color Print Soc, 77; and others. *Bibliog:* Miller & Swenson (auth), Lives and Works: Talks with Women Artists, Scarecrow Press, 81. *Mem:* Col Art Asn Am; Philadelphia Print Club; Calif Soc Printmakers; Boston Printmakers; Soc Am Graphic Artists; founding mem Coalition Women's Art Orgn. *Media:* Intaglio, Lithography. *Publ:* Auth, Some notes on women printmakers, Art J, summer 76; designed & publ, B J O Nordfeldt, Etchings, 77, Friends and Foes from A to Z, by Dorothea Greenbaum, 78 & Woman, A Portfolio, 78; auth, Rediscovering Women Printmakers: 1500-1850, Counterproof, spring 79; The Status of Women in Art, Feminist Collage, Columbia Teachers Col Press, 79. *Dealer:* Assoc Am Artists 20 W 57th St New York NY. *Mailing Add:* c/o Assoc Am Artists 20 W 57th St New York NY 10019

BRODSKY, STAN
PAINTER, EDUCATOR
b Brooklyn, NY, Mar 23, 25. *Study:* Univ Mo, BJour; Univ Iowa, with Jim Lechay & Byron Burford, MFA; Columbia Univ, EdD. *Work:* New York Univ & Port Authority, World Trade Ctr, New York; Heckscher Mus, Huntington, NY; ATT, Chicago, Ill; pvt collection of Dr James Watson, Cold Springs Harbor, NY; Wm A Farnsworth Mus, Rockland, Maine; Parrish Mus, Southampton, NY; Mus Fine Arts, St Petersburg, Fla. *Comn:* Electronic Abstract Symbols (lobby mural), PRD Electronics, Syosset, NY, 70. *Exhib:* Munic Gallery, Regensburg, Ger, 88; two-man show, June Kelly Gallery, 88, one-man show, 89 & 91; 20th Century Long Island Landscape Painting, Mus at Stonybrook, Long Island, NY, 90; Retrospective, Heckscher Mus, Huntington, NY, 91; Hopkins Gallery, Wellfleet, Mass, 92; and others. *Teaching:* Prof art, C W Post Col, Long Island Univ, 60-, prof emer, 91- *Awards:* Yaddo Fel, Saratoga Springs, NY, 87; Va Ctr Creative Arts, 89; Trustees Award Scholarly, Creative Achievement, C W Post, Long Island, NY, 92; and others. *Bibliog:* Ron Pisano (auth), Long Island Landscape Painting in the 20th Century, Little Brown & Co, 90; NY Review of Art, 4th ed, Krantz Pub Co, Chicago, 90; Dr J Collischan (auth), Transportation Into Color (catalog), Mus Retrospective, 91. *Media:* Oil, Casein. *Publ:* Illusr for poster, Enclosure VI, 2000 edition, Graphique de France, Boston, Mass, 88; Ionian Green IV, 500 Ed Color Q, Dayton, Ohio. *Dealer:* June Kelly Gallery 591 Broadway New York NY 10012. *Mailing Add:* 7 Glen-A-Little-Trail Huntington NY 11743

BRODY, ARTHUR WILLIAM
PRINTMAKER, PAINTER
b New York, NY, Mar 2, 43. *Study:* Harvey Mudd Col, BS, 65; Claremont Grad Sch & Univ Ctr, MFA, 67. *Work:* Southern Ill Univ, Carbondale; St Lawrence Univ, Canton, NY; Ariz State Univ, Tempe; Hist & Fine Arts Mus, Anchorage, Alaska; Portland Mus, Ore. *Exhib:* Boston Printmakers, 91; Queensborough Community Col, 91; Print Club, 91; Harper Nat, 92; Print Club Albany, 92; and others. *Teaching:* Instr printmaking, design, drawing, painting & art hist, beginning & advan; instr, Univ Alaska, 67-69; asst prof, Ripon Col, Wis, 70-75; from asst prof to assoc prof, 77-84, prof, 84-; printmaking & computer art, Univ Alaska. *Awards:* Holder Mem Award, Chantangua, 91; First Prize Printmaking, Harper Nat, 92; Second Prize Printmaking, Harrisburg Nat, 92. *Mem:* Col Art Asn; Print Club; World Print Coun; NW Printmakers. *Media:* Woodcut, Intaglio; Acrylic, Oil. *Publ:* Auth, Communications & Intent, Communications--Tyrant or Liberator?, Ripon Col, 74. *Mailing Add:* Dept Art Univ Alaska Fairbanks AK 99201

BRODY, BLANCHE
PAINTER, PRINTMAKER
b Brooklyn, NY. *Study:* Hunter Col, 41-44; Boston Univ, BS, 49, MEd, 51; San Francisco Art Inst, with Richard Diebenkorn, 57-59. *Work:* Itel, San Francisco, Calif; El Dorado Press, Berkeley, Calif; Rene di Rosa, Bay Area Figuratives Mus. *Comn:* Logo, Anti-Defamation League Biennale Brit, 88. *Exhib:* San Francisco Women Artists, San Francisco Mus Art, Calif, 57, 58, 60, 62, 63, 66 & 67; Calif Painters Ann, Oakland Mus, 58, 62-64; Painted Flower Invitational, Oakland Mus, Calif, 59 & 64; Jack London Square, Oakland Mus, Calif, 59-67; Mid Year Ann, Butler Inst Am Art, Youngstown, Ohio; West Coast Oil Painting Ann, Frye Art Mus, Seattle, Wash, 62, 63, 65 & 66; Natural & Supernatural, 64-66 & The Contemp Landscape, 68-69, San Francisco Art Inst, Calif. *Awards:* Second Prize, Oakland Mus, Jack London Square, 61; Ed Hill, El Paso, Tex; First Hon Mention, Biennale Int de Vichy, 64; First Prize, San Francisco Women Artists, 66-67; Hon Mention, Biennale Int del Deporter en las Bellas Artes, Barcelona, Spain, 67. *Bibliog:* James Normile (auth), The subject is children, Archit Dig, 11-12/73; Louis Chapin (auth), Looking west--to exuberance, Christian Sci Monitor, 10/25/78; Thomas Albright (auth), Art in the San Francisco Bay Area, 1945-1980. *Mem:* Artists Equity (mem bd 60-63); Valley Art Ctr. *Media:* Oil, Watercolor; Monotypes. *Dealer:* Allan Stone Gallery 48 E 86th St New York NY 10028; Manolides Gallery 89 Yessler Way Seattle WA. *Mailing Add:* 19 Vista Del Orinda Orinda CA 94563

BRODY, CAROL Z
PAINTER
b Brooklyn, NY, July 5, 41. *Study:* Brooklyn Col, BA(cum laude), 62; Parsons Sch Design, 82-84. *Work:* Staten Island Borough Hall, NY; Snug Harbor Cult Ctr, Staten Island, NY; St Vincents Med Ctr, Staten Island, NY; Kidder-Peabody Offices, New York, Carmel, Calif & Mich; Metrop Savings Bank, Brooklyn, NY. *Comn:* Cover design (portrait), Women in History Month, Staten Island Borough Hall, 84; collage & watercolor painting, Smith Kline Beecham Pharmaceuticals Co, Parsippany, NJ, 91; cover design (invitation), Staten Island Inst Arts & Scis, 92. *Exhib:* Ann Nat Exhib, Knickerbocker Artists, Salmagundi Club, New York, 83 & 92; Layerists: Level to Level, Johnson-Humrickhouse Mus, Coshocton, Ohio, 90; one-woman show, Recent Watercolors, AT&T Corp Educ Ctr, Hopewell, NJ, 90; Ga Watercolor Nat Exhib, Columbus Mus, 91; 167th Ann Exhib, Nat Acad Design, New York, 92; Biennial Juried Exhib, Staten Island Inst Arts & Scis, NY, 92. *Teaching:* Instr watercolor, Art Lab, Snug Harbor, Staten Island, NY 86- *Awards:* Hudson Valley Art Asn Award, Salmagundi Club, 88; Adriana Zahn Award, 90; First Place Solo Award, Pen & Brush Ann Mem, 90. *Mem:* Audubon Artists; Catherine Lorillard Wolfe Art Club; Salmagundi Club (jury awards, 89, admiss comt, 90-92); Soc Layerists Multi-Media; Pen & Brush (chmn watercolors, selection comt). *Media:* Watercolor. *Publ:* Illusr, Layering, An Art of Time and Space, Soc Layerists Multi-Media, 91. *Mailing Add:* 159 Fields Ave Staten Island NY 10314

BRODY, JACOB JEROME
EDUCATOR, MUSEOLOGIST
b Brooklyn, NY, Apr 24, 29. *Study:* Brooklyn Mus Art Sch, with Gross & Ferren, 46-50; Art Students League, with Groth, 47; Cooper Union, cert, 50; Brooklyn Col, 50-52; Univ NMex, BA, 56, MA, 64 & PhD, 71. *Collections Arranged:* Early Masters of Modern Art, Isaac Delgado Mus Art, New Orleans, La, 59; Indigo, Mus Int Folk Art, Santa Fe, NMex, 61; Myth, Metaphor & Mimbreno Art, Maxwell Mus Anthrop, Univ NMex, Albuquerque, 77; Between Traditions (auth, catalog), Univ Iowa Mus, 76; The Chaco Phenomenon (auth, catalog), Maxwell Mus Anthrop 83-85; Mimbres Painted Pottery (auth, catalog), Am Fedn Arts 83-85; Mimbres Pottery, Roswell Mus Fine Arts, 83; Beauty From the Earth; Anasazi & Pueblo Indian Pottery (auth, catalog), from Collection of Univ Pa Mus; A Bridge Across Cultures: Pueblo Painters in Santa Fe 1910-1932 (auth, catalog), Wheelwright Mus; and others. *Pos:* Cur art, Everhart Mus, 57-58; cur collection, Isaac Delgado Mus Art, 58-60; cur collection, Mus Int Folk Art, 61-62; dir & cur, Maxwell Mus Anthrop, NMex, 62-84; res cur, Sch Am Res 87-; res assoc Lab Anthrop, Mus Indian Art & Cul, 90- *Teaching:* Prof museology, Univ NMex, 63-, prof Am Indian art, 65- & emer status. *Awards:* Art Book Award, Border-Regional Libr Asn, 78; Hist Preserv Award, NMex Hist Soc, 78; Archaeol Soc NMex (honoree, 92); and others. *Bibliog:* Joyce Szabo (auth), J J Brody, Archaeology, Art and Anthropology, Papers in Honor of J J Brody, Archaeol Soc NMex, 92. *Mem:* Am Asn Mus; Soc Am Archaeol; Native Am Art Studies Asn; Am Rock Art Res Asn; Coun Mus Anthrop. *Res:* Native American art; Southwest Pueblo Indian prehistoric & historic arts, ethnic and modern art. *Publ:* Auth, Indian Painters and White Patrons, Univ NMex Press, 71; Mimbres Painted Pottery, Sch Am Res & Univ NMex Press, 77; coauth (with LeBlanc & Scott), Mimbres Pottery: Ancient Art of the American Southwest, Hudson Hills Press, 83; co-dir, Painted Earth, Program for Art on Film (film), Metrop Mus Art & Getty Found, 89; auth, The Anasazi, JACA Bks, Milan & Rizzoli, New York, 90; Anasazi and Pueblo Painting, USM Press & Sch Am Res, 91; plus many articles, etc. *Mailing Add:* Dept Art & Art Hist Univ NMex Albuquerque NM 87131

BRODY, JACQUELINE
EDITOR
b Utica, NY, Jan 23, 32. *Study:* Vassar Col, AB, 53; London Sch of Econ, 53-57. *Pos:* Ed, The Print Collector's Newsletter, 72- *Mailing Add:* c/o Print Collector's Newsletter 119 E 79th St New York NY 10021

BRODY, MYRON ROY
ADMINISTRATOR, SCULPTOR
b New York, NY, Apr 5, 40. *Study:* Nat Inst Fine Arts, Mexico City; Philadelphia Col Art, BFA, 65; Grad Sch Fine Art, Univ Pa, MFA, 68; Ateneum, Helsinki, Finland, 68-69; Univ Va, 70-71; Harvard Univ, 75. *Work:* Univ of Arts; Princeton Univ Art Mus, NJ; Univ Va Art Mus, Charlottesville; Mus Nac Bellas Artes, Rio de Janeiro; US Dept of State; and others. *Comn:* Polished bronze, N Patrol Sta, Kansas City Police Dept, Mo, 77; polished bronze, Prudential Insurance Co Am, Plymouth, Minn; polished bronze, Technical Audit Ltd, Surrey, Eng. *Exhib:* Nelson Gallery-Atkins Mus, Kansas City, Mo; Allan Stone Gallery, New York; Wichita Art Mus, Kans; Kans City Art Inst; Minneapolis Inst Arts; Dusseldorf Kunstakademie, Ger; Ark Art Ctr; and other group & one-person exhibs. *Pos:* Bd mem & pres, Mo USA/Para Brazil, Partners Americas & Kans City Arts Coun; sr consult, Arts Exchange Int; dir, consult, Global Assoc; EXPO 92, Seville, Spain; Nat Mus Woman Arts, Washington, DC. *Teaching:* Asst prof sculpture & design, Va Western Community Col, 69-76, chmn dept art, 69-72; adj prof ceramics, art educ & sculpture, Univ Va Sch Continuing Educ, 70-76; lectr sculpture, Hollins Col, Va, 75-76; chmn art dept & prof, Avila Col, Kans City, Mo, 76-85; chmn art dept & prof, Univ Ark, Fayetteville, 85-91. *Awards:* Va Comn Arts & Humanities Award, 75; Cert for Distinguished Serv, Mus Nacional de Belas Artes, Rio de Janeiro, 83; Fulbright-Hays Fels, Ger Govt, 91; and others. *Mem:* Col Art Asn; Nat Asn Arts Adminrs; Arts & Bull Soc Kansas City (founder); Ark Fulbright Fel, Alumni Asn (pres, 86-89 & 91-). *Media:* Multimedia. *Publ:* Contribr, Decorative Art in Modern Interiors, 73-74; New Designs in Ceramics, 70; Visual Art & The End Usuer: Who Uses Whom, Int Forum Design, Ulm, Ger, 90. *Mailing Add:* Dept Art FNAR 116 Univ Ark Main Campus Fayetteville AR 72701

BRODY, RUTH
PAINTER, PRINTMAKER
b New York, NY, Aug 11, 17. *Study:* Hunter Col, BA, 38; Columbia Univ, MA, 40. *Exhib:* 9th Ann, Knickerbocker Artists, New York, 56; Nat Soc Painters Casein & Acrylics, New York, 63-65, 67, 69 & 73; 14th New Eng Ann, Silvermine Guild, Conn, 63; Bronx Ann, Bronx Mus, NY, 69-70, 75, 77 & 80; Graphics & Crafts Show, Hudson River Mus, Yonkers, NY, 70 & 71; Westchester-Putnam Art Teachers Exhib, Neuberger Mus, Purchase, NY, 77; Am Soc Contemp Artists Ann Exhib, 83-88. *Teaching:* Instr art, Secondary Schs, New York, 40-53; chmn art dept, Roosevelt High Sch, Yonkers, NY, 67-79. *Awards:* Best in Show, Riverdale Neighborhood, 68; Second Prize, Bronx Coun Arts Paint Out, 75; Victor A Sachse Mem Award, Am Soc Contemp Artists. *Bibliog:* An artist is inspired, Riverdale Press, NY, 11/6/80. *Mem:* New York Artists Equity Asn; Found Community Artists; Bronx Coun Arts; Am Soc Contemp Artists. *Media:* Watercolor, Pen & Ink; Intaglio, Monoprints. *Publ:* Auth, Using artwork in the school yearbook, Columbia Scholastic Press Asn Advisers Asn Bull, 71; Chance and Choice: An art game for the creation of a mural, Nat Art Educ Asn, 75. *Mailing Add:* 3338 Giles Pl Bronx NY 10463

BROER, ROGER L
PAINTER, SCULPTOR
b Omaha, Nebr, Nov 9, 45. *Study:* Eastern Mont Col, BA, 74; Cent Wash Univ, 74-75. *Work:* Mus Native Am Cult, Spokane, Wash; US Dept Interior, Browning, Mont; Eastern Mont Col, Billings; Safeco Insurance Co Am, Seattle; Seafirst Bank Collection, Seattle; and others. *Exhib:* Fifty group and twenty-five solo shows including at Dept Interior, Washington, DC and Espace de Pierre Cardin, Paris. *Teaching:* Iowa State Arts Comn Workshop, 81; artist in schs, Arts Alaska Inc, 83-87; artist-in-residence, Wash State Arts Comn. *Awards:* Numerous awards in national shows, including Trail of Tears Show and the Red Cloud Show. *Bibliog:* Theo Nassar (auth), Western art has begun to take on some vast new meanings, Spokesman, 3/79; O J Parsons (auth), Western impressions, Spokesman, 6/79; and others. *Mem:* Puget Sound Group Northwest Painters; Indian Arts & Crafts Asn. *Media:* Mixed Media. *Publ:* Articles in various publications, including Contemp Western Artists and The Nebraskaland Mag. *Mailing Add:* 29621 154 Ave SE Kent WA 98042

BROIDO, LUCY
WRITER, DEALER
b New York, NY, Jan 19, 24. *Study:* Cornell Univ, 41-44; Teacher's Col, Columbia Univ, BS, 45; Adelphi Col, Garden City, NY, 50-51. *Exhib:* French Opera Posters, Mus Performing Arts, Lincoln Ctr, New York, 74. *Pos:* Pres, Lucy Broido Graphics, Ltd, 72-; dir, Arts Exchange Mag, 77-79. *Teaching:* Fac mem, The New School, New York, 81. *Mem:* Philadelphia Art Alliance; Appraisers Asn Am. *Res:* Nineteenth century graphic arts. *Specialty:* Nineteenth & twentieth century posters and related prints. *Publ:* Auth, French Opera Posters, 1868-1930, 76; Jules Chéret: Catalogue Raisonnée, 80, Dover Publ, expanded ed, 92. *Mailing Add:* 908 Wootton Rd Bryn Mawr PA 19010

BROKER, KARIN
DRAFTSMAN, PRINTMAKER
b Pa, July 27, 50. *Study:* Univ Iowa, Iowa City, BFA, 72; Atelier 17, Paris, with Stanley Hayter, 73; Univ Wis, Madison, with Warrington Colescott & Jack Damer, MFA, 80. *Work:* Cabo Frio Bienal Collection, Brazil; US Info Serv, Middle East; Brooklyn Mus Art, NY; Prudential Insurance, Fla & NJ; Boston Mus Fine Arts, Mass. *Comn:* Trophy (3-D drawing), InterFirst Bank & Houston Symphony, 83; RSVP, Bechtler Gallery, Charlotte, NC, 92. *Exhib:* World Print Four, San Francisco Mus Mod Art, 83241; Showdown, Alternative Mus, New York, 83; Int Exchange Exhib of Prints, Seoul, Korea, 83; 1986 New Orleans Triennial: The Centennial Exhibition, New Orleans Mus Art, La, 86; Shrines and Altars, John Michael Kohler Arts Ctr, Sheboygan, Wis, 86; Graphica Atlantica, Reykjavik, Iceland, 87; one-woman show, Univ Corpus Christi, 88, McMurtrey Gallery, Houston, Tex, 92; Figurative Graphics, Graphic Figures, Kurst Aus Den USA, Berufsverbard Bildener Kunstler, Koln, Ger, 91; Retrospective, Rice Univ, Sewell Art Gallery, Houston, Tex, 92. *Pos:* Pres, Southern Graphics Coun, 84-86; studio coordr, Col Art Asn Am Conf, Houston, Tex, 88. *Teaching:* Assoc prof, Rice Univ, Houston, Tex, currently. *Awards:* Nat Endowment Arts Visual Artist Fel, 85 & 87. *Bibliog:* Casey Rote (auth), essay, Corpus Christi State Univ, 88; David Brauer (auth), essay, Rice Univ, 92. *Media:* Drawing. *Publ:* Auth, Mad Artist-Printmaker (catalog), Tex Tech Univ, 83. *Dealer:* McMurtrey Gallery Houston TX. *Mailing Add:* Dept Art-Rice Univ PO Box 1892 Houston TX 77251

BROMM, HAL
DEALER, DESIGNER
Study: Pratt Inst, BA; Royal Col Art, 69; Attingham Sch, Eng, 71. *Pos:* Dir, Hal Bromm Gallery, New York. *Teaching:* Instr, Sch Visual Arts, 82-84. *Awards:* Victorian Soc Book Award for Texture of Tribeca. *Bibliog:* Sally Silliqi, (auth), Changing times in Tribeca, Metropolis, 9/89; Peter Blauner (auth), O Pioneers, NY Mag, 12/25/89; Brigitte Knauf (auth), Smarter Dealer, Ambiente, 5/90; Suzanne Stephens (auth), Historic District: Tribeca, Archit Dig, 11/90. *Mem:* Fine Arts Federation (bd dirs); Community Bd One; Am Friends Attingham; Historic Districts Coun (bd dirs); chmn, Wash Market Hist Dist. *Specialty:* Painting, sculpture, drawing, photography by contemporary American, European and Russian artists. *Publ:* Auth, Selections from Hal Bromm, Eaton/Shoen Gallery, 80-81; auth, Moving 77, Hal Bromm Gallery, New York, 78; Introduction in: Natalya Nesterova: Recent Works from Moscow, Sovart Inc, 88; auth, Introduction, In: The Texture of Tribeca, Tribeca, Community Asn, 89. *Mailing Add:* 90 W Broadway New York NY 10007

BROMMER, GERALD F
PAINTER, WRITER
b Berkeley, Calif, Jan 8, 27. *Study:* Concordia Teachers Col, BSc(educ), 48; Univ Nebr, MA, 55; Chouinard Art Inst; Otis Art Inst, Univ Southern Calif; Univ Calif, Los Angeles; Christ Col Irvine, DLitt, 85. *Work:* Howard Ahmanson Collection, Los Angeles; Hughes Labs, Malibu; Pac Telesis, San Fransisco; State of Calif Collection, Sacramento; Utah State Univ; Owensboro Mus of Fine Art, Ky; TRW, Sunnydale, Calif. *Comn:* Series watercolors, Hilton Hotels, Las Vegas & San Francisco, Intercontinental Hotel, Los Angeles. *Exhib:* Am Watercolor Soc, New York, 69, 72 & 73; Nat Acad Design, New York, 71; Watercolor USA, Springfield, Mo, 73, 75 & 76; Nat Watercolor Soc, Los Angeles, 74, 75 & 77-; Royal Watercolor Soc, London, 75; plus over 125 one-man shows. *Pos:* Chief designer, Daystar Designs, Inc, 63-73. *Teaching:* Chmn dept art, Lutheran High Sch, Los Angeles, 55-74; instr, workshops, US & abroad, 75-88. *Awards:* Landmark Purchase Award, Watercolor USA, 69; Crescent Cardboard Co Purchase Award, Nat Watercolor Soc, 72; Utah State Purchase Award, Watercolor West Invitational, 73. *Bibliog:* Article in SW Art Mag, 11/87; Elizabeth Leonard (auth), Painting the Landscape, Watson-Guptill, 84; article, Am Artist, 2/84. *Mem:* Nat Watercolor Soc (treas, 63, vpres, 65-66, 80-81, pres, 67-68, 81-82); W Coast Watercolor Soc; Nat Art Educ Asn; Watercolor USA Honor Soc; Rocky Mountain Nat Watermedia Soc. *Media:* Transparent Watercolor, Collage. *Publ:* Auth, Exploring Transparent Watercolor, 93, The Art of Collage, 78, Discovering Art History, 81, 3rd ed, 93 & Exploring Drawing, 87, Davis; Watercolor and Collage Workshop, Watson-Guptill, 86. *Dealer:* Esther Wells Collection 1390 S Coast Hwy Laguna Beach CA 92652; Fireside Gallery PO Box 3374 Carmel CA 93921. *Mailing Add:* 11252 Valley Spring Ln North Hollywood CA 91602

BRONER, MATHEW
PAINTER, EDUCATOR
b Detroit, Mich, Jan 26, 24. *Study:* Soc Arts & Crafts, 42; Wayne State Univ, 43-45; Cranbrook Acad Art, BFA, 48, MFA, 49. *Work:* Ill State Mus, Springfield; Cranbrook Mus, Bloomfield Hills, Mich; Manhattanville Col, NY. *Exhib:* Detroit Inst Art, Mich, 41-48; 4th Ann Paintings of the Year, Rochester Mem Gallery, Nat Acad Design, New York, Toledo Mus Art, Ohio & Corcoran Gallery Art, Washington, (traveling exhibs), 47-48; Biennial Exhib Contemp Am Art, Va Mus Fine Arts, Richmond, 48; San Francisco Mus Art, Calif, 48; one-person shows, Chuck Levitan Gallery, New York, 80, Manhattanville Col, Purchase, NY, 90; Whitney Counterweight 3, New York, 81; Landmark Gallery, 81, Air Gallery, 85, Broome St Gallery, New York, 91. *Pos:* Consult, Am Coun Arts Educ, 77. *Teaching:* Instr drawing & design, Syracuse Univ, NY, 49-52; prof painting, drawing, color, Manhattanville Col, Purchase, NY, 67-, chmn dept art, 74-76, 80-82 & 86-88. *Awards:* MacDowell Fel, 79; and others. *Bibliog:* Palmer Paroner (auth), rev, Artspeak, 12/18/80. *Mem:* Am Asn Univ Prof. *Media:* Acrylic on Canvas, Watercolor. *Mailing Add:* 66 Greene St New York NY 10012

BRONER, ROBERT
PRINTMAKER, PAINTER
b Detroit, Mich, Mar 10, 22. *Study:* Ctr Creative Studies, Detroit, 42-45; Wayne State Univ, BFA, 44, MA, 46; painting with Stuart Davis, 49-50; Atelier 17, New York, with S W Hayter, 49-52. *Work:* Guggenheim Mus, Mus

Mod Art & Metrop Mus Art, New York; Los Angeles Co Mus; Philadelphia Mus Art & Pa Acad Fine Arts; Bibliot Nat, Paris; Nat Collections, Smithsonian Inst, Washington, DC; Brooklyn Mus Art. *Comn:* Ed etchings, Detroit Inst Arts, 67; ed etchings & woodcut, London Arts Gallery, 67-69. *Exhib:* Eight shows, Brooklyn Mus Prints Nat, 51-76; Am Prints, Drawing & Watercolors, Metrop Mus Art, New York, 53; Young Am Printmakers, 54, Print Acquisitions, 59 & Pop Graphics, 70, Mus Modern Art, New York; Brit Int Print Biennale, 68, 70, 72 & 84; Salon de Mai, Mus Art Mod, Paris, 69 & Belgrade, 70; Silk Screen Hist, Philadelphia Mus Art, 72; Walker Art Ctr, Minneapolis, 73; Los Angeles Printmakers, Grunwald Mus Graphic Art, 82 & 84; one person show, Merging One Gallery, Santa Monica Calif, 87 & woodcuts, Israel, Mus, Jerusalem, 93; Maine Coast Artists, Rockport, Maine, 90; and others. *Teaching:* Prof emer art & art hist, Wayne State Univ, 64-86; adj prof printmaking, Cooper Union, 82-92. *Awards:* Print Purchase Prize, Brooklyn Mus, 64; Purchase Prize, Soc Am Graphic Artists, 69 & 85; Detroit Inst Award, 61 & 66; Los Angeles Co Mus Print Prize, Los Angeles Print Soc, 84; New York Found Arts Fel Award, 90; Mich Coun Arts Fel Award 83 & 86. *Mem:* Drawing & Print Club, Detroit Inst Art (bd dirs, 66-76); Mich Asn Printmakers (pres); pres, Nat Print Coun, 79-83; Philadelphia Print Club; Soc Am Graphic Artists (pres, 81-84). *Media:* Etching; Oil on Canvas. *Publ:* Auth, articles, Artforum, 9/80 & 1/81. *Mailing Add:* 40 W 22nd St New York NY 10010

BRONSON, A A (MICHAEL WAYNE TIMS)
POST-CONCEPTUAL ARTIST, WRITER
b Vancouver, BC, June 16, 46. *Work:* Nat Gallery Can, Ottawa; Art Gallery Ont, Toronto; Mus Contemp Art, Gent, Belg; Musee d'Art Contemporain, Montreal; van Abbemuseum, Eindhoven; Vancouver Art Gallery, Vancouver. *Comn:* Ursa Major and Taurus: Pavillion Fragments from the Starry Vault, Relief Mural, Toronto Stock Exchange, 83; Exterior Relief Sculpture, Ottawa Courthouse, 86. *Exhib:* Group exhibs, Venice Biennale, Can Pavilion, 80, Documenta 7 & 8, Kassel, WGer, 82 & 87, Neuberger Mus, State Univ New York, Purchase, 90-92, Words & #'s, Wright State Univ, Dayton, 91, David Clarkson, General Idea, Allan McCollum, S L Simpson Gallery, Toronto, Can, 92 & Grey Art Gallery & Study Ctr, New York Univ, 92-93; Vancover Art Gallery, Can, 84; Mus Contemp Art, Gent, Belg, 84; Kunsthalle Basel, Switz, 84; Van Abbemuseum, Eindhoven, Neth, 85; Musee d'art Contemporain, Montreal, 85; Albright Knox Art Gallery, Buffalo, 86; Contemp Art Mus, Houston, 87; New Mus Contemp Art, New York, 88; solo exhibs, General Idea's Yen Boutique, Dörrie-Priess Galerie, Hamburg, Ger, 89, Fin de siècle, Koury Wingate Gallery, New York, 90, PLAOEBO/ General Idea's Yen Boutique, Stampa Gallery, Basel, Switz, 91, Blue (Cobalt) PLAOEBO, Galerie Montenay, Paris, France, 92 & San Francisco Mus Mod Art, 92-93; Shut the Fuck Up, Span Television broadcast, 90; General Idea, Kölnischer Kunstverein, Cologne, Ger, 91; General Idea, Taormina Arte Video, Taormina, Italy, 92. *Pos:* Ed, File Mag, Toronto, 72-89. *Awards:* Can Coun Arts Awards, 68-83; Ont Arts Coun Award Art Criticism, 74; Gershon Iskowitz Award, 88; Toronto Arts Award, 89. *Bibliog:* Roberta Smith (auth), General Idea, NY Times, C-32, 3/24/90; Paolo Bianchi (auth), General Idea: Kunstlergruppen, Kunstforum, Cologne, 250-255, 11-12/91; Lois Nesbitt (auth), General Idea, Stux Gallery, Artforum, 98-99, 9/92. *Publ:* Auth, Menage A Trois, Gen Idea, 78; co-ed, Performance by artists, Art Metropole, 79; auth, Getting Into the Spirits Cocktail Book, Gen Idea, 80; co-ed, Museums by artists, Art Metropole, 83; Contribr, General Idea, 1968-84, Stedelijk Van Abbemuseum, Eindhoven, 84. *Mailing Add:* 136 Simcoe Toronto ON M5H 3G4 Canada

BRONSON, CLARK EVERICE
SCULPTOR
b Kamas, Utah, Mar 10, 39. *Study:* Art Instr Inst, 56-57; Univ Utah, 59. *Comn:* Hartford Stag (bronze), Hartford, Conn, 80; Chadwick Ram (bronze), Boone Crockett Buffalo Bill Hist Ctr, Cody, Wyo, 82. *Exhib:* Nat Acad Western Art, Nat Cowboy Hall Fame, 73, 74 & 75; Mzuri Safari Found Conf, Reno, Nev, 73 & 74; Mont Hist Soc, Helena, 78; C M Russell Art Show & Auction, Great Falls, Mont, 79-81; Nat Sculpture Soc, New York, 81. *Pos:* State of Utah Fish & Game Staff Artist, 60-63. *Awards:* First Prize, Nat Art Competition, Art Instr Inst, 57; Silver Medal (bronze sculpture), Nat Acad Western Art, 74, 75 & 77; Silver Medal (bronze sculpture), Nat Sclulpture Soc, 81. *Bibliog:* Don Jardine (auth), The continuing success of Clark Bronson, Illustrator, 71; Scott Dial (auth), Symbols of freedom, Southwest Art, 1/80; Richard P Christenson (auth), Bronson's love of life is forever frozen in bronze, Desert News, 9/81. *Mem:* Nat Acad Western Art; Nat Sculpture Soc; Soc Animal Artists; Wildlife Artists Int; Northwest Rendezvous Group. *Media:* Bronze sculpture and painting. *Publ:* Illusr, Nat Wildlife Mag, 63 & High Uintahs--Hi, 64, Album of North American Animals, 66, Album of North American Birds, 67 & Biography of a Grizzly, 69. *Mailing Add:* 17 Hitching Post Rd Bozeman MT 59715

BROOKE, DAVID STOPFORD
MUSEUM DIRECTOR
b Walton-on-Thames, Eng, Sept 18, 31. *Study:* Harvard Univ, AB, 58, AM, 63. *Pos:* Asst cur, Fogg Art Mus, Cambridge, Mass, 60-61; asst to dir, Smith Col Mus, Northampton, 63-65; chief cur, Art Gallery Ont, Toronto, 65-68; dir, Currier Gallery Art, Manchester, NH, 68-77; dir, Clark Art Inst, 77- *Mem:* Asn Am Art Mus Dirs. *Res:* British painting of the eighteenth and nineteenth centuries. *Publ:* Co-auth, James Tissot (catalog), Art Gallery Ont, 68; auth, Mortimer at Eastbourne and Kenwood, Burlington Mag, 68; James Tissot's amateur circus, Boston Mus Bulletin, 69; co-auth, The Dunlaps of New Hampshire, Antiques, 70; auth, Raeburn's portrait of John Clerk of Eldin, Currier Gallery Bulletin, 71. *Mailing Add:* 767 N Hoosac Rd Williamstown MA 01267

BROOKE, PEGAN
PAINTER
b Orange, Calif, July 19, 50. *Study:* Univ Calif, San Diego, BA, 72; Drake Univ, BFA(painting), 76; Univ Iowa, Iowa City, MA(painting), 77; Stanford Univ, MFA(painting), 80. *Work:* Guggenheim Mus; Univ Nebr Art Mus, Omaha; Iowa State Capitol Bldg, Des Moines; Bank Am Int Hq, San Francisco; San Francisco Mus Mod Art; and others. *Exhib:* solo exhib, Fuller Goldeen Gallery, San Francisco, 81, 83, 85 & 87, Scottsdale Ctr Arts, Ariz, 83, Saxon-Lee Gallery, Los Angeles, 89, Images Transformed, Oakland Mus, 92, Univ Calif Davis, 92; Emerging Northern California Artists, Orange Co Ctr Contemp Arts, Santa Ana, 82; New Perspectives in American Art, 83, Emerging Artists 1978-86, 88, Guggenhiem Mus; CA Directions in Painting, Alaska State Mus, 86; Survey of Calif Women Artists, Fresno Art Mus, 87; Landscape as Presence, San Jose Inst Contemp Art, 89. *Teaching:* Lectr, Univ Calif, Berkeley, 82, Davis, 83, Calif Col Art & Crafts, 83, Sonoma State Univ, 83 & San Francisco Art Inst, 84- *Awards:* Tiffany Found Fel Painting, 84; Marin Arts Coun Painting Grant, 92. *Bibliog:* Christine Tamblyn (auth), Pegan Brooke at Fuller Goldeen, Art News, 87; Mark Levy (auth), Pegan Brooke at Fuller Goldeen, Art in Am, 88; Suvan Geer (auth), Pegan Brooke, LA Times, 89; David Bonetti (auth), San Francisco Examiner, 92. *Mem:* Col Art Asn. *Media:* Oil. *Dealer:* 315 Sutter St San Francisco CA 94108. *Mailing Add:* PO Box 857 Bolinas CA 94924

BROOKINS, JACOB BODEN
SCULPTOR, PAINTER
b Princeton, Mo, Aug 28, 35. *Study:* Boise Jr Col, AA(painting); Univ Ore, BS(ceramics), MFA(metalsmithing & sculpture); also with Max Nixon, Jan Zach, Robert James & James Hanson. *Work:* Northern Ariz Univ, Univ Ore. *Exhib:* Ariz Comm Arts & Humanities Touring Exhib, 72-73; Southwestern Invitational, Yuma, Ariz, 72-73; Intermountain Crafts Exhib, Flagstaff, 73; Mus Northern Ariz, 77-79; Coconino Co Arts Ctr, 80-81; and others. *Collections Arranged:* Nat Coun Educ Ceramic Arts Conf '72 Exhib, 72; Intermountain Crafts Exhib, Ariz Designer Craftsmen, Flagstaff, 73. *Pos:* Dir, Mus Northern Ariz Art Inst, 75-79; founder, dir, Cosnino Inst, 79-; chmn, Cosnino Co Arts Comn, 81- *Teaching:* Instr jewelry, Univ Ore, 67-68; instr sculpture, Northern Ariz Univ, 69-75; instr ceramics, Yavapai Col, 79-80; volunteer instr applied crafts, US Peace Corps, Republic of Zaire, currently. *Awards:* Nat Endowment Art, 77 & 78. *Mem:* Nat Coun Educ Ceramic Arts; World Crafts Coun; Am Crafts Coun; Ariz Designer Craftsmen (mem bd dir, 70-75, state pres, 71-72); Nat Sculptors Conf; and others. *Media:* Metal, Ceramic. *Mailing Add:* 6351 Cosnino Rd Flagstaff AZ 86004

BROOKNER, JACKIE
SCULPTOR
b Providence, RI, Nov 20, 45. *Study:* Wellesley Col, BA, 67; Harvard Univ, MA, 70; New York Studio Sch, 76-77. *Work:* Dow Jones Collection; Becton Dickinson. *Exhib:* The New Spiritualism, Oscarsson Hood Gallery, New York & Univ Conn Gallery, Stoors, 81; Fifty National Women in Art, Edison Col Mus, Ft Myers, Fla, 82; Collection Gallery VI, McNay Art Inst, San Antonio, Tex, 82; solo exhibs, Oscarsson Hood Gallery, New York, 82 & 84 & Watson Art Gallery, Wheaton Col, Norton, Mass, 83; Varieties of Sculptural Ideas, Max Hutchinson Gallery, New York, 84; traveling exhib, New York/Beijing, Shanghai Art Mus, Beijing Art Inst & Hong Kong Arts Festival, 87-88; Pamela Auchincloss Gallery, New York, 91. *Pos:* Guest ed, Art J, Art & Ecology, Summer 92. *Teaching:* Instr sculpture, Parson Sch Design, New York, 78-; instr, Grad Sculpture Fac, Bard Col, 87; dean & instr, New York Studio Sch, 87. *Awards:* 90 New York Foundation Arts. *Bibliog:* Nancy Grove (auth), Jackie Brookner, Arts Mag, 2/82; Craig Mannister (auth), Jackie Brookner, Women Artist's News, 5/82; Stephen Westfall (auth), Jackie Brookner Arts Mag, 9/84; Steven Madoff (auth), Jackie Brookner, Art News, 10/84; G MacKenzie (ed), New York/Beijing: 22 American Artists, Coyote Press, 87; Michael Brenson (auth), The artist's hand, New York Times, 4/8/88; Michael Brenson (auth), Four sculptures with intense visions, New York Times, 4/17/88; Michael Brenson (auth), New York Times, Jackie Brookner, 6/91. *Mem:* Int Sculpture Asn; Col Art Asn. *Media:* Mixed Media. *Publ:* "Is Feminism An Issue for Students of the 80's and 90's?", Art Journal, 90; Guest editor, Art Journal on Art and Ecology, Summer 92. *Mailing Add:* 131 Spring St New York NY 10012

BROOKS, (JOHN) ALAN
PAINTER, INSTRUCTOR
b Burbank, Calif, Oct 11, 31. *Study:* San Jose State Col, MA, 60. *Work:* City San Francisco, Calif; Calif Canadian Bank; Scripps Inst, Calif; A T & T; Itel Corp; Pub Health League Calif; Hyatt Hotel Corp; and others. *Exhib:* Phelan Awards Biennial, San Francisco, 65, 67 & 69; one man shows, St Mary's Col, Calif, 67; John Bolles Gallery, San Francisco, 68-71; Newman Ctr, Univ Calif, Berkeley, 69; Van Doren Gallery, San Francisco, 74; Valley Art Ctr, Walnut Creek, Calif, 75. *Teaching:* Instr painting & drawing, City Col San Francisco, 71- *Awards:* Purchase Award, Calif State Fair, 60; First Prize Award, Mann Co Fair, 78 & San Mateo Co Fair, 81, Calif. *Media:* Oil, Watercolor; Pastel. *Publ:* Contribr, Sch Arts Mag, 71. *Dealer:* Van Doren Assoc 3800 Washington St San Francisco CA 94118. *Mailing Add:* Dept of Art City Col San Francisco 50 Phelan Ave San Francisco CA 94112

BROOKS, BRUCE W
PAINTER, SCULPTOR
b New York, NY, July 10, 48. *Study:* Pratt Inst, BFA(art educ), 70, MFA(painting), 75. *Exhib:* 415 W Broadway, New York, 78; William Patterson Col, NJ, 81; Miss Mus Art, 81; one-man shows, O K Harris, New York, 81 & 83 & Ron Hunnings, New York, 81. *Teaching:* Vis instr painting & drawing, Pratt Inst, 72-, asst to chmn dept, 72-74; adj asst prof painting, sculpture, art hist, design, LaGuardia Community Col, 77- *Mem:* Japan Soc; Japanese Sword Soc; Col Art Asn. *Media:* Alkyd, Paper. *Mailing Add:* 108 Wyckoff St Brooklyn NY 11201

BROOKS, ELLEN
PHOTOGRAPHER
Study: Univ Wis, Madison; Univ Calif, Los Angeles, BA, 68, MA, 70, MFA, 71. *Work:* Mus Mod Art, New York; Nat Mus Am Art, Washington, DC; Nat Gallery Can, Ottawa; Musee d'Art Contemporain Montreal, Can; Albright-Knox Mus, Buffalo, NY. *Exhib:* Solo exhibs, Polaroid Porject: Ellen Brooks, Vikky Alexander, Dorothy Goldeen Gallery, Santa Monica, Calif, 91, Wooster Gardens, New York, Vikky Alexander/Ellen Brooks, Ansel Adams Ctr, Friends Photography, San Francisco & Urbie et Orbie, Paris France, 92, Cleveland Ctr Contemp Art (traveling), Ezra & Cecile Zilkha Gallery-Wesleyan Univ, Middletown, Conn & Stux Gallery, New York, 93-94; Departures Photography 1923-1990 (traveling), Independent Curator's Inc, 92; Between Home and Heaven, Nat Mus Am Art, Washington, DC, 92; Bennington Col, Vt, 92; Concept/Construct: Photoghraphy in Los Angeles Art 1960- 1990, Laguna Art Mus, Calif, 93; Thomas Segal Gallery, Boston, Mass, 93. *Teaching:* Instr, San Francisco Art Inst, Calif, 73-82, Sch Visual Arts, New York, 85, Tisch Sch Arts, New York Univ, 84-92. *Awards:* Individual Fel, Nat Endowment Arts, 79 & 91; Phelan Award, Oakland, Calif, 72. *Bibliog:* Mary Ellen Haus (auth), Beyond Nature, Ellen Brooks, Tema Celeste, 1-2/89; Leslie Tonkonow (auth), Ellen Brooks, J Contemp Art, fall/winter 91; Carol Squires (auth), review, Artforum, 11/91. *Mailing Add:* 152 Wooster New York NY 10012

BROOKS, H(AROLD) ALLEN
HISTORIAN, LECTURER
b New Haven, Conn, Nov 6, 25. *Study:* Dartmouth Col, BA, 50; Yale Univ, MA, 55; Northwestern Univ, PhD, 57; Univ Nova Scotia, DEng(hon causa), 84. *Teaching:* Prof, Univ Toronto, Ont, 58-86; vis pro, Dartmouth Col, 69; Mellon chair, Vassar Col, 70-71; vis prof, Archit Asn Sch Archit, London, 77-82. *Awards:* Fels, Can Coun, 62, 75 & 78 & Guggenheim, 73; Alice Davis Hitchcock Book Award, Soc Archit Historians, 73; Fel, Victoria Univ, 83. *Mem:* Soc Archit Historians (pres, 64-66, dir, 61-64, 67-70 & 71-74); Soc Archit Historians Gr Brit; Soc Study Archit Can; Int Comt Monuments & Sites. *Res:* Frank Lloyd Wright & LeCorbusier. *Publ:* Auth, The Prairie School: Frank Lloyd Wright and His Midwest Contemporaries, 72 & ed, Prairie School Architecture: Studies from the Western Architect, 75, Univ Toronto Press; ed & contribr, Writings on Wright: Selected Comment on Frank Lloyd Wright, MIT Press, 81; The LeCorbusier Archive, 32 vols, Garland Publ, 82-84; auth, Frank Lloyd Wright and the Prairie School, Braziller, 83; ed & contribr, Le Corbusier, Princeton Univ Press, 87. *Mailing Add:* 9 River Ridge Rd Hanover NH 03755

BROOKS, HARRY A
GALLERY DIRECTOR, ART DEALER
Study: Princeton Univ, BA, 35; Inst Fine Arts, New York Univ, 46-48. *Pos:* Vpres, Knoedler & Co, 46-68; pres, Wildenstein & Co, Inc, New York, NY, 68- *Specialty:* Old and modern master paintings, drawings and sculpture. *Mailing Add:* Wildenstein & Co 19 E 64th St New York NY 10021

BROOKS, JOHN H
ADMINISTRATOR, EDUCATOR
b Cambridge, Mass, June 13, 35. *Study:* Princeton Univ, BA, 58; Columbia Univ, MA, 64. *Pos:* Staff lectr, Nat Gallery Art, Washington, DC, 64-68; assoc dir, Sterling & Francine Clark Art Inst, Williamstown, Mass, 68- *Teaching:* Lectr Am art, Univ Md Col, 67-68 & North Adams State Col, Mass, 71-75. *Awards:* Grace May Tilton Prize in Fine Arts, 58. *Mem:* Am Asn Mus; Int Coun Mus. *Publ:* Active connections: paintings and other arts, Prism, Mus Art, Carnegie Inst, 80; Highlights of the Sterling and Francine Clark Art Institute, Williamstown, Mass, 81; Monet in Massachusetts (catalog), 85; Clark as a Collector (video), 88. *Mailing Add:* 43B Gale Rd Williamstown MA 01267

BROOKS, LOUISE CHERRY
COLLECTOR, CERAMIST
b Phoenix City, Ala, Aug 28, 06. *Study:* Studied with Kelly Fitzpatrick, Charles Shannon & Wright Putney, Auburn Univ. *Exhib:* Leon Loard Gallery. *Pos:* Mem bd trustees, Montgomery Mus Fine Arts, Alabama Art Guild & Alabama Historical Asn, currently. *Awards:* Ala Art League & Nat Soc Arts & Lett. *Collection:* Early English Staffordshire figures; especially ceramic bird groups, egg-shell art. *Mailing Add:* 3604 Narrow Lane Rd Montgomery AL 36111

BROOKS, ROBERT
PAINTER
b Fall River, Mass, Oct 19, 22. *Study:* Swain Sch Design, New Bedford, Mass; Vesper George Sch Art, Boston, Mass, scholar. *Work:* Guild House, Barnstaple, Eng; First Nat Bank, Boston; Bass River Savings Bank, Hyannis; Gen Electric Corp, Framingham. *Comn:* Series of int scenes, Nationwide Insurance Co, Columbus, Ohio, 67-68; mural, Am Legion of Yarmouth, Mass, 77; series of paintings, comn by Arthur A Kaplan, Inc, New York, 77; mural, Cape Cod Synagogue, Hyannis, 78. *Exhib:* One-man shows, New Bedford Pub Libr, 46, Lincoln Savings Bank, New York, 75, Cape Cod Art Asn, Barnstable, 76 & Richards Gallery, Hyannis, Mass, 82 & 83; Acad Artists Asn, Springfield, Mass, 81. *Pos:* Illusr, Armed Forces, 43-46; designer, NE Stencil Engraving Co, New Bedford, 46-53; artist, Screencraft Prod, Yarmouth, 53-67; gallery dir, Robert Brooks Art Gallery, Hyannis, 69-80. *Teaching:* Art instr drawing, Swain Sch Design, 46-47; tutor design, Veteran's Admin, 47-49; instr painting, Cape Cod Community Col, summer 81-83. *Awards:* Copley Artist Award, Copley Soc Boston; First Prize in Watercolor, All New Eng Show, Cape Cod Art Asn, 81; Grumbacher Gold Medal, Acad Artist's Nat Exhib, Springfield, Mass, 81; First Prize in Watercolor, Cape Cod Art Asn, 83; Yankee-Sagendorph Award, 85. *Mem:* Cape Cod Art Asn; Soc Marine Painters; Acad Artist's Asn; Copley Soc Boston. *Media:* Watercolor. *Specialty:* Traditional landscapes and seascapes. *Dealer:* Market Barn Gallery Falmouth MA; Birdsey on the Cape Gallery Osterville MA. *Mailing Add:* 236 Bearse's Way Hyannis MA 02601

BROOKS, WENDELL T
PRINTMAKER, EDUCATOR
b Aliceville, Ala, Sept 10, 39. *Study:* Ind Univ, BS(art educ), 62, MFA(printmaking; Martin Luther King Jr Fel, scholar, Southern Fel), 71; Woodstock Artist's Asn, scholar, summer 61; Pratt Graphic Art Asn, scholar, 62; Univ Md, 65-66; Howard Payne Col, 66-67. *Work:* Libr of Cong, Washington, DC; Nasson Col; Mount Union Col; Carleton Col; Bethel Col; plus others including pvt collections. *Exhib:* A Return to Humanism, Burpee Art Mus, Rockford, Ill, 71; Social Comment in Recent Art, Concordia Teachers Col, Seward, Nebr, 71; The Black Experience in Prints, Pratt Graphic Ctr, New York, 72; Black Artists of America, NJ State Mus, Trenton, 72; Jew Jersey, 1972, 7th Ann Exhib, Trenton, 72; A Very Spec Invitational Show, McCarter Theatre, Princeton, NJ, 79; Black Artists/South, 79. plus many other group & one-man shows. *Teaching:* Instr printmaking, Ala A&M Univ, 67-68; asst prof printmaking & artist in residence, Nassan Col, 70; asst prof printmaking, Trenton State Col, 71-; lectr art at var art groups, cols & univs, 69-72. *Bibliog:* Article in Negro Heritage, 10/68; article in Chalkboard, 11/68; article in Christian Sci Monitor, 6/22/70; plus many other newspapers. *Mem:* Philadelphia Print Club. *Mailing Add:* Dept of Art Trenton State Col Hillwood Lakes Trenton NJ 08650

BROOME, RICK (RICHARD RAYMOND)
PAINTER
b Pueblo, Colo, Oct 13, 46. *Study:* Northrop Univ, 67-71; Northrop Inst Tech, 68. *Work:* USAF Acad, Colorado Springs, Colo; Naval Air Mus, Pensacola, Fla; Air Force Mus, Dayton, Ohio; San Diego Art & Space Mus, Calif; Northrop Univ, Inglewood, Calif. *Comn:* T-33/Colo Rocky Mountains, 74, F-105/Vietnam, 75, B-1/USAF Acad, 79, F-15/USAF Acad, 81 & T-Birds/USAF Acad, 82, USAF Acad Cadets, Colorado Springs. *Exhib:* JOC Aviation Art Show, Craig Air Force Base, Selma, Ala, 76 & Scott Air Force Base, Ill, 77. *Awards:* Best Cover/Year, Rocky Mountain Collegiate Asn, 75. *Bibliog:* Will Robinson (dir), From Time to Time (film), KRDO TV, 80 & 81; Gary Olson (auth), Airplanes in art: Broome a master, Weekend, Colo Springs Sun, 3/7/80. *Media:* Acrylic. *Res:* Created 1450 plus historically accurate aviation originals involving complete detailed research. *Publ:* Illusr, 12 covers of Frontier Mag, Inflight Publ, 74-82; illusr, 3 covers of Talon Mag, USAF Acad, 75-82; illusr, 2 covers of Check Points Mag, USAF Acad, 80; illusr, 3 covers of Aerospace Historian, Univ Kans, 79-82. *Dealer:* Kemper Galleries 1624 N Academy Blvd Colorado Springs CO 80915. *Mailing Add:* 2809 Old Broadmoor Rd Colorado Springs CO 80906

BROOMFIELD, ADOLPHUS GEORGE
PAINTER, DESIGNER
b Toronto, Ont, Aug 26, 06. *Study:* Ont Col Art, Toronto & Port Hope; studied with Lismer, MacDonald & Carmichael. *Work:* War Collection, Nat Gallery Can; Imperial War Col, Ottawa; Can Wire & Cable Co Collection, Toronto. *Exhib:* RCAF World Wide Exhib, Can & Eng, 45; Can Traveling Show, Montreal & Vancouver, 62; Royal Can Acad Arts, Nat Gallery Can, 65. *Bibliog:* L Schrag (auth), article, Broomfield, Globe & Mail, 64; Out of the wilderness, Can Crafts, 8/78; H Robertson (auth), A terrible beauty in Canada at War, James Lorimer Publ, 77. *Mem:* Royal Can Acad Arts. *Media:* Oil; Drypoint Etching, Heavy Textile Tapestry. *Publ:* Conserv, Tapestry Series, Out of Wilderness, 82. *Mailing Add:* Brackenwood 232 Isabella Ave Mississauga ON L5B 1A9 Canada

BROSK, JEFFREY
SCULPTOR
b New York, NY, Feb 15, 47. *Study:* Univ Pa, BA & BS, 70; Mass Inst Technol, MA(archit), 76. *Work:* Bank Am, San Francisco. *Comn:* IBM, Dallas, Tex. *Exhib:* Aldrich Mus Contemp Art; Hudson River Mus, Yonkers, NY, 78; solo exhibs, Max Hutchinson Gallery, New York, 83, Roanoke Mus Fine Arts, Va, 85, Fine Arts Ctr, Univ Mass, Amherst, 87, Stephen Rosenberg Gallery, New York, 88 & 90, Joan Robey Gallery, Denver, 91, Clark Univ, Worcester, Mass, 92 & Stephen Rosenberg Gallery, New York, 92; Construct Gallery, Chicago, 81; Galerie Alain Oudin, Paris, 81; Anne Reed Gallery, Ketchum Idaho, 90; Current Minimalists, Art Festival, Atlanta, Ga, 91; and many others. *Awards:* Grant, Pollock-Krasner Found, Inc. *Bibliog:* Hal Foster (auth), article, Artforum, 12/79; Michael Brenson (auth), Rev/Art, NY Times, 12/2/88; Stephen Westfall (auth), rev, Art Am, 4/89; Eleanor Heartney (auth), Rev, ARTnews, New York, 90; Mizue, Tokyo, Japan, 91. *Media:* All Media. *Dealer:* Stephen Rosenberg Gallery 115 Wooster St New York NY 10012. *Mailing Add:* 135 Spring St New York NY 10012

BROSS, ALBERT L, JR
PAINTER
b Newark, NJ, June 29, 21. *Study:* Art Students League, with Messrs Dumond, Bridgeman & McNulty. *Work:* NJ State Mus, Trenton; AT&T, New York; Roebling Collection; Springville Mus Art, Utah; Hanover Park High Sch. *Exhib:* Nat Arts Club Print Show, New York, 72; Hudson Valley Art Asn Regional Show, White Plains, NY, 72; Acad Artists Asn, Springfield, Mass, 72; Springville Mus Art, 72. *Awards:* Award, Am Asn Univ Women, 72; Lt Melvin D Brewer Mem Award, 76; Gold Medallion Miniature Art Soc, New Jersey, 90. *Mem:* Life mem Art Students League; Hudson Valley Art Asn; Assoc Artists NJ; Hunterdon Co Art Ctr, NJ; Miniature Art Soc, NJ. *Media:* Oil. *Dealer:* GWS Galleries 2600 Post Rd Southport CT. *Mailing Add:* Village Rd New Vernon NJ 07976

BROTHERS, BARRY A
PAINTER, MURALIST
b Brooklyn, NY, Jan 18, 55. *Study:* Brooklyn Col, City Univ NY, BS(photog & art), 77, MFA(painting), 80. *Work:* Herbert F Johnson Mus Art, Cornell Univ, NY; Brooklyn Col Collection, New York; Am Broadcasting Co, Inc; Capital Cities/ABC Inc, NY. *Comn:* 7 paintings, 6 photographs for portfolio, US oil refineries, for Fortune Mag, New York, 81; six murals (two triptychs), Am Broadcasting Co Inc, Brodcast Opers Complex, New York, 85-86; mural, Capital Cities/ABC, Inc, Corp Hq, New York, 89. *Exhib:* New Realists, Adelphi Univ, Garden City, NY, 82; Brooklyn 83 & 85, Brooklyn Mus, 83 & 85; The Brooklyn Landscape, Ammo Artists Space, Brooklyn, 84; 12 Year Retrospective, Brooklyn Mus, 84; 11th Ann Invitational, Henry Hicks Gallery, Brooklyn, 86; Printmaking at British Columbia, Mus Borough Brooklyn, NY, 87; In Search of the American Experience, Mus Nat Arts Found, 89. *Pos:* Independent graphic-advertising artist, 74-90; room screen furniture design, computer software develop, 89- *Awards:* DESI 9, Graphic Design, USA, 86; Landscape Painting Competition, Artists Mag, 87; In Search of the American Experience, Mus Nat Arts Found, 89. *Bibliog:* American Artists--Survey of Leading Cont Am (essay), 85 & The New York Art Review (essay), 89, Krantz Co; Art Product News Mag (article), Grady Publ Co, 3/87 & 4/87; Contemporary Graphic Artists (essay) Gale Research Co, Publ, Vol 2, 87. *Media:* Oil, Acrylic. *Publ:* Contribr, Print Mag XXXVIII:2, (article), 3/84 & 4/84; Gran Bazaar Maf, (essay), Milan, Italy, 85; Graphic Design: USA, Kaye Publ, Corp, 8/86. *Mailing Add:* 1922 E 18th St Brooklyn NY 11229

BROTHERTON, NAOMI
PAINTER, INSTRUCTOR
b Galveston, Tex. *Study:* Baylor Univ, Waco, Tex, BA(fine arts); Art Students League, with Edgar A Whitney, Milford Zornes, Gerry Peirce, Robert E Wood, John Pike, Rex Brandt, John C Pellew & Charles Reid. *Work:* S Ark Art Ctr, Eldorado; Baylor Univ Permanent Collection; Carlsbad Mus & Art Ctr, Carlsbad, NMex; Texas Instruments, Dallas; Republic Nat Bank, Dallas; and others. *Exhib:* Am Watercolor Soc, New York, 67; Southwestern Watercolor Soc, 64-88; Watercolor Okla, Oklahoma City, 75-76, 88, 90 & 91; Tex Watercolor Soc, San Antonio, 81 & 86; Western Fed Watercolor Soc, 89 & 90. *Teaching:* Instr adult watercolor painting, 62-; instr, Artisan's Studio-Gallery, Dallas, 62-; instr, Sul Ross State Univ, Tex, 80 & 81; instr, Workshops across US & Bermuda sponsored by art orgns. *Awards:* Merit Awards, Artists & Craftsmen Asn, 82 & 83; Coppini Acad Fine Arts, San Antonio, 83, 86, 88 & 90; First Place Representational Watercolor, Ann Tri-State, Carlsbad, NMex; Southwestern Watercolor Soc, 87 & 88; Nat Watercolor Okla, 90. *Bibliog:* Spotlight on the artist, SWS Scene, Southwestern Watercolor Soc, 3/77; video tapes, Tree Painting in Watercolor, Night Scenes in Watercolor, 85 & Painting Flowers in Watercolor, 88; Am Artist Mag, article about Night Scenes, 3/91. *Mem:* Okla Watercolor Asn (signature mem); Tex Watercolor Soc (signature mem); Southwestern Watercolor Soc (pres, 67-68, signature mem); Artists & Craftsmen Assoc, Dallas (signature mem). *Media:* Watercolor. *Publ:* Coauth, Variations in Watercolor, 81. *Mailing Add:* 4808 Oak Trail Dallas TX 75232

BROUDE, NORMA FREEDMAN
HISTORIAN, EDUCATOR
b New York, NY, May 1, 41. *Study:* Hunter Col, AB, 62; Columbia Univ, MA(Woodrow Wilson Found Fel), 64, PhD(Woodrow Wilson Dissertation Fel), 67. *Teaching:* Instr art hist, Conn Col, New London, 66-67; vis asst prof, Oberlin Col, Ohio, 69-70; asst prof art hist, Columbia Univ, New York, 72-73; vis asst prof, Vassar Col, Poughkeepsie, NY, 73-74; asst prof art hist, Am Univ, Washington, DC, 75-77, assoc prof art hist, 77-86, prof, 86- *Awards:* Nat Endowment Humanities Fel, 81-82; Mina Shaughnessy Scholar, 82; Bellagio Study & Conf Center Fel, Rockefeller Found, 91. *Mem:* Col Art Asn of Am; Women's Caucus Art. *Res:* Late 19th and early 20th century European painting. *Publ:* auth, The Macchiaioli: Italian Painters of the 19th Century, Yale Univ Press, 87; Degas and French Feminism Circa 1880, Art Bull, 88; auth & ed, World Impressionism: International Movement, 1860-1920, Harry N Abrams Inc, 90; auth, Impressionism, A Feminist Reading 91, Georges Seurat, 92 & gen ed, The Rizzoli Art Series, 92, Rizzoli; co-ed (with Mary D Garrard), the Expanding Discourse; Feminism and Art History, HarperCollins, 92. *Mailing Add:* c/o The Dept of Art Am Univ Mass & Nebr Ave NW Washington DC 20016

BROUDO, JOSEPH DAVID
EDUCATOR, CERAMIST
b Baltimore, Md, Sept 11, 20. *Study:* Alfred Univ, BFA, 46; Boston Univ, MEd, 50. *Work:* Int Mus Ceramics, Faenza, Italy; Prieto Collection, Mills Col, Calif; Joan Mannheimer Collection. *Exhib:* Int Exhib, Ostend, Belg, 60; Ten Boston Area Craftsmen, New York World's Fair, 64-65. *Teaching:* Dept head & prof art, Endicott Col, 46- *Awards:* Grand Prize, Int Exhib, Ostend, Belg, 60; Top Honors, Eastern States Expos & De Cordova Craftsmen Exhib; and others. *Mem:* Mass Asn Craftsmen (chmn, 55-56, dir, 72); Am Crafts Coun (exec coun, 71-72); Boston Soc Arts & Crafts (dir, 62-78); Cult Connection (dir, 87-90). *Mailing Add:* c/o Endicott College Dept Art Beverly MA 01915

BROUGH, RICHARD BURRELL
EDUCATOR, DESIGNER
b Salmon, Idaho, May 31, 20. *Study:* Chouinard Art Inst, Los Angeles, dipl; Witte Mem Mus, San Antonio, Tex. *Work:* Montgomery Mus Fine Arts, Ala; Birmingham Art Mus, Ala; Ford Motor Co, Dearborn, Mich; S Cent Bell, Blun, Ala. *Comn:* 12 hist paintings, Gulf States Paper Corp, 60; 14 paintings, Vulcan Mat Corp, Birmingham, Ala. *Exhib:* American Painting Today, Metrop Mus Art, New York, 50; US Variety Show, US Info Agency, traveling exhib to Mid East, 60; Ford Exhib, New York World's Fair, 64. *Teaching:* Prof graphics, Univ Ala, 48-87. *Awards:* Purchase Award, Ala Watercolor Soc, 74; Outstanding Commitment to Teaching Award, Univ Ala Alumni Asn, 85; Distinguished Career Award, Soc Fine Arts, Univ Ala, 92. *Bibliog:* Meet the artist, TV spec, Birmingham, Ala, 69. *Mem:* Birmingham Art Asn; Ala Watercolor Soc; Tex Watercolor Soc. *Media:* Watercolor, Acrylic. *Publ:* Illusr, 99 Fables, 65; Ford Times, 50-74. *Mailing Add:* 17 Elmira Drive Tuscaloosa AL 35405

BROUILLETTE, AL(BERT C)
PAINTER, INSTRUCTOR
b Holyoke, Mass, Jan 9, 24. *Study:* Ft Worth Art Ctr Sch, Tex. *Work:* Hermann Fine Arts Ctr, Marietta, Ohio; New York Transit Authority, Brooklyn; Univ Tex Sch Law, Houston; Hallmark, Kansas City, Mo; NMex Watercolor Soc; and others. *Exhib:* Southwestern Watercolor Soc, Dallas, 69-88; Tex Watercolor Soc, San Antonio, 69-75; Watercolor USA, Springfield, Mo, 74-75 & 77; Nat Acad Design, New York, 74-75 & 92; Am Watercolor Soc, New York, 75-86. *Pos:* Art dir, Dallas-Ft Worth Ad Agencies, 52-76. *Teaching:* Instr acrylics, workshops. *Awards:* Mary Pleissner Mem Award, 90; Clara Stroud Mem Award, Am Watercolor Soc, 91; The William A Payton Prize, Nat Acad Design, 92; and others. *Bibliog:* Nita Leland (auth), Exploring Color, 85; Al Brouillette (auth), The Evolving Picture, 87; M Stephen Doherty (auth), article, Watercolor 92, Am Artist, 92; Marilyn Hughey Phillis (auth), Watercolor techniques for releasing the creative spirit, 7/92; Bebe Raupe (auth), Award winning watercolors, Artist's Mag, 9/92; and others. *Mem:* Assoc Nat Acad Design; Southwestern Watercolor Soc (prof standards, 74-75); Allied Artists Am; Am Watercolor Soc; Nat Watercolor Soc; and others. *Media:* Acrylic, Watermedia Design. *Publ:* Article, Am Artist, 80. *Mailing Add:* 1300 Sunset Ct Arlington TX 76013

BROUN, ELIZABETH GIBSON
ADMINISTRATOR, CURATOR
b Kansas City, Mo, Dec 15, 46. *Study:* Univ Kans, BA, 68, MA, 69, PhD 76. *Collections Arranged:* Prints of Anders Zorn (auth, catalog), 79, Kansas Printmakers (auth, catalog), 81; Engravings of Marcantonio Raimondi (auth, catalog), 81-82; Prints and Drawings by Pat Steir (auth, catalog), 82; Patrick Ireland Drawings (auth, catalog), 85; Spencer Mus Art, Lawrence, Kans; Albert Pinkham Ryder, Nat Mus Am Art, Washington, DC, 90. *Pos:* Cur prints & drawings, Spencer Mus Art, Univ Kans, Lawrence, 77-83, actg dir, 82-83; chief cur, Nat Mus Am Art, Smithsonian Inst, Washington, DC, 83-89, actg dir 88-89, dir, 89- *Teaching:* Asst prof, Univ Kans, 80-83. *Res:* History of American art and graphic arts. *Publ:* Benton's Bentons, 80, Spencer Mus Art, Univ Kans, Lawrence; auth, Contents of Whistler's Art, Arts Mag, 87; auth, The Art of Lithography, Univ Houston, 87; auth, Benton, A Politician in Art, Smithsonian Studies in Am Art, spring 87; auth, Albert Pinkham Ryder, Smithsonian Press, 89. *Mailing Add:* 8620 Hempstead Ave Bethesda MD 20817

BROWN, ALAN M, JR
DEALER, CONSULTANT
b New Rochelle, NY. *Study:* Syracuse Univ, BS, 69. *Pos:* Dir, Alan Brown Gallery, Hartsdale, NY, 72- *Mem:* Coun Arts Westchester (trustee, currently); Westchester Pub Art (bd dirs). *Res:* Contemporary artists. *Collection:* Contemporary American art; folk art. *Mailing Add:* 210 E Hartsdale Ave Hartsdale NY 10530

BROWN, ALICE DALTON
PAINTER
b Danville, Pa, Apr 17, 39. *Study:* Acad Julian, Paris, 57; Cornell Univ, 58-60; Oberlin Col, Ohio, BA, 62. *Work:* Am Telephone, Telegraph Co, NY; Metrop Life Insurance Co & Bank of NY, New York; General Electric Co, Conn & NY; First Nat Bank & Trust Co, Chicago; American Express, New York. *Comn:* Painting, General Electric Co, 90. *Exhib:* Collectors Choice, McNay Art Inst, San Antonio, Tex, 81, 89 & 90; one-woman shows, A M Sachs Gallery, New York, 82, 83 & 84, Katharina Rich Perlow Gallery, New York, 85; Columbus Mus, Ohio, 85; Fishbach Gallery, New York, 87, 89 & 91; William Sawyer Gallery, San Francisco, 88. *Awards:* Purchase Award, The West Collection: Art & the Law, 85. *Bibliog:* James F Cooper (auth), article, New York Tribune, 6/13/83; Gerrit Henry (auth), article, Art News, 11/83; Susan Gill (auth), article, Arts Mag, 11/85; Calif Mag Review, 6/88. *Media:* Oil. *Dealer:* Fischbach Gallery 24 W 57th St New York NY 10019. *Mailing Add:* 305 E 24th St Apt 8G New York NY 10010

BROWN, BETTY ANN
EDUCATOR, CRITIC
b Oklahoma City, Okla, June 6, 49. *Study:* Southern Methodist Univ, BFA, 71; Univ Tex, Austin, MA, 73; Univ NMex, Albuquerque, PhD, 77. *Collections Arranged:* Faces of Fiesta, San Diego State Univ, 82; Susan Kleinberg, Univ Southern Calif, Davidson Conf Ctr, 82; Sensuous Surfaces, Univ Southern Calif, 82; Generations, Conejo Valley Art Mus, 83; Caretas Mexicanas, Mexican mask exhib, Southwest Mus, 83; Space (Artists Spaces), Occidental Col, 86; Roland Reiss Retrospective, 91. *Pos:* Dir visual arts prog, Col Continuing Educ, Univ Southern Calif, Los Angeles, 81-; art critic for weekly newspaper, Reader, 81-83; auth, monthly series of previews on Los Angeles art exhibs, Artscene, 82-; auth, monthly column, Arts Mag, 82-; ed, Visions Mag, 86-87. *Teaching:* Asst prof art hist, Ill State Univ, 77-79; asst prof, Calif State Univ, Northridge, 79-81 & 86-; adj prof, Univ Southern Calif, 81-85; assoc prof art, Calif State Northridge, 88- *Mem:* Art Table; Women's Caucus Art; Asn Latin Am Art (secy, 81-83); Inst Hispanic Media & Cult (bd

dirs, 82-83). *Res:* Contemporary Art, Ancient and contemporary arts of Latin America. *Publ:* Auth, numerous articles on Pre-Columbian art history and contemporary folk arts of Latin America; Exposures: Women and Their Art, 89; auth, numerous articles on contemp criticism. *Mailing Add:* Art Gen Studies Cal St Univ Northridge 18111 Nordhoff St Northridge CA 91330

BROWN, BRUCE ROBERT
PAINTER, SCULPTOR
b Philadelphia, Pa, July 25, 38. *Study:* Tyler Sch Art, Temple Univ, BFA(painting), 62, MFA(sculpture), 64. *Work:* Telfair Acad Arts & Sci, Savannah, Ga; Festival Arts Collection, Erie, Pa. *Exhib:* Carnegie Inst, 55-57; Nat Show, Pa Acad Fine Arts, Philadelphia, 62; Nat Show, Butler Inst Am Art, Youngstown, Ohio, 62-63; Am Acad Arts & Lett, New York, 68; 21st Ann Int Exhib, Beaumont, Tex, 72; and many others. *Teaching:* Instr, adult painting prog, Dept Recreation, Philadelphia, 61-64; instr ceramics & art, Philadelphia Pub Sch, 65-66; instr art, West Liberty State Col, 67-68; assoc prof art, Monroe Community Col, State Univ NY, 69- *Awards:* Award Painting, Appalachian Corridors: Exhibition I, Charleston, WVa, 68; Purchase Award, Arts & Humanities Coun WVa, 67; Purchase Award, Am Acad Arts & Lett, 68. *Mem:* Col Art Asn Am; Southern Sculptors Asn; Rochester Print Club; Artist's Equity Asn, New York. *Media:* Oil. *Publ:* Auth, Robert Henkes, Sport in Art (guide for beginning illus). *Mailing Add:* 17 Sedgewick Dr Honeoye NY 14771

BROWN, C W See Crow, Carol (Wilson)

BROWN, CAROL K
SCULPTOR, DRAFTSMAN
b Memphis, Tenn. *Study:* Univ Miami, BFA, 78; Univ Colo, MFA, 81. *Work:* Univ Colo, Boulder; Jacksonville Art Mus, Fla; Art Mus, Fla Int Univ, Miami; Percent Art Prog, Orlando, Fla; Tampa Mus Art, Fla; and others. *Comn:* Sculpture, Fla Int Univ, Miami, Dade Co Art Pub Places, Miami, Fla, 87, Univ of Fla, Gainesville, 88; Southeast Banking Corp, 89; Eastern Nat Bank, 90. *Exhib:* Solo exhibs, Contemp Arts Ctr, New Orleans, 79 & Bass Mus Art, Miami Beach, 86, Bacardi Sculpture Plaze & Gallery, Miami, Fla, 88, Ctr Fine Arts, Sculpture Plaza, 87; A Woman's Place, John Michael Kohler Arts Ctr, Sheboygan, Wis, 81; Great Plains Sculpture Exhib, Sheldon Mem Art Gallery, Lincoln, Nebr, 81; Denver Art Mus Invitational, 81; Art of Miami, Southeastern Ctr Contemp Art, Winston-Salem, NC, 85; Nat Endowment Arts-Fel Artists, Fla State Univ, Tallahassee, 85 & 86; The Hortt Exhib, Mus Art, Ft Lauderdale, Fla, 85, 86 & 87; and others. *Teaching:* Instr, Miami-Dade Community Col, 86, New World Sch Arts, 91- *Awards:* State Fla Fine Arts Fel, 83 & 92; Nat Endowment Arts Fels, 84 & 86; Southeastern Ctr Contemp Art Fel, 84. *Bibliog:* Helen Kohen (auth), Sculptor's work shows her mettle, Miami Herald, 1/12/86; Leslie Judd Ahlander (auth), A Potpourri of Excellence is Showing at Local Galleries, Miami News, 4/1/88; Elisa Turner (rev), Art News, 4/92. *Media:* Welded & Cast Metal; Drawing. *Dealer:* Gloria Luria Gallery 1033 Kane Concourse Bay Harbor Islands FL 33154; Nohra Haime Gallery 41 E 57th St New York NY. *Mailing Add:* 101 W Dilido Dr Miami Beach FL 33139

BROWN, CEE SCOTT
ADMINISTRATOR, CURATOR
b Yakima, Wash, Nov 4, 52. *Study:* Univ de Haute Bretagne, 71-72; Univ Wash, MFA, 76. *Pos:* Gallery dir, Holly Solomon Gallery, 80-85; proj assoc, VIART Corp, 85-86; exec dir, Creative Time, 87-; founding bd mem, Art Matters Inc. *Awards:* Curators award, Henry McCall Found, 90. *Mailing Add:* 90 W Broadway No 2A New York NY 10002

BROWN, CHARLOTTE
COLLAGE ARTIST, PAINTER
b Brooklyn, NY. *Study:* Pratt Inst Art, Brooklyn, NY, BFA, 56. *Work:* Fine Arts Mus Long Island, Hempstead, NY; Pratt Inst Art, Brooklyn, NY; Va Commonwealth Univ, Richmond; Long Island Univ, C W Post, Greenvale, NY; Pepsico, IBM, Citicorp, Xerox & HBO, New York & Conn. *Exhib:* Contemporary Reflections, Aldrich Mus Contemp Art, Ridgefield, Conn, 74; Works on Paper, Women Artists, Brooklyn Mus, NY, 75; Flower Garden, Mus Fine Arts Nassau Co, Roslyn, NY, 76 & 83; Alternate Imaging Systems, Everson Mus, Syracuse, NY, 79; Electroworks, Int Mus Contemp Art, Rochester, NY, 79 & Cooper Hewitt Mus, New York, 80; Prime Examples, Hechscher Mus, Huntington, NY, 83; New Imaging by Computer, Fine Arts Mus Long Island, Hempstead, NY, 86. *Pos:* Art dir, Woodbury Country Club Asn, NY, 65-70; vice pres & historian, Prof Artist Guild, Long Island, NY, 70-73; vis artist-in-residence, Nassau Co Mus Fine Arts, Roslyn, NY, 72-87. *Teaching:* Artist-in-residence printmaking, Syracuse Univ, NY, 79; vis artist printmaking, Va Commonwealth Univ, Richmond, 83. *Awards:* Graphic Fel, Creative Pub Serv Prog, New York, 76 & 82; Printmaking Fel, Nat Endowment Arts, Washington, DC, 77; Innovation Clay Grant, Collaborations Art, Sci & Technol, Syracuse, NY, 78. *Bibliog:* David Shirey (auth), Xerographic Originality, NY Times, 11/23/76; Tom Hoving (dir), Copy Art, Charlotte Brown Studio (film), ABC Television Network News, 80; Barbara Flug Cohn (auth), Gallery reviews, NY Arts J #24, 82. *Mem:* Nat Asn Women Artists. *Publ:* Contribr, Copy Art, Richard Marek, 78; New editions (phot, text), Art News, 84; Art in the World, Holt, Rinehart, Winston, 84 & 89; The Collage Handbook, Thames & Hudson, 85; Crafts, Contemp Design & Technique, Davis Publ, 86. *Dealer:* John Szoke 591 Broadway New York NY 10012; Joy Horwich 226 E Ontario Chicago IL 60611. *Mailing Add:* 11 Hunting Hill Rd Woodbury NY 11797

BROWN, CHARLOTTE VESTAL
MUSEUM DIRECTOR, HISTORIAN
b Siler City, NC, June 3, 42. *Study:* Univ NC, Greensboro, BA(with honors), 64; Univ NC, Chapel Hill, PhD, 75. *Collections Arranged:* West African Textiles, 85; North Carolina Vernacular Pottery: 1982-1986, 87; New Art/New Material, 89. *Pos:* City of Raleigh, Hist Preservation, 81-82. *Teaching:* Asst prof, Duke Univ, 71-79; asst prof mod archit, NC State Univ, 89-90. *Mem:* Am Asn Univ Profs; Soc Archit Hists; Royal Oak Found; Am Asn Mus; NC Preservation/Hist Preservation Found. *Res:* Architectural history and theory, 19th and 20th century; American and English. *Publ:* Coauth, The Humanities, D C Heath, 89; Architects and Builders in NC, Univ NC Press, 90. *Mailing Add:* NC State Univ Mus Art & Design Box 7306 Univ Student Ctr Raleigh NC 27695-7306

BROWN, CHRISTOPHER
PAINTER
b Camp Lejeune, NC, 1951. *Study:* Univ Ill, Champaign-Urbana, BA, 72; Univ Calif, Davis, MFA, 76. *Work:* San Francisco Mus Mod Art, Univ Art Mus, Fine Arts Mus San Francisco & Security Pac Nat Bank, Calif; Chase Manhattan Bank, Metrop Mus, New York Pub Libr, Grey Art Gallery & New York Univ, New York; Gen Mills, Walker Art Ctr, Minneapolis, Minn; Sheldon Mem Art Gallery, Lincoln, Nebr; Coca-Cola Corp, Atlanta, Ga. *Exhib:* One-person exhib, The Painted Room, Madison Art Ctr, Wis, 85-86, travel to: Matrix Gallery, Univ Art Mus, Berkeley, Calif, Des Moines Art Ctr, Iowa, 85-86, Univ Tex, Arlington, 88, Ctr Res Contemp Art, 88 & Gallery Paule Anglim, San Francisco, Calif, 90; Chicago Int Art Exposition, Ill, 86 & 88; traveled to San Francisco Art Inst, Calif, 86; Newport Harbor Art Mus, Calif, 86 & 87; Contemp Arts Ctr, Cincinnati, Ohio, 87; Am Acad & Inst Arts & Letters, New York, 88; Contemporary Landscape, Cumberland Gallery, Nashville, Tenn, 89; Blum Helman, Los Angeles, Calif, 89; 10 Plus 10: Contemporary Soviet & American Painters, traveling, 89-90; In the Realm of the Plausible, Shea & Baker Gallery, NY, 90; Edward Thorp Gallery, NY, 92. *Teaching:* Prof Art, Univ Calif Berkeley, 81-92. *Awards:* Fel, Nat Endowment Arts, 87; Award, Am Acad & Inst Art & Letters, 88. *Bibliog:* Kenneth Baker (auth), Christopher Brown, San Francisco Chronicle, 10/23/87; Bill Berkson (auth), Christopher Brown, Artforum, 1/88; Jan Alfred (auth), Christopher Brown, Flash Art, 2/88; Frances De Vuono (auth), Christopher Brown, ARTnews, 3/92. *Mailing Add:* 770 Camelia St Berkeley CA 94710

BROWN, CONSTANCE GEORGE
GALLERY DIRECTOR, ART DEALER
Study: Perry Normal Sch, Boston, Dipl, 54, Northeastern Univ, 73-76. *Collections Arranged:* F Ladd, 76, F Brown, 77, Ingersoll & Bloch, 77, Dr A Noonan, 79 & G White & A Brown, 85, Seventeen Wendell Street. *Pos:* Chair & mem adv bd, Nat Ctr Afro-Am Art Mus, 80-; mem, Local Site Comt, Mass Art & Humanities, 85 & Art Planning Coun, Lena Park Develop Corp, Boston, Mass, 86. *Mem:* Archives of Am Art. *Res:* Contemporary Black-American artists. *Mailing Add:* Wendell Street Gallery 17 Wendell St Cambridge MA 02138

BROWN, DANIEL
CRITIC, COLLECTOR
b Cincinnati, Ohio, Nov 4, 46. *Study:* Middlebury Col, AB, 68; Univ Mich, MA, 70. *Collections Arranged:* Constance McClure: A Retrospective & Rita Zimmerman: New Monoprints (guest cur), 86; New Art from Academe: An Overview, The Cent Exchange (guest cur), Kansas City, Mo, 88; Cincinnati Past & Present: The Golden Ages in the Visual Arts, Tangeman Fine Arts Gallery (guest co-cur), Univ Cincinnati, 88; Contemporary Landscape, KenCabCo (guest cur), 88; Figure It Out, Katz & Dawgs Gallery Inaugural Exhib (guest cur), Columbus, Ohio, 88; Lyrical Abstractions (guest cur), 89 & the Artist at Mid- Career: A Dialogue Between Cincinnati & Columbus (guest cur), 89-90,Katz & Dawgs Gallery, Columbus, Ohio; Arts Consortium, Cincinnati, Ohio; Interpretations of the Everyday Object, 91; Frescoes of Working People, 91; Landscape East and West, 91-92; Union Terminal, Cincinnati Multiculturalism: the Evolution and the Celebration Group Show, African-Am Mus, 91-92; Black Not White, in black and white, 92. *Pos:* Art critic, Cincinnati Mag, 79-82, Dialogue Art J, Columbus, Ohio, 83-, WCPO-TV, Cincinnati, 86- & Provincetown Arts, 88-; artist's model, Constance McClure, 84-, David Bumbeck, 84-85, Dan Boldman, 85-, Jerome Mussman, 85-, David DeVaul, 86 & Cole Carothers, 87-; art commentator, WKRC-TV, Cincinnati, 85; pres, Daniel Brown Inc, Independent Art Consultants; cur, The KZF Gallery, Cincinnati, 87-; regular guest columnist art issues, Cinncinnati Post, 91-; art critic, Cincinnati Herald, 92- *Teaching:* Guest lectr, Contemp Arts Ctr, Cincinnati, 84-86, Cincinnati Art Mus, 86 & Univ Cincinnati, 86; part-time lect printmaking, drawing & painting, Art Acad Cincinnati, currently. *Awards:* Winner, the Critics Purse, Dialogue Mag, 85. *Mem:* Contemp Arts Ctr, Cincinnati (trustee, 84-88); Enjoy the Arts, Cincinnati (trustee, 85-88, vpres, 86-88). *Res:* Psychoanalytic and political implications of contemporary art. *Collection:* Contemporary prints, drawings and paintings of both national and regional artists. *Publ:* Auth, David Bumbeck Prints: A Retrospective; auth, Tom Bacher, High Tech American Impressionist (catalog), Cincinnati Art Galleries, 89; The Universe Watching: The Art of Nancy Fletcher Cassell, (catalog), J B Speed Mus, Louisville, Ky, 90; Brad Austin Smith Introdution Essay to Artists Book, 92; Bukang Kim: Journey to the East (catalog), Gallery Yehyand, Seoul, Korea, 92. *Dealer:* Carl Solway Gallery 314 W fourth St Cincinnati OH 45202. *Mailing Add:* 3900 Rose Hill Ave Apt 401B Cincinnati OH 45229

BROWN, DAVID ALAN
HISTORIAN, CURATOR
b Bellevue, Ohio, July 25, 42. *Study:* Harvard Col, BA(magna cum laude), 64; Cambridge Univ, Fulbright fel, 64-65; Yale Univ, MA, 67, PhD, 73. *Collections Arranged:* Berenson and the Connoisseurship of Italian Painting, 79, From Leonardo to Titian: Italian Renaissance Paintings from the Hermitage, 79, Raphael and America, 83 & Leonardo's Last Supper: Before and After, 84, Nat Gallery Art, Washington, DC. *Pos:* Cur Italian Renaissance painting, Nat Gallery Art, Washington, DC, currently. *Teaching:* Lectr art hist, Yale Univ, New Haven, Conn, 73-74 & Smithsonian Assoc Prog, Washington, DC, 75- *Awards:* Finley Fel, Nat Gallery Art, 68-71; Fel Villa I Tatti, Harvard Ctr for Renaissance Studies, Florence, 69-70. *Mem:* Renaissance Soc Am; Col Art Asn. *Res:* Italian Renaissance painting; Leonardo Da Vinci; Correggio. *Publ:* Auth, articles on Leonardo Da Vinci and on Correggio, Mitteilungen des Kunst Historischen Inst, Florence, 71, Mus Studies, 72, Master Drawings, 74 & 75. *Mailing Add:* Kansas State Univ Manhattan KS 66506

BROWN, DAVID LEE
SCULPTOR
Study: Cass Tech, 57; NC Sch Design, 60; Cranbrook Acad Art, 62. *Work:* John Hopkins Univ, Baltimore, Md; De Cordova Mus, Lincoln, Mass; Hirshhorn Mus & Sculpture Garden, Washington, DC; Milwaukee Art Ctr, Wis; Chase Manhattan Bank, New York. *Comn:* Sculptures, Reynolds Aluminium Corp, Richmond, Va, 76, Xerox Corp (monumental), Stamford, Conn, 78, Warner Lambert Co, Morris Plains, NJ, 81, Lincorp Corp, Dallas, Tex, 85 & Fla Nat Bank, Jacksonville, 86. *Teaching:* Instr sculpture, Cranbrook Acad Art, 60-61; prof design, Pratt Inst, NY, 72- *Media:* Stainless Steel, All Media. *Dealer:* Grace Borgenicht Gallery 724 Fifth Ave New York NY 10019. *Mailing Add:* 621 Fireplace Rd East Hampton NY 11937

BROWN, DIANE
DEALER
b Cleveland, Ohio, Nov 23, 47. *Study:* Univ Wis, Madison, BA, 69; Univ Md, Col Park. *Pos:* Owner & dir, Diane Brown Gallery, 76- *Specialty:* Contemporary art with emphasis on sculpture. *Mailing Add:* 23 Watts St New York NY 10013

BROWN, EDITH RAE
SCULPTOR, MEDALIST
b Flushing, NY, Nov 9, 42. *Study:* Art Students League. *Work:* Smithsonian Inst, Washington, DC; Am Numismatic World Mus, Colorado Springs, Colo; Newark Mus, Newark, NJ. *Comn:* comn by pvt collectors. *Exhib:* Office Cult Affairs, New York; Nassau Co Mus Fine Arts; Salmagundi Art Club; St John's Univ; Am Artists Prof League; Nat Arts Club; Newark Mus, NJ; Fedn Int de la Medaille, Helsinki, Finland; Chesterwood, 89; Federal Plaza Foley Sq, 91; and others. *Pos:* Chmn sculpture exhibs; juror sculpture exhibs; lectr, demonstrate carving stone sculpture. *Teaching:* Stone carving. *Awards:* Award Excellence, Suburban Art League, 85, 91; Joel Meisner Casting Award, Hecksher Mus, 91; Award Excellence, St Johns Univ, 91. *Mem:* Salmagundi Art Club; Nat Arts Club; Hudson Valley Art Asn; Nat Asn Women Artists. *Media:* Stone, Bronze. *Publ:* Auth, Artist expresses her need to create, Intermountain Jewish News, 6/11/85; Contemporary Sculpture, Chesterwood, 89. *Mailing Add:* 38 Shadetree Lane Roslyn Heights NY 11577

BROWN, FREDERICK JAMES
PAINTER
b Greensboro, Ga, Feb 6, 45. *Study:* Southern Ill Univ, BA, 68. *Work:* Metrop Mus Art, New York; Nat Mus Am Art & The White House (Fed Arts Coun), Washington, DC; Brooklyn Mus, NY; Afro-Am Mus, Los Angeles, Calif. *Comn:* paintings (3), Gov of Liberia, Monrovia, 75. *Exhib:* Recent Acquisitions, 79 & 83 & the 1980's: A New Generation, 88, Metrop Mus Art, New York; Rufino Tamayo Mus, Mexico City, Mex, 84; Foundation Verraneman, Brussels, Belg, 86; Jan Turner Gallery, Los Angeles, Calif, 86; Nat Mus of Chinese Revolution, Tian An Men Square, Beijing, China, 88. *Bibliog:* Documentary of China Exhibition (TV review), CBS Sunday Morning Show, 7/88; Dorinda Elliot (auth), Paintings from the heart, Newsweek, 6/28/88; Christopher Lyon (auth), Frederick Brown: Marlborough, Artnews, 11/89. *Media:* Oil. *Mailing Add:* 120 Wooster St New York NY 10012

BROWN, GARY HUGH
PAINTER, EDUCATOR
b Evansville, Ind, Dec 19, 41. *Study:* DePauw Univ, Greencastle, Ind, BA, 63; Acad Belli de Arti, Rome & Florence, Italy, 63-64; Univ Wis-Madison, MFA, 66. *Work:* Elvehjem Art Ctr, Madison, Wis; Yale Univ, New Haven, Conn; Glenbow Art Mus, Alta, Can; Utah Mus Fine Arts, Salt Lake City; Tyler Mus Art, Tex; and others. *Comn:* Ltd ed paper suite, Source Gallery, San Francisco, publ by Twinrocker, Ind, 76; mural, Osaka Univ, 85. *Exhib:* One-man shows, Fleischer-Anhalt Gallery, Los Angeles, Calif, 68, de Saisset Art Gallery, Univ Santa Clara & Santa Barbara Mus Art, 71-72, Comsky Gallery, Beverly Hills, Calif, 75, United Arts Club, Dublin, Ireland, 75, Source Gallery, San Francisco, 76 & 78, Art/Life Gallery, Santa Barbara, 82 & Ventura Col, 91; Art-Space, Osaka-Tokyo, Japan, 85; Tokyo Munic Mus Art, 86. *Pos:* Artist-in-residence, Int Inst for Experimental Papermaking, Calif, 74, New Harmony, Ind, 76, Ateliershaus Worpswede, WGer, 82 & Artist Union, Nishinomiaya, Japan, 85. *Teaching:* Prof painting & drawing, Univ Calif, Santa Barbara, 66- *Awards:* Greenshields Found Grant for Europ Travel/Study, 63. *Mem:* Col Art Asn. *Media:* Drawing, Oil. *Publ:* Illusr, Peter Whigham's The Blue Winged Bee, Anvil, 69; John Logan (auth), Poem in Progress, Dryad, 75; The Santa Cruz Mountain Poems, Morton Marcus (auth), Capra, 75, 2nd ed, 92; The Music of the Troubadors, Ross-Erikson, 79; Electroworks, George Eastman House & Chanticleer Press, 80. *Mailing Add:* Art Studio Dept Univ Calif Santa Barbara CA 93106

BROWN, GILLIAN
PHOTOGRAPHER
Study: Brown Univ, Providence, RI, BA, 73; RI Sch Design, Providence, MAE, 77; Univ Calif, Los Angeles, MFA(photog), 80. *Work:* Addison Gallery Am Art, Andover, Mass; Art Mus, Princeton Univ; Bibliotheque Nat, Paris; Calif Mus Photog, Univ Calif, Riverside; Calif Inst Arts, Valencia. *Exhib:* Solo exhibs, Andover Gallery, Mass, 86, Gatehouse Gallery, Mt Vernon Col & Constructions, Kathleen Ewing Gallery, Washington, DC, 87, Howard Yezerski Gallery, Andover, Mass, 88, Notre Dame Col, Baltimore, Md, 90 & Jones, Troyer, Fitzpatrick Gallery, Washington, DC, 92; Options '90, Wash Proj Arts, 90; Photographic Installations, Photofest, Houston Ctr Photog, 90; Other Rooms, a Kunstraum proj, Morgan Annex, Washington, DC, 90; Bedrooms, Snug Harbor Cult Ctr, New York, 91; Concept/Construct: Photography in Los Angeles Art, 1960-1980 (traveling), Laguna Mus Art, Friends Photog, San Francisco, Des Moines Art Ctr, 92-94. *Awards:* Grant, Art Matters Inc, New York, 88; Nat Endowment Art Fel, 90; Md State Arts Coun Grant, 92. *Bibliog:* Michael Welzenbach (auth), Non-Stock options, Washington Post, 1/17/90; John Dorsey (auth), Local retrospective explores photography's illusionistic nature, Baltimore Sun, 10/10/90; Elaine Louie (auth), Artists give bedrooms a nautical motif, NY Times, 1/31/91. *Mailing Add:* 811 Haywood Ave Takoma Park MD 20912

BROWN, HILTON
PAINTER, EDUCATOR
b Momence, Ill, Sept 22, 38. *Study:* Goodman Theatre & Sch Drama, Art Inst Chicago, 56-58; Univ Chicago, 59; Skowhegan Sch Painting & Sculpture, Maine, summers 60 & 61; Art Inst Chicago, dipl fine arts(George T & Isabelle Brown foreign travel fel), 62, BFA, 63, MFA, 64; Univ Ill, Chicago, 62-63. *Work:* Baltimore Mus Art; Ball State Univ Art Collection; Macomb Co Community Col, Detroit; Goucher Col; Univ Md, College Park. *Comn:* Exterior wall paintings, City of Baltimore, 73-75; mural, T Johnson Sch, Baltimore, 79-80. *Exhib:* Chicago & Vicinity Show, Art Inst Chicago, 60; Nat Print Exhib, Brooklyn Mus, 64; Twelve Chicago Painters, Walker Art Ctr, Minneapolis, 65; 20th Mo Show, City Art Mus, St Louis, 66; Md Regional Exhib, Baltimore Mus Art, 75; Kornblatt Gallery, Baltimore, Md, 79; Leslie Lohman Gallery, New York, 80; Baltimore Mus Art, 86. *Pos:* Mem contemp art accession comt, Baltimore Mus Art, 68-78; contrib ed, Am Artist Mag, 81-86. *Teaching:* Instr color, drawing & design, Art Inst Chicago, 62-65; asst prof drawing & compos, Sch Fine Arts, Washington Univ, 65-68; chmn art dept & prof drawing, painting & printmaking, Goucher Col, 68-78; vis prof artists mat & tech, Winerthur Prog Conserv Art, Univ Del, 74-78, assoc dir, 78-80, prof art, art history and conservation, 78-, coordr, Ralph Mayer Ctr Artists Techniques, 84-88, Ralph & Bena Mayer prof, 84-88. *Awards:* Renfrow Art Award, City Art Mus, St Louis, 65; Berney Award Painting, Baltimore Mus Art, 70. *Bibliog:* Franz Schultz (auth), Chicago Art Inst, 3/67; John Brod Peters (auth), Art views: Hilton Brown: New directions, St Louis Globe Democrat, 8/12/67; Lincoln F Johnson (auth), Retrospective shows Brown growth, The Sun, Baltimore, 2/24/77; Hilton Brown, the artist comes out, The Gay Paper, Baltimore, 9/80. *Mem:* Col Art Asn Am; Am Inst Conserv; Artists Equity Asn; Am Soc Testing & Materials; Inter-Soc Color Coun. *Media:* Oil, Acrylic. *Publ:* auth, Looking at paintings: Joseph Stella and John Storrs silverpoint drawings, 5/81, Looking at paintings: Paul Cadmus' playground, 1/82, History of watercolor, 3/83 & History of landscapes painting, 2/84, Am Artist Mag. *Mailing Add:* Art Conservation Program 303 Old Col Univ of Del Newark DE 19716

BROWN, JAMES
PAINTER, GRAPHIC ARTIST
b Brooklyn, NY. *Study:* Long Island Univ, BA, 54; Brooklyn Col, MS, 55; NY Univ & Yeshiva Univ. *Work:* Corpus Christi Mus, Tex; New York City Tech Col; York Col City Univ NY; Tuscan Dairies, NJ; Municipal Bldg, Union, NJ; Medgar Evers Col, Brooklyn, NY. *Comn:* Portraits, New York City Pub Schs, 79; illus, Nat Asn Advan Colored People, New York, 80; illus, Revlon, USV Lab, 80; Black Winners (illus), comn by Melvin Douglas, 84; York Col, New York, 85; and others. *Exhib:* Minn Mus Art, Saint Paul, 79; Albrecht Art Mus, Saint Joseph, Mo, 80; Mus Philadelphia Civic Ctr, Pa, 80; Univ Mo, 80; Tulane Univ, La, 80; Rutgers Univ, NJ, 82; Queens Mus, NY, 84; Schenectady Mus, NY, 85; poster Shop Galerie, Martinique (WI), 86; Le Centre d'Arte, Haiti (WI), 88; Festival Arts, Port-au-Prince, Haiti, 89. *Pos:* Supervisor art, New York Bd Educ, 74-83. *Teaching:* Critic, New Jersey State Col, 75; instr drawing, painting & printmaking, Intermediate Sch, New York, 76-78; guest artist, Corpus Christi Mus, 78; lectr bus of art, Col New Rochelle, NY, 79; panelist, Artists as Agents of Social Change: Five Views, Heckscher Mus, Huntington, NY, 86. *Awards:* Purchase Award & First Prize, C of C, Union, NJ, 79; Award, Greater Patterson Arts Coun NJ, 80; Best in Show, Festival on the Green, NJ, 81; and others. *Bibliog:* A Aumis (auth), James Brown, France Antilles, Ft de France, Martinique, 11/30/86; Georges Paul Hector (auth), Atelier de Reflexion, Le Nouvelliste, Port-au-Prince, Haiti, 2/3/88; Michael Brenson (auth), Works for urban college raise hard questions, NY Times, 4/8/88; Georges Paul Hector (auth), Atelier de Reflexion: Conjonction ou itineraire a deux, Valcin II et James Brown, Le Nouvelliste, Port-au-Prince, Haiti, 11/11/89; and others. *Mem:* Coalition Black Artists (dir, 78-); Long Island Black Artists Asn (pres, 83-85); Jamaica Art Ctr Coop Gallery, Queens, NY; and others. *Media:* Oil, Pastel; Carbon Pencil. *Publ:* Contribr, Interracial Books for Children, Coun on Interracial Bks for Children, New York, 79; illusr, Ten Little Niggers, St Albans Printing, New York, 81; Black Winners, Nat Asn Advan Colored People, 84. *Dealer:* Dorsey's Art Gallery 553 Rogers Ave Brooklyn NY 11225; Festival Arts Distributors Port-au-Prince Haiti. *Mailing Add:* 117-54 219th St Cambria Heights NY 11411

BROWN, JAMES MONROE, III
MUSEUM DIRECTOR
b Brooklyn, NY, Oct 7, 17. *Study:* Amherst Col, BA, 39; Harvard Univ, MA, 46, Advan Mgt Prog, 58; Amherst Col, Hon MA, 54. *Pos:* Asst to dir, Inst Contemp Art, Boston, 41, asst dir, 46-48; asst to dir, Dumbarton Oaks Res Libr & Collection, Washington, DC, 46; dir, William A Farnsworth Art Mus, Rockland, Maine, 48-51; dir, Corning Glass Ctr, 51-63, dir pub affairs, 56-59, dir mgt develop, 59-61; pres, Corning Found, 61-63; pres, Corning Mus Glass, 61-63; dir, Oakland Mus, Calif, 64-67; dir, Norton Simon Inc Mus Art, 68-69; dir, Va Mus Fine Arts, Richmond, 69-76; emer dir, Soc Four Arts, Palm Beach; Retired. *Mem:* Am Asn Mus (pres, 70-72); Asn Art Mus Dirs; Int Exhibs Found. *Mailing Add:* RT 2 Box 2504 Brunswick ME 04011

BROWN, JOHN CARTER
MUSEUM DIRECTOR
b Providence, RI, Oct 8, 34. *Study:* Harvard Univ, AB, 56, MBA, 58; Munich Univ, 58, with Bernard Berenson, Florence, Italy, 58-59; Neth Inst Art Hist, 60; New York Univ Inst Fine Arts, MA, 62, Brown Univ, LLD, 70; Mt St Mary's Col, LHDm 74; Georgetown Univ, LHD, 75. *Pos:* Asst to dir, Nat Gallery Art, 61-63, asst dir, 64-68, dep dir, 68-69, dir, 69- *Awards:* Austrian Cross of Honor for Arts & Letts, 86; Gold Medal, Nat Inst Soc Sciences, 87; Comdr, Royal Order Polar Star, Sweden, 88. *Mem:* Asn Art Mus Dirs; Col Art Asn Am; Am Asn Mus; Soc Archit Historians; hon Am Inst Architects; Nat Geographic Soc (trustee); Fed Coun Arts & Humanities. *Res:* Seventeenth century Dutch art. *Publ:* Auth & dir, American Vision (film), 65. *Mailing Add:* c/o Nat Gallery Art 4th St & Constitution Washington DC 20565

BROWN, JOHN HALL
PAINTER, ARCHITECT
b Houston, Tex, June 6, 10. *Study:* Tex A&M Col, BA, 33, 35-36. *Work:* City Richardson Pub Libr, Tex; Art Soc Permanent Collection, Sherman, Tex. *Exhib:* Tex Fine Arts Soc Regional; Artists & Craftsmen Regional; Richardson Civic Art Soc Regional; Jefferson Arts Festival National, New Orleans, La; Tex Watercolor Soc Regional. *Awards:* Best Show, Richardson Civic Art Soc, 71; Second Prize, Nat Okla Watercolor, 77; 37 regional & local awards. *Mem:* Southwest Watercolor Soc (vpres, 70); Richardson Civic Art Soc (vpres, 72); Artists & Craftsmen; Tex Fine Arts Soc. *Media:* Watercolor. *Dealer:* Curl Gallery 4843 Massachusetts Ave NW Washington DC 20016. *Mailing Add:* 1221 W Campbell Suite 233 Richardson TX 75080

BROWN, JONATHAN
HISTORIAN
b Springfield, Mass, July 15, 39. *Study:* Dartmouth Col, AB, 60; Princeton Univ, PhD, 64, Guggenheim Mem Fel, 81-82. *Pos:* Dir, Inst Fine Arts, NY Univ, 73-78; vis mem, Inst Advan Study, 78-79. *Teaching:* Asst prof art hist, Princeton Univ, 65-71, assoc prof, 71-73; from assoc prof to prof, Inst Fine Arts, New York Univ, 73-84, Carroll & Milton Petrie prof, 84-; Slade prof fine art, Oxford Univ, 81-82. *Awards:* Arthur Kingsley Porter Prize, Col Art Asn Am, 71; Nat Endowment Humanities Fel, 78-79; Order of Isabel la Católica Award, 86. *Mem:* Spanish Inst (bd dir, 87-); Master Drawings, New York; Am Philos Soc; Real Accad de Bellas Artes de San Fernando (corresp mem). *Res:* Spanish art 16th-19th centuries. *Publ:* Coauth (with J H Elliott), A Palace for a King: The Buen Retiro and the Court of Philip IV, 80; El Greco and Toledo, In: El Greco of Toledo, 82; Velázquez, Painter and Courtier, 86; coauth (with R G Mann), Spanish Paintings of the Fifteenth through Nineteenth Centuries, Nat Gallery Art, 90; The Golden Age of Painting in Spain, 91; and others. *Mailing Add:* 1 E 78th St New York NY 10021

BROWN, JUNE GOTTLIEB
PAINTER
b Dunn, NC, June 21, 32. *Study:* With Leon Stacks, 64-70, Frederick Taubes, 73 & 75 & Robert F Calrow, 77 & 81. *Work:* DuPont & Co, Leland, NC; Dalton Collection, Charlotte, NC; Springs Mills, New York; United Carolina Bank, Southport, NC; Brunswick Co, Bolivia, NC; Fed Reserve Bank, Richmond, Va; J Arthur Dosher Memorial Hospital, Southport, NC; Fairley Jess & Isenberg, Southport, NC. *Exhib:* North Carolina Realism, Mint Mus, 74; Ann Open Exhib, Catharine Lorillard Wolfe Show, New York, 80, 82, 83, 86, 87, 88 & 89; Hoyt Nat Painting Show, Hoyt Inst Fine Arts, New Castle, Pa, 82; Allied Artists Am Ann Exhib, New York, 82 & 86; Nat Mid-Year Exhib, Butler Inst Am Art, 82 & 83; Salmagundi CLub Open Competition, New York, 83; Henley Southeastern Spectrum, Galleries 214, Winston-Salem, NC, 83; Marinters Museum, Mystic, CT, 89:. *Teaching:* Instr art, Brunswick Community Col, 78- *Awards:* Mae Berlind Bach Award, Catharine Lorillard Wolfe Show, 82; Emily Morse Mem Award, Salmagundi Club, 83; Traveling Show Award, Henley's Southeastern Spectrum, 83; Dorothy Watkeys Barberis Award, Catharine Lorillard Wolfe Show, 86:. *Mem:* Asn Artists Southport, NC (mem bd dirs, 70-, pres, 77-80); Asn Artists Winston-Salem, NC; Artists Fel Inc; Am Artists Prof League; Salmagundi Club; Catherine Lorillard Wolfe Art Club; Soc Painters Casein & Acrylic,; Int Soc Women Marine Artists; Am Soc Marine Artists. *Media:* Acrylic & Oil. *Dealer:* Colorworks Club Gallery Hilton Head Island SC. *Mailing Add:* 230 River Dr Southport NC 28461

BROWN, LARRY
PAINTER
b New Brunswick, NJ, June 1, 42. *Study:* Wash State Univ, Pullman, BA, 67; Univ Ariz, MFA, 70. *Work:* Walker Art Ctr; Indianapolis Mus Art; Minn Mus Art; Portland Mus Art; Newark Mus Art, NJ. *Exhib:* Drawing USA, Minn Mus Art, 71; Invitation: 74, Walker Art Ctr, 74; solo exhibs, RI Sch Design, 74, Carlo Lamagna Gallery, New York, 75, 86, 87, 89 & 90, O K Harris Works Art, 77, 79 & 82, Morgan Gallery, Kansas City, Mo, 78, 80, 85 & 92, Ivory/Kimpton Gallery, San Francisco, Calif, 88, G H Dalsheimer Gallery, Baltimore, Md, 88 & Elliot Smith Gallery, Saint Louis, Mo, 88; Carnegie Mus Art, Pittsburgh, 88; Ann Jaffe Gallery, Bay Harbor Island, Fla, 87 & 90; Edward Thorden Gallery, Gothenburg, Sweden, 89; Mind & Matter/New American Abstraction, Traveling Troughout SE Asia, 89-91; and others. *Teaching:* Vis artist painting, Mont State Univ, Bozeman, 78, Iowa State Univ, Ames, 82, Ohio State Univ, Columbus, 83 & 86, NTex State Univ, 85, Rutgers Univ, 87, State Univ NY, Stonybrook, 87 & 91, NMex State Univ, 88, Ariz State Univ 88, Syracuse Univ, 88 & Cooper Union, 91- *Awards:* Nat Endowment Arts Fel, 79-80. *Bibliog:* Leslie Luebbers (auth), Mind & Matter/New American Abstraction (exhib catalog), 87; John Caldwell (auth), Ten Americans (exhib catalogue), Carnegie Mus Art, 88; Curt Barnes (auth), Constructed painting, Art J, 91; and others. *Mem:* Calif Art Asn. *Media:* Oil. *Mailing Add:* 54 Franklin St Apt 4R New York NY 10013

BROWN, LAWRIE
PHOTOGRAPHER, EDUCATOR
b San Jose, Calif, Mar 11, 49. *Study:* San Jose State Univ, Calif, BA, 72; San Francisco State Univ, MA, 75. *Work:* Oakland Mus, Calif; San Francisco Mus Mod Art, Calif; Bibliotheque Nat, Cabinet Des Estampes, Paris, France; Ctr Creative Photography, Tucson; Stanford Univ Mus Art, Calif; Security Pac Bank; Polaroid Corp; Univ Tex, Austin. *Exhib:* Everson Mus Art, Syracuse, NY, 77; San Francisco Mus Mod Art, Calif, 78; Arco Ctr Visual Art, Los Angeles, 79; Il Diaframma-Canon, Milan, 82; Oakland Mus, Calif, 83; Boise Gallery Art, Idaho, 83; Hudson River Mus, Yonkers, NY, 84; Alternative Mus, New York, 84; Canon Photogallery, Amsterdam, 85; Friends Photog, Carmel, Calif, 85; Int Ctr for Photog, New York, 87; Houston Ctr for Photog, 87; Bank of Am, San Francisco. *Teaching:* dir, Photog Dept, Cabrillo Col, Calif, 79- *Awards:* Nat Endowment Photogrs Fel, 79; Polaroid Grants, 85, 86 & 87. *Bibliog:* Peter Hunt Thompson (auth), Untitled 6, Quarterly Friends Photog, 73; Hal Fischer (auth), Don Worth, Barbara Thompson, Lawrie Brown, Casey Williams, Art Week, 9/25/76; Leland Rice (auth), Contemporary California Photography, Camerawork Gallery, 78. *Mem:* Soc Photog Educ; Friends Photog. *Media:* Photography. *Publ:* Auth, Legacy of Light, Knopf, 87; contribr, Am Photog, 6/88; Il Diaframma, Fotofrafia Ital, No 256, 81; Darkroom Photog, San Francisco, 9-10/83 & 86. *Dealer:* Marcuse Pfeifer, New York; Robert Koch San Francisco. *Mailing Add:* 3403 Chardonnay Rd Soquel CA 95073-9743

BROWN, MARION B
PAINTER, INSTRUCTOR
b Brooklyn, NY, Oct 15, 13. *Study:* Pratt Inst, Sch Fine & Appl Arts, cert teaching; also with Edgar A Whitney. *Work:* Dimes Savings Bank New York, Brooklyn; First Nat City Bank, Syosset, NY; Long Island Lighting Co; IBM, New York. *Exhib:* Hudson Valley Art Asn, White Plains, NY, 61-91; Am Watercolor Soc, Nat Acad Design Galleries, New York, 62, 69, 71-74 & 76-78; Am Artists Prof League, New York, 66-91; Catharine Lorillard Wolfe Art Club, Nat Arts Club, New York, 67-86; Frye Mus, Seattle, Wash, 73, 76, 77 & 78; Columbia Mus Art, SC, 74 & 76; Mus Fine Arts, St Petersburg, Fla, 76; and others. *Teaching:* Watercolor workshops, Lynbrook, NY, 67-; instr watercolor, Garden City Community Club, NY, 67- *Awards:* Herb Olsen Award, Am Watercolor Soc, 71; Gold Medal, Hudson Valley Art Asn, 71; Gold Medal, Franklin Mint Gallery of Am Art, 73. *Mem:* Am Watercolor Soc; Hudson Valley Art Asn; Am Artists Prof League; Catharine Lorillard Wolfe Art Club; Art League Nassau Co. *Media:* Watercolor. *Dealer:* Garden City Galleries Ltd 923 Franklin Ave Garden City NY 11530. *Mailing Add:* 18 Nassau Ave Freeport NY 11520

BROWN, MARY RACHEL See Marais,

BROWN, MILTON WOLF
HISTORIAN
b Newark, NJ, July 3, 11. *Study:* New York Univ, BA, 32, MA, 35, PhD, 49; Courtauld Inst, summer 34; Univ of Brussels, summer 37; Harvard Univ, 38-39. *Collections Arranged:* Jacob Lawrence Retrospective, Whitney Mus of Am Art, New York, 74; Modern Spirit, American Painting & Photography, Arts Coun of Great Brit, 77; Masterpieces of American Painting from Washington DC Public Collections, Inst Contemp Art, Mexico City, 80. *Pos:* chmn bd, Brooklyn Col, NY, 64-70. *Teaching:* From instr to prof art hist, Brooklyn Col, NY, 46-70; prof art hist & exec off, PhD Prog in Art Hist, Grad Sch, City Univ New York, 71-79, resident prof, 79-; Zacks prof, Hebrew Univ, Jerusalem, 82. *Awards:* Sachs Fel, 38-39 & Fogg Mus Fel, 40-41, Harvard Univ; Sr fel, Williams Col Art Mus, 83-87; Phi Beta Kappa vis Scholar, 87-88; Samuel H Kress Professor, CASVA, Nat Gal Art, 89-90. *Mem:* Col Art Asn Am; Soc Archit Hist; Archives of Am Art (adv coun, 65-, chmn, 85-); Victorian Soc in Am. *Res:* American art, especially early 20th century, art nouveau. *Publ:* Auth, American Painting from the Armory Show to the Depression, Princeton Univ Press, 55; Story of the Armory Show, Hirshhorn Found, 63, second ed, Abbeville Press, 88; American Art to 1900, H N Abrams, 77; co-auth, American Art, H N Abrams, 79; Maurice B Prenderqast & Charles Prenderqast, Catalog Raisonne, Williams Col Mus Art, 90. *Mailing Add:* 15 W 70th St New York NY 10023

BROWN, PAMELA WEDD
PAINTER, PRINTMAKER
b Cauderan, Gironde, France, Nov 21, 28; US citizen. *Study:* Academie Julian, Paris, 46-50; Ecole des Beaux Arts, Paris, 50; studied with Motoi Oi, Tokyo, 57-59 & Sarah Baker, 67-73. *Work:* Smithsonian Inst, Mus Am Hist, Washington, DC; Libr Cong, Print Div, Washington, DC; Nat Mus Women in Arts, Washington, DC; Christopher Newport Col, Hampton Roads, Va;

Nat Inst Health (Cancer) Bethesda, Md. *Exhib:* Salon d'Automne, Musee de L'Art Moderne, Paris, 47; The Red Leaves, Ueno Mus, Tokyo, 59; Boston Arts Festival, Boston Common, Mass, 63; Grabados USA, Museo de Arte Moderno, Buenos Aires, 87; Int Prints 1, Int Monetary Fund, Washington, DC, 88; Winter Relief, Nat Mus Am Hist, Smithsonian Inst, 92. *Pos:* Artist in residence, The Art Barn, 86; exec dir, New Arts Ctr, (Washington Women's Arts Ctr), 87-88; pres, Washington Printmakers Gallery, 90-91. *Teaching:* Dir arts & crafts, Central YWCA, Toronto, Ont, Can, 50-51. *Awards:* Purchase Award, Junior League, 71; Equal Award, members exhib, Art League, 80, 82, 85 & 86; Honorable Mention, Artists' Equity, 88 & 92. *Bibliog:* Daniel Barbiero (auth), The Generic Figure, Wash Art Reporter, 86; Francis Chenot (auth), Gravure a L'Americaine, Lanterne Bruxelles, 88; Charlotte Clark (auth), article, Eye Wash, 90; Janet Wilson (auth), Galleries, Washington Post, 91; Mary Betts Anderson (auth), Eye Wash, 92. *Mem:* Artists Equity; The Art League; Wash Area Printmakers; Studio Gallery (co-pres, 92); Wash Proj Arts. *Dealer:* Studio Gallery 2108 R St NW Washington DC 20036. *Mailing Add:* 3500 Macomb St NW Washington DC 20016

BROWN, PEGGY ANN
PAINTER, COLLAGE ARTIST
b Ft Wayne, Ind, Mar 15, 34. *Study:* Marquette Univ, BS(jour); Ft Wayne Art Inst. *Work:* Ind Univ, Bloomington; Columbus Art Ctr, Ohio; Ricks Col, Rexburg, Idaho; Cooperstown NY Art Asn; Mus Art, Ft Wayne, Ind. *Comn:* Painting, Univ Mich; painting, NAm Van Lines; painting, General Electric; painting, The Upjohn Co; painting, Owens-Illinois. *Exhib:* Allied Artists Am, New York, 70-91; Nat Watercolor Soc, Los Angeles, 72-74, 76 & 79-85; Am Watercolor Soc, New York, 74, 76, 79 & 82; Nat Acad Design, 79 & 82; one-person shows, Ft Wayne Mus Art, Ind, Burpee Mus, Ill & Purdue Univ, 82. *Teaching:* Instr creative watercolor, Ind Univ, Ft Wayne, 74-82. *Awards:* Gold Medal Watercolor, Allied Artists Am, 78; Harrison Cady Award, Am Watercolor Soc, 79; Ranger Purchase Award, Nat Acad Design, 80. *Bibliog:* James Voirol (auth), Catalog, Ft Wayne Mus Art Publ, 75; Women in Design Compendium, 82; Watercolor 86, Am Artist Publ, 86. *Mem:* Nat Watercolor Soc; Allied Artists Am; Soc Layerists in Multi-Media; Am Watercolor Soc; Rocky Mountain Watermedia Soc. *Media:* Transparent Watercolor, Drawings. *Publ:* Auth, Watercolorist, Northlight Mag, 80. *Dealer:* Chameleon Gallery Plymouth MI; Brown County Art Guild Gallery Nashville TN. *Mailing Add:* RR 4 Box 1987 Nashville IN 47448

BROWN, PETER C
SCULPTOR, EDUCATOR
b Port Chester, NY, Oct 10, 40. *Study:* Ohio Wesleyan Univ, BFA, 63; Cranbrook Acad of Art, MFA, 65. *Work:* Dannheiser Found, New York; First Nat Bank Chicago, Ill; Sydney & Frances Lewis Found, Richmond, Va; The Prudential, New York, NY. *Exhib:* Contemporary Reflections, Aldrich Mus, Ridgefield, Conn, 76; Solo Exhibs, 55 Mercer Gallery, New York, 80 & 82, Harm Bouckaert Gallery, New York, 82 & 84, Queens Mus, Flushing, NY, 82, M-13 Gallery, New York, 87 & 88, Winston Gallery, Washington, DC, 87; Inside Spaces, Mus Mod Art, New York, 82; Sculptor's Drawings, Sculpture Ctr, New York, 84; Approaches to Abstractions, Shanghai Exhib Ctr, Shanghai, China, 86; Dwellings, Althea Viatora Gallery, New York, 87. *Teaching:* Asst prof fine art, Western Col, Oxford, Ohio, 65-70; instr painting, Philadelphia Art Mus, 71-72; prof fine art, LaGuardia Col, City Univ New York, 73- *Awards:* Creative Artists Pub Serv Prog Fel, NY State Coun Arts, 83-84; Fel, New York Found Arts, 85; Research Award, City Univ New York, 85, 88. *Bibliog:* Joseph Masheck (auth), Constructive issues in relief, Artforum, 11/82; J W Mahoney, rev, New Arts Examiner, 2/88; Corinne Robins, rev, Sculpture, 3/89. *Media:* Wood, Acrylics. *Dealer:* M-13 Gallery 72 Greene St New York NY 10012. *Mailing Add:* c/o M-13 Gallery 72 Greene St New York NY 10012

BROWN, PETER THOMSON
PHOTOGRAPHER, EDUCATOR
b Northampton, Mass, June 5, 48. *Study:* Stanford Univ, BA, 71, MFA, 77. *Work:* Mus Fine Arts, Houston; Stanford Univ Mus Art; Gernsheim Collection, Univ Tex, Austin; Santa Barbara Mus Art; Menil Collection, Houston. *Exhib:* Am Photogr Exhib, Andromeda Gallery, Buffalo, NY, 76; Tony Cronin Mem Exhib, Mus Fine Arts, Houston, Tex, 79; Emerging Texas Photographers, Laguna Gloria Mus, Austin, 81; Color from the Collection, Mus Fine Arts, Houston, 82; Art from Houston, Stavanger Mus, Norway, 82; one-man shows, Art Alliance, Philadelphia, Pa, 82, Art Ctr, Waco, Tex, 83, Canon Gallery, Amsterdam, Holland, 84, Alphaville Gallery, Piacenza, Italy, 84 & Tyler Mus, Tex, 85; Southwest 85, Santa Fe Mus Art, 85; Ten Texas Photographers, Abilene Mus Fine Art, 86; and others. *Teaching:* Lectr photog, Stanford Univ, 76-77; lectr photog, Rice Univ, 78- *Awards:* Nat Prize, Bicentennial Traveling Show, Mile Photo, 76; Grad fel, Carnegie Found, 77; Imogen Cunningham Award, 83. *Bibliog:* Joan Murray (auth), Words and images, Artweek, 5/21/83; Lynn McLanahan (auth), Photography in Houston, Artspace, spring, 85; Elliot Klein (auth), article, Palo Alto Weekly, 11/81. *Mem:* Soc Photog Educ. *Media:* Color, Black & White. *Publ:* Illusr, Learning to Die, Learning to Live, Fortress Press, 76; Popular Photography Annual, 76; photog & auth, At the races, Am Photogr, 6/82 & The bedrock of God's high school, 5/83. *Dealer:* Harris Gallery 1100 Bissonnet Houston TX 77006; Carson-Sapiro Gallery 2601 Blake Dr Denver CO 80205. *Mailing Add:* PO Box 23 Heath MA 01346

BROWN, REYNOLD
PAINTER, ILLUSTRATOR
b Los Angeles, Calif, Oct 18, 17. *Study:* Otis Art Inst, Los Angeles; Chouinard Art Sch; also with Will Foster. *Work:* Alamo Mus, San Antonio, Tex; Home Savings & Loan Collection, Los Angeles; Fort Hays Univ, Kans. *Comn:* Portrait of Col Dean Hess, US Air Force, 65; Portrait of Founder Sch Dentistry, Univ Calif, Los Angeles, 72, Portrait of Second Pres, 74. *Exhib:* San Gabriel All City Festival, 72-76; Ambassador Col, Pasadena, 77; City Lancaster Art Mus, 87; City Loveland, Colo, Art Mus, 89; USA Mid Am Arts Alliance; and others. *Pos:* Illusr, N Am Aviation, Los Angeles, 42-49; freelance advert illusr mag story & cover, New York, 49-55; illusr, all major motion picture co, 50-73. *Teaching:* Prof illus head & figure drawing, Los Angeles Art Ctr Col Design, 50-76. *Awards:* Purchase Award, Los Angeles All City Festival, 72; Best of Show, Buena Park All City Festival, 72 & 75 & San Gabriel All City Festival, 72, 75 & 80; Artist of the West, Am Indian & Cowboy Asn, 83. *Bibliog:* Remember Reynold Brown, Nebraskaland, 7/88; Legacy of a Master Instructor, Southwest Art, 10/88; Reynold Brown and the Western Tradition, The Western Horseman, 4/90. *Mem:* Master & fel Am Inst Fine Arts; Los Angeles Soc Illusr; San Gabriel Fine Art Asn. *Media:* Oil, Watercolor. *Publ:* Illus mags & cover stories for: Life, Cosmopolitan Popular Science, Boy's Life Mechanics Illus, Outdoor Life, Liberty, Motor Trends, 46-50. *Dealer:* Trailside Gallery Jackson WY 83001 & Scottsdale AZ 85251; Peppertree Western Art Show Santa Inez CA. *Mailing Add:* HC61, Box 61B Whitney NE 69367

BROWN, ROBERT DELFORD
CONCEPTUAL ARTIST
b Portland, Colo, Oct 25, 30. *Study:* Univ Calif, Los Angeles, BA, 52, with Howard Warshaw, 54-55, MA, 58. *Work:* Smithsonian Inst, Washington, DC; RCA Collection, New York; Archive, Sohm, Ger; Yale Univ; Polaroid Collection, Boston, Mass; Denver Art Mus, Colo. *Comn:* Meat Show, Nathan Romanoff, New York, 64; London St Happening, Robert Frazier Gallery, London, 66. *Exhib:* Ann Exhib Painting, Los Angeles Co Art Mus, Los Angeles, 58; Graphics, Brooklyn Mus, NY, 63; Altered Photog, M H de Young Mem Mus, San Francisco, 75; Victory Over Dumbness Day, New York, 76; NC Mus Art, Raleigh, 77; 15 Yr Retrospective, 1963-1978, Iran-Am Ctr, Tehran, Iran, 78; Osuna Gallery, Washington, DC, 80; Phyllis Kind Gallery, New York, 81; Moore Col Art, Philadelphia, Pa, 85; Special Project, PS 1, Long Island City, New York, 86; First National Church of the Exquisite Panic Inc 1964-1986, PS 1, Long Island City, NY, 86; Maps to Nevada, Leonard Perlson Gallery, NY, 86; Travelogues, Nahan Contemp, NY, 90; Ikons of the First Natioal Church of the Exquisite Panic Inc, Fondazione Mudima, Milan, Italy, 92. *Pos:* Founder, First Nat Church of the Exquisite Panic, Inc, 64 & Great Bldg Crack-Up, 67. *Awards:* Strangest Artist in the World, Olympics of Art, Donald Collender, 72. *Bibliog:* Lil Picard (auth), The work of art, Das Kunstwerk, Ger, 12/64; Lette Eisenhauer (auth), Portrait Bob Delford Brown, Art & Artists, London, 7/73; Contemporary Artists, St James Press, London & St Martin's Press, New York, 77. *Media:* Sight, Sound. *Publ:* Auth, Hanging, 67, First Class Portraits, 73, Ulysses by Robert Delford Brown, An Altered Plagiarism, 75 & Grand Opening Series, 78, First Nat Church of the Exquisite Panic Press; contribr, A D Coleman, ed, Grotesque Photography, Ridge Press, 77. *Mailing Add:* c/o Great Bldg Crack-Up 251 W 13th St New York NY 10011

BROWN, ROBERT K
DEALER
b Springfield, Mass, May 22, 42. *Study:* Boston Univ, BS; Annenberg Sch Commun, Univ Pa, MCommun Arts. *Pos:* Dir & co-owner, Reinhold-Brown Gallery, New York, currently. *Mem:* Antiquarian Booksellers Asn Am; Int League Booksellers. *Specialty:* Rare posters relating to the early avant-garde including constructivism, functionalism, art nouveau-deco, Vienna secession; rare books on 20th century art and architecture. *Publ:* Contribr, Art Deco Minneapolis Inst, 70; ed, Art in Design in Vienna, 72; auth, Art Deco Internationale, Quick Fox, 77. *Mailing Add:* 120 E 86th St New York NY 10028

BROWN, ROGER
PAINTER
b Hamilton, Ala, Dec 10, 41. *Study:* Am Acad Art; Sch Art Inst Chicago, BFA, 68, MFA, 70. *Work:* Corcoran Gallery Art, Nat Mus Am Art, Washington, DC; Am Tel & Tel, Metrop Mus Art, Mus Mod Art, Whitney Mus Am Art, New York; The Art Inst Chicago, First Nat Bank, Main Bank, Mus Contemp Art, Northern Trust Bank, Playboy Collection, The State of Ill Collection, Chicago, Ill; Akron Art Inst, Ohio; and many others. *Exhib:* One-person shows, Fendrick Gallery, 87, Hirshhorn Mus & Sculpture Garden, Washington, DC, 87-88, Asher/Faure Gallery, Los Angeles, 83 & 88, David Heath Gallery, Atlanta, Ga, 90, Arthur Roger Gallery, New Orleans, La, 88 & 90, Phyllis Kind Gallery, Chicago, 71, 73, 74, 76, 77, 79, 86, 88 & 91, Phyllis Kind Gallery, New York, 75, 77, 79, 81, 82, 84, 85, 87, 89 & 92; Extraordinary Realities, Whitney Mus Am Art, New York 89; Everson Mus, Syracuse, New York, 89; Contemp Art Ctr, Cincinnati, 89; Chicago Painters in Press: Brown, Paschke, Hull, Lostutter, Pasin-Sloan, Bramson, Wirsum, Landfall Press, 89 & 91, Birthday Cake, Hyde Park Art Ctr, 89, Death, State Ill Art Gallery, 89, Portraits of a Kind, Phyllis Kind Gallery, 90, Revelations: Artists Look at Religions, Sch Art Inst Chicago, Gallery 2, 91, From America's Studio: Twelve Contemporary Masters, Art Inst Chicago, 92, Face to Face: Self Portraits by Chicago Artists, Chicago Cult Ctr, Chicago, Ill, 92; 78th Ann Exhib: Chicago, Maier Mus Art, Randolph-Macon Woman's Col, Lynchburg, Va, 89; Recent Prints from the Landfall Press, San Antonio Art Inst, Tex, 89; A Certain Slant of Light: The Contemporary American Landscape, Dayton Art Inst, Ohio, 89; The Road Show: The Automobile in Contemporary Art, John Michael Kohler Arts Ctr, Wis, 89; The Alabama Artists Reunion, Ala Artists Gallery, Montgomery, Ala, 89; A Different War: Vietnam in Art, Whatcom Mus Hist & Art, Bellingham, Wash, 89-91; Home Again, Columbus Mus Art, Ga, 90; Speaking Out: Five Centuries of Social Commentary in Printmaking, Telfair Acad Arts

& Sci, Savannah, Ga, 90-91; Word As Image/American Art 1960-1990, Milwaukee Art Mus, Wis & traveling, 90-91; Spirited Visions: Portraits of Chicago Artists by Patty Carroll, State Ill Art Gallery & traveling, 91-93; My Father's House Has Many Mansions, Phyllis Kind Gallery, New York, 92; 500 Years Since Columbus, Triton Mus Art, Santa Clara, Calif, 92; Mind and Beast: Contemporary Artists and the Animal Kingdom, Leigh Yawkey Woodson Art Mus, Wausau, Wis & traveling, 92-93; Parallel Visions: Modern Artists and Outsider Art, Los Angeles Co Mus Art & traveling, 92-93. *Mailing Add:* Phyllis Kind Gallery 313 W Superior Chicago IL 60610

BROWN, SUZANNE GOLDMAN
GALLERY OWNER, COLLECTOR
b New York, NY, Sept 8, 29. *Study:* Radcliff Col, BA(cum laude; Am hist since 1785), 51; Harvard Law Sch, 51-52; Tufts Col, grad work in hist, 52-53; Ariz State Univ, 68-69. *Collections Arranged:* Numerous exhibs arranged through docent prog, Phoenix Art Mus, 60-63. *Pos:* Gallery owner, The Suzanne Brown Gallery & Art Images West, 68-; officer, Friends of Mex Art, Phoenix, 68-70; mem & docent, Phoenix Art Mus League, 69-73; pres, Main St Art Asn, 76-; mem bd, Ariz Theatre Co, 80-82. *Teaching:* Guest lectr, Ariz State Univ, Northern Ariz Univ, Phoenix Col, Scottsdale Ctr Arts & Art News Conf. *Awards:* Woman Yr Award, Ariz Women's Caucus Arts, 82. *Bibliog:* Articles in Ariz Republic, 80 & 81, Southwest Art Mag, 81 & Art Talk, 84. *Res:* Mexican art history with emphasis on Orozoco; in-depth study of history of Southwestern art from the 1830's; Aleschinsky; graphics. *Specialty:* Contemporary Southwestern art. *Publ:* Contribr, Southwestern Art, Craig Cornelius, 76. *Mailing Add:* The Suzanne Brown Gallery 7156 Main St Scottsdale AZ 85251

BROWN, THEOPHILUS
PAINTER
b Moline, Ill, Apr 7, 19. *Study:* Yale Univ, BA, 41; studied with Ozenfant, New York, 48 & with Leger, Paris, 49; Univ Calif, Berkeley, MFA, 52. *Work:* Metrop Mus Art, New York; San Francisco Mus Mod Art; Oakland Mus. *Exhib:* Solo exhibs, Univ Kans Art Mus, 67, Landau-Alan Gallery, New York, 68, Charles Campbell Gallery, San Francisco, 72, 75 & 78, Elizabeth Packard Smith Gallery, Univ Calif, Santa Cruz, 82, Tatistcheff, New York, 90, 91, Koplin, Los Angeles, 89, 91 & Harcourt, Theodaus Brown, San Francisco, 92; Drawings from the Figure, Calif State Univ, Hayward, 81; Contemporary Landscapes, Art Mus S Tex, Corpus Christi, 82; Figure Drawings, Charles Campbell Gallery, 82. *Teaching:* Instr, Univ Calif, Berkeley, 54-56, San Francisco Art Inst, 55-57, Univ Calif, Davis, 56-60 & 75-76, Univ Kans, Lawrence, 67 & Stanford Univ, 67. *Media:* Oil, Acrylic. *Dealer:* John Berggruen Gallery 228 Grant Ave San Francisco CA 94108. *Mailing Add:* 468 Jersey St San Francisco CA 94114

BROWNE, ROBERT M
COLLECTOR, PATRON
b Brooklyn, NY, Apr 12, 26. *Study:* Univ Rochester, NY, BA(with distinction), 46; Johns Hopkins Univ Sch Med, MD, 50. *Exhib:* Collection exhibited: Oceanic Arts, Honolulu Acad Arts, Hawaii, 67; Sculpture of Polynesia, Art Inst Chicago, 67 & Mus Primitive Art, New York, 68; Arts of Oceania, Dallas Mus Fine Arts, 70; Art of the Sepik River, Art Inst Chicago, 71; Art Collections in Hawaii, Univ Hawaii Art Gallery, 76; The Art of the Pacific Islands, Nat Gallery Art, 79-80. *Bibliog:* Terence Barrow (auth), The Art of Tahiti and the Neighbouring Societies, Austral and Cook Islands, Thames & Hudson, London, 79. *Mem:* Fel, Honolulu Acad Arts; Western Reciprocal Mus; Bishop Mus Asn; founder, Contemp Art Mus. *Interests:* Primative art; Japanese Mingei folkcraft; contemporary art. *Collection:* Oceanic and Pre-Columbian art; Japanese Mingei folkcraft. *Mailing Add:* 3625 Anela Pl Honolulu HI 96822

BROWNE, SYD J
PAINTER
b Brooklyn, NY, Aug 21, 07. *Study:* Pratt Inst; Art Student League; study under Eric Pape. *Work:* Libr Cong, Washington, DC; New Brit Inst, Conn; New York Pub Libr, NY; Staten Island Inst, NY; Fairleigh Dickinson Univ, NJ. *Awards:* Mischa Lempert Mem Purchase Prize, Salmagundi Club, 50; William Church Osborn Purchase Prize, Am Watercolor Soc, 50; Soc Am Artists Award, Salmagundi Club, 70. *Mem:* Nat Acad Design; Salmagundi Club. *Media:* Oil, Watercolor. *Dealer:* The Art Gallery, Winter Harbor, ME. *Mailing Add:* Main St Winter Harbor ME 04693

BROWNE, VIVIAN E
PAINTER, EDUCATOR
b Laurel, Fla, Apr 26, 29. *Study:* Hunter Col, BS, MFA; Art Students League; Pratt Graphics Ctr; New Sch Social Res. *Work:* City Chemical Bank, Bronx Hosp, Chase Manhattan Bank, Schomburg Collection Libr, New York; Southeast Ark Arts & Sci Ctr; Nat Westminster Bank NJ. *Exhib:* Mus Mod Art, New York, 68, 88; Rutgers Fac Exhib, 79; Soho 20 Gallery, 80, 84, 87, 89; Ill State Univ, 80-82; New Mus, New York, 81; Douglass Col, 83; Franklin Marshall Col, 83; Orlando Gallery, 85; Jane Vorhees Zimmerli Mus, 88; and many others. *Pos:* Prof Art, Rutgers Univ. *Teaching:* Asst prof painting, Rutgers Univ, Newark, 71-75, assoc prof painting, 75-, chmn, Dept Art, 75-78; vis prof, Univ Calif, Santa Cruz, 83-; prof, Rutgers Univ, 85- *Awards:* Distinguished Teacher of Art Award, Col Art Assoc, 89; Award of Hon, NYFAI, New York, 87; Artists and Influence, Hatch-Billops Collection, 85; MacDowell Colony Fel, 80; Achievement Award, Nat Assoc Business and Professional Women, Huntington Hartford Painting Fel. *Bibliog:* Archives of American Art, Smithsonian Inst, 69; Grace G Alexander (dir), Making more than one, WNYE TV Series on Printmaking, 71; Oakley N Holmes (dir), Black Artists (film), 75. *Mem:* Soho 20 Gallery; Col Art Asn; Heresies Collective Bd. *Media:* Oil, Acrylic; Intaglio, Lithography. *Publ:* Contribr, Eight by Ten Art Portfolio, Elohim Raman, 71-73; auth, Afro-American Art: An Annotated Bibliography, New York City Bd Educ, 72; contribr, Graphics Portfolio, Printmaking Workshop, 72; contribr, Attica Book, Benny Andrews & Rudolf Baranik, (auth), 72; contrib ed, Heresies Mag, 82. *Dealer:* Soho 20 469 Broome St New York NY. *Mailing Add:* 451 W Broadway #35 New York NY 10012

BROWNETT, THELMA DENYER
PAINTER, CONSERVATOR
b Jacksonville, Fla, Oct 26, 24. *Study:* Wesleyan Conserv, BFA(magna cum laude), 46, with Emile Holzhauer; Columbia Univ, 48, with Dr Edwin Ziegfield; Univ Ga, MFA, 52, with Lamar Dodd, James Johnson Sweeny & William Zorack. *Work:* Ga Mus Art, Athens; Gertrude Herbert Art Mus, Augusta, Ga; Atlanta Art Mus, Ga; Ringling Mus Art, Sarasota, Fla; also pvt collections in the US & abroad. *Comn:* Mural, Puppet Playhouse, Augusta, Ga, 51; hundreds of portraits, 56-; Reredos, St Peter's Church, Jacksonville, Fla, 58; Triptych, St Mark's Episcopal Church, Jacksonville, 63; mural, Off Bldg, San Jose Plaza, Jacksonville, 65. *Exhib:* High Mus Art, Atlanta; Ga Mus Art, Athens; Columbia Mus Art, SC; Beaumount Art Mus, Tex; Bradenton Art Mus, Fla; Retrospective Exhib, Kent Campus, Fla Jr Col, Jacksonville, 84. *Pos:* Dir, Gertrude Herbert Art Inst, 51-55; art comnr, State of Ga, 54-57; chmn visual arts, Arts Festival Eleven, Jacksonville, 68-69; dir & owner, Art Unlimited 92, Jacksonville, 75- *Teaching:* Chmn dept art, Augusta Col, 52-55 & Jacksonville Univ, 56-58; chmn dept art, Fla Jr Col, 65-70, prof art, 70-; restorer of paintings, pvt studio, 56-, Oxford Stained Glass Studio, 86- *Mem:* Asn Ga Artists (pres, 53-55); Fedn Fla Artists (bd dir, 57-59); Jackson Coun Arts (mem bd dirs, 69-); Fla Artist Group (secy-treas, 74-). *Media:* Oil Paints, Stained Glass. *Publ:* Auth, Painting, Student Handbook, 71, 75, 78 & 83; Painting, Studio Handbook, 78 & 83. *Mailing Add:* 4774 Apache Ave Jacksonville FL 32210

BROWNING, COLLEEN
PAINTER
b Fermoy, Co Cork, Ireland, 29; US citizen. *Study:* Slade Sch Art, London, Eng. *Work:* NY State Mus, Albany; Detroit Art Inst; Columbia Mus, SC; Milwaukee Art Ctr; St Louis Art Mus, Mo; Wichita Art Mus, Kans; Randolph Macon Woman's Col, Va. *Comn:* Olympic Editions 1976 (lithograph); Kent Bicentennial Portfolio (lithograph). *Exhib:* Five shows, Whitney Mus Am Art Contemp Ann, New York, 51-63; Art Inst Chicago, 54; ann shows, Nat Acad Design, New York, 57-78; Cleveland Mus, Ohio, 75; Indianapolis Mus, Ind, 76; solo exhibs, 7 at Kennedy Galleries, 68-89, Towson State Col, Md, 78 & Wichita Mus, 87; Butler Mus Am Art, 91. *Teaching:* Instr painting & drawing, City Col New York, 60-76; instr, Nat Acad Design, 79-81. *Awards:* Figure Composition Award, Stanford Univ, 56; Second Prize for oils, Butler Inst Am Art, 60 & 74; Adolph & Clara Obrig Prize, Nat Acad Design, 70; Art Medal Merit, Butler Art Inst, Ohio, 74. *Bibliog:* Jerry Tallmer (auth), NY Post, 76, 79 & 89; Greta Berman (auth), Arts Int, 8/84; Jim Auer (auth), article, Milwaukee J, 89. *Mem:* Academician Nat Acad Design (corresp secy, 72-73). *Media:* Oil. *Publ:* Illusr, Portrait of a Lady, Ltd Ed Club, 67; Every Man Heart Look Down, Crowell-Collier, 70; Downtown Is, McGraw-Hill, 72; Working Out a Painting, Watson-Guptill, 89; Can't Sit Still, Dutton Childrens Bks, 93. *Dealer:* ACA New York 40 East 57th St. *Mailing Add:* 100 LaSalle St New York NY 10027

BROWNING, DIXIE BURRUS
PAINTER, WRITER
b Elizabeth City, NC, Sept 9, 30. *Study:* Mary Washington Col; Richmond Prof Inst; and with Barclay Sheaks, Ray Prohaska & Ric Chin. *Work:* US Coast Guard Mus, New London, Conn; Statesville Mus Arts & Sci, NC; Duke Hosp Collection, Durham, NC; Wachovia Bank & Trust, Z Smith Reynolds Found, Winston-Salem. *Exhib:* Marine Exhib, James River Juried, Mariners Mus, Newport News, Va; Irene Leache Mem Biennial, Norfolk Mus Art, Va, 68; Regional Gallery Art, Boone, NC, 71 & 74; Manufacturers Hanover Trust Gallery, New York, 71; Southeastern Ctr for Contemp Art, Winston-Salem, 76. *Pos:* Founder & co-dir, Art Gallery Originals, Winston-Salem, 68-73; co-dir, Art V Gallery, Clemmons, NC, 74-75; pres, co-owner, Browning Artworks, Ltd, Frisco (Cape Hatteras) NC, 84- *Teaching:* Teacher watercolor & acrylics, Arts & Crafts Asn Inc, Winston-Salem, 67-73; watercolor lectr & demonstr in schs & art orgns, NC, currently. *Awards:* Three First Prizes & one Second Prize, Southport Art Festival, 67, 68 & 71; Best in Show, Assoc Artists NC, 71; Third Prize, Watercolor Soc NC, 76. *Bibliog:* Ola Mae Foushee (auth), North Carolina Artists, Univ NC; Anthony Swider (auth), Going to the Gallery, Winston-Salem & Forsyth Co Sch Syst, 69; Ward Nicholls (auth), Artists & Craftsmen in North Carolina, Wilks Art Guild, 74. *Mem:* Int Soc Artists; Assoc Artists Winston-Salem (vpres, 68-69); Watercolor Soc NC (co-organizer & pres, 72-73); Winston-Salem Arts Coun; Arts & Crafts Asn, Inc. *Media:* Watercolor, Chinese Ink. *Publ:* Illusr, North Carolina Parade, Univ NC, 66; contribr, Drawing & Painting the Natural Environment, Davis, 74; auth introd, Artists/USA 79-80, Found Advan Artists; auth film, Acrylics, The Contemporary Colors, Hunt Mfg Co. *Mailing Add:* 5316 Robinhood Rd Winston-Salem NC 27106

BROWNING, MARK DANIEL
PAINTER, SCULPTOR
b Miles City, Mont, Dec 26, 46. *Study:* Self taught. *Work:* Plains Art Mus, Moorhead, Minn; USDA/Human Nutrition Ctr & Univ NDak, Grand Forks, NDak; Custer Co Art Ctr, Miles City, Mont; Pillsbury Co/Corp Offs, Minneapolis. *Exhib:* Solo exhibs, Yellowstone Art Ctr, Billings, Mont, 81, Talley Gallery, Bemidji State Univ, Minn, 83, Plains Art Mus, Moorehead, Min, 84 & Bismark Art Gallery, NDak, 92; 113th Am Watercolor Soc,

Salmagundi Club, New York, 80; Watercolor USA, Springfield Art Mus, Mo, 82, 83 & 90; 10th Midwest Watercolor Soc, Neville Mus, Green Bay, Wis, 86; Collection of Mid-Am Artists, Art Ctr Minn, Wayzata, 87; and many others. *Pos:* Dir & bd dirs, Custer Co Art Ctr, 76-79; pres, Mont Inst Arts, 76-78, bd dirs, 76-81; studio artist & gallery owner, 79-; pres, Greater Grand Forks Arts & Humanities Asn, 86-88. *Awards:* Purchase Selection, Am Art, Pillsbury Co, 80; Honorable Mention, Midwest Watercolor Soc, Manitowoc, Wis, 80; Purchase Award, Midwestern Invitational, Plains Art Mus, 85. *Bibliog:* Sebby Wilson Jacobson (auth), Zaner gallery review, Times-Union, Rochester, NY, 85; Ron Netsky (auth), Art Agenda, Democrat & Chronicle, Rochester, NY, 85. *Mem:* Mont Arts Coun (fine arts adv panel, 76); Midwest Watercolor Soc; NDak Coun Arts (test prog comt mem, 84-88 & coun mem, 90-); and others. *Media:* Watercolor; Smooth Surface, Non-Traditional. *Mailing Add:* 22 N Fourth St Grand Forks ND 58203

BRUBAKER, JACK
SCULPTOR, KINETIC ARTIST
b Chicago, Ill, Aug 30, 44. *Study:* studied painting & drawing with Mary Brubaker, also at Art Inst Chicago, 64, Syracuse Univ, BFA, 66, Ind Univ, MFA, 68. *Work:* Joseph Hirshhorn Collection, Naples, Fla; Ind Univ Mus, Bloomington; and many others. *Comn:* Architectural hardware, Grammar Baptist Church, Ind, 79, Nashville State Bank & St Agnes Catholic Church, Nashville, Ind, 82; and many others. *Exhib:* Let There Be Light, Nat Ornamental Metal Mus, Memphis, Tenn, 84; Contemporary Iron 87, travelling show, 87-89; solo exhib, Indianapolis Mus Art, Ind, 87; and many others in US & Europe. *Awards:* Award for Excellence in Design, Cincinnati Crafts Fair, 83; Gold Trouser Button, Ctr for Metal Design, Aachen, WGer, 86. *Mem:* Artist Blacksmith Asn Am (pres, 83-88); Brit Artist Blacksmith Asn. *Publ:* Dir, Forging Stone Cutting Tools (video), Artist Blacksmith Am, 81; and many others. *Mailing Add:* c/o Hand of Man The Curtis Shops Lenox MA 01240

BRUCKER, EDMUND
PAINTER, EDUCATOR
b Cleveland, Ohio, Nov 20, 12. *Study:* Cleveland Inst Art, dipl(painting), 34-36; Wayman Adams Summer Sch, 44. *Work:* Cleveland Mus Art; Indianapolis Mus Art, Ind; Butler Inst Am Art, Youngstown, Ohio; Evansville Mus Arts & Sci, Ind; Dartmouth Col, Hanover, NH. *Comn:* Portrait of President, Ind State Univ, 75; Portrait of Chancellor, Taylor Univ, Ind, 80; Portraits of Mr & Mrs Anton Hulman, 500 Indianapolis Motor Speedway Hall Fame Mus, 82; Portrait of Former Coach, Depauw Univ, Ind, 82; Portrait of President, Purdue Univ, Ind, 83; and others. *Exhib:* Directions in American Painting, Carnegie Inst, Pittsburgh, Pa, 41; 145th Ann of Painting & Sculpture, Pa Acad Fine Arts, Philadelphia, 50; Metrop Mus Art, New York, 52; Cincinnati Mus Art, Ohio, 55; Herron Mus Art, Indianapolis, 63; La State Univ Int Drawing Invitational, Baton Rouge, 65; Contemp Ind Artists, Ind State Mus, Indianapolis, 75; 200 Years Ind Art, Indianapolis Mus Art, 76; 69th Indiana Artists Show, Indianapolis Mus Art, 83. *Pos:* Portrait cover artist, Ind Bus & Indust Mag, Culver, 60-71. *Teaching:* Instr drawing, Cleveland Inst Art, 36-38; instr drawing & painting, John Herron Art Sch, Indianapolis, 38-67; prof drawing & painting, Herron Art Sch, Ind Univ, Indianapolis, 67-83, prof emer, 83- *Awards:* First Prize in Oils, Ill State Fair 12th Prof Art Exhib, 58; Millikin Award for Artistic Achievement, Art Asn Indianapolis, 63; Best Show, 58th Ann Hoosier Salon, Indianapolis, 82. *Bibliog:* Jacob Getlar Smith (auth), The drawings of Edmund Brucker, Am Artist Mag, 56; Medium of the ancients, Indianapolis Star Mag, 59. *Mem:* Ind Artists Club (1st vpres, 70); Hoosier Salon Patrons Asn. *Media:* Oil. *Mailing Add:* 545 King Dr Indianapolis IN 46260

BRUDER, HAROLD JACOB
PAINTER, EDUCATOR
b Bronx, NY, Aug 31, 30. *Study:* Cooper Union, cert, 51; New Sch Social Res; Pratt Graphic Art Ctr. *Work:* NJ State Mus, Trenton; Sheldon Mem Gallery, Lincoln, Nebr; Hirshhorn Mus, Washington, DC; Univ NMex Mus. *Exhib:* Corcoran Gallery Biennale, Washington, DC, 63; Modern Realism & Surrealism, Am Fedn Arts Traveling Show, 64, The Realist Revival, 72-73; 22 Realists, Whitney Mus Am Art, New York, 70; Aspects of the Figure, Cleveland Mus Art, 74; Am Family Portraits, Philadelphia Mus Art, 76; one-man shows, Armstrong Gallery, New York, 84 & 86 & Contemp Realist Gallery, San Francisco, 88; and others. *Pos:* Artist-in-residence, Aspen Sch Contemp Art, summer 67. *Teaching:* Assoc prof art, Kansas City Art Inst, 63-65; vis lectr, Pratt Inst, 65-66; prof art, Queens Col, 65-, chmn art dept, 82-85. *Awards:* Purchase Prize, Am Acad Arts Letters, 78; PSC-BHE Fac Res Award, 76, 79 & 84; Nat Endowment Arts Grant, 85-86. *Bibliog:* Ralph Pomeroy (auth), Harold Bruder and immediate family, Art & Artists, 10/68; Alan Gussow (interviewer), A sense of place, Saturday Rev Press, 72; Ralph Pomeroy (auth), Harold Bruder's Metaphors, Arts, 10/82. *Mem:* Col Art Asn. *Media:* Oil. *Publ:* Auth, Notes from the Prado, Art J, fall 72; Monumental Miniatures: The Drawings of Pierre Bonnard & Edward Vuillard, Drawing, 3-4/92. *Dealer:* Contemp Realist Gallery San Francisco CA. *Mailing Add:* 165 West End Ave, No 3N New York NY 10023

BRULC, LILLIAN G
PAINTER, SCULPTOR
b Joliet, Ill. *Study:* Art Inst Chicago, MFA(George D Brown Foreign Travel Fel), 64; Univ Chicago, MFA, 64; also with Franz Gorse, Austria. *Work:* Major works in permanent architectural environments, smaller works in private collections. *Comn:* Life-size bronze, St Victor Church, Calumet City, Ill, 79; life-size bronze, mural, environ design, SVD Theologate, Chicago, 79-80; bronze relief, 83 & mural & mosaic, 86, Iron Range Interpretative Ctr, Chisholm, Minn; Holocaust Mem bronze & ceramic, Joliet Jewish Congregation Temple, Joliet, Ill, 89; bronze bas relief, Capitol Develop Bd, State of Ill, 92; and others. *Exhib:* Prints, Drawings & Watercolors 2nd Biennial by Ill Artists, Art Inst Chicago, 64; one-woman show, Drawings & Lithographs, Casa de Escultura, Panama City, 69; Murals for People (slide of Chicago works), Mus Contemp Art, Chicago, 71; Ljubljana, Yugoslavia, 85 & 88; Gallery Genesis, Chicago, 88, 89, 90, 91 & 92. *Pos:* Artist in residence, Chicago Archdiocese Panama Mission, San Miguelito, 65-70, art adv & part-time resident, 73-79; artist in residence, Archdiocesan Latin Am Comt, Chicago, 71-72 & SVD Theologate, Chicago, 79-80; consult, Gallery Genesis, Chicago, 88. *Teaching:* Asst instr lithography, Art Inst Chicago, 61-64; lectr theol & art, Divine Word Sem, Techny, Ill, 66-68; instr design, mat, portrait & drawing, Chicago Acad Fine Arts, 72-78. *Bibliog:* Charlando (TV presentation), Univ Chicago WGN-9, 68; Jorge Amado (auth), Perfiles, Cuem en Marcha, Panama City, 70; Edward Gobetz (auth), Lillian Brulc, Painter, Sculptor, Printmaker, Success Stories, SRCA, 81; Darja Groznik (auth), interview, JANA, Ljubljana, Yugoslavia, 88. *Mem:* Environ & Art Comt, Archdiocese of Chicago; Chicago Women's Caucus for Art. *Media:* Acrylic, Oils; Bronze. *Publ:* Illusr & auth, Make me a people, Bible Today Mag, 74; illusr, Thirsting For the Lord, Alba House, 76; auth, Visit with Franz Gorse in Carinthia, Austria, SRCA Publ, 78; illusr, Dream Visions, SRCA Publ; Old Testament Message (23 vols), Michael Glazier Inc. *Mailing Add:* L' Atelier 909 Summit Joliet IL 60435

BRUMER, MIRIAM
PAINTER, EDUCATOR
b New York, NY, Oct 7, 39. *Study:* Univ Miami, BA(art & eng); Boston Univ, MFA(painting). *Work:* Chase Manhattan Bank, New York; Citibank, New York; Boston Univ, Mass; Bell Labs, NJ; and many pvt collections. *Comn:* Painting for office, New York Bank Savings, 73. *Exhib:* Tweed Gallery, Plainfield, NJ, 82; Tossan-Tossan Gallery, New York, 82, Three Artists, Hankook Gallery, 82 & 83, Eight, ESTA Robinson Gallery, 83, New York; one-person show, Hankook Gallery, New York, 82; 37 Artists, Boston City Hall Gallery, Mass, 83; AIR Invitational, New York, 83, 84 & 85; More Than Meets the Eye Invitational, 22 Wooster Street Gallery, New York, 84; and others. *Pos:* Writer & ed, Feminist Art J, New York, 72-74; educator, Queens Mus, 87- *Teaching:* Asst prof studio art & art hist, NY Inst of Technol, Old Westbury, 69-75; lectr studio art & art hist, Marymount Manhattan Col, New York, 76-; instr, Hunter Col, 76-81; instr, NY Univ, 83- *Awards:* Ludwig Vogelstein Found Grant, 76-77; Comt Visual Arts Grants, 79 & 80; artist-in-res, NY Found Arts, 85. *Bibliog:* Kay Kenny (auth), Views by Women Artists, 82; Michele Kidwell (auth), Miriam Brumer, Arts Mag, (in prep); Diana Morris (auth), Eight, Women Artist News, 83; Michelle Kidwell (auth), Miriam Brumer, Arts Mag; Hedy O'Beil (auth), More than meets the eyes, Arts, 5/84. *Media:* Acrylic; Pencil. *Mailing Add:* 250 W 94th St New York NY 10025

BRUMER, SHULAMITH
SCULPTOR, INSTRUCTOR
b Russia, July 5, 24; US citizen. *Study:* Art Students League, with William Zorach; Columbia Univ, with Oronzio Malderelli. *Work:* Philbrook Art Ctr, Tulsa, Okla; Va Mus Fine Art, Richmond; State Univ NY, Plattsburgh. *Exhib:* One-man shows, Sculpture Ctr, New York, 65, 68, 73 & 79, Union Am Hebrew Congregations, 81, Pleiades Gallery, 86, 88 & 90, Mus Fine Arts, Plattsburgh, NY; Philbrook Mus, Tulsa, Okla; Nat Acad Design, New York; Riverside Mus, New York; Va Mus Fine Arts; Bergen Mus, NJ. *Teaching:* Instr stone & wood carving, Sculpture Ctr Art Sch, 71-80. *Awards:* Knickerbocker Prizes, 57, 76 & 80; Audubon Artists Awards, 58 & 62; Gold Medals, Allied Artists, 86 & Knickerbocker Artists, 87. *Mem:* Am Asn Contemp Artists; Nat Asn Women Artists; Audubon Artists; Allied Artists; Knickerbocker Artists. *Media:* Stone, Bronze. *Mailing Add:* 473 Franklin D Roosevelt Dr New York NY 10002

BRUMFIELD, JOHN RICHARD
PHOTOGRAPHER, WRITER
b Los Angeles, Calif, Apr 1, 34. *Study:* Los Angeles State Col, BA, 60, MA, 61; Univ Calif, Berkeley, MA, 70; Calif Inst Arts, MFA, 72. *Work:* Mus Mod Art, New York; Los Angeles Co Mus Art & Univ Calif, Los Angeles; San Francisco Mus Mod Art; Santa Barbara Mus Art, Calif; Minneapolis Inst Art, Mo. *Exhib:* One-man shows, de Saisset Mus, Santa Clara, Calif, 78, Washington Proj Arts, DC, 78 & Camerawork Gallery, San Francisco, 79; Attitudes of the 1970's, Santa Barbara Mus, Calif, 79; Southern Calif Invitational Retrospective, Univ Southern Calif, 79; Albright-Knox Mus, Buffalo, NY, 81; G Ray Hawkins Gallery, Los Angeles, 81; and others. *Pos:* Contribr photog, J Los Angeles Inst Contemp Art, 80-; consult photog, San Joaquin Valley Hist Proj, Calif State Col, Bakersfield, 80-; guest ed, photog issue, The Dumb Ox, 80-; vis artist, Art Inst Chicago, 81. *Teaching:* Assoc dean sch art & design, chmn photog prog & instr art, Calif Inst Arts, 70-; instr, Art Ctr Col Design, Pasadena, Calif, 79-80; instr, Visual Studies Workshop, Rochester, NY, summer 80. *Awards:* Nat Endowment Arts Photog Grant, 80. *Bibliog:* Hal Fischer (auth), Portraits in Sequence, Art Week, 79; Jim Hugunin (auth), Hot Shots, Afterimage, 79; Michael Starenko (auth), Photography and Language, New Art Examiner, 79. *Mem:* Col Art Asn. *Media:* Photography. *Publ:* Auth, Beneath the plot it thickens, In: Lew Thomas, ed, Structuralism and Photography, 78; Count Dracula in the olive grove, J Los Angeles Inst Contemp Art, 80; (et ego in Arcadia): Hortense Always was High Strung, Obscura, 81; The Americans and the Americans, Afterimage, 80; Photography, world order and other fictions, The New Art Examiner, 80. *Mailing Add:* c/o Art Ctr Col of Design 1700 Lida St Pasadena CA 91103

BRUMMEL, MARILYN REEDER
COLLAGE ARTIST, PRINTMAKER
b Syracuse, NY, Dec 29, 26. *Study:* Syracuse Univ, BFA, 48; also studied with Roberto De La Monica, 72 & Krishna Reddy, 78. *Work:* Newark Mus, NJ; Passaic Co Hist Soc, NJ; Govt Off Bldg (NJ State Coun Arts), Atlantic City; Nat Elec Rural Co-op Asn, Washington, DC; Pub Serv Elec & Gas Co, Bergen County, NJ. *Comn:* Odyssey (30 prints), Art Ctr NJ, Tenafly, 76; Cryogenic Landscape (print), Arde Inc, Norwood, NJ, 83. *Exhib:* Womens Show Invitational, Everson Mus, Syracuse, NY, 74; Nat Arts Club Show, New York, 74; Silvermine Guild Artists, New Canaan, 75; 1st Biennial NJ Artists, Newark Mus, 77; Print Club Ann, Philadelphia, Pa, 78; Audubon Artists Ann, Acad Design, New York, 81. *Awards:* Gold Medal Award, Catherine Lorrilard Wolfe Ann, 78; Director's Award, Bergem Community Mus, 89; Best Contemp Award, Kerygama Gallery, 90. *Bibliog:* David Speiegler (auth), Art Review, Bergen Record, 71 & 78; John Zeamon (auth), Art Review, Bergen Record, 89. *Mem:* Nat Asn Women Artist (chmn, membership extn), 92-93; Printmaking Coun NJ; Art Ctr Painting Affiliates (co-chmn). *Media:* Miscellaneous. *Dealer:* Prints Etcetera 1517 163rd St Whitestone NY 11357. *Mailing Add:* 1626 Buckingham Rd Teaneck NJ 07666

BRUNDAGE, SUSAN LOUNSBURY
DEALER
b Orange, NJ, June 18, 49. *Study:* Smith Col, BA, 71. *Work:* Paine Webber Inc, New York. *Pos:* Treas, White Columns, New York, 78-; dir, Leo Castelli Gallery, New York, currently. *Specialty:* Contemporary American & European art. *Mailing Add:* 448 W 23 St New York NY 10011

BRUNEAU, KITTIE
PAINTER, PRINTMAKER
b Montreal, Que, Can, Oct 12, 29. *Study:* Ecole Beaux Arts Montreal, EBA. *Work:* Mus d'Art Contemporain, Montreal; Mus Que; Univ Montreal & Que Libr; Art Gallery Ont, Toronto; Sir George William Univ. *Exhib:* Peintures Dessins, Mus d'Art Contemporain, Montreal, 66; Vancouver Print Int, 67; l'Expo Centenaire l'Ont, Toronto, 67; 2nd Biennale Gravure Cracovie, Pologne, 68; Foire Int Bale, Suisse, 72; Centre Culturel Can, Paris, France, 75; Thomas Moore Inst, Montreal, 76; Bibliothéque Nationale, Montreal, 77 & 78; 4 Graveurs, Libr Que, Paris, 80; and many other group & one-woman shows. *Bibliog:* Guy Viau (auth), Kittie Bruneau-peintre et sculpteur, Cite Libre, Montreal, 62; J de Roussan (auth), Kittie Bruneau, Lidec, Montreal, 67. *Mem:* Conseil de la Gravure du Que; Guilde Graphique. *Media:* Oil. *Mailing Add:* PO Box 733 Ste Adele PQ J0R 1L0 Canada

BRUNELL, RICHARD HOWARD
EDUCATOR, DESIGNER
b Pawtucket, RI, May 26, 16. *Study:* Pratt Inst, with Tom Benrimo, dipl(design), 39; RI Sch Design, with John Howard Benson & John Frazier, BFA, 46; Black Mountain Col, with Joe Albers, 47; Brown Univ, BA, 49. *Work:* Centre Georges Pompidou, Centre de Creation Industrielle, Paris. *Comn:* Nat traveling exhib Trademarks, US Trademark Asn, DC, 56. *Exhib:* Southeastern Ann, High Mus Art, Atlanta, Ga. *Collections Arranged:* Design Process, Mus Dirs Nat Asn, RI Sch Design, 47; Profession of Art, High Mus Art, Atlanta, 56. *Pos:* Art dir, GM Basford Advert, New York, 39-42 & 50-53; dean, Atlanta Art Inst, 56-58; dean, Kansas City Art Inst & Sch Design, 58-60. *Teaching:* Prof design, Univ Ga, Atlanta, 53-55; prof art, Wash Univ, St Louis, Mo, 60-82, chmn dept design, 70-82. *Awards:* Special Commendation, Combat Illus, US Eighth Air Force, 45; Gold Medals, Art Dirs Atlanta, 57 & Art Dirs St Louis, 64. *Bibliog:* Edward Gottschall (auth), Profile/Dick Brunell, Typographic, Vol 2, No 2, 70. *Mem:* Int Cong Graphic Design Asns. *Mailing Add:* 1834 Ridgeview Circle Dr Manchester MO 63021

BRUNER, LOUISE KATHERINE
CRITIC, WRITER
b Cleveland, Ohio, June 13, 10. *Study:* Denison Univ, BA; Bowling Green State Univ, MA. *Pos:* Art critic, Toledo Blade, 58-79; oral interviewer, Archives of Am Art, 73-; trustee, Univ Toledo Carlson Libr, 75- *Teaching:* Instr reviews & criticism, Univ Toledo, 72- *Awards:* Roy Neuberger Found Award, Am Fedn Arts Nat Coun Arts Criticism Workshop, 68; First Prize for Critical Writing, Ohio Newspaperwomen's Asn, 71; Alumni Citation, Denison Univ, 71. *Mem:* Toledo Artists Club; Toledo Mod Art Group; Arts Comn Greater Toledo; Presidents Coun Toledo Mus Art. *Publ:* Contribr, Arts Mag, 64-; contribr, Craft Horizons, 71; contribr, Am Artist, Art Gallery Mag & Antiques. *Mailing Add:* 4506 Indian Ridge Sylvania OH 43560

BRUNI, UMBERTO
PAINTER, GRAPHIC ARTIST
b Montreal, Que, Nov 24, 14. *Study:* With Guido Nincheri, Montreal, 30-37; Ecole Beaux-Arts, Montreal, grad prof, 37. *Comn:* Bust of Brother Andre, St Joseph Shrine, Montreal, 39; religious scene at church (fresco), Montreal, 58; historical scene (oil), Rougier et Freres, Montreal, 59; Da Giovanni (mosaic mural), Montreal, 60; religious mosaic mural, Ste Elizabeth Church, Ville Emard, Que, 61; portrait of ex-Prime Minister Sauve, Quebec Parliament. *Exhib:* Solo exhibs, Figuratif a L'Abstrait, Mus Beaux-Arts, Montreal, 61 & Giotto Art Gallery, Rome, Italy, 62; Can Artist in Paris, Maison Que, France, 62; Art Coun Can, O'Keefe Ctr, Toronto, 62; Univ Quebec, 77-86; and many others. *Pos:* Cur, Univ Que, Montreal, 70-80, founder & dir, Gallery, 74-80. *Teaching:* Prof, Ecole Beaux-Arts, Montreal, 47-69; prof, Univ Que, Montreal, 70-80; Retired. *Awards:* Fel to Rome & Paris, Art Coun Can, 61-62; Research Fel to Rome & Paris, Que Govt, 72. *Mem:* Royal Can Acad Arts; Acad Gentium Pro Pace, Rome; Int Inst Conserv Hist & Artistic Works. *Media:* All. *Interests:* Didactical presentation of exhibitions. *Publ:* Auth, Signatures, Marcel Broquet Ed, 81. *Mailing Add:* 1325 Blvd D'Auteuil Laval PQ H7E 3J4 Canada

BRUNKUS, RICHARD ALLEN
PRINTMAKER, CURATOR
b Cleveland, Ohio, Mar 31, 50. *Study:* Miami Univ, Oxford, Ohio, BFA(printmaking & painting), 72 & MFA(printmaking), 74. *Work:* Minot State Col, NDak; Univ Mich Mus, Ann Arbor. *Exhib:* Cincinnati Art Mus Print Invitational, Ohio, 74; 15th Nat Print Exhib, Bradley Univ Art Mus, 75; 17th Ann Nat Print & Drawing Exhib, Oklahoma City, Okla, 75; 3rd US Int Graphics Ann, Hollis, NH, 75; Colorprint US, Tex Tech Univ Art Mus, 76; 11th Dulin Nat Print and Drawing Competition, Knoxville, Tenn, 77; 4th Nat Hawaii Print Exhib, Honolulu Acad of Arts, 78; and others. *Collections Arranged:* Japanese Book Illustrations from the 18th and 19th centuries, 76; An American Image 1900-1950, 76; Architectural Prints of the 17th, 18th and 19th Centuries, 76; 20th Century Master French Prints, 77; Georges Rouault's Miserere Et Guerre, 77. *Pos:* Cur of print collection, Albion Col, 75- *Teaching:* Asst prof, Albion Col, Mich, 74-83, assoc prof visual arts, 83- *Awards:* Purchase Award, Colorprint US, Tex Tech Univ, 74, 15th Nat Bradley Print Exhib, Bradley Univ, 75 & 3rd Nat Hawaii Print Exhib, Honolulu Acad Arts, 75. *Mem:* Graphics Soc, Hollis, NH. *Media:* Engraving, Color Intaglio. *Collection:* Early 18th and 19th century Japanese woodblock prints of courtesans; prints by Giovanni Battista Piranesi, 18th century printmaker. *Dealer:* Miriam Perlman Gallery 474 N Lakeshore Dr Chicago Ill. *Mailing Add:* c/o Miriam Perlman Gallery 474 N Lakeshore Dr Chicago IL 60611

BRUNNER, JULIA See Castanis, Muriel (Julia Brunner)

BRUNO, PHILLIP A
DIRECTOR, LECTURER
b Paris, France. *Study:* Columbia Col, BA(hist fine arts & archit); Inst Fine Arts, New York Univ. *Comn:* Restored 17th century house on Martha's Vineyard, Mass, 64. *Collections Arranged:* Ralph Rosenborg Retrospective, Washington, DC, 52; Jose Luis Cuevas, Paris, 55; Elmer Livingston Macrae, Nashville, 63; Tschang-yeul Kim, 79 & Enrico Donati, 80, FIAC, Grand Palais, Paris; Tschang-yeul Kim/Wolfgang Kubach & Anna Marie Wilmsen, 81. *Pos:* Weyhe Gallery, New York, 50-51; co-founder & assoc dir, Grace Borgenicht Gallery, 51-55; dir, World House Gallery, New York, 56-60; dir, Am Exhibs for La Napoule Found, New York & France; dir, Staempfli Gallery, New York, 60-89, co-dir, 81, assoc dir, Marlborough Gallery, New York, 89-; adv bd mem, Ossabaw Island Found, Savannah, Ga, 78-; art consult, First Am Nat Bank, Nashville, 80-81; assoc dir, Marborough Gallery, New York, 89- *Teaching:* Guest lectr, Foreign Ministry Finland, Helsinki, 78 & Cornell Univ, 92. *Mem:* Hon life mem St Paul Art Ctr; hon mem Tenn Fine Arts Ctr Cheekwood, Nashville; Dukes Co Hist Soc, Edgartown, Mass; Munic Art Soc; Nat Trust Hist Preservation. *Collection:* Mainly mid-twentieth century American watercolors and drawings, ranging from Marin to Kline, including Lachaise, Demuth, Tobey, Bravo, Lopez-Garcia, Wunderlich; Selections of the collection have been exhibited at the Krannert Art Museum, Tennessee Fine Arts Center, Finch College Museum Art, Minn Mus, Vassar Art Col Gallery, Quqanheim Mus & The Phillips Collection. *Mailing Add:* 342 E 67th St New York NY 10021

BRUNO, SANTO M
PAINTER
Study: Tyler Sch Art, Temple Univ, Philadelphia, Pa, BFA, 69, MFA, 71; studies with David Pease, Romas Viesulas & Steven Green. *Work:* High Mus Art, Atlanta; Kilpatrick, Cody & Regenstein Collection; Stampe Nacional de Italia; Univ Osaka, Japan; Creiger Assocs, Boston. *Comn:* Five major painting-constructions, New Atlanta Hartsfield Int Airport, Ga, 80. *Exhib:* Solo shows, First Impressions of Atlanta, Image South Gallery, Atlanta, Ga, 72, Illusions of a Greek Spring, Gallerie Illien, 73, Crow Carter Presents Santo Bruno: A Five-year Select of Work, Crow-Carter & Assocs, 76, Recent Work, Javo Gallery, 77, A Selection of Work: 78-80, Atlanta Art Workers Coalition Gallery, 80; Flight Patterns, Forest Ave Consortium, Atlanta, 80; Artists and the Cyclorama Project, Colony Square, 82; Abstraction/Attraction, Newhouse Gallery, Staten Island, NY, 86; Bruce Lurie Gallery, New York, 87 & 88; Gotham Fine Arts, Ltd, 87; Dome Gallery, 88. *Pos:* Conserv contractor, Santo Bruno Fine Art, 83- *Teaching:* Instr painting, Tyler Sch Art, Temple Univ, Rome, Italy, 70-71; instr painting & drawing, Atlanta Col Art, 71-78, head dept painting, 77-78. *Bibliog:* Preview essay, Art Voices S, 1/78; Sherry Baker (auth), Interview with Santo Bruno, Off-Peachtree Mag, 2/78; Michael Fressola (auth), What's new at Newhouse, Staten Island Advance, 2/86. *Dealer:* Dome Gallery 578 Broadway New York NY 10012. *Mailing Add:* 67 Monroe Ave #3 Staten Island NY 10301

BRUNO, VINCENT J
HISTORIAN, ADMINISTRATOR
b New York, NY, Feb 8, 26. *Study:* Bard Col, 46-48; Academie Julian, Paris, cert painting, 49; Kenyon Col, BA(philos art), 51; Columbia Univ, MA, 62, PhD, 69; Kenyon Col, DFA, 84. *Teaching:* Instr art hist, Wellesley Col, 64-65; assoc prof, C W Post Col, Long Island Univ, 65-66; assoc prof, State Univ NY, Binghamton, 66-76, chairperson, 72-76; chmn dept art, Univ Tex, Arlington, 76-84, prof art, 76- *Awards:* John Simon Guggenheim Mem Fel, 78-; Am Coun Learned Soc Grant-in-Aid, 80; Am Philos Soc Grant-in-Aid, 82; Nat Endowment Humanities, Fel, 86-87; Getty Found Grant, 89. *Bibliog:* Martin Robertson (auth), The classical palette: Review of Formand Color in Greek Printing, Times Lit Suppl, London 8/5/77; S R Roberts (auth), Review of form and color in Greek painting, Art Bulletin LXII, 80; A O Koloski Ostrow (auth), Review of Hellenistic painting techniques, Am J Archeol 91, 87. *Mem:* Col Art Asn Am; Archeol Inst Am; Am Inst Nautical Archeol; Am Sch Classical Studies, Athens; hon fel Am Acad Rome (mem, adv comt). *Res:* Conducted excavations at Cosa under auspices of American Academy in

Rome and State Univ of New York at Binghamton, 68-72; ancient painting techniques. *Publ:* Auth, The Parthenon, Norton Critical Studies in the History of Art, 74 & Form and Color in Greek Painting, 77, W W Norton & Co; articles in the Am J of Archaeol, Archaeol Mag; Princeton Encyclopedia of Classical Sites, Int J Nautical Archaeol, In Memoriam Otto J Brendel; Hellenistic painting techniques: The evidence of the Delos fragments, Columbia Studies in the Classical Tradition, Vol XI, Leiden (monogr), 85. *Mailing Add:* Dept Art Univ Tex Arlington TX 76019

BRUS, GUNTER
CONCEPTUAL ARTIST, PRINTMAKER
b Ardning, Austria, 38. *Study:* Sch Arts & Crafts, Graz, Austria; Acad Applied Arts, Vienna, Austria. *Work:* Mus Mod Art, New York; Libr Cong, Washington, DC; Tate Gallery, London, Eng; Albertina Mus, Vienna, Austria. *Exhib:* Dokumenta V, 72 & Dokumenta VII, 82, Kassel, Ger; Bodyworks, Mus Contemp Art, Chicago, Ill, 75. *Media:* All. *Mailing Add:* c/o Crown Point Press 568 Broadway New York NY 10012

BRUSCA, JACK
PAINTER
b New York, NY, Nov 18, 39. *Study:* Univ NH; Sch Visual Arts, New York, with Alex Gottlieb, Alex Katz, Joe Tilson & Helen Frankenthaller. *Work:* Aldrich Mus Contemp Art, Ridgefield, Conn; Whitney Mus, New York; RI Sch Design; Albright-Knox Art Gallery, Buffalo, NY; Cleveland Mus Art, Ohio. *Comn:* Stage Set & Costumes, Lyon Opera Ballet, France, 86 & Gulbenkian Ballet, Lisbon, Portugal, 86; Cologne Opera Ballet, WGer, 89. *Exhib:* Plastic Presence, Jewish Mus, New York, 69; Flint Invitational, Mich, 70; Toledo Mus Art, Ohio, 70; Paintings & Sculptures of Today, Indianapolis Mus Art, Ind, 70; Highlights of the Season, Aldrich Mus Contemp Art, 70; Queens Mus, New York, 72; Fischbach Gallery, New York, 81. *Teaching:* PUC Univ, Rio de Janeiro, Brazil. *Media:* Acrylic. *Dealer:* Bonino Gallery 48 Great Jones St New York NY 10001; Fischbach Gallery 29 W 57th St New York NY 10019. *Mailing Add:* 109 W 26th St New York NY 10001

BRUSH, GLORIA (ELIZABETH) DEFILIPPS
PHOTOGRAPHER, EDUCATOR
b Chicago, Ill, Mar 29, 47. *Study:* Sch Art Inst Chicago, BFA, 68, MFA, 72; and asst to Sonia Landy Sheridan. *Work:* Polaroid Int Collection; Philadelphia Mus Art; Film in the Cities, St Paul, Minn; Minneapolis Inst Arts; Bryn Mawr Col; Los Angeles Co Mus of Art (Nash Collection); Tweed Mus Art, Duluth, Minn; Kresge Art Mus, Mich State Univ; and many private collections. *Exhib:* Santa Barbara Mus Art, 79, Photokina, Cologne, 92 & Los Angeles Co Mus Art, 91; Minn Mus Art, 82; Solo exhibs, Film in the Cities, St Paul, 84, Real Art Ways, Hartford, 85, Print Club, Philadelphia, 85, Contemp Arts Ctr, New Orleans, 87, Plains Art Mus, Moorhead, Minn, 88 & Clarence Kennedy Gallery, Cambridge, 88; Minneapolis Inst Arts, 85 & 86; Kohler Arts Ctr, 87 & 90; Ctr Photog, Woodstock, 88, The Light Factory, 91. *Pos:* arts policy adv, Charles K Blandin Found, 80-83; Arrowhead Regional Arts Coun, 81-83; bd mem, 89-; panel mem, Minn Artists Exhib Prog, 85-87. *Teaching:* Asst prof photog, Univ Minn, Duluth, 81-85, assoc prof & head, dept art, 85-; prof & dept head, 89- *Awards:* Minn State Arts Bd Grant, 82 & 87; Nat Endowment Arts Photogr Fel, 83; Bush Found Artist Fel, 84; Film in the Cities/McKnight Photo Fel, 85, 90. *Bibliog:* Ron Glowen (auth), article, Artweek, 2/5/83; Todd Maitland (ed), Making Art: Interviews with Ten Minn Artists, Minneapolis Inst Arts, 86; Chris Waddingotn (auth), rev, Artpaper, 4/88; Kelly Wise (auth), rev, Boston Globe, 12/1/88; Holt Confer (auth), article, Polaroid Photo Educ, Vol 6, No 1, 89. *Publ:* Auth, Photographing small scale objects: History, context & format, Leonardo, Vol XX, No 3, 87. *Mailing Add:* 2909 Jefferson St Duluth MN 55812

BRUSH, LEIF
SOUND SCULPTOR, INSTRUCTOR
b Bridgeport, Ill, Mar 28, 32. *Study:* Art Inst Chicago, dipl(fel), 70, MFA(fel), 72. *Work:* Mills Col Libr; Inst Recherche Coord Acoustique & Musique Libr; Audio Arts Libr, London; and others. *Comn:* Minn Dept Trans/State Arts Bd, Milaca, 86. *Exhib:* Minneapolis Inst Arts, 77, 79, 86 & 89; Walker Art Ctr, Minneapolis, 79 & 80; Neuberger Mus, Purchase, NY, 81; Suono/Ambiente/Musica, Milan, Italy, 82; Minneapolis Col Art & Design, 82; Hudson River Mus, New York, 82; Mail Music, Monza, Italy, 83; New Music Am, 80, 87; Yellow Springs Inst, Chester Sps, Pa, 87; The Aerial (cassette/CD), Nonsequitur, Issue 4, 92. *Pos:* Vis artist, Univ Victoria, 73, Univ Colo, 75, State Univ NY, Alfred, 76, Univ Md, Baltimore Co, 77, Wright State Univ, 78, Art Res Ctr, Kansas City, Univ NDak & ZBS Found, Fort Edward, NY, 79; res artist, Visual Studies Workshop, 84. *Teaching:* Instr audible constructs, Art Inst Chicago, 70-72; asst prof, Univ Iowa, Iowa City, 72-76; asst prof sculpture, Univ Minn, Duluth, 76-79, assoc prof, 79-87, prof, 87- *Awards:* Fels, Jerome Found, 82 & Nat Endowment Arts, 73 & 83; Bush Found, 80; Minn Percent for the Arts, 86. *Bibliog:* Oscar Brand (auth), Voices in the Wind, Nat Pub Radio, 75; Jerome Downs & Stewart Turnquist (dir), Leif Brush: Inside the Hidden Landscape (videotape), Minneapolis Inst Arts, 78; KTCA, New Music (videotape), Minneapolis, 80; Musicworks 30, Toronto, Ont, 85; Buma Stemra Mag, Holland, 10/85; David Moss (prod) Art You Can Hear, NPR, 86; New Music America, Am Pub Radio Network, 88; Soundviews: Sources, Nonsequitur, Santa Fe, 90. *Publ:* Contribr, Fifth Assembling, New York, 75; Soundings, Neuberger Mus, 81; Ear Mag, Vol IX, No 5, New York, 85; contrib, New Music America, Hartford, 84; Leonardo, Pergamon, Vol 17, 84 & Vol 23, Issue 20, 90; Musicworks, Toronto, 85; Experimental Musica Instruments, vol VII, no 5, 92. *Mailing Add:* 2909 Jefferson Ct Duluth MN 55812

BRUST, ROBERT GUSTAVE
PAINTER, WRITER
b Pittsburgh, Pa, Aug 14, 45. *Study:* Carnegie Mellon Univ, BA, 68, Conn Col, MA, 75. *Work:* Blue Cross Western Pa; Monroeville Pub Libr, Pa. *Exhib:* Three Rivers Arts Festival, Carnegie Mus Art, Pittsburgh, 80 & 90; Non Members Ann, Salmagundi Club, New York, 85 & 86; Nat Soc Painters in Casein & Acrylic Ann & Audubon Artist Ann, Nat Arts, 88; Westmoreland Art Nat, Westmoreland Co Community Col, Youngwood, Pa, 90; Associated Artists of Pittsburgh Ann, Carnegie Mus Arts, 92; W&J Nat Painting Show, Olin Fine Arts Ctr Gallery, Washington & Jefferson Col, Washington, Pa, 92. *Teaching:* Instr, painting, design & color, Pa Art Asn, Penn Hills, 82-83 & 87-89 & demonstr, acrylic & oil painting 83-92; demonstr, Suburban Artists League, Murrysville, Pa, 92. *Awards:* Best of Show, Penn Art Asn, 84, 85, 87, 89 & 90. *Bibliog:* Niles Campbell (auth), Photography influences perception of art, Pittsburgh Business Times, 7/88; Jane Crawford (auth), Painter brings nature's brilliance to light, Pittsburgh Post-Gazette, 8/88; Donald Miller (auth), Today at the arts festival, Pittsburgh Post-Gazette, 6/90. *Mem:* Penn Hills Arts Coun (bd mem, currently); Pa Art Asn (bd mem, pres 78-80); Artists Equity Asn, Pittsburgh Chap (bd mem, vpres 88-90); Pittsburgh Soc Artists; Assoc Artists Pittsburgh. *Media:* All Media. *Publ:* Coauth, Picture perception: An alternative view of reversible Figures, Arts Educ Int J, 73; E & A, Penn Art Asn Newsletter, 78-92; Interaction effects of picture & caption on humor ratings of cartoons, J of Social Psychology, 79; Humor & interpersonal attraction, J of Personality Assessment, 85. *Dealer:* Pittsburgh Ctr for the Arts 6300 Fifth Ave Pittsburgh PA 15232; Studio Z Gallery 1415 E Carson St Pittsburgh PA 15203. *Mailing Add:* 836 Hamil Rd Verona PA 15147-2926

BRUSTLEIN, DANIEL
PAINTER
b Mulhouse, France, Sept 11, 04; US citizen. *Study:* Ecole des Arts, Geneva, Switz, cert of capacity. *Work:* Centre Nat d'Art Contemp, Mus Pompidou, Paris, France; Ministere des Affaires Culturelles, Paris; Baltimore Mus. *Exhib:* Corcoran Gallery Ann, Washington, DC, 58; Nat Inst Arts & Lett, 67; Patricia Learmonth Gallery, New York, 77; Am Painters in the French Nat Collections, Centre Beaubourg, Paris, 77; A M Sachs Gallery, New York, 78 & 81; La Famille des Portraits, Mus des Arts Decoratifs with Mus du Louve, Paris, 79-80; Musée Cantini, Marseilles, France; La Famille des Portraits, Mus des Arts Decoratifs with Mus du Louvre, Paris, 79-80; Greenbaum Gallery, New York; Galerie Jocob, Paris; and others. *Awards:* Premiere Selection du Prix P L Weiller, Mus Marmottan, Paris, 71; Chevalier des Arts et des Lettres, Paris. *Bibliog:* Cover illus, 10/60 & Jack Tworkov (auth), Religious art without God, 11/64, Art News. *Mailing Add:* 8 rue de General Bertrand Paris 75007 France

BRUTOSKY, (SISTER) MARY VERONICA, CSJ
PAINTER, PRINTMAKER
b Connellsville, Pa, Apr 27, 32. *Study:* Otis Art Inst, Los Angeles, BFA, 75, Calif State Univ, Fresno, MA (painting), 84; Studied with Joseph Mugnaini, Emerson Wolfer & Charles White. *Comn:* Two ceramic side altars, Our Lady of Guadalupe Church, Hermosa Beach, Calif, 72; Wall sculptures, Abbey Press, St Meinrad, Ind, 73; Two etched glass doors (designs), Our Lady of Guadalupe Church, Los Angeles, 76; set of 10 calligraphic scripture cards for Printery House, St Louis, Mo. *Exhib:* Closer Than We Think, Los Angeles Artists Call Against Us Intervention in Central America, Univ Relig Ctr, Univ Southern Calif Contemp Art Galleries, West Hollywood, Calif, 72-80; Easter Light: New Life, West Bend Gallery, Wis, 92. *Pos:* Founder & dir, Int Registry for Religious Women Artists, 78-; dir, Art Space Gallery, 84-86. *Teaching:* Instr screenprinting, Calif State Univ, Fresno, 82-84; instr gallery practices, Fresno City Col, Cal, 84-86, writing, 84- *Bibliog:* Nena Bryans (auth), Full Circle, Schuyler Inst Worship Arts, 88. *Mem:* Midwest Area Relig Talent; Cath Fine Arts Soc. *Media:* Oil; Computer-Generated Serigraphy. *Publ:* Auth, Art Ministry (booklet), 78; Mining the Gold, Sisters Today, 1/91. *Dealer:* Polly Brewer Plums Contemp Arts Gallery Fresno CA. *Mailing Add:* 1315 N Van Ness Ave Fresno CA 93728-1937

BRYAN, JACK L
PAINTER, EDUCATOR
b Lawton, Okla, Aug 30, 42. *Study:* Univ Okla, BFA, 65, post-grad work, 73-74; Tulsa Univ, MA(art hist, hons), 67. *Exhib:* Handmade Book Exhibition, Cameron Univ Gallery, Lawton, Okla, 81; Artist's Books: From the Traditional to the Avant-Garde, Rutgers Univ, NJ, 82; Breaking the Bindings: American Book Art Now, Elvehjem Mus, Madison, Wis, 83; Objects in Transition: Contemporary Book Art, Temari Ctr, Honolulu, 84; Arts Festival 1985, Carrier Found, Belle Mead, NJ. *Teaching:* Chmn dept art, Cameron Univ, Lawton, Okla, 67- *Awards:* Teacher of the Year, Lawton Arts & Humanities Coun, 84. *Mem:* Nat Asn Sch Art & Design; Okla Summer Arts Inst; Leslie Powell Found (bd dirs). *Media:* Oil, Clay. *Publ:* Illusr, Meadowlark, 81, Cross Stitch, 82 & Southwest Pass, 83, Valentine Series, Hosanna Press, Chicago. *Mailing Add:* 10 NW 35th St Lawton OK 73505

BRYANS, JOHN ARMOND
INSTRUCTOR, PAINTER
b Marion, Ohio, July 21, 25. *Study:* Ringling Sch Art, Sarasota, Fla, 47-49; Burnsville Painting Classes, NC, 48-50; Jerry Farnsworth Studio, Sarasota, 50. *Work:* Columbus Mus, Ga; Abilene Mus & McMurray Col, Abilene, Tex; Muskingum Col, New Concord, Ohio; Appalachian State Univ, Boone, NC. *Comn:* Murals, Foundry Methodist Church, DC, 72 & 78, Coral Gables Methodist Church, Fla, 83. *Exhib:* 7th, 9th, 10th & 12th Ann Area Exhib, Corcoran Gallery Art, 52, 55, 56 & 58; Md Regional, Baltimore Mus, 57; Ga Watercolor Nat, 85 & 92; Irene Leach Mem, Chrysler Mus, Norfolk, 88;

Watercolor USA, Springfield Mus, 89; Aqueous Nat, Louisville, KY, 92; Adirondacks Nat, Old Forge, NY, 92; and others. *Teaching:* Instr drawing & painting, Hill's Art Sch, Arlington, Va, 52-77; head dept art, McLean Arts Ctr, Va, 65-73 & 78-; co-dir, Painting in the Mountains, Burnsville, NC, 65-83; instr watercolor, Md Col Art & Design, Silver Spring, 80-81. *Awards:* Award Winner, Seasoned Eye Three Competition, Mod Maturity Mag, 89; Awards, Va Watercolor Soc, 91 & 92; Second Award, Baltimore Watercolor Soc, Mid Atlantic Regional, 92. *Mem:* Southern Watercolor Soc; Potomac Valley Watercolorists; Va Watercolor Soc; Ky Watercolor Soc; Ga Watercolor Soc. *Media:* Watercolor, Acrylic. *Mailing Add:* 2264 N Vernon St Arlington VA 22207

BRYANT, EDWARD ALBERT
WRITER, CONSULTANT
b Lenoir, NC, July 23, 28. *Study:* Univ NC, Chapel Hill, BA(art), 50 MA(art hist) with Clemens Sommer, 55; Univ Pisa, Fulbright Grant, 54-55; Univ Ravenna, cert(Byzantine art), 55; Brooklyn Mus Training Prog, fel, 57-58. *Work:* Munson-Williams-Proctor Inst, Utica, NY. *Exhib:* Drawings USA, St Paul Art Ctr, Minn, 64; Nat Graphic Arts & Drawing Exhib, Wichita Art Asn, 67; Drawing & Small Sculpture Ann, Ball State Univ, 67; Piedmont Graphics, Mint Mus Art, Charlotte, NC, 67; Artists of Cent New York Ann, Munson-Williams-Proctor Inst, 72, 76 & 77; and many one-man exhibs. *Collections Arranged:* Beaumont Newhall & Willard Midgette, 81, Marion Faller, Scott Hyde, Ellen Carey, Bart Parker, Joan Lyons, Bonnie Gordon, Michael Bishop, John Pfahl, John Divola, James McGarrell, 82, Ana Mendieta, Carl Andre, Leon Golub, Nancy Spero, 83, Univ Art Mus, Univ NMex; Geometric Formalism in American Art; Concepts & Issues in Contemporary Art Series, 82-84, Univ Art Mus, NMex; and many others. *Pos:* Gen cur, Wadsworth Atheneum, Hartford, Conn, 59-61; assoc cur, Whitney Mus Am Art, New York, 61-65; dir, Univ Gallery, Univ Ky, 65-68, Picker Gallery, Colgate Univ, 68-80 & Univ Art Mus, Univ NMex, 80-84. *Teaching:* Asst prof art hist & studio courses, Univ Ky, 65-68; assoc prof, Colgate Univ, 68-80, chairperson dept fine arts, 76-77; prof, Univ NMex, 80- *Awards:* Mus Prof Fel Grant, Nat Endowment Arts, 74. *Mem:* Col Art Asn. *Media:* Watercolor, All Drawing Media. *Res:* 20th century artists, primarily Americans, Italians; 19th century sepulchral sculpture. *Publ:* Coauth, Forty Under Forty, 62; auth, Jack Tworkov, 84; Robert Broderson: 32 Drawings, Duke Univ, 64; contribr, Art in Educational Institutions in the United States, Scarecrow, 74; auth, Joseph Pennell's New York Etchings, Dover, 80. *Mailing Add:* 1400 Marron Circle NE Albuquerque NM 87112

BRYANT, LAURA MILITZER
WEAVER, PAINTER
b Detroit, Mich, Mar 3, 55. *Study:* Univ Mich Sch Art, BFA, 78. *Exhib:* Albright Knox Art Gallery, Buffalo, NY, 92; Craft Art in Wetern NY, Birchfield Art Ctr, Buffalo, 92; Fine Crafts at Matrix, Matrix Gallery, Sacramento, Calif, 92. *Teaching:* Lectr fabric design & color, State Univ Col Buffalo, 87-89. *Awards:* Grant, Nat Endowment Arts, 90; Vern Stein Fine Art Award, Albright Knox Art Gallery, 92. *Mem:* Am Craft Coun. *Media:* Acrylic, Oil. *Dealer:* Modern Art Gallery 49 In The Miramar Sarasota FL 34236. *Mailing Add:* 3376 Bayshore Blvd NE St Petersburg FL 33103

BRYANT, LINDA GOODE
ART DEALER, GALLERY DIRECTOR
b Columbus, Ohio, July 21, 49. *Study:* Spelman Col, BA, 72; City Univ New York, MA candidate. *Pos:* Dir, Just Above Midtown Gallery, New York, 74-86; dir educ, Studio Mus in Harlem, 74-75; panelist, NY State Coun on the Arts & DCA, 77-86; freelance artist. *Awards:* Grad Intern, Metrop Mus, 73, Rockefeller Fel, 73-74. *Bibliog:* Satterwhite (auth), Black Dealer/57th St, New York Post, 11/74; USA's Linda Bryant, African Woman, 76; Essence Woman, Essence Mag, 7/77. *Res:* American abstract art; theory on stylistic development in the 1970s termed contextures. *Specialty:* New and emerging artists working in contexturalist vein; utilizing materials not heretofore used as primary in art object (smoke, hair, clothes, nylon mesh). *Publ:* Co-auth, Contextures (American Abstract Art 1945-1978), Just Above Midtown, 78. *Mailing Add:* 215 W 90th St New York NY 10024

BRYANT, OLEN L
SCULPTOR, EDUCATOR
b Cookeville, Tenn, May 4, 27. *Study:* Murray State Col, BS; Cranbrook Acad Art, MFA; Inst Allende, San Miguel, Mex; Cleveland Inst Art; Art Students League. *Work:* Tenn Fine Arts Ctr Collection, Nashville; Hunter Gallery, Chattanooga, Tenn; Carroll Reece Mus, Johnson City, Tenn. *Comn:* Aura, St Phillips Episcopal Church, Franklin, Tenn, 87; The Actors, Tenn Performing Arts Ctr, Nashville, Tenn, 85; Sentinel, Austin Peay State Univ, Austin, 80 & Seeds, Libr, 87; Humanitarian Awards, Country Music Found, 86-89. *Exhib:* One-man shows, Tenn Fine Arts Ctr, 68 & 82, Hunter Gallery, 69, Evansville Mus, Ind, 70, Haas Gallery Bloomsburg, Pa, 71, Morehead Univ, 71 & Vanderbuilt Gallery, Nashville, 83. *Teaching:* Instr art, Shaker Heights Schs, Ohio, 58-61; instr art, Union Univ, 62-65; prof art, Austin Peay Univ, 66-91. *Mem:* Am Crafts Coun. *Media:* Wood, Clay. *Mailing Add:* 536 York St Clarksville TN 37040

BRYANT, TAMARA THOMPSON See Thompson, Tamara

BRYCE, EILEEN ANN
PAINTER
b Tulsa, Okla, June 8, 53. *Study:* Inst European Studies, Vienna, Austria, 73; Southern Methodist Univ, BFA, 75; Univ Tulsa, MA, 78. *Work:* Chautauqua Art Mus, New York. *Exhib:* Chautauqua Nat Exhib of Am Art, Chautauqua Art Mus, New York, 81; Art Ann Two, Okla Art Ctr, Oklahoma City, 81; Tex Fine Arts Asn Nat Exhib, Laguna Gloria Mus, Austin, 82; Alexandria Mus Visual Arts, La, 82; First Ann, Provincetown Art Mus, Mass, 83; Nat Print & Drawing Exhib, Lee Hall Gallery, Clemson Univ, 83. *Awards:* Purchase Prize, Chautauqua Nat Exhib Am Art, New York, 80; Plaque of Distinction, Marietta Nat Exhib Am Art, 81; Painting Award, Alexandria Mus Vis Arts Invitational, 82. *Bibliog:* Articles, Art Voices, 9-10/81 & Tulsa Mag, 6/82; Arts Chronicle, Okla Educ TV Authority, 82. *Media:* Oils, Acrylic. *Dealer:* Leslie Levy Gallery 7141 Main St Scottsdale AZ 85251. *Mailing Add:* 1732 S College Tulsa OK 74104

BRYCE, MARK ADAMS
PAINTER, PRINTMAKER
b San Francisco, Calif, July 4, 53. *Study:* Philadelphia Col Art, 69-71; Pa Acad Fine Arts, with Hobson Pitman, Morris Blockburn & Arthur DeCosta, 70-74. *Work:* Free Libr Philadelphia; Moore Col Art; FMC Corp. *Comn:* Portrait, comn by Marian Locks, Philadelphia, 76; Bishop White House-Independence Hall Trompe'l Oeil Comn, Philadelphia, Pa. *Exhib:* Earth Art, Philadelphia Civic Ctr Mus, 73; Int Competition, Philadelphia Print Club, 75; Currents, NJ State Mus, Trenton, 76; solo exhibs, Marian Locks Gallery, Philadelphia, 76, 78 & 85, Butcher & More, 81, Del Art Mus, Wilmington, 83 & Somerville-Manning Gallery 84 & 86; Philadelphia Painters, Southern Allegheny Mus Art, Pa, 82; Nat Mid-Year Show, Butler Inst Am Art, 82; group show, Reading Mus Art, 84; Allan Stone Gallery, New York, 88-89; Contemp Philadelphia Art, Philadelphia Mus Art, Pa, 90. *Teaching:* Instr drawing, Philadelphia Col Art, 80-82; lectr painting, Wilmington Soc Fine Arts, 83-84. *Awards:* Outstanding Painting, Earth Art, Philadelphia Civic Ctr Mus, 74; Charles Smith Endowment Prize, Woodmere Open, 76; Award Merit, Reading Art Mus, 83. *Bibliog:* David Fathergill Quinlan (auth), Raissónné (catalog), NJ, 85. *Media:* Oil, Pencil; Lithography. *Publ:* Am Artist, 90. *Mailing Add:* c/o Somerville Manning Art Gallery Greenville Ctr Suite E129 Greenville DE 19807

BRYCELEA, CLIFFORD
PAINTER, PRINTMAKER
b Shiprock, NMex, Sept 26, 53. *Study:* Ft Lewis Col, Colo, study with Mick Reber & Stan Englehart, BA(art), 75. *Work:* Los Angeles Athletic Club, Calif; Transcoe Co, Houston, Tex; Norwest Bank & Jackson David Bottling Co, Durango, Colo; Albuquerque Federal Savings And Loan Asn, NMex; Burns Nat Bank & Tamarron Resort, Durango, Colo; and others. *Comn:* Mural, The Indian Ctr, Ft Lewis Col, Colo, 73; mural, Ft Lewis Administration, Colo, 74; mural, The Indian Ctr, Durango, Colo, 74; Dulce High Sch, 83. *Exhib:* Gallup Ceremonial, Red Rock Park, NMex, 76-81; Am Inst Contemp Art Ann, San Dimas Exhib Hall, Calif, 80-82; Navajo Show, Mus Northern Ariz, Flagstaff, 80-82; Death Valley 49'ers Show, Mus Death Valley, Calif, 81; Indian Shows, Navajo Tribal Mus, Window Rock, Ariz, 82; Indian Market, Santa Fe, NMex, 80-92; IACA Markets, Denver & Mesa, Ariz, 87-92. *Awards:* Purchase Awards, NMex Watercolor Soc II, 76 & NMex State Fair, 77; Gold Medal Winner, Am Indian & Cowboy Asn Show, 81; 1st Place & Mem Award, Gallup Ceremonial Gallups NMex. *Bibliog:* Carey Vicanti (auth), Clifford Brycelea, Jicarilla Chirtain Newspaper, 6/81; Julie Pearson (auth), Southwest Art Mag, 6/92. *Mem:* Indian Arts & Crafts Asn; Am Indian & Cowboy Asn. *Media:* Acrylic, Watercolor; Stonelitho, Photoprint. *Publ:* Illusr, Am Way Mag, 77; contribr, Art Fever, Gallery West Inc, 81; contribr, Haunted Mesa, Bantam Books, 82; illusr, Pieces of White Shell, 84; Southwest Art Mag, 92. *Dealer:* Tohatin Gallery 145 W Nineth St Durango CO 81301; Ray Tracey Gallery 135 W Palace Ave Santa Fe NM 87501. *Mailing Add:* 1721 Montano St Santa Fe NM 87501

BRZOZOWSKI, RICHARD JOSEPH
PAINTER
b New Britain, Conn, Sept 9, 32. *Study:* Paier Art Sch, New Haven, Conn. *Work:* Grumbacher Collection, New York; Phoenix Mutual Inst, Hartford, Conn; Springfield Mus Art, Mass; CBT Bank, Hartford, Conn; Otis Elevator, Farmington, Conn. *Exhib:* Allied Artists, 91-92; Copley Soc, Boston, Mass, 91-92; Am Watercolor Soc, 83 & 86, 90; Adirondacks Nat Exhib Am Watercolors, 90 & 92; Watercolor USA, 91; Nat Acad Design, 92; and others. *Awards:* Grumbacker Gold Medal; Nat Soc Painters Casein & Acrylic, 90; Nicolas Reale Award, Allied Artists, 91; and others. *Mem:* Am Watercolor Soc (bd dirs, 87-88, corresp secy, 4th vpres); Conn Watercolor Soc (bd dirs, 69-70); Nat Soc Painters Casein & Acrylics (bd dirs); Allied Artists Am; Copley Soc Boston. *Media:* Watercolor, Acrylic. *Mailing Add:* 13 Fox Rd Plainville CT 06062

BUBA, JOY FLINSCH
SCULPTOR, ILLUSTRATOR
b Lloyd's Neck, NY, July 25, 04. *Study:* Eberle Studio, New York; Staedel Kunst Inst, Frankfurt, Ger; Art Acad, Munich, Ger; also with Theodor Kaerner & Angelo Yank. *Work:* Metrop Mus Art, New York; Florence Sabin, Statuary Hall, Capitol Bldg, Washington, DC; Nat Portrait Gallery, Washington, DC; John D Rockefeller, Jr, Rockefeller Plaza, New York; Pope Paul VI, Vatican Mus. *Comn:* Bust of Pope John Paul II, St Patrick's Cathedral, New York. *Exhib:* Roger Tory Peterson, Nat Sculpture Soc Exhib. *Mem:* Fel Nat Sculpture Soc. *Publ:* Illusr, Elephants, Proboscidea Memoir; Elephants, Rabbits, Frogs & Toads, Goldfish; Written in Sand; Lyrico, the Only Horse of His Kind. *Mailing Add:* 8 Wagon Trail Black Mountain NC 28711

BUBRISKI, KEVIN E
PHOTOGRAPHER
b North Adams, Mass, Nov 29, 54. *Study:* Bowdoin Col, BA. *Work:* Yale Univ Art Gallery, New Haven, Conn; Mus Mod Art, Met Mus Art, New

York; San Francisco Mus Mod Art, Calif. *Exhib:* Mus Photog Art, San Diego, Calif, 90; In Tibet, traveling exhib, 91; Introductions, Robert Koch Gallery, 91; Contemp Photo Journalism, ICP Uptown Gallery, New York, 91. *Pos:* Fine Art Photog. *Teaching:* Instr photog, Harvard Univ, summer 92. *Awards:* Fel of Film Studies Ctr, Harvard Univ, 85-88; Nat Endowment Arts, 88; Fulbright Award, 89-90. *Publ:* Auth, A Fine Art Book: Portrait of Nepal, fall 93. *Dealer:* Robert Koch 49 Geary St 5th Fl San Francisco CA 94108. *Mailing Add:* 817 Main St Bennington UT 05201

BUCH, GARY
PAINTER
b Harrisburg, Pa, Nov 5, 54. *Study:* Bloomsburg Univ, Pa, 72-76; Cent Wash Univ, Ellensburg, MFA(painting), 80; Skowhegan Sch Painting & Sculpture, 84. *Exhib:* 10th Annual Works on Paper Exhib, SW Tex State Univ, 79; Pacific NW Arts Festival, Bellevue Mus, Wash, 81; Maine Invitational, Bowdoin Col, Brunswick, Maine, 83; Inaugural Exhib, Barn Gallery, Ogunquit, Maine, 84; one-man shows, Hobe Sound Galleries, Portland, Maine, 84 & 87, Fla, 87 & Midtown Galleries, New York, 86; Maine Biennial, Portland Mus Art, 85. *Teaching:* Grad teaching asst painting & drawing, Cent Wash Univ, 78-80; vis artist, Salisbury Sch, Conn, 85- *Awards:* Marguerite Zorach Scholar, Skowhegan Sch Painting & Sculpture, 84; Sports Renault Award, 85. *Bibliog:* Douglas C McGill (auth), Personal art, the Skowhegan experience, NY Times, 9/84; Edgar Allen Beam (auth), Gary Buch has made it, Maine Times, 3/86; Lorraine Karafel (auth), Gary Buch, Art News, 5/86. *Dealer:* Midtown Payson Galleries 745 Fifth Ave New York NY 10151. *Mailing Add:* 1085 Washington Ave Portland ME 04103

BUCHANAN, JOHN EDWARD, JR
MUSEUM DIRECTOR, ADMINISTRATOR
b Nashville, Tenn, July, 24, 53. *Study:* Univ Col, Oxford Univ, England, 73; Univ South, BA(fine arts, hon), 75; Vanderbilt Univ, MA(art hist), 79. *Work:* Tenn State Mus, Nashville. *Collections Arranged:* The Passion of Rodin: Sculpture from the B Gerald Cantor Collection, 88; Heirs to Impressionism: Andre and Berth Noufflard, 88-89; The World of Toulouse-Lautrec featuring The Guardsmark Collection (auth, catalog); Louis XV and Madame de Pompadour: A Love Affair with Style (auth, catalog); Odilon Redon: The Ian Woodner Collection (auth, catalog). *Pos:* Coordr mus develop, Tenn State Mus, 78-80; mus assessment prog coordr, Am Asn Mus, Washington, DC, 80-82; exec dir, Lakeview Mus Arts & Sci, Peoria, Ill, 82-86; dir, The Dixon Gallery & Gardens, Memphis, Tenn, 86- *Mem:* Am Asn Mus; Asn Art Mus Dirs; Art Mus Asn. *Publ:* Auth, Resources for Small Museums and Historic Sites, Tenn State Mus, rev ed 79; Professional Concern Checklist, Am Asn Mus, 80; The new museum assessment program, Mus News, 7-8/80; An applicant's map to the museum assessment program, Hist News, 9/80. *Mailing Add:* c/o Dixon Gallery & Gardens 4339 Park Ave Memphis TN 38117

BUCHANAN, NANCY
VIDEO ARTIST, CONCEPTUAL ARTIST
b Boston, Mass, Aug 30, 46. *Study:* Univ of Calif, Irvine, BA, 69, MFA, 71. *Work:* Mus Mod Art, New York; Mus Contemp Art, La Jolla, Calif; Mus Art, Long Beach, Calif; Allen Mem Art Mus, Oberlin, Ohio. *Exhib:* API Nat Video Fest, Am Film Inst, Los Angeles, 84 & 91; Video Drive-in, Mod Art Center, Lisbon, Portugal, 89; New Television, WHET, KCET, KGBH, NY, Los Angeles & Boston, 89 & 90; The 90's various PBS stations, NY, Calif & Chicago, 91; New Calif Video, Long Beach Mus, 91; Committed Visions, Mus Mod Art, New York, 92. *Teaching:* Asst Prof non-static art, Univ Wis, Madison, 82-84; live action fac video production, Calif Inst Arts, Valencia, 85-92. *Awards:* Individual Artist's Fel (video), 83 & 89 & Western States Media Arts Fel, 87, Nat Endowment Arts. *Bibliog:* Nancy Grub (ed), Making Their Mark: Women Artists Move into the Mainstream, Abbeville Press, 89; Christine Tamblyn (dir) & Doug Hall & Sally Jo Fifer (eds), Significant Others, Illuminating Video, Aperture, 91. *Dealer:* Video Data Bank 37 S Wabash Chicago Ill 60603. *Mailing Add:* c/o San Francisco Art Institute Emanuel Walter & Atholl McBean Galleries 800 Chestnut St San Francisco CA 94133

BUCHANAN, SIDNEY ARNOLD
EDUCATOR, SCULPTOR
b Superior, Wis, Sept 12, 32. *Study:* Univ Minn, Duluth, BA, 62; NMex Highlands Univ, Las Vegas, MA, 63. *Work:* Sheldon Mem Art Gallery, Univ of Nebr, Lincoln; Joslyn Art Mus, Omaha, Nebr; Springfield Art Mus, Mo; Jacksonville Art Mus, Fla; City Art Gallery, Manchester, Eng. *Comn:* Sculpture, City of Omaha, Cent Park Mall, 82; sculpture, Wayne State Col, 83; sculpture (26'), Omaha Int Airport, 86; sculpture new bldg Omaha, Eurou Corp Am, 91; sculpture (46' high & 50 ton), Kutak Found Univ Nebr, Omaha, 92. *Exhib:* Midwest Biennial, 64-70 & Nebr 75, 75, Joslyn Art Mus, Omaha, Nebr; Mid-Am Exhib, William Rockhill Nelson Gallery of Art , Atkins Mus Fine Arts, Kansas City, Mo, 65-66; Colo/Nebr Exchange Exhib, Omaha & Denver, 67; Report on the Sixties, Denver Art Mus, 69; Northwestern Biennial, SDak Mem Art Ctr, 72; one-man shows, Turner Park, Nebr, 80 & Sheldon Mem Gallery, Univ Nebr, Lincoln, 86, Col St Mary, Omaha, 89-90. *Pos:* Vis sculptor, Manchester Col of Art & Design, Eng, 69-70; artist-in-residence, Southern Ill Univ, Edwardsville, 72, Bemidji State Col, Minn, 75 & Plattsburg State Univ, 78. *Teaching:* Prof sculpture, Univ of Nebr, Omaha, 64- *Awards:* Purchase Awards, Midwest Biennial, Joslyn Art Mus, Omaha, Nebr, 64-66 & Western Wash State Col, 67; Nat Endowment for the Arts Grant, 75. *Bibliog:* Dr Judith Van Wagner (auth), Metal Paintings, Leonardo Mag, Spring 77 & Award Winning Sculpture, Margaret Harold Publ, 67. *Media:* Steel, Aluminum. *Dealer:* Gallery 72 2709 Leavenworth Omaha NE 68105. *Mailing Add:* 1202 S 62nd St Omaha NE 68106

BUCHER, FRANCOIS
HISTORIAN, EDUCATOR
b Lausanne, Switz, June 11, 27; US citizen. *Study:* Univ Bern, Switz, PhD, 55; Brown Univ, Hon MA, 61. *Pos:* Mem exec comt, Acad Spoleto, 65- & Int Ctr Medieval Art, 68-; pres, Nautilus Found, Lloyd, Fla, 87- *Teaching:* From instr to asst prof art hist, Yale Univ, 54-60; assoc prof, Brown Univ, 60-63 & Princeton Univ, 63-70; prof, State Univ NY, Binghamton, 70-77, co-dir, Ctr Medieval & Early Renaissance Studies, 73-76; prof, Fla State Univ, Tallahassee, 78- *Awards:* Guggenheim Fel, 58; Am Coun Learned Soc Grant, 59; Inst Advan Studies Fel, 62-63; Pres Nautilus Found, Lloyd, Fla. *Mem:* Medieval Acad Am; Col Art Asn Am; Soc Archit Historians; fel Int Ctr Medieval Art. *Media:* History of Art, Writing. *Res:* Medieval architecture; contemporary art. *Collection:* Permanent collection World art and Prints, Nautilus Foundation, 91- *Publ:* Auth, Josef Albers, Despite Straight Lines, Yale Univ Press, 69, rev ed MIT Press, 77; The Pamplona Bibles, Yale Univ Press, 70; The Dresden sketch-book of vault projection, Acts 22nd Int Cong Art Hist, 71; Nature in the visual arts of the Middle Ages, Tenth Ann Conf Ctr Medieval & Early Renaissance Studies, State Univ NY Press, 78; Architector, Medieval Lodge-books, Abaris Press, 79; Ein Strahlendes Ende, Bertelsmann, Munich, 84. *Mailing Add:* Dept Art Hist Fla State Univ Tallahassee FL 32306

BUCHMAN, ARLES (ARLETTE BUCHMAN)
PAINTER, ASSEMBLAGE ARTIST
b Liverpool, England; US citizen. *Study:* Lycee Jules Ferry, Paris, France; Herne Bay Collegiate Sch, England; Silvermine Art Sch, Conn. *Work:* Randolph-Macon Col, NC; Guild Hall, Easthampton, NY. *Comn:* Mem portrait, Ardsley Sch, New York. *Exhib:* Parrish Art Mus, Southampton, NY; Monmouth Mus, NJ; Inst Mod Art, New York. *Pos:* Pres, Victor D'Amico Inst Art, 85-91. *Teaching:* Instr art, Mus Mod Art, 61-71; Metro Mus Art, 71-80; Victor D'Amico Inst Art, 63-90. *Awards:* First Prize, Westchester Art Soc, 70; Best Abstract, Nat Asn Woman Art, 89. *Bibliog:* Brian O Doherty (auth), Art, wide variety display, NY Times, 62; Robert Blaisdell (auth), An Artist-Teacher, Video VDIA, 90. *Mem:* Nat Asn Women Artists; NY State Teachers Asn; Mamaroneck Artists Guild; Jimmy Ernst Alliance. *Media:* Multi-media. *Publ:* Coauth, Assemblage, Mus Mod Art, 70; auth, Palate to Palate, Times Book, 78; contribr, Jardin des Modes, France, 82; auth, You're Never Too Thin or Too Rich, Southampton, 88. *Dealer:* Media-Loft 50 Webster Ave New Rochelle NY 10801. *Mailing Add:* Eight Wildwood Cir Larchmont NY 10835

BUCHMAN, JAMES WALLACE
SCULPTOR
b Memphis, Tenn, Dec 3, 48. *Study:* Dartmouth Col, BA; Skowhegan Sch Painting & Sculpture. *Work:* Mus Fine Arts, Springfield, Mass. *Comn:* 1980 Olympic Games, Lake Placid, NY; Gen Serv Admin, Pittsfield, Mass. *Exhib:* one-man shows, Sculpture Now Inc, 75, Max Hutchinson Gallery, 79 & 83 & Haenah-Kent, New York, 91; Sculpture Outdoors, Nassau Co Mus Fine Arts, Roslyn, NY, 75; Sculpture Invitational, Zabriskie Gallery, New York, 82; Rochester Polytechnic Inst, 87; Haenah-Kent, New York, 91. *Teaching:* Marlboro Col, 80-82; asst prof, State Univ NY, Albany, 83- *Awards:* Guggenheim fel, 77; Nat Endowment Arts, 80. *Bibliog:* Robert Hughes (auth), Working on the rock pile, Time Mag, 4/7/75; Ingeborg Hoesteret (auth), Buchman (Sculpture Now), Art Int, 6/15/75; Donald B Kuspit (auth), James Buchman at Sculpture Now, Art Am, 7-8/75; Alan Singer (auth), article, Arts Mag, 4/85. *Mailing Add:* 180 Duane St New York NY 10013

BUCHWALD, HOWARD
PAINTER
b New York, NY, 1964. *Study:* Cooper Union, BFA, 64; Hunter Col, MA, 72. *Work:* Whitney Mus Am Art. *Exhib:* Solo exhibs, French & Co, New York, 71, Galerie Farideh Cadot, Paris, France, 76 & 78, Janet Steinberg Gallery, San Francisco, 86 & Tomassulo Gallery, Union Col, Cranford, NJ, 90; Drawing Today in New York, travelling to univs in US, 76; Minneapolis Mus Art, Minn, 78; Weatherspoon Art Gallery, Univ NC, Greensboro, 83; Louis K Meisel Gallery, New York & Danforth Mus Art, Framingham, Mass, 85. *Pos:* Chair, dept painting & sculpture, Columbia Univ, 87-88. *Teaching:* Prof, Pratt Inst, 72-, Princeton 75-81, 91- & Columbia Univ, 82-92. *Awards:* Guggenheim Fel, 74; Nat Endowment Arts, 81 & 89; Creative Artists Prog Serv, 83. *Mailing Add:* c/o Nancy Hoffman Gallery 429 W Broadway New York NY 10012

BUCK, JOHN
SCULPTOR
b Ames, Iowa, 1946. *Study:* Kansas City Art Inst & Sch Design, BFA, 68; Univ Calif, MFA, 72. *Comn:* Sculpture, three Generations, comm by Principal Financial Group, Iowa, 89. *Exhib:* Mus Mod Art, New York, 72; solo exhibs, Univ Ky Art Mus, Lexington, 75, Carlo Lamagna Gallery, New York, 85, 86, 88 & Contemp Arts Ctr, Honolulu, Hawaii, 87; Denver Art Mus, Denver, Colo, 79-80, touring US; Madison Art Ctr, Madison, Wis, 82-83; Brooklyn Mus, NY, 86-87, touring US; Mus Contemp Art, Chicago, Ill, 90. *Teaching:* Sculpture instr, Humboldt State Col, 73-75 & Mont State Univ, 76- *Awards:* Nat Endowment Art, 80; Nat Artists Award, 84. *Mailing Add:* c/o Ann Kohs & Assoc 251 Post St, Suite 540 San Francisco CA 94108

BUCK, PORGE
PRINTMAKER
b Washington, DC, Jan 31, 31. *Study:* Richmond Prof Inst, Col William & Mary, Va, 49-51; Ill Wesleyan Univ, BFA, 53. *Work:* NCNB Corp, Charlotte, NC; Maine Nat Bank, Augusta. *Exhib:* Pennell Printmakers Exhib, Libr Cong, Washington, DC, 56; Corcoran Gallery Art, Washington, DC, 57;

Colburn Gallery, Kenyon Col, Gambier, Ohio, 83; Contemporary American Printmakers, The Print Club, Philadelphia, 83; Asheville Art Mus, NC, 85; Minneapolis Col Art & Design, Minneapolis, Minn, 88; and others; Intermont Col, Bristol, 89. *Pos:* Co-dir, Intaglio-Relief Soc, Asheville, NC, 78-; printer & dir, IRS Press Editioning, Black Mountain, NC, 92- *Mem:* NC Print & Drawing Soc; Southern Graphics Coun; Artists Equity Asn; Int Graphic Arts Found; Mid Am Print Coun. *Media:* Intaglio, Woodcut. *Mailing Add:* 309 Portman Villa Rd Black Mountain NC 28711

BUCK, ROBERT TREAT, JR
HISTORIAN, MUSEUM DIRECTOR
b Fall River, Mass, Feb 16, 39. *Study:* Williams Col, BA; New York Univ, with Dr Walter Friedlaender, MA. *Collections Arranged:* Sam Francis: Paintings 1947-1972 (with catalog), 72; Paintings by Auguste Herbin; Here and Now: 13 Young Americans; Modernist Painting; Pollock to the Present; Master Drawings from the Art Inst Chicago & Mus Mod Art; Homage to Albers; Max Bill, 74; Bradley Walker Tomlin: A Retrospective View, 75; Richard Diebenkorn: Paintings & Drawings 1943-1976, 76-77; Antoni Tapies: 33 Years of His Work, 77; Cleve Gray: Serial Paintings, 77; Sonia Delaunay: A Retrospective (with catalog), 80; and many others. *Pos:* Lectr-researcher, Toledo Mus Art, 64-65; asst cur & instr, Wash Univ, 65-67 & dir, Gallery of Art, 68-70; asst dir, Albright-Knox Art Gallery, Buffalo, 70-73, dir, 73-83; dir, Brooklyn Mus, 83- *Teaching:* Adj assoc prof mus training, Univ Toledo, 65-66; adj assoc prof mus training & 19th & 20th century art, Wash Univ, 66-70; adj assoc prof mus training, State Univ NY Buffalo, 72-73. *Awards:* NY State Coun Arts Traveling Fel, summer 71; Nat Endowment Arts Fel Mus Professional, summer 75. *Mem:* Int Coun Mus; Asn Art Mus Dirs (trustee, secy & treas); Brooklyn Arts Coun (mem bd, 83-); Arts Alliance, New York (mem bd, 84-); Pratt Art Inst (mem bd, 84-92). *Res:* Nineteenth century French painting; art of the twentieth century. *Mailing Add:* c/o The Brooklyn Museum 200 Eastern Pkwy Brooklyn NY 11238

BUCKLEY, MARY L (MRS JOSEPH M PARRIOTT)
PAINTER, EDUCATOR
b New Haven, Conn. *Study:* Yale Univ Art Sch; also with Victor Candell & Hans Hoffman. *Work:* Yale Art Mus; Heckscher Mus, Huntington, NY; Lake Erie Col, Painesville, Ohio; Pratt Inst, New York. *Comn:* Murals, Philip Johnson, Seagrams Bldg, New York, 59; Color & Design, Philip Johnson, New York World's Fair Pavillion, 64; People I (sculpture), Paragon Oil, Melville, NY; State Symbols Standards, People II (sculpture), NY State Legislature Bldg, Albany; color & design, Herman Miller. *Exhib:* Manhattan Community Col, 70; Nassau Community Col, 71; Midtown Gallery, New York, 77; Women's Inter-art Exhib, New York, 77; Munson Gallery, New Haven, Conn, 77-83; Prince Street Gallery, 91; St John The Devine Cathedral Gallery, New York, 92; Hutchins Gallery, Brookville, Long Island, 92. *Pos:* Dir, Margaret Gate Inst, 73-; consult, Herman, Miller, Inc. *Teaching:* Prof art & design, 58-, distinguished prof, 92, prof emer, Pratt Inst, 92; adj prof, Union Col, Antioch, Ohio, 75- *Awards:* Nat Endowment Arts Grant; Am Psychiatric Award, Ittleson Found; Gold Metal Award, Am Soc Interior Designers, 90. *Mem:* Nat Asn Women Artists; Indust Designers Soc of Am; Eastern Arts Asn; fel MacDowell Asn; fel Royal Soc Art; Nat Arts Club. *Media:* Oil, Plate Aluminum. *Publ:* Auth, Color Theory Bibliography, Gale Res; Color Glimpses, UR Brooklyn J, 76. *Mailing Add:* Bay Crest Huntington NY 11743

BUCKNALL, MALCOLM RODERICK
PAINTER
b Twickenham, Eng, Feb 1, 35. *Study:* Univ Viswa-Bharati, West Bengal, India, 54-55; Chelsea Art Sch, London, Intermediate Nat Dipl Design, 58; Univ Tex, Austin, BFA(hon), 61; Univ Wash, Seattle, MFA, 63. *Work:* Butler Inst of Am Art, Youngstown, Ohio; Okla Art Ctr, Oklahoma City; Univ of Va Art Mus, Charlottesville; Crescent Collection, Crescent Marketing Ctr, Dallas, Tex. *Exhib:* Artists Biennial, New Orleans Mus, La, 71, 75 & 77; Delta Show, Ark Art Ctr, Little Rock, 73, 74, 79, 80, 82, 83, 85 & 88-90; Betty Moody Gallery, Houston, Tex, 81; Graham Gallery, Houston, Tex, 85, 87 & 91; Third Coast Review, Aspen Art Mus, Colo, 87; Feather Fure Fin, Laguna Gloria Art Mus, Austin, 90; Texas Dialogues: Blue Star Art Space, San Antonio, Tex, 91; and others. *Teaching:* Instr drawing & design, Univ Wash, Seattle, 61-63. *Awards:* Nat Jury Show, Chautauqa Inst, New York, 72 & 74; Medal, Midyear Show, Butler Inst of Am Art, 72 & 76; Artist Fel, Nat Endownent Arts, 85-86. *Bibliog:* Lisa Tuttle (auth), Risky Artist Wins Worthwhile Gamble, Austin Statesman, 6/76; Patricia Sharpe (auth), Different Strokes, Tex Mo, 10/76; Melissa Hirsch (auth), Malcolm Bucknall: Apprehension of Mystery, Dart Mag, spring 83. *Media:* Oil, Watercolor. *Dealer:* Graham Gallery 1431 W Alabama Houston TX. *Mailing Add:* 808 West Ave Austin TX 78701

BUCKNER, KAY LAMOREUX
PAINTER, DRAFTSMAN
b Seattle, Wash, Dec 26, 35. *Study:* Sch of Art, Univ Wash, BA(art), 58; Claremont Grad Sch, MFA(painting), 61, study with Roger Kuntz & Phil Dike. *Work:* Olympic Col, Bremerton, Wash; First Nat Bank Ore, Portland; Ga-Pac Co, Portland, Ore; Emanuel Hosp, Portland, Ore; Great Western Nat Bank, Portland, Ore. *Exhib:* Frye Art Mus, Seattle, 79; Oregon Mus Art, Eugene, 81; NMex Int, Clovis, 81; Nat Landscape Art Exhib, Springfield Art Mus, Ill, 82; Clark Gallery, Rockford, Ill, 82; Nat Women Art Exhib, Springfield Art Mus, Ill, 83; Ward-Nasse Gallery, New York, 86 & 87; Jadite Galleries, New York, 88; Word Works, Seattle Ctr, 89; Contemp Works on Canvas, Md Fedn Art, Annapolis, 91. *Teaching:* Adj instr, Univ Ore, Eugene, 76-88. *Awards:* First Prize Painting, 18th Nat Greater Fall River Exhib, Mass, 76; First Prize, NMex Int Exhib, 81; Northwest Poets & Artists Calendar, Wash, 90. *Bibliog:* Diana Freedman (auth), The Richness of Kay Buckner, Artspeak, New York, 11/16/87; Miles Unger (auth), The Power of Metaphor, Manhattan Arts, June-July, 88; Dennis Wepman (auth), Kay Buckner's Luminous Vision, Manhattan Arts, 12/87. *Mailing Add:* 2332 Rockwood Ave Eugene OR 97405

BUCKNER, PAUL EUGENE
SCULPTOR, EDUCATOR
b Seattle, Wash, June 16, 33. *Study:* Univ Wash Sch of Art, BA(sculpture), 59; Claremont Grad Sch, MFA(sculpture), 61, study with Albert Stewart; Fulbright grant, Slade Sch, Univ Col, London, 61-62. *Work:* Olympic Col, Bremerton, Wash; Salem Civic Ctr, Ore; Ore Mus Art, Eugene; First Nat Bank Ore, Portland; Multnoma Athletic Club, Portland, Ore. *Comn:* Centennial Medallion, Univ Ore, Eugene, 76; wood carvings, carved doors, Sacred Heart Gen Hospital, Eugene, Ore, 82-83; Entry Court Sculpture, Eastern Ore Correctional Inst, Pendleton, Ore, 88; wood carvings, Mount Angel Abbey, St Benedict, Ore, 85-86; Two carved wood figure groups, Timberline Lodge, Ore, 90. *Exhib:* Northwest Artists, Seattle Art Mus, Wash, 64; solo exhib, Ore Mus Art, Eugene, 64; Sculpture 67, Seattle Art Mus, Wash, 67; Mainstreams Int, Marietta Col, Ohio, 71, 76 & 77; Sculptors of Ore, Ore Mus Art, Eugene, 74; Works in Wood by Northwest Artists, Portland Art Mus, Ore, 76; Mountain High III, Timberline Lodge, Ore, 81; Sculpture on the Green, Univ Portland, 82; retrospective, The Figure-Twenty-Five Years, Ore Mus Art, Eugene, 86. *Teaching:* Prof sculpture, Univ Ore, Eugene, 62- *Awards:* Nat Sculpture Rev Prize, Nat Sculpture Soc, 77; Award of Distinction, Mainstreams 77, Marietta Col, Ohio, 77. *Bibliog:* Lorraine Widman (auth), Sculpture: A Studio Guide, Concepts, Methods, and Materials, Prentice Hall, Englewood Cliffs, NJ, 89; Mary Balcomb (auth), Paul Buckner: Sculptor, Am Artist, 6/80; Charlotte Graydon (auth), Nationally known sculptor takes crisp view of wood, The Oregonian, 9/10/84. *Mailing Add:* 2332 Rockwood Ave Eugene OR 97405

BUDNY, VIRGINIA
SCULPTOR, WRITER
b Maui, Hawaii, April 15, 44. *Study:* Vassar Col, with Concetta Scaravaglione, AB, 65; Columbia Univ, with Peter Agostini, 65-66; Univ NC, Greensboro, with Peter Agostini, MFA, 70; Inst Fine Arts, New York Univ, MA, 88. *Work:* Smithsonian Inst; Vassar Col Art Gallery; Weatherspoon Art Gallery. *Exhib:* North Carolina Sculpture 79, Weatherspoon Art Gallery, Univ NC, Greensboro, 79; Am Porcelain Traveling Exhib, Renwick Gallery, 80-83; Illusion, Southeast Ctr Contemp Art, Winston-Salem, NC, 83; Contemporary Trompe l'Oeil Painting and Sculpture, Boise Gallery Art & traveling, 83-85; Equitable Gallery, New York, 84; Alternative Mus, New York, 85; Brenda Kroos Gallery, Columbus, Ohio, 85; Desires, A Personal Gallery, Greensboro, 88; Sculptors Draw the Nude, Luise Ross Gallery, New York, 90. *Teaching:* Asst prof sculpture, Univ NC, Greensboro, 73-80; instr art hist, Continuing Educ, Cooper Union, New York Univ, 87-88; lectr art hist, Parsons Sch Design, 91-92, instr, 92. *Awards:* Yaddo Found Fel, 81; Am Philos Soc Grant, 84; June & Morgan Whitney Fel, Metrop Mus Art, 92-93; and others. *Bibliog:* William Zimmer (auth), rev, Arts Mag, 1/77; Jane D Scholl (auth), article, Smithsonian Mag, 2/81; Vivien Raynor (auth), rev, NY Times, 1/11/85. *Res:* Leonardo da Vinci's creative process studied through his composition sketches. *Publ:* Auth, The poses of the child in the composition sketches by Leonardo da Vinci for The Madonna and Child With a Cat, Weatherspoon Gallery Asn Bulletin, 80; The sequence of Leonardo's sketches for The Virgin and Child with Saint Anne and Saint John the Baptist, Art Bulletin, 83. *Mailing Add:* 47-49 Greene St New York NY 10012

BUECHNER, THOMAS SCHARMAN
PAINTER, WRITER
b New York, NY, Sept 25, 26. *Study:* Princeton Univ, 44-45; Art Students League, 46-47; Ecole Beaux-Arts, Fontainebleau & Paris, France, 47-48; Levine-Shikler, 61-80. *Work:* Bowdoin Col, Maine; Metrop Mus Art, Brooklyn Mus, Cirnell Univ, New York; Nat Mus Am Art, Smithsonian Inst, Washington, DC. *Comn:* Portrait, Paul Sheaffer, Brooklyn Hosp, 65; portrait, Alice Tully, Lincoln Ctr; portrait, David Atwater, Grace Episcopal Church, 70; portrait, Joseph Hill, State Univ NY Downstate Med Ctr, 72; portrait, Alfred Gelhorn, Univ Pa; portrait, Robert Blum, Brooklyn Mus. *Exhib:* A M Adler Fine Arts, New York; Artists of Am, Denver, Colo, 80-90; Nat Acad Design; Heller Gallery, New York; Arnold Gallery, Newport; OK Harris, New York; Gallery M, Lindau, Ger, 89. *Collections Arranged:* Vincent Van Gogh, Metrop Mus Art, New York, 49; Glass 1959, Corning Mus Glass, 59; Levine-Shikler (catalog), Brooklyn Mus, New York, 71; Artist Am, Denver, Colo, 80-90; Exactitude, Metrop Mus Art, 88. *Pos:* Dir, Corning Mus Glass, 50-60, pres, 71-; dir, Brooklyn Mus, 60-71; pres, Corning Glassworks Found, 71; Rockwell Mus, 76-; Market St Restoration Agency, 78-; pres, Steuben Glass, 82-86; illustr, Book World & Dubbings Electronics, currently. *Teaching:* Head dept art, Corning Community Col, NY, 58-60; head painting & drawing, Heights Casino, Brooklyn, NY, 65-68; prof drawing arts & social change, Salzburg Sem Am Studies, 71; artist-in-residence, Haystack Mountain Sch, Maine; Pilchuck Glass Sch, Wash; landscapes & still life, Scottsdale Artist's Sch, Ariz, 87-; Bild Werk, Frauenau, Fed Repub Ger, 87-; landscape painting, Bild Werk, Frauenau, Ger, 88. *Awards:* Brooklyn Man of Year, Brooklyn Col, 63; Forsythia Award, Brooklyn Botanic Garden, 71; Gari Melcher's Gold Medal, Artist's Fel, 71; Bowdoin Col Award. *Bibliog:* Article in Art News, 12/85; Am Artist, 6/80; US Art, 7/88. *Mem:* Louis Comfort Tiffany Found (trustee, 71); fel Royal Soc Art. *Media:* Oil, Watercolor. *Res:* American illustration, emphasis on cover artists; glass history with emphasis on art glass. *Publ:* Auth, Glass Vessels in Dutch Painting in the 17th Century, 52; contribr, A Guide to the Brooklyn Museum, 67; auth, Norman Rockwell: Artist and Illustrator; Art of Ogdon Pleissner; Arts of David Levine. *Dealer:* O K Harris W Broadway New York NY; West End Gallery Market St Corning NY. *Mailing Add:* 11 N Rd Corning NY 14830

BUECKER, ROBERT
GALLERY DIRECTOR, PAINTER
b Pittsburgh, Pa, 1935. *Study:* Pa State; Carnegie Tech. *Exhib:* Solo exhibs, Richard Feigen Gallery, New York, 66 & 69 & Zolla/Lieberman Gallery, Chicago, 77; Other Ideas, Detroit Inst Arts, Mich, 69; Six Greek Crosses, 77 & Religious Work Retrospective, 79, Cathedral St John the Divine Mus Religious Art; and others. *Pos:* Owner, Buecker & Harpsichords, New York, 70- *Bibliog:* Suzy Gablic (auth), article, Art News, 1/64; Michael Andre (auth), article, Village Voice, 8/11/75; Tom Johnson (auth), article, Village Voice, 3/25/81. *Res:* Contemporary New York art history. *Specialty:* Contemporary American art. *Mailing Add:* 465 W Broadway New York NY 10012

BUERGER, JANET E
HISTORIAN, CURATOR
b Boston, Mass, May 30, 46. *Study:* Skidmore Col, BA, 68; Columbia Univ, MA, 69, PhD(art hist & archaeol), 78. *Collections Arranged:* French Daguerreotypes, 77, The Kodak Number 1: More than Just a Snapshot, 79, Pierre Petit, 80, George Eastman House, Int Mus Photog; Nineteenth Century Photography, 79-87; The Era of the French Calotype (auth, catalog), 82; Naya's Italy, 83; The Last Decade: Emergence of Art Photog in the 1890s (auth, catalog), 84; Dresden at Eastman House, 84; Daguerre: The Artist, 85; Early Am Photog, 89. *Pos:* Curatorial intern, George Eastman House, Int Mus Photog, 75-76, res cur & exec asst to dir, 76-79, actg cur 19th century photog, 79-81, from asst cur to assoc cur photog collections, 81-; mem ed bd, Image, 78- *Teaching:* Adj asst prof hist photog, Univ Rochester, 79-80, lect, Fine Arts, Harvard Univ Extension, 86. *Awards:* Comt to Rescue Ital Art Fel, 72-73 & Instituto Roberto Longhi Fel, 73-75, Florence, Italy; Mary Ingraham Bunting Inst Fel, Nat Endowment Humanities Fel, Radcliffe Col, 85-86. *Mem:* Col Art Asn; Am Asn Mus. *Res:* Nineteenth century French and American photography; the fin-de-siècle avant-garde. *Publ:* Auth, Ceramica smaltata tardo medievale della costa adriatica, Atti, Albisola, Convegno Int della Ceramica, 74; auth, Reperti dagli scavi di Santa Reparata, Archeol Medievale, 75; auth, Minor White 1908-76, 76 & Degas, solarized and negative photographs, 78, Image; auth, The medieval glazed pottery, Diocletian's Palace Joint Am-Yugoslav Excavations (part three), 79. *Mailing Add:* 18 Lowell Rd Concord MA 01742

BUGBEE-JACKSON, JOAN (MRS JOHN M JACKSON)
SCULPTOR, EDUCATOR
b Oakland, Calif, Dec 17, 41. *Study:* Univ Mont; San Jose State Col, BA & MA; Art Students League, with R B Hale; Sch of Fine Arts, Nat Acad Design; also with M Wildenhain, EvAngelos Frudakis, Joseph Kiselewski, Granville Carter & Adolph Block. *Work:* Cordova Pub Libr, Alaska; Pac Lutheran Univ, Anchorage, Alaska. *Comn:* Alaska's Wildlife (bronze medal), 80; two sculpture murals, Alaska State Capital Bldg, Juneau, Alaska, 81; Gruening & Bartlett busts, Alaska State Capitol Bldg, Juneau, 82; plaque, Armin F Koernig, 85; two portraits, comn by Mr & Mrs Robert B Atwood, 85; Cordova Fisherman's Memorial Statue, 85; bronze relief, Alaska's Five Govenors, Loussac Libr, Anchorage, 86; Charles E Bunnell Bronze Statue, Univ Alaska, Fairbanks, 88; bronze sitka, Alexander Baranof Monument, Alaska, 89; bronze plaque plaque, Wally Noerenberg, Prince Wm Sound, Alaska, 89; Russian-Alaskan friendship plaques, Kayakis & Cordova, Alaska, Vladivostok & Petropavlovsk-Kamchatskiyi, Russia, 91. *Exhib:* One-woman show, Springvale, Maine, 70; Nat Sculpture Soc Ann, New York, 70-73; Allied Artists Am Ann, New York, 70-72; Nat Acad Design Ann, New York, 71 & 74; Joan Bugbee, Retrospective, New York, 72; Cordova Womanart Show, 86, 87, 88. *Teaching:* Instr design, De Anza Col, Cupertino, Calif, 67-68; instr pottery & glaze chem, Greenwich House Pottery, New York, 69-71; instr pottery, Prince William Sound Community Col, Cordova, 72-88. *Awards:* Helen Foster Barnet Prize, Nat Acad Design, 71; Daniel Chester French Prize, Nat Sculpture Soc, 72 & C Percival Dietsch Prize, 73; Allied Artist Am Award, 72; Citation, Alaska State Legislature, 81. *Bibliog:* Jim Seay (auth), A move for inspiration, Anchorage Daily News, 8/13/72; New Issues, Alaskan Medal Series, The Numismatist, 1/81; Ron Dalby (auth), Cordova's contemporary realist, Alaska Mag, 86; Rebecca Hom (auth), Cordova's Sculptor, Rualite Mag, 9/88. *Mem:* fel Nat Sculpture Soc; Artists' Equity Asn. *Media:* Fired Stoneware Clay, Cast Bronze. *Publ:* Contribr, Nat Sculpture Review, winter 70-71, spring 71 & winter 81-82. *Mailing Add:* Box 374 Cordova AK 99574

BUITRON-OLIVER, DIANA
CURATOR, HISTORIAN
b Quito, Ecuador, Apr 17, 46; US citizen. *Study:* Smith Col, BA, 69; Inst of Fine Arts, New York Univ, MA, 72 & PhD, 76; Am Sch of Classical Studies, Athens, Greece, 72-73. *Pos:* Curatorial asst, Fogg Art Mus, Harvard Univ, 70-72; Andrew Mellon & Chester Dale Fel, Metrop Mus Art, New York, 73-75; cur Greek & Roman art, Walters Art Gallery, Baltimore, Md, 77-84; dir, Excavations in the Archaic Precinct, Kourion, Cyprus, 82-85; guest cur, Nat Gallery Art, Washington, DC. *Teaching:* asst prof classics, John Hopkins Univ, 82-83; vis lectr, Smith Col, 87; prof lectr, Georgetown Univ, 88-89. *Mem:* Archaeol Inst Am; Am Asn Univ Women; Ger Archaeol Inst. *Res:* Greek art, specializing in Greek vase painting & Cypriot archaeology. *Publ:* Ed, New Perspectives in Early Greek Art, Washington, DC, 91; The Odyssey and Ancient Art (catalog), Annandale-on-Hudson, 92; Excavations in the Archaic Precinct at the Sanctuary of Apollo at Kourion in Cyprus (in press); Auth, Attic Vare Painting in New England Collections, (Kerameus series), Douris (in press). *Mailing Add:* 3401 Rolling Ct Chevy Chase MD 20815

BUJESE, ARLENE
GALLERY DIRECTOR, PRINTMAKER
b Hillsdale, NJ, May 8, 38. *Study:* Corcoran Sch Art, 64-70; Hood Col, Md, AB, 75, MA, 78. *Work:* Parrish Art Mus, Southampton, NY. *Exhib:* Four Graphic Artists, Parrish Art Mus, 70; Nat Exhib Prints & Drawings, Okla Art Ctr, 72; 11 Contemp Printmakers, Int Monetary Fund, Washington, DC, 74; Printmakers of the Region, Guild Hall Mus, New York, 75; solo exhib, Arts Club Washington, DC, 84; NJ National Print Exhib, Hunterdon Art Ctr. *Pos:* Dir & vpres, Phoenix II Gallery, Washington, DC, 81-83; dir, Benton Gallery, Southampton, NY, 86- *Teaching:* Instr design, Hood Col, Md, 81- *Awards:* First Prize for Graphics, Ann Student Exhib, Corcoran Sch, 69; Best in Any Media, Guild Hall Ann, 80; Exhib Comt Prize, Arts Club Washington, DC, 82. *Mem:* Arts Club Washington, DC; Guild Hall; Smithsonian Assoc. *Media:* Etching. *Specialty:* Contemporary American artists, primarily first generation abstract expressionists and young emerging artists, New York school. *Publ:* Ed, 25 Artists: Hans Namuth and 24 Artists, Univ Publ Am, 82. *Mailing Add:* 40 Whooping Hollow Rd East Hampton NY 11937

BUJNOWSKI, JOEL A
PRINTMAKER, PAINTER
b Chicago, Ill, Dec 16, 49. *Study:* Western Ill Univ, BA, 72, MA, 74; Northern Ill Univ, MFA, 78. *Work:* State Ill Ctr Collection, Chicago, Ill; Lamar Dodd Art Ctr Collection, La Grange Col, Ill; Univ NDak Collection, Grand Forks; Univ Dallas Collection, Irving, Tex; Clemson Univ Collection, SC. *Exhib:* 11th Monroe Nat Art Exhib, Masur Mus Art, Monroe, La, 79; Wesleyan Int Exhib Prints & Drawings, traveling exhib, 80-81; 7th Univ Dallas Print Invitational, Tex & Gt Brit, 81-83; 79th & 80th Chicago & Vicinity Exhib, Art Inst Chicago, Ill, 81 & 84; New Am Graphics III, Mus in Europe, Africa & Asia, 83; 20th Ann All Media Exhib, Brea Civic Cult Ctr Gallery, Calif, 86; Int Biennial Print Exhib, Taipei Fine Arts Mus, Repub China, 87; solo exhib, Univ Ariz Mus Art, Tucson, 89; Third Biennial Exhib of Prints, Mus Mod Art, Wakayama, Japan, 89; 16th, 22nd, 23rd Bradley Nat Print & Drawing Exhib, Peoria, Ill, 77, 89 & 91. *Teaching:* Asst prof printmaking & drawing, Univ Hawaii, Manoa, Honolulu, 86-87; dir, Harper Col Nat Print & Drawing; adj fac, current. *Awards:* Award Excellence, Memphis State Univ, 85; Best of Show, Bradley Univ, 89; Arts Midwest & Nat Endowment Asn Regional, 90. *Bibliog:* Marcia Morse (auth), Fresh faces, new visions, Honolulu Sunday Star Bull, 9/14/86; Karl Moehl (auth), review, New Art Examiner, 90; Jerry Klein (auth), Peoria J Star, 90. *Dealer:* Chicago Ctr for Print 1509 Fullerton Chicago IL. *Mailing Add:* 2439 W Armitage Ave Chicago IL 60647

BUKI, ZOLTAN
CURATOR, ADMINISTRATOR
b Pecs, Hungary, Oct 26, 29; US citizen. *Study:* Acad de Belle Arti, Rome; Art Inst Chicago, BFA; Wayne State Univ Grad Sch; Tulane Univ Grad Sch, MFA. *Collections Arranged:* Responsive Environment, 72; For the Mind & the Eye, 77; Contemporary American Still-Life (auth, catalog), 86; Peter Stroud Retrospective, 88. *Pos:* Dir exhibs, Ark Arts Ctr, Little Rock, 63-68; chmn art dept, Humboldt State Col, 68-69; cur fine arts, NJ State Mus, 69- *Teaching:* Instr drawing & painting, Univ Southwestern La, 61-62; instr drawing & anat, Layton Sch Art, Milwaukee, 62-63. *Publ:* Coauth, The Trenton Monument Eakins Bronzes, 73. *Mailing Add:* Off Curator NJ State Mus 205 W State St Trenton NJ 08625-0530

BUKOVNIK, GARY
PAINTER, PRINTMAKER
b Cleveland, Ohio, Apr 10, 47. *Study:* Cleveland Inst Art, 66-68. *Work:* Metrop Mus Art, New York; Boston Mus Fine Art; Brooklyn Mus; Art Inst Chicago; Mus Art, Carnegie Inst, Pittsburgh, Pa; Fine Arts Mus of San Francisco. *Comn:* Image for Easter at the White House, Washington, DC, 84 & 86; watercolors, Peat, Marwick, Mitchell & Assocs, Atlanta, 86; watercolors, Bonaventure Hotel, Los Angeles, 86; watercolors, IBM, Atlanta, 86; image for poster, Metrop Opera, New York, 91. *Exhib:* Solo exhibs, Brooklyn Mus Art, New York, 84, Atlanta Botanical Garden, 87, Galerie Kutter, Luxembourg, 88, Kurts Bingham Gallery, Memphis, 90 & 91, Ansorena, Madrid, 91, de Saisset Mus, Santa Clara Univ, 91 & Garden Ctr Greater Cleveland, 92; group exhibs, Gene Baro Collects, Brooklyn Mus Art, 83; Flower Influenced Art, Arts Comn, San Francisco, Calif, 88; Bouquets to Art, M H De Young Mus, San Francisco, Calif, 90; Recent Acquisitions, Fine Arts Mus, San Francisco, 91; 20th Century Flower Painting, Ft Lauderdale Mus Art, 91; In the Garden, Bolinas Mus, 91; 50 Peintres en Hommage a Jean Lurcat, Abusson, France, 92; and others. *Awards:* George Bunker Award, Print Competition, Philadelphia Mus Art, 81; Award of Merit, Am Soc Mus Publ, 82 & San Francisco Arts Comn, 88. *Bibliog:* Anna Novakov (auth), Speaking of flowers, Art Week, 87; Judith Gordon (auth), Dream Weaver, SF Mag, 4/90; Painter of Perfection, El Punto de las Artes, Madrid, 1/18-24/91; and others. *Media:* Watercolor; Monotype, Lithograph. *Publ:* Flowers: Gary Bukovnik Watercolors & Monotypes, Harry N Abrams, 90; illusr, A Taste of San Francisco, Doubleday, 90; From a Breton Garden, Addison Wesley, 90. *Mailing Add:* 1179 Howard St San Francisco CA 94103

BULL, FRAN
PAINTER, EDUCATOR
b Orange, NJ, Sept 22, 38. *Study:* Bennington Col, Vt, BA, 60; State Univ NY, Stony Brook with Malcolm Morley, 71; NY Univ, MA, 80. *Work:* Baltimore Mus Art, Md; Brooklyn Mus Art, New York; Indianapolis Mus Art, Ind; NJ State Mus Art, Trenton; Speed Art Mus, Louisville, Ky. *Exhib:* Cincinnati Inst Contemp Art, 74; Indianapolis Mus Fine Arts, 74; Allentown Art Mus, Pa, 74; Contemp Images in Watercolor, Traveling Exhib, 76; Contemp Naturalism, 80 & The Animal in American Art, 81, Nassau Co Fine Arts, Roslyn, NY; The American Photo Realist--an Anthology, Fisher Fine Art

Gallery, London, Eng, 86. *Teaching:* Instr watercolor, New York Univ, 79-86; vis artist, Towson State, Md, 86-87; vis instr painting, Univ Wis, 88; Artist & Teacher, Vt Col of Norwich Univ, 92. *Bibliog:* Louis K Meisel (auth), Photo Realism, Harry Abrams, Inc, 80; David Bourdon (auth), Art: A painters aviary, Archit Digest, 81; Eileen Watkins (auth), Women paint women, Newark Star Ledger, 89. *Media:* Acrylic, Watercolor. *Publ:* Illusr, Science News, 82; Houston Symphony Mag, 84; Trade with Italy, 89; Mordant Rhymes for Modern Times, Middletown Press, 90. *Dealer:* Morgan Gallery 472 Delaware Suite A Kansas City MO 64105; Seraphim Gallery 32 N Dean St Englewood NJ 07631. *Mailing Add:* PO Box 442 Alpine NJ 07620

BULL, HANK (HENRY OSLER)
CONCEPTUAL ARTIST, VIDEO ARTIST
Can citizen. *Study:* New Sch Art, Toronto, Can, 69. *Comn:* Mural, McMaster Univ, Hamilton, Ont, 72. *Exhib:* HP Show, A Space, Toronto, 76; Dokumenta 8, Kassel, 87. *Pos:* Pres & dir, Western Front, 73-88. *Awards:* B Award, Canada Coun, 80 & 87. *Publ:* HP in a Pickle, 74. *Mailing Add:* c/o Western Front 303 E 8th Ave Vancouver BC V5T 1S1 Canada

BULLARD, EDGAR JOHN, III
MUSEUM DIRECTOR
b Los Angeles, Calif, Sept 15, 42. *Study:* Univ Calif, Los Angeles, BA, 65, MA, 68; Nat Gallery Art, Samuel H Kress Found Fel, 67-68; Harvard Univ Inst Arts Admin, 71; Loyola Univ, New Orleans, La, LHD, 87. *Collections Arranged:* German Expressionist Watercolors in American Collections, 69, Mary Cassatt 1844-1926, 70 & John Sloan 1871-1951 (auth, catalog), 71, Nat Gallery Art, Washington, DC; Richard Clague 1821-1873, 74 & Zenga & Nanga: Paintings by Japanese Monks & Scholars, 76, New Orleans Mus Art; The Contemp South: Photog, US Info Agency, 77; The Wild West: Paintings and Sculpture by Frederic Remington and Charles M Russell, 79, Robert Gordy: Paintings and Sculpture 1960-80, 81 & Edward Weston and Clarence John Laughlin: An Introduction to the Third World of Photography (auth, catalog), 82, New Orleans Mus Art; and others. *Pos:* Asst cur, J Paul Getty Mus, Malibu, Calif, 67; mus cur, Nat Gallery Art, 68-70, asst to dir, 70-71, cur spec projs, 71-73; dir, New Orleans Mus Art, 73-; trustee, Ga Mus Art, Univ Ga, 75-80; trustee, Knessel Hall Music Sch, Blue Hill, Maine, 86-, La SPCA, 86. *Awards:* Order Rep Egypt, 79; Louis Brandeis Humanitarian Award, 85. *Mem:* Am Asn Mus; Col Art Asn Am; Nat Arts Club; Asn Art Mus Dir. *Res:* Late 19th & 20th century American and European art. *Publ:* Auth, Mary Cassatt: Oils and Pastels, Watson-Guptill, 72; A Panorama of American Painting (exhib catalog), 75; American paintings from the John J McDonough Collection, Antiques, 11/77; Two visions of the wild west: Frederic Remington & Charles M Russell, Southwest Art, 12/79; The Kinetic Sculpture of Lin Emery (exhib catalog), 82; and others. *Mailing Add:* New Orleans Mus of Art PO Box 19123 New Orleans LA 70179

BULLOCK, JAMES BENBOW
SCULPTOR
b St Louis, Mo, Feb 6, 29. *Study:* Wesleyan Univ, Middletown, Conn, BA, 50; San Francisco Art Inst, 67. *Work:* Hakone Open Air Mus, Japan; Vallejo Pub Libr, Calif; Chapman Col, Orange, Calif; Art Inst Southern Calif, Laguna Beach; Schiller Int Univ, Strasbourg, France. *Comn:* Steel sculptures, Vallejo Times Herald, Calif, 88, Plaza Real Hotel, Santa Fe, NMex, 90; Aluminum Diptych, Del Amo Financial Ctr, Calif, 85. *Exhib:* Design Frontiers, Richmond Art Ctr, Calif, 85; Black & White, San Francisco Mus Mod Art, 85; San Francisco Art Festival, Civic Ctr Arts Comn, 86; 33rd Ann Juried Show, San Diego Art Inst, 87; Third Ann Sculpture Walk, Los Angeles Arts Coun, 89; Sixth Ann Henry Moore Exhib, Hakone Open Air Mus, Japan, 89; Ecole des Beaux Arts, Maubeuge, France, 92. *Awards:* Ueno Royal Mus Award, Hakone Open Air Mus, Japan, 89. *Media:* Metal. *Mailing Add:* 11 Sandy Beach Rd Vallejo CA 94590

BUMAS, JONATHAN MARK
PAINTER
b Forest Hills, NY, Aug 22, 57. *Study:* Princeton Univ, AB, 78; Pratt Inst, 78-81; Univ NMex, 81-82. *Work:* Graphic Arts Collection, Firestone Libr, Princeton Univ, NJ. *Exhib:* For Pastels Only, Nat Arts Club, New York, 87-92; Grand Nat Exhib, Salmagundi Club, New York, 88; Nat Works on Paper, Nassau Community Col, Garden City, NY 89; Interpreting the Figure, Alexander F Milliken Inc, New York, 90; Smile, Please, Graphic Arts Collection, Princeton Univ, NJ, 91; Pro Libris: Pictures & Studies, The Princeton Lib, New York, 92. *Awards:* Samuel Shellabarger Mem Creative Thesis Prize, Princeton Univ, 78; Mrs Sidney Kalikow Mem, Pastels Only, 87. *Bibliog:* Simon, Secin (auth), Pastel Soc Am--ARTspeak, 10/92. *Mem:* Pastel Soc Am; Soc Scribes; Graphic Artists Guild. *Media:* Pastel, Conte. *Publ:* Illusr, Roaring at One Hundred, Princeton, 84; Phonethics, Palaemon Press, 85; Poison Pen, Stuart Wright, 85. *Mailing Add:* 99-44 67th Rd Apt 6C Forest Hills NY 11375

BUMBECK, DAVID A
PRINTMAKER, EDUCATOR
b Framingham, Mass, May 15, 40. *Study:* RI Sch Design, BFA, 62; Syracuse Univ, with Robert Marx, MFA, 66. *Work:* New York Pub Libr; Metrop Mus Art, New York; Brooklyn Mus, NY; Wiggin Collection, Boston Pub Libr; Libr Congress, Washington, DC. *Exhib:* Boston Printmakers Nat Exhib, 67-86; Living Am Artists & the Figure, Mus Art, Pa State Univ, 74; 31st Nat Print Exhib, Brooklyn Mus, 78; Nat Print Exhib, Philadelphia Print Club, 79; Nat Exhib, Soc Am Graphic Artists, 79. *Pos:* Dir, Christian A Johnson Gallery, 73-85. *Teaching:* Instr painting & printmaking, Mass Col Art, Boston, 66-68; prof printmaking, Middlebury Col, 68- *Awards:* David Berger Mem Award, Boston Printmakers Nat Exhib, 68; Purchase Award, Soc Am Graphic Artists Nat Exhib, NY, 79; Acadamician Nat Acad Design, 92. *Mem:* Boston Printmakers (mem exec bd, 68-); Soc Am Graphic Artists. *Media:* Intaglio. *Dealer:* Mary Ryan Gallery 452 Columbus Ave New York NY 10024. *Mailing Add:* Drew Lane RD Three Middlebury VT 05753

BUMGARDNER, JAMES ARLISS
PAINTER, EDUCATOR
b Winston-Salem, NC, Mar 25, 35. *Study:* Univ NC; Salem Col, Winston-Salem; Richmond Prof Inst, BFA; also with Hans Hofmann. *Work:* NC Mus Fine Arts, Raleigh; Va Mus Fine Arts; Philip Morris & Co, Richmond; Chrysler Mus, Norfolk, Va; Sidney & Frances Lewis, Richmond, Va; and others. *Exhib:* Art USA, New York, 59; Va Artist's Show, var times, 59-77; Art Across America, New York, 65; Metarealities, Wash Proj Arts, 80; South Eastern Ctr Contemp Art Invitational, 81; Encuento Am Mus, Lima, Peru, 91; and others. *Pos:* Guest set designer, Va Mus Theater, Waiting for Godot, 80. *Teaching:* Prof drawing & painting, Va Commonwealth Univ, 58- *Awards:* Five Special Awards Painting, NC Mus Art, 57-62; four Cert of Distinction, Va Mus Fine Art, 59-63 & 77; Purchase Prize, Southeastern Ctr for Contemp Arts, 77; and others. *Bibliog:* Metarealities rev, New Art Examiner, Vol 7, No 7, 4/80 & Gallery K rev, 9/85; Beyond refinement, Images & Issue, Vol 3, winter 80-81; and others. *Media:* Oil, Pastel. *Dealer:* Gallery K 2010 R St NW Washington DC 20009; Zola Fine Art Inc 12204 Ventura Blvd Studio City CA 91604. *Mailing Add:* 406 N Allen Ave Richmond VA 23220

BUNIN, LOUIS
SCULPTOR
b Kiev, Russia, Mar 28, 04; US citizen. *Study:* Chicago Art Inst, 29; Acad Grande Chaumiere, Paris, 30-31; Art Educ Alliance, New York, 75-80. *Work:* Mid-Hudson Art Mus, Poughkeepsie, NY; Corcoran Gallery Art; Montreal Mus Fine Arts. *Exhib:* Retrospective, Younge Gallery, Chicago, 30; Wood Carvings, ACA Gallery, New York, 66; Sculpture in Motion, Lytton Ctr Art & Sci, Los Angeles, 75; Puppet Heritage, Pratt Inst Gallery, 78 & Corcoran Gallery Art, 80; Ideal Type Casting in Sculpture, Bronx Mus, 78; Mid-Hudson Art Mus, Poughkeepsie, NY, 81; Animation Film, Montreal Mus Fine Arts, 82. *Teaching:* Artist-in-residence sculpture, in animation film, Pratt Inst, 78-79; instr, Sch Visual Arts, 79- *Awards:* Elizabeth Erlanger Mem Award, Steel Dancer, Am Soc Contemp Art, 83; Brit Film Inst Archive (for Alice in Wonderland). *Bibliog:* Seymour Peck (auth), article in NY Times, 53; Derek Hudson (auth), Type casting in sculpture, Constable, London, 54; Seamas Culhane (auth), Sculpture in Animation, Dell, 83. *Mem:* Am Soc Contemp Artists (mem bd dirs, 79); Artists Equity; Sculptors Alliance; Int Sculpture Ctr. *Media:* Steel, Stone. *Publ:* Auth, 3-D forms in animation film, Theater Arts Mag, 39; article in Am Artist Mag, 11/81; Sculpture on films, Close Up Mag, 82; producer, Alice in Wonderland (film: sculpture in animation). *Mailing Add:* 790 Riverside Dr New York NY 10032

BUNN, DAVID
PHOTOGRAPHER
b Greensboro, NC, Apr 12, 50. *Study:* St Andrews Col, BA, 72; Univ Calif, Los Angeles, MFA, 84. *Work:* Los Angeles Co Mus Art, Los Angeles; Nat Mus Am Art, Smithsonian Inst, Washington, DC; San Francisco Mus Mod Art. *Comn:* Permanent Installation, Los Angeles Cent Libr. *Exhib:* One-man shows, Allied Arts Gallery, Las Vegas, 87, Sphere of Influence, Santa Monica Mus Art, 88 & 89, Deliberate Investigations, Los Angeles Co Mus Art, 89, Roy Boyd Gallery, Santa Monica, 90, Individual Realities, Sezon Mus, Tokyo & Tsukashin Hall, Osaka, 91 & Biennial III: Mapping Histories, Newport Harbor Art Mus, 91; 4-artists show, San Francisco Mus Mod Art, 89; Open Channels Five Year Survey of Video Fellowships, Long Beach Mus Art, 90; Biennial I, Calif Mus Photog, Riverside, 90; LA Times: A Survey of Recent Los Angeles Art, Boise Art Mus, Idaho, 91; The Chapman Market Show, Chapman Market, Los Angeles, 91; and others. *Awards:* Individual Artist Fel, Mass Artists Found, 81; Nat Endowment Arts, 88 & 89. *Bibliog:* Fran Colpitt (auth), Art in America, 1/90; Amy Gerstler (auth), rev, Art Forum, 9/90; Howard Singerman (auth), Lessons from David Bunn (catalog essay), Biennial III: Mapping Histories, Newport Harbor Art Mus, 91; and others. *Mailing Add:* 1547 Tenth St Santa Monica CA 90401

BUNNELL, PETER CURTIS
EDUCATOR, CURATOR
b Poughkeepsie, NY, Oct 25, 37. *Study:* Rochester Inst Technol, BFA, 59; Ohio Univ, MFA, 61; Yale Univ, MA, 65. *Collections Arranged:* Photography as Printmaking, 68, Photography into Sculpture, 70, Clarence H White, 71, Mus Mod Art, New York; Harry Callahan, US Pavillion, Venice Bienale, 78; Robert O Dougan Collection, 83; Minor White: The Eye That Shapes, 89; The Art of Pictorial Photography, 92. *Pos:* Cur photog, Mus Mod Art, New York, 66-72; cur photog, Art Mus, Princeton Univ, 72-, dir, 73-78. *Teaching:* Vis lectr hist photog, Dartmouth Col, 68 & Inst Film/TV, New York Univ, 68-70; McAlpin prof hist photog & mod art, Princeton Univ, 72-; vis lectr hist photog, Yale Univ, 73. *Awards:* Guggenheim Fel, 79; Asian Cult Coun, 84; George Wittenborn Award, Art Libraries Soc, 89. *Mem:* Soc Photog Educ (nat chmn, 73-77); Col Art Asn Am (bd dirs, 75-79); Friends of Photog (bd trustees, 74-86, pres, 78-87, chmn, 87-92). *Media:* Photography. *Res:* History of photography with primary emphasis on the 20th century. *Publ:* Auth, John Pfahl, 81, Emmet Gowin, 83, Clarence H White: The Reverence for Beauty, 87, Nina Alexander, 87, Minor White: The Eye That Shapes, 89; ed, A Photographic Vision, 89, Edward Weston on Photograpy, 83, The Art of Pictorial Photography, 92; auth, Degrees of Guidance, Cambridge Univ Press, 93. *Mailing Add:* Dept Art & Archeol Princeton Univ Princeton NJ 08544

BUNNEN, LUCINDA WEIL
PHOTOGRAPHER, COLLECTOR
b Katonah, NY, Jan 14, 30. *Study:* Atlanta Col Art, 70-71; also study with Michael Lesy, Minor White, Linda Connor, Duane Michaels & George Tice. *Work:* Mus Mod Art & Whitney Mus Am Art, New York; Pushkin Mus, Moscow; High Mus Art, Atlanta; R J Reynolds Industs, Winston-Salem, NC. *Comn:* 40 photographs, O'Hare Hyatt House, Chicago, 72; 40' mural & 5-screen slide show, High Mus Art, Atlanta, 74; film from slides, US Comn Civil Rights, Montgomery, 78; prints, Northside Hosp, Atlanta, 86. *Exhib:* Synthetic Color, Univ Southern Ill, Carbondale, 74; Portrait of America, Smithsonian traveling exhib, 75-79; Friends of Photography, Carmel, Calif, 76, 78 & 79; Women in the Arts, Soho 20, New York, 77; Movers and Shakers in Georgia, High Mus Art, Atlanta, 78; Central Wash State Univ, Ellensburg, 83; Atlanta in France, Angolene Art Ctr, Angolene, France, 85; Nexus Gallery, Atlanta, 85 & 86; one-woman shows, The Upstairs Art Space, Tryon, NC, 85, Columbia Mus Arts & Sci, SC, 88, Scoring in Heaven, Jackson Fine Art, Atlanta, Ga, 91, Arts Connection, Atlanta, Ga, 91, Wyndy Morehead Fine Arts, New Orleans, La, 91, Albany Mus Art, Ga, 91, Lamar Dodd Art Ctr, LaGrange, Ga, 92. *Collections Arranged:* Subjective Vision: The Lucinda Bunnen Collection of Photographs (with catalog), High Mus Art, Atlanta, 84. *Pos:* Bd dirs, High Mus Art, 78-, Image Film & Video, 82-, Art Papers, 82-. *Awards:* Outstanding Leadership Award, Am Asn Univ Women, 75; Governor's Award Arts, Ga, 86; First Place, 2nd Ann Photog Contest, Atlanta Women's News, 90. *Bibliog:* Steve Dollar (auth), Atlanta J, 3/6/91; Sarah Ferrell (auth), The Last Word, NY Times Bk Rev, 7/28/91; Picks & Pans, People Mag, 3/25/91. *Mem:* Friends of Photog; Int Ctr Photog; Eastman House; Visual Studies Workshop. *Media:* Photography, Video. *Collection:* Contemporary photography, painting & sculpture. *Publ:* Contribr, Southern Ethic, Nexus Press, 75; auth, Movers and Shakers in Georgia, Simon & Schuster, New York, 78; contribr, Family of Women, Ridge Press, 79; Visions, Environment. *Dealer:* Jackson Fine Art 515 E Paces Ferry Rd NE Suite 200 Atlanta GA 30305. *Mailing Add:* 3910 Randall Mill Rd NW Atlanta GA 30327

BUNTS, FRANK
KINETIC ARTIST, PAINTER
b Cleveland, Ohio, Mar 2, 32. *Study:* Yale Univ; Cleveland Inst Art; Case Western Reserve Univ, BA & MA. *Work:* Philadelphia Mus Art, Pa; Fine Arts Gallery, San Diego, Calif; Libr Cong, Washington, DC; Corcoran Gallery Art, Washington, DC; Cleveland Mus Art, Ohio; and others. *Exhib:* Cleveland Mus Art, Ohio; San Francisco Mus Art, Calif; One-man shows, Nat Acad Sci, Washington, DC, Catholic Univ Am, Washington, DC, 78, Plum Gallery, Washington, DC, 79 & Limelight Gallery, New York, 88; Corcoran Art Gallery, Washington, DC, 72; Indianapolis Mus Art, Ind; Brooks Mem Art Gallery, Memphis, Tenn, 73; Mus Mod Art, Rijeka, Yugoslavia; Guild Hall, East Hampton, NY; Christie's, New York. *Teaching:* Cleveland Inst Art, Ohio, 63-64; Ark State Univ, Jonesboro, Ark, 65-67; Univ Md, College Park, 67-77, dir, Grad Art Studio Prog, 71-77. *Awards:* Purchase Prize, Cleveland Mus Art, 62; Exhib Award, Nat Acad Sci, 76. *Bibliog:* American References, NY Art Rev, 88; American Drawings, Watercolors, Pastels & Collages, (catalog), Corcoran Gallery Art, 83; Cleveland Mus Art Bull 5/62 & 5/68. *Mem:* Archibr Am Art, New York. *Media:* Oil and organic resin on Canvas. *Dealer:* Flatiron Studio New York NY. *Mailing Add:* 15 W 24th St New York NY 10010

BUONAGURIO, EDGAR R
PAINTER, MURALIST
b Yonkers, NY, July 4, 46. *Study:* City Col New York, BA, 69; Teachers Col, Columbia Univ, MA, 72. *Work:* Joseph Hirshhorn Mus & Sculpture Garden, Washington, DC; Mint Mus Art, Charlotte, NC; Bronx Mus Arts, NY; Herbert F Johnson Mus Art, Cornell Univ; Everson Mus Art, Syracuse, NY. *Comn:* Fantail (mural), The Continental Group, Stamford, Conn, 80-81; Byzantine Dream, Continental Nat Bank, Ft Worth, 82; Labyrinth (mural), City Nat Bank, Baton Rouge, 83; Olympia & York, Inc, New York, 85; Develop Specialists, Inc, Chicago, Ill, 86. *Exhib:* Mint Mus Art, Charlotte, NC; Everson Mus Art, Syracuse, 83; Zolla-Lieberman Gallery, Chicago, Ill, 84; Gloria Luria Gallery, Bay Harbor Islands, Fla, 85; Jerald Melberg Gallery, Charlotte, NC, 85; Hadler/Rodriquez, Houston, Tex, 86; Oscarsson-Siegeltuch, New York, 87; and others. *Pos:* Critic, Arts Mag, New York, 77-80. *Teaching:* Instr painting, Hudson River Mus, Yonkers, NY, 69-74; instr art & art hist, Riverdale Country Sch, Bronx, NY, 69-79; adj prof painting, Westchester Community Col, 72, Col New Rochelle, 74. *Awards:* Creative Artists Pub Serv Prog Fel Painting, 81-82. *Bibliog:* Ellen Lubell (auth), Edgar Buonagurio at Andre Zarre, Art in Am, 83; Phillip Verre (auth), Recent painting by Edgar Buonagurio, Arts Mag, 84; Grace Glueck (auth), Edgar Buonagurio, NY Times, 84. *Media:* Acrylic, Canvas. *Dealer:* Oscarsson-Siegeltuch Gallery 568 Broadway New York NY 10012; Zolla-Lieberman Gallery 356 W Huron Chicago IL 60610. *Mailing Add:* 120 Vineyard Ave Yonkers NY 10703

BUONAGURIO, TOBY LEE
SCULPTOR
b Bronx, NY, June 28, 47. *Study:* City Col New York, BA(fine arts), 69, MA(art educ), 71. *Work:* Heckscher Mus, Huntington, New York; Everson Mus Art, Syracuse, NY; Mint Mus Art, Charlotte, NC; Alternative Mus, New York. *Exhib:* Solo exhibs, Gallery Yues Arman, New York, 82, Everson Mus Art, Syracuse, NY, 82, Bronx Mus Arts, NY, 83, Contemp Arts Ctr, New Orleans, 83, Jerald Melberg Gallery, Charlotte, NC, 85 & Fine Arts Gallery, State Univ NY, Stony Brook, 86; Contemp self-portraits, Allan Frumkin Gallery, New York, 83; and others. *Teaching:* Prof and dir undergrad study, art dept, State Univ NY, Stony Brook, 76- *Awards:* Creative Artists Public Service Fel for drawing, 80-81. *Bibliog:* April Kingsley (auth), Toby Buonagurio, Arts Mag, 80; Robert Lubar (auth), Toby Buonagurio, Arts Mag, 82; Thomas Piche (auth), Toby Buonagurio, Am Ceramics, 82; Ellen Lee Klein (auth), Toby Buonagurio: More optical bounce to the ounce, Arts Mag, 86; Ceramics Today: Toby Buonagurio USA (monogr), Editons Olizare, Geneva, Switz, 84; and others. *Mem:* Col Art Asn. *Media:* Ceramic; Mixed Media. *Publ:* Coauth, Ceramic directions: A contemporary overview, 83. *Mailing Add:* 1723 Holland Ave Bronx NY 10462

BURCH, CLAIRE R
PAINTER, WRITER
b New York, NY, Feb 19, 35. *Study:* Wash Sq Col, New York Univ, BA, 47. *Work:* Butler Inst Am Art, Youngstown, Ohio; Guild Hall, East Hampton, NY; Birmingham Mus, Ala; Brooklyn Mus, NY; Beth Israel Hosp, New York; North Shore Hosp; and others. *Comn:* Painting, Roche Image, 65. *Exhib:* One-man shows, Ruth White Gallery, New York, 63, Galerie L'Antipoete, Paris, France, 63, Southampton Col, 64-65 & Roko Gallery, 64; Maniacal Laughter, Westbeth Gallery, New York, 71 & 84; Berkeley Art Ctr, 81; Visual Art Prog, broadcast on bay area cable station, Calif, 89-92. *Pos:* Contrib ed, Network News, Life, Saturday Review, McCalls, Arts & Sci, NY Times Book Review, Madamoiselle, Good Housekeeping and others; exec dir art & educ media, Berkeley, Calif, currently. *Teaching:* Adj prof, Union Experimenting Col; workshop instr coun arts, Westbeth, New York. *Awards:* grant, Ctr Independant Living, Berkeley, Calif; grant; grant, City Berkeley; and others. *Mem:* New York Playwrights Cooperative. *Media:* Watercolor, Collage, Oil on Paper. *Publ:* Careers in Psychiatry, MacMillan; Stranger in the Family, Bobbs Merrill, 72 & 92; Notes of a Survivor, 72; illus, Shredded Millions, Alfonia, 82; Postscript to the Livermore Thousand, 83; James Baldwin (film), Entering Oakland (film), Thumbed a Ride to Heaven (film), Oracle Rising (film), Remembering the Summer of Love and Other Songs by Claire Burch (film), People's Part of Berkeley (film) & Homeless in the 80's (film); and others. *Dealer:* Regent Press Gallery 6020A Adeline Oakland CA 94608. *Mailing Add:* 2747 Regent St Berkeley CA 94705

BURCHARD, PETER DUNCAN
ILLUSTRATOR, PHOTOGRAPHER
b Washington, DC, Mar 1, 21. *Study:* Philadelphia Mus Sch Art, cert, 47. *Awards:* Guggenheim Fel, 66; Christopher Award, 73. *Mem:* Int PEN. *Media:* Black & White Color Film. *Publ:* auth & illusr, Whaleboat Raid, Coward McCann & Geoghegan, 77; illusr, Night Spell, Atheneum, 77; Ocean Race, 78 & Chinwe, 79, G P Putnam's Sons; auth & illusr , Sea Change, Farrar Straus Giroux; Venturing: An Introduction to Sailing, Little Brown and Co; and 80 books for major publ & mus revs and profiles of mus dirs for "Connoisseur". *Mailing Add:* 1192 W Main St Williamstown MA 01267-2622

BURCHESS, ARNOLD
PAINTER, SCULPTOR
b Chicago, Ill, June 7, 12. *Study:* City Col New York, BSS; also with George W Eggers & Robert Garrison. *Comn:* Three bas reliefs (with Robert Garrison), Radio City Music Hall, New York, 35; portrait in bronze of Senator Edmund S Muskie, State Capital, Augusta, Maine, 74. *Exhib:* Am Watercolor Soc, New York, 55-; Birmingham Mus Art, Ala, 55; one-man show, Van Dimant Gallery, Southampton, NY, 57; Mus Mod Art, New York, 59; Maine Art Gallery, Wiscasset, 75; Saddleback Col, Mission Viejo, Calif, 81. *Teaching:* Lectr, Shapes in Clay, Metrop Mus Art, New York, 39; prof fine art & chmn dept, Fashion Inst Technol, New York, 59-74; vis prof figurative sculpture, Bowdoin Col, 75; instr, Saddleback Col, Calif, 79- *Awards:* Watercolor Prize, Birmingham Mus Art, 55. *Bibliog:* Article in La Rev Mod, 56; Arnold Burchess-watercolorist, Am Artist Mag, 59; Norman Kent (auth), 100 Watercolor Techniques, Watson-Guptill, 70. *Mem:* Am Watercolor Soc; Audubon Artists. *Media:* Watercolor; Ceramic Clay, Slate. *Publ:* Coauth, The Human Form, Anatomy, Avery Publ, 81. *Dealer:* Challis Gallery Laguna Beach CA. *Mailing Add:* 5299 Cantante Laguna Hills CA 92653

BURCHETT, DEBRA
ADMINISTRATOR, CURATOR
b Bremerhaven, Ger, Sept 26, 55; US citizen. *Study:* Univ Ky, Lexington, 74-75; Univ Calif, Irvine, with Craig Kauffman, Alexis Smith & Tony DeLap, BFA, 77, independent res under Melinda Wortz, BA, 78. *Collections Arranged:* Clothing Constructions, 79, Michelangelo Pistoletto, 79, Barry Le Va, New York Artist, Nat Endowment Arts Exhib, 80, Architectural Sculpture, Nat Endowment Arts Mus Prog, 80, Il Modo Italiano, Nat Endowment Arts Mus Prog, 83-84 & others, Los Angeles Inst Contemp Art. *Pos:* Gallery asst, Univ Calif, Irvine & Newport Harbor Art Mus, Newport Beach, Calif, 76-77; ed, Jour: Contemp Art Mag, 77-80; cur, Main & Entrance Galleries, Los Angeles Inst Contemp Art, 79-84; develop asst, Fine Arts Gallery, Mount St Mary's Col, 81 & Calif State Univ, Los Angeles, 83; dir, sales & admin, Gemini-G E L (graphics ed ltd), Los Angeles, 84-92 & The Litho Shop Inc/Sam Francis, Santa Monica, Calif, 92-; advert rep, Art Forum Mag. *Awards:* Nat Endowment Visual Arts Mus Prog Grant, 79; Critics Residency Grant, 79 & Artist Residency Grant, 80, Nat Endowment Arts; and others. *Bibliog:* Jennifer Seder (auth), Closet art, Los Angeles Times, 6/8/79; Germano Celant (auth), Culture, L'Europeo, Rome, Italy, 8/79; Melinda Wortz (auth), Clothing constructions, Art News, 9/79. *Mem:* Nat Asn Artists' Orgn (founding bd dirs, 82-83); Graphics Arts Coun. *Publ:* Ed, Art and music, 70, issues 17-25, 77-80 & Another look at conceptualism, 79, J Southern Calif Art Mag; contribr, Visits: Kisch, Lere, Vogel & Scoops: Nordman, Irwin, Wheeler, 78 & ed spec issue, Art in Latin America (bilingual ed), 79, J Los Angeles Inst Contemp Art. *Mailing Add:* c/o The Litho Shop 2058 Broadway Santa Monica CA 90404

BURCHETT, KENNETH EUGENE
EDUCATOR, ADMINISTRATOR
b Stockton, Mo April 26, 42. *Study:* SW Mo State Univ, BS, 66; Univ Tulsa, MA, 70; Univ NTex, PhD, 80. *Exhib:* 47th Ann Ten State, Moody Art Ctr, Shreveport, La, 70; 39th Ann Ten State, Springfield Art Mus, Mo, 70; 30th Okla Ann, Philbrook Mus, Tulsa, 70; Drawing Mid-USA 1, Spiva Art Ctr, Joplin, Mo, 76; Fine Arts Ann, Dallas Mus Fine Art, Tex, 78; Nat Painting, Pensacola Col, Fla, 80; Mid-Four Regional, Nelson-Atkins, Kansas City, Mo, 84; Group Invitational, Ark Arts Ctr, Little Rock, 87. *Teaching:* Prof & chmn art, Col of the Ozarks, Branson, Mo, 72-85; prof & chmn art, Univ Central Ark, Conway, 85- *Mem:* Inter-Soc Color Coun; Nat Asn Sch Art & Design; Col Art Asn Am; Nat Art Educ Asn; Am Asn Univ Prof. *Res:* Color Theory: Attributes of Color Harmony, Color Design and Color Applications. *Publ:* Auth, Art Vocabulary, Mental Measurements Yearbook, Gryphon, 78; Twelve Books on Color, 89 & Color Harmony Attributes, 91, Color Research & Application, Wiley & Sons; Faber Birren, Leonardo JISAST, Pergamon, 90; Color Education, Inter-Soc Color Coun News, 91. *Mailing Add:* University of Central Arkansas Dept of Art McAlister Hall No 101 Conway AR 72032

BURCHFIELD, JERRY LEE
PHOTOGRAPHER, EDUCATOR
b Chicago, Ill, July 28, 47. *Study:* Calif State Univ, Fullerton, BA(photo-commun), 71, MA(art), 77, MFA, 90. *Work:* Los Angeles Co Mus, Calif; St Louis Mus Art, Mo; Bibliot Nat, Paris; Minneapolis Inst Arts, Minn; Denver Art Mus; plus others. *Comn:* Mixed media installation, Organge Co Ctr Contemp Art, 91; Mixed media installation, Calif Mus Photog, 92. *Exhib:* Studio Work, Los Angeles Co Mus Art, 82; Dreamscapes, Clarence Kennedy Gallery, Boston, Mass, 85; Photograms, John Michael Kohler Arts Ctr, Sheboygan, Wis, 85; Min Gallery, Tokyo, Japan, 88; Relevance of Narrative, Long Beach Mus, 89; Earth People, Organge Co Ctr Contemp Art, 91; Projections/Documentations, Calif Mus Photog, 92; and others. *Pos:* Asst dir, Newport Gallery, Newport Sch Photog, Calif, 73-75; dir/co-owner, BC Space, Photog Gallery, Laguna Beach, Calif, 73-87; coordr photog gallery, Cypress Col Calif. *Teaching:* Instr & lectr photog, Calif State Univ, Fullerton, 78-87; instr, Saddleback Col, Mission Viejo, Calif, 79- & Cypress Col, Cypress, Calif, 88-; instr, Orange Coast Col, 81-87. *Awards:* Photographer's Fel, Nat Endowment Arts, 81; Numerous Purchase Awards. *Bibliog:* Lauri Pelissero (auth), Jerry Burchfield, photographer, Air Calif Mag, 12/79; Elaine Dines (auth), Jerry Burchfield, Photo Bulletin, 6-7/81; Linda Bellon (auth), Jerry Burchfield: An interview, Obscura, fall 82. *Mem:* Soc for Photog Educ; Los Angeles Ctr for Photog Studies; Friends of Photog. *Media:* Photography. *Publ:* Auth, Color Solarization, 73 & Cameraless photography, 75, Peterson's Photogs; illusr/contribr, Basic Darkroom Book, Plume, 77; contrib ed, articles in Darkroom Photog Mag, Vol 1, No 3 & 6, 79; auth & illusr, Darkroom Art, Amphoto, 80; plus others. *Dealer:* TBA Gallery Santa Monica, CA. *Mailing Add:* 6 Meade Irvine CA 92720-2623

BURCKHARDT, RUDY
PHOTOGRAPHER, FILMMAKER
b Basel, Switz, Apr 5, 14; US citizen. *Study:* Ozenfant Sch, New York, 48; Brooklyn Mus Sch, 49; Acad Naples, 50-51. *Work:* Mus Mod Art, Metrop Mus Art, New York; Art Inst Chicago; Univ New Orleans; Contemp Arts Mus, Houston, Tex. *Exhib:* Brooke Alexander Gallery, New York, 75; Marlborough Gallery, New York, 81; Photographs, Houston, Tex, 88; Painting, Blue Mountain Gallery, New York, NY, 90; Retrospective (films), Mus Mod Art, New York, 87. *Teaching:* Lectr filmmaking, Grad Sch Art, Univ Pa, Philadelphia, 67-75, lectr painting, 75-84. *Awards:* Brendan Gill Award, 88. *Bibliog:* Alex Katz (auth), article, Art News, 63; Lucy Lippard (auth), article, Art in Am, 75; Thomas B Hess (auth), article, New York Mag, 75. *Publ:* Illusr, Mediterranean Cities, 55; illusr, Mobile Homes, Z-Press, 79. *Dealer:* Brooke Alexander Gallery 26 E 78th St New York NY 10021; Blue Mountain Gallery (Coop) 121 Wooster St New York NY 10012. *Mailing Add:* 50 W 29th St New York NY 10001

BURCKHARDT, YVONNE HELENE See Jacquette, Yvonne Helene

BURDEN, CARTER
COLLECTOR
b Los Angeles, Calif, Aug 25, 41. *Study:* Harvard Univ, BA(cum laude), 63; Columbia Univ Law Sch, LLB, 66. *Pos:* Trustee, New York Pub Libr; mem, vis comt, Fogg Art Mus, Harvard Univ. *Collection:* Works of the contemporary period, mainly American abstract paintings since 1950. *Mailing Add:* 630 Fifth Ave Rm 2030 New York NY 10111

BURDEN, CHRIS
CONCEPTUAL ARTIST, SCULPTOR
b Boston, Mass, Apr 11, 46. *Study:* Pomona Col, BFA, 69; Univ Calif, Irvine, MFA, 71. *Work:* Art Mus South Tex, Corpus Christi; La Jolla Mus Contemp Art, Calif; Magasin 3 Konsthall, Stockholm; Mus Contemp Art, Los Angeles; Mus Mod Art, New York; Newport Harbor Art Mus, Newport Beach, Calif; Lannan Found, Los Angeles; Los Angeles Co Mus Art. *Exhib:* Projects Video, Mus Mod Art, New York, 75; Painting and Sculpture in California: The Modern Era, San Francisco Mus Mod Art, 76; New Talent Award Winners '63-'76, Los Angeles Co Mus Art, 76; The Mus as Site: Sixteen Projects, Los Angeles Co Mus Art, 81; TV in Place, San Francisco Art Inst, 81; Eight Artists: The Anxious Edge, Walker Art Ctr, Minneapolis, Minn, 82; A Recent Survey of International Painting and Sculpture, Mus Mod Art, NY, 84; Modern Machines: Recent Kinetic Sculpture, Whitney Mus Am Art, Phillip Morris Br, 42nd St, New York, 85; solo exhibs, All the Submarines of the United States of America, Christine Burgin Gallery, NY, 87, Chris Burden: A Twenty-Year Survey, (traveling exhib), Newport Harbor Art Mus, Newport Beach, Calif, 88-89, Devil Drawings, Christine Burgen Gallery, 89, Chris Burden, Kent Fine Art, NY, 89, Sampson, Josh Baer Gallery, NY, 89, Chris Burden, Jurgen Becker Gallery, Hamburg, 90, Chris Burden, Daniel Buchholz Gallery, Cologne, 90; Committed to Print, Mus Mod Art, (traveling exhib), NY, 88-90; Just Pathetic, Rosamund Felsen Gallery, Los Angeles, 90; Seven Obsessions: New Installation Work, Whitechapel Art Gallery, London, 90; New Art for Newcastle, TSWA Four Cities Project, Eng, 90; New Works for New Spaces: Into the Nineties, Wexner Ctr Visual Arts, Columbus, Ohio, 90-91; Dislocations, Mus Mod Art, 91-92; Chris Burden, Lannan Found, 92; Helter Skelter, Mus Contemp Art, Los Angeles, 92. *Teaching:* Asst to vis prof, Carpenter Ctr Visual Arts, Harvard Univ, Cambridge, Mass, 64; San Francisco Art Inst, 78; full prof, Univ Calif, Los Angeles, 78- *Awards:* New Talent Award, Los Angeles Co Mus, 73; Nat Endowment Arts Individual Artist Grant, 74, 76, 80 & 83; John Simon Guggenheim Fel, 78. *Bibliog:* Mediamatic: Edge 90, 4:4, Edge Trust, London & Mediamatic Found, Amsterdam, summer 90, 198, 200, 201-202, 215, 216, 226; David Pagel (auth), Vexed Sex, Art Issues, Los Angeles, #9, 2/9, 11-16; 1989 Biennial Exhibition (catalog), Whitney Mus Am Art, NY, 89. *Media:* Broadcast Television. *Publ:* Auth & dir, Through the Night Softly (video), 73; Poem for LA (video), 75; Chris Burden (video), 76; Full Financial Disclosure (video), 77. *Mailing Add:* c/o Kent Fine Art Inc 41 E 57th St New York NY 10022

BURDOCK, HARRIET
HISTORIAN, PRINTMAKER
b Buffalo, NY, June 21, 44. *Study:* Univ NMex, with Garo Antresian, BFA, 66; Kean Col, Mass, 69; Pratt Graphics Ctr, New Sch Social Res, with Clare Romano & Federico Castellon. *Pos:* Lectr, NJ State Mus, Trenton, 67-68; asst, Art, Prints & Photog Div, New York Public Libr, 80- *Teaching:* Instr art hist, Bergen Co Col, Paramus, NJ, 78-79. *Mem:* Col Art Asn Am; Am Asn Mus; Int Coun Mus; Asn Hist Am Art; Print Club New York (founding comt, 92-). *Publ:* Auth, Notes from Russia, Graphic Arts Coun NY Newsletter, 77; auth, Woodcuts in China, Print Collector's Newsletter, 81. *Mailing Add:* c/o Art, Prints & Photog Div NY Public Libr New York NY 10018

BURFORD, BYRON LESLIE
PAINTER, PRINTMAKER
b Jackson, Miss, July 12, 20. *Study:* Univ Iowa, BFA & MFA. *Work:* Worcester Art Mus, Mass; Walker Art Ctr, Minneapolis; Nelson-Atkins Gallery, Kansas City, Mo; Sheldon Art Mus, Lincoln, Nebr; High Mus Art, Atlanta, Ga. *Exhib:* Solo exhibs, Babcock Galleries, 66, 67, 69 & 75; Am Acad Arts Ann, New York, 66, 72 & 79; Foxley/Leach Gallery, Washington, DC, 87; Venice Biennale, Italy, 68; Bienal Arte Coltejer, Colombia, 70; Kunsthaus, Zurich, Switz, 72; and others. *Teaching:* Prof painting, Univ Iowa, 47-86, prof emer, 86; Univ Minn & Univ Mass, 67. *Awards:* Guggenheim Found Fel, 60 & 61; Ford Found Award, 61, 62 & 64; Nat Inst Arts & Lett Grants, 67, 72 & 75; Midwest Arts Nat Endowment Regional Fel, 88. *Media:* Acrylic, Oil; Prints. *Dealer:* Foxley/Leach Gallery 3214 O St NW Washington DC. *Mailing Add:* 113 S Johnson Iowa City IA 52240

BURFORD, WILLIAM E
DEALER, ADMINISTRATOR
b Lubbock, Tex, May 16, 36. *Study:* Tex Tech Univ, BA. *Pos:* Pres, Tex Art Gallery, Dallas, 76-; vchmn, Tex Comn on the Arts & Humanities, Austin, 76, chmn, 77-78; mem, Dallas City Art Comn, 77- *Specialty:* Predominately contemporary Western art with Americana, wildlife, landscapes, books, prints, sculpture and porcelains. *Mailing Add:* Texas Art Gallery 5570 W Lovers Lane, Suite 396 Dallas TX 75209-4220

BURG, PATRICIA JEAN
PAINTER, PRINTMAKER
b Windsor, Ont, Can, Jan 9, 34; US citizen. *Study:* Otis Art Inst, Los Angeles, MFA, 66. *Work:* IBM Co, Los Angeles; Art in Embassies, White House Loan Collection; Standard Oil Co, New York. *Comn:* Oil paintings, Latham & Watkins, Los Angeles, 75 & 79, Allison Corp, Los Angeles, 75, Roberts Scott & Co, San Diego, 76 & Carson City Hall, Calif, 77. *Exhib:* Northwest Printmakers, Seattle Art Mus, Wash, 69; Affect-Effect Exhib, La Jolla Mus Art, Calif, 69; New Work-New Talent, Los Angeles Co Mus Art, Los Angeles, 74; Contemporaries 17-Security Pacific, Los Angeles, 80; International Exchange, Exchange Gallery; Fine Arts, Soeul, Korea, 88; US-UK Print Collection, Barbican Ctr, London, Eng, 89. *Pos:* Co-founder & dir, Triad Graphic Workshop, Los Angeles, 66-; co-owner, Art Source Gallery, Los Angeles, 75- *Teaching:* Instr drawing, Otis Art Inst-Parsons, Los Angeles, currently; instr drawing, Occidental Col, Eagle Rock, Calif. *Awards:* Purchase Awards, Home Savings & Loan, Los Angeles, 64, Mus Fine Arts, Boston, 68 & Otis Art Inst, Los Angeles, 69. *Bibliog:* Bentley Schaad (auth), The Realm of Contemporary Still Life, Reinhold Press, 65; Thelma R Newman (auth), Innovative Printmaking, Crown, 75. *Mem:* Los Angeles Inst Contemp Art; Los Angeles Printmaking Soc (bd dirs, 76-77, pres, currently); Artists Econ Action. *Media:* Etching. *Specialty:* Modern art with emphasis on graphics and paintings. *Mailing Add:* 3666 Longridge Ave Sherman Oaks CA 91423

BURGER, GARY C
MUSEUM DIRECTOR
b Greenville, SC, Nov 6, 43. *Study:* Williams Col, BA, 65; Williams Col, Clark Art Inst, MA, 76. *Pos:* Assoc dir, Mass Coun Arts & Humanties, 76-78; consult, New Eng Found Arts, 78-79; dir, The Berkshire Mus, 79-89; Williamstown Regional Art Conserv Lab, 89- *Mem:* New England Mus Asn (past pres); Mass Arts Advocacy Comt; Asn Regional Conserv Ctrs (pres); Williams Col Mus AA vis comt. *Publ:* Auth, 100 American Drawings from the J D Hatch Collection, Heim Galleries, 76. *Mailing Add:* 324 Oblong Rd Williamstown MA 01267-3043

BURGER, W CARL
EDUCATOR, PAINTER
b Baden, Ger, Dec 27, 25; US citizen. *Study:* NY Univ, BS, MA; Columbia Univ, prof dipl; Rutgers Univ; Parsons Sch Design. *Work:* Kean Col, NJ; Bergen Mus; Chubb Asn; Newark Mus & State Mus, NJ; Exxon, NJ; and others. *Comn:* Space Mural, Lockheed Electronics, Woodbridge, NJ, 60. *Exhib:* Somerset Col, Tri-State Show, Somerville, NJ, 78; Watercolor Show, Holyoke Mus, Mass, 78; Newark Mus Triennial, 82; American Drawing, Morris Mus, 85; Retrospecitve, NJ State Mus, 87; and others. *Pos:* Set designer, Capemay Playhouse, 54-55 & Hillson's Theatre Stars, Binghamton, NY, 56. *Teaching:* Prof of design & drawing, Kean Col of NJ, Union, 60- *Awards:* Jocelyn Mus Award, Ball State Drawing Ann, Jocelyn Mus, 73; NJ State Coun Arts Grant, 81; Grant for Watercolor, Kean Col. *Bibliog:* Article in Art News, 9/83; featured on NJ Artists Series, NJ Pub TV, 86. *Mem:* NJ Watercolor Soc; Hunterdon Art Ctr (trustee, 69-72); Audubon Artists; Assoc Artists NJ (past pres, 80-83); Phi Delta Kappa. *Media:* Watercolor, Ink Drawings. *Dealer:* Robin Hutchins Gallery Maplewood Ctr Maplewood NJ; Church Door Gallery Califon NJ 07830. *Mailing Add:* Beacon Light Rd Box 322 RR 1 Califon NJ 07830

BURGESS, DAVID LOWRY
ENVIRONMENTAL ARTIST
b Philadelphia, Pa, Apr 27, 40. *Study:* Pa Acad Fine Arts, Philadelphia; Univ Pa; Inst Allende, San Miguel, Mex. *Work:* Houghton Libr; Harvard Univ, Cambridge, Mass; Mus Fine Arts, Boston; Smithsonian Collection, Washington, DC; Archives, Boston Pub Libr; Pa Acad Fine Arts Mus, Philadelphia; Herning Mus, Herning, Denmark; De Cordova Mus, Lincoln, Mass. *Exhib:* Earth, Air, Fire, Water, The Elements, Mus Fine Arts, Boston, 71 & Master Drawings of the 19th & 20th Centuries, 72; CAYAC Traveling Exhib, Spain, Peru, Arg & Chile, 72; Multiple Interaction Team, Chicago, San Francisco, Cincinnati & Philadelphia; Art Transition, Mass Inst Technol; Documenta 6, Kassel, Ger; Vienna Biennial, Austria, 79; Sky Arts Conference (co-ed catalog), Mass Inst Technol, 81, Linz, Austria, 82 & Munich, WGer, 83; De Cordova Mus, 85; Monocle, Hamburg Kunsthalle, 85; Pa Acad Fine Arts Mus; Kunstuersin, Karlsruhe, WGer; Cone, Light, Churn, Herning Art Mus, Herning, Denmark. *Pos:* Fel & sr consult, Ctr Advan Visual Studies, Mass Inst Technol, 71- *Teaching:* Prof, Mass Col Art, Boston, 69-; Dean, Col Fine Arts, Carnegie Mellon Univ, Pittsburgh, currently. *Awards:* Am Acad Arts & Lett Award, 72; Guggenheim Award, 73; Nat Endowment Arts Individual Artist Grant, 77 & 86; Rockefeller Artist Grant, 79-80 & 86; Mass Artist Found Fel, 83. *Bibliog:* Baker & kepes (co-auth), articles, Environment, 72; Starpits Waiting for Light Planes, Leonardo, winter 75; articles, Boston Mag, 10/78, 11/85 & Art in Am, 2/86; T Frick (auth), article, Sacred Theories of the Earth, 2/86; Raymond Vezina (ed) Burgess, Burgess Teéarré, Montreal. *Mem:* Arts Educ Am (adv bd, 78-); Nat Humanities Fac. *Publ:* Auth, Fragments, 69, Looking and Listening, 72 & Memory, Environment & Utopia, 75; and others. *Mailing Add:* 185 Spring St Hull MA 02045

BURGESS, JOSEPH JAMES, JR
PAINTER, EDUCATOR
b Albany, NY, July 13, 24. *Study:* Hamilton Col, BA, 47; Yale Univ, MA, 48; Pratt Inst, 52-54; Cranbrook Acad Art, MFA, 54. *Exhib:* Recent Drawings USA, Mus Mod Art, New York, 56; Drawing Nat, Calif Palace Legion Hon, San Francisco, 59; two-person show, Flint Inst Art, 56-65 DeWaters Art Ctr, Flint, Mich 64; Calif Design Ten Show, Pasadena Art Mus, 68; First Ann City of Angels Int Exhib Photog, 74; Santa Fe Festival of Arts, 79; one-man exhib, Albany Inst Hist, Art,NY, 58 Ball State Teachers College, 58, Historic Costume of the Orient, Sante Fe, NMex, 83. *Pos:* Designer & co-owner, Origins, retail & K/B Designs, wholesale, Carmel, Calif, 66-75 & The Gold Persimmon, retail & K/B Designs, wholesale, Santa Fe, NMex, currently; dir, Blair Galleries, Ltd, Santa Fe, NMex, 76-79. *Teaching:* Asst prof fine arts & head dept, St Lawrence Univ, Canton, NY, 54-55; art instr, chmn dept & dir, DeWaters Art Ctr, Flint Community Jr Col, 56-65; asst prof design, Ariz State Univ, Tempe, 65-66; asst prof art, NMex Highlands Univ, 82-83; instr drawing & design, Santa Fe Community Col, NMex, 86-90; workshops at Valdes Inc, Sante Fe NMex, 87- *Media:* Mixed. *Specialty:* Painting, sculpture and graphics. *Publ:* Auth, Three Chinese Poems, Translations from Tang Dynasty poets, winter 61-62, Four Chinese poems, translations from T'ang poetry, fall 61 & Some thoughts on non-communication in the arts, spring 63, Mich Voices; auth, A random poem, translation from the T'ang Dynasty poet Wang Wei, 10/12/73, A shining legend, 9/10/74, Asia's first iron-clad warship, 5/19/75, Christian Sci Monitor; and many others. *Mailing Add:* PO Box 2151 Santa Fe NM 87504-2151

BURGESS, LINDA SUZANNE
PAINTER, PHOTOGRAPHER
b Coral Gables, Fla, May 14, 54. *Study:* Miami-Dade Community Col, AA, 74; Appalachian State Univ, BA, 77; Rutgers Univ, MFA, 79. *Work:* Polaroid Int Collection. *Exhib:* Solo exhibs, Southeastern Ctr Contemp Art, Winston-Salem, NC, 82 & 86; 16 Artists & Birmingham Biennial, 83, Birmingham Mus Art; New Orleans Triennial, New Orleans Mus Art, 83; End of the World: Contemporary Visions of the Apocalypse, New Mus, New York, 83; Laughing to Keep from Crying, Dark Humor in the South, Contemp Art Ctr, New Orleans Mus & Alexandria Mus, La, 84; Romantic Painting, Tracey Garet Gallery, New York, 84; Dreamscapes, Olin Kennedy Ctr, Cambridge, Mass, 85; Focus: Three Birmingham Photographers, Birmingham Mus Art, Ala, 85; Three Photographers, Marie Martin Gallery, Washington, DC, 86. *Teaching:* Asst prof art, Judson Col, 79-81; assoc prof art, Birmingham-Southern Col, Ala, 81- *Awards:* Award of Merit, Shreveport Art Guild Nat Exhib, 84. *Bibliog:* Suzi Gablik (auth), Art alarms: Visions of the end, Art in Am, Vol 72, 4, 4/84; James R Nelson (auth), Focus at the Art Museum is best photographic exhibit in recent memory, Birmingham News, 6/23/85; Rose Wojnar (auth), Spontaneously combusting photos catch fire for artist, Ala J & Advertiser, 4/20/86. *Mem:* Birmingham Art Asn. *Media:* Oil. *Mailing Add:* Winstone Press Inc PO Box 24482 Winston-Salem NC 27114

BURGGRAF, RAY LOWELL
PAINTER, EDUCATOR
b Mt Gilead, Ohio, July 26, 38. *Study:* Ashland Col, BS, 61; Cleveland Inst Art, BFA, 68; Univ Calif, Berkeley, MA, 69, MFA, 70. *Work:* Mint Mus Art; Western Ill Univ; Montgomery Mus Fine Arts; Greenville County Mus; Dekalb Col. *Comn:* Royal Caribbean Cruise Lines Inc, 85. *Exhib:* Artists of the Southeast & Texas, Isaac Delgado Mus Art, New Orleans, 71; The Great Buffalo Show, Cameron Univ Art Gallery, Lawton, Okla, 86; Ann Juried Exhib, Orlando Mus Art, Fla, 87; Four From Florida, Kennesaw State Col, Marietta, Ga, 90; Works on Paper, Nat Acad Sciences, Washington, DC, 90. *Teaching:* Asst prof painting & drawing, Fla State Univ, 70- *Awards:* First Nat Bank Award, Mobile Art Patrons League, Ala, 71. *Mem:* Col Art Asn Am. *Media:* Acrylic. *Mailing Add:* 1507 Marion Ave Tallahassee FL 32303

BURGUES, IRVING CARL
SCULPTOR, LECTURER
b Austria, Oct 16, 06; US citizen. *Study:* Vienna Arts Sch, BA(fine arts), 26; Brooklyn Mus; Sch of Indust Fine Arts, Newark, NJ; sculpture apprentice to Mollet, Paris; Art Students' League; Mod Sch of Art, New York. *Work:* White House Mus; Vatican; Kremlin; Smithsonian Inst, Washington, DC; Brooklyn Mus. *Comn:* New Testament mural, Rio de Janeiro, 30; Big Horn Sheep sculpture, State of Nev, 73; Am Wild Goat, State of Mont, 76. *Exhib:* Brooklyn Mus, NY, 35; Indianapolis Mus, 70; Mus of Sci & Indust, Chicago, 72; NJ State Mus, 74; Smithsonian Inst, 76. *Mem:* Artists Equity. *Mailing Add:* Burgues Porcelain 1433 Oakwood Ave Lakewood NJ 08701-1736

BURK, A DARLENE
DEALER, COLLECTOR
b Wheatland, Wyo, Dec 24, 29. *Study:* Calvin Goodman Sem, 76-80. *Pos:* Owner, Plaza Gallery, currently. *Mem:* Rotary; Watercolor Soc Las Vegas; Boulder City Chamber Commerce. *Specialty:* Western art, Indian culture, landscape and wildlife. *Collection:* Painting, John Hilton, Jeff Craven, Carol Harding; woodcarvings, Don Ely; bronzes, Jerry Anderson, Clyde Ross Morgan. *Mailing Add:* Burk Enterprises 505 Hotel Plaza Boulder City NV 84005

BURKE, BILL
CERAMIST
Work: Xerox Corp, Rochester, NY; Perdue Univ, Art Galleries, Perdue, Ind; Univ N Dakota, Univ Art Galleries, Fargo, N Dakota. *Exhib:* Xerox Invitational, Xerox Hall, Rochester, NY, 73; Ceramics Invitational 74, Pratt Inst Art, New York, NY; John Michael Kohler Art Ctr, Sheboygan, Wis, invitational, 79; GLOVE Exhib Nat Invitational, travelling, Valencia Community Col, Fla, 83; Works Gallery, South Hampton, NY, 86; Regional Ceramics Invitational, Univ Miami, New Gallery, Coral Gables, Fla, 87; 1989 Ann Juried Exhib, Orlando Mus Art, Fla, 89. *Teaching:* Grad asst, State Univ Col- New Paltz, New York, NY, 73, grad teaching asst, 73-74, instr design, 74; assoc prof, Fla Int Univ, Miami, Fla, 74- *Awards:* Fla Fine Arts Coun State Grant, 78-79 & 82; Merit Award, 30th Ann M Allen Hortt Exhib, Mus Art, Ft Lauderdale, Fla. *Mailing Add:* c/o Barbara Gillman Gallery 3886 Biscayne Blvd Miami FL 33137

BURKE, DANIEL V
PAINTER, EDUCATOR
b Erie, Pa, Apr 21, 42. *Study:* Columbus Col Art & Design, 60-62; Mercyhurst Col, BA(art), 69; Edinboro State Col, MEd(art), 72; MacDowell Colony, Peterborough, NH, 70 & 73. *Work:* Del Mar Col Art Gallery, Corpus Christi; Laguna Gloria Art Mus, Austin, Tex; Southern Utah State Col; IBM Corp, Austin; NC Nat Bank, Boone; and others. *Exhib:* 18th Nat Chautauqua Art Asn Show, NY, 75; Drawings USA, Minn Mus Art, St Paul, 75; one-man shows, Williams Col Mus Art, Mass, 81, Erie Art Ctr, Pa, 82 & Rike Ctr Gallery, Univ Dayton, Ohio, 83; Magahan & Penelecc Galleries, Allegheny Col, Pa, 84; Cummings Gallery, Mercyhurst Col, Pa, 85; Return to the Figure, Southern Alleghenies Mus Art, Loretto, Pa, 85. *Teaching:* prof art, Mercyhurst Col, 69-, dir dept art, 79- *Awards:* Best of Show, Greater New Orleans Int, 74; Purchase Award, Appalachian Nat Drawing Competition, 75; Chautauqua Art Asn Award, 18th Nat Show, 75; Visual Arts Fel, Pa Coun Arts, 86. *Mem:* Northwestern Pa Artists Asn (co-exec chmn, 75-). *Media:* Acrylic. *Mailing Add:* 223 E Sixth St Erie PA 16507

BURKE, JAMES DONALD
MUSEUM DIRECTOR, ADMINISTRATOR
b Salem, Ore, Feb 22, 39. *Study:* Brown Univ, AB, 62; Univ Pa, AM, 66; Fulbright-Hayes Fel, Holland, 68-69; Harvard Univ, PhD, 72. *Collections Arranged:* Charles Meryon (auth, catalog), 74-75. *Pos:* Cur, Allen Art Mus, Oberlin Col, 71-72; cur drawings & prints, Art Gallery, Yale Univ, 72-78; asst dir, St Louis Art Mus, 78-80, dir, 80. *Teaching:* Instr, Yale Univ, 72-78. *Awards:* Nat Endowment Arts Mus Fel, 73. *Mem:* Am Asn Mus; Col Art Asn; Print Coun Am. *Res:* Sixteenth and seventeenth century Dutch and Flemish art; contemporary and modern art. *Publ:* Auth, Jan Both: Paintings, Drawings & Prints, 75. *Mailing Add:* St Louis Art Mus Forest Park St Louis MO 63110

BURKERT, ROBERT RANDALL
PAINTER, PRINTMAKER
b Racine, Wis, Aug 20, 30. *Study:* Wustum Art Ctr, Racine; Univ Wis-Madison, with John Wilde & Alfred Sessler, 48-55; Jacques Desjobert Atelier, Paris, France, summer 70. *Work:* Metrop Mus Art, New York; Mus Fine Arts, Boston; Nat Collection Fine Arts, Washington, DC; Tate Gallery, London; Libr Congress Print Collection; plus others. *Comn:* Outdoor wall (with Derse Outdoor Advert), Mortgage Guarantee Ins Co, 72; Wall painting, Bradley Estate, 85. *Exhib:* Recent Drawings, USA Exhib, Mus Mod Art, New York, 56; Presentation Artist, Boston Printmakers, 62; Butler Art Inst Ann, 65; New Talent Graphics Show, Assoc Am Artists, New York, 66; Univ Ill Graphics Invitational, Champaign-Urbana, 70; Okla Printmakers, 77; Camden Art Ctr, London, 80; Travelling Exhib monoprints, Eng, 84; Retrospective, Wustum Mus, Racine, Wis, 85. *Pos:* Bd trustees, Milwaukee Art Mus. *Teaching:* Prof graphics & drawing, Univ Wis-Milwaukee, 56- *Bibliog:* James Schineller (auth), Art: Search and Self Discovery, Int Textbook Co, 69; Ross & Romano (auth), The Complete Printmaker, Macmillan Free Press, 72; Fritz Eichenberg (auth), Art of the Print, Abrams, 76; James Wautrous (auth), Am Printmaking, 85. *Dealer:* Rubiner Galleries 7001 Orchard Lake Rd W Bloomfield MI 48033; Bradley Galleries 2565 N Downer Ave Milwaukee WI 53211. *Mailing Add:* 3228 N Marietta Ave Milwaukee WI 53211

BURKHARDT, HANS GUSTAV
PAINTER, PRINTMAKER
b Basel, Switz, Dec 20, 04; US citizen. *Study:* Cooper Union, 25-28; Grand Cent Sch Art, 28-29; Arshile Gorky Studio, 29-36. *Work:* Moderna Museet, Stockholm, Sweden; Kunstmuseum Basel, Switz; Hirshhorn Mus, Washington, DC; Columbia Mus Art, SC; Guggenheim Mus, New York; plus others. *Exhib:* Solo exhibs, Pac Northwest Col Art, Portland, Ore, 84, Sid Deutsch Gallery, New York, 87, Cunningham Mem Art Gallery, Bakersfield, Calif, 87, Oakland Mus, Calif, 87, Muhlenberg Col, Allentown, Pa, 90, Laguna Art Mus, Calif, 90 & Galway Int Art Festival, Ireland, 90; Artists of Union Sq, Assoc Am Artists, New York, 87; Elders of the Tribe, FHP Hippodrome Gallery, Long Beach, 87; Unique Visions, Ace Gallery, Los Angeles, 88; New Acquisitions, Skirball Mus, Los Angeles, 89; Dealers Choice, Brand Libr Art Galleries, 89; No Stomach, Installation Gallery, San Diego, 89; Between Two Worlds, Credit Suisse, New York, 90; Turning the Tide: Early Los Angeles Modernists 1920-1956, traveling show, 90. *Teaching:* Prof painting & drawing, Univ Southern Calif, 59-60; asst prof, Univ Calif, Los Angeles, 61-63; assoc prof, Calif State Univ, Northridge, 63-73, emer prof, 73- *Awards:* Ala Story Purchase Award for Oil, Santa Barbara Mus Art, 58; First Purchase Award for Oil, Howard Ahmanson, 61; Hans Burkhardt Art & Humanities Ctr, Calif State Univ, Northridge, 89. *Bibliog:* Rabbi William Kramer (auth), Hans G Burkhardt: Artist and Patron of the Arts, Santa Susana Press, 82; Jack Rutberg (auth), Hans Burkhardt-The War Paintings, Santa Susana Press, 84; Gary & Sarah Legon (producers, Hans Burkhardt: The Artists World, Estate Films Inc, 87. *Media:* Oil, Pastel; Linocut. *Collection:* Arnoldo Pomadoro sculptures; deKooning watercolors and lithographs; numerous works of Mark Tobeys; also prints by Picasso, Kollwitz, Tamayo, Raphael Sawyer, Roualt and many others; large collection of Gorky oils and drawings. *Publ:* Rattlesnake August, 78, The Last Good Kiss, 84 & Husks of Wheat, 87, Santa Susana Press. *Dealer:* Robert Schoelkopf Gallery New York NY; Jack Rutberg Gallery Los Angeles CA. *Mailing Add:* 1914 Jewett Dr Los Angeles CA 90046

BURKHART, KATHE K
CONCEPTUAL ARTIST, PAINTER
b Martinsburg, WVa, June 18, 58. *Study:* Cal Arts, BFA, 82, MFA, 84. *Work:* Pvt collection of Helena Kontova & Giancarlo Politi, Milan; pvt collection of Rogier & Hilde Matthys, Ghent, Belg; pvt collection of Ellen & Richard Sandor, New York; pvt collection of Andre Willocx, Bruges, Belg; pvt collection of Carlo Pappruco, Turin, Italy; Ghent Mus, Belg. *Comn:* Banner, Los Angeles Contemp Exhib, 85. *Exhib:* Works on Paper from the Liz Taylor Series, Witzenhausen/Meijerink, Amsterdam, 91; Original Sin, Hillwood Art Mus, 92; Selected Works from the Liz Taylor Series, Shoshana Wayne Gallery, Santa Monica, 92; Reframing Cartoons, Wexner Ctr, Columbus, Ohio, 92; From Media to Metaphor: About AIDS, Musee d'Art Contemporain, Montreal, Que, 93; and others. *Pos:* Bookstore mgr, Los Angeles Contemporary Exhibs, 82-85; freelance graphic designer for var clients, 85- *Teaching:* Vis artist painting, Mason Gross Sch Art, Rutgers Univ, New Brunswick, NJ, 91-92. *Awards:* Change Inc, R Rauschenberg's Found, 90. *Bibliog:* Helena Kontova (auth), Bad girl made good, Flashart, 10-11/90. *Media:* Image and Text. *Publ:* Auth, From Under the 8 Ball, LINE, 85. *Dealer:* Shoshana Wayne Gallery 1454 Fifth St Santa Monica CA 90401. *Mailing Add:* 47 S Fifth St Brooklyn NY 11211

BURKO, DIANE
PAINTER, EDUCATOR
b Brooklyn, NY, Sept 24, 45. *Study:* Skidmore Col, BS, 66; Univ Pa Grad Sch Fine Arts, MFA, 69. *Work:* Philadelphia Mus Art; DeCordova Mus, Lincoln, Mass; Reading Pub Mus; Am Tel & Tel; Wells Fargo Bank; Pa Acad Fine Arts; IBM, Tucson, Ariz; CIGNA Corp. *Exhib:* One-person shows, Bucknell Univ & Pa Acad Fine Arts, 80, Allentown Art Mus, Everhart Mus, Mus Art Pa State Univ & Reading Pub Mus, 83, Hollins Col, 87, Marian Locks Gallery, 88 & 90 & Nat Acad Sci, Washington, DC, 91; Whitney Mus Am Art, 81; Art Inst Chicago, Ctr for the Arts, Wesleyan Univ & Albright Col, 83; Douglass Col, 84; Denver Mus Natural Hist & Art Mus Princeton Univ, 85; Tampa Mus Art, 86; Md Art Inst, 86; Colgate univ, 88. *Pos:* Pres & founder, Philadelphia Focuses on Women in Visual Arts, 73-75; Mayors Cult Adv Coun, 88-90; Art Comn Philadelphia, 92- *Teaching:* From asst prof drawing, painting & design to assoc prof, 69-85, Philadelphia Community Col, head art dept, 80-85, prof, 85-; vis prof, Princeton Univ, 85. *Awards:* Vis fel, Tamarind Inst, Albuquerque, NMex, 80 & 82; Pa Coun Arts Individual Artists Grant, 81; Nat Endowment Arts, 85-86; residence fel Giverny, Readers Digest Found, Apr-Sep 89; Individual Artist Grant, Pa Coun Arts, 89; Nat Endowment Arts Visual Arts Fel, 91-92. *Bibliog:* Edward J Sozanski (auth), Diane Burko of Marion Locks, Phildelphia Inquirer, 88-90; Michael Matza (auth), Impression: Paradise, Philadelphia Inquirer, 89; Judith Stein (auth), Burko at Locks, Art in Am, 91; Alexandria Anderson (auth), Burko-Locks, Art News, 91. *Mem:* Col Art Asn Am; Women's Caucus Art (treas adv bd, 77-78 & 82-85); Philadelphia Volunteer Lawyers for Arts, (bd mem 86-). *Media:* Oil, Acrylic. *Dealer:* Marian Locks 600 Wash Square S Ctr Philadelphia PA 19106. *Mailing Add:* 510 S 46th St Philadelphia PA 19143

BURKS, MYRNA R
PRINTMAKER, GALLERY DIRECTOR
b Chattanooga, Tenn, Oct 31, 43. *Study:* Ga State Univ, BFA, 71; Univ NMex, MA, 73, MFA, 76. *Work:* Hunter Art Mus, Chattanooga, Tenn; US Info Agency, var embassies; Univ NMex Fine Arts Mus, Albuquerque. *Exhib:* Third Hawaii Nat Print Exhib, Honolulu Acad Arts, 75; Northwest Int Small Format Print Exhib, Davidson Gallery, Seattle, Wash, 76; Women Artists '79: Paperworks, Art & Design Gallery, Univ Kans, Lawrence, 79; Selected Artists, Mulvane Art Ctr, Topeka, Kans, 79-80; Mo Works on Paper Traveling Exhib, 79-80; Texture in Prints, 81, Northwest Prints 82, Oregon Biennale, 85 & Western State Print Exhib, 85, Portland Art Mus; Northwest Print Coun Exhib, Galleri Norske Grafikere, Oslo, Norway, 85. *Collections Arranged:* Artists Choose Artists, Univ Mo-Kansas City, 79 & Missouri Artists: Works on Paper (auth, catalog), 80. *Pos:* Cur, Tamarind Inst, Univ NMex, 72-73, printer, 77; co-owner & printer, North Light Editions, Portland, Ore, 81- *Teaching:* Instr art & dir gallery, Univ Mo-Kansas City, 78-80. *Awards:* Ford Found Res Fel, 76; Best of Show Award, Women Artists: Paperworks, 79. *Bibliog:* Donald Hoffman (auth), The history of the world traced through its scars, Kansas City Star, 9/79; Jan Schmitz (auth), The personal lure of Myrna Burks, Forum/Kansas City Artists' Coalition, 10/79; Leonard Koenig (auth), A portfolio of artwork, New Lett, Univ Mo-Kansas City, 79-80. *Mem:* Col Art Asn; Women's Caucus Art (adv bd Kansas City chap, 78-80); Kansas City Artist's Coalition (adv bd, 79-80). *Media:* Lithography, Mixed. *Publ:* Auth, Women artists, Forum/Kansas City Artists' Coalition, 12/79. *Mailing Add:* 131 Avenue B New York NY 10009

BURLEIGH, KIMBERLY
PAINTER
b Meadville, Pa, April 1, 55. *Study:* Ohio Univ, Athens, BFA, 77; Ind Univ, Bloomington, MFA, 80. *Work:* Progressive Corp, Cleveland, Ohio; Com Nat Bank, Shrevesport, La; Dwinn Shaffer & Co, Chicago; Cincinnati Bell. *Comn:* Progressive Corp, Cleveland, Ohio. *Exhib:* Visiontelevision, Franklin Furnace Archive, New York, 85; one-person shows, Pittsburgh Plan for Art, Pa, 85 & Feature Gallery, Chicago, 86 & 87; Spaces, Cleveland, Ohio, 86; From the Files, Alternative Mus, New York, 87; Postmodernism: A Spectacle of Reflexivity, Milwaukee Art Mus, Wis, 87; Of Plato's Cave, Greathouse Gallery, New York, 88; Romancing the Stone, New York, 89; Double Take, Contemp Arts Ctr, Cincinnati, 89; Arts Ctr Gallery, Col Dupage, Glen Ellen, Ill, 89; Cleveland Ctr Contemp Art, Ohio, 90; Edinboro Univ, Pa, 90; Art Mus Miami Univ, Oxford, Ohio, 91; Hoyt Inst Fine Arts, New Castle, Pa, 91; Water Tower in Louisvile, Ky, 92. *Pos:* Vis artist, Murray State Univ, Ky, 83. *Teaching:* Vis asst prof painting, Univ Utah, Salt Lake City, 81-82 & Ohio Univ, Athens, 86-89; asst prof, State Univ Tex, Nacadoches, 82-83; assoc prof/grad prog dir fine art, Univ Cincinnati, 90- *Awards:* NJ State Coun Arts Grant, 81; Vis Fel Grant, Nat Endowment Arts, 87; Ohio Arts Coun Grant, 89. *Bibliog:* David McCracken (auth), Words help tell the message in painting, Chicago Tribune, 9/25/87; Barbara Gallati (auth), New work, Arts Mag, 11/81. *Mailing Add:* 3440 Telford No 15 Univ of Cincinnati, Col of Design Cincinnati OH 45220

BURLESON, CHARLES TRENTMAN
PAINTER, EDUCATOR
b Charlotte, NC, June 15, 52. *Study:* Philadelphia Col Art, BFA, 74; RI Sch of Design, MFA, 76. *Work:* NC Arts Soc, Raleigh; Surry Col, Dobson, NC; Providence Jour Collection, RI. *Comn:* Outdoor mural, RI State Coun Arts, Providence, 77; A Case for Boxes (house box), RI Sch of Design Mus, 80. *Exhib:* One-man shows, Central Falls, New York, 80, Gallery Z, New York, 86 & Virginia Lynch Gallery, Tiverton, RI, 88; group shows, Alan Stone Gallery, New York, 80, RI Sch of Design Mus Art, 90; Helander Gallery, New York, 90. *Pos:* Chief critic, EHP Prog, Rome, Italy, 85. *Teaching:* Assoc prof painting, RI Sch of Design, 76-90. *Awards:* Second Place Award, NC Arts Soc, 69; Purchase Award, Mint Mus Art, Charlotte, 74; Purchase Award, NC Mus Art, 75. *Bibliog:* Edward Sozanski (auth), Burleson's landscapes are striking, Providence J, 82; Edward Booth-Clibborn (auth), American Illustration, Abrams, 84; Drawings-Gallery Z, East Village Rev, 3-4/87. *Media:* Oil. *Mailing Add:* 87 Hope St Providence RI 02906

BURLEY, LINA
PAINTER
b Washington, DC, May 31, 22. *Study:* Univ Md, BS, 43; Art Students League, New York, with George Grosz, Edwin Dickinson, 56-61. *Work:* Bell Labs, Abex Corp & Summit Trust Co, Summit, NJ. *Exhib:* Nat Acad Ann, New York, 64; Am Watercolor Soc Ann, New York, 65; Hecksher Mus, Long Island, 64; Audubon Artists Ann Juried, New York, 66; NJ Watercolor Soc Ann, Morristown, NJ, 70-71. *Teaching:* Watercolor, Studio Workshop, Weekly, 76- *Awards:* Award Merit, M Grumbacher, 69; Medal Honor, Nat Asn Women Artists, 77; Cert Achievment, ISA First Juried Show, Int Soc Artists, 78. *Mem:* Nat Asn Women Artists; Boothbay Region Art Found (pres, 77-79, 87-88); Maine Art Gallery (vpres bd, 92). *Media:* Oil, Watercolor. *Dealer:* Mast Cove Gallery Rte 9 Kennebunkport ME 04544. *Mailing Add:* Rte 96 Box 782 East Boothbay ME 04544

BURNETT, BARBARA ANN
PAINTER
b Kansas City, Kans, May 7, 27. *Study:* Primarily self taught; La Tech, 82-83. *Work:* Barnard Libr, La Crosse, Kans; Pub Libr, Coffeyville, Kans; City of Mission & City of Prairie Village, Kans; Panhandle Eastern Pipeline Co. *Comn:* Mural, comn by Lloyd Wagner, Kans, 54; and numerous private & corporate comns. *Exhib:* Am Watercolor Soc & travel Show, 80; Century II Kans Tri-State, Wichita, 81; Midwest Watercolor Soc, Burpee Art Mus, Rockford, Ill, 81; Salmagundi Open Exhib, New York, 82, 84 & 85; Allied Artists Am, 82 & Catherine Lorillard Wolfe, 82-83, Nat Arts Club, New York; Wichita Art Mus; and many others. *Pos:* Founder & owner, Burnett Art Studio, 73-; writer, Sunshine Artists Mag, 79-83. *Teaching:* Instr, The Pallette, Leawood, Kans, 70-75; instr, workshops, Kans State Univ, Lawrence, 78, Sch Ozarks Col, Point Lookout, Mo & Sedalia State Fair Community Col, Sedalia, Mo. *Awards:* Hunt Award, Midwest Watercolor Soc, 81; Floral Still Life Awards, Catherine Lorillard Wolfe Club, 82 & 83; Florence Lonsford Award, Salmagundi Club; Metrop Mus Gift Award 86; and others. *Mem:* Kans Watercolor Soc; Signature mem, Catherine Lorillard Wolfe Art Club, New York; Whiskey Painters Am; Greater Kansas City Art Asn (bd mem, 73-82); Life signature mem Midwest Watercolor Soc; Images II, Kans City Mo, 88. *Media:* Watercolor, Miscellaneous. *Publ:* Auth, A Century in Story & Pictures, Rush Co, Kans, 76; A History in Painting, Jo Co, Kans, 77; Cover painting, Sunshine Artist Mag, 78. *Mailing Add:* 8916 Hadley Pl Shawnee Mission KS 66212

BURNETT, CALVIN
PAINTER, PRINTMAKER
b Cambridge, Mass, July 18, 21. *Study:* Mass Col Art, BFA & BS; Sch Boston Mus Fine Arts; Boston Univ, MFA; studied with George Lockwood & Lawrence Kupferman. *Work:* Boston Mus Fine Arts, Mass; Oakland Mus, Calif; Fogg Art Mus, Harvard Univ; Wiggins Collection, Boston Pub Libr; Wellesley Col; plus others. *Comn:* Illus comn by D C Heath; illus, Houghton Mifflin; illus, Scott Foresman; illus, Boston Globe; illus, Atlantic Publishers. *Exhib:* San Francisco Mus Art; Mus Fine Art, Boston; Smithsonian Inst Travelling Exhib; Taller de Graphico, Mex; Bazalel Nat, Israel; Brooklyn Mus. *Teaching:* Prof emer, Mass Col Art, 56- *Awards:* First Award Printmaking, Boston Printmakers, 64; Leipzig Int Book Illus Exhib Award, Ger, 65; First Award Painting, Atlanta Univ Ann, 66. *Bibliog:* M Holsen (auth), Introducing some Boston printmakers, The Connoisseur, London, 67; V E Atkinson (auth), Black Dimensions in Contemporary American Art, New Am Libr, 71; F van Almelo (auth), article, Tuesday Mag, 71. *Mem:* Boston Afro-Am Artists Asn; Northeastern Univ Afro-Am Master Artists in Residence Prog. *Media:* Oil; Mixed Drawing Media. *Publ:* Auth-designer, Objective Drawing Techniques, Van Nostrand Reinhold, 66; auth & illusr of children's bks; portfolios of fine prints, 68; impressions graphics workshop. *Dealer:* AAMARP 590 Huntington Ave Boston MA; Raymond A Liddel & Assoc Inc 186 South St Boston MA 02111. *Mailing Add:* 87 Fisher St Medway MA 02053-2232

BURNETT, DAVID GRANT
HISTORIAN, CURATOR
b Lincoln, Eng, Oct 1, 40; Can citizen. *Study:* Birkbeck Col, Univ London, BA, 65; Courtauld Inst of Art, MA, 67, PhD, 73, under M Kitson. *Pos:* Cur contemp Can Art, Art Gallery Ont, Toronto, 80-84. *Teaching:* Lectr art hist, Univ Bristol, England, 67-70; assoc prof art hist, Carleton Univ, Ottawa, Ont, 70-80. *Res:* Contemporary Art. *Publ:* Guido Molinari: Quantificateur, 79; auth, Guido Molinari: Drawings, 80; auth, Alex Colville, 83; auth, Contemp Canadian Art, 83; auth, Harold Town, 86; auth, Jeremy Smith, 88; auth, Gershon Iskowitz, 82; auth, Masterpieces of Canadian Art, Nat Gallery Can, 90. *Mailing Add:* 201 W Glengrove Ave Toronto ON M4R 1P4 Canada

BURNETT, PATRICIA HILL
PAINTER, SCULPTOR
b Brooklyn, NY. *Study:* Univ Toledo; Goucher Col; Corcoran Art Sch; Soc Arts & Crafts; Inst Allende, Mex; Wayne State Univ; Truro Sch Art; also with John Carroll, Sarkis Sarkisian, Wallace Bassford, Walter Midener & Seong Moy. *Work:* Detroit Inst Arts, Mich; Bloomfield Art Asn, Mich; Wayne State Univ; Wooster Col; Ford Motor Co Collection, Detroit. *Comn:* Oil portrait, Joyce Carol Oates, Windsor, Ont, 72; portrait, Benson Ford, Ford Motor Co, Detroit, 75; portrait of Gov William Milliken, State of Mich, 79; portraits of Indira Ghandi, Corazon Aquino & Margaret Thatcher, among others. *Exhib:* Butler Mus Nat Art Show, Cleveland, Ohio, 72; Ms & Masters, Midland Ctr Arts, Midland, Mich, 75; Forty-one one-woman shows. *Teaching:* Painting techniques, Univ Mich Exten Courses & sculpture techniques, Grosse Pointe War Mem, formerly. *Awards:* First Prize Painting, Figure Painting Show, Boston, 69; First Prize, Western Art Show, Albuquerque, NMex, 74; First Prize Painting, Scarab Club, 77; Ohio Hall of Fame, Jessup W Scott Sch, Toledo, 88. *Bibliog:* Christine Hinz (auth), Detroit artist: Feminist homemaker and painter, Daily News, Midland, Mich, 75. *Mem:* Mich Acad Arts; Detroit Soc Women Painters & Sculptors; Ibex Club (pres, 50-51); Sculptors Guild Birmingham; Portrait Club (US nat advisory bd, 77-). *Media:* Oil; Bronze, Clay. *Publ:* Contribr, Painting the Female Figure, Bassford, Watson-Guptill Founders Gallery, 73; auth, Will NOW and the Junior League ever meet?, Jr League Mag, 73; Have women artists been brushed aside?, Women in the Arts Mag, 75; The winds of change are blowing, Zonta Mag, Int, 75; Women today in Russia, Israel, India & Thailand, PHP Int Mag, Japan, 75. *Dealer:* Scarab Club 217 Farnsworth St Detroit MI 48202. *Mailing Add:* 18261 Hamilton Rd Detroit MI 48203

BURNHAM, JACK WESLEY
CRITIC, WRITER
b New York, NY, Nov 13, 31. *Study:* Boston Mus Sch, 53-54 & 56-57; Wentworth Inst, Boston, AE, 56; Sch Art & Archit, Yale Univ, BFA, 59, MFA(sculpture), 61. *Pos:* Contrib ed, Artforum Mag, 71-72; assoc ed, Arts Mag, 72-76; contrib ed, New Art Examr, 74- *Teaching:* Prof art, Northwestern Univ, 62-; Dana prof fine arts, Colgate Univ, Hamilton, NY, 75-76; Clark prof art hist, Williams Col, Williamstown, Mass, 80; prof art & chmn dept, Univ Md, 83- *Awards:* Guggenheim Fel, 73; Critics Award, Chicago Art Awards, 77 & 78. *Bibliog:* Albert Elsen (auth), Beyond modern sculpture, Artforum, 5/69; Tom Conley (auth), The radicality of modern art, Diacritics, spring 73; R Blazer (auth), Blazer on Burnham--great western salt works, Criteria, 11/74. *Res:* Contemporary criticism; art semiotics; the writings and art of Marcel Duchamp; semiotics, narrative structure in art. *Publ:* Auth, Beyond Modern Sculpture, Braziller, 68; Art in the Marcusean Analysis, Pa State Univ Press, 69; The Structure of Art, 71 & Great Western Saltworks, 74, Braziller; coauth, Hans Haacke: Framing and Being Framed, New York Univ Press, 75. *Mailing Add:* Dept Art Univ Md College Park MD 20742

BURNS, G JOAN
LIBRARIAN
b Belleville, NJ, Mar 6, 18. *Study:* Newark State Col, BA(art educ), 39; Columbia Univ, 42-44; Rutgers State Univ, MLS, 63. *Pos:* Draftswoman, Archit Forum, 42-45; free-lance archit illusr, Progressive Archit, Archit Forum, Holiday, and others, 45-57; principal art librn, Newark Pub Libr, 68-; reviewer art titles, Libr J, 70-75 & Am Reference Bks Ann, 72- *Mem:* Art Libr Soc North Am; Victorian Soc in Am. *Interests:* Twentieth century architectural history and design. *Publ:* Illusr, Forms & Functions of 20th Century Architecture, Columbia Univ Press, 52. *Mailing Add:* 99 Vreeland Ave Nutley NJ 07110

BURNS, JEROME
PAINTER, PRINTMAKER
b Brooklyn, NY, Mar 26, 19. *Study:* Art Students League, 36-39; Hans Hofmann Art Sch, New York, 42; Brooklyn Mus Art Sch, 49. *Work:* Okla Mus; C W Post Col Mus, Long Island Univ; Metrop Mus Art, New York. *Exhib:* Allied Artists Am, New York, 66; Nat Soc Painters in Casein & Acrylic, New York, 66-; Long Island Univ, 84; Mostyn Gallery, Llandudno, NWales; Broekman Gallery, chester,Eng; and others. *Pos:* Pres, Brownstone Gallery Inc, Brooklyn, 69-76. *Teaching:* Instr painting, Brooklyn Mus Art Sch, 60-61. *Awards:* Samuel F B Morse Medal, Am Nat Acad, 63; Tesser Mem Award, Audubon Artists, 64; Dir Award, Nat Soc Painters in Casein & Acrylic, 66, Memory of Ada Award, 78. *Mem:* Artists Equity Asn; MacDowell Colony Fels; Nat Soc Painters in Casein & Acrylic; Appraisers Asn Am. *Media:* Casein, Acrylic, Etching. *Mailing Add:* 248 Garfield Pl Brooklyn NY 11215

BURNS, JOSEPHINE
PAINTER
b Llandudno, North Wales, July 2, 17. *Study:* Cooper Union Art Sch, grad, 39, BFA, 76; Art Students League, 49 & 50. *Work:* C W Post Col Mus, Long Island Univ; Okla Mus Art, Oklahoma City; Bristol City Art Gallery, Whitworth Art Gallery, Manchester Univ, England. *Exhib:* Brooklyn & Long Island Artists, Brooklyn Mus, 58; one-woman show, Alonzo Gallery, New York, 66; Community Gallery, Brooklyn Mus, 76, 77 & 80; Bergen Co Community Mus, 82; Mostyn Art Gallery, NWales, UK, 82 & 85-92; Salena Gallery, Long Island Univ, 84; Broekman Gallery, Chester, UK; and others. *Pos:* Co-dir, Hicks Street Gallery, Brooklyn, 58-63; assoc dir, Brownstone Gallery, Brooklyn, 69-76. *Awards:* Resident Fel, MacDowell Colony, 60, 62, 64, 65 & 68; Resident Fel, Yaddo, Saratoga Springs, NY, 61. *Mem:* Artists Equity Asn, New York; MacDowell Colony Fels. *Media:* Oil, Pastel. *Dealer:* Kraushaar Galleries 724 Fifth Ave New York NY 10019. *Mailing Add:* 248 Garfield Pl Brooklyn NY 11215

BURNS, MARK A
CERAMIST
b Springfield, Ohio, Oct 5, 50. *Study:* Sch Dayton Art Inst, BFA, 72; Univ Wash, Seattle, MFA, 74. *Exhib:* Everson Mus Art, Syracuse, NY & Renwick Gallery, Smithsonian Inst, Washington, DC, 79; solo exhibs, The Hotel Lobby, Helen Drutt Gallery, Philadelphia, Pa, 76, The Vases, Helen Drutt Gallery, Philadelphia, Pa, 75, Fairy Tales, Helen Drutt Gallery, Philadelphia, Pa, 82, Happy Birthday Frank Furnets, Pa Acad Fine Arts, Philadelphia & Helen Drutt Gallery, Philadelphia, Pa, 84, A Decade in Pennsylvania: 1975-1985, Soc Art & Craft, Verona, Pa, 86, As Seen on TV, University Gallery, Calif State Univ, Chico, 86 & New Work, Helen Drutt Gallery, New York, 89; Mus Philadelphia Civic Ctr, travelling, 80; Contemp Artists: An Expanding View (with catalogue), Wellesley Col Mus, Mass, Monmouth Mus Art, Lincroft, NJ & Squibb Gallery, Princeton, NJ, 86; Am Ceramics Now: 27th Ceramic Nat Exhibit, Everson Mus Art, 87; Perch Int Crafts, Triennial Twenty Americans: American Figurative Ceramics, Art Gallery Western Australia, 89. *Pos:* Asst prof, Philadelphia Col Art, Pa, 75-83; asst prof, Tyler Sch Art, Temple Univ, Philadelphia, Pa, 81-82, Moore Col Art & Design, Philadelphia, Pa, 85 & Univ Nev Las Vagas, 91-; vis prof, Univ Ariz, Tucson, 82-83 & RI Sch Design, Providence, 89-91. *Awards:* Nat Endowment Arts, 76 & 88. *Publ:* Coauth (with Louis DiBonis), Fifties Homestyle: Popular Ornament of the USA, Harper & Row, 88. *Mailing Add:* 1721 Walnut St Philadelphia PA 19103

BURNS, MARSHA
PHOTOGRAPHER
b Seattle, Wash, Jan 11, 45. *Study:* Univ Wash, 63-65; Univ Mass, Amherst, 67-69. *Work:* Mus Mod Art, Metrop Mus Art, New York; Nat Mus Am Art, Smithsonian Inst, Libr Cong, Washington, DC; Ctr Creative Photog, Tucson, Ariz; Seattle Art Mus, City of Seattle Collection, Wash; Stedelijk Mus, Amsterdam; Dallas Mus Fine Art, Tex; San Francisco Mus Contemp Art, Fed Reserve Bank of San Francisco, Calif; and others. *Exhib:* One-woman shows, Marsha Burns Poloroids, Whatcom Mus Hist & Art, Bellingham, Wash, 89, Andrea Ross Gallery, Santa Monica, Calif, 90, Recent Photographs, Portland Sch Art, Ore, 90, Human Scenes, Univ Ill, Chicago, 91, Ministry Culture, Alden, Belg, 91; Charles Cowles Gallery, New York, 92 & Portraits from America, Susan Spiritus Gallery, Costa Mesa, Calif, 92; China 1989, One Path Three Vision, Italia, Seattle, Wash, 90; Western Women Photographers, Maveety Gallery, Portland, Ore, 90; Anniversary Show, Linda Farris Gallery, Seattle, Wash, 90; 1991 Nat Governors Asn Art Exhib, Wash State Convention & Trade Ctr, Seattle; People & Places, Northern Ill Univ Art Mus Gallery, Chicago, 91; SoHo at Duke, Five Artists from Charles Cowles Gallery, Duke Univ Mus Art, Durham, NC; To Collect the Art of Women: The Jane Reese Williams Collection of Photography, Mus NMex, Sante Fe, 92; Photographs: Jock Sturges, Plauto, Marsha Burns, Charles Cowles Gallery, New York, 92; and others. *Awards:* Photogr Fel, Nat Endowment Arts, 78; Awards in Visual Arts, Nat Mus Am Art, Southeastern Ctr Contemp Art, 81. *Bibliog:* Gerard Malanga (ed), Scopophilia: The Love of Looking, Alfred Van de Mark Ed & Harper & Row, 85; Chris Bruce (auth, catalog) Cities, Henry Gallery Mus, Univ Wash, 87; articles, Korper, Polaroid Corp, 88; and others. *Dealer:* Charles Cowles Gallery 420 W Broadway New York NY 10012. *Mailing Add:* 627 First Ave Seattle WA 98104

BURNS, MILLIE
PHOTOGRAPHER, PRINTMAKER
b Brooklyn, NY, Dec 25, 50. *Study:* Rochester Inst Technol; Parsons Sch Design; Sch Visual Arts. *Work:* NY Pub Libr; Can Inperial Bank Commerce, Haines Lundberg Waehler, St Vincent's Hosp, Price Waterhouse & Co, Mus Mod Art, New York; Brooklyn Mus, NY. *Comn:* 4 Toned & colored silver prints, City NY Parks & Recreation, 88; 8 toned silver prints, Los Sures. *Exhib:* Third Biennial Exhib, Newark Mus, NJ 81; Photosensitive, Libr Arts, Washington, DC, 89; A Decade of the Marketplace, Bronx Mus Arts, NY, 90; Photographs of Millie Burns, En Foco Inc, Bronx, NY, 90; Women in the Arts 1992, Smithtown Township Arts Coun, St James, NY, 92; Vision of Solitude, One Square Mile Gallery, Seacliff, NY, 92; and others. *Pos:* Gallery cur, Dance Theater Workshop, New York, 90- *Teaching:* Artist-in-residence photog, Childrens Mus Manhattan, 88-89; artist/instr photogr, Children's Art Carnival, New York, 89-90; guest instr artists bks, The Rotunda Gallery, Brooklyn, NY, 92. *Awards:* Artist Grants, Artist in the Marketplace, 86-87, Retrospection, 87-88 & Photographs from the Dorland Mountain, 90-91, Artists Space. *Bibliog:* Vivien Raynor (auth), Two shows at the Bronx Museum, NY Times, 6/14/87; Elizabeth Wix (auth), Women on different canvases, Newsday, 3/92. *Mem:* Am Soc Mag Photogr; Orgn Independent Artists. *Media:* Serigraphy. *Publ:* Auth, An Illustrated Bio-bibliography of Black Photographers. *Mailing Add:* 1024 Greene Ave Brooklyn NY 11221-2911

BURNS, SHEILA
PAINTER, LECTURER
b Scotland; US citizen. *Study:* Detroit Soc Arts & Crafts; Wayne State Univ, BA. *Work:* Grand Rapids Mus, Mich; Wayne State Univ; Founders Soc Gallery Loan Collection, Detroit Inst Art; Hillberry Theatre, Wayne State Univ, Detroit. *Comn:* Grosse Prep Acad, Am Spoon Foods; Children's Hosp Mich. *Exhib:* Mich Biennial Exhib Painters & Printmakers, Grand Rapids Mus; Mich Acad Sci, Art & Lett & Mich Regional Exhib, Univ Mich; Blue Water Int Exhib, US & Can, 74 & 75; Eastern Mich Int, 75; plus many others. *Teaching:* Instr, secondary schs. *Awards:* Purchase Award, Mich Biennial Painters & Printmakers, Grand Rapids Mus; Watercolor Awards, Scarab Club Detroit. *Mem:* Am Asn Prof Artists. *Media:* Watercolor, Oil. *Publ:* Illusr, Detroit Free Press; illusr, Are Nursery Rhymes for Children? by Dr Edward Southern; Centennial Poster (ltd-ed), and other ltd-ed posters. *Dealer:* Galerie de Boicourt Birmingham MI 48011. *Mailing Add:* 23036 Ardmore Park St Clair Shores MI 48081

BURNS, STAN
PAINTER, SCULPTOR
b Suitersville, Pa. *Study:* Wayne State Univ, BA & MA; Detroit Soc Arts & Crafts, with Reginald Bennett, Sarkis; Pewabic Pottery with Mary Chase Stratton. *Work:* Wayne State Univ; Ford Motor Co; Founders Gallery Loan Collection, Detroit Art Inst. *Comn:* Numerous pvt comns & portrait comns. *Exhib:* Mich Acad Sci, Art & Lett & Mich Regional Exhib, Univ Mich; Mich Artists Exhib, Detroit Inst Art; Mich Watercolor Soc; Blue Water Int Exhib, 73 & 74; Eastern Mich Int, 75; solo-invitational, Bacardi Gallery, Miami; plus many one-man shows including galleries in Dallas, Miami, Washington, DC, Detroit, Chicago & Kalamazoo. *Awards:* Board of Directors' Award, Scarab Gold Medal Show, Detroit; Blue Water Int Exhib, Port Huron Mus, Mich; Eastern Mich Int Exhib Award; Best of Show, Scarab Art Club; Gold Plaque, Detroit/Windsor Int Freedom Festival. *Mem:* Nat Asn Prof Artists; Scarab Club. *Mailing Add:* 23036 Ardmore Park St Clair Shores MI 48081

BURNSIDE, MADELEINE HILDING
CRITIC, MUSEUM DIRECTOR
b London, Eng, Oct 18, 48; US citizen. *Study:* Warwick Univ, Eng, BA, 70; Univ Calif, Santa Cruz, PhD, 76. *Collections Arranged:* Universal Limited Art Editions: The First 10 Years (auth, catalog), Islip Art Mus, 83 & Guild Hall Mus, 84; Preparation & Proposition (auth, catalog), 84, The Living Carousel, 84, The Writing on the Wall (auth, catalog), 85 & Myths & Rituals for the 21st Century (auth, catalog), 86, Islip Art Mus. *Pos:* Ed assoc, Art News Mag, 73-79 & Arts Mag, 79-80; dir, Islip Art Mus, 80- *Teaching:* Asst art hist, Univ Calif, 72-73; adj prof art hist, Dowling Col, 83- *Awards:* Fels, Harkness, 70, Ford Found, 73 & Helena Rubinstein, 75. *Res:* Contemporary art. *Publ:* Auth, Hard Line, Drawing as a Primary Medium, 84 & Luis Camnitzer, the Torture Series, 85, Islip Art Mus; coauth, Houston Conwill's St Matthew Passion, Alternative Mus, 86. *Mailing Add:* c/o Mel Fisher Maritime Heritage Soc 200 Greene St Key West FL 33040

BUROS, LUELLA
PAINTER, BOOK DESIGNER
b Canby, Minn. *Study:* Teachers Col, Columbia Univ, 29-30 & 33-34; Rutgers Univ, 31-32; Ohio State Univ, 34-35. *Work:* Newark Mus, NJ; Montclair Art Mus, NJ; City Cape May, NJ. *Exhib:* Five Watercolor & Print Exhibs, Pa Acad Fine Arts, Philadelphia, 37-47; Contemp Exhib Painting & Sculpture, Golden Gate Int Expos, San Francisco, 39; Corcoran Biennial Art, Corcoran Gallery Art, Washington, DC, 39, 43 & 45; Four Int Exhibs of Watercolors, Art Inst Chicago, 40-43; Contemp Am Art Exhib, Artists for Victory, Metrop Mus Art, New York, 43. *Awards:* First Prize Watercolor, Contemp Va Oil & Watercolor Exhib, Norfolk Mus Arts & Sci, 44-45; Medal Honor Oil, Nat Asn Women Artists, Nat Acad, 53. *Mem:* Nat Asn Women Artists. *Media:* Watercolor. *Mailing Add:* 4651 E Coachlight Ln Tucson AZ 85718

BURPEE, JAMES STANLEY
PAINTER, INSTRUCTOR
b Oakland, Calif, Feb 12, 38. *Study:* San Jose State Col, BA, 58; Calif Col Arts & Crafts, with James Weeks, MFA, 60. *Comn:* Painting, 13 x 4 ft, Dain Bosworth, Minneapolis, 92. *Exhib:* A Sense of Place: Artists & the American Land, Sheldon Mem Art Gallery, Lincoln, Nebr, 73-74; America 1976, Minneapolis Inst Arts, 77; one man shows, Col St Catherine, St Paul, Minn, 78, Nash Gallery, Univ Minn, 82 & 85, Artbanque Gallery, Minneapolis, 84, Katherine Nash Gallery, Univ Minn, 82 & 85, Flanders Contemp Art, Minneapolis, Minn, 93; Figurative Painting, Macalaster Col, St Paul, 79; American Art; The Challenge of the Land, Pillsbury Co Sponsor, 81; two person show, Meetings & Archetypes: Minn Artists exhib prog, Minneapolis Inst Arts, 87. *Teaching:* From instr to asst prof & chmn, Art Dept, Midwestern Univ, Wichita Falls, Tex, 60-67; from asst prof to prof painting & drawing, Minneapolis Col of Art & Design, 67-; vis artist painting, Kansas City Art Inst, 74 & Calif Col of Arts & Crafts, 74 & 75; guest lectr, Calif Col Arts & Crafts, 79-80; lectr, Wash Univ, St Louis, 84; lectr, Tour for Milton Avery Show, Walker Art Ctr, Minn, 83. *Awards:* Fel Residency Found Karolyi, Venice, France, 89; Nat Endowment Arts Artist-in-residence, Volcanoes Nat Park, Hawaii, 73-74; Fel, MacDowell Colony, 76. *Media:* Acrylic. *Publ:* Illusr, Visual Studies by Frank Young, Prentice-Hall, 84. *Mailing Add:* 3208 Aldrich Ave S Minneapolis MN 55408

BURR, HORACE
CURATOR, SCULPTOR
b New Castle, Ind, Feb 9, 12. *Study:* DePaun Univ, BA; Univ Southern Calif, MA; Acad Fine Arts, Florence, Italy, cert; studied with Alfred van Loen, New York, 50; Univ Parma, Italy, Hon Dipl Merit, 81; Sem Int Mod & Contemp Art, Maestro di Pittura, 82; Accad D'Europe, hon degree, 83. *Work:* James Madison Univ Mus Fine Arts. *Exhib:* Eleven one-man shows & 81 exhibs in 42 cities & 14 states; Nat Southern Arts Exhib. *Teaching:* Prof hist Japanese art, Univ Va, 74-77; cur fine arts & art consult, James Madison Univ, Harrisburg, 77-86. *Awards:* Golden Centaur Prize, 82; Nations Prize, 83; Gold Medal Int Parliament, 83; Statue of Victory World Cult Prize, 85; Golden Flame Award, 86; and others. *Bibliog:* The Ancient City (doc film), St Augustine Rec, 57; Sculpture of Horace Burr, 63; History of Contemporary Art, Accad Italia, 83. *Mem:* Albermarle Art Asn (pres, 55-65, emer pres, 65-); Accademia Italia. *Media:* Mixed Media, Stone. *Publ:* Seventy-six publications in fine arts. *Mailing Add:* Carrsgrove Stribling Ave Charlottesville VA 22902

BURR, LEE REYNOLDS
PAINTER, PRINTMAKER
b Los Angeles, Calif, Mar 15, 36. *Study:* Univ S Calif, BFA, 66. *Work:* Univ Notre Dame, South Bend, Ind; Miami Mus Art, Fla; Ga Art Mus, Atlanta; The Munic Gallery, Los Angeles; Kavai Mus, Hawaii. *Comn:* numerous comns for public area art. *Pos:* Chmn, bd of dirs, East Park Gallery, Los Angeles, 82- *Media:* Mixed Media on Canvas. *Dealer:* East Park Gallery 13310 Ralston Ave Los Angeles Calif. *Mailing Add:* 10433 Wilshire Blvd Los Angeles CA 90024

BURR, RUTH BASLER
PAINTER
b Chicago, Ill, Feb 12, 32. *Study:* Glendale Col; Pierce Col; UCLA; Laguna Beach Sch Art, Calif. *Work:* Calif Inst Technol, Pasadena; UCLA Med Ctr, Westwood, Calif; Glendale Fed, Glendale, Calif; Transamerica Corp, Los Angeles. *Comn:* Over 100 murals, 53-70, over 100 portraits, 68-72, People in Los Angeles Co, Calif; 3 large oils of ships, Robinson Develop Co, Newport, Calif, 79; 75 paintings, Trans Am Corp, Los Angeles, Calif, 80-84. *Exhib:* Brand II, Brand, Glendale, Calif, 70; one woman show, Descanso Gardens, Hospitality Mus, La Canada, Calif, 70-92; Art Expo Cal Ann, Conf Ctr, Los Angeles, 87-92; featured artist, Los Angeles Co Fair, 92; Artist of Year, Buena Park, Calif, 92. *Pos:* Co-chmn with Johnny Ray, Hear Found, Pasadena, Calif, 70-71; co-chmn, Art Under Oaks, Descanso Gardens Guild, 85-88. *Teaching:* Instr art, Los Angeles City Sch, 72-80; instr, Pasadena City Col, 75-80; instr, Brand Art Ctr, 80-86. *Awards:* Best of Year, 3 catagorys, Ebell, Ebell Club, 82; First Place, Under Oaks, Descanso Gardens, 90. *Media:* Watercolor. *Mailing Add:* 27071 Glenar FF Lane San Juan Capistrano CA 92675

BURRIS, BRUCE C
PAINTER, SCULPTOR
b Wilmington, Del, Dec 9, 55. *Study:* Nasson Col, Springvale, Maine, 77; San Francisco Art Inst, 87; Visual Art Access, 91. *Work:* San Jose State Photog & Video Archive, Calif; also many pvt collections. *Exhib:* One-man shows, Braunstein Quay Gallery, San Francisco, 90, Anton Gallery, Washington, DC, 90, Pavel Vavrys Gallery, Prague, Czech, 92, Urban Inst Contemp Art, Grand Rapids, Mich, 93; Janet Fleisher Gallery, Philadelphia, Pa, 82; Delaware Ctr Contemp Art, Wilmington, Del, 88. *Pos:* Theater prop designer, Theatre Divaldo Pod Pdmovka, Prague, Czech, 92. *Teaching:* Guest Lect, Charles Univ, Prague, Czech, 92. *Awards:* Painting Fel, Vt Studio Colony, Johnson, 87, 88 & 89. *Bibliog:* Chuck & Jan Rosenak (coauths), Mus Am Folk Art Encyclopedia of 20th Century Americal Folk Artists, 90; Michael S Bell (auth), The Burris Flash, Visions Art Quarterly, 9/91; Betsy Miller (auth), Every Picture Tells a Story, Inside Santa Cruz, 12/91. *Media:* Acrylic on canvas, Painted found objects. *Dealer:* Braunstein/Quay Gallery 250 Sutter St San Francisco CA 94108; Anton Gallery 2108 R St NW Washington DC 20008. *Mailing Add:* 121 Mesa Ln Santa Cruz CA 95060

BURROUGHS, MARGARET T G
LECTURER, PAINTER
b St Rose, La, Nov 1, 17. *Study:* Art Inst Chicago, BFA, 44, MFA, 48; Teacher's Col, Columbia Univ, 58-61; Lewis Univ, Hon PhD. *Work:* Atlanta Univ Art Collection; Howard Univ Art Collection; Ala A&M Univ Print Collection; Jackson State Col Art Collection, Miss; Johnson Publ Co. *Exhib:* One-woman shows, Mexico City, 52-53, USSR, 65, Poland, 65, South Side Art Ctr, 72, 74, 78 & 87, YWCA, 73, Nicole Gallery, Chicago, 86; Ten Outstanding Afro-Am Artists, Washington, DC, 80; Two Centuries of Afro-Am Art, High Mus, Atlanta, Ga, 80; Sapphire & Crystals, S Side Community Art Ctr, 87. *Pos:* Founder & dir, Du Sable Mus African-Am Hist, Chicago, 61-85; asst prof African-Am art hist, Art Inst Chicago, 68; prof African-Am art & cult, Elmhurst Col, 68, Barat Col, 69; prof humanities, Kennedy-King Col, Chicago, 69-79, retired, 79; lectr at numerous college & universities. *Teaching:* Art, Du Sable High Sch, Chicago, 46-69; teacher art hist, Art Inst Chicago, 68-69; teacher humanities, Kennedy-King City Col, 67-69, prof, 69- *Awards:* Progressive Black Woman's Award, Enverite Charity Club, 87; Chicago Youth Ctr Award, 87; Community Serv Award, Black Law Students Asn of John Marshall Law Sch, 87. *Mem:* founder Nat Conf Artists (chmn, 61); founder Southside Art Ctr; African-Am Heritage Studies Prog (dir, 80-). *Media:* Watercolor, Oil. *Publ:* Ed, Home, Charles Buroughs (auth), Broadside, 84; I, Child of the Promise, Gayle Goss Hutchinson (auth), 84; Home, Poems by Charles Burroughs, 85; Jazz Interlude (12 poems), Frank Marshall Davis (auth), 87; Poems by Gayle Goss Hutchison, 87. *Mailing Add:* 3806 S Michigan Ave Chicago IL 60653

BURROWS, SELIG S
COLLECTOR, HISTORIAN
b New York, NY, 1913. *Study:* Fordham Univ, grad, 33; NY Univ Law Sch, grad, 36. *Pos:* Trustee & chmn acquisitions comt, Norton Gallery, West Palm Beach, Fla, currently; trustee, Friends of Whitney Mus, currently; trustee, Armory Art Ctr, currently. *Mem:* Soc Four Arts, Palm Beach, Fla. *Collection:* Late nineteenth and twentieth century American art; German expressionist and modern French paintings. *Mailing Add:* 660 Park Ave New York NY 10021

BURSON, NANCY
PHOTOGRAPHER, CONCEPTUAL ARTIST
b St Louis, Mo, Feb 24, 48. *Study:* Colo Women's Col, 66-68. *Work:* San Francisco Mus Mod Art; Libr Cong, Washington, DC; Hallmark Collection, Kansas City, Mo; Victoria & Albert Mus, London. *Comn:* Aged celebrities, People Mag, New York, 82; Big Brother, CBS News Special, New York, 83; updates of missing children, FBI, Washington, DC, 84-86; Mick & Keith, Rolling Stone Mag, New York, 86; Aged Marilyn Monroe, Good Morning Am, New York, 86. *Exhib:* solo exhibs, Int Ctr Photog, New York, 85, Jayne Baum Gallery, New York, 90; Group shows, Photography of Invention: American Pictures of the 80's, Nat Mus Am Art, Washington DC, Whitney Mus Am Art, 90; Identity, Palais de Tokyo, Paris, 85; Stills: Cinema & Video Transformed, Seattle Art Mus, 86. *Teaching:* Vis artist photog, Kansas City Art Inst, Mo, 85; photog course, Tisch Sch Arts, New York Univ, 90- *Awards:* Nat Endowment Arts Grant-Photog, 91. *Bibliog:* Owen Edwards (auth), Portraits with Bursonality, 5/89; Elizabeth Hoyt-Atleins (auth), Art News Review, 5/90; Vince Aletti (auth), About Face: Redefining Normality with Nancy Burson, The Village Voice, 94, 4/21/92. *Media:* Computer Generated Photography. *Publ:* Photogr, Am Photogr, 85, Newsweek, 85, New York Post (cover), 85, Manipulator Mag, 85-86 & Smithsonian Mag, 86; Composites, William Morrow, 86; Faces: Nancy Burson, publ by CAM, Houston, essay by Lynn Herbert, 92. *Dealer:* Jayne Baum Gallery 588 Broadway New York NY 10012. *Mailing Add:* 548 Broadway New York NY 10012

BURT, DAN
PAINTER
b Owensboro, Ky, Aug 17, 30. *Study:* Ramon Froman Sch Art, Cloudcroft, NMex; Simon Michael Sch Art, Rockport, Tex; also with Harold Roney, Joy Carrington & William H Earle. *Work:* Texaco Corp, Houston; Brownsville Art League Mus, Tex; Methodist Hosp, San Antonio. *Exhib:* Knickerbocker Artists of Am, New York, 79, 84, 90 & 91; Allied Artists Am, 75 & 91, Nat Watercolor Soc, Brea, Calif, 87 & 89 & Audubon Artists, New York, 82, 89 & 90; Watercolor West, Glendale, Calif, 91. *Teaching:* Oil & watercolor painting, Hill Country Arts Foundation, Ingram, Tex, 76-82, 91 & 92. *Awards:* The Founders Award, Watercolor West 23rd Ann, Glendale, Calif, 91; Arjomari/Arches/Rives Paper Award, Knickerbocker Artist 41st Ann, New York; Gold Medal Honor (Watermedia), Allied Artists Am, 78th Ann, New York. *Bibliog:* Harry Reed (auth), article in Southwest Art, 3/78 & Art Voices S, 9-10-79. *Mem:* Nat Watercolor Soc Calif; Knickerbocker Artists New York; Allied Artists Am New York; Southwestern Watercolor Soc Dallas; Tex Watercolor Soc San Antonio. *Media:* Oil, Watercolor. *Dealer:* Tex Trails Gallery 245 Losoya San Antonio TX; The Greenhouse Gallery 2218 Breezewood San Antonio TX 78209. *Mailing Add:* 2110 B West Lane Kerrville TX 78028

BURT, DAVID SILL
SCULPTOR
b Evanston, Ill, Feb 20, 17. *Study:* Harvard Univ, BA, 40. *Work:* Fine Art Ctr, Univ Wis-Milwaukee; US Art in Embassies Prog, Stamford Mus. *Comn:* Harvey Hubbell Co, 74; Phelps Dodge Co, 81; Waterway Tower, Dallas, 81; Landmark Bldg, Stamford, Conn, 81; Excelsior Hotel, Tulsa, 81; Bradley Int Airport, Hartford, Conn, 86; Data Switch Corp, Shelton, Conn, 86; Philips Electronic Corp, Mahwah, NJ, 88; Chartwell Reinsurance Inc, Stamford, Conn, 90. *Exhib:* Pa Acad Fine Arts Exhib, 64; Northeast USA Exhib, 65, 67, 69, 70, 77, 80 & 81; 18 one-man exhibs, New York, Conn, RI, Colo, Tex & Ireland. *Pos:* Promotion writer, Archit Forum, Indust Design & Interiors. *Mem:* Sculptors League; Silvermine Guild Artists. *Media:* Hammered & Braised Sheet Metal. *Publ:* Auth, Detour to sculpture, Am Artist Mag. *Mailing Add:* 20 Covewood Dr Rowayton CT 06853

BUSCH, RITA MARY
PAINTER, SCULPTOR
b Middletown, RI, July 14, 26. *Study:* Watercolor workshops: Robert Wood, 72, Charles Reid, 75 & Doug Walton, 85. *Work:* Fidelity Nat Bank, Oklahoma City; Presby Hosp Found, Oklahoma City; Consolidated Insurance Co, Tulsa, Okla; Country Club Publ, Oklahoma City; Weyerhauser Corp Hq. *Comn:* Watercolor paintings, Dorothea Land, Oklahoma City, 86; watercolor painting, Preston Nichols, Moore, Okla, 86; pastel portrait, Mrs Jack J Wells, Oklahoma City, 86; watercolor painting, (World Neighbors, Commemorative Piece), Mr & Mrs Douglas Ormseth, New York, 87. *Exhib:* Okla Art Guild Juried Exhib, Penn Square Mall, Oklahoma City, 84-89; Okla Art Guild, North Park Mall, Oklahoma City, 84; Newport Art Festival, RI, 84 & 86; Nat League Am Pen Women, Pirates Alley, Oklahoma City, 86; Okla Watercolor Travelling Exhib, 86. *Pos:* Jr Art Coordr, State Fair Okla, 76-90. *Teaching:* Teacher, watercolor, St Lukes Sch Continuing Ed, Oklahoma City, 86, Geatches Art Sch, Oklahoma City, 86 & Arts Annex, Oklahoma City, 88-89; artist-in-residence, Skyview Elem Sch, Yukon, Okla, 90. *Awards:* Equal Merit Award, Okla Art Guild Juried Show, 84; First Place Watercolor & Oils, McAlester Art Fest, McAlester Art Guild, 81; First Place Pastel, Pen Women's Show, Nat League Am Penwomen, 86. *Mem:* Okla Art Guild (3rd vpres, 76-77, 2nd vpres Shows, 77-79, pres, 79-80); Okla Watercolor Asn; Nat League Am Pen Women, (pres, 90-92). *Media:* Watercolor, Pastels; Metal, Cast. *Dealer:* Margo K Shorney Shorney Gallery Fine Art 6616 N Olie Oklahoma City OK 73116. *Mailing Add:* 1220 N Glade Oklahoma City OK 73127

BUSH, CHARLES ROBERT See Robb, Charles

BUSH, DONALD JOHN
HISTORIAN, EDUCATOR
b San Francisco, Calif. *Study:* Ariz State Univ, BS, 59; Univ Notre Dame with Dr John Howett, MA(art), 64; Univ NMex with Clinton Adams, Van Deren Coke & Peter Walch, PhD(art hist), 73. *Teaching:* Teaching asst art, Univ Notre Dame, 63-64; chmn art dept, Univ Albuquerque, 64-75; assoc prof art hist & humanities, Ariz State Univ, 75-80; assoc prof design hist, Ariz State Univ, 80- *Mem:* Col Art Asn; Am Studies Assoc; Soc Architectural Historians; William Morris Soc. *Res:* Development of American industrial design and architecture; product semantics. *Publ:* Auth, Streamlining and American industrial design, autumn 74; auth, The Streamlined Decade, George Braziller, 75; auth, Thorstein Veblen's economic aesthetic, Leonardo Mag, autumn 78; auth, Futurama--World's Fair as utopia, Alternative Futures, fall 79; auth, How Objects Speak, Proceedings Interface, 87, and Numerous art exhib catalogs & book rev. *Mailing Add:* Dept of Design Sciences Ariz State Univ Tempe AZ 85281

BUSH, JILL LOBDILL
PAINTER
b Grand Island, Nebr, May 11, 42. *Study:* Tex Tech Univ, BA(adv art & design), 64. *Work:* Collection five paintings, First Fed Savings & Loan, Ft Smith, Ark; Holt Crock Clinic, Ft Smith, Ark, 80; Peace oil painting, Harris Methodist HEB Hosp, Ctr Women's Health, Bedford, Tex, 91. *Comn:* Dr O J Wallenman Jr mem portrait, St Joseph Hosp Drs, Ft Worth, 79; Marion Day Mullins DAR portrait, Ft Worth Woman's Club, 80; Brig Gen Victor Carey, portrait, Darby's Rangers Mus, Ft Smith, Ark, 80; Coach Indian Jim Malone, portrait, Southern La State Univ, Hammond, 80; Dr Paul Parham mem portrait, TCU Libr Asn, Ft Worth, 87. *Exhib:* Knickerbocker 29th Ann, Nat Arts Club, New York, 79; Pastel Soc Am Exhib, Copley Mus, Boston, 79; 1st Ann Main St Tex Invitational, Ft Worth, 86; Pastel Soc Am Invitational, 3rd Salon Des Pastellists, Lille, France, 87; PSA Invitational Exhib, Ashland Area Gallery, Ky, 89; and others. *Teaching:* Instr figure drawing & oil painting, Ft Worth Art Mus Sch, 65-70; instr figure drawing & oil painting, Ft Worth Jr Woman's Club, 73-76, instr oil, pastel & drawing, 74-79. *Awards:* Pastel Soc Am Award, San Marcus Nat, 79; Schwann Weber Award, Pastel Soc Am Eighth Ann, 80; First Place, Pastel Soc SW Ann, 85. *Bibliog:* Ann B White (auth), Making their marks, Aura Mag, 86; Madlyn-Ann Woolwich (auth), Jill Bush, Texas Portrait Artist, Pastelagram, Pastel Soc Am, 89; Madlyn-Ann Woolwich (auth), Pastel Interpretations, Northlight Bks, 92. *Mem:* Pastel Soc

Am. *Media:* Pastel, Oil. *Publ:* Contribr, Pastel Interpretations, Northlight Bks, 92-93. *Dealer:* Evelyn Siegel Art Gallery 3700 W Seventh St Ft Worth TX 76107; L L Gallery 216 N Fredonia Longview TX 75601. *Mailing Add:* 6440 Curzon Ft Worth TX 76116

BUSH, MARTIN H
MUSEUM DIRECTOR, HISTORIAN
b Amsterdam, NY, Jan 24, 30. *Study:* State Univ NY Albany, BA & MA, 58; Syracuse Univ, PhD, 66. *Collections Arranged:* Photo Realism: Rip-Off or Reality, 75; George Grosz, 75; Wayne Thiebaud, 75; Robert Goodnough, 75; Richard Pousette-Dart, 75; Duane Hanson, 76; W Eugene Smith, 77; Milton Avery, 78; Joan Miro, 78; Louise Nevelson, 78; Theodoros Stamos, 79; Kenneth Noland, 80; Figures of Contemporary Sculpture 1970-1990, 92; and many others. *Pos:* Dir, E A Ulrich Mus Art, Wichita State Univ, 71-89, vpres acad resource develop, 74-89; pres, ACA Galleries, 89- *Teaching:* Instr, Syracuse Univ, 63-65, asst dean, 65-70. *Mem:* Am Asn Art Mus; Col Art Asn; Art Dealers Asn Am. *Res:* 20th century American art. *Publ:* Auth, Duane Hanson, 76; Ernest Trova, 77; Robert Goodnough, Abbeville, 82; The Photographs of Gordon Parks, Ulrich Mus Art, 83; Philip Reisman: People are his passion, Ulrich Mus Art, 86; and many articles, brochures and catalogs. *Mailing Add:* ACA Gallery 41 E 57th St New York NY 10022

BUSH-BROWN, ALBERT
WRITER, EDUCATOR
b West Hartford, Conn, Jan 2, 26. *Study:* Princeton Univ, AB, 47, MFA(Woodrow Wilson Fel), 49, PhD, 58; Emerson Col, Hon LLD, 65; Providence Col, Hon HHD, 66; Mercy Col, Hon DFA, 76. *Pos:* Nat adv comt, Archives Am Art, 62-85; mem, Nat Coun on The Arts, White House, 64-70; dir-at-large, Nat Coun Arts in Educ, 65-71; managing dir, Metrop Opera, 78-85; dir, Barclays Bank, New York, 79-, chmn, 81-; pres, Nat Building Mus, 80-82; dir, US-Morocco Found, 81-, Hecksher Mus Art, 81-85 & Univ Andes Found, 82-; pres, AB-BA Assocs, 85-; sr coun, Hill & Knowlton, New York, 87- *Teaching:* Instr art & archaeol, Princeton Univ, 49-50; asst prof art & archit, Western Reserve Univ, 53-54; asst prof archit, Mass Inst Technol, 54-58, assoc prof & exec officer archit, 58-62; pres, RI Sch Design, 62-68; Bemis vis prof, Mass Inst Technol, 68-69; vpres, State Univ NY Buffalo, 69-71; chancellor, Long Island Univ, 71-85; vis lectr, currently. *Awards:* Howard Found Fel, Brown Univ, 59-60; Ford Found Fel, 68-69; fel, Harvard Univ, John F Kennedy Inst & Joint Ctr for Urban Studies, 68-69. *Mem:* Century Asn; hon mem Am Inst Architects; Conference Bd; Coun Foreign Relations. *Publ:* Auth, Louis Sullivan, 60; co-auth, The Architecture of America: a Social Interpretation, 61; auth, Books, Bass, Barnstable, 67; King Khalid Military City, Saudi Arabia, 78; Louis Sullivan, Japan, 79; numerous articles in encycl, art & archit jounals, 52-65. *Mailing Add:* Pine Lane Barnstable MA 02630

BUSHMAN, DAVID FRANKLIN
PAINTER, EDUCATOR
b Toledo, Ohio, Aug 2, 45. *Study:* Univ Wis, MA, 68 & MFA, 69; also with Al Leslie, Jack Beal, James Rosenquist & Richard Artschager. *Work:* Johnson Wax Co, Racine, Wis; Wis State J, Madison; Univ Wis-Madison; C M Bruckner Collection, New York; Madison Art Ctr, Wis; and others. *Comn:* Mural, Mr & Mrs G Lauderdale, Ft Lauderdale, Fla, 70; painting, H C Westerman, Brookfield Ctr, Conn, 73; portrait, Mr & Mrs S Crane, Chicago, 75; painting, Mr & Mrs James Stewart, Chicago, 75; painting, Racine Nat Bank, Wis, 80; and others. *Exhib:* Solo shows, Penn State Univ, State Col, 76, Gilman Galleries, Chicago, Ill, 78, Drawings by D F Bushman, Lakeview Mus Art, Peoria, Ill, 82; Realism Today, Evansville Mus Arts & Sci, Ind, 83; 14th Union League of Chicago Competition and Exhib, Artemesia Gallery & Union League Club, Chicago, 85; 1987 Nat Biennial, Sioux City Art Ctr, Iowa, 87; 72nd Hudson River Annual, Hudson River Mus, Yonkers, NY, 87; 1988 Mid America Biennial, Owensboro Mus Art, Ky, 88; Portland Art Mus, Ore, 83; and others. *Teaching:* Instr painting & drawing, Univ Wis-Madison, 67-69; asst prof painting & drawing, Univ Ill, Urbana-Champaign, 69-76, assoc prof, 76-; guest lectr, Louisville Art Ctr, Ky, 72; guest lectr, George Peabody Univ, 74, Univ Wis, 82. *Awards:* Cash Award, Nat Drawings, NY Univ, 69; Cash Award, Ill State Fair, 70; Award, Art Inst Chicago; and others. *Mem:* Col Art Asn; New Col Art Asn; Am Fedn Teachers. *Dealer:* Gilman Gallery 227 Ontario Chicago IL 60611. *Mailing Add:* 134 Fine Arts Bldg Dept Art Design Univ Ill Champaign IL 61820

BUSHNELL, KENNETH WAYNE
PAINTER, EDUCATOR
b Los Angeles, Calif, Oct 16, 33. *Study:* Univ Calif, Los Angeles, BA(art), 56; Univ Hawaii, MFA(painting), 60. *Work:* Honolulu Acad Art, Hawaii State Found Cult & Arts; Mich State Univ, East Lansing; Bibliotheque Nationale, Paris; Corcoran Gallery, Washington, DC. *Comn:* portrait of Dr Richard Lee, comn by Sch Publ Health, Univ Hawaii, 69; steel sculpture Pearl Ridge Ctr, Hawaii, 84; two 23 ft wall reliefs, Kaiser Clinic Honolulu, 86; Kalakaua Ctr Proj, five wall reliefs 20 ft x 9 ft, Honolulu, 89; Painting on glass, 9 ft x 16 ft, Japan Travel Bureau, Honolulu, 89; Four Panels 6 ft x 17 ft mural project, First Hawaiian Bank, Main Branch, Honolulu. *Exhib:* Painting USA: The Figure, New York Mus Mod Art, 62; Baltimore Mus Art, 62; Drawings USA, St Paul Art Ctr, Minn, 63; 158th Ann Exhib, Pa Acad Fine Arts, Philadelphia, 63; NW Printmakers Ann, Seattle Mus & Portland Mus, 64; New Talent in the West, Salt Lake City Art Ctr, 68; Calif-Hawaii Exhib, San Diego Mus, 70; Int Print Biennial, Krakow, Poland, 74; Int Print Biennial, Honolulu Acad Art, 78-82; solo exhibs, Contemp Arts Ctr, Honolulu, Hawaii, 65 & 86, Honolulu Acad Art, 68 & 73, Sande Webster Gallery, Philadelphia, 81, 85, 88 & 92, Meissner Editions, Hamberg, 84, Maghi Behini Gallery, Amsterdam, 84 & Karen Fesel Gallery, Dusseldorf, WGer, 90, Contem Art Ctr. *Pos:* Bd mem, Hawaii Artists League, 81. *Teaching:* Prof art painting, Univ Hawaii, 61-81; prof art painting, C W Post Ctr, Long Island Univ, 78-79 & 83; chairman, Department of Art Univ Art Manoa, 91- *Awards:* Purchase Award, Honolulu Acad Art, 68; First Award Painting, Calif-Hawaii Exhib, San Diego Mus, 74; John Wyatt Gregg Award, Honolulu Acad Art, 73; Hawaii State Found Purchase Awards, 75, 81, 84, 86 & 87. *Mem:* Honolulu Printmakers (pres, 71); Nat Arts Club New York; Hawaii Artists League. *Media:* Oil, Acrylic Polimer. *Dealer:* Fine Art Associates Ward Ctr Honolulu Hawaii 96814; Karen Fesel Gallerie Dusseldorf Ger. *Mailing Add:* 2081 Keeaumoku St Honolulu HI 96822

BUSINO, ORLANDO FRANCIS
CARTOONIST
b Binghamton, NY, Oct 10, 26. *Study:* State Univ Iowa, BA, 52. *Pos:* Cartoonist, Sat Eve Post, McCall's, Ladies Home J, Sat Rev, Look, True, Argosy, Boys' Life, Family Circle & other US & foreign mags. *Awards:* Best Mag Cartoonist of Year, Nat Cartoonists Soc, 65, 67 & 68. *Mem:* Nat Cartoonists Soc; Mag Cartoonists Guild. *Mailing Add:* 12 Shadblow Hill Rd Ridgefield CT 06877

BUSSABARGER, ROBERT FRANKLIN
SCULPTOR, PAINTER
b Corydon, Ind, Sept 17, 22. *Study:* Wittenburg Univ, with Ralston Thompson, AB, 44; Mich State Univ, with John de Martelli, Louis Raynor & Carl Schmidt, MA, 47; Ohio State Univ, with Paul Bogatay & Edgar Littlefield, 49-51. *Work:* Air India Collection, Bombay, India; Springfield Art Mus, Mo; Mo Hist Soc, Columbia; Columbia Art & Archeology Mus, Univ Mo. *Comn:* 33 ft Ceramic Mural, Col Arts Sci, Univ Mo in Columbia, 91. *Exhib:* Sculptors Gallery, St Louis, Mo, 66; Acad Fine Arts, Calcutta, India, 69; Am Cult Ctr, Bombay, India, 69; solo exhibs, Chemould Art Gallery, Bombay, India, 78 & 84 & Urja Art Gallery, Baroda, India. *Collections Arranged:* Univ Mo Fine Arts Gallery, 55-59 & 63-67; Indian art exhib based on Bussabarger & Robins Collections, Univ Mo, Stephens Col, Westminster Col & Carleton Col. *Teaching:* Teacher art, Benton Harbor Jr & Sr High Sch, Mich, 48-49; asst prof art, Stephen F Austin State Univ, Nacogdoches, Tex, 51-53; prof art, Univ Mo-Columbia, 53-91, chmn dept, 70-73, prof emer art, 91- *Awards:* Merit Award in Sculpture, 30th Springfield Ann, Mo, 60; Fulbright Fel India, 61-62; Hays Univ SAsia Ctr Fac Fel, 68-69; Univ Mo-Columbia Fac Alumni Award, 87. *Bibliog:* A B Pine (auth), Bussabarger & ceramic art, Mo Alumnus, 11/60; L Bhattacharia (auth), Robert Bussabarger, US Info Serv, 10/62; Bussabarger, Span Mag, Usis, India, 3/84; Bussabarger, Crafts Monthly, Seoul, Korea, 8/88. *Mem:* Mo Crafts Coun; Columbia Art League; Mid-Am Art Conf. *Media:* Ceramic, Metal; Pastel, Watercolor. *Publ:* Ed, John Sloans Etchings, Univ Mo, 67; coauth & illusr, The Everyday Art of India, Dover, 68; coauth, The Makara, Archaeology, 1/70; Folk images of Sanjhi Devi, Atribus Asiae, 7/75; Mirrored Images, Splendors of Tamil Nadu, Marg, 80. *Mailing Add:* 1914 Princeton Columbia MO 65203

BUSSCHE, WOLF VON DEM
PHOTOGRAPHER, PAINTER
b Ger; US citizen. *Study:* Columbia Col, studied art hist, 56-62; Columbia Univ Sch Painting & Sculpture, 59-62; Art Students League, 61-62; self-taught in photog. *Work:* San Francisco Mus Mod Art; Mus Mod Art, Int Ctr Photog, Metrop Mus, New York; George Eastman House, Rochester, NY; and others. *Exhib:* Vision & Expression, George Eastman House, Rochester, NY, 69; Soc Encouragement Contemp Art Award Exhib, San Francisco Mus Mod Art, 80; Int Triennial Exhib Photog, Musee d'art et d'hist, Fribourg, Switz, 81; Counterparts, Metrop Mus, New York 82; Pleasures & Terrors of Domestic Comfort, Moma, NY, 91; numerous one-man shows. *Awards:* Who's Who in the West, 91. *Bibliog:* Carole Kismaric (auth), article, Camera, No 10, 71; Jerome Tarshis (auth), article, Art in Am, 1/81; Thomas Albright (auth), article, Art News, 4/82. *Media:* All. *Mailing Add:* 841 Contra Costa Ave Berkeley CA 94707

BUSTO, ANA MARIE
PHOTOGRAPHER
Study: Barcelona, Spain, BA(journalism). *Exhib:* One-person shows, Cibachrome Photographs, Midtown Y Photog Gallery, 85, Studies on Color, White Columns, New York, 86, Entre Naturalezas, Forun, Tarragona, Spain, 92; Counter-Representations, Brooklyn Mus, 85, Dream Machinations in America, Minor Injury, Brooklyn, NY, 90; The Fairy Tale: Politics, Desire, and Everyday Life, Artist Space, 87, Update 1986-87, White Columns, 87, Female Re-Production, White Columns, 88, Contemporary Saints, Henry St Settlement & Longwood Arts Projs, PS 39, 90, Race and Culture, 494 Gallery & City Col NY, New York, 91; Urban Narrative-Evil Empires, Aljira, Newark, NJ & Longwood Arts Projs, PS 39, New York, 90. *Awards:* NY Found Arts, 90; Nat Endowments Arts, 90. *Publ:* Village Voice, New Observations, 85; NY Times, La Vanguardia, Spain, 89, El Pais, Spain, 90. *Mailing Add:* 107 Roebling Brooklyn NY 11211

BUSZKO, IRENE J
PAINTER
b Brooklyn, NY, Sept 22, 47. *Study:* Pratt Inst, BFA, 69; Queens Col, MFA, 72. *Work:* Lehman Brothers Collection; Lloyd's Bank Int, New York; Chemical Bank & Citibank, Citicorp Ctr, New York; Mitsubishi Int, New York. *Exhib:* 157th Ann Exhib, Nat Acad Design, New York, 82; one-woman shows, Tatistcheff & Co, New York, 82, 85, 89 & Plandome Gallery, NY, 92; Painted Light, 83 & 1st Eight Years, 84, Artist's Choice Mus, New York; Three Painters from New York, Bloomsbury Theater, London, Eng, 85; The Richmond Hill Series, Queens Mus, Flushing, NY, 86. *Teaching:* Instr painting, Nat Acad Design, 87-88. *Awards:* Creative Artist Pub Serv Grant, NY State Coun Arts, 76. *Mem:* New York Artists Equity. *Media:* Oil on Canvas. *Dealer:* Tatistcheff & Co 50 W 57th St New York NY 10019. *Mailing Add:* 652 Broadway New York NY 10012

BUTCHKES, SYDNEY
PAINTER, SCULPTOR
b Covington, Ky, Oct 13, 22. *Study:* Cincinnati Art Acad, Ohio; Art Students League; New Sch Social Res, New York. *Work:* Metrop Mus; Brooklyn Mus, NY; Cincinnati Art Mus; Wadsworth Atheneum, Hartford, Conn; Nat Collection Fine Arts, Smithsonian Inst, Washington, DC; and others. *Comn:* Sculpture for lobby of Financial Progs Bldg, Denver, 69; hanging sculpture for bar of Ritz Carlton Hotel, Boston, 69; painting for lobby of Skidmore, Owings, Merrill, Chicago, 70; paintings, World Trade Ctr, NY & Continental Tel Co, Washington, DC. *Exhib:* Art for the Collector, San Francisco Mus Art, 65; Painting Without a Brush, Inst Contemp Art, Boston, 65; Painting Out from the Wall, Des Moines Art Ctr, Iowa, 67; Plastic as Plastic, Mus Contemp Crafts, New York, 69; Mus Acquisitions, Colorado Springs Art Ctr, 69; Art, Design and the Modern Corp, Nat Mus Am Art, Washington, DC, 85. *Awards:* Am Crafts Coun Hon Fel. *Mem:* Abstr Am Artists. *Media:* Acrylic Paint; Wood. *Mailing Add:* Sagg Main St Sagaponack NY 11962

BUTERA, VIRGINIA FABBRI
CURATOR, HISTORIAN
b Norristown, Pa, Nov 15, 51. *Study:* Trinity Col, Conn, BA, 73; Johns Hopkins Univ, MA(art hist), 75; City Univ NY, PhD program, ongoing. *Collections Arranged:* The Graphic Side of the Second Empire, Philadelphia Mus Art, 78; The Great American Fan Show (auth, catalog), Lerner-Heller Gallery, New York, 81; The Folding Image: Screens by Western Artists of the 19th and 20th Centuries (coauth, catalog), Nat Gallery Art, Washington, DC & Yale Univ Art Gallery, 84-86; Contemporary Screens (auth, catalog), Contemp Arts Ctr, Cincinnati, Lowe Art Mus, Toledo Art Mus & City Gallery Contemp Art, Raleigh, 86-88. *Pos:* Fel, Nat Mus Am Art, Washington, DC, 76-77; asst, dept prints, drawings & photographs, Philadelphia Mus Art, 78-79, asst to dir, 79-81; co-chair & bd trustees, AIR Gallery, New York, 84-85; curatorial consult, Everything for Industry, Jersey City Mus, currently. *Awards:* Smithsonian Mus Fel, 76-77; Nat Endowment Arts Grant, 78-79; Mall Gallery Fel, City Univ NY, 84-86. *Mem:* Col Art Asn. *Res:* European and American painting and sculpture, 1860 to the present. *Publ:* Auth, The fan as form and image in contemporary art, 81 & Investigating Jim Jacobs' sculpture and painting, 86, Arts Mag; Contemporary screens, Art Mus Asn Am, 86; Jim Jacobs: Screens, Mus of Art, Ft Lauderdale. *Mailing Add:* 18 Fay Place Summit NJ 07901

BUTLER, BYRON C
JEWELER
b Carroll, Iowa, Aug 10, 18. *Study:* Univ Calif, Los Angeles, 36-39; Columbia Col Physicians & Surgeons, MD, 43, Columbia Univ, MedScD, 50; Gemological Inst Am, Santa Monica, 86, grad gemologist, jewelry sketching, 92. *Work:* Phoenix Art Mus, Ariz; NASA, Houston, Tex, Smithsonian Inst, DC; plus many others. *Comn:* Large canvas by R C Gorman of Hohokam Indians Masked Dancers, St Lukes Hosp, Phoenix, 71. *Exhib:* Am Indian Art Collection, Heard Mus, Phoenix, Oklahoma City Mus, Okla, Atlanta Mus, Ga, Northern Ariz Mus, Flagstaff & Millicent Rogers Mus, Taos, NMex, 57-73. *Collections Arranged:* Yaqui Indian Art, Heard Mus, 77. *Pos:* Pres & art dealer, Art Consultants, 55-79; mem, bd dirs, Heard Mus, 68-74; pres, World Gems, 80- *Bibliog:* Clara Lee Tanner (auth), Southwest Indian Paintings, Univ Ariz Press, 73; Guy & Doris Monthan (auth), Art and Indian Individualists, 75 & Doris Monthan (auth), R C Gorman Lithographs, 78, Northland Press. *Mem:* Gem Trade Asn; Int Colored Gemstone Asn; Jewelers Am; Ariz Jewelers Asn. *Mailing Add:* 6900 E Camelback Ste 700 Scottsdale AZ 85251

BUTLER, CHARLES THOMAS
MUSEUM DIRECTOR, CURATOR
b Pearisburg, Va, Apr 20, 51. *Study:* Univ Del, with William Inness Homer, BA(cum laude), 76; Univ NMex, with Beaumont Newhall & Tom Barrow, MA(abd), 76-78. *Collections Arranged:* Recent Graphics from American Print Shops (auth, catalog), 86; Michael Eastman: Color Photographs (auth, catalog), 88; Gardens of Paradise: Oriental Prayer Rugs (textiles), 89; Enduring Impressions: Prints, 1960-1990 (graphics), 90; Dick Arentz: Outside the Mainstream (photographs; auth, catalog), 91. *Pos:* Ass dir, Sioux City Art Ctr, Ind, 79-85; exec dir, Mitchell Mus, Mt Vernon, Ill, 85-88; dir, Huntington Mus Art, WVa, 88- *Mem:* Midwest Mus Conf; Am Asn Mus; Southeastern Mus Conf (exec comt, 89-); WVa Asn Mus (exec comt, 90-). *Media:* Photography, Graphics. *Publ:* Auth, New Talent, New York, Sioux City Art Ctr, 84; coauth, Edward McCullough: The Elegy Series, Mitchell Mus, 87. *Mailing Add:* 2033 McCoy Rd Huntington WV 25701

BUTLER, HIRAM
DIRECTOR
b Del Rio, Tex, 1951. *Study:* Univ Tex, Austin, BFA, 76; Williams Col, Williamstown, Mass, MA(art hist), 7. *Pos:* Asst cur iconography collection, Humanities Res Ctr, Univ Tex, Austin, 77; asst cur, Clark Art Inst, Williamstown, Mass, 78-79; intern, Nat Endowment Arts, Mus Mod Art, New York, 79-80; dir gallery, David Tunick Inc, New York, 80-81; dir, Delahunty Inc, Dallas, 81-84, Hiram Butler Gallery, Houston, Tex, 84- *Publ:* Auth, The Cranfill Collection of Latin America, 76; contribr, Drawings, Design and Collage: Fifty Contemporary American Works on Paper from the Collection of Mr & Mrs Stephen D Paine, 79; auth, Downtown in the fifties, Horizon: The Mag Arts, 6/81. *Mailing Add:* 4520 Blossom Houston TX 77007

BUTLER, JAMES D
PRINTMAKER, PAINTER
b Ft Dodge, Iowa, Aug 30, 45. *Study:* Omaha Univ, Nebr, BS, 67; Univ Nebr, Lincoln, MFA, 70. *Work:* Brooklyn Mus, NY; Brit Mus, London, Eng; Tamarind Inst, Albuquerque, NMex; Libr of Cong, Washington, DC; Smithsonian Inst, Washington, DC. *Comn:* First Ill Print Comn, Ill Arts Coun, 73. *Exhib:* Corp Collections Show, Minn Mus of Art, St Paul, 72; Prints: Midwest Invitational, Walker Art Ctr, Minneapolis, 73; 19th Nat Print Exhib, Brooklyn Mus, 74; Mod Printmaking Exhib of Contemp Prints, Bevier Gallery, Rochester Inst of Technol, NY, 74; New American Colorists, World Print Coun, San Francisco, 81; 30 American Printmakers, Columbus, Ohio, 82; and others. *Teaching:* Asst prof, Southern Ill Univ, Edwardsville, 70-76; assoc prof, Ill State Univ, Normal, 76-81, prof, 81- *Awards:* Robert Cooke Endowment Award, 1971 Mid-States Art Exhib, Evansville Mus of Arts & Sci, Ind, 71; First Place, Fine Art of Printmaking, Lexington, Ky, Nat Soc of Arts & Lett, 71; Nat Endowment Arts, 75-76 & 79. *Bibliog:* Clinton Adams & Susan Ellis (auths), Drawing Color Separations on Surfaced Mylar, Tamarind Tech Papers, 74; Experiments in affordable custom lithography, Print News, Vol 3, 2-3/81. *Mem:* Mid-Am Col Art Asn; Col Art Asn. *Media:* Lithography; Drawing, Oil. *Dealer:* Associated American Artists New York NY. *Mailing Add:* 102 Warner St Bloomington IL 61701

BUTLER, JOSEPH THOMAS
CURATOR, WRITER
b Winchester, Va, Jan 25, 32. *Study:* Univ Md, BS, 54; Univ Ohio, MA, 55; Univ Del, MA(Winterthur Fel), 57. *Exhib:* Am Furniture from Westchester Collections: 1650-1880, Katonah Gallery, Katonah, NY, 86; The Am Eagle: An Enduring Symbol, Katonah Gallery, Katonah, NY, 89; Amer Painted Furniture, Scarsdale Historical Soc, 90; Visions of Washington Irving, 91. *Collections Arranged:* Divided Loyalties, Philipsburg Manor, North Tarrytown, NY, 76-79 & Four Centuries of History, A Decade of Restoration. *Pos:* Cur & dir Collections, Hist Hudson Valley, Tarrytown, NY, 57-; Am ed, The Connoisseur, 68-78; ed bd, Art & Antiques, 78-83; adj prof art hist, Fashion Inst Tech, New York, 86- *Teaching:* Adj assoc prof archit, Columbia Univ, 71-81. *Mem:* Nat Arts Club; Furniture Hist Soc; Victorian Soc in Am; Am Ceramic Circle; The Century Asn. *Res:* American decorative arts and architecture. *Publ:* Auth, American Antiques, 1800-1900, 65; Candleholders in America, 1650-1900, 67; coauth, The Arts in America, the 19th Century, 70; auth, Washington Irving's Sunnyside, 75; Van Cortlandt Manor, 78; Sleepy Hollow Restorations: A Cross Section of the Collection, 83; Field Guide to American Antique Furniture, 85; American Painted Furniture, 90. *Mailing Add:* 222 Martling Ave Tarrytown NY 10591

BUTLER, MARIGENE H
ADMINISTRATOR, CONSERVATOR
b Ann Arbor, Mich, July 20, 31. *Study:* Mt Holyoke Col, AB, 53; Fogg Art Mus, Harvard Univ, 53-55; Art Inst Chicago, 66-68. *Pos:* Asst conservator, Art Inst Chicago, 68-70, assoc conservator, 70-73; dir & head training, Intermuseum Lab, Oberlin, Ohio, 73-78; head conserv, Philadelphia Mus Art, 78- *Mem:* Fel Int Inst Conserv Hist & Artistic Works; fel Royal Micros Soc; fel Am Inst Conserv Hist & Artistic Works. *Publ:* An investigation of the technique and materials used by Jan Steen, Bulletin, Philadelphia Mus Art, Vol 78, No 337-338, winter 82-spring 83; An Investigation of the materials and techniques used by Paul Cezanne, The Am Inst Conserv Hist & Artistic Works, Los Angeles, Calif, 5/87; Coauth with J R L van Asperen de Boer, The Examination of the Milan-Turin Hours with Infrared Reflectography, A Preliminary Report, In Actes du Colloque VII pour l'etude du dessin sous-jacent, 87; An Investigation of Two Paintings of the Stigmatization of Saint Francis thought to have been painted by Jan van Eyck, Actes du Colloque VIII pour Dessin Sous - jacent et copies, 89. *Mailing Add:* Philadelphia Mus of Art Box 7646 Philadelphia PA 19101

BUTT, HARLAN W
SILVERSMITH, ENAMELIST
b Princeton, NJ, Mar 30, 50. *Study:* Tyler Sch Art, with Stanley Lechtzin, BFA, 72; Southern Ill Univ, with Brent Kington, MFA, 74. *Work:* Southern Ill Univ, Carbondale. *Comn:* University mace & jazz band commemorative, NTex State Univ, Denton; University mace, Southwest Adventist Col, Keene, Tex. *Exhib:* Solo exhibs, Wichita Art Assoc, Wichita, Kans, 88, Seika-do Gallery, Kyoto, Japan, 82 & 85, Nat Ornamental Metal Mus, Memphis, 83 & Contemp Crafts Gallery, Portland, Ore, 86; International Exhibition Enameling Art, Ueno Royal Mus, Tokyo, 85; Enamels International, Long Beach Mus Art, Calif, 85; Biennale, La Maison des Arts, Laval, Can, 86. *Collections Arranged:* Kyoto Metal: An Exhibition of Contemporary Japanese Metalwork (auth, catalog), 83-84. *Teaching:* Lectr metalworking, San Diego State Univ, Calif, 75-76; prof metalworking, Univ NTex, Denton, 76- *Awards:* Merit Award, Int Exhib Enameling Art Comt, 85. *Mem:* Soc NAm Goldsmiths; Am Crafts Coun; NTex Enamel Guild; Enamel Guild West. *Media:* Metal. *Mailing Add:* Rt 2 Box 637 N Denton TX 76201

BUTTER, TOM
SCULPTOR, INSTRUCTOR
b Amityville, NY, Oct 19, 52. *Study:* Philadelphia Col Art, BFA, 75; Wash Univ, St Louis, Mo, MFA, 77. *Work:* Acad Fine Arts, Philadelphia; Metrop Mus Art, New York; Chase Manhattan Bank; Prudential Insurance Co Am; Indianapolis Mus Art, Ind; Albright-Knox Art Gallery, Buffalo, NY. *Exhib:* Solo exhibs, Lawrence Oliver Gallery, 83, 84, 85 & 86, Morris Gallery, Pa Acad Fine Arts, 85, Curt Marcus Gallery, 86, 88 & 91, Nina Freundenheim Gallery, Buffalo, NY, 87 & 92, John Berggruen Gallery, San Francisco, 87-, Pence Gallery, Los Angeles, 88; Transformation of the Minimal Style, Sculpture Ctr, NY, 84; Perspectives from Pennsylvania, Carnegie Mellon

Univ Art Gallery, Pittsburgh, 87; Sculpture Inside Outside, Mus Fine Arts, Houston, Tex, 88-89; The 1980's A New Generation, Metrop Mus Art, New York, 88; and many others. *Teaching:* adj, Parsons Sch Design. *Awards:* Nat Endowment Arts Grant, 80 & 82; NY Found Arts Grant 87. *Bibliog:* Wade Saunders (auth), article, Art Am, 3/83 & Interview with ten sculptors, 11/85; Kate Linker (auth), article, Artforum, 11/83; Benjamin Forgey (auth), Prismatic Showcase, Washington Post, 4/25/85; Huntington Richards, reviews in Buffalo Courier Express, 2/11/81 and 4/6/88; plus others. *Dealer:* Curt Marcus Gallery 578 Broadway New York NY 10013. *Mailing Add:* 34 Ave A New York NY 10009

BUTTERBAUGH, ROBERT CLYDE
SCULPTOR, EDUCATOR
b Freeport, Ill, May 28, 31. *Study:* Univ of the Pac, BFA, 54; Claremont Grad Sch, with Paul Darrow MFA, 62. *Work:* Sunderland Col Art, Eng. *Comn:* Sculpture relief (copper sheet), Temple Beth El, Salinas, Calif, 64; sculpture (welded corten steel), T Merrill Hall, Hartnell Col, Salinas, 65; fountain (redwood & cast bronze), Cent Plaza Bldg, 66; sculpture (redwood & plastic), Salinas City Hall Foyer, 68; sculpture group & low relief (cast concrete), Aquatic Complex, Hartnell Col, 73; Children's Playground (steel & concrete), Salinas, 80. *Exhib:* Midland Group Gallery, Nottingham, Eng, 69; Cerritos 70, Norwalk, Calif, 70; Form and the Inner Eye, Los Angeles, Calif, 71; Southern Ore Col Gallery, Ashland, 71; Univ Mich, Ann Arbor, 75; and others. *Teaching:* Prof art, Hartnell Col, 62-; lectr sculpture & drawing, Sunderland Col Art, 68-69. *Awards:* Fulbright-Hays travel grant, 68-69. *Media:* Plastics, Metals. *Mailing Add:* Dept Art Hartnell Col 156 Homestead Ave Salinas CA 93901

BUTTERFIELD, DEBORAH KAY
SCULPTOR
b San Diego, Calif, May 7, 49. *Study:* Univ Calif, Davis, BA, 71, MFA, 73. *Work:* Whitney Mus Am Art, New York; San Francisco Mus Contemp Art, Calif; Israel Mus, Jeusalem; Walker Art Ctr, Minneapolis, Minn; Metrop Mus Art, New York; Hirshhorn Mus, Washington, DC. *Comn:* Copley Square, Boston, Mass. *Exhib:* 2 Sculptors, Univ Mus Berkeley, Calif, 74; Whitney Biennial & The Decade in Review, Whitney Mus Am Art, New York, 79; 8 Sculptors, Albright-Knox Gallery, Buffalo, 79; Israel Mus, Jerusalem, 80; Arco Ctr Visual Art, 81; Walker Art Ctr, Minneapolis, 82; Dallas Mus Fine Arts, 82; Oakland, 83; Mile of Sculpture, Chicago, 85; Contemp Ar Ctr, Honolulu, 86. *Teaching:* Asst prof sculpture, Univ Wis-Madison, 75-76; asst prof sculpture, Mont State Univ, Bozeman, 79-81, adj prof, 81- *Awards:* Nat Endowment Arts Grant, 77 & 80; Guggenheim Grant, 80. *Bibliog:* Thomas Albright (auth), Unique balance of realism, art, San Francisco Chronicle, 6/15/74; Kay Larsen (auth), Behold a pale horse (or two), Village Voice, 11/26/79; Richard Martin (auth), A horse perceived by sighted persons, Vol 61, In: Arts, 1/87; Donald Kuspit, review, Art Forum, 3/87; Barry Schwabsky, review, Arts, 2/87. *Media:* Natural Materials, Steel. *Dealer:* Edward Thorp Gallery 103 Prince St New York NY 10012; Zolla Lieberman Gallery 368 W Huron Chicago IL 60610. *Mailing Add:* c/o Yellowstone Art Ctr 401 N 27th St Billings MT 59101

BUTTI, LINDA (BENINCASA)
PAINTER, EDUCATOR
b Brooklyn, NY, Jan 15, 51. *Study:* Brooklyn Col, New York, with Philip Pearlstein & William T Williams, BA, 72, MFA(painting), 75. *Work:* Brenau Permanent Collection of Am Art, Gainesville, Ga; Art Network, Staten Island, NY; Iona Col Permanent Collection of Art, New Rochelle, NY; Bell Atlantic, Atlanta, Ga; NBC Studios, New York. *Comn:* Watercolor (mural, 4' x 5'), Catholic Telecommunication, New York, 88; wall mural, Network of America; murals (two, 42" x 30"), Swanston Fine Arts Inc, Atlanta, Ga, 88. *Exhib:* Brooklyn '77 & Brooklyn '78, Brooklyn Mus, New York; solo exhibs, Newhouse Ctr Contemp Art, Snug Harbor Cult Ctr, New York, 85 & New Visions, Princeton Univ, NJ, 89; Members Exhib, Staten Island Mus, New York, 88; Contemporary Spiritual Art Nat, Paul VI Inst Arts, Washington, DC, 88; 51st Ann Artists Exhib, Guild Hall, Mus, Easthampton, NY, 89; Brenau Col Nat Exhib. *Teaching:* Asst prof, St Johns Univ, 81-82, Iona-Seton Col, 84-88 & LaGuardia Community Col, 88-90; lectr, Bronx Community Col, 83-85, Cultural Pluralism, LaGuardia Community Col, 89 & Saurat & European Art, Staten Island Mus. *Awards:* Independent Artists Grant, Artists Space, 80, 85 & 89; Woman of Acheivement Award, Nat Orgn Italian-American Women, 3/92; Staten Island Coun Arts Grant, 91. *Bibliog:* Craig Schneider (auth), In the Arts, S I Advance, 88; Eileen Watkins (auth), Women's Visions, Star Ledger, 89; M Fressola (auth), Best of Both Worlds, S I Advance, 92. *Mem:* Women in Arts Inc (bd mem, secy, 86-); Women's Caucus for Art; Col Art Asn. *Media:* Oil on Canvas. *Dealer:* Nancy Stein Gallery 340 W 57th St New York NY; Art South Gallery Philadelphia PA. *Mailing Add:* 1000 Clove Rd Apt 8L Staten Island NY 10301

BUTTS, H DANIEL, III
GALLERY DIRECTOR
b Pittsburgh, Pa, July 15, 39. *Study:* Yale Univ, BA, 60, BFA, 61; Pa State Univ, MA, 62. *Pos:* Dir, Arts & Crafts Ctr Pittsburgh, 65-68; dir, Mansfield Art Ctr, 68- *Teaching:* Instr hist art, painting & drawing, Shady Side Acad, Pittsburgh, 62-65. *Mailing Add:* 699 Sloane Ave Mansfield OH 44903

BUXBAUM, ROBERT
SCULPTOR
b Brooklyn, NY, July 7, 39. *Study:* Work & study in the studio of Frederick J Kiesler, 62 & 64. *Work:* Chase Manhattan Bank, Union Carbide Corp & Xerox Corp, New York, NY; Owens-Corning Fibenglass Corp, Toledo, Ohio; Best Products Co, Richmond, Va. *Exhib:* Solo exhibs, Warren Benedek, 75, O K Harris, 77 & 55 Mercer, 82, New York, NY; Abstraction: Alive & Well, Brainerd Hall, State Univ NY, Postdam, 75; Brookhaven Nat Lab, Brookhaven, NY, 79; Sculptural Works Incorporating Glass, New York Experimental Glass Workshop, New York, NY, 80; Diversity, Univ RI, Kingston, 85. *Bibliog:* Shoichiro Higuchi (auth), Robert Buxbaum - Metaphysics of Transparency, IDEA, 87. *Mailing Add:* 119 Spring St New York NY 10012

BYARD, CAROLE MARIE
SCULPTOR, ILLUSTRATOR
b Atlantic City, NJ, July 22, 41. *Study:* Fleischer Art Mem, sculpture with Aurelius Renzetti, 61-63; New York-Phoenix Sch Design, painting with Felix & Trini DeCosio, cert, 64-68; Westbeth Graphic Artist Workshop, with Hiromitsu Morimoto, 72. *Comn:* Religious mural, House of Light, Ibaden, Nigeria, 72; panel for Kwanza celebration, Studio Mus, Harlem, NY, 73 & 74; Praisesong for Charles Installation for Art Awareness, Lexington, NY, 88. *Exhib:* In Her Own Image, Fleischer Art Mem, Philadelphia, Pa, 74; Children of Africa, Am Mus Natural Hist, New York, 75; Sojourn: Carole Byard & Valerie Maynard, Gallery 1199, New York, 75; Spells & Spirits, Univ Mass, Amherst, 77; FESTAC Exhib, Nigeria, 77; InterGrafik 80 & InterGrafik 76, Berlin, Ger, 76 & 80; Prints and Drawings, Inst Int Educ, UN Plaza, NY, 80; Impressions-Expressions, traveling exhib, Studio Mus, NY, Howard Univ & Smithsonian Inst, Washington, DC, 79-84; Art Against Apartheid, Westbeth Gallery, Abyssinian Baptist Church, 84; Pickard Smith Gallery, Univ Calif, Santa Cruz, 85; Columbia Mus, SC, 85. *Pos:* Lectr & demonstrations, Univ Ibadan, Nigeria, 72, Pratt Univ, New York, 77, NC Cent Univ, Charlotte, 78, Mich State Univ, 85; artist-in-residence, Studio Mus Harlem, NY, 72-74; pres, Darshan, New York, 74-; mural artist, NJ State Coun on the Arts, 76. *Teaching:* Instr drawing & painting, New York-Phoenix Sch Design, 68-71, Metrop Mus Art, 74 & NY Found Arts, 83; instr found drawing, Maryland Inst Col Art, 83; Baltimore Sch Arts, 79-84; Parsons Sch Design, 88. *Awards:* Visual Arts Fel, Nat Endowment Arts, 86; Unique New Yorker Art Award, 77; Coretta Scott King Award for Africa Dream, 78; Coreeta Scott King Award for Cornrows. *Bibliog:* Barbara Cohen (auth), Careers (filmstrip), Harcourt Brace Jovanovich, 74; Marla Hoffman (auth), Two women who paint, World Mag, Long View Publ, 74; Helen King (auth), Carole Byard speaks with her art, In: What It Is, Let's Save the Children Inc; article, An artist's lifestyle, Black Enterprise Mag, 12/75; Blacks and the arts, New York Post, 2/7/76; E C Fax (auth), Black Artists of the New Generation, Dodd Mead Publ, 77. *Mem:* Westbeth Graphic Artist; Black Artist Guild; Coast to Coast: A Women of Color Nat Arts Organ; Women's Caucus for Art. *Media:* Oil; Lithography. *Publ:* Illusr, The Sycamore Tree, African Folktales, Doubleday, 74; illusr, Under Christopher's Hat, Scribners, 72; Arthur Mitchell, 75, auth, Africa Dream, 77 & auth, I Can Do It By Myself, 78, Crowell; Cornrows, Coward McAnn Publ, 79; Grandma's Joy, Collins World Publ, 80; Black Snowman, Scholastic, 89. *Mailing Add:* 463 West St Studio 951D New York NY 10014

BYARS, DONNA
SCULPTOR, COLLAGE ARTIST
b Rock Island, Ill. *Study:* Stephens Col, Columbia, Mo; Iowa State Univ, BA; Parsons Sch of Design, New York. *Work:* Va Mus of Fine Arts, Richmond; Bellevue Hosp Collection, New York; Pub Art Prog, Long Island Univ-C W Post; Franklin Furnace, New York. *Comn:* Site sculpture, Bard-Hudson Valley Studies, 78; site sculpture, New Wilderness Found, 78; site sculpture, Wave Hill, Bronx, NY, 79. *Exhib:* Solo exhibs, 55 Mercer, 75, AIR Gallery, 77, 79, 84 & 87 & Hudson River Mus, 89; Aldrich Mus Contemp Art, Ridgefield, Conn, 75-76; Alternative Mus, New York, 80; Lunds Konsthall, Lunds, 81, & Kulturhurst, Stockholm, 82, Sweden; Schweinfurth Mus, Auburn, NY, 82; Va Mus Fine Art, 88; The Nature of the Beast, Hudson River Mus, 89; Max Hutchinson's Sculpture Fields (outdoor installation), 88-92. *Pos:* Dir, Parsons Gallery, Parsons Sch Design, New York, 84-86. *Teaching:* Instr drawing, Parsons Sch Design, 76-92; instr collage, New Sch for Social Res, New York, 77- *Awards:* Artist-in-Residence Grant, Palisades Interstate Park, Am the Beautiful Fund, Washington, DC, 76; Creative Artists Pub Serv Program Fel, 82. *Bibliog:* Patricia Phillips, (auth) review, Artforum, 4/85; Gloria Orenstein (auth), The Reflowering of the Goddess, Pergamon Press; James J Kelly (auth), The Sculptural Idea, Arts Rev; and others. *Mem:* Women's Caucus Art, New York; Col Art Asn. *Dealer:* May Hutchinson. *Mailing Add:* Five Woodworth Ave Yonkers NY 10701

BYE, RANULPH
PAINTER
b Princeton, NJ, June 17, 16. *Study:* Philadelphia Col Art; Art Students League; studied with Henry 'C Pitz, Frank V Dumond & William C Palmer. *Work:* Munson-Williams-Proctor Inst, Utica, NY; Woodmare Art Mus; Reading Pub Mus, Pa; Smithsonian Inst, Washington, DC; Pa Hist & Mus Comn, Harrisburg, Pa. *Comn:* Mine Force (paintings of naval base), US Navy Dept, Charleston, SC, 66. *Exhib:* Nat Acad Design; Newman Galleries, Philadelphia, 77 & 80; Hahn Gallery, Philadelphia, 82, 84, 86, 88 & 90; Coryell Gallery, Lambertville, Pa, 87, 90 & 92; Bargeron Gallery, Washington Crossing, Pa, 89; and others. *Teaching:* Instr, Moore Col Art, Philadelphia, 49-79. *Awards:* Winsor & Newton Award, Audubon Artists, 89; Phillips Mill Award, New Hope, Pa, 89; Henry Gasser Mem Award, Allied Artists, 89. *Bibliog:* Wendy Buehr (auth), Station Closed, Am Heritage Press, 66. *Mem:* Salmagundi Club; Am Watercolor Soc; Allied Artists Am; assoc Nat Acad Design; plus others. *Media:* Watercolor, Oil. *Publ:* Auth, Seascapes and Landscapes, 56 & Watercolor Technique American Artists, 66, Watson-Guptill; The Vanishing Depot, Livingston, 73 & Haverford House, 2nd ed 83; Victorian Sketchbook, Haverford House, 80; Ranulph Bye's Bucks County, Bargeron Gallery, 88; Ranulph Bye's Buck County: A Selection of 100 Paintings, Bargeron Publ, 89. *Mailing Add:* PO Box 362 Mechanicsville PA 18934

BYERS, FLEUR
PAINTER, GRAPHIC ARTIST
b Washington, DC. *Study:* Pomona Col, Claremont, Calif; Univ Pa, Corcoran Gallery Art, Washington, DC, 51; Pa Acad Fine Arts, 59. *Work:* Salomon Brothers, New York; Polyclinic Hosp, Harrisburg, Pa; Bank America, Boston, Mass; Dauphin Deposit Bank, Harrisburg, Pa; NcNees, Wallace & Nurick, Harrisburg, Pa. *Exhib:* Two-person invited exhib, Wyomissing Inst Fine Arts, Pa, 92; Nat Drawing Exhib, Md Inst, Col Art, Baltimore, 92; Oil Pastel Asn 10th Int Juried Exhib, Watchung Art Ctr, NJ, 92; Catharine Lorillard Wolfe Juried Exhib, Lever House Gallery, New York, 92; Susquehanna Art Soc 9th Biennial Northeast Regional Juried Exhib, Selinsgrove, Pa, 92; and others. *Collections Arranged:* Arts for Peace & Justice Exhib, Galerie 110 Harrisburg, Pa, 90, 91 & 92. *Awards:* Philip Isenberg Award, 6th Int Juried Exhib Oil Pastel Asn, Pen & Brush Gallery, New York, 89; Unsung Heroine Award for Dedication and Excellence as an Artist and Activist for Peace and Justice, Int Womens Day Coalition, Harrisburg, Pa, 91; Pastel Soc Am Bronze Plaque for a Pastel of Exceptional Merit, 21st Ann Open Juried Exhib, York Art Asn, Pa. *Bibliog:* Muriel Wasserman (auth), Western Nassau art events, Sunstorm, Long Island, NY, 12/83; Karin Lipson (auth), Drawings--refined to raffish, Newsday, Long Island, NY, 5/20/88; Lester Hirsh (auth), Work of Pennsylvania Artist Fleur Byers, Frog Songs and Piano Dances, Bone and Flesh Publ, Concord, NH, 10/92. *Mem:* Catharine Lorillard Wolfe Art Club; Oil Pastel Asn; Pastel Soc Am; Nat Asn Women Artists. *Media:* Pastel, Oil; Pen & Ink, Charcoal. *Publ:* Coauth, A woman of artistic power, Levittown Tribune, NY, 4/ 2/87; auth, Woman of power, Women of Power Inc, spring 87. *Dealer:* Gallery Madison 90 1248 Madison Ave New York NY 10028; Veerhoff Galleries 1604 17th St NW Washington DC 20009. *Mailing Add:* 36 Drexel Pl New Cumberland PA 17070

BYNUM, E ANDERSON (ESTHER PEARL)
CURATOR, PRINTMAKER
b Henderson, Tex, Dec 19, 22. *Study:* Dallas Mus Fine Arts, 52; NTex State Univ, BA, 65; Univ Md, MA, 72, advan grad specialist cert, 73; also lithography with Tadeusz Lapinski. *Work:* US Civil Serv Bldg, Washington, DC; Montgomery Co Contemp Print Collection & Montgomery Co Pub Schs, Md. *Exhib:* New York Int Art Show, 70; Baltimore Mus, 73-74; Jersey City Mus, NJ, 74; 26th Ann Exhib, McNay Art Inst, San Antonio, 75 & 32nd Ann, 81, Tex Watercolor Soc; Lowe Art Mus, Univ Miami, Fla, 75. *Pos:* Cur, Four Oaks Gallery, Henderson, Tex, 80- *Teaching:* Instr art, Montgomery Co Pub Schs, Rockville, Md, 65-75, elem art coordr, 75-79; artist in educ, Longview Pub Sch, Tex Art Coun, 84-86. *Bibliog:* Articles in Henderson Daily News & Longview, Tex Arts Coun. *Mem:* Tex Watercolor Soc; Am Craft Coun; Graphics Soc. *Media:* Watercolor, Lithographs. *Publ:* Contribr, monthly visual arts article, Henderson Daily Newspaper. *Dealer:* Four Oaks Gallery 709 Hwy 43 Henderson TX 75652. *Mailing Add:* 711 Highway 43 Henderson TX 75652

BYRD, D GIBSON
EDUCATOR, PAINTER
b Tulsa, Okla, Feb 1, 23. *Study:* Univ Tulsa, with Alexandre Hogue, BA; Univ Iowa, MA. *Work:* Butler Inst Am Art, Youngstown, Ohio; Philbrook Art Ctr, Tulsa; Kalamazoo Art Ctr, Mich; Wright Art Ctr, Beloit Col; Madison Art Ctr, Wis. *Exhib:* Walker Art Ctr Biennial Exhib, Minneapolis, 58; 2nd Nat Drawing Exhib, Univ Wis-Green Bay, 70; Arts: USA II, Northern Ill Univ, 71; Wisconsin Directions, Milwaukee Art Ctr, 75; State of the Art: Wisconsin Painting and Drawing, Kohler Art Ctr, 82; and others. *Pos:* Dir, Kalamazoo Art Ctr, 52-55. *Teaching:* Prof art, Univ Wis-Madison, 55-; vis lectr, Sch Art Educ, Birmingham, Eng, 65-66. *Mem:* Col Art Asn. *Media:* Oil, Gouache. *Publ:* Auth, The artist-teacher in America, Col Art J, winter 63-64; Theodore Robinson (exhib monogr), Univ Wis, 64; Artist-teacher in America: John Sloan, Sch Arts Mag, 66; Visiting artists: thoughts & second thoughts, Visual Arts Educ, 70; Thomas Hart Benton (exhib catalog), Madison Art Ctr, 70. *Dealer:* Bradley Galleries 2565 N Downer Ave Milwaukee WI 53211; Edgewood Orchard Galleries Door County. *Mailing Add:* c/o Bradley Galleries 2639 N Downer Ave Milwaukee WI 53211

BYRD, JERRY
PAINTER
b Fullerton, Calif, Mar 6, 47. *Study:* Univ Calif, Irvine, BFA, 70, MFA, 72. *Work:* Mus Contemp Art, Melbourne, Australia; Crocker Art Mus, Sacramento, Calif; Newport Harbor Art Mus, Newport Beach, Calif; Laguna Beach Mus Art, Calif. *Comn:* Paintings on canvas, AT&T, San Francisco, 77, IBM, San Jose, 82, Carol Beadel, Santa Barbara, 84 & Peabody Hotel, Orlando, Fla, 86. *Exhib:* The First Decade, Fine Arts Gallery, Univ Calif, Irvine, 75; Painting and Sculpture Today, Indianapolis Mus Art, 76; Current Concerns, 76 & New Directions in Southern California Art, 78, Los Angeles Inst Contemp Art; Geometric Abstraction, Inst Art, Boston, 81; California Contemporary Artists, Laguna Beach Mus Art, Calif, 84. *Awards:* Fine Arts Patrons Award, Univ Calif, Irvine, 69; Nat Endowment Arts Fel, 74. *Bibliog:* Robert Hutchinson (auth), Scale and modern comfort, Archit Digest, 79; Clark Poling (auth), Geometric Abstraction: A New Generation, Boston Inst Contemp Art, 81; Suvan Geer (auth), Emphasis on formalism, Art Week, 84. *Media:* Oil, Acrylic. *Publ:* Illusr, College Algebra (auth, Louis Leithold), MacMillan Publ Co, Inc, New York, NY, 80. *Dealer:* Ivory-Kimpton 55 Grant Ave San Francisco CA 94108. *Mailing Add:* 1137 Palms Blvd Venice CA 90291

BYRD, ROBERT JOHN
ILLUSTRATOR, INSTRUCTOR
b Atlantic City, NJ, Jan 11, 42. *Study:* Philadelphia Mus Col Art, BFA(graphic arts), 66. *Work:* Free Libr Philadelphia; Philadelphia Col Art. *Exhib:* Soc Illusr, New York, 71-77; Graphis Press, Zurich, Switz, 74-77; Philadelphia Art Alliance, 74; Bologna Worlds Children's Book Fair, Italy, 75; Design & Illustration: USA, Teheran, Iran, 78; Graphis Poster & Ann, Zurich, 78-79. *Teaching:* Portfolio sem illusr, Philadelphia Col Art, 76-77; adj instr illus, Moore Col Art, Philadelphia, 77- *Awards:* Citation Merit, Soc Illusr, 76; Jr Lit Award for The Gondolier of Venice, 76 & The Detective of London, 78. *Bibliog:* Diana Klemin (auth), The portfolio of Robert Byrd, Am Artist, 71; Linda Munich & Marty Jacobs (producers), For Your Information, WKBS TV, 78. *Mem:* Philadelphia Children's Reading Round Table; Illusr Guild (Graphic Arts Guild). *Publ:* Illusr, Rebecca Hatpin, 73, Pinch Penny Mouse, 74, The Gondolier of Venice, 76 & The Detective of London, 78, Windmill Bks. *Mailing Add:* 409 Warwick Rd Haddonfield NJ 08033

BYRNE, CHARLES JOSEPH
CONSULTANT, GRAPHIC ARTIST
b Louisville, Ky, Oct 15, 43. *Study:* Univ Louisville, BS; Wayne State Univ. *Comn:* Various Exhib Designs, Detroit Inst of Arts, 73-80; Contemp Arts Ctr, Cincinnati, 81-84; Univ Calif, Berkeley. *Exhib:* Buckminster Fuller Portfolio, Gettler Paul Gallery, 81, New York Art Dir Club Ann Exhib, 82, 83 & 84; Archit Photog Exhib, CAGE Gallery, 82, Local Color Photog Exhib, Tangeman Fine Arts Gallery, Univ Cincinnati, 82, Advert Club Cincinnati Ann Exhib, 81-84, Cincinnati Art Dir Club Ann Exhib, 79-84, Poster, Brodie Gallery, Univ Cincinnati, 82 & 83, Color and Contract, Photog Exhib, Carl Solway Gallery, Cincinnati, 84; Cult Posters Exhib, Univ Louisville, 82, Posters, Portland Mus, Louisville, Ky, 84. *Pos:* Cur, Dept of Fine Arts, Univ Louisville, Ky, 63-66, asst univ designer, 66-70; chief designer graphics & signage, Smith, Hinchman & Grylls Assoc, Inc, Detroit, 70-76; owner, Colophon Design Studio, Cincinnati & Colophon, San Francisco, 78-84, Chuck Byrne Design, Oaklawn, 85-; contrib ed, Print Mag, 88- *Teaching:* Instr, Interior Designers Guild, San Diego, 77-78; instr, Cincinnati Acad Art, 80, Acad Art Col, San Francisco, 92-; adj fac, Univ Cincinnati, 81-84; assoc prof design, Calif Col Arts & Crafts, 88-91. *Awards:* Commun Arts Mag Award, 74, 81 & 85; Commun Graphics Award, Am Inst of Graphic Arts, 74, 75 & 82-85; Awards, Art Dirs Club Cincinnati, 79-83. *Bibliog:* Print Magazine Casebook 8, Environ Graphics, 90; Carol Stevens (auth), Chuck Byrne, Print Mag, Sept/Oct, 90; Gatta, Lange, Lyons (auths), Foundations of Graphic Design, Davis Publ Inc, Worcester, Mass, 90. *Mem:* Am Inst Graphic Arts; Int Design by Electronics Asn. *Media:* Print Graphics. *Publ:* Coauth, Computer Graphics, Mich Soc Archit Bull, 4/75; coauth, Downtown vs Suburban Shopping Centers: a Clear Case of Identity, Detroit Free Press Mag, 2/76; numerous articles for Print Magazine, 86- *Mailing Add:* 5528 Lawton Ave Oakland CA 94618

BYRNES, JAMES BERNARD
ART HISTORIAN, MUSEUM DIRECTOR
b New York, NY, Feb 19, 17. *Study:* Nat Acad Design, New York, 36-38; Am Artists Sch, New York, 38-40; Art Students League, 41-42; Univ Perugia; Istituto Meschini, Rome, 51-52. *Collections Arranged:* Edgar Degas, His Family & Friends in New Orleans (with catalog), 65; Odyssey of an Art Collector--The Collection of Mr & Mrs Frederick S Stafford, Paris (with catalog), 66; Arts of Ancient & Modern Latin America (with catalog), 68; Rothko (with catalog), 74; Artist as Collector--Ethnic Art (with catalog), 75. *Pos:* Cur mod & contemp art, Los Angeles Co Mus, 46-54; dir, Colorado Springs Fine Arts Ctr, 54-56; assoc dir, NC Mus Art, 56-58, dir, 58-60; dir, New Orleans Mus Art, 61-72; dir, Newport Harbor Art Mus, Newport Beach, Calif, 72-75; consult fine arts. *Teaching:* Vis prof hist 20th century art, Univ Southern Calif, 50, Univ Fla, 60-61. *Awards:* Knight in the Order of Leopold II, Belg Govt, 72; Hon Title, Dir emer, New Orleans Mus Art, 89. *Mem:* Sr mem, Appraisers Soc Am; Appraisers Asn Am; Am Asn Mus; Int Coun Mus; hon life mem Am Inst Designers; and others. *Res:* Nineteenth and twentieth century art; Edgar Degas; pre-Columbian and African art. *Mailing Add:* James B Byrnes & Assoc 7820 Mulholland Dr Los Angeles CA 90046

BYRON, CHARLES ANTHONY
DEALER
b Istanbul, Turkey, Dec 15, 19. *Study:* Ecole Libre Sci Polit, Paris, France; Univ Paris; Harvard Univ; BA, LLB & MA. *Pos:* Dir & owner, Byron Gallery, New York. *Mem:* Art Dealers Asn Am, Inc. *Specialty:* Modern paintings and Surrealist art. *Mailing Add:* 25 E 83rd St New York NY 10028

BYRON, MICHAEL
PAINTER
b Providence, RI, 1954. *Study:* Kansas City Art Inst, BFA, 76; Novia Scotia Col Art & Design, MFA 81. *Exhib:* Solo exhibs, White Columns, New York, 83, Aldrich Mus Contemp Art, Ridgefield, Conn, 87, Galeria Barbara Farber, Amsterdam, Neth, 87 & 89, Aldrich Mus Contemp Art, Ridgefield, Conn, 87, Luhring Augustine Hetzler, Santa Monica, Calif, 90 & Boymans van Beuningen Mus, Rotterdam, Netherlands, 91; Mus Mod Art, New York, 83; Boymans-Van Beuningen, Rotterdam, Neth, 86; Whitney Biennial, Whitney Mus Am Art, New York, 89; Maryland Inst Art, Baltimore, 91; Selections from the Permanent Collection, Phoenix Art Mus, Ariz, 92; Recent Donations & Acquisitions, Whitney Mus, New York, 92. *Teaching:* Vis artist, RI Sch Design, 85; Vis artist, Nova Scotia Col Art & Design, Halifax, 85 & 92; guest lectr, Sch Visual Arts, New York, 88; guest lectr, Hogeschool Hertenbosch voor Kunst, Den Bosch, Netherlands, 91; vis artist, Hogeschool voor Kunsten (graduate level), Arnhem, Netherlands, 91-92. *Bibliog:* Anna Tilroe (auth), Volkskrant, Een Kolossale Bruine Mandarijn, 11/1/91; Wouter Welling (auth), Het Poetische Theater van Michael Byron, Kunstbeeld, 91; Jurriaan Benchop (auth), Interview with Michael Byron, Metropolis M, 91. *Mailing Add:* c/o Echo Press 1901 E Tenth St Bloomington IN 47408

BYRUM, DONALD ROY
EDUCATOR, PRINTMAKER
b Hertford, NC, June 19, 42. *Study:* RI Sch Design, BFA, 67; Univ Mich, MFA, 69; spec studies in lithography with John Maggio, 79. *Work:* Minn Mus Art, St Paul; Chrysler Mus Art, Norfolk, Va; BYK Gulden Lomberg Chemische Fabrik GMBH, Konstanz, WGer; Am Embassy, Madrid, Spain; Yale Univ Art Gallery. *Comn:* Etching & aquatints, comn by Dryden Gallery, New York. *Exhib:* Minn Printmakers, Minn Arts Coun, 69-70; Talent Six, Minn Mus Art, St Paul, 73; Contemporary Master Prints, Winthrop Col Gallery, 76; Eastern US Print Exhib, Spirit Sq Art Ctr, NC, 79-81; Southeastern Ctr Contemp Art, Winston-Salem, NC, 80; Don Byrum-Reflections Portfolio Traveling Exhib, 81-82; Mint Mus Art, 81; New Am Graphics US State Dept Tour, 82-83; Southern Printmakers, Southern Graphics Coun, 84, 88 & 90. *Pos:* Dir & cur, Lincoln Art Gallery, Mankato State Univ, 69-74; chmn dept visual arts, Univ NC, Charlotte, 82-92; dir, Rowe Art Gallery, Univ NC, Charlotte, 83-85. *Teaching:* Asst prof printmaking, Mankato State Univ, 69-74; asst prof, 74-80, assoc prof, Univ NC, Charlotte, 80- *Awards:* Purchase Awards, Minn Printmakers, Minn Arts Coun, 70 & NC Artists, Asheville Mus, 77; Fayetteville Mus Art Award, 79; Purchase Award, Eastern US Print Exhib, Fac Res Grant Computer Graphics, 89 & 92 & Res Leave, Computer Graphics, fall 92; Outstanding Computer Curric Award, 89. *Mem:* Nat Coun Art Adminrs; State Bd, NC Art Ed Asn; Southeastern Col Art Asn (conf comm); Conf Comt, Southeastern Col Art Conf; Col Art Asn Am; NC Art Ed Asn (State bd). *Media:* Etching & Lithography. *Dealer:* Hodges Taylor Gallery 227 N Tryon St Charlotte NC 28202. *Mailing Add:* 4136 Woodgreen Terr Charlotte NC 28205

C

CABLE, MAXINE ROTH
SCULPTOR
b Philadelphia, Pa. *Study:* Tyler Sch Fine Art, Temple Univ, AA; Corcoran Sch Art, George Washington Univ, AB; Am Univ, with Hans Hofmann. *Work:* Allied Chem Corp Gallery, New York; Nat Acad Sci, Washington, DC; George Washington Univ. *Comn:* Environ sculpture, Allied Chem Corp, 69-70; sculpture, Wolf Trap Farm Performing Arts, Va, 73. *Exhib:* Area Exhibs, Corcoran Gallery Art, 55-67; Artists Equity Traveling Exhib, Columbia Mus, SC, 73-74; one-woman shows, Adams Morgan Gallery, Washington, DC, 64, Hodson Gallery, Hood Col, Frederick, Md, 69, Gallery Ten, Washington, DC, 75, 76, 79 & 83 & Art Dept, Cath Univ Am, 83. *Pos:* Dir, Glen Echo Graphics Workshop, Md, 75. *Teaching:* Consult art, Montgomery Co, Md, 57-65 & Head Start Prog, Washington, DC, 70. *Awards:* Sculpture Award, David Smith, Corcoran Gallery Art, 55; First Prize in Painting, Smithsonian Inst, 67. *Bibliog:* Washington Artists Today, Artists Equity Asn, 67; Art for Public Places, Dept Housing & Urban Develop, 73. *Media:* Mixed, Natural and Man-Made. *Dealer:* Gallery Ten Ltd 1519 Connecticut Ave Washington DC 20036. *Mailing Add:* c/o Gallery-10 Ltd 1519 Connecticut Ave NW Washington DC 20036

CABOT, HUGH
PAINTER, SCULPTOR
b Boston, Mass, Mar 22, 30. *Study:* Vesper George Sch Fine Arts; Boston Mus Fine Arts Sch; Col of Americas, Mexico City; Asmolean, Oxford Univ, Cambridge, England. *Work:* USN Dept Hist & Rec, USN Art Gallery, The Pentagon & Nat War Mus, Washington, DC; Harwood Found Art, Taos, NMex; Tucson Med Ctr. *Comn:* Great American Rodeo Cowboy (lifesize figure), Las Vegas Hilton Hotel, 85. *Exhib:* Korea, Mitsubichi Gallery, Tokyo, Japan, 58 & Tokyo Press Club; La Marine Americaine, Mus de la Marine, Paris, 63; Oper Palette, every major city in free world incl Nat Gallery Art. *Awards:* First, Second & Third Awards, Tex Tri State, 69; Artist of Yr, Scottsdale, Ariz, 78. *Bibliog:* Jim Newton (auth), Those Cabots, Phoenix Gazette, 74; Meet Hugh Cabot, Ariz Living, 75; Danny Medina (auth), Hugh Cabot, Ariz Art Talk, 82; David M Brown (auth), Tubac Artist---Hugh Cabot, Greyhawk Mag, 85; Allen Scott (auth), Cabots cowboy, Tucson Lifestyle, 86. *Mem:* Salmagundi Club. *Media:* Oil, Watercolor; Bronze. *Publ:* Auth-illusr, Korea one, Readers Dig, 54. *Mailing Add:* PO Box 1478 Tubac AZ 85646-1478

CADDELL, FOSTER
PAINTER, INSTRUCTOR
b Pawtucket, RI, Aug 2, 21. *Study:* RI Sch Design; pvt study with Peter Helck, Robert Brackman & Guy Wiggins. *Comn:* Off portraits of Sen Thomas J Dodd, Washington, DC & Judge L P Moore, US Circuit Ct Appeals, Second Dist, New York; portrait of Dr George S Avery, Brooklyn Botanical Gardens, NY; portrait of Carl Cuttler, Mystic Seaport Mus, Conn; relig paintings for many denominations incl Church of Eng; portraits of many bus & civic leaders. *Exhib:* Am Artists Prof League Grand Nat Exhib, 70-92; Am Watercolor Soc Ann, Nat Acad Galleries, 71; Slater Mus, Norwich Acad, 71-80; Nat Arts Club, New York, 73-80; one-man show, Slater Mem Mus, Norwich Free Acad, 76; Soc Rep Pastellistes De France & Inst Exhib, Lille, France, 87. *Pos:* Lithograph artist, Providence Lithograph Co, 39-52; artist with Far East Air Force, 43-46. *Teaching:* Instr, Foster Caddell's Art Sch, currently. *Awards:* Michael Guiheen Award, 75; Weber Wyeth Award, Int Soc Artists, 78; Award for pastel, Salmagundi Club, New York, 80; Best of Show, Conn Pastel Soc, 89; and others. *Bibliog:* David Lewis (ed), Oil Painting Techniques, Watson-Guptill, 83; The New American Impressionism, 91; Paster Interpretations & Foster Caddell's Solutions to Your Painting Problems, North Light Books, 93. *Mem:* Am Portrait Soc; Am Artists Prof League; Acad Artists Am; Salmagundi Club; Pastel Soc Am; and others. *Media:* Oil, Pastel. *Publ:* Illusr, series sports bks, Little, Brown & Co; auth & illusr, Keys to Successful Landscape Painting, 76, Keys to Successful Color & Keys to Painting Better Portraits, 82, Pitman & Sons, London & Watson-Guptill; David Lewis (ed), Landscape Painting Techniques & Oil Painting Techniques, Watson-Guptill, 84. *Mailing Add:* Northlight Rte 49 Voluntown CT 06384

CADE, WALTER, III
PAINTER, COLLAGE ARTIST
b New York, NY, Jan 17, 36. *Study:* Inst Mod Art, New York. *Work:* Southeast Banking Corp; City of Miami Beach, Fla; Va Beach Art Mus; Rockefeller Found; Bruce Mus; Fine Arts Mus of the South. *Exhib:* Art Ann, 69-70, Contemporary Black Artists in Am, 71, Whitney Mus Am Art, New York; Corcoran Gallery, Washington, DC, 72; Queens Cult Ctr Arts, New York, 73; one-man shows, Ocean Co Col, 77 & Jackson State Univ, 80; Miss Mus Art, Jackson, 81; Tampa Mus, Fla, 82; Tuscon Mus Art, Ariz, 83. *Awards:* First Prize, Fine Arts Mus South, Mobile, Ala, 82; Best in Show, Bruce Mus, Greenwich, Conn, 84. *Bibliog:* Jeanne Paris (auth), The ghetto sparkles, Long Island Sun Press, 5/7/72; article in New York Amsterdam News, 5/6/72; The Florida Arts Gazette, 5/80. *Media:* Acrylic, Collage. *Mailing Add:* c/o Studio Gallery 172-03 119th Ave Jamaica NY 11434

CADIEUX, MICHAEL EUGENE
EDUCATOR, PAINTER
b Missoula, Mont, June 15, 40. *Study:* Univ Mont, BA & MA. *Work:* Univ Mont Fine Arts Collection, Missoula; Yuma Fine Arts Asn, Ariz. *Exhib:* Spokane-Pac NW Ann, Cheney Cowles Mus, 66; SW Yuma Fine Arts, 66-68; Ariz Ann, Phoenix Art Mus, 67; Tucson Art Mus Ann, Ariz, 68; Mid-Am, Nelson-Atkins Mus, Kansas City, Mo, 72, 30 Miles, 75; Mid-Am, St Louis Art Mus, 72; Davidson Nat Drawing, Davidson Col Galleries, 75. *Collections Arranged:* Univ Wis Ctr Syst, 67; Univ Md, 67; Western Asn Art Mus Traveling Exhib, 69; fac shows, Spiva Art Ctr, Memphis Acad, 75-78; Mo Art Coun-Mid Am Arts Alliance Shows. *Pos:* Reviewer art publ, SE Asia in Rev, 76- *Teaching:* Instr painting & drawing, Ariz Western Col, Yuma, 66-69; assoc prof art hist, Kansas City Art Inst, Mo, 69- *Awards:* Third Place, 2nd Southwestern, Yuma Fine Arts, 67; Grant Study in India, US Off Educ, 71. *Bibliog:* Donald Hoffman (auth), Here's Art all in a row, Kansas City Star, 72 & Michael Cadieux, Kansas City Star, 77. *Media:* Painting Collage. *Res:* Cross-cultural art history. *Publ:* Auth, The mural tradition in Indian painting, SE Asia in Rev, 77. *Mailing Add:* Dept Art Hist Kansas City Art Institute 4415 Warwick Blvd Kansas City MO 64111

CADILLAC, LOUISE ROMAN
PAINTER, INSTRUCTOR
b Central City, Pa. *Study:* Univ Northern Colo, BA, 54, MA, 64; with Sylvia Glass, Calif, Gene Matthews, Colo & Chen Chi, New York. *Work:* Denver Public Libr Western Hist Div; Jefferson Sch Credit Union, Lakewood, Colo; Jewish Community Ctr, Denver; Ouray Art Asn, Colo. *Exhib:* Metrop Exhib, Denver Art Mus, 60; Rocky Mountain Nat Watermedia, Foothills Art Ctr, Golden, Colo, 74-90; Ky Watercolor Soc Ann, Owensboro Mus Fine Art, 83-85 & 87; Nat Watercolor Soc, Palm Springs Mus Fine Art, Calif, 82-90; solo exhib, Univ Northern Colo, 84; Nat Acad Design, New York, 86 & 88; Am Watercolor Soc, 92. *Pos:* Juror, Painting Competitions, Critic & Group Sessions. *Teaching:* Instr sec & elem art, Jefferson Co Pub Sch, Lakewood, Colo, 57-67, adaptive art specialist, 74-83; instr, Watermedia Workshops; Dillman's Sand Lake, Wis; Acapulco with J Morrell; Leech Studio, Sarasota, Fla; Nevada Watercolor Soc, Las Vegas, Nev. *Awards:* Rocky Mountain Nat Watermedia Top Award, Foothills Art Ctr, 91; Gold Medal of Honor, Am Watercolor Soc, 92; Leila Gardin Sawyer Award, Nat Acad Design, New York, 86 & 88. *Bibliog:* Watercolors for Grades 4, 5 & 6 (film), KRMA TV, Denver Pub Sch, 75. *Mem:* Nat Watercolor Soc; Rocky Mountain Nat Watermedia Soc; Soc Layerists in Multimedia; Ky Watercolor Soc; Soc Experimental Artists. *Media:* Watermedia, Mixed Media. *Publ:* Auth, Adaptive art for the multiply handicapped student, In: Viewpoints: Dialogue in Art Education, Univ Ill Col Fine Arts, 76; Miles Batt's Creative Watercolors, 88; Auth, Establishing meaningful content in painting, In: Watercolor, 89, Am Artist Mag, 88; Artists Mag, 92; Splash II, 93. *Dealer:* Alpha Gallery 959 Broadway Denver CO 80203; Edward Day Gallery Kingston Ont K7L 2Z4 Canada. *Mailing Add:* 880 S Dudley St Lakewood CO 80226

CADLE, RAY KENNETH
CRAFTSMAN, PAINTER
b Ravenswood, WVa, Aug 26, 06. *Study:* Dayton Art Inst; woodblock printing with Kiyoshi Saito & suiboku painting with Ryukyu Saito, Tokyo. *Exhib:* Hanga Group Exhib, Metrop Gallery, Ueno Park, Tokyo, 52; one-man shows, Int House Gallery, Tokyo, 54 & Centenary Col Gallery, Shreveport, La, 65; Morris Harvey Col, Charleston, WVa, 59; La State Mus, Shreveport, 75; Barnwell Art Ctr, Shreveport. *Pos:* Staff arts & crafts dir, Hq Fifth Air Force, Nagoya, Japan, 49-50, Hq Far E Air Forces, Tokyo, 50-57 & Hq Pac Air Forces, Honolulu, 54-58; command arts & crafts dir, Hq Second Air Force and Eighth Air Force, Barksdale AFB, La, 61-78. *Awards:* Nat Recreation & Park Asn Fel Arts & Crafts, 64; Sculpture Award, Men's Art Guild, Shreveport, 80 & 90, Painting Award, 90 & 91. *Mem:* Allied Artists, WVa; Honolulu Printmakers; Men's Art Guild, Shreveport (bd mem, 66-, pres, 79-80, secy hist, 90-); Int Suiboku Soc, Japan. *Media:* All. *Dealer:* C C Hardman 712 Texas St Shreveport LA 71101. *Mailing Add:* Towne House Apt 501 726 Cotton St Shreveport LA 71101

CADMUS, PAUL
PAINTER, PRINTMAKER
b New York, NY, Dec 17, 04. *Study:* Nat Acad Design, 19-26; Art Students League, with Joseph Pennell, 28. *Work:* Whitney Mus Am Art, New York; Metrop Mus Art, New York; Mus Mod Art, New York; Fogg Art Mus, Cambridge, Mass; Smithsonian Inst, Washington, DC. *Comn:* Costumes & scenery, Filling Station Ballet, Ballet Caravan, 38; mural, Parcel Post Bldg, Richmond, Va, 38. *Awards:* Flora Mayer Witkowsky Prize, Art Inst Chicago, 45; Nat Inst Arts & Lett Grant, 61; Purchase Prize, Norfolk Mus Arts & Sci, 67; Gerald Manley Hopkins Award, Fairfield Univ, Conn, 90. *Bibliog:* Philip Eliasoph (auth), Paul Cadmus-Yesterday & Today, Miami Univ Art Mus, 81; Lincoln Kirstein (auth), Paul Cadmus, Rizzoli, 86; Guy Davenport (auth), The Drawings of Paul Cadmus, Rizzoli, 89. *Mem:* Soc Am Graphic Artists; Am Acad & Inst Arts & Lett; academician Nat Acad Design. *Media:* Egg Tempera. *Dealer:* Midtown-Payson Galleries 745 Fifth Ave New York NY 10022. *Mailing Add:* PO Box 1255 Weston CT 06883

CADY, DENNIS VERN
CONSERVATOR, PAINTER
b Portland, Ore, Nov 10, 44. *Study:* Portland State Univ; Brooklyn Mus Art Sch, printmaking & drawing with Rubin Tam; Pratt Inst Graphic Ctr; Empire State Col, BS, plus independent study of tech aspects of paper restoration; Margo Fieden Galleries, New York, apprenticeship in restoration and preserv of works on paper, 74-77. *Comn:* Poster, 72, costumes for dance (with Frank Garcia), 74, costumes, 77, Phillis Lamhut Dance Co; poster, Emery Hermans Dance Theatre, 75. *Exhib:* Max Beckman Scholar Students Paintings, Brooklyn Art Mus, 69; one-man shows, Drawings & Prints, Renshaw Gallery, Linfield Col, Ore, 71 & Margo Fieden Gallery, New York, 76; South Street Seaport Mus, New York, 80; and others. *Pos:* Freelance restorer, New York, 77- *Awards:* Nat Scholastics Award, New York, 62. *Mem:* Portland Art Asn. *Media:* Oil, Watercolor. *Publ:* Auth, Block Prints by Dennis Cady, Hillside Ctr, Portland, Ore, 71. *Dealer:* Ellen Sragow 80 5th Ave New York NY 10003; Judith Selkowitz 65 E 55th St Suite 504 New York NY 10022. *Mailing Add:* 45 Orchard St New York NY 10002

CADY, SAMUEL LINCOLN
PAINTER, INSTRUCTOR
b Boothbay Harbor, Maine, July 21, 43. *Study:* Univ NH, Durham, BA, 65; Ind Univ, Bloomington, MFA, 67. *Work:* Addison Gallery, Andover, Mass; Chase Manhattan Bank, New York; Prudential Insurance Co, Newark, NJ; Pac Securities Int Bank, Los Angeles, Calif; Gen Elec, Fairfield, Conn. *Comn:* Mountain Landscape (oil on canvas), State of NH, 83. *Exhib:* Whitney Biennial (with catalog), Whitney Mus, New York, 75; Art on Paper, Weatherspoon Gallery, Greensboro, 77; Paintings By, Otis-Parsons Gallery, Los Angeles, 81; Material Illusions-Unlikely Materials, Taft Mus, Cincinnati, 83; Time Out: Sport & Leisure in Am Today (with catalog), Tampa Mus, Fla, 83; Viewpoint '84 Out of Square, Cranbrook Acad, Bloomfield Hills, Mich, 84; solo exhibs, Holly Solomon Gallery, New York, 76, 78-80, 83 & 84, Hampshire Col, Mass, 78, Capricorn Gallery, Bethesda, Md, 79, Castelli-Goodman-Solomon Gallery, E Hampton, NY, 82 & Fujii Gallery (with catalog), Tokyo, 84 & 88; retrospective exhib, 1966-1986, Addison Gallery Am Art (with catalog), 87; Gwenda Jay Gallery, Chicago, Ill, 89; Howard Yezerski Gallery, Boston, Mass, 90. *Teaching:* Instr drawing, painting & printmaking, Univ NH, Durham, 68-69; instr grad workshop, Sch Visual Arts, NY, 84- *Bibliog:* Mablen Jones (auth), Sam Cady: Iconography of the everyday, Arts Mag, 2/84; Richard Armstrong (auth), Sam Cady's Frugal Paintings, 1/87; Mary Sherman (auth), Preserving the richness of symbols, Boston Globe, 5/90. *Media:* Oil on Canvas, Silkscreen. *Publ:* Contrib, Inner/Urban, First St Forum, St Louis, Mo, 81; Time Out: Sport and Leisure in America Today, Tampa Mus, Fla, 83; Fujii Gallery (with catalog), Tokyo, Japan, 84 & 88; Addison Gallery Am Art Retrospective (with catalog) Andover, Mass, 87. *Dealer:* Howard Yezerski Gallery 186 South St Boston MA 02111. *Mailing Add:* PO Box 4518 Middletown NY 10940

CAFRITZ, ROBERT CONRAD
HISTORIAN, CRITIC
b New Haven, Conn, July 5, 53. *Study:* Columbia Col, Columbia Univ, New York, BA, 77, MA(art hist), 78. *Collections Arranged:* Okada, Shinoda & Tsutaka (ed, catalog), Washington, DC, Austin, Utica, 79-80; Leon Spilliaert (ed, catalog), Washington, DC, Metrop Mus Art, NY, 80; Sam Francis: The 50's (ed, catalog), Washington, DC, 80; Braque: Late Paintings (ed, catalog), Washington, DC, San Francisco, Minn & Houston, 82-83; Howard Hodgkin (co-ed, catalog), Washington, DC, New Haven, Conn, Hannover, Ger, London, Eng, 84, XLI Venice Biennale, Italy; John Marin (ed, catalog), Washington, DC; Odilon Redon: The Ian Woodner Collection (ed, catalog), Washington, DC, 88; The Pastoral Landscape, Nat Gallery, Washington, DC, 88. *Pos:* Asst cur, The Phillips Collection, Washington, DC, 78-83, assoc cur, 83-87, cur, 19th century art, 87-89, fine arts hist critic, adv & landscape designer, 89. *Res:* Renaissance art & architecture; twentieth century art. *Publ:* Auth, The Great Late Braque, The Connoisseur, 11/82; Georges Braque, Burlington Mag, NY, Goggeheim, Mus, 9/88; coauth, Places of Delight, Clarkson W Potter, Inc, 88; auth, Jed Perl, Paris without end, Burlington Mag, 9/89; Lettre de Washington, Muséart, 3/91. *Mailing Add:* 3014 Woodland Dr NW Washington DC 20008

CAHANA, ALICE LOK
PAINTER
b Budapest, Hungary, Feb 7, 29; US citizen. *Work:* US Holocaust Mem Mus, Washington, DC. *Exhib:* From Ashes to the Rainbow--A Tribute to Raoul Wallenberg, Skirball, Los Angeles, 87, Rotunda US Cong, 87, Pa Acad Fine Art, 88. *Mailing Add:* 9002 Ferris Houston TX 77096

CAHILL, JAMES FRANCIS
HISTORIAN, EDUCATOR
b Fort Bragg, Calif, Aug 13, 26. *Study:* Univ Calif, Berkeley, BA, 50; Univ Mich, with Max Loehr, MA(Louise Wallace Hackney Scholar, 50-52), 53, PhD(Fulbright Scholar, 54-55), 58. *Collections Arranged:* Guest-dir, The Art of Southern Sung China (with catalog), Asia House Gallery, New York, 62, Fantastics and Eccentrics in Chinese Painting (with catalog), 67 & Scholar-Painters of Japan: The Nanga School (with catalog), 72. *Pos:* Cur Chinese art, Freer Gallery Art, Washington, DC, 58-65. *Teaching:* Prof hist art, Univ Calif, Berkeley, 65- *Awards:* Louise Wallace Hackney Scholar, 50-52; Fulbright Scholar, 54-55; Guggenheim Fel, 72-73; Charles Eliot Norton Prof Poetry, Harvard Univ, 78-79. *Mem:* Col Art Asn Am. *Res:* Chinese and Japanese painting; Chinese bronzes. *Publ:* Auth, Chinese Painting, Skira, Geneva, Switz, 60; coauth, The Freer Chinese Bronzes, 67; auth, Hills Beyond a River: Chinese Painting of the Yuan Dynasty, 76; Parting at the Shore, Chinese Painting of the Early & Middle Ming Dynasty, 78. *Mailing Add:* 1515 Josephine St Berkeley CA 94703

CAIN, CHARLOTTE
PAINTER, TAPESTRY ARTIST
Study: RI Sch Design, BS, 63. *Work:* Rockefeller Collections, Chase Manhattan Bank, New York; Presidential Insurance Co Am, Wash, DC. *Comn:* Knitted hanging triptych, Iowa State Music Bldg, Ames; knitted hanging triptych, Gould Corp, Rolling Meadows, Ill, 79; Gould Corp, Rolling Meadows, Ill. *Exhib:* Des Moines Art Ctr, Iowa, 79; Fibre Structures Fabric Surface, Herron Gallery, Indianapolis, 79; Sun Valley Art Ctr, Ketchum, Idaho, 80; Nancy Lurie Gallery, Chicago, 80 & 90; Olson Larsen Gallery, Des Moines, 84, 85; Art Folio, 87; Nancy Lurie Discoveries, Chicago, 88, 89 & 92. *Teaching:* Instr, drawing & painting, Maharishi Int Univ, 73-79, assoc prof art dept, 79- *Awards:* Nat Endowment Arts Grant, 80-81; First Prize Crafts Show, McNeider Art Mus, 82. *Bibliog:* John Clark (auth), Charlotte Cain, Arts, 6/79; Gretchen E Woelfle (auth), article, Patterns of infinity, Fibre Arts, 7/79; W White (auth), article, Los Angeles Times, 5/82. *Media:* Oil, Watercolor; Gouache, Knitted Yarn. *Dealer:* Nancy Lurie Gallery Chicago. *Mailing Add:* c/o Maharishi Int Univ Fairfield IA 52556

CAIN, DAVID PAUL
PAINTER, PHOTOGRAPHER
b Indianapolis, Ind, Oct 14, 28. *Study:* Univ NMex, Albuquerque, 48-49; Earlham Col, Richmond, Ind, BA, 50; Madison Art Sch, Conn, 79. *Work:* Old Jailhouse Found, Austin, Tex; Int Ctr Photog, New York. *Exhib:* US Army Art Show, European Command, Munich, Germany, 52; one-man shows, Richmond, Ind, 53 & Yale Univ, New Haven, Conn, 81. *Mem:* Brush & Palette, New Haven; Copley Soc of Boston; Am Artists' Prof League; Madison Art Soc, Conn (pres, 81-); Mt Carmel Art Asn. *Media:* All; Black & White. *Mailing Add:* 162 Forest Hamden CT 06514

CAIN, JOSEPH ALEXANDER
PAINTER, EDUCATOR
b Henderson, Tenn, May 27, 20. *Study:* Univ Calif, Berkeley, BA, 47, MA, 48. *Work:* Butler Inst Am Art, Youngstown, Ohio; Nat Watercolor Soc Collection; Witte Mus, San Antonio, Tex; Univ Utah Permanent Collection; Laguna Gloria Mus, Austin, Tex. *Comn:* Oil mural, CofC, Corpus Christi, Tex, 59; mosaic mural, comn by Freeman Martin, Spohn Hosp, 62; mosaic murals, comn by Joe Williams, Buccanneer Bowl, 65. *Exhib:* Philadelphia Watercolor Club Exhib, Pa Acad Fine Arts, 65; Butler Inst Am Art Mid-Year Ann, 65; Southwestern Watercolor Soc Regional Show, Dallas, 69; Nat Watercolor Soc Ann, Los Angeles, 69; Watercolor USA, Springfield Art Mus, Mo, 73; Am Painters in Paris, 75; Nat Acad of Design, New York, 77-78. *Pos:* Critic, Art News and Reviews, Corpus Christi Caller-Times, 56-74. *Teaching:* Prof art, Del Mar Col, 50-82, chmn dept, 66-82. *Awards:* Juror's Award of Merit, Pa Festival Art, Pa State Univ, 79; Best in Show, 7th Ann Div Show, Corpus Christi Art Ctr; Top Award, 68th Ann Nat Show, Tex Fine Arts Asn. *Mem:* Fel Royal Soc Arts; Nat Watercolor Soc; Tex Fine Arts Asn (third vpres, 77-78); Tex Watercolor Soc (third vpres, 71-72); Nat Soc Painters Acrylics & Casein; Tex Fine Arts Asn (regional dir, 70). *Media:* Acrylic, Watercolor. *Publ:* Auth, The Ten, Art Voices-South, 3/78. *Mailing Add:* 402 Troy Dr Corpus Christi TX 78412

CAIN, MICHAEL PETER
SCULPTOR, PAINTER
b Boston, Mass, July 3, 41. *Study:* Art Students League, 61-62; Harvard Col, AB, 64; Yale Sch Art, BFA(painting), MFA(painting), 67. *Work:* Gould Corp, Rolling Meadows, Ill; CBS Collection, Los Angeles; IBM, Atlanta, Ga; Prudential Insurance Co of Am, Washington, DC; Arts Mag, AT&T, New York; McDonald's Corp, Chicago and Indianapolis; Des Moines Art Ctr; Guild Investment Corp, Malibu; Solar Sources, Greenwood, Ind. *Comn:* In the Wave (relief murals), Bullock's Corp Hq, Los Angeles, 83; Hyatt Regency Hotel Corp Hq, 84; Ames Residence, Rancho Mirage, Calif, 85; Hilton Hotel, Chicago, 85; Poly-America, Inc, Grand Prarie, Tex, 87. *Exhib:* Gallery, Yale Sch Art, 68, 70 & 72; Mus Mod Art, 70, Automation House, 71, Adam L Gimble Gallery, 82 & 83, Feature Gallery, 90, New York; Philadelphia Mus Art, 71; Calif Inst Arts, 71 & 72; Stella Polaris, Los Angeles, 81 & 82; Meredith Long Gallery, Houston, 83; Des Moines Art Ctr, 88, 89, 90 & 92; Midlands Invitational, Joslyn Art Mus, 90; CCA Gallery, Chicago, 90, 91 & 92; Sioux City Art Ctr, 92. *Teaching:* Res assoc & lectr, Yale Sch Art, 67-73; prof art, Maharishi Int Univ, 73- *Awards:* Pulsa Graham Found Res Grant, 68-72; Arts Midwest Grant, 89-90; Vis Artist Fel, Univ Minnesota, Minn, 89-90. *Bibliog:* Lucy Lippard (auth), Pulsa, Arts Can, 12/68; Gregory Battcock (auth), Politics of space, Arts, 2/70; Melinda Wortz (auth), Living the simple life, Art News, 2/82; Betty Ann Brown (auth), Michael Peter Cain

at Stella Polaris, Arts, 9/83; Anna & Lee Fergusson (auth), Iowa Artists 1988, New Art Examiner, 10/88. *Media:* Cast Bronze, Painted Wood Relief. *Dealer:* CCA 325 W Huron Chicago IL 60610 Tel: 312-944-0099. *Mailing Add:* Dept Art Maharishi Int Univ Fairfield IA 52556

CAISERMAN-ROTH, GHITTA
PAINTER, PRINTMAKER
b Montreal, Que, Mar 2, 23. *Study:* Parsons Sch Design, BA; Art Students League; Ecole Beaux-Arts, with Albert Dumouchel. *Work:* Montreal Mus Fine Arts; Vancouver Art Gallery, BC; Confederation Art Gallery, Charlottetown, PEI; London Pub Libr & Art Mus, Ont; Beaverbrook Art Gallery, Fredericton, NB; and others. *Comn:* Hommage a Dumouchel, Univ Que Press, 72; and others. *Exhib:* Expo '67, 67; Joint Int Exhib, Soc Can Etcher-Painters & Engravers & Can Soc Graphic Arts, 70; group show, Can Embassy, DC, 70; one-person show, Waddington Galleries, Montreal, 70; Dominion Gallery, Montreal, Can. *Teaching:* Instr art, Concordia Univ, 60, Queen's Univ, 63 & Saidye Bronfman Ctr, Montreal, 70; John Abbott Col, 88. *Awards:* Can Govt Centennial Medal, 67; Fel Eplor, Can Coun, 88; and others. *Mem:* Can Soc Painter Etchers; Can Soc Graphic Art; Royal Can Acad Art; Can Coun; Graphia 3710 Inc. *Media:* Acrylic; Mixed, Graphics. *Publ:* Auth, Ghitta Caiserman-Roth (paintings & drawings), 88. *Dealer:* Robertson Galleries Ottawa ON; Dominion Gallery Montreal. *Mailing Add:* 3475 Jeanne-Mance Rue Montreal PQ H2X 2J7 Canada

CAJORI, CHARLES F
PAINTER
b Palo Alto, Calif, Mar 9, 21. *Study:* Colorado Springs Fine Arts Ctr; Cleveland Art Sch; Columbia Univ; Skowhegan Sch Painting & Sculpture. *Work:* Corcoran Gallery Art; Mitchner Collection, Univ Tex, Austin; Walker Art Ctr, Minneapolis; Whitney Mus Am Art, New York; Metrop Mus, New York; Hirshhorn Mus, Washington, DC. *Exhib:* Solo exhibs, Tanager Gallery, 56 & 61,Howard Wise Gallery, 63, Landmark Gallery, 75 & 81, Ingber Gallery, 76, New York, Gross McCleaf Gallery, Philadelphia, 83 & 85, Am Univ, Washington, DC, 88 & New York Studio Sch, NY, 88; Decade of American Drawings, Whitney Mus Am Art, 65; Loeb Ctr, NY Univ, 70 & Artists Choice Mus, NY, 83 & 84; Conn Painters, Wadsworth Atheneum; Conn Artists, Bruce Mus, Greenwich; Connecticut Now, New Britain Mus. *Teaching:* Instr drawing & painting, Cooper Union Art Sch, 56-65; instr drawing & painting, New York Studio Sch, 64-; emer prof, Queens Col, Flushing, NY, 86- *Awards:* Award in Painting, Inst Arts & Letts, 70; Childe Hassam Purchase Award, 75, 76 & 80; Nat Endowment Arts, 81; Benjamin Altman Figure Prize, Nat Acad, New York, 83. *Bibliog:* L Finkelstein (auth), Cajori: figure in the scene, Art News, 63; Teaching drawing: Cajori, Drawing Soc Rev, 79; Interview in Transfer, fall-winter 89/90. *Mem:* Col Art Asn Am; Nat Acad Design. *Media:* Oil, Acrylic. *Mailing Add:* Litchfield Rd Watertown CT 06795

CALABRO, RICHARD PAUL
SCULPTOR, PAINTER
b Yonkers, NY, June 27, 37. *Study:* Univ Ga, BLA, 62; Sch Visual Arts, New York, 66; Pa State Univ, MFA, 68. *Work:* Pa State Univ Mus, State College, Pa; Univ Mass, Amherst; Mus Mod Art, New York; Venice video Libr, Italy. *Exhib:* Information, Mus Mod Art, New York, 70; solo exhibs, Henri Gallery, Washington, DC, 70, Max Hutchinson Gallery, New York, NY, 72 & Shippee Gallery, New York, 85 & 86; Categorizing (solo exhib), Moore Col Art, Philadelphia, Pa, 75; Lenore Gray Gallery, Providence, RI, 88. *Teaching:* Prof sculpture, Univ RI, 68- *Awards:* Fulbright Fel, 68; Nat Endowment Arts Grant, 77; RI State Arts Coun Grant, 79 & 88. *Dealer:* Shippee Gallery 41 E 57th St New York NY. *Mailing Add:* 119 Boon St Narragansett RI 02882

CALAMAR, GLORIA
PAINTER
b New York, NY, Sept 7, 21. *Study:* Otis Art Inst, Los Angeles, 39-43; Art Students League, scholar, 43-45, State Univ NY, New Paltz, BA(art hist), 69-70. *Work:* Santa Barbara Mus, Calif; Mt St Mary Col; Art Students League. *Exhib:* Solo exhibs, Mus Art Mod, Paris, 67, Univ Calif, Berkeley, 69, Georgetown Univ, 74, Paranassus Sq, Woodstock, NY, 78 & Ibiza, Balearic Islands, Spain, 78, Santorini, Greece, 80, Jerusalem, Israel, 81, Tunis, Tunisia, 81, Womens Community Ctr, Santa Barbara, Calif, 86; Los Angeles Co Mus Art, 54; Bertrand Russel Centenary Invitational, London, 72-73; Drawings & Watercolors of India, Swastika Gallery, Jaisalmer Gallery, 84; Victorian Houses, Humboldts Finest Gallery, Eureka, Calif, 88; Lighthouses, Starr King Gallery & Unitarian Church, San Francisco, Calif, 88; Santa Barbara Faulkner Gallery, 92-93. *Teaching:* Instr studio courses & art hist, Orange Co Community Col, 63-68 & Santa Barbara City Col, 75-79; art hist, Mt St Mary Col, New York, 68-69; instr drawing, Univ Calif, Santa Barbara, 79. *Awards:* Nat Endowment Arts Grant, 80-81; Residency Grant, Dorland Mountain Art Colony, Temecular, Calif; Santa Barbara Heritage Soc Award. *Bibliog:* A gift is indicated, Trumpeteer Mag, 49; Gloria Calamar has affinity for her subject, Am Artist Mag, 4/69. *Mem:* Woodstock Art Asn (life mem); Art Students League (life mem); Otis Art Asn Alumna, Los Angeles. *Media:* Watercolor, Oil. *Publ:* Auth, The Adventuress a Remarkable Travel Experience, Independent News Alliance, 69; Palette Talk, Grumbacker, Publ, #28. *Dealer:* George Furnemont 47 Rue Esperonniers Brussels Belg. *Mailing Add:* PO Box 844 Summerland CA 93067

CALAPAI, LETTERIO
PRINTMAKER, PAINTER
b Boston, Mass, Mar 29, 02. *Study:* Mass Sch Art; Sch Fine Arts & Crafts; Art Students League; Am Artists Sch; also with Robert Laurent, Ben Shahn & Stanley Hayter. *Work:* Metrop Mus Art, New York; Fogg Art Mus, Cambridge, Mass; Art Inst Chicago; Brit Mus, London; Bibliot Nat, Paris, France; Kyobashi Mus Mod Art, Tokyo, Japan; Collection Mod Relig Art, Vatican Mus. *Comn:* Presentation Print, Soc Am Graphic Artists, 78; bookplate, Thomas Wolfe Collection, Libr St Mary's Col, Raleigh, NC, 79. *Exhib:* Retrospective 20 years of graphic work, touring univs & cols throughout the US, 72-73, 50 years of Printmaking at Palazzo Venezia, Rome, Italian Ministry For Affairs, 86; Int Print Exhib, Rockford Col, 79; Selected Chicago Artists, Chicago Pub Libr & Cult Ctr, 79; 79th Nat Print Exhib, Univ Tex, Austin, 79; Boston Printmakers Exhib, Attleboro Mus, 79; plus many others. *Pos:* Founder-dir, Intaglio Workshop for Advance Printmaking, New York, 60-65. *Teaching:* Chmn graphic arts dept, Albright Art Sch, Univ Buffalo, 49-55; instr graphics, New Sch Social Res, 55-62, NY Univ, 62-65; vis assoc prof fine arts, Brandeis Univ, 64-65; instr, Univ Ill, Chicago Circle, 65. *Awards:* Tiffany Found grant, 59; Rosenwald Found, 60; Series of Intaglio, The Seven Last Words of Christ, collection mod relig art, Vatican Mus, 87; plus others. *Mem:* Soc Am Graphic Artists; Boston Printmakers. *Media:* Acrylic, Oil. *Publ:* Illusr, portfolio of 25 wood engravings inspired by Thomas Wolfe's Look Homeward, Angel Publ, 48. *Dealer:* Childs Gallery 169 Newbury St Boston Mass; M Lee Stone Fine Arts San Jose CA. *Mailing Add:* PO Box 158 344 Tudor Glencoe IL 60022

CALCAGNO, LAWRENCE
PAINTER
b San Francisco, Calif, Mar 23, 13. *Study:* Calif Sch Fine Arts, San Francisco, 47-50; Acad Grande Chaumiere, Paris, France, 50-51; Acad Delgi Belli Arte, Florence, Italy, 51-52. *Work:* San Francisco Mus Art; Whitney Mus Am Art, New York; Brooklyn Mus; Nat Mus Am Art, Smithsonian Inst, Washington, DC. *Exhib:* Albright Art Gallery, Buffalo, NY, 56; Am Pavilion, Brussels World's Fair, 58; Carnegie Inst Mus Int, 61; Mus Fine Arts, Houston, 65; Nat Collection Fine Arts, Smithsonian Inst, 68; Whitney Mus Am Art, 70; SITES, 73-75; traveling retrospective, 82-83; Nat Mus Am Art, Smithsonian Inst, Washington, DC, 85. *Teaching:* Vis Andrew Mellon prof painting, Carnegie-Mellon Univ, 65-68. *Awards:* Ford Found Grant, 65; USIA-USSR Cult Exchange Grant, 88. *Mem:* Artists Equity Assoc. *Media:* Acrylic, Oil. *Mailing Add:* 215 Bowery New York NY 10002

CALDWELL, BENJAMIN HUBBARD, JR
COLLECTOR, HISTORIAN
b Humboldt, Tenn, May 1, 35. *Study:* Vanderbilt Univ, BA, 57, MD, 60. *Exhib:* Permanent Collection of Tennessee Made Silver Print to 1860, Tenn State Mus; Collection of Eng & Am Silver, Cheekwood Mus, Nashville. *Collections Arranged:* Made in Tennessee, Tenn Fine Art Ctr, Cheekwood, 71; Gilbert Gaul painting, Tenn State Mus; Carrol Cloar Painting, Tenn State Mus; Collection Will Edmondson Sculpture, Cheekwood Mus; Chinese Export Silver, Peabody Mus, Salem, Mass. *Pos:* Acquisition Comt, Tenn State Mus & Belle Meade Mansion; Steering Comt, The Hermitage, Home of Andrew Jackson, Nashville. *Teaching:* Lectr, Winterthur Mus, 80 & 83, Tenn State Mus, 81 & Williamsburg Antique Forum, 84, Mus Early Southern Decorative Arts, 88 & 89, Natchez Antique Forum & Hermitage Forum, 93. *Res:* Tennessee silver; Tennessee silversmiths. *Collection:* Tennessee silver; 18th century American furniture; 19th and 20th century American art and American primitive art; American Folk or Outsider Art of South, Contemporary (20th cent) Folk Art; 19th & 20th century American painting; Presidential Silver (belonging to American presidents); English, American and Chinese Export Silver of 18th & 19th century. *Publ:* Auth, Tennessee Silver & Checklist of Tennessee Silversmiths, Antiques, 71; Tennessee Silversmiths, Univ NC Press, 89. *Mailing Add:* 4321 Chickering Lane Nashville TN 37215

CALDWELL, ELEANOR
JEWELER, EDUCATOR
b Kansas City, Mo, May 1, 27. *Study:* Southwest Mo State Univ, Springfield, BS in Educ, 48; Columbia Univ, MA, 53, EdD, 59. *Work:* Colo Women's Col, Denver; Ft Hays Kans State Col, Hays; Denver Pub Schs; Northern Ill Univ, DeKalb; Sheldon Mem Art Gallery, Lincoln, Nebr. *Comn:* Presidential medallion, Northern Ill Univ, 70. *Exhib:* Am Jewelry, Smithsonian Inst Travelling Exhib, 55-57; Handweaving II, Smithsonian Inst Travelling Exhib, Denver Art Mus, 58-59; Own Your Own Exhib, Denver Art Mus, Colo, 61-63 & 65-67; Jewelry & Precious Metalsmiths, Wichita Art Asn, 72; Toys Designed by Artists, Ark Art Ctr, Little Rock, 75 & 78; Am Metalwork 1976, Sheldon Mem Art Gallery, Lincoln, 76; The Metalsmith Int Exhib, Phoenix Art Mus, Ariz, 77; Metalsmith Int, Univ Kans, Lawrence, 81; Soc N Am Goldsmiths' Int, Cranbrook Acad Art, 87; Wichita Nat Decorative Arts, Wichita, 88; Contemp Jewelry Invitational, New York, 89; and many others. *Teaching:* Assoc prof jewelry & graphics, Ft Hays Kans State Univ, 54-57 & 64-67; assoc prof jewelry & graphics, Edinboro State Col, Pa, 60-62; prof jewelry & metals, Northern Ill Univ, 67-83, prof emer, 83-; prof jewelry & metals, Arrowmont Sch of Crafts, Univ Tenn, Gatlinburg, 74-77 & 82-88. *Awards:* Jewelry Award, 12th Nat Decorative Arts, Cent States Craftsmen's Guild, 57; Purchase Award, 5th Ann Own Your Own Exhib, Denver Pub Schs, 61; Res Grant, Northern Ill Univ Grad Sch, 68-82. *Bibliog:* Meg Torbert (ed), American Jewelry, Design Quart, Walker Art Ctr, 59 & 61; Lois E Franke (auth), Handwrought Jewelry, McKnight & McKnight, 62; Jon Nelson (auth), American Metalwork 1976 (slide set), Sheldon Mem Art Gallery, Lincoln, 76; Slide Bank, Phoenix Arts Comm, Ariz, 90. *Mem:* Soc of NAm Goldsmiths; Am Crafts Coun. *Media:* Jewelry and related objects in gold and silver. *Dealer:* Sanders Galleries 6420 N Campbell Tucson AZ 85718. *Mailing Add:* 5430 N Paseo Soria Tucson AZ 85718

CALDWELL, JOHN
CURATOR
b Nashville, Tenn, Nov 16, 41. *Study:* Harvard Col, AB(cum laude; Harvard Nat Scholar), 63; Hunter Col, MA, 73; Yale Univ. *Collections Arranged:* Carnegie Int, 85 & 88; Carnegie Mus Art, Pittsburgh; Christopher Wool, San Francisco Mus Mod Art, 89; Sismar Polke, San Francisco Mus Mod Art, 90. *Pos:* Andrew W Mellon Fel, Metrop Mus Art, 75-77; asst cur, Metrop Mus Art, 77-80; art critic, regional ed, New York Times, 80-83; cur contemp art, Carnegie Mus Art, 83-89; cur painting & sculpture, San Francisco Mus Mod Art, 89- *Res:* Jeff Koons, Sherrie Levine, Cody Noland, Georg Herold, San Francisco Mus Mod Art, 90. *Publ:* A New Generation, San Francisco Mus Mod Art, 90; auth, Baselitz in the seventies: Representation and abstraction, Parkett, no 11, 86; Six recent sculptures, In: Richard Deacon (exhib catalog), 88; The making of the 1988 Carnegie International, In: 1988 Carnegie International (exhib catalog), Carnegie Mus Art, 89. *Mailing Add:* c/o San Francisco Mus Mod Art 401 Van Ness Ave San Francisco CA 94102

CALDWELL, MARTHA BELLE
EDUCATOR, HISTORIAN
b Chapel Hill, NC, Dec 12, 31. *Study:* Cornell Univ, BA; Univ Miss, MA; Ind Univ, MA & PhD. *Teaching:* Instr art hist, Westhampton Col, Univ Richmond, 60-63 & Rice Univ, 66-68; from asst prof to prof art hist, James Madison Univ, 68- *Awards:* Award of Distinction, Southeastern Col Art Conf, 88. *Mem:* Southeastern Col Art Conf (pres, 84-87); Col Art Asn; Soc of Archit Historians; Am Comt for Irish Studies (mem exec bd, 81-83); Am Inst of Archaeol. *Res:* Nineteenth and twentieth century art and architecture. *Publ:* Auth, Alfred Charles Bossorn: Specialist in Bank Design, Alfred Charles Bossorn's American Architecture 1903-1926, Dennis Sharp (ed), London, 84. *Mailing Add:* Dept Art James Madison Univ Harrisonburg VA 22807

CALDWELL, SUSAN HAVENS
HISTORIAN, EDUCATOR
b Clinton, Okla, June 9, 38. *Study:* Washburn Univ, Topeka, Kans, BA, 61; Cornell Univ, Ithaca, NY, PhD, 74. *Teaching:* Asst prof art hist, Boise State Univ, 74-76; asst prof, Okla Sch Art, 76-81, assoc prof, 81- *Awards:* Regents Award for Superior Teaching, Univ Okla, 85. *Mem:* Col Art Asn Am; Midwest Art Hist Soc; Int Ctr Medieval Art; Am Soc Hispanic Art Hist Studies. *Res:* Medieval, specifically Spanish Romanesque; portal development, liturgical relationships to sculpture; contemporary criticism; medieval art patronage by women. *Publ:* Auth, Penance, baptism, apocalypse: The Easter context of Jaca cathedral's west tympanum, Art Hist, 80; Ken Dawson Little, Catalog of Works, 83; Reading Medieval Art Objects: Relationships Between Art and Liturgy in the Middle Ages, In: Songs of Glory: Medieval Art from 900-1500, 85; Urraca of Zamora and San Isidoro in León: Fulfillment of a Legacy, Woman's Art J, 86; And They Sang A New Song: Twenty-Four Musical Elders at Santiago de Compostela, video, 88. *Mailing Add:* Sch of Art Univ of Okla Norman OK 73019

CALFEE, WILLIAM HOWARD
SCULPTOR, PAINTER
b Washington, DC, 09. *Study:* Ecole Beaux-Arts, Paris, France; Cranbrook Acad Arts; Am Univ, LHD, 79 (hon). *Work:* Nat Collection Fine Arts, Washington, DC; Corcoran Gallery Art, Washington, DC; Honolulu Mus Art; Metrop Mus Art, New York; Baltimore Mus Art. *Comn:* Eight murals & two sculptures, Sect Fine Arts, US Treas Dept, 36-41; font, altar & candlesticks, St Augustine Chapel, Washington, DC, 69; sculpture, Civic Ctr, Rockville, Md, 79. *Exhib:* One-man shows, Southern Vt Art Ctr, Manchester, Vt, Baltimore Mus Art, Md & Corcoran Gallery Art, Washington, DC; Carnegie Int, Pittsburgh, Pa; Metrop Mus of Art, New York; Heritage of Am Art, Nat Archives; Nat Acad of Sci, Washington, DC; retrospective, Nat Acad Sci, 79; and numerous others. *Pos:* Instr painting & drawing, Phillips Gallery, Washington, DC; instr mural tech, Ctr Art, Port Au Prince, Haiti, 49. *Teaching:* Chmn dept painting & sculpture, Am Univ, 46-54 & adj prof, Am Univ; guest assoc prof painting, Univ Calif, Berkeley, 51. *Media:* All Media. *Mailing Add:* 7206 45th St Chevy Chase MD 20015

CALHOUN, LARRY DARRYL
CERAMIST, PAINTER
b Revere, Mo, Oct 9, 37. *Study:* Iowa Wesleyan, BA(art); Univ Iowa, MA(ceramics). *Work:* Bowling Green State Univ, Ohio. *Comn:* Outdoor sculpture, Ill Arts Coun for Decatur, Ill, 78. *Exhib:* Ann Crafts Exhib, Butler Mus Art, Youngstown, Ohio; Designer Craftsman Biennial, Columbus Mus Art, Ohio; Ann Crafts Exhib, J B Speed Mus, Louisville, Ky & Evansville Mus Art, Ind; Invitational, Akron Art Inst, Ohio; Marietta Crafts Regional, Ohio; Realism Today: Mitchell Mus Regional Exhib, Evansville Art Mus, Marion, Ill. *Pos:* Owner, Village Arts, 76-; Ill craftsman-in-residence, Ill Arts Coun, Decatur, 77-78. *Teaching:* Instr art, Westmar Col, Le Mars, Iowa, 61-63; asst prof art, Millikin Univ, Decatur, Ill, 63-70; assoc prof ceramics, Akron Univ, 70-76; from asst prof to assoc prof & chmn dept art, MacMurray Col, Jacksonville, Ill, 79- *Awards:* Prize, Ball State Univ Small Sculpture & Drawing Exhib. *Mem:* Woodrow Wilson Fel, 60-61. *Media:* Oil, Pastel. *Mailing Add:* 320 S Diamond Jacksonville IL 62650

CALIFF, MARILYN ISKIWITZ
PAINTER, DESIGNER
b Memphis, Tenn, Apr 27, 32. *Study:* Memphis Acad Arts, BFA; Memphis State Univ, MFA. *Work:* Memphis Brooks Mus Art, Overton Park. *Comn:* Glass mosaic murals (with Barbara Shankman), Memphis Hebrew Acad, 62, Baron Hirsch Synagogue, 66 & Memphis Jewish Community Ctr, 68. *Exhib:* 4th Nat Exhib, Tyler, Tex, 67; Ann Mid-South Exhib, Memphis Brooks Mus Art, Tenn, 62-73; Ball State Univ Drawing Exhib, 71; Memphis Ctr Contemp Art Inaugural Opening, 88; one-woman exhibs: Earth Art Gallery, West Palm Beach, Fla, 89, Univ Northern Ala, Florence, 91 & Oak Ridge Cult Arts Ctr, Tenn, 91. *Awards:* First in Oils, 13th Mid-South Exhib, Brooks League, 68; Three Purchase Prizes, First Tenn Artists & Craftsman Show, 72; Penwomen, Tenn State Art Competition First in Acrylics 89 & First in Mixed Media, 91, Jackson. *Mem:* Penwomen; Nat Mus Women Arts; Nature Conservancy. *Media:* Oil, Collage. *Publ:* Auth, Your First Quilt, 72; The Pillow Book, 73. *Mailing Add:* 5305 Denwood Ave Memphis TN 38119

CALKINS, KINGSLEY MARK
PAINTER, EDUCATOR
b South Lyon, Mich, May 13, 17. *Study:* Eastern Mich Univ, BS, 48; Univ Mich, MS, 49; Univ Mich & Detroit Soc Arts & Crafts, post grad study. *Work:* South Bend Mus, Ind; Dayton Mus Nat Hist; Ford Motor Co; Parke-Davis; Steelcase Corp. *Comn:* Watercolors, Ford Motor Co Publ, 65-75; murals, Mayflower Hotel, Plymouth, Mich; watercolor, Mich Heart Asn. *Exhib:* Col Art USA, Andover Acad; Audubon Artists, New York; Mich Show, South Bend, Ind; Mich Artists Ann; Mich State Fair. *Pos:* Coord, Medieval Fair, Ringling Mus, Sarasota, Fla, 80-85. *Teaching:* Instr adult educ, Univ Mich, 48-50; from instr to prof watercolor & head dept, Eastern Mich Univ, Ypsilanti, 50-79; adjunct prof, Univ Southern Fla, winter 81; Paris Prog Eastern Mich Univ, 83, 87, 89. *Mem:* Nat Asn Art Adminr; Mich Watercolor Soc; Mich Art Educ Asn; Ann Arbor Art Asn. *Media:* Watercolor, Acrylic. *Publ:* Illusr, The scarlet ibis, Lincoln Mercury Times & Ford Times. *Dealer:* Helen Hegener 637 40th St Sarasota FL 34234. *Mailing Add:* 1327 Collegewood Ypsilanti MI 48197

CALKINS, ROBERT G
HISTORIAN, EDUCATOR
b Oakland, Calif, Dec 29, 32. *Study:* W (auth), Sculpture as painting as sculpture, Artweek, 77. *Teaching:* prof hist art, Cornell Univ, 66- *Awards:* Grant, Am Coun Learned Soc, 73 & APS, 80. *Bibliog:* Morris Yarowsky (auth), article, Art in Am, 79; Richard Armstrong (auth), catalog, Modernism, 81. *Mem:* Int Ctr Medieval Art (mem bd adv, 71-, dir & vpres, 80-81, pres, 81-); Col Art Asn; Medieval Acad Am. *Publ:* Distribution of labor: The illuminators of the hours of Catherine of Cleves, Transactions Am Philos Soc, 79; Monuments of Medieval Art, Dutton, 79; Illuminated Books of the Middle Ages, Cornell Univ Press, 83 & 85; Programs of Medieval Illumination, Helen Foresman Spencer Mus Art, 84. *Dealer:* 104 Corson Pl Ithaca NY 14850. *Mailing Add:* Dept Hist Art 35 Goldwin Smith Hall Cornell Univ Ithaca NY 14853

CALLAHAN, AILEEN (AILEEN LOUGHLIN CALLAHAN)
PAINTER, MURALIST
b Dayton, Ohio. *Study:* Boston Univ, BFA, 68, MFA, 70; Skowhegan Sch of Painting & Sculpture, Summer Grants, 68 & 69; Escuela Nacional de Pintura y Escultura, Mexico City, Fel study with David Alfaro Siquieros & Juan O'Gorman, 70-72. *Work:* Hotel Camino Real, Mexico City; Boston Univ; Clinic Collection, City of Boston. *Comn:* Interior wall, Skowhegan Sch Painting & Sculpture, Maine, 69; interior mural (2 walls), Inst Contemp Art, Boston, 75; exterior wall, San Felipe Church, Albuquerque, NMex, 79. *Exhib:* Skowhegan Invitational, Galleries of Nat Acad Design, New York, 70; solo exhib, Nat Palace Fine Arts, Mexico City, 72; 38th NAm Print Exhib, DeCordova Mus, Lincoln, Mass, 86; Greater Midwest Int IV, Central Mo State Univ, 89; Nat Competition Exhib, Pindar Gallery, New York, 89; Small Works Nat Exhib, Amos Eno Gallery & Nat Affiliate Members Exhib, Soho 20 Gallery, New York, 90 & 91; Invitational Exhib, Pratt Manhattan Gallery, 91. *Teaching:* Lectr fine arts, Boston Col, 79- , Regis Col, Weston, Mass, 79- & Lesley Col, Cambridge, Mass, 88-91, Univ Mass, Boston, 91- *Awards:* Lincoln Fel to Mexico, Mexican Gov, 70-72; Blanche E Coleman Award, Coleman Trust, 84; Jurors Award, Small Works, Amos Eno Gallery, 90. *Mem:* Women's Caucus for Art. *Media:* Oil, Fresco. *Publ:* Auth, A painter's language: the color of wind, Regis Today Mag, 87; The Face of Art Once Removed, Regis Today Mag, 92. *Mailing Add:* 1200 Massachusetts Ave 41W Cambridge MA 02138

CALLAHAN, HARRY
PHOTOGRAPHER
b Detroit, Mich, Oct 22, 12. *Study:* Mich State Col, 31-33; self-taught; RI Sch Design, Hon DFA, 78; Atlana Col Art, Hon DFA, 90. *Work:* Int Mus Photog, George Eastman House, Rochester, NY; Metrop Mus Art, Mus Mod Art, New York; Nat Gallery of Can, Ottawa, Ont; Victoria & Albert Mus, London, Ont; and others. *Exhib:* Family of Man, Mus Mod Art, New York, 55; retrospective, Int Mus Photog, George Eastman House, 58 & Mus Mod Art, 76; Mod Mus, Stockholm, Sweden, 78; solo exhibs, Mass Inst Technol, 68, traveling exhib, George Eastman House, 71, Light Gallery, New York & Los Angeles, 80 & Colo Mountain Col, 81; The Magical Eye, Nat Gallery Can, Ottawa, 80; retrospective travelling exhib, Cardiff Photo Gallery, London, 85; represented US, Venice Bienale, 78. *Pos:* Head photog dept, Inst of Design, Ill Inst of Design, 49-61 & RI Sch of Design, 64-75. *Teaching:* Instr photog, Inst Design, Ill Inst Technol, Chicago, 46-49, photog dept head, 49-61, assoc prof, 61-64, prof, 64-77; chmn dept photog, RI Sch Design, 61-73; vis instr, Black Mountain Col, 51, Univ Calif Exten, Berkeley, 66 & Univ Mass, Boston, 74. *Awards:* Hon Photogr, Rencontres Int de la Photog, Arles, France, 77; Distinguised Career in Photogr, Friends Photog, 81; Branders Medal, 85. *Bibliog:* Sherman Paul (auth), The Photography of Harry Callahan, Mus Mod Art, 67; John Szarkowski (auth), Callahan, Mus Mod Art, Aperture, 76; Keith Davis (auth), New Color, Callahan Hallmark Cards, 88. *Mailing Add:* 153 Benefit St Providence RI 02903

CALLE, PAUL
PAINTER, WRITER
b New York, NY, Mar 3, 28. *Study:* Pratt Inst. *Work:* Thomas Gilcrease Inst Am Hist & Art, Tulsa, Okla; Nat Cowboy Hall Fame & Western Heritage Ctr, Oklahoma City; Nat Air & Space Mus, Washington, DC; NASA Fine Art Collection; US Dept Interior; and others. *Comn:* NASA, Cape Kennedy, Jet Propulsion Lab, Star City, Moscow, USSR, 68-75; Basic History of Iron & Steel, Basic Indust, 68-70; Nat Park Serv, Mesa Verde, Yosemite, Cape Hatterus, 70-74; Classics in Surgery, Schering Co, 71-73; and others. *Exhib:* 1st Convocation Western Art, Dallas, Tex; 2nd Convocation Western Art, Arlington, Tex; NASA Eyewitness to Space, Nat Gallery Art, Washington, DC, 70; NASA Apollo-Soyuz, Moscow, 75; 25 Year Retrospective, Thomas Gilcrease Mus, 92; and others. *Awards:* Hamilton King Award, Soc Illusr; Mill Pond Press Award, Northwest Rendezvous, 79 & 80; Silver Medal Drawing, Nat Acad Western Art, 92; and others. *Mem:* Soc Illusr; Northwest Rendezvous Group. *Media:* Oil, Pencil. *Publ:* Auth & illusr, The Pencil, Watson & Guptill, 75. *Mailing Add:* 149 Little Hill Dr Stamford CT 06905

CALLICOTT, BURTON HARRY
PAINTER, CALLIGRAPHER
b Terre Haute, Ind, Dec 28, 07. *Study:* Cleveland Sch Art, cert, 31. *Work:* Memphis Brooks Mus Art, Tenn; Tenn Art Comn, Nashville; Miss Art Asn, Jackson; Ark Art Ctr, Little Rock; Addison Gallery Am Art. *Comn:* Three mural panels, Pub Works Admin Proj, 34-35. *Exhib:* New York World's Fair Exhib Am Painting, 39; Iron Horse in Art, Ft Worth Mus Art, Tex, 58; one-man shows, Memphis Brooks Mus Art, 65 & 74, Miss Art Asn, 69 & Memphis Col Art, 71 & 85. *Teaching:* Prof drawing, painting & calligraphy, Memphis Col Art, 37-73. *Awards:* Purchase Award, Ark Art Ctr, 69 & Hors Concour Award, 70; Worthen Bank Award, Little Rock, 71; Tenn Govs Award, 86. *Bibliog:* Edward Faiers (auth), catalog foreword, Memphis Col Art, 61; Sherwin Simmons (auth), catalog foreword, Memphis Brooks Mus Art, Memphis, 74; Gary Witt (auth), article, Art Voices S, 78; Ronald Brister (auth), article, West Tenn Hist Soc, 84; James Kelly (auth), Landscape & Genre Painting in Tennesse, Tenn Hist Quart, 85; Ray Kass (auth), catalog essay, Memphis Brooks Mus Art, 91. *Media:* Oil. *Mailing Add:* 3395 Douglass Ave Memphis TN 38111

CALLIS, JO ANN
PHOTOGRAPHER
b Cincinnati, Ohio. *Study:* Univ Calif, Los Angeles, BA(art), 74; MFA(photog), 77. *Work:* Bibliotheque Nationale, Paris, France; Carnegie Inst, Pittsburgh, Pa; Ctr Creative Photog, Tucson, Ariz; Corcoran Gallery Art, Washington, DC; Denver Mus Art, Colo. *Exhib:* One-person exhibs, Gallery Min (with catalog), Tokyo, Japan, 86, Richard Green Gallery, Los Angeles, 87, New York, 88, Des Moines, Iowa, 89-90, Rewdex Gallery, Kyoto, Japan, 91, Dorothy Goldeen Gallery, Santa Monica, 91 & 92, Kyle Roberts Gallery, San Francisco, Calif, 91; Greenberg Gallery, St Louis, Mo, 90; Fantasies Fables and Fabrications: Photo-Works from the 1980's, Herter Gallery, Univ Mass, Amherst, 90; Los Angeles Artists, de Oude Kerk, Amsterdam, Neth, 91; de Persona, Oakland Art Mus, Calif, 91; Visions/Revisions, Selections from the Contemporary Collection, Denver Art Mus, 91; Individual Realities, Sezon Mus Art, Tokyo, Japan, 91; Pleasures and Terrors of Domestic Comfort, Mus Mod Art, New York, 91; The Nude in 20th Century Photography, Jan Kesner Gallery, Los Angeles, Calif, 92; (Basically) Black & White, Riverside Art Mus, Calif, 92; Patterns of Influence, Ctr Creative Photog, Univ Ariz, Tucson, 92. *Pos:* Panelist, Bush Artist Fel Preliminary, St Paul, Minn, 90. *Teaching:* Instr photog, Calif State Univ, Fullerton, 77-78, Univ Calif, Los Angeles, 77-, Calif Inst Arts, Valencia, 76- *Awards:* Photog Fel, Nat Endowment Arts, 80, 85 & 91; Awards in the Visual Arts, 89; Guggenheim Fel, 90. *Bibliog:* Susan Kandel (auth), Jo Ann Callis (rev), Arts Mag, 9/91; Janet Koplos (auth), Jo Ann Callis at Dorothy Goldeen (rev), Art Am, 12/91; Richard B Woodward (auth), Pleasures and Terrors of Domestic Comfort, Mus Mod Art, Artnews, 2/92. *Mailing Add:* c/o Dorothy Goldeen Gallery 1547 Ninth St Santa Monica CA 90401

CALLNER, RICHARD
PAINTER, EDUCATOR
b Benton Harbor, Mich, May 18, 27. *Study:* Univ Wis, BS(art); Art Students League; Acad Julian, Paris, France, cert; Columbia Univ, MAFA. *Work:* Philadelphia Mus Art, Pa; Chicago Art Inst; Cincinnati Art Mus; Detroit Inst Art; Mus Painting & Sculpture, Istanbul, Turkey. *Comn:* Tapestries, Mambush Tapestry Workshop, Ein Hod, Israel, 75-77. *Exhib:* Butler Inst Am Art Mid Yr Ann, Youngstown, Ohio, 57, 59, 61 & 62; Pa Acad Fine Arts Ann, Philadelphia, 58, 59, 61 & 63; De Cordova Mus, Lincoln, Mass, Ann Nat Print Exhib, Washington, DC; Watercolor Soc Ann, Washington, DC; Premio Int dell Arte, Sicily; one-man exhibs, US Info Serv, Italy, 67, Ger, 68 & 69 & Turkey, 73 & Bristol Mus, RI, 73; Lubljana Print Bienalle, Yugoslavia, 81, 83, 85 & 87. *Collections Arranged:* Kalamazoo Art Ctr, Mich, 64; Tyler Sch Art, 70; US Info Serv, Turkey, 73; Bristol Mus, RI, 75; State Univ NY Albany, 76. *Teaching:* Founding dir & prof painting, Tyler Sch Art, Temple Univ, Rome, Italy, 65-70; chmn dept art & prof painting, State Univ NY Albany, 75- *Awards:* Guggenheim Found Fel Painting, 59; Distinguished Fulbright Prof, 81. *Media:* Oil. *Mailing Add:* Art Dept State Univ NY 1400 Washington Ave Albany NY 12222

CALMAN, W(ENDY L)
PRINTMAKER, PHOTOGRAPHER
b New York, NY, Feb 23, 47. *Study:* Univ Pittsburgh, BA(art hist), 69; Tyler Sch Art, Temple Univ, MEd, 70, MFA(printmaking), 72. *Work:* Honolulu Acad Arts; Ark Art Ctr, Little Rock; Del Mar Col; Int Ctr Photog, George Eastman House, NY; House of Humor and Satire, Gabravo, Bulgaria. *Exhib:* Photography Unlimited, Fogg Art Mus, Harvard Univ, 74; Photographer's Choice, Witkin Gallery, New York, 76; Photo-Synthesis, Herbert F Johnson Mus, Ithaca, NY, 76; Uniquely Photographic, Honolulu Acad Arts, 79; 16th Joslyn Biennial, Joslyn Art Mus, 80; Photofusion, Pratt Manhattan Ctr Gallery, New York, 81; Sights Unseen, AIR Gallery, New York, 82; Works on Paper, America Haus, Hamburg, Ger, 87. *Teaching:* Instr drawing & printmaking, Univ Tenn, Knoxville, 72-76; assoc prof printmaking, Ind Univ, Bloomington, 76- *Awards:* Best Graphic Award, 16th Joslyn Biennial, Joslyn Mus Art, 80; Master Arts Fel, Ind Arts Coun, 85. *Bibliog:* K Wise (auth), Photographer's Choice, Addison House Found, 75; Thelma Newman (auth), Innovative Printmaking, Crown Publ, 77; Virginia Watson-Jones (auth), Contemporary American Sculptors, Oryx Press, 86. *Mem:* Col Art Asn; World Print Coun; Philadelphia Print Club. *Media:* All. *Mailing Add:* 500 S Hawthorne Dr Bloomington IN 47401

CALROW, ROBERT F
INSTRUCTOR, PAINTER
b Lansing, Mich, Oct 20, 16. *Study:* Minn Sch Art, St Paul; Univ Minn, BArch; Minneapolis Sch Art. *Comn:* Hist montage watercolor, Kraft Foods Inc, New York, 71. *Exhib:* Am Watercolor Soc Annuals, Nat Acad Gallery, New York, 70, 72, 77, 83 & 90; Acad Artists Annuals, Springfield Mus, Mass, 72 & 73; Ann Juried Shows, Stamford Art Asn, Stamford Mus, Conn, 74 & 76; Rockport Art Asn, 83; and others. *Pos:* Dir, Painting Workshops & Cruises, US, Puerto Rico & Ireland. *Teaching:* Teacher watercolor, Stamford & Greenwich, Conn & San Juan, PR, 68-75. *Awards:* Forbes Mag Award, 71; Gabriel Dante Luchetti Award, Conn Classic Artists, 72; Best of Show, Old Saybrook, Conn Art Festival, 75; First Prize, Rowayton, Conn Art Ctr Ann, 79 & 83; Medal of Merit Award, Knickerbocker Artists, New York, 79; Martha Moore Mem Award, Rockport Art Assoc, 83; Two Dimensional Award, 32nd Nat Juried Exhib, Mamaroneck Artist Guild, 85. *Mem:* Knickerbocker Artists, New York; Hudson Valley Art Asn; Rockport Art Asn; Am Watercolor Soc; Conn Watercolor Soc; Salmagundi Club, New York. *Media:* Transparent Watercolor, Ink. *Mailing Add:* 30 Glenbrook Rd Stamford CT 06902-2946

CALZOLARI, ELAINE
SCULPTOR
b Albertson, NY, Dec 30, 50. *Study:* Hofstra Univ, BA(magna cum laude), 73; studied sculpture in the Quarries; Sarah Lawrence Col & Lacoste, France, 72. *Work:* Mesa Col, Grand Junction, Colo; Piper, Jaffray & Hopwood Inc, Minneapolis, Minn; US West Inc, Denver, Colo; Denver Art Mus; Williams, Krell, Torrigan & Andrews & Kirth, Houston. *Comn:* The Sun Watchers (stone sculptures), comn by Rocky Mountain Energy Co, Broomfield, Colo, 81; Plume Portal (sculpture), Univ Colo Med Sch, Denver, 83; Cirrus Clouds (suspended wind sculptures), Mass Bay Transit Authority, Boston, 84; Astolat (sculpture garden), Linclay Corp, Denver, Colo, 85; Hogback, Parks & Recreation Dept, Denver, Colo, 90. *Exhib:* 6th Colorado Ann, 80, Colorado State of the Arts: Outdoor Sculpture Show, 82 & Artist of the Western Region, 86, Denver Art Mus; Southwest 85, Mus Fine Arts, Mus NMex, Santa Fe, 85; solo exhib, Aspen Int Humanistic Studies, Colo, 86; Sculpture 89, Aspen Art Mus, Colo, 89; Connemara 90, Connemara Conservancy, Dallas, Tex, 90. *Pos:* Artist design team, New Denver Airport, 90; pub art consult, City Time, 92; mem design team, Natural & Environ Sci Bldg, Colo State Univ, 92. *Awards:* Fel Visual Arts, Colo Coun Arts & Humanities, 86. *Bibliog:* Steve Rosen (auth), Women Are Reshaping the Field of Public Art, New York Times, 11/8/87; Arthur Williams (auth), Sculpture: Technique, Form, and Content, Davis Publ, Worchester, Mass, 89; Donna Michaels (auth), What's So Special About Stone Sculpture?, Art Talk, 1/90. *Mem:* Int Sculpture Ctr. *Media:* Stone; Light Diffraction Materials. *Mailing Add:* 1380 Poplar Denver CO 80220-3025

CAMARATA, MARTIN L
ARTIST, EDUCATOR
b Rochester, NY, June 10, 34. *Study:* NY State Univ, Buffalo, BA, 56; NY Univ, MA, 57. *Work:* Mus Belles Artes, Caracas, Venezuela; Univ of the Pac; Mus Palace of Legion Fine Arts, San Francisco. *Exhib:* Twenty-Second Painting Ann, Butler Inst Am Art, 57; Boston Printmakers Ann, 62-66; Philadelphia Print Club Ann, 65 & 66; Print-Drawing Ann, Pa Acad Fine Arts, 65, 66 & 68; Potsdam Ann Print-Drawing, NY, 74; one-man shows, McKissick Mus, Univ SC & Ore State Mus Fine Arts, Eugene, Ore. *Teaching:* Prof drawing & printmaking, Calif State Univ, Stanislaus, 64- *Awards:* First Prize Print, William J Keller Award, 56; Best of Show, Calif State Fair Art Exhib, 65; Fulbright Fel, Rome, Italy, 58-59. *Bibliog:* T Albright (auth), rev in San Francisco Chronicle, 72 & 75. *Publ:* Auth, Lithography at Collectors Press, Artists Proof Mag, 72. *Mailing Add:* 531 Meadowlark Dr Turlock CA 95380

CAMASTRO-PRITCHETT, ROSE
PAINTER
b Chicago, Ill, June 16, 42. *Study:* Quincy Col, Ill, BFA, 64; Western Ill Univ, Macomb, MS, 72. *Work:* Ohmodos City Mus, Cyprus. *Comn:* Middle Eastern Florals, Venables Inc, Cannes, Australia, 87; paintings Arab mystic, comn by Andrea Azar, Rastanura, Saudi Arabia, 87; florals, Earl Mont Guest House, Oxford, England, 87. *Exhib:* Ilmoian Midwest Ann, Quincy Art Ctr, Ill, 87, 88 & 89; Inscapes Nat Watercolor Show, LA Artcore Gallery, Los Angeles, Mo, 88; Watercolor USA, Springfield Art Mus, Mo, 88; 100 Years/100 Works: Women Artists of Today Salute Their Centennial, traveling, 89-90; Nat Asn Women Artists Traveling Show, 91-92. *Pos:* Co-owner, dir, Camastro/Pritchet Art Int, 87- *Teaching:* Camastro/Pritchett Art Int Painting Workshops, Wales, Cyprus, US, 87. *Awards:* Grumbacher Gold Medal Award, 39th Ilmoian Midwest, Quincy Art Ctr, 89; City of Quincy

Arts Award for Individual Artist, Ill, 89; Gehner Award, 90 & 92, Nat Asn Women Artist Exhib. *Bibliog:* Glyn Hughes (auth), Nightingales of Platres Meet Green Fields of Home, Cyprus Weekly, 89; Betsey Schein-Goldman (auth), Making Travel A Family Business, Am Artist Mag, 3/90; David Pritchett (auth), Let the Paint Do the Work, Leisure Painter Mag, 90; R Camastro (auth), Know your paints, 91 & Pictures on record, 92, Leisure Painter Mag; Glyn Hughes (auth), Platres signs (in paint) again, Cyprus Weekly, 91. *Mem:* Nat Asn Women Artists; Nat Watercolor Soc; Am Watercolor Soc; Chicago Artists Coalition; Lousiana Watercolor Soc. *Media:* Watercolor, Acrylic. *Dealer:* Mostyn Gallery 12 Vaughan St Llanduano Gwynedd N Wales UK LL301AB. *Mailing Add:* 41 Hickory Grove Quincy IL 62301

CAMBER, DIANE WOOLFE
MUSEUM DIRECTOR, CURATOR
b Miami Beach, Fla. *Study:* Barnard Col, Columbia Univ, BA(art hist); Boston State Col, MEd(visual arts); Mass Col Art. *Collections Arranged:* Chaim Gross: Sculpture & Drawings (auth, catalog), 82; Charmion von Wiegand: Her Art & Life (auth, catalog), 82; Origins of Modern Design in Art Nouveau & Art Deco (auth, catalog), 82; Frank Lloyd Wright: Decorative Objects, Prints, Drawings, Fla Projects (auth, catalog), 84; Mid Century Design: Decorative Arts 1940-1960 (auth, catalog), 85; French Art, Sackner Arch Visual & Concrete Poetry (auth, catalog), 87; Seventy Years of Miami Architecture (auth, catalog), 88; Richard Wagner's Bayreuth Festival Performance of the Ring Cycle Art, Costume & Scenery 1876-1988, 89. *Pos:* Mus lectr, Albright-Knox Mus, Buffalo, 62-64 & Mus Fine Arts, Boston, 68-69; mus educator, De Cordova & Dana Mus, Lincoln, 67-68; assoc dir, Miami Design Preserv League, 78-80; actg dir, Bass Mus Art, 80-82, exec dir, 82-; mem adv coun, Fla Cult & Educ Alliance. *Teaching:* Art specialist, Holliston Pub Sch, Mass, 70-74; instr art, Lafayette Pub Schs, La, 75-77; instr hist furniture design, Ft Lauderdale Art Inst, 78-79. *Bibliog:* Angel Hernandez (auth), Turning the Bass from bust to boom, Miami News, 6/81; Vicki Sanders (auth), Basking in Bass glory, 1/84 & Richard Capen (auth), Salute to South Florida's best, 12/84, Miami Herald. *Mem:* Miami Design Preserv League (bd dirs, 80-); Am Asn Mus; Dade Co Cult Exec Coun (vpres, 82-84, pres, 84-88, exec bd, 89); Fla Art Mus Dirs Asn (vpres, 84-86, pres, 86-). *Mailing Add:* Bass Mus Art 2121 Park Ave Miami Beach FL 33139

CAMERON, BROOKE BULOVSKY
EDUCATOR, PRINTMAKER
b Madison, Wis. *Study:* Univ Wis, Madison, BS(art educ; honors); Univ Minn summer art hist tour of Europe with Prof Lorenz Eitner; Univ Iowa, with Maruicio Lasansky, MA(printmaking); NY Univ, viscosity printing workshop with Krishna Reddy, 82-83; Pratt Manhattan Graphics Ctr, litho & photo litho with James Martin & Ryo Watanabe; studied with Vito Giacalone, China & Japan, 84. *Work:* Emory Univ, Atlanta, Ga; Univ Ga Mus Art; Springfield Art Mus, Mo; Ringling Mus, Sarasota, Fla; Rockford Col Dept Art Collection. *Comn:* Miss Willie, ed prints, Lakeside Studios, Mich, 77. *Exhib:* NDak Nat Print & Drawing Exhib, 83; 9th Independents Exhib Prints, Kanagawa, Japan, 83; Nat Print Exhib, Springfield Art Mus, Mo, 84; American Printmakers in England, W Surry Col Art & Design Invitational, 85; Cadaques Int Mini-Print Juried Exhib, Barcelona, Spain, 85; Shoot 3, Photo-Imagery, Survival Graphics, Madison, Wis, 85; Women Printmakers, Davis Art Gallery, Stephens Col, 89; Oregon Beach, Nat Print Exhib, Hunterdon Art Ctr, Clinton, NJ; Mo State Fair Prof Div, Sedalia, 90; 4 person show, Univ Art Life Prog, Columbia, Mo, 90. *Collections Arranged:* Heart of America Nat Printmaking Exhib, Univ Mo. *Teaching:* Instr art & art hist, Tex Christian Univ, Ft Worth, 66-67; from instr to assoc prof fine arts, Univ Mo, 67-, chmn dept art, 79-82. *Awards:* Printmaking Award, Crown Ctr Exhib Halls, Kansas City, Mo, 74. *Mem:* Col Art Asn Am; Women's Caucus Art; Wis Women Arts. *Media:* Intaglio, Photo-intaglio. *Dealer:* Lakeside Studios 150 S Lakeshore Rd Lakeside MI 49116; Chicago Ctr for the Print Chicago Ill. *Mailing Add:* 923 College Park Columbia MO 65203

CAMERON, DUNCAN F
MUSEUM DIRECTOR
b Toronto, Ont, Feb 1, 30. *Pos:* Sr adminr, Royal Ont Mus, Univ Toronto, 56-62; pres & chmn bd, Janus Mus Consult Ltd, Toronto, 62-71; nat dir, Can Conf Arts, Toronto, 68-71; dir, Brooklyn Mus, NY, 71-73; pres, P S Ross & Co, Mgt Consult, Toronto, 75-77; dir & chief exec officer, Glenbow-Alta Inst, Calgary, 77-88; dir emer, Glenbow-Alberta Inst, Calgary, 88-89; Chmn & pres, Tousley Consulting Ltd, 89- *Teaching:* Occasional lectr museology, Royal Ont Mus, Univ Toronto, 71-76; adj prof art criticism, Univ Western Ont, London, 76-77. *Awards:* Samuel H Kress Found Res Grant, 74; Merit Award, Can Mus Asn, 85; Chai Award, Calgary Jewish Community Coun & Can Jewish Cong, 86. *Mem:* Can Mus Asn; Can Asn Mus Dirs; Can Art Mus Dirs Orgn; Int Coun Mus; Commonwealth Asn Mus (past pres); fel, Glenbow Alta Inst, 90-; fel, United Kingdom Mus Asn, 90- *Publ:* Auth, The Arts in Canada 1975: A Viewpoint, Can Coun, 75; Gold for the Gods: A Review, Gazette, Quart Can Mus Asn, winter 77; An Introduction to the Cultural Property Export and Import Act, Dept Secy State, Govt Can, 77; and others. *Mailing Add:* 3438 Six St SW Calgary AB T2S 2M4 Canada

CAMERON, ELSA S
CURATOR, ADMINISTRATOR
b San Francisco, Calif, Nov 19, 39. *Study:* San Francisco State Univ, BA, 61 & MA, 65. *Collections Arranged:* Native American Ceramics: Contemporary Pueblo Works, 73, Works of Benemeno Serrano, 74, Food Show, 76, Foot Show, 76, Downtown Ctr & Downtown Dog Show, 78, M H de Young Mem Mus, San Francisco, Calif, The Right Foot 80, Lights, Chairs, Tools, S Fairport. *Pos:* Cur-in-charge, M H de Young Mem Mus Art Sch, Downtown Ctr, Fine Arts Mus of San Francisco, 66-80; chief cur exhib & art collections, San Francisco Int Airport, 80-; consult educ, Univ Art Mus, Berkeley; art consult, Gensler & Assoc Architects, San Francisco, 83, Heller & Leak, 89, Markmack, 90, Geraldines Interests, OM&M, Olympia, York, 86-90; dir, Comn Arts Inc for Art Proj(s) MIA, John Wayne Airport, Los Angeles, 88-90. *Teaching:* Asst prof art education, Univ Southern Calif, 82-83. *Awards:* Nat Endowment Arts Fel, 73 & 76-77. *Res:* Museum education and community arts. *Publ:* Contribr, Museum as educator, Univ Calif, Berkeley, 78. *Mailing Add:* San Francisco Int Airport Exhib Dept PO Box 8097 San Francisco CA 94128

CAMERON, ERIC
ADMINISTRATOR, PAINTER
b Leicester, Eng, Apr 18, 35. *Study:* Kings Col, Univ Durham, Newcastle, Eng, BA, 57, study with Lawrence Gowing, Victor Pasmore & Richard Hamilton; Courtauld Inst, Univ London, Acad Dipl(hist art), 59. *Work:* Art Gallery Ont, Toronto; Nat Gallery Can, Ottawa, Ont; Univ East Anglia, Norwich, Eng; Univ Leeds, Eng; Vancouver Art Gallery, BC. *Exhib:* Woods II, Nat Gallery Can, 71 & Woods I, Art Gallery Ont, 71; Videoscape, Art Gallery Ont, 74; Video Show, Serpentine Gallery, London, Eng, 75; Int Video Exhib, Aarhus, Denmark, 76; Paintings in Mixed Exhib, Art Gallery NS, Halifax, 77; Newspaper Paintings & Lawn, Anna Leonowens Gallery, Halifax, NS, 77; Keeping Marlene Out of the Picture--and Lawn, Vancouver Art Gallery, BC, 78; Divine Comedy, Nat Gallery Can, 90. *Pos:* Dir grad prog, NS Col Art & Design, Halifax, 76-87; head, Dept Art, Univ Calgary, 87- *Teaching:* Lectr art & art hist, Univ Leeds, Eng, 59-69; assoc prof painting & video, Univ Guelph, Ont, 69-76. *Awards:* Can Coun grant collective projs, 71; Can Coun travel grant, 74; Can Coun video grant, 75. *Mem:* Univs Art Asn Can (Ont rep, 72-73, secy-treas, 73-76 & 76, vpres, 76-); fel Royal Soc Arts; Col Art Asn Am. *Media:* Oil, Acrylic. *Publ:* Auth, Mac Adams: The Mysteries, 76, Dan Graham: Appearing in Public, 76, Art as Art and the Oxford Dictionary, Vanguard, 77 & Bill Beckley's Lies, 77, Artforum; Bent Ayis Approach, Nickle Arts Mus, Calgary, 84; Divine Comedy, Nat Gallery Can, 90. *Dealer:* Art Metropole 241 Yonge St Toronto ON Can. *Mailing Add:* Head Dept Art 2500 Univ Dr NW Calgary AB T2N 1N4 Canada

CAMFIELD, WILLIAM ARNETT
HISTORIAN
b San Angelo, Tex, Oct 29, 34. *Study:* Princeton Univ, AB, 57; Yale Univ, MA, 61, PhD, 64. *Teaching:* From asst prof to assoc prof mod Am & mod Europ art, Univ St Thomas, Houston, Tex, 64-69; from assoc prof to prof, Rice Univ, Houston, Tex, 69- & Joseph & Joanna Naziro Mullen Prof, 80. *Awards:* Am Philos Soc Grant, 65; Am Coun Learned Socs Grant-in-Aid, 68, Fel, 73-74; Nat Endowment Humanities Fel, 81; Guggenheim Fel, 88. *Bibliog:* F Will-Levaillant (auth), Picabia et la machine: symbole et abstraction, Rev l'Art, Paris, No 4, 69; Douglas David (auth), Big Dada, Newsweek, 9/70; Christopher Green (auth), Francis Picabia, his art, life and times, Burlington Mag, 11/81. *Mem:* Col Art Asn; founding mem Asn l'Etude Dada Surrealisme; co-founder, Tex Conf Art Historians. *Res:* Emphasis on Dada in Paris and art in France from about 1910 to 1925. *Publ:* Auth, Juan Gris and the golden section, 65 & The machinist style of Francis Picabia, 66, Art Bulletin; Philip Renteria, Pelham-von Stoffler Gallery, 76; Francis Picabia, Princeton Press, 79. *Mailing Add:* Dept Art & Art Hist Rice Univ PO Box 1892 Houston TX 77251

CAMHI, MORRIE
PHOTOGRAPHER, EDUCATOR
b New York, NY, Aug 16, 28. *Study:* Univ Calif, Los Angeles, BA, 56. *Work:* San Francisco Mus Mod Art; Ctr Creative Photog, Tucson; Oakland Mus; Israel Mus, Jerusalem; Magnes Mus, Berkeley. *Exhib:* Haiku, Camerawork, Christchurch, NZ, 76; Petaluma, San Francisco Art Inst, 77; Espejo, Ctr Contemp Photog, Chicago, 78, Oakland Mus, 78 & Ctr Creative Photog, Tucson, 83; Humanism, Consejo Fotografia, Mexico City, 79; Jews of Greece, Magnes Mus, Berkeley, 80; AD: Vantage, San Francisco Mus Mod Art, 83 & 85. *Pos:* Assoc ed, Photoshow Mag, 79-81. *Teaching:* Mem fac photog, San Francisco City Col, 69-; instr sem, Friends Photog & Univ Calif. *Awards:* Grants, Nat Endowment Arts, 77, Columbia Found, 78 & Magnes Mus, 80. *Bibliog:* Milton Meltzer (auth), Eye of Conscience, Follett Press, 74; Don Owens (auth), articles, Picture Mag, 78 & 80. *Mem:* Soc Photog Educ. *Res:* Nature of medium; marketplace; international overview. *Publ:* Auth, Photography in China, Darkroom Mag; Back to Basics, Camerawork Quart, 82; Innovation over tradition, 83 & Avedon and the Art Factory, Photo Metro, 86. *Dealer:* Cityscape Gallery 97 E Colorado St Pasadena CA 91105; MIN Gallery 402 Masa Ebisu Tokyo 150 Japan. *Mailing Add:* 95 Marshall Ave Petaluma CA 94952

CAMPANELLI, DAN
PAINTER
b Bronx, NY, Mar 18, 49. *Study:* Sch Visual Art, New York, grad, 69. *Work:* Portsmouth Mus Art, Va; NJ Bell Tel Collection; Atlantic County Fine Arts Comn, Atlantic City, NJ. *Exhib:* Am Drawings, El Paso Mus Art, Tex, 77, Albrecht Art Mus, St Joseph, Yellowstone Art Ctr, Billings, Mont, & Mint Mus Art, 78; Drawings, Smithsonian Inst Traveling Exhib, 77-79; Temple Univ, Pa, 81; Art Gallery, Univ Ala; Cedar Rapids Art Ctr, Iowa. *Awards:* Distinguished Service Award, Am Artists Prof League-Grand Nat, 72 & Gold Medal Graphics, 73; Purchase Award, Portsmouth Mus, Va, 76. *Bibliog:* Cover story, Colonial Homes Mag, 3-4/81; interviews, NJ Network Pub Broadcasting Serv prog, State of the Arts, 4/84 & cable television, Warren Co Video Mag, 7/88. *Media:* Watercolor. *Publ:* Limited & unlimited prints, NY Graphic Soc, 86. *Dealer:* Kerygma Gallery Ridgewood NJ; Golden Door New Hope PA. *Mailing Add:* 65 Route 627 Phillipsburg NJ 08865

CAMPANELLI, PAULINE EBLE
PAINTER
US citizen. *Study:* Ridgewood Sch Art, NJ, grad, 64; Art Students League, 65. *Work:* Colonial Carbon & Ribbon, Boca Raton, Fla; Page Industries, Hanover, NJ. *Comn:* Yankee Mag, Dublin, NH, 88. *Exhib:* Catherine Lorillard Wolfe Art Club, Nat Arts Club & Nat Acad, New York, 75 & 77; Channel 39 On the Air Auction, Allentown Mus, Pa, 78; two-person show, Temple Univ, Pa, 81. *Awards:* Gold Medal Oils, 71 & 75 & Still Life Award, 72, Catharine Lorillard Wolfe Art Club; Distinguished Service Award, Am Artists Prof League, 72; and many others. *Bibliog:* Cover article, Colonial Homes Mag, 81; interview, NJ Network, Pub Broadcasting Serv prog State of the Arts, 4/84; articles, Country Living Mag, 4/85 & 10/92; article, NY Times, 11/85. *Media:* Oils. *Publ:* Illusr, prints, NY Graphic Soc; feature article, US Art Mag, 1-2/89. *Dealer:* NY Graphic Soc PO Box 1469 Greenwich CT 06836-1469; Golden Door Gallery Parry Barn New Hope PA 18938. *Mailing Add:* 65 Route 627 Phillipsburg NJ 08865

CAMPBELL, DAVID PAUL
PAINTER
b Takoma Park, Md, Mar 31, 36. *Study:* Art Students League, 57-58 & 61. *Work:* Mus Fine Arts, Boston; Metrop Mus Art, New York. *Comn:* Painting, Gillette Co, Boston, 80. *Exhib:* A Sense of Place, Univ Nebr & Joslyn Mus, 73; Watercolor USA, Springfield Art Mus, 74; Directions in Realism, Danforth Mus, Framingham, Mass, 80; Brockton Art Mus Triennial, Mass, 80; Perspectives on Contemporary American Realism, Pa Acad Fine Arts, 82 & Art Inst Chicago, 83; Six From Around Town, Rose Art Mus, Waltham, Mass, 83; San Francisco Mus Mod Art, 85; Contemp Drawings from Boston Collections, Mus Fine Arts, Boston, 86-87; Boston Ann Drawing Show, 87, 88 & 91. *Teaching:* Instr life drawings, Montserrat Col, Beverly, Mass, 89; instr watercolor, NE Sch Art, Boston, 90, Jewish Community Ctr, Newton, Mass, 90- *Awards:* Purchase Award, Watercolor USA, Hallmark Inc, 74; Grant, Adolph & Esther Gottlieb Found, 87, Pollock-Krasner Found, 90. *Bibliog:* Peter Merchant, John Pennington & Wendy Mason (dirs), David Campbell, Words and Watercolors (videotape), Somerville Educ TV, 84; Frank H Goodyear Jr (auth), Perspectives on Contemporary American Realism, Pa Acad Fine Arts, 82; Alvin Martin (auth), American Realism, San Francisco Mus Mod Art & Henry N Abrams, 85. *Media:* Oil, Drawing. *Dealer:* Gerald Wunderlich & Co 50 W 57th St New York NY. *Mailing Add:* 1 Fitchburg Somerville MA 02145

CAMPBELL, DOROTHY BOSTWICK
PAINTER, SCULPTOR
b New York, NY, Mar 26, 1899. *Study:* Study with Eliot O'Hara, Washington, DC & Marilyn Bendell, Cortez, Fla. *Work:* Mystic Mus, Conn; Pioneer Gallery, Cooperstown Art Asn; and others. *Exhib:* Cooperstown Art Asn, var group & one-man shows, 65; var shows, Sarasota Art Asn, Fla & Pioneer Gallery, Cooperstown, 65, 74 & 88; Cortez Art Sch, Fla, 72; solo-show, 91. *Awards:* Purchase Prize Oil, Cooperstown Art Asn, 65; Merit Award for Oils, Cortez Sch Art Exhib, 72; Reasner Special, 75. *Mem:* Am Art League; Am Fedn Arts; Cooperstown Art Asn; Sarasota Art Asn; Longboat Art Asn, Fla. *Publ:* Auth & illusr, Passing Thoughts, Bks 1-17, 67-86. *Mailing Add:* 4315 Mangrove Pl Sarasota FL 34242

CAMPBELL, JEANNE BEGIEN
PAINTER, EDUCATOR
b Cincinnati, Ohio, Oct 21, 13. *Study:* Colorado Springs Sch Painting & Sculpture; Skowhegan Sch Painting & Sculpture; Richmond Sch Art, Col William & Mary. *Work:* Va Mus Fine Arts; Univ Richmond; Univ Va; Hollins Col; Roanoke Mus. *Exhib:* Va Mus Fine Arts; Phillips Gallery; Mint Mus Art. *Teaching:* From instr to assoc prof studio art, Univ Richmond, 44-83, cur, Marsh Gallery, 68-83, assoc prof emer, 83- *Awards:* Cite Artes, Paris, 68. *Media:* Acrylic, Oil. *Mailing Add:* 3715 Douglasdale Rd Richmond VA 23221

CAMPBELL, JEWETT
EDUCATOR, PAINTER
b Hoboken, NJ, Aug 10, 12. *Study:* Cooper Union; Art Students League; Skowhegan Sch Art, Maine; Hans Hofmann Sch of Art. *Work:* Mus Mod Art, New York; Va Mus Fine Arts, Richmond; Univ Va, Charlottesville. *Comn:* Mural, Va Educ Asn, Richmond, 50; mural, Chesapeake Corp, West Point, Va, 65. *Exhib:* One-man shows, Va Mus Fine Arts, Richmond, 43-70; Va Mus Fine Arts, Biennials, 48-70; Corcoran Biennial, Washington, DC; Art of the Armed Forces, Nat Gallery, Washington, DC, 44; retrospective, Anderson Gallery, Va Commonwealth Univ, 84. *Collections Arranged:* Avant-Garde Exhib, Richmond Artists Asn, 58. *Teaching:* Instr painting, Univ Richmond, 51-57 & Exten, Univ Va, 55-60; prof painting, Va Commonwealth Univ, 48-82, prof emer, 83-; retired. *Awards:* Purchase Awards, Va Mus, 40 & 60. *Media:* Oil. *Dealer:* Marc Moyens 2109 Paul Springs Rd Alexandria VA 22307; Gallery K 2032 P St NW Washington DC 20036. *Mailing Add:* 3715 Douglas Dale Rd Richmond VA 23221

CAMPBELL, KENNETH FLOYD
SCULPTOR, RESTORER
b Ogden, Utah, Sept 17, 25. *Study:* Univ Utah, BFA, 50, MFA, 51; Univ Iowa, MA, 53; Univ San Carlos, Guatemala, cert, 56; Univ Wis, Eau Claire, BA, 70; Oxford Univ, England, Dip Eth, 73, BLitt, 77, MLitt, 80, DPhil, 81. *Work:* W G Skelley Mem, Tulsa Fairgrounds; Okla Art Ctr; Philbrook Art Ctr, Tulsa; Nat Indian Hall Fame, Anadarko, Okla; Campus, Univ Wis, Eau Claire. *Comn:* Judge Tillman D Johnson Sculpture, Utah Bar Asn, Salt Lake City, 51; Gov Warren Knowles Sculpture, Friends Warren Knowles, Madison, Wis, 65; mall sculpture, Univ Wis, Eau Claire, 67; Old Abe Sculpture, Wilson Park Comn, Eau Claire, Wis, 69; Jim Thorpe Sculpture, Sac-Fox Tribal Coun, Shawnee, Okla, 79. *Exhib:* Eighth Midwest Biennial, Joslyn Art Mus, 64; Jewelry 64, Plattsburgh Col, NY, 64; Walker Art Ctr Biennial, 64; Okla Ann, Philbrook Art Mus, Tulsa, 67; 14th Ann Drawing & Small Sculpture Exhib, Ball State Univ, 68; Nat Exhib Painting & Sculpture, Jersey City Mus, NJ, 69 & 70; Nat Sculpture Invitational, Okla Art Ctr, 70. *Teaching:* Chmn art dept, E Cent State Col, 53-64; chmn art dept, Univ Wis, Eau Claire, 64-67, prof art hist, retired. *Awards:* Purchase Award Sculpture, Fifth Ann Southwest Exhib, 63 & All-Okla Exhib, 64, Okla Art Ctr & Okla Ann, Philbrook Art Ctr, 64; Excellence Scholar Award, Univ Wis, 86. *Bibliog:* Margaret Harold (auth), Prize Winning Graphics, 63 & Prize Winning Sculpture, 64, Margaret Harold Publ. *Mem:* Eau Claire Regional Arts Coun. *Media:* Stone, Bronze. *Res:* Skin-covered masks of Cross River region of Nigeria--Cameroun. *Publ:* Illusr, Men of Influence in Nuristan, Sem Press, London, 74; Nuristan, Akad Druck, Graz, Austria, 79; Le leopard, le serpent, et le crocodile, Arts d'Afrique Noire, France, 81; contribr, Kunst aus dem Alten Afrika, Staatlichen Mus, Munchen, Ger, 82; illus, Nsibidi actualise, Arts d'Afrique Noire, France, 83; AGWE, the Unique Masks of the Widekum, Arts d'Afrique Noire, France, 88. *Mailing Add:* 628 E Tyler Ave Eau Claire WI 54701

CAMPBELL, (JAMES) LAWRENCE
PAINTER, WRITER
b Paris, France, May 21, 14. *Study:* London Cent Schs Arts & Crafts; Acad Grande Chaumiere, Paris; Art Students League. *Work:* Joseph H Hirshhorn Mus & Sculpture Garden, Washington, DC. *Exhib:* One-man show, Contemp Arts, New York, 52, Tanager Gallery, 60, Kornblee Gallery, 65 & Green Mountain Gallery, 75; Am Fedn Arts Traveling Exhib, 55-56; Pa Acad Fine Arts Ann, Philadelphia; Weatherspoon Gallery, Univ NC; Realist Shows, circulated through State Univ NY, 70-72; plus others. *Pos:* Ed assoc, Art News Mag, 49-75; dir publ, Art Students League, 50-; contribr, Art in Am Mag, 81- *Teaching:* Vis assoc prof art hist, Pratt Inst, 67-; assoc prof studio art, Brooklyn Col, prof, 72-84, emer prof, 84- *Mem:* Int Asn Art Critics (mem, Am Sect); Art Students League; mem, Fedn Mod Painters & Sculptors, 54- *Media:* Oil, Watercolor. *Res:* 19th & 20th century European and American painting; Ruskin; history of Art Students League. *Publ:* Auth, Thomas Sills, 65; ed, The Elements of Drawing, Dover, 71; auth, articles, Art News & others. *Mailing Add:* 215 W 98th St Apt 5A New York NY 10025

CAMPBELL, NANCY B
PRINTMAKER
b Syracuse, NY, May 28, 52. *Study:* Syracuse Univ, BFA, 74; Univ Mich, MFA, 76. *Work:* Philadelphia Mus Art, Pa; Libr Cong, Washington, DC; Worcester Art Mus, Mass; Mt Holyoke Col Art Mus, South Hadley, Mass; Syracuse Univ Art Collection, NY. *Exhib:* A Graphic Muse: Prints by Contemporary American Women, Yale Univ Art Mus, New Haven, Conn, 87, Nelson Atkins Mus Art, Kansas City, Mo, 87 & Santa Barbara Mus Art, Calif, 87; Prints by Contemporary American Women Artists, Mary Ryan Gallery, New York, 88; Nancy Campbell: Prints & Drawings, Univ Dallas, Irving, Tex, 90; Collaboration in Print, Stewart & Stewart Prints: 1980-1990, Detroit Inst Arts, Mich, 91 & Kalamazoo Inst Arts, Mich, 91. *Pos:* Chairperson art dept, Mt Holyoke Col, South Hadley, Mass, 92- *Teaching:* Asst prof studio art, Oberlin Col, Ohio, 79-80 & Univ Hartford, Conn, 80-81; assoc prof studio art, Mt Holyoke Col, South Hadley, Mass, 81- *Awards:* Patron Award, Ralph E Cades Family Found, 63rd Int Exhib Print Club, Philadelphia, 87; Juror's Commendation, Boston Printmakers 43rd Am Print Exhib, 91; Award, Springfield Art League 72nd Ann Exhib, 91. *Bibliog:* Richard Field & Ruth Fine (auth), A Graphic Muse: Prints by Contemporary American Women, Hudson Hills Press, 87; Ellen Sharp, Collaboration in Print: Stewart & Stewart Prints: 1980-1990, Mich Coun Arts, 91; Gloria Russell (auth), Mediums Come Together at Art Exhibition, Sunday Republican, Springfield, Mass, 92. *Media:* Screenprinting, Lithography. *Dealer:* Mary Ryan Gallery 24 W 57 St New York NY 10019. *Mailing Add:* 369 Middle St Amherst MA 01002

CAMPBELL, RICHARD HORTON
PAINTER, PRINTMAKER
b Marinette, Wis, Jan 11, 21. *Study:* Cleveland Sch Art; Art Ctr Sch, Los Angeles; Univ Calif, Los Angeles. *Work:* Theater Guild Am, New York; Hilton Hotel, Denver. *Exhib:* Los Angeles Co Mus, Calif; Denver Mus; Frye Mus, Seattle, Wash; Oakland Art Mus, Calif; De Young Mus, San Francisco. *Pos:* Dir, Los Angeles Art Asn. *Awards:* Second Prize, Los Angeles All-City Exhib, 51; First Prize, Cleveland May Show, 54; First Prize, 7th Festival of Arts, Los Angeles, 58. *Mem:* Nat Watercolor Soc; Los Angeles Art Asn; fel Int Inst Arts & Lett. *Media:* Oil, Acrylic. *Mailing Add:* 643 Baylor St Pacific Palisades CA 90272

CAMPBELL, WILLIAM HENRY
PAINTER
b Philadelphia, Pa, Sept 14, 15. *Study:* La France Art Inst, 28-30; Fleisher Art Mem, 30-33; Univ Pa, 33-34; Philadelphia Col Art, with Earl Horter, Franklin Watkins & Alex Brodevitch, dipl, 37. *Work:* Univ Del, Newark; Harcum Col & Ithan Valley Sch, Bryn Mawr, Pa; Container Corp Am; Blue Cross, Philadelphia; Nat Mus Am Art, Washington, DC. *Exhib:* Pa Acad Fine Arts, Philadelphia, 35; Art Inst Chicago, 45; Philadelphia Sketch Club, 45-86; Philadelphia Art Alliance, 48 & 56; Philadelphia Mus Art, 62; Artist's Equity Asn, Civic Ctr, Philadelphia, 68, 71, 75 & 78; Nat Arts Club, NY, 84-90; Am Col, Bryn Mawr, 87 & 88. *Pos:* Art dir, Pa Railroad, Philadelphia, 53-58. *Teaching:* Instr illus, Moore Col Art, Philadelphia, 50-52; instr water media, Philadelphia Col Art, 63-65. *Awards:* Nat Soc Painter Casein & Acrylic Award, 84 & 86; Perkins Art Ctr, Moorestown, NJ, 87; Woodmere Art Mus, 88. *Bibliog:* Paul Theobald (auth), Modern art in advertising, Container Corp,

46; Egbert Jacobson (auth), Good design, Graphis, Vol 6, 50; article, Art Direction, 12/58; Art, Design & the Modern Corp, Nat Mus Am Art, 85. *Mem:* Life mem Pa Sketch Club; Philadelphia Watercolor Club; Nat Soc Painters Casein & Acrylic. *Media:* Gouache, Acrylic. *Mailing Add:* 552 N 23rd St Philadelphia PA 19130

CAMPOLI, COSMO
SCULPTOR, EDUCATOR
b South Bend, Ind, Mar 21, 22. *Study:* Art Inst Chicago, grad, 50, Anna Louise Raymond traveling fel to Italy, France & Spain, 50-52. *Work:* Mus Mod Art, New York; Va Mus Fine Arts; Unitarian Church, Chicago; City of Chicago Park Dist; Exchange Nat Bank, Chicago; and many pvt collections. *Exhib:* The New Images of Man, Mus Mod Art, New York, 59; US Info Agency Show, Moscow & Petrograd; The Chicago School Exhibition, Galerie due Dragone, Paris; Festival of Two Worlds (sculpture exhib), Spoleto, Italy; 30-yr retrospective, Mus Contemp Art, Chicago, 71; and many others. *Teaching:* Instr adult art group, Hull House, 47-49; instr sculpture, Contemp Art Workshop, Chicago, 52-69; assoc prof sculpture, Inst Design, Ill Inst Technol, 53-69, chmn dept sculpture, 55-69; vis prof, Univ Chicago, summers 63-65; lectr original artist-mkt-concept, Conf World Affairs, Univ Colo, 72. *Awards:* Bronze Medal, Deleg Nat Educ-Fisica, Madrid, 69; Automotive Asn Spain Award, An Expression of the Automobile Obsession, 69; Knight of Mark Twain, 71; and others. *Bibliog:* Harold Haydon (auth), article, Chicago Sun-Times, 5/19/71; Franz Schulze (auth), article, Chicago Daily News, 5/29/71; Rev of 30-yr Retrospective, Fr TV, 6/71; and many others. *Publ:* Auth, Artists Market, Alumni Asn Newspaper, Sch Art Inst Chicago, 71. *Mailing Add:* 1160 E 54th Chicago IL 60615

CAMPOPIANO, REMO
SCULPTOR
Study: Southeastern Mass Univ, North Dartmouth, BFA(sculpture, photog), 74-78; Cranbrook Acad Art, Bloomfield Hills, Mich, MFA(sculpture), 78-80). *Exhib:* Contemp Arts Forum, Santa Barbara, Calif, 89; List Visual Art Ctr, Mass Inst Technol, Boston, 89; Northern State Col, Aberdeen, SDak, 90; Glam Slam Exhib, Minneapolis, Minn, 91. *Pos:* Co-founder & develop dir, Visual Arts Info Serv, 80-88; developer, Criticism & the Art Market, 83-84; developer, Forum (supplement in Artpaper), Jerome, Bush & Northwest Area Found, 84-87; develop dir, Artifex Alternative Arts Mus, 91. *Teaching:* Guest speaker, Swain Sch Art, New Bedford, Mass, 83, St Paul Artists Collective, Minn, 84, Tweed Mus Art, Duluth, Minn, 84, Mid-Am Col Art Asn Conf, Minn, 87& DBAE Conf, 90; panelist, Jewish Community Ctr, Minn, 84, MCAD, Minneapolis, Minn, 91; artist-in-residence, Bethel Col, Minn, 88 & Mass Inst Technol, Boston, Mass, 89. *Awards:* Diverse Visions Grant, 90; Forecast Pub Art Affairs: R & D Stipend, 90; Nat Endowment Arts Fel, 90. *Mailing Add:* 110 W Grant St Suite 21K Minneapolis MN 55403

CAMPUS, PETER
PHOTOGRAPHER, VIDEO ARTIST
b New York, NY, May 19, 37. *Study:* Ohio State Univ, BS, 60. *Work:* Dallas Mus Art; Walker Art Ctr, Minneapolis; Met Mus Art, NY; Musee Nat d'Art Moderne, Paris; Stadisches Mus Abteiberg, Monchengladbach. *Comn:* Mass Inst Technol, 80. *Exhib:* Projected Art II, Corcoran Gallery Art, 71; Whitney Mus Am Art, 73, 75 & 76; Revision, Contemp Arts Mus, Houston, Tex, 73-74; Walker Art Ctr, 74 & 79; solo exhibs, Whitney Mus Am Art, 78 & 88, Paula Cooper Gallery, 81-83, 85, 86, 89, 90 & 91, New York, Galleria Civica D'arte Mod, Ferrara, Italy, 88, 80 Wash Galleries, New York Univ, 88, The High Mus Atlanta, Genovese Gallery, Boston, 89, 90, MIT List Visual Arts Ctr, Cambridge, 92; Extended Photography, Int Biennale, Asn Visual Artists, Vienna, Austria, 81; Post Minimalism, Aldrich Mus Contemp Art, Ridgefield, Conn, 82; Festival of the Arts, Ctr Arts, Muhlenberg Col, Pa, 83; Content, Hirshhorn Mus, Washington, DC, 84; Planes of Memory, Long Beach Mus Art, Calif, 88; Kolnisher Kunstverein, Koln, 89; Points of Departure: Origins in Video, Carnegie Mus Art, Pittsburgh, 90; Eye For I: Video self-portraits, Weathwespoon Art Gallery, Greensboro, 91; The Encompassing Eye: Photography as Drawing, Univ Akron, Ohio, 91; Voices for Choice, Soho 20, New York, 91; More than One Photography/Works since 1980 from the Collection, Mus Mod Art, New York, 92; Gifts and Acquisitions in Context, Whitney Mus Am Art, New York, 92. *Teaching:* Fel, Mass Inst Technol, Cambridge, 76-78; RI Sch Design, 82-83; assoc prof art, New York Univ, 83-. *Awards:* Guggenheim Fel, 75; Nat Endowment Arts Fel, 76; Fel, Ctr for Advan Visual Studies, Mass Inst Technol, Cambridge, 76-79. *Bibliog:* Bruce Kurtz (auth), Fields, Peter Campus, Arts Mag, 5/73; Roberta Smith (auth), About faces, the new work of Peter Campus, Art in Am, 3-4/77; Ingrid Sischy (auth), Inside out: Peter Campus, Art Forum, 3/85; Hearne Pardee (auth), Peter Campus, Arts Mag, 5/85. *Media:* Photographs; Video Tape. *Publ:* Auth, Campus on Campus, Studio Int, Vol 198, No 1008, 85. *Dealer:* Paula Cooper Gallery. *Mailing Add:* c/o Paula Cooper Gallery 155 Wooster St New York NY 10012

CANBY, JEANNY VORYS
ARCHAEOLOGIST, CURATOR
b Columbus, Ohio, July 14, 29. *Study:* Bryn Mawr Col, BA, 50, PhD, 59; Oriental Inst, Univ Chicago, MA, 54. *Collections Arranged:* Egyptian Collection (rearranged), Walters Art Gallery, Baltimore, 65, Ancient Near Eastern and Egyptian Collection (re-installed new wing), 74-75; special exhibits, Ancients Seals, Egyptian Sculptor's Models & Sculpture from Sumer and Akkad (with catalog), 70; In Search of Ancient Treasure, 78; Ancient Persia, Art of an Empire, 78; Jewelry, Ancient to Modern (Egyptian & Near Eastern), 79; Egypt's Golden Age, 82. *Pos:* Asst cur ancient art, Walters Art Gallery, 64-71, cur ancient Near Eastern & Egyptian art, 71-84. *Teaching:* Vis lectr, Near Eastern archaeol, Johns Hopkins Univ, Baltimore, 60-64. *Mem:* Archaeol Inst Am; Am Oriental Soc; Am Res Ctr, Egypt. *Publ:* Auth, Decorated garments in Ashurnasirpalis sculpture, XXXII: 31-53, & The Stelenreihen at Assur, Tell Halaf & Massebot, XXXVIII: 113-128, Iraq; auth, Some Hittite figurines in the Aegean, Hesperia, XXXVIII: 14-149; auth, Walters Gallery Cappadocian tablet and the Sphinx in Anatolia in the Second Millennium, BC, J Near Eastern Studies, Vol 34 (1975): 225-248; The jewelry of the ancient Near East & The jewelry of ancient Egypt, In: Jewelry Ancient to Modern, 80. *Mailing Add:* 616 Pembroke Rd Bryn Mawr PA 19010

CANCEL, LUIS R
MUSEUM DIRECTOR, PAINTER
b New York, NY, July 6, 52. *Study:* Pratt Inst, BFA, 75; New York Univ, MAA, 87; Harvard Univ, John F Kennedy Sch of Govt, MPA, 90. *Exhib:* Taller Boricua, Mus of the City of New York, 73; Galleria II, New York, 75; Brooklyn Mus, NY, 76; Cayman Gallery, Soho, NY, 76; Xerox Exhib Ctr, Rochester, NY, 77; Latin Excellence, Museo Al'Kasaba, Morocco, 82, 83 & 85. *Collections Arranged:* Devastion/Resurrection: South Bronx, 79; First, Second & Third Emerging Expression Biennials: Artists & the Computor, 86, 88 & 91; Latin American Spirit: Art & Artists in the US 1920-1970, 9/88. *Pos:* Dir, Cayman Gallery, 75-77 & Bronx Mus Arts, NY, 78- *Awards:* Distinguished Academic Achievment Award & Distinguished Publication Award, New York Univ Mus Mgt Prog, 87; Honorary Mem, Sociedad Bolivariana de Arquitectos, Caracas, Venezuela, 88; Distinguished Community Service Award in Computer Educ, Bd Educ, Bronx Tech Assistance Ctr, 88. *Mem:* Asn Art Mus Dirs; NY State & Am Asn Mus; Int Coun Mus (bd dirs, 89). *Media:* Multi-Media. *Publ:* Auth, Latin American Spirit: Art & Artist in the US 1920-70, Abrams, 88. *Mailing Add:* Bronx Museum of the Arts 1040 Grand Concourse Bronx NY 10456

CANDAU, EUGENIE
LIBRARIAN
b San Francisco, Calif, Jan 26, 38. *Study:* Fat City Sch Finds Art, MFA, 73; San Francisco State Univ, BA, 74; Univ Calif, Berkeley, MLS, 78. *Collections Arranged:* Kaethe Kollwitz, San Francisco Mus Art, 70; Hand Bookbinding Today, An International Art (traveling exhib), San Francisco Mus Mod Art, 78. *Pos:* Librn, Louise Sloss Ackerman Fine Arts Libr, San Francisco Mus Mod Art, 68- *Mem:* Col Art Asn; Art Libr Soc NAm (exec bd, 90-91); Pac Ctr Bk Arts (exec bd, 83-86); Berkeley Civic Arts Comn, 83-90; Berkeley Art Ctr (exec bd, 90-). *Interests:* Arts of the book; modern & contemporary art. *Publ:* Bibliographies for San Francisco Mus Mod Art publ: Edward Ruscha, Philip Guston, Sigmar Polke, and others, 70-; auth, articles and reviews in Fine Print and Art Week, 76-; Hand Bookbinding Today, An International Art (exhib catalog), 78; contribr, P Selz, In: Art in Our Times, Abrams, 81; and others. *Mailing Add:* 2108 Derby St Berkeley CA 94705

CANDIOTI, BEATRIZ A
PAINTER
Study: Col Nac, with Ramos Mejia, AA, 50; Univ Louisville, BA, 80, Univ KY, 86-90. *Work:* Nat Mus Am Art, Smithsonian Inst, Washington, DC; Floyd Co Art Mus, New Albany, Ind; Galerie Triangle, Washington, DC. *Exhib:* One-woman show, Galerie Triangle, Washington, DC, 83; James Hunt Baker Galleries, New York, 83; Kentucky Tradition in American Landscape Painting 1800 to the Present, Owensboro Mus Fine Art, Ky, 83; Capital Art from Kentucky, Lazenby Assoc, Washington, DC, 85; Kentucky Art Exhib, J B Speed Art Mus, Louisville, 86. *Awards:* First prize, Art Asn Harrisburg, Pa, 84; Catherine Lorillard Wolfe Award, 85; Kentucky Artist Award, Ky Gen Assembly, 90. *Mem:* Nat Asn Women Artists. *Mailing Add:* Lagerquist Gallery 3235 Paces Ferry Pl NW Atlanta GA 30305

CANNIFF, BRYAN GREGORY
DESIGNER, DIRECTOR
b Minneapolis, Minn, Dec 26, 48. *Study:* Minneapolis Col Art & Design, BFA, 71. *Collections Arranged:* Designer, The Life of Florence Ziegfeld (and 40 other maj shows), New York City Mus, 75 & Bicentennial Exhib, South St Seaport Mus, 76. *Pos:* Art dir, New York City Mus, 72-75; designer, South St Seaport Mus, New York, 75-76 & Mus Mod Art, New York, 76-79; art dir, Saturday Rev Mag Corp, New York, 79-80, Panorama Mag, 81 & Boating Mag, 81-83; graphics dir, Popular Mechanics Mag, 83- *Awards:* NY Directors Club Awards, 80 & 87; Desi Awards, 82-92; Am Inst Graphic Arts, 88. *Mem:* Soc Publ Designers; Art Dirs Club; Soc Illusr; Am Inst Graphic Arts. *Mailing Add:* 281 West 11th St New York NY 10014

CANNULI, RICHARD GERALD
PAINTER, GALLERY DIRECTOR
b Philadelphia, Pa, Feb 2, 47. *Study:* Villanova Univ, BFA, 73; Art Students League, 75; Pratt Inst, MFA, 79. *Comn:* Paintings, St Nicholas Tolentine Church, Bronx, 77-79, Assumption-St Paul Parish, Mechanicville, NY, 78 & St Augustine Prep Chapel, Richland, NJ, 80-81; Dedication Cross, Connelly Ctr, Villanova Univ, 80; Design the Chapel, Biscayne Col, Fla, 81. *Exhib:* Expressions, Earth Art, Mus Philadelphia Civic Ctr, 79; Creative Dimensions, Carrier Found, Bellmead, NJ, 79; Liturgical Art, Pavilion Gallery, Mt Holly, NJ, 81. *Teaching:* Instr studio art & hist, Msgr Bonner High Sch, Drexel Hill, Pa, 73-78; asst prof studio art & dir gallery, Villanova Univ, 79- *Media:* Oil, Fabric. *Mailing Add:* Dept Art & Art Hist Villanova Univ Villanova PA 19085

CANO, MARGARITA
LIBRARIAN, PAINTER
b Havana, Cuba, Feb 27, 32. *Study:* Univ Havana, PhD, 56, MLibSc, 62; studies in art hist & mus conserv with Helmut Ruheman from Nat Gallery, London, Eng. *Collections Arranged:* Cintas Fellows, Paintings by Cuban

Artists (auth, catalog), Miami-Dade Pub Libr, Fla, 77; The Romance of an Era, Colonial Art in Cuba, Main Libr, 80; The Miami Generation, Cuban Mus, Miami, 83; Art of the Bound Book, 85 & Some of Our Favorite Things, 86, Main Libr; Cintas Fellows Revisited, Main Libr, 88. *Pos:* Registr, Julio Lobo Found, Napoleonic Art Mus, 57-58; art librn, Miami-Dade Pub Libr, 63-80; art serv adminr, Main Libr, 80-82, community relations & special prog developer, 82; bd dirs, Cuban Mus, Miami & Cintas Found, NY & Miami Book Fair Int. *Teaching:* Instr contemp Latin Am art, South Campus, Miami-Dade Community Col, 77, instr hist Latin Am art, 82. *Awards:* Cintas Found Fel, 75-76. *Mem:* Art Libr Soc NAm; Am Libr Asn. *Media:* Encaustic, Tempera. *Res:* Contemporary Latin American art. *Publ:* Auth, How to Bridge the Art Gap, Art Libr Soc NAm, 76; Dictionary of Latin American Artists (bibliog), Cintas Found, 76. *Mailing Add:* 501 SW 24th Ave Miami FL 33135

CANO, PABLO D
SCULPTOR, EDUCATOR
b Havana, Cuba, Mar 11, 61; US citizen. *Study:* Miami-Dade Community Col, Wolfson Scholar, AA, 80; Md Art Inst, BFA, 82; Queens Col, Cintas Fel, MA, 86. *Work:* Miami-Dade Pub Libr & Miami-Dade Community Col, Miami; Cintas Found, New York. *Exhib:* Carnival of Critters, Main Libr Gallery, Miami, 81; The Miami Generation (with catalog), Cuban Mus Arts & Cult, Miami 83 & travelling nationally, 83-85; Celebration! The Holiday Tradition, Mus Art, Ft Lauderdale, Fl, 88; and many others in the US, Colombia & France. *Teaching:* Instr advan drawing, New World Sch Arts, 88; prof humanities, Miami Dade Community Col, Med Ctr Campus, 92. *Bibliog:* Helen Kohen (auth), Bright days for art in South Florida, Art News, 12/80; Giulio V Blanc (auth), Pablo Cano, Noticias de Arte, 9/81; and others in Miami Herald, Miami News, El Herald & Diario Las Americas, 80-81. *Media:* Miscellaneous. *Publ:* Illus, The Thorns are Green My Friend, Ediciones Universal, 88. *Dealer:* Marta Gutierez Fine Art Key Biscayne FL; NYE-Gomez Gallery Baltimore MD. *Mailing Add:* 501 SW 24th Ave Miami FL 33135

CANRIGHT, SARAH ANNE
PAINTER
b Chicago, Ill, Aug 20, 41. *Study:* Art Inst Chicago, BFA. *Work:* Kresge Found, New York; Art Inst Chicago; Nat Collection Fine Art, Washington, DC; Chase Manhattan Bank, London; AT&T Corp, Richmond, Va; and others. *Exhib:* Whitney Biennial, New York, 74; Phyllis Kind Gallery, Chicago, 74-79; Franklin Furnace, New York, 79-81; Pam Adler Gallery, New York, 79-81 & 83-84; Walker Art Ctr, Minneapolis, 81; Artemesia Gallery, Chicago, 86; Marvin Seline Gallery, Austin, Tex, 87; and others. *Teaching:* Instr, Princeton Univ, 78-; instr, Skowhegan Sch Painting & Sculpture, 80; sr lectr, Univ Tex, Austin, 82- *Awards:* Armstrong Award, Art Inst Chicago, 71; Nat Endowment Arts Fel Grant, 75 & 78-85; Creative Artists Public Serv Prog Grant, 77. *Bibliog:* Robert Storr (auth), article, Arts Mag 9/81 & Art in Am, 2/85; Douglas Cameron, (auth), article, Art News, 5/85; Mel McCombie (auth), article, Art News, 5/87. *Mem:* Am Abstract Artists. *Media:* Oil. *Dealer:* Pam Adler Gallery 37 W 57th St New York NY 10019. *Mailing Add:* 161 Mulberry St New York NY 10013

CANTINE, DAVID
PAINTER
b Jackson, Mich, June 7, 39. *Study:* Univ Iowa, BA, 62, MA, 64. *Work:* Mazur Mus, Monroe, La; Alta Art Found. *Exhib:* One-man shows, Univ Saskatchewan, Univ Alberta & Northern State Univ, 66, 67 & 69, Mazur Mus, 72 & Kraushaar Galleries, New York, 77 & 82 & 88. *Teaching:* Prof art, Univ AB, currently. *Mem:* Col Art Asn Am. *Media:* Oil, Acrylic Polymer. *Dealer:* Kraushaar Galleries 724 Fifth Ave New York NY. *Mailing Add:* 99 St Georges Crescent Edmonton AB T5N 3M7 Canada

CANTINI, VIRGIL D
MURALIST, SCULPTOR
b Italy, Feb 28, 20. *Study:* Carnegie Inst Technol, BFA, 46; Univ Pittsburgh, MA, 48; Duquesne Univ, Hon DFA, 81. *Work:* Wichita Mus Art, Kans; Carnegie Mus Art, Pittsburgh, Pa; Westmoreland Co Mus Art, Greensburg, Pa; Hillman Libr, Univ Pittsburgh; Point Park Col. *Comn:* Three sculptures & two tapestries, Hillman Libr, 69 & Nat Sci Bldg, 74, Univ Pittsburgh; Joy of Life (fountain sculpture), Urban Redevelop Authority, Pittsburgh, 69; Skyscape (enamel mural), Oliver Tyrone Co, Pittsburgh, 71; enamel murals, Univ Pittsburgh, 75 & 77. *Exhib:* Assoc Artists Pittsburgh, 45-70; Pittsburgh Int, Carnegie Mus Art, 61,64 & 67; one-man shows, Westmoreland Co Mus Art, 62, & Pittsburgh Plan for Arts, 62, 67, 72, 75 & 78; Enamels 50-80, Brookfield Craft Ctr Gallery, Conn, 81. *Pos:* Vpres, Pittsburgh Coun for Arts, 68-70. *Teaching:* Prof art & chmn dept studio arts, Univ Pittsburgh, 52- *Awards:* Guggenheim Fel, 58; Pope Paul VI Bishop's Medal, 64; Davinci Medal-Ital Sons & Daughters Am, Cultural Heritage Found, 68. *Bibliog:* Dorothy Sterling (auth), article, Am Artist, 52; Helen Knox (auth), article, Pitt Mag, 64; Lloyd Davis (auth), article, Appalachian, 67. *Mem:* Assoc Artists Pittsburgh (pres, 62-64); Arts & Crafts Ctr (vpres, 55-57); Pittsburgh Plan for Arts; Col Art Asn Am; Am Crafts Coun. *Media:* Enamel. *Mailing Add:* 205 S Craig St Pittsburgh PA 15213

CANTONE, VIC
CARTOONIST, LECTURER
b New York, NY, Aug 7, 33. *Study:* Sch Art & Design, New York, grad, 52; Art Inst Schs, Inc, Minneapolis, grad, 78; Nassau Col, Garden City, NY, AA(cum laude), 78; Hofstra Univ, with Prof John Wildeman, Hempstead, NY, BA, 79; post-grad, 85-; Fulbright Scholar, Japan, 87. *Work:* Mus Cartoon Art, Ohio State Univ; US Presidential Librs (Johnson, Ford & Reagan); Hofstra Univ Mus; Smithsonian Inst. *Exhib:* Int Pavillion Humor, Montreal, Can; Smithsonian Inst. *Collections Arranged:* Political Cartoons/Caricatures, Int Salon Cartoons, Montreal, 76-89; Reins of Power, Mus Cartoon Art, Portchester, NY, 79; Best Editorial Cartoons of the Year 1975-1992. *Pos:* Cartoonist, Newsday, Melville, NY, 54-59; political cartoonist, caricaturist, New York Daily News, 59-; ed art, Newsweek, 74-82; political cartoonist & caricaturist, King Features/North Am Syndicate, 91-; Wall Street Journal Report (nat tv), 82-83; cur & dir, Geo Graphics, Political Cartoons & The Environment, Hofstra Mus, 90; No Laughing Matter: Political Cartoonists on the Environment, Smithsonian Inst, 92. *Teaching:* Lectr, Nassau Col, 77, Hofstra Univ, 79 & 86, NY Press Club, 80 & 86, Asn Am Ed Cartoonists, 83, 84 & 86 & John Jay Col Criminal Justice, 85. *Awards:* Fourth Estate Award, Am Legion, 76; Recognition Award, Nat Conf Christians & Jews, 77; George Washington Honor Medal, Freedoms Found, 78; Golden Press Award, 79; plus others. *Bibliog:* Cover story, Vic Cantone, Editorial Cartoonist, Illusr Mag, 79; Reach Out, Cable & Satellite, 5/83; Faces & Places, NY Daily News, 85. *Mem:* Asn Am Ed Cartoonists; New York Press Club. *Media:* Print, Video. *Publ:* Auth & illusr, Topo the Mouse, T S Denison & Co, 69; The Sea Circus, Chicago Tribune, 70; newspaper articles; cartoonists themes, Ed & Publ Mag, 74 & 76. *Dealer:* Rothco Cartoons Syndicate 1463 44 St Brooklyn NY 11219; King Features/North Am Syndicate 235 E 45 St New York NY 10017. *Mailing Add:* PO Box 1039 New York NY 10116-1039

CANTOR, B GERALD
COLLECTOR
b New York, NY, Dec 17, 16. *Study:* NY Univ; Col of the Holy Cross, Hon DFA, 80; Gonzaga Univ, Hon DFA, 85; Long Island Univ, LHD, 86. *Pos:* Chmn, Cantor Fitzgerald, New York, Chicago, Boston, Dallas, Los Angeles, London & Tokyo; hon life trustee, Los Angeles Co Mus Art; mem pres coun, Col of the Holy Cross; trustee emer Metrop Mus Art, 85- *Awards:* Officer, Order of Rio Branco, Fed Repub Brazil, 80; Off of Arts & Lett, French Ministry of Cult, 84; Gertrude Vanderbilt Whitney Award for Patronage of the Arts, Showhegan Sch Painting & Sculpture. *Mem:* Am Fedn Arts; Fine Arts Soc San Diego; Bus Comt for the Arts; fel Metrop Mus Art; fel Cleveland Mus Art. *Interests:* Scholarships to museums and universities, patronage of 19th and early 20th century collections. *Collection:* World's largest private collection of Auguste Rodin sculptures; Nineteenth and early twentieth century paintings and sculpture. *Mailing Add:* c/o Cantor Fitzgerald & Co Inc One World Trade Ctr New York NY 10048

CANTOR, FREDRICH
PAINTER, PHOTOGRAPHER
b New York, NY, July 8, 44. *Study:* Pratt Inst, 62-64, 66 & 67; San Francisco Art Inst, 66; Cooper Union, 69; studied with Philip Pearlstein. *Work:* Pa State Mus; New Orleans Mus Art, La; Sheldon Mem Art Gallery, Univ Nebr, Lincoln; Univ Mass Mus Art, Amherst; Bibliot Nat & Mus Carnavalet, Paris, France; Musee Nicéphore Niépce, Chalon S/Saone, France. *Exhib:* City Landscape, Bibliot Nat, Paris, France, 74; one-man shows, Robert Schoelkopf Gallery, NY, 76, Sheldon Mem Art Gallery, Univ Nebr, Lincoln, 79, Galeria Diaframma, Milan, Italy, 80, Galerie Delpire, Paris, France, 80 & 82, La Galerie Le Trepied, Geneva, Switz, 81, Marcuse Pfeifer Gallery, New York, 81 & Musee Nicephore Niepce, Chalon, S/Saone, France, 85; Galerie Philippe Fregnac, Paris, 83; Am Ctr, Paris, 84; and others. *Teaching:* Special instr photographic printing, St Martin's Sch Art, London, Eng, 71; adj lectr photog, Brooklyn Col, NY, 74-76; instr photog & drawing, Sch Visual Arts, NY, 75-76, Parsons Sch Design, New York, 77-78. *Awards:* Fel, Va Ctr Creative Arts, 79, 80, 84 & 85; Fel, McDowell Colony, 80; Fel Grant, NY State Found Arts, photog, 87; and others. *Bibliog:* Hilton Kramer (auth), Fredrich Cantor, New York Times, 3/27/76 & 5/17/81; Janet Malcolm (auth), Fredrich Cantor, The New Yorker, 5/29/76; Carole Naggar (auth), Fredrich Cantor-Dictionnaire des Photographes, Editions Seuil, Paris, 83. *Mem:* Col Art Asn. *Media:* Silver Gelatin & Kodalith Prints; All. *Publ:* Auth, Rome: Vol 1, 77 & Paris: 1982, 82, pvt publ; illusr, Soul Survivors, Ticknor & Fields, 83. *Mailing Add:* 338 West 11th St New York NY 10014

CANTOR, MIRA
SCULPTOR, GRAPHIC ARTIST
b New York, NY, May 16, 44. *Study:* State Univ NY, Buffalo, BFA, 66; Univ Ill, Champaign-Urbana, MFA, 69. *Work:* Mus Fine Arts, Boston; Boston Pub Libr; Honolulu Acad Arts, Hawaii; State Found, Honolulu; Rose Art Mus. *Comn:* Portraits comn by Negroponte Family, Brookline, Mass, 78; portraits comn by Baumann Family, Dusseldorf, Ger, 79; portrait comn by Renate Bohmer, Essen, Ger, 79; portrait comn by Dieter Schroder, Dusseldorf, Ger, 79. *Exhib:* one-person show, Galerie Lohrl, Ger, 78, De Cordova Mus, 86, Tokyo Am Ctr, Japan, 87 & Northeastern Univ, 88, 90; Boston Invitational '78, Brockton Art Ctr, Mass, 78; Three Dimensional Possibilities, Rose Art Mus, Waltham, Mass, 79; Centerbeach, Ctr Advan Visual Studies, Mass Inst Technol, 79 & 80; Fitchburg Art Mus, 92. *Pos:* consult, Massport, 81-82; coordr visual arts, Northeastern Univ, 85-87; consult, Urban Arts, Boston, 89-90. *Teaching:* Instr painting & drawing, Univ Hawaii, Honolulu, 70-71; instr drawing, Mass Inst Technol, 78-80; instr, Northeastern Univ, Boston, 83-87, asst prof, 88-91, assoc prof, 91-; lecturer, Univ Alexandria, 91- *Awards:* Ctr Advan Visual Studies Fel, Mass Inst Technol, 78-80 & Artist Found Award, 79, State Mass; Artist-in-residence Award, Univ Hawaii, 82; Res & Develop Fund, Northeastern Univ, 89; Fac Exchange, Univ Alexandria, 91. *Bibliog:* Sammy Amalo (auth), Mira: The Sound and the Fury, Honolulu Advertiser, 3/71; Jean Charlot (auth), Art, Honolulu Star-Bulletin, 3/71; Mira Cantor zeigt Bilder und figuren aus Leinwand, Bild Niederrhein, Dusseldorf, 10/78; Dorothee Boeker (auth), Die amerikanische Kunstlerin Mira Cantor stellt din Betrachter von der Spiegel: Enrliche Figuren aus Leinwand, Rheinische Post, Dusseldorf, 10/78; Robert Taylor (auth), Show Yields Fresh Perspectives, 4/84, Christine Temin (auth), Mira Cantor:

Drawings that Dance, 5/88, Running Freeze 4/90, Boston Globe; Nancy Stapen (auth), New England Portraitists in 80's Keep Faces Fresh, 1/89, Artist Wasteland Embodies Life-and-Death Questions, 5/90, Boston Herald; Mira Cantor (article), Arts and Sciences Chronical, Northeastern Univ Col of Arts and Sciences, 3/90. *Mem:* Col Art Asn. *Media:* Soft Canvas Sculpture; Drawing. *Mailing Add:* 1129 Beacon St Brookline MA 02146

CANTOR, RUSTY
PAINTER
b New York, NY, Aug 6, 27. *Study:* Art Students League. *Work:* Inst Am Indian Art Mus, Santa Fe, NMex; Art in Embassies Prog, Washington, DC. *Exhib:* Inst Am Indian Art Mus, Santa Fe, NMex, 84; Brand Galleries, Los Angeles, Calif, 84; San Francisco Arts Comt Gallery, 87; Am Embassy, New Delhi, India, 90-92; Frank Lloyd Wright Gallery, San Raphael, Calif, 90; Sub-vers-ive Spirituality, Badé Mus, Berkeley, Calif, 92; The Golden Section, Calif Poly State Univ, San Luis Obispo, 92. *Teaching:* Nut's & Bolts, self-management for women artists, 92- *Bibliog:* Article in Calif Art Review, Am Reference Publ Corp, 89. *Mem:* Northern Calif Womens Caucus Art (pres, 89-92); Northern Calif Coun Nat Mus Women Artists (exec comt mem, 91-92); Nat Women's Caucus Art (bd dir, 90-93). *Media:* Acrylic, Glass. *Dealer:* Roth Waters HSW Gallery New Montgomery San Francisco CA. *Mailing Add:* 1870 Ralston St Belmont CA 94070

CANTRELL, JIM
PAINTER
b Sulpher, Okla, Nov 23, 35. *Study:* Univ Nebr, Lincoln, BFA, 58; Pa State Univ, 59; Univ Northern Colo, Greeley, MA, 65. *Work:* Sheldon Mem Art Gallery, Lincoln, Nebr; Albrecht-Kemper Mus Art, St Joseph, Mo; Owensboro Mus Fine Art, Ky; Austin Peay State Univ, Tenn; Miss Mus Art, Jackson; J B Speed Art Mus, Louisville, Ky. *Comn:* Canvas murals of the 12 Apostles and Holy Family, St Joseph Proto Cathedral, Bardstown, Ky, 85; 3 oil paintings, Abbey of Gethsemani, Trappist, Ky, 89; 7 oils (portraits of Abbots), St Meinrad Monastery, Ind. *Exhib:* One-man shows, Sheldon Mem Art Gallery, 70, Hunter Mus of Art, Chattanooga, Tenn, 73, Distelheim Galleries, Chicago, 75 & J B Speed Art Mus, 85; Sunne Savage Gallery, Boston, 79; Southern Realism, Miss Mus Art, Jackson, 79; Butler Inst Am Art, Youngstown, Ohio, 90; Albrecht-Kemper Mus Art, St Joseph, Mo, 91; Evansville Mus Arts & Sci, Ind, 92. *Pos:* Resident artist, Berea Col, 70-71; independent studio artist, Bardstown, Ky, 71- *Teaching:* Guest instr art, Univ Northern Colo, summer, 66; assoc prof art, John F Kennedy Col, 66-70; vis artist, Austin Peay State Univ, Tenn, 88. *Awards:* Purchase Award, Mid-America Biennial, Owensboro Mus Fine Art; Prof Development Grant, 87; Al Smith Fel, 92. *Bibliog:* Jim Cantrell: An artist not by choice but by providence, Ky Artist & Craftsmen Mag, 76; Thelma Newman (auth), The Container Book, Crown, 77; Watercolorists, Beaux Arts Mag, 12/80; Jim Cantrell, Am Artist Mag, 7/87. *Mem:* Ky Guild Artists & Craftsmen (bd trustees, 73-75 & 78-79). *Media:* Oil, Watercolor. *Publ:* Auth, Cut decoration, 75 & Studio management, 85, Ceramics Mo; Kentucky Reflected: a study in Character and Setting, J B Speed Mus, 5/85; The Fragmented Image, Nat Acad Sci, Wash, DC, 91. *Dealer:* Bardstown Art Gallery PO Box 417 Bardstown KY 40004; Malton Gallery 2709 Observatory Ave Cincinnati OH 45208. *Mailing Add:* PO Box 417 Bardstown KY 40004

CANTWELL, WILLIAM RICHARD
PAINTER, PRINTMAKER
b Philadelphia, Pa, July 24, 47. *Study:* Trinity Col, Conn, BA, 69; Sch Visual Arts, studied drawing & illustration with Jack Potter, 77-84; Pratt Inst & Manhattan Graphics Ctr, studied etching with David Finkbeiner, 85-86. *Comn:* Public Relations Booklet, Consolidated Edison, New York, 77; Citibank Bldg & New York Skyline (drawings), Citibank, New York, 78; portrait series, Fairbanks Rehabilitation Asn, Alaska, 85. *Exhib:* Solo exhib, The Five Oaks, New York, 77; Washington Sq Outdoor Art Exhib, 79-88; Carlyle Gallery, New York, 82; Hialeah Art Festival, Fla, 85; Key West Art Festival, Fla, 86, 87, 88; Westport Art Festival, Conn, 86, 87, 88; Mystic Art Festival, Conn, 86, 87, 88; Gracie Square Art Festival, New York, 86-88; Miami Beach Festival Arts, 87, 88; Maitland, Fla Art Fest, 87-88; Gasparilla Art Festival, Tampa, 89; Beaux Arts Festival, Coral Gables, 88-89; Wickford Art Festival, RI, 89-90. *Teaching:* Art therapist & painting instr, The Grove Sch, Madison, Conn, 69-70; instr graphics & photog, The Reece Sch, New York, 70-77. *Awards:* First Place, graphics, Washington Square Outdoor Exhib, New York, 79 & 85 & Key West Old Island Days Art Festival, 86; Philip Isenberg Award, Salmagundi Club, New York, 81; Rowland N Adfton Award for best show, 88; Second-Third Place, watercolor, Washington Square Art Exhib, 88. *Media:* Watercolor, Etching. *Publ:* Illusr, Around the system: We don't just work here, Consolidated Edison, New York, 77; Celebrity choice, Playbill Mag, New York, 83; Circling Manhattan, Dramalogue, Hollywood Co, New York, 83; Portraits, Fairbanks Rehabilitation Asn, Alaska, 85. *Mailing Add:* 201 West 92nd St #4B New York NY 10025

CAPA, CORNELL
PHOTOGRAPHER, MUSEUM DIRECTOR
b Budapest, Hungary, Apr 10, 18. *Study:* Madach Imre Gymnasium, Budapest, 28-36. *Exhib:* Margin of Life, Ctr of Inter-Am Relations, New York, 74; Johnson Mus, Cornell Univ, Ithaca, NY, 75. *Pos:* Staff & contrib photogr, Life Mag, New York, 46-67; mem photogr, Magnum Photos, New York & Paris, 54-; guest dir, The Concerned Photographer, Riverside Mus, New York, 66, The Concerns of Roman Vishniac, Jewish Mus, New York, 73, Behind the Great Wall: China, Metrop Mus Art, New York, 72 & The Concerned Photographer Two, Israel Mus, Jerusalem, 73; ed, The Concerned Photographer One & Two, Grossman/Viking, 69-72; exec dir, Int Ctr of Photog, 74- *Teaching:* Lectr photog, NY Univ, 68-72 & Int Ctr of Photog, 74- *Awards:* Honor Roll, Am Soc Mag Photogr, 75; Joseph A Sprague Mem Award, Nat Press Photogr Asn, 76; New York Mayor's Award of Honor, 78. *Bibliog:* Feature prof, Who Am I?, NBC Television, Channel 4, 71; Center of Concern, CBS Television, 77; Richard Whelan (auth), Cornell Capa's lighthouse of photography, Artnews, 4/79. *Mem:* Magnum Photogs (pres, 57-60); Overseas Press Club of New York (exec comn, 67-70 & 69-73); Am Soc Mag Photogr. *Publ:* Coauth (with Maya Pines), Retarded Children Can Be Helped, Channel Press, 57; coauth (with Matthew Huxley), Farewell to Eden, Harper & Row, 64; coauth (with J M Stycos), Margin of Life, 73 & ed, International Center of Photography Library of Photographers (first six titles), 74, Grossman Publ. *Dealer:* Magnum Photog Inc 261 Park Ave South New York NY 10036. *Mailing Add:* 275 Fifth Ave New York NY 10016

CAPES, RICHARD EDWARD
GRAPHIC ARTIST, INSTRUCTOR
b Atlanta, Ga, Nov 6, 42. *Study:* Univ Ga, Athens, BS, 65, MA, 69; Univ Ga, Cortona, Italy, 70. *Work:* Barnwell Mem Garden Art Ctr, Shreveport, La. *Comn:* 200 Years (painting), Collectors Wall Gallery, Sarasota, Fla, 76; graphic design, Laser Corp, Bradenton, Fla, 78; illus, Southside Sch, Sarasota, Fla, 83; graphic symbol of Venice, Fla, Chamber Commerce, 92. *Exhib:* Two Southern Draughtsmen, Addison Gallery Am Art, 72; Brooks Mem Art Gallery, 72; 32nd Ann Exhib, Jacksonville Art Mus, Fla, 81; 36th Ann Exhib, Lee Scarfone Gallery, Univ Tampa, Fla, 86; two person show, Creative Edge, Bradenton, Fla, 92; 43rd Ann Fla Artists Group Inc Show, Sarasota, Fla, 92. *Teaching:* Asst prof art educ, Univ Southern Miss, 71-73; asst prof art, Morehead State Univ, 73-74. *Awards:* Southeast Bank Award, 80 & Hamel Mem Award, 81, Fla Artist Group Inc; First Prize, Arvida State Fla, 83; First Place Art, United First Fed Savings & Loan, Fla, 86. *Bibliog:* Wayne Mayhail II (auth), Gulfcoast People, Gulf Coast Publ, 89; Ralph Montgomery (ed-auth), article,Bus Magiziner, 89. *Mem:* Manatee Art League; Sarasota Art Asn; Fla Artist Group Inc; Anna Maria Island Art League; Fla Watercolor Soc. *Media:* Ink, Watercolor. *Publ:* Illusr, Sarasota Scene - Historical, 4/90; illusr, cover, Bus Magazine Yearbook, 90; cover, SARASOTA: A Sentimental Journey, Libr Cong, 91. *Dealer:* Brittany Lore Galleries Sarasota FL. *Mailing Add:* 2116 Florinda St Sarasota FL 33581

CAPLAN, JERRY L
SCULPTOR, EDUCATOR
b Pittsburgh, Pa, Aug 9, 22. *Study:* Carnegie-Mellon Univ, BFA & MFA; Art Students League; Univ NC; Pittsburgh Film Makers. *Work:* NC State Art Gallery, Raleigh; Pittsburgh Bd Educ; Westinghouse Corp; US Steel; Alcoa; and others. *Comn:* Terra-cotta sculptures, Pittsburgh Parking Authority; ceramic mural, New Kensington Gen Hosp, North Kensington, Pa; terra-cotta, Kossman Group, Kossman Assocs, Pittsburgh, 72; bronze symbol, Deutchtown Fire Sta, Pittsburgh, Pa; mahogany screen, Temple Adat Ari El, North Hollywood, Calif. *Exhib:* Five shows, Butler Inst Am Art, 55-75; Carnegie Inst, 71; The Clay Place, Pittsburgh, Pa, 83, 85 & 91; Zanesville Art Ctr, Ohio, 87; Reynolds Gallery, Pittsburgh, 92. *Teaching:* Instr terra cotta, Pittsburgh Ctr Arts, 62-; pipe sculpture workshops, Logan, Ohio, 73-92 & Fremont, Calif, 79-91; emer prof art, Chatham Col, 88- *Awards:* Purchase Award, Assoc Artists Pittsburgh, 65; Soc Sculptors Award, 70; Pittsburgh Artist of the Year, 75; and others. *Bibliog:* Ceramics Monthly; Revista Ceramica. *Mem:* Assoc Artists Pittsburgh (pres, 65); Soc Sculptors (treas); Am Crafts Coun; Pittsburgh Craftsmen's Guild; Artists Equity; and others. *Media:* Terra-cotta, Wood. *Publ:* Auth, articles in Ceramic Mo, 9/76, 11/76 & 6/80. *Mailing Add:* 5819 Alder St Pittsburgh PA 15232

CAPLAN CIARROCHI, SANDRA
PAINTER, INSTRUCTOR
b Winnipeg, Man. *Study:* Univ Man, BFA, 57; Boston Univ, MFA, 60. *Work:* Winnipeg Art Gallery; J A MacAulay Collection, Toronto; Boston Mutual Life Insurance; Bellevue Hosp, New York; Connor Clark Inc, Toronto. *Exhib:* Landmark Gallery Invitational, New York, 73, 78 & 80; one-person exhib, Winnipeg Art Gallery, 74; Maine Coast Artists Exhibs, 74-77; Watercolor, Contemporary View, Fairleigh Dickinson Univ, 81; Views by Women Artists, Fordham Univ, 82, Gallery 53, Cooperstown, NY, Still Life-Landscape; Atlantic Gallery, 86; First Street Gallery, 89. *Teaching:* Instr art, Mus Mod Art, New York, 65-71, Village Community Sch, New York, 71-79, lenox Sch, New York, 79-89, & Town Sch 89- *Awards:* Can Coun Award, 61-62; Woodstock Art Asn Award Watercolor, 83; 3rd Prize Painting, Cooperstown Art Asn Nat Competition. *Bibliog:* John Graham (auth), article, Winnipeg Free Press, 74; John Perrault (auth), article, Soho Weekly News, 76; article, Artspeak, 1/86; David Daniel (auth), In the Galleries Art & Antiques, 4/89. *Media:* Oil, Pastel. *Publ:* Illusr, Fair Game--Hunter's Cookbook (Great American Cooking Schools), Irena Chalmers Cookbooks Inc, 83. *Dealer:* First Street Gallery New York NY. *Mailing Add:* 463 West St New York NY 10014

CAPLES, BARBARA BARRETT
PAINTER, PRINTMAKER
b Providence, RI, Oct 28, 14. *Study:* Smith Col, AB(magna cum laude), 36; Yale Univ Sch Fine Arts, 36-38; also with George Laurence Nelson & Ruth Starr Rose. *Work:* Smith Col Mus, Northampton, Mass; Univ Va, Charlottesville; Carlsbad Mus, NMex; Pushkin Mus, Moscow, Soviet Cult Found. *Exhib:* Soc Wash Printmakers, 66-78; Boston Printmakers, 71; one-man shows, Art League, Alexandria, Va, 70 & 86, Washington Printmakers Gallery, 88 & 90 & Carlsbad Mus, NMex, 82; Contemp Am Graphics, Pushkin Mus, Moscow, 92. *Teaching:* Instr art & art hist, Rye Country Day Sch, NY, 38-40; instr art, Walter Reed Hosp, Washington, DC, 43-45; instr serigraphy, Alexandria Community Y, 65-75. *Awards:* Numerous awards, Art League, Alexandria, 65-71; NVa Fine Arts Assoc, 71 & 72; and others. *Mem:*

Soc Wash Printmakers, 66-78; Art League, Alexandria (mem bd, 69); NVa Fine Arts Asn; Wash Printmakers Gallery. *Media:* Watercolor; Monotypes. *Dealer:* Washington Printmakers Gallery 2106 R St NW Washington DC 20008. *Mailing Add:* 1111 Roan Lane Alexandria VA 22302

CAPOBIANCO, DOMENICK
PAINTER, SCULPTOR
b St Louis, Mo, Dec, 22, 28. *Study:* Washington Univ, St Louis, Mo, BFA, 58; Skowhegan Sch Painting & Sculpture, 58 & 59. *Work:* Univ Dallas, Tex; Newark Public Libr, NJ; Mus Mod Art, Skopje, Academie des Beaux-Arts, Ljubljana, Yugoslavia; Graphische Sammlung Albertina, Vienna, Austria; Mus Contemp Art, Fredrickstad, Norway; Nat Mus Krakow, Poland; Weatherspoon Mus, Univ NC Greensboro; Musee Du Petit Format, Couvin, Belgium. *Comn:* Stage Sets: Experimental Death Unit #1, LeRoy Jones, St Marks Theatre, 64, Forensic & The Navigators, Sam Sheppard, Theatre Genesis, 67, Willy the Germ, Murray Mednick, Theatre Genesis, 68 & The Hunter, Murray Mednick, Theatre Genesis, 68. *Exhib:* Sky Piece over Soho (skywriting drawing), 74 & 76, 55 Mercer Gallery, New York (wall works-Invitational); 79, 80, 81, 82, 84, 85 & 86 Condeso/Lawler Gallery New York (painting); Brooklyn Mus Print Exhib, NY, 76; Brooklyn Mus, NY, 78; Kyoto Municipal Mus Art, Japan, 80; Gallery artists, Condeso/Lawler Gallery, New York, 83; Gathering of Avant-Garde, Lower East Side 1948-70, New York, 85; Himmelsschreiber: Diemensionen eines fluchtigen mediums, Kassel, 86; Maubeuge-Sculpt 87/III, France, 87; Of Paper, Pigment & Glass, Castle Gallery, Col New Rochelle, 87. *Teaching:* Instr painting, Washington Univ, St Louis, Mo, 57-58; lectr, Art Dept, Univ NC, Greensboro, 67; prof, Art Dept, Rutgers Univ, 67- *Awards:* Creative Artists Public Service Program Grant, 76; 2 Purchase Awards, Int Exhib Graphic Art, Ljubljana, Jugoslavia, 77; Guggenheim Fel Grant, 84-85. *Bibliog:* Allen Tannenbaum (auth), Soho Weekly News, 10/74; Tiffany Bell (auth), Arts Mag, 5/79; Peter Wallach (dir), film interview; A Life in Art/F Conway, 86; Joe Pollack (auth), article, St Louis Post-Dispatch, 8/31/86; and others. *Media:* Oil, Canvas; Mixed Media. *Dealer:* Mercer Gallery 55 Mercer St New York NY 10013; Galerie Al Lõwenstr 43B 7000 Stuttgart 70 Ger. *Mailing Add:* 133 Eldridge St New York NY 10002

CAPONI, ANTHONY
SCULPTOR, EDUCATOR
b Pretare, Italy, May 7, 21. *Study:* Univ Flore, Italy; Cleveland Sch Art; Walker Art Ctr, Minn; Univ Minn, BS & MEd. *Work:* Minneapolis Inst Art; St Cloud State Col; Minn Mus Art. *Comn:* Sculpture, columns & figures, St Joseph Sch, Red Lake Falls, Minn, St Mary's Church, Warroad, Minn; St John's Church, Rochester, Minn; wax models for all bronze motifs in Eisenhower Libr, Abilene, Tex; two bronze relief sculptures, Ascoli, Italy; plus others. *Exhib:* Walker Art Ctr, Minneapolis, 47-58; St Paul Gallery Art, 47-58; Iowa State Teachers Col, 58; Minneapolis Art Inst Ann; Augustana Col, Sioux Falls, SDak, 71; and other group & one-man shows. *Teaching:* Prof art & chmn dept, Macalester Col, 58- *Awards:* Ford Found Grant & Four Prizes, Minneapolis Inst Art, 47-59; six Awards, Minn State Fair, 48-65; Awards, St Paul Gallery Art, 49 & 55. *Mem:* Artists Equity Asn; Soc Minn Sculptors. *Media:* Stone. *Publ:* Auth, Boulders & Pebbles of Poetry & Prose, Independence Press, 72. *Mailing Add:* Dept Art MacAlester Col 1600 Grand Ave St Paul MN 55105

CAPONIGRO, PAUL
PHOTOGRAPHER
b Boston, Mass, Dec 7, 32. *Study:* With Benjamin Chin & Minor White. *Exhib:* Solo exhibs, Mus Mod Art, New York, 68, San Francisco Mus Art, 70, Art Inst Chicago, 73, Victoria & Albert Mus, London, 75, Albright-Knox Art Gallery, Buffalo, 76, Carl Siembab Gallery, Boston, 76, Mus Fine Arts, Santa Fe, 76, David Mirvish Gallery, Toronto, 77, Galerij Paule Pia, Antwerp, 81 & Photog Gallery, La Jolla, 81; American Masters, Smithsonian Inst, 74; Photography in America, Whitney Mus Am Art, 74; 14 American Photographers, Baltimore Mus Art & traveling, 75; Mirrors and Windows, Mus Mod Art, New York & traveling, 78-80; Color as Form: A History of Color Photography, Int Mus Photogr, George Eastman House, Rochester, NY; among other group and solo shows. *Pos:* Consult photo res dept, Polaroid Corp, Cambridge, 60-70. *Teaching:* Instr creative photography, NY Univ, 67-71; instr photography, Yale Univ, 71-86; lectr at numerous universities & art schools throughout the US. *Awards:* Guggenheim Fel, 66 & 75; Nat Endowment Arts Grant, 71, 74 & 75; Art Dirs Club NY Award, 74. *Bibliog:* Joan Murray (auth), Caponigro and Heyman, Artweek, 8/23/75; Rolf Koppel (auth), Caponigro: A respect for the activities of existence, Santa Fe Reporter, 10/28/76. *Mem:* Founder Am Heliographers Asn. *Publ:* Portfolio Two, 73; Sunflower, Film Haus Inc, 74; Landscape: Photographs by Paul Caponigro, McGraw-Hill, 75; Portfolio Three: Stonehenge, 77. *Dealer:* Andrew Smith Gallery 76 E San Francisco Santa Fe NM 87501. *Mailing Add:* Rte 3 Box 96D Santa Fe NM 87501

CAPORAEL, SUZANNE
PAINTER
b New York, NY, Aug 5, 49. *Study:* Otis Art Inst, Los Angeles Co, BFA, 77, MFA, 79. *Work:* Los Angeles Co Mus Art, Los Angeles; San Francisco Mus Mod Art; Art Inst Chicago, Ill; Carnegie Art Inst, Pittsburg; Nat Mus Women in the Arts, Washington, DC. *Exhib:* Suzanne Caporael, Newport Harbor Art Mus, Newport, 84 & Santa Barbara Mus Art, Calif, 86; Summer 1985, Mus Contemp Art, Los Angeles, 85; Avant Garde In The Eighties, Los Angeles Co Art Mus, Los Angeles, 87; Presswork, Nat Mus Women in the Arts, Washington, DC, 91; Individual Realities, Sezon Mus Art, Amagasaki, Japan, 91. *Awards:* Nat Endowment Arts, 86. *Mailing Add:* c/o John Berggruen Gallery 228 Grant Ave 3rd fl San Francisco CA 94108

CAPORASO, PAT MARIE
ART DEALER
b Englewood, NJ, Nov 27, 52. *Study:* Pratt Inst, Brooklyn, NY, BFA, 70-74. *Pos:* Dir, Castelli Galleries, New York, NY, 77-91; Pvt art dealer & consult currently. *Mem:* Art Dealers Asn Am (adv panel, 83-); Art Appraisers Assn Am. *Media:* Drawings, Prints. *Specialty:* Contemporary art, late 1950s to the present; modern art. *Publ:* Print Collector's Newsletter, NY Times. *Mailing Add:* 682 Broadway No 5B New York NY 10012

CAPPS, KENNETH P
SCULPTOR
b Kansas City, Mo, April 10, 39. *Study:* Univ Calif, San Diego, BA, 73, MFA, 75. *Work:* Aldrich Mus Contemp Art, Ridgefield, Conn; Storm King Art Ctr, Mountainville, NY; Sculpture Park Alfred Schmela, Düsseldort, Ger; Oakland Mus, Calif; San Diego Mus Contemp Art, La Jolla, Calif. *Comn:* Konoids, outdoor sculpture, San Diego Unified Port Dist, Calif, 85; sculpture, Garden Grove, Calif, 87. *Exhib:* Sculpture in the Fields, Storm King Art Ctr, Mountainville, NY, 73; Public Sculpture Urban Environment, Oakland Mus, Calif, 74; The Minimal Tradition, Aldrich Mus, Ridgefield, Conn, 79; Sculpture in Calif 1975-80, San Diego Mus, Calif, 80; Constructed Metal, Univ Calif Santa Barbara, 84; A San Diego Exhib, San Diego Mus Contemp Art, La Jolla, Calif, 85 & Sculpture Arenas, Mandeville Gallery, Univ Calif, La Jolla, 87,; Metered Atmosphere, Brandstater Gallery, Loma Linda Univ, Calif, 87; Metophor of Function, San Diego State Univ, Calif, 90. *Awards:* Fel, drawing, 83, sculpture, 87, Nat Endowment Arts, 86; Pollock-Krasner Found, 86; Engelhard Found, Boston, Mass, 88. *Bibliog:* Tara Collins (auth), Kenneth Capps, Arts Mag, 9/76; David Lewinson (auth), Forty-two Emerging Artists, San Diego Mus Contemp Art, 85; Francis Colpitt (auth), Art in Am, 5/87; Robert Pincus (auth), On the cutting edge with steel, San Diego Union, 87; Robert & Andrea Perine (auths), San Diego Artist, Artra Publ Inc, 88. *Dealer:* Vera Engelhorn Gallery 591 Broadway New York NY. *Mailing Add:* 1175 Hoover St Carlsbad CA 92008

CARBAJAL G, ENRIQUE See Sebastian

CARBONE, DAVID
PAINTER, CRITIC
b New York, NY, Nov 29, 50. *Study:* Skowhegan Sch Painting & Sculpture, with Laderman, Noland, Diao, Marden, Blaustein, Morley, Beal, 70; Sch Mus Fine Arts, Tufts Univ, with Feininger, Cox, Schwartz & Rubenstein, BFA, 71; Brooklyn Col(fel), with Holty, Holtzman, Bontecou, Stone, Ernst, Pearlstein, Russell & Groell, MFA, 74. *Exhib:* Boston Now: Figuration, 82 & Currents, 85-86, Inst Contemp Art, Boston; one-person shows, Zoe Gallery, Boston & David Brown Gallery, Provincetown, 86, Mass; American Art Today: Narrative Art, Art Mus Fla Int Univ, 88; Landscape Painting, 1960-1990, Spoleto Festival, Gibbes Mus & Baylu Mus, 90; Boston Now: 10, Inst Contemp Art, Boston, 91; Contemp Am Paiting, Wake Forest Univ, 91; New American Figure Painting, Contemp Realist Gallery & Clemson Univ, 92; and others. *Teaching:* Instr painting, Brooklyn Col, 74-75; lectr art hist, Boston Mus Sch, 75- & instr grad sem, 76-81; vis artist painting & art hist, Knox Col, 83; vis artist painting, Montserrat Art Sch, 85; vis assoc prof, Pratt Inst, 87, Stanford Univ, 90 & Parsons Sch Design, 91. *Awards:* Ingram-Merrill Award, 85; Charlene Engelhard Award, 86. *Bibliog:* John Hollander (auth), The Italian Tradition in American Art in Landscape Painting 1960-1990, 90; Jed Perl (auth), Art in New York, an altenate view, Modern Painters, 91; Thomas Bolt (auth), New American Figure Painting (catalog), 92; and others. *Mem:* Col Art Asn. *Media:* Oil. *Publ:* Auth, James Weeks Retrospective, Arts Mag, 78; The Field Beyond Chassy, Antaeus, 80; Francis Bacon, 9/90, Carlo Maria Mariani, 1/91, Susana Jacobson, 3/91, Eugene Leroy, 4/91 & Jim Knutt, 12/91, Art Antiques; Alfred Russell, Modern Painters, fall 91 & Art Antiques, 92; and others. *Dealer:* Contemporary Realist Gallery 23 Grant Ave 6th fl San Francisco CA 94108. *Mailing Add:* 260 Mott St New York NY 10012

CARD, ROYDEN
PAINTER, PRINTMAKER
b Cardston, Alta, Can, Aug 2, 52; US citizen. *Study:* Brigham Young Univ, BFA, 76, MFA, 79. *Work:* Springville Mus Art, Utah; Mus Fine Arts, Salt Lake City; Latter Day Saint Church Mus Hist & Art, Salt Lake City; Smithsonian Inst Libr, Washington, DC; Ill St Univ. *Exhib:* Mountain West Biennial Paperworks, Nora Eccles Harrison Mus Art, Logan, 88; Miniature Print Biennial John Szoke Graphics; New York, 89; two-person, Woodworks, Ariz St Univ, Tempe, 89, Canyons, Courtyard Gallery, Salt Lake City, Utah, 89; N Mountain Invitational, Kimball Art Ctr, Parkcity, Utah, 92. *Teaching:* Instr printmaking, Brigham Young Univ, 80-90, Univ of Utah, 90-; inst painting & drawing, Utah Valley Community Col, Orem, Utah, 92. *Awards:* Purchase Awards, Utah Arts Coun, 85; Cash Award, Utah Arts Coun, 84; Utah Works on Paper Purchase Award, Utah Arts Coun, 87. *Media:* Relief, Acrylic. *Publ:* Illusr, Dialogue, A Journal of Mormon Thought, Dialogue Found, Vol 18, No 1, 85; auth, Dale L Morgans Utah, Red Butte Press, Univ Utah Marriott Libr, Salt Lake City, Utah, 87; Vern Swanson, Robert Olpin, Utah Art Peregrine/Smith Press, Layton, Utah. *Dealer:* Ellie Sontag 132 North E St Salt Lake City Utah 84114. *Mailing Add:* 559 South 1150 West Orem UT 84058

CARDILLO, RIMER ANGEL
PRINTMAKER, SCULPTOR
b Montevideo, Uruguay, Aug 17, 44. *Study:* Nat Sch Fine Arts, Uruguay, MFA, 68; Weissenssee Sch Art & Archit, Berlin, Ger, 70; Leipzig Sch Graphic Art, Leipzig, Ger, 71. *Work:* Prints Cabinet of Berlin, EGer; Chicago Art Inst, Ill; Mus Mod Art, New York; Cabinet Des Estampes, Bibliotheque Nationale, Paris, France; Nat Mus Visual Arts, Montevideo, Uruguay. *Comn:*

Suite of prints, HMK Fine Arts, New York, 82; print, Carton de Venezuela, Caracas, Venezuela, 84; print portfolio, 86 & crystal sculptures, 88, Cretum Art, Gliavagen, Sweden; suite of bronze and cast iron sculptors, Galeria Latina, Montevideo, Uruguay, 90. *Exhib:* Int Biennial Graphic Art, Sakaide, Japan, 88; Europe and the Third World, Messepalast, Vienna, Austria, 88; Ceremony of Memory, Ctr Contemp Art, Santa Fe, NMex, 89; solo exhibs, Altares Intar Gallery, New York, 89; Arte dell Uruguay nel Novecento, Inst Italo-Latin Am, Roma, Italy, 89; La Tierra: Visiones de America Latina, Mus Contemp Hispanic Arts, New York, Mus de Bellas Artes, Caracus, Venezuela, 90; Echoes of the Spirit, Atlanta Col Art Gallery, 90. *Pos:* Artist-in-residence, Southern Ill Univ, 79-81; mem bd adv, Intar Gallery, New York, 82-. *Teaching:* Prof painting, Nat Circle Fine Arts, 72-74; prof graphics, State Univ NY, Purchase, 88-90; instr graphics, Printmaking Workshop, New York, 88-. *Awards:* Fel, Adolf and Esther Gottleib Found, 88; Spec Proj Fel, NY State Coun Arts, 89; fel, Pollock-Krasner Found, 90. *Bibliog:* Victor Zamudio-Taylor (auth), Ceremony of Memory (contemp commentary), Sante Fe Ctr Contemp Arts, 88; Susana Torruella Leval (auth), Identity and Change, The Latin American Challenge, Hispanic Art Tour III, 88-89; Amalia Mesa-Bains (auth), The Archaelogicalo Aesthetic of Rimer Cardillo, Stratum, Elements & process, Intar Gallery, 89. *Media:* All media. *Dealer:* Galeria Latina Sarandi 671 Montevideo Uruguay; Intar Gallery 420 W 42nd St New York NY 10036. *Mailing Add:* 508 W 53rd St 3rd Floor New York NY 10019

CARDINAL, MARCELIN
PAINTER
b Gravelbourg, Sask, Apr 26, 20. *Study:* Self-taught. *Work:* Quebec Mus, Que; Can Coun, Ottawa; Hirshhorn Mus, Washington, DC; Musee d'Art Moderne, Dunkerque, France; Musee d'Art Contemporain, Montreal. *Comn:* Mural, Metro St Michel, Montreal, CTCUM, 86. *Exhib:* Guggenheim Mus, New York, 54 & 58; Albright-Knox Art Gallery, Buffalo, NY, 60; 5th Int Art Fair, Basel, Switz, 74; Galerie Gilles Corbeil, Montreal, 75; Musee du Quebec, 76; Musee d'Art Moderne, Dunkerque, France, 77; Musee d'Art Contemporain, Montreal, 77 & 78; Don Stewart Gallery, Toronto, 82; Galerie Daniel Beauschene, Montreal, Can, 85. *Awards:* Creation et Recherche, Minister Cult Affairs, Quebec, 72, 73, 75 & 78. *Bibliog:* Christian Allegre (auth), article, Vie des Arts, 72; Profile: Marcelin Cardinal, Art Mag, 3/79; Germain Lefebvre (auth), Marcelin Cardinal, Temps, Espace Et Continuite--Vie Des Arts, 82. *Mem:* Soc Prof Artists Quebec (vpres, 72-73); Can Conf Arts; Can Artists' Representation. *Media:* Oil, Acrylic. *Mailing Add:* 4897 Queen Mary Rd Montreal PQ H3W 1X1 Canada

CARDOSO, ANTHONY
PAINTER, SCULPTOR
b Tampa, Fla, Sept 13, 30. *Study:* Univ Tampa, BS(art); Art Inst Minn, BFA; Univ SFla, MA; Elysion Col, PhD. *Work:* Minn Mus Art, St Paul; Suncoast Credit Union Bldg, Tampa, Fla; Ringling Mus Archives Sarasota, Fla; and others. *Comn:* Sports Authority, Tampa Stadium Off, 71; sports theme paintings, Leto High Sch & Pierce High Sch, Tampa, 71; two murals, Sun Coast Credit Union Bldg, Tampa, Fla, 75; and many others. *Exhib:* Drawings USA, Minn Mus Art, St Paul, 71; Rotunda Gallery, London, Eng, 72; Brussells Int, Belg, 73; Ringling Mus Archives, Sarasota, Fla, 78; Accademia Italia Exhib, Terma, Italy, 80-85; Centro Studi E Ricerche Della Nazioni, Italy, 86; and many others. *Pos:* Supt art, Hillsborough City Schs, 85-89, studio dir, 89-91 & gallery dir, 91-92. *Awards:* Gold Medal Award & Victory Statue; Accademia Italia Exhib, 80-85; Palma D'Oro D'Europa, Accademia D'Europa, 89; and others. *Bibliog:* Bertrand Sorlot (auth), article in La Rev Mod, 71; articles, Tampa Tribune, 75-92 & Accad Italia, 80-86. *Mem:* Fla Arts Coun; Ringling Art Mus Archives; Fla League Arts; Accad Italia, Italy; Tampa Art Coun. *Media:* Oil, Acrylic. *Publ:* Contribr, La Rev Mod, 71 & 72; Accad Italia, 80-86; Tampa Tribune, 83-92; St Petersburg Times, 92. *Dealer:* Art Studio I & Gallery 3208 Nassau St Tampa FL 33607; El Prado Art Gallery 4318 El Prado Blvd Tampa FL 33629. *Mailing Add:* 3208 Nassau St Tampa FL 33607

CARDUCCI, VINCENT A
CRITIC, CONCEPTUAL ARTIST
b Detroit, Mich, June 30, 53. *Study:* Mich State Univ, BFA, 75. *Work:* Blue Cross/Blue Shield, Mich; Standard Fed Bank, Mich; Franklin Furnace Arch Inc, New York. *Exhib:* Urbanology: Artists View Urban Experience, Ctr for Creative Studies, Detroit, 89; Text/Image, Detroit Artists Market, 92. *Pos:* Regional ed (Mich), New Art Examiner, Chicago, Ill, 84-; contribr, Art Forum, New York, 89-92. *Bibliog:* Gerhard H Magnus (auth), Vincent A Carducci at Creative Arts Gallery, New Art Examiner, 86; Joy Hakanson Colby (auth), The Art of the Real, Detroit News, 92. *Mem:* Detroit Focus Gallery (bd dirs). *Res:* Esthetic and social issues in contemporary art. *Publ:* Ikons & ideologies: corporate identity and the age of self, 87, City Arts Quart; Detroit: art and transmission, New Art Examiner, 87; Bielat: Sculpture (exhib catalog), CADE Gallery, 88; Late-Modern Abstraction (exhib catalog), Detroit Artists Market, 90; Seasons of Glass, Am Craft, 92; and others. *Dealer:* Dais Annis 7402 Azalea Ct West Bloomfield MI 48033. *Mailing Add:* 1305 E Fifth St Royal Oak MI 48067

CAREY, ELLEN
PHOTOGRAPHER
b New York, NY, June 18, 52. *Study:* Art Students League, NY, 70; Kansas City Art Inst, BFA, 75; State Univ NY, Buffalo, MFA, 78. *Work:* Albright-Knox Art Gallery; Fogg Mus; Mus Fine Art, Houston; Patrick Lannan Found, Palm Beach, Fla; Chase Manhattan Bank, New York; Lightworks, Syracuse, NY; Dannheiser Found, New York; Picker Art Gallery, Colgate Univ, Hamilton, NY; Brooklyn Mus, NY; and others. *Comn:* 7 Light Boxes, Madison Sq Garden, Exec Hq, New York, 90-93. *Exhib:* One-person exhibs, Zone, Springfield, Mass, 86, Real Art Ways, Hartford, Conn, 86, Art City, New York, 86, Simon Cerigo, New York, 87, Int Ctr Photog, New York, 87, John Good Gallery, New York, 89, Schneider, Bluhn & Loeb Gallery, Chicago, Ill, 90, Aetna Inst Gallery, Hartford, Conn, 91, Jayne H Baum Gallery, 92, Nat Acad Scis (catalog), Washington, DC, 92; Appropriation & Syntax: Uses of Photography in Contemporary Art, Brooklyn Mus, NY, 88; Departures: Photography 1923-1990 (catalog), Canor Art Gallery, Holy Cross Univ, Worcester, Mass, 90; Selections 5 (catalog), Bibliotheque Nationale, Paris, France, 90; Summer Group Show, Jayne Baum Gallery, New York, 90; 5 Person Exhibition, Vrej Baghoomian Gallery, New York, 90; Colt 4, Wadsworth Atheneum (catalog), Hartford, Conn. *Pos:* Cur, Vrej Baghoomian, Gallery, New York. *Teaching:* Asst, State Univ NY Buffalo, 76-78, instr, 77, 78; vis artist, instr, Int Ctr Photog, New York, 81-83; vis artist, Rhode Island Sch Design, Providence, 83; vis artist, Columbia Col, Chicago, Ill, 90; asst prof photog, Hartford Art Sch, Univ Hartford, Conn, 85-. *Awards:* Polaroid 20 X 24, Polaroid Corp, Boston, Mass & New York, 84-90; New Works Grant, Mass Coun Arts, Boston, 86; Coffin Grant, Univ Hartford, Conn, 90. *Bibliog:* Andy Grundberg (auth), Abstraction returns to haunt photography, NY Times, 2/26/90; Andy Grundberg (auth), Departures: Photography 1923-1990 (catalog); Selections 5, Photokina, Cologne, WGer, 90; Dwight V Gast (auth), Photos as Art Keep Value, Photog & Video, Int Herald Tribune, 9/16/92. *Mem:* Whitney Mus Am Art, New York; New Mus, New York; Brooklyn Mus, NY; Wadsworth Atheneum, Hartford, Conn; Mus Mod Art, New York. *Dealer:* Arthur Solway Inc PO Box 467 Prince St Sta New York NY 10012; Texas Gallery 2012 Peden Ave Houston TX 77019. *Mailing Add:* c/o Pace-MacGill 11 E 57th St New York NY 10022

CARIOLA, ROBERT J
PAINTER, SCULPTOR
b Brooklyn, NY, Mar 24, 27. *Study:* Pratt Inst Art Sch; Pratt Graphic Ctr. *Work:* Fordham Univ; De Pauw Univ; La Salle Col; Hofstra Col; Topeka Pub Libr, Kans. *Comn:* Metal mural, altar & artifacts for St Gabriel's Church, Oakridge, NJ, 70-71; murals, Walker Mem Baptist Church, Bronx, NY, 75; two chapel murals, Mt St Mary Cemetery, Queens, NY, 77; four chapel murals, paintings, St John's Mausoleum, Queens, NY; mural painting, Luthern Church, Merrick, NY. *Exhib:* Boston Mus Printmakers Exhib, 62; Corcoran Gallery Art, Washington, DC, 63; Pa Acad Fine Arts, Philadelphia, 63; Vatican Pavilion, New York World's Fair, 64; Nat Acad Design, New York, 70; one-man show, Long Beach Mus, Long Beach, NY, 85. *Pos:* Art consult, Cath Youth Orgn, Rockville Centre, NY, 67-; art coordr, St John's Cloister, Queens, NY, 72-74. *Teaching:* Instr art, La Salle Acad, Oakdale, NY, 63-65, Catholic Youth Orgn Summer Wkshop & Huntington Twp Art League, 71. *Awards:* First Prize Painting, John Kennedy Cult Ctr Bankers Trust Award, 71; Grumbacher Cash Award, Silvermine Guild Artists, New Canaan, Conn, 76; Best in Show Award, Bayshore C of C Art Festival, 79; First Prize Painting & First Prize Sculpture, Long Beach Mus, 84; Grantee, New York S Coun Arts, Creating Murals in Sch, Wantagh NY Sch Dist & a Mural in Senior Citizen Ctr. *Bibliog:* A V LesMez (auth), Cariola, Long Island Rev Mag, 64; balt Carlson (auth), Vatican Pavilion gets Long Island exhibit, New York Times, 8/27/64; Jeanne Paris (auth), Cariola's works on exhibit at Merrick Gallery, Long Island Press, 5/28/67. *Mem:* Prof Artists Guild (pres, 69-70); hon mem Cath Fine Arts Soc. *Media:* Acrylic. *Publ:* Illusr, Writers's Ann, 58; Sign Mag, 71; contribr, Liturgical Arts Mag, 71-72; Equine Images, fall 91. *Dealer:* Landing Gallery Woodbury NY; Soundview Gallery Port Jefferson NY. *Mailing Add:* 1844 Gormley Ave Merrick NY 11566

CARL, JOAN
SCULPTOR, PAINTER
b Cleveland, Ohio, Mar 20, 26. *Study:* Cleveland Sch Art; Chicago Art Inst; Mills Col; with Dong Kingman; Bordman Robinson; Carl Morris; apprenticeship, Albert Wein; New Sch Art, with Arnold Mesches & Ted Gilien. *Work:* NC Mus Art, Raleigh; Int Cult Ctr for Youth, Jerusalem, Israel; The Temple Mus, Cleveland, Ohio; Thomas Bros Maps, Irvine Calif; Judah Magnes Mus, Berkeley; NE Ohio Mus, Cleveland, Ohio. *Comn:* Bas relief, Capitol Nat Bank, Cleveland, Ohio; sanctuary, Temple Adat Ari El, North Hollywood, Calif; modular relief, Repub Savings & Loan, Los Angeles, Calif; welded fountain & mosaic wall, Mount Sinai Mem Park, Hollywood, Calif; Bronze Family Group, Neuropsychiatric Ctr, Brea, Calif; aluminum pillars, Zinkal Ltd, Tel Aviv, Israel; and others. *Exhib:* Laguna Beach Art Mus, 69; Fresno Art Mus, 71; Linden-Kicklighter Gallery, Cleveland, Ohio, 71 & 73; Muskegon Community Col, 73; Chai (graphics), Nat & Int Traveling Show, 74-75; Brand Libr Gallery, Glendale, Calif, 83; Feldhyme Libr Gallery, San Bernardino, Calif, 87; and other group & solo shows. *Pos:* Faculty, Valley Ctr of Arts, Los Angeles, 59-64; lectr Title III Prog, San Bernardino, Inyo & Mono Co, Calif, 67-69. *Teaching:* Instr, Univ Judaism, 84-88. *Awards:* Honorable Mention, Nat Orange Show, San Bernardino, 58 & Calif State Fair, Sacramento, 70 & 72; Design Award, Ceramic Tile Inst, 75. *Bibliog:* Will H Tagress (auth), Valley sculptor believes in reflecting world around her, The News, 74. *Mem:* Founding mem Calif Confederation Arts; Artist Equity Asn, Inc (past pres). *Media:* Multimedia. *Publ:* Illusr, A World of Questions and Things, 50; Discovery Unlimited, A Guide to Raising a Creative Child, 81. *Mailing Add:* 4808 Mary Ellen Ave Sherman Oaks CA 91423

CARLBERG, NORMAN KENNETH
SCULPTOR, INSTRUCTOR
b Roseau, Minn, Nov 6, 28. *Study:* Brainerd Jr Col, Minn, 47-49; Minneapolis Sch Art, 50; Univ Ill, Urbana, 53-54; Yale Univ, BFA, 58, MFA, 61. *Work:* Addison Gallery Am Art, Phillips Acad, Andover, Mass; Whitney Mus Am Art, New York; Schenectady Mus, NY; Pa Acad Fine Arts, Philadelphia; Hirshhorn Mus, Washington, DC; Guggenheim Mus, New York, NY. *Comn:* Modular screen, Baltimore City Hosp, 65; four modular sculptures, Baltimore

City Schs, Northern Parkway Jr High, 70-73 & for PS 39, 73-75; modular column, Harry Seidler, Trade Group Complex, Canberra, Australia, 73-75 & Black Widow (steel modular), 75-; Winter Wind, Painted Steel 26' x 26', Riverside Ctr, Brisbrane, Australia; Uno Y Dos, Steel 12' x 12' x 10', Milford Mills, Baltimore, Md. *Exhib:* Recent Sculpture USA, Mus Mod Art, New York, 59; Structured Sculpture, Galerie Chalette, New York, 60; one-man shows, Cath Univ, Santiago, Chile, 60 & Baltimore Mus Art, 68; Whitney Ann, Whitney Mus Am Art, 62. *Teaching:* Instr sculpture, Cath Univ, Santiago, 60-61; sculptor in residence, Rinehart Sch Sculpture, Md Inst Col Art, Baltimore, 61- *Awards:* Fulbright Teaching Grant, Santiago, Chile, 60; Purchase Award, Ford Found, 62; Mus Prize, Baltimore Mus Art, 66. *Bibliog:* Josef Albers (auth), The Yale School-Structured Sculpture, Art in Am, 61; George Rickey (auth), Constructivism, George Braziller, 67; Peter Blake (auth), Architecture for the New World, the work of Harry Seidler, Wittenborn & Co, 73. *Media:* All. *Mailing Add:* 120 W Lanvale St Baltimore MD 21217

CARLILE, JANET (HILDEBRAND)
PRINTMAKER, EDUCATOR
b Denver, Colo, Apr 26, 42. *Study:* Cooper-Union, BFA, 66; Pratt Inst, MFA, 72. *Work:* Brooklyn Mus, NY; Conn Pub Libr Print Collection, New Canaan; Brooklyn Col Print Collection, NY; Printmaking Workshop Print Collection, New York; Neuberger Mus, Purchase, NY; Hirshorn Collection, Washington, DC. *Comn:* Sneffel's Range (drawing), NY Health & Hosp Corp, 84; ed of prints, Woodstock Sch Art, NY, 84. *Exhib:* Soc Am Graphic Artists Show; Assoc Am Artists Gallery, New York, 71-84; 50 Years American Printmaking, 74 & American Landscape Paintings, 76, Brooklyn Mus, NY; solo exhib, Blue Mountain Gallery, New York, 80; Alpine Artists Show, Ouray Colo Arts Asn, 84; Woodstock Artists, Woodstock Artists Asn, NY, 82. *Pos:* Adv, Printmaking Workshop, 68-86 & Woodstock Sch Art, 80-86; asst dir, Brooklyn Mus Art Sch, 73; pres, Ouray Arts Asn. *Teaching:* Instr printmaking, Sch Visual Arts, 70-72 & Brooklyn Mus Art Sch, 71-80; assoc prof, dir printmaking, Brooklyn Col, NY, 71- *Awards:* Hirshhorn Purchase Award, Soc Am Graphic Artists, 72; Creative Artists Pub Serv Drawing & Printmaking Award, 80. *Bibliog:* Kaplan (auth), American landsacpe painting, Am Artist Mag, 84. *Res:* 2-D media. *Mailing Add:* 12 Bellows Lane Woodstock NY 12498

CARLIN, ELECTRA MARSHALL
DEALER
b Ft Worth, Tex. *Study:* George Washington Univ, BA. *Pos:* Dir, Carlin Galleries. *Mem:* Ft Worth Art Asn; Dallas Mus Art Asn. *Specialty:* American artists and craftsmen; Eskimo prints and carvings. *Mailing Add:* 2401 Warner Rd Ft Worth TX 76110

CARLIN, JAMES
PAINTER
b Belfast, Ireland, June 25, 10; US citizen. *Study:* Belfast Munic Col, grad; London Art Schs; Newark Sch Fine & Indust Art; apprenticeship stained glass painting studios with German, English & Irish instrs. *Work:* Montclair Art Mus, NJ; also in pvt collections of Dore Schary, Los Angeles & many others. *Comn:* Design of stained glass windows (in collaboration), Londonderry Guild Hall & several prominent churches in Ireland, 26-28. *Exhib:* 12th Brooklyn Mus Int, NY, 41; Victory Exhib, Metrop Mus Art, New York, 42; Allied Artists Am Exhib, New York, 45; Portrait of America, Pepsi-Cola Co, New York, 45; Allied Artists Am Oils Exhib, Nat Acad Galleries, New York, 46. *Teaching:* Mem fac, Queen's Col; instr fine arts & head dept, Newark Sch Fine & Indust Art, 46- *Awards:* First Award, Watercolor, 77 & Purchase Award, 77, NJ State Show; First Award, Oil, Am Tel & Tel; First Prize in Oils, Audubon Artists. *Bibliog:* Norman Kent (auth), The Artist Speaks His Mind, 69 & Wendon Blake (auth), Acrylic Watercolor Painting, 71, Watson-Guptill; Michael Jenson (auth), Carlin and nature, Newark News, 71. *Mem:* Am Watercolor Soc; Philadelphia Watercolor Soc; NJ Watercolor Soc; Audubon Artists; Assoc Artists NJ; plus others. *Media:* Oil, Watercolor. *Dealer:* Radann Gallery 790 Madison Ave New York NY. *Mailing Add:* 73 Cathedral Ave Nutley NJ 07110

CARLOS, (JAMES) EDWARD
PAINTER, ADMINISTRATOR
b Kingsville, Pa, Nov 8, 37. *Study:* Indiana Univ Pa, BS(art educ), 59; Colo Col, with Enrique Montenegro, summer 60; Cath Univ Am, with Ken Noland, Alexander Giampietro & Bernard Leach, MFA, 63; Univ Hawaii, with Gustav Ecke; Ohio Univ, fel & PhD. *Exhib:* Mainstreams '72, Marietta, Ohio, 72; Italy, Sweden & Scotland, 75; one-man show, Edinburgh Int Festival, Scotland, 76. *Pos:* Lectr various art groups & schs; Dir gallery & mus, Univ of the South, Tenn, currently. *Teaching:* Vis prof art, Portland State Col, summer 65; asst prof art, Western Ill Univ, 65-66; instr art, Ohio Univ, 67-69; from assoc prof to prof, Univ of the South, 69- *Awards:* Int Snapshop, East-Kodak, 71. *Media:* Oil. *Mailing Add:* Dept of Fine Arts Univ of the South Sewanee TN 37375

CARLSON, CYNTHIA J
PAINTER, EDUCATOR
b Chicago, Ill, Apr 15, 42. *Study:* Chicago Art Inst, BFA; Pratt Inst, MFA. *Work:* Va Mus Fine Art, Richmond; Guggenheim Mus, New York; Philadelphia Mus of Art; Metrop Mus Art, New York; Allem Mem Art Mus, Oberlin, Ohio. *Comn:* Mural, comn by Md State Arts Coun, Baltimore-Washington Int Airport, 85. *Exhib:* Artpark, 77; one-woman exhibs, Allen Mem Art Mus, Oberlin, Ohio, 80; Lowe Art Mus, Coral Gables, Fla, 82; Milwaukee Art Mus, Wis, 82; Albright-Knox Art Gallery, Buffalo, NY, 85; Queens Mus, Flushing Meadow, NY, 90. *Teaching:* Assoc prof art, Philadelphia Col Art, 67-81, prof, 81-86; prof, Queens Col, City Univ New York, 86- *Awards:* Nat Endowment Arts Grant, 75, 78, 80, 87; PSC-CUNY Res Award, 88, 90. *Bibliog:* Patricia Stewart (auth), High decoration in low relief, Art in Am, 2/80; April Kingsley (auth), Cynthia Carlson: The subversive intent of the decorative impulse, Arts Mag, 3/80; Regan Upshaw (auth), Cynthia Carlson: Memento Mori, Art in Am, 7/86. *Mem:* Col Art Asn (bd dir). *Media:* Acrylic, Oil. *Mailing Add:* 139 W 19th St New York NY 10011

CARLSON, GEORGE ARTHUR
SCULPTOR, PAINTER
b Elmhurst, Ill, July 3, 40. *Study:* Am Acad Art; Chicago Art Inst; Univ Ariz. *Work:* Indianapolis Mus Fine Arts & Eiteljorg Mus Am Indian & Western Art; Outdoor Mus Art, Englewood, Colo; Genesee Mus, Rochester, NY; also pvt collections of Harrison Eiteljorg, Senator Barry Goldwater, Daniel M Galbreath, Otis Parchman, Jr, Dr William Petersen, Eugene Adkins, Fritz Scholder, Daren Writer, Bill Cosby, Robert Mehi, Dr Bane Travis, Dr David M Smith & Dr N Jill Warren; Western & Wildlife Mus, Jackson Hole, Wyo. *Comn:* Monument of prospector, Washington Park, Denver, 77; portrait bust, comn by Bill Cosby, 79 & Bill Harrach, 81; Navajo John (bronze sculpture), Foreign Diplomat Coun, Washington, DC, 81; Paul Robeson, comn by Bill Cosby. *Exhib:* Nat Acad Western Art, Okla, 74-80; retrospective, Indianapolis Mus Fine Arts, Ind, 79-80; one man shows, Smithsonian Inst, Nat Hist Mus, Washington, DC, 82, The Tarahumara, Indianapolis Mus Art, Stremmel Galleries, Reno, Nev, 82 O'Grady Galleries, Chicago, Ill, 83 & Gerald Peters Gallery, Santa Fe, NMex, 85 & 88; Artist Am Show, Denver, 81-89; Nat Sculpture Soc, New York, 86-87; Kyoto World Expos Hist Cities, Traveling Show, 87; Ky Derby Mus, Lexington, 88; and many others. *Awards:* Gold Medals, 74, 78, 80 & 85, Prix de West, Best of Show, 75, Silver Medals, 76 & 81, Nat Acad Western Art. *Bibliog:* Linda Humphrey, Fred Albert & Michael Jensen (coauths), American Design: The Northwest, Bantam, 89; Arthur Williams (auth), Sculpture: Technique-Form-Content, Davis Publs Inc, 89; articles in numerous mags, including Art News, 9/89 & Ladies Home J, 12/89. *Mem:* Nat Acad Western Art; Nat Sculpture Soc. *Media:* Bronze; Mixed. *Publ:* Auth, The Tarahumara, pvt publ, 77. *Dealer:* Peters Corp 439 Camino del Monte Sol Santa Fe NM 87501. *Mailing Add:* c/o Peters Corp 439 Camino Del Monte Sol PO Box 908 Santa Fe NM 87504-0908

CARLSON, JANE C
PAINTER
b Boston, Mass, Sept 1, 28. *Study:* Art Students League; Mass Col Art; study with Charles Kinghan & Robert Davis. *Exhib:* Allied Artists Am, 69-83; Am Artists Prof League, 70-83; Am Watercolor Soc, Nat Acad Design, New York, 71-83; Audubon Artists, 73-83; Art for the Parks, Nat Exhib, 87. *Teaching:* Watercolor demonstrations. *Awards:* Gold Medals, Am Artists Prof League, 79 & 81; High Winds Medal, Am Watercolor Soc, 83 & 85. *Mem:* Am Watercolor Soc; Am Artists Prof League; Audubon Artists; Allied Artists Am; Hudson Valley Art Asn; Knickerbocker Artists. *Media:* Oil, Watercolor. *Dealer:* The Art Studio Pondfield Rd Bronxville NY 10708; The Edgartown Gallery Martha's Vinyard Mass. *Mailing Add:* c/o Edgartown Art Gallery S Summer St Edgartown MA 02539

CARLSON, LANCE R
CRITIC, EDITOR
b Los Angeles, Calif, Feb 5, 50. *Study:* Calif State Univ, Fullerton, BA, 71, MA, 80: Calif State Univ, Los Angeles, MA, 73. *Work:* San Francisco Mus Mod Art. *Exhib:* Solo exhib, B C Space Gallery, Laguna Beach, Calif, 85; The Theatre as Gesture, Los Angeles Ctr Photog Studies, 83; Anxious Interiors, Laguna Beach Mus Art, Calif, 84; The Implied Performance, San Francisco Mus Mod Art, 84; Facets of the Permanent Collection, San Francisco Mus Mod Art, 85; Randolph Street Gallery, Chicago, Ill, 87; DIA Art Found, New York, 88; The Photography of Invention, Smithsonian Inst, 89; and others. *Pos:* Proj dir, Los Angeles Photog Studies, 79-80; ed, Southern Calif, Artweek, 90. *Teaching:* Dean, arts & scis & prof art hist/photog, Rio Hondo Col, Whittier Col, Calif, 73-; vis artist, Sch Art Inst Chicago, 86-87; instr, Calif State Univ, 85. *Awards:* Nat Endowment Arts Grant, 82 & 88. *Bibliog:* Barbara De Genevieve (auth), Sex as subject, Exposure, 20:4, 82; Mark Johnstone (auth), Still photographs speak, Catskill Ctr Photog Quart, 86; Christopher Knight (auth), Experiencing Life Through Art's Filter, LA Herald-Examiner, 8/19/88. *Mem:* Los Angeles Ctr Photog Studies (bd mem, 77-83). *Publ:* Auth, A formal report, Afterimage, 83; Manipulating prints, 83, The humanism of the disabled, 84 & Bodies in water, 85, Artweek, Art Issues, 90, High Performance, 90; articles in Art Issues & High Performance, 90. *Mailing Add:* PO Box 830 Whittier CA 90608-0830

CARLSON, MARY
SCULPTOR
b Stevens Point, Wis, Mar 21, 51. *Study:* Sch Visual Arts, BFA, 73. *Work:* Chase Manhattan Bank, New York. *Exhib:* Solo exhibs, Curt Marcus Gallery, New York, 86, Michael Klein Inc, New York, 87 & Max Protetch Gallery, New York, 92; Desired Path, White Plains, NY, 88; Psychological Abstraction, Deste Found, Athens, Greece, 89; Something Strange, White Columns, New York, 90; Blood Remembering, Newhouse Gallery, Snug Harbor, Staten Island, New York, 90; Death and Desire, Tom Cugliani Gallery, New York, 90; The Interrupted Life, New Mus, New York, 91. *Bibliog:* William Zimmer (auth), Everyday Expectations With a Twist, NY Times, 12/23/90; Gretchen Faust (auth), New York in Review, Arts Mag, 2/91; Holland Cotter (auth), Art in Review, NY Times, 4/10/92. *Mailing Add:* 17 White St New York NY 10013

CARLSON, ROBERT MICHAEL
GLASS BLOWER, PAINTER
b Brooklyn, NY, Nov 19, 52. *Study:* City Col NY, 70-73; Pilchuck Sch, 81-82. *Work:* Corning Mus Glass, NY; Tucson Mus Art; Glasmuseum, Frauenau, Ger; Glasmuseum, Ebeltoft, Denmark; Davis, Wright, Tremain, Seattle. *Exhib:* Design Visions-International Directions, Art Gallery West Australia, Perth, 92; Clearly Art/Pilchuck Connection, Whatcom Co Mus, Bellingham, Wash, 92; Interglas Symposium Exhib, Crystalex, Novy Bor, Czech, 91; The Frozen Moment, Bellvue Art Mus, Wash, 91; Glass Inventions/Silica Dreams, Mus Craft & Folk Art, San Francisco, 89; and others. *Teaching:* Vis artist, glass art, Calif Col Arts & Crafts, Oakland, 89; fac, glass art, Pilchuk Sch, Stanwood, Wash, 89-90 & 92. *Awards:* Award of Merit, Ariz Bienniel, Tucson Mus Art, 86; Jurois Award, 5th Ann Capitol Invitational, The Glass Gallery, 86; Nat Endowment Arts, Fel, 90. *Bibliog:* Lisa Hammel (auth), 3 in crafts show, color, joy, NY Times, 89; Dick Weiss (auth), Robert Carlson, Class Work Mag, 90; Bonnie Miller (auth), Chronical Books, 91. *Mem:* Glass Art Soc (bd dirs 92-). *Media:* Multimedia. *Mailing Add:* PO Box 11590 Bainbridge Island WA 98110

CARLSON, WILLIAM D
SCULPTOR, GLASS BLOWER
b Dover, Ohio, Feb 18, 50. *Study:* Art Students League, 70; Cleveland Inst Art, BFA, 73; State Univ NY Col, Alfred, MFA, 76. *Work:* Metrop Mus Art, New York; Kyoto Mus Mod Art, Japan; Hokkaido Mus Mod Art, Sapporo, Japan; Cleveland Mus Art, Ohio; Los Angeles Cty Mus, Calif. *Comn:* Glass sculpture, Chicago Bd Options Exchange, 83-84; British Petroleum, Cleveland, Ohio, 89. *Exhib:* Poetry of the Physical, Am Craft Mus, New York, 89; New Forms in Glass, Evansville Mus Arts & Science, Ind, 89; Means to Ends: Process and Its Traces in Recent Sculpture, Rockland Ctr Arts, NJ, 90; Masterpieces of American Glass, Steuben Glass, Moscow, USSR, 90; Crafts Today USA, Am Crafts Coun, Int Traveling Exhib, Mus fur Kunsthandwerk, Frankfurt, WGer, Zacheta Gallery, Warsaw, Poland, Musee Des Arts Decoratifs, Lausanne, Switz, Mus Applied Arts, Moscow, USSR, 90; 30th Japan Contemp Arts & Crafts 1991, Metrop Mus, Tokyo; World Glass Now '91, Traveling Exhib (Japan); Craft Today, USA, Am Crafts Coun Int Traveling Exhib (Belg, Czech, Ger, Greece, Turkey), 91-92; Visions in International Glass, Traveling Exhib (Mexico), 92; L'Art Contemporain du Verde, Galerie Katia Granoff, Paris, 92. *Teaching:* Prof art, head crafts & undergraduate sculpture, Univ Ill, Champaign, 76-; instr glass, Penland Sch Crafts, 82 & Pilchuck Glass Ctr, 83; Haystack Mt Sch Art, Deer Isle, Maine & Appalachian Sch Crafts, Smithville, Tenn. *Awards:* Nat Endowment Arts Craftmen's Fel, 82; Ill Arts Coun Artist Fel, 85; Univ scholar, Univ Ill, 85. *Bibliog:* Edwin Ziegfield (auth), Art Today, Holt, Rinehart and Winston, 85; Chicago Board of Options Exchange, William Carlson Commission, Am Crafts, 3/85; Craft Today USA, Am Crafts Mus, NY, Philip Morris Int, Inc & US Info Agency. *Mem:* Glass Art Soc (bd dirs, 83 & 87, pres, 86-87); Creative Glass Ctr Am, NJ (bd dirs, 85-90); Renwick Gallery, Smithsonian Inst, Washington, DC (hon bd dirs, 86-90). *Media:* Glass. *Dealer:* Betsy Rosenfield Gallery 212 W Superior Chicago IL 60610; Heller Gallery 71 Greene St New Yory NY 10012. *Mailing Add:* 603 W Michigan Urbana IL 61801

CARLSTROM, LUCINDA
PAINTER, PRINTMAKER
b Jamestown, NY, Sept 8, 50. *Study:* Ringling Sch Art, Sarasota, Fla, 68-70; Atlanta Col Art, Ga, BFA, 74; Inst Allende, San Miguel, Mex, 73. *Work:* Contemp Hotel, Walt Disney World, Lake Buena Vista, Fla; DeKalb Jr Col, McClatchey, Cody Rodgers & Regenstein, Atlanta, Ga; Barnett Banks, Barnett Holding Co, Jacksonville, Fla; Eldorado Hosp, Tucson. *Exhib:* Walt Disney World, Lake Buena Vista, Fla, 74-79; New Orleans Mus Art, 75; US Info Agency Traveling Exhib, 76-78; High Mus Art Gallery, Atlanta, Ga, 79- *Awards:* Best Graphics, Space Coast Arts Festival, Cocoa Beach, Fla, 75; Best Watercolor, Southeastern Arts & Crafts Festival, Macon, Ga, 76; Second Award, Art Festival Atlanta, 79. *Mem:* Artists Equity Asn; Univ Mich Artists Guild; Ga Watercolor Soc. *Media:* Watercolor; Etching. *Mailing Add:* 1075 Standard Dr NE Atlanta GA 30319

CARMEAN, E A, JR
HISTORIAN, CURATOR
b Springfield, Ill, Jan 25, 45. *Study:* MacMurray Col, BA(hist art), hon PhD, 81; Univ Ill, with Allen Weller. *Collections Arranged:* The Collages of Robert Motherwell (with catalog); Friedel Dzubas (with catalog); Modernist Art 1960-1970 (with catalog); Morris Louis: Major Themes & Variations (with catalog); The Subjects of the Artist (with catalog); Mondrian: The Diamond Compositions (with catalog); Morton G Neumann Collection (with catalog); Picasso: The Saltimbanques (with catalog); Kadinsky: The Improvisations. *Pos:* Cur 20th century art, Mus Fine Arts, Houston, 71-74; cur 20th century art, Nat Gallery Art, 74-84; dir, Ft Worth Art Mus, Tex, 84-91. *Teaching:* Lectr art hist, Univ Ill, Urbana, 67-69; vis prof 20th century art, Rice Univ, 73-74; vis prof 20th century art, George Washington Univ, 75-76. *Awards:* Guggenheim Found Fel, 78-79. *Mem:* Col Art Asn; Am Asn Mus. *Res:* Picasso & cubism; abstract expressionism; modern sculpture. *Publ:* Auth, Braque the papier colles, 82; David Smith, 82; Je suis le cahier:The sketchbooks of Picasso, 87; Nancy Graves, 87; Helen Frankenthaler - A painting retrospective, 89. *Mailing Add:* 241 N El Camino San Mateo CA 94401

CARMICHAEL, DONALD RAY
PAINTER
b Elnora, Ind, Dec 26, 22. *Study:* Herron Art Inst, BFA, 51; Univ Tenn, Knoxville, MFA, 75; also with John Taylor & David Freidenthal, New York & Edwin Fulwider, Ford Times & Garo Antreasian, NMex. *Work:* Tenn State Mus, Nashville, Tenn; Jackson-Madison Co Pub Libr, Jackson, Tenn; Casey Jones Railroad Mus, Jackson, Tenn; Tarble Arts Ctr, Charleston, Ill; Bristol Art Ctr, Tenn. *Comn:* Life size statue, Carl Smith Agency, Jackson, 67; official seal (engraving), Jackson State Community Col, 67; five panel mural, History of Jackson, McDonalds, Inc, 68. *Exhib:* Three-man show, Lynn Kottler Galleries, New York, 71; 23rd Grand Prix Int, Deauville, France & Palace of Fine Arts, Rome, Italy, 72; Watercolor USA, Springfield Art Mus, 74-75; Southeastern Collection of Contemporary Art, Mich Artrain Tour, 74; and others. *Collections Arranged:* Lawrence Calcagno Retrospective, 82-83; Walter Sorge Retrospective, 83-84; Med Illustr, CIBA Collection, Frank Netter, Md, 84; Watercolor Ill, Fourth and Fifth Biennial, 83-85. *Pos:* Pres, Jackson Art Asn, 65-67; pres, Jackson Arts Coun, 68-70; chmn visual arts adv panel, Tenn Arts Comn, 72-75, field rep, 75-78; dir, Tarble Arts Ctr, Eastern Ill Univ, Charleston, 78-85, emer dir, 85-; bd mem, Cent Ill Arts Consortium, 78-84; mem rev comt, Art in Archit, Capital Develop Bd, Ill, 79-82; dir exhib, Venice Art Ctr, FL, 87. *Teaching:* Instr painting, Shelbyville Art League, Ind, 51-55; instr art appreciation, Union Univ, Tenn, 64-66, instr drawing, painting & composition, 66-74; grad asst, Univ Tenn, Knoxville, 74-75; instr evening classes, Dyersburg State Community Col, Tenn, 76-77; instr art theory, Eastern Ill Univ, Charleston, 80-84; instr watercolor, Venice Art Center, FL, 87. *Awards:* Purchase Award, Enjay Chem Nat, 66; Tennessee Painting Today Purchase Award, Tenn Arts Comn, 67; Tennessee Watercolor Soc Purchase Award, 75. *Bibliog:* Newman Jones (auth), Art leagues in small communities, Delta Rev, 68; William T Alderson (auth), Tennessee lives, Historical Rec Asn, 71; article, La Rev Mod, 72. *Mem:* Artists Equity Asn; Tenn Col Arts Coun; Tenn Watercolorist (dir & mem chmn, 71-); Southern Watercolor Soc; co-founder Tenn Watercolor Soc (pres, 74). *Media:* Watercolor, Oil. *Publ:* Contribr, Edward Betts, auth, Creative Seascape Painting, 81. *Dealer:* Tarble Arts Ctr Eastern Ill Univ Charleston IL 61920. *Mailing Add:* 860 Stewart Ave Englewood FL 33533

CARMICHAEL, JAE
PAINTER, SCULPTOR
b Los Angeles, Calif, Aug 22, 25. *Study:* Mills Col, 42-44; Univ Southern Calif, BFA, 51, PhD(cinematography & art hist), 72; Claremont Grad Sch, MFA, 55. *Work:* Long Beach Mus Art; Oakland Mus; Frye Mus; Tate Gallery, London; San Francisco Mus Mod Art; plus pvt collections. *Comn:* Arbor of Light, Stained Glass Ceiling, Mountain View Mausoleum, Altadena, Calif, 88. *Exhib:* Titanium One, Laguna Beach Art Mus, 71; Long Beach Mus & Palm Springs Mus, 79, 81 & 83; Edward-Dean Mus, 83; Mills Col Invitational, 88; and many others. *Pos:* dir, Wooden Horse Gallery, Laguna Beach, 62-66; dir, Pacificulture-Asia Mus, Pasadena, 72-75. *Teaching:* Art instr, Pasadena Art Mus, 53-60, Palos Verdes Community Art Asn, 66-88; instr drawing & painting, Pasadena Sch Fine Arts, 54-58 & 66-, dir, 70-; lectr art hist & cinema, Pasadena City Col, 68-71; lectr art hist & film, Otis Art Inst, Los Angeles, 70-75; adj prof cinema, Univ Southern Calif, 77- *Awards:* First Award Sculpture, 73, Pasadena Soc Artists; Gold Crown Award Artist Yr, Pasadena Arts Coun, 78. *Bibliog:* Southern California 100, Laguna Beach Mus, 77; Gordon T McClelland & Jay T Last (coauths), The California Style, California Watercolor Artists 1925-1955, 85; Robert Perine (auth), The California Romantics, 86. *Mem:* Nat Watercolor Soc (pres, 76 & 80); Pasadena Soc Artists (mem bd, 58-60, 62 & 63, pres, 70-72); Los Angeles Art Asn (mem bd, 65-); Los Angeles Art Asn (mem bd, 65-); Nat Arts Club, New York (60-); Am Watercolor Soc, (55-). *Publ:* Auth, The Rug Culture, 72 & auth, A Joint Exhibition, Los Angeles Printmaking Society and the Korean Printmaking Society, 73, Pacific-Asia Mus; auth, NWS the first half-century, Nat Watercolor Soc, 75; dir, Heritage of Hope (film), 76; auth, Lighting and art direction, Am Cinematographers Mag, 11/82. *Mailing Add:* Los Angeles Art Assoc 825 N La Cienga Blvd Los Angeles CA 90069

CARNWATH, SQUEAK
PAINTER
b Abington, Pa, May 24, 47. *Study:* Goddard Col, 69-70; Calif Col Arts & Crafts, MFA, 77. *Work:* Oakland Mus; San Francisco Mus Mod Art. *Exhib:* Oakland Mus, 74; Sculpture Now, California Clay Routes, San Francisco Mus Art, 79; one-person exhibs, San Francisco Mus Art, 80, Fuller-Goldeen Gallery, San Francisco, 82, Brentwood Gallery, St Louis, 83 & Palo Alto Cult Ctr, Calif, 83. *Teaching:* Guest instr studio art, Univ Calif, Berkeley, 82-83; prof, Univ Calif, Davis, 84- *Awards:* Nat Endowment Arts Grant, 80; Soc Encouragement Contemp Art Award, 80; Alice Baber Art Award, 90; John Berggruen Gallery Duerassi Artists Residence Fel, 92. *Bibliog:* S Winn (auth), Ramps & ghosts, Artnews, 11/80; S Boettger (auth), From the sunnyside, Art in Am, 1/83 & Impolite figure, Artforum, 10/83. *Media:* Oil. *Dealer:* Dorothy Goldeen Gallery santa Monica CA. *Mailing Add:* John Berggruen Gallery 228 Grant Ave San Francisco CA 94108

CARO, FRANCIS
DEALER
b New York, NY, Aug 22, 38. *Pos:* Dir, Frank Caro Gallery, New York, currently. *Specialty:* Antique arts of China, India and Southeast Asia. *Mailing Add:* c/o Frank Caro Gallery 41 E 57th St New York NY 10022

CARPENTER, ARTHUR ESPENET See Espenet,

CARPENTER, DENNIS WILKINSON (BONES)
PHOTOGRAPHER, EDUCATOR
b Meridian, Miss, June 7, 47. *Study:* Univ Ky, BArch, 72; Univ Fla, MFA, 79. *Work:* Jacksonville Art Mus, Fla; Polaroid Corp, Clarence Kennedy Gallery, Cambridge, Mass; Polaroid Int, Amsterdam, Neth; St Petersburg Mus Fine Art, Fla; Univ Fla, Gainesville. *Exhib:* Graphics Invitational, Mint

Mus, 80; solo exhib, Univ Denver, 82, Light Factory, Charlotte, NC, 83, Webster Univ, St Louis, 83 & Photogenesis Gallery, Albuquerque, 83; Photographers Choose Photographers, Name Gallery, Chicago, 83. *Pos:* 606-257-9000, Home: 606-254-5146. *Teaching:* Assoc prof photog, Univ Ky, Lexington, 73-; grad teaching asst, Univ Fla, Gainesville, 77-79; dir photog, Penland Sch Crafts, NC, 83. *Awards:* Best of Show, The Landscape, Crealde Sch Art, 81 & Each Image Unique, Catskill Ctr Photog, 81; Nat Endowment Arts Fel, 83. *Mem:* Soc Photog Educ; Col Art Asn; Friends Photog. *Media:* Mixed. *Mailing Add:* 403 Pennsylvania Ct Lexington KY 40508

CARPENTER, EARL L
PAINTER
b Long Beach, Calif, Nov 13, 31. *Study:* Chouinard Art Sch, 1 yr; Art Ctr Col Design, 4 yrs. *Work:* Mus Northern Ariz, Flagstaff; Valley Nat Bank Gallery Western Art, Valley Ctr, Phoenix; also in pvt collections of Olaf Weighorst, Sen Barry Goldwater, Walter Bimson, John P Sands, George Getz Jr & Scott L Libby. *Exhib:* Retrospective, Wyo State Arch & Hist Dept, 74; Gallery Western Art, Valley Nat Bank, Scottsdale, Ariz, 75; Grand Canyon Art, Northern Ariz Univ, Flagstaff, 78; Artist of the Rockies 10th Anniversary Exhib, Pueblo, Colo, 83; Nat Park Acad Art, Wyo, 87; Gov's Invitational, Cheyenne,. *Pos:* Tech illusr, Advert Art (Agency), 65- *Teaching:* Stable Art Gallery, Scottsdale, Ariz. *Awards:* Stacey Scholar, 67 & 69. *Mem:* Western Art Asn. *Media:* Oil, Gouache. *Publ:* Auth, My painting technique, Am Artist Mag, 68; illusr, paintings in Ariz Highways Mag, Phoenix, 73, 74 & 87; article, Southwest Art Mag, 1/81 & US Mag, 9/88; Art of the West, 4-5/90 & 11-12/92. *Dealer:* Legacy Art Gallery Scottsdale AZ 85251. *Mailing Add:* Earl Carpenter Studio Pinewood Munds Park AZ 86017

CARPENTER, GILBERT FREDERICK (BERT)
PAINTER, EDUCATOR
b Billings, Mont, July 14, 20. *Study:* Stanford Univ, AB; Chouinard Art Inst; Ecole Beaux Arts, Paris, France; Columbia Univ. *Work:* Honolulu Acad Art; Sheldon Mem Mus, Lincoln, Nebr; Weatherspoon Gallery, Univ NC, Greensboro; Kresge Found, Mich State Univ; Univ Mass, Amherst. *Comn:* 3 paintings, Fayetteville Pub Libr, NC, 86. *Exhib:* Honolulu Acad Art, 51 & 59-61; one-man shows, Calif Palace Legion Honor, 52, Joslyn Mus, Omaha, Nebr, 52 & 54, A M Sachs Gallery, 72, 77 & 80-83, Zabriskie Gallery, 70, 72 & 74, Joy Tash Gallery, Scottsdale, Ariz & Artists Space Gallery, New York, 85; Gruene Baum Gallery, New York, 88. *Pos:* Dir, Weatherspoon Gallery, 74-89. *Teaching:* Instr art, Columbia Univ, 54-60; head dept art, Univ Hawaii, 60-64; prof art & head dept, Univ NC, Greensboro, 64-74; prof art, Weatherspoon Gallery, 74-89. *Publ:* Art critic, Honolulu Star Bull, 61-62. *Dealer:* Joy Tash Gallery Scottsdale AZ. *Mailing Add:* 2505 W Market St Greensboro NC 27403

CARPENTER, LINDA BUCK
SCULPTOR, ASSEMBLAGE ARTIST
b Los Angeles, Calif, July 22, 52. *Study:* Immaculate Heart Col, Los Angeles, 71-72; Calif State Univ, Sacramento, BA, 80, MA, 87. *Work:* Sculpture Grebitus and Son Jewelers. *Comn:* Art in Pub Places Prog, Sacramento Co, 89. *Exhib:* Northern Calif Artists Competition, Open Ring Gallery, Sacramento, 81; Americans in Glass, traveling nationally and internationally, 84-86; Artists Working in Glass, Richard L Nelson Gallery, Davis, Calif, 84; Int Exhib Glass Craft, Kanazawa, Japan, 88 & 90. *Bibliog:* Karen Wilson (dir), Glass Artists, Arts Alive Program, KVIE-TV, Pub Broadcasting, 83; Suzanne Foley (auth), The measure of success, Am Craft, 84; Ellen Schlesinger (auth), Glass as texture, line, color, Sacramento Bee, 1/27/85; Victoria Dalkey (auth), Elegant Expressionism, Sacramento Bee, 5/31/87. *Media:* Flat Glass. *Dealer:* Artists Contemporary Gallery 542 Downtown Plaza Sacramento CA 95814. *Mailing Add:* c/o Artists Contemporary Gallery Hyatt Regency Plaza 1200 K St Mall No 9 Sacramento CA 95814

CARR, CAROLYN K
CURATOR, HISTORIAN
b Providence, RI, Feb 23, 39. *Study:* Smith Col, BA, 61; Oberlin Col, MA, 65; Case-Western Reserve Univ, PhD, 78. *Collections Arranged:* Ohio: A Photographic Portrait (auth, catalog), 80, The Image in American Painting and Sculpture 1950-1980 (auth, catalog), 82, Akron Art Mus, Ohio; Gaston Lachaise: Portrait Sculpture (auth, catalog), Nat Portrait Gallery, Washington, DC, 85; Then and Now: American Portraits of the Past Century (auth, catalog), Nat Portrait Gallery, 88. *Pos:* Art critic, Akron Beacon J, Ohio, 68-74; chief cur, Akron Art Mus, Ohio, 78-83; deputy dir, Nat Portrait Gallery, Washington, DC, 84- *Teaching:* Instr art hist, Kent State Univ, 63-65. *Mem:* Col Art Asn; Am Asn Mus. *Res:* Post 1945 American art; late ninteenth century American Art; photography. *Publ:* Auth, Ohio: A Photographic Portrait 1935-1941, Kent State Univ Press, 79; O Winston Link: Ghost Trains, Chrysler Mus, Norfolk, Va, 83; coauth, Gaston Lachaide: Portrait Sculpture, Smithsonian Inst Press, 85. *Mailing Add:* 4943 Hillbrook Lane NW Washington DC 20016

CARR, SALLY SWAN
SCULPTOR
b Minong, Wis. *Study:* New York Univ; advan sculpture, Phoenix Sch Design; life sketch, Clay Club; also with John Hovannes, Frederick Allen Williams & wax tech with Paul Manship; Art Students League. *Work:* Am Numismatic Soc, New York; Basketball Hall Fame, Springfield, Mass; Cayuga Mus Art & Hist, Auburn, NY; Florentine Craftsmen, New York. *Comn:* Great Seal of US (woodcarving), comn by M Ketchum, Jr, US Embassy, Rabat, Morocco, 59; Lion of St Marks (bronze relief), Marco Polo Club, Waldorf Astoria Hotel, New York, 60; Cardinal Virtues (cararra marble reliefs), Riverside Mem Park, St Joseph, Mich, 65; Dr A Schweitzer (bust), Town Hall, Kaysersburg & Gunsbach, France, 70; and others. *Exhib:* Nat Acad Design, Allied Artists, 69-70; Acad Artists, Springfield Mus Art, Mass, 70; Burr Artist, Metrop Mus Art, 77, Caravan Galleries, New York, 77; Goldboro Mus, NC, 77; Spec Award Winners Show, Nat Arts Club, New York, 78; Three Bronze Portraits, Basketball Hall of Fame, Springfield, Mass, 86; and others. *Awards:* A H Huntington First Prize Trophy, Catharine Lorillard Wolfe Art Club, 70, hon mem, 87; Founders Prize & Plaque, Pen & Brush Club, New York, 70 & Bronze Medal, 79; and others. *Mem:* Burr Artists (second vpres, 69-72); Catharine Lorillard Wolfe Art Club (first vpres, 66-71, pres, 71-74); Composers, Auth & Artists Am (dir & historian, 69-72); hon mem Smithsonian; assoc mem Nat Arts Club; Nat League Am Pen Women, Inc. *Media:* Stone, Wood. *Mailing Add:* 530 E 23rd St Apt 9A New York NY 10010

CARRERO, JAIME
PAINTER, EDUCATOR
b Mayaguez, PR, June 16, 31. *Study:* Polytechnic Inst, Columbia Univ, BA(art hist); Pratt Inst, MS. *Work:* Ponce Mus, PR; Mus Inst PR Art & Univ PR, San Juan; Inter-Am Univ Collection, San German. *Comn:* Illus for bk, Cuentos Puertorriquenos, 73. *Exhib:* Univ PR, San Juan, 60 & 65; Inst Cult PR, San Juan, 62; Acad Fine Arts, Calcutta, India, 65; Ateneo Puertorriqueno, San Juan, 66; Ponce Mus, 86; Springfield Mus, Mass, 90. *Teaching:* Prof painting, drawing & art hist, Inter-Am Univ, 57-; prof art hist, Rum, Mayaguez, PR, 74-75. *Bibliog:* Josemilio Gonzalez (auth), Jaime Carrero, Pintor, El Mundo, 60; Drawings by Jaime Carrero, El Corno Emplumado, Mex, Nos 26, 28 & 30, 64-66; Drawings: The San Juan Star. *Media:* Acrylic, Watercolor. *Mailing Add:* A-26 Urb Interamericana San German PR 00753

CARR-HARRIS, IAN REDFORD
SCULPTOR, CRITIC
b Victoria, BC, Can, Aug 12, 41. *Study:* Queen's Univ, Kingston, Ont, BA(hon), 63; Univ Toronto, Ont, BLS, 64; Ont Col Art, Toronto, AOCA, 71. *Work:* Nat Gallery Can, Ottawa; Can Coun Art Bank, Ottawa; Art Gallery Ont, Toronto. *Exhib:* Contemp Ont Art, Art Gallery Ont, 74; 9th Biennale of Paris, Mus d'Art Mod, Paris, 75; Another Dimension, Nat Gallery Can, 77; Kanadische Kunstler, Kunsthalle, Basle, 78; Confrontations, Vancouver Art Gallery, 79; Int Sculpture Conf, Washington, DC, 80; Fiction, Art Gallery Ont, 82; solo exhib, Dalhousie Art Gallery, Halifax, 82, 49th Parallel Gallery, 83 & Art Gallery Ont, 88; Venice Biennale, 84; Aurora Borealis, Montreal, 85; Luminous Sites, Vancouver, 86; Documenta 8, Kassel, 87; Sydney Biennale, 90. *Pos:* Chief librn, Ont Col Art, Toronto, 71-88, chmn, experimental arts, 88-90, chmn sculpture prog, 92- *Teaching:* Instr contemp art, Ont Col Art, Toronto, 76- *Awards:* Can Coun Proj Cost Grant, 72, 75 & 82; Can Coun Art Grant B, 76 & 80; Grant A, 90. *Bibliog:* P McGrath (auth), Ian Carr-Harris at Carmens, Vanguard, summer 81; D Nemiroff (auth), Ian Carr-Harris: A Demonstration, Parachute, winter 81; P Monk (auth), Ian Carr-Harris 1971-1977, Art Gallery Ont, 88. *Mem:* Univ Art Asn Can; Royal Can Acad Arts. *Media:* Text, Light. *Publ:* Contribr, Parachute, Montreal, 75 & 82-; Vanguard, Vancouver, BC, 82-; C Mag, Toronto, 83. *Mailing Add:* 68 Broadview Ave 4th Fl Toronto ON M4M 2E6 Canada

CARRINGTON, JOY HARRELL
PAINTER, ILLUMINATOR
b Jacksonville, Tex. *Study:* Kansas City Art Inst, three years; Am Acad Art, Chicago; Nat Acad Chicago; Chicago Art Inst, with Pougialis; Art Students League, four years; also with Frank Peyraud, Highland Park, Ill & Robert Brackman, Noank, Conn. *Work:* Long Barrack Mus, Alamo; First Methodist Church, Jacksonville; Alamo Libr; Coppini Acad Fine Arts, San Antonio, Tex; State Capitol Bldg, Austin. *Comn:* Portrait, Carmen Hicks, sister of former Gov John Connally; portrait, George W Vaught, then vpres B F Goodrich & Ms Vaught; portraits, Frank Folsum, then pres of Radio Corp Am & Mrs Folsum. *Exhib:* McNamara O'Conner Mus, Victoria, Tex; Univ Tex, San Antonio, 76-78; Springville Mus Art, Utah, 85; Frontier Times Mus, Bandera, Tex, 91-92; one-person exhib, oil portraits, Carrington Gallery, 92. *Pos:* Com artist for Frank Bros, San Antonio, Hartman Furniture Co & Handelan & Staff Shoe Agency, Chicago & Loesers, Brooklyn. *Teaching:* One day a week at Carrington Studio. *Awards:* Best of Show, & First Place Coppini Acad Fine Art, 82; First Place, Kerrville Art Club, 87; Second Place, Coppini Acad Fine Arts Ann, 90; and others. *Bibliog:* Glenn Tucker (auth), Arts Rev, San Antonio Light, 8/63; Herweck (auth), article in The Record, spring 72. *Mem:* Am Artists Prof League; Nat Soc Arts & Letts; Coppini Acad Fine Arts; Kerrville Art Club; San Antonio Watercolor Group. *Media:* Oil. *Dealer:* Carrington Studios. *Mailing Add:* T Anchor Ranch Rte 16 Box 30 Medina TX 78055

CARRINO, DAVID
PAINTER
b New York, NY, 19, 59. *Study:* New Sch Social Res, 78; Sch Visual Arts, New York, BFA, 81. *Exhib:* Scott Hanson Gallery, New York, 88 & Tony Shafrazi Gallery, New York, 89 & 91; Pace Eds, 91; A Passion for Art: Watercolours and Works on Paper, Tony Shafrazi Gallery, New York, 91-92; American Art Today: Surface Tension, Art Mus, Fla Int Univ, Miami, 92; Rena Branston, San Francisco, 92; Wooster Gardens, New York, 92; and many others. *Bibliog:* Joshua Decter (auth), New York reviews, Flash Art, 3-4/90; Collins & Milazzo (auths), Outside America: Going Into the 90's (exhib catalog), Fay Gold Gallery, Atlanta, 91; Ken Johnson (auth), Vogue Arts, Vogue, 8/91; The New Yorker, 10/14/91; Stephen Westfall (auth), American Art Today: Surface Tension (essay), Art Mus, Fla Int Univ, Miami, 92; and others. *Mailing Add:* c/o Tony Shafrazi Gallery 130 Prince St New York NY 10012

CARROLL, JAMES F L
PAINTER, SCULPTOR
b Postville, Iowa, Apr 4, 34. *Study:* Colo State Col, BA, 56, MA, 62; Univ Colo, Boulder, MFA, 66; also studied with Richard Ellinger, Sir Robin Phillipson, Joan Brown, Roland Reiss. *Work:* Butler Inst Am Art, Youngstown, Ohio; Kutztown Univ, Pa; St Mary's Col Md, St Mary's City. *Exhib:* One-man exhib, 112 Workshop, New York, 77; Modern Art Gallery, Vienna, Austria, 82; Underknown in New York, II, Hunter Fac Select, Hunter Col, New York, 88; Area Artist 1989, Lehigh Univ, Bethlehem, Pa, 89; 2nd Exhib, Sculpture Garden, Maria Feliz Gallery, Jim Thorpe, Pa, 90. *Pos:* Dir, founder, New Arts Prog, Kutztown, Pa, 72- *Teaching:* Prof fine arts, Kutztown Univ, Pa, 66- *Awards:* Exceptional Acad Serv, Commonwealth of Pa, 78; Nat Sculpture Show, Touring Exhib, Statesboro, Ga, 79; Community Spirit, Morning Call Newspaper, 89. *Bibliog:* Tim Higgins (auth), Carroll's NAP brings mtns, 8/5/86, Geoff Gehman (auth), Nature plays host to 43, Morning Call Newspaper, 8/26/90; Marilyn J Fox (auth), A solo new arts exhib, Eagle/Times Newspaper, 8/2/92. *Mem:* Am Asn Mus; Pa Arts Coalition; Int Sculpture Ctr; Am Asn Univ Prof; Lehigh Valley Arts Coun (bd mem, 89-92). *Media:* Paint; Wood. *Publ:* Contribr, 11th, 10th, Critical & 8th Assembling, Assembling Press, 78-81; In and Out of New York, Hunter Yoder, 80; auth, 71 Small Works on Paper, 1965-81, 81 & In and Out of Kutztown, 82, James Carroll. *Mailing Add:* 56 Wiltrout Rd Kutztown PA 19530

CARRON, MAUDEE LILYAN
PAINTER, SCULPTOR
b Melville, La. *Study:* Creative Arts Sch, Houston, scholar, with McNeill Davidson; Lamar Univ; also with Dr James McMurray; Lamar Univ Sch, Rome, summer 82. *Work:* Univ Tex Austin; Gulf-Chevron Collection; Beaumont Art League; Pvt collections of James Surls, JJ Sweeney Estate & Bert Long, Tex. *Comn:* Poster & stage sets for Glass Menagerie, Who's Afraid of Virginia Wolf? & Macbeth, Univ Tex Austin Drama Dept, 70 & 72. *Exhib:* 16 Southeastern States & Tex Exhib, New Orleans Mus, 63; Eight State Exhib, Okla Art Ctr, Oklahoma City, 68; one-man shows, Images, Univ Tex Fine Arts Gallery, 70, Environment 71, Univ Tex Austin, 71 & Et Cetera 3, Southwestern Univ, 72; All-Media Exhib 77, Univ Houston, 77; Sculpture; The Spectrum, Lawndale Art Performance Ctr, 87 & The Blue Star Complex, San Antonio, 87; Another Reality, Art Mus SE Tex, Houston. *Teaching:* vis instr, Dick Dowling Pub Sch, & Pa Montessori Sch, 79. *Awards:* Miller Award for Incognito, Beaumont Art Mus, 68 & two awards for A Dangerous Game in Archaic Form, 70; Award for A Temple for All Delights, Tex Fine Arts Asn, 69; Purchase Award, Empire of Am, Tex, 83 & Tri-State Exhib, Beaumont League Gallery, 86; Purchase Award, Mobil Oil Found, 85 & 86. *Mem:* Tex Watercolor Soc; Tex Prof Sculptors Soc; Graphic Soc, Lamar Univ. *Media:* Mixed Media; Wood. *Publ:* Auth, Thought-Crime, 89. *Dealer:* Kunstraum Galerie West Berlin Ger; Hooks-Epstein Galleries Houston TX. *Mailing Add:* Rte 6 Box 300 Beaumont TX 77705

CARSON, G B
CONSULTANT, ART DEALER
b Helena, Mont, Feb, 28, 50. *Study:* Univ Calif, Berkeley, BA(art hist), 77. *Collections Arranged:* Le Desert de Retz: An 18th Century French Folly Garden, Calif Palace Legion Hon, San Francisco, 91. *Mem:* Graphic Arts Coun, Fine Arts Mus, San Francisco; Asn Study of Dada & Surrealism. *Specialty:* California art of the 1960's. *Mailing Add:* PO Box 9571 Berkeley CA 94709

CARSWELL, JOHN
MUSEUM DIRECTOR, PAINTER
b London, Eng, Nov 16, 31. *Study:* Wimbledon Sch Art, Surrey Eng, 46-48; Royal Col Art, London, ARCA, 48-51. *Exhib:* One man shows, Hanover Gallery, London, 56 & Fischbach Gallery, New York, 66. *Collections Arranged:* Islamic Binding & Bookmaking (auth, catalog), 81-82; Blue & White: Chinese Porcelain & Its Impact on the Western World, (auth, catalog), 85. *Pos:* Cur, Oriental Inst Mus, Univ Chicago, 78-85, dir, David & Alfred Smart Gallery, 85- *Teaching:* Prof fine art, Am Univ Beirut, Lebanon, 56-76. *Media:* Oil, Paper. *Res:* Islamic art and architecture; Far eastern ceramics; cross-cultural contacts in Asian Art. *Publ:* Auth, Coptic Tattoo Designs, Am Univ Beirut, 58; New Julfa: Armenian Churches & Other Buildings, Oxford Univ Press, 68; coauth, Kutahya Tiles and Pottery in Armenian Cathedral of St James, Jerusalem, Oxford Univ Press, 72. *Mailing Add:* Islamic Dept 3425 New Bond St London W1 England United Kingdom

CARSWELL, RODNEY
PAINTER, EDUCATOR
b Carmel, Calif, Dec 15, 46. *Study:* Univ NMex, BFA, 68; Univ Colo, MFA, 72. *Work:* Univ NMex, Albuquerque; Univ Colo, Boulder; Ill State Mus, Springfield; Evansville Mus Art, Ind; Art Inst Chicago; Prudential, New York. *Exhib:* Chicago & Vicinity Show, Art Inst Chicago, 73, New Horizons in Art, Chicago, 73; one-man shows, Not in New York Gallery, Cincinnati, Ohio, 76, Roy Boyd Gallery, Chicago & Los Angeles, 78, 81, 85, 87-89 & 91-92 & Art Mus, Univ Oklahoma, Norman; The Chosen Object, Joslyn Mus, Omaha, Nebr, 77; Carl Solway Gallery, New York, 77; Surfaces: Two Decades of Chicago Painting, Seventies & Eighties, Terra Mus Am Art, Chicago, 87; Good Painting, Art Gallery, State Ill Bldg, Chicago, 88; Am Acad Arts & Letts, New York, 91. *Teaching:* Asst prof painting & drawing, Univ Ill, Chicago, 83- *Awards:* Nat Endowment Arts Midwest, 87; J S Guggenheim Fel, 89; Nat Endowment Arts Fel, 91; and others. *Bibliog:* William Wilson (auth), Rodney Carswell, Los Angeles Times, 3/13/87; Dennis Adrian (auth), Two Decades of Painting in Chicago, Beneath the Surfaces, Art Examiner, 12/87; Buzz Spector (auth), Rodney Carswell (exhib catalog), Art Mus, Univ Okla, 88. *Media:* Oil, Wax. *Dealer:* Roy Boyd Gallery 739 N Wells St Chicago IL 60610. *Mailing Add:* Dept Art Design M-C 036 Univ Ill PO Box 4348 Chicago IL 60680

CARTER, (CHARLES) BRUCE
PRINTMAKER, EDUCATOR
b North Adams, Mass, May 15, 30. *Study:* Albright Art Sch, Buffalo, NY, dipl, 51; State Univ NY Buffalo, BS, 52; Pa State Univ, University Park, MEd & DEd, 58. *Work:* Nat Hist Mus, Univ Oslo, Norway; Philadelphia Mus Art; State Art Mus, Raleigh, NC; Amarillo Art Ctr, Tex. *Comn:* Painted mural, Narvik City Coun, Norway, 62 & mosaic mural, 63; mosaic mural, Kiruna, Sweden, 62; Painted Mural, Nat Mus, Gettysburg, Pa; mosaic mural, Nordsland Banken, Leknes, Norway, 68. *Exhib:* Soc Am Graphic Artists, New York, 71; 2nd Triennial Int Exhib Contemp Xylography, Nat Mus Xylography, Carpi, Italy, 72; Hokkaido Print Asn Int Exhib, Sapporo, Japan, 72; 3rd Int Print Biennial Exhib, Art Mus, Epinal, France, 75; Return to the Crucible, The Pentagon, DC, 76; Wounded Knee: An Am Tragedy, Amarillo Art Ctr, Tex, 76; 6th Nat Print Exhib, Los Angeles, 78; Nat Hist Mus, Univ Oslo, Norway, 80; The Warsaw Woodcuts, Ghetto Fighters Mus, Israel, 81. *Pos:* Art consult, Poetry on the Buses, Pittsburgh, 76- *Teaching:* Prof printmaking-drawing, Carnegie Mellon Univ, Pittsburgh, 63- *Awards:* Purchase Prizes, Nat Mus Xylography, Carpi, Italy, 72 & Univ Wis-Madison, 75. *Mem:* Col Art Asn; Philadelphia Print Club; Artists' Equity Asn. *Media:* Woodcut, Lithography. *Publ:* Coauth, Wounded Knee: An American Tragedy (film), WQED-TV, 72. *Mailing Add:* Dept Art Carnegie Mellon Univ 5000 Forbes Ave Pittsburgh PA 15213

CARTER, CAROL A
PAINTER
b Sumter, SC, 1955. *Study:* Principia Col, Elsah, Ill, BA, 77; Washington Univ, St Louis, Mo, MFA, 84. *Work:* Boatmen's Nat Bank, St Louis, Mo; Nanjing Art Sch, China; St Louis Art Mus; Citicorp, Maui, Hawaii; Arjomari Arches, Rives Paper Inc. *Comn:* Edison Brothers, St Louis, Mo; Renaisance Ctr, Detroit, Mich. *Exhib:* One-woman shows, Keane-Mason Gallery, New York, 81, Strecker Gallery, Manhattan, Kans, 84, Mark Twain Bancshares Inc, St Louis, Mo, 85, B Z Wagman Gallery, 86 & 87, Messing Gallery, St Louis, 88 & Margaret Harwell Art Mus, Poplar Bluff, Mo, 90; Five State Watercolor, Wichita Art Mus, Kans, 90; Elliot Smith Gallery, St Louis, Mo, 91; Diane Nelson Gallery, Laguna, Calif, 90; Ethical Soc, St Louis, Mo, 92; and others. *Pos:* Gallery owner & operator, Rockport, Mass & St Louis, Mo, 76-79; asst, B Z Wagman Gallery, St Louis, 85-86. *Teaching:* Teaching assistantship, Wash Univ, St Louis, 83-84; watercolor instr, Fine Arts Inst, Wash Univ, 85-, drawing instr, Sch Archit, 89-91. *Awards:* Purchase Award, Nat Watercolor Show, 89; Kans Five State Watercolor, Wichita, Kans, 90; Purchase Award, Springfield Art Mus, 91. *Bibliog:* J P Wolf (auth), Introspective Reflections (cover article), Am Artist Mag, 10/89; Paul Harris (auth), Methphorical messages from Carol Carter, St Louis Post Dispatch, 12/90; Carol Shepvey (auth), Carol Carter has a story to tell, St Louis Post Dispatch, 5/92. *Media:* Acrylic, Watercolor. *Dealer:* Beverly Gordon Gallery 2404 Cedar Springs Rd Dallas Texas 75201; Elliot Smith Contemp Art. *Mailing Add:* 1709 Washington Ave St Louis MO 63101

CARTER, CLARENCE HOLBROOK
PAINTER, DESIGNER
b Portsmouth, Ohio, Mar 26, 04. *Study:* Cleveland Sch Art, 23-27; with Hans Hofmann, Capri, Italy, summer 27. *Work:* Metrop Mus Art; Mus Mod Art; Whitney Mus Art; Philadelphia Mus Art; Cleveland Mus Art; and others. *Comn:* Murals, sect painting & sculpture, Treasury Dept, Portsmouth, Ohio & Ravenna, Ohio Post Off & Cleveland Pub Auditorium. *Exhib:* One-man shows, Mus Art, Carnegie Inst, 40, Minneapolis Inst Arts, 49, NJ State Mus, 74 & Univ Tex Art Mus, 77; Painting and Drawings 1960-1988, Weitzenhoffer Gallery, New York, 88; plus many European, South American, Canadian & other museums. *Pos:* Dir, FAP for Northeastern Ohio, 37-38. *Teaching:* Asst prof painting & design, Carnegie Inst, 38-44; dir art, Chautauqua Inst, NY Univ, summer 42-43; guest instr painting, Cleveland Inst Art, summer 48; guest instr, Minneapolis Sch Art, fall 49, Lehigh Univ, 54, Ohio Univ, 55 & Atlanta Art Inst, 57; vis lectr, Lafayette Col, 61, artist-in-residence, 61-69; guest artist, Univ Iowa, spring 70, Iowa State, 75, Kent State 75. *Awards:* Honored by Ohio House of Reps and Gov Richard F Celeste, 84; Cert Merit, Am Watercolor Soc, 59 & 62; Governor's Arts Award presented by Thomas H Kean, 89. *Bibliog:* Gordon BIshop (auth), Gems of New Jersey, Star-Ledger; American Traum und Depression-1920/40, Berlin, NGKB, 80; Franz Geierhass & Brigitte Hellgath (coauths), The Creative Paths to Realization, 84; Clarence Holbrook Carter (foreward by James Michener), Rizzoli, 89. *Mem:* Assoc Nat Acad Design; Del Valley Art Asn (pres, 62-63); Am Watercolor Soc (bd dirs, 61-62, vpres, 62). *Publ:* Auth, chap, In: Work for artists; contrib, articles in Col Art J & Am Artist. *Dealer:* Sid Deutsch Gallery, 29 W 57th St New York NY 10019; Gimpel/Weitzenhoffer Gallery 415 W Broadway New York NY 10012. *Mailing Add:* 251 Shire Road Milford NJ 08848

CARTER, CURTIS L
CURATOR
b Iowa, Oct 10, 35. *Study:* Taylor Univ, Upland, Ind, 60; Spec student, Brandeis Univ & Harvard Univ, 61 & 66; Boston Univ, PhD, 71. *Collections Arranged:* Romanticism and Cynicism in Contemp Art & Photography on the Edge; Barbara Morgan: Prints, Drawings, Photographs, 89; Richard Lippold Sculpture, 90-91; Collaborative Photography/Nagatani & Tracy, 91-92; Contemporary American Folk Art, 92. *Pos:* Chmn, Marquette Univ, Comt Fine Arts, 77-84; dir, Haggerty Mus Art, Marquette Univ, 84; Pres, Dance Perspectives Found Inc, 87- *Teaching:* Asst prof aesthet & philos, Marquette Univ, 69-76, assoc prof aesthet & philos, 76-84 & prof aesthet & philos, 84- *Awards:* Wis Dance Coun Award, 92. *Mem:* Wis Alliance Arts Educ (co-chmn, 74-79); ARTREACH Milwaukee Inc (founding pres & bd mem 75-81, mem, presently); Nat Endowment Arts & Humanities (panelist & referee,

84-); Dance Perspectives Found (vpres 78-87, pres 87-). *Publ:* Ed & coauth exhib catalogs, Photography on the Edge, 88, Barbara Morgan: Prints, Drawings, Photographs, 89 & Images of Death in Contemporary Art, 90, Marquette Univ; Ed & contribr exhib catalogs, Richard Lippold Sculpture, 90 & Contemporary American Folk Art, 92, Marquette Univ; ed & auth, Contemporary Folk Art, 92; auth, Franta: The Body as a Metaphor for Human Suffering and Resistance, 92. *Mailing Add:* Marquette University Haggerty Museum of Art 13th & Clybourn St Milwaukee WI 53233

CARTER, DAVID GILES
CONSULTANT, MUSEUM DIRECTOR
b Nashua, NH, Nov 2, 21. *Study:* Princeton Univ, with C R Morey & A M Friend, AB, 44; Harvard Univ Grad Sch Arts & Sci, with P Sachs, C R Post, C Kuhn & others, MA, 49; Inst Fine Arts, New York Univ, 51, with W Cook, E Panofsky & G Schoenberger. *Collections Arranged:* Turner in America (with Wilbur D Peat), 56; The Young Rembrandt and His Times, 58; The G H A Clowes Collection, 59; Dynamic Symmetry, 61; El Greco to Goya (with Curtis Coley), 63; The Weldon Collection, 64; Masterpieces from Montreal, 66; The Painter and the New World, 67; Rembrandt and His Pupils, 69; Jan Menses, 76; and others. *Pos:* Curatorial asst, Metrop Mus Art, New York, 50-54; cur paintings & prints, John Herron Art Mus, 55-59; dir, Mus Art, RI Sch Design, 59-64 & Montreal Mus Fine Arts, 64-76. *Teaching:* Lectr, Ind Univ, Bloomington, 58-59. *Awards:* Gold Medal of Ital Cult, Ital Ministry Foreign Affairs, 63. *Mem:* ICOM; Mediaeval Acad; Grolier Club; Royal Soc Arts; plus others. *Res:* Northern Renaissance; secondary interest in Mannerist and Northern Baroque painting. *Publ:* Auth, Rencontre avec Valentin, l'Oeil, 70; The Winnipeg flagellation and the master of the View of St Gudule, Miscellanea in Memoriam Paul Coremans (1908-1965), Bull de l'Institut royal du Patrimoine artistique, xv, 75; Spanish itinerary, 5/76 & Northern Baroque and the Italian connexion, 5/76, Apollo; Montreal musee des beaux-arts, The Art Gallery, 4-5/76; and others. *Mailing Add:* 100 Edgehill Rd New Haven CT 06511

CARTER, DEAN
SCULPTOR, EDUCATOR
b Henderson, NC, Apr 24, 22. *Study:* Corcoran Sch Art; Am Univ, BA; Ogunquit Sch Painting & Sculpture; Indiana Univ, MFA; Ossip Zadkine Sch Art, Paris, France. *Work:* Cranbrook Acad Art, Mich; Charlotte Plaza, NC; Washington & Lee Univ; Wichita Art Asn Galleries, Kans; Harrisonburg Community Hosp, Va. *Comn:* Bronze portrait, Gropius, Col Archit, Va Polytech Inst, 65; welded bronze screen, Roanoke Mem Hosp, Va, 70; three piece bronze group, St Joseph's Preparatory Sch, Philadelphia, 70; welded bronze relief, First Colony Ins Co, Lynchburg, Va; bronze portrait, Stuart Cassell, Va Polytech Inst, 77; plus others. *Exhib:* Pa Acad Fine Arts, Philadelphia, 54; Cini Found, Venice, Italy, 64; Smithsonian Circulating Exhib, 69-71; one-man show, Artists' Mart, Washington, DC, 70; Contemp Gallery Art Ann Sculpture Show, Winston-Salem, 71. *Pos:* Mem art adv bd, Va Highlands Community Col, Abigdon, 69-71 & Mountain Empire Community Col, Wise, 71-75; consult, US Fine Arts Surv, 72. *Teaching:* Founder art dept, Va Polytech Inst & State Univ, 63-; artist in residence, USA Studies Abroad, Cortona, Italy. *Awards:* Sculpture Comn, Va/Md Sch Veterinary Med, 91; Allied Artist Award for Sculpture, 92; Odk G Burk Johnston Award for Outstanding Teacher-Adminr, 92; plus others. *Bibliog:* Ted Kliman (dir), A World of Sculpture (film), Va Polytech Inst & State Univ, 62; W M White, Jr (auth), Sculpturing by Dean Carter, Maelstrom, 66; W C Burleson (auth), On campus--Dean Carter, Context, summer 69. *Mem:* Soc Washington Artists; Southern Sculptors Asn (vpres, 66-68); Am Crafts Coun (state rep, 65); Col Art Asn Am; Am Fedn Art; plus others; Southeastern Col Art Conf (pres, 77). *Media:* Bronze, Wood. *Dealer:* Area Landscape 4118 Olley Lane Fairfax VA 22039. *Mailing Add:* 1011 Highland Circle Blacksburg VA 24060

CARTER, FREDERICK TIMMINS
PAINTER, ILLUSTRATOR
b Galveston, Tex, Sept 22, 25. *Study:* Franklin Sch Prof Art, New York, grad with hons, 45-48. *Comn:* Paintings, El Paso Natural Gas Co, Tex, Ford Motor Co, Dearborn, Mich. *Exhib:* Tex Ann Paintings Exhib, Dallas, Houston & San Antonio Mus; Audubon Artists Nat Exhib, Nat Acad Galleries, New York; Sun Carnival Nat Exhib, El Paso Mus Fine Art; Nat Soc Painters in Casein, New York. *Pos:* Staff artist, Wilkinson-Schiwetz & Tips, Houston; art dir, Mithoff Advert, El Paso, Frederick Carter Studio, 66- *Mem:* El Paso Co Hist Soc. *Media:* Acrylic. *Publ:* Illusr, Frank Mangan's Bordertown, El Paso, & Bordertown Revisited; illusr, Ford Times Mag; illusr, Fort Bliss History. *Dealer:* Frederick Carter Studio 5744 Beaumont El Paso TX 79912. *Mailing Add:* 5744 Beaumont Pl El Paso TX 79912

CARTER, GARY
PAINTER, SCULPTOR
b Hutchinson, Kans, Mar 12, 39. *Study:* Art Ctr Col Design, BFA, 71. *Work:* Nat Cowboy Hall Fame, Oklahoma City; C M Russell Mus, Great Falls, Mont; Mont Hist Soc, Helena; Gould Inc, Chicago; Cowboy Artists Am Mus, Kerrville, Tex. *Comn:* Mont Centennial Painting Comn (1889-1989), Pepsi-Cola Corp; mural, 1st Security Bank of West Yellowstone; mural, Big Sky Ski Resort. *Exhib:* Grand Central Art Gallery, Baltimore Gallery, New York, 78; Cowboy Artists of America, Phoenix Art Mus, 82-90; Nat Acad Western Art Show, Oklahoma City, 82, 88 & 89; Western Heritage, Shamrock Hilton, Houston, 84; Buffalo Bill Art Show, Cody, Wyo, 86; Cowboy Artists of Am miniature show, Kerrville, Tex, 4/90; Wildlife of the Am West Art Mus, Jackson, Wyo, 9/88, 89 & 90. *Teaching:* Taught Art Seminar, C Mus, Kerrville, Tex, 86. *Awards:* Award of Merit, Kans City Soc of Western Art; Best of Show, Western Rendezvous of Art, Helena Mt, 78; Artist of the West 1990, San Dimos Festival of Western Arts. *Mem:* Cowboy Artists Am (pres, 85-86). *Media:* Oil; Bronze. *Publ:* Auth, article, cover & feature Midwest Art Mag, 4/86; article, Outdoor Life Mag, 8-11/88; article, Western Horseman, 9/88. *Mailing Add:* PO Box 338 West Yellowstone MT 59758

CARTER, HARRIET (ESTELLE) MANORE
PAINTER
b Grand Bend, Ont, Mar 22, 29. *Study:* Dundas Valley Sch Fine Arts, Ont. *Work:* Sarnia Pub Libr & Art Mus, Ont; Art Gallery Brant, Brantford, Ont; Can Coun Art Bank; Hart House, Univ Toronto; Can Soc Painters Watercolour Diamond Jubilee Collection presented to her Majesty Queen Elizabeth II for the Royal Collection of Drawings and Watercolours at Windsor Castle; and many other pvt collections both in Can & US. *Exhib:* Traveling Exhib, 70-83 & Fifty Years, 75, Can Soc Painters Watercolour; On View Traveling Exhib, Ont, 76-77; Can Watercolour Soc Japan & Can Exhib, 76-77; Ont Soc Artists Ann Exhib, Oakville Centennial Gallery, 77; Cloud Flowers Traveling Exhib, 81-82. *Pos:* Commercial designer, Dominion Glass Co, Wallaceburg, Ont, 49-52. *Awards:* Hon Award, Can Soc Painters Watercolour, 69; Ont Soc Artists 100th Ann Exhib Awards, 72; Purchase Award, London Pub Art Gallery & Mus, 72. *Bibliog:* Tom Thompson Memorial Gallery Museum of Fine Art Show, Art Mag, 71; Kay Kritzwiser (auth), Four exhibits mind stretching style, Toronto Globe & Mail, 72; Lenore Crawford (auth), Manore Carter art gets message across, London Free Press, 73. *Mem:* Can Soc Painters Watercolour; Ont Soc Artists; Royal Can Acad Arts. *Media:* Watercolor. *Dealer:* Nancy Pooles Gallery 16 Hazelton Ave Toronto ON M5R 2E2. *Mailing Add:* 78 MacLennan Ave Hamilton ON L8V 1X6 Canada

CARTER, JERRY WILLIAMS
MOSAIC ARTIST, SCULPTOR
b Wichita, Kans, Apr 19, 41. *Study:* Univ Md, BA, 68; Chicago Art Inst, 69; Acad Fine Arts Finland, 70; Centro Int Studi L'Insegnamento Mosaico, cert, 70; L'Ecole Nat Superieur Beaux Arts Paris, with Pierre Singier, 71; Acad Belli Arti Ravenna, with Pomadoro, 72; Univ Studi Bologna, cert, with Bovini, 71; Nat Inst Design Finland, 73; Antioch Univ, Columbia Visual Arts Ctr, MFA, 81. *Work:* The Phillips Collection, Washington, DC; Pinacoteca Comunale Ravenna, Italy; Kunstgewerbemuseum der Stadt Köln, Cologne, Ger. *Comn:* Descent of the Holy Spirit (venetian glass mosaic), Church Holy Spirit, Forrestville, Md, 78; Cascade (ceramic & venetian glass mosaic sculpture), Vista Int Hotel, Washington, DC, 83; Second Genesis, American Peace/Ecology Monument (cast concrete relief & glass mosaic monument), comn by High Patronage of the Pres of Italy & European Parliament, Ravenna, Italy, 88; Flight of Fantasy (plastic & glass relief-mosaics), Montgomery Co Sch, Bethesda, Md, 86; Human Rights Monument (cast concrete monolith & glass mosaic), comn by City of Moscozo, Moscow, Russ, 92. *Exhib:* solo exhib, Layering in Stone & Glass, Am Asn Advan Sci, Washington, DC, 87; Tenth Anniversary Exhib Solidarnosc, Gadansk, Poland, 90; Spaso House, Moscow, USSR, 90; M'ysuri, Georgian Cultural Center, Moscow, USSR, 90; Galeria Esplanade (Metsovaara), Helsinki, Finland, 90; Amerika Hauser (USIS), Cologne, Munich, Ger, 90; and many others. *Collections Arranged:* Finnish Architecture Exhib, Am Inst Architects Headquarters, 77; Finnish Folk Art Exhib of 16th through 19th Century (auth, catalog), George Washington Univ, 78. *Pos:* art dir, ABC-TV, Washington, DC, 66-68; artist-in-residence, Iittala Nuutijärvi Glass Factory, Finland, 89-; tech art & forensic art consult, 84- *Awards:* Am Winner, Sign of Peace & Friendship Among Peoples Award, UNESCO, 83; Fulbright Italiana, 84; Medallion of Ravenna, presented by Mayor, Ravenna, Italy, 84; 100 Most Significant, Corning Glass Int Rev, 86; invited participant, Global Forum, Supreme Soviet & Soviet Acad Sci, Moscow, USSR, 90; invited guest-partic, Solidarnosc 10th Anniversary, Gadansk, Poland, 90. *Bibliog:* Jennifer Gibson (auth), Reflections in stone and glass, an American reinterprets the art of mosaics, In: The World and I, 10/87; Igor Ignatiev (auth), The creative process and creations of Jerry Carter, Echo of the Planet, Tass, Moscow, USSR, 10/88; C Frazier Smith (auth), Monumental mosaic, Baltimore Sun Mag, 11/88; I Wiman (auth), Expecting the unexpected: Some ancient roots to current perceptions of nature, Ambio, Royal Swedish Acad Sci Publ, Stockholm, Sweden, XIX, No 24, 90; T A Yasui (auth), Jerry Carter and the international mural mission, The Washington Post, 4/16/90; E Egoreva (auth), Artist Jerry Carter, Decorative Arts USSR, Moscow, USSR, 7/90; G Nicola (auth), Jerry W Carter-Glass Mosaic, Neues Glass, Freschen, Ger, 2/91. *Mem:* Helsinki Artists Union, Helsinki, Finland; Int Asn Contemp Mosaicists, Ravenna, Italy; MARS Gallery Asn, Moscow, Russ. *Media:* Glass, Stone. *Publ:* Auth, Mosaic: Medium for the Times, Presso il centro stampa del comune di Ravenna, Italy, 80. *Dealer:* J W Carter & Assoc 10502 Bucknell Dr Silver Spring MD 20902. *Mailing Add:* 10602 Bucknell Dr Silver Spring MD 20902

CARTER, KATHARINE TIPTON
PAINTER, EDUCATOR
b Tampa, Fla, Feb 21, 50. *Study:* Univ Fla, BA(art), 76; Univ SFla, MFA, 80. *Work:* Univ SFla Contemp Art Mus; Rockefeller Found, New York; Am Tele & Telegraph, NJ; Deutsche Bank, New York; Equilease Corp, New York; and many others. *Exhib:* Outside NY, New Mus Contemp Art, 78; Solo exhibs, PS 1, New York, 79, Hal Bromm Gallery, New York, 82 & 86, Henri Gallery, Washington, DC, 86, Univ NC, Chapel Hill, Robeson Ctr, Rutgers, 87, Mason Gross Sch Arts, 88 & AT&T, NJ 89; Art Aid, Sotheby's, New York, 86; Albright-Knox, Buffalo, NY, 87; Morris Mus, NJ, 87; Jeffrey Neale Gallery, New York, 87; Lintas Worldwide, New York, 88; At the Waters Edge, Tampa Mus Art Ctr for Arts, Vero Beach, Fla & Virginia Beach; Johnson & Johnson Corp, NJ, 90-92. *Pos:* Independent lectr on New York art trends, highlights of the New York Art Season, New York gallery reviews & professional

promotion, Professional Workshop Series at over 200 cols, art ctrs & mus nationwide, 85-; founder & dir, Career Consultation Individual Artist & professional ser div, 91- *Teaching:* Instr studio art, Univ South, Sewanee, Tenn, 82-83, Middlesex Co Col, NJ, 84-87, Rutgers Univ, 86- & Drew Univ, 87. *Awards:* Fla Arts Coun Exhib Grant, 79; NJ Artists Fel, 85; NJ Printmaking Fel, 89. *Bibliog:* William Zimmer (auth), Compelling mundanities in stone and paint, 3/10/85, Patricia Malarcher (auth), The incorporation of folk art, 4/14/85 & John Russell (auth), rev, 5/2/86, The New York Times; Robert Mahoney (auth), rev, in: Arts Mag, Vol 61, No 1, 9/86; Vivien Raynor (auth), The first rule is break the rules, The New York Times, 10/11/87; and others. *Mem:* Col Art Asn. *Media:* Acrylic. *Mailing Add:* 9 Bridgewater Dr No 4 Oceanport NJ 07757

CARTER, MARY
PAINTER, PRINTMAKER
b Hartsdale, NY. *Study:* Art Students League, with Reginald Marsh, Robert Beverly Hale & E Dickenson, 51-55; Hunter Col, 67, Sch Visual Arts, 68; Parsons Sch, 81. *Exhib:* Audubon Artists Ann, 54 & Nat Acad Design, New York, 56, 57 & 72; Hartford Atheneum Show, Conn, 56; Pa Acad Fine Arts, 57; Philadelphia Sketch Club, 58; Ball State Art Gallery, 58 & 63; Nat Competition, Springfield Art Mus, Mo, 66; Ann Drawings & Sculpture Show, Del Mar Col, Corpus Christi, Tex, 67; Hudson Guild Invitational, New York, 75- & solo show, 85- *Mem:* Art Students League. *Media:* Oil, Tempera. *Mailing Add:* 253 W 16th St New York NY 10011

CARTER, NANETTE CAROLYN
PAINTER, PRINTMAKER
b Columbus, Ohio, Jan 30, 54. *Study:* L'Accademia di Belle Arti, Italy, 75; Oberlin Col, Ohio, BA, 76; Pratt Inst Art, New York, MFA, 78. *Work:* Newark Mus, NJ; Herbert Johnson Mus Art, Cornell Univ, Ithaca, NY; Studio Mus, Harlem, New York; Morgan Guaranty, New York; MCI Telecommunications, Chicago, Ill. *Comn:* Mural, Dwight Englewood Sch, NJ, 80; Color poster for concert, Jazzmobile, Avery Fisher Hall, New York, 85; Color poster exhib, Black Women in the Arts 1990, Montclair State Col, NJ. *Exhib:* 25th Annual Exhibit, Parrish Art Mus, Southampton, NY, 78; Guild Hall Mus, East Hampton, NY, 79; Hudson River Mus, Yonkers, NY, 80; Enroute: Six Contemporary Artists, Studio Mus Harlem, New York, 81; Biennial Print Exhibit, Brooklyn Mus, New York, 81; Twentieth Century Afro-American Artists, Newark Mus, NJ, 85; Assoc Am Artists Gallery, NY, 85; Louisa McIntosh Gallery, Atlanta, Ga, 87; Mary Ryan Gallery, NY, 88; solo shows, Birmingham, Mich, 89, June Kelly Gallery, NY, 90; Nat Mus Women Arts, Washington, DC, 92. *Teaching:* Instr printmaking and drawing, Dwight Englewood Sch, Englewood, NJ, 78-87; prof, City Col New York, 92. *Awards:* Jerome Found Grant, 81; Nat Endowment Arts Grant, 81; NY State Coun Artist-in-residence, 84; New York Found Arts, 90. *Bibliog:* Evette Porter (auth) article, Essence Mag, 90; Ruth Bass (auth), rev, Art News, 2/91; Phyllis Braff (auth), rev, New York Times, 12/1/91. *Mem:* New York Artists Equity Asn, Inc. *Media:* Oils, Monoprints. *Publ:* Illusr (cover), Midnight Birds, Mary Helen Washington (auth), Japan, 82. *Dealer:* George R N'Namdi Gallery Detroit MI; June Kelly Gallery New York NY. *Mailing Add:* 788 Riverside Dr New York NY 10032

CARTER, SAM JOHN
PAINTER, SCULPTOR
b Des Moines, Iowa, Mar 20, 43; Can citizen. *Study:* Calif State Univ, Long Beach, BA, 65, MA, 82; Univ Toronto, BL Arch, 70; Ikenobo, Ikebana, Kyoto, Japan, 82. *Work:* Ont Sci Ctr & Ont Place, Toronto; Nat Gallery, Ottawa; Expo 86 & Artists Gallery, Vancouver. *Comn:* Flower Totoms, Govt Can, Vancouver, BC, 80; Vancouver Sea Flowers, Jonathan's Seafood, BC, 81; China Lion, Wons, Vancouver, BC, 82; Vancouver-Papal Visit, Pageant & Chair of Catholic Church, BC, 84; Parade, Theme Pageant, Expo 86, Vancouver, 86. *Exhib:* Summer Numbers, A Space, Toronto, 70; Ont Col Art Gallery, Toronto, 71; Spoleto Festival, Italy, 71; World Wildlife Event, United Nations Conf, Stockholm, Sweden, 71; Art-Subterranean, Mus Mod Art, Mexico City, 80; Kado-Flower Way, Contemp Fine Arts Gallery, Tokyo, Japan, 85. *Pos:* Sr designer, Ont Sci Ctr, 65-71; Chmn, found div, Emily Carr Col Art & Design, 73-86. *Teaching:* Instr cult probe, Ont Col Art, 70-71. *Bibliog:* Yamashita (auth), Gardens of the world project, Ikenodo J, Kyoto, 83-84; Rule (auth), Art in season, Western Living, Vancouver, 85; De Vecchi (auth), Fantasy as partner, Vogue Decoration, Paris, 4/86. *Mem:* Ikenobo Ikebana Soc; Craftsman's Asn BC; Vancouver Community Arts Coun; Circle Craft Cooperative. *Publ:* Auth, Celebration of Paper, Arts Coun, 80; Some Roads to Here, Can Soc For Educ through Art, 80; Art and the City, Peregrine, 80; Kado-World Garden, Ikenobo J, 83. *Dealer:* Dianne Farris Gallery BC Canada. *Mailing Add:* Emily Carr Col Art & Design 1399 Johnston St Vancouver BC V6H 3R9 Canada

CARTER, YVONNE PICKERING
PAINTER, EDUCATOR
b Washington, DC, Feb 6, 39. *Study:* Traphagen Sch, cert, 59; Howard Univ, AB, 62, MFA, 68. *Work:* NC Mus, Raleigh; Federal Reserve Bank, Richmond, Va; Gibbes Gallery, Charleston, SC; Miami-Dade Co Libr, Fla; Montgomery Co Print Collection, Md; Artery Orgn, Md. *Exhib:* An Am Album: Images by Women Artists, traveled to Nairobi, Kenya, Calif & Md, 85-86; Performance: Installation-Lament, Walters Art Gallery, Baltimore, Md, 88; Coast to Coast: A Women of Color Nat Artists' Book Project, traveled to New York, Baltimore, Chicago, Houston, etc, 88-90; Pillar to Post: Wall Works by Contemp Artists, Kenkeleba Gallery, New York, 89; Performance; Confessions, Nat Mus Women Arts, Washington, DC, 90; African-Am Contemp Art, Gibellina Museo Civico D'Arte Contemporanea, Palermo, 90; Introspectives: Contemp Art by Am & Brazilians of African Descent, Calif Afro-Am Mus, Los Angeles & Bronx Mus Arts, NY, 89-90; Continuing Traditions: Contemp African Am Craft Artists, New Visions Gallery, Atlanta, Ga, 90; and others. *Teaching:* Prof design & painting, Univ District of Columbia, Washington DC, 71- *Awards:* DC Comn Arts & Humanities Visual Arts Award, 81 & 82; Fac Res Grant, 84. *Bibliog:* Scott Lucas (auth), Washington Walkabout, New Art Examiner, 81; M Sunderland (auth), 3 Artists, 3 Ways, Ocular, fall 81. *Mem:* Col Art Asn; Washington Women's Art Ctr; Women's Caucus Art. *Media:* Watercolor. *Mailing Add:* 1337 Tenth St NW Washington DC 20001

CARTMELL, HELEN
PAINTER, DRAFTSMAN
b Bridgeport, Conn, Jan 6, 23. *Study:* Detroit Soc Arts & Crafts, scholar, 41; LaNapoule Art Found, 85; Fel France, 87; Wayne State Univ; Vt Studio Ctr, 91; also with Jack Beal & Sondra Freckelton. *Work:* Wayne State Univ Collection; Chrysler Corp, Detroit; Int Nickel Co, New York; Ford Motor World Hq; Avon Corp; and many others. *Exhib:* Detroit Inst Arts; Willistead Gallery, Ont, Can; Grand Rapids Art Mus; one-woman shows, Arwin Galleries, Detroit, 70 & 75, Lansing Art Gallery, 86, Belian Art Ctr, Troy, Mich, 87 & Preston Burke Gallery, Detroit, Mich, 89; Drawing Exhib, South Bend, Ind, 90; Ecole Du Fois, La Cerqueux, France, 89. *Pos:* Educ media art dir, Ctr Instrnl Technol, Wayne State Univ, 67-85. *Teaching:* Media Spec, Wayne State Univ, Detroit, Mich. *Awards:* Hon Mention, Graphics, HESCA/Network for Continuing Med Educ; Ferris Fitch Award, Purchase Award & 1st, 2nd Hon Mention, Mich Acad Arts, Sci & Letts. *Bibliog:* William Tall (auth), Detroit Free Press, 75; M Meilgaard (auth), The Eccentric, Birmingham, Mich, 87. *Mem:* Mich Watercolor Soc; Detroit Soc Women Painters. *Media:* Oil, Conti Pencil; Pen & Ink, Graphite. *Dealer:* Cary Galleries Rochester MI; Preston Burke Galleries Inc 240 E Grand River Detroit MI 48212. *Mailing Add:* 21700 Winshall Rd St Clair Shores MI 48081

CARTWRIGHT, CONSTANCE B & CARROLL L
COLLECTORS
. *Mem:* Mrs Cartwright, Mus Mod Art Int Coun; Mus Mod Art (drawing comt). *Collection:* Late 19th and 20th century drawings; Chinese blue and white porcelain; French antique furniture. *Mailing Add:* 435 E 52nd St New York NY 10022

CARTWRIGHT, ROY R
CERAMIST
Study: Mt San Antonio Col, Walnut, Calif, 55-56, 57-58; Univ Southern Calif, Los Angeles, 56-57; Calif Col Arts & Crafts, Oakland, BFA(ceramics), 61; Rochester Inst Technol, NY, MFA(ceramics), 63. *Work:* Cincinnati Bell System; Univ Fla, Miami; Cleveland Mus Art; Johnson Collection Am Crafts; Everson Mus, Syracuse, NY. *Exhib:* Solo shows, Art Asn Harrisburg, Pa, 89, Contemp Art Ctr, Cincinnati, Ohio, 89, Swindler Gallery, Royal Oak, Mich, 91 & Carnegie Art Ctr, Covington, Ky, 92; Carnegie Art Ctr, Covington, Ky, 90; Dawson Gallery, Rochester, NY, 90; Northeast Mo State Univ, Kirksville, Miss, 91. *Teaching:* Cleveland Art Inst, 63-64; Univ Ill, 64-65; Univ Cincinnati, 65-; lects, talks & panel discussions, var cols & univs, 76-91. *Awards:* Research Equip Award, Univ Res Coun, 90; Visual Artist Fel, Nat Endowment Arts, 90; Individual Artist Grant, Ohio Arts Coun, 91. *Bibliog:* Rev, Cincinnati Post, 5/89; rev, Panorama, 10/89; rev, Dialogue, 11-12/89; and others. *Mem:* Delta Phi Delta. *Mailing Add:* 2307 Ohio Ave Cincinnati OH 45219

CARULLA, RAMON
PAINTER, PRINTMAKER
b Havana, Cuba, Dec 7, 38; US citizen. *Study:* Self taught. *Work:* Detroit Inst Art, Mich; Mus Tamayo, Mexico; Cincinnati Art Mus, Ohio; Mus Fine Art, Montreal, Can; Mus Latin Am Art, Washington, DC. *Exhib:* One-man shows, Joy Moos Gallery, SoFa & Hostage Series, Miami, 85, VI Graphic Biennial, San Juan, PR & Malcolm Brown Gallery, 85, Bacardi Gallery, Miami, Fla & Le Grand le Jeunne Auhordi-Grand Palais, Paris, France, 88; Paper as a Medium, Fla Int Univ & Smithsonian Inst, 79-80; 20 Years After, Bacardi Gallery, Miami, 87; and others. *Teaching:* Guest lectr, Cranbrook Acad Art, Bloomfield Hills, Mich, Wayne State Univ, Detroit, 83 & Cleveland State Univ, Ohio, 85; private art instr. *Awards:* Sixth Biennial of Graphic Latin Am Artists, San Juan, PR; Silvia Daro Dawidowicz Award, Metrop Mus & Arts Ctr, Coral Gables, Fla, 82; Cintas Fel Grant, 73-74 & 79-80; plus others. *Bibliog:* Uva Clavijo (auth), Diario de las Americas, 80; R Pau Llosa (auth), The origins of Cuban art, Miami Herald, 10/81; Ramon Carulla and the Latin American Expression, Vanidades Mag, 10/82. *Mem:* Ctr Fine Arts, Miami, Fla. *Media:* Oil on canvas & paper. *Publ:* (Carulla) Schweyer-Galdo Editions, 85. *Dealer:* Barbara Scott Gallery 1055 Kane Concourse Bay Harbor Island FL 33154. *Mailing Add:* 4735 NW 184th Terr Miami FL 33055

CARVALHO, JOSELY
PRINTMAKER, PAINTER
b Sao Paulo, Brazil, Sept 21, 42. *Study:* Printmaking with Marcelo Grassman & Darel, 61-63, Woodcut with Shiko Munakata, 65, Sch Archit, Washington Univ, St Louis, Mo, BA, 67. *Work:* Casa de Las Americas, Havanna, Cuba; Mus Mod Art, New York; Bronx Mus Art, Bronx, NY; Mus de Bellas Artes, Caracas, Venezuela; Brooklyn Mus, NY. *Comn:* Spectacolor Board-Times Square, Pub Art Fund, New York, 88. *Exhib:* Latin Am Artists, Chrysler Mus, Norfolk, Va, 83; one-man show, Cheiro de Peixe, Mus da Imagem e do Som, Sao Paulo, Brazil, 85; II Bienal de La Habana, Mus Nat de Bellas Artes, Havanna, Cuba, 86; Committed to Print, Mus Mod Art, New York, 88; UP Tiempo, Mus del Barrio, New York, 88; Decade show, Mus Contemp Hispanic Art, New Mus Contemp Art & Studio Mus Harlem, New York, 90;

Diary of Images: It's Still Time to Mourn, Hillwood Mus, Brookville, NY, 91; Diario De Imagens: Dia Mater, Museu De Arte De Sao Paulo (MASP), Sao Paulo, Brazil, 92. *Teaching:* vis prof, Sch Archit, Nat Univ Mex, 71-73; vis prof silkscreen, State Univ NY, Purchase, 88; artist-in-residence, Franklin & Marshall Col, Lancaster, Pa, 88; vis artist painting, State Univ of NY, Purchase, 92. *Awards:* Nat Endowment Arts Fel, 75-76; NY State Coun Arts, 78-82; NY Found Arts Fel, 84, 85. *Bibliog:* Arlene Raven (auth), Rape, Ohio State Univ, 85; Lucy Lippard (auth), Following the Dots, Connecting Project/Conexus, 87; Deborah Wye (auth), Committed to Print, Mus Mod Art, 88. *Mem:* Heresies Collective; Women Caucus Art. *Media:* Silkscreen. *Publ:* Mothers, Mags & Movie Stars, Heresies Collective, 85 & Story of Elza; auth, The Meal, 86; coauth, with Conexus, Connection Project, 87; illusr, We Hold Our Ground, Ikon, 88; illusr (cover), Abortion and Woman's Choice, Northeastern Univ Press, 90. *Dealer:* Terne Gallery 38 E 57th St 6th fl New York NY 10022. *Mailing Add:* 216 E 18th St New York NY 10003

CASANOVA, ALDO JOHN
SCULPTOR, EDUCATOR
b San Francisco, Calif, Feb 8, 29. *Study:* San Francisco State Univ, BA, 50, MA, 51; Ohio State Univ, PhD, 57. *Work:* Whitney Mus, New York; San Francisco Mus Art; Sculpture Garden, San Diego Mus, Calif; Sculpture Garden, Univ Calif, Los Angeles; Joseph Hirshhorn Collection, Washington, DC. *Comn:* Skidmore, Owings & Merrill, Archit, San Francisco, 66; Atlantic-Richfield Co, Los Angeles, 69; Washington Mutual Savings Bank, Seattle, 69; Calif Inst Technol, Pasadena, 74; Univ Judaism, Los Angeles, 81. *Exhib:* Pa Acad Ann, Philadelphia, 62-67; Art Dealers Asn Am, Parke-Bernet Gallery, New York, 64; solo exhibs, Esther Robles Gallery, Los Angeles, 67, Santa Barbara Mus, 67 & Calif Inst Technol, 72; The New Vein, Smithsonian Inst, SAm travel tour, 68-70; New Acqusitions, Whitney Mus Am Art, New York, 70; State Univ NY, Albany, 81. *Pos:* Juror, New York, 64 & 74; sculptor in res, Am Acad, Rome, 75. *Teaching:* Asst prof sculpture, Antioch Col, 56-58; Asst prof sculpture, Temple Univ, 61-64, assoc prof sculpture, 68-70; prof sculpture, Scripps Col, 66-, chmn art dept, 71-73; summer fac, Skowhegan Sch Painting & Sculpture, Maine, 74, head summer fac, 75; vis prof sculpture, State Univ NY, Albany, 80-81; prof sculpture, Claremont Grad Sch, 82- *Awards:* Acad in Rome fel, 58-61; Louis Comfort Tiffany Award, 69. *Bibliog:* Anthony Parovano (auth), The Process of Sculpture, Doubleday & Co, 81; Jonathan Tslock & Jerry Leisure (auth), Understanding Three Dimensions, Prentice-Hall, 87. *Mem:* FARR, New York; Nat Acad Design, New York, 92. *Media:* Bronze, Casting; Carving, Stone or Wood. *Dealer:* Carl Schlosberg Fine Arts 15447 Valley Vista Blvd Sherman Oaks CA 91403. *Mailing Add:* 691 W 12th St Claremont CA 91711

CASARELLA, EDMOND
SCULPTOR, PRINTMAKER
b Newark, NJ, Sept 3, 20. *Study:* Cooper Union, BFA, 42; Brooklyn Mus Art Sch, 49-51. *Work:* Whitney Mus Am Art, Brooklyn Mus, New York & Mus the City of New York; Nat Gallery Australia, Canberra; NJ State Mus, Trenton; Speed Mus, Louisville, Ky; Libr Cong, Washington, DC; Nat Gallery, Athens, Greece. *Comn:* Sculpture, Northern Valley Bank, Cresskill, NJ; Unitarian Church, Louisville, Ky; RKO Century Bldg, New York; Harcourt, Brace & Jovanovich Hq, Orlando, Fla. *Exhib:* Brooklyn Mus, 52 & 58; Pa Acad Fine Arts, 53, 59 & 63; Libr Cong, 55, 56 & 58; Corcoran Gallery Art, 55; Boston Mus Fine Arts, 57; Victoria & Albert Mus, 59; Whitney Mus Am Art, 59 & 61-63; Los Angeles Co Mus Art, 63; solo exhibs, Speed Mus, 68-69, Landmark Gallery, New York, 77 & 80 & Sculpture Ctr, New York, 77; retrospective, Allegheny Col, 78 & Edward Williams Col, 79; Sylvan Cole Gallery, 88, 89 & 90; and many others. *Pos:* and many others. *Teaching:* Instr graphics, Brooklyn Mus Sch, 56-60, Norfolk Summer Art Sch, Yale Univ, 58, NY Univ, 62, Cooper Union, 63-70, Hunter Col, 63-, Columbia Univ, summer 63 & 64, Yale Univ, 64-, Rutgers Univ, 64-, Pratt Inst, 64-, Finch Col, 69-74, Manhattanville Col, 73-74 & Queens Col, 80. *Awards:* Fulbright Award for Graphics, Italy, 51-52; Tiffany Award Graphics, 55; Guggenheim Fel for Graphics, 59-60. *Bibliog:* Ross-Romano (auth), The Complete Printmaker, MacMillan Free Press; Una Johnson (auth), Am Prints & Printmakers; James Watrous (auth), Century of Printmaking; David Acton (auth), A Spectrum of Innocation Color in American Printmaking, 60-90. *Mem:* Sculptors Guild. *Media:* Steel, Bronze. *Dealer:* Sylvan Cole New York NY; Susan Teller New York NY. *Mailing Add:* 83 E Linden Englewood NJ 07631

CASAS, FERNANDO
PAINTER, DRAFTSMAN
b Cochabamba, Bolivia, Mar 25, 46. *Study:* Colo Col, BA; Rice Univ, MA, PhD; pvt training with Raul Prada. *Work:* Nat Mus Art, La Paz, Bolivia; Pinacoteca Nac, Cochabamba, Bolivia; Art of the Americas Collection (B Duncan), New York; Mus Fine Arts, Houston. *Comn:* Five paintings about Society, Baker World Trade, Houston, 80; mural, Hermman Hosp, Houston, 90. *Exhib:* One-man shows, Harriet Griffin Gallery, New York, 76 & Mus Nacional De Arte, La Paz, Bolivia, 88; Toni Jones Gallery, Houston, 79 & 80; Heritage Gallery, Los Angeles, 79; Duveen Gallery, Houston, 79; Galeria Emusa, Bolivia, 86; Blue Mt Gallery, New York, 89. *Awards:* First Nat Award Painting & First Nat Award Drawing, Concurso Nac de Artes Plasticas, Bolivia, 72 & 73. *Bibliog:* Itsuo Sakane (auth), The Asahi Shimbun, Japan, 8/83, 5/84 & others; Flocon (auth), Curvilinear Perspective, Univ Calif Press, 87; Pintura Boliviana del siglo XX, BHN Bolivia, 89. *Media:* Oil; Mixed. *Publ:* Auth, Flat sphere perspective, Vol 16, No 1, 83 & Polar perspective: A graphical system for creating two dimensional images representing a world of four dimensions, Vol 17, No 3, 84, Leonardo; and others. *Dealer:* Beowulf Fine Arts Ltd 12620 I-45 N Suite 218 Houston TX 77060 Tel: 713-872-1342. *Mailing Add:* 22214 Meadow Sweet Houston TX 77355

CASAS, MELESIO (MEL)
PAINTER, EDUCATOR
b El Paso, Tex, Nov 24, 29. *Study:* Univ Tex, El Paso, BA, 56; Univ of the Americas, Mex, MFA, 58. *Comn:* Jim & Ann Harithas, NY; Robert Wilson, Houston, Tex; Joe Nicholson, San Antonio, Tex; Todd Spites, Hondo, Tex. *Exhib:* Artists of the Southeast & Tex, Biennial Painting & Sculpture, 71; Tex Painting & Sculptures: 20th Century, 72; Mex-Am Art Symp, Trinity Univ, 73; 12 Tex Artists, Contemp Art Mus, Houston, 74; 1975 Biennial Contemp Am Art, Whitney Mus Art, 75; Dale Gas--Chicano Art of Tex, Contemp Arts Mus, Houston, 77; Showdown, Alternative Mus, New York, 83; Chicano Expression, INTAR, New York, 86; Ft Worth Art Festival, Tex, 86; One-man show, Lagunz Gloriz Mus, Austin, Tex. *Pos:* Book reviewer, Choice Mag, Am Libr Asn, 54-; panels, San Antonio Art Coun & Nat Endowment Arts, 86. *Teaching:* Prof art, design & painting, San Antonio Col, Tex, 61-90; retired. *Awards:* Purchase Prize, 59 & Cash Award, 64, El Paso Art Mus; Cash Award, San Antonio Art League, 66 & Ft Worth Art Festival, 86. *Bibliog:* Jacinto Quiarte (auth), The Art of Mexican Americans, Univ Tex, 73; article, Art News, 12/77; Mimi Crossley (auth), Dale Gas at the Contemporary Art Museum, Art in Am, 1-2/78. *Mem:* Founding mem Con Safo Painters; Fine Arts Comn, San Antonio, Tex. *Media:* Acrylic. *Mailing Add:* 6933 Border Brook No 1004 San Antonio TX 78238-4036

CASCIERI, ARCANGELO
SCULPTOR, INSTRUCTOR
b Civitaquana, Italy, Feb 22, 02; US citizen. *Study:* Sch Archit, Boston Archit Ctr, 22-26; Boston Univ, 32-36. *Work:* Boston Col; Holy Cross Col; Buffalo Courier Express Bldg; Parlin Jr High Sch, Everett, Mass; Lexington Jr High Sch, Mass. *Comn:* Am War Mem World War I, Belleau Woods, France & World War II, Margraten, Holland; exterior Mem Auditorium, Lynn, Mass; exterior Boys' Stadium, Franklin Field, Dorchester, Mass; sculpture on fountain, Parkman Plaza, Boston; Duxbury Art Complex Mus, Mass; and many others. *Exhib:* Sculpture Exhib, Boston Mus Fine Arts; Sculpture Exhibs, New Eng Sculpture Asn; one-man exhib, Sch Design, Harvard Univ; Lit Arts Soc Exhib, New York. *Pos:* Asst dir sculpture & wood carving, W F Ross Studio, Cambridge, 23-41; sculptor & asst dir, Schwamb Assocs Studio, Arlington, 41-46, sculptor & dir, 46-52; partner studio for sculpture & decorations, Boston, 52- *Teaching:* Pvt classes, Boston, 32-37; instr design & head sch archit, Boston Archit Ctr, formerly; instr, Craft Ctr Sch, Boston, 39-40; instr design, New London Jr Col, Conn, 41-43. *Awards:* First Commun Award, New Eng Sch Art & Design, Hon Alumnus, 79; Citation Boston 200, 75; Silver Medal for Distinguished Pub Serv in the Arts & Educ, Boston Univ Alumni Asn, 76. *Mem:* Fel Am Inst Archit; hon mem Dante Alighieri Soc; hon mem Naples Asn Inst Archit & Engineers; New Eng Sculptors Asn; Mass Asn Archit; and others. *Mailing Add:* 500 Concord Ave Lexington MA 02173

CASE, ELIZABETH
PAINTER, WRITER
b Long Beach, Calif, July 24, 30. *Study:* Fr Inst, New York, with Mr Lee, 46; Art Students League, with Vlascov Vytlacil, Robert Hale, Reginald Marsh & Harry Sternberg, 48-49; Elmira Col, 49-51; Syracuse Univ; Chaffey Col, Ont, with Doug McClellan, 54; Scripps Col, with Dr Schardt, 54. *Work:* USN Combat Art Collection, Washington, DC; Elmira Col Ford Mus, NY; Edgewater Pub Libr, NJ. *Comn:* View Through Trees (mural), pvt comn, New York, 75; Torpedo Loading, Homecoming of USS Skate & NROTC Ball, comn by Secy Navy Middendorf, USN Combat Art Collection, 75-76; Wall of Discovery (mural), Old Bridge Pub Libr, 77; History of Typography (mural), Graphic Technol Inc, New York, 85. *Exhib:* One-man shows, Inaugural Exhib, Ft Lee Libr, NJ, 75, Ridgefield Pub Libr NJ, 77 & Current Veiws, Eastern VA Med Ctr Exhib Facility, Norfolk VA, 84; Am Freedoms Caravan Mural Design Exhib, Nat Arts Club, New York, 75 & Wilmington Opera House, 76; Nat Exhib Miniature Paintings, Nutley, NJ, 75; and other group & one-man shows. *Pos:* Asst animator, Walt Disney Prod, 56-58; sr copywriter/designer spec proj, Prentice-Hall Col Advert Dept, Englewood Cliffs, 75-77; creative dir, Gadfly Productions, Edgewater, NJ, 77- & Echo, 88-; design/prom, Rutherford Mus, NJ, 79; sales prom mgr, M Grumbacher Inc, New York, 79-81; typography qual control, Graphic Technol Inc, New York, 84-; The Graphic Work, 90. *Teaching:* Instr basic drawing & painting, Ft Lee Adult Sch, 75-85. *Awards:* Second Award, Wyn Rogers Gallery, Cliffside Park, NJ, 64; Award & Citation for Outstanding Achievement, Elmira Col, 76. *Bibliog:* Thomas Oat (auth), article, Groton News, Conn, 75; Judy Plummer (auth), article, Dolphin Newspaper, New London, Conn, 75; Roberta Roesch (auth), There's Always a Right Job for Every Woman, Berkeley, 76; John Luke (auth), feature article, Gutenberg Family-Mag of Type Dir Asn, 85; Linda Skelly, 30 minute video interview, A Stroke of Color, Channel 10, Video Cable, NJ, 85. *Mem:* Nat Soc Mural Painters Inc (secy, 75). *Media:* Egg Tempera, Oil. *Publ:* Auth, Nat Soc Mural Painters Brochure, 73; illusr cover, Weidenbaum's Business, Government and the Public, Prentice-Hall, 76; illusr cover & part openings, Algren & Hackworth's Programmed Algebra, Vols I & II, 77, Vol III, 79 & R Kimble's Use and Misuse of Statistics, 78, Prentice-Hall; illusr & designer, What Do I Do With A Major In ? (by Dr L Malnids), Abbott, 85. *Mailing Add:* Fine Arts Studio PO Box 58 Edgewater NJ 07020

CASEBERE, JAMES E
PHOTOGRAPHER, SCULPTOR
b Lansing, Mich, Sept 17, 53. *Study:* Mich State Univ, 71-72; Minneapolis Col Art & Design, BFA, 76; Whitney Mus Independent Study Program, 77; Calif Inst Arts, MFA, 79. *Work:* Neuberger Mus, Purchase, NY; Walker Art Ctr, Minneapolis, Minn; Victoria Albert Mus, London; Tampa Mus, Fla; Mus Mod Art, New York; Mus Fine Art, Boston. *Comn:* Minn Hist Ctr, St Paul, 91. *Exhib:* Fabricated to be Photographed, San Francisco Mus Mod Art,

Albright-Knox Gallery, Buffalo, NY, Newport Harbor Art Mus, Newport Beach, Calif & Univ NMex, Albuquerque, 79-80; Photo, Metro Pictures, New York, 81; TV Generation, Los Angeles Contemp Exhibs, 86; Arrangements for the Camera: A View of Contemporary Photography, Baltimore Mus Art, Md, 87; Photography of Invention, Nat Gallery Am Art, Washington, DC, 89; Cross References Sculpture into Photog, Walker Art Ctr, Minn & Mus Contemp Art, Chicago; Photog & Art: Interactions Since 1946, Los Angeles Co Mus Art; This is not a Photograph: 20 Years of Large Scale Photog, Ringling Mus Art, Sarasota, Fla; solo exhibs: Mus Photog Arts, San Diego, 90, Urbi et Orbi, Paris, 90-91, Photog Resource Ctr, Boston, 91, Univ Iowa Mus Art, Iowa City, 91, Galerie Bruges La Morte, Brugge, Belgium, 91, Model Fictions, Birmingham Mus Art, Ala, 91, James Hockey Galery, WSCAD, Farnham, Eng, 91; Pleasures and Terrors of Domestic Comfort, Mus Mod Art, New York, 91; Not One Photography, Mus Mod Art, New York, 92; Constructing Images, Lieberman & Saul Gallery, NY, Tampa Mus Art & Ctr Creative Photog, Tucson, Ariz, 91-92; and others. *Teaching:* Asst prof photog, Rockland Community Col, 85-88; vis artist, Calif Inst Arts, 84, Boston Mus Sch, 89 & RI Design, 91. *Awards:* Visual Artist Fels, 82, 86 & 90, Nat Endowment Arts; Visual Artist Sponsored Proj Grant, NY State Coun Arts, 82; Fel, New York Found Arts, 85 & 89. *Bibliog:* Hal Foster (auth), Uncanny images, Art Am 11/84; Herbert Muschamp (auth), Nightlights, (catalogue), APAC, Nevers, France, 90; Stuart Morgan (auth), Broken Home, (catalogue), James Hockey Gallery, WSCAD, Farnham, 91. *Publ:* Auth, In the 2nd Half of the 20th Century, CEPA Gallery, Buffalo, 82. *Dealer:* Michael Klein Inc 611 Broadway New York NY 10012. *Mailing Add:* 175 Ludlow St New York NY 10002

CASELL, JOACHIM See Casellas, Joachim

CASELLAS, JOACHIM
PAINTER
b Gerona Prov, Spain, Aug 1, 27; US citizen. *Study:* Col Sacred Heart, Gerona, Spain, BA, 48; Inst Escobar. *Work:* Mus Provincial & Tossa Mus, Gerona, Spain. *Exhib:* Salon de Octobre, Galleria Leytana, Barcelona, Spain, 50; Brazil Biennial, Brazil, 51; Paris Group, Paris, France, 52; Art Who? Ocean Springs, Miss, 88; Casell Gallery, New Orleans, La, 88; Artist Showcase, New Orleans, La, 88. *Awards:* Merit Award, Ocean Springs Art Asn, 88; First Place, Fall Festival, Biloxi Art, 88. *Mem:* Ocean Springs Art Asn. *Media:* Pastel, Miscellaneous Media. *Mailing Add:* Casell Galleries 818 Royal St New Orleans LA 70116

CASEY, JACQUELINE SHEPARD
DESIGNER
b Quincy, Mass, Apr 20, 27. *Study:* Mass Col Art, BFA, 50; & Hon Dr Fine Arts, 90; study of drawing with Hyman bloom, 51-53. *Work:* Libr of Cong, Washington, DC; Mus Mod Art, Cooper Hewitt Mus, New York. *Exhib:* Direction 1968, Philadelphia Col Art, 68; Mass Inst Technol Hayden Gallery Corridor, Cambridge, Mass, 72, 79, 83 & 88; Images of an Era, The American Poster, 1945-1975, Corcoran Gallery Art, Washington, DC, 76; Warsaw Biennale, Poland, 80 & 84; Lahti IV Poster Biennale, Finland, 81, 83 & 85; Images Survival, The 40th Anniversary Bombing Hiroshima, 85; Cooper Union, New York, 86; Ten Pivotal Women Design, Chicago, 88; and others. *Collections Arranged:* Ann Design for Printing and Commerce, Am Inst Graphic Arts; Typomundus 20 & 20 II; Creativity on Paper; New York Type Directors Club. *Bibliog:* Jean Coyne (auth), MIT design services office, Commun Arts, 9-10/74; Stanley Mason (auth), Objective graphic design (MIT), Graphis, Zurich, Switz, 74-75; Rithsve Siegle (auth), American Graphic Designers: 30 Years of Design Imagery, McGraw Hill Bks, 84. *Mem:* Alliance Graphique Int; Am Inst Graphic Arts. *Publ:* Peace Posters, Dai-Nippon Printing Co, 85; Posters by Members of the Alliance Graphique Internationale, Rizzoli Int Publ Inc, 86; Thirty Centuries of Graphic Design, Watson-Guptill Publ, 87; Women Designers of America, Idea Mag, 88; Women in Design, Liz McQuiston, Rizzoli Int Publ Inc, 88. *Mailing Add:* Mass Inst of Technol Media Lab E-15, Rm 450, 77 Massachusetts Ave Cambridge MA 02139

CASEY, JOHN THAYER
PAINTER, SCULPTOR
b New London, Conn, June 27, 31. *Study:* Univ Ore, BA; Calif Col of Arts & Crafts, MFA with Nathan Oliveira & Harry Krell. *Work:* Univ Ore, Eugene; State of Ore, Salem & Pendleton; Coos Art Mus, Ore. *Exhib:* 68th Western Ann, Denver Art Mus, 62; The Painted Flower, Oakland Art Mus, Calif, 63 & 64; Supplement 66, Fountain Gallery, Portland, 66; Ore Artists Ann, Portland Art Mus, 67, 71-73, 75 & 77; 22nd Spokane Ann, Cheney Cowles Mus, Wash, 70, 72, 74 & 76; 32nd Ann NW Watercolor Exhib, Seattle Art Mus Pavilion, Wash, 71; and others. *Teaching:* Assoc prof drawing, painting & design, West Ore State Col, Monmouth, 65-88, emer prof. *Bibliog:* G E Guilbert (auth), The Art Forms Explosion, Spokane Spokesman-Rev, 7/72; Lorraine B Widman (auth), Sculpture: A Studio Guide to Concepts, Methods & Materials, Prentice-Hall, 90- *Media:* Acrylic, Watercolor; Miscellaneous Media. *Mailing Add:* 2125 Oak Grove Rd NW Salem OR 97304-9511

CASEY, TIM (TIMOTHY WILLIAM)
PAINTER
b Lawton, Okla, July 19, 47. *Study:* Art Acad Cincinnati, 65-68; RI Sch Design, BFA, 70, MFA, 72. *Work:* Chase Manhattan Bank, New York. *Comn:* Painting, Vera List for Jewish Mus, New York, 86. *Exhib:* Solo show, Gabrielle Bryers, New York, 85-86 & Tomoko Liguori, New York, 88; A Radical Plurality, William Paterson Col, Elizabeth, NJ, 86; Artists Space, New York, 90-91. *Teaching:* Instr drawing, RI Sch Design, 73-74; instr drawing & painting, State Univ NY at Purchase, Exten Sch, 86-89; artist in residence, Studio in a School, PS 11, 89- *Awards:* Studio Program, PS 1, The Clocktower, 86. *Bibliog:* John Russell (auth), Review, New York Times, 85; Grace Glueck (auth), Review, New York Times, 85; Stephen Westfall (auth), Review, Art in Am, 88. *Media:* Oil, Watercolor. *Mailing Add:* Margulies Taplin Gallery 1401 Brickell Ave Miami FL 33131

CASIDA, KATI
PRINTMAKER, SCULPTOR
b Viroqua, Wis, Mar 28, 31. *Study:* Univ Wis-Madison, BS(art educ), 53; New Sch Social Res, with Antonio Frasconi, New York, 55. *Work:* Syntex Corp, Palo Alto & City Percent Art Prog, Brea, Calif; Ore Art Comn, Salem; Int Paper Co, New York. *Comn:* Sculpture (steel), Spectrum Ctr, Criswell Co, Dallas, 83; sculpture (aluminum & steel), Lurie Co, San Francisco, 85; sculpture (wood & trees) Viroqua City Park, Wis, 87. *Exhib:* Sculpture, Hastings Col of Law, San Francisco, Calif, 84; Going Public, Walnut Creek Civic Arts Ctr, Calif, 85; Victor Fischer Galleries, Oakland, 85 & San Francisco; Oakland City Ctr, 88; New Leaf Garden Gallery, Berkeley, 91; and others. *Teaching:* Instr art & hist, Upsala Col, East Orange, NJ, 55-56. *Awards:* Am Asn Univ Women, La Crosse, Wis, 50; Open Proposals, City of Oakland, 91. *Bibliog:* Radio, Jonsok sculpture, Nat Norweg Broadcasting Co, 6/85; Andrea Workman (auth), Casida-modern sculptor, Viking Mag, Minneapolis, Minn, 12/85. *Mem:* Int Sculpture Ctr; Calif Soc Printmakers; Nat Women's Art Caucus; The Nat Mus of Women in the Arts, Washington, DC. *Media:* Woodcut; Metal. *Publ:* Coauth, Jonsok sculpture, Viking Mag, Minneapolis, Minn, 12/85; Sculpture for Missing Persons, Hellenic J, San Francisco, 3/92. *Mailing Add:* c/o Studio 1570 La Vereda Rd Berkeley CA 94708

CASLIN, JEAN
ARTS ADMINISTRATOR
b Washington, DC. *Study:* Boston Univ, BA(art hist, Eng lit), 74; Stanford Unvi, MA(art hist), 77. *Pos:* Exec dir, Houston Ctr Photog, 88- *Teaching:* Lectr photographic hist, Boston Col, 85-88; lectr, Univ Houston, 89-90. *Mem:* Soc Photog Educ. *Mailing Add:* c/o Houston Ctr for Photography 1441 W Alabama Houston TX 77006

CASS, BILL
PAINTER
b Chicago, Ill, 1954. *Study:* Univ Ill, Champaign-Urbana, BFA, 77; Art Inst Chicago, MFA, 81. *Work:* Krannert Art Mus, Champaign, Ill; Madison Art Ctr, Wis; Prudential Insurance, Chicago; Arthur Anderson & Co, Chicago; Container Corp, Chicago. *Exhib:* One-man exhibs, Mariane Deson Gallery, Chicago, 83, 85, 87, Freeport Mus, Freeport, Ill, 86, Trinity Christain Col, Palos Heights, Ill, 87, G W Einstein, New York, 88 and Roy Boyd Gallery, Chicago, 89; three-person exhib, Braunstein-Quay Gallery, San Francisco, 87; Saga(s), Carlo LaMagna Gallery, New York, 88; Internazionale d'Art Contemporanea, Milan Fair, Italy, 89; Selections from the Roy Boyd Gallery, Calder Fine Arts Center, Grand Valley State Univ, Allendale, Mich, 90; The Chicago Show, Chicago Cult Center, 90; and many others. *Teaching:* Vis artist, Art Inst Chicago, 82- *Awards:* Edward L Ryerson Traveling Fel, Art Inst Chicago, 81; Ill Arts Coun Fel Grants, 84, 85 & 88; Regional Visual Arts Fel, Arts Midwest/Nat Endowment Arts, 87; Fel, Chicago Artists Abroad, 88. *Bibliog:* Numerous articles in Artweek, New Art Examiner, Chicago Sun-Times, Art News and other publ. *Dealer:* Marianne Deson Gallery 340 W Huron Chicago IL 60610; Roy Boyd Gallery 739 N Wells Chicago IL 60610 Tel: 312-642- 1606. *Mailing Add:* 3608 N Tripp Ave Chicago IL 60641

CASSARA, FRANK
PAINTER, PRINTMAKER
b Partinico, Sicily; US citizen. *Study:* Colorado Springs Sch Fine Arts, Colo; Univ Mich, MS(design); also spec study, Atelier 17, Paris, France. *Work:* Libr Cong, Washington, DC; Bibliot Nat, Paris, France; Stedelijk Mus, Amsterdam, Neth; Detroit Inst Arts; Free Libr Philadelphia; Nat Mus Am Art, Smithsonian, Washington, DC; Owen Ill, Toledo, Ohio; and others. *Comn:* Murals, Ft Wayne, Detroit, Mich, 38, US Post Off, East Detroit, 39, Donald Thompson Sch (fresco), Highland Park, Mich, 39, US Post Off, Sandusky, Mich, 40 & Water Conditioning Plant, Lansing, Mich, 41. *Exhib:* Seventh Int Exhib Lithography & Wood Engr, Art Inst Chicago, 39; 1st Exhib Am Printmakers, Gallerie Nees Morphes, Athens, Greece, 65; 22nd Nat Exhib Prints, Libr Cong, 71; Atelier 17: A Retrospective, Elvehjem Art Ctr, Madison, Wis, 77; Toledo Mus Art, Ohio, 82; Mus Art, Univ Mich, Ann Arbor, Mich, 86; DeWaters Art Ctr, Flint, Mich, 90; and others. *Teaching:* Instr drawing, Detroit Soc Arts & Crafts, 46-47; prof printmaking, Univ Mich, 47-83, emer prof art, currently. *Awards:* Over 50 in national and regional exhibitions; Rackham Res Grants, Univ Mich, 61, 68, 74 & 75. *Media:* Oil; All. *Publ:* Contribr, Artists' Proof, A Collectors Edition, 71. *Mailing Add:* 1122 Pomona Rd Ann Arbor MI 48103

CASSELL, BEVERLY
PAINTER
b Montgomery, Ala, 1936. *Study:* Univ Ga, Athens, MFA(art & philosophy), 60 study with Lamar Dodd & Howard Thomas; NY Univ, New York, 63. *Work:* Disney Studios, Burbank, Calif; Ga Mus, Athens; Taiwan Mus Art, Taichung; US Embassy, Manila, Philippines; Univ House, Univ Calif, Santa Cruz. *Exhib:* Art Mus Santa Cruz County, Santa Cruz, Calif, 84 & 85; Art Source Los Angeles, Calif, 87; Thomas Jefferson Cult Ctr, Manila, Philippines, 89; Venice Art Walk Show, Los Angeles, Calif, 90; Dirs Guild Am, Los Angeles, Calif, 90; Los Angeles Co Mus Art, 92; Nagasaki Mus Art, Japan, 92; and others. *Pos:* Founder & dir, West Coast Artist Conf Network, 83-; dir, Los Angeles Inner City Youth Water Sculpture Proj, 92; bd dirs, Los

Angeles Artcore Gallery, 92. *Teaching:* Univ Colo, Denver, 67-69; Univ Calif Santa Cruz, 72-80; UCLA Exten, 86-89; Getty Mus Art Educ Ser, Los Angeles, 92. *Awards:* Los Angeles Cult Affairs Coun Grant for Los Angeles Inner City Youth Water Sculpture Proj. *Bibliog:* Article, Calif Art Review, 89; Visual arts crossroads, Univ Calif-Santa Cruz, 89; 4th International Contemporary Art Fair Catalog, Art LA, 89. *Mem:* West Coast Artist Conf Network; Los Angeles Artcore. *Media:* Oil, Gouache. *Mailing Add:* 2202 W 20th St Los Angeles CA 90018

CASSELLI, HENRY C, JR
PAINTER
b New Orleans, La, Oct 25, 46. *Work:* Libr Congress; New Orleans Mus; Hunter Mus, Tenn; Greenville Mus, SC; Albany Mus, Ga; Am Tel & Tel, New York; The White House, Nat Portrait Gallery, Washington, DC. *Comn:* La State Univ, Baton Rouge, 78; W C Bradley, Columbus, Ga; portrait of Pres R Reagan, Nat Portrait Gallery, Smithsonian Inst & The White House. *Exhib:* Solo exhibs, Lauren Rogers Mus, 72 & Greenville Co Mus, SC, 80; Smithsonian Traveling Drawing Exhib, 72-75; Hunter Mus, Tenn, 81; Am Watercolor Soc, New York, 71-86; and others. *Awards:* High Winds Medals, 76, 77, 79 & 88, Silver Medal, 86 & Gold Medal, 87, Am Watercolor Soc. *Bibliog:* Doreen Mangan (auth), Henry Casselli, Am Arts; Susan Meyer (auth), 20 Figure Painters, Watson-Guptill, 79; article, Southern Accent Mag, 81; Betty Harvey (auth), Henry Casselli, Art West Digest, 85; John Kemp (auth), Henry Casselli, Am Artist. *Mem:* Am Watercolor Soc (vpres, 79-); Nat Acad Design, New York. *Media:* Watercolor, Pastels. *Publ:* Contribr, The Natural Way to Paint, Davis, 78; Using Color, Dobie, Watson-Guptill, 86. *Dealer:* Tex Art Gallery, Dallas; Mongerson-Wunderlich, Chicago, IL. *Mailing Add:* 4015 N LaBarre Rd Metairie LA 70002

CASSIDY, MARGARET CAROL (MRS JOHN MANSHIP)
SCULPTOR
b Whitinsville, Mass. *Study:* Framingham State Col, BS, 44; Univ Mass, Amherst, MS, 49; Smith Col; Rosary Col Grad Sch Fine Arts, Florence, Italy, MA, 54. *Work:* Britain Mus Am Art, Conn; NY Univ Bobst Libr, Maryknoll, New York; Holy Cross Col Dinand Libr, Worcester, Mass; Framingham & Bridgewater State Col Librs, Mass; Vatican Collections, Rome. *Comn:* Madonna & St Joseph (sculpture), Holy Spirit Church, Kyoto, Japan, 61; Cardinal Newman, 63, Newman Ctr, Amherst, Mass, St Jude, 81; Risen Christ, St Anthony's Maronite Church, Springfield, 71 & St Mary's Church, Uxbridge, Mass, 75; stained glass, New Britain Mus of Am Art; L L Winship Medal for the Boston Globe; Three Medals, Newman Ctr, Univ Mass. *Exhib:* Nat Acad Design Ann, New York, 66 & 79; three-man show, New Britain Mus, Conn, 71; Burr Artists, Metrop Mus Art, New York, 76. *Teaching:* Asst prof art, Bridgewater State Col, 64; artist-in-residence, Univ Southern Ill, Edwardsville, 76 & Castleton S Col, Vt. *Awards:* Silver Medal, Pen & Brush Club, New York, 72; Bronze Medal, Catharine Lorillard Wolfe Art Club, New York, 72; Campidoglio D'oro, Burckhardt Acad, Rome, 78. *Bibliog:* Articles in Madmoiselle, 53, Boston Globe, 79 & Dict Am Sculptors, 84. *Mem:* Salmagundi Club; Catharine Lorillard Wolfe Art Club; Pen & Brush Club; Burr Artists; Rockport Art Asn. *Media:* Bronze. *Res:* Card catalog of all American artists. *Dealer:* Harbor Gallery 49 Main St Rockport MA 01966. *Mailing Add:* c/o John Manship 463 West St New York NY 10014

CASSILL, HERBERT CARROLL
PRINTMAKER, EDUCATOR
b Percival, Iowa, Dec 24, 28. *Study:* State Univ Iowa, BFA, 48, MFA, 50, with Mauricio Lasansky. *Work:* Mus Mod Art, New York; Cleveland Mus Art; Brooklyn Mus; Libr Cong, Washington, DC; Oakland Art Mus, Calif. *Exhib:* Libr Cong, 52, 54 & 60; six shows, Philadelphia Print Club, 53-60; Int Exhib Graphic Arts (shown in Europe), Mus Mod Art, 54, Modern Art in the USA (shown in Europe), 55; Soc of Am Graphic Artists Overseas Exhib, US State Dept, 60. *Pos:* head dept printmaking, Cleveland Inst Art, 57- *Teaching:* Instr printmaking, State Univ Iowa, 53-57. *Awards:* Tiffany Found Fel Printmaking, 53; Purchase Prize, Philadelphia Print Club, 56; First Prize, Print Show, State Univ NY, Potsdam, 61. *Media:* Intaglio, Wood. *Mailing Add:* 3084 Coleridge Rd Cleveland OH 44118

CASSYD, SYD
CURATOR, CRITIC
b NJ, Dec 28, 08. *Study:* Oxford Summer Inst, End, 29, Alliance Francaise, Paris, France, cert, 30; New Theatre Sch, 37; NY Univ, 43. *Work:* Theatre Arts Libr, Univ Calif, Los Angeles; Variety Arts Ctr. *Exhib:* TV 1930-1974, Beverly Hills Libr, Calif. *Pos:* Actg cur television collection, Univ Calif, Los Angeles, 60-61; television cur, Hollywood Mus, 60-65; dir, New Horizons Broadcasting Sch, Ventura, Calif, 69; cur television collection, Hollywood Chap, Acad Television Arts & Sci, 75-; auth, Weekly column for Beverly Press, 88- *Teaching:* Asst instr motion picture, New York Univ, Washington Sq Col, 42-44. *Awards:* Grant, 45, Pres Emmy, 56 & Gov Award Emmy, 55 & 71, Syd Cassyd Founder's Award, 91, Acad Television Arts & Sci; Dove Award, Friendship Day Camp, 60. *Mem:* Life mem Acad Television Arts & Sci (pres, 50); Acad Motion Picture Arts & Sci; Found Motion Picture Pioneers; Calif State Coun Arts (exec vpres, 62-65); Hollywood Foreign Press Asn (vpres, 79-80); Jewish Art Comn, Los Angeles Fedn. *Publ:* Auth, 100 feature articles in Boxoffice Mag, 63-75; An academy or a chamber of commerce, NAEB J, 64; Emmy Awards confidential--how TV moved from motion pictures, Acad TV Arts & Sci, 76; Peace has come to PBS, MAC Mag, 79; contribr (forward), Emmys, Penguin Bks, 92. *Mailing Add:* 917 S Tremaine Ave Los Angeles CA 90019

CASTANIS, MURIEL (JULIA BRUNNER)
SCULPTOR
b New York, NY, Sept 27, 26. *Study:* Self-taught. *Work:* New Sch Social Res, New York; Martin Margulies Collection, Coral Gables, Fla; Gordon Hanes Collection, Winston-Salem, NC; Norton Gallery Art, West Palm Beach, Fla; Sydney & Frances Lewis Found, Richmond, Va; and others. *Comn:* sculptures, 580 Calif St, San Francisco, 83; Prudential Life Ins, Newark, NJ, 88; State Univ of Arizona, Tempe, AZ 90; Montgomery Co, MD, 90; IBM, Atlanta, GA 90. *Exhib:* Solo exhibs, Douglass Col Art Gallery, Rutgers Univ, New Brunswick, NJ, 78, OK Harris Works of Art, New York, 80, 83, 85 & 87, City Univ New York Grad Ctr, New York, 84, Carpenter Ctr Visual Arts, Harvard Univ, Cambridge, Mass, 85, Tweed Courthouse, New York, 85, Trout Gallery, Dickinson Gallery, Carlisle, Pa, 86 & Broadway Windows, New York Univ, New York, 87; The Classic Tradition in Recent Painting and Sculpture, Aldrich Mus Contemp Art, Ridgefield, Conn, 85; Contemporary Sculpture from Florida Collections, Univ Gallery, Univ Fla, Gainesville, 87; Classical Concerns, Twining Gallery, New York, 87-88; Frontiers in Fiber: The Americans, int traveling exhib, NDak Mus Art, Grand Forks, NDak, 88-90; Architectural Art: Affirming the Design Relationship, traveling exhib, Am Craft Mus, New York, 88-90; Grace Hokin Gallery, Palm Beach, Fla 91; and others. *Teaching:* Instr advan sculpture, Cooper Union, New York, 78-79. *Awards:* Tiffany Found Sculpture Grant, 77; Award for Outstanding Design, Show Bus, 77; Award of Distinction, Va Mus Fine Art, 79. *Bibliog:* Grace Glueck (auth), article, New York Times, 8/7/81; Peter Carlson (auth), Design: American Craft Museum, Art News, 5/88; Carl Little (auth), Collaboration: art & architecture, Art New Eng, 5/88; and others. *Media:* Cloth. *Publ:* Contribr, Speak out the arts & Behind every art, Village Voice, 3/70; contribr, Her story, Know Inc, 73; contribr, Women in the Year 2000, Arbor Press, 74; contribr, Are you a closet collector, Heresies Collective, winter 78. *Dealer:* O K Harris Gallery 383 W Broadway New York NY 10012. *Mailing Add:* 444 Sixth Ave New York NY 10011

CASTANO, ELVIRA
GALLERY DIRECTOR, HISTORIAN
b Cincinnati, Ohio, July 23, 29. *Study:* Emerson Col, BLI; Villa Schifanoia, Florence, Italy, grad study; Univ Florence, Italy (audited classes). *Pos:* Dir, Castano Art Gallery, Needham, Mass. *Teaching:* Emmanuel Col, Boston, 52. *Res:* Italian Renaissance art and the Macchiaioli school of art. *Specialty:* Traditional and Renaissance art. *Collection:* American, Dutch and Italian art. *Mailing Add:* 245 Hunnewell St Needham Heights MA 02194

CASTELLETT, MARISA See Re, Marisa del

CASTELLI, LEO
DEALER
b Trieste, Italy, Sept 4, 07. *Study:* Univ Milan; Columbia Univ. *Collections Arranged:* Ninth Street Show, 51. *Pos:* Dir, Leo Castelli Gallery, 57-90; pres & owner, Castelli Graphics, 90- *Awards:* Mayor's Award of Honor for Arts & Cult, New York, 76; Manhattan Cult Awards Prize, 80;; Distinguished New Yorker Award, Bowery Savings Bank (150th Anniversary), 84; Honorable Mention, Chevalier de l'Ondre Nat de La Legion d'Honneur, Gov France, 87; Butler Medal Life Achievement Am Art, Butler Inst Am Art, 87. *Bibliog:* Danielle Gardner (auth), A Modern Medici: Leo Castelli: The Man Who Sold Europe on Contemporary American Art. *Mem:* Art Dealers Asn Am. *Specialty:* American vanguard painting and sculpture. *Mailing Add:* c/o Leo Castelli Gallery 420 W Broadway New York NY 10012

CASTER, BERNARD HARRY
PAINTER, ENAMELIST
b Wolcott, NY, May 27, 21. *Study:* Syracuse Univ, AA(fine arts), 56, BA, 60. *Work:* St Lawrence Univ; Newark Pub Libr, NY; Sch St Croixe de Neuilly, Paris, France. *Exhib:* 21st Ann Western NY Regional, Buffalo, 55; 19th Ceramic Nat, Syracuse Mus, 56; NY State Artists Exhib, NY State Fair, 58; The Kentucky Guild Train, 66; 14th Ann Rochester Festival of Religious Arts, 72. *Awards:* Marie Wilner Award, Cayuga Mus Hist & Art, Auburn, NY, 62, Ceramic Award, 64; Purchase Award, Four County Appleseed Collection, Wayne County Arts in Action, 83. *Media:* All. *Mailing Add:* Box 154 South Butler NY 13154

CASTERAS, SUSAN PAULETTE
CURATOR, EDUCATOR
b New Brunswick, NJ. *Study:* Vassar Col, BA, 71; Yale Univ, MA, 73, MPhil, 75 & PhD, 77. *Collections Arranged:* Substance or the Shadow: Images of Victorian Womanhood, Yale Ctr Brit Art, 82; Richard Redgrave (coauth, catalog), Victoria & Albert Mus, 88; Pocket Cathedrals, Yale Ctr Brit, 91. *Pos:* Asst cur, Yale Ctr Brit Art, 77-91 & cur painting, 91- *Teaching:* Adj prof, Hist Art Grad Prog, City Univ New York, 85-87; lectr art hist, Yale Univ, 78- *Awards:* Danforth Found Fel, 71; Am Coun Learned Soc Fel, 83; NEH Fel Univ Teachers, 91. *Mem:* Interdisciplinary Nineteenth-Century Studies (2nd vpres, 91-); Col Art Asn; Northeast Am Soc 18th-Century Studies. *Publ:* Contribr, Hard Times: Victorian Social Realism, Lund Humphries, 87; Auth, Images Victorian Womanhood in English Art, Assoc Univ Presses, 87; English Pre-Raphaelitism & Its Reception in America, Assoc Univ Presses, 90; Pocket Cathedrals: Pre-Raphaelite Book Illustrations, 91. *Mailing Add:* Yale Center for British Art 1080 Chapel St New Haven CT 06520

CASTILE, RAND
MUSEUM DIRECTOR
b North Carolina, July 15, 38. *Study:* Drew Univ, BA; Urasenke Tea Ceremony Hq, Kyoto, Japan; also study with Grand Master Sen Soshitsu, XV, diplomae. *Collections Arranged:* Four exhibs per yr, Japan House Gallery,

71-86. *Pos:* Lectr, Japanese art & tea ceremony, US & Japanese Univs & mus; dir, Japan House Gallery, Japan Soc Inc, New York, 70-86; consult-panelist, Nat Endowment Arts, 75; consult, Nat Endowment Humanities, 75-; bd adv, Japan Study Ctr, Columbia Univ; dir,The Brundage Collection, Asian Art Mus San Francisco, 86- *Awards:* Fulbright Scholar, 66-67; Mayor's Award of Honor for Arts & Culture, New York, 82. *Mem:* Asn Art Mus Dirs; Metrop Mus Art (vis comt); Am Fedn Arts (Nat Exhib Comt); Am Asn Mus; US-Japan Educ & Cult Conf. *Publ:* Auth, numerous articles in Art News, Geijutsu Shincho, Bijutsu Techo & Print Collector's Newslett, 63-; The Way of Tea, 72; Ikeda & Ida: Two Japanese Printmakers, 74; Japanese Art Now: Tadaaki Kuwayama & Rikuro Okamoto. *Mailing Add:* The Brundage Collection Asian Art Mus Golden Gate Park San Francisco CA 94118

CASTILLO, MARIO ENRIQUE
MURALIST, EDUCATOR
Study: Ill Inst Design, cert, 64; Sch Art Inst Chicago, BFA, 69; Sch Fine Arts, Univ Southern Calif Los Angeles, post grad studies, 69-70; Calif Inst Arts, Valencia, MFA, 72, post grad studies, 73-74; Pasadena City Col, 77; Calif State Univ Los Angeles, 80; East Los Angeles City Col, 81 & 82 & Univ Calif Dominguez Hills, 87 & 88; Nat Univ, Inglewood, Calif, 89. *Work:* Nat Mus Am Art, Washington, DC; San Francisco Mus Art; Denver Art Mus; Albuquerque Mus, NMex; Portland Art Mus, Ore. *Comn:* Metafisica (mural), 68 & Wall of Brotherhood (mural), 69, City of Chicago, Ill; mural (painting), El Mercado Co, Los Angeles, 82; four paintings, Latino Inst, Chicago, 91; two murals, Mex Am Fine Arts, Chicago, 92. *Exhib:* Sacred Images-New Visions, Riverside Art Mus, Calif, 89; solo exhibs, Inst Hispanic Cult Studies, Santa Monica, Calif, Orlando Gallery, Sherman, Okla, 89, Sangre De Cristo Arts Ctr, Pueblo, Colo, 91 & Prospectus Art Gallery, Chicago, 91-92; Day of the Dead, Mex Fine Arts Mus, Chicago, Ill, 90; Cara (travelling show), Fresno Art Mus, 91, Tucson Mus Art, 91 & Smithsonian Inst Nat Mus Am Art, 92. *Pos:* Artist/designer, Lukas & Assocs, 65-66; artist, City of Chicago, Bd of Educ, 67-68; artist/designer, El Mercado Co, Los Angeles, 81-83. *Teaching:* Art instr design, Santa Monica City Col, summer 73; asst prof fine arts, Univ Ill, Champaign-Urbana, 73-76; art instr design, Immaculate Heart Col, Los Angeles, 79-80; painting instr fine arts, Exceptional Childrens Found, Los Angeles, 85-86; art instr fine arts, Plaza de La Raza, Los Angeles, summer 89; fac mem fine arts, Columbia Col, Chicago, 90- *Awards:* First Place Painting, 74, First Place Drawing, 75 & First Place Photog, 75, Hispanic Art Exhib, Mus Sci & Indust, Chicago. *Bibliog:* Sebastian Rotella (auth), Ancient art inspires a modern man, LA Times, 12/8/89; Lyman Pitman (auth), Hands, feet, eyes, lead viewers to artist's mind, Chieftain, Pueblo, Colo, 4/28/91; Olga Herrera (auth), Castillo exhibit opens innovative local gallery, Lawndale News, Chicago, 10/24/91. *Media:* Acrylic. *Publ:* Contribr, Pictures For Writing, Bantam Books, 69; Mural Manual, Beacon Press, 75; Towards's A People's Art-The Contemporary Mural Movement, Dutton & Co, 77; Canto Al Pueblo Anthology, Penca Books, San Antonio, 78; Community Murals: The People's Art, Assoc University Presses, Cranbury, NJ, 82. *Dealer:* Prospectus Art Gallery 1210 W 18th St Chicago IL 60608. *Mailing Add:* 10101 S Ave M Chicago IL 60617

CASTLE, WENDELL KEITH
SCULPTOR
b Emporia, Kans, Nov 6, 32. *Study:* Univ Kans, BFA & MFA; Md Inst Art, Hon DFA; St John Fisher, Hon DHL. *Work:* Mus Fine Arts, Boston; Nordenfieldske Kunstindustrimus, Norway; Philadelphia Mus Art; Metrop Mus Art, New York; Renwick Gallery, Smithsonian Inst; and others. *Comn:* Clock sculpture, Pillar Bryton Partners, Orlando, Fla; commemorative piano, Steinway & Sons, Long Island, NY; outdoor clock sculpture, Hammerson Can, Inc, Toronto; art furniture, Cincinnati Art Mus; clock sculpture, Maccabees Mutual Life Insurance Co, Southfield, Mich. *Exhib:* Mem Art Gallery, Rochester, NY, 62, 65 & 86; Woodenworks, Smithsonian Inst, 72; Art & Relig, Vatican, Rome, 78; Fendrick Gallery, Washington, DC, 78, 80 & 86; Alexander E Milliken Gallery, New York, 81, 83, 85 & 86; Am Craft Mus, 81 & 86; Whitney Mus Am Art, New York, 85; Masterpieces of Time, Taft Mus, Cincinnati, Ohio, 85 & Renwick Gallery, Nat Mus Am Art, Smithsonian Inst, Washington, DC, 85-86; Rochester Inst Technol, 86, 88, 89; Eloquent Object, Oakland Mus, 87; Mus Fine Arts, Boston, 88; Milwaukee Art Mus, 88; Hokin Kaufman Gallery, Chicago, 88; Furniture of Wendell Castle, Detroit Inst Arts, 89, Delaware Art Mus, 90, Va Mus Fine Arts, 90; Peter Joseph Gallery, New York, 91. *Pos:* Bd dirs, Nat Mus Am Art & Rochester Mem Art Gallery, NY, 92. *Teaching:* Instr drawing, Univ Kans, 60-61; assoc prof furniture design, Rochester Inst Technol, 62-70; prof sculpture, Wendell Castle Workshop, 80-88; artist-in-residence, Rochester Inst Technol, 84- *Awards:* Louis Comfort Tiffany Found & NY State Grants, 72; Nat Endowment Arts Grants, 73, 75, 76 & 88; Civic Award-Culture & Arts, Rochester, NY, 83; Fel, NY Found Arts, 86; Golden Plate, Am Acad Achievement, 88. *Bibliog:* Machi (auth), Made in America, Pub Broadcasting System, 87; Robert Jensen (auth), Ornamentalism, Crown, 83; Diamondstein (auth), Handmade in America, Abrams, 83; Lucie-Smith (auth), American Art Now, Morrow, 85; Denise Domergue (auth), Artists Design Furniture, Abrams, 84; Giovannini (auth), Furniture by Wendell Castle. *Mem:* Am Craftsman Coun; NY State Coun Arts; Am Craft Coun (trustee, 86-); Nat Mus Am Art Comn; Renwick Gallery (hon(trustee, 90-). *Media:* Wood. *Publ:* Auth, George Sugarman, 68, Mike Nevelson, 69 & Wharton Esherick, 71, Craft Horizons; coauth, The Wendell Castle Book of Wood Lamination, Van Nostrand Reinhold, 80; coauth, The Fine Art of the Furniture Maker, Mem Art Gallery, 81. *Mailing Add:* 18 Maple St Scottsville NY 14546

CASTLEMAN, RIVA
CURATOR, HISTORIAN
b Chicago, Ill, Aug 15, 30. *Study:* State Univ Iowa, BA; Inst Fine Arts, New York Univ. *Collections Arranged:* Picasso Master Printmaker, Henri Matisse; Mus Mod 70; Jasper Johns, Lithographs, 70-71; Technics & Creativity: Gemini G E L, 71; The Prints of Edvard Munch, 73; Modern Prints Int Traveling Exhib, 73-75; Latin Am Prints from Mus Mod Art Int Traveling Exhib, 74-75; Impresario--Ambroise Vollard, 77; Modern Artists as Illustrators Int Traveling Exhib, 81-84; Printed Art: A View of Two Decades, 80; Prints from Blocks: Gaugin to Now (auth, catalog), 83; Jasper Johns, A Print Retrospective, 86; Prints of Andy Warhol, 90. *Pos:* Curatorial asst, Art Inst Chicago, 51-55; cur, Calif Hist Soc, San Francisco, 56-57; from curatorial asst to cur, Mus Mod Art, New York, 63-, dir Dept Prints & Illus Bks, 76-, deputy dir, curatorial affairs, 86- *Awards:* Fel, Corning Mus Glass & Tamarind Lithography Wkshp. *Mem:* Print Coun Am; Grolier Club; Cintas Found; Int Conf Graphic Art Cur. *Res:* Contemporary prints. *Publ:* Auth, Contemporary Prints, 73; auth, Prints of the Twentieth Century: A History, 76; American Impressions: Prints Since Pollock, Alfred A Knopf (in prep). *Mailing Add:* Mus Mod Art 11 W 53rd St New York NY 10019

CASTORO, ROSEMARIE
SCULPTOR
b Brooklyn, NY, Mar 1, 39. *Study:* Mus Mod Art, New York, scholar, 54-55; Pratt Inst, BFA(cum laude), 56-63. *Work:* Berkeley Mus, San Francisco; Woodward Found, Washington, DC; Chase Manhattan Bank; Mus Mod Art, New York; Newark Mus, NJ. *Comn:* Procession of Strokes, NY State Coun Arts, 72; Hexatryst, Gen Serv Admin, Topeka, Kans, 79; 24 Flashers, Art Park, Lewiston, NY, 79; Etherial Concrete Flasher, Athena Found, LIC, NY, 86. *Exhib:* Solo shows, Tibor de Nagy Gallery, New York, 71-73, 75, 76, 80, 81, 83, 85 & 89 & Hal Bromm Gallery, New York, 92; Highlights of the 70-71 Art Seasons, Aldridge Mus Contemp Art, Conn, 71; Otis Art Inst, Los Angeles, 76; Julian Pretto & Co, NY, 78 & 79; Painting & Sculpture Today, Indianapolis Mus Art, 78, 80 & 86; Eaton-Shoen Gallery, San Francisco, 84 & 86; Acquisitions, Mus Mod Art, NY, 85-86. *Teaching:* Boston Mus Sch, 85, Hunter Col, New York, 72, Calif State Univ, Fresno, 73, Philadelphia Col Art, 74, Mt Berry Col Art, Ga, 74, Syracuse Univ, NY, 75, Univ Colo, Boulder, 77, Stockton State Col, NJ, 83. *Awards:* Fel Guggenhein, 71;; NY State Coun Arts Grant, 72 & 74; Nat Endowment Arts Grant, 75 & 85; Tiffany Found, 77; Pollack-Krasner Grant, 89-90. *Bibliog:* E C Goosen (auth), Distillation, 11/66 & Lucy Lippard (auth), article, 5/72 & 2/74, Art Forum; Carter Ratcliff (auth), article, Art Int, 5/75; Joseph C Scrapits (auth), Strokes of genius, Attenzione, 6/86. *Media:* All. *Publ:* Auth, Artists transgress all boundaries, Art News, 1/72; ed, Art in the mind, 70 & Conceptual Art, 72; Tracks, 75. *Dealer:* Tibor de Nagy Art Gallery 41 W 57th St New York NY 10019; Hal Bromm Gallery 90 W Broadway New York NY 10007. *Mailing Add:* 151 Spring St New York NY 10012

CASTRO, GIOVANNI
PAINTER
b June 16, 46; Colombian citizen. *Study:* Andes Univ, BA, 71. *Work:* Univ Miami, Coral Gables, Fla; De Armas Group Collection & Mayor Xavier Suarez, Miami, Fla; UN High Comnr for Refugees, Lisbon, Portugal; Hugh B D'Annoux Collection, Paris, France. *Comn:* Poster, Red Cross, Bogota, Colombia, 83; oil painting, Univ Miami, Fla, 88; oil painting, Fla Int Univ, Miami, 88. *Exhib:* Peintres Naifs Du Monde Entier, Paris, France, 83; Inst Audiovisual Francais, Paris, France, 83; Sci Mus, Miami, 84; Salon D'automne, Gran Palais, Paris, France, 84; Colombian Consulate, Miami, 86; Cuttler Ridge Pub Libr, Miami, 87; Le Plus Grand du trois Ameriques-Aquitania, Tonne, 88. *Pos:* Instr art in anthrop, Javeriana Univ & Nat Univ, Bogota, 73-74. *Awards:* First Prize, Art Naive, Latina Am Art Exhib, Pamplona City, 83; First Prize, Art Naive, Gran Prix D'Aquitaine, Aquitaine City, 88. *Bibliog:* Dr Ariel Ramos (auth), Giovanni Castro's Art, 87; Gomez & Caceres (auths), Castro's Work, Ville de Paris, 88. *Mem:* Ctr Fine Arts, Miami, Fla. *Media:* Oil. *Mailing Add:* 999 S Bayshore Dr No 1102 Miami FL 33131-2931

CASWELL, HELEN RAYBURN
PAINTER, WRITER
b Long Beach, Calif, Mar 16, 23. *Study:* Univ Ore Sch Fine Arts. *Comn:* Murals, Federated Church, Saratoga, Calif, 65; Mem Paintings, San Jose Hosp, Calif, 67 & Emanuel Lutheran Church, Saratoga, 69. *Exhib:* De Young Mus Show, Soc Western Artists, 61; one-man shows, Northwest Mo State Col, 66 & Rosicrucian Mus, San Jose, 70; Montalvo Cult Ctr, Saratoga, 68. *Awards:* James D Phelan Award for Narrative Poetry, 58; San Francisco Browning Soc Award, 66. *Media:* Oil. *Publ:* Auth & illusr, A Wind on the Road, 64 & A New Song for Christmas, 66, Van Nostrand Reinhold; Shadows from the Singing House, Charles Tuttle, 67; auth & illusr, Thank You for Being You, Gibson, 73; auth, Never Wed an Old Man, Doubleday, 75; Growing in Faith Library, Abingdon, 89. *Dealer:* Gallery Americana Lincoln St & Sixth Ave Carmel CA 93921; Fisher Galleries 1509 Connecticut Ave NW Washington DC 20036. *Mailing Add:* 13207 Dupont Rd Sebastopol CA 95472

CASWELL, JIM (JAMES DANIEL CASWELL-DAVIS)
SCULPTOR, CERAMIST
b St Boniface, Man, Can, Nov 9, 48. *Study:* Calif State Univ, Northridge, with Peter Plagens, Walt Gabrielson, Karen Carson & Howard Tollefson, 66-71. *Comn:* Vases, Manufacture Nat de Sevres, Sevres, France, 86. *Exhib:* Scripps Ann, Lang Art Gallery, Claremont, Calif, 82; Pacific Currents, San Jose Mus Art, 82; Art and/or Craft, Kanazawa, Japan, 82; Clay for Walls, Renwick Gallery, 83; On and Off the Wall, Oakland Mus, 83; Triennale de la

Porcelaine, Nyon, Switz, 86; 27th Ceramic Nat Exhib, Everson Mus, Syracuse, NY, 87; American Ceramics Now, Am Craft Mus, New York, NY, 87; East-West Contemp Ceramics, Olympic Invitational, Seoul, Korea, 88. *Awards:* Nat Endowment Arts Fel, 83; Fel, Centre Nat des Arts Plastiques, 85 & 86. *Media:* Ceramic. *Dealer:* Jane Corkin Gallery 179 John St Suite 302 Toronto ON Canada. *Mailing Add:* 2208 Cloverfield Blvd Santa Monica CA 90405

CATALAN, EDGARDO OMAR
PAINTER, EDUCATOR
b Valparaiso, Chile; US citizen. *Study:* Sch Fine Arts, Vina Del Mar, Chile, with Hans Soyka, MA, 60; Calif Col Arts & Crafts, Oakland, 67; lithography with Carlos Gonzalez, Stade, Ger. *Work:* Museo Bellas Artes, Vina Del Mar; Fine Arts Gallery, San Diego, Calif. *Exhib:* Bradley Gallery, Santa Barbara, Calif, 78; Dresdener Bank, Ger, 81; Prism Gallery, Bovenden, Ger, 81; Daberkow Gallery, Frankfurt, Ger, 81; Int Monetary Fund, Washington, DC, 83; Univ Calif, Los Angeles, 85; Nat Mus Fine Arts, Santiago, Chile, 85; Arlington Gallery, Santa Barbara, Calif, 88; Running Ridge Gallery, Sante Fe, NMex, 89; Vina Del Mar, Chile, 91. *Teaching:* Prof painting & drawing, Acad Fine Arts, Vina Del Mar, Chile, 62-64; chmn fine arts dept, Thacher Sch, Ojai, Calif, 64-75; dir fine arts prog, Univ Valparaiso, Chile, 89- *Awards:* First Prize Painting, Autumn Salon, Mus Art, Valparaiso, 64; First Prize Poster, Cafe de Brasil, Brazilian Govt, 64; Calif Arts Coun Grant, Artist-in-Residence Prog, Santa Barbara Pub Schs; and others. *Media:* Oil, Watercolor. *Mailing Add:* c/o Rodrigo Catalan 838 N Cherokee Ave Los Angeles CA 90038

CATALDO, JOHN WILLIAM
EDUCATOR, CALLIGRAPHER
b Boston, Mass, Nov 28, 24. *Study:* Mass Col Art, BSEd; Columbia Univ, MA & EdD; Sch Am Craftsmen, Rochester, NY, with L Copeland; Univ Calif, Los Angeles, with J P Jones; Teachers Col, Univ Buffalo; Pa State Univ. *Work:* Wichita Art Asn, Univ Mo; Albright-Knox Art Gallery, Buffalo, NY; NY State Crafts Fair, Ithaca; Teachers Col, Columbia Univ; Munic Art Ctr, Long Beach, Calif. *Comn:* Films on art, Nat Educ Asn, 61; screen-divider, Sheraton-Palace Hotel, San Francisco, 62; sculpture, Lithuanian Social Ctr, DuBois, Pa, 65; 30 films, Nat Inst TV, Bloomington, Ind, 70-72; five bronze sculptures, Boston Archit Ctr, 78. *Exhib:* Young Americans, USA, Contemp Crafts Show, 56; Wichita Art Asn Sculpture & Jewelry Show, 56 & 61; Albright-Knox Art Gallery Show, 60; Graphic Design, Syracuse Univ, 61; Ball State Drawing & Sculpture Ann, 63-64; Calligraphy, Mass Inst Technol Sch Archit. *Pos:* Assoc ed, Art Educ, 60-63; ed, Sch Arts, 62-67. *Teaching:* Assoc prof art, Teachers Col, Columbia Univ, 60-61; assoc prof art, Pa State Univ, 61-65; dir art educ & prof art, Philadelphia Col Art, 65-70; acad dean & instr calligraphy, Mass Col Art, 70-, prof & chmn media & performing arts dept, currently. *Awards:* Lacey Print Prize, Western NY Ann, 56 & Ceramic Sculpture Prize, 58, Albright-Knox Art Gallery; Words & Calligraphy, selected for AIGA 50 Best Books Award, Van Nostrand Reinhold, 70. *Mem:* Nat Art Educ Asn (bd dirs, 66-70, pres, Eastern Region, 68-70); Educ Press Asn; Am Asn Univ Prof; Col Art Asn Am. *Publ:* Auth, Lettering--a Guide for Teachers, David Publ, 58; auth, Graphic Design & Visual Communication, Intext, 66; auth, Words & Calligraphy for Children, Van Nostrand Reinhold, 69; auth, Pen Calligraphy, Davis Publ, 80. *Mailing Add:* Mass Col Art 621 Huntington Ave Boston MA 02215

CATCHI
PAINTER, PRINTMAKER
b Philadelphia, Pa, Aug 27, 20. *Study:* Briarcliff Jr Col, 37; Commercial Illus Studios, 38-39; also with Leon Kroll, Harry Sternberg & Hans Hofman & with Angelo Savelli, Positano, Italy; Accademia Int Medicea Bella Arte Firenze, Italy, hon degree, 83. *Work:* Rosenberg Found; Hofstra Univ, Hempstead, NY. *Exhib:* One-person shows, Rayburn Hall, Washington, DC, 68 & 76, Gallerie Arte Spenetti, Florence, Gallery Coin d'Arte, Genoa, Wichita Fall Mus, Tex, 86 & Longview Art Mus, Tex, 87. *Pos:* Artist-in-Residence, Friends Acad, Locust Valley, NY, 84. *Awards:* Goldie Paley Award, Nat Asn Women Artists, 77; Winston Memorial Prize, 80; William Meyerowitz Memorial Prize, 82; and others. *Bibliog:* Nan Ickeringill (auth), Art & at home with Catchi, New York Times, 68; Doris Herzig (auth), She has painted since she was 12, Newsday, 68; Molly Sinclair (auth), Oil brush & canvas, Atlanta Constitution, 69. *Mem:* Nat Asn Women Artists (pres, 81-85); Audubon Artists; Int Platform Asn; New York Soc of Women Artists (pres, 84-86); Artists Equity, New York (bd, 86-90). *Media:* Oil, Watercolor; Stone, Cast Metals. *Publ:* Illusr (cover), La Revue Art Moderne Mag, France, 7/75 & 6/78; doc book, Int Sculpture Symp, Tex, 76. *Mailing Add:* 2 Gristmill Lane Manhasset NY 11030

CATE, BARBARA KAUFMAN
EDUCATOR, ART HISTORIAN
b New York, NY. *Study:* Cornell Univ, BA, 43; Columbia Univ with Millard Meiss, MA, 49. *Collections Arranged:* Art of Haiti (auth, catalog), 68; Louis Lozowick (auth, catalog), 73; Henry Gulick (auth, catalog); A Time to Reap (auth, catalog), 85. *Pos:* Dir, Folk Art Inst, Mus Am Folk Art, 85- *Teaching:* Prof art hist, Seton Hall Univ, South Orange, NJ, 65- *Res:* Folk art studies. *Publ:* Dir, Museum of American Folk Art Encyclopedia of Folk Art & Artists, Abbeville, 91. *Mailing Add:* Folk Art Inst of the Museum of Am Folk Art 61 W 62nd St New York NY 10023-7015

CATE, PHILLIP DENNIS
HISTORIAN, DIRECTOR
b Washington, DC, Oct 19, 44. *Study:* Rutgers Univ, BA(art hist), 67; Ariz State Univ, MA(art hist), 70. *Collections Arranged:* Meryon's Paris/Piranesi's Rome (with catalog), 71; The Ruckus World of Red Grooms (with catalog), 73; Japonisme: Japanese Influence on French Art, 1854-1910 (with catalog), 75; The Color Revolution, color lithography in France 1890-1900 (with catalog), 78; Circa 1800: The Beginning of Modern Printmaking, 1775-1835 (catalog), 80; Theophile Alexander Steinlen, 1859-1923 (auth, catalog), 82; The Circle of Toulouse-Lautrec (auth, catalog), 85; Matsukata Collection of Ukiyo-e Prints from Tokyo National Mus (auth, catalog), 88; Eiffel Tower: A Tour de Force (auth, catalog), 89. *Pos:* Asst to dir, Pa Acad Fine Art, 67-68; dir, Jane Voorhees Zimmerli Art Mus, Rutgers Univ, 70- *Mem:* Print Coun Am; Printmaking Coun NJ (adv bd, 74-); Asn Art Mus Dirs; Col Art Asn; Grolier Club. *Res:* 19th century French prints. *Publ:* Ed & essayist, The Graphic Arts & French Soc, 1871-1914, Rutgers Press, NB, 88; essayist, L'Estampe Originale: Artistic Printmaking in France 1893-1895, Van Gogh Mus, Amsterdam, 91; From Pissarro to Picasso; Color Etching in France, Bibliotheque Nationale, Paris, 92. *Mailing Add:* Jane Voorhees Zimmerli Art Mus Rutgers Univ New Brunswick NJ 08903

CATHCART, LINDA LOUISE
HISTORIAN
Study: Calif State Univ, Fullerton, BA(fine arts), 69; Hunter Col, City Univ New York, MA(art hist), 72; Courtauld Art Inst (Fulbright fel), London, postgrad study, 73-74. *Collections Arranged:* American Still Life 1945-1983, Richard Diebenkosn, Alfred Jensen, Cindy Sherman; Robert Rauchenberg, Melissa Miller, Robert Longo, Bruce Nauman, Edward Ruscha. *Pos:* Curatorial asst, Whitney Mus Am Art, New York, 71-73; coordr spec progs, Brooklyn Mus, NY, 74-75; cur, Albright-Knox Gallery, 75-79; dir, Contemp Arts Mus, Houston, formerly & Linda Cathcart Gallery, currently. *Awards:* Nat Endowment for the Arts & Humanities Award, 71-72; Fulbright Fel. *Mem:* Am Asn Mus; Am Asn Mus Dirs. *Mailing Add:* 924 Colorado Ave Santa Monica CA 90401

CATLETT, ELIZABETH
SCULPTOR, GRAPHIC ARTIST
b Washington, DC, Apr 15, 19; Mexican citizen. *Study:* Howard Univ, Washington, DC, BS(art), 36; State Univ, Iowa, MFA, 40; Art Inst, Chicago; Art Students League, New York; privately with Ossip Zadkine, New York, 44. *Work:* Metrop Mus Art, New York; Ist Nac Bellas Artes, Mexico, DF; New Orleans Mus Art, La; Nat Mus Am Art, Washington, DC; Mod Art Mus, New York; Mod Art Mus, Mex; Met Mus Art, Ny; High Mus, Atlanta, Ga. *Comn:* Olmec Bather (bronze), Nat Polytech Inst, Mexico, 66; Louis Armstrong (bronze), City Park, New Orleans, La, 75-76; bronze reliefs, Chemical Eng, Exxon Inc & Howard Univ, Washington, DC; life-size figures (2 bronzes), comn by Secy of Educ, Mexico, 81; marble carving, Fla A & M Univ, 89; bronze relief, Atlanta City Hall, Ga, 90; marble carving, Colgate, 92. *Exhib:* One-woman shows, Modern Art Mus, Mex, 70, Studio Mus Harlem, New York, 71-72, Saxon Summer Place, Dresden, 73 & New Orleans Mus Art, La, 83; retrospective print show; Mus African American Art, Los Angeles, Calif, 89; Committed to Print, Mod Art Mus, New York, 89; Presentation Exhib, Nat Mus Am Art, Washington, DC, 90; Miss Mus Art, Jackson, 90; Montgomery Mus Art, Ala, 91; Polk Mus Art, Lakeland, Fla, 91-92. *Teaching:* Head dept art, Dillard Univ, New Orleans, La, 40-42; head dept & prof sculpture, Nat Sch Fine Arts, Nat Univ, Mex, 58-73. *Awards:* Brit Coun Grant, 71; Alumni Award, Howard Univ, Washington, DC, 79; Nat Award, Women's Caucus Art, 81; Award, Nat Sculpture Conference, Works by Women, Cincinnati, OH, 87; Amistad Arts Award, New Orleans, 90; Art Award, Nat Counc 100 Black Women, New York 91. *Bibliog:* Juan Mora (dir), Elizabeth Catlett (film), Contemp Crafts, Los Angeles, Calif, 78; Samella Lewis (auth), The art of Elizabeth Catlett, Handcraft Studios, 84; Stephanie S Oliver (auth), Elizabeth Catlett, Essence Mag, 85. *Mem:* Hon life mem Women's Caucus Arts; Salon de La Plastica Mexicana. *Media:* Wood & Stone Carving. *Dealer:* Watson Hines III 626 Riverside Dr New York NY 10031; June Kelly Gallery 591 Broadway New York NY 10012. *Mailing Add:* Apartado Postal 694 Cuernavaca Morelos 62000 Mexico

CATLIN, STANTON LOOMIS
CURATOR, CONSULTANT
b Portland, Ore, Feb 19, 15. *Study:* Oberlin Col, AB; Acad Fine Arts & Charles Univ, Prague, Czech; Am Sch Classical Studies, Athens; Fogg Mus, fel mod art, Harvard Univ; Inst Fine Arts, NY Univ, MA, 67. *Pos:* Asst to dir circulating exhibs, Mus Mod Art, 39; secy comt art, Coordr Inter-Am Affairs, 41-42; supvr exhib contemp Am painting sent to S Am & Mexico by Mus Mod Art, 41; exec dir, Am Inst Graphic Arts, 46-50; from ed to cur Am art, Minneapolis Inst Arts, 52-58; asst dir, Yale Univ Art Gallery, New Haven, Conn, 58-67; dir art gallery, Ctr Inter-Am Rels, NY, 67-71; dir, Lowe Art Gallery & Grad Mus Training Prog, Syracuse Univ, 74-77. *Teaching:* Prof NAm art, Fac Fine Arts, Univ Chile, 42-43; lectr hist art, Yale Univ, 62-64; dir art of Latin Am since independence, Yale Univ-Univ Tex, 65-67; vis assoc prof art, Hunter Col, 72-73; prof art, Col Visual & Performing Arts, Syracuse Univ, 74-82; vis prof art, PhD prog art hist, grad ctr, City Univ New York, 88; Seminar, catalog Raisonné, rural painting, Orozco, Rivera, UNAM; Inst Investigaciones Estéticas, Nat Univ Mex, 92. *Bibliog:* J Canaday (auth), Art of Latin American exhibition, New York Times, 2/66; R Schaedel (auth), Pictures at an exhibition, Latin Am Res Rev, summer 66; S Goldman (auth), Identifying LA Art, Art Hist, fall 90. *Mem:* Grolier Club, NY; Am Asn Mus; Col Art Asn Am; Syracuse Univ Libr Asn. *Res:* History of modern Latin American art. *Publ:* Political Iconography in the Diego Rivera Frescos at Cuernavaca, Mass Inst Techol Press, 78; Mural Census (Diego Rivera retrospective), Detroit Inst Arts, 86; collabr, The Frescos of Diego Rivera (with Michael Camerini), film for Detroit Inst Arts, 86; auth, Traveler Reporter Artists and the Empirical Tradition in Post-Independence Latin Am Art, Hayward London, Gallery-Yale, 89; dir, Oral History Program, Archives Am Art (film), New York, 89-90. *Mailing Add:* 200 Warren St Fayetteville NY 13066

CATOK, LOTTIE MEYER
PAINTER
b Hoboken, NJ. *Study:* New York Sch Appl & Fine Arts; also with Guy Wiggins, W Lester Stevens & Robert Brackman. *Work:* Fla Southern Col, Lakeland; Smith Col, Northampton, Mass; Bay Path Jr Col, Longmeadow, Mass; founders portrait, Springfield Symphony, 84; portrait, Hall of Justice, 84; treas portrait, Bank of NE West, 85. *Comn:* Portraits of pres, Am Int Col, Springfield, 63, clergymen, churches & temples, 63-80, Ted Shawn (ballet), Jacob's Pillow, Lenox, Mass, 64, Med men, Med Ctr of Western Mass, 66-71, pres, Bay Path Jr Col, 80, Albert Santinelli, proprietor, Santis Salon, 87, Ralph Wener, dir, Jewish Home, 87; plus others. *Exhib:* Grand Cent Art Galleries, New York, 55-57 & 77; North Shore Art Asn, Gloucester, Mass, 63-81; Hudson Valley Art Asn, White Plains, NY, 69-79; Allied Artists Am, New York, 70; Am Artists Prof League, New York, 70-80; Salute to the Met, Metrop Mus, New York, 79. *Awards:* Portrait Awards, Acad Artists, 76, 78, 80 & 83; Figure Award, North Shore Art Asn, 81; Portrait Awards, Ogunquit Art Asn, 81 & 82; Salmagundi Club Award, New York, 84. *Bibliog:* Jack Steiner (auth), I know what I like, New York World Tel, 66. *Mem:* Copley Soc Boston; Royal Soc Art, London, Eng; Salmagundi Club; Acad Artists (pres, 69-70 & 75-80); Am Artists Prof League (dir, 75). *Media:* Oil, Watercolor. *Publ:* Contribr, Art News, 58; The Fifty American Artists' Book, 69; Robbins Reproductions, 69. *Mailing Add:* 45 May Fair Dr Longmeadow MA 01106

CATON, DAVID
PAINTER
b Pasadena, Calif, Sept 13, 55. *Study:* Univ Houston, BFA, 79; Yale Univ, MFA, 81. *Work:* Tex Commerce, Houston, Tex; Tex A&M Univ, Houston; First City Bank, Houston, Tex. *Exhib:* Wilhelm Gallery, Scottsdale, Ariz, 87 & 88; Bill Ross Gallery, Memphis, Tenn, 88; Bienville Gallery, New Orleans, 88; Harris Gallery, Houston, 90. *Awards:* Visual Arts Fel, Painting, Nat Endowment Arts, 85 & 87. *Dealer:* Harris Gallery 1100 Bissonnet Houston TX 77005. *Mailing Add:* 1918 Ridgemore Houston TX 77055

CATTANEO, (JACQUELYN A) KAMMERER
PAINTER, INSTRUCTOR
b Gallup, NMex, June 1, 44. *Study:* Tex Women's Univ, Denton, 62-64; studied with Frederick Taubes, 72-73, Sergei Bongart, 78, Bettina Steinke, 85, Ben Konis, 76-77, Daniel Greene, 84 & Everett Raymond Kinstler, 85. *Work:* Zuni Arts & Crafts Mus, NMex; C J Weimer Collection, Grand Prarie, Tex; Armand Hammer Private Collection, Los Angeles, Calif; Gallup Pub Libr Permanent Collection, NMex; NMex State Capitol, Gov & Mrs Bruce King Collection & Lt Gov & Mrs Casey Luna. *Comn:* Portrait of Calvin C Hall, Univ NMex; portraits, Sunwest Bank, First State Bank, City of Gallup & El Rancho Hist Hotel, Gallup, NMex. *Exhib:* Santa Fe Festival of the Arts Invitational, Sweeney Convention Ctr, 79; 12th Ann Pastel Soc Am Exhib, New York, 84; Images of America, Invitational Fine Arts Ctr, Taos, 84; 7th Ann Open Juried Exhib, Salmagundi Club, New York, 84; Best & the Brightest Invitational, O'Briens Art Emporium, Scottsdale, 86; Asn pour Du Promotion Du Patrimone Artistique Francias, Paris, France, 91; Catharine Lorrilard Wolfe Art Club, NY, 84-92; Int Nexus, 92 Fine Art Exhib, Trammell Crow Pavilian, Dallas, Tex; Women Reflect, Carlsbad Mus Fine Arts, Carlsbad, NMex, 92. *Pos:* Vchmn, Gallup Area Arts Coun & Coop Gallery, 70-88; comt mem, Gallup NMex Multi-Cultural Ctr, 87-88; memt Soviet Union Delegation to Leningrad, Moscow, Russia Kiev & Ukrania, 90; memt US Women Artists Middle East Delegation & Exchange Prog, Jerusalem, Ibillin, Tel Aviv, Isreal, Cairo & Egypt, 92; judge fine arts, Inter-tribal Ceremonial Gallup, NMex, 80, 84 & 92. *Teaching:* Instr art for children, Studio Corner, Gallup, NMex, 65-78; instr portraiture, Caprizo Lodge, Ruidoso, NMex, 78, San Juan Col, Farmington & Univ NMex, Gallup, 85-86. *Awards:* Women of Distinction, Artistic Accomplishments Soroptimists Int, Gallup, NMex, 90; Cert Participation & Contr Asn Pour Du Promotion Du Patrimone Artistique Francias, 91; NMex State Senate, 14th Legislature, 2nd Session Memorial #101 for Artistic Achievements, 92. *Bibliog:* Herbert Lieberman (auth), A Guide to Contemporary Art, 81. *Mem:* Am Portrait Soc; Catharine Lorillard Wolfe Art Club; Pastel Soc West Coast; Gallup Area Artists Coop Bd Dir (vchmn, 84); Gallup Area Arts Coun (vpres & secy, 88-). *Media:* Oil, Pastel. *Publ:* Contribr, Southwest Art, Pastel Society of West Coast Profile, 11/87; Artists of New Mexico Volumn III, Mountain Productions, Albuquerque, NMex, 90; Northlight, Northlight Book Club, Vol 23, No 162, 10/91. *Dealer:* Dallas & Associates Fine Art PO Box 817 Ruidoso NM 88345. *Mailing Add:* c/o Studio Corner 210 E Green Gallup NM 87301

CATTELL, RAY
PAINTER, DIRECTOR
b Birmingham, Eng, May 5, 21; Can citizen. *Study:* Birmingham Col Art, Eng; Univ Toronto. *Work:* London Art Gallery, Sarnia Art Gallery, Ont; Saskatoon Art Gallery, Alta; Windsor Pub Libr. *Exhib:* Royal Can Acad Art, 60-71; Ont Soc Artists, 60-71; Flint Inst Fine Arts, Mich, 65; Can Soc Painters in Watercolour, 66-72; Am Watercolor Soc, 72. *Pos:* Exec vpres, Royal Can Acad Art, 74-75. *Awards:* Watercolour Award, City of Toronto, 63; Hon Award, Can Soc Painters in Watercolour, 65, 68 & 72; Baxter Purchase Award, 66. *Mem:* Royal Can Acad Art; Ont Soc Artists (vpres, 67-68); Can Soc Painters in Watercolour (pres, 77); Arts & Lett Club; Art Dirs Club Toronto (pres, 64-65). *Media:* Acrylic, Watercolor. *Publ:* Auth, article on creativity, Marketing Mag, 60. *Dealer:* Allen Rubiner Gallery 621 S Washington Royal Oak MI. *Mailing Add:* 19 Green Valley Rd Willowdale ON M2P 1A4 Canada

CATTERALL, JOHN EDWARD
PAINTER, EDUCATOR
b Sheridan, Wyo, Jan 12, 40. *Study:* Univ Wyo, BA, 66; Wash State Univ, MFA, 68. *Work:* Brooklyn Mus, NY; Detroit Inst Arts, Mich; Cranbrook Acad Art; Univ Colo, Boulder; Tex Tech Univ. *Comn:* Triptych, Barnett Winston Co, Jacksonville, Fla, 78; diptych, R J Reynolds Corp, Winston-Salem, NC, 80; IBM Corp, Boca Raton, Fla, 86. *Exhib:* New American Graphics, Elvehjem Art Ctr, Madison, Wis, 75; Int Print Biennial, Ministry Cult & Art, Kracow, Poland, 76; Int Print Exhib, Cranbrook Acad Art, 80; solo exhib, Yellowstone Art Ctr, Billings, Mont, 80; Recent Acquisitions, Brooklyn Mus, 81; Western Skies--Western Eyes, Colo Inst Arts, Denver, 82; Int Print Invitational, Korean Print Soc, Seoul, 83. *Pos:* Bd dir, Artspace Mag, 86. *Teaching:* Asst prof painting & printmaking, Univ SFla, 71-75; prof & dir, Mont State Univ, 75-82; prof & dept head, NMex State Univ, 82-88; chmn & prof, Univ Fla, 88- *Awards:* Purchase Awards, Boston Printmakers Exhib, 70 & Potsdam Prints, State Univ NY, 75; Best of Show, Printmaking Exhib, Univ Colo, 75. *Bibliog:* Coke Van Deren (auth), The Painter & The Photographer, 72. *Mem:* Northwest Print Coun, Portland, Ore (bd mem, 80-82); World Print Coun; Col Art Asn; Nat Coun Arts Admin. *Media:* Acrylic, Oil. *Dealer:* Art Sources Jacksonville Fla; Adair Margo Gallery El Paso TX. *Mailing Add:* 1653 NW 14th Ave Gainesville FL 32605

CATUSCO, LOUIS
PAINTER, SCULPTOR
b Liberty, NY. *Study:* Brooklyn Mus Sch Art with John Ferren & Xavier Gonzalez, 47-50. *Work:* Santa Fe Mus Fine Art, NMex; US Bank Omaha Gallery, Nebr; Midland Bank, Denver. *Exhib:* Brooklyn Mus Fine Art; Mus Santa Fe Biennials, 64-76; Albuquerque Mus Fine Art, 66; Dallas Mus Fine Art, 66-70; Johnson Mus Fine Art, Albuquerque, 67; Joslyn Mus Fine Art, 70; El Paso Mus Fine Art, 70-73. *Awards:* Blumenschein, TAA Award Show, Helen Blumenschein, 66 & 67; Wurlitzer, TAA Award Show, Wurlitzer Found, 68; Gaspard Graphic, TAA Award Show, Dora Kaminsky Gaspard, 70-71. *Bibliog:* Tricia Jones (auth), The most private or lonely of men?, Southwest Arts Mag, 74 & Solitude is Catusco (objective), US Nat Bank of Omaha Art Gallery, 72. *Mem:* Taos Art Asn. *Media:* Acrylic, Oil; Construction, Wood. *Dealer:* Stables Art Gallery Taos NMex; Total Arts Gallery Taos NMex. *Mailing Add:* Ranchos De Taos Taos NM 87557

CAUDURO, RAFAEL
PAINTER, MURALIST
b Mexico City, Mex, Apr 18, 50. *Study:* Univ Iberoamericana, indust design, 69-74. *Work:* Mus Mod Art, Cuevas Mus, Alfa Cult Ctr, Mex. *Comn:* Postage stamp, Dept Communs, Mexico City, 85; Communications (mural), Dept Communs, Mexican, Vancouver, British Columbia, Can, 86; London Underground (mural), Paris Metro (mural), City Coun, Mexico City, 89. *Exhib:* One-man retrospective, Palace Fine Arts, Mexico City, 84; Painting Collage, Chrysler Mus, Norfolk, Va, 86; one-man shows, Alfa Cult Ctr, Monterrey, Mex, 87 & Mus Mod Art, Mexico City, 91; The Blessing of Spring, Casa de la Cultura Mex-Japan, Mexico City, 91; Images for the Children, Children's Mus Manhattan, 90; and many others. *Bibliog:* Jorge A Manrique (auth), Cauduro: cual realismo, La Jornada, 4/91; Alberto Hijar (auth), Cauduro y la posmoder, El Dia, 7/91; Raquel Tibol (auth), Rafael Cauduro simulacion y melan, Proceso Mag, 8/91. *Media:* Oil, Acrylic. *Publ:* Coauth, Rafael Cauduro, MoArt Mus, Mex, 91. *Dealer:* Louis Newman Galleries 322 N Beverly Dr Beverly Hills CA 90210. *Mailing Add:* c/o Saturno 12 Cuernavaca Morelos 62360 Mexico

CAVA, PAUL
ART DEALER, PAINTER
b Brooklyn, NY, May 15, 49. *Study:* Richmond Col, NY, BA, 72; Rochester Inst Technol, MFA, 75. *Work:* Free Libr Philadelphia, Pa; Biblioteque Nationale, Paris, France. *Exhib:* Drawings from the Collection of Milt Brutten & Helen Herrich, Ben Shahn Gallery, William Paterson Col, NY, 81; Still Modern After All These Years, Chrysler Mus, Norfolk, Va, 82; Photocollage, Contemp Arts Mus, Houston, Tex, 82; Contemporary Philadelphia Photographers, Pa Acad Fine Arts, 84. *Awards:* Artist Fel, Pa Coun Arts, 82. *Media:* All Media. *Specialty:* Contemporary art. *Dealer:* Jessica Berwind Gallery Philadelphia PA. *Mailing Add:* c/o Paul Cava Gallery 22 N Third St Philadelphia PA 19106

CAVALIERE, BARBARA
CRITIC, HISTORIAN
b New York, NY. *Study:* State Univ NY Stony Brook, BA, 75; Queens Col, City Univ New York. *Pos:* Contrib ed, Arts Mag, New York, formerly; contribr, Acad Am Encycl, 21 vols, Arete Publ Co Inc, Princeton, NJ, 78-80, Contemp Artists, St Martin's Press; prod ed, Metrop Mus, currently. *Awards:* Helena Rubenstein Fel, Whitney Mus Am Art, 75; Art Critic's Fel, Nat Endowment Arts, 80. *Mem:* Int Asn Art Critics (chmn, membership comt, 81-84, treas 84-90); Found Community Artists, New York; Nat Writer's Union. *Res:* 19th and 20th century art, especially abstract expressionism and contemporary art of 1940's to present. *Publ:* Auth, Theodoros Stamos in perspective, 12/77, auth, The making of omega, 10/80, auth, Vir heroicus sublimis: Building the idea complex, 1/81 & auth, Possibilities II, 9/81, Arts Mag; auth, Notes on Mark Rothko & auth, Early abstract expressionism: The 1940's, Flash Art, 1-2/79. *Mailing Add:* 245 E 25th St No 7H New York NY 10010

CAVALLI, DICK
CARTOONIST
b New York, NY, Sept 28, 23. *Exhib:* Punch Exhib Humor, London, 53. *Pos:* Cartoonist, Syndicated Comic Strip, Winthrop, Newspaper Enterprise Asn,

currently; mem founding fac, Famous Cartoonists Course, Famous Artists Schs. *Mem:* Nat Cartoonists Soc; Newspaper Comics Coun. *Publ:* Contribr cartoons, numerous bks, anthologies & cartoon collections; contribr cartoons in Sat Evening Poat, Collier's, Look, This Week, True & many other US & foreign mags. *Mailing Add:* 90 Braeburn Dr New Canaan CT 06840

CAVAT, IRMA
PAINTER, EDUCATOR
b New York, NY. *Study:* New Sch Social Res; Archipenko Art Sch; Acad Grande Chaumiere, Paris; also with Ozenfant, Paris & Hans Hofmann. *Work:* Mus Modern Art; Flint Mus; Art Inst Detroit; Delgado Mus. *Comn:* Mural, Vodun, Port-au-Prince, Haiti, 48; wall of portraits, Fac Club, Univ Calif, Santa Barbara, 68; mural, pvt hotel, Athens, Greece, 70; wall piece, Los Angeles, Calif, 70; Santa Barbara Mall & Ventura Mall, Calif, 76; Barry Berkus, Architect, Santa Barbara, Calif. *Exhib:* Festival of Two Worlds, Spoleto, Italy, 58-59; Ten Americans, Palazzo Venezia, Rome, 60; solo exhibs, Santa Barbara Mus, Calif & Phoenix Mus, Ariz, 66-67; Kennedy Galleries, 82 & 84; Feingarten Gallery, Los Angeles, 86; Preston Burke, Detroit, 87. *Teaching:* Prof painting & drawing, Univ Calif, Santa Barbara, 64- *Awards:* Yaddo Fel, Trask Found, 50; Fulbright Fels, 56-58; Creative Arts Inst Award, Univ Calif, 70; Humanities Award, Univ Calif, 88. *Media:* Oil, Mixed Media. *Dealer:* Kennedy Galleries New York NY; Preston Burke, Detroit, MI. *Mailing Add:* 802 Carosam Rd Santa Barbara CA 93109

CAVE, LEONARD EDWARD
SCULPTOR, EDUCATOR
b Columbia, SC, Oct 22, 44. *Study:* Furman Univ, BA; Univ Md, College Park, with Kenneth Campbell, MA. *Work:* Banker's Trust, Columbia, SC; Herbert F Johnson Mus Art, Cornell Univ, Ithaca, NY; George Meany Ctr for Labor Studies, Silver Spring, Md; Columbia Mus of Art, SC. *Comn:* Sculptural menorahs, Beth Torah Synagogue, Hyattsville, Md, 72; Duame Mem, Bells Mill Sch, Potomac, Md, 75. *Exhib:* Four Sculptors, Sid Deutsh Gallery, New York, 83; Carved Wood Sculpture, Sculpture Ctr, New York, 83; one-man show, Marsha Mareyka Gallery, Washington, DC, 84. *Teaching:* Asst prof art, Georgetown Univ, 70-77. *Awards:* Chaim Gross Sculptor's Exhib First Prize, Nat Young Sculptors Guild, 69; Alaska State Arts Coun Grant. *Bibliog:* William Bradley (auth), Art, Magic Impulse & Control, Prentice-Hall, 73; Dona Z Meilach (auth), Woodworking, The New Wave, Crown Publ Inc, 81. *Mem:* Sculptors Guild; Artists Equity, Washington, DC (vpres, 73-75); Washington Sculptors Group (pres, 83-86). *Media:* Stone; Wood. *Dealer:* Marsha Mateyka Gallery Washington DC; Sculpture Ctr 167 E 69th St New York NY 10021. *Mailing Add:* 1400 Tucker Lane Ashton MD 20861

CAVER, WILLIAM RALPH
SCULPTOR, PRINTMAKER
b Longview, Tex, Oct 11, 32. *Study:* NTex State Univ, BS; Univ Guanajuanto, MFA; Univ Barcelona. *Work:* Houston Mus Fine Arts; NTex State Gallery, Denton; Inst Allende Gallery, San Miguel de Allende, Mex. *Comn:* Sculpture, Louisville Libr, 71 & Texarkana Col Libr, Tex, 72; St James Church, Texarkana, Tex, 80. *Exhib:* Dallas Art Libr Exhib, 63 & 64; Inst Allende Ann Show, 66; Texarkana Regional Art Show, 67-69; Denton Regional Art Show, 71; Paris, Tex Regional & Four States Regional, 74, 87 & 91. *Teaching:* Instr art, Dallas Pub Sch Syst, 58-67; prof art, Texarkana Col, 67-; adj prof, E Tex State Univ,. *Awards:* First Prize, 83 & 85 & Second Prize, 84, Four States Regional; Second Prize, Four States Regional, 88 & 89. *Mem:* Tex Asn Art Schs. *Media:* Clay. *Dealer:* Casa Del Bosque Texarkana TX 75501; Alley Gallery Texarkana TX. *Mailing Add:* Rte 6 Box 453 Texarkana TX 75501

CAWEIN, KATHRIN
PRINTMAKER, ILLUMINATOR
b New London, Conn, May 9, 1895. *Study:* Art Students League, with George Bridgman, Allen Lewis & Harry Wickey; Oberlin Col Hon MA, 66; Pac Univ, Ore, Hon DFA, 81. *Work:* Metrop Mus Art, New York; Nat Gallery, Washington, DC; Oberlin Col, Ohio; Tampa Univ, Fla; Pa State Univ; and others. *Comn:* Illuminated manuscripts, St Marks Church, Van Nuys, Calif, St Andrew Church, Sarasota, Fla, Congregational Church, Colorado Springs, Colo, St John's Church, Pleasantville, NY & Pac Univ, Forest Grove, Ore. *Exhib:* Breezeway, Sarasota, Fla, 73; Tampa Univ, Fla, 73; Oberlin Col, 74; Berea Col, Ky, 76; Pac Univ, Forest Grove, Ore, 79-85; and many others. *Pos:* Instr etching, Westchester Co Workshop, White Plains, 35-36; instr children's drawing, pvt studio, 50-55 & Pac Univ workshop, 82. *Awards:* Prize non-mem, Soc Am Etchers; Etching Award, Nat Asn Women Artists; Hon Mention, Hudson Valley Women's Club, 52; Named Hon, Kathrin Cawein Gallery of Art, Pac Univ, Ore, 85. *Mem:* Art Students League; Nat Asn Women Artists, New York; Am Soc Graphic Artists. *Mailing Add:* 35 Mountain Rd Pleasantville NY 10570

CAWLEY, JOAN MAE
ART DEALER, PUBLISHER
b McKeesport, Pa. *Study:* Okla State Univ, BA, 48; Univ Okla, teaching cert, 52; Univ Mich, MA, 57. *Pos:* Docent prog chmn, Wichita Art Mus, 63-68; pres, Wichita Art Mus, 68-69. *Mem:* Santa Fe Gallery Asn; Scottsdale Gallery Asn. *Specialty:* Art of the southwestern United States; posterprints; Publ of posters and prints, 3 gallery locations, Santa Fe, NMex, Scottsdale, Ariz, Lenexa, Kans. *Mailing Add:* Joan Cawley Gallery Ltd 15500 College Blvd Lenexa KS 66219

CAWOOD, GARY KENNETH
PHOTOGRAPHER
b Chattanooga, Tenn, Jan 17, 47. *Study:* Auburn Univ, BArchit, 70; E Tenn State Univ, MFA, 76. *Work:* Baltimore Mus Art, Md; New Orleans Mus Art, La; Libr Cong; Amon Carter Mus, Fort Worth, Tex; Corcoran Gallery Art, Washington, DC. *Exhib:* Solo exhibs, Sarah Reynolds Gallery, Univ NMex, Albuquerque, 77, Contemp Art Ctr, New Orleans, 79, Workspace Gallery, Univ Colo, Boulder, 86 & Memphis Ctr Contemp Art, Memphis, Tenn; Works on Paper, Dallas Mus Art, Tex, 78; Photography in Louisiana, New Orleans Mus Art, 80; two-person exhibs, Ascherman Gallery, Cleveland, Ohio, 82 & Project Art Ctr, Cambridge, Mass, 82; Recent Acquisitions, Baltimore Mus Art, 83; New Orleans Mus Art, Triennial, 86; Living Things, Wash Proj for the Arts, 86; Recent Acquisitions, Corcoran Gallery Art, Washington, DC; Current Works, Soc Contemp Photog, Kansas City, 87-89; Obstacles (auth, catalog), travelling exhib. *Teaching:* Adj prof photog, Univ Del, 75-76; assoc prof, La Tech Univ, 76-85 & Univ of Ark, Little Rock, 85- *Awards:* Visual Artist Fel Grant, Nat Endowment Arts, 82; Eugene Feldman Award, Philadelphia Print Club, 85; Visual Artist Fel Grant, Arkansas Arts Coun, 90. *Bibliog:* Roger Green (auth), article, New Orleans Times/Picayune, 1/29/82. *Mem:* Soc Photog Educ. *Publ:* Contribr, Southern Eye, Southern Mind: A Photographic Inquiry, Memphis Acad Arts, 81; American Infra Red Survey, Photo Survey Press, 82; Century of Vision, SW Louisiana Univ Mus Art; Scenes Unseen, White Rose Press. *Mailing Add:* Dept of Art Univ Ark at Little Rock Little Rock AR 72204

CECIL, CHARLES HARKLESS
PAINTER
b Kansas City, Mo, May 12, 45. *Study:* Haverford Col, Pa, BA(with honors), 67; Yale Univ Grad Sch, 67-69; with R H Ives Gammell, Boston, Mass, 69-71 & Richard F Lack, Minneapolis, Minn, 72-73. *Work:* Haverford Col Libr, Pa; West Bend Gallery Fine Arts, Wis; Seashore House, Children's Hosp, Philadelphia, Pa; Am Philos Soc, Philadelphia, Pa. *Comn:* Portrait, Dr Gilbert White, past pres, Haverford Col, 72; portraits comn by Count & Countess Carl Klingspore, (Sweden), 88; portrait, Henry S Cecil MD, President Emeritus, Children's Seashore House, Children's Hosp, Philadelphia, Pa, 90; portrait, Jonathan Evans Rhoads, MD, past pres, Am Philos Soc, Philadelphia, Pa, 92. *Exhib:* Twin City Art Exhib, Minneapolis, Minn, 75; 154th & 155th Ann, Nat Acad Design, New York, 79 & 80; one-man show, Univ Club Chicago, Ill, 80; Boston Painters of the Light, Dallas, Tex, 84; American Realism Abroad, Colby Col, Waterville, Maine, Butler Inst Am Art, Youngstown, Ohio & Wichita Art Mus, Kans, 90. *Teaching:* Dir, Charles H Cecil Studios, Borgo San Frediano, Florence, Italy, currently; instr, British Inst, Florence, Italy, currently; co-dir, Studio Cecil-Graves, Florence, Italy, formerly; instr, Villa Schifanoia Grad Sch Fine Arts, Florence, Italy, formerly. *Awards:* Julius T Hallgarten First Prize for Oil Painting, 79, Benjamin Altman Second Prize Landscape, 80, Nat Acad Design; Grant for Painting, John F & Ann Lee Stacey Found, 80; three ann grants, Elizabeth Greenshields Found, Montreal; RHI Gammell Found Grant, 86. *Media:* Oil. *Publ:* Coauth, Realism in Revolution, The Art of the Boston Sch, 86. *Mailing Add:* Box 1108 Tryon NC 28782

CECILIA
EDUCATOR, PAINTER
b Indianapolis, Ind, Nov 27, 15; Italian & Am citizen. *Study:* Art Inst Chicago; Univ Chicago; studied with Oskar Kokoschka and Marino Marini; Pope Pius Inst, Florence; Art Inst Venice with Tito Guido. *Work:* Ill Bell Tel Co, Chicago; Art Inst Chicago; Civic Mus Revltella, Trieste, Italy. *Comn:* Sculpture in memory of John F Kennedy & Robert F Kennedy, Community of Milano, Italy, 69; stained glass windows, San Giorgio Maggiore, Benedictine Monastery, 73 & painting of St John Morosini, 77; stained glass windows, Cini Found & Benedictine M Nuovalese, 73; artistic glass sculpture of Murano for the best film presented at the VII Festival Int Film of Sch & Fiction, Trieste, 69. *Exhib:* Venice Biennale, 72 & 74; La Cappella, Art Ctr, Trieste, 75; The Women of Today, Italian Inst Cult, Vienna, 75; Engravings, Int Ctr Graphics, Venice, 75; Fourth Festival Films & Art, Asolo, Italy, 76; Hotel Londra, Venice, Italy, 88. *Collections Arranged:* Exhibition of the Nude, Art Inst Venice, 75; 34th, 35th & 36th Biennales, Int Art Exhib, Venice, 68, 70 & 72. *Teaching:* Prof painting, Mercyhurst Col, Erie, Pa, in Venice, 66-; prof glass sculpture, mosaics & art hist Venetian painters, New York Univ, Venice, 66- *Awards:* First Prize Int Painting & Sculpture, Fruili-Venezia Guilia, 71; Silver Medal for Painting, Pope Paul VI, 73. *Mem:* Arts Club Chicago; Renaissance Soc Univ Chicago; Artists Equity; Alumni Asn Sch Art Inst Chicago. *Media:* Multimedia. *Dealer:* Gallery La Cella Carpenedo Venice Italy; Centro Francescano di Cultura Piazza San Antonio 9-Marghera Venice Italy. *Mailing Add:* Piscina San Moise No 2053 San Marco 30124 Venice Italy

CEDERQUIST, JOHN
FURNITURE MAKER
b Altadena, Calif, Aug 7, 46. *Study:* Calif State Univ, BA, 69, MA, 71. *Work:* Renwick Gallery, Smithsonian Inst & MCI Corp World Hq, Washington, DC; Am Craft Mus, New York; Oakland Mus, Calif; Art Inst Chicago; Craft & Folkart Mus, Los Angeles. *Exhib:* Poetry of the Physical, Am Craft Mus, New York, 87; New American Furniture, Second Generation of Studio Furniture Makers, Mus Fine Art, Boston, Mass, 89; solo exhib, Franklin Parrasch Gallery (catalog publ), New York, 91 & 93; Circa 1990, 90, The Endowed Chair (with catalog), 92, California Dreaming, Franklin Parrasch Gallery, New York, 92. *Teaching:* Instr art, Saddleback Community Col, 76- *Awards:* Nat Endowment Arts Fel, 75, 77 & 86. *Bibliog:* Earnest Joyce (auth), Encyclopedia of Furniture Making, Sterling Publ Co, 87; Edward S Cooke Jr (auth), New American Furniture: The Second Generation of Studio Furniture Makers, Mus Fine Arts, Boston, Mass, 89; Patricia Conway (auth), Art for Everyday, Clarkson Potter Publ, New York, 90. *Mailing Add:* 34971 Calle Fortuna Capistrano Beach CA 92624

CEDERSTROM, JOHN ANDREW
PAINTER, CONSERVATOR
b Philadelphia, Pa, Apr 26, 29. *Study:* Univ Arts, study illus with Henry Pitz, painting with Gertrude Schell & watercolor with Ben Eisenstat; Pa Acad Fine Arts, study painting with Roswell Weidner. *Work:* Philadelphia Mus Art, Pa; Allentown Art Mus, Pa; UNICEF Collection, New York; Lehigh Univ, Bethlehem, Pa; Fed Reserve Bank, Philadelphia, Pa; Mus Fine Arts, Raleigh, NC; Noyes Mus, NJ. *Comn:* Corp logo, Am Medicorp, Riverside Gen Hosp, NJ, 76 & FOCUS Orgn, Wallingford, Conn, 76; posters & logo, Nat Coun Arts & Educ, New York, 77; sketches jungle idol, Blue Lagoon, Columbia Pictures Inc, Hollywood, 79; Price, Waterhouse Co, Philadelphia, Pa. *Exhib:* Ann Int, Pa Acad Fine Arts, Pa, 51; Regional Exhib, Philadelphia Mus Art, Pa, 54; one-man shows, Woodmere Art Mus, Philadelphia, Pa, 69 & Philadelphia Art Alliance, 79; Audubon Artists, Nat Acad Design, New York, 76-78; The Artist Views the City, 76 & Print Show, 76, Philadelphia Art Alliance. *Collections Arranged:* Friends Cent Collection 40th Anniversary: Ernest Lawson to Karel Appel, 71, Wildlife in Art: Benefit Philadelphia Zoo Wolf Woods, 73, A Child's World: Benefit Exhib, 74, Women in Art: 1776-1976, 76 & Surrealism, Fantasy & Sci Fiction: Dali to Miro, 77, Friends Cent Gallery, Philadelphia, Pa. *Pos:* chief conserv, Hahn Gallery, Philadelphia, 75-; chief conserv for Galleries, NJ, MD and Mass. *Teaching:* Dir art educ, Bryn Mawr Art Ctr, Pa, 53-63; chmn art & art hist, Friends Cent Sch, Philadelphia, Pa, 63-81. *Awards:* Charles K Smith Prize, 14th Ann Exhib, Woodmere Art Mus, Philadelphia, Pa, 54; First Prize, First Ann Etchers Show, Philadelphia Sketch Club, Pa, 54, 1975 Graphics Ann, First Prize, Environment, 90, Chester Co Art Asn, West Chester, Pa. *Bibliog:* Eleanor Cederstrom (auth), A Poetry and Painting Festival, Gloucester Daily Times, Essex Co News, 77; Charles Movalli (auth), John Cederstrom, Looking for the infinite connection, Am Artist, 79, Art Matters, Philadelphia 3/87, Philadelphia's Renaissance Man; Philadelphia's renaissance man, Art Matters. *Mem:* Artists Equity Asn, Philadelphia (vpres, 79-80); Am Color Print Soc; Philadelphia Watercolor Club; Am Artists Prof League; Trust Comt Fel Penn Acad Fine Arts. *Media:* Oil, silk screen. *Dealer:* Hahn Gallery 8439 Germantown Ave Philadelphia PA 19118. *Mailing Add:* 518 Prescott Rd Merion Station PA 19066

CELENDER, DON
CONCEPTUAL ARTIST
b Sharpsburg, Pa, Nov 11, 31. *Study:* Carnegie-Mellon Univ, BFA, 56; Univ Pittsburgh, MEd(highest hon student), PhD(A W Mellon Scholar), 63. *Work:* Centro Arte y Communicacion & Mus Arte Mod, Buenos Aires; Metronom, Madrid, Spain; Sol Lewitt Collection, Hartford, Conn; Nat Gallery of Art, Can; Los Angeles Co Mus Fine Arts; and others. *Comn:* Stained glass panels, Children's Hosp, Pittsburgh, 61; moving water sculpture, Nokomis Br, stained glass mural, Main Br, & Eva Rhodes Freeman Mem (stained glass mural), Lake St Br, Minneapolis Pub Libr, 67; mem (stained glass panels), St James Lutheran Church, Minneapolis, 68. *Exhib:* Solo exhibs, O K Harris Gallery, New York, 70-93, DeAnza Col, Cupertino, Calif, 74, Mus Mod Art, Sydney, Australia, 78-80, Stout, Gallery 209, Univ Wis, Menomonie, 80, Kiehle Gallery, St Cloud State Univ, Minn, 80, Mus Waregen, Belg, 80 & Hera Found, New Eng, traveling exhib, 84-85; Art Systems, Whitney Mus Am Art, New York, 76; Repeated Exposure-Photographic Imagery in the Print Media, Nelson Art Gallery/Atkins Mus, Kansas City, Mo, 82; from the collection of Sol Lewitt, Wadsworth Antheneum, Conn, 84; Offset: A Survey Artists Books, New Eng Found Arts, 84; Artists' Books, 87 & Just Plain Screwy, 92, Charles Wustum Mus Fine Arts, Racine, Wis; Articulated Thumbprints, Boca Raton Art Mus, 92. *Pos:* Cur, Nat Gallery Art, 61-63; dir educ & pub activities, Minneapolis Inst Arts, 63-64; Edith M Kelso prof art hist, Macalester Col, St Paul, Minn, 64-; art consult & appraiser, 64-; art juror, 64- *Teaching:* Edith M Kelso prof art hist, Macalester Col, 64- *Awards:* Nat Endowment Arts Fel, 74; Bush Found Fel Visual Arts, 78; Best Show in NY Gallery, Am Acad Design, 78. *Bibliog:* Karen B Tancill (auth), The book as art, J Times, 4/87; Humor in art, New York Times, 4/10/87; Claude Peck (auth), The artist who licks the stamps, Minneapolis, St Paul Mag, 12/89; Adrian McCoy (auth), The Celenders bring art and better breakfasts to America, Carnegie Mellon Alumni Mag, winter 92. *Mem:* Col Art Asn Am; Am Mus Asn; Delta Phi Delta; Minn Arts Forum; Minneapolis Soc Fine Arts. *Res:* Development of conceptual art movements and surveys. *Publ:* Musical Instruments in Art, Lerner Publs, 66; Observation & Scholarship Examination for Art Historians, Museum Directors, Artists, Dealers & Collectors, OK Harris, 75; Destiny of a Name, 78 & National Architects Preference Society, 79, OK Harris; Vermeer Paints a Picture, 81 & Reincarnation Study, 82; Questions About the Arts You May Never Have Thought to Ask, OK Harris, 92; and others. *Dealer:* O K Harris Gallery 383 W Broadway New York NY 10012. *Mailing Add:* Dept Art Macalester College St Paul MN 55105

CELENTANO, FRANCIS MICHAEL
PAINTER, EDUCATOR
b New York, NY, May 25, 28. *Study:* NY Univ Inst Fine Arts, MA, 57; Acad Fine Arts, Rome, Italy, Fulbright Fel, 57-58. *Work:* Mus Mod Art, New York; Albright-Knox Art Gallery, Buffalo; Fed Reserve Bank, San Francisco; Seattle Art Mus, Wash; Rose Art Gallery, Brandeis Univ, Waltham, Mass. *Comn:* Painting, Hwy Bldg, Wash State Hwy Dept, 70; mural, Port of Seattle, Seattle-Tacoma Airport, 71; mural, Seattle City Light, 74; mural, Lincoln Mutual Savings Bank, Seattle, 79. *Exhib:* The Responsive Eye, Mus Mod Art, New York, 65; Kinetic & Optical Art Today, 65 & Plus by Minus: Today's Half Century, 68, Albright-Knox Art Gallery; Whitney Ann, Whitney Mus Am Art, 67; Pacific Cities, Auckland City Art Gallery, New Zealand, 71; 1st Western States Bienniel Exhib, Nat Gallery Fine Arts, Washington, DC, 79; retrospective, Portland Ctr Visual Arts, Ore, 86. *Teaching:* Prof art, Univ Wash, 66- *Awards:* Int Artist's Sem Award, Fairleigh Dickinson Univ, 65; Nat Endow Arts Fel, 90; Western States Arts Fedn. *Bibliog:* Moore (auth), Letters from 31 Artists, Albright-Knox Art Gallery, 70; Kingsbury (auth), Art, Francis Celentano, 1/70, Seattle Mag, 1/70; Kangas (auth), Francis Celentano, transcendence & negation, exhib catalog, 81. *Media:* Acrylic on Plastic, Acrylic on Canvas. *Dealer:* Woodside/Braseth Gallery Seattle WA. *Mailing Add:* Dept Art-Bldg DM-10 Univ Washington Seattle WA 98195

CELLI, PAUL
PAINTER, EDUCATOR
b Boston, Mass, May 8, 35. *Study:* Mass Col Art, BFA, 60; RI Sch Design, MFA, 62. *Work:* Bank of Boston. *Exhib:* Providence Art Festival, RI, 61-69; New England Contemp Artists Asn, Boston, 63; Berkshire Mus, Pittsfield, Mass, 66; one-man shows, Bennett Col, Millbrook, NY, 67 & McIvor Reddie Gallery, Boston, 68 & 70; North Gallery, Boston, 85. *Teaching:* Prof 4D theory, Mass Col Art, 70- *Bibliog:* Horn (auth), Contemporary Graphic Artists, Vol 1, 85. *Media:* Oil, Acrylic. *Publ:* Auth, Ink Comics, Number 3: An Art Comic Book, Nat Distribution. *Mailing Add:* PO Box 109 Dover MA 02030

CELLINI, JOSEPH
ILLUSTRATOR
b Budapest, Hungary, June 13, 24; US citizen. *Study:* Acad Fine Art, Budapest, MA, 49. *Media:* Oil, Pencil. *Publ:* Illusr, The Great Adventure of Michelangelo, 65, illusr, The Miracle of Flight, 68 & illusr, Bayou Country, 69, Doubleday; illusr, Animal Fathers, Holiday House, 76. *Mailing Add:* 415 Hillside Ave Leonia NJ 07605

CENCI, SILVANA
SCULPTOR
b Florence, Italy, Aug 4, 26. *Study:* Manzoni Inst, Italy; Acad Fine Art, Italy, 49; Acad Grand Chaumiere, Paris, 49-50. *Work:* Uffizi Gallery Mod Art & Numero Gallery, Florence, Italy; Bundy Art Mus, Waitsfield, Vt; Metrop Boston Transit Authority; Merchants Bank, Manchester, NH; and others. *Comn:* Monumental sculpture, Pavilion Archit, New Haven, Conn, 61; two lions explosively formed, Graham Jr Col, Boston, 63; baptistry doors, Carter & Woodruff Archit, Keene, NH, 65; fountains, Western Front Restaurant, Cambridge, Mass, 67 & Sasha Montagu, Brookline, 69. *Exhib:* New England Art Today, Northeastern Univ, 62; Bristol Art Mus, RI, 67; New Eng Sculptors Asn, Boston City Hall, 69 & Contemporary Art-Italian Heritage, 75; ten-year retrospective, Bristol Art Mus, 77; and others. *Pos:* Artist-in-residence, City of Boston, 71-73. *Teaching:* Instr art, Brookline Art Ctr, 66-69. *Awards:* Gold Hammer Award, Medea, Italy, 58; First Honorable Mention, Design in Transit, Inst Contemp Art, 71; Blanche Coleman Award, 74; World Culture Prize, Salsomaggiore Terme, Italy. *Bibliog:* Al Kaliman (auth), Odyssey Implosion/Explosion, WBZ-TV, 64; John A Hughes (auth), Explosion in Northwood, NH Profiles, 64; Richard Hadley (auth), The state we are in, Channel 11 TV, NJ, 75. *Mem:* NH Art Asn; Artists Equity Asn. *Mailing Add:* Old Pittsfield Rd Northwood NH 03261

CENGLE
PAINTER
b Boston, Mass, July 1, 30. *Study:* Studied with Leonard Craske, 40's; Boston Mus Sch, 40's; Harvard Col, AB, 52. *Work:* Boca Raton Mus Art, Fla; Inst Contemp Art, Boston, Mass; D'orsay Mus, Paris, France; Mus Art, Ft Lauderdale; Royal Palace Mus, Palma de Mallorca, Spain. *Media:* Acrylic, oil. *Mailing Add:* c/o Gulfstream Equity Management 21301 Powerline Rd No 206 Boca Raton FL 33433

CENSOR, THERESE
SCULPTOR
b Antwerp, Belgium; US citizen. *Study:* Mus Mod Art, NY; New Scho Social Studies; Art Life Studio, New York. *Work:* Smithsonian Inst, Washington, DC; Mus Art, La Jolla, Calif; Bergman Collection, Israel Mus, Jerusalem; Butler Inst, Youngstown, Ohio. *Exhib:* Small Sculpture from USA, Int Arts Prog; US Comt Int Asn of Art, Helsinki, Finland; Princeton Univ, NJ; New England Shows, Silvermine Guild of Artists, New Canaan, Conn. *Mem:* Audobon Artists; Nat Asn Women Artists; NY Soc Women Artists; Artists Equity of New York; Hudson River Contemp Artists. *Media:* Welded Metal, Stone. *Mailing Add:* 525 E 86 St New York NY 10028

CERNUDA, PALOMA
PRINTMAKER
b New York, NY, Feb 18, 48. *Study:* Calif State Univ, BFA, 83; Hunter Col, MA, 85. *Exhib:* Selections 29, Drawing Ctr, New York, NY, 85; Underknown in New York, Leubsdorf Gallery, Hunter Col, 87; one-person show, AFR Fine Art, Washington, DC, 88; Lines of Vision: Drawings by Contemp Woman, traveling show, 89. *Awards:* Art Fel, New York Found Arts, 87; Residents Grant, Phillip Morris Fel, Yaddo, Saratoga Springs, NY, 87 & 88; Artists Fel, Nat Endowment Arts, 89. *Mailing Add:* 223 First Ave No 3 New York NY 10003

CERNUSCHI, ALBERTO C
DEALER, CRITIC
US citizen. *Study:* Univ Milan, PhD; Univ Lausanne, PhD; Kensington Univ, Calif, PhD. *Pos:* Founder, Cernuschi & Caravan de France Galleries, Paris, France, Tokyo & New York & Cernuschi Art Historian of Great Britain; trustee, Cernuschi Mus, Paris. *Teaching:* Lectr mod art, Ecole du Louvre, Mus Cernuschi. *Mem:* Appraisers Asn Am. *Specialty:* Modern art. *Publ:* Constructive Manifesto; Theory of Autodeism; Life and Voyages of Century. *Mailing Add:* Cernuschi Galleries 210 E 86th St New York NY 10028

CERVENE, RICHARD
PAINTER, CURATOR
b Ft Dodge, Iowa. *Study:* Grinnell Col, BA, 51; Univ Iowa, Iowa City, MFA, 53; Yale-Norfolk Art Sch, with Josef Albers, Nicholas Marsicano & Gabor Peterdi, 53; Yaddo Found Grant in painting, Saratoga Springs, NY, summer 63 & 74. *Work:* Des Moines Art Ctr; Joslyn Art Mus; Coe Col, Iowa; Grinnell Col Iowa. *Exhib:* Nat Midyear Ann, Butler Inst Am Art, 66; Tenth Midwest Biennial Exhib, Joslyn Art Mus, 75; 45th Ann 17 State Show, Springfield Art Mus, Mo, 75; Iowa Artist Exhib, Des Moines Art Ctr, 76; Contemp Am Art, Am Acad & Inst Arts & Lett, New York, 79; Am Artists Exhib, US Embassy, Oslo, Norway, 80-81; one-man show, Blanden Mem Art Mus, Ft Dodge, Iowa, 86; retrospective exhib, Grinnell Col Art Gallery, 91. *Collections Arranged:* Appel & Alechinsky, 81, Japanese Prints, 82, African Art: East & West, 83, 85, 88 & 90, Giovanni Battista Piranesi, 83, Grinnell Col. *Teaching:* Prof art, Grinnell Col, 56-; Cur, Permanent Art Collection, 72-86. *Awards:* First Award Painting, Iowa Artists Exhib, Des Moines Art Ctr, 65; Purchase Award, Tenth Midwest Biennial Exhib, Joslyn Art Mus, 68; Recipient Grinnell Col Alumni Award Distinguished Career Accomplishments, 91. *Mem:* Am Asn Art Mus; Am Asn Univ Prof; Col Art Asn Am; Am Soc Aesthetics. *Media:* Oil, Watercolor. *Mailing Add:* Dept Art Grinnell Col Grinnell IA 50112

CERVENKA, BARBARA
EDUCATOR, PAINTER
b Cleveland, Sept 28, 39. *Study:* Siena Heights Col, Studio Angelico, Adrian, Mich, 57-64, BA, 64; Wayne State Univ, Detroit, 67-69; Univ Mich, Ann Arbor, 69-71, MFA, 71. *Work:* Alumni Mem Mus & Univ Mich, Ann Arbor; Eastern Mich Univ, Sill Hall Art Collection, Ypsilanti; Jesse Besser Mus, Alpina, Mich; Clarke Col, Dubuque, Iowa; Dennos Mus, Traverse City, Mich. *Exhib:* Watercolor USA, Springfield, Mo, 69, 73 & 75; Mid-Mich Show, Midland, 71; Mich Watercolor Soc Show, 89, 90 & 91; Am Watercolor Soc Show, New York, 73; Toledo Area Artists Show, Ohio, 73. *Pos:* Asst dean, Sch Art, Univ Mich, currently. *Teaching:* Instr drawing & watercolor, Siena Heights Col, 71-78; adminr, Adrian Dominican Sisters, Mich, 78-82; instr watercolor drawing, Sch Art, Univ Mich, currently. *Awards:* Purchase Prize, Eastern Mich Univ, 71 & Watercolor USA, 73; First Prize, Toledo Area Artists Show, 73. *Mem:* Mich Watercolor Soc; Col Art Asn; Watercolor USA Hon Soc. *Media:* Watercolor. *Mailing Add:* Sch Art Univ Mich Ann Arbor MI 48109

CETÍN, ANTON
PAINTER, PRINTMAKER
b Bojana, Croatia; Sept 18, 36; Can citizen. *Study:* Sch Applied Arts, dipl, 59; Acad Fine Arts, Masters dipl, 64. *Work:* Imperial Oil & Ontario Collection, Toronto, Can; Sony Collection, Tokyo, Japan; Mus Art & Craft, Mus & Gallery Ctr and Nat & Univ Libr, Zagreb, Croatia; Can Cult Ctr, Nat Libr France, Paris; Univ Mich, Dearborn; Princeton Univ; and others. *Exhib:* One-man shows, Galerie Le Creuset, Brussels, Belgium, 74, Art Gallery Hamilton, Can, 78, Heritage Gallery, Los Angeles, 79, Galeria Juan Martin, Mex, 79, Salon XX, Bogota, Columbia, 81, Mannheimer Abendakademie, Ger, 81 & Gilman Galleries, Chicago, 83; Beverely Gordon Gallery, Dallas, 87; Pfarrzentrum der Stiftspfarre, Bonn, Ger, 87; Nat & Univ Libr, Zagreb, Croatia, 88; Oberhausmuseum, Passau, Ger, 90; Sony Plaza Art Gallery, Tokyo, Japan, 91; and many others. *Awards:* Artist of the Year, Toronto, Can, 86. *Bibliog:* Nanette Dillard Simpson (auth), Anton Cetín's Show in Texas, Art-Talk, Scottsdale, Ariz, 87; Tomislav Laden (auth), Cetín's Show at National University Library (catalog), Zagreb, Croatia, 88; Dr David Burnett (auth), Eve, Show at Oberhsuemuseum (catalog), Passau, Ger, 90 & Cetín (monogr), 90; Alexander K Shiroka (auth), Introduction Show at Oberhausmuseum (catalog), Passau, Ger, 90; Franz Geierhaas (auth), My muse: Eve, J Print World, Meredith, NH, summer 91; and others. *Media:* Oil, Acrylic; Etching, Aquatint. *Mailing Add:* 37 Hanna Ave 13A Toronto ON M6K 1W9 Canada

CHABOT, AURORE (MARTHA)
SCULPTOR
b Nashua, NH, July 30, 49. *Study:* Pratt Inst, BFA, 71; Univ Colo, Boulder, MFA, 81. *Work:* J M Kohler Art Ctr, Kohler Co; Taipei Fine Arts Mus; Tucson Mus Art; Pushkin Mus, Moscow; Mus Decorative Arts, Riga, Latvia. *Exhib:* Group exhibs, Gallery II: Nat Affil, AIR Gallery, New York, 91, Objects & Entities: Small Sculptures, Univ Art Gallery, NMex State Univ, 90, Int Ceramic Symp Exhib, Dzinteri, Latvia, 91, At Home in Tucson, New Acquistions & Permanent Collection Exhib, Tucson Mus Art, 92; Solo exhibs, Mary H Dana Women Artist Series, Mabel Douglas Libr, Douglass Col/Rutgers Univ, 90, Univ of Ariz Art Mus, 90. *Pos:* juror, Ariz Comn Arts Traveling Exhibits Panel, Ill Coun Arts Individual Artists Grants Panel, 90. *Teaching:* Asst prof, Art Dept, Univ Vt, Burlington; artist-in-residence, Artpark, Lewiston, NY, 84, J M Kohler Art Ctr Industry Prog, 85, Watershed Ctr Ceramic Arts, 87 & 88 & Banff Ctr, Sch Fine Arts, Canada, 87; assoc prof art dept, Uniz Ariz, 88-; guest artist, NCECA Nat Conf, Tempe, Ariz, 91; vis artist, Int Ceramic Symp, Dzinteri, Latvia, 91. *Awards:* Research in the Arts Award Grant, Univ Ariz, 89 & 90; Governors Arts Award Artist, Ariz, 90; Tucson/Pina Individual Artist Grant, 91, Int Travel Grant, Univ Ariz, 91. *Bibliog:* Susan Wechsler (auth), A house is not always a home, Am Ceramics, Vol 4, No 3, 85; Richard Zakin (auth), Ceramics: Mastering the Craft (photos), 206-207, 90; Joyce Tognini (auth), A Joviet Reunion, 6-7, 2-3/92. *Mem:* Col Art Asn; Am Craft Coun; Nat Coun Educ Ceramic Arts. *Media:* Ceramics, Mixed. *Publ:* Auth, articles, Nat Coun Educ Ceramic Arts Newslett, 84 & Nat Coun Educ Ceramic Arts J, 85, 87, 89 & 91-92. *Dealer:* Kyle Belding Gallery Denver CO; Margo Jacobsen Gallery Portland OR. *Mailing Add:* 823 52nd Ave Tucson AZ 85701

CHADBOURN, ALFRED CHENEY
PAINTER, INSTRUCTOR
b Izmir, Turkey, Oct 5, 21; US citizen. *Study:* Chouinard Art Inst, Los Angeles, 40-42; Ecole des Beaux Arts, Paris, 47-50; Academie de la Grande Chaumiere, Paris, 47-51. *Work:* Adelphi Univ & Nat Acad Design, New York; Portland Mus Art, Maine; Boston Mus Fine Arts; Chicago Art Inst. *Exhib:* Salon des Independents, Mus Mod Art, Paris, 48-50; Ann, Los Angeles Co Mus, 50; Art Inst Chicago, 53; Pa Acad, Philadelphia Mus, 53-57; Nat Acad Design, New York, 53-54, 56-60, 70, 72-81; Whitney Mus Art, New York, 56; Wadsworth Atheneum, Hartford, Conn, 58. *Teaching:* Instr, Queen's Col, New York, 53-56, Portland Sch Art, Maine, 56-58 & Westbrook Col, Portland, Maine, 73-81. *Awards:* Louis Comfort Tiffany Found, 59; Henry Ward Ranger Purchase Award, 64 & Emil & Dines Carlsen Award, 81, Nat Acad Design. *Mem:* Nat Acad Design. *Media:* Oil, Watercolor. *Publ:* Contribr, A direct approach to painting, N Light Publ, 80; Painting with a Fresh Eye, Watson-Guptill, NY, 87. *Dealer:* Frost Gully Gallery Portland ME; Munson Gallery Chatham MA. *Mailing Add:* 4 Church St Yarmouth ME 04096

CHADDLESONE, SHERMAN
PAINTER, SCULPTOR
b Lawton, Okla, June 2, 47. *Study:* Inst Am Indian Arts, Santa Fe, with Allan Houser, Fritz Scholder & Otellie Loloma, dipl, 67; Cent State Univ, Okla, with William Wallo, 72-73. *Work:* Dept Interior Bldg, Washington, DC; Southern Plains Indian Mus, Anadarko, Okla; Inst Am Indian Art Mus, Santa Fe; Mabee-Gerrer Mus, Shawnee, Okla; Mus NMex, Albuquerque. *Comn:* Murals, Kiowa Tribal Mus, Carnegie, Okla, 84; TC Cannon (bronze bust), Nat Hall of Fame for Famous Am Indians, Anardarko, Okla, 88. *Exhib:* Inst Am Ind Arts Student Exhib, NMex Fine Arts Mus, Santa Fe, 64; Scottsdale Ann Ivitational Exhib, Ariz, 65 & 66; Contemp Am Indian Art, Palace Fine Arts, San Francisco, 70; Inst Am Indian Arts Alumni Traveling Exhib, Amon Carter Mus Western Art, Ft Worth, New Orleans Mus Art & Okla Art Ctr, 73-74; Pintura Amerindia Contemporanea Traveling Exhib, US Communications Agency, SAm, 79; Ann Western Art Show & Auction, Mus Native Am Cult, Spokane, 82; Contemporary North American Indian Art, Smithsonian Inst, 82-83. *Collections Arranged:* New Kiowa Five, Inst Am Indian Arts Mus, 83. *Teaching:* Dir, Indian Arts Workshop, San Francisco Art Comn, 70-71. *Awards:* Best of Show, Art From the Earth, 81 & First Place, Ann Kiowa Show, 82, Galeria, Norman, Okla; Second Place Painting, Gallup Ceremonial, 83; Best of Category Sculpture, Ann Trail Tears Art Show, Cherokee Nat Mus, Tahlequah, Okla, 85. *Bibliog:* Maurice Boyd (auth), Kiowa Voices, Vol II, Tex Christian Univ Press, 82. *Media:* Acrylic, Pastel; Stone. *Publ:* Kiowa Murals, Southwest Art, 7/87. *Dealer:* Okla Indian Art Gallery 2335 SW 44th St Oklahoma City OK 73119. *Mailing Add:* Box 1732 Anadarko OK 73005

CHADEAYNE, ROBERT OSBORNE
PAINTER
b Cornwall, NY, Dec 13, 1897. *Study:* Colgate Univ; Art Students League; also with C K Chatterton, Henry Martin Hoyt, George Luks & John Sloan. *Work:* Columbus Gallery Fine Arts; Butler Inst Am Art; Schumacker Collection, Capital Univ; and others. *Comn:* Broad & High St 1920 (painting), 64 & Central Ohio (painting), 65, Trautman Off Bldg, Columbus, Ohio; cityscape, Huntington Nat Bank, Columbus, 70. *Exhib:* Art Inst Chicago Ann; Pa Acad Fine Arts Ann; Nat Acad Design Ann, New York; Corcoran Biennial, Washington, DC; Butler Inst Am Art Midyear Nat Exhib, Youngstown, Ohio, 65-70. *Teaching:* Dir drawing & painting, Columbus Art Sch, 27-42; prof fine arts, Ohio State Univ, 42-63. *Awards:* Norman Waite Harris Medal, Art Inst Chicago, 20; Purchase Prize, Pa Acad Fine Arts, 20; IBM Medal for Contribution to World of Art. *Mem:* Columbus Art League; Columbus Gallery Fine Arts. *Dealer:* Capricorn Galleries 8003 Woodmont Ave Bethesda MD 20014. *Mailing Add:* 5578 Riverside Dublin OH 43017

CHADWICK, WHITNEY
CRITIC, HISTORIAN
b Niagara Falls, NY, July 28, 43. *Study:* Middlebury Col, BA, 65; Pa State Univ, MA, 68, PhD, 75. *Teaching:* Assoc prof art hist, Mass Inst Technol, Cambridge, Mass, 72-78; prof art hist, San Francisco State Univ, 78- *Awards:* Grants-in-Aid, Am Coun Learned Soc, 76 & 81; Fel, Nat Endowment Humanities, 80-81; fel, Am Coun Learned Soc, 87; Nat Endowment Humanities, 88; Fel, Mary Ingraham Bunting Inst, 92. *Mem:* Col Art Asn; Women's Caucus Art. *Res:* Surrealism; contemporary art; feminism. *Publ:* Auth, Masson's Gradiva: The metamorphosis of a surrealist myth, Art Bulletin, 70; Eros or Thanatos: The surrealist cult of love reexamined, Artforum, 75; Myth in Surrealist Painting, 1929-1939, UMI Press, 80; The muse as artist, Art in Am, 85; Women Artists and the Surrealist Movement, Thames & Hudson, 85; Women Artists and the Politics of Representation, Feminist Art Criticism, 88; Toyen and the Surrealist Movement in Czechoslovakia, Symp, 89; Women, Art and Society, Thames and Hudson, 90. *Mailing Add:* Dept Art San Francisco State Univ 1600 Holloway Ave San Francisco CA 94132

CHAET, BERNARD
PAINTER, EDUCATOR
b Boston, Mass, Mar 7, 24. *Study:* Boston Mus Sch, with Karl Zerbe, 42-45; Tufts Univ, BS, 49; Md Inst, Col Art, Hon Dr Fine Arts, 85. *Work:* Fogg Art Mus, Harvard Univ; Univ Calif Art Gallery, Los Angeles; Brooklyn Mus, NY; Addison Gallery Am Art, Andover, Mass; RI Sch Design Mus, Providence. *Exhib:* Univ Ill Biennial Am Painting, 51, 53 & 60; Golden Years of American Drawing 1900-56, Brooklyn Mus, 56; Recent Drawings USA, Mus Mod Art, New York, 56; Corcoran Biennial Am Painting, Washington, DC, 62; Pa

Acad Fine Arts Ann, Philadelphia, 62; and 37 one-man exhibs. *Pos:* Auth mo article, Studio talk, Arts Mag, 56-69. *Teaching:* Prof drawing & painting, Yale Univ Art Sch, 51-, William Leffingwell prof painting, 79-90, emer prof, 90- *Awards:* Grant, Nat Found Humanities Arts, 66-67; Hassam & Speicher Fund Purchase Award, Am Acad & Inst Arts & Lett, 81; Distinguished Teaching Art Award, Col Art Asn, 86. *Bibliog:* Margaret Mathews (auth), article, Am Artist, 9/82; Janice C Oresman (auth), article, Arts Mag, 11/82. *Publ:* Auth preface, 20th Century Drawing (catalog), Yale Art Gallery, 55; Artists at Work, Webb, 61; The Art of Drawing, Holt, 71, 77, & 83; An Artist's Notebook: Techniques and Materials, Holt, 79. *Dealer:* Marilyn Pearl Gallery 29 W 57th St New York NY 10019; Alpha Gallery 121 Newbury St Boston MA 02116. *Mailing Add:* 141 Cold Spring St New Haven CT 06511

CHAFETZ, SIDNEY
PRINTMAKER, EDUCATOR
b Providence, RI, Mar 27, 22. *Study:* RI Sch Design, BFA, 47; Acad Julian, Paris, 47-48; L'Ecole Am Beaux Arts, Fontainebleau, 47; with Fernand Leger, Paris, 48 & S W Hayter, Atelier 17, 50-51. *Work:* Libr Cong, Washington, DC; Morgan Libr, NY; Dahlem-Staalische Mus; Philadelphia Mus Art; British Mus; Mus Art, New York. *Comn:* Dedication etching, Ohio State Univ Col Law, 64; Hawthorne Keepsake, Ohio State Univ, 64; Robert Lowell Poster, Int Poetry Forum, Pittsburgh, Pa, 67; F Scott Fitzgerald Keepsake, Fitzgerald Newsletter, Ohio State Univ, 68; Poor Richards Almanacks Original Woodblock Portrait, Imprint Soc, Barre, Mass, 70. *Exhib:* Ten Years of American Prints, 1947-57, Brooklyn Mus, NY, 57; Young American Printmakers, Mus Mod Art, New York, 58-59; 9th Int Expos Gravure, Switz, Norway & Sweden, 66; 1st Biennial Int Gravure Sur Bois, Banska Bystrica, Czech, 70; 2nd Triennial Int Graphica Contemp, Capri, Italy, 72; 30-Year Retrospective, Antioch Col & throughout Ohio, 78-79; Satire & Homage, Chafetz Graphics, 88. *Teaching:* Emer prof art, Ohio State Univ, 48-82, prof emer, 82-; vis prof art, Univ Ariz, spring 65, Univ Wis-Madison, summer 67 & Univ Denver, summer 71 & 79; Fulbright Sr lectr, Univ Belgrade, Yugoslavia, 80. *Awards:* Fulbright Fel, 50-51; Purchase Prize & Awards, 1st Biennial Int Gravure, Banska Bystrica, Czech, 70; MacDowell Colony Fel, 79; Governors Award, Ohio, 91. *Mem:* Soc Am Graphic Artists; Am Color Print Soc; Am Asn Univ Prof; Nat Acad Design. *Media:* Woodcut, Intaglio. *Publ:* Auth, Chafetz Graphics: Satire and Homage, The Ohio State Univ Pres, 88. *Dealer:* Susan Teller Gallery 568 Broadway New York NY 10012. *Mailing Add:* Dept Art Ohio State Univ Columbus OH 43210

CHAHROUDI, MARTHA L
CURATOR
b Chicago, Ill, Nov 3, 46. *Study:* Col Wooster, BA, 68; NY Univ, MA, 70; State Univ NY, Buffalo, MFA, 81. *Collections Arranged:* Ansel Adams: 100 Photographs, 79-80, August Sander: Photographs of an Epoch, 80, The Spirit of an American Place, 80-81, The New West: Photographs by Robert Adams, 81, American Frontiers: The Photographs of Timothy H O'Sullivan 1867-1874, 81-82, Danny Lyon: Pictures from the New World 1962-1982, 82, Frederick H Evans: The Desired Haven, 82, Minor White, 83 & Tibet: The Sacred Realm, Photographs 1880-1950, 83, Philadelphia Mus Art; The Golden Age of British Photography 1839-1900, 84-85; All American, photogr by Burk Uzzle, 84-85; Twelve Photographers Look at Us, 87; Emmet Gowin photogr, 90. *Pos:* Assoc cur photogr, 85. *Awards:* Visual Arts Prog Critics Fel, Nat Endowment Arts, 79. *Mem:* Soc Photog Educ. *Publ:* Auth, Tibet: The Scared Realm, Photographs 1880-1950, Millerton, 83; All American: Photographs by Burk Uzzle, St Davids, 84; Twelve Photographers Look at Us, Philadelphia Mus Art Bull, 84; Emmet Gowin Photographs, Philadelphia Mus Art, 90. *Mailing Add:* Philadelphia Mus Art PO Box 7646 Philadelphia PA 19101

CHAIKIN, ALYCE
GRAPHIC ARTIST, PAINTER
b New York, NY. *Study:* Parsons Sch Design, cert, 43; Silvermine Guild Ctr Arts, 79-81; Yale Univ Sch Art, with Robert Reed, 80-83. *Work:* Town of Fairfield, Conn; New Haven Paint & Clay Club, Conn; Univ Conn Health Ctr, Farmington; Mem Solan-Kettering Cancer Ctr, NY. *Exhib:* solo exhibs, Vassos Gallery, Silvermine Guild Ctr, Conn, 82 & Capricorn Galleries, Bethesda, 86; Prizewinners' Exhib, Audubon Artists, Lever House, New York, 86; Drawing, Ark Art Ctr, Little Rock, 86; Drawing Invitational, Huntsville Mus, Ala, 87; Philip Desind Collection Contemp Realism, Butler Inst Am Art, Youngstown, Ohio, 87; The Honorable Artist, Legislative Off Bldg, Hartford, Conn, 88; Connecticut Gallery, Invitational, Marlborough, Conn, 90; and others. *Awards:* Best in Show, Summer Showcase, Ridgefield Guild Artists, 79; Silvermine Guild Award, 32nd New Eng Exhib, 81; Audubon Artists 43rd Ann Louis Lozowick Award, 85. *Bibliog:* Paula Reens (auth), Silvermine 60th anniversary, Art New Eng, 10/82; Walter Zimmer (auth), Recognizable image, NY Times, 2/85; Philip Eliasoph (auth), Recognizable image, Greenwich Time, 2/85. *Mem:* Silvermine Guild Ctr Arts; New Haven Paint & Clay Club; Conn Women Artists. *Media:* Pencil, Silverpoint. *Dealer:* Capricorn Galleries 4849 Rugby Ave Bethesda MD 20814. *Mailing Add:* 192 Glengarry Rd Fairfield CT 06430

CHAIKLIN, AMY
PAINTER
b Newark, NJ, Oct 4, 55. *Study:* New York Studio Sch, Paris, France, studied with Elaine de Kooning, 76, Wash Univ, Sch Fine Arts, BFA, 77. *Work:* Mus Mod Art, libr, New York; Franklin Furnace Arch, New York; Visual Studies Workshop Arch, Rochester, NY; Art Circolo, E V, Munich, Ger. *Comn:* Eyes on You (mural), Fashion Moda, Bronx, NY, 83; Media Girls (mural), Eyes and Ears Found, San Francisco, Calif, 84; Girl with Pet Rat (mural), Limbo Gallery, New York, 84; Berlin Beauties (mural), Comn by Maria Makkaroni, Berlin, Ger, 84. *Exhib:* Women Art 77, Kansas City Art Inst, MO, 77; Smart Art, Too, Harvard Univ, Cambridge, Mass, 85; Purgatory & Paradise, Met Mus, New York, 86; Works on Paper, Galerie V Vertes, Munich, Ger, 89; Alumni Exhib, New York Studio Sch, New York, 90; solo exhibs, New Paintings, Galerie Schrill, Berlin, Ger, 90 & Sergei Diaghilev Art Ctr, Marble Palace, St Petersburg, Russia, 92; Fine Arts Mus Long Island, Hempstead, NY, 91; 37 Räume, Kunst-Werke Berlin, Ger, 91. *Awards:* Artist-in-Residence, Cite Int des Arts, Wash Univ, 88; Artist-in-Residence, Stiftung Starke, Berlin, Ger, 92-93. *Bibliog:* Vera Botterbusch (auth), Aktuell in Münchner Galerien, Süddeutsche Zeitung, 89; Elfi Kreis (auth), Amy Chaiklin in der Galerie Schrill, Der Tagesspiegel, 90; Andreas Quappe (auth), Vom Fussball platz in 37 Räume, Berliner Zeitung, 92. *Media:* Oil, Watercolor. *Mailing Add:* 26 Beaver St New York NY 10004

CHALKE, JOHN
CERAMIST, SCULPTOR
b Gloucestershire, Eng, Sept 28, 40; Can citizen. *Study:* Bath Acad Art, Wiltshire, Eng, teacher's cert art educ, 62. *Work:* Esso Resources; Massey Found; Alta Art Found; Can Coun Art Bank; Ceramics Monthly Collection; Charles Bronfman Corp Collection; Univ Alta Collection; Burlington Art Ctr Collection. *Exhib:* Int Exhib Ceramics, Victoria & Albert Mus, London, Eng, 72; First & Second Int Ceramic Exhib Taipei, Taiwan, 85 & 92; Second World Teriennial Exhib, Yugoslavia, 87; Third, Fourth & Fifth Nat Biennial Ceramics Trois Riviéres, Que, 88; over 170 nat & int ceramics exhibs. *Teaching:* Instr ceramics, var art schs in Southern Eng, 64-68; instr visual fundamentals, Univ Alta, Edmonton, 71-76; instr, Univ Calgary, Alta, 76-83; instr, Alta Col Art, Calgary, Alta, currently. *Awards:* Can Coun Grants, 72, 78, 82 & 84; Award of Excellence, Can Olympic Exhib, Montreal, 76; Alta Cult Grant, 83, 88 & 92. *Bibliog:* Hildegard Storr-Britz (auth), Contemporary International Ceramics, 78; Charlotte Speight (auth), Images in Clay Sculpture, 83; Robin Hopper (auth), The Ceramic Spectrum, 84; and thirteen other bks on ceramics. *Mem:* Acad Italia; Int Acad Ceramics; Can Crafts Coun; Alta Crafts Coun; Alta Potter's Asn. *Media:* Clay. *Publ:* Contribr, numerous photographs & articles, Ceramics Monthly Mag, 3/75-9/90; Ceramic Review, UK 2/75, 3/82, 11/87, 12/88 & 3/89, Am Craft, 1/86. *Mailing Add:* 429 12th St NW Calgary AB T2N 1Y9 Canada

CHALLIS, RICHARD BRACEBRIDGE
DEALER, LECTURER
b London, Eng, Aug 12, 20. *Study:* King's Col Sch, London, 34-37; Chelsea Col, 38-39. *Collections Arranged:* Roger Kuntz Retrospective, Laguna Beach Mus Art, Calif, 77; Moderator, The Ruth Stoever Fleming Collection, Newport Beach, 85; Publ, Newport-Mesa Unified Sch Dist. *Pos:* Founder & dir, Challis Galleries, 50-82; art dir, Los Angeles Home Show, 65-67; consult, Esther Wells Collection, 83- *Teaching:* Lectr, Marketing of Fine Art, Orange Co Dept Educ. *Mem:* Laguna Beach Festival Arts; Art Inst S Calif; life mem Laguna Art Mus. *Specialty:* 20th century paintings and sculpture. *Mailing Add:* 1390 S Coast Hwy Laguna Beach CA 92651

CHALMERS, E LAURENCE, JR
ADMINISTRATOR
b Wildwood, NJ, Mar 24, 28. *Study:* Princeton Univ, AB(psychol), 48, MA(exp psychol), 50, PhD(exp psychol), 51. *Pos:* Dean, Col Arts & Sci, Fla State Univ, 64-66, vpres, Acad Affairs, 66-69; chancellor, Univ Kans, 69-72; pres, Art Inst Chicago, 72-87; Pres, San Antonio Mus Asn, 87- *Mailing Add:* San Antonio Mus Assoc 3801 Broadway San Antonio TX 78299

CHAMBERLAIN, CHARLES
CERAMIST, EDUCATOR
b Brockton, Mass, Aug 7, 42. *Study:* Mass Col Art, BFA; Col Ceramics, Alfred Univ, MFA. *Work:* Smithsonian Inst, Washington, DC; Archie Bray Found, Helena, Mont; Mass Col Art, Boston; Col Ceramics, Alfred Univ, NY. *Exhib:* Artist, Craftsmen, Inst Art, Jacksonville, Fla, 73; one-man retrospective, NC Mus Art, Raleigh, 73; 27th Ceramics Nat, Everson Mus, Syracuse, NY, 74; Craft Multiples, Smithsonian Inst, Washington, DC, 75; North Carolina Clay, Raleigh, 92. *Pos:* Jury mem, Piedmont Craftsmen, Winston-Salem, NC, 74- *Teaching:* Instr ceramics, Worcester Art Ctr, Mass, 65 & Univ NH, 66-67; prof ceramics, East Carolina Univ, Greenville, NC, 67-, chmn design dept, 82-85. *Awards:* Best in Show, Mass Assoc Craftsmen, 65; Merit Award, Emerging Craftsmen of New Eng, 65; Hon Mention, Piedmont Craftsmen Ann, 71. *Mem:* Piedmont Craftsmen; Am Crafts Coun; Nat Coun Educ Ceramic Art. *Media:* Clay, Mixed Media. *Dealer:* ART Gallery Pollock St New Bern NC 28560. *Mailing Add:* 2307 E Third St Greenville NC 27834

CHAMBERLAIN, DAVID (ALLEN)
SCULPTOR, PAINTMAKER
b Canton, Ohio, Aug 11, 49. *Study:* Princeton Univ, with Joe Brown & James Seawright, BA(archit design), 71; Colo Col, 72; Univ Pa, with Robert Engman & Neil Welliver, MFA(sculpture), 77. *Work:* Johnson Mus Art, Ithaca, NY; Delaware Mus Art, Wilmington; Muskegon Mus Art, Mich; Nelson Mus Art, Kansas City, Mo; Portland Mus Art, Maine; Wadsworth Athenaeum, Hartford, Conn. *Comn:* Cantata, Horne Libr, Babson Col, Wellesley, Mass, 81; TORUS, Stratus Computer Inc, Marlboro, Mass, 86; A Une Passante, M C Wallace Libr, Wheaton Col, Norton, Mass, 91; Ballette, Southworth Libr, Canton Col, New York, 91; Eroica, Morgridge Auditorium, Univ Wis, Madison, 92. *Exhib:* Pucker/Safrai Gallery, Boston, Mass, 79-92; Arlene McDaniel Galleries, Simsbury, Conn, 85-92; Renjeau Gallery, Concord, Mass, 89-92; MacLaren/Markowitz Gallery, Boulder, Colo, 90-92; Joanne Lyon Galleries, Aspen, Colo, 89-91; one-man shows, Everson Mus Art, Syracuse, NY, 83, Gallerie Obussier, Nantucket, Mass, 85, Lyme Acad Fine

Arts, Old Lyme, Conn, 85 & 86, Gibson Gallery, SUNY at Postsdam, New York, 87, Pucker/Safrai Gallery, Boston, Mass, 81, 84 & 88, MacLaren/ Markowitz Gallery, Boulder, Colo, 91; one-man retrospective, The Art Complex Mus, Duxbury, Mass, 88, McKissick Mus Art, Columbia, SC, 90. *Teaching:* Co-dir & artist in residence, Arts Col House Prog, Univ Pa, 75-77; assoc prof, Univ SC, 90-91; adj prof, River Col, Nashua, Ntl, 91-39. *Awards:* Haas Fund Award, 74-75; Venture Fund Grant, Ford Found & Univ Pa, 75-77; Red Ribbon Award, Am Film Festival, 82. *Bibliog:* Search for Perfection (videotape), FIS/Pucker Safrai, 82; Melodic Form: The Sculpture of David Chamberlain, David Godine, 90; David Chamberlain: Artistry in Motion (film), SC-ETV, 92. *Mem:* Mus Fine Arts Council, Boston; New Eng Sculptors Asn. *Media:* Bronze, Mahogany. *Mailing Add:* c/o Pucker-Safrai Gallery 171 Newbury St Boston MA 02116

CHAMBERLAIN, JOHN ANGUS
SCULPTOR
b Rochester, Ind, Apr 16, 27. *Study:* Art Inst Chicago, 51-52; Univ Ill; Black Mountain Col, 55-56. *Work:* Albright-Knox Gallery, Buffalo, NY; Los Angeles Co Mus Art; Guggenheim Mus, Mus Mod Art, New York; Dallas Mus Fine Arts; and others. *Comn:* Coloured gates of Louisville: the inevitable return of the indefatigable Dr Fahey (wall relief), Ky Ctr Performing Arts, 88. *Exhib:* One-man shows, Guggenheim Mus, New York, 71 & Galerie Heiner Friedrich, Cologne, 79, Mus Contemp Art, Los Angeles, Galerie Pierre Huber, Geneva, 87-88, Margo Leavin Gallery, Los Angeles, 88, Pace Gallery, New York, 89 & Waddington Galleries, London, 90; Guggenheim Mus, 74; Whitney Mus Am Art, 79; Va Mus Fine Arts, Richmond; Mus Mod Art, New York; Corcoran Gallery Art, Washington, DC; Smithsonian Inst, Washington, DC; Cranbrook Acad Art Mus, Bloomfield Hills, Mich; Philadelphia Mus Art, Pa; Albright-Knox Art Gallery, Buffalo, NY; two-man show, Univ Calif Art Mus, Santa Barbara, 84; The Oliver-Hoffmann Collection: Three Decades, Mus Contemp Art, Chicago, 88-89; Lost and Found: The Object Transformed, Barbara Mathes Gallery, New York, 89; American Masters, Fabian Carlsson Gallery, London, 89-90; and many others. *Pos:* Artist-in-Residence, Skowhegan Sch Painting & Sculpture, Maine, 85; art dept, Am Acad & Inst Arts and Letters. *Awards:* Guggenheim Fels, 66 & 77; Creative Arts Awards, Brandeis Univ, 84. *Bibliog:* Duncan Smith (auth), In the Heart of the Tinman: An Essay on John Chamberlain, Art Forum, Jan 84; William Wilson (auth), The Galleries: La Cienega Area, Los Angeles Times, Mar 15, 85; Douglas C McGill (auth), Art People, NY Times, Aug 1, 86; David Lee (auth), article The Times of London, London, 4/24/87; Edward S Sozanski (auth), Work of four prominent sculptors, The Philadelphia Enquirer, 3/17/88; Jack Flam (auth), Making the gallery rounds, Wall Street Journal, 3/22/89; Peter Clothier, Living with Art, Artnews, 5/90; and many others. *Mailing Add:* c/o Pace Gallery 32 E 57th St New York NY 10022

CHAMBERLIN, SCOTT
SCULPTOR, CERAMIST
b Orange, Calif, Oct 14, 48. *Study:* Calif State Univ, San Francisco, BA(art), 73; NY State Col Ceramics, Alfred Univ, MFA(ceramic art), 76. *Work:* Dordrecht Mus, Holland; Ceramic Collections, Alfred Univ, NY; Denver Art Mus, Colo. *Exhib:* Clayworks Invitational, Carmel Col Art Gallery, Oxford, Eng, 78; North California Clay Routes: Sculpture Now, San Francisco Mus Mod Art, 79; solo exhibs, Dordrecht Mus Art, 80 & Exposorium Vriej Universiteit, Amsterdam, Holland, 81; New Works in Clay, Hadler-Rodriguez Gallery, New York, 83; California Art 1984, Laguna Beach Mus Art, Calif, 84; San Francisco Art Acad, 85; Craft Today: Poetry of the Physical, Am Craft Mus, New York & Denver Art Mus, 86; Ceramics Now: 27th Nat Exhib, Everson Mus Art, Syracuse, NY, 87; A Different Garden: Dorothy Weiss Gallery, San Francisco, 87; Arvada Ctr Arts & Humanities, Denver, Colo, 88. *Teaching:* Lectr ceramics, Camberwell Sch Art, London, Eng, 76, 78 & 83; asst prof fine art ceramics, Univ Colo, Boulder, 85- *Awards:* Soc Encouragement Art Award, San Francisco Mus Mod Art, 79; Artist Fel, Colo Coun Arts & Humanities, 86; Nat Endowment Arts Individual Artists Fel Grant, 86. *Bibliog:* C R Grant (auth), Keramishce objecten van Scoitch, Mus News, Holland, 80; Joanne Burstein (auth), Review of tall sculptural pots, Images & Issues Mag, 81; Wendy Dubin (auth), rev, Am Ceramics, 6/84; M F Parges (auth), review, Am Ceramics, winter 87. *Media:* Clay; Terra Cotta. *Publ:* Auth, Source & stimulus, Ceramic Rev Mag, London, Eng, 79. *Dealer:* Dorothy Weiss Gallery 254 Sutter St San Francisco CA 94108; Cydney Clayton Gallery 2544 15th St Denver CO 80211. *Mailing Add:* Dept Fine Arts Univ Colo Boulder Boulder CO 80309

CHAMBERS, BRUCE WILLIAM
DEALER, HISTORIAN
b Cincinnati, Ohio, June 22, 41. *Study:* Yale Univ, BA, 63; Univ Rochester, MA, 70; Univ Pa, PhD, 74. *Collections Arranged:* Selections from the Robert P Coggins Collection of American Painting (auth, catalog), Univ Rochester, 76; Charles Burchfield: The Charles Rand Penney Collection (coauth, catalog), Smithsonian Inst, 78; Uncommon Visions (coauth, catalog), Univ Rochester, 79; David Gilmour Blythe, 1815-65 (auth, catalog), Nat Collection Fine Arts, 80; Art and Artists of the South: The Robert P Coggins Collection (auth, catalog), Univ SC, 84; George DeForest Brush (coauth, catalog), Berry-Hill Galleries; Old Image: American Trompe L'Oeil, Image of Currency (auth, catalog), Berry-Hill Galleries, New York, 88- *Pos:* Asst dir curatorial serv, Mem Art Gallery, Univ Rochester, 76-, actg dir, 79-80; dir, Univ Iowa Mus Art, 80-81; assoc, Berry-Hill Galleries, New York, 82- *Teaching:* Asst prof art hist, Emory Univ, Atlanta, 70-76; adj prof, Univ Rochester, NY, 76-80. *Mem:* Col Art Asn; NY State Coun Arts. *Res:* Nineteenth and twentieth century American art and iconography. *Publ:* Auth, American Paintings in the High Museum of Art, High Mus Art, 75; Pythagorean puzzle of Patrick Lyon, Art Bulletin, 6/76; Thomas Cole and the ruined tower, Currier Gallery Bulletin, 11/83; Continuities: American Figure Painting, 1900-1950, Berry-Hill Galleries, 83; Southern artist and the Civil War, Southern Quart, fall-winter 85; Robert Henri's Street Scene with Snow, Yale Art Gallery Bull, winter 86. *Mailing Add:* c/o Artsist Chambers Inc 191 Glen Pkwy Hamden CT 06517

CHAMBERS, KAREN
HISTORIAN, CRITIC
b Madison, Ind, Sept 28, 48. *Study:* Wittenberg Univ, 66-70, BFA, 73; Case-Western Reserve Univ, study with Wolfgang Stechow; Univ Cincinnati, MA, 78. *Pos:* Cur asst, Dayton Art Inst, Ohio, 70-73; asst registr, Cincinnati Art Mus, 75; asst cur, Contemp Arts Ctr, Cincinnati, 75-77; asst dir, Sperone Westwater Fischer, New York, 77-79; asst dir, Droll/Kolbert, New York, 79-80; dir, Susan Caldwell, 81; ed, New Work, 83- *Mem:* Col Art Asn; Am Asn Mus; Glass Art Soc. *Res:* Glass arts. *Specialty:* Contemporary. *Publ:* Auth & ed, Selections from the Collection of the Vent Haven Museum, Contemp Arts Ctr, 77; auth, Jane Reece's portraits of artists, Exposure, 79; auth, Mission: Impossible--Dale Chihulu, spring 83 & Howard Bentre: An artist in time, summer-fall 83, New Work; auth, Fragments, Tangeman Ctr Fine Arts Gallery, Univ Cincinnati, 83. *Mailing Add:* 1 Sheridan Sq #3C New York NY 10014

CHAMBERS, PARK A, JR
SCULPTOR, EDUCATOR
b Wheeling, WVa, Oct 29, 42. *Study:* Kent State Univ, BFA, 68, MFA, 70. *Work:* The Chicago-Tokyo Bank & Shatkin Trading Company, Chicago, Ill; Johnson & Johnson, Elmhurst, Ill; Kent State Univ, Ohio. *Comn:* Wrist Sculpture, comn by Fred Gordon, Skokie, Ill, 73; Installation/Performance, Focus on the Arts, Highland Park, Ill, 75; Body Sculpture, Friedman Leather Fashions, New York, 79-80; Baby Sculpture, SSF Inc, Chicago, Ill, 75-88. *Exhib:* 51st Ann, The Cleveland Mus Art, Ohio, 69; 22nd Ann, Butler Inst Am Art, Youngstown, Ohio, 70; Form in Fiber, Deson-Zaks Gallery, Chicago, Ill, 72; Sculpture in New Media, Ill State Mus, Springfield, 73; Fiber Forms, Cincinnati Art Mus, Ohio, 78; Fiber as Art, Metrop Mus, Manila, Philippines, 80; Art for AIDS, Vopol Gallery, San Francisco, Calif, 86; Figure & Place, Artemisia Gallery, Chicago, Ill, 88. *Collections Arranged:* 6 X 6 Exhib, SAIC Gallery, 77, Extensions & Spirit & Image: Art of Vodoo, SAIC Gallery, 77, 86 & 87; SAIC, Idaho State Univ, Pocatello, 87. *Pos:* Juror, Univ Chicago, Ill, 72; lectr, Mus Contemp Art, 72; artist-in-residence, Highland Park High Sch, Ill, 74-75; vis artist, Ctr Creative Studies, Detroit, Mich & Univ Ariz, Tucson, Ariz, 88. *Teaching:* Instr metal & fiber, Kent State Univ, Ohio, 68-69; instr fiber, Akron Art Inst, Ohio, 69-70; assoc prof fiber & mixed media, Art Inst Chicago, Ill, 70- *Awards:* Research Grant, Kent State Univ Grad Sch, 69; Experiment Materials, Brunswick Corporation, Chicago, Ill, 69; Individual Grant, Nat Endowment Arts, 76. *Bibliog:* Judith Russi Kirshner (auth), The Art Gallery Mag, New York, 72; Franz Schulze (auth), Chicago Daily News, 72; Robert Glauber (auth), Skyline, Chicago, 72; E Chung & A Sandoval (coauth), The New Plastics, Vis Arts Ctr Alaska, 82; D Consentino (auth), Spirit & Image, Vol 21, No 1, African Arts, 87. *Media:* Rope, Wood. *Publ:* Contribr, Decorative Art in Modern Interiors, Studio Vista Limited, London, 71; contribr, Techniques of Rya Knotting, Van Nostrand Reinhold Co, 71; contribr, Soft Sculpture, Crown Publishers, 74; contribr, How to Create Your Own Designs, Doubleday & Co, 75; contribr, Hardcore Crafts, Ballantine Books, 76. *Mailing Add:* Sch Art Inst Chicago 37 S Wabash Ave Chicago IL 60603

CHAMBERS, WILLIAM MCWILLIE
PAINTER, ART DEALER
b Baton Rouge, La, Aug 6, 51. *Study:* Louisiana Tech Univ, Ruston, 69-71; Kans City Art Inst, Mo, BFA, 73; New York Studio Sch, with Leland Bell, 73-74. *Pos:* Vpres, Grace Borgenicht Gallery, 74-; co-curator Fifty Years of Canadian Landscape Painting, Grace Borgenicht Gallery, 86. *Mem:* Art Dealers Assoc Am, Bowery Gallery. *Media:* Oil. *Specialty:* 20th century American, Canadian & German Expressionists. *Publ:* Ed of numerous exhib catalogues, 74-; Jose de Rivera-Constructions, Taller Ediciones, Madrid, 80. *Dealer:* Grace Bórgenicht Gallery 724 Fifth Ave New York NY 10022. *Mailing Add:* 319 E 50th St New York NY 10022

CHANDLER, ELISABETH GORDON
SCULPTOR
b St Louis, Mo, June 10, 13. *Study:* Pvt study with Edmondo Quattrocchi; Art Students League. *Work:* Bronze, Columbia Univ Sch Law; Tonkin Gulf Memorial, (bronze releif), Aircraft Carrier USS Forrestal; Gov Dummer Acad Libr; John Jay, First Chief Justice, (bronze), Pace Univ Sch Law; and many others. *Comn:* Busts, Owen R Cheatham, Founder, Georgia Pac Corp, Albert A Michelson, Hall of Fame for Great Americans, NY Univ; Adlai E Stevenson High Sch, 74; Chief Justices Harlan Fiske Stone & Charles Evans Hughes, Columbia Univ; Queen Anne (statue), Queen Anne's Co Courthouse Sq, Centerville, Md, 77; St Frances Cabrini, St Patricks Cathedral, New York. *Exhib:* Mattatuck Mus, Waterbury Conn, 49; Nat Acad Design Ann, New York, 50-83; Nat Sculpture Soc Ann, 53-83; Allied Artists Am, New York, 61-82; Smithsonian Inst, Washington, DC, 63; Paul Mellon Art Ctr, Wallingford, Conn; Old State House, Hartford, Conn; and others. *Pos:* Trustee, Lyme Acad Fine Arts, 76-, Brookgreen Gardens, 89- *Teaching:* Instr portrait sculpture, Lyme Acad Fine Arts, Old Lyme, Conn, 76- *Awards:* Thomas R Proctor Prize, Dessie Greer Prize, Nat Acad Design, 60, 79, 85; Silver Medal Citation, Nat Sculpture Soc, 92; Gold Medal, Am Artists Professional League, 60, 69, 73, 75. *Mem:* Fel Nat Sculpture Soc (rec secy, 73-76); fel Am Artists Prof League (dir, 71-73); Nat Acad Design; Nat Sculpture Rev; Lyme Art Asn. *Media:* Bronze. *Mailing Add:* 2 Mill Pond Lane Old Lyme CT 06371

CHANDLER, JOHN WILLIAM
PAINTER, EDUCATOR
b Concord, NH, Sept 28, 10. *Study:* Exeter Sch Art, Boston; Manchester Inst Arts & Sci; St Anselm's Col, AB; Boston Univ, EdM(scholar), 60; Harvard Univ; Columbia Univ; study in Europe & with Aldro T Hibbard. *Exhib:* Pasadena Nat, 46; Currier Gallery Art Regional, 47; one-man show, Keene State Col, 51; De Cordova & Dana Mus, 52; Nebr Wesleyan Univ, 58. *Pos:* From asst to dir to actg dir, Currier Gallery Art, 42-52. *Teaching:* Exec dir & instr design & painting, Manchester Inst Arts & Sci, 33-46; assoc prof art & head dept, Lycoming Col, 52-70; instr painting, Concord Artists, Inc, 71-72; instr, Studio II, 72- *Awards:* First Watercolor Award, Currier Gallery Art, 47; Danforth Found Award, 52. *Mem:* Founding mem Concord Artists; charter mem NH Art Asn. *Publ:* Author various articles on glass & silver. *Mailing Add:* 2 Coolidge Ave Concord NH 03301

CHANDLER, MICHAEL ROBERT
PAINTER
b Denver, Colo, June 27, 50. *Study:* Univ Colo, BFA, 72. *Exhib:* Anniottanta, Galleria Comunale d'Art Moderna, Bologna, Italy, 85; Mus Art, Providence, RI, 85; Art--Made in the USA, Stadtische Mus, Regensberg, Ger, 88; Eco Art 92, Museo de Arte Moderna do Rio de Janeiro, Brazil, 92; Slow Art: Painting in New York Now, PSI, New York, 92. *Bibliog:* Michael Kimmelman (auth), article, NY Times, 1/10/92; Alfred Corn (auth), article, Art News, 4/92; Francesco Bonami (auth), article, Flash Art, 5-6/92. *Media:* Oil on Canvas. *Dealer:* Salvatore Ala 560 Broadway New York NY 10012. *Mailing Add:* 83 Canal St New York NY 10002

CHANNING, SUSAN ROSE
ADMINISTRATOR, PHOTOGRAPHER
b Englewood, NJ, Aug 16, 43. *Study:* Pa State Univ, BA(fine arts) & BA(gen arts & sci), 65; George Washington Univ, MFA, 67. *Work:* Polaroid Corp. *Exhib:* Eighteenth Ann Corcoran Gallery of Art Area Show, Washington, DC, 67; Camera Movements, Moore Col Art Gallery, Philadelphia, 83. *Collections Arranged:* Design in Transit, State Subway Station Competition, 71 & Points of View, Recent Work By Area Photographers (auth, catalog), 72, Inst of Contemp Art, Boston; Photography Fellowship Recipients, Enjay Gallery, Boston, 76; Prints & Drawings, Frank Tanzer Gallery, Boston, 77; Art of the State, Recipients & Finalists in Painting, Printmaking & Drawing, Rose Art Mus, Brandeis Univ, Waltham, Mass, 77 & 79; Photography Fellowship Recipients, Mass Inst of Technol Creative Photog Gallery, Cambridge, Mass, 78; and others. *Pos:* Performing arts prog coordr & art instr, Wadsworth Atheneum, Hartford, Conn, 68-70; dir urban action prog & spec proj, Inst Contemp Art, Boston, 70-72; asst dir, Mass Coun Arts & Humanities, Boston, 72-73; dir artists fel prog, Artists Found Inc, Boston, 73-82; consult, WGBH New TV Workshop, Boston, 78-79; dir, Prints in Progress, Philadelphia, 83-85; dir, Spaces Gallery, Cleveland, Ohio, 86- *Teaching:* Instr photog & serigraphy, Wadsworth Atheneum, Hartford, Conn, 68-70. *Publ:* Auth & ed, Art of the State--Massachusetts Photographers 1975-1977, Addison House, 78; ed, The Leather District and the Fort Point Channel, Artists Found, 82. *Mailing Add:* 2220 Superior Viaduct Cleveland OH 44113

CHAO, BRUCE
SCULPTOR
Study: Wayne State Univ, Detroit, Mich; RI Sch Design, Prividence, BFA, 73, MFA, 75; Univ Wis, Madison. *Work:* Corning Mus Glass, NY. *Exhib:* Contemporary Crafts of the Americas, Colo State Univ, Fort Collins, 75; New American Glass: Focus West Virginia, Huntington Galleries, WVa, 76; solo exhibs, An Invisible Barrier, 77 & Angels, 78, O K Harris Gallery, New York, Joslyn Art Mus, Omaha, Nebr, 81; Space Window, List Art Ctr, Brown Univ, Providence, RI, 77; Directions in Contemporary Glass, Univ Wis, Madison, 78; Americans in Glass, Leigh Yawkey Woodson Mus, Wausaw, Wis, 81; International Directions in Glass Art, Art Gallery W Australia, Perth, 82; Exposition Art Contemporain du Verre, Upper Normandy Regional Coun, Rouen, France, 91. *Teaching:* Asst prof, RI Sch Design, Providence, 82-88, assoc prof, 88-92. *Awards:* Fel Grant Sculpture, Nat Endowment Arts, 76, 81 & 90; RI Sch Design Fac Develop Grant, sculpture, 88; Finalist Award, sculpture, Mass Artists Fel Prog, 91. *Bibliog:* Patricia Malarcher (auth), The Beauty and Mystery of Glass, NY Times, 1/31/88; Carol Doran-Khewhok (auth), Glass: Another View, New Work, summer 87; Helmut Ricke (auth), Again - Glass and the Fine Arts, Neus Glas, 10-12/86. *Mailing Add:* 143 Summer St Rehoboth MA 02769

CHAPELLIN, HELENA See Wilson, Helena (Helena Chapellin Wilson)

CHAPIAN, GRIEG HOVSEP
PAINTER, CONSERVATOR
b Varna, Bulgaria, May 27, 13; US citizen. *Study:* Cooper Union, 30-31; Nat Acad Design, 31-36, with Leon Kroll, Karl Anderson, Charles C Curran, Arthur S Covey, Francis Scott Bradford, Jr, Gifford Beal, Charles S Chapman & Ivan Olinsky. *Work:* Eastern NMex Univ, Portales; NMex State Fair Permanent Collection, Albuquerque. *Comn:* Two murals for Auto Racing Syndicate, Johannesburg, SAfrica, 39. *Exhib:* Pa Acad Fine Arts, Philadelphia, 37; NMex State Fair Art Exhib, Albuquerque, 71; Grand Nat Exhib, Am Artists Prof League, New York, 72; Int Art Show, Univ Eastern NMex, Portales, 75; Bicenntenial Art Show, Am Artists Prof League, New York, 76; Mountain Rd Galleries, Albuquerque, 83. *Pos:* Founder & dir, Albuquerque Inst Art, 74-; pres, NMex Art League, 91-92. *Teaching:* Dir hist art & landscape, Murray Art Schs, Scranton & Wilkes-Barre, Pa, 48-50; dean & dir figure drawing & painting, Cooper Sch Art, Cleveland, 50-55; dean fashion illus & philos of art, Pan-Am Art Sch, New York, 60-66. *Awards:* First for Oils & Best of Show for Graphics, NMex Art League, Grand Prize & First for Oils, Local One, CIO, 44; Purchase Prize, NMex State Fair, 74; Purchase Prize, Los Altos NMex Art Exhib, 87; Best of Show Award, NMex Art League, 90; over 50 prizes won. *Bibliog:* Louise Bruner (auth), Commercial shows now rival fine art, Cleveland News, 12/15/51; Flo Wilks (auth), Magic realism in noted artist's work reflects his wide range of interests, Albuquerque J, 6/14/70; Lynn B Villella (auth), Chapian work top winner, Albuquerque Tribune, 9/12/74; article, Magic realism by Grieg Hovsep Chapian, Lib & Fine Arts Rev, Eastern NMex Univ, Portales, 82. *Mem:* Am Artists Prof League; Southwest Watercolor Soc; Artists Equity Asn, Albuquerque (pres, 73-74); Nat Art League; NMex Art League (mem bd dirs, 69-71). *Dealer:* Galeria on the Plaza PO Box 1017 Mesilla NM 88046. *Mailing Add:* 1850 Gretta St NE Albuquerque NM 87112

CHAPLIN, GEORGE EDWIN
PAINTER, EDUCATOR
b Kew Gardens, NY, Aug 30, 31. *Study:* Yale Univ Sch Art, with Josef Albers, BFA & MFA. *Work:* Yale Univ Gallery; State Univ NY Col Cortland; Trinity Col, Conn; World Bank, Washington, DC; Mattatuck Mus, Conn. *Exhib:* Carpenter Ctr, Harvard Univ, 74; Dept of State, Washington, DC, 76-80; New Britain Mus, Conn, 77; Conn 78 Invitational, Carlson Art Gallery, Univ Bridgeport; Mattatuck Mus, Waterbury, Conn, 78; Slater Mem Mus, Norwich, Conn, 81; Munson Gallery, New Haven, Conn, 91; and others. *Teaching:* Head dept painting, Silvermine Col Art, 65-71; dir studio prog, Trinity Col, Hartford, Conn, 72-91, prof fine arts, 78-88, Charles S Nutt prof emer fine arts, retired. *Awards:* David G Lyon Award, 31st New England Ann, Conn, 81; 1st Prize, 1st Faber Birren Color Award Exhib, Stamford Art Asn, Conn, 81. *Media:* Oil, Pastel. *Mailing Add:* Box 488 ORS Oxford CT 06483

CHAPLINE, CLAUDIA BEECHUM
PAINTER, ART CONSULTANT
b Oak Park, Ill, May 23, 30. *Study:* Corcoran Sch Art, 48-53; George Washington Univ, Washington, DC, AB, 53; Washington Univ, St Louis, Mo, MA, 56. *Work:* Crocker Mus Art, Sacramento; Univ Calif, Los Angeles; Downey Mus Art, Calif. *Comn:* Performance proj, Calif Arts Coun, Santa Monica, 79; performance proj, City Santa Monica, Calif, 81. *Exhib:* Solo exhibs, Brand Libr Art Ctr, Glendale, 74, Am River Col, Sacramento, 87; Soft, Stuffed & Stitched, Los Angeles Co Mus Art, 73; Laguna Beach Mus Art, 73; Long Beach Mus Art Invitational, 73; Collage & Assemblage, Los Angeles Inst Contemp Art, 73; Installation, IDEA, Sacramento, 90; Wilder Gallery, Los Gatos, 92. *Collections Arranged:* Performance Series 74-80 & Introductions, 85-86, Inst Dance Design & Experimental Art; San Francisco Civic Arts Festival, 88 & 89; Calif Arts Coun, Artists in Residence, 82 & Art in Pub Bldg, 84-90. *Pos:* Founder dir, Inst Design & Experimental Art, Calif, 74-87; coordr, Artists in Social Inst, Calif Arts Coun, Sacramento, 82-84; mgr, Art in Pub Bldgs, Calif Arts Coun, 84-90; Owner, Claudia Chapline Gallery, Stinson Beach, Calif, 87; dev dir, Bolinas Mus, 90. *Teaching:* Instr dance, Washington Univ, 53-56; asst prof, Univ Calif, Los Angeles, 60-67 & Calif State Univ, Northridge, 61-64. *Bibliog:* Salli Stevenson (auth), Claudia's World, Neworld, 78. *Mem:* Am Asn Mus; San Francisco Art Dealers Asn. *Media:* Acrylic, Assemblage. *Publ:* Auth, Tension-Line, High Performance, 78; editor numerous articles in Artists News, 81. *Mailing Add:* PO Box 946 Stinson Beach CA 94970

CHAPMAN, ROBERT GORDON
JEWELER, PAINTER
b Los Angeles, Calif, 26, 41. *Study:* Ventura Col; San Jose Univ, with Fred Spratt & J Richard Sorby, BA(painting), with David Hatch, John Leary & Dr Robert Coleman, MA(jewelry design), Pupil Serv Credential(career coun in visual arts). *Work:* Metal Arts Guild, San Francisco; San Jose State Univ Gallery; San Jose Art League. *Comn:* Moon Pendant (commemorating first lunar landing), 68; Ring, comn by David San Jose, 69; plus pendants, rings, pins & body adornment comn by various individuals. *Exhib:* Art '65, Univ Santa Clara; Calif Expos of the Arts, 66-69; Crafts 10, 67; Western US Traveling Exhib, 68; Triton Mus, Santa Clara, Calif, 69; Eastside Fac Show, 81. *Pos:* Dir, Group 21 Gallery, Los Gatos, Calif, 72-73; mem art educ screening comt, San Jose State Univ, 73-; past bd dirs, San Jose Art League. *Teaching:* Instr art & chmn dept, Piedmont Hills High Sch, San Jose, 64-74; instr jewelry & metalsmithing, West Valley Col, Saratoga, Calif, 66-; coun visual arts, Santa Teresa High Sch, San Jose, 74- *Awards:* Ellen Brucker Jewelry Award, 69; Achiever of the Year in Art, Nat Pen Women Asn, 69; San Jose Regional Art Second Award, 75. *Mem:* Metal Arts Guild San Francisco; Calif Art Educators Asn. *Media:* Aqueous; Silver, Gold. *Publ:* Auth, An Analysis of Photomicrography as a Design Source for Lost-Model Jewelry, 69. *Mailing Add:* 6060 Loma Prieta Dr San Jose CA 95123

CHAPMAN, WALTER HOWARD
PAINTER, ILLUSTRATOR
b Toledo, Ohio, Dec 7, 12. *Study:* Cleveland Inst Art; John Huntington Polytech, Cleveland; Art Students League; study portraiture with Rolf Stoll, Cleveland and figure painting with Jon Corbino, New York. *Work:* Toledo Fedn Art Collection, Toledo Mus Art; Zanesville Art Mus, Ohio; Springfield Mus Art, Mo; Univ Toledo; Toledo Trust Co, Ohio. *Comn:* Five portraits, Law & Sci Bldgs, Univ Toledo, 70 & 77; Bicentennial painting, Waterville Chamber of Commerce, Ohio, 76; three portraits, First Fed Bank, Toledo, 77; Portrait: Bishop Donovan, Holy Rosary Cathedral, Toledo OH, 90; Portrail, Univ of Toledo, 90. *Exhib:* Watercolor USA, Springfield Mus of Art, Mo, 72; Zanesville Mus of Art, 73 & Ella Sharp Mus, Jackson, Mich, 74; Springfield Art Ctr, Ohio, 74; Mid-Yr Ann, Butler Mus of Art, Youngstown, Ohio, 75; O'Briens Art Emporium, Scottsdale, Ariz; Toni Jones Gallery, Houston, Tex;

and others. *Pos:* Illusr, New York, 39-42; combat artist, US Army, 43-45; creative dir, Phillipps Assoc, Toledo, 46-80; owner, Chapman Art Gallery, Sylvania, 70- *Teaching:* Instr illus, Toledo Mus Sch Design, 55-89; instr portrait & figure, Toledo Artists Club 55-64, instr watercolor landscape-Lourdes Col, Sylvania OH 89-90. *Awards:* First Award, Summer Show, Salmagundi Club, New York, 72; First Prize & Purchase Award, Mainstreams Ann, Marietta Col, Ohio, 73; Award Distinction, Ohio Watercolor Soc, 92. *Bibliog:* Murray Kalis (auth), article in Art Rev, 68. *Mem:* Allied Artists Am; Salmagundi Club; Toledo Fedn Art Soc (pres, 54-56); Ohio Watercolor Soc (bd mem, 77); NW Ohio Watercolor Soc (pres, 71-72); Watercolor USA (honor soc, 86). *Media:* Watercolor, Oil. *Publ:* Contribr (cartoons), Stars & Stripes & Railsplitte, US Army newspapers, 45; illusr, Battle of Germany, Viking Press, 46; contribr ed cartoons, Toledo Monitor, 65; contribr, Prize Winning Art, Allied Publ, 66; contribr (cover art), Exhibit Mag, 67. *Dealer:* Chapman Art Gallery 5151 S Main St Sylvania OH 43560. *Mailing Add:* 6001 Gregory Dr Sylvania OH 43560

CHAPPELL, BERKLEY WARNER
PAINTER, PRINTMAKER
b Pueblo, Colo, Mar 21, 34. *Study:* Univ Colo, BFA, 56, MFA, 58. *Work:* San Francisco Mus Art; Henry Gallery, Univ Wash, Seattle; Tacoma Mus Art, Wash; Univ BC, Vancouver; Salishan Lodge, Gleneden Beach, Ore. *Exhib:* Young West Coast Artists, Pasadena, Calif, 59; Abstract Expressionism Today, San Francisco, 60 & Landscape Painting Today, 61; Am Printmaking Today, Ger, Greece, France, 69; Grand Gallerie, Seattle, 75. *Teaching:* Asst painting, Univ Colo, 56-58; instr to asst prof painting, Univ Puget Sound, Tacoma, 58-63; asst prof to prof painting & printmaking, Ore State Univ, Corvallis, 63- *Awards:* Purchase Awards, San Francisco Art Inst, 61 & Henry Gallery, Univ Wash, 64 & 69. *Media:* Oil; Engraving. *Mailing Add:* Dept Art Ore State Univ Corvallis OR 97331

CHAPPELL, MILES LINWOOD
HISTORIAN, EDUCATOR
b Norfolk, Va, June 6, 39. *Study:* Col William & Mary, BS, 60; Univ NC, Chapel Hill, with Philipp Fehl, Frances Huemer & Joseph Sloane, PhD(art hist), 71. *Collections Arranged:* Rubens in Prints (auth, catalog), Col William & Mary, 77; Arthur Strauss and the German Expressionists (auth, catalog), Col William & Mary, 78; Disegni dei Toscani a Roma 1580-1620 (coauth, catalog), Uffizi Gallery, Florence, 79; Drawings from the Herman Collection (auth, catalog), Muscarelle Mus Art, Col William & Mary, 83; Cristofano Allori (auth, catalog), Pitti Gallery, Florence, 84; Age of Caravaggio (catalog), New York, 84; Il Seicento Fiorentino (contribr, catalog), Florence, 86; Disegni di Lodovico Cigoli (auth, catalog), Uffizi Gallery, 92; Cigoli tra manierismo e barocco (intro, catalog), Pitti Gallery, 92. *Pos:* Assoc ed, Studies in Iconography, 76-81, ed, 81-82; art adv bd, Interlochen Ctr Arts, 90- *Teaching:* Prof fine arts, Col William & Mary, 71-, Chancellor Prof, 86-; assoc fel, Harvard Univ Ctr Italian Renaissance, Florence, 80. *Awards:* Nat Endowment Humanities Fel, 83. *Mem:* Col Art Asn Am; Southeastern Col Art Conf (mem bd dirs, 78-84); Renaissance Soc Am; Kunsthistorisches Inst, Florence. *Res:* Renaissance and Baroque art; old master drawings; British and Colonial American painting. *Publ:* Auth, Cristofano Allori's depictions of St Francis, Burlington Mag, 71; Cigoli, Galileo and Invidia, 75 & John Smibert's Italian sojourn, 82, Art Bulletin; Missing paintings by Cigoli, Paragone, 82; Identification of S Coccapani drawing collection mark, Master Drawings, 83; Fuseli: Antique and Nightmare, Burlington Mag, 86; Drawings by Cigoli, Master Drawings, 89. *Mailing Add:* Dept Fine Arts Col William & Mary Williamsburg VA 23185

CHAPPELL, WALTER (LANDON)
PHOTOGRAPHER, CURATOR
b Portland, Ore, June 8, 25. *Study:* Frank Lloyd Wright Taliesin Fel, Ariz, 53-54; Benson Polytech Sch; Ellison-White Conservatory Music; studied with Minor White, Rochester, NY. *Work:* Mus Mod Art, New York; Alfred Stieglitz Ctr, Philadelphia Mus Art, Pa; George Eastman House, Mus Photog, Rochester, NY; Smithsonian Inst; Ctr Creative Photography; Mus Art, Stanford Univ, Calif; Art Mus, Princeton Univ, NJ. *Comn:* Treepeonies on Estate, comn by William Gratwick, Pavillion, NY, 57-60; M Edmond Kara (sculpture) & portraits Richard Burton & Elizabeth Taylor, Big Sur MGM Studios, Culver City, Calif, 64; portraits Sharon Tate, Filmways, New York, 64-68. *Exhib:* Photography at Mid-Century, George Eastman House Mus, Rochester, NY, 59; The Sense of Abstraction, Mus Mod Art, New York, 60; solo exhibs, Mus de Ville de Paris, France, 72, The New Gallery, Taos, NMex, 82, Nicholas Potter Gallery, Santa Fe, NMex, Colo Photographic Art Ctr, Denver, Ctr Media Art of the Am Ctr, Paris, Grapestake Gallery, San Francisco, The Photography Gallery, La Jolla, Calif & The Am Ctr, Cairo, Egypt; Photography in America, 74 & Texture, A Photographic Vision, 75, Whitney Mus Am Art, New York; Mirrors and Windows, Mus Mod Art, New York, 79-81; 25 Years: Retrospective, Colo Ctr Photog Art, Denver, 80; Alfred Steiglitz Ctr, Philadelphia Mus Art; New Mexico Photographers, Santa Fe Festival Arts & Sarah Campbell Blaffer Gallery, Univ Houston, Tex; The New Spirit of Photography, Fashion Inst Technol, New York; Imogen Cunningham Centennial, Mus Art & Sci, San Francisco; Love & Eroticism: Photography, Gavin Collier & Co, Santa Fe, NMex; and many others. *Collections Arranged:* Return to the Bud, Minor White Retrospective, Eastman House, 59; Photography at Mid-Century, Eastman House Mus, 59; A Quest for Light: F Bruguiere, Eastman House Mus, 59; Under the Sun, Poindexter Gallery, New York, 60; Heliography 101 Prints, Lever House Gallery, 63. *Pos:* Dir exhib, Photog Workshop Inc, Denver, 55-57; co-ed, Aperture Quart, Rochester, 57-60; cur exhib, prints & traveling shows, George Eastman House Mus, 57-61; artist in residence, Volcanoes Nat Park, Volcano Art Ctr, Hawaii, 77-78. *Teaching:* Lectr & sem instr, var US locations, 72-; instr camera vision workshop, Visual Studies Workshop, Rochester, 73. *Awards:* Photog Fel in Hawaii, 77 & in NMex, 80 & 84, Nat Endowment Arts. *Bibliog:* Lyons, Labrot, Chappell Under the Sun, Brazillier, 60 & Aperture, 70; Arthur Ollman (producer), Walter Chappell (video), 76; George Shaub (auth), Poet of light, Photogr Forum, 83. *Res:* History of photography; psychology in human nature pertaining to image formation and expression in art. *Publ:* Auth, ed & illusr, Gestures of Infinity, Wittenborn, 57; auth & ed, Logue and Glyphs, Poems 1942 to 1951, Glyph Press, 51; contribr, Aperture Quart, 57-81; auth & illusr, Collected Light, The Body of Work, (in prep), Peregrine Smith, 84. *Dealer:* Andrew Smith 76 E San Francisco Santa Fe NM 87501. *Mailing Add:* PO Box 181 El Rito NM 87530

CHAPPELLE, JERRY LEON
CERAMIST, SCULPTOR
b Fredericktown, Mo, Nov 14, 39. *Study:* Murray State Univ, BS; Univ Minn, MFA. *Work:* High Mus Art, Atlanta, Ga; Greenville Co Mus Art, SC; Ga Coun Arts; La Sch Visual Impaired, Baton Rouge, La. *Comn:* Ceramic mural, Sally Julius Mem, Miller Libr, La Plume, Pa, 80 & Kelly Airforce Base, San Antonio, Tex, 85; ceramic & stucco mural, St Gregory's Episcopal Church, Athens, Ga, 81; mural, Mohasco Entrance, High Point, NC, 86; ceramic mural, Mus Arts & Sci, Macon , Ga, 90. *Exhib:* Fun and Fantasy, Xerox Corp Gallery, Rochester, NY, 73; Regional Invitational, Gallery Contemp Art, Winston-Salem, NC, 75; Hopkins Gallery Art, Ohio State Univ, Columbus, 80; Greenville Co Mus Art, SC, 81; Carrol Reece Mus, Johnson City, Tenn, 88. *Pos:* Dir, Scorpio Rising Workshops, 70-77; vis artist, Ohio State Univ, 80. *Teaching:* Instr ceramics, Univ Minn, 69-70; asst prof ceramics, Univ Ga, 70-76. *Awards:* Two First Prizes, Atlanta Arts Comt, 75; Second Prize, Covington Arts Exhib, Covington Art Ctr, 74; Artist Initiated Grant, Ga Endowment Arts, 89. *Bibliog:* Larry Smith (auth), Ceramic Art (film), Univ Ga, 74; Evolution of the Artist Craftsman in Georgia, Highlight of Contemporary Ceramics (film), Ga NEA-TV, 74. *Mem:* Am Crafts Coun; Piedmont Craftsmen Inc. *Media:* Clay, Glass. *Mailing Add:* 1210 Carson Graves Rd Watkinsville GA 30677

CHARLES, DURANT See Rizzie, Dan

CHARLESWORTH, SARAH E
PHOTOGRAPHER, CONCEPTUAL ARTIST
b East Orange, NJ, Mar 29, 47. *Study:* Barnard Col, BA, 69. *Work:* Stedelijk Van Abbemuseum, Eindhaven, Holland; Mus Mod Art, New York Pub Libr; Nat Mus Am Art Smithsonian Inst, Wash, DC; Princeton Univ Mus, NJ; Mus Fine Arts, Boston; Birmingham Mus Art, Ala. *Exhib:* Solo exhibs, Interim Art, London, Eng, 89, Jay Gorney Mod Art, New York, 89-91, S L Simpson Gallery, Toronto, Can, 86 & 90, Galerie Xavier Hufkens, Brussels, Belg, 91, Paley Wright Gallery, London, Eng, 91, The Queens Mus Art, Queens, NY, 92; The Photography of Invention: American Pictures of the 1980's, Nat Mus Am Art, Smithsonian Inst, Wash, DC, 89; A Forest of Signs: Act in the Crises of Representation, Mus Contemp Art, Los Angeles, Calif, 89; Culture Medium: A Notion of Truth, Int Center Photog, New York, 89; The Play of the Unsayable - Wittgenstein and the Art of the XXth Century, Vienna Secession, Austria, 89; Fauxtography, Art Center Col Design, Pasadena, Calif, 89; Camera Culture, Thomas Segal Gallery, Boston, Mass, 89; Vis-a-Vis: Aspects of Contemporary Art, Grita Insam Gallery, Vienna, Austria and Mus voor Hedendaagse Kunst Het Kruithuis, Hertogenbosch, Netherlands, 89; Abstraction in Contempory Photography, Emerson Gallery, Hamilton Col, Clinton NY and Anderson Gallery, Virginia Commonwealth Univ, Richmond, Va, 89; Moscow-Vienna-New York, Messepalast, Vienna, Austria, 89; Image World: Art and Media Culture, Whitney Mus Am Art, New York, 89; Int Ctr Photog, 90, The Interupted Life, New Mus Contemp Art, New York, 91; The Indomitable Spirit (with catalog), Los Angeles Munic Art Gallery, Los Angeles, Calif, 90; Figuring the Body, Mus Fine Arts, Boston, Mass, 90; Motion & Document-Sequence & Time: Eadward Muybridge & Contemporary American Photography (travelling show/ catalog), Nat Mus Am Art, Smithsonian Inst, Washington, DC, 91; Beyond the Frame, American Art 1960-1990, Setagaya Art Mus, Tokyo, Nat Mus Art, Osaka, Fukuoka Art Mus, Fukuoka, Japan, 91; Victoria & Albert Mus, London, Eng. *Pos:* Vis artist-lectr, Soc Photog Ed, 83; Artists Talk on Art, 83; guest lectr, Sch Visual ARts, 83; Int Center Photog, 83; vis artist-critic, RISD, Providence, RI, 83484. *Teaching:* Instr photog, NY Univ, 83-85; Rutgers Univ, New Brunswick, NJ, 83; vis lectr, Boston Univ, 86; Dept Fine Arts, New York Univ, 86; Tyler Col, Temple Univ, Philadelphia, Pa, 87; visiting artist & lecturer at numerous universities & museums. *Awards:* Creative Artists Pub Serv Fel, 77; Nat Endowment Arts Fel, 76, 80 & 83. *Bibliog:* Susan Weiley (auth), Sarah Charlesworth's Abracadabra, Art News (cover), 3/91; Michael Brenson (auth), Shifted Images of the Renaissance, New York Times, 3/22/91; Pierre Stiwer & Paul D Felice (auths), Sarah Charlesworth: L'Immaculee Conception (interview), Cafe Creme, Summer, 91. *Publ:* Contribr, Art in Am, 79 & Art Forum, 82; auth, glossolalia, Bomb Mag, spring 83; A Lovers Tale, Wedge Press, 84. *Dealer:* Jay Gorney Mod Art 100 Green St NY NY 10012; Jay Gorney Mod Art 100 Greene St New York NY 10012. *Mailing Add:* 31 Great Jones St New York NY 10012

CHARLOT, MARTIN DAY
PAINTER, MURALIST
b Athens, Ga, Mar 6, 44. *Study:* Apprenticeship with Jean Charlot & Ansel Adams. *Work:* Bishop Mus, Honolulu; State Found Cult & Arts, Honolulu; The Queen Emma Found, 91; Honolulu Police Dept, Oahu, 92. *Comn:* Murals, Konawaena High Sch, 76, Hawaii State Sr Ctr, 78, Kauai Intake Ctr, 80, Ala Moana Ctr, 83, 87 & 89, McDonalds Restaurants, Kaneohe, 85, Consolidated Theater Kahala; Koke Hanau Hou, Westin Kaui, Lihue, 87; tile murals, SS Constitution & SS Independence, Am Hawaii Cruises, Honolulu,

89; oil paintings & etched glass dividers, McDonald's Nimitz Restaurant, Oahu, Hawaii, 89; tile mural, Scully Rogers Ltd, 90. *Exhib:* One-man shows, De Mena Gallery, New York, 67, Hawaii State Libr, Honolulu, 72, Volcano Art Ctr, 76, Contemp Arts Ctr, Hawaii, 79, Kauai Libr, 80 & Hawaii Loa Col, 84; A Vision of America at Peace, The Concourse, San Francisco, 84; Have You Got a Minute?, Contemp Arts Ctr, 85; Hawaii Loa Col, 87; State Found Cult & Arts Retrospective, 87; Felesia, Kahuku Libr, Hawaii, 88; Penney's Ala Moana Ctr, Honolulu, 88; An Am Palette, a Dance Celebration of Am Art & Mus, Principia Col, Ill, 89; Brockman Gallery, Los Angeles, 89. *Pos:* Illusr, Collins Assoc, New York, 69; art dir, Bravura Films, Mountain View, Calif, 70; contribr, Ha'ilono Mele, 79-80; illusr, Honolulu Advertiser Progress Edition, 82. *Teaching:* Lectr art & film, Univ Hawaii, 62-; lectr filmmaking, St John's Univ, 69; teacher cinema, Honolulu Acad Arts, 70; artist-in-schools, Doe Sch Syst, Hawaii, 75. *Awards:* Akamai Business Award, Kaneohe Bus Group, 83. *Bibliog:* Anthony Huxley (auth) The Painted Garden, Wellfleet Press, 88; On paper gallery, Commun for Peace, Aqua Planet Inc, Japan, 89; Les Krantz (auth), Calif Art Rev, 89. *Mem:* Hawaii Painters & Sculptors League; Hawaii Film Bd; Pac Film Inst; mem Screen Actors Guild; Film Makers Coop, New York. *Media:* Oil, Acrylic. *Publ:* Auth & illusr, Once Upon a Fish Hook, Island Heritage Press, 72; illusr, How to Make Your Own Hawaiian Musical Instrument, Bess Press, Inc, 88; cover, White Bread, Hawaii Rev, Univ Hawaii, 89; J Am Planning Asn, Hunter Col, NY, 90; contribr, Kalapana Will Be Forever, film, 90. *Mailing Add:* PO Box 161 Kaneohe HI 96744

CHARMATZ, BILL (WILLIAM ADOLPHE)
ILLUSTRATOR, PAINTER
b New York, NY, Nov 15, 25. *Study:* Ecole Beaux Arts, Paris, 49; Ecole Grande Chaumiere, Paris, 51-52. *Comn:* Mural, Union DC 37, New York, 75. *Exhib:* Art Dirs Club, New York, 47-79; Soc Illusr, New York, 47-79; Am Inst Graphic Art, New York, 65-68 & 73-76; solo exhib, Soc Illusr, New York, 78. *Teaching:* Instr, Sch Visual Arts, New York, 63-68. *Bibliog:* Ernst Lehrner (auth), Bill Charmatz's line, Publimondial, Paris, 50; Kichi Okasaki (auth), Bill Charmatz, Idea, Tokyo, 65; Jo Yanow (auth), Bill Charmatz, Graphics Today, 79. *Mem:* Soc Illusr; Am Inst Graphic Arts; Graphic Artists Guild (vpres, 76-78). *Media:* Ink, Gouache. *Publ:* Auth & illusr, The Little Duster, 69, auth & illusr, The Cat's Whiskers, 73 & auth & illusr, Troy Street Bus, 77, Macmillan; co-auth & illusr, My Darling Mao, Grosset & Dunlap, 70; auth & illusr, Endeerments, Ballantine, 72. *Dealer:* Arthur Brown & Bro Inc 2 West 46th St New York NY 10036. *Mailing Add:* 25 West 68th St New York NY 10023

CHARNEY, MELVIN
SCULPTOR, ARCHITECT
b Montreal, Que, Aug 28, 35. *Study:* Sch Art & Design, Montreal Mus Fine Arts; McGill Univ, BA(archit), 58; Yale Univ, MA(archit), 59. *Work:* Nat Gallery Can, Ottawa, Ont; Art Gallery Ont, Toronto; Musée d'Art Contemporain, Montreal, Que; Musée du Que; Mus Contemp Art, Chicago, Ill. *Comn:* XXI Olympic Comt, Montreal, Que, 76; Musée d'Art Contemporain, 79; Mus Contemp Art, Chicago, Ill, 82; Visual Arts Ontario, Toronto, 82; Canadian Tribute to Human Rights, Ottawa, 86; Can Centre Archit, 89; City of Montreal, 90. *Exhib:* Melvin Charney-Other Monuments, Art Gallery of Ont, Toronto, 78; Melvin Charney, 1970-1979, Musée d'art Contemporain, Montreal, 79; Biennale de Paris, Ctr George Pompidou, Paris, France, 80; Melvin Charney, Mus Contemp Art, Chicago, Ill, 82; Canada in Berlin, Akademie der Kunst, Berlin, WGer, 82; Documenta Urbana, Documenta 7, Kassel, WGer, 82; Kunstler aus Kanada, Wurttembergisher, Kunstvereim, Stuttgart, WGer, 83; Melvin Charney: Canadian Pavilion, Venice Biennale, Italy, 86. *Teaching:* Prof archit, Univ Montreal, 64- *Awards:* Sr Arts Awards, Can Coun, 82 & 86; Berliner Kunstlerprogramme Award, Deutscher Akademischer Austauschdienst, 82. *Bibliog:* Mary Jane Jacob (auth), Melvin Charney, Mus Contlemp Art, Chicago, 82; Alexander Tzonis (auth), Melvin Charney 1970-1979, Cultural Affairs, Que, 79; Diana Nemiroff (auth), Melvin Charney, Nat Gallery Can, 86. *Mem:* Canadian Artists Representation; Royal Canadian Acad. *Media:* Steel Construction, Oil Pastel. *Publ:* Auth, Memo Series, Artform, 71; Pour une définition de l'architecture au Que, U d M Presses, 72; Art as Urban Activism, Architectural Design, 77; Melvin Charney 1981-83, Queens Univ Press, 83; Signs of recognition, ciphers of deception, Parachute, 84. *Dealer:* Rene Blouin Gallery Montreal; Sable-Castelli Gallery Toronto. *Mailing Add:* 3620 Marlowe Ave Montreal PQ H4A 3L7 Canada

CHASE, ALICE ELIZABETH
EDUCATOR, WRITER
b Ware, Mass, Apr 13, 06. *Study:* Radcliffe Col, with G H Edgell & P J Sachs, AB; Yale Univ, with Henri Focillon, Sumner Crosby & G H Hamilton, MA. *Pos:* Cur educ, Brooklyn Mus, 46-47. *Teaching:* Docent, Art Gallery, Yale Univ, 31-70, asst prof hist art, 46-70, emer prof, 70- *Awards:* Citations, Wilson Col & Radcliffe Col, 69. *Mem:* Archaeol Inst Am; Col Art Asn Am. *Publ:* Auth, Famous Paintings, An Introduction to Art for Young People, 51, 61 & 62 & Famous Artists of the Past, 64, Platt; Looking at Art, Crowell, 66 & 74. *Mailing Add:* 18 Pleasant St Ware MA 01082

CHASE, ALLAN (SEAMANS)
SCULPTOR, MURALIST
Study: Univ Ga, BFA. *Comn:* Brass on steel, Sherwood Theatre, Gainesville, Ga, 66 & Oxford Chem Co, Atlanta, 67; welded steel, Woodward Acad, College Park, Atlanta, 68; 17 steel & polyester murals, Fla, 71-75. *Exhib:* 5th Biennial Nat Relig Art Exhib, Bloomfield, Mich, 66; Southeastern Ann Exhib, Atlanta, 66 & 68; Piedmont Park Arts Festival, Atlanta, 66-72; Mus Arts & Sci, Macon, Ga, 67; C & S Bank, Atlanta, 75. *Pos:* Designer, Gi-Gi's Restaurants, Fla & Rochester, NY, 65- *Teaching:* Instr, DeKalb Community Col, 80-81. *Media:* Steel, Other Metals; Relief Painting on Hardboard. *Dealer:* Art Gallery 1200 Foster St NW Atlanta GA 30318. *Mailing Add:* 3779 Vermont Road NE Atlanta GA 30319

CHASE, DORIS (TOTTEN)
VIDEO ARTIST, SCULPTOR
b Seattle, Wash, Apr 29, 23. *Study:* Univ Wash; also with Mark Tobey. *Work:* Mus Mod Art, Kobe, Japan; Art Inst Chicago; Nat Collection Fine Arts & Smithsonian Inst, Washington, DC; Mus Fine Arts, Boston; Mus Mod Art & NY Univ, New York. *Comn:* Monumental kinetic sculpture, Expo '70, Osaka, Japan, Atlanta Sculpture Park, Ga, Kerry Park, Seattle, Wash, four ballets, Seattle Opera Asn, Wash & Lakeside Park, Anderson, Ind. *Exhib:* One-man shows, Western Mus Asn Circulating Exhib, 70-72 & Henry Gallery, Univ Wash, Seattle, 71 & 78; Metrop Mus Art, New York, 74; Kennedy Ctr, 77 & 90; Univ Mich, Ann Arbor, 77 & 80; Calif Palace Legion Hon, 78; Hirshhorn Mus, 77; Mus Mod Art, New York, 78 & 81; Georges Pompidou Ctr, Paris, 82-85; AIR Gallery, New York, 83; 911-Media Arts Ctr, 89 & 92; DC/TV '90, New York; Woodside/Braseth Gallery, Seattle, Wash, 90 &93; Seattle Art Mus, 92. *Awards:* Nat Endowment for Arts Fel, 76; NY State Coun Arts Grant, 80; Governors Art Award, State Wash, 92. *Bibliog:* Articles in Newsweek, 7/3/78, New York Times, 3/18/81 & Videography, 9/81, Sightlines, spring, 86; Robin Schanzenbach (dir), Doris Chase: Portrait of the Artist (documentary film), Pub Broadcasting Serv, 85; Doris Chase: Artist in Motion, Univ Wash Press, 92. *Mem:* Women/Artist/Filmmakers (pres, 78); Asn Independent Video & Filmmakers; NY Film Coun (bd mem); 911-Media Arts (bd mem). *Publ:* (Films), Circles II, 72, Doris Chase Dance Series, 72-81, Dance Frame, 78, Jazz Dance, 79 & Doris Chase Concepts Series, 81-83, Thulani, 84, Video Sculpture Series, 85, Table for One, 85, Dear Papa, 86, Sophi, 89 & By Herself (series), 90. *Dealer:* Mus Mod Art New York NY; Woodside/Braseth Gallery Seattle WA. *Mailing Add:* c/o Chelsea Hotel 222 W 23rd New York NY 10011

CHASE, JACK S(PAULDING)
SCULPTOR
b Burlington, Vt, Mar 4, 41. *Study:* US Military Acad, BS, 63; Univ Vt, Burlington, MS, 72. *Work:* Cathedral Church St Paul, Burlington, Vt; Champlain Valley Union High Sch, Hinesburg, Vt; Smithsonian Mus (Nat Zoological Park) & Am Cancer Soc, Washington, DC. *Comn:* Bronze tree, Heckler & Koch, Arlington, Va, 81; steel mobile, Security Arms Co, McLean, Va, 82; bronze mem trophy, Lake Champlain Yacht Club, Shelburne, Vt, 83; bronze tree, comn by Bishop Harvey Butterfield, South Burlington, Vt, 83; Welded Mem Sculpture, US Army For Sci & Technol Ctr, Charlottesville, Va. *Exhib:* Nat Vietnam Mem Design Winners, Am Inst Archit, Washington, DC, 81; Nat Defense Univ, Washington, DC, 86; US Army Intelligence Agency, Washington, DC, 88; US Army War Col, Carisle, Pa, 90. *Pos:* Owner, Chase Welded Sculpture, Jericho, Vt, 73-; co-owner & sr partner, Birch Pond Sculpture, Jericho, Vt, 82- *Awards:* Most Popular Sculpture Award, Exhib Vt Artists, Norwich Univ, 80 & 82; Phillippe Citation Distinguished Pub Serv Art, Gen Electric Found, 82. *Bibliog:* Donna Carpenter (auth), Yankee Artist, Monogram, Gen Electric Co, 83; Anne Brown (auth), Witness Trees, High Roads Folio, 85; Catherine Orr (auth), A man for all seasons: Jack Chase, Lookout Mag, 86. *Mem:* Vt Coun Arts. *Media:* Welded Metal, Miscellaneous. *Dealer:* Barbara Gilmore 9 Piedmont Dr Rutland VT 05701. *Mailing Add:* RFD 1 Snipe Island Rd Box 244 Jericho VT 05465

CHASE, JEANNE NORMAN
PAINTER
b Spokane, Wash, Feb 15, 29. *Study:* Calif State Univ, BFA, 59. *Work:* LaGrange Col, Ga; Ringling Sch Art & Design. *Exhib:* 30 Fla Women in Art, Edison Community Col, Fort Meyers; From the Shutter to the Palette, Tampa Mus Art, Fla, 88; Contemp Fla Women Artists Invitational, Rosendale, NY, 88; Contemp Fla Women Artists, Binnewater Arts Ctr, NY, 88; Jeanne Norman Chase at Sanibel, Phillips Gallery Art Ctr, Sanibel, Fla, 92; and others. *Pos:* Lectr, Women in the Arts. *Teaching:* Instr, figure drawing & painting & chmn fine arts, Ringling Sch Art, Fla, 79-90 & workshops, Wild Acres, NC, 84-87. *Awards:* First Prize, Southeastern Art Exhib, 76; Merit Awards, Longboat Art Ctr Nat & Daytona Mus Art, 79. *Bibliog:* Linda Sherbert (auth), She sees subjects larger than life, Ft Lauderdale News, 76; Lorraine Huber (auth), Jeanne Norman Chase, painter, Fiesta Mag, 76; Dorothy Stockbridge (auth), Jeanne Norman Chase, 10 women and their art, Skylight, St Augustine, Fla, 12/85; Alicia Caldwell (auth), Activist artist prepares series, Bradenton-Herald, Fla, 12/29/85. *Mem:* Artists Equity; Women's Caucus Arts; Fla Artists Group. *Media:* Pencil, Oil. *Publ:* Auth, Drawing in another dimension, Design Mag, 76; Artists and Their Cats, Midmarch Press, 90. *Dealer:* Mickelson Gallery 707 G St NW Washington DC 20001; Tatem Gallery 830 E Las Olas Blvd Ft Lauderdale FL 33301. *Mailing Add:* 1602 Bay Rd Sarasota FL 34239

CHASE, LOUISA L
PAINTER
b Panama City, Panama, Mar 18, 51; US citizen. *Study:* Syracuse Univ, BFA, 73; Yale Univ Sch Art, MFA, 75. *Work:* Mus Mod Art, Metrop Mus Art, Whitney Mus Am Art, New York; New York Public Libr; Morton Neumann Family Collection, Chicago, Ill; Newsweek, New York; Libr Congress, Washington, DC; Albright-Knox Art Gallery, Buffalo, New York. *Comn:* Silkscreen print, Lincoln Ctr, New York, 81. *Exhib:* Landscape, Seascape, Cityscape, New York Acad Art with Contemp Arts Ctr, New Orleans, 86; Whitney Biennial, Whitney Mus Am Art, New York, 81; Am Landscape, Whitney Mus, Fairfield Co, Conn, 81; New Visions, Aldrich Mus, Ridgefield, Conn, 81; one-person exhibs, Robert Miller Gallery, New York, 81, 82, 84 &

86, Harcus-Krakow Gallery, Boston & Galerie Inge Baker, Cologne, 83, Mira Goddard Gallery, Toronto 84 & 89, Paul Cava Gallery, Philadelphia, 84, Margo Leavin Gallery, Los Angeles, 85, Texas Gallery, Houston, 87 & Brooke Alexander, New York, 89; Landscape Painting in the East and West, Shizuoka Prefectural Mus Art & Kobe City Mus, Japan, 84; Since 1980: New Narrative Painting, Phoenix Art Mus, Ariz, 86; Ten Years of Collecting American Art, Selections from the Edward R Down Jr Collection, Wellesley Col Mus, Mass, 87; Selections from the Frederick R Weisman Collection, travelling exhib, 87; The New Generation, The 80s, American Painters and Sculptors, Metrop Mus Art, New York, 88; Making Their Mark, Women Artists Move into the Mainstream, 1979-85, traveling exhib, 89. *Teaching:* Instr painting, RI Sch Design, Providence, 75-79; instr painting, Sch Visual Arts, New York, 80-82. *Awards:* Nat Endowment Arts, 78-79 & 82-83; Creative Artists Public Serv Prog, 79-80. *Bibliog:* Margaret Moore (auth), Louisa Chase, Brooke Alexander, Artnews, summer 89; Richard Kalina (auth), Louisa Chase, Arts Mag, 5/89; Michael Brenson (auth), Works from nature, Louisa Chase, New York Times, 2/17/89. *Media:* Oil. *Dealer:* Robert Miller Gallery 724 5th Ave New York NY 10019. *Mailing Add:* 185 Lafayette St New York NY 10013-3219

CHASE, ROBERT M
ART DEALER, COLLECTOR
b Chicago, Ill, Dec 5, 40. *Study:* Univ Wis, BS. *Pos:* Pres & CEO, Merrill Chase Galleries, 64-; partner, Sculpture Group Ltd, currently. *Mem:* Am Soc Appraisers; Mus Contemp Art, Chicago; Art Inst Chicago. *Specialty:* American and European paintings: prints and sculpture of the 20th century including Rembrandt, Durer, Lautrec, Renoir, Robbe, Pissarro, Picasso, Matisse, Chagall, Miro, Hart, Likan, Leverett. *Publ:* Ed, Story of Prints, 77, Rediscovered Printmakers of the 19th Century, 78 & Manuel Robbe Catalog, Vol I, 79, Vol, II, 80, Merrill Chase Galleries. *Mailing Add:* Merrill Chase Art Galleries 835 N Michigan Ave Chicago IL 60611

CHASE, W(ILLIAM) THOMAS
CONSERVATOR
b Boston, Mass, May 31, 40. *Study:* Oberlin Col, Ohio, BA, 62; NY Univ, MA, 67, conserv cert, 67; Brit Coun Course on conserv of antiquities, 69. *Pos:* Wadsworth Atheneum, Hartford, Conn, 62 & 63; conservator to Nemrud Dagh Excavations, Adiyaman Villayet, Turkey, 64; Chester Dale Fel in Conserv Dept, Metrop Mus Art, New York, 66; asst conservator, Freer Tech Lab, 66-68, head conserv, 68-; adv to John D Rockefeller 3rd Fund for Thai Bronze Treatment Proj, 73-75. *Mem:* Fel Int Inst Conserv Hist & Artistic Works; fel Am Inst Conserv; Washington Conserv Guild (vchmn, 68-69, pres, 70). *Res:* Technical studies of Oriental art, particularly ancient Chinese bronzes and belt-hooks, mirrors and other objects; corrosion study and analysis. *Publ:* Coauth (with Gettens & Clarke), Two early chinese weapons with meteoritic iron blades, Freer Occasional Papers, 71; auth, Bronze Disease and Its Treatment, Dept Fine Arts, Thailand, 75; co-ed, Corrosion and Metal Artifacts, Nat Bur Stand, 77; co-auth (with U Franklin), Early Chinese Black Mirrors and Pattern-Etched Weapons Ars Orientals XI; coauth, Islamic metalwork, Fransan Gallery, 85. *Mailing Add:* c/o Freer Gallery of Art 1050 Independence Ave SW Smithsonian Inst Washington DC 20560

CHASE-RIBOUD, BARBARA
SCULPTOR, WRITER
b US, June 26, 39. *Study:* Temple Univ, BFA, PhD; Yale Univ, MFA. *Work:* Mus Mod Art, New York; Berkeley Mus, Univ Calif; Newark Mus, NJ; Beaubourg Mus, Paris; NY State Off Bldg; Metrop Mus Art, New York; Nat Collections, France; and others. *Comn:* Fountain, Kiron Arts & Communications, Paris, 92; multi-colored bronze sculpture, Lannan Found, Los Angeles; bronze & silk sculpture, Metrop Mus, New York. *Exhib:* One-man shows, Mass Inst Technol, Boston, 70, Berkeley Univ Mus, 73, Detroit Art Inst, 73, Indianapolis Art Mus, 73, Mus Mod Art, Paris, 74, Kunstmuseum, Dusseldorf, 74, Kunstmuseum, Baden-Baden, 79, Mussee Rlatu, Artes, 80 & Bronx Mus, New York, 81, Passadena Col Mus, Los Angeles, 90. *Pos:* Lectr, US State Dept, Tunisia, Senegal, Mali, Ghana, Ivory Coast, and others, currently. *Awards:* Nat Endowment Arts Individual Grant, 73; John Hay Whitney Fel; Carl Sandberg Prize, Best Am Poet, 88. *Bibliog:* Newton (auth), The Artist at Work, Los Angeles Times, 90; American Women Sculptors, Rubinstien, 91; Notable Black Women, Gale, 91. *Mem:* Century Asn, New York; PEN; Am Ctr New York. *Media:* Multicolored Bronze, Silk. *Publ:* Auth, Sally Hemings--A Novel, (French, Ger, Ital, Spanish & Swed transl), Viking, 79; Valide--A Novel(French, Ger, Ital transl), William Morrow, New York, 86; Portrait of a Nude Woman as Cleopatra, 88 & Echo of Lions, 89, William Morrow. *Dealer:* Kiron Art &Communications 10 rue de la Vocherie Paris 75011 France. *Mailing Add:* 3 Rou Auguste Comte Paris 75006 France

CHASIN, MARTIN
ART DEALER, CONSULTANT
b Brooklyn, NY, July 17, 38. *Study:* Brooklyn Col; Univ Pa; Oxford Univ; Free Univ Berlin. *Pos:* Registrar, Univ Pa Art Collection, 63-66; dir mktg, Ctr Art Galleries, Honolulu, Hawaii, 83-85; prin, Martin Chasin Fine Arts, Fairfield, Conn, 85- *Teaching:* Instr, Howard Univ, 66-69. *Mem:* Bridgeport Area Arts Coun, (vpres, 87). *Specialty:* Eighteenth to twentieth century paintings, graphics, engravings and etchings; English silver. *Publ:* Auth, The Jonathan Lees Clock, Libr Chron, 68; The Crusade of Varna, In: History of the Crusades, VI, Univ Wis Press, 90. *Mailing Add:* 1125 Church Hill Rd Fairfield CT 06432

CHATMAS, JOHN T
PAINTER
b Marlin, Tex, Nov 1, 45. *Study:* Univ Tex, Austin, BFA, 68; Pratt Inst, MFA, 70. *Work:* Univ Tex, Austin. *Exhib:* Artists Biennial, New Orleans Mus Art, 73; Southwest Tarrant Co Ann, Ft Worth Art Mus, 77; Southwest Fine Arts Biennial, Mus Fine Arts NMex, Santa Fe, 78; Made in Tex, Univ Tex, Austin, 79; NTex Invitational, NTex State Univ, 79; Small Works, 80 Washington Sq E Galleries, NY Univ, 80; New American Talent, Laguna Gloria Art Mus, Austin, 86; solo exhib, Baylor Univ, 92. *Teaching:* Instr art & art hist, McLennan Community Col, 70- *Awards:* First Place Award, The Art Ctr, Waco, Tex, 77; Fac Develop Leave Grant, McLennan Community Col, 85; Visual Artists Fel, Art Matters Inc, New York, 90. *Bibliog:* Gordon McConnell (auth), The paintings of John Chatmas, Cult Activities Ctr, Temple, Tex, 10/83. *Media:* Acrylic, Oil. *Mailing Add:* 1315 N 34th St Waco TX 76710

CHATTERJEE, JAY (JAYANTA)
ADMINISTRATION, EDUCATOR
b Calcutta, India, Mar 19, 36: US citizen. *Study:* Indian Inst Technol, BArch(hons), 58; Univ NC, MRP, 62; Harvard Univ, MArch, 65. *Pos:* Dean, Col Design, Archit, Art & Planning, Univ Cincinnati, 82- *Mem:* Am Planning Asn; Asn Collegiate Schs of Planning (pres, 83-85); ICFAD; NASAD. *Publ:* Contribr, Managing University Team in Partnership Planning, Sage, 82; Schools and the Private Sector in Partnership, Rutgers, 84. *Mailing Add:* Col Design Archit Art & Planning Univ Cincinnati Cincinnati OH 45221-0016

CHAVEZ, EDUARDO ARCENIO
PAINTER, SCULPTOR
b Wagonmound, NMex, Mar 14, 17. *Study:* Colorado Springs Fine Arts Ctr, Colo, with Boardman Robinson, Frank Mechau, Arnold Blanch & Peppino Mangravite; Tiffany Found painting grants, 48; Inst Int Educ, Italy, Fulbright grant, 51. *Work:* Libr of Cong Print Collection & Watkins Gallery, Washington, DC; Mus Mod Art, New York; Detroit Mus Art; Butler Inst Am Art, Youngstown, Ohio. *Comn:* Murals, Govt Art Com, Post Off, Center, Tex, 38, Post Off, Geneva, Nebr, Post Off, Glenwood Springs, Colo, West High Sch, Denver; mural, USA 200th Sta Hosp, Recife, Brazil. *Exhib:* Nat Inst Arts & Lett, New York; Whitney Mus Am Art, New York; Nat Acad Design, New York; Pa Acad Art Ann, Philadelphia; Am Art Exhib, Metrop Mus Art, New York. *Teaching:* Instr painting, Art Students League, 54-58; vis prof art, Colo Col, Colorado Springs, 59-60; prof art, Syracuse Univ Sch Art, 60-62. *Awards:* Tiffany Found Grant Painting, 48; Fulbright Grant Painting, 51; Childe Hassam Award for Painting, Nat Inst Arts & Lett, 53. *Mem:* Woodstock Art Asn; academician Nat Acad Design. *Mailing Add:* Box 370 John Joy Road Woodstock NY 12498

CHAVEZ, JOSEPH ARNOLD
SCULPTOR, INSTRUCTOR
b Belen, NMex, Dec 25, 39. *Study:* Univ Albuquerque, BS(art educ), 63; Univ NMex, MA(art educ), 67, MA(art), 71; Univ Cincinnati, 74. *Work:* Slide Libr Collection, Univ Southern Ala; plus numerous works in pvt collections across the nation. *Exhib:* One-man shows, Jonson Gallery, Univ NMex, 71 & 76; NMex Arts & Crafts Fair Ann, Albuquerque; Southwest Arts & Crafts Fair Ann; Southwest Crafts Biennial, Santa Fe Folk Art Mus, 74; State Fair Dallas, Tex, 75; Gallery A, Taos, NMex; Aldridge Gallery, Albuquerque; Hispanic Market, San Francisco Nat Mus, 90; Denver Art Show, 90. *Teaching:* Art, Lincoln Jr High, Albuquerque, 63-70; supvr student teachers art educ, Univ NMex, 70-71; teacher art, Sandia High Sch, Albuquerque, 71-; instr art, Univ Albuquerque, summer 70; supvr student teachers art educ, Univ Cincinnati, 74; artist in residence, Pueblo, Colo, 90. *Awards:* Sculpture, Festival in the Pines, Flagstaff, Ariz, 90; Second Place, Pottery & Sculpture Expos, Rio Grande Art & Crafts Fair, 74; Spec Merit, State Fair Tex, 75; Fourth Place, NMex State Fair Sculpture Exhib, 83. *Bibliog:* Dr Jacinto Quirarte (auth), Mexican-American Artists, Univ Tex, 73; The Man Who Fell to Earth, London Film Co, 75; Joseph Chavez (auth, videotape), The Art of Carving Stone. *Mem:* Designers & Craftsmen NMex (pres, 73); Art Advocacy. *Media:* Stone, Wood. *Publ:* Auth, Critique on art, Col St Joseph News, 64; auth, Space filled & fulfilled, Southwest Art, 4/82. *Dealer:* Gallery A Taos NM; Aldridge Gallery Albuquerque NM. *Mailing Add:* c/o Gallery A 105-107 E Kit Carson Rd PO Box 1221 Taos NM 87571

CHAVOOSHIAN, MARGE
PAINTER
b New York, NY, Jan 8, 25. *Study:* Art Students League, New York, 41-45; study with Reginald Marsh, 41 & Mario Cooper, 77. *Work:* Jesse Besser Mus, Alpena, Mich; Art Mus San Lazarre, Venice, Italy; Rider Col, Lawrenceville, NJ; NJ State Mus, Trenton; Morris Mus, Morristown; and others. *Comn:* Holiday design (reproduction), Multiple Sclerosis Soc, Trenton Chap, 73 & Nat Dist, 74; historic bldg series (30 paintings), NJ State Coun Arts, 80; holiday poster, Port Authority NY & NJ, New York, 81; painting (reproduction), Armenian Sisters Acad, Philadelphia, Pa, 81. *Exhib:* Solo exhibs, NJ State Mus, 81 & Trenton City Mus, 84 & 88; Frye Mus, Seattle, Wash, 83; Owensboro Mus Fine Art, Ky, 83; Allied Artists Am Nat Exhib, Salmagundi Club, New York, 83; 200 Years of American Drawings, Morris Mus, NJ, 84; Catherine Lorillard Wolfe Nat Exhib, Nat Arts Club, New York, 85; Nat Asn Women Artists, Jacob Javitz Fed Bldg, New York, 86; Philadelphia Watercolor Club 70th Ann Exhibit, Port of Hist Mus, 88. *Pos:* Consult art, teacher-student workshop, Trenton Pub Sch, NJ, 66-73; artist-at-large, NJ Chap Nat Orgn, Alliance Art Educ, 79-81; corresp secy, Trenton Artist Workshop Asn, 86- *Teaching:* Studio instr painting & drawing, Princeton Art Asn, NJ, 77-79; asst prof watercolor, Mercer Co Col, West Windsor, NJ, 85-91. *Awards:* Silver Medallion, Garden State Watercolor Soc,

Grumbacher, 81; Bermel Award Traditional Watercolor, Monmouth Mus, NJ Watercolor Soc, 84; Gold Medallion, 90 & Title of Fel, 91, Am Artists Prof League; and many others. *Bibliog:* William D Gorman (auth), Marge Chavooshian paints the cities, Artform Mag, NJ, 11/81; Nancy Alderman (auth), Woman of the month, Woman's Newspaper, Princeton, 9/84; Pat Van Gelder (auth), The Watercolor page, Am Artist, 10/88. *Mem:* Midwest Watercolor Soc; NJ Watercolor Soc; Nat Asn Women Artists; Am Artists Prof League; Philadelphia Watercolor Club; Allied Artists Am. *Media:* Watercolor, Pen & Ink. *Publ:* Contribr, Small town and villages, Hunterdon Art Ctr, 82; article, Hist Comn Newslett, 5/82; Travel tips from the pros, 3/85, Quick tips, 7/85 & The Watercolor Page, 10/88, Am Artist Mag. *Dealer:* The Gallery 21st St Barnegat Light NJ 08006; Lawrence Gallery Lawrenceville NJ 08648. *Mailing Add:* 222 Morningside Dr Trenton NJ 08618

CHE, CHUANG
PAINTER, PRINTMAKER
b Peking, China, Dec 12, 34. *Work:* Detroit Art Inst; Cleveland Art Mus; Hong Kong City Hall Mus; Nat Mus Hist, Taipei, Taiwan; Univ Mich Art Mus, Ann Arbor. *Exhib:* Bienal de Sao Paulo, Brazil, 59, 63 & 73; solo exhib (with catalog), Kalamazoo Inst Art, Mich, 84; retrospective show (with catalog), Nat Mus Hist, Taipei, Taiwan, 80; Modern Chinese Art, Grand Rapids Art Mus, Mich, 84; A Retrospective of Chinese Modern Art, Taipei City Art Mus, Taipei, Taiwan, 85. *Pos:* Assoc prof, Tunghai Univ, Taichung, Taiwan, 63-73 & Nat Inst Arts, Taipei, 85-86. *Awards:* Gold Medal, Hong Kong Int, Hong Kong Art Asn, 63; First Prize, Asian Leading Artists Show, Hong Kong Air Line, 65. *Mem:* Mus Mod Art, NY. *Publ:* An Essay on Modern Painting (auth), Bookworld Co,Taipei, Taiwan, 66. *Dealer:* Louis Newman 322 N Beverly Dr Beverly Hills CA 90210. *Mailing Add:* c/o Robert Kidd Gallery 107 Townsend St Birmingham MI 48011

CHEATHAM, FRANK REAGAN
PAINTER, DESIGNER
b Beeville, Tex, Feb 20, 36. *Study:* Art Ctr Col Design, BPA; Chouinard Art Inst; Otis Art Inst Los Angeles Co, study with Lorser Feitelson, Louis Danziger & Arthur Ames, BFA & MFA. *Work:* Los Angeles Co Mus Art; NMex Mus Fine Arts, Santa Fe. *Comn:* Catalog, Simon Rodia's towers in Watts, Los Angeles Co Mus Art, 62. *Exhib:* Los Angeles Munic Art Gallery Ann, Los Angeles Co Mus, 69; Sixth Ann Art Show, La Jolla Mus Art, 69; Ann Exhib, Long Beach Mus 70; Southwest Fine Arts Biennial, Mus NMex, 74. *Pos:* Creative dir, Porter, Goodman & Cheatham Design, Los Angeles, 61-73. *Teaching:* From assoc prof to prof design, Tex Tech Univ, Lubbock, 73- *Awards:* Cert of Merit, Art Dir Club New York, 60, 70 & 74; Award of Excellence, Am Inst Graphic Arts, 63, 65, 72 & 74; Purchase Award, Mus NMex Found, 74. *Mem:* Am Inst Arts; Am Craftsmans Coun. *Media:* Acrylic; Wood, Polychromed Ceramic. *Dealer:* Silvan Simone 11579 Olympic Blvd W Los Angeles CA 90064. *Mailing Add:* 2305 53rd St Lubbock TX 79412

CHEE, CHENG-KHEE
PAINTER, EDUCATOR
b Fujian, China, Jan 14, 34; US citizen. *Study:* Nanyang Univ, Singapore, BA, 60; Univ Minn, Minneapolis, MA, 64; studied watercolor painting with Dong Kingman & Edgar Whitney. *Work:* Univ Minn & 3-M Co, St Paul; Tweed Mus Art, Duluth, Minn; Purdue Univ, Calumet, Ind; Honeywell Inc, Minneapolis. *Comn:* Lakeshore Surf (painting), Lake Superior Paper Indust, Duluth, Minn, 88. *Exhib:* Minn Mus Art, St Paul, 76; Rocky Mountain Nat Watermedia Exhib, Foothills Art Ctr, Golden, Colo, 76, 78, 80, 84 & 90-92; Midwest Watercolor Soc Ann, 77-92; Allied Artists Am Ann, Nat Art Club, New York, 80, 82 & 91; Nat Watercolor Soc Ann, 83-85 & 92; Adirondacks Nat Exhib Am Watercolors, 82, 83, 86, 89, 91 & 92; and many others. *Pos:* Sr librn, Univ Minn, Duluth, 65-78. *Teaching:* Instr, Univ Minn, Duluth, 78-80, asst prof, 81-88, assoc prof, 88- *Awards:* Gold Medal, Allied Artists Am 67th Ann, 80; Gold Medal, Knickerbocker Artists Ann, 90; Silver Medal, Am Watercolor Soc Ann, 91; and others. *Bibliog:* Joni Danzl (auth), Strokes of light in the wilderness, Lake Superior Mag, 12/82; Shannon King (auth), Cheng-Khee Chee, East meets west, Midwest Art, 12/87; Marcia Brown (auth),The Eastern Mountain Walks on Water, Cheng-Khee Chee China Exhib (catalog), 87. *Mem:* Am Watercolor Soc; Midwest Watercolor Soc; Nat Watercolor Soc; Rocky Mountain Nat Watermedia Soc; Sumi-e Soc Am. *Media:* Watercolor, Chinese brush painting. *Publ:* Auth, Retrospective Exhibition, 1973-1982, 82; Cheng-Khee Chee Watercolors (portfolio), 84, 89 & 91; contribr, Watercolor Energies, 83; auth, Exhibition in the People's Republic of China, 1987-1988, 87; illusr, Old Turtle, 92. *Dealer:* J-Michael Galleries 3916 W 59th St Edina MN 55424. *Mailing Add:* 1508 Vermilion Rd Duluth MN 55812

CHEEK, RONALD EDWARD
PAINTER, INSTRUCTOR
b Greenville, SC, Dec 6, 42. *Study:* Ringling Sch Art & Design, BFA, 71; Art Students League, with Frank Mason, Theodoros Stamos & Charles Alston; New Sch Social Research, with Joseph Floch. *Work:* Columbia Mus Art & SC State Mus, Columbia; Augusta Mus, Ga; The Citadel Mus, Charleston, SC; Banks Haley Art Mus, Albany, Ga; Jasper Rand Art Mus, Westfield, Mass; Polk Mus Art, Lakeland, Fla; Sioux Indian Mus, US Dept Interior, Rapid City, SDak. *Comn:* Plant Remedies: Medicine of the American Indians, Blair-Murrah Exhibs, 91. *Exhib:* Prize Winning Paintings of West Coast, Long Boat Key Art Ctr, Fla, 78, 84 & 85; one-man shows, Jasper Rand Art Mus, Westfield, Mass, 79, Old Hyde Park Art Ctr, Tampa, Fla, 81, Cayuga Mus Hist Art, Auburn, NY, 81, Citadel Mus, Charleston, SC, 81, Sioux Indian Mus, Rapid City, SDak, 82, Manatee Community Col, Bradenton, Fla, 83 & Univ SFla, Sarasota, 85; Columbia Mus Art, SC, 86; Greenville Co Mus Art, SC, 89; Venice Art Ctr, Fla, 90; Anderson Co Art Ctr, SC, 91. *Teaching:* Art instr figure & drawing, Manatee Art League, Bradenton, Fla, 78-80; art instr all media & drawing, Manatee Area Vocational-Technical Ctr, 78-; art instr portrait & drawing, Sarasota Co Vocational-Technical Ctr, 78-90; art instr pastel painting & drawing, Sarasota Art Asn, 91- *Awards:* Golden Jubilee Award, Sarasota Art Asn, 76; First Place, Paul Dorfmuller Mem Pastel Compitition, 82; First Place, Pickens Co Mus Art Invitational, 88. *Bibliog:* Drawings by Ronald Cheek, Sioux Indian Mus & US Dept Interior, 82; Forty works at forty, Sarasota Herald Tribune, 83; South Carolina Art Collection, Columbia Mus Art, 86. *Mem:* Old Hyde Park Art Ctr, Tampa, Fla; Art Ctr, St Petersburg, Fla; Venice Art Ctr, Fla. *Media:* Pastel. *Mailing Add:* 2434 Hickory Ave Sarasota FL 34234

CHEMECHE, GEORGE
PAINTER, SCULPTOR
b Baghdad, Iraq, May 11, 34; US citizen. *Study:* Avni Sch Fine Arts, Tel Aviv, 56-59; Ecole des Beaux Arts, Paris, 60-63. *Work:* Guggenheim Mus, New York; Denver Art Mus; Fogg Mus, Boston; San Francisco Mus Mod Art; Herbert F Johnson Mus Art, Cornell Univ, Ithaca, NY. *Exhib:* Mus Mod Art, Paris, 63; Tel Aviv Mus, 66; Jerusalem Mus, 76; Jewish Mus, New York, 77; Aldrich Mus Contemp Art, Ridgefield, Conn, 80 & 81. *Awards:* Am-Israel Cult Found Award, 60. *Bibliog:* Jean Pierre Vandigaum (auth), Interview with the artist, Art Press, Paris, 77; John Perreault (auth), article, in: Soho News, 77; Ruth Bass (auth), article, in: Art News, 81. *Media:* Oil, Pastel; Metal. *Dealer:* Lillian Heidenberg Gallery 50 West 57th St New York NY 10024. *Mailing Add:* 222 West 23rd St #422 New York NY 10011

CHEN, HILO
PAINTER
b Taiwan, Repub of China, Oct 15, 42; US citizen. *Study:* Chong Yen Col, BS(archit). *Work:* Guggenheim Mus; Byer Mus, Evanston, Ill. *Exhib:* Wadsworth Atheneum, Hartford, Conn, 74; Indianapolis Mus of Art, 74; Pa State Mus of Art, 74; Baltimore Mus of Art, 75; Lafayette Natural Hist Mus & Planetarium, La, 75; Edwin Ulrich Mus, Wichita State Univ, Kans, 76. *Collections Arranged:* New-Photo Realism, Wadsworth Atheneum, 74. *Bibliog:* Robert Hughes (auth), An omniverous & literal dependence, Arts, 6/74; Andrea Mikotajuk (auth), American realists at LKM, Arts, 1/75; Dorothy Belden (auth), Realism exaggerated in Ulrich Art Exhibition, Wichita Eagle, 3/76. *Media:* Oil on Canvas, Watercolor on Paper. *Dealer:* Louis K Meisel 141 Prince St New York NY 10012. *Mailing Add:* 302 Bowery 3rd Floor New York NY 10012

CHENEY, LIANA DE GIROLAMI
HISTORIAN, CURATOR
b Milan, Italy, 1942; US citizen. *Study:* Univ Miami, BA, 68, MA(art hist), 70; Worcester Art Ctr, Mass, studied ceramics, 70; Wellesley Col, Mass, 71, post-grad study, Renaissance art; Boston Univ, PhD(Renaissance, Mannerism & Baroque art), 78. *Collections Arranged:* Karl May, 80, Thomas Nast, Illustrator, 84 & J Beuys, 84, Univ Lowell; Whistler, 84, Lawrence Kupferman, 85, Samuel P Howes, 86 & Photographs of Cambodia, 87, Whistler House Mus, Lowell; and many other exhibitions at Univ Lowell and Whistler House Mus, Lowell. *Pos:* Consult, Nat Endowment Humanities Art Hist Grants, 80-; cur, Whistler House Mus, Lowell, 84- *Teaching:* Instr art hist, Boston Col, 73-74; from instr to prof art hist, Univ Mass-Lowell, 74- & chairperson art dept, 83- *Awards:* Samuel H Kress Found Grants, 73, 73 & 74; Nat Endowment Humanities Grants, 77-78, 79-82, 89 & 92; Mass Coun Arts & Humanities Grant, 85-86; Am Learned Soc, 90. *Mem:* Col Art Asn Am; Renaissance Soc Am; Emblematic Soc; Victorian Soc Am; Visual Resource Asn. *Publ:* Auth, Religious Architecture of Lowell, Two vols, Landmark Publ, Lowell, 84; The Paintings of Casa Vasari, Garland Publ, New York, 85; Botticelli's Mythological Paintings, Univ Press Am, Md, 85; coauth (with P Marks), The Whistler Papers, 86 & The Whistler Notes, Lowell, 88; ed, Vanitas and Vanities: Symbols in the Arts, Edwin Mellen Press, 92; Pre-Raphaelitism, Edwin Mellen Press, 92. *Mailing Add:* 112 Charles St Boston MA 02114

CHENG, CARL F K, AKA JOHN DOE CO
ENVIRONMENTAL ARTIST, SCULPTOR
b San Francisco, Calif, Feb 8, 42. *Study:* Univ Hawaii, 63; Univ Calif Los Angeles, Dickson Art Ctr, BA, 63, MA, 67; Folkwang Art Sch, Essen, Ger, 64-65. *Work:* Fred Weisman Collection, Pepperdine Col, Malibu, Calif; Exploratorium, San Francisco; George Eastman House, Eastman Kodak, Rochester, NY; David Bermant Collection, Santa Barbara. *Comn:* Art & technol sculpture, Exploratorium, San Francisco; Seattle underwater sculpture, Seattle Arts Comn, 80-91; Santa Monica Art Tool, Calif, 88; lens tower sculpture, Kaiser Permananente Hosp, Los Angeles, 91; Sheriff's Facility sculpture proj, San Francisco, 92; Marine Station, Metro Railroad, Los Angeles Co Transit Comn, 93. *Exhib:* Studio Artist Exhib, Clocktower, New York, 87; Water Projects, ASG Gallary, Nagoya, Japan, 88; Impression of an Invisible Sculp, List Visual Arts, Mass Inst Tech, Cambridge, 88; 66 Percent Water, Capp St Projs, AUT, San Francisco, 89; 40 Years of Assemblage, Wight Gallery, Univ Calif Los Angeles, 89; and others. *Awards:* Nat Endowment Arts, 82 & 86; Getty Visual Arts Grant, Getty Mus, 90; Los Angeles Cult Arts Grant, 90. *Bibliog:* Shifra Goldman (auth), A Synthesis of Contradictions (catalog), 89; Michael Hall (auth), Art in the Public Interest, UMI Research Press, 89; Betty Klausner (auth), Interview with Carl Cheng, Contemp Arts Forum, 91. *Mem:* Los Angeles, Contemp Eds (exhib comt, 91); Mus Contemp Art, Los Angeles; Sculpture Inc. *Media:* Installations. *Mailing Add:* 1518 17th St Santa Monica CA 90404

CHENG, EMILY
PAINTER
b New York, NY, July 28, 53. *Study:* Rhode Island Sch Design, BFA, 75, New York Studio Sch of painting, Drawing & Sculpture. *Exhib:* Mutations, Annina Nosei Gallery, New York, 88; Solo exhib, Bronx Mus, 89; Mystery, New Visions Gallery, Ithaca, 89; Bevier Gallery, Rochester, 89; 100 Drawings by Women, Hillwood Art Gallery, Blum Helman, NY, 89. *Awards:* Nat Endow Arts Fel, 82-83. *Bibliog:* Michael Kimmelman (auth), New York Times, 12/2/88; Charles Hagen (auth), Artforum Mag, 3/89; Robert Mahoney (auth), Arts Mag, 90. *Media:* Oil. *Dealer:* Lang & O'Hara Gallery 568 Broadway New York NY 10003. *Mailing Add:* c/o Jonathan O'Hara Fine Art 41 E 57th St 13th floor New York NY 10022

CHENG, FU-DING
FILMMAKER, PAINTER
b Palo Alto, Calif, Feb 5, 43. *Study:* Sch Archit, Univ Southern Calif; Alliance Francaise, Paris; Univ Calif, Berkeley, BArch. *Exhib:* New Am Filmmakers, Whitney Mus Am Art, New York, 70; Yale Film Festival, 72; Belg Int Film Festival, 73; Asian-Am Film Festival, New York, 86; Tokyo Int Film Festival, 87. *Teaching:* Instr art, Univ Calif, Los Angeles, 76-82. *Awards:* independent grant, Film Proj, Am Film Inst, 77; First Place, Foothill Nat Film Festival, Foothill Col; Gold Prize, Int Festival, 90. *Mem:* Independent Feature Project, West. *Media:* Film video; Watercolor, Acrylic. *Publ:* Auth, Los Angeles Times Calendar, Brave New Artists Video, 87; auth, Video Lace, Urban Mystic, 87. *Dealer:* Cinergy Entertainment Santa Monica CA. *Mailing Add:* 209 Seventh Ave Venice CA 90291

CHEPP, MARK
ADMINISTRATOR
b Milwaukee, Wis. *Study:* Univ Wis, Milwaukee. *Collections Arranged:* Ralston Thompson--A Retrospective, 1933-74, Springfield Art Ctr & James Roy Hopkins, Ohio Artist, 1877-1969, 77 & 82; The Barnitz Triad, 78. *Pos:* Cur, Univ Wis, Milwaukee Art Mus, 74-91; dir, Springfield Mus Art, 91- *Mem:* Am Asn Mus; Ohio Mus Asn; Col Art Asn. *Mailing Add:* 107 Cliff Park Rd Springfield OH 45501

CHER, BEATRICE (BEATRICE MICHELLE CHER-KILLIGAN)
PAINTER, SCULPTOR
b Buenos Aires, Argentina; US citizen. *Study:* Estimulo Bellas Artes, Buenos Aires, Argentina, Cert Fine Arts, 65; L'Alliance Francaise, Paris, France, AA, 73; Miami Dade Community Col, Fla. *Work:* Thompson Tech, Paris, France. *Comn:* Charles Aznavour & Nourhan Fringian Fundation, Paris, France. *Exhib:* L'a Rentree Artistique a St Germaine, Galerie Hautefeuille, 89, Jeune Peinture-Jeune Expression, Galerie Nesle, 89, 90, 91, 92, Hommage a Van Gogh, 90 & Les Grands et Juenes d'Audjoudhui, 90, Grand Palais des Champs Elysees, all Paris, France; Interior Visions, Ariel Gallery, Soho, New York, 90. *Pos:* Dir, Gables Art Gallery, Miami, Fla, 78-82. *Awards:* Hon Mention, Armenian Allied Arts Asn, 88; First Prize Painting/Collages, Musee Paul Dumail, France, 88; First Grand Prize, Seigneurs De L'Art's-Les-Pins, France, 90 & 91. *Mem:* Salon Des Independants Oficial. *Publ:* Article, Interior Visions--Beatrice Chers Passion, Art Speak, 90; Astur Morsela (auth), Beatrice Cher in New York, Miami, 90; Beatrice Cher's Adagio in Paris, France, Aim Mag. *Mailing Add:* 66 Valencia Ave #903 Coral Gables FL 33134

CHERKAS, CONSTANTINE
PAINTER
b Sumi, USSR, Aug 05, 19; US citizen. *Study:* Moscow Academie Fine Arts, MFA, 36-41; Vienna Academie Fine Arts, 45; Munich Academie Fine Arts, Akademische Kunstmaler, 45-49; studied with Ilya Mashkov, Igor Grabar, Aristarch Lentulov, Alexandre Deineka. *Work:* Academie Fine Arts, Moscow, USSR; State Tretjakov Gallery, Moscow, USSR; Claremont Univ Gallery, Claremont, Calif; Tokyo Nat Mus Mod Art. *Exhib:* Bavarian Art Union Gallery, Munich, Ger, 49; Area Artists, Los Angeles Co Art Mus, Calif, 54; restrospective, 30 Years in America, Los Gatos Mus, Calif, 82. *Awards:* First Prize, Los Angeles County Mus, Calif, 54; First Prize, Friday Morning Club, 58; First Prize, Painters' and Sculptors' Club of Los Angeles, 58. *Bibliog:* Andre Cherkas (auth), In search of light, Southwest Art, 6/77; Int Communication Agency (auth), article, America (published for circulation in USSR), 6/80; M J Van Deventer (auth), article, Art Gallery Int, 4-5/86. *Media:* Oil. *Dealer:* Peter Cherkas 310 15th St Santa Monica CA 90402. *Mailing Add:* PO Box 241 Julian CA 92036

CHERMAYEFF, IVAN
DESIGNER, PAINTER
b London, Eng, June 6, 32; US citizen. *Study:* Harvard Univ, 50-52; Inst Design, Ill Inst Technol, four Moholy-Nagy scholar, 52-54; Yale Univ Sch Design, BFA(Mohawk Paper Co Fel), 55. *Work:* Mobil Oil Corp; Mus Mod Art, New York. *Comn:* Exploding Triangles (shaped canvases), IBM Data Processing Hq, Harrison, NY, 70; Dimensional Abstractions (plastic laminate wall constructions), Bartholomew Consol Sch Corp, Columbus, Ind, 71; Abstraction I (Aubusson tapestry), Westinghouse Elec Corp, Pittsburgh, 72; Abstractions II & III, Philip Morris Inc, Richmond; Construction (wall with painted steel components), Am Repub Ins Co, Des Moines, Iowa; Tapestry, Am Electrical Power, Columbus, Ohio. *Exhib:* Industry Sculpture Show, Butler Inst Am Art, Youngstown, Ohio, 71; Venice Biennale, 72; Va Mus Art, Richmond, 74; Jacksonville Art Mus, 75; Addison Gallery, Andover, Mass. *Pos:* Trustee & comt mem painting & sculpture, film, design, Mus Mod Art, New York, 65-85; vpres, Yale Arts Asn, 68-76; mem comt arts & archit, Yale Univ Coun, 71-; mem comt Visual & Environmental Studies, Harvard Univ Bd Overseers, 72-80; vpres, Am Inst Graphic Art. *Teaching:* Instr design, Brooklyn Col, 56-57 & Sch Visual Arts, 59-65; Andrew Carnegie prof design, Cooper Union; Joyce C Hall distinguished prof, Kansas City Art Inst. *Awards:* Pres Fel Award, RI Sch Design, 81; Yale Arts Medal, 85; Hon Doctorate Fine Arts, Corcoran Mus Art, Washington, DC & Univ Arts, Philadelphia, 91. *Bibliog:* Douglas Davis (auth), article, Newsweek Mag, 71 & 200 American leaders, Time Mag, 74. *Mem:* Am Inst Graphic Arts (vpres, pres & bd dirs, 60-); Int Design Conf Aspen (vpres & co-chmn bd dirs, 67 & 90); Indust Designers Soc Am; Alliance Graphique Int; Benjamin Franklin fel Royal Soc Arts. *Publ:* Auth, Observations on American Architecture, Viking, 72. *Dealer:* Ullysus Gallery Fuller Bldg Suite 1110 41 E 57 St New York NY. *Mailing Add:* 15 E 26th St New York NY 10010

CHERNICK, MYREL
SCULPTOR
Study: RI Sch Design, 70-72; Rutgers Univ, BA, 74; Art Inst Chicago, MFA, 76. *Exhib:* Messages to the Public, Spectacolor Lightboard, Times Sq, New York, 88; Washington Sq Windows, Grey Art Gallery, New York, 90; Collage: New Applications, Lehman Col Art Gallery, Bronx, NY, 91; Dirt and Domesticity: The Construction of the Feminine, Whitney Mus Am Art, New York, 92; Under Contract, Randolph St Gallery, Chicago, Ill, 93. *Awards:* Whitney Mus Independent Study Prog, 76; Creative Artists Pub Serv Prog Fel, 80; Nat Endowment Arts Visual Artist Fel, 89-90. *Bibliog:* Roberta Smith (auth), Dirt and Domesticity, NY Times, 6/26/92. *Mailing Add:* c/o Sculpture Space 12 Gates St Utica NY 13502

CHERNOW, ANN
PAINTER, PRINTMAKER
b New York, NY, Feb 1, 36. *Study:* Syracuse Univ, 53-55; NY Univ, BS, 57, MA, 69; with Irving Sandler, Jules Olitski, Hale Woodruff & Howard Conant. *Work:* New Britain Mus Am Art, Conn; Housatonic Mus Art, Bridgeport, Conn; US Art Embassies Collection; Nat Mus Women Arts, Washington, DC; Elvehjem Mus, Wis; Davison Art Ctr, Wesleyan Univ, Conn. *Comn:* Artist of the year, United Way, Tri-towns, Conn, 85; Friends of Music 91, Year of Mozart Celebration. *Exhib:* One-woman shows, Alex Rosenberg Gallery, New York, 82 & 84, & Stamford Mus, Conn, 85, Uptown Gallery, New York, 90; Munson Gallery, New Haven, 89; George Goodstadt, Ridgefield, Conn, 91; UFO Gallery, Provincetown, Mass, 92; Va Lust Gallery, New York, 92; and others. *Teaching:* Instr studio work, Mus Mod Art, New York, 66-70; instr painting & drawing, Silvermine Col & Silvermine Guild, 68-80; instr art hist, Univ Conn, 69; assoc prof, Norwalk Community Col, 82- *Awards:* Publ Award, Old Lyme Art Works, 83; Lithography Award, Print Club Philadelphia, 89; Conn Humanities Scholar, 89-; NCC Found Award, 91-92; Etching Award, Printmaking Coun NJ, 92. *Bibliog:* Hue Points Mag, spring-summer, 83; Janet Dickson (auth catalog), 88; Herbert Lust (auth catalog), 9/92. *Mem:* Silvermine Guild Art; Print Club Philadelphia; Soc Am Graphic Artists, New York; Nat Drawing Asn; Albany Print Club. *Media:* Oil; Miscellaneous Media. *Publ:* Auth, Reuben Nakian, sculptor, 69, Palette Mag, Conn Art Asn; Odd Man In, Krushenick Exhib (catalog), Housatonic Mus Art, Conn, 75; art ed & contribr, Communitas, New Eng, 79. *Dealer:* Virginia Lust Gallery 61 Sullivan St New York NY 10012; Uptown Gallery 1194 Madison Ave New York NY 10128. *Mailing Add:* Dept Art Norwalk Community Col 333 Wilson Ave Norwalk CT 06854

CHERNOW, BURT
WRITER, MUSEUM DIRECTOR
b New York, NY, July 28, 33. *Study:* NY Univ, BA, 58, MA, 60; with Lawrence Alloway, Jules Olitski, Irving Sandler & Hale Woodruff. *Work:* Jacksonville Mus, Fla; Bridgeport Mus Art, Sci & Indust, Conn; Col Art Mus, Hampton, Va; Le Mus de L'Art Contemporain, Skopje, Yugoslavia; Housatonic Mus Contemp Art, Bridgeport, Conn. *Exhib:* Loeb Student Ctr, NY Univ; Bridgeport Mus; UN Pavilion, New York World's Fair, 64-65; US Info Agency Traveling Exhib; Silvermine Guild, New Canaan, Conn. *Collections Arranged:* 20th Century American & European Contemporary Art (auth catalog), Housatonic Mus Art; Christo Exhib (auth catalog), Wadsworth Atheneum, Hartford, Conn, 78; Abe Ajay Retrospective (auth catalog), Neuberger Mus, Purchase, NY, 78; Will Barnet Retrospective (auth catalog), Neuberger Mus, 79-80. *Pos:* Consult & writer, Educ Directions, 68-; dir, Housatonic Mus Art, 68-, emer dir, 85; dir, Conn Fine Arts Gallery, Westport, 70-; pres, Westport Ctr Arts, 85-87. *Teaching:* Staff, Mus Mod Art, New York, 67-70 & Silvermine Guild Artists, 70-81; chmn art dept, Housatonic Community Col, Bridgeport, 68-85, emer prof, 85- *Awards:* First Prize (sculpture), Barnum Art Festival, Bridgeport Mus, 60. *Bibliog:* M Bishop (auth), For arts sake, Conn Mag, 3/72. *Mem:* Westport-Weston Arts Coun, Conn (bd dirs, 69-); Conn Art Asn (bd dirs, 64-65); Silvermine Guild Artists; Appraisers Asn Am; Int Art Critics Asn. *Publ:* Gabor Peterdi Paintings, Taplinger, 82; Drawings of Milton Avery, Taplinger, 84; Francisco Zuniga: The Complete Graphics, 85; Milton Avery Paintings, Miami Fine Arts Ctr, 87; Kandinsky, Westport Ctr Arts, 89; articles in Arts, Artnews, Intellect Mag, Craft Horizons, Conn Mag; and others. *Mailing Add:* 2 Gorham Ave Westport CT 06880

CHESHIRE, CRAIG GIFFORD
PAINTER, EDUCATOR
b Portland, Ore, Dec 31, 36. *Study:* Univ Ore, BA, 58, with David McCosh, MFA, 61; also with Francis Chapin. *Work:* Mus Art, Eugene, Ore; Univ Ore; Eastern Ore Col. *Exhib:* Northwest Artists Ann, Seattle; Artists of Ore Ann, 58-75; Northwest Painters, Smithsonian Inst Traveling Exhib, 59; Mus Art, Eugene, 61-74; Gallery West, Portland, 72; Visions & Perceptions Gallery, Eugene, 80; Littman Gallery, Portland State Univ, 87. *Teaching:* Assoc prof drawing & painting, Portland State Univ, 63-81, prof, 78- *Awards:* Ina McClung Award in Painting, 61 & Ore Develop Fel, 62, Univ Ore; Purchase Award, Mus Art, Eugene & Ore Arts Comn, 74. *Mem:* Portland Art Mus; Am Asn Univ Prof. *Media:* Oil, Watercolor. *Publ:* auth, David McCosh (monogr), Mus Art, Univ Ore, 85. *Mailing Add:* Portland State Univ Portland OR 97207

CHESLEY, PAUL ALEXANDER
PHOTOGRAPHER, GRAPHIC ARTIST
b Red Wing, Minn, Sept 10, 46. *Study:* Ariz State Univ; Univ Minn; Colo Mountain Col. *Work:* Bell Mus of Natural Hist, Minn; Honolulu Acad, Hawaii. *Exhib:* One-man shows, Ecuador, Colorado Springs Fine Arts Ctr, 74 & Gargoyle Gallery, Colo, 75; Nature, Nishi Ginza Galleries, Tokyo, Japan, 75; Indians of the Andes, Birmingham Mus Art, Ala & Sci Mus Minn, 75; retrospective, James Ford Bell Mus Natural Hist, Minn, 75; Nature, Honolulu Acad Art, Hawaii, 76. *Awards:* Photo Design Stock Award. *Bibliog:* Julia Scully (auth), Four photographers, Mod Photog, 7/77; Constance Brown (auth), It's always hot springs time in the Rockies, Smithsonian, 11/77 & Woman Alive, Quest, 11/77; and others. *Mem:* Am Soc Mag Photog. *Media:* Color Photography. *Publ:* Auth, Hot springs bathing in Japan, Geo Mag/Ger, 80; Along the Continental Divide, Nat Geographic Bk; Compass Guide to Colorado; Compass Guide to Hawaii; Day in the Life, II Bks. *Dealer:* Putney Gallery Aspen CO 81611. *Mailing Add:* Box 94 Aspen CO 81612

CHESNEY, LEE R, JR
PAINTER, PRINTMAKER
b Washington, DC, June 1, 20. *Study:* Univ Colo, BFA, 46; Univ Iowa, MFA, 48; Univ Michoacan, Morelia, Mex; also with James Boyle, James Lechay & Mauricio Lasansky. *Work:* Rosenwald Collection, Nat Gallery Art, Washington, DC; Mus Mod Art, New York; Tate Gallery Art, London; Bibliot Nat, Paris; Nat Gallery Art, Stockholm, Sweden. *Comn:* Honolulu Print Soc, 75 & 83; Honolulu Acad Art, 77; Univ Hawaii Centennial Comn, 82. *Exhib:* Six Artists in Paris, Am Cult Ctr, Paris, 64; Epinal Print Biennial, France, 70-71; Cite Int des Arts, Paris, France, 79; Contemp Arts Ctr, Honolulu, 80; 10 yr retrospective, Fisher Gallery, Univ of Southern Calif, 68; BMIC Galerie, Paris, 81; Salon de Mai, Paris, 82; Honolulu Acad of Art, 85; Portland State Univ Gallery, 88; Univ Fla Gallery, 89; Amon Carter Mus, Ft Worth Tex, 90; Worcester Art Mus, Mass, 91; Mona Bismark Fedn, Paris, France, 91; Spectrum of Innovation, Nelson-Atkins Mus, Kansas City, Mo, 90. *Teaching:* Univ Ill, 50-67; assoc dean fine arts, Univ Southern Calif, 67-72; faculty mem, Univ Hawaii, 72-84; Louis D Beaumont Vis Distinguished Prof, Wash Univ, 79; Lacoste Sch France, 89; UCLA, 89-90. *Awards:* Vera List Purchase Award, Soc Am Graphic Artists, 65; Univ Hawaii/Ford Found Fac Enrichment Award, Paris, 78-80; Fondation Gardilanne-Moffat Studio Award, Cite Intern des Arts, Paris, 78-83. *Bibliog:* Wayne Miyamoto (auth), Lee Chesney--25 years of printmaking. *Mem:* Soc Am Graphic Artists; Col Art Asn Am; Los Angeles Printmaking Soc (adv bd, 67-); Hawaii Artists League; Honolulu Printmaking Soc; NW Prints Coun; Southern Graphics Conf. *Media:* Oil; Acrylic. *Publ:* Contribr, Printmaking today, Col Art J, Vol XIX, No 2; A brief glance at Ukiyo-e and Hanga, Japan Print Quart, winter 67; Teaching in art grad progs, J Educ Perspectives, fall 77. *Dealer:* Williams/Lamb Gallery 102 W 3rd St Long Beach CA. *Mailing Add:* 5726 W Washington Blvd Los Angeles CA 90016

CHESNEY, LEE ROY, III
PRINTMAKER, EDUCATOR
b San Antonio, Tex, July 5, 45. *Study:* Univ Ill, with Dennis Rowan, Eugene Telez, BFA; Univ Calif, Los Angeles, with Ray Brown; Ind Univ, with Rudy Pozzatti, Marvin Lowe, MFA. *Work:* Honolulu Acad Arts; San Diego State Univ Mus; State Univ NY Potsdam; Dickinson State Col Mus, NDak; Graphic Chem & Ink Co Collection, Chicago. *Exhib:* Libr Cong, Nat Collection Fine Arts, Smithsonian, Washington, DC, 69 & 73; 1st Int Pratt Graphics, Bath, Eng, 73-74; Int Print Biennials, Epinal, France, 75 & 77; Boston Printmakers, 82; Prints USA, 82; Pratt Graphics, New York, 82; and others. *Pos:* Prog dir art dept, Univ Tex, 78-81, grad adv, 81-88. *Teaching:* Assoc instr printmaking, Ind Univ, Bloomington, 69-72; instr design & prints, Univ Tex, Austin, 72-75, asst prof printmaking, 75-78, assoc prof art, 78- *Awards:* Graphic Chem & Ink Purchase Award, Soc Am Graphic Artists, 73; Honolulu Acad Arts Purchase Award, 73; Prints from Am Univs Purchase Award, US Info Agency, 74. *Mem:* Col Art Asn Am; The Southern Graphics Coun; Soc Am Graphic Artists, New York. *Media:* Intaglio, Mixed Media. *Mailing Add:* 4206 Wildwood Rd Austin TX 78722

CHESTER, CHARLOTTE WANETTA
PAINTER, WRITER
b Columbus, Ohio. *Study:* Ft Wright Col, Wash, BFA; Capitol Univ; Oklahoma City Univ; Pa Acad Fine Arts, with Blackburn & Sloan; Philadelphia Col Art, with Niebert; also with Eric Irmer, Frankfurt, Ger, two years; numerous teachers and workshops in US and Europe. *Work:* Artist and Space, Nat Air & Space Mus, Smithsonian Inst, Washington, DC; The Barn, Millville, NJ; also art collections of Soovia Janis, New York, Katherine Gellhorn, Spokane, Wash & Mrs Ray, Spokane, Wash. *Comn:* Many paintings. *Exhib:* Frankfurt Ger Juried Exhib, 65; Atlantic City Art Ctr, NJ, 65-70; Cult Art Ctr of Ocean City, 68; Kerr Mus, Okla, 70; Frye Mus, Wash, 85; Corbin Art Ctr, 86, 87 & 88; Eugenia Stow Gallery, Spokane, Wash; plus numerous traveling exhibs. *Teaching:* Instr advan oil painting, Atlantic Community Col, 68-69; pvt art classes, 65-88. *Awards:* Numerous national and international awards. *Mem:* Am Fedn Art; League South Jersey Artist (pres, 68-70); Fed Art Asn NJ (chmn South Jersey, 71); Watercolor Soc London; Am Pen Women (pres, 88); Am Univ Women. *Media:* Watercolor, Collage. *Publ:* Contribr, Yearbook Ocean City, 68. *Mailing Add:* RT 1 Box 53 Reardan WA 99029

CHETHAM, CHARLES
MUSEUM DIRECTOR
US citizen. *Pos:* Dir, Smith Col Mus Art, currently. *Teaching:* Prof art, Smith Col. *Mailing Add:* 6 Cook St Provincetown MA 02657

CHEVINS, CHRISTOPHER M
PAINTER, DRAFTSMAN
b New York, NY, May 31, 51. *Study:* Yale Univ, BA, 73; Rutgers Univ, with Leon Golub, MFA, 81 (Teaching Fel). *Work:* Jane Voorhees Zimmerli Mus, Rutgers Univ, New Brunswick, NJ; Continental Insurance Co, Piscataway, NJ. *Exhib:* New Galleries of Lower East Side, Artists Space, New York, 84; Fusion, Paulo Salvador, New York, 84 & 85; Smart Art, Harvard Univ, Sert Gallery, Cambridge, Mass, 85; New Art New York, Lidewij Edelkoort, Paris, France, 85; Urban Mythologies, Fine Arts Ctr, Univ RI, Kingston, 86; 12 Emerging Artists, Hudson River Mus, 87-88. *Teaching:* Instr painting, Mason Gross Sch of Arts, 81-82. *Bibliog:* Joseph Masheck (auth), Smart Art, Willis, Locker & Owens, 84. *Mem:* Found Community Artists. *Media:* Oil on Canvas. *Mailing Add:* 10 Beach St Third Fl New York NY 10013-2425

CHEW, PAUL ALBERT
ADMINISTRATOR, LECTURER
b Norristown, Pa, Apr 22, 25. *Study:* Univ Pittsburgh, BA, 50, MA(Henry Clay Frick Fine Arts Dept Grad Asst), 52; Univ Manchester, England, PhD(fel), 57; St Vincent Col, Latrobe, Pa, Hon DFA, 81; Seton Hill Col, Greensburg, Pa, DLitt, 84. *Collections Arranged:* All at Westmoreland Mus Art, Greensburg, Pa:; Holiday Exhibs: Antique Toy Collection & Large Guage Model Train, 89, 90, 91 & 92; Winterlude: Invitational Regional Painters & Sculptors Exhib, 90 & Invitational Regional Craftsmen, Photographers & Printmakers, 91; James Preston: American Post-Impressionist Exhib, 90; Southwestern Pa Painters, Collection of Westmoreland Mus Art, 90 & 92; Paul Warhola: Exhib of Recent Work, 90; What Style is it? Exhib - Photographic Survey of Prominent Am Architectural Styles, 90; Stitches in Time: Quilts, Coverlets & Samplers, 91; J-Anne Bates, Prints, 91; Andy Warhol: The Early Years, 91; William Partridge Burpee, 1846-1940, Am Marine Impressionist, 91; Michael Lotenero, Paintings, 91; Recent Paintings: Charles W Gibbons, III, 92; Recent Acquisitions, 92; Whiskey Rebellion Bicentennial Exhib, 92; Acqueous Open '92, Nat Juries Watercolor Exhib; Selected works from Southwestern Pa pvt collections, 92; L Murray Jamison, Photographs, 92; A World Observed, The Art of Everett Longley Warner, 1877-1963, 92. *Pos:* Asst to dir, Carnegie Mus, 52-53; exec to dir circulating exhibs, Mus Mod Art, New York, 53-54; dir, Westmoreland Co Mus Art, 57-; adv comt mem, Gov Home, Harrisburg, Pa, 79-86; trustee, Woods-Marchand Found, currently; mem bd dir, Pa Fed Mus & Hist Orgns, 90-; mem grants rev bd, Pa Hist & Mus Comn, 90-91. *Teaching:* Instr art hist, Univ Pittsburgh, Greensburg, Pa, 63- *Awards:* Forbes Medal, Ft Pitt Assoc Inc, 83; Distinguished Graduate Medallion, Univ Pittsburgh, 84; Gold Medal (distinguished serv), Westmoreland Soc. *Mem:* Col Art Asn Am; Am Asn Mus; Nat Trust Hist Preserv. *Publ:* Ed, Permanent Collection of Westmoreland Museum of Art (catalog), 78; Southwestern Pennsylvania Painters, 1800-1945, 81; Southwestern Pennsylvania Painters, 89. *Mailing Add:* 208 N Maple Ave Greensburg PA 15601

CHI, CHEN
PAINTER
b Wu-sih, China, May 2, 12. *Study:* Study in China. *Work:* Metrop Mus Art, New York; Pa Acad Fine Arts, Philadelphia; Butler Inst Am Art, Youngstown, Ohio; Fort Worth Art Mus, Tex; Charles & Emma Frye Art Mus, Seattle. *Exhib:* American Watercolors, Drawings & Prints, Metrop Mus Art, 52; Whitney Mus Am Art Ann, New York, 54-63; 24th Biennial, Corcoran Gallery Art, Washington, DC, 55; Contemporary American Painting & Sculpture, Univ Ill, Urbana, 57; Brooklyn Mus 22nd Int Watercolor Biennial, 63; Today's Artist & the West, Nat Acad Design, Phoenix Art Mus, 72; Contemp Watercolor Exhib, Western Ill Univ, 73; Charles & Emma Frye Art Mus, Seattle, Washington; Columbus Mus Art & Sci, Ga, 80, 83 & 89; Butler Inst Am Art, Youngstwon, Ohio, 81-84 & 90; Pa Acad Fine Arts, 81-84; Brandon Mem Mus, Dodge, Iowa, 89; Gilcrese Mus, Tulsa, Okla, 92; Artists Am Show, Denver, Colo, 92. *Teaching:* Instr watercolor, St Johns Univ, Shanghai, 42-46; vis prof watercolor, Pa State Univ, 59-60; artist in residence, Ogden City Schs, Utah, 67 & Utah State Univ, 71. *Awards:* Nat Inst Arts & Letter Grant for Creative Work in Art, 60; Samuel Finley Breese Mose Medal, 61 & Saltus Gold Medal of Merit, 69, Nat Acad Design; Bicentennial Gold Medal, Am Watercolor Soc, 76; Medal, Benjamin West Clinedirst Fel, 76; Edmund Greacen Nat Art Honor Award; Award, Nat Acad Design, 82; Medal of Honor, Nat Mus Hist, Taiwan Mu Art, Taiwan, China; Gold Medal Watercolor, Cowboy Acad Western Art, Oklahoma City, 89, 90 & 91. *Mem:* Nat Acad Design (counr, 69-); Am Watercolor Soc (dir, 56-59); Audubon Artists (dir, 64-69 & 72-); Allied Artists Am (dir, 58-60); Nat Arts Club (gov, 72-); Chen chi Found (pres). *Media:* Watercolor, Oil. *Publ:* Auth, Acquerelles de Chen Chi, Shanghai, 42; illusr, A Single Pebble, Readers Digest Condensed Bks, 56; Pageantry of VIII Winter Olympics, Squaw Valley, Sports Illus, 60; auth, Two or Three Lines from Sketchbooks of Chen Chi, New York, 69; China from the Sketchbooks of Chen Chi, New York, 74; Chen Chi, Watercolors, Drawings, Sketches, New York, 80 & Shanghai, 81; Heaven and Water, New York, 84. *Dealer:* Grand Central Art Galleries 24 W 57th New York NY 10022. *Mailing Add:* 23 Washington Sq N New York NY 10011

CHIA, SANDRO
PAINTER
b Florence, Italy, 1946. *Exhib:* One-man exhibs, Gian Enzo Sperone, Rome, 79, Sperone, Westwater, Fischer, New York, 80, Gallery Bischofberger, Zurich, Switz, 81, James Corcoran Gallery, Los Angeles, 82 & Leo Castelli Gallery, New York, 83, Yoshimitsu Hijikata Gallery, Nagoya, Japan, 89 & 90, Fondazione Mudima, Milan, Italy, 90, Galeria G B Shells, Mexico City, 92; Homo Sapiens: The Many Images, Aldrich Mus Contemp Art, Ridgefield, Conn, 83; Painting & Sculpture, Anthony d'Offay, London, 83; Dracos Art

Ctr, Athens, Greece, 84; Works on Paper, Bayer Fine Arts, Provincetown, Mass, 85; A New Romanticism: Sixteen Artists from Italy, Hirshhorn Mus, Washington, DC, 85-86; Painting In Europe, Karl Pfefferle, Munich, 87; Fifty Years of Collecting: An Anniversary Selection; Painting Since World War II, Solomon R Guggenheim Mus, 87-88; City For Sale, Huntington Room, Nat Acad Design, NY, 88; Akira Ilceda Gallery, Nagoya, Japan, 89; ARCO 90 Art Fair, Madrid, Spain, 90; Blum Helman Gallery & Germans Van Eck Gallery, 90; Sperone Westwater, New York, 92; and many others. *Bibliog:* Claude Royer (auth) rev, Flash Art, No 117, 1/84; William Wilson (auth), rev, Los Angeles Times, 8/10/84; Vivien Raynor (auth), rev,The New York Times, 1/20/85; Mark Stevens (auth), rev, Newsweek Mag, 3/10/86; Charlotte Mosley (auth), Monte Carlo Sculpture 87, Art News, 10/87; Jack Gulla (auth), Chia At Sperone Westwater, Art/World, 3/18/88; David Hornung, Sandro Chia: Sperone Westwater, Art News, 2/90; and many others. *Mailing Add:* 521 W 23rd St New York NY 10011

CHIARA, ALAN ROBERT
PAINTER
b Cleveland, Ohio, May 5, 36. *Study:* Cooper Sch Art, Cleveland; Cleveland Inst Art. *Work:* Butler Inst Art, Youngstown, Ohio; Springfield Art Mus, Mo; Cent Nat Bank Cleveland; Bethany Col, Lindsborg, Kans; Nat Acad Design, New York. *Exhib:* Butler Inst Art, 68; Watercolor USA, Springfield, Mo, 68; Nat Art Exhib, Wichita, Kans, 70; Nat Acad Design, New York, 71; Am Watercolor Soc, New York, 72. *Pos:* Master designer, Am Greetings, Cleveland, 58-70; pres, Chiara Galleries, Cleveland, 69- *Awards:* Silver Medal Award, Am Watercolor Soc, 66; Adolph & Clara Obrig Prize, 67 & William A Paton Prize, 70, Nat Acad Design. *Mem:* Am Watercolor Soc; assoc Nat Acad Design. *Media:* Watercolor. *Specialty:* Living American artists. *Publ:* Auth, Watercolor page, Am Artist Mag, 11/67. *Mailing Add:* 5061 Marina Cir Boca Raton FL 33486

CHIARENZA, CARL
PHOTOGRAPHER, HISTORIAN
b Rochester, NY, Sept 5, 35. *Study:* Rochester Inst Technol, AAS, 55, BFA, 57; Boston Univ, MS, 59, AM, 64; Danforth Found Teacher Grant, 66-68; Harvard Univ, PhD, 73. *Work:* Los Angeles Co Mus Art; Nat Mus Mod Art, Washington, DC; Philadelphia Mus Art; Mus Mod Art, New York; Art Inst Chicago; Minneapolis Inst Arts; Mus Fine Arts, Boston & Houston; Int Mus Photog, George Eastman House, Rochester; Ctr Creative Photog, Tucson; Fogg Art Mus, Cambridge; and others. *Exhib:* One-person exhibs, Minneapolis Inst Arts, Int Ctr Photog, Sch Art Inst Chicago, RI Sch Design Mus Art, Krannert Art Mus, Scales Fine Arts Gallery, Wake Forest Univ, Paul Arts Ctr Univ NH & Tampa Mus Art, 92; Mus Mod Art; Mus Fine Arts, Boston; Nat Mus Am Art; Inst Contemp Art, Boston; Metrop Mus Art; Int Mus Photog, George Eastman House; Ctr Creative Photog, Houston; Yale Univ Art Gallery; Los Angeles Co Mus Art; RI Sch Design Mus Art; and many other one-person & group exhibs. *Pos:* Ed, Contemp Photogr, Boston, 66-69; co-founder, Imageworks Ctr & Sch, Cambridge, Mass, 71-73; trustee, Visual Studies Workshop, Rochester, 75-; chmn, Dept Art Hist, Boston Univ, 76-81. *Teaching:* Prof art hist, Boston Univ, 63-86; vis prof photog hist & theory, Visual Studies Workshop, Rochester, NY, 73-74; Harnish vis artist, Smith Col, 83-84; Fanny Knapp Allen prof art hist, Univ Rochester, 86-; vis prof, Cornell Univ, 91- *Awards:* Mass Arts & Humanities Foun Fel, 75-76; Nat Endowment Arts Fel, 77-78. *Bibliog:* Deborah Martin Kao (auth), Landscapes of the Mind, Views, Summer, 88; Estelle Jussim & Charles Millard (coauths), Chiarenza: Landscapes of the Mind, David R Godine, Boston, 88; George Craven (auth), Object & Image, 89; Estelle Jussim (auth), The Eternal Moment, 89; Merry Foresta (auth), Seven Settings (essay), Tampa Mus Art, 92; and others. *Mem:* Soc Photog Educ (bd dirs, 68-73); Photog Resource Ctr (bd trustees, 77-); Friends of Photog (adv trustee, 79-83). *Media:* Black and White Photography. *Res:* Twentieth century American photography. *Publ:* Auth, Notes toward integrated history of picturemaking, Afterimage, Vol VII, No 1/2, 79; Siskind: Pleasures and terrors, NY Graphic Soc, Boston, 82; coauth, Heinecken, Friends Photog, 80; auth, Eye & mind: The seriousness of wit, Kenneth Josephson, Mus Contemp Art, Chicago, 83; Gary Winogrand (essay), Image, vol 34, no 3-4 & vol 35, no 1-2, 92; and others. *Dealer:* Wooster Gardens 40 Wooster St New York NY 10013; Benteler-Morgan Galleries, 4200 Montrose, Houston, TX 77006. *Mailing Add:* 5 Edgemere Dr Rochester NY 14618

CHICAGO, JUDY
PAINTER, SCULPTOR
b Chicago, Ill, July 20, 39. *Study:* Univ Calif, Los Angeles, BA, 62, MA, 64. *Work:* Brooklyn Mus; San Francisco Mus Mod Art; Oakland Mus Art; Pacific Sci Ctr; Pa Acad Fine Arts, Philadelphia; Michael Reese Hosp, Chicago; Los Angeles County Mus Art; and numerous pvt collections. *Exhib:* One-person exhibs, Rolf Nelson Gallery, Los Angeles, 66, Kenmore Galleries, Philadelphia, 74, Ruth S Schaffner Gallery, Los Angeles, 76, 77 & 79, Parco Galleries, Tokyo & Osaka, Japan, 80, ACA Galleries, New York, 84, 85 & 86, Robertson Galleries Ltd, Ottawa, Ont, 84 & Marilyn Butler Fine Art, Santa Fe, NMex & Scottsdale, Ariz, 85; Sculpture of the Sixties, Los Angeles Co Mus Art & Philadelphia Mus Art, 67; West Coast Now, Seattle Art Mus & San Francisco Mus Art, 68; Color as Structure, Whitney Mus Am Art, 70; Univ Wash, Seattle, 72; de Saisset Mus, Santa Clara, Calif, 73; Univ NDak, Grand Forks, 73; Western Wash State Col, Bellingham, 74; Cerritos Col, Newark, Calif, 75; The Dinner Party, San Francisco Mus Mod Art, 79; Brooklyn Mus; and others. *Pos:* Fac mem, Calif Inst Arts, 71-73. *Teaching:* Instr, Feminist Studio Workshop, 73-74; asst prof, Calif State Univ, 69-71. *Awards:* Outstanding Woman Yr, Mademoiselle Mag, 73; Individual Artist Grant, 76 & Service to the Field Grant, 77, Nat Endowment Arts; Woman of Achievement of the World, Women's Pavilion, La World Expo, 84; Vesta Award, Woman's Bldg, Los Angeles, 90. *Bibliog:* Lucy Lippard (auth), exhib rev, Art Am, 4/80; John Perrault (auth), exhib rev, Soho News, 10/15/80; Jane Adams (auth), article, Horizon Mag, 3/81; and others. *Mem:* Women's Caucus Art. *Interests:* Porcelain painting. *Publ:* Auth, Through the Flower: My Struggle as a Woman Artist, Doubleday, 75 & 81; auth, The Dinner Party: a Symbol of Our Heritage, 79 & Embroidering Our Heritage: The Dinner Party Needlework, 80, Anchor/Doubleday; The Birth Project, Doubleday, 85. *Mailing Add:* PO Box 8138 Santa Fe NM 87504

CHICHURA, DIANE B
ADMINISTRATOR, ART DEALER
b Queens, NY. *Study:* Pratt Inst, BS, 54; Columbia Univ, MA, 57; Fordham Univ, PhD, 80. *Pos:* Dist dir, Related Arts, West Hempstead Pub Schs, 68-; co-owner, Isis Gallery, Ltd, Searingtown, NY, 82- *Teaching:* Instr reading & the arts, Fordham Univ Grad Sch, 77-79. *Mem:* Int Soc Educ Art; US Soc Educ Art; Nat Art Educ Asn; NY State Art Teachers Asn (prog chmn, 70, 74 & 82); Long Island Art Teachers Asn. *Publ:* Co-auth, Super Sculpture: Using Science, Technology and Natural Phenomena in Sculpture, Van Nostrand Reinhold, 74; contribr, Cognition and the Visual Art Experience, In: Tapestry: The Interrelationships of the Arts in Reading & Language Development, Collegium Book Publ, Elmsford, 79; coauth, Cognitive Model for Visual Arts Experience & Interactive Development of a Cognitive Curriculum for Visual Arts Experience-Based on the Dynamic Process of Equilibrium, Fordham Univ, 80. *Mailing Add:* 47 Dogwood Rd Searingtown NY 11507

CHIEF EAGLE, CHARLES LINCE
SCULPTOR
b Pine Ridge, SDak, Aug 19, 61. *Study:* Self taught. *Work:* Heritage Ctr, Holy Rosary Mission, Pine Ridge, SDak; Sioux Indian Mus, Rapid City, SDak; Haffenreffer Mus Anthrop, Brown Univ, Mt Hope Grant, Bristol, RI, 90; Minneapolis Inst Arts, Minn, 91. *Comn:* Smithsonians nat Mus Am Indian, New York, 91. *Exhib:* Lawrence Indian Arts Show, Kans, 90; Northern Plains Tribal Arts, Sioux Falls, S Dak, 90; Mus Am Indian, New York, 91; Oscar Howe Art Ctr, Mitchell, SDak, 91. *Teaching:* Art Instr, Beadwork, Standing Rock Coll, Ft Yates, NDak, 87. *Awards:* Governor's Award, Northern Plains Tribal Arts, SDak Governor and Centenial Comn, 89. *Mem:* United Tribes Indian Art Expo Artist Guild, 92. *Media:* Three Dimensional, Mixed Media. *Dealer:* Southwest Trading Co 211 West Main St Charles Il 60174. *Mailing Add:* Box 132 Oglala SD 57764

CHIEFFO, CLIFFORD TOBY
PAINTER, CONSERVATOR
b New Haven, Conn, July 23, 37. *Study:* Southern Conn State Univ, BS; Teachers Col, Columbia Univ, MA. *Work:* Baltimore Mus Art; Berkshire Mus Art; Georgetown Univ; US State Dept Art in Embassies Prog; Nat Mus Am Art, Washington, DC; plus others. *Exhib:* Corcoran Gallery Art, 63, 65 & 67; Baltimore Mus Art, 65 & 66; Four American Printmakers, Am Embassy, Ireland, 68; 45 group and one-man exhibs. *Pos:* Tech ed, Am Artist Mag. *Teaching:* Instr painting, drawing & silk-screen, Univ Md; Corcoran Sch Art; prof fine arts & cur, Georgetown Univ, currently. *Awards:* Distinguished Alumni Award, Southern Conn State Univ, 74; Nat Mus Art Grant, 76-77; Award, Univ Tenn, 79; and others. *Mem:* Col Art Asn Am; Washington, DC Conservators Guild; Am Inst Conservators Hist Artistic Works. *Media:* Oil, Graphic. *Publ:* Auth, Silk-Screen as a Fine Art, Van Nostrand-Reinhold, 67 & paperback, 78; Contemporary Oil Painters Handbook, Prentice-Hall, 76 & Van Nostrand Reinhold, 82. *Mailing Add:* 14 Riverwood Ct Potomac MD 20854

CHIEGO, WILLIAM J
DIRECTOR, CURATOR
b Newark, NJ, Sept 17, 43. *Study:* Univ Va, Charlottesville, BA(with distinction), 65; Case Western Reserve Univ, Cleveland, Ohio, MA(art hist), 68, PhD(art hist), Univ Fel, Bingham Travel Fel), 74; Mus Mgt Inst, 81; Resident Fel, Yale Ctr British Arts, 82. *Collections Arranged:* From Oregon Private Collections, 77; Master Prints from the Gilkey Collection, 80; The Phillips Taste in Portland, Portland Art Mus, Ore, 80; French Paintings from the Chrysler Mus, NC Mus Art, 86; Sir David Wilkie of Scotland, NC Mus Art, 87; mod & contemp art, Aberlin Alumni Collection, 89. *Pos:* Asst cur, Toledo Mus Art, Ohio, 73-74, assoc cur, 74-76; cur, Portland Art Mus, Ore, 76-82 & NC Mus Art, 82-86; dir, Allen Mem Art Mus, Oberlin Col, 86-91; dir, Marion Koogler McNay Art Mus, 91- *Mem:* Col Art Asn; Art Mus Asn; Decorative Arts Chap, Soc Archit Historians. *Res:* French art, 1750-1850; British and American art of the 18th and 19th centuries; David Wilkie. *Publ:* Auth, A boudoir scene by Le Prince, 74 & Two paintings by Fantin Latour, 74, Mus News, Toledo Mus Art; Gericault, Carle Vernet and sour grapes at the salon of 1912, Arts Mag, 82. *Mailing Add:* c/o McNay Art Mus 6000 N New Braunfels Ave San Antonio TX 78209

CHIHULY, DALE PATRICK
GLASS ARTIST, EDUCATOR
b Tacoma, Wash, Sept 20, 41. *Study:* Univ Wash, Seattle, BA 65; Univ Wis, Madison, MS, 67; RI Sch Design, Providence, MFA, 68; RI Sch Design & Univ Puget Sound, Tacoma, Wash, Hon Dr Art, 86; Calif Col Arts Crafts, Oakland, Hon Dr Art, 88. *Work:* Metrop Mus Art, New York; Seattle Art Mus; Wadsworth Atheneum, Hartford, Conn; Philadelphia Mus Art; Victoria & Albert Mus, London; Lobmyer Mus, Vienna, Austria; Nat Mus Am Art, Smithsonian Inst, Washington, DC. *Comn:* Frank Russell Co, Tacoma, Seattle Aquarium, Sheraton Hotel & Towers, Wash; Hyatt Hotel, Adelaide, Australia; Rainbow Pavilion, Rockefeller Ctr, NY; Tacoma Art Mus, Tacoma Financial Ctr, Wash; Fleet Bank, Providence, RI. *Exhib:* Habitat Gallery,

Detroit, 80-83; Charles Cowles Gallery, New York, 81-83; Betsy Rosenfield Gallery, Chicago, 81-83; World Glass Now, Hokkaido Mus Mod Art, Sapporo, Japan, 82; The Wisconsin Movement-Glass in Form, Priebe Art Gallery, Univ Wis, Oshkosh, 82; The Descendents, NDak Mus Art, Grand Forks, 83; 11th Ann Nat Invitational Contemp Am Glass, Columbus Col Art & Design, Ohio, 83; Solo exhibs, Israel Mus, Jerusalem, 89, Hudson River Mus, Yonkers, NY, 90, Contemp Mus, Honolulu, Hawaii, 90, Lakeview Mus Arts Sci, Peoria, Ill, 90, Nickle Arts Mus, Univ Calgary, Alta, 90, Mus Art, Ft Lauderdale, Fla, 90 & Azabu Mus, Tokyo, Japan, 90; Mus Arts & Crafts, Hamburg, 92. *Teaching:* Chmn dept glass blowing, RI Sch Design, 67-80, chmn dept sculpture, 76-77; educ coordr & co-founder, Pilchuck Glass Ctr, Stanwood, Wash, 71- *Awards:* Louis Tiffany Found Award, 67; Fulbright Fel, Murano, Italy, 68; Master Craftsman-Apprenticeship Grant, Nat Endowment Arts, 75; Individual Artists Grant, Nat Endowment Arts, 77; Gov's Art Award, Wash, 84 & 85, Gov's Writers Award, Wash, 87. *Bibliog:* David Manzella (auth), The Fluid Breath of Glass, Craft Horizons, 71; Roni Horn (auth), Dale Chihuly and the Glass Cylinders, Studio Potter, 76; Alexandra Anderson (auth), Bravura glass, Portfolio Mag, 82. *Media:* Glass. *Publ:* Chihuly: Glass, 82; Auth, Chihuly: Color Glass & Form, 86. *Dealer:* Charles Cowles Gallery 420 W Broadway New York NY 10012. *Mailing Add:* 1124 Eastlake Ave E Seattle WA 98109

CHILDERS, MALCOLM GRAEME
PRINTMAKER, PHOTOGRAPHER
b Riverside, Calif, Feb 19, 45. *Study:* Humboldt State Univ, Arcata, Calif, BA, 69; Fullerton State Univ, Calif, MA, 72. *Work:* Springfield Art Mus, Mo; Tenn State Mus, Nashville; Meadows Mus Art, Shreveport, La; Brooks Mem Art Gallery, Memphis, Tenn; Standard Oil Co-Ind, Chicago Corp Art Collection. *Exhib:* Appalachian Corridors Biennial Art Exhib 4, Charleston, SC 75; Bradley Print Show, Peoria, Ill, 75-76; La Grange Nat Competition II, Ga, 75-76 & 86; Tenn Bicentennial Exhib, Nashville, Tenn, 76; and others. *Teaching:* Instr printmaking, Loma Linda Univ, Calif, 72-74; asst prof drawing, painting & printmaking, Southern Missionary Col, Collegedale, Tenn, 74-86. *Awards:* Purchase Awards, La Grange Nat II, La Grange Art Mus, 75, Mid-South Biennial, Brooks Mem Art Gallery, 75 & Tenn Bicentennial, State of Tenn, 76. *Dealer:* Assoc Am Artists 663 Fifth Ave New York NY 10022. *Mailing Add:* 5571 Tucker Rd Ooltewah TN 37363

CHILDS, CATHERINE O See Catchi,

CHILTON, FRED
PAINTER
b Las Cruces, NMex, June 14, 44. *Study:* Ctr for Creative Studies, Detroit, Mich, 63-66. *Comn:* Mural (collabr with Roger Gillett & Ronald Brown), Mich Bell Tel Co, 74; mural, Lady of Guadalupe Cath Church, Tortugas, NMex, 85; vicariate banners, comm by Cath Diocese of Las Cruces, NMex, 85. *Exhib:* 50th Ann Mid-year, Butler Inst Am Art, Youngstown, Ohio, 86; Watermedia 86, Mont Watercolor Soc; Close to the Border, NMex State Univ, Las Cruces, 86; Rio Bravo Watercolor Exhib, El Paso Mus Art, 87; 121st Ann Exhib Am Watercolor Soc, 88; El Paso Art Asn Ann Exhib, Sierra Med Ctr, 92; and others. *Awards:* Bronze Medal Color Photog, Scarab Club of Detroit, 78; Grumbacher Gold Medal, Salamagundi Club, 82; Huthsteiner Purchase Award, 88; Silver Medal, El Paso Mus Art, 88; Best of Show, NMex Watercolor Soc, 92. *Mem:* El Paso Art Asn; NMex Watercolor Soc. *Media:* Oil. *Publ:* Contemp Western Artists, Southwest Art Publ, 82; NMex Mag, 5/92. *Dealer:* Adobe Patio Gallery PO Box 697 Mesilla NM 88046. *Mailing Add:* 5293 Mesa Dr Las Cruces NM 88001

CHIMES, THOMAS JAMES
PAINTER
b Philadelphia, Pa, Apr 20, 21. *Study:* Art Students League. *Work:* Philadelphia Mus Art; Mus Mod Art, New York; Ringling Mus Art, Sarasota, Fla; Wadsworth Atheneum, Hartford, Conn; Larry Aldrich Mus, Ridgefield, Conn. *Exhib:* Recent Acquistions, Mus Mod Art, New York, 62; retrospectives, Jacksonville Mus, Fla, 68 & Ringling Mus, 69; Biennial, Whitney Mus Am Art, New York, 75; Philadelphia/Houston Exchange, Inst Contemp Art, Philadelphia, 77; Tom Chimes-a compendium, Paley Gallery, Moore Col, Philadelphia, 86. *Awards:* Residency, Pa Coun Arts, 79; Fel, Nat Endowment Arts, 87. *Bibliog:* Karl Nickel (auth), Tom Chimes, Retrospective, Ringling Mus, 68; S Martin & S Berg (auths), Tom Chimes, Moore Col, 86. *Media:* Oil. *Publ:* ilusr, Cymbalum Mundi, Des Periers/Knapp, Bookman Assocs, 65; Antonin Artraud, Man of Vision, Knapp, David Lewis, 69. *Mailing Add:* 600 Washington Sq South Philadelphia PA 19106

CHIN, MEL
SCULPTOR
b Houston, Tex, 1951. *Study:* Peabody Col, Nashville, Tenn, BA, 75. *Work:* Birmingham Mus Art, Ala; Harold Washington Libr, Chicago, Ill; Menil Found, Houston, Tex; Mus Fine Arts, Houston, Tex; Prudential Service Corp, Newark, NJ. *Exhib:* Solo exhibs, Robinson Galleries, Houston, Tex, 76 & 77, Modus Operandi, Diverse Works, 85, Operation of the Sun Through the Cult of the Hand, Loughelton Gallery, New York, 87, Selected Weapons, Frumkin/Adams Gallery, 88, Directions: Mel Chin, Hirshhorn Mus & Sculpture Garden, Washington, DC, 89 & Viewpoints: Mel Chin, Queens Mus, New York, 90-91; Mel Chin, Eric Levine, Manuel Neri, BR Kornblatt Gallery, Washington, DC, 90; Aprile, Chin, Winters, Frumkin/Adams Gallery, New York, 90; Cruciformed: Images of the Cross since 1980, Cleveland Ctr Contemp Art, Ohio, travelled to Mus Contemp Art, Wright State Univ, Dayton, Ohio, Western Gallery, Western Wash Univ, Bellingham, Macdonald Stewart Art Centre, Guelph, Ont, Can, 91-92; Beyond Glory: RePresenting Terrorism, Md Inst, Col Art, Baltimore, 92; Fragile Ecologies: Contemporary Artists' Interpretations and Solutions, Queens Mus, 92-93. *Awards:* Nat Endowment Arts Grant, 88 & 91; Mid-Atlantic Art Found Residency, Pittsburgh Ctr Arts, Pa, 90; Penny McCall Found Award, 91. *Mailing Add:* c/o Loughelton Gallery 67 Prince St New York NY 10012

CHIN, RIC
LECTURER, PAINTER
b Hong Kong, July 16, 35; US & UK citizen. *Study:* State Univ NY, BA; Art Students League; Sch Chinese Brushwork, New York; also with Barse Miller, Cheng Dai-Chien & Wang Chi-Yuan; Normal Univ Taiwan, MFA. *Work:* Nat Palace Mus, Taiwan; Penang Mus, Malaysia; Manhattan Savings Bank, Eastchester, NY; Houston's Ethan Allen Gallery, Greensboro, NC; Wantagh Sch Syst, NY; and pvt collections. *Exhib:* Am Artists Prof League Grand Nat, Lever House, NY, 71-75; Nat Palace Mus Ann, Taiwan, 74; one-man shows, Winston-Salem Hyatt House, NC, 74 & Ctr Asian Studies, St John's Univ, NY, 75; United Va Bank; and others. *Pos:* Dir, Bertrick Assoc Artists Inc, Seaford, NY, 65-74. *Teaching:* Lectr Chinese cult & art, Long Island Univ, 70-71; instr Chinese brushwork, var workshops, Southeastern US & Nat Art League, Douglaston, NY; nat painting & cooking lectr tour in 78 cities & on 34 TV shows, 77-78. *Mem:* Salmagundi Club (mem bd dir, 74 & 75); Am Artists Prof League; Sumi-E Soc Am; Nat Art League; Art League Nassau Co; Va Beach Arts Ctr; Chinese Calligraphy Asn, NY. *Media:* Watercolor, Water-Ink. *Res:* Rice paper with controlled texture. *Mailing Add:* 902 W Market St Greensboro NC 27401

CHINNI, PETER ANTHONY
SCULPTOR, PAINTER
b Mount Kisco, NY, Mar 21, 28. *Study:* Art Students League; Acad Belle Arti, Rome, Italy; also with Roberto Melli, Rome & Felice Casorati, Turin. *Work:* Whitney Mus Am Art, New York; Mass Inst Tech; New Orleans Mus Fine Art, La; Nat Gallery Art, Smithsonian Inst, Washington, DC; Rockefeller Collection. *Comn:* Stainless steel sculpture, City of Columbia, Mo, 78; stainless steel sculpture, City of New York, 84; wood sculpture, St Patrick's Church, Yorktown Heights, NY, 84. *Exhib:* Carnegie Int, Pittsburgh, Pa, 64-65; Whitney Mus Am Art Ann, 64-65; New Sch Social Res, 69; Biennale Roma, 69; Gallery Mod Art, Rome, 70; Beeckestijn Mus, Velsen, Holland, 76; Ixelle Mus, Brussels, Belgium, 76. *Awards:* Award Comn for Columbia, Mo Outdoor Steel Sculpture, 79. *Mem:* Sculptors Guild, NY; Artist's Equity, NY; Int Sculpture Ctr, Washington, DC. *Media:* Bronze, Marble; Oil, Acrylic. *Dealer:* Novus Inc 116 B Bennett St NW Atlanta GA 30309. *Mailing Add:* 88 W Hyatt Ave Mt Kisco NY 10549

CHO, DAVID
DESIGNER, ASSEMBLAGE ARTIST
b Los Angeles, Calif, Aug 13, 50. *Study:* Calif State Univ, Los Angeles, BA, 72. *Work:* Long Beach Mus Art, Calif. *Exhib:* Long Beach Mus Art 10th Ann, 72; Small Environments, Southern Ill Univ & Wis Art Ctr, Madison, 72; The David Cho Show, Amerasia Gallery, Los Angeles, 74; Collage & Assemblage in Southern California, Los Angeles Inst Contemp Art, 75; William Grant Still Art Ctr, Los Angeles, Calif, 78; and others. *Bibliog:* Articles, San Francisco Chronicle, 71, Los Angeles Times Calendar Mag, 72 & Art Gallery Mag, 72. *Mailing Add:* 400 Burnside Ave Los Angeles CA 90036

CHO, Y(EOU) J(UI)
PAINTER
b Taiwan, China, Nov 3, 50; US citizen. *Study:* Nat Taiwan Normal Univ, BFA, 73; State Univ NY, Albany, MA, 77. *Work:* Hong Kong Fine Art Mus; Caravan Product Inc, Totowa, NJ; pvt collections of Martin Margulies, Coconut Grove, Fla & Max Palevesky, Los Angeles; Taipei Fine Art Mus. *Exhib:* Solo exhibs, O K Harris Works Art, New York, 86, 88 & 90, Hong Kong Inst Prom Chinese Cult, 88 & Frank Bernarducci Gallery, 89; New York Observed, Frank Bernarducci Gallery, New York, 89; Chinese Am Arts Coun, New York, 89; Contemp Drawing Exhib, Cheng Piin Gallery, Taipei, Taiwan, 90; Dual Cultures, Nassau Co Mus Art, Roslyn, NY. *Awards:* First Prize, Prov Mus Taiwan, 73. *Bibliog:* Alan Zie Yongder (auth), Y J Cho, Photog Art, 89; Nancy Chou (auth), A tenacious artist Y J Cho, Hsiung Shih Art Monthly, Taiwan, 10/91; Pei-Kai Cheng (auth), Y J Cho's search for real & history, Con-Temporary Monthly, Taiwan, 10/91; Bettie Johnson (auth), How to render wood, Airbrush Action, 1-2/92; Artists from the world, Artforum Japan, 4/92; and others. *Media:* Acrylic, Oil; Watercolor. *Dealer:* Frank Bernarducci 560 Broadway New York NY 10012; O K Harris Gallery 383 W Broadway New York NY 10012. *Mailing Add:* 74 Grand St 5F New York NY 10013

CHODKOWSKI, HENRY, JR
PAINTER, EDUCATOR
b Hartford, Conn, Mar 20, 37. *Study:* Univ Hartford, BFA, 61; Yale Univ, MFA, 63. *Work:* Nat Gallery Greece, Athens; Phillips Collection, Nat Collection Fine Arts, Washington, DC; Philadelphia Mus; DeCordova Mus, Mass. *Exhib:* One-man shows, J B Speed Art Mus, 68, 72 & 78, Duke Univ Mus, 72, Middendorf Gallery, Washington, DC, 75, Allan Stone Gallery, New York, 79 & The Hellenic-American Union, Athens, 85 & 91; Gallery Contemp Art, Winston-Salem, NC, 74; Hassam & Speicher Exhib, Am Acad & Inst Arts & Letters, New York, 82; Twenty-one American Artists on Paper, Warsaw Acad Fine Arts, Warsaw, Poland, 88. *Teaching:* Prof advan & grad painting, Univ Louisville, 73- *Awards:* Polaroid Corp Grant, 68; Award for Excellence in Teaching & Scholarship, Univ Louisville, 78; Al Smith Fel, KY Arts Coun, 89-90. *Bibliog:* Jay Kloner (auth), The precisionist paintings of Henry Chodkowski, 10/75 & Henry Chodkowski, 3/79, Arts Mag; Mary Machas (auth), Taosim and the Minoan Labyrinth, The Athenian, 5/85. *Media:* Acrylic. *Dealer:* Triangle Gallery 522 W Short St Lexington KY 40508. *Mailing Add:* 2015 Baringer Ave Louisville KY 40204

CHONG, PING
DIRECTOR, VIDEO ARTIST
b Oct 3, 46. *Study:* Pratt Inst, 64-66, Sch Visual Arts, 67-69. *Work:* Site-specific installations, Mass Inst Technol, Albert & Vera List Visual Arts Ctr, Cambridge, 85 & Three Rivers Arts Festival, Pittsburgh, 88. *Comn:* In the Absence of Memory (light installation), New England Found Arts, 89; Tempus Fugit, Haggerty Mus Art, Marquette Univ, Milwaukee, Wisc, 90. *Exhib:* Walker Art Ctr, Minneapolis, Minn; St Louis Art Mus, Mo; Carnegie Inst Art, Pittsburgh, Pa; Mus Contemp Art, Chicago; Haggerty Mus Art, Milwaukee, Wisc; Lafayette Col Gallery, Easton, Pa; Austin Ctr Arts, Hartford, Conn. *Pos:* Founder, dir, Ping Chong & Co. *Awards:* Five Nat Endowment Arts Fel, USA; USA Playwrights Award; Bronze Star Award, Sacramento Int Film & Video Festival, Calif, 89. *Publ:* Dir, Education of the Girl Child (video), 73; co-dir, Paris, KCTA-TV, 82 & Turtle Dreams, WGBH-TV, (videos), 87; dir, A M/A M--The Articulated Man (film), 82; Plage Concrete (video) WGBH TV Ser, 88; Snow (script), Plays in Progress. *Mailing Add:* 47 Great Jones St New York NY 10012

CHOO, CHUNGHI
SILVERSMITH, FIBER ARTIST
b Inchon, Korea, May 23, 38; US citizen. *Study:* Cranbrook Acad Art, Bloomfield Hills, Mich, MFA, 65. *Work:* Metrop Mus Art, Mus Mod Art, Am Craft Mus, Cooper Hewitt Mus, New York; Musee des Arts Decoratifs, au Louvre, Paris, France; Art Inst Chicago; Victoria & Albert Mus, London, Eng; and others. *Exhib:* Young Americans 1969, Mus Contemp Crafts, New York; one-woman show, Jack Lenor Larsen Show Rm, New York, 71; Fabric Vibrations, Eastern & Western Europe, Near & Far East & Pac Islands sponsored by Smithsonian Inst, 72-75; North American Goldsmith, Renwick Gallery, Washington, DC & travelling, 74-77; Forms in Metal: 275 years of Metalsmithing in America, Mus Contemp Crafts, New York & travelling, 75-76; Dyers Art, Mus Contemp Crafts, New York, 76; Int Fiberworks, Cleveland Mus Art, Ohio, 77; For the Table Top, Am Craft Mus, New York and travelling, 80-82; Craft Today: Poetry of Physical, Am Craft Mus, New York and travelling, 86-88; Beyond Craft: Celebration of Creativity, Visual Arts Mus, New York; Craft Today USA, Europ travelling exhib, Am Craft Mus & US Information Agency, 89-92. *Teaching:* Prof jewelry & metalsmithing, Sch of Art & Art Hist, Univ Iowa, 68- *Awards:* Nat Endowment Art Grant, 81; AMOCO Excellence in Teaching Award, 87. *Bibliog:* Jack Lenor Larsen (auth), Dyer's Art, Reinhold; Katherine Pearson (auth), American Crafts; Robert Rorex (auth), Chunghi Choo, works in Metal & Silk, 10/82. *Mem:* Distinguished Mem Soc NAm Goldsmiths; Am Crafts Coun. *Mailing Add:* 2 Glenview Knolls NE Iowa City IA 52240

CHOW CHIAN-CHIU,
PAINTER, HISTORIAN
b Canton, China, Dec 23, 10. *Work:* Tsing Hwa Univ, Peking; Hopkins Ctr Art Galleries, Dartmouth Col, NH; Cernuschi Mus, Paris; Lawrence Univ, Canton, NY. *Exhib:* Yugoslavia traveling exhib, Kansas State Univ, Univ Calif, Berkeley, Stanford Univ, Calif, Univ Pittsburgh, Pa, Univ Rochester, NY & others; Art Mus Seattle, Wash; Dartmouth Col, Hanover, NH; and others. *Teaching:* Pres, Int Studio Chinese Art, 52-67; instr Chinese art, Grove Art Sch, Miami Art Ctr, Fla, 68-70. *Awards:* Respect Award, Inst Chinese Cult, New York, 70; Gold Medal & Jin Ding Award, Cent Gov Republic China, 80; Oscar Award, D'Italia, 85. *Bibliog:* Walter Foster (auth), Chinese Art, film, Wilbur T Blume, 62. *Mem:* Chinese Artist Asn, Nanking; Chinese Artist Asn, Hong Kong; hon mem Miami Artist Asn. *Media:* Watercolor. *Publ:* Coauth, Easy Way to do Chinese Painting, 61; coauth, Chinese Painting No 2, 72; auth, The Biographies of Chinese Painting New School Founder in History, Libr Cong, 75; A Comprehensive Guide of Chinese Painting, 80; Chinese Painting, Poetry, Calligraphy, 90; Portflio Chinese Paintings, 90. *Mailing Add:* 2740 Le Jeune Rd Coral Gables FL 33134

CHOW LEUNG CHEN-YING,
PAINTER, CALLIGRAPHER
b Canton, China, Mar 20, 21. *Study:* Art Teacher Training Col, China. *Work:* Hopkins Ctr Art Galleries, Dartmouth, NH; Mus Cernuschi, Paris, St Lawrence Univ, Canton, NY; Fla Int Univ, Miami; Hong Kong Univ; Conn Col, New London. *Exhib:* Dartmouth Col, Hanover, NH, Art Mus Seattle, Wash, Kans State Univ, Manhattan, Stanford Univ, Calif & Univ Pittsburgh, Pa; and others. *Teaching:* Prof, Int Studio Chinese Art, 52-67; instr Chinese art, Grove Art Sch, Miami Art Ctr, Fla, 69-70; pres & prof, Chow Studio, 69-86. *Awards:* Gold Medal & Jin Ding Award, Cent Gov Republic China, 80; Oscar Award d'Italia, 85. *Bibliog:* Foster (auth), Chinese Art (film), Wilbur T Blume, 62. *Mem:* Chinese Artist Asn, Hong Kong; hon mem Miami Artist Asn; hon chmn, Canton Artist Asn, China. *Media:* Watercolor. *Publ:* Coauth, Easy Way to do Chinese Painting, 61; coauth, Chinese Painting No 2, 72; A Comprehensive Guide of Chinese Painting, 80; Chinese Painting, Poetry, Calligraphy, 90; Portfolio of Chinese Paintings, 90. *Mailing Add:* 2740 Le Jeune Rd Coral Gables FL 33134

CHOY, TERENCE TIN-HO
PAINTER, EDUCATOR
b Hong Kong, Nov 26, 41; US citizen. *Study:* San Francisco State Univ, BA; Univ Calif, Berkeley, with David Hockney, Elmer Bischoff & Earl Loren, MA. *Work:* Alaska State Coun Arts, Anchorage; Alaska State Mus at Juneau; Univ Alaska, Anchorage; Univ Alaska, Fairbanks. *Exhib:* M H de Young Mem Mus, San Francisco, 69; Honolulu Acad Art, Hawaii, 76; Woodson Art Mus, Wausau, Wis, 76; Nat Collection Fine Arts, Washington, DC, 78; Univ Minn, Minneapolis, 80; Wing Luk Mem Mus, 81. *Pos:* Photographer, Univ Calif, Berkeley, 68-70; gallery coordr, Art Galleries, Univ Alaska, Fairbanks, 71-75. *Teaching:* Instr art, de Young Mus Art Sch, San Francisco, 69-70; prof art, Univ Alaska, Fairbanks, 70- *Awards:* Nat Endowment Humanities Grant, 79; Alaska State Coun Arts Grant, 79; Mellon Found Grants, 80 & 81. *Mem:* Col Art Asn; Nat Art Educ Asn; Alaska Asn Arts; Visual Art Ctr Alaska. *Mailing Add:* 7627 Mandolin Way Rohnert Park CA 94928

CHRISTENBERRY, WILLIAM
PAINTER, EDUCATOR
b Tuscaloosa, Ala, Nov 5, 36. *Study:* Univ Ala, Tuscaloosa, BFA, 58, MA, 59. *Work:* Corcoran Gallery Art, Washington, DC; Mus Mod Art, Whitney Mus Am Art, New York. *Comn:* Southern Wall, US Gen Serv Admin, Washington, DC, 78; Cola Wall, Arnold and Porter, Washington, DC, 83; Potomac Wall, Phillip Morris Corp, 89. *Exhib:* Photographs, Corcoran Gallery Art, Washington, DC, 73 & 78; Drawings and Small Works, Washington Gallery Art, Washington, DC, 73; one-man exhibs, Baltimore Mus Art, 73 & Pace MacGill Gallery, New York, 85 & 92; Zabriskie Gallery, New York, 76; Montgomery Mus Art, Ala, 79; Middendorf/Lane Gallery, Washington, DC, 81; Inst Arts, Rice Univ, 82; Corcoran Gallery Art, Wash, DC, 83; Of Time & Place, Amon Carter Collection, Ft Worth, Tex, 92; Yellowstone Art Ctr, Billings, Mont, 92. *Teaching:* Assoc prof art, Corcoran Sch Art, Washington, DC, 68-74, prof, 74- *Awards:* Fel Nat Endowment Arts, 76; Lyndhurst Found Prize, 82-84; Fel, Guggenheim Found, 84. *Publ:* William Christenberry Southern Photographs, Aperture Inc, 83. *Mailing Add:* 2739 Macomb St NW Washington DC 20008

CHRISTENSEN, BETTY (ELIZABETH)
ILLUSTRATOR, PAINTER
b Collingdale, Pa. *Study:* Philadelphia Col Art, cert; Art Students League; Nat Acad, with Jack Pellew, Am Watercolor Soc. *Work:* Mattatuck Mus, Waterbury, Conn; Hoffman Fuel, Danbury, Conn. *Exhib:* Am Watercolor Soc Ann, Nat Acad, New York, 57-59, 61-63, 66, 69 & 78; 200 Years: Watercolor Painting in America, Metrop Mus Art, New York, 66; Invitational, 81 & Connecticut Classic Arts, 82, Mus Art, Sci & Indust, Bridgeport, Conn; Putman Arts Coun, Mahopac, NY, 81 & 85; Allied Artists Ann, Nat Arts Club, New York, 85; Conn Watercolor Soc Ann, New Haven, 85; Sheffield Art League Spring Show, Mass, 85 & 86; Catherine Lorillard Wolfe Art Club, New York; Art on the Mountain, Wilmington, Vt; Solo shows, Brooks libr, Brattleboro, Vt. *Awards:* Shortell Framing Award, Conn, 90; Volunteers Award, Art on the Mountain, 88; Third Prize Wis, Coun Classic Arts, 88; Best-in-Show, Soc Creative Arts, Newtown, Conn; Best-in-Show, Bethel Art League, 91. *Mem:* Am Watercolor Soc; Allied Artists; Conn Watercolor Soc; Kent Art Asn; Conn Classic Arts. *Media:* Watercolor. *Publ:* Illusr, A Few Thoughts on Trout, Simon & Schuster, 86. *Mailing Add:* PO Box 237 Newtown CT 06470

CHRISTENSEN, DAN
PAINTER
b Lexington, Nebr, 1942. *Study:* Kansas City Art Inst, BFA, 64. *Work:* Metrop Mus Art, Mus Mod Art, New York; Hirshhorn Mus, Washington, DC; St Louis Art Mus, Mo; Denver Mus Art; Guggenheim Mus, New York; Ludwig Collection, Wallraf-Richartz Mus, Cologne, Ger; Whitney Mus Am Art, New York. *Exhib:* Corcoran Biennial, Washington, DC, 69; Guggenheim Mus, New York, 69; Color & Field 1890-1970, Albright-Knox Gallery, Buffalo, NY, 70; The Structure of Color, Whitney Mus, New York, 71; Abstract Painting in the 70's, Boston Mus Fine Arts, 72; Douglas Drake Gallery, Kansas City, Kans, 81; Martha White Gallery, Louisville, Ky, 82; Ivory/Kimpton Gallery, San Francisco, 82; Miro in America, Mus Fine Arts, Houston, Tex, 82; 46th Ann Nat Midyear Show, Butler Inst Am Art, Youngstown, Ohio, 82; Philip Johnson: Selected Gifts, Mus Mod Art, New York, 85; Important Works on Paper, Meredith Long & Co, Houston, Tex, 89; Salander-O'Reilly Galleries, New York, 90; one-man shows, Ivory-Kimpton Gallery, San Francisco, 82, Salander-O'Reilly Galleries Inc, New York, 82, 83 & 84, Lincoln Ctr Gallery, New York, 83 & 84 & Edwin A Ulrich Mus Art, Wichita State Univ, 84. *Teaching:* Instr, Sch Visual arts, 78-82. *Awards:* Grant, Nat Endowment Arts, 68; Fel, Guggenheim Found, 69502; Theodoran Award, 69. *Bibliog:* Grace Glueck (auth), Like a beginning, Art in Am, 5-6/69; Emily Wasserman (auth), New York, Artforum, 9/69; Valentin Tatransky (auth), New Work in New York, Mus Mag, 7-8/81; Doanld Hoffman (auth), Masterly technique distilled, Kansas City Star, 5/23/82. *Publ:* Auth, Fine Young Artists Theodoron Awards, Guggenheim Mus, 69. *Mailing Add:* c/o Salander-O'Reilly Gallery 22 E 80th St New York NY 10021

CHRISTENSEN, DON B
PAINTER, COLLECTOR
b Gothenberg, Nebr, Mar 10, 48. *Study:* Univ Nebr, 68; Kansas City Art Inst, 69-70. *Awards:* Fel in Painting, Nat Endowment Art, 92. *Media:* Oil. *Mailing Add:* 81 Warren St New York NY 10007

CHRISTENSEN, LARRY R
PAINTER, INSTRUCTOR
b Manti, Utah, Jan 18, 36. *Study:* Utah Tech Col, cert, 2 yrs. *Work:* Vernal High Sch, Utah; Cliff Lodge, Snowbird, Utah; Salt Lake City Chamber Com, Vet Admin & Am Express, Salt Lake City. *Comn:* Idaho Telephone Dir Cover, 61, portrait of pres, 62, Mountain Bell. *Exhib:* Cody County Regional Art Exhib, Wyo, 67-81; Springville Mus Art Nat, Utah, 69-79; Cedar City Nat Exhib, Utah, 72-77; two-man show, Phillips Gallery, 73, 74, 76, 79 & 82; Univ Utah Mus Fine Art, 76-79; plus others. *Pos:* Art dir, Mountain Bell, 71-79; instr, Watercolor Workshop, Salt Lake City, 75, 76, 79 & 80; Div Continuing Educ, Univ Utah, 75, Photo Blue Workshop, 77- *Awards:* Silver 2nd Award, Utah State Expos, 70; First Place, Cody Country Art 70 & 81; Special Cash

Award, Utah, 81. *Mem:* Assoc mem Am Watercolor Soc; Utah Watercolor Soc; assoc mem Watercolor Soc Calif. *Media:* Watercolor, Pencil. *Publ:* Contribr, Art West, 72. *Dealer:* Kimball Art Ctr Park City Utah; Phillips Gallery 444 E 2nd Salt Lake City UT 84111. *Mailing Add:* 3534 Dover Hill Dr Salt Lake City UT 84121

CHRISTENSEN, NEIL C
PAINTER
b Imperial, Nebr, Oct 28, 47. *Study:* Univ Nebr, Lincoln, BFA, 78, MFA, 84. *Work:* Peru State Col, Nebr; Mus Nebr Art, Kearney; Sioux City Art Ctr, Iowa. *Exhib:* 18th Joslyn Biennial, Joslyn Art Mus, Omaha, Nebr, 84; People on Paper, Sheldon Mem Art Gallery, Lincoln, Nebr, 86; 37th Spiva Art Ctr, Joplin, Mo, 87; Ceremonial Gardens, Haydon Gallery, Lincoln, Nebr, 90. *Awards:* Vreeland Award, Univ Nebr, 84; Cash Award, 18th Joslyn Biennial, Joslyn Art Mus, 84; Purchase Award, 1987 Biennial, Sioux City Art Ctr, 87. *Media:* Oil on Panel. *Mailing Add:* Hardy Bldg Suite A 335 N Eighth Lincoln NE 68508

CHRISTENSEN, SHARLENE
PAINTER, INSTRUCTOR
b Fountain Green, Utah, Aug 24, 39. *Work:* Equitable Life & Casualty Utah Collection; Salt Lake Surgical Ctr, Am Express Co, First Interstate & Vet Admin, Salt Lake City; Salt Lake County Fine Arts Collection, 87; Salt Lake Chamber of Com. *Exhib:* Springville Mus Art, Utah, 69-90; Eccles Art Ctr, Ogden, Utah, 75, 79 & 88; Audubon Artists 38th Ann, New York, 80; Utah Watercolor Soc, 75-92; Watercolor West, Riverside, Calif, 80; San Diego Int Watercolor Exhib, 81; Kimball Art Ctr, Park City, Utah, 84, 89 & 92; Southam Gallery, 88-92; Am Watercolor Soc, New York; and many others. *Pos:* Artists-in-schs prog, Nat Found Arts & Utah Inst Fine Arts, 73-74. *Teaching:* Instr watercolor, Salt Lake Art Ctr, 72-84; Christensen Workshops, Summer Arts Inst, Kimball Art Ctr, Park City, Utah, 75-92; instr watercolor, subjects in nature, Kimball Art Ctr, 88; A Way of Seeing through Watercolor, 92. *Awards:* Award of Excellence, Utah Watercolor Soc, 78; Equitable Life & Casualty Utah Collection Purchase Award, 85; Jurors Choice Award, Loge Gallery, 85. *Bibliog:* Ann Poore (auth), article in Salt Lake Tribune, 3/88; George Dibble (auth), Art Scene, Salt Lake Tribune, 5/88. *Mem:* Am & Utah Watercolor Soc; assoc mem Am Watercolor Soc. *Media:* Transparent Watercolor. *Publ:* Contribr, Art West, 72; Dict Utah Artists; Robert Olpin, 80; Who's Who in the West; Who's Who Am Women. *Dealer:* Southam Gallery 50 E Broadway Salt Lake City Utah 84111. *Mailing Add:* 3534 Dover Hill Dr Salt Lake City UT 84121

CHRISTENSEN, TED
PAINTER, PRINTMAKER
b Vancouver, Wash, Mar 20, 11. *Study:* Art Ctr Sch, Los Angeles, with King & Feitelson; Mus Art Sch, Portland, Ore, with Givler & Bunce; Otis Art Inst, Los Angeles, with Hansen & Zornes. *Work:* Wurlitzer Found, Taos, NMex; Sausalito Collection & Sausalito Hist Mus, Calif; Harwood Found, Taos; St Johns Col, Santa Fe, NMex; Sonoma Co Mus, Santa Rosa, Kelly House Mus, Mendocino, Calif. *Exhib:* Los Angeles Co Mus Ann, Los Angeles, 45 & 46; Ore Soc of Artists, Portland Art Mus, 46 & 47; Painters & Sculptors Ann, Oakland Art Mus, Calif, 46-47 & 54; Int Ceramic Ann, Syracuse Mus of Art, NY, 49 & 50; one-man shows, Col of Marin, Kentfield, Calif, 54 & 63, Marin Mus, San Rafael, Calif, plus over 60 others. *Teaching:* Instr life drawing, Col of Marin, Kentfield, 52-60. *Awards:* First Prize, Ore Soc of Artists, Portland Art Mus, 46 & 47; First Prize, Marin Soc of Artists, Webb Gallery, Ross, Calif, 58; and fifty other awards. *Bibliog:* Susan E Myer (auth), 20 Landscape Painters & How They Work, Watson-Guptill, 77; Acrylic painting in North America, Artists Mag, London, 11/78; Catherine Littel (auth), Ted Christensen, Art of Calif Mag, Feb/Mar, 91. *Mem:* Marin Co Watercolor Soc. *Media:* Acrylic; Serigraph. *Publ:* Auth, Mendocino Sketchbook, pvt publ, 72; illusr, Kitchen Magic with Mushrooms, San Francisco Mycological Soc, 63. *Dealer:* Querca Gallery Dunians Mills CA 95430. *Mailing Add:* 573 Third St E Sonoma CA 95476

CHRISTENSEN, VAL ALAN
PRINTMAKER, GALLERY DIRECTOR
b Valentine, Nebr, Jan 26, 46. *Study:* Univ Nebr-Lincoln, with Thomas P Coleman, BFA, 68; Wichita State Univ, MFA, 70. *Work:* Sioux City Art Ctr, Iowa; Sheldon Mem Art Gallery, Lincoln, Nebr; Kearney State Col, Nebr; Hastings Col, Nebr. *Exhib:* Thirty-fifth Nat Graphic Arts & Drawing Exhib, Wichita Art Asn, Kans, 71; 29th Nat Print Exhib, Silvermine Guild of Artists, New Canaan, Conn, 72; 3rd Ann Nat Print Exhib, Ga State Univ, Atlanta, 72; 43rd Ann Art Exhib, Springfield Art Mus, Mo, 73; Nebraska 75, Joslyn Art Mus, Omaha, 75; one-person show, Sheldon Mem Art Gallery, Lincoln, 76. *Pos:* Artist-in-sch, Grand Island Cent Cath, 75-79; panel mem, Community Arts Prog, Nebr Arts Coun, Omaha, 77-79; dir, Spiva Atr Ctr, 79; asst prof of found prog, Mo Southern State Col, Joplin, 79- *Teaching:* Asst prof printmaking, Univ Nebr-Lincoln, 71-72; instr printmaking/drawing, Hastings Col, Nebr, 72-75; asst prof art, Mo Southern St Col, 79- *Awards:* Vreeland Award, Univ Nebr-Lincoln Found, 67; Purchase Awards, 40th Ann Art Exhib, Springfield Art Mus, Mo, 70 & 33rd Ann Fall Show, Sioux City Art Ctr, 71. *Mem:* Mid-Am Col Art Asn; Col Art Asn. *Media:* Intaglio prints. *Mailing Add:* Dept Art Missouri Southern State College Joplin MO 64801

CHRISTIANA, EDWARD
PAINTER, INSTRUCTOR
b White Plains, NY, May 8, 12. *Study:* Pratt Inst, dipl; Munson-Williams-Proctor Inst Sch Art, Utica, NY, with William C Palmer. *Work:* Currier Gallery Art, Manchester, NH; Syracuse Mus Fine Arts, NY; Worcester Mus, Mass; Albany Inst Hist & Art, NY; Cooperstown Art Asn, NY; Canajoharie Collection, NY; Columbus Mus Art, Ohio; Univ Conn Collection. *Exhib:* 53rd & 55th Watercolor & Drawing Ann, Art Inst Chicago, 42 & 44; Am Watercolor Soc Ann, New York, 45-50; Audubon Artists, New York, 50; 37th Allied Artists Am Ann, New York, 50; 146th Painting & Sculpture Ann, Pa Acad Fine Arts, Philadelphia, 51; Oils & Watercolors, Munson-Williams-Procter Inst & Mus of Art, Utica, 78; Distinguished Mid-Atlantic Artists: Four Decades of Growth, Univ Del, 80; Retrospective exhibition, Munson-Williams-Proctor Inst and Mus, Utiza, 89. *Teaching:* Instr painting, drawing & design, Munson-Williams-Proctor Inst Sch Art, Utica, 42-78, instr watercolor, 71-82, emer. *Awards:* William Church Osborn Purchase Prize, Am Watercolor Soc, 49 & 51; 27th Ann Exhib Award, Assoc Artists Syracuse, 54; 21st Ann Upper Hudson Exhib Award, Albany Inst Hist & Art, 56. *Mem:* Cooperstown Art Asn; Cent New York Watercolor Soc (pres, 85-86. *Media:* Watercolor. *Mailing Add:* 10 Steuben St Holland Patent NY 13354

CHRISTIANSEN, DIANE
PAINTER
b Grinnel, Iowa, Oct 27, 58. *Study:* Grinnel Col, Iowa, BA(antrhop), 81; Loyola Univ, Chicago, MSW, 90; Art Inst Chicago, MFA(painting), 90. *Work:* South Bend Art Ctr, Ind. *Exhib:* Solo exhibs Artemisia Gallery, Chicago, 85 & 91, Race St Gallery, Grand Rapids, 86, Ill Cent Gallery, Peoria, 88, World Tattoo Gallery, Chicago, 90, Chicago Cult Ctr, 92; Gigantic Women, Miniature Work, Gallery II, Chicago, 90; Itinerary, MWMWM Gallery, Chicago, 91; group show, Lannon Cole Gallery, Chicago, 91. *Awards:* Purchase Prize, Michiana Regional Show, South Bend, Ind, 86; Full Merit Scholarship, Art Inst Chicago, 88; Visual Arts Fel Award, Arts Midwest, Nat Endowment Arts Regional, 92. *Bibliog:* Susan Alexis Collins, Diane Christiansen, Walter Andersons, New Art Examiner, 12/91. *Media:* Oil on plaster. *Mailing Add:* 2022 W Crystal Chicago IL 60622

CHRISTIE, ROBERT DUNCAN
PAINTER
b Saskatoon, Sask, April 8, 46. *Study:* Univ Sask, BA, 67, hon degree(fine arts), 68, BEd, 70. *Work:* Mendel Art Gallery, Saskatoon, Sask; Edmonton Art Gallery; Norman Mackenzie Art Gallery, Sask Arts Bd, Regina; Can Coun Art Bank, Ottawa. *Exhib:* Canada X Ten, Edmonton Art Gallery, 74; Abstraction West, Nat Gallery Can, 76; solo exhibs, Edmonton Art Gallery, 78, Norman Mackenzie Art Gallery, Regina, Sask, 81 & Mendel Art Gallery, Saskatoon, 82. *Pos:* Gallery supvr, Univ Sask, Saskatoon, 73-82. *Teaching:* Lectr art, Univ Sask, Saskatoon, 83. *Bibliog:* Liz Wylie (auth), article, Artmag, Vol 12, No 50, 80; Nancy Tousley (auth), article, Calgary Herald, 82. *Media:* Acrylic on Canvas. *Dealer:* Can Art Galleries Calgary AB; Waddington & Shiell Galleries Ltd Toronto ON. *Mailing Add:* 725-13th St E Saskatoon SK S7N 0M1 Canada

CHRISTISON, MURIEL B
EDUCATOR, MUSEUM DIRECTOR
b Minneapolis, Minn. *Study:* Univ Minn, BA & MA; Univ Paris Inst Art & Archaeol, dipl art hist; Univ Brussels, dipl art hist. *Collections Arranged:* The Impressionist & Post-Impressionists, 51, Goya, 53, Masterpieces of Chinese Art, 55, Les Fetes Galantes, 55, Masterpieces of American Silver, 60 & Sport & the Horse, 60, Va Mus Fine Arts, Richmond; Art of India & Southeast Asia, 63 & For Your Home, 66 & 70, Univ Ill; plus many others. *Pos:* Cur researcher, Minneapolis Inst Arts, 36-42, head educ dept, 44-47; assoc dir, Va Mus Fine Arts, Richmond, 48-61; consult, Ark Art Ctr, 61; assoc dir & oper dir, Krannert Art Mus, Univ Ill, Champaign-Urbana, 62-71, dir, 71 & 75-82, dir emer, 82-; coun mem, Am Asn Mus, 72-82, sr examiner, 82-; interim dir, Muscarelle Mus, William & Mary Col, Williamsburg, Va, 84-85; evaluator, Univ Tex, Austin, 78, Wash Univ, St Louis, 80, Ohio Arts Coun, 84 & SC Arts Comn, 86. *Teaching:* Instr art in civilization & Am art, Univ Minn, Minneapolis, 45-47; dir grad prog art mus studies, Univ Ill, 72-82; vis prof art, Col William & Mary, 83- *Awards:* Carnegie Scholar, Inst Int Educ, 36; CRB Fel, Belg-Am Educ Found, 38; Distinguished Serv, Midwest Mus Conf, 82. *Mem:* Asn Art Mus Dirs; Col Art Asn; Am Asn Mus; Soc Preserv Va Antiquities; Soc Archit Hist (Va chap). *Publ:* Auth, Buffington Art Bulletin, 42; circular on mus educ: seven titles, 51-55; The artmobile, an experiment in education, Art J, 55; Le Museobus de Virginia Museum of Fine Arts, Mus, Unesco, 55; 25th anniversary in Virginia, 60 & The design game, 71, Mus News. *Mailing Add:* 37 Winster Fax Williamsburg VA 23185

CHRIST-JANER, ARLAND F
PAINTER, PRINTMAKER
b Garland, Nebr, Jan 27, 22. *Study:* Carleton Col, BA, 43, LLD, 67; Yale, BD, 49; Univ Chicago, JD, 52; Coe Col, hon LLD, 61; Monmouth Col, hon LHDm 67; Colo Col, hon LLD, 71; Curry Col, hon LHD, 72. *Work:* Am Repub Ins Co, Des Moines, Iowa; Bankers Trust Co, New York; Hershey Foods Corp, Pa; Montclair Art Mus, NJ; Motion Picture Asn Am, New York; Indianhead Mills, New York; and others. *Exhib:* Nat Print Competition, Auburn Univ, Ala; Nat Print & Drawing Exhib, NMex Univ; Columbia Art League, Mo, 76; one-man shows, Carleton Col, 80, Columbia Col, 81; plus others. *Pos:* Pres, Cornell Col, Boston Univ, New Col & Stephens Col, formerly & Ringling Sch Art & Design, Sarasota, Fla, 84-; dir, Sun Bank, Independent Col Univ Fla, Fla Independent Col Fund; trustee, New Col Found, John & Mable Ringling Mus Art. *Mem:* Am Acad Arts & Scis; Newcomen Soc N Am; Nat Asn Sch Art & Design (future's comt, 2 yrs). *Media:* Graphic. *Mailing Add:* Ringling Sch Art & Design 2700 N Tamiami Trail Sarasota FL 34234

CHRISTO
ARTIST
b Gabrovo, Bulgaria, June 13, 35. *Study:* Fine Arts Acad, Sofia, 52-56, Vienna Fine Arts Acad, Austria, 57. *Work:* The Whitney Mus Am Art, New York; Centre National d'Art et de Culture Georges Pompidou & Musee d'Art Moderne de la Ville, Paris; The Tate Gallery & Victoria and Albert Mus, London; The Hara Mus Contemp Art & The Seibu Mus, Tokyo; Nat Galerie, Berlin; Walker Art Ctr, Minneapolis; Albright-Knox Mus, Buffalo; Kaiser Wilhelm Mus, Krefeld, WGer; Rijks Mus, Kroller-Muller, Otterloo, The Netherlands; Stedelijk Mus, Amsterdam, The Netherlands; Boymans van Beumingen Mus, Rotterdam, The Netherlands. *Exhib:* Valley Curtain (1250-1368' x 185-365'), Grand Hogback, Rifle, Colo, 70-72; Running Fence (18' high, 24 1/2 miles long), Sonoma & Marin Counties, Calif, 72-76; The Wall, Wrapped Roman Wall, V Veneto & Villa Borghese, Rome, 74; Pont Neuf Wapped (440,000 sq ft woven polymide fabric & 42, 900' of rope), Paris, 75-85; Wrapped Walk Ways, Loose Park, Kansas City, Mo, 77-78; The Mastaba of Abu Dhabi, United Arab Emirates, 79; The Gates, Central Park, New York, 80; Surrounded Islands, Biscayne Bay, Miami, Fla, 80-83; The Umbrellas (1340 blue in Ibaraki, Japan & 1760 yellow in Calif), 84-91. *Bibliog:* David Bourdon, Otto Hahn & Pierre Restany (auths), Christo, Edizioni Apollinaire, Milan, 65; Sally Yard & Sam Hunter (auths), Christo: Ocean Front, Princeton Univ Press, NJ, 75; Maysles Brothers/Charlotte Zwerin (dirs), Running Fence (film), 77; Christo: Complete Editions, 1964-1982, Verlag Schellmann & Kluser, Munich/New York Univ Press, 82; Werner Spies (auth), Christo: Surrounded Islands, Biscayne Bay, Greater Miami, Florida, 1980-1983, Dumont Buchverlag, Cologne, WGer, 84; Dominique Laporte (auth), Christo, Art Press/Flammarion, Paris, 85; Maysles Brothers (dirs), The Pont Neuf (film), 86; and many other books and films. *Dealer:* Jeanne-Claude Christo 48 Howard St New York NY 10013. *Mailing Add:* 48 Howard St New York NY 10013

CHRYSSA
SCULPTOR
b Athens, Greece, 1933; US citizen. *Study:* Acad Grande Chaumiere, Paris, 53-54; Calif Sch Fine Art, 54-55. *Work:* Mus Mod Art, Whitney Mus Am Art, Guggenheim Mus, Metrop Mus, New York; Albright-Knox Art Gallery, Buffalo, NY; Walker Art Ctr, Minneapolis; plus others, incl major Europ mus. *Comn:* Skimore, Owings & Merill, Chicago. *Exhib:* One-man shows, Solomon R Guggenheim Mus, 61, Mus Mod Art, New York, 63, Pace Gallery, 66 & 67, Harvard Univ, 68, Galerie Rive Droite, Paris, 69 & Whitney Mus Am Art, New York, 72; Whitney Mus Am Art, New York, 72; Musee de l'Art Moderne de la Ville de Paris, France, 79; Kunsthaus, Zurich, 79; Urban Icons (with catalog), Albright-Knox Art Gallery, Buffalo, NY, 82-83; Leo Castelli, New York, 88 & 91. *Bibliog:* Lucy R Lippard (auth), Pop Art, Praeger, 66; Gregory Battcock (ed), Minimal Art: A Critical Anthology, Dutton, 68; Diane Waldman (auth), Chryssa: Selected Works 1955-1957, Pace Gallery, 68; Sam Hunter (auth), Chryssa, Verlag Gerd Hatje, Stuttgart, WGer, 74; Pierre Restany (auth), Chryssa, Harry Abrams, New York, 77. *Mailing Add:* 565 Broadway New York NY 10012

CHU, GENE
PRINTMAKER, PAINTER
b China, Dec 8, 36; Can citizen. *Study:* Ont Col Art; Art Students League, with Harry Sternberg & Edwin Dickerson; Claremont Grad Sch, MFA. *Work:* Tom Thomson Mem Gallery & Mus Fine Art, Owen Sound, Ont; McMaster Univ; Art Bank of Can Coun, Ottawa; Art Gallery Solvenj Gradec, Yugoslavia; Univ Guelph. *Exhib:* Rockford Int Print Competition, 79; Philadelphia Print Club Biennial Int Open Juried Exhib, 79; Boston World Art Exposition, 79; Ninth Int Miniature Print Competition, 83; Int Exhib Woodcuts & Small Wooden Sculptures, Art Gallery Solvenj Gradec, Yugoslavia, 86; 38th North Am Juried Print Exhib, 86. *Pos:* Assoc Prof. *Teaching:* Instr drawing & printmaking, Mary Washington Col, 68 & 69; assoc prof drawing & printmaking, Univ Guelph, 69- *Awards:* First Prize, Tom Thomson & Mem Gallery & Mus Fine Art Ann Exhib, 72; Purchase Award, Rockford Int Print Competition, 79; Jurors' Commendation Award, 38th NAm Ann Print Exhib. *Mem:* Ont Soc Artist; Print & Drawing Coun Can; Int Graphic Art Found; Asn Difusora Obra Gráfica Int. *Media:* Lithography; Watercolor. *Mailing Add:* Univ Guelph Guelph ON N1G 2W1 Canada

CHU, JULIA NEE
PAINTER
b Shanghai, China, Dec 10, 40 US citizen. *Study:* Univ Calif Los Angeles, BA, 78, MFA, 81. *Work:* Meyers Bianche McConnell Law, Merrill Lynch Investment, Sidly & Austin Law, Fred Silverman Productions, Lathan Watkin Law, Los Angeles, Calif; Hong Kong Mus, Sumitomo Co, Osaka, Japan; Trammel Crow Develop Co, Los Angeles; Gibraltar Savings, Houston, Tex; Cent Plaza Bldg, Hong Kong. *Exhib:* Turning to the Landscape, Univ Southern Calif, Santa Monica, 87; one-person show, Taipei Fine Arts Mus, Taiwan, 89; Am Cult Ctr, Taipei, Taiwan, 90; Sydney Univ, Australia, 92; Macau Mus Invitation Show, 92; and others. *Teaching:* Grad, Teaching fel, Univ Calif, Los Angeles, 80-81. *Awards:* Ford Found Grant, 80. *Bibliog:* Sylvia Moore (ed), Yesterday and Tomorrow: California Women Artists, Mid-March Arts, New York, 89; Peter Frank (forward), exhib catalog, Taipei Fine Arts Mus, 89. *Mem:* Asian Am Art Ctr, New York; Art Action, Hong Kong. *Media:* Acrylic, Oil. *Dealer:* Dunlap-Freidenrich Fine Arts Ltd 177 Riverside Dr Newport Beach CA 92663; Alisan Fine Arts Ltd 315 Princes Bldg 10 Chater Rd Hong Kong. *Mailing Add:* 1520 17th St Santa Monica CA 90404

CHURCH, C HOWARD
ADMINISTRATOR, EDUCATOR
b South Sioux City, Nebr, May 1, 04. *Study:* Art Inst Chicago, with Boris Ainsfeld, John Norton & William P Welsh, 28-32, BFA, 35; Univ Chicago, BA, 38; Ohio State Univ, MA, 39. *Comn:* Murals (including libr panel Canterbury Pilgrims), Morgan Park Mil Acad, Chicago, 32-36. *Exhib:* One-man shows, Mulvane Art Mus, Thayer Mus Art, Univ Nebr, Joslyn Art Mus & Kresge Art Ctr, East Lansing, Mich; and others. *Pos:* Dir, Morgan Park Sch Art, Chicago, 33-36; dir, Mulvane Art Mus, Washburn Univ, 40-45. *Teaching:* Head art dept, Washburn Univ, 40-45; head art dept, Mich State Univ, 45-60, prof, 60-72; retired. *Awards:* Mich Fine Arts Medal, 63 & Purchase Award, mem exhib, 66, Mich Acad Sci, Arts & Lett; Print Purchase Award, Mich Artists Exhib, Mich Educ Asn, 69 & 70; and others. *Mem:* Am Asn Univ Profs. *Media:* Painter, Printmaker. *Mailing Add:* 271 Lexington Ave East Lansing MI 48823

CHURCH, MAUDE
PAINTER, EDUCATOR
b Berkeley, Calif, June 15, 49. *Study:* Antioch Col, Yellow Springs, Ohio, 69-70; Calif Col Arts & Crafts, Oakland, BFA, 72; Byam Shaw Col Art, London, Eng, MA, 73. *Comn:* Red & Yellow (mural), Calif Sch Prof Psychology, San Francisco, Calif, 74; Curved Space (mural), comn by J V Ferrero Jr, Palos Verdes, Calif, 76; Oasis (triptych), comn by Pamela & Joe Bonino, Palm Springs, Calif, 84. *Exhib:* Retrospective, Riverside Art Mus, Calif, 78; Starburst: Maude Church, Bank Am World Hq, San Francisco, 80; Exchange Exhib: San Francisco-Berlin, Amerikahaus Gallery, Berlin, Ger, 81; California Artists, 81, Oakland Mus, Calif; 3rd Ann Women's Nat, Triangle Gallery, Washington, DC, 82; Marine Art, Coos Art Mus, Coos Bat, Oregon, 88. *Pos:* North Calif Artists Equity Asn, pres, 78-79; adv bd dir, Bay Area Lawyers Arts, 78-79; nat bd dirs, Women's Caucus for Art, 89-92. *Teaching:* Adj fac art, Calif Sch Prof Psychology, Berkeley, 74-90; assoc prof art, Lone Mountain Col, San Francisco, Calif, 75-76. *Awards:* Fine Art Merit Award, San Francisco Arts Festival, 77; Outstanding Young Woman of the Year, 79; Sculpture Award, small sculpture exhib, Medocino Art Ctr, Calif, 90. *Bibliog:* Arthur Bloomfield (auth), City's art in the right place, San Francisco Examiner, 9/28/78; Sylvie Roder (auth), Tight formats, Artweek, 10/15/83; Kim Anno (auth), A propensity for animals, Bay Area Reporter, 9/12/85. *Mem:* Women's Caucus Art; Artists Equity Asn (pres, 78-79); Pro Arts, Oakland, Calif. *Media:* Acrylic, Asemblage Artist. *Publ:* Illusr, covers, Cathexis J, Vol 1-3, 77-81 & album cover, Holly Near, Watch Out, 84; Two posters, The Nature Co, 87. *Mailing Add:* 5504 C San Pablo Oakland CA 94608

CHURCHILL, DIANE
PAINTER
b Bronxville, NY, Jan 8, 41. *Study:* Wellesley Col, BA(art hist); Brooklyn Mus Art Sch; Hunter Col, MA(painting). *Work:* Chase Manhattan Bank Collection, New York; Reliance Group Inc, Mass; Jay Hambridge Art Found, Rabun Gap, Ga; Weehawken Twp; Grolier Publ; Wellesly Col Collections. *Comn:* Geraldine Dodge Found. *Exhib:* Soho 20 Gallery, 76, 78 & 80; Stevens Inst Technol Libr Gallery, 79; NJ State Mus, Trenton, 80; Bronx Mus, New York; Air Gallery & Henry St Arts for Living Ctr, NY, 86; William Carlos Williams Ctr, Rutherford, NJ; St Peter's Church at Citicorp Ctr, NY. *Pos:* Artist catalyst, Brigade-In-Action, New York, 68-73; publ & ed, Fourth St, 71-73; field rep, Visual Arts Dept, NY State Coun Arts, New York, 76-77. *Teaching:* Teacher art, Hudson Sch, Hoboken, NJ, 79-88; instr art, Fieldston Sch, Riverdale, NY. *Awards:* Yaddo, 68; NJ State Coun Arts Fel, 79-80 & 85-86; Karoly Found, Vence, France, 88. *Bibliog:* Helen Harris (auth), Experimenting with the Purity of Pastels, New York Times, 11/16/86; Naomi Kenan (auth), First the Probing Blue Eyes Stop You, Gold Coast Mag, NJ, 3/88; Pat Van Gelder (auth), Animals as subjects in contemp art, Am Artist Mag, 5/89. *Mailing Add:* 267 Piermont Ave South Nyack NY 10960-4617

CHUTJIAN, SETA LEONIE See Injeyan, Seta L

CHWAST, SEYMOUR
GRAPHIC ARTIST, ILLUSTRATOR
b New York, NY, Aug 18, 31. *Study:* Cooper Union; Parsons Sch Design, Hon PhD. *Work:* Mus of Mod Art, New York; Cooper-Hewitt Mus, Smithsonian Inst; Libr Congress; Israel Mus; Gutenberg Mus, Mainz, Ger. *Exhib:* Musee Des Arts Decoratif, The Louvre, Paris, France, 71 & 73; A Century of Am Illus, Brooklyn Mus, 73; Galerie Delpire, Paris, 81; Kunstgerverbe Mus, Zurich, 81; Gutenberg Mus, Mainz, Ger; one-man shows, Cooper Union, New York, 86; Jack Gallery, New York, 87; Lustrare Gallery, New York, 91; Bradley Gallery, Milwaukee, 92. *Pos:* Publ & art dir, The Push Pin Graphic Bi-Monthly Mag, 56-80; dir, Push Pin Studios, New York, 75-82; partner, Pushpin Lubalin Peckolick, Inc, 82-86; pres & dir, Pushpin Group Inc, 82. *Teaching:* Instr design & illus, Cooper Union, 75-81. *Awards:* St Gardens Medal, Cooper Union; Several medals, NY Art Dir Club; Art Dir Club Hall of Fame, 83; Am Inst Graphic Arts Medal, 85. *Bibliog:* T Nishio (auth), Seymour Chwast, Shinkosha Publ, Tokyo, 74; Mann Mit Nase (man with nose): Seymour Chwast, Frankfurter Allgemeine Zeitung, 81. *Mem:* Am Inst of Graphic Arts; Art Dir Club of New York; Graphic Artists Guild; Alliance Graphique Internationale. *Publ:* Designer & illusr, Pancake King, Delacorte Press, 70 & Limerickricks, Random House, 72; designer, Sweetheart Book and Others, Avon Bks, 75; designer & illusr, Tall City, Wide Country, Viking Press, 83; co-ed, Art of New York, 83, Left Handed Designer, 85, Graphic Style, 88; Happy Birthday Bach, Doubleday, 85; auth, Harry's Bath, Bantam Press, 89. *Mailing Add:* c/o Push Pin Group Inc 215 Park Ave S New York NY 10003

CIANCIO, JUNE (KIRKPATRICK)
PAINTER, INSTRUCTOR
b Wilkinsburg, Pa, June 26, 20. *Study:* Carnegie-Mellon Univ, BFA, 42; Columbia Teachers Col; Hans Hoffman Sch; Art Students League, with Will Barnet. *Work:* Parrish Art Mus, Southampton, NY; Nassau Community Col, Garden City, NY; Citibank New York. *Exhib:* One-person shows, Parrish Art Mus, 74 & Long Beach Mus, NY; 38th Ann, Audubon Artists, New York, 80; 27th Ann, Nat Soc Painters Casein & Acrylic, New York, 80; 85th Ann, Catherine Lorillard Wolfe Art Club, New York, 81. *Teaching:* Instr watercolor, Parrish Art Mus, Southampton, NY, 76-79. *Awards:* Award of Excellence, Huntington Township Art League, 79; Grumbacher Silver Medal, Nat Soc Painters Casein & Acrylic, 80; Stefan Hirsch Award, Audubon Artists, 80; Paul Pazinas Award, Allied Artists Am, 83. *Mem:* Guild Hall; assoc mem Audubon Artists; Nat Soc Painters Casein & Acrylic. *Media:* Acrylic, Watercolor. *Dealer:* Gallery East 257 Montauk Highway East Hampton NY 11937. *Mailing Add:* 13 W Argonne Rd Hampton Bays NY 11946

CIANFONI, EMILIO
CONSERVATOR, PAINTER
b Rome, Italy, Oct 9, 46; US citizen. *Study:* Drawing, painting & restoration with Giustino Caporali, 58-63, Manieri Art Inst, 60-63, Accad di Belle Arti, 64-66; conserv of paintings at Inst Centrale del Restauro, 66-67, Rome; Art Students League, New York, 70-72; Baldwin Sch (glazes chemistry), New York, 73. *Comn:* Paintings, Lowenbrau Co, Munich, Bavaria, Ger, 67; painting & sculpture, comn by Pacifici Family, Rome, Italy, 67; mural, Church Hosp Comples, Vilalba, Italy, 69; Bicentennial Coins Competition, Metrop Mus of Art, New York, 74. *Exhib:* Galeria Modigliani, 63, 20th Century Competition, City Bldg, 64 & Mus of Mod Art, 65, Rome; New Talent (2 shows), Betty Parsons Gallery, New York, 74; Primitive & Contemporary Art, Tucson, Ariz, Betty Parsons Gallery, 75; UN Group Am Exhib, New York, Truman Gallery, 77. *Pos:* Design painter-conservator, Gucci Shops, Rome & New York, 68-70; sr craftsman, Alva Reproductions, New York, 70-72; restorer, Metrop Mus of Art, New York, 72-74; chief conservator, Vizcaya Mus & Gardens, 75- *Awards:* First Prize, 20th Anniversary of Italian Partisans Competition, Rome, 64; Second Prize, Ciac Poetry & Arts Competition, Rome, 66. *Mem:* Am Inst Conserv Hist & Artistic Work; Int Inst Conserv Hist & Artistic Work; Asn Preserv Technol. *Media:* Mixed. *Dealer:* Truman Gallery 38 E 57th St New York NY 10022. *Mailing Add:* 272 NW 36th St Miami FL 33137

CIARDIELLO, JOSEPH G
ILLUSTRATOR
b Staten Island, NY, July 22, 53. *Study:* Parsons Sch Design, with Maurice Sendak & Jim Spanfeller, BFA, 75. *Exhib:* Soc Illusrs Ann Exhib, New York, 74-92; Soc Publ Designers, New York, 79 & 86; Art Dirs Ann, Art Dirs Club, New York, 80 & 87; Graphic Art & Illustration, Quebec City, Can, 85; The Illustrator & The Environment, Soc of Illusrs, New York, 90; Sci/Fi & Fantasy, Soc Illusrs, 92. *Teaching:* Guest lectr illus, Fashion Inst Technol, Parsons Sch Design & Montclair State Col, 80- & Moore Col Art; adj prof illus, Montclair State Col, Upper Montclair, 81; co-instr illus, Parsons Sch Design, 87. *Awards:* Silver Award, Soc Publ Designers, 79; Silver Medal, Soc of Illusrs, 92. *Bibliog:* Tom Goss (auth), Mini-portfolio Joe Ciardiello, Print Mag, 84; Marion Muller (auth), Drawing pens & drumsticks, Upper & Lower Case, 84; Scott Gutterman (auth), article, How Mag, 1-2/87; article, Idea Mag, Japan, No 208, 88 & No 219, 90. *Mem:* Graphic Artists Guild; Soc Illustrators. *Media:* Pen & Ink, Watercolor. *Publ:* illus, Around the World in 80 Days, 88; Moby Dick, 89, 20,000 Leagues Under the Sea, 90, Dr Jekyll & Mr Hyde, 91, Reader's Digest; Art for Survival, Graphis Press, 92; The Savage Mirror: Contemporary Caricature, Watson Guftill, 92. *Mailing Add:* 2182 Clove Rd Staten Island NY 10305

CIARROCHI, RAY
PAINTER, EDUCATOR
b Chicago, Ill. *Study:* Chicago Acad Fine Arts; Wash Univ, BFA, with Fred Conway; Boston Univ, MFA. *Work:* Ciba-Geigy Collection, Ardsley, NY; Citibank, New York; Owens-Corning Glass Found; Am Tel & Tel; Brooklyn Mus. *Exhib:* One-man shows, Tibor De Nagy Gallery, 71, 72, 74, 76, 78, 80, 83 & 85, Fischbach Gallery, 86 & 89 & landscapes 1978-91, Marsh Gallery, Modlin Fine Arts Ctr, Univ Richmond, Va; Am Watercolors, 1800 to the Present, Brooklyn Mus, NY, 76; Works on Paper from the Ciba-Geigy Collection, Neuberger Mus, Purchase, NY, 77; The Face of the Land, Southern Alleghenies Mus Art, Loretto, Pa, 88; Painterly Realism, traveling exhib, Houston, Tex; and others. *Teaching:* Instr painting & drawing, Parsons Sch Design, New York, 66-71; adj prof, Sch Arts, Columbia Univ, 69-71 & 76- & Baruch Col, City Univ New York, 76-; instr painting, Md Inst Col Art, 71-72; instr, Brooklyn Col, 72-76. *Awards:* Fulbright Grant to Italy, 63-64; Tiffany Grant, 67; Ingraham Merrill Found Grant, 77 & 82-83. *Bibliog:* James R Mellow (auth) & Hilton Kramer (auth), rev in New York Times, 4/1/72 & 3/2/74; Richard Waller (auth), Ray Ciarrochi - Landscapes 1978-91. *Media:* Oil, Pastel. *Dealer:* Katharina Rich Perlow Gallery 560 Broadway New York NY 10012. *Mailing Add:* 55 Bethune St Apt D1004 New York NY 10014

CICANSKY, VICTOR
SCULPTOR
b Regina, Sask, Can, Feb 12, 35. *Study:* Univ Sask, Saskatoon, BEd, 64; Univ Sask, Regina, BA, 67; Univ Calif, Davis, MFA, 70, with Bob Arneson & Roy DeForrest. *Work:* Sask Govt Arts Bd; Can Coun Art Bank; Sacramento State Col; Mus of Mod Art, Tokyo, Japan; Mus of Mod Art, Montreal; Mus Fine Arts, Montreal; The Glenbow Mus, Calgary; and many others. *Comn:* The Grain Bin (group scultpure), Sask Olympics Art Comt, Montreal, 76; The Old Working Class (sculpture), Saskatoon, 77 & The New Working Class (sculpture), 81, Sask Govt; Regina-My World (sculpture), Co-op Life Insurance Co Bldg, Regina, Sask, 79; The Garden Fence (mural), Can Broadcasting Corp, 83-84; Founders Awards (sculpture), Sask Writer's Guild, 84; Heritage Seeds (sculpture), Sask Govt, 85. *Exhib:* Contemp Ceramics, Mus of Fine Arts, Kyoto, Japan, 71; Int Ceramics, Victoria & Albert Mus, London, Eng, 72; Trajectories 73, Musee de Art Moderne de Ville de Paris, France, 73; Espace 5, Montreal, Que, 74; Fired Clay Show, Greater Victoria Art Gallery, Victoria, BC, 75; New York Clay, Monique Knowlton Gallery, New York, 75; one-man show, MacKenzie Gallery, Regina, Glenbow Mus, Waterloo Art Gallery & Mendel Art Gallery, 83, Susan Whitney Gallery, 84, Woltjen/Udell Gallery, Edmonton, 85 & Grunwald Gallery, Toronto, 85; and many others. *Teaching:* From assoc prof art to prof, Univ Regina, Sask, 70-85. *Awards:* Can Coun grants/travel & work, 68, 69, 71, 74 & 83; Kingsley Ann Award/Sculpture, Sacramento, 69; Royal Albert Award, Ceramic Sculpture, Toronto, 71. *Bibliog:* Personal bests, Can Art, fall 85; Christopher Hume (auth), Voluptuous clay veggies set off titters at the Grunwald's, Toronto Star, 10/11/85; Karen Wilken (auth), Sculpture, Can Encyl, 85. *Media:* Clay. *Publ:* Contribr to Arts Mag, Fall 70, Mus of Mod Art J, Amsterdam, 4/71, Arts Can, 5/73; Art & Artists, 8/73, Time, 4/73 & ArtsCan, 230/231; Hand & Eye, Glorious Mud (television series), CBC Television, 2/16/84. *Mailing Add:* Dept Visual Arts Univ Regina Regina SK S4S 0A2 Canada

CICCONE, AMY NAVRATIL
LIBRARIAN
b Mich, Sept 19, 50. *Study:* Wayne State Univ, 72, BA(art hist); Univ Mich, 73, AMLS, specializing in art librarianship. *Collections Arranged:* Hidden treasures, The Chrysler Mus, 85-86; Samuel Johnson (auth), Univ Southern Calif, 88. *Pos:* Librn, Norton Simon Mus, Pasadena, Calif, 74-81; ed, Art Librs Soc of NAm Directory of Members, 75-77; chief librn, Chrysler Mus, Jean Outland Chrysler Libr, Norfolk, Va, 81-88; Archit & Fine Arts Libr, Univ Southern Calif; head librn, Archit & Fine Arts Libr, Univ Southern Calif, Los Angeles, 88- *Mem:* Art Libr Soc NAm (mem chmn, 75-77, mem coordr, 79, facilities standards comt, 86); Dec Arts Roundtable (coord, 91-). *Interests:* Decorative Arts, Medieval Art/Artichecture. *Publ:* Contribr, Art Libr Soc NAm Newsletter, 75-77; Art Documentation, 83-; contrib ed, Art Reference Serv Quarterly, 90- *Mailing Add:* 12718 Westminster Ave Mar Vista CA 90066

CICERO, CARMEN L
PAINTER
Study: Newark State Col, NJ, BS; Hunter Col, New York. *Work:* Guggenheim Mus, New York; Mus Mod Art, New York; Hirshhorn Mus, Washington, DC; Whitney Mus, New York; Metropolitan Mus Art, New York. *Exhib:* 6 Whitney Mus Anns, 55-66; one-man shows, Peridot Gallery; Premiere Bienale de Paris, France; Graham Gallery, New York; June Kelly Gallery, New York. *Teaching:* Mem fac, Sarah Lawrence Col, 59-68; instr, Montclair State Col, 60- *Awards:* Guggenheim Found Fel, 57 & 63; Purchase Prize, Ford Found, 65. *Media:* Oil, Acrylic. *Dealer:* June Kelly Gallery 591 Broadway New York NY 10012. *Mailing Add:* 268 Bowery New York NY 10012

CIFOLELLI, ALBERTA (ALBERTA CARMELLA LAMB)
PAINTER, EDUCATOR
b Erie, Pa, Aug 19, 31. *Study:* Cleveland Inst Art, dipl(painting), 53; Kent State Univ, BS(art educ), 55; Fairfield Univ, MA, 75 (commun). *Work:* Cleveland Art Asn Rental Collection, Cleveland Mus Art; Smithsonian Inst, Washington, DC; Housatonic Mus Art, Bridgeport, Conn; Stamford Mus; Nat Mus Women Arts. *Comn:* Mitsubishi Capital, Rockefeller Ctr. *Exhib:* one-woman shows, Noho Gallery, 82, Kaber Gallery, New York, 83, St Mary's Col Md, Univ Conn & Reece Galleries, New York; A State of Artists, Invitational, Aldrich Mus Contemp Art, Ridgefield, Conn; The Natural Image Invitational, Stamford Mus, Conn, 88; Harmon-Meek Gallery, Naples, Fla, 89; 400 Years of Women Artists, touring exhib, Nat Mus Women, Washington,DC; The Connecticut Biennial, Bruce Mus; and others. *Pos:* Vpres, Westport Weston Arts Coun, Conn, 78-79; dir, New Eng 31st Ann, New Canaan, Conn; chairwoman, Inst Visual Arts, 88-89; artists-in-residence, Djerassi Found, 86. *Teaching:* Instr painting & life drawing, Cleveland Inst Art, 67-70; prof life drawing & design, Sacred Heart Univ, 79-; prof, Grad Sch Painting, Col New Rochelle. *Awards:* Second Prize, Cleveland Mus Art, 59 & 65; Doris Kreindler Mem Award, Nat Soc Painters in Casein & Acrylic, 74; four grants, Conn Comn Arts; Residency to live and work at Djerassi Found, Woodside, Calif, Summer 86; Salute to Women Award, 88. *Bibliog:* Margaret Barnett (auth), Stamford Advocak 3/89; A Journal of Women, Running Press; Vivian Raynor (auth), Fullhouse at Gallery in Marlborough; and others. *Mem:* Visual Artist & Gallery Asn; Westport Weston Arts Coun (vis arts chmn, 76-); trustee Silvermine Guild Artists (bd dirs, 78-83); Women's Caucus for Art, NY Chap. *Media:* Oil, Pastel. *Dealer:* Reece Galleries New York NY; Branchville Soho Gallery Old Main Hwy Georgetown CT 06829. *Mailing Add:* 8 Plover Ln Westport CT 06880

CIKOVSKY, NICOLAI, JR
HISTORIAN, EDUCATOR
b New York, NY, Feb 11, 33. *Study:* Harvard Col, AB; Harvard Univ, AM & PhD. *Collections Arranged:* Sanford Robinson Gifford, Univ Tex Art Mus, 70-71; The White Marmorean Flock; Nineteenth Century American Women Neoclassical Sculptors, Vassar Col Art Gallery, 72; William Merritt Chase: Summers at Shinecock (catalog), 87; Raphaelle Peale Still Lifes (catalog), 88; Paintings, Manoogian Collection, 89. *Pos:* Dir, Vassar Col Art Gallery, 71-74; cur Am & Brit Painting Nat Gallery Art, Washington, DC, 83- , Dep Sr Cur,

90. *Teaching:* Assoc prof art, Vassar Col, 71-74; prof art, Univ NMex, 74-83. *Awards:* Guggenheim Fel, 78-79; Kress Sr Fel, Ctr Advan Study in Visual Arts, Nat Gallery Art. *Mem:* Col Art Asn. *Res:* Nineteenth & twentieth century American painting and sculpture. *Publ:* Auth, George Inness, 71 & Life & Work of George Inness, 77; ed, Samuel F B Morse's Lectures on the Affinity of Painting with the Other Fine Arts, 83; coauth, George Inness, 85; Winslow Homer, 90; Winston Homer Watercolors, 91. *Mailing Add:* Nat Gallery Art 4th St & Constitution Ave Washington DC 20565

CILELLA, SALVATORE G, JR
MUSEUM DIRECTOR, ADMINISTRATOR
b Chicago, Ill, Oct 19, 41. *Study:* Univ Notre Dame, BA, 63, MA, 66, State Univ NY, MA, 71. *Pos:* Asst to the dir, NY State Hist Asn, 73-76; develop officer, Smithsonian Inst, 81-87; exec dir, Columbia Mus Art, 87- *Mem:* Am Asn Mus. *Publ:* Auth, Tavern Signs in collections of NY State Hist Asn, The Clarion, 78; SFB Morse Paintings in collections of NY State Hist Asn, The Clarion, 78; 18th Century Views of Bethlehem Pa, Pa Heritage, 80; Emphasizing human elements in fund raising, Mus News, 87; Fundraising for small & mid-sized museums, Am Asn Mus 87. *Mailing Add:* Columbia Mus Art 1112 Bull St Columbia SC 29201

CIMBALO, ROBERT W
PAINTER, PRINTMAKER
b Utica, NY. *Study:* Pratt Inst, Brooklyn; Syracuse Univ; Socita Di Dante Alighari, Belle Arte & Univ Studi Roma, Rome. *Work:* Kirkland Art Ctr, Clinton, NY; Munson-Williams-Proctor Inst, Utica, NY; Syracuse Univ; State Univ NY Col Cortland; Pratt Inst. *Comn:* Portrait of Past Pres, Utica Col, NY. *Exhib:* Dante's Inferno Traveling Exhib to various cols and univs; many works included in public & private exhibs. *Teaching:* Assoc prof art hist & studio art, Utica Col, Syracuse Univ, 78- *Awards:* Targo D'oro Premio D'italia, 86. *Media:* Oil. *Publ:* Illusr, East Utica, Munson Williams Proctor Inst, fall 71; Frank, Catherine and Vito, Black Locust Press, 79. *Mailing Add:* 1602 Harrison Ave Utica NY 13501

CINTRON, JOSEPH M
PAINTER, EDUCATOR
b Ponce, PR, Aug 4, 21. *Study:* Univ Dayton, BA, 43; Ohio State Univ, 51; Cleveland Inst Art, dipl, 54; with Robert Brackman, Madison, Conn, 62; Art Students League, with Sidney Dickinson, David Leffel, Howard Sanden & Gustav Rehberger. *Work:* Univ Hospitals Cleveland; La Fortaleza, San Juan, Puerto Rico; First Federal Bank, Cleveland; The Cleveland Clinic, Ohio; Cleveland Play House; and others. *Comn:* Portrait, Eric Fromm, Case Western Reserve Univ, Cleveland, Ohio, 69; Potrait, Gov Luis a Ferre, La Fortaleza, San Juan, PR, 74; Potrait Dr Dudley Allen, Univ Hospitals, Cleveland, 80; Potrait Bishop Gregory Rozman, Klagenfurt, Austria, 85; Potrait Raymond O'Neill, Cleveland Playhouse, 86; and others. *Exhib:* Canton Art Inst Regional, 65-69; Cleveland Mus Art Regional, 69; Nat, Butler Inst Am Art, 70; Sch of Fine Arts, Willoughby, Ohio, 72; Inst Platform Asn, Washington, DC, 81-85; Northern Ohio Invitational, 83; Kuban Galleries, Cleveland, 84; and others. *Teaching:* Prof painting & drawing, Cleveland Inst Art, 56-, Cooper Sch Art, 63-82, Sch Fine Arts, Willoughby, Ohio, 82- *Awards:* Painting Award, Cuyahoga Valley Art Ctr, 67 & 68; First Place, 81, Popular Award, 83 & Second Place, 84, Int Platform Asn; and others. *Bibliog:* Marie Kirkwood (auth), Cintron trademark is realism, Sun Press, Cleveland, 8/5/71; Gloria Borras (auth), Pintar Rostros es Captar Almas, Puerto Rico Ilustrado, San Juan, 3/30/75. *Mem:* Int Platform Asn. *Media:* Oil, Pastels. *Dealer:* The Bonfoey Galleries Cleveland Ohio. *Mailing Add:* Cleveland Inst Art 11141 E Blvd Cleveland OH 44106

CIPRIANO, MICHAEL R
PAINTER, EDUCATOR
b Waterbury, Conn, Jan 15, 42. *Study:* Cent Conn State Col, BS, 67, MS, 69; Univ Conn, 70; Columbia Univ, EdD, 77. *Work:* New Brit Mus Am Art, Conn; Richard Judd Collection, Cent Conn State Univ, New Britain; Howell Cheney Vocational Inst, Manchester, Conn; Manchester Community Col, Manchester, Conn; Wheaton Col, Norton, Mass. *Comn:* Large painting canvas, 84 & installation six large mural paintings, Conn Comn on the Arts, Manchester, 84. *Exhib:* Conn Painters Four, New Britain Mus Am Art, 81; Wadsworth Atheneum, Hartford, Conn, 82; Works on Paper, Cartwright Hall Gallery, Bradford, Eng, 84; Aetna Inst Gallery, Hartford, 84; Hewlett-Woodmere Gallery, NY, 85; Atria Gallery, Hartford, 86; Watson Gallery, Norton, Mass, 89; Bushnell Gallery, Conn Artists Showcase & Conn Coun Arts, Hartford, 89. *Pos:* Bd dirs, Artworks Gallery, Hartford, 81-83 & New Brit Arts Coun, 80-; Univ Arts Coun, New York, 82; Fine Arts, Cent Conn State Univ, 88. *Teaching:* Prof fine arts, Cent Conn State Univ, 73-86, chmn dept art, 86- *Awards:* Best in Show, 84 & Gen Elec Prize, Conn Watercolor Soc; Purchase Award, Conn Comn on the Arts, 84. *Bibliog:* Bernard Hanson (auth), Museum of American Art, New Britain, Saltbox Gallery & West Hartford-Michael Cipriano, Art in New England, 81; William Zimmer (auth), Diverse show opens gallery, 11/25/84 & Charlotte Libov (auth), Public art thrives with State support, 4/27/86, New York Times; New abstracts display strength, Emotion in Manchester Exhib, Hartford Courant, 10/89. *Mem:* New Brit Arts Coun (bd dirs, 79-86); Artists Equity Asn. *Publ:* Auth, Artist, an unused resource, Sch Arts, 72; Arts: Frills or fundamentals, CAEA, 77. *Mailing Add:* 76 Pendleton New Britain CT 06053

CISNEROS, FLORENCIO GARCIA See Garcia, Frank

CITRON, HARVEY LEWIS
SCULPTOR
b New York City, June 26, 42. *Study:* Pratt Inst, Brooklyn, BFA, 65, Academia di Belli Arti, Rome, Italy, 68. *Comn:* St John Baptist, Archdiocese of Philadelphia, Pa, 76. *Exhib:* Contemp Am Realism Since 1960, travelling exhib in US & Europe, 81-83; Neo-objective Sculpture, Dart Gallery, Chicago, 82; Artists Choice: First 8 Years, Artists Choice Gallery, New York, 85; Works on Paper, Tianjin Acad Fine Arts, Tianjun, China, 85; Group Sculpture/Painting, Union Club, New York, 89; Works on Paper, Drawing Univ Arts, Phildelphia, 89; group exhib, Artists Notebook Preliminary Study, Univ Arts, Phildelphia, 91, Painting Sculpture Grad Sch Figurative Art, New York Acad Art, 92, 18 Sculptors, Philadelphia Art Alliance, Philadelphia, 92. *Teaching:* Adj assoc prof sculpture, Univ Arts, 81-89; assoc prof sculpture, NY Acad Art, 87-89. *Bibliog:* Hilton Kramer (auth), Five gallery realist show, New York Times, 80; F H Goodyear Jr (auth), Contemporary American Realism Since 1960, New York Graphic Soc, 81; A G Artner (auth), Dart displays contemporary view of human form, Chicago Tribune, 82. *Media:* Bronze, Clay. *Mailing Add:* 57 Warren St New York NY 10007

CIVALE, BIAGIO A
PRINTMAKER, PAINTER
b Rome, Italy, Aug 11, 35. *Study:* Acad Grande Chaumiere, Paris, 53-55; Fine Arts Acad, Rome, dipl(art educ), 58; NY Univ, 83-90; State Univ NY, Purchase, 84. *Work:* Gabinetto Naz Stampe, Rome; Mod Sacred Art Gallery, Montecatini Mus, Florence, Italy; Argenton-Sur-Creuse Mus, France; Mus Espanol Arte Contemp Madrid, Spain; Mod Mus, Stockholm; Sforza Castel Pub Collection of Prints, Milan, Italy. *Comn:* Large Panels for Ital Air Force Club, Cagliari, Italy, 58; Large Panels for NATO Ctr, Chateauroux, France, 62; Crucifixion for Sacrestia, Scarperia Church, Florence, Italy, 74; New Testament & Christmas, Dicomano Church, Florence, Italy, 75. *Exhib:* Naz Gioventu, Palazzo Barberini, Rome, 53-55 & 58; Ecole Francaise, Mus Beaux Arts, Paris, 55; Art Libre, Palais Beaux Arts, Paris, 55-57; 42 yr retrospective, Yonkers Educ & Cult Ctr, New York, 92; 40 yr retrospective, Palazzo Ranghiasci, Gubbio, 90; San Ban Kan Ginza Gallery, Tokyo, Japan, 92; Zhejang Acad Fine Arts, Hangzhou, Peoples Republic of China, 92. *Pos:* Art critic, 50-90; cur, 74-93. *Teaching:* Instr art educ, Roosevelt High Sch, Yonkers, NY, 79 & 80. *Awards:* Third place, Sea Heritage Marine Art, Southport, NY, 88. *Bibliog:* Marzio Bugatti (auth), monogr, 70 & Puck Kroese (auth), Civale's Graphics (monogr), 70, Bugatti Ed; Luigi Servolini (auth), Incisori D'Italia, EIA, Milano, 74; Biagio Civale, Woodcuts and Linocuts, 1950-1990, Edition Heliodor, Westbury, NY, 90. *Media:* Miscellaneous Media. *Dealer:* Castillon Fine Arts 159 Madison Ave New York NY 10016. *Mailing Add:* 311 Lee Ave Yonkers NY 10705

CIVITELLO, JOHN PATRICK
PAINTER
b Paterson, NJ, Aug 17, 39. *Study:* William Paterson Col, BA, 61; NY Univ, MA, 62. *Work:* Nat Mus Am Art-Smithsonian Inst, Washington, DC; Monterey Peninsula Mus Art, Calif; 3M Co, St Paul, Minn; NBC-TV, New York; Lloyd's Bank, Calif; Comput Sci Corp, Los Angeles. *Exhib:* 30th Biennial Am Art, Corcoran Gallery Art, Washington, DC, 67; What's Happening in Soho, Univ Md Art Gallery, 71; one-man show, Art Club Chicago, 74; Am Acad Arts & Lett Ann, 76; Drawing Today in New York, Sewall Art Gallery, Houston, Tex & Dayton Art Inst, Ohio; and others. *Pos:* Art project dir, Great Falls Historic District, Paterson, NJ, 78. *Awards:* Prix-de-Rome, Italy, 68-70; Creative Artists Pub Serv Grant, Cult Coun Found, 72; Childe Hassam Purchase Award, Am Acad Arts & Lett, 76. *Bibliog:* E Bilardello (auth), Pittori Americani a Roma, Margutta-Periodico d'Arte Contemporanea, Rome, 70; article in Arts Mag, 7/75. *Mem:* Am Acad Rome Alumni Asn; Foundation for the Community Artists, NY. *Media:* Acrylic. *Mailing Add:* 3239 N Arrowhead Ave San Bernardino CA 92405

CIVITICO, BRUNO
PAINTER, EDUCATOR
b Dignano D'Istria, Italy, Sept, 1, 42; US citizen. *Study:* Rutgers Univ, 60; Pratt Inst, BFA, 66; Ind Univ, MFA, 68. *Work:* Bayly Mus, Univ Va, Charlottesville; Boston Pub Libr; Chemical Bank & Claude Bernard Galleries, New York, NY. *Comn:* Silkscreen poster, NH Comn Arts, Theater by the Sea, Portsmouth, NH, 80. *Exhib:* Brooklyn College Faculty Past & Present, Davis & Long & Schoelkopf Gallery, New York, 77; Realism and Metaphor, USF Art Galleries, Tampa, Fla, 80; Narrative Painting, Alan Frumkin, New York, 81; Cleveland Mus Ann, Ohio, 83; one-man shows, Robert Schoelkopf Gallery, New York, 72, 74, 77, 80 & 84, Manchester Inst Art & Sci, NH, 87 & Contemp Realist Gallery, San Francisco, 90 & 92; and others. *Teaching:* Instr, Pratt Inst, 69; lectr, Brooklyn Col, 71, Princeton Univ, 72, Boston Univ, 79, Sch Art, Yale Univ, 82, Washington Univ, St Louis, 85 & New York Acad Art, 91; asst prof, Univ NH, 73-79; vis artist, Tyler Sch Art, Philadelphia, 80-81 & Cleveland Inst Art, 82-83; adj asst prof painting, Queens Col, NY, 83-85. *Awards:* Prize Painting, Louis Comfort Tiffany Found, 80; Nat Endowment Arts Fel, 81; Fel, Ingram Merill Found, 89; and others. *Bibliog:* Edward Lucie-Smith (auth), American Art Now, William & Morrow, 85; Charles Jencks (auth), Post Modernism, Rizzoli, 87; John L Ward (auth), American Realist Painting 1945-1980, UMI Res Press, 89. *Media:* Oil. *Publ:* Auth, An analysis of recent landscape and narrative paintings by Gabriel Laderman, Am Artist, 86. *Mailing Add:* 2 Wragg Sq Charleston SC 29403-6209

CLAGUE, JOHN ROGERS
SCULPTOR
b Cleveland, Ohio, Mar 14, 28. *Study:* Cleveland Inst Art, BFA. *Work:* Cleveland Mus Art; Art Gallery Ont; Princeton Univ Mus; Williams Col Mus; Smithsonian Archives Am Art. *Comn:* Israel (bronze sculpture), Jewish

Community Ctr, Cleveland, 61; kinetic sound-making sculpture (stainless steel), Ashland Col, Ohio, 72; stainless & lacquer relief, Lakewest Hosp, Willoughby, Ohio, 80; Beachwood Libr, Beachwood, Ohio, 84; Astra (suspended painted sculpture), Trumbell Mem Hosp, Warren, Ohio, 88. *Exhib:* Cleveland Mus Art May Show, 55-87; Whitney Mus Am Art Ann, New York, 64-65; Waddell Gallery, New York, 66; Highlights of 1966-1967 Art Season, Larry Aldrich Mus, 67; Int Monumental Sculpture Exhib, Blossom Music Ctr, 68. *Teaching:* Instr sculpture, Oberlin Col, 57-61 & Cleveland Inst Art, 56-71. *Awards:* Yale Norfolk Fel, 54; Catherwood Found Traveling Fel, 56; Nat Scholastic Mag Hall of Fame, 70. *Bibliog:* The Sculpture of the End of the 19th and the 20th Century, Editions Recontre, Paris; Nathan Knobler (auth), The Visual Dialogue, Holt, Rinehart & Winston, Inc; Richard Campen (auth), Outdoor Sculpture in Ohio, Summit Press. *Mem:* New Orgn for Visual Arts. *Media:* Stainless Steel, Bronze. *Mailing Add:* 11625 County Line Rd Gates Mills OH 44040

CLANCY, PATRICK
VIDEO ARTIST
b Hornell, NY, Oct 19, 41. *Study:* Pratt Inst, BS, 64; Yale Univ, BFA, 64 & MFA(painting), 67. *Exhib:* Spaces, Mus Mod Art, New York, 69 & 70; Works for New Spaces, Walker Art Ctr, Minneapolis, 71; Music with its Roots in Ether, Mills Col, Oakland, Calif, 71; Pulsa, Automation House, New York, 71. *Teaching:* Lectr & res assoc, Pulsa Sem, Yale Univ, 67-72; vis artist, Calif Inst Arts, 71 & 72; instr hist of cinema & environ art, Colgate Univ, NY, 73-80. *Awards:* Graham Found Grant, Advan Studies in Visual Arts, 68-72. *Publ:* Co-auth, Pulsa, Eye Mag, 5/68; auth, Proposal, Spaces Catalog, Mus Mod Art, 1/70; co-auth, Pulsa, radio interview, KPFA, Berkeley, Calif, 3/71; auth, The city as an artwork, Arts of the Environ, 72; Paseo video, anthology from the Center for Contemporary Music, Mills Col, 78. *Mailing Add:* 6 E 62nd St Kansas City MO 64113

CLAPSADDLE, JERRY
PAINTER, DESIGNER
b Hastings, Nebr, Dec 12, 41. *Study:* Drake Univ, Des Moines, Iowa, BFA, 64; Ind Univ, MFA, 66. *Work:* Chase Manhattan Bank, New York & Wilmington, Del; Student Loan Mktg Asn, Washington, DC; Washington Post; Hyatt Regency, Baltimore & Crystal City, Va; Swiss Bank Corp, World Trade Ctr, New York,. *Comn:* Mural, Artery Orgn, 82; mural wall & sidewalks, Bethesda Gateway Bldg, 86; print ed, Washington Area Lawyers for the Arts, 86; Stuart St Paving, Ballston Metrop Ctr, Arlington, Va, 90. *Exhib:* Pattern Painting, PS1, New York, 77; Max Protetch Gallery, 77 & Protetch-McIntosh Gallery, 77 & 79, Washington, DC; Maryland Biennial, Baltimore Mus Art, 78; The Emerging Generation, Washington Proj for the Arts, 79; McIntosh-Drysdale Gallery, Washington, 81 & 87; Am Inst Architects, Washington, 86 & 89; and many others. *Pos:* Exhib organizer, Fine Arts Ctr, Univ RI, Kingston, 71-74; dir, Fine Arts Ctr Gallery, State Univ NY, Oneonta, 74-76. *Teaching:* From instr to asst prof studio art & printmaking, Univ RI, Kingston, 67-74; asst prof painting, Univ Md, College Park, 76-80; assoc prof, Studio, George Mason Univ, Fairfax, Va, 81- *Awards:* Artists' Fel, 80 & Art in Pub Places Grant, 84, Nat Endowment Arts; Works in Progress Grant, Md State Arts Coun, 82. *Bibliog:* Paul Richard (auth), A decade's painted daydreams, 8/30/80 & Ben Forgey (auth), Jerry Clapsaddle at Montpelier, 4/11/83, Washington Post; Maeve Bee (ed), New faces-new images, Ocular, fall 80. *Mem:* Col Art Asn; Washington Proj Arts. *Media:* Acrylic, Brick. *Publ:* Designer of exhib catalogs, Linda Benglis: Physical & Psychological Moments in Time, 75, Michelle Stuart, 75, State Univ NY & Maurice Prendergast: Art of Impulse & Color, 76 & From Delacroix to Cezanne: French Watercolor Landscapes of the 19th Century, 77 & The Public as Patron, 79, Univ Md. *Dealer:* B R Kornblatt 406 7th St NW Washington DC 20004. *Mailing Add:* George Mason Univ 4400 University Dr Fairfax VA 22030

CLARK, CAROL
ART HISTORIAN, CURATOR
b New York, NY, July 21, 47. *Study:* Univ Mich, AB(with distinction), 69, MA, 71; Cleveland Mus Art, Kress Found Fel, 72-75; Case Western Reserve Univ, PhD, 81. *Pos:* Cur paintings, Amon Carter Mus Western Art, Ft Worth, Tex, 77-84; exec fel, Prendergast Proj, Williams Col Mus Art, 84-87. *Teaching:* Instr art hist & mus studies, Tex Christian Univ, Ft Worth, 75-77; lectr art hist, Williams Col, 85-87; assoc prof fine arts & Am studies, Amherst Col, 87-92, prof, 92- *Mem:* Col Art Asn; Am Studies Asn. *Res:* American 19th & early 20th century painting. *Publ:* Auth, Jean-Baptiste Simeon Chardin, still life with herring, Bull Cleveland Mus Art, 11/74; Thomas Moran's Watercolors of the American West, Univ Tex Press, 80; A Romantic Painter in the American West, Alfred Jacob Miller: Artist on the Oregon Trail, 82; Charles Deas, Am Frontier Life, 86; co-auth, Maurice Brazil Prendergast & Charles Prendergast, Catalogue Raisonne, 90. *Mailing Add:* Fine Arts Dept Amherst Col Amherst MA 01002

CLARK, CHARLES D
COLLECTOR, PATRON
b Peoria, Ill, May 28, 17. *Study:* Univ Mich, Ann Arbor, BA, LSA, 39. *Collections Arranged:* German Graphics of the 60s, 74, Swiss Concrete Art in Graphics, 75 & Finnish Constructivism, 79, Univ Tex Art Mus. *Pos:* Mem, Friends Coun, Univ Mich Mus, 68-75, Nat Comt, Art Mus, Univ Calif, Berkeley, 69-70 & Fine Arts Adv Coun, Univ Tex, Austin, 76- *Mem:* Am Fedn Arts; Arch Am Art. *Collection:* Contemporary prints. *Mailing Add:* 404 Lindberg Ave McAllen TX 78501

CLARK, CLAUDE
INSTRUCTOR, PAINTER
b Rockingham, Ga, Nov 11, 15. *Study:* Philadelphia Mus Sch Art, dipl; Barnes Found, painting fel, 42-44; Sacramento State Col, BA; Univ Calif, Berkeley, MA. *Work:* Pa Mus, Philadelphia; Atlanta Univ, Ga; Oakland Mus, Calif; Fisk Univ, Tenn; Nat Collection Art, Smithsonian Inst, Washington, DC; Hampton Univ, Va. *Comn:* Freedom Morning (canvas interpretation), Philadelphia Orchestra Asn, 44. *Exhib:* Negro Artist Comes of Age, Brooklyn Mus, 45; Black American Artists 1750-1950 traveling exhib, Los Angeles Co Mus, 76-; Black Artists-South, 79; Hidden Heritage: Afro-American traveling exhib, 85-; Choosing: Afro-Am Art, 1925-1985, Masters Art Exhib, Salvador-Bahia, Brazil, 88; Introspective: Contemporary Art by Americans & Brazillians of African Descent, Los Angeles, 89; Travelling 50 year retrospective of paintings, 90; and others. *Pos:* Artist, Fed Art Proj, Philadelphia, 39-42. *Teaching:* Assoc prof art, Talladega Col, Ala, 48-55; instr art, Alameda Co Schs, Calif, 59-68 & Merritt Col, 68-81. *Awards:* Carnegie Found Grants Res, Painting & Ceramic Res, 49-50 & 51. *Bibliog:* David Driskell (auth), Retrospective Exhib, Fisk Univ, 72. *Mem:* Am Soc Composers Authors & Publ; Nat Coun Arts; Am Asn Univ Prof. *Media:* Oil. *Res:* African and African American art history; African art and culture in Ghana; ancient Nile valley culture - Egypt. *Publ:* Auth, A Black Art Perspective, 70. *Mailing Add:* 788 Santa Ray Ave Oakland CA 94610

CLARK, EDWARD
PAINTER
b New Orleans, La, May 6, 26. *Study:* Art Inst Chicago, 46-51; Acad de la Grande Chaumiere, Paris, France, 52. *Work:* Aldrich Mus Contemp Art, Ridgefield, Conn; Centio des Arts Mod, Guadalajara, Mex; Mus Solidarity, Titograd, Yugoslavia; La State Univ, Baton Rouge. *Exhib:* Salon D'Automme, 52 & Salon des Realites Nouvelles, 55 & 85, Mus d'Art Mod, Paris; Prix d'Othn Friese, Mus des Arts Decoratifs, Paris, 55; The Brata Groupe, Mus Mod Tokyo, Japan, 60; Biennial, Whitney Mus, New York, 73; Bicentennial Banners, Hirshhorn Mus, Washington, DC, 76; Icarus Odyssey, Centro de Arte Moderno, Guadalajara, Mex, 79; retrospective, Studio Mus of Harlem, New York, 80; Realities Nouvelles, 1984, Grand Palais, Paris, 84. *Awards:* Creative Artists Pub Serv Award, New York, 59; Nat Endowment Arts Grant Painting, 72 & 81. *Bibliog:* Article, Edward Clark, pushbroom in action, Art Int, 70; Corrine Robbins (auth), Pluralist Era in American Art, Harper & Row, 83; article, Edward Clark, statement, Issue Mag, 85. *Mem:* Association des Anciens de la Cite Internationale des Arts, Paris. *Media:* All. *Dealer:* Larry Randall 82-30 138th St Kew Gardens NY 11435; Julia Hotton 202 E 76th St New York NY 10021. *Mailing Add:* 4 W 22nd St New York NY 10010

CLARK, EMERY ANN
PAINTER, ENVIRONMENTAL ARTIST
b New Orleans, La, Sept 12, 50. *Study:* Newcomb Col, BFA, 72; Sch Fine Arts, Boston Univ, 69; Skowhegan Sch Painting & Sculpture, 71; Tulane Univ, MFA, 81. *Work:* New Orleans Mus Art & Virlane Found, New Orleans, La; IBM, Washington, DC; Chase Manhattan Bank, Miami, Fla; Hunte Mus Art, Chatanooga, Tenn. *Comn:* NOMA Nile (29' 6" 45 mile color environmental installation), New Orleans Mus Art, La, 77; Art by the Yard (1000' x 5' painted canvas), Art Coun New Orleans, La, 82 & Barbara Gillman Gallery, Miami, Fla, 83; Sea Wall (environmental installation 40 x 41), Touro Med Off Bldg, New Orleans, La, 83; Art Plan for New Orleans Int Airport Expansion, 89-90; Arts Coun New Orleans & New Orleans Aviation Bd, 89-92. *Exhib:* Artists' Biennial, New Orleans Mus Art, La, 75 & 77; Louisiana Major Works, La World Expos, New Orleans, 84; The Art of New Orleans, Southeastern Ctr Contemp Art, Winston-Salem, NC, 84; Landscape, Cityscape, Seascape, Contemp Arts Ctr, New Orleans, La & New York Acad Art, New York, 86; Tampa Triennial, Tampa Mus Art, Fla, 88; 50th Ann Nat Exhib Contemp Am Paintings, Soc Four Arts, Palm Beach, Fla, 88; one-person show, Lowery Sims (with catalog), Alexandria Mus Art. *Teaching:* Vis artist, New Orleans Ctr Creative Arts, 74-76; instr, Tulane Univ, 79-81. *Awards:* Thomas J Watson Traveling Fel, 72; 1st Prize, 50th Ann Nat Exhib Contemp Am Painting; Spec Guest, Aspen Inst Humanistic Studies, Aspen Co, 74. *Bibliog:* John Kemp (auth), An artist's sense of place, Am Artist, Vol 52, 62-65, 6/88; Lowery Sims (auth), catalog, Alexandria Mus, 89. *Mem:* Contemp Arts Ctr New Orleans (bd mem, 76-89, co-chmn Arts Comt, 77, Arts Comt, 78-81 & 86-88, chmn Arts Comt, 80-81, vpres, 78 & 82-84); Women's Caucus Arts; College Art Asn; Nat Asn Artists Orgn; New Orleans Ctr Creative Arts Community (Liaison bd, 80-89, pres, 84-85). *Media:* Painting, Environmental Art. *Publ:* Bomb Mag, New York, No XXII, 46-47, fall 90. *Dealer:* Arthur Roger Gallery 432 Julia St New Orleans LA 70130; Arthur Roger Gallery 136 Prince St New York NY 10012. *Mailing Add:* 904 Hillary St New Orleans LA 70118

CLARK, GARTH REGINALD
DEALER, HISTORIAN
b Pretoria, Republic SAfrica, May 15, 47. *Study:* Royal Col Art, London with Lord Queensberry & Edwardo Paolozzi, MA, 76. *Exhib:* Hans Coper: A Retrospective, Gardiner Mus, Toronto, Can, 85. *Collections Arranged:* A Century of Ceramics in the US Traveling Exhib (auth, catalog), 79; The Contemporary American Potter Traveling Exhib (auth, catalog), Smithsonian Inst, 80; Michael Carden: A Portrait, NCECA Conference, 81; Ceramic Echoes: Historical References in Contemporary Ceramic Art (auth, catalog), Nelson Atkins Mus, 83. *Pos:* Dir, Inst Ceramic History, Los Angeles, 79-81. *Teaching:* Art historian ceramics, Univ Calif, Los Angeles, 78. *Awards:* Services to the Field, Nat Endowment Arts, 79; Art Critics Award, Nat Endowment Arts, 80; Morton Professor, Ohio Univ, 81; Eleventh Wittenborn Mem Award for Art Book of the Year, 89. *Mem:* Decorative Art Soc; Inst

Ceramic History; Art Libr Soc NAm. *Publ:* Co-auth, Potters of Southern Africa, G Struik, 73; ed, Ceramic Art: Comment & Review, E P Dutton, 78; auth, Century of Ceramics in the United States, 1878-1978, E P Dutton, 79; auth, American Potters, Watson Guptill, 81; auth, Ceramic echoes, Contemp Art Soc, 83; co-auth, American Potters Today, Victoria & Albert Mus, London, 86; auth, American Ceramics: 1876 to the Present, 87, The Eccentric Teapot, 89, The Mad Potter of Biloxi: The Life and Art of George E Ohr, 89 & The Book of Cups, 90, Abbeville Press; co-auth, American Ceramics in The Everson Museum, Rizzoli, 88. *Mailing Add:* c/o Garth Clark Gallery 24 W 57th St Suite 305 New York NY 10019

CLARK, JON FREDERIC
EDUCATOR, GLASS BLOWER
b Waterloo, Wis, Aug 13, 47. *Study:* Univ Wis, BSc; Royal Col Art, London, MFA. *Work:* Royal Col Art, London, Eng; Archie Bray Found, Helena, Mont; Portnoy Ltd, New York; Hadler Galleries, New York; Lannan Found, Palm Beach, Fla. *Exhib:* New Am Glass, Focus WVa, Huntington, 76; Contemp Art Glass, Lever House, New York, 76; Art of Craft, The Am View, Ill State Univ, Normal, 76; Nat Glass III, Univ Wis, Madison, 76; Nat Craft Exhib, Del Mus of Art, Wilmington, 76; Philadelphia Craft Show, Philadelphia Mus of Art, 77. *Collections Arranged:* Cup Show, Fritz Driesbach, 76 & Eisch Retrospective, Littleton Collection, 77, Tyler Sch Art, Temple Univ, Philadelphia. *Teaching:* Glass technician, Calif Col of Arts & Crafts, Oakland, 73; assoc prof, Tyler Sch Art, 73-82. *Bibliog:* Judith Stein (auth), Exhibition Review, Vol 3 (1) & Richard Avidon (auth), Exhibition Review, Vol 4 (1), Glass Art Mag. *Mem:* Am Crafts Coun; Glass Art Soc; Nat Coun on Educ for Ceramic Arts. *Media:* Glass, polyester. *Mailing Add:* Art Dept Temple Univ Beach & Primrose Ave Philadelphia PA 19122

CLARK, LYNDA K
MUSEUM DIRECTOR, EDUCATOR
b Miami, Fla. *Study:* Fla Atlantic Univ, BFA, 69; Calif State Univ, Long Beach, MA, 86. *Collections Arranged:* Maurice LeGrand LeSeuer Sullins (catalog), 87-88; Robert Lostutter, 89; New Work, John Balsley, 90; Eva Enderlein (photographs), 90. *Pos:* Asst cur, Long Beach Mus Art, Calif, 83-86; cur, Ill Sate Mus, Springfield, 86-88; dir, Niuart Mus, Dekalb, Ill, 89- *Awards:* Fel Nat Endowment Arts, 86; Fel Kellogg Found, 86. *Mem:* Am Asn Mus; Col Art Asn; Asn Col & Univ Mus & Galleries; Int Soc Appraisers; Asn Corp Art Cur. *Res:* The Bauhaus; comtemporary American artists; 20th century folk and outsider art. *Publ:* Auth, The Blue Four: Fianinger, Jawlensky, Kandinsky, Klee, Long Beach Mus Art, 85; Maurice LeGrand Leseuer Sullins: Paintings, Ill State Mus, 87; Folk Artists of Northern New Mexico, Robert Vogle, 89; The Work of Milton D Ratner: Assemblages, etc, Northern Ill Univ, 90. *Mailing Add:* PO Box 412 De Kalb IL 60115

CLARK, MARIE
SCULPTOR
b Philadelphia, Pa. *Study:* Univ Pa, BA; Tyler Sch Art; Philadelphia Mus Sch Art; study with I Sankowsky, G Utesche, Arlene Love & Joe Greenberg. *Comn:* Alabaster abstract, comn by F Wallace, Bordentown, NJ, 74; wood abstract, comn by J Thomas, Haddenfield, NJ, 75; wood abstract, comn by O Ryan, Philadelphia, Pa, 83; epoxy torso, comn by J Montague, 84. *Exhib:* Six Sculptors from 3 states to complement mod sculpture from the Guggenheim, Allentown Mus, 85; Touch to See, Kemerer Art Mus, Bethlehem, Pa, 85; Statton Art Festival, Vt, 85 & 90; Gov's Exhib of Paintings & Sculpture, Vt, 87; Sculpture to Touch (traveling), Children's Mus, Martin Luther King Mus, Washington, DC, and Loyda College Art Gallery, Baltimore, Md, 87; solo exhibs, Southern Vt Art Center, 85, Beside Myself Gallery, Vt, 86 & 90, Third St Gallery, Philadelphia, Pa, 88; and others. *Awards:* Woodmere Art Mus Sculpture Award, 78; 2nd Best in Show, Norwich Univ, 83; Best Sculpture, Southern Vt Art Ctr, 88. *Mem:* Philadelphia Acad Fine Arts; Vt Coun Arts; Philadelphia Art Alliance; Womens Caucus for Arts. *Media:* Wood, Stone, Bronze, Epoxy. *Publ:* Festival of the Arts, Southern Vt Art Center, 85; Contribr, Sculpture to touch, Gwendolyn Cafritz Grant, Washington, DC, 3/4/87; Around & About (J), Bill Reed, Vt, 7/25/90. *Dealer:* Third Street Gallery Philadelphia Pa; Ward Nasse Gallery NY. *Mailing Add:* 8620 Montgomery Ave Philadelphia PA 19118

CLARK, MARK A
CURATOR
b Dayton, Ohio, Jan 20, 31. *Exhib:* When the New Century Arrived: Art of 1900, 85; Art Pottery and Beyond: American Ceramics from the Chrysler Museum Collection, 86; Treasures for the Table, Silver from the Chrysler Mus (catalog), Chrysler Mus, Norfolk, Va, 89; Proud Possessions: A Community Collects (exhib catalog), Chrysler Mus, 92. *Collections Arranged:* The Lipton Collection of Antique Tea Silver, 58; Glass from Area Collections, 66; The Folger Collection of Antique Silver Coffee Pots, 67; Paul Storr Silver in American Collections (with catalog), 72; Vermeil Collection (cataloger), White House, 72; A Tricentennial Celebration: Norfolk, 1682-1982 (catalog), 82; American Silver--A Survey of the Chrysler Museum Collection, 82; English Silver from the Chrysler Museum Collection, 83. *Pos:* Mus registr, Dayton Art Inst, 57-61, assoc cur decorative arts, 61-68, cur decorative arts & mus registr, 68-; cur dec arts, Chrysler Mus, Norfolk, Va, 76- *Mem:* Decorative Arts Soc. *Mailing Add:* c/o The Chrysler Mus Olney Rd & Mowbray Arch Norfolk VA 23510

CLARK, MICHAEL VINSON
PAINTER, PRINTMAKER
b Tex, Nov 20, 46. *Work:* Corcoran Gallery Art, Nat Collection Fine Art, Nat Gallery Art & Phillips Collection, Washington, DC; Everson Mus, Syracuse, NY. *Exhib:* One-man shows, Mus STex, Corpus Christi, 78 & Harry Lunn Gallery, DC, 79; The Art of Organic Form, Smithsonian Inst, Washington, DC, 68; New Painting: Structure, Corcoran Gallery, 68; Nat Drawing Soc Show, Philadelphia Mus Art, Pa, 70; Ten Washington Artists 1950-1970, Edmonton Art Gallery, Can, 70; Washington Art: Twenty Years, Baltimore Mus of Art, 70; 75th Anniversary, Cooper-Hewitt Mus, New York, 77; Critics Choice 1977, Lowe Mus, Syracuse Univ, Syracuse, NY, 77; Dimock Gallery, George Washington Univ, DC, 79; Images of the 70's, Nine Washington Artists, Corcoran Gallery Art, DC, 80. *Awards:* Purchase Award, Nat Drawing Soc, Philadelphia Mus, 70; Purchase Award, 35th Corcoran Biennial Contemp Painting, 77. *Bibliog:* James Harithas (auth), Michael Clark, Everson Mus Art, 73. *Publ:* Illusr, The Art of Organic Form, Smithsonian Inst, 68. *Mailing Add:* c/o Gallery 1054 31st St NW Washington DC 20003

CLARK, NANCY KISSEL
SCULPTOR, CONSULTANT
b Joplin, Mo, Jan 27, 19. *Work:* Woodmere Art Gallery, Pa; Univ Del, Newark; Pa Military Col, Chester; Provident Nat Bank , Philadelphia. *Comn:* Steel sculpture, Walter Piel Mem, Corkran Gallery, Rehoboth, Del, 65; metal sculpture, Wood-Haven Kruse Sch, Wilmington, 66; Christ (5 ft), Notre Dame Brothers, St Edmond's Acad Chapel & Courtyard, Wilmington, 74; Holy Trinity Church, Dallas, 79; Design of Newman Chapel, Lafayette Col, Pa, 87; and others. *Exhib:* Nat Sculpture Soc Ann, New York, 71-73; Tex Sculpture Symp, Southern Methodist Univ Gallery, 78; Distinguished Mid-Atlantic Artists, Univ Del, 81; US Embassy Cult Exchange Touring Exhib, Mex & Cen Am; Mayors office, Del, 90; and others. *Teaching:* Lectr workshops at various learning insts, 81-92. *Awards:* First Binswanger Award, Philadelphia Mus, 66; First Award, Nat League Am Pen Women Biennial, Tulsa, Okla, 66; Artist of the Year Award, Wilmington Coun Churches, 69. *Bibliog:* Art in, National Competition, US Dept Housing & Urban Develop, 73; Archives, Am Art, Smithsonian Inst, 74 & Dallas Mus Fine Arts, Tex, 78; 100 Years: Time Capsul, Historical Mus, 90. *Mem:* Philadelphia Art Alliance; Artists Equity Asn, Philadelphia; mem-at-large Nat League Am Pen Women. *Media:* Welded Metal, Stained Glass. *Publ:* Legacy from Delaware Women; History of Joplin, Missouri; Nat Art Award Bk. *Mailing Add:* 1015 Overbrook Rd Wilmington DE 19807-2235

CLARK, ROBERT CHARLES
PAINTER, LECTURER
b Minneapolis, Minn, Aug 31, 20. *Study:* Minneapolis Sch Art; Walker Gallery Art Sch, Minneapolis. *Work:* Los Angeles Co Mus Hist, Sci & Art, Los Angeles; Norton B Simon Inc, Hunt's Foods & Industs Found, Los Angeles; Glendale Fed Collection of Calif Art. *Comn:* The Resurrection (mural), Forest Lawn Mem Park, Glendale, 65. *Exhib:* Artists of Los Angeles & Vicinity, Los Angeles Co Mus Art, 55-58; Illusion & Reality, Santa Barbara Mus Art, Calif, 56; one-man shows, Calif Palace of Legion of Honor, San Francisco, 56 & Rosicrucian Egyptian Mus, San Jose, 73; Charles & Emma Frye Mus, Seattle, Wash, 57-58. *Pos:* Background artist, Natural Hist Dept, Los Angeles Co Mus, 54-62. *Awards:* Artists of Los Angeles & Vicinity Award, Los Angeles Co Mus Art, 55; Purchase Award, Palos Verdes Estates Art Gallery, 56. *Bibliog:* Janice Lovoos (auth), The tempera paintings of Robert Clark, Am Artist, 12/69; William F Taylor (auth & producer), Robert Clark: An American Realist (film), 74; Elizabeth Rigby (auth), Robert Clark: A perfectionist's medium, Southwest Art, 1/79. *Media:* Tempera, Watercolor. *Dealer:* Zantman Art Galleries Ltd Sixth & Dolores Sts Carmel CA 93921; El Prado Gallery Art PO Box 1849 Sedona AZ 86336. *Mailing Add:* 2270 W 230th St Torrance CA 90501

CLARK, ROBERTA CARTER
PAINTER, WRITER
b St Louis, Mo, May 2, 24. *Study:* Purdue Univ; Ctr Creative Studies, Detroit, 48-51; Art Ctr Sch, Los Angeles, 53-54; Art Students League, with Hirsch, 59; also studied with John Terelak, Don Stone & Charles Reid. *Work:* Brookdale Col, Lincroft, NJ; Rutgers Univ, New Brunswick, NJ; Monmouth Med Ctr, Long Branch, NJ; Wash & Lee Univ, Lexington, Va; Seton Hall Univ, South Orange, NJ; and others. *Exhib:* Soc Western Artists, De Young Mus, San Francisco, 54; Midwest Watercolor Soc, 83-92; Am Watercolor Soc, 85, 87, 89 & 92; Nat Acad Exhib, New York, 90; Adirondacks Nat Exhib Am Watercolors, 90, 91 & 92; and others. *Teaching:* Instr workshops, Calif, St Louis, Hilton Head, Rockport, Mass, Vt & Pocono Pines, Pa. *Awards:* Silver Medals, NJ Watercolor Soc Ann, 78, 81 & 85 & Knickerbocker Artists, Grumbacher Inc, 82, 85, 87 & 88; Cent NY Watercolor Soc Award, Adirondocks Nat Exhib Am Watercolors, 90, Harold Coopersmith Award, 91 & Paul Mowrey Mem Award, 92; Warga Award, Garden State Watercolor Soc, 91; and othrs. *Mem:* NJ Watercolor Soc (secy, 76-78, pres, 79-82); Knickerbocker Artists; Rockport Art Asn; Allied Artists; Midwest Watercolor Soc. *Media:* All. *Publ:* Illusr, The Littles, thirteen bk ser, Scholastic Inc, 70-90; auth & illusr, How to Paint Living Portraits, North Light, 90; Painting Children's Portraits, North Light, 93. *Dealer:* Portraits Inc 985 Park Ave New York NY 10028. *Mailing Add:* 47B Cheshire Sq Little Silver NJ 07739

CLARK, TIMOTHY JOHN
PAINTER, INSTRUCTOR
b Santa Ana, Calif, June 30, 51. *Study:* Art Ctr Col Design, with Paul Marciel Souza & Harry Carmean, 69-70; Chouinard Art Inst, with Donald W Graham & Harold M Kramer, CFA, 72; Calif Inst Arts, BFA, 74; Calif State Univ, Fullerton, with Victor Joachim Smith, 75; Calif State Univ, Long Beach, with Joyce Wahl Treiman, MA, 78. *Exhib:* Rocky Mountain Nat Watermedia Exhib, Foothills Art Ctr, Golden, Colo, 80; Am Watercolor Soc Ann Exhib, Nat Acad Galleries, New York, 80; Nat Acad Design Ann Exhib, Nat Acad

Galleries, New York, 80; Salmagundi Club Ann, New York, 82 & 83; 11th Street Gallery, Santa Monica, Calif, 88-91. *Teaching:* Instr drawing & painting, Orange Coast Col, Costa Mesa, Calif, 74-79; instr drawing, Saddleback Col, Mission Viejo, Calif, 76-77; instr drawing & painting, Coastline Col, Fountain Valley, Calif, 76-; dir, Timothy J Clark Watercolor Workshops, Hawaii & Europe, 81-; instr watercolor, Univ Hawaii, 82. *Awards:* Mustard Seed Award, Rocky Mountain Watermedia Exhib, 80; Purchase Award, Nat Original Print Show, 83; Nominated for Emmy, Focus on Watercolor, PBS-TV, 89. *Bibliog:* Jane Summer (auth), The Art of Timothy J Clark, Showcase, The Santa Ana Register, 1/18/81; Joan Talmage Weiss (auth), Pastel colors and passionate song, Forum 50 Mag, 1/81; Mark Pinsky (auth), Nat TV exposure for artist, Los Angeles Times, 1/8/89. *Media:* Watercolor, Oil. *Publ:* Auth, Edges in Watercolor, Am Artist Mag, 84; contribr, Learning from the Pros, Watson Guptill, 85; Tips on analyzing your subject, Am Artist Mag, 87; Focus on Watercolor, Watson Guptill 87. *Dealer:* 1568 10th St Santa Monica CA 90404. *Mailing Add:* PO Box 2728 Capistrano Beach CA 92624

CLARK, VICKY A
HISTORIAN, CURATOR
b Atlanta, Ga. *Study:* Univ Calif, Los Angeles, BA, 72; Univ Calif, Davis, MA, 74; Univ Mich (teaching fel, 75-77), PhD, 79. *Collections Arranged:* Tom Otterness, Lothar Baumgarten, Contemp Women: Works on Paper, Jeff Wall, Meg Webster, Barbara Bloom, Carnegie Mus Art. *Pos:* Cur educ, Carnegie Mus Art, Pittsburgh, 81-89, assoc cur contemp art, 89- *Teaching:* Instr, Univ Toledo & Toledo Mus Art, 79; asst prof, Univ RI, 80 & Skidmore Col, Saratoga Springs, NY, 80-81; adj prof, Chatham Col, 87-, Univ Pittsburgh, 92. *Mem:* Am Asn Mus; Col Art Asn. *Res:* Contemporary art. *Publ:* Auth, Collecting from the internationals, Carnegie Mag, Vol LVI, No 5; Richard Serra in Pittsburgh, Carnegie Mag, Vol LVIII, No 4 8/86; Tom Otterness (exhib catalog), 86; On the Meaning of Art at the End of the Century in Carnegie International, Carnegie Mus Art, 88. *Mailing Add:* Carnegie Inst Mus Art 4400 Forbes Ave Pittsburgh PA 15213

CLARK, VICKY JO
PAINTER, MURALIST
b Lamesa, Tex, Sept 14, 37. *Study:* Abilene Christian Univ Tex, 56-59, studied with Ben Konis, Albert Handell, Daniel Greene. *Work:* Abilene Christian Univ, Tex; Seminole High Sch, Tex; First Int Bank, Houston, Tex; Plaines Nat Bank, Lubbock, Tex; Post Nat Bank, Tex. *Comn:* Mural, Primary Cafeteria, Seminole Pub Sch, Tex, 91. *Exhib:* Westcoast Pastel Soc, Sacramento Fine Arts Ctr, Carmichael, Calif, 88, 89 & 91; Midwest Pastel Soc, J Rosenthal Fine Arts Ltd, Chicago, Ill, 89, 90 & 91; Southeastern Pastel Soc, Northpark Town Ctr, Atlanta, Ga, 89; Degas Pastel Soc, World Trade Ctr, New Orleans, La, 90; Northwest Pastel Soc, Issaquah Gallery, Seattle, Wash, 90 & 91; Pastel Soc Am, Nat Arts Club Gallery, New York, 87, 88, 89 & 91; Salmagundi Club, New York, 88, 89, 90, 91 & 92; Catharine Lorillord Wolfe, Nat Arts Club, New York, 88, 89 & 90; Maryland Pastel Soc, Johns Hopkins Sch Med, Baltimore, 89 & 91; Paste Soc SW, Dallas, Tex, 90. *Teaching:* Workshops pastel, Tex & NMex. *Awards:* First Place, Southeastern Pastel Soc, 89; Purchase Award, A&A Guffuni, Pastel Soc Am, 89; Pastel Soc Am Plaque, Salmagundi, 89; Merit Awards in Chicago, 89, Dallas, 90 & Seattle, 91. *Mem:* Pastel Soc Am; Catherine Lorillard Wolfe. *Media:* Pastel. *Dealer:* Jones Virmar Gallery 2714 50th Lubbock TX 79413. *Mailing Add:* 607 SW Avenue 1 Seminole TX 79360

CLARK, WILLIAM ROGER
SCULPTOR, PAINTER
b Altoona, Pa, July 27, 49. *Study:* Md Inst, BA, 71; Temple Univ, Tyler, MEd, 74; Univ Idaho, MFA, 79; Mary Knoww Language Inst, Seoul, Korea, 85. *Work:* Am Forestry Asn, Washington, DC; Catholic Foreigh Mission Soc Am; Nat Wildflower Res Ctr, Austin, Tex; Nat Geog Soc, Washington, DC. *Comn:* mural, St Michaels the Archangel Church, Levittown, Pa, 83; sculpture, Cath Foreign Mission Soc Am, Seoul, Korea, 86. *Exhib:* Lorenzo IL Magnifico, Florence, Italy, 92; Christo Umbrella Project, St Cloud, Minn, 92; Columbus Again, Barcelona, Spain, 92. *Pos:* Cur, Cummings Gallery, Mercyhurst Col, Erie, Pa, 87-90. *Teaching:* Montgomery Co Col, Blue Bell, Pa, 90- & Bucks Co Community Col, Newtoun, Pa, 91- *Mem:* Col Art Asn; Nat Art Educ Asn; Pa Art Educ Asn. *Media:* Watercolor. *Publ:* Lithograph, Autumn Reflections, Doubleday Inc, New York, 83; Golden Reflections, Art Spectrum, 83; Illus, Maryknoll Mag, 10/85, 2/87 & 6/87. *Mailing Add:* 48 Kingswood Ln Levittown PA 19055

CLARK, WILLIAM W
HISTORIAN
b Tampa, Fla, Jan 17, 40. *Study:* Pa State Univ, BA(with hons); Columbia Univ, MA & PhD. *Pos:* Ed, Gesta, 88-; prof art, Queens Col, City Univ New York, 67- *Teaching:* Prof medieval archit, Queens Col & Grad Ctr, City Univ NY, Flushing, 67- *Awards:* Grants, Nat Endowment Arts, Am Coun Learned Soc & J Paul Getty Trust. *Mem:* Col Art Asn; Societe Francaise d'Archeologie; Int Ctr for Medieval Art; Centre des Recherches d'Archeologie Medievale; Medieval Acad Am. *Res:* Twelfth-century early Gothic architecture and sculpture in France and England. *Publ:* Auth, Spatial innovations in the chevet of Saint-Germain-des-Pres, J Soc Archit Historians, no 38, 1979; Laon Cathedral: Architecture, Harvey Miller Publ, London, vol 1, 83 & vol 2, 87; The first flying buttresses: A new reconstruction of the nave of Notre-Dame de Paris, Art Bull, no 66, 1984; Suger's church at Saint-Denis: The state of research, In: Abbot Suger and Saint-Denis, 86; Medieval Architecture, Medieval Learning, Yale Univ Press, New Haven, 92. *Mailing Add:* Dept Art Queens Col Flushing NY 11367

CLARKE, ANN
EDUCATOR, PAINTER
b Norwich, Eng, Aug 27, 44; Can citizen. *Study:* Slade Sch Fine Art, Univ Col, London, dipl fine art & design. *Work:* Can Coun Art Bank; Westburne Collection, Montreal; Hill Trust Fund Collection, Calgary, Alta; Prov Courthouse Collection, Edmonton, Can; Queensland Art Gallery, Brisbane, Australia. *Exhib:* Abstraction West: Emma Lake and After, Nat Gallery, Ottawa, Ont & Mendel Art Gallery, Saskatoon, Sask, 76; Beaverbrook Art Gallery, Frederickton, NB, 76; Mus d'Art Contemp, Montreal, Que, 76; Seven Prairie Artists, Art Gallery of Ont, 79; one-person shows, Edmonton Art Gallery, 77, Southern Alta Art Gallery, 79 & Gallery One, Toronto, 86; Heritage of Jack Bush, Oshawa, Ont & traveling throughout Can, 81; Threshold of Colour, Edmonton Art Gallery, 82; and others. *Pos:* Art coodr, Royal Ont Mus, Toronto, 85-86; artistic dir, Kingston Artists Asn Int, 88-90. *Teaching:* Asst prof art, NS Col Art & Design, Halifax, 75-76; lectr art, Univ Alta, Edmonton, 76-84 & Red Deer Col, 79-80, Grant McEwan Col, 80-84; lect art, Univ Guelph, Ont, 85-91; lectr art, Queen's Univ, Kingston, Ont, 88-91; asst prof art, Lakehead Univ, Thunder Bay, Ont, 92- *Awards:* Can Coun Art Bank Award, 73 & 76; Govt Alta Cult Award, 74; Can Coun Art Award, 78-79. *Bibliog:* Article, Ken Carpenter (auth), Ann Clarke, Art Mag, 6/81; David Burnett & Marilyn Schiff (auths), Contemporary Canadian Art, 83; Karen Wilkin (auth), Ann Clarke, Vie des Arts, 86. *Media:* Acrylic and Oils on Canvas. *Mailing Add:* 572 Oliver Rd Apt 3 Thunderbay ON P7B 2H3 Canada

CLARKE, BUD (WARREN F)
DESIGNER, PAINTER
b Windsor, Vt, Jan 10, 41. *Study:* Art Students League, 59-63; Sch Visual Arts, with Milton Glazer. *Pos:* Art dir, McCalls Corp, 68-70; art dir, McGraw Hill Inc, New York, 70-81; founder, Bud Clarke & Assocs, 81-84; pres, Clarke/Thompson Design, 84- *Teaching:* Instr mag design, 77-, instr media commun, 78-, Sch Visual Arts, New York. *Awards:* Cert of Merit, Art Dir Mag; Soc Publ Designers; Jesse H Neal Award, Am Bus Press, 80 & 82. *Bibliog:* Roy Paul Nelson (auth), Publication Design, William C Brown, 78. *Mem:* Soc Publ Designers; McGraw Hill Art Dirs Club (pres, 74-78). *Media:* Magazines, Printed Material; Watercolor, Mixed Medium. *Mailing Add:* 19 W 21st St Suite 902 New York NY 10010

CLARKE, JOHN CLEM
PAINTER
b Bend, Ore, June 6, 37. *Study:* Ore State Univ; Mexico City Col; Univ Ore, BFA, 60. *Work:* Whitney Mus Am Art, New York; Dallas Mus Art, Tex; Va Mus Fine Arts; Metrop Mus Art & Mus Mod Art, New York; Baltimore Mus Fine Arts, Md. *Exhib:* Bi-Ann, Whitney Mus, 67-73; Realism in Am, touring USA; Mus Mod Art, New York; Aspects of Realism, touring Can, 76-78; Illusion and Reality, touring Australia, 77-78; Art About Art, Whitney Mus, New York, 78; Contemp Am Realism Since 1960, Pa Acad Fine Arts, Philadelphia, 81; The Ponderosa Collection, Butler Inst Am Art, Youngstown, Ohio, 83. *Media:* Oil on Canvas. *Mailing Add:* 465 W Broadway New York NY 10012

CLARKE, JOHN R
HISTORIAN , CRITIC
b Pittsburgh, Pa, Jan 25, 45. *Study:* Georgetown Univ, AB, 67; Yale Univ, MA, 69, PhD, 73. *Teaching:* Asst prof hist art, Yale Univ, 75-80; asst prof, Univ Tex, Austin, 80-82, assoc prof, 82-87, prof, 88. *Mem:* Col Art Asn Am; Archaeol Inst Am. *Res:* History of Roman art; architecture; American art and art criticism, 1960 to present; methodology. *Publ:* Auth, Roman Black-and White Figural Mosaics, NY Univ Press, 79; Life-art-life, Quentin Crisp and Eleanor Antin: Notes on performance in the seventies, 79, Up against the wall, transavanguardia!, 82, Arts Mag; The Early Third Style at the Villa of Oplontis, Roemische Mitteilungen, 87; The Houses of Roman Italy, 100 BC-AD 250: Ritual, Space and Decoration, Univ Calif Press, 91. *Mailing Add:* Dept Art Univ Tex Austin TX 78712

CLARK-LANGAGER, SARAH ANN
GALLERY DIRECTOR, CURATOR
b Lynchburg, Va, May 14, 43. *Study:* Randolph-Macon Woman's Col, Lynchburg, Va, BA(art hist), 65; Univ Wash, Seattle, MA(art hist), 70; City Univ New York, Grad Ctr, PhD(art hist0, 88. *Collections Arranged:* Northwest Traditions (auth, catalog), Seattle Art Mus, 78; Sculpture Space: Recent Trends-Sculpture Space Utica (auth, catalog), Munson-Williams & Proctor Inst, 84; Order & Enigma: American Art Between Two Wars (auth, catalog), NY Consortium & Munson-Williams & Proctor Inst, 84; Private Art/Public Visions, Western Gallery, Western Wash Univ, 89; Sighted/Sited at Western: Drawings for Sculpture, Western Gallery, Western Wash Univ, 90. *Pos:* Assoc cur, modern art, Seattle Art Mus, 75-79; cur, 20th century art, Munson-Williams Proctor Inst, Utica, NY, 81-86; Gallery dir & cur of Outdoor Sculpture Collection, Western Gallery, Western Wash Univ, Bellingham, 88- *Teaching:* Assoc, Educ Dept, art history, Albright-Knox Art Gallery, Buffalo, 67-68; assoc, Educ Dept, art hist, Seattle Art Mus, Wash, 71-75; asst prof, art hist, Univ N Tex, Denton, 86-88. *Mem:* Wash Art Consortium, (vpres, 89-90, pres, 90-92); Am Asn Mus. *Publ:* Auth, The early works of David Hare, Arts Mag, 10/82; ed & contribr, Master Works of American Art from Munson-Williams & Proctor Institute, Munson-Williams & Harry Abrams, 89; auth, Intro; private art/public visions, Western Gallery, Western Wash Univ, 89; Audiophone Tour (Nat Endowment Arts funded) & Brochure, Outdoor Sculpture Collection, Western Wash Univ, 91. *Mailing Add:* 2970 N Shore Dr Bellingham WA 98226

CLAYBERGER, SAMUEL ROBERT
PAINTER, EDUCATOR
b Kulpmont, Pa, Mar 26, 26. *Study:* Chouinard Art Inst, Los Angeles; Jepson Art Inst; study with Don Graham, Rico Lebrun & Richard Haines. *Work:* Pasadena Art Mus, Calif. *Exhib:* One-man shows, Pasadena Art Mus, 60, Laguna Beach Mus Art, Calif, 67, Whittier Art Asn, Calif, 70 & Orange Coast Col, Costa Mesa, Calif, 73, Heritage Gallery, 88; Otis Art Inst Gallery, Los Angeles, 73. *Pos:* Designer-colorist, UPA Pictures Inc, Burbank, 53-58 & Jay Ward Prod Inc, Los Angeles, 59-64. *Teaching:* Instr design, Chouinard Art Inst, 60; instr design & painting, Otis Art Inst of Los Angeles Co, 63-69, asst prof drawing & painting, 69-79; instr drawing, Otis Parsons, 79- *Awards:* Nat Watercolor Soc, 56, 58, 60 & 69; Los Angeles All-City Exhib, Home Savings & Loan, 62. *Bibliog:* George De Groat (auth), Sam Clayberger eyes the human condition, Star News, Pasadena, 70. *Mem:* Artists Equity Asn. *Media:* Acrylic, Watercolor. *Mailing Add:* 486 Marvis Dr Los Angeles CA 90065

CLAYSON, S HOLLIS
HISTORIAN
b Itasca, Ill. *Study:* Wellesley Col, BA, 68; Univ Calif, Los Angeles, MA, 75, with T J Clark, PhD, 84. *Teaching:* Asst prof art hist, Wichita State Univ, 78-82 & Northwestern Univ, Evanston, 82-90; assoc prof art hist, Northwestern Univ, Evanston, 91- *Awards:* Grant, Fund Improvement Post-Sec Educ, Dept Educ, 82; Col Art Asn Teaching Award, 90; Am Coun Learned Soc Fel, 90-91. *Mem:* Col Art Asn; Midwest Victorian Studies Asn; Midwest Art Hist Soc; Asn Art Historians, Eng. *Res:* Social iconography of later 19th century French art. *Publ:* Auth, catalog for The Second Exhibition, 1876: A Failed Attempt, The New Painting, Impressionism 1874-1886, The Fine Arts Mus, San Francisco & The Nat Art Gallery Art, Washington, DC, pp 145-159, 86; rev of Pleasures of the Belle Epoque: Entertainment and Festivity in Turn-of-the-Century France (auth, Charles Rearick), Yale Univ Press, 85, in Art in Am, 11/86; Painted Love: Prostitution in French Art of the Impressionist Era, Yale Univ Press, 91; essay: The Sexual Politics of Impressionist Illegibility, Dealing with Iegas: Representations of Women and the Politics of Vision, Richard Kendall & Griselda Pollock (eds), London, 92. *Mailing Add:* Dept Art Hist Kresge Hall Northwestern Univ Evanston IL 60201

CLEARY, B J B See Cleary, Barbara B

CLEARY, BARBARA B
PAINTER, INSTRUCTOR
b Durant, Okla, Aug, 10, 35. *Study:* Univ Okla, BS, 58; Univ Central Okla, MA, 63; also studied with John Pike, Edgar Whitney & M Douglas Walton. *Work:* Muchnic Gallery, Atchinson, Kans; Winfield Art Ctr, Kans; City of Salina, Kans; City of Newton, Kans; Main Hurdman, Kans. *Exhib:* Kansas Watercolor Soc 5-State, Wichita Art Mus, 85, 86, & 88; Art Ann V,Cult Arts Ctr, Tulsa, Okla, 86; Southern Watercolor, Okla Art Ctr, Okla City, 87-88; National Watercolor Oklahoma, Okla Art Ctr, Oklahoma City, 88-89; 115th American Watercolor Soc, Nat Gallery, New York. *Teaching:* Ft Scott Community Col. *Awards:* Past Pres Award, Fall Nat, Bakersfield, Calif, 85; Patron Award, Kans Watercolor Soc 4-State, 85; Patron Arts Award, Southern Watercolor Soc, 87. *Mem:* Kans Watercolor Soc (bd dirs, 78-79, 84-85 & 86-87); Images II, Fine Arts (chmn, 88-90). *Media:* Watercolor; oil. *Publ:* Contribr, The Best of Kansas Arts and Crafts, State of Kans, 88. *Dealer:* Richard Hamilton 17201 E 40 Hwy Independence MO 64055. *Mailing Add:* 602 E Miami Paola KS 66071

CLEARY, FRITZ
SCULPTOR, CRITIC
b New York, NY, Sept 26, 14. *Study:* St John's Univ; Nat Acad Design; Beaux-Arts Inst, with Alexander Finta & Polyenotis Vagis. *Comn:* Presidential heads, Long Br Jr High Sch, NJ; Robert Mount Mem, Monmouth Col, NJ; World War II Mem, Point Pleasant, NJ; John F Kennedy Mem, Asbury Park, NJ; Rocco Bonforte Mem, Long Branch, NJ. *Exhib:* Nat Acad Design, New York; Pa Acad Fine Arts, Philadelphia; Oakland Art Mus, Calif; Nat Sculpture Soc, Allied Artists & Hudson Valley Art Asn Ann; also in col art mus & city mus in Eastern US. *Pos:* Art critic, Asbury Park Press, 45-62, Sun, 62-72; pres & cur mus, Asbury Park Soc Fine Arts, 66-; ed adv, Nat Sculpture Rev, 74-78, ed, 84-90. *Awards:* NJ Soc Archit Ann Award, 72; John Spring Award, Nat Sculpture Soc, 74; Anna Hyatt Huntington Award Sculpture, Hudson Valley Art Asn, 75; Gold Medal, Allied Artists Am, 70. *Mem:* Allied Am Artists; fel Nat Sculpture Soc (pres, 84-88); Salamagundi Club; Nat Arts Club; Asbury Park Soc. *Media:* Bronze. *Publ:* Auth & illusr, Sixty Days Around the World, 56; auth, editorials & articles, In: Nat Sculpture Rev, 72-90; and others. *Mailing Add:* 209 Windermere Ave Asbury Park NJ 07712

CLEARY, MANON CATHERINE
PAINTER, EDUCATOR
b St Louis, Mo, Nov 14, 42. *Study:* Wash Univ, BFA, 64; Temple Univ, MFA, 68. *Work:* Corcoran Gallery Art, Washington, DC; Mem Art Gallery, Univ Rochester, NY; Brooklyn Mus, NY; Ponce Mus, PR; Phoenix Art Mus, Ariz; Utah Mus Fine Arts, Salt Lake City; Nat Mus Women in Arts, Washington, DC. *Exhib:* Fine Arts Gallery Invitational Drawing Exhib, San Diego, Calif, 77; Images of the 70's: 9 Washington Realists, Corcoran Gallery Art, Washington, DC, 80; Taft Menagerie, Taft Mus, Cincinnati, Ohio, 81; An Am Bestiary, Inst Contemp Art, Richmond, Va, 81; Am Drawings in Black & White, Brooklyn Mus, NY, 81; Perspectives on Contemporary American Realism: Works of Art on Paper from the Collection of Jalane and Richard Davidson, Pa Acad Fine Art & Chicago Art Inst, 82-83; Twentieth Century American Drawings: The Figure in Context, traveling exhib, Int Exhib Found, Terra Mus Am Art, Okla Mus Art, Nat Acad Design, 84-85; Pintura e desenhode de Manon Cleary, Centro de Arte de Arte Moderna, Gulbekian Found, Lisbon, Portugal, 85. *Pos:* Guest artist, Herning Hoiskoke, Denmark, 80; artist-in-residence, Ucross Found, Wyo, 84. *Teaching:* Instr fine arts, State Univ NY, Oswego, 68-70; prof fine arts, Univ DC, Washington, DC, 70-93, actg chairperson art dept, 85-86 & 90-91 & assoc dean, Col Lib & Fine Arts, 92-93. *Awards:* Fac Res Award, Univ DC, 83 & 89. *Bibliog:* Gerrit Henry (auth), Manon Cleary at Iolas-Jackson, Art Am, summer 82; Paul Cunnings (auth), Twentieth Century American Drawings: The Figure in Context, Int Exhib Found, 84; Jose Sommer Ribeiro & Lee Fleming (auths), Pintura E Desenho de Manon Cleary, Gulbeukian Found, 85. *Mem:* Col Art Asn. *Media:* Oil, Graphite. *Dealer:* Osuna Gallery 406 Seventh St NW Washington DC 20004. *Mailing Add:* 1736 Columbia Rd NW Washington DC 20009

CLEARY, SHIRLEY (SHIRLEY CLEARY COOPER)
PAINTER
b St Louis, Mo, Nov 14, 42. *Study:* Washington Univ, St Louis, BFA, 64; Tyler Sch Art, Temple Univ, MFA, 68; The Corcoran Mus Sch, 69-71. *Work:* Fedn Flyfishers Int Mus, W Yellowstone, Mont; Washington State Art Pub Places Collections; Herning Højskole, Denmark; Arts for the Parks, Jackson, Wyo. *Comn:* Portrait of Gov Swinden, Sen Melcher, Sen Baucus, Cong Williams (medallion), comn by Mont Democratic Party, Helena, 85-90; Limited prints, Mont ambassadors, comn by State of Mont, Helena, 86; Poster, Montana Quality Month, Comn by State of Mont, 91. *Exhib:* Drawing USA, Minn Mus Art, Minneapolis, Minn, 75; solo exhib, Mont State Mus, Helena, 75 & Herning Højskole, Denmark, 81; C M Russell Mus, Great Falls, Mont, 83 & 86-92; Women in Wildlife Art, Nat Invitaional Exhib, Wild Wings Gallery, Minneapolis, 85 & 87; America in Paint & Bronze, Mo Hist Soc Mus, St Louis, 87; Western Wildlife Gallery, San Francisco, Calif, 88; Arts for the Parks (US Tour), 89; Women Artists of the West, Calif, 90 & 92. *Pos:* Bd mem, Mont Arts Coun, 73-82; guest artist, Herning Højskole, Denmark, fall 81; artist-in-residence, Rivermeadow, Jackson Hole, 89-92. *Awards:* Best of Show, 3rd Ann Miniature Exhib, El Dorado Gallery, Colo, 84; First Place Acrylic & Gouache Painting, Bosque Art Gallery, NMex, 84 & 85; First Place, Oregon Trout Stamp, 90; First Place, Asn NW Steelheaders Stamp, 92. *Bibliog:* Ann Geracimos (auth), Shirley Cleary-artist of the West, Am Artist Mag, 4/81; Vivian A Paladin (auth), Shirley Cleary-eclectic artist in the West, Art West, 7/81; Dennis Bitton (auth), Fishermen enjoy Shirley Cleary's art, Flyfishers, 7/88; Judy Hughes (auth), Feeling the Splash of the Water, The Angling Art of Shirley Cleary, 9/92. *Mem:* Miniature Art Soc NJ; Mont Miniature Art Soc; Col Art Asn; Women Artists of the West; Mont Asn Female Exec. *Media:* Gouache, Oil. *Publ:* Illusr, covers, Mont Outdoors & Mont Fish & Games, 81-86, 92 & Flyfisher's Mag Int Fedn Flyfishermen, 86; auth, Fishing for a subject, Artist Mag, 86; The Opaque Power of Gouache, Artist's Mag, 86; La Forza Opaca della Tempera, Disegnare & Dipingere, 11/87. *Dealer:* Wyoming Galleries 50 E Broadway Jackson WY; The Hole in the Wall PO Box 321 Ennis MT 59729. *Mailing Add:* 1804 Beltview Dr Helena MT 59601

CLEAVER, DALE GORDON
HISTORIAN, EDUCATOR
b Lafayette, Ind, June 24, 28. *Study:* Willamette Univ, BA, 50; Univ Chicago, MA, 52, Fulbright Res Grant Belg painting, 52-53, PhD, 55. *Pos:* Adviser, Dulin Gallery Art, Knoxville, 74-79; mem acquisitions comt, Hunter Mus, Chattanooga, 76-88. *Teaching:* Prof 19th & 20th century painting, sculpture & archit, Univ Tenn, Knoxville, 58-88; retired, 88. *Awards:* Lindsay Young Professorship Art Hist, 80; Outstanding Teacher Award, Univ Tenn Alumni, 81. *Mem:* Col Art Asn Am; Southeastern Col Art Asn. *Res:* Belgian 19th century painting; French landscape painting of the late 18th and early 19th centuries. *Publ:* Auth, Three combat scenes by Henri Leys, Bull Mus Royaux des Beaux-Arts de Belg, 6/53; The concept of time in modern sculpture, summer 63 & Girodet's deluge: A case study in art criticism, winter, 79, Art J; Art: An Introduction, 66, rev ed, 85 & coauth, Art and Music: An Introduction, 77, Harcourt Brace; Michallon et la theorie du paysage, Revue du Louvre, 12/81. *Mailing Add:* 2429 Lake Moor D Knoxville TN 37919

CLEMENT, ALAIN GERARD
PHOTOGRAPHER
b France. *Study:* Univ Dijon France, 68. *Work:* Menil Collection, Houston, Tex; Houston Mus Fine Art, Tex; Bibliotheque Nationale, Paris; Dallas Mus art, Tex; Musee Nicephore Niepce, Chalons/Saone, France. *Exhib:* Art from Houston in Norway, Stavanger Art Mus, Norway, 82; Constructions & Photographs, Art Inst, San Antonio, Tex, 84; Intersections, Gloria Laguna Mus, Austin, Tex, 86; Focus 87, Art Gallery of Ontario, Toronto, Can, 87; Recent Acquisitions, Mus Fine Art, Houston, Tex, 90; Works on Paper, McNeese Mus, Lake Charles, La, 90; Photography the Eighties: Discovery & Invention, Special Exhib Art Fair, Basel, Switzerland, 90. *Awards:* Creative Artist Program Award, Cult Arts Coun, 87; Nat Endowment Arts, 88. *Bibliog:* Edward Lucie-Smith (auth), American Art Now, William Morrow, 85; Anne Tucker (auth), Deep in the Heart of Texas, Am Photogr, 87; Mel McCombie (auth), Alain Clement, Art News, 88. *Dealer:* Graham Gallery 1431 W Alabama Houston TX 77006; Jane Corkin Gallery 179 John St Toronto Can. *Mailing Add:* 408 Archer St Houston TX 77009

CLEMENT, KATHLEEN (RUTH)
PAINTER, GRAPHIC ARTIST
b Ord, Nebr, May 28, 28. *Study:* Univ Nebr, BA, 50; with Frank Gonzalez, 67-69; Univ Am, with Toby Joysmith, 77-79; Mus Studies, Paris, 80. *Work:* Mus Mod Art, Isidro Fabela Cult Ctr & Inst North Am Cult Relations, Mexico; House of Humour & Satire, Gabravo, Bulgaria, 88. *Comn:* Paintings comn by, Co Minera Autlan, Elias Mussali & Jacobo Margolis; Rudolf Mosny; Embotelladora De Sinaloa. *Exhib:* solo exhib, Rossi Gallery, Morristown, NJ,

83, Mus Puebla, Mex, 91, Mus Fine Arts, Toluca, Mex, 92; Nat Mus Fine Arts, Mex, 88; Latin Am Art, Germany, Austria, 88; Biennal-Humour & Satire, Gabravo, Bulgaria, 89; Rafael Matos Gallery, Mex, 90; and others. *Awards:* Prize in Graphics, Nebr Reg Compt, 48; Delta Phi Delta; Purchase Prize, Bienal, Gabrovo, Bulgaria, 88. *Bibliog:* Jorge J Crespo de la Serna (auth), article, Novedades, 3/30/76; Berta Taracena (auth), article, Tiempo, 5/24/82; Gloria Bucco (auth), article, Vail Daily, 4/485; Unicorno Blanco, Mex, 90. *Mem:* SOMART; Foro de Arte Contemporanio. *Media:* Acrylic, Pen & Ink. *Dealer:* Sibley 19-01 21st Dr Astoria New York NY 11105. *Mailing Add:* Tulipan 359 Col El Toro Contreras Mexico 10610 DF Mexico

CLEMENT, SHIRLEY
PAINTER
b New York, NY July 7, 22. *Study:* Ringling Sch Art, two yrs; Amagansett Art Sch, Sarasota, Fla, two yrs. *Work:* Univ Fla, Gainesville; Davenport Munic Gallery, Iowa; Henry Ward Ranger Fund, New York. *Exhib:* Am Watercolor Soc, Nat Acad, New York, 50-; Watercolor Show, Phoenix Mus, 68; Winterpark Sidewalk Art Festival, Fla, 71; Disneys Festival of the Masters, Lake Buena Vista, Fla, 74; Nat Acad Show, New York & High Mus, 74; Allied Artists, Nat Arts Club, New York, 74. *Awards:* Salmagundi Award, Am Watercolor Soc, 69; William A Paton Award, Nat Acad Design, 74; Verda Karen McCracken Young Award, Am Watercolor Soc, 77. *Mem:* Am Watercolor Soc; Fla Artist Group; Fla Watercolor Soc; Sarasota Art Asn; Manatee Art League. *Media:* Watercolor, Acrylic. *Publ:* Auth, article on The watercolor page, Am Artist, 4/48. *Mailing Add:* 3951 Red Rock Lane Sarasota FL 34231

CLEMENTE, FRANCESCO
PAINTER
b Naples, Italy, 52. *Exhib:* Solo exhibs, Centro Cultural Arte Contemporaneo, 89-90, Salvador Riera Galeria D'Art, Barcelona, 89-90, Vrej Baghoomian Gallery, NY, 89-90, Sperone Westwater Gallery, NY, 90, Philadelphia Mus Art, 90; Pritns and Multiples, Krygier/Landau Contemporary Art, Santa Monica, Calif, 90; Numbeis One 1990, Galeria Daval Set, Barcelona, 90; Kunsthalle, Nurembers, Ger, 90; Artists for Amnesty, Blum Helman Gallery & Germans van Eck Gallery, NY, 90; Annual 2RC, Contemp Graphics Exhib Fiorella Ulbinati Gallery, Los Angeles, 90; retrospectives, Kunstmuseum Basel, Mus fur Gegenwartskunst, Switz, 92, Leccese Spruth Galerie, Cologne, 92, Gallery Bruno Bischofberger, Zurich, 92, Gagosian Gallery, New York, 92. *Bibliog:* Basel: Clemente Back to Front, FlashArt, Flash Art News, 1-2/92; Bernice Rose (auth), Allegories of Modernism: Contemporary Drawing, NY Mus Mod Art, 92; Michael Kimmelman (auth), Just What Is a Drawing? Definitions, Definitions, NY Times, 2/21/92; Allan Schwartzman (auth), The Big Chill, Connoisseur, 2/92. *Dealer:* Sperone Westwater 142 Greene. *Mailing Add:* 684 Broadway New York NY 10012

CLEMENTS, ROBERT DONALD
EDUCATOR, SCULPTOR
b Pittsburgh, Pa, Dec 24, 37. *Study:* Carnegie-Mellon Univ, BFA(painting), 59; Pa State Univ, MA(art), 62, PhD(art educ), 64. *Work:* Nat Mus Am Arts, Smithsonian Inst, Washington, DC; Jacksonville Mus Arts; AT&T; Chase Manhattan Bank; Coca Cola USA. *Comn:* Sculpture, Fifty Yuppies, Arts festival of Atlanta, 87; Indian Creek MARTA Sta, Atlanta; mobiles, OK Cafe, Atlanta. *Exhib:* One-man show, Totems to Southerners & the South, Hunter Mus Art, Montgomery Mus & Asheville Mus; Nat Sculpture '80; South Exhib, Palazzo Venezia, Rome, 84; Atlanta in France, Sorbonne, Paris & Toulouse, 85. *Pos:* Art consult, Arts & Humanities Prog, US Off Educ, 68-69. *Teaching:* Asst prof art, Ball State Univ, 64-68; assoc prof art, Univ Ga, 69-81, prof art, 81- *Awards:* Gen Sandy Beaver Teaching Prof, 85-88; Energy Art Award, 82; Univ Affiliated Fel, Ga VAP, 86-; Ga Endowment Arts, Artist Grant, 87. *Bibliog:* Cynthia Bickley Green (auth), Robert Clements, Art Papers, Vol 10, No 5, 86; Joy Lee (auth), Wood sculpture, Arts/Crafts, spring 80; Charlotte von Glasersfeld (auth), article, Art Papers, 11/83; Barbara Mackenzie (auth), Old & new blend in Clements' sculpture, Atlanta Constitution, 7/22/86. *Mem:* Nat Art Educ Asn; Ga Art Educ Asn; Southern Asn Sculptors; Int Sculpture Ctr. *Publ:* Auth, Metaphor in Art Education, Art Educ, 9/82; auth, The inductive method of teaching visual art criticism, J Aesthetic Educ, 7/79; auth, Modern architecture's debt to creativity education, Gifted Child Quart, summer 81; coauth (with Claire Clements), Art and Mainstreaming, Art Instruction for Exceptional Children in Regular Classrooms, Charles C Thomas, 84; coauth, Emphasis Art: A Qualitative Art Program for Elementary & Middle School, Harper Collins, 92. *Dealer:* Fay Gold Gallery 247 Buckhead Ave NW Atlanta GA 30305. *Mailing Add:* 155 Bar H Ct Athens GA 30601

CLERK, PIERRE
PAINTER, SCULPTOR
b Atlanta, Ga, Apr 26, 28. *Study:* Loyola Col; McGill Univ; Montreal Sch Art & Design; Acad Julian, Paris; Acad Grande Chaumiere, Paris. *Work:* Mus Mod Art, Guggenheim Mus & Whitney Mus Am Art, New York; Nat Gallery Can, Ottawa, Ont; Mus Contemp Art, Montreal. *Comn:* City Walls, NY; Com Bank of Kansas City; First Wis Develop Corp, Milwaukee; Marine Midland Bank, NY; sculpture, City Toledo, 83; and others. *Exhib:* One-man exhibs, Everson Mus Art, Syracuse, NY, 77, Waterside Plaza, NY, 77, Monumental Outdoor Sculpture, NY, 77-78, Iran-Am Ctr, Tehran, Iran, 78 & Metrop Mus, Manila, Philippines, 78; and others. *Awards:* US Info Serv Exhib Grant, 77; Munic Art Soc Grant, 77; US State Dept Travel Grant, 77-78; and others. *Mailing Add:* 70 Grand St New York NY 10013

CLEVELAND, ROBERT EARL
ADMINISTRATOR, EDUCATOR
b Union, Miss, June 8, 36. *Study:* Miss Col, BA; Univ Miss, MFA; Univ Tenn, EdD. *Work:* Univ Miss Fine Arts Ctr, University, Miss. *Comn:* Redwood sculpture, Carson-Newman Col, 76; redwood sculpture, First Nat Bank, 85; wood & fibre glass resin sculpture, First People's Bank, 85. *Exhib:* Second Nat Print & Drawing Exhib, Dulin Gallery Art, Knoxville, Tenn, 67; Tenn Watercolor Exhib, Cheekwood Mus, Nashville, 75; Quinlan Ann Art Exhib, Gainesville, Ga, 76; Carroll Reece Mus, Johnson City, Tenn, 77; Owensboro Mus Fine Arts, Ky, 79; Somerhill Gallery, Durham, NC, 80; Goldsboro Ann Art Exhib, NC, 85; Sacred Arts Seven Exhib, Wheaton, Ill, 85; Whiting Gallery, Fairhope, Ala, 86; 50-yr retrospective, Toledo Mus Art, 88. *Pos:* Artist-illusr, Ling-Temco-Vought Inc, Dallas, Tex, 61-62. *Teaching:* Instr art, Univ Miss, Oxford, 63-64; prof art & chmn dept, Carson-Newman Col, Jefferson City, 64- *Awards:* First Prize Painting, Morristown Art Competition, Tenn, 66 & Macon Ann Arts Exhib, Macon Arts Coun, 73; First Prize Drawing, Oak Ridge Relig Art Exhib, Oak Ridge Art Ctr, Tenn, 76; Second Prize, Centennial Photography Exhib, Knoxville, Tenn, 85. *Mem:* Nat Asn Schs Art; Nat Coun Art Adminrs; Southeastern Col Art Conf; Tenn Watercolor Soc. *Media:* Watercolor, Drawing. *Res:* Arts administration in higher education and art and law issues. *Publ:* Auth, Art and the Law, 77 & auth, The Art Department Chairperson: An Ambiguous Role, 78, Nat Coun Art Adminrs; The law: Public aid and the private sector, 78 & Art administration in pursuit of efficacy, 83, Fac Studies; Structured Models for Managing Conflict, Fac Studies, 85. *Mailing Add:* Box 1901 Art Dept Carson-Newman Col Jefferson City TN 37760

CLIFF, DENIS ANTONY
PAINTER, INSTUCTOR
b Victoria, BC, Aug 8, 42. *Study:* Univ Victoria, BEd, 65; New Sch Art, 66-67. *Work:* Nat Gallery Can, Art Bank Gallery, Ottawa; Charlottetown Confederation Ctr Arts, PEI; Univ Sask, Saskatoon; Art Gallery of Northumberland, Cobourg, Ont. *Comn:* Murals, Ostler Sch Nursing, Toronto, 70, Simcoe Bd Educ, Ont, 71, Eaton Ctr, Toronto, 78 & Fisher-Price, Toronto, 79; Parkdale Focus Mural, Toronto, 92. *Exhib:* New Blood, Rodman Hall Art Ctr, St Catherines, Ont, 73; Can Invitational, Can Consulate, Chicago, 77; Artists Coop Toronto at Nexus, Philadelphia, 78; Explorations, Thames Art Ctr, Chatham, Ont, 80; Toronto Exchange, Mem Univ, St Johns, Nfld, 81. *Pos:* Dir, Artist's Co-op, Toronto, 77-82; pres, Arts Sake Inc, 78-80; vpres, Workscene Co-op Gallery, 88-89. *Teaching:* Artist in residence, Canador Col, North Bay, Ont, 72-74 & Arts Sake, Toronto, 77-79; vis prof, York Univ, Toronto, 79-82; asst prof, Univ Victoria, 82-; instr, Toronto Sch Art, 85- *Awards:* Best Painting, 70 & Best in Show, 71, City Toronto Ann; Can Coun Grant, 79; Ontario Arts Coun Award, 88. *Bibliog:* Sandra Shaul (auth), Altered egos: An exhibition of drawings by Denis Cliff, 77; Diane Pugen (auth), article, 78, Art Mag; Margie Kelk (auth), Denis Cliff: Drawings, 92. *Mem:* Royal Can Acad Art. *Media:* Acrylic on Canvas, Drawing on Paper Collage. *Dealer:* Workscene Gallery 183 Bathurst St #302 Toronto Ont Canada. *Mailing Add:* 207A Cowan Ave Toronto ON M6K 2N7 Canada

CLIFFORD, JUTTA
DEALER, LECTURER
b The Hague, Holland; US citizen. *Study:* Univ Dallas, printmaking, 74 with Jurgen Strunck; Abitur Klosterscule, Hamburg, Ger, 64. *Pos:* Owner/dir, Clifford Gallery, 74- *Mem:* Dallas Print & Drawing Soc; Dallas Art Dealers Asn. *Specialty:* Contemporary art - fine prints, sculpture and paintings; eight exhibitions annually. *Mailing Add:* 9022 Lydgate Dr Dallas TX 75238

CLIFT, WILLIAM BROOKS
PHOTOGRAPHER
b Boston, Mass, Jan 5, 44. *Study:* Workshop Paul Caponigro, 59. *Work:* Metrop Mus Art, Mus Mod Art, New York; Art Inst Chicago; Mus Fine Arts, Boston; Nat Gallery, Canberra, Australia; Fogg Art Mus, Yale Univ; Mus Fine Arts, Santa Fe; Libr Congress, Washington, DC; Nat Mus Am Art. *Comn:* Photographs, Old City Hall, Boston, Mass Coun Arts, 70, American County Courthouses, Joseph Seagrams & Sons, New York, 75-76, American Images, Am Tel & Tel, New York, 78 & Hudson River, Readers Digest Asn, 85-88. *Exhib:* Solo exhibs, Old City Hall, Boston, Worcester Art Mus, Mass, 71, Landscapes, Mus Fine Art, Santa Fe, 79, Phoenix Art Mus, 81, Chicago Art Inst, 87 & Amon Carter Mus, Ft Worth, Tex, 87; Court House, 77, Mirrors and Windows, 78 & American Landscapes, 81, Mus Mod Art, New York; Counterparts, Metrop Mus Art, New York, 82; Landmarks Reviewed, Pensacola Mus Art, Fla, 83; one man shows, Boston Atheneum, Mass, Eclipse Gallery, Boulder, Colo, 83, Bank Santa Fe, NMex & Susan Harder Gallery, New York, 84; Western Spaces, Burden Gallery, New York, 85; retrospective, Equitable Gallery, New York, 93. *Awards:* Fels, Nat Endowment Arts, 72 & 79 & Guggenheim Found, 74 & 80. *Bibliog:* Erla Zwingle (auth), Romancing the stones, Am Photogr, 6/87. *Mem:* Charter mem Asn Heliographers; NMex Coun Photog. *Publ:* Coauth, American Images, McGraw-Hill, 79; contribr, American Photographers in the National Parks, Viking, 81; Counterparts-Form and Emotions in Photographs, Metrop Mus Art, 82; Landmarks Reviewed, Pensacola Mus Art, 83; Photographic Viewpoints, Boston Mus Fine Arts, 85; auth, Certain Places, William Clift Eds, 87; A Hudson Landscape, William Clift Eds, 93. *Mailing Add:* PO Box 6035 Santa Fe NM 87502

CLIFTON, MICHELLE GAMM
SCULPTOR, FILMMAKER
b Los Angeles, Calif, July 11, 44. *Study:* Yale Univ, summer scholar, 65; Univ Ill, Urbana, with Lee Chesney, BFA, 66; Pa State Univ, with Carol Summers, MFA, 68. *Work:* Mus City New York; Los Angeles Co Mus Art; Meany Ctr

for Labor Studies, Silver Spring, Md; State Univ NY Col, Potsdam; US Info Agency, Washington, DC. *Comn:* Soft New York Times, comn by Carey Peck, A O Sulzberger at New York Times, 76; Bathroom Faucet (3-D billboard), Pasco Hernando Community Col, Brookville, Fla, 79. *Exhib:* Libr Cong, Washington, DC, 69; Fun & Fantasy, Xerox Ctr, Rochester, NY, 73; Renwick Gallery, Smithsonian Inst, Washington, DC, 74-75; Dayton Art Inst, Ohio, 77; two-person show, Cordy Gallery, New York, 77; Whimsy, Taft Mus & Cincinnati Inst of Fine Arts, 78; one-person shows, Great Am Foot Show, Mus Contemp Crafts, New York, 78 & US Military Acad, West Point, 81; Mus Art, Carnegie Inst, Pittsburgh, 79; and others. *Pos:* Art dir, Hardtimes Movie Co, Garrison, 72-; art dir & vpres, Hudson River Film Co, Garrison, 77-; art dir & production mgr, Henry Hudson's River: A Biography (film), 79. *Teaching:* Asst drawing & printmaking, Pa State Univ, 66-68. *Awards:* Hon Mention as Art Dir, Emmy Winner Christina's World, 77; Cine Golden Eagle Award, 79; Grand Award, Houston Int Film Festival, 79. *Bibliog:* Steven Lindstedt (auth), Soft Sculpture, Family Creative Workshop, 76; Erica Brown (auth), ! unking in a barnyard, New York Times, 12/25/77; Carol Sama (auth), Michelle Gamm Clifton lives in a material world, Houston Home & Garden, 5/77. *Mem:* Am Crafts Coun; Nat Acad TV Arts & Sci. *Media:* Fabric, Stuffing. *Publ:* Illusr series, Gerald Ford's America, San Francisco Pub TV, 75; auth & illusr cover, New York City couch, Art Now Gallery Guide, summer 77. *Mailing Add:* South Mountain Pass Rd Garrison NY 10524

CLINE, CLINTON C
PRINTMAKER, EDUCATOR
b Granite City, Ill, Oct 21, 34. *Study:* E Los Angeles Col, AA, 62; Calif State Univ, Long Beach, BA, 65, MA, 68. *Work:* Univ Tex, Irving; Univ SDak; Downey Art Mus, Calif; Palm Springs Mus, Calif; Drake Univ, Des Moines, Iowa. *Exhib:* 15th Joslyn Biennial, Joslyn Art Mus, Omaha, Nebr, 78; 21st Nat Exhib, Okla Art Ctr, Oklahoma City, 79; Univ Tex Nat, Irving, 79; travelling group, Collagraph Problem Solving, 88-90; 16th Harper Col Nat, 92; 36th Ann, Unterdon Art Ctr, 92. *Collections Arranged:* 1975 Governor's Awards for the Arts and Humanities, 75; In Their Own Image, Southern Conn State Col, 76. *Teaching:* Lithography, Univ Colo, Boulder, 69-, full prof, currently. *Awards:* Purchase Awards, Los Angeles Printmaking Soc, 79 & Vermillion Nat Print & Drawing, 79. *Bibliog:* Leonard Edmundson (auth), Etching, Van Nostrand Reinhold, 73; Eldon L Cunningham (auth), biog, A Primary Form of Expression. *Media:* Lithography, Intaglio. *Publ:* Publisher, First National Colorado Print and Drawing, 74; Border to Border print publ, Univ SDak, Univ Colo, Univ Neb, Univ Minn; Int Juried, Univ SDak; First Nat Printmaking Slides & Video Exchange, E C Cunningham. *Dealer:* Emerson Gallery 23 E 74th St New York NY 10021. *Mailing Add:* Fine Arts Dept Univ Colo Boulder Boulder CO 80309

CLINEDINST, KATHERINE PARSONS
PAINTER, LECTURER
b Stamford, Conn, July 13, 03. *Study:* Pratt Inst, with Jessie Leigh; China Inst, with Prof Wang. *Exhib:* Smithsonian Inst, Washington, DC; Springfield Mus, Mass; Asbury Park Mus, NJ; Hammond Mus, South Salem, NY. *Pos:* Asst mgr, Boston Soc Arts & Crafts, New York, 23-24. *Awards:* Hudson Valley Art Asn Award for Dr Woodrow, White Plains, NY, 63; Meridan Art Asn Award, Conn, 67; Mt Vernon Art Asn Award, NY, 67; Cash Prize, NJ State Show, 85. *Mem:* Ocean Co Art Guild NJ; Asbury Fine Arts Asn; Nat League Am Pen Women (pres, Westchester Br, 59-61); Kent Art Asn, Conn; Monmouth Art Asn. *Media:* Watercolor, Oil. *Mailing Add:* 400 Locust Ave Lakewood NJ 08701

CLINTON, PAUL ARTHUR
PRINTMAKER, INSTRUCTOR
b Salem, Ore, Nov 1, 42. *Study:* Ore State Univ, BA, 68; Tamarind Lithography Workshop, master printer, 70; Univ SFla, MFA, 77. *Work:* Mus Mod Art, New York; Brooklyn Mus; Pasadena Art Mus, Calif; Tex Technol Univ, Lubbock; Gruenwald Graphics Art Found, Univ Calif, Los Angeles. *Comn:* Sculpture, City of Tacoma, 84. *Exhib:* Univ Wis, Madison, 75; Univ Dallas, Irving, 75; State Capitol Mus, Olympia, Wash, 78; Brooklyn Mus, 79; Okla Art Ctr, Oklahoma City, 81; Wash Painting & Sculpture, 83; and others. *Collections Arranged:* Collaboration, Prints by Major American Artists, Tacoma Art Mus, 81. *Pos:* Master printer, Tamarind Lithography Workshop, Los Angeles, 69-70; master printer, Gemini, Los Angeles, 70; master printer, Cirrus Ed, Los Angeles, 70-71; master printer, Graphicstudio, Univ SFla, Tampa, 71-76; proprietor, Arch Press. *Teaching:* Asst prof, Univ SFla, Tampa, 71-76; instr, Ft Steilacoom Community Col, Tacoma, Wash, 77- *Awards:* Printers Fel & Ford Found, 69. *Mem:* NW Print Coun; World Print Coun. *Media:* Lithography, Intaglio. *Publ:* Contribr, Printmaking: History and Process, Holt, Rinehart, Winston, 78. *Mailing Add:* 1603 Sequalish Steilacoom WA 98388

CLISBY, ROGER DAVID
CURATOR, HISTORIAN
b New York, NY, Feb 8, 39. *Study:* Pa State Univ, BA 61, MA, 68; Goethe Inst, 66, Univ Calif, Berkely, 84, certs. *Pos:* Dir, Artspace Alternative Space Gallery, Sacramento, 77-78; actg dir, Crocker Art Mus, Sacramento, 83 & chief cur, 83-85; deputy dir & chief cur, The Chrysler Mus, Norfolk, Va, 85-89, actg dir, 89. *Teaching:* Instr Northern Renaissance art, Univ Calif, Davis, 73; lectr gallery admn, Calif State Univ, Sacramento, 74-75. *Mem:* Calif Arts Coun (adv panel, 83-84); Norfolk Rotary Club; Va Comn Arts (grants panel, 87-88); Nat Endowment Arts (panelist, 87). *Res:* General research on Italian, German, Dutch, French painting and drawing from Renaissance to the present. *Publ:* Auth, Roy De Forest: Recent Painting, Drawings and Constructions (catalog), 80; Philip Menard: Retrospective of Paintings and Drawings (catalog), 81; Welcome to the Candy Store! An Exhibition of Paintings, Drawings and Sculpture from the Candy Store Gallery (catalog), 81; Masterworks of Photography from the Rubel Collection (catalog), 82; Wayne Theibaud: Landscapes and City Views (catalog), 83; Peter Vandenberge Recent Ceramic Heads (catalog), 85; Contempory American Monotypes (catalog), 85. *Mailing Add:* c/o Columbia Mus Art 480 E Broad St Columbus OH 43215

CLIVE, RICHARD R
PAINTER
b New York, NY, Jan 8, 12. *Study:* Nat Acad Design, 30; NY Univ, BFA, 35; also with Dan Greene & Harold Wolcott. *Work:* US Navy Combat Art Collection, Washington, DC; Munic Collection, Ossining, NY; Munic Collection, Gloucester, Mass; Addision-Gilbert Hosp, Gloucester, Mass; Fordham Univ Collection. *Comn:* WAVES at US Naval Training Ctr, Bainbridge, Md; Marines & Civilians, S Vietnam, Dept of Navy, Washington, DC. *Exhib:* Salmagundi Club Ann, 61-84; Am Friends Hebrew Univ Art Festival, 63-65; four presentations, Naval Art Coop & Liaison Comt, 63-72; Stevens Ctr Art Exhib, Stevens Inst Technol, 68; Society Animal Artists, 83; Oil Pastel Asn. *Teaching:* Elizabeth Seton Col. *Awards:* Portrait Prize, 67 & First Prize Graphic, 68, New Rochelle Art Asn; Lt Harry E Breng Award, Am Legion, 68; Purchase Award, Miniature Art Soc NJ. *Mem:* Hon mem Salmagundi Club (pres, 79-81); Am Artists Prof League; Acad Artists Asn; Pastel Soc Am; Miniature Art Soc NJ; Soc Animal Artists. *Media:* Oil, Pastel. *Mailing Add:* 19 Henry Ct Dobbs Ferry NY 10522

CLIVER, KENDRA-JEAN (KENDRA-JEAN CLIVER KRIENKE)
DEALER, PAINTER
b Plainfield, NJ. *Study:* Drew Univ, with Lee Hall & Peter Chapin, BA; Nat Acad Design, with Philip Isenberg, watercolor with Nicholas Reale. *Work:* Drew Univ Collection, Madison, NJ; Douglass Col Collection, New Brunswick, NJ; US Steel. *Comn:* Portrait of retiring dean, Douglass Col, 70; Portrait--US Steel, Coun Tennant, Summit, NJ, 70; Christmas Card Design, Spaulding for Children, Westfield, NJ, 72; Drawing of AT&T Bldg, AT&T Int Hq, Basking Ridge, NJ, 78; and others. *Exhib:* Group show, AT&T Hq Gallery, Basking Ridge, 79. *Collections Arranged:* 19th Century American Paintings, 82; American Paintings, Nabisco Gallery, 84; Fifty Years of 19th Century American Painting, Schering-Plough, 86; Childhood Enchantments, Mus Cartoon Art, 89. *Pos:* Free lance portrait artist, 70-75; art restorationist, Princeton Fine Arts; art restorationist, Whistler's Daughter Gallery, art dealer, framer & designer, 72-, art dealer, 74-; art dealer, Whistler Gallery, 84-90 & Kendra Krienke, 90-92. *Awards:* Purchase Award, Drew Univ, 68; Selection Award for Christmas Card, Spaulding for Children, 72 & Hon Mention, 73. *Bibliog:* Liz Matt (dir), State of the Arts (doc film), NJ Pub TV, 82 & 84; Bruce Gimelson (dir), What's It Worth (interview), New York cable TV, 88; Vivian Raynon (auth), Children's Illustrations: From 1880- 1940, NY Times, 5/7/89; Young at Heart, Colonial Homes Mag, 2/90; The seven hottest collectibles, Metrop Home Mag, 4/91. *Mem:* Soc Illusrs, 91- *Media:* Watercolor, Mixed Media. *Specialty:* Original Art By Illustrators For Children and Fantasy, 1880- 1950, including Arthur Rackham, Kay Nielsen, Jessie Willcox Smith, Fanny Young Cory, Harold Gaze, Ludwig Bemelmans, among others. *Publ:* Contribr, Art Lovers Cookbook, Summit Art Ctr, 75; American Illustrator Art, Random House, 91; ten full color exhib catalogs. *Mailing Add:* 230 Central Park W New York NY 10024

CLOAR, CARROLL
PAINTER
b Earle, Ark, Jan 18, 13. *Study:* Southwestern Memphis, BA; Memphis Acad Arts; Art Students League, MacDowell fel, 40; DH, Southwestern Memphis, 77; Southwestern Col, Hon Doc Arts, 78. *Work:* Metrop Mus Art, Mus Mod Art & Whitney Mus Am Art, New York; Brooks Mem Art Gallery, Memphis; Joseph H Hirshhorn Mus, Washington, DC; also pvt collections of Nelson Rockefeller, Laurance Rockefeller, John D Rockefeller III, Jack Lemmon, Dinah Shore, Stanley Marcus, Shelley Winters & others. *Exhib:* Retrospective, State Univ NY, Albany, Tenn State Mus, Nashville, 83; Pittsburgh Int; Metrop Mus Mod Art; Pa Acad Fine Arts Ann, Philadelphia; Brooks Mem Art Gallery, Memphis; one-man shows, Forum Gallery, New York, 79, 81, 83 & 85; Whitney Art Mus, New York. *Pos:* Bd trustees, Brooks Mem Art Gallery, 69-71. *Awards:* Guggenheim Fel, 46; Am Acad Arts & Lett Prize, 67. *Bibliog:* An Arkansas boyhood, Horizon, 11/58; Summer dies as slowly, Time Mag, 8/19/66; Growing up in the Arkansas Delta, Esquire, 6/69. *Media:* Acrylic, Oil. *Publ:* Auth, Hostile Butterflies & Other Paintings, Memphis State Univ Press. *Dealer:* Schmidt-Bingham 41 W 57th New York NY 10019. *Mailing Add:* 235 S Greer Memphis TN 38111

CLOSE, CHUCK
PAINTER
b Monroe, Wash, July 5, 40. *Study:* Everett Community Col, Wash, 58-60; Yale Summer Sch Music & Art, Norfolk, Conn, 61; Univ Wash Sch Art, Seattle, BA, 62; Yale Univ Sch Art & Archit, New Haven, Conn, BFA, 63, MFA, 64; Acad Fine Arts, Vienna, Austria, Fulbright grant, 64-65. *Work:* Mus Mod Art & Whitney Mus Am Art, New York; Walker Art Ctr, Minneapolis; Neue Gallerie, Aachen, Ger; Art Gallery Ont, Toronto; Albright-Knox Art Gallery, Buffalo; and many others. *Exhib:* 22 Realists, Whitney Mus Am Art, 70, Baltimore Mus Art, Md, 76, Wadsworth Atheneum Mus (with catalog), Hartford, Conn, 77-78, Contemp Arts Mus (with catalog) Houston, 85; one-man shows, Los Angeles Co Mus, 71, Mus Contemp Art, Chicago, 71 & Mus Mod Art, New York, 73, Artists Choice: Chuck Close, Mus Mod Art, NY, 91, Large Polaroids, Contemp Mus, Honolulu, 91 & Pace Gallery, New York, 91; Documenta V, Kassel, WGer, 72; George Pompidou Centre, Paris, 79; retrospective, Walker Art Ctr, Minneapolis, traveling, 80-81; Calif Mus Photog, Univ Calif, Riverside, 82;

Jacksonville Art Mus, Dec 82-Jan 83; Columbia Mus, S Carolina, 11/84-1/85; Pace/MacGill Gallery, New York, Jan & Feb/85; Aldrich Mus Contemp Art, Ridgefield, Conn, 4/87; Pace Gallery, New York, 9/88; Yokohama Mus Art, Japan, 89; group show, Whitney Biennial Exhib, Whitney Mus Am Art, New York; and others. *Teaching:* Instr art, Univ Mass Sch Art, Amherst, 65-67; Sch Visual Arts, New York, 67-71; NY Univ, 70-73. *Awards:* Infinity Award, Int Ctr Photogr, 90; Acad-Inst Awards in Art, Am Acad & Inst Arts & Lett, 91 & elected to Acad, 92. *Bibliog:* Barbara Harshman (auth), An interview with Chuck Close, 6/78, Kim Levin (auth), Chuck Close: Decoding the image, 6/78 & Lisa Lyons (auth), Close portraits, 80, Arts Mag; HH Annason (auth), History of Modern Art: Painting, Sculpture, Architecture, 3rd ed, New York, Harry N Abrams Inc, 86; Robert Storr & Lisa Lyons (coauth), Chuck Close, Rizzoli Int Publ, New York, 87; John Daxland (auth), Up Close and Personal, Daily News, 10/1/88 & Arlene Raven (auth), I to Eye, The Voice, 1/31/89; and many others. *Media:* All Media. *Dealer:* Pace Gallery 32 E 57th St New York NY 10022. *Mailing Add:* 271 Central Pk W New York NY 10024

CLOSE, DEAN PURDY
PAINTER, ART DEALER
b Holmesville, Ohio, Aug 15, 05. *Study:* Ohio Northern Univ; Ohio State Univ; also with Charles William Duvall. *Work:* Am Embassies, Japan & Ger & in many pvt collections. *Exhib:* Columbus Art League, Ohio, 38-50; Butler Art Inst Am, 40; Ogonquit, Maine, 40. *Pos:* Dir, Fifth Avenue Galleries, Columbus, Ohio, 61- *Media:* Oil, Acrylic. *Specialty:* American art. *Interests:* The status of American impressionism. *Collection:* Works of Croft, Leslie Cope, R Wagner and other fine American impressionists. *Mailing Add:* 3130 Glenrich Pkwy Columbus OH 43221

CLOSE, FRANK
STAINED GLASS ARTIST, SCULPTOR
b Dec 28, 47. *Study:* Univ Ky, BA, 71; stained glass with Casey Lewis & Peter Mollica, Berkeley, Calif, 75; glass design with Kenneth van Roenn, Univ Ky, 76 & Ludwig Schaffrath, Berkeley, Calif, 77; glass painting with Albinas Elskus, Washington, DC, 78; hot glass with Fred Mercer, Louisville Sch Art, Ky. *Comn:* entry piece, Oliver Wendell Holmes Libr, Phillips Acad, Andover, Mass, 89; lead & glass piece (5' x 5'), Costain Group, Lexington, Ky, 90; two works, (73" x 94" each), Office Ctr, Short Hills, NJ, 90; Totem MCMXCI, IBM Data Ctr, Rochester, NY, 91; Suspended Construction, Minn Percent Arts, Alexandria, 92. *Exhib:* Wood & Glass, 86 & Crafts Invitational, 87, Southeastern Ctr for Contemp Art, Winston-Salem, NC; Glass Invitational, Ind Univ Southeast, New Albany, 86; Glasswork, Ky Art & Craft Gallery, Louisville, 87; group shows, Triangle Gallery, Lexington, Ky, 88 & John Davis Gallery, New York, 88; 2e Salon Int du Vitrail 1989, Chartres, France. *Pos:* Cur, Waller Gallery exhibs, Lexington, Ky, 79-82; Henry Faulkner, Opera House Gallery, Lexington, Ky, 82; lectr, many univ & mus. *Teaching:* Instr, Univ Ky, Lexington, 70-83. *Bibliog:* Contemporary glass (catalog), Louisville Art Gallery, 86; New Work in New York, New Work, winter-spring 86; Glasswork (catalog), Ky Art & Craft Found Gallery, 87. *Mailing Add:* 397 W 12th St New York NY 10014

CLOSSON, NANCI BLAIR
PAINTER, COLLAGE ARTIST
b Durham, NC, Sept 5, 43. *Study:* Purdue Univ, BA, 65; Univ Ariz, grad studies ceramics, printmaking, 84-89. *Work:* Springfield Art Mus, Springfield, Mo; Ind Univ, Bloomington; Dopson Hicks, Inc, Tampa, Fla; Southwest Forest Industs, Phoenix, Ariz; Richard Houser & Assoc, Los Angeles. *Comn:* Painting (acrylic), Eli Lilly Corp, Indianapolis, Ind. *Exhib:* Watercolor USA, Springfield, Mo, 73-86; Nat Watercolor Soc, Los Angeles, Calif, 73-86; Am Watercolor Soc, New York, NY, 74-86; Watercolor USA Bicentennial Invitational, Springfield Art Mus, Mo, 77; Rocky Mountain Watermedia Exhib, Golden, Colo, 79-86; Arizona Biennial, Tucson Art Mus, 80, 82 & 84; West '83-Art and the Law, St Paul, Minn. *Awards:* High Winds Medal, Am Watercolor Soc, 84; Century Award, Rocky Mountain National, 84. *Bibliog:* Elizabeth Rigby (auth), Artist changed by the west, Southwest Art, 12/80. *Mem:* Am Watercolor Soc; Nat Watercolor Soc; Audubon Artists; Rocky Mountain Nat Watercolor Media; hon mem Watercolor USA. *Media:* Mixed Media. *Publ:* Contribr, Master Class in Watercolor by Edward Betts, 75 & Watercolor and Collage Workshop by G Brommer, 86, Watson-Guptill; Watercolor, the Creative Experience, by B Nechis, North Light, 78; New Spirit of Watercolor, M Ward, North Light. *Dealer:* Paul Willard Gallery Scottsdale AZ; Eleanor Jeck Tucson AZ. *Mailing Add:* c/o Eleanor Jeck Gallery 6336 E Broadway Tucson AZ 85710

CLOTHIER, PETER DEAN
WRITER, CRITIC
b Newcastle-on-Tyne, Eng, Aug 1, 36; US citizen. *Study:* Cambridge Univ, Eng, BA & MA; Univ Iowa, PhD. *Work:* Los Angeles Co Mus Art; Univ Southern Calif. *Pos:* Dean Col, Otis Art Inst, 76-79, actg dir, 77-79; dean, Col Fine & Communication Arts, Loyola-Marymount Univ, 81-85. *Teaching:* Asst prof comparative lit, Univ Southern Calif, Los Angeles, 68-76. *Awards:* Dart Award for Acad Innovation, Univ Southern Calif, 72; Art Critics Fel Grant, Nat Endowment for the Arts, 76-77; Rockefeller Found Humanities Fel, 80. *Bibliog:* Joseph E Young (auth), Re-evaluating the tradition of the book, Art News, 75; Peter Plagens (auth), Chiaroscuro by Peter Clothier, Art in Am, 86; Rebecca Solnit (auth), Dirty-Down by Peter Clothier, Artweek, 87. *Publ:* Auth, Magic of the possible, Artforum, 77; Bricks, barbells & brushes, 81 & Moving downtown, 81, Art in Am; Chiaroscuro, St Martin's Press, 84; Dirty-Down, Atheneum, 86; Sign Language, True Grit, Artnews, 89; At the Hard Edge: California Abstraction Then & Now, Artcoast, 89. *Mailing Add:* 2341 Ronda Vista Dr Los Angeles CA 90027

CLOUD, JACK L
GALLERY OWNER, PUBLISHER
b Fremont, Ohio, Mar 15, 25. *Pos:* Owner/pres, Litho-Graphics (publ), 72-80; owner/chmn bd, Odyssey Int Gallery, 75-80. *Mem:* Rockport Art Asn; Univ Mich Artist Guild; Int Platform Asn; Am Printing Hist Asn; Check Collector Round Table. *Specialty:* Contemporary American art and limited edition graphics and prints. *Mailing Add:* 4253 Brandywyne Dr Troy MI 48098

CLOUDMAN, RUTH HOWARD
CURATOR
b Oklahoma City, Okla, June 11, 48. *Study:* Washington Univ, St Louis, BA, 70; Bryn Mawr Col, Pa, MA, 73. *Collections Arranged:* A Rich Inheritance: Oriental Rugs of the 19th and Early 20th Centuries (auth, catalog), 74-75 & The Chosen Object: European and American Still Life (auth, catalog), 76-77, Joslyn Art Mus; Preston Dickinson, 1889-1930 (auth, catalog), Sheldon Mem Art Gallery, Univ Nebr, 79-80; Perspectives 4: Cindy Sherman (auth, catalog), Portland Art Mus, 86. *Pos:* Asst cur, Joslyn Art Mus, Omaha, Nebr, 73-75, chief cur, 75-78; guest cur, Sheldon Gallery, Univ Nebr, Lincoln, 78-79; assoc, Newhouse Galleries, New York, 80-84; sr cur, Portland Art Mus, 84- *Mem:* Col Art Asn; Am Asn Mus. *Res:* Early 20th century modernism; contemporary art. *Mailing Add:* J B Speed Art Mus 2035 S Third St Louisville KY 40208

CLOUGH, CHARLES SIDNEY
PAINTER
b Buffalo, NY, Feb 2, 51. *Study:* Pratt Inst, Brooklyn, NY, 69-70; Ontario Col Art, Can, 71-72. *Work:* Albright-Knox Art Gallery & Burchfield Ctr, State Univ Col, Buffalo, NY; Buscaglia-Castellani Art Gallery, Niagara Univ, NY; Brooklyn Mus, NY; Dayton Art Inst, Ohio; Commodities Corp, Princeton, NJ; Citibank, New York; Owens Corning Fiberglass, Toledo, Ohio; Prudential Insurance, Newark, NJ. *Comn:* Mural, Niagra Frontier Transportation Authority, 84; video, Music Television Network. *Exhib:* Solo exhib, Brooklyn Mus, NY, 85, Galeria Peccolo, Livorno, Italy, 86, Am Fine Arts Co, New York, 87, Nina Freuden heim Gallery, Buffalo, NY, 88, Scott Hanson Gallery, New York, 90, Barbara Gillman Gallery, Miami, 91, State Univ NY at Potsdam, 91. *Pos:* Co-Founder, Hallwalls Inc, Buffalo, NY, 74, pres bd dirs, 77-79. *Awards:* Painting Fel, Nat Endowment Arts, 82 & 89; Graphic Artists' Fel, Creative Artists Pub Serv Prog, 83. *Bibliog:* Michael Brenson (auth), Review: Charles Clough, New York Times, 2/27/85; Charlotta Yotik (auth), Grand Lobby Installation by Charles Clough, Brooklyn Mus Bulletin, 12/85; Holland Cotter (auth), Review: Charles Clough, Art in Am, 6/88. *Media:* Mixed. *Publ:* coauth (with Mimi Thompson), 2 Painters, New Mus, 11/87. *Dealer:* American Fine Art Co Inc 40 Wooster St New York NY 10012. *Mailing Add:* 124 Thompson St New York NY 10012

CLOUGH, ELEANOR
SCULPTOR
b St Albans, Vt, 1953. *Study:* Univ Vt, BS(art educ), 82; Art Inst Chicago, MFA(sculpture), 85. *Exhib:* Along the Y Axis, Art Inst Chicago, 85; A Forest Through the Trees, Glasgow Sch Art, Scotland, 88; Contemporary Cast Sculpture, Sch Art Inst Chicago, 89; Available Ingredients, Spaces Gallery, Cleveland, 90; Artists for ART, Erie St Gallery, Chicago, 91; Amalgamations, Gallery 2, Sch Art Inst Chicago, 91; Midwestern Sculpture Exhib, South Bend Regional Mus Art, Ind, 92; Evanston & Vicinity Show, Evanston Art Ctr, Ill, 92; Domestic (two-person show), Chicago Cult Ctr, Ill, 92. *Teaching:* Lectr sculpture, Barat Col, Lake Forest, Ill, 85; lectr sculpture, Art Resources in Teaching, 86-89; instr sculpture, Univ Vermont, summer, 87, 88. *Awards:* Honorable Mention, Travelling, Art Inst Chicago, 85; Fel, Ill Arts Coun, 87; Fel, Nat Endowment Arts, 88. *Bibliog:* Women's Art/Women's Lives, Brattleboro Mus, VT, 82; Raw Space, ARC Gallery, Chicago, 86-88; New on the Block, Governors Awards, 89. *Mem:* Col Art Asn. *Media:* Mixed media. *Mailing Add:* 4444 N Wolcott No 1A Chicago IL 60640

CLOWES, ALLEN WHITEHILL
COLLECTOR, PATRON
b Buffalo, NY, Feb 18, 17. *Study:* Harvard Univ, BS(fine arts), 39; Fogg Mus, with Chanler Post, Benjamin Rowland, Leonard Opdyke, Kuhn & Paul Sachs; Harvard Univ Grad Sch Bus Admin, MBA, 42; Franklin Col, Hon DFA, 64. *Pos:* Dir, Clowes Fund Collection Old Masters, Indianapolis Mus Art, 58-71, cur 71- *Collection:* Paintings by the Old Masters from the 14th to 19th Century, including Bellini, Bosch, Bruegel, Caravaggio, Clouet, Constable, Cranach, Duccio, Durer, El Greco, Goya, Hals, Holbein, Rembrandt, Rubens and Titian; Clowes Fund Collection originally formed by the late Dr G H A Clowes and now belongs to Clowes Fund, Inc, located in Clowes Pavilion, Indianapolis Museum of Art. *Mailing Add:* 3744 Spring Hollow Rd Indianapolis IN 46208

CLUTZ, WILLIAM
PAINTER, INSTRUCTOR
b Gettysburg, Pa, Mar 19, 33. *Work:* Mus Mod Art & Chase Manhattan Bank, New York; Joseph H Hirshhorn Collection, Washington, DC; Fogg Art Mus, Cambridge, Mass; Metrop Mus Art, New York; plus many others. *Comn:* Salomon Bros, New York; 3rd Nat Bank, Dayton, Ohio; Minn Mutual Life Insurance, St Paul; Mobil Corp; and others. *Exhib:* Recent Painting USA: The Figure, Mus Mod Art, New York, 62; Pa Acad Fine Arts Ann, Philadelphia, 64-66; one-man shows, Bertha Schaefer Gallery, 63, 64, 66 & 69 & Graham Gallery, 72; Alonzo Gallery, 77- 79; Tatistchaff & Co, New York, 81, 82 & 84; John C Stoller Co, Minneapolis, 83; and many others. *Teaching:* Instr, Parsons Sch Design, New York, 69- *Mailing Add:* c/o Tatischeff Gallery Inc 1547 10th St Santa Monica CA 90401

CLYMER, ALBERT ANDERSON
PAINTER
b Memphis, Tenn, Feb 16, 42. *Study:* Tex A&M Univ, with Joseph Donaldson, Napa Col with Frank Altamura. *Work:* White House, Washington, DC; Newport Mus Mod Art, Calif; Oakland Mus Mod Art, Calif; Berkeley Mus Mod Art, Calif; San Francisco Mus Mod Art, Calif; Leiv Straus, San Francisco, Nut Tree, Nut Tree, Calif. *Comn:* Ten paintings for Army Recruiting, US Army Reserve, Mountain View, Calif, 77; 30 paintings for Episcopal Homes Found, Santa Rosa, Calif, 77; 20 Abstract Indian Forms, Shorebirds, Tiburor, Calif, 87. *Exhib:* Dallas Mus Fine Arts, Tex, 65; Newport Mus Mod Art, 69; Exhib of Am Art, Chautauqua, NY, 69-71; Univ Berkeley Mus, Calif, 71; Mus Mod Art, Roseville, Calif, 72; Depot Gallery, Yountville, Calif, 90; Shore Birds, Tiburon, Calif, 90; Mesa Gallery, San Francisco, 90; plus 201 one-man-shows. *Pos:* Bd dir, Depot Gallery, Yountville, Calif, 81- *Awards:* First Prize in Mod Oil, Vintage 76 Int, 68 & Santa Rosa Statewide Ann, 71 & 72. *Bibliog:* Stephens (auth), Albert Anderson Clymer, La Rev Mod, Paris, 66 & 74; Paul Gillette (auth), The Single Man's Indispensable Guide Handbook, Playboy Press, 73; Artist of Northern California, Mountain Publ, 89. *Mem:* Berkeley Arts Crafts Coop. *Publ:* Illusr, Oakland Redevelopment Agency's Annual Report, Abby Press, 66; Bodega Bay, Nut Tree, 75; (catalog), Works by Albert Anderson Clymer, Arlene Lind Gallery, 78. *Dealer:* Depot Gallery in Vintage 1870 Yountville Ca 94599; Shore Birds On The Boardwalk Tiburon Ca 94920. *Mailing Add:* PO Box 2278 Yountville CA 94599

COATES, ANN S
CURATOR, PHOTOGRAPHER
b Louisville, Ky. *Study:* Univ of Louisville, BA, 63, MA, 69; New York Sch Interior Design, Cert, 65; Arrowmont Sch Arts Crafts, Tenn. *Work:* Brown-Forman Distillers Corp; James G Brown Regional Cancer Ctr; Actors' Theatre Louisville; Kentucky Fried Chicken, Brown & Williamson. *Exhib:* 80 Biennial Exhib of Piedmont Crafts, Mint Mus, Charlotte; Paper 90, Headley-Whitney Mus, Lexington, Ky; Southeast 81 Craft Competition, Lemoyne Art Found, Tallahassee; Thread and Fiber, Alexandria Mus, La; Handmade Paper Nat Invitational, Liberty Gallery, Louisville; Paradigmo of Perserverence, Louisville Visual Art Asn; and others. *Collections Arranged:* Edward Weston 1958-1968, 68; Kentucky Threads, Louisville Art Gallery. *Pos:* Cur slides, Univ Louisville, 69- *Teaching:* Instr mod art, Univ Louisville, 69-; lectr, Univ Ky, Lexington & Louisville Craftsmen's Guild. *Awards:* Bronze Medal, Great Quilts of America, Good Housekeeping, 78; Ky Found for Women Grant. *Bibliog:* Sarah Lansdell (auth), Paper works show uncovers artist's passion for the medium, The Courier, 7/20/80; Karen Hisle (auth), Ann Coates mixes work with pleasure, Scripps-Howard Press, 7/9/80; Fiber Arts Design Book, Hasting House, 80. *Mem:* Col Art Asn; Art Libr Soc NAm; Soc Archit Historians. *Media:* Fiber. *Res:* Paper Conservation; preservation; women artists. *Publ:* The Female Image in the Nineteenth Century (film), Univ Louisville, Women's Studies Ctr, 78. *Mailing Add:* 1819 Woodbourne Louisville KY 40205

COATES, ROSS ALEXANDER
HISTORIAN, PAINTER
b Hamilton, Ont, Can, Nov 1, 32. *Study:* Univ Mich; Art Inst Chicago, BFA; NY Univ, MA & PhD. *Work:* Chase Manhattan Bank, New York; NY Univ; Univ Calif, Berkeley; Schenectady Mus; City of Seattle. *Exhib:* Eastern Wash Univ, 79; Diablo Valley Col, Calif, 82; Whatcom Mus, Bellingham, 83; Space Gallery, Los Angeles, 84; Northwestern Artists Workshop, Portland Ore, 85; Art Gallery Hamilton, Ont, Can, 88; one-man shows, Thirteen Whirlwinds (installation), Gallery II, Wash State Univ, Pullman, WA, 90, Northview Gallery, Portland Community Coll, Ore, 90, Fisher Gallery, Cornish Sch Art, Seattle, 91, & UOP Gallery, McCaffrey Ctr, Univ Pacific, Stockton, Calif, 92, Getting From One Place, Fine Arts Ctr, Port Angeles, Wash, 91, Dreamtime, Pritchard Gallery, Univ Idaho, Moscow, 92; Some Assembly Required, Bumbershoot, Seattle, Wash, 89; Sun Valley Ctr Arts, Idaho, 91; Storie Naturali, Artists' Books, Genoa, Italy, 91; Come to Your Senses, collaborative pieces with Marilyn Lysohir, Bellevue Art Mus, Wash, 91; Dreams and Shields, Salt Lake Art Ctr, Utah, 92; Inter, Kunsthalle, Holstebro, Denmark, 92. *Teaching:* Art tutor, Canon Lawrence Col, Uganda, EAfrica, 68-70; prof dept fine arts, Wash State Univ, 77- *Awards:* Idaho Arts Comn Artists Grant, 90. *Mem:* Col Art Asn Am. *Media:* Oil. *Res:* Non-Western art, particularly Africa; occult and how it relates to contemporary art. *Publ:* Ed, Some Thoughts on thee Problems of Artists in Contemporary Africa, J African Studies, Univ Calif, LosAngeles, 78; Gard Okello in Six Artists, African Arts, Univ Calif, Los Angeles, 79; Gods Among Us: American Indian Masks, State Univ San Diego, 90. *Mailing Add:* Dept Fine Arts Wash State Univ Pullman WA 99163

COBB, JAMES
PAINTER
b La Mesa, Calif, 1951. *Work:* Frederick R Weisman Collection, Los Angeles, Calif; Henry Hopkins Collection, Los Angeles, Calif; Hal Bromm Collection, New York; Butler Collection, Dallas, Tex; San Antonio Mus Art, Tex. *Comn:* Mural, Centro de La Correspondensia, Tepoztlan, Morelos, Mex, 85; limited edition poster, Hal Bromm Gallery, New York, 88. *Exhib:* Solo exhibs, Ephrussi Gallery, San Antonio, Tex, Au Gallery, Nishinomiya, Japan & Gallerie Del Occhio, New York, 86, Blue Collar Gallery, Tex, 87, Read Stremmel Gallery, 89, Adams- Middleton Gallery, Dallas, Tex, 90 & Jansen-Perez Gallery, San Antonio, Tex, 91 & Los Angeles, Calif, 92; Texas II, San Francisco Mus Art Rental Gallery, Calif, 88; Contemporary Art for San Antonio, Blue Star III, Blue Star Art Space, San Antonio, Tex, 88; East Coast, West Coast, Third Coast, Locus Gallery, San Antonio, Tex, 88; Texas Triennial Exhibition, Contemp Arts Mus Houston, Tex, 88; Evidence: Contemporary Narrative Painters of the Southwest, San Antonio Mus Art, Tex, 89. *Awards:* Nat Endowment Arts Visual Artist Fel, 89. *Mailing Add:* 628 S St Mary's, Suite 101 San Antonio TX 78205

COBB, RUTH
PAINTER
b Boston, Mass, Feb 20, 14. *Study:* Mass Col Art, cert. *Work:* Boston Mus Fine Arts; Va Mus Fine Arts, Richmond; Butler Inst Am Art, Youngstown, Ohio; Munson-Williams-Proctor Inst, Utica, NY; Brandeis Univ, Waltham, Mass. *Exhib:* Am Watercolor Exhib, Metrop Mus Art, New York, 52; 22nd Biennial Int Watercolor Exhib, Brooklyn Mus, NY, 63; Am Watercolor Soc Ann, 68-77 & 80-83; Watercolor USA, Springfield Art Mus, Miss, 69; 35 Years in Retrospect, Butler Inst Am Art, 71; 45th Ann, Butler Inst Am Art, 81; and others. *Awards:* Purchase Award, Nat Acad Design, 68; Emily Lowe Award, 74 & Emily Goldsmith Award, 75, Am Watercolor Soc; Adolph Obrig Award, Nat Acad Design, 82. *Bibliog:* Article & reproductions in Am Artist Mag, 4/79; Artist at Work, Channel 5 TV, Boston, 81; and others. *Mem:* New Eng Watercolor Soc; American Watercolor Soc; Allied Artists Am; Nat Acad Design. *Media:* Watercolor. *Publ:* Auth, Watercolor Bold & Free, Watson Guptill, 80. *Dealer:* Francesca Anderson Gallery Lexington MA. *Mailing Add:* 38 Devon Rd Newton MA 02159

COBB, VIRGINIA HORTON
PAINTER, LECTURER
b Oklahoma City, Okla, Nov 23, 33. *Study:* Colo Univ; Community Col of Denver; additonal study with William Schimmel, Chen Chi & Edward Betts. *Work:* Foothills Art Ctr, Golden, Colo; Nat Acad of Design, New York; NMex Watercolor Soc, Albuquerque; St Lawrence Univ, Canton, NY. *Exhib:* Am Watercolor Soc, Nat Acad Galleries, New York, 73-85; Butler Inst Am Art, Youngstown, Ohio, 75; Nat Acad Design, New York, 78-85; San Bernadino Co Mus, 78; Nat Watercolor Invitational, 81; one-person exhib, Stuhr Mus, Grand Island, Nebr, 82; and others. *Teaching:* Lectr & demonstr, Emphasis-KRDO Channel 13, Colorado Springs, Colo, 77; instr, Crafton Hills Col Master Seminars, Yucaipa, Calif, 77, 78 & 81; instr, Univ Alaska, Anchorage, 81; lectr & demonstr, Pub Broadcasting Serv, KAKM, Anchorage, 81. *Awards:* Walter Biggs Mem Award, Nat Acad Design, 78 & 81; High Winds Medal, 81; Silver Medal Honor, Am Watercolor Soc, 83; Adolph & Clara Obrig Prize, 85. *Bibliog:* Southwest Art Mag, 11/79; Todays Art Mag, 3/79; Houston Home & Garden, 2/80. *Mem:* Assoc Nat Acad Design; Dolphin fel Am Watercolor Soc; Watercolor USA Honor Soc; Rocky Mountain Watermedia Asn. *Media:* Mixed Watermedia; Graphics. *Publ:* Contribr, Am Artist Mag, 1/79. *Mailing Add:* 208 S Avenue G Humble TX 77338

COBER, ALAN E
ILLUSTRATOR, PRINTMAKER
b New York, NY, May 18, 35. *Study:* Univ Vt, 52-54; Sch Visual Arts, 54-56. *Work:* Minn Mus Art, St Paul; Nat Air & Space Mus, DC; Albrecht Art Mus, St Joseph, Mo; New Britain Art Mus, Conn. *Comn:* Sketchbooks, Pres Campaign, Time, 80; mural, Mus Am Hist, Smithsonian Inst, 82; Pope's Tour USA, Rolling Stone, 87. *Exhib:* Drawings USA, Minn Mus Art, St Paul, 68 & 73; Century of Am Illus, Brooklyn Mus, NY, 72; Color, Whitney Mus Am Art, New York, 74; 200 Yrs Am Illus, NY Hist Soc, 76; Printmaking in Mod Am Illus, Pratt Graphic Ctr, New York, 79; solo exhibs, Ga Mus Art, 91, Auburn Univ, 92, Katonah Mus Art, NY, 92 & Burchfield Ctr, Buffalo, 93. *Teaching:* Pres fac illus & design, Illusr Workshop, Noroton, Conn, 74-88; distinguished vis prof illus & vis artist, State Univ NY, Buffalo, 87-; Lamar Dodd prof art, Univ Ga, spring 91. *Awards:* Gold Medals, Soc Illusr, 68-77 & Art Dirs Club, New York, 73, 76, 77 & 82; John Taylor Arms Award, Audubon Artists, 71. *Bibliog:* Dugald Stermer (auth), Alan E Cober: Illustrator, Reporter & Social Historian, Communication Arts, 1-2/75; Nick Meglin (auth), Alan E Cober, Graphis 192, Graphis Press, 11/77; Steven Heller (auth), Innovators of American Illustration, Van Nostrand, Reinhold, 86. *Media:* Pen and Ink, Watercolor; Etching. *Publ:* Illusr, The Forgotton Society, Dover, 75; illusr, The Trial (Kafka) Limited Editions Book Club, 77 & illusr, Exile and the Kingdom/Camus/Etchings, 80, Franklin Libr; auth & illusr, Cober's Choice, E P Dutton/Unicorn 79. *Mailing Add:* Croton Dam Rd Ossining NY 10562

COBURN, BETTE LEE
PAINTER, INSTRUCTOR
b Chicago, Ill, July 31, 22. *Study:* Grinwell Col, Iowa; Chicago Art Inst; Univ NC. *Work:* Fed Reserve Bank, Charlotte, NC; SC Arts Comn, State Art Col, Columbia; Greenville Co Mus Arts, SC; Univ SC, Columbia; Univ Ga, Athens. *Comn:* Painting, comn by Pres, Ivey's, Greenville, SC, 62; city seal, Greenville City Bd, SC, 65; painting, First Fed Bank, Henderson, NC, 68; State Governer's Comt, Columbia, SC 69; Astro Theatre's I & II, Greenville, SC, 73. *Exhib:* Atlanta High Mus Art, Ga, 69; Nat USA Travelling Exhib Oils, London Pub Art Mus, Ontario, 70; 23rd Grand Prix Int, Deuville Expo Mus, France, 72; retrospective, SC State Mus, Columbia, 88; Greenville Co Art Mus, SC, 88; Florence Mus Art, SC, 89; Invitational Exhib, State Mus Art, Columbia, SC, 89; Art's Symposium 2nd Exhib, Greenville Co Mus, SC, 89. *Teaching:* Instr painting, Greenville Co Art Mus Sch, 65-83. *Awards:* Purchase Award, Univ SC, 68; Grumbacher Award, Nat Asn Women Artists, NY, 74. *Bibliog:* Rene Borel (auth), Le Semaines International de La Femme, 69; Jack A Morris (auth), 39 Contemporary Artists of SC, 70; Elizabeth Montgomery (auth), Poet without words, Greenville Woman Mag, 5/87. *Mem:* Greenville Mus Art Sch (chmn, educ comt, 61-62); Greenville Artists Guild (pres, 65); Nat Asn Women Artists (mem comt, 70); SC State Arts Comn (selection comt, 74 & 75); SC State Artists Guild (pres, 81). *Media:* Egg Tempera. *Dealer:* Hampton III Gallery 10 Gallery Ctr Taylors SC 29687. *Mailing Add:* 436 Henderson Rd Greenville SC 29607

COBURN, RALPH (M H)
PAINTER
b Minneapolis, Minn, Aug 10, 23. *Study:* Mirski Art Sch, with Esther Geller, Carl Nelson, Barbara Swan & John Wilson, 46-49; Mass Inst Technol, 47; Acad Julian, 50. *Work:* Stedlijk Mus, Amsterdam; Mus Mod Art, Caracas, Venezuela; Brockton Art Mus, Mass; Chase Manhattan Bank, New York; Smithsonian Inst. *Exhib:* Mass Inst Technol, 54 & 76; Mirsks Gallery, 55. *Media:* Oil, Acrylic; Pen and Ink, Watercolor. *Dealer:* Alpha Gallery 14 Newbury St Boston MA 02116. *Mailing Add:* 1269 Washington St Gloucester MA 01930

COCKER, BARBARA JOAN
PAINTER, GALLERY DIRECTOR
b Uxbridge, Mass, Oct 16, 23. *Study:* Becker Jr Col, 43; Mt St Mary Col, 45; NY Sch Interior Design, 68. *Work:* Central Jersey Bank & Trust, Rumson, NJ; Midlantic Bank, Edison, NJ; President's House, Monmouth Col, West Long Branch, NJ; Riverview Hospital, Red Bank, NJ. *Comn:* Ocean paintings, comn by Judge William Kirkpatrick, Rumson, NJ, 69; ship painting, comn by William Crawford, Singer Island, Fla, 70; ocean paintings, comn by Dr J Putnam Brodsky, Rumson, NJ, 70; sea marsh painting, comn by Daniel Riley, Greenwich, Conn, 92. *Exhib:* Catharine L Wolfe Club, Nat Acad, New York, 70; solo exhibs, IBM Corp, Dayton, NJ, 77, S St Seaport Mus, New York, 77 & 80, Bell Lab, Holmdel, NJ, 82 & 86, AT&T, Holmdel, NJ, 87 & 88, Nantucket Art Asn, 88 & 91, Monmouth Co Libr, NJ, 91 & Art Alliance, Red Bank, NJ, 92. *Pos:* Owner & dir, Paintings of the Sea Gallery, Nantucket, Mass, 75-91. *Awards:* Woman of the Year, Zonta Int, 83; Spec Award, Pen & Brush Club, NY, 84; Blue Ribbon, Monmouth Arts Club, NJ, 92. *Bibliog:* Fran Merlino (auth), The sea around her, Becker Col Alumnus, 68; Carl Diegert (dir), Profiles of Professionals, Storer, NJ Cablevision, 83 & 87; Tom Saxton (dir), Paintings of the Sea, Nantucket Cablevision, 88; Capturing the surf, Art & Antiques, 89. *Mem:* Pen & Brush Club, New York; Catharine L Wolfe Art Club, New York; Southern Vt Art Ctr, Manchester, Vt; Artists Asn Nantucket (adv to the bd, 78-79); Am Artists Prof League, NJ. *Media:* Acrylic on Canvas. *Dealer:* Frank Lewis Gallery Killarney Ireland. *Mailing Add:* 3 Rumson Rd Rumson NJ 07760

COCKRILL, SHERNA
PAINTER, INSTRUCTOR
b Chicago, Ill. *Study:* Univ Ark, BA & MA; Malden Bridge Sch Art, 67 & 68; also study with R V Goetz, 65-69; with Albert Handell, 80-81. *Work:* Smithsonian Inst Archives Am Art, Washington, DC; Ozark Art Ctr, Springdale; First Nat Bank, Little Rock; Mid-Am Mus, Hot Springs, Ark; Arts Ctr Ozarks. *Comn:* Many portrait comn. *Exhib:* Greater New Orleans Nat Exhib, 73; Tex Fine Arts Asn Ann, Austin, 73-74; Governor's Distinguished Artists Exhib, 76; Five State, Univ Ark, 79-83; Art Expo '83, Dallas; Laguna Gloria Mus Austin, Tex Fiesta Exhib, 84, 86; Sequoya Exhib (Univ Ark), 80-86; Easton Rooms, Rye, E Sussex, Eng, 87; Romney Bay Gallery, Kent, Eng, 87; and others. *Teaching:* Instr oil painting, Ozarks Arts Ctr, 72-75; also pvt classes. *Awards:* Grand Prize, Arkansas State Festival Art, 73; First Prize in Art, Little Rock Ten State Arts Fair, State of Ark, 73; Top Award Ark Festival Art, 73 & 74 & Top Award Ark Festival & Art Invitational, 75; 5 State Competitive Award for Sequoia, Univ Ark, 86. *Mem:* Ozark Artists & Craftsmen (bd dir, 75-). *Media:* Oil, Acrylic. *Publ:* Auth, Women artists in mid-USA, Feminist Art J, Brooklyn, 74-75. *Dealer:* Frame Gallery 200 W Dickson St Fayetteville AR 72701. *Mailing Add:* Rt 8 Fayetteville AR 72701

CODE, AUDREY
PAINTER
b Pittsburgh, Pa, Oct 6, 37. *Study:* Carnegie Mellon Univ, with Balcomb Greene, BFA, 59, MFA, 61; Provincetown Workshop, Mass, 61. *Work:* Aldrich Mus Contemp Art, Ridgefield, Conn; Chautauqua Art Mus, NY; Fulton Co Arts Coun, Gloversville, NY. *Comn:* Murals, St John's Church, 62 & Sr Citizens Ctr, 75, Pittsburgh, Pa; mural, Cyclerama, Los Angeles, 70. *Exhib:* Contemporary Reflections, Aldrich Mus, Ridgefield, Conn, 78; Arte Fiera, Bologna, Italy, 78; PS1, New York, 78; solo show, Frank Marino Gallery, New York, 79, PSI, NY, 86; West End Gallery, Portland, Maine, 88, Los Angeles Nicola Gallery, Los Angeles, Calif, 88, Celebrity Ctr, NY, 88; Herbert F Johnson Mus, Ithaca, NY, 81; Alchemy, Hankook Gallery, New York, 83; Group Shows, Andre Zarre, New York, 86, Rabbett Gallery, New Brunswick, NJ, 89; More Than Meets the Eye, New York, 85; Rabbet Gallery, New Brunswick, NJ, 89. *Teaching:* Vis artist, San Francisco Art Inst, 79; lectr, Stuyvesant Group, New York, 80-88; Westchester Community Col, 88. *Awards:* Creative Artists Pub Serv Fel, NY State Coun Arts, 81. *Bibliog:* Corinne Robbins (auth), Audrey Code's drawings, F Marino, 79; Diana Morris (auth), Eight, Women Artists News, 83; Alchemy, Artspeak, 83; Sherry Miller (auth), West End Gallery, Oct 88. *Mem:* Women Arts; Women's Caucus Art. *Media:* Miscellaneous Media. *Publ:* Illusr, Life Forms of the 70's, Independent Press, 75; auth & illusr, Eggplants and Other Murders, Chrome Press, 82; auth, Alchemy, Chrome Press, 83. *Dealer:* Andre Zarre 379 West Broadway New York NY. *Mailing Add:* 70 Grand St New York NY 10013

CODELL, JULIE FRANCIA
HISTORIAN, ADMINISTRATOR
b Chicago, Ill, Sept 19, 45. *Study:* Vassar Col, AB, 67; Univ Mich, MA(English), 68; Ind Univ, MA(art hist), 75, cert(renaissance studies), 77, PhD(comparative lit & arts), 78. *Collections Arranged:* Montana Women Artists and the Environment (auth, catalog), Missoula Mus Arts, 82; Photographs of Edward S Curtis, Custer City Art Ctr, Miles City, Mont, 88; Postmodernism, Univ Mont, 89. *Pos:* Chair, Art Dept, Univ Mont, 88-90; dir, Sch Art, Ariz State Univ, Tempe, 91-; ed, J pre-Raphaelite Studies, 91- *Teaching:* Instr, Western Ill Univ, 68-71; asst prof art hist & criticism, Univ Mont, Missoula, 79-83, head slide libr, Dept Art, 79-90, assoc prof, 83-89, prof, 89-90; prof, Ariz State univ, 91- *Awards:* Distinguished Teaching Award, Univ Mont, 84; Travel-to-Collections Grant, 86 & 90, Summer Stipend, 88 & Summer Institute Grant, 89 & 91 Nat Endowment Humanities; William Nelson Prize, Renaissance Soc Am, 87; Fel for Col Teachers, Nat Endowment Humanities, 92. *Bibliog:* D McNamer (auth), Julie Codell, art historian, Missoulian, 80; Carol Woodruff (auth), From Renaissance to Robocop, Visions, 88. *Mem:* Col Art Asn; Midwest Victorian Studies Asn; Res Soc Victorian Periodicals; Midwest Art Hist Asn; Interdisciplinary Nineteeth-Century Studies. *Res:* Art criticism of the 19th and 20th centuries;; Victorian artists' professional lives and art world infrastructures. *Publ:* Auth, Expression over beauty: Facial expression and circumstantiality in the paintings of the pre-Raphaelite brotherhood, Victorian Studies J, 29, winter 86; Giotto's Peruzzi Chapel frescoes: wealth, patronage and the earthly city, Renaissance Quart, winter 88; Murphy's law/Robocop's body/capitalism's work, In: Jump Cut, A Review of Contemporary Media, fall 88; The Dilemma of the Artist in Millais's Lorenzo and Isabella: Phrenology, The Gaze and the Social Discourse, Art History, 3/91; Decapitation & Deconstruction: The Body of the Hero in Robert Bresson's Lancelot du Lac in Mancoff, ed, The Arthurian Revival, 92. *Mailing Add:* c/o Sch Art Ariz State Univ Tempe AZ 85827-1505

COE, ANNE ELIZABETH
PAINTER, VIDEO ARTIST
b Henderson, Nev. *Study:* Ariz State Univ, BA, 70, MFA, 80; Univ PR, 78. *Work:* Centro Arte Mod Guadalajara, Mex; NDak Mus Art, Grand Forks; Scottsdale Ctr Arts, Ariz; Smithsonian Inst; Fund Anthropologia El Ecuador, Quito; Columbus Mus Art, Ga. *Comn:* Mural & set design, Warner Brothers, Tempe, Ariz, 76. *Exhib:* Ariz Invitational, Centro Arte Mod Guadalajara, Mex, 82; Recent Works, Art West, Jackson, Wyo, 82; Continuing Frontiers, NDak Mus Art, Grand Forks, 82; Tucson Mus Art Biennial, 82; Whatever Happened to the Avant Garde, Ctr Contemp Art, Santa Ana, Calif, 83; Segal Gallery, New York, 85; American Art Now, Columbus, Ga, 85; Women of the American West, Bruce Mus, Greenwich, Conn, 85. *Pos:* Arts profucer, KAGT-TV, Phoenix, 77-80; artist-in-residence, Ariz Comn Arts, 81-83. *Bibliog:* Carol Kotrozo (auth), Four Arizona women, 82 & Donald Lock (auth), Arizona invitational, 82, Artspace; Robert Ewing (auth), Esthetic badness, Artweek, 82; Jon Stuart (auth), article, Southwest Art, 7/85. *Media:* Acrylic on Canvas. *Dealer:* Segal Fine Art 200 W 90 St New York NY 10024; Elaine Horwich Galleries Scottsdale AZ. *Mailing Add:* c/o Segal Gallery 200 W 90th St New York NY 10024

COE, HENRY
PAINTER
b Baltimore, Md, Oct 23, 46. *Study:* Roanoke Col, Salem, Va, BA, 69; Md Inst Col Art, MFA, 72. *Work:* Kanagawa Mus Mod Art, Japan; Acad Arts, Easton, Md. *Comn:* Mural, Baltimore City Sch System, Md, 78. *Exhib:* Maryland Art Place, Baltimore, Md, 88; Horizons, Maryland Landscapes, Md State Arts Coun & Md Hist Soc. *Awards:* Edward Maxwell Award, Md Biennial Exhib, Baltimore Mus Art, 80; Md State Arts Coun Grant, 92. *Bibliog:* John Dorsey (auth), Henry Coe's Fast Developing Landscapes, Baltimore Sun, 11/3/86; John Dorsey (auth), Coe's Experiments--, Baltimore Sun, 11/5/87; Joanne Dudziak, (auth), Heart Works, Baltimore Mag, 12/88. *Media:* Oil. *Dealer:* Grimaldis Gallery Baltimore MD; Harris Gallery Houston TX. *Mailing Add:* 2823 St Paul St Baltimore MD 21218

COE, MATCHETT HERRING
SCULPTOR
b Loeb, Tex, July 22, 07. *Study:* Cranbrook Acad Art, with Carl Milles; Lamar Univ. *Work:* US Navy C B Mus, Port Hueneme, Calif; Am Numismatic Soc & Metrop Mus Art, New York; Carnegie Mus, Pittsburgh; Corcoran Gallery Art, Washington, DC. *Comn:* Bronze statues, Dick Dowling, State of Tex, Sabine Pass, 36 & The Texan, Vicksburg Nat Mil Park, 60; entrance to zoo (stone relief), City Houston, 52; 75th Issue, Soc Medalists, New York, 67; Figure for family monument, Glenwood Cemetery, Houston, 92. *Exhib:* Nat Sculpture Soc 75th Anniversary Exhib, 68 & Medals by Mem Show, Smithsonian Inst, 68; Am Numismatic Asn Conv, San Diego, Calif, 68; Fidem Exhib, Lisbon, Portugal, 79. *Awards:* First Place, Dick Dowling Monument, Nat Competition; First Place, Frieze on New London Sch Mem, State Competition; selected by noted panel of sculptors to design 75th Issue, Soc Medalists. *Bibliog:* Emma Lila Fundaburk (auth), Art in Public Places in the United States, 75. *Mem:* Nat Sculpture Soc. *Media:* All. *Mailing Add:* 2554 Gladys St Beaumont TX 77702

COE, RALPH TRACY
MUSEUM DIRECTOR, CURATOR
b Cleveland, Ohio, Aug 25, 29. *Study:* Oberlin Col, BA, 53; Yale Univ, MA, 57. *Collections Arranged:* Many exhibs at Nelson Gallery, 59-79; Lost & Found Tradition Native American Art 1965-1985, traveling exhib, Am Fedn Arts, 86- *Pos:* Asst cur, Nat Gallery Art, 57-59; cur paintings & sculpture, Nelson Gallery Art, Kansas City, Mo, 59-82, asst dir, 65-77, dir, 77-82; freelance cur, 82- *Teaching:* Lectr, Univ Kans, 70-82, Univ NMex, 91. *Mem:* Asn Art Mus Dirs (trustee, 79-82, pres 81-82); Am Asn Mus; Am Fedn Arts (trustee, 77-82); Col Art Asn Am; Soc Archit Historians; Southwest Asn on Indian Affairs (trustee, 84- *Res:* French 19th century painting; modern art; ethnology. *Publ:* Auth, Impressionist and post-impressionist paintings in Washington, Burlington Mag, 59; co-ed, American Architecture and Other Writings, Harvard Univ, 61; auth, Pissarro's Jardin des Mathurins, Nelson Gallery Art & Atkins Mus Bulletin, 63; Sacred Circles: Two Thousand Years

of North AmericanIndian Art (catalog), 76; Dale Eldred: Sculpture into Environment, Regents Press of Kans, 78; Lost and Found Traditions: Native American Art 1965-1985 (catalog), 86. *Mailing Add:* 1701 Agua Fria Santa Fe NM 87501

COE, SUE
PAINTER
b Tamworth, Staffordshire, Eng. *Study:* Royal Col Art, London, Eng, 70-73. *Work:* Metrop Mus Art, Mus Mod Art & New York Publ Libr, New York; Nat Mus Am Art, Smithsonian Inst, Washington, DC. *Exhib:* Selections from the Eli Broad Family Collection, Kresge Art Mus, Mich, 88; Committed to Print, Mus Mod Art, New York, 88; Police State, traveling exhib, Mus Mod Art, Oxford, Eng, Orchard Gallery, Derry, Ireland & Herbe Gallery, Eng, 89; Porkopolis, traveling exhib, Portland, Maine, Bloomington, Ind & St Louis, Mo, 89-91. *Publ:* Auth, How to Commit Suicide in South Africa, Raw Books, 83; X (The Life & Times of Malcolm X), Raw Books, 86; Police State (catalog), Anderson Gallery, 87. *Mailing Add:* Gallery St Etienne 24 W 57th St New York NY 10019

COES, KENT DAY
PAINTER, DESIGNER
b Chicago, Ill, Feb 14, 10. *Study:* Grand Cent Sch Art, New York; Art Students League; NY Univ. *Work:* Montclair Art Mus, NJ; Holyoke Mus Fine Arts, Mass; Norfolk Mus Arts & Sci, Va; Nat Acad Design, NY; Museo de la Acuarela Mexicana, Mexico City. *Exhib:* Ann exhibs, Nat Acad Design, Allied Artists Am, Am Watercolor Soc, New York & Acad Artists Asn, Springfield, Mass; exchange exhibs, London, Mexico City, Ont, Can & Sydney, Australia. *Pos:* Art for several publ, McGraw-Hill, 47-75; dir, Splash (3 color repros), North Light Books, F & W Publ, Cincinnati, Ohio. *Awards:* Gold Medal Honor, Allied Artists Am, 59; Silver Medal, NJ Watercolor Soc, 73 & 91; Walser Greathouse Medal, Am Watercolor Soc, 85. *Bibliog:* Kent Day Coes insists, Am Artist Mag, 10/57; Norman Kent (auth), 100 Watercolor Techniques, 68 & Norman Kent & Susan Meyer (auth), Watercolorists at Work, 72, Watson-Guptill. *Mem:* Acadamecian Nat Acad Design (aquarelle); Am Watercolor Soc (dir, var terms 52-); Allied Artists Am (dir, secy, vpres, 50); NJ Watercolor Soc (founder-mem & pres, 47-48); Salmagundi Club, New York. *Media:* Watercolor. *Dealer:* Baker Gallery Fine Art 1301 13th St Lubbock TX 79408; Francesca Anderson Fine Arts 56 Adams St Lexington MA 02173. *Mailing Add:* 463 Valley Rd Upper Montclair NJ 07043

COFFEY, DOUGLAS ROBERT
PAINTER, EDUCATOR
b Cleveland Heights, Ohio, Dec 27, 37. *Study:* Cleveland Inst Art, dipl, 59; Univ Denver, BFA, 61; Western Reserve Univ, MA, 65. *Work:* Xerox Corp, New York; Kodak Corp, Rochester, NY; Cleveland Mus Art. *Exhib:* Butler Inst Am Art Exhib, Youngstown, Ohio, 63; Rochester Fingerlakes Exhib, 71; 13th Ann Rochester Festival of Relig Art, 71; 16th Nat Print Exhib, Hunterdon Art Ctr, 72; one-man show, Mem Art Gallery, 75. *Teaching:* From assoc prof fine arts to prof, Rochester Inst Technol, 67-82. *Awards:* Sullivan Award for Painting, Fingerlakes Exhib, 70; First Award, 13th Ann Festival of Relig Art, 71; Painting Award, Mem Art Gallery, 75. *Media:* Polymer, Oil. *Dealer:* Jo Sibley 9 Union St Nantucket MA 02554. *Mailing Add:* Rochester Inst Technol Rochester NY 14623

COFFEY, JOHN WILLIAM, II
CURATOR
b Raleigh, NC, Mar 12, 54. *Study:* Univ NC, Chapel Hill, BA, 76; Williams Col, MA(hist art), 78. *Collections Arranged:* Four artists: Biederman, Maddrell, Ross, Saganic (auth, catalog), 81, Maine Artists Invitationals, 82-84, Alex Katz: Small Works, 85 & Yvonne Jacquette: Tokyo Nightviews (auth, catalog), 86, Bowdoin Col Mus Art; Twilight of Arcadia: American Landscape Painters in Rome, 1830-1880 (auth, catalog), 87, Lucy Sallick: In the Vicinity of the Self (auth, catalog), 87 & New England Now: Contemp Art from Six States (coauth, catalog), 87, Bowdoin Col Mus Art; Referees: Dotty Attie, Christopher Hewat, John O'Reilly (auth, catalog), 90 & Making Faces: Self-Portraits by Alex Katz (auth catalog), 90, NC Mus Art; Finding the Forgotten: Landscape Paintings by John Beerman (auth, catalog), 91 & Moshe Kupferman: Between Oblivion and Remembrance (auth, catalog), 91, NC Mus Art. *Pos:* Asst to dir, Williams Col Mus Art, 78-79, actg dir, 79-80; cur, Bowdoin Col Mus Art, 80-88; mem adv comt, Maine State Comn Arts & Humanities, 82-85, Maine Coast Artists Gallery, 86 & Baxter Gallery, Portland Sch Art, 86-88; cur, Am & Mod Art, NC Mus Art, 88-; visual arts panel, NC Arts Coun, 90-91. *Teaching:* Instr art hist, Williams Col, 79-80. *Mem:* Maine Festival Arts (vpres, 82-83, pres, 83-84). *Res:* Nineteenth and twentieth century American art. *Publ:* Contribr, The Lawrence H Bloedel Collection of American Art, Int Exhibs Found, 81; Christine Woelfle (sculptor), Baxter Gallery, Portland Sch Arts, 87. *Mailing Add:* 2714 Van Dyke Ave Raleigh NC 27607

COGGINS, JACK BANHAM
INSTRUCTOR, PAINTER
b London, Eng, July 10, 14; US citizen. *Study:* Grand Cent Sch Art Students League, New York. *Work:* Reading Pub Mus & Art Gallery & Philadelphia Maritime Mus, Pa; Air & Space Mus, Smithsonian Inst, Washington, DC. *Exhib:* Pastel Soc Am Ann Show, New York, 85-90; Prof Artists Am Ann Show, New York, 88; Mystic Int Maritime exhib, 89-90. *Teaching:* Instr, Hunter Col, New York, 48-53; instr, Wyomissing Inst Fine Arts, Pa, 59-. *Mem:* Artist mem, Pastel Soc Am; Am Soc Marine Artists. *Publ:* Auth & illusr, Arms & Equipment of the Civil War, Doubleday, 62; Ships & Seamen of the American Revolution, Stackpole, 69; Campaign for Guadalcanal, Doubleday, 72; Campaign for North Africa, Doubleday, 80; Marine Painter's Guide, Van Nostrand Reinhold, 83. *Mailing Add:* PO Box 57 Boyertown PA 19512

COGSWELL, DOROTHY MCINTOSH
EDUCATOR, PAINTER
b Plymouth, Mass, Nov 13, 09. *Study:* Yale Univ, BFA & MFA. *Work:* Springfield Mus Fine Arts, Mass; Wisteriahurst, Holyoke Mus, Mass; Newport Art Asn; Mt Holyoke Col; Gordon Libr, Worcester Polytechnic Inst. *Comn:* Mural, Libr, 44, mural, Buckland Hall, 61 & mural & relief, Torrey Hall, 63, Mt Holyoke Col. *Exhib:* New Haven Paint & Clay Club, 29-; New York Watercolor Soc, 32-; Am Watercolor Soc, 33-; Conn Acad, 37; New York World's Fair, 39; restrospective, Mt Holyoke Art Mus, 74; and others. *Pos:* Dir collections, Mt Holyoke Col, 70-74. *Teaching:* Prof art hist, Mt Holyoke Col, 39-74, emer prof, 74- *Awards:* First Prize in Watercolor, Eastern States Exhib, 41; Fulbright lectr, Nat Art Sch, Sydney, Australia, 57-58; Purchase Prize, Holyoke Bicentennial, 76. *Mem:* Manatee Art League (vpres, 81-83); Mt Holyoke Friends Art (chmn, 47-60); Mount Holyoke Art Adv, 83- *Media:* Watercolor, Acrylic. *Publ:* Auth, A visitor's impressions of Australian art, Soc Artists, Sydney, 58; Mount Holyoke College art collection, Col Art J, 72. *Mailing Add:* 1700 Third Ave W Apt 1020 Bradenton FL 34205

COGSWELL, MARGARET PRICE
INSTRUCTOR
b Evanston, Ill, Sept 15, 25. *Study:* Wellesley Col, BA, 47; Pratt Inst; Art Inst Chicago; Columbia Univ; Art Students League, Georgetown Univ, MA, 89. *Collections Arranged:* Communication Through Art, 64; The American Poster (ed, catalog), 68; American Exhib, 34th & 35th Venice Biennales, 68 & 70; Explorations, 70; The Audio-Visual Mag, 72; George Catlin's American Indians, 74; Images of an Era: The American Poster (with catalog), 75. *Pos:* Head dept publ & assoc foreign exhib, Am Fedn Arts, 55-66; ed, The Am Artists Series, 59-63; chmn, 50 Bks of the Yr, Am Inst Graphic Arts, 64; dep chief, Off Prog Support, 66-80, Nat Collection Fine Arts, Smithsonian Inst, 66-, mem, Women's Coun, 77-81, vchmn, 79, deputy cur of educ, 81-84, coord special academic progs, 84- *Teaching:* Smithsonian Inst, 70. *Awards:* Gold Medal for Printmaking, Am Artist Mag, 53. *Mem:* Am Asn Mus; Col Art Asn. *Publ:* Ed, The Ideal Theater: Eight Concepts, 63; co-ed, The Cultural Resources of Boston, 64; ed, Sao Paulo 9, 67; Images of an Era: The American Poster 1945-75, 76; National Survey of Assembility in Museums, 89. *Mailing Add:* 2929 Connecticut Ave NW Washington DC 20008

COHAN, ZARA R
GALLERY DIRECTOR, EDUCATOR
b Elizabeth, NJ, Aug 11, 28. *Study:* Newark State Col, Union, NJ, MA(fine arts), 68-70; Kunsthistoriches Inst, Florence, Italy, with Dr U Middledorf, 71; Creative Arts Div, New York Univ, 72-74. *Collections Arranged:* Recent Acquisitions (auth, catalog), 80, Faculty Drawing: New Attitudes (auth, catalog), 83, Retrospective: John Button an American Painter (coauth, catalog), 84, & Let's Look at Pictures: 19th Century Museum Views (auth, catalog), 84, Kean Col Gallery, Union, NJ. *Pos:* Admin, Mus Mod Art, New York, 56-64; educ supv, NJ State Mus, Trenton, 66-68; dir, James Howe Gallery, Union, NJ, 70-91; chairperson, Small Mus Comt, Mid Atlantic Asn Mus, 81. *Teaching:* Asst prof mus training & art educ, Kean Col, NJ, formerly. *Awards:* Award of Recognition, NJ Hist Comn, 89. *Mem:* Am Asn Mus; Mus Coun NJ (treas, vp & pres, 77-79, bd trustees, 85-86, 87-91); Elizabeth Develop Co, 82; Mid Atlantic Asn Mus. *Mailing Add:* 118 Acme St Elizabeth NJ 07202

COHELEACH, GUY JOSEPH
PAINTER, SCULPTOR
b New York, NY. *Study:* Cooper Union, with Don Eckelberry, grad; Col William & Mary, Hon Dr Arts, 75. *Work:* Nat Wildlife Gallery, Washington, DC; Nat Audubon Soc; Am Mus Natural Hist; Beware, presented to President of US. *Comn:* Snowy Egrets, Nat Audubon Soc, 68; American Eagle, US Govt, presented to Vice President Agnew, 71; Elephant, African Safari Club, Washington, DC, for President of US, 72; Leopard & Elephant, World Wildlife Fund, 72. *Exhib:* Wildlife Art of America, Louisville, Ky, 68 & 72; Linnean Soc Exhib, Am Mus Natural Hist, New York, 69; Bird Artists of the United States, Graham Gallery, New York, 72; Bird Artists of the World, Tryon Gallery, London, 72. *Awards:* Guy Coheleach, Prints Mag, 79 & Mich Outdoors, 79; Master Artist, Leigh Yawkee Art Mus, Wis, 83. *Bibliog:* Roger Caras (auth), Quest: An Artist & His Prey; Terry Weiland (auth), Guy Coheleach, Briarpatch Press, 88. *Mem:* Soc Animal Artists (vpres); Explorer's Club; African Safari Club; Adventurer's Club. *Media:* Oil, Tempera. *Interests:* First occidental artist to exhibit in post-WWII Peking. *Publ:* Illusr, Sat Eve Post, 67; Nat Wildlife Mag, 67-; Readers Digest, 67-; Int Wildlife Mag, 71-; auth, The Big Cats-The Paintings of Guy Coheleach, Harry Abrams, 82. *Dealer:* Pandion Art Box 728 Jensen Beach FL 33457. *Mailing Add:* c/o Pandion Art PO Box 96 Bernardsville NJ 07924

COHEN, ADELE
SCULPTOR, PAINTER
b Buffalo, NY. *Study:* Art Inst Buffalo; Albright Sch Buffalo; Parsons Sch Art, New York. *Work:* Burchfield Ctr, Western NY Forum Am Art, State Univ NY Col Buffalo; Newark Mus, NJ; Univ Mass, Amherst; Charles Rand Penny Collection, Lockport, NY; State Univ New York, Buffalo. *Comn:* Fando & Lis stage sets, NY State Theatre, Buffalo Fine Arts Acad & Workshop Repertory Theatre, 67; Gorge Legend Arbor (sculpture), Art Park & Co, Lewiston, NY, 78; Chesterwood (sculpture), Nat Trust Hist Preserv, Stockbridge, Mass, 83, 86 & 90; sculpture, Sti-Co Ind, Orchard Park, NY. *Exhib:* Burchfield Ctr, Western NY Forum Am Art, State Univ NY Col Buffalo; Albright-Knox Art Gallery, Buffalo; Art Across Am Inst Contemp Art, Boston; Foreign Inst Group Exhib, Dortmund, WGer; Kanazawa Art Exhib Exchange Show, Japan; State Univ New York, Buffalo; 98th Annual Exhib, Nat Asn Women

Artists. *Teaching:* Instr drawing, State Univ NY Col Buffalo, 74-75. *Awards:* Buffalo Courier Express Award, 32nd Western NY Exhib, Albright-Knox Art Gallery, 69; Janet E Turner Prize, 88th Ann Exhib Nat Asn Women Artists, 77; Yaddo fel (sculpture & drawing) Saratoga, NY, 88. *Bibliog:* Jane Marinsky (auth), Adele Cohen: Tracing Her Inner Image, 77; Elaine Hancock Jones (auth), Adele Cohen: Gorge Legend Arbor, In Process, 78; Ethel Moore (auth), The Inner Image: Adele Cohen 1960-80, 80. *Mem:* Nat Asn Women Artists. *Publ:* Auth The Wayward Muse, Albright Knox (cat), Buffalo, NY, 87; Transforming Images, Poetry/Rare Books Collection, Univ of Buffalo, NY, 89. *Mailing Add:* 66 Burbank Dr Snyder NY 14226

COHEN, ALAN BARRY
PHOTOGRAPHER, EDUCATOR
b Harrisburg, Pa, Aug 28, 43. *Study:* NC State Univ, BS, 66; Ill Inst Technol/Inst of Design, MS(photography), 72. *Work:* Art Inst Chicago, Ill; High Mus Art, Atlanta, Ga; Baltimore Mus Art, Md; Nat Mus Am Art, Washington, DC; Metrop Mus Art, New York. *Exhib:* West/Midwest: New Photographs, Sander Gallery, New York, 88; Three Decades of Midwestern Photography, 1960-1990, Davenport Mus Art, 92; Milwaukee Art Mus, 92; Philadelphia Mus Art, 92; Harn Mus Art, Gainesville, 93. *Pos:* Bd dir, New Art Examiner, 90-92; reviewer, Nat Endowment Humanities, 80-85. *Teaching:* Instr photog, Ill Inst Tech, Chicago, 72-74; vis artist photo hist/photog, Columbia Col, Chicago, Ill, 76-86; vis artist photog hist, Sch Art Inst, Chicago, Ill, 86-; vis artists photog & photo hist, DePaul Univ, Chicago, Ill, 92. *Awards:* Grant & Fel Nat Endowment Arts & Nat Endowment Humanities, 78. *Bibliog:* Charles Traub (auth), The New Vision: 40 Years Of, Aperture, 82; Abigail Foerstner (auth), Project takes the pulse of art in Illinois, Chicago Tribune, 87; Mark Towner (auth), Three Decades of Midwestern Photography: 1960-1990, Davenport Mus Art, 92. *Publ:* coauth, From Pictorialism to Precisionism, A B Bookman, 84; JNO Cook: Radically recycled cameras, Mass Inst Tech, 90; interview (text) with Cook; The Black Trans-Atlantic Experience: The Photographs of Stephen Marc (inteview), Univ Ill Press, 92; Midwestern Photography: 1960-1990 (includes statement), Davenport Mus Art, 92. *Mailing Add:* 1255 S Wabash Ave, Studio No 404 Chicago IL 60605-2427

COHEN, ARTHUR MORRIS
PAINTER, GRAPHIC ARTIST
b New York, NY, Jan 2, 28. *Study:* Cooper Union, 48-50, Art Students League with Edwin Dickinson, 50 & 60. *Work:* Metrop Mus Art, New York; Brooklyn Mus; Hirshhorn Mus, Washington, DC; New York Hist Soc; Boston Mus Fine Art. *Exhib:* Solo exhibs, Munson Gallery, Chatham, Mass, 85, 88 & 89, Kornbluth Gallery, Fairlawn, NJ, 86, E End Gallery, Provincetown, Mass, 86 & 87, Phoenix Gallery, Provincetown, Mass, 88, New E End Gallery, Provincetown, Mass, 89 & 90 & Wellfleet Fine Arts Gallery, Mass, 90; Salute to the Great Bridge, New York Hist Soc, 83; Urban Graphics, New York, 83; Hudson Guild Gallery, New York, 84; Jewish Community Ctr, Bayonne, NJ, 84; Assoc Am Artists Inc, New York, 84; Provincetown Art Asn, 85 & 86; Kornbluth Gallery, Fairlawn, NJ, 88; and others. *Teaching:* Instr painting, Sch Agean, 87. *Awards:* Guggenheim Fel; Pollock-Krasner Fel; Gottlieb Fel. *Bibliog:* Gerrit Henry (auth), Art Am, 4/83; Carl Little (auth), Arts Mag, 6/83; Vivian Raynor (auth), New York Times, 4/27/86 & 5/8/88. *Mem:* Provincetown Art Asn. *Media:* Oil. *Publ:* Cover, House of Light, 90. *Dealer:* East End Gallery Provincetown, MA; Swansborough Gallery, Wellfleet, MA. *Mailing Add:* 55 Tiemann Place New York NY 10027

COHEN, BRUCE JOEL
PAINTER
b Santa Monica, Calif, Dec 26, 53. *Study:* Univ Calif, Santa Barbara, BA, 75. *Work:* Guggenheim Mus; San Diego Mus Art; Pacific Telesis Group, San Francisco; Atlantic Richfield Co, Calif; Philip Morris Inc, New York. *Exhib:* New Perspective in American Art, Guggenheim Mus, 83; Images of American Pop Culture Today, La Fouret Mus, Tokyo, 89; Frederick Weisman Found, Palm Springs Desert Mus, 84. *Bibliog:* William Wilson (auth), The galleries, Los Angeles Times, 1/83; Ronnie Cohen (auth), Bruce Cohen, Art Forum, 12/87; Cathy Curtis (auth), Los Angeles Times, 3/89. *Media:* Oil on Canvas. *Mailing Add:* c/o Cirrus Gallery 542 S Alameda St Los Angeles CA 90013

COHEN, CHARLES E
HISTORIAN, EDUCATOR
b New York, NY, July 11, 42. *Study:* Columbia Univ, AB, 63; Princeton Univ, MFA, 65; Harvard Univ, PhD, 71. *Teaching:* From asst to prof, Univ Chicago, 70-, chmn, Art Dept, 76-82 & 85-88. *Awards:* Delmas Found Fel, 80; Guggenheim Found Fel, 83-84; Nat Endowment Humanities Univ, Fel, 89-90. *Mem:* Col Art Asn Am; Midwest Art Hist Soc. *Res:* Venetian & North Italian painting and drawing in the Renaissance. *Publ:* Auth, Pordenone's painted facade on the Palazzo Tinghi in Udine, Burlington Mag, 74; I disegni di Pomponio Amalteo, GEAP, 75; Pordenone's Cremona Passion Scenes & German Art, Arte Lomberda, 76; The Drawings of Giovanni Antonio da Pordenone, La Nuova Italia, 80; Pordenone not Giorgione, Burlington Mag, 80. *Mailing Add:* 5540 S Greenwood Ave Chicago IL 60637

COHEN, CORA
PAINTER
b New York, NY, Oct 19, 43. *Study:* Bennington Col, with Paul Feeley, David Smith & Tony Caro, BA, 64, MA, 72. *Exhib:* Solo exhibs, State Univ NY, Oneonta, 77, Max Hutchinson Gallery, New York, 79, 80 & 84, Dunnel Steen Fine Arts, Greenwich, Conn, 81, Maples Gallery, Fairleigh Dickenson Univ, NJ, 83, Wolff Gallery, New York, 88 & Holly Solomon Gallery, New York, 90; Multiple Grounds, Sytsema Galleries, Baarn, Holland, 92; Sandra Gering Gallery, New York, 92; Painting Self-Evident: Evolutions in Abstraction, Piccolo Spoleto Festival, Charleston, SC, 92; An Esemplastic Shift, 92 & The Fetish of Knowledge, 92, A/C Project Room, New York; Contemporary surfaces, Pamela Auchcloss Galleryl, New York, 92; and many others. *Teaching:* Vis artist painting, Art Inst Chicago, 83, Univ Chicago, 84, Art Inst Chicago, 85, Boston Mus Sch Fine Arts, 85; lectr, New York Studio Sch, 89 & Tyler Sch Art, 90. *Awards:* Nat Endowment Arts Painting Fel, 87; NY Found Arts, 89; Gottleib Found Award, 90; and others. *Bibliog:* StephenWestfall (auth), Art Am, 6/89; Cora Cohen (auth), Bomb Mag, fall 91; Saul Ostrow (auth), Tema Celeste, autumn 91; Roberta Smith (auth), NY Times, 6/26/92; Holland Cotter (auth), NY Times, 8/7/92; and others. *Mem:* Col Art Asn. *Media:* Oil. *Mailing Add:* 287 Broadway New York NY 10007

COHEN, ELAINE LUSTIG
PAINTER, DESIGNER
b Jersey City, NJ, Mar 6, 27. *Study:* Tulane Univ, 45-46; Univ Southern Calif, BFA, 48. *Work:* Mus Mod Art, New York; Am Tel & Tel; Chase Manhattan Bank; Newark Mus; Atlantic Richfield, Calif. *Comn:* Graphic designs for Am Fedn Arts, Philip Johnson (architect), Lincoln Ctr, Fed Aviation Agency & Meridian Bks. *Exhib:* One-person exhibs, Janus Gallery, Los Angeles, 82 & 85, Gloria Luria Gallery, Bay Harbour Islands, Miami, Fla, 82, Carson Sapiro Gallery, Denver, Colo, 82, Exit Art, New York, 85; Watercolors: A Contemporary Survey, San Diego State Univ Art Gallery, Calif, 84; Drawings: New Dimensions, Nina Freudenheim Gallery, Buffalo, NY, 84; An Affair of the Heart: Artist's Valentines, Albright Knox Art Gallery, Buffalo, 85; Imagenes en Cajas Museo Rufino Tamayo, 85; Adornments, Bernice Steinbaum Gallery, New York, 85. *Pos:* Designer (with Alvin Lustig), until 55; freelance designer, 55-67; mem adv comt art & archit, Yale Univ Sch Design, 57-62. *Mailing Add:* 160 E 70th St New York NY 10021

COHEN, GEORGE MICHAEL
EDUCATOR
Study: Harvard Univ, AB, 55, AM, 58; Boston Univ, PhD, 62. *Teaching:* Prof, Hofstra Univ, 70- *Publ:* Auth, The bird symbolism of Morris Graves, Col Art J, 58; The paintings of Charles Sheeler, 59 & The lithographs of Thomas Hart Benton, 62, Am Artist; The sculpture of John B Flannagan, Artvoices, 65; The art of George Catlin, Art & Antiques, 81; and many others. *Mailing Add:* 80 Wintercress Lane East Northport NY 11731

COHEN, HAROLD
ARTIST-THEORIST, EDUCATOR
b London, Eng, May 1, 28. *Study:* Univ London, Diploma(fine arts), 51. *Work:* Tate Gallery, London; Stedelijk Mus, Amsterdam, Holland; Victoria & Albert Mus, London; Los Angeles Co Mus Art, Calif; Walker Art Ctr, Minneapolis, Minn. *Comn:* Wall hanging, Milan Triennale, 63; tapestry, Brit Petroleum Co, 65. *Exhib:* Documenta, Kassel, WGer, 64 & 77; 33rd Venice Biennale, 66; one-man shows, Mus d'Art Contemporain, Montreal, Que, 67, Victoria & Albert Mus, 68 & Stedelijk Mus, 77; Three Behaviors for the Partitioning of Space, Los Angeles Co Mus Art, 72; Retrospective, Scottish Arts Coun Gallery, Edinburgh, 76; Harold Cohen: Drawing, San Francisco Mus Mod Art, 79; Computers & the Visual Arts: The Research & Drawings of Harold Cohen, Sierra Nevada Mus Art, 79; and others. *Pos:* Vis scholar, Artificial Intelligence Lab, Stanford Univ, 73-75. *Teaching:* Instr art, Univ Col London, 61-65; prof art, Univ Calif, San Diego, 68-, chmn visual arts dept, 68-69, dir, Ctr Art/Sci Study, 74- *Awards:* Harkness Fel of Commonwealth Fund, 59-61; Purchase Award, Gulbenkian Found, 61; Nat Endowment Arts Workshop Grant, 76. *Publ:* Auth, The making of a tapestry, 67, Apropos work in progress, 68 & On purpose, 74, Studio Int; The material of symbols, First Ann Symposium onSymbols & Symbol Processing, Univ Nev, 76; What is an Image?, Int Joint Conf Artificial Intelligence, Tokyo, Japan, 79. *Mailing Add:* Dept Visual Arts Univ Calif San Diego La Jolla CA 92093

COHEN, HAROLD LARRY
DESIGNER, EDUCATOR
b Brooklyn, NY, May 24, 25. *Study:* Pratt Inst Art Sch, Brooklyn; Northwestern Univ; Inst Design, BA. *Pos:* Dir, Inst Behav Res, Silver Spring, Md, formerly; dean sch archit & environ design, State Univ NY, Buffalo, formerly, prof, currently. *Teaching:* Prof design, chmn dept & dir design res & develop, Southern Ill Univ, Carbondale, formerly. *Awards:* Five Good Design Awards, with Davis Pratt; Mus Mod Art Awards, 49-53. *Mailing Add:* Sch of Archit & Environ Design State Univ NY Buffalo NY 14214

COHEN, HY
PAINTER
b London, Eng, June 13, 01. *Study:* Nat Acad Design; City Col New York, BS. *Work:* Hirshhorn Mus. *Exhib:* Brooklyn Mus; Art Inst Chicago; Metrop Mus Art; St Louis Mus; Los Angeles Mus; Am Watercolor Soc; Washington Univ; Pa Acad Fine Arts; Carnegie Inst; Walker Art Ctr; Corcoran Gallery. *Pos:* Organized & moderated, Let's talk about art, weekly radio prog, 45-46. *Mem:* Artists Equity Asn New York (pres, 63-70, hon pres, 70-); life mem Am Watercolor Soc. *Mailing Add:* 166 W 72nd St New York NY 10023

COHEN, JEAN
PAINTER
b New York, NY, Aug 1, 27. *Study:* Pratt Inst, Brooklyn, 44-45; Cooper Union Art Sch, New York, 46-49; Skowhegan Sch Painting & Sculpture, Maine, summer 50. *Work:* Ciba-Geigy Corp, Ardsley, NY; Hampton Inst Mus, Va; Bocour Color Collection, Garnersville, NY; Colby Col Mus, Waterville, Maine; Wright State Univ Mus. *Exhib:* Contemp Artists, Riverside Mus, New York, 63; Pa Acad Regional, Philadelphia, 64; Visual R&D, Univ Tex Art Mus, Austin, 73; Contemp Am Painting, Randolph-Macon Col, 74; West Bronx Art League, Bronx Mus, 75. *Pos:* Consult, West

Bronx Art League, 69-75; founder, Landmark Gallery, New York; cur, Magic Circle Exhib, Bronx Mus Arts, 77. *Teaching:* Instr painting & design, Cooper Union, spring & summers, 51-63; lectr painting, Philadelphia Col Art, 62-69; lectr painting, Queens Col Art Dept, 72-75; Jersey City State Col, Philadelphia Col Art, 81-86 & La State Univ, spring 90. *Awards:* Landscape Painting Prize, Skowhegan Sch Painting, 50; Creative Artists Pub Serv Grant, 80; Adolph Gottlieb Grant, 84. *Mem:* Artists Equity; Am Abstract Artists. *Media:* Oil, Compressed Charcoal. *Dealer:* Cape Split Place Addison ME 04606. *Mailing Add:* 20 Cornelia St New York NY 10014

COHEN, JEAN R
CERAMIST, COLLECTOR
b Colorado Springs, Colo, Apr 13, 35. *Study:* Penland Sch Crafts; Maples Mills Sch Crafts; Arrowmont Sch Crafts; Visual Arts Ctr; also, study with Richard La Fean, Jane Peiser, Elsa Rady, Ralph Baccera, David Leach, Don Pilcher, Rudi Staffel, Catherine Hiersoux & Sally Silberberg. *Work:* Towson State Univ Gallery, Baltimore; Vessels Aesthetic, Taft Col, Calif. *Exhib:* Maryland Craft Coun Biennial Exhib, Maryland, 81 & 83; Contemp Crafts Exhib, Del Art Mus, Del, 82; Lloyd Herman Selects, Arlington Arts Ctr, Virginia, 82; Am Hand Inc, Washington, DC & New York, 83 & 84; Everson Mus Art, NY, 84; Crafts Nat, Buffalo State Col, NY, 85; Am Ceramic Nat, Calif, 86. *Teaching:* Teacher, Potters Guild Baltimore, Md, 77-82; Workshop Instr, Washington Kiln Club, 84, Santa Barbara State Col, 86. *Awards:* Purchase Award, Vessels Aesthetic, 83. *Mem:* Clayworks of Baltimore, Md; Potters Guild of Baltimore, Md; Am Craft Coun. *Publ:* Ceramics Monthly, 4/86. *Mailing Add:* 6104 Eastcliff Dr Baltimore MD 21209

COHEN, JOAN LEBOLD
HISTORIAN, PHOTOGRAPHER
b Highland Park, Ill, Aug 19, 32. *Study:* Smith Col, BA, 54. *Work:* Smith Col Mus Art; Harvard Law Sch; Atlantic Richfield Corp Collection. *Exhib:* LaChine, Centre Culturel De L'Ambassade De France, Peking, 81; Shadows of Mt Huang, Univ Art Gallery, Berkeley, Calif, 81; Detroit Inst Arts, 81; Univ Texas, Austin, 81; Art Mus, Princeton, 82; Alisan Fine Arts, Hong Kong, 87 & 89; Smith Col Alumnae House, 90. *Collections Arranged:* New York, The City and Its People, (photgr exhib; co-chair), Beijing, 85. *Pos:* Guest cur, Smith Col Mus Art, 82 & Sarah Lawrence Col Art Gallery, 87. *Teaching:* Lectr, Dept Pub Educ, Mus Fine Arts, Boston, 65-71; lectr Asian art & film, China, Japan & India, Sch of Mus Fine Arts, Tufts Univ, Boston, 68- *Awards:* Two awards for bk, China Today & Her Ancient Treasures, 74 & 75; Smith Col Medal, 90. *Res:* Asian film & art. *Publ:* Frequent contribr writing & photog, Artention Int, Hong Kong; auth, Painting the Chinese Dream, Chinese Art Thirty Years After the Revolution, 82; coauth & photogr, China Today and Her Ancient Treasures, Abrams, 74, rev eds, 80 & 86; auth & photogr, The New Chinese Painting, 1949-1986, Abrams, 87; Yunnan Sch, A Renaissance in Chinese Painting, Fingerhut, 88. *Dealer:* Jonathan Stein Assoc 353 E 77th St New York NY 10021; Photoresearchers 60 E 56th New York NY 10522. *Mailing Add:* 50 E 89th St New York NY 10028

COHEN, JONATHAN JACOB
DESIGNER, CRAFTSMAN
b Boston, Mass, Aug 13, 55. *Study:* Cornell Univ, studied with Dennis Ichiyama, BA, 78. *Comn:* Jones, Grey & Bailey Law Offices, Bellevue, Wash, 85; dining room, comn by Dr & Mrs S Wyte, La Jolla, Calif, 86; Pacific Dunkmann Co, Seattle, Wash, 87; Whitten residence, comn by Mr & Mrs G Whitten, Bellevue, Wash, 88. *Exhib:* Embellishment Upon Function, Henry Art Gallery, Seattle, Wash, 80; Nat Invitational, Am Crafts Gallery, Cleveland, Ohio, 84, 85 & 86; Furniture That Keeps Secrets, 84 & Nat Invitational, 87 & 88, NW Gallery of Fine Woodworking, Seattle, Wash; Wood Invitational, Signature Gallery, Boston, Mass, 85; one-man exhib, Dark Dancers, NW Gallery of Fine Woodworking, 89, Rain Forest Show, 92. *Teaching:* Visiting prof furniture design, Univ Wash, 87-92. *Awards:* (2) First Place Awards, Special Crafts Exhib, Bellevue Art Mus, Wash, 81. *Bibliog:* A V Chastain Chapman (auth), Fine Furniture Making, Am Craft, 12-84; Sharon O'Boyle (auth), Tomorrows Antiques, Wash Mag, 3-85; J Queener Shaw (auth), Enchanted Woods, Pacific NW Mag, 5-87. *Mem:* Am Crafts. *Publ:* Regular contribr to Fine Woodworking Mag, 83- *Dealer:* NW Gallery Fine Woodworking 202 First Ave S Seattle WA 98104. *Mailing Add:* 3410 Woodland Park Ave N Seattle WA 98103

COHEN, LYNNE G
PHOTOGRAPHER, INSTRUCTOR
b Racine, Wis, July 3, 44. *Study:* Slade Sch Art, London, 64-65; Univ Wis, Madison, BS(art), 67; Univ Mich, 68, Eastern Mich Univ, MA(art), 69. *Work:* Int Mus Photog, George Eastman House, Rochester, NY; Musse d'Art Moderne de la Ville de Paris, France; Nat Gallery Can, Ottawa; Victoria & Albert Mus, London, Eng; Mus Voor Fotografie, Antwerp, Belg. *Exhib:* Solo exhibs, Int Ctr Photog, New York, Interim Art, London, Eng, 88, Mus Gestaltung Zurich, Switz, 89, PPOW, New York, 92, FRAC Limousin, 92; Mus Mod Art, New York, 77; Musee des Beaux Arts, Montreal & traveling, 81; Victoria & Albert Mus, London, 89; Ehlers Caudill Gallery, Chicago, 90; Newport Harbor Art Mus, Calif, 91; Galerie Samia Saouma, Paris, 91; Galerie Rodololphe Janssen, 92; and others. *Teaching:* Lectr photog-art, Eastern Mich Univ, Ypsilanti, 68-73; from lectr to asst prof photog, Dept Visual Arts, Univ Ottawa, 74-; vis artist & prof, Art Inst Chicago, 84 & 92. *Awards:* Logan Award, 71st Chicago & Vicinity Show, Art Inst Chicago, 67; Can Coun Sr Arts Grant, 85; Ont Arts Coun Sr Arts Grant, 85. *Bibliog:* Owen Edwards (auth), article, Saturday Rev, 7/8/78; Thierry de Duve (auth), catalog essay, Galerie Gokelaeire & Janssen, Brusels, 90; Marc Freidus (auth), catalog & bk, Typologies, Nine Contemporary Photographers, Newport Harbor Art Mus. *Media:* Artist, Photographer. *Publ:* Contribr, Image, George Eastman House, 74; The Photographer's Choice, Addison House, 75; Creative Camera, 4/78; The Banff Purchase, John Wiley, 79; Photo Communique, winter 82. *Dealer:* PPOW 532 Broadway New York NY 10012; Galerie Samia Saouma 16 Rue Des Coutures St-Gervais 75003. *Mailing Add:* Univ Ottawa 600 Cumberland Ave Ottawa ON K1N 6N5 Canada

COHEN, MICHAEL S
CERAMIST, PHOTOGRAPHER
b Boston, Mass, Mar 7, 36. *Study:* Mass Col of Art, BFA, 57; Cranbrook Acad of Art, Bloomfield Hills, Mich, 61; Haystack Mountain Sch Crafts, Deer Isle, Maine, 61. *Work:* Mus of Mod Art, New York; Mus Contemp Crafts, New York; Johnson Collection Contemp Crafts, Wis; Everson Mus, Syracuse, NY; Addison Gallery, Andover, Mass. *Exhib:* Syracuse Int, Everson Mus, 62, 64 & 66; Am Studio Pottery, Victoria & Albert Mus, London, Eng, 63; 10th Int Exhib of Ceramic Art, Smithsonian Inst, Washington, DC, 65; one-man shows, Soc of Arts & Crafts, Lexington, Mass, 74 & Gallimaufry, Croton-on-Hudson, NY, 76; Objects USA, Mus Contemp Crafts, New York, 70; Crafts 1970, Boston City Hall, Mass; Potter's Wheel, DeCordova Mus, Lincoln, Mass, 76; and others. *Awards:* Nat Endowment Arts grant, 74; Master Craftsman grant, Nat Endowment Arts, 75; 2nd Int Symposium, Tenn, 75. *Bibliog:* Peter Sabin (auth), Studio Production, Studio Potter, 76. *Mem:* Am Crafts Coun; Mass Asn of Craftsmen; Asparagus Valley Potters Guild (pres, 75-89). *Media:* Stoneware. *Mailing Add:* RR 2 Amherst MA 01002

COHEN, MILDRED THALER
ART DEALER, GALLERY DIRECTOR
b New York, NY, Oct 30, 21. *Study:* Hunter Col, New York, BA, 42; Pratt Inst Libr Sch, Brooklyn, NY, BLS, 43. *Collections Arranged:* Women Students of William Merritt Chase, 73; Ethel Paxson, 76; New Choate Jones, 79; Frederic Taubes, 81; Three Generations of Wiggins: Carleton, Guy C, Guy A, 81; Robert Hallowell, 83; Eliot Clark, 88; Samuel Rothbort, 89; Rachel Hartley, 91; Frank Kleinholz, 92. *Pos:* Librn, Mus French Art, French Inst, New York, 43-45; dir, The Marbella Gallery, Inc, New York, 71- *Mem:* Appraisers Asn Am Inc. *Specialty:* Nineteenth and early twentieth century American paintings. *Mailing Add:* 28 E 72nd St New York NY 10021

COHEN, REINA JOYCE
GRAPHIC ARTIST, PRINTMAKER
b New York, NY, Mar 28, 31. *Study:* Cooper Union, NY, 51; The New School, 66. *Work:* Nassau Co Med Ctr, Hempstead, NY; Vitelco, St Thomas, US VI; St Laurence Univ, Canton, NY. *Comn:* Monoprints, Winrock Inn, Albuquerque, NMex, 90. *Exhib:* Firehouse Gallery, Nassau Comm Col, Hempstead, NY, 81; Space Group Korea, Seoul, 82 & 84. *Awards:* First Prize, Freeport Arts Coun, 79; Award of Excellence, Independent Art Soc, 84 & 90; Grant, Mid Atlantic Arts Found, Baltimore, Md, 91. *Mem:* Nat Asn Women Artists; Independent Art Soc. *Media:* Miscellaneous Media, Etching. *Dealer:* Art Rep Inc 279 Woodmere St Islip Terrace NY 11752. *Mailing Add:* 29 Farmstead Lane Brookville NY 11545

COHEN, RONNY
CRITIC, CURATOR
b New York, NY, Apr 19, 50. *Study:* Finch Col, BA, 72; Inst Fine Arts, MA, 74, PhD, 79. *Collections Arranged:* Energism, PS 1 Critical Perspectives, 82; New Spiritual Abstraction of the 1980's Nohra Haime Gallery, New York, 84; Alan Shields: A Survey of His Prints, Cleveland Ctr Contemp Art, 86; Nature In Art, Contemp Art at 1 Penn Plaza, New York; Meticulous Realist Drawing, Squibb Gallary, Princeton, NJ, 89; An Artist's Christmas, Midtown Payson Galleries, New York, 90; Watercolor Across the Ages, Bristol-Myers Squibb, Princeton, NJ, 91. *Pos:* Ed, The Art Dealer's Newsletter, 83-85. *Teaching:* Cooper Univ, 89. *Awards:* Danforth Found Fel, 72-79; Fulbright-Hays Fel, US & Italian Govt, 76-77. *Bibliog:* Owen Findsen (auth), Energism: Becomes a new buzz word for art, Artists, The Cincinnati Enquirer, 10/2/81; Roger Green (auth), Energism peps things up, Times-Picayune, New Orleans, 9/19/82; Art, The New Yorker, 12/31/90. *Mem:* New York Artists Equity Asn; Inst Fine Arts Alumni Asn; Int Asn Art Critics. *Publ:* Auth, Energism: An attitude, 9/80 & Alexandra Exter's designs for the theater, 9/81, Artforum; Drawing the meticulous realist way, 3/4/82; New abstraction V, PCN, 4/5/87; Minimal Prints, PCN, 6/90;; and others. *Mailing Add:* 521 E 82nd St New York NY 10028

COHEN, SOREL
CONCEPTUAL ARTIST, PHOTOGRAPHER
b Montreal, Que, Can. *Study:* Concordia Univ, Montreal, BFA, 74, MFA, 79. *Work:* Nat Gallery Can, Ottawa, Ont; Bibliot Nat, Paris; Mus d'Art Contemporain, Montreal Mus Fine Arts; Winnipeg Art Gallery, Manitoba. *Exhib:* An Extended and Continous Metaphor, PS 1, New York, 83; Productions and the Axis of Sexuality, Walter Philips Gallery, Banff, 84; Visual Facts, Third Eye Ctr, Glasgow, 85; Doppleganger/Cover, Galerie Aorta, Amsterdam, 85; et les ateliers de femmes, Mus d'Art Contemporain, Montreal, 86; Songs of Experience, Nat Gallery of Can, 86; Figures, Cambridge Darkroom, 87. *Pos:* bd mem, Galerie Optica, 80-88. *Awards:* Bourse du Quebec, Ministere des Affairs Culture, 83; Arts Grant B, Can Coun, 85; Duke & Duchess Award in Photogr, Can Coun, 88. *Bibliog:* R Graham & G Godmer (auths), monogr essays, Mus d'Art Contemporain, 86; Therese St Gelais, rev, Parachute, 86-87; Bob Wilkie (auth), Telling pictures, revealing histories, Afterimage, Vol 17, No 9, 4/90. *Dealer:* Wynick Tuck Gallery 80 Spadina Ave Toronto Ont M5V 2J3 Canada. *Mailing Add:* 631 Lansdowne Ave Montreal PQ H3Y 2V7 Canada

COHLON, WILLIAM
PAINTER
b Albany, NY, 1941. *Study:* Sch Visual Arts, 60-63; Sch Art & Archit, Yale Univ, BFA & MFA, 65-67. *Work:* Dallas Mus Fine Arts, Dallas, Tex; Everson Mus, Syracuse, NY; Albright-Knox Art Gallery, Buffalo, NY; AT&T & Lehman Brothers, NY. *Comn:* List Art Poster, Lincoln Ctr Performing Arts, New York, NY; Saatchi & Saatchi/DFS/Compton, Los Angeles, Calif. *Exhib:* Visual Arts Gallery, NY, 64; solo exhibs, Yale Univ Art Gallery, New Haven, Conn, 68, Reese Palley Gallery, NY, 70 & 72, Andre Emmerich Gallery, NY, 77, 80, 81, 85, 86 & 87 & Carnegie Inst Mus Art, Pittsburgh, Pa, 81; J L Hudson Gallery, Detroit, Mich, 70; Whitney Mus Am Art, NY, 72; Ralph Wilson Gallery, Lehigh Univ, Bethlehem, Pa, 77; Am Painting: The Eighties, A Critical Interpretation, int tour incl Austria, Japan, Hungary, Poland, etc, 79-83; Janie C Lee Gallery, Houston, Tex, 85; Hokin Gallery, Miami, Fla, 87. *Awards:* Nat Endowment Arts, 77. *Bibliog:* Carter Ratcliff (auth), The Whitney Annual, Part I, Art Forum, Vol X, 28-32, 4/72; Ellen Lubell (auth), Review, Sch Visual Arts, Arts Mag, 26, 10/77; Herbert Meltzer (auth), The Unexpected, The Sciences, Vol 18, No 3, 3/78. *Mailing Add:* c/o Hokin Gallery 245 Worth Ave Palm Beach FL 33480

COHN, BARBARA G See Bisgyer, Barbara G (Cohn)

COHN, FREDERICK DONALD
DEALER, APPRAISER
b Monroe, Mich, May 3, 31. *Study:* Univ Wis, BA, 54; Detroit Col Law, LLB, 57. *Pos:* Art dealer, Images Gallery, Toledo, Ohio, currently. *Mem:* Appraisers Asn Am; Toledo Mod Art Group (mem bd, currently); Toledo Mus Art, Pres Coun. *Specialty:* Nineteenth and twentieth century American painting, print and sculpture. *Mailing Add:* Images Gallery 3154 Markway Rd Toledo OH 43606

COHN, MARJORIE B
CURATOR, HISTORIAN
b New York, NY, Jan 10, 39. *Study:* Mt Holyoke Col, BA, 60; Radcliffe Col, AM, 61. *Collections Arranged:* Albrecht Durer, 1471-1528 (auth, catalogue), Mt Holyoke Col, 71; Wash & Gouache, Watercolor at Harvard, Fogg Art Mus, Harvard Univ, 77; Ingres Collection (auth, handbook), 81 & Gray Collection of Engravings (auth, handbook), 86, Fogg Art Mus; A Noble Collection: the Spencer Albums of Old Master Prints (auth, handbook), Fogg Art Mus, 92. *Pos:* Conservator works of art on paper, Fogg Art Mus, Harvard Univ, 62-89, curator prints, 89-, actg dir, 90-91; mem bd examr (paper), Am Inst for Conserv, 76-78, mem nominating comt, 77 & ed jour. *Teaching:* Guest lectr print hist, Boston Univ, 73; vis lectr print hist, Wellesley Col, 73; vis asst prof print hist, Brown Univ, 75; sr lectr fine arts, Harvard Univ, 77- *Mem:* Fel Int Inst for Conserv; fel Am Inst for Conserv. *Res:* History, materials & techniques of traditional graphic arts. *Publ:* Contribr, Technical Appendix, Ingres Centennial Exhibition, Fogg Art Mus, 67; A Note on Media and Methods, Tiepolo, A Bicentenary Exhibition, Fogg Art Mus, 70; Wash & Gouache: A Study of the Development of the Materials of Watercolor, Fogg Art Mus, 81; contribr, Pursuit of Perfection: Works by J A D Ingres, J B Speed Mus, 83; Francis Gallery Gary and Art Collecting for America, Harvard Unit Art Mus, 86. *Mailing Add:* Fogg Art Mus Harvard Univ Cambridge MA 02138

COHN, MAX ARTHUR
PAINTER, PRINTMAKER
b London, England, Feb 3, 03; US citizen. *Study:* Art Students League, New York, 21-25; Colarossi Acad, Paris, 27. *Work:* Nat Mus Am Art, Washington, DC; Metrop Mus, New York; Philadelphia Mus; William Rockhill Nelson Gallery Art, Kansas City; Dallas Mus, Tex; Boston Mus Fine Arts; Brit Mus, London, Eng; Univ Wis-Milwaukee; Mus City NY. *Exhib:* One-man shows, ACA Gallery, New York, 34, Delphic Studios, New York, 36, Couturier Galleries, Conn, 64 & Lucinda Galleries, NJ, 68; Biennial Watercolor, Brooklyn Mus, NY; Prints & Paintings, Mus Mod Art, New York. *Mem:* Life mem Art Students League; Del Valley Artists Asn (treas 47-62); Works Proj Artists Asn, New York. *Media:* Oil, Watercolor. *Publ:* Co-auth, Silk Screen Stenciling as a Fine Art, McGraw-Hill, 42; Silk Screen Techniques, Dover Press, 58. *Dealer:* Lyle Evans Gallery Lexington MA; Rosenfeld Galleries 50 W 57th St New York NY. *Mailing Add:* 311 W 24th St New York NY 10011

COHN, RICHARD A
DEALER
b New York, NY, Feb 20, 24. *Study:* Univ Wis. *Pos:* Pres, Richard A Cohn Ltd, New York, 65-; partner, Kimmel/Cohn Photography Arts, New York, 74- *Specialty:* Twentieth century German Expressionism. *Mailing Add:* Richard A Cohn Ltd One W 64th St New York NY 10023

COIT, M B
PAINTER, SCULPTOR
b New London, Conn. *Study:* Univ Conn, BFA, 68. *Comn:* Triptych, Mitsui Manufacturers Bank, Los Angeles, Calif, 83. *Exhib:* Images, Bowers Mus, Santa Ana, Calif, 87; LA Art, Gallery Q, Tokyo, Japan, 87; Designations, Los Angeles Co Mus Art, Calif, 87; one-man show, Branslater Gallery, Riverside, Calif, 89; Artist's Book, Anchorage Mus, Alaska, 90; traveling exhib, Southern California Decade 1980-89--Contemporary Artists, Univ Calif, Los Angeles, 90. *Bibliog:* Suzanne Muchnic (auth), Galleries downtown, LA Times, 11/2/84; Melinda Wortz (auth), article, Loma Linda Univ, 89; Roger Churches (auth), M B Coit: lucid lights, Loma Linda Univ, 89. *Media:* Acrylic, Oil; Plastic. *Mailing Add:* 702 Sixth Ave Venice CA 90291

COKE, F VAN DEREN
PHOTOGRAPHER, CURATOR
b Lexington, Ky, July 4, 21. *Study:* Univ Ky, BA; Ind Univ, MFA; Harvard Univ; Acad Art Co, San Francisco, LHD, 86. *Work:* Mus Mod Art, New York; Int Mus Photog, Rochester, NY; Nat Gallery Can, Ottawa, Ont; San Francisco Mus Mod Art; Sheldon Mem Art Gallery, Lincoln, Nebr. *Exhib:* Witkin Gallery, New York, 74; Oakland Mus, 75; Galerie die Brucke, Vienna, 75; Schoelkopf Gallery, New York, 76; Art Mus, Univ NMex, 82; Albuquerque Mus, NMex & Phoenix Art Mus, Ariz, 86. *Pos:* Dir, Univ NMex Art Mus, 62-67 & 72-79; dir, George Eastman House, 70-72; dir dept photog, San Francisco Mus Mod Art, 79- *Teaching:* Asst prof photog & art hist, Univ Fla, 58-61; assoc prof, Ariz State Univ, 61-62, adj prof, 83-; prof, Univ NMex, 62-70 & 72-79, chmn dept art, 62-70; lectr, St Martin's Sch Art, London, 71; prof art hist, Univ Rochester, 71-72; vis prof, Univ Calif, Berkeley, 73; distinguished vis prof, Univ Calif, Davis, 74. *Awards:* Int Competition Awards, Mod Photog Mag, 56 & US Camera Mag, 57, 58 & 60; New Talent USA Award, Art in Am, 60; Guggenheim Fel, 75. *Bibliog:* Joan Murray (auth), Two views of the West, Artweek, 1/22/72; A Frankenstein (auth), A creative photographer, San Francisco Chronicle, 1/13/72; Robert Routh (auth), An interview with Van Deren Coke, Peterson's Photo Mag, 4/11/76; Janzita Rover (auth), No party line: a conversation with Van Deren Coke, Exposure, Vol 20, 82; Liz Lufkin (auth), Van Deren Coke: Pied piper of the avant garde, Am Photogr, 6/85. *Mem:* Col Art Asn Am (bd dir, 72-76); Int Folk Art Found (bd dir, 68-76); Guadalupe Found (bd dir, 76-79); Soc Photog Educ (bd dir, 67-70). *Res:* The use of photographs by artists; twentieth century American painters; contemporary photographers. *Publ:* Auth, Joel-Peter Witkin, 75; Facets of Modernism, 76; Fabricated to be Photgraphed, 79; The Markers, 81; Avant-Garde Photography in Germany 1919-1939, 83; Bret Weston Photgraphs: 1925-1930 and 1980-1983, 83; Val Telberg, 83. *Mailing Add:* 1053 Governor Dempsey Dr Sante Fe NM 87501

COKENDOLPHER, EUNICE LORAINE
PAINTER, INSTRUCTOR
b Sonora, Tex, April 17, 31. *Study:* Tex Womans Univ, 48-50; studied with Don Stone, Edgar Whitney, Zoltan Szabo, George Cherepov, Bud Biggs, Naomi Brotherton & Howard Wexler, 75-89. *Work:* Southern Guild Artists & Craftsmen, Bowling Green, Ky; Baptist Med Ctr Found, Oklahoma City. *Comn:* Noah and the Ark, First United Methodist Church, Burkburnett, Tex, 81. *Exhib:* Tex Fine Arts Citation Exhib, Laguna Gloria Mus, Austin, Tex, 80; Aqueous 79', Ky Watercolor Soc, 79; The Best of Southwest Watercolor Soc, Brookhaven Col, Dallas, 81 & 84; Southern Watercolor Soc Seventh Ann, Asheville Art Mus, NC, 83; Ga Watercolor Soc Fifth Nat Exhib, Valdosta State Col Fine Arts Bldg, 84. *Teaching:* Instr watercolor, Wishing Well Studio, Burkburnett, Tex, 84. *Awards:* Award Merit, Aqueous 79, Ky Watercolor Soc Nat Exhib, 79; Mary Jo Weale Award, Southern Watercolor Soc Nat Exhib, 83; Second Place, Best of Southwest Watercolor Soc, 84. *Mem:* Southwestern Watercolor Soc. *Media:* Watercolor, Oil. *Mailing Add:* 1200 Clover Dr Burkburnett TX 76354

COKER, CARL DAVID
PAINTER, EDUCATOR
b Greensboro, NC, Feb 8, 28. *Study:* Art Students League with Robert Beverly Hale; Univ NC; Univ NMex with Raymond Jonson, Richard Diebenkorn & Enrique Montenegro, BFA & MA; Ill State Univ. *Work:* Philbrook Mus, Tulsa; Performing Arts Ctr, Tulsa; Univ Okla Mus, Norman; Jonson Gallery, Univ NMex, Albuquerque; Mus of NMex, Santa Fe. *Comn:* Welded steel altarpiece, Holloman Air Force Hosp Chapel, USAF, 67; painting, Farmers & Merchants Bank, Tulsa, 75; fiberglass painting, 76 & welded steel sculpture, 77, Hicks Park, City of Tulsa; stainless steel sculpture (36' high) Gerald Hines Int Redman Plaza, Tulsa OK, 83. *Exhib:* Tex Ann, Dallas Mus of Fine Arts, 60; Ill Print & Drawing Show, Art Inst Chicago, 63; Nat Drawing Show, Bucknell Univ, 65; Five NMex Artists, Pronaf Mus, Juarez, Mex, 65; NMex Sculptors, 66 & NMex Painters, 67, Mus of NMex, Santa Fe; Instituto Cultural Peruano Norte Americano, 79; Galeria Forum, Lima, Peru, 80; and others. *Teaching:* Instr painting, ETex State Univ, Commerce, 56-61; asst prof painting-sculpture, NMex State Univ, Las Cruces, 64-68; prof painting, Univ Tulsa, 68-; guest artist, Escuela Nacional de Bellas Artes, Lima, Peru, 79-80. *Awards:* First Prize Sculpture, 14th Ann, Quincy, Ill, 63; Grand Award, Okla Ann, Philbrook Mus, Tulsa, 73; Fulbright Teaching/Res Grant, Lima, Peru, 79-80; Gold Medal, Painting, El Paso Mus, 88. *Mem:* Taos Art Assoc; Asociacion Peruana de Artistas Plasticas. *Media:* Acrylic, Wood Sculpting. *Mailing Add:* PO Box 2661 Taos NM 87571

COLANTUONO, ANTHONY
HISTORIAN
b Somerville, NJ, May 5, 58. *Study:* Rutgers Univ, BA, 80; Johns Hopkins Univ, MA, 82, PhD, 87. *Teaching:* Vis asst prog art hist, Wake Forest Univ, 88-89; asst prof, Vanderbilt Univ, 89-90; asst prof southern baroque art, Univ Md, College Park, 90- *Res:* Theory and interpretation of Italian renaissance and Italian and French baroque art. *Publ:* Auth, Titians Tender Infants, I Tatti Studies, 89. *Mailing Add:* Rm 1211 Art/Sociology Bldg Univ Md College Park MD 20742

COLAO, RUDOLPH
PAINTER
b Peekskill, NY, Dec 26, 27. *Study:* Art Students League, with Frank V Dumond, Edwin Dickinson & Frank Mason, 49-52. *Work:* Springville Mus, Utah. *Exhib:* Ann Exhib, Hudson Valley Art Asn, White Plains, NY, 83; Allied Artists Am, New York, 84; Nat Acad Design, New York, 84; Western Heritage Fair, Houston, Tex, 84-85; Summer Exhib, Rockport Art Asn, Mass, 88. *Teaching:* Instr drawing & painting, Art Students League, NY, 84-87; instr

oil painting, Scottsdale Artists Sch, 87-88. *Awards:* Silver Medal, 81 & Gold Medal, 85, Rockport Art Asn; John Young Hunter Award, Allied Artists Am, 84. *Bibliog:* Herbert E Abrams (auth), The Teaching of Frank Dumond, Am Artist, 74; Jill Warren (auth), Rudolph Colao, Southwest Art, 82; Charles Movalli (auth), A Conversation with Rudy Colao, Am Artist, 84. *Mem:* Allied Artists NY; Knickerbocker Artists; Rockport Art Asn; Hudson Valley Art Asn. *Media:* Oil, Watercolor. *Mailing Add:* 15 W 67th St New York NY 10023

COLARUSSO, CORRINE CAMILLE
PAINTER, INSTRUCTOR
b Boston, Mass, Mar 22, 52. *Study:* Yale Summer Sch Art & Music, 72; Univ Mass, BFA, 73; Tyler Sch Art, Temple Univ, Philadelphia, MFA, 75. *Exhib:* Corcoran Gallery Art, Washington, DC, 75; Inst Contemp Art, Recife, Brazil, 76; O'Kane Gallery, Univ Houston, Tex, 77; 30 Women Artists, Peachtree Ctr, Atlanta, Ga, 78; one-person show, Oglethorpe Univ, Atlanta, 78; Personal Statements: Drawing, Southeastern Ctr Contemp Art, Winston-Salem, NC, 79; Atlanta Women's Invitational, Agnes Scott Col, 79. *Teaching:* Asst drawing, Univ Mass, Amherst, 72-73; grad teaching asst, Tyler Sch Art, 74-75; fac mem found design & drawing, Atlanta Col Art, 75-, dept head found studio, currently. *Awards:* MacDowell Colony Fel, 77 & 79; Fulbright-Hayes Res Grant, India /Nepal, 78. *Mailing Add:* Atlanta Col Art 1280 Peachtree NE Atlanta GA 30309

COLBY, BILL
PRINTMAKER, PAINTER
b Beloit, Kans, Jan 8, 27. *Study:* Univ Denver, BA, 50; Univ Ill, Champaign, MA, 54. *Work:* Libr Cong, Pennell Print Collection, Washington, DC; Seattle Art Mus; Wichita Art Mus, Kans; Portland Art Mus, Ore; Tacoma Art Mus, Wash. *Comn:* Painting, Kilworth Chapel, Univ Puget Sound, Tacoma, Wash, 67; prints, Weyerhauser Corp, Tacoma, 82. *Exhib:* Seattle Art Mus, Wash, 71; State Capitol Mus, Olympia, Wash, 74, 76, 78, 80 & 91; solo exhib, Kittredge Gallery, Tacoma, 79, 87 & 89; Art Alliance Gallery, Philadelphia, 79; Bellevue Art Mus, Wash, 79, 83 & 85; retrospective, Tacoma Art Mus, 86; and others. *Teaching:* Prof printmaking, Univ Puget Sound, Tacoma, Wash, 56-89, dir Kittredge Gallery, Univ Puget Sound, 58-65 & 83-89. *Mem:* Am Color Print Soc, Philadelphia; Puget Sound Sumi; Tacoma Arts & Crafts Asn; NW Printmakers. *Media:* Woodcut, Etching; Acrylic, Watercolor. *Mailing Add:* 3706 North Union Ave Tacoma WA 98407

COLBY, JEFF
SCULPTOR
b Staten Island, NY, Mar 26, 56. *Study:* Univ Tex, BFA, 78; Sch Art Inst, Chicago, MFA, 80. *Work:* Biegel & Sandler, Chicago, Ill; Authur Anderson Co, Chicago, Ill. *Exhib:* Fetish Art: Obsessive Expressions, Rockford Art Mus, Ill, 86; solo exhibs, Roy Boyd Gallery, Chicago, 87, J L Becker Gallery, Provincetown, Mass, 87, Univ Club, Chicago, 88, Union League Club, Chicago, 88 & Roy Boyd Gallery, Chicago, 88; Artists' liaison, Evanston Art Ctr, 88; 34th Ann Drawing & Small Sculpture Show, Ball State Univ, Muncie, Ind, 88; J L Beckor Gallery, Provincetown, Mass, 88; Internazionale d'Arte Contemporanea, Milan, Italy, 89; Objects, Moody Gallery, Houston, Tex, 90; Recent Work, A Montgomery Ward Gallery, Univ Ill, Chicago, 90. *Awards:* Ford Found Grant, 77 & 78; Visual Artists Fel, Nat Endowment Arts, 87; Pollack-Krasner Found, 90. *Dealer:* Roy Boyd Gallery 739 N Wells Chicago IL 60610. *Mailing Add:* 300 N Ogden, Apt 202 Chicago IL 60607

COLBY, JOY HAKANSON
CRITIC
b Detroit, Mich. *Study:* Detroit Soc Arts & Crafts; Wayne State Univ, BFA. *Pos:* Art critic, Detroit News, 50- *Awards:* Art Achievement Award, 83, Wayne State Univ; Detroit Press Club Award Arts Writing, 84; Award for Achievment, Ctr for Creative Studies, 89. *Mem:* Mich Coun Arts (adv, 72-79); Detroit Coun Arts; New Detroit Inc Arts Comt; Bloomfield Hills Arts Coun. *Publ:* Auth, Art & A City, 56; Arts and Crafts in Detroit, Detroit Inst Arts, 76. *Mailing Add:* Detroit News 615 W Lafayette Detroit MI 48231

COLBY, VICTOR E
SCULPTOR, EDUCATOR
b Frankfort, Ind, Jan 5, 17. *Study:* Corcoran Sch Art; Ind Univ, AB, 48; Cornell Univ, MFA, 50. *Work:* Ithaca Col Mus; Munson-Williams-Proctor Inst, Utica, NY; St Lawrence Univ, Canton, NY; State Univ NY Col Cortland; Roberson Mus, Binghamton, NY. *Comn:* Wall sculpture, Wilson Nuclear Physics Lab, Cornell Univ, 68. *Exhib:* One-man shows, Hewitt Gallery, 58, The Contemporaries, 66 & Hartley Gallery, 74. *Teaching:* Prof sculpture, Cornell Univ, 50-82; retired. *Media:* Wood. *Mailing Add:* 642 Peruville Rd Groton NY 13073

COLE, BRUCE
HISTORIAN, EDUCATOR
b Cleveland, Ohio, Aug 2, 38. *Study:* Western Reserve Univ, BA, 62; Oberlin Col, MA, 64; Bryn Mawr Col, PhD, 69. *Teaching:* Asst prof art hist, Univ Rochester, NY, 69-73; assoc prof art hist, Ind Univ, Bloomington, 73-77, prof, 77-88, distinguished prof, 88- *Awards:* Fel, Nat Endowment Humanities, 72-73, Guggenheim, 75-76 & Am Coun Learned Soc, 79-80. *Mem:* Accad Senese degli Intronati; Nat Coun on the Humanities. *Res:* Art of Renaissance Italy. *Publ:* Auth, Giotto & Florentine Painting 1280-1375, 76, Sienese Painting from its Origins to the Fifteenth Century, 80, The Renaissance Artist at Work, 83 & Italian Art 1250-1550, Harper; Agnolo Gaddi, Clarendon Press & Oxford Univ Press, 77; Masaccio and the Art of Early Renaissance Florence, 80 & Sienese Painting in the Age of the Renaissance, 85, Ind Univ Press; coauth, Art of the Western World, Summit Press, 89; Pieno della Francesca, Harper Collins, 91. *Mailing Add:* Dept of Fine Arts Ind Univ Bloomington IN 47401

COLE, DONALD
PAINTER
b New York, NY, Oct 31, 30. *Study:* Bucknell Univ, BS(civil eng); Univ Iowa, MFA. *Work:* Worcester Art Mus, Mass; Patrick Lannan Found, Palm Beach, Fla. *Exhib:* One-man exhibs, Nancy Hoffman Gallery, 73, 75, 78, Wake Forest Univ, Winston-Salem, 79, Va Commonwealth Univ, 81, Univ Ga, Athens, 81, Frank Marino Gallery, 81, 82, Adirondack Mus, Elizabeth Town, NY, 83 & State Univ NY, Plattsburgh, 86; Animals in American Art: 1880's-1980's, Nassau County Mus Fine Art, Roslyn, NY, 81; The Animal Within, Jay Gallery, NY; Galerie Bernard Jordan, Paris, 90; and others. *Teaching:* Pres, Parsons Sch Design, NY, 77- & Fashion Inst Technol, 83- *Awards:* Creative Artists Pub Serv Grant/Painting, NY State Coun on the Arts, 75; Artist-in-residence grant, Nat Endowment Arts, State Univ NY, Plattsburgh, 77, Artists Fel Grant, 78. *Bibliog:* Caril Dreyfuss McHugh (auth), Donald Cole, Arts Mag, 5/81; Ellen Lubell (auth), article in Arts Mag, 73, 75 & 78; Robert Berner (auth), Donald Cole, Arts Mag, 4/82. *Media:* Acrylic, Oil Stick. *Mailing Add:* 328 Grand Ave Brooklyn NY 11238

COLE, GRACE V
PAINTER, DRAFTSMAN
b Chicago, Ill. *Study:* Prarie State Col; Ecole Albert Du Fois, Vihers, France; Ted Seth Jacobs (Art Students League). *Work:* Bristol Meyers Gallery, Evansville, Ind; Medinah County Club Hall of Fame, Medinah, Ill; Espicopal Diocese, Chicago, Ill; Rockford Col, Ill. *Comn:* 4 portraits, Scharfman Orgn, New York, 87; 1 portrait, Rockford Col, Ill, 88; 2 portraits, Episcopal Diocese of Chicago, Ill, 88; 3 portraits, Bank of Louisville, Ind, 89-90; 10 portraits, Medinah Country Club, Ill, 88-90. *Exhib:* American Invitational, Clementi House Gallery Art, London, Eng, 88; Realism Today, Evansville Mus Art, Ind, 89; New Works - New Artists, J B Speed Art Mus, Louisville, Ky, 89; Real/Superreal/Surreal, Indianopolis Art League, Ind, 92; solo exhib: New Works, Union League Club, Chicago, 92. *Teaching:* Instr painting & drawing, Cole Studio, Chicago, Ill, 79-; instr painting & fine art, Prarie State Col, Chicago Heights, Ill, 85- *Bibliog:* Meet the Artist, Cox Cable, Park Forest, 5/83; Fritz Henning (auth), Portrait of a portrait artist, Artists Mag, 3/84; Karl Moehl (auth), Illinois artist, New Art Examiner, 9/86. *Mem:* Chicago Artists Coalition (bd mem, 87-90); The New Group of Mus Contemp Art, Chicago, Ill; Oil Plainters Am, Skokie, Ill. *Media:* Oil; Drawing Materials. *Dealer:* Portraits Inc 985 Park Ave New York NY 10028; Portraits/Chicago 780 Greenview Lake Forest, IL 60045. *Mailing Add:* 4342 N Clark St Chicago IL 60613

COLE, HAROLD DAVID
HISTORIAN, EDUCATOR
b Tulsa, Okla, Feb 28, 40. *Study:* Univ Tulsa, BA, MA(art criticism), with Alexander Hogue & Harry A Broadd; Ohio State Univ, MA(art hist), PhD, with Franklin Ludden & Maurice Cope. *Work:* Art Gallery, Univ Tulsa, Okla; Art Gallery, Baldwin-Wallace Col, Berea, Ohio; Art Gallery, Cumberland Col, Williamsburg, Ky; Art Gallery, Nicholls State Univ, Thibodaux, La. *Exhib:* 32nd Ann Springfield Ann Ten-State Exhib, Springfield Art Mus, Mo, 62; 12th Ann Own Your Own Exhib, Denver Art Mus, Colo, 68; 51st Ann May Show, Cleveland Mus Art, Ohio, 69; one-man shows, Cumberland Col, 70 & 72 & Nicholls State Univ, 71. *Collections Arranged:* Kenneth R Weedman Exhib (auth, catalog), 73. *Pos:* Mem visual art panel, Ohio Arts Coun, 77-79. *Teaching:* Prof art hist, Baldwin-Wallace Col, 66- *Awards:* Special Jury Mention, Cleveland Mus Art May Show, 69. *Mem:* Col Art Asn; Midwest Art Hist Asn; Int Ctr Medieval Art; Monument Historique. *Res:* Thirteenth century French sculpture and architecture; 19th century French painting. *Publ:* Auth, Kenneth R Weedman Sculpture Exhibition, Crafts Horizons, 72; coauth, Grant Reynard: His Life & Work, Baldwin-Wallace Col, 75. *Mailing Add:* Dept Art Baldwin Wallace Col Berea OH 44017

COLE, HERBERT MILTON
HISTORIAN, PHOTOGRAPHER
b Newton, Mass, Apr 15, 35. *Study:* Williams Col, BA, 57; Columbia Univ, MA, 64, Ford Found foreign area fel, 65-68, William B Cutting fel, 66-67, PhD, 68; Nat Endowment for Humanities fel, 71-72; Creative Arts fel, 74. *Collections Arranged:* African Arts of Transformation (auth, catalog), Univ Calif, Santa Barbara, 70; The Arts of Ghana (auth, catalog), Mus Cult Hist, Univ Calif, Los Angeles, 75-77; Igbo Arts: Community & Cosmos (coauth, catalog), Los Angeles, 84. *Pos:* Consult ed, African Arts, Univ Calif, Los Angeles, 70- *Teaching:* Prof African art hist, Univ Calif, Santa Barbara, 68- *Media:* Photography. *Res:* Arts of tropical Africa. *Publ:* Ed, African Art and Leadership, Univ Wis-Madison, 73; auth, The art of festival in Ghana, African Arts, Vol VIII, No 3, 75; auth, North American Indian, African and oceanic art, In: Art Through the Ages, sixth ed, 75; auth, The Arts of Ghana, Univ Calif, Los Angeles, 77; Mbari: Art and Life Among the Owerri Igbo, Ind Univ Press, 80; plus many others. *Mailing Add:* 3874 Crescent Dr Santa Barbara CA 93110

COLE, JEANETTE
PAINTER, INSTRUCTOR
b Lincoln, Nebr, Mar 29, 52. *Study:* Univ Nebr, BFA(art educ), 73; Tex Tech Univ, MFA, 79. *Work:* Shearson Lehman Am Express, New York; Liberty Fidelity Bank, Richmond, Va; Brush Gallery, St Lawrence Univ, Canton, NY; Tex Tech Univ Mus, Lubbock. *Exhib:* Solo exhibs, John Gibson Gallery, New York, 84-85, Introductions, Frumkin/Adams Gallery, New York, 88, Second St Gallery, Charlottesville, Va, 92; Virginia Biennial, Va Mus Fine Arts, Richmond, 83; Lower Manhattan Artists, Governor's Gallery, World Trade Ctr, New York, 85. *Teaching:* Vis prof painting, Murray State Univ, Ky, 80-81, St Lawrence Univ, Canton, NY, 81-82 & Franklin & Marshall Col, Lancaster, Pa, 83-88; asst prof, Univ Mass, Amherst, 89- *Awards:* Juror's

Award, 10th Ann Southwest, Mus Southwest, 76; Purchase Prize, Tex Col 6, Mountain View Col, Dallas, 79; Gold Medal, 8th Ann, Ocean City Art Asn, 80. *Media:* All. *Mailing Add:* PO Box 124 Canal St Station New York NY 10013

COLE, JOYCE
PAINTER
b New York, NY. *Study:* Finch Col, BA(art hist); Art Students League; Sch Visual Arts, MA; New York Univ, MA(telecommunications). *Work:* Aldrich Mus Contemp Art, Ridgefield, Conn; Guggenheim Mus; Oklahoma Art Ctr; Mobil, Warner Commun. *Exhib:* Andre Emmerich Gallery, NY, 72; Whitney Mus Am Art Biennial, New York, 73; Contemporary Reflections, Aldrich Mus Contemp Art, Conn, 73 & 80; Galerie Denise Rene, New York, 73; Soho Ctr Visual Arts, New York, 74; Susan Caldwell Gallery, New York, 77; Gloria Luria Gallery, Fla, 78; Adrich Mus Contemp Art, Conn, 80; Schiller Wapner Gallery, New York, 88. *Bibliog:* Lawrence Campbell (auth), Reviews & previews, Art News, 9/73; April Kingsley (auth), New York letter, Art Int, 10/73; Peter Frank (auth), article, Art News, 10/77; Archit Dig, 2/83. *Mem:* Artists Equity; Women's Caucus for the Am Arts Soc; Women's City Club. *Mailing Add:* 200 Central Park S New York NY 10019

COLE, JULIE KRAMER
PAINTER
b Springfield, Ohio, June 9, 42. *Study:* Colo State Univ, Fort Collins, 60-62; Colo Inst Art, Denver, grad, 63. *Work:* San Dimas City Hall, Calif; Home St Bank, Loveland, Colo. *Exhib:* Am Royal Western Art Show, Kansas City, 84 & 85; Governor's Western Art Show, North Platte, Nebr, 84-88; Am Indian and Cowboy Asn Show, San Dimas, Calif, 88-91; Minneapolis Western & Wildlife Show, Minn, 89, 90 & 92; Classic Am Western Art Show, Beverly Hills, Calif, 90 & 91. *Pos:* Freelance fashion illusr, 63-80; prof western artist, Cole Fine Art Inc, 81-; illustr, Antrock, 90, Johnson Creative Arts, 90 & Leanin' Tree Publ Co, 84-, Bradford Exchange, 92. *Awards:* Festival Choice, 88; Silver Medal, 89; Gold Medal, 90; Am Indian & Cowboy Asn Show Hall of Fame, Colo Inst Art, 92. *Media:* Pastel, Gouache. *Publ:* Auth, Western Horseman, 4/89; US Art, 4/91. *Mailing Add:* 2553 W County Rd 14 Loveland CO 80537

COLE, MAX
PAINTER
b Hodgeman Co, Kans, Feb 14, 37. *Study:* Univ Ariz, Tucson, MFA, 64. *Work:* St Paul Art Ctr; Santa Barbara Mus Art; Newport Harbor Art Mus; La Jolla Mus Contemp Art; Everson Mus; Dallas Mus; Utah Mus; Mus NMex; Louisiana Mus, Denmark; Nat Gallery Mod Art, New Delhi, India. *Exhib:* Whitney Mus Am Art Biannual, 75; New Abstract Painting, Los Angeles Co Mus, 76; 35th Biannual, Corcoran Gallery Art, 77; one-person exhibs, Sidney Janis Gallery, New York, 77 & 79, Los Angeles Louver Gallery, 79, 80 & 83, Miami-Dade Col, 82, Cologne Art Fair, Ger, 90, Kiyo Higashi Gallery, Los Angeles, 91, Kunstraum, Kassel, Ger, 91 & Mus Folkwang, Essen, Ger, 92; Oscarsson Siegeltuch Gallery, New York, 86; Zabriskie Gallery, New York, 87; Galerie Helene Grubair, Miami, 88; Haines Gallery, San Francisco, 88; Galerie Schröder, Mönchengladbach, WGer, 90; and others. *Teaching:* Asst prof painting, Pasadena City Col, Calif, 67-79; adj assoc prof, Columbia Univ, New York, 85- *Awards:* Nat Endowment Arts Fel, 83; Pollock-Krasner Fel, 86; Res Fel, Indo-US Subcommission, 88; and others. *Mailing Add:* 195 E Third St New York NY 10009

COLE, SYLVAN
DEALER, WRITER
b New York, NY, Jan 10, 18. *Study:* Cornell Univ, BA, 39. *Pos:* Pres & dir, Asn Am Artists, New York, 58-83; adv bd, Pratt Graphics Ctr, 64-86; pres & dir, Sylvan Cole Gallery, New York, 84- *Teaching:* Instr, Pratt Inst, 85-86. *Mem:* Appraisers Asn Am, 62; Art Dealers Asn Am, 63-, (dir 68-76); Int Fine Print Dealers Asn, 86- (vpres, 87-). *Specialty:* American fine prints. *Publ:* Auth, Raphael Soyer: Fifty Years of Printmaking, 67; The Graphic Work of Joseph Hirsch, 70; Will Barnet--Prints 1932-1972, 72, supplement, 73-79; The Lithographs of John Stuart Curry, A Catalog Raisonne, 76; The Lithographs of Grant Wood, 84; The Prints of Stuart Davis, 86. *Mailing Add:* 25 Sutton Place South New York NY 10019

COLEMAN, A(LLAN) D(OUGLASS)
CRITIC, LECTURER
b New York, NY, Dec 19, 43. *Study:* Hunter Col, Bronx, NY, BA, 64; San Francisco State Col, MA, 67; New York Univ. *Collections Arranged:* Silver Sensibilities, Snug Harbor Cultural Ctr, Staten Island, NY, 80 & Catskill Ctr Photog, 82; The Erotic in Photography: Contemporary Trends, Cameravision, Los Angeles, 82; Tisch Sch Arts, New York Univ, 85; Testimonies: Photography and Social Issues, Houston Fotofest, 90. *Pos:* Photog columnist, Latent Image, Village Voice, 68-73; photog critic, New York Times, 70-74; contrib ed, Camera 35, 75-82, Lens' on Campus, 83-87; vpres, Photog Media Inst, Inc, 77-; founder/organizer, Conf on Photog Criticism, 77-; bd dirs, Photog Resource Ctr, 78-82; critic-in-residence, Int Ctr Photog, New York, 79; founding ed, Views: A New Eng J Photog, 79-81; mem bd advisors, Ctr Photog Woodstock, 82- & Los Angeles Ctr Photog Studies, 82-; photog critic, New York Observer, 88-; columnist, Darkroom Photog, der Alltag, Switz European Photog, WGer, Fotografisk Tidskrift, Sweden, Cliches, Belgium & Photo Metro, 89- *Teaching:* Mem fac photog criticism, New Sch Social Res, New York, 70-71, 79-81; vis lectr, Col Art, Md Inst, 71-73; Instr photog, Dept Film/TV, New York Univ, 78-82, asst prof, Dept Photog, 83- *Awards:* Nat Endowment Arts Art Critics fel, 75. *Bibliog:* Video interview, Video Databank, Sch Art Inst Chicago, 77; Craig Morey & Ted Hedgpeth (auths), interview, San Francisco Camerawork Newsletter, 10/82; Video interview, Md Inst Col Art, 83. *Mem:* Int Asn Art Critics (exec vpres & chmn, membership comt, 87-); Authors Guild; PEN Am Ctr; Int Soc Gen Semantics; Nat Writers Union. *Res:* Hist of photog, examining the impact of the invention of the lens on Western culture between 1500 to present. *Publ:* Auth, The Grotesque in Photography: A Critical Survey, Ridge Press/Summit Books, 77; Light Readings: A Photography Critic's Writings, 1968-1978, Oxford Univ Press, 79 & Galaxy Paperback, 82; Lee, Model, Parks, Samaras, Turner: Five Interviews Before the Fact, Photographic Resource Ctr, 79; co-auth, The Photography A-V Program Directory, PMI, Inc, 80; auth, Depth of Field: Essays on Photography, Mass Media and Lens Culture, Univ NMex Press, 91. *Mailing Add:* 465 Van Duzer St Staten Island NY 10304

COLEMAN, CONSTANCE DEPLER
PAINTER
b Macomb, Ill, Sept 9, 26. *Study:* Dominican Col, San Raphael, Calif, 45-47; Calif Sch Fine Arts, San Francisco, with Mark Rothko & David Parks, 47-49; Cincinnati Art Acad, Ohio, with Paul Chitlaw, 63-65. *Comn:* All work commissioned by private clients. *Exhib:* James Huntbarker Gallery, Palm Beach, 79; Wondrous Wildlife, Int Wildlife Juried Show, Cincinnati, Ohio, 83; A B Crosson Jr Gallery, Cincinnati, Ohio, 84; Portraits for Commission, McIntosh-Drysdale Gallery (with Gifford Myers & Bruce Sharp), Washington, DC, 86. *Pos:* Designer & illusr, paper products, greeting cards & wall paper, portraying animals in human situations, 49-70; "Member of the Family" gift products, 88. *Teaching:* Dir, teacher & founder, Primary Art Dept, Cincinnati Country Day Sch, Ohio, 62-68. *Bibliog:* David Larsen (auth), Animal lover is Picasso of the pet set, Los Angeles Times, 7/28/83; Marcia Smith (auth), They pant for arf art, Dallas Times Herald, 5/14/84; article, Pet Portraits, Epcot Mag, Disney Cable-TV, 84; Julie Adams Church (auth), Joy in a Wooly Coat (exhib catalog), HJ Kramer Inc, 88. *Media:* Oil, Silverpoint. *Dealer:* Portraits Inc 985 Park Ave New York NY 10028. *Mailing Add:* 924-C Garden St Santa Barbara CA 93101

COLEMAN, EDWARD H
DEALER, COLLECTOR
b Allentown, Pa, Aug 6, 28. *Pos:* Bd of dirs, Lehigh Valley Ctr Performing Arts, 76-78; bd of trustees, Valley Arts Coun, 78- *Specialty:* 15th to 20th century sculpture, paintings, prints and watercolors. *Collection:* French impressionists, Mexican realists, native painters and social realists. *Mailing Add:* 1509 Hamilton St Allentown PA 18102

COLEMAN, FLOYD WILLIS
EDUCATOR, PAINTER
b Sawyerville, Ala, Jan 13, 39. *Study:* Ala State Univ, with Hayward L Oubre, BA, 60; Univ Wis, with Robert Burkert, MS, 62; Univ Ga, with Edmund B Feldman, PhD, 75. *Work:* Oakland Mus, Calif; High Mus Art, Emory Univ, Spelman Col, Atlanta Univ, Atlanta, Ga. *Exhib:* Am Drawing Ann, Norfolk Mus Arts & Sci, Va, 62; 18th Southeastern Ann, High Mus Art, Atlanta, Ga, 63; 30 Contemporary Black Artists, Minneapolis Inst Arts, Minn, 68; Spiral: Afro-American Art of the Seventies, Mus Nat Ctr Afro-Am Artists, Boston, 80; Recent Works on Paper, Last Stop Gallery, Richmond, Va, 88. *Teaching:* Asst prof, Clark Col, Atlanta, Ga, 65-71; assoc prof, Southern Ill Univ, Edwardsville, 76-80, prof, 81-83; prof & chair, Jackson State Univ, 83-87; prof & chair, Howard Univ, 87- *Awards:* Fels, Ford Found, 68-70, Esso Found, 71 & Nat Endowment Humanities, 76-77. *Mem:* Col Art Asn Am; Nat Conf Artists (co-chmn, 70-71). *Media:* Mixed-Media on Paper. *Res:* African continuities in Afro-American art; Mexican influences on Mayan architecture; Black artists of the South. *Publ:* Auth, African influences on Black American art, 76 & Toward an aesthetic toughness in Afro-American art, 78, Black Art Quart; auth, Popular images in Afro-American art, J Soc Ethnic & Special Studies, 80; coauth, Black Design: Systems, Elements, Applications, 84, Prentice-Hall. *Mailing Add:* Dept Art Howard Univ Washington DC 20059

COLEMAN, GAYLE
LECTURER, CONSERVATOR
b Allentown, Pa, Mar 15, 54. *Study:* Lehigh Univ, Bethlehem, Pa, BA; Art Restoration Tech Inst, cert & apprenticeship; Nova Law Sch. *Pos:* Art conservator, Lehigh Univ, Bethlehem, Pa, 76-; freelance art restorer, Pa; partner, Coleman Art Gallery, Allentown, 76-; lecturer at various colleges and universities. *Mem:* Am Inst for Conserv of Hist & Artistic Work; Asn for Preservation Technol; Am Bar Asn. *Res:* Microchemical analysis of art work; moral rights & art conservation. *Mailing Add:* 920 SW Seventh St Ft Lauderdale FL 33315

COLEMAN, JUDY
PHOTOGRAPHER
b New York, NY, 1944. *Study:* Cornell Univ, BA, 66; Univ Calif, Los Angeles, MFA, 83. *Work:* Newport Harbor Art Mus, Newport Beach, Calif; Seattle Art Mus; Laguna Mus Art, Laguna Beach, Calif; Grunwald Ctr Graphic Arts, Univ Calif, Los Angeles. *Exhib:* One-person exhibs, Swen Parson Gallery, Northern Ill Univ, De Kalb, 86, G Ray Hawkins Gallery, Los Angeles, 87, Fay Gold Gallery, Atlanta, Ga, 88, Laguna Mus Art, Laguna Beach, Calif, 89, New Work, G Ray Hawkins Gallery, Los Angeles, 89, Photo Exhib, Parco Gallery, Tokyo, Japan, 90 & Print Room, Fogg Art Mus, Harvard Univ, Cambridge, Mass, 91; Women Photographers in America, 1987, Los Angeles Munic Art Gallery, 87; A Visual Expedition: Fifteen Decades of Photography, Brea Gallery, Calif, 89; The Photography of Invention: American Pictures of the 1980's, Nat Mus Am Art, Smithsonian Inst, Washington, DC & Walker Art Ctr, Minneapolis, Minn, 89; Recent Acquisitions & Gallery Artists, G Ray Hawkins Gallery, Santa Monica, Calif, 90; Art 21 '90, Basel, Switz, 90. *Teaching:* Instr, Univ Calif, Los Angeles,

84-86. *Awards:* Nat Endowment Arts, Fel, 84-85 & 88-89. *Bibliog:* Elaine Dines-Cox (auth), Judy Coleman, Twin Palms Publs, Altadena, Calif, 89; Cathy Curtis (auth), The Galleries, Los Angeles Times, 12/8/89; Cynni Murphy (auth), Profile: Judy Coleman, Photog Forum, 11/90. *Media:* Gelatin Silver Prints, Oil Paint. *Publ:* Woman Photographers in America (exhib catalog), Los Angeles Munic Art Gallery, 8/87; auth, The Photography of Invention: American Pictures of the 1980's, Walker Art Ctr Calendar & Newsletter, 7-8/90. *Mailing Add:* 910 Colorado Ave Santa Monica CA 90401

COLEMAN, M L (MICHAEL LEE)
PAINTER, INSTRUCTOR
b Livingston, Mont, May 11, 41. *Study:* Univ Wyo, BS, 63; with James Disney, Loveland, Colo, 69 & 75, Hall Diteman, Billings, Mont, 77 & Wilson Hurley, Albuquerque, NMex, 85. *Work:* Northern Natural Gas, Omaha, Nebr; Iowa Beef Producers; several oil companies, Can; Webtrend Graphics, Vista, Calif. *Exhib:* Mus Native Am Cult Art Show & Auction, Spokane, Wash, 80 & 81; Sun Valley Western Art Auction & Exhib, Idaho, 80 & 81; Stockmen's Found Art Show & Auction, Calgary & Edmonton, Alta, 81; Art of the West, German Mus, Munich, 81. *Teaching:* Instr workshops, Sedona, Ariz & Calgary, Alberta, Can, currently. *Awards:* Best of Show, Stockmen's Found Art Show and Auction, Calgary, Alta, 81. *Bibliog:* Kathe McGehee (auth), M L Coleman's dramatic landscapes, Art West Mag, Vol III, No 6; Dale Burk (auth), A brush with the West, Mountain Press, 80; Peggy & Harold Samuels (auths), Contemporary Western Artists, SW Art Publ, 82. *Media:* Oil. *Dealer:* Crimson Shadows 450 N Hwy 89A Sedona AZ 86336. *Mailing Add:* 450 N Hwy 89A Sedona AZ 86336

COLEMAN, MICHAEL
PAINTER
b Provo, Utah, June 25, 46. *Study:* Brigham Young Univ. *Work:* Buffalo Bill Hist Mus, Cody, Wyo; Kennedy Gallery, New York; J N Bartfield Galleries, New York. *Comn:* Boone & Crockett Club; Alaska Prof Hunters Asn. *Exhib:* Springville Mus Nat; Nat Acad Western Art, Nat Cowboy Hall of Fame, Oklahoma City; Buffalo Bill Hist Ctr; Charlie Russell Mus; Kennedy Galleries; Wunderlich Gallery; Gerold Peters Gallery, Santa Fe, NMex; Artists Am, Denver; J N Bartfield Gallery, New York. *Bibliog:* Diane Cochrane (auth), Romantic Western landscapes, Am Artist, 1/75; Susan Myers (auth), Twenty American Landscape Painters; Romantic Western painter, SW Art Mag, 2/77; and others. *Media:* Oil. *Dealer:* J N Bartfield Galleries 30 W 57th St New York NY 10019. *Mailing Add:* 2822 Rolling Knolls Dr Provo UT 84604-4382

COLES, THELMA
EDUCATOR
b Portsmouth, Va, Aug 18, 52. *Study:* San Diego State Univ. *Exhib:* San Antonio Mus Art, Tex, 89; Mus Art, Univ Tex, El Paso, 89; Univ Southern Ill, Carbondale, 89; Yuma Art Ctr, 90. *Teaching:* Assoc prof art, Univ Tex, Austin, 78. *Awards:* Nat Endowment Arts, 77, 80, 84 & 86. *Publ:* Auth, The Art of Tenuous Affils, Matchsmith, Vol 6, No 3, summer 86. *Mailing Add:* Art Dept Univ Tex 23rd & San Jacinto Austin TX 78712

COLESCOTT, ROBERT H
PAINTER, INSTRUCTOR
b Oakland, Calif, Aug 26, 25. *Study:* Univ Calif, Berkeley, BA, 49 & MA, 52; with Fernard Leger, Paris, France, 49-50. *Work:* Metrop Mus Art & Mus Mod Art, New York; Seattle Art Mus, Wash; San Francisco Mus Mod Art; Boston Mus Fine Art, Mass; Corcoran Gallery Art, Washington, DC. *Exhib:* Art About Art, 78 & Biennial 83 & 84, Whitney Mus, New York; solo exhibs, Phyllis Kind Gallery, Chicago, Ill, 87, 89, 90 & 91, Recent Paintings, Greg Kucera Gallery, Seattle, Wash & Univ Tex, El Paso, 89, Arthur Roger Gallery, New Orleans, 90, New Work, Howard Yezerski Gallery, Boston, Mass & Linda Cathcart Gallery, Los Angeles, Calif, 90, Recent Work, Univ Colo Mus, Boulder, 91; Eight Black Am Artists, Va Mus Fine Arts, 80; La Foret Mus, Tokyo, 89; Black USA, Overholland Mus, Amsterdam, 90; The Art Advocacy, Aldrich Mus Art, Ridgefield, Conn, 91. *Pos:* Artist-in-residence, Am Res Ctr, Egypt, 64-65. *Teaching:* Assoc prof drawing & art educ, Portland State Univ, Ore, 57-66; assoc prof painting, Am Univ, Cairo, 66-67; prof art, Calif State Col, Stanislaus, 70-74, Univ Ariz, 88-89; lectr, Univ Calif, Berkeley, 74-79; instr, San Francisco Art Inst, 79-85; vis artist, Univ Ariz, Tucson, 83- & prof art, 85-90, regents prof art, 90- *Awards:* Nat Endowment Arts Grant for Creative Painting, 76, 80 & 83; Guggenheim Found Fel, 85. *Bibliog:* Davis Alam (auth), History Reawakened and Revisited by Artist, Colo Daily, 1/22/91; Charlie Ahern (auth), Colescott Parodies Race Crisis, City Sun, pg 16, 1-2/91; Brooks Adams (auth), Robert Colescott at Phyllis Kind, Art in Am, 7/91. *Mem:* Soc Independent Artists, New York. *Media:* Mixed. *Publ:* Auth, The Reimaging of America, New Society Publishers, 90. *Dealer:* Phyllis Kind Gallery 136 Greene St New York NY 10012. *Mailing Add:* Art Dept Univ Ariz Tucson AZ 85719

COLESCOTT, WARRINGTON W
PRINTMAKER, PAINTER
b Oakland, Calif, Mar 7, 21. *Study:* Univ Calif, Berkeley, BA & MA; Acad Grande Chaumiere, Paris; Slade Sch Art, Univ Col, London. *Work:* Metrop Mus Art, Mus Mod Art, New York; Brooklyn Mus, NY; Art Inst Chicago; Carnegie Mus, Pa; Whitney Mus Am Art. *Exhib:* Biennial Int, Ljubljana, Yugoslavia, 81, 83, 85 & 87; one-man shows, Tampa Mus Art, 87, Perimeter Gallery, Chicago, 88, 91 & 93 & 40 Years of Printmaking, Elvehjem Mus, Univ Wis, 88; Warrington Colescott Retrospective, Univ SDak Galleries, 92; Univ Ore Mus Art, 92; and others. *Pos:* Co-dir, Mantegna Press, Hollandale, Wis; chair, adv bd, Tandem Press, Univ Wis, 85-92. *Teaching:* Prof art, Univ Wis-Madison, 49-78, Leo Steppart chair prof, 79-84, prof emer, dept art, 86. *Awards:* Guggenheim Fel, 65; Nat Endowment Arts Artists Fel, 76, 79 & 83-84; Academican, Nat Acad Design, NY, 92; and others. *Bibliog:* Warrington Colescott's History of Printmaking, Madison Art Ctr, 79; Mathias Mende (auth), Durer A-Z, Verlag H Carl, Nurnberg, 80; Richard Cox (auth) Warrington Colescott: 40 years of Printmaking, Elvehjem Mus Art, Madison, 88; Richard Cox (auth), Warrington Colescott, the London Years, Tamarind Papers, Vol 14, 91-92; E C Cunningham(auth), Printmaking, Univ Colo Press, 91. *Mem:* Wis Acad Sci, Arts & Lett; Philadelphia Print Club; Mid Am Print Counc. *Media:* Etching; Watercolor. *Publ:* Illusr, Death in Venice, Aquarius Press, 71; illusr (covers), 30 Years of Printmaking, Brooklyn Mus, 76 & Art News Mag, 3/77; illusr, Since Man Began to Eat Himself, Perishable Press, Mt Horeb, Wis, 85; Improvisations, Dieu Donne Press, NY, 92. *Dealer:* Garver Gallery 230 State St Madison WI 53705; Perimeter Gallery 150 N Orleans Chicago IL. *Mailing Add:* Rte 1 Hollandale WI 53544

COLETTE
PAINTER, SCULPTOR
b Borain-Tunis, Tunisia, Oct 8, 52; US citizen. *Study:* William Paterson Univ, BA. *Work:* Ludwig Mus, Cologne, Ger; Brooklyn Mus, New York; Mus Mod Art, Montreal, Can; Gugenheim Mus, NY; Newport Harbor Mus, Calif; Weatherspoon Gallery, NC. *Exhib:* Camille (installation & sculpture), Mus Mod Art, New York, 77; Out of the House, The Last Stitch (installation), Whitney Mus Art, New York, 78; one-woman retrospective, 10-years of work, Kunstverein-Munster, Ger, 81, Ludwig Mus, Cologne, Ger, 86; Daniel Newburg Gallery, NY, 86-87; The Bavarian Adventure, Bonn Mus, Ger, 88; Dorsky Gallery, NY, 89-91; Carol Johnssen Gallery, Munich, 90-92; Rempire Gallery, NY, 91-92. *Teaching:* Instr painting, New York Univ, 83; guest prof sculpture, Yale Univ, Conn, 87; guest prof multi media, Inst Chicago, 87, Banff Ctr, Can, 85-87, Univ NC, 92. *Awards:* Fashion Innovator, 79; DAAD Fel, 84; Nat Endowment, 85. *Bibliog:* Colette - Ten Years of Work (monogr), Politi, 88; Colette - The Bavarian Adventure (monogr), Dumont, 85; Colette - New Paintings & Works (monogr), Kammerer, 85. *Media:* Mixed Media. *Mailing Add:* 213 Pearl St New York NY 10038

COLIN, GEORGIA T
COLLECTOR, DESIGNER
b Boston, Mass. *Study:* Smith Col; Univ Grenoble, Sorbonne, Paris, France; Ecole de Louvre. *Pos:* Pres, Talmey Inc, 54- *Mem:* Am Soc Interior Designers; Smith Col Mus Art (vis comt 51-70). *Collection:* With husband, Ralph F Colin, have for forty years collected paintings, sculpture, drawings and graphics mainly School of Paris 1890-1970. *Mailing Add:* 941 Park Ave New York NY 10028

COLINA, ARMANDO G
GALLERY DIRECTOR, EDITOR
b Veracruz, Mex, Mar 30, 35. *Study:* Univ Mex, BA. *Collections Arranged:* Carlos Merida: Graphic Works, Mus de Monterrey, Nuevo Leon, Mex & traveling to New York, Washington, DC, San Francisco, Coral Gables, Fla, San Antonio, Tex & Puerto Rico; Gunther Gerszo: A Retrospective; Diego Rivera: Col Dolores Olmedo; Rufino Tamayo: A Retrospective & An Hommage to Dr Alst, Museo de Monterrey, Mex; Diego Rivera: The Cubist Years, Phoenix Art Mus, Ariz; Francisco Zuniga: Ten Years of Graphic Work, Montreal, New York & Washington; Frida Kahlo, Japan and Australia; El Renacimiento Mex: Orozco, Siqueiros y Rivera, Japan; El Surrealismo entre Viejo y Nuevo Mundo, Las Palmas de Gran Canaria & Madrid, Spain; Carlos Merida: An Hommage, Museo de Arte Moderno, Guatemala; Imagen de Mex: Frankfurt Kunsthalle, Vienna & Dallas, Tex; Art in Latin Am: London, Stockholm & Madrid; Remedios Varo, Madrid & Monterrey, Mex; Francisco Toledo, Hommage to Jorge Luis Borges, Fantastic Zoology; Itinerant exhib 17 mus throughout world; Un panorama del arte Mex, Inst Cult Mex, Washington, DC; V Triennale Klein-plastik, Fellbach, Ger & Lehmbruck Mus Duisburg, Ger, 92; Mex Masters, CDS Gallery, NY, 90; Nat Homage to Carlos Merida, Fine Arts Palace Mus, Museo de Monterrey, Mex, 92-93; Voces de Ultramar, Las Palmas de Gran Canaria & Madrid, 92. *Pos:* Art consult, currently; owner, Arvil Art Gallery, currently; trustee, Mus Monterrey, NL, Mex; Museo Arte Contemporaneo, Oaxaea, Mex; greeting card operation consult, Unicef, 92. *Specialty:* Contemporary Latin American & Mexican Art. *Publ:* Illusr, Camara de Diputados/Historia de Los Recintos, 82; ed, Diego Rivera: Una libreta de apuntes, 1928, 88; Las Castas Mexicanas, 90; El Marco del Encuentro, 91; Gloria y Fama Mexica, 91. *Mailing Add:* c/o Galeria Arvil SA Cerrada de Hamburgo No 9 Mexico 6 DF Mexico

COLKER, EDWARD
PAINTER, GRAPHIC ARTIST
b Philadelphia, Pa, Jan 5, 27. *Study:* Philadelphia Col Art, grad; NY Univ, MA; spec study with E & J Desjobert, Paris. *Work:* Mus Art, Philadelphia; Univ Ariz, Tucson; New York Pub Libr Print Collection; Mus Mod Art, New York; New York Univ; and others. *Comn:* Lithography ed, Print Club, Philadelphia, 66, Int Graphic Art Soc, New York, 66 & 69 & Ill Arts Coun, 73. *Exhib:* Solo exhib, Kenyon Gallery, Chicago, 75, Ctr Book Artists, 85, Neuberger Mus, Purchase, 85-86 & Univ Ill, Chicago, 86; Stampe di due Mondi, Rome & Philadelphia Mus Art, 67; American Art Today, Pa Acad Fine Arts, Philadelphia, 68; Nat Collection Fine Arts, Washington, DC, 77; Works on Paper, Yugoslavia, 82; Univ of the Arts, 86. *Collections Arranged:* Spec exhibs, Symbol & Vision, Calif Painters & Sculptors, 70, Depth & Presence, Environmental Sculpture, Corcoran Gallery Art, Washington, DC, 71; Arts of the Book, Philadelphia, 88. *Pos:* consult, Works on Paper, US Int Commun Agency, 82. *Teaching:* Assoc prof fine arts, Univ Pa Grad Sch Fine Arts, 68-70; prof & dir, Sch Art & Design, Univ Ill, Chicago Circle, 72-78, res prof art, 77-80; dean, visual arts, State Univ NY, Purchase, 80-85; chmn dept art, Cornell Univ, 85-86; provost, Univ of the Arts, 86- *Awards:* Guggenheim

Fel, 61; Univ Ill Res Bd, 77; Graham Found, 77; Ill Arts Coun, 80. *Bibliog:* Zigrosser (auth), The Appeal of Prints (appreciation), 70; introd essay In: New York Landscape, 81. *Mem:* Col Art Asn Am; Caxton Club; Ctr for Book Arts; Grolier Club. *Publ:* Contribr, Pablo Neruda (lithos), 77; The Fall (lithos), 77; From South Dakota (lithos), 78; Aesthetique du Rale (lithos), 78; Selections, Essay on Nature, Emerson, Sky at Ashland, Anania (lithos), 85; and others. *Mailing Add:* 77th St New York NY 10003

COLLADO, LISA
COLLAGE ARTIST, PAINTER
b Washington, DC, June 24, 44. *Study:* Art Students League, 78-80; Empire State Col, State Univ NY, BA, 85; NY Univ, MA, 93. *Work:* Phillips Acad, Addison Gallery Art, Andover, Mass; Mead Art Mus, Amherst Col, Amherst, Mass; Everson Mus Art, Syracuse, NY; Washington Co Mus Fine Arts, Hagerstown, Mass; New Eng Community of Contemp Artists, Brooklyn, Conn. *Comn:* Hist placque, Egyptian Tourist Office, New York, 86; biography in college, F Aley Allen, New York, 86; Portrait, Calipha Al-Sabah, Kuwait, 89; glass sculpture, comn Nasser Al Nassir, New York, 89. *Exhib:* Emerging Women Artists, Nat Mus, Warsaw, Poland, 89; Women in the Arts, traveling, India, 88-89. *Awards:* Award Merit, Univ Del, 82. *Bibliog:* Cynthia Maris Dantzig (auth), Design Dimensions: An Introduction to the Visual Surface, Prentice-Hall, 89. *Mem:* New York Artists Equity Asn; Nat Asn Women Artists; Orgn Independent Artists; Lenox Hill Artists Forum; Nat Womens Studies Asn; and others. *Media:* Acrylic, Oil. *Publ:* Coauth, Nasser Ovissi, Editorial La Gran Enciclopedia Vasca, 88. *Mailing Add:* 920 Park Ave New York NY 10021

COLLERY, PAULA
PAINTER
b Glen Cove, NY, Dec 15, 54. *Study:* Tyler Sch Art, Temple Univ, Philadelphia, BFA(painting & photog), 78. *Work:* Dannheiser Found, New York. *Exhib:* Solo exhibs, Gracie Mansion Gallery, 82, 83 & Germans Van Eck Gallery, 85, New York, Gallery Six to Six, 87; Hats Off, New Mus, New York, 83; Totem Show, New York, 84; Chill Out, Kenkeleba Gallery, New York, 84; Bernice Steinbaum Gallery, New York, 84; Harm Bouchaert Gallery, New York, 85; Edinburgh Festival, Scotland, 85; Group nude show, Gallery Six to Six, New York, 90. *Awards:* Art Fel Residency Va Ctr Arts, 88, Cummington, 85; MacDowell Colony Residency, 84, 85. *Bibliog:* David Herhkovits (auth), Art in Alphabetland, Art News, 9/83; Ted Castle (auth), article, Art Monthly, London, 83; Vivien Raynor (auth), article, New York Times, 2/84. *Media:* Oil, Acrylic. *Mailing Add:* 100 St Mark's Place New York NY 10009

COLLETT, FARRELL REUBEN
PAINTER, EDUCATOR
b Bennington, Idaho, Nov 13, 07. *Study:* Brigham Young Univ, BA & MA; Sch Fine Arts, San Francisco; Art Inst Chicago; Am Acad Art, Chicago; Art Ctr Col Design, Los Angeles; Art Students League; and with Paul Bransom; Weber State Col, Hon PhD Humanities, 76. *Work:* Springville Mus Art, Utah; Brigham Young Univ; Grand Central Art Galleries, New York; Univ Calgary. *Comn:* Portrait of Pres, Weber State Col, 59; Wildlife-Cougars, Brigham Young Univ, 70; Ft Buenaventura (mural), Walker Bank, Ogden, Utah, 72; Wildlife, Va Bankshares, Richmond, 73; Wildlife-Bison, Franklin Mint, Pa, 73. *Exhib:* Utah State Inst Fine Arts Ann, 68-; Wildlife 71, Minneapolis, 71-72; Am Natural Hist Art Show, Univ Minn, Minneapolis, 71; Soc Animal Artists Ann, New York, 72; Dismal Swamp Art Exhib, Richmond, Va, 73. *Pos:* Chmn, Utah State Inst Fine Arts, 63-65. *Teaching:* Prof art, Weber State Col, 39-, chmn dept, 39-69; guest prof painting, Brigham Young Univ, summer 53; guest prof art hist & painting, Univ Calgary, summers 66 & 67. *Awards:* Best of Show for White Horse, Nat Invitational, Springville Mus Art, Utah, 63; Best of Show for Girl in the Black Hood, Ogden Outdoor & Sweepstakes Award, Prize-winning Paintings Only Exhib, Salt Lake City, 65; DH, Weber State Col, Ogden, Utah, 77; Collett Art Bldg and Gallery Weber St Col dedicated, 82. *Bibliog:* George S Dibble (auth), Collett's horses are exciting, Salt Lake Trib, 11/24/74; Donald Jardine (auth), Most unforgettable lecture, Illustrator; George Harrison (auth), Painting a bright future for Dismal Swamp, Nat Wildlife, 10-11/74; 100 Best Paintings, Arts fpr the Parks, 87. *Mem:* Soc Animal Artists. *Media:* Oil, Watercolor. *Publ:* Illusr, Pit Pony, Knopf, 46; illusr, Conserv Series Filmstrips, Chicago, 54; illusr, Annual report, Pepsi-Cola Co, 56; illusr, Calendar posters, Browning Ann, 59; auth, Felt tip diary, Illustrator, fall 69; illusr, Mammals of Interment, W Univ Utah Press, 87. *Mailing Add:* 1541 Navajo Dr St George UT 84770

COLLINGS, BETTY
SCULPTOR, WRITER
b Wanganui, NZ, Jan 15, 34. *Study:* Ohio State Univ, BFA, 71, MFA, 74. *Work:* Israel Mus. *Exhib:* Solo shows, Urdang Gallery, 79, 80, 83, 89 & 90, Antioch Univ, 82, Grad Ctr, City Univ New York, 83 & Ukraine Union Artists, Kiev, 92; Generative Systems, Wright State Univ, 79; Triple Helix, Ohio Univ, Lancaster, 83; Preparation & Proposition, Islip Art Mus, 84; TAO III, Ohio Wesleyan Univ, 89; The Figure's Edge, Akron Univ, 92; Art League Invitational, Fort Hayes, 92. *Collections Arranged:* Contemporary Collection of Ohio State Univ, 75-80. *Pos:* Dir, Ohio State Univ, Gallery Fine Arts, 74-80, ed acquisitions, 76-78; consult, Oberlin Col, 81-82; invited cur, Wright State Univ, 81-, Va Commonwealth Univ, 82, Bard Col, 82 & Cleveland Ctr Contemp Art 85; Int exhib consult, Ohio Arts Coun, China, 88-; cur, Kiev-US exchange, 92-93. *Awards:* Sculpture Fel, 81-82 & Critism Fel, 83-84, Ohio Arts Coun; Eight Misc Awards for Sculpture, 76-90. *Bibliog:* Madeline Burnside (auth), Betty Collings, Arts Mag, 9/79; Helen A Harrison (auth), article, NY Times, 9/23/84; Roberta Smith (auth), article, NY Times, 12/22/89. *Mem:* Col Art Asn; Int Asn Art Critics; NZ-US Arts Found (mem bd adv, currently); Artists' Orgn (pres, 85-87, dir prog, 87-). *Media:* Plastic, Clay. *Publ:* Auth, Apects of Perception, Va Commonwealth Univ & Bard Col, 84; Sculptural Views on Perceptual Ambiguity: Thomas Macaulay 1968-1986 (catalog), Dayton Art Inst, 86; Shaanxi-Ohio (posterlogue), The Artists Orgn, 90. *Mailing Add:* 1991 Hillside Dr Columbus OH 43221

COLLINS, CHRISTIANE C
HISTORIAN, LIBRARIAN
Study: Carleton Col, BA; Columbia Univ, MA & MLS. *Pos:* Cataloguing librn, Mus Mod Art, New York, 71-72; head librn, Parsons Sch Design, Adam L Gimbel Libr, New York, 73- *Awards:* Fulbright Teaching/Research Fel, Sch Archit City Planning, Technische Univ, Graz, Austria, 80-81. *Mem:* Art Libr Soc NAm; Soc Archit Historians; Col Art Asn. *Res:* City planning; late 19th century, contemporary, German expressionist architecture; 20th century design. *Publ:* Ed & coauth, Architecture of Fantasy, Praeger, 62; translr, Camillo Sitte's City Planning According to Artistic Principles, 65 & coauth, Camillo Sitte & the Birth of Modern City Planning, 65, Random House/Phaidon. *Mailing Add:* 448 Riverside Dr Apt No 1 New York NY 10027

COLLINS, DAN (DANIEL MCCLELLAN)
PAINTER
b Los Angeles, Calif, Aug 20, 54. *Study:* Ark State Univ, 76; Santa Monica Col, AA, 79; Art Center Col Design, Los Angeles, BFA, 83. *Comn:* Franklin & Argyle, Hollywood C of C, 86. *Exhib:* Mus Sci & Industry, Ontario, Calif, 83; Hollywood-Inside & Out, Los Angeles Munic Art Gallery, 86; Small Works, Jose Drudis-Biada Gallery, Los Angeles, 87; Group Exhib, Mus Neon Art, Los Angeles, 88. *Pos:* Dir-cur, Goski Gallery, Los Angeles, 84-86. *Media:* Wood, Oil. *Mailing Add:* c/o Lisa Sette Gallery 4142 N Marshall Way Scottsdale AZ 85251

COLLINS, GEORGE R
HISTORIAN, EDUCATOR
b Springfield, Mass, Sept 2, 17. *Study:* Princeton Univ, BA, 39, MFA, 42; Univ Barcelona, Dr Hon Causa, 77. *Pos:* Chmn, Urban Studies Program, Columbia Col, 80- *Teaching:* From instr to prof art hist, Columbia Univ, 46-, Mathews lectr, fall, 79. *Awards:* Guggenheim Fel, 62-63; Rockefeller Humanities Fel, 76-77. *Res:* Modern architecture and city planning; Spanish art and architecture. *Publ:* Coauth, Architecture of fantasy (transl & rev, Phantastische Architektur), 62; coauth, Camillo Sitte..., Random House & Phaidon, Eng, Vols I & II, 65; auth, The Drawings of Antonio Gaudi, 77; auth, Visionary Drawings of Architecture and Planning, 79; coauth, Fantastic Architecture, Abrams, 80. *Mailing Add:* Bob Jones Univ Greenville SC 29614

COLLINS, HARVEY ARNOLD
MURALIST, EDUCATOR
b High Springs, Fla, Aug 22, 27. *Study:* Univ Fla, with Fletcher Martin, BFA, 51; MFA, 52; LHD, 82. *Comn:* All Faiths Mural, St; 75 Year History of Olivet Col (mural), Bourbonnais, Ill, 82; mural, Nazarene Publ House, Kansas City, Mo, 83; Weakley Memorial Mural, Bradley Public Libr, Ill. *Pos:* Chmn dept art, Olivet Nazarene Univ, Bourbonnais, Ill, 71- *Teaching:* Instr painting, drawing & ceramics, Largo Jr High Sch, Fla, 58-71; prof painting & art hist, Olivet Univ, Bourbonnais, Ill, 71-91; art instr, Santa Fe Community Col, Gainesville, Fla. *Bibliog:* 75th Anniversary Mural (exhib catalog), Nazarene Publ House, Kansas City, Mo, 1/84. *Mem:* Mid-Am Col Art Asn; Nat Coun Art Adminr; Nat Art Educ Asn. *Media:* Acrylics, Oils. *Mailing Add:* 13310 NW 39th Ave Gainesville FL 32606-4719

COLLINS, HOWARD F
HISTORIAN
b Buffalo, NY, Oct 28, 22. *Study:* Albright Art Sch, Buffalo, with Charles Burchfield, Ralston Crawford & Isaac Soyer, dipl, 43; State Univ NY Col, Buffalo, BS, 47; Columbia Univ, MA, 54; Univ Pittsburgh, with William S Heckscher & Charles Seymour Jr, PhD, 70. *Teaching:* Assoc prof art hist, Kutztown State Col, 60-65; from assoc prof to prof, WVa Univ, 65-72, chmn div art, 69-71; prof, Univ Nebr, Lincoln, 72- *Mem:* Col Art Asn Am; Mid-Am Col Art Asn; Renaissance Soc Am; assoc Int Inst Conservation; Asn Historians Am Art. *Res:* Fifteenth century Venetian painting. *Publ:* Major narrative paintings by Jacopo Bellini, Art Bull, 9/82; The Cyclopean Vision of Jacopo Bellini, Pantheon, 82; Time, space and Gentile Bellini's Miracle of the Cross at Ponte S Lorenzo, Gazette Beaux Arts, 12/82; Pictorial space in Donatello's relief panels on the high altar of the santo in Padua, Arte Veneta, XLII, 87; The Decagonal Temples of Jacopo Bellini, Paragone, 9/90. *Mailing Add:* Dept Art & Art Hist Univ Nebr Lincoln NE 68588

COLLINS, JESS See Jess,

COLLINS, JIM
EDUCATOR, SCULPTOR
b Huntington, WVa, Sept 12, 34. *Study:* Marshall Univ, AB, 57; Univ Mich, Ann Arbor, MPH, 61; Ohio Univ, MFA, 66. *Work:* Wichita Art Asn, Kans; Univ SC, Columbia; Hunter Mus Art, Tenn; Am Repub Ins Co, Des Moines, Iowa; Milwaukee Art Ctr, Wis. *Comn:* Atmospheric sculpture, River Bend Festival, Chattanooga, Tenn; wood sculpture, Bearing Hq, Chicago, 85; Woodcut Print Series, Mason Co Mus, Ky, 86; The Family, five life-sized figures on a fountain, Market Ct, Chattanooga, 89; painting, The Honors Course, Chattanooga, 90. *Exhib:* Naples Art Gallery, Fla, 84; Sculpture at Heritage Village, Columbus, Ohio, 85; Works on Walls, Huntington Galleries, WVa, 86; one-man show, Hunter Mus Art, 87; Interpretations of the River, Hunter Mus Art, 90; Folk Art Gallery, New York, 90; J Rosenthal Fine Arts, Chicago, 91; and others. *Teaching:* Prof art, Univ Tenn, Chattanooga, 66-83.

Awards: Tenn Drawings, 74 & Tenn Bicentennial Art Exhib, 76, Tenn Arts Comn; Best of Show, Chiaha Nat, Rome, Ga, 78. *Bibliog:* A Catalogue of the American Collection, Hunter Mus Art, 85; PBS, Special Program, Interpretations of the River, 9/90. *Mem:* Southern Asn Sculptors (pres, 70-71). *Media:* Wood, Metals. *Publ:* Auth introd, A Handbook to British Landscape Painters, 70; auth, Women Artists in America, 18th Century to the Present, 75 & Women Artists in America II, 76. *Mailing Add:* 201 N Palisades Dr Signal Mountain TN 37377

COLLINS, LARRY RICHARD
PAINTER, EDUCATOR
b Spokane, Wash, July 15, 45. *Study:* Univ Okla, BFA, 67, Ind Univ, studied with James McGarrell, Mass Col Art, MFA, 80, La Napoule Art Found, studied with Jack Beal. *Work:* Sheldon Mem Art Gallery, Univ Neb, Lincoln; Mabee-Gerrer Mus Art, Shawnee, Okla; Mus Art Univ Okla, Norman; Dept Defense, Washington, DC; Boston Pub Libr, Mass. *Exhib:* Realistic Directions, Zoller Gallery, Pa State Univ, 83 & Recent Acquisitions, Sheldon Mem Art Gallery, Lincoln, Nebr, 83; one-man shows, Mabee-Gerrer Mus Art, Shawnee, Okla, 84 & New York Pub Libr, 87; Am Artist Mag: 50th Anniversary Exhib (traveling) 87. *Teaching:* Guest lectr, Anat, Boston Univ, Mass, 86; instr drawing Univ NH, Durham, 86-88; instr anat, Mass Col Art, Boston, 79- *Awards:* Travel Fel, Creative Arts Studies Found, 84; Individual Arts Fel, NH State Coun Arts, 88; Artists Opportunity Grant, NH State Coun Arts, 90. *Bibliog:* Jack N Kramer (auth), Human Anatomy & Figure Drawing, Van Nostrand, 84; John Stuart Engle (auth), Still Lifes, Am Artist, 6-87; Laurie Hurwitz (auth), Profiles: Larry R Collins, Am Artist, 6-87. *Media:* Oil. *Dealer:* Michael Allen Gallery 300 Harvard St Brookline MA 02146. *Mailing Add:* 3 Newbury Drive Atkinson NH 03811-2248

COLLINS, LOWELL DAUNT
PAINTER, DEALER
b San Antonio, Tex, Aug 12, 24. *Study:* Colorado Springs Fine Art Ctr, with B Robinson; Mus Fine Arts, Houston; Art Students League; Acad Grande Chaumiere, Paris; Univ Houston, BFA & ML. *Work:* Mus Fine Arts, Houston; Mus Fine Arts, Dallas; US Info Agency. *Comn:* Painting for Nelson Found. *Exhib:* Provincetown Arts Festival; New York World's Fair; Hemisfair, San Antonio; Columbia Biennial, SC; NZ Exchange Exhib; plus many others. *Pos:* Art ed, Tex Cancer Bull, 47-49; cur pre-Columbian art, Mus Nat Sci, Houston, 70-; dir, Lowell Collins Gallery, 70-; lectr, Int Conf Pre-Columbian Art, St Louis Univ, 77 & Chicago, 79; hon cur pre-Columbian Art, Houston Mus Natural Sci; bd dirs, African Am Heritage Mus. *Teaching:* Instr art & archit, Univ Houston, 51-58; dean art dept, Mus Fine Arts, Houston, 58-66; dir art sch, Lowell Collins Gallery, 66- *Mem:* Sr mem Houston Philos Soc; sr mem Am Soc Appraisers; hon mem Hanzen Col, Rice Univ; Oriental Ceramic Soc; Ima Hogg Ceramic Circle. *Media:* Oil. *Specialty:* Pre-Columbian art; African art; Oriental art. *Publ:* Illusr, Houston, Land of Big Rich, 51; Houston, The Feast Years, 61; The Galveston Era, 65; Unhappy Medium, 68. *Mailing Add:* 2903 Saint St Houston TX 77027

COLLINS, PAUL
PAINTER
b Muskegon, Mich, Dec 11, 36. *Study:* Self-taught. *Work:* Gerald R Ford Mus, Grand Rapids, Mich; Martin Luther King Jr Ctr Nonviolent Social Change, Atlanta, Ga; Joseph P Kennedy Found, Washington, DC; Puskin Mus, Moscow, USSR; Palace de la Presidence du Senegal, Dakar Senegal, Africa. *Comn:* Portrait of the pres of Senegal, US Embassy, 72; portrait of an African journey, Eerdmens Publ Co, Grand Rapids, Mich, 73; Black Struggle, Grand Rapids Pub Mus, 73; Portrait of Dr Martin Luther King, Dr Martin Luther King Ctr, Montgomery, Ala, 74; Life of the President of US, Kent Co Airport, 75; and many others. *Exhib:* American Artist, Butler Inst Art, Youngstown, Ohio, 71; Am Heritage Exhib, Corcoran Gallery, Washington, DC, 73; John F Kennedy Ctr Performing Arts, Washington, DC; Parthenon Mus, Nashville, Tenn; Mus Sci & Industry, Los Angeles; Children's Mus, Indianapolis, Ind; Avery Fisher Hall, Lincoln Ctr, New York; and many others. *Awards:* Spec Art Award, Stax Rec Co, 74; Award, Accademia della Arti e dell Lavoro, Italy, 80; and others. *Bibliog:* Bicentennial projects, Newsweek Mag, 75; Paul Collins painter of people, Am Artist, 75; and others. *Media:* Dry Oil, Own Media. *Publ:* Auth, Show down at Wounded Knee, Ebony Mag, 73; Twenty Figure Paintings and How They Work, Watson-Guptill, 79; and others. *Mailing Add:* 615 Kent Hills Rd NE Grand Rapids MI 49505

COLLINS, TRICIA See Collins & Milazzo, (Tricia Collins & Richard Milazzo)

COLLINS & MILAZZO, (TRICIA COLLINS & RICHARD MILAZZO)
CURATORS, CRITICS
Exhib: Hybrid Neutral, Independent Curators Inc traveling exhib, 89-90. *Collections Arranged:* Natural Genre, Fla State Univ Gallery & Mus, 84; The New Poverty, John Gibson Gallery, New York, 87; Art at the End of the Social, Rooseum, Malmo, Sweden, 88; The Last Decade: American Artists of the 80's, Tony Sha Frazi Gallery, New York, 90. *Pos:* Sr critics, Yale Univ, New Haven, Conn, 88-89; Am corresps, Kunstforum, Cologne, WGer, currently. *Bibliog:* Grace Glueck (auth), Tastemakers, New York Times, 9/87; Thomas McEvilley (auth), Sons of Sublime, Artforum, 88; Sarah Morris (auth), Collins & Milazzo, Flash Art, 89. *Mem:* White Columns. *Publ:* Coauths, Robert Longo: Static violence, Flash Art, 83; Radical consumption and the new poverty, New Observations, 87; Tropical codes, Kunstforum, 88; Ross Bleckner, Galeries Mag, 88. *Mailing Add:* 99 Spring St New York NY 10012

COLLYER, ROBIN
SCULPTOR, VIDEO ARTIST
b London, Eng, Mar 7, 49; Can citizen. *Study:* Ont Col Art, Toronto, 67-68. *Work:* Nat Gallery Can & Can Coun Art Bank, Ottawa; Art Gallery Ont, Toronto; Mus d'Art Contemporain, Montreal; Can Cult Ctr, Paris, France. *Exhib:* Carmen Lamanna Gallery, Toronto, Ont, 71, 72, 74, 76, 78, 79, 81 & 83, Mt Allison Univ, 76 & Etherington Art Ctr, 82; Nat Gallery Can, Ottawa, 73; Kunsthalle, Basel, Switzerland, 78; Seven Toronto Artists, Artists' Space, New York, 80; Frankfurter Kunstverin, Frankfurt; Akademie der Kunste, Berlin; Travelling Retrospective, Can & US, 82 & 84; Ctr Int d'Art Contemporain, Montreal, 85. *Teaching:* Instr, Ont Col Art, Toronto, 75; NS Col Art, Halifax, 77. *Awards:* Can Coun Grants, 69-71, 73, 74 & 76-69; Can Coun Sr Arts Grant,80. *Bibliog:* David Burett & Marilyn Schiff (auths), Contemporary Candian Art, Hurtig Publ, Edmonton, 83. *Mem:* Can Coun Adv Art Panel; Trinity Square Video (bd dirs, 79-82). *Media:* Mixed Media; Photography, Video. *Publ:* Contribr, Impulse, summer 80; co-prod & co-dir, The Girl Can't Fly It (film), A Space & Broadcast Serv, Toronto, 80; co-prod & co-dir, Darn These Hands (film), A Space & Rogers Cable TV, Toronto, 80; co-prod, Sculpture of Here and Now (film), Toronto. *Mailing Add:* 57 Pemberton Ave Willowdale ON M2M 1Y2 Canada

COLMAN, VIRGINIA O'CONNELL
SCULPTOR, GRAPHIC ARTIST
b Manhasset, Long Island, NY. *Study:* Columbia Univ, BS(art), 47; Teachers Col, Columbia Univ, MA(art), 68; sculpture with Minoru Niizuma, 74-80; watercolor with Edgar A Whitney & George Post. *Work:* Ambulatory Monitoring Inc, Ardsley, New York. *Exhib:* Painters & Sculptors Soc NJ, Jersey City Mus, 69 & 72-74; Nat Acad Galleries, New York, 74-75, 77 & 79; Silvermine Guild Artists, New Canaan, Conn, 75; Newark Mus, NJ, 77 & 79; solo exhib, Bergen Mus Art & Sci Ann, Paramus, NJ, Ann 78, 78, 83, 85, 90, 91 & 92, John Harms Ctr Arts, Englewood, NJ, 91, Paterson, NJ Mus, 91, Distinguished Alumni Exhib, Teachers Col, Columbia Univ, NY, 91, Broome Street Gallery, NY, 91, Sculpture Ctr, NY, Faculty Exhib, 91, Rockland Ctr Arts, W Nyack, NY, 91, William Carlos Wiliams Ctr Arts, Rutherford, NJ, 92, Blue Hill Cultural Ctr, Pearl River, NY, 88, 92, Artists Night Invitational, benefit Newark Mus, Hertz Corp, Park Ridge, NJ, 92, Graphic Eye Gallery, Port Washington, NY, 92, Jon Tanner Gallery, Westwood, NJ, 92; Morris Mus, Morristown, NJ, 83-; Monmouth Mus, Lincroft, NJ, 85, 88 & 90; Salmagundi Club, New York, 85 & 87; City Without Walls Gallery, Newark, NJ, 88; Trenton City Mus, Trenton, NJ, 90. *Pos:* Art ed & staff artist, Collier's Encyl, 49-52; art dir, Girl Scouts USA, New York, 52-56; promotion art dir, Macfadden Publ, New York, 56. *Teaching:* Instr stone carving, Sculpture Ctr, New York, summer 80 & 90. *Awards:* Silver Medal, Audubon Artists Ann, 79; Ida Becker Award, Catharine Lorillard Wolfe Art Club, NY, 86 & 88; Anna Hyatt Huntington Award, Snug Harbor Cultural Ctr, Catharine Lorillard Wolfe Art Club, NY, 91. *Bibliog:* Winnie Bonelli (auth), Union City Dispatch, 8/73; Eileen Watkins (auth), Newark Star-Ledger, 6/87 & 10/88. *Mem:* Sculptors Asn NJ (corresp secy, 74-78, rec secy, 88-92); Stone Sculpture Soc NY (corresp secy, 78-80, treas, 80-85); Catharine Lorillard Wolfe Art Club, NY (bd mem, 89-92). *Media:* Marble, Limestone. *Mailing Add:* 105 Leonia Ave Leonia NJ 07605

COLMER, ROY DAVID
PHOTOGRAPHER
b London, Eng; US citizen. *Study:* Hochschule fur Bildender Kunste, Hamburg, Ger, 60-65; New Sch/Parsons with George Tice, 78 & Lisette Model, 82. *Work:* Mus Mod Art, Mus City New York & Chase Manhattan Bank, New York, NY; Brooklyn Mus, NY; Mus d'Ixelles, Brussels, Belg; Mus Fine Arts, Houston; Biblotheque Nationale, Paris. *Exhib:* To-Day Art, Mus d'Ixelles, Brussels, Belg 75; Recent Acquisitions, Mus Mod Art, New York, 87; Contemporary American Photography, Kiek in De Kok Mus, Tallinn, Estonia, 88; Selected Photographs, Brooklyn Mus, NY, 89; The Human Presence, Yale Sch Art, New Haven, Conn, 89; Mean Streets: American Photographs From the Collection, 1940's-1980's, Mus Mod Art, New York, 91; Open Mind: The LeWitt Collection, Wadsworth Atheneum, Hartford, Conn, 91. *Teaching:* Asst prof painting, Univ Iowa, 70-71; vis lectr, Univ Cincinnati, Ohio, 71; instr photog, New Sch/Parsons, New York, 87- *Awards:* Guggenheim Fel, 88; Found Contemp Performance Arts Inc, 90. *Publ:* Contrib, Copy Art, Horseguard Lane Pro, 78; auth, Roy Colmer/Photographs, pvt publ, 87; contrib, The Human Presence, Yale Sch Art, 89. *Mailing Add:* 36 A Walker St New York NY 10013

COLOMBINI, SUSAN MURPHY See Murphy, Susan (Susan Avis Murphy Colombini)

COLOMBO, CHARLES
PAINTER
b Wilmington, Del, Nov 3, 27. *Study:* Pa Acad Fine Arts, Philadelphia; Art Students League with Charles DeFeo; privately with Frank E Schoonover. *Work:* Pvt collections throughout US & abroad including The Vatican, Rome, Italy, Prince Ranier, Monaco, former Vpres & Mrs Walter Mondale & Senator Joseph R Biden, Jr. *Comn:* Hagley Powder Mills, comn by State of Del for Pres J F Kennedy, 62. *Exhib:* Am watercolor Soc, 66-81; Nat Arts Club, New York, 66-75; Charles & Emma Frye Mus, Seattle, 75; Colonnade Des Artes Gallery; Lake Buena Vista, Disneyworld, Fla. *Awards:* Watercolor Award, Pa Acad Fine Arts, 49; Scholar Award, Pa Acad Fine Arts; Watercolor Award, Del Art Mus, Wilmington, 56. *Bibliog:* Frederick Kramer (auth), Brandywine Tradition Artists, Great Am Ed, New York, 71; Nancy Mohr (auth), Charles Colombo, a part of the Brandywine tradition, Delaware Today, Wilmington, 71; article, Art News, 5/83. *Mem:* Am Watercolor Soc; Rehoboth Art League. *Dealer:* Gallery At Greenville Wilmington DE; Maxwell Gallery San Francisco CA. *Mailing Add:* 101 13th St Wilmington DE 19801

COLP, NORMAN B
PHOTOGRAPHER, CURATOR
b Bronx, NY, Sept 3, 44. *Study:* Queens Col, Flushing, NY, BA(art), 67; Pratt Inst, Brooklyn, NY, 67; Parsons Sch Design, NY, 71. *Work:* La Bibliotheque Nat, Paris, France; Brooklyn Mus, NY; Int Center Photog, New York; Mus Mod Art: Libr Bookworks, New York; Victoria & Albert Mus, Nat Art Libr, London, England. *Comn:* Porcelain enamel signs, Creative Stas/MTA, New York, 91; zoetrope-B/W photo images with John Billingham, Nat Shopping Centers, Hamden, Conn, 91. *Exhib:* Artworks of Artforum, PS1 Mus, Long Island City, NY, 78; Artists' Postcards Series II, Cooper-Hewitt Mus, New York, 78; If you really must know, Int Center Photog, New York, 80; Artists' Books, Walker Art Ctr, Minneapolis, 81; Color in the Summer, Brooklyn Mus, 84; Typo-Graphism, Centre Georges Pomidou, Paris, France, 85; New York City, Mus Mod Art, 90; Ziggurat, Victoria & Albert Mus, London, Eng 91. *Collections Arranged:* Stories Your Mother Never Told You, White Plains Publ Libr, 82; Less is More, Pratt Graphics Ctr, 82; One Cubic Foot, Metrop Mus Art, 83; From the Beginning, Pratt Graphics Ctr, 84; The Impractical-Practical, White Plains Pub Libr, 84. *Pos:* Assoc cur, Alternative Mus, New York, 79-80; cur exhibs, Center Book Arts, New York, 80-83 & exhib coord, 83. *Teaching:* Instr, book art, Sch of Visual Arts, New York, 82-86 & Pratt Graphics Ctr, New York, 83-84. *Bibliog:* Don Williams (reporter), News 4 New York, WNBC-TV, 6/3/92; Cathy Courtney (auth), Private Views & Other Containers, estamp/London, 6/92. *Media:* Framed, Bookworks and Porcelain Enamel on Steel. *Publ:* Auth, The Thrice Told Tale, 77, private publ; An Old Saw, 82, A Primer on Art Criticism, 83, Crazy Hair, 83 & Freud's Recipe, 83, Hand & Mind Books. *Mailing Add:* 180 West End Ave 3R New York NY 10023

COLPACCI, VIORICA
SCULPTOR
b Romania, US citizen. *Study:* Inst Fine & Decorative Arts, Bucharest, Romania, MFA; NY Univ, MA. *Work:* Galati Mus, Romania; Romania-State Collections; Marrieta Col, Ohio. *Comn:* Mural, al fresco, Sch #24, Bucharest, Romania, 70. *Exhib:* First Int Exhib, Ertfurt Mus Art, Ger, 74; 16th Int Art Competition, Perugia Mus Art, Italy, 74; 32nd Int Competition Ceramics, Frenza, Italy, 74; Craft Nat, Marietta Col, Ohio, 80; Jubilee 50, Nat, League NH, Manchester, 81; group exhib, Bergen Mus, Paramus, NJ, 83; Galex 18 Int, Gallesburg Pub Art Ctr, Ill, 84; 2nd Int Shoebox Sculpture Exhib, Univ Hawaii Art Gallery, 85. *Awards:* Charles Murphy Award, Nat Asn Women Artists, 83. *Bibliog:* Karen Rychlewski (auth), Marrieta Craft Nat, Ceramics Monthly, 81; Sharon Webster (auth), The Greatest Show - V Colpacci, VanGuard Press, Vt, 8/85. *Mem:* Nat Asn Women Artists; Sculptor Guild. *Media:* Bronze & Welded Steel. *Mailing Add:* 60-71 70th Ave Ridgewood NY 11385

COLPITT, FRANCES
HISTORIAN, CRITIC
b Tulsa, Okla, Dec 19, 52. *Study:* Univ Tulsa, BFA, 74, MA, 77; Univ Southern Calif, PhD, 82. *Collections Arranged:* Constructed Metal: Modern Sculpture, Univ Calif, Santa Barbara, 84; Finish Fetish: LA's Cool School, Univ Southern Calif, 91; Knowledge: Aspects of Conceptual Art, Univ Calif, Santa Barbara, 92. *Pos:* Corresponding Ed, Art Am, currently. *Teaching:* Vis lectr & vis asst prof art hist, Univ Calif, Santa Barbara, 82-88; vis asst prof, Cornell Univ, 85-86, Univ Southern Calif, 88-90; asst prof, Univ Tex, San Antonio, 90- *Mem:* Int Asn Art Critics; Am Soc Aesthetics; Col Art Asn. *Res:* Contemporary abstract painting and sculpture; theories of 20th century criticism. *Publ:* Auth, Heizer's extracts, Art Am, 84; The issue of boredom: is it interesting?, J Aesthetics & Art Criticism, 85; coauth, Abstract Options, Univ Calif, Santa Barbara, 89; auth, Minimal art: The critical perspective, UMI Res Press, 90 & Univ Wash Press, 93; The Shape of Painting in the 1960s, Col Art J, 91. *Mailing Add:* Div Art & Archit Univ Texas San Antonio TX 78285-0642

COLT, JOHN NICHOLSON
PAINTER, EDUCATOR
b Madison, Wis, May 15, 25. *Study:* Univ Wis, BS & MS. *Work:* Whitney Mus Am Art; Milwaukee Art Ctr; Munson-Williams-Proctor Mus, Utica, NY; Le Centre d'Art, Port au Prince, Haiti; Beloit Col, Wright Art Ctr, Wis. *Comn:* Murals, Marquette Univ, 59 & First Wis Ctr, 73. *Exhib:* Butler Inst Am Art Exhib Am Painting, Youngstown, Ohio, 55; Whitney Ann Exhib Am Painting, Whitney Mus Am Art, New York, 60; one-man shows, Milwaukee Art Ctr, Wis, 62 & 69, Minneapolis Inst of Art, 70, Bradley Gallery, Milwaukee, 73, 75, 77, 79, 81 & 83, Neil Gallery, New York, 77 & 79-81, Cincinnati Acad Art, 81 & Perimeter Gallery, Chicago, 83, 86, 90 & 91; Chicago Vicinity, Art Inst Chicago, 62 & 64; Walker Biennial, Walker Art Ctr, Minneapolis, 62, 64 & 66; Art Across America, Knodler Gallery, New York, 68; Chicago Int, 87 & 88; 100 Years of Wisconsin Art, Milwaukee Art Mus, 88; Tory Folliard Gallery, Milwaukee, 92 & 93; Milwaukee Art Mus, Univ Wis, 93. *Pos:* Vis prof, Univ Saskatchewan, 59, Am Univ Beirut, Lebanon, 72. *Teaching:* Prof painting, Univ Wis-Milwaukee, 58-90, emer prof, 90- *Awards:* Medal of Honor, Milwaukee Art Ctr; Ford Found Award & Top Award, Walker Art Ctr. *Media:* Oil, Acrylic. *Dealer:* Perimeter Gallery 750 N Orleans Chicago IL 60610. *Mailing Add:* 8329 N Regent Rd Fox Point WI 53217

COLTON, JUDITH
EDUCATOR, HISTORIAN
b New York, NY, Mar 21, 43. *Study:* Smith Col, Northampton, Mass, BA, 63; Inst Fine Arts, New York Univ, MA, 65, PhD, 74. *Teaching:* Art hist, Bennington Col, 71-72; instr art hist, Queens Col, City Univ New York, 72-73; asst prof art hist, Yale Univ, 73-78, assoc prof, 78- *Awards:* James L Clifford Prize, Am Soc 18th Century Studies, 78; Ingram Merrill Found, 79-80; Fel, Am Coun Learned Socs, 82-83. *Mem:* Col Art Asn Am; Am Soc 18th Century Studies; Garden Hist Soc. *Res:* 17th and 18th century art in Italy, France and England; concentrating on the history of painting sculpture and garden design. *Publ:* Contribr, Architectura, 74; Eighteenth-Century Studies, 76; auth, The Parnasse Francois: Titon du Tillet and the Origins of the Monument to Genius, Yale Univ Press, 79; contribr, Studies on Voltaire and The Eighteenth century, 80; Art the Ape of Nature: Studies in Honor of H W Janson, 81. *Mailing Add:* Dept Hist Art 56 High St Yale Univ New Haven CT 06520

COLVILLE, ALEXANDER
PAINTER, PRINTMAKER
b Toronto, Ont, Aug 24, 20. *Work:* Nat Gallery Can; Mus Mod Art, New York; Wallraf-Richarts Mus, Cologne, Ger; Ctr Nat Art Contemporain, Paris; Boymans-Van Beuningen Mus, Rotterdam. *Exhib:* Gemeentmuseum Arnhem, Kunsthalle, Dusseldorf; Fischer Fine Art, London, 77; Art Gallery Ont, Toronto; Staatliche Kunsthalle, Berlin; Ludwig Mus, Cologne, 83; Teien Mus, Tokyo, 85. *Awards:* Companion Award, Order of Can, 82. *Bibliog:* David Burnett (auth), Colville, McClelland & Stewart, Toronto, 83. *Dealer:* Drabinsky Gallery 86 Scollard St Toronto ON M5R 1G2 Canada. *Mailing Add:* PO Box 550 Wolfville NS B0P 1X0 Canada

COLWAY, JAMES R
PAINTER
b Oneida, NY, Nov 12, 20. *Study:* Syracuse Univ Sch Art, 45-48, Univ Col, 46-48. *Work:* US Embassy Prog, Washington, DC; Butler Inst Am Art, Youngstown, Ohio; Lyman Allyn Mus, Univ Conn, New London; St Lawrence Univ, Canton, NY; Slater Mem Mus, Norwich, Conn; plus others. *Comn:* Painting reproductions, comn by Aaron Ashley & Hedgerow House, New York, NY. *Exhib:* Grumbacher Show, Grand Cent Art Gallery, New York, 64; one-man shows, Chase Gallery, New York, 69, St Lawrence Univ, 70, Grand Haven Art Ctr, Mich, 70 & 75 & Arvest Galleries, Boston, 76; Munson-Williams-Proctor Inst, Utica, NY; Schweinfurth Mus, Auburn, NY. *Pos:* Sr vpres & dir, Oneida Ltd, retired; pres, Colway Assocs, currently. *Bibliog:* Show rev in Art News, 5/69; Grumbacher's Palette Talk, 78. *Mem:* Am Artists Prof League; Cent NY Watercolor Soc; Artists Equity Asn. *Media:* Water Media, Oil. *Mailing Add:* 101 The Vineyard Oneida NY 13421

COLWELL, JUDITH KOGOD
CERAMIST
b New York, NY, Dec 16, 49. *Study:* George Washington Univ, BA, 71; Corcoran Sch Art; Inst Allende, Mex. *Work:* Am Asn Retired Persons. *Exhib:* American Ceramic National III, Downey Mus, Calif, 85; Beyond Function: New Directions in Decorative Arts, Washington, DC, 88; Washington Craft show, Smithsonian Mus, Washington, DC, 88-90; Art on the Table, Soc Art Crafts, Pittsburgh, Pa, 89; Designs for Dining, Smithsonian Mus, Washington, DC, 89; Wichita Nat, Wichita Art Asn, Kans, 89; Studio Ceramics Invitational, Berea Col, Ky, 90. *Awards:* Best in Clay, 18th Biennial Exhib Creative Crafts Coun, Rockville, Md, 88; Individual Artists Award in Crafts, Md State Arts Coun, 90 & 92. *Bibliog:* Nine Washington, DC area potters, Studio Potter Mag, Vol 9, No 1, 12/80; Connie Stapleton (auth), At Home with Commissions, Washington Mus Arts, 5-6/88; Pat Ross (auth), Formal Country, Viking, 89. *Media:* Clay. *Publ:* Auth, Portfolio: Washington Craft show, Sales Surprises, Ceramics Monthly, 88. *Mailing Add:* 7325 Takoma Ave Takoma Park MD 20912

COMÈS, MARCELLA (MRS RANDOLPH WINSLOW)
PAINTER, WRITER
b Pittsburgh, Pa. *Study:* Carnegie Sch Fine Arts, Pittsburgh; Accademia Della Belle Arte, Florence, Italy; also with A Kostellow & Knath, USA. *Work:* Brooklyn Mus; US Mil Acad, West Point; Cent Intelligence Agency; Naval Acad, Annapolis, Md; Georgetown Univ; Harvard Univ. *Comn:* Mural, Homewood Libr, Pittsburgh, Pa; mural, Stone Ridge Sch, Washington, DC; portrait Adm Nimitz, Nimitz Libr, Annapolis, 76; portraits for Eliot House, Harvard Univ: John Finley, 80, Walter Jackson Bate, 81 & Harry Levin, 82. *Exhib:* Corcoran Biennial, Washington, DC; 18 Pittsburgh Artists, Carnegie Inst, Pittsburgh, Pa; Mus de la Marine, Paris, France; one-woman show, Brooks Mus, Memphis, Tenn & Gallery on the Green, Lexington, Mass, 81; Tuscan Art, Florence, Italy. *Collections Arranged:* Travel tour, Washington Artists, 10 Southeastern Mus, 72. *Pos:* Nat ed, Artists Equity Newslett, 75-79. *Teaching:* Instr painting, Catholic Univ. *Awards:* Katherine Kuh Award, Soc Washington Artists, 61; Benedictine Art Award, Am Fedn Arts, 68; Jurors Award, Adelyn Breeskin Presents, 85. *Bibliog:* Phillis Theroux (auth), Marcella Comes, Washingtonian Mag, 77; Robert Taylor (auth), Painter to writer, Boston Globe, 81; A Washington life, Washington Post, 7/89. *Mem:* Artists Equity (nat vpres, 69-74). *Publ:* Illusr, Robert Frost portrait, Washington Post, 63; auth, art reviews, Carnegie Mag & Univ Pittsburgh Record; DC harbors underground painters, Art Scene Mag, 71; Shock of the old, AEA Newslett, 81. *Mailing Add:* 3106 P St NW Washington DC 20007

COMINI, ALESSANDRA
HISTORIAN, WRITER
b Winona, Minn, Nov 24, 34. *Study:* Barnard Col, with Julius Held, BA, 56; Univ Calif, Berkeley, with Herschel Chipp, MA, 62; Columbia Univ, PhD, 69. *Teaching:* Asst prof art hist, Columbia Univ, 69-74; vis prof, Yale Univ, 73; prof, Southern Methodist Univ,74-83, univ distinguished prof, 83- *Awards:* Charles Rufus Morey Book Award, Col Art Asn, 75; Outstanding Prof, Southern Methodist Univ, 79, 81, 83, 85, 86, 88, 89 & 90; Awarded Grand Medal of Honor for services to Austrian Republic, 90. *Mem:* Am Soc Composers, Auth & Publ; Tex Inst Letters. *Res:* Jugendstil and expressionism;

changing image of Beethoven; foreign artists in Rome 1750-1914; Gothic revival and German romanticism; images & idols of Brahms, images of Schoenberg, Berg & Webern; Alma Mahler and her Vienna. *Publ:* Auth, Egon Schiele's Portraits, Univ Calif Press, 74, 2nd ed, 90; Gustav Klimt, George Braziller, Inc, 75 & 88; Ego Schiele, George Braziller, Inc, 76 & 88; The Fantastic Art of Vienna, Alfred A Knopf, 78; The Changing Image of Beethoven, 1770-1918: A Study in Myth-Making, Rizzoli Int Publ, 87. *Mailing Add:* 2900 McFarlin Dallas TX 75205

CONAL, ROBBIE
PAINTER
b New York, NY, 1941. *Study:* Stanford Univ, MFA, 78. *Exhib:* Col Notre Dame Art Gallery, Belmont, Calif, 80; San Francisco Mus Mod Art, San Francisco, Calif, 81; UGA Fine Arts Gallery, Athens, Ga, 82; Gallery 500X, Dallas, Tex, 84; Cleveland Ctr Contemp Art Galleria, Ohio, 88; poster projects, False Profit, Los Angeles, New York, Washington, Houston, 88, Sex, Drugs & Rock & Roll, Los Angeles, New York, Chicago, San Francisco, Oakland, Berkeley, Washington, DC, 89 & Plan Ahead, Los Angeles, New York, New Orleans, San Francisco, Oakland, Berkeley, Washington, DC; The Armory Ctr for the Arts, Pasadena, Calif, 90. *Mailing Add:* c/o Robert Berman/B-1 Gallery 2730 Main St Santa Monica CA 90405

CONANT, HOWARD SOMERS
PAINTER, EDUCATOR
b Beloit, Wis, May 5, 21. *Study:* Art Students League, with Kunyiyoshi; Univ Wis, BS & MS(painting); Univ Buffalo, EdD. *Work:* Milton Col, Wis; CW Post Col, NY; Northern Ariz Univ, Flagstaff; Univ Ariz, Tucson; Univ Wis, Milwaukee Art Mus; and others. *Comn:* Mural painting, Molloy Col, Rockville Center, NY, 70; environmental mural, Sperry High Sch, Henrietta, NY, 71; Environmental painting, Valley Nat Bank, Tucson, 80; environmental painting, Good Samaritan Hosp, Phoenix, 81. *Exhib:* Kioso del Arte, Hermosillo, Mex, 78; Univ Cent Fla, Orlando, 79; Northern Ariz Univ, 80; Wash State Univ, 81; Western Ore State Col, 81; Pima Col, Tucson, 81; Kingsborough Col, Brooklyn, NY, 87; Amarillo Art Ctr, Tex, 89; Galeria Arte de Oaxaca, Mexico, 90; Armstrong State Col, Savannah, Ga, 90. *Pos:* Art ed, Intellect Mag, 72-76 & USA: Today, 76-85. *Teaching:* Prof art, State Univ NY, Buffalo, 47-55; prof & chmn, Dept Art & Art Educ, NY Univ, 55-76; head, Dept Art, Univ Ariz, Tucson, 76-86, prof painting, 86-87; prof artist, 87- *Awards:* Distinguished Serv to Art Educ, Nat Gallery Art, 66; Distinguished Alumnus, Univ Wis-Milwaukee, 68; Distinguished Fel, Nat Art Educ Asn, 85; Nat Endowment for the Arts Sr Fel Painting, 85. *Bibliog:* John Perreault (auth), Impressions of Arizona, Art Am, 4/81; Arizona Biennial 82 (exhib catalog), Tucson Mus Art, 82; Ron Schultz (auth), Tucson, a blue chip city, Pacific Southwest Airliner mag, 1/83. *Mem:* Int Asn Art Critics; Col Art Asn; Nat Asn Schs Art & Design; Partners of the Americas. *Media:* Acrylic, Ink. *Publ:* Auth & ed, Masterpieces of the Arts, 63; auth, Art Education, 64; Seminar on Elementary and Secondary School Education in the Visual Arts, 65; auth & ed, Lincoln Library of the Arts, 73; Art for schools: A study of children's responses to original works of art, Ctr Appl Res Educ; and others. *Dealer:* Art Source Inc Tulsa OK; Sol del Rio Gallery San Antonio TX. *Mailing Add:* 1721 Entrada Doce Tucson AZ 85718

CONANT, JAN ROYCE
TRADITIONAL PAINTER
b Boston, Mass, Sept 14, 30. *Study:* Boston Mus Sch Fine Arts, 48-51; Cincinnati Art Acad, 51-53. *Work:* Wyndham Rose Hall Hotel, Montego Bay, Jamaica, West Indies; Smith-Worthington Saddlery Co, Hartford, Conn; Chukka-Cove Farm, Ltd, St Ann, Jamaica, West Indies. *Comn:* 4 Paintings, Contract Art, Centerbrook, Conn; more than 275 commissioned paintings in pvt collections. *Exhib:* Solo exhibs, Conn Bank & Trust Co, Hartford, 71, Jamaica by Jan, Runaway Bay Hotel, West Indies, 80, Chester Art Gallery, 87 & Lyman Allyn Mus, New London, Conn, 89; Animals in Art, Salt Box Gallery, West Hartford, Conn, 81; Catherine Lorillard Wolfe Art Club, New York, 86; Am Soc Equine Art, Lexington, Ky, 87. *Mem:* Artists Equity Asn; Am Soc Equine Art; Lyme Acad Fine Arts; Conn Comn Arts. *Media:* Oil, Watercolor. *Publ:* Illusr, The Judge and the Junior Exhibitor, Duel, Sloan & Pearce, 64; auth & illusr, Half Pint and others, Book Press, 66; illusr, The Chronicle of the Horse, 68-79; Hunter Seat Equitation, Doubleday, 71; Designing Courses & Obstacles, Houghton Mifflin, 78. *Dealer:* The Crossroads of Sport Inc 5 E 47th St New York NY 10017; Cinamon Teal Essex CT. *Mailing Add:* Stonefield Farm Three Bridges Rd East Haddam CT 06423

CONAWAY, GERALD
SCULPTOR, PAINTER
b Manson, Wash, Feb 15, 33. *Study:* Everett Jr Col, Wash, ABA; Univ Wash, Seattle, with George Tsutakawa & Everett Dupen, BA(art educ), MFA(sculpture). *Work:* Anchorage Fine Arts Mus, Alaska; Alaska Methodist Univ, Anchorage; Nat Gallery Art. *Comn:* William H Seward (marble monument), Mutual Ins Co, New York & Anchorage Centennial, Anchorage, 67; concrete wall sculptures, Raymond Lawson, AIA, 73; aluminum sculptures, Gen Serv Admin Fed Bldg, Fairbanks, Alaska, 79 & Pub Safety Bldg, Fairbanks, Alaska, 81; Benny Benson Mem (aluminum), Anchorage, 83. *Exhib:* All Alaska, Anchorage, 65-70; Western Regional Craft Show, Portland, 67; Sculpture Northwest, Seattle, 68. *Pos:* Sign writer & artist, Univ Wash, 54-65; graphic artist, Boeing Airplane Co, 57. *Teaching:* Instr art, Northshore Sch Dist, Wash, 57-65; from assoc prof to prof art, Alaska Methodist Univ, 65-76. *Awards:* Sculpture Award, All Alaska, 65-70; Jewelry Award, Western Regional Craft Show, 67. *Mem:* Nat Art Educ Asn. *Media:* Wood, Stone. *Dealer:* Francine Seders Gallery 6701 Greenwood Ave N Seattle WA 98103. *Mailing Add:* 2457 Cottonwood St Anchorage AK 99508

CONAWAY, JAMES D
PAINTER, EDUCATOR
b Granite City, Ill, Oct 9, 32. *Study:* Southern Ill Univ, Carbondale, Ill, BA; Univ Iowa, Iowa City, MA, MFA. *Work:* Am Embassy Collection; Waterloo Munic Art Gallery, Iowa; Davenport Munic Art Gallery, Iowa; Gen Mills, Minneapolis, Minn; 3M Company, St Paul, Minn. *Comn:* Painting, Texaco Oil Co, Houston, 81. *Exhib:* Walker Biennial, Walker Art Ctr, Minneapolis, 67; Art for the Embassies, Smithsonian Inst, Washington, DC, 67; Midwestern Ann Competition, Joslyn Art Mus, Omaha, 73; Mid Year Biennial, Butler Inst Am Art, Youngstown, Ohio, 74; Manisphere, Winnepeg Art Ctr, 74; Marietta Int Painting Exhib, Ohio, 76; Palace of Fine Arts, Santiago, Chile. *Teaching:* Asst prof, Univ Wis, Stevens Point; prof painting & drawing, Anoka Ramsey Col, Minneapolis, currently; prof painting, Hamline Univ, St Paul, currently. *Awards:* Purchase Award, Davenport Munic Art Gallery, 63, Waterloo Munic Art Galleries, 65; Donors Prize, Walker Art Ctr Biennial, 66. *Bibliog:* James Conaway, Artists of the Rockies, Fall 80; By the time he got to Phoenix, Arizona Arts and Lifestyle, Spring 81; James Conaway (auth), Minneapolis-Santa Fe connection, Southwest Profiles, 5/83. *Mem:* Mid-Am Col Art Asn (treas, 77-78); Artist Equity. *Media:* Oil. *Dealer:* Suzanne Kohn Gallery 100 Second Ave N Minneapolis MN 55401; Harris Gallery 110 Bissonnet Houston TX 77005. *Mailing Add:* 2758 Benjamin St Minneapolis MN 55418

CONCANNON, ANN WORTH
ADMINISTRATOR
b Menominee, Mich, Aug 17, 46. *Study:* Univ Mich, BA, 64. *Exhib:* Stages: Images of Childhood, Art Ctr of Battle Creek, 12/85. *Pos:* Dir, William Bonifas Art Ctr, Escanaba, Mich, 75-78; dir, Art Ctr of Battle Creek, Mich, 81- *Mem:* Mich Mus Asn (pres, 88-90); Midwest Mus Conf; Mich Asn Community Arts Agencies; Mich Coun Humanities (bd dirs); Mich Cult Conserv Alliance. *Mailing Add:* 265 E Emmett St Battle Creek MI 49017

CONCANNON, GEORGE ROBERT
PAINTER
b Berkeley, Calif. *Study:* Stanford Univ, BA; Harvard Univ, MA; Can Col. *Work:* Gulbenkian Mus, Lisbon, Port; Woollahra Gallery, Sydney, Australia; Wind-Borne Gallery, Darien, Conn; Olga Dollar Gallery, San Francisco, Calif; Mayans Gallery, Santa Fe, NMex. *Media:* Oil on Canvas. *Mailing Add:* 2995 Woodside Rd Woodside CA 94062

CONCHA, JERRY
PAINTER
b Sacremento, Calif, 35. *Study:* San Francisco Art Inst, BFA, 70. *Work:* San Francisco Mus Mod Art; Seattle Art Mus; de Saisset Art Mus Gallery, Santa Clara, Calif; AT&T, New York; Mex Mus, San Francisco. *Exhib:* Solo exhib: Bank Am Hq, San Francisco, 80 & Palo Alto Cult Ctr, Calif, 84; World Print Three, San Francisco Mus Art,80; Paintings, Calif State Univ, Hayward, 81; Galeria de la Raza, San Francisco, 85; Lo del Corazon, Mex Mus, San Francisco, 86; Mano A Mano: Abstraction/Figuration 16 Mexican American & Latin American Painters, Univ of Calif, Santa Cruz & Oakland Mus, 88-89. *Awards:* Artist Yr, Oakland Mus, Calif, 83. *Bibliog:* Thomas Albright (auth), Art reviewer, San Francisco Chronicle, 6/22/83; Mark Van Proyen (auth), Art reviewer, Artweek, 89; Charles Santiago (auth), Mus Calif, 89. *Media:* Acrylic. *Mailing Add:* c/o Allrich Gallery 251 Post St San Francisco CA 94108

CONDESO, ORLANDO
PRINTMAKER
b Lima, Peru, Dec 31, 47. *Study:* Visual Arts, Lima; Pratt Graphics Ctr, New York. *Work:* Nat Mus Hist, Repub China; Harlem Art Collection, New York; Orgn Am States, Washington, DC; Braniff Int, Lima; Cult Peruvian NAm Inst, Lima. *Exhib:* Second Biennial of Latin Am Prints, San Juan, PR, 72; 2nd Int Print Exhib, Mus Mod Art, Sao Paulo, Brazil, 72; 18th Nat Print Exhib, Brooklyn Mus, NY, 72; Young Artists 1973, Int Play Group Inc, New York, 73; Calif Palace Legion Honor, San Francisco, 73; Nat Mus Hist, Repub China, 73; 2nd Miami Graphics Biennial, Fla, 75; one-man shows, Pensacola Art Ctr, Fla, 77, Ivone Briceno Gallery, Lima, Peru, 78, Usdan Gallery, Bennington, Vt, 79, Nobe Gallery, New York, 79, Forum Gallery, Lima, Peru, 81 & 85, Wilson Arts Ctr, Rochester, NY, 82 & Pancho Fierro Gallery, Lima, Peru, 91; NJCVA Fac Exhib, Schering-Plough Corp, Madison, NJ, 89; Printers of The Vinalhaven Press, Fogg Gallery, Vinalhaven, Maine, 89; Earth Works NJCVA, Sumit, NJ, 91. *Pos:* Co-owner, Condeso-Lawler Gallery, currently. *Teaching:* Photog tech printmaking, Lower East Side Printshop, NY, 82-84; etching instr, Cooper Union, NY, 83; etching instr, NJ Ctr Visual Arts, Summit, 89-90. *Awards:* First Prize, 5th Nat Print Competition, USA Embassy, Lima, 70; Award, 5th Ann Exhib, Pratt Graphics Ctr, 72; Purchase Award, 2nd Miami Graphics Biennial, 75. *Media:* Acrylic, Silkscreen. *Publ:* Art News, 3/71; Printshop Calendar, New York, 75; Who is Who in Am Art, 78-82; Escandalar Mag No 7, New York, 79; Art Gallery Scene, Jan Issue, 83. *Mailing Add:* 217 E 22nd New York NY 10010

CONE, GERRIT CRAIG
ART ADMINISTRATOR
b Denver, Colo, May 23, 47. *Study:* Univ NMex, 65-68; Long Beach City Col, AA, 69; Calif State Univ, Long Beach, BA, 72. *Pos:* Gallery coordr, Tucson Art Ctr, 72-73; actg dir, Tucson Mus Art, 73-74, cur collections & asst dir, 74-80. *Mem:* Am Asn Mus; Western Regional Conf Am Asn Mus (Ariz state rep, 74-76, first vpres); Western Asn Art Mus (first vpres); Arch Am Art; Art Libr Soc Ariz (chmn, 75-76); and others. *Publ:* Ed, Western Regional Conf Am Asn Mus Newslett, 75-77. *Mailing Add:* 4615 N Park Ave Suite 103 Chevy Chase MD 20815

CONESA, MIGUEL A
PAINTER, ILLUSTRATOR
b Ponce, PR, Sept 29, 52. *Study:* Jose Azaustre Acad, Ponce, PR, 67-68; Escuela Artes Plasticas, San Juan, PR, 72; Augusta Col, Ga, 75-77. *Work:* Carnegie Libr, Ex-Libris Collection, San Juan, PR; Libr Univ Rio Piedras, PR; Ponce Art Mus, Luis A Ferre Found, PR; McDuffie Co Mus, Thomson, Ga; and over 300 works in pvt collections in the US, Puerto Rico, Latin America & Europe. *Comn:* Homenaje a la Grandeza del Paisaje Puertorriqueno, assemblage-mixed media mural, Image Makers Corp, 84-88. *Exhib:* First Am Painters in Paris, Argraf Asn Paris, France, 75-76; South Eastern Artist, High Mus, Atlanta, Ga, 76; Retrospective, Ponce Art Mus, PR, 80; Ann Show, Inst Cultura, San Juan, PR, 80; Gallery II/RSVP, Charlottesville, Va, 83; Cayman Gallery, New York, 83; 14 Year Retrospective, Col Tech, Ponce, PR, 84; UNESCO, Ann Show, Museo Univ Puerto Rico, 84; Inter-Am Univ, Ponce, 85; Col Abogados de PR, Santurce, 88; Second Expo Arte Ponceno, Col Tech, Ponce, PR; and 7 works submitted to Sotheby's Latin Am auction, New York, 88. *Pos:* Post card designer, Graficas Nativas, Domingo Cabrera, Rio Piedras, PR, 71-72; illusr, Korsevish Advert Agency, Atlanta, Ga, 77-78; illusr, TASC Fed Govt, Ft Gordon, Ga, 81-83; creative dir, MC Studio Mod Design, Hato Rey, PR, currently; vpres, Avant Garde Productions, Ponce, PR, 84-85; pres, Graphitec, currently; pres & art instr, Taller Galeria San Jose, Ponce, PR, currently. *Awards:* Best of Show Scholar Award, Luis Ferre Found, 70-71; Best of Show, Ga Depot Art Festival, McDuffie, 75; Bailies' Award, Augusta Col, Bailies' Studio, Augusta, 75. *Bibliog:* Antonio Molina (auth), History of Painting in Puerto Rico, Gran Enciclopedia de PR, vol 8, 73; Fay Rice (auth), Profile on Miguel Conesa, Art Voices South, 5-6/81. *Mem:* Int Platform Asn, Cleveland; Ponce Art Mus, Ponce, PR; Image Makers Corp, Ponce, PR. *Media:* All. *Publ:* Auth, Museo de Arte de Ponce, Odicea Cultural, La Fuente Informativa, 3/86; El Digital, Western Digital Caribe, Ponce, PR, 88-89. *Dealer:* Euro-Am Consult Mems Group Inc Jean Daniel Etchevers Mutis 255 Ponce de Leon Ave Hato Rey PR 00919. *Mailing Add:* 2-709 2nd Ext Rambla Ponce PR 00731

CONE-SKELTON, ANNETTE
PAINTER, DEALER
b LaGrange, Ga, Oct 20, 42. *Study:* LaGrange Col, Ga; Atlanta Col Art, Ford Found scholar, BFA. *Work:* High Mus Art, Atlanta, Ga; Hunter Mus Art, Chattanooga,Tenn; Am Tel & Tel Collection, New York & Chicago; Herbert F Johnson Mus, Cornell Univ, Ithaca, NY; Emory Univ, Atlanta. *Exhib:* Southeastern Ann Exhib, High Mus Art, Atlanta, 67 & 68; Hunter Mus Art Ann, Chattanooga, 67, 70 & 76; Ga Artists Show, High Mus Art, Atlanta, 71, 72 & 74; 8th Grand Prix de Peinture, de la cote d'Azur, Paris, France, 72; 13th Atlanta Artists, Penha Gallery, Ft Lauderdale, Fla, 73; one-person shows, Image S Gallery, 74 & 75 & Heath Gallery, 77, 78, 79 & 80, Atlanta; Galleries Int, Winter Park, Fla, 75; 13 Women Painters, Festival of Women in the Arts, Ga State Univ, Atlanta, 75; 35 Artists in the SE, High Mus Art, Atlanta, 76, Birmingham Mus, Ala, 77, Greenville Co Mus, SC, 77, HunterMus, Chattanooga, Tenn, 78 & Southeastern Ctr Contemp Art, Winston-Salem, NC, 78; Mint Mus, Charlotte, NC, 79; Avant-Garde: 12 in Atlanta, High Mus Art, 79. *Pos:* Art consult, Arnold Gallery, Atlanta, 77-; managing ed, Contemp Art/SE, Atlanta, 77-79; dir, Heath Gallery, 79- *Awards:* Merit Award, Southeastern Ann, High Mus Art, Atlanta, 67; Merit Award, Ga Inst Technol, Atlanta, 68; Purchase Award, 15th Hunter Ann, Hunter Mus, Chattanooga, Tenn, 76. *Bibliog:* L'Art a l'Etranger, La Revue Mod, 71. *Dealer:* Heath Gallery Inc 416 E Paces Ferry Rd Atlanta GA 30305. *Mailing Add:* 1765 Peachtree St Suite C1 Atlanta GA 30309

CONFORTE, RENEE
DEALER
b Belgrade, Yugoslavia, US citizen. *Study:* Mt Holyoke Col, BA(magna cum laude); Univ Paris I, Sorbonne; Ecole du Louvre, Paris. *Pos:* Admin asst, Marlborough Gallery, New York, 68-72; dir & co-owner, David McKee Gallery, New York, 74- *Specialty:* Contemporary American art. *Mailing Add:* c/o McKee Gallery 745 Fifth Ave New York NY 10151

CONFORTI, MICHAEL PETER
HISTORIAN, CURATOR
b Bradford, Mass, Apr 3, 45. *Study:* Trinity Col, Conn, BA, 68; Harvard Univ, MA, 73, PhD, 77. *Pos:* Cur sculpture & decorative arts, Fine Arts Museums San Francisco, 77-80; chief cur & Bell Mem Cur, Minneapolis Inst Arts, 80-; cataloger, Sotheby & Co, London & NY, 68-71. *Teaching:* Adj prof art hist, Univ Minn, 86- *Awards:* Fel Art Hist, Am Acad Rome, 75-77; Robert Smith Award, 87; Getty Guest Scholar, 88. *Mem:* Am Asn Mus; Decorative Arts Soc; Am Ceramics Circle; Silver Soc; English Ceramic Circle; Soc Archit Historians. *Res:* Sculpture and decorative arts, 17th to 20th centuries. *Publ:* The Lateran Apostles, Memoirs Am Acad Rome, 80; coauth & ed, Sweden: A Royal Treasury 1550-1700, Nat Gallery Art, 88; American Craftsman and the European Tradition 1620-1820, Minn Inst Art, 89; Deaccessing in American Museums: Some Thoughts for England, Apollo, 8/89; Expanding the Canon of Art Collecting in Museums, Mus News, 9-10/89. *Mailing Add:* Minneapolis Inst Arts 2400 Third Ave So Minneapolis MN 55404

CONGDON, WILLIAM (GROSVENOR)
PAINTER, WRITER
b Providence, RI, Apr 15, 12. *Study:* Provincetown Sch Art, with Henry Hensche; Demetrious Sch Sculpture, Boston & Folly Cove, Mass. *Work:* Metrop Mus Art, Whitney Mus Am Art & Mus Mod Art, New York; Cleveland Mus, Ohio; Vatican Mus Contemp Art, Vatican City; and others. *Comn:* Bronze head, Stephen O Metcalf, RI Sch Design, Providence Mus, 39. *Exhib:* Landmarks, American Painting--50 years, Wildenstein Gallery, New York, 50; Painters under 35, Metrop Mus Art, 50; Biennale Venezia, 52 & 58; Carnegie Inst Int, Pittsburgh, Pa, 52 & 58; New Decade, Whitney Mus Am Art, 55; Palazzo, Diamanti, Ferrara, Italy, 81; and others. *Awards:* Temple Gold Medal, Pa Acad Fine Arts, 51; Purchase Prize, Univ Ill, 52; Clark Award, Corcoran Gallery Art, Washington, DC, 53. *Bibliog:* Dorothy Seiberling & George Hunt (auth), William Congdon, Life Mag, 4/30/51; Peggy Guggenheim (auth), Pittore di Venezia, Biennale Venezia, 2/53; Emily Genauer (auth), Congdon converted, New York Herald Tribune, 8/21/68; and others. *Mem:* Found Improving Understanding Arts. *Media:* Oil, Pastel. *Publ:* Auth, In My Disc of Gold, Reynal, 62; An Artist, His Art & the Christian Community, 72 & Esistenza-Viaggio di Pittore Americano, 75, Jaca Bk, Italy; Congdon: A Life, Selz Licht Balzaretti, 92. *Mailing Add:* Via Marconi 33 20090 Buccinasco Milan Italy

CONGER, CLEMENT E
CURATOR
b Rockingham, Va, Oct 15, 12. *Study:* Strayer Col, grad, 32; George Washington Univ, 33-34; Adjutant Gen Officer's Candidate Sch, grad, 43; Col William & Mary, DHL, 77. *Pos:* Cur, Diplomatic Reception Rooms, US State Dept, 61-92, White House, 70-86 & Blair House, 76-92; trustee, Va Mus Fine Arts, Richmond, formerly & Treasury Hist Asn, currently; chmn, Fine Arts Comt, US Dept State, 61- & Supreme Ct Hist Soc Acquisitions Comt, currently; pres, Va Trust Hist Preserv, currently. *Awards:* Award For Excellence, Decorative Arts Trust, 87; Henry Francis DuPont Award & Gold Medal, Winterthur, 92; Secy State's Distinguished Serv Award & Gold Medal, 92; and many others. *Mem:* Nat Trust Hist Preserv; Hist Comt Supreme Ct; Int Orgn Experts, Paris France; Soc of the Cincinnati; Lee-Jackson Found (vpres); and others. *Mailing Add:* 320 Mansion Dr Alexandria VA 22302

CONGER, WILLIAM
PAINTER, EDUCATOR
b Dixon, Ill, May 29, 37. *Study:* Art Inst Chicago, 56-57; Univ NMex, with Elaine deKooning, BFA, 61; Univ Chicago, MFA, 66. *Work:* Mus Contemp Art, Chicago; Art Inst Chicago; Ill State Mus, Springfield; Jonson Mus, Albuquerque; Portland Mus, Wash. *Comn:* Painting for IBM Corp, 86. *Exhib:* Chicago & Vicinity, Art Inst Chicago, 63, 71, 73, 78, 80-81 & 84-85; one-man shows, Krannert Ctr Performing Arts, Urbana, Ill, 76, Zaks Gallery, Chicago, 78, 80 & 83 & Boyd Gallery, Chicago, 85, 87, 90 & 92; Visions-Painting & Sculpture of Distinguished Alumni 1945 to present, Art Inst Chicago Sch Gallery, 76; Abstract Art in Chicago, Mus Contemp Art, 76; Chicago Connection, Nat Traveling Exhib, 76-77; Chicago: Some Other Traditions, Nat Traveling Exhib, 83-85; Conger, Paschke, Valerjo, Block Gallery, NWestern Univ, Evanston, Ill, 86; Chicago Abstractionists, Grae Gallery, St Louis, Mo, 87; Partners in Purchase, Lakeview Mus, Ill, 90; Albuquerque '50s, Univ Mus, Albuquerque, 90; Janus Gallery, Santa Fe, 92; and many others. *Pos:* Mem bd dirs, Oxbow, Saugatuk, Mich, 83-86; adv bd, Renaissance Soc, 88- *Teaching:* Prof art, DePaul Univ, Chicago, 71-85, chmn dept, 71-77 & 80-85; vis artist, Univ Southern Ill, 84, Sch of Art Inst Chicago, 85; prof & chmn dept art theory & practice, NWestern Univ, Evanston, Ill, 85- *Awards:* Bartels Prize, 71 & Cluseman Prize, 73, Art Inst Chicago; Ill Acad Fine Arts Award Nominee, Chicago, 92. *Bibliog:* C L Morrison (auth), article, Artforum, 76 & 78; M Gedo (auth), articles, Arts Mag, 82 & 83; C Lyon (auth), article, Art News, 84; C Moser (auth), article, Art in Am & Art News, 85; Lucie E Smith (auth), article, Am Art Now, 85; Michael Bonesteel (auth), William Conger, Art in Am, 11/85; M Gedo (auth), The meaning of artistic form & the promise of the psychoanalytic method, Vol 2, No 3, Art Criticism, 86; Carol Volk (auth), Art & Antiques, 4/92; and many others. *Mem:* Col Art Asn Am; Arts Club Chicago. *Media:* Acrylic, Oil. *Publ:* Looking & dreaming in New York & Chicago, No 1, Chicago/Art/Write, 85 & Abstract painting: Fact, fiction, paradox, No 2, & Art Limits, No 4, 87; Drawing, No 13, WhiteWalls, 86; The Journal of Eugene Delacroix, Psychoanalytic Studies of Biog, Int Univs Press Inc, 87. *Dealer:* Roy Boyd Gallery 739 N Wells St Chicago IL 60610; Janus Gallery 225 Canyon Rd Santa Fe NM 87501. *Mailing Add:* 3500 N Lake Shore Dr Chicago IL 60657

CONKLIN, ANDREW STERRETT
PAINTER
b Chicago, Ill, July 2, 61. *Study:* Am Acad Art, AFA, 82; Nat Acad Design, with Harvey Dinnerstein and Ronald Sherr, Cert, 84; Art Students League, 85. *Work:* Nat Acad Design Sch Fine Arts, New York. *Comn:* Portrait, Greek Orthodox Church of N & SAm, New York, 86; Princeton Univ, NJ, 92. *Exhib:* Ann Exhib, Union League, Chicago, Ill, 82; 73rd Ann & 74th Ann Exhibs, Allied Artists of Am, 86 & 87; 161st, 165th & 167th Ann Exhibs, Nat Acad Design, New York, 86 & 90; 48th Ann Exhib Aububon Artists, New York, 90; Acad-Inst Invitational Exhib, Am Acad & Inst Arts & Lett, 91; Century Collectors' Show, Century Asn, 92. *Teaching:* Instr, Parsons Sch Design, New York, 91- *Awards:* Elizabeth Greenshields Found Grant, 85 & 91; Paul Puzinas Award, Allied Artists of Am, 86; John F & Anna Lee Stacy Scholarship Award, 88; Julius Hallgarten Prize, Nat Acad Design, 92. *Bibliog:* Philip Eliasoph (auth), --Hasting takes academic bow, Advocate Greenwich Times, 5/25/86; Louise Neville Jones (auth), Artists work to achieve--, Review Press-Reporter, 3/2/89; Jonathon Phillips (auth), Realism at Frank Caro, Art World, 3/24/89. *Mem:* NY Artists Equity; Allied Artists Am. *Media:* Oil. *Publ:* Figures in an underground landscape, Am Artist Mag, 12/91. *Dealer:* Gitte Blass One Orchard Pl Bronxville NY 10708. *Mailing Add:* c/o Portraits Inc 985 Park Ave New York NY 10028

CONKLIN, GLORIA ZAMKO
PAINTER
b Detroit, Mich, Feb 6, 25. *Study:* Am Acad Art, Chicago, cert, 45; Art Inst Chicago, 46; Critique Professional Artists with Theodoros Stamos, 71-90; Art

Students League, 76. *Work:* Smithsonian Collection, Washington, DC; Peat, Marwick & Mitchell, New York; Johnson & Higgins, New York; Scarsdale Bank, Scarsdale, NY; Greenwich Develop Corp, Conn; Reichold Chemical Corp, White Plains, NBW Div, White Plains, NY; Reuben H Donnelley, Conn; Chase Manhattan Bank; Great Northern Nekoosa Corp. *Exhib:* Bruce Mus, Greenwich, Conn, 74; 23rd Ann Juried Exhib, White Plains, NY, 76; Bridge Gallery Westchester, White Plains, NY, 78; Ikones Group, Stamford Mus, Conn, 79; 155th Ann, Nat Acad Design, New York, 80; Nat Asn Women Artists, New York, 80, 83, 85, 87 & 89; Pindar Gallery, New York, 86. *Bibliog:* Helen Thomas (auth), article, Arts Mag, 10/77. *Mem:* Nat Asn Women Artists; Artists Equity New York. *Media:* Acrylic, Pastel. *Dealer:* The Wind Mueller Gallery 15 Chesterfield Rd Scarsdale NY 10583. *Mailing Add:* 104 Ellinson Ct Williamsburg VA 23185

CONLEY, ZEB BRISTOL, JR
COLLECTOR, GALLERY DIRECTOR
b Andrews, NC, Feb 12, 36. *Study:* Mars Hill Col, 55-57; Col William & Mary, 57-61; NMex Highlands Univ, 63. *Collections Arranged:* Alfred Murang Retrospective, Mus of the Southwest, Midland, Tex, 85. *Pos:* Dir, Jamison Galleries, Santa Fe, 73-, bd mem, 74-, pres, 81-; guest cur, Mus of the Southwest, Midland, Tex, 85. *Specialty:* Traditional Southwestern art, specializing in Taos and Santa Fe masters. *Mailing Add:* Jamison Galleries 111 E San Francisco St Santa Fe NM 87501

CONLON, JAMES EDWARD
SCULPTOR, HISTORIAN
b Cincinnati, Ohio, Dec 9, 35. *Study:* Ohio State Univ, BS(art educ), 59, MA(fine arts), 62. *Work:* Fine Arts Mus South Mobile; Fine Arts Mus of York, Ala; Symbiotic Series, Mobile Arts Coun; Moses, Springhill Ave Temple, Mobile, Ala. *Comn:* Three Angels (wall relief), Seventh Day Adventist Church, St Elmo, Ala, 82; design & execution of competition awards for Am Drug-Free Powerlifting Asn, 82; sculptural relief, Mobile, Ala Airport; Design & Execution of the Ceremonial Mace, Univ South Ala; Gateway, Cathedral Sq, Mobile Arts Coun & Mainstreet Mobile, Ala, 93. *Exhib:* Southern Asn Sculptors Traveling Exhib, Smithsonian Inst; Competition 75, Mobile, Ala, 75; two-person show, Fine Arts Mus South-Mobile, 77; Montgomery Mus Art, 78-79; Alabama Sculptors Invitational, 80. *Teaching:* Instr, Ind Univ, Bloomington, 62-65; from asst prof to assoc prof, Univ S Ala, Mobile, 65-73, prof, 74- *Awards:* Award to Develop the Ethnic Am Art Slide Libr, Samuel H Kress Found, 72-75; Award to Produce a Res Index of Afro-Am Art, Am Revolution Bicentennial Comn, 73; Univ Res Grant, 76-77. *Mem:* Southern Asn Sculptors; Southeastern Col Art Asn (vpres, 74-75). *Media:* Woods, Limestone; Cast & Laminated Plastics. *Res:* An investigation of stylistic development in Afro-American, Mexican American and Native American art from 1800 to the present; adaptation of the industrial process of cultured marble to the production of hollow-cast figurative forms 1983-1986. *Publ:* Coauth, An Afro-American slide project, Col Art Asn J, winter 70. *Mailing Add:* PO Box 781 Middle Earth Rd Citronelle AL 36522

CONN, DAVID EDWARD
PRINTMAKER, PAINTER
b Jersey City, NJ, Apr 10, 41. *Study:* Newark Sch Fine Arts, NJ; Md Inst Col Art, Baltimore, BFA, with Peter Milton; Univ Okla, Norman, MFA. *Work:* Ark Art Ctr, Little Rock; Ft Worth Art Mus, Tex; Modern Mus Art, Campinas Sao Paulo, Brazil. *Exhib:* 20th Exhib Southwestern Prints & Drawings, Dallas Mus Art, 75; 17th Int Biennial Graphic Art, Mus Modern Art, Ljubljana, Yugoslavia, 87; Texas Visions, Mus Art Am Southwest, Houston, 86; Joslyn Art Mus, 78; 1984 Int Art Competition, Los Angeles; 4th Int Exhib, Lodz, Poland; Int Prints II, John Szoke Graphics Gallery, New York, 88. *Pos:* Chmn dept art & art hist, Tex Christian Univ, 90- *Teaching:* Prof art-printmaking, Tex Christian Univ, 69- *Awards:* Ford Fel, Painting, 65; Purchase Award, Ark Print, Drawing & Crafts, Ark Art Ctr, 71; Visual Arts Fel, Nat Endowment Arts, 85-86. *Bibliog:* American Printmakers 74--Graphics Group, Arcadia, Calif, 74. *Media:* Intaglio, Oil. *Mailing Add:* Dept Art & Art Hist PO Box 30793 Tex Christian Univ Ft Worth TX 76129

CONN, LAURENCE
CURATOR, PAINTER
b Chicago, Ill, 1945. *Study:* Univ Ill, Chicago, 63-64; Chicago Acad Fine Arts, BFA, 64-68. *Work:* Jones, Day, Reavis & Pogue & First Nat Bank, Chicago; Billy Graham Ctr Mus, Wheaton, Ill; Burroughs Corp, New York; Ingersol Rand Corp, Rockford, Ill; Shea Archit, Minneapolis. *Exhib:* Wisconsin Directions II, Milwaukee Art Ctr, 78; System & Structure, UW Wis Green Bay, 83, Priebe Art Ctr, Oshkosh, 83,Burpee Art Mus, Rockford, Ill, 83, Ukranian Inst Mod Art, Chicago, 84; Contemp Spiritual Art, Washington DC, 88; Sacred Arts, Billy Graham Mus, Wheaton, Ill, 90; Univ NMex, Albuquerque, 90. *Pos:* Cur currently, Franklin Sq Gallery, Ancient Echoes Collection, Richard J Daley Col Gallery & Space 900. *Media:* Acrylic, Graphite. *Dealer:* Deson Saunders Gallery Chicago IL; Anderson & Anderson Gallery, Minneapolis MN. *Mailing Add:* 900 N Franklin Chicago IL 60610

CONN, RICHARD GEORGE
CURATOR
b Bellingham, Wash, Oct 28, 28. *Study:* Univ Wash, Seattle, BA, 50, MA, 55. *Collections Arranged:* Approx 40 temporary exhibs, EWash State Hist Soc, Spokane, 59-66; Robes of White Shell and Sunrise (auth, catalog), Denver Art Mus, 74; Circles of the World (auth, catalog), Denver Art Mus, 82; A Persistent Vision (auth, catalog), Denver Art Mus, 86; Les Indiens d'Amerique (auth, catalog), Paris, 87; Die Kultur der Indianer Nordamerikas (auth, catalog), Bonn, 87. *Pos:* Cur of native art, Denver Art Mus, 55-59 & 71; dir, EWash State Hist Soc, Spokane, 59-66; chief of human hist, Man Mus, Winnipeg, Can, 66-70. *Teaching:* Adj prof native Am art, Univ Colo, Denver, 73- *Awards:* John J McCloy Found fel, 79. *Mem:* Am Asn Mus. *Res:* Native American art, all geographic areas, with special emphasis on native clothing and decoration. *Publ:* Auth, Native American Art in the Denver Art Museum, 79. *Mailing Add:* Curator Native Arts Denver Art Mus 100 W 14th Ave Pkwy Denver CO 80204

CONNATSER, LARRY STUART
PAINTER
b Birmingham, Ala, Sept 17, 38. *Study:* Vanderbilt Univ, BA(Eng lit), 61. *Work:* High Mus, Atlanta; Telfair Acad Mus, Savannah, Ga; Columbia Mus Art, SC; Ga Inst Technol, Atlanta; Vanderbilt Univ, Nashville. *Comn:* 91 Exchange Place (mural), Atlanta Urban Walls, 76; Carriage House (mural), Savannah Hist Dist, Ga, 79; Decatur Marta Sta, Metrop Rapid Transit, Atlanta, 81; Libr mural, Savannah Col Art & Design, Ga, 82; mural ser, St Joseph Hosp, Atlanta, 91. *Exhib:* Chicago & Vicinity Show, Chicago Art Inst, Ill, 66; New Paintings, Newark Mus, NJ, 67; Chicago Paintings, Ga State Univ, Atlanta, 68; one-man shows, Telfair Acad, Savannah, Ga, 72, Columbia Mus, SC, 76, New Southern Painting Gallery, Savannah, Ga, 88 & Art View Gallery, Atlanta, 91; Ga Artists Show, High Mus Art, Atlanta, 75. *Awards:* Poster Design Award, Atlanta Arts Festival, 84; Best Show, Southern Homes Regional Invitational, Atlanta, 88. *Bibliog:* Carlyn Fisher (prod), Four Georgia Artists (film), Ga Pub Television, 75. *Media:* Acrylic. *Dealer:* New Southern Paintings 111 E Gwinnett Savannah GA. *Mailing Add:* c/o David Fraley PO Box 1123 Decatur GA 30031

CONNEEN, JANE W
PRINTMAKER, MINIATURIST
b Montclair, NJ, April 19, 21. *Study:* With George Parker, Emily Hatch, Sally Kugelmeyer & David Sander; Lehigh Univ. *Work:* Hunt Inst Botanical Doc, Pittsburgh, Pa; Mus City New York; Am Tel & Tel Long Lines, Bedminster, NJ. *Comn:* Drawings, Allentown Art Mus, Pa, 75 & Pa Chamber Commerce, Harrisburg, 76. *Exhib:* Solo exhib, Lehigh Univ & Kemerer Mus, Bethlehem, Pa, 85; Miniature Painters Sculptors & Gravers Soc, Washington, DC, 76-92; Philadelphia Print Club, 82; Royal Soc Miniature Painters, London, 83; 20-yr Retrospective Exhib, Lehigh Univ, 90. *Awards:* Best in Show & First in Graphics, Am Nat Miniature Show, Laramie, Wyo, 80; First in Graphics, Miniature Painters, Sculptors & Gravers Washington, DC, 83, Miniature Art Soc Fla, 84 & Miniature Art Soc NJ, 85; Distinguished Book award from The Miniature Book Soc, 90. *Bibliog:* Lee Whitfield (auth), Herbs in miniature, Whitchappels Herbal, 80; Louis Bondy (auth), Miniature Books, Sheppard Press, London, 81; Joan M Pursley (auth) A potpourri of prints, Miniature Collector, spring 89. *Mem:* Impressit-Printmakers Group; fel Int Guild Miniature Artisans; Printmaking Coun NJ; Philadelphia Print Club; Miniature Book Soc. *Media:* Hand-Colored Etchings; Pen and Ink, Watercolor. *Publ:* Auth, Member of the issue, Northlight Mag, 78; The Winding Roads of Ireland, 90; The Language of Herbs I & II (miniature bks), 91. *Mailing Add:* The Little Farm 820 Andrews Rd Bath PA 18014

CONNEEN, MARI M
PAINTER, PRINTMAKER
b Allentown, Pa, Dec 21, 46. *Study:* Self taught. *Work:* Lowe Art Mus, Miami, Fla; Pensacola Visual Arts Mus, Fla; Loch Haven Art Ctr, Orlando, Fla; Walt Disney World, Orlando, Fla; Hunt Botanical Inst, Pittsburgh, Pa. *Comn:* Two large watercolors of sea life, Song of Norway Cruise Line, Miami, Fla, 87. *Exhib:* Allied Artists of Am 85th Watercolor Exhib, Nat Arts Club, New York, 84; Adirondacks Nat Exhib, Old Forge Art Ctr, 84, 85, 86, 87 & 88; Watercolor Exhib, Mus on Hudson, 85; Int Exhib, Mathes Cult Ctr, Escondido, Calif, 87; Miss Watercolor Exhib, Mus Art Jackson, 87; Okla Watercolor Exhib, Okla Art Ctr, 87. *Awards:* Best of Show, Winter Park Art Festival & Coconut Grove Art Festival, 83; Experts Choice, Artist Soc Int, 84. *Mem:* Nat Mus Women in Arts; Am Artist Prof League; Guild Natural Sci Illusr; Southern Watercolor Soc; Nat Watercolor Soc. *Media:* Watercolor; Lithography. *Publ:* Auth, Watercolor '86, Am Artists, 86; Artists of Florida, Mountain Productions, 87, Southern Accents, 12/90. *Dealer:* J Lawrence Gallery 1010 E New Haven Ave Melbourne FL 32901; Grand Cent Art Galleries Inc 24 W 57th Ave New York NY 10019. *Mailing Add:* 441 N Harbour City Blvd No 1 Apt 14 C Melbourne FL 32935

CONNELLY, CHUCK
PAINTER
b Pittsburgh, Pa, 1955. *Study:* Tyler Sch Art, Philadelphia, Pa, BFA, 77. *Work:* Metro Mus Art, New York; Brooklyn Mus Art, New York; Portland Art Mus, Ore. *Exhib:* New Narrative Painting, Museo Tamayo, Mexico City, Mex, 84; solo exhib, Northern Ill Univ Art Gallery, Chicago, 84-85; Aldrich Mus Contemp Art, Ridgefield, Conn, 84 & 86; Painting & Sculpture Today, Indianapolis Mus Art, Ind, 86; Nassau Co Mus Art, Roslyn, NY, 91; Tucson Mus Art, Ariz, 92. *Bibliog:* Grace Glueck (auth), article, New York Times, 10/12/84; Michael Brenson (auth), article, New York Times, ll/29/85; Barry Schwabsky (auth), article, Arts Mag, 2/86; Eleanor Hartney (auth), article, Art in America, 5/92; Edith Newhall (auth), article, Artnews, 4/92. *Media:* Oil. *Dealer:* Lennon-Weinberg Inc 580 Broadway 2nd fl New York NY 10012. *Mailing Add:* c/o Lennon-Weinberg 580 Broadway 2nd fl New York NY 10012

CONNER, ANN
PRINTMAKER, PAINTER
b Wilmington, NC, Aug 11, 48. *Study:* Salem Col, NC, BFA, 70; Salem-Hofstra Summer Prog, Asolo, Italy, 70; Univ NC, Chapel Hill, MACT, 72,

MFA, 75. *Work:* Amon Carter Mus, Ft Worth, Tex; Calif Palace of Legion of Honor, San Francisco, Ca; Nat Gallery Art, Washington, DC; Equitable Life Insurance Ctr, New York; Libr Cong, Washington, DC; NY Pub Libr, New York; Philip Morris USA. *Comn:* Cinnamon, Philip Morris USA, Charlotte, NC, 81. *Exhib:* 17th Int Independante Exhib of Prints, Kanagawa Prefectural Gallery, Yokahama, Japan, 92; 11th Int Biennial Woodcuts, Cent Slovak Gallery, Banská Bystricia, Czech, 91; Woodcuts, Wenniger Graphics, Boston, 92; Bounty from the Block, Elvehjem Mus, Madison, Wis, 93; and others. *Teaching:* Prof painting, Univ NC, Wilmington, 72- *Awards:* Res & Develop Grant, Univ NC, Wilmington, 89-90 & 92; Emerging Artist Grand, NC, 90; NC Governor's Bus Award Ed, 91. *Bibliog:* Hedy O'Beil (auth), Arts reviews: Ann Conner, Arts Mag, 10/76; Judith Dunham (auth), Recent prints: Ann Conner, 11-12/84 & Woodcut joins the mainstream, spring 86, Print News. *Mem:* World Print Coun; Southern Graphics Coun; Los Angeles Printmaking Soc; Print Club, Pa; Print Consortium; Col Art Asn Am. *Media:* Woodcut; Acrylic, oil. *Publ:* The New York Art Review, Les Krantz, 88; Modern Graphics, Art of the 80's, Libr Congress, 89; Printworld Directory of Contemp Prints, 85-86, 88-89 & 93; The Complete Manual of Relief Printmaking, Kindersley, 88; Print News, Prints from Blocks, 85. *Dealer:* John Szoke Graphics Inc 164 Mercer St New York NY 10012. *Mailing Add:* 329 Stradleigh Rd Wilmington NC 28403

CONNER, BRUCE
GRAPHIC ARTISTS, COLLAGE ARTIST
b McPherson, Kans, Nov 18, 33. *Study:* Wichita Univ; Univ Nebr, BFA; Brooklyn Mus Art Sch; Univ Colo; San Francisco Art Inst, Hon DFA, 86. *Work:* Guggenheim Mus, Whitney Mus Am Art, Mus Mod Art, New York; Art Inst Chicago; Los Angeles Co Art Mus, Norton Simon Mus, Los Angeles; Rose Art Mus, Brandeis Univ, Waltham Addison Gallery, Andover, Mass; San Francisco Mus Mod Art, Calif. *Comn:* Poster, New York Film Festival, Am Fedn Arts, 65. *Exhib:* The Art of Assemblage, Mus Mod Art, New York, 60; Whitney Biannual, Whitney Mus Am Art, 82; Retrospective, Inst Contemp Art, Univ Pa, 67 & de Young Mem Mus, San Francisco, 74; American Sculpture of the Sixties, Los Angeles Co Art Mus, 67; Belly-Button Art of the Seventies, Newport Harbor Art Gallery, 72; Tyler Mus Art, Tex, 74; Smith-Andersen Gallery, Palo Alto, Calif, 74, 84 & 86; de Young Mem Mus, 75; one-person show, Northpoint Gallery, San Francisco, Calif, 81, Smith Andersen Gallery, Palo Alto, Calif, 84 & 86, Michael Kohn Gallery, Santa Monica, Calif, 90. *Pos:* Pres & founder, Rat Bastard Protective Asn, San Francisco, 58-61; dir, bd dirs, Canyon Cinema Coop, San Francisco, 69-72 & 85. *Teaching:* Instr film making, Calif Col Arts & Crafts, 65-66; undergrad sem, Wasted Time, San Francisco Art Inst, 66-67. *Awards:* Nat Endowment Arts, 84; Mus Contemp Art Grant, 84; Calif Tamarack Found Grant, 85. *Bibliog:* Carl Belz (auth), 3 films by Bruce Conner, Film Cult Mag, spring 67; Anthony Reveaux (auth), Bruce Conner (films), Film in the Cities, 81. *Mem:* Artists Equity. *Media:* Ink on Paper, Engraving Collage. *Publ:* Coauth, Bruce Conner/Mike McClure, Averhahn Press, 67; auth, The Dennis Hopper One-Man Show, Crown Point Press, Vols I-III, 71-73. *Dealer:* Michael Kohn Gallery 920 Colorado Ave Santa Monica CA 90401; Smith Andersen Gallery 200 Homer St Palo Alto CA 94301. *Mailing Add:* Smith Andersen Gallery 200 Homer Ave Palo Alto CA 94301

CONNER, LOIS
PHOTOGRAPHER
b Long Island, NY, Feb 12, 51. *Study:* Pratt Inst, BFA, 75; Yale Univ, MFA, 81. *Work:* Mus Mod Art & Metrop Mus Art, New York; Smithsonian Inst, Nat Mus Art, Washington, DC; Victoria & Albert Mus, London, Eng; Nat Gallery Victoria, Melbourne, Australia. *Comn:* Wave Hill, Botanical Gardens, New York, 90; The Cuyahoga River, Gund Found, Cleveland, Ohio, 91. *Exhib:* Photographs from the Collection, Victoria & Albert Mus, London, Eng, 87; Photographs of China, Canton Art Mus, China, 88; China, Cleveland Mus Art, Ohio, 88; Landscapes, Bombay Ctr Photog, Bombay, India, 90; In the Shadow of the Wall (auth, catalog), Taiwan Mus Art, Taichung, Rep China, 92; Between Heaven & Home, Smithsonian Inst, Washington, DC, 92; Mus Mod Art, New York, 92. *Teaching:* Adj prof photog, Fordham Univ, New York, & Cooper Union, New York, 91; asst prof photog, Yale Univ, New Haven, Conn, 91- *Awards:* Fel, Nat Endowment Arts, 83; Guggenheim Fel, 84; Fel, NY State Coun Arts, 79. *Bibliog:* Dang Ho Liu (auth), In the Shadow of the Wall, Taiwan Mus Art, 92. *Dealer:* Laurence Miller Gallery 138 Spring St New York NY 10012. *Mailing Add:* 36 Gramercy Park E No 4-E New York NY 10003

CONNETT, DEE M
EDUCATOR, PRINTMAKER
b Mulvane, Kans, May 25, 35. *Study:* Kans State Teachers Col, BS(art educ), 53; Wichita State Univ, MA, 64; Am Univ, Mex, 64; art sem, Florence, Italy & Athens, Greece, 84; England, 86. *Work:* Wichita Art Mus, Kans; Nebr Wesleyan Univ, Lincoln; Centre House, Swannanoa, NC; MacCray Gallery, Western NMex State Univ, Silver City. *Comn:* Paintings, Litwin Enterprises, Wichita, 70. *Exhib:* Juror's Selection Kans Post ACACK Series II & III, Topeka, 79-80; 15th Ann Nat Drawing & Small Sculpture Show, Del Mar Col, Corpus Christi, Tex, 81; Kans Artist's Comn finalist Touring Exhib, Topeka, 81; Juried Show for Kans Artists, 82 & 86; Tom Millea Photographic Competition, Danbury, Conn, 83; Kans Black & White Show, Wichita, 85; Juried Show, Kansas City Artist Coalition, 86; Nat Sacred Arts' (Ten shows), Wheaton, Fla, 88; Nat Invitational Computer Imagery Show, Silver City, NMex, 92. *Pos:* Mem, Fine Arts Coun Comt, Wichita, 66-81; bd mem, Wichita Art Mus, 66-91; mem, Century II Sculpture Planning Comt, Wichita, 70-72; mem, Metrop Arts Bd, Wichita, 78-81; bd mem, Wichita Artist Guild, 88-91; Hutchinston Art Asn bd, 92- *Teaching:* Instr art, Wichita Pub Schs, 57-64; chmn dept art & prof, Friends Univ, Wichita, 66-91, distinguished chair prof, 85-91, Wichita Art Mus, 69-70; chmn dept fine arts, Community Col, Hutchinson, 91- *Awards:* Outstanding Teacher of Year Award, Friends Univ, 70; Juried Show for Kans Artists Merit Award, 82; Distinguished Chair Prof, Friends Univ, 85. *Bibliog:* Dorothy Belden (auth), Wichita Eagle, 8/81; Reimer & Brooks (auth), Framing the Artist: A Social Portrait of Mid-American Artists, 82. *Mem:* Kans Artist-Craftsmen Asn; Hutchinson Art Asn Bd; Kans Arts Commun Arts Alliance Bd. *Media:* Silkscreen, Computer Graphics. *Publ:* Illusr, Errol Elliot's Sing the Faith, 75 & Deepening Stream, 82; Friends and the Visual Arts, 82; Mennonite Mag, Can, 83. *Dealer:* Reuben Saunders Gallery 825 N Washinton Wichita KS 67202. *Mailing Add:* 1817 E 24th Ave No 7 Hutchinson KS 67502-1151

CONNIFF, GREGORY
PHOTOGRAPHER, WRITER
b Jersey City, NJ, May 3, 44. *Study:* Columbia Univ, BA, 66; Univ Va Law Sch, LLB, 69; with William Weege (printmaker), 71-72. *Work:* Mus Mod Art, New York; Ctr Creative Photogr, Tucson, Ariz; Mus Fine Arts, Boston, Mass; Baltimore Mus Art, Md; Corcoran Gallery Art, Washington, DC. *Exhib:* Solo exhibs, Corcoran Gallery Art, Washington, DC, 79 Toledo Mus Art, 83, Akron Art Mus, 86, Ohio & Mus Contemp Photogr, Chicago, Ill, 86; Contemporary Photographs, Fogg Art Mus, Cambridge, Mass, 80; A Century of Landscape, High Mus Art, Atlanta, Ga, 81; The Lens in the Garden, Hudson River Mus, Yonkers, NY, 84; two-man show, Two Days in Louisiana, Milwaukee Art Mus, Wis, 89. *Pos:* Consult ed (landscape), Johns Hopkins Univ Press. *Awards:* Nat Endowment Arts Photog Fel, 80-81, 92-93; Wis Arts Bd Visual Arts Fel, 78, 84 & 90; Nat Endowment Arts Int Exchange Fel, 92-93. *Bibliog:* Jane Livingston (auth), Gregory Conniff, Corcoran Gallery Art, 79; David Tannous (auth), Gregory Conniff, Art Am, summer 80; Kent Williams (auth), In His Own Image, Isthmus, 11/24/89. *Publ:* Auth & illusr, Common Ground: Vol 1 of an American Field Guide, Yale Univ Press, 85. *Mailing Add:* 1426 Rutledge St Madison WI 53703

CONNOLLY, JEROME PATRICK
PAINTER, MURALIST
b Minneapolis, Minn, Jan 14, 31. *Study:* Univ Minn, BS(art educ); also with Francis Lee Jaques. *Work:* Diorama backgrounds & murals in 36 mus, incl Carnegie Mus, Pittsburgh, James Ford Bell Mus, Minneapolis, George C Page Mus, Los Angeles, Smithsonian Mus Nat Hist, Taipei Zoo Educ Bldg, Taiwan & many others. *Exhib:* Sportsman's Gallery of Art & Bks, New York; Crossroads of Sport, New York; Abercrombie & Fitch, New York & San Francisco; Petersen Gallery, Los Angeles; one-man show, Abercrombie & Fitch, New York, 72; and others. *Pos:* Staff artist, Ill State Mus, Springfield, 58-60, Natural Sci Youth Found, Westport, Conn, 60-65. *Media:* Oil, Acrylic. *Publ:* Illusr, Adelbert the Penguin, 69; The Deer Family, 69; Aise-ce-bon: a Raccoon, 71; Saga of a Whitetail, 81; 15 children's books & contribr, Audubon Mag, Nat Wildlife, Hartford Life Insurance Co calendar & Pa Game News. *Mailing Add:* 102 S US 11-15 Selinsgrove PA 17870

CONNOR, LINDA STEVENS
PHOTOGRAPHER, INSTRUCTOR
b New York, NY, Nov 18, 44. *Study:* RI Sch Design, BFA, with Harry Calahan; Inst Design, Ill Inst Technol, MS, with Aaron Siskind. *Work:* Boston Mus Fine Arts, Mass; Art Inst Chicago; Int Mus Photog, George Eastman House, Rochester, NY; Mus of Mod Art, New York; San Francisco Mus Mod Art, Calif. *Exhib:* one-person shows, Visual Studies Gallery, Rochester, NY, 76, Ctr Photographic Studies, 76 & de Young Mem Mus, San Francisco, 77, Art Inst Chicago, Ill, 88 & Spiral Journey Mus Contemp Photography Chicago, Ill, 89; Vision Gallery, Boston, 81; Light Gallery, New York, 81; Corcoran Gallery Art, Washington, DC, 82; Calif Mus Photog, Riverside, 83; San Francisco Mus Mod Art, 92. *Teaching:* Prof, San Francisco Art Inst, 69. *Awards:* Nat Endowment Arts Grant, 76, 88; Guggenheim Fel, 79; Peer Award, Friends of Photog, 86; Charles Pratt Memorial Award in Photog, 88. *Mem:* Soc for Photographic Educ; Friends Photog. *Media:* Photography. *Publ:* American Images, McGraw-Hill, 79; contribr, Linda Connor, Corcoran Gallery Art, 82; Calif Mus Photog Bul, Vol 2, No 2; Marks in Place, Univ NMex Press, 87; Spiral Journey, Contemp Mus Photog, Chicago, 90; Women in Photog, Abrams, 90. *Dealer:* Scheinbaum & Russek 328 Guadalupe Santa Fe NMex 87501; Greenberg Gallery 120 Wooster New York NY 10012. *Mailing Add:* 87 Rutherford San Anselmo CA 94960

CONOVER, CLAUDE
SCULPTOR, CERAMIST
b Pittsburgh, Pa, Dec 15, 07. *Study:* Cleveland Inst Art, grad cert. *Work:* Cleveland Mus Art, Ohio; Everson Mus Art, Syracuse, NY; Utah Mus Fine Arts, Salt Lake City; Philadelphia Mus Art; Newark Mus, Newark, NJ; and others. *Exhib:* Ann Exhib Works by Artists & Craftsmen of the Western Reserve, Cleveland Mus Art, 14 yrs; Ceramic Nat, Everson Mus Art, four biennials; Ann Ohio Ceramic & Sculpture Show, Butler Inst Am Art, Youngstown, Ohio (12 shows); Beaux Arts Designer-Craftsmen Biennial Exhibs, Columbus Mus Art, Ohio (4 shows); Objects USA Traveling Exhib, US & Europe; plus numerous one-man & invitational group exhibs. *Pos:* Graphic designer, several art studios in Cleveland, Ohio, 30-57; sculptor, 30-57; sculptor-ceramist, pvt studio, 57- *Awards:* Governor's Award, Columbus Mus Art, 68; 10 Spec Jury Awards, Ann Shows, Cleveland Mus Art; Visual Arts Award, Cleveland, 83. *Bibliog:* Roger Bonham (auth), Claude Conover, Ceramics Mo, 5/66. *Mem:* Am Crafts Coun. *Mailing Add:* 1860 Oakmount Rd Cleveland OH 44121-4046

CONOVER, ROBERT FREMONT
PRINTMAKER, PAINTER
b Trenton, NJ, July 3, 20. *Study:* Philadelphia Mus Sch Art; Art Students League; Brooklyn Mus Sch. *Work:* Smithsonian Inst, Libr Cong, Washington, DC; Mus Mod Art, New York Pub Libr, Whitney Mus Am Art, New York; Detroit Inst. *Comn:* Print ed, 200 woodcuts, 57 & 75 woodcuts, 61, Int Graphic Art Soc; print ed, 75 woodcuts, Hilton Hotels, 62; print ed, 30 woodcuts, Assoc Am Artists Galleries, 69; print ed, 60 relief prints, Ferdinand Roten Galleries, 71. *Exhib:* Painters of the 20th Century, Mus Mod Art, New York, 50; Whitney Mus Am Art Ann, 50-54; Carnegie Int, Pittsburgh, 54; Pa Acad Fine Arts Painting Ann, 54; one-man show, New Sch Social Res, New York, 68 & 74; Brooklyn Mus Print Biennial, 70 & 75. *Teaching:* Instr painting & graphics, New Sch Social Res, 51-; instr painting, Brooklyn Mus Sch, 60-; instr graphics, Newark Sch Fine & Indust Arts, 67- *Awards:* Purchase Prizes, Brooklyn Mus, 54, Soc Am Graphic Artists, Assoc Am Artist Gallery, 67 & Philadelphia Print Club; NY State Fel, Creative Artists Pub Serv, 76; Veras List Award, Ed of Twenty Nation Acad, 82 & 84. *Bibliog:* Article, Art in Am, 57; Seuphor (auth), Dictionary of Abstract Painting, 58; Jules Heller (auth), Printmaking Today, Holt, 72. *Mem:* Soc Am Graphic Artists; Am Abstract Artists. *Media:* Oil, Graphics; Woodcut. *Publ:* Auth, American Prints and Printmakers - Una Johnson, Doubleday. *Dealer:* Assoc Am Artists Gallery 663 Fifth Ave New York NY 10022. *Mailing Add:* 162 E 33rd St New York NY 10016

CONRAD, GEORGE
EDUCATOR, PRINTMAKER
b Newark, NJ, Feb 10, 16. *Study:* Newark Sch Fine & Indust Arts; NY Univ, BS; Columbia Univ, MA & EdD. *Work:* Butler Inst Am Art; La Jolla Mus Art; Univ Ga; Columbus Pub Libr, Ohio; Univ Ore; and others. *Comn:* Photography, Nat Gallery Art; photography, Metrop Mus Art, New York. *Exhib:* Artists from NJ, Newark Mus; Independent, New York; NJ Art in Cols, State Mus, NJ. *Pos:* Ed, The Arts, 62-72; mem, NJ Arts Coun, 66-71. *Teaching:* Prof art educ, Ill State Univ, 49-58; chmn dept art, Glassboro State Col, 58-73, prof art hist, 58-79, emer prof, 79- *Mem:* NJ Art Educ Asn (pres, 69); Eastern Arts Asn (coun, 69); Nat Art Educ Asn (state assembly, 69). *Media:* Multiprint, Photography. *Publ:* Auth, The Process of Art Education, Prentice-Hall, 64. *Dealer:* Dumont-Landis Princeton Corp Plaza Monmouth Junction NJ 08852. *Mailing Add:* 163 N Mansfield Blvd Cherry Hill NJ 08034

CONRAD, JOHN W
EDUCATOR, CERAMIST
b Cresson, Pa, Aug 3, 35. *Study:* Ind Univ of Pa, BS; Carnegie-Mellon Univ, Pittsburgh, MFA(ceramics); Univ Pittsburgh, PhD. *Work:* Mesa Col, San Diego, Calif. *Exhib:* Tiffany Invitational, New York, 65; one-man show, Sculpture Gallery, San Diego, Calif, 76; Small Sculptures: Nat Cypress Fine Arts Gallery, Cypress, Calif, 76; Ceramics Design 76, Sculpture Gallery, San Diego, 76; Soup Tureens--1976, Campbell Mus, Camden, NJ, 76. *Pos:* Pres, Ceramic Artists San Diego, 82- & Allied Craftsmen San Diego, 85- *Teaching:* Part time instr, Carnegie Mellon Univ, 60-63; prof ceramics & chmn dept, Mesa Col, San Diego, 66- *Mem:* Col Art Asn; Nat Coun Educ Ceramic Arts; Ceramic Artists San Diego. *Publ:* Auth, Ceramic Formulas: The Complete Compendium, MacMillan, 73; Contemporary Ceramic Techniques, Prentice-Hall, 77; Contemporary Ceramic Formulas, MacMillan, 80; Ceramic Windchimes, 85, Advance Ceramic Manual, 88 & Cone Six Ceramics, 93, Falcon Co; Studio Ceramic Dict, 90. *Mailing Add:* 770 Cole Ranch Rd Encinitas CA 92024

CONRAD, NANCY R
PAINTER
b Houston, Tex, Jan 29, 40. *Study:* Houston Mus Fine Arts; Randolph Macon Woman's Col, BA. *Work:* Randolph Macon Collection Am Women Painters, Harris Co Libr System, Houston, Tex; El Paso Mus Fine Arts, Tex; Continental Oil Co Collection & Dresser Indust Collection, Houston; Aviation Am Bldg, Love Field, Dallas; Allied Bank Group. *Comn:* Paintings, Tex Commerce Banks; Allied Bank Systems, First City Banks, 84-85; Stauffer Hotel, Trammel Crow Properties, Austin, Tex, 86. *Exhib:* Sun Carnival Exhib, El Paso Mus Fine Arts, 73-75; Tex Painting & Sculpture, Dallas Mus Fine Arts; 52nd Ann Nat Exhib, Shreveport, La, 74; Nat Women's Year Exhib, 79; Women & Their Work, touring show, 80-81; Staged & Stages, Blaffer Gallery, Univ Houston, 85; Texas Visions, 86. *Teaching:* Pvt instr, currently. *Awards:* Foley Award, Foley's of Houston, 70; First Place Jurors Choice, Assistance League of Houston, 73; Purchase Award, El Paso Mus Art, 73. *Bibliog:* Articles in Southwest Art Mag, Art Mag, Art Voices South, & Artweek Newspaper; San Francisco, Texas Artist, Vol II. *Mem:* Art League Houston (vpres, 74-75); Artists Equity Asn. *Media:* Watercolor, Oil. *Mailing Add:* 819 Wade Hampton Houston TX 77024

CONRAD, PAUL FRANCIS
CARTOONIST, SCULPTOR
b Cedar Rapids, Iowa, June 27, 24. *Study:* Univ Iowa, BA, 50. *Exhib:* Bronze sculptures & cartoons, Los Angeles Co Mus Art, 79. *Pos:* Ed cartoonist, Denver Post, 50-64, Los Angeles Times, 64-; cartoonist, Los Angeles Times Syndicate; lectr, Cooke-Daniels Lectr Tours, Denver Art Mus, 64. *Awards:* Sigma Delta Chi Award, 63, 69, 71, 81, 82 & 87; Pulitzer Prize Ed Cartooning, 64, 71 & 84; Overseas Press Club Award, 71 & 81; Robert F Kennedy Award, 85, 90 & 92; Fel, Soc Prof Journalists; Hugh Hefner First Amendment Award, Print Journalism, 90. *Media:* Pen, Ink; Bronze. *Publ:* Coauth (with Malcolm Boyd), When in the Course of Human Events, Sheed and Ward, 73; auth, The King and Us, Clymer Publ, 74; Pro and Conrad, Neff-Kane/Presido Press, 79; Drawn and Quartered, Harry N Abrams, 85. *Mailing Add:* Times Mirror Sq Los Angeles CA 90053

CONSAGRA, PIER
PAINTER
b Rome, Italy, 1954. *Study:* RI Sch Design, Brown Univ, BA. *Work:* US Trust, New York; Steven Paine, Boston, Mass; Progress Corp, Mayfield, Ohio; Jerry Speyer, New York. *Exhib:* Solo exhibs, Fluid Geometry, Conn Col, New Haven, 90 & Barbara Toll Mus, New York, 93; Vertical Slice, Cummings Gallery, New London, Conn, 92. *Teaching:* Adj asst prof sculpture, Columbia Univ, 92- *Awards:* NY Found for Arts Fel, 87; Nat Endowment Arts Fel, 89. *Bibliog:* Michael Benson (auth), article, NY Times, 6/1/90. *Media:* Miscellaneous Media. *Publ:* Contribr (cover), Sportsman of the Year Orel Hershiser, Sports Illus, 88. *Dealer:* Barbara Toll Fine Arts 146 Greene St New NY 10012. *Mailing Add:* 542 Broadway New York NY 10012

CONSEY, KEVIN E
MUSEUM DIRECTOR, ADMINISTRATOR
b New York, NY, Jan 15, 52. *Study:* Hofstra Univ, BA, 74; Univ Va, Charlottesville, 75; Univ Mich, Ann Arbor, MA(mus practice art history), 77. *Collections Arranged:* African Art (auth, catalog), Art Mus, Univ Mich, 76 & 77; Real, Really Real, Super Real, 81. *Pos:* Dir, San Antonio Mus Art, 80-83 & Newport Harbor Art Mus, 83-89, Mus Contemp Art, Chicago, 89- *Teaching:* Instr art hist, Univ Toledo, 75-76; asst prof & dir, Emily Lowe Gallery, Hofstra Univ, 77-80; vis prof, Univ Tex, San Antonio, 81-83. *Mem:* Asn Art Mus Dirs; Col Art Asn; Visual Arts Panel, Tex Comn Arts; Int Coun Mus. *Res:* Twentieth century European and American art. *Publ:* Coauth, Pompeii as Style, In: Pompeii as Source and Inspiration, Univ Mich, 77; ed, Art for the People--New Deal Murals on Long Island, Hofstra Univ, 78; Off the Wall--Environments and Installations, San Antonio Mus Art, 81. *Mailing Add:* 237 E Ontario St Chicago IL 60611

CONSTABLE, ROSALIND
COLLECTOR, CRITIC
Pos: Researcher, Fortune Mag, 38-47; cult corresp, Time, Inc, 48-67; free lance writer; trustee, Mus NMex Found; guest cur, Mus Fine Arts, Santa Fe. *Collection:* Contemporary art. *Publ:* Contribr, articles in, Life Mag, New Yorker, Bk Wk, New York & others. *Mailing Add:* 609 Old Taos Hwy Santa Fe NM 87501

CONSTANTINE, GREG JOHN
PAINTER, EDUCATOR
b Windsor, Ont, Can, Feb 14, 38. *Study:* Andrews Univ, Mich, BA; Mich State Univ with Angelo Ippolito, MFA; Univ Calif, Los Angeles. *Work:* Grand Rapids Art Mus, Mich. *Exhib:* Ark Nat, 69; Chicago & Vicinity, Chicago Art Inst, 71; Michigan Artists, Detroit, 71; Philbrook Art Ctr, Tulsa, Okla, 75; LaGrange Nat, Ga, 75. *Teaching:* Chmn dept painting & art hist & prof art, Andrews Univ, 63- *Awards:* W & B Clusman Prize, Chicago Vicinity Show, Chicago Art Inst, 71. *Bibliog:* J Heriksen (auth), Artist, Insight Mag, 70; O Young (auth), Editor, Focus Mag, 75. *Mem:* Mus Contemp Art, Chicago; Col Art Asn; Mid-Am Art Asn. *Media:* Acrylic; Photography. *Publ:* Auth, article, Spectrum Mag, 75. *Mailing Add:* Dept Art Andrews Univ Berrien Springs MI 49104

CONSTANTINE, MILDRED
HISTORIAN
b Brooklyn, NY, June 28, 13. *Study:* NY Univ, MA, 39. *Collections Arranged:* The Olivetti Company, 52, The Package, 59, The Object Transformed, 66, Word & Image, 68 & Wallhangings, 69, Mus Mod Art, New York; art collections for Am Tel & Tel & Union Camp. *Pos:* Asst keeper, Archiv Hispanic Cult, Libr Cong, Washington, DC, 40-42; assoc cur, Dept Archit & Design, Mus Mod Art, 49-71, spec asst to dir, 71; consult art, archit & design, 71- *Teaching:* Instr hist graphic design, Parsons Sch Design, 71-; vis fac, Banff Centre Arts, 79-85. *Awards:* Asian Cult Coun, 84; ISE Cult Coun, 86; Nat Endowment Arts Grant, 88. *Mem:* Col Art Asn; Latin Am Studies Asn. *Res:* Latin American art from pre-Columbian to modern; modern art, architecture and design. *Publ:* Coauth, Beyond Craft: The Art Fabric, Van Nostrand Reinhold, 73, second ed, Kodansha Int, 86; ed, Jack Lenor Larsen, Musee des Arts Decoratifs, Paris, 81; coauth, The Art Fabric: Mainstream, Van Nostrand Reinhold, 81, second ed, Kodansha Int, 86; auth, Tina Modotti: A Fragile Life, Rizzoli Int, second ed, 83, ed Japan, 86; Archit Art, 88; and others. *Mailing Add:* 307 East 44th St Rm 1218 New York NY 10017

CONTE, JEANNE LARNER
PHOTOGRAPHER, ENAMELIST
b Dallas, Tex, May 25, 28. *Study:* Lindenwood Col, St Charles, Mo, 46-47; Univ Ala, Tuscaloosa, 47-49; Ohio Domenican, Columbus, 65-66; Ohio State Univ Continuing Educ, 88 & 89. *Comn:* Celtic Cross, cloisonne enamel, comn by Dr & Mrs J Q Dorgan, Columbus, Ohio, 79; photos & text/brochure, comn by Mr James Burkhart, Upper Arlington, Ohio, 89; 22 color photos for book Columbus: City of Discovery, Windsor Publ, 91; Ohio Garden Slide Presentation, Dawes Arboretum, 91. *Exhib:* Liturgical Art Show II, 69 & Liturgical Art Show IV, 73, Schumacher Gallery, Capitol Univ, Bexley, Ohio, 69; Ohio Artists & Craftmen's Int, Massilon Mus, 76; Fine Arts, Folk Arts & Crafts Festival, Wagnalls Mem, Lithopolis, Ohio, 77; Invitational Exhib, Aaron Faber Gallery, 666 Fifth Ave, New York, 79. *Awards:* Honorable Mention, Art Exhibition 66, Ohio State Fair, 8/66; Blue Ribbon, Wagnalls Mem, 8/6/77; Honorable Mention, Columbus Dispatch, 12/88. *Bibliog:* Jacqueline Hall (auth), Art Show Critique, Columbus Dispatch, 72. *Mem:* Homer Hon Soc Int Poets. *Publ:* Auth & contribr, Angels!, Messenger, Padua, Italy, 89; Magical Classical Secret Garden in Columbus, Am Horticulturist, 90; Secret Sculptures, Cincinnati Homes, 90; The Teacher, World & I Magazine of the Washington Times; Gum Trees of Australia, Life Today, 92. *Mailing Add:* 1469 Kenwick Rd Columbus OH 43209

CONTINI, ANITA
ADMINISTRATOR, CURATOR
b Cleveland, Ohio, Jan 16, 44. *Study:* Cleveland Music Settlement, scholar, 60; Elizabeth Seton Col, Yonkers, NY, AAS, 64; Hofstra Univ, Long Island, NY, BA, 66. *Collections Arranged:* Ruckus Manhattan by Red Grooms (auth, catalog), 75-76, Ruckus Manhattan, 81 & Art on the Beach (auth, catalog), 82, Creative Time Inc. *Pos:* Exec dir & pres, Creative Time Inc, New York, 73-86; pres & bd mem, Athena Found Inc, New York, 78-; vpres & dir, World Finan Ctr Arts & Events Prog, 92. *Awards:* Certs Merit, Ruckus Manhattan, 76 & Masstransiscope, 81, Munic Art Soc. *Bibliog:* Deborah C Phillips (auth), New faces in alternative spaces, Art News, 11/81; Grace Glueck (auth), New home, new look for Ruckus Manhattan, New York Times, 12/18/81; Carrie Rickey (auth), Taking care of artists' business, Village Voice, 1/5/82. *Mem:* Arts & Bus Coun New York. *Mailing Add:* 200 Liberty St 18th Fl New York NY 10281

CONTINOS, ANNA
PAINTER, DESIGNER
b New York, NY. *Study:* Hunter Col, BA. *Work:* JFK Libr, Piscataway, NJ; Am Fuji Seal Inc, NJ; I E DuPont De Nemours & Co, Wilmington, Del; Bell Labs - Holmdel, Piscataway, NJ; Ctr for Health Affairs, Princeton, NJ; many pvt collections in the US, Can, Taiwan, S Africa, Spain, Eng, Ireland, Puerto Rico & Japan. *Exhib:* solo shows, Pentimento Galleria, Stone Harbor & Art Spirit Gallery, Clinton, 82, Ortho Pharmaceuticals Gallery, Raritan, NJ, 84, Zeta Gallery, Shrewsbury & New Brunswick Cultural Ctr, 85, Short Hills Art Gallery, 88; Trenton City Mus Invitational, NJ, 84; NJ Watercolor Soc 50th Anniversary Invitational, Noyes Mus, Oceanville, Montclair Mus & Monmouth Mus, 90-91; Nat Asn Women Artists Traveling Painting Exhib (7 locations), 91-92; 73rd Ann Philadelphia Watercolor Club, Noyes Mus, Oceanville, NJ, 92. *Awards:* Award for Excellence, Somerset Art Asn Ann, 80; Best Show, Princeton Art Asn Ann, Princeton Microfilm COrp, 83; Forbes Award, NJ Watercolor Soc Ann, Forbes Mag, 90. *Mem:* NJ Watercolor Soc; Catherine Lorillard Wolfe Art Club; Nat Asn Women Artists; Am Artists Prof League; Princeton Art Asn. *Media:* Watercolor. *Dealer:* Greenwich Village Art Gallery New York; Short Hills Art Gallery, NJ. *Mailing Add:* 315 Willowbrook Dr North Brunswick NJ 08902

CONVERSE, ELIZABETH
WRITER, PAINTER
b Springfield, Ill, Jan 17, 46. *Study:* Lake Forest Col, BA, 67; New York Univ, 70-72. *Work:* Provincetown Art Mus, Provincetown, Mass. *Comn:* Harvest Ball, pvt comn, Darien, Conn, 88; murals & paintiongs, Susan Chen, Zonshine Development, Los Angeles, 92; murals, Gooden Sch, Sierra Madre, Calif, 92; office of Dr John Talevich, Sierra Madre, Calif, 92. *Exhib:* Florence Film Festival, 83; Film in the Cities, Minneapolis Film Coun, Minn, 84; Film in All Forms, Epernay Coun, France, 84; Massenzio Summer Festival, Rome, 84; Provincetown Art Mus, Conn; Sound/Shore Gallery, Portchester, NY, 86-88; Gallarie Bonheur, Greenwich, Conn, 87. *Pos:* Writer, dir & actor, Alexyz Partnership, 78-83; vpres & creative dir, Productions Systems, Inc, 82-89; writer, Vision Mag, 90- *Teaching:* South Bay Contemp Art Mus, 92. *Awards:* Nat Endowment Arts Grant, 77. *Media:* All Media. *Mailing Add:* 225 N Lima No 1 Sierra Madre CA 91024-3026

CONWILL, HOUSTON E
SCULPTOR
b Louisville, Ky, Apr 2, 47. *Study:* Howard Univ, BFA, 73; Univ Southern Calif, MFA, 76; Niagara Univ, Hon LHD, 90. *Comn:* The Filmore Center, San Francisco, 90. *Exhib:* Just Above Midtown, New York, 78 & 83; Bronx Mus, 88; Williams Col Art Mus, 89; Mus Mod Art, New York, 89; Hirshhorn Mus & Sculpture Gardens, Washington, DC, 89. *Pos:* Vpres, Los Angeles Printmaking Soc, 78-80; artist-in-residence, St Mary's Col, 83, Notre Dame, 85, Fabric Workshop, Philadelphia, 86, Am Acad in Rome, 85-86, Brandywine Workshop, 88; bd dir, New York Found for the Arts, 87; lectr, Niagara Univ, Albright Knox Art Gallery, 89, Ctr Contemp Art, Cincinnati & J B Speed Mus, Louisville, 90; resident artist, Skowhegan Sch Painting & Sculpture, 90. *Teaching:* Adj prof, Calif State Univ, 76-80, State Univ NY, Old Westbury, 81-87. *Awards:* Nat Endowment Arts, 82 & 89; John Simon Guggenheim Fel, 82; Prix de Rome, Am Acad in Rome, 84; New York Found Arts Fel, 85; Distinguished Alumnus, Howard Univ, Col Fine Arts, 90. *Bibliog:* Kay Larson (auth), Houston Conwill's Installation at MOMA is Impressive, New York Mag, 12/4/89. *Mailing Add:* 65 Central Park W Apt 6F New York NY 10023

COOK, AUGUST CHARLES
PAINTER, PRINTMAKER
b Philadelphia, Pa, Mar 15, 1897. *Study:* Pa Acad Fine Arts; Harvard Univ. *Work:* La Salle Col, Philadelphia; Libr Cong; Butler Mus Am Art, Youngstown, Ohio; Gibbs Art Gallery, Charleston, SC; SC Art Comn Collection. *Exhib:* Pa Acad Fine Arts; Soc Am Graphic Artists; Libr Cong Print Exhib; Nat Acad Design, New York; Carolina 25th Ann, Gibbs Art Gallery. *Teaching:* Prof fine arts & head dept, Converse Col, Spartanburg, SC, 24-66, emer, 67- *Awards:* Purchase Prize, Furman Univ, Greenville, SC. *Bibliog:* Jack Morris (auth), Contemporary Artists of South Carolina, 70. *Mem:* Guild SC Artists. *Media:* Oil; Wood Engraving. *Mailing Add:* 438 S Fairview Ave Ext Spartanburg SC 29302

COOK, CHRISTOPHER CAPEN
ADMINISTRATOR, PAINTER
b Boston, Mass, May 28, 32. *Study:* Wesleyan Univ, BA, 54; Univ Ill, MFA, 59. *Work:* Fogg Mus; Addison Gallery Am Art. *Exhib:* De Cordova Mus, Lincoln, Mass, 64; Boston Fine Arts Festival, 64; Northeastern Regional Mead Corp, Smith Col Mus Art, 65; Mus Mod Art, New York, 70; Ctr Art & Commun, Buenos Aires, Arg, 70; Kyoto, Japan, 71; solo exhib, Inst Contemp Art, Boston, 73; Sch Mus Fine Arts, Boston, 78; Howard Yezerski Gallery, 87. *Pos:* Asst dir, Addison Gallery Am Art, Phillips Acad, Andover, Mass, 64-69, dir, 69-; dir, Inst Contemp Art, Boston, 71-72; visitor visual & environ studies, Harvard Univ, 74-79. *Teaching:* Instr art, Colby Jr Col, 56; instr art, Univ NH, 59-63, asst prof, 63-64; vis prof, Lesley Col, Cambridge, 75-78; vis artist teacher, Sch Mus Fine Arts, Boston, 78- *Mem:* Coun Mus & Educ in Visual Arts; Nat Humanities Fac; Archiv Am Art (adv bd, 72-76). *Publ:* Auth, Possibles, 69; Book of Instants, 70; Poem System-Anytime, 71. *Mailing Add:* Addison Gallery Am Art Phillips Acad Andover MA 01810

COOK, JOHN (ALFRED)
SCULPTOR, MEDALIST
b Excelsior, Minn, June 2, 30. *Study:* Ariz State Univ, BA(with distinction), 55; Univ Iowa, with H Albrizio, MFA(sculpture), 56; Akad Bildendenkuenste, Munich, with Kirchner, 62. *Work:* Brit Mus, London; Smithsonian Inst, Washington, DC; Estense Gallerie, Modena, Italy; Nat Gallery, Budapest; Am Numismatic Soc Mus, New York; and others. *Comn:* Atherton Sculpture Relief, 82, Eos Medal Merit, 83; Frivolity, Vanity (medal), Soc Medallists, Danbury, Conn, 81; Brookgreen Gardens, SC; Brit Art Medal Soc, London; Fed Int de la Medaille, Paris; Walters Courtyard Relief, 88. *Exhib:* Solo exhibs, Mus Art, Phoenix, Mus Art, Pa State Univ, Am Numismatic Soc Mus Retrospective, New York, 88 & Purdue Univ, Lafayette, Ind; The Medal as Art, Brit Mus, London, 89; Equestrian Medals from the British Mus, Neqishi Equine Mus, Yokohama, Japan, 90; Smithson Mus Am Hist, Washington, DC, 90; 22nd Int Medal Exhib, Helsinki, 90; and others. *Teaching:* Prof art, Pa State Univ, 64-90. *Awards:* Am Numismatic Asn Literary Guild Award, 85; Saltus Award for medallic design, 87; Gold Medal for Artistic Excellence, Am Numismatic Asn, 88. *Bibliog:* A medalist, The Numismatist, 3/84; John Cook, Un Enigma, Medaglia, Milano, 89. *Mem:* Am Medallic Sculpture Asn (mem bd dirs, 82-86); Fedn Int Medaille (mem exec coun, 83-86); life fel Am Numismatic Soc; fel emer Inst Arts & Humanistic Studies. *Media:* Cast Bronze. *Publ:* Contribr, Future American Directions, 1/84, The Amuletic Medal, 1/84, Medailles, Paris; auth, Larger Ideas in smaller format, The Medal, London, 2/84; Trivia or art, Medaille, London/Paris, 85; The emerging amulet, Beeldenaar, Amsterdam, fall 85; American medals in Fidem Biennial, Nat Sculpture Rev, New York, fall 85; American medals, Medallic Sculpture, fall 85. *Mailing Add:* PO Box 33682 Kerrville TX 78029-3682

COOK, JOSEPH S
PAINTER
b Glendale, Calif, Aug 5, 36. *Study:* Otis Art Inst, Los Angeles, 53-54; Chouinard Art Inst, Los Angeles, 55-58. *Exhib:* Solo exhib, Mt St Marys Col Gallery, Los Angeles; Watercolor USA, Springfield Art Mus, Mo; San Francisco Mus Modern Art; Laguna Beach Mus Art; Barker Collection, Joslyn Mus, Omaha, Nebr; National Watercolor Soc Ann, Palm Springs Mus & Tucson Mus Art, Calif. *Pos:* Asst art coordr, City of Los Angeles, 60-62. *Awards:* James Phelan Awards, Palace Legion Honor, San Francisco; Brugger Award & First Purchase Award, Nat Watercolor Soc; Watercolor USA First Award. *Mem:* Nat Watercolor Soc (pres, 76); Watercolor USA. *Media:* Watercolor, Acrylic & Oils. *Mailing Add:* 484B Washington St No 430 Monterey CA 93940

COOK, KATHLEEN L
PAINTER
b Amarillo, Tex, Mar 19, 49. *Study:* Amarillo Col, AA(sci), 69; Tex Tech Univ, BFA, 73; studied with Daniel Greene, 79; studied with Albert Handell, 82. *Work:* San Antonio Art League; San Marcos Telephone Co, Tex. *Comn:* 125 portrait comns in various cities, Tex, 82-92. *Exhib:* Amarillo Rotary Club Invitational Exhib, Amarillo Art Ctr, Tex, 86-88; Allied Artists of Am Ann Competition, New York, 86; Images, McAllen Int Mus, Tex, 86; solo exhib, About Light, Mus SW, Midland, Tex, 87; Plains Hist Mus, Canyon, Tex, 89-91; and others. *Pos:* Illusr, art dir, Hemphill-Wells, Lubbock, Tex, 70-80; bd dirs, Hill Country Arts Found, Ingram, Tex, 83-85. *Teaching:* Instr pastel-figure/still-life, Hill Country Arts Found, Ingram, Tex, 82-90; invitational one-week workshops, pastel, Dallas, Houston, McAllen, Midland, Amarillo & Lubbock, Tex. *Awards:* Silver Medal Pastel, Knickerbocker Artists, 86; First Place, Pastel Soc SW, 87; Best of Show, Pastel Soc W Coast, 89. *Bibliog:* Survey of contemporary art of the figure, Am Artist Mag, 2/85; Susan Embry (auth), Kathleen Cook, SW Art Mag, 8/89. *Mem:* Pastel Soc Am; Knickerbocker Artists. *Media:* Pastel, Oil. *Publ:* Coauth, Looking around the color wheel, Am Artist Mag, 92. *Dealer:* Greenhouse Gallery Fine Art 2218 Breezewood San Antonio TX 78209. *Mailing Add:* 625 Clay St Kerrville TX 78028

COOK, LIA
TAPESTRY ARTIST, EDUCATOR
b Ventura, Calif, 1942. *Study:* Univ Calif, Berkeley, BA, 65, MA, 73. *Work:* Am Craft Mus, New York; Galerie de la Tapisserie et d'Art Textile, Beauvais, France; Mus Mod Art, Metrop Mus Art, New York. *Comn:* Embarcadero Ctr, San Francisco, 74; City Hall, Fairfield, Calif, 76; Art in Archit Prog, US Gen Serv Admn, Richmond, Calif, 76; Rensselaer Polytechnic Inst, 79; Mercantile Bank, Tex, 86. *Exhib:* Solo exhibs, Renwick Gallery, Nat Mus Am Art, 80 & San Jose Mus Art, Calif, 80; The Art Fabric: Mainstream, San Francisco Mus Mod Art, traveling, 81-84; Celebration 25, 81 & The Pattern Show, 82, Am Craft Mus, New York; Jacquard Textiles, Cooper-Hewitt Mus, New York, 82; Fiber Directions, Brunnier Gallery and Mus, Iowa State Univ, 82; retrospective, Galerie Nat de la Tapisserie et d'Art Textile, Beauvais, France, 83. *Teaching:* Prof art, Calif Col Arts & Crafts, Oakland, 76- *Awards:* Fels,

Nat Endowment Arts, 74-75, 77-78 & 86; Special Proj Grant, Nat Endowment Arts, 81; Calif Arts Coun Artist Fel Grant, 90. *Bibliog:* Barbaralee Diamonstein (auth), Handmade in America: Conversation with Fourteen Craftsmasters, Harry M Abrams, New York, 84; Maureen Conner (auth), The tapestries of Lia Cook, Arts Mag, 2/85; Nancy A Corwin (auth), Lia Cook, Monograph from Nat Acad Sci Exhib, 90. *Media:* Rayon. *Publ:* Auth, Ed Rossbach as Educator: A Personal View, Ed Rossbach: 40 Years of Exploration and Innovation in Fiber Art, Textile Mus, Lark Bks, Washington, DC, 90. *Dealer:* Allrich Gallery 251 Post St San Francisco CA 94108; Bellas Artes Gallery 653 Canyon Rd Santa Fe NM 87501. *Mailing Add:* Calif Col Arts & Crafts Oakland CA 94618

COOK, MICHAEL DAVID
PAINTER, VIDEO ARTIST
b Ramey, PR, July 16, 53. *Study:* Fla State Univ, BFA, 75; Univ Dallas, MA, 76; Univ Okla, MFA, 78. *Work:* Mus Contemp Art, San Diego; Sandra Conn & Assoc, Chicago; World Book Corp, Chicago; Polaroid Corp, New York. *Exhib:* 77th Ann Exhib by Artists of Chicago & Vicinity, Art Inst Chicago, 78; New Dimensions--Time, Mus Contemp Art, Chicago, 80; Working Drawings, Hunter Gallery, New York, 81; War Games, Kitchen, New York, 82; solo exhibs, NAME Gallery, Chicago, 82, Grayson Gallery, Chicago, 83, Wenger Gallery, La Jolla, Calif, 84, Janet Steinberg Gallery, San Fran cisco, Calif, 86, Recent & Past Work, Art Mus, Univ NMex, Albuquerque, 89, Animal-Vegetable or Mineral?, Mus Fine Arts, Santa Fe, 90 & Charity, Shidoni Contemp,Tesuque, NMex, 90; The End of the World, New Mus Contemp Art, New York, 83-84; System and Structure, Allen Priebe Art Gallery & travelling, 83-84; Myth & Magic, Wenger Gallery, Los Angeles, 87; Social Space, Janet Steinberg Gallery, San Francisco, 88; 20 X 40, Jayne Baum Gallery, New York, 89; Playing with Fire, Ctr Contemp Arts, Santa Fe, 90-91. *Teaching:* Vis artist painting & drawing, Video Univ Ill, Champaign-Urbana, 78-80; asst prof, Univ Ill, Chicago, 80-83; vis lectr, Univ Calif, Berkeley, 83-85, Univ Calif, Davis, 85; Spec vis fac, San Francisco Art Inst, 85; asst prof painting & drawing, Univ NMex, Albuquerque, currently. *Awards:* Ford Found Fac Res Grants, 78 & 79; Ill Arts Coun Fel, 82; Nat Endowment Individual Artists Fel, 84-85; Teacher of Year Award, Univ NMex, 89-90. *Bibliog:* Janet Kutner (auth), Graf-feet-i, glitter and crab claws, Artnews, 79; Pat Tomson (auth), article, New Art Examiner, 82; Lynn Gumpert (auth), The End of the World (catalogue), New Museum, New York, 83; Kenneth Baker (auth), Filtering Apocalypse through illusions, San Francisco Chronicle, 5/13/86; Ina Russell (auth), Signs of the global village, Artweek, 2/6/88. *Publ:* Auth, Radiation Remains the Same, Phono Record, Grayson Gallery, 83. *Mailing Add:* 924 11th St NW Albuquerque NM 87102

COOK, R SCOTT
ART DEALER, CRITIC
Study: NY Univ, MA, 75. *Specialty:* 20th Century European paintings, sculpture & drawings; Latin American art. *Publ:* Auth, Space Shots, Art Am, 82; Bruce Conner, Artforum, 82; Andre Masson, Arnold Herstand, 84; The Brothers Duchamp, Arnold Herstand, 86; Rene Magritte, Arnold Herstand, 86. *Mailing Add:* 28 W 38th St New York NY 10018

COOK, ROBERT HOWARD
SCULPTOR, MEDALIST
b Boston, Mass, Apr 8, 21. *Study:* Demetrios Sch, 38-42; Beaux Arts, Paris, under Marcel Gaumont, 45. *Work:* Whitney Mus Am Art, New York; Pa Acad Fine Arts, Philadelphia; Va Mus Fine Arts, Richmond; Hirshhorn Collection, Washington, DC; State Univ NY, Oneida. *Comn:* Lifeline, Sun Co, Radnor, Pa, 78; Off the Water, Sun-Co, 79; Emerging, Saudi Arabia, 81; Camel, Saudi Arabia, 82; Stretch, Saudi Arabia, 82; Giant, Woodlands, Tex. *Exhib:* One-man shows, Inst Contemp Art, Boston, 51, Birmingham Mus Fine Arts, Ala, 67, Mint Mus Art, Charlotte, NC, 68, Va Mus Fine Art, Richmond, 68 & Schenectady Mus Art, NY, 77; Pa Acad Fine Arts; Whitney Ann; Nat Acad Design; Boston Art Festival; Univ Ill; Biennale Venezia, Italy, 51; and other group & one-man shows. *Awards:* Second Prize, Prix de Rome, Am Acad Rome, 42; Cash Award & Best-of-Show, Nat Acad Arts & Lett, 48; Tiffany Award, Tiffany Found, 48. *Bibliog:* Tracy O'Kates & Arnold Eagle (auth), World of Robert Cook (27-minute doc on his work), Beechtree Productions, 77. *Mem:* Sculptors Guild; Nat Sculpture Soc. *Media:* Bronze, Wood. *Publ:* Auth, Family Album in Bronze (photographs by Franco Romagnoli), 76, Twelve commissions, 78 & In motion, 80, Jasillo. *Dealer:* Henry Cook 79 St Rose St Jamaica Plain Boston MA 02130. *Mailing Add:* Piazza Borghese 91 Rome 00186 Italy

COOK, STEPHEN D
PRINTMAKER, DRAFTSMAN
b Jackson, Miss, Sept 10, 51. *Study:* Miss Col, BA, 73; Univ Miss, MFA, 75; Royal Col Art, London, cert, 76. *Work:* Victoria & Albert Mus, London; Southern Graphics Coun Print Arch, Oxford, Miss; Miss Sch Supply Co, Jackson; Meridian Mus Art. *Exhib:* One-man show, Janet Redmont Gallery, Millsaps Col, 87; Mid-South Biennial, Brooks Mem, Memphis, 74; one-man shows, Miss Art Asn Gallery, Jackson, 77 & Meridian Mus Art, 79; Comparisons & Contrasts, Soviet Union Tour, 79-81; Southeast Mo State Univ Nat Print Invitational Exhib, 81; Southern Graphics Council Member Touring Exhib, 86-88. *Pos:* Artist-in-residence, Tupelo, Miss, 77-78. *Teaching:* Chmn dept printmaking, Miss Mus Art Sch, 77-78; instr printmaking & drawing, Univ Miss, Oxford, 78; instr, Hinds Junior Col, Raymond, 80, Miss Col, Clinton, 83-90, asst prof, 90-; adj instr, Jackson Pub Schs, 82. *Awards:* Bellamann Mem Found Ann Award, 75; ITT Corp Int Fel, London, 75-76; Award of Merit, Miss Artists Competitive, 78. *Mem:* Southern Graphics Coun (vpres, 86-88, pres, 88-90). *Media:* Etching in Line & Aquatint; Charcoal, Pastel. *Publ:* Contribr, J Royal Col Art, 76; Interchange, ITT Fel Publ, 87. *Mailing Add:* 4561 Meadow Hill Rd Jackson MS 39206

COOKE, JODY HELEN
PAINTER, EDUCATOR
b Wind River, Wyo, Oct 25, 22. *Study:* Univ Calif, Berkeley, BA(fine arts); Univ Minn, MA; Calif Col Arts & Crafts, Calif State Univ, Hayward; Univ Ore, PhD with June King McFee, Gordon Kensler & Vincent Lanier, Calif State Univ, advert study. *Work:* Calif State Univ, Hayward; Alaska State Mus, Juneau; Anchorage Hist Fine Arts Mus; Laussac Libr, Anchorage, Alaska. *Exhib:* Three-man show, Allied Arts Gallery, Sacramento, 67; All Alaska Exhib, Alaska Hist & Fine Arts Mus, 76 & 77; Contemporary Arts of Alaska, Smithsonian Inst, Washington, DC, 78; one-man show, Anchorage Hist & Fine Arts Mus, 79; On and of Paper, Alaska, 81 & traveling exhib, 83-84; Civic Ctr Gallery, Fairbanks, Alaska; Stonington Gallery, Anchorage Hist & Fine Arts Mus, 85. *Teaching:* Head art dept, Col Siskiyous, 64-67; asst prof art & educ, Univ Iowa, 69-70 & Ore State Univ, 70-73; lectr art educ, Calif State Univ, Sacramento, 73-74; assoc prof & dir exhib, Univ Alaska, 74-88, chmn art dept, 76-78, prof art, 86-88. *Awards:* Merit Award, Auburn Arts Festival, Calif, 66; Purchase Awards, All Alaska Competition, 77 & Alaska State Bank, 81. *Bibliog:* Reid Hastie (auth), Encounter With Art, 61; J K McFee & R Degge (auths), Art Culture & Environment: A catalyst for teaching. *Mem:* Visual Arts Ctr Alaska; Anchorage Adv Arts Comn; Alaska Artists Guild; Anchorage Mus Asn. *Media:* Oil, Acrylic. *Collection:* Drawings, prints, paintings and pottery of contemporary artists. *Mailing Add:* 4271 Bridle Circle Anchorage AK 99517-1410

COOKE, JUDY
PAINTER
b Bay City, Mich, July 8, 40. *Study:* Boston Mus Sch Fine Arts, Hons dipl, 63; Tufts Univ, Medford, Mass, BFA, 65; Reed Col, Portland, Ore, MAT, 71. *Work:* Boston Mus Sch of Fine Arts; Portland Art Mus, Ore; Ranier Bank & Pac Northwest Bell, Seattle; Itell Corp, San Francisco; Bank Am, San Francisco; Hewlett Packard Co, Portland, Ore. *Exhib:* Prospect: Northwest 72, Seattle Art Mus Pavilion, 72 & Northwest Ann, 73 & 74; 80th Anniversary Invitational, Portland Art Mus, Ore, 73; Aesthetics of Graffiti, San Francisco Mus Mod Art, 78; San Jose Inst Contemp Art, 84; Blackfish Gallery 6th Anniversary Exhib, Portland, Ore; Expo 86, Vancouver, BC; Esther Saks Gallery, Chicago, Ill, 90. *Pos:* Founding mem, Blackfish Gallery, 79-84. *Teaching:* Assoc prof, Pac NW Col Art, Portland, Ore, 86- *Awards:* Purchase Award, Portland Art Mus, 73; Painting Award, Seattle Art Mus Pavilion, 73; Boston Mus traveling fel, 65 & 74; Visual Artist Fel Painting, Nat Endowment Arts, 89. *Bibliog:* Judy Cooke/Canvas Constructions, Portland Art Mus, 73; Lucy Lippard (auth), Northwest passage, Art in Am, 7-8/76; Bruce Guenther (auth), Fifty Northwest Artists, Chronicle Bks. *Media:* Oil Paint, Mixed Media. *Dealer:* Elizabeth Leach Gallery 207 SW Pine St Portland OR 97204. *Mailing Add:* c/o Pacific NW Col Art 1219 SW Park Portland OR 97205

COOKE, SAMUEL TUCKER
PAINTER, EDUCATOR
b Gainesville, Fla, Dec 4, 41. *Study:* Stetson Univ, with Fred Messersmith, BA; Univ Ga, with Lamar Dodd & Howard Thomas, MFA. *Work:* Asheville Art Mus, NC; Mint Mus Art, Charlotte, NC; Univ Ga Collection; Hunter Gallery Art, Chattanooga, Tenn; Davidson Col, NC. *Exhib:* Nat Drawing & Small Sculpture Exhib, Ball State Univ, 72-74; Davidson Col Nat Print & Drawing Exhib, 74-75; Gallery Contemp Art Realist, Winston-Salem, NC, 74-75; Southeastern Drawing Invitational, Mint Mus, Charlotte, 79; one-man shows, New Morning Gallery, Asheville, 78, Somerhill Gallery, Durham, 79 & 81 & Asheville Art Mus, 80. *Teaching:* Chmn dept art, Univ NC, Asheville, 68-79. *Awards:* 3rd Davidson Nat Drawing & Print Award, Knight Publ Co, 74; 39th Southeastern Painting & Drawing Award, Wachovia Bank NC, 74; Mint Mus Award for Realism in North Carolina, NC Arts Coun, 74. *Dealer:* New Morning Gallery 3 1/2 Kitchen Pl Asheville NC 28803; Somerhill Gallery 5504 Chapel Hill Blvd Durham NC 27707. *Mailing Add:* Dept Art & MusicUniv NC One University Heights Asheville NC 28814

COOLEY, ADELAIDE N
PAINTER, WRITER
b Idaho Falls, Idaho, Apr 18, 14. *Study:* Stephens Col for Women, Columbia, Mo, AA; Univ Wis-Madison, BS; Bradley Univ, Peoria, Ill. *Work:* Peoria Art Guild, 89; St Paul's Episcopal Cathedral Collection; Bradley Univ, Peoria, 89. *Comn:* Altar paraments, Univ United Methodist Church, Peoria, Ill, 67. *Exhib:* 24th Ann Invitational, Ill State Mus, 71; paintings & pottery with floral motifs, Peoria Pub Libr, 78; paintings & pottery, Western Ill Univ, Macomb, 79; retrospective exhib paintings, pottery & small sculpture, Peoria Art Guild, 79; Peoria Art Guild, 89. *Pos:* Art consult, Peoria Hist Soc, 83-; art critic, Appraisals, 83-; juror, Civic Ctr Exhib, Peoria Art Guild 25th Ann Fair, 87; bd dirs, Univ Ariz, 90-91. *Awards:* Outstanding Woman in Art, YWCA, Peoria, Ill, 73; Arts Award, YWCA, Peoria, Ill, 78. *Bibliog:* Barbara Mantz (auth), Getting to know Adelaide Nation Cooley, Peoria J Star, 1/6/74. *Mem:* Peoria Art Guild (pres, 61-63); Lakeview Mus Arts & Sci. *Media:* Oil, Watercolor. *Publ:* Auth, History of Art in Peoria, 1830-1975, Peoria Jaycees Mag, 75; Joseph Petarde, immigrant stone carver, Ill Mag, 76; The Monument Maker, Biography of Frederick Ernst Triebel, Expo Press, 78; Reviews of art exhibits, The New Art Examiner, Chicago, 81; Peoria's war memorial monument, Illinois Mag, 88; Peoria Women's Club, Ill Mag, 89. *Dealer:* Peoria Art Guild 1831 N Knoxville Peoria IL 61603. *Mailing Add:* 501 LaPosada Circle No 159 Green Valley AZ 85614

COOLIDGE, JOHN
HISTORIAN
b Cambridge, Mass, Dec 16, 13. *Study:* Harvard Univ, BA, 35; NY Univ, PhD, 48. *Pos:* Dir, Fogg Art Mus, Harvard Univ, 48-68; trustee, Mus of Fine

Arts, Boston, 48-77, pres bd, 76-77, emer pres bd, 77- *Teaching:* Prof fine arts, Harvard Univ, 47-85, emer prof, 85- *Mem:* Col Art Asn Am; Soc Archit Historians. *Res:* History of American architecture, Italian renaissance architecture. *Publ:* Auth, Mill & Mansion, 42; The Villa Guilea, Art Bulletin, 42; Patrons Archit, 89. *Mailing Add:* Fogg Art Mus 32 Quincy St Harvard Univ Cambridge MA 02138

COOPER, MARIO
PAINTER, INSTRUCTOR
b Mexico City, Mex, Nov 26, 05. *Study:* Otis Art Inst, Los Angeles, 24; Chouinard Art Sch, Los Angeles, 25; Grand Cent Art Sch, New York, 27-37; and with F Tolles Chamberlin, Louis Treviso, Pruett Carter & Harvey Dunn. *Work:* Metrop Mus Art; Col USAF; Butler Inst Am Art; NASA; and others. *Comn:* Painting of Atlas ICBM & planes, USAF, Marianas Hall, Armed Serv Staff Col, Norfolk, Va; comn by USAF to paint the capitals of Europe, 60; invited by Nat Gallery to doc flight Apollo 10 & 11 for NASA, 69. *Exhib:* Shows & exhibs in Japan, Gt Brit, Europe, Can, Mex & Australia. *Pos:* Deleg to US Comn, Inter-Am Press Asn, 54-; in charge team artists to Japan, Korea & Okinawa, USAF, 56 & in charge team artists to Japan, 57; art consult, USAF, 60. *Teaching:* Instr, Art Students League, 57-; instr, Nat Acad Design Sch Fine Arts, City Col New York, 61-68. *Awards:* Audubon Artists Gold Medal of Honor, 74; Samuel F B Morse Gold Medal, Nat Acad Design; Am Watercolor Soc High Winds Medal, 79 & 81. *Bibliog:* History of the American Watercolor Society, 69 & History of watercolor painting in America, USAF, 66; The romance in Mario Cooper's watercolors, article in Am Artist, 9/79. *Mem:* Academician Nat Acad Design; Am Watercolor Soc (pres, 59-); Audubon Artists (pres, 54-58); hon mem Royal Watercolour Soc Gt Brit; Century Asn. *Publ:* Auth, Drawing & Painting the City, 67 & Painting with Watercolor, 71, Van Nostrand Reinhold; illusr, short stories of, P G Wodehouse, Quentin Reynolds & many others; auth, Watercolor by Design, Watson-Guptill, 80; auth, Flower Painting in Watercolor & Painting in Watercolor, 81 & The Art of Drapery, 83, Van Nostrand Reinhold. *Mailing Add:* One W 67th St New York NY 10023

COOPER, PAULA
DEALER
b Mass, Mar 14, 38. *Study:* Pierce Col, Athens, Greece; Sorbonne, Paris; Goucher Col; Inst Fine Arts, NY Univ. *Pos:* Asst, World House Galleries, New York, 59-61; dir, Park Place Gallery, 65-67; dir, Paula Cooper Gallery, 68- *Mem:* Art Dealers Asn Am. *Specialty:* Contemporary art. *Mailing Add:* 155 Wooster St New York NY 10012

COOPER, RHONDA H
GALLERY DIRECTOR, CURATOR
b New York, NY, Nov 5, 50. *Study:* Hunter Col, BA, 71; Univ Hawaii, Honolulu, MA, 72; Cornell Univ, 74-75. *Collections Arranged:* The Asian Collection (auth, catalog), Dayton Art Inst, 79; World of Japanese Theater (auth, catalog), Queens Mus, 83; Carl Andre Sculpture (ed, catalog), 84, Toby Buonagurio Selected Works (auth, catalog), 86 & Eight Urban Painters, 86 & Permutation and Evolution: Edgar Buonagurio 1974-1988 (auth, catalog), 88, State Univ NY, Stony Brook; Robert Kushner: Silent Operas (auth, catalog), 89; Kit-Yin Snyder: Enrico IV (auth, catalog), 90. *Pos:* Cur Asian art, Dayton Art Inst, 76-79; cur exhibs, Queens Mus, NY, 82-83; dir, Univ Art Gallery, State Univ NY, Stony Brook, 83- *Teaching:* Instr Asian art, Univ Bridgeport, Conn, 74-76 & Art Inst Boston, 80-81; adj lectr Asian art & arts mgt, State Univ NY, Stony Brook, 84- *Mem:* Am Asn Mus. *Publ:* Auth, Orthodoxy & Eccentricity in 17th Century China, Dayton Art Inst, 78; Zeng Shanqing, Hsiung Shih Art Monthly, 9/91. *Mailing Add:* Fine Art Ctr Gallery State Univ NY Stony Brook NY 11794-5425

COOPER, RON
SCULPTOR
b New York, NY, July 24, 43. *Study:* Happy Valley Sch, Ojai, Calif, Chouinard Art Inst, Los Angeles. *Work:* Chicago Art Inst; Kaiser Wilhelm Mus, Krefeld, West Ger; Stedelijk Mus, Amsterdam, Netherlands; Whitney Mus Am Art, Solomon R Guggenheim Mus, New York. *Comn:* Floating Volume Atmosphere (sculpture), Libr Cong Dept Copyright & Artist, 68; Large Floating Volume of Light (drawing), Ft Worth, Tex, 71; Oasis (sculpture), Dallas, Tex, 85; sculpture, Frederick Weisman Found, Los Angeles, Calif, 88; bronze sculpture, Pacific Enterprises Corp, 90. *Exhib:* Whitney Ann Painting, 69; Theodoran Awards, Guggenheim Mus, 71; Documenta V, Kassel, WGer, 72; The State of California Painting, Brigham Young Univ Gallery, Utah, 73; Light, Lang Art Gallery, Scripps Col, Calif, 74; California Light, Cedars Sinai Med Ctr, Los Angeles, 77; Attitudes: Photography in the 70's, Santa Barbara Mus Art, 79; one-man exhib, La Jolla Mus Art, 73, Rosamund Felsen Gallery, Los Angeles, 79, 80 & 81, Peppers Art Gallery, Univ Redlands, Calif, 81, Advance Art Gallery, Rinconada, NMex, 83; Gallery 454, Los Angeles, Calif, 87 & 88; Gallerie Sena West, Santa Fe, NMex, 88 & 89; solo exhibs, Sena Gallery West, Santa Fe, NMex, 88, Pacific Enterprise Comn, Los Angeles, Calif, 89, Maguire Thomas Comn, Santa Monica, Calif, 90, Sena Galleries, Santa Fe, NMex, 91; Minimal, Cirrus Gallery, Los Angeles, 91. *Pos:* Bd dir, Los Angeles Inst Contemp Art, 81- *Awards:* Los Angeles Co Mus Art Purchase Award, 68; Nat Endowment Arts Award, 70 & 80; Theodoran Purchase Award, Guggenheim Mus, 71. *Bibliog:* Jane Livingston (auth), Two generations in LA, Art Am, Vol 57:95, 1/69; Colin Gardner (auth), Ron Cooper, Artforum, 12/85; Peter Clothier (auth), Ron Cooper at Ovsey, Art Am, 1/86. *Mem:* Artist Equity Asn (bd dir, 80-81). *Mailing Add:* c/o Sena Galleries West Plaza Mercado Upper Level 112 W San Francisco St Sante Fe NM 87501

COOPER, RUFFIN
CONCEPTUAL ARTIST, PHOTOGRAPHER
b Washington, DC, Jan 4, 42. *Study:* Univ Houston, 60-61; Boston Univ, BFA, 64. *Work:* Brooklyn Mus; Chase Manhattan Bank, Dean Witter & Co, New York; Bibliotheque Nationale, Paris; New Orleans Mus Fine Art. *Comn:* Photo Construction, Comedie Francaise, Paris, Warner Ctr, Los Angeles, Calif, 83; Ann Report, Fed Reserve Bank, Cleveland, Ohio, 84; Banners, Port Authority NY & NJ, New York, 85. *Exhib:* Church at Rancho de Taos, Amon Carter Mus, Ft Worth, Tex & Mus Fine Arts, Santa Fe, NMex, 82; Liberty, Brooklyn Mus, NY, 86; Galleria Bastille, Paris, 85; European Photos, de Saisset Mus, Santa Clara, Calif, 88; Nudes & House, Firenze Gray Hawkins, Los Angeles, 88. *Awards:* Merit Award, Camera Arts, NY Art Dirs Club, 82; Worlitzer Found Grant, Taos, NM, 89. *Bibliog:* Monica Cipnic (auth), Ruffin Cooper, Popular Photogr, 74; Al Frankenstein (auth), Ruffin Cooper, San Francisco Chronicle, 78; Joel LaRoche (auth), Ruffin Cooper, Zoom, 85. *Publ:* Coauth, article, Southwest Art, 78; Statue of Liberty, Am Heritage 81 & NY Times, 86; article, Interior Design, 82; Statuesque, Interview, 86. *Mailing Add:* 1076 Hampshire St San Francisco CA 94110-3426

COOPER, SUSAN
PAINTER, SCULPTOR
b Los Angeles, Calif, Apr 25, 47. *Study:* Univ Calif, Berkeley, BA, 68, MA, 70; Calif State Univ, Northridge. *Work:* Denver Art Mus, Colo; Kaiser Permanente, Colo; Westin Hotel, Cancuun, Mex; City & Co Denver; Denver Pub Libr; Denver Parks & Recreation Dept. *Comn:* Sculpture, Denver Parks & Recreation, 91; painting, Kaiser Permanente, 92; sculpture, Denver Pub Libr, 93; relief murals, City & County Buildings, 93. *Exhib:* Centennial Exhib, San Francisco Mus Mod Art, Calif, 71; Four Corners Biennial, Phoenix Mus Art, Ariz, 73; solo exhib, Roswell Mus, NMex, 73, Inkfish Gallery, Denver, Colo, 83, 85, 88 & 90; Colo Ann, 76 & 80 Recent Acquisitions, 83 & Mayor's Awards, 88, Denver Art Mus, Colo; retrospective, Jonson Gallery, Univ NMex, Albuquerque, 80; Nat Mus Women in Arts, Significant Colo Women Artists of 20th Century, 88; Henri Gallery, 89; Galeria Expositum, Mexico City, 92. *Pos:* Dir, Rocky Mountain Women's Inst, Denver, Colo, 77-80, pres, 83-84. *Teaching:* Instr drawing, Community Col of Denver, Red Rocks, Colo, 77; instr, painting & drawing, Metrop State Col, 87-; instr, Univ Colo, Denver, 89-90. *Awards:* Artist-in-Residence Grant, Roswell Mus & Art Ctr, 72-73; Guest Residency, Yaddo, Saratoga Springs, NY, 73; First Prize, Poster Competition, Colo Lawyers for the Arts, 86. *Bibliog:* Lindy Lyman Moore (auth), Susan Cooper, winter 78-79 & Katharine Smith-Warren (auth), Susan Cooper, fall 84, Artspace Mag; Irene Clurman (auth), Pastels at Inkfish, Rocky Mountain News, 1/18/83; Howard Rissoti (auth), Susan Cooper at Henri, Art Forum, 2/90; Jennifer Heath (auth), The Art is at Home, Rocky Mountain News, 1/8/88. *Mem:* Ctr for Idea Art, Denver (bd mem); Pirate, Contemp Art Oasis. *Media:* Wood, Steel. *Dealer:* Inkfish Gallery 1810 Market St Denver CO 80202; Henri Gallery 1500 21st St NW Washington DC 20036. *Mailing Add:* 1 Winwood Dr Englewood CO 80110

COOPER, THEODORE A
DEALER
b Cleveland, Ohio, Feb 20, 43. *Study:* Muskingum Col, BA, 65; Ind Univ, MA, 67. *Pos:* Asst dir, IFA Galleries, 68-70; dir, Studio Gallery, 70-71; pres & dir, Adams Davidson Galleries, Inc, 71-; mem art adv panel, Internal Revenue Serv. *Teaching:* Teaching asst introd art, Ind Univ, 65-67. *Mem:* Sr mem Am Soc Appraisers; Wash Art Dealers Asn (pres, 81-87, 91-93). *Specialty:* 19th & early 20th Century American Masters. *Mailing Add:* 3233 P St NW Washington DC 20007

COOPER, WAYNE
PAINTER, GRAPHIC ARTIST
b Depew, Okla, May 7, 42. *Study:* Valparaiso Univ; Famous Artist Sch; Gary Artist League, Cowboy Artists Am, Kerrville, Tex; American Atelier, New York. *Work:* Art Inst Gallery, Chicago; Ft Wayne Mus Gallery, Ind. *Comn:* Story of Flight (oil), Parkview Hosp, Ft Wayne, 65; Crucifix (oil), Assembly of God Church, Hebron, Ind, 66; Christ Descending (oil), Endtime Tabernacle, Tulsa, Okla, 69; Painting of Christ, Church of God, Depew, Okla, 74; lithograph ed, Am Express Co, New York. *Exhib:* Country Beautiful, Minn, 68; Nat Show, Tyler, Tex, 69; Ft Wayne Mus, 75; Valparaiso Univ, 75; Gilcrease Mus, Tulsa; One-man shows, Will Rogers Mus, Claremore, Okla, Ky Univ & Circle Galleries. *Awards:* Best of Show, Twas Bay Show, Gilcrease Mus, Tulsa, 76 & America Beautiful Miniature, Nat Small Painting Show, Albuquerque, 91; First Place for Oils, Southern Shores, Gary, Ind, 70; First Place for Watercolor, Ft Wayne Mus, 75. *Mem:* Mid-Am Art Asn; Ind Artists & Craftsmen; Am Artists Prof League; Fla Fedn Artists; Cowboy Hall of Fame. *Media:* Oil, Watercolor; Pencil, Charcoal. *Mailing Add:* Box 361 Hebron IN 46347

COOPERSMITH, GEORGIA A
MUSEUM DIRECTOR
b Phillipsburg, NJ, May 19, 50. *Study:* Syracuse Univ, 68-70, MFA, 77; Rochester Univ Technol, BFA, 73. *Exhib:* Expressionist Impulses in Recent American Art, 84; Variations on a Theme-Figurative Art, 85; The North Country Landscape, 86. *Pos:* Dir, Roland Gibson Gallery, Potsdam, NY, currently; asst cur, Mem Art Gallery, Rochester, 79-81. *Teaching:* Instr mus studies & gallery practices, State Univ & Col Arts & Science, Potsdam, 81- *Mem:* Am Asn Mus; Northeast Mus Conf; Col Art Asn; Williamstown Regional Art Conserv Asn (trustee); Tri-County Arts Coun (founder). *Publ:* Auth, Paintings & Photographs, Moholy-Nagy, Mem Art Gallery, 78; Drawings & Watercolor, Mem Art Gallery, 79; Sculpture from the Johnson Atelier, Brainerd Art Gallery, 82; The Twentieth Anniversary Exhibition of the Vogel Collection, 82. *Mailing Add:* Roland Gibson Gallery State Univ NY Potsdam NY 13676

COPE, LOUISE TODD
COLLAGE ARTIST
b Ventnor, NJ, June 17, 30. *Study:* Syracuse Univ, BA(fine arts); Indepent Textile Res, Guatemala, Scandinavia, Nepal, Bhutan & Thailand. *Work:* Australian Crafts Coun; NC Mus Art, Raleigh; Del Art Mus, Wilmington; Kutztown State Col Collection, Pa; Helen Drutt Collection; Pfannebecker Collection. *Exhib:* Invisible Artist, Philadelphia Mus Art, 73-74; Women's Work, American Art, Civic Ctr Mus, Philadelphia Nat Exhib, 74; 2nd & 3rd Int Miniature Exhib; Thread Poem Traveling Show, Australia, 78; NC Mus Hist, 83; collab with Marcia Plevin Dance Co, Two Survivors, NC Mus Art, 83; Silkworks, Gayle Willson Gallery, Southampton, NY, 84; Arvada Ctr Arts, Colo, 85-86; Wearable Art: A National Experience, Springfield, Ill, 85; Columbia Mus Art, 88-89. *Teaching:* Instr fibers, Haystack Sch Crafts, 69-89; chmn dept textiles, Moore Col Art, 70-74; teacher textiles, Penland Sch Crafts, NC, summers 70-72 & 81-86; tutor textiles, Wincester Sch Art, Eng, summer 73; teacher fibers, var workshops in US, Eng & Can. *Awards:* NC Mus Art Purchase Award, 71; Del Art Mus Purchase Award, 70; NC Mus Art Award, 83. *Mem:* World Crafts Coun; Am Crafts Coun. *Media:* Fiber. *Publ:* Auth, Thread Poems, 76 & Sleeves, A treasury of ideas, techniques & patterns, 88, Coat of Arms Press. *Mailing Add:* PO Box 1 Penland NC 28765

COPELAND, LILA
PAINTER, PRINTMAKER
b New York, NY, Apr 29, 22. *Study:* Art Students League, with George Grosz; Pratt Graphic Art Ctr. *Work:* Brit Mus, London, Eng; Bibliot Nat, Paris, France; Nat Collection Fine Arts, Washington, DC; Philadelphia Mus Art, Pa; Boston Mus Fine Arts, Mass; and others. *Exhib:* Art Inst Chicago; De Pauw Univ; Lincoln Ctr, New York; City Gallery, New York; Harbor Gallery, New York. *Awards:* Norman Waite Harris Bronze Medal & Prize, Art Inst Chicago. *Bibliog:* Joan Hess Michel (auth), Children--the drawings of Lila Copeland, Am Artist, 12/70; Joyce Hill (auth), Sketch of Lila Copeland, Lower Cape Newspaper, 12/12/72. *Media:* Pencil, Crayon; Lithography, Etching. *Dealer:* Harbor Gallery 24 W 57th St New York NY 10019. *Mailing Add:* 31 W Ninth St New York NY 10011

COPENHAVER-FELLOWS, DEBORAH (DEBORAH LYNNE FELLOWS) SCULPTOR, PAINTER
b Spokane, Wash, Jan 2, 48. *Study:* Holy Names Col, Fort Wright, BA(fine art), 70. *Work:* Bronze Stage Coach, Pro Rodeo Hall Fame, Colorado Springs, 81; Monumental Statue, Hecla Mining Co, Coeurdalena, Idaho, 91; Life Size Bronze Scout, Boy Scouts Am, Diamond Lake, Wash, 92; Frank Irwin Mem, Univ Tex, Austin, 86; BUSI Bronze Sculpture, Remington Park, Oklahoma City, 90. *Comn:* Vietman War Mem, Montana State, Missoula; Inland Pacific Vietnam War Mem, Spokane, Wash; Bing Crosby Mem, Gonzaga Univ, Spokane, Wash; Benny Binion Mem, Las Vegas; Korean War Mem, Wash State, Olympia. *Exhib:* Buffalo Bill Art Show, Whitney Mus, Cody, Wyo, 92. *Awards:* Best of Show Sculpture, Mus Native Am Cult, 85. *Bibliog:* Southwest Art Mag, 85. *Media:* Bronze; Oil. *Dealer:* BigHorn Gallery Copy WY; Alterman Morris Dallas TX. *Mailing Add:* Box 464 Bigfork MT 59911

COPLANS, JOHN (RIVERS)
PHOTOGRAPHER
b London, Eng, June 24, 20. *Work:* Metrop Mus Art, New York; Biblioteque Nat, Paris; San Francisco Mus Art; Minneapolis Inst Arts; Mus Mod Art, New York. *Exhib:* One-person shows, Art Inst Chicago, 81 & 88, Mus Mod Art, New York, 88, San Francisco Mus Mod Art, 88, Frankfurter Kunstverein, 90 & Mus Boymans van Beoningen, 90. *Pos:* Ed-at-large, Artforum Mag, 62-66, assoc ed, 66-70, ed, 71-; dir, art gallery, Univ Calif, Irvine, 65-68; cur, Pasadena Art Mus, 67-70; dir, Akron Art Inst, 78-81. *Teaching:* Distinguished vis prof, Am Univ, Cairo, Egypt, 84. *Awards:* Guggenheim Fel, 69 & 84; Frank Jewitt Mather, 74; Nat Endowment Arts Fel, 75 & 81. *Bibliog:* Jean-Francois Chevrier (auth), John Coplans Autoportraits, Photogaphies, Paris, 8/85; Susan Butler (auth), Body Politics: The Rebels and Rebellion of Age, Ten 8, London, 4/87; David Bonetti (auth), John Coplans Self Portraits, Art New Eng, Boston, 6/89. *Publ:* Auth, Serial Imagery, 70 & Andy Warhol, 70, New York Graphic; Roy Lichtenstein, Praeger, 72; Ellsworth Kelly, Abrams, 72; Decisions, Decisions, 75, Norton; Weegee: Tater und Opfer, Schirmer/Mosel, 78; contribr, Artforum, Art News, Art in Am, Art Int; and others. *Dealer:* Pace-McGill Gallery New York NY. *Mailing Add:* 125 Cedar St New York NY 10006

COPLEY, WILLIAM NELSON
PAINTER
b New York, NY, Jan 24, 19. *Study:* Self-taught; Yale Univ, 42; Phillips Acad, Andover, Mass. *Work:* Beaubourg Ctr, Paris; Whitney Mus Am Art, Mus Mod Art, New York; Chicago Art Inst; Pasadena Mus Art; Los Angeles Co Mus Art, Calif; Fine Arts Gallery, Univ Sydney, Australia; Nagaoka Contemp Art Mus, Japan. *Comn:* Murals, Gov Rm, New York Cult Ctr. *Exhib:* One-man shows, Brooks Jackson Gallery, New York, 80 & 81, Centre George Pompidou, Paris, 81, Phyllis Kind Gallery, Chicago, 77, 82, 90 & 91, New York, 81, 83, 85, 87 & 91, The Quay Gallery, San Francisco, 85 & New Mus Contemp Art, New York, 86; retrospective, Kundhalle Berne, Switz, 80; Ideal-The Fantastic, Whitney Mus Am Art, 80; Phyllis Kind Gallery, New York & Chicago; Int Ausstellung Westkunst, 1939-1981, Cologne, WGer, 81; Festival of the Arts, Muhlenberg Col, Allentown, Pa, 83; Auto & Culture, traveling exhib, Mus Contemp Art, Los Angeles & Detroit Inst Arts, Mich, 84; Paravents, Schloss Lorsfeld, Kerpen, Ger, 85; Conquante Ans des Dessins Amercains: 1930-1980, Ecole Nat Superiere des Beaux Arts, Paris & Stadtische Galerie im Stadelschen Dunsinstitut, Frankfurt am Main, 85-86. *Bibliog:* Articles by Roland Penrose, Patrick Waldberg & Robert Melville. *Media:* Multimedia. *Mailing Add:* Phyllis Kind Gallery 136 Greene St New York NY 10012

COPPEDGE, ARTHUR L
PAINTER, EDUCATOR
b Brooklyn, NY, Apr 21, 38. *Study:* Brooklyn Mus Art Sch, with David Levine & Isaac Soyer; Art Students League; Pratt Graphic Ctr. *Work:* Brooklyn Mus, NY; Studio Mus Harlem, New York; First Edition Inc; Chase Manhattan Bank NAm. *Comn:* Mural painting, Servo-Mation Corp, New York, 67; paintings & drawings, US Dept of Interior, DC, 75-76; paintings, Am the Beautiful, NY, 77. *Exhib:* Smithsonian Inst, DC; Ann Awards, Am Acad Arts & Letts, New York; Nat Gallery Jamaica, US Embassy, Jamaica, 83; Mus Contemp Art, San Francisco; one-man exhib, Schenectady Mus, NY, 88; Edward Hopper House, Nyack, NY, 90; Christie's, New York, 90. *Pos:* Bd mem, Found for Community of Artists, dir exhib dept, New Muse Mus, 76-78; consult, African-Am Caribbean Cult Ctr, Brooklyn, NY; bd mem, NY State Coun Human, currently; exec vpres bd mem, Artists Equity and Artists Welfare Fund, New York. *Teaching:* Instr portraiture, painting & drawing, Brooklyn Mus, 73-78; instr painting & drawing, Ethical Cult Soc, 76-; guest lectr, New Sch Social Res, Cornell Univ & Studio Mus, Harlem; instr drawing, Jamaica Sch Art, Jamaica, West Indies. *Awards:* Jerome Straka Award, Nat Arts Club, 77. *Bibliog:* Painting My World (film, 26 min). *Mem:* Art Students League; Allied Artists; Brooklyn Arts & Cult Asn (consult, 78, bd mem regrant prog, 81-82); Brooklyn Consortium Artists & Arts Inc. *Media:* Oil, Watercolor. *Publ:* Contribr, Attica Book; illusr, Intimate Portrait of Martin Buber, Viking Press; illusr, Essence Mag; auth, Found for Community of Artists; contribr, Cult Post, Nat Endowment Arts, Artspeak. *Dealer:* Brooklyn Consortium for Artists & the Arts 135 Eastern Parkway Brooklyn NY 11238. *Mailing Add:* 135 Eastern Pkwy Brooklyn NY 11238

COPT, LOUIS J
PAINTER
b, Emporia, Kans, Jan 29, 49. *Study:* Emoria State Univ, BA, 71; Art Students League (New York), 85; Univ Kans - Landscpace Class, 86. *Comn:* Grand Canyon (oil), Kans Geological Survey, Lawrence, Kans, 91; watercolor landscape, City of Lawrence, Kans, 91; Grand Canyon (oil), Mike Hayden (Asst Secy Interior), Washington, DC, 92. *Exhib:* Mid-4, Nelson-Atkins Mus, Kansas City, Mo, 87; Kans Watercolor Soc, Wichita Art Mus, 87-92; Kansas 9 - Kansas 8, Mulvane Art Mus, Topeka, 89-90. *Pos:* Pres, Lawrence Arts Comn, 85-86; bd mem, Asn Community Arts Kans, 91-; Kans Watercolor Soc, 85-93. *Awards:* Purchase Awards, Kans Watercolor Soc, 86, 89-90; Purchase Awards, Corporte Woods, 89-90; Am Artist Award, 5th Nat Midwest Pastel Soc, 90. *Bibliog:* Richard LeComte (auth), Artist scours landscape, Lawrence J World, 90; Jan Witkowski (auth), Craft art-survival, Topeka Capital J, 92; Louis Copt (auth), Winter watercolors, The Artist's Mag, 92. *Mem:* Kans Watercolor Soc; Assoc Arts Agencies of Kans; Lawrence Arts Comn (pres 85-86); Lawrence Art Guild (pres 84-85); Midwest Pastel Soc. *Media:* Oil, Watercolor. *Publ:* Auth, Finding color in the winter landscape, The Artists Mag, 92; illus, Battle for the prairie, Earthwatch, 92. *Dealer:* Kyle Garcia 2900 F Oakley Brookwood Ctr Topeka Kans 66614. *Mailing Add:* Eighth St Artists 619 E Eighth Lawrence KS 66044

CORAOR, JOHN E
MUSEUM DIRECTOR, ADMINISTRATOR
b Woodbury, NJ, Nov 30, 55. *Study:* Syracuse Univ, BFA, 77; Pa State Univ, MA, 81, PhD, 85. *Pos:* Managing ed, Museologist Quart, 80-83; exec dir, Tempe Arts Ctr, Ariz, 85-88; dir, Hecksher Mus, Hungtington, NY, 88-. *Teaching:* asst educ, H F Johnson Mus Art, Ithaca, NJ, 77-79; instr, Pa State Univ & State Col, 81-85. *Awards:* Northeast Mus Conf Fel, 80; Mayoral Proclamation in Recognition of Outstanding Service, City of Tempe, 88. *Mem:* Am Asn Mus; Mid-Atlantic Asn Mus (actg ed, 82-83, vchmn publs comt, 91-); Mus Asn Ariz (rep to exec bd, 87-88); Suffolk Co Cult Affairs Adv Bd, 90-; NY Soc Asn Mus (secy & counc, 92-); and others. *Publ:* Auth, Documentation, evaluation & dissemination: Museologist, 82; The perforative viewer: some pedagogical reflections from a phenomenological perspective, Pa State, 84; Fifty years of the museologist, Museologist, 85. *Mailing Add:* Heckscher Mus Prime Ave Huntington NY 11743

CORBIN, GEORGE ALLEN
HISTORIAN, WRITER
b Detroit, Mich, Oct 23, 41. *Study:* Oakland Univ, Rochester, Mich, BA(art hist), 63; Bucknell Univ, Lewisburg, Pa, MA, 68; Columbia Univ, MA(art hist), 71, PhD(primitive & pre-Columbian art), 76. *Teaching:* From asst to assoc prof & chair art, Lehman Col, New York, 69- *Mem:* Col Art Asn. *Res:* Art of the South Pacific Islands, particularly Melanesia and Polynesia; African, North American Indian and pre-Columbian art. *Publ:* Auth, The art of the Baining: New Britain, Exploring the Visual Art of Oceania, Univ Press Hawaii, 79. *Mailing Add:* Dept Art 250 Bedford Park Blvd W Herbert H Lehman Col Bronx NY 10468

CORBINO, MARCIA NORCROSS
CRITIC, WRITER
b Tulsa, Okla. *Study:* Duke Univ, BA, 49; Art Students League, 50. *Pos:* Writer & photogr, Sarasota Jour, 74-77; critic, Sarasota Herald Tribune, 77-82; consult, Corbino Galleries, 85- *Awards:* Nat Endowment Arts Critic fel, 80. *Mem:* Int Asn Art Critics. *Res:* Contemporary art. *Publ:* Contribr, Centennial Salute, New York Times, 83; Contemporary art criticism, Am Artist, 83; Mira & outside Cuba/Fuera de Cuba, Art Papers, 89; Photograph of Villamizar Sculpture, Arte en Columbia Internacional, 90; John Chamberlain, Contemp Masterworks, St James Press, 91. *Mailing Add:* 1111 N Gulfstream Ave No 6B Sarasota FL 34236

CORDINGLEY, MARY BOWLES
PAINTER
b Des Moines, Iowa, Jan 1, 18. *Study:* Minneapolis Sch Art & Design; Minneapolis Art Inst; Univ Minn; Colorado Springs Fine Arts Ctr; Mont State Univ; also with Steve Rettegi, New York, Hilton Leech, Fla, Paul Olsen, Minneapolis, Robert E Wood, Zoltan Szabo, Carleton Plummer & Tony Couch. *Work:* Great Falls Pub Libr, Mont; and over 300 pvt collections. *Exhib:* Traveling exhibs, 66, 67 & 86 & Print Show, 70, Mont Inst Arts; Nat League Am Pen Women Nat Biennial, Washington, DC, 67 & 70; Jr League Print Shows, Great Falls, Mont; and over 30 one-man shows incl C M Russell Mus, Great Falls, 67 & 71, C M Russell Auction, 77, Univ Mont Mus Rockies, 70 & Univ Minn; Nat Traveling Watercolor Show, 86; Kessel-Long Gallery, Scottsdale, Ariz; Gov Mansion Exhib, 90. *Pos:* Creator & owner, Orig Pioneer Prints Notepaper Co. *Mem:* Mont State Arts Coun; Mont Inst Arts; Prof Women Artists Mont; Sierra Artists' Network, 91-; Adv Bd, Sierra, Nev Col, 92. *Media:* Oil, Watercolor. *Publ:* Illus, The Tobacco Route Geological Society Guide Book,92; This I Believe, booklet, Illustrations. *Mailing Add:* 1618 Gainey Ranch Rd No 133 Scottsdale AZ 85258

CORDY-COLLINS, ALANA (KATHLEEN)
CURATOR, EDUCATOR
b Los Angeles, Calif, June 5, 44. *Study:* Univ Calif, Los Angeles, BA(art hist), 70, MA(archeol), 72, PhD(archeol), 76. *Pos:* Mem chmn, Archeol Inst Am, San Diego Chap, 77-78, pres, 79-81; cur, Latin Am Collections, San Diego MusMan, 79- *Teaching:* Instr archeol, Univ Calif, Los Angeles 72-74; instr art & archeol, Univ Calif, San Diego 74-79 & San Diego Mesa Col, Calif, 75-80; assoc prof anthrop, Univ San Diego, 80- *Awards:* Altman Art Award, Univ Calif, Los Angeles, 72. *Res:* Iconographic study of Chavin & Peru art; shamanic art; function of art in culture. *Publ:* Ed, Pre-Columbian Art History, Selected Readings, Vol 2, 82; auth, The Cerro Sechin massacre: Did it happen?, Mus of Man Ethic Technotes, No 18, 83; Ancient Andean art as explained by Andean ethnohistory: An historical review, 83 & coauth (with D D McClelland), Upstreaming along the Peruvian north coast, 83, Brit Archeol Reports; Mega-Ninos, Spondylos Shells, and the Chimor-Calangone Connection, J New World Archaeol, Inst of Archeol, Univ Calif, Los Angeles (in press). *Mailing Add:* Mus Man Balboa Park San Diego CA 92101

CORKERY, TIM (TIMOTHY JAMES)
PAINTER, EDUCATOR
b Washington, DC, Oct 30, 31. *Study:* Univ Chicago Univ Col, 55-59; Art Inst Chicago, BFA, 60; Inst Allende Univ Guanajuato, Mex, MFA, 64. *Work:* Baltimore Mus Art; Idaho First Nat Bank, Boise; Alcoa Aluminum Co, Pittsburgh; Johnson & Johnson Inc, Newark, NJ. *Comn:* Mural for pub housing, Dept of Housing & Community Develop, Baltimore, 73; indoor mural for Univ Baltimore, Mayor's Adv Comt for Art & Cult, 79; indoor mural for Arts Tower, Baltimore, 80. *Exhib:* Eighteenth Area Exhib, Corcoran Gallery Art, Washington, DC, 67; one-man shows, Royal Marks Gallery, New York, 69 & 70 & Max Hutchinson Gallery, New York, 73 & 74; Univ Md, Baltimore Co, 75; Univ Ore Mus Art. *Collections Arranged:* Seventeenth Area Exhib (cataloged), Corcoran Gallery Art, Washington, DC, 65; Washington 20 Years (cataloged), Baltimore Mus Art, 70; Mem Gallery, Albright-Knox Gallery, 70 & 75; New Washington Painting (cataloged), Hayden Gallery, Mass Inst Technol, 71; Washington Art, Richmond Mus Exten, 71; Artists Making Art, Baltimore Mus Art, 72; Synergy-Artists One Plus One Equals Three (cataloged), Thorpe Intermedia Gallery, Sparkill, NY, 82. *Teaching:* Instr fine arts & painting, Corcoran Sch Art, Washington, DC, 65-67; instr painting, Md Inst Col Art, Baltimore, 67-77; vis artist painting, Univ Ore, Eugene, 77-78 & Sch Art, Inst Chicago, 78. *Awards:* Purchase Awards, Baltimore Mus 70 & Macht Found, 70; Munic Art Soc Award, 72. *Bibliog:* Sidra Stich (auth), Five Washington artists, Art Int Mag, 12/71; Carter Ratcliff (auth), article, Art Spectrum Mag, 2/75; Ellen Lubell (auth), article, Arts Mag, 2/75. *Mem:* Col Art Asn Am. *Media:* Oil on Canvas. *Mailing Add:* 49 W 19th St No 5 New York NY 10011

CORMACK, MALCOLM
CURATOR, HISTORIAN
b Birmingham, Eng, Dec 6, 35. *Study:* Courtauld Inst Art Univ London, BA, 59; Cambridge Univ, Eng, MA, 65. *Pos:* Asst keeper, City Birmingham Mus & Art Gallery, Eng, 59-62; from asst keeper to keeper, Fitzwilliam Mus, Cambridge, 62-76; cur paintings, Yale Ctr Brit Art, 76- *Teaching:* Instr art hist, Cambridge Univ, 62-76; instr, Yale Univ, 76- *Mailing Add:* Va Mus Fine Arts 2800 Grove Ave Richmond VA 23221-2466

CORMIER, ROBERT JOHN
PAINTER, LECTURER
b Boston, Mass, May 26, 32. *Study:* R H Ives Gammell Studios, cert. *Work:* Maryhill Mus, Goldborough, Wash; Superior Courthouse, Cambridge, Mass; Univ Sch, Shaker Heights, Ohio; Salem Courthouse, Mass; Suffolk Co Courthouse, Boston, Mass. *Comn:* Portraits for St Michael's Church, Charleston SC; John Hancock Mutual Life Insurance Co, 81; Mass Appellate Court, Boston, 83; Mass Supreme Judicial Court, Boston, 90; Boston Col Law Sch, Newton MA, 90. *Exhib:* New Eng Artists Contemp Ann, 54-69; Guild of Boston Artists, 60-90; Boston Arts Festival, 62; Coun Am Artists Socs, New York, 66; Springfield Mus, Mass, 79. *Pos:* Mem, City Art Comn, Boston, 82- *Teaching:* Instr drawing & painting, Vesper George Sch Art, 69-83; pvt instr, studio & artasns. *Awards:* Grand Prize, Boston Arts Festival, 62; Gold Medal of Honor, Coun Am Artists Socs, 65; Greenshields Found Award, 70. *Mem:* Guild Boston Artists (secy, bd gov, 70-81 pres, 82-86); Copley Soc Boston (vpres, 70-77); Portraits, Inc. *Media:* Oil, Pastel. *Mailing Add:* 30 Ipswich St Boston MA 02115

CORN, WANDA M
HISTORIAN, EDUCATOR
b New Haven, Conn, Nov 13, 40. *Study:* Washington Square Col, New York Univ, BA, 63; Inst Fine Arts, New York Univ, MA, 65, PhD, 74. *Collections Arranged:* The Color of Mood: American Tonalism, 1880-1910, (auth, catalog), 72; The Art of Andrew Wyeth (auth, catalog), 73; American Art: An Exhibition from the Collection of Mr & Mrs John D Rockefeller 3rd, 76; Grant Wood: The Regionalist Vision (auth, catalog), 83-84. *Pos:* Vis cur, Fine Arts Mus, San Francisco, 72, 73, 76 & 84 & Minneapolis Inst Arts, 82-84; comnr, Nat Mus Am Art, Smithsonian, 88-; acting dir, Stanford Mus, 89-91; dir, Stanford Humanities Ctr, 92- *Teaching:* Lectr Am art, Univ Calif, Berkeley, 70 & 76; from asst prof mod Europ & Am art to assoc prof, Mills Col, 70-80; assoc prof Am art, Stanford Univ, 81-88, prof, 89-, chmn, 89-91. *Awards:* Smithsonian Fel, Nat Mus Am Art, 78-79; Fel, Woodrow Wilson Int Ctr Scholars, 79-80; fel, Stanford Humanities Ctr, 82-83; Am Coun Learned Soc Awards, 82 & 86; Regents Fel, Smithsonian Inst, 87. *Mem:* Col Art Asn (bd dir, 70-73 & 80-84); Women's Caucus Art (adv bd, 80-84); Am Studies Asn (nat coun, 86-89). *Res:* American art from the Civil War to the present. *Publ:* Auth, Coming of Age: Historical Scholarship in American Art, Art Bul, LXX, pp 188-207, 6/88. *Mailing Add:* Dept Art Stanford Univ Stanford CA 94305

CORNELL, DAVID E
CERAMIST, SCULPTOR
b Kalispell, Mont, Feb 24, 39. *Study:* Mont State Univ, BS(art); Archie Bray Found, with Kenneth Ferguson & David Shaner; Corcoran Sch Art, with Teuro Hara & Richard LaFean; Alfred Univ, MFA(ceramics), with Bob Turner, Val Cushing & Daniel Rhodes. *Work:* Greenville Art Mus, SC; Charles M Russell Gallery, Great Falls, Mont; Libby Dam, Treaty Tower, Vis Ctr, Libby, Mont; Archie Bray Found, Helena, Mont; Mont State Univ, Bozeman. *Comn:* Ceramic fountain fixtures, Mont State Univ Libr, 64; Treaty Panel (sculpture), US Army Corps 18 Engineers & Mont Hist Soc, 75. *Exhib:* Tenth Int Exhib Ceramic Art, Smithsonian Inst, Washington, DC, 66; Norfolk Mus Art, Va, 66; Harriman Gallery, Orange Co Community Col, Middletown, NY, 69; Handblown Glass Exhib, Corning Glass Ctr, NY, 69; Mint Mus Art, NC, 70; Appalachian Corridors: Exhib 2, Charleston, Wva, 70; NW Crafts Show, Henry Gallery, Seattle, Wash, 71; Cheney Cowles Mem Mus, Spokane, Wash, 73; Mont State Hist Soc Exhib, Poindexter Gallery, Helena, 75. *Pos:* Artist-in-residence, Penland Sch of Crafts, 69-70; dir, Archie Bray Found, 70-77; owner-mgr, Pear Blossom Pottery, Talent, Ore; pres, Clayfolk, Inc, 78-79. *Awards:* First Prize, Univ Exhib, Mont State Univ, 64; Jury Award, 11th Biennial NW Ceramics, Ore Ceramics Studio, 65; Best of Show, 11th Ann Own Your Own, Southern Colo State Col, 74. *Bibliog:* Mary Lou O'Neil (auth), Archie Bray Found, Mountain Lines, Mountain Bell Tel & Tel, 11/70; David Depew (auth), Archie Bray Found, Ceramics Mo, 5/72; Jerry Metcalf (auth), Today at the Bray, Mont Arts, Mont Inst Arts, 76. *Mem:* Helena Arts Coun (vpres, 73); Mont Art Gallery Dir Asn (secy, 75-76); Nat Coun Educ in Ceramic Arts; Am Crafts Coun; Glass Art Soc. *Media:* Ceramic. *Mailing Add:* 2316 S Pacific Hwy Talent OR 97540

CORNELL, THOMAS BROWNE
PAINTER, PRINTMAKER
b Cleveland, Ohio, Mar 1, 37. *Study:* Amherst Col, Mass, BA, 59; Yale Univ, 59-60. *Work:* Mus Mod Art, New York; Princeton Univ Libr; Lessing J Rosenwald Collection, Nat Collection Fine Arts, Washington, DC; Cleveland Mus Art, Ohio; Harvard Univ, Cambridge, Mass; and others. *Comn:* Mural, 64 & portrait, 79, Bowdoin Col, Brunswick, Maine; bronze plaques, Maine State Comn on Arts & Humanities, 68; Dionysus (bronze plaque), J Walter Thompson Inc, New York, 70; portrait, Va Engineering Found, 81; mural, John Hancock Mutual Life Insurance Co, Boston Mass, 86. *Exhib:* Contemp Painters & Sculptors as Printmakers, Mus Mod Art, New York, 66; Young New Eng Painters Traveling Exhib, 69; Living Am Artists & the Figure, Pa State Univ, 74; 30 Yrs of Am Printmaking, Brooklyn Mus, NY, 76; one-man shows, A M Sachs Gallery, New York, 79 & 81 & G W Einstein Co, NY, 86 & 89; Santa Barbara Mus Art, Calif, 80; Utopian Visions, Contemp Art Coun, Mus Mod Art, NY, 87 & 88; American Painting After the Death of Painting, Kuznetsky Most, Moscow USSR, 89. *Collections Arranged:* Thomas Cornell Drawings & Prints, 71, & Paintings--the Birth of Nature, 90, Bowdoin Col; and others. *Teaching:* Instr art, Univ Calif, Santa Barbara, 60-62; lectr visual arts prog, Princeton Univ, NJ, 69-71; prof present art & chmn art dept, Bowdoin Col, 63-82, prof art, currently. *Awards:* Louis Comfort Tifanny Award, 61; Nat Inst Arts & Lett Grant, 64; Nat Found Arts & Humanities Grant, 66-67; Fulbright Grant, 66; Ford Found Grant, 70; and others. *Bibliog:* Charles Jencks (auth), Post-Modernism: The New Classicism in Art & Architecture, Rizzoli, Publ, 87. *Mem:* Col Art Asn; Union of Maine Visual Artists; Nat Acad Design. *Media:* Oil, Pastel; Etching, Monotype. *Publ:* Illusr, The Monkey, pvt publ, 59; The Defense of Gracchus Babeuf, Gehenna Press, 64, Univ Mass, 67 & Schocken Press, 71; illusr & ed, Frederick Douglas, 64, illusr & ed, William Lloyd Garrison, 64 & illusr, Composed for Dying, 64, Tragos Press; illusr, Voiceprints, Romulus Eds, 89. *Mailing Add:* 305 Maine St Brunswick ME 04011

CORNETTE, MARY ELIZABETH
DEALER, PAINTER
b Russellville, Ky, Sept 9, 09. *Study:* Bowling Green Col Com, BS; Western Ky State Univ, MS; WTex State Univ, with Dr Emilio Caballero; also with Dirk Van Driest, Taos, NMex. *Pos:* Dir & pres, Canyon Art Gallery, Inc, Tex, 65- *Awards:* WTex CofC Cult Achievement Award, 72. *Bibliog:* Norman Nadel (auth), Mary Elizabeth Cornette brings Tenkei Tachibana wall screens to US as gift to people of US, Scripps-Howard Publs, 10/17/72. *Media:* Watercolor, Oil. *Specialty:* Representational art of Southwestern United States, especially of Texas. *Mailing Add:* Canyon Art Gallery 2710 Fourth Ave Canyon TX 79015

CORNIN, JON
PAINTER
b New York, NY, Mar 24, 05. *Study:* NY Univ; Art Students League; and with Raphael Soyer. *Exhib:* Palace of Legion of Honor, San Francisco; Los Angeles Co Mus; de Young Mem Mus, San Francisco; Sweat Mem Mus, Portland, Maine; J B Speed Mus, Louisville, Ky; San Francisco Mus Art; and others in US, Can & Japan. *Teaching:* Instr, Cornin Studio Wkshp, Berkeley & Oakland, Calif, 51-80. *Media:* Oil, Casein Tempera. *Publ:* Auth, Painter's Credo: Selected Notes, Stone House Press, Roslyn, NY, 85. *Mailing Add:* 812 Northvale Rd Oakland CA 94610

CORR, JAMES D
PAINTER, COLLEGE EDUCATOR
b Missoula, Mont, Feb 13, 31. *Study:* Western Mont Col, BS(art); Univ Mont, ME(art); also with Peter Volkous & Walter Hook. *Work:* Western Gallery & Co High Sch, Dillon, Mont; Univ Collection, Missoula; Copper City Mus, Anaconda, Mont. *Exhib:* Electra II, Helena, Copper Camp Festival, Butte, Mont; Mondak, Sidney, Mont. *Pos:* Gallery dir, Western Gallery, Dillon, Mont, 70. *Teaching:* Assoc prof art, Western Mont Col, 70-86. *Awards:* Mary Baker Emerick Art Chair. *Mem:* Mont Watercolor Soc; Mont Inst Arts; Beaver Head Watercolor Soc. *Media:* Multimedia. *Mailing Add:* 515 South Dakota Dillon MT 59725

CORREA, FLORA HORST
PAINTER
b Seattle, Wash, Feb 16, 08. *Study:* Univ Wash, BA(art); also with Kenneth Callahan, Sergei Bongart, Richard Yip, Raymond Brose, Mark Tobey & Rex Brandt. *Work:* Seattle First Nat Bank Collection; Craftsman Press, Seattle; Pac First Fed Savings & Loan Asn, Seattle; Rainier Bank, Seattle; Krusteaz Centennial Mills Collection, Oberto, Trident Seafoods. *Exhib:* Puget Sound Area Exhib, Frye Art Mus, 64-65, 67-68 & 75; Univ Ore Invitationals, 67 & 71-72; Northwest Watercolor Ann, Seattle, 64-67 & 72-75; Watercolor Exhib, Seattle Pac Col, 75; Grand Galleria Exhib, 75; Nat Biennial Exhib, Nat League Am Penwomen, 86. *Awards:* Excellence in Art Award, Older Womens League, 73-80; First & Second in Watercolor, 79 & 81, First & Second in Oils, 70 & 81, Penwomen's Wash State Biennial. *Bibliog:* Linda Plumb (auth), Flora Correa's distinctive collage art, View Northwest, 5/75. *Mem:* Northwest Watercolor Soc (secy, 67); Women Painters of Wash (pres, 69-70); Nat League Am Penwomen (vpres, Artist Div, Seattle Br, 74-77); Olympic Art Asn, Seattle (pres, 74-77). *Media:* Watercolor, Oil. *Mailing Add:* 919 109th Ave NE Bellevue WA 98004

CORSO, SAMUEL (JOSEPH)
STAINED GLASS ARTIST, PAINTER
b Monroe, La, Jan 11, 53. *Study:* La State Univ, Baton Rouge, BFA, 75, MFA, 77; studied mosaics, sumi-e & bronze sculpture with Paul A Dufour, 77, 78 & 79. *Work:* River Oaks Sq Arts & Crafts Ctr, Alexandria, La; Louisville Arts Club, Ky; Signal Corp, La Jolla, Calif; Duravent Corp, Redwood, Calif; Premier Bancorp, Baton Rouge, La. *Comn:* Mosaic & stained glass, St Francis Cabrini Hospital, Alexandria, La, 88; stained glass, St Mark's Catholic Church, Gonzalez, La, 89; mosaic mural, Sisters Charity Incarnate Word, Houston, Tex, 90; stained glass, Soc of Jesus Retirement Home, New Orleans, 90; bronze sculpture, Emmy Lou Biedenharn Found, Monroe, La, 90. *Exhib:* Mint Mus Art, Charlotte, NC, 78 & 80; Missoula Mus Art, Mont, 88; Materials, Hard & Soft, Denton, Tex, 88; La Festival Arts, Masur Mus Art, Monroe, 89; Texas & Neighbors Exhib, 90; Southeastern Juried Competition, Fine Arts Mus South, Mobile, Ala, 90; and others. *Teaching:* Instr, Arrowmont Sch Arts & Crafts, Gatlinburg, Tenn, 78, 81 & 88; asst prof drawing & design, La State Univ, Baton Rouge, 81, instr, 83-91. *Awards:* Am Crafts Coun Southeast, 86; Terrebonne Hist & Cult Soc, 88; New Orleans Art League, 88. *Bibliog:* Albert Lewis (auth), Stained glass goes to college, Glass Mag, Vol V, No 4, 78; Lisa Corbin (auth), A painter's viewpoint, Prof Stained Glass, 5/91; Robert Kehlmann (auth), Neus Glass. *Mem:* La Crafts Coun (bd dirs, 83-86); La State Arts Coun; La Watercolor Soc; Ala Watercolor Soc; Am Crafts Coun; and others. *Media:* European & Domestic Glass; Watercolor, Sumi-E. *Publ:* Contribr, Robert Jenson's & Patricia Conway's Ornamentalism, Clarkson N Potter, 81; auth, New glass review No 4, Corning Mus, 82; Spectrum, Glass Mag, 12/82; contribr, Experiments in Water, 88 & How to Make an Oil Painting, 90, Watson/Guptil Press. *Dealer:* Trinity Gallery 249 Trinity Ave Atlanta GA 30303; Baton Rouge Gallery 1440 City Park Dr Baton Rouge LA 70808. *Mailing Add:* 615 Steele Blvd Baton Rouge LA 70806

CORTESE, DON F
PRINTMAKER, INSTRUCTOR
b Chicago, Ill, Dec 30, 34. *Study:* Art Inst Chicago, BFA; Syracuse Univ, MFA. *Work:* Libr Cong, Washington, DC; Art Inst Chicago; Boston Pub Libr; Houghton Libr, Harvard Univ; Uffizi Gallery, Florence, Italy. *Comn:* Intaglio Print, Impressions Workshop, Boston, Mass, 71; etching on experimental paper, Boise Cascade, 80; 60th Int Paper Conf, Ottawa, Can, 85; 25th Anniversary Syracuse Pulp & Paper Found, 85; 120th Anniversary King & King Architects, Handmade paper & print, Syracuse, NY, 88. *Exhib:* The 58th Conn Acad Fine Arts Exhib, Wadsworth Atheneum, Hartford, 68; Nat Print & Drawing Exhib, Northern Ill Univ, 70; Int Print Competition, Seattle Art Mus, Wash, 71; Graphics 71 Nat Print Exhib, Western NMex Univ, 71; Artists of Cent NY, Munson-Williams-Proctor Inst Mus, Utica, NY, 76; Breaking the Bindings-American Book Art Now, Elvehjem Mus, Univ Wis, 83; Self-portraits, American Artists, Uffizi Gallery, Florence, Italy, 83. *Collections Arranged:* New England Land Grant Universities Workshop, 81; June Exhib of Visiting Printmakers, Herter Gallery; Univ Mass Botany of Papermaking Invitational, Mo Botanical Garden Libr, St Louis, 81. *Teaching:* Prof hand papermaking & book arts printmaking, Sch Art, Syracuse Univ, NY, 65- *Awards:* Purchase Prize, Nat Print Competition, Western NMex Univ, 71; Ford Found Grant, Hand Papermaking, Print & Book, 80; First prize, Common Threads Exhib, Schweinfurth Art Ctr, Auburn, NY, 88. *Mem:* Empire State Crafts Alliance; Friends of Daro Hunter Paper Mus. *Mailing Add:* Dept Art Syracuse Univ Syracuse NY 13210

CORTESE, EDWARD FORTUNATO
ADMINISTRATOR, ILLUSTRATOR
b Philadelphia, Pa, Jan 11, 22. *Study:* Temple Univ, 50; Philadelphia Col Art, with Henry Pitz, BFA, 51. *Exhib:* Bk Fair, Pa Acad Fine Arts, Philadelphia, 55. *Pos:* Art dir, John C Winston Co-Holt Rinehart Winston, Philadelphia, 50-60, Pa Lithographic Co, Philadelphia, 61-62, Curtis Publ Co, Philadelphia & Indianapolis, 63-79 & Benjamin Franklin Lit & Med Soc Inc, Indianapolis, 79- *Teaching:* Instr illus, Philadelphia Col Art, 65-70. *Media:* Watercolor, Ink. *Publ:* Illusr, The Lost Colony, A Boy for a Man's Job, To Beat a Tiger, 57-58; The Adventures of Tom Sawyer, Robinson Crusoe, King Arthur, Black Beauty & To the Shores of Tripoli, 58-59, John C Winston Co, Philadelphia; A Visit to the White House, Curtis Publ Co, 64; Dinosaurs, Curtis Publ Co, 79. *Mailing Add:* 2719 Embassy Row Indianapolis IN 46224

CORTOR, ELDZIER
PAINTER, PRINTMAKER
b Richmond, Va, Jan 10, 16. *Study:* Art Inst Chicago, 36 & 41; Inst Design, Ill Inst Technol, 42-43; Columbia Univ, New York, 47. *Work:* Nat Gallery Am Art, Washington, DC; Mus Mod Art & Am Fedn Art, New York; Mus du Peuple Haitien, Port au Prince, Haiti; Art Inst Chicago; Portland Art Mus, Ore. *Comn:* Painting, comn by Julius Rosenwald Fel, Chicago, 45-47; painting, comn by John Simon Guggenheim Fel, New York, 49-50. *Exhib:* Reality Expanded, Studio Mus, New York, 73; Jubilee, Boston Mus Fine Art, 75; Migrations, Museo de Arte Moderno LaTertulia, Cali, Columbia, 76; Southern Heritage, Columbia Mus Art, SC, 80; Three Masters, Kenkeleba Gallery, 88; and others. *Teaching:* Instr, Ctr Art, Port au Prince, Haiti, 49-51 & Pratt Inst, Brooklyn, NY, 72-74. *Awards:* Bertha A Florsheim Award, Am Artists, 45 & William H Bartels Award, Chicago Artists, 46, Art Inst Chicago; Hon Mention, Painting USA, Carnegie Inst, Pittsburgh, 47. *Bibliog:* Cedric Dover (auth), American Negro Art, New York Graphic Soc, 60; Elton C Fax (auth), 17 Black Artists, Dodd Mead Co, 71; Elso Honig Fine (auth), The Afro-American Artist, New York. *Mem:* Artist Fel, Inc; Soc Am Graphic Artists. *Media:* Oil. *Dealer:* Assoc Am Artists 663 Fifth Ave New York NY 10022. *Mailing Add:* 35 Montgomery St New York NY 10002

CORTRIGHT, STEVEN M
ASSEMBLAGE ARTIST, CONCEPTUAL ARTIST
b Long Beach, Calif, Mar 18, 42. *Study:* Stanford Univ, BA & MA; Univ NMex, Tamarind Workshop artist-teacher fel. *Work:* Mus Mod Art, New York; Int Mus Photog, Rochester, NY; Victoria & Albert Mus, London; Brooklyn Mus, NY; Albright-Knox Mus, Buffalo, NY. *Exhib:* One-man shows, Franklin Furnace, New York, 78, Univ RI, Kingston, 81, Western Wash Univ, Bellingham, 85 & Santa Barbara Mus Art (with catalog), Calif, 86; Fifth & Eighth Int Brit Print Biennale, Braford, Eng, 76 & 83; Dokumenta VI (with catalog), Kassell WGer, 77; Not Just for Laughs (with catalog), The New Mus, New York, 81; Visual Paradox (with catalog), Kohler Arts Ctr, Sheboygan, Wis, 88. *Teaching:* Prof art, Univ Calif, Santa Barbara, 67- *Awards:* Tamarind Lithography Workshop Artist/Teacher Fel, Univ NMex, Albuquerque, 65; Individual Artists Fel, Nat Endowment Arts, 80-81 & 87-88. *Bibliog:* Judith Hoffberg (auth), review of Steven Cortright: California Viewpoints, High Performance, Los Angeles, spring 87. *Publ:* Auth, East-West: A Book of Fortune, Chicago Bks, New York, 86. *Mailing Add:* c/o Santa Barbara Contemp Arts Forum 653 Paseo Nuevo Santa Barbara CA 93101

CORWIN, SOPHIA M
PRINTMAKER, PAINTER
b New York, NY. *Study:* Nat Acad Sch Fine Arts; Art Students League; Hoffman Sch; Archipenko Sch; Phillips Gallery Art Sch, Washington, DC, with Karl Knaths, scholar, 45; NY Univ, BA & MA(creative arts). *Work:* Middlesex Univ Hosp, New Brunswick, NJ. *Exhib:* One-woman shows, Capricorn Gallery, Creative Art Gallery, NY, Colony Gallery, O Street Gallery, Washington, DC & Hansen Gallery, 89-90, NOHO Gallery, 92 & Visual Art Wooster Street, NY; Baltimore Mus Art; Mus in the Mall, Bridgeport & Silvermine Guild, Conn; Corcoran Gallery Art, Nat Collection Fine Arts & Phillips Mem Gallery, Washington, DC; Bergen Mus & Middlesex Gen Hosp, NJ; City Ctr Gallery; Aegis Gallery; Union Col; and many other group shows. *Teaching:* Grad asst related arts, NY Univ, 61-62; from instr to dir, Studio Workshop, Bronx House, NY, 62-73; lectr art hist, Coop Col Ctr Westchester, State Univ NY Col Purchase, 71-73; lectr art, New York City Drug Rehabilitation Ctr & Bedford Hills Women's Prison, 73-81. *Awards:* Nat Sculpture Competition Award, US Dept Housing & Urban Develop; Painting Award, Nat Asn Women Artists, 85; Honorarium for Sculpture, Queens Mus Art. *Mem:* Nat Soc Women Artists; Am Soc Contemp Artists; Women's Caucus on Art; Sculptors League. *Media:* Steel, Marble; Oil, Acrylic. *Publ:* Auth, article, Women's Studies Arts, Sculptors League, 78; article, Nat Community Arts Prog Forhud, 78; article, Women Artists, 78. *Dealer:* Bill Ratner 2386 Silver Ridge Rd Los Angeles CA 90039. *Mailing Add:* 79 Franklin Ave Yonkers NY 10705

COSGROVE, STANLEY
PAINTER
b Montreal, PQ, Dec 23, 11. *Study:* Beaux-Arts, Montreal; Art Asn Montreal; also with Orozco, Mex. *Work:* Nat Gallery Can; Vancouver Art Gallery; Mus

Mod Art, New York; Winnipeg Art Gallery; Beaverbrook Art Gallery, NB, Canada; Quebec Mus; Edmonton Art Gallery; and others. *Exhib:* Yale Univ; UNESCO; Montreal Mus Fine Arts; Quebec Provincial Mus; Nat Gallery Can, Ottawa, Ont; and others. *Teaching:* Ecole des Beaux Arts, Montreal, 44-58. *Awards:* Medal, Beaux-Arts, Montreal; Provincial Govt Scholar, Mex, 40-44; Travel Scholar in France, Fed Govt, 53. *Bibliog:* Jacques de Rousson (auth), Cosgrove-Dessins, Rousson Ed Inc, 89. *Mem:* Royal Can Acad Arts. *Media:* Oil, Pastel. *Publ:* Cosgrove, Collection Signatures, Eds Marcel Broquet. *Mailing Add:* 57 Mount Victoria Hudson PQ J0P 1H0 Canada

COST, JAMES PETER
PAINTER
b Philadelphia, Pa, Mar 3, 23. *Study:* Univ Calif, Los Angeles, BA, 50; Univ Southern Calif, MS, 59. *Work:* R W Norton Mus, Shreveport, Mass; Monterey Mus Art; Reader's Digest Collection. *Comn:* Numerous commissions internationally. *Exhib:* Artists Guild Gallery Am, Carmel, Calif, 61-63; Mus Fine Arts, Springfield, Mass, 65 & 73; Nat Arts Club, New York, 66; one-man shows, Northwood Inst, Midland, 71 & R W Norton Gallery, Shreveport, 71; plus others. *Pos:* Owner, James Peter Cost Gallery, 64-88. *Teaching:* Instr art, Los Angeles City Sch Dist; lectr art, Northwood Insts, Midland, Mich & Dallas, 71. *Awards:* Gold Medal, Franklin Mint, 75. *Mem:* Carmel Art Asn. *Mailing Add:* 27 Heaaula Place, Haiku Maui HI 96708

COSTA, EDUARDO
CONCEPTUAL ARTIST, SCULPTOR
b Buenos Aires, Argentina. *Study:* Univ Buenos Aires, MA; studied with Eng & Am Lit with Jorge L Borges. *Work:* Costume Inst, Metrop Mus Art, New York; New York Univ Libr; Columbia Univ Libr; Yale Univ Libr. *Exhib:* Eminent Immigrants, Snug Harbor's Newhouse Gallery, Staten Island, NY, 86; Fashion and Surrealism, Fashion Inst Tech, NY, 87 & Victoria & Albert Mus, London, Eng, 88; Latin-American Spirit, Bronx Mus Arts, NY, 88-89. *Teaching:* Guest artist & lectr, Cooper Union, 84-88. *Bibliog:* Jeff Weinstein (auth), All fashion involves ideas,Village Voice, 10/5/82; Gary Indiana (auth), Home, Village Voice, 7/8/86; Deborah Drier (auth), Obession, Art in Am, 2/88. *Media:* Mixed Media. *Publ:* Auth, The Shower Curtain, Even, Village Voice, 12/22/87; I have before me a letter, Sulfur Mag, spring 88. *Dealer:* Carla Stellweg Gallery 87 E Houston St New York NY 10012. *Mailing Add:* 167 Bleecker St, No 15 New York NY 10012

COSTAN, CHRIS
PAINTER
b Chicago, Ill, Sept 18, 50. *Study:* Univ Ill, Chicago, BA, 73, Santa Reparata Print Workshop, Florence, Italy, 74, Univ Wis, Madison, MA/MFA, 75. *Work:* Grand Rapids Mus Art, Mich; Brooklyn Mus, NY; Nelson-Atkins Mus Art, Kansas City, Mo; Dayton Art Inst, Ohio; Newark Mus, NJ. *Exhib:* New Work, New York, Seattle Art Mus, Wash & Spencer Mus Art, Lawrence, Kans, 88; Committed to Print, Mus Mod Art, New York, 88; Art by Chance, Nelson-Atkins Mus Art, Kansas City, 89; solo exhibs, Univ Wis, Madison, 74 & 75, Windows on White, New York, 85, Ave B Gallery, New York, 85, 86 & 87, Peter Miller Gallery, Chicago, 87, Germans Van Eck Gallery, New York, 88; Print Selections from the Permanent Collection, Brooklyn Mus, NY, 90; Intaglio Printmaking in the 1980's (catalog), 90, Hot off the Press (catalog), 91, Zimmerli Art Mus; Presswork: The Art of Women Printmakers (catalog), Nat Mus Women Arts, Washington, DC, 91; Apocalypse & Resurrection (catalog), Gallery 30, New York, 92. *Awards:* Nat Endowment Arts, 89-90. *Bibliog:* Yoshiko Ebihara (auth), New York art scene is a survival game, Brutus, 8/15/89; Joy Hakanson Colby (auth), Collect Calling, Detroit News, 11/6/90; Kay Larson (auth), Art/Kay Larson, New York Mag, 3/9/92. *Media:* Acrylic, Watercolor. *Publ:* Auth, Art by Chance (exhib catalog), Nelson-Atkins Mus Art, 89; Intaglio Printmaking in the 1980's (exhib catalog), 90; Presswork: The Art of Women Printmakers (exhib catalog), 91. *Mailing Add:* 303 Park Ave S, No 515 New York NY 10010

COSTANZA, JOHN JOSEPH
SCULPTOR, CERAMIST
b New York, NY, June 24, 24. *Study:* Tyler Sch Fine Arts, Temple Univ, BFA, 49; Univ Pa, cert, 43. *Work:* Philadelphia Col Performing Arts; Harcum Jr Col, Bryn Mawr, Pa. *Comn:* Ceramic murals, University City High Sch, Philadelphia Sch District, Pa; Paragon Industry, West Orange, NJ, Ampacet Corp, Mt Vernon, NY; Monsanto Corp, Montvale, NJ; Rauch, Duban & Venturi, Architects & Shubert Theatre, Philadelphia. *Exhib:* Nat Ceramic Competition, Everson Mus Art, Syracuse, NY, 58, 60, 62 & 64; New York World's Fair Invitational, 64-65; Smithsonian Drawing Nat, Washington, DC & traveling, 64-67; Painting, Drawing & Sculpture Invitational, Univ Del, Newark, 66-68; Philadelphia Regional Art Show, Philadelphia Mus Art, 67; Ceramics Invitational, Philadelphia Civic Ctr Mus, 67, 70 & 73; Ceramics Invitational, Mus Contemp Crafts, New York, 68, 75 & 77. *Pos:* Designer, Potters of Wall St, New York, 50-51. *Teaching:* Art, Devereux Sch, Devon, Pa, 51-53 & Sayre Jr High Sch, Philadelphia, 53-57; teacher ceramics, West Chester High Sch, Pa, 57-63; prof ceramics, Moore Col Art, Philadelphia, 63-73. *Awards:* Purchase Award, Univ Del Art Show, 65; Purchase Prize, Temple Univ Alumni Show, 68; First Prize, Sculpture, William Penn Mem Mus, Harrisburg, Pa, 71. *Bibliog:* Jack Bookbinder (dir), Black History, The Making of a Mural (film), Philadelphia Sch District, 75; Dr Burton Wasserman (auth), Exploring the Visual Art, Davis Publ, 76; Louis G Redstone (auth), Public Art-New Directions, McGraw Hill, 80. *Mem:* Artists Equity Asn; Am Craftsman Coun. *Media:* Clay. *Publ:* Ed, Gerry Williams's Nine Philadelphia Potters, Daniel Clark Found, 73. *Dealer:* Hahn Gallery 8439 Germantown Ave Philadelphia PA 19118. *Mailing Add:* 737 Polo Rd Bryn Mawr PA 19010

COSTELLO, CYNTHIA ANN
PAINTER, GRAPHIC ARTIST
b St Paul, Minn, Jan 26, 52. *Study:* Knox Col, BA(art), 74; Brooklyn Col (Charles A Shan Mem Scholar), MFA, 80; Fashion Inst Technol, ASS (textile design), 82. *Work:* Prince Street Gallery & Covington Fabrics, New York; Blue Cross Blue Shield Office, Philadelphia, Pa; Russell Reynolds Assoc; Pan Am Bldg, New York; Dewey Ballantine, Inc, New York. *Exhib:* 30 New York City Painters, Houghton House Gallery, Hobart & William Smith Cols, Geneva, NY, 82; Soho in the South, Archie Wolfe & Assoc, Memphis, Tenn, 83; Great Swamp XXV, Somerset County Environ Educ Ctr, Basking Ridge, NJ & Nabisco Brands Inc Gallery, East Hanover, NJ, 85; Summerscape II, Gross McCleaf Gallery, Philadelphia, 86; Montauk Club, Brooklyn, NY 88; one-woman show, Prince Street Gallery, 83, 86 & 89. *Pos:* Textile designer, Waverly Fabrics, 81-83; textile designer, Covington Fabrics, 84; textile designer & stylist, Anju Woodridge, New York, 85-89; textile wallcovering stylist, Schumacher & Co, 89- *Teaching:* Cur asst art hist, Brooklyn Col, NY, 78-80, asst instr painting, 80; instr drawing, Brooklyn Skills Exchange, NY, 79. *Awards:* Scholar, Skowhegan Sch Drawing & Sculpture, Maine, 80; Residency, Va Ctr Arts, Sweet Briar, 86. *Bibliog:* Paintings reproduced for contemporary interiors, Mod Living Mag, Japan, 83; Breda Joy (auth), Painting the Irish landscape, The Kerryman, Ireland, 84; article, New York Art Review. *Mem:* Graphics Artists Guild; Women's Art Registry, Minneapolis, Minn. *Media:* Oil, Pastel. *Dealer:* Gross McCleaf Gallery 1713 Walnut St Philadelphia PA 19103. *Mailing Add:* c/o Prince St Gallery 121 Wooster St New York NY 10012

COSTIGAN, CONSTANCE FRANCES
PAINTER, EDUCATOR
b NJ, July 3, 35. *Study:* Boston Mus Sch Fine Arts; Simmons Col, BA; Am Univ, MA; Univ Va; Univ Calif, Berkeley. *Work:* Phillips Collection, Washington, DC; Hirshhorn Mus, Washington, DC; Univ Iowa Mus; Dimock Gallery, George Washington Univ; also pvt collections in US & Gt Brit. *Exhib:* 19th Area Exhib, Corcoran Gallery Art, 74; Barbara Fiedler Gallery, Washington, DC, 79 & 82; 25 Washington Artists, Realism & Representation, Foundry Gallery, Washington, DC, 80; Del Mus Art, Wilmington, 80; Surface/Structure: Fiber Innovations, Arlington Arts Ctr, Va, 82; 10 Years, A Retrospective, Northern Va Community Col, 83; Franz Bader Gallery, Washington, DC, 85 & 90. *Collections Arranged:* Elements of Art: line (auth, catalog), Arlington Arts Ctr, Va, 80. *Pos:* Exhib designer, Smithsonian Inst, 57-59. *Teaching:* Instr studio art & crafts, Arlington Co Pub Sch, 70-76; instr drawing, design & painting, Smithsonian Inst, Washington, DC, 70-76; prof, George Washington Univ, 76-; distinguished vis prof, Am Univ in Cairo, Egypt, 80-81. *Awards:* Grant Award, Lester Hereward Cooke Found, Washington, DC, 78; GSAS Facilitating Fund, George Wash Univ, Washington, DC, 80. *Bibliog:* Lenore Miller (auth), Constance Costigan, Phillips Collection, Washington, DC, 77. *Mem:* Am Crafts Coun; fel Royal Soc Arts; fel MacDowell Colony; fel Ossabow Island Project; Col Art Asn. *Media:* All Media. *Dealer:* Franz Bader Gallery 1701 Pennsylvania Ave NW Washington DC 20006. *Mailing Add:* Dept Art George Washington Univ Washington DC 20050

COSTIN, FRANK
DEALER
Can citizen. *Study:* Univ Guelph, Can, BA. *Pos:* Dir, Gallery One, 80-86; dir, Costin & Klinworth Gallery, Toronto, currently. *Specialty:* Contemporary Canadian painting and sculpture. *Mailing Add:* 30 Glouster Toronto ON M5R 1G4 Canada

COSTLEY-JACOBS, AVERILLE ESTHER
DEALER, GALLERY DIRECTOR
b Washington, DC, Mar 24, 47. *Study:* Univ DC, 70-74; Northeastern Univ, Boston, 74-75. *Pos:* Art dealer & asst gallery dir, Galerie Triangle, Washington, DC, 78-; cur, First Am Bank Washington, DC, 82-84; visual arts panelist, DC Comn Arts & Humanities, 85-86. *Teaching:* First Class Inc,. *Bibliog:* Andre Shashaty (auth), Swann Street's Galerie provides an alternative, Rock Creek Monitor, 6/26/80; Delmar Lipp (auth), A reporter-at-large, Hill Rag, 5/1/81; Schroeder Cherry (auth), Home galleries, Palavra Arts Publ, winter 81-82. *Specialty:* Contemporary American traditional arts in all media. *Publ:* Contribr, Building an art collection for less, Sol, Julia Jones, 83; Are Washington artists disenchanted with Washington galleries?, Wash Mus News, 84; How to buy art intelligently, Int Women Artists Arch News, 86. *Mailing Add:* 3701 14th St NW Washington DC 20010

COTE, ALAN
PAINTER
b Windham, Conn, 37. *Study:* Sch Mus Fine Arts, Boston, MA, 60. *Work:* Solomon R Guggenhim Mus, Mus Mod Art, Whitney Mus Am Art, Paine Webber Group Inc, New York; J Patrick Lannan Found, Palm Beach, Fla; Suermondt Mus, Collection Ludwig, Ger. *Exhib:* Drawings, Recent Acquisitions, Whitney Mus Am Art, New York, 73 & 74; New York Artists, Albright-Knox Art Gallery, Buffalo, NY, 74; Biennial, Corcoran Gallery Art, Washington, DC, 75; American Drawing in Black and White, Brooklyn Mus, NY, 80; Three American Painters, Axiom Gallery, Melbourne, Australia, 81; Recent Aquisitions: Paintings and Sculpture, Mus Mod Art, New York, 83; Big Abstract Drawings, Pratt Inst Gallery, New York, 86. *Teaching:* Prof, art-painting, Bard Col, Hudson, NY, 70- *Awards:* Fel, Mus Fine Arts, Boston, 61-64; Guggenheim Award, 84; Painting Award, Nat Endowment Arts, 89. *Media:* Acrylic, Oil. *Mailing Add:* c/o Washburn Gallery 41 E 57th St 8th Floor New York NY 10022

COTHREN, MICHAEL WATT
EDUCATOR
b Nashville, Ark, Apr 9, 51. *Study:* Vanderbilt Univ, BA, 73; Columbia Univ, MA, 74, PhD, 80. *Teaching:* Prof art hist, chmn dept art, Swarthmore Col, 78- *Mem:* Int Ctr Medieval Art; Medieval Acad Am; Soc Francaise d'Archeologie; Corpus Vitrearom USA. *Res:* Gothic art & architecture, especially stained glass. *Publ:* Auth, The Iconography of Theophilus Windows in the First Half of the Thirteenth Century, Speculum 59, 84; The Choir Windows of Agnieres (Somme) and a Regional Style of Gothic Glass Painting, J Glass Studies 28, 86; The Twelfth-Century Crusading Window of the Abbey of Saint- Denis: Praeteritorum enim Recordatio Futurorum est Exhibitio, with Elizabeth A R Brown, Journal of the Warburg and Courtauld Institutes 49, 86; The Seven Sleepers and the Seven Kneelers: Prolegomena to a Study of the 'Belles Verrieres of Rouen Cathedral, Gesta 25, 86. *Mailing Add:* Dept Art Hist Swarthmore Col Swarthmore PA 19081

COTT, JEAN CAHAN
PAINTER
b Brooklyn, NY. *Study:* Pratt Inst, Brooklyn, NY, 29; Columbia Univ, BS, 36, MS. *Work:* Malkan Collection, Ft Worth, Tex. *Exhib:* Int Watercolor Show, Brooklyn Mus, NY, 39; Acad Arts & Letters, Childe Hassam Purchase Found, New York, 58; Nat Asn Women Artists Travel Show, Eng, France & Scotland, 64; Am Soc Contemp Artists Travel Show, Bergen Co Mus, NJ, 83; Purdue Univ, West Lafayette, Ind, 84; Springfield Art Mus, Mo. *Teaching:* Inst Fine arts, Julia Richman High Sch, NY, 36-42, advan painting, 58-74. *Awards:* Medal of Honor, Nat Asn Women Artists, 67; Watercolor Prize, Nat Asn Women Artists, 72 & Am Asn Contemp Artists, 88. *Bibliog:* Carol Campana (auth), review, Vassar Miscellany News, 64; Janice Bandyk (auth), Arts Review, Arts Mag, 77. *Mem:* Nat Asn Women Artists (adv bd, 84-85); Am Soc Contemp Artists. *Media:* Watercolor. *Mailing Add:* 165 E 66th St New York NY 10021

COTTER, HOLLAND
CRITIC, HISTORIAN
Study: Harvard Col, AB, 70; Columbia Univ. *Pos:* Ed, New York Arts J, 76-80; contrib ed, Art in America; ed assoc, Art News. *Mem:* Int Asn Art Critics. *Publ:* NY Times; Art in America; Art News; Arts Mag; Flash Art. *Mailing Add:* 91 Payson Ave Apt 6E New York NY 10034

COTTER, JAMES EDWARD
SCULPTOR, DESIGNER
b Corning, Iowa, Mar 13, 44. *Study:* Wayne State Col, BFA, 67; Univ Colo, 68; Univ Wyo, MA, 69. *Work:* Nat Broadcasting Corp, New York; Wayne State Col, Wayne, Nebr; Blount Found, Montgomery, Ala; McDonald's Corp, Oak Brook, Ill; Mr & Mrs Gerald Ford, Vail, Colo. *Exhib:* Midwest Biennial, Joslyn Art Mus, Omaha, Nebr, 64; Denver Art Mus, Denver, Colo, 69, 79 & 86; Artists Working in Metal, Sheldon Mus, Lincoln, Nebr, 76; Nat Ornamental Metal Mus, Memphis, Tenn, 79; Copper 2, Mus Art, Tucson, Ariz, 80; solo exhib, Nat Ornamental Metal Mus, Memphis, Tenn, 80; The Great American Cowboy, traveling exhib, Libr Cong, 83-84. *Pos:* Mem, Design Rev Bd Comt, Town of Vail, Colo, 74; mem adv bd, Colo Mountain Col, Vail, Colo, 74-80; adminr, Summer Vail Workshops Symp, Vail, Colo, 75-76. *Teaching:* Instr metalsmithing, Colo Mountain Col, Vail, Colo, 71-76; instr jewelry, Pendland Sch, Pendland, NC, 78. *Bibliog:* Murray Bovin (auth), Jewelry Making, 67; Lee & Jay Newman, Electroplating & Electroforming, Crown Publ. *Mem:* Soc N Am Goldsmiths Conf. *Media:* Metal & Stone; Mixed Media. *Dealer:* J Cotter Gallery 234 Wall St Vail Co 81657. *Mailing Add:* Box 385 234 E Wall St Vail CO 81657

COTTINGHAM, LAURA JOSEPHINE
CRITIC, WRITER
b Alexandria, Ky, Feb 4, 59. *Study:* Univ Chicago, BS, 81; Whitney Mus Independent Study Program. *Pos:* Managing ed, Art & Auction, 86-89; contrib ed, Contemporanea, Venice, Italy, currently; adv bd NY, Balcon, Madrid, Spain, currently. *Res:* Contemporary art, Feminism. *Publ:* Auth, The Feminist De-Mystique, Flash Art, 89; Why Second Wave Feminism Failed, Silent Baroque, 89; Thoughts Are Things: What is a Woman?, Contemporanea, 90; The Prison House of Language, Contemporanea, 90; Critical Poetics, Contemporanea, 90. *Mailing Add:* 172 E Fourth St No 8H New York NY 10009

COTTINGHAM, ROBERT
PAINTER, PRINTMAKER
b Brooklyn, NY, Sept 26, 35. *Study:* Pratt Inst, New York, 59-63, AA, 62. *Work:* Guggenheim Mus Art, Whitney Mus Am Art, Metrop Mus Art, Mus Mod Art, New York; Art Inst Chicago; Philadelphia Mus Art; Baltimore Mus Art, Md; Birmingham Mus Art, Ala; Butler Inst Am Art, Youngstown, Ohio; Fogg Art Mus, Harvard Univ, Cambridge, Mass; Honolulu Acad Arts, Hawaii; Hunter Mus Art, Chattanooga, Tenn; Libr Cong, Washington, DC; Milwaukee Art Mus, Wis; St Louis Art Mus, Mo; Tate Gallery, London, Eng; Utah Mus Fine Arts, Univ Utah, Salt Lake City; Va Mus Fine Arts. *Comn:* Permanent Public Installation of 12 enamel panels deplicting American Railroad Imagery, Union Station, Hartford, Conn. *Exhib:* Recent Acquistions, Whitney Mus Am Art & Hirshhorn Mus & Sculpture Garden, 77; Photo Realist Statement: Recent Painting by Robert Cottingham, Wichita Art Mus, 83, Fendrick Gallery, Washington, DC, 84 & Springfield Art Mus, Mo, 84; Photo Realism Painter, Printmaker, Art Guild, Farmington, Conn, 85, Abilene Christian Univ, Tex, 85, Ramsay Gallery, Chicago, 85 & Reynolds House Mus Am Art, Winston-Salem, NC, 85; A Print Retrospective, 1972-1986, Springfield Art Mus, Mo, 86; Photo Realism, Mus Art Sci & Indust, Bridgeport, Conn, 86, Karl Oskar, Westwood Hills, Kans, 86 & Brenda Kross Gallery, Columbus, Ohio, 86; one-man exhibs, Rolling Stock Series, Marisa Del Re Gallery, New York, 90, Brenda Kroos Gallery, Cleveland, Ohio, 92 & Butler Inst Am Art, Youngstown, Ohio, 92, Rahr-West Art Mus, Maritowoc, Wis, 90, Lyman Allyn Art Mus, New London, Conn, 91 & Harcourts Contemp, San Francisco, Calif, 91; retrospective, 1972-1989, Paine Art Ctr & Aboretum, Oshkosh, Wis, 90; and others. *Pos:* Art dir, Young & Rubicam Advertising, New York, 59-64 & Los Angeles, 64-68. *Teaching:* Instr, Art Ctr Col Design, Los Angeles, 69-70; artist-in-residence, Wesleyan Univ, Middletown, Conn, 87-92. *Awards:* Nat Endowment Arts Grant, 74-75; Artist of the Year Award, Fairfield Chamber Com, Fairfield, Conn, 88; Walter Gropius Fel, Huntington Mus Art, WVa, 92. *Bibliog:* Udo Kultermann (auth), New Realism, Tubingen, Ger, 72; Peter Schjeldahl (auth), Too easy to be art, New York Times, 5/74; Toni Del Renzio (auth), Robert Cottingham--the capers of the signscape, Art & Artists, London, 2/75; Jane Cottingham (auth), Techniques of three photorealist painters, Am Artist, 2/80. *Mem:* Nat Acad Design. *Media:* Acrylic, Oil; All Media. *Dealer:* Marisa del Re Gallery 41 E 57th St New York NY 10022. *Mailing Add:* 16 Blackman Rd PO Box 604 Newtown CT 06470-0604

COUCH, URBAN
PAINTER, EDUCATOR
b Minneapolis, Minn, Apr 27, 27. *Study:* Minneapolis Sch Art, BFA, 51; Skowhegan Sch Painting & Sculpture, 51; Cranbrook Acad Art, MFA, 59; Kyoto, Japan, 64-66. *Work:* Minneapolis Inst Arts; Walker Art Ctr, Minneapolis; Sioux City Art Ctr, Iowa; Cranbrook Mus, Bloomfield Hills, Mich; Hirshorn Collection, Washington DC; plus 167 others. *Exhib:* Walker Art Ctr, 59; Neville Mus Invitational, Green Bay, Wis, 67; Art in the Embassies, US State Dept, Sophia, Bulgaria & Canberra, Australia, 68-71; Minneapolis Inst Arts, 68; Difference of a Decade, Lee Nordness Galleries, New York, 69; plus 43 others. *Pos:* Graphic designer, USN, Calif, 45; alumni dir, Minneapolis Col Art & Design, 57; design consult, Control Data Corp, 60-62; consult-examiner prog, Comn on Cols & Univs, Chicago, 62-63; consult & examiner, NASAD Asn, 63-, chmn div art, 71-81; dir, Galleries & art collections, WVa Univ, 81-92, chmn div art, 87-89. *Teaching:* Instr art, Minneapolis Col Art & Design, 55-70, chmn found prog, 59-62, actg dir, 62-63, asst to dir, 63-64, actg chmn fine arts div, 65-66, chmn painting dept, 68-71; instr advan painting, Walker Art Ctr, 57-61; instr art, Kingswood Sch, Bloomfield Hills, Mich & Bloomfield Hills Art Ctr, 58-59; grad workshop, Univ Minn, 59-61; instr advan painting, Minnetonka Art Ctr, Minneapolis, 59-61; artist in residence, Minn Jr Cols, summers 67-69; instr grad painting, Calif Col Arts & Crafts, summer 70; prof painting, WVa Univ, 71-92; hon prof, WVa Univ, Discovery Lab, 92- *Mailing Add:* 1160 Charles Ave Morgantown WV 26505

COUGHLIN, JACK
PRINTMAKER, SCULPTOR
b Greenwich, Conn, Feb 19, 32. *Study:* Art Students League; RI Sch Design, BFA, 54, MS, 61. *Work:* Metrop Mus Art & Mus Mod Art, New York; Norfolk Mus Arts & Sci, Va; Staedelsches Kunst Inst, Frankfort, Ger; Nat Collection Fine Arts, Washington, DC; Mus Mod Art, New York. *Comn:* Ed original prints, Assoc Am Artists, 62-79, Int Graphic Arts Soc, 66 & 68, Silvermine Guild Artists, New Canaan, Conn, 67, Graphic Studio, Dublin, Ireland, 71 & Franklin Mint, Pa, 77, Springfield Mus, 83. *Exhib:* Nat Inst Arts & Lett, 70-92; Soc Am Graphic Arts, NY, 71-92; Nat Acad Design Ann Exhib, 74-92; 4th Int Graphic Biennial, WGer, 76; 3rd Norwegian Int Print Biennale, Norway, 76; Fifth Int Print Exhib, Barcelona, Spain, 85, 88. *Teaching:* Prof drawing & printmaking, Univ Mass, Amherst, 60- *Awards:* Nat Exhib Award for etching, Soc Am Graphic Artists, 77 & 81; Nat Exhib Awards for drawing & printing, Nat Acad Design, 80, 82 & 83; NDak Am Drawing Biennial, 90. *Bibliog:* Robin Skelton (auth), Imagination of Jack Coughlin, 70, Jack Coughlin: Irish portraits, 72 & Jack Coughlin: A Perspective View, 80, Malahat Rev, Univ Victoria, BC; article, Am Artist Mag, 6/86. *Mem:* Nat Acad Design; Soc Am Graphic Artists; Boston Printmakers. *Publ:* Illusr, Mnemosyne Lay in Dust, 66 & Synge-Petrarch, 71, Dolmen Press, Dublin, Ireland; Grotesques, 20 Etchings by Jack Coughlin, Aquarius Press, 70; 13 Irish Writers, Etchings, Godine Press, 73; Impressions of Bohemia, Pac Rim Galleries, 86. *Dealer:* Golden Cod Galleries E Commercial St Wellfleet MA 02667; Michaelson Gallery S Pleasant St Amherst MA 01002. *Mailing Add:* N Leverett Rd Montague MA 01351

COUPER, CHARLES ALEXANDER
PAINTER, INSTRUCTOR
b Portsmouth, NH, Feb 19, 24. *Study:* Vesper George Sch Art, Boston, cert; Cape Sch Art, Provincetown, Mass, with Henry Hensche; Ernest Lee Major Studio, Boston. *Work:* Greenshields Mus, Montreal; Attleboro Mus, Mass; Heritage Mus, Provincetown, Mass. *Comn:* Pastel portrait, Judge Phillip, Wolaver QC, NS, Can, 80. *Exhib:* One-man shows, Cape Cod Art Asn, 73, Soratoga Gallery-Bridgetown, NS, 92 & Guild Boston Artists, 73; Allied Artists Am, New York, 74; Grande Prix Int, Cannes, France, 74; Deauville Int, France, 75. *Pos:* Mem, Provincetown Art Comn, Mass, 78-79. *Teaching:* Instr life drawing & painting, Vesper George Sch Art, 55-; instr, Swain Sch Design, New Bedford, Mass, 65-68. *Awards:* Gloria Layton Mem Award, Allied Artists Am, 68; Elizabeth T Greenshields Found Mem Grant, Montreal, 69; Medal of Distinction, Grande Prix Int de Pientre de la Cote Azur, 75; and others. *Bibliog:* Critical rev in La Rev Mod, Paris, 69. *Mem:* Pastel Soc Can; Artist de Peintre de La Cote d'Azur; Visual Arts NS. *Media:* Oil, Pastel. *Dealer:* Duke of Argyle Gallery Halifax NS Can. *Mailing Add:* RR 1 Bear River NS B0S 1B0 Canada

COUPER, JAMES M
PAINTER, EDUCATOR
b Atlanta, Ga, Nov 21, 37. *Study:* Atlanta Art Inst; Ga State Univ; Fla State Univ. *Work:* Fla State Univ; Miami Art Ctr; John & Mable Ringling Mus Art; Ft Lauderdale Mus, Fla; Dept Natural Resources, Fla; Blount Collection, Ala; IBM, Inc; Art-in-Pub Places, Fla; and others. *Comn:* Mural, 20th Century Fox, 68. *Exhib:* Isaac Delgado Mus Art Nat, New Orleans, 66; Drawings 72, Ft Lauderdale, Fla, 72; Fla State Dept, 72; one-man shows, Fornal Gallery, New York, 78 & Metrop Mus & Art Ctrs, Fla, 81; Fla Int Univ, 82; Virginia Miller Gallery, Miami, 86; Gallery Z, NY, 87; Barbara Gillman Gallery, Miami, 91. *Collections Arranged:* Art of the Asian Mountains, 69; The Artist & The Sea, 69; Art of Italy, 69; Up & Out, 69-70. *Pos:* Asst to dir, Miami Art Ctr, 67-70; gallery dir, Fla Int Univ, 77-80. *Teaching:* Instr painting, Miami-Dade Jr Col, 64-68; instr painting, Miami Art Ctr, 65-72; from instr to prof painting, Fla Int Univ, 72-, chmn art dept, 77-78. *Awards:* Hand Hollow Fel, 81; Fla Int Univ Found Grant, 81; Fla Fine Arts Coun Grant, 81 & 90; Yaddo Fel, 87, Hambidge Ctr Fel, 90, 91. *Bibliog:* Reviews, Art News, 12/80, Miami News & Miami Herald, 4/80, American Artists, 10/86, Art News, 87, Miami Herald, 86, 87, 88, 89, 90, 91 & 92. *Media:* Oil. *Dealer:* Barbara Gilman Gallery 270 NE 39th St Miami FL. *Mailing Add:* 7845 SW 118th St Miami FL 33156

COURTNEY, BARBARA WOOD
PAINTER
b Pratt, Kans, Nov 12, 29. *Study:* Okla State Univ, 47-49; Famous Artist Course, cert, 67; with John C Pellew, 81-83, William Reese, Claude Croney Charles Reid & Albert Handel. *Work:* Ponca City Art Asn, Okla; Phillips Petroleum Co, Bartlesville, Okla; Salina City Off, Kans; CCI Bldg, Utica Nat Bank, Tulsa; Franks & Sons Trucking, Big Cabin, Okla. *Comn:* Private portraits, Tulsa, Okla; mural, Grove, Okla. *Exhib:* Okla Mus Art, Oklahoma City, 80 & 83; Mayfest, Tulsa Arts & Humanities Coun, 81-83; Arts, Crafts & Design Fair, Montessori Soc, Little Rock, Ark, 81-83; Wichita Falls Spring Fling, Wichita Falls Art Mus, Tex, 81-83; Austin Fine Arts Mus Festival, Tex, 82-83; one-man shows, First Fed Savings & Loan, Oklahoma City, 85 & Bartlesville Art Asn, Bartlesville, Okla, 87; La Guna Gloria, Austin, Tex, 91. *Teaching:* Instr workshops in Bartlesville, 86, Grove, Okla, 87, Wimberly, Tex, 92 & Eureka Springs, Ariz, 92. *Awards:* Best of Show, Okla Mus Art, 80 & Eastern Trails Art Show, Uinita Okla Art Asn, 82; First Bartlesville Ann Award, 85; Johnson D Hill Mem, Grove, Okla, 88. *Mem:* Bartlesville Art Asn; Grove Art Asn; Allied Artist Am, 88. *Media:* Oil. *Mailing Add:* RR 1 Box 150 C Eucha OK 74342

COURTNEY, KEITH TOWNSEND
ADMINISTRATOR
b Oshawa, Ont, July 23, 49. *Study:* Waterloo Lutheran Univ, BA(English & art hist). *Pos:* Cur, Art Gallery Hamilton, Ont, 74-77, community relations officer, 77- *Mem:* Ont Asn Art Galleries; Hamilton Pub Relations Asn. *Mailing Add:* c/o Art Gallery Hamilton 123 King St W Hamilton ON L8P 4S8 Canada

COURTNEY, SUZAN
PAINTER, PRINTMAKER
b Mobile, Ala, Sept 6, 47. *Study:* Tulane Univ, 68-69; Kingston-Upon-Hull Col Art, Hull, Eng, dipl art & design, 73; Whitney Mus Independent Study Prog, 74-75; Yale Univ Sch Art, MFA, 77. *Work:* Insurance Co NAm, Ericson Gallery & Davis, Markel and Edwards, New York; Gasperi Gallery, New Orleans; Fine Arts Mus of the South, Mobile, Ala. *Exhib:* Solo exhibs, Univ SFla, 77, Fine Arts Mus of the South, Mobile, Ala, 87, Gasperi Gallery, New Orleans, La, 89 & Galerie Gordon Pym & Fils, Paris, 92; Two Decades of Abstraction, traveling nationally, 79; Five New York City Artists, Ericson Gallery, New York, 81; Invitational Exhib, Bristol Art Mus, Eng, 81; Perspectives South, 82 & Invitational, 84, Ericson Gallery, New York,; Urban Spirit, City Without Walls, Newark, NJ, 85; New Urban Artists, Int Monetary Fund, Washington, DC, 85-86; Folk-Funk Show, Gasperi Gallery, New Orleans, La; Small Works, Parsons Sch Design, 89; Europa - America, 360 E-Venti, New York - Rome, Pino Molica Gallery, 92; Miauhaus, New York, 92. *Pos:* Visiting artist, Princeton Univ, Rutgers Univ & Spring Hill Col, 84-86, Reading Univ & Slade Sch Art, London, Eng, 86. *Teaching:* Instr painting & drawing, RI Sch Design, Providence, 79-83 & Univ South Fla, Tampa, currently; adj prof painting & drawing, Southampton Col, NY, 83-84; adj prof color theory, Rutgers Univ, NJ, 85-92; adj prof drawing, Parsons Sch Design, 87-92. *Awards:* Skowhegan Sch Painting Fel; Susan Whedon Prize Painting, Yale Sch Art, 75; Edward Albee Studio Award, Montauk, NY, 80. *Media:* Oil on Canvas. *Publ:* New York Art Review, 88. *Dealer:* Gasperi Gallery New Orleans LA. *Mailing Add:* 530 Canal St Studio 2E New York NY 10013

COURTRIGHT, ROBERT
COLLAGE ARTIST, PAINTER
b Sumter, SC, Oct 20, 26. *Study:* St John's Col, Annapolis, Md; New Sch Social Res, New York, 47-48; Art Students League, 48-52. *Work:* Phillips Collection, Washington, DC; Metrop Mus Art, New York; Thyssen-Bornemisza Collection, Lugano, Switzerland; Wadsworth Atheneum, Hartford, Conn; Collection de l'Etat, Paris, France. *Exhib:* Smithsonian Inst, Washington, DC, 56; Mus Mod Art, New York, 57; Carnegie Int, Carnegie Inst, Pittsburgh, Pa, 59; Festival Int de la Peinture, Cagnes-sur-Mer, France, 76; Am & Europe, A Century Mod Masters from Thyssen-Bornemisza Collection, traveled in Australia & NZ, 79-81. *Bibliog:* Calvin Tompkins (auth), Robert Courtright, Andrew Crispo Gallery, NY, 79; Ralph Pomeroy (auth), Light and substance: The collages of Robert Courtright, Arts Mag, 12/79; Jeffrey Robinson (auth), Robert Courtright: Collage-Masks, Andrew Crispo Gallery, NY, 81. *Media:* Papier Mache, Acrylic. *Mailing Add:* 80 Varick St New York NY 10013

COUTURIER, MARION B
DEALER, COLLECTOR
US citizen. *Study:* Univ Lausanne, Switz, cert de Francais et Langues; Univ Dijon; Columbia Univ. *Pos:* Owner, Couturier Gallery, 61-; art consult, currently. *Specialty:* Consultant, major private, museums & corporate collections, impressionists, post impressionists & contemporary art. *Interests:* Work with major private and museum collections, selecting works from the modern to the contemporary. *Collection:* Contemporary artists in all media; Latin American artists for merit and variety of their work. *Mailing Add:* c/o Couturier Gallerie 1814 Newfield Ave Stamford CT 06903

COVE, ROSEMARY
SCULPTOR, PAINTER
b New York, NY, Jan 11, 36. *Study:* Parsons Sch Design, 54-56; Art Students League, 64-65; with Knox Martin, 66-70. *Work:* Weatherspoon, NC; New York Times; Grenoble Knitwear Inc; Tallix Inc; CIBA Geigy, NY. *Exhib:* Works on Paper, Brooklyn Mus, 75; Ingber Gallery, 84, 86 & 88; Thompsen Gallery, 90; Lincoln Ctr, 92; Grahm Modern, 92; and others. *Awards:* Residency Grant, 84, Theater Grant, 86, Nat Endowment Art; Ford Foundation Award. *Bibliog:* Allen Ellingswieg (auth), Rosemary Cove, 75 & Natalie Edgar (auth), Rosemary Cove, 78, Arts Mag; Dorothy Beskind (auth), Rosemary Cove (film), 77; Ed McCormack, auth, Art Speak. *Mem:* Women in the Arts. *Media:* Terra-Cotta, Corten Steel; Oil, Ink. *Mailing Add:* 71 Waller Ave White Plains NY 10605

COVELL, ALAN CARTER
HISTORIAN, CURATOR
b Yonkers, NY, Feb 10, 52. *Study:* State Univ NY, Albany, BA, 82; South Baylor Univ, Garden Grove, Calif, MA, 83, PhD, 86; Brigham Young Univ, Provo, Utah, MA, 88. *Res:* Korean and Japanese art history, with emphasis on religious motivations. *Publ:* Auth, Ecstacy: Korean Shamanist Painting, 82 & Shamanist Folk Painting, 83, Hollym Publ; coauth, Japan's Hidden History, Hollym Publ, 84; auth, Folk Art and Magic: Korea Shamanist Painting, 85; coauth, The World of Korean Ceramics, Si-sa-yong-O-sa Pub, 86; also auth of two other books. *Mailing Add:* 9200 Westminster Westminster CA 92683

COVI, DARIO A
HISTORIAN
b Livingston, Ill, Dec 26, 20. *Study:* Eastern Ill State Col, BEd, 43; State Univ Iowa, MA, 48, with William S Heckscher; NY Univ, with Richard Offner, PhD, 58. *Pos:* Mem exec comt, Ky Arts Comn, 65-70. *Teaching:* From instr to prof art hist, Univ Louisville, 56-70; prof, Duke Univ, 70-75; Hite prof, Univ Louisville, 75-, prof emer, 91- *Awards:* Am Coun Learned Socs Fel, 64; Fulbright-Hays Fel, 68-69; Gladys Krieble Delmas Found Grant, 79. *Mem:* Col Art Asn Am; Southeastern Col Art Conf; Renaissance Soc Am; Midwest Art Hist Soc. *Res:* Italian Renaissance art. *Publ:* Auth, Prints from the Allen R Hite Art Institute Collection (exhib catalog), 63; contribr, McGraw-Hill Dict Art, Art Bull, Burlington Mag, Renaissance Quart & other nat art publ; auth, The Inscription in Fifteenth Century Florentine Painting. *Mailing Add:* Hite Art Inst Univ Louisville Louisville KY 40292

COVINGTON, HARRISON WALL
PAINTER, EDUCATOR
b Plant City, Fla, Apr 12, 24. *Study:* Univ Fla, 42-43; Hiram Col, 43; Univ Fla, BFA(hons), 49, MFA, 53. *Work:* Herron Mus Art, Indianapolis, Ind; Everson Mus Art, Syracuse, NY; John & Mable Ringling Mus Art, Sarasota, Fla; Jacksonville Mus Art, Fla; Nat Gallery Art, Washington DC. *Comn:* Portrait, Gov State of Fla, 55; portraits of pres, 70, 76 & 84, sculpture bas relief, Univ South Fla, 75; sculpture bas relief, Fla Fed Savings & Loan, 74; Sculptured Figures, Int Shrine Hq, 80. *Exhib:* Museum Director's Choice, throughout Southeastern US, 56-59; Painting USA: The Figure, Mus Mod Art, New York, 62; New York World's Fair, 64; Florida 17, Pan-Am Union, Washington, DC, 68; Graphic Studio USF, Brooklyn Mus, 78; Tampa Mus Art, 87. *Teaching:* Instr art, Univ Fla, 49-61; prof art, Univ SFla, 61-82, chmn visual arts prog, 61-67, dean, Div Fine Arts, 67-72, dean, Col Fine Arts, 77-82, emer prof, 82- & emer dean, 82- *Awards:* Sloan Found Grant, 47; Guggenheim Fel, 64. *Bibliog:* Gene Baro (auth), Graphic Studio USF: An Experiment in Art and Education (exhib catalog), Brooklyn Mus, 78. *Media:* Acrylic, Plastic. *Mailing Add:* 11809 Vera Ave Tampa FL 33618

COWAN, AILEEN HOOPER
SCULPTOR, PAINTER
b Windsor, Ont, June 11, 26. *Study:* Univ Toronto, BA; Queen's Univ, Kingston, Ont; Univ Toronto. *Work:* Univ Western Ont; Robert McLaughlin Gallery, Oshawa, Can. *Comn:* J Gush, Toronto; Govt of Ont. *Exhib:* Art Gallery Hamilton, 73; Agnes Etherington Gallery, Queen's Univ, Kingston, Ont, 74; Merton Gallery, Toronto, 79; McDowell Gallery, Toronto, 80; Sculptors Soc BC, Robson Sq Media Ctr, Vancouver, 80; J Aird Gallery, Toronto, 89 & 90; and many others. *Collections Arranged:* Arranged & curated permanent coll of Sculptor's Soc of Can, (traveling exhib), 81. *Pos:* Curator, permanent collection, Sculptor's Soc Can. *Teaching:* Univ Toronto, Ont. *Awards:* Augusts Kopmanis Mem Award, 80. *Bibliog:* Article, Athens News, Greece, 7/72; article, Art Mag, Toronto, Vol 5, No 15, 73. *Mem:* Sculptors Soc Can (past pres). *Media:* Bronze, Acrylic. *Publ:* Earth and You, Vol XVI, 87. *Dealer:* Gallery, Helena, Toronto. *Mailing Add:* 277 Strathallan Wood Toronto ON M5N 1T7 Canada

COWAN, RALPH WOLFE
PAINTER
b Pheobus, Va, Dec 16, 31. *Study:* Art Students League, New York, 51. *Work:* The Marcos Years Mus, Malacanans Palace, Manila, Philippines; Carter

Presidential Ctr, Atlanta, Ga; Portsmouth Mus, Va; Royal Palace Monaco, Monte Carlo; Graceland, Memphis, Tenn. *Comn:* 12 family portraits, comn by Mrs Ferdinand Marcos, Philippines, 82-85; Palace Collection, comn by King Fahd, Saudi Arabia, 84; 3 portraits, comn by King Hassan II, Morocco, 84; 18 portraits, comn by HM Sultan Hassanal Bolkiah, Brunei, 85; 2 portraits, comn by Pres Augusto Pinochet, Chile; 4 portraits, comn by Pres Sheik Zayed, United Arab Emirates. *Exhib:* One-man retrospective, Portsmouth Mus, Va, 84; Ft Lauderdale Mus Art, Fla. *Awards:* Portsmouth Notable, Portsmouth Hall of Fame, Va, 87; Best in Show, Norton Mus Art, Norton Artist Guild, 88. *Bibliog:* Doug Stewart (auth), Making Faces is a hard dasy Fight, Smithsonian Mag 11-5-88; Linda Marx (auth), Painter Fights Back, People Mag, 9/4/89. *Mem:* Art Students League; Portrait Inst; Am Portrait Soc; Am Soc Artists. *Media:* Oil. *Publ:* Auth, A Personal Vision, self published, 88. *Mailing Add:* 243 29th St West Palm Beach FL 33407

COWIN, EILEEN
PHOTOGRAPHER
b Brooklyn, NY, Aug 17, 47. *Study:* State Univ NY, New Paltz, BS, 68; Ill Inst Technol, with Aaron Siskind & Arthur Siegel, MS, 70. *Work:* Mus Mod Art, New York; Los Angeles Co Mus Art; Newport Harbor Art Mus; Fogg Mus; Brooklyn Mus; Nat Mus Am Art, Smithsonian Inst, Washington, DC; Polaroid Corp. *Exhib:* California Photography, Mus Art; The Diaristic Mode, Univ NMex Art Mus, Albuquerque, 83; The Image Scavengers, Inst Contemp Art, Philadelphia, 83; Mus Mod Art, Paris, 83; Whitney Biennial, Whitney Mus Art, 83; Los Angeles Co Mus Art, 85; La Jolla Mus Contemp Art, 85; Viviane Esders Gallery, Paris, 85; The Photography of Invention, Nat Mus Am Art, 89; Odalisque, Jayne H Baum Gallery, New York, 90; Pleasures and Terrors of Domestic Comfort (catalog), Mus Mod Art, NY, 91; de-Persona (catalog), Oakland Mus, Calif, 91; Erotic Desire (catalog), Perspektief, Rotterdam, Neth, 91; one-person exhibs, Jayne H Baum Gallery, New York, 91, Roy Boyd Gallery, Santa Monica, Calif, 91, Mus Contemp Photog, Chicago, Ill, 91. *Teaching:* Prof art, Calif State Univ, Fullerton, 75-; vis artist photog, Art Inst Chicago, 80. *Awards:* Nat Endowment Arts Fel, 79, 82 & 90; Public Art Fund, Pa Sta Proj, 90. *Bibliog:* Mark Johnstone (auth), Eileen Cowin, Min Gallery, Tokyo, 87; Max Kozloff (auth), The Privileged Eye, Univ NMex Press, Albuquerque, 87; Judi Freeman (auth), Eileen Cowin, Darryl Curran The Photographic: Two Points of View, Calif State Univ, Fullerton, 89. *Mem:* Soc Photog Educ. *Dealer:* Jayne H Baum Gallery 588 Broadway New York NY 10012; Roy Boyd Gallery 1547 Tenth St Santa Monica CA. *Mailing Add:* c/o Roy Boyd Gallery 1547 10th St Santa Monica CA 90401

COWLES, CHARLES
ART DEALER, COLLECTOR
b Los Angeles, Calif, Feb 7, 41. *Study:* Stanford Univ, 63. *Pos:* Pres & publisher, Artforum Mag, 65-79; cur mod art, Seattle Art Mus, 75-79; art dealer, Charles Cowles Gallery, 80-; chmn, bd trustee, New York Studio Sch. *Bibliog:* Laura de Coppett & Alan Jones (coauths), The Art Dealers, Potter. *Mem:* Art Dealers Asn Am. *Specialty:* Modern and contemporary art. *Collection:* Contemporary Art and Japanese Folk Art. *Mailing Add:* Charles Cowles Gallery 420 West Broadway New York NY 10012

COWLES, FLEUR
PAINTER, WRITER
Study: Pratt Inst, New York; Elmira Univ, LLD. *Work:* Seattle Art Mus, Wash; Museu Arte Mod, Sao Paulo, Brazil; Fisher Found, Iowa; Dart Indust, Orlando, Fla. *Comn:* Murals, Hotel Hilton, London, Eng & Athens, Greece. *Exhib:* 43 one-man exhibs, including: Seattle Mus Art, 70, Museu de Arte Mod, Sao Paulo, 72, Cranbrook Mus, Bloomfield Hills, NJ, 74, Singer Mus, Laren, Holland, 77, Hammer Galleries, New Yor0, 78 & Partridge Galleries, London, 83; El Paseo Mus, Tex, 86; Gallery Kanasawa, Kyoto, Japan, 88; Galeria de Arte Grife Barcolors, Spain, 90; Chris Brettes Gallery, London, 90; Art Miami, Fla, 92; and others. *Pos:* Assoc ed, Look Mag, 48-55; ed-in-chief, Flair Mag, 50-52. *Awards:* Queen's Coronation Medal, Gt Brit, 53; Comdr Order Bienfasence, Greece, 70; Ribbin of LaDama, Order Isabella Catolica, Spain, 76; Comdr Order Southern Cross, Brazil, 80; Fleur Cowles Fel Humanities, Tex Univ, Austin, 92; and others. *Mem:* Royal Soc Arts; Univ Art Mus Coun, Berkeley, Calif; Coun Am Mus, Bath, Gt Brit. *Media:* Acrylic. *Publ:* Robert Vaura (auth), Painter, Tiger Flower, 69, Lion and Blue, 74, Romany Free, 77, The Love of the Tiger Flower, 81 & Take a Unicorn, 88; The Flower Game, 83; Flower Decorations, 85; People as Animals, 86; An Artists Journey, 88. *Dealer:* Portals Ltd 230 W Huran Chicago IL 60610. *Mailing Add:* A5 Albany Piccadilly London England United Kingdom

COWLEY, EDWARD P
PAINTER, EDUCATOR
b Buffalo, NY, May 29, 25. *Study:* Albright Art Sch; Buffalo State Col, BS, 48; Columbia Univ, MA, 49; Nat Col Art, Dublin, Ireland, Ford Found Fel, 55. *Work:* Albany Inst Hist & Art, NY; Schenectady Mus, NY; Smith Col, Northhampton, Mass; Colgate Univ, Hamilton, NY; Berkshire Mus, Pittsfield, Mass. *Teaching:* Prof art & chmn dept, State Univ NY Albany, 56-75, prof art, 76-88. *Awards:* State Univ NY Res Grant, 66 & 74. *Media:* Pastels, Stained Glass. *Mailing Add:* Box 198 Altamont NY 12009

COX, E MORRIS
COLLECTOR
b Santa Rosa, Calif, Feb 5, 03. *Study:* Univ Calif, AB; Harvard Univ Grad Sch Bus, MBA. *Pos:* Pres, San Francisco Mus Contemp Art, 55-60, trustee, currently; treas, Calif Acad Sci, 63-67, chmn bd trustees, 67-70; dir, Bay Area Educ TV Asn, formerly; trustee, Univ Calif Berkeley Found, currently. *Collection:* Contemporary sculpture and painting. *Mailing Add:* c/o Dodge & Cox Inc Sansome St 35th Fl San Francisco CA 94104-4405

COX, ERNEST LEE
SCULPTOR, EDUCATOR
b Wilmington, NC, June 1, 37. *Study:* Col of William & Mary, BA(fine arts); Cranbrook Acad of Art, Bloomfield Hills, Mich, MFA(sculpture); Mich State Univ, Oakland. *Work:* St Petersburg Pub Libr, Fla; Eckerd Col, St Petersburg; Univ SFla, Tampa; 1st Nat Bank of Atlanta, Ga; 1st Nat Bank of Tampa, Fla. *Comn:* Steel sculptures, 64, Fed Deposit Ins Corp, Washington, DC, 65 & Gulf Life Ins Co, Jacksonville, 67. *Exhib:* The 17th Va Artists Exhib, Va Mus Fine Arts, Richmond, 58; 24th Ann NC Artists Exhib, NC Mus Fine Arts, Raleigh, 61; 20th-22nd Southeastern Ann Exhibs, High Mus Art, Atlanta, Ga, 65-67; Fla 17, Pan Am Union, Washington, DC, 68; 15 Fla Artists Sculpture Exhib, Gallery Contemp Art, Winston-Salem, NC, 70; solo exhibs, Jacksonville Mus of Art, Fla, 73 Fla Art Fellows Exhib, Mus Fine Arts, St Per; 15 Fla Artists Sculpture Exhib, Gallery Contemp Art, Winston-Salem, NC, 70; one-man show, Jacksonville Mus Art, 73; Fla Art Fellows Art Exhib, Mus Fine Arts, St Pertersburg, Fla, 82 & Fla Art Fel Exhib, Norton Gallery Art, Palm Beach, 89. *Teaching:* From instr to prof sculpture, Univ SFla, Tampa, 62-, chmn art dept, 71-73. *Awards:* Second Prize, Fla Sculptors 7th Ann Exhib, 63; First Prize, Fla State Fair Fine Arts Exhib, 65; Purchase Prize, Southeastern Sculpture Exhib, Atlanta Chamber of Commerce, 69; Fla Art Fel, 82 & 89. *Media:* Welded, Forged Steel. *Mailing Add:* 7309 Bozman Neavitt Rd Bozman MD 21612

COX, MARION AVERAL
PAINTER, INSTRUCTOR
b Washingtonville, Ohio. *Study:* With H Gauguin, W Goodrich, H Radio, B I Payne, C Wallace, J M Jehu, N Bel Geddes, Max Reinhardt (Ger), and many others. *Exhib:* Sixty Text Books, Am Inst Graphic Arts, Grand Cent Palace, 44 & 54; 13th Ann Ohio Artists & Craftsmen, Massillon Mus, 48; 14th New Years Show, Butler Art Inst, 49; American Painting Today, Metrop Mus Art. *Pos:* Art dir, Universal Studios, Universal City, Calif, 28-30; tech illusr, My Own Studio & Gallery, Salem, Ohio, 38-52; architect, Translux Construct, 50-; author, Readex Book Exchange, Cave Creek, Ariz, 68- *Teaching:* Teacher art theory & practice, Art-O-Technix Inst, Carefree, Ariz, 75- *Mem:* Am Asn Advan Sci. *Media:* Mixed. *Publ:* Illusr, E T Smith (auth), Exploring Biology, 38. *Mailing Add:* Box 325 Cave Creek AZ 85331

COX, RICHARD WILLIAM
HISTORIAN, WRITER
b Los Angeles, Calif, July 13, 42. *Study:* Univ Calif, Los Angeles, BA(hist), 64, MA(hist), 66; Univ Wis, Madison, MA(art hist), 70, PhD(art hist), 73. *Teaching:* Instr Am art, Univ Wis, River Falls, 71-74; from asst prof to prof Am art & hist prints, La State Univ, 74- *Awards:* Solon Buck Award for Best Article, Minn Hist, 75; Nat Endowment Humanities Fel, 75. *Bibliog:* Matthew Baigell (auth), The American Scene: American Painting of the 1930s, Praeger, 74; James Dennis (auth), Grant Wood, A Study in Art & Culture, Viking, 75. *Mem:* Col Art Asn; Art Educ Asn; La Hist Soc. *Res:* American painting and graphic arts in 1900-1945 period; contemporary art. *Publ:* Art Young: Cartoonist from the middle border, Wis Mag Hist, 77; Caroline Durieux: The lithographs of the 1930's and 1940's La State Univ Press, 77; Adolf Dehn--jazz age satirist, Arch Am Art J, 78; Southern works on paper, 1900-1950, Southern Arts Fedn, 80; coauth (with Clinton Adams), Adolf Dehn, Catalogue Raisonne of the Lithographs, Minn Hist Soc Press, 87; (with Carlton Overland), Warrington Colescott, Forty Years of Printmaking, A Retrospective, Elvehjem Mus Art, Univ Wis, 89. *Mailing Add:* Sch Art La State Univ Baton Rouge LA 70803

COYLE, TERENCE
PAINTER
b Williamstown, Mass, Sept 7, 25. *Study:* Columbia Univ, 46-48; Hunter Col, 50; Art Students League, 64-70. *Work:* Mus City of New York; Fordham Univ, Lincoln Ctr, New York; Billy Rose Collection, NY Libr Performing Arts; NY State Mus, Albany; Chubb & Son Inc, New York. *Exhib:* Am Artists Prof League, Lever Brothers Bldg, New York, 76; Nat Arts Club, Nat Arts Gallery, New York, 81; Last Days of the Helen Hayes Theatre, Sharon Creative Arts Found, Conn, 83; Places Please, Astor Gallery, Lincoln Ctr, New York, 84; Curtain Call at the Helen Hayes, Fordham Univ, Lincoln Center, New York, 86. *Teaching:* Instr oil painting, Art Students League, 74-; lectr artistic anatomy, Nat Acad Design, Sch Fine Arts, New York, 79-; instr figure portrait painting, Scottsdale Artists Sch, Ariz, ann workshop, 85. *Awards:* Award for graphic design, Communications Art Exhib, Am Inst Graphic Design, 79; Silver Medal, Nat Art League, 83. *Bibliog:* Artist chronicle's theatre demise, Lakeville J, Conn, 9/1/83; Richard Nielson (auth), The skin's game art/rev, Ariz Republic, 2/14/87; article, Hazelton Standard, 3/20/89. *Mem:* Life mem, Art Students League; Am Artists Prof League; Artist's Equity; Nat Art League. *Media:* Oil. *Publ:* Coauth, Anatomy Lessons From the Great Masters, Watson-Guptill, 77; Albinus on Anatomy, Watson-Guptill/Dover, 79 & 88; auth, Master Class in Figure Drawing, Watson-Guptill, 85. *Mailing Add:* 305 E 72nd St New York NY 10021

COYNE, JOHN MICHAEL
PAINTER, EDUCATOR
b St Stephen, NB, Can, 1950. *Study:* Mt Allison Univ, BFA, 75; Univ Regina, MFA, 77. *Work:* Art Gallery NS, Halifax; Husky Oil, Calgary; Placer Dome, Inc, Toronto; Midland Doherty, Xerox Canada, Abitibi Price, Toronto; Air Canada, Toshiba Canada; Bank of NS, Toronto; Govt, Nfld & Labrador. *Exhib:* Art Gallery NS, Halifax, 80; Acadia Univ Art Gallery, Wolfville, NS, 83; Edmonton Art Gallery, Alberta, 84; St Mary's Univ, Halifax, 84; Mira Godard Gallery, Toronto, 86; Grenfell Col, Corner Brook, Nfld, 87 & 89; Gallery 78, Fredericton, NB, 88; Mem Univ Art Gallery, 90; Emma Butler Gallery, St John's, Nfld, 90. *Teaching:* Asst prof, Acadia Univ, Wolfville, NS,

77-84, assoc prof & head art dept 83-86; head dept visual arts Mem Univ, Grenfell Col, Corner Brook, Nfld, 86-92, prof, 91- *Awards:* Grant, Greenshield's Found, Montreal, 76. *Bibliog:* C MacLauglin (auth), Atlantic lines, Heritage Can Mag, 2/79; Dr Helen J Dow (auth), Michael Coyne: A Retrospective, Acadia Univ Art Gallery, 83; Arts Atlantic Winter 85, 87 & 91; Colleen O'Neill (auth), Michael Coyne, Sir Wilfred Grenfell Col Art Gallery, 90. *Mem:* Col Art Asn; Visual Arts Ont. *Media:* Oil, Acrylic. *Dealer:* Mira Godard Gallery 22 Hazelton Ave Toronto Ont. *Mailing Add:* Dept Visual Art, Mem Univ Sir Wilfred Grenfell Col Corner Brook NF A2H 6P9 Canada

COYNE, PETAH E
SCULPTOR, PHOTOGRAPHER
b Oklahoma City, Okla, Sept 30, 53. *Study:* Art Academy Cincinnati, Grad, 77; Kent State Univ. *Work:* The Brooklyn Mus, NY; San Diego Mus Contemp Art, La Jolla, Calif; The Speed Mus, Louisville, KY. *Exhib:* Elements, Whitney Mus Am Art, New York, 88; Grand Lobby Installation, Brooklyn Mus, NY, 89; Unmaking of Nature, Whitney Mus Am Art, New York, 90; Art Contemporain Vision 90, Centre International d'Art Contemporaine, Montreal, CN, 90; Award in the Visual Arts, Hirshhorn Mus, Washington, DC, 91; Coyne-Hurtman Collaboration, Neuberger Mus, Purchase, NY, 92; Petah Coyne Sculpture, Contemporary Mus, Honolulu, Hawaii, Cleveland Ctr Contemp Art, Ohio, Ctr Contemp Art Santa Fe, NMex, 92-93. *Teaching:* Grad Faculty Painting/Sculpture, Sch Visual Arts, 90-92. *Awards:* Guggenheim Mem Foun, Guggenheim Found, 89; Awards in the Visual Arts, AVA 10, Southeastern County/Contemp Arts, 90; Nat Endowment Arts, Fellow Sculpture, 90. *Bibliog:* Lasse Antonsen (auth), Installation by Petah Coyne, Massachusetts Contemp, 91; David Rubin (auth), Petah Coyne, Cleveland Ctr Contemp Art, 92; Tony Carlson (auth), Beauty and the Beast (film), 92. *Mem:* Skowhegan Sch Painting & Sculpture, New York (bd gov 88-92); Orgn Independent Artist (bd dirs 88-92); Sculpture Ctr, New York (bd dir 90-92). *Dealer:* Jack Shainnan Gallery 560 Broadway New York NY 10012; Diane Brown Gallery 23 Waits St New York NY 10013. *Mailing Add:* 477 Broome Street New York NY 10013

CRABLE, JAMES HARBOUR
MULTI-MEDIA ARTIST, INSTRUCTOR
b Bronx, NY, Aug 30, 39. *Study:* State Univ NY Col Buffalo, BS, 62; Rochester Inst Technol, NY, MFA, 66; Chelsea Sch Art, London, Eng, HDA, 70. *Work:* Adolph Coors Co; Bell South Corp; AT&T Collection, Washington, DC; Equitable Life Assurance Soc Am; State Univ NY Art Collection, Albany; IBM Collection; Chrysler Mus, Norfolk, Va; Everson Mus, Syracuse, NY. *Exhib:* 35 Artists in the Southeast, High Mus Art, Atlanta, Ga, 76-77; one-man shows, Va Mus Fine Arts, Richmond, 76, Southeastern Ctr Contemp Art, Winston-Salem, 78 & Gallery K, Washington, DC, 79 & 82, Monterey Penninsula Mus Art, Monterey, Calif, 89, Interform Gallery, Osaka, Japan, 89, Fresno Metrop Mus Art, Calif, 90 & Photo Forum, Pittsburgh, Pa, 90; Continuum VII, Dulin Gallery Art, Knoxville, 82; Artscape 85, Md Inst, Baltimore; Selections from the Bequest of Nancy Hanks, Duke Univ, NC, 85; Over the Blue Ridge, Roanoke Fine Art Invitational, Va, 87; Collage: Four Directions, San Jose Mus Art, Calif, 88. *Teaching:* Assoc prof art survey, drawing & art educ, State Univ Col Brockport, NY, 66-69; lectr found studies, Croydon Col Art, Surrey, Eng, 70-71; prof drawing & art survey, James Madison Univ, Harrisonburg, Va, 73- *Awards:* Fel, Nat Endowment Arts Southeastern Fel, 79; Best in Show Award, Light Images 83, Chrysler Mus, Norfolk, Va, 83; Gold Medal, Los Angeles Inter Art Competition, 84; Visual Arts The Southeast Award, Ga State Univ, Atlanta, 86; Va prize in visual arts, presented by Gov Gerald Baliles, 87. *Mem:* Col Art Asn Am; Va Art Educ Asn. *Media:* Photo-collage. *Mailing Add:* 261 Green St Harrisonburg VA 22801

CRAFT, DAVID RALPH
PAINTER, PHOTOGRAPHER
b Elberton, Ga, July 31, 45. *Study:* ETenn State Univ, BS, 67. *Work:* Appalachian State Univ; Blount Inc, Montgomery, Ala; Tenn Arts Comn, Nashville; Hunter Mus Art; Tenn Valley Authority. *Exhib:* Nat Print & Drawing Competition, Davidson Col, NC, 74 & 75; Art USA: The South, New Orleans Mus, 75-77; Smithsonian Inst, touring, 76; 11th Ann Nat Drawing & Small Sculpture Competition, Del Mar Col Art Ctr, 77; Am Drawings I, II & IV, Portsmouth Arts Ctr, 78 & 82; More Than Land and Sky: Art from Appalachia, Nat Mus Am Art, Washington & touring, 82-84; Landscape & Genre Painting Tennessee, 1810-1985 Travelling Exhib. *Teaching:* Instr, Hunter Mus Art, 75-84; teacher photog Girls Prep Sch, 84- *Awards:* Purchase Awards, Dulin Gallery Nat, 76, Mt Holyoke Nat, 76 & Lauren Rogers Regional, 79. *Media:* Acrylic, Oil. *Dealer:* Margaret Townsend Gallery 406 High St Chattanooga TN 37403. *Mailing Add:* 1109 1/2 Mississippi Ave Chattanooga TN 37405

CRAFT, DOUGLAS D
PAINTER, EDUCATOR
b Greene, NY, Oct 20, 24. *Study:* Univ Iowa; Univ Chicago; Art Inst Chicago, BFA; Syracuse Univ; Univ NMex, MA. *Work:* Mus Mod Art & Whitney Mus Am Art, New York; Art Inst Chicago; Univ Ky, Lexington; Newark Mus, NJ; Univ Calif, Santa Cruz; Warner Lambert World Hq, Morris Plains, NJ. *Comn:* Paintings, comn by Mr & Mrs Daniel Weinstein for Edward Weinstein Ctr Performing Arts, Nat Col Educ, Evanston, Ill, 72. *Exhib:* One-man shows, Royal Col Art Galleries, London, Eng, 64, Traverse Festival Gallery, Edinburgh, Scotland, 65, Mus Art, Carnegie Inst, Pittsburgh, Pa, 68, Twentieth Century West Galleries, Ltd, New York, 68, Fischbach Galleries, New York, 73 & Jersey City Mus, 78, 55 Mercer Gallery, New York, 80 Col Ctr Art Gallery, New Rochelle, NY, 90, Bratton Gallery, Inc, New York, 90; Rose Fried Gallery, New York, 68; Three Person Show, Studio K, Long Island City, NY, 85; Montclair Art Mus, Montclair, NJ, 84; Contemporary Syntax, Rutgers Univ, NJ, 87; Collage at NAME, NAME Gallery, Chicago, 88. *Pos:* Vis artist in residence, Univ Ky, 64; Am artist in residence, Royal Col Art, London, Eng, 64-65; vis artist-critic, Sunderland Col Art, Eng, 65 & Gloucestershire Col Art, Cheltenham, Eng, 65; cur, Fourteen Women Artists, Castle Gallery, New Rochelle, 82 & cur of Paper, Pigment & Glass, Castle Gallery, New Rochelle, 87. *Teaching:* Assoc prof painting, Art Inst Chicago, 55-66 & Carnegie Inst Technol, 66-69; vis artist, Cooper Union, 69-71 & Sch Visual Arts, New York, summer 88; prof painting, Col New Rochelle, 71- *Awards:* Harry Allison Logan Mem Award, Chautauqua Inst, NY, 63; Logan Bronze Medal & Prize, Art Inst Chicago, 66; Jury Award/Distinction in Painting, Mus Art, Carnegie Inst Int, 68. *Bibliog:* Max Wykes-Joyce (auth), Douglas Craft, Arts Rev, London, 64; Cordelia Oliver (auth), Exhibitions at Edinburgh, Guardian, 65; D L Shirey (auth), Douglas Craft Show in Jersey City, New York Times, 78; Vivien Raynor (auth), A magnetic group of 8 in Jersey City, New York Times, 80; Vivien Raynor (auth), Show of collages opens new exhibit hall in New Rochelle, New York Times, 88. *Media:* Acrylic, Oil. *Mailing Add:* PO Box 245 Jeffersonville NY 12748

CRAFT, JOHN RICHARD
MUSEUM DIRECTOR
b Uniontown, Pa, June 15, 09. *Study:* Phillips Acad, Andover, Mass; Yale Univ; Art Students League; Univ Paris, 36-38; Acad Julien; and with Andre l'Hote; Am Sch Classical Studies, Athens, Greece, 37-39; Johns Hopkins Univ, MA & PhD. *Pos:* Dir, Washington Co Mus Fine Arts, Hagerstown, Md, 40-49; dir, Columbia Mus Art, SC, 50-77, dir emer, 77- *Mem:* Am Asn Mus; Southeastern Mus Conf (pres, 52-55); SC Fedn Mus (pres, 70-71); Am Inst Designers. *Mailing Add:* 712 Kipling Dr Columbia SC 29205

CRAIG, SUSAN V
LIBRARIAN
b Newton, Kans, Nov 11, 48. *Study:* Univ Kans, BA, 70; Emporia State Univ, MLS, 71. *Pos:* Indexer, Art Index, H W Wilson Co, New York, 71-74; art hist & classics librn, Univ Calif, Berkley, 75-81; art librn, Univ Kans, 81- *Teaching:* Instr art bibliog, Univ Calif, Berkeley, 81. *Mem:* Art Libr Soc NAm (secy 75-77, chmn, 86). *Res:* Kansas artists; art librarianship. *Mailing Add:* 1717 Indiana Lawrence KS 66044

CRAMER, DOUGLAS S
COLLECTOR, PATRON
b Louisville, Ky. *Study:* Northwestern Univ, 49-50; Sorbonne, Paris, 51; Univ Cincinnati, BA, 53; Columbia Univ, MFA, 54. *Pos:* Co-chmn, Entertainment Art Alliance, Los Angeles County Mus Art, 84-87. *Bibliog:* Grace Glueck (auth), Artful LA, NY Times Mag, 11/23/86; Peter Clothier (auth), Douglas Cramer: Passionate Perfectionist, Art News, 2/87; Bob Colacello (auth), At Home on the Ranch, Vanity Fair, 4/88. *Mem:* Mus Contemp Art (pres bd trustees), Los Angeles; Ctr Theater Group (bd dir 85-90); Int Coun Mus Mod Art; Am Ballet Theater (Nat Bd Dir). *Collection:* Approximately 600 works of contemporary American art from 1960 to the present. *Mailing Add:* 5700 Wilshire Blvd, Suite 575 Los Angeles CA 90036

CRAMER, PETER
DIRECTOR, PHOTOGRAPHER
b Bennington, Vt. *Study:* Skidmore Col, Sch Am Ballet with Stanley Williams & Richard Rapp, 78; Manhattan Sch Dance, with Margaret Craske & Sallie Wilson, 78-82. *Work:* New York Libr Performing Arts; Libr Cong, Washington, DC. *Exhib:* Artist's Call Against US Intervention in Central America, Charas-El Bohio, New York, 84; ABC No Rio: The First Five Years, City Gallery, New York, 85. *Pos:* Co-dir, Allied Prods, Inc, 82-85 & ABC No Rio, New York, 83-86. *Awards:* Interarts Grant, Nat Endowment Arts, 88. *Bibliog:* Rosalyn Deutsche & Cara Gendel Ryan (auths), The Fine Art of Gentrification, 10/84; Jolinda Lewis (auth), POOL at St Mark's Danspace, Dance Mag, 85. *Media:* Film, Performance. *Mailing Add:* ABC No Rio 156 Rivingston St New York NY 10002

CRAMER, RICHARD CHARLES
PAINTER, EDUCATOR
b Appleton, Wis, Aug 14, 32. *Study:* Layton Sch Art, BFA; Univ Wis-Milwaukee, BS, Univ Wis-Madison, MS, 61, MFA, 62. *Work:* Pa Acad Fine Arts; Everhart Mus, Scranton, Pa; Everson Mus, Syracuse, NY; Univ Wis; Philadelphia Mus; plus others. *Comn:* Mosaic mural, Temple Univ, Student/Fac Ctr, 81. *Exhib:* Drawings Biennial, Norfolk Mus Art, 65; Drawings, Smithsonian Inst traveling exhib, 65; one-man shows, Gloria Cortella Gallery, New York, 77-78, Barbara Fiedler Gallery, Washington, DC, 77 & Pa Acad Fine Arts, Philadelphia, 78; Chromatic Structure, Philadelphia Col Art, 80; Geometric-Abstractions, Inst Contemp Art, Boston, 81; American Abstraction, Mieisel Gallery, New York, 85. *Teaching:* Prof painting & drawing, Tyler Sch Art, Temple Univ, 66- *Awards:* Prizes, Milwaukee Art Inst, 54, Syracuse Allied Artists, 64 & Munson-Williams-Proctor Inst, Utica, NY, 65; and others. *Media:* Acrylic, Oil. *Publ:* Reconstructivist painting, Artspace, 3-4/90; Drawing in the 80's, White Walls, spring 86. *Mailing Add:* 159 Rivington St 3rd Flr New York NY 10002

CRANDALL, JERRY C
PAINTER, HISTORIAN
b La Junta, Colo, Apr 1, 35. *Study:* Woodbury Col, Los Angeles, Calif, 60. *Work:* Favell Mus, Klamath Falls, Ore; Koshare Indian Mus, La Junta, Colo; Bianchi Mus, Temecula, Calif. *Comn:* Robert Conrad as Pasquinelle in Centennial, comn by Robert Conrad, Malibu, Calif, 78; Wild Bill Hickock, Petersen Publ Co, Beverly Hills, Calif, 75; Custer's Last Stand, comn by Dr

Larry Frost, Monroe, Mich; Luftwaffe aircraft for private Ariz collector. *Exhib:* Round Up of Western Art Ann, Saddleback Western Art Mus, Santa Ana, Calif, 74-; John Selmon Mem Art Show, Stamford, Tex, 76-77, 79 & 84; Portraits from Life, Art Cottage, Corona, Calif, 82 & 83; C M Russell Show, Great Falls, Mont, 83 & 84; O S Ranch Art Exhib, Post, Tex, 83 & 84; Rotary Club Amarillo, 84-86; Tulsa Gilcrease Mus Art, 84-; Western Art in the Grand Traditon, 86-; Champlin Mus Art Show, 90 & 91. *Pos:* Historical technical adv, Universal Studios filming of Centennial, 78 & Columbia Pictures filming of The Mountain Men, 79; speaker, Professional Motivation in the Arts, Univ Calif, Riverside, 80-81, Forum Am Soc Aviation Artists, 90. *Awards:* Gold & Silver Medals, Western Artists Am Ann Exhib & Sale, 81. *Bibliog:* Jerry Crandall of Riverside, Art Voices South, 2/80; Phyllis Barton (auth), Creative credibility, Southwest Art, 10/80; Historical authenticity in art, In: Man at Arms, 11/83; Air Classics, 3/92 & 12/92. *Mem:* Little Big Horn Asn; Am Fighter Aces; Tailhook; Am Soc of Aviation Artists; Los Angeles Soc Illusr. *Media:* Oil, Acrylic. *Publ:* Illusr, Marsielles, Star of Africa, 69 & Battle of Britain, 70, JWC Publ; Guns of the Gunfighters (cover), Petersen Publ Co, 75; General Custer and the Battle of the Little Big Horn, Garry Owen Press, 76; Aviation a History through Art, p-51, (cover). *Dealer:* Eagle Editions Ltd PO Box 1830 Sedona AZ 86336. *Mailing Add:* PO Box 2606 Sedona AZ 86336

CRANDALL, JUDITH ANN
GALLERY DIRECTOR, WRITER
b Milwaukee, Wis, Aug 20, 48. *Study:* El Camino Jr Col, Univ Ariz. *Collections Arranged:* Eleventh Ann Membership Show for Women Artists of the American West, 83; Phoenix Forum Am Soc Aviation Artists, 88; Champlin Mus Aviation Art Show, 90 & 91; Air Aces Symp, Mesa, Ariz & Atlanta, Ga, 92. *Pos:* Staff writer, Southwest Art Mag, Houston, 74-; dir, Saddleback Western Art Gallery, Calif, 78-80; owner, Eagle Ed, Sedona, Ariz, currently; ed, Aerobrush, Am Soc Aviation Artists, 99-90; guest ed, Great Am Aviation Artists, Challenge Publ, Calif. *Publ:* Auth, The Custer centennial, 76, Retrospective view of the year, 80 & Women artists of the American West, 82, Southwest Art; plus auth of over 40 artists biography profiles publ in Southwest Art Mag as a freelance writer; Little Chief, Air Classics Mag, 88; Ed, Great Am Aviation Artists; The artist's wife, AeroArt Mag, 88. *Mailing Add:* PO Box 2606 Sedona AZ 86336

CRANE, BARBARA BACHMANN
PHOTOGRAPHER, EDUCATOR
b Chicago, Ill, Mar 19, 28. *Study:* Mills Col, with Alfred Neumeyer, 45-48; NY Univ, BA(art hist), 50; Inst of Design, Ill Inst Technol, with Aaron Siskind, MS(photog), 66. *Work:* Libr Cong, Washington, DC; Int Mus Photog, George Eastman House, Rochester, NY; Art Inst Chicago; Mus Mod Art, New York; Getty Mus, Malibu, Calif. *Comn:* 26 photomurals, Baxter Travenol Labs, Deerfield, Ill, 75; Chicago Epic (photomural), Chicago Bank Commerce, Standard Oil Bldg, Chicago. *Exhib:* One-woman shows, Friends of Photog, Carmel, Calif, 69 & 75, Herbert E Johnson Mus Art, Cornell Univ, Ithaca, NY & Tweed Mus Art, Univ Minn, Duluth, 86; People of North Portal, Mus Sci & Indust, Chicago, 72, Univ Iowa Mus, Iowa City, 73 & 75 & Int Mus Photog, George Eastman House, Rochester, NY, 83; retrospective exhib, Ctr Creative Photog, Univ Ariz, Tucson, 80 & traveling; Polaroid traveling exhibition program, 85; San Francisco Mus Mod Art (with catalog), 85. *Pos:* Mem, educ adv bd, Polaroid Corp, 85; Visual arts panel, MacDowell Colony, 89-90. *Teaching:* Prof photog, Sch Art Inst Chicago, 67-; vis prof photog, Philadelphia Col of Art, 77, Sch Mus Fine Arts, Boston, 79 & Cornell Univ, Ithaca, NY, 83, Bezalet Acad Art & Design, Jerusalem, Israel, 87. *Awards:* Nat Endowment Arts Grant, 74 & 88; Guggenheim Found Fel in Photog; Polaroid Corp Assistance Grant, 79-; Ill Arts Coun Grant, 85; Young Women's Christian Asn Outstanding Achievement Award, Art, 87. *Bibliog:* Mary Sherman (auth), rev, Chicago Sun Times, 3/25/88; Alice Thorson (auth), rev, Washington Times, 2/9/89; JoAnn Lewis (auth), rev, Washington Post, 2/11/89; Bernard Welt (auth), rev, New Art Examiner, 4/89. *Mem:* Soc Photog Educ (mem bd, 72-76); Friends of Photog (trustee, 75-81). *Media:* Various Photographic Processes. *Publ:* Auth, Barbara Crane Photographs, 1948-1980 (monogr), Ctr Creative Photog, 81; auth, Barbara Crane: The Evolution of a Vision, (exhib catalogue), Albin O Kuhn Libr & Gallery, Univ Md, 83; American Photography, A Critical Record, 1945 to the Present, Harry N Abrams Co, New York, 84; Landscape as Photograph, Yale Univ Press, 84; Instant Projects, Polaroid Corp, 86; Masters of Photog Series, In: Europ ean Photog, Vol 8, Issue 4, 7-8/84; Wipe Outs, In: European P hotog, Vol 6, Issue 4, 10-11-12/87; Swimmers, Aperture Bks, 88. *Mailing Add:* 1230 W Washington Chicago IL 60607

CRANE, BONNIE L
ART DEALER, GALLERY DIRECTOR
b Minneapolis, Minn, Aug 24, 30. *Study:* Sweet Briar Col, Va, BA, 50; Bryn Mawr Col, Pa, MA, 72. *Collections Arranged:* Blanche Ames, Artist & Activist (auth, catalog), Brockton Art Mus, 82; Crane Collection: Special Exhibitions, Boston Sch, 85-86; Bruce Crane, Am Tonalist, 10-11/86; Tonalism, 10 & 11/87; Inspiration Cape Ann, summer 88; Gentle Art of Still Life, 89; Theresa Bernstein Centennial Exhib, 90; Interiors, 92. *Pos:* Cur & dir educ, Brockton Art Mus, Brockton, Mass, 81-82; cur, Clark Gallery, Lincoln Station, Mass, 81-85; owner, Crane Collection, Boston, Mass, 85-. *Teaching:* Lectr Am painting, Mus Fine Arts Sch, Houston, Tex, 75-76 & Rice Univ, 76; studio teacher drawing & painting, Cairo Am Col, Egypt, 78-79. *Mem:* Archives Am Art; Nat Acad Design; Artcetera (bd mem); Handel & Haydn Soc (bd mem); Friends of Art, Sweet Briar Col (bd mem, 92). *Specialty:* American painting of the 19th & early 20th centuries, especially Hudson River School, New England landscapes & the Boston School. *Publ:* Auth, Artist & activist Blanche Ames, Brockton Art Mus & Smith Alumnae Quart, 82. *Mailing Add:* Crane Collection 121 Newbury St Boston MA 02116

CRANE, DAVID FRANKLIN
CERAMIST, EDUCATOR
b Hamilton, Ohio, Aug 16, 53. *Study:* Northern Ariz Univ, Flagstaff, BFA, 76, Ill State Univ, Normal, Ill, MFA, 78. *Work:* IBM Corp, Charlotte, NC; Souran Bank, Roanoke, Va; Fred Marer Collection, Los Angeles, Calif; Neville Pub Mus, Greenbay, Wis; Ill State Univ, Normal; Southern Progress Corp. *Exhib:* Marrietta Col Crafts Nat, Grover Herman Fine Arts Ctr, Ohio, 78; Clay and Fiber: Fifteen ViewPoints, Charles Wustain Mus, Racine, Wis, 78; Young Americans Clay/Glass, Mus Contemp Crafts, New York, 78; Biennial Exhib Crafts, Mint Mus Art, Charlotte, NC, 79; 36th Annual Nat Ceramics Invitational, Lang Art Gallery, Scripps Col, Claremont, Calif, 80; Earthenware USA, Hand & Spirit Gallery, Scottsdale, Ariz, 81; Southeast Seven 9, Southeastern Ctr Contemp Art, Winston-Salem, NC, 86; Clay Az Art, Crafts Mus, Helsinki, Finland, 87; Running Ridge Gallery, 89; Uncommon Vessels, Fla Gulf Coast Art Ctr, 90. *Pos:* Artist-in-Residence, Ford Found, Univ Ga, Athens, 78-79; dir, Armory Art Gallery, Va Tech, 89. *Teaching:* Visiting instr, art-ceramics, Univ Ga, Athens, 79-80; instr, ceramics, Callanwolde Fine Arts Ctr, Atlanta, Ga, 79-80; assoc prof art-ceramics, Va Tech, Blacksburg, Va, 80- *Awards:* Award of Excellence, Radford Univ, 84; Secca-Seven Art Fel, RJ Reynolds Corp, 86; Va Mus Fel, 89. *Bibliog:* Mark Erikson (auth), Sophisticated Clay, Va Gazette, 84; Patricia Mattews (auth), David Crane, Am Ceramics, 5/88. *Mem:* Nat Coun Educ Ceramic Arts. *Publ:* Contrib, Low-Fire: Other ways to work in clay, Davis, 80; Images of Clay Sculpture, Harper & Row, 83. *Dealer:* Schneider Bluhm Loeb Gallery 230 Superior St Chicago IL. *Mailing Add:* 1449 Lusters Gate Rd Blacksburg VA 24060

CRANE, JEAN
PAINTER
b Battle Creek, Mich, July 25, 33. *Study:* Syracuse Univ, BFA, 55. *Work:* Wustum Art Mus, Racine, Wis; Madison Art Ctr, Wis; The Kemper Collection; Northwest Mutual Life Collection; Miller Brewery Collection. *Exhib:* Watercolor USA, Kohler Art Ctr; Wisconsin Biennale; Am Watercolor Soc, New York; Paine Art Ctr, Wis; Layering: An Art of Time and Space, Albuquerque Mus Art, 85; and others. *Awards:* First Place, Wustum Art Mus, 89; Emily Lowe Award, Am Watercolor Soc, New York, 81. *Bibliog:* Review, New Art Examiner, Chicago, 3/81. *Mem:* Wis Watercolor Soc; Wis Painters & Sculptors. *Media:* Watercolor. *Dealer:* Katie Gingrass Gallery 241 N Broadway Milwaukee WI 53202; Leslie Levy Gallery 7135 Main St Scottsdale AZ 85251. *Mailing Add:* N64 W5691 Columbia Rd Cedarburg WI 53012

CRANE, JIM (JAMES G)
PAINTER, CARTOONIST
b Hartshorne, Okla, May 21, 27. *Study:* Albion Col, BA; State Univ Iowa, MA; Mich State Univ, MFA. *Work:* Walker Art Ctr, Minn; Joslyn Mus, Omaha; Wis State Univ, River Falls; St Cloud State Col, Minn. *Exhib:* 28th Biennial, Corcoran Gallery Art; 149th Ann, Pa Acad Fine Arts, Philadelphia; Mich Artists, Detroit Art Inst; Painting of the Year, Smithsonian Inst; Ringling Mus, Sarasota; Centro Colombo Americano, Cali, Colombia; Walker Art Ctr, Minneapolis; Arts in Embassies Prog, Lima, Peru & Katmandu, Nepal. *Teaching:* Prof art, Eckerd Col, currently. *Awards:* Awards, Fla State Fair, 65, Soc Four Arts, Palm Beach, Fla, 67 & Tampa Mus, Tampa Bay, 82; plus others. *Media:* Acrylic Collage, Acrylic Painting. *Publ:* Auth, On Edge, 65, Great Teaching Machine, 66 & Parables, 71, John Knox; auth, Inside Out, 67; illusr, A Funny Thing Happened on the Way to Heaven, 69; plus others. *Mailing Add:* Dept Art Visual Arts Eckerd Col PO Box 12560 St Petersburg FL 33733

CRANE, MICHAEL PATRICK
MUSEUM DIRECTOR, CURATOR
b St Louis, Mo, Dec 24, 48. *Study:* Art Inst Chicago, MFA(design & commun), 76. *Work:* Jean Brown Arch, Tyringham Inst, Mass; Arch Sohm, Markgroningen, WGer; Mus Contemp Art, Univ Sao Paulo, Brazil; Mod Mus, Stockholm, Sweden. *Exhib:* 03-23-03, Nat Gallery Can, Ottawa, Ont, 77; Open Ring Gallery, Sacramento, 79; Berry Col, Mt Berry, Ga, 79 & 80; Union Gallery, San Jose, 80; La Mamelle, San Francisco, 81; and others. *Pos:* Original mem & co-dir, Name Gallery, Chicago, 73-74; ed, Running Dog Press, San Jose, 74-; adminr, All the Chicago Fog Performance Gallery, Chicago, 75-76; res fel, Inst Advan Studies in Contemp Art, San Diego, Calif, 77-78; gallery dir, Calif State Univ, Sacramento, 78-79; gallery dir, San Jose State Univ, 79-83; gallery & mus dir, Arvada Ctr Arts & Humanities, Colo, 83-86; gallery dir, Univ Colo, 86- *Teaching:* Vis artist, Univ Chicago & Calif State Univ, Sacramento, 77; vis artist, San Diego State Univ, 78; lectr, Calif State Univ, Sacramento, 78-79; vis artist, Sch Art Inst, Chicago, 79; vis artist, Ariz State Univ, 79; lectr, San Jose State Univ, 79-83; asst prof, Univ Colo, 86- *Publ:* Contribr, Anti-Object Art, Northwestern Univ Press, 74; auth, Fill in This Space, 75 & Landscapes I'd Love to Perform/Do, 76, Running Dog Press; ed, Correspondence Art, Contemp Arts Press, 83. *Mailing Add:* CU Art Galleries Univ Colo Box 318 Boulder CO 80309-0318

CRARY, JONATHAN KNIGHT
ART HISTORIAN
b New Haven, Conn. *Study:* San Francisco Art Inst, BFA, 73; Columbia Univ, BA, 75, MA, 78, PhD, 87. *Pos:* Found ed, Zone, 85. *Teaching:* Vis lectr, Univ Calif, San Diego, 83 & 85; asst prof, Columbia Univ, 87. *Awards:* Mellon Fel in Humanities, 87-89; J P Getty Fel Art Hist & Humanities, 90-91; Guggenheim Fel, 91. *Res:* Contemporary art and culture. *Publ:* Auth, Passage from virgin to bride, 77 & Real estate opportunities, 78, Arts Mag; Delirious operations, 78, Artforum; Eclipse of the Spectacle, Art After Modernism, 84; Techniques of the Observer, MIT Press, 90. *Mailing Add:* 310 W 106th St New York NY 10025

CRASH (JOHN MATOS)
PAINTER, PRINTMAKER
b Bronx, NY, Oct 11, 61. *Work:* Ludwig Mus, Aachen, Germany; Mus Mod Art, New York; Frederick Weissman Found, Los Angeles, Calif; Mus of Arte, Bolognia, Italy; Groninger Mus, Netherlands. *Comn:* Set designs, Twyla Tharp, New York, 81; spectacolor billboard, Pub Art Fund, NY, 82; float design, Contemp Art Ctr, New Orleans, La, 83; mural installation (interior), Mus Mod Art, Paris, France, 84. *Exhib:* Graffiti, Groninger Mus, Groninger, Netherlands, 84 & La Mus Art, Humblebeck, 84; Graffiti, La Mus Art, Humblebeck, 84; The Big Car Show, Indianapolis Ctr Art, Ind, 85; Ludwig Collection, Forte Belvedere, Florence, Italy, 87; American Art Today, The Art Mus, Fla, 90. *Bibliog:* Richard Goldstein (auth), Enter the anti-space, Village Voice, 11/80; Grace Blueck (auth), The new collectives, NY Times, 81; Kim Levin (auth), The 57th St stop, Village Voice, 12/83. *Media:* Spray Paint. *Dealer:* Sidney Janis Gallery 110 W 57th St New York NY 10019. *Mailing Add:* c/o Sidney Janis Gallery 110 W 57th St New York NY 10019

CRAVEN, DAVID JAMES
PAINTER, COLLAGE ARTIST
b London, Ont, Dec 18, 46. *Study:* Univ Western Ont, BA, 69; Ont Col Art, 71-73. *Work:* Nat Gallery Can, Ottawa, Ont; Art Gallery Ont, Toronto; Vancouver Art Gallery; Montreal Mus Fine Art; Winnipeg Art Gallery. *Exhib:* One-man shows, Musée d'Art Contemporain, Montreal, Que, 78 & Vancouver Art Gallery, BC, 78; Paris Biennale, Musée d'Art Moderne de la Ville de Paris, 80; Material Matters, Clocktower, New York, NY & Norton Mus, Palm Beach, Fla, 80; Canada in Birmingham, Ikon Gallery, Birmingham, Eng, 81; Psychodrama, Philadelphia Art Alliance, Pa, 85. *Bibliog:* Peter White (auth), David Craven: Recent Work, Southern Alta Art Gallery, 78; Sandra Shavl (auth), David Graven: The Signification of Collage, Parachute Mag, 79; Stephen Westfall, David Craven, Art in Am, 84. *Media:* Acrylic on Board. *Dealer:* Sable-Castelli Gallery 33 Hazelton Ave Toronto ON M5R 2E3 Canada. *Mailing Add:* c/o Biher-Larkin 597 Broadway New York NY 10012

CRAVEN, ROY CURTIS, JR
EDUCATOR, MUSEOLOGIST
b Cherokee Bluffs, Ala, July 29, 24. *Study:* Univ Chattanooga, BA, 49; Art Students League, 49-50, with George Grosz, Yasuo Kuniyoshi & Byron Browne; Univ Fla, MFA, 56. *Work:* Va Mus Art, Richmond; Mus Arqueolgia y Etnologia Guatemala, Guatemala City; Esso Standard Oil Collection, New York; New Col, Sarasota, Fla; Chattanooga Art Asn, Tenn. *Comn:* Archit relief, Jacksonville Civic Auditorium. *Exhib:* American Prints & Watercolors, Metrop Mus Art, New York, 50; Forecast, 57-58 & Painting of the Year, 61-62, Am Fedn Arts touring exhibs, US; Delgado Mus, New Orleans, La; Four Arts Club, Palm Beach, Fla. *Pos:* Dir Univ Gallery, Univ Fla, 66-86 & dir, Ctr Latin Am & Tropical Arts, 72- *Teaching:* Prof art, Univ Fla, 54- *Awards:* Am Philos Soc Res Travel Grant, India, 76; Guest of Gov of India, 82; Lifetime Achievement Award, Fla Art Mus Dirs Asn, 90. *Mem:* Int Coun Mus Southeastern Mus Conf (bd mem, ed jour, 67-); Asia Soc; Asn Asian Studies; fel Royal Soc Arts; fel, Royal Asiatic Soc. *Res:* Publications in ancient and contemporary art of India; pre-Columbian art. *Publ:* Auth, A Concise History of Indian Art, London, 76; Ramayana, Pahari Paintings, Bombay, 90; L'Art Indien, Paris, 91. *Mailing Add:* 6818 NW 65th Ave Gainesville FL 32601

CRAVEN, WAYNE
HISTORIAN, WRITER
b Pontiac, Ill, Dec 7, 30. *Study:* John Herron Art Sch, Indianapolis, Ind; Ind Univ, BA, 55, MA, 57; Columbia Univ, PhD, 63. *Collections Arranged:* Co-cur, Exhib Celebrating the Creative American (sculpture sect), White House, Washington, DC, 65; guest cur, 200 Years of American Sculpture, Whitney Mus Am Art, New York, 76. *Pos:* Mem bd ed, The Am Art J, New York, 74-; mem adv bd, Daniel Chester French Papers, Nat Trust, Washington, DC, 75- *Teaching:* Instr art hist, Wheaton Col, Norton, Mass, 58-60; prof art hist, Univ Del, Newark, 60- *Mem:* Col Art Asn; Victorian Soc in Am (mem adv comt, 72). *Res:* Eighteenth and nineteenth century American painting and sculpture. *Publ:* Auth, Sculpture in America, T Y Crowell, Co, New York, 68; co-auth, Britannica Encycl Am Art, Chanticlair Press, 74; plus many jour articles on Am art. *Mailing Add:* Art Hist Dept Univ Del Newark DE 19716

CRAWFORD, BILL (WILBUR OGDEN)
ILLUSTRATOR, ADMINISTRATOR
b Northfield, NJ, Oct 5, 41. *Study:* Hussian Sch Art, AST, 65. *Work:* Philadelphia Mus Art; Smithsonian Inst, Washington, DC; Am Bank. *Comn:* Paper sculpture, Ann Poster for Exhib to Benefit the Philadelphia Aids Task Force, 90 & 92. *Exhib:* Bakers Art, Mus Contemp Crafts, New York; Christmas Exhib, Smithsonian Inst; Illustration, Philadelphia Art Alliance & Soc Illusr, New York; Design, Art Dir Show, New York; Int Design Exhib, Brussels, Belg, Japan & France; New York Art Dirs Ann. *Pos:* Pres, Artist Guild Del Valley. *Teaching:* Instr advert design, Hussian Sch Art, 65-88, asst dir design, 74-88, vpres dir educ, 81-88 & asst dir bus art, 83-88; lectr & consult, graphic design & illus; lectr paper sculptures, Art Careers Portfolio Develop. *Awards:* Gold Award, Philadelphia Art Dirs Ann, 90; Gold & Silver Award, Int 3D Illus exhib, 90 & 92; Gold & Best of Show Award, Philadelphia Artists Guild, 91. *Bibliog:* Raymond Ballinger (auth), Design with Paper, Van Nostrand Reinhold, 82. *Mem:* Philadelphia Watercolor Club; Artist Guild Del Valley (pres, 74-75, exec off, 76-90); Art Dir Club Philadelphia; Int Coun Design Sch. *Media:* Paper Sculpture, Calagraphs. *Publ:* Contribr, Cookies and Breads--The Bakers Art, Van Nostrand Reinhold, 67; Illustrator 20, Hastings House, 78. *Mailing Add:* 90 Bethel Rd Glen Mills PA 19342

CRAWFORD, CATHERINE BETTY
PAINTER
b Ingersoll, Ont, Can, Feb 5, 10. *Study:* Univ Toronto, BA; summer study with Eliot O'Hara & at Doon Sch & Queen's Univ; also study with Gordon Payne, E H Varley & Carl Schaeffer; painting groups in England, Ireland & Philippines. *Work:* London Art Gallery, Ont; Arch Can Painter-Etchers, Hamilton, Ont; Woodstock Art Gallery, Ont. *Exhib:* Western Art League Shows, London, Ont & Soc of Can Painter-Etchers, var yrs; one-man shows, London, Burlington & Woodstock, 48-67 & London, 73; Brantford, 73; retrospective show, Ingersoll, 86; Seven Painters, Woodstock Gallery, 89; Public Art Gallery, 89. *Awards:* Purchase Award, London Women's Comt at Gallery, 53; First Prize for Watercolor, Western Fair, London, 64, Woodstock Gallery, 74; Govt Grant Purchase Award, Ingersall Theatre Performing Arts, 92. *Media:* Watercolor. *Mailing Add:* One Duke Lane Ingersoll ON N5C 2L1 Canada

CRAWFORD, THOM COONEY
PAINTER, SCULPTOR
b Boston, Mass, Sept 23, 44. *Study:* Provincetown Workshop, 63 & 64; Spring Hill Col, Mobile, Ala, BS, 66-62; Syracuse Univ, MFA, 66-67; RI Sch Design, 69. *Work:* Univ Pa; Everson Mus; Prudential Insurance Co; Rockford Art Mus, Ill; Amoco Products. *Comn:* Interior & Exterior (painting & sculpture), Prickly Mt Architectural Project, Warren, Vt, 67; Exterior (painting & sculpture), Bundy Art Mus, Waitesfield, Vt, 69; Mem stone sculpture, Allassio, Italy, 90. *Exhib:* One-man exhibs, Galerie Libre, Montreal, Can, 69, Middlebury Col, Vt, 73, Tibor de Nagy Gallery, New York, 81 & 82, PS 1 Project Room, Long Island City, 83 Sculpture Ctr, New York, 87, M-13 Gallery, New York, 87, 89 & 90, Fendrick Gallery, Washington, DC, 88, Lafayette Col, 90, M-13 Gallery, 91 & Ramnarine Gallery, 93; Post Modernism Metaphors, Alternative Mus, New York, 81; New Visions, Aldrich Mus Contemp Art, Ridgefield, Conn, 81; New York Visions, Janus Gallery, Los Angeles, 83; Queens Mus, 83; PS 1, Proj Rm, New York, 83; Monique Knowlton Gallery, New York, 84; M-13 Gallery, New York, 86; Basel Art Fair, Switz, 87. *Teaching:* Asst prof sculpture, LaFayette Col, 90. *Awards:* Creative Artists Pub Serv Prog Fel, 82-83; Nat Endowment Arts Fel, 85. *Bibliog:* Ruth Bass (auth), rev, Art News, 11/89; William Zimmer (auth), Origins (catalog essay), 90; Janie Welker (auth), The Express, 91; and others. *Media:* Bronze, Mixed Media. *Publ:* Auth & illusr, Raising of the Heart, Limited Ed, Queen City Eds, 72; auth, Alpha Omega (print portfolio), Graphico Uno, 88. *Dealer:* Ramnarine Art Gallery 25-20 43rd Ave Long Island City NY 11101. *Mailing Add:* 18 Mattes Lane Easton PA 18042

CREECH, FRANKLIN UNDERWOOD
SCULPTOR, GRAPHIC ARTIST
b Smithfield, NC, Oct 14, 41. *Study:* Univ NC, Chapel Hill, summers 63 & 64; Duke Univ, BA, 64; Fla State Univ, MS, 66; Det Danske Selskab, Holbaek, Denmark, printing with Hugo Arne Bock. *Work:* Duke Univ Art Mus; NC Nat Bank; Appalachian State Univ; Rauch Indust; Mint Mus, Charlotte, NC. *Exhib:* 1971 Crafts Exhib, Gallery Contemp Art, Winston-Salem, NC, 71; 8th Int Grand Prix du Cote d'Azur, Cannes, France, 72; 1972 Regional Painting Exhib, Lauren Rogers Mus Art, Laurel, Miss, 72; dedication of the Storyteller, Gastonia, NC, 78; solo exhib, Goldsboro Arts Ctr, 80; and others. *Pos:* Chmn, Johnston Community Col, 80- *Teaching:* Instr pottery, design & graphics, Gaston Col, Dallas, NC, 66-, chmn dept, 69-77; vis instr, Duke Univ, spring, 81; instr, Atlantic Christian Col, 81; chmn commercial art dept, Johnston Tech Col, currently. *Awards:* Purchase Award, Piedmont Drawing & Graphic Show; First Place, Appalachian Nat Drawing Competition, 77; Second Place, First Sofa Exchange, 77. *Bibliog:* Artist in the 33rd North Carolina Artists exhibition, La Rev Mod, 10/71; feature in Profiles, Art Voices of the South, 78 & NC State Mag, 12/79. *Mem:* Am Crafts Coun; World Crafts Coun; Nat Art Educ Asn. *Media:* Multi-Media. *Publ:* The development of art departments in the community college, Art Teacher Mag, 1/76. *Mailing Add:* 312 S Fourth St Smithfield NC 27577

CREECY, HERBERT LEE
PAINTER, SCULPTOR
b Norfolk, Va, Aug 14, 39. *Study:* Atlanta Col Art, 64; Southwest Hayter-Atelier 17, Paris, France, 64-65. *Work:* Whitney Mus Am Art, New York; High Mus Art, Atlanta, Ga; Akron Mus Art, Ohio; Indianapolis Mus Art, Ind; Norton Gallery Art, West Palm Beach, Fla; and others. *Exhib:* Herb Creecy: Recent Work, High Mus Art, Atlanta, Ga; 35th Biennial Exhib Am Painting, Corcoran Gallery Art, Washington, DC, 77; Abstraction, Southeastern Ctr Contemp Art, 85; Painting & Things, Nexus Contemp Art Ctr, 88; Painting: 70's - 80's, Lamar Dodd Art Ctr, 88. *Teaching:* Lectr, Univ Ga; Studies Abroad Program, Cortona, Italy; vis lectr, Univ Tenn, Knoxville. *Awards:* Governor's Grant, Ga Coun Arts. *Media:* Acrylic, Oil; Miscellaneous. *Publ:* Artforum Int, summer 88; Southern Homes, 5-6/89; Southern Accent, 1-2/90; Veranda, summer 90. *Mailing Add:* 27 Market St Barnesville GA 30204

CREESE, WALTER LITTLEFIELD
EDUCATOR
b Danvers, Mass, Dec 19, 19. *Study:* Brown Univ, AB; Harvard Univ (fel 44-45), MA & PhD; Columbia Univ. *Pos:* Ed, J Soc Archit Historians, 50-53; chmn, Louisville & Jefferson Co Planning & Zoning Comt, 54-55; dean sch archit & allied arts, Univ Ore, 63-68. *Teaching:* Instr, Wellesley Col, 45; asst prof & prof, Univ Louisville, 46-58; prof achit & chmn archit hist, Univ Ill, Urbana, 58-63 & 68-87; vis prof, summer sch, Harvard Univ, 61-63. *Awards:* Cult Achievement Award, US Dept Interior, 79; Excellence in Educ Award, Am Inst Architects, Ill Coun, 87; Lewis Munford Prize, Am Soc for City & Regional Planning Hist, 91; and others. *Bibliog:* John S Garner (ed), Midwest

in American Architecture: Essays in Honor of Walter L Creese, Univ Ill, 91. *Mem:* Col Art Asn Am (dir, 51-55); hon mem Am Inst Archit; Soc Archit Historians (pres, 58-59). *Publ:* Auth, Search for Environment, Yale, 66, 2nd ed Johns Hopkins, 92; Legacy of Raymond Urwin, Mass Inst Technol, 67; Crowning of the American Landscape, Princeton Univ, 85; TVA's Pub Planning, Univ Tenn, 90. *Mailing Add:* 1817 Moraine Dr Champaign IL 61821

CREEVY, BILL
PAINTER, WRITER
b New Orleans, La, May 24, 42. *Study:* La State Univ, New Orleans, BA(hist), 65, Baton Rouge, MFA, 68; Brooklyn Mus Art Sch, 69 (Max Beckmann Scholar). *Comn:* Paintings of New York, Munic Asst Corp, NY, 81. *Exhib:* 161st Ann Exhib, Nat Acad Art, New York, 85; Am Artist Mag Golden Anniversary Nat Art Competition, San Francisco, St Louis & New York, 87; Int Exhib, Pastels Only, Soc Pastelistes de France, Lille, France, 87; 38th Art of NE USA, Silvermine Guild Arts Ctr, New Canaan, Conn, 87; 16th Ann Open Exhib, Pastel Soc Am, New York, 88. *Pos:* Art dir, Brooklyn Pub Libr, New York, 69-; asst dir, First Street Gallery, New York, 76- *Teaching:* Asst graphics & drawing, La State Univ, 66-68; instr painting, Brooklyn Mus Art Sch, 69. *Awards:* J Klimberger Mem Award for Still Life, Pastel Soc Am, 87; C R Gibson Award for Mixed Media, Silvermine Guild Arts Ctr, 87; Nat Arts Club Award for Excellence, Pastel Soc Am, 88. *Bibliog:* Golden Anniversary winners, Am Artist, 87; Eileen Myles (auth), Bill Creevy at First Street, Art in Am, 88. *Mem:* Pastel Soc Am. *Media:* Pastel, All. *Publ:* Auth, What counts is what's underneath: Pastel techniques by Bill Creevy, Artist's Mag, 3/88, rev ed; The Pastel Book, Bill Creevy, 91 & The Oil Painting Book, 93, Watson Guptill. *Dealer:* First Street Gallery New York NY. *Mailing Add:* 6 Greene St New York NY 10013

CRELLY, WILLIAM RICHARD
HISTORIAN
b St Louis, Mo, Mar 15, 24. *Study:* Washington Univ, St Louis, Mo, BA, 49; Fulbright Scholar Study in Paris, 50-51; Am Coun Learned Soc, 58; Inst Fine Arts, NY Univ, PhD, 58; Morse Fel Study in Italy, 61-62. *Pos:* Lectr & instr, Washington Sq Col, NY Univ, 52-56; from instr to assoc prof, Yale Univ, 56-65; prof art hist, Emory Univ, Atlanta, Ga, currently. *Mem:* Col Art Asn Am. *Res:* Marcello Giovanetti, poet of the Roman baroque. *Publ:* Auth, Simon Vouet's allegory of victory, Bulletin John Herron Art Inst, 61; auth, The Painting of Simon Vouet, Yale Univ Press, 62; contribr, French Art of Sixteenth Century (exhib catalog), Cummer Gallery Art, Fla, 6/64; contribr, The Iconography of the Elian Graces (essays in hon of Walter Friedlaender), Marysas Mag, 65; contribr, Two allegories of the seasons by Simon Vouet and their iconography, In: Art the Ape of Nature, Prentice-Hall, 81. *Mailing Add:* 1852 Merrimac Ct Atlanta GA 30329

CRENSHAW, KAREN BRUCE
CONSERVATOR
b Baltimore, Md, Oct 29, 52. *Study:* Univ Del, Newark, BA(art hist & chem), 74; Intermuseum Laboratory, Oberlin, Ohio, cert, 77; Oberlin Col, Ohio, MA(art conserv), 79. *Pos:* Asst painting conservator, Cleveland Mus Art, Ohio, 77-81; conservator, Mus Art, Carnegie Inst, Pittsburgh, Pa, 81-; sr conservator, The Baltimore Mus Art. *Awards:* Historic Deerfield Summer Fel, Mass, 74; Andrew W Mellon Fel, Conservation of Paintings, Cleveland Mus Art, 79-81. *Mem:* Prof assoc mem Am Inst Conserv Hist Artistic Works; assoc mem Int Inst Conserv Hist Artistic Works; Midwest Regional Conserv Guild. *Res:* Conservation research, study of 18th and 19th century American painting techniques and materials. *Publ:* Auth, A Study of Texture Modifications, Interlining Materials, Support Fabrics, and Cushioning Materials, 78 & A Study of George Inness' Painting Technique, 81, Am Inst Conserv Hist Artistic Works. *Mailing Add:* 160 Ave L Pittsburgh PA 15221

CREPS, GERALD A
ENVIRONMENTAL ARTIST, EDUCATOR
b Roaring Springs, Pa, Feb 24, 39. *Study:* Studied with Hugh Laidmain, 64-74; Pratt Inst, Brooklyn, BA, 76; Columbia Univ, New York, MA, 78. *Work:* Carter Presidential Libr, Atlanta, Ga; Pratt Inst, Brooklyn, NY. *Comn:* Custom wallcovering, The White House, 78; murals, Blue Ridge Parkway, Va, Nat Park Serv, 84; paintings, Blue Ridge Parkway, NC, Eastern Nat Parks & Monuments Asn, 85; wild life & nature paintings, Corp Exec offices, Fortune 500. *Exhib:* All major regional & nat wildlife art shows & competitions along the east coast, 80- *Collections Arranged:* Great Waterfalls of the World (over 40 original paintings), River Gallery, Atlanta, Ga, 88; Neo Hudson River paintings of NY great Adirondack wilderness, 42 paintings, ICA Gallery, Sioux Falls, SDak, 92. *Pos:* Owner, Living Hist & Diorama Exhib Co, Asheville, NC, 80-86. *Teaching:* Instr art, Genesee Community Col & Medialle Col, NY prisons, 88-; North Country Community Col, NY prisons, 88-91,educ consult specializing in seminars to bus & non-profit organizations to foster the commodity of creativity, 91- *Awards:* Personal letter from White House, 82; Mountain of the Holy Cross, accepted into the permanent collection of Mus of Pratt Inst. *Mem:* Nat Asn Interpretation; Nat Col Arts Asn; Correctional Educ Asn. *Media:* Oil, Watercolor. *Publ:* Auth, There Is a Dead Horse in the Creek, Pratt Inst, 74. *Dealer:* Barbara Volkman/Berdow Assoc 345 86th St New York NY 10028. *Mailing Add:* PO Box 2441 Wilton NY 12866

CRESPIN, LESLIE A
PAINTER, ASSEMBLAGE ARTIST
b Cleveland, Ohio, Sept 30, 47. *Study:* Univ Capetown, 68-69; Hiram Col, 69-70; also apprenticed under Ray Vinella. *Work:* Harwood Found Mus Art, Taos, NMex; Carlsbad Fine Arts Mus, NMex; Monsanto Int, New York, St Louis; Midland Savings & Loans, Denver; Johnson-Humrick House Mus, OH; Maytag, New York & Santa Fe. *Comn:* 4-Monsanto Int, New York & St Louis, 88, 89 & 90; Rolm Corp Div of IBM Corp, Dallas; Santa Fe Contract Design, Odessa, Tex. *Exhib:* Western Reserve Exhibition, Cleveland Mus Art; Roanoke Fine Arts Mus; Vinella-Crespin, Amarillo Art Ctr, Tex, 83 & Carlsbad Fine Art Mus, NMex, 85; Coos Art Mus, Ore, 84; 21st Annual Tri-State, Carlsbad Fine Arts Mus, NMex, 85; De Los Muertos, Millicent Rogers Mus, Taos, NMex, 85; Beachwood Mus, Ohio, 85; Russian Icon Exhib, Fechin Inst, Taos, 86; Recent Paintings, Harwood Found, Mus Taos Art, 87 & 89; North Miami Mus Ctr Contemp Arts, Miami, FL, 89; Johnson-Humrick House Mus OH, 90; Carson Co Square House Mus TX, 90-91; Ctr Arts Southwest, Santa Fe, NM, 90. *Teaching:* Instr design, Taos Sch Fine Art, NMex, 77. *Awards:* Best of Show, & 1st Prize, Nonrepresentational, 21st Tri-State, Carlsbad Fine Arts Mus, NMex, 85; Masterfield Award, North Coast Collage Soc, 85 & 87; Best of Show, The Spectral Pallette of Taos Art, Taos Art Asn, 88. *Bibliog:* Peggy Ridgeway (auth), Creating art from the emotion, Art Gallery, 83; V Forman (auth) Energized at Tracy Felix, Artspace, Springs Mag CO, 85; American Artists: An Illustrated Survey of American Contemporaries, The Krantz Co, 85; S Parlo (auth) Lights Up On Taos, Southwest Profile Mag, NMex. *Mem:* Fechin Inst; Albuquerque United Artists; North Coast Collage Soc; Soc Layerists Multi-Media. *Dealer:* The Fenix Gallery 228-B Paso Del Pueblo Norte TaosNM 87571. *Mailing Add:* c/o The Fenix Gallery 228B N Pueblo Rd Taos NM 87571

CRESPO, MICHAEL LOWE
WRITER, PAINTER
b New Orleans, La, Jan 3, 47. *Study:* La State Univ, BA; Queens Col, MFA. *Work:* New Orleans Aquarium, Meilhenny Collection La State Univ, City Nat Bank Collection, Baton Rouge, La. *Exhib:* Simms Fine Art, New Orleans, La; Mesur Mus, Monroe, La; McMurtrey Gallery, Houston, Tex; Transco Energy Tower Gallery, Houston, Tex; Kurts Bingham Gallery, Memphis, Tenn; Artists' Choice Mus, New York; Contemp Art Ctr, New Orleans, La. *Pos:* Dir, Sch Art, La State Univ. *Teaching:* Instr painting, Univ Southwestern La, 71; prof, La State Univ, 71-; vis artist painting, Purdue Univ, 74. *Awards:* La Div Arts Artist Fel. *Media:* Oil on Canvas, Watercolor. *Publ:* Auth, Watercolor Day by Day, Watson-Guptill, New York, 87; Experiments in Watercolor, Watson-Guptill, New York, 88; How to Make An Oil Painting, Watson-Guptill, New York, 90. *Mailing Add:* 535 Cornell Ave Baton Rouge LA 70808

CRESS, GEORGE AYERS
PAINTER, EDUCATOR
b Anniston, Ala, Apr 7, 21. *Study:* Emory Univ; Univ Ga, BFA, MFA. *Work:* Tenn Fine Arts Ctr; High Mus, Atlanta, Ga; Ford Motor Co; Birmingham Mus, Ala; Mint Mus, Charlotte, NC; plus many others. *Exhib:* Pa Acad Fine Arts; Springfield Watercolor Ann; one-man shows, Grand Cent Moderns, NY, Addison Gallery Am Art 20 Yr & 50 Yr Retrospective, Hunter Gallery & var southeastern mus; Nat Mus Am Art, Washington DC; Bampton Arts Centre, Oxon, Eng; and others. *Pos:* Pres SE Col Art Conf, 56, 66 & 83; chmn, Tenn Col Arts Coun, 66-68. *Teaching:* Instr art, Judson Col, Marion, Ala, 45-46, Mary Baldwin Col, Staunton, Va, 46-47, Univ Md, 47-48, Univ Ga, 49, 65 & 69, Univ Tenn, 49-51, Ont Dept Educ, 63 & Univ SC, 67; Guerry prof art, painter-in-residence, Univ Tenn, Chattanooga, 51-84. *Awards:* Southeastern Ann, Birmingham Mus Ann & Atlanta Arts Festival; plus many others. *Mem:* Southeastern Col Conf (pres, 56, 66 & 83). *Media:* Oil, Watercolor. *Mailing Add:* c/o UTC Art Gallery Fine Arts Ctr Vine & Palmetto St Univ Tenn Chattanooga TN 37403

CRETARA, DOMENIC ANTHONY
PAINTER, EDUCATOR
b Chelsea, Mass, Mar 29, 46. *Study:* Boston Univ Sch Fine Arts, BFA(magna cum laude), 68, MFA, 70, Tanglewood Inst, summer 68. *Work:* Metrop Mus Art; Duxbury Art Complex, Mass; McBall Corp, Chicago, Ill. *Exhib:* Contemporary Naturalism, Doll and Richards Gallery, Cambridge, Mass, 80; Selections 21, Drawing Ctr, New York, 84; Works on Paper, travelling, Weatherspoon Art Gallery, Greensboro, NC, 84; solo exhibs, Segal Gallery, New York, 84 & 85, Koplin Gallery, Los Angeles, 86, Victor McNeil Gallery, New York, 88, Koslow Gallery, Los Angeles, 90, John Thomas Gallery, Los Angeles, 91 & Alon Gallery, Boston, 91; Sherry French Gallery, New York, 88; Triton Mus Art, Santa Clara, Calif. *Teaching:* Instr painting & design, DeCordova Mus Art, Lincoln, Mass, 71-74; chmn dept fine arts & prof painting & drawing, Art Inst Boston, 73-86; prof painting, Calif State Univ at Long Beach, 86- *Awards:* Fulbright-Hayes grant, Italian & US govts, 74-75; Camargo Found Grant Artist-in-Residence, Cassis, France, 78-79; Boston Padua Sister Cities Grant, 84. *Bibliog:* Articles, Arts Mag, 12/84, Artweek, Los Angeles, 4/87 & 4/90 & Los Angeles Times, 4/87 & 4/90; A course in figure drawing, Artist's Mag, 6/90; Article, Am Artist Mag, 12/92. *Mem:* Boston Visual Artist's Union; Asn Artist Run Galleries. *Media:* Oil, Charcoal. *Publ:* Contribr, Figure Drawing, 76, The Art of Responsive Drawing, rev ed, 77 & Painting: Perceptual and Technical Fundamentals, 79, Prentice Hall; One Hundred American and European Drawings, Prentice Hall, 82; auth, A course in life drawing, Artist's Mag, 6/90. *Dealer:* John Thomas Gallery 602 Colorado Ave Santa Monica CA 90401; Alon Gallery 1665A Beacon St Brookline MA. *Mailing Add:* Dept Art Calif State Univ 1250 Bellflower Blvd Long Beach CA 90840

CRILE, SUSAN
PAINTER
b Cleveland, Ohio, 1942. *Study:* Bennington Col, BA, 65; Hunter Col, 71-72. *Work:* Metrop Mus Art, New York; Phillips Collection, Hirshhorn Mus, Washington, DC; Brooklyn Mus, NY; Albright-Knox Art Gallery, Buffalo,

NY; Cleveland Mus Art, Ohio. *Exhib:* Whitney Ann Exhib Am Paintings, Whitney Mus Am Art, New York; solo exhibs, Ivory Kimpton Gallery, San Francisco, 81 & 84, Nina Freudenheim Gallery, Buffalo, 80, Cleveland Ctr Contemp Art, Ohio, 84, Graham Modern, 85, 87, 88 & 90, Gloria Luria Gallery, Bay Harbor Island, FL, 87,; Works on Paper, Va Mus Fine Arts, Richmond, 75; Geometric Abstraction: A New Generation, Inst Contemp Art, Boston, 81; solo exhibs, Ivory Kimpton Gallery, San Francisco, 81 & 84, Nina Freudenheim Gallery, Buffalo, 80, Cleveland Ctr Contemp Art, Ohio, 84, Graham Modern, 85, 87, 88 & 90 & Gloria Luria Gallery, Bay Harbor Island, Fla, 87; After Matisse, traveling exhib, 86; IBM Gallery & Neilsen Gallery, New York, 89; Nat Gallery Art, Washington, DC, 90; Detroit Inst Art, Mich, 91; Nat Mus Women Arts, Washington, DC, 91. *Pos:* Vis critic, Univ Pa, Philadelphia, 80. *Teaching:* Instr painting, Princeton Univ, 74-76, Sch Visual Arts, New York, 76-82 & Sarah Lawrence Col, 76-78; Barnard Col, 83-86; assoc prof, Hunter Col, 82- *Awards:* Ingram Merrill Found Grant, 72; Fel Nat Endowment Arts, 82, 89-90; Res painting, Amer Acad in Rome. *Bibliog:* Hearne Pardee (auth), Susan Crile, Artnews, 10/90; Ronny Cohen (auth), Susan Crile, Artforum, 10/90; Robert Mahoney, Susan Crile, Arts, 9/90, p101. *Media:* Oil, Pastel. *Publ:* Ralph Humphrey: Voices (catalog), Ralph Humphrey, The Late Paintings on Paper, Hunter Col City Univ NY, 91. *Mailing Add:* 168 W 86th St New York NY 10024

CRIMI, ALFRED D
PAINTER, INSTRUCTOR
b San Fratello, Italy, Dec 1, 1900; US citizen. *Study:* Nat Acad Design; life drawing with Ivan Olinsky, Beaux Arts Inst; Preparatory Sch Ornamental Arts; fresco painting & Pompeian encaustic with Prof Venturini Paperi, Rome, Italy. *Work:* Ulrich Mus Art, Wichita State Univ, Kans; Butler Inst Am Art, Youngstown, Ohio; Smithsonian Inst, Washington, DC; Syracuse Univ, NY; Springfield Mus Fine Arts, Ma; and others. *Comn:* Fresco Mural, Rutgers Presbyterian Church, New York City, Nat Competition, 38; Fresco, Post Off Dept, Washington, DC, 37-38; oil mural, Northampton, Mass, 38-39; mosaic, comn by New York Bd Educ, Einstein Jr High Sch, 66-67 & Adlai Stevenson High Sch, 68-69. *Exhib:* Mus Mod Art, New York, 36; Art Inst Chicago, 36; Whitney Mus Am Art, 46 & Metrop Mus Art, New York, 52-53; First Int Exhib Liturgical Art, Trieste, Italy, 61. *Teaching:* Instr, City Col New York, 47-53; Pratt Inst, 48-51; Pa State Univ, 63; also instr, lectr & critic, cols & univs, 44- *Awards:* Mainstream Int, Marietta Col, Ohio, 69 & 70; top purchase award, Butler Inst Am Art, 69; Gold Medal of Honor, Audubon Artists, 71; plus others. *Bibliog:* Mechanical brains (artist's drawings of war machinery), Life Mag, 1/21/44; Carrie Timpano (photographer & collabr), The making & fascination of fresco painting (color film), 57-59. *Mem:* Audubon Artists; Allied Artists Am (bd dir, 47-72); Am Watercolor Soc; Fedn Mod Painters & Sculptors. *Media:* Oil, Watercolor. *Publ:* Auth, articles in, Am Artist Mag, 1/57 & 2/62; The Art of Abstract Dimensional Painting, Grumbacher Libr Publ, 77; autobiography, A Look Back-A Step Forward, Ctr for Migration Studies, 88. *Mailing Add:* 615 Pelham Pkwy N Bronx NY 10467

CRIMMINS, JERRY (GERALD GARFIELD)
ASSEMBLAGE ARTIST, PAINTER
b Minneapolis, Minn, Feb 9, 40. *Study:* Minneapolis Col Art, BFA, 65; Pratt Inst, MFA, 67. *Work:* Philadelphia Mus Art; Minneapolis Inst Arts; Pratt Inst, Brooklyn, NY; Southern Ill Univ, Carbondale; Rotterdamse Kunstichting, Neth. *Exhib:* The Artists' Book, Univ Calif, San Diego at La Jolla, 77; Selections from the Collection of Richard Brown Baker, Squibb Gallery, Princeton, NJ, 79; Words & Images, Philadelphia Col Art, 79; Southern Alleghenies Mus, Pa; one man shows, Hansen Fuller Goldeen Gallery, San Francisco, Calif, 80, Touchstone Gallery, New York, 80 & Rodger LaPelle Galleries, Philadelphia, Pa, 82, DC Armory, Washington, 81, Moore Col Art, 86; Imaginary Lands, Rotterdam Arts Found, Neth, 83; Return of the Narrative, Palm Springs Desert Mus, Calif, 84; group exhibs, Fleisher Mus, Palm Springs Desert Mus, Tyler Sch Art, Southern Alleghenies Mus. *Teaching:* Instr, Tyler Sch Art, Philadelphia, 67-68; prof basic arts & sculpture, Moore Col Art & Design, Philadelphia, 68- *Awards:* Purchase Award, So Ill Univ, 72 & Philadelphia Mus Art, 80; Men of Achievement Award, Cambridge, Eng, 81 & 82; Nat Endowment Arts Grant, 83; Pollock-Krasner Found Grant, Pa Coun Arts, 90. *Bibliog:* Jo Ann Lewis (auth), article, Washington Post, 9/11/81; John Russell (auth), article, New York Times, 4/21/80; Peter Frank (auth), Artists' stamps and stamp images, Art Express, 11/7/81. *Media:* Multimedia, Sculpture. *Publ:* Auth & illusr, Anatomical Notes, pvt publ, 75; Thicker than Blood, Cold Chair Press, 76; The Song of the Fair Haired, pvt publ, 77; Visitors Guide to La Republique de Reves, Synapse Art Press, 80; The Secret History of La Republique de Reves, Reverian Govt, 83; contrib to other professional publications, 58-61. *Dealer:* Jeffrey Fuller Gallery The Studio Lehman Lane Philadelphia PA. *Mailing Add:* Fine Arts Moore Col 20th & Parkway Philadelphia PA 19103

CRIMMINS, JERRY See Thompson, Jack

CRIMP, DOUGLAS
CRITIC, HISTORIAN
b Coeur d'Alene, Idaho, Aug 19, 44. *Study:* Tulane Univ, BA(art hist), 68; City Univ New York, MPhil, 83. *Pos:* Curatorial staff, Solomon R Guggenheim Mus, 68-71; ed assoc, Art News, 71-76; guest cur, Visual Arts Gallery, New York, 72 & Artists Space, New York, 77; managing ed, October, 77-83, exec ed, 83-86, ed, 86-90; series ed, October Bks, MIT Press, 88-90. *Teaching:* Instr art hist, Sch Visual Arts, New York, 70-76; vis instr, Dept Art Hist, NS Col Art & Design, Halifax, 82, Visual Arts Prog, Princeton Univ, 86, Mason Gross Sch Arts, Rutgers Univ, 88 & Cooper Union, New York, 88, Calif Inst Arts, Valencia, spring 89 & 90, Sarah Lawrence Col, 90-91. *Awards:* Art Critics Fel, Nat Endowment Arts, 73 & 84; Chester Dale Fel, Ctr Advan Study Visual Arts, Nat Gallery Art, 83-84; Frank Jewett Mather Award, for distinction in art criticism, Col ARt Asn, 88. *Mem:* fel Inst Archit & Urban Studies; Int Asn Art Critics; Col Art Asn. *Publ:* Auth, Richard Serra: Sculpture exceeded, fall 81, The new French culture: An interview with Guy Hocquenghem, winter 81 & Fassbinder, Franz, Fox, Elvira, Erwin, Armin and all the others, summer 82, October; auth, Drawings for sale, Arq, Quebec, 7-8/82; auth, Appropriating appropriation, In: The Image Scavangers: Photography, Inst Comtemp Art, Philadelphia, 83; The art of exhibition, October, fall 84; The postmodern museum, Parachute, spring 87; The end of art and the origin of the museum, The Art J, winter 87; This is not a museum of art (essay), In: Marcel Broodthaers, Walker Art Ctr, Minneapolis, 89; The boys in my bedroom, Art in Am, 2/90; Art acts up: A graphic response to AIDS, Out/look, summer, 90. *Mailing Add:* 93 Nassau St New York NY 10038

CRISPO, DICK
PAINTER, PRINTMAKER
b Brooklyn, NY, Jan 13, 45. *Study:* Ariz Sch Art; Carmel Art Inst; Monterey Peninsula Col; Hartnell Col; St Sophia Divinity Sch; also with Victor DiGesu, Sam Colburn, Jan Hannah, Alexander Napote, Kay Rodgers & others. *Work:* Libr Cong, Washington, DC; Bibliot Nat, Paris, France; Inst Nac de Bellas Artes, Mexico City, Mex; Mus Western Art, Tokyo, Japan; Nat Libr Ireland, Dublin; plus others. *Comn:* Ecology (mural), Monterey High Sch, Calif, 72; Ecology, Robert Louis Stevenson Sch, Pebble Beach, Calif, 72; Spirit of Youth, Carmel Youth Ctr, Calif, 73; History of the Migrant Worker (mural), Opportunity Indust Ctr, Salinas, Calif, 74; Twelve Master Teachers of the World (mural), Church of Antioch, Pacific Grove, Calif, 75. *Exhib:* Calif State Fair, Sacramento, 64; Small Painting Biennial, Purdue Univ, 68; Univ Calif, Berkeley, 72; Pan-Am Graphics, Mexico City, 72; Western Graphics, Tokyo, 73; and others. *Pos:* Chmn, Fine Arts Div, Monterey County Fair, 72-74; co-founder, Mus on Wheels, Monterey, 74-; exhib dir, Pacific Grove Art Ctr, 74-; art counr, Monterey Co Probation Dept, 75-; Am cult specialist to Latin Am for USIS. *Teaching:* Instr arts & Crafts, York Sch, Monterey, 71-73; instr folk & ethnic arts, Monterey Peninsula Col, 74-75; instr folk & ethnic arts & art hist, St Sophia Divinity Sch, Pacific Grove, 75-; vis lectr, Univ Calif, Santa Cruz, Interdisciplinary Studies Dept, Porter, Col. *Awards:* All Calif Watercolor Competition Third Prize, Pacific Grove, 67; San Juan Bautista Invitational Second Prize, Calif, 68; Gold Medal, Acad Italy, 79; plus others. *Bibliog:* Pat Griffith (auth), An artist with a sense of humor, Carmel Valley Outlook, Carmel, Calif, 72; Robert Miskimon (auth), Social consciousness of art, Pine Cone, Carmel, 73. *Mem:* Artists Equity; Carmel Art Asn; Pacific Grove Art Ctr; Pac Art Asn (chmn); Art Workers United. *Media:* All. *Res:* Eclectic study of world folk art. *Collection:* Folk and eccentric art from over 40 countries. *Publ:* Auth, Contemporary Print Making Renaissance in Japan, 69; dir, Dick Crispo Maker of Images, Frasconi-Selzer Films. *Mailing Add:* c/o 417 Cannery Row Monterey CA 93940

CRIST, C JEFFREY
DIRECTOR, CURATOR
b Jamestown, NY, Apr 22, 55. *Study:* State Univ NY, Fredonia, NY, BA(art, summa cum laude), 78. *Exhib:* Invitational Alumni Exhib, Rockefeller Art Ctr, Fredonia, NY, 79; Jeffrey Crist: Polyethylene & Fire, Alternate Space Gallery at W Broadway, New York, 80; Three Artists, Colonade-Chautauqua Inst, New York, 88; CAA Mems Exhib, (contribr, catalog), CAA Galleries, 89 & 90, Tri-State; Invitational, 89, Chautauqua, NY. *Collections Arranged:* Chautauqua Nat Exhib Am Art, 89 & 90; Women Artists Am, 90; Chautauqua Int Exhib Art, 91; Nat Renaissance: Arts Alive in Am, 91; Traditions & Alternatives in Realism, 92. *Pos:* Artist, Jeff Crist Studio, Jamestown, NY, 78-88; dir, CAA Galleries, Chautauqua Inst, NY, 88-90; dir & founder, Mus Without Walls Int, Bemus Point, NY, 90-92. *Teaching:* Teacher art studio & appreciation, Levant Christian Sch, Falconer, NY, 85-88; lectr accessibility in visual art, CAA Galleries Chautauqua Inst, NY, 89-90; instr painting, Mus Without Walls Int, Bemus Point, NY, 91- 92. *Bibliog:* Anthony Bannon (auth), CAA Exhibition is Bold & Aggressive, Chautauqua Daily, 7/89; Juliet Borne (auth), Museum Director Advocates making Art Accessible, 7/90 & Prize Winning Art Work Raises Questions, Chautauqua Daily, 6/90. *Mem:* Arts Council Chautauqua Co; Chautauqua Art Asn. *Publ:* Auth & illustr, From the Outside Out, Mus Press, 91; auth, 1991 Mus without Walls Int Exhibs, Mus Press, 92. *Mailing Add:* 3816 E Lake Rd Bemus Point NY 14712

CRIST, WILLIAM GARY
VISUAL ARTIST, EDUCATOR
b Pocatello, Idaho, Jan 17, 37. *Study:* Univ Wash, Seattle, BA(art educ), 66; Cranbrook Acad Art, Detroit, MFA(sculpture), 71; study with Michael Hall, Julius Schmidt, Joseph Beuys, Nam June Paik & Klaus Rinke; Staatliche Kunstakademie, Dusseldorf, WGer, 81 & 83. *Work:* Cameron Univ, Lawton, Okla; Univ Mo, Kansas City; Gen Serv Admin, Washington, DC. *Exhib:* Noho Gallery, New York, 79 & 80; Staatliche Kunstakademie, Dusseldorf, WGer, 81; XVth Ann Int Electronic Music Festival, 85; Randolph Street Gallery, Chicago, 86; Oppression/Expression, Contemp Arts Ctr, New Orleans, 86; Pleiades Gallery, 10th Ann Juried, New York, 92. *Teaching:* Asst prof art, Wesleyan Col, Macon, Ga, 71-72; instr art, Cameron Univ, Lawton, Okla, 72-74; asst prof art, Univ Mo, Kansas City, 74-81, assoc prof art, 81-88, chair, dept art & art hist, 85-89 to prof art, 88-; dir 2 and 3D computer graphics, Univ Mo Video Network, 89- *Awards:* Interdisciplinary Arts Fel Prog, Rockefeller Found & Nat Endowment Arts, 86; Southwestern Bell Telephone Found, 92. *Mem:* Kansas City Artists Coalition; Col Art Asn. *Media:* Mixed Media, Electronics. *Res:* Computer art; synthesis of various technologies into visual art; visual and audio relationships of space and time. *Publ:* Auth, article, High Performance Mag, Issue 32; Coherent light and electronics as creative mediums, Okla State Arts Comn, 73; interview with Joseph Beuys, 82 & interview with Nam June Paik, Forum Mag, 5/86; auth, Underground art in Poland, Col Art Asn, Toronto. *Mailing Add:* Dept Art & Art Hist Univ Mo Kansas City MO 64110

CRITE, ALLAN ROHAN
PAINTER, ILLUSTRATOR
b Plainfield, NJ, Mar 20, 10. *Study:* Boston Mus Fine Arts Sch; Mass Sch Art; Boston Univ, CBA; Harvard Univ, BA; Suffolk Univ, Hon DH, 79. *Work:* Boston Mus Fine Arts; Spelman Col, Atlanta, Ga; Addison Gallery Am Art, Andover, Mass; Marine Hosp, Carville, La; Villanova Col, Pa; and others. *Comn:* Insignia, USS Wilson; mural, Grace Church, Martha's Vineyard, Mass; stations of the cross, Holy Cross Church, Morrisville, Vt, 57; Allan Crite Wing, Blackstone Sq Community Sch, Boston; and others. *Exhib:* One-man shows, Boston Mus Fine Arts, Fogg Mus Art & Farnsworth Mus Art; Religious Art Festival, Brandon, Vt, 61; Festival Arts, Ecumenical Youth Assembly NAm, Ann Arbor, Mich, 61; and others. *Pos:* Artist-historian, Semitic Mus, Harvard Univ, formerly. *Teaching:* Lectr Christian art, Oberlin Col, 58 & Regis Col, formerly. *Awards:* Boston Mus Fine Arts Sch & Seabury Western Theol Sem Award, 52; Fourth Prize, Franklin Mint Bicentennial Medal Design; HDH, Suffolk Univ, 79. *Publ:* Auth & illusr, Cultural heritage of the United States, 68 & Were you there when they crucified my Lord, McGrath, 69; contribr to magazines, bulletins & religious books. *Mailing Add:* 410 Columbus Ave Boston MA 02116

CRIVELLI, ELAINE
ENVIRONMENTAL ARTIST, SCULPTOR
b Philadelphia, Pa, Dec 4, 50. *Study:* Westchester Univ, BFA, 78; Univ Del, with Joe Moss, MFA, 82. *Comn:* Sculpture installations, Univ NC, Chapel Hill, 82 & Gotham Design, Dobbs Ferry, NY, 88; Movement Int Theater, 87; Please Touch Mus, Philadelphia, Pa, 90. *Exhib:* What Color Is Your Space, Del Art Mus, Wilmington, 81; Regional Trends in 3 Dimensions, Stockton State Col, NJ, 81; Painted Lyrics (solo exhib), Marion Locks Gallery, Pa, 82; Woven Rhythms (solo exhib), Artpark, Lewiston, NY, 82; Sculpture: Penn's Landing, Port of Hist Mus, Philadelphia, 84; Invitational Group Exhib, Tianjin Fine Arts Col, China, 86; Artists by Themselves, Sushi Gallery, San Diego, Calif, 87; Altered Sites, Fairmount Park, Philadelphia, 88. *Pos:* Gallery dir, Painted Bride Art Ctr, Philadelphia, 84-87. *Teaching:* Lectr 3-D design, Philadelphia Col Art, 83-; prof design & drawing, Philadelphia Col Textiles & Sci, 87-; prof, Chestnut Hill Col, Pa, 87-89; prof, Savannah Col Art & Design, Savannah, Ga, 89- *Awards:* Fel, Univ Del, 80. *Bibliog:* Ronnie H Cohen (auth), Artpark, Artforum, 82; Deborah Curtis (auth), Introduction to Visual Literacy, Prentice Hall, 86; Edward J Sozanski (auth), On galleries, Philadelphia Inquirer, 2/26/87; Beth Wilcox (auth), Creating Art at Artpark, Sculpture Mag, 89. *Mem:* Sculptors Int; Col Art Asn. *Media:* Mixed Media. *Mailing Add:* 413 E Front St Media PA 19063

CROCKETT, GIB (GIBSON M)
CARTOONIST, PAINTER
b Washington, DC, Sept 18, 12. *Study:* Studied watercolor under several nationally known artists; illustration with Harry Anderson. *Work:* Represented in many pvt collections. *Comn:* Many commissions of local and political figures. *Exhib:* Landscape painting in local & nat exhibs. *Pos:* Mem staff, Washington Eve Star, 33-75, ed cartoonist, 47-75, sport cartoonist, 40-46; free lance illusr, 43-; art dir, Am Publ Co, Washington, 45-85; Retired. *Teaching:* Instr, pvt portrait painting classes. *Awards:* Cartoon Awards from Headliner Asn & Freedoms Found; over 20 awards for watercolor paintings from local and area competitions. *Mem:* Wash Soc Landscape Painters; Ed Cartoonists Asn; Baltimore Watercolor Soc. *Mailing Add:* 4713 Great Oak Rd Manor Club Rockville MD 20853

CROFT, MICHAEL FLYNT
CRAFTSMAN, EDUCATOR
b Minneapolis, Minn, Oct 11, 41. *Study:* Univ NMex, Albuquerque, BFA; Southern Ill Univ, Carbondale, MFA. *Work:* Southern Ill Univ Art Mus, Carbondale; Renwick Gallery, Smithsonian Inst, Washington, DC; Tucson Art Mus, Ariz. *Comn:* Offertory basin, All Saints Episcopal Cathedral, Indianapolis, 65. *Exhib:* Craft Multiples, Renwick Gallery, Smithsonian Inst, Washington, DC; The Art of Personal Adornment, Am Craft Mus, NY; Young Americans-1969, Am Craft Mus, NY; Pure Gold, Winston-Salem, NC; and many others. *Pos:* Dir, Copper, Brass & Bronze Competition, Univ Ariz Art Mus, Tucson, 77 & 80; vpres, Acad Affairs, Swain Sch Design, New Bedford, Mass, 86-87; pres, Soc NAm Goldsmiths, 85-87. *Teaching:* Prof art, jewelry & metalsmithing, Univ Ariz, 72- *Awards:* Nat Endowment Arts Grants, 76, 79 & 80; Fac Achievement Award, Univ Ariz, 83; Oral Hist Collection, Columbia Univ, New York 88; and others. *Bibliog:* James Schineller (auth), Art: Search & Self Discovery, Int Textbook Co, 2nd ed, 68; Oppi Untracht (auth), Jewelry Concepts and Technology, Doubleday, 82; Tim McCreight (auth), Custom Knifemaking, Stackpole Books, 85. *Mem:* Soc NAm Goldsmiths; Am Crafts Coun; Artists Blacksmiths Asn NAm Soc Am Silversmiths. *Media:* Precious Metals. *Mailing Add:* 1441 N Day Rd Tucson AZ 85715-5633

CRONBACH, ROBERT M
SCULPTOR
b St Louis, Mo, Feb 10, 08. *Study:* St Louis Sch Fine Arts, with Victor Holm, 25-26; Pa Acad Fine Arts, with Charles Grafly & Albert Laessle, 27-30; Cresson scholar to Europe, 29-30. *Work:* Nat Collection Art, Smithsonian Inst, Washington, DC; St Louis Art Mus; Springfield Art Mus, Mo; Walker Art Ctr, Minneapolis; Mus Fine Arts, Skopje, Yugoslavia; Colby Col, Maine; and others. *Comn:* Fountain, Fed Off Bldg, St Louis, 63; fountain, Kanawha Co Pub Libr, Charleston, WVa, 66; Tribute to Leroy Grumman (stainless steel sculpture), Long Island Asn Hall Fame, 72; fountain, Libr Cong, Washington, DC, 74; 18 ft sculpture (bronze), Fashion Inst Technol, NY, 76; outdoor hwy sculpture, East Hills, NY, 81; and others. *Exhib:* Whitney Mus; HemisFair, San Antonio, Tex; Pa Acad Fine Arts; Houston Mus Fine Arts; Brooklyn Mus; Retrospective, Humphy Gallery, New York; and many other group & one-man shows. *Pos:* Chmn bd gov, Skowhegan Sch Painting & Sculpture; mem, Mayor's Comt Beautification of New York. *Teaching:* Instr, Adelphi Univ, 48-62, vis assoc prof, 74 & 75; instr, N Shore Community Arts Ctr, 50-55 & Skowhegan Sch Painting & Sculpture, 59-60, 64-65 & 72, chmn bd gov, formerly, bd mem, 83- *Awards:* Reynolds Metals Sculpture Trophy, 61; Henny Hering Mem Medal, Nat Sculpture Soc, 85 & 91; Audubon-Artists, 90; and others. *Bibliog:* John I H Baur (auth), Revolution and Tradition in Modern American Art, Harvard Univ Press, 59; Minor L Bishop (auth), Fountains in contemporary architecture, Am Fedn Arts, 65; Louis G Redstone (auth), Art in Architecture, McGraw-Hill, 68. *Mem:* Sculptors Guild; Munic Art Soc; Fedn Mod Painters & Sculptors. *Media:* Welded Metal, Clay-Terra Cotta. *Publ:* Auth, New New Deal Art Projects, An Anthology of Memoirs, Smithsonian Inst Press, 72. *Mailing Add:* 420 E 86th St New York NY 10028

CRONE, RAINER F
EDUCATOR, CURATOR
b Hamburg, Ger, July 6, 42. *Study:* Univ Hamburg, Berlin, Bonn, Freiburg & Paris, Free Univ Berlin, PhD, 74. *Collections Arranged:* Peter Blake Retrospective, Stedelijk Mus, Amsterdam, Neth, 73; Warhol Drawings 1942-1976, Kunstverein Stuttgart, WGer, 76; Numerals, Yale Art Gallery, New Haven, Conn, 78; Francesco Clemente Pastels, Nat Gallery, Berlin, Ger, 83; Similia/Dissimilia, Kunsthalle Dusseldorf, Ger & Wallach Art Gallery, Columbia Univ, New York, 87; BiNational: Ger Art of the Late 80s, Kunsthalle/Kunstammlung Düsseldorf & Mus Fine Art/ICA, Boston, Mass, 88; Objet/Objectif, Galerie Templon, Paris, France, 89; Painting Along, Pace Gallery, New York, 90. *Pos:* Directors Fel, Am Film Inst, Los Angeles, 79-81; Chief cur, Kunsthalle Dusseldorf, 87- *Teaching:* Asst prof, art hist, Yale Univ, New Haven, Conn, 76-79; assoc prof, Columbia Univ, New York, 84-; prof, Univ Munich, Ger, 91- *Res:* Abstraction as allegory: Paul Klee and Kasimir Malevich; Contemporary Art: Francesco Clemente. *Publ:* Auth, Malevich and Friedrich Nietzche, RES, 85; Francesco Clemente: Pastels 1974-84, Prestel, 84; The Art of Michael Heizer, Mus Contemp Art, 84; Donald Judd, Stedelijk Mus, Eindhoven, 87; coauth, Climax of Disclosure: Kasimir Malevich, Univ Chicago Press, 91. *Mailing Add:* 133 Greene St New York NY 10012

CRONIN, ROBERT (LAWRENCE)
SCULPTOR
b Lexington, Mass, Aug 10, 36. *Study:* RI Sch Design, BFA, 59; Cornell Univ, MFA, 62. *Work:* Worcester Art Mus, Mass; Boston Mus Fine Arts; Brooklyn Mus; Mus Art, RI Sch Design; Mus Art, Univ Okla, Norman; Springfield Mus Fine Arts, Mass. *Comn:* On Speculation (sculpture), Lippincott Co, 81-; R S Reynolds Mem Award, 82. *Exhib:* Inst Contemp Art, Boston, 71; Gimpel Fils, London, 82; Gimpel & Weitzenhoffer Ltd, New York, 82 & 84; Watson DeNagy, Houston, 83; Gimpel-Hanover & Andre Emmerich Galerien, Zurich, 83; Klonaridis Gallery, Toronto, 84 & 86; Janet Steinberg Gallery, San Francisco, 85; Galerien Esperanza, Montreal, 85. *Teaching:* Instr painting, Bennington Col, 66-68; instr art, Sch Worcester Art Mus, 71-79. *Awards:* First Prize in Painting, Boston Fine Arts Festival, 63; Mass Arts & Humanities Grant, 75; Mass Artists Found Grant, 79. *Bibliog:* Hilton Kramer (auth), New talent, New York Times, 6/17/73; Hilton Kramer (auth), article, New York Times, 9/21/74; Max Wykes-Joyce (auth), Robert Cronin, Gimpel Fils, London Arts Rev, 4/9/82. *Media:* Light Metals, Wire. *Mailing Add:* c/o Helander Gallery 350 S County Rd Palm Beach FL 33480

CROOKS, W SPENCER
PAINTER, LECTURER
b Ireland, July 26, 17; US citizen. *Study:* RI Sch Design, cert, Shrivenham Am Univ, Eng, cert; summer sem with Edgar Whitney; RCA Scholar (scenic design), Berkshire Music Ctr, Roger Williams Col, Hon DFA, 86. *Work:* RI Sch Design Fine Art Mus; Boston Symphony Hall, Mass; Pawtucket Boys Club, RI; Mayor's Office, City Hall, Providence, RI. *Comn:* Watercolor, covers for RI Providence J, 61-65; watercolor, Old Colony Banks, RI, 71-73; watercolor, Indust Leasing Corp, Indust Nat Bank, Providence, RI, 72; Irish Cult Exchange Comn RI, 82. *Exhib:* Watercolor USA, Springfield, Mo, 64; Am Watercolor Soc Ann, Nat Acad Art Gallery, 67, 72 & 75; Springfield Mus Fine Arts, 75; one-man show, Rockport Art Asn, 75 & Trinity Col, Dublin, Ireland, 82; Ireland's Nat Art Gallery, Dublin, 84. *Pos:* Creative artist, Hallady, Inc, Providence, RI, 52-58 & Hassenfeld Inc, Central Falls, 59-60; art dir, Cardono Inc, Pawtucket, 60-61; demonstr, watercolor, Grumbacher's Palette Talk, 75. *Teaching:* Instr Watercolor, Brown Univ Exten Sch, 68-74, Cranston East High Sch (adult educ), 65-68 & URI-NARR-Bay Campus, 90-; teacher graphic art, RI Col, 72- & instr watercolor, 74-75. *Awards:* Travel Award, Washington Sq Show, New York, Forbes Mag, 67; James G Geddes Mem Award, Rockport Art Asn, 71; RI Heritage Hall Fame, 86. *Mem:* Providence Watercolor Club, Rockport Art Asn, Mass; Cape Cod Art Asn, Barnstable, Mass; Philadelphia Watercolor Club; Am Watercolor Soc; RI Heritage Hall Fame (bd dirs, 87). *Media:* Watercolor; Pen, Ink. *Publ:* Illusr, Providence J Mag Sect, 61-65; ed, DeCordova Mus Gallery (catalog), 62; RI Sch Design Alumni Bull, 75; illusr, Palette Talk, Grumbacher Artist Material, NY, 75; Yankee Mag, Dublin, NH, 82. *Dealer:* Bert Gallery Omni Biltmore Hotel Kennedy Plaza Providence RI 02903. *Mailing Add:* 84 Davis Ave Cranston RI 02910

CROPPER, M ELIZABETH
HISTORIAN, LECTURER
b Dewsbury, Yorkshire, Eng, Aug 11, 44. *Study:* Newnham Col, Univ Cambridge, BA(hon), 67; Bryn Mawr Col, PhD, 72. *Pos:* Dir, Villa Spelman, 85; painting comt, Philadelphia Mus Art. *Teaching:* Prof art hist, Temple

Univ, 73-; prof, Johns Hopkins Univ, 85- *Awards:* Leverhulme Trust Res Fel, Univ Cambridge, 71-72; Arthur Kingsley Porter Prize, 76; fel, Villa I Tatti, Harvard Univ & Leopold Schepp Found, 78-79. *Mem:* Col Art Asn; Renaissance Soc Am; vis mem, Inst Advanced Study, Princeton, 89. *Res:* Italian Renaissance and Baroque art. *Publ:* Auth, Bound theory and blind practice, 71 & Virtue's wintry reward, 74, J Warburg & Courtauld Insts; auth, On beautiful women, 76 & Poussin and Leonardo, 80, Art Bulletin; auth, The Ideal of Painting, Princeton Univ Press, 84; Pietro Testa 1612-50, Philadelphia Mus Art, 88. *Mailing Add:* 3906 St Paul St Baltimore MD 21218

CROSBIE, HELEN BLAIR See Blair, Helen

CROSBY, RANICE W
MEDICAL ILLUSTRATOR, EDUCATOR
b Regina, Sask, Can, Apr 26, 15. *Study:* Conn Col, AB; Johns Hopkins Med Sch, under Max Broedel; also under Robert Brackman; Johns Hopkins Univ, MLA. *Pos:* Illusr for N J Eastman, Johns Hopkins Hosp, currently. *Teaching:* Assoc prof & dir emer, dept art as appl to med, Johns Hopkins Med Sch, 44- *Awards:* Asn Med Illusr: Fel, Lifetime Achievement Award; William P Didusch Award, Am Urological Asn. *Mem:* Asn Med Illusr; Am Asn Univ Prof. *Publ:* Illustrator for medical textbooks and journals; Max Brödel: The Man Who Put Art into Medicine, Springer/Verlag. *Mailing Add:* 3926 Cloverhill Rd Baltimore MD 21218

CROSMAN, CHRISTOPHER BYRON
MUSEUM DIRECTOR, WRITER
b Chicago, Ill, June 25, 46. *Study:* Washington & Lee Univ, BA, 68; Oberlin Col, 70-72. *Collections Arranged:* Painterly Panels: Jonathan Santlofer & Arlene Slavin; James Brooks: 25 Years of Work, 63-88; An Eye For Adornment; Shared Visions: American Landscapes; Voyages of the Modern Imagination; By Land and Sea: Selected Works from the Collection of Andrew & Betsy Wyeth; and others. *Pos:* Cur educ, Albright-Knox Art Gallery, 80-84; peer rev panel, NY State Coun Arts, 82-84; dir, Heckscher Mus, 84-88 & Farnsworth Libr & Art Mus, 88-; field revs (reader), Inst Mus Servs, 85-86. *Teaching:* Instr art hist, Empire State Col, Buffalo, NY, 79-81. *Publ:* Exhib Catalogs & video interviews with artists. *Mailing Add:* PO Box 466 Rockland ME 04841

CROSS, WATSON, JR
PAINTER, VIDEO ARTIST
b Long Beach, Calif, Oct 10, 18. *Study:* Chouinard Art Inst, scholar, 38-42. *Work:* US Air Force Permanent Collection, Washington, DC. *Comn:* Illustrations of Air Bases, USAF, Alaska, 63. *Exhib:* San Francisco Mus Art Ann, 47-48; Los Angeles Co Mus Art Ann, 53-54; seven video performance pieces, Calif State Univ, Northridge, 80-84; All Mem Nat Watercolor Soc Show, 86, 87 & 88; Past Pres Nat Watercolor Soc, Brand Mus, 87; Santa Barbara Mus, 88; Retrospective drawings, pvt studio, Eva Margueritte Studio, 11/90; and others. *Teaching:* Prof drawing & painting, Chouinard Art Inst, 44-71; assoc prof, Calif State Univ, Northridge, 75-85; instr drawing, Art Ctr Col of Design, Pasadena, Calif, 75-79; instr, Otis Art Inst of Parsons Sch Design, Los Angeles, 80-86. *Awards:* Hon Mention Video USA, Eastern Tenn State Univ, 85. *Mem:* Life mem Nat Watercolor Soc (secy, 51-53, pres, 53-54). *Media:* Watercolor, Oil. *Publ:* Contribr, Content of Watercolor, Van Nostrand Reinhold, 69; illusr (cover), Westways Mag, 8/78; contribr, The California Style, McClelland-Last, Hillcrest Press, Beverly Hills, Calif, 85; The California Romantics: Harbingers of Watercolorism, Artra Publ, 86; Regionals: The California View, Santa Barbara Mus, 88. *Mailing Add:* 1238 E Workman Ave West Covina CA 91790

CROSS, YVONNE
ARTIST
Study: Accademia di Belli Arti, Florence, Italy, diploma 78. *Exhib:* Touchables, Ga Tech, Univ Gallery, Atlanta. *Mem:* ISC Washington DC. *Mailing Add:* 8644 Wilshire Blvd Beverly Hills CA 90211

CROSSGROVE, ROGER LYNN
PAINTER, EDUCATOR
b Farnam, Nebr, Nov 17, 21. *Study:* Kearney State Col; Univ Nebr, BFA; Univ Ill, MFA; Univ Michorcan, Mex. *Work:* Butler Inst Am Art, Youngstown, Ohio; Montclair Art Mus, NJ; Des Moines Art Ctr, Iowa; New Britain Mus Am Art; Inst Mex-Norteamericano Relac Cult, Mexico City. *Exhib:* Whitney Mus Am Art, New York, NY, 56; Pa Acad Fine Arts, Philadelphia, 64; Audubon Artists, New York, 68; Conn Watercolor Soc, Wadsworth Atheneum, Hartford, Conn, 70; Monotypes, Pratt Graphics Ctr, New York, 72; New Am Monotypes, SITES, 78; William Benton Mus Art, Storrs, Conn, 91. *Pos:* Contribr & ed, Artists Proof, 67- *Teaching:* Prof art & assoc chmn dept graphic arts, Pratt Inst, 52-68; prof art, Univ Conn, 68-88, prof emer, 88. *Awards:* Emily Lowe Award, 51; Gold Medal, Nat Arts Club, 67; Am Watercolor Soc Award, 67. *Bibliog:* Henry N Rasmusen (auth), Printmaking with Monotype, Chilton, 60. *Mem:* Conn Acad Arts; Conn Watercolor Soc; Artworks Gallery, Hartford, Conn. *Media:* Monotype, Watercolor. *Publ:* Contribr, Paperbound Books in Print, 63. *Mailing Add:* 362 Gurleyville Rd Storrs CT 06268

CROTTO, PAUL
PAINTER, SCULPTOR
b New York, NY, Oct 24, 22. *Study:* Art Students League; Beaux-Arts, Florence, Italy; also with Fernand Leger, Paris. *Work:* Villeneuve-sur-Lot Mus, France; Mus Art Int, San Francisco; Galerie Grave, Munich, Ger. *Comn:* Portraits, L E Kaplan, New York & Robert Aries, Paris. *Exhib:* Mostra Artisti Am, Florence, 51; Mostra Int, Bordighera, Italy, 53; Am Painters in France, Galerie Craven, Paris, 53; Salon Automne, Paris, 56; Salon Comparaisons, Mus Mod Art, Paris, 68. *Awards:* Prix Int de Peinture, Villeneuve-sur-Lot, 63. *Bibliog:* T Ehrenmark (auth), American Artist in Sweden, Dagens Nyheter, 63; A Blasco Ibanez (auth), American artist in Paris, Los Angeles Herald Examiner, 68; Betty Werther (auth), Art, Time-Life, Paris, 69. *Mem:* Soc Coop Entre Aide Artistes. *Media:* Oil; All. *Mailing Add:* 19 Rue Cauchois Paris F-75018 France

CROUCH, NED PHILBRICK
SCULPTOR, CURATOR
b Nashville, Tenn, Mar 14, 48. *Study:* Austin Peay State Univ, Clarksville, Tenn, BS(art), 72; Cranbrook Acad Art, Bloomfield Hills, Mich, MFA(sculpture), 74. *Work:* Tenn Fine Arts Comn, Nashville; Cheekwood Fine Arts Ctr, Nashville; Ark Arts Ctr, Little Rock; Montgomery Bell Acad, Nashville; Austin Peay State Univ, Clarksville. *Exhib:* Michigan II, Flint Inst Arts, Flint, Mich, 74; Mid-South Biennial, Brooks Mem Art Gallery, Memphis, Tenn, 75; Artists Biennial, New Orleans Mus Art, 75; Nat Sculpture USA, Huntsville Mus Art, Ala, 75; 18th Ann Delta Exhib, Ark Arts Ctr, Little Rock, 75; Tenn Bicentennial, Brooks Mem Art Gallery, Memphis, 76; Invitational, Southeastern Ctr Contemp Art, Winston-Salem, NC, 77. *Pos:* Guest cur, Am Folk-Exhib of 20th Century Quilts, Drawings & Sculpture, Vanderbilt Univ, Nashville, 76-; consult spec proj, Cheekwood Fine Arts Ctr, Nashville, 77- *Teaching:* Instr sculpture, Austin Peay State Univ, Clarksville, 74-75. *Awards:* Hon Mention, Delta Exhib & Purchase Award, Toys by Artists, 75, Ark Arts Ctr, Little Rock; Purchase Award, Tenn Bicentennial, Tenn Fine Arts Comn, 76. *Mem:* Col Art Asn Am; Midwest Regional Conservation Guild. *Media:* Welded Steel, Wood. *Mailing Add:* 114 E Glenwood Dr Clarksville TN 37040

CROUSE, MICHAEL GLENN
EDUCATOR, PRINTMAKER
b Grand Rapids, Mich, June 20, 49. *Study:* Kendall Sch Design, Grand Rapids, dipl, 70; Atlanta Col Art, BFA, 77; Univ Mich, Ann Arbor, MFA, 79. *Work:* Ga Dept Educ, Atlanta; Huntsville Mus Art. *Exhib:* Serial Imagery, Huntsville Mus Art, Ala, 82; Southeastern Graphics Int, Mint Mus Art, 82; Wesleyan Second Int Exhib Prints & Drawings, Macon Mus Arts & Sci, Ga, 82; Ninth Int Miniature Print Competition, Pratt Graphics Ctr, New York, 83; Second Int Miniature Print Exhib, Space Group Seoul, SKorea, 83; Red Clay V, Huntsville Mus Art, Ala, 83. *Teaching:* Instr art, Ill Col, 79-80; asst prof printmaking, Univ Ala, Huntsville, 80- *Awards:* Charles Brand Machinery, Pratt Graphics Ctr Int Miniature Print Competition, 79; Purchase Award, LaGrange Nat VI, LaGrange Col, 81 & 24th NDak Print & Drawing Show, Univ NDak, 81. *Mem:* Col Art Asn; Southeastern Col Art Conf. *Media:* Mixed Media. *Dealer:* Absteins Gallery Art & Framing 1139 Spring St Atlanta GA 30309. *Mailing Add:* Dept Art & Art History Roberts Hall Rm 313 Univ Ala Huntsville AL 35899

CROUTON, FRANCOIS (LAFORTUNE)
PHOTOGRAPHER
b Montreal, Que, Can, Mar 9, 21. *Study:* Col Montreal, BA & DLibrarianship. *Work:* Municipal Libr Montreal; Libr Can Inst, Quebec; Pub Libr Serv, Quebec; Quebec Mus; Musee Nicephore Niepce, de Chalon-Sur-Saône, France. *Exhib:* Toronto Univ, 49; Laval Univ; Municipal Libr Montreal, 50; All Art Ctr, Que; V U Gallery, Que. *Pos:* Librn, Municipal Libr Montreal, 48-52; chief librn, Libr Can Inst, Quebec, 53-60; asst dir, Pub Libr Serv, Quebec, 60-75; conservator, Quebec Mus, 75-86; retired, 87. *Awards:* Min Aff Culturelles du Que. *Publ:* Auth, Ou La Lumiere Chante, Laval Univ with Toronto Univ, 66; Les Photographes--Photographies, Crouton; La Photograpie Dans Le Monde Musee Niepce, Chalon-Sur-Soane, France, 92. *Mailing Add:* 893 Ave de Levis Quebec PQ G1S 3E2 Canada

CROW, CAROL (WILSON)
SCULPTOR
b Christiansburg, Va, July 31, 15. *Study:* Columbia Univ, with Oronzio Maaldareli, 58; Beartsi Foundry, Italy, 65; Univ Calif, with Peter Vaulkos, 68. *Work:* Cannery Row, Monterey, Calif; Rose Garden Am, La. *Exhib:* Fine Arts Asn Show, Ft Worth Art Ctr, Tex, 60; Tex General Art Competition, Dallas Mus, 60-62; Tex General, Laguna Gloria Mus, Austin, Tex, 61; Pennisula Artists, Mus Fine Arts, Calif, 70; Invitational Sculpture Show, San Francisco Mus, Calif, 70; Houston Art Women, Alley Theater Gallery, Tex, 79; Fire, Contemp Art Mus, Houston, 80; Images of Childhood, Houston Mus Fine Arts, Tex, 81. *Teaching:* Sculpture, Sunset Ctr, 69-71; portraits, Art League Houston, 79-81. *Awards:* Bute Award, Mus Fine Arts, 52; First Prize, Monterey Jazz Festival, 69-70. *Mem:* Artists Equity of Houston; Tex Soc Sculptors; Women's Caucus Art (bd dirs, 80). *Media:* Clay, Bronze. *Mailing Add:* 1601 S Shepherd No 115 Houston TX 77019

CROWN, KEITH ALLEN
PAINTER
b Keokuk, Iowa, May 27, 18. *Study:* Art Inst Chicago, 36-40, 45-46, BFA, 46. *Work:* Mus of Albuquerque, NMex; Phillips Collection, Washington, DC; Springfield Mus, Mo; Univ Tex Art Mus, Austin; Gerald Buck Collection, Laguna Hills, Calif. *Exhib:* California Artists, Witte Mus, San Antonio, Tex, 65; Painting as Painting, Univ Tex Art Mus, Austin, Tex, 68; Lyric View, Lang Gallery, Scripps Col, 74; Looking at a Strange Land, Mus Fine Arts, Santa Fe, NMex, 77; one-man shows, Ariz State Univ Mus Art, Tempe, 78, Univ Utah Mus Art, Salt Lake City, 78, Va Polytech Inst & State Univ & Univ Ariz Mus Art, Tucson; Retrospectives, Los Angeles Municipal Art Gallery, 87; Palos Verdes Art Ctr, Palos Verdes, Calif, 88; Fine Arts Gallery, Riley Mus, Kans State Univ, Manhattan, 89. *Teaching:* Prof painting & drawing, Univ Southern Calif, 46-83, prof emer, 83-; prof painting, Univ Ill, 70-71 & 77-78

& Univ NC, 79. *Awards:* Purchase Awards, Nat Watercolor Soc, 60, 63 & 71; Purchase Award, Watercolor USA, Springfield Mus, Mo, 74. *Bibliog:* Article, Am Artist Mag, fall 1978; Sheldon Reich (auth), Keith Crown Watercolors, Univ Mo Press, 86. *Mem:* Artists Equity Asn (LA bd dirs, 49-50); Nat Watercolor Soc (vpres, 58, pres, 59). *Media:* Watercolor, Oil. *Publ:* Contribr, Content of Watercolor, Van Nostrand Reinhold; Master Class in Watercolor, 75, Mastering Color and Design in Watercolor, 80 & Watercolor Bold and Free, 81, Watson-Guptill; Cover, Watercolor of the Huntington Libr, San Marino, Calif for Am Libr Mag bicentennial issue, 76. *Dealer:* J Noblette Gallery PO Box 1777 Boyes Hot Springs CA 95416. *Mailing Add:* 819 Edgewood Ave Columbia MO 65203

CROWN, ROBERTA LILA
PAINTER, CONCEPTUAL ARTIST
b New York, NY. *Study:* Queens Col, MA, 70. *Exhib:* Ann Exhib, Queens Mus, Flushing, NY, 84; Best Ann, Queens Mus, Flushing, NY, 89; solo exhib, Queens Col Art Ctr, Flushing, NY, 89; A Salute to Women, Nat Mus Women Arts, Washington, DC, 91. *Pos:* Exec coordr, Women Arts Found Inc, 80- *Teaching:* Fine arts, Corlears JHS, 56-69- *Awards:* Mary K Karasick Mem Award, 91 & Leila Sawyer Mem Award, 92, Nat Asn Women Artists. *Mem:* Women Arts (exec coordr, 80-); Women's Caucus Art; Artists Equity; Nat Women's Asn Women Artists; New York City Art Teachers Asn. *Media:* Oil on Canvas. *Publ:* Contribr, Triangle Annual, Triangle, 87; IBM Nachrichton-Excellence, IBM, 89. *Dealer:* Terori 30 E Third Ave San Mateo CA 94401. *Mailing Add:* 1175 York Ave New York NY 10021

CROYDON, MICHAEL BENET
SCULPTOR, EDUCATOR
b Woodford, Eng, July 2, 31. *Study:* Goldsmiths Col Art, London, 50-51; Ealing Col Art, London, 51-53; Royal Col Art, London, with John Nash, ARCA, 56. *Work:* Victoria & Albert Mus, London; Nat Collection of Kenya, Nairobi; Royal Col Art, London; Ill State Mus, Springfield; First Nat Bank Chicago. *Comn:* Bronze mem figure, by Gen Ojukwu, Lagos, Nigeria, 75; 65 ft cor ten & stainless steel monument, Fogelson Co Inc, Chicago, 76-; lithographs for Plucked Chicken Press, Chicago, 85; bronze, St Joseph, St James Church, Highwood, Ill. *Exhib:* Brit Art from African Collections, Sorsbie Gallery, Nairobi, 64; 3 Sculptors, Suburban Fine Arts Gallery, Highland Park, Ill, 73; New Horizons in Sculpture, 500 N Michigan, Chicago, 73-74; Prof Mem Show, Arts Club Chicago, 74; Recent Sculpture & Drawings by Michael Croydon, Sonnenschein Gallery, Lake Forest, Ill, 88. *Collections Arranged:* Graven Image--the Prints of Ivan Albright (auth, catalog), Lake Forest Col, 79; First & Second Int Holography Exhibs, Chicago, 82 & 85. *Pos:* Art reviews-radio, Voice of Kenya, Nairobi, 64-67; dir pub TV, Voice of Kenya (two programs), Nairobi, 64-68; design consult, Ministry Com & Indust, Govt of Kenya, 67-68. *Teaching:* Head dept design, Univ EAfrica, Nairobi, Kenya, 62-68; prof art, Lake Forest Col, Ill, 68-, artist-in-residence, 69-71. *Awards:* Sculpture Prize, Ealing Col Art, London, 53; Inland Steel-Ryerson Award, 81. *Bibliog:* Carol Ray (dir), Michael Croydon (doc film), Voice Kenya TV, 64; Laura Watters (auth), Artist's sculptural reality, The Herald, 11/16/77; Garrett Holg (auth), Michael Croydon--Richard Hunt, New Art Examiner, 6/9/82. *Mem:* Arts Club Chicago; Col Art Asn Am. *Media:* Bronze, Terra-cotta. *Publ:* Auth, Ivan Albright, Abbeville Press, 78; contribr, Colliers Encycl, Humanities, McMillan Educ Corp, 79. *Dealer:* Grayson Gallery 833 N Orleans Chicago IL 60610. *Mailing Add:* 950 Benson Lane Green Oaks IL 60048

CROZIER, RICHARD LEWIS
PAINTER, EDUCATOR
b Honolulu, Hawaii, Dec 28, 44. *Study:* Univ Wash, Seattle, BFA(painting), 68; Univ Calif, Davis, with Wayne Thiebaud, MFA(painting) 74. *Work:* J B Speed Mus, Louisville, Ky; Am Embassy, Zaire. *Comn:* Paintings Juvenile Court Bldg, Charlottesville-Albemarle Comt Arts, Va, 80-81; Cover, Am Libr Asn J, Chicago, 75; painting, Brown-Forman Corp, Louisville, 91. *Exhib:* Calif Landscape, Oakland Mus, 75; Va Artists, Va Mus Fine Arts, Richmond, 77; Sacramento Valley Landscape, Univ Calif, Davis, 79; Realist Invitational, Southeastern Ctr Contemp Art, Winston-Salem, 79 & 81; New York Realists 1980, Thorpe Intermedia Gallery, Sparkill, 80; Am Realism since 1960, Pa Acad Fine Arts, Philadelphia, 81; Contemp Landscape PTG, Mem Art Gallery, Univ Rochester, NY, 89; The Landscape Observed, Md Inst, Baltimore, 90. *Teaching:* Prof studio art, Univ Va, 74- *Awards:* Purchase Award, Southeastern Ctr Contemp Art, 77. *Bibliog:* Thomas Bolt (auth), Richard Crozier, Arts Mag, 1/86; John Arthur (auth), Spirit of Place, Bulfinch, 89; R Crozier & Thomas Bolt (coauths), Inventing the Landscape, Watson Guptill, 89. *Media:* Oil. *Dealer:* Peter Tatistcheff 50 W 57th St New York NY 10022. *Mailing Add:* 624 Preston Pl Charlottesville VA 22903

CROZIER, WILLIAM K, JR
CRAFTSMAN, DESIGNER
b Stanwood, Wash, Mar 23, 26. *Study:* Wash State Univ, BFA; Univ Wash, MFA(silversmithing, design). *Exhib:* Contemp Craftsmen of the Far West Mus Contemp Crafts, 61 & Craftsmen USA 66, 66; Northwest Craftsmen's Exhib, Henry Gallery, Seattle, 61, 65, 67, 71 & 77; The Kentucky Guild Train, State Ky, 67; Calif Crafts VI Pac Dimensions, E B Crocker Art Gallery, Sacramento, 69; Am Crafts Coun NW Metal Traveling Exhib, 73-75; NW Designer Craftsmen, Seattle, Spokane & Portland, 78-88. *Pos:* Cur slides & visuals, Sch Art, Univ Wash, 59-61; chmn dept art, Ore State Univ, 72-75. *Teaching:* Asst prof design, jewelry, Ore Col Educ, 61-66; prof silversmithing, Thundering Seas Sch Fine Crafts, 84-; prof emer, Ore State Univ. *Awards:* Nat Merit Award, Am Crafts Coun, 66; Ore State Univ Grad Sch Res Grant, 70, Gen Res Grant, 77; Spec Recognition Award, Ore Summer Festival Arts, 74; Stewart Fel, Ore State Univ, 84. *Bibliog:* Paul Soldner (auth), Craftsmen USA '66/pt 2, Crafts Horizons, 66; R Phillips (ed), Faculty Section, Ore State Univ Summer Bull, 72. *Mem:* Northwest Designer Craftsmen; Am Crafts Coun; World Crafts Coun; Soc NAm Goldsmiths; Thundering Seas Found (bd mem & pres). *Media:* Sterling Silver; Gold, Pewter. *Mailing Add:* Dept Art Ore State Univ Corvallis OR 97331

CRUM, DAVID
PAINTER
b Peoria, Ill, Dec 6, 38. *Study:* Independently with John Chamberlain. *Work:* Long Beach Mus, Calif; Baruch Col Gallery, New York. *Exhib:* Newport Beach Mus, Calif, 66; Paintings on Paper, Glassboro Col Gallery, NJ, 72; Recent Acquisitions, Aldrich Mus, Ridgefield, Conn, 74; New Directions in Contemporary Art, Santa Barbara, Calif, 82. *Teaching:* Vis assoc prof painting, La State Univ, 84. *Bibliog:* Peter Frank (auth), article, Soho Weekly News, 76; Sam Hunter (auth), New Directions in Contemporary Art, Princeton, NJ, 81; Judith Stern (producer), Fresh air, Nat Pub Radio, 81. *Mem:* Artists Equity; Nat Arts Club. *Media:* Acrylic. *Mailing Add:* 492 Staten Ave Oakland CA 94610

CRUM, KATHERINE B
GALLERY DIRECTOR, EDUCATOR
b Palo Alto, Calif, Dec 10, 41. *Study:* Stanford Univ, BA, 62, MA, 64; Hunter Col, NY, MA(art hist), 74; Columbia Univ, PhD(art hist), 84. *Collections Arranged:* Richard Ruben & Michael Goldberg, 84, George Mayocole, Lynn Mayocole & Bill Taggart, 84, Color Abstraction in the 1980's, 85, Figurative Art of the New York School, 85, Women Artists of the Surrealist Movement, 86, Bradley Walker Tomlin, 89, Baruch Col Gallery, City Univ New York & Clyde Connell, Mills Col Art Gallery, 92. *Pos:* Dealer & owner, Nicholas Wilder Gallery, Los Angeles, 64-69; cur, exhibs, Inst Res Hist, New York, 80-83; dir, Baruch Col Gallery, City Univ New York, 83-89 & Mills Col Art Gallery, Oakland, Calif, 91- *Teaching:* Adj asst prof art hist, Baruch Col, City Univ New York, 74- 89. *Mem:* Col Art Asn; Inst Res Hist (dep dir, 80-82); Am Asn Mus. *Res:* 20th century art; 13th & 14th century Italian painting. *Publ:* Ed, Places of Origin, Inst Res Hist, 80; contribr, Western Civilization, Houghton Mifflin, 81; auth, The Cudner-Hyatt House, Scarsdale Hist Soc, 82; Figural Art of the New York School, Baruch Col, 85. *Mailing Add:* c/o Mills Col Art Gallery 5000 MacArthur Blvd Oakland CA 94613

CRUMP, WALTER MOORE, JR
PRINTMAKER, PAINTER
b Winston-Salem, NC, Mar 18, 41. *Study:* Gilford Col, NC, 61-64; Harvard Univ Exten, 64-66; Boston Univ, BFA, 70. *Work:* DeCordova Mus, Lincoln, Mass; Philadelphia Mus Art; Nat Mus Am Art, Smithsonian Inst; Libr Congress Print Collection; NC Mus Art, Raleigh; New York Pub Libr; Citicorp World HQ; RJ Reynolds World HQ. *Exhib:* Davidson Nat Drawing & Print Exhib, NC, 73; Color Print USA, Tex Tech Univ, Lubbock, 75; Artists Under 36, DeCordova Mus, 76; Int Miniature Print Exhib, Pratt Graphics Ctr, New York, 77; Boston Printmakers Nat Exhib, Mus Fine Arts, Boston, 75-88 & DeCordova Mus, 77 & 79; Korean Exchange Print Exhib, Seoul, 78; Silvermine Nat Print Exhib, New Canaan, Conn, 78, 80 & 83; one-man shows, Plum Gallery, Washington, DC, 80, 82 & 88; Tacer Gallery Tort, Spain, 85; Wauz Gallery, 86 & 87. *Teaching:* Chmn art dept & instr printmaking, Commonwealth Sch, Boston, 72-; lectr & slide presentations, DeCordova Mus, 78 & Nat Collection of Fine Arts, Washington, DC, 79. *Awards:* Purchase Prize & First Prize, Dulin Nat Print & Drawing Competition, Knoxville, Tenn, 78 & 79; A P Hanks Mem Purchase Prize, Print Club Int Biennial, Philadelphia, 79; Purchase Prize, Boston Printmakers Exhib, 76-79. *Mem:* Boston Visual Artists Union; Boston Printmakers. *Media:* Intaglio; Oil. *Mailing Add:* 73 Delle Ave Boston MA 02120

CRUTCHFIELD, WILLIAM RICHARD
PAINTER, SCULPTOR
b Indianapolis, Ind, Jan 21, 32. *Study:* Herron Sch Art, Ind Univ, Indianapolis, BFA, 56; Tulane Univ, La, MFA, 60. *Work:* Mus Mod Art, New York; Art Inst Chicago; Philadelphia Mus Art; Libr of Cong, Washington, DC; Los Angeles Co Mus Art. *Comn:* Countdown II (watercolor), Skylab II, NASA, 73; Alphabet Spire VI (laminated wood sculpture), Westfarms, West Hartford, Conn, 74; Countdown (wood sculpture), Newark, NJ, 80; Punctuation Spire (wood sculpture), Los Angeles, 81; The Importance of Being a Bubble (painted wood relief), Ft Lauderdale Int Airport, 89; and others. *Exhib:* Minneapolis Inst Art, 67; Ft Lauderdale Mus Arts, 71; NJ State Mus, Trenton, 71 & 72; California Prints 1972, Mus Mod Art, New York, 72; Dorsky Gallery, New York, 72, 73 & 75; Arco Ctr Visual Art, Los Angeles, 79. *Teaching:* Instr drawing, painting & design, Herron Sch Art, Indianapolis, Ind, 63-65; asst prof & chmn found studies, Minneapolis Col Art, Minn, 65-67. *Awards:* Mary Milliken Award for Travel in Europe, Herron Sch Art, Ind Univ, Indianapolis, 56; Fulbright Scholar, State Art Acad, Hamburg, Ger, 61; Mayor's Award for Outstanding Achievement in the Arts, Los Angeles, 88. *Bibliog:* William Crutchfield, Sage of Machine Wit, KCET television (emmy nomination), Los Angeles, 73; Crutchfield: A Recollection of the Future, WPBT television, Miami, 77; Los Angeles: An Artist's View, Channel 2, television, Los Angeles, 80. *Mem:* Educ Coun, Mus Ctr Los Angeles Co, 92. *Media:* Mixed. *Publ:* Auth, Crutchfield phenomena, Art Am, 71; Art & Technology, A Report on the Art & Technology Program of the Los Angeles County Museum of Art 1967-1971, Viking Press Inc, 71; William Crutchfield: Wicken Innocence, Dorsky Galleries Catalog, 72; Transports of Delight and other Contraptions, Horizon Mag, 73; Sage of Machine Wit, Studio Int, 74. *Mailing Add:* PO Box 591 San Pedro CA 90733

CRUZ, EMILIO
PAINTER
Work: Albright Knox Gallery, Buffalo, NY; Hirshhorn Mus, Washington, DC; Mus Mod Art, New York; Nat Gallery Art, Washington, DC; many other public & private collections. *Exhib:* Nat Collection, Smithsonian Inst, Washington, DC, 68; Mus Contemp Art, Chicago, 76; Tradition and Conflict, Studio Mus in Harlem, New York (& traveling), 84; Martha Jackson Mem Collection, Nat Mus Am Art, Washington, DC, 85; Directions, Newport Art Mus, RI, 90; Artistas Latino y Afro Americanos en USA, Mus Nat de Bellas Artes, Santiago, Chile, 91; Gallery Revue, Porter Randall Gallery, La Jolla, Calif, 92; Anita Shapolsky Gallery, New York, 86 & 90, Studio Mus Harlem, New York, 87, Calif African Am Mus, Los Angeles, 88, Robeson Ctr Gallery, Robeson Ctr Rutgers Univ, Newark, NJ, 88, Kingsborough Col, Brooklyn, NY, 89, Galerie Francoise et Ses Freres, Baltimore, Md, 91; many other group & solo shows throughout the US. *Pos:* Founder & artistic dir, Spectacle Inc. *Teaching:* Prof painting & drawing, Art Inst, Chicago, 70-82; vis artist, SUNY, Purchase, NY, 87; assoc prof, Parsons Sch Design, 88; assoc prof, Cooper Union, 88. *Awards:* Fulbright Scholar, 64; Fel, Nat Endowment Arts, 70 & 87. *Bibliog:* Bernard Evslin (auth), Monsters of Mythology, Geryon, 87, Monsters of Mythology, Cerberus, 87, Chelsea House Publ; John Howell (auth), Elle Decor Mag, 90. *Publ:* Contribr, Free Spirit Mag, 88. *Mailing Add:* 300 Broadway New York NY 10013

CRUZ, PURA (PURA ISABEL CRUZ)
PAINTER, CURATOR
b Santurce, Puerto Rico. *Study:* Stony Brook Univ, BA, 88. *Work:* Melville Libr, Stony Brook Univ. *Exhib:* Islip Art Mus, NY, 89 & 90; Innovations, 89 & Culture Shock, 90, Discovery Art Gallery, Glen cove, NY; The Figure as Form, Clary-Miner Gallery, Buffalo, NY, 89; Annual Show, Fine Arts Mus of Long Island, Hempstead, NY, 89; Original Sin, Hillwood Art Mus, Brookville, NY, 91. *Pos:* Gallery asst, Morin-Miller Galleries, New York, 87-88; proj coordr, Mus Contemp Hispanic Art, Soho, New York, 88; cur, Humor with Cours, Union Gallery, SUNY at Stonybrook, 92. *Teaching:* Instr children's workshop, Islip Art Mus, NY, 89. *Awards:* Third Nat Award, Clary-Miner Gallery, 89. *Bibliog:* Helen A Harrison (auth), Diverse view of Hispanic ethnicity, 3/25/90, Long line of fabulists adds new names, 5/20/90, NY Times & Putting the blame on Adam and Eve, 2/10/91. *Mem:* Col Art Asn; Smithtown Twp Arts Coun (bd dirs, 90-91). *Publ:* Contribr, Images/ Latina Style, Freesia!, 89; illustr, The Deal of Art, La Nuez, 90; contribr, Culture Shock, La Tirbiuna, 90. *Mailing Add:* 2 Quincy St New York NY 11776

CRYSTAL, BORIS
PAINTER
b Poland, Dec 25, 31; US citizen. *Study:* Plocer's Sch Fine Arts, 62-63; Acad Fine Arts, Israel, 63-64. *Work:* Israel Mus, Tel-Aviv; Journalist House Art Gallery, Tel-Aviv; Herzl Inst, New York; Nicholas Roerich Mus, New York; Mus Mod Art, New York; and numerous other museums. *Exhib:* Journalist House Art Gallery, Tel-Aviv, 66; Herzl Inst Art Gallery, New York, 68; Nicholas Roerich Mus, New York, 70; Mus Mod Art, New York, 72; Lerner Art Gallery, New York, 75; La Galerie Mouffe, Paris, France, 77; and numerous others. *Collections Arranged:* Herzl Int Exhib USA, 65; Human Relations Coun in Coop with Art League USA, 68; Int Group Exhib of Paintings, Sculpture & Graphics, New Haven, Conn, 71. *Awards:* Int Award, Crown Art Gallery, 71; Vallombreuse Prize, Biarritz, France, 76; Gold Medal, Accad Italia, 80. *Bibliog:* Max Founry (auth), article, Art News, 69. *Mem:* Artists Equity Asn; Art League New York. *Media:* Oil, Watercolor. *Dealer:* Ella Lerner 241 E 76th St New York NY 10021. *Mailing Add:* 70-20 108th St Forest Hills NY 11375

CSERNUS, TIBOR
PAINTER
b Kondoros, Hungary, June 28, 27; French citizen. *Study:* Acad Fine Arts, Budapest, dipl, 52. *Work:* Collection Thyssen - Bornemisza, Basel, Switz; Hirshhorn Mus, Washington, DC; Mus Fine Arts, Budapest, Hungary. *Exhib:* Biennal de Paris, Mus D'Art Mod, France, 59; Realismus und Realität, Kunsthalle, Darmstadt, 75; Mythologies Quotidiennes II, Mus d'Art Mod, Paris, 77; Representation Abroad, Hirshhorn Mus, Washington, DC, 85; one-man shows, Mücsarnok, Budapest, 89. *Bibliog:* Gerald Gassiot-Taiabot (auth), Tibor Csernus, 64; Jean Clair (auth), Tibor Csernus, L'Art Vivant, Paris, 71; Jack Beal (auth), A letter to Tibor Csenus, Arts Mag, 5/85. *Media:* Oil. *Dealer:* Galerie Claude Bernard 7 Rue DesBeaux Arts Paris 75006 France. *Mailing Add:* 6 rue Garreau Paris 75018 France

CUEVAS, JOSE LUIS
DRAFTSMAN
b Mexico City, Mex, Feb 26, 34. *Study:* Sch Painting & Sculpture (La Esmeralda, Inst Nac Bellas Artes), Mexico City. *Work:* Mus Mod Art & Solomon R Guggenheim Mus, New York; Brooklyn Mus, NY; Mus of Albi & Lyons, France; Metrop Mus Art, New York. *Exhib:* Biennial Venize, Italy, 72; Palais Beaux Arts, Brussels, Belg, 74; Warsaw Gallery, Poland, 75; Ludwig Mus, Cologne, Ger, 78; Mus Mod Art, Mexico City, 79; World Print Awards, San Francisco Mus Art, 83; Frederick S Wight Art Gallery of UCLA, 84; Mus Mod Art, Mexico City, 85; Musee d'Art Moderne de Liege, Belgium, 86; Alvar Alto Mus, Helsinki, Finland, 86; Pinacoteque Nationale Musee Alexandre Soutzos, Athens, Greece, 87; Orangerie Palais Auersperg, Vienna, Austria, 87. *Teaching:* Resident artist, Philadelphia Mus Sch Art, 57; lectr art, San Jose State Col, 70, Fullerton Col, 75 & Wash State Univ, 75. *Awards:* First Int Prize for Drawing, V Biennial of Sao Paulo, Brazil, 59; First Int Award, Mostra Bianco e Nero, 62; Award Excellence, 29th Ann Exhib, Art Dir Club, Philadelphia, 83. *Bibliog:* Carlos Fuentes (auth), Los mundos de Jose Luis Cuevas, Misrachi Gallery, Mexico City, 70; Daisy Ascher (auth), Revelando a Jose Luis Cuevas, Madero, Mex, 79; J B Ponce (auth), Jose Luis Cuevas: Genio O Farsante?, Ed Signos, 83; J M Tasende (auth), Tasende Gallery - 1982, La Jolla, Calif, 82. *Publ:* Illusr, Crime by Cuevas, Lublin Ed, 68; Homage to Quevedo, 69 & Cuevas Comedies, 71, Collectors Press; Roberto Sanesi, Jose Luis Cuevas, Centro Arte/Zarathustra, Milano, Italy, 78; J M Tasende, Jose Luis Cuevas Letters, 82, Peter Selz, Intolerance, 83 & J M Tasende, Twenty five years with Jose Luis Cuevas, La Jolla, Calif, 92, Tasende Gallery; Carlos Fuentes, The Buried Mirror, Houghton Mifflin, NY, 92. *Mailing Add:* c/o Tasende Gallery 820 Prospect St La Jolla CA 92037

CULBERTSON, JANET LYNN (MRS DOUGLAS KAFTEN)
PAINTER, ENVIRONMENTAL ARTIST
b Greensburg, Pa, Mar 15, 32. *Study:* Carnegie Inst Technol, BFA, 53; Art Students League, 54; NY Univ, MA, 63; Pratt Graphic Arts Inst, 64-65. *Work:* Univ Mass Mus Collection, Amherst; AT&T, Chicago; Westinghouse Corp, Pittsburgh; Heckscher Mus, Huntington, NY; Guild Hall, East Hampton, NY; and others. *Exhib:* One-woman shows, Lerner-Heller Gallery, new York, 71, 73, 75 & 77, Aronson Gallery, Atlanta, Ga, 72 & 82, Benson Gallery, Bridgehampton, NY, 78, 81, 83, & 89, Nardin Gallery, New York, 81; Visitors to Arizona, Pheonix Art Mus & Tucson Mus Art, 80; Animals in the Arsenal, Dept Parks, New York, 81; The Fine Line: Drawing with Silver in America, Norton Mus, West Palm Beach , 85-86; Harrisburg State Mus, Pa, 88; Guild Hall Mus Invitational, E Hampton, NY, 89,; Islip Mus, NY, 90 & 92; C W Post Hillwood Mus, Brookville, NY, 90. *Teaching:* Instr art, Pace Col, 64-68; adj prof, Pratt Art Inst, 73-74 & Southampton Col, NY, 76. *Awards:* Creative Artists Pub Serv Prog Graphics Award, 79; NY Abstract Award, Guild Hall, 79; Mixed Media Award, 92, Guild Hall, 92. *Bibliog:* Helen Harrison (auth), article, New York Times, 6/1/80, 11/9/80 & 5/20/90; Joan Marter (auth), article, Arts Mag, 2/81; Phyllis Braff, (auth), NY Times, 8/16/87, 8/27/89 & 4/8/90; and others. *Mem:* Womens Caucus Art; Women Mus; Greenpeace; Sierra Club; Earthwatch. *Media:* Acrylic, Oil. *Publ:* Auth, articles in Feminism and Ecology, 81; article in Women Artists Newsletter; article, Gallerie, Vol 8, 90. *Mailing Add:* 46 Hilo Dr PO Box 455 Shelter Island Heights NY 11965

CULBRETH, CARL R
SCULPTOR
b Mineola, NY, Dec 2, 52. *Study:* Nassau Community Col, AA(studio art), 73; Univ Vt, BS(art educ), 75; Univ Del, MFA(ceramic sculpture), 79. *Work:* Syracuse Univ; Roberson Ctr Arts & Sci, Binghamton, NY. *Exhib:* Ten Artists Under 30, Fine Arts Mus Long Island, Hempstead, NY, 81; Wards Island Sculpture Site, New York, 81; Brooklyn Mus, 81; East Coast Clay, Sculpture Ctr, New York, 82; The Figure: New Form, New Function, Arrowmont Sch Gallery, Gatlinburg, Tenn, 83; Ancient Inspirations, Contemporary Interpretations, NY State Mus, Albany, 83; Three Dimentions, Univ Tex, El Paso. *Pos:* Resident ceramist & gallery dir, Clayworks Studio Workshop, New York, 79-80; dept head, Terra Cotta, MJM Studios, Hoboken, NJ, 85- *Teaching:* Adj assoc prof art, Long Island Univ, 80-85; coordr ceramics prog, Parsons Sch Design, 80-84. *Bibliog:* Donna Harkavay (auth), article, Am Ceramics, 8/82; Martin Ries (auth), article, Re-Dact, 11/83. *Mem:* Am Crafts Coun; Nat Coun Educ Ceramic Arts; Col Art Asn. *Media:* Clay. *Mailing Add:* 189 Upper Mountain Ave Montclair NJ 07042

CULHANE, SHAMUS H
FILMMAKER, WRITER
b Ware, Mass, Nov 12, 08. *Study:* Walt Disney Art Sch, 35-39; Chouinard Art Sch, 42-47. *Work:* Montreal Mus, Que. *Exhib:* Golden Age of Animation, Whitney Mus, New York, 81; Animation Drawings, Montreal Mus, 82; retrospectives, Am Film Inst, 76, Cineforum, New York, 84, ASIFA, New York, 85 & Reg Hartt, Toronto, 86, Mus Mod Art, 91; Animator, Snow White and the Seven Dwarfs, 38, Pinnochio, 39, Disney Studios, Hollywood, Calif, Gullivers Travels, 40, Mr Bug Goes to Town, 41, Fleischer Studios, Miami, Fla. *Pos:* Animator, Walt Disney Productions, 35-39; dir, Walter Lantz Studio, 43-46; pres & producer, Shamus Culhane Productions, 47-88. *Awards:* Outstanding Television Commercials, NY Art Dir Award, 48-58; Golden Award, Motion Picture Cartoonists, 84; Annie Award, Asn Int du Film d'Animation. *Bibliog:* John Canemaker (auth), Filmmakers Newsletter, 74; Gene Langley (auth), Animated life of Shamus Culhane, Christian Sci Monitor, 7/86; John Gross (auth), Talking animals, New York Times, 7/86. *Mem:* Asn Int du Film d'Animation (pres, 67-72, exec bd, 76-88); Dirs Guild Am. *Media:* Animation. *Publ:* Auth, Talking Animals and Other People, St Martin's Press, 86; Animation from Script to Screen, St Martin's Press (in prep). *Mailing Add:* 325 West End Ave New York NY 10023

CULKIN, JOHN MICHAEL
ADMINISTRATOR, EDUCATOR
b Brooklyn, NY, June 21, 28. *Study:* Woodstock Col, STL, 61; Harvard Univ, EdD, 64. *Pos:* Dir, Ctr for Commun, Fordham Univ, 63-69; dir & founder, Ctr for Understanding Media, New York, 69- & Media Studies Prog, New Sch for Social Res, 74- *Teaching:* Asst prof commun, Fordham Univ, New York, 63-69; lectr media studies, New Sch for Social Res, New York, 74- *Mem:* Am Film Inst (trustee, 68-73); Media Educators Asn (founder, 70); Art, Educ & Americans (media adv). *Publ:* Auth, A Schoolman's Guide to Marshall McLuhan, Saturday Rev, 67; ed, Trilogy--An Experiment in Multi-Media, Macmillan, 68; contribr, Summerhill--For and Against, Hart, 68; coauth, Films Deliver, Citation, 69; auth, The New Literacy: From the Alphabet to Television, Media & Methods, 77. *Mailing Add:* 69 Horatio St NO 1 New York NY 10014

CULLING, RICHARD EDWARD
PAINTER, COLLAGE ARTIST
b Detroit, Mich, Dec 5, 51. *Study:* Wayne State Univ, BFA, 74, Univ Mich Sch Art, MFA, 88. *Work:* Univ Mich Permanent Collection, Ann Arbor. *Exhib:* 11th Mich Biennial, Kresge Art Mus, E Lansing, 88; Figuring It Out, Calvin Col, Grand Rapids, Mich, 88; What's New in Art, Galesburg Civic Ctr, Ill, 88; Animal Art, United Auto Workers, Gen Motors Resource Bldg, Auburn Hills, Mich, 88; Two Person, Univ Mich, Flint, 88; A Matter of Painting, Detroit Focus, Mich, 88. *Teaching:* Instr painting, Univ Mich, 86-88; instr painting, Paint Creek Ctr Arts, 88. *Awards:* Artist Grant, Mich Coun Arts, 84; Guggenheim Award, 85; Res Fel Award, Univ Mich, 87. *Bibliog:* Marsho Miro (auth), 2 Artists find there's no place like home, Detroit Free Press, 1/16/83. *Mem:* Col Art Asn. *Media:* Oil. *Dealer:* Mary C Wright 568 N Woodward Birmingham Mich 48154. *Mailing Add:* 38798 Kingsbury Livonia MI 48154

CULVER, MICHAEL L
PAINTER, CURATOR
b Louisville, Ky, Sept 10, 47. *Study:* Univ Louisville, BA(sculpture), 72, MA(painting), 77 & PhD(art hist), 86. *Work:* Mus Art Ogunquit, Maine; Owensboro Mus Fine Art, Ky; Univ Louisville, Brown & Williams Tobacco Co & Humana Corp, Louisville, Ky. *Comn:* Poster & program cover, Louisville Ballet, 83. *Exhib:* Ogunquit Art Asn, 84; Nat Arts Club Gallery, New York, 87; solo-exhibs, Headley-Whitney Mus, Lexington, Ky & Owensboro Mus Fine Arts, Ky, 88; Nat Show, Viridian Gallery, New York, 88. *Collections Arranged:* Art of Marguerite & William Zorach, 88; John Heliker: Works from 1950-1990, 90; Dozier Bell Exhib, 91; Walt Kuhn: American Master, 92; The Art of Jack Levine, Mus Art Ogunquit, Maine, 92. *Pos:* Pres, Ky Art Educ Asn, 79; cur, Mus Art Ogunquit, 83- *Teaching:* Instr human Am studies, Univ Louisville, Ky, 81-82. *Media:* Acrylic. *Res:* Twentieth century American art. *Publ:* Auth, Examination of illustrations for pound's a draft of XVI Cantos, Paideuma J, Univ Maine, 83; Realistic art of Henry Strater (exhib catalog), Washington & Lee Univ, 86; Henry Strater an American original (exhib catalog), Owensboro Mus Fine Arts, 88. *Dealer:* PS Gallery PO Box 1559 Ogunquit ME 03907; Park Gallery 3932 Chenoweth Sq Louisville, KY 40207. *Mailing Add:* Shore Rd PO Box 815 Ogunquit ME 03907

CUMMENS, LINDA TALABA See Talaba, L (Linda Talaba Cummens)

CUMMING, GLEN EDWARD
GALLERY DIRECTOR
b Calgary, Alta, Can, July 2, 36. *Study:* Alberta Col Art, 4 yr dipl. *Collections Arranged:* Nine Out of Ten, A Survey of Contemporary Canadian Art 1974-75; Ontario Now: A Survey of Contemporary Art 1976; Karel Appel, The Complete Graphic Collection (1957-1977), 77; Contemp Art of Senegal, 79; Viewpoint Twenty-nine by Nine, 81 & 82. *Pos:* Cur, Regina Pub Libr Art Gallery, Sask, 67-69; dir, Kitchener-Waterloo Art Gallery, Kitchener, Ont, 69-72; dir, Robert McLaughlin Gallery, Oshawa, Ont, 72-73; dir, Art Gallery Hamilton, Ont, 73-; dir 49th Parallel Gallery, Contemp Can Art, 89. *Awards:* Queen Elizabeth Prize, Govt Alberta, 60. *Mem:* Int Asn Art Critics. *Publ:* Auth, The Graphic Work of Karel Appel, 77-89; Contemporary Art of Senegal, 79; Viewpoint: 29 by 9, 81; El Dorado, Gold from Ancient Colombia, 82; Living Imprssions, Contemp Can Art, 89. *Mailing Add:* 60 E 8th St New York NY 10003

CUMMING, ROBERT H
ARTIST, PHOTOGRAPHER
b Worcester, Mass, Oct 7, 43. *Study:* Mass Col Art, Boston, BA, 65; Univ Ill, Champaign, MFA, 67. *Work:* Mus Fine Arts, Houston; Mus Mod Art, New York. *Comn:* Outdoor sculpture, Walker Art Ctr, Minneapolis, Minn, 70; Nation's Capitol Documentation, Corcoran Gallery, Washington, DC. *Exhib:* Art by Telephone, Mus Contemp Art, Chicago, 69; 9 Artists-9 Spaces, Walker Art Ctr, Minneapolis, Minn, 70; 24 Young Los Angeles Artists, Los Angeles Co Mus, 71; Narrative Art, Palais des Beaux Arts, Brussels, Belg, 75; Whitney Biennial, New York, 77 & 81; Paris Biennale, Mus d'Art Mod, France, 77; Mirrors and Windows, Mus Mod Art, New York; and others. *Teaching:* Instr painting & drawing, Univ Wis, Milwaukee, 67-70; lectr photog,Univ Calif, Los Angeles, 74- *Awards:* Frank Logan Prize, Chicago Art Inst, 69; Nat Endowment Arts Awards, 72, 74 & 83; Guggenheim Fel, 80. *Bibliog:* M Jochimsen (auth), Story Art, Mag Kunst, Mainz, Ger, 2/74; C Hagen (auth), Robert Cumming's Subject-Object, Artforum, summer 83. *Media:* Multimedia. *Publ:* Auth, Picture Fictions, Anaheim, Calif, 71; The Weight of Franchise Meat, Anaheim, Calif, 71; A Training in the Arts, Toronto, Can, 73; A Discourse on Domestic Disorder, Irvine, Calif, 75; Equilibrium and the Rotary Disc, Meriden, Conn, 80. *Mailing Add:* c/o The Print Club & Gallery Store 1614 Latimer St Philadelphia PA 19103

CUMMINGS, DAVID WILLIAM
PAINTER
b Okmulgee, Okla, July 15, 37. *Study:* Kansas City Art Inst, Mo, BFA, 63; Univ Nebr, Lincoln, MFA, 67. *Work:* Whitney Mus Am Art, New York; Los Angeles Co Mus Art, Los Angeles, Calif; Phoenix Art Mus, Ariz; Mus Contemp Art, Antwerp, Belg; Aldrich Mus Contemp Art, Ridgefield, Conn; and others. *Exhib:* Lyrical Abstraction, Philadelphia Mus Art, Pa, 70 & Whitney Mus Am Art, 71; 20th Century Am Artists, Corcoran Gallery Art, Washington, DC, 71; Contemporary Reflections, Aldrich Mus Contemp Art, 71-72; one-man shows, Allan Stone Gallery, New York, 74-77 & 82, Gallery Alexandra Monett, Bruxelles, Belg, 75, 77, 79 & 82, Ericson Gallery, New York, 80 & Shahin Requicha Gallery, Rochester, NY, 83, Gallery Jupiter, Little Silver, NJ, 87; Galerij Tremerie, Huise, Belg, 79; AMB Galleries, Hoboken, 89; Cabrillo Col, Aptos, Calif, 91. *Pos:* Vis artist, Ohio State Univ, Columbus, 74, Univ Iowa, Iowa City, 76 & Univ NDak, Grand Forks, 81; coordr painting symposium, Colo Mountain Col, Vail, 76-78. *Teaching:* Instr, State Univ NY, 67-71; assoc prof, City Univ New & York, 71-89; prof, St Peters Col, Jersey City, NJ, 85. *Awards:* John Lehmann Award, St Louis Mus Art, Mo, 65; Woods Found Fel, Univ Nebr, 66-67; Painting Fels, NJ State Coun of the Arts, 85 & 91. *Bibliog:* Jacques Meuris (auth), David Cummings Plus Minus Zero, 11/79; Theodore F Wolff (auth), The colorist's art, The Christian Sci Monitor, 9/10/80; Susan Dodge Peters (auth), A master of color, Rochester City News, 4/28/83. *Media:* Oil, Pastel. *Dealer:* Richard Roepke 592 Hillside Ave Rochester NY 14610. *Mailing Add:* 106-108 Hopkins Ave Jersey City NJ 07306

CUMMINGS, MARY T
ADMINISTRATOR, CONSULTANT
b Minneapolis, Minn, May 22, 51. *Study:* Univ Minn, BA(art hist), 73; Univ Mich, MA(art hist), 76; Ind Univ, MA(arts admin), 81. *Pos:* Lectr, Minneapolis Inst Arts, 77-78; asst to dir, Tweed Mus, Duluth, Minn, 78-79; dir, Missoula Mus Arts, Mont, 81-89; assoc dir, Minn Mus Art, St Paul, 89- *Teaching:* Instr art hist, Macalester Col, St Paul, 77-78 & Univ Minn, Duluth, 78-79; vis prof art hist, Univ Mont, Missoula, 88- *Mem:* Am Asn Mus; Women Mus Dir & Admin Caucus; Mont Art Gallery Dir Asn (pres, 83-86); Asn for Asian Studies. *Res:* Impact of museums on small communities; approaching art and visual images for the layman; nature of museums; Asian art (various topics). *Publ:* Auth, The Lives of the Buddha in the Art and Literature of Asia, Univ Mich, 85; Asian Di-Visions: A Contrast Between China and Japan (exhib catalog), 82 & The Primal Plastic Pool: Contemporary Art of the West (exhib catalog), 85, Missoula Mus; The artist and the museum: Some mutual expectations, The Crafts Report, 86; On learning to look and the function of museums, Mus Studies J, 88. *Mailing Add:* Minn Mus Art 75 W Fifth St St Paul MN 56304

CUMMINGS, PAUL
EDITOR, WRITER
Study: Univ Minn; Univ London;. *Collections Arranged:* David Smith: The Drawings (auth, catalog), 79-80 & Willem de Kooning: Retrospective (auth, catalog), 83, Whitney Mus Am Art; 20th Century Drawings (auth, catalog), Whitney Mus Am Art, 85. *Pos:* Consult, var corporations & foundations, 62-; dir oral hist, Arch Am Art, 67-78, ed jour, 74-78; founder, Print Collectors Newslett, 70; adj cur drawings, Whitney Mus Am Art, 76-87; pres, Drawing Soc, 78-, ed, Drawing, 79-; publ, Catchword Papers, 83- *Res:* Twentieth century American art & drawing. *Publ:* Auth, American Drawings: The Twentieth Century, Viking Press, 76; Artists in Their Own Words, St Martin's Press, 79; Irving Petlin, Pastels, Kent Fine Art Inc, 88; Joseph Goldyne, Univ Wash Press, 89. *Mailing Add:* 420 E 72nd St New York NY 10021

CUMMINS, KAREN GASCO
ADMINISTRATOR, MUSEOLOGIST
b Trenton, NJ, Jan 30, 45. *Study:* Goucher Col, BA; Temple Univ, MEd; NY Univ. *Collections Arranged:* NJ traveling art exhibs, Intaglio Printmaking, Planographic Printmaking, Relief Printmaking, Merci (prints & posters by Ben Shahn), For the Sake of a Single Verse (by Ben Shahn), Olympic Games Posters, The Dreigroschen Film, Eleven Pop Artists & two portfolios by John Randolph Carter. *Pos:* Sr mus technician, NJ State Mus, Trenton, 67-68, coordr traveling exhib & pub info officer, 68-73, asst to dir, 73- *Mem:* Mus Coun NJ (chmn, 73-75); Northeast Mus Conf; Am Asn Mus. *Mailing Add:* NJ State Hist Mus 205 W State St Trenton NJ 08625

CUNINGHAM, ELIZABETH BAYARD (MRS E W R TEMPLETON)
ART DEALER
b New York, NY. *Study:* Bronxville Sch, NY; Vassar Col, Poughkeepsie, NY; Finch Col, NY, BA; Hunter Col, New York, MA(art hist). *Pos:* Exec secy, Olana Preserv Inc, New York, 65-66; dir publicity, Comt to Rescue Italian Art, New York, 66-67; asst to pres, Nat Trust for Hist Preserv, 68-70; asst dir, Reese Palley Art Gallery, New York, 70-72; pres, Cuningham Ward Inc, 72-78; Betty Cuningham Gallery, 78-82; Hirsch & Adler Modern, New York, 82- *Mem:* Drawing Soc Inc (exec comt, 70-80); Art Dealers Asn, 79-81. *Specialty:* Contemporary painting. *Mailing Add:* 321 E 43rd St New York NY 10017

CUNNICK, GLORIA HELEN
PAINTER
b New York, NY. *Study:* Art Students League; New York Univ; Long Island Univ, C W Post, BFA, 87. *Work:* Fine Arts Mus Long Island, Hempsted, NY; Eight pvt collections in NY. *Exhib:* Traveling exhib Southwest, Nat Asn Women Artists, 91-92; Nat Asn Women Artists, Fed Plaza, New York, 92; solo exhib, Berger Art Ctr, East Hills, 92; H T A L, Hecksher Mus, Huntington, 92; North By South, Nassau Co Mus Art, Roslyn, 92; and others. *Awards:* Grand Prize Winner, Berger Art Ctr, North Shore YWHA, 92; Krusos Award, Heckscher Mus, Denis & Catherine Krusos, 92; William Meyerowitz Award, Fed Plaza, Teresa Bernstein Meyerowitz, 92. *Bibliog:* Zoltan Hegyes (auth), Spiritual Geometry, Artspeak, 91; Helen Harrison (auth), A Few Standouts in Large Juried Show, NY Times, 91; Betty Ommerman (auth), Artist Math Equals Award, NewsDay, 1/26/92. *Mem:* Nat Asn Women Artists; Long Island Network Women Artists; Manhasset Art Asn Inc; Artist Network Great Neck; and others. *Media:* Acrylic, Encaustics. *Mailing Add:* Three Orchard Farm Rd Port Washington NY 11050

CUNNINGHAM, (CHARLES) BRUCE
PAINTER
b Bayonne, NJ, Mar 30, 43. *Study:* Baylor Univ, BFA; Univ Tex, Austin; Univ Calif, Berkeley, MA & MFA; also with Erle Loran, Elmer Bischoff & David Simpson. *Work:* Aldrich Mus Art, Ridgefield, Conn; Am Tel & Tel Co, NJ; Oppenheimer & Co, New York; Dallas Mus Fine Art, Tex; Gen Instrument Corp, New York. *Exhib:* One-man shows, Projects II, Dallas Mus Fine Arts, 75, Watson de Nagy Gallery, Houston, 77, Contemp Gallery, Dallas, 77, Inst for Art & Urban Resources, PS 1, New York, 79, Soho Ctr Visual Arts, New York, 81, 55 Mercer St Gallery, New York, 82, 85, 86, 87, 88, Dome Gallery, New York, 88; plus others. *Pos:* Artist-in-residence, Tex Comn Arts & Humanities, Longview Mus & Arts Ctr, 74-75, Southwestern Univ, Georgetown, Tex, 81 & John Dewey High Sch, Brooklyn, NY, 81-82. *Teaching:* Instr painting & drawing, Baylor Univ, 72-74; asst prof painting & drawing, Univ Tex, Arlington, 75-77; vis prof painting, Univ Tex, Austin, 80-81. *Awards:* Nat Endowment Arts Fel, 75; Amarillo Two-Dimensional Three State Exhib Cash Award, Amarillo Art Mus, 75; First Award in Painting, Southwest/Tarrant Co Ann, Ft Worth Art Mus, 76. *Bibliog:* Stephen Westfall (auth), Bruce Cunningham at 55 Mercer, Art Am, 7/85; Vered Lieb (auth), Bruce Cunningham Dome Gallery, Arts Mag, p 109, Summer, 88. *Media:* Oil, Charcoal. *Mailing Add:* 40 Great Jones St No 2N New York NY 10012

CUNNINGHAM, E C (ELDON LLOYD CUNNINGHAM)
PRINTMAKER, EDUCATOR
b Colby, Kans, Mar 2, 56. *Study:* Wichita State Univ, Kans, BFA, 79; Univ Colo, Boulder, MFA, 82. *Work:* Kaiser Med Found, US W Denver, Univ Colo, Metrop State Col, Boulder, Colo. *Exhib:* Parkside Nat Print Exhib, Univ Wis, Kenosha, 88; Works on Paper, Ill Wesleyan Univ, Bloomington, 88; Recent Works, Kans State Univ, Manhattan, 90; Western Travel, W Tex State Univ, Canyon, 91; Color Print USA, Tex Tech Univ, 91; and others. *Pos:* Master printer, Master Eds Ltd, Englewood, Colo, 82-84. *Teaching:* Assoc prof printmaking, Metrop State Col, Denver, 83- *Awards:* Best of Show, Works on Paper, Reuben Saunders Gallery, 80, Communications 1988, 1999 Broadway Gallery, 88. *Mem:* Col Art Asn; Nat Asn Schs Art Design; Southern Graphics Coun. *Media:* All Media. *Publ:* Auth, National Printmaking Slide/Video Exchange, Metrop State Col, 90; Printmaking A Primary Form of Expression, Univ Press Colo, 92. *Dealer:* Alpha Gallery 909 Broadway Denver CO 80203. *Mailing Add:* Metrop State Coll, Dept Art 1006 11th St Denver CO 80204

CUNNINGHAM, FRANCIS
PAINTER, INSTRUCTOR
b New York, NY, Jan 18, 31. *Study:* Art Students League, with Edwin Dickinson & Robert Beverly Hale. *Work:* Berkshire Mus, Pittsfield, Mass; Royal Theatre, Copenhagen; Security Pac Nat Bank, San Francisco; General Foods, Minneapolis; E P Dutton, NY; and other. *Exhib:* one-man shows, Hirsch & Adler Galleries, 68, 70 & 75, Berkshire Mus, Pittsfield, Mass, 69, Distelheim Galleries, Chicago, 70 & Mickelson Gallery, Washington, DC, 71 & Marsh Gallery, Univ Richmond, Va, 89; two-man exhib, Forum Gallery, 79; New Brooklyn Sch, NY, 82; and others. *Pos:* Co-founder & dir, NY Acad Sch Art, 80-85. *Teaching:* Instr painting & drawing, Brooklyn Mus Art Sch, 62-80, Art Students League, New York, 80-83 & New Brooklyn Sch, 80-85. *Awards:* Berkshire Art Asn Purchase Award, Berkshire Mus, 68; Louis Comfort Tiffany Found Grant, 73; Joseph Raskin Mem Award, Audubon Artists, 85; and others. *Mem:* Art Students League; Audubon Artists. *Media:* Oil, Pencil. *Publ:* Coauth, Polykleitos' Diadoumenos: Measurement & animation, Art Quart, summer 62; illusr, Fundamentals of Roentgenology, 64. *Mailing Add:* 789 West End Ave New York NY 10025

CUNNINGHAM, J
SCULPTOR
b Greenwich, Conn, Sept 18, 40. *Study:* Kenyon Col, BA, 62; Yale Sch Art & Archit, BFA, 63 & MFA, 65. *Work:* and others and many pvt collections. *Exhib:* One-man show, Art of the Pyramids, Shick Gallery, 86, Walk Like an Egyptian, Skidmore Col, 87. *Teaching:* Prop Art, Skidmore Col, Saratoga Springs, 67- *Awards:* Fel in Sculpture, Univ Pa, 66. *Publ:* Techniques of pyramid-building in Egypt, Nature, 3/3/88. *Mailing Add:* c/o PMW Gallery 530 Roxbury Rd Stamford CT 06902

CUNNINGHAM, SUE
PAINTER, ILLUSTRATOR
b Newton, Ill, Oct 19, 32. *Study:* Southern Ill Univ, Carbondale; Millikin Univ, Decatur, Ill; study with Irving Shapiro, Zoltan Szabo & Maxine Masterfield. *Work:* Mead Johnson & Co; US Coast Guard, Washington, DC; Quaker Oats Co, Danville, Ill; Bristol Myers Corp, Evansville, Ind; Hillside Acad, Hillside, Ill. *Comn:* Eight watercolor paintings, V A Kibler & Assoc, Architects, Newton, Ill, 81 & 85; eleven watercolor paintings, Comfort Inn, Vandalia, Ill, 85. *Exhib:* Mid-Am Biennial, Owensboro Mus Fine Art, Ky, 82 & 86; Nat Watercolor Soc Travel Show, 84; Ky Watercolor Soc Aqueous, 84; Adirondacks Nat Exhib Am Watercolors, 84 & 92; Am Watercolor Soc, 85; La Watercolor Soc, New Orleans, 85; Nat Arts Club Watercolor Open, New York, 86; Allied Artists Am, New York, 86; Nat Watercolor Okla, Okla Art Ctr, 86 & 87; Watercolor USA, Springfield, Mo Mus Art, 87; Gov Exec Mansion, Ill, 87. *Pos:* Regional Rep, Nat Watercolor Soc; Official Coast Guard Artist. *Teaching:* Art marketing seminars; instr, watercolor workshops. *Awards:* First Place Watercolor, Ill State Fair Prof Art Exhib, 84; Award of Excellence, St Louis Art Affair, West Port Plaza & West Co Art Asn, 85; Juror's Award, Realism Today, Evansville Ind Mus Art, 89; St Louis Artists Guild, 86 & 87; Watercolor Ill Biennial, 85, 87 & 90. *Bibliog:* William Michael (auth), Self-portrait makes "watercolor page", Herald & Rev, Decatur, Ill, 9/18/86. *Mem:* Signature Mem, Nat Watercolor Soc; St Louis Artists' Guild; Assoc Am Watercolor Soc; Assoc Key Watercolor Soc. *Media:* Watercolor. *Publ:* auth & illusr, Watercolor page, Am Artist Mag, 9/86. *Mailing Add:* 112 Manchester Dr Decatur IL 62526

CUPPAIDGE, VIRGINIA
PAINTER
b Brisbane, Queensland, Australia, Aug, 14, 43; US citizen. *Study:* Orban Art Sch, Sydney, Australia, 62; Mary White Sch Fine Art, Sydney, Australia, MFA, 65. *Work:* Neuberger Mus, Purchase, NY; Art Gallery New South Wales, Australia; Chase Manhattan Bank, New York; Whitney Commun, New York; Kingsborough Commun Col, Brooklyn, NY. *Comn:* Mural, Brisbane Grammar Sch, Queensland, Australia, 84. *Exhib:* Solo exhib, Gallery A, Sydney, Australia, 74-82, Susan Caldwell Gallery, NY, 75, Penrith Regional Gallery, New South Wales, 83, Stephen Rosenberg, New York, 86-89 & 93, Bloomfield Galleries, Sydney, Australia, 85-87. *Teaching:* Vis artist painting, Univ Calif, Berkeley, 75 & Santa Barbara, 84; guest lectr, Pratt Inst, Brooklyn & Lehman Col, Bronx, 77-82; assoc prof, Lehman Col Art, 92. *Awards:* CAPS Award, New York, 75; Macdowell Colony Fel Peterborough, NH, 75; Guggenheim Fel, 76. *Bibliog:* Art News, 90; Art in America, 90; Australian Weekend Mag, 92. *Media:* Acrylic, Oil. *Dealer:* Stephen Rosenberg Gallery 115 Wooster St New York NY 10012. *Mailing Add:* 66 Grand St New York NY 10013

CURLEY, DONALD HOUSTON
PAINTER, LECTURER
b Halifax, NS, Apr 4, 40. *Study:* Nova Scotia Col Art & Design, 58; Art Students League, New York, 59-61 & 66-68; Royal Acad, London, 69-70; also study with Dean Cornwell & Frank Reilly, New York. *Work:* Art Gallery NS & NS Art Bank, Halifax, NS; Mus Natural Sci, Ottawa; many corporate collections, internationally. *Comn:* Cover, painting, World Wildlife Annual Publication, 82; Cover, Painting, The Art of Survival, 88. *Exhib:* Canadian Nature Art, Mus Natural Sci, Canada & Eng, 81; The Spirit of the Wild, World Wildlife Fund, Toronto, 82; Canadian Prints, Art Gallery NS, Halifax, 85; The Illustrated Bird in Canada, Mus Natural Sci & traveling, Canada, 86; Wildlife, Royal Ont Mus, Toronto, 87; Friends of the Wild, Can Nat Tour on Behalf of Endangered Spaces, World Wildlife Fund, 90. *Pos:* Dir, WVancouver Acad Fine Art, 64-66. *Teaching:* Lectr art hist, Dalhousie Univ, Halifax, NS, 73. *Bibliog:* Roma Senn (auth), Don Curley paints the animals, Atlantic Insight, 81; David M Lank (auth), The wilderness art of Donald Curley, Arts Atlantic, 83; Alexandra Thompson (auth), The Art of Don Curley, Art Impressions, 8/91. *Mem:* Visual Arts NS. *Media:* Oil. *Publ:* Illusr, The Spirit of the Wild, World Wildlife Fund, 83; Islands at the Edge, Douglas & McIntyre, 84; Nature Canada, Can Nature Fedn, 86; The Art of Survival, Can Wildlife Assoc, 88; Cover & Featured Article, Art Impressions, 8/91. *Dealer:* Galerie De Bellefeuille 1212 Ave Greene Montreal PQ Can; Beckett Gallery 142 James St S Hamilton Ont Can. *Mailing Add:* 101 Queen St Chester NS B0J 1J0 Canada

CURMANO, BILLY
CONCEPTUAL ARTIST, SCULPTOR
b 1949; US citizen. *Study:* Univ Wis, Milwaukee, BFA, 73, MS, 77; Art Students League, 82. *Work:* Franklin Furnace Arch, New York; Temple Univ, Philadelphia; Milwaukee Art Mus, Wis; Munic Mus, Ourense, Spain; Univ Hawaii, Honolulu; and others. *Exhib:* Artists Proposals, Milwaukee Art Mus, 71; Eighth Tyler Nat, Tyler Mus Art, Tex, 72; Triangulation, Dean Gallery, Minneapolis, 74; Vienna Grapikbiennale, Secession, Austria, 77; 23rd Chautauqua Nat, NY, 80; Irretrievable Statements, Krasl Art Ctr, St Joseph, Mich, 81; Orange County 16th Ann, Brea Civic Cult Ctr, Calif, 82; 10th Small Works, New York Univ, 86; Oppresion/Expression, The Contemporary, New Orleans, 86; The Drought, Minneapolis Inst Arts, 88; and others. *Awards:* Mayor's proclamation: Billy X Curmano Day, St Louis, Mo, 92. *Bibliog:* Don Morrison (auth), Curmano kidding on square, Minneapolis Star, 8/15/74; In depth performance, Assoc Press, 9/18/83; Reggie McLeod (auth), River rapping, Chicago Tribune, 8/1/88. *Media:* Mixed. *Publ:* Contribr, Libres D'Artista--Artists Books, Metronom, 81; Mail Art Book, Japan Artists Union, 82; High performance, Astro Artz, 81-83; Swimmin', Part II: The Drought, Minneapolis Inst Arts, 88; Art Journal, Col Art Asn, New York, 92. *Dealer:* Art Works USA Rushford MN 55971. *Mailing Add:* Rt 1 Box 116 Rushford MN 55971

CURRAN, DARRYL JOSEPH
PHOTOGRAPHER, PRINTMAKER
b Santa Barbara, Calif, Oct 19, 35. *Study:* Ventura Col, AA, 58; Univ Calif, Los Angeles, BA, 60 & MA, 64. *Work:* Mus Mod Art, New York; Nat Gallery Can, Ottawa; Int Mus Photog, George Eastman House, Rochester, NY; Royal Photog Soc, Bath, Eng. *Exhib:* Vision & Expression, George Eastman House, 68; Photog into Sculpture, Mus Mod Art, New York, 70; Photog into Art, Brit Arts Comn, 73; one-man shows, Focus Gallery, San Francisco, Calif, 74, Midway Studios, Univ Chicago, 75, Art Space, Los Angeles, 78 & Chaffey Col, 82. *Collections Arranged:* Graphic/Photographic (auth, catalogue), Art Gallery, Calif State Univ, Fullerton, 71; 24 From LA (auth, catalogue), San Francisco Mus Mod Art, 73; Photo Visionaries, Floating Wall Gallery, Santa Ana, Calif, 76; Los Angeles Perspectives, Secession Gallery, Victoria, BC, 76. *Pos:* Bd dir, Los Angeles Center for Photog Studies, 73-77, pres, 80-, juror & chmn, Los Angeles Olympic Organizing Comt Photog Comn Proj for 1984 Olympic Games. *Teaching:* Prof creative photog, Calif State Univ, Fullerton, 67-; vis artist photog, Sch of Art Inst Chicago, spring 75. *Awards:* Phelen Award in Photog, James Phelan Trust, Oakland Mus, 71; First Place in Photog, 76 Calif Art Expo, Calif State Fair, 76; Nat Endowment Arts Photographers Fel, 80; Calif Mus Photog Award, Career Achievement, 86.

Bibliog: Robert Stuart (auth), Light & Substance, Univ NMex, Coke/Barrow, 74; Lewis/Alger (auth), Darryl Curran Photographs 1967-1981 (exhib catalog), Chaffey Col, 82; Judy Freeman (auth), The Photographic: Two Points of View (exhib, catalog), Calif State Univ, Fullerton. *Mem:* Soc Photog Educ (bd dir, 75-79). *Publ:* Contribr, Revolution in a Box, Univ Calif, Riverside, contribr, Untitled 11, Emerging Los Angeles Photographers, Friends of Photog, Carmel, Calif; Object, Illusion, Reality, Calif State Univ, Fullerton, 79; L A Issue, Los Angeles Ctr Photog Studies, 79. *Dealer:* G Ray Hawkins Gallery 7224 Melrose Ave Los Angeles CA 90060. *Mailing Add:* 10537 Dunleer Dr Los Angeles CA 90064

CURRAN, DOUGLAS EDWARD
PHOTOGRAPHER, WRITER
b Seaforth, Ont, Can, Aug 7, 52. *Study:* Ryerson Polytech Inst, Toronto, BAA, 77; Banff Sch Fine Arts, Alta, scholar, 79. *Work:* Nat Film Bd Can, Ottawa; Alta Art Found, Edmonton; Walter Phillips Gallery, Banff Ctr, Alta; Olden Camera Gallery, New York; Edmonton Art Gallery; Winnipeg Art Gallery, Man. *Comn:* Alberta 1980, PhotoProject, Alta 57th Comn, Edmonton, 80; Metis Settlements of Alberta, Fedn Metis, Edmonton, 81; Structured Paradise: The National Park Experience, Banff Ctr, Parks Can & Whyte Mus, Alta, 85. *Exhib:* Recent Acquisitions, Nat Film Bd Can, Ottawa, 79; Seven, Walter Phillips Gallery, Banff, Alta, 81; Folk Concepts of Outer Space, Edmonton Art Gallery, 81 & traveling, 81-83; Primary Colour, Harbourfront, Toronto, 82; Document, Nat Film Bd Can, Ottawa, 83; Nat Touring Exhib, Edmonton Art Gallery, 85. *Teaching:* Sessional instr photog, Univ Alta, Edmonton, 83-84. *Awards:* Grants, Can Coun, 77 & 78; Alta Writers Guild Non Fiction Award, 85. *Bibliog:* Doug Clark & L Wedman (auth), Keepsake, Artswest Publ, 82; Metisism: A Cultural Identity, Fedn Metis Settlements, 82; Contemporary Photographs, Nat Film Bd Can, Hurtig Publ, 84. *Publ:* Auth & photogr, In Advance of the Landing: Folk Concepts of Outer Space, Abbeville Press, 86. *Mailing Add:* 2046 Curling Rd North Vancouver BC V7P 1X4 Canada

CURRIE, BRUCE
PAINTER, PRINTMAKER
b Sac City, Iowa, Nov 27, 11. *Work:* Nat Acad Design, New York; State Univ NY Albany; Butler Inst Am Art, Youngstown, Ohio; Colorado Springs Fine Arts Ctr; Kalamazoo Inst Arts, Mich. *Exhib:* Butler Inst Am Art, Ann Exhibs, 53-74 & 78;; Audubon Artists, 62-92; Albany Inst Hist & Art, 65, 68, 70, 75 & 76; Nat Acad Design, 69-92; Colorado Springs Fine Arts Ctr, Colo, 71; Am Acad & Inst Arts & Letts, 77; plus many others incl one-man shows. *Teaching:* Artist-in-Residence, Syracuse Univ, 79. *Awards:* Benjamin Altman Figure Prize, Nat Acad Design, 79; Audubon Artists Medal of Honor, 62 & 82; Smith Co Award, Adirondack Nat Exhib Am Watercolor, 90. *Mem:* Nat Acad Design; Am Watercolor Soc; Audubon Artists; Woodstock Artists Asn. *Media:* Oil, Acrylic; Woodcuts. *Dealer:* Midtown Payson Galleries 745 Fifth Ave New York NY 10151. *Mailing Add:* 120 Boggs Hill Woodstock NY 12498

CURRIE, STEVE
SCULPTOR
b Flint, Mich, Sept 1, 54. *Study:* Univ Mich, BFA, 77; Yale Univ, MFA, 84. *Work:* Metrop Mus Art, New York; Walker Art Ctr, Minneapolis, Minn; Albright-Knox Art Gallery, Buffalo; Des Moines Art Ctr, Iowa; Brooklyn Mus, NY. *Comn:* American Narrative Painting & Sculpture: the 1980's, Nassau Cty Mus Art, Roslyn Harbour, NY, 91. *Exhib:* The 1980's: A New Generation of American Painters & Sculptors, Metrop Mus Art, New York, 88; Innovations in Sculpture, Aldrich Mus Contemp Art, Ridgefield, Conn, 88; Spring Aquisitions, Weatherspoon Art Gallery, Greensboro, NC, 90; Height, Width, Length: Contemporary Sculpture from the Weatherspoon Collection, Weatherspoon Art Gallery, Univ NC, Greensboro. *Awards:* Igor Found Grant, 86; Nat Endowment Arts Award for Sculpture, 88; NY Found Arts Award for Sculpture, 90. *Media:* All Media. *Dealer:* Grace Borgenicht Gallery 724 Fifth Ave New York NY 10019. *Mailing Add:* 106 Franklin St Brooklyn NY 11222

CURRY, DAVID PARK
CURATOR, WRITER
b Independence, Mo, July 24, 46. *Study:* Univ NDak, BA, 68; Univ Kans, MA, 74; Yale Univ, PhD(hist art), 81. *Collections Arranged:* Monument: The Connecticut State Capitol (auth, catalog), Hartford, Conn, 79; James McNeill Whistler, Freer Gallery of Art, 84; Winslow Homer: The Croquet Game, Yale Univ & traveling, 84; Contemplating the American Watercolor (auth, catalog), Denver, 85. *Pos:* Asst to dir, Univ Kans Mus Art, 73-76, asst dir, 76; cur Am art, Freer Gallery, Smithsonian Inst, Washington, DC, 81-83 & Denver Art Mus, Colo, formerly. *Teaching:* Teaching fel, Yale Univ, 80-81, lectr 19th century art & archit, 81-82. *Awards:* Nat Mus Act Grant, Advan Acad Degree Prog, 76-78; 6th Nat Film & Video Competition Winner, Nat Trust Historic Preserv, 79; Spec Merit Award, New Eng Book Fair, 85. *Res:* 19th century art; architecture and decorative arts; cross currents between media; material culture's effect upon visual presentation. *Publ:* Auth, Charles Lang Freer and American Art, Apollo, 8/83; Winslow Homer: The Croquet Game, Yale Univ, 84; James McNeill Whistler at Freer Gallery of Art, W W Norton, 84; Whistler and Decoration, Antiques Mag, 11/84; Total Control: Whistler at an Exhibition, Nat Gallery Art, 86. *Mailing Add:* 3001 Veazey Terr NW No 316 Washington DC 20008

CURRY, KEVIN LEE
CURATOR, DIRECTOR
b Louisville, Ky, Feb 2, 57. *Study:* Centre Col Ky, BA, 79; Univ N Tex, 86. *Work:* Univ NTex, Denton. *Comn:* Installation, Cliff & Jody Cohen, Atlanta, Ga, 86; Installation, Murray Camp, Austin, Tex, 90. *Exhib:* 2nd Big Name Invitational, 500 Exposition Gallery, Dallas, 79; Accountrements of Power, DW Gallery, Dallas, 86; Learning to Live with our Mistakes, Univ Tex-Dallas, Richardson, 86; Life in Airports, 2633 Commerce, Dallas, 87; Installed, 2633 Commerce, Dallas, 88; Kevin Curry, Jeff Elrod, Paul Meinel, 2633 Commerce, Dallas, 88; Critics Choice, D-Art Visual Art Ctr, Dallas, 88. *Collections Arranged:* Distinctive Vision I-IV, 7-8/87, 8/88, 7/89, Distinctive Vision V, 9/89, Pivotal Signals, 7/90, Counter Signals, 8/90, Contemp Tex Art; Stars Over Texas, James Pace, Hills Snyder, Frank Tolbert, 3/90; Trance Medial: Mysticism and Technology in Contemporary Texas Art, 3/91; Substance and Subversion: New Political Art, 9/91; Joe Allen and Drew Deleo, 9/91; Small Works and Installations, 6/92. *Pos:* Gallery mgr, Foster Goldstrom, Dallas, Tex, 83-86; co-dir, Distinctive Vision Dallas & Austin, Tex, 87-91; dir, Univ NTex, Denton, 88-89; co-dir, Curry/Camp Exhibs, Dallas & San Antonio, 91-; dir, Dallas Artists Res & Exhib, Tex, 91- *Teaching:* Grad fel, Drawing I & II, 86-88. *Bibliog:* Charles Dee Mitchell (auth), Staying Power, Dallas Observer, 7/90; Janet Kutner (auth), DARE selects Kevin Curry as first director, Dallas Morning News, 4/91; Shannon Dawson (auth), The Right Direction, Dallas Observer, 4/91. *Specialty:* Contemporary Texas art. *Mailing Add:* 2514 White Oak Lane Arlington TX 76012-4849

CURTIS, DAVID
PAINTER, EDUCATOR
b Chester, Pa, Sept 26, 49. *Study:* E Carolina Univ, BFA, 75; Univ NC, Greensboro, MFA, 80; Hollins Col, CAS, 90. *Work:* Greenville Mus Art, NC; NC Dept Natural Resources, Raleigh; Roanoke Mus Fine Art, Va; Dominion Bank Corp Collection, Roanoke, Va; Coleman-Adams Const Group, Lynchburg, Va; and others. *Comn:* Hickory Wind (painting), Susan B Reeves Pub Libr, Sanford, NC, 84. *Exhib:* 38th Ann NC Artist Exhib, NC Mus Art, Raleigh, 75; 1980 Am Art Exhib, Owensboro Mus Fine Art, Ky, 80; 48th Exhib, Southeastern Ctr Contemp Art, Winston-Salem, NC, 82; Art on Paper, Weatherspoon Art Gallery, Greensboro, NC, 82; Energy Art Exhib, Foothills Art Ctr, Golden, Colo, 83; Watercolor USA '84, Springfield Mus Art, Mo, 84; Greater Midwest Int Exhib, Cent Mo State Univ, Warrensburg, Mo, 87; Adirondack Nat Exhib Am Watercolors, 90; 13 solo exhibs, 75-92. *Teaching:* Vis artist, NC Community Col System, 80-84; prof art dept head, Va Western Community Col, Roanoke, 84- *Awards:* Judges Award, Marietta Nat, 79; Artist/Fel, Atlantic Ctr Arts, Fla, 83; Award Merit, Alliance Arts, Va, 91. *Mem:* Southeast Col Art Conf. *Media:* Oil, Watercolor. *Dealer:* Gallery III Ltd Roanoke VA. *Mailing Add:* 3436 Rosewood Ave SW Roanoke VA 24015

CURTIS, DOLLY POWERS
SCULPTOR, WEAVER
b Bronx, NY, April 25, 42. *Study:* Pa State Univ, BS, 60-63; NY Univ, MA, 63-65; Brookfield Craft Ctr, Conn, 73-86. *Work:* Southern Conn State Univ; Choate Sch Art Dept; Marymount Col; Gov Residence, State Conn; Smithsonian Inst Archives Am Art. *Comn:* Knotted sculpture, Landplan Partnership, Southport, Conn, 77; numerous comns for private residences, northeast US, 77-; woven wall, Richard Bergmann Architects, New Canaan, Conn, 80; weavings, Naperville Corp Ctr, Ill, 82; woven hanging, Coopers & Lebrand CPA, Hartford, Conn, 83; and others. *Exhib:* Solo exhibs, Woven Folds--Fabric Drawing in Space, Pindar Gallery, New York, 80, 81 & 82 & Woven Environmental Sculpture, Wesleyan Univ, Conn, 82; Art in Craft Media Traveling Exhib, 81-83; Pa State Univ Mus Art, 82; Fiber: The Artist's View, C W Post Ctr, Long Island Univ, 83; The Newport Art Mus, RI, 85; Mus Art, Sci & Industry, Conn, 85; and others. *Pos:* Owner, Archit Textiles, Easton, Conn, 73- *Teaching:* Instr weaving, Brookfield Craft Ctr, Conn, 77, Haystack Mt Sch, Deer Isle, Maine, 77. *Awards:* State Conn Grant, 76; Outstanding Achievement Design, Women in Design Int, 83; Best in Fiber, Soc Conn Craftsmen, 85; and others. *Bibliog:* Patricia Hubbell (auth), Her weavings soar thru space & Kossia Orloff (auth), Reforming fabric, Women Artists News, fall 82; Martha B Scott (auth), article, Art Voices, 1-2/81; Donna Clemson (auth), Weaving Magician, The Penn Stater, 82; article on videotape, Dolly Curtis--Fiber artist, Crafts Report, 5/86. *Mem:* Artists Equity Asn; Am Crafts Coun; Women's Caucus Art; Surface Design Asn; Artist-Craftsmen New York. *Media:* Fiber, Textiles. *Publ:* Auth, State grant: A two way street, Shuttle, Spindle, Dyepot, fall 77; contribr, Architectural Ornament, Van Nostrand Reinhold, 82; Designing for Weaving, Hastings House Publ, 82; Fiberarts Design II, Lark Publ, 83; Women Working Home, Rodale Press, 83. *Dealer:* Silvermine Galleries New Canaan Conn; Atria Architects Hartford Conn. *Mailing Add:* 35 Flat Rock Rd 1037 Silvermine Rd Easton CT 06612

CURTIS, MARY CRANFILL
PRINTMAKER, PAINTER
b Ft Worth, Tex, Aug 6, 25. *Study:* Columbia Univ, BS, 46; Southern Methodist Univ, MFA, 73. *Work:* Dallas Mus Art, Tex; Okla Art Ctr, Oklahoma City; Southern Methodist Univ; Mobil Oil Collection; Heard Mus Natural Hist, McKinney, Tex; and others. *Comn:* Portraits, Austin Col, 57; designed rug & glass murals, 65, Grayson Co Bank, Sherman, Tex. *Exhib:* Davidson Nat Print & Drawing, NC, 74; Int Miami Graphics Biennial, Fla, 75 & 77; Libr Cong & Nat Collection Fine Arts Nat Exhib Prints, Washington, DC, 75; Los Angeles Printmaking Nat, 75; three-person show, Masur Mus Art, Monroe, La, 76; Print Exhib, Visual Arts Ctr Alaska, Anchorage, 79; Texas Printmakers Exhib, Meadows Mus, Southern Methodist Univ, Dallas, 90. *Teaching:* Instr art Austin Col, Sherman, Tex, 55-57 & 65-67, Sch Continuing Educ, Southern Methodist Univ, Dallas, 68-75. *Awards:* Midwestern Graphics Purchase Award, Tulsa City-Co Libr, Okla, 75; Juror's Commendation, Boston Printmakers, 75. *Bibliog:* Feature: Miniature Showcase, July, 88; Biography: Texas Printmakers '90. *Mem:* Print Consortium, St Joseph, Mo. *Media:* Etching; All. *Dealer:* Assoc Am Artists 663 Fifth Ave New York NY 10022; Murray Smither 1934 Kessler Pkwy Dallas TX 75208. *Mailing Add:* 328 Sutton Pl Richardson TX 75080

CURTIS, PHILIP CAMPBELL
PAINTER
b Jackson, Mich, May 26, 07. *Study:* Albion Col, BA, 30; Univ Mich Law Sch; Yale Univ Sch Fine Arts, cert, 35; Harvard Univ, 41; Albion Col, hon DFA, 71; Ariz State Univ, hon doctorate, 79, DHL, 81. *Work:* Curtis Room, Phoenix Art Mus. *Exhib:* San Francisco Mus Art, Calif, 49; Calif Palace Legion Hon, 66; Galerie Krugier, Geneva, Switz, 67; Amon Carter Mus, Ft Worth, Tex, 70; Univ Calif, Los Angeles, 72; one-man show, Galerie Ariadne, Vienna, 74, Marylan Butler Gallery, Scottsdale, Ariz & Santa Monica, Calif, 90, Albion Col; Phillips Collection, Washington, DC, 78; Nat Mus Am Art; Mus Mod Art, New York; Rose Mus, Brandeis Univ; Des Moines Art Ctr; Paul Nix Art Mus, Pax, Ariz; Univ Northern Ariz. *Pos:* Supvr mural painting, Works Progress Admin Proj, New York, 35; founder & first dir, Phoenix Art Ctr & Phoenix Art Mus, Ariz, 36-39; Designer, WPA Art Proj Exhib, DeYoung Mus, San Francisco, Calif, 38; mem staff, Des Moines Art Ctr, 39-41. *Awards:* Governor's Award, Artist of the Year, 83; Distinguished Alumni Award & Philip C Curtis Visual Arts Grant, Albion Col, 91. *Bibliog:* Jose Bermudez (auth, film), The Time Freeze, 74; article, Esquire Mag, 12/82. *Mem:* Benjamin Franklin fel, Royal Soc Arts. *Media:* Oil. *Publ:* Illustr, The Work of Philip C Curtis (calalog), Garland Press, 93. *Mailing Add:* 109 Cattle Track Scottsdale AZ 85253

CURTIS, ROBERT D
SCULPTOR
b Susanville, Calif, Mar 28, 48. *Study:* Univ Ariz, BFA(sculpture), 70; Ariz State Univ, MFA(sculpture & design), 72. *Exhib:* Wis Directions 2, Milwaukee Art Mus, 78; Anita J Welch Mem Nat Competition & Sculpture Exhib, Scottsdale Ctr Arts, Ariz, 79; Wis Sculpture, Wustum Mus Fine Arts, Racine, 79; two-person exhib, Arts Club Chicago, Ill, 82; one-person exhib, Kit Basquin Gallery, Milwaukee, 82; Int Art Expo, Navy Pier, Chicago, 82 & 83. *Pos:* Consult restoration & installation of large scale sculpture, Bradley Family Found, Milwaukee, Wis, 78-; consult restoration & installation of large scale sculpture, Milwaukee Art Mus, 79. *Teaching:* Instr design & sculpture, Univ Wis, Milwaukee, 72-73; instr drawing, 3-D design, sculpture, Mt Mary Col, 75- *Awards:* Shapes of 77 Stainless Steel Sculpture Competition, Vollrath Co, Wis, 77; Grant-in-Aid, Wis Arts Bd, 78; First in Sculpture Competition, City Madison, 83. *Bibliog:* Judith M Kaiser (auth), New Dimensions in Wisconsin Art: Robert Curtis, Exclusively Yours, The Patten Co, 80; Karen Thorsen-Collins (auth), Opening exhibition: Kit Basquin Gallery, New Art Examiner, 12/81. *Mem:* Int Sculpture Ctr; Col Art Asn; Wis Painters & Sculpture Inc (pres, 76-78). *Media:* Steel, Stone. *Mailing Add:* 4109 Edgevale Ct Chevy Chase MD 20815

CURTIS, ROGER WILLIAM
PAINTER, DEALER
b Gloucester, Mass, Dec 20, 10. *Study:* Exten courses, Boston Univ, Harvard Univ, Mus Sch Boston; pvt study with Aldro T Hibbard; Burdett Col. *Work:* Cape Ann Hist Mus; Raytheon Corp; Nat Shawmut Bank, Boston; Eastern Gas & Fuel, Boston; Mellon Bank, Pittsburgh, Pa; and others. *Exhib:* Jordan Marsh Exhib, 45-75; Arts Atlantic Exhib, NShore Arts Asn, Gloucester, 47-75; Sheldon-Swope Mus, Terre Haute, Ind; Symphony Hall Exhib, Boston, 65-70; Acad Artist Asn, Springfield, Mass, 72-75; Attleboro Mus, Mass, 84. *Pos:* Treas, Guild Boston Artists, Mass, 64-; adminr, Ledgendsea Gallery & Riverview Gallery, formerly. *Teaching:* Instr painting, pvt classes, 53- *Awards:* North Shore Arts Mem, 80; Gordon Grant Mem, 81; Saunders Award, 83; A J McCarthy Award, 84; Reinert Award, 85. *Mem:* NShore Arts Asn (pres, 52-58, treas, 65-); Am Artists Prof League (vpres, secy-treas, 50-); Cape Ann Festival Arts (treas); co-founder, Coun Mass Art Asn; Acad Artists Asn; and others. *Media:* Oil. *Publ:* Auth & illusr, How to Paint Successful Seascapes, 75 & Color in Outdoor Painting, 77, Watson-Guptill. *Mailing Add:* c/o New England Artists 30 Riverview Rd Gloucester MA 01930

CURTIS, TERRY WAYNE
PAINTER, SCULPTOR
b Moorehead, Ky, Dec 3, 51. *Study:* Univ Cincinnati, studied under Frank Herman, 77; Cincinnati Art Acad. *Work:* Trisolini Gallery, Ohio Mus Art, Athens; Tampa Mus Art, Fla; Nat Univ Mex Gallery, Cuernavaca; Foster Harmon Galleries of Am Art, Sarasota, Fla; E P Gallery, Dusseldorf, Ger; and others. *Comn:* Acrylic wall sculpture, Panamanian Embassy, Tokyo, Japan, 86; large canvas, Critikon Inc, Tampa, Fla, 86; 2 large canvases, B R Starnes Develop Co, Ft Lauderdale, Fla, 87; The Wentworth Collection (6 paintings), Tarpon Springs, Fla; Major Exterior Sculpture of Stainless Steel & Granite Titled Quintessence, USX Corp, Sand Key Beach, Fla, 92; and others. *Exhib:* Major Fla Artists, Foster Harmon Galleries Am Art, Sarasota, 82-90 & Tampa Mus Art, 86; one-man shows, Ohio Mus Art, 86 & Nat Univ Mex, 84; Expression Landscapes, Fla State Capitol Exhib, Tallahassee, 87; FA/AIA State Fla Conf Off Poster, 90. *Bibliog:* Charles Benbow (auth), Pinellas artist encounters critical praise while abroad, St Petersburg Times, 84. *Mem:* Pinellas Co Arts Coun, Fla; Arts Coun Hillsborough Co, Fla; Int Sculpture Asn, Washington, DC. *Media:* Acrylic, Oil; All media. *Dealer:* Foster Harmon Galleries 1415 Main St Sarasota FL 33577. *Mailing Add:* 287 Cypress Trace Tarpon Springs FL 34689

CURTIS, VERNA P
CURATOR
Study: Univ Calif, Berkeley, BA, 67; Ariz State Univ, Tempe, 70-72; Univ Wis, Milwaukee, MA(art hist), 74. *Collections Arranged:* Walker Evans from the Collection of Arnold H Crane, 81, Lewis W Hine: Child Labor Photographs (auth, catalog), 82, Art in the Streets: 19th Century French Posters, 83, Atget's Paris, 84, Toulouse-Lautrec Prints from the Permanent Collection, 86 & La Tauromaquia: Goya, Picasso and the Bullfight, 86, Milwaukee Art Mus, Wis. *Pos:* Cur asst, Art Hist Galleries, Univ Wis-Milwaukee, 74; asst cur, Milwaukee Art Mus, 74-76, assoc cur, collections & exhibitions, 77-80, assoc cur, prints, drawings & photographs, 81-85, cur, 86- *Teaching:* Inst print connoisseurship, Univ Wis-Milwaukee, 79, instr photog hist, 84; instr print hist, Milwaukee Art Mus, 83. *Awards:* Nat Endowment Arts Grants, 82 & 84; Govt of Spain Grant, 86; Getty Trust Grant, 86. *Mem:* Print Coun Am. *Publ:* Auth, The Photograph and the Grid, 84 & Nic Nicosia's Realities, 85, Milwukee Art Mus; Warrington Colescott, Perimeter Gallery, Chicago, 85. *Mailing Add:* 4109 Edgevale Ct Chevy Chase MD 20815

CUSACK, MARGARET WEAVER
ILLUSTRATOR, SCULPTOR
b Chicago, Ill, Aug 1, 45. *Study:* Pratt Inst, BFA(cum laude), 68. *Comn:* Hanging & poster, Am Express Co, New York, 84; hanging, Culinary Inst Am, Hyde Park, NY; hanging, Seagram's Bldg, New York; hanging, Yale New Haven Hosp, Conn. *Exhib:* 20th Century Images of George Washington, Fraunces Tavern Mus, New York, 82; The Christmas Carol Sampler, Art Dir Club, New York, 83; New York Soc of Illustrators Exhib to Japan (traveling), Tokyo, Japan, 84; Contemp Illustr, Col D'Enseignement General et Professionel, Quebec, Can, 85; Looking at Earth, Smithsonian Nat Air & Space Mus, Washington, DC, 86; and many others. *Awards:* Soc of Illusr Award, 74, 81, 82, 84 & 85; Art Ann Award, Communication Arts Mag, 76 & 81; Alumni Achievement Award, Pratt Inst, 88. *Bibliog:* Amerika Mag, Usia, 2/89; Art Product News, 10/89; Step by Step Graphics Mag, 7/92. *Mem:* Graphic Arts Guild; Am Crafts Coun. *Media:* Fabric Collage, Woodcuts; Soft Sculpture. *Publ:* The Christmas Carol Sampler, Harcourt Brace Jovanovich, 83. *Mailing Add:* 124 Hoyt St Brooklyn NY 11217-2215

CUSICK, NANCY TAYLOR
PAINTER
b Washington, DC. *Study:* Am Univ, BA, 59, MA, 61, with Gates, Calfee, D'Artista and Summerford; Corcoran Art Sch, 68; Univ Calif, 71, with Lindgren, 71. *Work:* Mus Fine Arts, Pangborn Corp, Hagerstown, Md; Am Univ, Libr Cong, Nat Mus Women in the Arts, Corcoran Gallery Art, Washington, DC; US Embassy, Madagascar; Turkish-Am Assoc, Ankara & Izmir, Turkey; Helenic-Am Union, Athens, Greece; Museo de Arte Moderno, Buenos Aires, Arg. *Exhib:* Washington Artists Ann, Smithsonian Inst, 60-69; Area Exhib, Corcoran Gallery Art, 67; Southeastern Museums Tour, Corcoran Gallery Art, 73; solo exhibs, Anne Hathaway Gallery, Folger Libr, Washington, DC, 83, Catholic Univ Am, Washington, DC, 84, Mus Fine Arts, Hagerstown, Md, 85, Antalya Mus Painting & Sculpture, Turkey, 90, Univ Calif, Los Angeles, 90, Gallery 10 Ltd, Washington, DC, 90, Goldman Art Gallery, Rockville, Md, 91; Feminism & Religious Experience, Cornell Univ, Ithaca, NY, 85; Grabadores USA, Museo de Arte Moderno, Buenos Aires, Arg, 87; Int Prints, Int Monetary Fund, Washington, DC, 88; A Salute to Women, Nat Mus Women in the Arts, Washington, DC, 91. *Pos:* Exec dir, Washington Women's Arts Ctr, DC, 79-80; contrib ed, Women Artists News, New York, 80-; Wash coordr, Int Festival Women Artists, UN Mid-Decade Conf Women, Copenhagen, Denmark, 80; proj dir, Focus Int-Am Women in Art, UN Decade Conf, Nairobi, Kenya, 85; pres, Gallery 10 Ltd, 91-92; arts caucus rep, Nat Women's Conf Comt, 91-92. *Teaching:* Instr painting & art hist, Dunbarton Col Holy Cross, 66-72; instr art, Prince George's Col, 72-77; lectr & workshop dir, Dokuz Eylul Univ, Izmir, Turkey, 89, Hacettepe Univ, Ankara, Turkey, 89, Bilkent Univ, Ankara, Turkey, 89. *Awards:* First Prize Painting, Soc Washington Artists, 66; Best in Show, Hagerstown Mus, 67. *Bibliog:* Jean R Murphy (auth), Nancy Cusick, Evening Times, Pawtucket, RI, 9/85; Daniel Barbiero (auth), Art Spirit at R Street Gallery, Wash Reporter, 11/86; Terry Parmelee (auth), Nancy Cusick, All Things Considered, Eyewash, 5/90; Michael Welzenbach (auth), Dramas in Dark Detail, Nancy Cusick at Gallery 10, 5/90; Lesley Phillips (auth), All Things Considered, Women Artists News, 9/90; Krystyna Wasserman (auth), A Salute to Women, Nat Mus of Women in the Arts, 2/91; Mal Johnson (auth), A Salute to Women, UNIFEM, USA, 4/91. *Mem:* Artists Equity Asn; Col Art Asn; Coalition Women's Art Orgn; Women's Caucus Art; Soc Washington Artists. *Media:* Mixed Media, Oil. *Mailing Add:* 2439 Villanova Dr Vienna VA 22180

CUTFORTH, ROGER
CONCEPTUAL ARTIST, PAINTER
b Lincolnshire, Eng, 1944. *Study:* Nottingham Col Art, Eng, 62-63; Ravensbourne Col Art, Eng, 63-66. *Work:* Walraf-Richartz Mus, Cologne, Ger; Metrop Mus Art, New York; Mus Abteiberg, Monchengladbeck, Ger; Mus Mod Art, New York. *Exhib:* Mus Mod Art, New York, 70 & 80; Int Cult Ctr Mus, Antwerp, Belg, 75; Contemp Art Mus, Zagreb, Yugoslavia, 76; Vienna Int Biennale, Austria, 81; Sydney Biennale, Australia, 81; Trouble in Paradise, A & M Artworks, New York, 82; Randolf Macon Women's Col, Lynchburg, Va, 83; Contemporary Triptychs, Edith C Blum Art Inst, Bard Col, Annandale-on-Hudson, NY, 84; Houston Ctr Photog, Tex, 86; solo exhib, Bauer House, Univ Tex, Austin, 88; Dos Amigos Gallery, Terlingua, Tex, 88 & 90; Work From The Seventies, Hall Bromm Gallery, New York, 90; San Angelo Mus Fine Arts, Tex, 91. *Teaching:* Instr intro photog, New York Univ, 84. *Awards:* Visual Artists Fel, Nat Endowment Arts, 84. *Bibliog:* Valentin Tatransky (auth), article, Arts Mag, 78; Loredana Parmesani (auth), article, Segno, 79; Jean Fisher (auth), article, Aspects, 81; Grace Glueck (auth), The triptych lives on in modern variations, New York Times, 7/1/84. *Media:* Color Photographs; Watercolor. *Publ:* Auth, The Empire State Building, private publ, 69; The Visual Book, private publ, 70; Cleopatra's Needle/Eiffel Tower/Empire State Building, private publ, 71. *Dealer:* Hal Bromm Gallery 90 W Broadway New York NY 10007. *Mailing Add:* HC 65 Box 2760 Alpine TX 79830-9801

CUTHBERT, VIRGINIA
PAINTER
b West Newton, Pa, Aug 27, 08. *Study:* Syracuse Univ, BFA, 30; Acad Grande Chaumiere, Acad Colarossi, Paris, France & Chelsea Polytech Inst, Eng, Augusta-Hazard fel, 30-31; study with George Luks, 32; Univ Pittsburgh, 33-34; Carnegie Inst Technol, 34-35. *Work:* Albright-Knox Art Gallery, Buffalo, NY; Princeton Univ Art Mus, NJ; Rutgers Univ Libr Collection, NJ; Burchfield Ctr, Buffalo, New York; Everson Mus, Syracuse, NY; and others. *Comn:* Fortune Mag covers, 51 & 56; Southwestern Rev cover, 52; State Univ New York, Buffalo; Marine Midland Bank. *Exhib:* Metrop Mus Art, New York, 43, 44 & 50; 7 Whitney Mus Am Art Ann, New York, 44-53; South Western Pa Paintings, Greenburg; Retrospective, Burchfield Ctr, Buffalo, NY, 71; Members Gallery, Albright-Knox Gallery, Buffalo, NY. *Pos:* Art columnist, Buffalo Courier Express, 54-55. *Teaching:* Instr painting, Albright Art Sch, 42-54; instr painting, Univ Buffalo, 42-54; instr painting, State Univ NY Buffalo, 54-66. *Awards:* First Prize, Western NY Exhib, Albright-Knox Art Gallery, 46-52; Nat Inst Arts & Lett Grant for Painting, 54; Small Paintings USA, 74. *Media:* Oil, Watercolor; Drawing. *Publ:* Auth, spec art rev in, Buffalo Eve News, 54-56. *Mailing Add:* c/o Nina Freudenheim Gallery 300 Delaware Ave Buffalo NY 14202

CUTLER, BESS
ART DEALER
b Salem, Mass, Dec 13, 49. *Study:* Brandeis Univ, BA, 71; Sch Mus Fine Arts, Tufts Univ, MFA, 76. *Pos:* Partner, Cutler-Stavandis Gallery, Boston, 78-82; owner & dir, Bess Cutler Gallery, New York, 83- *Specialty:* Contemporary artists. *Mailing Add:* 593 Broadway New York NY 10012-3211

CUTLER, ETHEL ROSE
PAINTER, DESIGNER
b New York, NY. *Study:* Hunter Col, BA; Columbia Univ, MA; Sch Prof Arts, cert advert & interior design; NY Univ; Univ Mo; Inst Design, Ill Inst Technol; Am Artist Sch; New Sch Social Res, with Yasuo Kuniyoshi & Alexei Brodovitch; Walden Univ, Inst Advan Studies, PhD, Fashion Inst Technol (computer graphic). *Work:* Permanent collections of New York Univ, Gray Art Gallery Study Ctr & Jewish Mus. *Exhib:* New York City Ctr Gallery; Young Am Artist Group, New York; Lynn Kottler Galleries, New York; Artist Equity Exhib, New York; East Galleries, NY Univ; and others. *Pos:* Design consult, artist & designer, 50. *Teaching:* Instr fine arts, Women's Col, Univ NC, Greensboro, 43-47; instr, Adelphi Col, 47-50; asst prof interior design & related arts, Univ Mo-Columbia, 50-55; asst prof surface design, RI Sch Design, 55-59. *Awards:* Award for Boats, New York City Ctr Gallery, 59; Award for Brothers, Macy's Gallery; Grant, Metrop Mus Art, New York, 68 & Walden Univ. *Mem:* Col Art Asn Am; Artists Equity Asn; Women in Design; Am Soc Interior Designers; Art Dir Club. *Media:* All. *Res:* Techniques of William Morris and the arts and crafts movement of the Beaux Arts, the Bauhaus and other influences of the 19th century; the garden as an aesthetic experience, its influence on selected artists. *Mailing Add:* 230 E 88th St New York NY 10028

CUTLER, GRAYCE E
PAINTER, WRITER
b Salt Lake City, Utah. *Study:* Univ Utah; Art Students League, New York, with Kuniyoshi & Morris Kantor; New York Sch Design, cert; Hans Hofmann Sch Art, Provincetown, Mass; also with Eliot O'Hara; poetry with John Ciardi. *Work:* Granite Schs Admin Art Collection, Salt Lake City; Pollard Collection, Greater Victoria Art Gallery, BC; Royal Family, Saudi Arabia; Utah State Arts Coun Collection; Springville Art Mus, Springville, Utah. *Exhib:* Soc Western Artists Ann, De Young Mus, San Francisco, 66, 68 & 69; one-woman shows, Rosicrucian Egyptian Mus & Gallery, San Jose, 68 & 71 & Kimball Art Ctr, Park City, Utah, 81 & 86; Watercolor West, Utah State Univ, Logan, 73; Metrop Mus Art, New York, 78; Bertha Eccles Gallery, Ogden, Utah; Park City, Utah, 81; Mormon Art Mus, Salt Lake City, 85. *Awards:* First Prize, watercolor, Utah State Fair; Watercolor Award of Honor, Intermountain States Traveling Exhib, Utah State Inst Fine Arts; Watercolor Gold Award, Nat League Am Pen Women Biennial, Washington, DC; plus others. *Bibliog:* Articles in Rosicrucian Digest, 68 & 71, Relief Soc Mag, 69 & Women Artists Utah, 84. *Mem:* Soc Western Artists; Am Soc Interior Designers (pres, Utah Chap, 73-74); Nat League Am Pen Women; Asn Utah Artists; Utah Watercolor Soc. *Media:* Watercolor, Oil. *Res:* Early writings and drawings as an art form. *Publ:* Auth, Panorama Poetry, 83 & 86-88 & Utah Sings, 85, Utah State Poetry Soc. *Mailing Add:* 777 E S Temple St Apt 8A Salt Lake City UT 84102

CUTLER, RONNIE
PAINTER
Study: Columbia Univ Art Sch, 57; Brooklyn Mus Art, Art Sch, 58; Art Students League, 59-60. *Work:* Art Students League Collections, New York; Commerce Bank, Memphis, Tenn. *Exhib:* Artists of Manhattan, Whitney Mus, New York, 54; 54th Ann Competition, Delgado Mus, New Orleans, La, 55; 5th Ann Competition, Berkshire Mus, Pittsfield, Mass, 56; Alumni Show, Brooklyn Mus, New York, 56 & 58; Casein Soc, Riverside Mus, New York, 57; Audubon Artists, Nat Acad Design, New York, 58 & 84; one-woman shows, Bodley Gallery, New York, 79, Ronrich Gallery, New York, 89, 90 & 91. *Awards:* Alumni Purchase Award, Art Students League, 60; Best of Show, Southern Berkshire Community Arts Coun, 79 & 80; Silvermine Guild Artists, New Canaan, Conn; First prize in Oil, Painters & Sculptors Soc, New York; First prize in Oil, Sheffield Art Asn, Mass, 86, 87 & 88. *Media:* Oil. *Mailing Add:* 175 W 12th St New York NY 10011

CUTLER-SHAW, JOYCE
CONCEPTUAL ARTIST, EDUCATOR
b Detroit, Mich. *Study:* New York Univ, BA, 53; Columbia Univ, 53-54; Univ Calif, San Diego, MFA, 72. *Work:* Mus Mod Art, New York; Teylers Mus Harlem, The Netherlands; Mus Natural Hist, San Diego; Johnson Mus, Cornell Univ; Univ Calif, San Diego; New York Pub Libr, Special Collections. *Comn:* Namewall for Los Angeles Int Airport, Los Angeles Bd Airport Commissioners, Calif, 74; Charity Namewall for New Orleans Charity Hospital, New Orleans Downtown Development District, La, 80; Volt Corp Park, Orange, Calif, 87-88 Carlsbad Water Stories, Magee Park, Calif, 90; Carlsbad Water Stories, Magee Park, Calif, 90. *Exhib:* Three Directions, Newport Harbor Art Mus, Calif, 76; Am Narrative Art, Contemp Art Mus, Houston, Tex, 77; Un Espace Parle, Galerie Gaetan, Geneva, Switz, 78; Other Child Book, Palace of Culture and Sci, Warsaw, Poland, 79; Arteder 82, Bilboa, Spain, 82; Nat Acad Sci, Washington, DC, 86; Herbert/Johnson Mus, Cornell Univ, Ithaca, NY, 86; Intersection, San Francisco, Calif, 88; Teylers Mus, Haarlem, The Netherlands, 90; Nat Mus Women in the Arts, Washington, DC, 92; Calligraphia USA/USSR, Int Typeface Corp, Traveling Minsk, etc, USSR & USA, 90-93. *Pos:* Dir, Art & Artists: Video/Audio Archive, 74-80; TV interviewer/project dir, Art & Artists, KPBS-TV, San Diego, Calif, 79-80; chairwoman, Pub Art Adv Coun, San Diego,Calif, 78; vis scholar (artist & residency), Sch Med, Univ Calif, San Diego, 92-93. *Teaching:* Vis fac contemp art, San Diego State Univ, Calif, 78-80; vis fac contemp art, Univ Calif, Irvine, 79-80. *Awards:* Project Patronage, Survival/Evolution, UNESCO, 79-80; Art & Artists Project Grant, San Diego State Univ Art Coun, 79-80; Nat Endowment Arts Media Grant, Video Portrait, 81-82; Nat Endowment Arts Grant, 85-87; Alphabet of Bones Poster, Purchase Prize, SUNY, New York. *Bibliog:* Moira Roth (auth), An Interview with Joyce Cutler-Shaw, Univ Southern Calif, 76, Catalog essay, Johnson Mus, 86; Lucy Lippard (auth), Three Directions, Newport Harbor Mus, 76; M Vogel (auth), Die Dame und der Vogel, Vaterland Luzern, Switzerland, 10/4/79; catalogue essay, Johnson Mus, Cornell Univ, 86. *Mem:* Col Art Asn; Woman's Caucus Arts; Landmark Art Projects (founding mem, secy, 78-84 & pres, 85- 92); Adv Coun, SanDiego City Architect, 90-92. *Media:* Multi-Media. *Publ:* Auth, We The People: Proposal for an Artwork, self publ, 75; auth, Survival--Evolution Proposal for a Public Art Project, self publ, 77; auth, The Lady and the Bird, self publ, 77-79; Alphabet of Bones, Kretschmer & Grossman, Frankfurt, WGer 87; Three Cages, Ctr for Book Arts, New York, 92. *Mailing Add:* 7245 Rue De Roark La Jolla CA 92037

CUTRONE, RONNIE BLAISE
PAINTER
b New York, July 10, 48. *Study:* Sch Visual Arts, 70. *Work:* Mus Mod Art, New York; T'Venster Mus Arts Coun, Rotterdam, Holland; Patrick Lannen Collection, Fla; Morton Neumann Family Collection, Kalamazoo, Mich; Eli Broad Found, Santa Monica, Calif. *Exhib:* One-man show, Venster Arts Coun, Rotterdam, Holland, 83, Venice Biennale, Italy, 84; From the Streets, Greenville Co Mus, NC, 83; Impressionism to New Wave, High Mus Art, Springfield, Ill, 86; Sacred Images in Secular Art, Whitney Mus, New York, 86; Comic Iconoclasm, ICA, London, Eng, 87; Avant Garde in the 80's, Los Angeles Co Mus, Calif, 87. *Bibliog:* Robert Becker (auth), article, Interview Mag, 82; Jeanne Silverthorne (auth), article, Art Forum, 83; Tommaso Trini (auth), article, Flash Art, 84. *Media:* Acrylic, Watercolor; Silkscreen. *Publ:* Auth, Ronnie Cutrone Watercolors, Salvatore Ala Gallery, 84; Ronnie Cutrone, Tony Shafrazi Gallery, 85; New Used and Improved Art for the 80's, Abbeyville, 87. *Mailing Add:* 176 Christopher St New York NY 10014

CUTTLER, CHARLES DAVID
HISTORIAN, LECTURER
b Cleveland, Ohio, Apr 8, 13. *Study:* Ohio State Univ, BFA & MA; Inst Art & Archeol, Paris, France; Univ Bruxelles; Inst Fine Arts, NY Univ, PhD. *Exhib:* Cleveland May Show, Ohio, 35-36; Philadelphia Watercolor Ann, Pa, 37. *Pos:* Guest lectr, Sem Europ Art & Civilisation Belg, Ghent, summer, 69, Tokyo, 81, Brussels, 88. *Teaching:* Asst instr art hist, Ohio State Univ, 35-37; from instr to asst prof art hist, Mich State Univ, 47-57; from assoc prof to prof, Univ Iowa, 57-83, res prof, 65-75, emer, 83- *Awards:* CRB Fel, Brussels, 53-54; Fulbright-Hays Sr Fel, Brussels, 65-66; Assoc mem, Royal Belgian Acad, 87. *Mem:* Col Art Asn Am; founding mem Midwest Art Hist Soc; Renaissance Soc Am; Medieval Acad Am; Int Ctr Medieval Art; life mem Hist Netherland Art. *Res:* Netherlandish and German art of the 14th to 16th centuries; art of Hieronymus Bosch. *Publ:* Lisbon Temptation of St Anthony by Jerome Bosch, 57; Northern painting, from Pucelle to Bruegel, XIVth, XVth & XVIth Centuries, 68, 73 & 91; Auth, Further Grünewald sources, Zeitschrf Kstgesch, 87; Errata in Netherlandish art: Jan Mostaert's New World Landscape, Simiolus, 89; Exotics in Post-Medieval Art: Giraffes and Centaurs, Artibus et Historiae, 91. *Mailing Add:* 1691 Ridge Rd Iowa City IA 52245

CYPHERS, PEGGY K
PAINTER, PRINTMAKER
b Baltimore, MD, April 19, 54. *Study:* Maryland Inst Col Art; Towson State Univ, BFA, 77; Pratt Inst, MFA, 79. *Work:* Chase Manhattan Bank, Prudential Life Insurance, New York; Best Products, Ashland, Va; Aldrich Mus, Conn; Mus Modern Art, New York. *Exhib:* Recent Acquisitions, Aldrich Mus, Conn, 86; group shows, Baltimore Mus Art, Md, 88, Betsy Rosenfield Gallery, Chicago, 90 & 92; New Painting, Hudson River Mus, New York, 88; Peggy Cyphers, E M Donahue Gallery, New York, 88, 90 & 91, Mincher/Wilcox, San Francisco, 89; New Generations: New York, Carnegie Inst Gallery, Carnegie Mellon, Pittsburgh, Pa; Transmodern, Baumgardner Gallery, Washington, DC. *Pos:* Auth, New York in Review (monthly article), Arts Mag, 88-90. *Teaching:* Instr, painting & drawing,

Parsons Sch of Design, 88, Pratt Inst, 89-92, New York Univ, 90-92. *Awards:* Ford Found Award, 79; Igor Found Grant, 88; Nat Endowment Artists Fel, 89-90. *Bibliog:* Andy Grunberg (auth), Peggy Cyphers, NY Times, 4/20/90; Jed Perl (auth), Peggy Cyphers, Gallery Going: Four Seasons in the Art World, Harcourt Brace Jovanovich, 231-233, 91; Ellen Handy (coauth), Peggy Cyphers, Art Mag, 2/92. *Mem:* Col Art Asn. *Media:* Acrylic, Oil; Miscellaneous Media. *Publ:* Ed, Progress (mag), New Observations, 58. *Mailing Add:* 315 Broadway #5 New York NY 10007

CZACH, MARIE
HISTORIAN, CURATOR
b Chicago, Ill. *Study:* Sch Art Inst Chicago, BAE, 67; Columbia Univ, New York, MA, 68; Univ Ill at Urbana-Champaign, PhD, 85. *Pos:* Res assoc, George Eastman House, Rochester, NY, 68-70; asst cur photog, Art Inst Chicago, Ill, 70-72; dir, Mus Gallery, Western Ill Univ, Macomb, 74-78 & Sioux City Art Ctr, Iowa, 85. *Teaching:* Dir studies, hist & criticism of photog & contemp art, Columbia Col, Chicago, 72-74. *Res:* Nineteenth-century art criticism; contemporary American art; history of photography. *Publ:* Auth, A Directory of Early Illinois Photographers, Western Ill Univ, 77. *Mailing Add:* 14312 La Salle St Riverdale IL 60627-2743

CZARNIECKI, M J, III
MUSEUM DIRECTOR
b San Francisco, Calif, May 28, 48. *Study:* Xaverius Col, Antwerp, Belg, dipl, 67; Wabash Col, Ind, BA, 71; Art Inst Chicago, 71-72; Columbia Col, Chicago, 73; Middlebury Col, Vt, 78; Salzburg Seminars, Austria, 89. *Collections Arranged:* Masters of Twentieth Century Photography (co-cur), Ringling Mus, 76; Before It's Too Late: The Photography of Edward S Curtis (cur, catalog), 78 & Dance Image: A Tribute to Serge Diaghilev (dir), 79, Miss Mus Art; Southern Realism (dir), Miss Mus Art/Southern Arts Fedn, 78-81; Russian Stage Designs: Scenic Innovation, 1900-1930 (dir), Miss Mus Art, 82; Paul Manship: Changing Taste in America (dir, Catalog), Minn Mus Art, 85-88; A Lighter Shade of Pale: Photographic Influences in Other Media, Minn Mus Art, 89; Cuba-USA: The First Generation, Fondo del Sol Visual Arts Ctr with Minn Mus Art, 92. *Pos:* Dir, Miss Mus Art, 76-83; consult, Nat Endowment Arts & Inst Mus Services, 78-88; cur-in-residence, US Info Agency, Sofia, Bulgaria, 82; dir, Minn Mus of Art, 83-; bd dir, Intermedia Arts, Minn, 85-91; bd dir, Pub Art, St Paul, 88-; bd dir, Concourse Arts, 89-; chair, Minn Archit Designer Selection Bd; visual arts chair, Minn/Cuba Proj, 85- *Teaching:* Instr photog, Wabash Col, Ind, 70-71; lectr hist photog, Art Inst Chicago, 72-74; dir educ, Ringling Mus Art, 74-76; lectr MBA arts prog, State Univ NY, Binghampton, 83-88, 90-92; lectr, Arts Admin, Metrop State Univ, Minn, 87. *Awards:* Am Field Serv Scholar, 66-67; Raymond Fund Grantee, 73; Honor Award, Am Inst Archit, St Paul Chapter, 87; McKnight Found Fel, 89; Fel, Salzburg Seminars, 89. *Mem:* Miss Inst Arts & Letters (founding dir, 79-83); Am Asn Mus (mem chair, 87-90); Int Coun Mus; Assoc Art Mus Dir. *Media:* Photography, Conceptual Art. *Publ:* Through the Sky in the Lake (photogs), Milkweed Editions, 90. *Mailing Add:* Minn Mus Art Landmark Ctr St Paul MN 55102-1486

CZARNOPYS, THOMAS J
PAINTER, SCULPTOR
b Grand Rapids, Mich, Dec 17, 57. *Study:* Sch Art Inst, BFA(art educ), 82. *Work:* Mus Contemp Art, Chicago; Wexner Ctr Arts, Columbus, Ohio; Milwaukee Art Mus, Wis; Grand Rapids Art Mus, Mich. *Exhib:* Solo exhibs, Grand Rapids Mus, Mich, 87, Contemp Arts Ctr, Cincinnati, Ohio, 88, Mus Contemp Art, Chicago, 88 & 89 & Va Mus Fine Arts, Richmond, 89; A Certain Slant of Light: The Contemporary American Landscape, traveling, Dayton Art Inst, Ohio, 89; Singular Spaces, Phenomenal Places, Contemp Arts Ctr, Cincinnati, Ohio, 89 & 91; The Nature of Sculpture, Jacksonville Art Mus, Fla, 91; About Landscape, Wexner Ctr Arts, Columbus, Ohio, 91; and others. *Teaching:* Vis artist, Sch Art Inst Chicago, 88 & Mich State Univ, East Lansing, 90. *Awards:* Nat Endowment Arts Fel Grant, 90; Ill Arts Coun Grant, 90. *Bibliog:* Lynne Warren (auth), Options 35: Tom Czarnopys, Mus Contemp Art, 88; Kathryn Hixson (auth), Latitudes: Focus on Chicago, Aspen Art Mus, 88; Sarah Rogers-Lafferty (auth), About Landscape, Wexner Ctr Arts, 91. *Media:* Mixed, Bronze. *Mailing Add:* c/o Zolla/Lieberman 325 W Huron Chicago IL 60610

CZESTOCHOWSKI, JOSEPH STEPHEN
MUSEUM DIRECTOR
b Brooklyn, NY, Aug 8, 50. *Study:* Univ Ill, Champaign-Urbana, BA, 71, MA, 73; Jagiellonian Univ, Cracow, Poland, dipl, 71. *Collections Arranged:* A Question of Regionalism, American Collections, Brooks Mem Art Gallery, Memphis, Tenn, 75; Arthur B Davies Retrospective, M Knoedler & Co, Inc, New York, 75; Polish Graphic Art & Design, Baltimore, 78; Charles Burchfield - Charles Rand Penney Collection, Mem Art Gallery, Rochester, 78; Marvin D Cone--Retrospective, Cedar Rapids Mus Art, 80; Atelier 17--New Directions, Cedar Rapids Mus Art, 81; Mauricio Lasansky, Cedar Rapids Mus Art, 82; Maurice Lasansky Collection-Selected Works, Cedar Rapids Art Asn, 86-87; James Swann-A Catalog Raisonne Chicago Soc Etchers, Prairie Print Makers, Woodcut Soc, Cedar Rapids Art Asn, Iowa, 89; Grant Wood & Marvin Cone Collection, Cedar Rapids Mus Art, 90; Mervin D Cone: Art As Self Portrait, Cedar Rapids Mus, 90; Grant Wood: Prints & Drawings, Cedar Rapids Art Asn, 91. *Pos:* Student asst, Krannert Art Mus, Univ Ill, 72; art ed, Perspectives Inc, Washington, DC, 72-75; cur collections, Brooks Mem Art Gallery, Memphis, Tenn, 73-75; dir, Decker Gallery, Md Inst, Col Art, 75-78; exec dir, Cedar Rapids Mus Art, 78- *Awards:* Fel Comt Relig & Art in Am, 76; Smithsonian Inst Foreign Currency Prog Res Award, 76-; Nat Endowment Arts, 1A Arts Coun, 78-; First Nancy Hanks Mem Award, Am Asn Mus, 85; Nat Endowment Arts Mus Fel, 86. *Bibliog:* Iowa's Young Successes, Des Moines Register, 8/7/83; Museum interview, Cedar Rapids Gazette, Iowa, 10/11/85; Building on a legacy, Horizon Mag, 3/86; Rev, Des Moines Regist, 12/3/89; Interview, The Iowan, fall 90. *Mem:* Am Asn Mus (sr examiner, Accreditation Comn); Am Asn Art Mus Dirs (mem, Future Directions Comt); Col Art Asn; Int Coun Mus; Am Coun Arts; Kosciuszko Found (exec finance comt & trustee); Polish Inst Arts & Sci in Am (trustee). *Res:* Nineteenth & early twentieth century American paintings, drawings and prints; contemporary American painters and printmakers; Polish art. *Publ:* Auth, Hassam Prints, Dover, 80; John Stewart Curry & Grant Wood, Univ Mo, 81; Am Landscape Tradition, E P Dutton, 82; Gerald Geerlings Graphics Catalogue, Cedar Rapids Mus Art, 83; Midwest sublime, Art News, 9/83; Marvin D Cone-An American Tradition, E P Dutton Inc, New York, 85; Graphics Catalogue Raisonne Arthur B Davies, Univ Del, 88; Robert Vickery, Kennedy Galleries, 10/90. *Mailing Add:* Cedar Rapids Museum Art 410 Third Ave SE Cedar Rapids IA 52401

CZIMBALMOS, MAGDOLNA PAAL
PAINTER, INSTRUCTOR
b Esztergom, Hungary. *Study:* Art Schs, Hungary & Ger. *Work:* Staten Island Mus, NY; Mus Int Inst, Detroit; Carnegie Inst Int Centennial, NY; Nat Gallery Budapest, Hungary; City Mus, Esztergom, Hungary. *Comn:* Portraits, Most Rev Daniel Ivancho & Nicholas Elko, Bishops, Msgr Ernest Dunda, Jacqueline Kennedy & family of Congressman John M Murphy, NY. *Exhib:* One-man shows, UN Plaza, New York, Pulitzer Gallery, New York, Univ Del, 80 & Le Salon, Paris & Monaco; and other group and one-man exhibs in US and abroad. *Pos:* Founder & dir, Hungarian Doll & Handicraft Factory, Reichenbach, Bavaria, formerly. *Teaching:* Czimbalmos Pvt Art Sch, 65- *Awards:* Staten Island Mus Gold Medal, 58, 62, 63, 66 & 69; Italian Cult Award, 67; Szinnyei Merse Gold Medal, New York, 71; City Award Esztergom, Hungary, 86. *Mem:* Pannonia World Orgn of Hungarian Artists (dir, currently); Staten Island Mus (dir exec bd, currently). *Mailing Add:* Czimbalmos Art Studio 31 Bayview Pl Ward Hill Staten Island NY 10304

CZIMBALMOS, SZABO KALMAN
PAINTER, EDUCATOR
b Esztergom, Hungary, 1914. *Study:* Royal Hungarian Acad Fine Arts, Budapest, grad, 36; also with J Haranghy & E Domanowsky, Vienna, Prague, Munich, Paris, London & Rome. *Work:* Nat Gallery Budapest; City Mus Esztergom, Hungary; Staten Island Mus, NY; Staten Island Community Col. *Comn:* Murals 32 churches US; Hungarian Govt & pvt owners. *Exhib:* Pulitzer Art Gallery, NY; Int Inst, Detroit; Univ Del, 80; Staten Island Mus; Le Salon, Paris; one-man shows & group exhibs in Hungary, Germany, France & Monaco. *Pos:* Owner, Czimbalmos Art Studio, Esztergom, 37-38, studio, Reichenbach, Ger, 45-49 & Staten Island, NY, 50-; art dir & partner, Hungarian Doll & Handcraft Factory, Reichenbach, formerly; art dir, Hungarian Relief, New York, 50; dir, Czimbalmos Pvt Art Sch, 55- *Awards:* Hungarian Art Award, Budapest, 34; Staten Island Mus Prize, 62, 64, 67 & 71; St Stephan Gold Medal, Pannonia Exhib, 71; City Award, Esztergom, Hungary, 85. *Mem:* Bavaryan Fine Art Soc; Staten Island Mus Art (vpres art sect, 61-62, pres, 63-64, exec bd, 63-75); Pannonia World Orgn Hungarian Artists (chmn bd dirs, 67-). *Media:* All. *Mailing Add:* Czimbalmos Art Studio 31 Bayview Pl Ward Hill Staten Island NY 10304

CZUMA, STANISLAW J
HISTORIAN, CURATOR
b Warsaw, Poland, Oct 26, 35; US citizen. *Study:* Jagiellonian Univ, BA & MA; Paderewski Found Scholar studies in India, 58-60; Nat Defense Foreign Lang Fel studies in India, 65-67; Banares Hindu Univ, with Vasudeva S Agrawala; Univ Calcutta, with S K Saraswati; Sorbonne, with Louis Renou; Univ Mich, with Walter Spink, PhD, 68. *Collections Arranged:* Cambodian Art, Asia Soc Gallery, New York (with catalog), 69; Permanent Indian Gallery, Brooklyn Mus; Indian Art from the George P Bickford Collection, Cleveland Mus (with catalog), 75; Kushan Sculpture, Seattle Mus (with catalog), 85-86 & Cleveland Mus & Asia Soc Gallery. *Pos:* Ford Found curatorial trainee, Cleveland Mus, 68-69; cur Oriental art, Brooklyn Mus, 69-72; cur Indian & Southeast Asian Art, Cleveland Mus, 72- *Teaching:* Res asst Oriental art, Univ Mich, Ann Arbor, 62-64; adj prof, Case Western Reserve Univ, 72- *Mem:* Asn Asian Studies; Asia Soc. *Res:* Art of India and early southeast Asia, especially Kushan, Gupta & Early Medieval India. *Publ:* Auth, Gupta style bronze Buddha, 2/70, A masterpiece of early Cambodian sculpture, 4/74, Mathura sculpture in the Cleveland Mus Collection, 3/77 & Mon-Dvaravati Buddha, 9/80, The School of Kashmiri Ivories, 10/88, Bulletin Cleveland Mus. *Mailing Add:* Cleveland Mus Art Asian Art Dept 11150 East Blvd Cleveland OH 44106

D

DABLOW, DEAN CLINT
PHOTOGRAPHER
b Superior, Wis, Aug 26, 46. *Study:* Univ Wis, Stevens Point, BS(educ), 69; Univ Iowa, MA, 72, MFA, 74. *Work:* New Orleans Mus Art, La; Kansas City Art Inst, Mo; Mus Art, Univ Okla; Corcoran Gallery, Washington, DC; Baltimore Mus Art. *Exhib:* One-man shows, Sioux City Art Ctr, Iowa, 79 & Project Art Ctr, Cambridge, Mass, 82; Photography in Louisiana 1900-1980, New Orleans Mus Art, 80; US Biennial, Mus Art, Univ Okla, 82; Louisiana Major Works, La World's Fair, 84; traveling exhib, A Century of Vision: La Photography 1884-1984; LaGrange Nat XI, Ga, 86; and others. *Teaching:*

Prof art, La Tech Univ, Ruston, 76- *Awards:* Artist Fel Grant Color Photog, La Arts Coun, 82; Purchase Award, 16th Ann Prints, Drawings & Crafts, Ark Art Ctr, 83 & LaGrange Nat XI, Ga, 86; Southern Arts Fedn/Nat Endowment Arts, Regional Photog, Fel, 87. *Bibliog:* Natalie Canavor (auth), Popular Photography, 4/83; Turner Browne & Elaine Partnow (ed), Photographic Artists & Innovators, MacMillan, NY, 83. *Mem:* Soc Photog Educ; Friends of Photog. *Media:* Silver Gelatin Photographs, Type C Color Photographs. *Publ:* Contribr, Creative Camera International Yearbook, Coo Press, London, 77; contribr, New Photographics/78 (cover), Cent Wash State Col, 78; contribr, Camera, C J Bucher Ltd, Lucerne, Switz, 9/81. *Mailing Add:* La Tech Univ Ruston LA 71272

DA CUNHA, JULIO
EDUCATOR, PAINTER
b Colombia, South Am, Mar 18, 29; US citizen. *Study:* Nat Univ Bogota, Colombia; Univ Fla, Gainesville, BA(archit), 52; Cranbrook Acad Art, Bloomfield Hills, Mich, MFA, 54. *Work:* Bloomsburg State Col, Pa. *Exhib:* Ann Regional Exhib, Del Art Mus, Wilmington, 56- & Univ Del, 61-; Four Del Artists, Del Art Mus, 64; Am Painters in Paris Bicentennial Exhib, France, 76; retrospectives, Haas Gallery, Bloomsburg State Col, Pa, 76 & Del Art Mus, 77. *Teaching:* Prof art, Univ Del, 56-91, prof emer, 91- *Awards:* Purchase Award, Univ Del, 63 & Del Art Mus, 62. *Bibliog:* A Profile: J Da Cunha, 71 & Clint Collins (auth), Paradoxes of J Da Cunha, 77, Del Today Mag. *Media:* Acrylic, Charcoal. *Mailing Add:* Univ Delaware Rm 001 413 Academy St Newark DE 19716

D'AGOSTINO, PELER
VIDEO ARTIST, EDUCATOR
b New York, NY, July 29, 45. *Study:* Acad Fine Arts, Italy, 65; Sch Visual Arts, New York, BFA, 68; San Francisco State Univ, MA, 75. *Work:* Artists Museum, Lodz, Poland; Long Beach Mus Art, Calif; Palais des Beaux-Arts, Charleroi, Belg; Nat Gallery Can, Ottawa; Mus Mod Art, New York. *Comn:* Performances: Angel Island, San Francisco Mus Mod Art, 77; Alpha Week of Int Performances, Mus Mod Art, Bologna, Italy, 77; San Francisco BART, San Francisco Mus Mod Art, 78; DC Metro, Washington Proj for Art, 79; Teletapes, TV Lab, WNET, New York, 81; STRING Cycles, Inst Contemp Art, Boston. *Exhib:* Solo exhibs, Mus Mod Art, San Francisco, 77, Mus Mod Art, New York, 79, Kitchen Ctr Video, Music & Dance, New York, 82, Franklin Furnace, New York, 83, Univ Art Mus, Berkeley, Calif, Inst Contemp Art, Boston, Philadelphia Art Mus; Time/Space/Sound: 1970's, San Francisco Mus Mod Art, 80; 1981 Biennial, Whitney Mus Am Art; Art Video: Perspectives and Retrospectives, Palais Beaux Arts, Belg, 83; Long Beach Mus Art, Calif, 84; Am Acad Rome, 86; Philadelphia Mus Art, 87; Electronic Arts Festival, Rennes, France, 88; Construction in process, Lodz, Poland, 90; Art NOW, Inst Contemp Art, Philadelphia, 91. *Pos:* Dir, Temple/London, 88; artist in residence, Television Laboratory WNET/Thirteen. *Teaching:* Instr art, Lone Mountain Col, 73-76 & San Francisco Art Inst, 76-77, San Francisco; asst prof art & art hist, Wright State Univ, Dayton, Ohio, 77-80; vis prof art, Univ NC, Chapel Hill, 82; prof commun, Temple Univ, 82-; fel, Ctr Advan Visual Studies, Mass Inst Technol, 83-85; vis artist, Am Acad Rome, 86; prof commun, Temple Univ, Philadelphia, currently. *Awards:* Nat Endowment Arts Awards, 74, 77, 79, 85 & 89; NY State Coun Arts Grant, 81; Pa Arts Coun Fel, 83 & 85; Japan Found Fel, 92; Pew Fel, Inst Arts, 92-93. *Bibliog:* Hal Fischer (auth), Cinematic Structures, Afterimage, summer 78; Paula Marincola (auth), Peter D'Agostino, review, Artforum, 11/87; David Tafler, (auth), The Circular Text: Interactive Video, Reception and Viewer Participation, Journal of Film and Video, summer 88. *Mem:* Col Art Asn Am; Int Network Arts. *Media:* Video, Film Photography. *Publ:* Contribr, Photography and Language, 76 & co-ed, Photography: The Problematic Model, 80, NFS Press; ed, Alpha, Trans, Chung: Semiotics, Film and Interpretation, Wright State Univ Press, 78; co-ed, The Un/Necessary Image, Mass Inst Technol-Tanam Press, 83; ed, Transmission, Tanam Press, 85; Essays, Alumination, 90. *Dealer:* Electronic Arts Intermix 536 Broadway New York NY 10012. *Mailing Add:* 523 Shoemaker Rd Elkins Park PA 19117

DAHILL, THOMAS HENRY, JR
PAINTER, EDUCATOR
b Cambridge, Mass, June 22, 25. *Study:* Tufts Col, BS, 49; Harvard Univ, summer 53; Sch Mus Fine Arts, Boston, dipl, 53, cert, 54; Skowhegan Sch Painting & Sculpture; Am Acad in Rome, fel, 55-57; Max Beckmann Gesellschaft, Murnau, Ger, resident, 56; Emerson Col, AM, 67. *Comn:* Mural, Unitarian Church, Brockton, Mass, 58; film strips, ser of paintings on Old & New Testaments, 61-62; film strip, life of George Washington Carver, 61; portrait, Dr Richard D Pierce, 74; drawing series on Madagascar, 83 & Bali, 85. *Exhib:* Boston Art Festival, 55, 56 & 63; Archit League, NY, 58; Int Bienale Relig Art, Salzburg, Austria, 58-59; Emerson Col, 64 & 67; Drawings of NAfrica exhibited through Mus Fine Arts Boston to galleries of New Eng prep schs, 67-69; St Botolph Club, 90. *Teaching:* Lectr gen art hist & contemp use of art in churches; instr hist art, Tufts Univ, 54-55 & 60-65; instr dept drawing, Sch Mus Fine Arts, Boston, 58-71; prof fine arts & chmn dept, Emerson Col, 67-, summer sch abroad, Europe, Africa & Asia, 67-82; guest, Minister of Cult, Moscow, USSR, summer, 74. *Awards:* Abbey Mem Fel to Am Acad in Rome, 55-57. *Mem:* MacDowell Colonists; Boston Ctr Arts; Soc Fel Am Acad in Rome; Medici Soc (dir, currently). *Media:* Acrylic on Canvas. *Mailing Add:* Emerson Col 100 Beacon St Boston MA 02116

DAHL, STEPHEN M
PHOTOGRAPHER
Study: Univ Wis-Eau Claire, BA, 71-75; Univ Wis-Madison, MA (social work), 78-79; Minneapolis Col Art & Design, Minn, 84-85; Film in the Cities, St Paul, Minn, 84-87; Visual Studies Workshop, Rochester, NY, 85. *Exhib:* Manifest Destiny, Unsettling America's Family Farmers, Light Factory, Charlotte,NC, 87; Time of the American Farm, Evanston Art Ctr, Ill, 88; Photograph as Document, Downey Mus Art, Calif, 89; Flashback: Ten years of Photography, Northfield Arts Guild Gallery, Minn, 90; Heartland: Regionalist Vision of the American Farm, Univ Art Mus, Univ Minn, 90; Black & White Photographs from My Goodhue Co Farm Family Documentary, 93. *Pos:* Social worker, Waushara Co Dept Social Servs, Wautoma, Wis, 75-78 & Hopkins Sch Dist, Minn, 79- *Awards:* Bush Artist Fel, St Paul, Minn, 90; Visual Arts Fel, Nat Endowment Arts, Washington, DC, 90; Minn State Arts Bd Photography Fel, St Paul, Minn, 92. *Mailing Add:* 1015 W 33rd St Minneapolis MN 55408

DAHLSTROM, NANCY GAIL
PRINTMAKER, PAINTER
b Buffalo, NY, Nov 29, 48. *Study:* State Univ NY, Buffalo, BFA, 70; Ohio Univ, MFA, 73. *Work:* Roanoke City Civic Ctr & Hollins Col, Roanoke, Va; Fed Reserve Bank Gallery & First & Merchants Bank, Richmond, Va; US Govt, 10 Foreign Embassies. *Exhib:* Solo exhib, Yard Quilts, Roanoke Mus Fine Art, 77; Papermaking & Paper Using, Southeast Ctr Contemp Art, Winston-Salem, NC, 79-80; 4 With Paper, traveling in Va, 79-80; Atelier Nord Etchers, Gallery F15, Jeløya Island, Norway, 82; Paperworks, Va Mus, Richmond & traveling, 82-84; Albright-Knox Gallery, Buffalo, NY, 85; Atelier Nord: 20 Years (with catalog), Galleri Aktuell Kunst, Oslo, 85; Contemporary Sculpture by Virginia Artists, Portsmouth Mus, Va, 85. *Teaching:* Assoc prof art, printmaking & drawing, Hollins Col, Roanoke, Va, 73- *Awards:* 2nd Place Printmaking, Allentown Exhib, Buffalo, NY, 72; 1st Prize Printmaking, Roanoke Mus Fine Art, Va, 75; Cabell Fel, One Year Travel & Art in Paris, Greece, Norway, 87-88. *Bibliog:* Heller (auth), Printmaking Slide Set, Crystal Publ, Aspen, Colo, 83; Annie Cheatham & Mary Clare Powell (auths), This Way Day Break Comes, New Soc Publ, 86. *Mem:* Col Art Asn. *Publ:* Illusr, article, in: Hand Papermaking Manual, Roanoke Valley Arts Coun, 79. *Mailing Add:* Dept Art Hollins Col Hollins College VA 24020

DAIGNEAULT, GILLES
CURATOR, CRITIC
b Montreal, Que, Apr 20, 43. *Study:* Univ D'Aix-Marseille, Doctorate es lettres, 70. *Collections Arranged:* L'art au Quebec Depuis Pellan, Musée Quebec, 88; F Sullivan & D Moore, Musée de Rimooski, 89; Montreal 1942-1992, Galerie de L'ugam, 92; Art Actuel-Présences Quebecoises, Château Biron, France, 92. *Pos:* Art critic, Soc Radio-Can, 78-89 & LeDevoir, Montreal, 82-88. *Mem:* Asn Int des Critiques D'Art (depuis, 80). *Publ:* Coauth, La Gravure au Quebec 1940-1980, Héritage, Montreal, 81; auth, L'Art au Quebec Depuis Pellan, Musée du Que, 88; coauth, Art Actuel-Présences Quebecoises, Paris, 92; coauth, Montreal 1942-1992, L'Anarchie Resplendissante de la Peinture, Univ du Que, 92. *Mailing Add:* 4596 Christophe Colomb Montreal PQ H2J 3G6 Canada

DAILEY, CHUCK (CHARLES ANDREW)
MUSEOLOGIST, PAINTER
b Golden, Colo, May 25, 35. *Study:* Univ Colo, BA(art), 61; study in Western Europe, 62-63. *Work:* Mus NMex Permanent Collection, Santa Fe; Vincent Price Collection, Hollywood, Calif; US Dept Interior, BIA Collection, Washington, DC. *Exhib:* Fiesta Biennial, 64 & 65 & Southwest Biennial, 68, Mus NMex; NMex State Fair, Albuquerque, 68; one-man show, Gallery 5, Santa Fe, 64; J F Kennedy Performing Art Ctr, Washington, DC, 73. *Collections Arranged:* Afro-Arabic World, 66-67, New Mexican Santero, 70-71 & World of Folk Costume, 71-72, Mus Int Folk Art, Three Culture-Sculpture Exhib & Rain Cloud Callers (Indian art), Fine Arts Mus & Spanish Endure (Spanish hist in Southwest), Palace of Governors, Mus NMex; Indian Arts & Crafts, J F Kennedy Ctr Performing Arts, Washington, DC, 73; One with the Earth traveling exhib, US & Can, 76- *Pos:* Mus preparator, Univ Colo Mus, Boulder, 59-61; exhibs tech, Mus Northern Ariz, Flagstaff, 62-63; cur-in-charge exhib div, Mus NMex, 64-71; mus workshop presentations, NMex, Alaska, Okla, Ariz & Wash & Smithsonian Inst. *Teaching:* Mus training dir, Inst Am Indian Arts, Santa Fe, 71- *Bibliog:* Catherine Wenzell (auth), Artists of Santa Fe, privately publ, 68. *Mem:* NMex Asn Mus; Am Indian Mus Asn; Am Asn Mus; Midwest Mus Asn; Far West Mus Asn. *Media:* Acrylic. *Publ:* Auth, Creating a Crowd, NMex Asn Mus, 72; auth, Bringing a unique perspective to museum work, Mus News, 5-6/77; auth, A selection of contemporary art by Native Americans from the Museum of the Institute of American Indian Arts, Ohio Univ Press, 81; auth, Major influences in the development of 20th century Native American art, 82 & Many ways of seeing: The anniversary of the Institute of American Indian Arts, 83, IAIA Press. *Mailing Add:* 64 Apache Ridge Rd Santa Fe NM 87505

DAILEY, DAN (DANIEL OWEN)
SCULPTOR, EDUCATOR
b Philadelphia, Pa, Feb 4, 47. *Study:* Philadelphia Col Art, BFA(glass), 69; RI Sch Design, MFA(glass), 72. *Work:* Corning Mus Glass, Metrop Mus Art, NY; Smithsonian Mus, Washington DC; Nat Gallery Victoria, Melbourne, Australia; Nat Mus Mod Art, Kyoto, Japan; High Mus Art, Atlanta, Ga; Philadelphia Mus Art; Los Angeles Co Mus Art; Boston Mus Fine Arts. *Comn:* Orbit cast glass relief (mural), Rainbow Room Rockefeller Ctr, 87; cast glass relief (mural), Marietta Mem Hosp, Ohio, 88; Parkman vase (glass & bronze) commemorating discovery Rubella vaccine comn by Paul Parkman, Kensington, MD, 88; Birds in Clouds (glass murals), comn by Dreyfus Corp, Swanke Hayden Connell Architects, 90; Sea Grass in Wind (12' x 16' cast glass mural), Northern Essex County Courthouse, 91. *Exhib:* One-man shows, Mass Inst Technol Gallery, 75 & 77, Theo Portnoy Gallery, New York, 77

& 79-82, Habatat Galleries, Detroit, Mich, 81, 83, 89 & 90, Heller Gallery, New York, 85, Betsy Rosenfield Gallery, Chicago, Ill, 86, 88 & 90, Habatat Galleries, Boca Raton, Fla, 87, 89 & 91, Rosenwald/Wolf Gallery, Philadelphia Col Art, Renwick Gallery, Smithsonian Inst, Washington, DC, 87, Kurland/Summers Gallery, Los Angeles, 88 & 90 & Kaplan Gallery, New York, 90; Craft Today USA, European Tour, Am Craft Mus, 89-90; Glass Now, Yamaha Corp Am, touring Japan, 90; 18th Ann Int Glass Exhib, Habatat Galleries, Farmington Hills, Mich; Lamporama, Bank of Boston Gallery and Artists' Found Gallery, Houston, 90; 1990 Economic Summit of Industrialized Nations, Rice Univ, Houston; The Venetians, Muriel Karasik Gallery, New York, 90; and others. *Pos:* Guest designer, Fabrica Venini, Murano, Venice, Italy, 72-73; designer & freelance artist, Cristallerie Daum, Nancy, France, 77- & Steuben Glass, New York, 82. *Teaching:* Teaching fel glass, RI Sch Design, Providence, 70-72; assoc prof glass, Mass Col Art, Boston, 73-, chmn three-dimensional fine arts dept, 74-79, dir glass prog, 74-; res fel sculpture & glass, Mass Inst Technol, 75-80; Pilchuck School, Stanwood, Wash, 77-; prof, Mass Col Art, currently. *Awards:* Fulbright-Hays Grant as Designer, Fabrica Venini, Murano, Italy, 72-73; Nat Endowment for the Arts Fel, 79; Masters Fel, Creative Glass Ctr Am, 89. *Bibliog:* Christine Temin (auth), The Art of the Lamp, The Boston Globe, 2/90; Karen Chambers (auth), Dan Dailey - A Designing Character, Neues Glas, 1/90; Marsha Miro (auth), Two approaches to glass: one sophisticated the other sophomoric, Detroit Free Press, 6/90; Jane Holtz Kay (auth), Architects expand use of glass art, New York Times, 7/90. *Mem:* Glass Art Soc Am (bd dirs, pres, chmn bd, 80, 81-82); Haystack Mt Sch of Crafts (bd trustees, 84-). *Media:* Glass, Metal. *Dealer:* Kurland/Summers Gallery 8742 A Melrose Ave Los Angeles CA 90069; Betsy Rosenfield Gallery 212 W Superior Chicago IL 60610. *Mailing Add:* 2 North Rd Kensington NH 03833

DAILEY, JOSEPH CHARLES See Jocda,

DAILEY, MICHAEL DENNIS
PAINTER, EDUCATOR
b Des Moines, Iowa, Aug 2, 38. *Study:* Univ Iowa, BA & MFA. *Work:* Smithsonian Inst, Washington, DC; Munic Gallery Mod Art, Dublin, Ireland; Seattle Art Mus, Wash; Mercyhurst Col, Erie, Pa; Mus of Mod Art, New York. *Exhib:* Art Across Am, San Francisco Mus Art, 65; Ultimate Concerns Drawing Exhib, Ohio Univ, Athens, 65; one-man shows, Tacoma Art Mus, Wash, 66 & 75, Fountain Gallery, Portland, 71, 73, 77, 81 & 84, Francine Seders Gallery, Seattle, 71, 74, 76, 78, 84, 87 & 90, William Sawyer Gallery, San Francisco, 72, 74, 76 & 82; Drawings USA, St Paul Art Ctr, Minn, 66 & 68; 73rd Western Ann, Denver Art Mus, Colo, 71; Art of the Pacific Northwest, Smithsonian Inst, 74; Am Acad & Inst Arts & Lett, New York, 86. *Teaching:* Prof drawing & painting, Univ Wash, 63- *Awards:* Purchase Award, Mercyhurst Nat Graphics Exhib, Erie, Pa, 65; First Place Award Painting, Wash State Ann Art Exhib, 67; Northwest Watercolor Soc Award, 30th Ann Northwest Watercolor Exhib, Seattle Art Mus, 70. *Media:* Acrylic, Oil. *Mailing Add:* c/o Francine Sedars Gallery 6701 Greenwood Ave N Seattle WA 98103

DAILEY, VICTORIA KEILUS
DEALER
b Los Angeles, Calif, Jan 21, 48. *Study:* Univ Calif, Los Angeles, BA, 70. *Collections Arranged:* Chemical Printing: The Invention of Lithography (auth, catalog), 80; The Poltroon Press: 10th Anniversary Retrospective (auth, catalog), 80; Joby Baker: Prints, Drawings Monotypes (auth, catalog), 80; Auguste Lepere Wood engravings (auth, catalog), 81; Terry De Lapp: Recent Still Life Paintings, 81. *Mem:* Printing Historical Soc; Bibliographical Soc Am; Rounce and Coffin Club, Los Angeles; Graphic Arts Coun; Antiquarian Booksellers Asn Am (bd govs, 80-). *Specialty:* 19th century prints and drawings, mainly French and English; art and illustrated books. *Publ:* Ed, Frijoles Canyon Pictographs, Pegacycle Press, 81; Henri Riviere, Peregrine Smith, 83. *Mailing Add:* 8216 Melrose Ave Los Angeles CA 90046

DAILY, EVELYNNE MESS
PAINTER, PRINTMAKER
b Indianapolis, Ind, Jan 8, 03. *Study:* Herron Sch Art, Ind Univ; Art Inst Chicago; Butler Univ; Ecole Beaux Arts, Fontainebleau, France, dipl; Wayman Adams Sch Portrait Painting, New York; also Bauhaus with Moholy-Nagy, Chicago; Colo State Christian Col, Hon PhD, 73. *Work:* Indianapolis Mus Art; Ft Wayne Mus; Richmond Art Asn; Libr Cong, Washington, DC; Philadelphia Mus Art. *Exhib:* Nat Acad Design, New York; Pa Acad Fine Arts; Brooklyn Mus, NY; Libr Cong Exhib Prints; Los Angeles Mus. *Teaching:* Instr drawing & painting, pub & pvt schs, Indianapolis, 40-60; instr painting & printmaking, Oxbow Acres Summer Art Sch, Brown Co, Ind, 64-80; etching & lithography, Wagmau Adams Summer Art Sch, Elizabethtown, NY. *Awards:* Honorable Mention, Ind State Art Exhibit, 80; Watercolor Prize & Print Prize, Ind Artist Club; J I Holcomb Prize for Painting, Herron Mus Art. *Bibliog:* Biography of George Jo Mess and Evelynne Mess Daily, Ind Hist Soc, 85. *Mem:* Nat Soc Arts & Lett; Ind Artists Club; Nat League Am Pen Women Inc; Hoosier Salon; Brown Co Art Gallery Asn Inc. *Media:* All. *Mailing Add:* 6237 Central Ave Indianapolis IN 46220

DALE, RON G
CERAMIST, SCULPTOR
b Spruce Pine, NC, Jan 26, 49. *Study:* Penland Sch, 71, 74 & 78; Goddard Col, Plainfield, Vt, BA, 77; La State Univ, Baton Rouge, MFA, 79. *Work:* John Michael Kohler Arts Ctr, Sheboygan, Wis; Asher-Faure Gallery, Los Angeles; Lockerbie Manufacturing Inc, Los Angeles. *Exhib:* Westwood Clay National, Downey Mus, Calif, 81; Betty Asher's Cups, Triton Mus, Santa Clara, Calif, 82; Still Lifes, Asheville Art Mus, NC, 83; solo exhib, Southeastern Ctr Contemp Art, Winston-Salem, NC, 83; Lagrange National, Lamar Dodd Art Ctr, Ga, 84; National Furniture Invitational, Am Crafts Coun, Tupelo Arts Ctr, Miss, 85. *Teaching:* Asst prof ceramics, Univ Miss, Oxford, 80-; vis instr ceramics, Penland Sch, NC, summer 85. *Bibliog:* Bova (auth), Ron Dale: Emerging talent, Nat Coun Educ Ceramic Arts J, 8/83; article, Ron Dale, Ceramics Monthly, 3/84; article, Paint on clay, Am Craft. *Mem:* Nat Coun Educ Ceramic Arts; Craftsmen's Guild Miss. *Media:* Clay, Wood. *Publ:* Auth, George E Ohr: Mad Biloxi Potter, Univ Miss, 83; George Ohr exhibition, Nat Coun Educ Ceramic Arts J, 83. *Dealer:* Martha Schneider Gallery 2055 Green Bay Rd Highland Pk IL 60035; Mario Villa Gallery 3988 Magazine St New Orleans LA 70115. *Mailing Add:* Rt 5, Box 76AA Oxford MS 38655

DALE, WILLIAM SCOTT ABELL
HISTORIAN, EDUCATOR
b Toronto, Ont, Sept 18, 21. *Study:* Univ Toronto, BA & MA; Harvard Univ, PhD. *Pos:* Res cur, Nat Gallery Can, Ottawa, Ont, 51-57; cur, Art Gallery Toronto, 57-59; dir, Vancouver Art Gallery, BC, 59-61; asst dir, Nat Gallery Can, 61-66, dep dir, 66-67; chmn, visual arts dept, Univ Western Ont, 67-75, 85-87. *Teaching:* Prof art hist, Univ Western Ont, 67-87. *Mem:* Col Art Asn Am; Medieval Acad Am; Royal Soc Arts; Int Ctr Medieval Art. *Res:* Romanesque ivories; sculpture of Chartres West; Exeter Cathedral. *Publ:* Contribr, Arts in Canada, 58; Oxford Companion to Art, 70; The British Museum Yearbook, 76. *Mailing Add:* Dept of Visual Arts Univ of Western Ontario London ON N6A 5B9 Canada

D'ALESSIO, GREGORY
CARTOONIST, PAINTER
b New York, NY, Sept 25, 04. *Study:* Art Students League, New York, with Walter Jack Duncan, Kimon Nikolaides & George Bridgman. *Work:* Syracuse Univ, NY; Univ Ill; Ohio State. *Exhib:* Metrop Mus of Art, New York; Gallery of Mod Art, New York; Mus of the City of New York. *Pos:* Vpres, Art Students League, New York, 37-44; syndicated cartoonist, These Women, 40-62. *Teaching:* Instr drawing, anat & compos, Art Students League, New York, 62- *Awards:* Am Soc Graphic Arts Award, 51; Reuben Award, Nat Cartoonists Soc, 61. *Mem:* Life mem Art Students League New York; life mem Soc Illusr New York; Nat Cartoonists Soc, New York (secy, 46-48); Soc Classic Guitar (vpres, co-ed, illusr, writer & Guitar Rev, 46-92. *Media:* Multimedia. *Publ:* Cartoonist & illusr, New Yorker, Esquire, Saturday Evening Post, Colliers, Look NY Times & many others; auth, Old Troubadour-Memoir Carl Sandburg, (Walker, 88). *Mailing Add:* 8 Henderson Pl New York NY 10128

D'ALESSIO, HILDA TERRY See Terry, Hilda

D'ALESSIO, NATALIE MARINO
PAINTER
b Elizabeth, NJ. *Study:* New York Univ, BA, 71; New Sch Social Res, 74; Summit Art Ctr, cert, 81; NJ Ctr Visual Arts; study with Philip Sherrod, Street Painters, New York; Accademia Bedriancense, Calvatone, Italy, Master Acad Art, 82. *Work:* Essex Co Div Aging, Orange, NJ; US Tang Soo Do Moo Duk Kwan Fedn Inc Mus, Springfield, NJ; Div Cult Affairs Essex Co, Newark, NJ; Soo Bahk Do Asn Hist Mus, Seoul, Korea. *Exhib:* European Banner Arts, Accad d'Europa, Calvatone, Italy, 84; Port History Museum Triennial, Philadelphia, 84; Nabisco Brands Inc Invitational, NJ, 85; Florence Art Gallery, Dallas, Tex, 86; Rosalyn Sailor Fine Arts, Philadelphia, PA & Margate, NJ, 90, 91 & 92. *Pos:* Cur & dir, Corridor Case Exhibition, Summit Art Ctr Mus, NJ, 79-81, dir, art forum, 80-86. *Teaching:* Instr advan painting, Union Col Cont Educ, Cranford, NJ, 81-82, Riker Hill Art Park, Livingston, NJ, 83-86; instr art, Union Bd Educ, Union Co, NJ, 84-86. *Awards:* Bee Co Award, Pastel Soc Am, 81; Gold Medal, European Banner Arts, Calvatone, Italy, 84; Ludwig Vogelstein Found Grant, 85-86; Union County Art Grant NJ State Coun Arts, 89. *Bibliog:* R DuBois (auth), D'Alessio brings feeling to the 2-Dimensional canvas, Art Voices South, 3-4/79; Rochelle Holt (auth), D'Alessio on cities and nudes, Art Workers News, 4/79; E Forman Singer (auth), rev, World Press, 81. *Mem:* Artists Equity; Women's Caucus Art; Riker Hill Art Asn, Livingston, NJ (steering comt, 84-86, secy, 85-86). *Media:* Pastel, Oil. *Publ:* Contribr, Masters Published in Gold, Nat Res Study Ctr, Calvatone, Italy, 83; illusr, Valhalla 6 Lifespan, Merging Media. *Mailing Add:* PO Box 225 Springfield NJ 07081

DALEY, WILLIAM P
CERAMIST
b Hastings-on-Hudson, NY, Mar 7, 25. *Study:* Mass Col Art, BS; Columbia Univ Teachers Col, MA. *Work:* Philadelphia Mus Art; St Louis Mus, Mo; Everson Mus Art, Syracuse; Los Angeles Co Mus; Victoria & Albert Mus, London. *Comn:* Ceramic screen abacus, comn by Int Bus Machines Corp, Seattle World's Fair, 61; ceramic & copper modular wall, SAfrican Airlines, New York, 70; ceramic wall, Fairfield Maxwell Corp, New York, 72; ceramic screen (10ft x 20ft), Ritz Theatre, Philadelphia, 78; Baptismal font, St Pauls, Elkon Park, Pa, 89. *Exhib:* Philadelphia: Three Centuries of Am Art, Philadelphia Mus Art, 76; A Century of Ceramics in the United States, Everson Mus, Syracuse & Renwick-Smithsonian, DC; American Ceramics Now, Everson Mus, 88; Craft Today USA, Mus des Art Decoratifs, Paris, France, 89; Hartland Gallery, Philadelphia, Pa, 90. *Pos:* Mem adv bd clay studio, Philadelphis & Haystack Sch Crafts, 90. *Teaching:* Prof ceramics & design, Philadelphia Col Art, 57-, chmn crafts dept, 66-69, prof emer; guest prof ceramics, Univ NMex, 72. *Awards:* Distinguished Achievement Arts Award, Mass Col Art, 80; First distinguished university professor, Univ Arts, Philadelphia Col Arts & Design, 89; Distinguished Teaching of Art Award, Col Art Asn of Am, 91. *Bibliog:* Garth Clark (auth), American Potters - the

work of twenty modern masters, Keramik der Welt, Gottfried Borman, 81; Peter Dormer, article in The New Ceramics, 86; article in Am Ceramics, 8/2/90. *Mem:* Hon life mem, Nat Coun Educ Ceramic Arts. *Media:* Clay. *Publ:* Auth, Notes on sources: A presentation, Nat Coun Educ Ceramic Arts J, Vol 1, No 1, 80; On drawing, Am Ceramics, Vol 1, No 1, 82; The geometry of residence, Nat Coun Educ Ceramic Arts J, Vol 4, 83. *Dealer:* Drutt Gallery 1721 Walnut St Philadelphia PA 19103; Drutt Gallery 724 50th Ave New York NY 10010. *Mailing Add:* 307 Ashbourne Rd Elkins Park PA 19117

DALGLISH, JAMIE (JAMES PARSONS)
PAINTER, VIDEO ARTIST
b Bryn Mawr, Pa, May 7, 47. *Study:* Art Acad Cincinnati (scholar), 70; RI Sch Design, BFA, 74; Nat Ctr Experiments TV, San Francisco, Calif, 74. *Work:* Chase Manhattan Bank, New York; Sydney & Francis Lewis Wing, Va Mus, Richmond. *Comn:* Painting, comn by Mr & Mrs Stephen Abramson, New York, 82. *Exhib:* Eight from New York, State Univ Stony Brook, NY, 80; solo exhib, Port Washington Pub Libr, NY, 80; Signs, Semiotics, Behavior (video), Mus Art, RI Sch Design, Providence, 82; Video-USA, Centre d'Art Contemporain, Geneva, Switz, 84; King Lear's High Theatre of Sovereign Immunity-Come (T) Here (video), Limelight, New York, 86. *Bibliog:* Attanasio di Felice (auth), Jamie Dalglish, Flash Art, 1-2/81; Robert Kleyn (auth), The shadow reflected, ZG, fall 84; Gary Indiana (auth), New & different, Village Voice, 1/7/86; Jerome Davis (auth), Talking heads, Vintage Mag Series, 86. *Mem:* ASCAP. *Media:* All. *Dealer:* O K Harris Gallery 383 W Broadway New York NY 10012. *Mailing Add:* 52 Bond St New York NY 10012

DALGLISH, MEREDITH RENNELS
SCULPTOR, EDUCATOR
b Bryn Mawr, Pa, Apr 15, 41. *Study:* Goddard Col, Plainfield, Vt, BA, 65; Claremont Grad Sch, Claremont, Calif, MFA, 83. *Work:* Gallery Contemporanea, Jacksonville, Fla; Deland Mus Art, Fla; Albertson-Peterson Gallery, Orlando, Fla; Stetson Univ, Deland, Fla. *Comn:* Mementoes in In-Laws (film), Los Angeles, Calif, 80; sculptures, Sheraton, Scottsdale, Ariz; sculptures, comn by Ralp Rudin, Los Angeles, Calif, 84, & Bill Bailey, Beverly Hills, Calif, 85; wall sculptures, Design Continuum, Atlanta, Ga, 90. *Exhib:* Westwood Ceramics Invitational, Downey Mus, Calif, 82; Ceramics Nat Invitational, Scripps Col, Claremont, Calif, 84; Dimensions, Los Angeles Co Mus Art, Calif, 85; Sculpture Carved & Forged, Tampa Mus, Fla, 87; 100 Year Nat Asn Women Artists Celebration, Jacob Javits Ctr, New York, 89; Spotlight '89, Univ Fla, Gainesville, 89. *Pos:* Co-dir, Venice Ceramics Gallery, Calif, 77-78; dir, Ibis Fine Arts Gallary, Pasadena, Calif, 84-85; dir/cur, Ormond Mem Art Mus, Ormond Beach, Fla, 86-87; founder, dir, Inst Women & Creativity. *Teaching:* Assoc prof, ceramics, Rio Hondo Col, Whittier, Calif, 84; prof, ceramics, Daytona Beach Community Col, Fla, 87-88; art specialist, art appreciation, Volusia Co Schs, Deland, Fla, 89-90; prof, Miami-Dade Community Col, Fla, 90-92. *Awards:* Award Merit, Elizabeth Kittrell, Westport, Conn, 60; Artistic Merit, Ruth Chenven, New York, 89. *Bibliog:* Judy Chicago (auth), The Dinner Party, Anchor Doubleday, 79; Mac McCloud (auth), Trends in clay, Artweek, 8/82; J Demetrakas (dir), Right Out of History: The Making of the Dinner Party (film). *Mem:* Nat Asn Women Artists, New York; Women's Caucus Arts; Nat Soc Multi-Layerists; Nat Coun Educ Ceramic Arts; Col Art Asn. *Media:* Mixed-media. *Publ:* Contribr, Old Market Craftsmen Cookbook, Ree Schonlau, 82; auth, Ron Fondaw (catalog), Ormond Mus, 87; Art in America, Letters, 7/92. *Dealer:* Albertson-Peterson Gallery 329 Park Ave S Winter Park FL 32789. *Mailing Add:* 8860 SW 112 St Miami FL 33176

DALLAS, DOROTHY B
PAINTER, PRINTMAKER
b New York, NY. *Study:* Watercolor study with Ed Whitney, 78-80; Pratt Inst, Brooklyn, NY, BFA, 79, MFA, 81. *Work:* Bergen County Freeholders, Courthouse, Hackensack, NJ. *Exhib:* Solo show, NJ Artists Series, Johnson & Johnson World Hq, NB, 88; Landscapes by Member Artists, Katonah Mus Art, NY, 88; 100 Years/100 Works Centennial Traveling Exhib, Islip Mus & others, 89; Hudson River Regional Watercolor Exhib, Woodstock Art Asn, NY, 89; NJ Watercolor Soc 50th Ann Exhib, Montclair Mus, NJ, 89. *Pos:* Guest cur, watercolor exhib, Art Ctr N NJ, Ordell, 76. *Awards:* Grumbacher Medallion, Nat Asn Women Artists 99th Ann, Colo, 88; First Prize, Hudson River Regional Watercolor Exhib, Woodstock Art Asn/Ulster County Art Asn, 89; Adrienna Lahn Best Floral Painting Award, Catharine Lorillard Wolfe Art Club, 89. *Mem:* Art Ctr Watercolor Affiliates (founder, 78, secy, 78-86, pres, 86-90); New Jersey Watercolor Soc (prospectus chmn, 81-); Catharine Lorillard Wolfe Art Club, Inc (bd dirs, 82-88, 1st vpres, 88-89, pres, 89-92); Nat Asn of Women Artists (corresp secy, 85-89). *Media:* Watercolor. *Mailing Add:* 378 Eastwood Ct Englewood NJ 07631

DALLMANN, DANIEL FORBES
PAINTER, PRINTMAKER
b St Paul, Minn, Mar 21, 42. *Study:* St Cloud Univ, BS, 65; Univ Iowa, MA, 68, MFA, 69. *Work:* Nat Collection Fine Arts, DC; Art Inst Chicago; Yale Univ Art Mus, New Haven, Conn; Chemical Bank, New York; J B Speed Art Mus, Louisville, Ky; and others. *Exhib:* Solo exhibs, Robert Schoelkopf Gallery, New York, 80-87, Recent Figure Works, The Cols, Geneva, NY, 88 & J Rosenthal Fine Arts, Chicago, 89; Contemporary Self Portraits, Allan Frumkin Gallery, New York, 82; New Vistas: Contemporary American Landscape, Hudson River Mus, NY & Tucson Mus Art, Ariz, 84; Conjuring Reality: The Paintings and Drawings of Daniel Dallman and Paul Wiesenfeld, J B Speed Mus Art, Louisville, Ky, 84; American Realism: Twentieth Century Drawings & Watercolors, San Francisco Mus Mod Art, 85; Realism Today, Nat Acad Design, New York, 88; The Landscape Observed, Md Inst, Baltimore, 90. *Teaching:* Prof drawing & printmaking, Tyler Sch Art, 69- *Awards:* Visual Arts Fel, Pa Coun Arts, 87. *Media:* Acrylic, Oil; All Media. *Dealer:* Tatistcheff & Co 50 W 57th St New York NY 10019. *Mailing Add:* 205 Oakland Pl North Wales PA 19454

D'ALMEIDA, GEORGE
PAINTER
b Paris, France, June 30, 34; US citizen. *Exhib:* Rolly-Michaux Gallery, New York, 79, 81, 83 & 86 & Boston, 80, 82 & 86; one-man exhib, Venice Biennial, 88; Galleria Rotta, Genoa, 77, 80 & 89; Galleria La Bussola, Turin, 89; and others. *Media:* Acrylic, Watercolor. *Dealer:* Galleria Schneider Rampa Mignanelli 10 Rome Italy; Fairweather Hardin Gallery 101 E Ontario Chicago IL 60611. *Mailing Add:* Casina di Selvole 53017 Radda in Chianti Siena Italy

DALY, KATHLEEN (KATHLEEN DALY PEPPER)
PAINTER
b Napanee, Ont, May 28, 1898. *Study:* Ont Col Art, assoc, with Arthur Lismer, J E H MacDonald & J W Beatty; Acad Grande Chaumiere, Paris; Ont Col Art; also woodcuts with Rene Poitier, Paris. *Work:* Nat Gallery Can, Ottawa, Ont; Art Gallery Ont, Toronto; Banif Libr & Archive Can Rockies, Ont; McMichael Mus, Kleinburg, Ont; Dept Northern Affairs, Ottawa. *Comn:* Portraits, comm by Dr Thomas Cullen, Baltimore, 41, Premier Herbert Greenfield, 46 & Senior Hach, Tetuan, Morocco. *Exhib:* Group of Seven, 31; Brit Empire Exhib, 37-38; Great Lakes Exhib, 38-39; New York World's Fair, 39; Ann, Ont Soc Arts, Royal Can Acad & Can Group Painters. *Awards:* Gold Medal, Academia Italia delle Arti e del Lavoro, 81. *Bibliog:* Life in Eskimoland, London Press, 62. *Mem:* Royal Can Acad; Ont Soc Artists; Toronto Helicomian Club; Zonta Club Toronto; Can Group Painters. *Media:* Oil, Crayon; Lithograph. *Publ:* Co-illusr, Kingdom of Saguenay, 36; illusr, North, Dept Northern Affairs, 62; auth, Morrice, Clarke, Irwin, Toronto, 66. *Mailing Add:* 561 Avenue Rd Apt 1101 Toronto ON M4V 2J8 Canada

DALY, NORMAN
PAINTER, SCULPTOR
b Pittsburgh, Pa, Aug 9, 11. *Study:* Univ Colo, BFA; Ohio State Univ, MA; grad study, Paris, Inst Fine Arts & NY Univ. *Work:* Rochester Mem Art Gallery, NY; Herbert F Johnson Mus Art, Ithaca, NY; Everson Mus Art, Syracuse; Univ Wash, Seattle; St Paul Mus Art, Minn; Wooster Col & Oberlin Col, Ohio; Munson-Williams-Proctor Inst, Utica, NY; Ithaca Col, NY. *Comn:* Stained glass windows, Mt Savior Monastery, Pine City, NY; bas-relief, Meditation Rm, Student Union, NY State Univ Col Cortland. *Exhib:* One-man shows, Akron Art Mus, 72; Indianapolis Art Mus, 73; Römisch-Germanisches Mus, Cologne & City Hist Mus, Boctium, Ger,74; Inst Contemp Art, Univ Pa & Tyler Sch Art, Temple Univ, 80 & 81, Philadelphia; Roberson Art Ctr, 82; Rotterdam Coun Arts Touring Exhib, Holland, 83; Rochester Mem Art Gallery, NY; State Univ NY, Albany. *Teaching:* Prof art, Cornell Univ, 42- *Awards:* Yaddo Fel, 71 & 76; Nat Endowment Arts Fel, 74; Cornell Distinguished Teaching Award, 81; and others. *Bibliog:* Charles Michener (auth), The fabulous Llhuroscians, Newsweek, 2/28/72; Kenneth Evett (auth), Llhuros, New Repub, 1/12/72; David Galloway (auth), The Civilization of Llhuros, Cleveland, 9/72. *Publ:* Illusr, Epoch, 71; contribr, Abrazas Press, 72; auth, The Civilization of Llhuros, 72; Llhuros-Eine Entdeckte Kiltur-1974; Leonardo, Pergamon Press, Oxford, Eng, Vol 3, 91. *Mailing Add:* 110 N Quarry St Ithaca NY 14850

DALY, STEPHEN JEFFREY
SCULPTOR, EDUCATOR
b Governors Island, NY, July 4, 42. *Study:* San Jose State Univ, Calif, BA, 64; Cranbrook Acad Art, Mich, MFA(sculpture), 67. *Work:* Oakland Art Mus, Calif; Tex A&M Univ; Am Acad Rome, Italy; Bank San Antonio; Shasta College, Redding, Calif; McNey Mus, San Antonio, Tex. *Exhib:* 85th San Francisco Art Inst Ann, M H DeYoung Mem Mus, Calif, 65; Objects USA, Smithsonian Mus, Washington, DC, 69; The Metal Experience, Oakland Art Mus, Calif, 71; one-man shows, Am Acad, Rome, 75, Triton Mus, Santa Clara, Calif, 77, William Campbell Contemp Art, Ft Worth, Tex, 87 & 89-91 & McNay Art Mus (catalog), San Antonio, Tex, 88; Group shows, Texas Currents, San Antonio Art Inst, 86 & New Sites-New Work, San Jose Inst Contemp Art, 86, The Blue Star Exhib, Blue Star Space, San Antonio, Tex, 86, Third Coast Review, Aspen Art Mus, Aspen, Colo, 87, The Art of Cast Iron, Univ Ala, Birmingham, 88, Another Reality (catalog), Hooks-Epstein Galleries Inc, Houston, Tex, 89 & A Century of Sculpture in Tex (catalog), Archer M Huntington Art Gallery, Univ Tex, Austin, 89; Hooks-Epstein Galleries, Houston, Tex, 91; & many others. *Pos:* Art & archit Panel, Tex Comn Arts, Austin, 80-82; coordr, 4th Tex Sculpture Symposium, 81-83. *Teaching:* Univ Minn, Minneapolis, 67-69, Humboldt State Univ, 69-79, Univ Tex, San Antonio, 79-81, Univ Tex, Austin, 81- *Awards:* Prix de Rome, Am Acad Rome, Italy, 75; Louis Comfort Tiffany Award Sculpture, 77; Centennial Fel Fine Arts, Univ Tex, Austin, 83-84 & 88-91. *Bibliog:* Howard Smagula (auth), Texas Currents (catalog), San Antonio Art Inst, 85; Annette Carlozzi (auth), Third coast rev: a look at Tex art, Aspen Art Mus, Colo, 88; Susie Kalil (auth), Stephen Daly, McNey Mus (exhib catalog), 88. *Media:* Metals, Cast. *Mailing Add:* Univ Tex Dept Art Austin TX 78712-1285

DAMAST, ELBA CECILIA
PAINTER
b Pedernales, Venezuela, Aug 11, 44. *Study:* Escuela Eloy Palacios, Maturin, Venezuela, BA, 59; Escuela Arturo Michelena, Valencia, MFA, 62. *Work:* Escuela Arturo Michelena, Gobernacio DF, Caracas, Biblioteca Del Estado, Valencia & Galeria El Parke, Valencia, Venezuela; Venezuelan Consulate, New York. *Exhib:* Salon Arturo Michelena, Valencia, 71; Joven Actualidad

Venezolana, Studio Actual, Caracas, Venezuela, 71; 24th New Eng Exhib, Silvermine Guild, New Canaan, Conn, 73; Spanish Am Painters & Sculptors, Bronx Mus, New York, 74, Brooklyn Mus, 75 & Metrop Mus Art, New York, 76; NY Bot Garden Mus Show, Bot Garden, New York, 76. *Awards:* Premio, Arturo Michelena, Cristobal Rojas, 71. *Bibliog:* Tibisay Useche (auth), Talentos d Emitierra, Carabobeno, Venezuela, 70; Rafael Rondon Tarchetti (auth), Arte en New York, Valencia, 76. *Media:* Acrylic. *Mailing Add:* 253 W 28th St New York NY 10001

D'AMATO, JANET POTTER
ILLUSTRATOR, CRAFTSMAN
b Rochester, NY. *Study:* Pratt Inst; Harriet FeBland Workshop. *Exhib:* Art Dir Club, New York, 89. *Awards:* Merit Award, Dimensional Illusr Inc, 89. *Bibliog:* Anne Commire (auth), Something About the Author, Gale Publ, 75; Carmel Marchionni (auth), Lifestyles, Westchester Gannett Publ, 75 & 77; D Russo (auth), article, Westchester Spotlight. *Media:* Acrylic, Collage; Paper Sculpture. *Res:* Primitive and folk art and crafts, American Indian and African. *Publ:* Auth & illusr, Gifts to Make for Love or Money, Golden, 73; Colonial Crafts for You to Make, Messner, 75; Quillwork, Craft of Paper Filigree, 75 & Italian Crafts, 77, Evans; Indians, 79; Horns, Bones and Antlers, Messner, 82; illusr, Ecology Basics, Prentice Hall, 86. *Mailing Add:* 32 Bayberry St Bronxville NY 10708

DAMAZ, PAUL F
WRITER, ARCHITECT
b Portugal, Nov 8, 17; US citizen. *Study:* Ecole Speciale Archit, Paris, France, BA(arch); Inst Urbanisme, Sorbonne, Paris, MA(town planning). *Pos:* Coun mem, Arts Acquisition Comt, State Univ NY Stony Brook, 70; dir, Fine Arts Fedn New York, 72-75. *Teaching:* Design critic archit, Columbia Univ, 52-53. *Awards:* Arnold Brunner fel, Archit League New York, 58. *Bibliog:* Anne Le Crenier (auth), Names, Archit & Eng News, 67. *Mem:* Am Inst Archits; Am Inst Planners; Ordre Architectes, France; Archit League New York; Munic Arts Soc. *Res:* Integration of art in modern architecture; art in public spaces. *Collection:* Contemporary art, mostly North and Latin American. *Publ:* Auth, Art in European Architecture, 56 & Art in Latin American Architecture, 62, Van Nostrand Reinhold. *Mailing Add:* 302 E 88th St New York NY 10028

DAN, LARS
PAINTER
b Copenhagen, Denmark, Feb 27, 60. *Study:* Royal Danish Sch Art, 79-84. *Work:* State Art Found, Denmark; State Mus Art, Denmark; N Jutland Mus Art, Denmark. *Exhib:* One-man shows, Himmerlands Art Mus, Aars, Denmark, 90, Gallery XII, Stockholm, Sweden, 91-92, Hall Fine Arts, Copenhagen, Denmark, 91, Int Art Expo, Hamburg, Ger, 91, Aalborg Hist Mus, Denmark, 92, Gallery Anette Gullberg, Cologne, Ger, 92 & Gallery Scag, Copenhagen, Denmark, 92; Fiac, Grand Palais, Paris, France, 87-88; 17 Artristes Danois, Camler Found, Paris, France, 88; Vejen Art Mus, Denmark, 90; N Jutlands Mus Art, Aalborg, Denmark, 92; and others. *Media:* All. *Publ:* Illusr, Desire, 83, A Place in the Unknown, 87, auth, Feberfrost, 89, Brudulje, 90, Lars Dan, Ninka, 91 & illusr, Selected Poems, 92, Borgen. *Mailing Add:* c/o Rodi Karkazis Gallery 168 N Michigan Ave No 300 Chicago IL 60601

DANBY, KEN
PAINTER, PRINTMAKER
b Sault Ste Marie, Ont, 1940. *Study:* Ont Col Art, Toronto, 58-60. *Work:* Nat Gallery Can, Ottawa, Ont; Mus Mod Art, New York; Montreal Mus Art, PQ; Art Inst Chicago; Univ Calif Art Gallery, Berkeley. *Comn:* Designer Series III Can Olympic Coins 1976 Olympics, Montreal. *Exhib:* Living Am Artists & the Figure, Pa State Univ, 74; 3rd Bienal Americana de Artes Graphicas, Colombia, 76; Aspects of Realism, Rothman's Touring Can Exhib, 76-78; Can Sport Art Collection, Olympics, Montreal, 76; 1st Bienniel Am Graphics, Maracibo, Venezula, 77; and others. *Pos:* Bd dirs, Can Coun, 85-91; bd trustees, Nat Gallery Can, 91-94. *Awards:* First Recipient of R Tait McKenzie Chair for Sport 1975, Nat Sport & Recreation Ctr, Ottawa; Ont Arts Coun Eds Award, 76; Queen's Can Silver Jubilee Medal, 77. *Bibliog:* Rex Bromfield (producer), Ken Danby (film), 71; Paul Duval (auth), High Realism in Canadian Art, Clarke-Irwin, 74; Paul Duval (auth), Ken Danby, Clarke-Irwin, 76. *Mem:* Royal Can Acad Arts. *Media:* Egg Tempera, Watercolor; Serigraphy, Silkscreen. *Mailing Add:* RR No 4 Guelph ON N1H 6J1 Canada

DANCE, ROBERT BARTLETT
PAINTER, PRINTMAKER
b Tokyo, Japan, May 31, 34; US citizen. *Study:* Philadelphia Col Art, with Henry C Pitz & W Emerton Heitland. *Work:* NC Mus Fine Art, Raleigh; R J Reynolds Indust, Winston-Salem, NC; Hanes Dye & Finishing, Winston-Salem; Miss Mus Art, Jackson; Wachovia Bank & Trust, Winston-Salem. *Exhib:* Mystic Int, Conn, 86; Arts for the Parks, Smithsonian Inst, Washington, DC, 87; Artist's Sketchbooks, Southeastern Ctr Contemp Art, 88; one-man retrospective, Southeastern Ctr Contemp Art, 91; Mystic 100, Conn, 92. *Awards:* First Place, NC Watercolor Soc, 73, 74 & 77, Assoc Artists Winston-Salem, 72, 73 & 74; Smithsonian Inst, Washington, DC, 87. *Bibliog:* Susan E Meyer (auth), 40 Watercolorists and How They Work, Watson-Guptill, 76 & Sir Isaac Pitman & Sons Ltd, Great Brit, 76; Wendon Blake (auth), The Alkyd Painting Book, Watson-Guptill. *Mem:* NC Watercolor Soc; Assoc Artists Winston-Salem. *Media:* Watercolor, Alkyd; Woodcut. *Publ:* Illusr, Things Invisible to See, Advocate Publ Group, 79; The Medium is the Message, Am Artist, 79; Yankee Mag, 9/80; Printing Atmospheric Effects, Am Artist, 85; Artist Mag, London, Eng, 1-2/88; plus others. *Dealer:* Southeastern Ctr for Contemp Art 750 Marguerite Dr Winston-Salem NC 27106; Mystic Seaport Gallery Mystic CT. *Mailing Add:* 320 Anita Dr Winston-Salem NC 27104

D'ANDREA, JEANNE
CONSULTANT, EDITOR
b Chicago, Ill, Dec 9, 25. *Study:* Art Inst Chicago; Colo Col, with Rico Lebrun; Univ Chicago, with Joshua Taylor, Ulrich Middledorf & Carlos Castillo, PhB & MA. *Collections Arranged:* Gericault, Los Angeles Co Mus Art, 71; Women Artists: 1550-1950, 76; Treasures of Mexico, 78; and others. *Pos:* Designer sets, costumes, Turnau Opera Co, NY & Arlington Opera Theatre, Arlington, Va, 59-72; head dept educ, Ringling Mus Art, Sarasota, Fla, 60-62; coordr exhibs & publ, Los Angeles Co Mus Art, 69-81, ed & design consult, 81- *Mem:* Col Art Asn Am. *Mailing Add:* 547 Alandele Ave Los Angeles CA 90036

DANE, BILL (WILLIAM THATCHER DANE)
PHOTOGRAPHER, PAINTER
b Pasadena, Calif, Nov 12, 38. *Study:* Univ Calif, Berkeley, BA(art & polit sci), 64 & MA(painting), 68. *Work:* Mus Mod Art, New York; Nat Gallery Can, Ottawa. *Exhib:* One-man shows, Painting, Sculpture, Snapshots, Reese Palley Gallery, San Francisco, 70, Unfamiliar Places, A Message from Bill Dane, Mus Mod Art, New York, 73, Ctr Creative Photog, Univ Ariz, Tucson, 76 & De Young Mus, San Francisco, 77; Landscape Discovery, Hofstra Univ, Long Island, NY, 73; Recent Am Still Photog, Edinburg Art Ctr, Scotland, 76; Concerning Photog, Photogr Gallery, London, 77. *Awards:* Fel in Photog, Guggenheim Mem Found, 73-74 & 82; Nat Endowment for the Arts photog fel, 76-77. *Publ:* Contribr, The Snapshot, Aperture Publ, 74; contribr, On Time, Mus Mod Art Calendar, 75. *Mailing Add:* 1065 Talbot Ave Albany CA 94706

DANE, WILLIAM JERALD
LIBRARIAN
b Concord, NH, May 8, 25. *Study:* Drexel Inst Technol, MLS; NY Univ Inst Fine Arts; Sorbonne, Paris, France; Attingham Park Summer Sch, Eng; Palladio Studies, Vicenza, Italy, 80; Victorian Soc Summer Sch, London, 81, Philadelphia, 83, Glasgow, 91. *Collections Arranged:* Fine Print Collection, Newark Pub Libr; 150 Years of Graphic Art in New Jersey; Silkscreen, A Survey Show of Serigraphs & Screenprints for the NJ State Coun on Arts; Prints by Joseph Pennell; Posters & Prints form Puerto Rico, 1950-1990; Contemp Am Prints, 1989; Hidden Treasures: Japanese Art Libr, 91; Glorious World Bk Illus, 92. *Pos:* Supvr art & music libr, Newark Pub Libr, 67-90; supvr spec collections, Newark Pub Libr, 91- *Mem:* Victorian Soc Am (nat bd mem, 74-80, chmn NY chap, 72-74); Victorian Soc (co-chair educ comm, 90); Newark Arts Coun (bd mem, 81-90); Art Libr Soc NAm (treas, 86-88); ARLIS; NJ State Coun Arts (Essex Co block grant juror, 88-). *Publ:* Auth, Picture Collection Subject Headings, 69; contribr, Arts in America: A Bibliography, Smithsonian Inst Press, 79; auth, Networking and the art library, Drexel Libr Quart, fall 83; John Cotton Dana: A Contemporary Appraisal of his Contributions & Lasting Influence on the Library & Museum Worlds, 90; The History of Fine Printing in Newark, 88. *Mailing Add:* Five Washington St Newark NJ 07101

DANHAUSEN, ELDON
SCULPTOR, EDUCATOR
US citizen. *Study:* Art Inst Chicago, James Nelson Raymond Foreign Traveling Fel, BFA, 47. *Work:* Hackley Art Gallery, Muskegon, Mich; Civic Ctr, New Orleans, La; Standard Club Chicago; Roosevelt Univ, Chicago. *Comn:* Sculpture, Int Minerals & Chem Corp, Skokie, Ill, 60; sculpture, Home Mutual Appleton, Wis, 63; sculpture, WOC TV, Davenport, Iowa, 64; sculpture, Civic Ctr, New Orleans, 67; sculpture, 150 N Wacker Dr Bldg, Chicago, 71. *Exhib:* Downtown Gallery, New York; Chicago Ann Show, Art Inst Chicago, 45-60; Rivinia Festival Art Exhib, 57, 59 & 60; American Business & the Arts, San Francisco Mus Art, 61; Sculpture 70, Art Inst Chicago, 70. *Teaching:* Prof emer, Art Inst Chicago, currently. *Awards:* Linde Co Prize, Chicago Ann Show, Art Inst Chicago, 60; Citation for Art in Architecture, Am Inst Archit Iowa Chap, 63. *Bibliog:* Meilach & Kowal (auth), Sculpture Casting, Crown; Meilach (auth), Contemporary Stone Sculpture, Crown; Meilach (auth), Creative Carving, Reilly & Lee. *Publ:* Auth, Art in the market place, sculptor's viewpoint, Chicago Mkt Scene, 3/70; contribr, Contemporary Stone Sculpture, Crown. *Mailing Add:* 1418 N LaSalle Dr Chicago IL 60610

DANIELS, ASTAR (CHARLOTTE LOUISE DANIELS)
PAINTER, STAINED GLASS ARTIST
b Fostoria, Ohio, Nov 27, 20. *Study:* Toledo Mus Sch of Design, 50-52; pvt study with colorist, Emerson Burkhart, Columbus, Ohio, 52-54; Univ Cincinnati, Ohio, AA(summa cum laude), 77. *Work:* Gallery of Findlay Col, Ohio; Gallery of Anne T Case Sch, Akron, Ohio; Gallery of Brown Univ, Providence, RI; Gallery of Defiance Col, Ohio; Ohio Youth Bldg, Columbus, Ohio. *Comn:* Bapistry mural, comn by Mr & Mrs W J Poorman, Forest, Ohio, 53; choir loft mural, Buckland Congregational Christian Church,Ohio, 54; hereford mural, comn by Mr Jason Miller, Forest, Ohio, 57; outside mural, comn by Mr & Mrs Joseph Newhard, Carey, Ohio, 58. *Exhib:* Toledo Area Artists' Exhib, Toledo Art Mus, Ohio, 52-55; Columbus Art League Exhib, Columbus Art Mus, Ohio, 53; First Duo-Sister Show Gallery 8, Toledo Art Mus, Ohio, 55. *Pos:* Dir of art, Ohio State Fair, Columbus, Ohio, 55-57. *Teaching:* Private lessons in Forest & Cincinnati, Ohio, 50-66; dir/instr art, Defiance COl, Ohio, 56-57; instr art/drama, Methodist summer camp, Sabina, Ohio, 60-64. *Bibliog:* Emma Fundaburk & Thomas Davenport (coauths), Art in Public Places in the United States, Bowling Green Univ Popular Press, 75. *Media:* Oil; Leaded Stained Glass. *Publ:* Auth & illusr, Aiming in His Direction, Capozzolo, 71. *Mailing Add:* 3740 Drakewood Dr Cincinnati OH 45209

DANIELS, DAVID M
COLLECTOR, PATRON
b Evanston, Ill, Apr 10, 27. *Study:* Yale Univ; Curtis Inst Music. *Pos:* Trustee & accessions comt, Minneapolis Inst Fine Arts, 65-; pres, Drawing Soc, 71-79. *Collection:* 19th Century drawings paintings & sculpture. *Publ:* Contribr, Drawings of Morris Graves, New York Graphics, 73. *Mailing Add:* 4 Sutton Pl New York NY 10022

DANIELS, LINDA
PAINTER
b Tampa, Fla, Sept 16, 54. *Study:* Calif Col Arts & Crafts, Oakland, BFA, 75. *Exhib:* Solo exhibs, fiction/nonfiction, New York, 88, 89, 91 & 93; There is a Light that Never Goes Out, Amy Upton Gallery, New York, 91; Bedroom Pictures, Asher-Faure Gallery, Los Angeles, 92. *Awards:* Fel Painting, Nat Endowment Arts, 91. *Bibliog:* Shirley Kaneda (auth), Painting and Its Others: In the Realm of the Feminine, Arts Mag, p 58-64, summer 91; Alisa Tager (auth), Colors, Lapiz Int Art Mag, no 80, p 62-65, 91; Robert Mahoney (auth), There is a light that never goes out, Arts Mag, 4/92. *Mailing Add:* c/o fiction/nonfiction 21 Mercer St New York NY 10013

DANIELSON, PHYLLIS I
ADMINISTRATOR, TAPESTRY ARTIST
b Marion, Ind. *Study:* Ball State Univ, BA(art), 53; Mich State Univ, MA, 60, EdS, 66; Ind Univ, EdD, 68; Kendall Col Art & Design, Hon DFA, 89. *Work:* Mint Mus Art, Charlotte, NC. *Exhib:* Weatherspoon Gallery, Greensboro, NC, 69 & 70; Stitchery, Pa, 71 & Iowa, 75; Matrix Gallery, Bloomington, Ind, 72; one-person shows, Jewish Community Ctr, Indianapolis, Ind, 72 & Eye-Opener Gallery, Cincinnati, Ohio, 72; Mint Mus Art, 74; Herron Art Gallery, Indianapolis, 74; Sloane O'Stickey Gallery, Cleveland, Ohio, 74; Women in Art, West Bend, Wis, 76. *Pos:* Pres, Kendall Col Art & Design, Grand Rapids, 76-; consult, mus & arts orgns, Danielson/Gillie & Assoc. *Teaching:* Asst prof art, Ball State Univ, Muncie, Ind, 66-67; asst prof art educ, Univ NC, Greensboro, 68-70; assoc prof educ & art, Herron Sch Art, Indianapolis, 70-76. *Awards:* Mich Woman of the Yr Arts Award, 84. *Bibliog:* Kathleen Fisher (auth), Women in Action. *Mem:* Nat Art Educ Asn; Nat Coun Art Adminr; Nat Asn Sch Art; Col Art Asn. *Media:* Fabric, Fiber. *Publ:* Auth, Art for the Second & Third Grades, Kimball/Hunt, 66; Paper mache and the elementary teacher, Arts & Activities, 12/70; Selected teacher characteristics of art student teachers , Studies Art Educ, winter 71; The woman administrator in art, Col Art J, 76; and others. *Mailing Add:* 6137 Chamonix Ct SE Grand Rapids MI 49516

DANK, LEONARD D
ILLUSTRATOR, CONSULTANT
b Birmingham, Ala, Dec 21, 29. *Study:* Cornell Univ, BA, 52; Sch Med Illus, Mass Gen Hosp, Boston, cert, 55; Art Students League; Jules Laurents Studio, New York. *Work:* McGraw-Hill Publ Co, New York; Stravon Educ Press Inc, New York; H S Stuttman Co Inc, Conn; Proj-in-Health, NJ; Doubleday & Co Inc, New York; PW Communications, NJ; Contemp Orthopaedics, Calif. *Comn:* The Brain in Hypertension Parts I & II (animated films), Merck, Sharp & Dohme, 78; Drug Induced Movement Disorders (animated film), Dupont Pharmaceuticals, 83; health & fitness posters, Esquire Mag, 85-88. *Exhib:* Art of Medicine Exhib, Soc of Illustr, 86. *Pos:* Staff artist, Plastic Surgery Clin, Manhattan Eye & Ear Hosp, New York, 55-57 & Eye Bank for Sight Restoration, New York, 57-59; owner, Leonard Dank Studio, New York, 59-61; owner, Medical Illus Co, New York & Cutchogue, NY, 61-; consult med illusr, St Luke's-Roosevelt Hosp Ctr, New York, 61-83, Contemp Orthopaedics Publ, 81-83; consult med illusr, Harper & Row, Publ, NY, 82-, PW Commun Inc, NJ, 82-86, Esquire Mag Health & Fitness Clinic, NY, 85-88 & Whittle-Time Commun Inc, 88- *Awards:* First Prize Motion Picture, Am Col Surgery, 59 & 62; Better Teller Award, Asn Indust Advertisers, 73; Outstanding Children's Sci Book Award, Nat Sci Teachers Asn, 82; Cert Merit, Soc of Illus, 86. *Mem:* Asn Med Illusr; Guild Natural Sci Illusr. *Media:* Multi. *Publ:* Coauth, Clinical Obstetrics & Gynecology, 73-76, Gynecologic Operations, 78, Harper & Row; illusr, The Male His Body, His Sex, Anchor Press/Doubleday, 79; Dr Fishbein's Illustrated Medical Encyclopedia, 79 & Every Woman's Health 80, 82, & 85, Doubleday & Co; Electromagnetic Spectrum 79, Jupiter 81 & Space Colony 82, elsever-Nelson; Principles of Human Anatomy, 83, 86, 90 & 92, Principles of Anatomy & Physiology, 84, 87, 90 & 92, Introduction to Human Body, 88, 90 & 92, Harper Collins. *Mailing Add:* PO Box 944 Cutchogue NY 11935

DANLY, SUSAN
CURATOR, HISTORIAN
b Chicago, Ill, July 27, 48. *Study:* Univ Wis, Madison, BA, 71; Brown Univ, MA, 77, PhD, 83. *Collections Arranged:* The Railroad in the American Landscape (with catalog), 81; Shadow Catchers: Photographs of Native Americans from the Huntington Collections (with catalog), 85; Prints & Drawings American West, 85; The Modern Poster: American Graphic Design in the 1890's, 85; Early Pasadena Artists, 86. *Pos:* Asst cur am art, The Huntington Libr, 84-86, assoc cur, 86- *Teaching:* Vis fac am art, Univ Calif, Los Angeles, 85. *Mem:* Col Art Asn; Am Studies Asn. *Res:* 19th Century American Art with speciality in history of photography. *Publ:* Auth, Edward Weston in Los Angeles, Huntington Libr, 86; The Railroad in American Art, MIT Press, 87. *Mailing Add:* Pennsylvania Acad Fine Arts 118 N Broad St Philadelphia PA 19102

DANOFF, I MICHAEL
MUSEUM DIRECTOR, WRITER
b Chicago, Ill, Oct 22, 40. *Study:* Univ Mich, BA, 62; Univ NC, Chapel Hill, MA, 64; Syracuse Univ, PhD, 70. *Collections Arranged:* Art in Our Time, travelling exhib, 80; Image in American Painting & Sculpture: 1950-1980 (co-auth, catalog), Akron Art Mus, 81; Cindy Sherman, Inc, 83; Robert Mangold, 84; Jeff Koons (auth, catalog), 88; Gerhard Richter: Painting (co-auth, catalog), Mus Contemp Art, Chicago, 88; Peter Halley Paintings, Des Moines Art Ctr, Ind, 92. *Pos:* Cur collections, Dickinson Col, 70-73; cur, Michener Collection, Univ Tex, 73-74; cur collections & exhibs, Milwaukee Art Ctr, 74-80; assoc dir chief cur, Milwaukee Art Mus, 74-80; dir, Akron Art Mus, 80-84, Mus Contemp Art, Chicago, 84-88, San Jose Mus Art, 88-91 & Des Moines Art Ctr, 91- *Teaching:* asst prof 19th & 20th Century & contemp art, Dickson Col, 70-73, Univ Tex, Austin, 73 & Univ Wis-Milwaukee, 75-80. *Awards:* Nat Endowment Arts Mus Prof Fel, 73. *Bibliog:* Rev, NY Times, 10/2/77; Helen Cullinan (auth), Italianate-Palazzo-Post Office, Art News, 9/81; Hilton Kramer (auth), An audacious inaugural, NY Times, 9/20/81; cover story, Arts & Books section, San Jose Mercury News, 11/20/88. *Mem:* Col Art Asn Am; Midwest Art Hist Soc; Am Asn Mus; Asn Art Mus Dir; Ill Arts Alliance (trustee, 86-88). *Res:* Contemporary art history & criticism. *Publ:* Auth, Gallery Guides to Collections, Milwaukee Art Ctr, 74-75; Mary Nohl: sophisticated naive, Midwest Art, 75; Europe in the Seventies, Art in Am, 1/78; Paintings that make your retinas dance, Art News, 11/81; Art and Commodities, Affinities and Intuitions: The Gerald S Elliott Collection of Contemporary Art, The Art Institute of Chicago/Thomas & Hudson, Chicago/New York, 90. *Mailing Add:* Des Moines Art Center 4700 Grand Ave Des Moine IA 50312

DANTZIC, CYNTHIA MARIS
EDUCATOR, PAINTER
b Brooklyn, NY, Jan 4, 33. *Study:* Bard Col, 50-52; Yale Univ, with Josef Albers & Jose de Rivera, BFA, 55; Pratt Inst, MFA, 63. *Work:* Brooklyn Mus; Adelphi Univ Gallery; Univ Mass Gallery, Amherst; Edson Tool Bldg, Belleville, NJ. *Comn:* Modular paintings, New York Soc Gen Semantics, 68 & Springbok Ed, Kansas City, Kans, 74; stained glass windows, Church Resurrection, Lakeland, Fla, 75; portrait Mary Susan Miller, Berkeley Inst, Brooklyn, 79; Above and Beyond (ed photog collages), Brooklyn Art & Cult Asn, 83. *Exhib:* Solo exhibs, Modular Paintings, East Hampton Gallery, New York, 66 & The Expanded Field, Resnick Gallery, Long Island Univ, 83; The Wit of It, Delgado Mus, New Orleans, 72; Affect-Effect, La Jolla Mus Art, 79; Interior-Exterior, 80 & 100 New Acquisitions, 81, Brooklyn Mus; Common Ground: New York Abstract, Galerie Arts Visuels, Que, 82. *Collections Arranged:* Art Festival for NAACP Legal Defense (auth, catalog), Brooklyn Mus, 63. *Teaching:* Asst prof art, Brooklyn Ctr, Long Island Univ, 65-70, assoc prof, 70-75, prof, 75-, dir dept, 77-79, chmn, 80-86; assoc prof (adj), Cooper Union, 92. *Awards:* Stipend Award Animation, Brooklyn Art & Cult Asn, 82; Newton Award for Excellence in Teaching, 88; Trustee Award for Scholarly Achievement, Long Island Univ, 90. *Bibliog:* Talk of the town, New Yorker, 5/28/66; Marie Avona (auth), Cynthia Dantzic, multi-media artist, Pratt Reports, 6/79; Herbert Keppler (auth), Expand your view: Cynthia Dantzic's photo collages, Mod Photog, 1/84. *Mem:* Col Art Asn; Am Asn Univ Prof. *Media:* Acrylic, Pencil. *Publ:* Auth, A teacher of art looks at education, Gen Semantics Bulletin, 64; auth & illusr, Stop Dropping Bread Crumbs on My Yacht, 74, Sounds of Silents, 76 & Design Dimensions: An Introduction to the Visual Surface, 90, Prentice-Hall; auth, An invitation to the butterfly ball, New York Times Book Rev, 5/76; illusr, Biography, Confrontation, Long Island Univ, 79. *Mailing Add:* 910 President St Brooklyn NY 11215

DANZIGER, AVERY C
PHOTOGRAPHER
b Chapel Hill, NC, June 25, 53. *Work:* Bibliot Nat, Paris; Corcoran Gallery Art & Nat Mus Am Art, Washington, DC; Mus Mod Art, New York; Stedelijk Mus Mod Art, Amsterdam. *Exhib:* Hot Shots, Southeastern Ctr Contemp Arts, Winston-Salem, NC, 79; New Acquisitions, Corcoran Gallery, 81; Color as Form: A History of Color Photography, Int Mus Photog, Rochester, NY, 82; 20th Century Contemp Photog, Seibu Mus, Tokyo, 83; one-man shows, Arco Ctr Visual Arts, Los Angeles, 83 & Ctr Contemp Arts, Santa Fe, 83. *Teaching:* Instr photog, Los Angeles Harbor Col, 81-82, East Los Angeles Community Col, 81-82 & Univ Calif, Los Angeles Exten, 82. *Awards:* Purchase Award, 39th Ann Artists Exhib, NC Mus Art, 76; Nat Endowment Arts Fel, 79; Photog Competition Award, Reynolds Industries, 79. *Bibliog:* Suzanne Muchnic (auth), Avery Danziger's art about art, Los Angeles Times, 2/1/80; Neal Menzies (auth), Visions of empathy, Artweek, 10/31/83; MaLin Wilson (auth), article, Art Lines, 10/83. *Mem:* Soc Photog Educ. *Media:* Cibachrome. *Dealer:* McLain/Davis Gallery 2818 Kirby Dr Houston TX 77098. *Mailing Add:* PO Box 30169 Columbia MO 65205

DANZIGER, FRED FRANK
PAINTER
b Pittsburgh, Pa, Feb 24, 46. *Study:* Pa Acad Fine Arts, cert, 70. *Work:* Philadelphia Mus Art; Pa Acad Fine Arts, Philadelphia; Ashville Mus Art, NC; Wichita Art Mus, Kans; Woodmere Art Mus, Philadelphia. *Exhib:* Art & the Law, Minn Mus Art, Minneapolis, 79; Recent Acquisitions, Noyes Mus, Oceanville, NJ, 86; Fel Ann, Pa Acad Fine Arts, Philadelphia, 88; Fel Ann, Michener Mus, Doylestown, Pa, 90; Recent Acquisitions, Woodmere Art Mus, Philadelphia, Pa, 92; Statewide Ann, State Mus Pa, Harrisburg, 92. *Awards:* Tiffany Grant, Nat Competition, Tiffany Found, 73; Alexander Prize, Painting Ann, Cheltenham Art Ctr, 89; Coyne Prize, Woodmere Painting Ann, Woodmere Mus, 92. *Bibliog:* Nicholas Roukes (auth), Acrylics Bold & New, Watson-Guptil, 87; Anna B Francis (auth), The road to recognition, Am Artist Mag, 91; Edward Sozanski (auth), On art's healing edge, Philadelphia Inquirer, 91. *Mem:* Fel Pa Acad Fine Arts (treas, 80-84). *Media:* Acrylic, Oil. *Publ:* Auth, The Alone Ranger & Other Paintings, pvt publ, 79; What does big art have against nature, Philadelphia Inquirer, 91. *Dealer:* Rodger PaPelle Galleries 122 N Third St Philadelphia PA 19106. *Mailing Add:* RD No 7 211 Lafayette Rd Coatesville PA 19320

DANZIGER, JOAN
SCULPTOR
b New York, NY, June 17, 34. *Study:* Cornell Univ, BFA, 54; Art Students League, 54-55; Acad Fine Arts, Rome, cert art, 56-58. *Work:* Nat Mus Am Art, Smithsonian Inst, Washington, DC; Jacksonville Mus Arts & Sci, Fla; Nat Mus Womens Art, Washington, DC; NJ State Mus, Trenton; New Orleans Mus Art, La. *Comn:* Suspended sculpture, Md Fine Arts Comn & Frostburg State Col, Md, 75; two sculptures, AFL-CIO Labor Studies Ctr, Silver Springs, Md, 76; three sculptures, Convention Ctr, Washington, DC, 85; five sculptures, comn by George Taylor, Dist Ct, Md, 90; Columbia Hosp, Wash. *Exhib:* 26th St Playground Show, Baltimore Mus Art, 72; Suspended Sculptures, New Orleans Mus Art, 73; one-man shows, Jacksonville Mus Art & Sci, 79, Fendrick Gallery, Wash, 79, Terry Dintenfass Gallery, New York, 80, Joy Horwich Gallery, Chicago, 82, NJ State Mus, Trenton, 82, Benjamin Mangel Gallery, Philadelphia, 84, La World Expos, New Orleans, 84, Textile Mus, Wash, 85, Nat Mus Women Arts, 87, San Antoio Art Ctr, 87; Images of the Seventies, 9 Washington Artists, Corcoran Gallery, DC, 80; A New Bestiary, Va Mus Fine Arts, Richmond, 81; Animal Images-Contemporary Objects & The Beast, Nat Mus Am Art, Washington, DC, 81; NJ State Mus, Trenton, 82; Joy Horwich Gallery, Chicago, 82; Rutgers Univ, New Brunswick, NJ, 83; La World Exposition, New Orleans, 84; Ben Mangel Gallery, Philadelphia, Pa, 84; Textile Mus, Washington, DC, 85; Osuna Gallery, Washington, DC, 90. *Pos:* Visual arts panelist, DC Comn Arts & Humanities, 74-80. *Teaching:* Vis artist, lectr, Smithsonian Inst, 80-82; artist-in-residence, AFL-CIO Labor Studies Ctr, 75; visual arts panelist, DC Community Arts & Humanities, 74-79, 84-85; sculpture panelist, NJ State Coun Arts, 82. *Awards:* Nat Endowment Arts Grant, 75; Int des Arts, Paris, Grant, 86. *Bibliog:* Constance Dodge (auth), Fantasy Sculpture, Albany News, NY, 78; Maryse Pailla (auth), Profile, Art Voices, 81; Joanna Shaw Eagle (auth), American women in sculpture, Harpers Bazaar, 81; Cynthia Nadelman (auth), article, Art News, 80; Michael Welzenbach (auth), The Magical Menagerie, Washington Post, 84; Virginia Watson-Jones (auth), Contemporary American Women Sculptors, 86. *Mem:* Artists Equity; Washington Sculptors Group; Int Sculpture Ctr; Sculpture Source. *Media:* Mixed-Media Sculpture. *Dealer:* Osuna Gallery 1919 Q St NW Washington DC 20036; Benjamin Mangel 1714 Rittenhouse Sq Philadelphia PA 19103. *Mailing Add:* 2909 Brandywine St NW Washington DC 20008

DAPHNIS, NASSOS
PAINTER, SCULPTOR
b Krokeai, Greece, July 23, 14; US citizen. *Work:* Mus Mod Art, New York; Whitney Mus Am Art, New York; Albright-Knox Gallery Art, Buffalo; Carnegie Inst, Pittsburgh; Hirshhorn Mus. *Comn:* Wall paintings, City Walls Inc, 70 & Nat Endowment Arts, 71; art environment, Arlen Realty Develop Corp, 71. *Exhib:* One-man exhibs, Mint Mus, Charlotte, NC, 49, Leo Castelli Gallery, New York, 59-, Work Since 1951, Albright-Knox Mus, Buffalo, NY, 69, Everson Mus, 69 & Andre Zarre Gallery, New York, 74 & 76; Corcoran Gallery Biennial, 59, 63 & 69; Ann Exhib Painting, Whitney Mus Am Art, 59, 61, 64, 65 & 67; Purist Painting, 61 & Geometric Abstraction in America, 62, Walker Art Ctr; Am Abstract Expressionists & Imagists, Guggenheim Mus, 61; Ann Exhib Sculpture & Drawing, Whitney Mus Am Art, 62; Highlights of the 68-69 Season, Aldrich Mus, 69; Pittsburgh Int, Carnegie Inst, 70; Birmingham Festival Art, Birmingham Mus Art, 76; Provincetown Painters 1890s-1970s, Everson Mus Art, 77; and many other one-man shows. *Awards:* Nat Found Arts & Humanities Award, 66; Nat Endowment Arts Grant, 71; Guggenheim Mem Found Fel, 77. *Bibliog:* Hilton Kramer (auth), The Corcoran Biennial, 2/23/69 & 12 artists join in an uncommon show, 3/18/71, NY Times. *Mem:* Am Abstract Artists. *Media:* Epoxy, Plexiglas. *Dealer:* Leo Castelli Gallery 420 W Broadway New York NY 10012. *Mailing Add:* 362 W Broadway New York NY 10013

DAR, DINA
PAINTER
b Poland, Feb 1, 39, US citizen. *Study:* Calif State Univ, Northridge, BA; Art Ctr Col Design, Los Angeles; Otis Art Inst, Los Angeles (painting); Chouinard Art Sch, Los Angeles (ceramics); Inst Psychology Jean Jacques Rosseau, Univ Geneva with Jean Piaget. *Work:* Balch Inst Ethnic Studies, Philadelphia; Int Mus Photg, George Eastman House, Rochester, NY; Hebrew Union Col, Skirball Mus, Los Angeles & Cincinnati; Museo Int de Electrografia, Cuenca, Spain. *Comn:* 300 Xerography Prints/Electroworks, Xerox Corp, Rochester, NY, 79; Xerography Prints-commemorating Martin Luther King, City Los Angeles, Dept Cult Affairs, 86. *Exhib:* Biennial Int Copy Art, Univ Valencia, Spain, 88; 20th Bienal Int, Sao Paulo, Brazil, 89; Group A-Z Electro Images, Mus Vasarely, Budapest, Hungary, 91; California Artists Books, Armory Ctr Arts, Pasadena, 91; solo exhib: A Loop of Fate, Skirball Mus, Los Angeles, 92; and others. *Awards:* First Prize, Painting, Anniversary of Israel, 73; Master Artist, Pasadena, Geisen Trust, 82. *Bibliog:* A D Coleman (auth), Light readings, Camera Mag, 2/80; Klaus Urbans (auth), Copy Art, DuMont Buchverlag Koln, Ger, 91; Suzanne Muchnic (auth), Dina Dar fashions Life's Fateful Loop into Art, Los Angeles Times, 5/3/92. *Media:* All. *Publ:* Contribr, Loop of Fate (catalog), Hebrew Union Co, Skirball Mus, 92. *Mailing Add:* 3573 Adamsville Ave Calabasas CA 91302

DARBOVEN, HANNE
CONCEPTUAL ARTIST, GRAPHIC ARTIST
b Munich, Ger, Apr 29, 41. *Study:* Hochscule for Bildende Kunst, Hamburg. *Work:* Stedelijk Mus, Amsterdam, Holland; Kaiser Wilhelm Mus, Krefeld, WGer. *Exhib:* Eight Contemp Artists, Mus Mod Art, New York, 74; one-person shows, Leo Castelli Gallery, New York, 73-75, 78 & 80, Kabinett fur Akutelle Kunst, Bremerhaven, Kunstmuseum, Basel, Switz, 74-75, Stedelijk Mus, 75 & Kunstmuseum Lucerne, Switz, 75; Projekt 74, Kunsthalle, Cologne, 74; and others. *Bibliog:* J Collins (auth), Reviews: Hanne Darboven, Castelli Downtown, 9/73, Lucy R Lippard (auth), Hanne Darboven: Deep in numbers, 10/73 & Max Kosloff (auth), Transversing the field: eight contemporary artists at Museum of Modern Art, Artforum, 12/74. *Publ:* Contribr, 6 Manuskripte 69, Kunstzeltung, Dusseldorf, 69; auth, Ein Jahrhundert, Amsterdam, 71; Words, Avalanche, springm 72. *Mailing Add:* c/o Leo Castelli Gallery 420 W Broadway New York NY 10012

D'ARCANGELO, ALLAN M
PAINTER
b Buffalo, NY, June 16, 30. *Study:* Univ Buffalo, AB(hist), 52; City Col New York; Mexico City Col. *Work:* Whitney Mus Am Art, Mus Mod Art, New York; Albright-Knox Mus, Buffalo; Gemeente Mus, The Hague; Joseph H Hirshhorn Mus, Washington, DC; Mus Mod Art, Nagaoka, Japan; Musees Royaux des Beaux-Arts de Bruxelles, Belgium; Wolrasf-Richardt Mus, Cologne, Ger; Metrop Mus Art, New York. *Comn:* mural, New York Worlds Fair, 63; mural, Bullfinch Bldg, Boston, Mass, 70; poster, Olympic Games, Munich, 72; Paintings US Dept Interior, 73; Bicentennial poster & print, Mobil Oil, 75. *Exhib:* One-man show, Albright-Knox Art Gallery, Buffalo, NY; New Forms, Stedelijk Mus, Amsterdam, Holland, 66; L'art Vivant Am, Found Maeght, St Paul de Vence, France, 69; Inaugural exhib, Va Mus Fine Arts, Richmond, 85-86; Pop Art: USA-UK, Odakyu Grand Gallery, Tokyo, Japan, 87; Made in USA: Art from the 50s & 60s, Univ Art Mus, Berkeley, Calif, 87. *Teaching:* Instr painting, Sch Visual Arts, New York, 63-68, Cornell Univ, 68, Syracuse Univ, 71 & Univ Wis, 72; prof art & grad fac, Brooklyn Col, 73-; grad fac, Sch Visual Art, 83- *Awards:* Artist-in-residence, Aspen Inst Humanistic Studies, 65 & 67; Nat Inst Arts & Lett Ann Award, 70; John Simon Guggenheim Fel, 1987-88. *Bibliog:* N Calas (auth), Icons and Images of the Sixties, Dutton, 71; Dore Ashton (auth), A Reading in Modern Art, Case Western Reserve Univ, 69; Lawrence Alloway (auth), Topics in American Art since 1945, Norton, 75. *Mem:* Soc Am Graphic Artists; City Walls Inc. *Media:* Acrylic, Oil. *Mailing Add:* PO Box 33 Kenoza Lake NY 12750

DARLING, SHARON SANDLING
MUSEUM DIRECTOR, HISTORIAN
b Mitchell, SDak, Feb 28, 43. *Study:* NC State Univ, BA; Duke Univ, MAT; Winterthur Summer Inst, Am Dec Arts. *Pos:* Cur dec arts, Chicago Hist Soc, 75-86; dir, Motorola Mus, 86- *Awards:* Charles F Montgomery Prize, Decorative Arts Soc, 85. *Res:* Decorative arts of Chicago and the Midwest; industrial arts. *Publ:* coauth (with Gail Farr Casterline), Chicago Metalsmiths, 77; Chicago Ceramics and Glass, 80; Chicago Furniture, 84; TECO: Art Pottery of the Prairie School, 89. *Mailing Add:* c/o Motorola Museum 1307 E Algonquin Rd Schaumburg IL 60194

DARR, ALAN PHIPPS
CURATOR
b Kankakee, Ill, Sept 30, 48. *Study:* Northwestern Univ, BA, 70; Inst Fine Arts, NY Univ, MA, 75, PhD(art hist), 80; Metrop Mus Art, cert mus training, 76; Univ Calif, mus mgt, 80; Harvard Univ, Ctr Italian Renaissance Studies, Villa I Tatti, Florence, postdoctoral fel, 88-89. *Pos:* Grad intern, Metrop Mus Art, New York, 76; asst cur, Detroit Inst Arts, 78-80, assoc cur, 80-81, cur in charge European sculpture & decorative arts, 81- *Teaching:* Instr, NY Univ, 76; adj prof, Wayne State Univ, Detroit, 82- *Awards:* Fel, Ford Found, 75-78; fel, John J McCloy, 80-81; fel, Nat Endowment Arts Mus Profs, 83. *Publ:* Contribr, articles to prof journals. *Mailing Add:* c/o Detroit Inst Arts 5200 Woodward Ave Detroit MI 48202

DARRIAU, JEAN-PAUL
EDUCATOR, SCULPTOR
b New York, NY, Nov 24, 29. *Study:* Pratt Inst, 47-48; Brooklyn Col, BA, 51; Univ Minn, MFA, 54. *Work:* Hirshhorn Mus & Sculpture Garden; Ind Univ Fine Arts Mus; Colorado Springs Art Ctr; Minneapolis Inst Art; Albert List Collection; Interracial Movement/Entrance to City, City of Bloomington, Ind. *Comn:* Man and Woman (aluminum), Jersey City State Col, 69; Adam and Eve I (bronze), 68, Adam and Eve II (bronze), 73 & four portrait busts, 76, Ind Univ Campus; Red, Blond, Black and Olive (limestone), City Bloomington, Ind, 80. *Exhib:* One-man show, Grippi Gallery, New York, 62; Sculptors Guild, New York, 70-72; FAR Gallery, New York, 72-73; Privileges and Silences, Ind Univ, Bloomington, 82 & Univ Chicago, 83; Sch Fine Arts, Ind Univ, 84; Mussavi Arts Ctr, NY, 85. *Teaching:* Instr, State Col, Arkadelphia, Ark, 53, Oberlin Col, 54 & Colo Col, 57-61; instr, Ind Univ, Bloomington, 61-, head sculpture dept, 61-72. *Awards:* Fulbright Grant, 55-57 & 66-67; res grants, Colo Col, 59 & Ind Univ. *Mem:* Col Art Asn; CAA Gay/Lesbian Caucus (bd mem). *Publ:* Contribr, Visions and Voice of the New Midwest, James A Rock & Co, 78; self-publ catalogs, 83 & 88. *Mailing Add:* Sch Fine Arts Ind Univ Bloomington IN 47405

DARROW, PAUL GARDNER
PAINTER, EDUCATOR
b Pasadena, Calif. *Study:* Colorado Springs Fine Art Ctr; Claremont Grad Sch & Univ Ctr. *Work:* Pasadena Art Mus, Calif; Times-Mirror Collection, Los Angeles; US Navy, Washington, DC; Lytton Savings & Loan Collection, Los Angeles; Long Beach Mus Art, Calif. *Comn:* Murals, Air France, Los Angeles, 61, Balboa Yacht Club, 63 & Newport Bank, Calif, 71; Wells Fargo Bank, Costa Mesa, Calif, 78. *Exhib:* Los Angeles Co Mus Art, 51-54; San Francisco Mus Art, 52 & 53; Seattle Art Mus, 53; Butler Inst Am Art, 53 & 54; Pa Acad Fine Art, 54; Denver Art Mus, 54; Corcoran Gallery, 54; Smithsonian Inst, 55; Oakland Art Mus, Calif, 64; solo exhibs, Newport Harbor, 72 & Gallerie Forma, El Salvador, 75; retrospective, Scripps Col, 73; Southern California 100, Laguna Beach Mus Art, 77; California Photographers, Claremont

Galleries, 78; and many others. *Teaching:* Prof art & chmn dept, Scripps Col, 60-; prof art, Claremont Grad Sch, 70- *Awards:* Purchase Award, Pasadena Art Mus, 58; Res Grant, Ford Found, 69; Nat Endowment Humanities Grant, 73. *Bibliog:* Bently Schaad (auth), The Realm of Contemporary Still Life Painting, 62 & Edmondson (auth), Printmaking, 72, Van Nostrand Reinhold. *Mem:* Calif Watercolor Soc; founding mem Los Angeles Printmaking Soc. *Media:* Graphic. *Publ:* Illusr, Aldous Huxley, Paris Rev, 62; The Concrete Wilderness, Meredith, 67; The Guide for the Married Man, Price Stern, 68; Psychological Perspectives, C G Jung JG Jung Inst, 70. *Dealer:* Art Connection 23811 Aliso Crk Rd Lagun Wiguez CA 90405. *Mailing Add:* 690 Cuprien Way Laguna Beach CA 92651

DARROW, WHITNEY, JR
CARTOONIST
b Princeton, NJ, Aug 22, 09. *Study:* Princeton Univ; Art Students League. *Pos:* Cartoonist, New Yorker Mag, 33- *Media:* Pencil, Charcoal. *Publ:* Auth, You're Sitting On My Eyelashes, 43, Please Pass the Hostess, 49 & Stop Miss, 57, Random House; Give Up, Simon & Schuster, 66; illusr, Walter, the Homing Pidgeon, Harper & Row, 81; and others. *Mailing Add:* 331 Newtown Turnpike Wilton CT 06897

DARTON, CHRISTOPHER
PAINTER
b New York, NY, Dec 9, 45. *Study:* New York Inst Technol, BFA, 69; Pratt Inst Grad Sch, MFA, 71. *Exhib:* Daniel Weinberg, San Francisco, Calif, 79; Mary Boone Gallery, 80. *Media:* Acrylic Paint. *Publ:* Auth, Matter as subject, Arts Mag, 11/77. *Mailing Add:* 9 E 16th St 4th Floor New York NY 10003

DASENBROCK, DORIS (NANCY) VOSS
DESIGNER, PAINTER
b Horicon, Wis, Nov 6, 39. *Study:* Wis State Univ, Oshkosh, BS, 62; Fla State Univ, Tallahassee, MFA, 67; Univ Md, College Park, BS, 89. *Work:* Fla State Univ Fine Arts Collection, Tallahassee; Mus Art, Ft Wayne, Ind; US House Rep, Washington, DC. *Comn:* Contemporary design, St Matthew's Episcopal Church, St Petersburg, 69; altar, Bowie, Md, 70, stained glass designs, 79, All Saints Lutheran Church, Bowie, Md. *Exhib:* Am Acad Arts & Lett, New York, 69 & 70; West Bend Galley Fine Art, Wis, 76; St Paul Mus Art, Minn, 77; Tweed Mus Art, Duluth, Minn, 77; South Alleghenies Mus, Loretto, Pa, 78; Mus Tex Tech Univ, Lubbock, 78; Fed Bldg, Washington, DC, 79. *Collections Arranged:* Artists Today Traveling Exhib, Prince George's Col, Marlboro Gallery, 79; Photography 79, Capital Ctr Gallery, 79. *Pos:* Exhib specialist, Capital Park Planning Comn, Riverdale, Md, 78-79; designer & illusr, Sterling Inst, Washington, DC, 79; media designer & coordr, Am Genetics Corp, Bethesda, Md, 79-; dir advert, GTCO Corp, Rockville, Md, 85-87, advert & mktg consult, 87- *Teaching:* Instr, Montgomery Col, Takoma Park, Md, 69-70; instr, Bowie State Col, Md, 75-76, George Mason Univ, Fairfac, Va, 78-79. *Awards:* Childe Hassom Purchase Award, Am Acad Arts & Lett, 69; Art Purchase Award, Benedictine Corp, 76; Award Excellence, Simpson Paper Co, 80. *Bibliog:* Brian Abbott (auth), Artist profile, Bowie Blade, Md, 6/3/76. *Mem:* Washington Women's Art Ctr; Women's Caucus Art; Artists Equity Asn; Md Fedn Art; Southern Watercolor Soc. *Media:* Watercolor, Oil; Pen & Ink. *Publ:* Illusr, Probing the physical world: Excursions, Fla State Univ, Tallahassee, 67; Air Conditioning - Refrigeration and Heating, Nat Radio Inst, Washington, DC, 73; Householder's Appliance Repair Course, McGraw-Hill, 74; Job Assessment and Career Development Guide, Sterling Inst, 79; Photography, McGraw-Hill, CEC, 88. *Dealer:* Jansson Art Gallery Rte 6A Barnstable MA 02637. *Mailing Add:* 1407 Pennington Lane Bowie MD 20716

DASH, HARVEY DWIGHT
ADMINISTRATOR, PAINTER
b Brooklyn, NY, June 28, 24. *Study:* Pratt Inst; Tyler Sch Fine Arts, Temple Univ, BFA, BSEd & MFA; Rutgers Univ; Columbia Univ; Montclair State Col. *Work:* Temple Univ. *Exhib:* Pa Acad Fine Arts, Philadelphia; Temple Univ; one-man shows, Fairleigh Dickinson Univ, Brighton Gallery, New York & Ridgewood Art Gallery, NJ, 64. *Pos:* Supvr art, Bound Brook Bd Educ, 48-51; dir creative arts, Paramus Sch Syst, 63-67; dir, Lighthouse Art Gallery, Nyack, NY, 67-69; dir, Dash Sch of Art (formerly Lighthouse Sch Art), Grandview, NY, 67-78. *Teaching:* Instr fine art, Temple Univ, 46-47; chmn dept art, Tenafly High Sch, 51-57 & Paramus High Sch, NJ, 57-67. *Awards:* Paramus Bd Educ grants, 65 & 66; Berley Grant, 62. *Bibliog:* New York Art Rev, 88. *Mem:* Nat Art Educ Asn. *Media:* All. *Mailing Add:* 16345 Bassett Ct Ramona CA 92065

DASH, ROBERT (WARREN)
PAINTER
b New York, NY, June 8, 34. *Work:* Brooklyn Mus, NY; Hirshhorn Mus, Washington, DC; Pittsburgh Mus Art; Joslyn Art Mus, Omaha, Nebr; Philadelphia Mus Art; Parrish Mus, Southhampton, NY; Heckscher Mus, Huntington, NY; Guggenheim Mus. *Comn:* Centennial, Cheseborough-Pond's Inc. *Exhib:* The New York Season, 60-61; Yale Univ Exhib, 61; Landscapes by Five Americans, Festival of Two Worlds, Mus Mod Art Traveling exhib, 66; Inform & Interpret, Am Fedn Arts Traveling Exhib, 68; The New Realism, Hirschl & Adler Galleries, New York, 81; New Acquisitions, Hirshhorn Mus, 83; Earthly Pleasures, Fort Wayne Mus, 88. *Pos:* Writer, bi-weekly column, East Hampton Star & monthly column, Long Island Monthly. *Teaching:* Adj prof advan painting, spring 70, 75, 77 & 81 & Master Wkshp, 85 & 86, Southampton Col; vis prof, State Univ NY, Stony Brook, 88. *Bibliog:* Gerrit Henry (auth), The making of the new Utopia, Art Int, spring 73; article, Am Artist, spring 74; The new realists, Art in Am, 9-10/81; An artist's garden, House & Garden, 87; Caroline See Bohm: Private Landscape, Clarkson Potter; Rosemary Verey (auth), The American Man's Garden, Little-Brown. *Mem:* Garden Bk Club (adv bd); Nature Conservancy (trustee); Peconic Land Trust (adv). *Media:* Oils, Pastels. *Mailing Add:* Sagg Main Sagaponack NY 11962

DASKALOFF, GYORGY
PAINTER
b Sofia, Bulgaria, May 15, 23; US citizen. *Study:* Acad Fine Arts, Sofia, grad. *Work:* Metrop Mus Art, New York; Nat Mus, Sofia; Royal Libr, Brussels, Belg; Butler Inst Am Art, Youngstown, Ohio. *Comn:* Mural, comn by ARA, Ann Arbor, Mich; portrait of Judge Theodor Levin, Detroit Bar Asn, 71; An American Family (mural), comn by Amos Cahan, New York, 73. *Exhib:* Bulgarian Art in Berlin, 58, Moscow, 59 & Prague, 59; Int Biennial Graphic Arts, Ljubliana, 59; Int Exhib Graphics, Leipzig, 60; Comparisons, Paris, 65-67. *Awards:* First Prize for Graphics, Bulgaria, 54 & 59. *Bibliog:* Pierre Rouve (auth), article, Arts Rev, London, 6/3/61; L L Sosset (auth), article, Les Beaux Arts, Brussels, 5/6/65; Pierre Lubecker (auth), article, Politiken, Copenhagen, 5/25/67. *Media:* Oil. *Mailing Add:* 46 Great Jones St New York NY 10012

DASS, DEAN ALLEN
PRINTMAKER, PAINTER
b Hampton, Iowa, Nov 16, 55. *Study:* Univ Northern Iowa, Cedar Falls, BA, 78; Tyler Sch Art, Temple Univ, MFA, 80. *Work:* Nat Collection Poland, Krakow; Brooklyn Mus, NY; Walker Art Ctr, Minneapolis; Kans State Univ, Manhattan; Univ Dallas, Irving, Tex; IBM Corp, Free Libr, Philadelphia Mus Art. *Exhib:* Nat Print Exhib, 81 & Artist as Printmaker, 83, Brooklyn Mus, NY; 59th Ann Int Exhib, Print Club, Philadelphia, 83; Impressions: Experimental Prints, Inst Contemp Art, Richmond, Va, 83; New Acquisitions, Walker Art Gallery, Minneapolis, 86; solo exhibs, Dolan Maxwell Gallery, Philadelphia, 86 & 89, Projects of Portfolios, Brooklyn Mus, 89, Danville Mus, Va, 90 & Schmidt/Dean Gallery, Philadelphia, 91; Bradford Biennial, Eng, 89; Graphic Triennial, Alvar Ralto Mus, Finland, 89; 1708 Gallery, Richmond, Va, 90; and others. *Teaching:* Instr printmaking & drawing, Kutztown Univ, 83-84; asst prof, Univ Va, Charlottesville, 85-90, assoc prof, 91- *Awards:* Purchase Award, Charlotte Printmakers Soc, NC, 83; Artist's Fel, Pa Coun Arts, 85; Va Prize in Printmaking, Va Comn Arts, 88. *Bibliog:* Ann Jarmusch (auth), Philadelphia: Dean Dass, Art News, 5/83; John Russell (auth), article, New York Times, 11/20/83; article, Print Collector's Newslett, 1-2/84; Edward J Sozanski (auth), article, Philadelphia Inquirer, 11/5/84. *Media:* Etching, Collage, Gouache, Natural Pigments. *Mailing Add:* Univ Va 2601 Jefferson Park Circle Charlottesville VA 22903

DATER, JUDY
PHOTOGRAPHER, WRITER
b Hollywood, Calif, June 21, 41. *Study:* Univ Calif, Los Angeles, 59-62; San Francisco State Univ, BA, 63, MA, 66. *Work:* San Francisco Mus Mod Art; Ctr Creative Photog, Tucson, Ariz; Bibliot Nat, Paris; Boston Mus Fine Arts; Mus Mod Art, New York; Albin O Kuhn Libr & Gallery, Univ Md, Baltimore; Fogg Art Mus, Harvard Univ, Cambridge, Mass; Int Ctr Photog, New York. *Exhib:* Solo exhibs, Spectrum Gallery, Fresno, Calif, 81 & Yuen Lui Gallery, Seattle, 82, Recent Photographs, Santa Monica, Calif, 89, New Works, Blatant Image, Silvereye, Pittsburgh, Pa, 89, Options Gallery, Odessa Col, Tex, 90, Cycles, Matsuya Dept Store, Ginza, Tokyo, Japan, 92; Photography in America, Whitney Mus, 74; Women of Photography, San Francisco Mus Art, 75; Mirrors and Windows Traveling Exhib, Mus Mod Art, New York, 78-80; Spirit of Women, Albin O Kuhn Gallery, Baltimore, 88; Similar Images/Dissimilar Motives, Sonoma State Univ Gallery, 90; Odalisque, Jane Baum Gallery, New York, 90; Suburban Home Life: Tracking the American Dream, Whitney Mus Am Art, New York, 90; retrospective, Stockton State Col Art Gallery, Ponona, NJ, 91; and others. *Collections Arranged:* Imogen Cunningham: A Portrait Traveling Exhib, (auth, catalog), New York Graphic Soc, 79. *Pos:* Freelance artist/photo & workshops, presently. *Teaching:* Instr, Univ Calif Exten, San Francisco, 66-74; instr photog, San Francisco Art Inst, Calif, 74-78; guest instr, Kans City Art Inst, 85; instr, Int Ctr Photog, 87-90. *Awards:* Nat Endowment Arts Fel, 76 & 88; J S Guggenheim Mem Found fel, 78; Indiv Artists Grant, Marin Arts Coun, 87. *Bibliog:* Gilles Walinski (auth), Judy Dater and Jack Welpott, Zoom, Paris, 11-12/79; Richard S Street (auth), Judy Dater, Pac Sun, 2/1/80; Emmanuel Cooper (auth), Fully Exposed: The Male Nude in Photography, Unwin Hyman Ltd, 90. *Mem:* San Francisco Camerawork; Soc Photog Educ. *Publ:* Coauth, Women and Other Visions, Morgan & Morgan, 75. *Dealer:* Collected Images PO Box 5154 Berkeley CA 94705; Witkin Gallery New York NY. *Mailing Add:* c/o Photogr Gallery Palo Alto 540 Romona St Palo Alto CA 94301

DAUB, MATTHEW FORREST
PAINTER, GRAPHIC ARTIST
b New York, NY, Aug 29, 51. *Study:* Southern Ill Univ, Carbondale, BA, 81, MFA, 84. *Work:* Metrop Mus Art & Mus City, New York, NY; Evansville Mus Arts & Sci, Ind; Mitchell Mus, Mt Vernon, Ill; Sheldon Swope Art Mus, Terre Haute, Ind. *Exhib:* Watercolor USA, 81, 82 & 83 & Watercolor USA, 1986: Monumental Image, 86, Springfield Art Mus, Mo; solo exhibs, Evansville Mus Arts & Sci, Ind, 83, Sherry French Gallery, New York, 84, 86, 88, 91, Jan Cicero Gallery, Chicago, Ill, 87, 89; The Recognizable Image: Sixteen Contemporary Realists, Bruce Mus, Greenwich, Conn, 85; Nightworks, Bronx Mus Arts, Bronx, NY, 87; Exactitude: New Acquisitions, Met Mus Art, New York, 87-89; Trains & Planes: The Influence of Locomotion in American Painting, Nat Acad Scis, Washington, DC, 89 & 90. *Teaching:* Assoc prof fine arts, Kutztown Univ Pa, 87- *Awards:* Purchase Awards, 35th & 36th Ann Mid-States Art Exhib, Evansville Mus, 82 & 83; Ill Arts Coun Fel, 86; Pollock-Krasner Fel, 92. *Bibliog:* Dan Wood (auth), The

Craft of Drawing, Harcourt Brace Javonovich; Gerrit Henry (auth), Signs of the Times (catalog essay), American Watercolors, Engagement Calendar, Metrop Mus Art, 91. *Media:* Watercolor, Conte Crayon. *Publ:* Auth, The watercolor page, Am Artist, 82; Auth, Carolyn Plochmann: A Charmed Vision, Evansville Mus Arts & Sci, 90; Auth, Carolyn Plochman, Am Artist, 90. *Dealer:* Sherry French Gallery 24 W 57th St New York NY 10019. *Mailing Add:* 920 N Richmond Fleetwood PA 19522

DAUDELIN, CHARLES
SCULPTOR
b Granby, Que, Can, Oct 1, 20. *Study:* Ecole du Meuble de Montreal, 41-43; with Fernand Leger, New York, 43-44, Paris, 46-48; with Henri Laurens, Paris, 46-48. *Work:* Nat Gallery Can, Ottawa; Mus D'Art Contemp, Montreal; Mus ou Quebec; Art Gallery Ont, Toronto; Musēe Des Beaux-Arts De Montreal. *Comn:* Iron fountain sculpture, Prov Govt, Charlottetown, PEI, 66; Nat Art Ctr (bronze), Ottawa, 69; Chaos (corten fountain), Quebec, 73; bronze mural, Notre Dame Church, Montreal, 82; Fontaine (bronze), St Germain-des-Pres, Paris, 84. *Exhib:* Innovation 65, Art Gallery Mus Beaux Arts, Montreal, 65; Naissance D'Une Sculpture, Art Contemp Mus, Montreal, and traveling, 69-72; Panorama de la Sculpture 45-70, Mus Art Contemp, Montreal & Musēe Rodin, Paris, 70; Biennale Middelheim, Anvers, Belgium, 71; retrospectives, Art Contemp Mus, Montreal, 74 & Mus Quebec, 74; Serv Cult, Du Quebec, Paris, 84; La Sculpture Au Quebec 1946-1971, Musēe Du Quēbec, 92. *Teaching:* prof allied arts, Univ Que, Montreal, 64-68 & 73-, Univ Que, Chicoutimi, 71-73. *Awards:* Lynch-Staunton Grant, Can Coun, 72; Allied Arts Award, Royal Archit Inst Can, 73; Prix Paul-Emile-Borduas, Les Prix du Quebec, 85. *Bibliog:* Louis Jacques Beaulieu (auth), Daudelin A Paris, Vie des Arts, 3/85; Charles Daudelin, ESPACE Sculpture, Ēte, 88; Pierre Moretti (dir), Bronze (film), Nat Film Bd, Montreal, 69. *Mem:* Royal Can Acad Arts; Conseil de la Sculpture du Quebec. *Media:* Bronze, Stainless Steel. *Dealer:* Michel Tetreault Montreal PQ Can; Galerie Esperanza 2144 Mackay Montreal PQ Can H3G 2J1. *Mailing Add:* 17166 Chemin Ste-Marie Kirkland PQ H9J 2K9 Canada

DAUGHERTY, MICHAEL F
EDUCATOR, SCULPTOR
b Seattle, Wash, Sept 30, 42. *Study:* Univ Wash, Seattle, 60-62; Univ Barcelona, Spain, 64-65; Univ Wash, Seattle, BA(sculpture), 69; Univ Tenn, Knoxville, MFA(sculpture), 71. *Comn:* Outdoor fountains, comn by Walter H Stevens, Knoxville, 70, Genevieve Stoughton, Oak Ridge, 71, Alvin Rotenberg, Baton Rouge, 73, Janice Sachse, Baton Rouge, 74 & Derwood Facundus, Baton Rouge,, 76. *Exhib:* 16th Joslyn Biennial, Joslyn Art Mus, Omaha, Nebr, 80; Nat Drawing and Sculpture Exhib, Del Mar Art Gallery, Corpus Christi, Tex, 81; Nat Sculpture Exhib, Westwood Ctr Arts, Los Angeles, Calif, 81; Biennial Five State Exhib, Fine Arts Gallery, Port Arthur, Tex, 81; Art for Arts Sake, Contemp Arts Ctr, New Orleans, La, 81; and many others. *Teaching:* Asst, Univ Tenn, 69-71; instr, Art Ctr, Oak Ridge, Tenn, 70; assoc prof sculpture, La State Univ, 71- *Awards:* Purchase Award, Tenn Sculpture 1970, Tenn Arts Comn, 71; Purchase Award, 7th Ann Mobile Art Exhib, Mobile, Ala, 72; Second Place Award, Biennial Five State Exhib, Port Arthur, Tex. *Mem:* Southern Asn Sculptors; Col Art Asn; Int Sculpture Ctr; Southeastern Col Art Asn. *Dealer:* Adelle M Taylor Gallery 3317 McKinney Ave Dallas TX 75204. *Mailing Add:* 5246 N Chalet Ct Baton Rouge LA 70808

DAUGHTERS, ROBERT A
PAINTER, PRINTMAKER
b Trenton, Mo, Feb 17, 29. *Study:* Kansas City Art Inst & Sch Design, Dipl, 53. *Work:* Koshore Indian Mus, Lajunta, Colo; Valley Nat Bank, Phoenix, Ariz; NMex State Fair, Albuquerque; Maytag Found, New York. *Exhib:* NMex State Fair, Albuquerque, 72; Taos 6 Exhib, Philbrook Mus, Tulsa, Okla, 76; Western Heritage Sale, Shamrock Hilton Hotel, Houston, Tex, 78; The Driscol Collection Am Western Art, Beijing Exhib Ctr, China, 81; Western Images, New York. *Pos:* Partner, Moyer Crandall Art Studio, Kansas City, Mo, 54-70. *Awards:* Best of Show & Gov Purchase Award, NMex State Fair, 72. *Bibliog:* Elizabeth Rigby (auth), 1980, Southwest Art (Anniversary Issue), 5/81; Don H Jones (auth), Robert Daughters, artist, Santa Fean Mag, 12/82; Trica Hurst (auth), Robert Daughters-Contemporary American Impressionist, NMex Mag, 8/83; and others. *Mem:* Nat Soc Art Dir. *Media:* Oil. *Publ:* Illusr, New Mexico Magazine's Distinguished Artist Calendar-84, Works by Robert Daughters, 84. *Dealer:* Meyer Gallery Santa Fe NM; Taos Art Gallery Taos NM. *Mailing Add:* 704 San Antonio PO Box 1754 Taos NM 87571

DAUTERMAN, CARL CHRISTIAN
CONSULTANT, LECTURER
b Newark, NJ. *Study:* Newark Sch Fine & Indust Art; Newark Mus Apprentice Training Course; NY Univ, BA; Columbia Univ, MA(art hist). *Collections Arranged:* Numerous exhibs in decorative arts, especially ceramics. *Pos:* Mgr spec exhibs, Cooper Union Mus Arts of Decoration, 38-42; catalog writer decorative objects, Parke-Bernet Galleries, 46-53; spec admin consult to the dir, Metrop Mus Art, 53-55, from assoc cur to cur Western Europ arts, 55-73, emer cur, 73-; consult & trustee, The Campbell Mus, 72- *Teaching:* From lectr to adj prof Europ & Am decorative arts, Columbia Univ, 51-85; vis prof art hist, Winterthur Mus, Univ Del, 73-74 & Cooper-Hewitt Mus Master's Degree Prog, 83- *Awards:* Guest archaeologist, Mex Govt Field Exped, Monte Alban, Oaxaca, 36; Award for Outstanding Achievement, Sch Gen Studies, Columbia Univ, 75. *Mem:* Am Friends Attingham Summer Sch; Am Ceramic Circle; Wedgwood Int Sem; Decorative Arts Chap, Soc Archit Historians; Am Soc 18th Century Studies. *Res:* Extensive analysis in 18th century archives of Manufacture Nationale de Sévres. *Publ:* Auth, Sévres, 69; coauth (with Sir Francis Watson), Catalogue of the Wrightsman Collection III: Furniture, Snuffboxes, Silver, 70; auth, Catalogue of the Wrightsman Collection IV: Porcelains, 70; Sévres Porcelain: Makers and Marks, 18th Century, Metrop Mus Art, 86. *Mailing Add:* 1326 Madison Ave New York NY 10128

DAVENPORT, RAY
PAINTER, PRINTMAKER
b Rockville Centre, NY, May 5, 26. *Study:* Pratt Inst, cert(advert design), 48; Univ SC, Columbia, 80. *Work:* SC Permanent Collection, Columbia; Ronald Reagan Libr; Stone Container Corp, Chicago, Ill; SC Nat Bank, Sumter & Columbia; Chernoff/Silver & Assocs, Columbia, SC. *Comn:* oil painting, First Fed Savings & Loan, Sumter, SC, 75; oil painting, Black River Elec Coop, 89. *Exhib:* 14th Hunter Ann, Hunter Mus Art, 74; SC Watercolor Soc First Ann, Columbia Mus Art, SC, 78; Am Artists First Nat Art Competition, Circle Galleries, Soho, New York, 78; Allied Artists Am 70th & 72nd Ann, Nat Arts Club, New York, 83 & 85; Capricorn Galleries, Bethesda, Md, 90; JF Kennedy Ctr Performing Arts, Washington,DC, 91; and others. *Awards:* Atto Newer Award, Allied Artists Am 70th Ann, 83 & Gloria Benson Stacks Award, 72nd Ann, 85; Merit Award, Modern Maturity National Seasoned Eye Competition, 90. *Mem:* Nat Soc Painters Casein & Acrylic; Allied Artists Am; Guild SC Artists (secy & treas, 77-78, pres, 88-89); mem with excellence, SC Watercolor Soc. *Media:* Acrylic, Oil; Lithography. *Dealer:* Country Art Gallery Locust Valley Long Island NY 11560; Capricorn Galleries Bethesda MD 20814. *Mailing Add:* 274 Keels Rd Sumter SC 29154

DAVENPORT, REBECCA READ
PAINTER, LECTURER
b Alexandria, Va, June 29, 43. *Study:* Pratt Inst, Brooklyn, NY, BFA(with honors), 66-70; Univ NC, Greensboro, MFA, 70-73. *Work:* Baltimore Mus Art, Md; Corcoran Gallery Art, Washington, DC; Chrysler Mus, Norfolk, Va; Federal Reserve Bank, Richmond, Va. *Exhib:* Selected 20th Century Nudes, Harold Reed Gallery, New York, 78; Mus d'Art Mod de la Villes de Paris, France, 78; Taft Menagerie, Taft Mus, Cincinnati, Ohio, 80; Images of the 70's, Corcoran Gallery Art, Washington, DC, 80; Inside Out, Newport Harbor Art Mus, Newport Beach, Calif, 81; Real, Really Real, Super Real, San Antonio Mus, Tex, 81; Contemp Am Realism Since 60, Pa Acad Fine Art, Philadelphia, Pa, 81. *Awards:* Cert of Distinction, Va Mus, Richmond, 73; Third Gold Palette, IV Festival IX de la Peinture, Cagnes Sur Mir, France, 77; Artist Fel, Nat Endowment Arts, 79. *Bibliog:* Theodore F Wolff (auth), Solving the mystery of the missing subject, Christian Sci Monitor, 10/1/80; Aubyn Kendall (ed), Real, Really Real, Super Real, San Antonio Mus Asn, 81; Frank H Goodyear (auth), Contemporary American Realism Since 1960, New York Graphic Soc, 81. *Media:* Oil. *Dealer:* Osuna Gallery 406 Seventh St NW Washington DC; Aberbach Fine Arts 988 Madison Ave New York NY. *Mailing Add:* 4100 38 St NW Washington DC 20016

DAVEY, RONALD A
HISTORIAN, EDUCATOR
b United Kingdom. *Study:* Wallasey Sch Art; Courtauld Inst, Univ London; Ecole Hautes Etudes, Univ Paris. *Teaching:* Asst lectr art, Slade Sch Fine Art, Univ London, 54-58; lectr, Univ Newcastle upon Tyne, 58-64; principal, West Sussex Col Art, 64-67; prof art & design, Univ Alta, 67-90, chmn, 67-76, prof emer, 90- *Mem:* Fel Royal Soc Arts. *Mailing Add:* 11527 77th Ave Univ Alta Edmonton AB T6G 0M2 Canada

DAVID, CYRIL FRANK
GRAPHIC ARTIST
b London, Eng, July 13, 20; US citizen. *Work:* Metrop Mus Art, New York, NY; Nat Mus Am Art, Washington, DC; Ark Art Ctr, Little Rock. *Exhib:* Art of Drawing, Staempfli Gallery, New York, 80, 84-89; Members Selections, Corcoran Gallery Art, Washington, DC, 80; Staempfli Gallery, New York, 86; one-man show, Ark Art Ctr, 84, 85 & 86. *Awards:* Nat Endowment Arts Fel, 80; Best Miniature Work, Guild Hall Mus, 82; Creative Artists Pub Serv Fel, NY State Coun Arts, 83. *Media:* Pencil. *Dealer:* Capricorn Galleries 4849 Rugby Ave Bethesda MD 20814. *Mailing Add:* PO Box 100 Sag Harbor NY 11963

DAVID, DON RAYMOND
PAINTER, INSTRUCTOR
b Springbrook, Ore, May 2, 06. *Study:* Fresno State, Calif, 28-29; Art Ctr Col Design, Los Angeles, 41-43; Chouinards, Los Angeles, 44; Hans Hoffman Sch, New York, 53-56. *Work:* Corcoran Gallery Art, Washington, DC; Ciba Geigy Corp; IBM Corp. *Exhib:* One-man shows, Webb Gallery, Los Angeles, 47, Camino Gallery, New York, 56, 58 & 60, New Sch Social Res, New York, 65, Baruch Col, 72 & Alonzo Gallery, New York, 69, 70, 72 & 78; The New American Still Life, Westmoreland Co Mus Art, Greensburg, Pa, 79; one-man show, Open Gallery, Parsons Sch Design, New York, 87. *Pos:* Art dir, Robinson's, Los Angeles, 42-46, Filenes, Boston, Mass, 48-50, Franklin Simon, 50-53, Helena Rubinstein, 53-58 & Burlington Mills, 58-72; chmn, Camino Cooperative Gallery, New York, 56-61. *Teaching:* Instr drawing, Art Ctr Sch Los Angeles, 46-48; instr hist pictorial art & illus, Newark Sch Fine & Indust Art, NJ, 68-; instr, Parson's Sch Design, New York, 83. *Bibliog:* Article in Am Artist Mag, 8/79. *Mem:* Col Art Asn. *Media:* Acrylic, Watercolor. *Dealer:* Barbara Tamerin Fine Arts 120 E 81st St New York NY 10028. *Mailing Add:* 521 East 14th St Apt 9B New York NY 10009

DAVIDEK, STEFAN
PAINTER, PRINTMAKER
b Flint, Mich, May 15, 24. *Study:* Flint Inst Arts, with Jaroslav Brozik; Art Students League, with Morris Kantor; Cranbrook Acad, with Fred Mitchell.

Work: Detroit Inst Arts, Mich; Flint Inst Arts, Mich; Muskegon Community Col & Hackley Art Mus, Mich; Albion Col; McClaren Hosp, Flint, Mich; Women's League, Univ Mich. *Comn:* sanctuary wall, Luke M Powers Sch, Flint, 70; interior murals, Zehnders, Frankenmuth, Mich, 80 & 81; chapel wall, MaClaren Hosp, Flint, Mich; ceiling decoration, St Paul, Flint, Mich. *Exhib:* Flint Ann, 46-90; Butler Midyear Show, 59; Pa Acad Fine Art 9; Buckham Art Space, Flint, Mich; Alma Col Print Ann, 89-91. *Awards:* Founder's Prize, 61 & Lou R Maxon Prize, Detroit Inst Art; Purchase Award, Alma Print Show, Mich, 91. *Media:* Oil, Watercolor; Serigraphy, Silkscreen. *Dealer:* De Graaf Fine Art 300 W Superior Chicago IL. *Mailing Add:* 5391 W Coldwater Rd Flint MI 48504

DAVIDOVICH, JAIME
PAINTER, VIDEO ARTIST
b Buenos Aires, Arg, Sept 27, 36; US citizen. *Study:* Nat Col, Buenos Aires, Arg, 54-58; Univ Uruguay, 59-61; Sch Visual Arts, New York, 63. *Work:* Mus Mod Art, Buenos Aires, Arg; Mus Belas Artes, Rio de Janiero, Brazil; Dayton Art Inst, Ohio; Everson Mus Art, Syracuse, NY; Akron Art Inst, Akron, Ohio. *Comn:* Carroll Wall Proj, John Carroll Univ, Cleveland, Ohio, 71. *Exhib:* One-man show, Retrospective 1962-1972, Drake Univ, Des Moines, Iowa, 71, Am Mus of Moving Image, 90; Exp in Art & Technol Show, Lake Erie Col, Ohio, 71; Five Artists, New Gallery, Cleveland, Ohio, 72; Arte de Sistemas, Mus Mod Art, Buenos Aires & Mus Fine Arts, Santiago, Chile, 72; Akron Art Inst, Ohio, 72-73; Whitney Mus Am Art, New York, 76; Long Beach Mus Art, Los Angeles, 81; Ctr Media Arts, Paris, France, 82; Video & Television Festival, Maastrich, Holland, 82; TV on TV, Tex Tech Univ, 84; Exit Art, New York, 86. *Pos:* Rep to US, DiTella Found Art Ctr, Buenos Aires, Arg, 65; founder & mem bd dirs, New Orgn Visual Arts, Cleveland, Ohio, 72-73; pres, Artists Television Network, 77-83; bd dirs, Artists Television Proj, Univ Iowa, 87; res fel, Sch Art & Art Hist, Univ Iowa, 87. *Teaching:* Prof painting, Sch Visual Arts, Bahia Blanca, Arg, 61-62. *Awards:* Grand Prize, Adhesive Tape Proj, Dayton Art Inst, Dayton, Ohio, 74; Creative Artists Pub Serv Prog grants, NY State Coun Arts, 75 & 82; Visual Arts Fels, Nat Endowment Arts, 78, 84 & 90; Video 81, San Francisco Video Festival, 81. *Bibliog:* Ellen Stern (auth), The inner tube, New York Mag, 4/17/78; TV finds its place among fine art, Plain Dealer, 5/29/80; Video artists still seek a showplace for their work, New York Times, 6-19-83; 16 Autumn, Real Life Mag, 86; and others. *Mailing Add:* 152 Wooster New York NY 10012

DAVIDSON, ABRAHAM A
ART HISTORIAN, PHOTOGRAPHER
b Dorchester, Mass, June 27, 35. *Study:* Harvard Univ, AB(cum laude), 57; Hebrew Teachers Col, Boston, BJed, 60; Boston Univ, MA(art hist), 60; Columbia Univ, PhD(art hist), 65. *Work:* Cigna Corp; Bank Leumi; Pub Libr Newark, NJ; Villanova Univ; Lehigh Univ; Sheldon Mem Art Gallery, Univ Nebr. *Exhib:* One-man shows, Paley Libr, Temple Univ, 72 & 81, Painted Bride Art Gallery, Philadelphia, 74, Burlington Co Community Col, NJ, 78, Gloucester Co Col, NJ, 79 & Villanova Univ, 82. *Teaching:* Vis lectr, Univ Iowa, 63; instr art hist, Wayne State Univ, 64-65; asst prof, Oakland Univ, 65-68; from asst prof to prof, Tyler Sch Art, Temple Univ, 68- *Awards:* Group 17 Prize for Photog, Detroit Inst Arts, 69; Travel Grant, Nat Endowment for the Humanities, 85. *Bibliog:* Burt Wasserman (auth), People and places come to life in collection of photographs, NJ Courier Post, 11/10/79; Burt Wasserman (auth), Abraham Davidson, New Art Examiner, 4/83; Victoria Donohoe (auth), A photographer takes a scholarly approach, Philadelphia Inquirer, 2/27/87. *Res:* History of 19th and 20th century American painting and sculpture. *Publ:* Auth, The Story of American Painting, Abrams, 74 & rev ed, 79; The Eccentrics & Other American Visionary Painters, Dutton, 78; Demuth's poster portraits, Artforum, 11/78; Early American Modernist Painting 1910-1935, Harper & Row, 81, rev ed 86; Art and Insanity, one case: Blakelock at Middletown, Smithsonian Studies in Am Art, summer 89. *Mailing Add:* Tyler Sch Art Temple Univ Beech & Penrose Aves Elkins Park PA 19126

DAVIDSON, ELIZABETH H DONNALLY
DEALER
b Newport, RI, Mar 28, 48. *Study:* Reed Col, BA, 70, MA, 71; Harvard Univ, arts mgt cert, 77; Portland State Univ. *Pos:* Dir mem & develop, Portland Art Mus, Ore, 75-78; dir artist-in-residence, Ore Arts Comn, Salem, 1/78-9/78; dir, Blackfish Gallery, Portland, 79-; owner, Donnally Books, Seattle, currently. *Specialty:* Seattle artist Peter Millett; artist made books. *Mailing Add:* 2924 72nd Ave SE Mercer Island WA 98040-2623

DAVIDSON, HERBERT LAURENCE
PAINTER, PRINTMAKER
b Green Bay, Wis, Sept 6, 30. *Study:* Art Inst Chicago, Anna Raymond Foreign Traveling Fel, 56. *Work:* Kemper Ins Co; Playboy Mag; Pullman Bank of Chicago; Rahr West Mus, Manitowoc, Wis; Walter Heller Corp, Chicago; Signode Corp, Glenview, Ill. *Exhib:* Butler Inst Am Art, Youngstown, Ohio, 65; Alta Col of Art, Calgary, 76; Mendel Art Gallery, Saskatchewan, Can, 77; Chicago Cult Ctr, 79; Syracuse Univ, Lubin Hall, 80; Sao Paolo Mus, Brazil; and others. *Bibliog:* Article, Am Artist Mag, 7/80. *Mem:* The Arts Club Chicago. *Media:* Oil; Lithography. *Dealer:* Wadle Galleries 128 W Palace Santa Fe NM. *Mailing Add:* 406 W Webster Ave Chicago IL 60614

DAVIDSON, IAN J
COLLECTOR, PATRON
b Toronto, Ont, July 21, 25. *Study:* Univ BC, BA;. *Pos:* Dir, Vancouver Art Gallery, 70-74; mem adv art comt, Can Coun, 75-; dir, Community Arts Coun, Vancouver. *Teaching:* Archit at Univ Toronto, Univ BC, Carleton Univ & Bezalel Acad, Jerusalem, Israel. *Awards:* Awards in architecture in every major design award program. *Mem:* Assoc Royal Can Acad Art; fel Royal Archit Inst Can. *Interests:* Commissioning original works by major artists in the non-objective and conceptual fields. *Mailing Add:* 405-1600 Howe St Vancouver BC V6Z 2L9 Canada

DAVIDSON, JEAN
PAINTER
b New York, NY. *Study:* Study with Moses Sawyer, 53; New Sch Social Res, with Peggy Bacon, 54; also with DeHirsh Margules, 54-59. *Work:* Corcoran Gallery, Washington, DC; Greenville County Mus Art, SC; Elvehjem Mus Art, Madison, Wis; IBM, New York; Hist Soc Woodstock, NY; Metrop Mus Art, New York. *Exhib:* Artists by Artists, Capricorn Gallery, New York, 67; New York Studio Sch Drawing Benefit, 72; 300 Artists to the Support of the New York Studio Sch, Xavier Fourcade Gallery, New York, 76; Unknown Universes, Pace Univ, New York, 79; Chelsea Artweek 1980, Cult Found, New York, 80; Albright-Knox Members Gallery, Buffalo, NY, 81; Gathering of the Avant Garde 1948-1970, Kenkeleba Gallery, New York, 85. *Awards:* Esther & Adolph Gottlieb Found Grant, 80. *Bibliog:* Gordon Brown (auth), revs, Arts Mag, 76; Will Grant (auth), The past is always present, Artspeak, 84; Lawrence Campbell, Special Feature: Painting of Kaldis by Jean Davidson, Art Now, New York Gallery Guide, 11/89. *Media:* Oil. *Dealer:* Emily Harvey Artworks 537 Broadway New York NY. *Mailing Add:* 205 W 19th St No 11R New York NY 10011

DAVIDSON, MAXWELL, III
DEALER
b New York, NY, Feb 8, 39. *Study:* Williams Col, BA(art hist), 61. *Pos:* Owner, Maxwell Davidson Gallery, 76- *Mem:* Art Dealers Asn Am. *Specialty:* 19th & 20th century masters and contemporary painters. *Mailing Add:* Maxwell Davidson Gallery 415 W Broadway New York NY 10012

DAVIDSON, NANCY
PAINTER
b Chicago, Ill. *Study:* Univ Ill, Chicago Circle, BA, 72; Art Inst Chicago, MFA, 75. *Comn:* Wall installations, City Chicago, 80, A T & T, 81 & IBM, 85. *Exhib:* Abstract Art in Chicago, Mus Contemp Art, Chicago, 76; Ten Painters, Walker Art Ctr, 77; 100 Years 100 Artists, Art Inst Chicago, 79; New Dimensions Surface, Mus Contemp Art, Chicago, 79; Works on Paper, Albright-Knox Gallery, 80; Berkshire Mus, Mass, 83. *Teaching:* Asst prof, Univ Ill, Champaign, 77-79, Williams Col, Mass, 80-84 & State Univ NY Purchase, 84- *Awards:* Fels, Nat Endowment Arts, 78, Yaddo Found, 80 & Mass Coun Arts, 81 & 84. *Publ:* Ed, NAME Book I: Artists Statements on Art, Name Gallery, 77. *Dealer:* Richard Anderson Gallery 63 Thompson St New York NY 10012. *Mailing Add:* 137 Duane St NW New York NY 10013

DAVIDSON, SUZETTE MORTON
PATRON, COLLECTOR
b Chicago, Ill, Aug 24, 11. *Study:* Vassar Col, AB, 34; Art Inst Chicago, 36-40. *Exhib:* Printing Design by Suzette Morton Zurcher (former name), Chicago Pub Libr, Albion Col, Mich & Univ Calif, Santa Barbara. *Pos:* Life Trustee, Art Inst Chicago; life trustee, Newberry Libr; trustee, Morton Arboretum, Lisle, Ill; owner, The Pocahontas Press, 37-; trustee, Santa Barbara Mus Art. *Awards:* Five Selections, 50 Bks of the Year Award, Am Inst Graphic Arts, 42-67. *Mem:* Am Fedn Arts. *Collection:* From classical antiquity to Picasso, with emphasis on seventeenth century Italian painting, pre-Raphaelite paintings and drawings; pre-Columbian gold. *Publ:* Designer numerous exhib catalogs, Art Inst Chicago. *Mailing Add:* 780 Riven Rock Rd Montecito CA 93108

DAVIDSON, THYRA (CLAIRE THYRA WEXLER)
DRAFTSMAN, SCULPTOR
b Brooklyn, NY, Oct 15, 26. *Study:* Nat Acad Design, with John Corbino, 43-45; Brooklyn Mus Art Sch, with Milton Hebald, 45; New Sch Soc Res, with Robert Gwathmey, 45-47. *Work:* Albany Inst Hist Art, NY; State Univ NY Art Gallery, Albany. *Exhib:* Artists of Mohawk-Hudson Region, NY, 71-75 & 80; New York Figurative Painting & Sculpture, First St Gallery, 71; Brooklyn Col Art Dept, Davis Long & Schoel Kopf Galleries, New York, 77; First St Gallery, New York, 79 & 82; 19th & 20th Century Woodcarvers, Schoelkopf Gallery, 86; and others. *Teaching:* Adj lectr sculpture, Brooklyn Col, NY, 72-76. *Awards:* Purchase Prize, Albany Inst, 73; State Univ NY, Albany, 89. *Bibliog:* Gabriel Laderman (auth), Unconventional realists, Artforum Mag, 71. *Media:* Pastel; Bronze. *Mailing Add:* 359 Springtown Rd New Paltz NY 12561

DAVIEE, JERRY MICHAEL
ADMINISTRATOR, PAINTER
b Oklahoma City, Okla, Mar 29, 47. *Study:* San Francisco Art Inst, 65-66; Oklahoma City Univ, BA, 69; Univ Tex, Austin, MA, 77, San Francisco Art Inst, MFA, 89. *Exhib:* San Francisco Arts Comn Gallery, 88; Gallery Sanchez, San Francisco, 89; Fort Mason Ctr, San Francisco, 89. *Collections Arranged:* Argentine Painting & Drawing, Univ Tex Art Mus, 75; Young Texas Artists Series, 77-78, Amarillo Competition, 79 & Jack Boynton: Retro-Spectrum, 80, Amarillo Art Ctr, Tex; Manuel Neri: Drawings & Bronzes, 81 & Sam Francis: Paintings on Paper & Monotypes, 83, Art Mus Asn, San Francisco. *Pos:* Registr, Univ Tex Art Mus, Austin, 74-77; cur, Amarillo Art Ctr, Tex, 77-80; cur, Art Mus Asn Am, San Francisco, 80-81, exhib prog dir, 80-83, planning & develop dir, 83-86; Grants officer, Oakland Mus, 89- *Teaching:* Instr painting & drawing, San Francisco Art Inst, summer 88, Core Studio Program, San Francisco Art Inst, spring 89. *Bibliog:* H J Wilson (auth),

A sequence of choices, Artweek, Vol 19, No 43, 12/17/88. *Mem:* Am Asn Mus; Col Art Asn. *Media:* Acrylic, Oil. *Res:* Contemporary art. *Publ:* Auth, American Paintings 1900-1970, 79 Nancy Chambers, 80, Before Columbus, 80 & Jack Boynton, 80, Amarillo Art Ctr, Tex; Stanton Macdonald-Wright, Art Mus Asn Am, 82. *Mailing Add:* c/o Oakland Mus 1000 Oak St Oakland CA 94607-4892

DAVIES, HARRY CLAYTON
PAINTER, PHOTOGRAPHER
b Wilmington, Del, Mar 3, 40. *Study:* Columbia Univ, BS, 66, MA, 69; Adelphi Univ, MA, 80. *Work:* Adelphi Univ, Garden City, NY; Washington Co Mus Fine Art, Hagerstown, Md; Fine Arts Mus Long Island, NY. *Exhib:* Long Island Faculty, Fine Arts Mus Long Island, Hempstead, 81; 2nd Invitational Show, Long Island Univ, Greenvale, 82; Eight by Ten, Washington Co Mus Fine Arts, Hagerstown, Md, 86; Heckscher Mus, Huntington, NY, 90. *Teaching:* Prof painting & drawing & chmn dept art, Adelphi Univ, 81- *Bibliog:* Long Island Look Ahead (interview), WSNL Channel 67, Smithtown, NY, 6/82. *Mem:* Huntington Township Art League (bd trustees, 85-); Col Art Asn, New York. *Media:* All. *Mailing Add:* Adelphi Univ Garden City NY 11530

DAVIES, HAYDN LLEWELLYN
SCULPTOR, PAINTER
b Rhymney, Wales, Nov 11, 21; Can citizen. *Study:* Ont Col Art, AOCA, 47. *Work:* Mus d'Arte Mod, Venice, Italy; Ctr Arts, Vero Beach, Fla; Galleria Nazionale d'Arte Mod e Contemporanea, Rome, Italy; Mus Royaux des Beaux-Arts de Belgique Art Mod, Brussels, Belg; Nat Mus Wales, Cardiff; Victoria & Albert Mus, London, Eng; Art Mus SE Tex, Beaumont; Gov Ontario, Toronto. *Comn:* Homage (laminated cedar), Lambton Col Arts & Technol, Sarnia, Ont, 74; Space Composition for Rebecca (fabricated aluminum), Burlington Cult Ctr, Ont, 78; Space Composition Red (fabricated aluminum), Govt Ont, Windsor, 78; Space Composition (fabricated aluminum), Trinity Sq, Bell Can, 84; Composition with Five Elements (fabricated welded steel), Gulf Can Ltd, Toronto, 80; Honda of Canada Mfg Inc, Alliston, Ont, 86 & 87. *Exhib:* Contemporary Sculpture at the Guild, Can Acad Arts, 80; Bridges Exhib, Pratt Inst, New York, 83; Ontario Art on View, Ont House, Paris, 82/84; Community Sculpture'85, 9 sculpture exhib, Cambridge, Ont, 85; Royal Can Acad Arts, Toronto, 87; solo exhibs, Planar Constructions, 87-89: Burlington Cult Ctr, Ont, 89, Stratford Art Gallery, Ont, 89, Ctr for Arts, Vero Beach, Fla, 90, Anita Shapolsky Gallery, New York, 91; Art Mus SE Texas, Beaumont, 92 & Asheville Art Mus, NC, 93; and others. *Teaching:* Artist-in-residence, Indian River Community Col, 82-83 & Ctr Arts, Vero Beach, Fla, 86; guest lectr, Sculpture Univ Toronto, 74 & Lambton Col Art & Technol, 75. *Awards:* Sculptor's Soc Can Award, On View, 76; Grants, Can Arts Coun, 78 & 80, Ont Arts Coun, 80, 81, 82 & 89 & Can Dept of External Affairs, 90. *Bibliog:* Nick Roukes (auth), Masters of Wood Sculpture, Watson-Guptill Publs, New York, 80; Jeanne Parkin (auth), Art in Architecture, Visual Arts, Ont, 82; Fern Bayer (auth), The Ontario Collection, Fitzhenry & Whiteside, Toronto, 84; Arthur Williams (auth), Sculpture/Technique, Form, Content, Davis Publications, Worcester, Mass, 89; Bryce Kanbara (auth), Haydn, Llewellyn Davies, Planar Constructions (exhib catlogue), 91. *Mem:* Royal Can Acad Arts. *Media:* Wood, Steel. *Dealer:* Anita Shapolsky 99 Spring St New York NY 10012. *Mailing Add:* 10 Rose Park Crescent Toronto ON M4T 1P9 Canada

DAVIES, HUGH MARLAIS
HISTORIAN, MUSEUM DIRECTOR
b Grahamstown, SAfrica, Feb 12, 48; Brit citizen. *Study:* Princeton Univ, AB, MFA & PhD. *Collections Arranged:* Artist & Fabricator (auth, catalog), 75, Richard Fleischner (auth, catalog), 77, Stephen Antonakos (auth, catalog), 78, Sam Gilliam (auth, catalog), 78, Al Souza (auth, catalog), 79, John Walker (auth, catalog), 79, George Trakas (auth, catalog), 80, Prints of Barnett Newman (auth, catalog), 83, Martin Puryear (coauth, catalog), 84; at Univ Gallery, Univ Mass, Amherst; Sitings: Alice Aycock, Richard Fleischner, Mary Miss & George Trakas (auth, catalog), La Jolla Mus Contemp Art, 86; Richard Long (auth, catalog), La Jolla Mus Contemp Art, 89. *Pos:* Asst dir, Monumenta Int Sculpture Exhib, Newport, RI, 74; dir, Univ Gallery, Univ Mass, Amherst, 75-83, San Diego Mus Contemp Art, 83- *Teaching:* Vis asst prof, Amherst Col, Mass, 80-83. *Awards:* Nat Endowment Arts Fel, 81-82. *Mem:* Asn Art Mus Dirs; Col Art Asn; Art Mus Asn Am. *Res:* 20th century American and European painting, sculpture, photography, design and architecture. *Publ:* auth, Francis Bacon: The Early and Middle Years, 1928-1958, Garland Press; coauth (with Horton Davies), Sacred Art in a Secular Century, Liturgical Press; auth (intro) to: Living with Modern Sculpture, Princeton Univ Art Mus-Princeton Univ Press, 82; coauth, Francis Bacon, Abbeville, 86. *Mailing Add:* c/o San Diego Mus Contemp Art 700 Prospect St La Jolla CA 92037

DAVIES, KENNETH SOUTHWORTH
PAINTER, INSTRUCTOR
b New Bedford, Mass, Dec 20, 25. *Study:* Mass Sch Art, Boston; Yale Sch Fine Arts, BFA, 50; New Eng Sch Law, Hon DFA, Boston. *Work:* Wadsworth Atheneum, Hartford, Conn; New Britain Mus Am Art, Conn; Detroit Inst Arts; Springfield Mus Fine Arts, Mass; Univ Nebr, Lincoln. *Comn:* US Postage Stamp commemorative for pharmacy, US Postal Serv, 72, chemistry, 76; Metrop Opera, 83. *Exhib:* American Symbolic Realism, London, Eng, 50; Carnegie Inst Int, 52; Whitney Mus Am Art Ann, 52; Univ Ill Ann, 52; 25 yr retrospective exhib, New Britain Mus Am Art, 71. *Teaching:* Sr Portfolio, Paier Col Art, Hamden, Conn, 53-81, vis prof & dean emer, 81-91. *Awards:* Louis Comfort Tiffany scholar, 50; Purchase Award, Berkshire Mus, Pittsfield & Springfield Mus, Mass, 50. *Mem:* Conn Acad Fine Arts (coun mem, 70, pres, 74-76). *Media:* Oil. *Publ:* Auth, Painting Sharp Focus Still Lifes, 75 & Ken Davies-Artist at Work, 78, Watson-Guptill. *Mailing Add:* PO Box 526 Madison CT 06443

DAVIES, THEODORE PETER
PAINTER, PRINTMAKER
b Brooklyn, NY, Oct 9, 28. *Study:* Sch Mod Photog, New York, 52; Art Students League, with George Grosz & Harry Sternberg, John Sloan Merit Scholar, 57-60. *Work:* Mus Mod Art, New York; Nat Gallery Art, Washington, DC; Philadelphia Mus Art; Art Students League; Queens Mus, NY; Guild Hall, East Hampton, NY. *Comn:* Six woodcuts on process of papermaking, Scott Paper Co, 60; three ed, woodcuts of New York financial dist, Picture Decorator, 68. *Exhib:* Silvermine Guild Ann; The Sense of Abstraction, Mus Mod Art, New York, 59; East End Arts Coun, NY, 80; Romana Kramoris Gallery, Sag Harbor, NY, 80; Parrish Art Mus, Southampton, NY, 80; Guild Hall, East Hampton, NY, 80; and others. *Awards:* First Prize Graphics, Atlantic City Ann Art Exhib, 59; Creative Artists Pub Serv Fel in Graphics, 73-74; Best in Show, 44th Ann Artists-Mem Exhib, Guild Hall Mus, East Hampton, NY. *Bibliog:* Laurence Campbell (auth), article, Art Students League News, 12/61; Gene Paris (auth), article, Long Island Press, 4/23/67; and others. *Mem:* Life mem Art Students League; Guild Hall, East Hampton, NY; Parrish Art Mus, Southampton, NY. *Media:* Multimedia; Woodcut, Serigraphy. *Publ:* Contribr, Woodcuts, 60; Realistic Abstract Drawing, 60; illusr, Picture Framing, 60. *Dealer:* Susan Teller Gallery Rm 405A 568 Broadway New York NY 10012; Benton Gallery 365 County Rd 39 Southampton NY 11968. *Mailing Add:* 2461 Town Line Rd Sag Harbor NY 11963

DÁVILA, MARITZA
PRINTMAKER, EDUCATOR
b Santurce, PR, Apr 18, 52. *Study:* Univ PR, BA, 74; Pratt Graphics Ctr, with Andrew Stasick & Margot Lovejoy, 74, Pratt Inst, MFA, 77. *Work:* Nat Libr, Paris; Printmaking Workshop, New York; Mus Univ PR, San Juan; Univ Tenn, Knoxville; Taller Galeria Fort Cadaques, Spain; and others. *Comn:* Reimpression of Thomas Hogarth plate, comn by A G Burkhart, Memphis, 85, 88 & 92. *Exhib:* Museo del Grabado, Instituto de Cultura Puertorriquena, San Juan, PR, 89; Textural Dimensions, Albers Fine Arts Gallery, Memphis, Tenn, 90; Coast to Coast, Flossie Martin Gallery, Radford Univ, Va, 90; Printmaking Symposium, Occidental Col Gallery, Los Angeles Printmaking Soc, Calif, 90; Delta State Univ Gallery, Cleveland, Miss, 91; and others. *Pos:* Bd, Memphis Books Mus Art Print Club, 87; mgr, Printmaking Workshop. *Teaching:* Instr art, Am Mus Natural Hist, New York, 79-81; artist-in-residence, Bd Educ, New York, 80; asst prof printmaking, Memphis Col Art, Tenn, 82- *Awards:* Printmaking Medal of Hon, Nat Asn Women Artists, 87; Purchase Award, Moravian Col, Bethlehem, Pa, 84; Award Printmaking, Ateneo Puertorriqueno, 85. *Bibliog:* Reuben Abruna (dir), Myths and Creations (film), New York Univ, 80; Davila to Conduct Workshop, Art Show at DSU Art Center, Bolival Commercial, Miss, 11/91; Fredric Koeppel Rev, Miss Coun Arts Fac Show, Commercial Appeal, 91. *Mem:* Los Angeles Printmaking Soc; Southern Graphic Coun; Memphis Print Club. *Media:* Mixed. *Dealer:* Albers Fine Arts Gallery 1027 Yates Rd Suite 101 Memphis TN 38119; Galeria Botello, San Juan Puerto Rico. *Mailing Add:* 3233 N Waynoka Circle Memphis TN 38111

DAVIS, ALONZO JOSEPH
VISUAL ARTIST, ADMINISTRATOR
b Tuskegee, Ala, Feb 2, 42. *Study:* Pepperdine Univ, BA, 64; Otis Art Inst, Los Angeles, BFA, 71, MFA, 73. *Work:* Afro-Am Studies Ctr, Univ Calif, Los Angeles; Libr Collection, Calif Polytechnic Inst, Pomona. *Comn:* Group mural, 50th & Crenshaw, Los Angeles, Calif, 73-75; sculpture, Rogers Recreational Ctr, Los Angeles, 74; mural-retainer wall, Santa Monica Freeway underpass at La Brea, Los Angeles, 75; west wall mural, Watts Towers Neighborhood Arts Ctr, 76; north wall mural, Brockman Gallery Productions, Los Angeles, 82. *Collections Arranged:* Brockman Gallery, Los Angeles, ten month installations, 67-73. *Pos:* Exec dir, Brockman Gallery Productions, Los Angeles, 73-82. *Teaching:* Instr African art, Calif State Univ, Northridge, 76-78; instr, Otis Art Inst, 78-79. *Bibliog:* J Edward Atkinson (auth), Black Dimensions in Contemp Am Art, 71; Lewis & Waddy (auth), Black Artists on Art, Vol II, Pub Contemp Crafts Inc, 71; Elton Fax (auth), Black Artists of the New Generation, Dodd Mead, 77. *Mem:* Artists for Econ Action; Calif Confedn of the Arts (bd mem); Nat Conf of Artists; Am Mus Asn; Smithsonian Assoc. *Publ:* Auth (catalogue introd), Varying Directions of Contemporary Black Artists, State of Calif, 75. *Dealer:* Sol Del Rio Gallery 1020 Townsend Ave San Antonio TX 78209. *Mailing Add:* c/o San Antonio Art Inst 6000 N New Braunfels Ave San Antonio TX 78209

DAVIS, BEN
PHOTOGRAPHER, PAINTER
b Syracuse, NY, June 5, 47. *Study:* Stetson Univ, Fla, ABA; Univ Fla, BS(commun); Fla State Univ, MFA. *Work:* Ctr Creative Photog, Univ Ariz, Tucson; Mus Mod Art, New York; Ctr Advan Visual Studies, Mass Inst Technol, Cambridge; Lomholt Formular Archive, Falling, Denmark. *Exhib:* Light Gallery, New York, 77; Art Inst Boston, 80; Mass Inst Technol, 81; Mail Art, Pieter Brattinga Gallery, Amsterdam, Neth, 81; Sky Art Conf, Munich, 83; Other Cinema, Syracuse Univ, 84; Ars Electronica, Stadt Mus, Linz, Austria, 86; Biennale Venice Int Art Exhib, 86; Boston Computer Mus, 87. *Pos:* Illusr, Fla State Archives & Mus, 74-75; dir, Senoj, Inc, Atlanta, Ga, 76-; dir, Visual Computing, MIT, 86-91; res assoc, MIT Ctr Educ Computing, 91- *Teaching:* Head dept video & photo, Atlanta Col Art, 75-86; Mass Inst Technol, 83-84; MIT Media-Lab, MIT Visual Arts Prog, 86-90. *Awards:* Fel, Nat Endowment Arts, Alternative Spaces, 77-78; Fel, Ctr Advan Visual Studies, 83-84. *Bibliog:* Steven Gowin (auth), The emperor's new videodisc, Videography Mag, 1/86; Infra-Thin Multimedia, Visual Resources Mag, 6/91; Image Learning, Teachers Col Press, 89. *Mem:* IMAGE Film & Video, Atlanta, Ga; Int Interactive Communications Soc, Atlanta, Ga. *Media:* Photo

Electronic Media, Paint. *Publ:* Auth, Role of the artist, Community TV Rev, 4/81; Sky Disc: Implications, Ctr Adv Visual Studies, Mass Inst Technol, 84; The age of computer art, Atlanta Art Papers, 1-2/86. *Mailing Add:* 168 Norfolk St Cambridge MA 02139

DAVIS, BERTHA G
PAINTER
b Vilno, Lithuania, July 15, 18; US citizen. *Study:* San Miguel Allende Pan Am Col, 60-61; with Fred Samuelson, Harold Phenix 72-73, Ed Whitney, 78 & Ed Betts, 79. *Work:* Lewisville City Bank, Tex; Shell Oil Co, Houston, Tex; La Ciudadela, Mex; Inst de Relaciones Culturales, Mex; and 150 pvt collections. *Comn:* Paintings, Arthur D Andersen Co, Houston; paintings, Transco Towers, Houston. *Exhib:* One-woman shows, Univ Tex Health Sci Ctr, Dallas, 79, Jewish Community Gallery, 81, Wichita Falls Art League, NTex Fed Gallery, 85 & First City Bank, Houston, Tex, 89; retrospectives, Jewish Community Ctr, Houston, 86, Richards Gallery, Galveston, 92 & Buteras, Houston, 92; El Paso Art League, Tex; Am Painters in Paris, France, 76; O'Kane Gallery, Univ Houston, Tex, 88; Jewish Community Ctr, W, 90; and others. *Awards:* Am Painters in Paris, France, 76; Signature Mem, Southwest Watercolor Soc, 81; Second Prize, Tex Fine Arts, 83. *Mem:* Southwest Watercolor Soc, Dallas; Texas Fine Art Asn; Western Art Asn; Watercolor Art Soc, Houston. *Media:* Acrylic, Watercolor. *Publ:* Contribr, La Revue Moderne des Artes de La Vie, 65, 68 & 69; Art in Jewish Life, Nat Coun Art, Dallas, 76; Repartorium Artists Guide European des Beaux Arts, 66-67 & Vision Mag, 82; Open Dallas-76 Nat Coun Art in Jewish Life, New York, 83. *Dealer:* Nimbus Gallery 1135 Dragon St Dallas TX 75207. *Mailing Add:* 8803 Jackson St Houston TX 77036

DAVIS, BRAD (BRADLEY DARIUS)
PAINTER
b Duluth, Minn, Apr 24, 42. *Study:* St Olaf Col, 61; Univ Chicago, 62; Art Inst Chicago, 63; Univ Minn, BA, 66; Hunter Col, 70. *Work:* Neue Galerie, Sammlung Ludwig, Aachen, WGer; Walker Art Ctr, Minneapolis; Whitney Mus Am Art, Mus Mod Art, New York; Saarland Mus, Saarbracken, WGer; and others. *Exhib:* Biennial, 64 & two-person show, 66, Walker Art Ctr, Minneapolis; Ann Exhib, 72 & Am Drawings '63-'73, 73, Whitney Mus Am Art; solo exhibs, Holly Solomon Gallery, New York, 75, 79, 81 & 83; The New Bestiary: Animal Imagery in Contemp Art, Inst Contemp Art, Va Mus, Richmond, 81; Friends of Corcoran Gallery 20th Anniversary Exhib, Corcoran Gallery Art, 81; New Work in Black and White, 81 & A Penthouse Aviary, 81, Art Lending Serv, Mus Mod Art, New York; Decoration and Representation, Alta Col Art Gallery, Can, 82; New Decorative Works from the Collection of Norma & William Roth, Loch Haven Art Ctr, Orlando & Jacksonville Art Mus, Fla, 83; New Decorative Art, Berkshire Mus, Pittsfield, Mass, 83; Back to the USA Traveling Exhib, Kunstmus, Lucerne, Switz, Rheinische Landesmus, Bonn & Kunstverein, Stuttgart, Ger, 83-84; and many others; Landscape/Cityscape, Art Gallery, State Univ NY Potsdam, 78; Pattern & Decoration, Sewall Art Gallery, Rice Univ, 78; Green Magic, Rutgers Univ Gallery, 79; Dekor, Kunstverein, Mannheim, Ger, 80; Am Drawings, Venice Biennale, Italy, 80; and many others. *Awards:* First Prize & Spec Jury Award, Minneapolis Inst Art Biennial, 65; Second Prize & Purchase Prize, Walker Art Ctr, 66. *Bibliog:* Alexandra Anderson (auth), Clay gardens, Portfolio, 3-4/82; Klaus Ahrens (auth), Schreie und Flustern, Stern Mag, Hamburg, Ger, 5/83; Klaus Honnef, New York Aktuelle, Kunstforum Int, 5/83. *Media:* Mixed. *Mailing Add:* c/o Holly Solomon Gallery 724 Fifth Ave New York NY 10019

DAVIS, CHARLES BURDIS, III
ART DEALER, COLLECTOR
b Raleigh, NC, Apr 4, 45. *Study:* Univ NC, BA, 70. *Exhib:* African Art from New Orleans Collections, 89; Wild Spirits, Strong Medicine, 89; Voruba, Nine Centuries of African Art and Thought, 90; Icons, Ideals and Power in the Art of Africa, 90. *Collections Arranged:* Nigerian Sculpture, Birmingham Mus, Ala, 84; Igbo Arts, Univ Calif, Los Angeles, 85; A Human Ideal in African Art, Smithsonian Inst, Washington, DC, 86; Bamana Figurative Sculpture, Metrop Mus Art, New York, 86; other works exhibited at the St Louis Mus Art, Cleveland Mus, New Orleans Mus Art & De Young Mus, San Francisco. *Pos:* Prin, Davis Gallery, New Orleans, currently. *Awards:* Beaux Arts Award, Contemp Arts Ctr, 88. *Mem:* New Orleans Contemp Arts Ctr (adv bd, 84, 85, 86 & 90); Wyes Art Auction, New Orleans (adv bd, 83-86). *Specialty:* African art. *Collection:* African and contemporary art and photography. *Publ:* Auth, The Animal Motif in Bamana Art, Davis Gallery, 81. *Mailing Add:* 3964 Magazine St New Orleans LA 70115

DAVIS, D JACK
EDUCATOR, ADMINISTRATOR
b Canton, Tex, May 17, 38. *Study:* Baylor Univ, BA, 59, MA, 61; Univ Minn, PhD, 66, studies with Reid Hastie, Paul Torrance & Malcolm Myers. *Pos:* Assoc dir & dir evaluation, Aesthetic Educ Prog, Arts in Gen Educ Proj, Cemrel Inc, St Louis, Mo, 69-71; ed, Studies in Art Educ, Nat Art Educ Asn, 75-77. *Teaching:* Instr art, Wayland Col, Plainview, Tex, 61-63; prof art, Tex Tech Univ, 65-69; prof, vprovost & assoc vpres acad affairs, Univ NTex, Denton, 71- *Awards:* Distinguished Fel, 89 & Lowenfeld Award, 90, Nat Art Educ Asn; Tex Art Educator Year, 91. *Mem:* Life mem Nat Art Educ Asn (chmn higher educ div, 73-75); Tex Art Educ Asn (pres, 87-89); Nat Coun Art Adminrs; Tex Asn Sch Art; Nat Soc Study Educ. *Publ:* Coauth, The Artist in the School, Cemrel Inc, 70; auth, Research in art education, Art Educ, 71; ed, Behavioral Emphasis in Art Education, Nat Art Educ Asn, 75; The visual arts: A classroom myth or an accountable program?, Nat Asn Sec Sch Principals Bulletin, 11/79; auth, Research on Teacher Education, Teacher Education in Visual Arts, Macmillan, 90. *Mailing Add:* 2007 Locksley Lane Denton TX 76201

DAVIS, DAVID ENSOS
SCULPTOR
b Rona de Jos, Romania, Aug 27, 20; US citizen. *Study:* Beaux Arts, Paris, France, 45; Cleveland Inst Art, BFA(scholar), 48; Case Western Reserve Univ, MA, 61. *Work:* Akron Mus Art, Ohio; Cleveland Mus Art, Ohio; Kenneth Beck Cult Ctr, Cleveland, Ohio; Kent State Univ; Bell Tel Co, Cleveland, Ohio. *Comn:* David-Berger Monument, Jewish Community Ctr, Cleveland, 73; outdoor sculpture, Progressive Insurance Co; outdoor sculpture, Van Wezel Performing Arts Hall, Sarasota, Fla; outdoor sculpture, Case Western Reserve Univ, 82. *Exhib:* May Show Ann, Cleveland Mus Art, 72-89; Ohio Painting & Sculpture, Dayton Art Inst, 74; Mats & Techniques of 20th Century Artists, Cleveland Mus Art, 77; Ten Collages & One Sculpture in the Harmonic Grid, Akron Inst Art, Ohio, 78; Recent Sculpture & Collages, New Gallery Contemp Art, Cleveland, 78; Brevard Art Ctr & Mus, Melbourne, Fla, 88; Polk Mus, Lakeland, Fla, 88; Cleveland Ctr Contemp Art, Ohio, 89. *Awards:* Major Sculpture Cash Prize, May Show, Cleveland Mus Art, 77; Individual Artist Award, Ohio Art Coun, 78; Cleveland Art Prize, 80. *Bibliog:* Prof Carol Nathason (auth), The Harmonic Grid, Case Western Reserve, 75; Edward B Henning (auth, catalog), 1984 Distinguished Alumnus, Cleveland Inst Art; Joseph Jacobs (auth, catalog), David E Davis: New Sculptures, 87-88. *Mem:* Trustee Cleveland Inst Art; Sculptors Guild, New York. *Media:* Mixed. *Mailing Add:* 12204 Euclid Ave Cleveland OH 44106

DAVIS, DOUGLAS MATTHEW
ARTIST, CRITIC
b Washington, DC, Apr 11, 33. *Study:* Abbott Art Sch, Washington, DC: Am Univ, BA, 56; Rutgers Univ, NJ, MA, 58. *Work:* Metrop Mus Art, New York; Ludwig Mus, Cologne, Ger; Dahlem Mus, WBerlin; Venice Biennale Archive, Italy; Hirshhorn Mus & Sculpture Garden, Washington, DC; Walker Art Ctr, Minneapolis; Wadsworth Atheneum, Hartford, Conn. *Exhib:* retrospective, Everson Mus, Syracuse, 72; Projekt 74, Kunstverein & Kunsthalle, Cologne, Ger, 74; San Francisco Mus Art, 75; Projected Video, Whitney Mus Am Art, New York & San Paulo Biennale, 75; Documenta 6, Kassel, WGer, 77; Arbeiten, Works 1970-1977, Berlin 1977-78; Neuer Berline Kunstverein (with catalog), 78 & Neue Galerie, Aachen, WGer, 78; Centre Georges Pompidou, Paris, 81; Whitney Mus Am Art, 81; Salon Sztuki (with catalog), Lodz, Poland, 82; Guggenheim Mus, New York, 88; solo exhibs, Solomon R Guggenheim Mus (with catalog), New York, 88, Contemp Arts Ctr, Cincinnati, Ohio, 88, Col Art Asn, Little Rock, Ark, 89, Kunstverein Cologne, Ger, 89, Centro de Arte y Communicacion, Harrod's en Arte, Buenos Aires, 91, Redness: A New Room, Ronald Feldman Fine Arts, New York, 92; Kunstverein, Cologne, 89; Menage A Trois, Satallite TV Performance, 89; Ronald Feldman Fine Arts, New York, 91. *Collections Arranged:* Wallraf-Richartz Mus, Cologne; Finch Col Mus, New York; De Saisset Art Gallery, Calif; Everson Mus Art, NY; Panza di Biuma, Milan. *Pos:* Critic/sr writer archit & photog, Newsweek, 69-88; dir, Int Network Arts, 79-; visual arts policy panel, Nat Endowment Arts, 80-83; advisor archit & design, Art in Embassies Prog, US Dept State, 86-88; consult in media, Rockfeller Found. *Teaching:* Vis artist, Corcoran Sch Art, 70 & 71, State Univ NY, Buffalo, 73; art critic in residence, NY Univ, 75; regents lectr, Univ Calif, San Diego, 76; instr advanced video & performance, Int Network Arts, State Univ NY Purchase, Philadelphia Col Art, 76-, Columbia Univ, Univ Calif, Los Angeles; vis prof, Artcener Col, Pasadena, 88-90; vis prof art & design, Univ Calif, Los Angeles, 90-91. *Awards:* Nat Endowment Arts Grants, 70 & 75; NY State Coun Arts Grant for Creative Work in Mixed Media, 70; Chairman's Grant, Nat Endowment Arts, 81 & Nat Pub Radio, 83; Intermedia Arts, Boston, 88; Trust for Mutual Understanding, 89; Rockefeller Found Grant, 90. *Bibliog:* Irving Sandler (auth), Questions NY-Moscow, San Francisco Mus Mod Art, 76. *Mem:* Artists Equity; Authors Guild. *Media:* Videotape, Printmaking. *Publ:* Auth, Media-art-media, Arts Mag, 9/71; Video obscura, 4/72 & What is content, 10/73, Artforum; Art and the Future, Praeger, 73; Fragments for a new art of the future, 75; co-ed, The New Television, Mass Inst Technol Press, 76; auth, Artculture: Essays on the Post-Modern, Harper & Row, 77; Photography as fine art, 83. *Dealer:* Ronald Feldman Fine Arts 31 Mercer St New York NY 10013. *Mailing Add:* 80 Wooster St New York NY 10012

DAVIS, ELLEN N
HISTORIAN
b Hackensack, NJ, July 20, 37. *Study:* Inst Fine Arts, NY Univ, with Peter H Von Blanckenhagen, PhD, 73. *Teaching:* Assoc prof ancient art hist, Queens Col, City Univ New York, 66- *Awards:* Arlt Award, Coun Grad Studies. *Mem:* Archaeol Inst Am; New York Soc (pres, 80-83); New York Bronze Age Colloq. *Res:* Aegean metalworking, painting and connections with Egypt. *Publ:* Auth, The Vapheio cups: one Minoan & one Mycenean?, Art Bulletin LVI, 74; ed, Symposium on the Dark Ages, Archaeol Inst Am, 74; auth, The Vapheio Cups and Aegean Metalware, Garland Press, 76; The icongraphy off the Thera Ship Fresco, In: Greek Art and Icongraphy, Univ Wis Press, 83; Youth and age in the Thera Frescoes , Am J Archaeol, 86. *Mailing Add:* 225 E 76th St New York NY 10021

DAVIS, HARRY ALLEN
PAINTER, EDUCATOR
b Hillsboro, Ind, May 21, 14. *Study:* Herron Sch Art, Ind Univ-Purdue Univ, Indianapolis, BFA, 38; Am Acad Rome, FAAR, 41. *Work:* Butler Inst Am Art, Youngstown, Ohio; Springfield Art Mus, Mo; Evansville Mus Arts & Sci, Ind; Grover M Hermann Fine Arts Ctr, Marietta Col, Ohio; Carroll Reece Mus, Johnson City, Tenn; plus others. *Comn:* Union Station, Bank One, 73; Pathology Building, Surgeons' College, Ind Mus Med Hist, Indianapolis, 74; History of Clay County (mural), Brazil, Ind, 79; four historic landmarks, Lafayette Life Insurance Co, 80; 29 Courtyard Am United Life Bldg, 89.

Exhib: Eight Butler Midyear Exhibs, Youngstown, 61-78; fifteen Watercolor USA, Nat Watercolor Exhibs, Springfield, Mo, 65-92; Mainstreams Int Exhibs, Marietta, Ohio, 68-77; Bicentennial Traveling Show, Ind State Mus, Indianapolis Mus Art, plus others, 76-77; The Italian Influence Traveling Exhib, 83; and others. *Teaching:* Artist in residence, Beloit Col, 41-42; prof painting & drawing, Herron Sch Art, Ind Univ-Purdue Univ, Indianapolis, 46-83, prof emer, 83- *Awards:* Second Medal, Butler Midyear Exhib, 78; Best of Show, Anderson Five-State Winter Show, 82; Best of Show, Hoosier Salon, 88 & 89. *Mem:* Fel Am Acad Rome; Ind Artists Club (pres, 55-56, dir, 72); charter mem, Watercolor USA Hon Soc; Ind Acad; and others. *Media:* Multi. *Mailing Add:* 6315 Washington Blvd Indianapolis IN 46220

DAVIS, JACK R
PAINTER, EDUCATOR
Study: Cent State Univ, Okla, BA; Univ Okla, MFA(painting & printmaking). *Work:* State of Okla Collection & Traveling Exhib; Okla Univ Col Nursing; Christ the King Church; Okla State Health Asn; and many others. *Exhib:* Kans State Univ Exhib to Grad Midwestern Univs, 69; one-man shows, Painting Prints & Vacuum Forms, Contemp Arts Found, Oklahoma City, 70, Graphic Retrospective, Emporia, Kans, 70 & Ten-O-One Gallery, Oklahoma City, 81-82; 31st Ann Exhib Okla Artists, Philbrook Art Ctr, Tulsa, 71; State of Okla Art Collection Exhib, Okla Art Ctr, 82; Okla Oil Men's Asn, 81; Chumming's Gallery, Edmond, Okla, 82; two-man exhib, Kirkpatrick Mus, 86. *Teaching:* Instr art, Okla Arts & Sci Found, 67-70; prof art, Oklahoma City Univ, 69-; instr art, state supported art classes for all fifth graders in Oklahoma City Pub Sch Syst, 71-72; instr, Okla Art Ctr, currently. *Awards:* Graphics Awards, 30th & 31st Ann Exhib Okla Artists, Tulsa, 70-71 & 57th Ann Tulsa Regional Exhib, 71. *Media:* Mixed. *Mailing Add:* Dept Art Oklahoma City Univ 2501 N Blackwelder Oklahoma City OK 73106

DAVIS, JAMES GRANBERRY
PAINTER
b Springfield, Mo, 31. *Study:* Wichita State Univ, Kansas, Mo, BFA, 54, MFA, 60. *Work:* Metrop Mus Art, New York; Nat Mus Am Art, Washington, DC; Univ Ariz Mus Art, Tuscon; Ariz State Univ Mus Art, Tempe; Mulvane Art Ctr, Kans. *Comn:* Large painting, Container Corp Am, New York, 65. *Exhib:* Arizona's Finest, Tempe Art Ctr, 82; 38th Corcoran Biennial, Washington, DC, 83; Solo exhibs, Germans Van Eck Gallery, New York, 84, Basil Art Fair, Switz, 85, Hans Redmann Gallery, Berlin, WGer, 86, 88 & 89, Marilyn Fine Arts, Santa Fe, NMex, 87, Shoshana Wayne Gallery, Santa Monica, Calif, 87, Etherton Gallery, Tucson, Ariz, 87 & Andrea Ross Gallery, Santa Monica, Calif, 89; Modern American Printmaking, Am-Haus, Ger, 85; The Neo-Figure, Riva Yares Gallery, Scottsdale, 85; Artists Who Teach, Nat Mus Art, Washington, DC, 87; 25 Year Retrospective, Tucson Mus Art, 88; Evidence, San Antonio Mus Art, Tex, 89; The Hunger Project, Scottsdale Ctr Arts, 89. *Teaching:* Assoc prof, Wichita state Univ, Kans, 59-62; instr painting & printmaking, Univ Mo, Columbia, 67-69; asst prof painting, Univ Ariz, Tucson, 79-70, assoc prof, 70- *Awards:* Purchase Award, Kans Artists Ann, 62, Topeka Art Ctr, 66, Eastern Mich Univ, 68 & Tucson Art Ctr, 74. *Bibliog:* Anita Winegate (auth), James G Davis, Artspace, 1/79; Barbara Cortright (auth), Interview with James G Davis, Phoenix Mag, 1/80; Carol Cratoza (auth), James G Davis, Art Voices S, 3/80. *Media:* Oil; Lithography, Monotype. *Mailing Add:* c/o Riva Yares Gallery 3625 Bishop Lane Scottsdale AZ 85251

DAVIS, JAMES ROBERT
CARTOONIST
b Marion, Ind, July 28, 45. *Study:* Ball State Univ. *Pos:* Artist, Groves & Assoc Advert, Muncie, Ind, 68-69; asst to cartoonist, Tumbleweeds (comic strip), 69-78; adv bd, Calif Mus Cartoon Art, 85- *Awards:* Emmy Award for Writing Best Animated Special, 85; Distinguished Alumni Award, Am Asn State Col & Univ, 85; Segar Award for All Round Excellence, 85 & Best Humor Strip Cartoonist, 86, Nat Cartoonist Soc. *Mem:* Nat Cartoonists Soc; Newspaper Comics Coun. *Publ:* Auth, Garfield Mix & Match Storybook, 82 & Garfield the Knight in Shining Armor, 82, Random House; Garfield Takes the Cake, 82, The Garfield Treasury, 82 & Garfield Weighs In, 82, Ballantine. *Mailing Add:* c/o United Media 200 Park Ave New York NY 10166

DAVIS, JAMES WESLEY
PAINTER, WRITER
b Los Angeles, Calif, Oct 9, 40. *Study:* Calif Col Arts & Crafts, BA(educ) & BFA; Univ Colo, MA & MFA(Inst Arts & Humanities Fel), 67. *Work:* Minn Mus Art; Ill State Mus; Alberta Col Art; Mulvane Art Mus; Laguna Gloria Mus; and others. *Exhib:* Mid-America 4, St Louis Art Mus & Nelson/Atkins Mus, 72; Smithsonian Inst Traveling Show, 73-74; Calgary Int Biennial, Alta Col Art Gallery, 74; Mid-Year Ann, Butler Inst Am Art, 74 & 75; 19th Mid-South Biennial, Brooks Mem Gallery, 75; Irwin Collection, Kvannert Mus, 80; Watercolor USA, Springfield Mus, 85; 6th Alabama Works on Paper, Int Auburn Art Assoc, 85; Am Watercolors, Chateau de Tours, France, 87. *Pos:* Assoc dean creative arts & dir special progs & inter-arts, San Francisco State Univ, 89-; dir, Creativity Inst, San Francisco, presently. *Teaching:* Instr painting & art hist, Univ Ark, 67-69; prof painting & drawing, Western Ill Univ, 69-81; vis prof, Univ Colo, 82; head art dept, ETex State Univ, 83-80; chmn art dept, Ind State Univ, 88-89. *Awards:* Sworovski Int Award, Sworovski of Belg, 67; James D Phelan Award, 73. *Bibliog:* S W Semaj (auth), Memories, Structure, Vol 2, No 3; Alfred Frankenstein (auth), Visual, surreal acrobatics, San Francisco Chronicle, 1/74; Sylvia Brown (auth), Editorial highlights, City Mag, 2/16/74. *Mem:* Col Art Asn Am. *Media:* Acrylic, Watercolor. *Publ:* Auth, Self-actualized sculpture, Sculpture Int, Vol 3, No 2; Unified drawing by means of hybrids and grids, Leonardo, Vol 5, No 1; Some perceptual considerations on Vermeer and op art, Studies in the 20th Century, 73; Revival in the slumbering cornfield, Art J, fall 74; On mounds, Studio Int, 4/74. *Mailing Add:* 37 Noe St San Francisco CA 94114

DAVIS, JERROLD
PAINTER
b Chico, Calif, Nov 2, 26. *Study:* Univ Calif, Berkeley, BA, 53, MA. *Work:* Carnegie Inst Int, Pittsburgh; Santa Barbara Mus Art, Calif; Los Angeles Mus Art; San Francisco Mus Art; Oakland Mus Art; and others. *Exhib:* One-man shows, Calif Palace of Legion of Honor, 60-64, Flint Art Inst, 64, Newport Harbor Art Mus, Newport Beach, Calif, 73 & retrospective, Richmond Art Ctr, Calif, 80; Especially for Children, Los Angeles Co Mus, 65; Univ Ariz, 67; Lytton Ctr, Los Angeles, 67 & 68; A Sense of Place, 74; and others. *Teaching:* Instr, Univ Calif, summer 67. *Awards:* Guggenheim Fel, 58-59; Am Fedn Arts-Ford Found artist in residence grant, Flint, Mich, 64; Prizes, Calif Palace Legion Honor, 60 & 62; and others. *Mailing Add:* 66 Twain Ave Berkeley CA 94708

DAVIS, KEITH FREDERIC
CURATOR, HISTORIAN
b Middletown, Conn, June 29, 52. *Study:* Drew Univ, 70-72; Southern Ill Univ, BS(cinema & photog), 72-74; Univ NMex, MA(art hist), 79. *Collections Arranged:* Edward Weston: One Hundred Photographs (auth, catalog), Nelson-Atkins Mus Art, Kansas City & traveling; Andre Kertesz: Form and Feeling, Sheldon Mem Art Gallery, Lincoln, Nebr & traveling, 83-86; Harry Callahan: New Color, Photographs 1978-1987 (auth, catalog), Nelson-Atkins Mus Art, Kansas City, Mo & traveling, 88- 89; Todd Webb: Photographs of New York and Paris, 1945-1960 (auth, catalog), Nat Ctr Photog, Bath, Eng & traveling, 88; Pictorialist Photography, Akron Art Mus, Ohio & traveling, 88-89; Night Light: A Survey of Twentieth Century Night Photography, Nelson-Atkins Mus Art & traveling, 89-91; and others. *Pos:* Intern, Int Mus Photog, Eastman House, Rochester, NY, 78-79; cur, Fine Art Collections, Hallmark Cards Inc, Kansas City, Mo, 79- *Awards:* Beaumont Newhall History of Photography Award, Univ NMex, 77; Nat Endowment Humanities Fel, 86-87. *Bibliog:* Big business: photography's angel in the wings, Popular Photog, 6/81; Gloria Baker Feinstein (auth), Keith Davis: an interview, Forum, 3/82; Donald Hoffman (auth), Picturing a perfect exhibition, Kansas City Star, 5/3/87. *Mem:* Soc Photographic Educ (bd dirs, 84-87). *Res:* History of 19th and 20th century photography. *Publ:* Auth, Desire Charnay: Expeditionary Photographer, Univ NMex Press, 81; George N Barnard: Photographer of Sherman's Campaign, Hallmark Cards, Inc, 90; Clarence John Laughlin: Visionary Photographer, Hallmark Cards, Inc, 90. *Mailing Add:* Hallmark Cards Inc Fine Arts Progs No 284 Kansas City MO 64108

DAVIS, KIMBERLY BROOKE
GALLERY DIRECTOR, ART DEALER
b Los Angeles, Calif, Nov, 25, 53. *Study:* Pratt Inst, BFA, 74. *Pos:* Admin asst, Inst Art & Urban Res, 75; admin asst, Guggenheim Mus, 76; assoc dir, Judith Selkowitz Fine Arts, 76-79; dir, Bernard Jacobson Gallery, Los Angeles, 79-84 & New York & Los Angeles, 83; dir, LA Louver Gallery, Venice, Calif, 85- *Mem:* Mod & Contemp Arts Coun Los Angeles Co Mus; Int Fine Art Print Dealers Asn. *Specialty:* Painting and sculpture by leading American and European contemporary artists, fine art prints. *Mailing Add:* LA Louver Gallery 55 N Venice Blvd Venice CA 90291

DAVIS, L CLARICE
BOOK DEALER, ART LIBRARIAN
b Akron, Ohio. *Study:* Univ Akron, BA(fine arts), 55; Univ Calif, Los Angeles, MLS, 61, MA(art hist), 68. *Pos:* Chief librn, Los Angeles Co Mus Art, 63-68; owner & mgr, Davis Art Book Store & Gallery, Los Angeles, 71-79, partner, Davis & Schorr Art Books, 79-91, L Clarice Davis, Fine & Applied Art Books, 91-; actg unit head, Art Libr, Univ Calif, Los Angeles, 73-75; art reference librn, Beverly Hills Pub Libr, 88- *Teaching:* Asst prof mod art hist, Calif State Univ, Northridge, 61-63 & 68-69; lectr, Otis Art Inst, Los Angeles, 69-70. *Mem:* Art Libr Soc NAm; Antiquarian Booksellers Asn Am. *Specialty:* Out of print art books and exhibition catalogues. *Publ:* Contribr bibliog catalog, R B Kitaj, 65 & Peter Voulkos, Sculpture, 65, Los Angeles Co Mus Art; contribr introd, Pornography in Fine Art From Ancient Times, Los Angeles Elysium, 69; auth, Annuals of auction sales, Art Libr Soc NAm Newsletter, 12/76. *Mailing Add:* PO Box 56054 Sherman Oaks CA 91413

DAVIS, MARIAN B
HISTORIAN, CURATOR
b St Louis Co, Mo, Sept 24, 11. *Study:* Washington Univ, BA, 32, MA, 35; Radcliffe Col, MA, 39, PhD, 48. *Collections Arranged:* Sch of Fontainebleau, 65; plus many others. *Pos:* Chief cur & actg dir, Art Teaching Gallery, Univ Tex, Austin, 63-78; instr art hist, Worcester Art Mus, 41-44. *Teaching:* From instr to prof, Univ Tex, Austin, 44-78, emer prof, 78- *Mem:* Col Art Asn (dir, 51-55); Soc Archit Historians; Archaeol Inst Am; Renaissance Soc; Nat Trust Hist Preserv. *Res:* Italian Renaissance; United States architecture. *Publ:* Auth, Two eighteenth century paintings, Worcester Art Mus Ann V, 46; Summer travel for students, Col Art J, 54; Some first impressions of Sicily, Tex Trends Art Educ, autumn 59; Art history--contribution to understanding, Western Arts Asn Bull, 61. *Mailing Add:* 2701 Wooldridge Dr Austin TX 78703

DAVIS, MEREDITH J
GRAPHIC ARTIST, EDUCATOR
b Pittsburgh, Pa, May 15, 48. *Study:* Pa State Univ, BS, 70, MEd, 74; Cranbrook Acad Art, with Katherine & Michael McCoy, MFA, 75. *Work:* Mead Libr Ideas, Dayton, Ohio; Am Inst Graphic Arts, New York. *Exhib:* Am Inst Graphic Arts, New York, 75, 82-83, 85 & 88; Mead Ann Report Competition, New York, 80; Soc Typographic Arts, Women in Design, Chicago, 81 & 88; New York Art Dir Club, 81 & 83; New York Type Dir Club, 82-85; 88; Ryder Gallery, Chicago, 85; Am Asn Mus, 84 & 87. *Pos:* Cur

educ, Hunter Mus Art, 75-76; partner, Communication Design Inc, Richmond, Va, 79-89; ed, Am Ctr Design, currently. *Teaching:* prof communication arts & design, Va Commonwealth Univ, 76- 89; dept head & prof graphic design, NC State Univ, 89- *Awards:* Excellence in Ann Report Design, Mead Libr Ideas, 81; Excellence Visual Communication, Designers Choice, Indust Design Mag, 82 & Creativity 13, New York Art Dir, 83; Gold Medalist, Washington AA Directors, 85; Silver & Gold Medalist, Case Cover Competition, Washington, DC, 85. *Bibliog:* Annual reports: Business as usual?, Art Direction Mag, 81. *Mem:* Am Inst Graphic Arts; Graphic Design Educ Asn (pres, 86-88 & 92-94, vpres, 90-92); Am Ctr Design (bd dirs, 90-94). *Publ:* Coauth, Problem Solving in the Man-Made Environment, Cranbrook Environmental Educ Proj, 75; contribr, Trends in Annual Reports, S D Warren Co, 83; The role of education in research, Design J, 83. *Mailing Add:* NC State Univ Box 7701 Raleigh NC 27695

DAVIS, PAUL
PAINTER, EDUCATOR
b Providence, RI, Dec 2, 46. *Study:* Boston Univ, BFA, 73, studied with Phillip Guston and James Weeks, MFA, 75. *Work:* Utah Mus Fine Arts, Salt Lake City; Salt Lake Art Ctr; Springville Mus Art, Utah. *Comn:* Ten paintings, Fremont Indian Mus, Salina, Utah, 87; Designs for 14 stations of the cross, St Elizabeth's Church, Richfield, Utah, 92. *Exhib:* 2-D Nat Competition, San Diego, 84; Diamonds Are Forever, Utah Mus Fine Arts & Smithsonian Inst, Salt Lake, Utah, 89; solo exhib, Salt Lake Art Ctr, Utah, 89. *Pos:* Chair, art dept, Univ Utah, 82-88. *Teaching:* Instr drawing, Art Inst Boston, 73-76; instr painting, Regis Col, Weston, Mass, 75-76; prof painting/drawing, Univ Utah, Salt Lake City, 76- *Awards:* Purchase Prize, Utah '80, 80; Utah Arts Coun/Visual Arts Fel, Utah Arts Coun, 86; Western States Arts Fel, Nat Endowment Arts, 88. *Bibliog:* Terry Melton (auth), 15 Artists in Print & Draw, Western States Arts, 88; Will South (auth), Paul Davis/Recent Work, Salt Lake Art Ctr, 89; Olpin/Swanson/Seifrit (auths), Utah Art, Gibbs Smith Publ, 91. *Media:* Oil. *Dealer:* Olga Dollar Gallery 210 Post St 2nd fl San Francisco CA 94108; Coda Gallery Paseo Dr Palm Desert CA. *Mailing Add:* 1202 Windsor St Salt Lake City UT 84105

DAVIS, PHILIP CHARLES
PHOTOGRAPHER, WRITER
b Spokane, Wash, Oct 15, 21. *Study:* Albright Art Sch, Buffalo, NY, cert. *Work:* Mus Art Inst Chicago; Int Mus Photog, Rochester, NY; Detroit Art Inst; Mus Mod Art, New York. *Comn:* Outdoor exhib photos, Univ Mich Sesquicentennial Comt, 66. *Exhib:* One-man show photographs, Kalamazoo Art Ctr, Mich, 62; The University, Univ Mich, Ann Arbor, 66; three-man show photographs, 831 Gallery, Birmingham, Mich, 71; Group Invitational, Kresge Art Ctr, Mich State Univ, 72 & 79; Midwest Invitational, Walker Art Ctr, Minneapolis, Minn, 73-74; The Art of the Photogravure, Colo Photog Arts Ctr, Denver, 79. *Teaching:* From instr to prof art, Univ Mich, Ann Arbor, 48- *Awards:* Gold Medal, 59, Silver Medal, 60 & Bravo Gold Medal, 61, Art Dirs Club Detroit. *Bibliog:* Irving Desfor (auth), Camera Angles, Assoc Press Newsfeatures, 72. *Mem:* Soc Photog Educ. *Publ:* Auth & illusr, The university, 67, Take Photography Step by Step, 70, Photography, 72, revised 79 & The Dexter Portfolio (50 set ed), 72. *Dealer:* The Halstead Gallery 560 N Woodward Birmingham MI 48011. *Mailing Add:* 7373 Webster Church Rd Whitmore Lake MI 48189

DAVIS, ROBERT
PAINTER
b New York, NY, May 8, 33. *Study:* Parsons Sch Design, cert, 55; Cranbrook Acad Art, Mich, 57; study with Ezio Martinelli. *Exhib:* Solo exhib, Mus Northern Ariz, Flagstaff, 80; Mich Focus Exhib Detroit Inst Arts & Flint Inst Arts, 75; Mich Artists Exhib, Univ Mich, Ann Arbor, 76; 44th Pac Northwest Prof Arts Exhib, Bellevue Art Mus, Wash, 90. *Media:* Acrylic, Gouache-Vinyl. *Mailing Add:* 2500 E Discovery Pl Langley WA 98260

DAVIS, RONALD
PAINTER, PRINTMAKER
b Santa Monica, Calif, June 29, 37. *Study:* San Francisco Art Inst, 60-64. *Work:* Los Angeles Co Mus; Mus Mod Art, New York; Tate Gallery, London; Albright-Knox Art Gallery, Buffalo; San Francisco Mus Art. *Exhib:* A News Aesthetic, Washington Gallery Mod Art, DC, 67; Documenta 4, Kassel, Ger, 67; Whitney Mus Am Art Ann, New York, 67; Color, Univ Calif, Los Angeles Art Galleries, 69; Venice Biennial, Italy, 72; Four Contemp Painters, Cleveland Mus Art, 78; and others. *Teaching:* Instr, Univ Calif, 67. *Awards:* Nat Endowment Arts, 68. *Bibliog:* M Fried (auth), Ronald Davis: Surface and illusion, Artforum, 4/67; R Hughes (auth), Ron Davis at Kasmin, Studio Int, 176, 12/68; B Rose (auth), American painting, Vol 2, 70. *Media:* Cel-Vinyl, Acrylic, Canvas; Computer Graphics. *Collection:* Contemporary art. *Dealer:* Blum Helman Gallery 916 Colorado Santa Monica CA 90401. *Mailing Add:* PO Box 276 Arroyo Hondo NM 87513-0276

DAVIS, STEPHEN
PAINTER
b Ft Worth, Tex, 45. *Study:* Claremont Grad Sch, MFA, 71. *Work:* San Francisco Mus Art; Oakland Mus; Univ Art Mus, Berkeley, Calif; Addison Gallery Am Art, Andover, Mass; Mus Contemp Art, Los Angeles, Calif. *Exhib:* Solo exhib, Hansen-Fuller Gallery, San Francisco, Calif, 72, 74 & 76, Hudson River Mus, Yonkers, NY, 79-80, Malinda Wyatt Gallery, New York, 85, Gallery Paule Anglim, San Francisco, Calif, 87 & Jernigan Wicker Gallery San Francisco, 92; New York, Fla State Univ & Phoenix Art Mus, Ariz, 82; Student Select, Yale Univ, 83; Jacob & His Twelve Sons, Addison Gallery Am Art, Andover, Md, 90; The Mattress Factory, Pittsburgh, Pa, 90; group shows, American Abstraction at the Addison, Addison Gallery Am Art, Andover, Mass, 91; and others. *Pos:* Cur & Four Berkeley Artist, Hansen-Fuller Gallery, 70; Lansdowne Lect, Univ Victoria, Can, 91. *Teaching:* Lectr, Univ Santa Clara, Calif, 75-77, Univ Calif, Santa Barbara, 78, Sarah Lawrence Col, New York, 79-80, State Univ NY, Purchase, New York, 82; Artist-in-Residence, Wright State Univ, Dayton, Ohio, 77; asst prof, Hunter Col, New York, 86- *Awards:* SECA-VESA Grant, San Francisco Mus Art, 77; Tiffany Found Grant, 83; Pollock-Krasner Found, 91-92. *Publ:* Stephen Davis (auth), Paintings, Washington Project for the Arts, (catalog), 86; Stephen Davis (auth), Jacob and His Twelve Sons, Addison Gallery Am Art, (catalog), 90; Stephen Davis (auth), 70's, 80's, 90's, Jernigan Wicker Fine Arts (catalog), 92. *Mailing Add:* 70 Thomas St New York NY 10013

DAVIS, THELMA ELLEN
PAINTER
b Las Animas, Colo, Sept 1, 25. *Exhib:* Allied Artists, Salmagundi Club, New York, 82; Catherine Lorillard Wolfe Art Club, New York, 82; one-woman Show, Rosicrucian Mus, San Jose, Calif, 83; Pastel Soc Am Ann, Nat Arts Club, 90; Pastel Soc West Coast Ann, Sacramento Fine Art Ctr, Sacramento, Calif, 92; Soc Western Artists Ann, Hall Flowers, San Francisco, 92. *Awards:* Margery Ryerson Mem, Catherine Lorillard Wolfe Art Club, 82; Best of Show, Pastel Soc West Coast, 86; Honorable Mention, Soc Western Artists, 92. *Mem:* Pastel Soc Am; Pastel Soc West Coast; Soc Western Artists; Gold Country Artists. *Media:* Pastel, Oil. *Mailing Add:* 6666 Acorn Hill Placerville CA 95667

DAVIS, WALTER LEWIS
PAINTER, COLLAGE ARTIST
b Americus, Ga, Jan 12, 37. *Study:* NY Community Col; Abracheff Sch Art, New York. *Work:* Detroit Bd Educ, Mich; NY State Brookdale Hosp, Brooklyn; NY State Lincoln Hosp, Bronx; Schomburg Ctr for Research in Black Culture, NY; Studio Mus, Harlem, NY. *Exhib:* One-man shows, Arts Extended Gallery, Detroit, Mich, 66-67 & 71 & Mt Vernon Coop Col Ctr, NY, 74; Childe Hassam Found Purchase Exhib, Am Acad Arts & Lett, New York, 69; Contemp Black Artists Am, Whitney Mus, 71; Univ of Conn, Stamford, 80; Wilson Arts Ctr-The Harley Sch, Rochester, NY, 85. *Awards:* Purchase Award Painting, Okinawa Art Ctr, 57; First Place, Greenwich Art-Music Festival, Conn, 80. *Bibliog:* William Tall (auth), Walter Davis' Totems for Charlie Parker, Detroit Free Press, 71; Lynn Moody Igoe (auth), 250 Years of Afro American Art, 81; The Art of Jazz, NY Publ Libr, 83. *Mem:* NY Artists Equity Asn. *Media:* Oil, Acrylic. *Mailing Add:* 801-12 Tilden St Bronx NY 10467

DAVIS, WILLIAM D
EDUCATOR, PRINTMAKER
b Erie, Pa, Oct 6, 36. *Study:* Edinboro State Col, BS(art educ), 59; Pa State Univ, MFA, 80. *Work:* Milton Shoe Collection Contemp Am Prints & Drawings, Pa; Sanford Gallery, Marwick-Boyd Fine Arts Ctr, Clarion, Pa; Kipp Gallery, Ind Univ, Pa; Bruce Gallery, Edinboro Univ, Pa; Lock Haven Univ Gallery, Pa. *Comn:* Lithograph, Friends Mus Art, Pa State Univ. *Exhib:* Drawing Exhib, Haslem Gallery, Washington, DC, 77; one-person shows, Butler Inst Am Art, 80, Babcock Galleries, New York, 90; Traditions: The Region, The World, Mich Art Train, Detroit, 81; 25-yr retrospective, Southern Alleghenies Mus Art, Loretto, Pa, 86. *Collections Arranged:* Living American Artists and the Figure (auth, catalog), 74, Materials Dominant (auth, catalog), 77, Intimate Worlds of Faust and Titolo (auth, catalog), 79, Sidney Goodman Paintings, Drawings, Graphics, 1959-1979, 80 & Jerome Witkin Paintings and Drawings: A Decade of Work, 83, Mus Art, Pa State Univ. *Pos:* Asst dir, Mus Art, Pa State Univ, 72-82, assoc dir, 82-83, interim dir, 83-85; exhib designer, 72-85; dir, Art Dept Slide Libr, 86- *Teaching:* Art, Pa pub schs, 59-60 & 62-71; asst prof art, Shippensburg Univ, formerly, prof art, 86- *Awards:* Graphics Award, Cent Pa Festival Arts, 69, 73 & 79; Purchase Award, Art Alliance, State Col, Pa, 74. *Bibliog:* Gerrit Henry (auth), article, Art News, 9/77; Michael Allison (auth), 25 year Retrospective (exhib catalog), Southern Alleghenies Mus Art, 86; Donald Miller (auth), article, Pittsburgh Post-Gazette, 8/1/86. *Mem:* Col Art Asn; Pa Art Educ Asn; Am Asn Mus; Northeast Mus Asn; Nat Art Educ Asn. *Media:* Graphite, Intaglio. *Dealer:* Babcock Galleries 724 Fifth Ave New York NY 10019. *Mailing Add:* 265 Newville Rd Shippensburg PA 17257

DAVISON, BILL
EDUCATOR, PRINTMAKER
b Burlington, Vt, Sept 23, 41. *Study:* Albion Col, BA, 63; Univ Mich, MFA, 66. *Work:* Libr Cong, Washington, DC; Dartmouth Col, Hanover, NH; Univ Southern Calif, Los Angeles; Franklin Furnace Arch, New York; Wesleyan Univ, Middletown, Conn; and many others. *Exhib:* Boston Printmakers 20th Ann Nat Exhib, Boston Mus Fine Arts, 68; one person exhibs, The Univ Gallery, Univ S Calif, Los Angeles, 77, Fla Ctr Arts, Univ S Fla, Tampa, 77, Davison Art Ctr, Wesleyan Univ, Middletown, Conn, 78, Kathryn Markel Gallery, New York, 78, Roy Boyd Gallery, Chicago, 79, Colby-Sawyer Col, New London, NH, 83 & Albany Acad Gallery, Albany, NY, 85; Nat Print Exhib, 77 & Thirty Years of Am Printmaking, 77, Brooklyn Mus, NY; High Tech/High Touch: Computer Graphics in Printmaking, Pratt Manhattan Gallery, New York, 87; Int Exhib Prints, Print Club, Philadelphia, 88; Post Industrial Expression, Sordoni Gallery, Wilkes Col, Wilkes-Barre, Pa, 88; Univ Dallas Nat Print Invitational, Tex, 89; Light Aberrations: A National Exhib of Photographs & Prints, Univ Tex, San Antonio, 90; Int Symposium Electronic Art, Croningen, Holland, 90; Exhin Electronic Art, Art Centre, Punkaharju, Finland, 91; Dakotas Int: Works on Paper, Univ S Dak, Vermillion, 91; 10th Int Conference on Computer Graphics (SIGGRAPH), Chicago, 92. *Teaching:* Assoc prof, Univ Vt, Burlington, 68-81, prof, 90- *Awards:* Indiv Grant, Vt Coun Arts, 70-71 & 78-79; Artist's Fel, Nat

Endowment Arts, 74-75; Vis Artist's Fel, Brandywine Workshop Offset Inst, Philadelphia, 88; MacDowell Colony Fel, Peterborough, NH, 89; Award of Distinction, PRIX ARS Electronica 90, Linz, Austria, 90. *Bibliog:* A Class Portrait, Arts Mag, 10/81; Print News, 12/81; New Images, Ocular, winter 82; Sculptors find new ways with wood, NY Times, 12/2/84; Bill Davison: New screenprints - John Cage: New etchings, Art New Eng, 6/90. *Publ:* Art & Technology (catalog), Lehigh Univ, Bethlehem Univ, Pa, 83; The Ways of Wood (catalog), Org of Independent Artists, Inc, New York, 84; Visual Proceedings - SIGGRAPH 1992 (catalog), Chicago, 92. *Mailing Add:* c/o Dept Art 304 Williams Hall Univ Vermont Burlington VT 05405

DAVY, WOODS
SCULPTOR
b Washington, DC, Oct 6, 49. *Study:* Univ NC, Chapel Hill BFA(Morehead Scholar), 72; Univ Ill, Champaign/Urbana, MFA, 75. *Work:* Palm Springs Desert Mus, Calif; Laguna Beach Mus Art, Calif; Fed Reserve Bank, San Francisco; Calif State Univ, Long Beach; Los Angeles Co Mus Art; Long Beach Mus Art; and others. *Comn:* 4 sculptures, steel & stone, Edward J DeBartolo Corp, Palm Springs, Calif, 86; William O Douglas Outdoor Classroom, Los Angeles, 88; Carnation Co, Glendale, Calif, 90; Sterling Drug Co, Collegeville, Pa; Xerox Corp, New York; and others. *Exhib:* Solo exhibs, Security Pacific Bank Plaza, Los Angeles, 80 & McIntosh/Drysdale Gallery, Houston, 84-86; Sculpture 1975, national traveling exhib, 75; Six Los Angeles Sculptors, Fed Reserve Bd, Washington, DC, 80; New Art of Downtown Los Angeles, nat traveling exhib, 82-84; The Forgotten Dimension, nat traveling exhibition, 82; New Public Art, Otis Art Inst, Los Angeles, 84; Monuments To, Univ Art Mus, Long Beach, Calif, 85; Arco Sculpture Garden, Am Film Inst, Los Angeles, 86; New Sculpture, Works Gallery, Long Beach, Calif. *Pos:* Bd dirs, Los Angeles Contemp Exhibs, 84-85; arts adv coun, Cedars Sinai Hosp, Los Angeles, 84- *Bibliog:* William Wilson (auth), How real is the downtown phenomenon? Los Angeles Times, 9/20/81; Carol Everingham (auth), Critic's choice, Houston Post, 5/3/85; JoAnn Lewis (auth), Woods Davy's sculptures, Washington Post, 2/8/86. *Media:* Steel and Stone in combination. *Dealer:* Works Gallery Long Beach & Costa Mesa CA. *Mailing Add:* 562 San Juan Ave Venice CA 90291-3327

DAWDY, DORIS OSTRANDER
WRITER, HISTORIAN
Study: MacPhail Sch Music, Minneapolis; Colo State Univ; Los Angeles City Col. *Bibliog:* Contemporary Authors; Lois Swan Jones (auth), Art Research and Resources/A Guide to Finding Art Information. *Mem:* Western Hist Asn; Orgn Am Historians. *Res:* American Indian paintings; artists of the American West born prior to 1900. *Publ:* Auth, Annoted Bibliography of American Indian Painting, Heye Found, 68; Artists of the American West, Swallow, 74 & 80, Vol II, 81 & Vol III, 85 & 87, Ohio Univ Press; The Wyant Diary: An Artist with the Wheeler Survey in Arizona 1873, Ariz and the West, Univ Ariz Press, 80. *Mailing Add:* 3055 23rd Ave San Francisco CA 94132

DAWLEY, JOSEPH WILLIAM
PAINTER
b Nashville, Ark, June 19, 36. *Study:* With Raymond Froman, 58-61; Southern Methodist Univ, BFA, 59; Dallas Mus Fine Arts, 60; Art Students League, 61. *Work:* Mus Arts & Crafts, Columbus, Ga; Davenport Mus Art, Iowa; Southern Methodist Univ, Dallas, Tex; Notre Dame Univ; The Mayo Clinic. *Comn:* Official portrait, Mother Elizabeth Ann Seton, comn by St Patricks Cathedral, 75. *Exhib:* Allied Artists Show, New York, 69 & 70; Acad Artists Show, Springfield, Mass, 69 & 70; Hudson Valley Art Show, White Plains, NY, 69 & 70; Am Artists Prof League, New York, 69-71; Salmagundi Club Show, New York, 70 & 72. *Pos:* Creator comic strip, Chief, 64-67; owner, Joseph Dawley Gallery, 77-87. *Teaching:* Instr, DuCret Sch of Arts, Plainfield, NJ. *Awards:* Figure or Portrait Anonymous Award, Acad Artists, 69; William Collins Award, Hudson Valley Art Asn, 69; Jane Peterson Portrait Award, Allied Artists, New York, 70. *Bibliog:* Kolbe (auth), Dawley reasserts realism, Am Artist Mag, 70; Singer (auth), Meet the artist--Joseph Dawley, Suburban Life Mag, 70; Calaway (auth), Bringing sanity back to art, Southwest Scene Mag, 70. *Mem:* Allied Artists Asn; Hudson Valley Art Asn; Am Artists Prof League; Acad Artists. *Media:* Oil. *Publ:* Auth, Character Studies in Oil, 72, The Painters' Problem Book, 73, Painting Western Characters, 75 & Painters' Problem Book II, 78, Watson-Guptill. *Dealer:* Calvert Collection 2301 Calvert St NW Washington DC 20009; The Artful Deposit Nine N Main St PO Box 203 Allentown NJ 08501. *Mailing Add:* 13 W Holly St Cranford NJ 07016

DAWSON, BESS PHIPPS
PAINTER, GALLERY DIRECTOR
b Tchula, Miss. *Study:* Belhaven Col; Southwest Miss Jr Col; workshops, Allisons Art Colony, Way, Miss & Miss Art Colony, Utica, Miss. *Work:* Art in Embassy Prog, Taiwan; Old Capitol Hist Mus & Miss Art Asn Gallery, Jackson, Miss; Lauren Rogers Mus, Laurel, Miss; First Nat Bank Miss Collection, Jackson. *Comn:* Murals, Church God, McComb, 58, Delta Elec Co, Greenwood, 58, First Nat Bank, McComb, 59 & Hankins Container Corp, Houston, Tex, 59; painting, Order Eastern Star, Jackson, 69. *Exhib:* Delgado Mus Art, New Orleans, La, 67; Brooks Mem Gallery, Memphis, Tenn, 69; Ark Arts Ctr, Little Rock, 70; Lauren Rogers Mus, Laurel, Miss, 80; Secy State Building, Jackson, Miss, 80; Cottonlandia Mus, Greenwood, Miss; Pike Co Arts Coun, Miss, 87; Miss Mus Art, Jackson, 88; Miss Gov Mansion, 90; Municipal Gallery, Jackson, Miss, 91. *Pos:* Owner & dir, Gulf South Galleries, 71-; dir, Miss Art Colony, 77-90. *Teaching:* Supvr art, McComb Pub Schs, 68-71. *Awards:* Miss Art Colony Awards, 76, 84 & 87; Purchase Award, Cottonlandia Mus, Greenwood, Miss, 86; George Orr Award, Craftsman Guild Miss, 86; Holiday Inn Award, McComb, Miss, 87. *Bibliog:* ETV-Documentary 90 Interviews, 91 & 92. *Mem:* Southwest Miss Art Asn (secy, 66-70); Miss Art Colony (bd dirs, 62-); Miss Art Asn (coordr state bd, 68-69); Pike Co Art Coun. *Specialty:* Mississippi artists in all media. *Publ:* Coauth, Manual for classroom teachers, 69 & illusr, Elementary Art (TV doc), 69, McComb Pub Schs. *Dealer:* Gulf South Galleries 1413 Aston Ave McComb MS 39648. *Mailing Add:* PO Box 32 Summit MS 39666

DAWSON, DOUG
PAINTER, INSTRUCTOR
b Oak Park, Ill, Aug 23, 44. *Study:* Macalester Col, St Paul, Minn, BS, 66, Drake Univ, Des Moines, Iowa, 69. *Work:* Blue Cross/Blue Shield Collection, Denver, Colo; US Senate Off, Washington, DC; Coutts Mus Art, El Dorado, Kans. *Comn:* World Relief, Guaranty Bank, Queen Anne Inn & Littleton Med Clinic, Colo. *Exhib:* Allied Artist Exhib, New York, 82 & 91; Knickerbocker Artists, New York, 83, 84 & 87; Denver Art Mus, Colo, 83; Palais Rameau in Lille, Paris, France, 87; solo exhib, Frye Mus, Seattle, Wash, 89; and others. *Pos:* Founding bd mem, Denver Art Students League, 87; consult, Summer Inst Linguistics, S Am, 88- *Teaching:* Instr painting, drawing, anat, Colo Inst Art, Denver, 78-; instr, Denver Art Students League, 87-; instr, pastels, Museo del Quijote, Guarajuato, Mexico, 90. *Awards:* Master Pastelist, Pastel Soc Am, New York; Emily Goldsmith Award, Am Watercolor Soc, New York. *Bibliog:* Articles Art Gallery Int, 1/86, Artists Mag, 4/86 & 9/87, Southwest Art Mag, 7/86, Western Art Digest, 9/86 & Focus/Santa Fe Mag, 8/89 & 2/92. *Mem:* Am Watercolor Soc; Pastel Soc, Am & Southwest; Knickerbocker Artists. *Media:* Pastel. *Publ:* Capturing Light & Color with Pastel, North Light, 8/91. *Dealer:* Ventana Fine Art 211 Old Santa Fe Trail Santa Fe NM 87501; Saks Gallery 3019 E Second Ave Denver CO 80206. *Mailing Add:* 8622 West 44th Place Wheat Ridge CO 80033

DAWSON, JOHN ALLAN
PAINTER, SCULPTOR
b Joliet, Ill, Sept 12, 46. *Study:* Northern Ill Univ, BFA, 69; Univ NMex; Ariz State Univ, MFA, 74. *Work:* Ulrich Mus Art; Phoenix Art Mus, Ariz; Ark Art Ctr, Little Rock; Okla Art Ctr, Oklahoma City. *Exhib:* Segal Gallery, New York; Ariz Invitational 75, Phoenix Art Mus, 75; one-man shows, Ark Art Ctr, Little Rock, 79, Okla Art Ctr, Oklahoma City, 79, Springfield Mus Art, Mo, 80 & Sheldon Mem Collection, Univ Nebr, Lincoln, 80; Wedding Series, Elaine Horwitch Gallery, Scottsdale, Ariz, 82; over 50 one man shows. *Pos:* Artist-in-residence, Mesa Pub Schs, Ariz Comn Art, 74. *Awards:* Purchase Award, Del Mar Col, 73 & El Paso Mus Art, 75. *Bibliog:* C D Kotrozo (auth), article, Art Voices South, 5/79; A Johns (auth), The wedding series, Ariz Arts & Lifestyle, winter 82; Claude Marks (ed), World Artists, 80-90. *Media:* Oil; Bronze. *Dealer:* Mangel Gallery Philadelphia PA; Radliff-Williams Gallery Sedona AZ. *Mailing Add:* 10246 E Brown Rd Mesa AZ 85207

DAY, BURNIS CALVIN
PAINTER, EDUCATOR
b Hepsibah, WVa, Dec 27, 40. *Study:* Ctr Creative Studies-Col Art & Design; Famous Artists Sch, 68; Oakland Comm Col Art, 69. *Work:* Detroit Inst Art, Mich; Las Vegas Art Mus, Nev; Museo de Arte de Ponce, PR; Mus Northern Arizona, Flagstaff; Univ Utah Mus Fine Arts. *Comn:* Painting, Tom Davis Agency, Detroit & Cleveland, Ohio; Detroit Bus & Civic League, Mich; mural of 4 sporting events, Detroit Recreation Dept, Mich, 78. *Exhib:* Original Paintings by Michigan Artists, Detroit Inst Arts, Mich, 76; 9th Ann Nat Small Painting Exhib, NMex Art League, Albuquerque, 79; 4th Ann Nat Am Show, Laramie Art Guild, Wyo, 79; Cult Exchange Trends, Gallery Tanner, Los Angeles, Calif, 84; Int Platform Asn, Mayflower Hotel, Washington, DC, 89. *Pos:* Art assoc, Cal Summers' House of Art, Detroit, Mich, 71-77; art dir, Urban Screen Process, Detroit, Mich, 72-73; freelance artist, 77- *Teaching:* Instr life drawing, Pittman's Gallery Inc, Detroit, Mich, 73-74; painting, Detroit Recreation Dept, Mich, 85; mixed media, Wayne Co Community Col, Detroit, Mich, 85-; art instr drawing & painting, Chrysler/UAW Nat Training Ctr, Detroit, Mich, 92- *Awards:* 1st & 2nd Place, US Tank Automotive, 77; Cert of Recognition, US Zone Comt, 77; Semi-Finalist, United Auto Workers 50th Anniversary Poster, 86. *Bibliog:* George B Eichorn (auth), Recreation center new sports mural, Detroit News, 4/78; Lora Frankel (auth), National Young Audiences Week, YAMD Newsletter, Winter 79; Marie Teasley (auth), Burnis Day in DIA Collect, Michigan Chronicle, 12/87. *Mem:* Detroit Inst Arts; Degas & Assocs (Diversified Visual Commun). *Media:* Acrylic, Oil. *Publ:* Auth, A Description of Neogeometric/Burnis C Day, private publ, 85; Article, Art, artists & my paintings, Projected Int/Burnis C Day, 89; The work book, Scott & Daughters Publishing, 90; Am Artist, Survey of Leading Contemps, American References, 89. *Dealer:* G R N'Namdi Galleries Inc 161 Townsend Birmingham MI 48009. *Mailing Add:* 15424 Lesure Detroit MI 48227

DAY, CHON
CARTOONIST
b Chatham, NJ, Apr 6, 07. *Study:* Art Students League, with Boardman Robinson & John Sloan. *Exhib:* Metrop Mus Art, 42; Pa Acad Fine Arts. *Awards:* Best Gag Cartoonist, Nat Cartoonists Soc, 56, 61 & 70. *Mem:* Nat Cartoonists Soc. *Publ:* Auth & illusr, I Could Be Dreaming, 45, What Price Dory, 55, Brother Sebastian, 57, Brother Sebastian Carries On, 59 & Brother Sebastian at Large, 61; contribr cartoons, New Yorker, Good Housekeeping, Ladies Home J & others. *Mailing Add:* 22 Cross St Westerly RI 02891

DAY, GARY LEWIS
PRINTMAKER, PAINTER
b Great Falls, Mont, Sept 29, 50. *Study:* Mont State Univ, BA, 75; Fla State Univ, MFA, 76. *Work:* Ariz State Univ, Tempe; Trenton State Col, NJ;

Sheldon Mem Gallery, Lincoln, Nebr; Joslyn Art Mus, Omaha, Nebr. *Exhib:* one person show, Sheldon Mem Gallery, Lincoln, Nebr, 84, William Jewell Col, Kansas City, Mo, 88; Thirty Years of American Printmaking, Brooklyn Mus, NY, 76; 62nd Ann Int Competition, Print Club, Philadelphia, Pa, 86; Nat drawing 87, Trenton State Col, NJ; Midlands Invitationals, Joslyn Art Mus, Omaha, Nebr, 90. *Collections Arranged:* Drawing Invitational (auth, catalog), Univ Nebr, Omaha, 79. *Teaching:* Instr art, Metrop Tech Community Col, Omaha, 77-79; vis lectr lithography, Creighton Univ, Omaha, 79; assoc prof drawing, Univ Nebr, Omaha, 79- *Awards:* Purchase Award, Appalachian Nat Drawing Competition, 79; Res Fel, Univ Nebr, 85; Purchase Award, Nat Drawing Exhib, Trenton State Col, 87; Visual Artists Fel Grant, Nat Endowment Arts, 87-88. *Bibliog:* The Picture Show, Nebr Educ TV doc, 85. *Media:* Intaglio, Lithography. *Publ:* Contribr, Colleagues: An Inter-Media Anthology of Artists, Pittore Euforico, 79; Another Normal Conception, Univ Ill, 80; An American Portfolio, Univ Ariz, 81. *Mailing Add:* Dept Art & Art Hist Univ Nebr 102 Richards Hall Tenth & T St Lincoln NE 68588

DAY, HOLLIDAY T
CRITIC, CURATOR
b Nashville, Tenn, Dec 25, 36. *Study:* Wellesley Col, Mass, BA, 57; Univ Chicago, MA, 79. *Collections Arranged:* Siah Armajani, 80; Martin Puryear, 80; George Sugarman retrospective, 81; Jennifer Bartlett, 82; Joyce Kozloff, 82; Elyn Zimmerman, 85; New Art of Italy, 85; Art of the Fantastic: Latin Am 1920-1987, 87; Power: Its Myths & Moves in American Art 1961-1991, 91. *Pos:* Writer, New Art Examiner, Chicago, 76-79, contrib ed, 79; cur Am art, Joslyn Art Mus, Omaha, Nebr, 80-85; cur contemp art, Indpls Mus Art, 85- *Awards:* Nat Endowment for the Arts critic's travel grant, 78-79; Am Mus Assoc Merit Award, 81; Chicago Book Show Award, 89. *Bibliog:* Article, Print Collectors Newsletter, 6/84; article, Indianapolis Star, 12/15/86; article, New York Times, 10/24/91. *Mem:* Col Art Asn. *Res:* Surfaces of David Smith's sculpture. *Publ:* Auth, Fotografia Polska, 1839-1979, Indianapolis, Cincinnati & Dayton, Art in Am, summer 79 & 1/80; I-80 Series: 14 catalogs, 80-82, Shape of Space: The Sculpture of George Sugarman, 81, Elyn Zimmerman: Images of the City, 85, The New Art of Italy, 85 & Joslyn Art Museum: Painting & Sculpture, 87, Joslyn Art Mus; Art of the Fantastic: Latin America, 1920-1987, IMA & Ind Univ Pr, 87; ed, Collection Handbook, IMA, 88; Power: Its Myths & Moves in American Art 1960-90 (catalog), IMA & Ind Univ Press, 91. *Mailing Add:* 18 South Park St Hinsdale IL 60521

DAY, LARRY (LAWRENCE JAMES)
PAINTER, EDUCATOR
b Philadelphia, Pa, Oct 29, 21. *Study:* Tyler Sch Fine Arts, Temple Univ, BFA & BS(educ). *Work:* Philadelphia Mus Art, Philadelphia Col Art, Fleischer Art Mem & Pa Acad Fine Arts, Philadelphia; Miami-Dade Col, Fla; Corcoran Gallery Art, Washington, DC; Nat Gallery Art, Washington, DC. *Comn:* Med Col Philadelphia. *Exhib:* Realism Now, Vassar Col; The Figure in Recent Am Painting Traveling Show (coauth, catalog), Westminster Col, Pa, 74; The Realist Revival, Am Fedn Arts Travelling Show; Bicentennial Exhib, Philadelphia Mus Art, 76; Realism Today, Nat Acad Design, New York. *Teaching:* Prof painting, drawing & theory, Philadelphia Col Art, Pa, 53-; prof emer, Univ Arts, Philadelphia. *Awards:* Temple Univ Alumni Cert Honor, 80; Hazlett Award for Excellence in the Arts, Pa, 82; Ingram-Merrill Found Grant, 84-85; Citation, City of Philadelphia, 88; Gene Durwood/Oscar Williams Award, 90. *Mem:* Col Art Asn. *Media:* Oil, Watercolor, Graphite. *Publ:* Coauth, American Figure Drawing (catalog), Victorian Col Art, Melbourne, Australia, 76; and others. *Dealer:* The More Gallery Inc 1630 Walnut St Philadelphia PA 19103; Jane Haslem Gallery 2025 Hillyer Place NW Washington DC 20009. *Mailing Add:* 19 Philadelphia Ave Takoma Park MD 20912

DEADERICK, JOSEPH
PAINTER, EDUCATOR
b Memphis, Tenn, Jan 17, 30. *Study:* Univ Ga, BFA, 52; Cranbrook Acad Art, MFA, 54; Ind Univ, 58-59. *Work:* Kalamazoo Col, Mich; numerous pvt collections. *Comn:* Ceramic tile mural, Univ Wyo, Laramie, 68; faceted glass window, Lutheran Campus Ctr, Laramie, 68. *Exhib:* Sixth Midwest Biennial, Joslyn Art Mus, Omaha, Nebr, 60; Brooklyn Mus Biennial Print Show, 64; Drawing USA Traveling Show, St Paul, Minn, 66-68; one-man show, Colorado Springs Fine Arts Ctr, 67; Fedn Rocky Mountain States Traveling Show, 66-72; 20 yr retrospective, Univ Wyo Art Mus, 78. *Teaching:* Instr design, Ind Univ, Bloomington, 56-59; prof art, Univ Wyo, Laramie, 59- *Awards:* First Place Award Design, Franklin Mint, 72; Nat Award Excellence in Design, Printing Indust Am Graphic Arts Competition, 72. *Media:* Multimedia. *Publ:* The Stage: A Series of Poetic Drawings by Joseph Deaderick, Univ Wyo, 78. *Mailing Add:* 2462 Park Laramie WY 82070

DEAL, JOE
PHOTOGRAPHER, EDUCATOR
b Topeka, Kans, Aug 12, 47. *Study:* Kansas City Art Inst, BFA, 70; Univ NMex, MA, 74, MFA, 78, study with Van Deren Coke. *Work:* Mus Mod Art, New York; Mus Fine Arts, Houston; Int Mus Photog at George Eastman House, Rochester, NY; Ctr Creative Photog, Tucson; Oakland Mus; Mus Contemp Art, Los Angeles, J Paul Getty Trust. *Comn:* Photogs const mus, Mus Contemp Art, Los Angeles, 84-86; site photogs New Mus, J Paul Getty Trust, 84-89. *Exhib:* New Topographics: Photographs of a Man-Altered Landscape, Int Mus Photog at George Eastman House, Rochester, Princeton Univ & Otis Art Gallery, Los Angeles, 75-76; Contemp Am Photographs, Mus Fine Arts, Houston, 77; American Images: Photography 1945-1980, Barbican Art Gallery, London, 85; Joe Deal: Men and Women, St Louis Art Mus, 91; Joe Deal: Southern California Photographs, 1976-1986, (exhib catalog), Los Angeles Munic Art Gallery, 92. *Teaching:* Lectr photog, San Francisco Art Inst, summer, 76; prof art, Univ Calif, Riverside, 76-89; Dean, Washington Univ, Sch Fine Arts, St Louis, 89- *Awards:* Nat Endowment Arts Photogr Fel, 77 & 80; Guggenheim Fel, 83. *Bibliog:* Carter Ratcliff (auth), Route 66 revisited: The new landscape photography, Art in Am, 1-2/76; Joe Deal: New Topographics, Northlight Five, Ariz State Univ, 77; Estelle Jussim & Elizabeth Lindquist-Cock (auths), Landscape as Photograph, Yale Univ, 85. *Mem:* Col Art Asn. *Mailing Add:* 324 Melville Ave St Louis MO 63130

DEAN, JAMES
PAINTER
b Fall River, Mass, Oct 14, 31. *Study:* Swain Sch Design, New Bedford, Mass. *Work:* Nat Aeronaut & Space Admin, Dept Interior & Smithsonian Inst, Washington, DC. *Comn:* Contemp Christmas stamps, US Postal Serv, 85 & 87. *Exhib:* American Artists & Water Reclamation, Nat Gallery Art, Washington, DC, 72; Smithsonian Inst Traveling Exhib, 72-73; Corcoran Gallery Art, Washingon, DC, 74; 107th Ann, Am Watercolor Soc, New York, 74; Washington Area Art, US Info Agency Worldwide Tour, 75-76; Nat Air & Space Mus, Washington, DC, 81-83; Foster Harmon Galleries Am Art, Sarasota, Fla, 83-90; Eyewitness to Apollo II, Nat Air & Space Mus, Washington, DC, 89. *Pos:* Dir fine arts prog, Nat Aeronaut & Space Admin, 61-74; cur art, Nat Air & Space Mus, 74-80. *Awards:* Cert Merit, Nat Acad Design, NY, Award of Excellence, Com Arts Mag, 76 & 77; Citation of Excellence, Am Inst Graphic Arts, 76-77. *Bibliog:* R J Williams (auth), James Dean painter of the past, Southern Living Mag, 6/73; Alice Laurich (auth), James Dean, Focus Mag, 9-10/75; Jack Perlmutter (auth), Duality of James Dean, Art Voices South, 7-8/79. *Mem:* Hereward Lester Cooke Found (bd trustees, 73-); Torpedo Factory Artists Asn (pres, 83-84). *Media:* Watercolor. *Publ:* Coauth, Eyewitness to Space, Abrams, 72; auth, Artist and space, Interdisciplinary Sci Rev; Artist and the space shuttle, NASA, 81; illusr, Liftoff, Grove, 88. *Dealer:* Foster Harmon Galleries Am Artist 1415 Main St Sarasota FL 33577; Prince Royal Gallery 204 S Royal St Alexandria VA. *Mailing Add:* 4804 King Richard Dr Annandale VA 22003

DEAN, NAT(ALIE CAROL)
PAINTER, SCULPTOR
b Redwood City, Calif, Jan 13, 56. *Study:* Calif Inst Arts, 71-76; Cooper Union Advancement Sci Art, 75; San Francisco Art Inst, BFA, 77; Capricornus Sch Bookbinding & Restoration, 77-81. *Work:* Fukuoka Cult Ctr, Japan; San Francisco Mus Mod Art; Aratex Ara Art Prog, Calif; San Jose State Univ, Union Gallery, Calif; and others. *Comn:* Box-Book, Jean Brown Archive, Tyringham, Mass, 82. *Exhib:* Aesthetics of Graffitti, San Francisco Mus Mod Art, 78; Bookworks, Walker Art Ctr, 81; Architecture, Metrop Mus Art, 85; Galerie Anton Meir, Geneva, Switz, 88; Ruth Bachofner Gallery, Santa Monica, Calif, 90; Orange Co Ctr Contemp Art, Santa Ana, Calif, 90; Memorial/Remembrance, Ctr Gallery, Wolfson Campus, Miami-Dade Community Col, Fla, 91; Book as Art, Boca Raton Mus Art, Fla, 91; Gods, Devils & Clowns, Los Angeles Contemp Exhibs, Calif, 91. *Pos:* Owner/designer, Ruta Zinc/Fine Arts, San Francisco & Los Angeles, Calif, 78-90; dir/owner, Artist Tools & Resources Survival, Calif & Fla, 89-; dir, career planning & placement & coop educ & internships, Inst Arts, Valencia, Calif, 86-89; dir, Ctr Career Servs, Ringling Sch Art & Design, Sarasota, Fla, 89-92. *Teaching:* Instr artist survival skills & bus art, Col New Rochelle, 80, Sch Visual Arts, 81, San Francisco Art Inst, 81 & 82, State Univ NY, Potsdam, 82, Calif Col Arts & Crafts, 84-87 & Calif Inst Art, 88 & 89; guest lectr, Humbolt State Univ, 87 & 90, Calif Col Arts & Crafts, 88-93, Chapman Col, Orange, Calif, 89, Pac Northwest Col Art, Portland, Ore, 89, San Diego State Univ, Calif, 89 & Univ SFla, Tampa, 91; sem presenter, Los Angeles Convention Ctr, 88-93; guest lectr & artist, Calif Inst Arts, Valencia, 88-93; guest lectr & consult, Savannah Col Art & Design, 88 & 89; adj fac & lectr, Ringling Sch Art & Design, Sarasota, Fla, 89-92. *Awards:* Wash State Arts Comn Artist Resource Bank, 88; Fla Arts Coun Vis Artists Roster, 90-93; Ringling Sch Art & Design Prof Develop Grant, Sarasota, Fla, 90; and others. *Bibliog:* Revs, LA Times, Calif, 87 & 90; revs, LA Weekly, Calif, 88; interview, La Bete Mag, Miami, Fla, 92; and others. *Mem:* Col Art Asn; Women's Caucus Arts; Nat Asn Artist Orgns; Nat Artists Equity Asn; Am Coun Arts; and others. *Media:* Acrylic; Mixed Media. *Publ:* Contribr, Whitewalls: a magazine of writings by artists (visual piece), Whitewalls, 83; Visions (column), Ringling Sch Art & Design, 89-92; For the Working Artist, 89. *Mailing Add:* 4511 Exposition Blvd Los Angeles CA 90016

DEAN, NICHOLAS BRICE
PRINTMAKER, PHOTOGRAPHER
b Huntington, NJ, July 20, 33. *Study:* Dartmouth Col; Harvard Col, with Ansel Adams & Minor White. *Work:* Int Mus Photog, George Eastman House, Rochester, NY; Mus Mod Art, New York; Univ Calif, Los Angeles; Portland Mus Art, Maine; Lessing J Rosenwald Col, Jenkintown, Pa. *Comn:* Poster, Maine State Comn on the Arts & Humanities, 70; poster, Maine Film Alliance, Augusta, 77. *Exhib:* Photog at Mid-Century, 59, Photog, 63 & Three Photogr, 63, George Eastman House; The Sense of Abstraction, Mus Mod Art, New York, 60; Sixth Minn Biennial, Minn Art Inst, 67; Photo in the 20th Century, Nat Gallery Can, Ottawa, Ont, 67; Into the Seventies, Ohio Art Inst, Akron, 70; Realists Invitational, SE Ctr for Contemp Art, Winston-Salem, NC, 73; one-man show, Univ Ga, Athens, 75. *Pos:* Res craftsman, Penland Sch Crafts, 72-73; artist-in-residence, Sandhills Community Col, Southern Pines, NC, 73-74. *Teaching:* Head photog dept, Portland Sch Art, Maine, 68-72; instr photog, Penland Sch Crafts, NC, summers 69, 71, 72, 78 & 79; instr graphics, Haystack Sch Crafts, Deer Isle, Maine, summer 72, 78 & 79. *Media:* Silkscreen, Intaglio; Silver Print. *Publ:* Illusr, Bulfinch's Boston, Oxford Univ Press, 64; auth, Lubec, Identity, Cambridge, Mass, 67; co-auth

(with Jonathan Williams), Blues & Roots/Rue & Bluets, Grossman, New York, 71; illusr, A Social History of the Boston Private Clubs, Barre, 71; illusr, Portland, Greater Portland Landmarks, 72. *Dealer:* Carl Siembab Gallery 172 Newbury St Boston MA. *Mailing Add:* River Rd Edgecomb ME 04556

DEAN, PETER
PAINTER
b Berlin, Mont, July 9, 39. *Study:* Cornell Univ; Univ Wis, BA; Pratt Graphic Art Ctr; also with Andre Girard. *Work:* Madison Art Ctr, Wis; Mus Mod Art, New York; Chicago Art Inst; Los Angeles Co Mus; Nat Collection Washington, DC. *Comn:* NDak Mus Art, Grand Forks, 89; Alternative Mus, NY, 90. *Exhib:* One-man shows, Allan Stone Gallery, New York, 70, 73, 78, & 80 & Alexandre Monett Gallery, Bruxelles, 76, 78 & 80; 32nd Corcoran Biennial Am Painting, Washington, DC, 71; Madison Art Ctr, Wis, 78; Semaphore Gallery, New York, 80 & 86; Darthea Speyer Gallery, Paris, 81; Venice Biennele, 84; Struve Gallery, Chicago, 84; Galeri Bellman, New York, 84, Koplm Gallery, Los Angeles, 84, 87 & 89, San Antonio Art Inst, 88 & NDak Mus Art, 89; Rena Bransten Gallery, San Francisco, 87 & 89; R H Love Gallery, Chicago, 89 & 92; Univ Ariz Mus Art, 91; Univ Wis Art Mus, Milwaukee, 92. *Pos:* Artist-in-residence, La State Univ, 74. *Teaching:* Vis artist, Yale Univ, Colgate Univ, NDak Univ, Univ Wis, Princeton Univ, Univ Tex, Tulane Univ, Cranbrook Acad, Univ Wash. *Awards:* NY Coun Arts Grant, 76; Nat Endowment Arts Fel Grant, 81 & 87. *Media:* Oil, Watercolor. *Dealer:* Bienville Gallery 1800 Hasting Pl New Orleans LA 70130. *Mailing Add:* 2 Spring St New York NY 10012

DE ANDINO, JEAN-PIERRE M
DEALER, COLLECTOR
b San Juan, PR, June 11, 46. *Study:* George Washington Univ; Univ NC. *Pos:* Pvt dealer, 72-77; dir-vpres, Osuna Gallery, Washington, DC, 77-81; pres, Crowley de Andino & Holmes Inc, Washington, DC, 81-82; pres, de Andino Fine Arts, currently; mem bd dirs, New Art Examiner, Washington, DC, 84-89. *Mem:* Am Soc Appraisers. *Specialty:* Nineteenth and twentieth century masters and contemporary art. *Collection:* Unique images on paper. *Mailing Add:* De Andino Fine Arts 1609 Connecticut Ave NW Suite 300 Washington DC 20009

DEANGELIS, JOSEPH ROCCO
SCULPTOR
b Providence, RI, Apr 22, 38. *Study:* RI Sch Design, BFA, 66; Syracuse Univ, NY, MFA, 68. *Work:* Art Gallery London, Ont. *Comn:* Windsor Pub Libr, Ont, 75; City North Vancouver, BC, 77; Essex Civic Ctr, Ont, 77; Prov Ont Govt Bldg, Windsor, 78; painted wall mural, Ciocaro Club, Windsor, Ont, 84-85. *Exhib:* Ontario Now, traveling, 76; Spectrum Canada, Montreal Olympics, 76; London Art Gallery, Ont, 77; Canadian Place, Toronto, Ont, 77; New Canadian Sculpture, The Windsor Symposium, Art Gallery Windsor, 85; Agnes Etherington Gallery, Kingston, Ont, 81; and others. *Teaching:* Lectr, Univ Mich, Ann Arbor, 69-70; assoc prof, Univ Windsor, Ont, 70- *Awards:* Sculpture Award, Art Gallery London, 75; Ont Arts Coun Grants, 77 & 84. *Bibliog:* Ann Rosenberg (auth), Wood sculpture of the Americas, Capilano Review, No 12, 77; Arthur Perry (auth), Vancouver: Wood sculpture of the Americas, Art Mag, 10-11/77; David Quintner (auth), Angelic sculptural work suspends tactile senses, Windsor Star, 3/81. *Mem:* Visual Art Ont. *Media:* Mixed. *Mailing Add:* 1690 Front Rd La Salle ON N9J 2B6 Canada

DE ARMOND, DALE B
PRINTMAKER, ILLUSTRATOR
b Bismark, NDak. *Study:* Study with Dannie Pierce, Carol Summers & Jules Heller. *Work:* Alaska State Mus; Anchorage Hist & Fine Arts Mus, Alaska Methodist Univ, Anchorage. *Exhib:* Charles & Emma Frye Art Mus, Seattle, Wash, 70; Alaska State Mus, Juneau, 75; Anchorage Hist & Fine Arts Mus, 77; Mus of Sci, Boston, 78. *Awards:* Purchase Award, Alaska Centennial, 67; First Prize Woodblock, All-Alaska Show, Exxon Corp, 75. *Bibliog:* Pat McCullough (auth), Alaskan Artist, Alaska J Hist & Art, 76; article, Am Artist, 4/82. *Media:* Woodblock, Wood Engraving. *Publ:* Auth, Juneau A Book of Woodcuts, 73, Raven, 75 & Dale De Armond, A First Book of Prints, 79, Northwest Publ; Berry Woman's Children, Greenwillow Bks, 85. *Dealer:* Rie Munoz Gallery 210 Ferry Way Juneau AK 99801. *Mailing Add:* 120 Katlian St Sitka AK 99835

DEATS, MARGARET
ART DEALER, WRITER
b Houston, Tex, May 27, 42. *Study:* Univ Houston; Univ St Thomas, Houston. *Collections Arranged:* Gulf Coast Invitational Sculpture Exhib, 76; Houston Festival Sculpture Invitational, 79; group exhib, Lovett Inn, Houston, 89; H J Bott's D-O-V 20th Anniversary exhib, 92. *Pos:* Fine Arts writer, Galveston Daily News, 71-75; owner-pres, Loft-on-Strand Gallery, 71-78; pvt dealer, 78- *Bibliog:* Gay McFarland (auth), Living on The Strand, Sculptor & Wife Preserve Old Building, Houston Post, 5/73; Dancie Perugini (auth), Loft-on-Strand, Houston Town & Country Mag, 4/76. *Mem:* Galveston Co Cult Arts Coun (bd mem, 73-74). *Specialty:* Contemporary paintings, sculpture, conceptual art and process installations. *Publ:* Auth, Painter Frank Freed mirrors human foibles, Galveston Daily News, 72; Nancy Hanks, the gentle persuader brings art to all people, United Press Int, 73; Piled sugar, sacrificed painting are Michael Tracy's statements, Galveston Daily News, 74; The arts of Galveston, Galveston Mag, 75; Carol Gerhardt Photos, FOTOFEST 90 (catalog). *Mailing Add:* 719 Leverkuhn Suite 102 Houston TX 77007-5745

DE BLASI, TONY
PAINTER, EDUCATOR
b Alcamo, Italy, Jan 1, 33; US citizen. *Study:* Art Students League, with Sidney Dickenson, Univ RI, BA; Ind Univ, Bloomington, with William Bailey, James McGarrell, Henry Hope & Albert Elsen, MFA. *Work:* Riverside Mus Collection, Rose Art Mus, Brandeis Univ; Wichita State Univ Mus Fine Arts, Kans; Detroit Art Inst; Ind Univ, Bloomington; Best Products Co Inc, Richmond, Va. *Exhib:* Midyear Show Contemp Am Art, Butler Inst, Youngstown, Ohio, 67; Mus Mod Art, New York, 68; one-man shows, Spectrum Gallery, New York, 68, 69, 71 & 73, Detroit Art Inst, 72, Razor Gallery, New York, 75 & 77 & Louis K Meisel Gallery, New York, 85, 87, 88, 89 & 91; 33rd Corcoran Biennial Contemp Am Painting, Corcoran Gallery, Washington, DC, 73; Wake Forest Univ, Winston-Salem, NC, 80; Hokin Kaufman Gallery, Chicago, Ill, 88; Hokin Gallery, Bay Harbor Islands, Fla, 90; and others. *Teaching:* Chmn & artist-in-residence, Washington & Jefferson Col, 63-66; prof painting & drawing, Mich State Univ, 66-86; instr, Sch Visual Arts, 88-90. *Awards:* Louis Comfort Tiffany Found grant, 66-67; Founders Purchase Prize, Detroit Art Inst, 70; Individual Artist Grant, Mich Coun Arts, 83. *Bibliog:* Emily Wasserman (auth), rev, In: Artforum, 4/68; Atirnomis (auth), rev, In: Arts Mag, 12-1/70; Gene Baro (auth), The 33rd Corcoran Biennial (catalog), 73; and others. *Mem:* Art Students League. *Media:* Acrylic. *Dealer:* Louis K Meisel Gallery 141 Prince St New York NY 10012. *Mailing Add:* 376 Broome St 3 Fl New York NY 10013

DE BOSCHNEK, CHRIS (CHRISTIAN CHARLES)
PAINTER, PRINTMAKER
b Cannes, France, Apr 24, 47; US citizen. *Study:* Cleveland Art Inst; Akron Univ. *Work:* Weiskoff, Silver & Co, New York; Newark Mus, NJ; Kelly, Drye & Warren, Stamford, Conn; US Steel Co, Pittsburgh, Pa; Sherman & Sterling, New York. *Exhib:* One-man shows, Akron Art Inst, Ohio, 71, Kathryn Markel Gallery, New York, 82, Queens Mus, NY, 88 & Elizabeth McDonald Gallery, New York, 88; Tibor de Nagy Gallery, New York, 73; OK Harris Gallery, New York, 79; Lerner Heller Gallery, New York, 82; Edith C Blum Art Ctr, Annandale on Hudson, 84; Hallwalls, Buffalo, NY, 85; Richard Green Gallery, New York, 86; and others. *Awards:* Yaddo Fel, 80. *Publ:* Articles in Cover Mag, spring 80 & winter 81, Arts Mag, 3/82, 9/86 & 2/88 & Artnews Mag, 4/82. *Mailing Add:* 66 S Fourth St Brooklyn NY 11211

DE BRETTEVILLE, SHEILA LEVRANT
DESIGNER, EDUCATOR
b Brooklyn, NY, Nov 4, 40. *Study:* Barnard Col, Columbia Univ, BA(art hist); Yale Sch Art & Archit, MFA(graphic design). *Work:* Victoria & Albert Mus, London; Design Collection, Mus Mod Art, New York; Pub Libr, Los Angeles & New York. *Comn:* 40 under 40 show, Archit League, New York, 65; spec issue design, Art Soc Wis, 70; Frederick Weisman Found Art, 85. *Exhib:* Communications Graphics, Am Inst Graphics Art, 72; 5e Biennale des Arts Graphiques, Brno Czech, 72; Color, Am Inst Graphic Arts, Whitney Mus, 74; Poster from the Vietnam Years, New York, 75; At Home, Long Beach Mus Art, 84; Let's Play House, Bernice Steinbaum Gallery, 86. *Pos:* Typographer, Yale Univ Press, New Haven, Conn, 65-68; designer, Olivetti, Milan, Italy, 68-69; designer, Calif Inst Arts, 69-74; co-founder & pres, Woman's Bldg Community Gallery, 73-; juror, Nat Endowment Arts-Civil Serv Comn, 75; co-founder, ed & designer, Chrysalis Mag, 77-; design dir, Los Angeles Times, 78-81; chmn, Dept of Commun, Design & Illus, Otis Art Inst of Parsons Sch of Design, Los Angeles, 81- *Teaching:* Dir inst & graphic design dept, Calif Inst Arts, 70-74; chmn, dept commun design, Otis/Parsons Univ; lectr at var cols & univs; dir grad studies graphic design, Yale Univ Sch Art. *Awards:* Grand Award Excellence, Soc Publ Designers, 71; Communication Graphics Awards, 72 & five Gold Medals, Calif 2 Exhib, Am Inst Graphic Arts; IBM Fel, Int Design Conf, Aspen, 74. *Bibliog:* Gilles de Bure (auth), Right on Sheila, Creations Recherches Esthetiques Europeenes, 73; articles Commun Arts, 6/83. *Mem:* Am Inst Graphic Arts; Internat Alliance Theatrical Stage Employees; Col Art Asn. *Media:* Paper, Stone. *Publ:* Ed, Calif Inst Arts: Prologue to a community, Vol 7 No 2 & A reexamination of some aspects of the design arts from the perspective of the women designer, Arts Soc, 74; auth, A reevaluation of design, Icographic 6, 73; Habitability, In: Proc of the Calif Chap Am Inst Archit, 74; Feminist Design, Space & Soc, 6/83. *Mailing Add:* 52 Lyon New Haven CT 06511

DEBROSKY, CHRISTINE A
PAINTER
b Kingston, NY, Dec 10, 51. *Study:* Albert Handell, pastel workshops, 80; Woodstock Sch Art (Art Students League), 90. *Work:* Key Corp Collection, Albany, NY; Standard & Poor's, New York; Riverside Women's Health, Poughkeepsie, NY; Altman & Selvaggi Inc, New York. *Comn:* Residence mural project, Anderson Sch, Staatsburg, NY, 82; pastel landscape/diptych, Key Corp/Greenhut Galleries, Albany, NY, 92. *Exhib:* Pastel Soc Am Ann, Nat Arts Club, New York, 89, 90 & 91; La Watercolor Int, World Trade Ctr, New Orleans, 91; Adirondacks Nat Watercolor, Arts Ctr/travelling, Old Forge, NY, 91; Midwest Pastel Soc Nat, Dellona Norris Cult Ctr, St Charles, Ill, 92; Pastel Soc Am, Harmon/Meek Gallery & Gallery on Venetian Bay, Naples, Fla, 92; and others. *Awards:* Am Artist Award, La Watercolor Int, 5/91; Scott Award/landscape, Barbara & Gary Scott, Pastel Soc Am Ann, 9/91. *Bibliog:* Mikhail Horowitz (auth), Art at the culinary institute of america, Woodstock Times, 89; Leslie Urbach (auth), Artists of the Hudson/Mohawk, Albany Ctr Galleries, 89; Bonnie Langston (auth), feature, 101 Donations, Daily Freeman, 9/91. *Mem:* Hudson River Watercolor Soc (founding mem/secy, 86-); Woodstock Artists Asn; Pastel Soc Am. *Media:* Pastel, Watercolor. *Mailing Add:* RD 1 Box 156 Tillson NY 12486

DEBRUYCKER, DIRK H A
PAINTER
b Ghent, Belg, 1955. *Study:* St Lucas Inst Fine Arts, Ghent, Belg, 73-77; Tamarind Inst, Univ NMex, Albuquerque, 79-80, with Garo Antresean (non-degree), 80-81. *Exhib:* Gallery 41, Antwerp, 81; one-man shows, Gallery ADG, Ghent, 83 & 85, Gallery XXI, Antwerp, 86, H & S DeBuck Gallery, Ghent, Belg, 89, 91 & 92, Kay Gurvey Gallery, Chicago, Ill, 90 & 92, Conlon Gallery, Santa Fe, NMex, 91, Jan Weiner Gallery, Kansas City, Mo, 91, Lowe Gallery, Atlanta, Ga, 92; Six Flemish Artists, The Art Soc Int Monetary Fund, Wash, DC, 86; Anne Reed Gallery, Ketchum, Idaho, 88; Out of Towners, Wright Gallery, New York, 88; Double Vision, Conlon Gallery & Linda Durham Gallery, Santa Fe, NMex, 91; Inst Am Indian Arts Mus, Faculty Exhib, 91; A Room of One's Own, Linda Durham Gallery, Santa Fe, NMex, 92. *Awards:* Young Belgian Graphic Art, Antwerp, Belg, 78; Laureate Provincial Award of Fine Arts, Ghent, Belg, 82-; Visions of Excellence, Albuquerque United Artists, 88. *Mailing Add:* Conlon Gallery 125 N Guadalupe Santa Fe NM 87501

DECAPRIO, ALICE
PAINTER, PHOTOGRAPHER
b Marshall, Mich, Feb 10, 19. *Study:* Mich State Univ, AB; Northwestern Univ, MA; also watercolor with Gerald Brommer, Nicholas Reale and Valfred Thelin. *Work:* Ocean Co Col, NJ; US Navy; RCA Corp Hq, New York; Chatham Savings & Loan; Ringling Mus, Sarasota, Fla. *Comn:* Drawings, Ringling Mus, Sarasota, Fla, 78 & 80; US Navy-NY Harbor Oper Sail activities, 76-77; Navy Women at Work on Board USS Vulcan, 79; brochure, Albaz Corp, Riyadh, Saudi Arabia, 81; and others. *Exhib:* One-person shows, Nat Arts Club, 77, S Vt Art Ctr, 77 & Sarasota Centennial Comt, Kress Int Plaza, Fla, 86; AT&T Corp Hq, NJ, 80 & Friends of Arts & Sci, Sarasota, Fla, 80; Heritage Plantation, Sandwich, Mass, 81; Plymouth Harbor, Women's Res Ctr (photog), Sarasota, 91. *Teaching:* Instr watercolor, Madison-Chatham Adult Sch, 68-76, instr outdoor sketching, 70-81, Creative Learning Workshop, Rockport, Mass, 77-82; instr sketching, Hilton Leech Studio Wkshps & Travelling Two-Arts Wkshps, 85-90. *Awards:* Exhib Comn Award, Nat Arts Club Open Watercolor Show, 75; Grumbacher Award, NJ Watercolor Soc, 77; Naval Art Coop & Liaison Comt Bronze Medal for Achievement in Watercolor, Salmagundi Club, 78; First Prize, Black & White Show, Manatee Art League, 85. *Mem:* Salmagundi Club; Int Soc Marine Painters; Fla Watercolor Soc; NJ Watercolor Soc; Nat League Am Pen Women. *Media:* Watercolor; Photography. *Dealer:* Art Uptown 1367 Main St Sarasota FL 34236. *Mailing Add:* 3963 Country View Dr Sarasota FL 34233

DECARAVA, ROY RUDOLPH
PHOTOGRAPHER, EDUCATOR
b New York, NY, Dec 9, 19. *Study:* Cooper Union Art Sch, 38-40; RI Sch Design, Hon PhD, 85; Md Inst Col Art, Hon PhD(art), 86. *Work:* Metrop Mus Art, Mus Mod Art, New York; Mus Fine Arts, Houston; Ctr Creative Photog. *Comn:* The Nation's Capitol in Photographs, Corcoran Gallery Art, 76; American Images, Am Tel & Tel, New York, 78. *Exhib:* Always the Young Strangers, Mus Mod Art, New York, 53; The Family of Man, Mus Mod Art, New York, 53; The Photographers Eye, Mus Mod Art, New York, 64; Photography in the Fine Arts, Metrop Mus Art, New York, 64; Thru Black Eyes, Studio Mus Harlem, 69; Photography in America, Whitney Mus Am Art, 74; solo exhibs, Mus Fine Arts, Houston, 75, Clarence Kennedy Gallery, Boston, 82 & Ziikha Gallery, Wesleyan Univ; Mirrors & Windows, Mus Mod Art, New York, 78; Silver Sensibilities, Newhouse Gallery, Staten Island, 80; The Sound I Saw, Studio Mus Harlem, 83. *Teaching:* Dir photog, Kamoinge Workshop, New York, 63-66; adj instr, Cooper Union Art Sch, 69-72; prof, Hunter Col, 75-; app distingued prof, Art, 88. *Awards:* Guggenheim Fel Photog, 52-53; Outstanding Achievements in Photography, Int Black Photogr, 79; Spec Citation Photojournalism, Am Soc Mag Photogr, 83. *Bibliog:* A D Coleman (auth), Roy DeCarava, Popular Photog, 70; Elton Fax (auth), Seventeen Black Artists, Dodd, Mead Co, 73; Pat Leighton (auth), Roy DeCarava, Photograph, Vol 1, No 3, 77. *Mem:* Friends Photog (mem bd trustees, 82-); Photo Resource Ctr. *Publ:* Coauth (with Langston Hughes), The Sweet Flypaper of Life, Simon & Schuster, 55, republ, Howard Univ Press. *Dealer:* Witkin Gallery 415 W Broadway New York NY 10012. *Mailing Add:* Hunter Col CUNY 695 Park Ave New York NY 10021

DE CASTRO, LORRAINE
SCULPTOR, CERAMIST
b Rio Piedras, PR, July 19, 46. *Study:* Univ PR, BA, 72, studied welding with John Balossi, 77; New York Univ, grad studies, 82-84. *Work:* Museo de Arte de Ponce, PR. *Exhib:* Clay and Fire: Seven Ceramists, Inst Cult, San Juan, 86; Growing Beyond, Women Artists from Puerto Rico, Orgn Am States, Washington, DC, Mus del Barrio, New York & Caribe Gallery, Puerto Rico, 87-88; Ceramics From Puerto Rico, EuroAmerican Gallery, Caracas, Venezuela, 90; Women Artists: Protagonists of the 80's, Museo delas Casas Reales, Dominican Republic, Mus Contemp Art, San Juan, PR, 90; Weaving Images, Normandie Gallery, San Juan, PR, 91, 25 Anniversary: Art League of San Juan, PR, 92; and others. *Teaching:* Prof ceramics, Art Students League of San Juan, 80-; prof, Univ PR, 89- *Bibliog:* Charlotte Speight (auth), Images in Clay Sculpture, 83. *Mem:* Mujeres Artistas de PR, Inc; Sculptors Asn PR. *Media:* Clay. *Dealer:* Botello Gallery Cristo St Old San Juan PR 00936. *Mailing Add:* G-16 Granada St Vistamar Marina Carolina PR 00983

DE CHAMPLAIN, VERA CHOPAK
PAINTER, PRINTMAKER
b Ger; US citizen. *Study:* Art Students League; spec studies with Edwin Dickinson. *Work:* Butler Inst Am Art, Youngstown, Ohio; Slater Mus, Norwich, Conn; Ga Mus Art, Athens; Evansville Mus Art & Sci, Ind; Smithsonian Inst Arch Am Art, Washington DC; and others. *Comn:* Portrait, Liederkranz Found, New York, 79 & 91; priv portraits & landscapes comns. *Exhib:* Metrop Mus Art, New York, 79; Muriel Karasik Gallery, Westhampton, NY, 80; B Altman Gallery, New York, 82; Consulate General of Fed Republic of Ger, 86; Traveling exhib, 88-89; Broome St Gallery, Soho, NY, 91-92; and others. *Teaching:* Art dir & instr oil painting, Emanu-El Ctr, New York, 68- *Awards:* Twilight & Onteora Club Award, Haines Falls, NY, 65; US Investor Award, 69; First Prize-World Award, Acad Italia, Parma, 85,87. *Bibliog:* Samuel M La Corte (auth), Creative images, Clifton Leader, 70. *Mem:* Fel Royal Soc Arts; Artists Equity Asn New York; Kappa Pi; Nat Soc Arts & Lett (art chmn Empire State, 69-); Art Students League; and others. *Media:* Oil, Watercolor; All. *Publ:* Auth, article, ArtSpeak, 3/86; article, Marketletter from Rosenthal & Co, 3/24/86. *Mailing Add:* 230 Riverside Dr New York NY 10025

DECHAR, PETER
PAINTER
b New York, NY, Apr 19, 42. *Work:* Mus Mod Art & Whitney Mus Am Art, New York; Larry Aldrich Mus, Conn; Walker Art Ctr, Chicago; Fiberglass Tower Art Collection. *Exhib:* Highlights from the 1967 Season, Larry Aldrich Mus, Conn, 67; Contemp Painting & Sculpture, Krannert Art Mus, 67; Whitney Mus Am Art Ann, New York, 67 & 69; one-man shows, Cordier & Ekstrom Gallery, New York, 67, 69 & 75; Twentieth Century Art from the Rockefeller Collection, Mus Mod Art, New York, 69. *Media:* Oil. *Mailing Add:* 455 Carroll St Brooklyn NY 11215

DE COUX, JANET
SCULPTOR
b Niles, Mich. *Study:* Carnegie Inst Technol, two yrs; NY Sch Indust Design; RI Sch Design; Art Inst Chicago; asst to C Paul Jennewein, A B Cianfarani, Gozo Kawamura, Alvin Meyer & James Earl Fraser. *Comn:* William Penn, William Penn Mem Mus, Harrisburg, Pa; Madonna (black granite), Manhasset, Long Island, NY; St Benedict, St Vincent's Archabbey, Latrobe, Pa; St Benedict sculpture proj, Liturgical Art Soc; five pieces sculpture, St Scholastica's Church, Aspinwall, Pa; plus many others. *Exhib:* One-man show, Carnegie Inst; Artist of Year Show, Arts & Crafts Ctr, Univ Pittsburgh. *Teaching:* Resident instr art, Cranbrook Acad Art, 42-45. *Awards:* Guggenheim Fel; Widener Gold Medal, Pa Acad Fine Arts; Lindsay Mem Prize, Nat Sculpture Soc. *Mem:* Nat Acad Design; Nat Sculpture Soc. *Media:* Stone, Wood. *Mailing Add:* 3930 Dickey Rd Gibsonia PA 15044

DE CREEFT, LORRIE J See Goulet, Lorrie

DECTER, BETTY EVA
PAINTER, SCULPTOR
Birmingham, Ala, 1927. *Study:* Self taught & Otis Art Inst. *Comn:* Painting, comn by Mr & Mrs Norman, Pauma Valley, Calif, 86. *Exhib:* Solo exhibs, Crocker Bank, Beverly Hills, Calif, 80, Roger Morrison Gallery, Los Angeles, Calif, 85, Bonwit Tellers, Beverly Hills, Calif, 86, Ivey's Dept Store, Gainesville, Fla, 86, Brand Libr Art Gallery, Glendale, Calif, 88, Riverside Co Mus, 89 & San Francis Gallery, Crossroads Sch Arts & Scis, Santa Monica, 92; Artists Equity Bienale Exhib, Brand Libr Art Gallery, Glendale, Calif, 87; Loyola Law Sch, SCalif Women's Caucus Art, 88; 16th Ann Multi Media Juried Art Show, Creative Arts Ctr Gallery, Burbank, Calif, 91. *Awards:* Cash Award, Assocs Brand Libr Award, Creative Arts Ctr Gallery, Burbank, Calif, 91. *Bibliog:* Women's Caucus Art, Feisty Women (video), 2/89; Mary Alice Cline (auth), Colors & Cultures Weigh in at a Ton of Kimonos, Press Enterprise, 4/16/89; Rita Townsend & Ann Perkins (coauths), Bitter Fruit, Hunter Publ Co, 92. *Mem:* Women's Caucus Art; Artists Equity. *Publ:* Contribr, Contemporary Women Artists Calendar & Datebook, Cedco Publs, 92; Mutiny and Mainstream, Midmarch Press, 92. *Mailing Add:* 5412 W Washington Blvd Los Angeles CA 90016

DE CUNTO, JOHN GIOVANNI See Giovanni,

DEDINI, ELDON LAWRENCE
CARTOONIST, GRAPHIC ARTIST
b King City, Calif, June 29, 21. *Study:* Hartnell Col, AA; Chouinard Art Inst, Los Angeles. *Work:* Achenbach Collection, Legion of Honor, San Francisco; Libr of Cong, Washington, DC; NY Univ. *Exhib:* Int Cartoonale, Heist-Duinbergen, Belg, 64-66; Three Cartoonists Show, Richmond Art Mus, Calif, 68; Three Cartoonists Show, Monterey Peninsula Mus Art, 83; Galerie Bartsch & Chariau, Munich, 89. *Pos:* Cartoonist, Salinas Index-Jour, Calif, 40-42; story cartoonist, Disney Studios, Burbank, Calif, 44-46; cartoonist-gagman, Esquire, Inc, Chicago, 46-50; cartoonist, New Yorker Mag, 50-92; Playboy, Inc, Chicago, 60-92. *Awards:* Best Mag Cartoonist, Nat Cartoonists Soc, 58, 61, 64 & 89. *Bibliog:* Paul Coker, (auth), Cartoonist Profiles, 6/73; Richard Calhoun (auth), Contemporary Graphic Artists, Vol 1, Gale Research Co, 86. *Mem:* Nat Cartoonists Soc; Cartoonists Asn, New York. *Publ:* Auth, The Dedini Gallery, 61 & illusr, La Clef, 70, Holt; A Much, Much Better World, Microsoft Press (Harper & Row), 85. *Mailing Add:* PO Box 1630 Monterey CA 93942

DE DONATO, LOUIS
PAINTER, INSTRUCTOR
b New York, NY, Aug 29, 34. *Study:* Art Students League, with Frank Reilly, 55-61. *Work:* Abe Sharp Found, Maine; Navy Art Combat and Laison, Washington, DC. *Exhib:* Allied Artists Am 68th Ann, Nat Arts Club, New York, 81; Soc Animal Artists Exhib, Acad Natural Sci, Philadelphia, 82 & Topeka, Kans, 83; Am Artists Prof League, New York, 83; Greenwich

Workshop Gallery Miniature Show, 83. *Teaching:* Instr life drawing & painting, Salmagundi Club, New York, 72- *Awards:* First Prize, NY & Conn Am Artists Prof League Show, 79; Maggie Bower Award, Knickerbocker Artists Asn, 80; Franklin B Williams Fund Prize, Salmagundi Club, 83. *Mem:* Salmagundi Club (bd dirs, 70-86); Allied Artists Am; Soc Animal Artists (bd dirs, 76-86); Am Artists Prof League; Hudson Valley Artists Asn. *Media:* Oil. *Publ:* Illusr, Nat Inst of Art & Design, Northwest Sch, Inc, 64. *Dealer:* Hobe Sound Galleries Hobe Sound FL; Husberg Fine Arts Gallery Sedona AZ. *Mailing Add:* 400 E 77th St Apt 105 New York NY 10021

DEE, ELAINE EVANS
HISTORIAN
b Cleveland, Ohio, Jan 11, 24. *Study:* Oberlin Col, with Wolfgang Stechow, BA, 45; Radcliffe Col, with Jakob Rosenberg, MA, 51. *Collections Arranged:* Views of Florence & Tuscany, Washington, DC, 68; Master Printmakers from the Cooper-Hewitt Mus (auth, catalog), New York, 70; Winslow Homer, A Selection from the Cooper-Hewitt Mus (auth catalog), Washington, DC, 72; An American Mus of Decorative Art & Design (contribr, catalog), Victoria & Albert Mus, London, Eng, 73; Etchings of the Tiepolos, Ottawa, Ont, 75; Nineteenth-Century American Landscape Drawings in the Cooper-Hewitt Collections (auth), 82; Versailles: The View from Sweden (coauth, catalog), Cooper-Hewitt Mus, 88; Under Changing Skies; Landscapes of Frederic E Church (auth), 92. *Pos:* Asst cur drawings, Fogg Art Mus, Harvard Univ, 45-51 & 52-53; asst cur drawings & prints, Cleveland Mus Art, Ohio, 51-52 & Pierpont Morgan Libr, New York, 61-68; cur drawings & prints, Cooper-Hewitt Mus Design, New York, 68-91. *Awards:* Samuel H Kress Found Traveling Fel, 73; Nat Endowment Arts Mus Prof Fel, 76. *Mem:* Int Comt Cur Pub Collections Graphic Arts; Am Fedn Arts; Print Coun Am; Am Mus Asn. *Res:* Eighteenth century French and Italian drawings, particularly the artists Gilles-Marie Oppenord and Guiseppe Zocchi. *Publ:* Contribr, One Hundred Master Drawings, Harvard Univ Press, 49. *Mailing Add:* c/o Cooper-Hewitt Mus Nat Mus Design Two E 91st St New York NY 10028

DEE, LEO JOSEPH
PAINTER, GRAPHIC ARTIST
b Newark, NJ, July 8, 31. *Study:* Newark Sch Fine & Indust Art, with Hans Weingartner, Benjamin Cunningham, James Rosati & Ruben Nakian, dipl. *Work:* Newark Mus Art, NJ State Mus, Trenton; Springfield Mus Art, Mass; Columbus Mus Art, Ohio; Yale Univ Art Gallery. *Exhib:* Drawing Soc Regional, Philadelphia Mus, Drawing Soc Nat, circulated by Am Fedn Arts, 65-66; Meticulous Realism, Tawes Art Ctr, Univ Md, 66; NJ State Mus, Trenton, 66-70; 4th Invitational Painting & Sculpture, Van Deusen Gallery, Kent State Univ, 70; one-man show, Coe Kerr Gallery, 75, NJ State Mus, Trenton, 78, Nat Portrait Gallery, 80, Nat Acad, NY, 87, Noyes Mus, NJ, 92. *Teaching:* Instr drawing & painting, Newark Sch Fine & Indust Art, 58- *Awards:* Purchase Awards, NJ State Mus, Trenton, 70, Newark Mus, 81; Cannon Prize, Nat Acad, New York, 87. *Bibliog:* William H Gerdts (auth), Painting & sculpture in New Jersey, Van Norstrand, 64; Theodore E Stebbins (auth), American master drawings & watercolors, Harper & Row, 76; Marvin Sadik & Harold F Pfister (auths), American portrait drawings, Smithsonian Inst Press, 80; Bruce Weber (auth), The front line, Norton Gallery, 85. *Media:* Oil. *Dealer:* Coe Kerr Gallery 49 E 82nd St New York NY 10028. *Mailing Add:* 38 Ridgewood Terr Maplewood NJ 07040

DEEM, GEORGE
PAINTER
b Vincennes, Ind, Aug 18, 32. *Study:* Sch of the Art Inst of Chicago, BFA, 58, with Paul Wieghardt & Boris Margo. *Work:* Indianapolis Mus Art, Ind; Mus Ludwig, Koln, WGer; Evansville Mus Arts & Sci, Ind; Albright-Knox Art Gallery, Buffalo, NY; Allen Mem Art Mus, Oberlin Col, Ohio. *Comn:* Painting, Nutter, McClennen & Fish, Boston, 88; painting, Paul, Weiss, Rifkind, Wharton & Garrison, New York, 90. *Exhib:* Solo shows, Indianapolis Mus Art, 74-75 & Witte Mem Mus, San Antonio, Tex, 75; Whitney Mus Am Art, New York, 78; Evansville Mus of Arts & Sci, Ind, 79; Wilhelm-Lehmbruck Mus, Duisburg, WGer, 78; Pa Acad Fine Arts, Philadelphia, 81; Allentown Art Mus, Pa; Fort Wayne Mus Art, Ind, 84; Chicago Int Art Expo, 85-86; Indianapolis Ctr for Contemp Art, 88, 90. *Pos:* Artist-in-residence, Evansville Mus Arts & Sci, 79; secy exec comt, MacDowell Colony Fels 82, 86; vis artist, Ill State Univ, Normal, 82. *Teaching:* Instr, Sch Visual Arts, New York, 65-66; instr painting, Leicester Polytech, Eng, 66-67 & Univ Pa, Philadelphia, 67-68. *Bibliog:* Ronald Vance (auth), Painting lists, Art & Artists, London, Eng, 2/68; Edgar Buonagurio (auth), George Deem, Arts Mag, New York, 11/77; Udo Kultermann (auth), Vermeer and contemporary American painting, Am Art Rev, Los Angeles, 11/78. *Media:* Oil on Canvas; Mixed. *Publ:* Auth, AANABABCAC, Sun & Moon, fall 79; A Painting For Babies, Benzene, fall 81; Extra Genre, White Walls, summer 81; Actual Size, Benzene, fall-winter 83-84; Drawing, White Walls, spring 86. *Dealer:* Nancy Hoffman Gallery 429 W Broadway New York NY 10012. *Mailing Add:* 10 W 18th St New York NY 10011

DE FAZIO, JOHN
SCULPTOR
b Reading, Pa, Jan 23, 59. *Study:* Philadelphia Col Art, BFA, 81; San Francisco Art Inst, MFA, 84. *Work:* Los Angeles Contemp Exhibs, Los Angeles. *Exhib:* One man shows, Fun Gallery West, San Francisco, Calif, 85, B-Side Gallery, New York, 86, Ohio State Univ, Gallery Fine Arts, Columbus, 87, La Luz De Jesus Gallery, Los Angeles, Calif, 88 & Garth Clark Gallery, New York, 92; NCECA Exhib, Contemp Crafts Gallery, Portland, Ore, 88 & Philadelphia Col Art, Pa, 92; Against Nature, Los Angeles Contemp Exhibs, Calif, 89; Serious Fun Festival, Lincoln Ctr, New York, 90; Post Pop and Beyond, Bess Cutler Gallery, Los Angeles, Calif, 91; Off the Wall, Am Craft Mus, New York, 92. *Teaching:* Artist in residence, Mont State Univ, currently. *Awards:* Change Inc, Visual Arts Grant, 90; Empire State Craft Allience, Artist Grant, 91; New York Found Arts Fel, 91. *Media:* Clay. *Mailing Add:* 107 Chrystie St New York NY 10002

DEFAZIO, TERESA GALLIGAN
PAINTER, GALLERY DIRECTOR
b Philadelphia, Pa, May 5, 41. *Study:* Moore Col Art, with Paulette VanRoekins, Dolya Goutman, Ranulph Bye & Leonard Nelson, BFA, 63; Pennsylvania Acad Fine Arts, with Louis Sloan & Glen Rudderow, 89-90. *Work:* Rosemont Collection, Radnor Twp Sch Dist, Radnor/Wayne, Pa. *Exhib:* Ann Exhib Small Oils, Philadelphia Sketch Club, 91 & 92; Ann Juried Exhib, The Plastic Club, Philadelphia, 91 & 92. *Pos:* Mgr, Newman Galleries, Bryn Mawr, Pa, 74-77, Art Space Gallery, Philadelphia, 90-; dir, Newman Galleries, Philadelphia & Bryn Mawr, 85-90. *Mem:* Fel Pa Acad Fine Arts; Philadelphia Art Dealers Asn (secy 87-89); Moore Col Art Alumnae Asn (secy, treas, vpres, pres, during 70s). *Media:* Oil. *Publ:* Coauth & ed, Moore Col Art Alumnae J, 70s; Kenneth R Nunamaker, 1890-1957, 84, Joe Brown-A Retrospective Exhibitions, 87, John Folinsbee-Following His Own Course, Newman Galleries, 90. *Mailing Add:* 695 Sproul Rd Bryn Mawr PA 19010

DE FOREST, ROY DEAN
PAINTER, SCULPTOR
b North Platte, Nebr, Feb 11, 30. *Study:* Yakima Jr Col, 48-50; Calif Sch Fine Arts, 50-52; San Francisco State Col, BA, 52-53, MA, 56-58. *Work:* San Francisco Mus Art; Art Inst Chicago; Joslyn Art Mus, Omaha, Nebr; Philadelphia Mus Art; Whitney Mus Am Art, New York; plus others. *Exhib:* Albright-Knox Gallery, 63; Walker Art Ctr, 63; solo exhibs, Hansen-Fuller Gallery, 71, 73, 75 & 78, Darthea Speyer Gallery, 74, 77 & 87 & Clark/Benton Gallery, Santa Fe, 77 & 81, Fuller Goldeen Gallery, 81, 82, 84 & 86 & Struve Gallery, 88; Extraordinary Realities, Whitney Mus Am Art, 73; retrospective, San Francisco Mus Art, 74; Painting and Sculpture in California: The Modern Era, San Francisco Mus Art, 76; 6 from California, Wash State Univ, 76; New in the Seventies, Univ Tex, Austin, 77; Roy de Forest, Robert Hudson, Inst Contemp Art, Boston, 77; Dog Images through the Century, Downtown Ctr, San Francisco Mus Art, 78; Skowhegan Visiting Artist Exhib, Colby Col Mus, Maine, 85; American Art Today: The Figure in the Landscape, Art Mus, Fla Int Univ, Miami, 86; The Importance of Drawing, Fuller Goldeen Gallery, San Francisco, 87; Animal Images: Roy DeForest/Lisbeth Stewart, Pittsburgh Ctr Arts, 87; The Call of the Wild, Rhode Island Sch Design, Providence, 87; Creatures Great and Small, Schmidt Bingham Gallery, New York, 87. *Pos:* Dir, Larsen Gallery, Yakima Jr Col, 58-60. *Teaching:* Instr, Calif Col Arts & Craft, Oakland, 64-65; from asst prof to assoc prof, Univ Calif, Davis, 65-82, prof, 85- *Awards:* Nealie Sullivan Award, San Francisco Art Asn, 64; Purchase Prize, La Jolla Art Mus, 65; Nat Endowment Arts Grant, 72. *Bibliog:* Thomas Albright (auth), Wildest of funk art, San Francisco Chronicle, 2/6/69; Charles Johnson (auth), The new symbolism, Sacramento Bee, 4/13/69; Grace Glueck (auth), Of beasts and humans: Some contemporary views, New York Times, 11/14/82; Helen L Kohen (auth), An affair with the land, Miami Herald, 1/17/86. *Mem:* San Francisco Art Asn. *Dealer:* Allan Frumkin Gallery 50 West 57th St New York NY 10019. *Mailing Add:* PO Box 47 Port Costa CA 94569

DEGENEVIEVE, BARBARA
PHOTOGRAPHER, EDUCATOR
b Wilkes-Barre, Pa, May 21, 47. *Study:* Wilkes Col, Wilkes-Barre, Pa, BFA, 69; Southern Conn State Col, New Haven, MS(art educ), 73; Univ NMex, Albuquerque, studied with Betty Hahn, Sandi Fellman, Van Deren Coke and Beaumont Newhall, MFA(photog, teaching asst), 80. *Work:* Univ NMex Fine Arts Mus, Albuquerque; Independent Press Archive, Visual Studies Workshop, Rochester, NY; State of Ill Art Acquistion Collection, Chicago & Ellensburg; Erie Art Ctr, Pa; Calif Inst Arts, Valencia; Tokyo Met Mus Photog. *Exhib:* Personal/Political: Sexuality Self Defined, Gallery 2 & Photography: Inventions & Innovations, Art Inst Chicago, 90; Self Portraits of Contemporary Women, Tokyo Metrop Mus Photog, Japan, 91; Parents, Mus Contemp Art, Dayton, Ohio, 92; Photobiographers, Atlanta Gallery Photog, Ga, 92; solo exhibs, Etherton/Stern Gallery, Tucson, Ariz, 92, Univ Colo, Denver, 93. *Collections Arranged:* Women in the Southwest (auth, catalog), 78 & 79; Intimate Statements, 79; Work by Women, 81; Altered States (auth, catalog), 82. *Pos:* Cur, Reimaging Masculinity, WORKS Gallery, San Jose, Calif, 91; cur, Articulated Disparities: Renegotiating Masculinity, Gallery 1, San Jose State Univ, Calif, 9-10/91; cur, No More Heros: Unveiling Masculinity, SF Camerawork Gallery, 10-11/91 & bd dirs, Exhib Comt, 91. *Teaching:* Asst prof, Univ Ill, Champaign, 80-89, chairperson photog, 83- 89; vis artist, Sch Art Inst Chicago, 85-86; assoc prof Calif State Univ, San Jose, 89-; vis artist, San Francisco Art Inst, 90-93. *Awards:* 1st Prize, No Dumb Photographs, Calif Inst Arts, 81; 3rd Award, Midwest Mus Am Art, 81; Univ Ill Faculty Res Bd Grant, 82 & 84; William & Flora Hewlett Summer Int Res Grant, 87; Ill Arts Coun Artists Fel, 87; Visual Artists Fel, Nat Endowment Arts, 88. *Bibliog:* Terry Barrett (auth), Criticizing Photographs: An Introduction to Understanding Images, p 135, 90; Self-Portraits of Contemporary Woman: Exploring the Unknown Self, Tokyo, p 46-51, 153, 159, 91; Parents, Mus Contemp Art (catalog), Dayton, Ohio, 92; PhotoVision, Barcelona, Spain, No 23, 91. *Mem:* Soc Photog Educ. *Publ:* Auth, Sex as subject, Exposure, Vol 20, No 4, 83; The Photographs of Anne Noggle (catalog essay), Photog Gallery, London, UK, 88; ed, No More Heros, SF Camerawork Quart, summer/fall 91. *Dealer:* Catherine Edelman Gallery 300 W Superior Chicago IL 60610. *Mailing Add:* 227 1/2 E Lincoln PO Box 888 Joseph IL 61873

DE GROAT, DIANE
ILLUSTRATOR, DESIGNER
b Newton, NJ, May 24, 47. *Study:* Pratt Inst, 65-69, BFA. *Comn:* Children's Book Council. *Exhib:* Soc Illusr Ann Nat Exhib, New York, 72 & 75; Insides, 74 & Ann Bk Show, 77, Am Inst Graphic Arts, New York; Poster USA/74, Art Dir Club, 74 & 85; Master Eagle Gallery, New York, 81, 83-85; Southeast Ohio Arts Ctr, 90; Kimberly Gallery, New York, 90. *Pos:* Designer & art dir, Holt, Rinehart & Winston, New York, 69-72; lectr, Pelham Art Ctr, New York, 81. *Bibliog:* Upcoming illustrator, Art Dir Mag, 74; article, New York Times (Westchester), 8/29/82; article, Westchester Spotlight, 6/83. *Mem:* Soc of Illus; Graphic Artists Guild. *Media:* Watercolor, Charcoal. *Publ:* Amanda and April, Morrow, 86; The Great Ideas of Lila Fenwick, Dial, 86; Bears in Pairs, Bradbury, 88; Where is Everybody?, Simon & Schuster, 89; auth-illusr, Annie Pitts, Artichoke, Simon & Schuster, 92; and 65 other titles. *Mailing Add:* Bristol Place Chappaqua NY 10514

DE GROAT, GEORGE HUGH
PAINTER, PRINTMAKER
b Newark, NJ, Jan 7, 17. *Study:* Newark Sch Fine Arts, 34-38; Newark Prep Col, BA, 40; Art Sch Detroit Soc Arts, 54-56. *Work:* Monterey Penninsula Mus Art, Calif; Downey Mus Art, Calif. *Exhib:* Solo exhibs, Monterey Peninsula Mus Art, 72 & 82 & Loyola Marymount Univ, 74; Faculty Exhib, Otis Art Inst, Los Angeles Co, 72; San Bernardino Co Mus Art, 82; Brand Gallery, Glendale, Calif, 82. *Pos:* Art critic, Pasadena Star-News, 68-70; artist-in-residence, Monterey Peninsula Mus Art, 77- *Teaching:* Instr painting, Calif State Col, San Diego, 66-67; instr painting, Art Ctr Col Design, Los Angeles, 68-71; instr life drawing & painting, Otis Art Inst, Los Angeles Co, 68-78. *Awards:* First Prize, Fourth Ann Southern Calif Exhib, Long Beach Mus Art, 66; McBride Award, Pasadena Art Mus, 69; Ford Found Grant Color Field Painting, 77. *Bibliog:* Mugnaini (auth), Drawing--A Search for Form & Oil Painting Techniques, Van Nostrand-Reinhold. *Mem:* Am Asn Univ Prof; Los Angeles Art Asn (bd gov, 70-); Carmel Art Asn, 69. *Media:* Oil on Canvas; Intaglio on Copper Plates. *Publ:* Auth, article, Am Artist Mag, 73. *Dealer:* Carmel Gallery of Modern Art Carmel CA 93921; Phyllis Lucas Gallery Second Ave New York NY. *Mailing Add:* PO Box 306 Carmel Valley CA 93924

DE GUATEMALA, JOYCE (JOYCE BUSH VOURVOULIAS)
SCULPTOR
b Mexico City, Mex, Feb 25, 38; Guatemalan citizen. *Study:* Univ Mex, 58; Univ Wis, 59; Silpakorn Univ, 60-62. *Work:* Mus Mod Art Mex City, Chapultepec/Mexico City, Mex; Orgn Am States & Mus Mod Art Latin Am, Washington, DC; Nat Mus Hist & Fine Arts, Escuela Nac De Bellas Artes & Guatemalan Chamber Indust, Guatemala City; Open Air Sculpture Symposium & the World Invitational Open Air Sculpture Exhib commemorating the 24th Summer Olympic Games, Olympic Park, Seoul, Korea. *Comn:* The Nat Fine Arts Sch of Guatemala, Guatemala City, 75; OAS & Mus Mod Art Latin Am, Washington, DC, 77; Exmibal-El Estor, Exmibal, Guatemala, 77; Kensington Town House Project, Redevelopment Authority of Philadelphia, Pa, 81; Elkins Park Free Library, Elkins Park, Pa, 85. *Exhib:* Solo exhibs, XIII Int Biann Sao Paulo, Brazil, 75, QxQ Checkmate, 88 & Medicine Wheel, 90, 14 Sculpturs Gallery, Soho, NY, Marian Locks Gallery, Philadelphia, 91; Ofrendas: Spirituality & Celebration in Latin Am, Temple Gallery, Temple Univ, Tyler Sch Art, Philadelphia, 88; Guggenheim Mus/Olympiad of Art, Seoul, Korea, 88; 2nd Intl Ephemeral Sculpture Exhib, Fortaleza, Brazil; Pipe Dreams: A Sited Collab, 14 Sculpturs Gallery, Soho, NY, 89; Sculpture of the Ams into the Nineties, Mus Mod Art Latin Am, Washington, DC, 90; Altars & Symbols, Cult Anthrop, 14 Sculpturs Gallery, Soho, NY, 90; Artists Choose Artists, Inst Contemp Art, Univ Pa, Philadelphia, 90; and others. *Pos:* Vpres, Asociacion Tikal, 68-73; dir, Fine Art Comt, Patronato de Bellas Artes, 72-75. *Awards:* Hon Mention for Sculpture Certamen Permanente Centro Americano, Guatemala; Miguel Gracia Granados Medal, Guatemala City, Guatemala, 76; VLI Corp Fel, Djerrasi Found Artist-in-Residence Grant, Woodside, Calif, 85. *Bibliog:* Deborah Victoria Curtis (auth), Visual Literacy, 85; Gallery Hyundai (ed), Olympic Sculpture Park Guide, Seoul Olympic Organizing Comt, 88; Ante Glibota (ed), Olympiad Art Catalogue, Seoul Olympic Organizing Comt, 88; Virginia Watson-Jones (auth), Contemporary American Women Sculptors, Oryx Press, 86. *Mem:* Woman Caucus Arts; Asn Tikal; Philadelphia Art Alliance. *Media:* Stainless Steel, Wood. *Dealer:* Marian Locks Gallery 600 S Washington Sq Philadelphia PA 19106; Barbara Gillman Gallery 3886 Biscayne Blvd Miami FL 33137. *Mailing Add:* 200 Fairview Rd Glenmoore PA 19343

DE GUZMAN, EVELYN LOPEZ
PAINTER, PRINTMAKER
b New York, NY, June 14, 47. *Study:* City Univ New York, BA, 70; Hunter Col, Grad Sch, MA, 74; Pratt Inst; Parsons Sch Design. *Work:* Museo del Barrio & Bronx Mus, New York; Museo de Arte y Historia, San Juan, PR; Museo de Ponce, PR; Mus Contemp Hispanic Art, New York; US Am Art Collection. *Exhib:* Museo del Barrio, New York, 78; Bridge Between Islands, traveling, New York, 78; Puerto Rican Artists, Bronx Mus, New York, 81; Mus Contemp Hispanic Art, New York, 84 & 85; Project America, Villa Taverna (traveling worldwide), New York, Washington, DC; Latin Roots, Nat Coun La Raza, Washington, DC, 90; Journeys, Martin Luther King Libr, Washington, DC, 92. *Teaching:* Instr, high school & elementary systems. *Bibliog:* Grace Glueck (auth), Art: Puerto Rican show in the Bronx, New York Times, 1/26/79; Elaine Wechsler (auth), Space: The inside, the outside, Artspeak, 11/81; Juan Bujan (auth), La Geometria Dinamica de Evelyn Lopez de Guzman, La Voz, 12/3/81. *Mem:* Women Arts; Women's Caucus Art; Asn Artist Run Galleries; Brooklyn Arts Cult Asn Inc. *Media:* Acrylic, Paste; Mixed Media. *Publ:* Contribr, New York Art Yearbook, Noyes Art Books, 75-; Puerto Rico: Its people, its artists, Lightsource, 77. *Dealer:* Noho Gallery 168 Mercer St New York NY 10012; MOCHA 584 Broadway New York NY 10012. *Mailing Add:* Two Hamilton Ct Stirling VA 22170

DE HEUSCH, LUCIO
PAINTER
b Sherbrook, Quebec, 1946. *Study:* Univ du Quebec et Montreal & Ecole des Beaux-Arts de Montreal, Quebec, 66-69. *Work:* Muse d'Art Contemporain, Musee des Beaux-Arts de Montreal, Univ Quebec, Montreal, PQ; Musee de Quebec; Calif Col of Arts & Crafts; Can Coun Art Bank; Ministry of External Affairs, Ottawa, Ont. *Exhib:* Solo exhibs, Galerie Graff, Montreal, 85 & 88, Kitchner-Waterloo Art Gallery, Kitchner, Ont, 86, Ayot-De Heusch, Galerie, Champlain, Univ Bishop, Lennoxville, PQ, 87; Art 16, Bale, Switz, 85; L'Art Pense, Galerie d'Art de l'Univ de Sherbrooke, Quebec, 85 & traveling throughout Canada; Ouevres Charnieres, Galerie Graff, Montreal, 86; Graff: 20 Ans d'Affiches, Place des Arts, Montreal, 86. *Awards:* Research Grant, Canadian Arts Coun, 74, 75 & 77; Ministry of Cult Affairs, Quebec Govt, 75 & 77; Materials Assistance Grants, Can Arts Coun, 81 & 84; Accessibilite Grant, 85, Bourse du Quebec, 85, Quebec Govt. *Bibliog:* Articles, La Presse, Montreal, 84, PEI, 85; articles, Le Devoir, Montreal, 10/5/85, 1/24/86 & 1/25/86; John Bentley May (auth), article, Globe & Mail, 12/17/87. *Mailing Add:* c/o Olga Korper Gallery 17 Morros Ave Toronto ON M6R 2H9 Canada

DEHNER, DOROTHY
SCULPTOR, PRINTMAKER
b Cleveland, Ohio, Dec 23, 01. *Study:* Univ Calif, Los Angeles; Skidmore Col, BS; Art Students League, with Nicolaides, K H Miller & Jan Matulka; Atelier 17, New York; Skidmore Col, Hon Degree, 82; Womans Art Caucus, Hon Degree, 83. *Work:* Metrop Mus Art & Mus Mod Art, New York; Seattle Art Mus, Wash; Minn Art Mus, Minneapolis; Cleveland Mus Art, Ohio. *Comn:* Aluminum grill, 59 & bronze room divider, 61, James Marston Fitch, Stony Point, NY; plexiglas relief, NY Med Col, Valhalla, 72; bronze sculpture, Union Camp Corp, Wayne, NJ, 72; bronze sculpture, Rockefeller Ctr, New York; bronze sculpture, AT&T, Basking Ridge, NJ. *Exhib:* Carnegie Inst Ann, 63; one-woman retrospective, Jewish Mus, New York, 65; Boston Mus Fine Arts; Baltimore Mus Art; Dallas Mus Contemp Art; San Francisco Mus Art; Los Angeles Co Mus; Rutgers Univ Mus, 84; solo exhibs, Phillips Collection, Washington, DC, 89, State Univ, Brit Mus, New Paltz, New York, Cleveland, 90 & Twining Gallery, New York, 87-91; Malcolm Brown Gallery, Cleveland; Whitney Mus; Chicago Art Inst; Perimeter Gallery, Chicago, 92. *Awards:* Sculpture Prize, Art USA, 68; Tamarind Lithography Inst Artist in Residence, 70-71; Yaddo Found Fel, 71. *Bibliog:* Voau Martee (auth), article, Womans Art Mag, 80. *Mem:* Sculptor's Guild (bd mem, 60-62); Fedn Mod Painters & Sculptors; Artists Equity Asn. *Media:* Bronze, Wood; Paper. *Publ:* Auth, Making & fabricating Plexiglas sculpture, 68 & John Graham, 69, Leonardo; Forward for John Graham's System & Dialectrics of Art, John Hopkins Press, 71; David Smith's medallions, Art J, 1/78; contribr, Jake Matulka Catalogue, Whitney Mus & Nat Gallery. *Dealer:* Associated American Artists 663 Fifth Ave New York NY 10022; A M Sachs 29 W 57 St New York NY 10019. *Mailing Add:* 33 Fifth Ave New York NY 10003

DEITCH, JEFFREY
CONSULTANT, CURATOR
b Hartford, Conn, 1952. *Study:* Wesleyan Univ, BA, 74, Harvard Bus Sch, MBA, 78. *Collections Arranged:* Lives, Fine Arts Bldg, New York, 75; Cultural Geometry (auth), 88, Artificial Nature (auth, catalog), 90, Deste Found, Athens, Greece; Strange Abstraction, Touko Mus, Tokyo, 91; Post Human, Castello di Rivoli, Torino, 92. *Pos:* Asst Dir, John Weber Gallery, New York, 74-76; cur, De Cordova Mus, Lincoln, Mass, 78-79; vpres, Citibank art adv serv, 79-88; principal, Jeffrey Deitch Inc, 88- *Awards:* Art critics fel, Nat Endowment Arts, 79. *Publ:* Auth, Keith Haring, Stedelijk Mus, 85; Figuration Libre, Arc, Paris, 85; The Art Industry, Metropolis, Berlin, 91. *Mailing Add:* 721 Fifth Ave New York NY 10022

DE KERGOMMEAUX, DUNCAN
PAINTER, EDUCATOR
b Premier, BC, July 15, 27. *Study:* Banff Sch Fine Art; Inst Allende, Mex; Hans Hofmann Sch Fine Art. *Work:* Nat Gallery Can; London Pub Art Gallery; Art Gallery of Ontario; Can Coun Art Bank; and others. *Comn:* Exterior wall mural, Vanier Post Off, Dept Pub Works, Can, 70; Man Centennial Caravan, Dept Secy State & Man Govt, 70; shaped banners, Schoeler, Heaton Archit, Univ Ottawa, 71; mall environment, Schoeler, Heaton Archit, Garneau Sch, Orleans, Ont, 71; and others. *Exhib:* 3rd & 6th Biennials Can Art, Nat Gallery Can, Can Painting, Albright Knox Gallery, 66; DeKergommeaux-DeNiverville Touring Exhib, Nat Gallery Can, 67-68; London Pub Art Gallery, 71 & 80; Loranger Gallery, Toronto, 80 & 81; Take Two Touring Exhib, 80-84; An Art of Ordered Sensations, London Regional Art Gallery, 86; and others. *Pos:* Dir, Can Pavilion Art Gallery, Expo 67, Montreal, 66-67; chmn dept visual arts, Univ Western Ontario, 81-84. *Teaching:* Prof drawing & painting, Univ Western Ont, 80-; vis prof drawing & painting, Banff Sch Fine Arts, summer 74-75; vis prof, NS Col Art, summer 80. *Awards:* Monsanto Can Art Competition, 57; Purchase Award, Minneapolis Biennial, Boutels, 58; Art Wall Competition, Benson & Hedges, 71. *Bibliog:* Groves (auth), DeKergommeaux at the Blue Barn, Can Art, 63; M Teitlebaum (auth), An Art of Ordered Sensations (exhib catalog), 86. *Mem:* Univ Art Asn Can; Royal Can Acad Arts. *Dealer:* Mira Goddard Gallery 22 Hazelton Ave Toronto ON. *Mailing Add:* 35 Woodgate Ct London ON N6K 4A4 Canada

DE KNIGHT, AVEL
PAINTER
b New York, NY, 1933. *Study:* Ecole Beaux-Arts, Acad Grande Chaumiere & Acad Julien, Paris. *Work:* Metrop Mus Art, New York; Walker Art Inst, Minneapolis, Minn; Norfolk Mus Arts & Sci, Va; Springfield Art Mus, Mo; Massillon Art Mus, Ohio. *Exhib:* Afro-American Artists, Boston Mus Fine Arts, 70; Black American Artists, Ill Arts Coun, 71; Projected Art/Artists at Work, Finch Col Mus, New York, 71; Nat Acad Design, 72 & Mus Mod Art, 72, New York. *Pos:* Art critic, France-Amerique, 58-68. *Teaching:* Instr painting, Nat Acad Design, currently. *Awards:* Gold Medal Grand Award, Am Watercolor Soc Centennial, 67; William A Paton Prize, 71; Palmer Mem Prize, 78. *Mem:* Academician Nat Acad Design; Am Watercolor Soc. *Media:* Gouache, Oil. *Dealer:* Babcock Galleries 20 East 67th St New York NY 10021. *Mailing Add:* c/o Soho Graphic Arts Workshop 433 W Broadway New York NY 10012

D'ELAINE
PAINTER, EDUCATOR
b Puyallup, Wash, Mar 19, 32. *Study:* Cent Wash Univ, BFA, 54; Univ Wash, MFA, 56; Univ London, research of sea hist. *Work:* Nova Scotia Art Mus, Can, 62; Prince/Princess Eleski, Russia; Int Foreign Govt, Japan, Sweden & Germany; Vancouver BC Mus, Can; Whatcom Mus, Bellingham, Wash. *Comn:* Wall mural, New York Life, Seattle, Wash, 58; sea books illus, comn by Dept Navy for USS Bremerton submarine; Rosicrucian Order, New Zealand. *Exhib:* Seattle Art Mus, 62; Featured Artist, Whatcom Mus, Bellingham, Wash, 75-82, State Capital Mus, Olympia, Wash, 76-80, Shoreline Mus, Wash, 78-80, Vancouver BC Maritime Mus, Can, 82, Corvallis State Univ, 82; Int Grand Prix XV, France, 86; Ore State Chautagua, 86; Newport Mus, Ore; Centre Int d'Art Contemp, France, 86; 13th Ann Puget Sound Exhib, Fry Art Mus, 88; Feature artist, Rosicrucian Egyptian Mus, San Jose, Calif; touring exhib in major mus of BC, Can, 89. *Teaching:* Instr drawing & painting, Mus Hist & Industry, 54-56, Edmonds Adult Classes, 54-59 & Seattle Pub Schs, 54-78. *Awards:* award, Thirtieth Ann Puget Sound Area Exhib, Fry Art Mus, Seattle, Wash, 88; award, Nat League Am Pen Women, Fry Art Mus, Seattle, Wash, 89; first recipient Pen Women Art Scholar, Nat League Am Pen Women, 90. *Bibliog:* Feature stories in Seattle Times, Seattle Post Intelligencer & Nat Art Mag; Prince George Citizen, British Columbia, Can, San Jose, Calif News Repartor. *Mem:* Kappa Pi; Nat Artist Equity Asn; Nat Women's Studies; Int Platform Asn; Am Coun Arts; Nat Pen Women. *Media:* Self-evolved Waterbase, mixed media. *Dealer:* Pisces Studio 16122 72nd Ave W Edmonds WA 98020. *Mailing Add:* 16122 72nd Ave W Edmonds WA 98026-4517

DE LAITTRE, ELEANOR
SCULPTOR, PAINTER
b Minneapolis, Minn, Apr 3, 11. *Study:* Boston Mus Fine Arts, 30-31; study with George Luks, 32 & John Sloan, 33, New York. *Work:* NJ State Mus, Trenton; Phillips Gallery, Washington, DC; Walker Art Ctr, Minneapolis, Minn; McCrory Corp, New York, NY; Univ Minn, St Paul. *Exhib:* The Independent Exhibition in Grand Central Palace, New York, 34; Golden Gate International Exhib, San Francisco World's Fair, 36; Fedn Mod Painters & Sculptors Exhibs, New York, 51-70; solo exhibs, Santa Barbara Mus,Calif, 57, Walker Art Ctr, Minneapolis, 58, Esther Bear Gallery, Santa Barbara, 75, Martin Diamond Gallery, New York, 84 & Univ Southern Calif, Santa Barbara, 87; Beyond the Plane-American Construction 1930-1965, NJ State Mus, Trenton, 83; Univ Calif, Santa Barbara, 88. *Mem:* New York Artists Equity. *Media:* Metal; Egg-oil, Acrylics. *Dealer:* Graham Gallery 1014 Madison Ave New York NY 10021. *Mailing Add:* 1988 Inverness Lane Santa Barbara CA 93108

DELAMONICA, ROBERTO
PRINTMAKER, EDUCATOR
b Ponta Pora, State of Mato Grosso, Brazil, 33. *Study:* Sao Paulo & Rio de Janeiro. *Work:* Mus Mod Art, Rio de Janeiro & New York; Nat Mus La Paz, Bolivia; Stedelijk Mus, Amsteram, Holland; Metrop Mus Art, New York; and others. *Exhib:* Brazilian Art Today, Royal Col Art, London, Eng, 64; New Talent in Printmaking, Assoc Am Artists Gallery, New York, 67; one-man shows, Pan Am Union, Washington, DC, Walker Art Ctr, Minneapolis, Minn & Columbia Mus, SC. *Teaching:* Instr graphics, Mus Mod Art, Rio de Janeiro, Nat Sch Fine Arts, Lima, Peru, Univ Santiago, Chile, Cath Univ, Santiago, Sch Fine Arts, Valparaiso, Chile, Minneapolis & Pratt Graphics Ctr, New York, formerly; instr, Art Students League, currently. *Awards:* Best Brazilian Printmaker, Seventh Sao Paulo Biennale; Grand Prize, Second Biennale of Santiago, Chile, 65; Guggenheim Fel, 65. *Mailing Add:* Dept Art Art Students League 215 W 57th St New York NY 10019

DELANEY, JANET CLARE
PHOTOGRAPHER
b Los Angeles, Calif, Aug 26, 52. *Study:* San Francisco State Univ, BA, 75; San Francisco Art Inst, MFA, 81. *Exhib:* Solo exhibs, San Francisco Art Comn Gallery, 80, NS Col Art & Design, 81, Form Follows Finance, Camerawork Gallery, San Francisco, 81, Nicaragua: A Grandmother's Story, Rutgers Univ, NJ, 87, Col Bakersfield, Calif, 87 & Univ Pac, Stockton, Calif, 88; Social Issues, Banff Ctr Sch Fine Arts, Can, 84; Feminist Photographics, Hunter Col, New York, 86; The Situated Image, Univ Calif, San Diego, 87; Stories of the City, Ctr Arts, San Francisco, Calif, 92; and others. *Pos:* Co-Owner, Duck Soup Color Darkroom, 79-91; bd dirs, San Francisco Camerawork Gallery, 82-84. *Teaching:* Instr color photog, Col San Mateo, 80-91; instr photojournalism, Santa Clara Univ, 86-93; instr color, Univ Calif, Berkeley, 88-93; instr, The View Camera, San Francisco Art Inst, 91. *Awards:* James D Phelen Award in Photog, 79; Photog Survey Grant, 79 & Photog Fels, 82 & 86, Nat Endowment Arts. *Publ:* Contribr, Fiction International, Central American Writings, San Diego Univ Press, 86; San Francisco Observed, Chronicle Books, 86; Valiant Women in War and Exile, City Lights Books, 87. *Mailing Add:* 2110 Byron St Berkeley CA 94702

DELAP, TONY
SCULPTOR, EDUCATOR
b Oakland, Calif, Nov 4, 27. *Study:* Menlo Jr Col, Calif; Calif Col Arts & Crafts, Oakland; Claremont Grad Sch, Calif. *Work:* Mus Mod Art, Whitney Mus Am Art, New York; Walker Art Inst, Minneapolis; San Francisco Mus Art; Tate Gallery, London, Eng. *Comn:* Thirteen sculptures, Carborundum Abrasive Mkt Awards, Niagara Falls, NY, 69; sculpture-fountain complex, CCH Bldg, San Rafael, Calif, 70. *Exhib:* Whitney Mus Am Art, 64; Chicago Art Inst, 64; Mus Mod Art, New York, 64, 65 & 67; solo exhibs, Robert Elkan Gallery, 65-, Newport Harbor, 77, Casat Gallery, La Jolla, 77, Calif State Col, Chico, 79 & Janus Gallery, Venice City, 79; Contemporary American Sculpture, Whitney Mus Am Art, 66; American Sculpture of the Sixties, Los Angeles Co Mus Art, 67; California Painting and Sculpture: The Modern Era, San Francisco Mus Art, 76; Corcoran Biennial, 78; and others. *Teaching:* Lectr fine arts, Univ Calif, Davis, 63-64; prof fine arts, Univ Calif, Irvine, 65-. *Awards:* Am Fedn Arts & Ford Found Grants, Mus in Residence Prog, Haverford, Pa, 66; Purchase Prize, Long Beach Mus Art, 69; First Prize Sculpture, Los Angeles Dept Airports, 76. *Bibliog:* Alan Solomon (auth), Tony DeLap: The Last Five Years, Univ Calif, Irvine, 68; Gene Cooper (auth), DeLap, The Edge as Form and Metaphor, 77. *Dealer:* Janus Gallery 8000 Melrose Ave Venice CA 90046; Robert Elkon Gallery 1063 Madison Ave New York NY 10028. *Mailing Add:* c/o Jan Turner Gallery 9006 Melrose Ave Los Angeles CA 90069

DE LARIOS, DORA
SCULPTOR
b Los Angeles, Calif, Oct 13, 33. *Study:* Univ Southern Calif, BFA, 57. *Work:* Oakland Art Mus, Calif; Craft & Folk Art Mus, Los Angeles; Security Pacific Bank Collection. *Comn:* Ceramic mural (8ft x 40ft), Compton Co Libr, Calif, 73; cement mural (8ft x 10ft), Security First Nat Bank, 76; ceramic mural (8ft x 16ft), Norwood Co Libr, Calif, 77; ceramic mural (5ft X 20ft) & 2 ceramic panels (3ft X 6ft), Makaha Inn Resort, Oahu, Hawaii, 79; Friendship Patterns (6ft X 26ft cement mural), Cent Park Develop, Nagoya, Japan, 79; porcelain mural (7ft X 40ft), Hilton Hotel, Anaheim, Calif, 84; porcelain mural with lacquered & patina wood sects (5'6ft X 15'6ft), Huntley Hotel, Santa Monica, Calif, 85; and many others. *Exhib:* Am Crafts at the White House, Renwick Gallery, Smithsonian Inst, Washington, DC, 77 & Contemp Craft Mus, New York, 77; Craft & Folk Art Mus, Los Angeles, 77; Kohler Art Ctr, Wis, 77; Everson Mus, Syracuse, NY, 77; Indianapolis Mus Art, Ind, 78; Southern Alleghenies Mus Art, St Francis Col, Loretto, Pa 82; Western Regional Conf, Logan, Utah, 82; one-woman retrospective, Wooster Col, Ohio, 83; Los Angeles Munic Art Gallery, Barnsdall, Calif, 84. *Teaching:* Vis instr ceramics, Univ Southern Calif, Los Angeles, 58, & Univ Calif, Los Angeles, 79. *Awards:* Purchase Award for Ceramic Sculpture, Calif State Fair, 61; Certificate of Honor, Women in Design Int. *Bibliog:* Elain Levin (auth), Dora De Larios, Ceramic Monthly, Vol XXVI, No 8, 10/78; Lorelei McDevitt (auth), Art & artisan-public spaces, Designer West, Vol XXVIII, No 1, 11/80; article, Dora De Larios, Ceramica, Madrid, Spain, Vol V, No 17, 83; Lorelei McDevitt (auth), Art & artisans-the evolving mask of Dora De Larios, Designers West, Vol XXXI, No 10, 8/84; Monika Guttman (auth), An artist who needs her Space-Dora De Larios, Santa Monica Evening Outlook Newspaper, 8/85. *Media:* Clay, Wood, Cememt. *Mailing Add:* 8560 Venice Blvd Los Angeles CA 90034

DE LA TORRE, DAVID JOSEPH
MUSEUM DIRECTOR
b Santa Barbara, Calif, June 14, 48. *Study:* Univ San Francisco, BA, 70. *Collections Arranged:* Rockefeller Collection of Mexican Folk Art (auth catalog), Mex Mus, 86; FRIDA, 87; Diego Rivera, 88. *Pos:* Curatorial asst, Fine Arts Mus San Francisco, 77-81; Develop dir, Triton Mus Art, 81-84; Exec Dir, Mex Mus, 84; consult, Hawaii State Found Cult & Arts, 91-; panelist NEA, 84-89, 92. *Mem:* Am Fed Arts. *Publ:* Contribr, The Art of Rupert Garcia, Mex Mus Chronicle Books, 86; Nelson A Rockefeller Collection of Mexican Folk Art, Mex Mus Chronicle Books, 85; The Marvelous/The Real: Carmen, La Man Gaza, 87. *Mailing Add:* Honolulu Acad Arts 900 S Beretania St Honolulu HI 96814

DELAURO, JOSEPH NICOLA
SCULPTOR, EDUCATOR
b New Haven, Conn, Mar 10, 16. *Study:* Yale Univ, BFA(Alice Kimball Fel, Tiffany Fel & Elizabeth Pardee Scholar), 41; Univ Iowa, MFA, 47; also in Italy, 53, 62, 66 & 71. *Work:* In private collections of Dr D Corradini, Quito, Ecuador, Dr B Clemente, Akron, Ohio, Rev Ralph Kowalski, Detroit & Bishop Ernest Primeau, Manchester, NH. *Comn:* Mankato stone sculpture, St Columba Cathedral, Youngstown, Ohio, 59; glass & plastic mural, Windsor Bd Educ, Ont, 64; bronze sculpture, Hiram Walker & Sons, Ltd, Ont, 67; bronze sculpture, Detroit Pub Libr, Mich, 67; bronze sculpture, Jewish Community Centre, Windsor, Ont, 70. *Exhib:* Walker Gallery, Minneapolis, 47; Mich Regional Exhib, Detroit, 48; Ecclestical Art Guild, Detroit, 50; Fine Arts Dept Fac Exhib, Art Gallery Windsor, Ont, 70-72; Biannale de Fiorino, Florence, Italy, 71. *Teaching:* Prof sculpture & drawing, Marygrove Col, Detroit, 47-59; prof, Univ Windsor, formerly. *Mem:* Fel Royal Soc Arts; Nat Sculpture Soc; Col Art Asn Am; Mid Am Col Art Asn; Univ Art Asn Can. *Media:* Bronze, Marble. *Mailing Add:* 7560 Bircklan Dr Canton MI 48187

DE LA VEGA, ANTONIO
PAINTER, DESIGNER
b El Paso, Tex, July 13, 27. *Study:* NY Univ; Art Students League; also study in Mex, Spain, France, Italy & Port. *Exhib:* Pintores Nuevos, Galeria Ciga, Buenos Aires, Arg, 60; Antonio de la Vega, Galeria Fuentes, Mexico City, Mex, 61; Spanish Impressions, Galeria Gran Via, Madrid, Spain, 62; Portugal Viejo, Galeria Sesimbra, Lisbon, 66; de la Vega, Galeria Botto, Rome, Italy, 68; Rockland Col, 88; Bronx Mus Art, 89. *Pos:* Art dir & designer, Cushing & Nevell, Inc, New York, 51-62 & Persons Advertising Inc, New York, 63-74; free-lance art dir, designer & illusr advert, 74- *Mem:* Nat Asn Portrait Painters; Am Artists Prof League; Am Inst Graphic Arts; Artists Guild New York (vpres, 64-65); Southwest Art Found. *Media:* Oil, Acrylic. *Mailing Add:* 209 Brentwood Ave Jacksonville NC 28540

DE LA VEGA, ENRIQUE MIGUEL
SCULPTOR, DESIGNER
b Los Angeles, Calif, June 13, 35. *Study:* Los Angeles City Col, AA, 60; Los Angeles Co Art Inst, MFA, 64; study of sculpture with Renzo Fenci and of drawing & design with Joe Magnani. *Comn:* Two monumental symbolic forms, South West Produce Ctr, Nogales, Ariz, 65; Resurrection (22 ft monument), Nat Shrine of the Millenium, Doylestown, Pa, 67; bronze equestrian monument, Robert Atkinson Mem Park, Cascade, Mont, 68; Birds in Flight (bronze forms), Air Force Village, San Antonio, Tex, 72; 15 ft sculpture/mosaic design, St Francis of Assisi Church, South Windsor, Conn, 75. *Exhib:* Group Exhib, Simon Patrich Gallery, Los Angeles, 67; one-man show, Galeria Teatro Casa de la Paz, Mexico City, Mex, 69; Valyermo Ann Art Festival (relig art), St Andrew's Priory, Valyermo, Calif. *Pos:* Art ed, Larchmont Chronicle, Hancock Park, Los Angeles, Calif, 65-70. *Awards:* Harriman Jones Portrait Award, Harriman Jones Clinic, Long Beach, Calif, 65; Nat Design Award, St Francis of Assisi Church, South Windsor, Conn, 75. *Bibliog:* Obras del la Vega, Am Embassy Mag, Mexico City, 68; Enrique de la Vega, Designers West Mag, 69; The Siesta Is Over (sculptures by de la Vega), KNX-TV Interview, Los Angeles, Calif, 72. *Mem:* Artists Equity Asn. *Media:* Miscellaneous Media. *Mailing Add:* 2016 Ridge Point Way Boise ID 83712

DE LA VERRIÉRE, JEAN-JACQUES See J J (De La Verriére)

DEL CHIARO, MARIO A
HISTORIAN
b San Francisco, Calif, Apr 22, 25. *Study:* Univ Calif, Berkeley, Ba, 50, MA, 51, PhD, 56. *Pos:* Chmn art hist, Univ Calif, Berkley, 69-70, 79-80. *Teaching:* Assoc prof, 62-66, prof, 66- *Awards:* Metrop Mus Art Fel, 53-54; Prix de Rome, Am Acad Rome, 58-60; Nat Endowment for the Humanities Fel, 77; Order of Merit of the Ital Repub, Cavaliere Officale. *Mem:* Archeol Inst Am, Studi Etruschi ed Italici, Florence; Archeol Inst, Berlin; Archeol Inst (German), Rome; Europ Acad Sci & Art, Salzburg. *Media:* Archeology. *Res:* Ancient art; archeology. *Publ:* The Genucilia Group, Berkeley, 57; auth, Etruscan Red-Figured Vase-Painting at Caere, Berkeley, 74; The Etruscan Funnel Group, Florence,74; Classical Art at the Santa Barbara Mus Art: Sculpture, 84; Studies in Honor of DA Amyx, 86. *Mailing Add:* c/o Univ Calif Dept Art Hist Santa Barbara CA 93106

DE LEEUW, LEON
PAINTER, SCULPTOR
b Paris, France, May 5 5, 31; US citizen. *Study:* Art Students League; NY Univ, with Philip Guston; also with Hans Hofmann. *Exhib:* One-man shows, Fairlong Libr, 71, Rivercel Gallery, 75 & NJ Inst Technol, Newark, 76; Fullerton Gallery, 78-81; Montclair Mus, 82; and others. *Teaching:* Instr painting & sculpture, Wilson Col, 59-60; assoc prof painting & drawing, Montclair State Col, 63- *Dealer:* Fullerton Gallery 13 S Fullerton Ave Montclair NJ 07042. *Mailing Add:* Montclair St Col Upper Montclair NJ 07043

DELEHANTY, SUZANNE E
HISTORIAN, MUSEUM DIRECTOR
b Worchester, Mass, July 18, 44. *Study:* Skidmore Col, BA(art hist) 65; Univ Pa, grad study (art hist), 66-88, with Frederick Hartt & John McCoubrey and specialized in ancient art with Richard Brilliant. *Collections Arranged:* Nancy Graves: Sculpture & Drawing 1970-72, 72; Agnes Martin (with catalog), 73; Six Visions (with catalog), 73; Robert Morris/Projects, 74; Cy Twombly: Paintings, Drawings, Constructions 1951-1974 (with catalog), 75; Video Art (with catalog), 75; George Segal: Environments, 76; Pieces & Performances, 76; Improbable Furniture (with catalog), 77; Paul Thek/Processions (with catalog), 77; Dwellings, 78; On Sculpture/Christo, di Suvero, Irwin & Segal, 79; Richard Artschwager/Themes (with catalog), 79; Soundings (with catalog), 81; Roni Horn/Space Buttresses, 86; David von Schlegell/Recent Work, 89; Fred Sandback/Sculpture, 89. *Pos:* Curatorial asst, Inst Contemp Art, Univ Pa, 68-71, dir, 71-78; dir, Neuberger Mus, State Univ NY, Purchase, 78-88;; consult, Art Comt, Chase Manhattan Bank, 85-91; rev, Interarts Prog, Nat Endowment Arts, Washington, DC, 85; dir, Contemp Arts Mus, Houston, 89- *Awards:* Outstanding Young Women Am, 80. *Bibliog:* The alchemy of mind and hand, Art Int, 3/76 & Arts Va, 6/77; On Soundings, Sound by Artist, Toronto, 88. *Mem:* Am Asn Mus Dir; Am Fedn Arts; NY Gallery Coun; Asn Art Mus Dir; Inst Coun Mus. *Publ:* Auth, Ann Wilson, In: Butler's Lives at 88 Pine Street, Creative Time Inc, 77; The Artist's Window, In: The Window in Twentieth Century Art, Neuberger Mus, State Univ NY, Purchase, 86. *Mailing Add:* c/o Contemp Art Mus 5216 Montrose Blvd Houston TX 77006-6598

DELEVORYAS, LILLIAN GRACE
PAINTER, DESIGNER
b Chicopee Falls, Mass, Jan 3, 32. *Study:* Pratt Inst, Brooklyn, NY 50-53; Cooper Union, New York, BFA, 56; Japan, 57. *Work:* Victoria Mus, Melbourne, Australia; Int Atomic Energy Comn, Vienna, Austria; Temple Newsham House, Leeds, UK; Guildford Coun Chambers, Surrey, UK. *Comn:* Wallhanging for Lady Pamela Harlech, London, Eng, 73; mural, comn by Andrew Gordon, London, 75; wallhanging, Victoria & Albert Mus, Arts Coun, Queens Jubilee, London, 77; Sisters of Mercy Convent, Brentwood, Essex, 78; altarpiece wallhanging, Our Lady of Ransome Church, Rayleigh, Essex, 81. *Exhib:* Univ Calif, Berkeley, 61; Calif Palace of Legion of Hon & De Young Mus, San Francisco, 62; Arts of San Francisco, San Francisco Mus Art, 62; New Talent-New York, New York Univ, 65; Threads of History, Royal Col Art, UK, 77, Queen's Jubilee Exhib, Victoria & Albert Mus, 77 & Royal Academy Summer Exhib, 86, London, Eng; and others. *Pos:* designer, Designers Guild Textile Collections, Elgin Court Cards, UK. *Teaching:* Lectr design, Elsa Williams Sch Needlework, WTownsend, Mass, 79; lectr painting & design, Gawthorpe Hall, Burnley, Eng, 85; lectr, Gloucestershire Col of Art, UK. *Awards:* Louis Comfort Award, Tiffany Found, 65; Apprenticeship Grant, Arts Coun, Eng, 72-79; Gold Award, Art Dir Club 57th Ann Exhib, 78. *Bibliog:* Ursula Robertshaw (auth), For collectors, Illustrated London News, 76; Elizabeth Williamson (auth), Lillian Delevoryas blossoms into print, Daily Telegraph, 81; Celia Haddon (auth), Artists & gardens, Sunday Express, Eng, 86. *Mem:* Copley Society, Boston. *Media:* All media. *Publ:* Auth, The World of the Makers by Edward Lucie-Smith, Paddington Press, 75; Country gardens, Crafts Mag, 75; illusr, International Design Yearbook, Abbeville & Thames & Hudson, 86. *Dealer:* Copernican Connection Garton-on-the-Wold E Yorkshire UK; Wenniger Graphics Boston MA. *Mailing Add:* 275 High Rd Newbury MA 01951

DELGYER, LESLIE
ENVIRONMENTAL ARTIST, PAINTER
b Plainfield, NJ, Sept 11, 46. *Study:* duCret School of the Arts with Dudley V DuCret & Marjorie Van Emburgh, 68. *Comn:* Conservation stamp collection: New Zealand Tuatara, 90, African Mountain Zebra, 90, Egyptian Caracal, 91 & Asian Goitered Gazelle, 92, World Wildlife Fund Int. *Exhib:* Pastel Soc Am, Copley Mus, Boston, 79 & Queens Mus, Flushing, NY, 82; Soc Animal Artists, Acad Natural Scis, Philadelphia, 81, Cincinnati Mus Natural Hist, 82 & Headley Whitney Mus, Lexington, Ky, 85. *Awards:* Margaret Sussman Award, Pastel Invitational, Pen & Brush Club, New York, 86 & 90; George Inness Memorial Award, Open Invitational, Salmagundi Club, New York, 90; Philip Eisenberg Award, Pastel Invitational, Pen & Brush Club, New York, 91. *Mem:* Pastel Soc Am, Nat Arts Club, NY; Soc Animal Artists (hist & parliamentarian 87 & asst secy exec bd, 89); duCret Sch (bd trustees, 85 & vpres bd trustee, 87; Nat Mus Women Arts, Washington, DC; Pen & Brush Club, NY. *Media:* Pastel. *Mailing Add:* 168 Westervelt Ave North Plainfield NJ 07060

DE LISIO, MICHAEL
SCULPTOR
b New York, NY. *Work:* Joseph H Hirshhorn Mus, Washington, DC; Minneapolis Inst Arts; Wichita Mus, Kans; Christ Church Col, Oxford Univ; Smith Col Mus Art, Mass; Mus City of New York; Addison Gallery Am Art, Andover, Mass. *Exhib:* One-man shows, Minneapolis Inst Arts, 71 & Brooke Alexander Gallery, New York, 78; Addison Gallery Am Art, Andover, Mass, 73; Princeton Univ Libr, 73; Smith Col Mus Art, Northampton, Mass, 74; Zabriskie Gallery, New York, 86; and others. *Bibliog:* Anthony Clark (auth), Michael de Lisio, Minneapolis Inst Arts Catalogue, 1/71; Robert Phelps (auth), article, Life Mag, 1/29/71; Martha Saxton (auth), article, Connoisseur, 9/85; Helicon Nine, J Women's Arts & Lett, 88. *Media:* Terra Cotta, Bronze. *Mailing Add:* 32 E 64th St New York NY 10021

DELL, ROBERT CHRISTOPHER
SCULPTOR, SCENIC ARTIST
b Nyack, NY, Feb 22, 50. *Study:* NY State Univ Col, Oneonta, BS(educ), 72; NY State Univ Col, New Paltz, MFA(sculpture), 75. *Work:* Syracuse Univ, NY; State Univ NY; MacDowell Colony, Peterborough, NH; Mus Fine Arts, Springfield, Mass; Iceland US Educ Commn, Reykjavik, Iceland; Reykjavik Munic Dist Heating Serv, Iceland; and others. *Comn:* Sculpture, Arts Coun Rockland, Spring Valley, NY, 78; and others. *Exhib:* Solo Exhibs, Vorpal Gallery, Chicago, 78, New York, 81 & 88, New Acquisitions Gallery, Syracuse, NY, 83, Vorpal Gallery, San Francisco, 85, Blue Hill Cult Ctr, Pearl River, NY, 87, Am Cult Ctr, Reykjavik, Iceland, 88 & Mid-Hudson Arts & Sci Ctr, Poughkeepsie, NY, 92; Sculpture 1980, Meyerhoff Gallery, Md Art Inst, Baltimore, 80; Everson Mus, Syracuse, NY, 84; 14 Sculptors Gallery, New York, 85; MIT Mus, Mass Inst Technol, Cambridge, Ma, 90-91; Perlan, Reykjavik, Iceland - permanent geothermal sculpture installation, 91-; Lehigh Univ, Bethlehem, Pa, 91-92. *Pos:* Mem, Archit and Community Appearance, Bd of Review, Town of Orangetown, 79-, vice chairman, 87-; Master Scenic Artist, Am Broadcasting Co, New York, 88- *Awards:* Artist-in-Residence, Vriesland West Hudson Art Ctr, Pearl River, NY, 80; MacDowell Colony Fel, Peterborough, NH, 80; New York State Coun Arts Grant, 86; Fulbright Res Grant, 88; Partners of the Americas Grant, 92. *Bibliog:* Articles in Spotlight Mag, 87; Joseph Merkel (auth), Artspeak, New York, 88; Bragi Asgeirsson (auth), Morgungladid, Reykjavik, Iceland, 88. *Media:* Geothermal Sculpture, Mixed Media. *Publ:* Robert Dell (video, 45 minute documentary of 1st geothermal sculpture), State Television, Reykjavik, Iceland, broadcast 11/88; video, Hitavaetur, Circumstantial Productions, 91. *Dealer:* Vorpal Gallery 465 W Broadway New York NY 10012 & San Francisco CA 94102. *Mailing Add:* 421 Washington St Tappan NY 10983

DELLA-VOLPE, RALPH EUGENE
PAINTER, EDUCATOR
b NJ, May 10, 23. *Study:* Nat Acad Design; Art Students League. *Work:* Chase Manhattan Bank Collection, New York; Treas Bldg, Washington, DC; Slater Mus, Norwich, Conn; Pennell Collection, Libr of Cong, Washington, DC; Wichita Art Asn, Kans. *Exhib:* Pa Acad Fine Arts, Philadelphia, 52; Butler Inst Am Art, Ohio, 63; Final, Nat Inst Arts & Lett, New York, 63 & 64; Columbia Mus, SC, 76; Seattle Art Mus, Wash; Berkshire Mus, Pittsfield, Mass; Grand Cent Galleries, New York. *Teaching:* Prof drawing & painting & artist in residence, Bennett Col, 49-77; prof drawing & painting, Marist Col, Poughkeepsie, 77-79. *Awards:* Libr of Cong Purchase Award, 52; Berkshire Mus Drawing Prize, 54; MacDowell Fel, MacDowell Art Colony, 63. *Media:* Oil. *Mailing Add:* South Road Box 51 Millbrook NY 12545

DELLER, HARRIS
CERAMIST
b Brooklyn, NY, Jan 28, 47. *Study:* Calif State Univ, Northridge, BA, 71; Cranbrook Acad Art, Mich, MFA, 73. *Work:* Ill State Mus, Springfield; Univ Mus Southern Ill Univ, Carbondale; Evansville Mus Art, Ind; Hong-Ik Univ Mus Seoul, S Korea; Cranbrook Mus Mich; Hallmark, Kansas City; Philip Morris, New York; Everson Mus, Syracuse, NY; Ariz State Univ, Tempe. *Exhib:* American Porcelin, Renwick Gallery, Smithsonian Inst, 80; solo exhibs, Int Commun Agency, Seoul, S Korea; Cranbrook Ceramics: 1950-1980, Cranbrook Mus, Mich, 83; The Service of Tea, Cooper-Hewett Mus, New York, 84; American Clay Artist, Port of Hist Mus, Philadelphia, 85; Poetry of the Physical, Am Craft Mus, New York, 86; Mus Southeast, Beaumont, Tex; Crafts Today, Musee des Beau Arts, Paris. *Teaching:* Vis instr Ceramics, Sch of Art Inst Chicago, 73; instr, Ga Southern Col, Statesboro, 73-75; prof ceramics, Southern Ill Univ, Carbondale, 76- *Awards:* Fulbright Hays Fel, Coun Int Exchange of Scholars, 81; Artist Fel, Ill Arts Coun, 86, 87 & 89 & Prog Completion Grant; Artist Fel, Arts Midwest, 90. *Bibliog:* Peter Lane (auth), Studio Porcelin, Chilton Book Co, 80; Axel & McCready (coauths), Porcelin: Traditions and New Versions, Watson-Guptill, 81; Pat Degner (auth), Deller's Witty, Unpretentious Ceramics, St Louis Post Dispatch, 12/7/84; Nancy Gardner (auth), Harris Deller, American Ceramics, vol 6, no 4, summer 88; Harris Deller, Ceramics Monthly, vol 36, no 6, 88. *Mem:* Fulbright Alumni Asn; Nat Coun Educ in Ceramics Arts (publ chair, 94). *Media:* Porcelain. *Dealer:* Esther Saks Gallery 311 W Superior St Chicago IL 60610; Garth Clark Gallery, New York, NY. *Mailing Add:* Sch Art Southern Ill Univ Carbondale IL 62901

DELLIS, ARLENE B
MUSEOLOGIST, CRAFTSMAN
b Brooklyn, NY, Apr 12, 27. *Study:* Antioch Col; Univ NC, Greensboro, BA. *Pos:* Head lending serv, Brooklyn Mus, NY, 49-55; head traveling exhibs & registr, Solomon R Guggenheim Mus, New York, 55-63; registr, Gallery Mod Art, New York, 64; registr, Marlborough-Gerson Gallery, New York, 64-67; registr, ed, Inst of Contemp Art, Boston, 67-68; registr, ed-designer & dir circulating exhibs, Bernard Danenberg Galleries, New York, 69-72; asst to dir, La Boetie Gallery, New York, 72-77; assoc dir, Helios Gallery, 78-79; fine leather designer craftsman, 76-79; registr, Lowe Art Mus, Univ Miami, Coral Gables, Fla, 79-82; registr, Ctr for Fine Arts, Miami, Fla, 82- *Publ:* Ed, Max Weber Drawings, 72; Kurt Seligman: His Graphic Work, 73; ed & designer, Hans Bellmer: Graphic Work, 74; auth, Kurt Seligmann Graphics, Mus Fine Arts, Springfield, Mass, 74. *Mailing Add:* Registrar Ctr Fine Arts 101 W Flagler St Miami FL 33130

DELONEY, JACK CLOUSE
PAINTER, ILLUSTRATOR
b Enterprise, Ala, Nov 2, 40. *Study:* Auburn Univ, BFA, 64. *Work:* First Nat Bank, Montgomery, Ala; First Ala Bank, Birmingham; Coca Cola Co, Montgomery, Ala; Pope & Quint Co, Mobile, Ala; Fla Gas Corp, Winter Park, Fla. *Exhib:* Seventh Juried Art Exhib, Mobile Art Mus, 72; Mainstreams 73 & 76; Hudson Valley 46th Nat, 74; WTex Watercolor Asn Nat, 75; Rocky Mountain Nat Watermedia, Colo, 76; Okla Nat Watercolor Exhib, Okla Mus Art, 76; and group and one-man shows. *Pos:* Book designer, Methodist Publ House, Nashville, Tenn, 64-65; illusr & painter, Ft Rucker, Ala. *Awards:* Purchase Award, People's Bank & Trust, Tupelo, 72; Best Landscape, NJ Miniature Art Soc, 73; Purchase Award, Bluff Park Show, Birmingham, Ala, 77. *Mem:* Ala Watercolor Soc; La Watercolor Soc; Southern Watercolor Soc; assoc mem Am Watercolor Soc; assoc mem Allied Artists of Am. *Publ:* article, North Light, 4/78. *Mailing Add:* c/o Deloney Studios PO Box 1627 Ozark AL 36361

DE LOOPER, WILLEM
PRINTMAKER, CURATOR
b The Hague, Neth, Oct 30, 32. *Study:* Am Univ, BA, 57. *Work:* Phillips Collection, Corcoran Gallery Art, Hirshhorn Mus & IBM, Washington, DC; Fed Reserve Bank, Richmond, Va & Miami, Fla; Nat Sci Found; Nat Gallery Art. *Comn:* Serigraph, Smithsonian Resident Assocs, 88. *Exhib:* One-man exhibs, Jefferson Place Gallery, 66-68, 70, 72 & 74, Max Protetch Gallery, 75-78, Catholic Univ Am, 78, Washington, DC, Galerie L, Hamburg, Ger, 79, Montgomery Col, Takoma Park, Md, 74, 78 & 85; Washington: Twenty Years, Baltimore Mus Art, 70; Corcoran Gallery Art, 80, 85 & 86; Shippee Gallery, New York, 88; Jones-Troyer-Fitzpatrick Gallery, Washington, DC, 89, 91 & 92; Atrium Gallery, St Louis, 90 & 92; Smith-Anderson Gallery, Palo Alto, Calif, 91. *Collections Arranged:* Franz Kline: The Paintings in Color, 78; Philip Guston: The Last Works, 81; Morris Graves: Vision O/T Inner Eye, 83; Exhibits on Kimura, 84, Arthur Dove, 85, Guillermo Roux, 87, John Graham, 88, Howard Ben TrÉ & William Willis, 89 & Gene Highstein, 92. *Pos:* Cur, Phillips Collection, Washington, DC, 82-87 & consult cur, 87- *Bibliog:* Articles & rev, Washington Star, 66-79, Washington Post, 66- 92, Art Forum, 67-89, Art Am, summer 74 & 2/88, Art News, 74, 79 & 92, Die Welt (Hamburg), 10/79, Washington Times, 83, 87 & 92 & St Louis Dispatch, 90-92; An interview with Willem de Looper, Art Int, 12/77; cover story, Interior Design Mag, 7/86. *Media:* Acrylic Emulsion. *Dealer:* Jones-Troyer-Fitzpatrick 1614 20th St NW Washington DC 20009; Atrium Gallery 815 Olive St St Louis MO 63101. *Mailing Add:* 2219 California St NW Washington DC 20008

DE LORY, PETER
PHOTOGRAPHER, INSTRUCTOR
b Cape Cod, Mass, Oct 2, 48. *Study:* San Francisco Art Inst, BFA(photog), 71; Univ Colo, MFA(photog), 74. *Work:* Minneapolis Inst Art; William Hayes Fogg Art Mus, Harvard Univ, Cambridge, Mass; Mass Inst Technol, Cambridge; Nat Gallery Can, Ottawa, Ont; Addison Gallery Am Art, Andover, Mass; Nat Mus Am Art, Smithsonian Inst, Washington, DC; Seattle Mus Art; San Francisco Mus Mod Art. *Comn:* Wash State Art Comn (3' X 20' color mural), S Kitsup High Sch, Port Orchard, 85. *Exhib:* One-man show, Addison Gallery Am Art, 74; Carl Siembab Gallery Photog, Boston, Mass, 76; Sheldon Mus Art, Lincoln, Nebr, 77; The West: Real & Ideal, Univ Colo, 77; Univ Ore, Eugene, 82; Southern Alta Art Gallery, Can, 83; Gallery Interform, Usaka, Japan, 86; Scheinder Mus Art, Ashland, Ore, 87; Santa Monica Col, Calif, 88. *Pos:* Dir photog dept, Sun Valley Ctr Arts & Humanities, 75-79. *Teaching:* Instr photog, Ctr Eye Sch, Aspen, 69-71; asst photog, Minor White Workshop, Hotchkiss, Conn, 72-73; instr advan photog, Sun Valley Ctr Arts & Humanities, Idaho, 74-78; instr, Sch Art Inst Chicago, 80 & 84, Univ Wash, Seattle, 82, Portland Sch Art, Maine, 83, State Univ Calif, San Jose, 86-90 & San Francisco Art Inst, 87. *Awards:* Western States Art Found Fel, Boise Art Gallery, 76-77; Nat Endowment Arts Photogr Fel, 79; Artist Fel, Calif Art Coun, 90. *Bibliog:* Alex Sweetman (auth), Peter deLory Photographs, An Afterimage, Visual Studies Workshop, Rochester, NY, 11/76. *Mem:* Soc Photog Educ. *Publ:* Contribr, Aperture, Inc, 73; Creative Camera, English, 12/73; Auth, The Wild and the Innocent, Calif Mus Photog, Riverside, 87. *Mailing Add:* 333 Fifth St San Francisco CA 94107

DELOYHT-ARENDT, MARY
PAINTER
b Independence, Mo, Mar 10, 27. *Study:* Christian Col, AA, 46; Univ Mo, BFA, 49. *Work:* Empire Machinery; Valley Nat Bank; Thunderbird Bank; Giant Indust, First Interstate. *Comn:* Watercolors Ariz Mountains, IBM, 81-82; Michael R Ellis Inc, Phoenix, Ariz, 88; Ariz Biltmore, Phoenix, 91; Merriott's Camelback Inn, Scottsdale, 92. *Exhib:* Western Fedn Watercolor Soc, Houston, Tex, 79; Southwest Watercolor Soc, Dallas, Tex & 79, Ardmore, Okla, 80; solo show, Mammen Gallery II, Scottsdale, Ariz, 82-89; Artists of the West Invitational, Ariz Bank, Phoeniz, 85-90; Nat Watercolor Soc, Brea, Calif, 85-87; and others. *Teaching:* Instr watercolor, Phoenix Art Mus, Ariz, 78-79; watercolor workshops, Tex, Calif, Okla, Colo, NMex, Alamos, Mex, Oxford, Eng & Scottsdale Artist Sch,Ariz & Kans, 78-92. *Awards:* Best of Show, Ariz Watercolor Asn, 80 & 81; Grumbacher Silver & Gold Medallion, Ariz Watercolor Soc, 84. *Bibliog:* DeLoyht-Arendt, Southwest Art Mag, Houston, Tex, 1/83; Introduction to Three Watercolor, Omni Art Rev, Dallas, Tex, 11/85; Deborah Wilbert (auth), National Watercolor Show, Gonzaga Univ, Spokane Rev, 3/86. *Mem:* Ariz Artis Guild (pres, bd dir); Ariz Watercolor Asn (bd dir); Western Fedn Watercolor Soc, Nat Watercolor Soc; 22X30 Prof Watercolor Critique Group. *Media:* Watercolor, Oil. *Publ:* Illusr, Mark of the Nails, Yellow bird, St Paul, Minn, 73; Desert Pot Luck, Runbeck Graphics, Phoenix, 82; poster, publ by Classic Printers, Prescott, Ariz, 86 & Romm Ltd, NY, 87-92, card, Polytint, Maidenhead, Eng. *Dealer:* O'Brien's Art Emporium Scottsdale & Phoenix AZ; Waterhouse Gallery Santa Barbara CA. *Mailing Add:* 2617 N 58th St Scottsdale AZ 85257

DELSON, ELIZABETH
PAINTER, PRINTMAKER
b New York, NY, Aug 15, 32. *Study:* Pa Acad Fine Arts; Smith Col, BA, 54; Hunter Col, MA, 72. *Work:* New York Pub Libr; Boston Pub Libr; Univ Southern Ill; Columbia Univ; Brooklyn Mus. *Comn:* Etchings comn and distributed by Assoc Am Artists, Collector's Guild Ltd, Landmarks Collection & Framemakers, Ltd, The Calvin Collection. *Exhib:* 100 Artists Honor the Prospect Park Centennial, 66; one-man shows, Hicks Street Gallery, 64, Paerdegat Libr, 72 & 74, Park Gallery, 73, Brownstone Gallery, 74 & Long Island Univ, 74; Brooklyn Mus Nat Print Biennials. *Teaching:* Instr printmaking, Pratt Inst, 62-66. *Awards:* Audubon Artists Medal of Honor for Graphics, 61. *Mem:* Soc Am Graphic Artists; Contemp Artists Guild (vpres, 71-75). *Media:* Oil Reliefs, Etchings. *Mailing Add:* 625 Third St Brooklyn NY 11215

DE LUCA, JOSEPH VICTOR
EDUCATOR, PAINTER
b Niagara Falls, NY, Mar 1, 35. *Study:* Bowling Green State Univ, BS, 57 & MA, 58; Mich State Univ, Clifton McChesney & Angelo Ippolito, MFA, 65. *Work:* Renaissance Ctr, Detroit, Mich; Toledo Mus Art, Ohio; Univ Omaha, Nebr; Grand Rapids Mus, Mich; Ford Motor Company, World Headquarters, Dearborn, Mich; Bowling Green State Univ, Ohio; Western Mich Univ, Kalamazoo; and others. *Comn:* Cyma & Silver Square (oils & aluminum on canvas), Renaissance Ctr, Detroit, Mich, 76; Pierre Marquet Hotel, Minneapolis, Minn, 89; Northwestern Nat Life Insurance Co, Minneapolis, Minn, 89. *Exhib:* One-man shows, Century Ctr, South Bend Art Ctr, Ind, 78, Bim Haus, Amsterdam, Neth, 80; two-person exhib, Gallery Artemus, Ghent, Belg, 81; Midwest Sculptors & Painters, Krannert Mus, Univ Ill; Mich Artists,

Southwest Regional, Kalamazoo Inst Arts, Mich, 80; Estoril-Auto, Mt Estoril, Port, 86; Anderson & Anderson Gallery, Minneapolis, Minn, 86, 88, 90 & 92. *Collections Arranged:* Works by George Ortman (auth, catalog), 69; Works by Angelo Ippolito (auth, catalog), 70; Works by Harry Brorby (auth, catalog), 71; Works by Clifton McChesney (auth, catalog), 72; Works by Graduates & Undergraduates, Bowling Green, Western Mich Univ, 73. *Pos:* Gallery dir (part time), Gallery Two, Western Mich Univ, Kalamazoo, 67-71; Danforth Assoc, Nat Invitational Educators Asn, 76-84. *Teaching:* Instr art, Findlay High Sch, Ohio, 58-62; instr drawing, painting & art educ, Central Mich Univ, Mount Pleasant, 62-66; prof drawing & painting, Western Mich Univ, Kalamazoo, 66- *Awards:* Individual Artists Grant, Mich Coun Arts, 80; First Award, South Bend Art Ctr, 76; Purchase Award, Krasl Art Ctr, 83; Director's Choice Award, Kalamazoo Art Inst, 88. *Bibliog:* Jeffrey Kastner (auth), New Art Examiner, summer 89; Anderson & Anderson Gallery (exhib catalog), Night Gate, 88; Articles in Art Am, 87-88. *Mem:* Arch Am Art, Smithsonian Inst; Kalamazoo Inst Arts. *Media:* Mixed. *Mailing Add:* c/o Anderson & Anderson Gallery 414 First Ave N Minneapolis MN 55401-1702

DELUIGI, JANICE CECILIA WEIL LEFTON See Cecilia

DELVALIE, EDUARDO See Gomez, Mirta & Eduardo Delvalie

DEL VALLE, CEZAR JOSE
PHOTOGRAPHER, PAINTER
b Washington, DC, Apr 14, 45. *Study:* Self taught. *Work:* Kinsey Inst, Ind Univ, Bloomington; Tampa Mus Art, Fla. *Exhib:* New Artists at Madison Sq Garden, New York, 81; Transamericia's Celebrate The Athlete (conjunction with the 84 Olympics), Calif, 84; Noyes Mus, Oceanville, NJ, 90; Small Impressions II, Monmouth Mus, Lincroft, NJ, 92; Small Impressions, Newark Mus, NJ, 92; and others. *Pos:* Co-owner, Talking of Michaelangelo Gallery, 73; pr dir, Park Slope Artist's Coun, 84; bd dirs, Nebruko Theatre Co, 84-85. *Teaching:* Lectr Holography, Mus Holography, New York, 88-92. *Awards:* Grant, Long Island Univ, Artist's Space, 90. *Bibliog:* Alexandra Shaw (auth), Cezar Del Valle, Manhattan Arts, 85. *Mem:* Printmaking Coun NJ; New Haven Arts Coun; Orgn Independent Artists; Art Initiatives, New York; Artist Network, New York. *Media:* Hand Tinted Photographs. *Publ:* Auth, Newspaper arts reviewer, Alexandria Port Packet, 75; Steely-eyed Workaholics, InfoWorld, 82; Best of Photography, Photog Forum, 82. *Mailing Add:* 433 16th St New York NY 11215

DEL VALLE, JOSEPH BOURKE
DESIGN CONSULTANT
b New York, NY, Feb 6, 19. *Study:* Cooper Union Art Sch, cert; Fulbright Grant Painting & Graphic Design, Paris; Inst Fine Arts, NY Univ. *Pos:* Design Consult, Metrop Mus Art; sr designer, Orgn Comt, XIX Olympic Games, Mex, 68; design consult, Philadelphia Mus Art; design consult, Mus Mod Art, New York. *Awards:* 50 Best Bks (three awards), Am Inst Graphic Arts; My Best Work, Mead Libr Ideas, 71; Award of Excellence, Mus Design Competition. *Publ:* Designed: In Pursuit of Beauty, Posters of the 1890's, Fragonard, Paul Klee: the Berguran Coll, Masterpieces of Impressionism & Post-Impressionism, the Annenberg Coll, Mus Mod Art; Western Collection, Stark Mus of Art, Orange, Tex, 78; The Smithsonian Illustrated Library of Antiques (15 vols), Cooper-Hewitt Mus, 83. *Mailing Add:* 41 Union Square W New York NY 10003

DEMANCHE, MICHEL S
PAINTER, PHOTOGRAPHER
b Ft Worth, Tex, Aug 16, 53. *Study:* Univ Tex, Arlington, BFA, 75; North Tex State Univ, MFA, 80. *Work:* Wise Co Heritage Mus, Decatur, Tex; North Tex State Univ Collection, Denton; Grant Arnold Collection, State Univ Oswego, NY. *Comn:* Frito Lay Corp; Robert Crill. *Exhib:* Showdown, Alternative Mus, New York, 83; Visions of Childhood, Whitney Mus Am Art, New York, 84; Introductions, Judy Yoven Gallery, Houston, Tex, 88; Holiday Pictures, Frito Lay, Dallas, Tex, 88; Texas Women Artist, Nat Mus Women Art, Washington, DC, 88; Artscape 90, Mount Royal Sch Art, Baltimore, MD, 90. *Pos:* Asst prof Art, Univ Md, Eastern Shore. *Awards:* Second Place Multi-Media, Art Quest, 86. *Bibliog:* Dr Mark Thistlewaite (auth), Michel Demanche, Artspace, spring 84; Wade Wilson (auth), Captain Midnight vs the forces of evil, Dallas Arts Rev, No 20, 86; Gary McKay (auth), New Wave of Texas Artist, Ultra, 3/88. *Mem:* Washington Proj Arts; Col Art Asn; Women in Photogr. *Media:* Miscellaneous. *Dealer:* William Campbell Contemp Art 4935 Byers Fort Worth TX 76107; Wade Wilson Gallery Chicago, IL. *Mailing Add:* c/o William Campbell Contemp Art 4935 Byers Ft Worth TX 76107

DEMAREE, BETTY (ELIZABETH ANN)
PAINTER, INSTRUCTOR
b Denver, Colo, Oct 19, 18. *Study:* Cooper Union Sch Art; with Robert E Wood, & Rex Brandt, Calif; with Edgar A Whitney, & Mario Cooper, New York; also with Milford Zornes, Utah & Charles Reid, Conn. *Work:* Kissinger Oil Bldg, Int Athletic Club & James Insurance Co, Denver; Van Schack, Littleton, Colo; Marathon Oil Bldg, Littleton; Los Alamos Nat Lab; Rocky Mountain Energy Co, Broomfield, Colo; Combs Gates Airport & Natkin & Co, Denver, Colo; Harris Bank & Trust, Scottsdale, Ariz; Utah State Univ, Logan; Jefferson Bank, Lakewood, Colo. *Comn:* Ceramic plaque of oil scene, Indust of Lowell Williamson, Calgary, Can, 62; ceramic, Off Gov of Colo, 62; watercolor scenes of Denver bldgs, Cassidy Paint & Hilb & Co, 69-72; Old Main (painting), Colo State Univ, Ft Collins, 70; watercolor portraits of children, James F Kuhns, Dallas, Tex, 71-72; James Insurance Co, Denver, Colo; Mason Reuler & Peek, Atty, Denver; Better Health Ctr, Denver; Jefferson Nat Bank, Lakewood, Colo. *Exhib:* Southwestern Watercolor Soc, Dallas, 69-75 & Albuquerque, NMex, 72; Am Watercolor Soc traveling exhib, 76-79; Watercolor West traveling exhib, Utah State Univ, 77-79; Allied Artists Am, New York, 78-90; Audubon Artists, New York, 79; Ky Watercolor Soc Aqueous, 84 & 91; Catharine Lorillard-Wolfe Art Exhib, New York, 84. *Teaching:* Instr pvt classes, 68-; lectr demonstrations & workshops, 75- *Awards:* Emily Lowe Mem Award, Am Watercolor Soc, New York, 76; John Young-Hunter Award, Allied Artists Am, 77, Winsor & Newton Award, 78; First Place Award, Colo Artists Asn, Denver, 80; Travelling Show Award, San Diego Watercolor Exhib, 84; Strathmore Paper Co Award, 84. *Bibliog:* Four demonstrations (video), Master Watercolor Video, Cave Creek, Ariz. *Mem:* Elected mem Allied Artists Am, New York; Colo Watercolor Soc; signature mem Southwestern Watercolor Soc; elected mem Active Am Watercolor Soc, New York; Audubon Artists, New York; Nat Watercolor Soc, Calif. *Media:* Watercolor, Pastel. *Publ:* Palette Talk & The Incredible Variety of Watercolor, 81, M Grumbacher. *Dealer:* Gallery A East Kit Carson Rd Taos NM 87571; Cason Gallery Seven N Last Chance Gulch Helena MT. *Mailing Add:* 4725 W Quincy No 1403 Denver CO 80236

DE MARIA, WALTER
SCULPTOR
b Albany, Calif, Oct 1, 35; US citizen. *Study:* Univ Calif, Berkeley, BA(hist) & MA(art), 53-59. *Work:* Mus Mod Art, Whitney Mus Am Art, New York; Basel Kunstmuseum, Basel, Switz; Mus Boymans-van Beuingen, Rotterdam. *Comn:* New York Earth Romm (earth, peat & bark), Dia Art Found, New York, 77. *Exhib:* Sculpture of the 60's, Los Angeles Co Mus, 67; Whitney Mus Am Art Sculpture Ann, 68; Information, Mus Mod Art, New York, 70; Vertical Earth Kilometer, Kassel, Ger, 77; Broken Kilometer, New York, 79; one-man exhibs, Dia Art Found, New York, 79 & 80, Kunsthaus Zurich, 92; Pier & Ocean, Hayward Gallery, London, 80; Venice Biennial, 80; Akron Art Mus, 92; Va Mus Fine Arts, Richmond, 92; and others. *Awards:* Guggenheim Fel, 69-70; Mather Sculpture Prize, 72nd Ann Exhib, Art Inst Chicago, 76; Inauguration of sculpture on the occasion of the Bicentennial, Bur Nat Assembly, Paris, 91. *Bibliog:* D Bourdon (auth), Walter De Maria, the singular experience, Art Int, 12/68. *Media:* Earth. *Publ:* Contribr, Hard core (land film ed 100), 69. *Dealer:* Gagosian Gallery 980 Madison Ave New York NY 10021. *Mailing Add:* 421 E Sixth St New York NY 10009

DEMARTIS, JAMES J
PAINTER
b Corona, NY, Mar 30, 26. *Study:* Acad Fine Arts, Florence, Italy, 50-54. *Work:* Pvt collections in Europe & US. *Exhib:* One-man shows, Ward Eggleston Gallery, Ruko Gallery, Marcaleo Gallery, Artemis East Gallery & Hicks St Gallery. *Awards:* Emily Lowe Award Painting, 61. *Mem:* Artists Equity. *Dealer:* Brownstone Gallery 76 Seventh Ave Brooklyn NY 11217. *Mailing Add:* 329 E Main St North Adams MA 01247

DEMATTIES, NICK
PAINTER
b Honolulu, Hawaii, Oct 19, 39. *Study:* Cal St Univ, Long Beach, BA, 64; Inst Design, Chicago, with Misch Kohn, MS, 67. *Work:* Los Angeles Co Mus Art; Brooklyn Mus Art; Cabinet Estampes, Bibliot Nat Paris; Libr Cong; San Francisco Mus Mod Art. *Comn:* Swengle-Robbins, 87. *Exhib:* Biennial, Tucson Mus Art, 84; Invitational, Missoula Mus Art, Mont, 85; New American Talent, Laguna Gloria Mus, Austin, Tex, 85; Invitational, Portland Art Mus, Oregon, 85; Nat Exhib, Owensboro Mus Art, Ky, 86. *Pos:* Founder & dir, Pac Northwest Graphics Workshop, 70-75; Pres Arts Resource Conservancy, 90. *Teaching:* Instr, San Diego State Col, 67-69; asst prof, Mt St Mary's Col, Calif, 69-70; vis prof, Univ Ore, 72; Asst Prof, Albion Col, Mich, 73-74; asst prof, Ariz State Univ, Tempe, 74-76, assoc prof, 77- *Awards:* Cash Award, Laguna Gloria Mus, Austin, TX, 84 & Biennial, Tucson Mus Art, AZ 85 & 88. *Bibliog:* Articles, Phoenix Gasette, 2/8/90, Artspace, winter 84 & 85 & Scottsdale Progress, 4/4/86; Articles, Art Voices S, 11-12/79 & 9-10/81 & Portfolio Mag, 7-8/81; and others. *Media:* Acrylic, Oil. *Dealer:* The Studio 2337 N Tenth St Phoenix AZ 85006. *Mailing Add:* 2337 N Tenth Phoenix AZ 85006

DEMETRION, JAMES THOMAS
MUSEUM DIRECTOR
b Middletown, Ohio, July 10, 30. *Study:* Miami Univ, BS, 52, Simpson Col, Hon, 84, UCLA, Univ Vienna. *Collections Arranged:* Egon Schiele & The Human Form, 71; Paul Klee, 73; 25 Yrs Am Painting 1948-1973, 73; European Art: The Postwar Years 1945-1955, 78; Giorgio Morandi: Retrospective, 81; Francis Bacon, 89. *Pos:* Cur, Pasadena Art Mus, Calif, 64-66, dir, 66-69; dir, Des Moines Art Ctr, Iowa, 69-84; mem mus adv panel, Nat Endowment for the Arts, 73-76; mem int adv comt, Stuart Found, La Jolla, 81-90; dir, Hirshhorn Mus & Sculpture Garden-Smithsonian Inst, 84-; art comm, First Nat Bank, Chicago, currently. *Mem:* Asn Art Mus Dir (treas, 76-77, 1st vpres, 78-79, pres, 79-80). *Mailing Add:* Hirshhorn Mus & Sculpture Garden Independence Ave & Eighth SW Washington DC 20560

DE MILLE, LESLIE BENJAMIN
PAINTER, SCULPTOR
b Hamilton, Ont, Apr 24, 27; US citizen. *Study:* Art Students League, New York. *Work:* Portraits, two US Pres; Death Valley 49ers Collection; Navy Art Mus, Washington, DC; Five past Pres, Whittier Col Collection, Calif. *Comn:* Portrait, Ronald Reagan, Calif, 67; portrait, Richard M Nixon, Washington, DC; paintings, US Sixth Fleet, Mediterranean (naval combat artist), 72 & Pearl Harbor, Hawaii painting, 73; portrait, Anchor Hocking Co, Ohio, 80; bronze sculpture, Pres Reagan & Gorbachev, 88; bronze monument, Hillside, Sedona, Ariz, 91. *Exhib:* Death Valley 49ers Exhib, Calif, 69-; Grand Nat Ann

Exhib, Am Artists Prof League, New York, 71-; and others. *Teaching:* Organizer, dir & instr, sem for art orgn in US, 66-; instr, Nat Portrait Seminar, 81; fac instr, Scottsdale Artists Sch, Ariz, currently; workshop tour, Hawaii, 92. *Awards:* Best Show, 71 & Gold Medals, 76, 79 & 80, Am Artists Prof League, New York; Best Show, Death Valley 49ers Inc, 80; and others. *Bibliog:* Portraits in Pastel (series of half-hour programs), Pub Broadcasting System, 81-; Feature article, SW Art Mag, 10/81. *Mem:* Am Inst Fine Arts; Am Artists Prof League; Coun Traditional Artists Soc; Death Valley 49ers Inc; Pastel Soc Am; Salmagundi Club. *Media:* Oil, Pastel. *Publ:* How to Draw Cats and Kittens, Walter Foster, 79; Portraits in Pastel, PBS Pub, 81; Painting with Pastels, Foster Art Libr Ser, 84. *Mailing Add:* Fine Portraits & Paintings 50 Cathedral Lane Sedona AZ 86336

DEMING, DAVID LAWSON
SCULPTOR, EDUCATOR
b Cleveland, Ohio, May 26, 43. *Study:* Cleveland Inst Art, with William McVey & John Clague, BFA; Cranbrook Acad Art, with Julius Schmidt, MFA. *Work:* Ft Worth Nat Bank, Tex; San Antonio Mus & Pub Libr Austin, Tex; Longview Mus Art, Tex; First City Ctr, Austin, Tex; Ark Art Ctr; Columbus Mus Art. *Comn:* Bronze Bust Winthrop Rockefeller for Winrock Int; Barbara Jordan Award Medalion; Harold Russell Award Medalion. *Exhib:* One-man exhib, Adams-Middleton Gallery, Dallas; Kouros Gallery Group Shows, New York; Int Chicago Art Expos at Navy Pier. *Teaching:* Instr sculpture, Sch Fine & Appl Arts, Boston Univ, 67-68; instr sculpture & drawing design, Univ Tex, El Paso, 70-72; prof sculpture & drawing, Univ Tex, Austin, 72-; chmn, Dept Art & Art Hist, 92. *Awards:* Am Inst Archit Award of Honor. *Mem:* Tex Sculpture Asn; Int Sculpture Asn. *Media:* Steel, Bronze. *Mailing Add:* 2504 Baxter Dr Austin TX 78745

DE MONTE, CLAUDIA
SCULPTURE, PAINTER
b Astoria, NY, Aug 25, 47. *Study:* Col Notre Dame, Md, BA; Cath Univ Am, MFA. *Work:* Mus Mod Art, New York; Indianapolis Mus Art, Indiana; New Orleans Mus; Del Mus; Ft Lauderdale Mus; Brooklyn Mus. *Comn:* Prudential Life Insurance, NJ, 81; Hyatt-Regency, Va, 81; City of New York, 90. *Exhib:* 19th Area Exhib, 74 & Plus One, 76, Corcoran Gallery Art, Washington, DC; 7th International Encounter on Video, Centre d'Estudio d'Art Contemporani, Barcelona, Spain, 77; Contemp Arts Ctr, New Orleans, La, 78; one-person shows, Corcoran Mus Art, Washington, DC, 76, Miss Mus Art, Jackson, 80, Ft Worth Art Mus, Tex, 80, Marion Locks Gallery, Philadelphia, 80 & Gracie Mansion Gallery, New York, 84, 85, 88 & 89; New York Now, Gothenberg Mus, Sweden; Biennial Paper Art, Dupen Mus, Ger; and others. *Pos:* Dir, Art Wkshops, New Sch Social Res, New York, 80-82. *Teaching:* Prof, Univ Md, Col Park, 72- *Awards:* Fel in Sculpture, New York Found. *Bibliog:* G Henry (auth), Claudia De Monte, Art Am, 9/84; article, Claudia De Monte, New York Times, 9/27/85. *Media:* Acrylic, Oil. *Publ:* Contribr, Women in the Arts, American Women and Social Change & Visual Arts, US Info Agency, 75; Public Poet: Tom Jones & Andy Warhol's Interview, 1/77; coauth, The Height Report, 83. *Mailing Add:* 96 Grand St New York NY 10013

DE MONTEBELLO, PHILIPPE LANNES
ADMINISTRATOR, MUSEUM DIRECTOR
b Paris, France, May 16, 36. *Study:* Harvard Col, BA(magna cum laude), 58; New York Univ Inst Fine Arts, BA, 63, MA 76; Lafayette Col, Hon LLD, 79; Bard Col, Hon LLD, 81. *Collections Arranged:* Greek Art of the Aegean Islands, 11/79; Clyfford Still, 11/79; Horses of San Marco, 2/80; Seventeenth Century French Painting, 6/82; Cimabue, 1/82; Vatican, 1/83; Manet, 9/83; Liechtenstein: the Princely Collections, 10/85, Van Gogh in Saint-Remy and Auvers, 11/86, Zurbaran, 9/87, Degas, 10/88, Canaletto, 11/89, Velazquez, 10/89, From Poussin to Matisse: The Russian Taste for French Painting, 5/90. *Pos:* Asst cur to assoc cur Europ paintings, Metrop Mus Art, 63-69, vdir curatorial & educ affairs, 74-77, actg dir mus, 77-78, dir, 78-; dir, Mus Fine Arts, Houston, Tex, 69-74; bd trustees, exec comt, Am Fedn Arts; bd trustees, Inst Fine Arts, New York Univ. *Teaching:* Lectr, Curatorial Studies, New York Univ Inst Fine Arts. *Awards:* Woodrow Wilson Fellow, New York Inst Fine Arts, 61-62; Alumni Achievement Award, New York Univ, 78; Gallatin Medal & Fel, New York Univ, 81. *Mem:* Coun Mus & Educ Visual Arts; Am Asn Mus; Am Asn Mus Dirs; Skowhegan Sch Painting & Sculpture (adv comt). *Publ:* Auth, Peter Paul Rubens, McGraw, 68; contribr, Metrop Mus Art Bull & others. *Mailing Add:* Metrop Mus Art Fifth Ave at 82nd St New York NY 10028

DE MOURA SOBRAL, LUIS
HISTORIAN, CRITIC
b Viseu, Port, June 24, 43; Can citizen. *Study:* Univ Louvain, Belg, MA(art hist), 73, PhD, 76. *Collections Arranged:* Le surrealisme portugais (auth, catalog), Galerie UQAM, Montreal, 83. *Pos:* Cur, Montreal Mus Fine Arts, 71-75; ed, Racar, 83- *Teaching:* Asst prof, Univ Montreal, 76-81, assoc prof, 81-87, full prof & chair, 87- *Mem:* Am Soc Hispanic Art Hist Studies; Univ Art Asn Can; Int Coun Mus; Asn Port Mus. *Res:* Baroque painting; Portuguese baroque painting; Iberoamerican colonial art; painting & poetry in the baroque age. *Publ:* Bento Coelho da Silveira y la pintura hispánica e hispanoamericana, Relaciones artísticas entre la Península Ibérica y América, Actas del V Simposio Hispano-Portugués de Historia del Arte, Univ Valladolid, 90; Josefa de Obidos e as gravuras: problemas de estilo e de iconografia, Josefa de Obidos e o Tempo Barroco, Lisbon, Palácio Nacional da Ajuda, 91; critical study, Luís Nunes Tinoco, Elogio da Pintura, Galeria de Pintura do D Luís, 91; L'estampe anversoise et la peinture portugaise au début du XVIIe siécle: le "Missel Pontifical" de Goncalves Neto, Portugal et Flandres, Visions de l'Europe, Bruxels, Musées royaux des Beaux-Arts de Belgique, Musée d'Art Ancien, 9-12/91; and others. *Mailing Add:* Dept Hist Art Univ Montreal PO Box 6128 Sta A Montreal PQ H3C 3J7 Canada

DEMPSEY, BRUCE HARVEY
MUSEUM DIRECTOR
b Camden, NJ, July 4, 41. *Study:* Fla State Univ, BA, MFA; study exten sch, Florence, Italy; Mozarabic manuscripts with Gulnar Bosch. *Collections Arranged:* Photons-Phonons (elec sculpture), 71; Lewis Comfort Tiffany, 72; Realizations and Figurizations, 72; Karl Zerbe Mem Exhib, 73; Photo Phantisists, 73; Colors (photog exhib), 74; Talent USA, 76; Elizabethan Portraiture, Nat Portrait Gallery, London, 76; New Realism, 77; New Floridians No 1, 77; The Florida Connection: Jim Rosenquist & Robert Rauschenberg, 77; Helen Frankenthaler, 77; New Floridians No 2, 78 & No 3, 79; The Flowing Word: Chinese Calligraphy, 79; Contemporary Stained Glass, 79; Duane Hanson, 80; Currents: A New Mannerism, 81; Joseph Raffael: Recent Works, 82; Calligraphy, Ming Dynasty, 82; Arakawa: Graphic Works, 82; Master Craftsmen, 83; Empress Dowager Forbidden City, 83; Masami Teraoka, 83; Ramses II: Pharaoh & His Time, 87. *Pos:* Dir art gallery, Fla State Univ, 68-74; dir, Jacksonville Art Mus, 75- *Teaching:* Instr fundamental art & art hist, Fla State Univ, 66-74. *Awards:* Fla Arts Recognition Award, State of Fla, 86-87. *Mem:* Am Asn Mus. *Publ:* Auth, Lewis C Tiffany-Beauty in Many Mediums, 72. *Mailing Add:* Jacksonville Art Mus Inc 4160 Boulevard Center Dr Jacksonville FL 32207

DE NAGY, EVA
PAINTER
b Hungary. *Study:* Acad Royal Beaux-Arts, Brussels, Belg. *Work:* Color slides, Guild Libr, Church Archit Guild Am, Washington, DC. *Exhib:* Painters & Sculptors Soc NJ, 61-62; Am-Hungarian Art Asn, New York, 62 & 63; Catharine Lorillard Wolfe Art Club, 62 & 64; Provincetown Art Asn & Mus, 60-86; West 80's Art and the Law Traveling Exhib, Minn Mus Art, 80-81; and others. *Pos:* Owner-dir, Eva de Nagy Gallery, Provincetown, Mass, currently; state art chmn, NJ Fedn Women's Clubs, 60 & 62; mem art comn, Trenton State Mus, 60 & 62; chmn, Roebling-Boehm art scholar, 62 & 64. *Awards:* Prizes, NJ State Fedn Women's Club, 54 & 59; Bronze Medal, Seton Hall Univ, 56; Prize, NJ State Med Asn Convention Art Exhib, 58 & 60; plus others. *Mem:* Provincetown Art Asn; Cape Cod Art Asn. *Mailing Add:* 427 Commercial St Provincetown MA 02657

DE NAGY, TIBOR (J)
DEALER, COLLECTOR
b Debrecen, Hungary, Apr 25, 10; US citizen. *Study:* DEcon & PhD; Univ Frankfurt; Kings Col, Cambridge, Eng & Owens Col, Manchester; Univ Basel, Switz. *Pos:* Pres & dir, Tibor de Nagy Gallery, Inc, New York, 50- *Awards:* Arts Award, Col Visual Arts, Syracuse Univ. *Mem:* Art Dealers Asn Am; Mus Mod Art. *Specialty:* Pioneer work to start out and promote contemporary talents, most of whom are Americans. *Collection:* Contemporary Americans. *Publ:* Auth, Die Ungarische National Bank, Duncker & Humboldt, Munich, 31; The integrity of the artist, dealer and gallery, In: Business of Art, Prentice-Hall. *Mailing Add:* Tibor de Nagy Gallery 41 W 57th St New York NY 10019

DENES, AGNES
ENVIRONMENTAL ARTIST, CONCEPTUAL ARTIST
b Budapest, Hungary; US citizen. *Study:* City Univ New York; New Sch Social Res, New York; Columbia Univ. *Work:* Metrop Mus Art, Mus Mod Art, Whitney Mus Am Art, NY; Nat Collection Fine Arts, Washington, DC; Moderna Museet, Stockholm, Sweden; and many others. *Comn:* Wheatfield--A Confrontation (wheat planted, downtown Manhattan), 82; Marble Sculptures, Stelae, Dept Cult Affairs, Genova, Italy, 86; Bioscapes-A Biopark, Int Ctr for the Preserv of Wild Animals, Ohio, 90-93; Hypersphere, Equitable Ctr, New York, 87; Flying Pyramids, Art Pub Places, Miami Airport, 87-89; North Waterfront Park Master Plan, City of Berkeley, Calif, 88-90. *Exhib:* Whitney Mus Am Art, 71, 73 & 76, Brooklyn Mus, 72, 76 & 80, Mus Mod Art, 73 & 77, New Mus, 80, NY; solo exhibs, Corcoran Gallery Art, 74, Ctr Cult American, Paris, France, Ikon Gallery, Birmingham, 78, Inst Contemp Art, London, Eng, 79, Hayden Gallery, Mass Inst Tech, Cambridge, 80, Master of Drawing Invitational, Nurnberg, Ger, 82, Univ Hawaii, 85, Agnes Denes Concept into Form, Works 1970-90, Arts Club Chicago, Ill, 90 & Agnes Denes: A Retrospective, traveling, Herbert F Johnson Mus, Ithaca, NY, 92; Biennal of Sydney, Australia, 76; Venice Biennale, Italy, 78 & 80; Seibu Art Mus, Tokyo, 79; Musee Nat d'Art Mod, Centre Georges Pompidou, Paris, 80; Museo Arte Contemp, Sao Paulo, Brazil, 80; Nat Mus Am Art, Smithsonian Inst, Washington, DC, 83 & 85; Moderna Museet, Stockholm, Sweden, 85; Cleveland Ctr Contemp Art, Ohio, 85; Kolnischer Kuntsverein, Cologne, Ger, 87; Cincinnati Art Mus, 89; New Orleans Art Mus, 89; Denver Art Mus, 89; Rose Art Mus Brandeis Univ, Waltham, Mass, 91; Mus Contemp Art, Helsinki, Mus Tempere, Findland, 92; Expo '92, Andalucia Pavilion, Convento de Santa Clara, Moguer, Spain, 92; Hofstra Mus, Hempstead, NY, Dallas Mus Natural Hist, Tex, Laumeier Sculpture Park & Gallery, St Louis, Mo, 93; plus other international group shows. *Teaching:* Instr fine arts, Sch Visual Arts, New York, 74-79; instr, Skowhegan Sch Painting & Sculpture, Maine, 79; guest lectr in numerous universities, museums & art centers in the US & Eur. *Awards:* Creative Artists Pub Serv Grant, 72, 74 & 80; Nat Endowment Arts Grant, 74-75 & 81; DAAD Fel, Berliner Kunstlerprogramm, 78; Hassam & Speicher Fund Purchase Award, Am Acad Art & Letters, 85; The Eugene McDermott Achievement Award Mass Inst Technol, 90. *Bibliog:* Peter Selz (auth), Agnes Denes: The visual presentation of meaning, Art in Am, 3-4/77; Donald Kuspit (auth), Agnes Denes: The ironies of comprehension, Arts Mag, 12/81; Agnes Denes (auth), A Monograph, Herbert F Johnson Mus Art, Cornell Univ, 92. *Media:* Mixed. *Publ:* Auth, Sculptures of the Mind, Univ Akron Press, 76; Paradox & Essence, Tau/Ma Publ, Rome, Italy, 77; Isometric Systems in Isotropic Space: Map Projections, 79 & Book of Dust: The Beginning and the End of Time and Thereafter, 86, Visual Studies Workshop. *Mailing Add:* 595 Broadway New York NY 10012

DE NIKE, MICHAEL NICHOLAS
SCULPTOR, WRITER
b Regina, Sask, Sept 14, 23; US citizen. *Study:* Nat Acad Fine Arts; also with Jean de Marco & Carl Schmitz. *Work:* Dernick Resources, Houston, Tex. *Comn:* Albert Payson Terhune Mem, Collie Fanciers Am, Paramus, NJ, 71; Medallion, Int Chef's Asn, New York, 72; Stations of the Cross, Christ Church, Pompton Lakes, NJ, 75; Bicentennial Mural, Twp Wayne, NJ, 75; Young St Francis (bronze), St David's in Kinnelon, NJ; and others. *Exhib:* Nat Acad Design, New York, 64; Audubon Artists, 65; Knickerbocker Artists, 65; Nat Sculpture Soc Ann, 66; Am Artists Prof League, 74; and others. *Pos:* Dir & founder, Am Carving Sch, Wayne, NJ, 74-90. *Teaching:* Instr woodcarving, Fair Lawn Adult Educ, 68-74; adj fac, Essex Co Col, Newark, NJ, 74-75; Am Woodcarving Sch, 74-89; Passaic Co Col, 76-80. *Awards:* Dr Ralph Weiler Award, Nat Acad Design, 64; Herald-News Award, Passaic-Clifton, NJ, 69; Allied Artists Am Award, 75. *Mem:* Am Artist Prof League; Nat Sculpture Soc; Knickerbocker Artists. *Media:* Wood, Stone. *Mailing Add:* 2343 Hamburg Turnpike Wayne NJ 07470

DENKER, SUSAN A
HISTORIAN, CRITIC
b New York, NY, Apr 2, 48. *Study:* Harvard Univ, BA, 66; Wellesley Col, MA, 79; Brown Univ, ABD, 82. *Teaching:* Lectr art hist, Tufts Univ, 76-; studio fac & chmn art hist, Sch of Mus Fine Arts, Boston, 80- *Awards:* Res Grant, French Govt, 69; Fel, Samuel Kress Found, 77-78; Russell T Smith Award, Boston Mus Sch, 92. *Mem:* Col Art Asn. *Res:* Modern European art, 1880 to present; American art, 1940 to present; Mondrian's relationship to European and American avant-garde art; women film directors. *Publ:* Coauth, Europe in Torment: 1450-1550, 74 & French Watercolors & Drawings: 1800-1910, 75, RI Sch Design Mus Art; auth, Sandi Slone: A Retrospective Exhib 1972-1981, Watson Gallery, 81; De Stijl: 1917-1931, Visions of Utopia, Art J, fall 82. *Mailing Add:* 361 Harvard St Apt 7 Cambridge MA 02138

DENMAN, PATRICIA PRICE (PAT DENMAN)
PAINTER
b Paterson, NJ, 1932. *Study:* Van Emburgh Sch Art, 50-51; study with Maxwell Stewart Simpson, 60-64, Nicholas Reale, 73-76. *Work:* Hershey Chocolate Corp, Pa; AT&T, Bedminster, NJ; NJ Bell, Somerville, NJ; US Trust Co, New York; Chubb Corp, Bridgewater, NJ. *Exhib:* Grand Nat Exhib, Salmagundi Club, New York, 83 & Am Watercolor Soc, 87-91; Audubon Artists, 87-89; Nat Arts Club, 87-89; Nat Acad Design, 88, 90 & 92; Allied Artist Am, 89; amd ptjers. *Pos:* Dir, trustee & instr, Somerset Art Asn, Inc, Far Hills, NJ, 71-74; Juror of Selection Awards. *Teaching:* Watercolor Workshops, Somerset Art Asn, Inc. *Awards:* Mary S Litt Medal, Am Watercolor Soc, 87; Adolph & Clara Obrig Prize, Nat Acad Design, 90; Merwin Altfeld Award, Nat Watercolor Soc, 91. *Mem:* Am Watercolor Soc (asst corresp secy, 90-91); NJ Watercolor Soc (vpres, 86-89 & pres, 90-92); Audubon Artists; Nat Asn Women Artists; Nat Watercolor Soc. *Media:* Watercolor. *Publ:* American Artist, Watercolor Page, 9/92. *Dealer:* Gallery Nine Main St Chatham NJ; Left Bank Gallery Wellfleet Cape Cod MA. *Mailing Add:* 29 Beechwood Rd Basking Ridge NJ 07920

DENNETT, LISSY W
SCULPTOR
b Vienna, Austria, May 3, 26; US citizen. *Study:* Brooklyn Col, BA, 48; Haber Sch Sculpture. *Exhib:* Salmagundi Art Club, New York, 80; Nat Asn Women Artists Ann Juried Show, New York, 89; New Rochelle Art Asn Ann Juried Show, 90; Village Arts Club, Rockville Ctr, 90. *Pos:* Pres, Sculptors Inc, Port Washington, NY, 86-90, vpres 90-; pres, Artists Network Great Neck, NY, 90- *Teaching:* Instr, sculpture, Great Neck Adult Educ, 88- *Awards:* Cera Cast Foundry Award, Mamaronek Art Guild, 86; Best in Show, Freeport-South Nassau Unitarian Gallery, 88; Suburban Art League Award Merit, sculpture, 89. *Mem:* Prof Sculptors Guild; Artists Network Great Neck (vpres 86-90, pres 90-); Nat Asn Women Artists (Centennial Comt); Visual Arts Alliance Long Island (recording scy 88-); Mamaronek Art Guild. *Media:* Stone, Clay. *Mailing Add:* 59A Nassau Great Neck NY 11021

DENNEY, JIM (JAMES DAVID)
PAINTER
b Greenville, SC, May 13, 53. *Study:* Univ Ore, Eugene, BFA, 78; Univ Kans, Lawrence, MFA(Lockwood Fel), 80. *Exhib:* Solo exhib, Carnegie-Mellon Univ, 82; Urban Pulses--The Artist & the City, Frick Fine Arts, Pittsburgh, 83; Nature, Sch No 33 Art Ctr, Baltimore, 33; Zaner Galery Nat, Rochester, 83; Three Painters, NAME Gallery, Chicago, 84; Young Pittsburgh, Carnegie Mus Art, Pittsburgh, 84; and others. *Teaching:* Asst prof art, Carnegie-Mellon Univ, 81- *Awards:* Proj Award, Urban Pulses, Vera Heinz Found, 83; Visual Arts Fel, Pa Coun Arts, 84. *Bibliog:* Elaine King (auth), article, New Art Examiner, 6/82; Harry Schwalb (auth), Teacher, teacher, Pittsburgh Mag, 3/83; William Homisak (auth), article, New Art Examiner, 11/83. *Media:* Oil. *Mailing Add:* c/o Lane Community Col Art Gallery 4000 E 30th St Eugene OR 97405

DENNIS, CHARLES HOUSTON
CARTOONIST
b Springfield, Mo, Nov 11, 21. *Study:* Art League Calif, San Francisco; Acad Art, San Francisco. *Pos:* Staff artist, Springfield Leader & Press, 39-42; free-lance mag cartoonist, 50- *Publ:* Contribr, numerous mags, 50-; auth, cartoon gag writing principles and techniques, 55. *Mailing Add:* 1831 Magnolia Way Walnut Creek CA 94595

DENNIS, DON W
PAINTER, INSTRUCTOR
b Reading, Pa, Jan 21, 23. *Study:* Kutztown State Col, Pa, BS(art educ), 51; Pratt Inst, Brooklyn, NY, 51-52; with Edgar A Whitney 65-68; also with Barse Miller, 69-70 & 72. *Work:* Miami Univ, Oxford, Ohio; First Nat Bank of Cincinnati, Madeira, Ohio; Reading Mus, Pa; Utstein Kloster, Norway; Bell Telephone; General Electric; Provident Bank, Cincinnati. *Comn:* 12 paintings (offshore oil rigs), Phillips Petroleum, Stavanger, Norway, 79. *Exhib:* One-man shows, Reading Mus & Art Gallery, Pa, 68 & Wyannie Malone Mus, Hopetown, Bahamas, 85 & 86; Am Watercolor Soc Ann, Nat Acad, New York; Cincinnati Art Mus Invitational, Ohio, 77; All-Ohio Watercolor Show, Massillon Mus, Ohio, 78; Ohio Watercolor Soc Ann, Ohio, 79, 80, 81, 82, 83, 84, 85 & 86; Group show - Kulturhus, Grimstad, Norway, 87. *Pos:* Art dir, Gibson Greetings, Cincinnati, 68-73; conductor watercolor workshops, Maine, Martha's Vineyard, Bahamas & Norway, 73-88; self-employed artist-teacher, 73- *Teaching:* Guest instr, Miami Univ, Oxford, Ohio, Wine Country Workshops, Napa Valley, Calif, 87-88. *Awards:* Emily Lowe Mem Award, 80, Walser Greathouse Medal, 82, Am Watercolor Soc; M Grumbacher Bronze Medallion, Ohio Watercolor Soc, 81; and others. *Bibliog:* The Watercolor Page, Am Artist, 8/82. *Mem:* Am Watercolor Soc (Midwest vpres, 76-77); Cincinnati Art Club (pres, 71-73); life mem Ohio Watercolor Soc (trustee, 80-85); Cincinnati MacDowell Soc; assoc Nat Acad Design. *Media:* Watercolor. *Publ:* Contribr, Master Color & Design in Watercolor, Watson-Guptill Publ; Exploring Color, Light Publ; Making Color Sing. *Mailing Add:* 731 Brooks Ave Cincinnati OH 45215

DENNIS, DONNA FRANCES
SCULPTOR, PRINTMAKER
b Springfield, Ohio, Oct 16, 42. *Study:* Carleton Col, BA, 64; Col Art Study Abroad, Paris, 65; Art Students League, with Stephen Greene, 66. *Work:* Geneva Art Mus, Switzerland; Neue Galerie-Sammlung Ludwig, Aachen, WGer; Walker Art Ctr, Minneapolis, Minn; Brooklyn Mus, New York; Chase Manhattan Bank. *Comn:* Entrance maze, Musical Theater Lab, Kennedy Ctr, Washington, DC, 77; Mad River Tunnel (outdoor sculpture), Dayton City, Ohio, 81; Moccasin Creek Cabins (outdoor sculpture), Aberdeen, SDak, 83; Steel Fence & ceramic medallions, PS 234, New York, 88. *Exhib:* Scale & Environment, Walker Art Ctr, Minn, 77; Biennial Exhib, 79, Developments in Recent Sculpture, 81, Whitney Mus Am Art, New York; Directions, 79, Content, 84, Hirshhorn Mus, Washington, DC; Painting & Sculpture Today, Indianapolis Mus Art, Ind, 80; New York Now, Kestner Ges, Hannover, WGer, 82; Artists Architecture, Inst Contemp Art, London, 83; New Art, Tate Gallery, London, 83; Ornamentalism, Hudson River Mus, Yonkers, 83; Night Stops, Neuberger Mus, Purchase, NY, Tunnel Tower, 92; Deep Station, Univ Mass, Amherst, 85, Brooklyn Mus, 87, Del Art Mus, Wilmington, 88, Madison Art Ctr, Wis, 89 & Indianapolis Mus Art, 91. *Teaching:* instr Skowhegan Sch Art, Maine, 82, Sch Visual Arts, NY, 83-89 & Princeton Univ, NJ, 84 & State Univ NY, Purchase, 84-88; assoc prof, State Univ NY, Purchase, 90- *Awards:* NY State Creative Artist Public Service Grant, 75 & 82; Nat Endowment Arts Grant, 77, 80 & 86; John Simon Guggenheim Found Fel, 79; Art Award, Am Acad & Inst Arts & Lett, 84; Grant, NY Found Arts, 85 & 92; Award for Excellence in Design, Art Commission New York, 87; Bard Award of Merit in Architecture and Urban Design, City Club New York, 89; Community Service Award for Excellence in Urban Design, Parks Coun New York, 89; Distinguished Achievement Award, Carleton Col and Carleton Alumni Asn, 89. *Bibliog:* James Jordan (auth), Light: Adams, Dennis & Sonneman, Dialogue, 3-4/80; Robert Jensen & Patricia Conway (auths), Ornamentalism: The New Decorativeness in Architecture and Design, Clarkson N Potter, 82; Edward Lucie-Smith (auth), American Art Now, William Morrow & Co, 85; James Wines (auth), De-Architecture, Rizzoli Int Publ, 87; Michael Brenson (auth), New York Times, 7/23/89; Carey Lovelace (auth), Intimate Immensity, Arts, 6/88. *Mem:* Bd Govs, New York Found Arts, 88- *Media:* Mixed. *Publ:* Illusr, Hotels, Z Press, 74; auth, The presence of the past, Domus Mag, 10/80; coauth (with K Elmslie), 26 Bars, Z Press, 87. *Mailing Add:* 131 Duane St New York NY 10013

DENNIS, GERTRUDE WEYHE
DEALER
Pos: Dir, Weyhe Gallery, New York, currently. *Mem:* Art Dealers Asn Am. *Specialty:* American prints & drawings, 1920s & 1930s. *Mailing Add:* 101 W 57th St Apt 8H New York NY 10017-2205

DENNIS, ROGER WILSON
PAINTER
b Norwich, Conn, Mar 11, 02. *Study:* Art Students League of Hartford, Frank Bicknell, Guy Wiggins, George Bruestle, James McManus, John Carlson, Allen Cochran. *Work:* Lyman Allyn, Mus; Florence Griswold Mus; New Britain Mus Am Art; Pfizer Inc; Hyatt Corp. *Exhib:* Lyme Art Asn; Lyman Allyn Mus; Old Lyme Art Works, Shippee Gallery; Mystic Art Gallery. *Pos:* Conservator painting, Lyman Allyn Mus, New London, Conn, 45-78; retired. *Awards:* General Retrospective Exhib at the Lyman Allyn Mus, New London Connecticut, 79. *Bibliog:* Edward Feit, (auth), Am Artist, BPI Communications, 88; Bethe duFresne, (auth), The New London Day, 92. *Mem:* Lyme Art Asn; Lyme Hist Soc. *Media:* Oil, Watercolor. *Dealer:* Patricia Shippee Fine Art Old Lyme Ct. *Mailing Add:* 9 Columbus Ave Niantic CT 06357

DENNISON, KEITH ELKINS
CONSULTANT, CURATOR
b Oakland, Calif, Sept 20, 39. *Study:* San Francisco State Univ, BA; grad studies, Dr Ernest Mundt; spec training, M H de Young Mem Mus, San Francisco. *Collections Arranged:* Horizons, A Century of California

Landscape Painting; La Pendule Francaise, A Selected Survey of French Clocks 1750-1900; Ecclesiastical Arts 13th Through 17th Centuries. *Pos:* Asst cur educ, M H de Young Mem Mus, 68-70; visual arts adv, Calif Arts Comn, Sacramento, 70-71; dir, Haggin Mus, Stockton, Calif, 71-86; fine arts consult, 86- *Teaching:* Instr museology, Univ of the Pac, 74- *Publ:* Auth, Horizons, a century of California landscape painting, 70. *Mailing Add:* 3631 Portsmouth Circle N Stockton CA 95209

DENNISTON, DOUGLAS
PAINTER, EDUCATOR
b Cornwall-on-Hudson, NY, Nov 19, 21. *Study:* Col William & Mary, cert, 42; Univ NMex, BFA, 45, MA, 48. *Work:* Va Mus Fine Arts, Richmond; Denver Art Mus; Tucson Mus Art & Univ Ariz Mus Art, Ariz; Jonson Gallery, Albuquerque, NMex. *Comn:* Painting, Tucson Airport Authority, 88. *Exhib:* Am Watercolors, Prints & Drawings, Metrop Mus Art, New York, 52; Young Am Printmakers, Mus Mod Art, New York, 53; 18th Ann Watercolor Exhib, San Francisco Art Mus, 54; 67th & 73rd Western Ann, Denver Art Mus, 61 & 71; Southwestern Prints & Drawings, Dallas Mus Fine Arts, 52-62; Southwest Fine Arts Biennial, Mus Fine Arts, Santa Fe, NMex, 76. *Teaching:* Prof art, Univ Ariz, 59-83, prof emer, 83- *Awards:* Purchase Awards, Denver Artists Ann, Denver Art Mus, 53, Fifth & Seventh Southwestern, Yuma Art Ctr, Ariz, 70 & 72. *Media:* Watercolor, Oil. *Publ:* Illusr, Calendar, Baleen Press, 72. *Mailing Add:* 1844 N Vine Ave Tucson AZ 85719

DENSON, G ROGER
CRITIC, WRITER
b Buffalo, NY, Feb 2, 56. *Study:* State Univ Col Buffalo, BA(arts & humanities), 78, with Paul Sharits & Hollis Frampton. *Pos:* Performance, video, 78-80 & exhibs dir, 80-82, Hallwalls, Buffalo, NY. *Mem:* Gallery Asn NY State (bd dirs, 81-87); Alternative Mus (bd dirs, 87-91). *Res:* Cultural studies and the critical analyses of the languages and values of criticism, cross-cultural relations and gender politics. *Publ:* Auth, Philip (Taaffe) of Naples and the educative geometry of history, 90 & Skeptic and sophist, Sigmar Polke doubts, 91, Parkett; Bad boy sublimations: John Miller & Andres Serrano, Contemporanea, 11/90; Rupturing the modernist gland: Lydia Dona, Artscribe, 1/91; coauth, Interview with Renée Green, Flash Art, 10/91. *Mailing Add:* 131 W 15th St, Suite 23 New York NY 10011

DENTON, PATRY
PAINTER, INSTRUCTOR
b Scottsbluff, Nebr, July 20, 43. *Study:* Art Students Tour, Europe, 60; Univ Kans, 61; Univ Denver, cert painting, 62; studied with Virginia Cobb, Charles Reid, Lee Weiss, Carol Barnes, Alex Powers & Don Andrews. *Work:* Wind River Collection; Mus Tex Tech Univ; Hospital Building & Equipment, St Louis, Mo; United Banks Colo, Denver; Synergen, Inc, Boulder; and many in pvt collections. *Exhib:* solo shows, W Nebr Art Ctr, 75, 81 & 90 & Foothills Art Ctr, 74 & 78; Am Watercolor Soc 125th & traveling show, New York, 92-93; Western Fed Watercolor Soc, Alburquerque, NMex, 92; Watercolor Art Soc, Houston, 92; Grand Nat All Media Exhib, Akron, 92; Nat Watercolor Soc, 92; and many other group & one-man shows. *Teaching:* Instr workshop, Wind River Artists Guild, Dubois, Wyo & GI Sketch Club, Aurora, Nebr; Colo Inst Art, 83-85; Lamar, Colo, 91-92. *Awards:* Brown Williamson Award, Ga Watercolor Soc, 88; Ruth Roseneau Silver Medallion, Adirondack Nat Watercolor, 91; Georgia Nat Watercolor, 88 & 92; Award of Distinction, New England Watercolor Soc. *Bibliog:* B Hosicowa (auth), Art of Pat Denton, Empire Mag, Denver Post, 11/12/72; Susan Thurston (auth), Leafprints, Today's Art, 5/84. *Mem:* Foothills Art Ctr; Southwestern Watercolor Soc; Colo Watercolor Soc; Niagra Frontier Watercolor Soc; Okla Watercolor Soc; Georgia Watercolor Soc. *Media:* Watercolor, Miscellaneous Media. *Publ:* The Artists Mag, 3/88 & 3/92. *Dealer:* Vern Stein Fine Art Buffalo NY; Paint Horse Gallery Breckenridge CO. *Mailing Add:* 2948 Pierson Way Lakewood CO 80215

DEO, MARJOREE NEE
PAINTER
b Escanaba, Mich, Aug 27, 07. *Study:* Univ Wis, BA, 28; Grand Chaumiere, Paris, 32-33; Phillips Gallery Art Sch, with Karl Knaths, 44-45; Am Univ, with Boris Margo & Jack Tworkov, 46; Fine Arts Inst, Sarasota, Fla, with Afro, Guston, Marca-Relli, Rivers & Brooks, 64-67. *Work:* Corcoran Gallery Art; Univ Wis, Madison; Regis Col, Colo; Wagner Col, NY. *Comn:* Paintings, Bancroft Sch & Camp, Haddonfield, NJ & Owl's Head, Maine, 68, 70 & 73, Groom & Nordberg Attorneys, Washington, DC, 75, 77 & 80, Marco Island Hotel, Fla, 76, Tierra Verde Hotel, St Petersburg, Fla, 79 & Ellis Bank & Trust, Sarasota, Fla, 82. *Exhib:* Baltimore Mus Regional, 55, 57, 59 & 61; Turkey Imagined Traveling Exhib, Turkey & Washington, DC, 58-59; US Info Agency Int Tours, Europe, 59-60; Butler Inst Am Art Ann, 59-62; Pa Nat, Pa Acad Fine Arts & Detroit Mus, 60; Corcoran Gallery Art Biennial, 63; US Embassy Prog, 67- *Teaching:* Guest lectr, Workshops-Mount Vernon Col, Washington, DC, 47; Studio Talks, Selby Libr, 82-83 & 86; Univ Carolina, 83-83 & 86. *Awards:* Fla Artists Group Ann Award, 68-73 & 84; Award, Sarasota Boy's Club, 85; Prize, Art Forms Exhib, 91. *Mem:* Artists Equity Asn; Sarasota Art Asn; Fla Artists Group. *Media:* Acrylic. *Dealer:* Surrounding Gallery Center Sandwich NH 03227; Ann Angle Charlottesville VA 22901. *Mailing Add:* 700 John Ringling Blvd No 503 Sarasota FL 34236-1505

DE PALMA, BRETT
PAINTER, SCULPTOR
b Lexington, Ky, June 19, 49. *Study:* Peabody Col, Nashville, TN, BA, 70; Boston Sch Mus Fine Arts, BFA, 72; Tufts Univ, Medford, Mass, MFA, 73. *Work:* Kunsthalle, Malmo, Sweden; Tenn State Mus, Nashville; Smithsonian Health & Hosp Orgn, New York. *Comn:* Paintings, Metro/Nashville, Tenn, 86. *Exhib:* One-person exhibs, Emilio Bazzoli Gallery, Modena, Italy, 82 & 83, Anders Tornberg Gallery, Lund, Sweden, 88, Fawbush Gallery, New York, 88 & 89; Phillipe Brit Gallery, New York, 89, Colleen Greco, New York, 90, Tenn State Mus, Nashville, 90 & Jacob Karpio, San Juan, Costa Rica, 90; Documenta 7, Kassel, WGer, 82; Correspondences, New York Art Now, Laforet Mus, Harajuku, Tokyo, Japan, 85; Contemporary American Collage, 1960-85, Univ Mass, Amherst, 87; Recent Acquisitions, Kunsthalle, Malmo, Sweden, 88; Robert Thompson Gallery, Minneapolis, Minn, 90; Indiana Univ, Bloomington, Ind, 90; Echo Press, Ft Wayne Mus, Ind, 90; Tenn Art Comn, Nashville, 90; Montebello Mansion, Nyack, NY, 90. *Teaching:* Vis fel painting, Princeton Univ, NJ, 89-90; lectr, painting, Sch Visual Arts, New York, 89-90. *Awards:* Nat Endowment Arts Grant, 87. *Bibliog:* Edward Lucie-Smith (auth), American Art Now, William R Morrow, New York, 85; Mario Diacono (auth), Social Icons, private publ, Boston, Mass, 85; Donald Kuspit (auth), review, Artforum, summer 88. *Media:* Oil, Acrylic; Assemblage, Mixed Media. *Mailing Add:* 262 Mott St New York NY 10012

DE PAOLA, TOMIE
DESIGNER, ILLUSTRATOR
b Meriden, Conn, Sept 15, 34. *Study:* Pratt Inst, BFA, 56; Calif Col Arts & Crafts, MFA, 69; Lone Mountain Col, Doctoral Equivalency, 70; also with Ben Shahn & Richard Lindner; Colby-Sawyer Col, LHD, 85. *Work:* Kerlan Collection, Univ Minn, Minneapolis; Worcester Art Mus, Mass; Osborne Collection, Toronto. *Comn:* Mural, Dominican Sisters Retreat House Chapel, Schenectady, NY, 58; two murals, Conception Abbey Retreat House, Mo, 59; renovation, design & murals, St Sylvester's Church, Graniteville, Vt, 61; murals, Glastonbury Monastery, Hingham, Mass, 62; altar painting, Newman Cult Ctr, Rensselaer Polytech Inst, 68. *Exhib:* Children's Bk Illusr, Everson Mus, 77; Art and the Alphabet, 78 & A Peaceable Kingdom: Animals in Art, 82, Houston Mus Fine Arts; The Original Art Ann, Master Eagle Gallery, New York, 80-83; A Decade of the Original Art of the Best Illustrated Children's Books, 1970-1980, Univ Conn Libr, Storrs, 82; Illustrators Exhib, Metrop Mus Art & New York Pub Libr, 82-83; and others. *Collections Arranged:* Kerlan Collection, Univ Minn, Minneapolis, 81. *Pos:* Designer & tech dir speech & theater, Colby-Sawyer Col, 73-76. *Teaching:* Asst prof design & painting, Newton Col of Sacred Heart, Mass, 62-66; asst prof design, Lone Mountain Col, San Francisco, 67-70; instr art, Chamberlayne Jr Col, 72-73; assoc prof, Colby-Sawyer Col, 73-76; assoc prof illus & graphic design, New Eng Col, Henniker, 76-79. *Awards:* Caldecott Honor Bk Award, Am Libr Asn, 76; Regina Medal, Cath Libr Asn, 83. *Bibliog:* Z Sutherland (auth), Children & Books, Scott Foresman, 5th ed, 77; Twentieth Century Children's Writers, St James-Macmillan, 83; Something About the Author, Volume 59, Gale Res, 90; Children's Literature Review, Volume 24, Gale Res, 91; Major Authors and Illustrators for Children and Young Adults, Gale Res, 92. *Mem:* Authors Guild; Soc Children's Bk Writers. *Media:* Mixed. *Publ:* Auth & illusr, The Clown of God, Harcourt Brace Jovanovich, 78; illusr, Tomie de Paola's Mother Goose, 85, Tomie De Paola's Books of Poems, 88, Bonjour, Mr Satie, 91, Jingle, the Christmas Clown, 92 & Jamie O'Rourke and the Big Potato, 92, G P Putnam's Sons. *Mailing Add:* 300 County Rd New London NH 03257

DE PEDERY-HUNT, DORA
SCULPTOR, DESIGNER
b Budapest, Hungary, Nov 16, 13. *Study:* State Lyceum, Budapest, 32; Royal Sch Appl Art, Budapest, MA, 43. *Work:* Nat Gallery Can, Ottawa; Art Gallery Ont, Toronto; Smithsonian Inst; Royal Cabinet Medals, Brussels, Belg & The Hague, Netherlands; Mus Contemp Crafts, Charlottetown, PEI; and others. *Exhib:* Can Pavillion, Expo '67; Sculpture Symposium, Toronto, 78; Prince Arthur Gallerie, 78; Hamilton Art Gallery, 79; Gallery Stratford, 79; and others. *Awards:* Purchase Prizes, Uno-a-Erre, Arezzo, Italy, 64-66; Can Govt Centennial Medal, 67; Queen's Jubilee Medal, 72; and others. *Mem:* Royal Can Acad; Sculptors' Soc Can; Ont Soc Artists. *Mailing Add:* 360 E Bloor St No 902 Toronto ON M4W 3M3 Canada

DEPILLARS, MURRY N
ADMINISTRATOR, ILLUSTRATOR
b Chicago, Ill, Dec 21, 38. *Study:* Kennedy-King Community Col, AA(fine arts); Roosevelt Univ, BA(art educ) & MA(urban studies); Pa State Univ, University Park, PhD (art educ). *Work:* Paul Roberson Cult Ctr, Pa State Univ, University Park; Inst Positive Educ, Chicago, Ill; Consolidated Bank, Richmond; Stucko Mus, Harlem, NY. *Comn:* Mural, African & African-Am Studies Ctr, Univ Mich, Ann Arbor, 71; illusr, J Negro Educ, Howard Univ, 74; illusr, Destruction of Black Civilizations, 74 & Steps to Break the Circle, 75, Third World Press; illusr, Story of Kwanza, Inst Positive Educ, Chicago, 75. *Exhib:* Mus Sci & Indust, Chicago, 70; The Indignant Eye, Whitney Mus Am Art, New York, 71; Am Greeting Card Gallery, New York, 72; Rainbow Sign Gallery, Los Angeles, 74; World Expo '74, African-Am Pavilion, Spokane, 74; Huntsville Mus Art, 79; Miss Mus Art, Jackson, 80; Heckscher Mus, Huntington, NY, 86; NY State Mus, Albany, 87; Alfred & David Smart Galleries, Univ Chicago, Ill, 87; Fay Gold Gallery, Atlanta, Ga, 88; Geme Festival of Culture, SERMAC, Ft DeFrance, Martinique, 88; Lee Hall Gallery, Clemson Univ, 90; Mus Sci & Indust, Chicago, 92. *Pos:* Asst dir, Educ Asst Prog, Univ Ill, Chicago, 68-71, Asst Dean, Sch Arts, Va Commonwealth Univ, 71-76, dean, 76- *Teaching:* Instr, Chicago Comt of Urban Opportunity, 68; asst prof art, Va Commonwealth Univ, 71-76, assoc prof 76-84, prof, 84- *Awards:* Man of Excellence Plaque, Rep China, 80; Nat Endowment Arts, 81, 82 & 83; Alumni Fel, Penn State Univ, 90; and others. *Bibliog:* F D Cossitt (auth), DePillars is Artist with message, Richmond Times Dispatch Newspaper, 6/15/70; Semella Lewis & Ruth Waddy (auth), Black artists on art, Contemp Crafts, Inc, Vol II; Robert Doty (auth), Contemporary

Black Artists in America, Whitney Mus Am Art, 72. *Mem:* Nat Conf Artists (pres, 73-); Nat Art Educr Asn; Pan African Artists Alliance; Afri-Cobra; and others. *Media:* Acrylic, Oil. *Publ:* Illusr, A People of the Sun, 73; auth, Emerging Voice of the Black Visual Artists, Black Art, 76; Art history and Black culture, 77 & Renaissance to Renaissance, 80, Minority Voices; Wanted: A role for the Black visual artists, Western J Black Studies, 82; Multiculturalism in Visual Arts Education: Are America's Educational Institutions Ready for Multiculturalism, Art, Cult & Ethnicity, 90; The Visual Arts: Obsession of Indifference and Intolerance, The Washington Review, 91. *Dealer:* Third World Press 7524 S Cottage Grove Chicago IL 60619. *Mailing Add:* Va Commonwealth Univ 325 N Harrison St Box 2519 Richmond VA 23284-2519

DE POL, JOHN
WOOD ENGRAVER, DESIGNER
b New York, NY, Sept 16, 13. *Study:* Art Students League; Sch Technol, Belfast, Northern Ireland. *Work:* Libr Cong; New York Pub Libr; Metrop Mus Art; Syracuse Univ Libr; Bucknell Univ Libr. *Comn:* Presentation prints, Woodcut Soc, 52, Miniature Print Soc, 53 & Albany Print Club, NY, 58-59. *Exhib:* One-man exhibs, Albany Print Club, Bucknell Univ, Syracuse Univ & Lycoming Col; Nat Acad Design Ann, 72. *Pos:* Free-lance art dir & design consult for var corp; illusr, Franklin Keepsake Ann Ser, ret, 81; free-lance wood engraver, 81- *Teaching:* Instr wood engraving, Bowne & Co South Street Seaport Mus, 81-83, Fairleigh Dickinson Univ, Madison, NJ, 81-83 & Univ Nebr, Omaha, 85, Mills Col, Oakland, Calif, 87. *Awards:* Albany Print Club Purchase Prize, 68; John Taylor Arms Mem Prize, Nat Acad Design, 68; Nat Arts Club Purchase Prize, 68. *Bibliog:* P K Thomajan (auth), John De Pol, wood engraver, Print Mag, 8/54; Norman Kent (auth), The wood engravings of John De Pol, 3/56 & William Caxton, Jr (auth), A new chiaroscuro wood engraving by John De Pol, Am Artist, 2/68. *Mem:* life mem Art Students League; academician Nat Acad Design; laureate, New York Printers Hall Fame, 80; hon mem Rowfant Club & The Typophiles. *Media:* Wood. *Publ:* Auth, Ireland Remembered, Fairleigh Dickinson Univ, 82; Patterns: Drawn & Engraved on Wood by John De Pol, The Yellow Barn Press, Council Bluffs, Iowa, 86; From Dark to Light, Sixty Engravings by John De Pol, The Stone House Press, Roslyn, NY; The Engraved Work of John De Pol by Renee I Weber, Matrix 6, 86; Reminiscences of a Wood Engraver, Book Club of Calif Quart Newsletter, spring 88. *Mailing Add:* 280 Spring Valley Rd Park Ridge NJ 07656

DE PUMA, RICHARD DANIEL
HISTORIAN
b DuBois, Pa, May 15, 42. *Study:* Swarthmore Col, BA(art hist), 64; Bryn Mawr Col, MA(archeol), 67, PhD(archeol), 69. *Collections Arranged:* Etruscan & Villanovan Pottery (auth, catalog), Univ Iowa Mus Art, 71; Roman Portraits (auth, catalog), Univ Iowa Mus Art, 88. *Pos:* Res assoc, Field Mus Natural Hist, Chicago, Ill, 84-; Adv bd, Am J Archaeol, 85- *Teaching:* Instr classical art, Univ Iowa, Iowa City, 68-69, from asst prof to assoc prof, 69-86, prof, 86- *Awards:* Nat Endowment Humanities Grant, 85; Getty Trust Publ Grants, 85 & 86; Dr M Aylwin Cotton Found Award, 85; Am Inst Indian Studies, 87. *Mem:* Archeol Inst Am; Col Art Asn; Soc Promotion Roman Studies. *Res:* Etruscan pottery & bronzes; Greek vase painting; mosaics. *Publ:* Auth, A Prenestine Mirror with Telephos and Orestes, Romische Mitteil, 80; Etruscan Tomb-Groups: Ancient Pottery and Bronzes in Chicago's Field Museum of Natural Hist, Mainz, 86; Corpus Speculorum Etruscorum, USA 1: Midwestern Collections, Ames, 86; Co-ed, Rome and India: The Ancient Sea Trade, Madison, 91. *Mailing Add:* 409 Hutchinson Ave Iowa City IA 52240

DERBY, MARK
CERAMIST
b E Lansing, Mich, Jan 1, 60. *Study:* Calif State Univ, Long Beach, BFA, 84 & MFA, 89. *Work:* Mus Ceramic Art Alfred, NY State Col Ceramics; San Angelo Mus Art, Tex; Nora Eccles Harrison Mus Art, Utah State Univ, Logan. *Exhib:* American Ceramics Now, Everson Mus Art, Syracuse, NY, 87; Monarch Tile Ceramic National, San Angelo Mus Art, Tex, 89; Whimsy, Clay Studio, Philadelphia, Pa, 90; Chicago INternational New Art Forms Exposition, Navy Pier, Lill St Gallery, 91 & 92; NCECA Clay National, Ariz State Univ Mus Art, Tempe, 91; Seventh Ann San Angelo Ceramic Nat, San Angelo Mus Fine Arts, 92. *Awards:* Outstanding Thesis Proj Award, Sch Fine Arts, Calif State Univ, Long Beach, 89; Individual Fel, Nat Endowment Arts, 90; Individual Fel, Ariz Comn Arts, 91. *Bibliog:* Jimmy Clark (auth), Whimsical Clay, Ceramics: Art & Perception, issue 5, 91; Harriet Brisson (auth), NCECA Clay National 1991, NCECA J, 91-92; Keely Coghlan (auth), Quiet Symmetry Speaks Volumes in Ceramics, San Angelo Standard Times, 4/17/92. *Mailing Add:* PO Box 3434 Eugene OR 97403

DERGALIS, GEORGE
PAINTER, SCULPTOR
b Athens, Greece, Aug 31, 28; US citizen. *Study:* Painting with DeChirico & Morandi, 48-50; Accad Belle Arti, Rome, MA, 51; Sch Mus Fine Arts, Boston, dipl, 58. *Work:* De Cordova Mus, Mass; Camara de Comercio & Museo de Arte, Medellin, Colombia; and others. *Comn:* Nine watercolors, Boston, 78 & mural, Norwood, 78, Neworld Bank; sculpture, Ames residence, Brookline, 81; portrait, Worcester Acad, 88; portrait, Adam Reimer, 89. *Exhib:* Galesburg Civic Art Ctr, 85; Boston Pub Libr, 88; Danforth Mus, 88-90;; Through the Looking Glass traveling show, 89-90; Fantasy, Boston Pub Libr, 92; and others. *Pos:* Artist-in-residence, Partners of the Americas, 79; master, Copley Soc Boston, 81. *Teaching:* Instr painting, De Cordova Mus, 61-; art instr, Sch Mus Fine Arts, Boston, 61-70; pvt art classes, Wayland, Mass, 69- *Awards:* Gold Medal, Accad Italia delle Arti e del Lavoro, 80; Merit Award, Throught the Looking Glass, Mus Fine Arts, Boston, 89. *Mem:* Int Sculpture Ctr, DeCordova Mus. *Media:* All. *Publ:* Combat Art of the Viet Nam War, McFarland & Co, 86; It's All in your Head, B B & K Communs, 91. *Mailing Add:* 72 Oxbow Rd Wayland MA 01778

DE RICCO, HANK
SCULPTOR, ENVIRONMENTAL ARTIST
Jersey City, NJ, May 28, 46. *Study:* William Paterson Col, 65-67; Pratt Inst, Brooklyn, NY, 67-69; Empire State Col, State Univ NY, BFA, 80. *Comn:* Site sculptures, Morris Mus, Morristown, NJ, 81, East Hampton Ctr, NY, 84, San Francisco State Univ, 87 & Univ Calif, Bakersfield, 88. *Pos:* Sculptor, Rockland CETA Arts Prog, 78-79. *Awards:* Louis Comfort Tiffany Grant, 82; CAPS Grant, 83; Pollock-Krasner Found Grant, 87. *Bibliog:* Vivien Raynor (auth), Art as anything but itself, New York Times, 7/5/81; Alan Wallach (auth), CAPS Sculptors, Arts Mag, 12/83; Phyliss Braff (auth), Sculpture inspired by site, New York Times, 5/12/85. *Mem:* Artists Equity Asn. *Dealer:* 55 Mercer Street Gallery 55 Mercer St New York NY 10013. *Mailing Add:* 68 Bergen St Brooklyn NY 11201

DERN, F CARL
SCULPTOR
b Salt Lake City, Utah, Apr 24, 36. *Study:* San Francisco Art Inst, with Richard Shaw & Fletcher Benton, 69; Univ Calif, Berkeley, with Robert Hudson & James Melchert, 71-72. *Work:* In many pvt collections. *Exhib:* San Francisco Art Inst Centennial Exhib, de Young Mus, 70; New Mus Mod Art, Oakland, 70-73; 1st & 2nd Soap Box Derby, San Francisco Mus Mod Art, 75 & 78; San Jose Mus Art, 78; Syntax Corp Outdoor Sculpture Exhib, 79-80; San Mateo Arts Coun, Proarts Gallery, Oakland, 80; Richmond Art Ctr, 81; and others. *Teaching:* Lectr sculpture, Univ Calif, Berkeley, 75 & Univ Calif, Davis, 83; lectr art, Sonoma State Univ, 77 & 78. *Awards:* Anne Bremer Prize in Art, Univ Calif, Berkeley, 69 & 72; First Prize, 1st Int Contemp, Jon Morehead Gallery, Chico, Calif, 71; Hand Hallow Found Fel, 82 & 83. *Mem:* Artists Equity. *Mailing Add:* c/o San Francisco Mus of Mod Art Rental Gallery Bldg A Ft Mason CA 94123

DERNOVICH, DONALD FREDERICK
PAINTER, EDUCATOR
b Rock Springs, Wyo, April 9, 42. *Study:* Univ Wyo, BA(art educ), 66, MA(art), 67; Ft Hays State Univ, MFA(painting), 83. *Work:* Birger Sandzen Mem Gallery, Lindsborg, Kans; Halseth Co Community Arts Ctr, Rock Springs, Wyo; Wayne State Col, Wayne, Nebr; Farmer's State Bank & Trust Co, Hays, Kans; Mus Nebr Art, Kearney. *Comn:* Two watercolors, Law Enforcement Acad, Douglas, Wyo, 85; painting, Chadron St Col, Chadron, Nebr. *Exhib:* Audubon Artists 38th Ann, Nat Arts Club, New York, 80; Rocky Mountain Nat Watermedia Exhib, Foothills Arts Ctr, Golden, Colo, 80 & 82; Kans Three Art Exhib, Mulvane Art Ctr, Washburn Univ, Kans, 83; Nat Watercolor Soc 64th Ann Brea Civic Cult Ctr, Brea, Calif, 84; Watercolor West Ann Juried XVI, Riverside Arts Ctr, Redlands, Calif, 84; Watercolor USA, Springfield Art Mus, Springfield, Mo, 89. *Pos:* Dir, McCook Area Arts Coun, 75-78; Exhib bd, Asn Nebr Arts Clubs, 86-90. *Teaching:* Art dir & instr, McCook Community Col, Nebr, 75- *Awards:* Best of Show, 80, Five State North Platte Valley Art Guild, 82 & Rock Springs Nat, Halseth Co Community Arts Ctr, 83; Purchase Awards, Prairie Lights Arts Showcase, Mus Nebr Art, 89. *Mem:* Asn Am Watercolor Soc; life mem McCook Art Guild; Nat Watercolor Soc; and others. *Media:* Watercolor, Oil. *Publ:* Watercolor Page, Am Artist Mag, 10/92. *Mailing Add:* Box 163 210 Taylor Culbertson NE 69024

DEROSA, MICHAEL LOUIS
PAINTER
b Bartlesville, Okla, July 6, 65. *Study:* Okla State Univ, BA, 87; Ill State Univ, MS 89, MFA, 92. *Work:* Ill State Univ, Bone Student Ctr; Amoco CCorp; Price Waterhouse. *Comn:* Amoco Corp; painting, comn by Danell Dovoark; painting, comn by Alfonsa & Jean Lirani. *Exhib:* solo exhibs, Ill State Univ, 89 & 92, Up Front Gallery, 89, Peoria Art Guild, 90; New Horizons, North Shore Art League, 90; Quincy's 40th Ilmoian Art Show, 90; Up Front Gallery, 91. *Pos:* Asst, Universal Ltd Art Eds, West Islip, Long Island, NY; studio asst for artists Jasper Johns, Susan Rothenburg, Terry Winters & Bill Jenson. *Teaching:* Teaching asst drawing I, Ill State Univ. *Media:* Charcoal on paper, Oil on canvas. *Mailing Add:* NW Art Associates 1109 W Main Collinsville OK 74021

DEROUX, DANIEL EDWARD
PAINTER, SCULPTOR
b Juneau, Alaska, Oct 25, 51. *Study:* NS Col Art & Design, Halifax, Can, 74-75. *Comn:* Drawing, Juneau Centennial Comn, Alaska, 79. *Exhib:* San Francisco Mus Mod Art, 79-80; 15th Ann Nat Small Sculpture & Drawing Exhib, Corpus Christi, Tex, 81; Collage & Assemblage, traveling exhib, 81-82; Los Angeles Int Art Competition, 88; NY Int Art Competition, 88; and others. *Pos:* Cur visual arts, Alaska State Mus, 78-79. *Awards:* Best of Show, Calgene W Coast Art Competition, Davis, 84; Third Place, NY Int Art Competition, 88; and others. *Bibliog:* Margaret Firmin (auth), Only painting what he sees, Alaska Advocate, 2/79; art ed (auth), Whimsical images are his delight, Anchorage Times, 2/79; Marianna Woodward (auth), Dan DeRoux Juneau buckaroo, Alaska J, 1/80. *Mailing Add:* c/o Stonington Gallery 415 F St Anchorage AK 99501

DERRICKSON, STEVE BRUCE
SCULPTOR
b Baltimore, Md, March 21, 52. *Study:* Ohio Univ, BFA, 74; Tyler Sch Art, Temple Univ, MFA, 77. *Work:* Bank of Am; Principal Financial Group; Univ

NC; Security Pac Bank. *Exhib:* 500 Expos Gallery, Dallas, Tex, 81 & White Columns, New York City, Sept, 85; Off the Wall: Environments & Installation, San Antonio Mus Art, 81; Commissioner Works, Huntington Art Galleries, Univ Tex, Tex Sculpture Symposium, Austin, Tex, 83; New Works, Laguna Gloria Art Mus, Austin, Tex, 83; Three Artists, Soho Ctr Arts, New York, 86; Selections 33, Drawing Ctr, New York, 86; Cinemaobject, City Gallery, Dept Cult Affairs, New York, 86; Movietone Muse, New York, 87; A Romantic Distance, Jeffrey Neale Gallery, New York, 88; Text Is Not Explained, Stux Gallery, Boston, Mass, 88; solo exhib, Stephen Wirtz Gallery, San Francisco, 89; Sue Spaid Fine Art, Los Angeles, Calif, 90; cur, Insect Politics, Body Horror, Social Order, Hallwalls, Buffalo, NY, 90; Invitational, Berland/Hall Gallery, New York. *Teaching:* Instr, art, Univ Tex, Austin, 77-80; asst prof art, Univ Tex, Austin, 80-84; vis artist, Ohio State Univ, Columbus, Ohio, 87. *Awards:* Hon Mention, Small Works, New York Univ, 80; Purchase Award, Appalachian Nat Drawing Competition, 79; Univ Res Inst Special Grant, Univ Tex, 80; Installation for Text Sculpture Symp, Tex Comm Arts, Austin, 83; Fel, Nat Endowment Arts, 87-88; Residency, MacDowell Colony, Petersborough, NH, 91. *Bibliog:* Dan Cameron (auth), Ten to Watch, Arts Mag, 9/86; Eleanor Heartney (auth), Art & the Electronic Fishbowl, Art News, 12/86; Kate Linker (auth), Review of Cinemaobject, Artforum, 12/86; Robert Mahoney (auth), Review of a Romantic Distance, Arts Mag, 5/88. *Mailing Add:* 247 Water St Brooklyn NY 11201

DE SANTO, STEPHEN C
PAINTER
b Louisville, Ky, May 27, 51. *Study:* Huntington Col, BA(art), 74; Ball State Univ, MA(art), 78. *Work:* Wichita Art Mus, Kans; Anderson Fine Arts Ctr, Ind. *Exhib:* Mid-Year Show, Butler Inst Am Art, Youngstown, Ohio, 80-82; Am Watercolor Soc Traveling Exhib, 10 museums across the US, 80, 82 & 85; 157th Ann Exhib, Nat Acad Design, New York, 82; Navy Pier Int Art Expo, Chicago, 85-88. *Pos:* Full-time Fine Artist for 12 yrs. *Awards:* Ed Whitney Award, 80 & High Winds Award, 85, Am Watercolor Soc Ann Exhib; Merit Award, Watercolor USA Ann, 85. *Bibliog:* Don Walker (auth), The dignity of photorealism, Artists Mag, 3/84; Greg Albert (auth), Splash-America's Best Contemporary Watercolors, North Light Books, 90. *Media:* Acrylic, Mixed Media. *Mailing Add:* 1325 Kensington Blvd Ft Wayne IN 46805

DESCHAMPS, FRANCOIS
PHOTOGRAPHER
b Nov 18, 46. *Study:* Sorbonne, Paris, 64-65; Univ Ill, Champaign, BS (phi beta kappa), MS, ABD (mathematics), 65-70; Ill Inst Technol, Inst Degisn, MS (photog), 72. *Work:* Mus Contemp Art, Chicago; Metropolitan Mus; Houston Mus Fine Arts; Mus Mod Art, New York; Brooklyn Mus. *Teaching:* Aegean Sch Fine Arts, Paros, Greece, 73; Bradley Univ, Peoria, Ill, 72-80; teacher & dir Photog Option, State Univ NY at New Paltz, 80- *Awards:* Nat Endowment for Arts, Photog Fel, 83 & 87; Friends of Imogene Cunningham Award, 84; Residency at Visual Studies Workshop, Rochester, 86; Sponsored Proj Grant, NY Coun Arts, for publ of The Return of the Slapstick Papyrus; Photgr's Fel, NY Found Arts, 88. *Publ:* Auth, Life in a Book, USW Press, 86; coauth, Particle Theory, Nexus Press, 91. *Mailing Add:* 120 Harsbrouck Rd New Paltz NY 12561

DESIDERIO, VINCENT
PAINTER
b Philadelphia, Pa, 1955. *Study:* Haverford Col, BA(Fine Arts/Art History), 77, Acad di Belle Arti, Florence, Italy, 77-78, Pa Acad Fine Arts, cert, 79-83. *Work:* Sammlung Ludwig Neve Galerie, Aachen, WGer; Denver Art Mus; Everson Mus, Syracuse, NY; Metrop Mus Art, New York. *Exhib:* Solo exhibs, Lawrence Oliver Gallery, Philadelphia, 86, Lang & O'Hara Gallery, New York, 87, 89 & 90, Greenville Mus, SC, 88, Metro Ctr for Arts, Denver, Colo, 91 & Marlborough Gallery, New York, 93; Morality Tales: Hist Painting in the 1980s, travelling exhib to Grey Art Gallery, NY Univ, 87; Visions/ Revisions, Marlborough Gallery, New York, 88; Kunst der Letzten 10 Jahre, Mus Moderner Kunst, Vienna, 89; Polyptyques et Paravents un Siecle de Creation 1890-1990, Galerie Bellier, Paris, 90; American Art Today: The City, The Art Museum, Florida Int Univ, 90; Runkel-Hue-Williams Ltd, London, 90; In the Looking Glass: Contemporary Narrative Painting, Mint Mus Art, Charlotte, NC, 91. *Awards:* Awarded Studio, Inst for Art & Urban Resources, PS 1, 84 & 85; Pollock/Krasner Found Grant, 87; Fel, Nat Endowment Arts, 87. *Bibliog:* Steven Rosen (auth), Modern 'History Painter' depicts grim views of life, Denver Post, 2/15/91; Carol Dickinson (auth), Touched by Desiderio's Allegorical Largess, Rocky Mountain News, 2/24/91; Ken Johnson, (auth) Reviews: Vincent Desiderio at Lang & O'Hara, Art Am, 3/91. *Media:* Oils. *Mailing Add:* c/o Lang & O'Hara Gallery 568 Broadway New York NY 10012

DESIND, PHILIP
DEALER, COLLECTOR
b New York, NY, Feb 28, 10. *Study:* City Col New York, BS, 34, MS, 38; Columbia Univ, currently. *Pos:* Dir, Capricorn Galleries, Bethesda, Md, 64- *Teaching:* Instr, Cath Univ & Univ Md, formerly; adj prof, Am Univ, Washington, DC, currently. *Specialty:* Contemporary American realism. *Publ:* Auth, Jewish and Russian Revolutionaries Exiled to Siberia. *Mailing Add:* 4849 Rugby Ave Bethesda MD 20814

DESJARLAIT, ROBERT D
PAINTER, ILLUSTRATOR
b Red Lake Chippewa Reservation, Redlake, Minn, Nov, 18, 46. *Study:* Self taught. *Work:* NDak Mus Art, Grand Forks; Meridel Le Sueur Libr, Augsburg Col, Minneapolis. *Comn:* Murals, Red Lake High Sch, Red Lake, Minn, 88; illus, 88-89 & murals, 91, Minn Indian Women's Resource Ctr, Minneapolis; illus, Anoka-Hennepin Am Indian Lang & Cult Prog, 89-90; mural, Saturn Sch Tomorrow, St Paul, 92. *Exhib:* Homecomings, NDak Mus Art, Grand Forks, 85; Minn Chippewa Art Exhib, Am Indian Community House Gallery,New York, 86; In Defense of Sacred Lands, Harcus Gallery, Boston, Mass, 87; Pictures from Home: Minnesota Illustrators of Children's Books, Univ Art Mus, Minneapolis, 88; Metaphorical Fish, Univ Art Mus, Minneapolis, 90. *Pos:* Art dir/curric specialist, Northern Winds Arts Educ Proj, Minneapolis, 92- *Teaching:* Art instr, Am Indian Art Hist & Drawing, Heart of the Earth Survival Sch, Minneapolis, 89-90. *Awards:* First Place, Drawing, Ojibwe Art Expo, Minneapolis, 88; Percy Fearing Award for Illus, Minn Coun Teaching of Foreign Lang, Minneapolis, 88. *Bibliog:* John Boler (auth), Understanding American Indian art, Art Bus News, 87; Kathy Thornes (auth), DesJarlait depicts Ojibwe vision, Red Lake Times, 87; Interview with Robert DesJarlait (video), Northern Lights & Insights, Hennepin Co Libr, Minneapolis, 92. *Mem:* Native Cult Arts Prog/Native Arts Circle. *Media:* Acrylic, Graphite Pencil. *Publ:* Auth & illusr, O-do-i-daym Ojibway: Clans of the Ojibway, 89 & illusr, The Spirit Within, 92, Minn Indian Women's Resource Ctr Press, Minneapolis; illusr, The First American Series, 88-90, auth, & illusr, Ni-mi-win: A History of Ojibway Dance, 90 & illusr, Traditional Indian Stories, 92, Anoka-Hennepin Press, Coon Rapids. *Dealer:* Art Lending Gallery 2500 Groveland Terr Minneapolis MN. *Mailing Add:* 5901 Rhode Island Ave N Crystal MN 55428

DESMARAIS, CHARLES JOSEPH
MUSEUM DIRECTOR, WRITER
b New York, NY, Apr 21, 49. *Study:* Western Conn State Col, 67-71; State Univ NY, Buffalo, BS, 75, MS, 77; Mus Mgt Inst, cert, 83. *Exhib:* Retrospective, Laguna Art Mus, Laguna Beach, Calif, 93. *Collections Arranged:* The Portrait Extended (auth, catalog), Mus Contemp Art, Chicago, 80; Mark Berghash: Jews and Germans: (auth, catalog), Calif Mus of Photog, 84, Why I Got into TV & Other Stories: The Art of Ilene Segalove, Laguna Art Mus, 90. *Pos:* Asst ed, Afterimage, Rochester, NY, 75-77; ed, Exposure: Quart J Soc Photog Educ, 77-81; dir, Chicago Ctr Contemp Photog, Columbia Col, 77-79; dir, Calif Mus Photog, Univ Calif, Riverside, 81-88; art columnist, Riverside (CA) Press-Enterprise, 87-88; dir, Laguna Art Mus, Laguna Beach, Calif, 88- *Awards:* Art Critics Fel, Nat Endowment Arts, 79. *Bibliog:* interview, Museum dreams of future, Los Angeles Times, 7/5/81; New director focuses in on Laguna Art Mus, Orange County Register, 7/3/88; Mus chief hopes to erase narrow image, 7/10/88 & Laguna Mus job takes a good listener, (interview), 11/5/89, LA Times. *Mem:* Soc Photog Educ (bd dir, 79-83); Col Art Asn; Am Asn Mus; Asn Art Mus Dir; Orange Co Arts Coun (chmn, 89-91). *Res:* Contemporary art and architecture, media arts (photography, film, video). *Publ:* Auth, Roger Mertin: Records 1976-78, 78 & Michael Bishop, 79, Columbia Col, Chicago; On Art (bi-weekly column), Riverside Press-Enterprise, Calif, 87-88; The Seventies, in: Decade by Decade (James Enveart, ed), Little, Brown, 89; Why I Got into TV & Other Stories: The Art of Irene Segalove, 90. *Mailing Add:* Laguna Art Mus 307 Cliff Dr Laguna Beach CA 92651

DE SMET, LORRAINE
PAINTER
b Passaic, NJ, May 5, 28. *Study:* Art Students League, study with Issac Soyer, Harvey Dinnerstein, David Leffel, Hillary Holmes, Ted S Jacobs, 79-84; Montclair Art Mus, 86. *Work:* US Coast Guard Collection; Union Trust, Stamford, Conn. *Exhib:* Salmagundi Non-Members, Salmagundi Club, New York, 87; Focus on Art, NJ, 88, 89 & 90; Vet Foreign Wars-COGAP, Chicago Hilton Hotel, Ill, 88; Ridgewood Art Inst, 89-90; Caldwell Col, 90 & 91; and others. *Awards:* Solo Show Award, Pen & Brush, New York, 84; First Place, Livingston Art Asn, 87 & 88; Slottman Award, Pen & Brush, 87. *Bibliog:* Joseph Merkel (auth), article, Artspeak, 84; Will Grant (auth), article, Artspeak, 87; Howard Farber (auth), Artspeak, 90. *Mem:* Pen & Brush Club (bd dirs, 85-92, brush chmn, 87-89, vpres, 89-92); US Coast Guard Art Prog; Art Students League NY; Am Artists Prof League; West Essex Art Asn (bd gov, 92-). *Media:* Oil. *Mailing Add:* 33 Campbell Rd Fairfield NJ 07004

DESMETT, DON
CURATOR, GALLERY DIRECTOR
b Philipsburg, Pa, May 20, 54. *Study:* Univ Mass, Amherst, MFA, 84. *Collections Arranged:* Power Struggle Exhib (catalog), Spaces Gallery, 90; Jerry Kearns: Deep Cover (auth, catalog), Tyler Sch Art, 91; The Price of Power, (auth, catalog), Cleveland Ctr Contemp Art, 91; Michele Blondel, Tyler Sch Art, 92. *Pos:* Dir, Tyler Galleries, Tyler Sch Art, 90- *Teaching:* Instr Mus Studies, Tyler Sch Art, currently. *Mailing Add:* Temple University, Tyler School of Art, Temple Gallery 1619 Walnut St Philadelphia PA 19103

DESMIDT, THOMAS H
PAINTER, EDUCATOR
b Sheboygan, Wis, Sept 6, 44. *Study:* Lincoln Col, AA; Layton Sch Art, BFA; Syracuse Univ, MFA. *Work:* Milwaukee Art Inst, Wis; Francis & Sidney Lewis Collection Contemp Art; F&M Corp, Richmond, Va; Miller Brewing Co, Milwaukee, Wis; Everson Mus Art, Syracuse; and others. *Exhib:* Solo exhibs, Mem Art Gallery, Univ Rochester, 72, Everson Mus, 73 & Va Mus Fine Arts, 78; James Yu Gallery, New York, 73 & 74; 19th Corcoran Biennial, Washington, DC, 74; Va Artists, Va Mus, Richmond, 77. *Teaching:* Instr painting, Va Commonwealth Univ, 70-73, dir, Art Found, 73-76, asst prof art, 73-, asst dean, 76- *Awards:* One-Man Exhib Award, Rochester Mem Gallery, 70; Fac Res Grant, Va Commonwealth Univ, 73. *Media:* Canvas, Acrylic. *Dealer:* OK Harris Works of Art 383 W Broadway New York NY 10013; James Yu Gallery 393 W Broadway New York NY 10012. *Mailing Add:* c/o Aaron Gallery 1717 Connecticut Ave NW Washington DC 20009

DESOTO, LEWIS D
CONCEPTUAL ARTIST, EDUCATOR
b San Bernardino, Calif, Jan 3, 54. *Study:* Univ Calif, Riverside, BA, 78; Claremont Grad Sch, Calif, MFA, 81. *Work:* Los Angeles Co Mus Art, Calif; San Jose Mus Art; Mus Modern Art, New York; Video Art Collection, Long Beach Mus Art, Calif; Bank Am, Los Angeles. *Comn:* Sculpture, Nine-one-one, Seattle, 87; photomural, San Francisco State Univ, 88 & 89; sculpture, Phoenix Art Comn, 90 & 91. *Exhib:* One-man show, Los Angeles Munic Gallery, Calif, 85, Intersection for the Arts, San Francisco, 87, Maryhill Mus Art, Goldendale, Wash, Headlands Ctr Arts, 90, Univ Art Mus, Berkeley, 91, Artists Space, New York, 91, Pétúkmiyat Pé Túkmiyat, San Jose Mus Art, 91; Photographic Memory, Seattle Art Mus, 88; Waterworks, Long Beach Mus, 90; Biennial 1, Calif Mus Photo, Riverside, 90; The Spatial Drwe, New Mus Contemp Art, New York, 92. *Teaching:* Instr photogr, Otis Art Inst, Parsons Sch Design, Los Angeles, Calif, 83-85; chmn, Art Dept, Cornish Col Arts, Seattle, Wash, 85-88; assoc prof, Art Dept, San Francisco State Univ, 88. *Awards:* Solo Exhib Award, Orange Co Ctr Contemp Art, 84; Affirmative Action Award, San Francisco State Univ, 89 & 90 & Meritorious Prof promise & achievement, 90; Fel in Installation, Calif Arts Coun, 92. *Bibliog:* David Pagel (auth), Myth Modernized, LA Times, 10/3/91; Rebecca Solnit (auth), Living Places, Art Space, 92; Jean Fisher (auth), Fragments of a Fictional Body/Lewis Desoto, Turning the Map (UK), 92. *Mem:* San Francisco Cameraworks (bd mem); Yerba Buena Ctr Arts (bd mem). *Media:* Installation Artist, Sculpture. *Publ:* Auth, Moving Toward Future Skills, Artweek, 5/84; Tahualtapa project, 9-1-1 Seattle, 5/86; Líaypatak, Witness, Kansatsusha, San Francisco Arts Comn, 90; coauth (with Rebecca Solnit), Kingdoms, 92. *Dealer:* Christopher Grimes Gallery 1644 17th St Santa Monica CA 90404. *Mailing Add:* 96 Panorama Dr San Francisco CA 94131

DESOTO, RAFAEL M
PAINTER, ILLUSTRATOR
b Aguadilla, PR. *Study:* Columbia Univ, 25; Pratt Inst, 33; Art Students League, 35-37; also with G Bridgeman, E Dickerson & I Soyer. *Work:* Bishop Mus, Bradenton, Fla; State Capitol Fla, Tallahassee; Mus Fine Arts, San Juan; State Univ NY, Greenly Mem Gallery, Farmingdale. *Comn:* Mural (fresco painted), Lens of Life, Westchester Med Ctr, NY, 38; mural, New World, Knights of Columbus Hall, Patchogue, NY, 66; monument, Lady of the Island (with Rock of Ages, Barry, Vt), comn by Montfort Fathers, Manorville, NY, 75. *Exhib:* Nat Soc Painters in Casein & Acrylic, Nat Arts Club, Gramercy Park, NY, 72; Am Artists Prof League, Lever House Bldg, New York, 72-74; solo exhibs, Ponce Mus Art, PR & San Juan Inst Cult, Mus Fine Arts, PR, 74; Lincoln Ctr for Performing Arts, Avery Fisher Hall, 75-79; and others. *Pos:* Illusr, various mag, pocket books, 33-60; asst art dir, Pop Publ Inc, 37. *Teaching:* Pvt instr, 58-; assoc prof art & design, State Univ NY Col Farmingdale, 62-82, prof emer, 82- *Awards:* Nat Poster Art Alliance Award, NY State Armory, 25; Great Seal State Fla, Former Gov Haydon Burns, 65; Emily Griffin Award, Nat Arts Club, 72; Second Place, Statewide Portrait Inst Compos; Fourth Place, Cert Merit, Int Portrait Seminar Competition. *Mem:* Am Artists Prof League; Nat Arts Club; South Bay Art Asn. *Media:* Multimedia. *Mailing Add:* PO Box 564 Bellport NY 11713-0530

DESPORTES, ULYSSE GANDVIER
PAINTER, HISTORIAN
b Winnsboro, SC, Apr 12, 20. *Study:* Richmond Prof Inst, Col William & Mary, with Julien Binford, Marion Junkin & Theresa Pollack, BFA; Ecole Normale Superior Beaux-Arts, Paris, France, with Maurice Brianchon; Inst Art & Archeol, Univ Paris, with Pierre Lavedan & Andre Chastel. *Work:* Va Mus Fine Arts, Richmond; Washington & Lee Univ, Lexington, Va; Va Commonwealth Univ, Richmond. *Exhib:* Va Artists 1961 & Va Artists 1963, Va Mus Fine Arts; SC Artists, Gibbs Art Mus, Charleston, 62. *Pos:* Dir catalogues, Kende Galleries, New York, 46-48; dir, Florence Mus, SC, 57. *Teaching:* Asst prof art hist & painting, Hollins Col, 57-62; prof art & chmn dept, Mary Baldwin Col, 62- *Awards:* Second Prize, SC Artists Asn, 62; Cert of Merit, Va Mus Fine Arts, 63. *Media:* Oil. *Res:* Neoclassic art; sculptor Guiseppe Ceracchi; painter Louis David. *Publ:* Contribr, Bulletin Mus Bernadotte, 62; Princeton Libr Chronicle, 62; Art Quart, 63 & 64; Antiques Mag, 69. *Mailing Add:* 322 N New St Staunton VA 24401

DESSER, MAXWELL MILTON
PAINTER, DESIGNER
b New York, NY. *Study:* Queens Col, with Barse Miller; Pratt Inst; Cooper Union. *Work:* Sun Oil Co, Radnor, Pa; Brooklyn Jewish Hosp, NY; Nat Acad Design; pvt collections. *Exhib:* Am Watercolor Soc Show, Nat Acad Design, New York, 68-81, Allied Artists of Am Exhib, 73-81 & Nat Acad Design Exhib, 76-81; Knickerbocker Artists Exhib, Nat Arts Club, New York, 75-81; Am Watercolor Soc Exchange with Mus in Australia, 76; Nat Soc Painters in Casein & Acrylic, Am Acad & Inst Arts & Lett, New York, 79; Salmagundi Club Mus Exhib, New York, 79-81. *Pos:* Free-lance filmstrip producer, McGraw-Hill Bk Co, New York, 55-; free-lance art dir, Dun & Bradstreet, New York, 55- & Pace Univ,. *Awards:* Silver Medal of Honor, Am Watercolor Soc, 75; Silver Medals of Honor, Allied Artists of Am, 76 & Audubon Artists, 79; Gold Medal of Honor, Knickerbocker Artists, 87; Gold Medal of Honor, Allied Artists of Am, 89; Certif of Merit, Nat Acad Design, 90. *Mem:* Am Watercolor Soc; Allied Artists Am; Audubon Artists (dir, 75-78 & 80); Nat Soc Painters in Casein & Acrylic; Salmagundi Club; Assoc Nat Acad; and others. *Media:* Acrylic, Watercolor. *Mailing Add:* 85-28 168th Pl Jamaica NY 11432

DESSNER, MURRAY
PAINTER
b Philadelphia, Pa, Nov 11, 34. *Study:* Pa Acad Fine Arts, William Emlen Cresson Traveling Scholar, 65 & J Henry Schiedt Traveling Scholar, 66; also with Franklin C Watkins & Hobson Pittman. *Work:* Pa Acad Fine; Pittman Collection, Bryn Mawr Col, Pa; Pa Fed Collection; Cornell Fine Arts Ctr Mus; Philadelphia Mus Art. *Exhib:* One-man shows, Peale Galleries, Pa Acad Fine Arts, 70, Marion Locks Gallery, Philadelphia, 72, 75, 78 & 84, Barbara Gillman Gallery, Miami, 83, Vorpal Gallery, New York, 84 & 86 & Levy Gallery, Philadelphia, 91. *Teaching:* Instr painting, Pa Acad Fine Arts. *Awards:* Philadelphia Mus Art Purchase Prize, Cheltenham Art Ctr, 69; Pa Acad Fine Art Purchase Prize, Philadelphia, 91. *Bibliog:* Two Philadelphians, Time Mag, 69; article, Art News, 69. *Media:* Acrylic. *Dealer:* Vorpal Gallery W Broadway New York NY. *Mailing Add:* 802 Sansom St Philadelphia PA 19107

DETMERS, WILLIAM RAYMOND
PRINTMAKER, EDUCATOR
b Pontiac, Mich, June 20, 42. *Study:* Miami Univ, Ohio, BFA, 64, MEduc, 68; Cranbrook Acad Art, MFA, 70; Univ Cincinnati, EdD, 78. *Work:* Miami Univ, Oxford, Ohio; Univ Southern Colo, Pueblo; Herron Sch Art, Indianapolis; Univ Hawaii, Manoa; Culver-Stockton Col, Canton, Mo; and others. *Comn:* Drawings, Methodist Church, Fredericktown, Ohio; drawings, Methodist Church, Canton, Mo; and others. *Exhib:* Ann Midyear Show, Butler Inst Am Art, Youngstown, Ohio, 64; one-man shows, Bd Room, Nova Scotia Col Art & Design, 70, Gallery, Southern Colo State Col, Pueblo, 73, Litho Constructs, Matrix Gallery, Ind Univ, Bloomington, 79, Mabee Foundation Gallery, Culver-Stockton Col, 91 & Keokul Art Ctr, Iowa, 92; Wakonda Art Guild Group Shows, Mo, 88-92; Juried Exhib, Novinger, Mo, 89 & 90; Hannibal Arts Club, Mo, 90-92; Quad States Art Exhib, Quincy, Ill, 91-92; Images 92, Highland CC, Kans; and others. *Teaching:* Art Teacher, Preble Co Schs, Ohio, 65-68; vis instr printmaking, Nova Scotia Col Art & Design, summer 70; instr printmaking & art educ, Southern Colo State Col, 70-73; art teacher, Fredericktown, Ohio Schs, 73-74; vis lectr, Ind Univ, Bloomington, 76; prog chmn art educ, Herron Sch Art, Ind Univ-Purdue Univ, Indianapolis, 76-80; area head art educ, La State Univ, 80-85; art educ, Univ Hawaii, Manoa, 85-88; assoc prof art, Culver-Stockton Col, 88- *Awards:* Educ Improvement Fund Grant, Univ Hawaii, 86-87; Fac Devt Awards, Culver-Stockton Col, 89-92. *Bibliog:* Mildred Monteverde (auth), Art display limited to plastic and wood, Pueblo Star J, 73; Lauretta Fox (auth), Litho Constructions and other prints by Detmers, Mt Vernon News, 75. *Mem:* Nat Art Educ Asn; Mo Art Educ Asn; Wakonda Art Guild; Canton Area Arts Coun, Mo (past pres); Quincy Art Club, Ill. *Media:* Lithography, Intaglio. *Publ:* Auth, A Conceptual Model for the Planning of Curricula for the Visual Arts in Higher Education, Dissertation Abstracts Int, 79; A Conceptual Model for Curriculum Planning and Evaluating in Visual Arts, Studies in Art Educ, 80; AV Reviews, Sch Arts, Davis Publ; Red Line Group Recommendations, Teachers Arts, La State Univ, 85; coauth (with K Marantz), The liberal education component of art teacher education: a response, Visual Arts Res, spring, 88. *Mailing Add:* Dept Art Educ c/o Culver Stockton Univ Canton MO 63435

DE TURCZYNOWICZ, WANDA (MRS ELIOT HERMANN)
PAINTER
b Krakow, Poland, June 16, 08; US citizen. *Study:* Study with Earl of Tankerville, Northumberland, Britain; with Hetherington, La Jolla, Calif; Ont Col Art, Toronto, with Beach. *Work:* Art Mus Juarez; Vancouver Mus Art; Victoria, BC; and many pvt collections. *Comn:* Costume designs & sets for operas, San Diego Community Chest, Calif, 25-26, Gilbert & Sullivan, La Jolla, 25-26, Toronto Univ Opera, 27-29 & Victoria Opera, 30-34. *Exhib:* Vancouver Mus Art, 30-35; Sun Carnival Shows, El Paso Mus Art, 40-60; El Paso Mus Art, 60's & 77-83; Santa Fe Bicentennial, NMex, 60's. *Pos:* Prog chmn, El Paso Art Asn, 45 & 64, vpres, 55 & 57, pres, 56; chmn, 6th Ann Sun Carnival, El Paso Mus Art, 62. *Teaching:* Pvt lessons all media, 30-; instr painting, drawing & sculpture, Boy Scouts Am, 61-83. *Awards:* Three Best of Show, 6 Firsts, Don Purchase Prize, 79, El Paso Mus Art. *Bibliog:* Hudson Bay Co news coverage, Winnipeg, Can, 33; article in Hermosa Beach Women's Club Mag, Calif, 37; rev in Western Rev, Western NMex Univ, 67. *Mem:* El Paso Arts Alliance; founder & life mem El Paso Art Asn. *Media:* Oil, Watercolor. *Mailing Add:* 4215 Santa Rita El Paso TX 79902

DEUTSCH, DAVID
PAINTER
b Los Angeles, Calif, 43. *Study:* Univ Calif, Los Angeles, AB, 66; Calif Inst Arts, 68. *Work:* Boston Mus Fine Arts, Mass; Brooklyn Mus, Mus Mod Art, Whitney Mus, New York; Los Angeles Co Mus Art, Calif; Walker Art Ctr, Minneapolis; and others. *Exhib:* New Talent, Los Angeles Co Mus Art, 70; New Acquisitions, Los Angeles Co Mus Art, 76; one-man exhibs, Annina Nosei Gallery, New York, 81 & 82, Gallery 5, Stockholm, Sweden, BlumHelman Gallery, New York, 85, 87 & 89, Massimo Audiello, New York, 87, Galerie Montenay, Paris, 88, Ezra & Cecile Zikha Gallery, Wesleyan Univ, 89 & Christine Burgin Gallery, New York, 92; Great Big Drawings, Hayden Gallery, Mass Inst Technol, Cambridge, 82; Young Talent Awards, Los Angeles Co Mus Art, 83; 2-man show, Hayden Gallery, Mass Inst Technol, Cambridge, 83; An International Survey of Recent Painting and Sculpture, Mus Mod Art, New York, 84; American Neo-Expressionists, Aldrich Mus Contemp Art, Ridgefield, Conn, 84; 50th Nat Midyear Exhib, Butler Inst Am Art, Youngstown, Ohio, 86; New Visions in Contemporary Art: the RSM Company Collection, San Francisco Mus Mod Art, 86; A Contemporary View of Nature, Aldrich Mus Contemp Art, Ridgefield, Conn, 86; Selections from Roger and Myra Davidson Collection, Art Gallery Ont,

Can, 87; The New Romantic Landscape, Whitney Mus Am Art, Stamford, Conn, 87; The New Romantic Landscape, Drawings from the Eighties, Whitney Mus Am Art, Stamford, Conn, 87; Nocturnal Visions in Contemporary Painting, Whitney Mus Am Art at Equitable Ctr, New York, 89; The Library, Josh Baer, New York, 91; Romance and Irony in Recent American Painting, Parrish Art Mus, Southampton, New York, 91; 3-man show, Blum Helman Gallery, New York, 92; Drawings, Stuart Regan Gallery, Los Angeles, 92; and others. *Bibliog:* The Library, New Yorker, 6/91; Nicholas Jenkins (auth), The Library, ARTnews, 10/91; Romance and Irony in Recent American Art, 91; and others. *Mailing Add:* 225 W 13th St New York NY 10011

DEUTSCH, RICHARD
SCULPTOR
b Los Angeles, Calif, 53. *Study:* Univ Calif, Santa Cruz, BA(art), 76. *Work:* Patrick J Lannon Foun, Los Angeles; Renwick Gallery, Smithsonian; Mill's Col, Oakland; McDonald's Corp, Chicago; Shell Oil Corp, Houston. *Comn:* Terrazza sculpture/Ocean View Park, Santa Cruz Arts Comn, Calif, 84; Marble sculpture Shelton Police Acad, Wash State Arts Comn Art in Pub Places, Shelton, 87; Terrazzo pavement medallion, San Francisco Arts Comn Pub Places, 88. *Exhib:* Renwick Gallery, Smithsonian, Washington, DC, 80; Gray Art Mus, NC, 82; Monterey Peninsula Mus Art, Calif, 82; San Jose Inst Contemp Art, Calif, 83; Art Mus Santa Cruz, Calif, 85; Jewish Community Mus, San Francisco, 87; Palo Alto Cult Ctr, Calif, 88. *Awards:* Exemplary Arts Education Residency, Calif Arts Coun, 83; Visual Artist Fel, Nat Endowment Arts, 84; Vis Sculptor, Am Acad Rome, 87. *Bibliog:* Paul Sutor (auth), Artist in the development process, Urbanland, 9/2/91; Elizabeth Broadrup (auth), Richard Deutsch: motion, Sculpture Mag, 11/12/92. *Media:* Marble. *Mailing Add:* c/o The Allrich Gallery 251 Post St San Francisco CA 94108

DEUTSCHMAN, LOUISE TOLLIVER
DEALER, CURATOR
b Taylorville, Ill, Sept 6, 21. *Study:* MacMurray Col, BA; Northwestern Univ Sch Journalism, Univ Paris. *Collections Arranged:* Seven Decades of Twentieth-Century Art From the Sidney and Harriet Janis Collection, Mus Mod Art & Sidney Janis Gallery Collection, La Jolla Mus Contemp Art & Santa Barbara Mus Art, Calif, 80. *Pos:* Assoc dir, Waddell Gallery, New York, 66-74; assoc cur, Sidney Janis Gallery, New York, 75-78 & 80-; dir, Alex Rosenberg Gallery, New York, 78-80. *Specialty:* Contemporary art; 20th century masters, American & European. *Mailing Add:* 36 E 68th St No 3B New York NY 10021

DEVINE, WILLIAM CHARLES
DEALER, COLLECTOR
b Brooklyn, NY, Aug 22, 32. *Study:* Union Col, Cranford, NJ. *Pos:* Owner, D Fine Arts Inc, Westfield, NJ, currently. *Specialty:* Eighteenth and nineteenth century paintings and bronzes; Alois LeCoque; Harry Devlin. *Collection:* Work by Alois LeCoque, Thomas Gainsborough, J R Grabach, H Gasser, Eugene Gauss, Grant Wood, Louis Lozowick, Ben Sahn, Waldo Pierce & William Palmer. *Mailing Add:* D Fine Arts Inc 133 Harrison Ave Westfield NJ 07090

DEVLIN, HARRY
PAINTER, CARTOONIST
b Jersey City, NJ, Mar 22, 18. *Study:* Syracuse Univ, BFA, 39; studied with Hans Hoffman, New York; Kean Col NJ, LHD. *Work:* Midlantic Bank; Crum & Foster; First Atlantic Bank; Corp Hq, City Fed Savings, Hillsboro, NJ, 77. *Exhib:* Am Cartoonists, Metrop Mus Art, New York, 54; Am Children's Bk Illusr, Voorhees Zimmerli Art Mus, Rutgers Univ, 76 & 90; one-man shows, Portraits of American Architecture, Morris Mus, NJ, 79, Gen Elec World Hq Gallery, Fairfield, Conn, 80, Union League Club, New York, World Hq AT&T, NJ & Schering Plough, NJ, 86. *Pos:* Trustee, Morris Mus Arts & Sci, 82- *Teaching:* Instr hist fine arts, Union Col, Cranford, NJ, 70-74, instr hist Am domestic archit, 76- *Awards:* Arents Medal for Art & Lit, Syracuse Univ, 77; Chairman's Medal, Soc Illusrs Ann Exhib, 81; Artist of the Year, Art Educators NJ, 92; and others. *Bibliog:* TV doc, Kean Forum. *Mem:* Soc Illusrs; Artists Equity; Nat Cartoonists Soc (pres, 56-57, hon chmn, 88, chmn Milton Gross Fund, 88); Dutch Treat Club; NJ Coun Arts (vice & grants chair, 70-79); Asn Artists NJ (pres, 83-85); NJ Comt Humanities, 84-; Gov Kean's Task Force on Literacy in the Arts. *Media:* Oil. *Publ:* Coauth & illusr, Old Black Witch, 63, auth & illusr, To Grandfather's House We Go: A Roadside Tour of American Homes, 67, What Kind of House Is That?, 69, coauth & illusr, Cranberry Thanksgiving, 71 & auth & illusr, Tales of Thunder & Lightning, 75, MacMillan Press. *Mailing Add:* 443 Hillside Ave Mountainside NJ 07092

DEVLIN, WENDE
PAINTER
b Buffalo, NY, Apr 27, 18. *Study:* Syracuse Univ, BFA, 40. *Work:* Midlantic Bank Collection, Edison, NJ; Central Jersey Trust Collection, Freehold, NJ. *Comn:* Portraits, Roy Forsberg & L Greisemer, Westfield, NJ, 70, Joan Topp, Conn, 72, Marion Pfalz, Summit, NJ, 82 & Elizabeth Brown, Leesburg, Va, 87. *Exhib:* One-person show, Schering Plough, Kenilworth, NJ, 86; City of Trenton Mus, Trenton, NJ, 87; Schering Plough, Madison, NJ, 88. *Awards:* Arents Award Art & Lit, Syracuse Univ, 77. *Bibliog:* Jean Turner (auth), Mother of seven writes books, Paints, Elizabeth Daily J, 8/29/68; Adele deLeeuw (auth), Devlins of Mountainside, New York Times, 6/19/77; Rita Edelman (auth), Newark Star Ledger, 6/22/88. *Mem:* Assoc Artists NJ; Woman Days Club, New York. *Media:* Acrylic, Oil. *Dealer:* Swain Gallery 703 Watchung Ave Plainfield NJ. *Mailing Add:* 443 Hillside Ave Mountainside NJ 07092

DE VORE, RICHARD E
CERAMIST
b Toledo, Ohio, 1933. *Study:* Univ Toledo, Ohio, BE, 55; Cranbrook Acad Art, Mich, MFA, 57. *Work:* Yale Univ Art Gallery, New Haven, Conn; Victoria & Albert Mus, London, Eng; Philadelphia Mus Art, Pa; Los Angeles Co Mus Art, Calif; Cleveland Mus Art, Ohio. *Exhib:* Solo exhibs, Hill Gallery, Birmingham, Mich, 87, Max Protetch Gallery, New York, 87, 89 & 91 & Greenberg Gallery, St Louis, Mo, 88; East-West Contemporary Ceramics, Seoul,Korea, 88; Ten American Ceramicists, US Embassy Exhib, Univ Hong Kong, 89; De Vore, Price, Turner, Hill Gallery, Birmingham, Mich, 90; 28th Ceramic Nat Exhib, Everson Mus Art, Syracuse, NY, 90; and others. *Awards:* Nat Endowment Arts Grant, 76, 80 & 86. *Bibliog:* Garth Clark (auth), American Potters, Watson-Guptill, New York, 81; Florence Rubenfeld (auth), Pottery of Richard De Vore, Am Craft, 83; Janet Kopolos (auth), article, Art Papers, Vol VIII, No 2, 84; Sarah Bodine & Michael Dumas (coauth), Am Ceramics, 89. *Publ:* Auth, Ceramics of Betty Woodman, Craft Horizon, 78; Color, Texture & Light, Studio Potter, 86. *Dealer:* Max Protech 560 Broadway New York NY 10012. *Mailing Add:* 1617 Sheely Dr Ft Collins CO 80526

DE WAAL, RONALD BURT
COLLECTOR, PATRON
b Salt Lake City, Utah, Oct 23, 32. *Study:* Univ Utah, BS, 55; Mexico City Col, summer 55 & 58; Univ Denver, MA, 58. *Collections Arranged:* Beethoven in the Arts, Univ Utah, 65 & Colo State Univ, 66, 67, 70, 83 & 85. *Pos:* Humanities librn & exhibs chmn, Colo State Univ, Ft Collins, 66-88. *Awards:* John H Jenkins Award for best work of bibliography published in US during 74; Colo Libr Asn Lit Award, 87. *Mem:* Beethoven Soc; Col Art Asn Am; Nat Sculpture Soc. *Collection:* Beethoven statuary and paintings; pewter, porcelain, and wood figure sculptures; Sherlock Holmes statuary, paintings and prints. *Publ:* Auth, The World Bibliography of Sherlock Holmes and Dr Watson, New York Graphic Soc, 74; Bramhall House, 77; The International Sherlock Holmes, Shoe String Press, 80; Universal Sherlock Holmes. *Mailing Add:* 638 12th Ave Salt Lake City UT 84103

DE WAN-CARLSON, ANNA
PRINTMAKER
b Dec 29, 49. *Study:* Art Inst Pittsburgh, 71; Syracuse Univ; Univ Col, Syracuse. *Work:* Carrier Corp-UTC; Print Club Albany; Onondaga Savings Bank; Onondaga Hist Asn; Maria Regina Col. *Exhib:* Print Club Albany 17th Nat Competition, NY; Space Group Korea 6th Int Miniature Print Biennial, Seoul, Korea; Ball State Ann Drawing & Small Sculpture Exhib, Muncie, Ind; Art Ctr Grand Prairie Nat Miniature Exhib, Stuttgart, Alaska; Fine Arts Inst San Bernardino Co Mus 27th Ann Exhib, Redlands, Calif. *Collections Arranged:* Proof of the Print-Syracuse Printmakers, A Retrospective Exhib, Onondag Hist Asn, Syracuse, NY, 92. *Pos:* Exhib cur, Syracuse Printmakers; contrib writer, J of the Print World, 92; guest cur, Onondaga Hist Asn, Syracuse, NY, 92. *Teaching:* Artist in residence, Marie Regina Col, 75-76. *Awards:* Best in Show-Graphics, Women's Art Gallery, New York; First Prize-Graphics, Allentown Festival Arts, Buffalo, NY; First Prize, Popular Photog Mag. *Mem:* Syracuse Printmakers (past pres); Print Club Philadelphia; Everson Mus; Print Club Rochester; Print Club Albany. *Media:* Serigraph; Miscellaneous Media. *Publ:* Proof of the Print-Syracuse Printmakers, J of the Print World: Vol 15, No 2, spring 92. *Mailing Add:* 145 Avon Rd Syracuse NY 13206

DHAEMERS, ROBERT AUGUST
SCULPTOR, EDUCATOR
b Luverne, Minn, Nov 24, 26. *Study:* Calif Col Arts & Crafts, BFA, 52, MFA, 54. *Work:* City San Francisco Art Comn, Calif; First Christ Lutheran Church, Burlingame, Calif; San Jose State Col; Mills Col, Oakland, Calif; St Catherine Indian Sch, Santa Fe, NMex. *Comn:* Wrought iron wall mural, Jerry's Restaurant, San Leandro, Calif, 60; sculpture crucifix, First Christ Lutheran Church, 61; fountain, Frank Hunt Archit, Oakland, Calif, 63; Sundial Cor-Ten (steel 2 ton), Sci Complex, Mills Col, 70; bronze tabernacle, Holy Cross Hosp, San Fernando, Calif, 77. *Exhib:* Am Fedn Arts Traveling Exhib of New Talent, 59; San Francisco Art Comn, Calif Palace Legion, 61; M H DeYoung Mus, San Francisco, 62; Columbia Univ, 64; Mus Contemp Crafts, Creative Casting, NY, 64; Bertrand Russell Centenary Int, Nottingham, Eng, 73; Brigham Young Univ, Utah, 76; 12th Int Sculpture Conf, Mills Col, 82; Public Sculpture Exhib, San Francisco Art Comn, 85-86; Brigham Young Univ, Utah, 76; and others. *Pos:* Adv, Kala Inst, 81-88. *Teaching:* Asst prof art, Calif Col Arts & Crafts, 51-56; assoc prof art, Mills Col, 57-75, prof, 75-, actg head dept art, 63-64, head dept, 73-76 & 79-80. *Awards:* First Award Sculpture Gold Metal, Oakland Mus Art, 52; First Award Metal Work, Calif State Fair, 62; Mellon Found Grant, 77, 80 & 83; Nat Endowment Arts Grant, 88-89. *Bibliog:* New Talent, Art Am, 66. *Mem:* Western Col Asn (accreditation comt, 69-); Western Asn Schs & Cols; Accrediting Comn Sr Cols & Univs; Int Sculpture Asn; Bay Area Consortium Visual Arts (steering comt, 87-89). *Media:* Metal, Etching. *Res:* Linear form and computer graphics. *Publ:* Coauth, Simple Jewelry Making for the Classroom , 58; contribr, Metal Techniques for Craftsmen, 68; Craftsmen of the Southwest, 65 & The Crafts of the Modern World, 68; Lunar Suite I, The Hamptons Publ Dans Papers Ltd, 7/81; Sculpture 12, Int Sculpture Ctr, 82; Calif Art Review, 88. *Mailing Add:* Mills Col Box 9924 Oakland CA 94613

D'HARNONCOURT, ANNE
HISTORIAN, MUSEUM DIRECTOR
b Washington, DC, Sept 7, 43. *Study:* Radcliffe Col, BA, 65; Courtauld Inst Art, Univ London, MA, 67. *Collections Arranged:* Marcel Duchamp, Philadelphia Mus Art, Mus Mod Art & Art Inst Chicago, 73-74; Philadelphia:

Three Centuries of American Art, Philadelphia Mus Art, 76; Eight Artists, Philadelphia Mus Art, 78; Violet Oakley, Philadelphia Mus Art, 79; Futurism and the International Avant-Garde, Philadelphia Mus Art, 80; John Cage: Scores and Prints, Whitney Mus Am Art, Albright-Knox Mus, Philadelphia Mus Art, 82. *Pos:* Cur asst, dept painting & sculpture, Philadelphia Mus Art, 67-69, asst cur, 20th century painting, 71-72, cur, 20th century art, 72-82; asst cur, 20th century art, Art Inst Chicago, 69-71; dir, The George D Widener & Philadelphia Mus Art, currently. *Awards:* Chestnut Hill Col Medal, 87; James D Burke Prize Fine Arts, St Louis Art Mus, 87; Women's Hist Award, Mayor's Comn Women, 88. *Mem:* Fairmont Park Art Asn Philadelphia; Grad Sch Fine Arts, Univ Pa, bd overseers; Col Art Asn; Am Asn Mus; Int Coun Mus. *Publ:* The first of Boccioni meets Miss FlicFlic ChiapChiap, Art News, 11/80; contribr, Futurism and the International Avant-Garde (exhib catalog), Philadelphia Mus Art, 80; Marcel Duchamp, Notes, G K Hall & Co, Boston, 83; Marcel Duchamp, Manual of Instructions for Etant Donnes, Philadelphia Mus Art, 87. *Mailing Add:* Philadelphia Mus Art PO Box 7646 Philadelphia PA 19101-7646

DIAL, GAIL
METALSMITH, EDUCATOR
b Tulsa, Okla, Aug 23, 47. *Study:* Pittsburg State Univ, Kans, MA, 71; Ind Univ, Bloomington, with Alma Eikerman, MFA, 74. *Work:* Mus Plains Ind, Browning, Mont; Idaho First Nat Bank, Boise; Ind Mus Fine Arts, Bloomington; Pittsburg State Univ, Kans. *Exhib:* Goldsmith: 74, Renwick Gallery, Smithsonian Inst, Washington, DC, 74; Forms in Metal: 275 Years of Metalsmith, Mus Contemp Crafts, NY, 74; Contemp Crafts Am, Colo State Univ, Ft Collins, 75; Crafts for Am, Phillipines Design Ctr, Manila, 77; Copper, Bronze & Brass, Tuscon, Ariz, 77; Lake Superior Nat, Duluth Art Inst, Minn, 81. *Collections Arranged:* Marilyn Levine: Ceramics, 79; William Wiley Prints, 80. *Teaching:* Prof metal & crafts, Idaho State Univ, Pocatello, 74- *Awards:* Cash Awards, Indianapolis Mus, 73 & Boise Art Gallery, 75 & 76. *Mem:* Prof mem Soc North Am Goldsmiths; Northwest Designer Craftsmen. *Media:* Gold, Silver. *Publ:* Contribr, Contemporary Jewelry, Holt Rinehart, 75; Contemporary Crafts of the Americas: 1975, Regnery, 75. *Mailing Add:* 533 Appaloosa Ave Pocatello ID 83201

DIAMOND, JESSICA
ARTIST
b June 6, 57. *Study:* Sch Visual Arts, NY, BFA, 79; Columbia Univ, MFA, 81. *Exhib:* Solo exhibs, Hallwalls, Buffalo, NY, 85, Am Fine Arts Co, New York, 89-90 & 92, Artspace Annex, San Francisco, 91, Jablonka Galerie, Koln, Ger, 91 & Galerie Fahnemann, Berlin, Ger, 91; On View, New Mus Contemp Art, New York, 86; Nostalgia as Resistance, Pop Project IV, Clocktower, New York, 88; Just Pathetic, Rosamund Felsen Gallery, Los Angeles, 90; Biennial, Whitney Mus Am Art, New York, 91; Nachtregels/Nightlines, Central Mus, Ultrecht, Holland, 91. *Bibliog:* Susan Morgan (auth), and that's the way it is--the works of Applebroog, Diamond, Wegman, Artscribe, 6-7/86; Thomas Lawson (auth), Nostalgia as Resistance, Modern Dreams: The Rise and Fall and Rise of Pop, Mass Inst Technol Press, 88; Lydia Dona (auth), The memo on the wall: recent works by Jessica Diamond, Arts Mag, 10/90. *Media:* Graphics. *Mailing Add:* c/o American Fine Arts 40 Wooster St New York NY 10013

DIAMOND, PAUL
PHOTOGRAPHER
b Brooklyn, NY, June 20, 42. *Study:* Pratt Inst, BFA, 65; Purdue Univ, MA, 80. *Work:* Int Mus Photog, George Eastman House, Rochester, NY; Nat Gallery Can, Ottawa, Ont; Fogg Art Mus, Cambridge, Mass; Boston Mus Fine Arts. *Exhib:* 60s Continuum, George Eastman House, 72; one-man shows, Sq Bromides, Gallery Optica, Montreal, Que, 73 & Floating Found of Photog, New York, 74; Peculiar to Photog, Univ NMex, 76; Five, St Charles on the Wazee, Denver, Colo, 77; Contemp Photog, Fogg Art Mus, 77. *Teaching:* Instr photog, Calif Col Arts & Crafts, Oakland, 77-78; guest lectr photog, Univ Colo, Boulder, 77; instr, Moore Col Art, Philadelphia, currently. *Awards:* Guggenheim Found Fel, 75-76; Nat Endowment for the Arts Grant, 78. *Mem:* Soc Photog Educ. *Publ:* Contribr, Photographer's Choice, Addison House, 75, Ctr for Creative Photog, Vol 4, Univ Ariz, 77 & Grotesque in Photography, Ridge Press, 77. *Dealer:* Witkin Gallery 41 E 57th St New York NY 10022. *Mailing Add:* 21 Saint James Pl Brooklyn NY 11205

DIAMOND, STUART
PAINTER
b Brooklyn, NY, Apr 8, 42. *Study:* Pratt Inst, BFA, 59-63. *Work:* Mus Mod Art, New York; Mus Contemp Art, Chicago. *Exhib:* Howard Wezreski Gallery, Boston, 89; Victoria Munroe Gallery, New York, 90-91; one-man exhibs, Grace Gallery, New York Community Col, 71, Rabinovitch & Guerra Gallery, New York, 75, David McKee Gallery, New York, 77, 79, 82, 84, 86 & 92, Drawings, Hayden Gallery, Mass Inst Tech, Cambridge, 79 & Dart Gallery, Chicago, 80; Cork Gallery, Lincoln Ctr, New York, 91; Great Wall Gallery, Toronto, 91; Japan Arts Gallery, Tokyo, 91; Baltimore Co Campus Fine Arts Gallery, Univ Maryland, 92. *Teaching:* Assoc prof art, Cooper Union, New York, 88-; instr painting, Parsons Sch Design, New York, 88- *Awards:* Solomon Guggenheim Fel, 87-88; Nat Endowment Arts Fel, 87-88; Receives Guggenheim Fel, 87. *Publ:* Auth, John Yau, Stuart Diamond's Fictions, Arts, 2/85; Kay Larson, Stuart Diamond, New York Mag, 4/28/86; Robert Olivio, Jewels Among the Glitter, New York Native, 5/12/86; Joan Crowder, New York Art comes to Auchincloss Gallery in a Classy Exhibition, Santa Barbara News-Press, 7/19/86; Dana Saulnier, Stuart Diamond, Q: A J of Art, Dept Art Col Archit, Art, & Planning, Cornell Univ, 5/90. *Dealer:* David McKee Gallery 745 5th Ave New York NY 10151. *Mailing Add:* 454 Broome St New York NY 10013

DIAMONSTEIN, BARBARALEE
WRITER
Study: New York Univ, PhD, 63; Baltimore Col Art, LHD, 90. *Collections Arranged:* Buildings Reborn: New Uses, Old Places, traveling, 76-; American Architecture Now (auth, catalog), Leo Castelli Gallery, New York, 80; Visions and Images, Int Ctr Photog, New York, 81-; Handmade in America, Leo Castelli Gallery & Metrop Mus Art, New York, 83; The Landmarks of New York (auth, catalog), 88; 8 Wonders of the NY World, 92. *Pos:* Staff asst, The White House, 63-66 & first dir cult affairs, 66-71; writer, Sat Rev, 65-68 & Harpers Bazaar, 69-71; spec proj ed, Art News, 74-, Ladies Home J, 77-81, Int Commun Agency, 78, Partisan Rev, 78-79 & Interiors, 80; interviewer & producer, ABC-ARTS Cable Network, CBS-TV, WNYC-TV, Manhattan Cable Television & Arts & Entertainment Network; comnr, New York Landmark Preserv Comt, 72-88, Cult Affairs Coun, 74-86, conservancy vice-chairperson, 83- , chmn, 87-; assoc, Am Craft Mus, 81-; dir, Munic Arts Soc, New York, 73-83 & Fresh Air Fund, 87-; adv comt hist & theory of design, Grad Sch Design, Harvard Univ, 90. *Teaching:* Adj assoc prof, City Univ New York, Hunter Col, 74-77; vis prof, New Sch-Parsons Design, 76-82, Duke Univ, 78. *Awards:* Award, Am Archit Now; J Clawson Mills Fel, 80-81; Ralph Menapali Award for Distinguished Civic Achievment, 90; and others. *Mem:* Municipal Art Soc (mem bd dirs, 72-); New York Landmark Conserv (bd gov); Am PEN Women's Forum. *Publ:* Auth, Interior Design, 3/81; American photographers on photography, 11/81; Handmade in America, Harry N Abrams Publ, 83; American Architecture Now, Part I & II, 84; Fashion: The Inside Story, 85; Remaking America, 86; auth, The Landmarks of New York, 89. *Dealer:* Leo Castelli Gallery 420 W Broadway New York NY. *Mailing Add:* 720 Park Ave New York NY 10021

DIAO, DAVID
PAINTER
b Sichuan, China, Aug 7, 43; US citizen. *Study:* Kenyon Col, AB, 64. *Work:* Whitney Mus Am Art, New York; San Francisco Mus; Art Gallery Ont, Toronto; Va Mus, Richmond; High Mus, Atlanta, Ga; Nat Collection, France; Danforth Art Mus; Litchener Col; Hirshhorn Mus; Mod Mus Art, France. *Exhib:* Postmasters Gallery, NY, 85, 86, 88 & 89, Galeria Westersingel 8, Rotterdam, Holland, 88, Musee d'Art Moderne, Saint Etinne, France, 89, Galerie Joseph Dutertre, Rennes, France, 89, Provincial Museum voor Moderne Kunst, Oostende, Belg, 90, Het Kruithuis, Museum voor Hedendaagse Kunst, 's-Hertogenbosch, Holland, 90, Claire Burrus Gallery , Paris (upcoming), 90; Annual Exhibition, Whitney Mus Am Art, New York, 89; Avant-Garde in the 80's, Los Angeles County Mus Art, Calif, 87; Generations of Geometry, Whitney Mus Art at Equitable Ctr, New York, 87; Post-Abstract Abstraction, Aldrich Mus, Ridgefield, Conn, 87; Wind and Matter: New American Abstraction, USIA traveling exhib to Asian capitals, 89; Jet Lag, Turon Travel, Inc, 89; Postmasters Gallery, NY, 89; one-man shows, Provincial Mus voor Mod Kunst, Oostende, Belg, 90, Het Kruithuis, Mus voor Hedendaagse Kunst, Holland, 90, Claire Burns Gallery, Paris, 90, Selections 1972-1991, Cherng Piin Gallery, Taipei, Taiwan, 91; Slow Art: Painting in New York Now, PS1 Mus, Queens, NY, Philippe Staib Gallery, New York, 92. *Teaching:* Instr independent study prog, Whitney Mus, New York, 70- *Awards:* Guggenheim Fel, 73-74; Creative Artists Pub Serv Award, 78; Nat Endowment Arts, 80 & 87. *Bibliog:* Kees Broos (auth), David Dio (essay catalog), Museum voor Hedendaagse Kunst Het Kruithuis, 's-Hertogenbosch, Netherlands & Provinciaal Museum voor Moderne Kunst, Oostende, Belg, 90; Richard Kalina (auth), David Diao at Postmasters (review), Art Am, 3/92; Marjorie Welish (auth), Abstraction, Advocacy of, Tema Celeste, 1-21/92. *Dealer:* Postmaster Gallery 80 Greene St New York NY 10012. *Mailing Add:* 72 Franklin New York NY 10013

DIAZ, LOPE MAX See Max, Lope (Diaz)

DIBBLE, GEORGE
PAINTER, WRITER
b Laie, Hawaii, Mar 29, 04; US citizen. *Study:* Art Students League with George Bridgman, Ivan Olinski & Howard Giles; Columbia Univ with Charles Martin, Arthur Young & Sallie Tannahill, BS & MFA. *Work:* Utah State Div Fine Arts, Salt Lake City; Univ Utah Mus Fine Arts; Utah State Univ, Logan; Southern Utah State Col, Cedar City; Granite Dist Sch & Davis Dist Sch, Utah. *Comn:* Watercolor collections of Hawaii, United Airlines, San Francisco Airport, Calif. *Exhib:* Utah Biennial, Salt Lake Art Ctr, 50; one-man show, Ogden Eccles Art Ctr, 67 & Phillips Gallery, Salt Lake City, 87; Watercolor W, Utah State Univ, 74-76; Centennial Exhib, Utah Artists, Salt Lake City Art Ctr, 76; two-man show, Art Gallery, Univ Utah, 76; Eight-State Regional--Watercolor, Utah State Inst of Fine Arts; Mus of Art, Taipei, Taiwan, 86; and others. *Pos:* Auth, weekly column, Art Scene, Salt Lake Tribune, 57- *Teaching:* Assoc prof watercolor, Univ Utah, 47-57, prof watercolor, 57-72, emer prof, 72- *Awards:* First Purchase Awards, Utah State Fair Asn, 35 & 38 & Utah State Inst of Fine Arts Watercolor, 52. *Bibliog:* One Hundred Years of Utah Painting, James Haseltine Salt Lake Art Ctr, 65. *Mem:* Fel, Utah Acad Sci, Arts & Lett; life mem, Salt Lake Art Ctr. *Media:* Watercolor, Oil. *Publ:* Auth, Art and the Unadjusted School Child, Art Educ Today, Columbia Univ, 36; auth, Watercolor, Materials and Techniques, Holt, Rinehart & Winston, 66. *Mailing Add:* 2049 Wilmington Ave Salt Lake City UT 84124

DIBERT, RITA JEAN
PAINTER, PHOTOGRAPHER
b Flint, Mich, Feb 25, 46. *Study:* Flint Community Jr Col, AA(art), 66; Univ Mich, Flint Col, 66, Ann Arbor, BFA, 69, MFA, 71; also studied with Gerome Kamrowski, Albert Mullen & Ted Ramsey; Univ Calif, Los Angeles, 67-68. *Work:* Detroit Inst Art; Calif Mus Photog, Riverside; Munson-Williams-

Proctor Inst; Polaroid Corp, Cambridge, Mass; WDIV-TV, Detroit; Pratt Art Inst; and many others. *Comn:* Hyatt Hotels; Hayworth Furniture; Detroit Renaissance Ctr Restaurant; Blue Cross/Blue Shield, Mich; Raddison Hotels; and others. *Exhib:* One-man shows, Space Gallery Western Mich Univ, 90, Artist Trait Gallery, Claremont, Calif, 87 & 90, Odessa Col Gallery, Tex, 91, Orange Coast Photog Gallery, Costa Mesa, Calif, 91, Upper Catskill Coun Art, 91, Clausen Gallery, Chicago, 91 & Saginaw Mus Art, Gallery 53, Cooperstown, NY, 91; Polaroid Group Show, Level 3 Gallery, Philadelphia, Pa, 91; Regional Photo Invitational, Artists Cent NY, Munson Williams Proctor Inst, Utica, 91; Booknotes/Notebooks, Cortland Arts Coun Mus, NY, 91; Hist Crosscuts, Buckham Fine Arts, Flint, Mich, 92; Regional Painting Invitational, Arnot Mus, Ithaca, NY, 92; and other one-man & group exhibs. *Teaching:* Lectr & area coordr photog & printmaking, Residential Col, Univ Mich, Ann Arbor, 72-74; asst prof, Hartwick Col, 74-79; asst prof & artist-in-residence, Pomona Col & Claremont Grad Sch, 79-86; asst prof arts, Claremont Grad Sch, 79-86; vis assoc prof, Hartwick Col, Oneonta, NY, 89-90; adj, State Univ New York at Brockport, 92-93. *Awards:* America the Beautiful Award, Photo Documentation, Upper Catskill Arts Coun, 76; Fac Res Grant, Pomona Col, 80-86; Materials Grant, Polaroid Corp, 83-92; Ruth Chenven Found Painting Grant, 90; New York State Coun Arts Decentralization Grant, 91. *Bibliog:* Article, Trends Section, Time-Life, 82, Popular Photog Ann, 86; Series of 5 Detroit full color 24x30 Lithographs, Univ Lithoprinters, Ann Arbor, Mich. *Mem:* Col Art Asn; Women's Caucus Art; Soc Photog Educ; Arts Greater Rochester, Pyramid Gallery. *Media:* Acrylic, Oil. *Publ:* Illusr, Infrared photography, Rangefinder Mag, 12/81; illusr back cover, European Photography, Polaroid Corp, 83; illusr, infrared photog, Photo District News, 3/91; illusr, infrared photog, Pop Photo Discoveries, 7/92. *Dealer:* Xochipilli Gallery Birmingham MI; Gallery 53 Cooperstown NY. *Mailing Add:* 1237 Main St E Rochester NY 14609-6941

DICE, ELIZABETH JANE
CRAFTSMAN, EDUCATOR
b Urbana, Ill, Apr 3, 19. *Study:* Univ Mich, BDesign, 41, MDesign, 42; Ind Univ, MA, 66; Int Sch Art, Mex; Inst Allende, Mex; Columbia Univ Teachers Col; Norfolk Art Sch; painting with Jerry Farnsworth; Penland Sch Crafts, 71 & 73. *Comn:* Woven Hanging, Carrier Chapel, Miss Univ for Women (Gift of class of 82). *Exhib:* Miss Art Asn, 48-51, 67 & 68; Nat Crafts Exhib, Wichita, Kans, 50; Nat Watercolor Show, Jackson, Miss, 51; New Orleans Art Asn, 55; Craftsmen's Guild Miss, 75; Path of the Weaver, Memphis, 78 & 80; and many others. *Teaching:* Assoc prof art, Miss State Col Women, 45-79, prof, 80-82; retired; Weaving Workshop for Chimmneyville Weavers, Jackson, Miss, 85. *Awards:* Prizes, Jackson, Miss, 46 & 51; Miss River Craft Exhib Award, 63; Horn Lake Libr Purchase Award. *Mem:* Archaeol Inst Am; Handweavers Guild Am (state rep, 72-77); Miss Mus Art; Southeastern Col Art Conf; Columbus Art Asn. *Mailing Add:* 134 King St Columbus MS 39701

DI CERBO, MICHAEL
PAINTER, PRINTMAKER
b Paterson, NJ, 1947. *Study:* Pratt Inst, BFA & MFA. *Work:* Brooklyn Mus, Pratt Inst & Columbia Univ, New York; NJ State Mus, Trenton; Victoria & Albert Mus, London; and others. *Comn:* Mural, Next City Corp, 82 & In Business Corp, 82. *Exhib:* Brooklyn Mus, 78; Print Club, Philadelphia, 80 & 85; Sotheby Park Bernet, New York, 81, 82, 83, & 84; solo exhib, Union St Gallery, San Francisco, 82; World Print Coun, San Francisco, 82; Kanagawa Prefectural Mus, Yokohama, 82, 84, 85, 88, & 90; Albany Inst Art Hist, NY, 86; De Cordova Mus, Lincoln, Mass, 86 & 90; Taipei Fine Arts Mus, 87 & 89; Schweinfurth Mem Art Ctr, Auburn, NY, 89; Aldrich Mus Contemp Art, Ridgefield, Conn, 90. *Pos:* Pres, Soc Am Graphic Artists 89- *Teaching:* Prof art, Seton Hall Univ, South Orange, NJ, 92. *Awards:* Boston Printmakers Award, 86; Purchase Award, SAGA 63rd Nat, 89; Profile Award, Manhattan Arts Mag, 92; and others. *Bibliog:* Art Am, 6/82; J Print World, fall 89; Articles, New York Times, 5/6/90. *Mem:* Soc Am Graphic Artists; Boston Printmakers & Artists Equity. *Media:* Acrylic, Watercolor, Etching. *Publ:* Architectural Fantasies, Symmetry 2, VCH, 89. *Dealer:* Corp Art Directions 41 E 57 St New York NY 10022. *Mailing Add:* 277 W 10th St Apt 5a New York NY 10014

DICKERSON, BRIAN S
PAINTER
b Middleburgh, NY, May 3, 51. *Study:* Private study with Charles Jahnke, 69-73; Pa Acad Fine Arts, 71-72. *Exhib:* One-man show, Del Co Community Col, Marple, Pa, 80; Nat Acad Design, New York, 80; Woodmere Gallery, Philadelphia, 80 & 81; Butler Mus Am Art, Youngstown, Ohio, 81; Hahn Gallery, Philadelphia, 82; Inst Man & Sci, Rensselaerville, NY, 83; and others. *Pos:* Artist, Inst Man & Sci, Rensselaerville, NY. *Awards:* First Prize, Woodmere Gallery; Medal of Merit, Nat Soc Painters Casein & Acrylic, 80. *Media:* Oil, Pastel. *Mailing Add:* 151 W Durham St Philadelphia PA 19119

DICKERSON, DANIEL JAY
PAINTER, EDUCATOR
b Jersey City, NJ, Dec 22, 22. *Study:* Cooper Union Art Sch, 41-43 & 45-46; Cranbrook Acad Art, BFA, 47, MFA, 49. *Work:* Joseph H Hirshhorn Collection; Adelphi Univ Mus; Ill Wesleyan Mus; Corcoran Gallery; Weatherspoon Gallery, Univ NC. *Comn:* Nue Bank mural, Leonia, NJ; art prog, US Coast Guard. *Exhib:* Whitney Mus Am Art Ann, 47; Pa Acad Fine Arts, 53; Audubon Artists Exhib, 64; Nat Inst Arts & Lett, 68; Nat Acad Design, 74; and others. *Teaching:* Lectr art, Manhattanville Col, 65-69; chmn dept art, Finch Col, 69-78; instr, Nat Acad Design Sch Art, 77-88 & Art Students League, 78-90. *Awards:* First Prize, Springfield Art Mus, 54; Emily Lowe Award for Painting, Audubon Artists, 64; Henry Ward Ranger Purchase Award, Nat Acad Design, 74; and others. *Mem:* Artists Fel; US Coast Guard Artists. *Media:* Acrylic, Oil. *Mailing Add:* 104 High St Leonia NJ 07605

DICKERSON, EDWARD TED
PAINTER, PRINTMAKER
b South Haven, Mich, June 10, 32. *Study:* Western Mich Univ, Kalamazoo, BS(art), 54; Univ Wis, Madison, MS(painting & printmaking), 57. *Work:* Smithsonian Inst, Washington, DC; Philadelphia Mus Art; St Louis Art Mus, Mo; Kalamazoo Inst Art, Mich; Charles A Wustum Mus Fine Arts, Racine, Wis. *Exhib:* Pa Acad Art, Philadelphia, 57; Contemporary American Prints, Libr Cong & US Info Agency, European tour, 57; Soc Washington Printmakers Nat Exhib, Smithsonian Inst, Washington, DC, 57 & 64; Atkins Mus Fine Art, Kansas City, Mo, 58; Univ Kans Mus Art, Lawrence, 58; Philadelphia Print Club, 62; Art Inst Chicago, 63 & 67; Butler Inst Am Art, Youngstown, Ohio, 64. *Pos:* Inventor, Dickerson Combination Press. *Teaching:* Instr art, Univ Mo, Columbia, 56-58; instr painting, Univ Wis, Madison, 58-60; asst prof, Wis State Univ, Whitewater, 60-62; asst prof, Sch Art Inst Chicago, 63-65. *Awards:* 1st Prize, Philadelphia Print Club Nat Exhib, 56; Pennel Fund Purchase Award, Washington Printmakers Soc Nat Exhib, 57; Jenkins Mem Award, 70th Exhib Art Inst Chicago, 67. *Mem:* South Haven Community Art Orgn. *Media:* Oil, Watercolor; Miscellaneous Media. *Mailing Add:* c/o Dickerson Studios Inc PO Box 8 South Haven MI 49090

DICKERSON, VERA MASON
PAINTER, INSTRUCTOR
b Radford, Va, July 28, 46. *Study:* Radford Univ, BFA, 68; Am Univ, MFA, 70; studied with Wayne Thiebaud & Daniel Greene (workshop). *Work:* Miller Brewing Co, Eden, NC; Gannett Publ Co, Arlington, Va; Dominion Bankshares Corp & Marriott Corp, Roanoke, Va. *Comn:* Portraits, Fed Judges James Hill, Atlanta, Ga, Adrian Spear, San Antonio, Tex & John Jamison, Fredericksburg, Va, comn by Bar Asn, Darlington Co, SC, 81-83; portraits, Gen Marion Kinon, Dillon, SC, 85 & Clara Black, comn by Roanoke City Schs, Va, 86. *Exhib:* Traveling Exhib, Over the Blue Ridge, Roanoke Mus Fine Arts, Va, 81; More Than Land or Sky, Nat Mus Am Art, Washington, DC, 81; Southeast Print & Drawing Show, Belle Air Gallery, Fla, 82; Va Mus Fine Arts, Richmond, 83; After Her Own Image, Salem Col, Winston-Salem, NC, 85; Henley Spectrum, Winston-Salem, NC, 92; and others. *Pos:* Artist-in-residence pastel drawing, Va Mus Fine Arts, Richmond, 83-84; dir, Sketchbook Tour Scotland, 90. *Teaching:* Asst prof art, Va Western Community Col, Roanoke, Va, 72-78, dept art chmn, 78-81; founded The Studio Sch, Roanoke, Va, 90- *Awards:* Best in show, Highland Festival, Abingdon, Va, 68 & 76; Shenandoah Award, Shenandoah Life Insurance, 75; Nat Endowment Arts Grant, 81; Best in show, Kaliedoscope Festival, 88, & Showcase for the Arts, 87, 88. *Bibliog:* Linda Forshey (auth), Jene Highstein, La Jolla Mus, Calif, 87; Jean Feinberg (auth), Jene Highstein at Wave Hill, Wave Hill, 89; Jene Highstein Gallery/Landscape, Santa Barbara Contemp Arts Forum, 91. *Mem:* Va Watercolor Soc (found mem, bd dirs). *Media:* Oil, Mixed. *Mailing Add:* Rd 1 Box 120 Troutville VA 24175

DICKERSON, WILLIAM J
ART DEALER
b Lexington, Ky, July 7, 43. *Pos:* Pres, O'Brien's Art Emporium, 78- *Specialty:* Contemporary-traditional American art. *Mailing Add:* O'Brien's Art Emporium 7122 Stetson Dr Scottsdale AZ 85251

DICKINSON, DAVID CHARLES
PRINTMAKER, PROFESSOR
b Hendon, Middlesex, Eng, Jan 3, 40. *Study:* Chelsea Sch Art, London, 56-61; Statens-Kunst-og-Handverks Industrie Skoolen, Oslo, Norway, 61-62; Rochester Inst Technol, MFA, 72. *Work:* Southampton Civic Ctr, Eng; Mem Art Gallery, Rochester, NY; Sheldon Mem Art Gallery, Lincoln, Nebr; Kansas City Art Gallery. *Comn:* Portfolio of Prints, Cold Cream Alley, Rochester, 73; EGR Commun, Rochester, 73 & 74. *Exhib:* Epinale International, France, 75 & 77; two-man shows, Univ Mo, Columbus, 76 & Shoe String Gallery, Rochester, 86; Printmaker's Invitational, Rochester Inst Technol, NY, 78; State Univ NY, Geneseo, 82; Shoestring Gallery, 88. *Teaching:* Prof Computer Art Prog, Rochester Inst Technol, 72- *Awards:* Purchase Award, Comn Arts, Atlanta, 71; Purchase Award, Finger Lakes Regional Exhib, 73; Hon Mention, MacWorld Art Contest, 88; and others. *Mem:* Rochester Printmakers. *Media:* Intaglio, Non-Silver Photographic Processes; Computer Art. *Mailing Add:* 6825 Rte 408 Mt Morris NY 14510

DICKINSON, ELEANOR CREEKMORE
PAINTER, VIDEO ARTIST
b Knoxville, Tenn, Feb 7, 31. *Study:* Univ Tenn, with C Kermit Ewing, BA, 52; San Francisco Art Inst, with James Weeks, 61-63; Univ Calif, 67, 71 & 81; Academié de la Grande Chaumière, Paris, France, 71; Calif Col Arts & Crafts, MFA, 82; Golden Gate Univ, 84. *Work:* Libr Cong, Nat Mus Am Art, Corcoran Gallery Art, Washington, DC; San Francisco Mus Mod Art; Fine Arts Mus San Francisco; and others. *Comn:* Wall installation (bronze), Univ San Francisco, 91. *Exhib:* Solo exhibs, Santa Barbara Mus, 66, Judah Magnes Mus, Berkeley, 68, Fine Arts Mus, San Francisco, 69 & 75, Knoxville Mus Art, Knoxville, 70, Corcoran Gallery Art, 70 & 74, Poindexter Gallery, New YOrk, 72 & 74, J B Speed Art Mus, Louisville, Ky, 72, Wash State Mus, 75, Cheney Cowles Mus, Spokane, Wash, 75, Triton Mus, Santa Clara, 75 &77, Smithsonian Inst Travelling Exhib, 75-81, Huntsville Mus Art, 77, Montgomery Mus Fine Arts, 78 & Oakland Mus, 79, Menil Mus/Screen Memories Gallery, Houston, Tex, 88; William Sawyer Gallery, 70 & 75; Tenn State Mus, 75, 81 & 82; Women's Inter Art Ctr, New York, 80; Screen Memories, Menil Mus, Houston, 88; Diverse Works Gallery, Houston, Tex, 90; Michael Himovitz Gallery, 91 & 93; and many others. *Pos:* Trustee, San Francisco Art Inst, 63-66; art critic, San Francisco Rev Bks, 75-78; dir galleries, Calif, Col Arts & Crafts, Oakland, 76-86; columnist, Visual

Dialogue, 75-79; writer, Women Artists News, NY, 79-; co-cur, Oakland Mus, 79-80 & Int Sculpture Symp, 82; cur, Inter Art Ctr, 80, Tenn State Mus, 80-91 & Graham Ctr Mus, 84-85. *Teaching:* Vis lectr drawing & painting, Univ Calif, 65, 70, 71 & 73; prof drawing & gallery mgt, Calif Col Arts & Crafts, Oakland, 71-; vis prof, Univ Calif Ext, Davis, 83, 84 & 85, Solano State Univ, 83, Fresno State Univ, 83 & Davis & Elkins Col, WVa. *Awards:* Graphics Prize, City of San Francisco, 73 & 75; Master Drawing Award, Nat Soc Arts & Lett, 83; Distinguished Alumni Award, San Francisco Art Inst, 84; Award in Graphics, Art Comn, San Francisco, 75; and others. *Bibliog:* Aline Saarinen (dir), Revival!, NBC Today Show, 70; James R Mellow (auth), Eleanor Dickinson, New York Times, 72; Walter Hopps (auth), Introduction to Revival!, Harper, 74; Dr Alfred Frankenstein (auth), Celebrated women in art-at the Legion, San Francisco Chronicle & Examiner, 75; Helga Epstein (auth), Eleanor Dickinson: social historian and artist, Am Artist, 80; Marsha Maguire (auth), Confirming the word: artist and social documentarian, Quarterly J Libr Cong, 81; Dr Peter Selz (auth), San Francisco: Eleanor Dickinson at Hatley Martin, 89. *Mem:* Artists Equity Asn (nat vpres); Women's Caucus Art (chap adv coun mem); Col Art Asn; Calif Lawyers Arts (state vpres). *Media:* Mixed Media. *Res:* Southern Appalachian Mountains Revival Meetings. *Publ:* Auth, Tennessee revival services, Libr Cong Arch Folk Song, 71; illusr, Complete Fruit Cookbook, Scribner, 72 & Human Sexuality: A Search for Understanding, West Publ, 84; coauth (with B Benziger), Revival!, 74 & illusr, That Old Time Religion, 75, Harper & Row; and others. *Dealer:* Rebecca Cooper 903 Park Ave New York NY 10021; Hatley Martin Gallery 41 Powell St San Francisco CA 94102. *Mailing Add:* 2125 Broderick St San Francisco CA 94115

DICKINSON, NORMAN
PAINTER
b Liverpool, Eng, May 8, 21. *Study:* Liverpool Col Art, 35-39; Royal Col Art, London, ARCA, 46-49. *Comn:* Portrait, Snyder IV, Pittsburgh, 72; portrait, Tony O'Reilly, Pittsburgh, 73; portrait, Trammell Crow, Dallas, Tex, 84; portrait, David Rockefeller, New York, 85; portrait, Arthur K Watson, IBM, New York, 87. *Media:* Oil. *Mailing Add:* Wensley, Bulstode Way Gerrards Cross Bucks Sl9 7QU England United Kingdom

DICKSON, JANE LEONE
PAINTER
b Chicago, Ill, May 18, 52. *Study:* Sch of Boston Mus Fine Arts, dipl, 76; Harvard Univ, BA(magna cum laude), 76. *Work:* Metrop Mus Art & Mus Mod Art, New York; Chicago Art Ins, Ill; Victoria & Albert Mus, London, Eng; Libr Cong, Washington, DC. *Comn:* City Maze (labyrinth), NY Bd Educ, Bronx, 81; Ann's White Gloves (sets for play), Nat Endowment Arts, New York, 85; A Tear in Time - ballet sets, Nederlands Dans Theatre, 88; Life Under Neon, Moore Col of Art, Philadelphia PA, 89; MTA Arts for Transit Poster, New York City, 90. *Exhib:* Content: A Contemporary Focus 1974-1984, Hirshhorn Mus, Washington, DC, 85; On 42nd Street, Whitney Mus-Philip Morris, New York, 84; Biennial Exhib, Whitney Mus, New York, 85; Correspondences: NY Art Now, La Foret Mus, Tokyo, Japan, 85-86; solo exhib, Brooke Alexander Gallery, New York, 86, 88 & 90, Joe Fawbosh Gallery New York, 83; Public & Private: American Prints Today, Brooklyn Mus, NY, Carnegie Inst, Pittsburgh & Walker Art Ctr, Minn, 86-87; A Graphic Muse, Prints By Contemp Am Women, Yale Univ Art Gal, Mt Holyoke Col MA & Richmond VA, 87-88; Ean Keuze/A Choice KunstRai Amsterdam, 88; Portraying the Night, Kansas City Art Inst, 88. *Teaching:* Sch Visual Arts New York 88-89, Temple Univ, Tyler Sch of Art, Philadelphia PA, 90. *Awards:* Grants, Nat Endowment Arts, Washington, DC & Ariana Found, 85; Dewars Young Artist Award, 90. *Bibliog:* John Russell (auth), In the arts: Critics choices, 11/27/83 & Vivien Raynor (auth), Jane Dickson & Dick Miller, 2/21/86, NY Times; Cynthia Nadelman (auth), Artists the critics are watching, Art News, 11/84. *Media:* All. *Dealer:* Brooke Alexander Gallery 59 Wooster St New York NY 10036. *Mailing Add:* 276 W 43rd St New York NY 10036

DICKSON, JENNIFER JOAN
PHOTOGRAPHER, PRINTMAKER
b Piet Retief, Repub SAfrica, Sept 17, 36; Can citizen. *Study:* Goldsmith's Col Sch Art, Univ London, 54-59; Atelier 17, Paris, with S W Hayter, 60-65. *Work:* Victoria & Albert Mus, London; Nat Gallery Can, Ottawa; Metrop Mus Art, New York; Montreal Mus Fine Arts; Smithsonian Inst; and many others. *Comn:* The Secret Garden (collabr: Henry J Kahanek & Ray Van Dusen), 76 & Paradise, 80, Nat Film Bd Can. *Exhib:* Salon des Realites Nouvelles, Musee d'Art Moderne, Paris, 62 & 66; Biennale de Paris, Mus Mod Art, Paris, 63; Modern Prints, 65 & Contemporary Prints, 66, Victoria & Albert Mus, London; Salon Internationale de la Gravure, Montreal Mus Fine Arts, 71; Folio Seventy Three Traveling Exhib, San Francisco Mus Art, 74; Forum 76, Montreal Mus Fine Arts, 76; Celebration of the Body, Agnes Etherington Art Centre, Queen's Univ, Ont; Tendances Actuelles au Quebec, 79 & L'estampe au Quebec 1970-1980, 80, Musee d'Art Contemporain, Montreal; 14th Int Biennial of Graphic Art, Ljubljana, Yugoslavia, 81; solo exhibs, Il Tempo Classica, Saidye Bronfman Centre, Montreal, 82, A Journey to Cythere, Wallack Art Ed, Ottawa, 82, Jennifer Dickson: A Continuum, Edward Monaghan Art Consult, Ottawa, 83 & Versailles: Through the Crystal Wall, Wallack Galleries, Ottawa, 83. *Collections Arranged:* Imprint 76 (current Can graphic art), Ont Arts Coun. *Teaching:* Vis prof fine arts, Univ Wis, Madison, 72; vis artist fine arts, Queen's Univ, Kingston, Ont, 77-78; instr dept visual arts, Univ Ottawa, currently. *Awards:* James A Reed Award, Can Painters-Etchers & Engravers, 73; Special Purchase Award, World Print Competition, San Francisco Mus Art, 73; Prize, 5th Norwegian Int Print Biennale, 80; and others. *Bibliog:* Michael Rothstein (auth), Frontiers of Printing, Studio Vista, 70; Anthony Gross (auth), Etching, Engraving & Intaglio Printing, Oxford Univ Press, 72; Edward-Lucie Smith (auth), Art in Seventies, Phaidon/Cornell Univ Press, 80; and others. *Mem:* Academician Royal Acad Arts; Print & Drawing Coun Can; Can Artists Representation; academician Royal Can Acad Arts; fel Royal Soc Painter-Etchers & Engravers. *Media:* Etching. *Dealer:* Wallack Galleries 203 Bank St Ottawa ON K2P 1W7 Can. *Mailing Add:* 20 Osborne St Ottawa ON K1S 4Z9 Canada

DICKSON, MARK AMOS
PAINTER, PRINTMAKER
b Boulder, Colo, Mar 4, 46. *Study:* Metrop State Col, BA, 69; Pratt Inst, 69-70; Univ Denver, MFA, 73. *Work:* Plains Art Mus, Morehead, Minn; Colo Graphic Arts Ctr, Denver, Colo; Denver Ctr Performing Arts, Colo. *Comn:* Oil on canvas, Texaco Oil, White Plains, NY; oil, American Airlines; oil, Kennedy Int Airport, New York; oil, Hakodate Hotel, Tokyo, Japan. *Exhib:* Nat Audubon, Nat Acad Design, New York, NY, 70; Artist Exchange, Joslyn Art Mus, Omaha, Nebr, 73; Arts 80, Nat Boulder Arts Ctr, 80; Colorado Print Invitational, Colo Graphic Arts Ctr, Denver, Colo, 84; Draw 82, Boulder Arts Ctr, Colo, 82; Creativity 86, Art Direction Mag, New York, 86; Graphics 86, Am Inst Graphic Arts, New York, 86; Artist of Taos, Stables Art Ctr, Taos, NMex, 87; Downtown Ctr Visual Art, 25 Years, 25 Artists, Metrop State Col, Denver, Colo, 90; Near North & Northwest Art Coun Gallery, Printmakers Coop Ann Exhib, Chicago, 92. *Teaching:* Instr printmaking, Univ Denver, Colo, 73; assoc prof fine art, St Thomas Col, Denver, 75-79; instr painting, Rocky Mountain Col Art, Denver, Colo, 87. *Awards:* Research & Travel Grant, Am Asn Theological Schs, 79; Award of Merit, Graphics 86, Inst Graphic Arts, 86; Award of Distinction, Creativity 86, Art Direction Mag, 86. *Bibliog:* Mystique Mag Northern NMex, 8/84; Where Chicago Mag, 9/91; Colorado Expression Mag, summer 92. *Media:* Oil; All Media. *Dealer:* Mary Bell Gallery Chicago IL; Friesen Gallery Seattle WA. *Mailing Add:* 101 Ash Denver CO 80220

DI COSOLA, LOIS
PAINTER, PRINTMAKER
b Brooklyn, NY, Jan 23, 35. *Study:* Early Master classes, Mus Mod Art, NY, grant, 51, BFA, 53; New Sch, R Pousette-Dart, 59; Pratt Graphics Ctr, 73-75; State Univ NY, Bachelor of Prof Studies for life's work in art, 85. *Work:* Guild Hall Mus, East Hampton, NY. *Exhib:* Prints by Pratt Printmakers, 5th Ann Exhibs Prints, traveling show, Butler Inst Am Art, Youngstown, Ohio, 73-76; Paula Cooper Gallery, NY, 74; Prints from the Permanent CollAction, Guild Hall Mus, Easthampton, NY, 80; Born to Survive, Mus Het Toreke, Belg, 84; Body Conscience, Selections from the Nat Drawing Asn, Elaine Benson Gallery, Brideghampton, NY, 89 & 91; Mailart 20th Century Anniversary, Cult Ctr, Genk, Belg, 89; and others. *Pos:* Bd mem, Nat Drawing Asn, 89- *Awards:* St Gauden's Medal for Draftsmanship, 53; Printmaking Award, Carnegie Inst Fine Art, 52; Art Dir's Club Award, 54; Painting & Drawing, Guild Hall Mus, Harold Rosenberg, 63; Guggenheim Mus Curator's Award, 64; Whitney Mus Curator's Award, 64. *Media:* All. *Dealer:* Aldona M Gobuzas 215 E 79th St New York NY 10020. *Mailing Add:* 25 Arch Lane Hicksville NY 11801

DIDOMENICO, NIKKI
CONCEPTUAL ARTIST, ASSEMBLAGE ARTIST
b Newark, New Jersey, June 8, 48. *Study:* Douglas Col, BA, 71; d'Ecole de Beaux Art Paris, 71-72; Scuola di Torano, Carrara, Italy, Masters, 73-78. *Work:* Pagani Found, Milano, Italy; Banco di Lavoro, Carrara, Italy. *Comn:* Sculptures, comn by J Blum, San Francisco, 76, E Marucci, New Jersey, 85. *Exhib:* Salon du Mai, Palais Royale, Paris, 73; Incontri, Pietrasanta, 76; Biennale della Spezia, The City, La spezia, 75. *Awards:* Recognition, Icontri, I Noguchi, 76. *Bibliog:* Laura Grahm (auth), Avanti, 80; Mirko Puccerelli (ed), Arte Now, 84. *Mem:* Artist Equity, New York; Il Gruppo, Italy; Art Police (co-pres, 88-). *Media:* Mixed Media. *Dealer:* Stephen H Jones 357 W 54th St New York NY 10019. *Mailing Add:* 252 W 21 St New York NY 10011

DIEBENKORN, RICHARD
PAINTER
b Portland, Ore, Apr 22, 22. *Study:* Univ Calif, 43-44; Calif Sch Fine Arts, 46; Stanford Univ, BA, 49; Univ NMex, MA, 52. *Work:* Art Gallery of Ontario; Corcoran Gallery Art, Washington, DC; Albright-Knox Gallery, Buffalo; Metrop Mus Art, New York; San Francisco Mus Art; and many others. *Exhib:* One-man shows, Wash Gallery Mod Art, DC, 64, Pa Acad Fine Arts, Philadelphia, 67, San Francisco Mus Mod Art, 72 & 83, Albright-Knox Art Gallery, Buffalo, NY, 76, Sheldon Mem Art Gallery, Lincoln, Nebr, 85, Mus Mod Art, NY, 88-89, Hara Mus Contemp Art, Japan, 89 & Whitechapel Art Gallery, London (also traveling), 91-93. *Pos:* Artist-in-residence, San Francisco Art Inst, 61-66, Stanford Univ, 63-64. *Teaching:* Prof art, Univ Calif, Los Angeles, 66-73. *Awards:* Purchase Prize, Olivet Col; Gold Medal, Pa Acad Fine Arts, 68; Skowhegan Medal Painting, Skowhegan Sch Art, 79; Edwin MacDowell Medal, 78. *Bibliog:* Richard Diebenkorn: Works on Paper, Houston, 87; Richard Diebenkorn, Rizzoli, 87; The Drawings of Richard Diebenkorn, Newton, 88. *Mem:* Am Acad Arts & Lett; Am Acad Design; Nat Inst Arts & Lett; Nat Coun Arts. *Media:* Acrylic, Oil. *Publ:* Auth, Drawing, 65; Ocean Park, Art Now, No 24, 1/80. *Mailing Add:* c/o M Knoedler & Co 19 E 70th St New York NY 10021

DIEHL, GUY LOUIS
PAINTER, INSTRUCTOR
b Pittsburgh, Pa, Feb 1, 49. *Study:* Calif State Univ, Hayward, BA, 73; San Francisco State Univ, MA, 76. *Work:* City Hall Bldg, Oakland, Calif; Redding Mus, Calif; Clark Co Libr, Las Vegas; Princeton Univ, NJ; Zimmerli Mus, Rutgers Univ, NJ. *Comn:* Barnes & Noble Bookstores Inc, New York;

Coldwell Banker, West Palm Beach, Fla; Robinson's Escondido, Calif; Hyatt Regency Alicante, Garden Grove, Calif. *Exhib:* One-man shows, Hank Baum Gallery, San Francisco, Calif, 79, 80, 82 & 84, 901 Market, Lurie Company, San Francisco, 86, Jeremy Stone Gallery, San Francisco, 86, 88 & 90, Hunsaker/Schlesinger Gallery, Los Angeles, 87, Magic Theatre, Fort Mason, San Francisco, 88, Univ Pacific, Stockton, Calif, 89; group exhibs, Northern California Realist Painters, Redding Mus, 82, Three Bay Area Painters, Diablo Valley Col, Calif, 83, Sun & Surf, Art Prog Inc, San Francisco & Los Angeles, 7-8/84, Gallery Artists, Jeremy Stone Gallery, San Francisco, 85; Allan Stone Gallery, New York, 90; Calif Contemp Realism, John Wayne Airport, Costa Mesa, Calif, 91; The Palm Tree Show-Modernism, San Francisco, 91. *Teaching:* Instr painting, Diablo Valley Col, Pleasant Hill, Calif, 77-82; instr painting, Chabot Col, Livermore, Calif, 80; Las Positas Col, Livermore, Calif, 80-90; Fort Mason Art Ctr, San Francisco, 92- *Awards:* Purchase Award, Alameda Co Art Commission, 72. *Bibliog:* Kenneth Baker (auth), San Francisco Chronicle, 9/20/86 & 6/17/91; Susan Hinton (auth), A relationship with photography, Artweek, 1/23/88; Ann Novarak (auth), West Coast Artists Exhibit Contemporary Still Lifes, Art Gallery Int, 5-6/88. *Media:* Acrylic, Watercolor. *Dealer:* Modernism 685 Market St San Francisco CA 94105; Hunsaker/Schlesinger Gallery 812 N La Cirenega Blvd Los Angeles CA 90069. *Mailing Add:* 188 W Blithedale Ave Mill Valley CA 94941

DIEHL, HANS-JURGEN
PAINTER
b Hanau, Germany, May 22, 40. *Study:* Ecole Nationale Supérieure des Beaux-Arts, Paris; Akademie der bildenden Künste, Munich; Hochschule fur Bildende Künste, Berlin, 59-66. *Work:* Mus Preusischer Kulturbesitz, Nat Gallery, Berlin, Ger; Ulmer Mus, Ulm, Ger; Sprengel Mus, Hannover, Ger; Kunsthalle Kiel, Kiel, Ger; Mus Witten, Witten, Ger. *Exhib:* Solo shows, Ulmer Mus, Ulm, Ger, 77, Kunsthalle, Berlin Ger, 85; Ugly Realism, Inst Contemp Arts, London, 78; Utopian Visions in Modern Art: Dreams and Nightmares, Hirshhorn Mus, Washington, DC, 83; Stationen der Moderne, Berlinische Galerie, Berlin, Ger, 89; Hugh Lane Munic Gallery Mod Art, Dublin, 91. *Teaching:* Prof painting, Hochschule der Künste, Berlin, 77. *Mem:* Deutscher Künstlerbund. *Dealer:* Galerie Limmer Maria-Theresia Strasse 15 7800 Freiburg Germany. *Mailing Add:* 47 Clinton St New York NY 10002

DIEHL, SEVILLA S
PAINTER
Study: Fleisher Art Mem, Philadelphia, 35-37; Philadelphia Mus Sch, 66-67; Barnes Found, 66-68; pvt studies with Hobson Pitman, Chinese brush painting with Phoebe Shih, mixed media with Ithzak Sankowsky & watercolor with Edgar Whitney. *Work:* Thomas Jefferson Univ; Widener Col; RCA Radio Corp, Washington, DC. *Exhib:* Woodmere Art Gallery 31st Ann Exhib, Chestnut Hill, Pa, 71; Catharine Lorillard Wolfe Art Club 66th Ann Show, Gramercy Sq, New York, 72; Nat Soc Painters in Casein & Acrylic 18th Ann, 72; three woman show, Philadelphia Art Alliance, 73; and numerous others. *Awards:* Shiva Artists Colors Award, Catharine Lorillard Wolfe Art Club, New York, 72; Best of Show, 74 & Jury Selection Award, 74, Main Line Ctr Arts, Haverford. *Bibliog:* Dorothy Grafly (auth), articles, Philadelphia Sunday Bulletin, 8/2/70 & Art-in-Focus, Philadelphia, 1/75. *Media:* Mixed. *Mailing Add:* 227 Swedeland Rd King of Prussia PA 19406

DIETRICH, BRUCE LEINBACH
MUSEUM DIRECTOR, ADMINISTRATOR
b Reading, Pa, Oct 10, 37. *Study:* Kutztown Univ, BS, 60; Univ Denver, 61; Temple Univ, 62-67; Millersville Univ, 67, State Univ NY, MS, 70; George Washington Univ, 81-83; Am Legal Inst/Am Bar Asn, 81-87; Kellog Proj/ Smithsonian Inst, 84, 85 & 87. *Collections Arranged:* The Sea, 76, Winter Winds, 78, Master Prints, 78, Spectrum, 78 & Director's Choice, 83, Reading Pub Mus & Art Gallery; Fractal Dimension, 88. *Pos:* Cur space sci, Reading Pub Mus & Art Gallery, 67-69, mus dir, 76-92; dir, Reading Planetarium, 69-; mus management consult, 92- *Mem:* Middle Atlantic Planetarium Soc; Asn Planetariums Can; Asn Sci Mus Dirs; Am Asn Advan Sci; and others. *Mailing Add:* 1546 Dauphin Ave Wyomissing PA 19610-2118

DIETZ, CHARLES LEMOYNE
MUSEUM DIRECTOR, PAINTER
b Zanesville, Ohio, Aug 8, 10. *Study:* Ohio Wesleyan Univ, 28-30; Carnegie Inst Technol, BFA, 35; Ohio State Univ, MFA & PhD, 56. *Work:* Zanesville Art Ctr, Ohio; Butler Art Inst, Youngstown, Ohio. *Comn:* Around the World, Hotel de Regulier, Amsterdam, Holland, 50; glass mosaic, stained glass windows & chandelier, St Stephens Church, Columbus, Ohio, 56; sculptural medalion, City of Zanesville, Ohio, 58; 4 stained glass windows, St James Episcopal Church, Zanesville, Ohio; stained glass rondel, St Thomas Activity Ctr, Zanesville, Ohio; and others. *Exhib:* Butler Annual, Butler Inst Am Art, Youngstown, Ohio, 60; Ohio Artists Exhib, Cleveland Mus Art, 62; Columbus Art Asn, Columbus Mus, 63-65; one-man show, Zanesville Art Ctr, Ohio; Ohio Artists, Johnson-Humrick House, Roscoe Village. *Pos:* Dir, Zanesville Art Ctr, Ohio, 55- *Teaching:* Dir, art dept, Westminster Col, New Wilmington, Pa, 49-53; asst prof art appreciation, Ohio State Univ, Columbus, 52-56; prof art hist & appreciation, Denison Univ, Granville, Ohio, 55-58. *Awards:* Distinguished Educator Award, 83; Secret Award Arts, Ohio Art Educ Asn, 86. *Media:* Watercolor, Stained Glass. *Mailing Add:* Zanesville Art Ctr 620 Military Rd Zanesville OH 43701

DI FATE, VINCENT
ILLUSTRATOR, PAINTER
b Yonkers, NY, Nov 21, 45. *Study:* Phoenix Sch Design, cert, 67; Sch Visual Arts, 68; Art Students League, 68-70. *Work:* NASA Mus, Cape Canaveral, Fla; NASAM, Smithsonian Inst, Washington, DC; Soc Illusr, New York; Univ Kans; New Brit Mus, Conn. *Exhib:* Solo shows, Reading Pub Mus, Pa, 78 & Mus Sci & Natural Hist, St Louis, Mo, 82; New Brit Mus Am Art, Conn, 80; Bronx Mus Arts, NY, 80; Stadthalle Limburg, WGer, 80; Am Mus-Hayden Planetarium, 88. *Teaching:* Instr, Univ Bridgeport, Conn, 79. *Awards:* Hugo Award, World Sci Fiction Asn, 78; Frank R Paul Award, Nashville Sci Fiction Asn, 78; Skylark Award, New Eng Sci Fiction Asn, 87. *Bibliog:* George Magnan (auth), Science fiction art, Today's Art & Graphics, 3/81; Ellen Datlow (auth), Stellar technician, Omni Mag, 5/81; Brian M Fraser (auth), All the colors of space and time, Questar Mag, 10/81. *Mem:* Soc Illusr; Graphic Artists Guild; Int Asn Astronomical Artists; Am Soc Aviation Artists. *Media:* Acrylic, Oil. *Publ:* Co-auth & illusr, Di Fate's Catalog of Science Fiction Hardware, Workman Publ, 80; contribr, The Science Fiction Reference Book, Starmont House, 81. *Mailing Add:* 12 Ritter Dr Wappingers Falls NY 12590

DIFRANZA, AMERICO M
PAINTER
b Boston, Mass, Feb 24, 19. *Study:* Mass Col Art, BFA, 42; Art Students League NY & Nat Acad Design, 73-78. *Work:* Readers Digest, Pepsico Inc, Union Carbide. *Comn:* Corp portraits, CPC Int, Englewood Cliffs, NJ, 85, Port Morris Corp, Bronx, NY, 87. *Exhib:* Pastel Soc Am Ann, Nat Arts Club, New York, 76-88; Hudson Valley Art Asn, Co Ctr, White Plains, NY, 76-83; Salmagundi Ann Open, New York, 78-80; Audubon Artist Ann, Nat Acad, New York, 78-80; Berkshire Art Asn Ann, Berkshire Mus, Pittsfield, Mass, 79 & 80; New Eng Art Exhib, Silvermine Guild Ctr, Conn, 80 & 81; Ann Invitational Exhib, Katonah Gallery, NY, 82, 83, 86 & 88; one man shows, Scarborough Gallery, 84-86 & 88. *Teaching:* Art Students League of NY, 84-; workshops, Nat Arts Club, 87-88; classes & demonstrations, Barrett House, Poughkeepsie, NY, 88; Nat Arts Club, New York, 88; painting workshops, Hudson River Valley, Greenville, NY, 90. *Awards:* Stefan Hirsch Mem Award for Portraiture, Audubon Artists Ann, 77; Award for Excellence in Any Medium, Hudson Valley Art Asn, Ann, 84; Master Pastelist, Pastel Soc Am, 85; Silverman Memorial Award for Landscape, Pastel Soc Am Ann, 86. *Bibliog:* Ron Lister (auth), Drawing with Pastels, Prentice-Hall, 82; article, Am Artist Mag, 8/89. *Mem:* Art Students League NY (bd control, 78-79, vpres, 80-81, pres & chmn bd, 81-83); Pastel Soc Am; Artists Fel Inc, NY; Knickbocker Artists, New York; Hudson Valley Art Assoc, White Plains, NY. *Media:* Pastels, Oils. *Publ:* Gannett Papers, White Plains, NY, 84; Master Pastelist Catalog, 86-87; auth & illusr, Am Artist, 89. *Dealer:* Scarborough Gallery 28 N Greeley Ave Chappaqua NY 10514; Katonah Gallery 28 Bedford Rd Katonah NY 10536. *Mailing Add:* 57 Chestnut St Rhinebeck NY 12572

DI GIACINTO, SHARON
PAINTER
b Chula Vista, Calif, Apr 13, 60. *Study:* Ohio Univ, Athens, BFA, 81; Tex Woman's Univ, Denton, MFA, 83. *Work:* Hill Country Arts Foundation, Ingram, Tex; Glendale Pub Libr, Ariz; Paradise Valley Community Col, Phoenix, Ariz; Glendale Community Col, Ariz; Peru State Col, Nebr. *Exhib:* Arizona Biennial, Tucson Mus Art, 88; Stockton Nat Print & Drawing Exhib, Haggin Mus Art, Calif, 92; 34th Ann Nat Exhib, San Diego Art Inst, Calif, 88; 64th Ann Nat April Salon, Springville Mus Art, Utah, 88; 23rd Ann Nat Exhib, San Bernardino County Mus, Redlands, Calif, 88; 53rd Ann Nat Midyear Exhib, Butler Inst Am Art, Youngstown, Ohio, 89; Hoyt Nat Painting & Drawing Exhib, Hoyt Inst Fine Arts, New Castle, Pa, 89; solo exhib, Sun Cities Art Mus, Sun City, Ariz, 89, The Return to Animal Imagery, Visual Arts Gallery, Phoenix, Ariz, 90; two person exhib, Chandler Ctr Arts, Ariz, 91; Am Realism Competition, Parkersburg Art Ctr, WVa, 92; 35th Chautauqua Nat Exib Am Art, NY, 92. *Pos:* Co-chmn, Peoria Arts Comn, 88-91. *Teaching:* Instr, painting & color theory, Phoenix Col, 83-84; Instr, drawing & color theory, Glendale Community Col, 85-88. *Awards:* Purchase Award, City of Mesa, 87; First Prize, St Hubert Giralda Animal Imagery Nat Exhib, 87; Best of Show, Don Ruffin Mem Statewide Exhib, 89. *Mem:* Col Art Asn of Am. *Media:* Oil, Graphite. *Mailing Add:* 6741 W Cholla Peoria AZ 85345

DIGIORGIO, JOSEPH J
PAINTER
b Brooklyn, NY, Jan 1, 31. *Study:* Cooper Union, BFA, 58. *Work:* 3-D Int, Houston; Bank of Calif, San Francisco; Security Pac Bank, Los Angeles; Western Elec, NJ; Shell Oil Co, Houston. *Comn:* Cherry Blossoms (oil), AT&T, Basking Ridge, NJ; Sierra Nev Mountains, comn by Victor Shaio, New York; Calif Coastline, Blue Cross of Calif, Los Angeles; After the Storm, comn by Victor Nevhaus, Houston. *Exhib:* US-Japan Exchange, US State Dept, Tokyo, 63; Biennial Exhib, Whitney Mus Am Art, 75; Large Scale Paintings, Security Pac Nat Bank, Los Angeles, 76; A Cur Collects, Art Inst Chicago, 77; 6 Sensibilities', Cornell Univ, Ithaca, NY, 78; A M Sachs, 80 & 81; Minn Art Mus, St Paul; and others. *Teaching:* Instr drawing, New York Univ, 80. *Awards:* Va Ctr Creative Arts Fel, 82 & 84. *Bibliog:* John Russell (auth), Whitney finds this land is its land, New York Times, 75; John Gruen (auth), Michael Walls exhibit, Soho Weekly News, 75; Tram Combs (auth), Arts Mag, 81. *Mem:* Artists Equity, New York. *Media:* Oil, Watercolor. *Mailing Add:* 269 Bowery New York NY 10002

DIGNAC, GENY
SCULPTOR, ENVIRONMENTAL ARTIST
b Buenos Aires, Arg, June 8, 32; US citizen. *Work:* Mus Mod Art, Cali, Colombia; Galeria Banco Cent, Quito, Ecuador; Latin Am Art Found, San Juan, PR. *Exhib:* Some More Beginnings, Exp in Art & Technol, Brooklyn Mus, NY, 68; IX Festival of Art, Cali, Colombia, 69; Earth, Air, Fire, Water,

Elements of Art, Boston Mus Fine Arts, 71; Arte de Sistema, Centro de Arte y Communicacion, Mus Mod Art, Buenos Aires, 71; III Biennial of Art Coltejer, Medellin, Colombia, 72; many one-woman shows, 67-71 & produced 27 fire gestures, US, Europe & SAm, 70-89. *Awards:* Uranus II (light & plastic sculpture), IX Festival of Art, Mus Mod Art, Cali, 69. *Bibliog:* J Bermudez (producer), Dignac, 67-68 & Three fire gestures (films), 70-71; R Osuna (producer), D Dig Dignac (film), 68; Salt River Fire Gesture, KAET (PBS), Tempe, Ariz, 80. *Media:* Light, Plastics; Fire, Temperatures. *Publ:* Auth, Three Fire Gestures, 70. *Dealer:* Osuna Gallery 1919 Q St NW Washington DC 20009. *Mailing Add:* 4109 E Via Estrella Phoenix AZ 85028

DILAURENTI, MARCO ITALO
ART DEALER, COLLECTOR
b Milan, Italy, Aug 8, 33. *Collections Arranged:* Reuben Nakian, Sculpture & Drawings, 85, Leon Polk Smith, New Works, 86, Alberto Burri, Eighteen Paintings, 1932-1986, 86 & Lowell Nesbitt, Secret Gardens, 86, DiLaurenti Gallery, New York. *Pos:* Pres, DiLaurenti Gallery, New York, currently. *Specialty:* Historic masters; established contemporary artists. *Collection:* Post Impressionists, modern masters, contemporary masters; painting and sculpture. *Mailing Add:* PO Box 330, Print Sta New York NY 10012

DILL, GUY GIRARD
SCULPTOR, EDUCATOR
b Duval Co, Fla, May 30, 46. *Study:* Chouinard Sch Art, Los Angeles, BFA. *Work:* Guggenheim Mus, Mus Mod Art, Whitney Mus Am Art, New York; Calif State Univ, Long Beach; Long Beach Mus Art, Calif; Mus Contemp Art, Los Angeles, Calif; Newport Harbor Art Mus, Calif. *Comn:* Prudential Ins Co, Canoga Park, Calif, 77; Fed Bldg, Huron, SD, 79; Pac Corp Towers, El Segundo, Calif, 86-87; Hughes Ctr, Las Vegas, Nev, 91; Sony Music Campus Arboretum in Santa Monica, Lowe Develop, Los Angeles, Calif, 92; and many pvt comns. *Exhib:* Guggenheim Mus, 71; Ace Gallery, Los Angeles, 71, 73 & 77; Felicity Samuel Gallery, London, Eng, 72; Pace Gallery, New York, 74 & 76; Biennial Show, Whitney Mus Am Art, 74; Sculpture Made in Place, Walker Art Ctr, Minneapolis, Minn, 76; Calif Sculpture Show, Bordeaux, France, 84 & Mannheim, Ger, West Bretton, Eng & Hovikodden, Norway, 85. *Teaching:* Instr & head sculpture dept, Univ Calif, Los Angeles, 77-82; instr, Wright State Univ, Dayton, Ohio, 77. *Awards:* Theodoron Award, Guggenheim Mus, 71; Nat Endowment Arts Fel, 74 & 81; First Prize, Am Show, Chicago Inst Art, 74. *Bibliog:* Bill Packer (auth), Interview with Guy Dill, Art & Artists, London, 72; Peter Frank & Phyllis Tuchman (auths), Guy Dill, Black Innes (catalog), p 1-20; Jan Butterfield (auth), About the Collection Artists, Art Collection of Pacific Enterprises (catalog), p 36, 111 & 186; Jan Butterfield (auth), Guy Dill sculpture is about proof, Artspace, p 55-57 & 71, 9-10/92. *Mem:* Calif Art Coun; Cedars Sinai Med Ctr, Los Angeles, Calif (adv coun arts, 85-92). *Media:* Mixed. *Mailing Add:* 1317 Innes Venice CA 90291

DILL, LADDIE JOHN
PAINTER, SCULPTOR
b Long Beach, Calif, Sept 14, 43. *Study:* Chouinard Art Inst, BFA, 68. *Work:* Mus Mod Art, New York; Norton Simon Mus, Pasadena, Calif; San Francisco Mus Mod Art, Calif; Smithsonian Inst, Washington, DC; Oakland Mus Art, Calif; Chicago Art Inst. *Exhib:* One-man shows, Pasadena Mus Mod Art, Calif, 71, Portland Univ Gallery, Ore, 71, Sonnabend Gallery, New York, 72, Calif Inst Technol, 82, Laica, 82 & Charles Cowles, 83; Recent Acquisitions, Pasadena Mus Mod Art, 71; 15 Abstract Artists, Santa Barbara Mus Art, Calif, 74; The Mod Era, San Francisco Mus Mod Art, 76 & Smithsonian Inst, Washington, DC, 77; Calif Painting & Sculpture, San Francisco Mus Mod Art, 77; Painting of the 70's, Albright-Knox Gallery, Buffalo, 78-79; Corcoran Biennial, 83-84. *Teaching:* Lectr painting, Univ Calif, Los Angeles, 75- *Awards:* Nat Endowment Arts Grant, 75 & 82; Guggenheim Fel, 80. *Bibliog:* Robert Hughes (auth), Los Angeles, Time Mag, 71; Judy Goodman (auth), Laddie Dill new work, Arts Mag, 75; Michael Smith (auth), Laddie John Dill, Baxter Art Gallery, Calif Inst Technol, Pasadena, 78. *Media:* Cement, Polymer, Glass; Oil on Canvas. *Dealer:* James Corcoran Gallery 1327 Fifth St Santa Monica CA. *Mailing Add:* 1625 Electric Ave Venice CA 90291

DILL, LESLEY
PAINTER, CURATOR
b Bronxville, NY, 1950. *Study:* Skidmore Col, 68-70; Trinity Col, BA(English, cum laude), 72; Smith Col, MA(art educ), 74; Md Inst Art, MFA(painting), 80. *Work:* ABC Motion Pictures, New York; Best Products Inc, Richmond, Va; Whoopi Goldberg, Los Angeles, Calif; Prudential Insurance Co Am, Newark, NJ; Zaner Corp, Rochester, NY. *Exhib:* Solo exhibs, 55 Mercer St Gallery, New York, 83, Galerie Taub, Philadelphia, Pa, 85, Carlo Lamagna Gallery, New York, 87 & 89, G H Dalsheimer Gallery, Baltimore, Md, 87 & 90 & Gracie Mansion Gallery, New York, 91; World AIDS Day, Manhattan Community Col, New York, 90; The Art of Drawing, Lehman Col, City Univ New York, 90; Sculptor's Drawings, E Hampton Ctr Contemp Art, Long Island, NY, 90; Sense of Self, Triplex Gallery, Manhattan Community Col, New York, 90; American Art Today: New Directions, Fla Int Univ, Miama, 91. *Pos:* Cur, Fall Show, Condeso/Lawler Gallery, New York, 84; cur, Traps: Elements of Psychic Seduction, Carlo Lamagna Gallery, New York, 87. *Teaching:* Instr art, St Ann's Sch, Brooklyn, NY, 84-91; Parsons Sch Design, 90-91. *Awards:* Zaner Corp Purchase Award, Small Works 83, Patterson Sims, 83; Sculpture Fel, Nat Endowment Arts, 90. *Bibliog:* Louise Sheldon (auth), Lesley Dill's Sculptures are Sensual and Spiritual, Baltimore Chronicle, 1/3/90; David Hirsh (auth), AIDS: Challenging Art, NY Native, 1/29/90; Rose Slivka (auth), From the Studio, E Hampton Star, 11/15/90. *Mailing Add:* 6 Greene St New York NY 10013

DILLINGHAM, RICK (JAMES RICHARD), II
CERAMIST, DEALER
b Lake Forest, Ill, Nov 13, 52. *Study:* Calif Col Arts & Crafts, Univ NMex, BFA; Scripps Col, MFA. *Work:* Mus Albuquerque, NMex; Los Angeles County Mus Art, Calif; Brooklyn Mus, New York; Victoria and Albert Mus, London; Mus NMex, Santa Fe. *Exhib:* Garth-Clark Gallery, New York; Ceramic Echoes, Nelson-Atkins Mus Art, Kansas City, Mo, 83; Gibbes Art Gallery, Charleston, SC, 84; Salon d'Automne, Le Grand Palais, Paris, 84; 13th Chunici Int Exhib Ceramic Art, Nagoya, Japan, 85; Contemp Am Prints & Ceramics, Brooklyn Mus, New York, 85; 3rd Western States Exhib, Brooklyn Mus, New York, 86; Craft Today: Poetry of the Physical, Am Craft Mus, New York, 87; Surface & Form, Nat Mus Ceramic Art, Baltimore, Md, 89; Raku: Transforming the Tradition, Kansas City Contemp Arts Ctr, Mo, 89. *Collections Arranged:* Pueblo Pottery & Demonstration, Dewey-Kofron Gallery, Santa Fe, NMex, 77; Seven Families in Pueblo Pottery (auth, catalogue), Maxwell Mus Anthrop, Univ NMex, 74; The Vessel, 12 Contemp Ceramic Artists, Delahunty Gallery, Dallas, Tex, 80; The Red and the Black: retrospective of Margaret Tafoya (auth, catalog), Wheelwright Mus, Santa Fe, NM; I am Here, Mus Indian Art & Culture New Mex (auth, catalog), 87; Pueblo Pottery: selections from the collection of Rick Dillingham, Nat Mus Ceramic Art, Baltimore, Md. *Teaching:* Asst prof ceramics, Calif Col Arts & Crafts, 76, 79 & 80; ceramics workshops, Tucson Mus Art, Ariz, 76, Univ Iowa, 77, The Boulder Potter's Guild, Colo, 79, Raku Ho'Alaule'A, Honolulu, 80; and numerous other workshops and seminars. *Awards:* Best of Show & Purchase Award, Craft 5, Mus Albuquerque, 75; Purchase Award, Pottery 5, Calif Polytech State Univ, San Luis Obispo, 75; Nat Endowment Arts Craftsman's Fel, 77-78 & 82-83. *Bibliog:* Susan Wechsler (auth), Low fire ceramics, Am Craft Mag, 11/81; Katharine Pearson (auth), American Crafts, Stuart, Tabori & Chang, New York, 83; Erin MacLellan (auth), The inspiration of New Mexico at the Salon d'Automne, Paris, Artspace Mag, spring 84. *Mem:* Am Crafts Coun. *Media:* Ceramics. *Specialty:* American Indian art. *Collection:* American Indian art, contemporary ceramics and lithography. *Publ:* Nine Pueblo potters, Studio Potter, 77; The pottery of Acoma Pueblo, Am Indian Art, 77; The ceramics collection of the School of American Research, Santa Fe, NMex, Studio Potter, Vol 12, No 2, 6/84. *Mailing Add:* 1713 Agua Fria St Box 2601 Santa Fe NM 87501

DILLON, C DOUGLAS
PATRON, COLLECTOR
b Geneva, Switz, Aug 21, 09. *Study:* Harvard Univ, AB, MCL, Harvard, Princeton, Penn, Columbia, New York Univ, LLD. *Pos:* Trustee Emer, Metrop Mus Art, 51-, pres, 70-78, chmn, 78-83; mem bd, Nat Mus Servs, 78-83, chmn, 82-83; mem bd, Nat Counc Arts, 83-89. *Collection:* French impressionist painting; 18th century French furniture and decorative objects; old Chinese paintings. *Mailing Add:* 1270 Ave of the Americas Rm 12300 New York NY 10020

DILLON, MILDRED (MURPHY)
PRINTMAKER
b Philadelphia, Pa, Oct 12, 07. *Study:* Philadelphia Col Art, 25-28; Pa Acad Fine Arts, 28-29; Barnes Found, with Henry McCarter & Earle Horter, 29-31. *Work:* Philadelphia Mus Art, Free Libr & Am Colorprint Soc Collection, Philadelphia; Barnes Found, Merion, Pa; Arch Can Painters & Etchers. *Exhib:* Libr Cong Nat, 57; Contemp Graphics Overseas, Mus Bellas Artes, Caracas, Venezuela, 60; Color Prints of the Americas, NJ State Mus, 70; one-man show, Philadelphia Art Alliance, 75, & Woodmere Art Gallery, 82; and others. *Pos:* Vpres, Am Color Print Soc, Philadelphia, 55-; chmn, Rittenhouse Sq Outdoor Exhib, 58-70; demonstr, Print Club Philadelphia, 61-70. *Awards:* Harrison Morris Prize, Pa Acad Fine Arts, 53; George Lear Mem Prize, Woodmere Mus, 58; Klein Prize, Print Club Philadelphia, 67. *Mem:* Philadelphia Art Alliance (mem bd dirs, 60-73); Pa Acad Fine Arts. *Media:* Serigraphy, Woodcut. *Mailing Add:* 6445 Germantown Philadelphia PA 19119-2345

DILLON, PAUL SANFORD
PAINTER
b Newport, Vt, Aug 5, 43. *Work:* Los Angeles Co Mus Art, Los Angeles, Calif; La Jolla Mus Art, Calif; Cheney Cowles Mus, Spokane, Wash; Security Pac Bank Collection, Los Angeles; Prudential Insurance Co Collection, Los Angeles. *Exhib:* Los Angeles Six, Los Angeles Co Mus Art, 74; Biennial of Am Painting, Whitney Mus Am Art, New York, 75 & Corcoran Gallery Art, Washington, DC, 77; Los Angeles Painting, Mus Mod Art, New York, 77; Collector's Choice, Los Angeles Inst Contemp Art, 77; San Francisco Mus Mod Art; one-man shows, Jack Glenn Gallery, Newport Beach, Calif, 75, Tortue Gallery, Los Angeles, 77 & 78, Iolas Gallery, New York, 78 & 79 & Newport Harbor Art Mus, 79. *Awards:* New Talent Award, Los Angeles Co Mus Art, 74; Purchase Award, Contemporary Painting, Cheney Cowles Mus, 77. *Mem:* Los Angeles Inst Contemp Art. *Media:* Acrylic, Collage. *Mailing Add:* 1316 S Fourth Ave Los Angeles CA 90019

DILLOW, NANCY E (NANCY ELIZABETH ROBERTSON)
ADMINISTRATOR, HISTORIAN
b Toronto, Ont, June 26, 28. *Study:* Univ Toronto, BA. *Collections Arranged:* J E H MacDonald, RCA, 1873-1932 (with catalog), 65; Piet Mondrian and the Hague School of Landscape Painting (with catalog), 69; Saskatchewan: Art and Artists (with catalog), 71; Marilyn Levine-Donovan Chester (with catalog), 74; Frank Nulf (with catalog), 76; Transformation of Vision, H Eric Bergman (catalog), 83, Tony Tascona (catalog), 84. *Pos:* From asst cur to cur exten & educ, Art Gallery Ont, 56-67; dir, Norman Mackenzie Art Gallery, 67-79; chief cur, Winnipeg Art Gallery, 80-86. *Teaching:* Prof hist Can art, Univ Regina, 72-79. *Mem:* Fel Can Mus Asn (coun, 67-70). *Res:* Canadian art history. *Mailing Add:* 99 Estelle Ave Toronto ON M2N 5H4 Canada

DI MEO, DOMINICK
PAINTER, SCULPTOR
b Niagara Falls, NY, Feb 1, 27. *Study:* Art Inst Chicago, four year dipl, 50, BFA, 52; Univ Iowa, MFA, 53. *Work:* Art Inst Chicago; Whitney Mus Am Art, New York; Ill Bell Tel Co, Chicago; Univ Mass, Amherst; Nat Collection Am Art, Smithsonian Inst. *Exhib:* Ann Exhib Contemp Am Painting, Whitney Mus Am Art, 67-68; Fantasy & Figure, Am Fedn Arts, New York & Traveling Show, 68-69; Violence in Recent American Art, Mus Contemp Art, Chicago, 68-69; The Crowd: Exhibit of Sculpture, Paintings & Graphics, Arts Club Chicago, 69; Visions/Painting & Sculpture: Distinguished Alumni 1945-Present, Art Inst Chicago, 76; 16th Joan Miro Int Drawing Prize Competition, Barcelona, Spain & Sala de Cult de la Caja de Ahorros de Navarra, Pamplona, 77; 100 Artists--100 Years, Alumni of the School of the Art Institute of Chicago, Centennial Exhibition, Art Inst Chicago, 79-80; Momento Mori, Centro Cultural/Arte Contemp, Mexico City, Mex, 86-87. *Teaching:* Instr, Chicago Acad Fine Arts, 67-69; vis artist, Art Inst Chicago, 77. *Awards:* Guggenheim Mem Found Fel Graphics, 72-73; Nat Endowment Arts Sculpture Fel, 82-83. *Bibliog:* Whitney Halstead (auth), Introd, In: Di Meo, Work: 1959-1966, Galaxie, 67. *Media:* Mixed. *Mailing Add:* 429 Broome St New York NY 10013

DIMONDSTEIN, MORTON
SCULPTOR, PAINTER
b New York, NY, Nov 5, 20. *Study:* Am Artists Sch, New York, 37-39; Art Students League, 39-41; Otis Art Inst, Los Angeles, 45-48; Inst Nac, Mexico City, Mex, 50-51. *Work:* World Bank, Washington, DC; Libr Cong; Pushkin Art Mus, Moscow, USSR; Seattle Art Mus, Wash; Portland Art Mus, Ore. *Exhib:* Solo exhibs, Jacqueline Anhalt Gallery, Los Angeles, 67-72, James Willis Gallery, San Francisco, 75-76, Roko Gallery, New York, 77, Gallery Nuance, Amsterdam, 80, Heritage Gallery, Los Angeles, 86 & Gallerie Ana Izac, Beverly Hills, 89. *Pos:* Staff artist, Patzcuaro, Mex, 52-53. *Teaching:* Instr all media, Sch Fine Art, Los Angeles, 63-72; instr drawing & sculpture, Univ Southern Calif, 64-68. *Awards:* Winner, Am Contemp Art Gallery, Nat One-Man Show Competition, New York, 51. *Mem:* Soc Am Graphic Artists. *Publ:* Mexico (portfolio of woodcuts), Posada Graphics, 54. *Dealer:* Heritage Gallery 718 N La Cienega Blvd Los Angeles CA 90069; Roko Gallery 257 East 7th St New York NY 10009. *Mailing Add:* 749 Longwood Ave Los Angeles CA 90005

DIMSON, THEO AENEAS
DESIGNER, ILLUSTRATOR
b London, Ont, Apr 8, 30. *Study:* Ont Col Art, Toronto, 50. *Work:* Typomundus 20, France. *Exhib:* Am Inst Graphic Arts, New York; Montreal Art Director's Show, 51-75; Graphica Club Toronto; Graphica Club Montreal; Int Poster Art, Bulgaria; one-man poster show, Toronto, 78; Posters Biennial, Warsaw, Poland, 80; Lahti Poster Biennial, Finland, 81; 1st Int Tirennial of Posters, Japan, 85; Int Litfass Biennial, Munich, Ger, 92. *Pos:* Vpres creative design, Art Assocs Ltd, Toronto, 59-65; pres & creative dir, Theo Dimson Design, Inc, Toronto, 65- *Awards:* Medal Awards, Arts Directors Club, Toronto & Montreal; Award of Excellence, Am Inst Graphic Arts; First Winner, Usherwood Award for continuous outstanding contribution to the Visual Arts, Can, 86. *Bibliog:* Hara (auth), Designers, Graphic Design Mag, 62; Republic of Childhood, Oxford Univ, 67. *Mem:* Royal Can Acad; assoc of Ont Col Art; Alliance Graphique Int; fel Graphic Designers Can; Art Dirs Club. *Media:* Graphic. *Publ:* Illusr, The Sunken City, 60 & The Double Knights, 63, Oxford; Rubaboo Five, Gage, 65; auth, Great Canadian Posters, Oxford Univ Press. *Mailing Add:* Box 358 Mt Albert ON L0G 1M0 Canada

DINC, ALEV NECILE
PAINTER, DESIGNER
b Turkey; US citizen. *Study:* Inst Technol, Ankara, Turkey, 56-61; Ridgewood Art Sch, NJ, 68; Fashion Inst Technol, New York, 69. *Work:* Turkish Embassy, NY; Kismet Furniture, Paterson, NJ. *Exhib:* Nat Turkish Art Show, Ankara Yenlgehir, Turkey, 60; In Between Two World, Int Market, Paterson, NJ, 66; World of Fantasy (No 2), Fine Arts Ctr, Passaic, NJ, 86; World of Fantasy (No 1), Nabisco Brands Gallery, Fairlawn, NJ, 86; Dreams and Visions, Broadway Gallery, Paterson & Union Camp Corp, Wayne, NJ, 87; International Art Show, Morin Miller Galleries, New York, 87; International Exhib, Mussavi Arts Ctr, New York, 88; Spring Bouquet White Gallery, Frankling Lakes, NJ, 89; group shows, Nathans Gallery, West Paterson, NJ, 89, Salute to Women Artists in New Jersey, Wayne, 90, ARTMH, Fine Arts Ctr, Passaic, NJ, 90, Presbyterian Church, Franklin Lakes, NJ, 90, Northern NJ Arts Ctr, New Milford, 91 & Int Cult Prog, Paramus, NJ, 91. *Awards:* First Prize, Turkey, 60; Danielle Ruebel, Mental Health Orgn, 89. *Bibliog:* Abraham Ilein (auth), Art Review, Artspeak, 87. *Mem:* Salute to Women in the Arts; Essex Phoenix Artist Asn; Art for Mental Health. *Media:* Oil, Acrylic; Watercolor. *Publ:* Auth, articles, N Jersey Herald New, Encyclopedia of Living Artist in America, 88. *Dealer:* White Gallery 777 Frankling Ave Frankling Lakes NJ 07417. *Mailing Add:* 90 Day St Apt G-4 Clifton NJ 07011

DINE, JAMES
PAINTER, SCULPTOR
b Cincinnati, Ohio, June 16, 35. *Study:* Univ Cincinnati; Boston Mus Sch; Ohio Univ, BFA, 58; studied drawing with Frederick Leach. *Work:* Whitney Mus Am Art, Mus Mod Art, New York; Tate Gallery, London, Eng; Nat Collection Fine Art; Albright-Knox Art Gallery, Buffalo; Stedelijk Mus, Amsterdam, Neth; Centre Pompidou, Paris, France; Western Australian Art Gallery, Perth, Australia; Solomon R Guggenheim Mus, New York; Metrop Mus Art, New York. *Comn:* Mural, Nuveen Co, Chicago, 85; Double Boston Venus, Boston, 87; Cincinnati Venus, Cincinnati, 88; Sculpture, Tishman Speyer Trammel Crow Ltd Partnership, NY; Rosehaugh Stanhope Develop PLC, Broadgate, London; Seibu Dept Store, Tokyo. *Exhib:* Happenings and Fluxus, Galerie 1900-2000, Paris, 89; Solo exhibs, Pace Gallery, New York, 90, Nelson-Atkins Mus Art, Kansas City, 90, Joanne Chappell Gallery, San Francisco, 90, Augun Gallery, Portland, 90, Blum Helman Gallery, Los Angeles, 90, Isetan Mus, Tokyo, 90-91 & Mus Art, Kintetsu (Osaka), 90-91; Galeria Enrico Navarra, Paris, 90; GegenwartEwigKeit, Martin-Gropius-Bau, Berlin, 90; Pop on Paper, James Goodman Gallery, New York, 90; Portrait of an American Gallery, Galeria Isy Brachot, Brussels, 90; Defining Modernism: Art of the 20th Century, Fairfield Univ, 90; Selected Works, Galeria Kaj Forsblom, Helsinki, 90; A Claim to Primacy, Lowe Art Mus, Univ Miami, 90. *Teaching:* Vis prof, Oberlin Col, 65 & Cornell Univ, 67; artist-in-residence, Williams Col, Williamstown, Mass, 76. *Awards:* Norman Harris Silver Medal & Prize, Art Inst Chicago, 64. *Bibliog:* Geraldine Norman (auth), Kings of the art jungle, Independent, 4/20/90; Sara Pearce (auth), Pullout cost CAC $65,000, Enquirer (Cincinnati), 5/30/90; Ann Seymour (auth), Frankly fun, Nob Hill Gazette, 7/90; The Nikon-toting Boswell of the Rolling Stones, Daily Telegraph, 7/6/90. *Mem:* Am Acad Inst Arts & Letts, New York. *Publ:* Illusr, The Poet Assassinated, 68; auth & illusr, Welcome Home Lovebirds, 69; coauth, Work from the Same House, 69; co-auth & illusr, The Adventures of Mr & Mrs Jim & Ron, 70. *Mailing Add:* c/o The Pace Gallery 32 E 57th St New York NY 10022

DINGUS, PHILLIP RICK
PHOTOGRAPHER, DRAFTSMAN
b Appleton City, Mo, Jan 3, 51. *Study:* Univ Calif, Santa Barbara, BA, 73; Univ NMex, MA, 77, MFA, 81. *Work:* Ctr Creative Photog, Tucson, Ariz; Mus Mod Art, Metrop Mus Art, New York; San Francisco Mus Mod Art; Mus Fine Arts, Houston, Tex; and others. *Exhib:* James Gallery, Houston Int Foto Fest, 88 & 90; Phoenix Art Mus, Ariz, 90; Dine'tah-Hajiinei: Place of Emergence, SW Mus, Los Angeles, Calif, 91; Between Home & Heaven, Smithsonian Inst, Washington, DC, 92; Dickinson State Univ, NDak, 92; plus many others. *Teaching:* Grad Teaching asst art photogr & fundamental, Univ NMex, 76-79; lectr photogr drawing & art hist, NMex Tech, 79-81; vis lectr, Univ Colo, Boulder, 81-82; assoc prof, Tex Tech Univ, 82- *Awards:* Nat Endowment Art/Mid Am Art Alliance Reg Fel, 87; Proj Grant photog India, 87-88; plus many others. *Bibliog:* Michael Costello (auth), Alternate views: A recent film by Roger Sweet and Rick Dingus, Artspace, summer 78. *Mem:* Soc Photog Educ; Friends Photog. *Publ:* Auth, The Photographic Artifacts of Timothy O'Sullivan, 82, Second View: The Rephotographic Survey Project, 84, Marks in Place, 88, Between Home & Heaven: Contemporary American Landscape Photo, 92, NMAA, Smithsonian, Univ NMex Press. *Dealer:* James Gallery 2930 Revere Suite 200 Houston TX 77098; Etherton/Stern Gallery 135 S Sixth Ave Tucson AZ 85701. *Mailing Add:* 4702 62nd St Lubbock TX 79414

DINHOFER, SHELLY MEHLMAN
WRITER, HISTORIAN
b Brooklyn, NY, May 29, 27. *Study:* Brooklyn Col, BA, 49, BS, 51, MA, 75; City Univ NY-Grad Ctr, doctoral candidate, 78. *Collections Arranged:* Celebrating the Gershwins, 82; Brooklyn Themes: Art in the Years of Roosevelt & La Guardia (auth, catalog), 82; Crossing Brooklyn Ferry: The River & The Bridge (auth, catalog), 83; Politics in Art: The Art of Politics (auth, catalog), 84; Brooklyn's Bounty: Natural Splendor and Domestic Opulence (auth, catalog), 85; From Brooklyn to the Sea: Ships, Seafarers and New York Harbor (auth, catalog), 85; Now Reposing in Green-Wood Cemetery: Artists, Heroes, Villains & Other Illustrious Residents (auth, catalog), 86; Tides of Immigration: Romantic Visions and Urban Realities (auth, catalog), 86; The Grand Game of Baseball And the Brooklyn Dodgers (auth, catalog), 87. *Pos:* Dir, Mus Borough Brooklyn, 82-87; spec adv art & tourism, NY State Assembly, 89-92. *Teaching:* Instr art hist, Brooklyn Col, 75-76, coordr, Mus Progs & Studies, 81-82; adj assoc prof, Yeshiva Univ, 79-81 & City Univ NY, 80-81. *Awards:* Brooklyn Woman of the Year, 84. *Mem:* Col Art Asn; Am Asn Mus; Am Asn Col Profs. *Res:* 19th Century American art; 19th century French academic art; 19th-20th century Art of baseball; 19th-20th century Art of politics. *Collection:* African and pre-Columbian sculpture; Japanese prints; 19th century American decorative arts, contemporary art. *Publ:* Auth, Fun and Fantasy: Brooklyn's Amusement Parks and Leisure Areas, 84; Art of Baseball, Crown Publ, 90. *Mailing Add:* 114 Westminster Rd Brooklyn NY 11218

DINNERSTEIN, HARVEY
PAINTER
b Brooklyn, NY, Apr 3, 28. *Study:* With Moses Soyer, 44-46; Art Students League, 46-47; Tyler Art Sch, Temple Univ, cert art, 50. *Work:* Metrop Mus Art (Lehman Collection) & Martin Luther King Labor Ctr, New York; New Britain Mus Art, Conn; Fleming Mus, Univ Vt, Burlington; Nat Mus Am Art, Washington, DC; Butler Inst Am Art, Youngstown, Ohio. *Exhib:* Contemp Am Paintings, 55 & Contemp Drawings, 64, Whitney Mus Am Art, New York; Childe Hassam Award Exhib, Am Acad & Inst of Arts & Lett, New York, 74, 78 & 87; Living Am Artists & the Figure, Pa State Univ Mus Art, University Park, 74; 3 Centuries of Am-Nude, New York Cultural Ctr, 76; Bicentennial Exhib of Am Illus, New York Hist Soc, 76; one-man show, Sindin Galleries, New York, 83; plus many others. *Pos:* Academician, Nat Acad Design, New York, 74. *Teaching:* Instr drawing & painting, Sch Visual Arts, New York, 63-80, Nat Acad Design, 74-, Art Students League, 80- *Awards:* Temple Gold Medal, Pa Acad Fine Art, 50; Hassam & Spelcher Purchase Award, Am Acad & Inst of Arts & Lett, 74 & 78; Ranger Purchase Award, Nat Acad Design, 76; Obrig Prize, Nat Acad Design, 86. *Bibliog:* Susan E Meyer (auth), 20 Figure Painters and How They Work, Watson-

Guptill, 79; How We Lived, Esquire Mag 50th Anniversary Issue, 6/83; The Seasons, Am Artist Mag, 8/83. *Mem:* Audubon Artists; Allied Artists. *Media:* Oil, Pastel. *Publ:* Coauth, New look at protest, the eight since 1908, Art News, 2/58; illusr, Drawings of the Montgomery Bus Boycott, 12/64 & illusr & auth, The face of protest, 12/68, Esquire Mag; illusr, A Portfolio of Drawings, Kenmore Press, 68; illusr & auth, Harvey Dinnerstein--Artist at Work, Watson-Guptill, 78; On pastel, Am Artist Mag, 5/88. *Dealer:* Capricorn Galleries 4849 Rugby Ave Bethesda MD 20814. *Mailing Add:* 933 President St Brooklyn NY 11215

DINNERSTEIN, LOIS
HISTORIAN, LECTURER
b New York, NY, Oct 24, 32. *Study:* NY Univ Wash Sq Col, BA, 53; NY Univ Inst Fine Arts, MA, 60; City Univ New York Grad Ctr, PhD, 79. *Pos:* Res cur, Benjamin Sonnenberg Collection, New York, 57-58, Daniel & Rita Fraad Collection, New York, 62-63 & Montclair Art Mus, NJ, 75-76. *Teaching:* Instr art hist, Vassar Col, 59-61, City Univ New York, Brooklyn Col, 64-77; adj prof, Brooklyn Ctr, Long Island Univ, 82-84; adj prof, Am Civilization Prog, Grad Sch Arts & Sci, NY Univ, 88; lect, Art Students League, 90-91. *Awards:* Rockefeller Found fel, City Univ New York, 77. *Mem:* Asn Historians Am Art. *Res:* Eighteenth and 19th century American art. *Publ:* Auth, Thomas Eakins' Crucifixion as Perceived by Mariana Griswold Van Rensselaer, 5/79, The iron worker and King Solomon: Some images of labor in American art, 9/79, Beyond revisionism: Henry Lerolle's The Organ, 1/80 & The industrious housewife: Some images of labor in American art, 4/81, Arts Mag; John Singleton Copley's Portrait of Elizabeth Allen Stevens (art mus catalog), Res Supplement, Montclair, 79; Artists in their studios, Am Heritage, 2/83; When Liberty was Controversial, In Support of Liberty: European Paintings at the 1883 Statue of Liberty Pedestal Fund Art Loan Exhibition (exhib catalog), Parrish Art Mus, Southampton & Nat Acad Design, New York, 86; and others. *Mailing Add:* 933 President St Brooklyn NY 11215-1603

DINNERSTEIN, SIMON A
PAINTER
b Brooklyn, NY, Feb 16, 43. *Study:* City Col New York, BA, 65; Brooklyn Mus Art Sch, with David Levine & Louis Grebenak, 64-67; Hochschule für Bildende Kunst, Kassel, Ger, Fulbright fel, 70-71. *Work:* Munson-Williams-Proctor Inst, Utica; Univ Md Art Mus, College Park; Minn Mus Art, St Paul; Albrecht Mus, St Joseph, Mo; Univ Mo, Columbia; Palmer Mus Art, Pa State Univ, University Park; Sara Roby Found; Nat Mus Am Art, Smithsonian Inst; Martin Luther King Labor Ctr, New York. *Exhib:* Childe Hassam Mem Exhib, Am Acad Arts & Lett, 75-78; New Sch, 76 & 79; one-man shows, Staempfli Gallery, 75, 79 & 88, Inst Int Educ, 76-77 & 79, Am Acad in Rome, 77 & New Sch, 81; Gallery 1199, 85; St Paul's Sch, Concord, NH, 91. *Teaching:* Instr painting, Brooklyn Mus Art Sch, 71-72; instr painting & drawing, The New Sch, New York, 75-; instr, New York City Tech Col, 79-; lectr & instr, Am Acad Rome, 77-78, US Info Serv, Spain, 79 & Pa State Univ, 84; vis prof, Pratt Inst, 86-87. *Awards:* Ingram Merrill Award for Painting, 78-79; Stefan Hirsch Mem Award, Audubon Artists, 84; Artists Fel, New York Found Arts, 87. *Bibliog:* Museum acquires triptych, Centre Daily Times, Pa, 12/16/82; Looking at one's artwork, Am Artist, 4/86; The Art of Simon Dinnerstein (monogr), Univ Ark Press, 268 pps, 140 reproductions, 90. *Mem:* Soc Fellows Am Acad Rome; Elected Mem Nat Acad Design, 92. *Media:* Miscellaneous, Oil. *Publ:* auth, The Art of Simon Dinnerstein, Univ Ark Press, 90. *Dealer:* Staempfli Gallery New York NY. *Mailing Add:* 415 First St Brooklyn NY 11215

D'INNOCENZO, NICK
SCULPTOR, DESIGNER
b Rochester, NY, Dec 12, 34. *Study:* State Univ NY Buffalo, BS(art educ), 60; Cranbrook Acad Art, MFA(sculpture/design), 63. *Work:* State Univ NY Buffalo; Smith-Corona-Marchant Corp, Syracuse, NY. *Comn:* Welded bronze reliefs, State Univ NY Col Oswego, City of Oswego & Oswego Co Savings Bank; 2 O'clock-Tower, 80' Fountain, State Univ NY. *Exhib:* Artists of Finger Lakes, Mem Art Gallery, Rochester, NY, 65-; Graphics USA, NY State Fairgrounds, Syracuse, NY, 70; Mirrors, Motors & Motion, Albright-Knox Art Gallery, Buffalo, 71; Artists of NY, Everson Mus, Syracuse, 75; Univ Artists, State Univ NY Albany, 76; Artists of NY State, State Fairgrounds, Syracuse, 81 & 89. *Teaching:* Prof sculpture & design, State Univ NY Col Oswego, 63- *Awards:* Chancellor's Award for Excellence in Teaching, State Univ NY, 79; First Prize Sculpture, Oswego Art Guild, 89 & Rochester, Mich. *Bibliog:* George Stark (auth), Artists/Teachers, Sch Arts, 66. *Mem:* NY State Art Teachers Asn; Int Sculpture Ctr. *Media:* Steel, Mixed Media. *Mailing Add:* Edwards Circle RD 3 Oswego NY 13126

DINSMORE, STEPHEN PUL
PAINTER
b Omaha, Nebr, July 7, 52. *Study:* Univ Nebr, Lincoln, BA, 74. *Work:* Neb Mus Art, Kearney. *Exhib:* Solo shows, Donald Wren Gallery, New York, 87, Honeywell Corp Gallery, Minneapolis, 87, Gallery 72, Omaha, 88, Samuel Dividson Gallery, Seattle, 90 RVS Fine Art, Southampton, NY, 89-92 & Lydon Fine Art, Chicago, 92; Robischon Gallery, Denver, 91-92; Susan Conway Gallery, Washington, DC, 92; Gallery Camino Real, Boca Raton, Fla, 92; Morgan Gallery, Kansas City, Mo, 92; Groveland Gallery, Minneapolis, 92; and others. *Awards:* Artist Residency, Bemis Found, Omaha, Nebr, 92. *Media:* Oil. *Publ:* article, Country Home Mag, 6/91; article, Omaha World Herald, 4/92; Article, Chicago Tribune, 4/2/92. *Mailing Add:* 99 Commercial St Brooklyn NY 11222

DINTENFASS, TERRY
DEALER
b Apr 4, 20. *Pos:* Dir, Terry Dintenfass, Inc. *Mem:* Art Dealer Asn Am. *Specialty:* Contemporary American & English art. *Mailing Add:* 50 W 57th St New York NY 10019

DIPASQUALE, DOMINIC THEODORE
SILVERSMITH, EDUCATOR
b Buffalo, NY, Feb 21, 32. *Study:* State Univ NY Col Buffalo, BS(art educ); Sch Am Craftsmen, Rochester Inst Technol, MFA(metal design). *Work:* First Methodist Church, Oswego, NY; Syracuse Diocese; and others. *Comn:* Inaugural medallion, State Univ NY Col Oswego, 66 & Worcester State Col, Mass, 75; Coat of Arms, comn by Bishop J F Cunningham, Syracuse Diocese, NY, 75. *Exhib:* Silversmiths of NY, Univ Mex, 75; 2nd Biennial Int Exhib, Tweed Mus, Duluth, 75; Nat Art Slide Competition, Fla, 75; Enamels 78, Torpedo Factory, Arlington, Va, 78; Prof Produce Invitational, Craftsmens Gallery, Scarsdale, NY, 79; Cooperstown Nat Art Exhib; Invitational, Kipp Gallery, Indiana, Pa; and others. *Teaching:* Prof jewelry & metals, State Univ NY Col Oswego, 63-, chmn dept art, 74- *Awards:* First Prize, Las Vegas Nat Art Round-Up, Nev, 69 & NY State Fair, Syracuse, 73; Jurors Award for Most Provacative in Show, Arnot Gallery, Elmira, NY, 79. *Mem:* Soc NAm Goldsmiths; York State Crafts Asn; Buffalo Craftsmen; Am Crafts Coun; Col Art Asn Am. *Media:* Gems, Precious Metals. *Publ:* Auth, Jewelry Making: An Illustrated Guide to Technique, 75. *Dealer:* Hanover Gallery Irving St Syracuse NY. *Mailing Add:* RR 5 No 139 Oswego NY 13126

DIPERNA, FRANK PAUL
PHOTOGRAPHER, INSTRUCTOR
b Pittsburgh, Pa, Feb 4, 47. *Study:* Ctr of the Eye, Aspen, Colo, with Gary Winogrand, 71; Visual Studies Workshop, Rochester, NY, with Ralph Gibson, Syl Labrot, Nathan Lyons & Alice Wells, 71-72; Goddard Col, MA(photog), 77. *Work:* Polaroid (Europa), Amsterdam, The Netherlands; Libr Cong, Smithsonian Inst, Corcoran Gallery Art, Washington, DC; Bibliot Nat, Paris; Nat Mus Am Art, Washington, DC; and others. *Exhib:* Va Photogr, Va Mus Fine Arts, 73 & 75; one-man shows, Bushes, 74 & Color Photographs, 77, Corcoran Gallery Art, Photographs, Diane Brown Gallery, Washington, DC, 77 & 81, Color Photographs, Sebastian Moore Gallery, Denver, Colo, 78, Kathleen Ewing Gallery, Washington, DC, 82 & 84 & Color Landscape Photographs, Rice Univ, Houston, Tex, 86; One of a Kind (traveling exhib), Mus Fine Arts, Houston, Univ Ariz, Los Angeles Inst Contemp Arts & Art Inst Chicago; Eye of the West: Camera Vision & Cult Consensus, Hayden Gallery, Mass Inst Technol, Cambridge, 77; Washington Photography: Images of the Eighties, 82, Terra Sancta, (with catalog) 90, Corcoran Gallery Art, Washington, DC; Light Work, Photography Over the 70s and 80s, Everson Mus Art, Syracuse, NY, 85; Comfort Gallery, Haverford Col, Pa, 86; Rice Univ, Houston, Tex, 86; Kathleen Ewing Gallery, Washington, DC, 89; Between Home and Heaven, Contemp Am Landscape Photog, Nat Mus Am Art, Wash, DC; Carnegie Mus Art (with catalog), Pittsburgh, Pa. *Teaching:* Instr photog, Northern Va Community Col, Alexandria, 73-78; instr photog, Corcoran Sch Art, 74-78, asst prof & chmn dept, 78-81, asst prof, 81-84, assoc prof & chmn dept, 84-87, assoc prof 87- *Awards:* Cert of Distinction, Va Photog, 73; Artist-in-Residence Fel, Camargo Found, Cassis, France, Lightwork, Syracuse, NY, 82. *Bibliog:* David Taunous (auth), Frank DiPerna at the Corcoran, Mark Power at Diane Brown, Art in Am, 1-2/78; Owen Edwards (auth), SX-70: Land's painless epiphany machine, Sat Rev, 7/22/78; Jo Ann Lewis Galleries, The Washington Post, 4/89. *Publ:* Auth, Color Photographs, Corcoran Gallery Art, 77; One of a Kind: Recent Polaroid Color Photography, Godine; SX-70, Lustrum Press, 79; contribr, Washington Photography: Images of the Eighties (catalog), Corcoran Gallery Art, 82. *Dealer:* Kathleen Ewing Gallery 1609 Connecticut Ave NW Washington DC 20009. *Mailing Add:* Rt 2 Box 836 Purcellville VA 22132

DIRKS, JOHN
SCULPTOR, CARTOONIST
b New York, NY, Nov 2, 17. *Study:* Art Students League, New York, 36; Boston Sch Practical Art; Yale Univ, BA, 39; Columbia Univ Painting & Sculpture, 45. *Work:* Ogunquit Mus Am Art. *Comn:* Over 400 pvt comns in 40 states (sculptures), 66- *Pos:* Dir, Ogunquit Mus Am Art, 88-92. *Mem:* Ogunquit Art Asn, Maine, 60-92; Lyme Acad Fine Arts, Old Lyme, Conn (trustee 83-91). *Media:* Non-Ferrous Metal with water. *Dealer:* Ogunquit Mus Am Art 181 Shore Rd Box 815 Ogunquit ME 03907. *Mailing Add:* 10 Hillwood E Old Lyme CT 06371

DIRUBE, ROLANDO LOPEZ
PAINTER, SCULPTOR
b Havana, Cuba, Aug 14, 28; US citizen. *Study:* Univ Havana Col Archit & Eng, 48; Art Students League, with George Grosz & Kuniyoshi, 49; Brooklyn Mus Art Sch, with Gabor F Peterdi & Max Beckman, 50; Escuela Nac Artes Graficas, Madrid, Spain, 51-52. *Work:* Metrop Mus Art, New York; Philadelphia Univ, Pa; Nat Mus, Havana, Cuba; Mus Mod Art, Madrid, Spain; Ponce Mus, PR. *Comn:* Nat Asn Architects, 56; Nat Theatre & Nat Sport Coliseum, Cuban Govt, Havana, 58; Int Theatres, GHG Enterprises, San Juan, PR, 70; One Biscayne Tower, GHG Enterprises, Miami, Fla, 72; outdoor sculpture, comn by Am Govt, Perrine Park, Fla. *Exhib:* I Bienal Hispanoamericana Arte, Madrid, 51; Lateinamerikanische Kunst Gegenwart, Ger, 51; II Bienal Sao Paulo, Brazil, 53; Int Colour Woodcut Exhib, Victoria & Albert Mus, London, 54-55; IX Biennale Int Art Menton, France, 72; one-man show, Mus Contemp Art, Caracas, Venezuela, 77. *Teaching:* Prof design anal, Inter-Am Univ PR Sch Archit, 64-65; lectr design, Sch Archit, Univ PR, San Juan, 67; prof painting, Art Students League, San Juan, 68- *Awards:* First

Prize Woodcut, I Bienal Hispanoamericana Arte, 51; Gold Medal in Painting & Gold Medal in Woodcut, Univ Tampa, 51; First Prize Sculpture, R J Reynolds Tobacco Co, 79. *Bibliog:* R Guastela (auth), Dirube painter & sculpture (film), Viguie Guastela, 68; J Gomez Sicre (auth), San Juan muralists, Pan Am Union Rev Am, 71; R Pau Llosa (auth), Dirube, Ala Art Editions. *Publ:* Illusr, En la Habana ha muerto un turista, 63; illusr, Los combatientes, 68. *Mailing Add:* 124 West Ocean Dr Bay View Catano PR 00632

DISKA, (P)
SCULPTOR
b New York, NY. *Study:* Vassar Col, BA; Acad Jullian, Paris. *Work:* Cornell Art Mus, Ithaca, NY; Mus Art & Indust St Etienne, France; Int Sculpture Parks, Austria, Israel, Czech, Yugoslavia & France; Palm Springs Desert Art Mus, Calif; Paris Open-air Sculpture Mus; French Ministry Cult; and others. *Comn:* Over 20 commissioned works in stone, wood, cast iron and brick for public spaces in France, including eight fountains & seven sculptures; Monument to the French Resistance, cast iron on rough-cut stones, St Ouen, Paris, 85. *Exhib:* One-man shows, Galerie Suzanne de Coninck, Paris, 65, Galerie Les Contards, Lacoste, 65, Southern Methodist Univ, Dallas, Tex, 65, Galerie Jacques Casanova, Paris, 66, Ruth White Gallery, New York, 69; Munic Mus, Mainz, WGer, 86; Ecole Des Hautes Etudes Commerciales, France, 88; Galerie Hansma, Paris, 92. *Teaching:* Instr sculpture, Sarah Lawrence Summer Sch, Lacoste, France, 74 & 75. *Awards:* Competition for fountain, New Town Melun-Senart, France, 79; Portes-les-Valence, France, 83. *Bibliog:* Virginia Watson Jones (auth), Contemporary American Women Sculptors, Oryx Press, 88; Charlotte Streier Rubinstein (auth), Women Sculptors of America, G K Hall, Boston; Dr Penny Dunford (auth), Biographical Dictionary of Women Artists in Europe and America Since 1850, Harvester/Wheatsheaf (Eng), Univ Pa Press, 89. *Mem:* Maison des Artistes, France; Réalités Nouvelles, France. *Media:* Mixed. *Mailing Add:* 84710 Lacoste Vaucluse 90 75 82 79 France

DI SUVERO, MARK
PAINTER, SCULPTOR
b Shanghai, China, 33. *Study:* San Francisco City Col, 53-54; Univ Calif, BA, 56. *Work:* Wadsworth Atheneum, Hartford, Conn; Whitney Mus Am Art; Hirshhorn Mus; Dallas Mus Fine Arts; Art Inst Chicago. *Exhib:* Solo exhibs, John Berggruen Gallery, San Francisco, 83, Oil & Steel Gallery, New York, 83 & 85, Storm King Art Ctr, Mountainville, NY, 85, Hill Gallery, Birmingham, Mich, 86, Akira Ikeda Gallery, Tokyo, 87, Wurttembergischer Kunstverein, Stuttgart, 88 & Retrospective de L'Oeuvre de Mark di Suvero, Musee d'Art Contemporain, Nice, France, 91; Germans Van Eck Gallery, New York, 87; John Berggruen Gallery, San Francisco, 87; Socrates Sculpture Park, Long Island, 87; Oil & Steel Gallery, Long Island, 87-88; Solomon R Guggenheim Mus, New York, 88; Gov State Mus, Park Forest, Ill, 80; Landmark Ctr, Minn Mus Art, St Paul, 80; San Diego Mus, 80; Nat Col Fine Art, Washington, DC, 80; ConStruct, Chicago, 80; and others. *Awards:* Longview Found Grant; Walter K Gutman Found Grant; Art Inst Chicago Award, 63. *Bibliog:* Robert Hughes (auth), Truth amid steel and elephants, Time, 7/71; Carter Ratcliff (auth), article, Artforum, 11/72; E C Baker (auth), Mark Di Suvero's Burgundian Season, Art Am, 5-6/74. *Mailing Add:* c/o Oil & Steel Gallery 3030 Vernon Blvd Box 2218 Long Island City NY 11102

DITZION, GRACE
SCULPTOR, PAINTER
b Montreal, Que; US citizen. *Study:* Hunter Col, BA, 33; NY Univ, MA, 36; Art Students League; Mus Mod Art. *Work:* Grad Ctr, City Univ NY; Univ Hawaii, Hilo; City Milford, Fine Arts Coun, Milford, Conn; Cayuga Co Community Col; Horace Mann-Bernard pvt collection. *Comn:* Sculptures (marble), comn by Joseph Borome, New York, 77 & Bernard Zelechow, Toronto, 79; Jacket cover for the book, Club, oil portrait of author Earl Conrad, 82. *Exhib:* Allied Artists Am, 76 & 78 & Ann Exhib Nat Acad Design, 78, Nat Acad Design, New York; solo exhib, Salmagundi Club, New York, 78; solo exhib, 80th Anniv Firts Prize Winner's Art Exhib, Nat Arts Club, New York; Hudson Valley Art Asn, Westchester Co Ctr, New York, 80; and others. *Pos:* Consult, Woman Art Gallery, 76-79 & 83-85. *Teaching:* Horace Mann-Bernard, 89-90; judge, Am Artists Prof League, Salmagundi Club; chairperson, Wash Soc Outdoor Art Exhib, 79-92. *Awards:* First Prize, Nat Art League, 82; Purchase Prize, Milford Fine Arts Coun, 86; Award of Excellence, Composers Auths & Artists Am, 88; and others. *Bibliog:* Patricia Keane-Mason (producer & interviewer), One-Woman Exhibit (TV show), Mus of Air, Channel D, Cable TV, New York, 10/75; Richard Roffman (producer), Richard Roffman Focus Show, Channel C & D, Cable TV, New York, 6/17/77; Bill Boggs (interviewer), Mid-Day Live Prog, WNEW TV, New York, 5/12/78. *Mem:* Salmagundi Club; Am Artists Prof League; Am Portrait Soc; Hudson River Contemp Artists; Composers, Artists & Authors. *Media:* Marble, Alabaster; Oil, Pastel. *Publ:* Auth, Rebirth of a widow, Hallandale Digest, 2/1/79; The cloud of uncertainty, Asn Human Relations Publ, 4/23/81; The creative impulse, Wash Sq Outdoor Art Exhib 50th Anniversary Issue, 5/25, 81; Symphony of the arts and sciences, Composers, Authors & Artists, Inc, vol 40, 11/1/85; Opposite Worlds, Am Poetry Anthology, 9/85; and others. *Dealer:* Gloria Salm Inc 35 Sutton Pl New York NY 10022. *Mailing Add:* 3635 Johnson Ave Bronx NY 10463

DIVOLA, JOHN MANFORD, JR
PHOTOGRAPHER
b Santa Monica, Calif, June 6, 49. *Study:* Calif State Univ, Northridge, BA, 71; Univ Calif, Los Angeles, MA, 73, MFA, 74. *Work:* Mus Mod Art, New York; Int Mus Photog, George Eastman House, Rochester; New Orleans Mus Art; Fogg Mus Art, Mass; Univ Calif, Los Angeles. *Comn:* 11 photographs, US Info Agency, 74. *Exhib:* 24 from Los Angeles, San Francisco Mus Art, 73; Mirrors & Windows, Mus Mod Art, New York, 78; New Presences at the Fogg, Fogg Mus Art, Mass, 78; Madison Art Ctr, Wis, 79; one-man shows, Vision Gallery, Boston, 79, Blue Sky Gallery, Portland, Ore, 79, Freidas Gallery, New York, 80, New Image Gallery, Harrisonburg, Va, 80, Photographers Gallery, Melbourne, Australia, 80 & Los Angeles Munic Art Gallery, Calif, 85; Young Hoffman Gallery, Chicago, 80; 1981 Biennial Exhib, Whitney Mus Am Art, NY; La Jolla Mus Comtemp Art, Calif, 85; group exhib, Calif Photography: Remaking Make Believe, Mus Mod Art, New York, 89. *Teaching:* Prof, Art Dept, Univ Calif, Riverside; instr photog, Calif Inst Arts, 78-88; prof, Univ Calif, Riverside, 88-91. *Awards:* Nat Endowment Art Grants 73, 76 & 79; Guggenheim Fel, 87. *Bibliog:* Photography Year 1980, Time-Life, 80; Andy Grundberg & Julia Scully (auths), Currents: American photography today, Mod Photog, 10/80; Mark Johnstone (auth), article in Camera, 11/80. *Mem:* Soc Photog Educ. *Publ:* Illusr, Three images reproduced, New West Mag, 11/6/78. *Dealer:* Jayne Baum Gallery 588 Broadway New York, NY 10012. *Mailing Add:* 245 Ruth Ave Venice CA 90291

DIXON, JENNY (JANE HODLEY)
ADMINISTRATOR
b Montreal, Que, Oct 1, 50; US citizen. *Study:* Univ Colo, BFA, 72; Univ Stranieri, Perugia, Italy, 72. *Collections Arranged:* Adminr & organizer of temporary installations of large-scale sculpture by: Jean Dubuffet, Isamu Noguchi, Jeffrey Owen Brosk, Mrvin Torffield, Richard Serra, Linda Howard & Sandro Martini; also assisted in installation of work by: Arthur Weyhe, George Sugarman, Pierre Clerk & others. *Pos:* Dir, Pub Art Fund Inc, formerly; moderator & producer of weekly radio prog, Artists in the City, WNYC-AM, 79-; exec dir, Lower Manhattan Cultural Council, New York, currently. *Publ:* Ed, Walking tour guide of public art in Lower Manhattan, Pub Arts Coun, 76. *Mailing Add:* c/o Lower Manhattan Cultural Council One World Trade Ctr New York NY 10048

DIXON, KEN
PAINTER
b St Clair, Mo, May 30, 43. *Study:* Drury Col, Springfield, Mo, BA, 65; SW Mo State Univ, Springfield, 66; Univ Ark, Fayetteville, MFA, 68, with David Durst & Howard Whitlach. *Work:* Nelson-Atkins Mus, Kansas City, Kans; San Antonio Mus Art, Tex; Kalamazoo Inst Arts, Mich; Mus Mod Art, Miami, Fla; US Govt, Dept Treasury; plus others. *Exhib:* One-man shows, Camden Inst, London, 73, Kalamazoo Inst Arts, 75 & Univ Ky Gallery, 90; Rutgers Nat Works on Paper, 84; Tex Fine Arts Nat, 84; Words as Images, 84 & Texas Currents, 85, San Antonio Inst; 10th Ann Nat Drawing Invitational, Emporia, Kans; and others. *Pos:* Gallery dir, Baldwin-Wallace Col, 69-72 & Tex Tech Univ, 77- 90. *Teaching:* Instr painting, Kalamazoo Col, 66-69 & Baldwin-Wallace Col, 69-72; prof painting, Tex Tech Univ, 75-. *Awards:* Purchase Award, Miami Graphics Inst Mus Mod Art, Fla, 77; Outstanding Emerging Artist Nat Competition, Galveston Art Ctr, 84; Tex Award, Mid-Am Arts Alliance. *Media:* Acrylic, oil. *Dealer:* Campbell Gallery Ft Worth TX. *Mailing Add:* 1920 32nd St Lubbock TX 79411

DIXON, SALLY FOY
DIRECTOR
Pos: Dir, Bush Artist Fel, Bush Found, St Paul, Minn, 80- *Teaching:* Macalester Col, St Paul, Minn, 81; lectr, Asn Univ Women, Minneapolis, Minn, 83, numerous other Univs & insts. *Mem:* Fel Roundtable; Am Fedn Arts, New York; Media Study (adv bd), Buffalo, NY. *Mailing Add:* c/o Bush Foundation E-900, First National Bank Bldg Saint Paul MN 55101

DIXON, WILLARD
PAINTER
b Kansas City, Mo, Mar 31, 42. *Study:* Cornell Univ; Brooklyn Mus Sch; San Francisco Art Inst, MFA, 69. *Work:* Metrop Mus Art, New York; Oakland Mus, Calif; Utah Mus Fine Art, Salt Lake City; San Francisco Mus Mod Art; San Francisco Int Airport, Calif. *Comn:* Death Valley (mural), Shell Oil Res & Develop Div, Houston, Tex, 82; Storm Source (mural), Oakland Mus, Nat Hist Dept, Calif, 84; Fire Road, Trans America Corp, 88; Pac Gas & Elect Co, San Francisco, 91. *Exhib:* SECA Contennial Exhib, San Francisco Mus Mod Art, Calif, 70; Western Landscape Painters, Mus West, Houston, Tex, 84; Large Scale, Harris Gallery Houston, Tex, 85; Landscape, Seascape, Cityscape, Contemp Arts Ctr, New Orleans, La, 86; Contemporary Landscapes, William Sawyer Gallery, 88; The Modern Pastoral, Robert Scholekopf Gallery, New York; The Landscape in Twentieth Century American Art, Metro Mus Art, 92; and others. *Teaching:* Instr, Calif State Univ, Hayward, 71-72, Calif Col Arts & Crafts, 73-76 & San Francisco State Univ, 89-90. *Awards:* Purchase Award, San Francisco Art Festival, 76 & 77; Fel, Nat Endowment Asn, 89. *Media:* Oil on Canvas. *Dealer:* Fischbach Gallery New York; Contemporary Realist Gallery San Francisco CA. *Mailing Add:* 5 Belloreid San Rafael CA 94901

DIXSON, WENDY FAY
PAINTER, GRAPHIC ARTIST
b London Eng, Sept 18, 31. *Study:* Regent St Polytech Sch Art, London, 48-51; Boston Mus Sch Art, 53; Corcoran Sch Art, 72 & 77. *Work:* Nat Mus Women in the Arts & Nat Mus Am Art, Smithsonian Inst, Washington, DC; Montgomery County Collection, Rockville, Md; The Frederick & Lucy S Herman Found, Norfolk, Va. *Exhib:* Label Women, Nat Women's Caucus for Art, Fed Bldg, 79; Southern Graphics, traveling, 83-85; 1st Ann Artists Equity Show, Washington, DC, 85; Focus International: UN Women's Conf, Nairobi, Kenya, 85. *Awards:* First Prize Drawing, Md County Art Exhib, 79; Citation, Am Album, 86. *Mem:* Philadelphia Print Club; Artists Equity;

Coalition Washington Artists; Montgomery County Arts Coun. *Media:* Silverpoint, Mixed Media. *Dealer:* Franz Bader Gallery 1701 Pennsylvania Ave Washington DC 20006. *Mailing Add:* 15 Baynard Cove Rd Hilton Head Island SC 29928

DMYTRUK, IHOR R
PAINTER, EDUCATOR
b Ukraine, Feb 11, 38; Can citizen. *Study:* Univ Alta; Vancouver Sch Art. *Work:* Alta Art Found; Univ Calgary, Alta; Ukranian Inst Mod Art, Chicago; Art Gallery, Windsor, Ont; Art Bank, Can Coun; plus others. *Exhib:* Alta Contemp Drawings, Edmonton Art Gallery, 73; one-man shows, 75 & 77 & Commonwealth Games Visual Arts Proj Exhib, 78, Latitude 53 Gallery, Edmonton; Alberta Art Found, Hokkaido Mus Mod Art, Japan, 79; Painting in Alberta: A Historical Survey, Edmonton Art Gallery, 80; Recent Acquisitions by Alta Art Found, Beaver House Gallery, 84; Artists of Ukrainian Heritage-Past and Present, Can Mus & Arch, Edmonton, 92. *Teaching:* Instr drawing & painting, Fac Exten, Univ Alta. *Awards:* All Alberta 1966 Award, Reeves & Sons Ltd; Can Coun Travel Grant, 66 & Arts Grant, 72 & 74. *Bibliog:* Myra Davies (auth), Recent work by Ihor Dmytruk, 10-11/71, Arts Can; Karen Wilkin (auth), Painting in Alberta-An Historical Survey, Edmonton Art Gallery Publ, 80; V Kubijovyč (ed), Encyclopedia Ukraine, vol 1, 84. *Media:* Multimedia. *Mailing Add:* 9801-92 Ave Edmonton AB T6E 2V4 Canada

DO, KIM V
PAINTER, EDUCATOR
b New York, May 23, 54. *Study:* New York Studio Empire State Col, 75; State Univ NY, BFA, 76; Univ Pa, MFA, 79. *Work:* Cargill Int; Johnson & Johnson, NJ; Mid Atlantic Bank, NJ; Reader's Digest, NY; Citicorp, NY. *Exhib:* Bodies and Souls, Artists Choice Mus, New York, 83; 167th Ann Exhib, Nat Acad Design. *Teaching:* Lectr painting, State Univ NY, Purchase 82-83; head dept drawing & painting, Horace Mann Sch, New York, 85- *Bibliog:* Ronny Cohen (auth), Kim Do, Artforum, 4/91; M Stephen Doherty (auth), Exploring One Location, Am Artist, 7/91; Gerrit Henry (auth), Kim Do, Art In Am, 1/92. *Mem:* Col Art Asn. *Media:* Oil, Gouache. *Dealer:* Tatistcheff & Co 50 W 57th Street New York NY 10019. *Mailing Add:* 53 Spring St New York NY 10012

DOBARD, RAYMOND GERARD
HISTORIAN, PAINTER
b New Orleans, La, Sept 13, 47. *Study:* Xavier Univ La, with Numa Rousseve, BA, 70; Johns Hopkins Univ, with Penelope Mayo, MA, 73 & Phoebe B Stanton & Charles F Stuckey, PhD, 75. *Work:* Tougaloo Col Gallery, Miss; Howard Univ Gallery, Washington, DC; Prairie View, A&M Univ Tex; Amerika Haus Hamburg, Ger; City of Lubeck, Ger. *Exhib:* Ann Fac Exhib, Gallery Art, Howard Univ, 76-90; one-man shows, Evans-Tibbs Gallery, Washington, DC, 80 & Washington Cathedral, 84; Kunstgalerie Signos, Lubeck, Germ; Hamburg Media Ctr, Ger, 87; Black Hist Resource Ctr, Alexandria, Va, 92. *Teaching:* Assoc prof art hist, Howard Univ, Washington, DC, 75-88. *Awards:* Mellon Scholar in Residence, Tougaloo Col, 81; artist in residence, Thomas Mann Fel, Lrübeck, Germany, 86. *Mem:* Col Art Asn; Am Quilt Study Group; Nat Quilters Asn. *Media:* Watercolor, Oil. *Res:* Death iconography in the works of Kaethe Kollwitz; German expressionism; iconography of Romare Bearden; quilts & the African-American Heritage. *Publ:* Contribr, This Place: Works by Doris Colbert, Howard Univ, 79; Lila O Asher Grafik, Denmark, 82; Art on Campus at Howard University, US Info Serv, Bonn, Ger; Lady's Circle-Patch Work Quilts Mag, 9-10/91. *Mailing Add:* 3816 Davis Pl NW Washington DC 20007

DOBBS, JOHN BARNES
PAINTER
b Passaic, NJ, Aug 2, 31. *Study:* Skowhegan Sch with Gregorio Prestopino & Jack Levine. *Work:* Syracuse Mus Art, NY; Fairleigh Dickinson Univ; Butler Inst Am Art, Youngstown, Ohio; Univ Mass; Springfield Mus Art, Mass; and others. *Exhib:* One-man shows, ACA Gallery, New York, 64, 66, 68, 70, 72, 75, 80 & 83, Long Island Univ, 71 & Wesleyan Univ, 71; Nat Acad Design, New York, 67, 68, 71, 74, 75 & 78; Nat Inst Arts & Lett, New York, 68-71 & 77; Washington Irving Gallery, New York, 82. *Teaching:* Instr, Brooklyn Mus Art Sch, 56-59; instr, New Sch Social Res, 65-; instr, City Col New York, 70-71; prof, John Jay Col Criminal Justice, 72-, Art Students League, 82-83. *Awards:* Ranger Fund Purchase Prize, Nat Acad Design, 74 & 80; Thomas Proctor Prize, 74 & Benjamin Altman Prize, 78, Nat Acad Design. *Mem:* Academician Nat Acad Design. *Media:* Oil. *Publ:* Illusr, Death and Justice Frescoes, 70; Fortune Mag, 70; Liberation Mag, 4/72; Common Elligies, 78 & What Rhymes with Cancer, 82, New Rivers Press. *Dealer:* Babcock Gallery 724 5th Ave New York NY. *Mailing Add:* 463 West St New York NY 10014

DOBIE, JEANNE
PAINTER, INSTRUCTOR
b Philadelphia, Pa. *Study:* Philadelphia Col Art; Rangemark Masterclass, Maine, with Barse Miller, Edward Betts & Chen Chi. *Work:* Lewis Univ, Lockport, Ill; NC Nat Bank; Frye Mus, Seattle; NMex Watercolor Soc Collection, Albuquerque; Wyeth-Beckman Pharmaceutical Labs, Philadelphia Headquarters, Pa. *Exhib:* Watercolor USA, Springfield Mus, Mo, 72, 74, 75 & 87; Midwest Watercolor Soc, Neville Mus, Wis, 84, 85, 87, 88, 89, 91 & 92; Nat Acad Design Ann, NY, 79; Rocky Mountain Natl Watermedia Exhib, 81 & 90; Watercolor West, Riverside Mus, Calif, 87; Contemp Japanese Rosohkai Watermedia Soc Exhib, Meguro Mus, Tokyo, 92; and others. *Teaching:* Instr watercolor, Rangemark, Maine, summers 74-77; instr watercolor workshops throughout US, Hawaii & Europe, 76-; mem fac, Moore Col Art, Philadelphia, 79-81. *Awards:* High Winds Medal, 80, Mary S Litt Medal, 85, Am Acad Art, 85, Du Page Award, 87, Edgar Whitney Award, 89 & Door Co Award, 92, Midwest Watercolor Soc; Quaintance Award, Rocky Mountain Nat Watermedia Exhib, 90; Best of Show, 88 & Grumbacker Gold Medallion, 92, Philadelphia Watercolor Club. *Bibliog:* East West Mag, 2/87; How artists live & work, Am Artist Mag, 2/87. *Mem:* Am Watercolor Soc (juror, 86); Nat Watercolor Soc; Philadelphia Watercolor Club (juror, 92); Midwest Watercolor Soc (juror, 84 & 88); S Africa Watercolor Soc (juror, 93). *Media:* Watercolor. *Publ:* Auth, Painting with watercolor, 80, What is a paint-escape?, 3/85 & cover, Watercolor, 91, fall issue, Am Artist; auth & illusr, Making Color Sing, Watson-Guptil Publ, 86; contribr, Recent Images, Recent Concerns, Watercolor, 91 fall issue; Splash II, North Light Publ, 93. *Mailing Add:* 160 Hunt Valley Circle Berwyn PA 19312

DOBKIN, JOHN HOWARD
MUSEUM DIRECTOR
b Hartford, Conn, Feb 19, 42. *Study:* Yale Univ, BA, 64; Inst d'Etudes Politiques, Paris, France, 65; NY Univ, JD, 68. *Collections Arranged:* Paintings of the Figure, Nat Acad Design, 79; Landscape Paintings, Nat Acad Design, 80; Edwin Dickinson: Draftsman Paints, 81; Artists by Themselves, 83. *Pos:* Exec asst to secy, Smithsonian Inst, Washington, DC, 68-71; adminr, Cooper-Hewitt Mus Design, 71-78; dir, Nat Acad Design, New York, 78-; adv comt, Archives Am Art, New York; bd dir, Municipal Art Soc, Arthur Ross Found & Sch Am Ballet. *Awards:* Exceptional Serv Award, Smithsonian Inst, 71. *Mailing Add:* Historic Hudson Valley 150 White Plains Rd Tarrytown NY 10591

DOCKSTADER, FREDERICK J
CONSULTANT, HISTORIAN
b Los Angeles, Calif, Feb 3, 19. *Study:* Ariz State Univ, AB & MA; Western Reserve Univ, PhD. *Work:* Cleveland Mus Art, Ohio. *Exhib:* Cranbrook Acad Art, Bloomfield Hills, Mich, 48; Cleveland Mus Art, 49-51. *Collections Arranged:* Specialized in exhib installation & reorganization at Cranbrook Inst Sci, Dartmouth Col Mus & Mus Am Indian. *Pos:* Staff ethnologist, Cranbrook Inst Sci, 46-53; cur anthrop, Dartmouth Col Mus, 53-56; asst dir, Mus Am Indian, 56-59, dir, 59-75; comnr, US Indian Arts & Crafts Bd, 56-68, chmn, 61-68. *Teaching:* Instr silversmithing, Cranbrook Acad Art & NH League Arts & Crafts, 52-55; prof art & archaeol, Columbia Univ, 61-64, mem adv coun, 61-; lectr silversmithing, American Indian art & arts & crafts; distinguished vis prof art dept, Ariz State Univ, 82, adj prof, 83-; res staff, C G Jung Found Analystic Psychological Inc, Div Arch Res Archetypal Symbolism, 85- *Awards:* Silver Medal, Leipzig Book Fair, 89; Hartwick Coll, Oneonta, NY, 91; Univ SDak, Vermillion, 92. *Mem:* Cosmos Club, Washington, DC; Century Club, New York. *Publ:* Auth & illusr, The Kachina and the White Man, 54 & 84; Indian Art in America, 61, Indian Art in Middle America, 64, Indian Art in South America, 67, Indian Art of the Americas, 73 & North American Indian Weaving, 78, Song of the Loom, 87; contribr, articles on arts & crafts to various nat publ. *Mailing Add:* 165 W 66th St New York NY 10023

DODD, ERIC M
GALLERY DIRECTOR, EDUCATOR
Can citizen. *Study:* Univ Durham, BA, 49, dipl(educ), 50; Ohio State Univ, MA, 51. *Teaching:* Prof art, Univ Calgary, 60-, head dept, 68-73. *Mailing Add:* 2007 Rattenbury Pl Victoria BC V8P 1Y4 Canada

DODD, LAMAR
PAINTER, EDUCATOR
b Fairburn, Ga, Sept 22, 09. *Study:* Ga Inst Technol, 26-27; Art Students League, with George Luks, Boardman Robinson, John Steuart Curry, Jean Charlot & George Bridgeman, 29-33; LaGrange Col, LHD, 47; Univ Chattanooga, DFA, 59; Fla State Univ, DFA, 68. *Work:* Atlanta Art Inst; Art Inst Chicago; Metrop Mus Art; Montclair Art Mus; Pa Acad Fine Arts; Nat Gallery, Washington, DC; Metrop Mus, New York. *Exhib:* Am Acad Arts & Lett; Am Fedn Arts; Art Inst Chicago; Am Watercolor Soc; Brooklyn Mus; plus others. *Pos:* Pres, Col Art Asn Am, 54-56; mem, US Dept State Comt Arts Tour, India, Thailand, Belg, Japan, Korea, Manila & others, 58; NASA artist, Apollo 7 & 10, 68-69. *Teaching:* Lectr, US, Denmark, Ger, Turkey, Italy, Austria & Greece; assoc prof art, Univ Ga, 37-29, head dept art, 38-73, regent's prof art, 48-76, chmn fine arts div, 60-76, Lamar Dodd prof art, 70-76, regent's prof emer art, chmn emer fine arts div & Lamar Dodd prof emer, 76-; lectr, United Chap Phi Beta Kappa, 67-68. *Awards:* Award, Nat Arts Club, 54; Purchase Prizes, Pa Acad Fine Arts & Whitney Mus Am Art, 58; plus others. *Bibliog:* Monroe Wheeler (auth), Painters and Sculptors of Modern America, Crowell, 42; Ray Bethers (auth), How Paintings Happen, Norton, 51; John I H Baur (auth), Revolution and Tradition in American Art, Harvard Univ, 59; plus others. *Mem:* Nat Acad Design; Col Art Asn Am; Southeastern Art Asn; Asn Ga Artists; Athens Art Asn; plus others. *Publ:* Illusr, The Savannah and the Santee, Rivers of Am Series; contribr, Col Art J, Bk Knowledge & others. *Mailing Add:* 590 Springdale St Athens GA 30606

DODD, LOIS
PAINTER, EDUCATOR
b Montclair, NJ, Apr 22, 27. *Study:* Cooper Union, with Byron Thomas & Peter Busa. *Work:* Cooper Union Mus, First Nat City Bank, Chase Manhattan Bank Collection, AT&T, New York; Kalamazoo Art Ctr, Mich; Ciba-Geigy Chem Corp, Ardsley, NY; RJ Reynolds, Winston-Salem, NC; Commerce Bank Shares, Inc, Kansas City, Mo; Security Pac Nat Bank; Nat Acad of Design; Metrop Life Insurance Co; Reader's Digest, Pleasantville, NY; Museo dell'Arte, Udine, Italy. *Exhib:* Tanager Gallery, 54, 57-58 & 61-62; Green Mountain Gallery, New York, 69-71 & 74-76; Cape Split Place, Maine,

77, 79 & 83; Fischbach Gallery, New York, 78, 80-82, 86, 88-90 & 92; Lyman Allyn Mus, New London, Conn, 80; NJ State Mus, Trenton, 81; Anne Weber Gallery, Georgetown, Maine, 87; Caldbeck Gallery, Rockland, Maine, 90; Dartmouth Col, Hanover, NH, 90; Rider Col, Lawrenceville, NJ, 92. *Pos:* Co-founder, Tanager Gallery, New York, 52-62; bd of gov, Skowhegan Sch of Painting & Sculpture, 80, chmn, 86-88. *Teaching:* Instr, Wagner Col, 63-64, Philadelphia Col Art, 63 & 65; instr, Brooklyn Col, 65-72, assoc prof, 75-85, prof, 85- *Awards:* Ital Govt Study Grant, 59-60; Longview Found Purchase Award, 62; Ingraham, Merrill Found Grant, 71; Am Acad & Inst Arts & Letters Award, 86; Nat Acad of Design, 87 & 90; Cooper Union, Distinguished Alumni Citation, 87. *Bibliog:* Patricia Mainardi (auth), article, Arts Mag, 81; Madeleine Keller (ed) Bench Press Series on Art, 85; Am Artist Mag, 4/91; Yankee Mag, 4/92. *Media:* Acrylic, Oil. *Dealer:* Fischbach Gallery 29 W 57th St New York NY 10019. *Mailing Add:* 30 E Second St New York NY 10003

DODD, M(ARY) IRENE
PAINTER, EDUCATOR
b Athens, Ga, Dec 30, 41. *Study:* Duke Univ, AB, 64; Univ Ga, with Lamar Dodd, Howard Thomas, Irving Marantz Everett Kinstler and others, MFA, 67. *Work:* Smithsonian Art & Space Mus, Washington, DC; High Mus Art, Atlanta, Ga; Macon Mus Arts & Sci, Ga; Univ Tenn, Martin; Ga Mus Art, Athens. *Exhib:* Solo exhibs, Lamar Dodd Art Ctr, LaGrange, Ga, 85 & 88 & Swan Gallery, Atlanta, 87; Hay House, Macon, Ga, 84; Fifty Outstanding American Artists, Foster Harmon Galleries, Sarasota, Fla, 84; Woodruff Art Ctr, Atlanta, Ga, 84; Valdosta State Col, Ga, 84; Southern Watercolor Exhibition, Jackson, Miss, 85; Georgia Watercolor Exhibition, Macon Mus Arts, Ga, 86; Nat Arts Club, New York, 86-90. *Teaching:* Prof hist, painting & drawing, Valdosta State Col, 67-, dept head, 72-80. *Awards:* Prize, Ga Watercolor Exhibition, 84; Prizes, Southern Watercolor Exhibition, 84 & 85. *Mem:* Nat Arts Club; Southern Watercolor Soc; Ga Watercolor Soc; Southwest Watercolor Soc. *Publ:* Illusr, Darien, The Death and Rebirth of a Southern town, Mercer Univ Press, Macon, Ga, 81. *Mailing Add:* 316 Oak Trace Dr Valdosta GA 31602

DODDS, ROBERT J, III
COLLECTOR, MUSEUM DIRECTOR
b San Antonio, Tex, Sept 19, 43. *Study:* Yale Univ, BA, 65; Univ Pa Sch Law, LLB, 69. *Pos:* Term trustee, Mus Art, Carnegie Inst, 71-82; pres, Pittsburgh Plan Art, Pa, 82-85; trustee, Westmoreland Co Mus Art, Greensburg, Pa, 83-; chmn, Carnegie-Mellon Univ Art Gallery, Pittsburgh, Pa, 85-91. *Collection:* Post-minimal and conceptual art. *Mailing Add:* 787 Avenida Primera S Santa Fe NM 87501

DODGE, JOSEPH JEFFERS
PAINTER, LECTURER
b Detroit, Mich, Aug 9, 17. *Study:* Sch Fine Arts, Harvard Col, BS(hons), 40; also study with Yasuo Kuniyoshi, Woodstock, NY, 44. *Work:* Fla State House; Am Express; Southern Bell; Cummer Gallery of Art; Univ Hosp. *Comn:* Delius Asn. *Exhib:* Artists of the Upper Hudson, Albany Inst Hist & Art, NY, 42-61; 64th Am Art Exhib, Art Inst Chicago, 61; Realist Invitational, Gallery Contemp Art, Winston-Salem, NC, 69; Florida Creates, var mus, 71-72; retrospective, Cummer Gallery Art, 75; plus others. *Pos:* Cur, Hyde Collection, 41-62; dir, Cummer Gallery Art, 61-72; treas, Art Celebration I and II, 73-74 & 81. *Teaching:* Instr drawing & painting, Hyde Collection, 41-62; substitute prof art hist, Hamilton Col, 47; instr art hist, Adirondack Community Col, 61-62; Hist Drawing, Univ North Fla, 88. *Bibliog:* Cover & article, Am Artist, 6/83; chap, In: Painting Faces and Figures, 86, Kalliope, 88. *Media:* Oil, Acrylics; Pencil. *Collection:* Nineteenth century realists and academic; drawings; art nouveau; small sculpture; contemporary. *Mailing Add:* 6910 Silver Lake Terr Jacksonville FL 32216

DODGE, ROBERT G
PAINTER, SCULPTOR
b Boston, Mass, Aug 14, 39. *Study:* Univ Pa, BA, 63, BFA, 65, MFA, 66. *Work:* McDonalds Corp, Chicago, Ill; TRW Corp, IBM & Equitable Corp, New York; James A Michener Mus. *Exhib:* Philadelphia Furniture, Pa Acad Fine Arts, 91; In Our Circle, James A Michener Mus, Doylestown, Pa, 91; New Abstraction, Rabbet Gallery, New Brunswick, NJ, 92; Sansar Gallery, Washington, DC, 92; Furniture of the 90's, Am Soc Furniture Arts, Houston & Parsons Sch Art, New York, 92. *Teaching:* Prof drawing & sculpture, Bucks Co Community Col, 68- *Awards:* Prix de Rome Sculpture, Am Acad, Italy, 74-76. *Bibliog:* Portfolio, Am Craft, 88; Collaboration sparks creativity in wood, New York Times, 8/9/87; An exhibit fills a mansion, Philadelphia Inquirer, 8/21/87. *Media:* Mixed. *Dealer:* Sansar Gallery 4200 Wisconsin Ave Washington DC 20016; Rabbet Gallery 120 Georges Lane New Brunswick NJ 08901. *Mailing Add:* PO Box 235 Newtown PA 18940

DODRILL, DONALD LAWRENCE
PAINTER, WRITER
b Richwood, Ohio, Aug 28, 22. *Study:* Marion Bus Col, cert, 41; Ohio State Univ, Columbus, BFA(cum laude), 49; Syracuse Univ, MFA(illus), 75. *Work:* Schumacher Gallery, Capital Univ; Zanesville Art Ctr, Ohio; Wagnall Found Gallery, Lithopolis, Ohio; Ger Village Soc Hist Mus, Columbus; First Methodist Church, Hilliard, Ohio; St Anthony Med Ctr, Columbus. *Comn:* Union Station (painting), Ohio Bell Tel, Columbus, 78; Neil House (painting), Columbus Dispatch, 81; paintings, Huntington Bank, Washington Court House, Ohio, 81, E V Bischoff Co, Columbus, 83 & Borden Co, Columbus, Ohio, 83; Marysville Methodist Church, 87; Newark Advocate, Newark, Ohio, 91; Licking County Hospital, Newark, Ohio, 92. *Exhib:* Ohio Watercolor Soc Exhibs, 74-87; Nat Waterclor Soc Exhib, Palm Springs Desert Mus, Calif, 81 & Laguna Beach Mus Art, Calif, 82; Midwest Watercolor Soc, Neville Mus, Green Bay, Wis, 84; Am Watercolor Soc, Salmagundi Club, NY, 86, 87, 88 & 92; Miss Watercolor Soc, Jackson, Miss, 91; and others. *Pos:* Partner, Dodrill Design, 54-; dir, Windon Gallery, 79- *Teaching:* Instr graphic design, Capital Univ, 76-83; instr watercolor, Adult Educ Prog, 77-, Upper Arlington, Ohio. *Awards:* Smithe Schnacke Award, Ohio Watercolor Soc, Cincinnati, 85; Hardy Gramatky Mem Award, Am Watercolor Soc, 86 & Ogden Pleisner Mem Award, 87; Karl Wolfe Award, Miss Watercolor Soc, Miss Mus Art, Jacksonville, 91. *Bibliog:* Jacqueline Hall (auth), Dodrill blends sensitivity, realism, Columbus Dispatch, 1/27/85; Susan Porter (auth), Book Dedicated to Local Cancer Victim, Worthington News, 9/27/89; Susan Stonick (auth), For Watercolor Artist Everything is a Subject, Dublin News, 9/20/89. *Mem:* Watercolor Soc, Nat, Ohio & Ky; Cent Ohio Watercolor Soc (vpres, 68, pres, 69); Bexley Area Art Guild (pres, 80); Ohio Watercolor Soc (bd dirs, 83-85); Am Watercolor Soc. *Media:* Watercolor. *Publ:* Illusr cover, Columbus Bus Forum, 75 & 76, Better Living Mag, 75 & 76 & Ohioana Libr Quart, 76-86; auth, The Transparent Touch, Watson Guptill, New York, 89; and others. *Dealer:* Windon Gallery 17 Aldrich Rd Suite C Columbus OH 43212. *Mailing Add:* 4853 Nugent Dr Columbus OH 43220

DODWORTH, ALLEN STEVENS
CONSULTANT, CURATOR
b Long Beach, Calif, Nov 19, 38. *Study:* Stanford Univ, BA(fine arts & design), 62; Portland State Univ; Univ Utah. *Collections Arranged:* Ann Exhibs for Artists of Idaho, 69-75, Painters of the Idaho Scene, 72 & American Masters in the West, 74, Boise Gallery Art; Am Abstracts, 76; The Grand Beehive, Salt Lake Art Ctr, 80; V Douglas Show Retrospective, Utah Mus Fine Arts, 93. *Pos:* Chmn, White Gallery, Portland State Univ, 67-69; dir, Boise Gallery Art, Boise Art Asn, 69-76; dir, Salt Lake Art Ctr, 76-81; dir, Western Colo Ctr Arts, 81-85; freelance art appraiser, Salt Lake City, Utah, currently. *Awards:* Mus Prof Fel, Nat Endowment Arts, 73. *Mem:* Salt Lake Art Dealers Asn; Utah Lawyers for the Arts (bd dirs); Am Soc Appraisers. *Mailing Add:* 1013 S 13th E St Salt Lake City UT 84105-1549

D'OENCH, ELLEN GATES
CURATOR, EDUCATOR
b New York, NY, Oct 2, 30. *Study:* Wesleyan Univ, BA, 73; Yale Univ, PhD, 79. *Collections Arranged:* Darkness into Light (with catalog), Yale Univ Art Gallery, 76; The Conversation Piece: Arthur Davis & Contemporaries (auth, catalog), Yale Ctr Brit Art, 80; Five Hundred Years of Master Prints in Davison Art Ctr, Wesleyan Col, 81; Jim Dine Prints 1977-1986 (coauth, catalog), Wesleyan Univ, national tour, 86. *Pos:* Cur, Davison Art Ctr, Wesleyan Univ, 79- *Teaching:* Adj prof hist prints & photog, Wesleyan Univ, Middletown, Conn, 79- *Mem:* Print Coun Am; Asn Am Mus. *Res:* 18th century French and British prints; contemporary prints. *Publ:* Coauth, Rembrandt in 18th Century England, Yale Ctr Brit Art, 83; auth, Robert F Sheehan: Color Photography 1948-1955, Davison Art Ctr-Wesleyan Univ, 87; coauth with Sylvia Plimack, Mangold: Words on Paper 1968-1991, Davison Art Ctr-Wesleyan Univ, 92. *Mailing Add:* Davison Art Ctr-Wesleyan Univ 301 High St Middletown CT 06457

DOGANCAY, BURHAN CAHIT
PAINTER, SCULPTOR
b Istanbul, Turkey, Sept 11, 29. *Study:* Acad Grande Chaumiere, Paris, France. *Work:* Guggenheim Mus, New York; Ga Mus Art; Brooklyn Mus; Mus Mod Art, New York; Los Angeles Co Mus Art; St Petersburg; Moscow Collection, Moscow. *Comn:* Alucobond Shadow Sculpture, Zurich, 83. *Exhib:* The State Russian Mus, St Petersburg; Palais des Beaux-Arts, Brussels, 82; Gallery Engstrom, Stockholm; Galerie Baukunst, Cologne, 82; Centre Georges Pompidou, Paris, 82; Seibu Mus-Yurakucho Art Forum, Tokyo, 89; The State Russian Mus, St Petersburg, 92; Artists' Union, Moscow, 92; and many others. *Awards:* City New York Cert Appreciation, 64; Tamarind Lithography Workshop Fel, 69; Golden Palette Award, Turkey, 83. *Bibliog:* Louise Schultz (auth), Dogancay and His Work, 71; E G Bowles & Tonny Russell (auth), This Book is a Movie, 71; Dogancay (monogr), Hudson Hills Press, New York, 86. *Media:* Acrylic, Gouache. *Publ:* LES MURS D'AMOUR, Editions Syros Alternatives, 92. *Mailing Add:* 220 E 54th St New York NY 10022

DOHANOS, STEVAN
ILLUSTRATOR, PAINTER
b Lorain, Ohio, May 18, 07. *Study:* Cleveland Sch Art. *Work:* Whitney Mus Am Art, New York; Cleveland Print Club; Avery Mem, Hartford, Conn; New Britain Inst; Dartmouth Col. *Comn:* Murals, Charlotte Amalie, St Thomas, VI, Forest Serv Bldg, Elkins, WVa & US Post Off, West Palm Beach, Fla. *Exhib:* New Britain Mus Am Art, Conn, 72. *Teaching:* Founding fac mem, Famous Artists Sch, Westport, Conn. *Awards:* Medal, Philadelphia Watercolor Club; Art Dirs Club; Hall of Fame, Soc Illusr New York, 71. *Mem:* Soc Illusr (pres, 61-63); Am Watercolor Soc. *Mailing Add:* 271 Sturges Hwy Westport CT 06880

DOHERTY, MICHAEL STEPHEN
EDITOR, PRINTMAKER
b New Orleans, La, Mar 9, 48. *Study:* Knox Col, Galesburg, Ill, BA, 70; Cornell Univ, Ithaca, NY, MFA, 72. *Work:* Smithsonian Inst. *Exhib:* Young Printmakers, Herron Sch Art, Indianapolis, Ind, 70; Bradley Nat Print & Drawing, Bradley Univ, Peoria, Ill, 77; Drawing Biennial, Muscarelle Mus, Col William & Mary, Wiliamsburg, Va, 88. *Pos:* Art critic, WHCUAM, Ithaca, NY, 72-76; copy supervisor & ed, Advance Process Supply Co, 77-78; ed in chief, Am Artist Mag, New York, 79- *Teaching:* Adj prof art, Tompkins-Cortland Community Col, 73-76; instr art & art hist, Knox Col, Galesburg,

Ill, 76-77. *Mem:* Am Soc Mag Ed; Col Art Asn. *Media:* Screen Printing. *Res:* Artist profiles; printmaking. *Publ:* Auth, Techniques of photo screen printing, Graphics, 79; The romance in Mario Cooper's watercolors, 79, Robert Cottingham: An unabashed realist, 79 & Working with light-sensitive materials, 80, Am Artist Mag; Dynamics of still-lifes in watercolor, 83; Paul Ortlip: his heritage & his art, 83; Developing ideas in artwork, 88. *Mailing Add:* Am Artist Mag 1515 Broadway New York NY 10036

DOKOUPIL, JIRI GEORG
PAINTER
b Krnov, Czech, June 3, 54. *Study:* Cooper Union, New York, 76-78; also studied in Cologne & Frankfurt. *Work:* Fundacio Caixa de Pensiones, Barcelona, Spain; Nat Galerie, Berlin; Van Abbemuseum, Eindhoven, Ger; Mus Folkwang, Essen, Ger; Boymans-van Beuningen, Rotterdam, Neth. *Exhib:* Retrospective, works from 1981-1984, Mus Folkwang, Essen, Ger, 84; one man shows, Galerie Beauborg, Paris, 89, Robert Miller Gallery, 89, 90 & 92, Galeria Leyendecker, Santa Cruz de Tenerife, 90, 91 & 92. *Teaching:* Guest teacher art, Kunstakademie Dusseldorf, 83-84 & Circulo de bellas Artes, Madrid, 89. *Bibliog:* Francisco Rivas (auth), Dokoupil, Fundacion Caja de Pensiones, Madrid, 89; Dokoupil Drawings, Vol I-III Galerie Leyendecker, Santa Cruz de Tenerife, Spain, Nickolaus Soone, Berlin Massimo Minini Gallery, Grescia, Italy, 89; Dokoupil, Robert Miller Gallery, 89; Dokoupil Fruit Paintings, Fruit Architect, Candle Paintings, Galene Krinzinger, Vienna, 91. *Media:* Multi media. *Mailing Add:* Robert Miller Gallery 41 E 57th St New York NY 10022

DOLAN, MARGO
ART DEALER
b Philadelphia, Pa, Mar 19, 46. *Study:* Conn Col, BA(art hist). *Pos:* Docent, Univ Mus, Philadelphia, Pa, 68-70; asst dir, Print Club, 70-73, dir, 73-77; dir, Asn Am Artists, Philadelphia, 78-84; co-owner, Dolan-Maxwell Gallery, Philadelphia, 84- & New York, 88- *Mem:* Int Fine Print Dealers Asn; Philadelphia Art Dealers Asn (vpres, 82-84 & pres, 84-85). *Specialty:* Modern and contemporary art. *Mailing Add:* Dolan/Maxwell 2046 Rittenhouse Sq Philadelphia PA 19103

DOLL, CATHERINE ANN
PAINTER, DESIGNER
b San Jose, Calif. *Study:* San Jose City Col, with Joseph Zirker, 72; Univ Wis, 82. *Work:* United Auto Workers Regional Hq, Milwaukee, Wis. *Exhib:* Wisconsin Directions, Milwaukee Art Mus, 82-84; 10th Year Anniversary, ARC Gallery, Chicago, Ill, 85; Haggerty Mus of Art, Milwaukee, 88; Topeka Gallery, Chicago, Ill, 88; Edinburgh Festival, 369 Galley, Scottland, 89; Tokyo Art Fair, Japan, 90; Lloyd Shin Gallery, Chicago, Ill, 90. *Collections Arranged:* Art by Auto Workers, United Auto Workers, Local 72, Kenosha, Wis, 81; Products of Society, NAB Gallery, 83 & ARC Gallery, 85, Chicago, Ill; Furniture/Furniture, Haggerty Mus, 88. *Pos:* Independent artist-designer, 82-; artist-designer hand painted clothing, workshop Very Special Art Fair, Ctr Learning Disabilities, Waukegan Ill & Univ Wis, Kenosha, 85; vpres, ARC Gallery, Chicago, Ill, 85-86. *Awards:* First Place Awards, Art by Auto Workers, United Auto Workers Union, 81 & 82; Assistance Grant, Chicago Off of Fine Arts, 85. *Bibliog:* Barry Benson (reporter), Six O' Clock News, NBC, 5/83; Anne Beaton (auth), Unemployed paint painful picture, 5/83 & Margaret Hawkins (auth), Weekend plus, 12/85, Chicago Sun Times; Marlo Danato (auth), Chicago Tribune, 89; Ginny Holbert (auth), Chicago Sun Times, 90. *Mem:* Chicago Artist Coalition; Artists Residents Chicago. *Media:* Mixed. *Publ:* Contribr, United Auto Workers Calendar, 80 & 81; cover, Law & Justice, Nelson-Hall, 87; Lloyd Shin Gallery, Selected Works (catalog). *Mailing Add:* 1917 S Halsted Chicago IL 60608

DOLL, DONALD ARTHUR
EDUCATOR, PHOTOGRAPHER
b Milwaukee, Wis, July 15, 37. *Study:* St Louis Univ, BA, MA. *Work:* Sheldon Art Gallery, Lincoln, Nebr; Mid-Am Arts Alliance, Kansas City, Mo; Rochester Inst Technol, NY. *Exhib:* Crying for a Vision, A Rosebud Sioux Trilogy (traveling exhib), Nat Endowment Arts, 76-78. *Teaching:* From assoc prof photog to prof, Creighton Univ, 69-, chmn fine & performing arts dept, 76-88. *Awards:* World Understanding Through Photog, Univ Mo Sch Journalism, Nat Press Photog Asn & Nikon, 76. *Mem:* Soc Photog Educ; Nat Press Photog Asn. *Publ:* Coauth & ed, Crying for a Vision, Morgan & Morgan, 76; contribr, Photojournalism, Nat Geographic & Nikon, 76. *Mailing Add:* Dept Fine & Performing Arts Creighton Univ Omaha NE 68178

DOLL, LINDA A
PAINTER, INSTRUCTOR
b Brooklyn, NY, May 5, 42. *Study:* Palomar Col, AA; San Diego State Univ, BA(art), 77; Univ Calif, San Diego Extension, cert(teaching), 78; studied with Rex & Joan Irving Brandt, Millard Sheets & Robert E Wood. *Work:* Scripps Hosp, La Jolla, Calif; Redlands Hospital, Riverside, Calif; Campbell River Community Coun, Campbell River, BC, Can. *Exhib:* San Diego Int Exhib, 78, 79, 82, 83 & 84; La Int Exhib, New Orleans, 82; Nat Arts Club Ann Exhib, New York, 82; Allied Artist Ann Exhib, Salmagundi Club, New York, 82; Adirondacks Nat Exhib Am Watercolors, Old Forge, NY, 83; Watercolor West Annual Exhib, Riverside, Calif, 82, 84 & 85-88; Rocky Mountain Nat Exhib, Golden, Colo, 84, 85; Nat Watercolor Soc Ann Exhib, Brea, Calif, 84, 85 & 88; Am Watercolor Soc Ann Exhib, New York, 85-90; Watercolor West Members Ann, Calif, 87 & 88. *Pos:* US Coast Guard Artist, 85- *Teaching:* Instr workshops & sems, Calif, 78-; instr drawing & painting, Poway Unified Sch Dist, 78-82 & Palomar Col, 80- *Awards:* Harry Hulett Jr Award, Watercolor Okla, 84; E Gene Crain Purchase Award, Watercolor West Ann Exhib, 85; Elsie & David Wu Ject-Key Award, Am Watercolor Soc Ann Exhib, 88. *Bibliog:* article, An American Artist, Watercolor; 2/86; Artists in Southern Calif, 88. *Mem:* Elected life mem, San Diego Watercolor Soc (pres, 80-81); La Jolla Art Asn (vpres, 79-80); Am Watercolor Soc, New York; Nat Watercolor Soc, Calif; Watercolor West (bd dirs, 86-); elected life mem, Fedn Can Artist, Vancouver. *Media:* All Media. *Dealer:* Painter's Perspective PO Box 270017 San Diego Ca. *Mailing Add:* PO Box 160494 Big Sky MT 59716

DOMINGUEZ, EDDIE
CERAMIST
b Tucumcari, NMex, Oct 17, 57. *Study:* Cleveland Inst Art, BFA, 81; Alfred Col Ceramics, MFA, 83. *Work:* Ariz State Univ, Tuscon; Albuquerque Mus Fine Art, NMex; Mus Fine Art, Santa Fe, NMex; Cooper-Hewitt Mus, New York. *Exhib:* Erie Arts Mus, Pa, 85; Roswell Arts Ctr & Mus, NMex, 86, 87; Scottsdale Ctr Arts, Ariz, 88; Montery Mus Art, Calif, 88; Mus Mex Art, New York, 89; solo exhibs, Mariposa Gallery, Albuquerque, NMex, 88 & 90, Greenwich House Pottery, New York, 89, Pro Art Gallery, St Louis, Mo, 89 & 90, Mobilia Gallery, Cambridge, Mass, 90, Munson Gallery, Santa Fe, NMex, 90 & 92, Joanne Rapp Gallery, Scottsdale, Ariz, 91, Felicita Found, Escondido, Calif, 91; Mus NMex, 91; Mus Fine Art, Santa Fe, NMex, 91; Plains Art Mus, Moorhead, Minn, 92; Kavesh Gallery, Sun Valley, Idaho, 92; Bradley Gallery, Milwaukee, Wis, 92. *Pos:* Lectr, Southern Ill Univ, Carbondale, 91; Eastern NMex Univ, Clovis, 91; Cleveland Inst Art, Ohio, 92. *Teaching:* Artist in residence & lectr, Ohio State Univ, 84; Cleveland Inst Art, Ohio, 86; Univ Mont, Missoula, 88. *Awards:* Fel, NEA, 86 & 88; Artists in Res, Roswell Mus & Art Ctr Grant, 87. *Media:* Clay, Metal. *Publ:* Contr, Ceramics Month. *Mailing Add:* 608 W Railroad Tucumcari NM 88401

DOMINIQUE, JOHN AUGUST
PAINTER
b Virserum, Sweden, Oct 1, 1893; US citizen. *Study:* Portland Art Asn Sch, 13; San Francisco Inst Art, 15-16; Van Sloan Sch Painting, 17; Santa Barbara Sch Arts, 21 & 27-29; also with Colin Campbell Cooper, Armin Hanson & Carl Oscar Borg. *Work:* Univ Va Art Gallery. *Exhib:* Portland Art Mus, Ore, 36; Oakland Art Mus, Calif, 41; Los Angeles Art Mus, Calif, 44; Calif Watercolor Soc, Pasadena Art Mus, 61; Charles & Emma Frye Art Mus, Seattle, Wash, 62; California Plein Air Painting (solo exhib), Kerwin Galleries, Burlingame, Calif, 88. *Awards:* Painting Award for Covered Bridge, Ore State Fair, 40, Painting Award for Oregon Landscape, 41; Painting Award for Peach Tree in Bloom, Glendale Art Asn, 50. *Bibliog:* Arthur Millier (auth), article in Los Angeles Times, 10/8/33; Maxine Buren (auth), article in Ore Statesman, 10/9/38; Melba Meredith (auth), article in Ojai Valley News, 7/5/62; Painting with a vision, Ojai Valley News, 7/25/88; Charlotte Berney (auth), The landscapes of John A Dominique, Antiques & Fine Arts, 10/88. *Mem:* Nat Watercolor Soc. *Media:* Oil, Watercolor. *Dealer:* Kerwin Galleries 1107 California Dr Burlingame CA 94010. *Mailing Add:* 216 N Pueblo Ave Ojai CA 93023

DOMIT, MOUSSA M
MUSEUM DIRECTOR, HISTORIAN
b Lebanon, May 24, 32; nat US. *Study:* Ohio State Univ, BA(art hist); Southern Conn State Col, MS(art hist); Yale Univ. *Collections Arranged:* Sculpture of Thomas Eakins, Corcoran Gallery Art (with catalog), 69; Art of Wilhelm Lehmbruck, Nat Gallery Art, Washington, DC, 72; and others. *Pos:* Cur intra-univ loan collection & registrar collections, Yale Univ Art Gallery, 66-68; assoc dir, Corcoran Gallery Art, 68-70; mus cur, Nat Gallery Art, 70-72; assoc dir, NC Mus Art, Raleigh, 72-74, dir, 74-80; bd adv, Univ Ga Mus Art, Athens, 77-80; freelance consult, 81-; dir, Dixon Gallery & Garden, Memphis, Tenn, 82-86 & Appleton Art Mus, Ocala, Fla, 86-88, freelance consult, 88- *Teaching:* Instr hist art, Columbus Col Art & Design, Ohio, 62-64; lectr art appreciation, Corcoran Sch Art, Washington, DC, 68-70; lectr art hist, Hood Col, 71-72, adj prof art, Univ NC, Chapel Hill, 76-77. *Mem:* Asn Art Mus Dir; Am Asn Mus; Nat Soc Lit & Arts. *Res:* American impressionist painting. *Publ:* Auth, George Lee: Recent Color Photography, Corcoran Gallery Art, 69; American Impressionist Painting, Nat Gallery Art, 73; Art of Saliba Douaihy, NC Mus Art, 78. *Mailing Add:* 304 W Aycock St Raleigh NC 27608

DOMJAN, JOSEPH (SPIRI)
PAINTER, GRAPHIC ARTIST
b Budapest, Hungary, Mar 15, 07. *Study:* Hungarian Royal Acad Fine Arts, BFA & MA; also study in Italy, Ger & France. *Work:* Metrop Mus Art, New York; Nat Mus Mod Art, Paris; Brit Mus, London; Smithsonian Inst & Libr of Cong, Washington, DC; Mus Mod Art, Tokyo; 175 museum collections. *Comn:* Cards & calendar, UNICEF, 60-63; Fifteen Battles (bd & album of originals), Limited Ed Club, 69 & 70; silver snowflake & gold star, 71-75, silver & gold heart, 78 & angel, rooster, hearts, 83-84, Metrop Mus Art. *Exhib:* Retrospective, NJ State Mus, Trenton, 66 & 73; Triennale Int Xilografia, Carpi, Italy, 69 & 72; Print Club, Albany, NY, 68; US Capitol; Int Exhib Exlibris, Marlboro, 75; Mint Mus Art, Charlotte, NC, 78; 500 one-man shows on four continents. *Teaching:* Vis lectr, coast to coast, 56- *Awards:* Rockefeller Found Grant, 58; George Washington Award, 70; Bela Bartok Commemorative Medal, 81; and others. *Bibliog:* Pierre Mornand (auth), Domjan in the Forest of the Golden Dragon, Opus, 73; Evelyn Domjan (auth), Edge of Paradise, 79 & Pavologia, 84. *Mem:* Fel Metrop Mus Art; Soc Illusr; Soc Am Graphic Arts; Soc Encouragement Progress, Paris; Nat Acad Design. *Media:* Oil; Wood, Tapestry. *Publ:* Illusr, Faraway Folk Tales, Holt, Rinehart & Winston, 72; Artist and the Legend, 75; Wing Beat, Eagle Woodcuts, Domjan, 76; Eternal Wool, 80; Sun Gates, 80. *Dealer:* Domjan Studio W Lake Rd Tuxedo Park NY 10987. *Mailing Add:* W Lake Rd Box 114 Tuxedo Park NY 10987

DOMROE, BARBARA
PRINTMAKER, PAINTER
b Brooklyn, NY, July 27, 39. *Study:* Brooklyn Mus, Cert, 55; Pratt Inst, Scholar, 57, BFA, 61. *Comn:* Xerox; General Electric; Humana; HIP. *Awards:* Soc Illusrs Award, 57; France Lieber Mem Prize Award, Nat Asn Women Artists, 82. *Bibliog:* Article Print Mag, 64; articles in various Long Island papers, 75-80. *Mem:* Nat Asn Women Artists. *Media:* Mixed media monotype; watercolors. *Mailing Add:* Ten Chatham Rd Commack NY 11725

DONAHUE, PHILIP RICHARD
PAINTER, EDUCATOR
b Detroit, Mich, Apr 1, 43. *Study:* St Peters Col, AB(art hist), 69; Spring Hill Col, MA, 72; Grad Theological Union, PhD, 83. *Comn:* Donahue Painting Series, Soc Jesus, New Orleans, La, 70-82; St Ignatius Mural, St Charles Col, Grand Coteau, La, 72; Presidential Series, Spring Hill Col, Mobile, Ala, 74; Ordination Card Series, Jesuit Sch Theology, Berkeley, Calif, 74-82; covers (Japanese poetry bk), Tokyo, 82-83. *Exhib:* Allied Arts Competition, Metrop Mobile Mus, Ala, 74; The Holy in Art, St Alberts Col, Oakland, Calif, 75; Religious Art Ann, Grad Theological Union, Berkeley, Calif, 75-82; Emergence Art Xian Thought, Grace Cathedral, San Francisco, Calif, 76; one-man show, Jesuit Art Ctr, Baltimore, Md, 78; Ann US Exhib, AT Gallery, Tokyo, 82-; Graduate Theological Union, Berkeley, 83. *Collections Arranged:* Artworks 82, Int Hunger Project, 82; Link Art Int, Tokyo, Osaka, Hiroshima, 82 & Hakuhodo, Sapporo, 83. *Pos:* Artist-in-residence, St Charles Col, Grand Coteau, La, 70-72; artist-in-residence, Jesuit Sch Theology, Berkeley, Caalif, 74-82; dir special events & art educ, Link Art Int Ltd, Oakland, 82-; writer, Meaning in Painting, Finearts, 91- *Teaching:* Asst instr art hist & drawing, St Peters Col, Jersey City, NJ, 64-68; asst prof painting, Spring Hill Col, Mobile, Ala, 72-74. *Awards:* Full Patronage, Soc Jesus, 70-82; First Place, Asn Educ Tech, 72; First Place, Allied Artist Coun, 74. *Bibliog:* C J McNaspy (auth), American Jesuits in the Arts, The Jesuit, fall 76; K G Connolly (auth), Art & belief, New Catholic World, 1-2/80; T Anzai & A Donahue (auth), Link art international, Motions, Tokyo, 11/81. *Mem:* Am Soc Aesthetics, 76- *Media:* Oil, Slides. *Res:* Iconological hermeneutics: symbolic interpretation of the levels of meanings in paintings. *Publ:* Illusr, Bom Pastor, Brazil, Catholic Voice, 77; auth, Iconological Hermeneutics, Am Acad Religion, 80; Visual Art, Society & Religion, New Catholic World, 80; auth, Greco-Roman Influences in Early Xian Iconology, Calif Classic Asn, 81. *Dealer:* Link Art Int Ltd 3700 Virden Ave Oakland CA 94619. *Mailing Add:* 3700 Virden Ave Oakland CA 94619

DONALDSON, JEFF R
PAINTER, ADMINISTRATOR
b Pine Bluff, Ark, Dec 15, 32. *Study:* Univ Ark, Pine Bluff, BA(studio art); Ill Inst of Technol, MS(art educ); Northwestern Univ, PhD(art hist). *Work:* Studio Mus in Harlem, New York; Corcoran Gallery of Art & Nat Collection of Fine Art, Washington, DC; Fisk Univ, Nashville, Tenn; Univ Ark, Pine Bluff. *Comn:* P B S Pinchback portrait, State of Ill Hist Soc, 63; Wall of Respect, Miles Col, Birmingham, Ala, 69; portrait, Hoyt Fuller, Cornell Univ, 85. *Exhib:* Mus la Tertulia, Cali, Colombia, 71; Studio Mus in Harlem, New York, 75; Nat Ctr for Afro-Am Art, Boston, Mass, 75; Southside Art Ctr, Chicago, 75; Herbert Johnson Mus, Cornell Univ, Ithaca, NY, 76; Howard Univ, Washington, DC, 76; Afro-Am Hist-Cult Mus, Philadelphia, Pa, 77; Washington Proj for Arts, DC, 85. *Collections Arranged:* Directions in Afro-Am Art, Johnson Mus, Cornell Univ, 75. *Pos:* Bd dir, Nat Ctr for Afro-Am Artists, 70-; vpres USA-Can zone, FESTAC 77, Lagos, Nigeria, 75-; art dir, Jazz Am Marketing, 81- *Teaching:* Chmn art dept, Howard Univ, Washington, DC, 70-76, assoc dean Col Fine Art, 85- *Awards:* First Place-Painting, Art & Soul Exhib, Westside Gallery, 68; First Place-Painting, Black Expressions, Southside Art Ctr, Chicago, 69; E Catlett-Mora Award, Nat Conf of Artists Ann, 77; Fac Res Grant, Howard Univ, 86-87. *Bibliog:* Harold Hayden (auth), Right On Art Lovers, Chicago Sun-Times, 9/70; Edward S Spriggs (auth), Africobra; Paul Richard (auth), A Bright New School, Washington Post, 3/76. *Mem:* Nat Conf of Artists; Africobra-Farafindugu. *Media:* Watercolor, Mixed Media. *Publ:* Auth, Civil Rights Yearbook, Henry Regenry, 63; illusr, Riot, 68 & Book of Life, 74, Broadside Press; ed, Directions 69, Ill Art Educ Asn, 69; illusr, Blues Journeys Home, Lotus Press, 86. *Mailing Add:* 504 T St NW Washington DC 20001

DONATI, ENRICO
PAINTER, SCULPTOR
b Milan, Italy, Feb 19, 09; US citizen. *Study:* Univ Pavia, Italy, Dr, 29; Art Students League, 40; New Sch Social Res, New York, 41. *Work:* Albright-Knox Art Gallery, Buffalo, NY; Univ Art Mus, Univ Calif, Berkeley; Mus Mod Art, New York; Whitney Mus Am Art, New York; Baltimore Mus Art. *Exhib:* Eight Carnegie Int Exhibs, 45-61; Embellished Surfaces, Mus Mod Art, New York, 53-54; Younger American Painters, Solomon R Guggenheim Mus, 54-55; Palais des Beaux-Arts, Brussels, Belg, 61; Friends Collection, Whitney Mus Am Art, 64, Staempfli Gallery, New York, 62-82 & Grand Palais, Paris, 80. *Pos:* Mem adv bd, Brandeis Univ, Waltham, Mass, 56-72; mem pres coun arts & archit, Yale Univ, 62-72; chmn nat comn, Univ Art Mus, Univ Calif, Los Angeles, 70-72. *Teaching:* Vis lectr & critic, Yale Univ, 62-72. *Bibliog:* John Gruen (auth), Enrico Donati, Mus de Poche, 65. *Dealer:* Gimpel & Weitzen Hoffer 1040 Madison Ave New York NY 10021. *Mailing Add:* 222 Central Park S New York NY 10019

DONATO, DEBORA E
ADMINISTRATOR, CURATOR
b Whittier, Calif, Oct 7, 51. *Study:* San Jose State Univ, BA, 79, MFA, 82. *Collections Arranged:* Fluxus and Friends (auth, catalog), Wright Mus Art, 84; Liars: A Question of Reason, Work by Mitchel Kane, Mike Love, Tony Tasset & Jonathan Waterbury, 87; Adivina Latino Chicago Expressions (auth, catalog), Mex Fine Art Ctr & Museo de Arte Moderno, Mex, 88; Good Painting (auth, catalog), State of Ill Art Gallery, 88. *Pos:* Cur, Union Gallery, San Jose State Univ, 79-83; dir, Wright Mus Art, Beloit Col, 83-85; adminr, State Ill Art Gallery, 85- *Teaching:* Asst prof art criticism, Beloit Col, Wis, 83-85. *Mem:* Am Asn Mus; Midwest Mus Conf, Cult Network. *Mailing Add:* 5310 N Magnolia St Chicago IL 60604

DONHAUSER, PAUL STEFAN
SCULPTOR, PAINTER
b Berlin, Ger, May 6, 36; US citizen. *Study:* Univ Wis-Milwaukee, BS(art); Univ Wis-Madison, MS(art); Ill State Univ, PhD(art). *Work:* Int Mus Ceramics, Faenza, Italy; Nat Mus Art, Gdansk, Poland; Maison des Metiers d'Art Francais, Paris; Everson Mus Art, Syracuse, NY; Univ Wis-Oshkosh, Reeve Union. *Comn:* Relief mural (6ft x 15ft), Student Union, Wis State Col, Oshkosh, 71; series of five free standing outdoor sculptures, Univ Wis Campus, 78; Ceramic mural (6 ft x 40 ft), Hughes Hall, Winn City Health Ctr, 84; Paintings (4 ft x 8 ft), Columba Correctional Inst, Portage Wis. *Exhib:* Wis Directions, Milwaukee Art Ctr, 76; Landscape: New Views, Johnson Mus, Cornell Univ, Ithaca, NY, 78; Int Biennial Exhib of Ceramic Sculpture, Vallauris, France, 78; Clay & Fiber, Wustum Fine Arts Mus, Racine, Wis, 78; Donhauser Retrospective: 1957-1977, Paine Art Ctr, Oshkosh, 77; Int Ceramics Exhib, Tejimi, Japan. *Teaching:* Instr ceramic sculpture, Madison Area Tech Col, Wis, 60-63; instr drawing & ceramics, Ill State Univ, Normal, 63-65; prof ceramic sculpture, Univ Wis, Oshkosh, 65- *Awards:* Nat Award for Ceramic Sculpture, 8th Miami Ceramic Nat Exhib, Coral Gables Art Asn, Fla, 72; Grand Prize of Faenza, 35th Int Exhib of Ceramics, Int Mus of Ceramics, 76; Nat Endowment Arts, Visual Artist Fel, 84. *Bibliog:* Sergio Cavina (auth), Emilia Romagna, Regione, Bologna, Italy, 9/76; Linda Witt (auth), Donhauser wins Italy's top ceramic prize, People Weekly, 10/11/76; James Auer (auth), Uncommon clay, Milwaukee J, 9/77. *Mem:* Int Acad of Ceramics, Geneva, Switz; Am Crafts Coun; Wis Designer Craftsmen. *Media:* Acrylic, Ceramics. *Publ:* Co-auth, New Ceramics, St Martins, London, 74; auth, History of American ceramics, The Studio Potter, Kendall/Hunt, 78. *Dealer:* Ruth Volid Gallery 225 W Illinois St Chicago IL 60610. *Mailing Add:* c/o Neville Pub Brown County 210 Museum Pl Green Bay WI 54303

DONLEY, ROBERT MORRIS
PAINTER, EDUCATOR
b Cleveland, Ohio, July 5, 34. *Study:* Sch Art Inst, BFA, 60, MFA, 66. *Work:* Springfield Mus, Ill; Ill State Univ, Normal; Northern Ill Univ, DeKalb; Mobil Oil Corp, New York; Smithsonian Inst, Washington, DC. *Exhib:* Los Angeles Mus Ann, Los Angeles Co Mus, 59-61; Nat Traveling Exhib Chicago Artists, Crocker Mus Art, Sacramento, Calif, 76; 76th & 77th Exhib Artists Chicago & Vicinity, Art Inst Chicago, 77 & 78; New Visions, Aldrich Mus Contemp Art, Ridgefield, Conn, 81; Crimes of Compassion, Chrysler Mus, Norfolk, Va, 81; 36th Ill Invitational, Ill State Mus, Springfield, 84; Intersections: Artists View of the City, Laguna Gloria Art Mus, Austin, Tex, 86; Fetish Art: Obsessive Expressions, Rockford Art Mus, Ill, 86. *Teaching:* Prof painting & drawing, De Paul Univ, Chicago, Ill, 67- *Awards:* Nat Endowment Arts Grant, 80; Pauline Palmer Prize, Chicago Show. *Bibliog:* Carrie Rickey (auth), Chicago, Art in Am, 7-8/79; Judith Wilson (auth), The last detail, Village Voice, Vol XXV, No 49, 80; Michele Vishny (auth), Robert Donley, Arts Mag, 10/83. *Media:* Oil, Mixed Media for Drawing. *Dealer:* Hokin/Kaufman 210 W Superior St Chicago IL 60610. *Mailing Add:* Depaul Univ 25 E Jackson Blvd Chicago IL 60604

DONNELLY, MARIAN CARD
HISTORIAN, EDUCATOR
b Evanston, Ill, Sept 12, 23. *Study:* Oberlin Col, AB, 46, MA, 48; Yale Univ, PhD, 56. *Pos:* Art librn, Univ Rochester, 51-53; res assoc, Art Inst Chicago, 56-57. *Teaching:* Instr art hist, Upsala Col, 48-50; from asst prof to prof art hist, Univ Ore, 66-; retired. *Mem:* Archaeol Inst Am; Soc Preserv New Eng Antiquities; Royal Soc Arts, London; Soc Archit Historians (dir, 64-67, 78-, second vpres, 72-74, first vpres, 74-76, pres, 76-78). *Res:* Vernacular and technological architecture in North Europe and America, particularly during the sixteenth, seventeenth and eighteenth centuries. *Publ:* Theaters in the Courts of Denmark & Sweden, J Soc Archit Historians, 84; New England Meeting Houses of the Seventeenth Century, Wesleyan Univ Press, 68; Materials in Early New England, Old Time New Eng, 71; A Short History of Observatories, Univ Ore Bks, 73; Architecture in the Scandinavian Countries, MIT Press, 92. *Mailing Add:* 2175 Olive St Eugene OR 97405

DONNESON, SEENA
SCULPTOR, GRAPHICS ARTIST
b New York, NY. *Study:* Pratt Inst; Art Students League, with Morris Kantor; Pratt Graphic Arts Ctr, with Michael Ponce de Leon. *Work:* Mus Mod Art, New York; Phillip Morris Int, NY; Los Angeles Co Mus Art; Smithsonian Mus, Washington, DC; Fort Lauderdale Mus Art. *Comn:* Ed of prints, Touchstone Press; tapestry design, Equitable Life & Insurance Co, New York, 76; ed prints, Ft Lauderdale Mus Fine Arts, Fla, 77; Outdoor sculpture for Snug Harbor Cult Ctr, Grow-Kiewit-Mk, New York, 79; outdoor sculpture, Jersey City State Col, NJ, 81. *Exhib:* Projected Art: Artists at Work, Finch Col, 71; Reflections/Refractions, Ft Lauderdale Mus Fine Art & New England Art, Part III, paintings on paper, DeCordova Mus Art; Sculpture in Color, New York, 78; Greenville Mus Art, 87; The Collograph, Pratt Graphic Arts traveling exhib, NY State Coun Arts; Material & Metaphor, Wm Patterson Col, Ben Shahn Gallery; Norfolk Mus Arts & Scis; Ann City Mus Art Gallery, Hong Kong. *Pos:* App mem, Nassau Co Fine Arts Comn, 70-; exhib coordr, Dept Parks, Recreation & Cult Affairs, New York, 71-74. *Teaching:* Lectr hist mod art, NY Univ, 61-63; in-sch-artist, Nassau Co Cult

Coun, 71-79; lectr, Nassau County Off Cult Develop, 71-79, New Sch Social Res, 74-, & painting & drawing, New Hampshire Col, 80-83. *Awards:* Fel, MacDowell Found, 63, 64; Clayworks, New York, 81; Creative Artists Serv Prog Grant, NY State Coun Arts, 83-84. *Bibliog:* John Perreault (auth), Up the river, Soho Weekly News, 78; Grace Glueck (auth), Sculpture under a city sky, New York Times, 78; Mary Anne Pennington (dir), Seena Donneson, Relief Sculpture, Greenville Mus Art, NC, 87. *Mem:* Artists Equity Asn NY; Nat Asn Women Artists; Long Island City Artists Inc. *Media:* Metals, Homemade paper; Collographs, Etchings. *Dealer:* Jayne Baum 588 Broadway New York NY 10012; Quietude Sculpture Gallery Garden Fern Rd East Brunswick NJ. *Mailing Add:* 43-49 Tenth St Long Island City NY 11101

D'ONOFRIO, BERNARD MICHAEL
GLASS BLOWER, SCULPTOR
b Medford, Mass, Jan 7, 51. *Study:* Univ Mass, Amherst, BFA, 73; Pilchuck Sch, Stanwood, Wash, 81, 82; Kent State Univ, MFA, 83. *Work:* Detroit Inst Art; Moderne Int Glaskunst, Ebeltoft, Denmark; Pilchuck, Stanwood, Wash; Headley Whitney Mus, Lexington, Ky; Michner Mus, Kent State Univ, Ohio. *Comn:* Bank One, Akron, Ohio, 82; Network World, Framingham, Mass, 90. *Exhib:* New Art Forms, Betsy Rosenfield Gallery, Chicago, 88; Boston Now, Inst Contemp Art, Boston, Mass, 89; Contemporary Glass, Milwaukee Art Mus, Wis, 90; International Exhibition of Glass, Kanazawa, Japan, 90; one-man exhib, Snyder Gallery, Philadelphia, Pa, 90 & Sanske Gallery, Zurich, Switzerland, 92; 10th Anniversary Exhibition, Helander Gallery, West Palm Beach, Fla, 91; World Glass Exhibition, Gallery Nakama, Tokyo, Japan, 91. *Teaching:* Instr design, Cranbrook Sch, Bloomfield Hills, Mich, 73-80; vis lectr glass, Mass Col Art, Boston, 83-92; vis artist glass, Tokyo Glass Art Inst, Japan, 92. *Awards:* Finalist Award, Mass Artists Fel, 89; Visual Artist Fel, Nat Endowment Arts, 90. *Bibliog:* Michal Lemar (auth), Boston Diary, New Work, 88; Susan Barahal (auth), Sculptural perspectives, Art New England, 88; Paul Hollistr (auth), Delicate and bold, NY Times, 89. *Mem:* Glass Art Soc. *Media:* Glass. *Dealer:* Snyderman Gallery 317 South St Philadelphia PA 19147. *Mailing Add:* 299 Village St Millis MA 02054

DONOHOE, VICTORIA
HISTORIAN, CRITIC
b Philadelphia, Pa. *Study:* Rosemont Col, BA; Univ Pa Grad Sch Fine Arts, MFA; Pius XII Inst Fine Arts Advan Study, Florence, Italy, cert(scholar), 53; Am Fedn Arts Workshop Art Criticism, scholar, 68. *Collections Arranged:* Religious & Liturgical Art from the Eastern US, Philadelphia Civic Ctr, 63. *Pos:* Art critic, Standard & Times, Philadelphia, 59-62; art critic, Philadelphia Inquirer, 62-; guest cur, Into Storage Exhib, Univ Mus, Univ Pa, 74; corresp, Art News, 75-; dir for selection, Exhib Liturgical Art, 41st Int Eucharistic Cong, Philadelphia, 76; adv, Philadelphia Craft Show, 77; adv fac, Franklin & Marshall Col, 79. *Teaching:* Lab asst studio art & art hist, Rosemont Col, 50-52, lectr, 54-55. *Awards:* Award, Catholic Fine Arts Soc, 76. *Mem:* Int Asn Art Critics/Am Sect; Soc Archit Historians; Irish Georgian Soc, Dublin; Medieval Acad Am; Am-Italy Soc. *Res:* Late 19th & early 20th century American sculpture; figurative painting & sculpture; contemporary crafts; American architecture. *Publ:* Contribr, Sculpture of a City: Philadelphia's Treasures in Bronze and Stone, 74; contribr, Knight-Ridder Newswire, 73-; also contribr to anthologies, mags, encyclopedias & Sunday supplements. *Mailing Add:* 34 Narbrook Park Narberth PA 19072

DOO DA POST (EDWARD FERDINAND HIGGINS III), III
PAINTER, MAIL ARTIST
b LaCrosse, Wis, Nov 11, 49. *Study:* Western Mich Univ, Kalamazoo, BA(art), 72; Univ Colo, Boulder, MFA, 76. *Work:* Electroworks Collection, Eastman House, Rochester, NY; US Post Off, Boulder, Colo; Univ Mich, Ann Arbor; Artists Stamps & Stamp Images, Simon Frasier Univ Gallery, Burnaby, BC; Jean Brown Arch, Shaker Seed House, Tryingham, Mass. *Comn:* business Face Issue (portrait), Paul Schorr; portrait & sheets, Doo Da Stamps of Portrait, Sue Blair. *Exhib:* Fourteenth Midwest Joslyn Art Mus, Omaha, Nebr, 76; Timbres, Et Tampons, E' Artistes Cabnet des Extampes, Mus d'Art & d'Histoire, Geneva, Switz, 76; 4th Denver Metro Show, Denver Art Mus, 76; Electroworks, Eastman House Photog Mus, Rochester, 79-80; Firecracker Paintings, Max Fish Gallery, Ludlow, NY, 89. *Collections Arranged:* First New York City Stamp Invite (auth, catalog), 34 Artists' Stamp Images, 77; Commonpress Number 18 (auth, catalog), 79; Third Int Doo Da Stamp Invite (catalog in prep), 384 Artists stamps. *Teaching:* Prof, painting, Rivington Sch Artists, New York. *Bibliog:* Peter Frank (auth), Artists Stamps, Art Express 1, Vol 1, 81; Alexandra Anderson (auth), Portfolio 3, Vol 3, 5-6/81; Ronnie Cohen (auth), article, Art News, 12/81. *Mem:* Rivington Sch. *Media:* Acrylic; Color Xerox. *Publ:* Auth & illusr, To Grow an Asparagus (under pen name Sam Scotland), 70, & A Piece of Licorice and Other White Elephants, 72, Glotco; contribr, The Rubber Stamp Album, Workman Publ, 78; auth, Artists' stamps, Print Collectors' Newslett, 11-12/79. *Dealer:* Sam Davidson Gallery, Seattle, Wash. *Mailing Add:* 153 Ludlow New York NY 10000

DOOLEY, HELEN BERTHA
PAINTER, DEALER
b San Jose, Calif, July 27, 07. *Study:* San Jose State Col, AB, 28; Douglas Donaldson Sch Design, 30; Calif Sch Fine Arts, San Francisco, 32; Chouinard Art Inst, Los Angeles, 35; Univ Calif, Berkeley, 37-38; Claremont Grad Sch, MA, 39; Teachers Col, Columbia Univ, 48. *Work:* Univ Pac; Shimizu Mus, Japan; Liquid Paper Corp & Great Western Savings, Carmel; Monterey Peninsula Mus Art, Monterey, Calif. *Comn:* Portrait of Dr D Elton Trueblood (oil), 55-56; portrait of Mrs Lloyd Bertholf (oil), Stockton, 56; portrait of Dr Irving Goleman (oil), Irving Goleman Libr, Univ Pacific, Stockton, 62. *Exhib:* Pa Acad Fine Arts, Philadelphia, 41; Soc Western Artists, De Young Mus, San Francisco, 51 & 66; Am Watercolor Soc, Nat Acad Galleries, New York, 63; Lord & Taylor Galleries, New York, 69; Los Angeles Co Art Exhib & West Coast Watercolor Soc, Sacramento, Calif, 71 & 75; Carmel Art Asn Galleries, 73, 79 & 80; Royal Watercolor Soc, London, 78; plus others. *Pos:* Owner, Dooley Gallery, Carmel, Calif, 64- *Teaching:* Instr art, Oakland City Schs, 28-30; adult educ instr art, San Jose City Schs, 33-37; instr art, Scripps Col, 37-39; supvr art, Kern Co Schs, Bakersfield, Calif, 39-47; prof art, Univ Pac, 48-68, San Jose State Univ, 55-56. *Awards:* Award for Mist on the Bay (watercolor), Soc Western Artists, 51; Award for How Green the Valley (oil), Calif State Fair, 65; Award for Festival (oil), Monterey Peninsula Mus Art, 67. *Bibliog:* Article, in: The California Style, McLelland & Last, Hillcrest Publ, Inc, Beverly Hills, Calif, 85. *Mem:* Carmel Art Asn; West Coast Watercolor Soc. *Media:* Oil, Watercolor. *Publ:* Auth, Figure Drawing Teaching Charts, 48-49; Elementary Crafts in a Nutshell, 63. *Mailing Add:* Dooley Gallery Box 5577 Carmel CA 93921

DOOLIN, JAMES LAWRENCE
PAINTER
b Hartford, Conn, June 28, 32. *Study:* Philadelphia Univ rts, BFA, 54, with Henry Pitz; Univ Calif, Los Angeles, MFA, 71, with Richard Diebenkorn. *Work:* Long Beach Mus of Art, Calif; Loyola Law Sch, Los Angeles, Calif; Nat Gallery of Victoria, Melbourne, Australia; Contemp Art Mus, Honolulu, Hawaii; Australian Nat Gallery, Canberra. *Comn:* Mural, Homart Devt Corp, Los Angeles, 87; painting, Jonathan Club, Los Angeles, 90. *Exhib:* Solo exhibs, Los Angeles Munic Gallery, 77, Shopping Mall--A Conceptual Perspective, traveling exhib, 78-79 & Univ S Calif Atelier Gallery, Santa Monica, 85; Laguna Art Mus, Calif, 86; Power Gallery Contemp Art, Sydney, 87; Contemp Art Mus, Honolulu, 88; California Cityscapes, San Diego Mus Art, Calif, 91; From the Studio: Recent Painting & Sculpture by 20 Calif Artists, Oakland Mus, Calif, 92; and others. *Teaching:* Instr drawing & painting, Prahran Tech Col, Melbourne, Australia, 65-66; lectr painting & drawing, Univ Calif, 72-80; instr drawing & painting, Otis-Parsons Art Inst, Los Angeles, 77 & 79-80, Art Inst Southern Calif, 92; instr drawing, Cerro Coso Col, Ridgecrest, Calif, 82-83; instr painting, Santa Monica Col, 84-86. *Awards:* Guggenheim Found Fel, 80; Nat Endowment Arts Grant, 81, 85 & 91. *Bibliog:* Santa Monica Mall: Jim Doolin, Dumb Ox Mag, fall 77-spring 78; review, Art Am, 9/84; Edward Lucie-Smith (auth), Am Art Now, William Morrow, 85. *Media:* All Media. *Dealer:* Koplin Gallery 1438 Ninth St Santa Monica CA 90401. *Mailing Add:* 2020 N Main, No 232 Los Angeles CA 90031

DORAY, AUDREY CAPEL
PAINTER
b Montreal, Que, June 4, 31. *Study:* McGill Univ, Montreal,with John Lyman & Arthur Lismer, BFA, 52; Atelier 17, with SW Hayter, Paris, France,56. *Comn:* Electronic mural, Mazda Motors, Vancouver, BC, 73; two paintings, Mandarin Hotel, Vancouver, 84. *Exhib:* Solo exhib, Vancouver Art Gallery, 61; Nat Art Gallery, Ottawa, Ont, 66; Intermedia Nights, 68 & Inaugural Show, 83, Vancouver Art Gallery; Vancouver Print Show, Heidelberg, Ger, 69; Mus Contemp Crafts, NY, 72; Arteder '82, Bilbao, Spain, 82. *Teaching:* Instr painting & graphics, Vancouver Art Sch, 59-62. *Awards:* Bursary Award, Can Coun, 68-70. *Bibliog:* Tony Emery (auth), The Vancouver explosion, Art Int, 10/68; Michael Rhodes (auth), Audrey Capel Doray, Arts Can, 12/68; Doris Shadbolt (auth), Canadian Art Today, Studio Int, 70. *Media:* Acrylic on canvas, Paper. *Dealer:* Bau Xi Gallery 3045 Granville St Vancouver BC V6H 3J9 Canada. *Mailing Add:* 4441 W First Ave Vancouver BC V6R 4H9 Canada

DOREN, A(RNOLD T)
PHOTOGRAPHER, EDUCATOR
b Chicago, Ill, July 29, 35. *Study:* Rochester Inst Tech, AAS, 59, BFA, 61. *Work:* George Eastman House Photog, Rochester, NY; Mus Mod Art, New York; Mass Inst Technol, Cambridge, Mass; Dallas Mus Art, Tex; Phillip Morris, Cabarrus Co, NC. *Exhib:* American Images, Osaka Univ, Japan, 61; Photographs of the New Generation, Milan, Italy, 61; Photography 63, Kodak Pavillion, New York World's Fair & George Eastman House Photog, Rochester, NY, 63; Photography as Printmaking, Mus Mod Art, New York, 68; Light 7, Mass Inst Technol, Cambridge, 68, Be-ing Without Clothes, 70 & Celebrations, 74, Mass Inst Tech, Cambridge; The Expanded Photograph, Philadelphia Civic Ctr Mus, 72; Photography Circle, Athens, Greece, 90; Photographic Ctr of Athens, 90. *Teaching:* Asst prof photog, Univ NC, Greensboro, 78-84, assoc prof, 84- *Awards:* Purchase Award, Perspectives, R J Reynolds Collection, 79; Purchase Award, Art on Paper, Dillard Paper Co, 84; First Prize, Human Interest B/W, NWest Int Exhib Photog, Puyallup Fair, 88. *Mem:* Soc Photog Educ; NC Ctr Creative Photog. *Publ:* Celebrations, Aperture Mag, 74; The Human Figure, World Gallery Photog, 83; Best of Photography Annual, Photogrs Forum, 86; Fabrications of Italy-Photographs & Literature, Rizzoli, 88; Il Nudo D'rte Parte Terza, Gruppo Editoriale Fabbri. *Mailing Add:* Univ NC 162 McKiver Bldg Greensboro NC 27412

DOREN, HENRY J T
EDUCATOR, PAINTER
b New York, NY, May 20, 29. *Study:* Sch Educ, NY Univ, BS, 48; Faculty of Arts, Ottawa Univ, MA, 59; Art Students League, 59-62; Frank Reilly Sch Art, New York, 62-64; Inst Allende, Univ Guanajuato, San Miguel de Allende, Mexico, MFA, 65. *Work:* Mother and Child, Polish Mother's Hosp Gallery, Lodz, Poland; Environment & 20th Century Man, Dom Polonii Mus, Pultusk Castle, Poland. *Exhib:* Recent Works, Student Ctr Gallery, Seton Hall Univ, S Orange, NJ, 71; Rutherford Mus, NJ, 78; showcase, Theatre Gallery, Montclair State Col, NJ, 83; Riker Hill Artists, Schering-Plough Gallery, Madison, NJ, 88; Polish-American Artists, Galleria del Arte, Petroleas Mexicana, Mexico City, 89. *Pos:* Ed, P S Arts, County Col of Morris Libr,

Randolph, NJ, 76-83; publ, NJ Artform, 79-83. *Teaching:* Assoc prof art, County Col of Morris, Randolph, NJ, 68-83. *Awards:* First Prize, Westfield Art Asn, 69; Fulbright Comn, Madrid, Spain, 71; Exchange Scholar Grant, Polish Acad Sci, Warsaw, 74-75. *Bibliog:* Ester Singer (auth), Doren show is forceful, Jersey J, 12/4/71; Dr W Carl Burger (auth), Doren, the humanist view, NJ Artform,; Madison artist honored, Independent Press, 12/89. *Mem:* Life mem, Art Students League; Polish American Artists Soc, New York. *Media:* Acrylic, Oil. *Publ:* Contribr, NJ Music & Art Mag, 70-71; auth, Tresures of Polish Art, Interpress, Warsaw, Poland, 76. *Mailing Add:* 17 Madison Ave No 61 Madison NJ 07940

DORETHY, REX E
ADMINISTRATOR, EDUCATOR
b Macomb, Ill, Mar 14, 38. *Study:* Ill State Univ, MS, 65, PhD, 72; Univ Ill, PostGrad, 68. *Pos:* Faculty & head dept, Art Ball State Univ, 72-84; chair dept of art/design, Univ Wis, 84-92; asst to dean, Coll Fine Arts, Univ Wis, 92- *Teaching:* Asst prof, Art Educ, Ill State Univ, 67-72; prof, Ball State Univ, Muncie, Ind, 72-84; prof art, Univ Wis, Stevens Point, 84- *Mem:* Nat Art Educ Asn; Wis Art Educ Asn; Nat Arts Policy Coun; Col Arts Asn. *Publ:* Auth, Teacher Action-Student Response, 70 & Motion Parallax in Spatial Abilities of Young Chile, Studies Art Educ, 78; coauth, Mental Function, Perceptual Differences, Achievement in Art, Studies Art Educ, 78; auth, Research Priorities in Visual Arts Educ, Rev Res Visual Arts, 81; Questions/ Positions Concerning the Gifted in Art, Viewpoints: Art Educ, 83. *Mailing Add:* 124 Maple Bluff Rd Stevens Point WI 54481

DORFMAN, BRUCE
PAINTER, COLLAGE ARTIST
b New York, NY, Aug 15, 36. *Study:* Art Students League, with Yasuo Kuniyoshi, Arnold Blanch; Univ Iowa, BA, 58. *Work:* Butler Inst Am Art, Youngstown, Ohio; Arco Ctr Visual Art, Los Angeles; Com Trust Co Found; Rockefeller Found; Govt Israel; Smithsonian Inst, Washington, DC; and others. *Comn:* Rockefeller Found, 79; mural, Dutchess County Art Asn, NY State Coun on the Arts, 80; Stedman Collection, Houston, Tex, 88. *Exhib:* Butler Inst Am Art, 71-72 & 75; New Sch Soc Res, 81 & 87; Arras Gallery, New York, 82, 86 & 88; Albright-Knox Art Gallery, Buffalo, NY, 87-88; Collector's Choice, Nat Asn Pvt Art Found Nat Traveling Exhib, 87-89; Hunter Mus, Tenn, 87-88; Addison-Ripley Gallery, Washington, DC, 90; and others. *Teaching:* Guest artist, Norton Mus, W Palm Beach, Fla, 62-64, Schenectady Mus, 65-66, Everson Mus, Syracuse, NY, 72; resident artist, Syracuse Univ, 71; mem fac, art workshops, New Sch Soc Res, 79- & Art Ctr Northern NJ, New Milford, 83-; instr, Art Students League, New York, 64-; Master Class, New York, 80- *Awards:* New York World's Fair Exhib Award, State of Fla, 64; Friends of Am Art Purchase Award, Butler Inst Am Art Ann, 72; Arts East Found Individual Grant, 88 & 90; and others. *Bibliog:* Lois Katz (auth), monograph, 88; Alexandra Enders (auth), article, Art & Antiques, 5/90; Gerrit Henry (auth), Catalog, 90. *Mem:* Life mem Art Students League; Fedn Mod Painters & Sculptors. *Media:* All Media. *Publ:* Color Mixing, Grosset & Dunlap, 67. *Dealer:* Hal Katzen Gallery New York NY 10012; Images Gallery 3154 Markway Dr Toledo OH 43606. *Mailing Add:* Art Students League 215 W 57th St New York NY 10019

DORFMAN, ELSA
PHOTOGRAPHER, WRITER
b Apr 26, 37. *Study:* Tufts Univ, Medford, BA, 59; Boston Col, Chestnut Hill, Mass, MEd, 62. *Work:* Portland Mus Art, Maine; Wellesley Col, Mass; Mus Fine Arts, Boston; San Francisco Mus Art, Calif; Princeton Univ, NJ; Fogg Art Mus-Harvard Univ. *Exhib:* Portraits of Women, Everson Mus, Syracuse, NY, 73; Women of Photog, San Francisco Mus Art, Calif, 75; Boston Artists, Boston Mus Fine Arts, 78 & 81 & 90; Boston Now, Inst Contemp Art, Boston, 83; Self Portraits, Zurich Art Mus, Switz, 85 & Lausanne Art Mus, Switz, 85; American Photog, Fogg Mus, 86; Big Apple Circus Portraits, Fogg Mus. *Pos:* Portrait photogr at own studio in Cambridge, Mass, currently. *Teaching:* Lecturer at various US universities & colleges. *Awards:* Bunting Fel, Radcliffe Col, 74. *Mem:* Am Civil Liberties Union. *Interests:* Rare Polaroid 20x24. *Publ:* Auth, Elsa's Housebook, Godine, 74; article, Womens Rev Books, Wellesley Col, 85-90; article, Views, Photog Resource Ctr; Here We Are, Here We Are, Zoland Bks, 90. *Dealer:* Brent Sikkema Fine Art 40 Wooster St New York NY 10013. *Mailing Add:* 607 Franklin St Cambridge MA 02139

DORFMAN, FRED
ART DEALER, GALLERY DIRECTOR
b Chicago, Ill, Feb 19, 46. *Study:* Am Univ, 69; Chicago Art Inst, 71-72. *Pos:* Owner, Dorfman Gallery, currently. *Mem:* Visual Artist & Gallery Asn; Int Art Dealers Asn. *Specialty:* Contemporary American art; sculpture, drawings, paintings and multiples. *Publ:* Article, New York Arts J, 79. *Mailing Add:* Dorfman Gallery 123 Watts St New York NY 10003-1725

DORN, PETER KLAUS
DESIGNER, GRAPHIC ARTIST
b Berlin, Ger, June 30, 32; Can citizen. *Study:* Journeyman compositor, Berlin; Ont Col Art, Toronto; Hochschule für Grafik & Buch Kunst, Leipzig. *Work:* Toronto Pub Libr Fine Arts Sect; Douglas Libr, Kingston. *Comn:* 200 Anniversary Commemorative Postage Stamp, New Brunswick; Canada, XIII Biennale di Venecia (catalogue), 86. *Exhib:* Royal Can Acad, 70; Agnes Etherington Art Ctr, Kingston, 71; Look of Books, 74, 76 & 77; Design Can, 75; Spectrum Can, 76; Group Exhib, Toronto, 79; and others. *Pos:* Proprietor, Heinrich Heine Press, Toronto, 63; typographer, Univ Toronto Press, 66-71; dir, Graphic Design Unit, Queen's Univ, 71; dir, Graphic Serv, King Abdulaziz Univ, Camberley, Eng, 82-83. *Teaching:* Teaching master typography, St Lawrence Col, Kingston, 78-; guest lectr, NS Col Art & Design, Univ Man, Sheridan Col, 80. *Awards:* Awards, Ont Asn Art Galleries, 80-83; Awards, Am Inst Graphic Arts, 80 & 83; Distinguished Serv Award, Queen's Univ, 91. *Bibliog:* Applied Arts Quart, Vol 3, No 1, spring 88. *Mem:* Royal Can Acad; Guild Hand Printers (dir); fel Graphic Designers Can (nat past pres, Kingston past pres); Am Inst Graphic Arts; Pittsburgh Hist Soc (exec). *Mailing Add:* Graphic Design Unit Queens Univ Rideau Bldg 207 Stuart St Kingston ON K7L 3N6 Canada

DORN, RUTH (DORNBUSH)
PAINTER
b Leipzig, Ger, Feb 16, 25; US citizen. *Study:* Studied in Ger & Bolivia; Brooklyn Mus; Brooklyn Col; Nat Acad Fine Arts. *Exhib:* Brooklyn Mus, 69 & 77; Artists League of Brooklyn, Metrop Mus Art, New York, 77; Brooklyn Come to the Met, Hudson Valley Art Asn, 77; Nat Arts Club, New York; Allied Artists of Am, 78; Cork Gallery, Lincoln Ctr, New York, 78; Union Carbide Corp, New York, 78; Permanent Collection Ctr Arts, Vero Beach, Fla. *Awards:* First Prize, 74 & Nell Van Hook Memorial Prize, 75, Composers, Authors & Artists Am. *Mem:* Composers Authors & Artists Am; Am Artists Prof League; Burr Artists; Deerfield Valley Art Asn; Leverett Craftsmen & Artists, Mass. *Media:* Oil. *Mailing Add:* 1890 Sandpiper Rd E Vero Beach FL 32963

DOROSH, DARIA
ENVIRONMENTAL ARTIST, PAINTER
b Ukraine, Mar 21, 43; US citizen. *Study:* Fashion Inst Technol, AAS, 63; Cooper-Union Sch Art & Archit, cert, 68. *Exhib:* Purchase Fund Exhib, Am Acad Arts & Letts, New York, 73; New Art II: Textures and Surfaces, Mus Mod Art, New York, 81; AIR Group, Kunsthalle, Lund, Sweden, 81; Patterns, San Jose Inst Contemp Art, Calif, 81; Photo Start, Bronx Mus, New York, 82; Homeless at Home, Storefront for Art Archit, New York, 86; Competition Diomede, Clocktower Gallery, New York, 89. *Teaching:* Instr painting, Parsons Sch Design, New York, 76-85; asst prof drawing, Fashion Inst Technol, 69-92. *Awards:* Nat Endowment Arts Grant, 86; NY State Coun Arts Grant, 88. *Bibliog:* Patricia Phillips (auth), review, Art Formum, 5/84; N F Karlins (auth), Tribeca sidwalk sculpture gets Soho Gallery preview, Battery News, 4/88. *Media:* Mixed Media. *Publ:* Auth, Art And Context: A personal view, Leonardo J Int Soc Arts, Sci & Technol, Pergmamon Press, 88. *Mailing Add:* c/o AIR 63 Crosby St New York NY 10012

DORRA, HENRI
HISTORIAN, EDUCATOR
b Alexandria, Egypt, Jan 17, 24; US citizen. *Study:* Univ London, BSc, 44; Harvard Univ, MS & MA, 50, PhD, 53, Student Fel, Metrop Mus Art, 51-52. *Collections Arranged:* Visionaries and Dreamers & Ryder, Corcoran Gallery Art, San Francisco Mus Art & Cleveland Mus Art, 55-60; Years of Ferment, Univ Calif, Los Angeles, 65. *Pos:* Asst dir, Corcoran Gallery Art, 54-61; Philadelphia Mus Art, 61-62; exec vpres, Indianapolis Art Asn, 62-63; trustee, Santa Barbara Mus Art. *Teaching:* mem fac, Univ Calif, Los Angeles, 63-65; prof art, Univ Calif, Santa Barbara, 65- *Awards:* Bowdoin Prize, Harvard Univ, 49; Nat Endowment Humanities Fel, 75; Guggenheim Fel, 78-79. *Mem:* Col Art Asn Am. *Publ:* Auth, Seurat, Beaux-Arts, Paris, 60; The American Muse, Viking, 60; Art in Perspective, 73; contribr, Gazette Beaux-Arts, Burlington Mag & Metrop Mus Art. *Mailing Add:* Dept Art History Univ Calif Santa Barbara CA 93106

DORRIEN, CARLOS GUILLERMO
SCULPTOR
b Buenos Aires, Arg, Oct 8, 48; US citizen. *Study:* Univ de la Plata, Arg, 67; Lowell Technol Inst, Mass; Montserrat Sch Visual Art, Mass, BFA, 73. *Work:* Bentley Col, Waltham, Mass; John Hancock Insurance Co, Boston; Mus 20th Century, Medellin, Colombia. *Comn:* Portal (sculpture), Bentley Col, Waltham, Mass, 78; Cutting Object (marble), City Medellin, Colombia,81; Granite Ribbon, Mass Transit Authority, Porter Sq Sta, Cambridge, Mass, 82. *Exhib:* Arts on the Line, Hayden Gallery, Mass Inst Technol, Cambridge, 79; Art in Public Places, Carpenter Ctr, Harvard Univ, Cambridge, Mass, 80; Biennial Art Medellin, Colombia, 81; Mus 20th Century, Colombia, 81; Brocton Art Mus Trienial, Mass, 83. *Pos:* Guest sculptor, City Medellin, Colombia, 81. *Teaching:* Lectr, Sch Mus Fine Arts, Boston, 80-81; instr sculpture, Art Inst Boston, 82-86. *Awards:* Traveling Grant, Partners Am, 81; Purchase Award, IV Biennial Art Medellin, Colombia, 81; WBZ-TV Fund for the Arts Grant, 83. *Bibliog:* Mary Sullivan (auth), Carlos Dorrien: An interview, Back Bay View, Vol 3, 78; Gerald Ryan (auth), Sculptures for business, Boston Today, 9/79. *Media:* Granite, Bronze. *Dealer:* Clark Gallery Lincoln Sta Lincoln MA 01773. *Mailing Add:* 156 Weston Rd Wellesley MA 02181-5739

DORSEY, DEBORAH WORTHINGTON
PAINTER
b Alexandria, Va. *Study:* Radcliffe, BA; Columbia Univ, MA MPhil; Nat Acad Sch Design. *Work:* Int Investors Inc, New York; Sears, Roebuck, Chicago, Ill. *Exhib:* Invitational Exhibition Former Prize Winners, Nat Arts Club, New York, 78; Adirondack Nat Exhib Am Watercolors, Community Arts Ctr, Old Forge, NY, 82; Am Watercolor Soc, Nat Acad Design & Salmagundi, New York, 82 & 88; one-man shows, Philadelphia Art Alliance, Pa, 89, Magenta Gallery Princeton, New Jersey, 91; Henri Gallery, Washington, DC, 90; Portrait Group Gallery, Washington, DC, 90; Art Network Gallery, Atlanta, 92; Newman Gallery, Philadelphia, 92; For Us and About Us, Nat Asn Women Artists, ARC Gallery, Chicago, 92. *Pos:* Art critic, Art News, 71-72; art researcher, Time Life Films, 70-73; writer, Filmstrip House, 74- *Teaching:* Adj prof art hist & painting, C W Post & Long

Island Univ, 74-78 & 82; instr drawing, State Univ NY-New Paltz, 82-83; instr portrait painting, Craft Students League, New York, 83-85. *Awards:* First Prize, 83 & Portrait Prize, 87, Ann Mem Exhib, Nat Arts Club, New York; Mem Award Portrait, Nat Asn Women Artists, Elizabeth Stanton Blake, 90. *Bibliog:* Cathy Viksjo (auth), Magenta Art Gallery a gem, Trenton Times, 3/4/90. *Mem:* Nat Asn Women Artists; Women in the Arts. *Media:* Watercolor. *Dealer:* Newman Gallery Walnut St Philadelphia PA; Art Network Peachtree St Atlanta GA. *Mailing Add:* 156 E 74th St New York NY 10021

DORSEY, LUCIA IANNONE
ADMINISTRATOR
b Buffalo, NY, Nov 23, 59. *Study:* Wesleyan Univ, Middletown, Conn, BA(art hist), 80; Univ Pa, 82-83. *Collections Arranged:* Goya/Los Caprichos (catalog), 81; Comedy & Revolution: Satire From Hogarth to Daumier (with catalog), 81; Neil Welliver: Recent Studies, 87; Francoise Gilot: Inner Voices, 89. *Pos:* Coordr, Arthur Ross Gallery, Univ of Pa, Philadelphia, 84-; cur asst, Yale Art Gallery, New Haven, Conn, 80-82. *Publ:* Auth, Goya/Los Caprichos (exhib catalog essay), Yale Art Gallery, 81; Comedy & Revolution: Satire from Hogarth to Daumier (exhib catalog essay), Wesleyan Univ, 81; contribr, the Spread of Durer's Woodcut Style (catalog essay), Yale Art Gallery, 81. *Mailing Add:* Univ Pa Arthur Ross Gallery Furness Bldg 220 S 34th St Philadelphia PA 19104

DORSEY, MICHAEL A
PAINTER, ADMINISTRATOR
b Findlay, Ohio, July 31, 49. *Study:* Eastern Ill Univ, BS, 71; Bowling Green State Univ, MA 72, MFA, 73. *Work:* Miss Mus Art, Jackson; Meridian Mus Art, Miss; Cotton Landia Mus Art, Greenwood, Miss; Southeast Ark Arts & Sci Ctr, Pine Bluff, Ark; Bowling Green State Univ, Ohio; Univ Perugia, Italy; Burroughs Wellcome Company, NC. *Exhib:* 17th Ann Piedmont Graphics, Greenville Mus Art, SC, 81; Of On & About Paper, Columbia Mus Art & Sci, SC, 82; SPAR Nat, Barwell Art Ctr, Shreveport, La, 83; 26th Ann Delta Exhib, Ark Art Ctr, Little Rock, 84; 19th Ann Nat Exhib, Coos Art Mus, Coos Bay, Ore, 84; 9th Ann Nat Southern Watercolor Soc, Miss Mus Art, Jackson, 85; Nat Ark Exhib, Ark Arts & Sci Ctr, Pine Bluff, 85; Artists Who Teach, Fed Reserve Bldg, Washington, DC, 87; solo exhibs, Swope Art Mus, Terre Haute, In, 89, Hinds Jr Col, Jackson, Miss, 90, Albers Art Gallery, Memphis, Tenn, 90, Miss State Univ, 92 & East Carolina Univ, 93. *Teaching:* Prof & dean, Sch Art, East Carolina Univ, 91-; assoc prof & dept head, Miss State Univ, 82-86, prof & dept head, 86-91. *Awards:* 2nd Place Award, Nat NFla Competition, Fla State Univ, 86; Outstanding Alumni, Bowling Green State Univ, 89; Outstanding Art Alumni, Eastern Ill Univ, 92. *Bibliog:* Paul Grootkerk (auth), The beauty parlor mirror, J Am Cult, 88 & Historical permanence of Fantastic, 89. *Mem:* Col Art Asn; Miss Watercolor Soc (pres, 86-88); Nat Art Educ Asn; Miss Art Asn. *Media:* Mixed Media, Drawing. *Mailing Add:* East Carolina Univ Sch Art Greenville NC 27858-4353

DORSKY, MORRIS
HISTORIAN, EDUCATOR
b New York, NY, July 8, 18. *Study:* Brooklyn Col, BA, 40; NY Univ, MA, 66. *Pos:* Chmn dept art, Brooklyn Col, City Univ New York, 70- *Teaching:* Prof art hist, Brooklyn Col, City Univ New York, 48- *Res:* Ben Shahn. *Mailing Add:* 120 W 70th St New York NY 10023

DORSKY, SAMUEL
ART DEALER
b Brooklyn, NY, May 7, 14. *Specialty:* 20th century art. *Mailing Add:* c/o Dorsky Art Gallery 379 W Broadway New York NY 10012

DORST, CLAIRE V
PAINTER, PRINTMAKER
b Plymouth, Wis, June 4, 22. *Study:* Beloit Col, BA, 49; Univ Iowa, MA, 53; Univ Wis-Madison, United Lutheran Church Am Scholar, 62-63, MFA, 63. *Work:* Univ Iowa; Univ Wis; also in pvt collections; Disney; McDonald's Corp. *Exhib:* Wisconsin at Work, 50 & Wisconsin Painters & Sculptors Ann, 64, Mem Mus, Milwaukee; Fla State Fair Show, Tampa, 65; Nat Exhib Contemp Painting, Soc Four Arts, Palm Beach, Fla, 66, 70 & 85; Hortt Mem Exhib, Mus Arts, Ft Lauderdale, Fla, 68, 70 & 87. *Pos:* Chmn Art Depts, Carthage Col & Fla Atlantic Univ; Indpendent watercolor workshop leader, 91- *Teaching:* Asst prof studio art, Wayne State Col, 53-59; prof art & art hist & chmn dept art, Carthage Col, 59-64; prof studio art, Fla Atlantic Univ, 64-, chmn Dept Art, 68-84, emer prof, 91. *Awards:* Tellus Madden Award, Wis Spring Show, 63; First Prize in Painting, Winter Park Art Fair, 65; Atwater Kent Award, Soc Four Arts Nat Exhib, 66; over 100 awards in major art fairs, 67- *Mem:* Hon mem Palm Beach Watercolor Soc (founding pres, 83); Fla Watercolor Soc, 91- *Media:* Oil, Watercolor; Etching. *Publ:* Auth, Artists Guide to Sidewalk Exhibiting, Watson/Guptill, 80. *Mailing Add:* Dept Art Fla Atlantic Univ Boca Raton FL 33431

DORST, MARY CROWE
GRAPHIC ARTIST, CRAFTSMAN
Study: Beloit Col, BA(art; cum laude); Northern Ill Univ, MA(drawing). *Work:* McDonald Corp; other pvt collections. *Exhib:* Hortt Mem Exhib, Ft Lauderdale Mus Arts, 69, 84 & 89; Piedmont Crafts Exhib, Mint Mus, Charlotte, NC, 71-75; Nat Exhib, Soc of the Four Arts, Palm Beach, Fla, 83, 85, 86, 89 & 91; Contemp Women Artists of the Gold Coast Traveling Exhib, 83-86; Landscape II Invitational, Vero Beach Ctr for the Arts, 90; 3 person exhib, Broward Community Col South, 93; & others. *Collections Arranged:* The Other Side of the Generation Gap, Constructions in Flexible Materials, Printmakers of the Americas & Edward S Curtis, Fla Atlantic Univ Art Gallery, 73-77; Florida Heritage, Contemporary Women Artists of the Gold Coast & Art in Fiber and Clay, Palmetto Gallery. *Pos:* Gallery dir, Fla Atlantic Univ, 73-77; art reviewer, Boca Raton News, Fla, 75-76 & 85-86; art dir, Palmetto Gallery, NCNB Banks, Boca Raton, 79-87; art/writer for local publ, 88-89. *Teaching:* Instr art, Marymount Col, Fla, 65-67, & Broward Community Col, Fla, 73-75; Palm Beach Jr Col, 75-83; adj instr, Atlantic Univ, Fla, 87- *Awards:* Hon Mention, Nat Exhib Am Painting, Soc Four Arts, 83; Spec Award, Palm Beach Watercolor Soc, 87 & 92; Broward Art Guild, 90 & 91. *Bibliog:* Featured artist (calendar), Broward Arts Coun, 86. *Mem:* hon mrm Fla Craftsmen (area dir, 75-78 & 82-84); Am Crafts Coun; Palm Beach Co Coun Arts; hon mrm Palm Beach Watercolor Soc (pres 89-91). *Media:* Drawing, Fiber. *Publ:* Auth, A Day in Mino, Crafts Horizons, 6/71; contribr, art articles, local monthly mag; Reviews in Art Voices, South. *Mailing Add:* 618 NW High St Boca Raton FL 33432

DOTY, ROBERT MCINTYRE
ADMINISTRATOR
b Rochester, NY, Dec 23, 33. *Study:* Harvard Univ, AB; Univ Rochester, MA. *Collections Arranged:* Photo-Secession, 1960; Photography America, 65 & 74; Whitney Ann, 66-71; Adolph Gottlieb, 68; Human Concern/Personal Torment, 69; Contemporary Black Artists of America, 71; Lucas Samaras, 72; American Folk Art in Ohio Collections, 76. *Pos:* Dir, Currier Gallery Art, currently. *Mailing Add:* 2172 Elm St Manchester NH 03104

DOUDERA, GERARD
PAINTER, EDUCATOR
b Sharon, Conn, Dec 29, 32. *Study:* Hartford Art Sch, BFA 56; Univ Ill. *Work:* Wadsworth Atheneum, Hartford; Butler Inst Am Art, Youngstown, Ohio; New Britan Mus, Conn. *Exhib:* One-man shows, DeCordova & Dana Mus, Lincoln, Mass, 59, Conn Comn Arts' Showcase Gallery, Hartford, 85, Conn Community Arts Gallery, Hartford, 85, Slater Mus, Norwich, Conn, 89, Pindar Gallery, New York, 89 & 90, Mus Art, Univ Conn, 90 & Kerygama Gallery, Ridgewood, NJ, 91; New Britain Mus Am Art, Conn, 61; Univ Hartford, 71. *Teaching:* Prof painting, Univ Conn, 62-87, head art dept, 74-77; emer prof art, Univ Conn, 87-; artist-in-residence, Camargo Found, Cassis, France, 87; vis artist, Weir Farm Heritage Trust, 92-93. *Awards:* First CAFA Award, Conn Artists Ann, Slater Mus, Norwich, 86. *Bibliog:* C Libov (auth), A Painter's World in Bigelow Hollow, Conn Sect, NY Times, 8/18/85; J Brodsky (auth), A Landscape Sensibility, Gerard Doudera A Retrospective (catalog), William Benton Mus, Univ Conn, 90. *Mem:* Conn Acad Fine Arts (pres, 81-86). *Media:* Oil, Watercolor. *Dealer:* Kerygma Gallery 38 Oak St Ridgewood NJ. *Mailing Add:* 490 Lewis Hill Rd Coventry CT 06238

DOUENIAS, NATALIE
PAINTER
b Brooklyn, NY, Jan 12, 40. *Study:* Empire State Col, BFA & BS(psychol), 78; Roslyn Sch Painting, 78-82; Post Col, with Robert Yasuda, 84-86; Pratt Inst (MA prog-art therapy), 88- *Exhib:* Long Island Artists Exhib, Islip Mus, NY, 85, 87 & 88; Long Beach Mus Art, NY, 85 & 86; Heckscher Mus, Long Island, NY, 85-87; Adelphi Univ, Garden City, NY, 87; Wunsch Art Ctr, Glen Cove, NY, 87-88; Phoenix Gallery, New York, 88; and others. *Awards:* Excellence Award, Long Island Artists Exhib, Heckscher Mus, Long Island Trust Co, 86; Grumbacher Art Award, Long Beach Mus Open Competition, NY State Coun Arts, 86; Mixed Media Award, Nat Asn Women Artists Ann Exhib, Martha Reed Mem, 86; Honorable Mention, Islip Art Mus, 88. *Bibliog:* Sidney Stiebel (auth), Opposites unite at Peri-Renneth Show, 9/83 & Madeleine Burnside (auth), Linda ViVona, Nola Zirin, Natalie Douenias, 6/85, Sunstorm; Helen A Harrison (auth), Celebrating an expansion, NY Times, 2/12/84; Karen Lipson (auth), 4-Gallery exhibition showcases 100 artists, 6/12/87 & Surprises among the prizes, 4/8/88, Newsday; Helen A Harrison (auth), What the jurors chose for Islip Museum Show, NY Times, 4/19/87. *Mem:* Nat Asn Women Artists Inc; Nat League Am Pen Women; Hempstead Harbor Artists Asn. *Media:* Acrylic, Mixed Media. *Mailing Add:* 20 Birchwood Lane Kings Point NY 11024

DOUGHERTY, PATRICK T
SCULPTOR
Study: Univ NC, Chapel Hill, BA, 67; Univ Iowa, Iowa City, MA, 69. *Exhib:* Solo exhibs, Spirit Square Art Ctr, Charlott, NC, 86, Second St Gallery, Charlottsville, Va & New York Univ, Broadway Windows, 88, St Andrew's Gallery, Sewanee, Tenn & NC Mus Art, Raleigh, 89; High Mus, Atlanta, Ga, 89; Huntsville Mus Art, Ala, 89; Memphis Brooks Mus Art, Tenn, 89; Durham Arts Coun, Pub Arts Conference, NC, 89; North Art Ctr, Atlanta, Ga, 89. *Awards:* NC Artist Fel Award, NC Arts Coun, 86; NC Arts Coun Matching Grant, Mint Mus, 87. *Mailing Add:* Rte 10 Box 70 Chapel Hill NC 27516

DOUGHERTY, RAY (RAYMOND EDWARD)
PAINTER, INSTRUCTOR
b Wildwood, NJ, June 15, 42. *Study:* Pa Acad Fine Arts, dipl, 68; Univ Pa Grad Sch Fine Arts, BFA, 70. *Work:* Ocean City Art Ctr, NJ; Noyes Mus, Ocean View, NJ; NJ Univ of Med & Dentistry, Camden; Atlantic Co Special Serv Sch Dist, Hostler Hall, NJ. *Exhib:* 27th Nat Soc Painters Casein & Acrylic, Am Acad & Inst Arts & Lett, New York, 79-90; 111th Am Watercolor Soc, Nat Acad Design, New York, 78; 2nd Biennial, NJ State Mus, Trenton, 79; Audobon Artist Ann, Nat Arts Club, New York, 80-89; NJ Art Educ Exhib, Trenton State Col, 82. *Collections Arranged:* 20th, 21st & 22nd Nat Traveling Exhib, Nat Soc Painters in Casein & Acrylic, 77-80; Old Bergen Art Guild, Bayonne, NJ Group Nat Tour, 79-80. *Teaching:* Instr fine arts, NJ Pub Schs, 70-78, Am Inst Ment Studies, Vineland, NJ, 79 & Secondary Parochial School System, 80; instr art, Helmbold Educ Ctr, 84;

instr, Atlantic Co Special Serv Dist, 90. *Awards:* Lotos Club Exhib Award Paintings, 90-91; Cert Merit, Nat Soc Painter in Casien & Acrylic, 91; Morecai Newman Mem Award, 85. *Mem:* Cape May Co Art League (pres, 77-78); Nat Soc Painter Casein & Acrylic (bd dirs, 79, vpres, 84, pres, 89-); Audubon Artists; Nat Artists Equity; Painters & Sculptors Soc NJ; and others. *Media:* Oil & Acrylic; Demonstration & Criticism. *Mailing Add:* 932 Main St Erma Park NJ 08204

DOUGLAS, EDWIN PERRY
PAINTER, INSTRUCTOR
b Lynn, Mass, June 18, 35. *Study:* RI Sch Design, BFA; San Francisco Art Inst, MFA. *Work:* Montreal Mus Fine Arts, Can; San Francisco Art Inst Art Bank; Dayton Art Mus, Ohio; Cincinnati Art Mus; Lincoln Land Community Col Art Mus, Springfield, Ill; Portland Mus Art. *Exhib:* San Francisco Art Inst Nat Painting & Sculpture Tour, 63; 81st Ann Spring Exhib, Montreal Mus Fine Arts, 64; 31st Ann Can Soc Graphic Art, Kingston, Ont, 64; Cincinnati Biennial, Cincinnati Art Mus, 69; Portland Mus Art, Maine, 74; Walt Kuhn Gallery, Maine, 83; Joan Whitney Payson Gallery, Maine, 84; Papendrecht Mus Contemp Art, Neth, 85; Icon Gallery, Brunswick, Maine, 90; Greenhut Gallery, Maine, 91. *Teaching:* Instr painting, Univ Man Sch Art, 63-64; instr drawing & painting, Cincinnati Art Acad, Ohio, 64-68; vis prof art, Wash Univ Sch Fine Arts, 69-72; vis lectr painting, Univ Cincinnati, 72-73; prof, Portland Sch Art, 73-, head painting dept, 73-; guest lectr, Joan Whitney Payson Gallery, Maine, 84 & Mt Holyoke Col, Mass, 88. *Awards:* Convocation & Commencement Addresses, 84 & 85. *Bibliog:* Dialogue on Painting (film), Miami Univ TV, 67. *Media:* Oil. *Mailing Add:* Portland Sch of Art 97 Spring St Portland ME 04101

DOUGLAS, L J
PAINTER, WRITER
b Sellersville, Pa, Dec 16, 48. *Study:* Philadelphia Col Art, with Ree Morton & Cynthia Carlson, BFA, 75; Sch Art Inst Chicago, MFA, 77. *Work:* Mus Contemp Art, Chicago. *Exhib:* Mythology and Religion in Art, NAME Gallery, Chicago, 84; Head Show, Randolph St Gallery, Chicago, Ill, 84; Looking at Men, Artemesia Gallery, Chicago, 85; Convergence, Mind, Myth & Material, Peter Miller Gallery, Chicago, 85; Krannart Mus, Champaign, Ill, 86. *Pos:* Critic, New Art Examiner, currently. *Bibliog:* Michael Segard (auth), Chicago's new expression, 1/85 & A Thorsen & J Yood (coauth), Who follows the hairy who?, 3/85, New Art Examiner. *Media:* Oil. *Publ:* Auth, Speakeasy, 2/84 & A message in darkness, 6/84, New Art Examiner. *Dealer:* Marianne Deson Gallery 340 W Huron Chicago IL 60610. *Mailing Add:* c/o CCA Gallery 325 W Huron St Chicago IL 60610

DOUGLAS, TOM HOWARD
PAINTER, SCULPTOR
b Lexington, Tenn, Nov 23, 57. *Study:* Austin Peay State Univ, BFA, 80; Univ Miss Oxford, MFA, 83. *Work:* Tenn State Mus, Nashville; Parthenon Mus, Nashville; Tupelo Artist Guild Gallery, Tupelo, Miss; Univ Miss, Oxford; Austin Peay State Univ, Clarksville, Tenn; Nashville Int Airport, Tenn. *Exhib:* Mid Am Exhib, Owensboro Fine Arts Mus, Owensbor, Ky, 80; Two Visions of Landscape, C W Woods Gallery, Hattiesburg, Miss, 85; Recent Works, Margaret F Treahorn, Clarksville, Tenn, 85; A Glimpse of the South, Brent Wood Gallery, St Louis, Mo, 86; ICC Faculty Show, Univ Ark at Littlerock, 88; Numbers Invitational, Cooper Ave Gallery, Memphis, Tenn, 88; 2 x 4, Carnegie Arts Ctr, Leavenworth, Kans, 88; Constellations, Ark State Univ, Jonesboro, 89; Oratory, Robinson-Willis Gallery, Nashville, Tenn, 89. *Pos:* Artist-in-Residence, Itawamba Co (Miss Arts Commn, NEA), 84-85. *Teaching:* Chair, dept art, painting, Itawamba Community Col, 83- *Awards:* Best of Show, Crossties, Crossties Asn, 85; Best of Show, Redlands Festival, 87; Best of Show, Gum Tree Arts Fair, Gum Tree Asn, 88. *Bibliog:* Alec Clayton (auth), Review, Art Papers, 3-4/86. *Media:* Acrylic, Enamel on Wood, Tin. *Mailing Add:* 1043 Blair Tupelo MS 38801

DOUKE, DANIEL W
PAINTER, EDUCATOR
b Los Angeles, Calif, Sept 18, 43. *Study:* Pasadena City Col, AA, 66; Calif State Univ, Los Angeles, BA, 70, MA, 71. *Work:* Minnesota Art Mus; Calif State Univ Art Mus, Long Beach; Am Friends Israel Mus, Jerusalem; Speed Mus, Louisville, Ky. *Exhib:* Oakland Mus Art, Calif, 73; State Univ NY Col, Potsdam, 74; one-man shows, OK Harris, New York, 79-89, Tortue Gallery, Santa Monica, Calif, 79-89; Mus Mod Art, New York, 76; Los Angeles Inst Contemp Art, 77. *Collections Arranged:* Douglas Bond: Twelve Year Survey (auth, catalog), Calif State Univ, 78. *Pos:* Visual arts specialist, Cult Arts, Los Angeles Co, 73-75; gallery dir, Calif State Univ, Los Angeles, 75- *Teaching:* Instr painting, Calif State Univ, Los Angeles, 75- *Awards:* James D Phelan Award in Painting, Oakland Mus, San Francisco Found, 73. *Mem:* Col Art Asn. *Media:* Acrylic. *Publ:* Auth, Project Outreach, Nat Endowment for the Arts, 74; coauth, Ceramic Conjunction, Co of Los Angeles, 74-75; contribr, Bradley Smith, auth, Erotic Art of the Masters, Lyle Stuart, 75; Gregory Battcock, auth, Super Realism, Dutton, 75; Udo Kultermann, auth, New Painting 2nd Edition, Wasmuth, 76. *Dealer:* O K Harris Works of Art 380 W Broadway New York NY 10012. *Mailing Add:* c/o Tortue Gallery 2917 Santa Monica Blvd Santa Cruz CA 90404

DOUMATO, LAMIA
LIBRARIAN, HISTORIAN
b Aug 26, 47; US citizen. *Study:* RI Col, BA; Pa State Univ, MA(art hist); Simmons Col, Boston, MLS; Boston Univ; Columbia Univ; George Washington Univ. *Exhib:* Retrospective 1972-1982, Women's Caucus for Art, Moore Col Art, 83. *Collections Arranged:* Rhode Island Architecture, Providence Pub Libr; Raphael, Nat Gallery Art Libr, 81; American Architecture: Hist View, Nat Gallery of Art Libr, 84. *Pos:* Art librn, Providence Pub Libr, 70-71; ref librn, Boston Univ Libr, 71-74; ref librn, Mus Mod Art Libr, New York, 74-78; reference librn, Nat Gallery Art, Washington, DC, 81-88, head of reader servs, 88- *Teaching:* Teaching asst art hist, Pa State Univ, 70; prof & head, Art & Archit Libr, Univ Colo, Boulder, 78-81; teacher res methods, Univ Colo, 79-81. *Awards:* Coun Creative Work Grants, Univ Colo, 79-81. *Mem:* Col Art Asn; Art Librn Soc NAm; Art Librn Soc Washington, DC; Asn Archit Librn. *Interests:* Illuminated manuscripts, architectural bibliography and women architects; History of Jewelry. *Publ:* auth, Museum Design, Chicago Coun Planning Librn, 80; Women in literature of art, Oxford Art J, Vol 3, 4/80; contribr, The Comfortable House, Mass Inst Technol Press, Cambridge, 86; Architecture and Women, Garland Pub, 88; Architecture a Place for Women, Smithsonian Press, 89. *Mailing Add:* 3001 Yeazey Terrace NW Washington DC 20008

DOVE, TONI
PAINTER, PRINTMAKER
b New York, NY, May 1, 46. *Study:* RI Sch Design, BFA, 68. *Work:* Mus Fine Arts, Boston, Mass; Worcester Art Mus, Mass; Achenbach Found Graphic Arts, Fine Arts Mus, San Francisco, Calif; Santa Cruz Co Art Mus, Calif; Bank Am Corp Collection, San Francisco & New York. *Exhib:* Fugitive Concepts (slides), Corcoran Armand Hammer Gallery, Washington, DC, Granary Books, New York, 89; Mesmer, Art in the Anchorage, Brooklyn, NY, 90. *Teaching:* Vis critic & lectr, Brown Univ, 74, Worcester Art Mus Sch, 74 & 79, Mass Col Art, Boston, 78, 81, 82 & 85 & Sch of Mus Fine Arts, Boston, 78, 81 & 82; instr studio arts, Pine Manor Jr Col, 75-79 & Boston Col, Mass, 79-86. *Bibliog:* reviews, High Performance, winter 89, Roberta Smith, 7/27/90, Kay Larson 8/13/90, NY Times & Raissa Lerner, Brooklyn Paper Publ, 7/27/90; Kay Larson (auth), The unique watercolors of Toni Dove, Decade Mag, 79. *Mailing Add:* 150 Duane St New York NY 10013

DOW, HELEN JEANNETTE
HISTORIAN, EDUCATOR
b Ottawa, Ont, June 13, 26. *Study:* Univ Col, Univ Toronto, BA, 49; Bryn Mawr Col, Pa, MA, 51, PhD, 55, Int Univ Found, Malta, Hon Dr Art, 87. *Collections Arranged:* Selections (auth, catalog), Owens Collection, Montreal Mus Fine Art, 63; Works of Alex Colville (auth, catalog), Univ Alta, 70; Alex Colville Collection of Helen J Dow (auth, catalog), Univ Guelph, 74; Exhib of Works of Alex Colville, Lynwood Arts Ctr, Simcoe, Ontario, 76; Alex Colville: The Dow Gift, Art Gallery of Ontario, Toronto, 87; Canadian Realists, Macdonald Stewart Art Centre, Guelph, Ont, 88. *Pos:* Cur, Owens Mus, Mt Allison Univ, NB, 61-64. *Teaching:* Lectr, Bryn Mawr Col, Pa, 57-58; asst prof, Reed Col, Portland, Ore, 58-60; acting chmn art dept, Sweet Briar Col, Va, 60-61; cur, asst prof, Mt Allison Univ, Sackville, New Brunswick, 61-64; assoc prof, State Univ New York, New Palz, 64-65, Univ Iowa, Iowa City, 65-66 & Univ Alta, Edmonton, 66-71; assoc prof art hist, Univ Guelph, 71-73, prof, 73-88, chmn, Dept Fine Art, 73-74. *Awards:* Bronze Peace Medal, Albert Einstein Int Acad, Levasy, Mo, 86; Woman of the Year, 90, Grand Ambassador of Achievement, 92, Am Biog Inst; Golden Acad Award, Lifetime Achievement Acad, 92. *Mem:* life mem Nat Art Collections Fund Gr Brit, 71; founder, Macdonald Stewart Art Ctr, Guelph, Ont, 82; life mem, World Inst of Achievement, Raleigh, NC, 86; Grand founder, Art Gallery of Ont, Toronto, 87; Lifetime Achievement Acad, Raleigh, NC, 92. *Res:* Medieval architecture and sculpture; Canadian painting. *Collection:* Works of Alex Colville; North American Indian art; Canadian Realists. *Publ:* Auth, Andre Beauneveu and England, Peregrinatio, 71; The Art of Alex Colville, McGraw-Hill Ryerson, 72; The apse mosaic of San Apollinare in Classe, PMR Proceedings, 79; The Uniqueness of Michael Coyne in Michael Coyne: A Restrospective, Acadia Univ, 83; The Equanimity of D P Brown: D P Brown Twenty Years, 85; The Sculptural Decoration of the Henry VII Chapel, Westminster Abbey, Pentland, 92. *Mailing Add:* 52 First Ave No 2 Ottawa ON K1S 2G2 Canada

DOW, JIM D
PHOTOGRAPHER
b Boston, Mass, July 26, 42. *Study:* RI Sch Design, BFA, 65, MFA, 68. *Work:* Addison Mus Am Art, Andover, Mass; Art Inst Chicago, Ill. *Comn:* New Eng Sports Mus, Boston; Yale Univ Law Sch; Polaroid Corp & Close-Up Mag; Los Angeles Olympic Arts Festival, Mus Contemp Art; Robert Freidus Gallery Publ. *Exhib:* One-person exhibs, Janet Borden Inc, New York, 90 & 93, James Madison Univ, Harrisonburg, Va, 90, Univ Md, 92, Oriole Park at Camden Yards, Baltimore, Md, 92, Univ Rochester, NY, 92; Smithsonian Inst Travelling Exhibs, Nat Touring Exhib of minor league baseball park panoramas, 93-94; Sales Gallery, Metrop Mus Art, New York, 90; Baseball Exhibit, Am Express Co, Englewood, Colo, 90; Collection Notes, Rose Art Mus, Brandeis Univ, Waltham, Mass, 90; Addison Mus Am Art, Andover, Mass, 91; Zoe Gallery & Photog Resource Ctr, Boston, Mass, 91; Site Work: Architecture in Photography Since Early Modernism, The Photog Gallery, London, Eng, 91; Cambridge MultiCultural Ctr, Cambridge, Mass, 92; Sharon Arts Centre, Sharon, NH, 92. *Teaching:* Art hist/hist photog, Mus Sch, Tufts Univ, 73-; photog, Sch Mus Fine Arts, Boston, Mass, 73-; numerous lectures & workshops since 1982. *Awards:* Mellon Found, 88; Maine Photog Workshop Grant, 89; Nat Endowments Arts Fel, 72, 79 & 90. *Bibliog:* Andrian Kreye (auth), The Game of American Summers, Frankfurter Allgemeine Mag, 4/26/91; Kohtaro Tizawa & Natsuki Ikezawa (auths), New Landscape, Tokyo, Japan, 91; Sports Stadiums, Saison J, Tokyo, Japan, 7/15/92. *Dealer:* Janet Borden Inc 560 Broadway New York NY 10012; Bonni Benrubi Fine Arts 148 E 74th St New York NY 101021. *Mailing Add:* 95 Clifton St Belmont MA 02178

DOWD, JACK
SCULPTOR
b New York, NY, Mar 23, 38. *Study:* Adelphi Univ, art educ, 60. *Work:* PGA Golf Hall Fame, Pinehurst, NC; David Cohen Symphony Hall, Sarasota, Fla. *Exhib:* Expressions, Art & Cult Ctr Mus, Hollywood, Fla, 90; Artstravaganza, Asn Visual Artists, Chattanooga, Tenn, 91; All Fla Juried Exhib, Boca Raton Mus Art, 92; The Fla Nat, Fla State Univ Mus, Tallahassee, 92; Brevard Art Mus, Melbourne, Fla, 93, Montgomery Mus Fine Arts, 92. *Pos:* Chmn, Sarasota Pub Art Comt, 91-92. *Teaching:* Artist-in-Residence, Asn Visual Artists, Cattanooga, Tenn, 92. *Awards:* First Place Sculpture, Coconut Grove Arts Festival, 90-92; Best of Show, Artstravaganza, 91; Artist Yr, Sarasota Art Asn, 92. *Mailing Add:* 1331 Tenth St Sarasota FL 34236

DOWD, ROBERT (O'DOWD ROBERT)
PAINTER, SCULPTOR
b Grand Rapids, Mich, May 1, 37. *Study:* Soc Arts & Crafts/Ctr Creative , studied with Sarkis Sarkisian, Detroit, 57-59. *Work:* Johnson Mus Art, Ithaca, NY. *Comn:* Sculpture: Cooper/Wood, Cornell Univ, Ithaca, NY, 72. *Exhib:* New Paintings of Common Objects, Pasadena Art Mus, Calif, 62; Pop Art, Oakland Art Mus, Calif, 63; Ann Exhib, Long Beach Mus Art, Calif, 63; The Painter & the Photograph, Univ NMex (traveling), Albuquerque, NMex, 64; solo exhibs, Santa Barbara Mus, Calif, 64, White Mus Art, Ithaca, NY, 72; Retrospective, Riverside Art Mus, Calif, 87; LA Pop of the Sixties, Newport Harbor Art Mus, Calif, 89. *Bibliog:* John Coplans (auth), New paintings of common objects, Artforum, 62; Louis Fox (auth), Pop arts forgotton paragon, Artweek, 87; Dr Anne Ayres (auth), LA Pop of the Sixties (exhib catalog), Newport Harbor Mus, 89. *Media:* Oil, Acrylic. *Publ:* Auth, The Painter and The Photograph (exhib catalog), Univ NMex, 64; auth, Pop Art, Praeger, 66; auth, The New Painting, Praeger, 69; auth, article, Gazette des Beaux Arts, 73; auth, article, Cash Art, Art Am, 88. *Mailing Add:* c/o David Stewart Galleries 748 N La Glenega Blvd Los Angeles CA 90069

DOWDEN, ANNE OPHELIA TODD
ILLUSTRATOR, WRITER
b Denver, Colo, Sept 17, 07. *Study:* Univ Colo; Carnegie Inst Technol, BA, Art Students League; Moore Col Art, Hon Dr Fine Arts, 88. *Work:* Hunt Botanical Libr, Pittsburgh, Pa; New York Botanical Garden; Brooklyn Botanical Garden. *Comn:* Paintings for reproduction as facsimile prints, Frame House Gallery, Louisville, Ky, 69-79; painting, three azaleas, Callaway Gardens, Pine Mountain, Ga, 71; painting, tulip tree flowers, New York Botanical Garden, 72; painting, rhododendron, Holden Arboretum, Cleveland. *Exhib:* American Textiles, Metrop Mus Art, New York, 48; one-man shows, Hunt Botanical Libr, 65, New York Pub Libr, 83 & Brooklyn Botanical Gardens, 57, 77 & 85; Int Group Shows, Hunt Botanical Libr, 64, 68, 72 & 77; and other group & one-man shows. *Teaching:* Instr drawing, Pratt Inst, 30-32; head dept art, Manhattanville Col, 32-53. *Awards:* Tiffany Found Fel, 29-31. *Bibliog:* Who's Who Am Women, Marquis, 76; Ronald King (auth), Botanical Illustration, Potter, 78; Something About the Author, Vol 10, Gale Research Inc, 90. *Media:* Watercolor. *Publ:* Auth & illusr, Look at a Flower, 63, Wild Green Things in the City, 72, The Blossom on the Bough, 75, & From Flower to Fruit, 84, The Clover and the Bee, 90 Crowell; This Noble Harvest, Collins, 77; illusr, Wild Flowers and the Stories Behind their Names, Scribner, 77; and many others. *Mailing Add:* 350 Ponca Place Boulder CO 80303

DOWELL, JOHN E, JR
EDUCATOR, PRINTMAKER
b Philadelphia, Pa, Mar 25, 41. *Study:* Temple Univ Tyler Sch Art, BFA(printmaking, ceramics), 63; John Herron Art Inst, Indianapolis, advan lithography with Garo Antreasian, 63; Tamarind Lithography Workshop, Los Angeles, artist-printer fel, 63 & sr-printer fel, 66; Univ Wash, Seattle, MFA(printmaking, drawing), 66. *Work:* Mus Mod Art, New York; Brooklyn Mus Art, NY; Boston Mus Fine Art, Mass; Art Inst Chicago; Corcoran Gallery Art, Washington, DC; and many others. *Exhib:* One-man shows, Venice Biennale, 70, Corcoran Gallery Art, DC, 71 & Ft Worth Art Mus Ctr, Tex, 72; Whitney Biennial, 75 & Printmaking New Forms, 76, Whitney Mus Am Art; Recent Am Drawings, Mus Mod Art, New York, 76; 30 yrs Am Printmaking, Brooklyn Mus Art, NY, 76; Three Centuries Am Art, Philadelphia Mus Art, 76; Drawings of the 70's, 35th Exhib of Soc Contemp Art, Art Inst Chicago, 77; Collectors Collect Contemp: A Selection from Boston's Collections, Inst Contemp Art, Boston, 77; A J Wood Galleries, Philadelphia, 80; and many others. *Teaching:* Assoc prof art & printmaking, Tyler Sch Art, Temple Univ, Rome, Italy, 71-74, Philadelphia, 74-76, prof, 76-82. *Awards:* Univ Ill, Champaign Fac Summer Fel, 70; Nat Endowment Arts Fel Painting, 74-75; Temple Univ Res Grant, 75-77; and others. *Bibliog:* Henry Martin (auth), Scribble, Art Int, 3/73; Donna Stein (auth), Musicianly painting, Art News, 11/73; John Dowell's sound perspective, Arts Exchange, 5/77; and others. *Mailing Add:* 1516 N 15th St Philadelphia PA 19121

DOWLER, DAVID P
SCULPTOR, DESIGNER
b Pittsburgh, Pa, Feb 1, 44. *Study:* Syracuse Univ, BID, 69. *Work:* Leigh Yawkey Woodson Mus Art, Wausau, Wis; Corning Mus Glass, NY; Hokkaido Mus Mod Art. *Exhib:* Mus Mod Art, Kyoto, Japan, 81; Americans in Glass, Leigh Yawkey Woodson Art Mus, Wausau, Wis, 81 & Cooper-Hewitt Mus, New York, 81; Good As Gold, Smithsonian Inst, Washington, DC, 81; Production Lines, Philadelphia Col Art, 83; Glass Now, Hokkaido Mus Mod Art, 83. *Awards:* Furniture Design Award, Progressive Archit Mag, 82. *Bibliog:* Elliot Erwit (auth), Assignment in Glass (film), 78. *Mailing Add:* 120 E Third St Corning NY 14830

DOWLEY, JENNIFER
DIRECTOR
Study: Denison Univ, Granville, Ohio, BA(theater arts), 70, grad studies. *Pos:* Apprentice, Film Study Ctr, Mus Mod Art, New York, 69; asst dir, Nat Cinemas, Dublin, Ireland, 71-72; admin asst, Mus Children, Denver, Colo, 73-74; fundraising consult, Boston Ballet, Mass, 75; assoc dir, Artists Fel Prog, co-dir, Taking Care Bus Artists Found, Boston, Mass, 75-78; dir, Arts Line, Cambridge Arts Coun, Mass, 78-81 & Headlands Ctr Arts, Saulsalito, Calif, 86-; coordr, Art Pub Places Prog, Sacramento Metrop Arts Comn, 81-86. *Publ:* Contribr, Money Business: Grants and Awards to Creative Artists, 1st ed, 78; Arts on the Line-a case study for the Urban Mass Transportation Administration, 80; Sculpture Sacramento (catalog), 82. *Mailing Add:* Headlands Center for the Arts 934A Fort Barry Sausalito CA 94965

DOWNES, RACKSTRAW
PAINTER, CRITIC
b Kent, Eng, Nov 8, 39; US citizen. *Study:* Cambridge Univ, Eng, BA, 61; Yale Univ, BFA, 63, MFA, 64. *Work:* Hirshhorn Mus, Washington, DC; Pa Acad, Philadelphia; Whitney Mus Am Art, Brooklyn Mus, New York; Chase Manhattan Bank, New York; Witherspoon Mus, NC; Metrop Mus Art, New York; Equitable Life Insurance, New York; Carnegie Inst, Pittsburgh. *Comn:* Painting, US Dept Interior, 76. *Exhib:* Artist's Choice Mus Show, six NY Galleries, 79; 20 Artists Yale Sch Art, Yale Univ Art Gallery, Conn, 81; The Animal in Am Art, Nassau Co Mus, NY, 81; 1981 Biennial, Whitney Mus, New York, 81; The Americans, the Landscape, Contemp Arts Mus, Houston, 81; Real, Really Real, Super Real, San Antonio Mus, 81; Contemp Am Realism, Pa Acad, Philadelphia, 81; Carnegie Int, Carnegie Inst, 83; New Narrative Painting: Selections from the Collection of the Metropolitan Museum of Art, Tamayo Mus, Mexico City, 84; The Realist Landscape, Rutgers Univ, New Brunswick, NJ, 85; Drawing and Drawings, Hudson River Mus, Yonkers, NY, 86. *Pos:* Gov, Skowhegan Sch Painting & Sculpture, 81. *Teaching:* Asst prof fine arts, Univ Pa, Philadelphia, 67-79. *Awards:* Creative Artists Public Service Award, 78, Individual Grant, Ingram Merrill Found, 75; Individual Grant, Nat Endowment Arts, 80. *Bibliog:* Linda Nochlin (auth), article, Art in Am, 1/76; Hilton Kramer (auth), Return of Realism, New York Times, 3/12/78; Peter Schjeldahl (auth), Realism on the comeback trail, Village Voice, 11/81; Robert Storr (auth), Rackstraw Downes: Painter as Geographer, Art in Am, 10/84. *Mem:* NY Artists Equity Asn. *Media:* Oil. *Publ:* Auth, What the sixties meant to me, Art J, 74; The Meaning of the Landscape, Parenthese, 75; Post-modernist painting, Tracks, 76; ed, Fairfield Porter: Art in its Own Terms, Taplinger, 79; auth, Claude's sermon on the mount, Art News, 10/81; What realism is to me, Mus Calif, 5-6/82. *Dealer:* Hirschl & Adler Modern 420 W Broadway New York NY 10012. *Mailing Add:* 16 Greene St New York NY 10013

DOWNEY, JUAN
VIDEO ARTIST, ARCHITECT
b Santiago, Chile, May 11, 40. *Study:* Sch Archit, Cath Univ Chile, BA(archit), 61; Atelier 17, Paris, 63-65, printmaking with S W Hayter; Pratt Inst, 67-69. *Work:* Mus Mod Art, New York; Casa Americas, Havana, Cuba; Tel Aviv Mus, Israel; Bibliot Nat, Paris; Nat Collection Fine Arts, Washington, DC; and others. *Exhib:* Lucht-Kunst, Stedelijk Mus, Amsterdam, 71; Art & Science, Tel Aviv Mus, 71; Contemp Art Mus, Houston, Tex, 76; Whitney Biennial, Whitney Mus Am Art, New York, 75, 83 & 85; Everson Mus Art, Syracuse, NY, 77; Documenta 6, Kassel, WGer, 77; Anthology Film Archives, New York, 77; Mus Arte Contemporaneo, Caracas, Venezuela, 77; Venice Biennale, US Pavilion, Venice, Italy, 80; solo exhibs, Corcoran Gallery Art, Washington, DC, 69, Howard Wise Gallery, New York, 70, Contemp Art Mus, Houston, Tex, 76, Univ Art Mus, Berkeley, Calif, 78, Schlesinger-Boissante Gallery, New York, 82, Galeria Plastica 3, Santiago, Chile, 84 & San Francisco Mus Mod Art, 85. *Teaching:* Asst prof archit, Pratt Inst, New York, 70- *Awards:* Guggenheim Found Fel 71 & 76; Mass Inst Technol Fel, 73; Nat Endowment Arts Grants, 74-76, 80, 82, 84 & 85. *Bibliog:* Howard Wise (auth), Pollution Robot (film), 70. *Publ:* Video Tapes: The Laughing Alligator, 79, More than Two, 78, The Circle of Fires, 79, Venus and her Mirror, 80, The Looking Glass, 81, Information Withheld, 83, Siange, 83, Chicago Boys, 84 & Shifters, 86; and many others. *Dealer:* Electronic Arts Intermix 536 Broadway New York NY 10012. *Mailing Add:* 146 W 26th St New York NY 10001

DOWNIE, ROMANA ANZI
SCULPTOR
b Rome, Italy, May 9, 25; US citizen. *Study:* Liceo Artistico Accademia Belle Arti, maturita, 45; San Francisco State Univ, BA(cum laude), 61, MA, 63; Univ Calif, Berkeley. *Work:* Museo de Roma, Italy; San Francisco Libr, Mus Photog & San Francisco State Col, San Francisco; Bidwell Libr, Southern Methodist Univ, Dallas. *Comn:* Portrait, Free Masons of Rome, 45; F DeBellis (portrait), comn by DeBellis Found, San Francisco, 68; George Moscone (portrait) & Harvey Milk (portrait), comn by Joseph Dee, San Francisco, 78 & 82; mural, Herrick's Hospital, Berkeley, Calif, 81; bronze statuette, Sammy Davis Jr, comn by Joseph Dee-Brooks, Mus Photography. *Exhib:* 1st Women's Show, Palazza Brancaccio, Rome, 47; San Francisco Art Festival, 64-81; Italian American Artists, Mus Italo Americano, San Francisco, 79-82. *Bibliog:* Michael Robertson (auth), A sculptor caught in the politics of art, San Francisco Chronicle, 7/9/82; Lucy Harris & Stephanie Johnson (auths), Artist extraordinaire, Viewpoint, Oakland, 2/84; Mark Luca (auth), Italian American artists in the Bay Area, Il Caffe, Sacramento, 2-3/86. *Media:* Clay, Wax. *Dealer:* Gallery of Mendocino CA PO Box 128 Mendocino CA 94560. *Mailing Add:* 27800 N Hwy One Ft Bragg CA 95437

DOWNS, DOUGLAS WALKER
SCULPTOR
b Pomona, Calif, May 30, 45. *Study:* Whittier Col, BA, 67; Claremont Grad Sch, 67-68, study with Aldo Casanova & Jean Ames; Ariz State Univ, 69-70. *Work:* King Karl Gustav XVI, Stockholm, Sweden; The White House; King Don Juan Carlos I & Queen Sofia, Seville, Spain; Long Island Chess Mus, Commack, NY. *Comn:* Bust of a Scholar (bronze), Collier Art Corp, Los Angeles, 74; Abstract Family (bronze), Am Asn Marriage & Family Therapy, Washington, DC, 75; Hawk on Rock (bronze), Tor House Found, Carmel, Calif, 79; Joseph Smith (bronze), 83 & Emma Smith (bronze), 85, Monterey Sculpture Ctr, Calif; Eagle gates (bronze), Ronald M Abend Inc, 89. *Exhib:* Solo exhib, Southwestern Arts Ltd, Carmel, 78; Favell Mus, Klamath Falls, Ore, 77; George Phippen Mem Exhib, Prescott, Ariz, 77; Westerman and Downs, Galerie de Tours, San Francisco, Calif, 84; The New Masters, May Gallery, Scottsdale, Ariz, 86; Artists of the West, Trails West Gallery, Laguna Beach, Calif, 88; California Comes to Arizona, May Gallery, Scottsdale, Ariz, 88. *Awards:* 1st Prize, Sculpture, 10th, 12th, 13th, 15th, & 16th Ann Nat Miniature, Gallery La Luz, NMex, 84-90; Col Archibald King Award, Sculpture, 52nd & 56th Ann Int Exhib, Miniature Painters & Sculptors Soc, Washington, DC, 85 & 89; Juror's Choice Award, Ninth Ann Int Show, Billings, Mont, 87; 1st Prize, Sculpture, 6th Ann Int Show, Marietta-Cobb Mus Art, Ga, 91. *Bibliog:* D W Armstrong (auth), Bronze artist Douglas Downs, Acquire, 5/74; L Longstaff (auth), Sculptor of 1000 faces, Southwest Arts, 11/77; H Sutliff (auth), Sculpture by Douglas Downs, Key, 9/79; A survey of the state's museums, galleries and leading artists, 88. *Mem:* Carmel Art Asn (bd dirs, treas, 83-84 & 87-88); Int Sculpture Soc. *Media:* Bronze. *Mailing Add:* 405 Alder St Pacific Grove CA 93950

DOWNS, LINDA ANNE
CURATOR, EDUCATOR
b Detroit, Mich, May 30, 45. *Study:* Monteith Col, Wayne State Univ, PhB, 69; Univ Mich, MA(hist of art), 73; Mus Mgt Inst, Univ Calif, Berkeley, 79. *Collections Arranged:* Student Art Exhibs, 69-77; Barbara Chase Ribaud Sculpture, 72; Diaghilev & Russian Stage Design, 72; Caravaggio's Conversion of the Magdalene: An Analysis of the Painting, 73; African Art of the Dogon, 74, Detroit Inst of Arts; The Rouge: The Image of Industry in the Art of Charles Sheeler and Diego Rivera (auth, catalog), Detroit Inst Arts, 78; Diego Rivera: A Retrospective (auth, catalog), Detroit Inst of Arts, 86. *Pos:* Spec asst, Proj Outreach, Detroit Inst Arts, Mich, 68-69, jr cur educ, 69-73, asst cur educ, 73-76, cur educ, 76-89; head, education div, Nat Gallery of Art, Washington, DC, 89- *Teaching:* Adj asst prof art hist, Wayne State Univ, Detroit, Mich, 76- *Awards:* Best Cult Film Award for Only Then Regale My Eyes, Midwest Pub Broadcasting Serv, 76; Cine Golden Eagle for the Frescoes of Diego Rivera film, 86. *Mem:* Am Asn Mus; Col Art Asn. *Publ:* Auth, Claes Oldenburg's Giant Three-Way Plub and Chrysler Airflow, Bull Detroit Inst Arts, 71; producer, Only Then Regale My Eyes (60 minute color film produced for the exhib, French Painting 1774-1830: The Age of Revolution), WTVS, Detroit, 75; auth, Diego Rivera's Portrait of Edsel Ford, Bulletin Detroit Inst of Arts, 79; coauth, The Rouge: The Image of Industry in the Art of Charles Sheeler and Diego Rivera, Detroit Inst Arts, 78, Diego Rivera's Portrait of Edsel Ford, Bulletin of Detroit Inst Arts, 79, The Annual School Art Exhibition: Detroit's Unique Tradition, Sch Arts, 84, Diego Rivera: A Retrospective, Detroit Inst Arts, 86; Los frescos de la Industria de Detroit: una interpretacion de la tecnología moderna, Diego Rivera Hoy, 86; Gallery Activities for Unguided Groups, Mus News, 89; Diego Rivera, International Dictionary of Art and Artists, London, 90. *Mailing Add:* Nat Gallery Art Washington DC 20565

DOWNS, STUART CLIFTON
ADMINISTRATOR, EDUCATOR
b Arlington, Va, Nov 11, 50. *Study:* Hampden-Sydney Col, BA, 73; Western Ky Univ, MA, 77; Univ NC, Chapel Hill, cert, 85. *Collections Arranged:* Folios, Quartos & Costumes: From the Folger Shakespeare Libr, 84; Philip Pearlstein: Personal Selections, 86. *Pos:* Dir, Sawhill Gallery, James Madison Univ, Harrisonburg, VA, 83- *Teaching:* Instr, introd to mus work & mus studies, James Madison Univ, 79-, internship art, 81- *Mem:* Am Asn Mus; Va Asn Mus (bd mem, 84-). *Mailing Add:* 52 Weaver Ave Harrisonburg VA 22801

DOYLE, JOE
PAINTER, EDUCATOR
b Manhattan, NY, Feb 27, 41. *Study:* San Francisco State Univ, Calif, BA, 69, MFA, 71. *Work:* Oakland Mus, Calif. *Comn:* Dallas, Tex. *Exhib:* Option 73/30, Contemp Art Ctr, Cincinnati, Ohio, 73; Interstices, Cranbrook Acad Art, Bloomfield Hills, Mich, 75; 6 EBay Painters, Oakland Mus, Calif, 77; Aesthetics of Graffiti, San Francisco Mus Art, 78; one-man show, San Jose Mus Art, Calif, 79, Foster Goldstrom Fine Arts, San Francisco, 83 & 85, Route 66 Gallery, Philadelphia, J Rosenthal Fine Arts, Chicago, 86, Ill Metrop Ctr, Chicago, 86, Merging One Gallery, Santa Monica, 87 & Harcourt's Contemp Gallery, San Francisco, 88; Reality of Illusion, Denver Art Mus, Colo, 79; Three Bay Area Painters, Chico State Univ, Calif, 79; Selections from the Contemp Art Collection of the Oakland Mus, Kaiser Ctr, Calif, 80; Midwestern Mus Art, Elkhorn, Ind, 81; Icons of Contemp Art, Foster Goldstrom Fine Arts, Oakland, Calif, 83; The Gallery Collection, J Rosenthal Fine Arts, Chicago, 84; Shadows, Univ Calif, Davis, 85; Dallas Collects, Concord Bank, Tex, 86; Merging One Gallery, Santa Monica, Calif, 87; The Goldstrom Collection, Davenport Art Ctr, Davenport, Iowa, 88. *Teaching:* Instr painting, Laney Col, Oakland, Calif, 71-73; co-chmn fine arts, Acad Art, San Francisco, 75-76; adj prof fine arts, Univ San Francisco, 75-76; instr, spray painting, Calif Col Arts & Crafts Exten Prog, Oakland, 79-80, painting, drawing, figure drawing, San Francisco Acad Art, 78-79,. *Bibliog:* David Berreth (auth), Art Museum, Miami Univ, Oxford, Ohio, 9/85; Thomas Albright (auth), Art in the San Francisco Bay Area 1945-1980, Univ Calif Press, 85; Daniel E Stetson (auth), New Acquisitions, Davenport Mus Art, Davenport, Iowa, 4/88. *Mem:* Calif Fedn Art Teachers. *Media:* Mixed. *Dealer:* Harcourts Contemporary 535 Powell St San Francisco CA 94108. *Mailing Add:* 4545 Toyon Pl Oakland CA 94619

DOYLE, JOHN LAWRENCE
PRINTMAKER, PAINTER
b Chicago, Ill, Mar 14, 39. *Study:* Art Inst Chicago, BAE, 62; Northern Ill Univ, MA, 68. *Work:* Libr Cong; Smithsonian Inst Collection Traveling Exhib; Art Inst Chicago; Cody Mus Western Art; Midwest Mus Am Art. *Comn:* Poster, Denver Mus Natural Hist. *Exhib:* 22nd Boston Printmakers Exhib, De Cordova Mus, Lincoln, Mass, 70; Images on Paper, Miss Art Mus, Jackson, 70; Prints & Drawings, Los Angeles Co Mus Art, Los Angeles, Calif, 73; Rahr W Mus, Manitowoc, Wis, 79; Scottsdale Art Ctr, Ariz, 79; Harvard Med & Law Libr, Cambridge, Mass; Nat Libr Med, Bethesda, Md; Nat Gallery Art, Wash DC; Milwaukee Art Ctr; Welcome Inst, London; and others. *Awards:* Eisendrath Prize, 73rd Chicago Show, Art Inst Chicago, 72; Purchase Prizes, 24th Am Drawings Biennial, Norfolk Mus Arts & Sci, 72 & Images on Paper, Miss Art Mus, 72. *Bibliog:* Mendelowitz (auth), Drawings (Illustration), Univ Iowa, 76; Ben Dallas (auth), Mysticism through visual metaphor, SW Arts Mag, 77; Scott E Dial (auth), John L Doyle, Art Voices S, 11/79. *Media:* Lithograph; Watercolor. *Dealer:* Fishy Whale Press 411 Lincoln Ave Rockford IL 61102. *Mailing Add:* RR 7 Box 85 Burnsville NC 28714

DOYLE, MARY ELLEN
PAINTER
b Hartford, Conn, Oct 8, 38. *Study:* Vassar Col, 56-58, study with Alton Pickens & Rosemarie Beck; Boston Univ Sch Fine Arts, BFA, 62, study with Walter Murch; Columbia Sch Painting & Sculpture, 64-65, study with John Heliker. *Work:* Bankers Trust Co, New York; Prudential Life Insurance Co, Newark, NJ; New Britain Mus Am Art; Vassan Col Art Gallery; Nat Mus Women in the Arts, Washington, DC. *Comn:* Desegregation pamphlet, NAACP Legal Defense & Educ Fund, Jackson, Miss, 66. *Exhib:* Solo exhibs, The New Sch Social Res, New York, 82 & 89, Richard Humphrey Gallery, New York, 89 & Susan Conway Gallery, Washington, DC, 92; Guild Hall, Easthampton, NY, 73, 87, 88, 90, 91 & 92; Parrish Art Mus, Southampton, NY, 76, 81, 84 & 88; Elaine Benson Gallery, Bridgehampton, NY, 83, 88 & 92; The Art Museum of the Museums, Stony Brook, NY, 90. *Teaching:* Instr studio art, Barnard Col, New York, 62-65; instr children's art classes, Mus Mod Art, New York, 63-71; instr drawing, The New Sch Social Res, New York, 78- *Awards:* Judge's Award, Collage-paintings, Parrish Art Mus, Southampton, NY, 76; Grumbacher Award, 77-78; Walter Biggs Mem Award, Nat Acad Design, 89; Best work on paper, Guild Hall, Easthampton, 90. *Bibliog:* Jane Andrews Aiken (auth), Mary Ellen Doyle, Arts Mag, 10/82; William Henry (auth), Perspectives: Galleries boost harbor art world, Southampton Press, 4/86; Ronald Pisano (auth), Long Island Landscape Painting, Volume II: the twentieth century, Buefinch Prso/Little Brown Co, 90; Janet Wilson (auth), Galleries: Mary Ellen Doyle and the beauty of the beach, Long Island Lights, Washington Post, 1/92. *Media:* Watercolor. *Mailing Add:* 41 Union Sq W New York NY 10003

DOYLE, TOM
SCULPTOR, EDUCATOR
b Jerry City, Ohio, May 23, 28. *Study:* Ohio State Univ, BFA, 52, MA, 53, with Roy Lichtenstien & Stanley Twardewicz. *Work:* Carnegie Inst, Pittsburgh; Kley Collection, Ger; City Beautiful Project, Dayton, Ohio; Allentown Cedar Parkway, Allentown, Pa, 87. *Comn:* Fiberglass sculpture, Pub Arts Coun, City of New York, 72; Fed Bldg & Courthouse, Fairbanks, Alaska, 80; Cooper Sq Housing, NY, 85. *Exhib:* Kunsthalle, Bern, Switz, 64; Kunsthalle, Dusseldorf, Ger, 65; Dwan Gallery, New York, 66 & 67; Sculpture of the Sixties, Los Angeles Co Art Mus, Calif, 67; Primary Structures, Jewish Mus Mus, New York, 67; Hammarskjold Plaza, New York, 82; Vanishing Points, Moderna Museet, Stockhom, Sweden, 84; The Ways of Wood, Queens Col, Flushing, NY, 84; Artist Toys, Vanderwoude Gallery, New York, 84 & 85; Diversity New York Artist, Univ RI, Kingston, 85; Am Abstract Artist 50th Anniversary Celebration, Bronx Mus, NY, 86; Sculpture Ctr, New York, 88; Idiomidella Scultura Contemporanea Z, Sommacompagne, Verona, Italy, 89; Portes Ouvertes, Foundation d'-Art De Lanapoule, Lanapoule, France, 89. *Teaching:* Instr sculpture, Brooklyn Mus Art Sch, 60-68; instr sculpture, New Sch Social Res, 61-68; assoc prof sculpture, Queens Col, 70-82, prof sculpture, 82. *Awards:* Guggenheim Fel, 82; City Univ New York Research Award, 89-90; Nat Endowment Arts, Fel Sculpture, 91-92. *Bibliog:* Lucy R Lippard (auth), Tom Doyle, Kunsthalle, Dusseldorf, 65 & Space embraced: Tom Doyle's recent sculpture, Arts, 4/66; Robert Pincus-Witten (auth), Tom Doyle: Things patriotic and union blue, Arts, 9/79; and others. *Mem:* Am Abstract Artists. *Media:* Wood, Bronze. *Mailing Add:* 130 W 18th St New York NY 10011

DRAKE, JAMES
PRINTMAKER, SCULPTOR
b Lubbock, Tex, Sept 12, 46. *Study:* Art Ctr Col of Design, fel, BFA with Hons, 69, MFA, 70. *Work:* El Paso Mus Art, Tex; Phoenix Art Mus, Ariz; Univ NMex Art Mus, Albuquerque; Univ Tex, El Paso; Mathews Art Ctr, Ariz State Univ, Tempe. *Exhib:* New Visions, Amarillo Art Ctr, Tex, 81; one-man exhib, Galveston Arts Ctr on the Strand, Tex, 82; Southern Fiction, Contemp Art Mus, Houston, 83; New Orleans Triennal, New Orleans Mus Art, 83; and others. *Teaching:* Instr life drawing, Art Ctr Col of Design, Los Angeles, 69-70 & Univ Tex, El Paso. *Bibliog:* Barbara Cortright (auth), Sculpture & graphics, Art Week, 2/76. *Mailing Add:* 5028 Love Rd El Paso TX 79922

DRAKE, PETER
PAINTER, DRAFTSMAN
b Garden City, NY, July 29, 57. *Study:* Pratt Inst, BFA, 79. *Work:* Mus Contemp Art, Los Angeles, Calif; Los Angeles County Mus, Calif; Mus Mod Art Mexico, Mexico City; Phoenix Mus Art, Ariz; J Patrick Lannen Found, Miami, Fla. *Exhib:* East Village Art in Berlin, Zellermayer Gallery, Berlin, 84; Nueva Pintura Narrativa, Mus Tamayo, Mexico City, 84; Blue Condition, Greenville County Mus, SC, 85; New York/Seattle, Seattle Ctr Contemp Art, Wash, 85; Romanticism/Cyncism in Contemp Art, Haggerty Mus, Milwaukee, Wis, 86; Avant Garde in the 80's, Los Angeles County Mus, Calif, 87. *Pos:* Artist/consult, The Drawing Ctr, New York, 84-; staff writer, Flash Art, 86. *Awards:* Nat Endow Arts, 87. *Bibliog:* Michael Kohn (auth), Romantic Vision, Flash Art, 85; Michael Cone (auth), Peter Drake, Flash Art, 86; Michael Brenson (auth), The ink drawing of Peter Drake, NY Times, 87. *Media:* Oil. *Dealer:* Curt Marcus Gallery 578 Broadway New York NY 10012. *Mailing Add:* c/o Curt Marcos Gallery 578 Broadway 10th floor New York NY 10012

DRAPELL, JOSEPH
PAINTER, SCULPTOR
b Humpolec, Bohemia, Czech, Mar 13, 40; Can citizen. *Study:* Cranbrook Acad Art, with Donald Willett & George Ortman, MFA, 70. *Work:* Guggenheim Mus; Mus Fine Arts, Boston; La Jolla Mus Contemp Art; Brit Mus, London; Art Gallery Ont, Toronto. *Comn:* Outdoor sculpture, Halifax, NS; mural, Cineplex Odeon Theatres, Toronto, Ont. *Exhib:* New Acquisitions, Guggenheim Mus, 72; New Abstract Art, Edmonton Art Gallery, Alta, 77; Color Abstractions, Mus Fine Arts, Boston, 79; The New Generation, Andre Emmerich Gallery, New York, 80; The Threshold of Color, Edmonton Art Gallery, Alta, 82; retrospective, Art Gallery Windsor, Ont, 84; Island Paintings, Shippee Gallery, New York, 88; New Acrylic Painters, Mus Art, Ft Lauderdale, Fla, 91; New Acrylic Painters, Ctr Arts, Vero Beach, Fla, 91, Galerie Gerald Piltzer, Paris, 92, Gallery One, Toronto, 92. *Teaching:* Instr artistic methods, York Univ, Toronto, 70-71; vis artist in residence, Syracuse Univ, 73; guest artist, Triangle Artists' Workshop, Pine Plains, NY, 84, Emma Lake Artists' Workshop, Univ Saskatchewan. *Awards:* Can Coun Grant, 71; Ont Arts Coun Grants, 75 & 76. *Bibliog:* Ken Carpenter (auth), Joseph Drapell: Re-inventing abstraction, Art Int, Switz, 12/78; Kenworth Moffett (auth), The New Generation, Rhineburgh Press, 80; Karen Wilkin (auth), The Recent Work of Joseph Drapell (catalog essay), New York, 86. *Media:* Acrylic on Canvas; Bronze. *Dealer:* Galerie Gerald Piltzer 78 Avenue des Champs-Elysees 75008 Paris; Gallery One Toronto. *Mailing Add:* 123 Bellwoods Ave Toronto ON M6J 2P6 Canada

DRAPER, JOSIAH EVERETT
PAINTER, WRITER
b East Orange, NJ, Oct 17, 15. *Study:* Pratt Inst, Brooklyn, advert design & illus; Grand Cent Sch Art, New York, with Harvey Dunn; also with Edgar Whitney, Paul Strisik & John Pike. *Work:* Cummer Gallery Art, Jacksonville, Fla; Jacksonville Univ; US Navy; City of Bahia Blanca, Arg; Jacksonville Mus of Arts & Sci; and others. *Comn:* Painting, Jacksonville Area Chamber of Commerce, 72 & 81; ten paintings, Sea Pines Co, Amelia Island, Fla, 73; 5 paintings, Indian River Plantation, Stuart, Fla, 81; painting, District Court Appeals, Daytona Beach, Fla. *Exhib:* Am Watercolor Soc Ann, New York, 62-74; one-man shows, Fla Gulf Coast Art Ctr, Clearwater, 73 & Jacksonville Art Mus, 74; District Court Appeals, Tallahassee, Fla, 82; Indian River Plantation, Stuart, Fla, 83; and many others. *Pos:* Artist, Prudential Ins Co Am, 35-50, art dir, 51-72; retired; pres, J E Draper, AWS, Inc, 81. *Teaching:* Instr watercolor technique, Jacksonville Art Mus, 70-88; spec watercolor workshops in US, West Indies, Europe & Mexico. *Awards:* Ann Traveling Exhib, Am Watercolor Soc, 66 & 69 & Carolyn Stern Award, 69. *Mem:* Am Watercolor Soc; Fla Watercolor Soc (bd dirs, 72-, pres, 77-78); St Augustine Art Asn (pres, 72-74, bd dirs, 75-81); Jacksonville Watercolor Soc (dir); Salmagundi Club, NY. *Media:* Transparent Watercolor. *Publ:* Auth, Putting People in Your Paintings, 85, People Painting Scrapbook, 88, contribr, Basic Drawing Techniques, 91, Basic Watercolor Techniques, 91 & Splash II, 92, North Light. *Dealer:* Ponte Vedra Club Ponte Vedra Beach FL 32082. *Mailing Add:* PO Box 12 Ponte Vedra Beach FL 32004

DRAPER, WILLIAM FRANKLIN
PAINTER, INSTRUCTOR
b Hopedale, Mass, Dec 24, 12. *Study:* Harvard Univ, 31-32; Nat Acad Design, 31-34; Grande Chaumiere, Paris, France, 35; Art Students League, 37; also with Jon Corbino, Leon Kroll & Henry Hensche. *Work:* Nat Portrait Gallery; Pavilion, Music Ctr, Los Angeles; Off Housing & Urban Develop; US Central Intelligence Agency; and others. *Comn:* 5 portraits, Paul Mellon, 74-77; portrait, Ambassador Walter Annenberg, 79; portrait, James Michener, 79; portrait, Pres Richard M Nixon, comn by Nat Portrait Gallery, 81; portrait, Mayor John V Lindsay for City Hall, NY, 81; and others. *Exhib:* Metrop Mus Art, 45; Cent Asn Ann; Graham Gallery, New York, 69 & 71; Palm Beach Gallery, Fla, 72; Far Gallery, 77-79; Wally Findlay Gallery, New York, 90; and others. *Teaching:* Instr, Art Students League, 65-82. *Mem:* Boston Allied Artists; Century Asn; Knickerbocker Club; Allied Artists Am; Artists' Fel. *Media:* Oil. *Dealer:* Portraits Inc 41 E 57th St New York NY 10022; Grand Central Art Galleries Madison Ave at 43rd St New York NY 10017. *Mailing Add:* 160 E 83rd New York NY 10028

DR BRUTE (ERIC WILLIAM METCALFE)
VIDEO ARTIST
b Vancouver, BC, Aug 22, 40. *Study:* Univ Victoria, BFA, 70. *Work:* Art Bank Can, Ottawa; Nat Gallery Can; Akad Kunst, West Berlin; Univ Calgary, Alta; Art Gallery Ont. *Comn:* Multi-media performance, 78 & video performance, 83, Music Gallery, Toronto. *Exhib:* Chair Show, Art Gallery Ont, 74; From This Point of View, Vancouver Art Gallery, 77; Off the Wall, A Space, Toronto, 77; Chair Show, And/Or, Seattle, 79; Manner SM, Vancouver Art Gallery, 82; Okanada, Akad Kunste, West Berlin, 83. *Pos:* Dir & cur performance art, Western Front, 73- *Awards:* Bursary, 73 & Video Production Award, 77, 80 & 83, Can Coun; JVC Corp Third Video Festival Award, 80. *Bibliog:* Balkind Shadbolt (auth), Visions, Douglas & McIntyre, 83; Peggy Gane (auth), Parachute, Colour Video, 83. *Media:* Video, Performance. *Mailing Add:* Western Front Soc 303 E Eighth Ave Vancouver BC V5T 1S1 Canada

DREIBAND, LAURENCE
PAINTER, LECTURER
b New York, NY, Nov 8, 44. *Study:* Chouinard Art Inst, Los Angeles, 61; Art Ctr Col Design, Los Angeles, BFA(with distinction), 67, fel & MFA, 68. *Work:* Home Savings & Loan Collection; Container Corp Am Collection; Chase Manhattan Bank. *Comn:* Great Ideas of Western Man, Container Corp Am, 70. *Exhib:* West Coast 70, E B Crocker Art Gallery, Sacramento, Calif, 70; Beyond the Actual, Pioneer Mus, Stockton, Calif, 70; one-man shows, David Stuart Galleries, 70-72, Los Angeles Inst Contemp Art, 80 & Allen Stone Gallery, New York, 81; California Artists, Long Beach Mus Art, 71; Galerie Quatres Mouvements, 74; Janus Gallery, 83. *Teaching:* Instr painting & photog, Art Ctr Col Design, 70-, chmn dept fine arts, 72- *Awards:* First Prize, Fine Arts Gallery San Diego, 70; Great Ideas of Western Man Purchase Award, Container Corp Am, 70; 19th All City Festival Purchase Award, Munic Art Gallery, Los Angeles, 71. *Bibliog:* Joseph Young (auth), Los Angeles artist--Laurence Dreiband, Art Int, 70; Barbara Witus (auth), Paintings of Laurence Dreiband, Los Angeles Free Press, 3/31/72; Udo Kulterman (auth), New Realism, New York Graphic Soc, 72. *Media:* Oil, Acrylic. *Publ:* Auth, Laurence Dreiband, Paintings and Drawings, David Stuart Galleries, 72. *Mailing Add:* Art Ctr Col Design 1700 Lida St Pasadena CA 91109

DREIKAUSEN, MARGRET
PAINTER
b Cologne, Germany, Jan 9, 37. *Study:* Fashion Inst Technol, AAS, 67; Hunter Col, BA, 75, MA, 78, study with Robert Swain, Mary Miss & Robert Morris. *Work:* Staedtische Mus Heilbronn, Heilbronn, Germany; IBM Corp; Westchester & Sterling Forest, NY; Citibank, Long Island City, NY; Hong Kong & Shanghai Banking Corp, NY. *Exhib:* Ten LIC Artists, Queensborough Community Col, Bayside, NY, 87; Small is Big, Parsons Exhib Ctr, New York, 89; Nature, Fact & Fantasy, Rockland Ctr Arts, West Nyack, NY, 89; Stadtbuecherei, Heilbronn, Ger, 91; Nat Art Competition, Northeast Mo State Univ, Kirksville, Mo, 92; and others. *Teaching:* Instr design, Parsons Sch Design, 79- *Awards:* Second Prize, Nat Art Competition, Northeast State Univ, Kirksville, Mo. *Bibliog:* Barbara Haag (auth), Die Erde von oben gesehen, 4/10/84; Ten Artists (catalog), Second Long Island City Open Studios; Heilbronner Stimme (auth), Das Truegerische im Foto, 1//10/91 & Landschafts-Design, 1/17/91. *Mem:* Col Art Asn Am; Long Island City Artists Inc. *Media:* Miscellaneous Media. *Publ:* Auth, Aerial Perception, The Earth as Seen From Aircraft and Spacecraft and its Influence on Contemporary Art, Art Alliance Press, Philadelphia, 85; contribr, Essays on Creativity and Science, ed by Diana DeLuca, Hawaii Coun Teachers English, Honolulu, 86. *Mailing Add:* 141 E 62nd St New York NY 10021

DREISBACH, CLARENCE IRA
PAINTER
b Union Hill, Pa, Jan 28, 03. *Study:* Federal Schs, dipl, 31. *Work:* Reading Pub Mus & Art Gallery, Reading, Pa; Bucks Co Sch, Doylestown, Pa. *Exhib:* Allentown Art Mus, Pa, 47; Mus Fine Arts, Boston, Mass, 54; Nat Arts Club, New York, NY, 57; Burr Art Gallery, New York, 60; Norton Gallery, West Palm Beach, Fla, 69. *Teaching:* Instr landscape, Allentown Community Col, 48-55, Baum Art Sch, Allentown, 53-57 & Wyomissing Inst Fine Arts, Reading, Pa, 63. *Mem:* Lehigh Art Alliance. *Media:* Oil. *Mailing Add:* Luther Crest, Bldg A-133 800 Hausman Rd Allentown PA 18104

DRESDNERE, SIMON
ART DEALER, PUBLISHER
b Romania, Nov 16, 20; Can citizen. *Study:* Univ Vienna, BA, 48. *Pos:* Dir & owner, Dresdnere Gallery, Montreal, 56-67, Toronto, 61- *Specialty:* Contemporary and classic European graphics, paintings and sculpture, formerly; contemporary Canadian, currently. *Publ:* Auth, Miller Brittain: In Focus, Simon Dresdnere Publ, Inc, 82; The Automatists: Then and Now (catalog), 86 & Borduas and other Rebels (catalog), 88, Galerie Dresdnere, Toronto. *Mailing Add:* Galerie Dresdnere 12 Hazelton Ave Toronto ON M5R 2E2 Canada

DRESKIN, JEANET STECKLER
PAINTER, EDUCATOR
b New Orleans, La, Sept 29, 21. *Study:* Newcomb Col, Tulane Univ, with Will Henry Stevens, BFA, 42; John Hopkins Univ, med art cert, 43; John McCrady Sch, New Orleans; Clemson Univ, MFA, 73; Art Students League, New York. *Work:* Nat Mus Am Art, Smithsonian Inst, Washington, DC; Ga Mus Art, Athens; Greenville Co Mus Art, SC; Guild Hall Mus, East Hampton, NY; State Art Collection, SC State Mus, Columbia. *Comn:* seals & plaque, SC State Bd Health, Columbia, 57; McDonald Corp, Chicago, 82; Merrill Lynch, Atlanta, Ga, 85; painting, Nat Mus Illus, New York, 86; Fed Reserve Bank Richmond, Charlotte, 88. *Exhib:* Chautauqua Exhib Am Art, NY, 70; 38th Ann Mid-Year Show, Butler Inst Am Art, Youngstown, Ohio, 74 & 83; Art in Medicine, Nat Mus Illus, New York, 86; Nat Print & Drawing Exhib, Rudolph Lee Gallery, Clemson Univ, SC, 87 & 89; traveling show, Centennial

Exhib, Nat Asn Women Artists, 89- 90, Invitational Drawing Exhib USA, MidAm Arts Alliance, Kansas City, Mo, 89-91; Nat Women's Exhib, India, 89-90; National Works on Paper, Univ Miss, Oxford, Mass, 91; many others. *Pos:* Staff artist, Am Mus Nat Hist, New York, 43-45; staff artist, Univ Chicago Med Sch, 45-50. *Teaching:* Painting & graphics, Greenville Co Mus Sch Art, 50-52 & 62-, head sch, 68-74; adj prof art, Univ SC, 73-92, Governor's Sch, 81-92. *Awards:* Owen H Kenan Mem Award of Merit, Am Contemp Exhib, Soc Four Arts, Fla, 68; W J Kaplan Award, Nat Exhib Painters in Casein & Polymer, 64; Merit Award, Int Grand Prix, Cannes, France, 73; Award, Southern Watercolor, Univ Miss, 85; and others. *Bibliog:* Jack A Morris, Jr (auth), Contemporary Artists of South Carolina, Tricentennial Comn, 70; Patricia Robbins (auth), Jeanet Dreskin, Art Voices S, 5-6/79; Feature, Art's the Thing, SC Educ TV, 87; and others. *Mem:* Guild SC Artists (mem bd, 55-, treas, 68, vpres, 71, pres, 72); Nat Asn Women Artists (mem comt, 71-); SC Watercolor Soc (pres, 83-84); Nat Asn Med Illusr; Southern Graphics Coun (secy-treas, 74-76, treas, 88-90, mem bd, 74-92); plus others. *Media:* Polymers, Oils. *Publ:* Illusr, Anatomy of the Gorilla, Am Mus Nat Hist, Columbia Univ, 43-46; What's New, Abbot Labs (& Latin Am ed), 46, 47 & 49; Surgery of Repair, Lippincott, 50; Williams Obstetrics, Stander-Appleton, 50; Surgical Anatomy, BC Decker, 90; many others. *Dealer:* Hampton III Gallery Ltd 11 Hampton Ctr Taylors SC 29687; Fay Gold Gallery 247 Buckhead Ave Atlanta Ga 30305. *Mailing Add:* 60 Lake Forest Dr Greenville SC 29609

DREWAL, HENRY JOHN
HISTORIAN, EDUCATOR
b Brooklyn, NY, Mar 11, 43. *Study:* Hamilton Col, BA; Inst African Studies, Columbia Univ, cert, MA, PhD. *Collections Arranged:* Dimensions in Black Art, African, Afro-American & Afro-Brazilian Art at Cleveland State Univ, 75 & African Fabrics: Tradition and Change, 76, Cleveland State Univ; Traditional Art of the Nigerian Peoples: the Ratner Collection (auth, catalog), Mus African Art, 77; African Artistry: Technique and Aesthetics in Yoruba Sculpture (auth, catalog), High Mus Art, Atlanta, 80; Object and Intellect: African Art from the Neuberger Mus, State Univ NY, Purchase, 86; Shapes of the Mind: African Art from Long Island Cols (auth, catalog), Hofstra Univ; Yoruba: Nine Centuries of African Art & Thought, (auth, catalog), 89; African Permanent Collection, Cleveland Mus Art, 90. *Teaching:* Asst prof African, Oceanic, Am Indian & Afro-Am art, Cleveland State Univ, 73-77, assoc prof, 77-81, chmn dept, 82-85, prof, 82-90; consult African Art, Cleveland Mus Art, 88-90; Erjue-Bascom prof art hist, Univ Wis, Madison, 90- *Awards:* Cleveland State Univ Res Grants, 74, 75, 76, 79, 80, 81 & 89; Nat Endowment Humanities Grant, 77-78, 81, 85, 89 & 90; Andrew W Mellon Fel, Metrop Mus Art, 85-86, 86-87; Rockefeller Found Grant, 88; NY State Coun on Arts, 89; Univ Wis-Madison, Fac Grants, 91. *Mem:* Col Art Asn; Triennial Symp Traditional African Art; Midwest Art Hist Asn; Soc Study Visual Anthrop; Art Coun African Studies Asn; Soc Africanist Archeologists. *Res:* History of art among the Yoruba, Fon and Ewe of West Africa and the African Diaspora of Brazil and Cuba; principles of performance aesthetics; iconology. *Publ:* Flaming Crowns, Cooling Waters: Masks of the Fjebu Yoruba, 86; Art and Divination Among the Yoruba, Design and Myth, 87; Mermaids, Mirrors, and Snake Charmers, Igbo Mami Wata Shrines, 88; Beauty and Being: Aesthetics and Ontology in Yoruba Body Art, 88; Performing the Other: Mami Wata Worship in West Africa, The Drama Rev, 88; Art or Accident: Yoruba Body Artists and their Deity Ogun, 89; The Meaning of Osugbo Art, Man does not go naked, 89; Yoruba: Nine Centuries of African Art and Thought, 89; Yoruba Art and Aesthetics, 91. *Mailing Add:* Dept of Art Cleveland State Univ Cleveland OH 44115

DREXLER, LYNNE
PAINTER
b Newport News, Va. *Study:* Richmond Prof Inst, BFA; Hunter Col; Col William & Mary; Hans Hoffman Sch Fine Arts, scholar. *Work:* Prentice Hall Collection, Englewood Cliffs, NJ; Ciba-Geigy Collection, Hudson River Mus; Tamarind Print Collection, Mus Mod Art, New York; Univ Mass, Amherst. *Exhib:* One-man show, Tanager Gallery, 59; Norfolk Mus Regional Show, 60; Galleria, San Miguel de Allende, Mex, 62; Tetra-Centennial, Va Mus Fine Arts, Richmond, 66; Traveling Show, mus in West & South, 66; plus others. *Dealer:* Alonzo Gallery 26 E 63rd St New York NY 10021; Aldona Gobujas Degdras Ltd 215 E 79th St New York NY 10021. *Mailing Add:* Box 14 Monhegan ME 04852

DREYER, CLARICE A
SCULPTOR
b Missoula, Mont, 46. *Study:* Mont State Univ, BFA(art educ), 79; Univ Calif Berkeley, MFA, 81. *Exhib:* Solo shows, Marilyn Butler Gallery, Santa Monica, Calif, 90, Cheney Cowles Mus, Spokane, Wash, Owings/Dewey Fine Art, Santa Fe, NMex & South East Ctr Contemp Arts, Winston Salem, NC, 91; Arvada Ctr Arts, Colo, 91; Boise Art Mus, Idaho, 91; Boulder Art Ctr, Colo; and others. *Awards:* Pub Sculpture Comn Finalist, Mill Valley Sculpture Fountain, Calif, 84; Nat Endowment Arts Fel, 84 & 90; Pub Art Comn, Arvada Ctr Arts, Colo, 91. *Bibliog:* Lyn Smallwood (auth), Art, Seattle Post-Intelligencer, 7/15/88; Doloris Targan Ament (auth), At the edge, Seattle Times, J3, 7/17/88; Chris Schnoor (auth), Ordinary people, Reflex, 20, 9-10/88; and others. *Mailing Add:* 4750 Jordon Spur Rd Bozeman MT 59715

DREYER, GAY
SCULPTOR
b Christiansburg, Va, July 31, 15. *Study:* Art Students League, with William Zorach, 33; Beaux Art Inst, with Eugene Steinhof, 34; Baylor Univ, BS, 57; Iowa Univ, MFA, 59. *Work:* Chrysler Mus, Norfolk, Va; Hermitage Foundation, Norfolk, Va. *Comn:* Eve at Gate of Paradise (bronze), Norfolk, Va, 82. *Exhib:* Pa Acad, Philadelphia, 40; Brooklyn Mus, NY, 62; Smithsonian Inst, Washington, DC, 63; Silvermine Guild, New Canaan, Conn, 64; Old Dominion Univ Gallery, Norfolk, Va, 81. *Teaching:* Instr sculpture, Baylor Univ, 54-59; chmn, Art Dept, Old Dominion Univ, Norfolk, Va, 69-79. *Awards:* Purchase Award, Southwestern Art Show, Dallas, 59; Best in Show, Womens Club, White Plains, NY, 63; Best in Show, Norfolk Festival Art, 81. *Media:* Mixed. *Dealer:* David Johnson 765 Grandy Norfolk VA 23501. *Mailing Add:* 1355 Bolling Ave Norfolk VA 23508

DRIESBACH, DAVID FRAISER
PRINTMAKER
b Wausau, Wis, Oct 7, 22. *Study:* Univ Ill, Beloit Col; Univ Wis; Pa Acad Fine Arts; State Univ Iowa; Atelier 17, with S W Hayter, 69. *Work:* Seattle Mus, Wash; Dayton Art Inst, Ohio; Columbus Gallery Fine Arts, Ohio; Bibliot Nat, Paris, France; Boston Mus Fine Arts. *Comn:* Fiscal Flight (ed, 150 color etchings), Sears Roebuck Co, 67; series of bronze reliefs, Assoc Am Artists, NY, 68; color intaglio ed, Checker Cab Co, Kalamazoo, Mich, 74; color intaglio, Soc Am Graphic Artists; color viscosity, Gemarts, Knoxville, Tenn. *Exhib:* Young Printmakers of America, Mus Mod Art, New York, 53; Ten Printmakers of USA, Purdue Univ, 66; One-man show travels Yugoslavia 5 months with US Info Agency, 85; Grafica Contemporanea Americana, Venice, Italy, 77; retrospective show, Univ Md, Baltimore Co, 79; Seventh British Int Print Biennale, Bradford, England, 82. *Teaching:* Prof printmaking, Northern Ill Univ, 64-91 (ret). *Awards:* Ford Found Purchase Prize for Intaglio, 60; 10th Ann Colorprint USA Purchase Prize, Tex Tech, 83; Second Int Exhib of Prints & Drawings Award, Wesleyan Col, Macon, Ga. *Bibliog:* Bob White (auth), David Driesbach, Chicago Art Scene, 1/68; The complex world of David Driesbach, Northern Alumnus, 3/68; David Driesbach Retrospective (catalog), Northern Ill, Univ, Dekalb. *Mem:* Midwest Col Art Asn; Soc Am Graphic Artists; Boston Printmakers. *Media:* Intaglio. *Dealer:* Edenside Gallery Louisville, KY; Wenniger Graphics Inc Boston MA 02116. *Mailing Add:* 810 Lawnwood Ave De Kalb IL 60115

DRIESBACH, WALTER CLARK, JR
SCULPTOR, INSTRUCTOR
b Cincinnati, Ohio, July 3, 29. *Study:* Sch Dayton Art Inst, 47-52, with Robert Koepnick; studio asst to Joseph Kiselewski, New York, 54-55; Art Acad Cincinnati, 55-56, with Charles Cutler. *Work:* Xomox Inc; Bell Tel Co; Gen Elec Co; Raymond Walters Col; Cincinnati Bel Info Systems, Inc. *Comn:* St Anthony of Padua (limestone relief), St Anthony of Padua Church, Cincinnati, 59; Life of St Teresa (limestone entablature), St Teresa Church, Cincinnati, 62; The Lord's Supper (walnut relief), Good Shepherd Church, Cincinnati, 64; Fireman Monument (granite figure), Cincinnati, 68; Immaculate Conception (oak figure), St Charles Borromeo Church, Dayton, Ohio, 81. *Exhib:* Ohio Sculptors, Akron & Canton Art Insts, 60; Northwest Territory Sculpture Show, Cincinnati Art Mus & John Herron Inst Art, Indianapolis, Ind, 61; Univ Cincinnati Regional Sculpture, 68; Invitational Exhib, Cincinnati Art Mus, Ohio, 72 & 81; Figure '82, Contemp Art Ctr, Cincinnati, 82; plus others. *Teaching:* Instr drawing & sculpture, Memphis Acad Arts, 56-58, Wilmington Col, 63-66, Thomas More Col, 70-71 & 78-; instr sculpture, Dayton Art Inst Evening Sch, 58-60 & Col Mt St Joseph, 72; instr sculpture, drawing & 3-D design, Univ Dayton, 66-72; instr sculpture, 3-D design & found, Art Acad Cincinnati, 70-87; instr wood carving, Communiv, Univ Cincinnati, 80-81. *Awards:* Fleischmann Purchase Prize, Zoo Arts Festival, Cincinnati, 64; First Prize, Prof Sculpture Div, Ohio State Fair Fine Arts Exhib, 66, Second Prize, 68. *Mem:* Cincinnati Carvers' Guild. *Media:* Wood, Cast Bronze. *Publ:* Contribr, Contemporary Stone Sculpture, 70 & Creating Small Wood Objects as Functional Sculpture, 76, Crown; Masters of Wood Sculpture, Watson-Guptill, 80; Sculpture: Technique-Form-Content, Davis Publ, 89. *Mailing Add:* 2541 Erie Ave Cincinnati OH 45208

DRIESSEN, ANGELA KOSTA See Kosta, Angela

DRISCOLL, ABIGAIL JULIA HANNAH
ADMINISTRATOR, CONSERVATOR
b Boston, Mass, Sept 12, 58. *Study:* Hamilton Col, Clinton, NY, BFA, 80. *Collections Arranged:* A Spirt & Myth--Adirondack Sporting Art (late 19th century). *Pos:* Exec dir, Tri-County Arts Coun. *Bibliog:* Jo Yanow Schwartz (auth), Old and looking old is new, Art Bus News, 6/12/86; Watertown Daily Times. *Mem:* Am Hist Print Collectors; Col Art Asn; Friends of Emerson Gallery; Friends of Gibson Gallery. *Specialty:* American and English historical prints; 19th and 20th century engravings; lithographs and chromolithographs. *Publ:* coordr, current, J of N Country Action. *Mailing Add:* Rt 2 Box 189 Hale Rd Canton NY 13617

DRISCOLL, EDGAR JOSEPH, JR
CRITIC
b Boston, Mass, Sept 1, 20. *Study:* Cambridge Sch Weston; Univ Iowa, with Grant Wood; Yale Univ Sch Fine Arts. *Pos:* Art critic, Boston Globe, 46-73; Boston corresp, Art News, 73- *Mailing Add:* 75 Hancock St Boston MA 02114

DRISCOLL, ELLEN
SCULPTOR
Comn: Manhattan Community Arts Fund 6th St & Ave B Oper Greenthumb Garden, New York, 85; Mid-Atlantic States Arts Consortium Virginia Ctr Creative Arts, Sweet Briar, Va, 86; Oliver Ranch, Geyserville, Calif, 88; Ellyn & Saul Dennison, Bernardsville, 90; Mr Robert Orto, La Jolla, Calif, 91. *Exhib:* Solo exhib, Hudson D Walker Gallery, Provincetown, Mass, 84 & 85, Damon Brandt Gallery, New York, 86 & 88, Paulo Salvador Gallery, New York, 86, Stavaridis Gallery, Boston, Mass, 87, The Loophole of Retreat,

Installation, Whitney Mus Am Art at Phillip Morris, NY, 91-92, Contemp Art Ctr, Cincinnati, 92; Brockton Art Mus, Mass, 85; Mayor's Off Cult Affairs, City Gallery, New York, 86; Aldrich Mus Contemp Art, Ridgefield, Conn, 86; 1980: A New Generation, Metrop Mus, New York, 88; Innovations in Sculpture, Aldrich Mus Contemp Art, Conn, 88; Sculpture on the Edge, DeCordove & Dana Mus & Park, Lincoln, Mass, 89; Means to Ends: Process and its Traces in Recent Sculpture, Rockland Ctr Arts, NY, 90; Alchemy, Fayerweather Gallery, Univ Va, Charlottesville, 91; Suzanne Biederberg Gallery, Amsterdam, Neth, 92. *Teaching:* Asst dir admissions, Parsons Sch Design, 80-83; dir, Parsons Sch Design, 85-89; vis lectr sculpture, Princeton Univ, 91; sophomore & jr sculpture, Sch Mus Fine Arts, 92. *Awards:* Chesterwood Award, Solomon R Guggenheim Mus, New York, 87; Guggenheim Mem Found, 87; Bunting Fel, Radcliffe Col, 90-91. *Bibliog:* Eleanor Heartney (auth), Artnews, 10/90; Phillip Morris (auth), Whitney Mus Am Art, 91; Goings on About Town/Art, New Yorker, 2/10/92. *Mailing Add:* 101 First Ave No 5 New York NY 10003

DRISCOLL, JOHN PAUL
DEALER, ART HISTORIAN
b Madison, Minn, Oct 28, 49. *Study:* Univ Minn, BA, 71; Pa State Univ, MA, 74, PhD, 85. *Exhib:* Organized with catalogues: Mitchell Siporin: The Early Years, 90; Keith Jacobshagen, 90; Edwin Dickinson: A Vision of Coast & Sea, 90; Seymour Lipton: Major Late Sculpture, 91; Thomas Eakins: Art and Archive, 92. *Collections Arranged:* Charles Sheeler: Works on Paper (catalog), 74, Checklist of the Permanent Collection, 77, American Paintings from Collection of Daniel J Terra, 77, Arthur B Davies from the Brill Collection, 79 & All That Is Glorious Around Us, 81, Pa State Univ Mus Art; Paintings from William H Lane Foundation, Munson-Williams-Procter Inst, 78; Contemporary British Ceramics, Fitchburg Art Mus, 82; John F Kensett: An American Master, Worcester Art Mus, 85. *Pos:* Registr, Pa State Univ Mus Art, 75-78; cur, William H Lane Found, 78-82; guest cur, Kensett Exhib, Worcester Art Mus, 83-85; owner, Driscoll & Walsh Fine Art, Boston, 83-88 & Babcock Galleries, 86- *Teaching:* Instr, Fitchburg State Col, 79-84. *Awards:* Alumni Achievement Award, Pa State Univ. *Bibliog:* Hilton Kramer (auth), Charles Sheeler, NY Times, 4/13/74; Outstanding exhibitions, Apollo Mag, 6/74. *Mem:* Col Art Asn; Am Asn Mus; Am Antiqn Soc; Am Numismatic Asn; Archives Am Art. *Res:* Emphasis on American art with current focus on John F Kensett and Edwin Dickinson. *Specialty:* 19th and 20th century American painting and sculpture, including contemporary. *Publ:* Auth, William Trost Richards' woodland scene rediscovered, Am Art J, 78; John F Kensett Drawings (exhib catalog), Pa State Univ Mus Art, 78; Charles Sheeler's early work: Five rediscovered paintings, Art Bull, 80; A Marsden Hartley of 1908, Am Art J, 80; John Stuart Ingle: Paradigms of reality, Am Artist, 82; John F Kensett: An American Master, Norton, 85. *Mailing Add:* Babcock Galleries 724 Fifth Ave New York NY 10019

DRISKELL, DAVID CLYDE
PAINTER, EDUCATOR
b Eatonton, Ga, June 7, 31. *Study:* Skowhegan Sch Painting & Sculpture, with Jack Levine & Henry V Poor, scholar, 53; Howard Univ, with James A Porter & Morris Louis, BA, 55; Cath Univ Am, with Nell Sonnemann & Ken Noland, MFA, 62; Riksbureau voor Kunsthistorisches Documentatie, The Hague, Neth, cert, 64. *Work:* Corcoran Gallery Art, Smithsonian Inst, Washington, DC; Birmingham Mus Art; Corcoran Gallery Art, Washington, DC; Carl Van Vechten Gallery Fine Arts, Fisk Univ, Nashville, Tenn; Ark Fine Arts Ctr, Little Rock; and others. *Comn:* Mountain and Tile Suite (10 woodcuts-color), Tenn Arts Comn, 72. *Exhib:* Baltimore Mus Area Exhib, 65; Corcoran Area Exhib, 66; Birmingham Festival Exhib, 72; Cent South Ann, Nashville, 72; Mid-South Exhib, Memphis, 75; and others. *Pos:* Mem bd adv, Mus African Art, 67-; mem visual arts adv panel, Tenn Arts Comn, 69-, mus adv bd, 73-; guest curator, Smithsonian Inst, 72; guest curator, Los Angeles Co Mus Art, 74-76; mus adv panel, Nat Endowment Arts, 74-77; bd gov, Skowhegan Sch Painting & Sculpture, 75- *Teaching:* Prof painting & art hist, Talladega Col, 55-62; prof painting & art hist, Howard Univ, 62-66; prof art & chmn dept, Fisk Univ, 66-76; vis prof, Univ Ife, Nigeria, 70; vis prof, Bowdoin Col, 73; vis prof, Bates Col, 73; prof art, Univ Md, College Park, 76-82, chmn dept art, 78-82. *Awards:* John Hope Award in Art, Atlanta Univ, 59; Museum Donor Award, Am Fedn Art, 62; Graphics Art Award, Corcoran Gallery Art, 65. *Mem:* Col Art Asn Am; Nat Conf Artists; Am Mus Asn; Am Fedn Art. *Media:* Oil, Tempera. *Res:* Role of the black artist in American society and traditional African art, its impact on Afro-American art. *Mailing Add:* 4206 Decatur St Hyattsville MD 20781

DROEGE, ANTHONY JOSEPH, II
PAINTER, DRAFTSMAN
b Philadelphia, Pa, Sept 22, 43. *Study:* Pa State Univ, BA, 65; Univ Iowa, MA, 67, MFA, 68. *Work:* Kemper Ins Co Collection, Long Grove, Ill; Clara Eagle Gallery, Murray State Univ, Ky; Art in the Embassy Prog, US State Dept; Indianapolis Mus Art, Ind; South Bend Art Ctr, Ind; and others. *Comn:* Numerous pub & pvt portrait comns. *Exhib:* Mid-Year Show, Butler Inst Am Art, Youngstown, Ohio, 70; Mainstreams, 5th Ann Marietta Col Int Competitive Exhib, Ohio, 72; The Emerging Real, Storm King Art Ctr, Mountainville, NY, 73; New Realism Re-Visited, Brainerd Hall Art Gallery, State Univ NY Col Potsdam, 74; Living American Artists & the Figure, Pa State Univ Mus Art, 74; The Big Show, J B Speed Art Mus, Louisville, Ky, 75; Am Painters in Paris, 76; Ind-Ill Bicentennial Painting Exhib, 76; Panorama Am Art, Midwest Mus Am Art, Elkhart, Ind, 79; Thirteenth Union League Club, Chicago Art Show, 81; 68th Ind Artists Show, Indianapolis Mus Art, 81; Master-Apprentice: The Indiana Art Tradition Carries On, Ind State Mus, 85; Realism Today, Evansville Mus Arts & Sciences. *Teaching:* Instr painting & drawing, Murray State Univ, Ky, 68-71; prof painting & drawing, Ind Univ, South Bend, 71- *Awards:* Commendation from Elmer Bishoff, Mid-Am Show, Joslyn Art Mus, Omaha, 68; First Place Painting, 7th Biennial Michiana Regional Art Competition, South Bend Art Ctr, 72; Best of Show at 8th Biennial Michiana Regional Art Competition, First Bank & Trust Co, 74. *Bibliog:* Byron Burford (auth), View from the Midwest, Readers & Writers, summer 68; Gene Porter (auth), Mirrors repeated in Droege paintings, Ft Wayne News-Sentinel, 4/73; Dennis Shapiro (auth), article, New Art Examiner, Chicago, 4/75. *Media:* Oil, Gouache; Pastel, Oil Pastel. *Mailing Add:* 202 S Filbert St New Carlisle IN 46552

DROHOJOWSKA, HUNTER
WRITER, EDUCATOR
b Schenectady, NY, Sept 5, 52. *Study:* Ohio State Univ, Columbus, 70-72; Ariz State Univ, Tempe, 73-75; Inst Allende, San Miguel de Allende, Mex, BFA, 76. *Pos:* Art ed, Los Angeles Weekly, Calif, 80-84; columnist, Los Angeles Herald Examiner, 83-86; W Coast corresp, Artnews, 85-; contribr, Archit Dig, 87-; chair, Dept Lib Arts & Sci, Otis Art Inst, Parsons Sch Design, 87- *Mem:* Int Asn Art Critics; Col Art Asn. *Res:* Biography of Georgia O'Keeffe. *Publ:* Auth, numerous articles in Artnews, Artforum & the Los Angeles Times, 86-92; Timothy Hawkinson, Concrete Metaphors, Artnews, 12/89; Ruscha Today, LA Style, 6/90; The Playground of Modern Desire, essay included in Monograph; Tempest in a Teapot, The Ceramic Art of Peter Shire, Rizzoli, spring, 91. *Mailing Add:* 844 18th St Santa Monica CA 90403

DROWER, SARA RUTH
PAINTER, CRAFTSMAN
b Chicago, Ill, Oct 15, 38. *Study:* Roosevelt Univ, BS, 59; Univ Ill, Chicago, MS, 61; Art Inst Chicago. *Work:* Ill State Mus, Springfield; Minn Mus Art, Minneapolis; Borg-Warner Corp, DePaul Univ, Standard Oil, Chicago. *Exhib:* Inedible Cakes & Souvenir Shows, 82, American Politics, 84, Renwick Gallery, Smithsonian Inst; New Elegance, Newark Mus, NJ, 84-85; Artwear '85, Bellevue Art Mus, Wash; Designed to Wear, Ore Art Mus, Arts & Crafts, 85-86; Wearable Fibers A Revolution Bodywear, Milwaukee Art Mus, 86; plus many others. *Pos:* Sci illusr, Turtox-Biol Supply, 62-64. *Awards:* First Prize Watercolors, Union League Club, Chicago, 72; Ill Coun Grant: Crafts, 86; Best of Show, Fine Art Exhib, Artists Guild Chicago, 74. *Mem:* Surface Design; Am Crafts Coun. *Media:* Miscellaneous Media. *Mailing Add:* 127 Laurel Wilmette IL 60091

DRUM, SYDNEY MARIA
PAINTER, PRINTMAKER
b Calgary, Alta, Can, Nov 20, 52. *Study:* Univ Calgary, BFA(with distinction in art), 74; York Univ, MFA, 76. *Work:* Mus Mod Art, New York; Philadelphia Mus Art, Pa; Nat Mus Am Art, Washington, DC; Univ Nebr, Lincoln; Can Coun Art Bank, Ottawa, Ont. *Comn:* Pope, Ballard, Shepard & Fowle, Chicago, 82; Zimmerli Mus, Rutgers Univ, New Brunswick, NJ, 89; Harmann-Reimer Corp, New York, 90. *Exhib:* One-woman shows, Name Gallery, Chicago, 79, Getter/Pall Gallery, New York, 81, Hart House Art Gallery, Univ Toronto, Ont, 81, Gallery Pascal, Toronto, Ont, 81 & Jan Cicero Gallery, Chicago, 82; World Print III, San Francisco Mus Mod Art, Calif, 80; Five Years of Prints, traveling exhib, US Embassy, Yugoslavia, 83; Neither/Nor, New York, 86; Bau-Xi Gallery, Toronto, Ont, 87, 90 & 92; Northwestern Univ, Evanston, Ill, 87. *Teaching:* Sessional lectr studio art, Univ Alta, Edmonton, Can, 76-77; instr studio art, Nova Scotia Col Art & Design, Halifax, Can, 77-78; asst prof studio art, Univ Ill, Chicago Circle, 78-83; univ lectr studio art, Governors State Univ, Ill, 83-84; asst prof studio art, Rutgers Univ, 84-87. *Awards:* Can Coun Arts Grant, 76-77; A-N-W Prof Prize, 55th Ann Members Show, Print Club, Philadelphia, Pa, 79; Artist Fel, Yaddo Found, 80. *Bibliog:* Nancy Tonsley (auth), Sydney Drum, Artscanada, 5-6/79; Joyce Zemans (auth), Beyond the border at Harbourfront Art Gallery, Artmag, 2-3/80; Liz Wylie (auth), Sydney Drum at Gallery Pascal & Hart House Art Gallery, Artmag, 5-6/81. *Mem:* Col Art Asn Am; Print Club; Printmaking Coun NJ. *Dealer:* Burns Fine Art New York; Bau-Xi Gallery Toronto. *Mailing Add:* 138 W 120th St New York NY 10027

DRUMM, DON
SCULPTOR, CRAFTSMAN
b Warren, Ohio, Apr 11, 35. *Study:* Hiram Col; Kent State Univ, BFA & MA. *Work:* Cleveland Mus Art; Bowling Green State Univ; Columbus Gallery Fine Arts; Pan Am Airlines; Goodyear Tire & Rubber Co; and others. *Comn:* Reliefs, walls, aluminum & steel sculpture & fountains, Alcoa Co, Pittsburgh, Episcopal Diocese, Sao Paulo, Brazil, Richard Gossar Mem Sculpture, Toledo, Ohio, Curtain Bluff Hotel, Antigua BWI & City of Akron, Ohio; 2 cement murals, Bowling Green State Univ, Ohio, 66; corten steel sculpture, Baltimore, Md & Miami, Fla, 75; corten steel sculpture, City of Miami, Fla, 75; 14 cement wall relief murals, Quaker-Hilton, Akron, Ohio, 80; and many others. *Exhib:* Group shows, 64 & 65 & Traveling Exhib circulated by Am Fedn Arts, 65-67 & 72, Mus Contemp Crafts, New York; Cleveland Mus Art, 64-68; Columbus Gallery Fine Arts, 66 & 67; and others. *Pos:* Owner, Don Drumm Studios & Gallery, Akron, Ohio, 71- *Teaching:* Artist in residence, Bowling Green State Univ, 66-71; instr, Penland Sch Crafts, 66-79. *Awards:* Purchase Prize, Cleveland Mus Art, 64; Prize, Nat Soc Interior Design, 65; Prize, Columbus Gallery Fine Arts. *Mem:* Ohio Designer Craftsmen; Am Craftsmen's Coun; Fine Arts Comn, Akron, Ohio. *Media:* Cast Metals, Miscellaneous Media. *Res:* Investigation into the use of contemporary materials and construction techniques to create urban sculpture specializing in the use of cast aluminum and concrete. *Dealer:* Don Drumm Studios & Gallery 437 Crouse St Akron OH 44311. *Mailing Add:* c/o Studio Gallery 133 S Salina St Syracuse NY 13202

DRUMMER, WILLIAM RICHARD
GALLERY DIRECTOR
b Ottawa, Ohio, Feb 17, 25. *Study:* Ohio State Univ, BA, 50, MA, 57. *Exhib:* Piranesi, Miss State Mus, Jackson, 80-81 & Brooks Mem Art Gallery, Memphis, 82; Pensacola Art Mus, Fla, 83; New Orleans Mus Art, La, 84; Mario Villa Gallery, New Orleans, La, 89. *Pos:* Dir, Gallery 539, New Orleans, 75- *Specialty:* Japanese woodblock prints, Piranesi etchings, fine architectural prints and drawings, rare architectural books. *Mailing Add:* 539 Bienville St New Orleans LA 70130

DRUMMOND, SALLY HAZELET
PAINTER
b Evanston, Ill, June 4, 24. *Study:* Rollins Col, 42-44; Columbia Univ, BS, 48; Inst Design, Chicago, 49-50; Univ Louisville, MA, 52. *Work:* Mus Mod Art, Metrop Mus Art, Whitney Mus Am Art, New York; Hudson's Dept Store, Detroit; J B Speed Mus Art, Louisville; Weatherspoon Art Gallery, Univ NC, Greensboro; Corcoran Gallery Art, Hirshhorn Mus, Washington, DC; and others. *Exhib:* Am Artists Ann, Whitney Mus Am Art, New York, 60; Americans 63, Mus Mod Art, New York, 63; one-man shows, Fischbach Gallery, New York, 72 & 78, Aldrich Mus, Ridgefield, Conn, 81, Artists Space, Mark Rothko Found, New York, 89, Springfield Art Ctr, Ohio, 88, Cornell Fine Arts Ctr, Rollins Col, Winter Park, 89, George D & Harriet W Cornell Fine Arts Ctr, Rollins Col, 89 & Louisville Visual Art Asn, Ky, 89; Retrospective, Corcoran Gallery Art, Washington, DC, 72; American Art, American Women, Stamford Mus, Conn, 86; The Kentuckians, Owensboro Mus Fine Art, Ky & Nat Arts Club, New York, 87; Art on Paper, Weatherspoon Art Gallery, Univ NC, Greensboro, 87; Connecticut Artists, Stamford Mus & Nature Ctr, 88; Surface & Proportion, Margaret Roeder Gallery, New York, 90; and many other one-man & group exhibs. *Teaching:* Instr, Skowhegan Sch Art, 73. *Awards:* Fulbright Grant, Venice, 52; Guggenheim Grant, France, 67. *Bibliog:* Lawrence Campbell (auth), Dotted light, Art News Mag, 4/72. *Media:* Oil. *Dealer:* Margaret Roeder Gallery 545 Broadway New York NY 10012. *Mailing Add:* RR 3 Box 510 B Red Hook NY 12571-9447

DRUTT, HELEN WILLIAMS
DEALER, LECTURER
b Winthrop, Mass, Nov 19, 30. *Study:* Tyler Sch Art, Temple Univ, BFA; Barnes Found; Moore Col Art, Philadelphia, hon DA, 90. *Collections Arranged:* Two British Goldsmiths, Ramshaw & Watkins, 73; UICA: Craft Faculty, 74; Soup Tureens: 1976 (ed, catalog), 76; Olaf Skoogfors Retrospective (ed, catalog), 79; Robert Arneson: Self-Portraits 1966-1978 (ed, catalog), 79; Ruth Duckworth & Claire Zeisler (ed, catalog), 79; Contemporary Ceramics: A Response to Wedgewood (ed, catalog); Robert L Pfannebecker (ed, catalog); Claus Bury (ed, catalog); Contemporary Arts: Aneypanding View (catalog), 86. *Pos:* Curatorial consult, Mus Philadelphia Civic Ctr, 67, 70 & 73; exec dir, Philadelphia Coun Prof Craftsmen, 67-73; dir, Helen Drutt Gallery, 74-; gallery consult, Moore Col Art, 78; consult, Nat Endowment Arts, 79-; cur many pub inst, 69-86; selected panelist & juror for numerous exhibs, 68-89. *Teaching:* Mod craft hist, Philadelphia Col Art, 72-80; prof, Moore Col Art, Philadelphia, 74-84 & prof hist art, 82 & 87; vis scholar, Am Academy, Rome, Italy. *Awards:* Merit Dedicated Serv Crafts, Philadelphia Col Art, 72; Award Advan Mod Ceramics, Int Ceramics Symp, 81; Grant, Pa Coun Arts, 85-88. *Bibliog:* Carol Saline (auth), Crafty lady, Philadelphia Mag, 75; Professional Women (film), ABC-TV, Philadelphia, 76. *Mem:* Collab 20th Century, Philadelphia Mus Art; Am Crafts Coun (Pa state rep, 75-); Pa State Coun on the Arts (crafts panel, 75-78). *Specialty:* Twentieth century work in fiber, ceramics & metal; contemporary crafts. *Publ:* Contribr, Craft Horizons, Am Crafts Coun, 70. *Mailing Add:* c/o Helen Drutt Gallery 1721 Walnut St Philadelphia PA 19103

DRUTZ, JUNE
PAINTER, EDUCATOR
b Toronto, Ont, Feb 14, 20. *Study:* Cent Tech Sch; Ont Col Art, grad(hons), 65. *Work:* McMaster Univ, Hamilton, Ont; Univ Waterloo, Ont; Royal Can Art Collection, Nat Gallery, Ottawa; Univ Guelph, Ont; London Trust Co, Ont; Citibank, Toronto; Hudson Bay Co, Toronto; and many others. *Comn:* Seeds of Spring Returning (serigraph ann print), Glenhyrst Art Asn, Brantford, Ont, 68-69. *Exhib:* One-man shows, Rebecca Sisler Gallery, Toronto, 78 & Prince Arthur Gallery, Toronto, 79; Ont Soc Artists, 80; Univ Ind, Elkhart, 80; Can Soc Painters Watercolor, 81; Latcham Gallery, Stouffville, Ont; and many others. *Teaching:* Instr, Ont Col Art, Toronto, 67-86, Ont Dept Educ, summers 68-72, Ryerson Polytech Inst, Toronto, 72-73 & Toronto Art Sch, 66-75, retired. *Awards:* Purchase Award, Graphex-3, Brantford, Ont, 75; Ian Griffiths Award Watercolor, 80 & Joseph E Seagrams Purchase Award, 80, Ont Soc Artists; Honor award, Can Soc Painters Watercolor, 89. *Bibliog:* Robert Myers (auth), The youth cult maidens of June Drutz, Art Mag, Vol 6, No 22, 75. *Mem:* Royal Can Acad; Ont Soc Artists; Can Soc Painters Watercolor; Print & Drawing Coun Can; Can Soc Graphic Artists. *Media:* Tempera, Watercolor. *Dealer:* Contemp Fine Art Consultants & Serv Toronto Ont; Geraldine Davis Gallery Toronto Ont. *Mailing Add:* 430 Annette St Toronto ON M6P 1R9 Canada

DRYSDALE, NANCY MCINTOSH
PATRON, DEALER
b Chicago, Ill, July 22, 31. *Study:* Northwestern Univ, BS, 53. *Pos:* Dir, McIntosh/Drysdale Gallery, currently. *Mem:* Washington, DC Art Dealers Asn. *Specialty:* Contemporary art, painting, drawing, sculpture; European and American. *Interests:* Integration of visual arts with the other arts and architecture. *Mailing Add:* 2103 O St NW Washington DC 20004

DUBACK, CHARLES S
PAINTER, PRINTMAKER
b Fairfield, Conn, Mar 10, 26. *Study:* Whitney Sch Fine Arts, New Haven, Conn; Newark Sch Fine & Indust Arts, NJ; Skowhegan Sch Painting & Sculpture, Maine; Brooklyn Mus Art Sch. *Work:* Corcoran Gallery Art, Washington, DC; Emory Collection, Emory Univ, Atlanta, Ga; Columbia Mus Art, SC; Butler Mus Am Art; Am Tel & Tel, New York; and others. *Exhib:* Prints & Drawings, 53, Trends in Watercolor Today, 57, 20th Biennial Int Watercolor Exhib, 59 & Print Show, 70, Brooklyn Mus, NY; Whitney Ann Exhib of Contemp Am Painting, New York, 59-60; Mus Mod Art, New York, 62; 20th Ann Exhib Contemp Am Painting, Lehigh Univ, Bethlehem, Pa, 74; Works on Paper, Weatherspoon Art Gallery, Greensboro, NC, 75; Ft Wayne Mus of Art, Ind, 76; one-man show, Landmark Gallery, 79-82, Susan Gross Gallery, Philadelphia, Pa, 85, Anne Weben Gallery Georgetown, Maine, 86; New Dimensions in Drawing, Aldrich Mus, Conn, 81; two-man show, Farnsworth Mus, Rockland, Maine, 84; Art in Embassies, US Govt, 85; Austin Peny State Univ, Clarksville, Tenn, 87. *Collections Arranged:* Ten Painters of Maine, Landmark Gallery, New York, 77. *Bibliog:* Connie Smith (auth), A sentimental journey, Village Voice, 4/76; Laura Pipune (auth), Window exhibit at museum, Ft Wayne Jour-Gazette, 10/76; Holland Cotter (auth), Charles DuBack, Arts Mag, 11/77. *Media:* Multimedia. *Mailing Add:* 457 W Broadway New York NY 10012

DUBANIEWICZ, PETER PAUL
PAINTER
b Cleveland, Ohio, Nov 17, 13. *Study:* Cleveland Inst Art, grad(scholar), 35; Agnes Gund Traveling Scholar, 35; Mus Sch Fine Arts, Boston, Mass; Albert Whitin Traveling Fel, France, Ger & Italy, 38. *Work:* Ohio Bell Tel Co; Cleveland Mus Art; Ford Motor Co; St Paul's Episcopal Church; Butler Inst; plus many other pub & pvt collections. *Comn:* Mural, New Eastman Br Libr, Cleveland, 80. *Exhib:* Metrop Mus Art, New York; Ten-Thirty Art Gallery, Cleveland; Corcoran Gallery, Washington, DC; Springfield Mus, Mass; 39th Ann Mid Year Show, Butler Inst Am Art; plus many others. *Teaching:* Instr, Boston Mus Sch Fine Art, 38-41; instr, Cleveland Inst Art, 45-81, prof emer, 81-; lectr, Skowhegan Sch Painting & Sculpture; instr, Oberlin Col, winter 72. *Awards:* Buffalo Art Club Prize, 63; Second Prize, Int Platform Asn Show, 66; H M Newman Relig Art Show, Cleveland, Ohio, 70; Hon Mention, Orange Arts Coun, Ohio, 86; Second Prize, Orange Arts Coun, Ohio, 87; First Prize, Watercolor, Orange Arts Coun, Ohio, 90. *Publ:* Illusr, color cover, Cleveland Plain Dealer. *Mailing Add:* 132 S Strawberry Lane Chagrin Falls OH 44022-1271

DUBASKY, VALENTINA
PAINTER, SCULPTOR
b Washington, DC, Mar 1, 51. *Study:* Goddard Col, BA, 74, MA, 77. *Work:* Newark Mus, NJ; Aldrich Mus Contemp Art; Seattle Art Mus; Jane Voorhees Zimmerli Art Mus, Rutgers Univ; Prudential Life Insurance Co, New York, NY. *Exhib:* Solo exhibs, Robert L Kidd Gallery, Detroit, Mich, 83, Gloria Luria Gallery, Miami, Fla, 85, Van Stratten Gallery, Chicago, Ill, 85 & Oscarsson-Hood Gallery, New York, 85; McNay Art Inst, Austin, Tex, 83; Albright-Knox Mus, Buffalo, NY, 83; Painting Invitational, Robeson Ctr Gallery, Rutgers Univ, 84. *Awards:* Artists Grant, Ariana Found Arts, 83; Pollock-Krasner Found, 86. *Bibliog:* Ronny Cohen (auth), New editions, Art News, 83; William Zimmer (auth), review, Arts Mag, 83; Gerrit Henry (auth), review, Art in Am, 86. *Media:* Oil on Canvas, Sculpture. *Mailing Add:* 253 E Tenth St New York NY 10009

DUBINSKIS, ANDA
PAINTER
b Bethesda, Md, 1952. *Study:* Cooper Union, New York, BFA, 74; Univ Pa, Philadelphia, 77. *Comn:* Bus stop poster, Philadelphia Art Now, Pa, 89. *Exhib:* Contemporary Philadelphia Painting (with catalog), Philadelphia Art Alliance, Pa, 86; A Telling Impulse, Morris Gallery, Pa Acad Fine Arts, Philadelphia, 87; Made in Philadelphia 7 (with catalog), Inst Contemp Art, Univ Pa, 87; Perspectives in Pennsylvania, Carnegie Mellon Univ, Pittsburgh, Pa, 87; two-man show, Williamsburg Mus, Va, 90; Janet Fleisher Gallery, Philadelphia, Pa, 91; Expressive Moment, Kutztown Univ, Pa, 91; Contemp Visual Art Invitational, Rock Island, Ill, 91; Fricke Gallery, Belfast, Maine, 92. *Teaching:* Instr advanced figure drawing, Moore Col Art, Philadelphia, Pa, 85-86; instr drawing, La State Univ, Baton Rouge, 89; instr art, Kutztown Univ, Pa, 91-92. *Awards:* Pa Coun Arts Fel for Painting, 85; Nat Endowment Arts Grant for Painting, 89 & Award, 91. *Bibliog:* Searching Out the Best, Morris Gallery, Philadelphia Fine Arts, Pa, 88. *Mem:* Col Art Assoc. *Media:* Oil on Wood Panel. *Dealer:* Janet Fleisher Gallery Philadelphia PA. *Mailing Add:* c/o Janet Fleisher Gallery 211 S 17th St Philadelphia PA 19103

DUBLAC, ROBERT REVAK
PAINTER
b Farmington, Conn, Nov 28, 38. *Study:* Hartford Art Sch, Univ Hartford, BFA(painting, cum laude), 63 & grad study, 68; Yale Univ, with Scully & Nodleman, 67; Temple Univ, Rome, Italy, with Richard Callner, Roger Anliker, Barbara LaPenta & Dmitri Hadzi, 68-69. *Work:* Tyler Sch Art-Temple Univ, Rome, Italy, 68; Hartford Insurance Group Gallery, 69; Sharon Creative Arts Found, Sharon, Conn, 80; Up-River Gallery, Hadlyme, Conn, 83; Beverly Gallery, Dallas, Tex, 84; Aries East Gallery, Brewster, Mass, 85; City First Bank, Dallas, Tex; Vanveldon Ltd, London, Eng; Marriott Hotel Corp; Cigna Corp, Hartford, Conn; Aetna Insurance Co, Hartford, Conn; Procter & Gamble, Cincinnati, Ohio; A S Hansen Inc, Dallas, Tex; Bank of Hartford, Con; and many pvt collection in US, Canada, Italy, Ger, France & Eng. *Exhib:* One-man exhibs, Up-River Gallery, Hadlyme, Conn, 83, Beverly Gallery, Dallas, Tex, 84, Images Art Gallery, Briarcliff Manor, NY, 85, Aires

E Gallery, Brewster, Mass, 85, Portfolio Gallery, Stamford, Conn, 86, Saugatuck Gallery, Westport, Conn, 86 & Unionville Mus, Farmington, Conn, 88; Portfolio Gallery, Stamford, Conn, 86; The Saugatuck Gallery, Westport, Conn, 86; The Unionville Mus, Unionville-Farmington, Conn, 88; Images Gallery, Toledo Ohio, 89; Wadsworth Atheneum, Hartford, Conn; and others. *Pos:* Chmn art dept, Avon High Sch, Conn, 65-67 & Litchfield High Sch, Conn, 69-80; co-dir, Fortman Studio, Florence, Italy, 77-78; self-employed artist/painter, 80- *Teaching:* Art instr, Avon High Sch, Conn, 65-67, adj prof art hist, 67; art instr, Litchfield High Sch, Conn, 69-80. *Awards:* Resident, Millay Colony Arts Inc, Steepletop, Austerlitz, NY, 88; Award, Beth El Show, West Hartford, Conn, 89; Grant, Adolph & Esther Gottlieb Found, 90; and others. *Media:* Watercolor, Oil. *Mailing Add:* 62 Cottage St Unionville CT 06085

DUBOIS, ALAN BEEKMAN
CURATOR, ADMINISTRATOR
b Forest Glen, NY, Dec 14, 35. *Study:* State Univ NY, New Paltz, BS, 58; Ind Univ, MFA, 66. *Work:* Ringling Mus Art, Sarasota, Fla; New Orleans Mus Art. *Exhib:* Light Seven, Mass Inst Technol. *Collections Arranged:* Pachner: Landscaes, 83; Murano Glass in the Twentieth Century, 83; Steuben Glass: The Carder Years, 84; The Old Masters of Taos: Selections from the Collection of Harrison Eiteljorg, 84; Aaron Siskind: Photographs, 84; Collector's View: Painting, Sculpture and Drawings from Collections in Central Florida, 86; European Studio Glass: Thirteen Artists from Eight Countries, 86; Eighteenth Century Porcelain from the Collection of Gertrude J & Robert J Anderson, 88; Fansala Mode, 88; Masterpieces of American Photography, 1899-1982, 89, Good, Better & Best: Decorative Arts from Mid-American Museum Collections, 90; European Fans 1700-1920 from the Colin Johnson Collection, 91; Color-Cut-to-Clear and Engraved Glass, 91; Elsa Freund: An American Studio Jeweler, 91; American Art Jewelers: 1950s, 91; National Objects Invitational, 91; American Glass: Carder and Stenben, 92; Flights of Fancy: Audubon Prints and Porcelain Birds, 92. *Pos:* Dir, Wash Co Mus Fine Arts, 64-66; asst dir, Mus Fine Arts, St Petersburg, Fla, 66-; asst dir, Orlando Mus Art, Fla, 84-89; cur decorative arts, The Ark Arts Ctr, Little Rock, 89- *Teaching:* Adj prof photog & art hist, Eckerd Col, St Petersburg, Fla, 84- *Awards:* Nat Endowment Arts Fel, 72 & 75. *Mem:* Col Art Asn; Am As Mus. *Res:* Photography; Objects in craft media. *Publ:* Auth, Andre Kertesz, Maitland Art Ctr, 81; Photo Collages of the 1920s, Tabloid, Tampa & New York, 83; Artists in Florida, Essays in Fla Hist, Fla Endowment Humanities, Tampa, 87; Photography: A Changing Expression, Eight Florida Photographers: A Photography Invitational, Cornell Fine Arts Mus, Winter Park, Fla, 88; Elsa Freund: An American Studio Jeweler & National Objects Invitational, Ark Arts Ctr, Little Rock, 91. *Mailing Add:* Arkansas Arts Ctr Little Rock AR 72203

DUBOIS, DOUGLAS J
PHOTOGRAPHER
Study: Hampshire Col, Amherst, Mass, BA(film & photog), 83; San Francisco Art Inst, Calif, MFA(photog), 88. *Work:* Mus Mod Art, New York; San Francisco Mus Mod Art, Calif. *Exhib:* Solo exhibs, Diego Rivera Gallery, 86, San Francisco Camerawork, 88, Calif, Midtown Y Photography Gallery, New York, 89, BCC Fine Arts Gallery, Ft Lauderdale, Fla & Dartmouth Col, Hanover, NH, 90 & Hampshire Col, Amherst, Mass, 92; Human Presence, Yale Univ, New Haven, Conn, 89; Twenty Promising Photographers, PARCO Gallery, Tokyo, Japan, 90; American Scene: Contemp Am Photogs, Rena Bransten Gallery, San Francisco, 91; Pleasures and Terrors of Domestic Comfort, Mus Mod Art, New York, 91, Baltimore Mus Art, Md & Los Angeles Co Mus Art, 92; Parents, Mus Contemp Art, Dayton, Ohio, 92. *Teaching:* Vis lectr, Col Marin, 87, San Francisco Camerwork, 88, Univ Calif-San Francisco, 88, San Francisco Art Inst, 89 & Calif Inst Arts, Valencia, 92; asst prof art, NMex State Univ, 89- *Awards:* Fine Arts Fel, San Francisco Found, 87; Visual Artist Fel, Nat Endowment Arts, 90; Arts & Sci Res Grant, NMex State Univ, 92. *Publ:* Contribr, Edge, Pub Television, 10/91; Pleasures and terrors of domestic comfort, Mus Mod Art, New York, 91 & Artnews, 2/92; Parents (catalog), Dayton Art Inst, Ohio, 92; The sun, Japan, 5/92; Flesh and Blood: Photographers' Images of Their Own Families, The Picture Project, NY, 92. *Mailing Add:* Box 4317 U P B Las Cruces NM 88003

DUBOIS, MACY
ARCHITECT, DESIGNER
b Baltimore, Md, Dec 20, 29; Can citizen. *Study:* Md Inst; Tufts Univ, BSE; Harvard Univ, MArch. *Comn:* Ont Pavilion, Expo 67, Ont Govt, 66; Lakehead Sci Bldg, Lakehead Univ, 66; Albert Campbell Libr, Scarborough Pub Libr Bd, 73; George Brown Col Applied Arts & Technol, Toronto, 73; Govt Can Bldg, North York, Ont, 78. *Exhib:* Toronto City Hall Competition, 58; Sao Paolo Exhib, 64; Massey Medals for Archit, 64 & 67; Amsterdam City Hall Competition, 69. *Pos:* Archit critic, Can Architect, 63- *Mem:* Ont Asn Architects; fel Royal Archit Inst Can; academician Royal Can Acad Arts. *Mailing Add:* 175 Carlton St Toronto ON M5A 2K3 Canada

DUCA, ALFRED MILTON
PAINTER, SCULPTOR
b Milton, Mass, July 9, 20. *Study:* Pratt Inst, 38-41; Boston Mus Fine Arts, 43-44. *Work:* Addison Gallery Am Art, Andover, Mass; Fogg Mus & Divinity Sch, Cambridge; Worcester Art Mus, Mass; Munson Procter Inst, Utica, NY; Boston Univ Sch Basic Studies; and others. *Comn:* Sculptures, Prudential Ins Co, Boston, 68-69, Standard Oil Co Ind Res Ctr, 71-72 & Computer Sphere, J F Kennedy Post Off, Boston, 71-72; steel screen, Proj 57, Boston, 71-72; sculpture, bronze screen, John McCormack Bldg, Boston, 75-76; Collaborative work, sculptural fountain (with Richard Duca), New England Bio Labs, Beverly, Mass, 88. *Exhib:* Local, regional & nat exhibs, 58-72. *Pos:* Beaux art dir, Brandeis Univ, 52-53; vis lectr, Boston Univ, 57-58; res assoc, Mass Inst Technol, 58-65; consult, White House Conf Children & Youth, 70-71; auth-dir, Dissemination network syst, Channel One; founder-prog dir, Gloucester Experiment & Channel One Prog. *Awards:* Grants, Rockefeller Found, 58 & Ford Found, 60; New Eng Res Ctr Educ Award, 72; Life Schievement Award, Gov Michael Dukakis, 89. *Bibliog:* Arch Am Art, Smithsonian Inst. *Mem:* Mass Coun Arts & Humanities; Gloucester Coun Arts & Humanities, Mass; Community Fellows Prog (adv bd), Mass Inst Tech. *Media:* Polymer; Metal. *Res:* Development of polymer processes for painters and sculptors; development of the foam vaporization process for casting metal for sculpture. *Publ:* Auth, Polymer Tempera, Significant Teaching Aid, 54; Art casting, Mass Inst Technol J, 62; coauth, Plastics as Art Form, Newman, 64; coauth, Synthetic Painting Media, Jensen, 64; ed & contribr, Facilitator's guide to channel one programming, 81. *Mailing Add:* 8 Arlington St Gloucester MA 01930

DUCKWORTH, RUTH
SCULPTOR, CERAMIST
b Hamburg, Ger, Apr 10, 19; Brit & US citizen. *Study:* Liverpool Sch Art, 36-40; Hammersmith Sch Art, 55; Cent Sch Art & Crafts, London, 56-58; De Paul Univ, Hon Dr, 81. *Work:* Windsor Castle, Eng; Smithsonian Inst, Washington, DC; Philadelphia Mus Art; Art Inst Chicago; Utah Mus Fine Arts; and others. *Comn:* Wall panel, St Mary's Church, Walsingham, Eng; porcelain wall panels, Perkins & Will, Architects, Chicago, 81; wall mural, Chicago Bd Options Exchange, 81; Beth Israel Synagogue, Hammond, Ind, 82; mural, Animal Care Ctr, Chicago, 83; and others. *Exhib:* One-woman shows, Hadler Gallery, New York, 78, Boyman's Mus, Rotterdam, 79 & Exhib A, Chicago, 80; Century of Ceramics, Traveling Exhib, 79; Am porcelain, Renwick Gallery, Washington, DC, 80; and many others. *Teaching:* Instr ceramics, Cent Sch Arts & Crafts, London, 59-64; asst prof ceramics, Midway Studio, Univ Chicago, 64-77. *Awards:* Third Prize, Int Crafts, Instanbul, Turkey, 67; First Prize for Foreign Craftsmen, Nippon Gendai Kohgei Bijutsuka, Kyokai, Japan, 68. *Bibliog:* Tony Birks (auth), The Art of the Modern Potter, Country Life, 67. *Mem:* Arts Club Chicago; Am & World Crafts Couns. *Media:* Stoneware, Porcelain. *Dealer:* Thea Burger 223 E State St Geneva IL 60134. *Mailing Add:* 3845 N Ravenswood Ave Chicago IL 60613

DUERWALD, CAROL
PAINTER, ILLUSTRATOR
b Brooklyn, NY, USA. *Study:* Studied with artist William C Kautz, 75-81; Parson Sch Design, 76; Huntington Art League, New York, 85-89. *Comn:* Mural, comn by Mr & Mrs B Cohen, Oyster Bay, NY, 89; portrait, comn by Mr & Mrs T Brennan, Chester, NJ, 91; portrait, comn by Mr & Mrs G Baker, Oyster Bay, NY, 92; portrait, comn by Mrs D Coleman, Charlottesville, Va, 92; portrait, comn by Mrs M Geenman, Upper Brookville, NY, 92. *Exhib:* Rochester Art Club Open Juried Exhib, Mem Art Mus, Rochester, 84; Huntington Township Art League Open Juried Exhib, Heckscher Mus, Huntington, NY, 85; Pastel Soc Am Juried Open, New York, 89-92; Am Artists Prof League Grand Nat, 91 & Salmagundi Open Juried Exhib, Salmagundi Club, New York, 92; and others. *Pos:* Sketch & design artist, Blum Folding Paper Box, Rosedale, NY, 56-57; sketch & design artist, Cellucraft Inc, New Hyde Park, NY, 57-61; illus & design, freelance, 65-70. *Teaching:* Instr drawing, Pittsford High Sch, NY, 83-84; instr pastel painting, Pittsford Art Club, NY, 83-84; instr pastel portraits, Penny Sch, Cutchoque, NY, 88. *Awards:* Best Painting in Show, Am Artist Prof Grand Nat League, 91; George Innes Mem Award for Pastel, Salmagundi Club Open Exhib, 92; Hon Mention, Am Artist Prof NJ & others. *Mem:* Pastel Soc Am; Am Artist Prof League; Huntington Township Art League; Somerset Art Asn; Morris Co Art Asn. *Media:* Pastel. *Publ:* Contribr, Dan's Papers, 88; Hampton Scene, 89; Observer Tribune, 91; Currier News, 91; Star Ledger, 92. *Mailing Add:* 50 Mile Dr Chester NJ 07930

DUESBERRY, JOELLYN
PAINTER
b Richmond, Va, June 30, 44. *Study:* Smith Col, BA(art hist), 66; Inst Fine Arts, New York Univ (Woodrow Wilson fel), MA, 67; Art Students League, New York, 69-79; Pietrasanta, Italy, 74-77. *Work:* A T & T, New York; Chemical Bank, New York; Shearson-Lehman Brothers, New York; First Bank Boston, Mass; Security Pac Bank, Los Angeles; and numerous pvt collections; Denver Art Mus. *Exhib:* Solo exhibs, 71, Tatistcheff & Co, New York, 82, 83 & 85, Reynolds-Minor Gallery, Richmond, Va, 84, Gerald Peters Gallery, Santa Fe, NMex, 86 & 88, Graham Mod, New York, 89 & Joellyn Duesberry: Landscapes 1972-1992, Denver Art Mus, 92-93; Contemporary Realism, Mus Gallery, NY State Coun Arts, White Plains, 82; DuPont Galleries, Mary Washington Col, Fredericksburg, Va, 83; The New American Scene, Squibb Gallery, Princeton, NJ, 85; Contemporary Romantic Landscape Painting, Orland Mus Art, Loch Haven, Fla, 86; The Landscape Observed, Md Inst Col Art, 89; Hubbard Mus Invitational, Ruldoso, NMex, Soviet Union, WGer & Japan, 90. *Awards:* Woodrow Wilson Fel, 66-67; Nat Endowment Arts Grant, 85-86; Finalist, Hubbard Mus Art Award Excellence, 90, Resident fellow, Rocky Mountain Nat'l Park 1991. *Bibliog:* May Brawley Hill (auth), Joellyn Duesberry, Arts Mag, 9/85; Michael Brenson (auth), Joellyn Duesberry, New York Times, 10/18/85; Carl Little (auth), Duesberry at Graham Modern, Art in Am, 3/92. *Dealer:* Graham Modern New York 10021; Mongerson-Wunderlich Gallery Chicago 60610. *Mailing Add:* 2800 Williamette Lane Littleton CO 80121

DUEZ-DONATO, DEBORA See Donato, Debora E

DUFF, ANN MACINTOSH
PAINTER, PRINTMAKER
b Toronto, Ont, Can. *Study:* Cent Tech Sch; Queen's Univ Summer Sch Fine Arts. *Work:* Nat Gallery Can, Ottawa; Art Gallery Ont, Toronto, Agnes Etherington Gallery, Queen's Univ; City Toronto Arch; Ore State Univ, Corvallis. *Comn:* Watercolor painting, Reader's Digest for Expo 67, Montreal. *Exhib:* Five Toronto Painters, Montreal Mus Fine Art; Six Ways with Watercolor, London Art Gallery, Ont; Can Soc Painters in Watercolour & Am Watercolor Soc Joint Exhib, 72; Fifty Years of Watercolour, Art Gallery, Ontario, 75; Watercolours Japan-Canada, Tokyo-Montreal, 76-77; fifteen one-woman shows in Toronto. *Awards:* Curry Award, 80 & 81; Loomis & Toles Award, 84; Hon Award, Can Soc Painters Watercolour, 84. *Bibliog:* Frances Duncan Barwick (auth), Pictures from the Douglas M Duncan Collection, Univ Toronto, 75; Rebecca Sisler (auth), Passionate spirits, Clarke Irwin, Toronto, 80. *Mem:* Royal Can Acad Arts; Can Soc Painters Watercolour (exec, 70-75); Can Soc Graphic Art (treas, 67-69); Print & Drawing Coun of Can. *Media:* Watercolor. *Dealer:* Lake Galleries 624 Richmond St W Toronto Canada M5V 1Y9. *Mailing Add:* 133 Imperial St Toronto ON M5P 1C7 Canada

DUFF, JAMES H
MUSEUM DIRECTOR, ADMINISTRATOR
b Pittsburgh, Pa, Oct 11, 43. *Study:* Washington & Jefferson Col, BA, 65; Univ Mass, MA, 70. *Collections Arranged:* Wildlife in Art, Brandywine River Mus, Chadds Ford, Pa, 73; Maxfield Parrish: Master of Make-Believe, 74; Harvey Dunn, 74; Peter Hurd, 77; The Collection of Amanda K Berls & Ruth A Yerion, 80; An American Vision: Three Generations of Wyeth Art (auth, catalog), 87. *Pos:* Dir, Mus Hudson Highlands, 66-73; consult, NY State Coun Arts, 70-72; dir, Brandywine River Mus, 73- & Nat Mus Serv Bd, 86- *Mem:* Asn Art Mus Dirs; Am Asn Mus; Mid-Atlantic Asn Mus (pres, formerly). *Publ:* Auth, Not for Publication: Landscapes, Still Lifes and Portraits by N C Wyeth, Brandywine River Mus, 82; An American Vision, Little, Brown, 87. *Mailing Add:* PO Box 297 Chadds Ford PA 19317

DUFF, JOHN EWING
SCULPTOR
b Lafayette, Ind, Dec 2, 43. *Study:* San Francisco Art Inst, BFA, 67; with Manuel Neri, Paul Harris & Ron Nagle. *Work:* Kaiser Wilhelm Mus, Krefeld, Ger; Guggenheim Mus Art, Whitney Mus Am Art & Mus Mod Art, New York; Inst Contemp Art, Boston, Mass; Metropolitan Mus, New York. *Exhib:* Anti-Illusion, Procedures & Materials Show, Whitney Mus, 69, David Whitney Gallery, 70 & 71, John Meyers Gallery, 72 & 73 & Willard Gallery, 75, 76, 77 & 78, New York; Irving Blum Gallery, Los Angeles, 72; Daniel Wienburg Gallery, 73, 75, 77, 79 & 81; Margo Leavin Gallery, Los Angeles, Calif, 81; Development in Recent Sculpture, Whitney Mus Am Art, 81 & Enclosing the Void, 88; Blumhelmar Gallery, 86 & 88. *Awards:* Theodor Award, Guggenheim Mus, 77; Brandis Award for Visual Arts, 87. *Bibliog:* Barbara Rose (auth), Where we are & what we like, New York Mag, 4/72 & 4/75; John Russell (auth), current shows in New York Times, 3/75; J Tannenbaum (auth), rev in Arts Mag, 6/75. *Media:* Fiberglas, Wood. *Publ:* Contribr, Art Now: New York, 72. *Mailing Add:* 5 Doyers New York NY 10013

DUFFY, BETTY MINOR
DEALER
Pos: Dir, Bethesda Art Gallery. *Mem:* Int Fine Print Dealers Asn. *Specialty:* American fine prints from the first half of the 20th century. *Publ:* Howard Cook (auth, catalog), Raisonne; J Jay McVicker (auth, catalog), Graphic Works. *Mailing Add:* PO Box 722 Glen Echo MD 20812

DUFFY, MICHAEL JOHN
PAINTER, PRINTMAKER
b Chicago, Ill, Dec 29, 45. *Study:* Colo Col, Colorado Springs, BA, 72. *Work:* Denver Art Mus; Mesa Col, Grand Junction; Colo Col, Colorado Springs; Columbia Mus Art, SC. *Exhib:* Solo exhibs, Colo Col Packard Gallery, Colorado Springs, 83, Glastonbury Gallery, San Francisco, 85 & Columbia Mus Art, SC, 90; Reflections of Vietnam, Washington Proj Arts, Washington, DC, 83; 46th Ann, Soc Four Arts, Palm Beach, Fla, 84; Chicago Print Show, Northwestern Univ, Evanston, Ill, 85; Small Paintings & Sculpture, Univ Denver, 87; and others. *Awards:* Atwater Kent Award, 46th Ann Soc Four Arts, 84; Best of Show, Colorado Springs Fine Art Ctr, 85. *Bibliog:* Max Price (auth), Topping our show, Denver Post, 86; Irene Clurman (auth), Intensity intact, Rocky Mountaint News, 5/30/86; New prints, Print Collectors Newsletter, 7/87. *Mem:* Chicago Art Inst; Chicago Art Coalition. *Media:* Oil. *Mailing Add:* 193 Country Commons Cary IL 60013

DUFOUR, PAUL ARTHUR
PAINTER, DESIGNER
b Manchester, NH, Aug 31, 22. *Study:* Univ NH, BA, 50; Yale Univ, BFA, 52; also with Takahiko Fujita & Ikuo Hirayama, Japan, 64. *Work:* Masur Mus Art, Monroe, La; Springfield Art Mus, Mo; La State Collection, Baton Rouge; La Bicentennial Collection; Centraplex Munic Collection, Baton Rouge. *Comn:* Stained glass sculpture & mosaic, St Joseph Prep Sch, Baton Rouge, La, 68; stained glass windows, Holy Ghost Church, Hammond, La, 74; stained glass windows & bronze sculpture, Our Lady of Mercy, Baton Rouge, 74; stained glass, St Patrick Church, Lake Providence, La; glass windows & bronze doors, St Mary of Pines, Shreveport, La, 79; and many others. *Exhib:* Stained Glass Invitational, Mus Fine Arts, Jacksonville, Fla, 79; 20 Year Retrospective, La State Univ Art Gallery, 79; Glaskunst, Int Expo of Glass, Kassel, Ger, 81; Vicointer, Glass Invitational Expo, Valencia, Spain, 83; A Rebirth of A Medium, Nat Glass Invitational, Univ Tex, San Antonio, 83; 21st through 34th Ann State Exhib Prof Artists, 66-79; Contemporary Glass, Corning Mus, 79 & 80; Southeast Craft, Lemoyne Art Found, 80; Am Glass Invitational, Kansas City, Mo, 80; Int Glass Art Exposition, Kassel, Germany, 80; and many others. *Pos:* Supvr educ, Currier Gallery Art, Manchester, NH, 52-55; artist in residence, Viterbo Col, 68. *Teaching:* Asst prof painting, St John's Univ, 55-58; vis prof design, Sienna Heights Col, 57; prof design & stained glass, La State Univ, Baton Rouge, 58- *Awards:* Top Award, La Int Watercolor Exhib, 69; First Purchase Award, 4th Int Watercolor, 72; Hon Mention, Vicointer, Valencia, Spain, 83. *Bibliog:* Corning Mus Glass Microfiche Prog, 78; New Glass Rev I, Corning Mus Glass, 80; Jensen & Conway (auths), Ornamentalism, Potter, 82. *Mem:* Am Glass Guild; Col Art Asn; Am Craft Coun; La Watercolor Soc. *Media:* Multimedia. *Dealer:* Baton Rouge Gallery 205 N Fourth St Baton Rouge LA 70801; Matrix Gallery 912 W 12th St Austin TX 78713. *Mailing Add:* 20535 Narrow Rd Covington LA 70433

DUFRESNE, ISABELLE COLLIN See Ultra Violet,

DUGAN, KAREN VERNON See Vernon

DUGMORE, EDWARD
PAINTER
b Hartford, Conn, Feb 20, 15. *Study:* Hartford Art Sch, scholarship, 4 years; Calif Sch Fine Arts; Univ Guadalajara, Mex, MA. *Work:* Albright-Knox Art Gallery, Buffalo; Ciba-Geigy Corp, Ardsley, NY; Walker Art Inst, Minneapolis; Des Moines Art Ctr, Iowa; Hirshhorn Mus, Washington, DC. *Exhib:* Solomon R Guggenheim Mus, New York, 61; San Francisco Mus Art, Calif, 63; Albright-Knox Permanent Collection Show, 72; A Period of Exploration, San Francisco 1945-50, Oakland Mus, 73; one-man shows, Stable Gallery, 53, 54 & 56, Howard Wise Gallery, 61, 62 & 63, Green Mountain Gallery, 71 & 73, Carlson Gallery, San Francisco, 90 & Manny Silverman Gallery, Los Angeles, 91; Painting & Sculpture in Calif, The Modern Era, San Francisco Mus Mod Art, 76; Nat Collection of Fine Arts, Smithsonian Inst, 77; plus others. *Teaching:* Vis artist, Mont Inst, Great Falls, 65, Univ Minn, Minneapolis, spring 70 & Des Moines Art Ctr & Drake Univ, 72; instr painting, Pratt Inst, Brooklyn, NY, 64-72 & Md Inst Col Art, Baltimore, Md, 73-82. *Awards:* Nat Endowment Arts Fel, 76-77 & 85-86; Award, Am Acad Inst Arts & Letters, 80; Ingram Merrill Found Award, 92; and others. *Bibliog:* Harold Rosenberg (auth), Art on the Edge, Macmillan, 75; Mary Fuller McChesney (auth), A Period of Exploration San Francisco 1945-1950; Irving Sandler (auth), Painters and Sculptors of the Fifties, Harper & Row, 78; plus others. *Media:* Oil. *Dealer:* Manny Silverman Gallery 800 N La Cienaga Blvd Los Angeles CA 90069. *Mailing Add:* 118 W 27th St New York NY 10001

DUHME, H RICHARD, JR
SCULPTOR, EDUCATOR
b St Louis, Mo, May 31, 14. *Study:* Pa Acad Fine Arts, 32-38; Univ Pa, 34; Barnes Found, Marion, Pa, 40-41; Am Sch Classical Studies, Athens, Greece, summer 51; Wash Univ, BFA, 53. *Work:* Steinberg Gallery, Wash Univ, St Louis, Mo; Smith-Wilkes Libr, Chautaugua, NY. *Comn:* Chautaqua New York Centennial Medallions (silver & bronze), 74; Airmen (bronze sculpture), US Air Force Mus, Dayton, Ohio, 80; St John Baptist De La Salle (cold cast bronze), Christian Brothers, St Louis, 80; Lion Cub Fountain, Mycenae, Greece; The Bears (monumental bronzwe group), Washington Univ, St Louis, Mo, 91; many other portrait busts and medals. *Exhib:* Pa Acad Fine Arts Ann, Philadelphia, 38-41 & 50; Metrop Mus Art Summer Sculpture Show, New York,42; St Louis City Art Mus Group Show, 49-50 & 52; Cincinnati Art Mus, Ohio, 61; Expos Int Medaile Contemporaine, Nat Mus, Athens, Greece, 66. *Teaching:* Prof sculpture, Wash Univ, 47-82, prof emer, 82-; head dept sculpture, Chautauqua Inst Summer Schs, 53-85; head dept sculpture, Syracuse Univ Chautauqua Ctr, 53-69. *Awards:* Cresson Foreign Travel Award, 35, Lewis S Ware Foreign Fel, 38 & May Audubon Post Prize Fel, 41, Pa Acad Fine Arts; First Hon Mention, Prix de Rome, Am Acad Rome, 39. *Mem:* Fel Nat Sculpture Soc; Allied Artists Am. *Media:* Bronze, Stone. *Mailing Add:* 8 Edgewood Rd St Louis MO 63124

DUIS, RITA
PAINTER
b New York, NY. *Study:* Nat Acad Design; Art Students League; Banff Sch Fine Arts, Univ Alta; China Inst; also with Rex Brandt, Edgar Whitney, George Post & Robert Wood. *Exhib:* Smithsonian Inst, Washington, DC, 63; Watercolor USA, Springfield, Ill, 70; Am Watercolor Soc, 71, 73, 76, 78 & 81; Hammond Mus, NY, 74; Jersey City Mus, NJ, 75; American Fortnight, Hong Kong, 75; Tweed Mus, Duluth, Minn, 77-78; Am Cult Ctr, Jerusalem, Israel, 81; Am Cult Ctr, Cairo & Alexandria, Egypt, 81; Am Cult Ctr, Cairo & Alexandria, Egypt, 81; and many others. *Awards:* Gold Medal, Catherine Lorillard Wolfe Art Club, 69; Bronz Medal, Nat Arts Club, 71; First Prize, Am Artists Prof League, 81; Merit Award, Salmagundi, 92; and many others. *Mem:* Salmagundi Club; Nat Arts Club; Am Watercolor Soc; Nat Asn Women Artists; Am Artists Prof League. *Media:* Watercolor, Oil. *Mailing Add:* The Belmont Apt 610 3170 N Sheridan Rd Chicago IL 60657

DU JARDIN, GUSSIE
PAINTER, PRINTMAKER
b San Francisco, Calif, Feb 19, 18. *Study:* Univ Colo, BA; Univ Iowa, MA. *Work:* NMex Mus Art, Santa Fe; NMex Highlands Univ; Univ Iowa; Roswell Mus, NMex; Univ Colo Mus; Mus NMex, Albuquerque. *Exhib:* Butler Inst Am Art 26th Ann, 61; NMex Biennial, 71, 73 & 75; Mus NMex Southwest Biennial Exhib, 72, 74 & 76, Invitational, 78; one-woman exhibs, Roswell Mus, 78 & 92, Gov Gallery, NMex State Capitol, Santa Fe, NMex, 79, Western State Col, Gunnison Colo, 91. *Pos:* Artist-in-Residence Prog, Roswell Mus, 77- *Awards:* First Purchase Award, Mus NMex, 61. *Media:* Acrylic, Oil. *Mailing Add:* 1403 W Berrendo Rd Roswell NM 88201

DUKE, LEILANI LATTIN
ADMINISTRATOR
b Aug 27, 43. *Study:* Denison Univ, BA, 65; Syracuse Univ, MA, 66; Arts Admin Inst, Harvard Univ, 78. *Pos:* Res asst, Onondoga City, Syracuse, NY, 66-69; staff asst, US Senate Labor & Public Welfare Comt, Washington, DC, 68-69; fed aid coordr, Senator Jacob Javits, US Senate, Washington, DC, 69-71; exec secy, Fed Coun Arts & Humanities Nat Fdn on Arts & Humanities, 71-78; coordr, Design Educ Prog, Nat Endowment Arts, 71-76, Spec Constituencies Prog, 76-78; exec dir, Calif Confederation Arts, 79-81; prog develop officer, J Paul Getty Trust, 81-; dir, Getty Ctr Educ Arts, 83- *Mailing Add:* 401 Wilshire Blvd Santa Monica CA 90401-1455

DUKES, CAROLINE
PAINTER, PRINTMAKER
b Ujpest, Hungary; Can citizen. *Study:* Sigiesmund de Strobl Studio, Hungary; Acad Fine Arts, Budapest; Sch Art, Univ Man, Winnipeg, dipl, 72, with Ivan Eyre. *Work:* Winnipeg Art Gallery; NDak Mus Art; Yad Vashem Art Mus, Jerusalem, Israel; Can Coun Art Bank, Ottawa; Montreal Mus Fine Art. *Comn:* Mosaic: A Journal for the Comparative Study of Literature and Ideas (cover & 11 reproductions), 77; No Longer Two People (cover), Turnstone Press, 79; Print edition, Winnipeg Art Gallery, Man, 81 & 88; Prairie Fire (Can mag), 92. *Exhib:* Yad Vashem Art Mus, Jerusalem, Israel, 87; Contemp Art in Manitoba, Winnipeg Art Gallery, Art Gallery NS, Halifax, Nickle Art Mus, Alberta, MacDonald Stewart Art Ctr, Guelph, Ont, 87-89; All Over the Map: Women & Place, Plains Mus, Moorehead, Minn, 91; Introductions: The Artists Who Live Among Us, NDak Mus Art, 91; solo exhibs, Building Series, Melnychenko Gallery, Winnipeg, At the Focus of Forces, Winnipeg Art Gallery, 91 & Remember, Relate, Retell, Plug in Gallery, Winnipeg, Can, 92. *Pos:* Juror (art). *Teaching:* Mentor, Manitoba Artist Women's Art, currently. *Awards:* Outstanding Painting Award, Winnipeg Art Gallery, Man Soc Artist, 76; B Grant, Canada Coun, 90; Winnipeg Arts Adv Coun Grant, 90. *Bibliog:* Doug Whiteway (auth), Message conveyed in Duke's art, Winnipeg Free Press, 3/85; Tom Lovatt (auth), The Trellis of Memory, Recent Drawings by Caroline Dukes, Border Crossings, winter 90-91; Randal McIlroy (auth), Dukes' new WAG exhibit explores human spirit in the Holy Land, 1/91, New technique enhances powerful Dukes paintings, 3/91 & Exhibit delivers feminist impact, 4/91, Winnipeg Free Press. *Mem:* Can Artist Representation; Plug In Inc; Manitoba Printmaking Asn; Ace Art; Main/Access. *Media:* Acrylic, Oil; Charcoal, Linocut. *Publ:* Gallerie, Women's Art, 12/89. *Dealer:* Brian Melnychenko Gallery 250 McDermot Avenue Winnipeg Canada R3B 0S5. *Mailing Add:* 736 Waverley St Winnipeg MB R3M 3L7 Canada

DUMAIS-BERUBE, YVETTE
PAINTER
b St Joseph de Lepage, Que, Can, July 18, 30. *Study:* Teachers Training Col, 49; scholarship cert(interior design), 68. *Work:* Govt of Can, Hon Benoit Bouchard, Ottawa; Hydro-Quebec, Denis St-Pierre, Montreal, Que; Govt of Que, Lavoie-Roux; Quebecor, Pierre Péladeau, Montreal, Que. *Exhib:* Nat Expos Ctr, Jonquiére, Que, 80; Immensité, Fjord Mus, Ville de la Bai, Can, 86; Aux Racines du Temps, Shawinigan Cult Ctr, Royal Ont Mus, Can, 87; Isis-déesse de la Vérité, Louis-Hémon Mus, Péribonka, Que, 89; Morin-Miller Galleries, New York, 88. *Awards:* Gold Medal, Collective & Trophy of Excellence, Nat Circle of Artists & Painters, 86; Bourse for solo exhib, Minister of Culture, 87. *Bibliog:* Esther Girard (auth), Yvette Damais-Bérubé, Univ Que, 81; Guy Fournier (auth), Yvette Dumais-Bérubé se distingue Progréis-Dimanche, 86; Marjo Moisan (auth), Analyse d'une Huile sur Papyrus, Laval Univ, 90. *Mem:* Asn of Well Known Artists of Visual Arts; Counc Que Painters; Regional Culture Coun; Int Asn Plastic Arts. *Publ:* Auth, Guy-Marc Fournier, Mieux Connaitre, Mieux Connaitre Inc, 86; auth & ed, Jean-Claude Larouche, Yvette Dumais-Bérubé Exprime son Art sur Papyrus, Editions JCL, 90. *Dealer:* Morin-Miller Galleries 233 Greenwood Ave Trappe PA 19426-2707. *Mailing Add:* 112 Ave Gagne Roberval PQ G8H 1E5 Canada

DUMAS, ANTOINE
PAINTER, EDUCATOR
b Quebec City, Que, Can, Dec 8, 32. *Study:* Col des Jesuites, Quebec City, Baccalaureate Rhetorique, 53; Ecole des Beaux-Arts, Quebec City, dipl, 58; Acad Art Col, San Francisco, 69-70; Ecole des Arts Visuels, Univ Laval, Titular, 81. *Work:* Imperial Oil Art Collection, Toronto, Ont; CIL Art Collection, Rothman Permanent Collection, Montreal; Mus du Sem, Mus du Que, Quebec City; Dupont Can, Toronto; Corp City of Toronto; Collection Alcan, Montreal. *Comn:* Stained glass mural, Dorval Airport, Montreal, 60; painted mural, RSW & Assoc Consult Engineers, Montreal, 75; four stamps, Can Post, Ottawa, 76, 78 & 79; tapestry, Aetna Can Bldg, Montreal, 83. *Exhib:* Forum 76, Montreal Mus Fine Arts; Traveling Exhib, Nancy Poole's Studio, Toronto, 80, Rodman Hall, St Catharines, 80, Laurentian Univ Mus, Sudbury, 80, & Univ Western Ont, 80; Livres d'Artistes, Bibliot Nat du Que, Montreal, 82; and others. *Teaching:* Prof graphic design, Ecole des Beaux-Arts, Quebec City, 62-65; dir, prog commun arts, Ecole des Arts Visuels, Univ Laval, 70-73, prof illus design, 70- *Awards:* Lt Gov's Silver Medal, Ecole des Beaux-Arts, Que State Dept, 58. *Bibliog:* Germain Lefebvre (auth), catalog, Ed Chema, 80; Michele Marchand (auth), Painters Series (film), Can Broadcasting Corp TV, 81; Roland Bourneuf (auth), Antoine Dumas, Ed Int Stanke, 83. *Mem:* Hon mem Soc Graphistes du Que; Royal Can Acad Art; Hon mem, Quebec Garrison Club. *Media:* Oil, Acrylics. *Publ:* Auth, A l'Enseigne d'Antan, Ed Pelican, 70. *Dealer:* Galerie Bernard Desroches 1444 Sherbrooke W Montreal PQ Canada H3G 1K4; Nancy Poole's Studio 16 Hazelton Toronto On M5R 2E2 Canada. *Mailing Add:* 1100 Marguerite Bourgeoys Sillery PQ G1S 3X9 Canada

DUNBAR, JILL H
CRITIC, WRITER
b New Haven, Conn, Feb 10, 49. *Pos:* Mem staff, Betty Parsons Gallery, New York, 75-76 & Truman Drawing Inc, 76-78; art critic, The Villager, Byron Publ, 76-; contrib ed, 57th St Rev, 76-77 & Art World, 76-78; contribr, Womanart Mag & Phoenix, 77-; contribr, Phoenix, 77- *Mailing Add:* 250 W 12th St New York NY 10014

DUNBAR, MICHAEL AUSTIN
SCULPTOR, ADMINISTRATOR
b Santa Paula, Calif, Sept 21, 47. *Study:* Ill State Univ, Normal, BS, 71, MS, 78; Sangamon State Univ, Springfield, MA, 74. *Work:* Ill State Mus; Ill Bell Collection, Chicago; Eastern Ill Univ, Charleston; Southern Ill Univ, Carbondale; Ill State Univ, Normal; and others. *Comn:* Western Ill Univ, Macomb; Eastern Ill Univ, Charleston; Gov Art Award Comn & Ill Arts Coun, Chicago, 79; Sedquicentennial Comn, City of Springfield, Mich. *Exhib:* Mayor Byrne's Mile of Sculpture, Ill, 79; solo exhib, Zaks Gallery, Chicago, 86; New Traditions in Sculpture, 85 & Il Bronzetto, Hyde Park Art Ctr, Chicago; Sculpture Tour, Univ Tenn, Knoxville, 85-86; Chicago Sculpture, Rockford Col, Ill, 85; New Traditions in Sculpture, Ill Art Coun, Chicago; Sculpture in the Landscape, Paine Art Ctr, Oshkosh, Wisc. *Pos:* Exec dir, Galesburg Arts Coun, 75-76. *Teaching:* Drawing instr, Lincoln Land Community Col, 78 & 86. *Bibliog:* Alumni news, Ill State Univ, 9/91. *Mem:* Chicago Sculpture Soc; Asn Corp Art Curs. *Media:* Steel, Bronze. *Dealer:* Struve Gallery 309 W Superior St Chicago IL 60610. *Mailing Add:* 912 S Park Springfield IL 62704-2341

DUNCAN, HARRY ALVIN
PRINTER, DESIGNER
b Keokuk, Iowa, Apr 19, 16. *Study:* Grinnell Col, BA, 38, Hon DLitt, 73; Hawthorn House, apprenticeship, 41. *Work:* Amherst Col Libr, Mass; Sheldon Mem Art Gallery, Lincoln, Nebr; Pierpont Morgan Libr, New York; Houghton Libr, Cambridge, Mass; Univ Nebr, Omaha Special Collection. *Comn:* I Rise in Flames, collab with Paul Wightman Williams New Directions, Norfolk, Conn, 51, Terence Illustrated, Chapin Libr, Williamstown, Mass, 55 & Dickens in Italy, Pierpont Morgan Libr, New York, 56; Journey to a Known Place, comn by J Laughlin, Norfolk, Conn, 61; The Poets Go Along, comn by Charles Antin, New York, 65. *Exhib:* Fifty Books of the Year, Am Inst Graphic Arts, New York; Cummington Press, Book Club Calif, San Francisco, 64 & Grolier Club, New York, 76; one-man show, Grinnell Col, Iowa, 73; Abattoir Ed/Cummington Press, Sheldon Mem Art Gallery, Lincoln, Nebr, 79; Ctr Bk Arts, New York, 89; Pub Libr, New York, 90. *Pos:* Founder, dir & pres, Cummington Press, Omaha, 42-; founder, dir & ed, Abattoir Ed, Omaha, 72- *Teaching:* Prof typography, Univ Iowa, Iowa City, 56-72; prof fine art arts press, Univ Nebr, Omaha, 72-86. *Awards:* Outstanding Research & Creative Activity, Univ Neb, 81. *Bibliog:* Mary L Richmond (auth), The Cummington Press, Books at Iowa, 69; K K Merker & Kay Amert (auth), Harry Duncan, Maker of Books, Fine Print, 78; Joseph Blumenthal (auth), The Printed Book in America, 143-144, David R Godine, 77. *Publ:* Auth, The Cummington Press, New Colophon, 51; The Technology of Hand Printing, Abattoir, 80; contribr, Collegiate Book Arts Presses, Fine Print, 82; auth, Doors of Perception, Essays in Book Typography, Austin, 83. *Mailing Add:* 1803 S 58th St Omaha NE 68106

DUNCAN, RICHARD (HURLEY)
DRAFTSMAN, PRINTMAKER
b Daytona Beach, Fla, Feb 11, 44. *Study:* Southern Ill Univ, BA, 66, MFA, 73. *Work:* Aukland City Art Gallery, NZ; Springfield Civic Collection, Ill; Southeast Ctr Contemp Art, Winston-Salem, NC; Printclub Albany, Cooperstown Art Asn, NY; Dulin Gallery, Knoxville, Tenn; Barnett Bank and Sunbank, Fl. *Comn:* Two lithographs, Verein Originalgraphik, Switz, 74. *Exhib:* 35 Artists of the Southeast, High Mus & travelling, 76-78; Worldprint 77, San Francisco Mus Mod Art, 77; one-person exhibs, Hunter Mus, 77 & Ritter Art Gallery, Fla Atlantic Univ, Boca Raton, 85; 25th Nat Exhib Prints, Nat Collection Fine Arts & Libr Cong, 77-78; 100 Worldprints, Smithsonian Travelling Exhib, 77-79; 40 Artists of the South, Russia-US Exchange, 80-82; Nat Painting & Drawing Exhib, Soc Four Arts, Palm Beach, Fla, 81 & 83; Honolulu Nat Print Exhib, Hawaii, 82; 62nd Nat Print Exhib, Soc Am Graphic Artists, New York, 86-87. *Teaching:* Instr printmaking, Univ South, 73-78; assoc prof printmaking & drawing, Fla Int Univ, 78- *Awards:* Ford Found Grants, 74 & 77; Merit Award, 18th Nat Printmaking & Drawing Exhib, 81; Nat Endowment Arts Grant, 85; S Fla Cult Consortium Grant, 85. *Bibliog:* Coleman, Richardson & Smith (auths), Basic Design: Systems, Elements, Applications, Prentice-Hall, 83. *Mem:* Col Art Asn Am; Worldprint Soc; Southeast Print Coun. *Media:* Etching, Pastels. *Mailing Add:* 8700 SW 149th Terr Miami FL 33176

DUNCAN, RUTH
PAINTER
b Greeley, Colo, Feb 19, 08. *Study:* Stephens Col, AA; Univ Okla, BFA; and with Harold A Roney, Simon G Michael & Warren Hunter. *Work:* Stephens Col, Columbia, Mo; San Antonio Col Libr, Tex; Royal Bldg, Dallas; Bexar Co Court House, San Antonio; NCNB Bank, San Antonio; and others. *Comn:* Many. *Exhib:* 50 one-man shows & many group shows; Smithsonian Institution, Nat Galleries; Witte Mem Mus, San Antonio; Haley Mem Mus, Midland, Tex; Nat Western Invitational; and others. *Awards:* Order of the Rose Award for Achievement & Success in Chosen Field with nat & int acclaim, Delta Gamma Sorority, 73; Artist of the Year, San Antonio Express News, 73; Medal of Honor, Coppini Acad Fine Arts, 79. *Mem:* Fel Am Artists Prof League; life mem River Art Group, San Antonio; Soc Western Artists, San Francisco. *Media:* Oil, Watercolor. *Publ:* PEO Record & Delta Gamma Anchora; San Antonio Light; San Antonio Express News. *Mailing Add:* 4040 High Ridge Circle San Antonio TX 78229

DUNHAM-GRIGGS, MARGARET
PAINTER, SCULPTOR
b Atlanta, Ga, May 30, 22. *Study:* Finch Col, New York, with Leon Kroll, 42; Art Students League, with Yasuo Kuniyoshi, 44; Columbia Univ, with John Heliker, 57. *Work:* Hudson River Mus, Yonkers, NY. *Comn:* Mural, comn by L Abernathy, Mt Kisco, NY, 57. *Exhib:* Wadsworth Atheneum Ann, Hartford, Conn, 68; Ann Invitational, Finch Mus, New York, 69; Gallery at Hastings-on-Hudson, NY, 82 & 85; solo exhibs, Hudson River Mus, Yonkers, NY, 67-86, Maine Art Gallery, Wiscasset, Maine, 75 & Maine Coast Artists, Rockport, 85; Lever House, New York, 87; and others. *Awards:* First Prize Painting, 5th Ann Adirondack Exhib, W Adams Sch Art, 58, Westchester Art Soc Nat Exhib, 68 & Nat Exhib, White Plains, Whitney Mus, 71. *Bibliog:* Suzanne Kiplinger (auth), Margaret Dunham, Village Voice, 58; Eve Medoff (auth), River scene, Herald Statesman, 67; K Beale (auth), On-the-line, Gannett Papers, 85. *Mem:* Maine Art Asn; Hudson River Contemp Artists; Union Maine Visual Artists. *Media:* All. *Dealer:* Stark Gallery 594 Broadway New York NY 10012. *Mailing Add:* RFD 2 - Box 2230 Brunswick ME 04011

DUNIGAN, BREON NINA
SCULPTOR
b New York, NY, Apr 13, 61. *Study:* Atlanta Col Art; Mass Col Art, BFA, 84; Rutgers Univ, NJ, MFA, 86, with W Gary Kuehn. *Exhib:* Provincetown Group Gallery, 90, 91 & 92; Better Homes & Monuments Show, Brooklyn, NY, 91; Berta Walker Gallery, Provincetown, Mass, 92. *Pos:* Freelance sculptor; carpentry. *Awards:* Nat Endowment Arts Grant, 90; Pollock-Krasner Grant, 91. *Mem:* Provincetown Art Assoc. *Media:* Miscellaneous. *Dealer:* Provincetown Group Gallery 288 Bradford St Provincetown MA 02657; PO Box 2360. *Mailing Add:* 429 S 5th St New York NY 10009

DUNITZ, JAY
PHOTOGRAPHER
b Reading, Pa, Feb 4, 56. *Study:* Kansas City Art Inst, 74; San Francisco Art Inst, BFA, 78. *Work:* Mus Mod Art, Int Ctr Photog, New York; Nat Mus Am Art, Corcoran Gallery Art, Washington, DC; Cornell Univ Art Mus; Indianapolis Mus Art, Ind; Cincinnati Art Mus, Ohio; Santa Barbara Mus Art, Calif; Newport Harbor Art Mus, Newport Beach, Calif. *Exhib:* New Acquisitions in Graphic Arts, Nat Mus Am Art, Washington, DC, 88; Present Tense, Los Angeles Munic Art Gallery, 88; solo exhibs, Santa Monica Col Photog Gallery, Calif, 88 & Fitchburg Art Mus, Fitchburg, Mass, 90; Photographs from EF Hutton Collection, Contemp Art, New York, 88; Photographs from the Collection, Corcoran Gallery Art, Washington, DC, 89; Ansel Adams Gallery, Yosemite Nat Park, Calif, 92. *Teaching:* Lectr, Santa Monica Col, Calif, Calif State, Long Beach, Rochester Inst Technol, Nat Aeronautics & Space Admin. *Bibliog:* Kathryn Livingston (auth), Making found objects, Am Photog, 9/84; Dinah Berland (auth), Dunitz zaps steel for light series, Los Angeles Times, 11/29/85; Larry Stein (rev), Arts LA, KCRW-FM, Nat Pub Radio, Santa Monica, 10/31/88. *Publ:* Auth, Pacific Light, Light Press, Inc, 89; illusr, A current affair, Confetti, 90. *Dealer:* Lumina 251 W 19th St 7-B New York NY 10011; Susan Spiritus Gallery 3333 Bear St Costa Mesa CA 92626. *Mailing Add:* 20110 Rockportway Malibu CA 90265

DUNKELMAN, LORETTA
PAINTER
b Paterson, NJ, June 29, 37. *Study:* Douglass Col, BA, 58; Accad Belle Arti, Florence, Italy, 60-61; Hunter Col, MA, 66. *Work:* Chase Manhattan Bank; Bellevue Med Ctr, New York; Dana Art Ctr, Colgate Univ; Univ Cincinnati; Univ Kans Art Mus, Lawrence. *Exhib:* Whitney Biennial Contemp Art, 73 & Am Drawings 1963-73, Whitney Mus Am Art, New York; AIR Gallery, New York 73, 74, 78, 81, 83 & 87; Waves: An Artist Selects, Cranbrook Acad Art, Bloomfield Hills, Mich, 74; Cornell Artists Past & Present, Johnson Mus, 77; New York Now, Phoenix Art Mus, 79; Structure, Narrative, Decoration, McIntosh-Drysdale Gallery, Washington, DC, 80; Konsthall, Lund, Sweden, 81; Let's Play House, Bernice Steinbaum Gallery, New York, 86; Michael Walls Gallery, New York, 89; and others. *Teaching:* Vis artist, Univ Cincinnati, 74; asst prof art, Univ RI, 74-75; asst prof art, Cornell Univ, 77-80; vis artist, Ohio State Univ, 84; asst prof painting, Virginia Commonwealth Univ, 86-88; vis artist, Sch Art Inst Chicago, 90. *Awards:* Am Asn Univ Women Fel, 76-77; Adolph & Esther Gottlieb Found Individual Grant, 91; NY Found for the Arts, Artist's Fel, 91. *Bibliog:* Ellen Lubell (auth), article, Arts Mag, 5/74; Peter Frank (auth), Gifts of the imagi, Village Voice, 1/8/79; Tiffany Bell (auth), article, Arts Mag, 2/79; Robert Merritt (auth), Romantic Views: Light and dark, Richmond Times Dispatch, 10/3/87. *Media:* Oil, All Media. *Mailing Add:* 151 Canal St New York NY 10002

DUNKELMAN, MARTHA LEVINE
HISTORIAN, EDUCATOR
b Cincinnati, Ohio, May 17, 47. *Study:* Wellesley Col, BA, 69; NY Univ, Inst Fine Arts, with Irving Lavin, MA, 71, with H W Janson, PhD, 76. *Pos:* Chair, Col Bd Advan Placement Art His Develop Comt, 90-93. *Teaching:* Instr art hist, Rider Col, Trenton, NJ, 75-76; asst prof, Wright State Univ, Dayton, Ohio, 76-80, assoc prof, 81-84; asst prof, SUNY at Buffalo, NY, 86, adj assoc prof, 86- *Awards:* Alumni Asn Award for Teaching Excellence, Wright State Univ, Dayton, Ohio, 79. *Mem:* Col Art Asn; Renaissance Soc Am; Ital Art Soc. *Res:* Italian fifteenth century painting and sculpture. *Publ:* Auth, Michelangelo's Earliest Drawing Style, Drawing, 79; Donatello's influence on Mantegna's early narrative scenes, Art Bulletin, 80; coauth, Italian Renaissance Sculpture in the Time of Donatello, Detroit Inst Arts, 85; auth, Central Italian Painting 1400-1465, G K Hall, 86; A New Look at Donatello's St Peter's Tabernacle, Gazette des Beaux Arts, 91. *Mailing Add:* Dept Art Hist SUNY Buffalo NY 14260

DUNKLE, JOAN OSBORN
PAINTER, PRINTMAKER
b Boston, Mass. *Study:* Bradford Col, 51-52; Sch Practical Art, 52-53; also spec pvt study, 80-91. *Work:* First Nat Bank Boston; DataQuest Inc, Menlo, Calif; Prime Computer Corp, Natick, Mass; Kidder Peabody & Co, Boston; Shawmut Bank Boston. *Comn:* Lebonan War Office (painting), Town of Lebonan, Conn, 60; Centenial Hall (painting), Town of North Hampton, NH, 92. *Exhib:* Am Watercolor Soc, New York, 80-91; Midwest Watercolor Exhib, 83; Laura Knott Gallery, Bradford Col, Mass, 87; New England Watercolor Soc Nat Open Show, Boston, 88, 90 & 92; Rocky Mountain Nat Watermedia Exhib, Golden, Colo, 90; and others. *Pos:* Co-owner, head nat workshops, Needham Art Ctr, Mass, 75-84; bd dir, New England Watercolor Soc, 82-92; principle dir & organizer, Art East Inc/Art East Teaching Guild & Gallery, Hampton, NH, 89-92; bd dirs, Oqunquit Art Asn, 92. *Teaching:* Instr watermedia, Needham Art Ctr, 75-84; vis instr watermedia, pvt schs, art asns, 75-92; instr watermedia, Art East Inc/Art East Teaching Guild & Gallery, 89-92. *Awards:* Nels Brosted Mem Award, Midwest Watercolor Soc, 83; Silver Medal, New Eng Watercolor Sco, 85; Derry Award, Attleboro Mus, 88. *Bibliog:* Judith Campbell-Reed (auth), Basic Watercolor Painting, North Light Publ, 82; Ann Schector (auth), Imaginative Works by Two Innovators, Lowell, 89; Jack Savage (auth), A gallery on the Move, NH Seacoast Sunday, 90. *Mem:* Oqunguit Art Asn; NH Art Asn; New Eng Watercolor Soc (bd dir); Copley Soc Boston; Monotype Guild New Eng; Providence Art Club. *Media:* Watermedia. *Publ:* Contribr, Basic Watercolor Painting, North Light Publ, 82. *Dealer:* Art III 44 West Brook St Manchester NH 03101. *Mailing Add:* Seven Pond Path North Hampton NH 03862

DUNLAP, LOREN EDWARD
PAINTER, INSTRUCTOR
b Anderson, Ind, Feb 2, 32. *Study:* Herron Art Sch, BFA; Oqunquit Sch of Painting & Sculpture; Tulane Univ, MFA. *Work:* Addison Gallery Am Art, Andover, Mass; Santa Barbara Mus, Calif; Univ Calif Collection; New York Times Bk Collection, Notre Dame Univ; Fine Arts Ctr, Anderson, Ind. *Comn:* Mural, comn by Jane Blaffer Owen, Blaffer Trust, New Harmony, Ind, 65; three panel paintings, comn by Jane Arneberg, New York, 70; painting, Pfizer Chemical Co, New York, 74; mural, comn by Kenneth Owen, New Harmony, Ind, 90; mural, comn by Joan Quillin, Palm Beach, Fla, 92. *Exhib:* One-man shows, Purdue Univ, West Lafayette, Ind, 59 & Santa Barbara Mus Art, Calif, 63; Drawing Ann, Norfolk Mus, Va, 60; Albright-Knox Art Gallery, Buffalo, NY, 60; Boston Mus Contemp Arts, Mass, 60; Univ Calif Fac Show, 63; 10 Year Retrospective, Columbia Club, Indianapolis, Ind, 85; and others. *Teaching:* Instr studio & art hist, Herron Sch, Indianapolis, 58-62; lectr studio & art hist, Univ Calif, Santa Barbara, 63-65. *Awards:* Louis Comfort Tiffany Grant, 55 & 65. *Media:* Oil. *Publ:* Auth, Traditions of the East, Revolutions of the West, Herron J, 60. *Mailing Add:* Box 332 Sagg Rd Sagaponack NY 11962

DUNN, CAL
PAINTER, FILMMAKER
b Georgetown, Ohio, Aug 31, 15. *Study:* Cincinnati Art Acad, 27; Cent Acad Commercial Art, 32-34. *Work:* NMex Mus Fine Art, Santa Fe; Albuquerque Mus Art; El Paso Mus Art; US Dept Interior; Barry Goldwater Collection. *Exhib:* Am Watercolor Soc Exhibs, New York, 54-56 & 58-59; Chicago & Vicinity Exhib, Art Inst Chicago, 56-58; 100 American Watercolorists, Royal Gallery, London, 63; Santa Fe Festival Arts, NMex, 80-81; traveling shows to most major US cities, Europe, the Middle East, Asia & Latin America. *Pos:* Art dir, Sarra Inc, 44-47; chief exec officer, Cal Dunn Studios, Chicago, 47-; illusr watercolor story assignments, Ford Times--Lincoln Mercury Times, Ford Motor Co, 50-62. *Awards:* Emmy Award for TV art direction; over 125 art awards and honors; and over sixty major film awards. *Mem:* Am Watercolor Soc; hon mem Artist Guild Chicago (pres, 55-57); Dir Guild Am; hon mem New Mexico Watercolor Soc. *Media:* Watercolor, Acrylic; Film, Video. *Publ:* Contemporary Western Art, Southwest Art Publ, 82. *Mailing Add:* Rt 9 Box 86L Santa Fe NM 87505

DUNN, FONTAINE
PAINTER, PHOTOGRAPHER
Study: Tulane Univ, New Orleans, BFA, 70, State Univ NY, Fredonia, 72, Whitney Mus Am Art, 73, Carnegie-Melon Univ, MFA, 74. *Exhib:* One-person shows, Art Latitude Gallery, New York, 80 & 81, Gray Art Gallery, Jenkins Fine Arts Ctr, E Carolina Univ, Greenville, NC, 85 & Condeso-Lawler Gallery, New York, 86; New Abstract Paintings, Cork Gallery, Avery Fisher Hall, New York, 86; Abstract Images, Art in General, New York, 87; Dwellings, Althea Viafora Gallery, New York, 87; Five Painters, PS 122, New York, 88; group show, 48 Laight Gallery, New York, 88; New Abstraction, Weatherspoon Art Gallery, Winston-Salem, NC, 89. *Teaching:* Guest lectr painting, Sarah Lawrence Col, Bronxville, NY, 86-89; vis lectr painting, Princeton Univ, NJ, 86 & spring 90; adj instr painting, Trenton State Col, NJ, spring 90. *Awards:* Nat Endowment Arts Fel in Drawing, 87; Adolph & Esther Gottlieb Found Grant, 88; Pollock-Krasner Found Grant, 88. *Bibliog:* Ken Sofer (auth), An exhibition of abstract painting, Artnews, 11/82; Valentin Tatransky (auth), Art in general, rev, Arts Mag, 10/85; Stephen Westfall (auth), rev of one-person show at Condeso-Lawler, Arts Mag, 5/87; Ellen Handy (auth), Abstract painting, Arts Mag, summer, 87. *Mem:* Col Art Asn. *Mailing Add:* 60 Cooper St 3-G New York NY 10034

DUNN, PHILLIP CHARLES
EDUCATOR, ADMINISTRATOR
b Chicago, Ill, Mar 1, 47. *Study:* Univ Ill, BFA(art educ), 68; Inst Design, Ill Inst Techol, MS(visual educ), 70; Ball State Univ, EdD(art educ), 78. *Comn:*

Sculpture, Univ SC, Spartanburg, 83, 85 & 87. *Exhib:* Photog 79, Ariz State Univ Gallery, Tempe, 79; four-person show, Presbyterian Col, Clinton, SC, 79; two-person show, McKissick Mus, Columbia, SC, 79; Columbia Col Gallery, SC, 80; one-person show, USC Coastal Gallery, Conway, SC, 82. *Pos:* Prog officer, Getty Ctr Educ Arts, 88-90 (vis appointment). *Teaching:* Instr photog, Col DuPage, 71-76; vis prof photog, St Xavier Col, 74-76; assoc prof art educ, Univ SC, 78-, dir grad studies in art, 80-85. *Awards:* Mary J Rouse Award, 81; Higher Educator of the Year, SC Art Educ Asn, 81; Southeastern Art Educator of Year, Nat Art Educ Asn, 87. *Mem:* Nat Art Educ Asn; Guild SC Artists; Columbia Artist Guild; SC Art Educ Asn (treas, 80-82). *Publ:* Coauth, Bridging the gap between teaching and research in art, Sch Arts, 82; coauth, Finding A Job in Art Education, 83; auth, Help! My principal just burst my you gotta have art balloon, Design Mag, 85; co-ed, A True Likeness: The Black South of Richard S Roberts, 1920-1936, Algonquin Press, 86; auth, Promoting School Art: A Practical Approach, Nat Art Educ Asn Press, 86. *Mailing Add:* Dept Art Univ SC Columbia SC 29208

DUNN, ROGER TERRY
HISTORIAN
b Bethesda, Md, Feb 24, 46. *Study:* Am Univ, Washington, DC; Pa State Univ, BA(art hist & painting); Pratt Inst, MFA(painting), 70; Northwestern Univ, PhD(art hist), 78. *Collections Arranged:* Quilts from the Plymouth Antiquarian Soc, 74; John J Enneking: American Impressionist (ed, catalog), 75; The Boston Painting Invitational, 75, Michael Mazur: Vision of a Draughtsman, 76; Craftforms (ed, catalog), 76; American Pastimes (ed, catalog), 77; On the Threshold of Modern Design: The Arts and Crafts Movement in America (auth, catalog), Danforth Mus, 84. *Pos:* Cur, Brockton Art Ctr, Mass, 74-77; dir, Gallery at OUI, Boston, 76-80. *Teaching:* Prof art hist, Bridgewater State Col, 80- *Mem:* Col Art Asn. *Res:* Monet, Rodin and their symbolist circle; exhibition research on 19th century American art. *Publ:* Auth, Lawrence Kupferman: A Retrospective Exhibition, 74; ed, Landscape and Life in 19th Century America, 74; The Ikat weavings of Joan Hausrath, Fiberarts, 11/81. *Mailing Add:* c/o Dept Art Bridgewater State Col Bridgewater MA 02324

DUNNIGAN, MARY CATHERINE
LIBRARIAN
b Shawvers Mill, Va, May 7, 22. *Study:* Mary Washington Col, BA; Columbia Univ, MLS. *Pos:* Librn, Col of Archit, Va Polytech Inst, Blacksburg, 66-73; librn, Fiske Kimball Fine Arts Libr, Univ Va, Charlottesville, 73-87. *Mem:* Soc Archit Historians; Art Libr Soc NAm; Asn Archit Sch Librn (pres, 80-81); Spec Libr Asn Arts & Humanities Div (chmn mus, 73-74). *Res:* Inventory-computation: Architectural drawings of University of Virginia buildings. *Interests:* Development of research library for support of art, architecture and drama curriculum. *Mailing Add:* 1643 Rugby Ave Bayly Dr Univ of Va Charlottesville VA 22901

DUNOW, ESTI
PAINTER, HISTORIAN
b New York, NY, June 12, 48. *Study:* Brandeis Univ, BA, 66-70; Skowhegan Sch Painting & Sculpture, 71; New York Studio Sch, with Phillip Guston & Mercedes Matter, 70, 70-72, New York Univ-Inst Fine Arts, with Robert Goldwater, Gert Schiff, Robert Rosenblum, William Rubin, 70-81. *Exhib:* One-person show, Bowery Gallery, NY, 81, 83, 85, 87 & 90. *Pos:* Coauthor, Chaim Soutine Catalog Raisonne, 76-78, 84- *Awards:* Ford Found Fel in Mus Work, Inst Fine Arts & Metrop Mus Art, 72; Mus Training Fel, Nat Endowment Arts, 76-77. *Bibliog:* Freddy Kaplan (auth), Regional landscapes, Artist, 2/84; Gerrit Henry (auth), New York reviews, Art News, 2/86; Jed Perl (auth), Houses, fields, gardens, hills, The New Criterion, 2/86. *Media:* Oil. *Res:* Early twentieth century painting; School of Paris, emphasis on Chaim Soutine. *Publ:* Auth, Chaim Soutine (exhib catalog) Arts Coun of Great Britain, 82; Soutive Galleri, exhib catalog, Bellman, NY, 84. *Mailing Add:* 209 W 86th St No 801 New York NY 10024

DUNWIDDIE, CHARLOTTE
SCULPTOR
b Strasbourg, France. *Study:* Acad Arts, Berlin, Ger, with Wilhelm Otto; also with Mariano Benlliure y Gil, Madrid, Spain & Alberto Lagos, Buenos Aires, Arg. *Work:* Cardinal's Palace, Buenos Aires; Church of Good Shepherd, Lima, Peru; Marine Corps Mus, Washington, DC; Mus Brookgreen Gardens, SC; Mus New Britain, Conn. *Exhib:* Salon Bellas Artes, Buenos Aires, 40-45; Allied Artists Am, 56-72; Nat Sculpture Soc, 58-72; Am Artists Prof League, 59-70; Nat Acad Design, 59-80. *Awards:* Speyer Award, 69, Artists Fund Prize Best Show, 72 & 74, Nat Acad Design; Lindsey Mem Prize, 82, Nat Sculpture Soc, 70; Herbert Adams Mem Medal, Nat Sculpture Soc, 90; and 15 gold medals. *Mem:* Academician & fel Nat Sculpture Soc (vpres, 79-81, pres, 81-); Royal Soc Arts; Am Artists Prof League (dir, 60-); Allied Artists Am. *Mailing Add:* 35 E Ninth St New York NY 10003

DU PEN, EVERETT GEORGE
SCULPTOR, EDUCATOR
b San Francisco, Calif, June 12, 12. *Study:* Univ Southern Calif, with Merril Gage; Yale Univ Sch Fine Arts, with George Eberhard, George Snowden & Alexander Archipenko, BFA(Tiffany Fel, Clara Kimball English Traveling Fel), 37. *Work:* Seattle Art Mus; Washington Mutual Savings Bank, Seattle; Safeco Insurance, Seattle; Aberdeen City Hall, Wash; Bell Telephone Co. *Comn:* DuPen fountain, Seattle Ctr, 61; Crucifix & wall carving, St John Episcopal Church, Seattle, 63; carved walnut screens, Munic Bldg, City of Seattle, 63; heroic bronze portrait, pres Univ Wash, 73; bronze group, Dallas, Tex, 82; bronze, Edmonds, Wash, 83-84. *Exhib:* Nat Acad Design, New York, 50, 59, 72 & 76-77; Seattle Art Mus Northwest Ann, 47-63; Pa Acad Fine Art, 50, 54 & 58; Nat Sculpture Soc, 50, 59, 72, 75 & 77; Mainstreams 72, Marietta Col, 72; one-man shows, Seattle Art Mus, 50, Seattle Mutual Bank, 78 & 79. *Pos:* Sculpture mem, Munic Art Comn, Seattle, 59-64; sculpture adv, Art Adv Bd Seattle World's Fair, 60-62. *Teaching:* Asst sculpture, Carnegie Inst Technol Art Sch, 39-40; asst sculpture, Wash Univ Art Sch, 40-42; from instr to prof sculpture, Univ Wash Sch Art, 45-82, prof emer, 82- *Awards:* Saltus Gold Medal, Nat Acad Design; Univ Wash Grad Sch Grants, 55 & 57. *Bibliog:* Minor L Bishop (auth), Fountains in contemporary architecture, Am Fedn Arts, 65; Louis G Redstone (auth), articles in Art Archit, 68 & Nat Sculpture Rev. *Mem:* Fel Nat Sculpture Soc; academician Nat Acad Design. *Media:* Wood, Bronze. *Mailing Add:* 1231 20th Ave E Seattle WA 98112

DUREN, STEPHEN D
PAINTER
b Fairfield, Calif, Apr 8, 48. *Study:* San Francisco Art Inst, BFA, 74; Calif State Univ, Sacramento, MA, 77. *Work:* Grand Rapids Art Mus, Mich; Muskegon Mus Art, Mich; Yergeau-Musee Int d'Art, Quebec. *Comn:* Paintings, Steelcase Inc; drawings, Herman Miller, Inc; poster design, Grand Rapids Arts Coun, Mich. *Exhib:* Solo exhibs, Muskegon Mus Art, Mich, Battle Creek Art Ctr, Mich, Creative Art Ctr Central Mich Univ & Grand Rapids Art Mus, Mich; group exhib, Corp Blockbusters, Grand Rapids Art Mus Nat Exhib American Art, Chautauqua Art Assoc, New York, Kresge Art Mus, Lansing, Mich & Laguna Gloria Art Mus, Tex; Between Dreams, Zola/Lieberman Gallery, Chicago. *Teaching:* Asst prof, Kendall Col Design, Mich, 79-84. *Awards:* Artist's Grant, Mich Coun Arts, 87; Artist Residency Fel, Ucross Found, Wyo, 88; Artist's Grant, Adolf & Esther Gottlieb Found, NY, 88. *Bibliog:* Openings, Art Calif, Mag, 60, 9/89; Duren, Grand Rapids Press, 12/90; Artist at work, Mich Coast Mag, 22-27, 36, 4/92. *Media:* Oil. *Dealer:* Harleen/Allen Fine Art 427 Bryant San Francisco CA 94107; Studio 11080 68th Ave Allendale MI 49401. *Mailing Add:* 11080 68th Ave Allendale MI 49401

DURHAM, JEANETTE R
PAINTER
b Plainfield, NJ, June 17, 45. *Study:* Montclair State Col, BA, 67; Art Students League with Bruce Dorfman, 71-72; Westchester Art Workshop with Gregory Lysun, 80-81; S U Col Onconta, MSEd, 91. *Work:* Peoples Daily Newspaper, Beijng; Kingsley Sch, Boston; Opto Generic Devices, Van Hornesville, NY. *Exhib:* Solo exhibs, A Hilly Place, Gallery 57, Cambridge Arts Coun, Mass, 84 & Birds of the Air and Other Phenomena, Gannett Gallery, State Univ NY, Utica, 88 & Waterfalls, South Shore Arts, Little Falls, NY, 91; 37th Art of Northeast USA, Silvermine Guild, New Canaan, Conn, 86; WHMT Exhib, NY State Mus, Albany, 88; 56th Ann Nat Exhib, Cooperstown Art Asn, 91; Coast to Coast, Pleindes Gallery, New York, 91; 56th Ann Nat Midyear, Butler Inst Am Art, 92. *Teaching:* Instr painting, drawing, Mohawk Valley Ctr Arts, Littel Falls, NY, 83; instr art, Owen D Young C S, VanHornesville, NY, 87-92. *Awards:* Best in Show, MVCA Invitational, 83; William Meyerowitz Mem Award, Nat Asn Women Artists, 91. *Bibliog:* Christine Temin (auth), Discovering art off the beaten path, Boston Globe, 11/15/84; Jonas Kover (auth), Durham's paintings appear lighter than air, Observer Dispatch, 1/24/88. *Mem:* Nat Asn Women Artists; New York Artists Equity. *Media:* Oil. *Dealer:* Pleiades Gallery 164 Mercer St New York NY 10012. *Mailing Add:* RD 1 Box 123 Jordanville NY 13361

DURHAM, WILLIAM
PAINTER, SCULPTOR
b Flint, Mich, Mar 14, 37. *Study:* Mich State Univ, BA, 60; painting with Morris Kantor, Boris Margo & Abraham Rattner. *Work:* Guild Hall, East Hampton, NY; Warnaco Inc, Park Ave, New York; Mich State Univ, East Lansing; Kidder Peabody Inc, New York; Butler Inst Am Art. *Comn:* Painting, New York World's Fair, 64. *Exhib:* One-man shows, Benson Gallery, Bridgehampton, NY, 67, 71, 72 & 74 & Art Placement Int, New York, 81; Am Acad Arts & Lett, New York, 74; Heckscher Mus, Huntington, NY, 74; Artist of the Hamptons, Guild Hall, Easthampton, NY, 75; Chicago Art Inst. *Bibliog:* Article, New York Herald Tribune, 64 & New York Times, 64-75; Art in America. *Media:* Acrylic; Aluminum. *Dealer:* Vered Gallery East Hampton NY 11937. *Mailing Add:* Main St Amagansett NY 11930

DURR, PAT (PATRICIA BETH)
PAINTER, PRINTMAKER
b Kansas City, Mo; Can citizen. *Study:* Univ Kans, BA(educ), 61; Univ Southampton, 62; Kansas City Art Inst, 63; Ottawa Sch Art, with Duncan deKergommeaux, 65. *Work:* Can Coun Visual Art Bank, Esso Resources, Calgary, Alta; Robert McLaughlin Pub Art Gallery, Oshawa, Ont; Ont Ministry Govt Serv, Toronto, Ont; City of Ottawa Art Collection; Nickle Art Mus, Univ Calgary, Alta. *Comn:* Mural, Ottawa Sch Bd, First Ave Sch, Ont, 79; Serigraph, 75th Anniversary Portfolio, Royal Trust Co, Ottawa, Ont, 80; mural, City of Ottawa Heron Rd Multiservice Ctr, 90; mural & frieze, Churchill Alternative Sch, Ottawa Bd Educ, 91; patterned concrete walkways & mural, Ottawa/Carleton Transpo Heron Rd Transitway Sta, 92-93. *Exhib:* Royal Canadian Acad House Gallery, Toronto, 87; Confederation Ctr Art Gallery, Charlottetown, PEI, 89; Cornwall Regional Gallery, Ont, 90; Sixteen Ottawa Painter, Arts Court Gallery, 90; Art Gallery Algoma, Sault Ste Marie, Ont, 90; solo exhibs, Woodland Cult Ctr, Brantford, Ont, 91, Owatonna Art Ctr, Minn, 91, Okanata, A-Space & Workscene Galleries, Toronto, 91, MacLaren Art Ctr, Barrie, Ont, 92. *Pos:* Consult, Mayor's Adv Comt Arts & Cult, 79-82, Revenue Can Visual Arts Adv Bd Customs Regulations, 80-82, Ottawa Visual & Performing Arts Ctr Steering Comt, 81-84, vchmn, Health & Welfare Can Adhoc Comt Health Hazards Arts & Crafts, 82 & 86 & chmn, Munic Ottawa Visual Arts Adv Comt, 86-90; vchmn, Ottawa Arts Ctr Found, 87-88; cur, Govt Can Persons Award Exhibition 87-88; consult, Arts-Peat

Marwick, 89; art comn adv, Ottawa/Carleton Regional Govt, 92. *Teaching:* Fine arts coordr, Algonquin Col Visual Art, Ottawa, Ont, 75-78, teaching master painting, 79-82; guest lectr, Univ Manitoba, NS Sch Art & Design, 82, Ottawa Sch Art, 86, Alberta Col Art, 87, Banff Ctr, 87, Holland Col Sch Visual Arts, PEI, 89, Georgian Col, Ont, 92; drawing & painting inst, Alpen Sch Art, summer 87; guest lectr, Holland Col Sch Visual Arts, PEI, 89, Georgian Col, Ont, 92. *Awards:* Victor Tolgesy Arts Award, City of Ottawa, Ont, 89; Ont Arts Coun Individual Artists Grant, 92; Regional Munic Ottawa/Carleton Artist's "A" Grant, 92. *Bibliog:* Pat Durr, Gallerie Publ, 88 ann; Mayo Graham (auth) catalog statement, Dreams of Black Rainbows, Confederation Ctr Art Gallery, Charlottetown, PEI, 89; Claudia McKnight (auth), Pat Durr, Extension, spring, 92, Huronia, 2/92. *Mem:* Can Artists Representation-Les Front des Artistes Canadians (pres, Ottawa, 79-80, nat vpres, 80-82, pres, 82-84); Visual Arts Ont; Print & Drawing Coun Can; Visual Arts Ottawa (activities chmn, 74-76); Royal Can Acad Arts (exec coun, 85-87, 90-91). *Media:* Acrylic & Mixed Media; Wooden Wall Relief. *Publ:* Auth, Canada Council Art Bank today, CARFAC News, 2-3/83; The not so impossible dream, Artviews, Vol 9, No 3, 83; Death & taxes, Parallelogamme, Vol 9, No 3, 2/84; The Ottawa Arts Court Project, Recreation Canada, Vol 46, No 4, 11/88; Peter Powning, Arts Atlantic 39, Vol 10, No 3, 91. *Dealer:* Ufundi Gallery 541 Sussex Dr Ottawa Ont Canada K1N 6Z6; Geraldine Davis Gallery 225 Richmond St W Toronto Ont Can. *Mailing Add:* 167 First Ave Ottawa ON K1S 2G3 Canada

DUSARD, JAY
PHOTOGRAPHER, WRITER
b St Louis, Mo, Feb 18, 37. *Study:* Univ Fla, BArch, 61. *Work:* J C Penney; Eastman Kodak; Ctr for Creative Photog; Fed Reserve Bank San Francisco, Los Angeles; Snell & Wilmer, Phoenix, Tucson, Irvine. *Exhib:* Addison Gallery Am Art, 75; New Landscapes Part I, Friends Photog, Carmel, Calif, 80; The North American Cowboy: A Portrait, Phoenix Art Mus, 82, Glenbow Mus, Calgary, Alta, 84 & Colorado Springs Fine Arts Ctr, 84; Ctr Creative Photog, Ariz; La Frontera, Centro Cultural de Tijuana, Mexico City, 87; Consejo Mexicano de Fotografia, Mexico City, 88; The Cowboy West: 100 Years of Photography, C M Russell Mus, Great Falls, Mt, 92. *Pos:* Designer & lithographer, Northland Press, Flagstaff, Ariz, 66-68. *Teaching:* Asst prof photog, Prescott Col, Ariz, 68-74. *Awards:* Guggenheim Mem Found Fel Photog, 81; The Show Silver Award, Art Dirs & Copywriters Club Minn, 85; Four Corners Book Award for Nonfiction for La Frontera, Northern Ariz Univ, Flagstaff, 88. *Bibliog:* David Featherstone (auth), New Landscapes, The Friends of Photog, 81; Michael Saltz (producer), segment, MacNeil-Lehrer News Hour (TV film), PBS-TV, 83; Sheilah Britton (producer), Arizon Artforms: The Art of Jay Dusard (TV film), KAET-TV, Tempe, Ariz, 90. *Mem:* Ctr for Photog Arts, Carmel (adv bd); Mad Dog Writers Consortium. *Publ:* Auth & illusr, Visions from the Southwest, Plateau Mag, Mus Northern Ariz, 80; auth & illusr, The North American Cowboy: A Portrait, Consortium Press, 83; illusr, La Frontera: The United States Border with Mexico, Harcourt Brace Jovanovich, 86; Contribr, Photographers & Their Images, Conran Octopus, London, 88; auth & illusr, Land & People, Camera & Darkroom Mag, Beverly Hills, Calif, 92. *Dealer:* Andrew Smith Gallery 76 E San Francisco St Santa Fe NM 87501; Etherton/Stern Gallery 424 E Sixth St Tucson AZ 85705. *Mailing Add:* 2221 View Dr Prescott AZ 86301

DUSENBERY, WALTER
SCULPTOR
b Alameda, Calif, 1939. *Study:* San Francisco Art Inst, 61; ceramics with Marguerite Wildenhain, 62-66; Calif Col Arts & Crafts, MFA, 71. *Work:* Carnegie Inst, Pittsburgh; Columbus Mus Art, Ohio; Guggenheim Mus & Metrop Mus Art, New York; San Francisco Mus Mod Art. *Comn:* Sculpture, Justice Ctr, Portland, Ore, 83; sculpture, Dept Art, Univ Northern Iowa, in prep. *Exhib:* One-man exhib, Univ Northern Iowa, Cedar Falls, 85, Fendrick Gallery, Wash, DC, 86 & 88, Barbara Fendrick Gallery, New York, 89; Metrop Mus Art, New York, 79; Int Sculpture Conf, Washington, DC, 80; Yorkshire Sculpture Park, Bretton Hall, England, 81-82; Hamilton Gallery, New York, 81; Grad Sch Design, Harvard Univ, 82; Anderson Gallery, Va Commonwealth Univ, 83; Laumeier Sculpture Park, St Louis, 83; Pratt Mus Art, New York, 87; and others. *Teaching:* Instr ceramic sculpture, Univ Calif, San Francisco, 69; vis sculptor, Sch Landscape Archit, Grad Sch Design, Harvard Univ, 79- *Awards:* Grants, Creative Artists Pub Serv, 80 & Nat Endowment Arts, 80. *Bibliog:* Nina French-Frazier (auth), Walter Dusenbery, Arts Mag, 6/78; David L Shirey (auth), Creations that bridge the passage of time, NY Times Long Island Ed, 9/13/81; Ann Sargent-Wooster (auth), Dusenbery at the Nassau County Museum, Art in Am, 1/82. *Mem:* Artists Equity Asn; Archit League. *Publ:* Auth, The Story of the Bed, Natoma Soc, Santa Barbara, Calif, 70; Dusenbery interviewed by Howard Greenfeld, 57th St Rev, 1/76. *Mailing Add:* Rte 1 Box 7 Fly Creek NY 13337

DUTTON, ALLEN A
PHOTOGRAPHER, PAINTER
b Kingman, Ariz, April 13, 22. *Study:* Art Ctr Schs, Los Angeles; Ariz State Univ, BA, MA, 49. *Work:* Mus Mod Art, New York; Bibliot Nat, Paris; Tokyo Col Photog Mus, Japan; Il Diaframma, Milano, Italy; Santa Barbara Mus Art; Northlight Ariz State Univ, Tempe; Ctr Photog Univ Ariz, Tucson; Univ NMex, Albuquerque; Univ Ky, Louisville. *Exhib:* Solo exhibs, Il Diaframma Gallery, Milano, Italy, 71, Northlight Gallery, Ariz State Univ, 79, 80-88, Photog Southwest Gallery, Scottsdale, Ariz, 79, Shinju Gallery, Tokyo, 79, Nagase Photo Salon, Tokyo, 84, Hayden Libr, Ariz State Univ, 85 & Hal Martin Fogle Gallery, Scottsdale, Ariz, 92. *Pos:* Art ed & photog head, Phoenix Point West Mag, 63-66. *Teaching:* Prof photog & head dept, Phoenix Col, Ariz, 61-82; prof, Tokyo Col Photog, Japan, 72-73. *Awards:* John Hay Fel, 60. *Bibliog:* A D Coleman (auth), Grotesque in Photo, Ridge Press, 78; Jim Stone (auth), Darkroom Dynamics, Curtain & London, 79. *Mem:* Soc Photog Educ. *Publ:* Auth, The Great Stone Tit, Little Wonder Press, 72; A A Dutton's Compendium, Buse Press, 74; coauth, Arizona Then and Now, AG2 Press, 82; Phoenix Then and Now, First Interstate Bank Press, 85; Mythology for the 21st Century, Zeckwough Press, 90. *Dealer:* Etherton Gallery 424 E Sixth St Tucson AZ 85705. *Mailing Add:* 15235 N 11th St Phoenix AZ 85022

DUVEEN, ANNETA
SCULPTOR, DESIGNER
b Brooklyn, NY, May 21, 24. *Study:* Adelphi Acad, watercolor with Anna G Morse, 38-41; Columbia Univ, sculpture with Oronzio Maldarelli, 42; also graphics with Charles L Goslin, 63; St Francis Col, Pa, DHH, 86. *Work:* Civic Ctr, Brooklyn; Mt Scott, Cape Palmas, Liberia WAfrica. *Comn:* John W Olin Memorials, Olin Corp, Stamford, Conn & East Alton, Ill, 72; St Maximilian Kolbe, The Vatican, 82; Francis Cardinal Cooke, Cardinal Cooke Guild, New York, 85; Christopher Columbus, Ital Heritage Ctr, Portland, Maine, 93; 45 stained glass window designs, St Anthony's Sanctuary, Brasilia, 93. *Exhib:* God's Minstrel: St Francis of Assisi, The Walters Art Gallery, Baltimore, 82; retrospective, Santa Croce Basilica Mus, Florence, Italy, 85 & MMC Gallery, Marymount Manhattan Col, New York, 86; Artiste, Dante Alighieri Soc, Palazzo Firenze, Rome, Italy, 86. *Mem:* Greenwich Art Soc. *Media:* Bronze. *Publ:* Illusr, McGraw Hill Encyclopedia of Sci & Technol, 71-86; coauth & illusr, Essentials of Astronomy, Columbia Univ Press, 77. *Mailing Add:* Rye Rd Greyrock Park Port Chester NY 10573

DUZY, MERRILYN JEANNE
PAINTER, LECTURER
b Los Angeles, Calif, Mar 29, 46. *Study:* Pvt study with Vern Wilson, Los Angeles; Calif State Univ, Northridge, BA, 74; Otis Art Inst, MFA 88. *Exhib:* Women Artists in History, Tampa Mus Art, Fla, 86; Contemp Expressions from Los Angeles, Taipei, Taiwan, 89; Of Nature & Nation Yellowstone Summer of Fire, Los Angeles, 90; Elements, Woodland Hills, Calif, 90; Women Artists in History, Platt Gallery, Los Angeles, 91; and others. *Collections Arranged:* Erotic Visions, George Sand Gallery, Los Angeles, 77; Autobiographies, Palos Verdes Art Ctr, Calif, 78; Erotica 88, Gorman Fine Arts, Santa Monica, CA. *Pos:* Founder & pres, Fla Chapter, Women's Caucus Art, 83-84, adv bd mem, Nat Women's Caucus Art, 84-87 & vpres, new chapters, 86-88. *Teaching:* Educator, Artspace Gallery, City of Los Angeles, 91- *Awards:* First Place, Nat Women's Caucus Art, Lehigh Univ, Pa, 84. *Bibliog:* Linda Saul (auth), Walking through history, Tampa Mus Newlett, 5/86; Laurel Paley (auth), Merrilyn Duzy & Margaret Lazzari, Artweek, 5/90; Steve Appleford (auth), Artspace's larger view of portraits, Los Angeles Times, 91; Nancy Kapitanoff (auth), Art notebook, Los Angeles Times, 91; and others. *Mem:* Women's Caucus Art; Artists Equity. *Media:* Oil, Pastel. *Collection:* Contemporary women artists; erotica; Vern Wilson, Bruno Bruni, Leonor Fini & Mario Casilli. *Publ:* Contribr, Contemporary Women Artists-Datebook, Bo-Tree, 87. *Mailing Add:* 8356 Capistrano Ave West Hills CA 91304

DVERIN, ANATOLY
PAINTER, ILLUSTRATOR
b Dnepropretrovsk, Ukraine, July 23, 35; US citizen. *Study:* Art Col, Dnepropetovsk, Ukraine, BA, 50-55; Com & Indust Arts Inst, Leningrad, 55-56; Kharkov Inst Fine Arts, Ukraine, MFA, 56-62. *Work:* Paintings approved, selected & purchased by the govts & comts of the former USSR and/or Ukraine for public display at different mus & galleries, locations unknown. *Comn:* Soldiers Dream (oil), 67, Songs of the Civil War, 69, Ministry Cult USSR, Moscow, Russia; New England (oil), Delta Airlines, 87; Portrait of John Adams (oil), John Adams Venture Capital, Boston, 89. *Exhib:* All-Union Art Exhib, Cent Exhib Hall, Moscow, Russia, 64-67, 70-71 & 74; Pastel Soc Am 19th Ann Open Exhib, New York, 91-92; Second Biennial Nat Exhib, Pensacola Mus Art, Fla, 92; NAm Artists Summit Exhib, Webb Gallery, New Haven, Conn, 92; 15th Ann Exhib, Salmagundi Club, New York, 92. *Awards:* Award of Excellence, Pastel 92, 2nd Biennial Nat Exhib, Pastel Soc NFla, 92; Third Place, NAm Artist Summit Exhib, 92. *Mem:* Pastel Soc Am; Pastel Soc NFla; Rockport Art Asn. *Media:* Soft Pastel, Oil. *Publ:* Illusr, When Animals Used to Speak, Childrens Bks, Kieve, USSR, 67; contribr, Don Lister, Drawing with Pastel, Prentice-Hall Inc, 82; contribr, Designing Greeting Cards & Paper Products, by Ron Lister, Prentice-Hall Inc, 84; illusr, Spirit of the Hills, Dan O'Brien (auth), Pocket Bks, 88. *Mailing Add:* Nine Oak Dr Plainville MA 02762

DWORZAN, GEORGE R
PAINTER
b New York, NY, Mar 28, 24. *Study:* Cooper Union, with Morris Cantor; Art Students League, with Harry Sternberg; Acad Grande Chaumiere, Paris, France; Acad Leger, Paris, with Fernand Leger. *Work:* NY Univ; Chase Manhattan Bank, New York; Univ Mass, Amherst; Ohio State Univ; Herron Mus Art, Indianapolis, Ind. *Exhib:* Salon Realities Nouvelles, Mus Art Mod, Paris, 48-49; Art USA, Coliseum, NY, 59; Nat Print Competition, AAA Gallery, New York, 60; Contemp Arts Soc Ann, Herron Mus, 64 & 68; Univ NC Ann, Chapel Hill, 68. *Teaching:* Asst prof painting & drawing, NY Univ, currently. *Media:* Mixed. *Dealer:* East Hampton Gallery 305 W 28th St New York NY 10025. *Mailing Add:* 17 Bleecker St New York NY 10012

DWYER, EUGENE JOSEPH
HISTORIAN
b Buffalo, NY, Sept 14, 43. *Study:* Harvard Univ, BA(classics, cum laude); NY Univ Inst Fine Arts, MA, 67, PhD, 74. *Teaching:* Prof art hist, Kenyon Col, Gambier, Ohio, 73- *Awards:* Tatiana Warsher Award for the Archaeol

of Pompeii, Herculaneum & Stabia, Am Acad Rome, 73-74; Nat Endowment Humanities Fel, 80-81, 87-88. *Mem:* Col Art Asn Am; Archaeol Inst Am; Am Numismatic Soc. *Res:* Greek and Roman art and classical tradition. *Publ:* The subject of Durer's four witches, Art Quart, 71; Augustus and the Capricorn, Roemische Mitteilungen, 73; auth, Sculpture and its display in houses of Pompeii, In: Pompeii and the Vesuvian Landscape, 79; auth, Pompeian Oscilla Collections, Roemische Mitteilungen, 81; auth, Pompeian Domestic Sculpture, 82; The Temporal Allegory of the Tazza Farnese, Amer J Arch, 92. *Mailing Add:* Dept of Art Hist Kenyon Col Gambier OH 43022

DWYER, JAMES
PAINTER, EDUCATOR
b Tulsa, Okla, Oct 24, 21. *Study:* Art Inst Chicago, BFA, 47; Acad Grande Chaumiere, Paris, 47-48; Syracuse Univ, MFA, 50; Univ Chicago; De Paul Univ; study with Boris Anisfeld. *Work:* Everson Mus, Syracuse, NY; Munson-Williams-Proctor Inst, State Univ, Utica, NY; Syracuse Univ, NY; Ashland Col, Ohio. *Comn:* 3100 sq ft mural decoration, Onondaga Co Civic Ctr, Syracuse, NY, 76. *Exhib:* Art Inst Chicago, 47; Metrop Mus Art, New York, 51; City Ctr Gallery, New York, 55; Silvermine Guild Artists Conn, 56; Univ Maine, Portland-Gorham, 74; Lubin House, New York, 77; solo exhib, Krasner Gallery, New York, 81; and others. *Teaching:* Prof painting & drawing, Syracuse Univ, NY, 49-82; retired. *Media:* Acrylic. *Mailing Add:* 223 Deforst Rd Syracuse NY 13214

DYCK, PAUL
PAINTER, DIRECTOR
b Chicago, Ill, Aug 17, 17. *Study:* With Johann Von Skramlik, Florence, Italy, Prague, Czech, Rome, Italy & Paris, France, 26-33; Univ Mont, LHD, 89. *Work:* Phoenix Art Mus, Ariz; Mus Northern Ariz, Flagstaff; Whitney Gallery Western Art, Cody, Wyo; Franklin Inst, Philadelphia; Tucson Mus Art, Ariz; and pvt collections in US, Can & Europe. *Comn:* Indians of the Overland Trail (painting), sponsored by pub mus, 56; Flame of Man (painting), F O Hess, Franklin Inst, Philadelphia, 70. *Exhib:* 65 One-man exhibs, incl, Southwest Mus, Los Angeles, Calif, Mont Hist Soc, Helena, Chicago Mus Nat Hist, Phoenix Art Mus & Ariz State Univ Mus. *Pos:* Dir, Paul Dyck Res Found Am Indian Cult; reviewer, Am Indian Quarterly, Journal Am Indian Studies, Native Am Studies Prog, Univ Calif Berkeley. *Awards:* Artist Commendation, US Navy, 45. *Mem:* Life mem Buffalo Bill Hist Ctr, Cody, Wyo; Manuscript Soc; Appraisers Asn Am. *Media:* Oil; Sumiye Watercolor. *Publ:* Auth, Brule, Sioux People of the Rosebud, 69; contribr, Montana, Mag of Western Hist, 72; Buffalo Bill Hist Ctr, 72; Persimmon Mag, 83. *Dealer:* Rosequist Galleries 1615 E Fort Lowell Rd Tucson AZ 85719. *Mailing Add:* PO Box 217 Rimrock AZ 86335

DYENS, GEORGES MAURICE
SCULPTOR
b Mar 18, 32; Fr & Can citizen. *Study:* Ecole Nat Superieure Beaux Arts, Paris, dipl, 61; Concordia Univ, Montreal, MFA; Premier Grand Prix Rome, New York Holographic Lab. *Work:* Mus Mod Art & Hotel Hilton, Paris; Mus Art Contemp, Montreal; Mus Quebec; Mus Holography, New York; Permanent outdoor installations in Montreal & Quebec City. *Exhib:* Symp Eur Sculptors, Berlin, 62; Biennial Int Piccolo Bronzo, Padova, Italy, 64-66; Mus Rodin, Paris, 66; Int Biennial New Delhi, India, 68; solo exhib, Mus Que, 81; Alternative Mus, New York, 88; Images du Futur, Montreal, 87, 89 & 92. *Pos:* artist-in-residence, Mus Holography, New York. *Teaching:* Prof sculpture, Univ Que, Montreal, 69- *Awards:* Ger Critic Prize, Berlin, 62; Prix Susse, Bienniale Paris, 63. *Bibliog:* Diulio Morosini (auth), La Revincita Della Vita, Paese Sera, Rome, 7/1/65; Gerald Gassiot-Talabot (auth), Dyens, Arts, Paris, 10/20/65; Yves Robillard (auth), Les metamorphoses lentes, Vie des Arts, Montreal, 6/80. *Mem:* Asn Sculptors Que, Montreal; Asn Arts & Techniques Holographics, Paris; Mus Holography, New York. *Media:* Multi Media. *Mailing Add:* CP 8888 Succ A Dept Plastic Arts Univ Que Montreal PQ H3C 3P8 Canada

DYER, CAROLYN PRICE
TAPESTRY ARTIST, EDITOR
b Seattle, Wash, Dec 19, 31. *Study:* Univ Wash, Seattle; Mills Col, Oakland, Calif, BA, 53, MA, 55; studied with Alfred Neumeyer, Ilse Schultz Hiller & Katherine Caldwell. *Comn:* Suns on a Wide Horizon, Tokio Marine, 80; Gen Electric logo, EPCOT, Fla, 83; Ocean Edge, Pepperdine Univ, 83; Santa Barbara Sunshine, Advan Comput Communications, 85; Carnation Field, Nestle USA Inc, Glendale, Calif, 86; Paper Gown, Huntington Mem Hosp, Pasadena, Calif, 90. *Exhib:* Craft & Folk Art Mus, Los Angeles, 68; China--A Personal View, Pac Asia Mus, Pasadena, 79; Travel Documents (two-person), Blue Heron Ctr Arts, Vashon, Wash, 89; Tapestry Artists of Puget Sound, Frye Mus, Seattle, Wash, 91; L'art dans la mode (with exhib catalog), Wignall Mus, Rancho Cucamonga, Calif, 91; Woven Documents (solo), Kennedy-Douglass Ctr Arts, Florence, Ala, 92; Form & Object, Univ Wyo (nat juried traveling exhibit), 92; and others. *Pos:* Founder & dir, Stone Court Gallery, Yakima, Wash, 58-65; ed, publ, lineup art newsletter, 78-; contrib ed, Fiberarts, 78-; guest cur, Surface & Structure: Concepts in Fiber, Blue Heron Ctr Arts, Vashon, Wash, 91; writer, Am Craft, Artweek, Crafts Report, HALI, Oriental Rug Rev, Visual Dialog, and others. *Teaching:* Instr art hist, Los Angeles Trade/Tech Col, 69-76. *Awards:* Textiles/Tapestries Awards, NW Craftsmen's Exhib, Seattle, 64 & Pac NW Arts & Crafts Exhib, Bellevue, Wash, 68; Gold Crown Award, Pasadena Arts Coun, 83. *Bibliog:* Judy Haddad (auth), Carolyn Dyer, Tapestries (videotape), Pasadena City Col, 76; Terry Pace (auth), From Coats to Documents: Dyer considers herself correspondent of art, Times Daily, 3/29/92. *Mem:* Am Crafts Coun; Pasadena Soc Artists; Textile Mus Assocs; Calif Fibers; Tapestry Artists of Puget Sound. *Media:* Natural Fibers, Paper. *Publ:* Auth, A kaleidoscopic tour of Turkey, Fiberarts, 80; Towards new horizons, Designers West, 80; London carpeted in Oriental gardens, Fiberarts, 84; Tracing the Silk Road, Fiberarts, 86; Inspired by the Oriental Carpet: Contemp Art Textiles, Fiberarts, 11/90. *Mailing Add:* 270 N Orange Grove Blvd Pasadena CA 91103-3536

DYER, M WAYNE
PAINTER, GRAPHIC ARTIST
b Roanoke, Va, Aug 6, 50. *Study:* Va Western Community Col, AAS, 70; James Madison Univ, BS, 73; Radford Univ, MFA. *Work:* Lykes Enrichment Ctr, Brooksville, Fla; Ctr for New Creation, Nashville, Tenn; Slocumb Galleries, Johnson City, Tenn; Flossie Martin Gallery, Radford, Va; DuPont Gallery, Fredericksburg, Va. *Exhib:* Solo Exhibs, Va Art Inst, Charlottesville, Va, 74, Roanoke Mus Fine Arts, 74, Kent Gallery, Radford, 83, Harding Mott Gallery, Univ Mich, Flint, 85, Watkins Inst Art, Nashville, 88, Tempo Gallery, Brooksville, Fla, 88 & Lincoln Mus, Harogate, Tenn, 90. *Pos:* Tenn Arts Commission, Media Panel, 85-89, chmn 87-89. *Teaching:* Assoc prof, East Tenn State Univ, 83- *Awards:* Award of Merit, First Tenn Exhib, Johnson City Area Arts Coun, 86; Award of Merit, First American Exhib, Kingsport, Tenn, 87; Best in Show, Cabaret VI, Johnson City Area Arts Coun, 88. *Mem:* Col Art Asn; Southeastern Ctr Contemp Art; Johnson City Area Arts Coun; Am Inst Graphic Design. *Media:* Acrylic, Oil. *Mailing Add:* East Tenn State Univ Slocumb Galleries Dept Art Box 23740A Johnson City TN 37614

DYSON, BRIAN
CURATOR, WRITER
b Leeds, Eng, Oct 4, 44. *Study:* Leeds Col Art, with Derek Hyatt, dipl AD, 66. *Exhib:* Remade Readymades & related work, Artons, Calgary, Alta, 77, toured Poland, 78; Canadians Nat touring, Mt Allison Univ, NS, 78; Artists' Polaroid NAm touring, Open Space, Victoria, BC, 78. *Collections Arranged:* One Eye Open, One Eye Closed, Photo: Belloq Krims (cataloged), 76; Mac Adams, Bill Beckley, James Collins, Photo-Narrative (ed, catalog), Alta Col Art, 77, Marcel Duchamp: a European Investigation (ed & contribr, catalog), 79 & Videonet, International Video/Performance (ed & co-auth, catalog), 79. *Pos:* Cur, Alta Col Art Gallery, Calgary, 75-80; juror, Video Sect, Can Coun, 79; founder/dir, Syntax, Calgary/Int Artists Contact Ctr. *Teaching:* Photog, Simon Fraser Univ, British Columbia, 70. *Awards:* Can Coun Travel Grant, 78; Can Coun Project Cost Grant, 79. *Bibliog:* Paul Woodrow (auth), Brian Dyson--Remade Readymades, Centerfold, 78 & Brian Dyson--Looking Both Ways at Once, Parachute, 78. *Media:* Mixed Media. *Publ:* Ed, Jan Swidzinski--Art, Society and Self-Consciousness, Alta Col Art Gallery, 79; ed, Les Levine, Media: the Biotech Rehearsal for Leaving the Body, 80. *Mailing Add:* 430 11 A St NW Calgary AB T2N 1Y1 Canada

DYYON, FRAZIER
PAINTER, SCULPTOR
b Ft Meyers, Fla, May 2, 46. *Work:* Mus Mod Art & Whitney Mus Am Art, New York; Larry Aldrich Mus, Conn; Case Western Reserve Univ. *Exhib:* Cleveland Top Artists, In Town Club, 69; Int Exhib Art, Cleveland, 70; Whitney Mus Am Art Ann, 72; Reflections, Larry Aldrich Mus, 72-73; one-man show, Mather Gallery, Case Western Reserve Univ, 83. *Awards:* T R Montalbano, 79; Printmaker Workshop Bd Scholar, New York, 82. *Mailing Add:* 155 W 73rd St New York NY 10023

DZIERSKI, VINCENT PAUL
PAINTER, DESIGNER
b Pittsburgh, Pa, Jan 1, 30. *Study:* Studied drawing & painting with Armando Del Cimuto, 48-52. *Pos:* Creative dir, Town Studios, Inc, 70- *Mem:* Art Dirs Soc Pittsburgh. *Media:* Egg Tempera, Oil. *Mailing Add:* c/o Town Studios Inc 717 Liberty Ave Clark Bldg Pittsburgh PA 15222

DZIGURSKI, ALEX
PAINTER
b Stari Becej, Vojvodlina, Yugoslavia, May 15, 11; US citizen. *Study:* Sch Art, Belgrade, Yugoslavia; Acad Art, Munich, Ger. *Work:* Boston Mus Fine Arts; Norton Gallery, Shreveport, La; Franklin Mint Am Art, Pa; Okla Art Ctr, Oklahoma City; Belgrade Art Mus, Yugoslavia. *Comn:* Altars in Serbian churches, Cleveland, Ohio, 52, Aliquippa, Pa, 55 & Canton, Ohio, 56; interior church & altar, St Sava Serbian Church, Milwaukee, Wis, 58; altar in Serbian church, Kansas City, Kans, 59. *Exhib:* Soc Western Artists Exhib, De Young Mus, San Francisco, 72 & 73; Findlay Galleries, Chicago, Ill, 74. *Awards:* Gold Medal, Biennale Venice, Italy, 48; First Prize, Popular, Soc Western Artists, De Young Mus, San Francisco, 65; Gold Medal, Franklin Mint Bicentennial, Pa, 73. *Mem:* Prof League Am Artists; Soc Western Artists; fel Fine Art Inst, Los Angeles. *Media:* Oil. *Dealer:* Findlay Galleries 814 N Michigan Chicago IL 60611. *Mailing Add:* c/o Simic Galleries San Carlos & Sixth St PO Box 5687 Carmel-By-The-Sea CA 93921

DZUBAS, FRIEDEL
PAINTER
b Berlin, Ger, Apr 20, 15; US citizen. *Work:* Metrop Mus Art, Solomon R Guggenheim Mus, New York; Boston Mus Fine Arts, Mass; Mus Fine Arts, Houston; Nat Mus Am Art, Hirshhorn Mus, Washington, DC; Edmonton Art Gallery, Alta. *Comn:* Nat Shawmut Bank, Boston, 75. *Exhib:* Color and Field, Albright-Knox Gallery, Cleveland Mus & Dayton Art Inst, 70-71; Abstract Painting in the 70's, Boston Mus Fine Arts, 72; retrospectives, Mus Fine Arts, Houston, 74 & Boston Mus Fine Arts, 75; 34th Biennial, Corcoran Gallery, Washington, DC, 75; New Works in Clay, Everson Mus, 76; solo exhibs, John Berggruen Gallery, San Francisco, 77, 79 & 83, M Knoedler & Co, New York, 77-80, 82, 83, 84, 85 & 86, Kunsthalle, Bielefeld, 77, Dart Gallery, Chicago, 78, Nassau Co Mus Fine Art Asn, NY, 87, Herbert F Johnson Mus Art,

Cornell Univ, Ithaca, NY, 87; Stamford Mus & Nature Ctr, Conn, 87; Am Acad & Inst Arts & Lett, New York, 87; and others. *Pos:* Vis artist/critic, Sarah Lawrence Col, 68-69, Cornell Univ, 70-73. *Teaching:* Artist in residence, Dartmouth Col, 62, Sch Mus Fine Arts, Boston, 80-86; vis artist critic, Inst Humanistic Studies, 65-66; vis artist critic, Univ Pa, 68-69; vis artist critic, Cornell Univ, 69-74. *Awards:* Guggenheim Fel, 66 & 68; Nat Coun Arts Award, 68. *Bibliog:* John Russell (auth), Art: Friedel Dzubas, New York Times, 3/29/85; Charles Millard (auth), Dzubas' paintings: Interview with the artist, Art/World, 1/86; Kenworth Moffet (auth), Review of show, Vol II, No 4, Moffet's Artletter, 4/87. *Media:* Acrylic; Oil. *Publ:* Auth, Statement & color plate, Art in Am, 67 & Art Now, 72. *Dealer:* Mirvish Gallery 596 Markham St Toronto ON Canada; André Emmerich Gallery 41 E 57th St New York NY 10022. *Mailing Add:* c/o Andre Emmerich 41 E 57th St New York NY 10022

E

EADES, LUIS ERIC
PAINTER, EDUCATOR
b Madrid, Spain, June 25, 23; US citizen. *Study:* Bath Sch Art, Eng; Slade Sch, Univ London; Inst Polytech Nac, Mexico City, Mex; Univ Ky, Lexington, BA. *Work:* Whitney Mus Am Art, New York; Mus Fine Arts, Houston; Dallas Mus Fine Arts; Ft Worth Art Ctr; Mus Fine Arts, Holyoke, Mass. *Comn:* Airport mural, Govt Honduras, Toncontin, Tegucigalpa, 48. *Exhib:* Recent Painting USA: The Figure, Mus Mod Art, New York, 62; Forty Artists Under Forty, Whitney Mus Am Art, 62; State of Man, New Sch Social Res, New York, 64; 2nd Intermountain Biennial Exhib, Salt Lake Art Ctr, Utah, 65; Colorado Springs Fine Arts Ctr, 69. *Teaching:* Prof painting & drawing, Univ Tex, 54-60; prof painting & drawing, Univ Colo, 61- *Media:* Oil, Acrylic. *Publ:* Illusr, The Precipice, Univ Tex, 69. *Dealer:* Carlin Galleries 710 Montgomery Fort Worth TX 76107; Carson-Sapiro Gallery 2601 Blake St Denver CO 80202. *Mailing Add:* 1627 Fifth St Boulder CO 80302

EAGEN, CHRISTOPHER T
DIRECTOR
b Ohio, Feb 18, 56. *Study:* Kansas City Art Inst, BFA, 78. *Collections Arranged:* Beyond the Surface: Abstract Illusionists, 82, Art of the Emotionally Disturbed Adolescents, 83, Sculpture from the Ceiling, 84, Live TV: Television as It Happened, 86, Tangeman Fine Arts Gallery, Cincinnati, Ohio. *Pos:* Dir publicity, Contemp Art Ctr, Cincinnati, 78-79; pres, Cincinnati Artists Group Effort, 79-80; asst dir, Tangeman Fine Arts Gallery, Cincinnati, 80-81. *Teaching:* Instr & gallery internship art appreciation, Univ Cincinnati, 82-86. *Publ:* Contribr, Fragments, 83-84, coauth, Contemporary African Sculpture, 84, contribr, Emeritae, 85 & Art Deco Cincinnati, 85, Univ Publ, Univ Cincinnati. *Mailing Add:* Palm Beach Community Col Mus Art 601 Lake Ave Lake Worth FL 33460

EAGERTON, ROBERT PIERCE
PAINTER
b Florence, SC, Mar 17, 40. *Study:* Atlanta Sch Art, BFA; Acad Fine Arts, Vienna, Austria; Cranbrook Acad Art, Bloomfield Hills, Mich. *Work:* Nat Collection Fine Art, Smithsonian Inst, Washington, DC; Art Inst Chicago; Lessing J Rosenwald Collection, Jenkintown, Pa; Sheldon Swope Gallery Art; Norman McKenzie Mus Art, Regina, Sask; Lincoln Conf Ctr, Indianapolis, Ind. *Exhib:* One-man show, Norman McKenzie Mus Art; Lithographs de la Collection Mourlot, PR, 71; Prints: USA 1974, Univ Pittsburgh; Image South Gallery, Atlanta, Ga, 81; Ruschman Gallery, Indianapolis, Ind, 88 & 90; and others. *Pos:* Co-founder, Transfigurations Press, Sarasota, Fla, 64-66. *Teaching:* Prof painting, Herron Sch Art, Ind-Purdue Univ, Indianapolis, 66-88; guest artist printmaking, Univ Ill, Champaign, 70; vis prof printmaking, Tyler Sch Art, summer 72; vis artist, Univ Sask, Regina, 73, Univ Mich, Ann Arbor, 77, Louisville Sch Art, Ky, 79, Cincinnati Sch Art, Ohio, 81 & Emma Lake Wkshp, Regina. *Bibliog:* Robert Eagerton (video), Indiana Univ, 90. *Media:* Oils. *Publ:* Contribr, Horizon, 87. *Dealer:* Ruschman Gallery 421 Massachusetts Ave Indianapolis IN 46204. *Mailing Add:* 3001 N New Jersey St No 3 Indianapolis IN 46205

EAMES, JOHN HEAGAN
ETCHER, PAINTER
b Lowell, Mass, July 19, 1900. *Study:* Harvard Univ, AB, 22; Royal Col Art, with Malcolm Osborne & Robert Austin, 33, 35 & 37. *Work:* Metrop Mus Art, New York; Libr of Cong, Washington, DC; Albany Inst Hist & Art, NY; Bates Col, Lewiston, Maine. *Exhib:* Royal Acad, London, Eng, 35, 37 & 40; New York World's Fair, 39; Int Print Exhib, Art Inst Chicago, 39; Biennial Exhib, Venice, Italy, 40; Contemp Am Drawings, Metrop Mus Art, New York, 42 & 52; Retrospective Exhib Bates Col, Lewiston, Maine, 92. *Awards:* Kate W Arms Mem Prize, Soc Am Graphic Artists, 52, 54 & 57, John Taylor Arms Prize, 53, Henry B Shope Prize, 57. *Mem:* Soc Am Graphic Artists; Nat Acad Design; Royal Soc Painters-Etchers, London, Eng. *Mailing Add:* Boothbay Harbor ME 04538

EARDLEY, CYNTHIA
SCULPTOR
b Trenton, NJ, Mar 18, 46. *Study:* Douglass Col, Rutgers Univ, New Brunswick, NJ, BA (with honors), 68; Sch Visual Arts, New York, 68-69. *Comn:* Peeling Wall, comn by pres Sydney Lewis, Best Products Inc, Richmond, Va, 72. *Exhib:* Buildings for Best Products, Mus Mod Art, New York, 80; Younger Artists: Figurative Art, Artist's Choice Mus, New York, 80 & 83-84; Monique Knowlton Gallery, New York 83-85; Precious Objects, 84 & Contemporary Pedestal Sculpture, 86, Univ Galleries, Univ South Fla, Tampa; New Talent, New York, Sioux City Art Ctr, Iowa, Univ Northern Iowa, Cedar Falls, 85 & Univ Wis, Menonomie & Green Bay, 85 & 86; Contemporary Pedestal Sculpture, Moody Gallery Art, Univ Ala, Tuscaloosa, 85 & Huntsville Mus Art, 86, Ala; Auction Preview Exhibs, New Mus Contemp Art, NY, 88 & 89; The Figure Now, Cork Gallery, Lincoln Center, New York, 90; Salena Gallery, Long Island Univ, Brooklyn, 90; Sally Hawkins Gallery, New York, 90; The Power of Scale, Art Mus S Tex, Corpus Christi, 91. *Pos:* Co-dir, Site Inc, New York, 69-73. *Awards:* First Place Award, Enviro-Vision, Everson Mus, 72; Semi-finalist, Municipal Servs Bldg Plaza Competition, Philadelphia, 92. *Bibliog:* John Russell (auth), Art: Cynthia Eardley, NY Times, 5/20/83; Gerrit Henry (auth), Cynthia Eardley: Monique Knowlton Gallery, 10/83 & Cynthia Nadelman (auth), The new American sculpture, 1/84, Art News; P Freeman (ed), New Art, Harry N Abrams, 84; Gail Mishkin (auth), Small Scale, International Sculpture, 12/86; Roberta Smith (auth), Sculpture in the City, New York Times, 4/20/90. *Media:* Bronze, Ceramic. *Dealer:* Sally Hawkins Gallery 448 West Broadway New York NY. *Mailing Add:* 115 W Broadway New York NY 10013

EARL, JACK EUGENE
CERAMIST
b Unioplis, Ohio, Aug 2, 34. *Study:* Bluffton Col, BA, 56; Ohio State Univ, MA, 64. *Work:* Butler Mus Art, Youngstown, Ohio; Milwaukee Art Mus, Wis; Mus Contemp Crafts, New York, NY; Nat Mus Am Art, Smithsonian, Wash, DC; Chicago Art Inst; and others. *Comn:* Mural, Kohler Co, Kohler, Wis, 76. *Exhib:* Int Exhib Ceramics, Victoria & Albert Mus Art, London, Eng, 72; Clay Things, Whitney Mus Am Art, New York, 74; one-man shows, Am Craft Mus, New York, 88, Charles A Wustum Mus, Racine, Wis, 88, Octagon Ctr, Ames, Iowa, 88, Perimeter Gallery, Chicago, Ill, 88, Kansas City Art Inst, Mo, 89, Miami Univ, Oxford, Ohio, 90 & Dorothy Weill Gallery, San Francisco, Calif, 90-92; American Clay Artists 1989, Port Hist Mus & Clay Studio, Philadelphia, Pa, 89; group show, Sybaris Gallery, Royal Oak, Mich, 89; 1989 Perth International Crafts Triennial, Art Gallery Western Australia, 89; Helen Dratt Gallery, New York, 90; and others. *Collections Arranged:* Objects USA, 68; The Plastic Earth, John Michael Kohler Arts Ctr, Sheboygan, Wis; Decade of Ceramic Art, San Francisco Mus of Art, Calif, 73. *Teaching:* Instr ceramics, Toledo Mus Art, 64-72; from asst prof to assoc prof ceramics, Va Commonwealth Univ, 72-78. *Awards:* Merit Award, Louisville Art Ctr, 68-70; Purchase Award, Columbus Gallery Fine Arts, 72; Nat Endowment Arts Award, 75-89; Ohio Coun Arts Award, 81, 83, 85 & 90; and others. *Bibliog:* Down Home, Arts in Va, 74; Art in industry, Crafts Horizon, 74; Lee Nordness (auth), Jack Earl - The Genesis and Triumph, Survival of an Underground Ohio Artist, 86; and others. *Mem:* Hon mem Nat Coun Educ Ceramic Arts. *Mailing Add:* 11173 Lake Dr Lakeview OH 43331

EARLE, EDWARD W
CURATOR, HISTORIAN
b New Orleans, La, Aug 19, 51. *Study:* Univ Notre Dame, BA, 74; Visual Studies Workshop, State Univ NY, Buffalo, MA(mus studies), 78. *Collections Arranged:* Points of View (ed, catalog), 79; Hand Camera in History, 82; The Orient Viewed, 82; Philip Brigandi, Photographer, 83; Prof Joseph Jastrow, 84. *Pos:* Cur, Visual Studies Workshop, Rochester, NY, 77-79; librn & archivist, Photog Resource Ctr, Boston, 80-82; cur, Calif Mus Photog, Univ Calif, Riverside, 82- *Teaching:* Instr photog, Swain Sch Design, New Bedford, Mass, 79-80; instr hist photog, Boston Col, Chestnut Hill, 82-83. *Mem:* Col Art Asoc; Soc Photog Educ; Am Cult Asn. *Res:* History of photography, relating aesthetic trends to social and cultural conditions. *Publ:* Contributing articles in Afterimage and New England J Photog, 77-; Points of View, The Stereograph in America: A Cultural History, VSW Press, 79; ed, Philip Brigandi, Calif Mus Photog Bulletin, 83; contribr, The Photographic Vision (TV ser), KOCE-TV for PBS. *Mailing Add:* Calif Mus Photogr Univ Calif Riverside CA 92521

EARLS, PAUL
ENVIRONMENTAL ARTIST
b Springfield, Mo, June 9, 34. *Study:* Eastman Sch Music, BM(cum laude), 55, MM, 56; Univ Rochester, PhD, 59. *Comn:* City Ring, Boston 200, 75; Augenmusik, Boston Musica Viva, 86. *Exhib:* Electra, Mus Mod Art, Paris, 83; Mehr Licht, Hamburger Kunsthalle, Ger, 85; Computers & Art, IBM Gallery, New York, 88; Images du Futur, Montreal, 90; Liberty Sci Ctr, 92; and others. *Pos:* Fel, Ctr Advan Visual Studies, Mass Inst Tech, 70- *Teaching:* Assoc prof music, Duke Univ, 65-72; vis prof, Univ Calif, 72, Univ Lowell, 77 & Harvard Univ, 90; lectr sound, Mass Col Art, 72-78; lectr environ art, Mass Inst Technol, 78- & Univ Indust Art, Helsinki, 92. *Awards:* Premier Award, Bienale Coltejar, Colombia, 73; Gold Medal, Dreamstage, Am Psychiatric Asn, 78; First Int Water Sculpture Competition Award, LA World Exposition, 82. *Media:* Music, Lasers. *Publ:* Auth, Sounding Space, Musical Sculpture, UAG, Can, 74. *Mailing Add:* 40 Massachusetts Ave Cambridge MA 02139

EARLS-SOLARI, BONNIE
CURATOR
b Fallbrook, Calif, Oct 4, 51. *Study:* Univ Calif, Berkeley, BA, 73. *Pos:* Asst cur, Univ Art Mus, 74-77; prog coordr, Cooper Hewitt Mus, 77-78; cur, dir, art prog, Bank Am Corp, 79- *Mem:* Asn Prof Art Adv; Graphic Arts Coun; Foto Forum; Art Table (Women Visual Arts). *Mailing Add:* BankAmerica Corporation Art Program 3021 PO Box 37000 San Francisco CA 94137

EASTCOTT, ROBERT WAYNE
PRINTMAKER, PAINTER
b Trail, BC, July 20, 43. *Study:* Emily Carr Col Art & Design, (Vancouver Sch Art), with J Shadbolt, D Jarvis & R Kiyooka, Senior Cert (painting & printmaking, hons), 66. *Work:* Nat Gallery, Ottawa; Art Gallery Greater Victoria, BC; Winnipeg Art Gallery, Man; Robert MacLaughlin Gallery, Oshawa, Ont; Kanagawa Prefectural Gallery, Yokohama, Japan. *Comn:* Portfolio of 5 editions, Generation 84 Youth Soc, Vancouver, BC, 83; portrait of Mr Belzberg (serigraph), New Play Ctr, Vancouver, 83; Edition of 125 (serigraph), Adovocat Structured Settlements; wall relief on riveted aluminum, Rienhard Derreth Graphics Ltd, Vancouver, BC, 89. *Exhib:* Modern Galerija (with catalog), Ljubljana, Yugoslavia, 76; Canada House, London, Eng, 78; Artists '79, United Nations, New York, 79; 10 Canadian Artists (with catalog), Tochigi Mus-Fuji TV Gallery, Tokyo, Japan, 80; History of Printmaking in British Columbia 1889-1983 (auth, catalog), Art Gallery Greater Victoria, BC, 84; Fomento de las Artes Decoratives, Barcelona, Spain, 85; Burnaby Art Gallery (with catalog) BC, 88; North of the Border-Contemporary Canadian Art, Watcom Co Mus, Wash, 90. *Pos:* Founding mem & pres, Dunderave Print Soc, 71-76. *Teaching:* Instr painting, Vancouver Sch Art, BC, 65-70; head dept printmaking, Capilano Col, NVancouver, BC, 71- *Awards:* Can Coun Grant, 68. *Bibliog:* Glenn Allison & E Hunning (auths), Four Canadian Artists, Mod Galeria, Lyublyana, Yugoslavia, 76; A Perry & K Kritzweiser (auths),Wayne Eastcott, Okui Assoc, Tokyo, Japan, 79; The Printed Painting-Ted Lindberg Burnaby Art Gallery, 88. *Mem:* Royal Can Acad Arts; Dunderave Print Soc; World Print Coun; Can Print & Drawing Soc; Malaspina Printmakers. *Media:* All Media; Acrylic, Enamel. *Dealer:* Yueko Okui 905 Parkside Heights 2-5-8 Shiba Minato-Ku Tokyo Japan. *Mailing Add:* c/o Patrick Doheny Fine Arts 1811 W First Ave Vancouver BC V6J 4M6 Canada

EASTERWOOD, HENRY LEWIS
EDUCATOR, TAPESTRY ARTIST
b Villa Rica, Ga, Oct 29, 34. *Study:* West Ga Col, 53-55; Memphis Acad Arts, BFA, 58, spec studies in Europe & Scandinavia, 65. *Work:* Memphis Brooks Mem Gallery Art, Tenn; Miss Art Asn, Jackson; State of Tenn Collection of Crafts, Nashville; Fall Creek Falls State Park, Tenn; Dulin Gallery Art, Knoxville, Tenn. *Comn:* Tapestry, Vanderbilt Univ, 74; four tapestries, Memphis Mem Gardens, 74; Fed Home Loan Bd, Washington, DC, 77; Baptist Mem Hosp, Memphis, 80; US News & World Report, Washington, DC, 83; IBM, Washington, DC, 84. *Exhib:* Fiber, Clay & Metal, St Paul Mus, Minn, 59, 61 & 63; Craftsmen USA, Mus Contemp Crafts, New York, 66; Miss Art Asn, 72; Signature Shop & Galleries, Atlanta, 85; Premonitions, Cheekwood Mus, Nashville, 85; Alice Bingham Gallery, Mem. *Pos:* Craft adv, Tenn Arts Comn, 70. *Teaching:* Assoc prof textiles & chmn dept, Memphis Col Art, 59- *Awards:* Miss River Crafts Award, 65, 67 & 69; Nat Merit Award, Am Craftsmen's Coun, 66; Am Inst Archit Gold Medal, 69; and others. *Mem:* Am Craftsmen's Coun (Tenn rep, 63-65); Tenn Craftsmen's Asn; hon mem Memphis Weavers Guild. *Media:* Tapestry, Fiber Arts. *Dealer:* Jean Efron & Associates 2440 Virginia Ave NW Washington DC 20037. *Mailing Add:* Dept Art Memphis Col Art Overton Park Memphis TN 38112

EASTMAN, GENE M
PAINTER
b Council Grove, Kans, Jan 1, 26. *Study:* Univ Kans, BFA; Art Inst Chicago; Univ Iowa, with Stuart Edie, MFA. *Exhib:* Houston Mus Fine Arts, Tex, 58 & 61; Dallas Mus Fine Arts Ann, 59, 63 & 66; Seven States Artists Ann, Delgado Mus, New Orleans, 61; Watercolor USA, Springfield, Mo, 64; 24-64 Nat Exhib Small Paintings, Purdue Univ, 64. *Teaching:* Prof drawing & painting, Sam Houston State Univ, 58-, chmn art dept, 72-79; guest instr drawing & painting, Mus Fine Arts Sch, Houston Mus Fine Arts, Tex, 68-70. *Awards:* First Prize, Painting, Tex Fine Arts Asn, 58; Purchase Award, Okla Printmaker Soc, 64; First Prize, Painting, Tri-State Exhib, Beaumont Mus, Tex, 67. *Media:* Oil, Watercolor. *Mailing Add:* 24004 S Sam Houston Ave Huntsville TX 77340

EASTON, ROGER DAVID
PAINTER, JEWELER
Douglaston, NY, Jan 4, 23. *Study:* Albright Art Sch, State Univ NY, BS, 49; State Univ Iowa, MA, 51; Univ Denver, EdD, 58. *Exhib:* Drawing & Small Sculpture show, Ball State Univ Art Gallery, Muncie, Ind, 59-81; Ann Regional Artists Exhib, Ft Wayne Art Mus, Ft Wayne, Ind, 59-81; Smithsonian Inst Crafts Exhib, nat traveling exhib, 60-62; Festival of the Arts, Tubac Ctr Arts, Tubac, Ariz, 87 & 88; Don Raffin Mem Art Exhib, Paradise Valley Community Col Gallery, Paradise Valley, Ariz, 88; Southern Ariz Watercolor Guild, Univ Ariz Gallery, Tucson, Ariz, 88. *Teaching:* Teaching fel, art hist, State Univ Iowa, Iowa City, Iowa, 50-51; from instr to assoc prof, art hist & educ, State Univ, New York, Cortland, NY, 51-58; prof, Ball State Univ, Muncie, Ind, 58-85. *Awards:* Awards, Regional Artists Exhib, Ft Wayne Mus Art, 59, 61 & 63; Hon Mention, Wabash Valley Exhib, Sheldon Swope Gallery, Terre Haute, Ind, 79 & 80; Juror's Spec Recognition Award, Spring Members Show, Ctr Arts, Tubac, Ariz, 87. *Bibliog:* Articles, Design Quart, Walker Art Gallery, 55 & 59; Murray Bovin (auth), article, Jewelry Making, 59. *Mem:* Southern Ariz Watercolor Guild; Nat Art Educ Asn; Ariz Art Educ Asn. *Media:* Acrylic, Watercolor. *Publ:* Auth, But is it art?, NY State Educ, Vol 41, No 5; Student questions on aesthetics, Col Art J, 54; coauth, A forward look at art and art education, Southern Zone, Art Educ NY, 57; auth, Guernica, Off Pub Info Serv, Ball State Univ, 69. *Mailing Add:* 3371 Placita Esconces Green Valley AZ 85614

EATON, PAULINE (FRIEDRICH)
PAINTER, INSTRUCTOR
b Neptune, NJ, Mar 20, 35. *Study:* Dickinson Col, Carlisle, Pa, BA, 57; Northwestern Univ, Evanston, Ill, MA, 58; seminars with Ed Betts, Glenn Bradshaw & Alex Nepote. *Work:* Butler Inst Am Art, Youngstown, Ohio; St Mary's Col, Md; Redlands Community Hosp, Calif. *Comn:* Paintings, Empire Savings Banks, Colo, 77-79; landscapes, Host Inns, Phoenix Airport, Ariz, 78; six paintings, Mercy Hosp, San Diego, 81. *Exhib:* Nat Acad Design, New York, 75 & 77; solo exhib, Nat Arts Club, New York, 77; San Diego Mus Art, 77-79 & 81; Butler Inst Am Art, Youngstown, Ohio, 77-79 & 81; Laguna Beach Mus Art, Calif, 78 & 80; Palm Springs Desert Mus, Calif, 79; solo show, Marin Civic Ctr, 84 & 88; St Supery Winery, 92. *Teaching:* Lectr & demonstr, San Diego Art Inst, San Diego & Watercolor Soc, 77-; instr, Miracosta Col, Oceanside, Calif, 80-81, Idyllwild Sch Mus & Arts, 83- & Marin Arts Guild, Belvedere, Calif, 84-87; pvt instr & workshops, currently. *Awards:* Golden Award, Foothills Art Ctr, Colo, 78; Strathmore Award, Butler Inst Am Art, 81; Third Award, Western Fedn Exhib, 82. *Bibliog:* Barbara Nechis (auth), Creative Watercolor, 79 & Edward Betts (auth), Creative Seascape Painting, 80, Watson-Guptill; Martin E Peterson (auth), On view: Pauline Eaton, Applause Mag, 80; Watercolor, Am Artist Mag, 87. *Mem:* Nat Watercolor Soc; San Diego Watercolor Soc (pres, 76-77); Nat Soc Painters Casein & Acrylic (western regional chmn, 80-81); Artists Guild San Diego Mus Art (pres, 82-83); Watercolor West (bd mem, 79-); West Coast Watercolor Soc (pres, 89-). *Media:* Watercolor, Acrylic. *Publ:* Auth, Crawling to the Light, 87. *Mailing Add:* Ten Alta Mira Ave Kentfield CA 94904

EATON, THOMAS NEWTON See Eaton, Tom

EATON, TOM
CARTOONIST, WRITER
b Wichita, Kans, Mar 2, 40. *Study:* Univ Denver, 58; Univ Kans, BFA, 62. *Comn:* Mag covers, Boy's Life, Scholastic Voice, Scholastic Scope, Child Life, and others; posters, Scholastic Mag Inc, 74-79; plus others. *Pos:* Artist-writer Contemp Cards dept, Hallmark Cards, Inc, Kansas City, Mo, 62-66; art ed, Scholastic Mag Inc, New York, 66-68; free lance cartoonist-writer, 68-; regular contrib comic features, Boys' Life Mag, 84- *Awards:* Cert of Excellence for Cover, Catch the Eye, 75, Am Inst Graphics Arts. *Bibliog:* Eleanor Van Zandt (auth), A cartoonist looks at the comics, Practical Eng Mag, 68. *Mem:* Nat Cartoonists Soc; Am Mensa; Am Anti-Vivisection Soc. *Media:* Pen, Ink. *Publ:* Auth & illusr, Flap, Delacorte Press, 72; Tom Eaton's Book of Marvels, 76, Holiday Greeting Cards, 78 & Super Valentines, 79, Scholastic Bk Serv; Rufus and the Earth Patrol, Sat Eve Post, 78; plus numerous others. *Mailing Add:* 911 W 100th St Kansas City MO 64114

EBERLE, EDWARD SAMUEL
CERAMIST, DRAFTSMAN
b Tarentum, Pa, Oct 3, 44. *Study:* Edinboro State Col, BS, 67; NY State Col Ceramics, Alfred Univ, MFA, 71. *Work:* Ariz State Univ, Tempe; Mus Art, Carnegie Inst, Pittsburgh, Pa; Detroit Inst Art; Cranbrook Acad Art Mus. *Comn:* Ceramic tile mural, City of Pittsburgh, 83; ceramic tile mural, Westinghouse Elec Corp, Monroeville, Pa, 86. *Exhib:* Contemp Ceramic Sculpture, WH Ackland Mem Mus, Chapel Hill, NC, 77; one-man show, Mus Art, Carnegie Inst, Pittsburgh, Pa, 80 & 91; Poetry of the Physical, Am Crafts Mus, New York, 86; Collecting Contemp Ceramics, Mus Art, Carnegie Inst, Pittsburgh, Pa; 28th Ceramic Nat Exhib, Everson Mus Art, Syracuse, NY; The Narrative Vessel, Kohler Arts Ctr. *Teaching:* From instr to asst prof ceramics, Philadelphia Col Art, 71-75; from asst to assoc prof, Carnegie-Mellon Univ, Pittsburgh, Pa, 75-85. *Awards:* Fel, Nat Endowment Arts, 87; Fel, Pa Coun Arts, 86 & 89. *Bibliog:* Gary Wells (auth), A mythic realm in black and white, Am Ceramics, 6/1/87; Michael Odom (auth), Edward Eberle: in the realm of myth, Am Craft, 5-6/92. *Dealer:* Garth Clark Gallery 24 W 57th St New York NY 10019. *Mailing Add:* 2100 E Ohio St Pittsburgh PA 15212

EBERLY, VICKIE
PAINTER
b Washington, DC, May 28, 56. *Study:* Md Inst Col Art, BFA(painting), 78; City Univ New York, Queens Col, NY, MFA(painting), 81. *Work:* Image Communications Inc, New York. *Exhib:* Queens Community Mus, New York, 81; Queens Col Gallery, City Univ New York, 81; Ball State Univ Art Gallery, Ind, 82; El Paso Mus Art, Tex, 82; Barrett House, Poughkeepsie, NY, 85; Central Hall Gallery, New York, 86; 22 Wooster Gallery, New York, 87; Tradition 3 Thousand Gallery, New York, 87. *Media:* Oil on Canvas, Mixed Graphics. *Dealer:* Tradition 3 Thousand Gallery 273 E 10th St New York NY 10009. *Mailing Add:* 84-21 110th St Richmond Hill NY 11418

EBIE, WILLIAM DENNIS
ADMINISTRATOR, PAINTER
b Akron, Ohio, Feb 7, 42. *Study:* Akron Art Inst Sch Design, scholar, 60, Univ Akron & Akron Art Inst Sch Design, BFA, 64; Calif Col Arts & Crafts, scholarships, 67-68, MFA, 68. *Work:* Calif Col Arts & Crafts Gallery. *Exhib:* The Figure: An Invitational Painting Exhibition, Kans State Col Gallery, Pittsburg, 75; Territorial Gallery, Roswell, NMex, 76 & 78; 20th Nat Sun Festival, El Paso Mus Art, Tex, 79; Santa Fe Festival of Arts, 79; Upstairs Gallery, Albuquerque, NMex, 80; Albuquerque United Artists Downtown Ctr Arts, NMex, 81; Fine Arts Gallery, NMex State Fairgrounds, Albuquerque, 85; Stables Art Gallery, Taos, NMex, 86; Carlsbad Art Mus, NMex, 88. *Pos:* Ceramic specialist, Peace Corps, Cuzco, Peru, 64-66; graphic artist, Alameda Co Health Dept, Oakland, Calif, 67-68; asst dir, Roswell Mus & Art Ctr & managing dir, Roswell Mus Artist in Residence Prog, 71-; dir, Roswell Mus & Art Ctr, 87- *Teaching:* Instr painting, Fla A&M Univ, 69-70; instr painting, Roswell Mus Adult Educ, NMex, 71-78. *Mem:* NMex Asn Mus; Mountain Plains Mus Asn. *Mailing Add:* 909 N Lea Roswell NM 88201

EBSEN, ALF K
CALLIGRAPHER, GRAPHIC ARTIST
b Berlin, Ger, July 29, 08; Can citizen. *Study:* Kunstgewerbeschule, Hamburg, Ger. *Work:* Canadian Royal Legion hq, Kentsbut, Ottawa. *Comn:* Honour scrolls, IBM Can, STELCO & many prof orgn; design of advert, Volkswagen AG, Ger; Medieval Studies Advertising, Univ Toronto. *Exhib:* Continual exhibs in Ontario. *Pos:* Dir graphic arts, Eddy Match Co, Ontario, 55-63. *Teaching:* Instr calligraphic design at community cols in Ontario & Alberta; lectr, Univ Toronto, 68-70; instr, Queen's Univ, Kingston & Hamilton Sch Fine Arts, Sir Samford Fleming Col, 84-86. *Bibliog:* The Review, Vol 62, no 2, Issue 340, Imperial Oil Ltd, 78; Applied Arts, fall 87. *Mem:* Calligraphic Arts Guild of Toronto (founder, 76); Royal Can Acad Arts. *Media:* Paper, Vellum. *Publ:* Auth, Calligraphy Practice Book of the Canadian System, pvt publisher; From the Farthest Hebrides, McMillan of Can. *Mailing Add:* 21 Edgewater Dr Roseneath ON K0K 2X0 Canada

ECHOHAWK, BRUMMETT
PAINTER, ILLUSTRATOR
b Pawnee, Okla, Mar 3, 22. *Study:* Sch Arts & Crafts, Detroit, 44; Art Inst Chicago, 44-48. *Work:* Gilcrease Mus Am Hist & Art, Tulsa. *Comn:* Truman Mem Libr (mural, with Thomas Hart Benton), Independence, Mo, 59-60. *Exhib:* Gilcrease Mus, Tulsa; Amon Carter Mus, Ft Worth, Tex; M H De Young Mem Mus, San Francisco; Imperial War Mus, London; Karl May Theater Mus, Bad Segeberg, WGer; Art Through the Embassies, US State Dept, Pakistani, India. *Pos:* Auth & illusr, articles in Western Horseman, Colorado Springs, 50-, Tulsa Sunday World, 50- & Okla Today, 60-; bd mem, Gilcrease Mus Am Hist & Art, Tulsa, 80- *Bibliog:* Whose Children Are These (film), ABC-TV Network, New York. *Media:* Oil, Tempera. *Publ:* Auth & illusr, Blue book, McCalls Mag, 49. *Mailing Add:* 2525 W Easton Tulsa OK 74110

ECKART, CHRISTIAN
PAINTER
b Calgary, Alta, Can, Jan 9, 59. *Study:* Hunter Col, City Univ New York, MFA, 86. *Work:* Mus Mod Art, New York; Chicago Art Inst; List Visual Art Ctr, Mass Inst Technol; New Sch Soc Res, New York. *Exhib:* Paul Kuhn Fine Art, Calgary, Can, 84; Massimo Audiello Gallery, New York, 86, 88 & 89; Rhona Hoffman Gallery, Chicago, 87 & 89; Galerie Tanit, Munich, Ger, 89, 92; Galerie 'T Venster, Rotterdam, Neth, 88; Galerie Thaddaues Ropac, Paris & Salzburg, 90 & 91; Rubin Spangle Gallery, New York, 90 & 92; Eli Broad Family Found, Santa Monica, Calif, 92. *Teaching:* Nova Scotia Col Art & Design, Halifax, NS, Can, 89, Art Ctr Col Design, Pasadena, Calif, 90, Univ Hartford Dept Art, Conn, 91, Alta Col Art, Calgary, Can, 91, Int Art His Conf, New York, 91, Aldrich Mus Contemp Art, Ridgfield, Conn, 92, Univ RI, 92, Sch Visual Arts, NY, 92. *Bibliog:* Alexander Puhringer (auth), 9 Fragen am Christian Eckart, Noema Mag, 4/91; Hiromi Honda (auth), Christian Eckart, Agora Mag, 6/91; Balcon Mag, Andachtsbild Dtudies, No 7, 12/91. *Dealer:* Rubin Spangle Gallery 395 W Broadway New York NY 10012. *Mailing Add:* 438 Bedford Ave Brooklyn NY 11211

ECKE, BETTY TSENG YU-HO See Tseng Yu-ho

ECKELBERRY, DON RICHARD
PAINTER
b Sebring, Ohio, July 6, 21. *Study:* Cleveland Inst Art. *Comn:* Bird postage stamp, British Honduras, 62; murals, Adirondack Mus, 60. *Exhib:* One-man shows, New York, 43, 46 & 56 & Louisville, Ky, 70; Cleveland Inst Art, 70. *Pos:* Staff artist, Nat Audubon Soc, 43-45; free lance artist, 45- *Mem:* Fel Am Ornithol Union; Audubon Artists Soc; Cooper Ornithol Soc; Soc Animal Artists; Wilson Ornithol Soc. *Mailing Add:* 180 Woodsome Rd Babylon NY 11702

ECKERSLEY, THOMAS CYRIL
EDUCATOR, PHOTOGRAPHER
b Detroit, Mich, Nov 23, 41. *Study:* Ohio Univ, with Clarence White, Jr, BFA, 66, MFA, 69. *Work:* Erie Art Ctr, Pa; Univ Calif; Marine Midland Bank; Ohio Univ; and others. *Comn:* Numerous commissions for individuals, businesses and organizations. *Exhib:* Brownsville 18th Int Art Show, 89; E Tex State Univ, 90; Lake Worth 49th Nat, 90; New York State Fair Photog Exhib, 91; State Univ NY-Cobleskill, 91; and others. *Pos:* Studio mgr & admin asst, Josten's Am Photog, 67-68; photogr, WOSU-TV, Ohio State Univ, 68-69. *Teaching:* Instr photog, Columbus Col Art & Design, 69-70; prof art, State Univ NY Col Oswego, 70-, chmn art dept, 77-86 & 92. *Awards:* First Prize, Oswego Art Guild, 75; 2nd Prize, New York State Fair Photog, 91; 3rd Prize, New York State Fine Arts, 91. *Mem:* Lepidopterists Soc. *Publ:* Coauth, Jewelry Making: An Illustrated Guide to Technique, 75. *Mailing Add:* Box 44 Hannibal NY 13074

ECKERT, LOU
PAINTER
b Lancaster, Pa, Jan 27, 28. *Study:* Univ Rochester, with John Mennihan, BA; workshops under Jan Horton, Univ Nebr, Ida Kohlmeyer, Univ New Orleans, Richard Brough, Univ Ala & Stuart Purser, Univ Fla; also with Marie Hull, Jackson, Miss Andrew Bucci, Washington, DC. *Work:* Miss Art Asn Munic Gallery, Jackson; Greater Gulf Coast Art Asn Collection, Biloxi, Miss; and others. *Exhib:* Mid-South Ann, Brooks Mem Art Gallery, Memphis, Tenn, 65 & 69; one-man shows, Percy H Whiting Art Ctr, Fairhope, Ala, 69, New Orleans Theatre Performing Arts, 77 & Gulf South Galleries, McComb, Miss, 79-83 & Second Greater New Orleans Nat Exhib, 72; ann two-man shows, Gulf South Galleries, McComb, Miss, 78; and others. *Pos:* Owner & operator, Two Plus Two Ltd Gallery, New Orleans, 73. *Awards:* First Nat Bank Award (Miss Collection), 67; Purchase Award, Grand Hotel, Biloxi, 75. *Bibliog:* Jan Horton (auth), Art for the Day (film), ETV Ctr, Jackson, 70. *Mem:* Miss Art Asn, Jackson; La Watercolor Soc, New Orleans. *Media:* Oil, Watercolor. *Mailing Add:* 3631 Post Oak Ave New Orleans LA 70131

ECKERT, WILLIAM DEAN
PAINTER, HISTORIAN
b Coshocton, Ohio, Oct 10, 27. *Study:* Ohio State Univ, BA(with distinction), BFA(cum laude) & MA; Univ Iowa, PhD. *Work:* Butler Inst Am Art, Youngstown, Ohio; State Hist Soc Mus, Columbia, Mo; Bristol-Myers, Pharmaceutical Collection, Evansville, Ind; The Theodora Pottle Collection, Macomb, Ill (catalog), 78. *Exhib:* 22nd Delta Art Exhib, Ark Art Ctr, Little Rock, 79; Biennial Exhib, 87 & 48th Ann, 89, Sioux City Art Ctr, 87; Realism Today Exhib, Evansville Mus, 87; Mid-Four Exhib, Nelson Gallery, Kansas City, 87; Art St Louis VIII, 91; and others. *Teaching:* Assoc prof art hist, Western Ill Univ, Macomb, 59-65 & Union Col, Schenectady, NY, 65-68; prof art hist emer, Lindenwood Cols, 68-91, chmn art dept, 75-78 & 80-91. *Awards:* Third Award in Painting, Quincy Art Ctr Regional, Ill, 71; Twentieth Century Art Club Ann prize, St Louis Artists' Guild, 88; Bader Prize, St Louis Artists' Guild, 91; and others. *Mem:* Art St Louis; Soc Archit Historians; St Louis Artists Guild; Decorative Arts Trust. *Media:* Acrylic. *Res:* Renaissance stage in Italy; evolution of the perspective scene. *Publ:* Contribr, The college gallery & the liberal arts, Symposium, summer 67. *Mailing Add:* 1302 Musket Hollow St Charles MO 63303

ECKHARDT, FERDINAND
HISTORIAN, MUSEUM DIRECTOR
b Vienna, Austria, April 28, 02; Can citizen. *Study:* Univ Vienna, hon LLD; Univ Man, 71. *Pos:* Head educ, State Mus, Vienna; dir, Winnipeg Art Gallery, 53-74, emer dir, 74. *Awards:* Austrian Cross of Honor for Sci & Art, 72; Order of Canada, Can Govt, 76. *Mem:* Can Mus Asn; Can Art Mus Dirs Asn; Int Coun Mus, Can; Am Asn Art Mus Dirs. *Publ:* Auth, Das Graphische Werk von Walter Gramatte, Leipzig, 32; Das Betrachten von Kunstwerken, Wien, 48; Walter Gramatte, Three Vols, Winnipeg, 81; Ferdinand Eckhardt (father), ein Wiener Graphiker, Winnipeg, 82; Auswahl der Briefe von Walter Grammatte, Berlin, 83; and others. *Mailing Add:* 54 Harrow St Winnipeg MB R3M 2Y7 Canada

ECKLIN, SISTER M IRENITA
PAINTER
b Lancaster, Pa, Dec 6, 08. *Study:* Moore Col Art, Philadelphia, Pa, BFA, 39; watercolor with J A F Everett, artist, Salt Lake City, 41-45, Univ Utah, MFA, 54. *Exhib:* Art Inst, Heyburn, Idaho, 50; solo exhibs, Bridge Art Gallery, Washington, DC, 75 & Demuth Found Gallery, Lancaster, Pa, 86; Springfield Ohio Art Asn, 72; and others. *Teaching:* Prof, Col St Mary Wasotch, Salt Lake City, 40-55; prof art & painting, Dunbarton Col, Washington, DC, 55-73, chairperson, 58-73. *Bibliog:* Robert Le Min (auth), rev, 3/14/86 & Dawn Lightop Gable (auth), Lifestyle, 3/28/86, Lancaster Intelligencer. *Mem:* Nat League Am Pen Women; Washington Watercolor Asn; Montgomery County Art Asn. *Media:* Watercolor. *Publ:* Auth, Techniques of American Watercolor, John Singer Sargent, Univ Utah, 54. *Dealer:* Country Framery 6 N Sturgis Lane Lititz PA 17543. *Mailing Add:* 5000 Strathmore Ave Kensington MD 20895

ECKSTEIN, RUTH
PAINTER, PRINTMAKER
b Nuremberg, Ger, May 11, 16; US citizen. *Study:* New Sch Social Res, New York, with Stuart Davis; Art Students League, with Harry Sternberg, Julian Levy & V Vitlacyl; Pratt Graphic Ctr, New York, with Seong Moy & Roberto Delamonica. *Work:* Philadelphia Mus Art; Brooklyn Mus; Solomon R Guggenheim Mus; Israel Mus, Jerusalem; Metrop Mus Art, Mus Modern Art, New York. *Exhib:* One-woman shows, Alonzo Gallery, New York, 68, 70, 72, 75 & 77 Kunsthalle, Nuremberg, 74-75, Nassau Co Ctr Fine Arts, 75, Benson Gallery, NY, 76 & 81, Galeria de Arte 9, Lima, Peru, 80; Art of Northeast USA, 87; A Living Tradition, Int Travelling Exhib Abstract Art, Eastern Europe, 88-92; Benton Gallery, 88; Neuberger Mus at SUNY, 89; Andrée Zarre Gallery, New York, 92; and others. *Awards:* Village Art Ctr Award, New York, 63; Audubon Artists Awards, 77, 78 & 85; Art of Northeast USA Award, 83. *Bibliog:* Art Int, 72; Art News, 72; review, New York Times, 80, 83, 84, 85, 90 & 91. *Mem:* Am Abstr Artists (secy, 70-80); Soc Am Graphic Artists; Art Students League; Silvermine Guild Artists. *Media:* Acrylic; Woodcut and Mixed Mediums Prints. *Dealer:* Anita Shapolsky Gallery 99 Spring St New York NY 10013. *Mailing Add:* 5 Cricket Lane Great Neck NY 11024

ECONOMOS, MICHAEL E
EDUCATOR, PAINTER
b Athens, Greece, March 13, 36; US citizen. *Study:* Worcester Art Mus Sch, 59; Yale Art & Architecture, BFA, 61, MFA 64. *Work:* Michigan Univ Mus, Ann Arbor; Goutcher Col Mus, Baltimore, Md; Republic of China, Peking; Yale Collection, New Haven, Conn. *Comn:* Street mural, City of Baltimore, Md, 88. *Exhib:* Solo exhib, Baltimore Mus, Md, 70; Light Sound and Motion, Hudson River Mus, New York, 72. *Collections Arranged:* Art Scape (with catalogs), 86, 87 & 88. *Teaching:* Prof painting drawing printmaking, Md Inst Col Art, 62- *Awards:* Fullbright Grant, 62-63; Ford Found Grant, 83; Nat Endowment Arts, 89-90. *Bibliog:* Bernard Chaet (auth), The Art of Drawing, Holt Rinehart & Winston, 79. *Publ:* Gregory Battock, Super Realism--A Cultural Anthology, E P Dutton & Co. *Mailing Add:* c/o Richard Gasperi Gallery 320 Julia St New Orleans LA 70130

EDDY, DON
PAINTER
b Long Beach, Calif, Nov 4, 44. *Study:* Univ Hawaii, Honolulu, BFA, 67, MFA, 69; Univ Calif, Santa Barbara, 69-70. *Work:* Cleveland Mus Art, Ohio; Toledo Mus Art, Ohio; St Etienne Mus, France; Neue Galerie, Aachen, Ger; Williams Col Mus Art, Williamstown, Mass. *Exhib:* Fogg Art Mus, Harvard Univ, Cambridge, Mass, 73; Storm King Art Ctr, Mountainville, NY, 73; New York Avant-Garde, Saidye Bronfman Centre, Montreal, Que, 73; Hyper-realisme Americaine, Realism Europ, Centre Nat d'Art Contemporain, Paris, 74; Wadsworth Atheneum, Hartford, Conn, 74; Tokyo Biennial, Japan, 74; Baltimore Mus Art, Md, 76; Realist & Illusionist Art Traveling Exhib, Australia, 77; and others. *Bibliog:* Udo Kulterman (auth), New realism, NY Graphic Soc, 72; Peter Sager (auth), Realismus, Verlag M DuMont Schauberg. *Media:* Acrylic. *Dealer:* Nancy Hoffman Gallery 429 W Broadway New York NY 10012. *Mailing Add:* 543 Broadway New York NY 10012

EDELHEIT, MARTHA
PAINTER, FILMMAKER
b New York, NY. *Study:* Columbia Univ Teachers Col, BS, 56; Univ Chicago. *Exhib:* Sons & Others, Queens Mus, New York, 75; Three Centuries of the Am Nude, New York Cult Ctr, 75 & Minneapolis Inst Arts, Minn, 75; Works on Paper, Brooklyn Mus, NY, 75; Portland Mus, Ore, 76; Brooklyn Mus, 77; Mus Mod Art, New York, 77; Collaborations & Amplifications, Sets by Artists, Salt Lake City Art Ctr, Utah, 79; BLAM!, Whitney Mus, 84; group show, Paper in Particular, Columbia Col, Md, 89 & 90, Installation Exchange, Kulturforum, Monchengladbach, Ger, 89-90, Galerie Be'19, Helsinki, Finland, 91 & 92. *Teaching:* Vis artist, Feminist Art Prog, Calif Inst of the Arts, 73; artist-in-residence painting, Wilson Col, Chambersburg, Pa, 75; artist-in-residence film, Univ Cincinnati, Ohio, 76; artist-in-residence painting & drawing, Art Inst Chicago, 76; guest lectr film, New Sch Social Res, New York, 77. *Awards:* Second Prize, Juried Invitational Lehigh Univ, Pa, 84. *Bibliog:* Barbara Haskell (auth), Blam (catalog), Whitney Mus, 84; Rob Edelman (rev) Art Am, 2/86; Grace Glueck (auth), Artist and models, NY Times, 6/86; Maria-Terttu Kivirinta (auth), Helsingin Sanomat, 5/6/92. *Mem:* Women/Artist Filmmakers Inc (vpres, 74, pres, 75-77); Women in the Arts; Women's Caucus Art; Col Art Asn. *Media:* Mixed. *Publ:* Contribr, Women in the Year 2000, Arbor House, 74; Anonymous Was a Woman, 74 & Art: A Woman's Sensibility, 75, Calif Inst of the Arts; auth, The Invention of the Albino Queen, ANIMA, Conococheague Assoc, 75; Georgia O'Keefe: A reminiscence, Woman Artists Newsletter, 12/77. *Mailing Add:* 393 W Broadway New York NY 10012

EDELL, NANCY
PAINTER, PRINTMAKER
b Omaha, Nebr, Nov 12, 42; Can citizen. *Study:* Univ Nebr Omaha, BFA, 64; Univ Bristol, Eng, studied film with George Brandt, 68-69. *Work:* Can Coun Art Bank, Ottawa, Ont; Art Gallery Nova Scotia, Halifax; Robert McLaughlin Art Gallery, Oshawa, Ont; Winnipeg Art Gallery, Man; Mt St Vincent Univ Art Gallery, Halifax, NS; Dalhousie Univ Art Gallery, Halifax, NS. *Exhib:* Moosehead Press: 10 Years, traveling exhib, Winnipeg Art Gallery, 87-88; Innovation: Subject & Technique, Univ Toronto, Scarborough, Ont, 87; 80/20: 100 Years of NSCAO, Art Gallery Nova Scotia, Halifax, 88 & Subject Matter: Contemporary Painting & Sculpture in NS, 92; solo shows, Univ Nebr Omaha Art Gallery, 88, Univ Moncton Art Gallery, NB, 89 & Art Nuns: Recent Work by Nancy Edell, Art Gallery NS (touring), 91; 4th Int Biennial Print Exhib, Taipei, Taiwan, 90; Boston Printmakers, 42nd NAm Print Exhib, Fitchburgh Art Mus, 90; and others. *Teaching:* Adj prof, NS Col Art & Design, 82-92; vis artist printmaking, St Michael's Printshop, St Johns, Nfld, 87; vis fac visual art, Banff Sch Fine Arts, Banff, Alta, 88. *Awards:* Can Coun grant, 74, 80, 84, 87, 88, 90 & 92; Manitoba Arts Coun Grant, 77 & 78; Can Coun, Paris Studio, 90. *Bibliog:* Robert Pope (auth), Charlotte W Hammond & Nancy Edell, Arts Atlantic, fall 88; Cliff Eyland (auth), Art Nuns: Recent Work by Nancy Edell, AGNS, Canadian Art, vol 8, no 4, winter 91; Anna Fiarello (auth), 3 Approaches to Contemporary Rug Hooking, Fiberarts, 91. *Mem:* Can Artists Representation (secy, 84-85); Visual Arts NS; NS Printmakers Asn (secy-treas, 87-88). *Media:* Miscellaneous Media. *Dealer:* Studio 21 Gallery 5435 Spring Garden Rd Halifax NS B3J 1G1 Can. *Mailing Add:* 6051 Welsford St Halifax NS B3K 1G3 Canada

EDELMAN, ANN
PAINTER, LECTURER
b New York, NY. *Study:* Brooklyn Col, NY; Am Univ, Washington, DC; spec study with Leon Berkowitz & Jacob Kainen. *Work:* US Dept Transportation. *Exhib:* Area Show, Corcoran Gallery Art, Washington, DC, 56; Society of Washington Artists, Smithsonian Inst, Washington, DC, 59; Maryland Artists, Baltimore Mus Art, Md, 70 & 71; Corcoran Gallery Art, Washington, DC, 73. *Teaching:* Lectr contemp art, Exten Course, Univ Md, 72-78, Am Univ, Washington, DC, 79. *Awards:* First Prize, Soc Washington Artists, 72. *Mem:* Artists Equity; Washington Womens Art Ctr. *Media:* Acrylics, Oil. *Mailing Add:* 12919 Crisfield Rd Silver Spring MD 20906

EDELMAN, RITA
PAINTER
b New York, NY, Nov 2, 30. *Study:* Traphagen Sch Design, cert, 51; Silvermine Col Art, 67; also with Victor Candell, Leo Manso & Robert Reed. *Work:* General Electric, Fairfield, Conn; Fairfield Univ, Conn; Gen Foods, White Plains, NY; Deloitte Haskins & Sells, Stamford, Conn; Wichita State Univ, Kans. *Exhib:* Stamford Mus, Conn, 73, 77, 78, 82, 90 & 91; Art of the Northeast USA, New Canaan, Conn, 76, 80, 81, 83, 89, 90 & 92; solo exhibs, Silvermine Guild Galleries, New Canaan, Conn, 76 & 81, Pindar Gallery, New York, 78, 80, 82, 85 & 87 & Stamford Mus, Conn, 90; Butler Inst Am Art, Youngstown, Ohio, 79; Grey Galleries, New York, 80; Aldrich Mus Contemp Art, Ridgefield, Conn, 81; and others. *Awards:* Judges Choice, Greenwich Art Soc, 72; First Prize, New Haven Paint & Clay Club, 75; Painting Award, New Eng Exhib Painting & Sculpture, Silvermine Guild Artists, 80. *Bibliog:* George Albert Perret (auth), essay, 10/80 & Robert Yoskowitz (auth), review, 12/80, Arts Mag; Cynthia Nadleman (auth), rev, Art News Mag, 1/81. *Mem:* Westport Weston Arts Coun; New Haven Paint & Clay Club; Silvermine Guild Artists. *Media:* Oil, Acrylic. *Dealer:* Pindar Gallery 127 Greene St New York NY 10012. *Mailing Add:* Seven Manitou Ct Westport CT 06880

EDELSON, GILBERT S
ADMINISTRATOR, LECTURER
b New York, NY, Sept 15, 28. *Study:* NY Univ, BS, 49; Columbia Univ Sch Law, LLB, 55. *Pos:* Officer, Art Dealers Asn Am; mem, Common Art Law, Asn Bar, City New York, 64-67, 72-75, 84-87 & 89, chmn, 92; dir, Col Art Asn, 69-89, Artforum Mag, 70-77 & Art Quart, 78-80. *Mem:* Am Fedn Art (trustee, mem exec comt, 82-); Archives Am Art (trustee); Int Found Art Res (trustee); NY Studio Sch (trustee). *Mailing Add:* 575 Madison Ave New York NY 10022

EDELSON, MARY BETH
PAINTER, SCULPTOR
b East Chicago, Ind. *Study:* Art Inst Chicago, 53-54; DePauw Univ, BA, 55; NY Univ, MA, 59. *Work:* Guggenheim Mus Art, New York; Mus Contemp Art, Chicago; Corcoran Gallery Art, Washington, DC; Indianapolis Mus Art; Detroit Inst Art; Danforth Mus; Nat Collection, Washington, DC; and others. *Comn:* Mural, Danforth Mus, 86; mural, Musee du Quebec, Can 87; mural, London Regional Gallery, 87; mural, Mendel Gallery, 88; mural, WPA, 89; mural, Gilford Col, 90. *Exhib:* The Presence of Nature, Whitney Mus Am Art, 79; International Feministiche Kunst, Stichting de Appel, Amsterdam, Holland, 79; one-woman shows, Albright-Knox Gallery, Buffalo, 80, Elise Meyer, New York, Max Hutchinson Gallery, New York, 81, AIR Gallery, New York, 75, 77, 79, 81 & 83, Resistance or Submission, Mendel Gallery, Musee du Quebec, Phillips Gallery, Can, 86-88, Classical Myths and Imagery in Contemporary Art, Queens Mus, NY, 84, Fish in the Sky, Danforth Mus, Boston, 85 & Phases of the Loon, PS 1, New York, 86; Musee de Art Contemporanes, Sao Paulo, Brazil, 80; New Dimensions in Drawing, 1950-1980, Aldrich Mus Contemp Art, 81; Contemporary American Landscapes, Whitney Mus Am Art, 81; A Photographic Survey of Mary Beth Edelson's Work Traveling Exhib, Wright State Univ, NAME Gallery, Chicago & Herron Gallery, Indianapolis, 81; A Path Without Shores, Cologne, WGer, 83; Feminist & Misogynist Together at Last, Avenue B Gallery, New York, 85; Salvage Utopia, New York, 91; Between the Sheets, PPOW, New York, 92; Hallwalls, New York, 92; A/C Projects Space: In Your Face, 92; Shape Shifters, Amy Lipton Gallery, New York, 92; and many others. *Teaching:* Instr, Corcoran Sch of Art, 71-76; lecturer in 45 colleges and universities in the US, Canada & Iceland, 77-86; artist-in-residence, Univ Ill, Chicago, 82 & 88, Univ Tenn, 83, Ohio Univ, Columbus, 84, Md Inst Art, 85 & KC AI, Kansas City, 86. *Awards:* Visual Artist Grant, Nat Endowment Arts, 81; Creative Artists Pub Serv Grant, NY, 82; Original Collective Mem Heresies, Women Artists Coalition. *Bibliog:* Jack Burnham (auth), Mary Beth Edelson's great goddess, Arts Mag, 11/75; Karen Peterson & J J Wilson (coauths), Women Artists, Harper & Row, 76; Lucy Lippard (auth), From the Center, E P Dutton & Co Bks, NY, 76; Overlays: Cont Art & AR of Prehistory, Pantheon Bks, 83; Jeanne Silverthorne (auth), Is Polyanna perverse?, Rev, Artforum, 1/84; Mark Levy (auth), The Shuman is a Gifted Artist, High Performance, fall 88; M B E (auth), Open Letter to Thomas McEvilley, New Art Examiner, 4/89; Adain Wienberg (auth), Vanishing Presence, Rizzoli Walker Art Ctr, 89. *Mem:* Founder Conf Women in Visual Arts, Washington, DC. *Media:* Mixed Media, Photography. *Publ:* Auth & publr, Seven Cycles, 80 & Seven Sites, 88; To Dance: Painting with Performance in Mind, 85; Shape Shifters: Seven Mediums, 90. *Mailing Add:* 110 Mercer St New York NY 10012

EDELSTEIN, J M
LIBRARIAN, LECTURER
b Baltimore, Md, July 31, 24. *Study:* Johns Hopkins Univ, AB, 47; Fulbright travel grant to Italy, 49-50; Univ Mich, MALS, 53. *Pos:* Chief librn, Nat Gallery of Art, 72-86; sr bibliographer & resource coordr, Getty Ctr Hist Art & Humanities, 86- *Teaching:* Lectr rare bks, Univ Calif Los Angeles, 66-72 & Cath Univ, DC, 75-83. *Awards:* Herzog August Bibliot Fel, Wolfenbüttel, WGer, 85; John Simon Guggenheim Fel, 86-87. *Mem:* Bibliog Soc Am (ed, 64-81); Jargon Soc (bd dirs, 76-85); Wallace Stevens Soc (ed, 76-); Am Libr Asn; Art Libr Soc NAm. *Publ:* Auth, Bibliographical Checklist of Writings of Thornton Wilder, Yale Univ, 59; ed, A Garland for Jake Zeitlin, Dahlstrom-Marks, 67 & Books from Library of Don Cameron Allen, Univ Calif San Diego, 68; auth, Wallace Stevens: a Descriptive Bibliography, Univ Pittsburgh, 74; A Jargon Society Checklist 1951-79, Books & Co, 79. *Mailing Add:* Getty Ctr Hist Art & Humanities 401 Wilshire Blvd Suite 400 Santa Monica CA 90401

EDELSTEIN, TERI J
MUSEUM DIRECTOR, HISTORIAN
b Johnstown, Pa, June 23, 51. *Study:* Univ Pa, BA, 72, grad fel, Stouffer Col House, 72-74, teaching fel hist art, 73-75, Penfield scholar, 75-76, MA, 77, PhD, 79. *Pos:* Asst dir dept acad prog, Yale Ctr Brit Art, New Haven, Conn, 79-83; dir, Mt Holyoke Col Art Mus, 83-90; dir, David & Alfred Smart Mus Art, Univ Chicago, 90- *Teaching:* Lectr art hist, Univ Guelph, Ont, 77-79.

Awards: Nat Endowment for the Arts, Fel for Mus Prof, 88; Resident Fel, Yale Ctr for British Art, 88; Trustee, Williamstown Regional Conserv Lab, 89. *Mem:* Col Art Asn; Am Soc Eighteenth-Century Studies. *Res:* Iconology of British art. *Publ:* Auth, The yellow-haired friend--Rosetti and sensation novel, Libr Chronicle, 79; They sang the song of the shirt, the visual iconography of the seamstress, Victorian Studies, 79; Vauxhall Gardens (exhib catalog), Yale Ctr Brit Art, 83; Augustus Egg's Egg's triptych: A narrative of Victorian adultery, Burlington Mag, 83; Donald Cooper Photographs of the Classic British Theatre (exhib, catalog), Mount Holyoke Col Art Mus, 87; ed, Perspectives on Berthe Marisot, Nudson Nillis Press, New York, 90. *Mailing Add:* c/o Art Inst Chicago Michigan Ave at Adams St Chicago IL 60603

EDEN, BRONSON B
PAINTER
b New Haven, Conn, Apr 26, 49. *Study:* Sch Visual Arts, with Malcolm Morley & Eva Hesse. *Exhib:* Int Art Forum, Zurich, Switz, 84; London Art Fair, Eng, 85; East Village, Bronfman Ctr, Montreal, Can & Seattle, Wash, 85. *Bibliog:* Von Werner Kruger (auth), Der Gaul Galoppiert Ins Gluck, Kolner Stadt-Anzeiger, 7/84; Timothy Cohrs (auth), Bronson Eden, Arts Mag, 9/85. *Media:* All. *Mailing Add:* RR 10 Box 642A Waco TX 76708

EDEN, F(LORENCE) BROWN
COLLAGE ARTIST, PAINTER
b Jericho Center, Vt, Oct 10, 16. *Study:* Univ Fla, 53-55; Univ Mich, spec studies with Frank Cassara, 62-63. *Work:* Jacksonville Art Mus & Southern Bell Collection, Jacksonville, Fla; Fed Reserve Bank of Atlanta; Coopers and Lybrand, Jacksonville Fla; Barnett Banks Collection, Fla. *Comn:* Landscape watercolor, Atlantic Nat Bank, Jacksonville; landscape watercolor pair, Touche Ross, Jacksonville. *Exhib:* solo exhibs, Ga Inst Technol, Atlanta, 72, Le Moyne Found Art, Tallahassee, Fla, 75, Alexander Brest Mus, Jacksonville, Fla, 69, 70, 71 & 78, Daytona Art Ctr, Daytona Beach, 80 & Gallery Contemporanea, Jacksonville, 85; American Painters in Paris, Ctr Int Paris, France, 75; Contemporary American Paintings, Soc Four Arts, Palm Beach, Fla, 77; Nat Soc Painters in Casein & Acrylics, Nat Arts Club, New York, NY, 80; Betty Parsons Exhib, City Hall, Naples, Fla, 80; Mus Arts & Sci, Macon, 82 & 86 & Mem Art Ctr, Atlanta, 83, Ga Nat Watercolor Exhibs IV, V & VII; Major Fla Artists, Harmon Galleries of Am Art, Sarasota, 83, 86 & 88; Audubon Artists 42nd Ann Exhib, Nat Arts Club, New York, 84; Southeastern Watercolorists, Deland Mus, Fla, 84 & 89; The Museum Collection, Jacksonville Art Mus, Fla, 85; Barnett Banks Collection, Polk Mus, Winter Haven, Fla, 86; Fla Competitive, Ctr Arts, Vero Beach, Fla, 87; Ala Nat Watercolor Exhib, 89. *Teaching:* Painting, City Club, Ann Arbor, Mich, 62-63 & Art Mus, Jacksonville, Fla, 63-68; instr printmaking, Art Mus, Jacksonville, 68-69. *Awards:* First Award, Ann Juried Exhib, Fla Artist Group, 71 & 79; McDaniel Painting Award, Major Fla Artists, Harmon Galleries, 79. *Bibliog:* Elihu Edelson (auth), JU show classy and complete, Fla Times Union, 12/14/79; Rex Allyn (auth), Works by a dozen women artists, Sarasota Herald Tribune, 8/21/83; Ann Hyman (auth), Well-done exhibits can be evocative, Fla Times Union, 3/18/88. *Mem:* Audubon Artists Am; Ga Watercolor Soc; Fla Watercolor Soc; Soc Painters in Casein & Acrylics; Fla Artist Group (area chmn, 68-85). *Media:* Polymer Collage; Watercolor. *Dealer:* Harmon Galleries of Am Art 1415 Main St Sarasota FL 33577; Gallery Contemporanea 526 Lancaster St Jacksonville FL 32204. *Mailing Add:* 5375 Sanders Rd Jacksonville FL 32211

EDEN, GLENN
DRAFTSMAN,PAINTER
b Atlanta, Ga, 1951. *Study:* DeKalb Community Col, AA, 71; Ga State Univ. *Work:* High Mus, Atlanta, Ga; Gibbes Mus, Charleston, SC; Columbia Mus, SC; Huntsville Mus, Ala; Mus Arts & Sci, Macon, Ga. *Comn:* Painting, Mariott Marquis, Atlanta, Ga, 85; drawing, Coca-Cola Co, Atlanta, Ga, 86; painting, Wilma, Atlanta, Ga, 87. *Exhib:* Wizard of Oz Drawings, Mint Mus, 76; Artists in Ga, High Mus Art, Atlanta, 81; The Human Figure, New Orleans Contemp Art Inst, La, 82; Ten Pens, Southern Arts Fedn, Atlanta, Ga, 82; Narrative Drawings, Nexus Gallery, Atlanta, 83. *Awards:* Atlanta Bureau of Cultural Affairs Grant, 82; Outstanding Alumnus, Dekalb Col, 85; Artists Fel Southeastern Ctr Contemp Art, Winston-Salem, NC, 87-88. *Bibliog:* Jeff Kipnis (auth), Glenn Eden at the Gibbes, Art in Am, 81; Jeff Kipnis (auth), Profile, Art Voices, 81. *Media:* Ballpoint Pen, Prisma Color; Oil on Canvas. *Mailing Add:* 639 Cooledge Ave NE Atlanta GA 30306

EDER, JAMES ALVIN
PRINTMAKER, PAINTER
b Buffalo, NY, Jan 9, 42. *Study:* State Univ NY, Buffalo, BS, 63; Univ Nebr, Lincoln, MS, 66; Northern Ariz Univ, Flagstaff, MA, 75. *Work:* Valley Nat Bank, Mesa, Ariz; First Interstate Bank, Honeywell Corp & Talley Industries, Phoenix, Ariz; Quanex Corp, Houston, Tex; Albuquerque Mus; Nelson Art Ctr, Ariz State Univ; Hunt Inst Botanical Doc, Carnegie Mellon Univ; Sky Harbor Airport, Phoenix, Ariz; US Embassies, Moscow & Conakry & Guinea. *Exhib:* One-man shows, Univ Ariz, Tucson, 80 & Scottsdale Community Col, Ariz, 81, Ariz State Capitol, Phoenix, 90, Sedona Arts Ctr, 91, Scottsdale Col, 91; 19th & 21st Southwestern Invitational, Yuma Arts Ctr, Ariz, 85 & 87; Eder-Kollasch, touring southwest, 86-88; Contemporary Nature (travelling), Tempe Arts Ctr, 89-90; Northern Ariz Images, Coconino Arts Ctr, Flagstaff, 90; 7th Int Exhib Botanical Art & Illustr, Hunt Inst Botanical Doc, Carnegie Mellon Univ, 92. *Teaching:* Instr art, Evening Div, Phoenix Col, 78-81 & Scottsdale Community Col, 87-92. *Awards:* First Place Printmaking, Ariz State Fair, 76, 77 & 81. *Bibliog:* Jim Eder: A unique western artist, Sedona Life Mag, winter 78; Mary Carroll Nelson (auth), James A Eder (profile), Art Voices, 9-10/81; Mary Carroll Nelson (auth), Jim Eder: Making woodcut prints, Am Artist, 11/81; The Geologic Art of Eder & Kollasch, Ariz Highways, 11/87. *Media:* Woodcut, Collagraph; Acrylic. *Publ:* Auth, Capturing the Realism of Rocks, Artists Mag, 3/85. *Dealer:* Agnisiuh Gallery Box 910 Hillside Ctr Sedona AZ 86336; Impressions II 2990 N Swan Suite 147 Tucson AZ 85712. *Mailing Add:* 1026 E Carter Dr Tempe AZ 85282

EDGE, DOUGLAS BENJAMIN
SCULPTOR, PAINTER
b Fennimore, Wis, Aug 4, 42. *Study:* San Fernando Valley State Col, BA. *Work:* Mus Mod Art, New York; Arco, Washington, DC; Security Bank, Los Angeles; Patrick Lannon Mus, Fla. *Comn:* Constructionist Pagoda, Imperial Bank, Costa Mesa, Calif, 79. *Exhib:* West Coast Now, Seattle Art Mus, 68; Violence in Am Art, Mus Contemp Art, Chicago, 69; Continuing Surrealism, La Jolla Mus Art, 71; Calif Prints, Mus Mod Art, New York, 72; Separate Realities, Los Angeles Munic Art Gallery, 73; Santa Barbara Mus, 77. *Teaching:* Instr sculpture, Calif Inst Art, Valencia, 70-72; instr painting workshop, Art Ctr Sch Design, Los Angeles, 73-74; lectr sculpture & drawing, Univ Calif, Santa Barbara, 75-76. *Awards:* Cassandra Found Grant, 70. *Bibliog:* Thomas Garver (auth), rev, 10/69 & Peter Plagens (auth), rev, 11/73, Artforum; Milinda Terbell (auth), Art News, 10/73. *Mailing Add:* 2020 N Main No 228 Los Angeles CA 90031

EDGREN, GARY ROBERT
PAINTER, CRAFTSMAN
b Chicago, Ill, Jan 27, 47. *Study:* Southern Ill Univ, BA 70, MFA, 72. *Work:* State of Ill Ctr, Chicago; Byer Mus Art & Nat Hist, Evanston, Ill; Ill Art Mus, Springfield; Univ Galleries, Southern Ill Univ, Carbondale; Kemper Insurance Corp, Chicago, Ill. *Exhib:* Painting & Sculpture, mid-west fac, Univ Ill, Champaign, 76; one-man shows, Deson-Zaks Gallery, Chicago, 75, Krannert Art Gallery Univ Ill, 76, Zaks Gallery, Chicago, 79 & 83 & Univ Galleries Southern Ill Univ, 84; George Irwin Collection, Krannert Art Mus, 79; 29th Ill Invitational, Ill State Mus, Springfield, 79; Survey of 16 Abstract Artists, Springfield Art Asn, 84. *Pos:* Self employed artist, 72-; owner, Special Effects Painting. *Teaching:* Consult acquisition, Univ Galleries Southern Ill Univ, 74-75, vis artist painting & drawing, 77, instr, 77-78. *Media:* All. *Dealer:* Sonia Zaks-Zaks Gallery 620 N Michigan Ave Chicago, IL. *Mailing Add:* RRI Box 368 Buncombe IL 62912

EDMISTON, SARA JOANNE
EDUCATOR, DESIGNER
b Independence, Mo, June 21, 35. *Study:* Univ Kans, BAE; ECarolina Univ, MA. *Work:* NC Mus Art, Raleigh; NC Nat Banks, several cities in NC; Wachovia Banks, several cities in NC; Duke Univ. *Comn:* Door knocker, NC Nat Bank, Charlotte, 74; and others. *Exhib:* NC Mus Art, Raleigh, 65-67, 71, 73 & 76; Enamels 70 Nat, Crafts Alliance, St Louis, Mo & William Rockhill Nelson Gallery Art, Kansas City, Mo, 70; Piedmont Crafts, Mint Mus Art, Charlotte, 70-73; Crafts Invitational, Jacksonville Mus, Fla, 72; Southeastern Crafts Exhib, Greenville Co Mus, SC, 74; New Directions in Fabric Design, Fine Arts Gallery, Towson State Univ, 76; and others. *Teaching:* Prof textiles & design, ECarolina Univ, 66- *Awards:* Purchase Award, 5th Ann Piedmont Graphics Exhib, Mint Mus Art, 69; Purchase Award, 39th Ann NC Artists Exhib, NC Art Soc, 76. *Mem:* Surface Design Asn (treas & nat mem chmn, 76-80); Am Crafts Coun; Piedmont Craftsmen Inc; Carolina Designer-Craftsmen; NC Crafts Asn (mem bd dirs, 76-79). *Media:* Dye, Enamel. *Dealer:* Piedmont Craftsmen Inc Sales Gallery 936 West Fourth St Winston-Salem NC 27101. *Mailing Add:* Dept Art East Carolina Univ Greenville NC 27834

EDMONDSON, LEONARD
PRINTMAKER
b Sacramento, Calif, June 12, 16. *Study:* Univ Calif, Berkeley, AB, 40, MA, 42. *Work:* Metrop Mus Art, New York; Bibliot Nat, Paris, France; New York Pub Libr; San Francisco Mus Art; Pasadena Art Mus. *Comn:* Edition of etchings, Int Graphic Arts Soc, NY, 60, Hilton Hotel, NY, 62, Ferdinand Roten Galleries, Inc, NY, 66 & US Info Agency, Washington, DC, 67; Edition of etchings, James B Lansing Sound Inc, 77. *Exhib:* American Watercolors, Drawings & Prints, Metrop Mus Art, 52; Younger American Painters, Guggenheim Mus, 54; American Prints Today, Print Coun Am, 62; Int Triennial of Original Colored Graphics, Switz, 64; Graphics '71 West Coast USA, Univ Ky, 71; Painting & Sculpture, The Modern Era, San Francisco Mus Art, 76; Nat Watercolor Soc Invitational, Brand Libr, Glendale, Calif, 87. *Teaching:* Prof art, Calif State Univ, Los Angeles, 64-74; chmn dept printmaking, Otis Art Inst, Los Angeles, 74-76; prof art, Calif State Univ, Los Angeles, 76-86. *Awards:* Purchase Prize for Oil, Univ Ill, 55; Purchase Prize for Etching, Brooklyn Mus, 56 & Pasadena Art Mus, 58. *Bibliog:* Mugnaini (auth), Oil Painting, Techniques & Materials, 69 & Reep (auth), The Content of Watercolor, 69, Van Nostrand; Heller (auth), Printmaking Today, Holt, 71. *Publ:* Auth, Etching, Van Nostrand, 73. *Mailing Add:* 719 Gretta Ave West Covina CA 91790

EDMONSON, RANDALL W
CERAMIST, PAINTER
b Washington, DC, Jan 30, 47. *Study:* Drury Col, BA, 69; Univ Mo, Columbia, MA, 76; Southern Ill Univ, Carbondale, MFA, 78. *Work:* Monterey Peninsula Mus Art, Calif; Evansville Mus Arts & Sci, Ind; Owensboro Mus Fine Arts, Ky. *Exhib:* Mid-American Biennial, Owensboro Mus Fine Art, Ky, 82; Nat Works on Paper Exhib, 2nd Street Gallery, Charlottesville, Va, 83; Painting Southeast, Fla Gulf Coast Art Ctr, Belleair, 83; Clay USA, Martin Gallery, Radford Univ, Va, 86; Saltglaze 86, Handworks Kammer Koblenz, WGer, 86. *Teaching:* Assoc prof art, Longwood Col, Farmville, Va, 79- *Awards:* Purchase Award, Owensboro Mus Fine Arts, Ky, 82; Cash Award, Va Watercolor Ann, Mead Corp, 83; Hon Mention, 11th Ann Works on Paper, 2nd Street Gallery, Charlottesville, Va, 83. *Mem:* Am Crafts Coun; Nat Coun Educ Ceramic Arts; Va Watercolor Asn. *Media:* Clay, Acrylic. *Mailing Add:* Visual & Performing Arts Longwood Col Farmville VA 23901

EDMONSTON, PAUL
EDUCATOR, EDITOR
b Newton, Mass, Nov 15, 22. *Study:* Mass Sch Art, with Ernest L Major & Cyrus Dallin; Boston Univ, AB(Eng lang & lit), with George Levitine, William Jewell, Edgar Brightman, Gerald Brace & Edward A Post; Fla State Univ, MA(art educ), with Karl Zerbe & Ivan Johnson; Ohio State Univ, PhD(fine art), with Hoyt Sherman, Sydney Chafetz, Manuel Barkan, Jerome Hausman & Ross L Mooney; Post Doctoral Fel, South India, 68; Univ Pa, SAsian studies, 72-73; 20th Century Dutch Painting, Univ Nijmegen, Fulbright scholar, 92. *Work:* Sch Visual Arts, Ohio State Univ; Kenyon Col. *Exhib:* One-man shows, Kenyon Col Gallery, 60, Ohio State Fine Arts Gallery, 64, Lowe Gallery, Univ Miami, 65, Fla A&M Gallery, 66, Art Gallery, Pa State Univ, 70, 74, 75 & 76 & Monhegan Themes, Visual Arts Gallery, Univ Ga, 86; 8th Ann Drawing/Small Sculpture Show, Ball State Univ, 62, 63 & 64; Drawing USA, St Paul Art Ctr, Minn, 63; Cent Pa Artists, State Mus, Harrisburg, Pa, 63; Sacred Arts X, Wheaton, Ill, 89; National Exposures 90, Winston-Salem, NC, 90; Photographer's Forum Ann, 90-91. *Pos:* Ed, Apelles: Ga Art J, 79-; assoc ed, Sch Arts, 62-65; ed, Monograph Series, Vols 1-7, Pa State Papers in Art Educ, 68-74 & An Anthology of Faculty Papers, Pa State Univ, 77. *Teaching:* Instr art/Eng, Manatee Co High Sch, Bradenton, Fla, 49-51; instr art, Fla State Univ, 51-55 & Ohio State Univ, 56-60; from assoc prof to prof art appreciation, printmaking & art ed, Pa State Univ, 60-77; prof art appreciation, drawing & painting & art educ, Univ Ga, 77-88 & prof emer art, 88- *Awards:* Gen Beaver Teaching Prof Award, Univ Ga, 82-85; Gov's Award, Ga, 83; Southeast Region Higher Educ Award (Teacher Yr), Nat Art Educ Asn, 87; and others. *Mem:* US Soc for Educ Through Art (vpres, 79); Nat Art Educ Asn (res sem, 70-); Asn for Asian Studies; Ga Art Educ Asn (pres, 81-83); Int Soc Educ Art; and others. *Media:* Watercolor; Brush & Ink on Rice Paper. *Res:* Studio way of learning, visual and artistic intelligence & nature of creative teaching; cross cultural studies; pre-Muslim art and architecture of South India; rasa theory of Indian aesthetics; English romantic watercolor painters. *Publ:* Auth, A conceptual model of creative visual intelligence, J Creative Behavior, 75; Myth and symbol in Indian art, Australia Soc Educ Art Bul, 77; A proposal for a curriculum in the visual arts, J Art & Design Educ, 82; Participant observation and visual documentation as modes of inquiry in the visual arts, Visual Arts Res, 83; On witnessing a name-giving ceremony of the Oglala Sioux, S Cross-Cult Res Art Educ, 86. *Mailing Add:* 100 Torrey Pine Pl Athens GA 30605

EDMUNDS, ALLAN LOGAN
PRINTMAKER, ADMINISTRATOR
b Philadelphia, Pa, June 7, 49. *Study:* Tyler Sch Art, Temple Univ, Philadelphia & Rome; also with Romas Viesulas & John Dowell, BFA & MFA, Cardiff Art Sch, Wales, UK. *Work:* Philadelphia Mus Art; Nat Collection of Fine Art, Libr of Cong; Pa Acad Fine Arts; Yale Univ; Studio Mus Harlem. *Comn:* Photosilkscreen ed, Philadelphia Mus Art, 71-72. *Exhib:* Silkscreen: History of a Medium, Philadelphia Mus Art, 71-72; Expanded Photograph, Philadelphia Civic Ctr Mus, 72; one-man show, Univ Md, Baltimore Co, 72; Second World Black & African Festival Art & Cult, Univ Pa Mus, 74; Nat Invited Print Exhib, Cent Wash State Univ, 75; traveling exhib, Smithsonian Inst, 81-82. *Pos:* founder-pres, Brandywine Graphic Workshop, Inc, 72-; visual arts panelist, Ohio, Fla, Md & Pa Coun Arts, 82-91; vis artist, Bloomsburg State Col, 80-, Ariz State Univ, 92; mem adv panel, William Penn Mus Fine Arts Collection, 81; Assoc, A L Edmunds Assoc, 81. *Teaching:* Instr graphics, Haystack Mountain Sch Crafts, Maine, 74; lectr printmaking, Philadelphia Col Art, 75; art coordr, Parkway Prog Sch Dist Philadelphia, 72-; adj instr, Philadelphia Col Art, 80- *Awards:* Res Assoc, Cardiff Art Sch; Visual Artist's Fel, Pa Coun, 90; Nat Endowment Arts Fel, 91. *Bibliog:* Choosing Mus Sci and Industry, Chicago, 86; Int Rev African Am Art Vol 7, No 4, 88; Artists Choose Artists, Contemp Art, Philadelphia, 91. *Mem:* Brandywine Workshop, Greater Philadelphia Cult Alliance; Arts & Cult Coun, Greater Philadelphia Chamber of Com; Mayor's Cult Adv Coun. *Res:* Continuous research project on the history of the Black graphic artist; collection of slides, manuscripts and original works as well as developing video documentation. *Dealer:* Hahn Gallery 8439 Germantown Ave Philadelphia PA 19118. *Mailing Add:* 1520-22 Kater St Philadelphia PA 19146

EDOUARD, PIERRE (PIERRE EDWARD MAUSSION)
PAINTER
b Oct 28, 59; French citizen. *Study:* Ecole nationale superieur des Arts decoratif, Dipl, 81; study painting with Zoa Wonki. *Exhib:* Musee des arts Decoratif, Paris, France, 84; Autoportraits, Mussee de la Seita, Paris, France, 86. *Awards:* Prinde dessin des Salon de Montrouge, 80. *Bibliog:* Pierre Cahonne (auth), Granite et intersite, Elle, 3/89; Jean Marie Tasset (auth), Le style des cimes, Le Figaro, 3/89. *Media:* Oil, Egg Tempera. *Mailing Add:* c/o Claude Bernard 9 Rue des Beaux Arts Paris 75006 France

EDSON, GARY F
MUSEOLOGIST, MUSEUM DIRECTOR
b Bethany, Mo, Sept 5, 37. *Study:* Kansas City Art Inst, BFA(sculpture), 60; Newcomb Art Sch, Tulane Univ, MFA(ceramics), 62. *Work:* Stifel Fine Arts Ctr, Wheeling, WVa; WVa Univ, Morgantown; Newcomb Art Sch, Tulane Univ, New Orleans. *Comn:* Ceramic art, Ft Benjamin Harrison Hosp, Indianapolis, 73; sculpture, Robert Borns Assocs, Indianapolis, 74; ceramic art, Fairmont Hotel, New Orleans, 74; sculpture, Pickwick Place Development, Indianapolis, 75; ceramic art, Mignon Faget Ltd, New Orleans, 75-78. *Exhib:* Crosscurrents, Stifel Fine Arts Ctr, Wheeling, WVa, 83; Texas Tech Univ Museum, Lubbock, 85; Univ North Dakota, Grand Fork, 85; Gallery Eighty-Six, Belfast, Maine, 85; Texas 2-D Competition, Tex A&M Univ, College Station, Tex, 85; Univ NMex, Albuquerque, 85; Edson, Kreneck & Murrow, Lubbock Fine Arts Ctr, Tex, 86. *Collections Arranged:* Mochawa: Indian Pottery, Gatlinburg, Tenn, 72; Mexican Market Pottery, Indianapolis, 77 & Morgantown, WVa, 81. *Pos:* Chmn, div art, WVa Univ, Morgantown, 80-84; chmn, dept art, Tex Tech Univ, Lubbock, 84-86; exec dir, the Mus Tex Tech Univ, Lubbock, 86- *Teaching:* Prof art & ceramics, Herron Sch Art, Indianapolis, 70-80; prof art, drawing & printmaking, Tex Tech Univ, Lubbock, Tex, 84- *Mem:* Nat Asn Sch Art & Design (bd mem, 86-); Nat Coun Arts Adminrs (bd mem, 86-); Tex Asn Sch Art (res comt, 86-); Am Asn Mus; Art Mus Asn Am. *Publ:* Auth, Open pit firing, 72 & Silla pottery, 73, Ceramics Monthly; Mexican Market Pottery, Watson-Guptill, 79. *Mailing Add:* Dept Art Tex Tech Univ Lubbock TX 79409

EDVI ILLES, EMMA
DEALER, PAINTER
b Budapest, Hungary; US citizen. *Study:* NY Sch Interior Design, 58; Int Asn Color Consults, dipl, 59; Sogetsu Sch Flower Design Tokyo, prof degree, 62. *Work:* Atlanta Decorative Arts Ctr; pvt collections in Munich, Rome, Caracas, Boston & Atlanta. *Exhib:* Watermelon Art Exhib, Miami Circle, Curran & Assoc, 91; one-woman shows, Buckhead Towne Club, Atlanta, 91, Bureau Int Ltd, 91; Int Art Rage, Soapstone Gallery, Atlanta, 91; Realty Network Spec Showing, 91. *Pos:* Owner & founder, Academia de Decoration, Caracas, Venezuela, 56; lectr & consult, Channel 2 & 4 TV, Caracas, 58-66. *Teaching:* Instr, Academia De Decoracion, Caracas. *Awards:* Dipl de Honor, Ministerio de Educ, Caracas, 66; diploma, Bd Two Thousand Women Achievement, 70. *Media:* Miscellaneous. *Publ:* Auth, Teoria de Color, 2 vols, 59; auth, Commercial Flower Design, 2 vols, 61. *Dealer:* 130 26th Peachtree St Suite 211 Atlanta GA 30309. *Mailing Add:* 130 26th St NW Apt 407 Atlanta GA 30309

EDWARDS, ELLENDER MORGAN
PRINTMAKER, PHOTOGRAPHER
b Hagerstown, Md. *Study:* Tyler Sch Art; pvt study art hist in Europe; Md Inst Col Art, BFA, 58; Art Students League, with Jean Liberte; Hunter Col, grad study; Corcoran Art Sch, George Washington Univ; also with Reuben Kramer & Victor D'Amico. *Exhib:* 29th & 30th Cumberland Valley Artists, Washington Co Mus Art, Hagerstown, Md, 61 & 62; Md Regional, Baltimore Mus Art, 61 & 76; 21st Ann Life in Baltimore, Peale Mus, Md, 61; Denim Art, Mus Contemp Crafts, New York, 74; Focus 76 Photo Competition, Amarillo Civic Ctr, Tex, 76; Bicentennial Competition, Goldman Fine Arts Gallery, 76. *Pos:* Secy, Montgomery Co Art Educators Asn, Rockville, Md, 70-73, treas, 73-75; treas, Glen Echo Graphics, 73-76. *Awards:* Second Prize Watercolor, Waterford Found, Inc, Va, 60; First Prize Graphics, Shepherd Col, 71; Hon Mention, Int Platform Asn, 73 & 74 & Goldman Fine Arts Gallery, 76; plus others. *Mem:* Nat League Am Penwomen. *Mailing Add:* PO Box 6402 Annapolis MD 21401-0402

EDWARDS, ETHEL
VISUAL ARTIST
b New Orleans, La. *Study:* Newcomb Col Art Sch; Student of Xavier Gonzalez. *Work:* Chase Manhattan Bank, IBM, New York; Commerce Trust Bank, Kansas City; Baltimore Mus Art, Md; Nat Gallery Art, DC; Newark Mus, NJ; Univ Nebr; Tex Eastern Co, Houston. *Comn:* Ser paintings, comn by Dept Interior, Colo & NMex. *Exhib:* Whitney Mus Am Art, 64 & 65; Watercolor: USA, Springfield, Ill, 67-69; Cape Cod Art Asn, 69; Nat Gallery, Washington, DC; Am Embassy, Paris; Galerie Jeanne Boucher, Paris; Mus Mod Art, New York; Pa Acad, Philadelphia. *Teaching:* Instr, Truro Ctr Arts & mem exec comt. *Awards:* Larry Aldrich Prize, Silvermine Guild Artists; Prizes, Watercolor: USA, Springfield, Ill, 67 & Ball State Univ, Muncie, Ind, 67; Nat Arts Club Ann, New York. *Mem:* Fel McDowell Colony; Cosmopolitan Club, New York. *Media:* Oil, Mixed Media. *Mailing Add:* c/o Rising Tide Gallery 494 Commercial St Provincetown MI 02657

EDWARDS, JAMES F
PAINTER, EDUCATOR
b New York, NY, July 25, 48. *Study:* Univ Calif, Santa Barbara, BA, MFA. *Work:* Everson Mus Art, Syracuse, NY; SC State Arts Collection; Am Consulate, Osaka, Japan; Am Embassy, Oman, Jordon; IBM Corp, Gaitherburg, Md. *Comn:* Collage, Huntsville Mus Art; mural, Atlanta Festival of Art, Atlanta Legal Aid, 88; painting, Embassy Suites Corp, Deerfield, Mich. *Exhib:* One-man shows, Greenville Co Mus Art, SC, 76 & Everson Mus Art, Syracuse, 77; Huntsville Mus Art, Ala, 81; Southeastern Ctr Contemp Art, Winston-Salem, NC, 81; Heath Gallery, Atlanta, 85; Hodges Taylor Gallery, Charlotte, 86; Southern Exposure, The Alternative Mus, NY, 85; Portrait of the South, Palazzo Venezia, Rome; and others. *Pos:* Div head, Studio Art, currently. *Teaching:* Prof drawing & painting, Univ SC, 78- *Awards:* Nat Endowment Arts Fel, 74-75; Proj Grant, SC Arts Comn, 76-77; Individual Artist Fel, SC Arts Comn, 81; and others. *Bibliog:* Kenneth Friedman (auth), James Edwards video tapes, Grossmont Col, El Cajon, Calif; Jane Kessler (auth), James Edwards: Profile, Art Papers, Atlanta, 1-2/82. *Media:* Miscellaneous. *Publ:* Auth, Getting into video, Contemp Art-Southeast, 77; Art, language and criticism, Contemp Art-Southeast, Vol II, Number 4-5. *Dealer:* Hodges-Taylor Gallery 227 N Tryon St Charlotte NC 28202. *Mailing Add:* Dept Art Univ SC Columbia SC 29208

EDWARDS, LINDA (LINDA MARGARET WEISS EDWARDS)
SILVERSMITH, GOLDSMITH
b Detroit, Mich, Dec 6, 51. *Study:* Cent Mich Univ, BFA(magna cum laude), 73; Univ Wash, BFA, 75; Cranbrook Acad Art, travel grant to Eng, 76 & 78, MFA, 77. *Work:* Cranbrook Art Mus, Bloomfield Hills, Mich; also several pvt collections. *Comn:* Cloisonne enamel & rosewood, Wiseway Corp, Chicago, 78; 18 karat gold neck piece, comn by Mr & Mrs Norman Stewart,

Birmingham, Mich, 78; jewelry, comn by Mr & Mrs Douglas Steakley, Carmel, Calif, 80; sterling silver & 14 karat gold kiddush cup, comn by Congregation Shir Hadash, Los Gatos, Calif, 80; Bronze holloware, comn by Mark Bloome Enterprises, Los Angeles, Calif, 83; 18K Gold Vase, comn by Mr & Mrs Albert Weiss, Detroit, Mich, 83; and others. *Exhib:* Three & One-Half Decades: Metalsmithing at Cranbrook, Cranbrook Art Mus, Bloomfield Hills, Mich, 82; Continuing Traditions in Silver, Argentum Galleries, San Francisco, 83; Current Directions: Metal Arts of the 80's, Monterey Peninsula Mus Art, Monterey, Calif, 83; Group shows, Elaine Potter Gallery, San Francisco, 83-88; Soc NAm Goldsmiths Exhib, Mitchell Mus, Mt Vernon, Ill, 84; Jewelers of Am, Designer Group, Jacob Javits Ctr, New York, 86-90; Calif Metal Forms '90, Calif Crafts Mus, San Francisco, 90; Fall Pac Jewelry Show, Contemp Designers Showcase, San Diego Convention Ctr, 90-92; Recent Acq to Permanent Collection, Cranbrook Acad Art Mus, Bloomfield Hills, Mich, 91; Metals Now 1992, Downey Mus Art, Downey, Calif, 92. *Pos:* Bd dirs, Mich Silversmiths Guild, 76-78; designer, goldsmith & mgr, McLean & Co, Goldsmiths, Sausalito, Calif, 78-81; partner, Weiss/Edwards Designs, Sausalito, Calif, 79-; jewelry design consult, Boring & Co, San Francisco, currently. *Teaching:* Vis artist metalsmithing & jewelry design, Univ Mich, Ann Arbor, 77; vis artist silversmithing & metalsmithing, Calif Col Arts & Crafts, Oakland, 79-80; prof, Acad Art Col, San Francisco, 81. *Awards:* Merit Award, The Calif Craftsman, Monterey Mus Art, 78; Merit Awards, 1978 Designer Craftsman & 1981 Designer Craftsman, Richmond Art Ctr, Richmond, Calif; Award for Artistic Excellence, Merlins Found, Fairfax, Calif, 83; T A P Plastics Award for Excellence in Craft, Marin Soc Artists, Ross, Calif, 92. *Bibliog:* Laurie Haig Glass (auth), Designer-craftsmen '78, Artweek, 11/18/78; Murray Bovin (auth), Jewelry Making for Schools, Tradesmen, Craftsmen, Bovin Publ, New York, 79; The Goodfellow Catalog of Wonderful Things No 3, Goodfellow Catalog Press, Berkeley, 81; and others. *Mem:* Soc NAm Goldsmiths; Am Crafts Coun; Marin Arts Coun; Metal Arts Guild, San Francisco. *Media:* Metals. *Publ:* Auth, Health hazards in the field of goldsmithing, Goldsmiths J, Soc NAm Goldsmiths, 78; Amerikanische Schmuckkugstler, Goldschmiede Veitung/European Jeweler, 6/83; Weiss/Edwards - High energy Artists, Jewelers Circular Keystone, 1/86; Regional shows offer fashion and fun, Nat Jeweler, 7/16/90. *Dealer:* Union St Goldsmiths San Francisco CA. *Mailing Add:* PO Box 1032 Sausalito CA 94966

EDWARDS, PAUL BURGESS
PAINTER, EDUCATOR
b Moulton, Iowa, Feb 18, 34. *Study:* Iowa Wesleyan Col, with S Carl Fracassini, BA, 55; Wichita Art Asn Sch Art, with Jack Pharo, 57; Wichita State Univ, with Robert Kiskadden, MA, 59. *Work:* Wichita Art Mus; Iowa Wesleyan Col; Wichita State Univ; Citizens Libr, Washington, Pa. *Comn:* Mosaic mural, Sisters St Joseph, Halstead, Kans, 58; mural, Tasco Mining Co, Washington, Pa, 79. *Exhib:* Nat Small Painting Show, Purdue Univ, 66; 19th Ann Nat Decorative Arts Show, Wichita Art Asn, 66; Second Nat Polymer Exhib, Eastern Mich Univ, 68; solo exhib, Spectrum Gallery, New York, 70; 36th Ann Midyear Show, Butler Inst Am Art, 72; 13th Ann Three Rivers Arts Festival, Gateway Ctr, Pittsburgh, Pa, 72. *Collections Arranged:* W & J Nat Painting Show, 68- & Malcolm Parcell Retrospective, 82, Olin Art Ctr; L Evans Parcell-Retrospective, Olin Art Ctr, 11/85. *Teaching:* Instr ceramics, Wichita State Univ, summer 62; asst prof sculpture, West Liberty State Col, 63-65; chmn & prof art, Washington & Jefferson Col, 65- *Awards:* First Prize Painting, Bethany Col Ann, 64; First Prize, Oglebay Inst Summer Show, 64; Best of Show Award, Huntington 180, Huntington Gallery, 65 & Juror's Award, 66. *Mem:* Am Asn Art Adminr; Arts Coun Washington, Pa (pres, 69-72); Washington Coun Hist Soc; Am Asn Univ Prof; Am Inst Hist & Artistic Works (AIC) Fel. *Media:* Acrylic, Oil. *Publ:* Contribr, Topic: 17 A liberal arts miscellany, Topic Mag, 69; illusr, Nonverbal Communication, Marcel Dekker Inc, 74. *Mailing Add:* 65 Dewey Ave Washington PA 15301-6306

EDWARDS, PAUL BURGESS See Pablo

EDWARDS, STANLEY DEAN
PAINTER
b Joliet, Ill, Dec 5, 41. *Study:* Art Inst Chicago; Univ Chicago; BFA; Saugatuck Summer Sch. *Work:* Smithsonian Inst, Washington, DC; Corcoran Gallery; Am Embassy, Oslo, Norway. *Comn:* Crain Commun, 87; Duchossois Industs, 90; Walter Netsch, 91. *Exhib:* 12 Chicago Painters, Walker Art Ctr, 65; Corcoran Biannual, Washington, DC, 65; Protest & Hope Group Show, New Sch Social Res, 67; Violence in Art, Mus Contemp Art, Chicago, 69; Arts Club Chicago, 91; David Anderson Gallery, Buffalo, NY; and others. *Teaching:* Instr design, Chicago Acad Fine Arts, Ill, 74-75; instr, Columbia Col, Chicago, 75-76 & 84-85; asst prof art, Winthrop Col, Rock Hill, SC, 85-86; prof, Int Acad Design, 90-92. *Awards:* Purchase Prize, Corcoran Gallery, 65; Vanderbilt Purchase Fund, 69. *Bibliog:* Whitney Halsted (auth), article in Artforum, 66; Franz Schultz (auth), articles in Panorama Mag & Chicago Daily News, 65-69. *Media:* All. *Publ:* Chronicles, J Am Cult, Rockford Inst Publ, 90, 91 & 92; Lincoln Legal Found, 92. *Mailing Add:* 3813 N Oakley St Chicago IL 60618

EDWARDS, SUSAN HARRIS
CURATOR, HISTORIAN
b Baltimore, Md, Sept 26, 48. *Study:* Univ SC, BA, 79, MA, 83; Grad Ctr, City Univ NY, MPh, 90. *Collections Arranged:* Hunter College Permanent Collection, 87; Systems and Abstraction, 88; New York Area MFA Exhibition, 90; Formulation & Representation , 90; Physical Relief, 91; Contemporary Icons, 92. *Pos:* Managing ed, Sheep Meadow Press, Riverdale, NY, 84-85; asst dept paintings & sculpture, Brooklyn Mus, NY, 82-84; cur, Hunter Col, City Univ NY, 87- *Teaching:* instr art hist, Newberry Col, SC, 81; instr, Queens Col, City Univ New York, 86-89, New York Univ, 90- *Awards:* Helena Rubenstein Scholar, 86-87. *Bibliog:* Joshua Dector (auth), Systems & Abstraction, Arts Mag, 3/89; Roger, Denson (auth), A Feminism without Men, Tema Celeste 4-5/92. *Mem:* Col Art Asn; Am Asn Mus; Artists & Homeless Collaborative (bd). *Publ:* Auth, A Debate on Abstraction, 88, Formulation and Representation in Recent Abstract Art, 90, Hunter Col. *Mailing Add:* 419 E 82nd St New York NY 10028

EDWARDS-TUCKER, YVONNE (LEATRICE YVONNE TUCKER)
CERAMIST, EDUCATOR
b Chicago, Ill, Jan 19, 41. *Study:* Univ Ill, Urbana, BFA(art educ; summa cum laude), 62; Univ Calif, Los Angeles, 62-64; Otis Art Inst, BFA, MFA, 68; studied with Charles White, Michael Frimkess & Helen Watson; numerous other workshops. *Work:* Fisk Univ, Nashville, Tenn; Otis Art Inst; Hampton Univ, Va; Syracuse Univ, New York; Fla A&M Univ, Tallahassee. *Exhib:* Contemporary African-American Crafts, Brooks Mem Art Mus, 79; Power Objects: Ancient & to the Future, Howard Univ Art Gallery, 80; Dimensions & Directions: Black Artists of the South, Miss Art Mus, 80; Forever Free: Art by African-American Women, 1862-1980, Joslyn Art Mus, Montgomery Mus Fine Arts, Indianapolis Mus, & Univ Md, 81-82; Magic of Clay, Calif Mus Afro-Am Hist & Cult, Los Angeles, 82; Traditional Crafts, Mus Nat Ctr Afro-Am Artists, Boston, 82; Surrealism and the Afro-American Artist, Evans-Tibbs collection, Washington, DC, 83; Voices: Afro-American Ceramics, Syracuse Univ, 88; JB Speed Mus, Louisville, Ky, 88; Ceramic Traditions, NCECA, Contemp Art Ctr, Kansas City, Mo, 89; African Images in American Craft, Folk Art Ctr, Asheville, NC, traveling, 92-93. *Collections Arranged:* Florida Craftsmen, 73, Impact 79: Afro-American Women Artists, 79 & Tallahassee Tribute, 81, Fla A&M Univ Art Gallery; Harambee at Lemoyne, 85; Harambee Invitational II, 86; Fla A&M Univ Centennial Art Exhib, 87; Celebration of African-American Art. *Teaching:* Asst prof ceramics & drawing, Miami-Dade Community Col, 68-73; adj prof art, Miami Exten, Shaw Univ, 72-74; prof ceramics & art, Fla A&M Univ, 73- *Awards:* Award Ceramic Sculpture, Fiftieth Anniversary Exhib, Otis Art Inst, 69; Best in Show, Clay Works 72, Grove House Gallery, Miami, 72; Purchase Award, Syracuse Univ Ceramics Collection, New York, 87. *Bibliog:* Ellen A Ashdown (auth), Afro-Raku: The ceramics of Yvonne & Curtis Tucker, Black Art Int Quart, winter 79 & The ceramics of Yvonne & Curtis Tucker, Art-Craft, 2-3/80; Arna Bontemps (ed), African-American Art History: The Feminine Dimension, In: Forever Free, Stephen Sun Inc. *Mem:* Nat Conf Artists; Nat Conf Educ Ceramic Arts; founding mem Harambee Arts Coun; Fla Folk Life Coun; Fla Craftsmen. *Media:* Clay, Raku Clay, Mixed Media. *Res:* African and Afro-American folklore; Black Art of the South; Black aesthetics; folk art. *Publ:* Illusr, Le theme de la violence, African Arts, Arts d'Afrique, Vol 1, No 1, 67; Auth, African, Indian & Oriental Influences in the Aesthetics of Two Contemporary Craftspeople: First National African-American Crafts Conference: Shelby State Community Col, 80; John T Scott & the black aethetic, Int Review African Am Art, Vol 6, No 2, 85; Afro-Raku Ceramics & Y&C Tucker, NCECA J, Vol 10, 51-54, 89-90. *Dealer:* Gallery Antigua 5138 Biscayne Blvd Miami FL 33134. *Mailing Add:* 3007 Kevin St Tallahassee FL 32301

EGBERT, ELIZABETH FRANCES
SCULPTOR, EDUCATOR
b Charleston, WVa, May 10, 45. *Study:* Mt Holyoke Col, South Hadley, Mass, BA, 67; New York Univ, MA, 70. *Work:* Lab Theater, Mt Holyoke Col; Nassau County Mus Fine Arts, Roslyn, NY; Biblioteque Nationale, Paris, France; Foreign Arts Mus, Sofia, Bulgaria. *Comn:* Courtyard design, Third St Music Sch, New York, NY, 79; Play Sculpture, New York Dept Cult Affairs, Community Arts Develop Fund & NY State Coun Arts, New York, 84-85. *Exhib:* Contemporary Reflections, Aldrich Mus, Ridgefield, Conn, 77; Sculpture on Shoreline Sites (outdoor installation), Roosevelt Island, NY, 80; one-person shows, Women's Interart Ctr, New York, NY, 81, Nassau County Mus Fine Art, Roslyn, NY, 83 & Sculpture Ctr Gallery, New York, 83; Four Sculptors, Sid Deutsch Gallery, New York, 83; one-person show, Seven Year Survey, Snu g Harbor Cultural Ctr, Staten Island, NY, 85. *Pos:* Educ & exhib consult, Jacques Marchais Ctr Tibetan Ctr, Staten Island, NY, 85-86; assoc bd mem, Snug Harbor Cultural Ctr, Staten Island, 85-88. *Teaching:* Instr sculpture, Sch Continuing Educ, New York Univ, 78-79; instr sculpture, Philadelphia Col Art, Pa, 85-87. *Awards:* Individual Artists Award, Staten Island Coun Arts, 84 & 85; Public Art Award, NY State Coun Arts, 85. *Bibliog:* Michael Brenson (auth), What's new around town in outdoor sculpture, 7/19/85 & A bountiful season in outdoor sculpture, 7/18/86, New York Times; Tsipi Ben-Haim (auth), Letter from New York, Int Sculpture, 11-12/85. *Mem:* Sculptors Guild (secy, 85-86); Orgn Independent Artists, New York. *Publ:* Ed & photogr, Shopping center art, On Site, 71. *Mailing Add:* 354 Van Duzer St Staten Island NY 10304

EGELI, CEDRIC BALDWIN
PAINTER, INSTRUCTOR
b Shady Side, Md, Aug 10, 36. *Study:* Principia Col, AA, 55; studied with Bjorn Egeli, 55-84; Corcoran Sch Art with Edmund Arden, 56; Art Students League, New York with Sidney Dickenson, Frank Mason & Frank Reilly, 57-60; Cape Sch with Henry Hensche, summers 78-87. *Work:* Pentagon, Alexandria, Va; John Hopkins Hosp, Baltimore, Md; State Capitol, Annapolis, Md; US Dist Ct, Washington, DC. *Comn:* Portrait, Arleigh Burke, Am Ordinance Asn, Washington, DC, 67; portrait, Stanfield Turner, CIA, Washington, DC, 79; portrait, Jackie Presser, Teamsters Union, Washington, DC, 83; portrait, Morris Abrahm, Brandeis Univ, Boston, 84; portrait, H Keith Brody, Duke Univ, Durham, NC, 90. *Exhib:* Nat Portrait Sems, New York, Washington, DC & Chicago hotels, 80-83; Egeli Family Exhib, Md Life

Bldg, Baltimore, 86. *Pos:* Pres, Md Portrait Soc, 84-86 & 90-92. *Teaching:* Portrait painting & figure drawing, Md Hall Creative Art, Annapolis, 79-87; outdoor portrait painting, Cape Sch Art, Provincetown, Mass, summers, 89-92. *Awards:* Best in Show, Grand Prize, Nat Portrait Sem, John Howard Sanden, 79; Gold Medal for Oil, 80 & Grumbacher Award, 81, Am Artists Prof League. *Bibliog:* Pappen Fuse (auth), History of Maryland, State of Md, 78; Steven Doherty (auth), Artists & sons, Am Artist, 88; Portraits as Art, Dossier, 89. *Mem:* Md Portrait Soc (pres, 84-86 & 90-92); Am Artists Prof League; Art Students League; Charcoal Club, Baltimore; Beachcomers Club, Provincetown, Mass. *Media:* Oil. *Dealer:* Wohlfarth Gallery 3418 Ninth St NE Washington DC 20017. *Mailing Add:* 37 Pearl St Provincetown MA 02657-1503

EGELI, PETER EVEN
PAINTER, ILLUSTRATOR
b Miami, Fla, Apr 19, 34. *Study:* Corcoran Sch Art; Md Inst, BFA; Art Students League; George Washington Univ; 3 yrs study with Jacques Maroger. *Work:* US Dept Agriculture; US State Dept; US District Court, Washington, DC; Maryland State Capitol; US Naval Dept; US Dept Energy. *Comn:* Portrait of John Block, US Dept of Agriculture, 87; Adm James D Watkins, USNI, 85; portrait, comn by William A Ball III, USN Dept, 90; portrait of Winston Lord, comn by Coun Foreign Relations, 86; portrait of Walter C McCarthy, Jr, Detroit Edison, 90. *Exhib:* one-man show, Bendann Art Galleries, Baltimore, 74; Mystic Int Marine Art Shows, Mystic, Conn, 81-84; Mariners Mus, Newport News, Va, 85; Egeli Family Exhib, Baltimore, Md, 85. *Pos:* Illusr, Marine Corps Inst, Washington, DC, 53-56; pres Am Soc Marine Artists, 86-89. *Teaching:* Instr painting, St Mary's Col of Md, 61-67. *Awards:* Best of Show, Mystic Int Marine Art Show, 81. *Bibliog:* Rebecca Smith (auth), The marine paintings of Peter Egeli, Nautical Quart Mag, 85; Ann Powell (auth), Artists Home on the St Mary's River, Mid-Atlantic Country Mag, 6/88; Amiad J Finkel (auth), Captured on Canvas, Chief Exec, Nov/Dec 88. *Mem:* Am Soc Marine Artists (pres, 86-89). *Media:* Oil, Watercolor. *Res:* 17th century English ships, 19th and early 20th century Chesapeake Bay craft. *Publ:* Auth/Illusr of seven prints of maritime subjects. *Dealer:* Mystic Seaport Musuem Gallery Mystic CT; Portraits Inc 41 E 57th St New York NY 10022. *Mailing Add:* Westbank Drayden MD 20630

EGLESTON, TRUMAN G
PAINTER
b Westfield, Mass, Oct 14, 31. *Study:* Mass Col Art, BFA, 58; Calif Col Arts & Crafts, MFA, 59. *Work:* Mus Fine Arts & Wellington Collection, Boston; Framingham State Col, Mass; Salem State Col. *Exhib:* Painting & Sculpture, 58 & Drawing, 59, San Francisco Mus Fine Arts; Boston Arts Festival, Boston Common, 64; Boston Now, Inst Contemp Art, 83; one-man exhib, Ann Plumb Gallery, 89; 3-man exhib, Space Attitudes, Holly Solomon Gallery, 91. *Teaching:* Asst prof drawing & painting, State Univ NY, Fredonia, 60-63; prof, Boston State Col, 64-82 & Univ Mass, Boston, 82-87. *Bibliog:* Neil Jenney (auth), retrospective exhib catalog, Univ Calif Press, 79; Robert Becker (auth), Neil Jenney, Interview Mag, Vol XIII No 5, 5/83; Paul Gardner (auth), Portrait of Jenney, Art News, 12/83. *Media:* Oil. *Mailing Add:* 160 Bleecker St New York NY 10012-1425

EGLITIS, LAIMONS
PAINTER, EDUCATOR
b Asite, Latvia, Nov 15, 29; US citizen. *Study:* With Joblovskis, 46-47; Tyler Sch Art, BFA, 69, MFA(fel), 71. *Work:* Philadelphia Mus Art; Virginia Beach Art Ctr Collection; Ottawa Art Collection; Albright Col Collection; Latvian State Mus, Riga. *Exhib:* New Directions, Civic Ctr Mus, Philadelphia, 71; New Acquisitions, Philadelphia Mus Art, 71; Baltimore Film Festival Invitational, Baltimore Mus Art, 75; Md Regional Water Color, Johns Hopkins Univ, 75 & 80; Bicentennial Events, Univ Pa Mus, 76; Overseas Artists, Riga Mus, Latvia, 81; Global Latvian Art Exhib, State Mus, Riga, 90. *Teaching:* Assoc prof art, Catonsville Community Col, 71-; adj prof, Maryland Inst Col Art, 85- *Awards:* Hon Award Visual Arts, Latvian Global Cult Found, 73; Gold Medal, Maryland Regional Watercolor Exhib, 86; and many others. *Bibliog:* Arnolds Treibergs (auth), Laimons Eglitis--a painter in exile, Latvju Maksla, Latvian Inst, 12/75. *Media:* Oils, Watercolors. *Mailing Add:* Visual & Performing Arts Catonsville Community Col 800 S Rolling Rd Catonsville MD 21228

EGRI, TED
SCULPTOR, PAINTER
b New York, NY, May 22, 13. *Study:* Master Inst Roerich Mus, dipl, 31-34; Duncan Phillips Mem Gallery Art Sch, 42; Hans Hofmann Sch Art, New York & Provincetown, Mass, 48. *Work:* William Rockhill Nelson Mus, Kansas City, Mo; Mus NMex, Santa Fe; Simon Wiesenthal Holocaust Mus, Los Angeles; Roswell Mus, NMex; Northern Iowa Univ; Carlsbad NMex Mus; and others. *Comn:* Fountain, Exec Life Bldg, Beverly Hills, Calif, 66; monument on pedestal, City Albuquerque, NMex, 69; 10 sculptures, Temple B'Nai Israel, Albuquerque, 79; 20ft fiberglass sculpture, Southwest Tex State Univ, San Marcos, 89; 6ft outdoor Saint Mary Ave Maria Parish, Parker, Colo, 88. *Exhib:* Colorado Springs Fine Arts Ctr, Colo, 50 & 52; Stables Gallery, 53-88; Pa Acad Fine Arts Ann, Philadelphia, 53; Art: USA 58, Madison Sq Garden, New York, 58; Religious Art Western World, 58 & Southwestern Art Show, 60, Dallas Mus Fine Arts, Tex; Roswell Mus, NMex, 58, 72 & 81; Shidoni 6th, 7th & 8th Ann Outdoor Show, Tesuque NMex, 80, 81 & 82; and others. *Teaching:* Instr oil painting & life drawing, Kansas City Art Inst, 48-50; lectr art sculpture, life drawing & painting, Univ Wyo, 59-60; instr painting, Philbrook Art Ctr, 5/56 & 5/57; vis lectr art, Univ Ill, Champaign, 60-61; vis artist teacher sculpture, Northern Iowa Univ, summer 63 & 64; lectr, Las Palomas Educ Convention Ctr, Taos, NMex, 82- *Awards:* A I Friedman Award, Audubon Artists Ann, 47; Top Award for Sculpture & Honorable Mention for Drawing, Mus NMex, 65; Top Award for Sculpture, Mus NMex Five-State Regional, 69. *Bibliog:* Louis G Redstone (auth), Art in Architecture; John Baldwin (auth), Contemporary Sculpture Techniques; John Rood (auth), Sculpture with a Torch; and others. *Mem:* Nat Artists Equity Asn Inc; Taos Art Asn, NMex; Nat Mus Women in Arts, Washington, DC. *Media:* Sculpture, Painting. *Publ:* Contrib 7 illus, Ted Egri: the survival of a sculptor, Am Artist, 6/77; 6 illus, Ted Egri: Sculptor of symbols, Southwest Art, 2/79; cover and 9 illus, Sculptured sentinels, Now Mag, 5/11/80; Art in Agriculture, Louis G Redstone; Contemporary Sculpture Techniques, John Baldwin. *Dealer:* New Directions Gallery Taos NM 87571. *Mailing Add:* PO Box 263 Taos NM 87571

EHLERS, CAROL A
ART DEALER
b Birmingham, Mich, May 10, 52. *Study:* Wheaton Col, Norton, Mass, BA, 74. *Pos:* Asst dir, Allan Frumkin Gallery-Photographs Inc, Chicago, 75-78, dir, 78-79; Pres & dir, Carol Ehlers Photographs Inc, 88-90; dir, Ehlers Caudill Gallery, 90. *Mem:* Asn Int Photog Art Dealers (vpres, 82-86). *Specialty:* 20th century photographs. *Mailing Add:* Ehlers Caudill Gallery Ltd 750 N Orleans Chicago IL 60610

EHRESMANN, DONALD LOUIS
HISTORIAN, EDUCATOR
b Newark, NJ, Oct 11, 37. *Study:* Rutgers Univ, BA, 59; NY Univ, MA, 63, PhD, 66; study with Willibald Sauerlander & Wolfgang Lotz. *Teaching:* Asst prof & chmn dept art hist, Bloomfield Col, NJ, 64-69; assoc prof art hist, State Univ NY Col Brockport, 69-71; assoc prof art hist, Univ Ill, Chicago Circle, 71-, chmn dept art hist, 73-77. *Awards:* Fritz Thyssen Found Res Fel, Ger Nat Mus, Nurenberg, WGer, 63-64; Alexander von Humboldt Found Res fel, Ger Nat Mus, Nurenberg, WGer, 67-68. *Mem:* Col Art Asn Am; Mid-West Art Hist Soc. *Res:* Medieval art and architecture; fine arts bibliography. *Publ:* Auth, articles & rev, Art Bull, Art J & Art Quart, 68-; auth, Fine Arts--A Bibliographic Guide to Basic Reference Works, Histories and Handbooks, 75, 2nd ed, 79, 3rd ed, 90 & auth, Applied and Decorative--A Bibliographic Guide to Basic Reference Works, Histories and Handbooks, 77; auth, Architecture--a bibliographic guide to basic reference works, Histories & Handbooks, 83. *Mailing Add:* Univ Ill Hist Arch & Art Dept 303 Jefferson Hall M/C 033 Box 4348 Chicago IL 60680-4348

EHRLICH, GEORGE
HISTORIAN
b Chicago, Ill, Jan 28, 25. *Study:* Univ Ill-Urbana, BS, 49, MFA, 51, PhD, 60. *Pos:* Chmn dept art & art hist, Univ Mo-Kansas City, 64-75. *Teaching:* Prof art hist, Univ Mo-Kansas City, 54-92. *Mem:* Soc Archit Historians (pres, Mo Valley chap, 71 & 72); Landmarks Commission, Kansas City, Mo. *Res:* Architectural history of Kansas City, Missouri; interrelationship of art to science and technology. *Publ:* Auth, George Caleb Bingham as ethnographer: A variant view of his genre works, Am Studies, fall 78; Kansas City, Missouri: An Architectural History, 1826-1990, Univ Mo Press, rev ed, 92; Partnership practice & the professionalization of architecture in Kansas City, Mo, Mo Hist Rev, 7/80; The Bank of Commerce by Asa Beebe Cross: A building of the latest architecture, J Soc Archit Historians, 5/84; The 1807 Plan for an illustrated edition of the Lewis & Clark expedition, The Pa Mag Hist & Biog, 1/85; coauth (with Sherry Piland), The Architectural Career of Nelle Peters, Mo Hist Rev, 10/89. *Mailing Add:* 5505 Holmes Kansas City MO 64110

EICHEL, EDWARD W
PAINTER, DRAFTSMAN
b Brooklyn, NY, June 8, 32. *Study:* Art Inst Chicago, BFA(G & I Brown Fel), 58; Oskar Kokoschka Acad, Salzburg, Austria, 59. *Work:* Lyman Allyn Mus, New London, Conn; New York Drawing Soc. *Exhib:* Young Painters Int Biennale, Mus Mod Art, Paris, France, 61; Animal Drawings from the 15th to 20th Centuries, Seiferheld Gallery, New York, 62; Drawing & Print Club Exhib, Detroit Inst Art, Mich, 66; Painters & Sculptors 27th Ann, Jersey City Mus, NJ, 68; Drawings: A Reinvestigation, Joseloff Gallery, Univ Hartford, Conn, 75; 156th Ann Exhib, Nat Acad Design, New York, 81; 43rd Anniversary Exhib, Fedn Mod Painters & Sculptors, 83. *Teaching:* Instr painting & drawing, Eastern Mich Univ, Ypsilanti, 65-66; instr drawing & illustration, Hartford Art Sch, Univ Hartford, Conn, 81-82. *Awards:* Tiffany Found Grant, 67; 27th NJ Ann Medal Merit, Syndicate Mag, 68. *Bibliog:* Sketches of a journey: Israel on the line of a pen, L'Arche, Paris, 7/61; Stuart Hilton (auth), Medal of merit in New Jersey Annual, Today's Art, 12/68. *Mem:* Fedn Mod Painters & Sculptors; Westbeth Artists Community; Creativity Laboratories (dir, 70-); Am Artist-Therapist Asn (hon bd mem, 79-). *Media:* Oil, Watercolor; Pencil, Pen & Ink. *Publ:* Illusr, The Glass Cage: The Eichmann Trial, Hakibbutz Hameuchad, 62; Israel Sketchbook, Dvir, 62; The Beast Book, Harper & Row, 64; The Perfect Fit: How to Achieve Mutual Fulfillment and Monogamous Passion through the New Intercourse, Donald I Fine Inc, 92. *Dealer:* Allan Stone Gallery 48 E 86th Street New York NY 10028. *Mailing Add:* Studio A-1106 463 West St New York NY 10014

EICKHORST, WILLIAM SIGURD
EDUCATOR, ART DEALER
b Hackensack, NJ, Mar 4, 41. *Study:* Parsons Sch Design, BFA(advert graphics), 62; Montclair State Col, BA(art educ), 69, MA(art educ), 70; Ball State Univ, EdD(art educ), 72; Univ Mo, Kansas City, 85; Kansas City Art Inst, 86 & 87. *Work:* Nelson-Atkins Mus Art, Kansas City, Mo; Albrecht Art Mus, St Joseph, Mo; Portland Mus Art, Ore; Spencer Mus, Lawrence KS; Quincy Art Ctr, Quincy I. *Exhib:* Art Horizons, Art 54 Gallery, New York, 88; 41st Ann Midstates Exhib, Evansville Mus Art, 88; 19th Biennial Jury

Show, Muscatine Art Ctr, 88; 18th Nat Works on Paper, Minot State Univ, 88; 3rd Ann Fla Nat, Fla State Univ, 88; Kansas 13th Nat, Fort Hays State Univ, 88; 5th Ann Maritime Nat, Univ Maine, 88; William Eickhorst, Albrecht Art Mus, 89. *Pos:* Founder & exec dir, Print Consortium, St Joseph, Mo, 83-; vpres, Gallery on the Square, Kansas City, Mo, 85-86. *Teaching:* Prof art educ & studio art, Frostburg State Col, Frostburg, Md, 72-75; head, grad & undergrad art educ progs, Univ Maine, Orono, 75-78; chmn art dept & prof art theory & criticism, Mo Western State Col, St Joseph, Mo, 78- *Awards:* Juror's Award, 38th Spiva Ann Competitive, 88; Cert of Excellence, Int Art Competition, 88; Mus Purchase Award, Central Sgtates Exhib, 89; and others. *Mem:* Boston Printmakers; Nat Art Educ Asn; Mo Art Educ Asn; Mo Alliance Arts Educ (bd dirs, 81-82); Soc Am Graphic Artists; and others. *Media:* Mixed Media, Photography. *Specialty:* Contemporary American graphics by established and emerging artists. *Publ:* Auth, rev of Children's Art Judgment by Gordon S Plummer, Art Teacher, 75; Art education and the seventeen years war, 77, Science explains modern art, 85, rev of Art Law by Leonard DuBoff, 85 & From abacus to art, 86, Art Educ-Nat Art Educ Asn. *Mailing Add:* 6121 NW 77th St Kansas City MO 64151

EIDE, JOHN
PHOTOGRAPHER
b Minneapolis, Minn, Jan 28, 43. *Study:* Lawrence Univ, BA; Univ Minn, MFA; also with Jerome Liebling, Elaine Mayes & Allan Downs. *Work:* Portland Mus Art. *Exhib:* One-man shows, Wentz Gallery, Portland Art Inst, Ore, Photo Gallery, Portland Sch Art, 79 & Brockton Arts Ctr, Mass, 80; Cyanotypes--Boston Visual Artists Union; Thayer Acad, Braintree, Mass; Worchester Art Mus, Bowdoin Col, Brunswick, Maine, 79; and others. *Pos:* Hon cur photog, Portland Mus Art; dir, Photo Gallery, Portland Sch Art, currently. *Teaching:* Prof, area head photog, Portland Sch Art, 70- *Mem:* Soc Photog Educ. *Publ:* Contribr, Io Mag, Earth Geog Issue, No 2, 72. *Mailing Add:* 10 Channel Rd South Portland ME 04106

EIDELBERG, MARTIN
HISTORIAN
b New York, NY, Jan 30, 41. *Study:* Columbia Univ, BA, 61; Princeton Univ, PhD, 65. *Pos:* Ed, Decorative Arts Soc Newslett (quart mag), 78-80. *Teaching:* Prof art hist, Rutgers Univ, New Brunswick, 64- *Awards:* Robert C Smith Award, Decorative Arts Soc, 82; Charles F Montgomery Prize, Decorative Arts Soc, 84; George Wittenborn Mem Award, Art Libr Soc NAm, 91. *Mem:* Decorative Arts Soc, Soc Archit Historians. *Res:* 18th century French painting and drawing; modern decorative arts. *Publ:* Coauth, The Arts and Crafts Movement in America, 1876-1916, Princeton Univ, 72; Japonisme-Japanese Influence on French Art, 1854-1910, Cleveland Mus, 75; auth, Watteau's Drawings: Their Use and Significance, Garland Press, 77; E Colonna, Dayton Art Inst, 82; coauth, Cranbrook, A Vision of Design in America, Abrams, 82; Eva Zeisel, Designer for Industry, Montreal Mus Decorative Arts, 84; ed & coauth, Musée des Arts Décoratisf de Montréal, Abrams, 91. *Mailing Add:* Dept Art Hist Rutgers Univ New Brunswick NJ 08903

EIKERMAN, ALMA
JEWELER, DESIGNER
b Pratt, Kans. *Study:* Kans State Col; Kans Univ; Columbia Univ, MA; spec study with Karl Gustav Hansen (silversmith), Baron Eric Fleming (metalsmith), Ossip Zadkine (sculptor) & Michael Wilm (goldsmith); Hon DFA, Univ Ohio, Miami, Ohio. *Work:* Smithsonian Inst, Washington, DC; Mus Contemp Crafts, New York; Sheldon Gallery Art, Univ Nebr, Lincoln; Hans Hansen Solvemedie, Kolding, Denmark; Home Galleries, Toulouse, France. *Comn:* Sterling silver plaque honoring Dean Wilfred Bain's yrs of serv to Ind Univ Music Sch, Bloomington; plus pvt comns. *Exhib:* Midwestern Crafts Exhib, Art Inst Chicago, 58; Soc NAm Goldsmiths Show, Minn Mus of Art, St Paul, 70, Renwick Gallery, Washington, DC, 74 & Henry Gallery, Univ Wash, Seattle, 77; 4th Int DeBijoux d'Art Contemporain, Toulouse, France, 73-74; Forms in Metal, 275 Yrs of Metalsmithing, Mus Contemp Crafts, New York, 75; Outstanding Jewelry Sch in USA, Nat Goldsmiths Show, Melbourne, Australia, 76; Objects USA, Smithsonian Traveling Exhib, Europe, 68-72. *Collections Arranged:* Creative Silversmithing Workshop I & II, summer 55 & 56 & Carnegie Grant for Graduate Student Experimental Silversmithing Project (with booklet & film), 68, Fine Arts Ctr, Ind Univ, Bloomington. *Teaching:* Asst prof design & jewelry, Kans State Univ, Wichita, 41-43, 45-46; head jewelry dept, Ind Univ, 47- *Awards:* Nat Endowment for the Arts Craft Award, 75; numerous travel grants for res. *Bibliog:* Lee Nordness (auth), Objects USA, Viking, 70; Phillip Morton (auth), Contemp Jewelry, Holt Rinehart & Winston, 76; Oppi Untracht (auth), Contemporary Craftsman, 78. *Mem:* Nat Soc Am Goldsmiths; Am Asn Univ Prof; Nat Soc Arts & Lett; Col Art Asn; Ind Craftsmen. *Media:* Gold, Silver; Copper, Brass. *Collection:* African sculpture, small Oriental and contemporary bronzes, enamel, ceramics, contemporary glass, paintings and prints. *Mailing Add:* 2007 E Second Bloomington IN 47401

EILERS, FRED (ANTON FREDERICK)
PORTRAIT PAINTER, DESIGNER
b Wilmington, NC. *Study:* William & Mary Col, BS; Richmond Prof Inst, with Theresa Pollack & workshop with Elaine De Kooning. *Work:* Evansville Mus, Ind; Owensboro Mus, Ky; Old Nat Bank, Citizens Bank, Evansville; Southern Ind Univ; Permanent Fed Bank; and others. *Comn:* Mural, Colonial Nat Bank, 69, Bustler Enterprises, 80. *Exhib:* One-man shows, Univ Evansville, Old Gallery, Evansville, Hoosier Gallery, Indianapolis & Thor Gallery, Louisville; one-man retrospective, Evansville Mus, 87; and others. *Pos:* Art restorer (oils), currently. *Teaching:* Instr portrait painting, Univ Evansville, 42-88, instr figure drawing, 50-82; guest artist, Fla Sch Arts; workshops, Fla, Ind & Ky, 89-92. *Awards:* Bronstein Purchase Award, 60 & Graphics Purchase Award, 68, Evansville Mus; Hoosier Salon Merit Award, 65. *Media:* Oil. *Dealer:* Risley Evansville IN 47708; Perigo-Moore Gallery Evansville IN 47708. *Mailing Add:* 2140 E Chandler Ave Evansville IN 47714

EINO
SCULPTOR
b Mynamaki, Finland, Feb 6, 40; US citizen. *Work:* Libr Congress, Washington, DC; City of Toronto; City of Santa Monica; City of Los Angeles. *Comn:* Christ, Ga Marble Co, Tate, 66; mem portrait, Univ Southern Calif, Los Angeles, 73; freeform marble, Sculpture Garden, Church of Perfect Liberty, Japan, 73; Sunset Vine Tower, 80; Valio, Helsinki, Finland, 80. *Exhib:* Gallerie Juarez, Los Angeles & Palm Springs, 70; Calif Expos, Sacramento, 71; Pepperdine Univ, 73 & 88; Opening Exhib, Palm Springs Desert Mus, Calif, 76; one-man exhib, Nat Endowment Arts, Century City, Calif, 78; Calif Inst Technol, 79; Scandinavia Today, Los Angeles City Hall, 83; Norman F Feldheym Libr Galleries, San Bernardino, 86; Sports Mus Helsinki, Finland, 88. *Teaching:* Instr sculpture, Pepperdine Univ, 69; instr TV credit course, Theta Cable, 71. *Awards:* Outstanding Sculptor, Finlandia Found, 84. *Bibliog:* Stan Pantovic (auth), The earth is shaking (Eino), The Geijutsu Seikatsu, Japan, 75; Stan Pantovic (auth), Eino: more than marble, Small World, winter, 80-81; profile, Fred Anderson Show, KNBC-TV, Los Angeles, 85; profile, Pub Broadcasting Serv, Videologe, 85-86. *Media:* Marble. *Mailing Add:* 530 Venezia Ave Venice CA 90291

EINREINHOFER, NANCY ANNE
CURATOR, MUSEUM DIRECTOR
b Paterson, NJ, Sept 8, 43. *Study:* Univ Leicester, PhD(Mus Studies). *Collections Arranged:* Five Views (auth, catalog), William Paterson Col, 79; Bladen, Kipp, Witkin (auth, catalog), 79; Illusion and Material (auth, catalog), 79; New New York (auth, catalog), 80; Language in the Visual Arts (auth, catalog), 81; Painting About Painting (auth, catalog), 81; Anti-Apocalypse (auth, catalog), 82; The Vogel Collection (auth, catalog), 82; Aspects of Contemporary Realism (auth, catalog), 83; The Great Illusionists (auth, catalog), 83; Legacy of Surrealism (auth, catalog), 88; Hand, Body, House (auth, catalog), 90. *Pos:* Dir, Ben Shahn Gallery, William Paterson Col, Wayne, NJ, 79- *Teaching:* Instr gallery & mus studies, William Paterson Col, currently. *Res:* Contemporary art; museum interpretation. *Publ:* Auth, Nineteenth Century Painting of the New Jersey Landscape, 85, Nineteenth Century Maritime New Jersey, 86, Ninteenth Century New Jersey Collection, 88 & Ninteenth Century New Jersey Architecture, 89, William Paterson Col Press. *Mailing Add:* Ben Shahn Gallery William Paterson Col Wayne NJ 07470

EINS, STEFAN
CONCEPTUAL ARTIST, MUSEUM DIRECTOR
b Prague, Bohemia; Austrian citizen. *Study:* Univ Vienna, Austria, MA, 64; Acad Fine Arts, Vienna, BA, 67. *Work:* Ōsterreichische Galerie, Vienna; New Mus, New York. *Collections Arranged:* John Ahearn, 79, Jenny Holzer, 79, Graffiti, Art Success, 80 & Keith Haring, 81, Fashion Moda Mus; Fashion Moda (auth, catalog), New Mus, New York, 80-81 & Documenta 7, Kassel, WGer, 82; Lady Pink, Lady Heart, 83; Ron English, 87. *Pos:* Founder & exec dir, 3 Mercer, New York, 72-79 & Fashion Moda Mus, Bronx, 78-84 & 88-; pres, Collab Proj Inc, 88. *Awards:* Nat Endowment Arts Fel, 80 & 87. *Bibliog:* Grace Glueck (auth), The new collectives, New York Times, 2/1/81; Calvin Tomkins (auth), The artworld, The New Yorker Mag, 12/26/83; Carey Lovelace (auth), S Bronx art, Los Angeles Times, 9/2/84; Karin Kuoni (auth), Stefan Eins: Fashion Moda, Kunstforum Bd 112, 3-4/91. *Mem:* Collab Proj Inc. *Media:* Ideas, Liquids. *Publ:* Ed, Some posters from Fashion Moda by Ingrid Sischy, Artforum, 1/81; auth, Francesca Alinovi-Arte di Frontiera, (Italian ed), Flash Art, 2/82; Gabriele von Arnim-Atelier in Den Slums, Art, Ger, 4/82; Lucy Lippard-Get the Message, Dutton, 84; Alan Moore & Marc Miller-ABC No Rio Dinero, ABC No Rio, 85; One/Steffan Eins Exhibitions Catalog, Ōsterreichische Galerie, Vienna, 91. *Mailing Add:* PO Box 33 New York NY 10013

EINSTEIN, GILBERT W
DEALER
b New York, NY, June 27, 42. *Study:* Columbia Univ, AB, 63, MBA, 68. *Pos:* Pres, G W Einstein Co, Inc, New York, 70- *Specialty:* Twentieth century American art. *Mailing Add:* G W Einstein Co Inc 591 Broadway New York NY 10012

EISENBERG, JEROME MARTIN
DEALER, COLLECTOR
b Philadelphia, Pa, July 6, 30. *Study:* Boston Univ, AB, 51; Columbia Univ, with Otto Brendel, Edith Porada & Henry Fischer, 60-63; Pa State Univ, with Jiri Frel, 69-71, PhD, 83. *Pos:* Dir, Royal-Athena Galleries, 58-; founder, Eisenberg Mus Biblical Archeol, Louisville, 61; chmn, Herodium Archeol Expedition Fund, 62. *Teaching:* Lectr forgery & fraud in ancient art, NY Univ, 69-70. *Bibliog:* Barbara Pollack (auth), Royal-Athena: Access to antiquities, Collectors Quart, 63. *Mem:* Archeol Inst Am; Appraisers Asn Am; patron Am Numismatic Soc. *Specialty:* Egyptian, Near Eastern, Greek, Roman, Pre-Columbian, Oriental, European and Tribal art. *Collection:* Ancient Egyptian faience figurines; Egyptian stone vessels; South Italian pottery; Roman glass; Pre-Columbian and tribal art. *Publ:* Auth, A Guide to Roman Imperial Coins, 57; Art of the Ancient, World, 65, 67 & 85. *Mailing Add:* Royal-Athena Galleries 153 E 57th St New York NY 10022

EISENBERG, MARC S
PAINTER, SCULPTOR
b New York, NY, Feb 17, 48. *Study:* Sch Visual Arts, BFA, 71. *Work:* Chase Manhattan Bank, New York; Prudential Life Insurance Co, Edison, NJ; Equitable Life Insurance Co, New York; Berley & Co, New York; Weatherspoon Art Gallery, Greensboro, NC. *Exhib:* 19th Nat Print Exhib, 76 & Decade of American Drawing, 81, Brooklyn, NY; Paper as Medium, Smithsonian Inst, Washington, DC, 78; Painting & Sculpture Today, Indianapolis Inst Art, Ind, 79; Art on Paper, Weatherspoon Mus, Greensboro, NC, 86. *Bibliog:* Corrine Robbins (auth), Works of Marc Eisenberg, Arts Mag, 76; Ronnie Cotrone (auth), Spotlight, Interview Mag, 76; Charles Gatewood (auth), Outlaw artists, Gallery Mag, 85. *Media:* Miscellaneous. *Mailing Add:* 40-60 Douglaston Pky Flushing NY 11363

EISENBERG, MARVIN
HISTORIAN, EDUCATOR
b Philadelphia, Pa. *Study:* Univ Pa, BA, 43; Princeton Univ, MFA, 49, PhD, 54. *Pos:* Mem, Inst for Advan Study, winter 70; mem adv comt, Ctr Advanced Study Visual Arts, Nat Gallery, Washington, DC, 79-83; mem vis comt, Freer Gallery Art, Washington, DC, currently & Dept Fine Arts, Harvard Univ, 75-80; ed, Bulletin Mus Art & Archeol, Univ Mich, 78-88. *Teaching:* Instr art hist, Univ Mich, 49-53, from asst prof to assoc prof, 54-61, prof, 61- & chmn dept, 61-69, prof emer, 89; vis prof, Stanford Univ, 73; Berg prof, Colo Col, 90. *Awards:* Guggenheim Fel, 59; Star of Solidarity, Ital Govt, 61; Distinguished Teaching in Art History, Col Art Asn Am, 87. *Mem:* Col Art Asn Am (pres, 68-69); Benjamin Franklin Fel Royal Soc Arts; Medieval Acad Am; Renaissance Soc Am. *Res:* Italian late medieval painting. *Publ:* Auth, articles on early Italian painting in journals and museum bulletins; Lorenzo Monaco, Princeton Univ Press, Princeton, 89. *Mailing Add:* Dept of Hist of Art Univ of Mich Ann Arbor MI 48109

EISENBERG, SONJA MIRIAM
PAINTER
b Berlin, Ger, June 10, 26; US citizen. *Study:* NY Univ, BA, 54; Nat Acad Sch Fine Arts, with Leon Kroll, 61; also with Daniel Dickerson, 62-68 & Sidney Delevante, in 60's. *Work:* Palm Spring Desert Mus; Fordham Univ Mus, New York; Archives Am Art, The Jewish Mus, New York; the Cathedral Saint John the Divine, NY. *Comn:* Designer, WF UNA Cachet, UN Water Conf, 77; designer mag cover, Our Planet Earth, Planetary Citizens, UN, 78; designer cover, Discovering Fire for the Second Time, Nat Conf of Christians & Jews, New York; designer cachet for United Nations, Int Year Disabled Persons; book, Seeing the Gospel According to St John, (text & 41 paintings), The Cathedral Saint John the Divine, New York. *Exhib:* One-woman shows, Galerie de Sfinx, Amsterdam, 74 & Am Mus Hayden Planetarium, New York, 80; Am Watercolor Soc 108th Ann Exhib, New York, 75; Archives of Am Art, Smithsonian Inst, 78; Betty Parsons Gallery, 81; Cathedral St John the Divine, New York, 83 & 85; The 14th Int Art Friendship Exhib, Tokyo Metrop Art Mus, Tokyo, Japan, 89. *Pos:* Artist-in-residence, Cathedral St John the Divine. *Awards:* Accademia Italia delle Arti e del Lavoro, Medaglio d'Oro, 81; Gold Medal for artistic merit, Int Parliament Safety & Peace, 83; World Prize for Culture; Palma d'Oro d'Europa, 86. *Bibliog:* Jan deCarpentier (auth), Kijk's kunst, De Typhoon, 6/74; Gordon Brown (auth), Sonja Eisenberg, Art Mag, 4/75; Nina Brodsky (auth), Miniature Collector, 4/82; Ray Fashora (auth), Taconic Newspapers, 6/89. *Mem:* Res Bd Adv, The Am Biog Inst. *Media:* Oil, Watercolor; Pastel. *Dealer:* Cathedral St John the Divine New York NY 10025. *Mailing Add:* 1020 Park Ave New York NY 10028

EISENSTAT, BENJAMIN
PAINTER, ILLUSTRATOR
b Philadelphia, Pa, June 4, 15. *Study:* Fleisher Art Mem; Pa Acad Fine Arts; Albert Barnes Found. *Work:* Philadelphia Mus Art, Fleisher Art Mem & Woodmere Mus, Philadelphia; Glassboro Univ, NJ; Noyes Mus, Oceanville, NJ. *Comn:* Official painting of nuclear ship Savannah, US Maritime & NY Ship Comn, Washington, DC, 59; mural, First Bank NJ, Philadelphia, 60; mural, Provident Mutual Life Ins Co, Philadelphia, 62; mural, Burlington Co Trust Co, Moorestown, NJ, 63; mural, Oreland Episcopal Church, Pa, 70. *Exhib:* Artists for Victory, 45 & Nat Drawing Show, 55, Metrop Mus Art, New York; Watercolor USA, Springfield, Mo; Nat Acad Design Ann, New York; Am Watercolor Soc Ann, New York; Rutgers Nat Drawing Show, Rutgers Univ, Camden, NJ, 77; Ann, New York Soc Illusr, 79 & 80; and others. *Teaching:* Assoc prof painting & drawing, Philadelphia Col Art, 46-69, prof painting & drawing & chmn illustrating dept, 69-80, prof emer, 80-; instr watercolor, Philadelphia Mus Art, 62-66; instr illus, Cambridge Col Arts & Technol, Eng, 76; lectr Am illus, Royal Col Art, London, Eng, 76; lectr hist Am illus, Parsons Sch Design, NY, 76-81 & Syracuse Univ, Masters Prog, 81; teacher hist of illus, Acad Art, San Francisco, 86; vis lectr, Art Ctr Col Design, Pasadena, Calif, 87; Moore Col Art & Univ Arts, Philadelphia, Pa, 4/88. *Awards:* Ann Medal Achievement, Philadelphia Watercolor Club, 62; Harrison Morris Prize, Fel, Pa Acad Fine Arts; Watercolor USA Prize, 72. *Bibliog:* Hugh Scott (auth), Mural on Market Street, Today Mag, 6/12/60; Henry Pitz (auth), Documentary drawings of Benjamin Eisenstat, Am Artists, 12/65. *Mem:* Am Watercolor Soc; Philadelphia Watercolor Club; fel Pa Acad Fine Arts (bd dirs, 55-60). *Media:* Acrylic, Oil. *Collection:* Original illustrations. *Publ:* Auth, Jessie Wilcox Smith, 9/87; Coauth (with Jane Sperry Eisenstat), articles on Master of the Past, Step by Step Graphics, 88; Illustration In America 1880-1890, article, Graphis, 7-8/90; Henry Raleigh, 5/91; The Visions of Rockwell Kent, 5/92. *Dealer:* Newman Gallery 1625 Walnut St Philadelphia PA 19103; Bingham Gallery 170 S Market St San Jose CA 95113. *Mailing Add:* 3639 Bryant St Palo Alto CA 94306

EISENSTEIN, (MR & MRS) JULIAN
COLLECTORS
Mr Eisenstein b Warrenton, Mo, Apr 3, 21. *Study:* Mr Eisenstein, Harvard Univ, BS, 41, MA, 42, PhD, 48. *Pos:* Mr Eisenstein, Nat res fel, Oxford, 52-53; physicist, Nat Bureau Standards, 57-66; pres & trustee, Washington Gallery Mod Art, 61-65. *Teaching:* Mr Eisenstein, instr, Univ Wis, 48-52; from asst prof to assoc prof, Pa State Univ, 53-57; prof, George Washington Univ, 66- *Collection:* Contemporary art. *Mailing Add:* 82 Kalorama Circle NW Washington DC 20008

EISENTRAGER, JAMES A
PAINTER
b Alvord, Iowa, Sept 3, 29. *Study:* Augustana Col, Sioux Falls, SDak, BA, 51; Univ Md in Wiesbaden, Ger, 52-53; Univ Northern Iowa, 55; Univ Iowa, Iowa City, MFA, 61; with Stewart Edie, Byron Burford & Mauricio Lasansky. *Work:* Univ Iowa, Iowa City; Sheldon Mem Art Gallery, Lincoln, Nebr; Millersville State Univ, Pa. *Exhib:* Ann Exhib, Springfield Art Mus, Mo, 64-72; one-man shows, Sheldon Mem Art Gallery, 66, Univ Del, Newark, 75 & Northern Ariz Univ Art Gallery, Flagstaff, 77; 31st Mid-Yr Show, Butler Inst Am Art, Youngstown, Ohio, 66; Mid-Am Exhib, William Rockhill Nelson Gallery of Art, Kansas City, Mo, 66 & 70; Mid-W Biennial, Joslyn Art Mus, Omaha, Nebr, 66 & 70; Ten Artists W of the Mississippi, Colorado Springs Fine Art Ctr, 67. *Teaching:* Prof painting, Univ Nebr-Lincoln, 61-; prof & lectr, Vail Summer Workshop, Colo, 71-76; vis prof art, Univ Colo, Boulder, summer 67. *Awards:* Purchase Award, May Show, Sioux City Art Ctr, Iowa, 63; Best Painting Purchase Award, Images on Paper Nat Competition, Springfield Art Asn, Ill, 73; Jesse Loomis Award, Waterloo Ann, Waterloo Munic Gallery, Iowa, 73. *Mem:* Mid-Am Col Art Asn. *Media:* Polymer, Oil. *Mailing Add:* Dept Art Univ Nebr at Lincoln Lincoln NE 68583

EISINGER, HARRY
PAINTER
b Berlin, Ger, Apr 23, 32; US citizen. *Study:* Calif Sch Fine Arts, San Francisco, 57-59; also with Ralph Putzker, Nathan Oliveira & Wayne Thiebaud. *Work:* Slides, Whitney Mus, New York. *Comn:* Drawings, Territorial Gazette, San Francisco, 59; posters, Marin Co Art Ctr, Calif, 60. *Exhib:* One-man shows, Panoras Gallery, New York, 73 & Gallery 84, 77; 32nd & 33rd Nat Audubon Exhibs, Nat Acad Galleries, 74 & 75 & Allied Artists Am Exhib, 75; Gallery 84, New York, 75 & 77. *Awards:* Spinaker Award, Sausalito Mayor, Calif, 60. *Bibliog:* Herb Caen (auth), article, San Francisco Chronicle, 60. *Mem:* Allied Artists Am; Audubon Artists. *Media:* Oil. *Dealer:* Gallery 84 30 West 57th St New York NY 10019. *Mailing Add:* 330 E 19th St New York NY 10003

EISNER, CAROLE SWID
PAINTER, SCULPTOR
b New York, NY, Oct 30, 37. *Study:* Syracuse Univ, AB, 58; study with Ethel Schwabacher, 63 & Marge Walzer, 69-78; Int Sch Photog, 76-78. *Work:* Guggenheim Mus & Knoll Int, New York; Syracuse Univ; Southeast Banking Corp, Miami; Northstar Reinsurance Co, Seattle; Nat Assocs Inc; and others. *Comn:* Set designs for four plays, Theater XII, New York, 78. *Exhib:* Solo exhibs, Segal Gallery, 84-86 & Jack Gallery, New York, 87 & 88; Maquettes, Rutgers Univ, Newark, NJ, 80; New Year Invitational, Gallery Schlesinger-Boisante, New York, 80-81; Art of the Northeast, Silvermine Guild, New Canaan, Conn, 83; Recent Acquisitions, Guggenheim Mus, New York, 86; Images Gallery, Norwalk, Conn, 86; Sculpture by Guild Artists, Silvermine, Conn, 88; New American Art Invitational, London, 88; First Womens Bank, 88. *Awards:* Rosenthal Award, Outdoor Sculpture, All New Eng Show, Silvermine, Conn, 78; Sculpture Award, Champion Int, 80; Finalist, Johnson Atelier Nat Sculpture Competition, Princeton, NJ, 80. *Bibliog:* William Pellicone (auth), article, Artspeak, 5/21/81; Jacqueline Moss (auth), article, Arts Mag, 10/84; Will Grant (auth), article, Artspeak, 7/1/86. *Mem:* Silvermine Guild Artists; Weston-Westport Arts Coun. *Media:* Acrylic; Welded Metal. *Publ:* Contribr, Contemporary Women Artists Calendar, Bo Tree Productions, 67 & 87; The Antiques J, 6/79 & 2/80. *Dealer:* David Findlay Gallery 984 Madison Ave New York NY 10021. *Mailing Add:* 1107 5th Ave New York NY 10028

EISNER, ELLIOT WAYNE
EDUCATOR
b Chicago, Ill, Mar 10, 33. *Study:* Roosevelt Univ, BA; Ill Inst Technol, MS; Univ Chicago, MA & PhD. *Teaching:* Instr art educ, Ohio State Univ, 60-61; asst prof educ, Univ Chicago, 61-65; prof educ & art, Stanford Univ, 65- *Awards:* Hon Doct, Univ Oslo, 86; Hon Doct, Hofstra Univ, 88; hon Doct, Maryland Inst Col Art, 89. *Mem:* Hon fel Nat Art Educ Asn (pres, 77-79); Am Educ Res Asn; Int Soc Educ Through Art (pres, 87-90); Am Educ Res Asn (pres, 92-93). *Res:* Children's artistic development; the uses of art criticism for the study and evaluation of educational practice. *Publ:* Auth, The Educational Imagination, MacMillan, 78; Cognition and Curriculum, Longmans, 82; The Art of Educational Evaluation, Falmer, 85; Qualitative Inquiry: The Continuing Debate (with Alan Peshkin), Teachers Col Press, 90; The Enlightened Eye: Qualitative Inquiry and the Enhancement of Educational Practice, Macmillan, 91. *Mailing Add:* Sch of Educ Stanford Univ Stanford CA 94305

EITELJORG, HARRISON
COLLECTOR, PATRON
b Indianapolis, Ind, Oct 1, 04. *Study:* Ind Univ Law Sch. *Mem:* Indianapolis Mus Art; Ind Art Comn; Contemp Art Soc; Decorative Arts Soc; Am Asn Mus. *Interests:* Sponsor of museum of western artifacts. *Collection:* Abstract

and modern American art; School of Paris; Western painting and bronzes; American Indian artifacts; African and oceanic. *Publ:* Treasures of the American West-Selections from the collection of Harrison Eiteljorg. *Mailing Add:* 4567 Cold Spring Rd Indianapolis IN 46208

EITNER, LORENZ E A
HISTORIAN, MUSEUM DIRECTOR
b Brno, Czech, Aug 27, 19; US citizen. *Study:* Duke Univ, AB, 40; Princeton Univ, MFA, 48, PhD, 52. *Collections Arranged:* Masterdrawings, Guggenheim Mus, New York & Univ Gallery, Univ Minn, 60; Gericault, Los Angeles Co Mus, Detroit Inst Art & Philadelphia Mus Art, 71-72; numerous art exhibs at Stanford Mus. *Pos:* Dir, Stanford Mus, 63- *Teaching:* Prof art, Univ Minn, 49-63; prof art & chmn dept, Stanford Univ, 63- *Awards:* Mitchell Prize, 84; Charles Rufus Morey Prize, 85. *Mem:* Col Art Asn Am (vpres, dir, 56-71 & 76-). *Res:* European painting of the latter half of the eighteenth century and the beginning of the nineteenth century. *Publ:* Auth, Introduction to Art, Burgess, 60; Gericault, Univ Chicago, 60; Neoclassicism and Romanticism, Prentice-Hall, 69; Gericault's Raft of the Medusa, Phaidon, 72; Gericault, His Life and Work, Cornell Univ Press, 83. *Mailing Add:* Dept of Art Stanford Univ Stanford CA 94305

EKDAHL, JANIS KAY
LIBRARIAN
b Topeka, Kans, Dec 7, 46. *Study:* Occidental Col, BA, 68; Columbia Univ, MLS, 69. *Pos:* Art librn, Vassar Col, Poughkeepsie, NY, 71-81; asst dir, Mus Mod Art Libr, New York, 81- *Mem:* Art Libr Soc North Am (Eastern regional rep, 81-83); Art Libr Soc New York; Col Art Asn; Am Libr Asn. *Interests:* Modern and contemporary art; sculpture; American art and architecture. *Publ:* Auth, American sculpture: A guide to information sources, Gale, 77. *Mailing Add:* 107 W 86th St No 11 D New York NY 10024

ELA, PATRICK H
DIRECTOR
b Oakland, Calif, June 20, 48. *Study:* Occidental Col, Los Angeles, BA, 70; Grad Sch Art Hist, 70-71; Anderson Sch Mgt, MBA, 73, Univ Calif, Los Angeles. *Pos:* Admin dir, Craft & Folk Art Mus, Los Angeles, 76-84, dir, 85-; int consult, 84- *Teaching:* Prof, arts mgt, Calif State Univ Fullerton, 78-80; Instr, sociology of art world, Occidental Col, 80. *Mailing Add:* Craft & Folk Art Museum 6067 Wilshire Blvd, 4th Fl Los Angeles CA 90036

ELDER, DAVID MORTON
SCULPTOR
b Windsor, Ont, July 3, 36; US citizen. *Study:* Wittenberg Univ, BA, 57; Ohio State Univ Grad Sch, MA, 61. *Work:* Denver Art Mus, Colo; Long Beach Art Mus, Calif. *Comn:* Sculpture (metal), Gloria Christi Chapel, Valparaiso Univ, 62, St Paul Lutheran Church, Glenn Bermie, Md, 63, Coconut Grove Ambassador Hotel, Los Angeles, 69 & Barnsdall Park, Los Angeles, 74; sculpture (resin), Pac Home Burbank, 74. *Exhib:* Long Beach Mus Art, 66, 70 & 71; Calif Sky Scape Show, Calif Col Arts & Crafts, Oakland, 69; Calif Landscape Show, La Jolla Mus Art, 69; San Francisco Centennial Show, De Young Mus, 71; Last Plastics Show, Calif Inst Arts, Valencia, 72. *Teaching:* Asst prof sculpture, Calif State Univ, Los Angeles, 68-71; prof sculpture, Calif State Univ, Northridge, 71-, chmn dept 3-D art, 72-, assoc dean, Sch Arts, 74- *Awards:* Fourth Ann Long Beach Mus First Prize, 66; Purchase Award Comn, Southwestern Col, 67; Artist of the Year, Pasadena Arts Coun, 71. *Media:* Bronze, Polyester Resin. *Dealer:* Orlando Gallery 17037 Ventura Blvd Encino CA 91316. *Mailing Add:* Dept, Art 3-D Media, Calif State Univ 18111 Nordhoff St Northridge CA 91330

ELDER, MULDOON
PAINTER, DEALER
b Los Angeles, Calif, June 24, 35. *Work:* Long Beach Mus Art; Downey Mus Art; Pentagon Collection; Syntex Collection. *Exhib:* Long Beach Mus Art, 57; Houston Mus, 58; Dallas Mus Art, 58; Downey Mus Art, 60; San Francisco Mus Art, 69. *Pos:* Owner, Vorpal Gallery, presently. *Awards:* Purchase Awards, Long Beach Mus Art, Pentagon Collection & Downey Mus Art. *Media:* Multimedia. *Mailing Add:* c/o Vorpal Gallery 393 Grove St San Francisco CA 94102

ELDER, R BRUCE
FILMMAKER, CRITIC
b Hawkesbury, Ont, Can, June 12, 47. *Study:* McMaster Univ, Hamilton, Can, BA(hons), 69; Univ Toronto, Can, MA, 70; Ryerson Polytechnic Inst, Toronto, BAppArt, 72-76; Univ Film Studies Ctr, Amherst, Mass, with Ed Emshwiller, Shirley Clarke & Standish Lawder, summers 73-75; modern dance with members of Merce Cunningham Co; political theology of language, with Jacques Derrida, summer, 86. *Work:* Numerous prints of films in public lending libraries, schools & universities. *Exhib:* The Art of Worldly Wisdom, Mus Mod Art, New York, 81; retrospectives, Art Gallery Ont, Toronto, 85 & La Cinematheque Quebecoise, Montreal, 86, Can, Anthology Film Archives, 88; Illuminated Texts, Mus Mod Art, New York, 86; Toronto Festival of Festivals, 88 & 91; Museo Reina Sofia, Madrid, 90; and numerous solo shows in Europe, US & Can. *Collections Arranged:* The Photographic Image (auth, catalog), Toronto World Film Festival, 84; Film from Three Continents, Art Gallery Ont, 86; Osnabrück Experimental Media Festival, 88; Int Experimental Film Cong, Toronto, 89; and others. *Pos:* Independent critic aesthet, photog & film, 78-; independent cur avant-garde film, 80- *Teaching:* Prof human figure & film, Ryerson Polytechnic Inst, Toronto, Can, 72-; adj prof grad film studies, Dept Film-Video, York Univ, Toronto, Can, 84- *Awards:* Best Experimental Film, Can Film Awards Found, 76; Best Independent Film, Los Angeles Film Critics Asn, 81; Study Tour Award, Auswartiges Amt, Govt Fed Repub Ger, 86. *Bibliog:* Lianne McLarty (auth), The films of R Bruce Elder, Take Two, Irwin Publ, 84; Loretta Czernis (auth), Elder: Artaud after Telsat, Can J Political & Social Theory, Vol X, No 1-2, 86; Bart Testa (auth), monograph, Bruce Elder Anthology, Film Archives, 88. *Mem:* Film Studies Asn Can (exec comt, 76 & 83-85); Forth Interest Group; Toronto Semiotic Circle. *Res:* Art and technology; Canadian film, especially the avant-garde in its philosophical context; aesthetics; international avant-garde cinema. *Publ:* Auth, All things in their times: On Michael Snow's Back and Forth, Cine-tracts, Vol 3, No 1, 80; Jack Chambers: From painting into cinema, J Can Studies, Vol 16, No 1, 81; Redefining experimental film: Postmodernist practices in Canada, Parachute, No 27, 82; Image: Representation and object, Akad der Kunste, Berlin, 82 & Take Two, Irwin Publ, 84; Thoughts remade around silence, Descant, No 5, 85; Image and Identity Reflections on Canadian Film and Culture, WLU Press; The Body in Film, Art Gallery Ontario, 89. *Dealer:* Canadian Filmmakers Distribution Ctr 67A Portland St Toronto ON Can M5V 2M9; New York Film-makers' Cooperative 175 Lexington Ave New York NY 10016. *Mailing Add:* 692 St Clarens Ave 10 Toronto ON M6H 3X1 Canada

ELDERFIELD, JOHN
HISTORIAN, CURATOR
b Yorkshire, Eng, Apr 25, 43. *Study:* Univ Leeds, BA & MPhil; Courtauld Inst Art, Univ London, PhD. *Collections Arranged:* Morris Louis (auth, catalog), London Arts Coun Gt Brit, 74; The Wild Beasts: Fauvism and Its Affinities (auth, catalog), 76, European Paintings from Swiss Collections: Post-Impressionism to World War II (auth, catalog), 76, Matisse in the Collection of the Museum of Modern Art (auth, catalog), 78, The Masterworks of Edvard Munch (auth, catalog), 79 & New Work on Paper (auth, catalog), 81, Mus Mod Art, New York; Contrasts of Form: Geometric Abstract Art 1910-1980, 85-86. *Pos:* Harkness fel, Yale Univ, New Haven, Conn, 70-72; Guggenheim Found Fel, 72-73; contrib ed, Artforum, 72-74 & Studio Int Mag, 73-75; cur painting & sculpture, Mus Mod Art, New York, 75-, dir dept drawings, 80-, cur Matisse exhib, 91- *Teaching:* Lectr hist art, Winchester Sch of Art, Eng, 66-70; instr art hist, Univ Leeds, Eng, 73-75. *Mem:* Int Asn Art Critics; Col Art Asn; Fel Royal Soc Arts. *Res:* Twentieth century art. *Publ:* Ed, Hugo Ball (auth), The Flight from Time--A Dada Diary, Viking, 75; auth, The Cutouts of Henri Matisse, Braziller, 78. *Mailing Add:* c/o Mus Mod Art 11 W 53rd St New York NY 10019

ELDREDGE, BRUCE B
MUSEUM DIRECTOR, ADMINISTRATOR
b Van Wert, Ohio, July 1, 52. *Study:* Ohio Wesleyan Univ, Delaware, BA, 74; Tex Tech Univ, Lubbock, MA(mus admin), 76; State Univ Albany, NY, 80-81. *Pos:* Dir, Geneva Hist Soc, 76-78, Schenectady Mus, 78-80, Frederic Remington Art Mus, Ogdensburg, 81-84, NY & Muskegon Mus Art, Mich, 84-87; coordr arts & humanities, Capitol Dist Humanities Prog, State Univ Albany, NY, 80-81; dir, Tucson Mus Art, Tucson, Az, 87- *Mem:* Am Asn Mus. *Mailing Add:* Portsmouth Lighthouse Mus PO Box 248 Portsmouth VA 23705

ELDREDGE, CHARLES CHILD, III
HISTORIAN
b Boston, Mass, Apr 12, 44. *Study:* Amherst Col, BA, 66; Univ Minn, PhD, 71. *Collections Arranged:* The Arcadian Landscape: Nineteenth Century Am Painters in Italy (coauth & ed, catalog), 72; Marsden Hartley Lithographs & Related Works (auth, catalog), 72; Gene Swenson: Retrospective for a Critic (contribr & ed, catalog), 71; John Ward Lockwood, 1894-1963 (auth, catalog), 74; Am Imagination & Symbolist Painting (auth, catalog), 79; Charles Walter Stetson: Color and Fantasy (auth, catalog), 82; Helen Foresman Spencer Mus Art, Univ Kans, Lawrence; Art in New Mexico, 1900-1945 (co-auth, book), Nat Mus Am Art, 86; Pacific Parallels: Artists And The Landscape In New Zealand (auth, catalog), NZ-US Arts Found, 91. *Pos:* Cur collections, Univ Kans Mus Art, Lawrence, 70-71, dir & chief cur, Helen Foresman Spencer Mus Art (formerly Univ Kans Mus of Art), 71-82; dir, Nat Mus Am Art, 82-88; assoc ed, Art J, 79-81; Hall distinguished prof american art, Univ Kansas, 88-; Smithsonian Res Assoc, 88; dir, Georgia O'Keeffe Found, 89- *Teaching:* Prof art hist; Univ Kans, 70-82 & 88- *Awards:* Smithsonian Fel, 79; Fulbright Scholar-New Zealand, 83; Outstanding Achievement Award, Univ Minn, Minneapolis, 86. *Mem:* Asn of Art Mus Dirs (treas, 81-82, trustee, 87-88, hon mem, 90-); Col Art Asn; Mid-Continent Am Studies Asn (mem ed bd, 73-77); Am Studies Assoc. *Res:* American and 19th-20th century European art. *Publ:* Contribr, Works by John Rood: A Memorial Exhibition, Univ Minn, 74; contribr, The Spiritual in Art: Abstract Painting, 1890-1985, Los Angeles County Mus, 86; co-auth, American Originals: Selections from Reynolds House, Mus Am Art, Abberville, 90; Georgia O'Keefe, Abrams, 91; contr, Georgia O'Keefe: Natural Issues 1918-1924, Williams Col, 92. *Mailing Add:* American Art Dept Art History University of Kansas Lawrence KS 66045

ELDREDGE, MARY AGNES
SCULPTOR
b Hartford, Conn, Jan 21, 42. *Study:* Vassar Col, with Concetta Scaravaglione & Juan Nickford, BA; Pius XII Inst, Florence, Italy, with Josef Gudics, MFA. *Work:* Hood Mus Art, Dartmouth Col. *Comn:* Ambry, (sanctuary lamp stand), Shrine of the Most Blessed Sacrament, Washington, DC, 81-82; organ frontals, St Boniface Church, San Francisco, 85-87; Stations of the Cross, crucifix, St Joseph Church, Farmington, Maine, 89; Mary the Mother of Us All, Our Lady of the Snows Church, Woodstock, Vt, 90; Mary and Child, Christ the King Cath Community, Las Vegas, Nev, 91. *Exhib:* Nat Arts Club Religous Art Exhib, New York, 66; Acad Artists Asn Nat Exhib, Springfield, Mass, 67; Modern Art and the Religious Experience, Fifth Ave Presby

Church, New York, 68; 6th Biennial Nat Religious Art Exhib, Cranbrook Acad Art, 69; 42nd Nat Interfaith Conf Relig, Art and Archit, Chicago, 81; and others. *Pos:* Dir, Springfield Art & Hist Soc, Vt, 88. *Awards:* Therese Richard Mem Prize, Nat Arts Club, 66; Staten Island Chamber Com Award, 77; Southern Vt Artists Miller Award for Sculpture, 90. *Bibliog:* Virginia Watson-Jones (auth), Contemporary American Women Sculpturs, Oryx Press, 86. *Mem:* Southern Vt Artists, Inc; Vt Coun on the Arts; Int Sculpture Ctr; Springfield Art & Hist Soc. *Media:* Miscellaneous media. *Dealer:* Contemp Christian Art Inc 217 E 66th St New York NY 10021; Gallery 2 Woodstock VT 05091. *Mailing Add:* 408 Parker Hill Rd Springfield VT 05156

EL HANANI, JACOB
PAINTER
b Casablanca, Morocco, Mar 14, 47. *Study:* Aveni Sch Arts, Tel Aviv, Israel, 66-69; Ecoles des Beaux Arts, Paris, 69-71. *Work:* Guggenheim Mus, Mus Mod Art, Metrop Mus Art, New York; Centre Georges Pompidou, Paris, France; Nat Gallery Art, Washington, DC. *Exhib:* New Acquistions, Guggenheim Mus, New York, 77; Constructivism and the Geometric Tradition, Albright Knox Gallery, 77; Micrography, Israel Mus, Jerusalem, 81; Printing and Writing, Cooper-Hewitt Mus, New York, 82; New Acquisitions, Hirshhorn Mus, Washington, DC, 86; Trends in Geometric Abstract Art, Tel Aviv Mus, 87. *Media:* Ink. *Dealer:* Gallery Gilbert Broanstone 9 rue St-Gillies Paris France. *Mailing Add:* 473 Broadway New York NY 10013

ELIAS, HAROLD JOHN
PAINTER, EDUCATOR
b Cleveland, Ohio, Mar 12, 20. *Study:* Art Inst Chicago, BFA, 50, MFA, 61; Mich State Univ; DePaul Univ; Univ Mich; Hamilton State Univ, Hon Dr, 73. *Work:* Ill State Mus, Springfield; Massillon Mus, Ohio; Univ Idaho, Moscow, Idaho; Univ Ill, Champaign; Upjohn Collection, Kalamazoo, Mich. *Comn:* Michigan Scenes (painting), Fraternal Order Eagles Lodge, Muskegon, Mich, 53; Michigan Scenes (painting), Round Lake Lodge, Watervliet, Mich, 64; Medical Mobile, Mercy Hospital, Benton Harbor, Mich, 66; Trilogy Mobile, Catholic Church, Muskegon Heights, Mich, 67; wall murals, mobile & construction, Kilgore Col, Longview, Tex, 79. *Exhib:* American Art Today, Metrop Mus Art, New York, 50; Pittsburgh Int, Pa Acad Art, 51; Int Sculpture Competition, Brussels Mus, Belgium, 53; Baltimore Nat, Baltimore Mus, Md, 53; Detroit Exhib, Detroit Inst Art, Mich, 55; Creative Gallery Nat, New York, 55; US Embassies, worldwide, 76-78; over 200 one-man shows from coast to coast. *Pos:* Asst & acting dir, Hackley Art Gallery, Muskegon, Mich, 52-57; comnr, Tex Comn Arts, 70-77; chmn, Tandy Corp Employee Ann Art Exhib, Fort Worth, Tex, 88, 89 & 90. *Teaching:* Asst prof art, Ambassador Col, Tex, 73-77, Stephen F Austin State Univ, 77-78; instr drawing, watercolor & advert art, Kilgore Col, Tex, 78-80; instr drawing & painting, Tarrant Co Jr Col, Tex, 80. *Awards:* Best of Show, Western Mich Artists, Grand Rapids Art Gallery, Mich, 52; Schiller Award, Mich Exhib, South Bend Art Gallery, Ind, 65. *Bibliog:* Esquire Exhib rev, Art News, 50; New talent, Art Am, 57. *Mem:* Tex Fine Arts Asn. *Media:* Oils, Watercolor. *Mailing Add:* 2612 High Oak Dr Arlington TX 75601

ELIAS, SHEILA
PAINTER
b Chicago, Ill. *Study:* Art Inst Chicago, 60-68; Columbus Col Art & Design, BFA, 74; Calif State Univ, Northridge, MA, 78. *Work:* Brooklyn Mus, NY; Chase Manhattan Bank, New York; First Los Angeles Bank; Kunsan Contemp Mus, Korea; Laguna Beach Mus Art, Calif. *Comn:* Hilton Hotel, Barbara Dorn & Assoc, Newark, Calif, 83; Exec Life Corp, Los Angeles Co Mus Art Rental & Sales, 84; Jeffries Residence, comn by Pasqualle Vazzana, Laguna, Calif, 74; Spago Restaurant, comn by Wolfgang Puck & Barbara Lazaroff, Tokyo, Japan, 85; Segerstrom Residence, Balboa, Calif, 85. *Exhib:* Solo exhibs, Ratner Gallery, Chicago, Ill, Paula Allan Gallery, New York, Anne Jaffee, Bay Harbor, Fla, Univ NC, Chapel Hill, NY Univ, New York, San Jose, Calif, Kunsun Comtemp Art Mus, Korea, 85; Liberty: The Official Exhibition Commemorating the Centenary of the Statue of Liberty, NY Pub Libr & Louvre, Institude des Decoratifs, Paris, France, 86; The Embellishment of the Statue of Liberty, Cooper-Hewitt Mus, New York, 86. *Awards:* Metro Art Int Medal, New York, 86; Women of Year, Chamber Commerce, Tarzana, Calif, 86. *Bibliog:* Gregory Galligan (auth), Arts Mag, 6/88; Alan Artner (auth), article, Chicago Tribune, 7/6/90; Sophie Burnhan (auth), Woman Artists, New Woman, 6/90. *Mem:* Artists Equity (mem bd dirs, 81); Col Art Asn; Women's Caucus Art. *Media:* Miscellaneous. *Dealer:* Ratner Gallery 750 N Orleans #403 Chicago IL 60610. *Mailing Add:* c/o Anne Jaffe Gallery 1088 Kane Concourse Bay Harbor Islands FL 33154

ELIASOPH, PHILIP
HISTORIAN, CRITIC
b New York, NY. *Study:* Adelphi Univ, BA, 72; State Univ NY, Binghamton, MA, 75, PhD, 79, study with Kenneth C Lindsay. *Collections Arranged:* Paul Cadmus: Yesterday and Today (auth, catalog), Miami Univ & traveling, 81; Robert Vickrey: Lyrical Realist, ACA Galleries & traveling, 82; Frederick Shrady: Invisible Made Visible, Fairfield Univ, Conn, 84; Stevan Dohanos: Images of America, New Britain Mus Am Art, 85; American Art: Past & Present, Kennedy Galleries, 88; Images of the Divine: Religious Art from the Rojtman-Berkman Collection, 91; Human Conditions: American Art from Midtown Payson Galleries, 92. *Pos:* Educ consul, Art of the Western World (TV ser), Pub Broadcasting System, 87-; Conn ed, Art New England (mo) 84-87; alternate mem & art adv comt, Stamford, Conn, Pub Arts, 86-88. *Teaching:* From instr to prof art hist & art criticism, Fairfield Univ, Conn, 75-77, chmn fine arts dept, 84-89; dir, Walsh Art Gallery, Quick Ctr Arts, 89- *Awards:* Fac Res Grant, Fairfield Univ, 84; CINE Golden Eagle (Robert Vickrey: Lyrical Realist), Int Film Jury, 86. *Mem:* Col Art Asn Am; Int Asn Art Critics. *Res:* 20th century American art; Italian renaissance painting; propaganda; art & politics; mass media & criticism. *Publ:* producer, Robert Vickrey: Lyrical Realist and Steven Dohanos: Images of America (doc films), 86; Valor & Vainglory: French Military Art, Forbes Mag Collection, 87; Mastering egg tempera-techniques of Robert Vickrey, Artist's Mag, 11/87; co-auth, Art of the Western World Faculty Guide, Pub Broadcasting System & Annenberg Found, 89; Robert Cottingham: Rolling Stock Series (exhib catalog), Harcourt's Contemp Art, San Francisco, 91; and others. *Mailing Add:* c/o Fine Arts Fairfield Univ Fairfield CT 06430

ELIOT, LUCY CARTER
PAINTER
b New York, NY. *Study:* Vassar Col, BA; Art Students League with Bridgman, Brackman, Raphael Soyer, William Von Schlegell & Kantor; Columbia Univ, with Ralph Mayer. *Work:* Rochester Mem Art Gallery, NY; Munson-Williams-Proctor Inst, Utica, NY. *Exhib:* Pa Acad Fine Arts, Philadelphia, 46, 48-50, 52 & 54; Va Biennial, 48; Corcoran Biennial, Washington, DC, 47 & 51; Ringling Bros Mus, Sarasota, Fla, 58; Nat Acad Design, New York, 71, 78 & 90; Butler Inst, Youngstown, Ohio, 65, 67, 69, 70, 72, 74 & 81; Upland Idyll, Everson Mus, Syracuse, NY, 76; Cooperstown Art Asn, 78, 81 & 90. *Pos:* Mem bd, Artists' Tech Res Inst, 75-79. *Teaching:* Instr painting & drawing, Dept Occupational Therapy, Bronx Vet Hosp, New York, 50-52. *Awards:* Liquitex Art Award, Spring Oil Exhib, 89 & 90; Cecilia Cardman Mem Award, Spring Oil Exhib, 91; Audubon Artists: The Elaine & James Hewitt Award, 91. *Mem:* Artists Equity Asn; Cooperstown Art Asn; Am Soc Contem Artists; Nat Asn Women Artists; Pen & Brush Club. *Media:* Oil, Casein. *Mailing Add:* 131 E 66th St New York NY 10021

ELISCU, FRANK
SCULPTOR
b New York, NY, July 13, 12. *Comn:* Inaugural medal, Pres Ford & Vpres Rockefeller; Astronauts, Headley Mus, Lexington, Ky; Cascade of Books (heroic bronze), James Madison, Libr Cong, Washington, DC; John & Mable Ringling (portrait busts), Ringling Mus, Sarasota, Fla; Shark Diver, Brook Green Gardens, SC; and others. *Exhib:* Pa Acad Fine Arts; Conn Acad Fine Arts; Cleveland Mus Art; Springfield Mus Art; Detroit Inst Art; plus others. *Teaching:* Instr sculpture, Nat Acad Design, currently. *Awards:* Prize, 55 & Silver Medal, 58, Archit League New York; Henry Hering Award, 60; Medal Hon, Nat Sculpture Soc, 87; plus others. *Mem:* Fel Nat Sculpture Soc (pres, 67-70); academician Nat Acad Design; Archit League New York. *Media:* Bronze-Slate. *Publ:* Auth, Sculpture: Three Techniques--Wax, Slate, Clay; Direct Wax Sculpture. *Mailing Add:* 4707 Ocean Blvd Sarasota FL 34242

ELKIN, BEVERLY DAWN
DEALER, GALLERY DIRECTOR
b Chicago, Ill, Apr 23, 33. *Study:* Univ Ill, BA, 55, MA, 65. *Pos:* Co-owner & co-show mgr, House of Art, Champaign, Ill, currently. *Mem:* Prof Picture Framers Asn. *Specialty:* Contemporary midwestern American artist; painting, sculpture and ceramics. *Mailing Add:* 1103 W Green Champaign IL 61821

ELKIN, ROWENA CALDWELL
SCULPTOR
b Ft Worth, Tex, Jan 8, 17. *Study:* Tex State Col Women, BS, 38; studies in Europe & Egypt, 77-85. *Work:* Mus Art, Los Alamos Col, NMex; Clarksville Lib, Tex; Tex Woman's Univ, Denton. *Exhib:* Am Asn Univ Women Centennial, Boston Univ, 81; Common Ground Women Caucus Art, Dallas City Hall, 88; travelling show, One Hundred Years of Sculpture in Texas, 1879-1979; The Power of Enduring Presence, War & Peace, Austin, Tex & touring, 91-92; traveling exhib: Women & Their Work; and others. *Awards:* First in sculpture, Tex Fine Arts Asn, Region II, Dallas, 65 & 78. *Mem:* Women's Caucus Art, Dallas, Tex; Tex Visual Arts Asn, Dallas; Int Sculpture Conf; Tex Sculpture Asn; charter mem Women's Mus, Washington, DC. *Media:* Metal, Wood. *Publ:* Virginia Watson (auth), Contemporary American Women Sculptors, Oryx Press, 86; Dr Eleanor Tufts (auth), American Women Artists, Garland Publ Co, 89. *Dealer:* Ruth Wiseman Gallery 2526 Elm St Dallas TX 75226. *Mailing Add:* 6623 Orchid Lane Dallas TX 75230

ELKINS, (E) LANE
EDUCATOR, CERAMIST
b McDonald Co, Mo, Mar 26, 25. *Study:* Southwest Mo State Col, BSEd(with hon), 49; Columbia Univ, MAFA & FAEd, 50; with Marquerite Wildenhain, 56 & 63; Cranbrook Acad Art, MFA, 62. *Work:* Springfield Art Mus, Mo. *Comn:* Pottery and jewelry comns for individuals. *Exhib:* Springfield Art Mus Ann Regional Show, 53-72; Wichita Art Asn Galleries Decorative Arts & Ceramics Exhib, 60 & 62; Ann Drawing & Sculpture Show, Ball State Univ Art Gallery, 63; American Jewelry Today, Ala Mus Fine Arts, 64; Am Craftsmen Show, Smithsonian Inst, 70. *Teaching:* Prof ceramics, Southwest Mo State Univ, 50-82, prof art, 82-; retired. *Awards:* Protective Image (cast bronze) Award, Edmund F Ball, Nat Sculpture Show, 63. *Mem:* Am Craftsman Coun; Mo Craftsman Coun. *Media:* Clay, Metals. *Publ:* Contribr, Walker Art Quart, spec issue, 59. *Mailing Add:* RR 3 No 198 Rogerville MO 65742

ELKINS, TONI MARCUS
PAINTER, DESIGNER
b Tifton, Ga, Feb 22, 46. *Study:* Boston Univ, 65-66; Univ Ga, ABJ, 68; Columbia Col, 78-80. *Work:* Parthenon Gallery, Nashville; Nancy Miller Gallery & Tance Designs, Columbia, SC. *Exhib:* Birmingham Watercolor Show, Birmingham Mus, 81; Ga Watercolor Soc, Macon Mus, 82; Rocky Mountain Nat, Foothills Art Ctr, Golden, Colo, 83; Watercolor West, 84; San

Diego Watercolor Soc Int, 84 & 85; SC State Mus traveling exhib, 85; and others. *Collections Arranged:* SC First Miniature Show (auth, catalog), Cameo Gallery, 80. *Pos:* Superintendent fine arts, SC State Fair; exec dir, SC Crafts Asn. *Awards:* President's Award, Soc Watercolor Painters, Joshua, Tex, 92; Meyer Hardware Award, Rocky Mountain Nat, Golden, Colo, 92; Howard B Smith Award, SC Watercolor Ann, Marion, 92; and others. *Media:* Watercolor, Photograph; Mixed Media. *Publ:* Contribr, Miles Batl's Complete Guide to Creative Watercolor; Les Krantz (auth), The New York Art Rev, 89; Community Tour Mag (cover), SC Arts Comn, 92; Who's Who Southwest; Who's Who Am Photog; and others. *Mailing Add:* 1511 Adger Rd Columbia SC 29205-1407

ELLENZWEIG, ALLEN BRUCE
CRITIC, CURATOR
b New York, NY, Nov 4, 50. *Study:* Cooper Union, with Dore Ashton, BFA, 73; New York Univ, MFA(dramatic writing), 85. *Collections Arranged:* Private Myths: Unearthings of Contemporary Art (auth, catalog), Queens Mus, NY, 78; Visual Diaries: A Personal Use of Words and Images (auth, catalog), Alex Rosenberg Gallery, 80; Prejudice & Pride: The New York City Lesbian & Gay Community, World War II-Present (auth, catalog), Tweed Gallery, City Hall, New York, 88. *Pos:* Contribr ed, Arts Mag, New York, 74-79; contribr reviewer, Art Am, 80-86; moderator, Artists Talk on Art, Landmark Gallery, New York, 81; lectr, Mois de la Photo, Am Ctr, Paris, 84; lectr & panelist, The History of Homoerotic Themes in Photography, Ethics & Evidence in Lesbian & Gay Studies, Ctr for Lesbian & Gay Studies, City Univ New York Grad Ctr, 89; moderator & panelist, The Homoerotic at Risk: Censorship of Gay Sensibility in Photography, 4th Ann Lesbian, Bisexual & Gay Studies Conf, Harvard Univ, 90; panelist, Gay & Lesbian Sensibility in Photography, 1991 Ann Conf, Col Art Asn, Washington, DC. *Awards:* Writer in residence, Michael Karolyi Mem Found, Vence, France, 72 & Edward Albee Found, Montauk, NY, 79. *Bibliog:* John Russell (auth), When art imitates anthropology, 4/9/78 & Grace Glueck (auth), Visual diaries, 2/22/80, NY Times; Carrie Rickey (auth), Dear diary, Village Voice, 2/11/80. *Mem:* Nat Writers Union; Publishing Triangle; Col Art Asn. *Res:* Male homoerotic themes throughout the history of photography. *Publ:* Auth, A Selection of American Art: The Skowhegan School 1946-1976, Inst Contemp Art, Boston, 76; The Homosexual Aesthetic, Am Photogr, 80; Photo fever on the Seine, Art Am, 4/83; Picturing the Homoerotic: Gay Images in Photography, OUTLOOK, winter 90; The Homoerotic Photograph: Male Images from Durieu/Delacroix to Mapplethorpe, Columbia Univ Press, 92. *Mailing Add:* 200 W 15th St New York NY 10011

ELLER, EVELYN (EVELYN ELLER ROSENBAUM)
COLLAGE ARTIST, PAINTER
b New York, NY, Apr 17, 33. *Study:* Art Students League, NY, with Morris Kantor & W Barnet, 51-54; Acad De Belle Arte, Rome Italy, 54-55; Sch for Visual Arts, New York, 89. *Work:* Indianapolis Mus Fine Art, Ind; Del Art Mus; Queens Col, City Univ New York; Prudential Insurance Co; Sackner Archive Concrete & Visual Poetry. *Exhib:* Works on Paper, Brooklyn Mus, New York, 75; Collage, The State of the Art, Bergen Mus Arts & Sci, NJ, 85; Book as Art IV, Nat Mus Women Arts, Washington, DC, 91; Artist Book, Islip Art Mus, Long Island, NY, 91; My Vision, Sumner Sch Mus, Washington, DC, 91; Diversity & Vision, Snug Harbor Cult Ctr, NY, 92; and others. *Pos:* Admin asst, Art Sch Mus Mod Art, NY, 58-59. *Teaching:* Workshop & sem instr, Alliance Queens Artists, NY, 89-92. *Awards:* Fulbright Fel to Italy, US Govt, 54; Resident at Yaddo Saratoga Springs, NY, 57; Juror Award, Small Works Ann, 83; Showcase Award, Queens Borough Pub Libr, New York, 85. *Bibliog:* John Arthur Shanks (auth), Evelyn Eller, techniques of landscapes collage, Artists Mag, 4/84; John & Joan Digby (auth), The Collage Handbook, Thames & Hudson, 85; B Ommerman (auth), Around Town, Newsday, 4/7/91. *Mem:* Artists Equity; Alliance Queens Artists; Orgn Independent Artists; Ctr Bk Arts. *Media:* Acrylic. *Mailing Add:* 71-49 Harrow St Forest Hills NY 11375

ELLINGER, ILONA E
PAINTER, EDUCATOR
b Budapest, Hungary, June 12, 13. *Study:* Royal Hungarian Univ Sch Art, MFA; Royal Swedish Art Acad; Johns Hopkins Univ, with David M Robinson & W F Albright, PhD; Univ Freiburg; Univ Wis. *Exhib:* Soc Washington Artists; one-man show, Am-Brit Art Ctr, George Washington Univ, 50; Silver Spring Art Gallery, 51; Corcoran Gallery Art, 58; Batiks, Gallery N, Setauket, 77; and others. *Teaching:* Prof art & head dept, Trinity Col, Washington, DC, 43-78, Fulbright prof hist art & archit, Nat Col Arts, Lahore, W Pakistan, 63-64; vis prof, State Univ NY Stony Brook, 69-79; prof, SUNY, 79-85. *Mem:* Soc Washington Artists; Archaeol Inst Am; Phi Beta Kappa. *Mailing Add:* 67 Quaker Path Stony Brook NY 11790

ELLINGSON, WILLIAM JOHN
EDUCATOR, PRINTMAKER
b Forrestburg, SDak, Mar 29, 33. *Study:* Minneapolis Sch Art & Design, Minn, BFA, 60; Skowhegan Sch Sculpture & Painting, Maine; State Univ Iowa, Iowa City, MFA, 63; postgrad work, Univ Minn, Minneapolis. *Work:* Nelson Gallery, Kansas City, Mo; Springfield Art Ctr, Mass; Col S Idaho, Twin Falls; Permanent Collection, Hamline Univ, Minneapolis; plus numerous pvt collections in Denmark, Japan, Can, Ger & Eng. *Comn:* Ltd ed etching, Minn State Arts Coun, Minneapolis, 67 & New Eng Life Insurance Co, Wichita, Kans, 75-77; ltd ed silkscreen, Denmark Prog, St Cloud State Univ, 76. *Exhib:* Audubon Artists Inc, New York, 67; Pa Acad Fine Arts; 142nd Ann Exhib, Nat Acad Design, New York; Conn Acad Fine Arts, Hartford; Boston Printmakers 19th Ann, Boston, Mass; Nat Drawing Exhib, Okla Mus Arts; one-man shows, Ingolstadt, WGer, 85 & Aallborg, Denmark, 86; plus many others. *Teaching:* Prof print media, St Cloud State Univ, Minn, 63-; vis artist, Univ Saskatoon, Sask, 77. *Awards:* Edna Stauffer Award, Audubon Artists, Inc, 67. *Mem:* Nat Graphic Soc. *Media:* Etching; Lithography; Woodcut; Silkscreen. *Dealer:* Fairweather Hardin Gallery 101 E Ontario Ave Chicago IL 60611. *Mailing Add:* 1723 Seventh St St Cloud MN 56301

ELLINGTON, HOWARD W
ART DEALER, ARCHITECT
b Anthony, Kans, Mar 2, 38. *Study:* Univ Kans, BA(archit), 61. *Pos:* Owner, Gallery Ellington, Wichita, Kans, currently. *Specialty:* 20th century realism; prints by Prairie Print Makers (1930-1965); other regionalists. *Publ:* Auth, The Prairie Printmakers, Gallery Ellington, 84. *Mailing Add:* Gallery Ellington 350 N Rock Rd Wichita KS 67206

ELLIOT, CATHERINE J
CERAMIST, PAINTER
b New York, NY, July 26, 47. *Study:* Sarah Lawrence Col, BA, 69; Creative Arts Workshop, New Haven, Conn, 73; Otis Art Inst, Los Angeles, 76-77; Univ Col Los Angeles, 80. *Work:* BBDO Advert; Cutter's Restaurant; New West Corp. *Comn:* Large outdoor sculpture, comn by Keith Williamson, Los Angeles. *Exhib:* Moon St Gallery, Westport, Conn, 74; Am Ceramics Soc, Brand Art Gallery, Los Angeles, 75 & 88; Otis Art Inst Group Show, Los Angeles, 77; one-man shows, RGA Gallery, Los Angeles, 77 & 26th St Gallery, Santa Monica, Calif, 79; 4th Annual Great Lakes Show, Chicago, Ill, 90; The Fifth Monarch Tile Nat Ceramic Competition, San Angelo Mus Fine Arts, Tex, 90. *Teaching:* Instr ceramics, Moon St Pottery, Westport, Conn, 73; instr pvt ceramics lessons, 74-77. *Awards:* Purchase Award, Am Ceramic Soc Group Show, 75. *Bibliog:* Carole Katchen (auth), Artist's Mag, 90; Sara Scribner (auth), Faces, Designer's West Mag, 90. *Mem:* Am Ceramic Soc; Artists Equity Asn. *Media:* Clay; Miscellaneous Media. *Mailing Add:* 530 Tigertail Rd Los Angeles CA 90049

ELLIOT, JOHN THEODORE
PAINTER, WRITER
b London, Eng, May 25, 29; US citizen. *Study:* Acad Fine Arts, Italy, 47-50; NY Univ, Film Sch, 51-54; Sch Visual Arts, 58-59; also pvt study in Europe. *Work:* Chesterwood Mus & Naumkeag, Trustees of Reservations, Stockbridge, Mass; Ala Space Ctr, Huntsville; Nat Trust Hist Preserv, Washington, DC; Newark Mus (file), NJ. *Comn:* DC French Public Monument (film), Nat Endowment Arts & Humanities; Hist Preserv, comn by Mrs Onassis, K Hepburn, A Baxter & Nat Trust, New York, Los Angeles & DC; Thomas Watson Tribute, David Rockefeller & Adv Coun, New York; set design, Noonan's, A Coupla White Chicks Sitting Around Talking, 83 & Other People's Money, Antrim Theatre, 92; mural, Thomas J Lipton Inc, Englewood Cliffs, NJ, 83; and others. *Exhib:* French Retrospective, Metrop Mus Art, New York, 76, Nat Collection Fine Arts, Smithsonian Inst, 77, Detroit Inst, Mich, 77 & Fogg Art Mus, Cambridge, Mass, 78; 20th Ann Int, Soc Illustr, New York, 77; Knickerbocker Nat, Nat Arts Club, New York, 79; Pastels Only, Copley Soc, Boston, 79; and others. *Pos:* Pres visual commun, Graphics for Industry Inc, Dover, Del & Tenafly, NJ, 67- *Teaching:* Workshops and videotapes, The Total Pastelist, Art & Design in Action & Tools of the Trade. *Awards:* Gold Medal, Freedoms Found Valley Forge, 70; Ten Best Awards, Soc Illustrators, 77; numerous nat exhib awards. *Bibliog:* Freedom to innovate, Indust Photog, 7/70; G McConnell (ed), Illustrators XX, Hastings House, 79; Working with oil pastel, Am Artist, 83; contrib ed, numerous articles, The Artist's Mag. *Mem:* Pastel Soc Am; Soc Illustrators; PSA Nat Arts Club; Oil Pastel Asn (pres); Salmagundi Club. *Media:* Pastel and Oils. *Publ:* Auth, The Night the Animals Talked, Am Broadcasting Co, 75; American Phenomenon, Nat Found, 77; Learning from the Pros, Watson/Guptill, 84; Introduction to Oil Pastels, 87; Pastels & the Portrait, 88; Painting Solutions, Hands, Faces & Figures, Quarto, 90; coauth, Pastels & the Landscape, 90; auth, Painting Solutions, Hands, Faces & Figures, Quarto, 90. *Mailing Add:* c/o Highmount Studios 304 Highmount Terr Upper-Nyack-on-Hudson NY 10960

ELLIOT, SHEILA
ADMINISTRATOR, WRITER
b Philadelphia, Pa, Mar 25, 46. *Study:* Vassar Col, AB, 67; Fairleigh Dickenson Univ, MA, 79; studied and New York Univ & Columbia Univ, NY. *Pos:* Dir pub relations, Pastel Soc Am, NY, 81-83; exec dir, Oil Pastel Asn NY, 83-; ed, Art & Artists USA, 83-; contrib ed, The Artist's Magazine, 86-; publicity dir, Pen & Brush Inc, NY, 87-90. *Res:* Working methos and procedures of current American artists. *Publ:* Contribr, Painting for the Pros, Watson-Guptill, 83; coauth, Introd to Oil Pastel, Holbein, 86 & Pastels & the Portrait, 88; numerous articles, The Artists' Mag, 85-; Decorative Artist's Workbook, 90; Pastels & the Landscape, 90. *Mailing Add:* 304 Highmount Terr Upper Nyack NY 10960

ELLIOTT, ANNE
SCULPTOR, PAINTER
b Pittsburgh, Pa, Aug 9, 44. *Study:* Sarah Lawrence Col, BA, 66; Art Students League, 67; Parson Sch Design, 69; Pratt Inst, Cert, 92. *Work:* Westmoreland Mus, Greensburgh, Pa; Alternative Mus, New York. *Exhib:* One-person exhibs, Graham Gallery, New York, 78 & 80, Westmoreland Mus Art, Greensburg, Pa, 82, Summerfare, Ctr Arts, State Univ NY Purchase, 83 & 84, Pittsburgh Public Theater, Installation for Production of K2, 84, Hewlett Gallery, Carnegie-Mellon Univ, 84, Johnston Art Mus, Johnstown, Pa, 88 & Blair Art Mus, Hollidaysburg, Pa, 88; Originals, Graham Gallery, New York, 80 & Selections from Gallery Artists, 83; Exchanges III, Abrons Art for Living Ctr, Henry St Settlement, New York, 81; Candidates for Awards, Am

Acad & Inst Arts & Letters, New York; Nature: Images & Metaphor, Views by Women Artists, Greene Space Gallery, New York, 82; Papyrus Abstractus, Westport-Weston Art Alliance, Westport, Conn, 82; The New Explosion: Paper Art, Fine Arts Mus Long Island, Hempstead, NY, 82, Byer Mus Arts, Evanston, Ill, 83; Seven New Artists, Pittsburgh, Today, The Carnegie, Pittsburgh, 84; Sculpture by Women in the Eighties, UP Gallery, Pittsburgh, 85; Columns by Artists, 14 Sculptors' Gallery, New York, 86; Paper: Form & Substance, NJ Ctr Vis Arts, Summit, NJ. *Awards:* Fel, Pa Coun Arts, 85. *Bibliog:* Hilton Kramer (auth), Art at Guggenheim: Niche for Favorites, New York Times, 5/31/80; John Perrault (auth), Anne Elliot, Westmoreland Mus, Gettyburg, Pa, 82; John Caldwell (auth), Seven New Artists, Pittsburgh Today, The Carnegie, 84. *Media:* Aluminum Mesh & Paper; Acrylic, Oil. *Dealer:* Leslie Ava Shaw 110 W 87th St New York NY. *Mailing Add:* 7 Cleveland Lane Princeton NJ 08540

ELLIOTT, BETTE G
PAINTER, INSTRUCTOR
b Mansfield, Ohio, Sept 22, 20. *Study:* Otterbein Col, BFA & BA, 42. *Work:* Canton Art Inst, Ohio; N Canton Libr, Ohio. *Comn:* 26 paintings for Gordon, Formet & Clevenger, Canton, Ohio. *Exhib:* Butler Mus, Youngstown, Ohio, 70; one-women shows, Duke Univ Libr, Durham, NC, 80, Ashtabula Art Ctr, Ohio, 88, Mansfield Art Ctr, Ohio, 88 & Zanesville Art Ctr, Ohio, 88; Marietta Regional, Marietta Col, Ohio, 89; Watercolor Ohio '89, Brit Petroleum Atrium, Cleveland; Pittsburgh Aqeous, Arts & Crafts Ctr, Cleveland, Ohio, 89; Art Expo, 92. *Teaching:* Instr watercolor, Alliance Art Ctr, 69-79, Canton Art Inst, 74-80; instr drawing, Wayne Gen, Orville, Ohio, 80-81; studio instr, 80-92. *Awards:* 1st Place, Pittsburgh Aqueous, 89. *Mem:* Ohio Watercolor Soc (show coordr, 82 & 86, vpres, currently); Assoc mem, Am Watercolor Soc. *Media:* Watercolor, Acrylic. *Publ:* Am Artist Mag, 7/92; Cover of Fla Eye Bank Ann Report; Ohio Artist Catalog, 92. *Mailing Add:* 806 Portage St North Canton OH 44720

ELLIOTT, DOROTHY BADEN
CONSERVATOR
b Brookfield, Md, July 18, 14. *Study:* Mt Holyoke Col, hons in course, AB, 36; Brooklyn Mus, prof training by Caroline Keck, 60-63. *Pos:* Asst to conservator, Whitney Mus, 61-62; assoc conservator, Brooklyn Mus, 62-63; conservator painting pvt studio, Sarasota, Fla, 63-; assoc conservator, Walters Art Gallery, Baltimore, 66-79. *Mem:* Fel Am Inst Conserv; fel Int Inst Conserv; Am Asn Mus; Int Coun Mus. *Mailing Add:* 700 John Ringling Blvd No 314 Sarasota FL 34236

ELLIOTT, JAMES HEYER
ADMINISTRATOR, CONSULTANT
b Medford, Ore, Feb 19, 24. *Study:* Willamette Univ, BA, 47, Hon DFA, 85; Univ de Paris, 47-48; l'Ecole du Louvre, 48; Harvard Univ, MA(hist art), 49; Fulbright scholar to Europe, 51-52, San Francisco Art Inst, Hon DFA, 90. *Pos:* Chief cur & actg dir, Walker Art Ctr, 53-56; cur mod art & asst chief cur, Los Angeles Co Mus, 56-63, chief cur, 63-66; dir, Wadsworth Atheneum, Conn, 66-76; mem adv panel, Nat Endowment Arts, 74-77; trustee, San Francisco Art Inst, 78-90; dir, Univ Art Mus, Univ Calif, Berkeley, 76-88, chancellor's cur, 88-90; dir emer, Univ Art Mus, Univ Calif, 90; trustee, Marcia Simon Weisman Found, Los Angeles, 91- *Teaching:* Teaching fel art hist, Harvard Univ, 50-51; assoc prof hist of art mus, Hunter Col, 66-67; adj prof Univ Calif Berkeley, 76-90; vis prof, San Francisco Art Inst, 88. *Mem:* Am Asn Mus; Asn Art Mus Dirs; Conn Comn on the Arts (comnr & vpres, 70-76); Col Art Asn; Int Comt Mus. *Publ:* Auth, Premiere, Bulletin, Los Angeles City Mus Art, 62 Vol 14 No 3; title essay for catalog, Pierre Bonnard Exhibition, 65; ed & coauth, Museums: Their New Audience, Am Asn Mus, 72; auth, title essay for catalog, James Lee Byars Exhibition, 90. *Mailing Add:* Univ Art Mus PO Box 4840 Berkeley CA 94704

ELLIOTT, LILLIAN
WEAVER, TAPESTRY ARTIST
b Detroit, Mich. *Study:* Wayne Univ, BA; Cranbrook Acad Art, Bloomfield Hills, Mich, MFA. *Work:* Mus Contemp Crafts, New York; Detroit Inst Arts; San Francisco City Art Collection; Objects, USA--Johnson's Wax Collection, Smithsonian Inst Traveling Exhib, 70-72; Univ Art Collections, Ariz State Univ, Tempe. *Exhib:* Calif Design Exhibs, Pasadena Art Mus, 62-71; Fabric Collage Invitational, Mus Contemp Crafts, New York, 65; Collagen--Collage Invitational Exhib, Kunstgewerbe Mus, Zurich, Switz, 68; Objects, USA--Johnson's Wax Collection, Smithsonian Inst Traveling Exhib, 70-72; Tapestry, Tradition & Technique Invitational, Los Angeles Co Mus Art, 71. *Pos:* Fabric designer, Ford Motor Co Styling Div, Dearborn, Mich, 56-59. *Teaching:* Instr art, Univ Mich Col Archit & Design, Ann Arbor, 59-60; lectr textiles, Univ Calif, Berkeley, 66-76. *Awards:* San Francisco Art Festival Purchase Award, 65 & 69; Founder's Soc Purchase Award, Mich Craftsmen's Show, Detroit Inst Arts, 69; Calif Arts Coun Grant/Artist in Residence, 79-80. *Media:* Textile. *Publ:* Auth, Chap, In: The New American Tapestry, Van Nostrand Reinhold, 68. *Mailing Add:* 1775 San Lorenzo Ave Berkeley CA 94707

ELLIOTT, SCOTT CAMERON
ART DEALER, CURATOR
b Chicago, Ill, Aug 6, 41. *Study:* Art Inst Chicago, 59-60; Art Students League, New York, 60-61; Yale Drama Sch, studied scene design with Donald Oenslager, 62-64. *Collections Arranged:* Frank Lloyd Wright and the Prairie School, Cooper-Hewitt Mus, New York, 83. *Pos:* Asst dir, La Boetie, New York, 68-72; dir, Helios Arts, Inc, New York, 75-79, Kelmscott Gallery, Chicago, 80- *Specialty:* Architectural drawings and objects by Frank Lloyd Wright and the Chicago and Prairie Schools. *Publ:* Auth, Frank Lloyd Wright, 81 & Frank Lloyd Wright and Viollet Le-Duc, 86, Kelmscott. *Mailing Add:* 4611 N Lincoln Chicago IL 60625

ELLIS, ANDRA
CERAMIST, PAINTER
b New York, NY, Mar 3, 48. *Study:* Queens Col, City Univ New York, BFA, 71. *Work:* Mint Mus Art, Charlotte, NC; Karen Johnson Boyd, Racine, Wis; Sanford Besser, Little Rock, Ark; Luwa Corp, Charlotte, NC; Nations Bank, Charlotte, NC. *Exhib:* Spotlight '91, Miss Mus Art, Jackson, 91; The Collector's Eye, Am Craft Mus, New York, 91; one-person exhibit, Hodges Taylor Gallery, Charlotte, NC, 92; and others. *Pos:* Dir/producer, Int Clay Film Festival, West Side YMCA & Greenwich House Pottery, New York & travelled to NY State Col Ceramics, Alfred, NY, 81-85; spec projs coord, Greenwich House Pottery, New York, 82-84; proj designer & dir, Children's Mural/Children's Law Ctr, Charlotte, NC, fall 91. *Teaching:* Lectr, Viewpoints: Four Artists on Art, Mint Mus Art, Charlotte, NC, 91; lectr, Surface Exploration in Clay, Sawtooth Ctr Visual Arts, Winston-Salem, 91-92 & Queens Col, Charlotte, NC, 91-92. *Awards:* Nat Endowment Arts Visual Artists Fel, 90-91; NC Arts Coun Artist Proj Grant, 92-93. *Bibliog:* Vanessa Lynn (auth), Andra Ellis, Am Ceramics, winter 89; Pamela Blume Leonard (auth), Figurative clay, Art Papers, 11-12/91; John Rodger (auth), Andra Ellis, Art Papers, 9-10/92. *Dealer:* Helen Drutt Gallery 724 Fifth Ave New York NY 10019; Fay Gold Gallery 247 Buckhead Ave Atlanta GA 30305. *Mailing Add:* 7141 Knightswood Dr Charlotte NC 28226

ELLIS, GEORGE RICHARD
MUSEUM DIRECTOR
b Birmingham, Ala, Dec 9, 37. *Study:* Univ Chicago, BA & MFA, Univ Calif, Los Angeles, candidate in PhD prog. *Pos:* Art supvr, Jefferson Co Schs, 62-64; former asst dir, Birmingham Mus Art; dir develop & asst dir, Mus Cult Hist, Univ Calif, Los Angeles, presently; dir, Honolulu Acad Arts. *Mem:* Los Angeles Ethnic Art Coun; Am Mus Asn; Art Mus Dirs Asn; Hawaii Mus Asn; Pac Arts Asn. *Mailing Add:* Honolulu Acad Arts 900 S Beretania St Honolulu HI 96814

ELLIS, LOREN ELIZABETH
PRINTMAKER, PHOTOGRAPHER
b Binghamton, NY, Dec 12, 53. *Study:* Univ SFla, BA, 74; Fla State Univ, MFA, 77. *Work:* Eastman Kodak Collection, Pharmaceutical Br, Philadelphia, Pa; House of Reps, Capitol Bldg, Tallahassee, Fla. *Comn:* Mural, Hillsborough Parks Dept, 82,; mural, Johnson & Johnson Co, 83; mural, Tampa Electric Co, 83; mural, Fund for Dance, 20th Anniversary, NY; mural, Lee County Electric Co, Ft Myers, Fla, 84. *Exhib:* Solo exhib, Hillsborough County Mus, Tampa, Fla, 74 & M Ingban Gallery, Soho, NY; Professional Women Artists, Lowe Art Mus, Miami, Fla, 74; Tampa Mus Art, 79, 80 & 82 and Nostalgia, Tampa Mus W, 84, Fla; Museums Choice, Lock Haven Arts Ctr, Orlando, Fla, 81; traveling show, Mus Mod Art, New York, 86. *Pos:* Art cur, Photo Exhib, Youth Mus Charlotte Co, Fla, 77 & Womerns Survival Ctr, 82-83. *Teaching:* Inst art & photomontage, Parsons Sch Design, New York, 89- *Awards:* Fine Arts Coun Fel, Fla, 77; Merit Award, Tampa Mus, 78; Grants, Arts Coun Tampa & Hillsborouhg Com 90. *Bibliog:* Articles in Art South & Tampa Times. *Mem:* Prof Women Photogrs. *Media:* Photographic painting. *Publ:* Contribr, cover art, Tampa Bay Mag, 79 & Organic Mag, 89. *Dealer:* Art S 4401 Cresson St Philadelphia PA 19127. *Mailing Add:* 2350 Broadway 629 New York NY 10024

ELLIS, RAY
PAINTER, LECTURER
b Philadelphia, Pa, Apr 24, 21. *Study:* Philadelphia Mus Sch Art, 39-42. *Work:* Farnsworth Mus, Rockland, Maine; Columbus Mus Art, Ga; Telfair Acad Art, Savannah, Ga; Morris Mus Arts & Sci, Morristown, NJ; Charles Russell Mus, Great Falls, Mont; Heckscher Mus, Huntington, NY; Univ Nebr Mus, Lincoln, Nebr; Harrisburg Art Mus, Pa; Cooperstown Hall of Fame Mus, NY. *Comn:* One Man's Island (watercolor), McGraw-Hill Co, New York, 67; series of watercolors, Midlantic Bank, Newark, NJ, 68; Polo (watercolor), Dun & Bradstreet, New York, 73; River Man (watercolor), AT&T Co, Bedminster, NJ, 77; Island Overlook, Allied Corp, Morristown, NJ; After Colors, Johnson-Higgins Inc, New York. *Exhib:* One-man shows, Pa Acad Fine Arts, Philadelphia, 47, Columbus Mus Art, Ga, 72, Columbia Mus Art, SC, 72, Charles Russell Mus, Great Falls, Mont, 74, Morris Mus Arts & Sci, Morristown, NJ, 76 & MacCullough Mus, Morristown; Am Watercolor Soc, Nat Acad Design, New York, 65-71; Nat Arts Club Ann, New York, 72-77; Chris Beatles Gallery, London, Eng, 87, 89, Audubon Artists, 69-74. *Teaching:* Instr workshops, Ga, Mass, Montana, NJ, Leicester Polytech - UK, NY & Fla, Miss Watercolor Soc. *Awards:* Grumbacher Award, Am Watercolor Soc, 69; Winsor & Newton Medal, Audubon Artists, 72; Gold Medal of Honor, Hudson Valley Art Asn, 74. *Bibliog:* Norman Kent (auth), Watercolors of Ray G Ellis, Twin City Press, 71; Susan Meyer (auth), Watercolorists at Work, Watson-Guptill, 72; Dr Allan McNabb (auth), Ray G Ellis Paintings, Morris Mus, 76; Walter Cronkite (auth), South by Southeast, 83 & North by Northeast, 86. *Mem:* Am Watercolor Soc; NJ Watercolor Soc (pres, 66-67); Salmagundi Club (first vpres, 72-73); Artists Fel Found (pres, 72-73); Philadelphia Watercolor Club Century Asn; Nat Arts Club; Lotus Club. *Media:* Watercolor, Oil. *Publ:* Contribr, Yachting, SxSe, 6/84; Sail, NxNE paintings, 9/86; Downeast SxSE paintings, 9/86; Southern Accents, 9/86; Yankee, 5/87; Cape Cod Mag, 6/87. *Mailing Add:* c/o Ray Ellis Gallery-Compass Prints Inc 205 W Congress St Savannah GA 31401

ELLIS, RICHARD
PAINTER, ILLUSTRATOR
b New York, NY, Apr 2, 38. *Study:* Univ Pa, BA. *Work:* New Bedford Whaling Mus, Mass; Philadelphia Zoological Garden; Denver Mus Natural Hist; Kendall Whaling Mus; Sea Life Park, Hawaii. *Comn:* Mural of whales, Denver Mus Natural History, 78; mural of Moby Dick, New Bedford Whaling

Mus, Mass, 86. *Exhib:* Whale paintings, New Bedford Whaling Mus, 75, Mystic Seaport, 75 & Am Mus Natural Hist, 76; Animal Art Show, Los Angeles Co Mus, 77; shark paintings, Am Mus Natural Hist, 78; Acad Natural Sci, Philadelphia, 81. *Pos:* Exhib designer, Am Mus Natural Hist, 65-68. *Teaching:* Lectr, Am Mus Natural Hist, 82-83. *Bibliog:* T Walker Lloyd (auth), Richard Ellis, Am Artist Mag; Steve Blount (auth), Richard Ellis, Sport Diver Mag; Derek S B Davis (auth), Richard Ellis, Pa Gazette. *Mem:* Soc Animal Artists; Explorers Club; Century Asn. *Media:* Mixed. *Publ:* Auth & illusr, The Book of Sharks, Grosset & Dunlap, 76; The Book of Whales, Knopf, 80; Dolphins and Porpoises, Knopf, 82; Men and Whales, 91; Great White Shark, 91; and others. *Dealer:* Sportsman's Edge Ltd 136 E 74th St New York NY 10021; Coast Gallery Hwy One Big Sur CA 93920. *Mailing Add:* 17 E 16th St No 9 New York NY 10003

ELLIS, ROBERT M
PAINTER
b Cleveland, Ohio, 1922. *Study:* Western Reserve Univ, Sch Archit, 40-42; Cleveland Sch Art, 46-48 (grad); Mexico City Col, Mexico City, BA, 49; Univ Southern Calif, MFA, 52. *Work:* Amoco Production Co, Houston; Mus Albuquerque; Mus Fine Arts, Santa Fe; Robert Walz & Assocs, Hollywood, Calif; numerous pvt collections. *Exhib:* Occidental Col Art Gallery, Los Angeles, 57; one-man shows, Pasadena Art Mus, Calif, 61, Hollis Gallery, San Francisco, 64, James Yu Gallery, New York, 75, Hills Gallery, Santa Fe, NMex 77, Wildine Gallery, Albuquerque, 81, Kauffman Galleries, Houston, 86, Retrospective, Univ NMex Art Mus, Albuquerque, 91; Greenhill Gallery, Fort Lauderdale, Fla, 73; Santa Barbara Mus Art, Calif, 79; Jill Youngblood Gallery, Los Angeles, 84. *Pos:* Cur educ, Pasadena Art Mus, 56-64; asst dir, Univ Art Mus, Univ NMex, 64-68, dir, 68-71; interim dir, The Harwood Found, Taos, NMex, 90. *Teaching:* instr dept art & art hist, Univ NMex, 64-87, prof emer, currently. *Bibliog:* Vivian Milford (auth), Review, Albuquerque Journal, 12/81. *Mailing Add:* PO Box 1449 Taos NM 87571

ELLIS, SALLY STRAND See Strand, Sally (Sally Strand Ellis)

ELLIS, STEPHEN
PAINTER
b High Point, NC, 1951. *Study:* Cornell Univ, Ithaca, NY, BFA, 73. *Exhib:* One-man shows, Koury Wingate Gallery, New York, 89 & 90, Galerie Ascan Crone, Hamburg, Ger, 90 & 92, Elizabeth Koury Gallery, New York, 91 & 92, Baumgartner Gallery, Washington, DC, 92; Mars Gallery, Tokyo, Japan, 92; Annina Nosei Gallery (with catalog), New York, 92; Shoshana Wayne Gallery, Santa Monica, Calif, 92; Evelyn Aimis Gallery, Boca Raton, Fla, 93. *Awards:* Painting Grant, NY Found Arts, 85; Painting Grant, Nat Endowment Arts, 91. *Bibliog:* Brooks Adams (auth), Art in Am, 163, 4/91; Demetrio Paparoni (auth), Tema Celeste, 48, 3-4/91; Steven Henry Madoff (auth), A New Lost Generation, Artnews, 73, 4/92. *Dealer:* Koury Gallery 89 Greene St New York NY 10012. *Mailing Add:* 44 White St New York NY 10013

ELLISON, ROBERT W
SCULPTOR
b Detroit, Mich, Dec 13, 46. *Study:* Mich State Univ, BFA, 69, MFA, 71. *Work:* Mich State Univ & Universal Steel Co, Lancing; City & Co San Francisco. *Comn:* Universal Steel, Lansing, Mich, 69; X Position, Wash State Univ, Pullman, 76; Slice, Syntex Corp, Palo Alto, Calif, 79. *Exhib:* New Ideas Expos, 70, Exhibs for Mich Artists, 70-72, Detroit Mus Art; 21st Ann All Calif Show, Laguna Beach Mus Art, 75; Outdoor Sculpture Exhib, Richmond Art Ctr, Calif, 75. *Collections Arranged:* Bourborbygmi, 28th Ann San Francisco Art Festival, 74; Grey Streak, 21st Ann Calif Show, 74; Riccochet, Palo Alto Outdoor Sculpture Exhib, 77; Four Times Daily, San Francisco Civic Ctr Plaza, 79; Arch Tworain, Donut Diorama, San Francisco Redevelopment Agency, 81. *Teaching:* Instr sculpture design & drawing, Mich State Univ, 70-71; instr sculpture design & drawing, Col Marin, Kentfield, Calif, 72-77. *Awards:* First Place, 21st Ann All Calif Show, 75. *Bibliog:* Gordon J Hazlitt (auth), Barometer of the unknown, Art News, 10/75; Four Times Daily (film), Bravura Films, 79; Donut Diorama (film), Chris Robson, 81. *Mem:* Artists Equity NCalif Region. *Media:* Welded Steel. *Mailing Add:* 6480 Eagle Ridge Rd Penngrove CA 94951

ELLIS-TRACY, JO
PAINTER, DEALER
Study: Univ Southern Calif, BFA; Stanford Univ, 64. *Work:* Philbrook Art Mus. *Comn:* 20 Drawings for Apollo 17 Mission, CBS, New York; Female Athlete (sculpture), Calif Sports Inc, The Forum, Los Angeles; Bronze Man Walking (sculpture), Conn Gen Life Insurance, Hartford; Space Life (painting & film), Nat Aeronautics & Space Admin, Goddard Space Ctr, Md; Commemorative Award (steel plaque), Armco Steel Corp, Ohio; Corp Imagery & Commun Proposals & Models. *Exhib:* Calif Design Show, Pasadena Art Mus; Calif Artists Group, Newport Harbor Art Mus, Newport Beach; Fisher Gallery, Univ Southern Calif, Los Angeles; Philbrook Art Mus, Tulsa, Okla. *Pos:* Founder, Jet-Art, New York, 66; critic, Pasadena Star News; pres & creative dir, The Eye Int Group, Inc, New York, Eye Int Gallery, Fine Arts Bldg, 89. *Bibliog:* Jo Ellis Tracy-Variations on a theme of the dance, KCET Television, Los Angeles; Jo Ellis Tracy-Artist, Pasadena Mag; Jo Ellis Tracy-American Artist, London Times. *Media:* Mixed Media, Oil. *Publ:* Illusr, Exquisite visions on a theme of Balanchine, Forbes Mag, 86 & American Business & the Arts, brochure, Forbes, 86. *Mailing Add:* 30 E 70th St New York NY 10021

ELLOIAN, CAROLYN AUTRY See Autry, Carolyn

ELLOIAN, PETER
GRAPHIC ARTIST
b Cleveland, Ohio, Apr 20, 36. *Study:* Cleveland Inst Art, BFA; Univ Iowa, MFA; Pratt Graphic Ctr. *Work:* Toledo Mus Art; Libr Cong, Washington, DC; Philadelphia Mus of Art; Okla Art Ctr, Oklahoma City; Mus of Mod Art Gallery, Yerevan, Armenia; Yugoslav Portrait Gallery, Tuzla, Yugoslavia. *Exhib:* Nat Exhib Prints, Libr Cong, 71 & 73 & 77; Int Biennal Graphic Art, Ljubljana, Yugoslavia, 81, 83, 85 & 87; Int Print Exhib, Taipei City Mus, Republic of China, 83, 85 & 89; Premio Int Biella, Italy, 84, 87 & 90; Drawings & Prints, Am Cult Ctr Gallery, Belgrade, Yugoslavia, 86; Inst per la Cultura e l'Arte, Catania, Sicily, 87; Int Print Biennale, Varna, Bulgaria, 89 & 91; Kochi Int Triennial Exhib Prints, Japan, 90. *Teaching:* Instr, Village des Arts en France, Lacoste, France, 84 & 87; prof printmaking & drawing, Art Dept, Univ Toledo at Toledo Mus Art, 87- *Awards:* Grand Diploma, Second Int Biennial Portrait Drawings & Graphics, Tuzla, Yugoslavia, 82; Ismet Mujezinovic Award, Fourth Int Biennial Portrait Drawings & Graphics, Tuzla, Yugoslavia, 86; Lynd Ward Mem Award, Print Nat, Hunterdon, NJ, 92; and others. *Mem:* Soc of Am Graphic Artists; Boston Printmakers. *Media:* Drawing, Printmaking. *Mailing Add:* 26114 West River Rd Perrysburg OH 43551

ELOUL, KOSSO
SCULPTOR
b Jan 22, 20; US citizen. *Study:* Art Inst Chicago, 39-43; sculptor symposiums, Austria, 60, Yugoslavia, 61, Italy & Israel, 62, Berlin, Ger, 63, Montreal, 64 & Long Beach, Calif, 65. *Work:* Shalom 7 (painted steel), Rose Mus, Brandeis Univ; Art Gallery Ont, Toronto; Mus d'Art Contemp, Montreal; Mus Tel Aviv, Israel; Bezalel Mus, Jerusalem, Israel. *Comn:* Alat (sculpture), Greenwin of Toronto, 72; Swink Advert Head Off, Marion, Ohio, 73; Constella, J D S Investments, North York, Toronto, 75; Braha (stelcology), Steinberg's Miracle Food Mart, Rexdale, 76; Hommage to the Bull (Stelco steel), Bridlebrook Farms, Guelph, Ont, 78; and many others. *Exhib:* Calif Artists in US Mus, Lytton Art Ctr, Los Angeles, 67; The Sculpture Walk, Nat Arts Ctr, Ottawa, 78; Subterranea, Mus Arte Carillo Gil, Inst Nac Bellas Artes, Mexico City, 79; one-man shows, Koffler Ctr Arts, Toronto, 79 & Kosso Eloul: Celebration of the Arch, Art Gallery Hamilton, 80; and others. *Teaching:* Artist in residence sculpture, Calif State Univ, Long Beach, 65-66; artist in residence form & space, Univ Toronto Sch Archit, 69-70. *Awards:* Can Coun Sr Art fel, 76; Medal of Accomplishment, Mexico City, 78; and others. *Bibliog:* T H Heinrich (auth), The razor's edge, Vol 156/157 & Gilles Hemault (auth), article, Artscanada; Fernande St Martin (auth), Lettre de Montreal, Art Int, 11/64; Curt Oplinger (auth), article, Artforum, 1/66. *Mem:* L'Accademia Tiberina, Rome, Italy; hon fel Royal Acad Fine Art The Hague; Royal Can Acad Arts. *Media:* Stainless Steel, Concrete. *Dealer:* Arras Gallery 29 W 57th St New York NY 10019; Godard Mira Gallery 22 Hazelton Toronto ON Can. *Mailing Add:* 288 Sherbourne St Toronto ON M5A 2S1 Canada

ELOWITCH, ANNETTE
DEALER
b Portland, Maine, Dec 24, 42. *Study:* Boston Univ, 61; Westbrook Col, Portland, Maine, AA, 63; Univ Maine. *Pos:* Co-owner, Barridoff Galleries, 75- *Specialty:* Nineteenth and twentieth century paintings. *Mailing Add:* Barridoff Galleries PO Box 9715 Portland ME 04104-5015

ELOWITCH, ROBERT JASON
DEALER, PATRON
b Portland, Maine, Apr 8, 43. *Study:* Amherst Col, BA. *Pos:* Drama/film critic, Portland Press Herald & Eve Express, 67-69, Maine Times, 70-75; owner, Barridoff Galleries, 75- *Mem:* Maine State Comn Arts & Humanities (comnr, 73-75); Skohegan Sch Painting & Sculpture (dir, 68-80); Portland Sch Art (sch comt mem, 74-75); United Portland Regional Orgn of Arts Resources (vchmn, 74). *Specialty:* 19th and early 20th century American oils and contemporary regional oils, watercolors, etc. *Interests:* Promotion and support of the arts in the state of Maine; purchase and sale of American and European art of the 18th, 19th & 20th centuries. *Mailing Add:* PO Box 9715 Portland ME 04104-5015

ELOZUA, RAYMON
SCULPTOR, PHOTOGRAPHER
b Ger, 1947; US citizen. *Study:* Univ Chicago, 65-69. *Work:* Cranbrook Mus Art, Bloomfield Hills, Mich; Am Craft Mus, New York, NY; San Francisco Mus Mod Art, Calif; Wadsworth Atheneum, Hartford, Conn; Mint Mus Art, Charlotte, NC; and others. *Exhib:* New Visions, Aldrich Mus Contemp Art, Ridgefield, Conn, 81; Brooklyn 1984, Brooklyn Mus, NY, 84; solo exhibs, Carlo Lamagna Gallery, New York, 88, Braunstein/Quay Gallery, San Francisco, Calif, 88 & 89, Cleveland Ctr Contemp Art, The Galleria, Ohio, 89 & Ariz Mus Art, Tucson, 90; Digs: Archaeology & Social Criticism, Chicago Ctr Ceramic Art, Ill, 87; American Art Today: The City, Fla Int Univ Art Mus, Miami, 90; American Myths, Procter Art Ctr, Band Coll, Rhinebeck, NY, 90; Art and the Law: 15th Ann Exhib, West Publ Co, St Paul, Minn, 90; and others. *Pos:* Properties designer, Julliard Theatre, New York, 71-73; designer & photog, Daniel Negrin Film & Dance, New York, 74-75; independent designer, Am Craft Coun, Baltimore, Md, 75-77. *Teaching:* Fac, grad sem, RI Sch Design, Providence, RI, 83-84; instr, grad sem, Pratt Inst Design, Brooklyn, NY, 84-85; fac, ceramic sculpture, New York Univ, New York, 82-86. *Awards:* Fels, Nat Endowment Arts, 80, 81 & 87 & NY Found Arts, 88. *Bibliog:* Robert Mahoney (auth), The decay of the urban landscape, Arts Mag, 86; Lucy Lippard (auth), Home Scrap, Carlo Lamaguna Gallery, 87; Susan Snodgrass (auth), Digs: Archeology & Social Criticism, New Art Examiner, 1/88. *Media:* All. *Mailing Add:* Braunstein/Quay Gallery 250 Sutter St San Francisco CA 94108

ELSE, ROBERT JOHN
PAINTER, EDUCATOR
b Wayne, Pa, Nov 26, 18. *Study:* Columbia Univ, BS & MA. *Work:* Crocker Art Mus, Sacramento; Univ of Calif-Los Angeles Libr; Calif State Libr Prints Rm. *Comn:* City Hall, Sacramento, 87. *Exhib:* 4th Print Ann Exhib, Brooklyn Mus, 50; Kingsley Ann Exhib for Northern Calif Artists, Crocker Art Gallery, 50-64; Oakland Art Gallery's Ann Exhib, 51; Survey of Pac Coast Painting, Walnut Creek, Calif, 51; 17th Ann Watercolor Exhib, San Francisco Mus of Art, 53; retrospective, Crocker Art Gallery, 77, Robert Else Gallery, Calif State Univ, Sacramento, 90; Sacramento Valley Landscapes, Univ Calif, Davis, 79. *Pos:* Coun mem, Comt on Art Educ, Mus of Mod Art, 49-52; mem joint bd trustees, Crocker Art Mus, 73-75; mem, Sacramento Metrop Arts Comn, 80-82. *Teaching:* Prof art pract, painting & drawing, Calif State Univ, Sacramento, 50-79, emer prof, 79- *Awards:* Purchase Award, 1st Int Biennial of Contemp Color Lithography, Cincinnati Mus of Art, 50; First Prize Oil Painting, Kingsley Club, 64. *Media:* Acrylic, Watercolor. *Mailing Add:* 5871 Shepard Ave Sacramento CA 95819

ELSEN, ALBERT EDWARD
HISTORIAN
b New York, NY, Oct 11, 27. *Study:* Columbia Col, AB; Columbia Univ, MA & PhD; Dickinson Con, Hon DFA, 80. *Teaching:* Asst prof art hist, Carleton Col, 52-58; prof art hist, Ind Univ, Bloomington, 58-68; prof art hist, Stanford Univ, 68-75, Haas prof art hist, 75- *Awards:* Fulbright Fel, 49-50; Guggenheim Fel, 66-67; Nat Endowment Humanities Sr Fel, 73-74. *Mem:* Col Art Asn Am (bd dirs, 66-70, secy, 70-72, vpres, 72-74, pres, 74-76). *Res:* Modern art, principally modern sculpture. *Publ:* Auth, Origins of Modern Sculpture: Pioneers and Premises, 74; coauth (with John Merryman), Law, Ethics & the Visual Arts, 79, 87-; auth, Modern European Sculpture, 1918-1945, 79; In Rodin's Studio, 80; The Gates of Hell by Auguste Rodin, 85; and others. *Mailing Add:* Dept Art Hist-Cummings Bldg 117 Stanford Univ Stanford CA 94305

ELY, TIMOTHY CLYDE
BOOK ARTIST
b Snohomish, Wash, Feb 9, 49. *Study:* Western Wash Univ, Bellingham, BA(drawing & printmaking), 72, Univ Wash, Seattle, MFA(design), 75. *Work:* Victoria & Albert Mus, London, Eng; Libr Cong, Washington, DC; John Paul Getty Mus, Los Angeles, Calif; Spencer Collection, New York Pub Libr, NY; Rijksmuseum Meermanno-Westreenianum Den Haag, Neth; Mus Mod Art, Brooklyn Mus, The Grolier Club, NY; Yale Univ, Princeton Univ & Harvard Univ. *Comn:* Artist Book, Polar Rare Book Rm, Univ Alaska, Fairbanks, 84; Book of Roses, Sony Music, New York. *Exhib:* Solo exhibs, Eaton/Shoen, San Francisco, 84, NY Acad Sci, 87, Contemp Crafts Gallery, Portland, Ore, 88, Granary Bks, NY, 89 & 91, Minn Ctr for Bk Arts, Minneapolis, 89, Victoria & Albert Mus, London, Eng, 89; Folger Libr, Washington, DC, 87; Univ Arts, Philadelphia, Pa, 88; Ctr for Bk Arts, NY, 88-92; Maison du Livre de l'Image et du Son, Ville de Villeurbanne, France, 88; Am Craft Mus, New York & Boston Athenaeum, Mass, 88; Cult Ctr, Boulogne-Billancourt, France, 89; Biblioteque de l'Arsenal, Paris, France & Bibliotheca Wittocklana, Brussels, Bel, 90; Grolier Club, New York, 91; Anchorage Hist & Fine Arts Mus, Alaska, 91; Princeton Univ, NJ, 92; Gallery Tinka, San Jose, Costa Rica, 92; Nat Col Art & Design, Bergen, Norway, 92. *Teaching:* Instr book art, Ctr for Book Art, New York, 84- *Awards:* Visual Artists Fel, Nat Endowment Arts, 82; Pollack-Krasner Found Grant, 86; Art Matters Grant, 88 & 90. *Bibliog:* Roy Harley Lewis (auth), Fine Bookbinding in the Twentieth Century, Arco Publ, 85; Martha Bergman (auth), An interview with Timothy C Ely, The New Bookbinder, UK, 87; Lois Allan (auth), Complex and simple mysteries, Artweek, 5/88. *Mem:* Designer Bookbinders, Eng. *Media:* Painting, Drawing. *Publ:* Auth, Portfolio (article), Am Crafts Mag, 6/86; Martina Margetto (auth), International Crafts, Thames & Hudson, 91. *Mailing Add:* 255 W 84th St Apt 2C New York NY 10024

ELZEA, ROWLAND PROCTER
MUSEUM DIRECTOR, CURATOR
b Columbia, Mo, Sept 19, 31. *Study:* Univ Mo, BA & MA; Hunter Col, MSEd; also with Esteban Vicente, New York; Fel Mus Prof, Nat Endowment Arts, 80. *Work:* Del Art Mus, Wilmington. *Collections Arranged:* Golden Age of American Illustration: 1880-1914 (with catalog), 72; Howard Pyle: Diversity in Depth (with catalog), 73; Jean Dubuffet, 74; Avant-Garde Painting and Sculpture in America, 1910-1925, 75-; The Pre-Raphaelite Era: 1848-1914 (with catalog), 76, The Am Mag, 1890-1940 (with catalog), 79; John Sloan: Spectator of Life (with catalog), 88. *Pos:* Chief cur, Del Art Mus, 58-, assoc dir, 80- *Teaching:* Pres, Sch Art & Design, Philadelphia, 69-70, instr art hist & painting, 69-71. *Awards:* Art Book of the Year, Univ Del Press, 88; Hon Res Fel Univ Galsgow, 92. *Res:* John Sloan, American Illustration, Pre-Raphaelites. *Publ:* Auth, Howard Pyle Collection, 71; auth, Samuel and Mary R Bancroft English Pre-Raphaelite Collection, 78; ed, The Correspondence Between Samuel Bancroft, Jr and Charles Fairfax Murray, 80; auth, John Sloan's Oil Paintings, A Catalogue Raisonné, 92. *Mailing Add:* 2013 Baynard Blvd Wilmington DE 19802

EMBREY, CARL RICE
PAINTER, INSTRUCTOR
b Hamilton, Tex, Oct 28, 38. *Study:* Univ Tex, Austin, BFA, 63, with Everett Spruce, MFA, 64. *Work:* Contemp Art Mus, Houston; Marion Koogler McNay Mus, San Antonio; San Antonio Art League, Tex. *Exhib:* One-man show, Marion Koogler McNay Art Inst, San Antonio, 74 & fifteen-year survey-San Antonio Art Inst, 88; Am Arts Nat Exhib, Butler Inst, Youngstown, Ohio, 65; Artists of the Southeast & Tex, Isaac Delgado Mus, New Orleans, 67; 60 Tex Artists, Inst Texan Cult, San Antonio, 68; Tex Artists Invitational, Longview Mus, Tex, 68-70; Art Teachers, Witte Mem Mus, 77; and other group & one-man shows. *Collections Arranged:* Paintings of Carl Embrey (cataloged), Five Year Retrospective, 74. *Teaching:* Prof painting & drawing, San Antonio Art Inst, 64- *Awards:* Onderdonk Mem Award, San Antonio Art League, 65; Honorable Mention, Arts Nat, Tyler Mus, 67; Merit Award, Tex Artists Invitational, Longview Art League, 72. *Bibliog:* Gail Falbo Smith (auth), Embrey--A Documentary, Trinity Univ, 78; Nanette Simpson (auth), Carl Embrey, Southwest Art, Houston, 79; Dan Goddard (auth), Carl Embrey, Southwest Art, Houston, 89. *Mem:* Tex Fine Arts Asn. *Media:* Acrylic Emulsion, Pencil. *Dealer:* Meredith Long & Co 2323 San Felipe Rd Houston TX 77019. *Mailing Add:* 9319 Nona Kay Dr San Antonio TX 78217

EMERICK, JUDSON J
HISTORIAN
b Kingston, NY, July 3, 41. *Study:* Hope Col, Holland, Mich, BA, 63; Univ Mich, Ann Arbor, MA, 65; Univ Pa, Phd, 75. *Teaching:* Instr art hist, Pomona Col, 73-75, asst prof art hist, 75-80, assoc prof, 80-, chmn dept art, 80-87. *Awards:* Samuel H Kress Found Fel, 71-73; Nat Endowment Humanities Fel, 81. *Mem:* Col Art Asn; Soc Archit Historians. *Res:* Late antique and medieval art with special emphasis on Italian architecture and painting. *Publ:* Coauth, Early Sixth Century Frescoes at San Martino ai Monti in Rome, Römisches Jahrbuch für Kunstgestichte, Vol XXI, 84. *Mailing Add:* 1421 N Guadalajara Dr Claremont CA 91711

EMERSON, ROBERTA SHINN
MUSEUM DIRECTOR
b Indianapolis, Ind, Feb 14, 22. *Study:* Northwestern Univ; Univ Chicago; Marshall Univ. *Collections Arranged:* WVa Artists on the Move (traveling exhib), 67; A Room Full of Ropes, 72; Ancient Art of Middle America, 74; New Am Glass: Focus WVa, 76; The Mining Life: Coal in Our History and Culture, 81; Beverly Pepper in Situ, Huntington Galleries, 83; Late Twentieth Century Art from Sydney and Frances Lewis Foundation, 84; Selections from the Collection of the Alex Hillman Family Foundation, 84; Selections from the Sara Roby Foundation Collection, 85. *Pos:* Interim dir, Huntington Galleries, 67, dir, 71-88, dir emer, 88- *Teaching:* Asst prof art appreciation, Marshall Univ, 68-69. *Awards:* Outstanding Contribr Arts, State WVa, 84. *Mem:* River Cities Cultural Coun. *Mailing Add:* 706 Ridgewood Rd Huntington WV 25701

EMERSON, WALTER CARUTH
PAINTER, EDUCATOR
b Dallas, Tex, Jan 24, 12. *Study:* Aunspaugh Sch Art; with Olin Travis; Southwestern Sch Theatre; with John Knott; Southern Methodist Univ, BA. *Work:* Tex State Mus, Washington-on-the-Brazos, Tex; Herman Brown Libr, Burnet, Tex; also in private collections. *Comn:* Pvt portrait & caricature commissions, 33-; life size full figure of Indian Chief Quanah Parker, Metrop Fed Savings, Dallas, 69; portraits of pres, Repub Tex & portrait of Gen Santa Anna, Tex State Mus, 72; murals, Prestonwood, Dallas, 82; murals, Prudential Bldg, Irving, Tex, 84. *Exhib:* Rainbowman Gallery, Santa Fe, NMex, 69; one-man show, Quadrangle Galleries, Dallas, 70, 72 & 79 & Tex State Mus, 73; Cushing Gallery, Dallas, 71. *Pos:* Founder & dir, art dept, Pollock Paper Corp, Dallas, 37-52; founder & officer in chg, Art Dept, USN, Washington, DC, 41-45; art dir, Food & Drug Div, Hunt Oil Co, Dallas, 63-69; caricaturist, Plaza Americas, Dallas, 82- *Teaching:* Course designer, instr art & art hist, Southern Methodist Univ, 40-63; conception, production & illustration, Pencil Personalities (TV series), 58; course designer, instr, art & art hist, Christian Col Southwest, 69-70, Dallas Co Community Col Dist, 72-74 & Dallas Co Jail, initiated instruction, leading to Col degrees in art, for inmates, 73-74; founder & dir, Art Acad Dallas, 74-; nat lectr, Kim Dawson Agency, 77- *Awards:* Best in Class, Cherokee Nat Mus, 76. *Bibliog:* Keith Kathan (auth), Walter Emerson Portraitist, Dallas Times Herald, 70; William Payne (auth), Portraits by Walter Caruth Emerson, Dallas Morning News, 73; Lorraine Haacke (auth), A guide to Dallas art galleries, Parade Mag, 74. *Media:* Miscellaneous Media. *Publ:* Editorial cartoons, Nationally Distributed, 37-56, Dallas Times Herald, 36, Dallas Morning News, 41, NY Daily Mirror, 56-58; auth, American tragedy at Brussels, Am Mercury Mag, 10/58; auth & illusr, The Truth About Santa Anna, 73, 75 & 85; auth, Art Alive (column), syndicated internationally, 79- *Mailing Add:* 3637 Haynie Ave Dallas TX 75205-1203

EMERY, LIN
SCULPTOR, KINETIC ARTIST
b New York, NY. *Study:* Ossip Zadkine Studio, Paris; Sculpture Ctr, New York. *Work:* Nat Collection Am Art, Washington, DC; New Orleans Mus of Art; Norton Art Galleries, West Palm Beach, Fla; Huntington Mus Art, WVa; Walter P Chrysler Mus, Norfolk, Va; Mus Foreign Art, Sofia Bulgaria; Fine Arts Mus South, Mobile, Ala; Brevard Art Mus, Melbourne, Fla. *Comn:* kinetic sculpture, Civic Ctr Lawrence, Kans, 82; Magnetmobile, SCent Bell, Birmingham, Ala, 72; kinetic & musical sculpture, InterContinental Hotel, New Orleans, 83; kinetic sculpture, Marina Ctr, Singapore, 86; kinetic sculpture, City of Virginia Beach, 89; City of Oxnard, Calif, 90; Hofstra Univ, NY, 90; Sterling Drug Co, Collegeville, Pa; Daytona Beach Airport, Fla. *Exhib:* solo shows, Contemp Arts Ctr, New Orleans, 78 & 81 & Max Hutchinson Gallery, New York, 82; Int Sculpture Conference Exhib, 80; GSA Art in Archit, Nat Collection Fine Art, 80; World Expo, Brisbane, Australia, 88; Alexandria Mus, La, 89; Mus SE Tex, Beaumont, 91; Brevard Art Mus, Melbourne, Fla, 92; Arthur Roger, New York, 93. *Pos:* Vis critic, Tulane Univ Sch Archit, 67-68; fel, Va Ctr Creative Arts, 81. *Teaching:* Vis artist, Newcomb Art Sch, Tulane Univ, 81 & Univ Maine, 88. *Awards:* Mayor's Award Excellence in the Arts, New Orleans, 80; Louisiana Woman of

Achievement, State of La, 84; Distinguished Louisiana Artist, NOCCA, 88; Young Womens Club Am Role Model Award, 89; Lazlo Aranyi Award Honor, Pub Art, 90. *Bibliog:* Moore & Allen (auth), Metal that moves, La Mag, 67; Pierce (auth), Lin Emery's aquamobiles, Art Int, 69; Roger Green (auth), The kinetic sculpture of Lin Emery, Arts Mag, 12/79; Bill Goliahtly (auth), Tubular Bells, Horizon, 4/85; Josef Marker (auth), Lin Emery, InSite, 90; V Watson-Jones (auth), Contemp Am Woman Sculptors; Charlotte Rubenstein (auth), Am Women Artists. *Mem:* Sculptors Guild New York. *Media:* Kinetics, Metals. *Publ:* Co-auth, Kinesone I, Leonardo, Vol 19, Issue No 3. *Dealer:* Kouros Gallery 23 E 73rd St New York NY 10021; Arthur Roger Gallery 432 Julia St New Orleans LA 70130. *Mailing Add:* 7520 Dominican St New Orleans LA 70118

EMIL, ARTHUR D
COLLECTOR
b New York, NY, Dec 29, 24. *Study:* Yale Univ; Columbia Law Sch. *Mem:* Int Coun Mus Mod Art; Am Fedn Arts. *Collection:* Modern painting; ancient sculpture. *Mailing Add:* 599 Lexington Ave New York NY 10022

EMMERICH, ANDRE
DEALER, WRITER
b Frankfurt, Ger, Oct 11, 24. *Study:* Amsterdam Lyceum, Neth; Kew Forest Sch, New York; Oberlin Col, BA, 44. *Pos:* Pres, Andre Emmerich Gallery, New York, 54- *Awards:* Distinguished Citizen's Award, Nassau Co Mus Fine Art Asn, 87. *Mem:* Art Dealers Asn Am (pres, 72-74, 91-); Century Club, New York; Sculptor Int (ed adv comt); Am Friends Israel Mus (bd dirs). *Specialty:* Contemporary art; classical antiquities. *Publ:* Auth, Art Before Columbus, Simon & Schuster, 63, 71, 78 & 83; auth, Sweat of the Sun and Tears of the Moon--Gold and Silver in Pre-Columbian Art, Univ Wash Press, 65 & 77; also numerous articles in Art Am, Arts, Am Heritage, Wash Post and many others. *Mailing Add:* 41 E 57th St New York NY 10022

EMMERT, PAULINE GORE
PAINTER
b Marks, Miss, July 1, 23. *Study:* Long Island Univ, BA, 70, MA, 78. *Work:* Long Island Univ, Greenvale, NY; New York Univ Hosp, NY; Daniel Gale, Sotheby Parke Bernet, & Sammis Real Estate Cold Spring Harbor, NY; N Shore Med Group, Huntington, NY. *Comn:* Lloyd Harbor (painting), comn by Mrs D Kent Gale, Huntington, NY, 78; Centerport Harbor (painting), comn by Capt & Mrs Victor Grubbs, Monroe, Ga 83; Cold Spring Harbor (painting), comn by Dr & Mrs Richard H Sand, Huntington, NY, 89; No--Five Cordwainer Lane, comn by Mr & Mrs Harold Paul family. *Exhib:* Sense of Place--Space, Whaling Mus, Cold Spring Harbor, NY, 81; Fine Arts Mus Long Island, 83; Miss Mus Art, Jackson, 84; Nat Asn Women Artists Travelling Show, 88, 90, 92, 93; 100 Years, 100 Artists, Nat Asn Women Artists, traveling ten states, 89; Cold Spring Harbor Community Ctr, 90. *Pos:* Lectr, Art Relig-Cult, Huntington Methodist Church, 78-79; Cur, TianJin Art Col, Huntington, NY, 83; Lectr, Nat Assn Univ Women, Huntington, NY, 84. *Teaching:* Studio, Huntington, NY Pub Schs, Cold Spring Harbor Dist II. *Awards:* Award of Excellence, Huntington Art League, Abraham & Strauss, 79; Elizabeth Erlanger Memorial-Award, Nat Assn Women Artists, 81; Martha Moore Memorial-Award, Nat Assn Women Artists, 87 & 89. *Bibliog:* David Shirey (auth), Nuances of Seasons, NY Times 81; Ronald Pisano (auth), Long Island Landscape Painting, Little Brown, 90. *Mem:* Nat Asn Women Artists (judge oils, 86-88); New York Artists Equity; Viridian Space (parliamentarian, 81-82); Huntington Township Art League. *Media:* Oil, Watercolor. *Mailing Add:* 3 Mux Lane Lloyd Neck Huntington NY 11743

ENDERS, ELIZABETH MCGUIRE
PAINTER
b New London, Conn, Feb 18, 39. *Study:* Conn Col (writing with William Meredith), BA, 62; Sch Visual Arts, 83-85; New York Univ, MA, 87. *Work:* Addison Gallery Am Art, Andover, Mass; Daimler-Benz Holding Co North Am, Inc; Graham Gund, Cambridge, Mass. *Exhib:* Art in Support of Art, Boston, Mass, 82; Small Works, New York Univ, New York, 83; Alumni Art Exhib, Conn Col, New London, Conn, 88; Maps and Madness, Bronx Coun Arts, Longwood Arts Gallery, 91-92; Marine Midland Bank, 92; Putt Modernism, Artists Space, New York, 92; one-woman show, Ulysses Gallery, New York, 92. *Bibliog:* An Auction with a Difference: Hole-Sale Art, Flash Art, 10/92. *Mem:* Artists Space (bd trustees, 86-); Col Art Asn; Drawing Soc. *Media:* Oil, Acrylic. *Publ:* Co-auth, Elizabeth Enders, John Sailer Ulysses, 92. *Mailing Add:* 530 E 86th St New York NY 10028

ENGEL, MICHAEL MARTIN, II
PAINTER
b New York, NY, Mar 20, 19. *Study:* With A Katchemakoff; Art Students League, with Kimon Nicolaides & George Picken; Am Sch Design, with Cherkasoff. *Work:* Parrish Art Mus, Southampton, NY; St Lawrence Univ, Canton, NY; US Navy Combat Art Collection; Antioch Col, Yellow Springs, Ohio. *Exhib:* Hofstra Col Invitational, 59; Audubon Artists Ann; Suburban Art League, NY; Nat Arts Club, New York. *Mem:* Audubon Artists (historian, 45-79, pres, 62-63); Int Asn Arts (vpres, 70-73); Artists Fellowship (trustee, 63-, pres, 77-80); Nat Arts Club; life fel Royal Soc Arts; Artists Equity NY. *Media:* Watercolor, Acrylic. *Dealer:* Clayton-Liberatore Gallery Bridgehampton NY. *Mailing Add:* 22 Lee St Huntington NY 11743

ENGEL, WALTER F
CRITIC, DEALER
b Vienna, Austria, June 11, 08; Can citizen. *Study:* Art & art hist with Oscar Lichtenstern, Vienna, 25-27; Joseph Floch, Paris, 28; Ludwig H Jungnickel, Vienna, 29-30. *Pos:* Art critic, Revista de las Indias, 41-51, El Tiempo, 44-55, Art Mag Plastica, 56-60 & El Espectador, 60-65, Bogota, Colombia; co-founder, critic & adv bd, Art Mag, Toronto, 69-79. *Bibliog:* Walter Jelen (auth), Walter Engel, Toronto: friend of the arts, promotor of the artists, Der Aufbau, New York, 3/23/79. *Mem:* Int Asn Art Critics; hon Soc Can Artists. *Res:* Twentieth century Latin American art, Canadian art, surrealism, and expressionism. *Specialty:* Contemporary art, with preference for Canadian, European and Latin American art, surrealism and figurative expressionism; Anishnawbe, Ontarian-Indian painting. *Publ:* Auth, Social Problems in the Visual Arts, 46; The Painter Fernando Botero, 52; Contemporary Colombian Paintresses, 59; Wiedemann, 59; The World of Frans Masereel (catalog), Art Gallery Windsor, Ont, 81 & Art Gallery Ont, Toronto, 82; Shlomo Schwartz, an Integral Artist (catalog), Aviv Fine Art Gallery, Great Neck, NY, 89. *Mailing Add:* 350 Lonsdale Rd Suite 201 Toronto ON M5P 1R6 Canada

ENGELHARDT, THOMAS ALEXANDER
EDITORIAL CARTOONIST
b St Louis, Mo, Dec 29, 30. *Study:* Denver Univ, 50-51; Ruskin Sch Fine Arts, Oxford Univ, 54-56; Sch Visual Arts, New York, 57. *Work:* State Hist Soc Mo, Columbia. *Comn:* Mural (humorous animals), Pediat Assoc, Mo, 73. *Exhib:* One-man shows, Fontbonne Col, Mo, 72 & Decade of the Environment 1970-1980, Old Courthouse, St Louis, 81 & Mark Twain Bank, St Louis, 88; Sch Visual Arts Alumni Exhib, Hansen Gallery, New York, 75; plus numerous group shows. *Pos:* Free-lance cartoonist, New York, 57-60; ed cartoonist, Newspaper Enterprise Asn, Cleveland, Ohio, 60-61 & St Louis Post-Dispatch, 62- *Awards:* Ethical Humanist of the Year, St Louis Ethical Soc, 87. *Media:* Pen & Ink, Crayon. *Publ:* Auth, Cartoonist Profiles, 69; Dateline 1976, Overseas Press Club, 76; Cartoonist Profiles, 91. *Mailing Add:* 900 N Tucker Blvd St Louis MO 63101

ENGELSON, CAROL
PAINTER
b Seymour, Ind, 1944. *Study:* Carnegie-Mellon Univ, Pittsburgh, Pa, BFA, 66. *Work:* Calouste Gulbenkian Found, Lisbon; Aldrich Mus, Ridgefield, Conn; Found Art This Century, Paris; San Diego Art Ctr; Chase Manhattan Bank, New York; Carnegie-Mellon Univ, Pittsburgh, Pa. *Exhib:* Solo exhibs, 112 Workshop, Inc, New York, 77, Ruth Schaffner Gallery, Santa Barbara, Calif, 78, Oscarsson-Hood Gallery, New York, 80 & Univ Conn, Hartford, 85; Third Annual Contemp Reflections, Aldrich Mus, Ridgefield, Conn, 74; Selections from the Aldrich Mus, Am Fedn Arts Traveling Exhibition, 74-77; New Dimensions in Drawing, 1950-1980, Aldrich Mus, Ridgefield, Conn, 81; Nat & Int tour, American Painting the 80's, 79-83; Color Abstraction in the 1980's, Baruch Col Gallery, NY, 85; Spiritual Landscape, Biota Gallery, Los Angeles, 91; Minus 40 Plus, Haenah Kent Gallery, New York, 91. *Teaching:* Vis lectr painting, Carnegie-Mellon Univ, 78, Univ Wis-Milwaukee, 82, Univ Conn, Hartford, 85, Pratt Inst, 87 & Parsons Sch Design, 88. *Awards:* Edward MacDowell Colony Fel, 71, 72, 74 & 75; Grant, Comt Visual Arts, New York, 74; Nat Endowment Arts Grant, 77-78; Am Acad Arts & Lett Grant, 83. *Bibliog:* Annette Nachumi (auth), Carol Engelson, Arts Mag, 11/80; John Yau (auth), Carol Engelson and Rick Klauber at Oscarsson-Hood, 3/81 & Deborah Rosenthal (auth), First underground show, fall 84, Art in Am; Vivien Raynor (auth), The gathering of the avant garde: The Lower East Side, NY Times, 85; Claire Gravel (auth), A Baie Saint-Paul, l'Art Contemporian Descend dans l'Arene, Le Soleil, 8/20/88; Barbara Rose (auth), Autocritique, 88; Hilton Kramer (auth), American painting the eighties, NY Times, 1/90; Grace Gluck (auth), New Debates on Jackson Pollock, New Biography. *Media:* Oil on Canvas, Pastel on Paper. *Publ:* Auth, Jackson Pollock, The Man and the Myth, J of Art, Vol 2, No 3, 12/89, 28. *Dealer:* David Anderson Gallery Martha Jackson Pl Buffalo NY 14214. *Mailing Add:* 131 Allen St New York NY 10002

ENGERAN, WHITNEY JOHN, JR
PAINTER, EDUCATOR
b New Orleans, La, Feb 1, 34. *Study:* Spring Hill Col, BA & MA; St Louis Univ, STL; Art Students League. *Work:* Cunningham Mem Libr, Terre Haute, Ind; Vincennes Univ; Harold E Simon Collection; Hugh Kohlmeyer Collection. *Comn:* Fire ritual mural, St Marys Col, 62; suffering servant mural, Martin Army Hosp, Columbus, Ga, 66; Terre Haute First Nat Bank, 74; sci ctr mural, WVa Inst Technol, 88. *Exhib:* Hands On--Hands Off (Review of 20 Yrs of Paintings & Drawings), Art Gallery, St Mary of the Woods Col, Terre Haute, Ind, 77; Tondo Paintings; Turman Gallery, Terre Haute, Ind, 80-86; Circling the Apocalypse, Tondi paintings, Pierce Gallery, Montgomery, WVa, 88; painting, Wholely, Holy, Wholely, Bicentennial Art Mus Paris, 90; and others. *Collections Arranged:* Ida Kohlmeyer Retrospective, 72, Images of Our Time, 73 & American 6 Pak: Sic Bicentennial Exhibits, 74-75, Turman Gallery, Terre Haute; I Kohlmeyer Retrospective, Mint Mus, 82-84. *Pos:* Cur permanent collection & dir, Turman Gallery, 71-75. *Teaching:* Asst prof aesthet & chmn dept art, Loyola Univ, 66-68; assoc prof aesthet, Stephens Col, 68-71; prof art theory & criticism, Ind State Univ, Terre Haute, 71-, chmn dept, 71-78. *Awards:* First Prize Watercolor, Kans Artists' Exhib, 62 & 65. *Bibliog:* Margaret Harold (ed), Prize Winning Watercolors of America, Allied Publ, 63; Jason Berry (auth), Rev, Ida Kohlmeyer: 30 years, New Orleans Mag, 19-20, 1/85. *Mem:* Col Art Asn Am; Nat Coun Art Adminr; Mid-Am Col Art Asn. *Media:* Enamel, Acrylics. *Publ:* Auth, Ida Kohlmeyer: A Retrospective Exhibition (catalog), High Mus, Atlanta, 12/71; article, Arts Mag, 4/78; article, Arts Update, 2/83; Ida Kohlmeyer (catalog), Mint Mus, 12/83; article, Full circle for Dick Hay--sculptor in clay, Butlleti Informatiu de Ceramica, Barcelona, Spain, 86. *Dealer:* Diane Mann and Assoc RR1 Box 116 Merom In 47861. *Mailing Add:* 1509 S Center St Terre Haute IN 47802

ENGGASS, ROBERT
HISTORIAN, EDUCATOR
b Detroit, Mich, Dec 20, 21. *Study:* Harvard Univ, AB, 46; Univ Mich, MA, 50, PhD, 55. *Teaching:* Instr, Bryn Mawr, 55-56; asst prof, Williams Col, 56-57; assoc prof art hist, Pa State Univ, 58-65, prof art hist, 66-71; prof & chmn art dept, La State Univ, 65-66; prof art hist, Univ Kans, 71-78; Callaway prof art, Univ Ga, 79-88; distinguished vis prof, Virgina Commonwealth Univ, 89. *Awards:* Grants-in-Aid, Am Coun Learned Socs, 58, 70 & 76; Fulbright Res Scholar, Univ Rome, 63-64; Univ Kans Res Grants, 66-70. *Mem:* Col Art Asn; Royal Soc Arts; Am Asn Univ Prof; Am Soc Eighteenth Century Studies. *Publ:* Auth, The Painting of Baciccio, Pa State Press, 64; coauth, Sources and Documents in the History of Art: Italy and Spain 1600-1750, Prentice-Hall, 70; Hortus Imaginum: Essays in Western Art, 75; auth, Early Eighteenth Century Sculpture in Rome: An Illustrated Catalogue Raissone, Pa State Univ Press, 76; coauth, Vatican Libr, edition of Pio's Vite di pittori, 77; Malvasia's Life of Guido Reni, 82 & Ridolfi's Life of Tintoretto, 84, Pa State Press; and many others. *Mailing Add:* 903 W University Pkwy No 401 Baltimore MD 21210

ENGLANDER, GERTRUD
CERAMIST
b Ger, Jan 29, 04; US citizen. *Study:* Kunstgewerbeschule Cologne; Craft Students League, YWCA, New York; NY Univ. *Exhib:* Designer-Craftsmen USA 1960, Mus Contemp Crafts, 60, Am Craftsmen's Coun Touring Exhib, 61; Craftsmen of Northeastern States, Worcester Art Mus, 63; Artist Craftsmen New York Ann, Lever House, 71. *Teaching:* Instr ceramics, Craft Students League YWCA, New York; instr ceramics, Little Art Workshop, New York, 53-55. *Awards:* Award of Merit for Outstanding Craftsmanship, Artist Craftsmen New York, 71; Award of Merit, Invitation Pen & Brush Club Show, 77. *Mem:* Artist Craftsmen New York; Am Craftsmens Coun; Craft Students League YWCA. *Mailing Add:* 345 E 52nd St New York NY 10022

ENGLE, CHET
PAINTER
b Danville, Ill, June 25, 18. *Study:* Am Acad Art, Chicago; Art Ctr Sch Design, Los Angeles. *Work:* Calif State Collection Art, Sacramento; Air Mus, Smithsonian Inst, Washington, DC. *Exhib:* Paintings in the United States, Carnegie Inst Fine Arts, Pittsburgh, 49; Los Angeles Co Mus, 47, 50 & 55; one-man shows, Cowie Gallery, Los Angeles, 58, Manhattan Gallery, Pasadena, 59 & 60 & Maxwell Galleries, San Francisco, 63. *Pos:* Instnl advert artist, Lockheed Aircraft Corp, Burbank, Calif, 50-73. *Awards:* First Prize, Servicemans Show, Butler Inst Art, Youngstown, Ohio, 43; First Prize, Calif State Exhib, Sacramento, 49. *Media:* Oil, Tempera. *Publ:* Illusr, Lockheed Horizons, 65-70. *Dealer:* Jones Gallery Green Dragon Colony La Jolla CA 92037; Taos Art Gallery Inc PO Box 1007 Taos NM 87571. *Mailing Add:* PO Box 267 Manchester CA 95459

ENGLE, STEVE (STEPHEN E)
SCULPTOR
b Honolulu, Hawaii, Dec 27, 50. *Study:* Santa Barbara Art Inst, Calif, BFA(sculpture), 71-73; Ind Univ, Bloomington, MFA(sculpture), 77-80; Pa Acad Fine Art, Philadelphia, figure painting class, 82-84. *Work:* Microsoft Corp, Redmond, Wash; First Hawaiian Bank, Honolulu; Wash State Arts Comn; Sch Dist, Lacey, Wash; Seattle Arts Comn. *Exhib:* Printmakers Ann, Honolulu Acad Art, Hawaii, 82; solo exhibs, Passing Through, 90 & Figurative Compulsions, 92, Lisa Harris Gallery, Seattle, Wash; From the Woods: Washington Wood Artists, Whatcom Mus, Bellingham, Wash State Univ, Pullman & Bellevue Art Mus, 91; Thirty Years of the Honolulu Advertiser Gallery 1961-1991, Honolulu Advertiser Gallery, 91; Exhibition 6, Microsoft Corp, Redmond, Wash, 92; Spirit of the West, A Celebration of the Arts, WestOne Bank, Wash, Ore & Idaho, 92. *Awards:* Visual Artists Fel Sculpture, Nat Endowment Arts, 90; Seattle Artists Proj Grant, Seattle Arts Comn, 90; Wash State Arts Comn Slide Registry, Olympia, 91. *Bibliog:* Karen Mathieson (auth), Passing through, Seattle Times, 3/29/90; Gretchen Faust (auth), Syncretism: art of the 21st century, Arts Mag, 5/91. *Dealer:* Lisa Harris Gallery 1922 Pike Place Seattle WA 98101. *Mailing Add:* 10807 41st Ave Seattle WA 98146

ENGLER, KATHLEEN GIRDLER
SCULPTOR
b Indianapolis, Ind, Jan 30, 51. *Study:* John Herron Sch Art, Ind Univ, 69-70; Univ Ga, 80; Med Col of Ga, 80; Augusta Col, BFA, 81. *Work:* Southern Bell Corp Collection, AFCO Corp Collection, Atlanta, Ga. *Comn:* Cultural Triad (bronze fountain), Maxwell Performing Arts Theater, Augusta, Ga, 86; Bronze Women of Excellence Awards, 88-92; The Graduate (bronze), Med Col of Ga, 89; Madame Butterfly (bronze), Augusta Opera, 91. *Exhib:* Sculpture by Indiana Artists, Indianapolis Mus Art, Ind, 84; Callanworde Art Ctr, Atlanta, Ga, 85; Ward-Nasse Gallery, New York, 88; Gertrude Herbert Art Inst, Augusta, Ga, 89; Altarpiece Exhib, Int Marian Res Inst, Dayton, Ohio, 92; 10th Anniversary Exhib, McIntosh Gallery, Atlanta, Ga, 92. *Media:* Bronze. *Dealer:* H L Stine Fine Arts Ltd Suite 2B Tula 75 Bennett St NW Atlanta GA 30309; Andries Van Dam Fine Arts Inc 2738 Devine St Columbia SC 29205. *Mailing Add:* 753 Aumond Rd Augusta GA 30909-3258

ENGLISH, HAL (HAROLD J ENGLISH)
PAINTER
b Buffalo, NY, Nov 21, 10. *Study:* Albright Art Sch, Univ Buffalo. *Exhib:* Pastels Only-Pastel Soc Am, Nat Arts Club, New York, 79-84 & 86-91, PSA Master Pastelist, 87; Pastels USA, Sacramento Fine Arts Ctr, Carmichael, Calif, 87-89 & 91; National Small Paintings Exhib, NMex Art League, Albuquerque, 82-90; Artists of America, Colo Hist Mus, Denver, 83 & 90; Ann Exhib-Oil Painters Am, Prince Gallery, Chicago, 92. *Pos:* Advert, 35-65. *Teaching:* Instr design, State Univ Col Buffalo, 65-66; artist-in-residence drawing, Hilbert Col, Hamburg, NY 74-76. *Awards:* Russell Award, Pastels Only, Pastel Soc Am, 80; Best of Show, Nat Small Paintings Exhib, NMex Art League, 82-83 & 89; Best of Show, 2nd Nat, Pastel Soc, NFla, 92. *Bibliog:* Dale C English & Pat Yungbluth (coauths), Hal English, Artists Rockies, 84. *Mem:* Pastel Soc Am; Acad Artists Asn; Fine Arts League Buffalo (pres, 90-92). *Media:* Pastel. *Mailing Add:* 136 Heather Hill Dr West Seneca NY 14224

ENGLISH, HELEN WILLIAMS DRUTT See Drutt, Helen Williams

ENGLISH, JOHN ARBOGAST
PAINTER
b Trenton, NJ, Nov 7, 13. *Study:* Trenton Sch Indust Art; Trenton State Col, BS. *Comn:* Numerous marine paintings & yacht portraits comn by pvt individuals. *Exhib:* Miami Int Boat Show Marine Exhib, 74-75; Am Soc Marine Artists Ann Show, 78-79; Greenwich Workshop Ann Marine Show, 79; Mystic Seaport Ann Marine Show, 79; 3rd Ann Exhib, Am Soc Marine Artists, 81; and others. *Pos:* Publ lithographic reproductions marine subj, Riverside Studio, Island Heights, NJ. *Awards:* Gold Medal, Franklin Mint; First Award Oil Painting, Ocean Co Artist Guild; Second in Show, Miami Int Boat Show Exhib. *Mem:* Ocean Co Artist Guild; Grove House, Miami; Am Soc Marine Artists. *Media:* Oil. *Dealer:* Newman Galleries 1625 Walnut St Philadelphia PA 19103. *Mailing Add:* 236 Ocean Ave Island Heights NJ 08732

ENMAN, TOM KENNETH
PAINTER, MUSEUM DIRECTOR
b Salt Lake City, Utah, Feb 22, 28. *Study:* Univ Wash, Exten, 48-49; Chicago Acad Fine Arts, cert, 52; Cape Sch Art, Provincetown, Mass, scholar, 52; Calif Col Arts & Crafts, Oakland, 53-54; Univ Calif, Los Angeles, Exten, 58-61; Laguna Beach Sch Art, Calif, 69; also with Alex Villumsion & Playa Del Ray, Calif, 62. *Exhib:* 19th Newport Ann, Newport Beach, Calif, 64; Laguna Beach Art Gallery Ann Fall Mem, 64; All Calif Exhib, Laguna Beach, 65; 7th Nat Ann Art Round Up, Las Vegas, 66; Laguna Beach Art Asn Graphic & Drawing Exhib, 67. *Pos:* Dir, Artist Guild Laguna Beach, 64-65; dir, Laguna Beach Mus Art, 65-80; consul, Plein Air Painters, 82 & 86. *Awards:* First in Graphic (pen & ink), 64 & hon mention in oil, 65, Laguna Beach Art Asn. *Mem:* Laguna Beach Art Asn (dir); Monterey Hist & Art Asn, Calif. *Media:* Oil, Watercolor. *Res:* American artist from 1890-1940. *Dealer:* Redfern Gallery 1540 South Coast Hwy Laguna Beach CA 92651; Maureen Murphy Fine Arts 1187 Coast Village Rd Montecito CA 93108. *Mailing Add:* 2160 S Coast Hwy Laguna Beach CA 92651

ENRIQUEZ, GASPAR
PAINTER, METALSMITH
b El Paso, Tex, July 18, 42. *Study:* East Los Angeles Jr Col; Univ Tex, El Paso, BA; printmaking with Loren Janzen & jewelry with Walt Harrison; NMex State Univ, metalsmithing with Kate Wagle & Peter Voris, MA. *Work:* State Nat Bank; Univ Tex, El Paso; NMex State Univ Gallery; Southwestern Bell. *Exhib:* Fresno Art Mus, 91; San Francisco Mus Art, 91; Albuquerque Mus, 91; Denver Art Mus, 91; Plains Art Mus, Fargo, NDak; Univ Minn Art Mus, Minneapolis; Nat Mus Am Art, Washington, DC; and others. *Awards:* Hon Mention, El Paso Designers Craftsmen, 79-80; Hon Mention, El Paso Int, 85; Juniors Award, Tex Fine Arts Asn Exhib, 87. *Mem:* Juntos Art Asn (pres); Int Designers Craftsman; Am Craft Coun. *Media:* Acrylic, Oil; Precious Metals. *Dealer:* Mi Casa Studio Gallery San Elizario TX 79849; Abbey Lane Gallery Box 27 Creed CO 81130. *Mailing Add:* Box 17112 El Paso TX 79917

ENSRUD, WAYNE
PAINTER, PRINTMAKER
b Albert Lea, Minn, Apr 4, 34. *Study:* Minneapolis Col Art & Design, BFA, 56; with Oskar Kokoschka, 56-79; with Ben Shahn, Joseph Albers & Vaclav Vitlacyl. *Work:* Bristol Mus Art, RI; New England Ctr Contemp Art, Brooklyn, Conn; French Inst Gallery, New York; Gallery Collection of the Governor of Trinidad, West Indies; Galleria of Contessa Borghese, Rome, Italy. *Comn:* Moses on Mt Sinai, Temple Emmanuel, Great Neck, NY, 77; life-size etched mirrors, Le Premier--Robert Pascal, New York, 77; engraved lucite wall, Nanni Il Valetto, New York, 78; The Last of the Blue Devils, Newport Jazz Festival, New York, 80; poster, Concert Management, New York, 80. *Exhib:* New England Ctr Contemp Art, Brooklyn, Conn, 81; Univ Conn, Storrs, 82; Buffalo Mus Sci, NY, 82; Slater Mus, Conn, 82; Old State House Mus, Hartford, Conn, 82; and others. *Pos:* Art dir, Univ Calif, Berkeley, 58-61; exec art dir, Channel 13 TV, New York, 64; art dir, Gemini Space Program, ABC, New York, 65-66. *Teaching:* Instr film animation, Pratt Inst, New York, 67-72; instr painting & drawing, Cumberland Sch, Great Neck, NY, 67-79; guest prof figure painting, Simon's Rock Early Col, Great Barrington, Mass, 78. *Awards:* Second Award in Oils, Christian Themes Lever House, 66. *Bibliog:* Monika Pichler (auth), Wayne Ensrud: Life of an artist, In: Work in Progress, 81. *Mem:* Coffee House Club. *Media:* Oil, Watercolor; Lithography, Etching. *Mailing Add:* 65 Central Park West New York NY 10023

ENSTICE, WAYNE
ASSEMBLAGE ARTIST, WRITER
b Irvington, NJ, Dec 16, 43. *Study:* Pratt Inst, BFA, 65; Univ NMex, MA, 69. *Work:* Univ NC, Chapel Hill; Univ Ark, Art Gallery, Fayetteville; Ariz Arts Comm, Phoenix; Roswell Mus & Art Ctr, NMex; Library of Congress, Washington, DC;; Tucson Art Museum, Ariz;; Univ NMex, Albuquerque. *Exhib:* Collage & Assemblage, Nat Touring Exhibit; Alternative Mus, New

York, 83; Diverse Works Gallery, Houston, 83; Drawing Ctr, New York, 84; SPACE Gallery, Los Angeles, 87 & 90; Ctr Contemp Art, Santa Fe, NMex, 87; Tacoma Art Mus, Wash, 88; Contemp SW Art, Roland Gibson Gallery, Potsdam, NY, 88; Univ Mont, Missoula, 89; 313 Gallery, New York, 92. *Teaching:* Prof, chmn, Dept Art, Ind State Univ, Terre Haute, 90. *Awards:* Artist-in-Residence Grant, Roswell Mus & Art Ctr, 84-85. *Bibliog:* Robert Murdock (auth), essay, Univ Ark Press, 79; William Peterson (auth), article, Artspace, 80; John Perreault (auth), rev, Art in Am, 81; Peter Frank (auth), essay, Roswell Mus & Art Ctr Catalog, 85. *Publ:* Auth, Performance Art's Coming of Age, Performance Art, Dutton Press, 84; Prologue: The Splash Factor, Re-Dact, Willis, Locker, Owens Press, 84; coauth, Drawing/Space, Form and Expression & Contemporary Drawing: 1986-1988, 90, Prentice-Hall; Jazz Spoken Here, La State Univ Press, 92. *Mailing Add:* RR 32 Box 701 Terre Haute IN 47803

ENTERLINE, SANDRA
JEWELER
b Oil City, Pa, 1960. *Study:* Rochester Inst Technol, Sch Am Craftsmen, AD, 80; RI Sch Design, BFA(jewelry & metalsmithing), 83. *Work:* Oakland Mus Art, Calif. *Exhib:* Quadrum Gallery, Chestnut Hill Mass, 87; Wita Gardiner Gallery, San Diego, Calif, 88; Am Craft Mus, New York, 88; Univ Tex, El Paso, 89; Drake Univ, Des Moines, Iowa; Americky Sperk (with catalog), Mus Decorative Arts, Prague, Czech, 91; Good as Gold, The Hand & The Spirit Gallery, Scottsdale, Ariz, 92. *Teaching:* Vis artist, Mass Col Art, Boston, 91; vis prof, Sch Mus Fine Arts, Boston, 91-92. *Awards:* Visual Arts Fel, Nat Endowment Arts, 88. *Publ:* Auth, article, Jewelers Circular Keystone, 1/86; Metalsmith Mag, Fall 88 & 91. *Dealer:* Susan Cummins Gallery 12 Miller Ave Mill Valley CA 94941. *Mailing Add:* c/o Susan Cummins Gallery 32 Miller Ave Mill Valley CA 94941

ENYEART, JAMES LYLE
HISTORIAN, DIRECTOR
b Auburn, Wash, Jan 13, 43. *Study:* Kansas City Art Inst, BFA, 65; Univ Santiago, Chile, cert(Orgn Am States Fel), 66-67; Univ Kans, MFA, 72. *Work:* Int Mus Photog, George Eastman House, Rochester, NY; Bibliot Nat, Paris, France; Sheldon Mem Gallery, Univ Nebr, Lincoln; Albrecht Mus Art, St Joseph, Mo; Nat Mus Am Art. *Comn:* Nineteenth Century archit of St Joseph, 74 & stained glass windows of St Joseph, 75, Albrecht Mus Art, St Joseph, Mo. *Pos:* Staff photog, Nelson Gallery Art, Kansas City, Mo, 65-66; charter dir, Albrecht Gallery Art, St Joseph, Mo, 67-68; cur photog, Helen Foresman Spencer Mus Art, Univ Kans, Lawrence, 68-76; dir, Ctr Creative Photog, Univ Ariz, 77-89, ed, The Archive, 77-89, Inter Mus Photog at Geo Eastman House, Rochester, 89-; leader hist sect, Rencontres Int de la Photog, Arles Festival, France, 79, Friends of Photog, Carmel, Calif, 76-77; consult, Polaroid Corp, 83-; ed, Image, 89- *Teaching:* Instr drawing & design, Mo Western State Col, Univ MO, 67-68; lectr art hist, Univ Kans, 68-70, asst prof, 69-75, assoc prof, 76, instr photog, 71-75; adj prof art, Univ Ariz, 77- *Awards:* Photokina Obelisk Award for photog contrib, Cologne, WGer, 82; John Simon Guggenheim Mem Fel, writing, 87; Josef Sudek Medal, Ministry of Culture, Prague, Czechoslovakia, 89. *Bibliog:* Bonnie Yochelson (auth), The picture is what you can do with the subject, Village Voice, 1/19/78; Photography's essential sixty, Am Photogr, 6/83; M Woodbridge Williams (auth), Enyeart Moves from CCP to Eastman House, Photo District News, 7/89. *Mem:* Nat Soc Photog Educ (bd dirs, 78-82); Friends Photog (exec dir, 76-77, vpres, 78-81). *Res:* Conservation and restoration of photographs; nineteenth and twentieth century photographers. *Publ:* Auth, Edward Weston's California Landscapes, New York Graphic Soc & Ctr Creative Photog, 84; introd to Andreas Feiginger: A Retrospective, Harry N Abrams, Inc, 86; Judy Dater: Twenty Years, Univ Ariz Press & Univ Santa Clara, 86; co-ed, Henry Holmes Smith: Collected Writings 1935-1985, Ctr Creative Photog, 86; ed, Decade by Decade: A Survey of Twentieth Century American Photography, Little Brown/Bullfinch Press, 89, Yasu Suzuka, Gallery Min, Tokyo, 91. *Mailing Add:* 6731 W Main Rd Lima NY 14485

EPSTEIN, BETTY O
SCULPTOR, PAINTER
b New York, NY, Oct 20, 20. *Study:* Pratt, Sch Visual Arts, BA-MA, 50; Paris with Hane Hoffman, Bur Hases & Herb Kallem. *Work:* Lavaggi Gallery, Roko GG Gallery, Sch Music & Arts, New York; Mus, Allentown, Pa; Am Cult Ctr, Tel Aviv, Beersheba Askelon, Jerusalem & Egypt. *Comn:* Ammand Hammer, New York, 80; Mus Mod Art, New York, 81. *Exhib:* Art Dirs, Art Educ of the Nation, Asken Sch Contemp Arts, 62; Allentown Art Mus, 63; Sculpture, Visual Arts, 67; Audabon Arts, 70; Art Exhib, Distelhein Gallery, Chicago, 91. *Awards:* Pauline How Prize, Sculpture, 83; Amelia Peabody Award, Sculpture, 84; Elsie Jack Key, Nat Arts Club, 92. *Mem:* Stone Sculpture Soc; VIP, Painters in Career & Acrylics; Contemp Artists Guild; bd mem, Nat Soc Women Artists; Painters & Sculptors, NJ. *Media:* All Media; Acrylic, Oil. *Mailing Add:* 39 Gramercy Park N New York NY 10010

EPSTEIN, MITCH (MITCHELL D)
PHOTOGRAPHER
b Holyoke, Mass, Aug 23, 52. *Study:* Union Col, Schenectady, NY, 70-71; RI Sch Design, 71-72; Cooper Union, New York, with Garry Winogrand, 72-74. *Work:* Australian Nat Gallery, Canberra; Bibliot Nat, Paris, France; Corcoran Mus Art, Washington, DC; Mus Mod Art, New York; Mus Fine Arts, Boston, Mass. *Exhib:* Recent Acquisitions, Boston Mus Fine Art, Mass, 80 & Corcoran Gallery Art, Washington, DC, 80; Creative Artists Public Service Program Photog Traveling Exhib, NY State, 80; The New Color, Int Ctr Photog, New York, 81; Color Photography, Mus Mod Art, New York, 84 & 87; Addison Ripley Gallery, Washington, DC, 85; Hallmark Photog Collection, Wanderlust, Kans City, Mo, 87; Contemp Group Am Photog, Cult Palace, Canton, China, 88; one-man shows, Galerie Watari, Tokyo, Japan, Lieberman & Saul Gallery, 87, Burden Gallery, New York, 88, Sandra Berler Gallery, Washington, DC, 88, Santa Barbara Mus Art, Calif, 89, Fogg Art Mus, Cambridge, Mass, 91, Cleveland Mus Art, Ohio, 91; The Indomitable Spirit, Int Ctr Photog, New York, 90; Romance of the Taj Mahal, Los Angeles Co Mus Art, Calif, 90-91; Reveries and Wanderings, Metrop Life Insurance Co Gallery, New York, 91. *Teaching:* Lectr color photog, Carpenter Ctr, Harvard Univ, 77. *Awards:* Individual Photog Grant, Nat Endowment Arts, 78 & NY State Coun Arts, 80. *Bibliog:* Klaus Fabricius & Red saunders (auth), 24-Hour in the Life of Los Angeles, Alfred Van der Marck Editions, 84; Mitch Epstein (auth), In Pursuit of India, Aperture, 87; photog, Caribbean Wind, Jonathan Cape, London, 12/91. *Publ:* Contribr, The New Color, 81 & Annie On Camera, 82, Abbeville Press. *Dealer:* Lieberman & Saul Gallery 155 Spring St W Broadway New York NY 10001. *Mailing Add:* 6 Rivington St No 2 New York NY 10002

EPSTEIN, YALE
PAINTER, PRINTMAKER
b New Haven, Conn, Jan 26, 34. *Study:* Brooklyn Mus Art Sch, 55-58 & Rosenthal Scholar, 59; Brooklyn Col with A O Reinhardt & Marc Rothko, MFA, 58; Pratt Graphics Ctr, 72-75. *Work:* Brooklyn Mus, NY; Albright-Knox Gallery, Buffalo, NY; Biblioteque Nat, Paris, France; City of Chicago; Univ Wis; Yale Univ. *Comn:* Hyatt Hotel, New York, NY; Marriot Hotel, Palm Springs, Calif. *Exhib:* Art 14, Basel Int, Switz, 83 & 90; Prints USA, Univ Wis, La Crosse; Woodstock Artists Asn; Hudson River Mus, Yonkers, NY; Brooklyn Col. *Teaching:* Instr art, Brooklyn Col, NY, 76-83 & Sch Visual Arts, 82-90. *Awards:* First Prize Graphics, Hudson River Mus, 84. *Bibliog:* Rev, Print Collector's Newslett, 9/81. *Mem:* Nat Art Educ Asn; Col Art Asn; Artists Equity; Woodstock Artists Asn. *Media:* Pastel; Etching, Serigraph. *Publ:* Auth, article, Art J, Col Art Asn, winter 67-68; Tom Boutis, rev, Arts Mag, 6/80; Artspeak, 6/16/88; Aspects of Nature, Domberger Stuttgart WGer Publ, 90. *Dealer:* Orion Editions 270 Lafayette St New York NY 10012; Summa Gallery 527 Amsterdam Ave New York NY 10024. *Mailing Add:* 135 Hudson St New York NY 10013

EPTING, MARION AUSTIN
PRINTMAKER, EDUCATOR
b Forrest, Miss, Jan 28, 40. *Study:* Los Angeles City Col, AA; Los Angeles Co Art Inst, Otis, MFA, 69; also with Ernest Freed, Lee Chesney, Shiro Ikegawa & Charles White. *Work:* Oakland Mus, Calif; Seattle Art Mus; Libr Cong, Washington, DC; Achenbach Found, DeYoung Mus, San Francisco; Whitney Mus, New York; Smithsonian Inst; and others. *Comn:* Intaglio prints comn by John Wilson, Lakeside Studios, Mich, 72 & 74. *Exhib:* 1st Nat Print Exhib, San Diego Fine Arts Soc, 69; Northwest Printmakers, Seattle Art Mus, 69; Oakland Art Mus, 73; traveling exhib, Western Asn Art Mus, 73-75; Smithsonian Inst Traveling Exhibs, 80-84. *Collections Arranged:* Black Untitled III, Western Asn Art Mus; Chico Group, Old Bergen Art Guild, NJ. *Pos:* Resident artist, Lakeside Studios, Mich, 70-; art dir, J-Squared B-Squared Consult, Los Angeles, 71- *Teaching:* Prof art, Calif State Univ, Chico, 69- *Awards:* Calif South 7 Best of Show, San Diego Fine Arts Guild, 69; Northwest Printmakers Purchase Award, Seattle Art Mus, 69; First Place for Graphics, Cal Expo, Del Mar, Calif, 69. *Bibliog:* J Edward Atkinson (auth), Black Dimensions in Contemporary American Art, Times Mirror, 71; Theresa Dickason Cederholm (auth), Afro American Artists, Boston Pub Libr, 73; Wadpy Lewis (auth), Art: African American, Harcourt Brace Jovanovich, 78. *Media:* Intaglio, Serigraphy. *Mailing Add:* Art Dept Calif State Univ Chico CA 95929

ERBE, GARY THOMAS
PAINTER
b Union City, NJ, Sept 2, 44. *Study:* Self-taught. *Work:* Butler Inst Am Art, Youngstown, Ohio; New Britain Mus Am Art, Conn; NJ State Mus, Trenton; Montclair Art Mus, NJ; Woodmere Art Mus, Philadelphia, Pa. *Exhib:* Solo Exhibs, Summit Art Center, NJ, 76, New Britain Mus Am Art, Conn, 76, Alexander Gallery, New York, 82 & 85, NJ State Mus, Trenton (with catalog), 83, Butler Inst Am Art, Youngstown, Ohio (with catalog), 85 & Sordini Art Gallery, 85; Newark Mus, NJ, 76, Montclair Art Mus, NJ, Canton Art Inst, Ohio, Westmoreland Mus, Pa, Woodmere Art Mus (with catalog), Philadelphia, 88; 163rd Ann Inv, Nat Acad Design, New York; Baseball Hall Fame, Cooperstown, NY, 91; NJ Fine Arts Ann, Noyes Mus, Oceanville, 92. *Awards:* Julius Hallsarten Award, Nat Acad Design, New York, 75; Gold Medal of Honor, 75 & 84, John-Young Hunter Mem Award, 82 & 86, Allied Artists Am, New York; Gold Medal of Honor, Allied Artists Am, NY, 91. *Bibliog:* Levitational realism, Am Artist, 74; Gary T Erbe, Arts Mag, 82; An artist who captures the eye, then the mind, New York Times, 83; Local heroes, NJ Monthly, 84. *Mem:* Allied Artists Am; Assoc Artists NJ; Conn Acad Fine Arts; Audubon Artists. *Media:* Oil. *Publ:* NY Art Review & Am Artists, Krantz Pub. *Dealer:* Alexander Gallery 996 Madison Ave New York NY 10021. *Mailing Add:* 539 42nd St Union City NJ 07087

ERBE, JOAN
PAINTER
b Baltimore, Md, Nov 1, 26. *Study:* Md Inst Col Art. *Work:* Munic Court, Washington, DC; Peale Mus, Baltimore; Baltimore Mus Art; Morgan Col. *Exhib:* Peale Mus, 51-61; seven shows, Baltimore Mus Art, 54-65; Smithsonian Inst, 56; Corcoran Gallery Art, 57-60; 20 one-person shows, IFA Galleries, Washington, DC, 58-82; Butler Inst Am Art, 60 & 61; Am Acad Arts, 76; Acad Arts, Easton, Md, 86; Rehoboth Art League, 87; Partners Gallery, Bethesda, Md, 88. *Teaching:* Pvt lessons, 70- *Awards:* Artists Equity Asn, 60 & 61; Corcoran Gallery Art, 60 & 62; Baltimore Mus Art, 63, 64 & 66; plus others. *Media:* All media. *Dealer:* Nye Gomez Gallery 836 Leaden Hall St Baltimore MD 21230; Originals An Art Gallery Del Mar Plaza Del Mar CA 92014. *Mailing Add:* 103 Woodlawn Rd Baltimore MD 21210

ERBES, ROSLYN MARIA See Rensch, Roslyn

ERDELAC, JOSEPH MARK
COLLECTOR, PATRON
b Cleveland, Ohio. *Exhib:* Ohio Collectors, A Nations Legacy, Toung, Japan. *Mem:* Life mem Cleveland Mus Art, Butler Inst Am Art, Youngstown, Ohio & Royal Photographic Soc Brit. *Interests:* Donor of art works to local and national museums, universities, schools and educational television. *Collection:* Oils, watercolors and graphics by local and national Washington Project for the Arts artists; oils, watercolors, drawings and graphics by Rockwell Kent; watercolors, drawings and collages by Stephen Longstreet; also work by Henry Miller, Charles Bukowski, Kenneth Patchen and Udinotti. *Mailing Add:* 19630 Center Ridge Rd Cleveland OH 44116

ERDLE, ROB
PAINTER, EDUCATOR
b Selma, Calif, Aug 17, 49. *Study:* Reedley Col, Calif, AA; Calif State Univ, Fresno, BA; Bowling Green Univ, Ohio, MFA. *Exhib:* Ala Nat Watercolor Exhib, Birmingham Mus Art, 75-76; Toledo May Show, Toledo Mus Art, Ohio, 75-76; Southern Watercolorist Nat Exhib, Cheekwood Arts Ctr, Nashville, Tenn, 77; Rocky Mountain Nat Watercolor Exhib, Foothills Arts Ctr, Golden, Colo, 77; one-man show, Del Mar Col, Corpus Christi, Tex, 77; Tex Fine Arts Nat Exhib, Laguna Gloria Art Mus, Austin, 77; and others. *Pos:* Dir, Chautauqua Inst Art Gallery, Chautauqua, NY, currently. *Teaching:* Asst prof watercolor works on paper, NTex State Univ, 76-80, assoc prof, 80- *Awards:* Outstanding Painting Award, May Show, Toledo Mus Art, 75 & 76; First Prize Purchase Award, Ala Nat Watercolor Exhib, Birmingham Mus Art, 76; Watercolor USA, Springfield Art Mus, 77. *Mem:* Nat Watercolor Soc, Los Angeles; Tex Watercolor Soc, San Antonio; Watercolor Soc Ala, Birmingham; Southern Watercolor Soc, Memphis; Southwestern Watercolor Soc, Dallas. *Media:* Mixed. *Mailing Add:* Dept Art North Tex State Univ Denton TX 76203

ERES, EUGENIA
PAINTER
b Winiza, Ukrania, Apr 28, 28; US citizen. *Study:* Fine Art Sch, Sao Paulo, Brazil, with Prof Murillo, 54-58; Famous Artists Sch, Westport, Conn, with Norman Rockwell, Fletcher Martin & Doug Kingman, 66-69; Nat Acad Fine Arts, New York, with Hugh Cumpel, 70-71. *Work:* Galleria de Artes IV Centenario, Sao Paulo; Russian Am Hist Mus, Lakewood, NJ; pvt collection of Jacqueline Kennedy-Onassis, H Bartow Farr Jr Dep Gen Counsel, and others. *Exhib:* One-man show, Galleria de Artes IV Centenario, Sao Paolo, Brazil, 56-58, Int Art Expo New York Coliseum, 83-85, Int Art Expo, Wash, DC, 83, Hommond Mus North Salem, NY, 68; Am Artists Prof League Grand Nat, 68-89; Nat Art League, New York, 74-81; Knickerbocker Artists, 74-81; Hudson Valley, 76-89; Pen & Brush, 77-79; Salmagundi Club, 77-78; Custom House Mus Area, World Trade Ctr, New York, 79-81; Le Salon des Nations, Paris, 83. *Awards:* First Prize, Russian Am Soc, 75-78; Gold Medal of Honor, Nat Art League, 77; Gold Medal, Accademia Italia, 79; and others. *Mem:* Life fel Am Artists Prof League; Knickerbocker Artists; Nat Art League; Catharine Lorillard Wolfe Art Club; Accademia Italia; Hudson Valley Art Asn. *Media:* Oil, Lithographs. *Interests:* Traditional impressionist. *Mailing Add:* 109-10 Park Line S No 810 Richmond Hill NY 11418

ERICKSON, JOY M
PAINTER, GRAPHIC ARTIST
b Princeton, Ill, June 18, 32. *Study:* Northern Ill Univ, with Jack McCarthy, 61; Univ Ill, with William J Kennedy, 62. *Work:* Rotunda, United Methodist Bldg, Capitol Hill, Washington, DC; Funderburg Libr, Manchester Col, North Manchester, Ind; Everett Free Libr, Pa; Int Serv Ctr, Md. *Comn:* Beauty in Aging, mural, comn by the directors, Fahrney Keedy Chapel, Boonesboro, Md, 73; Ashton 1910, hist mural, Ashton Hist Soc, Ill, 74; portrait of Dorothy Johnson, comn by Dr John Baker, Juniata Col, Huntingdon, Pa, 89; portrait, Elizabeth Baker, comn by John Baker, Ohio Univ, Athens, 91; portrait, Dr C C Ellis, comn by Dr Calvert N Ellis for Juniata Col, Huntingdin, Pa, 92; portrait, H B Brumbaugh, comn by Harold Brumbaugh for Juniata Col, Huntingdin, Pa, 92. *Exhib:* Images of Refugees, Rotunda, Cannon Bldg, Washington, DC, 82; Nat Asn Women Artists, Jacob Javitts Fed Bldg, New York City, 85, 86 & 89; Women Artists Invitational, Hodson Gallery, Hood Col, Frederick, Md, 86; Nabisco Figurative Show, Corporate Gallery, Morristown, NJ, 87; NAPCA, Nat Arts Club, New York, 86, 87 & 90; Arts Invitational, City Hall Gallery, Frederick, Md, 88. *Pos:* Pres & publ ed, Nat Asn for the Arts, Elgin, Ill, 73-83; interim dir arts & relig, Church of the Brethren, Elgin, Ill, 77-78; vpres communs, NRPRC of Washington, DC, 83-86. *Awards:* Sauk Valley Col Best of Show, Town & Co Arts, 67, 68 & 69; Best of Show, Phidian Art Club Ann Exhib, 71; Northern Ill Univ Blue Ribbon, Town & Country Dist. *Bibliog:* David Boul (auth), Find out about refugees in art, Baltimore Sun, 12/11/81; Susan Mix Schank (auth), Art that reflects the spirit, Church Woman, 12/86; Linda Greely (auth), Fine arts highlight invitational, Frederick News Post, 5/88. *Mem:* Nat Asn Painters in Casein and Acrylic; Nat Asn Women Artists. *Media:* Acrylic. *Publ:* Auth, In Straw and Story, 77, illusr, A is for Angels, 78 & ed, Let Not the Music that is in Us Die, 78, Brethren Press. *Dealer:* G L Gannett 3652 Allenwood St Sarasota FL 34232. *Mailing Add:* 3652 Allenwood St Sarasota FL 34232

ERICKSON, MARGARET JANE See Goodwill, Margaret

ERICKSON, MARK D
PAINTER
b Hollywood, Calif, 1955. *Study:* Art Ctr Col Design, Los Angeles, Calif, 68-70; Ore Sch Arts & Crafts, Portland, Ore, 83-84. *Exhib:* Contemporary Wood '90, Banaker Gallery, Walnut Creek, Calif, 90; The Shapes & Colors of Wood 1990, ACCI Gallery, Berkeley, Calif, 90; solo exhibs, New Work, Meredith Gallery, Baltimore, Md, 90, Western Colo Ctr Arts, Grand Junction, Colo, 92; Top of the Table, Virginia Breier Gallery, 90, Calif Crafts Mus, Ghiradelli Sq, San Francisco, Calif, 92; Benchmark: Studio Furniture for the Nineties, travelling exhib, 90; Multimedia Southwest, Ten Arrow Gallery, Cambridge, Mass, 90; Richmond Art Ctr, Calif, 90-91; New American Furniture, Oakland Mus, Calif, 91; Gallery Fair, Mendocino, Calif, 90 & 92. *Teaching:* Ore Sch Arts & Crafts, Portland, 84-85; lectr & woodshop technician, 85-90. *Awards:* Nat Endowment Arts, 88; First Place: Golden Bear Award, Calif Works, Sacramento, 88; First Place Award, Sun Gallery Exhib, Hayward, Calif, 88. *Media:* Acrylic. *Publ:* Numerous articles in various magazines, 86-90. *Mailing Add:* 722 W Mesa Ave Grand Junction CO 81505

ERICKSON, MARSHA A
DIRECTOR, ADMINISTRATOR
b Ancon, Panama, Feb 1, 45; US citizen. *Study:* Univ Hawaii, Manoa, 63-65. *Exhib:* Hawaiian Quilts, Mus Am Folk Art, New York, 78. *Pos:* Founder, Volcano Art Ctr, Hawaii, 74, prog dir, 74-81, exec dir, 81-86; Kokée Natural Hist Mus, 87- *Bibliog:* Thelma & Jay Newman (auths), Container Book, 77 & Barbara Stephan (auth), Decorations for Holidays & Celebrations, 78, Crown Publ. *Mem:* Arts Coun of Hawaii (mem bd, 85-86); State Found on Cult & Arts (comt mem, 80-86); Nat Asn Interpretation; co-founder, Hawaii Environ Educ Asn. *Res:* Intersection of arts and sciences. *Specialty:* Hawaiian landscapes, cultures and world views. *Publ:* Ed, The Volcano Gazette, Volcano Art Ctr, 74-84. *Mailing Add:* Kokee Nat Hist Mus PO Box 400 Waimea Kauai HI 96796

ERICSON, BEATRICE
PAINTER
b Paris, France; US citizen. *Study:* With Morris Davidson & Boris Margo, Provincetown, Mass; also with Max Schnitzler, New York. *Work:* NY Univ Fine Arts; Marist Col, Poughkeepsie, NY; Miami Mus Mod Art; Gov Nelson A Rockefeller Collection. *Exhib:* Silvermine Guild Artists, New Canaan, Conn; Norfolk Mus Arts & Sci; one-man shows, Letters to the Unknown, Brata Gallery, 67, Archaic Past, Caravan House, 72 & 77 & Gallery 84, 81, 83 & 88, New York. *Bibliog:* Leo Soretsky (auth), article, FM Guide, 4/72; Leo Soretsky (auth), article, FM Guide, 4/72; ArtSpeak, 10/81; Park E, 10/81. *Media:* Acrylics, Ink. *Dealer:* Gallery 84 50 W 57th St New York NY 10021. *Mailing Add:* 14 Watkins Ave Middletown NY 10940

ERICSON, KATE See Ziegler, Mel(vin) and Kate Ericson

ERIKSEN, GARY
SCULPTOR, MEDALIST
b Jackson, Mich, Sept 11, 43. *Study:* Oberlin Col, BA, 66; Kent State Univ, MA, 68; Univ Chicago, 71-73; Accad Belle Arti Roma, 73-77; Scuola Dell'Arte Medaglia, Rome, dipl licenza, 77. *Work:* Nat Gallery Art, Budapest; Smithsonian Inst Numismatics Collection; Cooper-Hewitt Mus; Zecca Roma, Italy; Am Numismatic Soc, New York. *Comn:* American Eagle, Kurt Wayne Inc, New York, 80; Church God in Christ, New York & Memphis, 81; thirty bas-relief portraits, Basketball Hall Fame, Springfield, Mass, 85; Gate Relief, Erasmus Hall High Sch, Brooklyn, NY, 87. *Exhib:* Fedn Int Editeurs Medailles Int Biennial, Palazzo Medici Riccardi, Florence, 83; First Ann Open Sculpture Exhib, Salmagundi Club, New York, 82; Carnegie Mansion Embellishments, Cooper-Hewitt Mus, New York, 83; Am Numismatic Asn, Colorado Springs, 87. *Pos:* Consult hand tools design, Sculpture House Inc, New York, 81-82. *Awards:* First Prize, Salmagundi Club First Ann Open Sculpture Exhib, 82; Fountains Proj Grant, NY State Coun Arts, 82. *Bibliog:* Ed Reiter (auth), article, New York Times, 8/15/82. *Mem:* Am Medallic Sculpture Asn (pres, 82-83, mem bd dirs, 82-87); Col Art Asn; Visual Artists & Galleries Asn. *Media:* Bronze, Terra Cotta. *Publ:* Illus, Village Voice, 5/1/84; auth, Alex Ettl, master artisan, Sculpture Rev, Fall 84; co-auth, Medals to the fore, Sculpture Rev, Fall 86. *Mailing Add:* PO Box 3994 New York NY 10163

ERLA, KAREN
PAINTER, PRINTMAKER
b Pittsburgh, Pa, Nov 17, 42. *Study:* Carnegie Tech, 58-59; Boston Univ, 60-62; George Washington Univ, Washington, DC, BFA, 65; Parsons Sch Design, NY, 79-81; Pratt Inst, NY, 80-82; independent study with printmaker John Ross, 80-82; New York Univ, 83. *Work:* Metrop Mus Art & Brooklyn Mus Art, NY; Philadelphia Mus Art, Pa; Los Angeles Co Mus Art, Calif; Baltimore Mus Art, Md; Australian Nat Gallery. *Comn:* Three large canvases, Gen Elec Co, New York, 85. *Exhib:* Group exhib, Fay Gold Gallery, Atlanta, 87; Boston Printmakers 37th Nat Exhib, Mass, 85; Jane Voorhees Zimmerli Mus, New Brunswick, NJ, 85; Fine Arts Mus Long Island, Hempstead, NY, 85; Int Miniature Exhib, Printmaking Coun NJ, North Branch Sta, 85; Women's Studio, Rosedale, NY, 85; Works on Paper, Nat Mus Am Art, Washington, DC, 85; solo exhib, E L Stark Gallery, New York, 88, Bennett-Siegal Gallery, New York, 90 & Queens Col, New York, 91; Australian Nat Gallery, 89. *Bibliog:* Sasha Grishin (auth), Collection has world significance, Canberra Times, 8/5/89; Jane Wollman (auth), New Yorker to watch: An artist on the move, Newsday, 9/10/89; International Print Acquisitions 1985-1989 (article), Australian Nat Gallery, 5-10/89. *Mem:* Los Angeles Printmaking Soc; Printmaking Coun NJ; World Print Coun; Col Art Asn. *Media:* Mixed. *Dealer:* Van Straaten Gallery 361 W Superior St Chicago IL 60610; E L Stark Gallery New York. *Mailing Add:* Old Orchard St White Plains NY 10604

ERLEBACHER, MARTHA MAYER
PAINTER
b Jersey City, NJ, Nov 21, 37. *Study:* Gettysburg Col, Pa, 55-56; Pratt Inst, Brooklyn, NY, BID, 60, MFA, 63. *Work:* Philadelphia Mus Fine Art, Pa; Pa Acad Fine Arts; Art Inst Chicago, Ill; NJ State Mus, Trenton; Libr Congress, Washington, DC. *Comn:* Portrait, Most Reverend Joseph McShea, Allentown, Pa, 80; portrait, Dr Eric Walker, Pa State Univ, State Col, 81; portrait, Dr William Hagerty, Drexel Univ, Philadelphia, Pa, 84; portrait, Drs Hilary & Irena Koprowski, comn by family, Wynnewood, Pa, 89; portrait, Dr Willys Silvers, Univ Pa Med Sch, Philadelphia, 90. *Exhib:* Philadelphia-Three Centuries Am Art, Philadelphia Mus Art, Pa, 76; Contemp Am Realism Since 1960, Pa Acad Fine Arts, Philadelphia, 81; Representational Drawing Today: A Heritage Renewed, Univ Art Mus, Santa Barbara, Calif, 83; Am Realism: 20th Century Drawings & Watercolors from the Glenn C Janss Collection, San Francisco Mus Mod Art, Calif, 85-86; Philadelphia Collects Art Since 1940, Philadelphia Mus Art, Pa, 86; Modern Myths, Boise Gallery Art, Idaho, 87; Realism Today: American Drawings from the Rita Rich Collection, Nat Acad Design, New York, 87-88; The Figure, Ark Arts Center, Little Rock, 89-90. *Teaching:* Univ Arts, Philadelphia, 66- *Awards:* Ingram Merritt Found Grant, 78; Sr Fel, Nat Endowment Arts, 82; Pa Coun Arts, Fel visual arts, 88. *Bibliog:* Anne D'Harmoncourt (auth), Philadelphia: Three Centuries Am Art, Philadelphia Mus Art, Pa, 76; Frank H Goodyear, Jr (auth), Contemp Am Realism Since 1960, NY Graphic Soc, 81; Charles Jencks (auth) Past Modernism, the New Classisism in Art and Achit, Rizzoli, NY, 87. *Media:* Oil. *Dealer:* Koplin Gallery 1438 Ninth St Santa Monica CA 90401; J Rosenthal Fine Arts Ltd 230 W Superior Chicago IL 60610. *Mailing Add:* 7733 Mill Rd Elkins Park PA 19117

ERMAN, BRUCE
PAINTER, EDUCATOR
b Los Angeles, Calif, Mar 14, 45. *Study:* Univ Calif, Berkeley & Los Angeles, BArch, 63-69; San Francisco Art Inst, 75-76; Calif Col Arts & Crafts, Oakland, with Arthur Okamura, Jason Schoener & Ronald Dahl, MFA, 75-79. *Work:* Clorox Corp, Oakland, Calif; Calif Col Arts & Crafts, Oakland; Davidson Col, Davidson, NC. *Comn:* Nicacio Elementary School Mural, 82 & Black Mountain Theatre, 83, comn by Youth-in-Arts, Greenbrae, Calif; Favorite Toy & Under the Sea (murals), comn by San Francisco Montessori Sch, Calif, 81; Alamo Square Victorians (mural), comn by Synergy Sch, San Francisco, 90-91. *Exhib:* One-person exhibs, Time Pieces, Calif Col Arts & Crafts, Oakland, 77, New Work, Davidson Col Art Gallery, NC, 80, Dwellings and Details, San Mateo Co Arts Coun, Belmont, Calif, 81, New Work-The Same Old Paintings, Art Space, Clark Co Community Col, Las Vegas, Nev, 83, New Work, Valley Art Gallery, Walnut Creek Art Ctr, Calif, 85 & Unreal Estate, Christa Faut Gallery, Davidson, NC, 91; Rainbow Show, De Young Mus Art, San Francisco, Calif, 75; All California '84, Laguna Beach Mus Art, Calif; Layering/Connecting, Zanesville Art Ctr, Ohio & Stifel Fine Arts Ctr, Wheeling, WVa, 87; 27th Ann, Fairfield, Calif, 89; and others. *Pos:* Guest cur, Calif Col Arts & Crafts, Oakland, 77 & Chabot Col, Hayward, 80, Calif. *Teaching:* Lectr painting, Calif Col Arts & Crafts, Oakland, 79 & 85, exten fac, dept painting, 83-87. *Awards:* First Prize Painting, Univ Calif Los Angeles, Westwood, 64; Jurors Award, Fairfield, Calif, 27th Ann, 89. *Bibliog:* Thomas Albright (auth), The crock at the end, Currant Mag, 75; Cathy Curtis (auth), Undeveloped premises, Artweek, 82; Harriet Leman (auth), Bruce Erman-Paintings (calendar), Montalvo Ctr Arts, Saratoga, Calif, 82. *Mem:* Col Art Asn, New York; San Mateo Co Arts Coun, Belmont, Calif. *Media:* All. *Publ:* Art Workshop, Berkeley Monthly, 74; Introduction to Woodcarving Tools, Whole Earth Epiloque & Co-Evolution Quar, 74. *Dealer:* Christa Faut Gallery Davidson NC 28036; San Francisco Mus Mod Art Rental Gallery Bldg A Ft Mason San Francisco CA 94123. *Mailing Add:* 546 Shotwell San Francisco CA 94110

ERMAN, GERALDINE
SCULPTOR
Study: Wayne State Univ, Detroit, Mich, BFA, 75; Cranbrook Acad Art, Bloomfield Hills, Mich, MFA, 78. *Exhib:* One-woman shows, Space Framed IV, Harvard Grad Sch Design, 87, Kingsborough Col Gallery, Brooklyn, NY, 89, Petrosino Park, outdoor installation, Lower Manhattan Cult Coun & NYSCA, 90, Watson Gallery, Wheaton Col, Mass, 93; Boston Now Ten, Inst Contemp Art, Boston, 91; The Pop Body, Sally Hawkins Gallery, New York, 92; Emerging Sculptors, Sculpture Ctr, New York, 92. *Teaching:* Vis artist, RI Sch Design, 85 & 91, Sarah Lawrence Col, 90, Temple Univ/Tyler Sch Art, Rome, 91; instr 3-D design, Cooper Union Sch Art, 92. *Awards:* Fel Grant Sculpture, Nat Endowment Arts, 86; Pollock-Krasner Found, 88-89; Rome Prize Fel Sculpture, Am Acad in Rome, 90-91. *Bibliog:* Peter Walsh (auth), A Delicate Balance, rev, Art New Eng, 5/90; Roberta Smith (auth), Three Group Shows, NY Times, 5/92; Catherine Liu (auth), The Pop Body, Flash Art, 10/92. *Mailing Add:* 91 Java St Brooklyn NY 11222

ERNSTROM, ADELE MANSFIELD
HISTORIAN
b Scranton, Pa, June 25, 30. *Study:* Univ Utah; Univ Calif, Los Angeles, BA, PhD. *Pos:* Co-ed, RACAR (Revue d'art canadienne/Canadian Art Review), 90-93. *Teaching:* Asst prof, Hamline Univ, St Paul, Minn, 66-68; asst prof, State Univ NY Col, Brockport, 68-71; asst & assoc vis prof, Univ Guelph, Ont, Can, 75-77; assoc prof & chairperson, Bishop's Univ, Lennoxville, Que, 77-82, prof, 82- & chairperson, 82-88, 90-92. *Awards:* Am Coun Learned Soc One-Yr Res Fel, 71-72; Res Grants, Bishop's Univ, 79 & 80; Social Scis & Humanities Res Coun Can Grant, 83 & 85; and others. *Mem:* Col Art Asn; Univ Art Asn of Can. *Res:* History of art history and criticism, including contributions of women; the work of Anna Jameson. *Publ:* Auth, John Sell Cotman, Brit Mus Publ, 78; co-ed (with M Y Ashcroft), John Sell Cotman in the Cholmeley Archive, Co Rec Off, Northallerton, Yorkshire, Eng, 80; co-ed & auth, Women as Interpreters of the Visual Arts, 1820-1979, Greenwood Press, 81; auth, Anna Jameson: The first professional English art historian, Art Hist, 83; Anna Jameson on Women Artists, Woman's Art J 87/88; Equally Lenders and Borrowers in Turn: The Working and Married Lives of the Eastlakes, Art Hist, 93. *Mailing Add:* c/o Dept Fine Arts Bishop's Univ Lennoxville PQ J1M 1Z7 Canada

ERTMAN, EARL LESLIE
HISTORIAN, EDUCATOR
b Parma, Ohio, Nov 13, 32. *Study:* Univ Southern Miss, BS, 65; Case Western Reserve Univ, MA, 67; Cleveland Mus, Egyptian art with John D Cooney, 67-71; Univ Akron, classics with T T Duke, 67-70. *Pos:* Art historian & field photogr, Johns Hopkins Exped to pyramid area, Giza, Egypt, summer 72 & 74, Tell el Rataba, 78; art historian/site supervisor, Univ Ariz, Egyptian Exped to W Valley of the King's, summer 92. *Teaching:* Instr Western art, Dept Art Hist & Educ, Cleveland Mus Art, 65-67; prof art hist, Univ Akron, 67-, dir sch art, 81- *Bibliog:* Edward K Werner (auth), The Amarna period of 18th dynasty Egypt, bibliography supplement, 76, Am Res Ctr Egypt Newsletter, Numbers 101-102, 77; Pauline Albenda (auth), Landscape bas-reliefs in the Bit-Hilani of Ashurbanipal, Am Sch Oriental Res Bulletin, 77; Arielle Kozloff (auth), Nefertiti beloved of the living disk, Bulletin Cleveland Mus Art, 11/77. *Mem:* Egypt Explor Soc; Archaeol Inst Am; Am Res Ctr Egypt; Int Asn Egyptologists; Soc Study Egyptian Antiquities, Toronto. *Res:* Iconographic and stylistic analysis of ancient Egyptian and Urartian art documentation of these objects in personal and public collections. *Publ:* Auth, The oldest known three-dimensional representation of the God Ptah, J Near Eastern Studies, 72; A manuscript fragment by the Parisian miniaturist Honore in Cleveland, Ohio, Sciptorium, Paris-Brussels, 73;; The cap-crown of Nefertiti: Its function and probable origin, J Am Res Ctr Egypt, 76; contribr, Recording & documentation of minor collections in the United States, 1st Int Cong Egyptology, Inst Hist & Archaeol, Munich, 76; Is There Visual Evidence of A King Nefertiti?, Amarna Letters, II, fall 92; and others. *Mailing Add:* Sch Art Univ Akron Akron OH 44325

ERVIN, KATHEY
CERAMIST
b Raymond, Wash, Nov 10, 52. *Study:* Peinsula Col, 72-74; Kansas City Art Inst, BFA (ceramic art), 81; Univ Ill, Champaign-Urbana, MFA, 83. *Exhib:* Solo exhib, Merwin Gallery, Ill Wesleyan Univ, Bloominton, Ill, 85; Pewabic Pottery, Detroit, Mich, 85, 86 & 87; A Spote O' Tea, The Clayhouse, Santa Monica, Calif, 87; Dinner at Eight, Gallery Eight, La Jolla, Calif, 87; At the Table, Soc Arts & Crafts, Boston, Mass, 87; The Teapot: Form & Functions, Artworks, Seattle, Wash, 87; The form of Fuction, Nat Clay Invitational, Creative Arts Workshop, New Haven, Conn, 88; Form and Fuction: Teapots, Craft Alliance, St Louis, Mo, 88. *Teaching:* Instr, Kansas City Art Inst, Mo, 79-81, Thornburn Community Ctr, Champaign, Ill, 83, Penland Arts & Craft Ctr, NC, 91. *Awards:* Creative & Performing Arts Fel, Univ Ill, 81-83; Nat Endowment Arts Grant, 86. *Bibliog:* Article, Am Craft Mag, 12/86; Art, money and the NEA, Ceramics Monthly, 2/87; Kathey Ervin (auth), Limitations adn focus, Ceramics Monthly, 2/88. *Mailing Add:* 330 Carlsborg Rd Sequim WA 98382

ERWIN, FRAN (FRANCES SUZANNE)
PAINTER
b Stockton, Calif. *Study:* St Mary's Col, Walnut Creek, Calif, certificate, 75-76; Thomas Leighton Acad Fine Art, San Francisco, Calif, 76-82; Can Fed Watercolor Artists, Salt Spring, 77. *Work:* Rosecrucian Egyptian Mus, San Jose, Calif; Nat Maritime Mus, Fort Bragg, Ky; Alameda Co Court House, Calif; Diocese of Oakland, Calif; Hayward Area Recreation Dept Off & Facilities, Calif. *Exhib:* Pastel Soc West Coast, Sacramento Fine Arts Ctr, Calif, 87-88 & 91-92; Pastel Soc Am Ann, Nat Arts Club, New York, 89 & 92; Invitational, City of Quincy Mus, Ill, 89; solo exhibs, Amador Hist Soc Mus, Pleasanton, 90 & San Ramon Community Ctr, Calif, 92; Soc Western Artists, Hall of Flowers, San Francisco, Calif, 90; Calif State Fair, Sacramento. *Teaching:* Lectr, portraiture, Merced Col, Calif, 91. *Awards:* Best of Show, Rosecrucian Mus, Soc Western Artists, 88; best of show, Alameda Co Fair, Air Comt, 89. *Bibliog:* Eleanor Chroman (auth), Lifestyles, Castro Valley Forum, 89; Pastel Artists, Southwest Art, 89; Noted Artist showing work at Mus , San Ramon Times, 90. *Mem:* Pastel Soc West Coast (chmn exhibs & events, 85-86, vpres, 87-88, pres, 89-); Pastel Soc Am (signature mem); Knickerbocker Artists, New York (signature mem); Nat League Am Penwomen (active mem); Soc Western Artists (signature mem); Allamo/Danville Art Soc. *Media:* Pastel, Oil. *Mailing Add:* c/o Harold Coursey , 610 Main St Pleasanton CA 94566

ESAKI, YASUHIRO
PAINTER, PRINTMAKER
b Omuta, Japan, June 8, 41. *Study:* Acad Art Col, BFA, 72; Lone Mountain Col, MFA(painting), 75, MFA(printmaking), 78. *Work:* Achenbach Found, Fine Art Mus, San Francisco; Boston Mus Fine Arts; Brooklyn Mus; Cincinnati Art Mus; Metrop Mus & Art Ctr, Miami, Fla. *Comn:* Etching, Mark Hopkins Hotel, San Francisco, 78. *Exhib:* MIX Graphic I, San Francisco Mus Mod Art, 73; Acquisition Shows, Achenbach Found, Fine Art Mus, San Francisco, 75, 78 & 79; Nat Drawing Exhib, Rutgers State Univ, Camden, 77; Third Int Graphic Biennial, Metrop Mus & Art Ctr, Miami, Fla, 77; Contemp Am Artist Exhib, Cent Mus, Tokyo, 78; 2nd Nat Drawing Competition, Miami Univ Mus, Oxford, Ohio, 78; 21st Nat Print Exhib, Brooklyn Mus, 79. *Teaching:* Instr printmaking, Acad Art Col, San Francisco, 78- *Awards:* Grand Prize, Third Miami Int Graphic Biennial, Metrop Mus & Art Ctr, 77; Purchase Prize, Belknap Mem Int Print Competition, Columbia-

Greene Community Col, 78; Purchase Prize, Stockton Nat '78, Univ Pac & Pioneer Mus & Haggin Art Gallery, 78. *Bibliog:* Robert McDonald (auth), Drawing by Yasuhiro Esaki, Artweek, 77; Nancy C Pierce (auth), Third Miami graphic biennial, Graphics, 78; Gene Baro (auth), Twenty-First National Print Exhibition, Brooklyn Mus, 79. *Mem:* Calif Soc Printmakers. *Media:* Acrylic, Color Pencil; Etching. *Mailing Add:* 499 Archer St Monterey CA 93940

ESAU, ERIKA
EDUCATOR, HISTORIAN
b Santa Barbara, Calif, Apr 1, 49. *Study:* Colo Women's Col, Denver, BA, 71; Univ Denver, MA, 72; Bryn Mawr Col, Pa, PhD, 85. *Pos:* Asst humanities librn, Portland State Univ, Ore, 72-73; librn, Deutscher Werkbund, Darmstadt, Ger, 74; slide librn, Univ Tex, San Antonio, 75-77; librn, Kimbell Art Mus, Ft Worth, Tex, 81-84. *Teaching:* Asst prof art hist & cur, Lawrence Univ, Appleton, Wis, currently. *Awards:* Fulbright Scholar, Darmstadt, Ger, 73-74; Kress Fel, Vienna, Austria, 80-81. *Mem:* Art Libr NAm. *Res:* Nineteenth-century Austrian art; Dada; German expressionism. *Publ:* Auth, Index, Werk & Zeit Mag 1965-1977, Deutscher Werkbund, 78; coauth, The mermaid in Mexican folk art, Southwest Folklore, 5/81; contribr, Schwitters, Macmillan Encycl Archit, 82; International Art Periodicals, Greenwood Press (in prep). *Mailing Add:* 212 McKinley St Appleton WI 54915

ESCALET, FRANK DIAZ
PAINTER, SCULPTOR
b Ponce, PR, Mar 16, 30. *Study:* Self taught. *Work:* Naprstek Mus, Nat Gallery, Prague, Czech; Union Artists, Moscow, Russia; Bratslavia Primitive Mus, Slovakia; Frydek-Mistek Mus, Northern Moravia. *Exhib:* Solo exhibs, Naprstek Mus, Prague, 90-91, Union Artists, Moscow, 91-92. *Awards:* Award of Excellance, Manhattan Arts Mag, 92; Represented USA at the Meeting of Two Worlds Exhib, Prague, Czech, 92. *Bibliog:* Subject of numerous television progs, 78-89; Manhattan Arts Mag, Rene Phillips Assoc, 91. *Publ:* Contribr, New York Art Review--An Illustrated Survey of the City's Museums Galleries & Leading Artists, Les Krantz Publ, 90. *Dealer:* House of Escalet Studios 13 Fletcher St Kennebunk ME 04043-1901. *Mailing Add:* 13 Fletcher St Kennebunk ME 04043-1901

ESCOBAR, MARISOL See Marisol,

ESCOBEDO, HELEN
ENVIRONMENTAL ARTIST
b Mexico City, Mex, July 28, 36. *Study:* Univ Motolinia, BA(humanities); ARCA, 3 yr scholar. *Work:* Mus Mod Art, Mex; Prague Nat Gallery, Czech; Palacio de Bellas Artes, Mexico City; also in pvt collection of Stanley Marcus, US; Ordrup Samlung, Copenhagen. *Comn:* Gateway to the Wind (concrete), Mex Olympic Games, Friendship Rte, 68; Signals (aluminum), Auckland, Golden Jublilee, NZ, 71; Coatl (steel), Univ Mex, 80; Reaseguradora Patria Bldg, 80; Barda Caida, Univ Mex, 81; The Great Cone (steel), City of Jerusalem, Israel, 86; El Reposo del Sol, Santiago, Cuba, 88. *Exhib:* One-man shows, Prague Nat Gallery, 69, Park Lazienkowsky, Warsaw, Poland, 70 & Mus Mod Art, Mexico City, 75; Kunstindustri Mus, Oslo, Norway, 70; Middelheim Sculpture Bienale, Antwerp, Belg, 71; Festival Cervantino, Guanajuato, Mex, 88; Ordrupgaard Mus, Copenhagen, 90. *Pos:* Dir, Dept Mus & Galleries, Nat Univ Mex, 61-77; tech dir, Mus Nat Arte, Mex, 82; dir, Mus Arte Mod, Mex, 83. *Teaching:* Artist in residence, Tulane Univ, 76, Hartnell Col, 77, Newcomb Col, 81, Kunsterhaus Betanien, Berlin, 81, Scripps Col, 83; res fel, Fac humanities, Ctr Sculptural Space, Univ Mex, 78. *Awards:* Acad Sci Letts et Beaux Arts, Belgium, 88; Guggenheim Fel, 91. *Bibliog:* Alfredo Gurrola (dir), Helen Escobedo - Ambients Totales (film), Color Mex; Rita Eder (auth), Helen Escobedo, Nat Univ Mex; Escobedo Derouin, Musée Du Que, Can. *Mem:* Int Nat Sculpture Ctr, Washington, DC (mem bd, 71-); Int Coun Mus (mem bd, 75-); Sculptor's Guild, NY; Academie Royale de Sciences Lettres et Beaux Arts, Belgium. *Media:* Multimedia. *Dealer:* 1a Cerrada de San Jeronimo 19 Lidice Mexico DF 10200. *Mailing Add:* AV San Jeronimo 162 Mexico DF 20 Mexico

ESHOO, ROBERT
PAINTER
b New Britain, Conn, Apr 27, 26. *Study:* Boston Mus Fine Arts Sch Mass, cert & dipl; Vesper George Sch Art, Boston; Syracuse Univ, BFA & MFA. *Work:* Boston Mus Fine Arts; Wadsworth Atheneum, Hartford, Conn; Currier Gallery Art, Manchester, NH; Munson-Williams-Proctor Inst, Utica, NY; Addison Gallery Am Art, Andover, Mass; and others. *Exhib:* Recent Drawings USA, Mus Mod Art, New York, 56; Chicago Art Inst Ann, 57; Young Artists, Whitney Mus, 57; Selections 1959, 59 & View 1960, 60, Inst Contemp Art, Boston; American Painting 1962, Va Mus Fine Arts, Richmond, 62; The Dana Collection, 62 & Potlatch, 63, Inst Contemp Art, Boston; 28th Biennial, Corcoran Gallery, Washington, DC, 63; Northeastern Regional--Art Across America, 65 & Art for Embassies, 66, Inst Contemp Art, Boston; one-man shows, Rigelhaupt Gallery, 68, Pucker-Safrai Gallery, Boston, 72 & 75 & Manchester, NH, 76 & 79 & Currier Gallery Art, 81 & 86 & Dartmouth Col, 86, St Paul's Sch, 88, New England Col, 89, Hatfield Gallery, Manchester, NH, 90. *Teaching:* Sch Mus Fine Arts, Boston, 54-55, Syracuse Univ, 56-57, Phillips Acad, Andover, 60 & 62-64 & Derryfield Sch, 65-80; supvr, Currier Art Ctr. *Bibliog:* New Talents USA, Art in Am, 2/56; American artists coming to the fore, Harper's Bazaar, 3/60; Emerging reputations, Art in Am, summer 62. *Media:* Oil, Watercolor. *Mailing Add:* 47 Amoskeag Pl Manchester NH 03101

ESLER, JOHN KENNETH
PRINTMAKER, PAINTER
b Pilot Mound, Man, Jan 11, 33. *Study:* Univ Man, BEd, Univ Man Sch Art, BFA. *Work:* Mus Mod Art, New York; Victoria & Albert Mus, London; Albright-Knox Gallery, Buffalo; Nat Gallery Can, Ottawa; Montreal Mus Fine Arts. *Comn:* Amoco Can Petroleum Ltd, Calgary Head Off. *Exhib:* Third Biennal Am Grababo, Santiago, Chile, 68; Third Int Gravure, Krakow, Poland, 70; Second Int Print Biennale, Bradford, Eng, 70; Premio Int Biella, Italy, 71; Int Buchkunst-Ausstellung, Leipzig, 71. *Teaching:* Assoc prof printmaking, Alta Col Art, Calgary, 64-68 & Univ Calgary, 68-80. *Awards:* C W Jeffories Award, Can Soc Graphic Arts, 68; First Purchase Award, Burnaby Biennial Print Exhib, 69; First Purchase Award, Graphic Exhib, Art Alliance Cent Pa, 70. *Mem:* Life mem, Print & Drawing Coun Can. *Media:* Etching, Collagraph. *Publ:* Auth, Printmaking in Alberta: Bente Roed Cochran, Univ Alta Press. *Mailing Add:* Box 2 Site 7 SS 1 Calgary AB T2M 4N3 Canada

ESMAN, ROSA
GALLERY DIRECTOR, DEALER
b New York, NY, Nov 29, 27. *Study:* Smith Col, BA. *Work:* Mus Mod Art, New York Int, Whitney Mus Am Art, Metrop Mus Art, New York; Brit Arts Coun, London. *Pos:* Pres & dir, Tanglewood Press, New York, 64-69 & 72-; dir, Abrams Original Editions, 69-72; pres & dir, Rosa Esman Gallery, 72- *Mem:* Art Dealers Asn Am; Art Table. *Specialty:* Contemporary American and European paintings, drawings and sculpture; Russian avant-garde material, 1911-1923; American art, 1950 to present. *Publ:* Ed, Seven objects in a box, 66 & New York, 10/69, Ten from Leo Castelli, 67, 9 Pyramios, Sol Lewitt, 91. *Mailing Add:* 575 Broadway New York NY 10012

ESPENET
CRAFTSMAN, LECTURER
b New York, NY, Jan 20, 20. *Study:* Dartmouth Col, BA. *Work:* City of San Francisco, Calif; San Francisco State Univ; Mus of Sci & Indust, Chicago; Oakland Mus, Calif; Johnson Wax Collection. *Comn:* Furniture, Stan Sobel, 70, Old St Mary's, 71, San Francisco; furniture, Mill Valley Libr, Calif, 72; furniture, Bishop O'Dowd Chapel; dais, Coun Chamber, Mt View, Calif. *Exhib:* Inst of Contemp Art, Boston, 49; Good Design Show, Mus of Mod Art, New York, 50-54; Mus of Contemp Crafts, New York, 56 & 66; Magnani Mem Craft Collection, San Francisco State Univ, 66; Wooden Works, Smithsonian Inst, Washington, DC, 72; E B Crocker Art Gallery, Sacramento, Calif, 73; Craft Multiples, Smithsonian Inst, 75; Living Treasures of California, Crocker Mus, 85. *Teaching:* Lectr furniture, San Francisco State Univ, Univ Calif, Berkeley & Anderson Ranch Arts Ctr, Snowmass, Colo, 78-86. *Awards:* Nat Endowment Arts Fel, 76 & Teaching Apprentice, 81; Fulbright, 85; Am Crafts Coun Col of Fel, 88; Living Treasure Calif, 85. *Bibliog:* Articles, Am Craftsm 7/82, Fine Woodworking, 11/82 & Britannica Encyl Am Art. *Mem:* Bolinas Craft Guild (pres, 77). *Media:* Wood. *Publ:* Auth, Eames Furniture, Craft Horizons, 73; Artiture, Fine Woodworking, 2/83. *Mailing Add:* Lower County Rd Bolinas CA 94924

ESPENSCHIED, CLYDE
PAINTER
b St Louis, Mo. *Study:* With Valentine Vogel portrait painter, 44-46; St Louis Sch Fine Arts, Washington Univ, 46-49; Am Acad, Rome, Italy, 55. *Work:* Peat Marwick Montvale Art Collection, Montvale, NJ; Bulgari, New York. *Exhib:* St Louis Mus, Mo, 49; Omaha Mus, Nebr, 60; Audubon Show, Nat Acad, New York, 62; Trenton Mus, NJ, 66, 68 & 74; Millhouse-Bundy Arts Ctr, Waitsfield, Vt, 83; Heidi Jones Gallery, New York, 84; one-person shows, Noho Gallery, New York, 84, 86, 88 & 91 & Mukaida Fine Arts Gallery, 91; Three Rivers Art Festival, Pittsburgh, Pa, 86 & 88; Morris Mus Fel Show, NJ, 87. *Awards:* Nat Endowment Arts Fel Grant, 85; NJ Coun Arts Grant, 85; Honorable Mention, Three Rivers Art Festival, Pittsburgh, Pa, 86. *Bibliog:* Vivien Raynor (auth), article, Arts Mag, 60; Frederic Schwartz (auth), article, Artspeak, 84; Mark Brennan (auth), article, Art & Oxygen, 84; Sanford Sivit Shaman (auth), Pa State Univ, 87. *Media:* Oil on Canvas, Pastel on Paper. *Dealer:* Noho Gallery 168 Mercer St New York NY 10012. *Mailing Add:* 265 Main St Spotswood NJ 08884

ESSER, JANET BRODY
HISTORIAN
b New Haven, Conn. *Study:* Univ Iowa, with John Rosenfield & William Heckscher, BFA, 51; Kent State Univ, BS, 53; Calif State Univ, Long Beach, MA, 70; Univ Calif, Los Angeles, with Rubin & Nicholson, PhD, 78. *Collections Arranged:* San Diego Collects: African Art, 78; Faces of Fiesta: Mexican Masks in Context, 80; sr consult, Behind the Mask in Mexico, Mus Int Folk Art, Santa Fe, 88-90. *Teaching:* From asst prof to assoc prof, San Diego State Univ, 75-83, prof, 83- *Awards:* Nat Endowment Humanities Summer Inst Fel, 78, 92; Hubert B Herring Mem Award for Best Scholarly Bk on Latin Am, 88. *Mem:* Col Art Asn Am; Latin Am Studies Asn; Latin Am Art Historians Asn; African Studies Asn; Ethno-Hist Soc; Pac Coast Coun on Latin Am Studies. *Res:* Pre-Columbian, European and African antecedents of masking traditions in contemporary rural Mexican cummunities; African imagery in Iberia; Social History of Mexican Folk Art. *Publ:* Auth, Mascaras rituales de la sierra tarasca, Michoacan, Inst Nac Indigenista, Mex; ed, Behind the Mask in Mexico, Mus NMex, Santa Fe, 88; Tarascan Masks of Women as Agents of Social Control, Univ BC Press, Vancouver, 83; The Functions of Folk Art in Michoacan, Memphis State Univ, 84; Mask Making and Mask Use in Michoacan, Mex Fine Arts Ctr Mus, Chicago, 90. *Mailing Add:* Dept Latin Am Hist San Diego State Univ San Diego CA 92182

ESSLEY, ROGER HOLMER
PAINTER, GRAPHIC ARTIST
b Rochester, NY, Jan 11, 49. *Study:* Syracuse Univ, 66-69; Goddard Col, MA, 81. *Work:* Metrop Mus Art, New York; Indianapolis Mus Art, Ind; Joslyn Art Mus, Omaha, Nebr; Ind Univ Mus Art, Bloomington; Mem Art Gallery, Rochester, NY. *Exhib:* One man show, Southeastern Ctr Contemp Art, Winston-Salem, NC, 84; Large Figurative Drawing, Va Mus Fine Arts, Richmond, Va, 85; The Figure in 20th Century Art, Nat Acad Design, New York, 85-86; Motion & Arrested Motion Contemporary Figure Drawing, Chrysler Mus, Norfolk, Va, 87; Contemp Wing, Metrop Mus Art, New York, 87-88; Uncommon Ground, Va Mus Fine Arts, Richmond, 90. *Awards:* Regional Fel, Works on Paper, Mid Atlantic Arts Found, 88; Va Prize for the Visual Arts, 90. *Bibliog:* Paul Richard (auth), Together again, Washington Post, 84; Edward Lucie-Smith (auth), Am Art Now, Phaidon Pr, 85. *Dealer:* Barbara Fendrick Gallery 568 Broadway New York NY 10012. *Mailing Add:* 2404 Terrett Ave Alexandria VA 22301

ESTABROOK, REED
PHOTOGRAPHER, EDUCATOR
b Boston, Mass, May 31, 44. *Study:* RI Sch of Design, BFA, 69; Art Inst of Chicago, MFA, 71. *Work:* Mus Mod Art, New York; Art Inst Chicago; Int Mus Photog, Rochester, NY; RI Sch Design, Providence; Minneapolis Inst Arts, Minn. *Comn:* San Jose Mus Mod Art. *Exhib:* Photo Synthesis, H F Johnson Mus, Cornell Univ, 76; Great West/Real: Ideal (travelling exhib), Univ Colo Mus of Art, Boulder, 77; Mirrors & Windows, Mus Mod Art, New York, 78; Attitudes, Santa Barbara Mus Art, Calif, 79; Hand Colored Photog, Philadelphia Col Art, 79; New American Nudes, Minneapolis Inst Arts, Minn; one-man shows, Sioux City Art Ctr, Iowa, 81, Klein Gallery, Chicago, 82 & James Madison Univ, Harrisburg, Va, 83. *Teaching:* Instr photog, Univ Ill, Urbana-Champaign, 71-74; asst prof photog, Univ Northern Iowa, 74-78, assoc prof, formerly; photog chmn, Kansas City Art Inst, formerly, coordr photo, Art Dept, San Jose State Univ, currently. *Awards:* W R French Fel Competition, Art Inst Chicago, 71; First Place, Am Photographics, Andromeda Gallery, Buffalo, 76; Photog Fel, Nat Endowment Arts, 76. *Mem:* Soc for Photog Educ. *Publ:* contribr, Aura, Vol 1, 76 & Vol 2, 77, Andromeda Gallery; contribr, Creative Camera, Coos Press, Vol 153 (77); contribr, Darkroom Dynamics, Curtis & London, 79; contrib, New American Nudes, Morgan & Morgan, 81; contrib, Picture Mag No 17, 81. *Mailing Add:* 155 S 17th Street San Jose CA 95112

ESTERN, NEIL
SCULPTOR
b New York, NY, Apr 18, 26. *Study:* Barnes Found, 46-47; Temple Univ, BFA & BS(educ), 47. *Work:* Brooklyn Mus; LaGuardia Community Col; Midwood High School. *Comn:* Portraits of LaGuardia, J Robert Taft, Danny Kaye, John F Kennedy, J Edgar Hoover, Pres Carter, Prince Charles, Lady Diana & Jack Nicholson; portrait bust of John F Kennedy, Kennedy Mem, Grand Army Plaza, Brooklyn, 65; Franklin D Roosevelt Memorial, Washington, DC. *Exhib:* Numerous one-man and group shows in Conn, New York, New Jersey, Philadelphia, NH & Italy. *Awards:* John Gregory Award, 66; Samuel F B Morse Gold Medal, 70; Award, Kent Art Asn, 81; Lindsey Morris Prize, 84; Mildred Vincent Prize, 88. *Mem:* Fel Nat Sculpture Soc; Nat Acad Design; Century Club. *Media:* Clay, Bronze. *Mailing Add:* 82 Remsen St Brooklyn NY 11201

ESTEROW, MILTON
EDITOR, PUBLISHER
b New York, NY, July 28, 28. *Study:* Brooklyn Col, NY. *Pos:* Asst cult news dir, New York Times, 63-68; ed & publ, ARTnews, 72-; publ, ARTnewsletter, 75-; Corp ARTnews, currently. *Teaching:* Lectr art, museums, colleges & universities. *Awards:* Silurians Award, 78; George Polk Award, 81; Nat Mags Award, 81; Clarion Award, 81 & 84; Investigative Reporters & Editors Award, 84; Page One Award, 85; Nat Headliner Award, 85; Silurians Award, 90; and others. *Publ:* Contribr, Art News, New York Times Mag & Atlantic Mag. *Mailing Add:* ARTnews 48 W 38th St New York NY 10018

ESTES, RICHARD
PAINTER
b Ill, 1932. *Study:* Chicago Art Inst, 52-56. *Work:* Whitney Mus Am Art & Mus Mod Art, New York; Rockhill Nelson Mus, Kansas City, Mo; Toledo Mus, Ohio; Art Inst Chicago; Des Moines Art Ctr; Hirshhorn Mus, Washington, DC. *Exhib:* Documenta V, Kassel, Ger, 72; Venice Biennale, Italy, 72; Whitney Mus Ann, 72; Twelve American Painters, Va Mus Fine Arts, Richmond, 74; Trends in Contemp Realist Painting, 75 & The Urban Landscape, 78, Boston Mus Fine Arts; Allen Stone Gallery, 83; and others. *Bibliog:* Peter Schjeldahl (auth), Flowering of the super-real, 3/2/69 & John Canaday (auth), Realism-waxing or waning, 7/13/69, New York Times; Mary Lou Kelly (auth), Popart inspired objective realism, Christian Sci Monitor, 4/1/74; John Perrault and Lou Meisel (auths), bk, Abrams, 86. *Media:* Oil. *Mailing Add:* 300 Central Park W New York NY 10028

ETCHISON, BRUCE
CONSERVATOR, PAINTER
b Washington, DC, Dec 19, 18. *Study:* Am Univ, BA; Yale Univ Sch Fine Arts, BFA & MFA. *Work:* Washington County Mus Fine Arts, Hagerstown, Md; Chesapeake Bay Maritime Mus, St Michaels, Md; Merrick Art Gallery, New Brighton, Pa. *Pos:* Dir, Washington Co Mus Fine Arts, 50-64; dir, Abby Aldrich Rockefeller Folk Art Collection, 64-66; conservator for pvt collectors mus, univs, cols, hist soc & the State of Pa, formerly; currently retired. *Mem:* Int & Am Insts Conserv Hist & Artistic Works; Washington Conserv Guild. *Media:* Oil, Etching. *Publ:* Coauth, Roentgen Examination of Painting, 60; auth, Radiant Heat for Vacuum Tables, 69. *Mailing Add:* 6221 Greenbriar Terr Fayetteville PA 17222

ETROG, SOREL
SCULPTOR, PAINTER
b Jassy, Romania, Aug 29, 33; Can citizen. *Study:* Tel Aviv Art Inst, Israel, 53-55; Brooklyn Mus Art Sch, 58. *Work:* Nat Gallery Can, Ottawa; Art Gallery Ontario & Hart House, Univ Toronto; Tate Gallery of London; Musee en Plein Air & Musee d'Art Moderne, Paris; Mus Mod Art & Guggenheim Mus, New York; Hirshhorn Mus, Washington, DC; Storm King Art Ctr, Mountainville, NY; Montreal Mus Fine Arts; and many others. *Comn:* EXPO, Montreal, 67; Olympia & York Ctr, Toronto, 72; Bow Valley Sq, Calgary, 75; Sunlite Ctr, Toronto, 84; Olympic Park, Soeul, Korea, 88; and others. *Exhib:* Solo exhibs, Walter Moos Gallery, 59, 61, 63, 65, 67, 81, 84 & 90 & Dominion Gallery, Montreal, 63, 67, 73 & 89; one man retrospective, Retrospective 1958-68, Pallazzo Strozzi, Florence, 68; Etrog - A Decade, 15 Ont Cols touring exhib, 68-69; City Hall, Toronto, 72; Dunkelman Gallery, Toronto, 70, 71 & 72; Fine Arts Mus, Montreal, 68; Winnipeg Art Gallery, Man, 71; 4th Int Exhib Contemp Sculpture, Mus Rodin, Paris, 71; and many others. *Bibliog:* William Withrow (auth), Etrog: Sculpture, Wilfred, Toronto, 67; Theodore A Heinrich (auth), The Painted Constructions 1952-1960, Staempfli et Cie, Berne, 68. *Mem:* Royal Can Acad Arts. *Publ:* Contribr, Imagination Dead Imagine, Calder, London, 72; auth, Dream Chamber (Joyce & the Dada Circus), Black Brick Press, London, 82; Hinges, a play, Calder, London, 83; L'Aquilone/The Kite, All'insegna del pesce d'oro, Milan, 84. *Mailing Add:* PO Box 5943, Sta Terminal A Toronto ON M5W 1P3 Canada

ETTENBERG, FRANKLIN JOSEPH
PAINTER, PRINTMAKER
b Brooklyn, NY, May 7, 45. *Study:* Univ Mich, BS(design), 66, with Milton Cohen, Fred Bauer & John Stephenson; Univ NMex, MA, 71, with John Kacere. *Work:* Detroit Inst Art; Univ NMex Fine Arts Mus, Albuquerque; Roswell Mus & Art Ctr, NMex; Fine Arts Mus, Santa Fe; Minnesota Mus Art, St Paul; Albuquerque Int Airport; Albuquerque Mus. *Comn:* Paired Paintings, NMex Arts Comn, 78; Taos Watershed Mural, Mary Medina Bldg, Taos, NMex, 78. *Exhib:* Solo exhibs, Janus Gallery, Santa Fe, 84, 86 & 88 & Wright Gallery, Dallas, 84 & 85; Taos to Tucson, Foundations Gallery, New York, 82; Southwest 85, Mus Fine Art, Santa Fe, 85; purchase exhib, Am Acad Arts & Lett, New York, 87; Conlon Gallery, Santa Fe, 89; Artists Discover Columbus, Castillo Ctr, New York, 92. *Pos:* Exec comt, Advocates for Contemp Art, Santa Fe, 73-75; cert graphoanalyst, Int Graphoanalysis Soc, Chicago, 77. *Teaching:* Instr, Santa Fe Workshops of Contemp Art, summer, 74; pvt painting instr, 79- *Awards:* Roswell Mus Artist in Residence Grant, NMex, 71; Southwest 85, purchase award, monotype, merit award, painting, Mus fine Art, Santa Fe, 85; Tamarind Inst Scholar, 87. *Bibliog:* W Peterson (auth), Critique of painted low-reliefs, spring 82, W Peterson (auth), review, fall 86, Abstract painting in New Mexico, fall 88, Artspace; W Clark (auth), Artist profile, Sunday Arts, Albuquerque J, 3/6/88. *Media:* Oil; Monotype on Rives BFK. *Publ:* Contribr, Santa Fe Fine Arts Calendar, 93. *Dealer:* Peyton Wright 128 Marcy St E Santa Fe NM 87501; Robischon Gallery 1740 Wazee St Denver CO 80202. *Mailing Add:* 2001 Ft Union Dr Santa Fe NM 87501

ETTER, HOWARD LEE
PAINTER, LECTURER
b Moberly, Mo, Jan 22, 31. *Study:* Art League Calif, San Francisco; Acad Art, San Francisco. *Work:* Butler Inst Am Art, Youngstown, Ohio. *Exhib:* 37th & 39th Midyear Show, Butler Inst Am Art, 73 & 75; Nat Painting Show, Washington & Jefferson Col, 74; 17th Ann Delta Art Exhib, 74. *Teaching:* Lectr drawing, painting & watercolor, Lawrence Inst Technol, 68-77. *Awards:* Spec Jurors Award, Washington & Jefferson Col Painting Show, 74; 39th Butler Inst Midyear Show Purchase Award, Friends Am Art, 75. *Mem:* Artist Equity Asn. *Media:* Watercolor, Egg Tempera; Acrylic. *Publ:* Auth, Perspective for Painters, Watson-Guptill Publ, 90; Everything You Ever Wanted to Know about Watercolor, Watson-Guptill Publ. *Dealer:* Massachusetts House Lincolnville ME. *Mailing Add:* PO Box 740 Camden ME 04843

ETTING, EMLEN
PAINTER, ILLUSTRATOR
b Philadelphia, Pa, Aug 24, 05. *Study:* Harvard Univ, BS, 28; Grande Chaumiere & Andre Lhote, Paris. *Work:* Whitney Mus Am Art, New York; Pa Acad Fine Arts, Philadelphia; Addison Gallery Am Art, Andover, Mass; Philadelphia Mus Art; Atwater Kent Mus, Philadelphia. *Comn:* Philadelphia Industries (oil), Market St Nat Bank, 47; oil, Italian Consulate, Philadelphia, 55. *Exhib:* Whitney Mus; Carnegie Inst, Pittsburgh; Corcoran Gallery Art, Washington, DC; Pa Acad Fine Arts; San Francisco World's Fair; Retrospectives, Fla Southern Col, Lakeland, 73 & Allentown Art Mus, Pa, 74. *Pos:* US artist-deleg, Second Int Cong Plastic Arts, Dubrovnik, 57. *Teaching:* Instr painting & drawing, Sch Indust Art, Philadelphia Mus Art; Philadelphia Col Art & Tyler Sch Art, Temple Univ. *Awards:* Chevalier, Legion d'Honneur, Fr Govt; Star Solidarity, Italian Govt. *Bibliog:* Mary Rupert (auth), Emlen Etting, Paintings of an American Romantic, London Studio, 39. *Mem:* Artists Equity Asn (nat pres, 55-58, hon pres & pres, Philadelphia Chap, 50-53, hon pres); Nat Soc Mural Painters; Century Asn; Philadelphia Art Alliance; Alliance Francaise (hon pres); plus others. *Media:* Oil, Acrylic. *Publ:* Illusr & translr, Valery, Le Cimetiere Marin, Centaur Press, 32; illusr, Amerika & Ecclesiastes, New Directions, 40; illusr, Born in a Crowd, Crowell-Collier; auth & illusr, Drawing the Ballet, Studio Bks, 44. *Dealer:* Midtown Payson Galeries 745 Fifth Ave New York NY 10151. *Mailing Add:* 1927 Panama St Philadelphia PA 19103

ETTINGER, SUSI STEINITZ
PAINTER, LECTURER
b Berlin, Ger, July 29, 22; US citizen. *Study:* Univ Louisville, BFA(cum laude art hist), 43; with Dr Justus Bier. *Work:* Springfield Art Mus, Mo; State Hist Soc Mo, Columbia; Sch of the Ozarks, Point Lookout, Mo; Greenwood Lab Sch, Springfield; Margaret Harwell Art Mus, Poplar Bluff, Mo. *Exhib:* Women Artists 77 Exhib, Kansas City, Mo Univ, 77; Watercolor USA, 79; one-artist shows, Springfield Art Mus, 75, Southwest Mo Univ, 80, Sch Ozarks, 87, Mabee Art Ctr, Drury Col, 84; Springfield Area Artists Exhib, Springfield Art Mus, 90; and many others. *Teaching:* Dir children's art classes, Springfield Art Mus, 60-66; lectr art, Southwest Mo State Univ, 64-84, emer prof, 84- *Awards:* Regional Ten State Competition Purchase Award, 69 & Purchase Award, Watercolor USA, 90, Springfield Art Mus; First Prize Painting, Mo Col Fac Show, 70; Award in recognition of creative accomplishments in the visual arts, Am Asn Univ Women, 74. *Media:* Acrylic, Collage. *Mailing Add:* 2020 S Ventura Ave Springfield MO 65804

ETTL, GEORG
PAINTER, SCULPTOR
b Nittenau, Ger, Mar 3, 31. *Study:* Sorbonne, Paris, France, 63-65; Wayne State Univ, BA, 65, MA, 67, MFA, 68. *Work:* Mus Abteiberg, Möchen Gladbach, Ger; Kaiser Wilhelm Mus, Krefeld, Ger. *Comn:* Amphitheater, 81 & Murals for City Co Bldg, Vierson, Ger, 83-84. *Exhib:* All Mich Exhib, Flint Inst Arts, 72; solo exhib, Mus Abteiberg, Mönchen Gladbach, Ger, 77-78; With a Certain Smile, Zurich, Switz, 79; Kick Out the Jams: Detroit's Cass Corridor 1963-77, Detroit Inst Arts & Mus Contemp Art, Chicago, 81; With a Certain Smile, Krefeld, Ger, 83. *Awards:* Purchase Prizes, 58th Exhib Mich Artists, Detroit Inst Arts, 70 & All Mich Exhib, Flint Inst Arts, 72. *Bibliog:* Johannes Cladders (auth), Georg Ettl, Städtisches Mus Mönchen Gladbach, 77; Julian Heyden (auth), Georg Ettl: Hausordnung, Krefelder Kunstmus, 83; Nena Dimitrijevic (auth), Sculpture and Its Double, Sculpture Show, Greater London Coun, 83. *Media:* All. *Mailing Add:* c/o Feigenson/Preston Gallery 796 N Woodward Birmingham MI 48009

ETTLING, RUTH (DROITCOUR)
PRINTMAKER, PAINTER
b Pittsburgh, Pa, Mar 30, 10. *Study:* RI Sch Design; Marshall Univ, BA; spec study with Charles Burchfield, Arnold Blanch, William Thon, Fletcher Martin, Victor Candell & Walter Murch. *Work:* Charleston Gallery Sunrise, WVa; Dayton Art Inst, Ohio; Hunterdon Co Art Ctr, Clinton, NJ; Huntington Galleries, WVa; WVa Arts & Humanities Collection, Charleston. *Exhib:* Hunterdon Co Nat Print Show, Clinton, 62; Ohio Printmakers, Dayton, 62; Ruth Ettling's Recent Prints, Huntington Galleries, 71; solo show, Ashland Area Art Gallery, Ashland, Ky, 85. *Teaching:* Instr drawing & painting, Huntington Galleries, 52-66, summer dir, print workshop, 72. *Awards:* Purchase Award, Tri-State Exhib, Huntington Galleries, WVa, 82; Merit Award, Cardinal Valley Show, Ashland, Ky, 83; Purchase & Mixed Media Awards, River Festival Exhibit, Fr Art Colony, Ohio, 85. *Mem:* Tri-State Arts Asn (pres, 72); Nat Art Educ Asn. *Publ:* Illusr, Dear Bob, Love Mother, 67. *Mailing Add:* 1475 Spring Valley Circle Huntington WV 25704

EVANS, BOB (ROBERT JAMES)
MUSEUM DIRECTOR, PAINTER
b Chicago, Ill, May 2, 44. *Study:* Parsons Col; Univ Iowa; Northeast Mo State Univ, BEd; Drake Univ; Southern Ill Univ, Carbondale, MFA. *Work:* Southern Ill Univ, Carbondale; Western Ill Univ, Macomb; Ill State Univ, Normal; Quincy Art Club; Lakeview Mus Arts & Sci; Rockford Art Mus, Ill. *Comn:* Subscription print series, Plucked Chicken Press, Evanston, Ill, 86. *Exhib:* 16th Midwest Biennial, Joslyn Art Mus, Omaha, Nebr, 80; Irwin Collection, Krannert Art Mus, Univ Ill, 80; Watercolor USA, Springfield Art Mus, Mo, 80; one-man shows, Zaks Gallery, Chicago, Ill, 81 & 84; Chicago Int Art Expos, 82 & 87; Fabrications, Chicago Sculpture Soc, 83; Sound/Light, ARC, Chicago, 87. *Collections Arranged:* Emergence of Modernism in Illinois 1914-1940, 76; Illinois Photographers 1978, 80; Illinois Invitationals, 71-84; Contemporary American Photography, 88; White Mountain Painters, 92. *Pos:* Res asst, Univ Galleries, Southern Ill Univ, Carbondale, 69-70; cur art, Ill State Mus, Springfield, 70-, head dept art, 81-85; gallery dir & dept chmn, Rockford Col, 85-88; Dir, Danforth Mus Art, Farmingham, MA, 88- *Teaching:* Instr drawing & painting, Springfield Art Asn, Ill, 71-76; adj asst prof arts mgt, Sangamon State Univ, 73-78; assoc prof, Rockford Col, 85-88; adj fac Farmingham State Col, Mass, 88- *Awards:* Best in Show, Quincy Art Club Ann Exhib, 72 & 78; Governors Art Award, Ill Arts Coun, 80; Merit Award, Miss Corridors, Davenport Art Mus, Iowa, 81. *Bibliog:* David Elliott (auth), article, Chicago Sun Times, 6/21/81; Alan G Artner (auth), article, Chicago Tribune, 7/3/81. *Mem:* Col Art Asn; Chicago Artists Coalition. *Media:* Mixed, Painting. *Publ:* Auth, articles in Living Mus, 70- & Craft Horizons & Mus News; plus numerous exhib catalogs. *Mailing Add:* 10 Lyman Rd Framingham MA 01701

EVANS, BRUCE HASELTON
MUSEUM DIRECTOR, HISTORIAN
b Rome, NY, Nov 13, 39. *Study:* Amherst Col, BA; NY Univ Inst Fine Arts, MA. *Collections Arranged:* The Paintings of Edward Edmondson, 72;; Jean-Leon Gerome--The Paintings (with catalog), 72. *Pos:* Cur asst to dir, Dayton Art Inst, 65-67, chief cur, 68-72, asst dir, 72-74, dir, 75-91, Mint Mus Art, Charlotte, NC, 91- *Mem:* Am Asn Mus; Ohio Mus Asn (pres, 82-85); Asn Art Mus Dirs (pres, 86-87). *Publ:* Auth, Fifty Treasures of the Dayton Art Institute, 69; Edward Edmondson--A Biography and Critical Study of His Paintings, 72; and numerous articles in museum bulletins and exhibitions catalogs. *Mailing Add:* PO Box 941 Dayton OH 45401

EVANS, BURFORD ELONZO
PAINTER, LECTURER
b Golinda, Tex, July 20, 31. *Study:* Sorbonne Univ, cert 55. *Work:* Mus Fine Arts, Lubbock, Tex; Black Arts Ctr, Waco, Tex; Northwood Inst, Midland, Mich; Bishop Col, Dallas, Tex. *Comn:* Josephite Black Arts Calendar, Josephite Pastoral Ctr, Washington, DC, 74. *Exhib:* Mobile Arts Festival, Ala, 70; Discovery 70, Nat Black Arts Festival, Cincinnati, Ohio, 70; Nat Black Arts Festival, Normal, Ill, 73; one-man show, State Capitol, Austin, Tex, 73; Tex Fine Arts Festival, Houston, 74. *Awards:* Second Award, Dimension IV Houston Art League, Humble Oil Co, 68; Betty McGowan Award, Mobil Arts Festival, 70; Distinguished Artist Award, Nat Coun Negro Women, 72. *Bibliog:* James Kennedy (auth), Ethnic American Art, Slide Libr, Univ Ala, 70-75; Charolette Phelen (auth), Evans remembers June tenth, Houston Chronicle, 71; Theresa Dickason Cederholm (auth), Afro American Artist, Boston Pub Libr, 73. *Mem:* Art League Houston; Tex Fine Arts Asn; Contemp Arts Asn. *Media:* Multimedia. *Mailing Add:* 5327 Knotty Oaks Trail Houston TX 77045

EVANS, DICK
SCULPTOR, PAINTER
b Roswell, NMex, July 10, 41. *Study:* Tex Tech Univ, Lubbock, 59-62; Univ Utah, Salt Lake City, BFA, 64, MFA, 66. *Work:* Nat Mus Am Art, Smithsonian Inst; Sheldon Mem Art Gallery, Univ Nebr, Lincoln; Milwaukee Art Mus, Wis; Ariz State Univ, Tempe; Herbert F Johnson Mus Art, Cornell Univ, Ithaca, NY; and others. *Comn:* ceramic murals, Deloitte, Haskins & Sells, 86, Warshafsky, Rotter, Tarnoff, Gesler & Reinhardt, 86 & Milwaukee Art Comn, 88, Milwaukee, Wis; RTE Corp, 87; First Wis Corp, 87. *Exhib:* Solo shows, Bradley Galleries, Milwaukee, 76, 78 & 80, Kohler Art Ctr, Sheboygan, 83, Michael H Lord Gallery, Milwaukee, Wis, 84 & 89 & Elaine Horwitch Galleries, Santa Fe, NMex, 90; Landscape: New Views, Johnson Art Mus, Cornell Univ, Ithaca, New York, 78; American Porcelain: New Expressions in an Ancient Art Travling Show, Smithsonian Inst, 80-84; Poetic Image, Elements Gallery, New York, 80; two-person show, Sheldon Mem Art Gallery, Univ Nebr, Lincoln, 82; and other group & one-man shows. *Teaching:* Instr ceramics, Texas Tech, Lubbock, 66-70; asst prof ceramics, Univ Tenn, Knoxville, 71-72 & Univ NMex, Albuquerque, 72-75; prof ceramics, Sch Fine Arts, Univ Wis, Milwaukee, 75-87, assoc dean, 81-83. *Bibliog:* Susan Peterson (auth), Slices from the heartland, Airbrush Digest, 11-12/83. *Dealer:* Elaine Horwitch Galleries 129 W Palace Ave Santa Fe NM 87501. *Mailing Add:* c/o Michael H Lord Gallery 420 E Wisconsin Ave Milwaukee WI 53202

EVANS, GROSE
HISTORIAN, EDUCATOR
b Columbus, Ohio, Dec 14, 16. *Study:* Ohio State Univ, BFA, 38, MA, 40; Inst Fine Arts, NY Univ, 41-43 & 45-46; Johns Hopkins Univ, PhD, 53. *Pos:* From lectr to assoc cur, dept educ, Nat Gallery Art, 46-60, cur exten serv, decorative arts & index Am design, 60-70, cur exhibs & loans, 70-73, cur decorative arts, 73. *Teaching:* Prof lectr Baroque-mod art, George Washington Univ, 53-61, adj assoc prof art hist, 73-90; prof lectr Am painting, Johns Hopkins Univ, 65; curric dir art teachers' training, George Washington Univ & Nat Gallery Art, 66 & 67; Retired. *Res:* Anglo-American art of the eighteenth century. *Publ:* Auth, Benjamin West and the Taste of His Time, Southern Ill Univ Press, 59; Vincent Van Gogh, McGraw, 68. *Mailing Add:* 2308 Glasgow Rd Alexandria VA 22307

EVANS, HENRY
PRINTMAKER
b Superior, Wis, May 16, 18. *Work:* Albertina, Vienna; Libr Cong, Washington, DC; Hunt Botanical Inst, Pittsburgh; Clark Libr, Los Angeles, Calif; Oakland Mus, Calif. *Exhib:* One-man shows, Royal Horticultural Soc, London, 65, Hunt Botanical Inst, 66, Biomed Libr, Univ Calif, Los Angeles, 68, Calif Acad Sci, San Francisco, 70 & Oakland Mus, 71; Vallejo Mus, Vallejo, Calif, 88. *Awards:* Silver Medal of Commonwealth Club; Fel, Calif Acad Sci, 87. *Bibliog:* staff, Henry Evans, printmaker (doc film), KQED, 69; Johan Kooy (auth), Henry Evans, printmaker, Pac Discovery, 12/70; Ruth Haskell (auth), Henry Evans: artist in the garden, Flower & Garden, 10/88; & others. *Publ:* Illusr, Champagne and shoes, Peregrine Press, 62; Hortulus, 66; Flower pot gardens, Crowell Collier, 67; auth, illusr & printer, State flowers, Vol 1-5, Peregrine Press, 68-72; auth, Botanical Prints with Excerpts from the Artist's Notebooks, Freeman & Co, 77; auth & illusr, California Native Wildflowers, 85. *Dealer:* Qumps 250 Post St San Francisco CA 94108. *Mailing Add:* c/o Henry Evans Library PO Box 640 1124 Pine St St Helena CA 94574

EVANS, JOHN
COLLAGE ARTIST
b Sioux Falls, SDak, Aug 24, 32. *Study:* Art Inst Chicago, BFA, 61, MFA, 63. *Exhib:* Pa Acad Fine Art Ann, 64; one-man shows, Eastern Mont State Univ, Billings, 80 & Arts Club, Chicago, 82; Castle Gallery, New Rochelle, NY, 87; 100 Years Art on the Lower Eastside, New York, 88; Works on Paper, 128 Rivington Gallery, 88; Gracie Mansion Gallery, New York, 90; Artstar, Los Angeles, 91; and others. *Pos:* artist-in residence, Decenter, Glumso, Denmark, 71; artist-in-residence, Villa Arson, Nice, France, 86. *Awards:* Nat Endowment Arts Grant, 85; Pollack-Krasner Grant, 89. *Bibliog:* Susan Grace Galassi (auth), article, Arts Mag, 3/80; Vivien Raynor (auth), A show that requires reading too, 3/23/80 & articles, 10/4/85 & 5/24/87; Lynn Zelevansky (auth), Art & Auction, 10/84; Victoria Donohue (auth), Philadelphia Inquirer, 2/28/87. *Mem:* Artist's Equity. *Publ:* Auth, Collection of 38 Collage Books, privately publ, 76; Remnants of an Unknown Woman-with Ursule Molinero, Red Dust Press, 87. *Mailing Add:* 199 E 3rd St 2B New York NY 10009

EVANS, JUDITH FUTRAL
PAINTER
b Ft Smith, Ark. *Study:* Univ Ark, Fayetteville, BA, 61; Univ Iowa, Iowa City, MFA, 64. *Work:* Dewey, Ballantine, Bushby, Palmer & Wood, Hunter Col, New York; E F Hutton & Co, New York; Cedar Crest Col, Pa. *Comn:* After Diego Rivera, comn by Al Solokov & Co, New York. *Exhib:* Blue Mountain Gallery, New York, 81, 85, 87, 90 & 92; Nat Mid-Year Am, Butler Inst Am Art, Ohio, 85, 88 & 92; Elaine Benson Gallery, Bridgehampton, NY, 88 & 92; Salmugundi Club, New York, 88; Nat Soc Painters Casein & Acrylic, New York, 89; Ark Women Artists, Washington, DC, 91; and others. *Pos:* Founder, Blue Mountain Gallery, New York, 79- *Mem:* United Scenic Artists, Local 829, New York. *Media:* All. *Mailing Add:* 34 Plaza St Apt 808 Brooklyn NY 11238

EVANS, RICHARD
PAINTER, EDUCATOR
b Chicago, Ill, Oct 1, 23. *Study:* Otis Art Inst, dipl; Calif Col Arts & Crafts; Studio of George Miller, New York; Univ Wyo, MA; Stacey Found Fel, 47; Tiffany Found Fels, 48 & 50. *Work:* San Francisco Fine Arts Comn; Univ Wyo; Col Southern Utah. *Comn:* Tile mural, Univ Wyo, 68; portrait of Sam S Knight, Univ Wyo Geol Mus; twenty sculptures of prominent personages for private comns. *Exhib:* one-man show, Yellowstone Art Ctr, Billings, Mont, 74; Retrospective, Univ Wyo Mus, 76; Santa Fe Art Festival, 77; Directions Gallery, Colo State Univ, 79; 57th Mid-Year, Butler Inst, 81; Drawing Ann, Rutgers Univ, 81; and others. *Teaching:* Instr drawing, Calif Col Arts & Crafts, Oakland, 50-52; instr drawing & painting, Miami Univ, Oxford, Ohio, 56-57; prof printmaking, drawing & painting, Univ Wyo, 57- *Awards:* Ford Found Grants, 64 & 66; 26th Cedar City Invitational Purchase Award, 66; Anonymous Donor Award, Otis Art Inst 50th Anniversary Exhib, 68. *Bibliog:* Victor Flach (auth), The Making of Ikon 13 (film & TV tape), Univ Wyo, 70; Victor Flach (auth), By these presents: Richard Evans, A retrospective, 76. *Media:* Oil, Acrylic; Intaglio. *Publ:* Auth, On large scale prints, Am Artist, 11/62. *Mailing Add:* PO Box 81 Centennial WY 82055

EVANS, ROBERT GRAVES
EDUCATOR, SCULPTOR
b Rawlins, Wyo, Nov 19, 44. *Study:* Atlanta Sch Art, BFA; French Govt Fel, Paris, 69; with Stanley Hayter; Tulane Univ, with Julius Struppeck, MFA. *Work:* Evansville Mus Arts & Sci, Ind; Sheldon Swope Art Mus, Terre Haute, Ind; Indiana State Univ, Terre Haute; Central Michigan Univ, Mt Pleasant; The Univ of the South, Swanee, Tenn. *Comn:* Man of Year Award (sculpture), Atlanta, Ga, 69; Film Festival Award (sculpture), Atlanta, Ga, 69; bronze bust of Pres Rankin, Ind State Univ, 75; outdoor sculpture, Cent Mich Univ, 75; outdoor monumental sculpture comn, Indianapolis, Ind, 82. *Exhib:* Mid-States Art Exhib, Evansville Mus Arts & Sci, Ind, 78; New Harmony Gallery of Contemp Art, New Harmony, Ind, 82; Wabash Col, Outdoor Sculpture Exhib, Crawfordsville, Ind, 85; Solo Sculpture Exhib, Herr-Chambliss Fine Arts Gallery, Hot Springs Nat Park, Ark, 90; Sculpture Exhib at Mid-America Mus, Hot Springs Nat Park, Ark, 91. *Teaching:* Prof sculpture, Ind State Univ, Terre Haute, 72-78, assoc prof art, 78-84, prof art, 84- *Awards:* Sculpture Acquisition, Swope Art Gallery, 77; Mus Guild Purchase Award, Evansville Mus Arts & Sci, 78; Beautification Award, Terre Haute CofC, 81. *Mem:* Southern Sculpture Asn; Arts Illiana; Col Art Asn. *Media:* Bronze, Aluminum. *Mailing Add:* Dept of Art Ind State Univ Terre Haute IN 47809

EVANS, TOM R
PAINTER
b St Paul, Minn, June 4, 43. *Study:* Univ Minn, BA, 65, MFA, 68. *Work:* Grey Gallery, New York Univ; Chase Manhattan Bank, London, Eng; Gen Mills, Minneapolis, Minn; IBM, White Plains, NY. *Exhib:* Walker Biennial, Walker Art Ctr, Minneapolis, Minn, 68; Contemporary Reflections, 71 & Best of Contemporary Reflections, 73, Aldrich Mus, Ridgefield, Conn; one-person exhibs, John Bernard Myers Gallery, New York, 73 & 74 & Max Hutchinson Gallery, New York, 79; group shows, New Work-New York, The New Mus, New York, 81, Gimpel & Weitzenhoffen Gallery, New York, 86. *Media:* Oil on Canvas or Linen. *Mailing Add:* 115 West Broadway New York NY 10013

EVAUL, WILLIAM H, JR
PAINTER, PRINTMAKER
b Philadelphia, Pa, July 2, 49. *Study:* Fleischer Mem Sch Art, Syracuse Univ, Pratt Inst, BFA, 81. *Work:* Provincetown Art Asn & Mus, Mass; Sunrise Art Mus, Charleston, WVa. *Exhib:* Provincetown & the Art of Printmaking, Smithsonian Inst Traveling Exhib, 90-92. *Pos:* Dir/cur, Provincetown Art Asn & Mus, 86-90; guest cur, Cape Mus Fine Arts, 92. *Teaching:* Asst inst lithography, Pratt Graphics Ctr, 80-82; instr printmaking, Truro Ctr Arts, 92-; guest lectr, Ga Mus Art, Ogleby Inst & others. *Awards:* Fel, Fine Arts Work Ctr, Provincetown, 70-72. *Bibliog:* Ann Brigham (auth), Contemporary artists, Orthodox traditions, Antiques & Arts, 1/90. *Mem:* Asn Am Mus; Nat Artists Equity; Art Fedn Am. *Media:* Oil, Woodcut. *Publ:* Auth, The Genesis of a unique woodcut tradition, Pratt Graphics Ctr, 84; The Eye of the Collector, Cape Mus Fine Art, 92. *Mailing Add:* PO Box 958 Truro MA 02666

EVEN, ROBERT LAWRENCE
EDUCATOR
b Breckenridge, Minn, June 7, 29. *Study:* Valley City State Col, BS; Univ Minn, MA & PhD; Art Inst Chicago; Minneapolis Col Art & Design. *Teaching:* Instr art, Univ Minn, 52-54; prof art, Northern Ill Univ, 63-, chmn dept, 74- *Awards:* Res Grant, State Ill, 64 & Dean's Fund, Northern Ill Univ, 65 & 73. *Mem:* Col Art Asn Am; Mid-Am Col Art Asn; Nat Coun Art Adminr; Nat Asn Sch Art. *Mailing Add:* 413 Fairmont Dr De Kalb IL 60115

EVERGON
PHOTOGRAPHER
b Niagara Falls, Ont, Dec 28, 46. *Study:* Mt Allison Univ, Sackville, NB, BFA, 70; Rochester Inst Technol, MFA (photog), 74. *Work:* Nat Gallery Can, Can Mus Contemp Photog & Can Art Bank, Ottawa, Ont; Found Cartier pour l'Art Contemp, Jouy-en-Josas, France; Mus de Que, Quebec City. *Exhib:* Solo exhibs, Galerie Séquence, Chicoutimi, Québec, Can, 89, Recent Works by Evergon, Glenn/Dash Gallery, Los Angeles, 89, Evergon 1971-1987 Traveling Exhib, 89-90, Richard Feign Gallery, Chicago, Ill, 90, Art 45, Montreal, Que, Can, 90, Recent Polaroids, Jack Shainman Gallery, New York, 90; Photographies: Pour célébrerle 150e anniversaire de la naissane de la photographie, Found Cartier pour l'art contemporain, Jouy-en-Josas, France, 90; The Photography of Invention: Am Pictures of the 80's, Nat Mus Am Art, Washington, DC, 89; Prospest Photographie, Frankfurt Kunstverein, Frankfurt, WGer, 89; Andreas Serrano, Andrea Rugieri Gallery, Washington, DC, 90; Selection III, Polaroid Collection, Houston Foto Fest, Tex, 90; Selections V, Polaroid Collection, Photokina, Stuttgart, Germany, 90; PRET, Collection D'Oeurves D'Art, Mus du Que, Can, 90; and others. *Teaching:* Lectr photog, Louisville Sch Art, Ky, 72-73; part-time lectr photog, drawing & design, Univ Ottawa, 74-90. *Awards:* Ont Arts Coun Grants, 80 & 89; Can Coun Arts Grants, 82-90; Can Coun Art A Grant, 90. *Bibliog:* Peter Weiermair (auth), Evergon-Homo Barocco, Cliches, No 48, Belg, 88; Chritsie Day (auth), The wit and wisdom of a remarkable Canadian artist, Can Photog, No 1, Toronto, Can, spring 90; Martin B Pendersen (auth), Graphis Photo 90, Graphis Corp, Zurich, Switz, 90. *Mem:* Can Artists Representative, Ont & Ottawa; Visual Arts Ont. *Media:* Polaroid, Holography. *Publ:* Contribr, Artifacts at the End of a Decade, 80; Canadian Portfolio, 80; Ottawa Portfolio 1983, The Company of Artists and Patrons, 83; The New Photography: A Guide to New Images, Processes and Display Techniques, Prentice-Hall, 85. *Dealer:* Art 45 2155 Guy St Montreal PQ H3G 1K4 Canada; Jack Shainman Gallery 560 Broadway New York NY 10012. *Mailing Add:* c/o Jack Shainman Gallery 560 Broadway New York NY 10012

EVERHART, DON, II
SCULPTOR, MEDALIST
b York, Pa, Aug 19, 49. *Study:* Kutztown State Univ, BFA(painting), 72. *Work:* Smithsonian Inst; Brit Mus; Franklin Mint Mus; Scott Paper Co; Am Numismatic Soc; and others. *Comn:* The Dance of the Dolphins (art medal), Soc Medallists, 82; bicentennial medal, Georgetown Univ, 88; Twenty-Five Coin of the Realm (legendary WWII aircraft), Marshall Islands, 90-91; Hermit Crab (art medal), Brookgreen Gardens, SC, 91; 22 installed sculptures, Georgetown Univ, Washington, DC, 92-; and others. *Exhib:* Reliefs & Medals Expos, Nat Sculpture Soc, New York, 85; Am Medallic Sculpture Asn, Newark Mus, NJ, 90; Nat Sculpture Soc Juried Show, Fairfield, Conn, 90; Traveling Show, Am Medallic Sculpture Asn, Univ Hartford, Conn, Cast Iron Gallery, New York & Bryant Libr, Roslyn, NY, 92; 23rd World Expos Fedn Int de la Medaille, Brit Mus, London, 92; and others. *Pos:* Illusr, Int Design Orgn, Moorestown, NJ, 72-73; sculptor in residence, Franklin Mint, 73-80; freelance sculptor & medalist, 80- *Teaching:* Instr sculpture, Chester Co Art Asn, 85-88. *Awards:* First Prize, Nat Sculpture Soc, 85; First Prize, Juried Sculpture Show, Chester Co Art Asn, 90; Second Prize, Sculpture, Franklin Mint Creative People Art Show, 91; and others. *Bibliog:* Carol Overstreet (auth), A young man's search for his art, Franklin Mint Almanac Mag, 76; MTB unveils liberty coins, Coin World, 9/82; Jed Stevenson (auth), Medal sculpture, NY Times, 3/92. *Mem:* Am Medallic Sculpture Asn (pres, 92-); Fedn Int de la Medaille; Int Sculpture Ctr; Knickerbocker Artists; Am Artists Prof League; and others. *Media:* Lost Wax & Bonded Bronze, Clay; Plaster, Urethane. *Publ:* Illusr cover, To Touch the Deer, Westminster Press, 81; The Secret of the 100 MPG Automobile, Crest Serv, 81; illusr bas-relief cover, Mefoxin--A Comprehensive Summary, Merck, Sharpe & Dohme, 83. *Mailing Add:* 1047 Niels Lane W West Chester PA 19382-7176

EVERSLEY, FREDERICK JOHN
SCULPTOR
b Brooklyn, NY, Aug 28, 41. *Study:* Carnegie Inst Technol, BSEE, 63; Inst Allende, San Miguel de Allende, Mex. *Work:* Smithsonian Inst, Nat Acad Sci, Nat Mus Am Art & Nat Air & Space Mus, Washington, DC; Whitney Mus Am Art & Solomon R Guggenheim Mus, New York; Thyssen-Bornemisza Collection, Castagnola, Switz; Mus Contemp Art, Los Angeles. *Comn:* Plastic sculpture, San Francisco Int Airport, Calif, 70 & Lenox Sq Ctr, Atlanta, Ga; plastic sculpture fountain, Dallas Hyatt-Regency Hotel; kinetic stainless steel sculpture, Miami Int Airport, Fla; laser beam sculpture, Detroit Gen Hosp; oil fountain sculpture, Saudi Pavilion, Expo 92, Seville, Spain. *Exhib:* Solo exhibs, Pepperdine Univ Art Gallery, Malibu, Calif, 82, Braunstein Gallery, San Francisco, 83, Bacardi Art Gallery, Miami, Fla, 84, Loyola Marymount Univ, Los Angeles, 85 & Hokin Gallery, Palm Beach & Bal Harbor, Fla, 88; Juda Rowan Gallery, London, 84 & 87; Light Games, Angels Gate Cult Ctr, San Pedro, Calif, 85; Artwalk 87 Salvo, Merging One Gallery, Santa Monica, 87; Newport Harbor Art Mus, Calif, 88; Highlights of the Simon Guggenheim Mus Collection, Columbia Mus Art, SC, 88; Constructivist Art, Mus Ludwig, Koln, WGer, 88; and others. *Pos:* Tech consult, Art & Technol Exhib, Los Angeles Co Mus Art, 71; first artist-in-residence, Nat Air & Space Mus, Smithsonian Inst, Washington, DC, 77-80. *Awards:* Purchase Prize, Tenth Ann Southern Calif Exhib, Long Beach Mus, 72; First Artist-in-Residence, Smithsonian Inst, Washington, DC, 77-80; Individual Artist Fel Grant, Nat Endowment Arts, Washington, DC. *Bibliog:* Kristine McKenna (auth), Eversley revives the finnish fetish mode, Los Angeles Times, 10/2/85; Joan Hugo (auth), Pick of the week, LA Weekly, 10/4-10/85; Susan Price (auth), Behind studio doors, Los Angeles times Sunday Mag, 5/24/87. *Media:* Multicolored Cast Transparent Plastic, Stainless Steel. *Mailing Add:* c/o Engineered Aesthetics 1110 W Washington Blvd Venice CA 90291

EVERTS, CONNOR
PAINTER, PRINTMAKER
b Bellingham, Wash, Jan 24, 26. *Study:* Chouinard Art Inst, Los Angeles; El Camino Col, Calif, AA; Univ Wash; Mexico City Col, BA; Courtauld Inst, Univ London. *Work:* Mus Mod Art, San Francisco; Mus Mod Art, New York; Mus Mod Art, Tokyo, Japan; Pushkin Mus, Moscow, Soviet Union; Chicago Art Inst. *Comn:* Collage mural, El Camino Col, 58; mural, Goldwater Bldg, Calif, 63. *Exhib:* Brand Art Ctr, Calif, 73; Cranbrook Art Mus, 80; World Print Coun Exhib, San Francisco, 82; Retrospective, Los Angeles Munic Art Gallery, 83; Orange County Ctr for Contemp Art, 86; Whatcom Mus, Hist & Art, 87; and others. *Teaching:* Chmn graphic dept, Calif Inst of Art, 60-64; guest artist painting, San Francisco Art Inst, 64-65; head printmaking dept, Crambrook Acad Art, 76-81. *Awards:* Painting Award, Los Angeles Artists & Vicinity, Los Angeles Co Mus, 55; Prize, 4th Int Young Artists Exhib, Tokyo, 67; Purchase Award, Southern Calif, Muckenthaler Found, 74. *Bibliog:* D Brewer (auth), The Studies of Connor Everts, Brand Art Ctr, 73; Lorend Sims (auth), Connor Everts-Transitions, Los Angeles Munic Art Gallery, 83; Donald Brewer (auth), Connor Everts-Selected Works, Whatcom Mus Hist & Art, 87. *Mem:* Nat Adv Bd Print; Los Angeles Printmaking Soc (pres, 63-64); Nat Asn Univ Prof. *Media:* Aqua Paint; Collage. *Dealer:* Ruth Bachofner Gallery 926 Colorado Ave Santa Monica CA 90401; Joy Emory 131 Rancheval Ave Grasse Point Farms MI. *Mailing Add:* The Market 2351 Sonoma Torrance CA 90501

EVETT, KENNETH WARNOCK
PAINTER
b Loveland, Colo, Dec 1, 13. *Study:* Colo State Col, AB; Colo Col, MA; also with Boardman Robinson, George Biddle & Henry V Poor. *Work:* Amon Carter Mus, Ft Worth, Tex; Colorado Springs Fine Arts Ctr, Colo; Herbert Johnson Mus, Cornell Univ, NY; Joslyn Mus, Omaha; Wichita Mus, Kans. *Comn:* Three murals for rotunda of Nebr State Capitol, 54. *Exhib:* Pa Acad Fine Arts, 52; Whitney Mus Am Art Ann, 52-54; Metrop Mus Art, 53; Corcoran Gallery Art Biennial, 54; Art Inst Chicago Biennial, 54; Nat Mus Am Art, 81; ten one-man exhibs, Kraushaar Galleries, 48-83. *Pos:* Art critic, New Republic, 72-77. *Teaching:* Prof art, Cornell Univ, 48-79, chmn dept, 74-77. *Awards:* Drawing Prize, Norfolk Mus, 66; Drawing Prize, Rochester Mus, 68; Purchase Prize, Munson-Williams-Proctor Inst, 68. *Media:* Watercolor, Oil. *Publ:* Auth, The New Realism, 72 & Literature and liberalism: 75 years of the New Republic, New Republic Mag. *Dealer:* Antoinette Kraushaar Galleries 724 Fifth Ave New York NY 10028. *Mailing Add:* 402 Oak Ave Ithaca NY 14850

EVILO, See Austin-Nuhfer, Olive H

EWALD, ELIN LAKE
WRITER
b Raleigh, NC. *Study:* Art Students League with Edwin Dickinson; Am Acad Art; Art Inst Chicago; grad prog, New York Univ & Metrop Mus Art; doctoral candidate, New York Univ. *Pos:* Assoc, Gallery Mayer, New York; free-lance art writer, 70-72; pres, O'Toole-Ewald Art Assoc Inc, 74- *Awards:* Am Soc Arts, NY; Am Soc Appraisers. *Mem:* Nat Asn Rev Appraisers; Am Soc Appraisers (pres & bd dirs, NY Chap); Am Asn Mus; Int Coun Mus; Costume Soc Am; Am Arbitration Asn;; Am Bankruptcy Inst;; Corp Art Mgt. *Specialty:* Consultants and fine art/antiques appraisers, specialists in damage/loss/fraud reports. *Interests:* For over 60 years, firm has appraised and assembled private collections for individuals, corporations and museums; additionally, it has arrangrd donations of individual works of art and collections to museums; specialists in damage/loss reports and appraisals of corporate collections. *Publ:* Auth, Hester Bateman and English Women Silversmiths of the 18th Century, Ms Mag, 76; auth, articles In: Valuation Mag & Fairshare; contrib ed, Personal Property J. *Mailing Add:* 1133 Broadway New York NY 10010

EWEN, PATERSON
PAINTER, EDUCATOR
b Montreal, Que, Can, Apr 7, 25. *Study:* Montreal Mus Sch Fine Art & Design, Can, dipl with high standing in painting, drawing & the teaching of child art; McGill Univ, Montreal, Univ Western Ont, hon DLitt, 89, London, Ont, hon DLett, 89; Concordia Univ, Montreal, hon LLD, 89. *Work:* Nat Gallery Can & Can Coun Art Bank, Ottawa, Ont; Amsterdam Civic Mus; Art Gallery Vancouver, BC; Mus de la Province de Que; Art Gallery Ont. *Comn:* Mural, Performing Arts Ctr, Univ Lethbridge, 81. *Exhib:* One-man shows, Carmen Lamanna Gallery, Toronto, 69, 72-74, 78, 80, 82, 84, & 86-90, Critical Works & Works on Paper, Art Gallery of Hamilton, 92, Equinox Gallery, Vancouver, 92; Rutgers Univ Art Gallery, 75; Mt Allison Univ, 75; retrospective, London Pub Art Gallery, London, Ont, 77, Art Gallery, Hamilton, 92; Paterson Ewen: Recent Works Traveling Exhib, Nat Gallery Can, 77-78; Biennale Venezia, Venice, 82; Ten Canadian Artists in the 1970's Traveling Show, Art Gallery Ont, 80-81; 20th Century Canadian Painting Traveling Show, Nat Gallery Can, 81; Dalhousie Univ, Halifax, Nova Scotia, 84; Pour la Suite du Monde et La Collection, Tableau Inaugural, Mus Contemp Art, Montreal, 92, L'Anarchie resplendissante de la peinture, Galerie de l'UQAM, Montreal & Baldacci-Daverio Gallery, New York, 92. *Pos:* Prof emer, Univ Western Ont, 88- *Teaching:* Asst prof painting & drawing, Univ Western Ont, London, 72-87. *Awards:* Sr Can Coun Award Can Coun, 71, 87; Donald Cameron Medal, Banff Sch Fine Art, 87; Toronto Arts Award, Arts Found Greater Toronto, 88. *Mem:* Royal Can Acad; Can Artists' Rep. *Media:* Mixed Media. *Publ:* Paterson Ewen: Recent Works, Vancouver Art Gallery (catalog), 5/77; Paterson Ewen: Phenomena Paintings 1971-1987, Art Gallery Ont, (exhib catalog), Toronto, 1/88; Paterson Ewen: The Montreal Years, Mendal Art Gallery (exhib catalog), Saskatoon, Can, 11/87; Startled Wonder: The Phenomenascapes of Paterson Ewen, Carmen Lamanna Gallery, Toronto, 89; rev, Paterson Ewen, Mus Fine Arts, Montreal Artforum, 90. *Mailing Add:* 1015 Wellington Street London ON N6A 3T5 Canada

EWING, EDGAR LOUIS
PAINTER
b Hartington, Nebr, Jan 17, 13. *Study:* Art Inst Chicago, grad, 35, Edward L Ryerson fel, 35-37 & also with Boris Anisfeld; two years European travel and study. *Work:* Richmond Mus Fine Arts, Va; Los Angeles Co Mus Art; Santa Barbara Mus; De Young Mem Mus, San Francisco; Nat Gallery, Athens, Greece; San Diego Mus; Univ Nebr; Raleigh Mus. *Exhib:* Sao Paulo Mus Art Int, Brazil; Carnegie Mus Int, Pittsburgh; Art Inst Chicago; Metrop Mus Art, New York; Pa Acad Fine Arts, Philadelphia; one-man shows, Greek Nat Gallery, 73, Munic Gallery, Los Angeles, 74 & Fisher Gallery, Univ Southern Calif, 78; 20 Yrs Retrospective, Palm Springs Desert Mus, 76-77; Santa Barbara Mus; De Young Mus, San Francisco. *Teaching:* Instr painting, Art Inst Chicago, 37-43; prof fine arts, Univ Southern Calif, 46-78, emer prof, 78-, distinguished emer prof, 87; Andrew Mellon prof painting, Carnegie Mellon Univ, 68-69. *Awards:* Purchase Award, 52 & Samuel Goldwyn Award, 57, Los Angeles County Mus Art; Jose Drudis Fund Grant, 67; Los Angeles Libr Asn Award, 76; Floresheim Award, Art Inst Chicago; 100 Artists, 100 Years, Art Inst Chicago, 11/79-1-80. *Bibliog:* Schaad (auth), The Realm of Contemporary Still Life Painting, 62 & Mugnaini (auth), Oil Painting--Techniques and Materials, 69, Van Nostrand. *Mem:* Am Asn Univ Prof; Nat Watercolor Soc (pres); Col Art Asn; Los Angeles Mus Asn. *Media:* Oil. *Dealer:* Studio Athens Greece Odos Piraeus 10431. *Mailing Add:* 4226 Sea View Lane Los Angeles CA 90065

EYRE, IVAN
PAINTER
b Tullymet, Sask, Can, Apr 15, 35. *Study:* Univ Sask, 52; Univ Man, BFA, 57; Univ NDak, 58. *Work:* Nat Gallery Can, Ottawa, Ont; Montreal Mus Fine Arts, Que; Vancouver Art Gallery, BC; Winnipeg Art Gallery, Man; Art Bank, Ottawa, Ont. *Comn:* Resurrection, (painting) Can Cath Conf, Ottawa, Ont, 76; Black Arrow Plain, (painting) Can Indust & Com Bank, Edmonton, Alta, 80; North Northwest (painting) Teron Int, Ottawa, Ont, 86. *Exhib:* 6th & 7th Biennial Can Painting, 65 & 67, New Landscapes, 74 & Landscape Can, 76, Nat Gallery Can, Ottawa, Ont; one-man shows, Nat Gallery Can, Ottawa, Ont, 78, 88, Robert McLaughlin Gallery, Ivan Eyre Expos, Oshawa, Ont, 80 (Travelled To Paris, London & Edinburgh) 81, Art Gallery Greater Victoria Traveling, 82 & Winnipeg Art Gallery, Winnipeg, 82 & 88; Mira Godard Gallery, Toronto, 81, 90 & 92; Ivan Eyre: Personal Mythologies: Images of the Milieu Nat, Gallery Can, Ottawa, Ont, 88; and others. *Teaching:* Prof drawing & painting, Univ Man, Winnipeg, 59-93; prof painting, Banff Centre, Alta, summer 73. *Awards:* Sr Arts Awards, Can Coun, 66 & 78; Queens Silver Jubilee Medal, Gov Gen of Can, 77; Univ Man Jubilee Award, 82. *Bibliog:* E Zuk (producer), Visual Thinker (film), CBC, Winnipeg, 81; George Woodcock (auth), Ivan Eyre, Fitzhenry & Whitside, 81; Doug Whiteway (auth), Out of sight, out of mind--the art of Ivan Eyre, Alumni J, Univ Man, autumn 82; Visions (film), TV Ont, 83; and many other films & articles in various mags. *Mem:* Royal Can Acad Arts. *Media:* Acrylic, Multimedia. *Dealer:* Mira Godard Gallery 22 Hazelton Ave Toronto On Canada M5R 2E2; Equinox Gallery 1525 W Eight Vancouver BC V6J 1T5 Can. *Mailing Add:* 1098 Trappistes St Winnipeg MB R3V 1B8 Canada

F

F(ORD), LISA COLLADO
COLLAGE ARTIST, PAINTER
b Washington, DC, June 24, 44. *Study:* Radcliffe Col, 62-63; Art Students League, New York, with Edward Giobbi, Leg Manso & Xavier Gonzales, 79-82; Empire State Col, NY, BA, 85. *Work:* Washington Co Mus Fine Arts, Hagerstown, NY; C W Post Col, Greenvale, NY; Everson Mus, Syracuse, NY; Eureka Col, Ill; NECCA Mus, Brooklyn, Conn; Addison Gallery, Andover, Mass; Mead Art Mus, Amherst, Mass; Rutgers Univ, New Brunswick, NJ; Museo de Arte Contemporaneo, Buenos Aires; Permanent Mission of the State of Qatarto, United Nations. *Comn:* Exxon Corp, 83 & F Aley Allan, 84, New York. *Exhib:* Hemisferia, Cultural Olympics Mexico City, San Antonio, Tex, 68; 2nd Ann Juried Show, Mus Hudson Highlands, Cornwall-on-Hudson, NY, 83; New Brunswick Arts Pride Week, Nat Endowment Arts, NJ, 85; Women Artists Series, Rutgers Univ, New Brunswick, NJ, 85; Nat Mus Art, Warsaw, Poland; Art Soc Int Monetary Fund, Washington, DC, 87; St Peter's Church, New York, 87; Am Sch Found, Mexico City, Mex, 88; Emerging Women Artists Series, AIR Gallery, New York, 89; Jehangir Gallery, Bombay, India, 89; Cornell Med Libr, 90; Lenox Hill Artists Forum, 90. *Awards:* Control Bd, 80 & Merit Scholar, 81, Art Students League, New York; Award of Merit, 20th Ann Juried Exhib, Univ Del, 82; Elizabeth Morse Gerthus Found, 89. *Bibliog:* Dr Ahmet Ali Arslan (dir), interview, Voice Am, 6/26/86; Kryptonita (auth), article, Arte Al Dia, Summer 88; Cynthia Man's Dantzig (auth), Design Dimensions an Introduction to the Visual Surface. *Mem:* Artists Equity Asn, New York; Nat Asn Women Artist; Orgn Independent Artists; Americanos Group, Lenox Hill Artists' Forum; Nat Women's Studies Asn. *Media:* Mixed Media. *Mailing Add:* 920 Park Ave Apt 2A New York NY 10028

FABBRI, ANNE R
MUSEUM DIRECTOR
b Norristown, Pa. *Study:* Radcliffe Col, AB(cum laude); Bryn Mawr Col, MA(art hist), 71; Univ Calif, Berkeley, 79; Princeton Univ, NEH Scholar, Dept of Art & Archaeol, 80. *Collections Arranged:* Seven Afro-American Artists of the Delaware Valley (auth, catalog), 81; Tradition and Innovations, 81; Five Hispanic Artists of Pennsylvania (auth, catalog), 82; Social Realism and the Figure, 82; Celebration of New Jersey Artists (auth, catalog), 83; Landscapes Here and Now, 87; Gerald Lynch, Sculptor, 88; Recent Oil Paintings by Glenn Rudderow, 89; Recent Sculpture by Charles Searles, 89; Artists' Gardens, 90; The Urban Scene, Philadelphia Through the Eyes of Its Artists, 92; What a Beautiful View, Ten Different Approaches to Nature, 92. *Pos:* Art critic & art ed, The Drummer, Philadelphia, 76-79; art critic, The Bull, Philadelphia, 79-80 & WXPN Express, 80-81; dir & cur, Alfred O Deshong Mus, Widener Univ, Chester, Pa, 80-82, Noyes Mus, Oceanville, NJ, 82- *Teaching:* Lectr hist art, Villanova Univ, Pa, 71-73 & Drexel Univ, Philadelphia, 74-76. *Bibliog:* Article, Art Matters, 6/83. *Mem:* Print Club, Philadelphia (bd govs); MUSE Found Visual Arts; Int Asn Art Critics; Am Asn Mus; Col Art Asn; Amici, Ctr Italian Studies (bd adv); VOICES, (bd trustees). *Res:* Art theory; Mannerist art and iconography. *Publ:* Auth, Patience pays at Dr Barnes's Bks & Arts, 1/80; Three sculptors, 1/80, Harry Bertoia, 2/80 & Judith Ingram, 3/80, Arts Mag. *Mailing Add:* 642 Valley View Lane Wayne PA 19087

FABE, ROBERT
PAINTER, EDUCATOR
b Chicago, Ill, May 24, 17. *Study:* Art Acad Cincinnati, cert fine art, 38; Art Students League, with George Grosz, Arnold Blanch & Raphael Soyer, Out of Town Scholar, 38-39. *Work:* Cincinnati Art Mus; Univ Cincinnati; Miami Univ, Ohio; Procter & Gamble, Cincinnati; and other pub & pvt collections. *Comn:* Murals, Shrimp Boat Restaurant, Dayton, Otter Bein Press, Dayton & Highland Towers, Marvin Warner Corp, Cincinnati. *Exhib:* Butler Inst Am Art, Youngstown, Ohio, 40-68; Cincinnati Ann, 40-70 & Laser Art Exhib, 71, Cincinnati Art Mus; one-man shows, Mt St Joseph Col, Cincinnati, 70 & Ohio State Capitol, 71; and many other group & one-man shows. *Teaching:* Prof, Col Design Archit & Art, Univ Cincinnati, 58- *Awards:* Dayton Art Inst Purchase Award; Butler Inst Am Art Purchase Award; Ohio Univ Show Award. *Mem:* MacDowell Soc (pres, 70-72); Cincinnati Prof Artists (pres, 70-72). *Media:* Tempera, Watercolor. *Mailing Add:* C E C E 120 McMicken Hall (ML 19) Cincinnati OH 45221

FABERT, JACQUES
PAINTER, SCULPTOR
b Paris, France, Apr 24, 25; US citizen. *Study:* Ecole Nat Super des Beaux Arts, Paris, grad, 46. *Work:* Butler Inst Am Art, Youngstown, Ohio; Norfolk Mus Art, Va; Univ Calif, Berkeley; Wash Munic Court Art Fund; Stedman Gallery, Rutgers Univ, Camden, NJ. *Comn:* Painting, San Francisco Theol Sem, Calif, 69; paintings, City San Francisco, 70; mural, Dr Boonswang, Easton, Pa, 78; paintings, Metromedia Corp; painting, IBM Corp. *Exhib:* Invitational Shows, Calif Palace of the Legion of Honor, San Francisco, 62, 63, 67 & 75; one-man shows, E B Crocker Mus Art, Sacramento, Calif, 69 & Carroll Reece Mus, E Tenn State Univ, Johnson City, 74; Nat Inst Arts & Lett Exhib, New York, 70; Nat Drawing '79, Stedman Gallery, Rutgers Univ, Camden, NJ, 79 & 81; and others. *Pos:* Dir, Mex Studies, Mex Exten, Calif Col Arts & Crafts, Morelia, Mex, 69-72; designer of tapestries for Beverly Godfrey Weaving Studios, 91- *Teaching:* Prof fine arts, San Francisco Acad Art, 63-70; prof fine arts, Calif Col Arts & Crafts, Oakland, 63-70; prof fine arts, Princeton Art Assocs, NJ, 79- *Awards:* Purchase Awards, Butler Inst Am Art, 68, Childe Hassam Fund, 70 & Stedman Gallery, Rutgers Univ, 79. *Bibliog:* Arthur Bloomfield (auth), article, San Francisco Chronicle, 67-69; Alfred Frankenstein (auth), article, San Francisco Examiner, 67-69. *Media:* Multimedia. *Dealer:* Langman Gallery 218 Old York Rd Jenkintown PA 19046; Genest Gallery Lambertville NJ. *Mailing Add:* PO Box 103 2682 Rte 413 Buckingham PA 18912

FABIAN FABIANO, DIANE
PAINTER
b Winthrope, Mass, Oct 7, 52. *Study:* Calif Col Arts & Crafts, BA(summa cum laude, painting), 76. *Work:* Ventura Mus, Calif; Laser Inst, Van Nuys, Calif; San Francisco Arts Comn Gallery, Calif; Calabasas Art Pub Places Gallery, Calif; Mass Gen Hosp, Boston. *Comn:* Site specific painting, Trade Wind Tours Hawaii, Las Vegas, Nev, 80; six site specific paintings, Benjamin Jay Stores & Salons, Woodland Hills, Calif, 90-91. *Exhib:* Group shows, LA Valley Col Gallery, Van Nuys, Calif, 86 & Aubes 3935 Gallery, Montreal, Can, 86; Work of the 80's, Tarsh Gallery, Woodland Hills, Calif, 88; The Planets, The Queens of Space, Palm St Gallery, Ventura, Calif, 91; Dangerous/Endangered Animals, Circa 9 Gallery, San Diego, Calif, 91; Endangered Species & Rainforests, Calabasas Art Pub Places Gallery, Calif, 92. *Pos:* Art dir, Eara Advert Resources, 90-91. *Bibliog:* Lisa McKinnon (auth), Planet myths, symbols mix (2 page interview), Press-Courier, 2/91; Art pick of the week, Ventura Co & Coast Reporter, 2/91; Lisa McKinnon (auth), Walking on the art side, Star Free Press, 5/92. *Mem:* City of Calabasas, Parks, Rec & Cult Comt (arts coun liaison, 91); Artist Equity Asn; Womens Caucus Arts; Show Coalition; World Affairs Coun. *Media:* Mixed. *Publ:* Contribr, Encyclopedia of Living Artists, Directors Guild Publ, 87; California Artists Review, Am References, 89; Who's Who In American Women, Macmillan/Marquis, 91-92; auth, The Planets, The Queens of Space, Golden Era Legacy Prod, 92; contribr, Art/Life Mag, Art/Life Eds, 2/92. *Dealer:* Deborist Dory-Burke 5790 Cherry Ridge Dr Camarillo CA 93012. *Mailing Add:* 5624 Las Virgenes Rd Studio 16 Calabasas CA 91302

FACCI, DOMENICO (AURELIO)
SCULPTOR, PAINTER
b Hooversville, Pa, Feb 2, 16. *Study:* Roerich Acad Arts, 36. *Work:* Norfolk Mus Arts & Sci, Va; Fla Southern Col, Lakeland; Polk Mus Art, Lakeland, Fla, 92. *Comn:* cartouche for lobby, Am Express Bldg, New York, NY, 78; cartouche for bronze doors, St Peter's Cathedral, Philadelphia, Pa, 78; bronze sculpture, Pub Sch 147, Bronx, NY, 85; bust, Bob Hope, Calif, 86; 100 feet of plaques on the Brooklyn Bridge, Building the Brooklyn Bridge on 17 Plaques on the Walkway at the North Tower, 92. *Exhib:* First Int Art Exhib, Fla Southern Col; Artists Equity Exhib, Whitney Mus Am Art; Butler Inst Am Art; Nat Acad, 78; Nat Sculpture Soc, 68; ann exhibs, Knickerbocker Artists, 78-; ann exhibs, Audubon Artists, 78-; and numerous others. *Teaching:* Vis prof sculpture & stone carving, Fla Southern Col, 52-; instr sculpture & stone carving, Ridgewood Art Sch, NJ, 61-65; instr sculpture & stone carving, Craft Student League, New York, 66-72; pvt instr, 73- *Awards:* Albert Dorne Prize, Audubon Artists, 56-61 & Cash Award, 78; Gold Medal, Knickerbocker Artists, 78; and numerous others. *Bibliog:* Domenico Facci, sculptor (film), WEDO-TV, Tampa, Fla, 70. *Mem:* Audubon Artists (pres, 66-77 & 82-84); Am Soc Contem; Sculptors League; assoc Nat Acad; fel, Nat Sculpture Soc. *Mailing Add:* 240 W 4th St New York NY 10014

FACCINTO, VICTOR PAUL
PAINTER, FILMMAKER
b Albany, Calif, Oct 30, 45. *Study:* Calif State Univ, Sacramento, BA, 69, MA, 72; Creative Artists Pub Serv Prog Fel, NY, 77, NC Artist Fel, 80, 86. *Work:* Film Study Collection, Mus Mod Art, New York; Philip Morris Inc, Cabarrus, NC. *Exhib:* New Am Filmmakers, Whitney Mus Am Art, New York, 72-74; Cineprobe, Mus Mod Art, New York, 75; Circulating Film Program, Am Fedn Arts, New York, 72-; American Experimental Cinema 1905-1984, Pompidou Ctr, Paris, 85; one-man show, NC Mus Art, 86, Phyllis Kind Gallery 1980, New York, 82, 87, Bruce Helander Gallery, New York, 90. *Collections Arranged:* Gladys Nilsson Retrospective, Wake Forest Univ Art Gallery, 79. *Pos:* Gallery dir, Wake Forest Univ, 78- *Teaching:* Instr multimedia, Wake Forest Univ, Winston-Salem, NC, 81-82; lectr art, painting & drawing, 84- *Awards:* NC Visual Artist Fel, 81 & 86. *Bibliog:* Grace Glueck (auth), New York Times, 4/4/80; Kay Larson (auth), Village Voice, 4/7/80; Victoria Lautman (auth), Exhibition review, Chicago Sun Times, 4/17/87. *Media:* Oil Acrylic; Film, Video. *Publ:* Co-producer & photographer, Howard Finster: Stranger from Another World, Abbeville Press, New York, 89. *Dealer:* Phyllis Kind Gallery 136 Greene St New York NY 10012; Helander Gallery 125 Worth St Palm Beach FL 33480. *Mailing Add:* Dept Art Wake Forest Univ Winston-Salem NC 27109

FACEY, MARTIN KERR
PAINTER, EDUCATOR
b Colorado Springs, Colo, Apr 25, 48. *Study:* Univ Calif, Los Angeles, with William Brice & Charles Garabedian, BA, 71, with Richard Diebenkorn, MA, 73, MFA, 74. *Work:* Security Pacific Bank Collection, Los Angeles, Calif; Bank Am Collection, San Francisco, Calif. *Exhib:* Solo exhib, Los Angeles Munic Gallery, 79, Ivory-Kimpton Gallery, San Francisco, 81, 83-85, 87, Tortue Gallery, Santa Monica, 80, 82-83, 86 & 88, Univ Art Mus, Albuquerque, NMex, 87; two-person show, Claremont Grad Sch Gallery, 85; Jean Albano Gallery, Chicago, 88 & 91; Zimmerman-Saturn, Nashville, Tenn, 89; Sena East Gallery, Santa Fe, NMex, 90. *Teaching:* Instr painting & drawing, Santa Monica Col, Calif, 78-85; vis lectr painting & drawing, Univ Calif, Los Angeles, 83-85; assoc prof painting & drawing, Univ NMex, 86- *Awards:* Gugenheim Fel in Painting, 82-83; Burlington Northern Found Award for Meritorius Teaching, Univ NMex, 87. *Bibliog:* Judith Spiegel (auth), Revitalizing abstraction, Artweek Mag, 6/25/88; Michael Laurence (auth), Martin Facey at Tortue, Artscribe Int, 10/86; David Winter (auth), Martin Facey at Ivory-Kimpton, Art News, 1/86; Peter Frank (auth), Pick of the Week, Los Angeles Weekly, 6/16/88; Sandy Ballatorxe (auth), Painter Centers Himself in Images. *Mem:* Col Art Asn; Los Angeles Contemp Exhib; Albuquerque United Artists. *Media:* Oil. *Dealer:* Sena East Gallery 125 East Pl Santa Fe NM 87501; Works Gallery 106 W 3rd St Long Beach CA 90802. *Mailing Add:* c/o Jean Albano Gallery 311 W Superior Chicago IL 60610

FADEN, LAWRENCE STEVEN
PAINTER, SCULPTOR
b Brooklyn, NY, Oct 21, 42. *Study:* Brooklyn Mus student scholar; Sch Visual Arts; NY Studio Sch; and with Nicholas Carone. *Work:* Chase Manhattan Bank, New York; Smith Kline Beckman Corp, NJ. *Exhib:* New Images, Figuration in Am Painting, Queens Mus, 74; Artists Choice Figurative Art in New York, Bowery Gallery, 76-77; one-man shows, G W Einstein Gallery, 80, 85 & 92; The 80's: A Post Pop Generation, Southern Alleghenies Mus Art, 90; 167th Ann Nat Acad Design Exhib, 92; and others. *Teaching:* Instr, Educ Alliance Art Sch, 82-84; vis artist, Parson Sch Design, 92. *Bibliog:* Alfred Frankenstein & Ann Van Devanter (co-auth), The American Self Portrait?, Praeger, 75; Carter Ratcliff (auth), monogr, 85; Brett Busang (auth), Am Artist Mag, 92. *Mem:* Alliance Figurative Artists (prog dir, 75). *Media:* Windsor Newton Oil; Terra Cotta Clay. *Dealer:* G W Einstein Co 591 Broadway New York NY 10012. *Mailing Add:* 184 E Seventh St No 7 New York NY 10009

FAGALY, WILLIAM ARTHUR
MUSEUM DIRECTOR, HISTORIAN
b Lawrenceburg, Ind, Mar 1, 38. *Study:* Ind Univ, Bloomington, BA, 62, MA, 67. *Collections Arranged:* Louisiana Folk Painting, Mus Am Folk Art, New York, 73; Art USA: The South, Cent & South Am, 75-78; David Butler: Louisiana Environmental Folk Sculptor, 76 & Five From Louisiana, 77, New Orleans Mus Art; Nat Endowment Arts Nat Site Works, Arts Festival

Atlanta, 88; 41st Biennial Exhib of Contemp Am Painting, Corcoran Gallery Art, Washington, DC, 89; Preacher Art, Arthur Roger Gallery, New Orleans, 90. *Pos:* Registrar, New Orleans Mus Art, 66-67, cur collections, 67-72, chief cur, 73-80, asst dir art, 81- *Teaching:* Assoc prof art hist, Delgado Col, 67-69; vis assoc prof, Univ New Orleans, 80. *Awards:* Nat Endowment Arts Mus Prof Fel. *Bibliog:* Joan Caldwell (auth), William A Fagaly Chief Curator of New Orleans Museum of Art, Arts Quart, vol 1, issue 2, 78; Bunny Matthews (auth), From New Orleans to Africa, Wavelength, 3/88; D Eric Bookhardt (auth), Interviewing William Fagaly, Art Papers, Vol 13, No 4, 15-18, 7-8/89. *Mem:* Arts Coun of African Studies Asn; Ctr African & African American Studies (adv bd). *Res:* African art; contemporary art; American contemporary folk art. *Publ:* Coauth, Southern fictions, In: Southern Fictions, Contemp Art Mus, Houston, 83; auth, An historical overview of Louisiana women's achievements in art, In: Louisiana Women in Contemporary Art, Univ Mus, Southern Ill Univ, 83; auth, Shapes of Power, Belief and Celebration, African Art from New Orleans Collections, New Orleans Mus Art, 89; Ida Kohlmeyer (exib catalog essay) Allene Lapides Gallery, Santa Fe, 92; Gumbo, Ya/Ya, and Hey Pocky Way: Willie Birch's New Orleans and African Americans Making It What is is, Willie Birch: A Personal View of Urban America, (exbih catalog essay), Exhib Art, New York, 92. *Mailing Add:* New Orleans Mus Art PO Box 19123 City Park New Orleans LA 70179

FAGAN, ALANNA
PAINTER
b New Bedford, Mass, 39. *Study:* Silvermine Guild Sch Art, New Canaan, Conn, painting & sculpture; studied privately with painters, Charles Reid, Daniel Greene, et al. *Comn:* Portrait, pres, Istituto Geografico de Agostini, Novara, Italy, 81; portrait, founder, Cohen & Wolf, PC, Bridgeport, Conn, 83; portrait, Ctr Creative Leadership, Wilmington, NC, 84; portrait, former dean, New Eng Sch Law, Boston, Mass, 84; portrait, retired pres, Harvard Club, New York, 91. *Exhib:* American Painters in Paris, Palais de Congrés, France, 75; Pastel Soc Exhib, Copley Mus, Boston, 79; Painters of St Barthelemy, Cent Falls Gallery, New York, 84; Group of 5, Galerie du Musée, Paris, France, 85; 161st Ann Exhib, Nat Acad Design, New York, 86; and others. *Teaching:* Instr portrait & pastels, Silvermine Guild Sch, 77-81. *Mem:* Allied Artists Am; Pastel Soc Am; Salmagundi Club; Silvermine Guild Artists. *Media:* Oil, Pastel. *Publ:* Auth & illusr, Drawing People (filmstrip) & Drawing Animals (filmstrip), Troll Assocs, 81. *Dealer:* Greene Art Gallery 29 Whitfield St Guilford CT 06437; La Galerie, St Barthelemy, French West Indies. *Mailing Add:* 73 Housatonic Dr Milford CT 06460

FAGER, CHARLES J
CERAMIST, SCULPTOR
b Osage City, Kans, Feb 3, 36. *Study:* Kans State Univ, Manhattan, BArch, 59; Univ Kans, Lawrence, MFA(ceramics), 63. *Work:* Nat Collection Fine Art; Nat Mus Am Art, Smithsonian Inst. *Comn:* Ceramic installation, Tampa Pub Libr, 70; ceramic wall, Arbor Off Ctr, Clearwater, Fla, 73; hanging sculpture instalation, GTE Fla, Tampa, 83; Sculpture, Florida Department of Law Enforcement Regional Crime Lab, Jacksonville, Fla, 87; hanging sculpture installation, Opus South Corporation, Tampa, Fla, 89. *Exhib:* Piedmont Craftsman, Mint Mus, Charlotte, NC, 76; Ceramics Conjunction, Long Beach Mus Art, Calif, 77; Craftsmen of the Southeast Invitational Exhib, Birmingham Mus Art, Ala, 78; American Porcelain: New Expressions in an Ancient Art, Renwick Gallery, Smithsonian Inst, 81; Cast Clay, Nat Invitational Exhib, Pinch Pottery, Northhampton, Mass, 85; Tampa Triennial, Tampa Mus Art, Fla, 85; and numerous other group & one man shows. *Pos:* Consult archit, Rowe Holmes Assoc Archits Inc, Tampa, Fla, 73-74. *Teaching:* Art instr, Kans State Univ, Manhattan, 60-61; grad asst instr, Univ Kans, Lawrence, 61-63; prof art, Univ S Fla, Tampa, 63- *Awards:* Irving Hill First Award for Ceramics, Ninth Ann Kans Designer-Craftsman Exhib, Lawrence, 62; Ceramics Purchase Award, Wichita Nat Decorative Arts & Ceramics Exhib, Wichita, 62; Award of Excellence, Ann State Fla Craftsmen Exhib, 76; Fla Individual Artist Fel Award, 87-88. *Bibliog:* Lloyd E Herman (auth), American Porcelain: New Expressions in an Ancient Art, 80; Charlotte F Speight (auth), Images, In Clay Sculpture, 83; Charlotte F Speight (auth), Images of Clay Sculpture, 83; Donald Frith (auth), Mold making for ceramics, 85. *Media:* Clay, Metal. *Res:* Application of industrial clay form processes to art; slip casting ceramic figures from life; photoceramics. *Mailing Add:* c/o Albertson-Peterson Gallery 329 Park Ave S Winter Park FL 32789

FAHLEN, CHARLES C
SCULPTOR
b San Francisco, Calif, 1939. *Study:* Calif State Univ, San Francisco, BA, 62; Otis Art Inst, Los Angeles, MFA, 65; Slade Sch, Univ London, Eng, 67. *Work:* Denver Art Mus, Colo; Mus Mod Art, New York; Oakland Mus, Calif; Philadelphia Mus Art. *Comn:* General Grant, comn by Dan & Jenny Dietrich, Chester Springs, Pa, 78. *Exhib:* One-man shows, Richard Feigen Gallery, New York, 71, Henri 2, Washington, DC, 74, Marianne Deson Gallery, Chicago, 79, Lawrence Oliver Gallery, Philadelphia, 89 & ICA, Philadelphia, 91; Untitled, Artpark, Lewiston, NY, 76; Mus Contemp Art, Chicago, 80; Cleveland Ctr Arts, Cleveland, 85; Lawrence Oliver Gallery, Philadelphia, 88; Inst Contemp Art, Philadelphia, 90. *Teaching:* Instr sculpture, Moore Col Art & Design, Philadelphia, Pa, 67- *Awards:* Nat Endowment Arts, 80 & 88; Hazlett Mem Award for Excellence in the Arts, Pa Coun on the Arts, 85. *Bibliog:* Artists try new directions, The Philadelphia Inquirer, 6/25/88; Ron Glowen (auth), Port Townsend: Tidal Park Revives Old Port, Public Art Review, Winter/Spring, 89. *Dealer:* Lawrence Mangel Fine Art Philadelphia PA 19103. *Mailing Add:* 945 N Randolph St Philadelphia PA 19123

FAHLMAN, BETSY LEE
HISTORIAN
b Wolfeboro, NH, July 18, 51. *Study:* Mt Holyoke Col, Mass, BA, 73; Univ Del, Newark, MA, 77, PhD, 81. *Teaching:* Lectr art hist, Franklin & Marshall Col, 77-79; asst prof art hist, Old Dominion Univ, Norfolk, Va, 80-88; assoc prof art hist, Ariz State Univ, 88- *Mem:* Col Art Asn; Soc Indust Archaeol; Soc Archit Historians; Victorian Soc Am. *Res:* American Art, 1850-1930, architecture, painting & sculpture. *Publ:* Auth, Pennsylvania Modern: Charles Demuth of Lancaster (exhib catalog), Philadelphia Mus Art, 83; Women art students at Yale, 1869-1913: Never a true son of the university, Woman's Art J, Vol 12, No 1, spring/summer 91; Art displays in New Haven: Edward Sheffield Bartholomew & Yale's exhibition of 1858, J New Haven Colony Hist Soc, Vol 38, No 1, fall 91; A plaster of paris antiquity: Nineteenth century cast collections, Southeastern Col Art Conf Rev, Vol 12, No 1, 91; The Spirit of the South: The Sculpture of Alexander Galt (1827-1863) (exhib catalog), Muscarelle Mus Art, Col William & Mary, 10-11/92. *Mailing Add:* Sch Art Ariz State Univ Tempe AZ 85287

FAIRBANKS, JONATHAN LEO
CURATOR
b Ann Arbor, Mich, Feb 19, 33. *Study:* Brigham Young Univ & Univ Utah, BFA, 53; Univ Pa & Acad Fine Arts, MFA, 57; Univ Del, MA(Winterthur Fel), 61; Inst Patologia Libro, Rome, cert conservation, 68. *Pos:* Cur asst, Winterthur Mus, 61-62, asst cur, 62-67, assoc cur, 67-; Katharine Lane Weems Cur, Am decorative arts & sculpture, Mus Fine Arts, Boston, 71-; app Comt Preservation The White House. *Teaching:* Teaching fel, Pa Acad Fine Arts, 55-57; adj prof, Univ Del, 61-70 & Am & New Eng Studies Prog, Boston Univ, 71- *Awards:* Mural Award, Acad Natural Sci; Robert H Lord Award Excellence Hist Studies, Emmanuel Col, 83. *Mem:* Hon mem New Eng Chap, Am Soc Interior Designers; Soc Archit Historians; fel Am Inst Conserv; fel Pilgrim Soc; Colonial Soc Mass; hon fel, Am Crafts Coun, 86. *Publ:* Auth, forward, Art and Commerce: American Prints of the Nineteenth Century, Univ Press Va, 78; ed, Boston Furniture of the Eighteenth Century, Colonial Soc Mass, Vol 48; coauth, American Furniture 1620 to the Present, Richard Marek Inc, 81; coauth, New England Begins, The Seventeenth Century, Boston Mus Fine Arts, 82; auth introd, Sam Maloof, Woodworker, New York, 83; and others. *Mailing Add:* Mus of Fine Arts 465 Huntington Ave Boston MA 02115

FAIRFIELD, RICHARD THOMAS
PRINTMAKER, EDUCATOR
b Peoria, Ill, Aug 7, 37. *Study:* Bradley Univ, BFA, 61; Univ Ill, MFA, 63. *Work:* Howard Univ, DC; St John's Univ, Jamaica, NY; B Carroll Reece Mem Mus, E Tenn Univ, Johnson City; Ball State Univ, Muncie, Ind; Albion Col, Mich. *Exhib:* Northwest Printmakers, Seattle Art Mus, 70; Ball State Small Sculpture & Drawings, Ball State Univ, Muncie, Ind, 73; Am Miniature Printmaker, San Diego State Univ, Calif, 88; Interprint LVIV 90, LVIV Mus Hist Relig & Atheism, USSR, 90-92; Int Independents Exhib Prints, Kanagawa, Japan, 90; Paper Invitational, John F Kennedy Mem Union Art Gallery, Univ Dayton, Ohio, 90; solo exhib, Albion Col, Mich, 91; and others. *Teaching:* Prof printmaking, Eastern Mich Univ, Ypsilanti, 63- & Santa Reparata, Florence, Italy, spring 74; Paris, France, spring 87 & 89; Florence, Italy, spring 90; Madrid, Cardoba, Barcelona, Spain, spring 92. *Awards:* Purchase Awards, NDak Ann, Univ NDak, 66, Imprint, Kutztown State Col, 67 & Drawing USA, St Paul Art Ctr, 67; Alma Col, 88. *Media:* Etching, Screen. *Mailing Add:* Dept Art Eastern Mich Univ Ypsilanti MI 48197

FAIRWEATHER, SALLY H
ART DEALER
b Chicago, Ill, Sept 29, 17. *Study:* Art Students League, 36; Art Inst Chicago, BA, 39. *Pos:* Co-dir & owner, Fairweather-Hardin Gallery, Chicago, 47-91, Art Dealers Asn Am, 62-63 & Found Arts Scholar, Chicago, 64-; co-founder, Chicago Art Dealers Asn, 66. *Teaching:* Instr life drawing, Katherine Lord Sch, Evanston, Ill, 39-43. *Specialty:* Modern paintings, graphics and sculpture. *Publ:* Auth, Picasso's Concrete Sculpture, Hudson Hills Press, 82. *Mailing Add:* 101 E Ontario St Chicago IL 60611

FAISON, SAMSON LANE, JR
HISTORIAN, MUSEUM DIRECTOR
b Washington, DC, Nov 16, 07. *Study:* Williams Col, BA, 29; Harvard Univ, MA, 30; Princeton Univ, MFA, 32; Williams Col, Hon LittD, 71. *Collections Arranged:* The New England Eye, 83, and other permanent collections & temporary exhibs, Williams Col Mus Art. *Pos:* Exec secy, Comt on Visual Arts, Harvard Univ, 54-55; dir, Williams Col Mus Art, 48-76; Trustee, Bennington Mus, Vt, Hancock Shaker Village, Inc, Mass & Hancock Shaker Mus, Pittsfield, Mass, 78-; art vis comt, Mt Holyoke Col, Mass. *Teaching:* From instr to asst prof art, Yale Univ, 32-36; from asst prof to prof art, Williams Col, 36-76, chmn dept, 40-69; vis prof, Univ Pa, NY Univ, Columbia Univ, Univ Calif, Berkeley & Harvard Univ, summers; vis res prof, Univ Ga, spring 68. *Awards:* Chevalier, Legion of Honor, Fr Govt, 47; Guggenheim Fel, 60-61. *Mem:* Col Art Asn Am (pres, formerly); Asn Art Mus Dirs; Int Asn Art Critics; Mass Coun Arts & Humanities. *Res:* German eighteenth century architecture; nineteenth and twentieth century French and American painting. *Publ:* Auth, Dominikus Zimmermann, Mag Art, 52; Manet, Abrams, 53; Guide to Art Museums of New England, Harcourt Brace, 58; Art Tours and Detours in New York State, Random House, 64; Art Musems of New England, Godine, 82. *Mailing Add:* Scott Hill Rd Williamstown MA 01267

FALFAN, ALFREDO
PAINTER, PRINTMAKER
b Mexico City, Mex, June 8, 36. *Study:* Escuela Nac De Arts Plasticas, 53-60; with Diego Rivera & Antonio Rodriguez Luna; Pratt Inst, Graphics Workshop, 69-70. *Work:* Mus Mod Art & Museo Rufino Tamaya, Mexico City. *Exhib:* Mus Mod Art, Paris, 66; Museo Genaro Perez, Cordoba, Argentina, 66; Mus Mod Art, Mexico City, 66 & 80; Museo Carrillo Gil, Mexico City, 78; Mus Art Boca Raton, Fla, 90. *Teaching:* Prof painting, Escuela Nac De Artes Plasticas, 80- *Awards:* Spec Prize, Am Biennial III, Mus Genaro Perez, 66 & Gold Medal, Cordoba Munic Cult Mgt, 66; Purchase Prize, Excuela Mexicana, Nat Inst Fine Arts, Mexico City, 67. *Bibliog:* Toby Joysmith (auth), Iconographer of life's meaning, News, Mexico City, 3/17/68. *Mem:* Salon de la Plastica Mexicana; Asn Mexicana de Artes Plasticas; Washington Art Asn. *Media:* Oils. *Mailing Add:* c/o Oleary-Jacobson Fine Art Gallery 342 E 65th St New York NY 10021

FALKENSTEIN, CLAIRE
SCULPTOR
b Coos Bay, Ore. *Study:* Univ Calif, Berkeley. *Work:* Addison Gallery Am Art, Andover, Mass; Baltimore Mus Art; Boston Mus Fine Arts; Solomon R Guggenheim Mus, New York; Los Angeles Mus Art. *Comn:* Floor to ceiling stair railing for Gallery Sapzio, Milan, Italy & for Gallery Stadler, Paris, France; fire-screen for Baron de Rothschild's chateau; fountain, Wilshire Blvd, Los Angeles; stained glass windows, rectory screen & doors, St Basil's Cath Church, Los Angeles; copper & fused glass fountain, Calif Fed Savings Bldg, Los Angeles. *Exhib:* Il Segno Gallery, Rome, Italy, 58; Inst Contemp Art, Boston, 59; Art for Use, Louvre, Paris, 62; Carnegie Inst, Pittsburgh, 64; Whitney Mus Am Art, New York, 64. *Mem:* Woman Caucus Art. *Media:* Glass. *Dealer:* Martha Jackson Gallery 32 E 69th St New York NY 10021. *Mailing Add:* c/o Jack Rutberg Fine Arts 357 N La Brea Los Angeles CA 90036

FALLER, MARION
PHOTOGRAPHER, EDUCATOR
b Wallington NJ, Nov 5, 41. *Study:* Hunter Col, City Univ New York, BA; State Univ NY-Visual Studies Workshop, Rochester, MFA. *Work:* Carnegie Mus Art, Pittsburgh, Pa; Int Mus Photog, George Eastman House, Rochester, NY; Mus Fine Arts, Houston; Light Work, Inc, Syracuse, NY; Albright-Knox Art Gallery, Buffalo, NY; and others. *Exhib:* Locations in Time, 77 & Acquisitions: 1973-1980, 80, Int Mus Photog, George Eastman House, Rochester, NY; one-person show, Menschel Gallery, Syracuse Univ, NY, 88, Univ Art Mus, Univ of NMex, 82, CEPA Gallery, Buffalo, NY, 85 & 88 & Ctr for Contemp Art, Santa Fe, NMex, 87; Reclaiming Paradise: American Women Photograph the Land, Tweed Art Mus, Univ of Minn, 87 & traveling exhib; and many others. *Collections Arranged:* Edward S Curtis (auth), Photogravures--Volumes I & III from the North American Indian, 76 & Upstate Color: Photographs by Bishop, Block, Pfahl, 77, Everson Mus Art, Syracuse, NY; Common Denominater: Work by Eder, Lentini, Kindermann, Rowe, Widmer, 84 & New Work: Photography, Bethune Art Gallery, 86, State Univ NY-Buffalo. *Pos:* Asst prof art dept, State Univ NYk, Buffalo, 82-89, assoc prof, 89- *Teaching:* Lectr photog, Dept Art, Hunter Col, New York, 71-74; lectr photog, Dept Art, Marymount Manhattan Col, New York, 73-74; asst prof photog & hist photog, Dept Fine Arts, Colgate Univ, Hamilton, NY, 74-82; asst prof photog & hist photog, State Univ NY-Buffalo, 82- *Awards:* Photogr's Grant, Light Work Visual Studies, Inc, Syracuse, NY, 76; Creative Artists Pub Serv Prog fel, NY, 77; NY Found Arts Photog Fel, 85. *Bibliog:* Marion Faller, A Portfolio of Photographs, Creative Camera Mag, London, 7/74; Connections: An invitational portfolio of images and statements by 28 women, Exposure, 81; Dana Asbury (auth), Observations of domestic realities, Popular Photography, 6/82. *Mem:* Soc for Photog Educ; Photog Hist Soc NY. *Media:* Color. *Publ:* Auth & illusr, A Resurrection of the Exquisite Corpse, Visual Studies Workshop Press, Rochester, 78; and others. *Dealer:* Visual Studies Workshop Gallery 31 Prince St Rochester NY 14607. *Mailing Add:* 75 Greenfield St Buffalo NY 14214

FALSETTA, VINCENT MARIO
PAINTER, EDUCATOR
b Philadelphia, Pa, Nov 5, 49. *Study:* Temple Univ, Philadelphia, Pa, BA, 72; Tyler Sch Art, Philadelphia, Pa, 72-73; Tyler Sch Art, Rome, Italy, MFA, 74. *Work:* Sheldon Swope Art Gallery, Terre Haute, Ind; United Bank Denver, Los Angeles; Utah Mus Fine Arts, Salt Lake City; Exxon Corp; Belo Corp, Dallas. *Exhib:* Solo exhibs, OK Harris Works of Art, New York, 86, 87 & 90 & Longview Mus, Tex, 92; Contemporary Trends, Utah Mus Fine Arts, Salt Lake City, 77; Works on Paper: Southwest, Dallas Mus Fine Arts, Tex, 78; Made in Texas, University Art Mus, Austin, 79; Patterns in Contemporary Art, Laguna Gloria Mus, Austin, 84; Gateway Experience, Dallas Mus Art, 84; USA Printworks, Traveling Exhib in Africa, 87-89; Mostra 91: Six Italian American Artists, Museo Italo Americano, San Francisco; Chaos to Order, Art Mus Southeast Tex, Beaumont, 92. *Teaching:* Asst prof painting & drawing, Ind Univ, Bloomington, 74-75; instr, Univ Utah, Salt Lake City, 75-77; asst prof, Univ NTex, Denton, 77-84, assoc prof, 84-92, prof, 92- *Awards:* Vis Artist Fel Brandywine Workshop, Philadelphia, Pa, 83,89; Fac Develop Grant, Univ NTex, 88; Res Grant, NTex State Univ, 80, 82, 85, 87. *Bibliog:* Robert Raczka (auth), Tackling a difficult game, Artweek, 1/17/81; Janet Kutner (auth), preview, Dallas Morning News, 10/4/85; Charles Dee Mitchell (auth), Dallas Ft Worth letter, Artspace, winter 85-86. *Media:* Acrylic. *Dealer:* OK Harris Works of Art 338 W Broadway New York, NY; Rosenfeld Gallery Philadelphia PA. *Mailing Add:* 202 Forest St Denton TX 76201

FALSETTO, MARIO
EDUCATOR
b Italy, May 17, 50; Can citizen. *Study:* Carleton Univ, Ottawa, Can, BA, 71; NY Univ with Jay Leyda, Annette Michelson, Stan Brakhage, Manny Farber, VF Perkins & P Adams Sitney, MA, 76, PhD, 90. *Pos:* Chmn dept cinema & photog, Concordia Univ, 81-84 & asst dean, Fac Fine Arts, 84-87; assoc & acting dean, Fac Fine Arts, 87-90. *Teaching:* Lectr film studies, Univ Manitoba, Winnipeg, Can, 77-78; lectr film studies, Concordia Univ, Montreal, Can, 78-82, asst prof, 82-87, assoc prof, 87- *Mem:* Film Studies Asn Can (pres, 85-87); Soc for Cinema Studies; L'Association Quebecois des Etudes Cinematographiques. *Res:* Recent American and experimental films; Films of Stanley Kubrick & Nicolas Roeg. *Publ:* Auth, William K Everson's, American Silent Film, Take One, 78; Production Guide Canada (Montreal), Millimeter, 79; The Mad & the Beautiful: A Look at Two Performances in the Work of Stanley Kubrick in making visible the invisible, Scarecrow Press, 90. *Mailing Add:* Dept Art 1455 DeMaisonneuve Montreal PQ H3G 1M8 Canada

FANE, LAWRENCE
SCULPTOR
b Kansas City, Mo, Sept 10, 33. *Study:* Harvard Univ, AB, 55; Boston Mus Sch, 56; with George Dimetrios, 56-59. *Work:* Corcoran Gallery; Univ Mass Mus, Amherst; Mus Contemp Art, Udine, Italy; New York City Bd Educ; De Cordova Mus, Boston; Weatherspoon Gallery, Univ NC, Greensboro; Univ Mo Mus. *Comn:* Bronze & concrete fountain, comn by Villa Sam Lorenzo, Assisi, Italy, 66; portrait, Union of Am Hebrew Congregation, New York, 67; concrete sculpture, Trent Univ, Peterboro, Ont, 71; 8ft outdoor sculpture, comn by Nichol Home, Milwaukee, 74; steel & concrete sculpture, Secker & Warburg Publ, London, 78. *Exhib:* One-man shows, Zabriskie Gallery, New York, 69, Marilyn Pearl Gallery, New York, 76, 78, 82 & 85, Spazio Oolp, Turin, Italy, 80, Duke Univ & Bard Col, 77, Washington Art Assoc, 85; group shows, Orgn Independent Artists, Wards Island, NY, 77, Arte Contemp Am, Rome, Italy, 80, Four Artists and a Writer, Fed Hall, NY, 82, Aspects of Abstraction, Colby Col Mus, 83, Nat Acad Design, 84, The Ways of Wood, NY, 84, Between Abstraction and Reality, Marilyn Pearl Gallery, 85, Working in Bronze, Univ Conn, 86, New York by Old Friends, De Cordova Mus, Boston, 86, Courtyard Sculpture, Hudson River Mus, Yonkers, NY, 88, Bi- Coastal Sculpture, San Francisco, Calif, 89 & The Significant Surface, Philadelphia Art Alliance, 90; Large Scale, Bill Bale Gallery, 91; Southamton Sculpture Fields, 92. *Teaching:* Instr design, RI Sch Design, Providence, 66-69; prof sculpture, Queens Col, NY, 69- *Awards:* Prix de Rome, 60-63; Fels, Ingram Merrill Found, 73 & 84, Dept Housing & Urban Develop, 74; Res Found, City Univ New York, 81; CUNY Res Found, 87. *Bibliog:* Michael Brenson (auth), Lawrence Fane, NY Times, 86; Hearne Pardee (auth), Arts Mag, 86; E Sozanski (auth), The Significant Surface, Philadelphia Inquirer, 90; and others. *Mem:* Am Acad Rome (exec comt, 79-); Sculptors Guild. *Media:* Steel, Bronze. *Dealer:* Bill Bace Gallery Two Bond St New York NY 10012. *Mailing Add:* 355 Riverside Dr New York NY 10025

FANGOR, VOY
PAINTER
b Warsaw, Poland, Nov 15, 22; US citizen. *Study:* Warsaw Acad Fine Arts, MFA. *Work:* Guggenheim Mus, New York; Mus Mod Art, New York; Univ Calif Art Mus, Berkeley; Muzeum Sztuki, Lodz, Poland; Stedelijk Mus, Amsterdam, Holland. *Exhib:* The Responsive Eye, Mus Mod Art, 65; 34th Biennale Venezia, Padiglione Centrale, 68; Guggenheim Mus, 70. *Teaching:* Asst prof painting, Warsaw Acad Fine Arts, 53-61; prof painting, Fairleigh Dickinson Univ, 65. *Bibliog:* R C Kennedy (auth), Notes on Fangor, Art Int, 66; Jay Jacobs (auth), Pertinent and impertinent: illusionist, Art Gallery Mag, 69; John Canaday (auth), Fangors romantic op, New York Times, 2/15/70. *Media:* Oil. *Mailing Add:* 2006 Conejo Dr Santa Fe NM 87501

FARAGASSO, JACK
ILLUSTRATOR, PAINTER
b Brooklyn, NY, Jan 23, 29. *Study:* Art Students League, with Frank J Reilly, 48-52. *Work:* George Washington Carver Mus, Tuskegee Inst, Ala. *Exhib:* Gallery Mod Art, New York, 69; Am Artists Prof League, 69-71 & 73-79; The Nude in Fine Art, O'Brien's Emporium, Scottsdale, Ariz, 91-92; Modern Masters of Figuative Painting, Leslie Levy Gallery, Scottsdale, Ariz, 92. *Pos:* Illusr, many book co, 57- *Teaching:* Instr drawing, painting & illus & dir, treas & trustee, Frank Reilly Sch Art, New York, 67-68; instr drawing, painting & illus, Art Students League, 68-; instr drawing & painting, Woodstock Sch Art, 81 & Scottsdale Artist Sch, Ariz. *Mem:* Art Students League; fel Am Artists Prof League; Am Portrait Soc; Artists Fel Inc. *Media:* Oil. *Publ:* Auth, The Students Guide to Painting, North Light Publ, 79. *Mailing Add:* 340 E 55th St New York NY 10022

FARBER, AMANDA
PAINTER, SCULPTOR
b New York City, May 13, 57. *Study:* Cooper Union, BFA, 78; Univ Calif, San Diego, MFA, 86. *Exhib:* One-woman shows, Mandeville Annex Gallery, Univ Calif, San Diego, 84 & Patty Aande Gallery, San Diego, 86 & 87; Santos-Dumont Aerostation of Aviation, San Diego, 87; Artists Invitational, Southwestern Col, 87; Group Show, Gwydion Gallery, La Jolla, 88. *Teaching:* Asst teacher, Walden Sch, New York, 79-81; teaching asst, Visual Arts Dept, Univ Calif, San Diego, 83-86; art teacher, The Child's Primary Sch, San Diego, 86-88; instr, San Diego State Univ, 88-89. *Awards:* Grand Recipient, Art Matters Inc, 89; Nat Endowment Arts, 89. *Bibliog:* At the galleries, Los Angeles Times, 11/8/85, 1/3/86, 3/27/87, 3/3/88. *Mailing Add:* PO Box 126243 San Diego CA 92112

FARBER, DEBORAH
GALLERY DIRECTOR, ART DEALER
b Iowa City, Iowa, Jan 26, 49. *Study:* Ind Univ; Purdue Univ, BA(art), hons, 72. *Exhib:* Celebration, Ohio Designer Craftsman, Columbus, 83; Barrington Arts Exhib, Ill, 85; Build a Better Box, Loho Gallery, Louisville, Ky, 86; Fountain Sq Arts Festival, Evanston, Ill, 86; Old Orchard Craft Festival, North Shore Art League, Chicago, Ill, 86. *Pos:* Adv bd mem, Crafts Report, Seattle, Wash, 80-; adv, Nat Crafts Planning Cong & Nat Endowment Arts, 83; co-dir, Mindscape Gallery, Evanston, Ill, currently. *Bibliog:* Sheila Flanagan (auth), A professional approach to fine crafts, Decor Mag, 79; Kim Russell (auth), Portrait of a gallery owner, Working Craftswoman, 83; Marvin David (auth), The Gallery as Art Form, Craft Marketing Yearbook, 84. *Mem:* Am Craft Coun; Evanston Arts Coun; Evanston Arts Alliance; Ill Arts Coun. *Specialty:* Contemporary American crafts 1969-; mixed media. *Publ:* Coauth, Craftshop design & display marketing techniques, Craft Market News, 78; Publicity: A gallery's point of view, Ceramics Monthly, 80; Reaching new markets through public relations & stalking the collector, Crafts Report, 85; Glass: The seductive media, Am Ceramic Soc, 86; Marketing series, Wis Designer Craftsman, 87; Why crafts, Crafts Report, 88. *Mailing Add:* Mindscape Gallery & Studio 1506 Sherman Ave Evanston IL 60201

FARBER, DENNIS H
PAINTER, PHOTOGRAPHER
b Pittsburgh, Pa, Mar 8, 46. *Study:* Trinity Col, BA, 68; Claremont Grad Sch, MFA, 75. *Work:* Brooklyn Mus, New York; Carnegie Mus Art, Pittsburgh, Pa; Mus Fine Arts, Houston, Tex; Baltimore Mus Art, Md; Mus Mod Art, NY; and others. *Comn:* Mural painting, Prince Kuhio Hotel, Honolulu. *Exhib:* Solo exhibs, Arco Ctr Visual arts, Los Angeles, Calif, 84 Laurence Miller Gallery, New York, 85 & 86, Queens Mus, Flushing, NY, 86, Jon Oulman Gallery, Minneapolis, Minn, 87 & 88, Univ Art Mus, Univ NMex, Albuquerque, 88, Maloney-Butler Gallery, Santa Monica, Calif, 89, Centric 34, Univ Art Mus, Calif Sate Univ, Long Beach, 89; Evoling Abstraction in Photography, Anita Shapolsky Gallery, New York, travelled to Univ Bridgeport, Conn, 89; Jon Oulman Gallery, Minneapolis, Minn, 90; Lang & O'Hara Gallery, New York, 90; Selections 5, Photokina, Cologne, Germany, 90. *Teaching:* Asst prof painting, Claremont Col, 75-76 & 82-83 & Md Inst, Coll Art, 91-92, 92-93. *Awards:* Exhib award, Hawaii-Calif Biennial, San Diego Mus, 79 & From Santa Barbara to San Diego, 82; Polaroid Grant, Polaroid Corp, 88 & 90; Individual Artists' Fel, New York Found Arts, 89. *Bibliog:* The Galleries, Los Angeles Times, 4/14/85, Creativity, 11/14/89; Art Review, New York Times, 7/6/90, 7/7/91 & 1/31/92. *Media:* Acrylic. *Mailing Add:* c/o Lawrence Miller Gallery 138 Spring St New York NY 10012

FARBER, MAYA M
PAINTER
b Timisoara, Rumania, Jan 24, 36; US citizen. *Study:* Pratt Inst, privately with Edwin Oppler; Hunter Col; Hans Hoffman Sch; Art Students League, with Reginald Marsh. *Work:* Butler Inst Am Art, Youngstown, Ohio; Int Tel & Tel, New York; Columbia Mus Art, SC; Ga Mus Art, Athens; Jacksonville Art Mus, Fla. *Exhib:* One woman shows, Rockefeller Ctr, New York, 79, Mountain Top Gallery, 80, Ugarit Gallery, Tel Aviv, Israel, 80 & NY State Fair, 84-85, River House, New York, 84 & 86, Nelli Aman Gallery, Tel Aviv, Israel, 92; Group shows, Great Expectations, Madison Ave, 78, Mountain Top Gallery, Windham, NY, 79 & Twilight Part Art Asn, Collage, 79; Chase Gallery, New York; Salon D' Automne, Lyon, France, 80; Flora & Fauna Show, Greene Co Coun Arts, New York; North Coast Collage Soc, 86; 1990 Ann Leonard Gallery, Woodstock, NY,86; Collage 88, N Light Gallery, Evertt, Wash, 88; Approaches to Still Life, Amerika Hause, Munich, Ger, 91. *Awards:* Second Prize, Jamaica Festival Art, 67. *Media:* Collage, Acrylic. *Dealer:* Chase Gallery Inc 31 E 64th St New York NY 10021. *Mailing Add:* 435 E 52nd St New York NY 10022

FARES, WILLIAM O
PAINTER
b Compton, Calif, July 16, 42. *Study:* San Francisco Art Inst, BA & MFA. *Work:* Chase Manhattan Bank; Va Mus Fine Arts; State Univ NY Col Purchase; Yale Art Gallery; Muhlenberg Ctr for the Arts, Allentown, Pa; Guggenheim Mus & Mus Mod Art, New York. *Exhib:* Biennial, Whitney Mus Am Art, New York, 75; Albright-Knox Art Gallery, Buffalo, NY, 75; Paperworks, Mus Mod Art, New York, 76; Am Drawing 1927-1977, Minn Mus Art, St Paul, 77; one-man exhib, Zolla/Lieberman Gallery, Chicago, 77; Stamford Mus, Conn, 78; Va Mus Fine Arts, 79; Jefferson Co Hist Soc, Watertown, NY, 79; Tex Gallery, 79; and many others. *Awards:* Nat Endowment Arts Grant, 79-80. *Bibliog:* David Bourdon (auth), article, The Village Voice, 12/6/76; Barbara Cavaliere (auth), article, Arts Mag, 2/77; Kenneth Whal (auth), On abstract literalist works, Arts Mag, 4/77; articles in: Art in Am & Art Forum. *Media:* Acrylic. *Dealer:* Dannenburg 44 Broone St New York NY 10012. *Mailing Add:* 110 W 26th St New York NY 10001

FARHI, JEAN CLAUDE
SCULPTOR
b Paris, France, Feb 11, 40. *Study:* Sch Beaux Arts, Nice, France, 68. *Work:* Mus Contemp Art, Antwerp, Belg; Mus Mod Art, Beaubourg Mus, Paris, France. *Comn:* Monumental sculpture, Palace Cong, Nice, France, 85; monumental sculptures, Atalanta Capitol, New York, 86; monumental sculpture, comn by Nathan Senota, Long Island, NY, 87; monumental sculpture, comn by Martin Sosnoff, New Canaan, Conn, 88; bldg facade, City of Nice, France, 88. *Exhib:* Solo exhibs, Maeght Found, St Paul, France, 73 & FIAC, Paris, France, 86; Silverman Collection, Cranbrook Acad Art Mus, Mich, 81; Les Mains Regardent, Mus Picasso, Antibes, France, 81; Chicago Int Art Fair, 84; Intermedia Between Painting & Sculpture, 84 & Innovation in Sculpture, 1985-1988, 88, Aldrich Mus Contemp Art, Ridgefield, Conn; Antwerp Mus Contemp Art, Belg, 87. *Awards:* Young Sculptor First Prize, Prix de Jeune Sculpture, Mediterranean Union Mod Art, 64. *Bibliog:* William Zimmer (auth), Three shows, three styles, New York Times, 84; Rene Predal (dir), Farhi Plastique Broadway 561, Nice Cinema, 85; Farhi-Sculptor, Tele-Monte-Carlo, Italy, 88. *Media:* Methacrylate. *Publ:* Auth, Iris Time, Pendel, 78; ed, Larousse Dictionary of Painting, Larousse, 80; Grand Dictionary-Encyclopedia Larousse, Vol VIII, Larousse, 85; auth, New York Face A Son Patrimoine, Pierre Mardgha, 86; Notre Observatoire, Martano. *Dealer:* Galerie Beaubourg 21 Rue de Ronard Paris France. *Mailing Add:* Rte de Perastasse Touretts Loup 06410 France

FARIAN, BABETTE S
PAINTER, DESIGNER
b New York, NY, June 6, 16. *Study:* New York Sch Fine & Appl Art, two years; Cooper Union, three years; Art Students League, three months, with Bridgman; Mus Mod Art, three years; additional study with Donald Stacy, Addison Lamar, Joseph Margulies & Morris Kantor. *Work:* Brooklyn Botanic Garden, NY; Tamassee DAR Sch Gallery; US Fine Arts Registry; Women's Fine Arts Mus; Sloan-Kettering Mem Ctr; also in many pvt collections. *Exhib:* Metrop Mus 81 St Gallery, New York, 77; Flushing Coun Culture & Arts, 86; Lever House, 88; Audubon Artists Nat Asn painters in casein & acrylic, 89, Kataine Lhorilard, 90, Nat Arts Club, 88 & 91; Queens Col, 91; Queensbore Community Col, 92; and others. *Pos:* Color consult, Addison Lamar, 37-40; designer, Krasom Co, New York, 55-57; freelance designer, 58-59; asst head studio, Manhattan Shirt Co, New York, 60-65; designer, Hanscom Fabrics. *Teaching:* Instr color & design, Cooper Union Art Sch, 40-41; pvt classes, 73-74. *Awards:* Award of Merit, Nat League Am Pen Women, 79 & Jackson Hts Art, 89; First Prize Short Story, 81 & First Prize Watercolor, 83, Composers, Authors & Artists Am; First Prize Oil, Jackson Hts Art Club 89- & Hon Mention, 90. *Bibliog:* article & photos in Vineyard Gazette, 74; Articles & photos in World Mag, 89 & Catholic Fine Arts Mag, 90. *Mem:* Burr Artists (vpres); Nat Asn Am Pen Women; Nat Arts Club; Composers, Authors & Artists Am; Artists Space; and many others. *Media:* Acrylic, Watercolor. *Publ:* Auth, The pendulum of time and the arts, 68; article, Artist's Equity Mag, 75, 86 & 88; auth, First Prize Short Story: Composers, Authors, Artists; Am Mag, 81. *Mailing Add:* 34-48 81st St Jackson Heights NY 11372

FARIS, BRUNEL DE BOST
PAINTER, EDUCATOR
b Oklahoma City, Okla, Aug 9, 37. *Study:* Univ Okla, BFA & MFA. *Work:* Univ Okla Art Mus, Norman; State Okla Collection; Philbrook Art Ctr, Tulsa, Okla; Barkouras Found, Los Angeles, Calif; Privatklinik-Diabetiker, Bad Lauterberg, WGer; Okla City Art Mus, Okla; Tulsa Performing Arts Ctr, Tulsa, Okla. *Exhib:* Mid-Am Ann, Nelson Gallery Art, Kansas City, Mo, 65; 35th Ann Exhib, Springfield Art Mus, 65; 8 State Exhib Southwestern Art, Okla Art Ctr, Oklahoma City, 68 & 71; Okla Ann, Philbrook Art Ctr, Tulsa, 69 & 75; one-man shows, Univ Okla Art Mus, 74 & Barkouras Found, Okla, 77; Kirkpatrick Gallery, Okla. *Pos:* Art dir, Okla Sci & Arts Found, 66-69; dir, Hulsey Gallery, Norick Art Ctr, Oklahoma City Univ, 85- *Teaching:* Instr art, Tulsa Pub Schs, 61-64 & Oklahoma City Pub Schs, 65-66; prof art & chmn dept, Oklahoma City Univ, 69-83. *Mem:* Okla City Art Mus; Okla City Arts Coun (bd mem); Okla City Arts Comn. *Media:* Collage, Assemblage. *Mailing Add:* 1012 N W 39th St Oklahoma City OK 73118

FARIS, PETER KINZIE
WRITER, HISTORIAN
b Washington, DC, Oct 7, 43. *Study:* Nat Col Art, Lahore, Pakistan, 62; Colo State Univ, Ft Collins, BA, 65; Univ Colo, Boulder, MFA, 70. *Exhib:* 1974 All-Calif Exhib, Laguna Beach Art Mus; One-man show, Hatton Gallery, Colo State Univ, Ft Collins, 79; Aspen Art Found Exhib, Colo, 75; Assistance League All-Media Competition, Houston Art Mus, Tex, 76; 8-West Biennial, Western Colo Ctr for the Arts, Grand Junction, Colo, 76; and others. *Collections Arranged:* Pattern and Sources of Navajo Weaving, Navajo Rug Exhib, 77; Life on the High Plains (auth, catalog), Hist Photos from Black Hills, 78. *Pos:* Gallery dir & educ progs coordr, Arvada Ctr for Arts & Humanities, Colo, 76-78; exec dir, Western Colo Ctr for Arts, Grand Junction, 78-81,; exec dir, Inst Archeoesthetics, 84- *Teaching:* Instr fine arts, Prestonburg Community Col, Ky, 70-72; asst prof studio art, Chapman Col, Orange, Calif, 72-74; instr, Univ Colo, Denver, 84- & Redrocks Community Col, Lakewood, Colo, 85-90. *Mem:* Colo Archeol Soc; Col Art Asn. *Publ:* Auth, A fertility cermony illustrated in The Cave of Life, Petrified Forest National Park, Arizona, Southwestern Lore, 3/86; Postclassic vernal abstraction: The evolution of a unique style in Late Fremont rock art in Dinosaur National Monument, Utah, Southwestern Lore, 3/87; auth, chapt In: Design Aspect in Uinta and San Rafael Fremont rock art; compiled paper, In: Rock Art of the Western Canyon, Johnson Publ & Colo Archeol Soc & Denver Mus Natural Hist, 89. *Mailing Add:* 7317 W Fremont Dr Littleton CO 80123

FARM, GERALD E
PAINTER, SCULPTOR
b Grand Island, Nebr, Mar 8, 35. *Study:* Famous Artist Sch, Westport, Conn; Nebr State Col, BA(educ). *Work:* Deming Fed Savings, NMex; Olney Savings & Loan, Tex; Bank of Beaver City, Okla; plus many pvt collections. *Comn:* First Nat Bank, Uvalde, Tex. *Exhib:* C M Russell Auction, Great Falls, Mont, 73 & 75; The Real Show, Grand Cent Art Galleries, New York, 79; Mus Nebr Art, Kearny, Nebr, 88; Nat Finals Art Auction, Las Vegas, Nev; Cheyenne Frontier Days Art Show, Wyo, 91 & 92; Miniatures, Fine Arts Mus, NMex,

92; Celebrate Am Realism, San Diego, 92; Western Rendezvous of Art, Helena, Mont, 92. *Bibliog:* Byron Jones (auth), The story teller's art of Gerald Farm, Southwest Art, 79; Patti Jones Morgan (auth), G Farm, tinged with nostalgia, Southwest Art, 88; Patricia O'Connor (auth), Gerald Farm-Accentuating the Positive, Art of the West, 92. *Media:* Oil. *Dealer:* Trailside Gallery Scottsdale AZ & Jackson, WY; Settlers West Gallery Tucson AZ. *Mailing Add:* 5609 Foothills Dr Farmington NM 87402

FARMER, JOHN DAVID
HISTORIAN, ADMINISTRATOR
b Washington, Ga, Jan 25, 39. *Study:* Columbia Univ, BA, 60; Univ NC, Chapel Hill, MA, 63; Princeton Univ, MFA, 65, PhD, 81. *Collections Arranged:* Virtuouso Craftsman (with catalog), 69; Concepts of the Bauhaus (with catalog), 72; German Master Drawings of the 19th Century (with catalog), 72-73; Rubens and Humanism (with catalog), 78; Rowing/Olympics (with catalog), 84. *Pos:* Curatorial asst, Worcester Art Mus, Mass, 67-69; cur, Busch-Reisinger Mus, Harvard Univ, 69-72; cur earlier painting, Art Inst Chicago, 72-75; dir, Birmingham Mus Art, 75-79; exec dir, Fulbright Comn, Belg, 79-80; dir, Univ Art Mus, Univ Calif, Santa Barbara, 81-90; dir exhibs, Am Fedn Art, 90- *Teaching:* Instr art hist, Clark Univ, 68-69; lectr, Harvard Univ, 71; adj prof, Univ Calif, Santa Barbara, 81-90. *Mem:* Col Art Asn; Am Asn Mus; Asn Art Mus Dirs. *Res:* Art of the Northern Renaissance, especially painting and decorative arts of early Sixteenth Century Low Countries. *Publ:* Coauth, Catalogue of European paintings, Worcester Art Mus, 74; auth, Gerard David's lamentation and an anonymous St Jerome, Mus Studies, 75; Ensor, Braziller, 77. *Mailing Add:* 233 E 35th St New York NY 10016

FARNHAM, ALEXANDER
PAINTER, WRITER
b Orange, NJ, May 5, 26. *Study:* Art Students League, with George Bridgeman, W C McNulty & Frank Vincent DuMond; also with Van Dearing Perrine & Anne Steel Marsh. *Work:* Newark Mus, NJ; Nat Arts Club, New York; Monmouth Col; James A Michener Collection; Morgan Guaranty Trust Co, New York. *Comn:* Murals, Naval subjects, Naval Repair Base, New Orleans, 45; portrait of dir, Am Found for Blind, 50; painting of off bldg, NJ Mfrs Ins Co, Trenton, 69; Washington Crosses the Delaware (pewter plate design), Franklin Mint, 76. *Exhib:* Methods and Materials of the Painter, Montclair Art Mus, circulated in Can, 54; Nat Acad Design 135th Ann Exhib, New York, 60; Eastern States Art Exhib, Springfield, Mass, 65-67; NJ Award Artists Exhib, Montclair Art Mus, 66; NJ Artists, Newark Mus Invitational, 68. *Pos:* Artist, US Navy, 45-46; writer, Maine Antique Digest, 76-92. *Awards:* Purchase Award, Newark Mus, 68; NJ State Coun Arts Fel, 80; First Award, Summit Art Ctr Nat Exhib, 81. *Bibliog:* Diane Hamilton (auth), Painters of the Valley, Country Mag, 12/81; Palette Talk #51, M Grumbacher, Inc, 82. *Mem:* Assoc Artists NJ (pres, 72-77; Hunterdon Art Ctr. *Media:* Oil. *Publ:* Auth & illusr, Tool collectors handbook, 70, 72 & 75; auth, Architectural patterns, subjects for the artists brush, 74; Early Tools on NJ & the Men Who Made Them, 84; Search for New Jersey Toolmakers, 92. *Dealer:* The Coryell Gallery 8 1/2 Coryell St Lambertville NJ. *Mailing Add:* 78 Tumble Falls Rd Stockton NJ 08559

FARNHAM, EMILY
PAINTER, WRITER
b Kent, Ohio, May 27, 12. *Study:* Kent State Univ, BSc(educ); Art Students League; Cleveland Sch Art; Hans Hofmann Sch Fine Arts; Ohio State Univ, MA & PhD. *Work:* Alice Collection, Utah State Capitol; NC Nat Bank; Mary Baldwin Col, Va; Gray Gallery, Greenville, NC; Provincetown Art Asn & Mus. *Comn:* Murals, Cine Sonora, Hermosillo, Sonora, Mex, 47. *Exhib:* one-man shows, Art Ctr, Salt Lake City, 40 & Univ Va, Charlottesville, 58; 6th Nat Exhib, Okla Printmakers Soc, Oklahoma City, 64; Traveling Show, Assoc Artists NC, 68; Outermost Gallery, Provincetown, 81; 2nd Ann Nat Prize Competition, Provincetown Art Asn, 84; Jacob Fanning Gallery, Wellfleet, 87; Eye of Horus Gallery, Provincetown, 89. *Pos:* Gov bd mem, NC Mus Art, 73-80. *Teaching:* Asst & instr design, Ohio State Univ, Columbus, 34-37, asst prof watercolor, 54-55; instr painting, Mich State Univ, East Lansing, 37; instr art, Utah State Univ, Logan, 38-41; head dept art, Stout State Col, Menomonie, Wis, 42-45; asst prof painting & drawing, Southern Ill Univ, Carbondale, 47-53; prof painting & art hist, Mary Baldwin Col, Staunton, Va, 56-62; prof painting & art hist, E Carolina Univ, Greenville, NC, 62-77, chmn art hist dept, 68-73. *Awards:* Res Grants, Res Coun Univ Ctr, Va, 57 & 59; nominated for Nat Book Award, Charles Demuth, Behind a Laughing Mask, 72. *Bibliog:* Douglas MacAgy (auth), Charles Demuth: behind a laughing mask by Emily Farnham, Sat Rev, 5/71. *Mem:* PEN; Provincetown Art Asn. *Media:* Mixed Media, Acrylics. *Res:* Abstract form resident in the great paintings of the past; notes taken in Hans Hofmann classes. *Publ:* Auth, Charles Demuth's Bermuda landscapes, Art J, New York, 65; Charles Demuth: Behind a Laughing Mask, Univ Okla Press, Norman, 71. *Dealer:* Jacob Fanning Gallery Wellfleet MA. *Mailing Add:* 616 Commercial St, No 10 Provincetown MA 02657

FARNSWORTH, HELEN SAWYER See Sawyer, Helen

FARRENS, JUANITA G
PAINTER, SCULPTOR
b Philippine Republic; US citizen. *Study:* Bukidnon Inst, Mindanao, Philippines, BSE, 39; Md Univ Exten, Ankara, Turkey, 53-54; La Tech Univ, 83-86, 87 & 88; Univ New Orleans, 88-92; Delgado Community Col, 88-92. *Work:* Westminster Abbey, Spencer, Mass; St Alphonso Church, Philippine Republic; St Dominic Church, Mother Cabrini High Sch & Knights of Columbus, New Orleans; Colo Gold Mine Sch, Golden; New Orleans Mus Fine Arts. *Comn:* Garden scene, comn by Joe Barhill, Boulder, 60; landscape, Shepherd Ctr, Mt Carmel Acad, New Orleans, 82; Knight Columbus, New Orleans, La, 84; Joseph Clementine, New Orleans, 85; William Sork, New Orleans, 85. *Exhib:* Biennial Exhib Piedmont Painting & Sculpture, Mint Mus Art, 77-79; Joslyn Art Mus Ann, 78; Pastel Soc Am Ann, Nat Arts Club, New York, 78-80 & 83; Ga Second Ann Exhib, Columbus Mus Arts & Sci, 81; Aqueous, J B Speed Art Mus, 82; First Patron Watercolor Gala, Kresge Fine Art Ctr, Oklahoma City, 83; Springville Mus Fine Art, Utah, 84-85; 47th Contemp Am Art, West Palm Beach, Fla, 85; Kans Pastel Soc Nat, 85-86; Degas Pastel Soc First Open Nat, New Orleans, La, 86; 45th Nat Watercolor, Birmingham Mus Art, Ala, 86. *Teaching:* Instr art, Farrens Art Sch, New Orleans, 60- & Sheperd Ctr, Mt Carmel Acad, New Orleans, 78-83; lectr & demonstr painting, New Orleans Art Asn, 64-83 & Holy Cross Col, 68. *Awards:* Merit Award, Tenth Nat New Orleans Art Asn, 84; Pastel Soc Award Excellence, 86. *Mem:* Allied Artists Am; Am Portrait Soc; founding mem La Watercolor Soc (vpres, 71-72); New Orleans Art Asn; Am Pastel Soc. *Media:* Watercolor, Pastel. *Publ:* New York Art Review, American Publishing Corp, 10/88; article, Times Picayune, 85-86. *Dealer:* Archieves Nat Found New York NY; Art South Inc PA. *Mailing Add:* 6164 Marshal Foch New Orleans LA 70124

FARRIS, JOSEPH
CARTOONIST, PAINTER
b Newark, NJ, May 30, 24. *Study:* Art Students League; Biarritz Univ; Whitney Sch Art. *Work:* Paintings in private collections. *Exhib:* One-man show, Ward Eggleston Gallery, New York; and many group exhib. *Pos:* Contract artist, New Yorker. *Awards:* Emily Lowe Award. *Mem:* Cartoonists Asn. *Media:* All. *Publ:* Contribr cartoons & covers to The New Yorker, Sat Eve Post, True, Ladies Home J, Playboy, Penthouse, New Woman, Punch & other nat mag; illusr, Slave boy in Judea; bk jackets for others; auth & illusr, Phobias & Therapies (cartoon bk), Grosset & Dunlap; contribr, Pilgrim's Progress (cartoon book), Thomas More Press; The New Yorker 1975-1985 Anniversary Album; illusr, The Latin Riddle Book; cartoon collections, They're a Very Successful Family, 89 & Just a Cog in the Wheel, 89; cartoon strip, Phipps, United Media, 89- *Mailing Add:* Long Meadow Lane Bethel CT 06801

FARRIS, LINDA B
DEALER
b San Francisco, Calif, Mar 29, 44. *Study:* Univ Calif, Berkeley, BA, 66. *Collections Arranged:* Eight Seattle Artists, Los Angeles Inst Contemp Art, 81; Self Portraits, Los Angeles Munic Art Gallery, 83. *Pos:* Mem bd dirs, Henry Gallery, Univ Wash, 77- & Dance Theatre Seattle, 78-79; adv bd, Factory Visual Arts, Seattle, 78- *Bibliog:* Matthew Kangas (auth), Decade of excellence at Linda Farris, Argus, 8/10/79; article, Working Woman, 3/83; Farris Gallery celebrates 13 years of success, Seattle Times, 5/27/83. *Mem:* Contemp Art Coun; Henry Gallery Asn; Seattle Art Mus; Art Dealers Asn. *Specialty:* Seattle and nationally known artists of museum calibre; innovative works by Seattle artists; major exhibitions of Robert Rauschenberg, Louise Nevelson, Sherry Markovitz, Christopher Brown, Ginny Ruffner & Sam Francis. *Mailing Add:* 322 Second Ave S Seattle WA 98104

FARROW, PATRICK VILLIERS
SCULPTOR
b Los Angeles, Calif, Nov 27, 42. *Study:* Univ Calif, Los Angeles; Loyola Univ; study under Archemedes Giocomantonio. *Work:* Norton Simon Mus, Pasadena, Calif; Middlebury Col, Vt; City of Rutland, Vt; City of Ishidoriya, Japan. *Comn:* Sculpture, City Rutland, 84; presentation piece, Crossroads Arts Coun, 86; Middlebury Col, 88; City Ishidoriya, Japan, 89. *Exhib:* Nat Art Club; Nat Acad Design, 77; Nat Sculpture Soc Ann, New York, 78-92; Am Acad Arts & Lett, New York, 80-; Am Soc Interior Designs, 85; Audubon Artists, New York, 86; and others. *Awards:* Award of Distinction, 77 & Memoriam Award, 85, Allied Artists Am; Bronze Medal, 78 & Edith & Richmond Proskauer Award, 80; Pietro Montana Mem Prize, 88; Nat Sculpture Soc. *Bibliog:* Rex Reed (auth), article, Cosmopolitan, 68; Theodora Morgan (auth), articles, Nat Sculpture Rev, 78, 80 & 83, 84 & 86. *Mem:* Nat Sculpture Soc; Allied Artists Am; Rutland Area Art Asn (bd dirs, 83-88). *Media:* Steel, Bronze. *Publ:* Contribr, NY Daily News, 79, NY Post, 80, People Mag, 5/80, Sculpture Rev, 83, Southern Vt Mag, 86, Boston Globe, 89, New York Rev, 88, Time Mag, 89 & NY Times, 89; House & Garden Mag, 91. *Dealer:* Peel Gallery Danby VT 05739; Foster Harmon Galleries of Am Art Sarasota FL. *Mailing Add:* 61 Killington Ave Rutland VT 05701

FARRUGGIO, REMO MICHAEL
PAINTER
b Palermo, Sicily, Mar 29, 06; US citizen. *Study:* Nat Acad Design, Beaux Arts Inst, Educ Alliance & Indust Art Sch, New York. *Work:* Metrop Mus Art, New York; Butler Inst Am Art, Youngstown, Ohio; Portland Mus Art, Ore; Santa Fe Art Mus, NMex; NMex Art Asn; Smithsonian Inst. *Exhib:* Blues and Other Paintings, Julien Levy Gallery, New York, 39; Galleria Art Mod, Mexico City, 50; John Heller Gallery, New York, 55, 56 & 58; Schneider Gallery, Rome, Italy, 57; Nuovo Sagitario Gallery, Milano, Italy, 73-74. *Teaching:* Instr painting, Fedn Artists, Detroit, Mich, 40; teacher painting, Portland Mus Art Sch, 54-55. *Awards:* Award for Dear Old Southland, Detroit Art Inst, 43; Butler Inst Am Art Award, 57; Award for Rocks, Hyannis Art Asn, Mass, 70. *Mem:* Artists Equity; Am Fedn Arts & Lett. *Media:* Mixed. *Mailing Add:* 208 E Tenth New York NY 10003

FARVER, SUZANNE
ADMINISTRATOR, COLLECTOR
b Pella, Iowa, Feb 22, 55. *Study:* Grinnell Col, BA(phi beta kappa), 78; Univ Denver, JD, 83. *Pos:* Trustee, Denver Art Mus, 88-; dir develop & pub affairs,

Anderson Ranch Arts Ctr, Snowmass Village, Colo, 90-92; dir, Aspen Art Mus, Aspen, 92- *Collection:* Contemporary Art, paintings, sculptures & photography including Joseph Cornell, Donald Judd, Ed Ruscha & Louise Bourgeois. *Mailing Add:* Aspen Art Museum 590 N Mill St Aspen CO 81611

FARWELL, BEATRICE
HISTORIAN, EDUCATOR
b Santa Barbara, Calif, Oct 9, 20. *Study:* Knox Col, BA(art), 42; NY Univ, MA(art hist), 65; Univ Calif, Los Angeles, PhD(art hist), 73. *Pos:* Mem bd trustees, Santa Barbara Mus of Art, 71-76. *Teaching:* Lectr & sr lectr, Metrop Mus Art, New York, 43-66; vis lectr art hist, Univ Calif, Santa Barbara, 66-67, lectr, 67-74, assoc prof, 74-77, prof, 77- *Mem:* Col Art Asn (bd dir, 77-81); Southern Calif Art Historians (vpres, 80-81); Arch Am Art. *Res:* French 19th century painting and graphic art; emphasis on realism and popular imagery. *Publ:* Auth, A Manet masterpiece reconsidered, Apollo, 7/63; Courbet's Baigneuses & the rhetorical feminine image, Art News Ann, 72; Manet's Nymphe Surprise, Burlington Mag, 4/75; French Popular Lithographic Imagery 1815-1870, Vols 1-9, Univ Chicago Press, 81-90; Manet and the Nude, Garland Press, 81; and others. *Mailing Add:* 4523 Auhay Dr Santa Barbara CA 93110

FASNACHT, HEIDE ANN
SCULPTOR
b Cleveland, Ohio, Jan 12, 51. *Study:* RI Sch Design, BFA, 73; New York Univ, MA. *Work:* Chase Manhattan Bank; Detroit Inst Art; Norton Collection, Fla; High Mus, Atlanta; Santa Barbara Mus Art; Brooklyn Mus, NY; Dallas Mus Art; and others. *Comn:* Prudential Bache, NY. *Exhib:* Solo exhibs, Hill Gallery, Birmingham, MI, 84 & 86, Saxon-Lee Gallery, Los Angeles, CA, 87, Germans von Eck Gallery, New York, 88-90 & 92, Dorothy Goldeen Gallery, Los Angeles, 89 & 91, Eugene Binder Gallery, Dallas, 91, Wilkey Fine Art, Seattle, Wash, 91 & Ram Galerie, Rotterdam, Neth, 92; Sculpture on the Wall, Aldrich Mus Contemp Art, Ridgefield, CN, 86-87; New Spiritual Abstraction of the 1980's, Nohra Haime Gallery, NY, 84; Figurative Impulses: Six Contemporary Sculptors, Santa Barbara Mus Art, CA, 88; Enclosing the Void, Whitney Mus Am Art at Equitable Ctr, 88; Making Their Mark: Women Artists Move Into the Mainstream 1970-1985, Cincinnati Art Mus, New Orleans Mus Art, Denver Art Musw & PaAcad Fine Arts, 89; Contemporary Collectors, La Jolla Mus Contemp Art, CA, 90; Contemp Collectors, La Jolla Mus Contemp Art, Calif, 90; Breaking Ground, Contemp Arts Ctr, Cincinatti, OH, 87; and other one-man shows. *Teaching:* Adj prof sculpture & drawing, State Univ NY, Purchase, 81; artist-in-residence, Bennington Col, Vt, 81 & 86; lectr, Yale Univ, 81,RI Sch Design, 87, 91 & 92, Parsons Sch Design, 89 & Whitney Mus Am Art, 90; vis artist & lectr, Cleveland Inst Arts, 81, Md Inst Col Art, 85 & RI Sch Design, 85; vis lectr, Princeton Univ, 87 & 92. *Awards:* Yaddo Fel, 80, 85 & 90; MacDowell Colony Fel, 81-82 & 86-87; Guggenheim Grant, 90; and others. *Bibliog:* Steven Henry Mado (auth), Sculpture unbound,Art News, 1/84; Stephen Westfall (auth), rev, Arts Mag, 2/86; Nancy Princenthal (auth), rev, Art Am, 1/86 & 11/88; Michael Kimmelman (auth), Critics picks, NY Times, 6/2/89; Elizabeth Hayt-Atkins (auth), The anxiety of influence contemporanea, 4/90; and others. *Mem:* Col Art Asn; Int Sculpture Soc. *Media:* Mixed Media. *Dealer:* Germans Van Eck Gallery New York NY. *Mailing Add:* 4 White St New York NY 10013

FASOLDT, SARAH LOWRY
DIRECTOR, ART DEALER
b Evanston, Ill, Feb 7, 50. *Study:* Ecole du Louvre, Paris, 69; Univ Colo, Boulder, BA, 72. *Pos:* Cur Homstead, Farnsworth Art Mus, Rockland, Maine, 83; dir, Maine Coasts Artists, Rockport, 84- *Specialty:* Advancement of contemporary art in Maine. *Publ:* Auth, But is it art?, 1/81 & Monhegan: 100 years of island painting, 8/84, Down East Mag. *Mailing Add:* c/o Maine Coast Artists Gallery Box 147 Rockport ME 04856

FAUBION, S MICHAEL
ADMINISTRATOR
b Tex, May 10, 52. *Study:* Univ Tex, BA, 74, LBJ Sch Pub Affairs, MPA, 76. *Pos:* Asst dir visual arts, Nat Endowment Arts, Washington, DC, 85-88. *Mailing Add:* 1422 Q St, NW Washington DC 20009

FAUDE, WILSON HINSDALE
DIRECTOR, CURATOR
b Hartford, Conn, Feb 20, 46. *Study:* Hobart Col, BA, 69; Trinity Col, MA. *Work:* Wadsworth Mus, Hartford, Conn; Mark Twain Memorial, Hartford, Conn; Old State House, Hartford, Conn. *Pos:* Exec dir, Old State House, 85-; cur, Mark Twain Mem, 71-79. *Mailing Add:* Old State House 800 Main St Hartford CT 06103

FAUDIE, FRED
PAINTER, ILLUSTRATOR
b DuBois, Pa, May 29, 41. *Study:* Cornell Univ, AB(art hist), 63; Univ Iowa, Iowa City, MA(painting), 65, photogr with John Schulz, 67-68; Syracuse Univ, MFA(illus), 79. *Work:* Addison Gallery Am Art; Lincoln Co Heritage Trust; Lincoln State Monument. *Exhib:* Brockton Triennial, Brockton Art Mus, Mass, 81 & 84; Billy the Kid, Lincoln Co Heritage Trust, 84; Something Human, Univ Mass, 87; Ninth Ann Boston Drawing Show, 88; Black in the Light, Genovese Gallery, Boston, 88; New England Impressions, Art of Printmaking, Fitchburg Art Mus, Mass, 88. *Teaching:* Prof painting & drawing, Univ Mass Lowell, 68-, chairperson art dept, 80-83. *Bibliog:* Allara (auth), New Editions, Vol 81, No 9, Art News, 9/82; Billy, the myth and image, Print Collectors Newsletter, Vol 13, No 3, 1983; Erdman (auth), Fred Faudie: Mixed themes, Art New Eng, Vol 9, No 2, 2/88. *Mem:* Boston Visual Artists Union; Lowell Art Asn. *Media:* Oil, Acrylic. *Mailing Add:* 38 Wannalancit St Lowell MA 01854

FAULCONER, MARY (FULLERTON)
PAINTER, DESIGNER
b Pittsburgh, Pa. *Study:* Pa Mus Sch Art; also with Alexei Brodovitch. *Work:* Paul Mellon pvt collection; Duchess of Windsor pvt collection; plus many others. *Comn:* paintings, Steuben Glass; designed six stamps, US Postal Serv, 74; designed Rose stamp, US Postal Serv, 78; designed Love stamp, US Postal Serv, 82; Franklin Mint, 84. *Exhib:* Alex Iolas Gallery, New York, 55, 58 & 61; Philadelphia Art Alliance, 62; Bodley Gallery, New York, 64, 66, 69 & 72; Tenn Fine Arts Ctr, Nashville, 67; De Mers Gallery, Hilton Head, SC, 71-72. *Pos:* Art dir, Harper's Bazaar Mag, 40; art dir, Mademoiselle Mag, 45. *Teaching:* Instr advert, Philadelphia Mus Sch Art, 36-40. *Awards:* Distinctive Merit Award, 54, 57 & 61, Silver Medal, 58 & 59, Art Dir Club; Gold Medal, Am Rose Soc, 78. *Media:* Gouache. *Mailing Add:* 20 Beekman Pl New York NY 10022

FAULDS, W ROD
ADMINISTRATOR, DESIGNER
b Rexdale, Ont, May 28, 53; US citizen. *Study:* Humbolt State Univ, BA, 77; Calif State Univ, Fullerton, MA, 80. *Pos:* Dir, Brattleboro Mus & Art Ctr, 81-84; assoc dir, Williams Col Mus Art, 84- *Mem:* Am Asn Mus; New Eng Mus Asn; Asn Col Univ Mus Galleries (NE rep, 86-89); Northern Berkshire Coun Arts (hon bd mem, 89-90). *Res:* Contemporary art with emphasis in sculpture and photography. *Publ:* Coauth, Object/Illusion/Reality-12 American Photographers, Calif Univ, Fullerton, 79; contribr, Mary Cassatt: The Color Prints, Abrams, 89; Black Photographers Bear Witness: 100 Years of Social Protest, Williams Col Mus Art, 89; Stitching Memories: African American Story Quilts, Williams Col Mus Art, 89. *Mailing Add:* 134 Bridges Rd Williamstown MA 01267

FAULKNER, FRANK
PAINTER
b Sumter, SC, July 27, 46. *Study:* Univ NC, Chapel Hill, BFA, 68, MFA, 72. *Work:* Hirshhorn Mus, Washington, DC; Nat Collection of Fine Arts, Washington, DC; Albright-Knox Art Gallery, Buffalo, NY; Smith Col, Northampton, Mass; Chase Manhattan Bank, New York. *Comn:* Urban wall proj, South Eastern Ctr Contemp Arts-Nat Endowment Arts, Winston-Salem, NC, 74; Orlando Int Airport, 81. *Exhib:* Whitney Mus Am Art Biennial, New York, 75; Material Dominant, Univ Pa, Philadelphia, 77; Southeast 7, Southeastern Ctr Contemp Art, Winston-Salem, NC, 77; Painters & Sculptors SE, High Mus Art, Atlanta, Ga, 77; Slocumb Gallery, Univ Tenn, 76; one-man shows, Knowlton Gallery, 76-81. *Awards:* Individual Artist Grant, Nat Endowment Arts, 75; Regional Artist Grant, South Eastern Ctr Contemp Arts-Nat Endowment Arts, 76; NC Architects Award, 76. *Bibliog:* William Zimmer (auth), Frank Faulkner, Arts Mag, 10/76. *Media:* Acrylic, Mixed Media. *Dealer:* Monique Knowlton Gallery 19 E 71st St New York NY 10021. *Mailing Add:* c/o Arden Gallery 129 Newbury St Boston MA 02116

FAUNCE, SARAH CUSHING
MUSEUM CURATOR
b Tulsa, Okla, Aug 19, 29. *Study:* Wellesley Col, BA; Washington Univ, MA; Columbia Univ. *Collections Arranged:* New Black Artists, 69; Peruvian Colonial Painting, 71; Pearlman Collection of Post-Impressionist Painting, 74; Anne Ryan Collages (auth, catalog), 74; Folk Sculpture USA (contribr, catalog), 76; Belgian Art 1880-1914 (contribr, catalog), 80; The Edith and Milton Lowenthal Collection of Modernist American Art (contribr, catalog), 81; Northern Light: Realism and Symbolism in Scandinavian Painting 1880-1910, 82; Carl Larsson (contribr, catalog), 82; Malcolm Morley, 84; Jennifer Bartlett, 85; Courbet Reconsidered (contribr, catalog), 88. *Pos:* Cur art collections, Columbia Univ, 65-69; exhib consult, Jewish Mus, 68-70; cur painting & sculpture, Brooklyn Mus, 69- *Teaching:* Lectr art theory & criticism, Barnard Col, 64. *Mem:* Col Art Asn Am; Am Asn Mus; Int Coun Mus; Cobly Col Art Adv Coun. *Publ:* Auth, Sewat & the Soul of Things, Belgian Art, 80; Modern French painting: Collecting in the 1920s, Apollo, 4/82; auth, The domestic art of Carl Larsson, In: Carl Larsson, 82; Eugene Delacroix, In: European Writers, the Romantic Century, Vol 1, 85; Reconsidering Courbet, In: Courbet Reconsidered, 88. *Mailing Add:* c/o Brooklyn Museum Eastern Pkwy Brooklyn NY 11238

FAURER, LOUIS
PHOTOGRAPHER
b Philadelphia, Pa, Aug 28, 16. *Work:* Mus Mod Art, New York; New Orleans Mus; Seagram Collection, New York; Metrop Mus Art, New York; Bibliotheque Nationale, Centre National des Arts Plastiques, Paris; Art Inst Chicago; Australian Nat Gallery, Canberra. *Exhib:* Then and Now, 52, In and Out of Focus, Family of Man, Photographs from the Mod Mus Collection, 59 & Self Portraits, 86, Mus Mod Art; one-man shows, Marlborough Gallery, New York, 77, Univ Md Art Gallery, 81, Light Gallery, New York, NY, 81, Howard Greenberg/Photofind Gallery, New York, 90, Bibliotheque Nationale, Paris, 90 & Zelda Cheatle Gallery, London, 91; New Acquisitions, Mus Fine Arts, Houston, Tex, 81; Los Angeles Coun Mus, Calif, 81; Bologna Arts Fair, Italy, 83; Appearance Fashion Photography Since 1945, Victoria & Albert Mus, London, 91. *Teaching:* Instr photog sem, Parsons Sch Design, New York, 75-77; instr, New Sch for Social Res, New York, 77; vis lectr, Univ Md, College Park, 81, Yale Univ, Conn, 83 & 85; vis prof, Univ Va, Charlottesville, 83-84; lectr, McIntire dept art, Univ Va & Cooper Union, New York, 84 & 90. *Awards:* Creative Artists Pub Serv Grant, New York, 77-78; Guggenheim Mem Found Fel, 79-80; Nat Endowment Art, 78, 81 & 82. *Publ:* Auth, Louis Faurer: Photographs of Philadelphia & New York 1937-1973, Univ Md Art Gallery, 81; Columbia Daily Spectator, 81; The Genius of Charles James, Holt Rinehart & Winston, 82; Fashion Photography Since 1945, Jonathan Cape Publ, 91. *Dealer:* Deborah Bell 137 E 26th St New York NY 10010. *Mailing Add:* c/o Westbeth Group 463 West St Suite H-520 New York NY 10014

FAUSETT, (WILLIAM) DEAN
PAINTER, MURALIST
b Price, Utah, July 4, 13. *Study:* Brigham Young Univ; Art Students League; Beaux Art Inst Archit Educ, Colorado Springs Fine Arts Ctr, Eastern Ill Univ, LHD, 82. *Work:* Metrop Mus Art; Mus Mod Art; Whitney Mus Am Art; Whitney Gallery of Western Art, Cody, Wyo; Toledo Mus Art. *Comn:* Murals, US Post Off, West New York, NJ, Bldg for Brotherhood, New York, US Air Acad, Colorado Springs, Colo, Global Power, USAF & 4-H Nat Ctr, Washington, DC; Flight Through Aurora Borealis, Pentagon, DC; Katzenbach Sch for the Deaf, Trenton NJ; plus many others. *Exhib:* Seven shows, Whitney Mus Am Art Ann, 32-46; retrospect, Harris Art Ctr, Brigham Young Univ, Provo, Utah, 58; one-man shows, Palm Springs Desert Mus, 69-70, Colorado Springs Fine Art Ctr, 70, Univ Ariz, Tucson, 71, Utah State Univ, Logan, 71, Inaugural Exhib, Tarble Art Ctr, 78; Eastern Ill Univ, Charleston, Ill, 82; Bennington Mus, Vt. *Pos:* Pres, Southern Vt Art Ctr, Manchester, Vt, 59-60. *Awards:* Prize, Salmagundi Club, 46; Distinguished Serv in Art Award, Brigham Young Univ, 69; Gold Medal & Cash Award, Franklin Mint, 76; and others. *Bibliog:* Monogram, Franklin Mint, Franklin, PA. *Mem:* Nat Soc Mural Painters (pres, 79-84); Southern Vt Art Asn (pres, 58-60); Found Preserv Traditional Values Fine Arts. *Media:* All. *Publ:* Auth, Address--special ceremony in Statuary Hall, US Capitol, Cong Rec, No 132, Part II, 9/21/82. *Mailing Add:* RR No 1, Box 865 Dorset VT 05251

FAUST, JAMES WILLE
PAINTER, SCULPTOR
b Lapel, Ind, May 22, 49. *Study:* Herron Sch Art, Indianapolis, Ind, BFA, 71, Univ Ill, Champaign-Urbana, MFA, 74. *Work:* Minn Mus Art, St Paul; Snite Mus Art, South Bend, Ind; Ind Univ Art Mus, Bloomington; Indianapolis Mus Art, Ind; Emporia State Univ, Kans. *Comn:* Absolut/Carillon Importers Ltd; Herb & Diane Meyer Simon; Melvin Simon & Assocs; Eli Lilly & Co; structured steel sculpture, SMT Realty/Allison Pointe, Indianapolis, Ind. *Exhib:* Brazil Works on Paper Partnership Int, Mus De Arte Do Rio Grande Do Sul, Porto Allegre, S Am, 84; solo show, Indianapolis Mus Art, 85 & 92; Contemp Am Drawing, Wichita Mus Art, Kans, 87; Am Drawing Biennial, Muscarelle Mus Art, Williamsburg, Va, 88; Chicago Int New Art Forms Expos, Navy Pier, Ill, 89; and others. *Awards:* Krannert Creative & Performing Arts Fel, Univ Ill, 73; Purchase Awards, 28th & 31st Ann Drawing & Small Sculpture Show, Ball State Univ Art Mus, 82 & 85; John Gordon Mem Award, 45th Ann Exhib Contemp Am Paintings, 83. *Bibliog:* A Conversation with James Faust (documentary), Indianapolis Art League; Absolut Indiana, Absolut Statehood Campaign, USA Today, 7/23/91. *Media:* Acrylic, Graphite & Prismacolor Pencils. *Publ:* Illusr, The American Story, Sat Evening Post, 75; Sat Evening Post Cover 3/76; Rock & Romance (record album), Faith Band, Village Records, Inc, 78; Arts Indiana (magazine cover), 6/88. *Dealer:* Kay Garvey Gallery 230 W Superior Chicago IL 60610; Ruschman Gallery 421 Massachusetts Ave Indianapolis IN 46204. *Mailing Add:* 8457 Union Chapel Rd Indianapolis IN 46240

FAUST, VICTORIA
PRINTMAKER
b Ohio, 1944. *Study:* Cleveland Art Inst, 63-64; Antioch Col, 64-65; Sch Mus Fine Arts, Boston, 69-72. *Work:* Security Pac Nat Bank, San Francisco, Calif. *Comn:* Illus, Atlantic Monthly fiction sect, 9/82. *Exhib:* Narration, Inst Contemp Art, Boston, Mass, 78; Art of the State, Hayden Gallery, Mass Inst Technol, Cambridge, 78; solo exhibs, Harcus Krakow Gallery, Boston, Mass, 81, 83, 86 & 88, Univ Art Mus, Calif State Univ, Long Beach, 86 & Stephen Wirtz Gallery, San Francisco, 90; Monterey Peninsula Mus Art, Monterey, Calif, 88; Hirschl & Adler Mod, New York, NY, 90; Group Show, Stephen Wirtz Gallery, San Francisco, Calif, 91; Transparency, Luise Ross Gallery, New York, 92; and others. *Awards:* Clare Bartlett Traveling Fel, Sch Mus Fine Arts, Boston, Mass, 78; Nat Endowment Arts Award, 89. *Bibliog:* Steven Jenkins (auth), Unsettling landscapes, Artweek, San Francisco, Calif, 3/22/90; Kenneth Baker (auth), One gallery's finale, another's new space, San Francisco Chronicle, 3/22/90; Phyllis Braff (auth), Experimentation in still life, NY Times, 5/6/90; and others. *Mailing Add:* c/o Ruggieohenis 215 W Broadway 5th fl New York NY 10012

FAVRO, MURRAY
SCULPTOR
b Huntsville, Ont, Dec 24, 40. *Study:* H B Beal Tech Sch, London, Ont, 58-64. *Work:* Art Gallery Ont, Toronto; Nat Gallery Can, Ottawa, Ont; Can Coun Art Bank, Ottawa, Ont. *Comn:* Sculpture, Ministry Transport Bldg, Cornwall, Ont, 78. *Exhib:* Solo shows, Carmen Lamanna Gallery, 68, 71-73, 76, 77, 80, 82 & 83; Musee d'Art Mod Ville, Paris, 73; Mt Allison Univ & Rutgers Univ Art Gallery, 75; Changing Visions: The Canadian Landscape (with catalog), Travelling Show), Europe, 80; London Art Gallery, Ont, 76; Ten Canadian Artists in the 1970's (with catalog), travelling exhib, Europe, 76; A Retrospective, Art Gallery Ont, 83; Outdoor Sculpture Exhib, Quebec City, 84; 49th Parallel, New York, 86; Havana, Cuba, 89; McKenzie Gallery, Saskatoon, Sask, 91; Obscure Gallery, Quebec City, Que, 92. *Awards:* Can Coun Grants, 68-72; Can Coun Senior Grant, 74, 78, 80 & 83. *Bibliog:* France Morin (auth), Icarus: The Vision of Angels, 86. *Mem:* Can Artists Representation; Royal Canadian Acad. *Publ:* Auth, Heart of London, Ottawa, 68; Biographical Information About the Influences on My Work, 71, Windmill Electric Generator, 75 & The Flying Flea and Henri Mignet Its Designer, 77, Carmen Lamanna Gallery, Toronto. *Mailing Add:* 783 Queens Ave London ON N5W 3H7 Canada

FAX, ELTON CLAY
PAINTER, WRITER
b Baltimore, Md, Oct 9, 09. *Study:* Syracuse Univ Col Fine Arts. *Work:* US Navy & Marine Corps Exhib Ctr, Washington, DC. *Awards:* Louis E Seley Naval Art Coop & Liaison Comt Award, 72; Coretta Scott King Award, 72; Arena Players Award, 72. *Bibliog:* Brawley (auth), The Negro genius, 36; Locke (auth), The Negro in art, 37; Dover (auth), American Negro art, 61. *Mem:* Salmagundi Club (Naval Art Coop & Liaison Comt); Author's Guild Am; Poets, Essayists & Novelists. *Publ:* Auth, Seventeen black artists, 71; auth, Garvey, 72; auth, Through Black eyes, Dodd Mead & Co, 74; auth, Black Artists of the New Generation, Dodd Mead & Co, 77; auth, Hashar (illusr with drawings & paintings by the auth), Progress Publishers, Moscow, 80; auth & illusr, Soviet People as I Knew Them, Progress Publ, 88. *Mailing Add:* 51-28 30th Ave Apt 4C Woodside NY 11377

FAY, MING G
SCULPTOR, PAINTER
b Shanghai, China, Feb 2, 43; US citizen. *Study:* Columbus Col Art & Design, dipl, 65; Kansas City Art Inst, BFA, 67; Univ Calif, Santa Barbara, MFA, 70. *Work:* Columbus Art Mus, Ohio; Hong Kong Mus Art; Sidney Lewis Found, Va; Mobile Hq, New York. *Comn:* Conrad Hilton, Hong Kong, 90. *Exhib:* Solo exhibs, The Hong Kong Inst for Promotion of Chinese Cult, Hong Kong, 86, Gallery Triform, Taipei, Taiwan, 88 & Alternative Mus New York, 88, Squibb Gallery, Princeton, NJ, 89, Chinese Am Arts Coun, Gallery 456, New York, Petrosino Pk (outdoor installation), New York, D D Fine Art Space, Taipei, Taiwan, 90, Images From Beyond, Butters Gallery, Portland, Ore, 91 & Nature Reborn: From Archaeology to Science Fiction, Exit Art, New York, 91; Paperworks, Castle Gallery, Col New Rochelle, NY, 91; Artists of Conscience, Alterative Mus, New York, 91; The Hybrid State, Exit Art, New York, 91; Bronze, Frumkin/Adams Gallery, New York, 91. *Pos:* Adv bd, Asian Am Art Ctr, NY, 88-92; artist adv bd, New Mus, NY, 90-92; bd, Alternative Mus, NY, 91 & Chinese Am Arts Coun, NY, 92. *Teaching:* Inst, Chinese Univ Hong Kong, 68-69; Columbus Col Art and Design, Ohio, 70-71; Univ Pittsburgh, Pa, 71-74; Hong Kong Polytechnic, Hong Kong, 75; Pratt Inst, Brooklyn, New York, 78-80; Semester at Sea, UCIS, Univ Pittsburgh, 82; William Patterson Col, Wayne, NJ, 83-90 7/30/89. *Awards:* Workspace Prog, Dieu Donne Papermill, Inc, New York, 90; Art Grant, William Paterson Col, 91; Lila Wallace-Reader's Digest Grant, 92; Prudential Ins Co, Los Angeles. *Bibliog:* Michael Brenson (auth), Ming Fay, New York Times, 2/23/90 & 2/15/91; Gerald Haggerty (auth), Ming Fay, Arts Mag, Summer 91; Robert Taplin (auth) Ming Fay at Exit Art, Art Am, 10/91. *Mem:* Epoxy Art Group; Overseas Chinese Renaissance Soc. *Media:* Mixed Media; Metal. *Publ:* Auth, Midnite Porridge, Artist Bk, 88. *Dealer:* Exit Art NY; Butter Gallery Portland OR. *Mailing Add:* 830 Broadway New York NY 10003

FEAR, DANIEL E
DEALER, GALLERY DIRECTOR
b Tacoma, Wash, Mar 28, 49. *Pos:* Dir & pres, The Silver Image Gallery Inc, 73- *Mem:* Founding mem Asn Int Photog Art Dealers, Inc; Friends Photog; Soc Photog Educ; Photog Coun, Seattle Art Mus. *Specialty:* Contemporary photography; nudes & traditional landscapes. *Publ:* Northwest Photographer's Resource Guide, 90; Creating a Successful Career in Photography, 92. *Mailing Add:* Silver Image Gallery 318 Occidental Ave S Seattle WA 98104

FEARING, WILLIAM KELLY
EDUCATOR, PAINTER
b Fordyce, Ark, Oct 18, 18. *Study:* La Tech Univ, BA; Columbia Univ, MA. *Work:* Dallas Mus Fine Arts; Ft Worth Art Ctr; Old Jail Art Ctr, Albany, Tex; Mus Fine Arts Houston; Inst Contemp Arts, Boston; Marion Koogler McNay Art Mus, San Antonio; Milwaukee Art Mus; Archer M Huntington Art Gallery, Univ Tex, Austin. *Exhib:* Solo exhib, Witte Mem Mus, San Antonio, Tex, 69; Du Bose Gallery, Houston, Tex, 77; L & L Gallery, Longview, Tex, 78; Spencer Gallery, Fine Arts Ctr, Univ Ark, Monticello, 81; Mary Moffett Gallery, La Tech Univ, 81; A Retrospective of Drawings and Other Works on Paper 1945-1985 (with catalog), Old Jail Art Ctr, Albany, Tex, 85 & Marion Koogler McNay Art Mus, San Antonio, 86; Valley House Gallery, Dallas, Tex, 92; Prints of The Fort Worth Circle 1940-1960, Archer M Huntington Art Gallery, Univ Tex, Austin, 92. *Teaching:* Prof art, Univ Tex, Austin, 47-87, Ashbel Smith, 83-87, pro emer, 87-92. *Awards:* Archives Am Art, Smithsonian Inst, Washington, DC, 84. *Bibliog:* New talent USA, Art in Am, 62; John Palmer Leeper (auth), The Texas hill country: Interpretations by 13 painters, Texas A & M Press, 81; Cathy Nordstrom (auth), Prints of the Ft Worth Circle, Archer M Huntington Art Gallery, Univ Tex, Austin, 92. *Mem:* Nat Soc Lit & Arts; lifetime mem Tex Art Educ Asn. *Media:* Multi. *Publ:* Coauth, Our expanding vision, 60, The creative eye, 2nd ed, 79 & Art and the creative teacher, 71, Benson; ed, Creativity and the human spirit, Tex Quart, spring 73 & spec issue, 75; coauth, Helping children see art and make art, Vol I & II & The Way of Art, Vol I & II, 86, Benson. *Dealer:* Valley House Gallery Spring Valley Rd Dallas TX 75240. *Mailing Add:* 914 Calethea Austin TX 78746

FEATHERSTONE, DAVID BYRUM
CRITIC, CURATOR
b Iowa City, Iowa, Jan 23, 45. *Study:* Univ Calif, Berkeley, AB, 67; Univ Ore, Eugene, MA, 71. *Exhib:* Celebrations, Hayden Gallery, Mass Inst Technol, Cambridge, 74; Northwest Invitational, Seattle Art Mus, Wash, 75; Attitudes: Photog in 70's, Mus Art, Santa Barbara, Calif, 80; Oh Well, Orwell, Monterey Peninsula Mus Art, Calif, 84. *Collections Arranged:* Bernard Freemesser, A Retrospective Exhib, 78; Photographs by Vilem Kriz (auth, catalog), 79; The Diana Show, Pictures Through A Plastic Lens (auth, catalog), 80; Aerial

Photographs by William Garnett, 80; Photographs by Marsha Burns (auth, catalog), 81; Mount St Helens, the Photographer's Response, 83; Point Lobos: Place as Icon, 84; The Painted Image: Applied Color in Photography, 85; Edward Weston: A Mature Vision, 86; Holly Roberts - Painted Photographs (auth, catalog), 90; Yosemite: A Lifetime, Photographs by Ansel Adams, 90. *Pos:* Cur photog, Historical Photog Collection, Univ Ore Libr, Eugene, 74-76; exec assoc, The Friends Photog, Carmel, Calif, 77-87, dir publs, 87- *Awards:* Art Critics Fel, 76 & 78 & Mus Prof Fel, 82, Nat Endowment Arts; Residency Fel, Wurlitzer Found, Taos, NMex, 82. *Mem:* Soc Photog Educ; Am An Mus; Oracle Conference of Photog Curators; Houston Fotofest (Int Adv Bd). *Res:* Contemporary photography. *Publ:* Auth, Doris Ulmann: American Portraits, Univ NMex Press, 85; Photographs of Mother Teresa's Mission's of Charity in Calcutta, Friends of Photog, 85; ed, Close to Documentary Photographers, 89 & Of Time and Place: Walker Evans and William Christenberry, 90, Friends of Photography. *Mailing Add:* 1820 Vallejo St No 114 San Francisco CA 94123

FEBLAND, HARRIET
PAINTER, SCULPTOR
b New York, NY. *Study:* Pratt Inst; NY Univ; Art Students League; Am Artists Sch; Atelier 17, Paris. *Work:* Westchester Co Court House, White Plains Civic Plaza; Cincinnati Art Mus; Emily Lowe Mus, Coral Gables, Fla; Metromedia, Los Angeles, Calif; Hempstead Bank of Long Island Collection of Am Art; Pepsico Corp, Purchase, NY; State Univ NY, Potsdam; Hudson River Mus, Yonkers, NY; and many others. *Comn:* Sculpture, Haverly Collection, NY; sculpture, comn by Hon & Mrs Irwin Davidson collection, New Rochelle, NY. *Exhib:* Solo retrospectives, Hudson River Mus, NY, 63, Silvermine Guild, Conn, 73, Bridge Gallery, Munic Art Ctr, White Plains, NY, 76 & Brainerd Art Gallery, State Univ NY, 86; partial solo exhibs, Riverside Mus, NY, 65, Katonah Gallery, 70 & 86, Vincent Price Gallery, Chicago, 71, Rutgers Gallery, NJ, 75 & Va Ctr Creative Arts, 91; group invitationals, Cincinnati Art Mus, 68, Mus des Art Mod, Paris, 70, Alwin Gallery, London, 70, Hudson River Mus, 70-83, Woman Choose Women, NY Cult Ctr, 73, Potsdam Plastics, State Univ NY, 74 & Carnegie Inst; and others. *Pos:* Harriet FeBland Art Workshop (painting), Chelsea Sch Art, London Univ, 85; artist-in-residence (printmaking), State Univ NY, Potsdam, 86; Bennington Col, Vt, 88. *Teaching:* Instr & lectr, NY Univ, 60-62; instr & dir, Harriet FeBland Art Workshop, Pelham Art Ctr, NY, 62-; instr, Westchester Art Workshop, White Plains, 65-72. *Awards:* Andrew Nelson Whitehead Award, Am Soc Contemp Artists, 85, 87 & 89; Elizabeth Morse Genius Found Award, Nat Asn Women Arist, 86 & 88. *Bibliog:* Newman (auth), Plastics as sculpture, 74 & Plastics as an art form, Chilton; Dona Meilach (auth), Collage and Assemblage, Doubleday, 75; Harriet FeBland (film), A K Haverly Found, 83; and others. *Mem:* NY Artists Equity Asn (vpres, 70-76, pres, 89-90, chmn & prog dir,); Am Soc Contemp Artists (pres, 81-83, pres emer, 83-); Int Art Asn (secy, 80-82); Nat Asn of Women Artists; Fine Arts Fedn NY (deleg). *Media:* Acrylic, Oil; All. *Mailing Add:* 245 E 63rd St Apt 1803 New York NY 10021

FECHTER, CLAUDIA ZIESER
MUSEUM DIRECTOR, LIBRARIAN
b New York, NY, Mar 14, 31. *Study:* Case Western Reserve, AB, 52; Columbia, MA, 54. *Collections Arranged:* The Loom and the Cloth, Fabrics of Jewish Life (catalog), Temple Mus, 88; Sacred Landmarks, Cleveland State Univ Gallery, 90; Sephard: A Continuing Heritage, 92. *Pos:* Dir, Temple Mus, 84- *Mem:* Coun Am Jewish Mus (steering comt); Northeast Ohio Mus Coun. *Res:* Judaic ritual fabrics. *Interests:* Judaica and antiquities of the Holy Land region. *Publ:* Auth, The Loom and the Cloth, Temple Mus, 88; Custom, costume & ceremonial cloth, Creative Needle, 9/88; The fabric of Jewish Life, Vol XVIII, No 1, Coun Am Embroideres, 2/89; From Generation to Generation: Fabrics of Jewish Lif, 88. *Mailing Add:* 1855 Ansel Rd University Circle at Silver Park Cleveland OH 44106

FEDELLE, ESTELLE
PAINTER, LECTURER
b Chicago, Ill. *Study:* Art Inst Chicago; Northwestern Univ; Inst Design; Am Acad Fine Arts; Colo State Christian Col, hon PhD, 73. *Work:* Lutheran Gen Hosp & W Clement Stone Insurance Co, Chicago. *Exhib:* Grand Central Galleries, New York; Barron Galleries, Chicago & Las Vegas; Kenosha Pub Mus, Wis; Chicago Pub Libr; Visual Arts Ctr; and others. *Pos:* Dir, Fedelle Art Studio, Chicago & Park Ridge, Ill; auth, weekly column, The Leader Newspapers, 74- *Teaching:* Lectr, eastern & midwestern US on style & techniques in oil painting and demonstration of procedures. *Mem:* Life fel Royal Soc Arts London; Park Ridge Art League; Nat League Am Penwomen; Regent Art League (hon dir); Munic Art League; and others. *Media:* Oil, Water. *Publ:* How to Begin Painting for Fun, 65. *Mailing Add:* 1500 S Cumberland Park Ridge IL 60068

FEDER, BEN
DESIGNER, PAINTER
b New York, NY, Feb 1, 23. *Study:* Parsons Sch Design; Vet Ctr, Mus Mod Art, with Prestopino. *Exhib:* Stamford Mus Art, Conn, 60; Bodley Gallery, NY, 64; Inst Allende, San Miguel Allende, Mex. *Pos:* Designer & graphic arts consult, New Bk Knowledge, Grolier Inc; pres, Ben Feder Inc, New York; owner & design consultant, Clinton Vineyards Dutchess Co, NY. *Mem:* Am Soc Enologists. *Media:* Guache, Acrylic. *Mailing Add:* 1025 Fifth Ave New York NY 10028

FEDER, PENNY JOY
PRINTMAKER, LECTURER
b New York, NY, Oct 13, 49. *Study:* C W Post Col, Long Island Univ, Brookville, NY, with James Lewicki & Harry Hohen, BA(art educ), 71 & with Arthur Leipsig & Alfred van Loen, MA(printmaking), 75; Brooklyn Mus Art Sch, printmaking, 72. *Work:* Nynex Corp; Cunard Lines Int; Holland Amer Shipping Lines Int. *Comn:* Catalog cover & poster design, Washington Sq Outdoor Art Exhib, New York, 75; woodcut, Collectors Guild, New York, 76; woodcut, Calhoun's Collectors Soc, Minneapolis, 81. *Exhib:* Ann, Philadelphia Print Club, 78 & 83; Long Island Printmakers, Galerijzolder, Belgium, 80 & Mus Düren, Ger, 80; Ann, Audubon Artists Soc, Inst Arts & Letts, 80; Nat Acad Design, 81; Knickerbocker Artists, Nat Arts Club, New York, 81; Brooklyn Mus, 85; Fed Plaza, New York, 86. *Teaching:* Lectr-demonstr, Suffolk Co Sch System, NY, 70 & Salamagundi Club, New York, 79; and at various other art groups in NY. *Awards:* John Taylor Arms Award, Audubon Artists 39th Ann, 81; Knickerbocker Award, 32nd Knickerbocker Artists Ann, 83; Gold Medal, Salmagundi Club, 83. *Bibliog:* Jeanne Paris (auth), Diaries of creativity & Malcolm Preston (auth), Flourishing symbiosis, Newsday Newspaper, Long Island, NY, 2/77. *Mem:* Philadelphia Print Club; Audubon Artists Soc. *Media:* Woodcuts, Etchings. *Mailing Add:* 302 7th St Brooklyn NY 11215

FEDERE, MARION
PAINTER, GRAPHIC ARTIST
b Vienna, Austria, 19; US citizen. *Study:* Studied with Frances Haendel; Charles Seiden's workshop, 58-60; Inst San Miguel De Allende, Mex, 58; Brooklyn Mus Beckman Scholar Classes, 60-62; Pratt Graphic Ctr, New York & several summer schs in US abroad, 49-72. *Work:* Butler Inst, Youngstown, Ohio; Philathia Mus Mod Art, London, Ont, Can; and others. *Exhib:* Brooklyn Mus Community Gallery, 72-86; Cork Gallery, Lincoln Ctr, New York, 75-92; Salmagundy Club Ann, 79-80; World Trade Ctr Mus, New York, 80; Lowenstein Gallery, Fordham Univ, Lincoln Ctr, 82; Jacob Javits Fed Bldg, 83; and many others. *Pos:* Treas, of two art groups, 75-85. *Awards:* Contemp Artists Award, Am Soc Contemp Artists, 81; Purchase Award, Chemical Bank, 84; Artist Equity Award, 89 & 90; and others. *Bibliog:* Hedy O'Beil (critic), Art Mag, 81; reviews in newspaper & mag articles & on radio & TV; reviews, UN Paper, 72-92. *Mem:* New York Artists Equity Asn; Am Soc Contemp Artists (mem bd dirs, 81-92); Metrop Painters & Sculptors; Contemp Artists Guild (treas); UN Art Club, 76-92. *Media:* Oils, Acrylics; Mixed Media. *Mailing Add:* 2277 E 17th St Brooklyn NY 11229

FEDERIGHI, CHRISTINE M
SCULPTOR, EDUCATOR
b San Mateo, Calif, June 22, 49. *Study:* Cleveland Inst Art, BFA, 72; Alfred Univ Col Ceramics, NY, MFA, 74. *Work:* Ariz State Univ Mus, Tempe; Nora Eccles Harrison Mus, Logan, Utah; Mus Art, Little Rock, Ark; John Michael Kohler Jr Collection, Sheyboygan, Wis; Ft Lauderdale Mus Art, Fla. *Comn:* Art State Pub Bldgs, 89; Fla Inst Univ Libr N Miami. *Exhib:* Perth Triennial, Art Gallery Western Australia, 89; group exhib, Palo Alto Cult Ctr, Calif, 89; Surreal Ceramics, John Michael Kohler Art Ctr, Sheyboygan, Wis, 90; Figures in Ceramics, La State Univ Gallery, Baton Rouge, 90; Ceramic Sculpture, Ore Sch Arts & Crafts, Portland, 90. *Teaching:* Prof ceramics/design, Univ Miami, 74- *Awards:* Grant, Fla Fine Arts Coun, 83, 79 & 91; Nat Endowment Arts, 88 & 89; Virginia A Groot Fdn, 90. *Bibliog:* Ann Prospero Reban (auth), article, Am Ceramics, Vol 5, 86; Frank Boyden (auth), 18 Ceramic Artists, Studio Potter, 88; Ricardo Pav-Louza (auth), Miami Artists, Art Int, 89. *Mem:* Nat Coun Educ Ceramic Arts. *Media:* Ceramics. *Publ:* Auth, Is anybody home?, New Art Examiner, 85; Bombs & Oranges, Discovering Miami's Explosive Art Scene, Arts Mag, 11/90; Helen Koher, Miami Herald, 1/11/91; Ceramics Monthly (cover & article), 2/92. *Dealer:* Esther Saks Gallery 3400 N Lake Shore Dr Chicago IL 60657; Bellas Artes 584 Broadway New York NY 10012. *Mailing Add:* 4351 SW 12 St Miami FL 33134

FEENEY, SANDRA BENEDICT
PHOTOGRAPHER
b Fargo, NDak, Oct 16, 36. *Study:* Goddard Col, BFA, 80. *Work:* Bibliot Nat, Paris, France. *Exhib:* The Finished Print, Art Guild, Farmington, Conn, 85; Alternatives '86, traveling exhib, Ohio State Univ, 86; Bristol Art Mus, RI, 86; Year of the Arts, Newport Art Mus, RI, 87; Images of Women, Lawrence Art Ctr, Univ Kans, 87. *Pos:* Assoc dir, Bristol Workshops in Photog, 85-92; ed, Photographic Insight, 87-92. *Awards:* Nat Endowment Arts fel photog, 86; Individual artist fel, RI State Coun Arts, 86. *Mailing Add:* 10 Cooke St Providence RI 02906

FEHL, PHILIPP P
PAINTER, HISTORIAN
b Vienna, Austria, May 9, 20; US citizen. *Study:* Art Inst Chicago; Stanford Univ, BA & MA; Univ Chicago, PhD. *Work:* Neue Galerie Joanneum, Graz, Austria; NC State Mus of Art, Raleigh; Krannert Art Mus, Univ Ill, Champaign. *Exhib:* One-man shows, Mt Holyoke Col, 79, Univ Tel Aviv, 81, Dante Soc, Venice, 81, Wolfenbuettel Lib, 82, Kiel Univ, 83, Univ Va, 86, Univ Del, 87, Univ Utah, 88 & Univ Ill, 90 & 91. *Pos:* Vis prof, Univ Calif, 60 & 63, Brown Univ, 67 & Tel Aviv Univ, 82; dir, Cicognara Prog, Univ Ill & Vatican Libr, 88-; Hebrew Univ Jerusalem, 92; Central European Univ, Prague, 93. *Teaching:* Prof hist art, Univ NC, Chapel Hill, 63-69 & Univ Ill, Urbana-Champaign, 69-90, prof emeritus, 90- *Awards:* Corresponding Member, Ateneo Veneto, 88-; Res Assoc Ctr Adv Study, Univ Ill, 90-; Braun Schiveigische Wissenschaftliche Gesellschaft, 92- *Bibliog:* Wilfried Skreiner (auth), Capricci by Philipp Fehl, Neue Galerie, Graz, 71; Maurice Cope (auth), Birds of a Feather, Univ Ill Press, 91. *Mem:* Col Art Asn Am (bd dirs,

68-71); Renaissance Soc Am; Am Soc Aesthetics & Art Criticism; Midwest Art Hist Soc; Int Surv Jewish Monuments (pres); Central Renaissance Soc. *Media:* Watercolor, Ink. *Res:* Renaissance art; history of the classical tradition in art; history of art criticism. *Collection:* Prints, Renaissance to modern. *Publ:* Illusr, The bird: a series of capricci, Finial Press, 70; auth, The classical monument, NY Univ Press, 72; ed, Franciscus Junius, Literature of Classical Art, Univ Calif Press, 90; auth, articles in Art Bull, Burlington Mag, J Warburg & Courtauld Inst, Gazette Beaux Arts & others; illusr, Voyager, Lillabulero & other mags; auth, Decorum and Wit: The Poetry of Venetian Painting, Biblioteca Artibus et Historial, Vienna, 92. *Mailing Add:* Sch Art Univ Ill 408 E Peabody Champaign IL 61820

FEIFFER, JULES
CARTOONIST, WRITER
b New York, NY, Jan 26, 29. *Study:* Art Students League, 46; Pratt Inst, 47-51. *Pos:* Asst to syndicated cartoonist, Will Eisner, 46-51; cartoonist, Village Voice, 56-; cartoons publ weekly, London Observer, Eng, 58-66 & 72-80 & Playboy Mag, 59-; syndicated nationally, 59- *Awards:* Acad Award Animated Cartoon, Munro, 61; George Polk Mem Award, 62; Pulitzer Prize for Editorial Cartoons, 86. *Bibliog:* Lisa Schwarzbaum (auth), Jules Feiffer in season, Daily News Mag, 3/5/89; Maralyn Lois Polak (auth), interview, Philadelphia Inquirer, 10/15/89; John Douglas (auth), Grand Rapids Press, 10/6/1. *Mem:* Authors Guild. *Publ:* Auth, 11 collections cartoons including, Feiffer's Marriage Manual, 67, Feiffer on Nixon, 67, Tantrum: A Cartoon Novel, 79, Jules Feiffer's America: From Eisenhower to Nixon. 82 & Marriage is an Invasion of Privacy, 84; Fieffer's Children, 86; and plays & novels. *Mailing Add:* Universal Press Syndicate Promotions Dept 4900 Main St 9th fl Kansas City MO 64112

FEIGEN, RICHARD L
DEALER, COLLECTOR
b Chicago, Ill, Aug 8, 30. *Study:* Yale Univ, BA, 52; Harvard Univ, MBA, 54. *Pos:* Chmn & dir, Richard L Feigen & Co, Inc, 57-; trustee, John Jay Homestead, Katonah, NY & Lincoln Univ, Pa, 82-90. *Mem:* Life fel Metrop Mus Art; life fel Minneapolis Soc Fine Arts; Art Dealers Asn Am (dir); Gov Life mem Art Inst Chicago. *Specialty:* European and American paintings, drawings and sculpture, 1400 to the present. *Collection:* Old Master paintings and drawings; Beckmann, Ernst, Tanguy, Cornell, Dubuffet, Rosenquist. *Publ:* Contribr, Arts Mag, 67; auth, Dubuffet and the Anticulture, 69; contribr, Office Design, 70; auth, George Grosz: Dada Drawings, 72. *Mailing Add:* 49 E 68th St New York NY 10021

FEIGIN, MARSHA
PRINTMAKER, PAINTER
b New York, NY, June 17, 48. *Study:* City Col New York, BA; Univ Hawaii, MFA; Cooper Union; Syracuse Univ. *Work:* Brooklyn Mus; State Found Cult & Arts, Hawaii; De Cordova Mus, Mass; Nat Mus, Poland; Minneapolis Inst Arts; Nat Art Mus of Sports, Conn; IBM, NJ. *Comn:* Etching, Creative Artists Pub Serv Prog, New York, 75 & Pratt Graphics Ctr, 81. *Exhib:* 22nd Nat Exhib Prints, Libr Cong, 71; 18th & 20th Nat Prints Exhib, Brooklyn Mus, 72 & 76; 10th & 11th Biennial Graphic Art, Ljubljana, Yugoslavia, 73 & 75; 5th, 6th & 8th Int Biennial Graphic Art, Crakow, Poland, 74, 76 & 79; Printmaking: New Forms, Whitney Mus Am Art, 76; Am Graphics in Venice, Galleria Bevilacqua La Masa, Venice, Italy, 77; Art Today: USA, Iran-Am Soc, Teheran, Iran, 77; Sports Art, Nabisco Corp Gallery, NJ, 84; and others. *Pos:* Master-printer, Printmaking Workshop, New York, 71-72. *Teaching:* Teaching asst printmaking, Univ Hawaii, 69-71; instr life drawing & painting, Bishop Mus, 71; guest lectr printmaking, Rutgers Univ, 73; guest lectr, Fla Technol Univ, 77; instr printmaking, San Jose State Univ, 78-79 & NY City Pub Sch System, 85-86. *Awards:* Creative Pub Serv Prog Printmaking Grant, NY State Coun Arts, 73 & 75; Nat Endowment Arts Printmaking & Drawing Grant, 75. *Mem:* Artists Equity Asn; Women's Caucus Art; Col Art Asn; Graphic Arts Coun of NY; Printmaking Workshop, New York. *Media:* Mixed. *Dealer:* Assoc Am Artists 663 Fifth Ave New York NY 10022. *Mailing Add:* 200 E 84th St New York NY 10028

FEIN, B(ARBARA) R
EDUCATOR, PAINTER
b Brooklyn, NY, Dec 11, 41. *Study:* Brooklyn Col, BA, 62; Univ Md, 64-66; City Univ New York, MA, 67, PhD, 69; Univ NH, 70-80. *Work:* New York Pub Libr; Seacoast Regional Coun Ctr, Portsmouth, NH; York Co Coun Ctr, Sanford, Maine; Deaconess Hosp, Boston; Kittery Art Asn, Maine; Harber Home, Maine. *Comn:* Child at a Circus (mural), USN Hosp, Portsmouth, 71. *Exhib:* Copley Soc, Boston, 69-75, Walt Kuhn Mem-Norton Hall Gallery, Cape Neddick, Maine, 69-76; Drawings '71, Minn Mus Art, Minneapolis, 71; 6th Ann Drawing & Small Sculpture Exhib, Del Mar Col, Corpus Christi, Tex, 72; Wadsworth Atheneum, Conn Acad Fine Arts, Hartford, 72; 33rd & 34th Ann Nat Art Exhib, Southern Utah State Col, Cedar City, 73 & 74; Mike Levitan Gallery, NY, 86. *Pos:* PS Gallery, Ogunquit, Maine, 87 & 88. *Teaching:* Guest lectr abstract painting, Univ Maine, Orono, 71; vis lectr drawing, oil painting & watercolor, Univ NH, Durham, 73-87; prof visual studies, NH Vocational Technol Col, Stratham, 82- *Awards:* Third Place Prof, Manchester Art Asn, NH, 70; First Place Oil-Acrylic & Hon Mixed Media, Newbury Port Art Asn, Mass, 71; Graphics Award, York Art Asn, Maine, 71, 73, 76 & 79. *Mem:* Maine State Art Asn (bd dir, 73-74); Copley Soc; York Art Asn (pres, 88-90). *Media:* Watercolor; Pencil. *Publ:* Illusr, Dora Young's Tatting Manuals, 74 & 75; illusr, Single's Circle, 74; illusr, MCAT: New Medical Admissions Test, Barnes & Nobles, 81. *Dealer:* Kennedy Gallery New York NY; Fry Gallery York ME. *Mailing Add:* Art & Sciences, NH Vocational Technol Col 101 Technol Dr, 277 R Portsmouth Ave Stratham NH 03885

FEIN, STANLEY
PAINTER, DESIGNER
b Brooklyn, NY, Dec 21, 19. *Study:* Parsons Sch Design; NY Univ. *Work:* NY Univ Collection; pvt collection Dr Timothy Costello, Pres Adelphi Univ; The Bank of New York Collection. *Comn:* NY History (paintings), 71, Cities of NY (paintings), 72, Historic Interiors (paintings), 78 & Colleges of NY (paintings), Bank NY. *Pos:* Art dir, Doremus & Co, formerly; creative dir, Pesin Sydney & Bernard, formerly, Stanley Fein, Advertising, currently. *Teaching:* Instr design & color, Pratt Inst, 56-58. *Awards:* Art Dirs Club NY, 56-65; Wall Street Art Asn, 60; Soc Illusrs, 70 & 71. *Media:* Multimedia. *Dealer:* Phoenix Gallery 30 W 57th St New York NY. *Mailing Add:* 313 DeGraw St Brooklyn NY 11231

FEINBERG, ELEN
PAINTER, EDUCATOR
Study: Cornell Univ, Ithaca, New York, BFA, 76; Indiana Univ, Bloomington, MFA, 78. *Work:* Los Angeles Co Mus Art; Israel Mus, Jerusalem; Milwaukee Mus, Wis; Univ Calif, Santa Cruz Art Mus; Fresno Art Ctr, Calif; Morgan Guarantee Trust, New York; IBM, Atlanta, Ga. *Exhib:* Solo exhib, Watson Gallery, Houston, Tex, 85 & 89, Roswell Mus & Art Ctr, NMex, 86, Roger Ramsay Gallery, Chicago, Ill, 87, Mekler Gallery, Los Angeles, 84, 86, 88 & 89, & Bill Bace Gallery, New York, 90; Fifty Years, Roswell Mus, Albuquerque, NMex, 87; Van Straaten Gallery, Chicago, Ill, 87; GW Einstein Gallery, New York, 87; Los Angeles Contemporary Art Fair, 89 & Chicago Int Art Expo, 90, Ruth Siegel Gallery; Contemporary Realist Gallery, San Francisco, 89; Fresno Art Mus, Calif, 89; Mus Fine Arts, Santa Fe, NMex, 90; Albuquerque Mus, NMex, 92; Mulvane Art Mus, Topeka, Kans, 93. *Pos:* Assoc prof, Art Univ NMex, currently; vis assoc prof, Art Wash Univ. *Awards:* Award in Painting, Ingram Merrill Found, New York, 88; Burlington Fel, 91; Ruth Chenven Found Award in Painting, NMex, 91. *Bibliog:* Peter Frank & Emily Kass (coauth), Elen Feinberg (catalog), Mekler Gallery, Los Angeles, Calif, 88; Clinton Adams (auth), Printmaking in New Mexico, Univ NMex Press, 91; Drs Jules & Nancy Heller (auth), Entry: Leonard Lehrer, Garland Publ, NY, 92. *Mailing Add:* 613 Ridge Place NE Albuquerque NM 87106

FEINBERG, JEAN
PAINTER
b New Rochelle, NY, 1948. *Study:* Skidmore Col, BS, 70; Hunter Col, MA, 77. *Exhib:* Art in Public Spaces, O I A Exhib, 26 Fed Plaza, New York, 77; Mary Boone Gallery, New York, 78; New Drawings, Bette Stoler Gallery, New York, 79; one-man shows, Rosa Esman Gallery, New York, 80, 81 & 84, Univ RI, Kingston, 81, John Davis Gallery, Akron, Ohio, 84, 85 & 87 & Victoria Munroe Gallery, New York, 89; Invitational, Bennington Col, Bennington, Vt, 81; Abstract Painting, Art Galaxy, New York, 82; Selected Drawings, Jersey City Mus, Jersey City, NJ, 83; Current New Abstractions, Milwaukee Mus Fine Art, Milwaukee, WI, 84; A Decade of Visual Arts at Princeton, Princeton Univ Art Mus, Princeton, NJ, 85; Invitational, Condeso Lawler Gallery, New York, 86; Romantic Science, One Penn Plaza, New York, 87; Victoria Munroe Gallery, New York, 88. *Awards:* MacDowell Colony Fel, 77; Nat Endowment Arts, 78, 83 & 89; Edward Albee Found Residence, 79. *Bibliog:* Dan Cameron (auth), Report from the Front, Arts Mag, 6/86; Barry Schwabsky (auth), Jean Feinberg at John Davis, Arts Mag, 5/87; John Yau (auth), Jean Feinberg, Victoria Munroe Gallery, Artforum, 3/90. *Mailing Add:* Ten Leonard St New York NY 10013

FEININGER, ANDREAS B L
PHOTOGRAPHER, WRITER
b Paris, France, Dec 27, 06; US citizen. *Study:* Bauhaus, Ger, 22-25; Bauschule, Ger, dipl(archit; summa cum laude), 28; studied with Le Corbusier, 32-33. *Work:* Metrop Mus Art, Mus Mod Art, New York; Baltimore Mus Art; Victoria & Albert Mus, London; Bibliot Nat, Paris; Mus Folkwang, Essen, Ger; Smithsonian Inst, Washington, DC; New Orleans Mus Art; Center of Creative Photography, Univ Ariz. *Exhib:* One-man show, Shells, Am Mus Natural Hist, New York, 72, New York in the Forties, New York Hist Soc, 78 & Hamburg, Mus Kunst & Gewerbe, Ger, 80; retrospective, Int Ctr Photog, New York, 76, Mus Folkwang, Essen, Ger, 81 & Ctr Creative Photog, Tucson, 81. *Pos:* Staff photogr, Life Mag, 43-62. *Teaching:* Instr creative photocommunication, NY Univ, winter 72-73. *Awards:* Robert Leavitt Award, 66 & Lifetime Achievement Award, 86, Am Soc Mag Photogr; Lifetime Achievement Award, Int Ctr Photogr, JCP, NY, 91. *Bibliog:* Fritz Gruber (auth), Grosse Photographen unseres Jahrhunderts, Econ, Dusseldorf, 64; Peter Pollack (auth), The Picture History of Photography, Abrams, 2nd ed, 69; Ralph Hattersley (auth), Andreas Feininger, Morgan & Morgan, 73; Harry N Abrams (auth), Andreas Feininger Photographer, 86. *Mem:* Charter mem Am Soc Mag Photogr. *Publ:* Auth, Feininger on Photography, Ziff-Davis, 49; auth, The Anatomy of Nature, Crown, 56; auth, The Complete Photographer, Prentice-Hall, 65; auth, Trees, 68 & The Mountains of the Mind, 77, Viking; In A Grain of Sand, Sierra Club Books, 86; Nature in Miniature, Rizzoli, 89. *Dealer:* Bonnie Benrubi Fine Arts 150 E 74th St New York NY 10021. *Mailing Add:* 5 E 22 St Apt 15P New York NY 10010

FEININGER, T LUX
PAINTER, WRITER
b Berlin, Ger, June 11, 10; US citizen. *Study:* Bauhaus, Dessau, Ger, 26-32; stage design with Oskar Schlemmer; also with Paul Klee, W Kandinsky & Josef Albers, dipl, 29; Inst Fine Arts, NY Univ, with Salmony, Lopez-Rey, Cook & Friedlaender, 46-47. *Work:* Mus Mod Art, New York; Busch-Reisinger Mus & Fogg Art Mus, Harvard Univ; Altonaer Mus, Hamburg, Ger. *Exhib:* American Realists and Magic Realists, Mus Mod Art, New York, 43;

Revolution and Tradition in Modern American Art, Brooklyn Mus, 51; Whitney Mus Am Art Ann, New York, 51; Four American Painters, Mass Inst Technol, 54; Retrospective, Busch-Reisinger Mus, 62; Wheaton Col, 73; Wamsutta Club, New Bedford, Mass, 74; Photographs of the 20's & 30's, Prakapas Gallery, NY, 80; Gallery on the Green, (with essay), Lexington, Mass, 86 & 88. *Teaching:* Instr design, Sarah Lawrence Col, 50-52; lectr drawing & painting, Harvard Univ, 53-62; instr, Boston Fine Arts Mus Sch, 62-75; retired. *Awards:* Hon mention, Arts & Crafts Club, New Orleans, 48; hon mention, Cambridge Art Asn, 63. *Bibliog:* Thomas B Hess (auth), Profile, Art News, 2/47; Feininger family, Life Mag, 11/51; E Bitterman (auth), Art in modern architecture, Van Nostrand Reinhold, 52. *Mem:* Westport Art Group. *Publ:* Auth, The Bauhaus: evolution of an idea, Criticism, summer 60; Lyonel Feininger: city at the edge of the world, Praeger, 65; Address on modern art, Harvard Art Rev, 66; The heritage of Lyonel Feininger, Am-Ger Rev, 66. *Mailing Add:* 22 Arlington St Cambridge MA 02140

FEINMAN, STEPHEN E
DEALER
b New York, NY, Sept 29, 32. *Pos:* Pres, Gary Arts Ltd, 65-72; pres, Multiple Impressions Ltd, 72- *Specialty:* Twentieth Century European and American prints, drawings and paintings. *Mailing Add:* c/o Multiple Impressions 128 Spring St New York NY 10012

FEINSTEIN, RONI
CURATOR, HISTORIAN
New York, NY. *Study:* Northwestern Univ, BA, 75; Inst Fine Arts, MA, 81; Inst Fine Arts, New York, PhD, 90. *Exhib:* The Junk Aesthetic: Assemblage of the fifties and sixties, Whitney Mus Am Art, Fairfield County & Equitable, 89; Robert Rauschenberg: the Silkscreen Paintings 1962-1964, Whitney Mus Am Art, 90; With the Grain: Contemporary Panel Painting, Whitney Mus Am Art, Fairfield County & Philip Morris, 90. *Pos:* Lectr, Education dept, Mus Modern Art, 78-84; br dir, Whitney Mus Am Art, 85-92. *Awards:* Robert Goldwater Fel, Inst Fine Arts, 82-83; Chester Dale Fel, Metrop Mus Art, 83-84; Clawson Mills Fel, Metrop Mus Art, 84-85. *Mem:* Am Asn Mus; Col Art Asn. *Res:* American art since 1945 with a specialization in the art of Robert Rauschenberg. *Publ:* Auth, Frank Stella's Prints 1967-1982, 3/83, Jim Dine's early work, 3/84, The Unknown Earyl Rauschenberg: The Betty Parsons exhib, 1/85, The Early Work of Robert Rauscheberg: The White Paintings, etc, 9/86, Arts; auth, Robert Rauschenberg: The Silkscreen Paintings 1962-1964, Whitney Mus Am Art, 90; Behind the screens (on Rauschenberg's Silkscreen Paintings), Antique Collector, London, 3/91. *Mailing Add:* 10612 Mendocino Lane Boca Raton FL 33428

FEIST, HAROLD E
PAINTER, SCULPTOR
b San Angelo, Tex, 1945. *Study:* Univ Ill, Champaign-Urbana, BFA, 67; Col Art, Md Inst, MFA, 69. *Work:* Mus Fine Arts, Boston; Edmonton Art Gallery, Alta; Art Gallery Hamilton, Ont; Mendel Art Gallery, Saskatoon, Sask; Mem Univ Newfoundland Arts & Cult Ctr. *Exhib:* 25 Canadians, Birmingham Arts Festival, Ala, 79; The New Generation: A Curator's Choice, Andre Emmerich Gallery & travelling, 80-82; The Hines Collection, Univ Place, Boston, 84; Abstraction X Four, Can House, Can High Comn, London, toured Europe, 85; Toronto 3, Eva Cohon Gallery, Highland Park, Ill, 86; Curator's Choice: A Ten Year Retrospective--Feist, Drapell, Sutton, Buschlen-Mowatt Gallery, Vancouver, 88; solo exhibs, Virginia Christopher Gallery, Calgary, 82 & 90, Gallery One, Toronto, 82-91, Galerie Elca London, Montreal, 83-86, 88 & 90, Buschlen-Mowatt Fine Art, Vancouver, 84 & 90, Eva Cohon Galleries, Chicago & Highland Park, Ill, 88, Agnes Etherington Art Centre, Queens Univ, Kingston, Ont, 88-90 & Kathleen Laverty Gallery, Edmonton, 90. *Teaching:* Mem fac, Alta Col Art, Calgary, 68-74, Univ Saskatchewan, Regina, 74-75 & Mt Allison Univ, Sackville, NB, 75-78, Univ Guelph, Ont, 78-80, Sheridan Col, Brampton, Ont, 79-80. *Bibliog:* Gary Michael Dault (auth), Paint, Can Art, fall 84; Karen Wilkin (auth), Harold Feist: Genesis of an image, Artpost, spring 88; Karen Wilkin (auth), Harold Feist: Genesis of an Image (exhib catalog), Agnes Etherington Art Centre exhib, 88. *Media:* Acrylic on Canvas; Acrylic Sheet, Wood. *Dealer:* Gallery One 121 Scollard St Toronto ON; Galerie Elca London Montreal. *Mailing Add:* 374 Delaware Ave Toronto ON M6H 2T8 Canada

FEIST, WARNER DAVID
DESIGNER, PAINTER
b Augsburg, Ger, Dec 3, 09; Can citizen. *Study:* Bauhaus, Dessau, Ger, with Joseph Albers, Paul Klee, Oscar Schlemmer, Josef Schmidt & photog with Walter Peterhaus. *Work:* Concordia Univ, Montreal, Que; Montreal Mus Fine Arts; Mus Modern Art, San Francisco; Folkwang Mus Essen; Mus Contemp Art, Montreal. *Exhib:* One-man show, Goethe Inst, Montreal, 74 & 86; Early Photos, San Francisco Mus Mod Art; Mus Mod Art, New York; Mus Contemp Art, Montreal, 85. *Pos:* Art dir, Harold F Stanfield Ltd, Montreal, 51-58 & Vickers & Benson Ltd, Montreal, 58-66; pres, Art Dir Club, Montreal, 58-60; design consult, Int Civil Aviation Orgn Bulletin, Int Air Transport Asn, 68- *Teaching:* Lectr basic principles art, Sir George Williams Univ, 63-68; lectr hist design, Concordia Univ, 82-87. *Media:* Acrylic. *Mailing Add:* 592 Luck Ave Montreal PQ H4X 1S4 Canada

FEITELSON, HELEN LUNDEBERG See Lundeberg, Helen

FEJES, CLAIRE
PAINTER, WRITER
b New York, NY, Dec 14, 20. *Study:* Art Students League with Jose de Creeft & Saul Balzerman; Univ Alaska, Dr Humanities. *Work:* Anchorage Mus, Alaska; Univ Alaska, Fairbanks; Alaska State Mus, Juneau; Noel Wien Libr, Fairbanks, Alaska; Archer Huntington Mus, Tex; Nagoya Gakium Univ, Japan; Michener Collection. *Comn:* Noelwein Libr, Alaska. *Exhib:* Solo exhibs, Frye Art Mus, 59 & 73, Charles Bowers Mus, Calif, 68, Norfolk Mus, Va, 69, Alaska State Mus, 71 & 82, Wash State Mus, 73, Bear Gallery, Fairbanks, Alaska, 78 & 83, Tokyo Metrop Mus, Japan, 83-84 & 85; Contemporary Art from Alaska, Smithsonian Exhib, 78; Cork Gallery, Lincoln Ctr, 81; Anchorage Art Mus, 83; Univ Alaska Mus0 Fairbanks, 91. *Teaching:* Instr art, Fairbanks Public Sch, Alaska; instr art, Univ Alaska. *Awards:* Gold Medal for Excellence, Inst Human Potential, Philadelphia, Pa, 81. *Bibliog:* Nina Mollet (auth), Clair Fejes, Alaska Mag, spring 79; Leslie Barber (auth), Southwest Art Article, Claire Fejes, 90; Mary Goodwin (auth), Fejes Retrospective, 91. *Mem:* Artists Equity. *Media:* Oil, Watercolor. *Publ:* Auth & illusr, People of the Noatak, Alfred A Knopf, 66; Enuk My Son, Pantheon, 69; illusr, Eskimo Story Teller, Univ Tenn, 75; auth, Villagers, Random House, 81. *Dealer:* Sindin Gallery 79th & Madison Ave New York NY 10021; Stonington Gallery Anchorage AK. *Mailing Add:* 924 Kellum St Fairbanks AK 99701

FEKETE, BRIAN
PAINTER
b Dearborn, Mich, June 10, 55. *Study:* Wayne State Univ, BFA, 79, MFA, 92. *Work:* Miller, Canfield, Paddock & Stone, Detroit, Mich; Mr & Mrs S Brooks Barron, Southfield, Mich; Mr & Mrs Frank Piku, Mich; Dick Goody & Michelle Stamler, Royal Oak, Mich,; Robert Kobetis & Patricia Miller, Detroit, Mich. *Exhib:* Premier Exhib, Nawara Gallery, Walled Lake, Mich, 86; Other Spaces: An Exhibition of Recent Art Work, Detroit Artists Market, Brookfield Off Park, Farmington Hills, Mich, 86; Alumni Exhib, Wayne State Univ, Detroit Mich, 86; Mich Ann XIV, The Art Ctr, Mt Clemens, 86; Mich Artists/Recent Work, The Detroit Focus Gallery, 87; Detroit Expressionists, Nawara Gallery, Walled Lake, Mich, 87; Choices: Twenty Painters from the Midwest, Minneapolis Col Art & Design, Minn, Travelling exhib, 87; From Artists Studios/Current Work, Artemisia Gallery, Chicago, Ill, 88; Art for Life Exhib, Southfield, Mich, 90; Exchange Exhib, Vox Populi Gallery, Philadelphia, Pa, 90. *Teaching:* Part-time instr painting, Wayne State Univ, 90-91. *Awards:* Proj Grant, Mich Coun Arts, 85 & 88; Visual Arts Fels, Nat Endowment Arts, 86 & 88; Alumni Teaching Fel, Wayne State Univ, Detroit, Mich, 90. *Bibliog:* Manon Meilgaard (auth), Detroit expressionists' filled with energy, Observer-Eccentric Papers, 9/24/87; Marsha Miro (auth), Eye on art, Pontiac Art Ctr, The Detroit Free Press, 4/87; Joy Hakanson Colby (auth), Oil & gas pair up in Pontiac, The Detroit News, 4/87. *Media:* Oil. *Publ:* Annual Guide to Galleries, Museums, Artists, Art in Am, 86 & 87; Wayne State Univ in Michigan, Alumni Exhib, 86; Other Space: An Exhibition of Recent Art Work, Detroit Artist Market, 86; Choices: Twenty Painters from the Midwest, Minneapolis Col Art & Design; Art for Life, 90. *Mailing Add:* 4456 Bishop Detroit MI 48224

FEKNER, JOHN
CONCEPTUAL ARTIST, ENVIRONMENTAL ARTIST
b New York, NY, Oct 6, 50. *Study:* NY Inst Tech, BFA, 72. *Work:* Mus Mod Art, New York; Milwaukee Art Mus; Malmo Mus, Sweden; Va Mus Fine Arts, Richmond; Heidelberg Mus, Ger. *Exhib:* Selections-Dissections, Moderna Musett, Stockholm, 86; Committed to Print, Mus Mod Art, New York, 88; Against the Wall, Heidleberg Mus, 89; The Technological Muse, Katonah Mus, NY, 90; Word as Image: American Arts 60-90, Milwaukee Art Mus, 91; and others. *Teaching:* Asst prof computer graphics, C W Post, Long Island Univ, Brookville, NY, 89- *Awards:* Multi Media, Arts, 87; Nat Endowment Arts Grant, 78. *Bibliog:* Lois Nesbitt (auth), John Fekner Exit Art, Artforum, 5/92; Nancy Princenthal (auth), John Fekner Exit Art, Art Am, 7/92. *Media:* Multimedia. *Publ:* Auth, Danger, Live Artists, Wedgepress & Cheese, Sweden, 82; Cassette Gazette, B-Sellers, Tokyo, Japan, 85; Beauty's Only Screen Deep, Wedge Press, New York, 85. *Dealer:* Anders Tornberg Gallery Kungsgatan 4 Lund Sweden 22350. *Mailing Add:* 31-14 80th St Jackson Heights NY 11370

FELD, AUGUSTA
PAINTER, PRINTMAKER
b Philadelphia, Pa, Apr 18, 19. *Study:* Fleisher Art Mem & Music Settlement Sch, Philadelphia; Philadelphia Col Art, BA; Tyler Sch Fine Arts, Temple Univ; Pa Acad Fine Arts, MA. *Work:* Acad Fine Arts, Hahnemann Hosp, Sch Dist Permanent Collection, Woodmere Art Mus, Philadelphia; Marple-New Town Libr, Broomall, Pa; Widerner Col, Chester, Pa; and others. *Comn:* Tree of Life (mural of wood inlays, gold paint and vinyl, with Joseph Brahim), Delaware Co Community Ctr, Springfield, Pa, 64; dance mural (oil painting), Melita Dance Studio, Philadelphia, 68; also portraits & murals comn by individuals. *Exhib:* Woodmere Art Mus, 61-88; Artist Equity Asn, Philadelphia, 74; Philadelphia Art Alliance, 74-75; Philadelphia Civic Ctr, 74 & 80; Cheltenham Art Ctr, Pa, 79-88; Abington Art Ctr, Jenkintown, Pa, 79-88; Beaver Col, Glenside, Pa, 84-85; Philips Mill Art Ctr, New Hope, Pa, 87-88; and others. *Pos:* Dir art, Hillview-Trout Nursery Sch, Broomall, Pa, 61-; art coordr, Abington Art Ctr, Jenkintown, 79-87. *Teaching:* Instr art, Philadelphia Sch Dist, 54-65, Wallingford Art Ctr, Pa, 63-64 & Haverford, Pa, 63-65. *Awards:* First Prize for oils, Atlantic City C of C, 68; First Prize, print exhib, Cheltenham Art Ctr, 71; First Prize in Portraiture, La Lomita Mus, Mission, Tex, 79; Best in Show, Perkiomen Valley Art Ctr, 84; First Prize in Oil Painting, Cheltenham Art Ctr, 85; Painting Award, Phillips Mill Art Exhib, New Hope, Pa, 88; First Prize (graphics), Doylestown Art Ctr, 90. *Bibliog:* Article, La Rev Mod, 64. *Mem:* Philadelphia Watercolor Soc; Philadelphia Watercolor Club; Doylestown Art League; Woodmere Art Mus; fel Pa Acad Art. *Media:* All Media. *Mailing Add:* 103 Forrest Ave Elkins Park PA 19117

FELD, MARIAN PARRY See Parry, Marian

FELD, STUART PAUL
DEALER
b Passaic, NJ, Aug 10, 35. *Study:* Princeton Univ, AB, 57; Harvard Univ, AM, 58. *Collections Arranged:* Three Centuries of American Painting, 65 & 200 Years of Watercolor Painting in American, 66, Metrop Mus Art; American Paintings & Historical Prints from the Middendorf Collection, Metrop Mus Art & Baltimore Mus Art, 67; and many others. *Pos:* Var curatorial positions leading to assoc cur-in-charge, Dept Am Paintings, Metrop Mus Art, 61-67. *Interests:* American and European art of 18th, 19th and 20th centuries. *Publ:* Coauth (with Albert Ten Eyck Gardner), American Paintings: Painters Born by 1815 (Catalogue of the Permanent Collection of the Metropolitan Mus of Art), Vol 1, NY Graphic Soc, 65; and more than fifty exhibition catalogues and articles about American paintings, decorative arts and architecture. *Mailing Add:* c/o Hirschl & Adler Galleries Inc 21 E 70th St New York NY 10021

FELDHAUS, PAUL A
EDUCATOR, PRINTMAKER
b Cincinnati, Ohio, July 19, 26. *Study:* Cincinnati Art Mus; Miami Univ, Oxford, Ohio, BFA, 50; Bradley Univ, Peoria, Ill, MA, 52; study with Edwin Fulwider & Ernest Freed, printmakers. *Work:* Carroll Reece Mus, ETenn State Univ; Friends Meeting House, Boston, Mass; Montgomery Mus Fine Arts, Ala; Mobile Pub Lbir, Ala; Ford Times Col; Achenbach Found, San Francisco; Turner Print Gallery, CSU, Chico; Art Gallery, Calif State Poly Univ, Pomona; Chico Art Center, Calif. *Comn:* Mural, Mastin Sch Nursing, Mobile, Ala, 66; mural, Woman's Clinic, Mobile, Ala, 67. *Exhib:* Int Biennial Graphic Art, Mus Mod Art, Ljubljana, Yugoslavia, 75; Int Exhib Graphic Art, Frechen, WGer, 76; Seventh Premio Int Biella of Printmaking, Italy, 76; US Embassy Travelling Exhib, Yugoslavia, 83; Crocker-Kingsley Exhib, Sacramento, 83; one-man print exhibit, Chico Art Ctr, Calif, 89; US-UK Print Connections travelling exhib, Eng, 89-90; Invitational Woodcut Print show, Goldenwest Coll, Huntington Beach, Calif, 89; and others. *Teaching:* Assoc prof art, Spring Hill Col, Mobile, Ala, 52-71; prof printmaking & drawing & coordr printmaking dept, Calif State Univ, Chico, 71-91, prof emer, 91- *Awards:* First Place Purchase Award, Dauphin Island Nat Competition, 65, 66, 68 & 70; Flack Purchase Prize, 7th Dixie Print Ann, Montgomery Mus of Art, 66; First Place Graphics, Mobile Watercolor & Graphic Arts Show, 69; Purchase prize, Ink & Clay XVI, Cal State Poly, Pomona, 90. *Mem:* Col Art Asn; Graphics Soc; Ala Art League (pres, 69-70); Calif Soc Printmakers, 71-; Los Angeles Printmaking Soc, 71- *Media:* Lithography, Engraving. *Publ:* Univ J, CSU, Chico woodcut or linocut included in every publ 85-91 with commendation & award, 90. *Mailing Add:* Dept Art Calif State Univ Chico Chico CA 95929

FELDMAN, ARTHUR MITCHELL
MUSEUM DIRECTOR, ART AND ANTIQUES DEALER
b Philadelphia, Pa, Dec 22, 42. *Study:* Villanova Univ, BS, 64; Univ Pa with George Tatum; Univ Mo, MA(art hist & archaeol), 70. *Pos:* Vis cur, Victoria & Albert Mus, London, Eng, 70-71; assoc cur & asst adminr, Renwick Gallery, Smithsonian Inst, Washington, DC, 71-73; dir, Spertus Mus of Judaica, 73-85; exec dir, Jewish Mus Chicago, 86-; pres, Arthur M Feldman Gallery, Highland Park, 86- *Teaching:* Lectr, Col Lake County, 86- *Mem:* Am Asn of Mus; Ethnic Preserv Coun. *Publ:* Auth, Jewish Artists of the 20th Century, 75, The Hill Page Collection, 75, The Jews of Yemen, 76 & Faith and Form: Synagog Architecture of Illinois, 76, Spertus Col Press; The Sons of Zebulan: Jewish Maritime History, 79. *Mailing Add:* 1815 St Johns Ave Highland Park IL 60035

FELDMAN, BELLA
SCULPTOR, EDUCATOR
b New York, NY. *Study:* Queens Col, City Univ New York, BA; Calif Col Arts & Crafts; Calif State Univ, San Jose, MA. *Work:* Oakland Mus, Calif; Berkeley Art Mus, Univ Calif. *Comn:* Sculptures, Marshal Tulin, Hydronautics Inc, Silver Spring, Md, 64, Sasaki-Walker Landscape Architects, Newport Shopping Ctr, Newport Beach, Calif, 65, Royston Hanamoto Landscape Architects, Potrero Park, Richmond, Calif, 66 & Fountain Fed Home Loan Bank, San Francisco, Calif, 90. *Exhib:* Palace Legion Honor, San Francisco, 61; Summer Series, San Francisco Mus, 64; San Francisco Art Inst, 75; San Jose Mus Art, 82; Calif Mixed Media Traveling Exhib, Japan, 82-83; Fibre/Espace Biennale, Lausanne, Switzerland, 83; Gallerie Bernard Letu, Geneva, 83; and others. *Pos:* Cult specialist, US Info Agency to Uganda, 90. *Teaching:* Prof, Calif Col Arts & Crafts, 64-, grad dir, 75-79; lectr art, Makerere Univ Col, Fine Art Sch, Uganda, 68-70. *Awards:* Calif Mus Trustees Award, 67; First Prize, San Francisco Women Artists, 67; E L Cabot Trust Fund Award, Harvard Univ, 75; Nat Endowment Arts Grant, 86-87. *Bibliog:* Gloria Frym (ed), Second Stories, Chronicle Bks; Kate Regan (auth), Possibility and paradox, Mus of Calif Mag, 9/87 & 10/87. *Mem:* Women's Caucus Art; Committee-West, East Bay; Col Art Asn. *Media:* Welded Medal, Cast Medal. *Dealer:* Jan Baum Gallery 170 S La Brea Los Angeles CA 90036; Barclay Simpson Gallery 3669 Mt Diablo Blvd Lafayette CA 94549. *Mailing Add:* Dept Fine Arts Calif Col Arts & Crafts 5212 Broadway Oakland CA 94618

FELDMAN, EDMUND BURKE
EDUCATOR, CRITIC
b Bayonne, NJ, May 6, 24. *Study:* Newark Sch Fine & Indust Arts, with John R Grabach & Emile Alexay, dipl, 41; Syracuse Univ, BFA, 49; Univ Calif, Los Angeles, with Karl With, Stanton MacDonald Wright & Abraham Kaplan, MA(art hist), 51; Columbia Univ, with Lyman Bryson & George Counts, EdD, 53. *Pos:* Cur paintings & sculpture, Newark Mus, 53. *Teaching:* Assoc prof art, Livingston State Col, 53-56; assoc prof painting, sculpture & design, Carnegie-Mellon Univ, 56-60; chmn art div, State Univ NY Col New Paltz, 60-66; prof art, Ohio State Univ, summer 66; prof art, Univ Ga, 66-; vis prof, Univ Calif, Berkeley, winter 74. *Awards:* Named Alumni Found Distinguished Prof Art, Univ Ga, 73. *Mem:* Kappa Pi; Col Art Asn Am; Nat Art Educ Asn (pres-elect, 79-81 & pres , 81-83). *Res:* Art history and criticism. *Publ:* Auth, Art as Image and Idea, 67, Becoming Human Through Art, 70, The Artist, 82 & Thinking About Art, 85, Prentice-Hall; Varieties of Visual Experience, Prentice-Hall & Abrams, 72, second ed, 81, third ed, 87, fourth ed, 93. *Mailing Add:* 140 Chinquapin Pl Athens GA 30605

FELDMAN, FRANKLIN
PRINTMAKER, WRITER
b New York, NY, Nov 12, 27. *Study:* Columbia Law Sch, LLB, 51; Art Students League (study with Howard Trafton, Ivan Olinsky & Byron Browne); New Sch Soc Res, Parsons Sch Des (study with John Ross). *Work:* Archival Collection, Nat Portrait Gallery, Washington, DC; Lynd Ward Mem Collection, Portland Art Mus. *Exhib:* Silvermine, Prints Int, 90; Int Miniature Show, 90. *Teaching:* Lectr law, Columbia Law Sch, 79- *Awards:* Fel, Yaddo, Saratoga Springs, NY, 83. *Mem:* Int Found Art Res (dir, 71-, pres, 71-76); Grolier Club; Coun, Nat Acad Design; Century Asn. *Media:* Etching, Painting. *Res:* Legal aspects of art. *Publ:* Coauth, Art Works: Law, Policy, Practice, Practising Law Inst, 74; Art Law, Little, Brown & Co, 86; also, various articles in legal publications relating to art & law. *Mailing Add:* 15 W 81st St New York NY 10024

FELDMAN, ROGER LAWRENCE
SCULPTOR, PAINTER
b Spokane, Wash, Nov 19, 49; US citizen. *Study:* Univ Wash, Seattle, BA, 72; Claremont Grad Sch, Calif, MFA, 77. *Work:* Washington State Arts Comn. *Comn:* Bronze Sculpture, East Hill Community Ctr, Gresham, Oregon, 79-80; Site spec steel sculpture, Wash State Arts Comn Rental Vocational Tech Inst, Renton, 87-89. *Exhib:* Cheney Cowles Mus, Spokane, Wash, 80 & 83; Visual Arts Ctr Alaska, Anchorage, 84; Lynn McAllister Gallery, Seattle, Wash, 86; Los Angeles Munic Satellite Gallery, 90; Connemara, Dallas, 91; Westbend Gallery, Wis, 92. *Teaching:* Assoc Prof sculpture, Biola Univ, La Mirada, Calif. *Awards:* Fel, Nat Endowment Arts, 86; King Co Arts Comn Fel, 88; Fel, Connemara Found, 91. *Bibliog:* Ron Glowen (auth), Roger Feldman, Vanguard, 11/84; Janet Kutner (auth), Nature has a hand in it, Dallas Morning News, 3/91; Steve Scott (auth), Third Way, Exeter, Eng, 8/92. *Mem:* Christians in Visual Arts; Int Sculpture Ctr. *Media:* Metal, Welded; Miscellaneous Media. *Mailing Add:* 1217 Newcastle Lane Fullerton CA 92633

FELDMAN, RONALD
DEALER
Pos: Co-owner, Ronald Feldman Gallery, New York, currently. *Specialty:* Contemporary artists; European and American masters, painting, sculpture and prints from Impressionism forward. *Mailing Add:* 31 Mercer New York NY 10013

FELDMAN, WALTER (SIDNEY)
PAINTER, PRINTMAKER
b Lynn, Mass, Mar 23, 25. *Study:* Yale Univ Sch Fine Arts, BFA, 50, Sch Design, MFA, 51; also with W de Kooning, Stuart Davis & Josef Albers. *Work:* Addison Gallery Am Art, Andover, Mass; Metrop Mus Art, New York; Fogg Art Mus, Cambridge, Mass; Israel Mus, Jerusalem; Mus Mod Art, New York. *Comn:* Mosaic pavements, Temple Beth-El, Providence, RI, 57; stained glass windows, Sugarman Mem Chapel, Providence, RI, 61; World's Fair poster, IBM Corp, 63; Quezalcoatl (mural), Pembroke Col, Brown Univ, 66; 32 panel mural, Temple Emanu-El, Providence, RI, 68. *Exhib:* American Watercolors, Drawings and Prints, Metrop Mus Art, 52; Recent Drawings USA, Mus Mod Art, New York, 55; Mostra Int, Milan, Italy, 57; 26th Biennial, Corcoran Gallery, Washington, DC, 59; Nat Inst Arts & Lett, New York, 61; one-man show, Hopkins Ctr, Dartmouth Col, 78. *Pos:* Dir, Brown/Ziggurat Press, 90. *Teaching:* Instr painting & design, Yale Univ Sch Design, 50-53; prof painting & printmaking, Brown Univ, 53-; vis prof drawing, Harvard Univ, 68; artist in residence, Hopkins Ctr, Dartmouth Col, 78. *Awards:* Metrop Mus Art Award, 52; Gold Medal, Mostra Int, Milan, Italy, 57; First Painting Award, Boston Arts Festival, Mass, 64; Governor's Award for Art, RI, 80. *Bibliog:* G Y Loveridge (auth), Providence practitioner of ancient art, The Rhode Islander, 4/25/54; Michael Forster (auth), The color of Mexico is black, Nivel 41, German P Garcia (Mexico City), 5/25/62; Jane Shelton (auth), Walter Feldman, Harvard Art Rev, spring 66. *Mem:* Am Color Print Soc. *Media:* All. *Publ:* Coauth (with J Schevill), Ghost Names, Ghost Numbers (woodcuts), Handmade Bks. *Mailing Add:* 107 Benevolent St Providence RI 02906

FELISKY, BARBARA ROSBE
PAINTER
b Chicago, Ill, Mar 24, 38. *Study:* Univ Mich, studied drawing under Frederick O'Dell, BA, 60; Laguna Sch of Art, with Hans Burchardt, 75. *Work:* City of Orange Civic Ctr, Calif; City of Brea Civic Ctr, Calif. *Comn:* Murals, Home Savings & Loan, Los Angeles, 84, Gen Tel Co, Sacramento, 84, Breakers Hotel, Long Beach, 85, Off Nat Educ, Irvine, 86; Folding Screen, New Seoul Hotel, Los Angeles. *Exhib:* California Traditionalist, Redlands Mus, Calif, 80; Catharine Lorillard Wolfe, Nat Arts Club, New York, NY, 82; The Traditionalist's Exhib, Brea Civic Ctr Gallery, Calif, 84; 51st Int Exhib, Arts Club of Washington, DC, 84; Int Miniature Art Shows, Min Art Soc of Fla & NJ, 85. *Teaching:* Teacher & consult, pvt studio, 76- & City of Orange Sch Dist, 76-84; teacher oil painting, YWCA, Santa Ana & Orange, Calif, 74-80. *Awards:* First Place Still Life, In Miniature Ann Exhib, 79; First Place

Landscaping, Nat Western Small Painting Show, NMex, 83; Purchase Award, City of Brea, 84. *Mem:* Artist mem Laguna Mus; Miniature Art Soc Washington, DC; Miniature Art Soc NJ; Miniature Art Soc Fla. *Media:* Oil, Monotype. *Publ:* Contribr, Flower painting then and now, Am Artist, 5/84; Illusr, Los Angeles Times Home Mag, 4/28/85; auth, The Search for Levitan, Am Artists, 7/88. *Dealer:* Renoir Gallery 7001 Scottsdale Rd Scottsdale AZ 85253; Art Angles Gallery 3403 E Chapman Ave Orange CA 92667. *Mailing Add:* 2942 Lake Hill Dr Orange CA 92667

FELKER, DAVID LARRY
SCULPTOR, GALLERY DIRECTOR
b Spokane, Wash, July 6, 40. *Study:* Eastern Wash Univ, BA, 75; Wash State Univ, MFA, 78. *Work:* Anchorage Mus Hist & Art, Alaska; Mus Judetean, Bistrita, Romania. *Exhib:* Solo exhibs, Intersections of Time & Space, 82, Three Coordinates Plus Time, 86, The Arc, Anchorage Mus Hist & Art, 87, Arc of the Alembic Current, Goldsmith's Mus, London, Eng, 90, Generator Bistrita, Mus Judetean, Generator Bucharest, Univ Bucharest Mus, Romanis, 90 Alaska Generator, Visual Arts Ctr, Anchorage, 92; US Cult Exhib, Magadan Mus Art, Russia, 92. *Collections Arranged:* International (sculpture), 84; Dennis Oppenheim (drawing/sculpture), 85; Colour (paintings), 86, Altered Images, Eng, 92; Interaction 20 (paintings/sculpture), Europe, 90. *Pos:* Dir of Sculpture, Visual Arts Ctr Alaska, 81; Dir Int Gallery Comtemp Art, 85- *Teaching:* Instr, drawing, Chapman Col, Alaska, 79-86; asst prof painting, drawing & sculpture, Univ Alaska, Anchorage, 86, instr, 87- *Awards:* Alaska State Fel, Anchorage Mus, 85; Nat Endowment Arts Fel 1989, Arc Alembic Current Goldsmith's, London, 90, Theurgic Helmet, VACA, 92. *Bibliog:* David Lewinson (critical rev), Los Angeles Times, 89; Colin Dan (critical rev), Art Romania, 90; Ron Glowen (critical rev), Artweek, 91. *Media:* All. *Mailing Add:* 3905 Carolina Dr Anchorage AK 99517

FELLER, ROBERT L
CONSERVATION SCIENTIST
b Newark, NJ, Dec 27, 19. *Study:* Dartmouth Col, AB, 41; Rutgers Univ, MS, 43 & PhD, 50. *Pos:* Head, Nat Gallery Art Res Proj, Carnegie-Mellon Inst Res, Pittsburgh, 50-76, dir, Ctr on the Materials of the Artist & Conservator, 76-88, dir emer, 88-; ed, Int Inst Conserv Hist & Artistic Works, Am Group Bulletin, 60-74. *Teaching:* Vis scientist, Conserv Ctr, NY Univ Inst Fine Arts, spring 61. *Awards:* Fel, Illum Eng Soc, 75; Pittsburgh Award, Am Chemical Soc, 83; Col Art Asn/Nat Inst Conserv Award, Distinction in Scholar & Conserv, 92. *Mem:* Fel Int Inst Conserv Hist & Artistic Works (pres, Am Group, 64-66); Int Coun Mus, Comt Conserv (pres, 69-78); Nat Conserv Adv Coun (pres, 76-79); Inter Soc Color Coun; Fedn Soc Paint Technol; and others. *Res:* Picture varnishes; effects of light on museum objects; analysis of pigments in works of art. *Publ:* Coauth, On Picture Varnishes and Their Solvents, 59, rev ed, 71; ed, Artists' Pigments, Vol I, Cambridge Univ Press, 85. *Mailing Add:* Carnegie-Mellon Inst Res 4400 Fifth Ave Pittsburgh PA 15213

FELLOWS, ALICE
PAINTER
b Atlanta, Ga, Sept 14, 35. *Study:* Syracuse Univ, BFA, 57; Antioch Univ, MAP, 92. *Work:* NC Mus Art, Raleigh; Southeastern Ctr Contemp Art (SECCA), Winston-Salem, NC; Mint Mus Art, Charlotte, NC; Eli Broad Corp Collection, Los Angeles; Norton Family Collection, Los Angeles. *Exhib:* Works of Candidates for Awards, Acad Arts & Letters, New York, 74; Alice Fellows: Recent Drawings, Mint Mus Art, Charlotte, NC, 74; A Look at Seeing, Barnsdall Gallery, Los Angeles, 80; Directions 1986, Hirshhorn Mus, Washington, DC, 86; Alice Fellows: Psychic Terrain, Santa Monica Col Gallery, Calif, 88; A Sense of Being, Claremont Grad Sch Gallery, Calif, 91. *Awards:* Visual Artists Fel, WESRAF/Nat Endowment Arts, 90; Fel Painting, Getty Trust, 90; Nat Endowment Arts Fel Painting, 91-92. *Bibliog:* Phillis Rosenzweig (auth), Painting into Nature, 86 & Directions 1986, catalog, 86, Hirshhorn Mus; Howard Fox (auth), 1990 Regional Fellowships, WESTAF-Nat Endowment Arts, 90. *Mailing Add:* 656 Copeland Ct Santa Monica CA 90405

FELLOWS, DEBORAH LYNNE See Copenhaver-Fellows, Deborah (Deborah Lynne Fellows)

FELLOWS, FRED
PAINTER, SCULPTOR
b Ponca City, Okla, Aug 15, 34. *Comn:* Portfolio of prints, Winchester on the Frontier, Winchester Firearms; Paintings/Bronze Sculptures for Nat Finals Rodeo, Pro Rodeo, Hesston Corp. *Exhib:* Cowboy Artists Am Show, Phoenix & Okla, 68-; Cowboy Hall of Fame; Whitney Gallery; Gran Palais, Paris; First Western Art Show, China; Los Angeles Co Mus Art; Cowboy Artists Am Mus, Kerrville, Tex. *Pos:* Commercial artist & art dir. *Teaching:* Painting workshops for Cowboy Artists of Am Mus. *Awards:* Award for Contrib to Fine Art in Am, Grumbacher, 76; Silver Medal, Cowboy Artists of Am, 78; Gold Medal Sculpture and Best of Show, Cowboy Artist Asn Ann Exhib, 91. *Bibliog:* Brave New Cowboy (doc), Nat Pub TV; Great Plains Massacre (doc), BBC; article, Southwest Art, 10/82. *Mem:* Cowboy Artists Asn (secy-treas & vpres, 74-75, pres, 75-76, dir, 92-). *Publ:* Auth, Saddles of the early west, Mont Hist Soc Mag, 68; Art of the West, 6/92. *Mailing Add:* Box 464 Bigfork MT 59911

FELSEN, ROSAMUND
ART DEALER, GALLERY DIRECTOR
b Pasadena, Calif, Feb 28, 34. *Pos:* Owner, Rosamund Felsen Gallery, Los Angeles, currently. *Specialty:* Contemporary art. *Mailing Add:* 8525 Santa Monica Blvd Los Angeles CA 90069

FELTER, JAMES WARREN
PAINTER, PRINTMAKER
b Bainbridge, NY, Aug 25, 43; Can citizen. *Study:* Univ S Fla, Tampa, BA(painting), 64; Univ Wash. *Work:* City of Vancouver, BC; BC Prov Collection, Can; Manawatu Art Gallery, NZ; Mildura Arts Centre, Australia; Mus Contemp Art, Quito, Ecuador; and others. *Comn:* Trademark, OCEPA-Ecuadorian Handcrafts, Quito, 65; posters, Seattle Opera Asn, Wash, 67; Simon Fraser Univ Arts Centre, Burnaby, BC, 70 & 72. *Exhib:* The Seventies, Mus Mod Art, Sao Paulo, Brazil, 76; 37th Venice Biennale (ECART Invitational), Italy, 76; Four Can Artists, Moderna Galerija, Liubljana & touring Yugoslavia, 76-77; Sixth Int Miniature Print Competition, Pratt Graphics Ctr, New York & touring US, 77-78; Cabo Frio Int Print Biennial, Brazil, 82; Images du Futur, Montreal, 87. *Collections Arranged:* Simon Fraser Collection, Simon Fraser Univ; The British Columbia Craft Exhibition (with catalog), Vancouver, BC, 72; Artist's Stamps and Stamp Images (circulated 1975-80), 74. *Pos:* Dir, Galeria de Ocepa, Quito, Ecuador, 65-66; cur-dir exhib, Simon Fraser Univ, 70-85. *Teaching:* Vis artist, Escuela de Bellas Artes, Univ Cent Ecuador, 66; resident visual arts, Simon Fraser Univ, 69. *Awards:* Finalist-Major Work of Art Competition, Univ Calgary, Alta, 74; Winner, Trademark Competition, Craftsmen's Asn BC, 75; Can Coun grant, 79. *Bibliog:* Article, La Rev Mod, Paris, 8/63; Mario Leon Meneses (auth), James W Felter en la Galeria Siglo XX, El Comercio, Quito, 2/24/66; Francoise Le Gris (auth), article, Vie des Arts 69, Montreal, 73; article, Vie des Arts, Montreal, 6/86. *Mem:* Western Can Art Asn (chmn, 75-76 & 78-80); Can Mus Asn; Int Coun Mus; bd dir, W Vancouver Community Arts Coun. *Media:* Ink, Acrylic. *Res:* Pre-Columbian and indigenous arts. *Publ:* Auth, 450 Desinos Del 500 DC, Span, Quito, 66; ed, Paul Rand 1896-1970, Vancouver, BC, 72; contribr, Contemporaries of Emily Carr in British Columbia, Vancouver, 74; contribr, Vehicule Art: in Transit, Montreal, PQ, 75. *Mailing Add:* 2707 Rosebery Ave West Vancouver BC V7V 3A3 Canada

FELTER, JUNE MARIE
PAINTER, PRINTMAKER
b Oakland, Calif, Oct 19, 19. *Study:* Oakland Art Inst, Calif, 37-40; Calif Sch Arts & Crafts, Oakland, 37-40, Calif Sch Fine Arts, San Francisco, with Richard Diebenkorn, 60-61. *Work:* Achenbach Found, Palace of the Legion of Honor, San Francisco; Int House, Berkeley, Calif; Oakland Art Mus; San Francisco Art Comn; Am Fedn Arts, New York. *Comn:* Suite of six etchings, comn by Dana Reich & Brian Jones, San Francisco, 81; three ed lithographs, Meridien Hotel, San Francisco, 83; plus 200 portraits comn by various indiviuals 54-58 & stage sets for various school programs in the 50's. *Exhib:* De Young Mus, San Francisco, 59; The Painted Flower, Oakland Art Mus, Calif, 60; Calif Soc Etchers, 63 & Nat Drawing Show, 70, San Francisco Mus Art; Elegant Miniatures, Kyoto, Japan, 83 & San Francisco Mus Mod Art, 84; Calif Soc Printmakers traveling show, 84-86; Japan-California Print Show, Tokyo, 86; 871 Fine Arts Gallery, San Francisco, 87, 89 & 90. *Teaching:* Instr watercolor, painting & figure drawing, San Francisco Mus Mod Art, 64-79; instr painting, Univ Calif, San Francisco, 79-80. *Awards:* Purchase Award, Oakland Art Mus, 60; Purchase Award Oil Painting, San Francisco Art Comn, 64. *Bibliog:* Susan Felter (dir), June Felter, A Painter (film), Univ Calif, Los Angeles, 69-70; Arthur Bloomfield (auth), A stir at the beach, San Francisco Chronicle, 8/3/78; Thomas Albright (auth), Art in the San Francisco Bay Area 1945-80, Univ Calif Press, Berkeley, 85. *Mem:* Calif Soc Printmakers (coun mem, 83-84). *Media:* Acrylic, Watercolor. *Publ:* Contribr, Prize Winning Paintings, Allied Publ, 66; auth, Musicality with poet Barbara Guest & illusr June Felter, Kelsey St Press, Berkeley, Calif, 88. *Dealer:* Adrienne Fish 871 Fine Arts Gallery 250 Sutter St San Francisco CA 94108. *Mailing Add:* 1046 Amito Ave Berkeley CA 94705

FELTUS, ALAN
PAINTER, EDUCATOR
b Washington, DC, May 1, 43. *Study:* Tyler Sch Fine Arts, Temple Univ, Philadelphia, 61-62; Cooper Union, New York, BFA, 66; Sch Art & Archit, Yale Univ, MFA, 68. *Work:* Univ Va Art Mus; Nat Mus Am Art, Am Med Asn & Hirshhorn Mus, Washington, DC; NJ State Mus. *Comn:* Murals, Am Med Asn, 85. *Exhib:* Washington Figurative Painters, Corcoran Gallery Art, Washington, DC, 73-74; Forum Gallery, New York, 76, 80, 83, 86 & 91; Nat Acad Design, 77, 78, 82, 86, 88 & 90; Am Acad & Inst Arts & Lett, New York, 77, 79 & 81; Okla Art Ctr, 78; Washington Painting, Corcoran Gallery Art, 82; Wichita Art Mus, 87. *Teaching:* Instr art, Dayton Art Inst, Ohio, 68-70; assoc prof art, Am Univ, Washington, DC, 72-84. *Awards:* Rome Prize Fel Painting, Am Acad Rome, 70-72; Tiffany Found Grant, 80; Nat Endowment Arts Individual Grant, 81. *Bibliog:* Charles Jencks (auth), Post-Modernism, New York, Rizzoli, 87; Alan Feltus (auth), Inside the painter's mind, the Artist's Mag, 1/92; Alan Feltus (auth), Living and working in Italy, Am Artist Mag, 8/92; Howard DaLee Spencer (auth), Alan Fedltus in Italy, Am Arts Quar, winter, 92. *Media:* Oil. *Dealer:* Forum Gallery 745 Fifth Ave New York NY. *Mailing Add:* c/o Forum Gallery 1018 Madison Ave New York NY 10021

FENCI, RENZO
SCULPTOR
b Florence, Italy, Nov 18, 14; US citizen. *Study:* Royal Inst Art, Florence. *Work:* Permanent Gallery Mod Art, Florence; Santa Barbara Mus Art, Calif; Cedars Sinai Med Ctr, Los Angeles. *Comn:* Nine banks in Los Angeles area, Home Savings & Loan Asn; Dr Charles Leroy Loman Mem, Orthopedic Hosp, Los Angeles, 68; George C Page Bldg, Children's Hosp, Los Angeles, Calif, 76; portrait of Edwin Lester, Music Ctr, Los Angeles, 77; Kilroy Indust, Sea-Tac, Seattle, 80; Southwest Gas Corp, Las Vegas, Nev, 88. *Exhib:* Art Inst Chicago, 41; Calif State Fair, 50; Los Angeles Co Mus Art, 55; Nat Exhib Contemp Arts US, Pomona, Calif, 56; one-man show, Santa Barbara Mus Art,

68. *Teaching:* Instr sculpture, Univ Wash, Pullman, 42; asst prof sculpture, Univ Calif, Santa Barbara, 46-54; prof sculpture & head dept, Otis Art Inst, 54-77. *Awards:* Calif State Fair Award, 47, 49 & 50; Los Angeles Co Mus Art Award, 55; Santa Barbara Mus Biennial Show Award. *Bibliog:* Bette Howell (auth), Twelve California sculptors, Am Artist Mag, 68; Dialogues in Art, ABC-TV, Los Angeles, 69. *Media:* Bronze. *Mailing Add:* 3206 Deronda Dr Los Angeles CA 90068

FENDELL, JONAS J
EDUCATOR, PRINTMAKER
b Brooklyn, NY. *Study:* New Sch Social Res; Brooklyn Mus Art Sch; Syracuse Univ, BFA & MFA. *Work:* Print collection, Mus Mod Art, New York; painting, Baltimore Mus Art; print, Syracuse Univ; print, Univ Maine; IBM Collection; Southern Graphic Artists. *Exhib:* Butler Inst Am Art; Brooklyn Mus Print Show; Baltimore Mus Art; Whitney Mus Am Art; Mus Mod Art; Univ Md, 81; Syracuse Mus; Corcoran Gallery, Washington, DC; Chryler Mus. *Pos:* Asst dir, Syracuse Mus, 57-58. *Teaching:* Prof design, painting & printing, Hurdell/Designs, 56-57; instr design & materials, Md Inst Col Art, 58-; instr materials, Essex Col, 68- *Awards:* Purchase Award, Mus Mod Art, New York; Purchase Prize, Baltimore Mus Art; Artist of Distinction Award, Univ Md, 81. *Mem:* Col Art Asn Am. *Publ:* Costa Rican Sun, 4/87. *Dealer:* Dark Horse Gallery Towson MD. *Mailing Add:* 1905 Dixon Rd Baltimore MD 21209-3507

FENN, (FRANCES) ELIZABETH
PAINTER, GRAPHIC ARTIST
b Toronto, Ont, Can, Oct 15, 14; US citizen. *Study:* Sch Indust Art, Philadelphia, with Alexy Brodovitch, BA, 36; with Wallace Harrison, New York, 45-49; with Fernand Leger, 52 & William Hayter, 54-56, Paris; with Samuel Adler, New York, 71-72. *Work:* Folger Shakespeare Libr, Washington, DC; Mus Haitian Art, Port-Au-Prince; US Trust Co, New York; Bally Shoes, Switz; Chamber de Compensation des Instruments Financiers de Paris, France, 87. *Comn:* Oil painting, Diptych, General Electric, Stanford, Conn, 84; oil portrait, Jacques Heari David, Paris, France, 85; oil portrait, Eleanor Kingsbury, principal, Springside Sch, Philadelphia, 6/90; 2 charcoal & pastel portraits, Isabelle DuPasquier, Paris, France, 92. *Exhib:* 68th Ann, Hudson River Mus, Yonkers, NY, 83; solo exhib, Cimaises Ventadour, Paris, 87 & Alliance Francaise, Greenwich, Conn, 91; Salon Int de Paris, 87; Glass Gallery, New York, 87, 88 & 90; West Side Arts Coalition, Lever House, 88; Three Artists, Country Art Gallery, Locustvalley, NY, 89. *Pos:* Art dir, Elizabeth Arden, 38-43 & J D Tarcher & Co, New York, 43-45; art dir & fashion illusr, Publicis, Paris, 56-63; art dir, fashion consult & illusr, Elvinger, Paris, 63-66. *Awards:* Prize for Best Artist, Salon Int de Paris, 87; Margaret Sussman Award, Oil, Pen & Brush, spring, 91; Ada Rosario Cecere Award, Graphics, Pen & Brush, 92; and others. *Bibliog:* Emile de Bongnie (auth), Au Centre Culturel de Parly II: Elizabeth Fenn, J de Versailles, 11/4/76; Dorothy Friedman (auth), Paintings by Fenn, sculptures by Flanagan, Greenwich Times, 11/30/83. *Mem:* Artists Equity, NY; Pen & Brush Club, NY. *Media:* Oil, Oil Pastel; Charcoal, Lead Pencil. *Dealer:* Marianne Wyman 84 Round Hill Rd Greenwich CT 06830. *Mailing Add:* 51 W 81st St Apt 9G New York NY 10024

FENSCH, CHARLES EVERETTE
ADMINISTRATOR, EDUCATOR
b Mansfield, Ohio, Dec 11, 35. *Study:* Kent State Univ, Ohio, BS(art), 58; Wayne State Univ, Detroit, Mich, MAE, 65; Univ Mich, Ann Arbor, Mich, MFA, 75. *Work:* Univ Tex, El Paso. *Comn:* Mural series, Kent State Univ, Ohio, 58. *Exhib:* Michigan Craftsmen, Detroit Inst Art; Fourth Invitational, Henry Ford Col, Dearborn, Mich; 16th Regional Exhib, Univ Mich, Ann Arbor; 15th Ann Exhib, Canton Inst Art, Ohio; Michigan-Indiana exhib, Nazareth Col, Ind; Brigham Young Univ, Provo, Utah. *Teaching:* Prof art, Eastern Mich Univ, 65-81; prof & chmn, Dept Art & Theatre Arts, Univ Tex, El Paso, 82-, assoc dean. *Awards:* Artist Teacher Yr, State Mich, 73; Best in Show, Mich Artists Exhib, Mich State Comn, 74. *Mem:* Nat Art Educ Asn (vpres); Mich Art Educ Asn (pres); Tex Asn Sch Art (bd dir); Nat Coun Arts Adminr (sec & treas); Col Art Asn. *Publ:* Auth, Art, a return to structure, E'lan; Art conference proposals, Art Educ, Nat Art Educ Asn. *Mailing Add:* Dept Art Univ Tex El Paso TX 79968

FENTON, ALAN
PAINTER, INSTRUCTOR
b Cleveland, Ohio, July 29, 27. *Study:* Pratt Inst, BFA; Art Students League; New Sch Social Res; also pvt study with Adolph Gottlieb & Jack Tworkov; Cleveland Sch Art. *Work:* Corcoran Gallery Art, Washington, DC; Hirshhorn Mus Art, Washington DC; Central Intelligence Agency, Washington DC; Herbert F Johnson Mus Art, Cornell Univ, Ithaca, NY; Norton Mus Art, West Palm Beach, Fla. *Exhib:* Pace Gallery, 63, 64, Fifth Ann Soc Encouragement Contemp Art Show, San Francisco Mus, 63; one-man exhibs, Larry Aldrich Mus, Ridgefield, Conn, 68, B Fiedler Gallery, Washington, DC, 73-80, New York Cult Mus, 74, Houston Mus Art, 77,Isatan Gallery, Tokyo, Japan, 79 & Phillips Collection, Washington, DC, 80; Corcoran Gallery Art, 71-72; Ft Wayne Mus, Ind, 83; Washes Retrospective of 1970's, Munich, WGer, 86; Painting retrospective by Vincent Melzac Collector, Washington, DC, 88; and others in Tokyo, Munich, Rome, Bern, Switzerland. *Teaching:* Instr drawing, Pratt Inst, 69- & Housatonic State Col, 71-73; spec asst, Cleveland Inst Art, Ohio, 77-78. *Awards:* First Prize, Cleveland Mus Art, 60-61. *Bibliog:* Alan Fenton, Phillips Collection Catalog, 77; Contemp Art Mus Houston, Catalog, 77; also articles in New York Times, New York Post, Village Voice, New York & Art Int. *Mailing Add:* 333 Park Ave S New York NY 10010

FENTON, CHARLES E H
ART DEALER, CONSERVATOR
b Rutland, Vt, Oct 21, 43. *Study:* Univ NH, BA, 65; Univ Kans, MA, 67. *Collections Arranged:* Life and Work of Irwin Hoffman, 84; Life & Work of Stephen Parrish, 87; InterArt Moscow, 91. *Pos:* Dir, Woodstock Gallery & Design Ctr, Vt, currently. *Teaching:* Instr, Dartmouth Col, NH, 67-71. *Mem:* A I C. *Media:* Painting, Paper. *Specialty:* American figurative painting & sculpture. *Mailing Add:* Gallery Place Woodstock VT 05091

FENTON, HOWARD CARTER
PAINTER, EDUCATOR
b Toledo, Ohio, July 2, 10. *Study:* Chouinard Art Inst; Univ Calif, Los Angeles, BA & MA; also with S McDonald Wright; also studies in Japan, Eng, & Italy. *Work:* Santa Barbara Mus Art Calif; Univ Calif, Santa Barbara; Univ Ill. *Exhib:* One-man shows, Santa Barbara Mus Art, 61 & 64, Esther Bear Gallery, 66 & 75, Univ Calif Art Galleries, 67, 74 & 90, Galleria Piazza di Spagna, Rome, 68 & Alwin Gallery, London, 68. *Teaching:* Prof art, Univ Calif, Santa Barbara, 48-78, emer prof, 78- *Bibliog:* David Gebhard (auth), Howard Fenton, Haagen Press, 68; Phyllis Plous (auth), Howard Fenton, Bollinger & Peters, 90. *Media:* Oil, Watercolor. *Collection:* Contemporary American artists. *Mailing Add:* 1000 Ladera Lane Montecito CA 93108

FENTON, JULIA ANN
CONCEPTUAL ARTIST, EDITOR
b Tupelo, Miss, Feb 11, 37. *Study:* Millsaps Col, Jackson, Miss, BA(relig), 58; Pa State Univ, grad study in philos & visual arts, 62-65; Atlanta Col of Art, 70-74. *Exhib:* Transcripts for Justine, High Mus Art, Heath Gallery, 77; Encuentro Int de Video 1977, Museo de Arte Contemporaneo de Caracas, Venezuela, 76-77; The Avant-Garde: 12 in Atlanta, High Mus Art, 79; Atlanta Women's Invitational, Agnes Scott Col, 79; Atlanta Women's Art Collective at AIR Gallery, New York, 80; solo shows, Reductions, Atlanta Women's Art Collective, 80, Perspective, Atlanta Art Workers Coalition, 80 & Julia A Fenton, Redmont Gallery, Jackson, Miss, 83; Twice Time, Atlanta Col Art, 84; About, Itawamba Jr Col, Miss, 86; You Are Here, Callanwolde Art Ctr Gallery, Atlanta, GA, 90. *Pos:* Ed & vpres ed affairs & mem bd dirs, Contemp Art/Southwest, 76-77; dir activities & ed newspaper, Atlanta Art Workers Coalition, 77-78, dir info resources & bd dirs, 79-80, Southeastern Women's Caucus Art (prog chairperson, 79); ed, Contemporary Art-Southeast Mag, 75-77; ed, Atlanta Art Workers Coalition Newspaper, 77-78; acting co-dir, Nexies Contemp Art Ctr Gallery, Atlanta, GA, 89-90; dir, Chastain Gallery, Atlanta, Ga, 90- *Bibliog:* John Howett (auth), Julia Fenton at the Atlanta women's art collective, Art in Am, 4/81; Robert Detweiler (auth), Julia Fenton: Reductions, Art Papers, 3-4/81; Catherine Fox (auth), Show puts area's art history in perspective, Atlanta J-Constitution, 12/2/84. *Media:* Multi-Media and Site Specific Installations. *Publ:* Contribr, John Y Fenton (ed), Theology and Body, Westminster, 74; ed, Thirty Six Women Artists, Atlanta Women's Art Collective, 4/6/78. *Mailing Add:* City Gallery at Chastain Suwanee GA 30174

FENWICK, ROLY (WILLIAM ROLAND)
PAINTER, EDUCATOR
b Owen Sound, Ont, Can, Feb 4, 32. *Study:* Mt Allison Univ, NB, with Alex Colville & Lawren Harris Jr, scholar, 54. *Work:* McIntosh Gallery, Univ Western Ont; Owens Mus, Mt Allison Univ, NB; London Regional Art Gallery, London Free Press, Ont; Sir George Williams Univ, Montreal. *Exhib:* Image of Man, McIntosh Gallery, London, Ont, 78; Masterworks on Paper, London Regional Art Gallery, 78; Take Two, Hart House Gallery, Toronto, 83; Three Artists, Bau-Xi Gallery, Toronto, 83; retrospective, London Regional Art Gallery, Ont, 78. *Pos:* Art dir, Simpsons-Sears, Toronto, 56-66. *Teaching:* Assoc prof art, Univ Western Ont, formerly. *Mem:* Univ Art Asn Can; Royal Can Acad; Ont Soc Artists. *Media:* Oil. *Publ:* Illusr, War and Other Measures, House Anansi, 77; Wintering Over, Quadraut Ed, 80. *Dealer:* Bau-Xi Gallery 340 Dundas St W Toronto ON M5T 1G5. *Mailing Add:* 755 Maitland St London ON N5Y 2W4 Canada

FERBER, LINDA S
CURATOR, HISTORIAN
b Suffern, NY, May 17, 44. *Study:* Barnard Col, New York, BA, 66; Columbia Univ, New York, MA, 68 & PhD(Wyeth Endowment Am Art fel), 80. *Pos:* Cur Am painting & sculpture, Brooklyn Mus, New York, 76-85, chief cur, 85- *Teaching:* Adj prof art hist, Columbia Univ, 78- *Awards:* Phi Beta Kappa, 66. *Mem:* Col Art Asn; Am Asn Mus; Int Found Art Res (adv coun); Archives Am Art. *Res:* Am art with a special interest in painting and sculpture of the nineteenth century. *Publ:* Auth, William Trost Richards (1833-1905): American Landscape and Marine Painter, 80; auth, Tokens of a Friendship: Miniature Watercolors by William T Richards, The Metrop Mus Art, 83; coauth, The New Path: Ruskin and the Am Pre-Raphaelites, The Brooklyn Mus, 85; auth, Never at Fault: The Drawings of William Trost Richards, The Hudson River Mus, 86; coauth, Albert Bierstadt: Art & Enterprise, The Brooklyn Mus in assoc with Hudson Hills Press, Inc, 91. *Mailing Add:* Dept Paintings & Sculpture Brooklyn Mus 200 Eastern Pkwy Brooklyn NY 11238

FERENCE, CYNTHIA See Kelly, Cynthia Ference

FERGUSON, CHARLES B
MUSEUM DIRECTOR, PAINTER
b Fishers Island, NY, June 30, 18. *Study:* Williams Col, AB; Art Students League, painting with Frank Dumond & graphics with Harry Sternberg; Trinity Col, MA. *Work:* New Britain Mus Am Art, Conn; Mattatuck Mus, Waterbury, Conn; DeCordova Mus, Lincoln, Mass; Amerind Found, Ariz; Scoville Corp, Waterbury, Conn. *Comn:* Stained glass window, Fishers Island,

71; murals, Williston Acad, East Hampton, Mass, Renbrook Sch, West Hartford, Conn, pvt home, Fishers Island, NY & Henry L Ferguson Mus, Fishers Island, NY. *Exhib:* Conn Acad Fine Arts; Conn Watercolor Soc; Greater Hartford Civic Arts Festival; Williams Col Mus, Williamstown, Mass, 91; Red Barn Gallery, Fishers Island, NY. *Collections Arranged:* Aaron Draper Shattuck, 70; Robert B Brandegee, 71; William T Richards, 73; Dennis Miller Bunker, 78; Three Generations of Wiggins, 1870's-1970's, 79; Three Centuries of Connecticut Art, 81; Allan Butler Talcott, Painter of Landscapes, 83. *Pos:* Dir, New Britain Mus Am Art, Conn, 65-84; trustee, Hillstead Mus, Farmington, Conn, currently; pres, Henry L Ferguson Mus, Fishers Island, NY, currently; dir, Emeritus New Brit Mus; art adv, to Hartford Steam Boiler Insurance Co, Conn. *Teaching:* Instr hist art & studio painting, Trinity Col & Loomis Sch. *Awards:* New Britain Herald Prize, 70; Sanford Low Prize, Conn Acad Fine Arts, 71; First Place in Oil, Int Maritime Exhib, Mystic, Conn, 78; First Prize for Oils, Mystic Marine Exhib, Conn, 81. *Mem:* Conn Acad Fine Arts. *Mailing Add:* 33 Farmstead Lane Farmington CT 06032

FERGUSON, GERALD
PAINTER
b Cincinnati, Ohio, Jan 29, 37. *Study:* Wilmington Col, Ohio, BS, 62; Ohio Univ, Athens, MFA, 66. *Work:* Mus Mod Art, New York; Mus Stuzki, Lodz, Poland; Art Gallery Ont, Toronto; Glenbow Mus, Calgary, Alta; Art Gallery NS, Halifax. *Comn:* Sculpture, Halifax Commons, 69. *Exhib:* Mus Mod Art, New York, 70; solo shows, Anna Leonowens Gallery, Halifax, NS, 74 & Art Gallery Ont, Toronto, 76 & 77; Galeria Foksal, Warsaw, Poland, 77; Glenbow Mus, Calgary, Alta, 81; Dalhousie Art Gallery, Halifax, 84; and others. *Teaching:* Asst prof, Kansas City Art Inst, 67-68; prof, NS Col Art, Halifax, 68-; mentor art, Calif Inst Arts, Valencia, 73-74. *Bibliog:* Eric Cameron (auth), Gerald Ferguson, Studio Int, spring 75; Dennis Young (auth), Task Oriented Art, Dalhousie Univ, 76 & Speculate to Appreciate, Vanguard, 85. *Media:* Miscellaneous Media. *Publ:* Auth, The Standard Corpus of Present Day English Language Usage by Word Length, 70; publ, Cleophas and his Own, Marsden Hartley (auth), 82. *Mailing Add:* Dept Art NS Col Art & Design 5163 Duke St Halifax NS B3J 3J6 Canada

FERGUSON, KATHLEEN ELIZABETH
SCULPTOR, LECTURER
b Chicago, Ill, Jan 31, 45. *Study:* Stephens Col, Columbia, Mo, 63-64; Layton Sch Art, Milwaukee, Wis, BFA, 69; RI Sch Design, Providence, MFA, 71. *Work:* Russell Courthouse, Atlanta. *Comn:* J B Speed Mus, 87. *Exhib:* One-person shows, Smithsonian Inst, Washington, DC, 72, Jan Cicero Gallery, Chicago, 79 & 84 Ctr Contemp Art, Univ Ky, 80, Univ Cincinnati, 81, High & Mus Art, Atlanta, Ga (with catalog), Kozmic Kingdom, An Environmental Installation, J B Speed Mus, Louisville, Ky, 87; Va Mus Fine Arts, Richmond, 73; Drawing Invitational, Rutgers Univ, NJ, 75; Biennial of Contemp Am Art, Whitney Mus Am Art, New York, 75; Season Review, McNay Art Inst, San Antonio, Tex, 84; Works by Women, Nat Juried Sculpture Exhib, Carnegie Art Ctr, Corington, Ky, 87; Southern Abstractions, traveling to Contemp Arts Ctr, New Orleans. *Pos:* Dir, Art Acumer Educational Systems. *Teaching:* Vis artist, Conn Col, 79; asst prof, Univ Ky, 80-82. *Awards:* Ky Arts Coun Grant; Fel, Helene Wurlitzer Found, Taos, NMex; Ky Found for Women Grant, Sally Bingham, La. *Bibliog:* David Shirey (auth), article, New York Times, 78; John Yau (auth), article, Art Am, 79; William Zimmer (auth), article, Soho Weekly News, 79; Grace Glueck (auth), article, New York Times, 85. *Mem:* Col Art Asn Am. *Media:* Cast Metal; Mixed. *Publ:* Contribr, Milton Klonsky (auth), Speaking Pictures, Crown, 74; auth & illusr, Natti's Navigations, pvt publ, 78. *Mailing Add:* PO Box 6419 Taos NM 87571

FERGUSON, LARRY SCOTT
PHOTOGRAPHER, CURATOR
b North Platte, Nebr, May 16, 54. *Study:* Univ Nebr, Lincoln, BFA, 77; Rochester Inst Technol, NY, sem 78. *Work:* Sheldon Mem Art Gallery, Lincoln, Nebr, Libr of Cong, DC; Western Heritage Mus, Omaha, Nebr; Univ Okla, Norman; Murray State Univ, Ky; and others. *Comn:* Photograph, collab Sachio Yamashita, Metrop Arts Coun, Omaha, Nebr, 79 & photograph, murals & sculpture, 79; photograph, Bldg Reborn, Smithsonian Inst, DC, 79; photograph, Tube Walkway, Omaha Airport Auth, Nebr, 80. *Exhib:* Am Vision, Nat Artists Alliance, NY Univ, 79; Juried Exhib, Friends of Photog Gallery, Carmel, Calif, 79 & Diana Camera Show, 80; Omaha: Then & Now, Western Heritage Mus, 79, Omaha: Then & Now II, 80 & Omaha: Then & Now III, 81; one-man shows, Sheldon Mem Art Gallery, Lincoln, Nebr, 79 & Southern Light Gallery, Amarillo, Tex, 80; Walker Art Ctr, Minneapolis, 81; and others. *Pos:* Cur photographs, Adams Co Hist Soc, Hastings, Nebr, 77-78, Nebr Arts Coun & Nat Endowment for Arts artist-in-residence grants & cur photographs, Bostwick-Frohardt Collection, Western Heritage Mus, Omaha, 78-81. *Teaching:* Instr photography, Univ Nebr, Omaha, 81-, Bellevue Col, 82- *Awards:* Jurors Award, Nat Artists Alliance, 79; Jurors Award, 2nd St Gallery, Charlottesville, Va, 80; Artist in residence Grant, Nebr Arts Coun, 81-82. *Bibliog:* Shawn P Leary (auth), Arts scan, 79 & Art Simmering (auth), Dodge Street, 80, Omaha Mag; Joanne Stanwick (auth), Suitable for framing, Omaha Mag, 81; article, Artweek, 9/5/81; and others. *Mem:* Soc Photog Educ; Friends of Photog; Visual Studies Workshop, Rochester, NY. *Publ:* Contribr, Twelve Photographers: A Contemporary Mid-America Document, Mid-Am Arts Alliance, 78; contribr, Self-Portrayal: The Photographers Image, 79 & Untitled Number 21, by Jim Alinder, 80, Friends of Photog; Object and Image, by George Craven, Prentice-Hall, 82. *Mailing Add:* 1701 Vinton St Omaha NE 68108-1432

FERHOLT, ELEANORE HEUSSER See Heusser, Eleanore Elizabeth (Eleanore Heusser Ferholt)

FERIOLA, JAMES PHILIP
PAINTER, DESIGNER
b Great Notch, NJ, July 4, 25. *Study:* Phoenix Sch Design, New York, grad. *Work:* Nassau Co Mus, Syosset, NY; R Peerman Corp & H Butt Corp, Corpus Christi, Tex; Country Art Gallery, Locust Valley, NY; Forbes Mag. *Exhib:* Smithsonian Inst; Nat Acad Design, New York; New York World's Fair Fine Arts Pavilion; Hammond Mus; Prince Rainier III Palace, Monaco. *Pos:* Supvr art & exhib dept, Nassau Co Mus, presently. *Awards:* Gold Medal of Honor, Smithsonian Inst; Travel Grant to Europe, Greenwich Village Art Show; Silver Medal Honor, Am Vet Soc Artists. *Bibliog:* Famous People of Hempstead, NY (film). *Mem:* Am Watercolor Soc; Hudson Valley Artists; Am Artists Prof League; Am Vet Soc Artists; Art League of Nassau Co. *Media:* Watercolor, Acrylics. *Mailing Add:* 226 Perry St Hempstead NY 11550

FERN, ALAN MAXWELL
MUSEUM DIRECTOR
b Detroit, Mich, Oct 19, 30. *Study:* Univ Chicago, AB, 50, MA, 54 & PhD, 60; Courtauld Inst, Univ London, res scholar. *Collections Arranged:* Diverse print, poster & photo shows, Libr Cong, 62-; Leonard Baskin, Nat Collection Fine Arts, Smithsonian Inst, 70. *Pos:* From asst cur to cur, asst chief to chief, Prints & Photographs Div, Libr Cong, 61-76, dir, Res Dept, 76-78, dir, spec collections, 78-82; dir, National Portrait Gallery, Smithsonian Inst, 82- *Teaching:* From asst to asst prof, Univ Chicago, 52-61. *Awards:* Chevalier, Ordre de la Couronne, Belgium, 80; Chevalier, Ordre des Arts et des Lettres, France, 85; Commander, Royal Order of Polar Star, Sweden, 88. *Mem:* Print Coun Am (dir, 63-69, pres, 69-71); Col Art Asn Am (dir, 84-88); Am Antiquarian Soc; Asn Art Mus Dir; Double Crown Club, London. *Res:* History of prints, posters, book design, 19th and 20th century art. *Publ:* Auth, A note on the Eragny Press, Cambridge Univ Press, 57; coauth, Art nouveau, 60 & Word and image, 69, Mus Mod Art, New York; Leonard Baskin, Smithsonian Press, 70; Revolutionary Soviet film posters, Johns Hopkins Press, 74; Arnold Newman's Americans, Little Brown, 92. *Mailing Add:* Nat Portrait Gallery Smithsonian Inst Washington DC 20560

FERNIE, JOHN CHIPMAN
SCULPTOR
b Hutchinson, Kans, Oct 22, 45. *Study:* Colo Col, 63-65; Kansas City Art Inst, BFA, 68; Univ Calif, Davis, grant, 69, teaching fel & MFA, 70. *Work:* San Francisco Mus Art; Univ Calif Mus, Berkeley. *Exhib:* One-man shows, Nova Scotia Col Art, 74 & John Gibson Gallery, 77; group shows, Documenta 5, Kasel, Ger, 72; 8th & 9th Biennale de Paris; Israel Mus, 76; Houston Mus of Contemp Art, 77; Whitney Mus, New York, 78; Denver Art Mus, 78; Boulder Art Ctr, Colo, 79; plus others. *Teaching:* Asst, Univ Calif, Davis, 69; instr sculpture, Calif Col Arts & Crafts, 70-72, Stephens Col, 72-75 & Nova Scotia Col Art & Design, 75- *Bibliog:* Richardson (auth), article in Arts Mag, 2/71; Albright (auth), Exciting, compelling show, San Francisco Chronicle, 7/1/71; Jochimsen (auth), Magazin Kunst, 7/74. *Media:* Wood, Cardboard, Photo, Plaster. *Publ:* Auth, Petit trianon, twikkel, I worship you, God bless your symmetry, 70; Masters survey, 70. *Mailing Add:* Po Box 453 Nederland CO 80466

FERRARA, JACKIE
SCULPTOR
b Detroit, Mich. *Work:* Chase Manhattan Bank, Mus Mod Art & Metrop Mus Art, New York; Lannon Found, Los Angeles; Dallas Mus Fine Art. *Comn:* Wash Conv & Trade Ctr, Seattle, 89; Stuart Collection, Univ Calif, San Diego, 91; Pittsburgh Int Airport, 92. *Exhib:* Biennial Exhib, Whitney Mus, 73 & 79; Drawings: The Pluralist Decade, Venice Biennale, Italy, 80; Painting & Sculpture Today, Indianapolis Mus Art, 80; solo exhibs, Univ Mass, Amherst, 80, Lowe Art Mus, Coral Gables, Fla, 82, Moore Col Art, Philadelphia, 87, San Antonio Art Inst, 87; Connections, Inst Contemp Art, Philadelphia, 83; Recent Acquisitions, Mus Mod Art, New York, 83; Hokin Collection, Mus Contemp Art, Chicago, 85; Sculpture of the Eighties, Queens Mus, NY, 87; Retrospective: Ringling Mus, Sarasota, Fla, 92, Indianapolis Mus Art, 92, Rose Mus, Brandeis Univ, Waltham, Mass, 92. *Awards:* Grants, NY State Coun Arts, 71 & 75 & Nat Endowment Arts, 73, 77 & 87; Guggenheim Found Fel, 76; Award for Excellence in Design, art comn city NY, 88; Inst Honor, Am Inst Architects, 90. *Bibliog:* Kate Linker (auth), Jackie Ferrara's illusions, Artforum, 11/79; Phil Patton (auth), Jackie Ferrara: Sculpture the mind can use, Artnews, 3/82; Nancy Princenthal (auth), Placemakers, Jackie Ferrara's Public Art (catalog essay), Ringling Mus, 92. *Publ:* Jackie Ferrara Drawings, 6 & 7/77, Lapp Princess Press, New York, 77; Jackie Ferrara Sculpture, A Retrospective, Ringling Mus, Sarasota, 92. *Dealer:* Michael Klein Inc 594 Broadway New York NY 10012. *Mailing Add:* 121 Prince St New York NY 10012

FERRARI, VIRGINIO LUIG
SCULPTOR, EDUCATOR
b Verona, Italy, Apr 11, 37. *Study:* Scuola d'Arte, with N Nani; Acad Cignaroli, Verona. *Work:* Biennale Nazionale di Verona; High Mus Art, Atlanta, Ga; Univ di Parma Mus, Italy; Ravinia Park, Highland Park, Ill. *Comn:* Bronzes, Pick Hall for Int Studies, Univ Chicago, 71; Vanderbilt Univ Med Ctr Hosp, 80; Being Born (sculpture), City of Chicago, 83 & Revenue Bldg, Springfield, Ill, 85. *Exhib:* Brooklyn Mus, 68; Art Inst Chicago, 68; traveling exhibs, State Ill Arts Coun, 69, Ill Bronzetto Ital, 71, Int Art Expo, Chicago, 81-86 & Mile of Sculpture, 82-84; Sears Tower Bank, Chicago, 77; Seven Sculptors, DePaul Univ, 78; retrospective, Paris Art Ctr, France & Cult Ctr, Ill, 85; and others. *Pos:* Sculptor in residence, Univ Chicago, 66-76. *Teaching:* Asst prof sculpture, Univ Chicago, 67-76. *Awards:* Nostra Ministero Publica, Istruzione Roma, Italy, 64; Biennale Nazionale di Verona,

65; Ill Coun of Am Inst Architects Award, 77; Man of the Year, Ital Cult Ctr, Ill, 86. *Bibliog:* Arturo Quitavalle (auth), Ferrari Gocce d'Amor Pop, Univ di Parma, 70; article, Cimaise Mag, 82; V Ferrari sculpture, Paris Art Ctr, Rizzoli Publ, 85. *Mem:* Sindacato Artisti; Arts Club Chicago; bd mem Hyde Park Art Ctr. *Media:* Metal, Marble. *Mailing Add:* c/o corp Art Source 900 N Franklin St Suite 200 Chicago IL 60610

FERREIRA, ARMANDO THOMAS
EDUCATOR, SCULPTOR
b Charleston, WVa, Jan 8, 32. *Study:* Chouinard Inst; Long Beach City Col; Univ Calif, Los Angeles, BA & MA. *Work:* Wichita Art Mus; State Calif Collection; Univ Utah Art Mus. *Exhib:* Los Angeles Co Mus, 58, 60 & 66; Pasadena Mus Art, 68; Univ Calif, Santa Barbara, 73; Northern Ill Univ, 86; Beckstrand Gallery, Palos Verdes, Calif, 87; Univ Madrid, 92; and other group & one-man shows. *Teaching:* Prof ceramic sculpture, Calif State Univ Long Beach, 57-85, assoc dean, Sch Fine Arts, 85-91, acting dean, Col Arts, 91-; Fulbright lectr, Brazil, 81. *Awards:* Purchase Awards, Calif Expos, 61 & Wichita Art Asn, 66. *Mem:* Nat Asn Schs Art Comn Accrediting; Int Video Art Network. *Media:* Clay, Mixed. *Mailing Add:* c/o State Univ Dept Art 1250 N Bellflower Blvd Long Beach CA 90840

FERRELL, CATHERINE (KLEMANN)
SCULPTOR
b Apr 27, 47; US citizen. *Study:* Fla Atlantic Univ, BA, 69; Univ Miami, MA, 72; Fritz Van Eden, 90. *Work:* Delray Beach Pub Libr, Fla. *Comn:* Black African Stone Fish, John H Surovek Fine Arts, Palm Beach, Fla, 82-83; Flight Form (stone), comn by Perry Offshore Inc, for presentation to Bennex Techol, Norway; Alabaster Self-Portrait, comn by Artine Artinian, Palm Beach, Fla, 83; Mythical Fish, comn by Mr & Mrs Gunter Schulz-Franke, Osnäbruck, WGer, 83; archit sculpture & wall reliefs, comn by Sally Gingras, West Palm Beach, Fla, 83 & 84; Sea Form (stone), comn by Bethesda Mem Hosp. *Exhib:* Directions 1-Emering Fla Artists, Helender Gallery, Palm Beach, Fla, 87; Lighthouse Gallery, Ann Celebration of Arts, 88; Prof Artists Guild Ann, Boca Raton Mus Arts Ann Competition, 89; group exhib, Emerging Realism, Trade St Gallery, 90; solo exhib, Helen Hill Inc, Delray Beach, Fla, 90. *Awards:* First Prize Sculpture, Delray Art League, 82 & 83; Artfest Award, Artist's Prof League, 91; Pen & Brush Award, Pen & Brush Exhib New York, 92. *Bibliog:* Nancy Miller (auth), Hands, heart and head all work to create beauty, Delray Beach News-J, 4/15/82; Gary Schwan (auth), New exhibits worth taking in, Palm Beach Post, 2/6/83; Pam Harbaugh (auth), Stone comes to life in hands of Merritt Island sculptor, Fla Today, 2/9/92. *Mem:* Catherine Lorilland Wolfe Art Club, New York; Prof Artists Guild, Boca Raton Mus Arts, Fla; assoc mem Audubon Artists Am, New York; Artist's Forum, Brevard, Fla; Salmagundi Club, New York; and others. *Media:* Stone, Metals. *Mailing Add:* One Stockton Dr Merritt Island FL 32952

FERRER, RAFAEL
PAINTER, SCULPTOR
b Santurce, PR, 1933. *Study:* Saunton Military Acad, Va, 48-51; Syracuse Univ, NY, 51-52; Univ PR, Mayaquez, with E Granell, 52-54. *Work:* The Ackland Art Mus, Chapel Hill, NC; Albright-Knox Art Gallery, Buffalo, Mus Mod Art, Metrop Mus Art, Whitney Mus Am Art, New York; Philadelphia Mus Art, Pa; Museo de Ponce, PR; Denver Art Mus, Colo; Va Mus Fine Arts, Richmond. *Exhib:* Art of Latin Am, Pa Acad Fine Arts, Philadelphia, 67; Op Losse Schroven, Stedelijk Mus, Amsterdam, 69; Info, Mus Mod Art, New York, 70 & 84; Whitney Mus Am Art Ann, New York, 70, 84 & 85; Depth & Presence, Corcoran Gallery Art, Washington, DC, 71; Biennial of Medellin, Colombia, SAm, 72; Whitney Biennial, 73; one-man shows, Philadelphia Mus Art Pa, 70, Whitney Mus, 71, Nancy Hoffman Gallery, New York, 74, 75, 77, 78, 82, 84, 86 & 88- 90, Mus Mod Art, New York, 74, Frumkin & Struve, Chicago, 80 & 82, Mangel Gallery, Philadelphia, Pa, 88; Nancy Hoffman Gallery, New York, 82-84, 85 & 86; Metrop Mus Art, New York, 83-86; Musee d'Art Contempporain, Montreal; Butler Art Inst, Youngstown, Ohio, 86; Philbrook Art Center, Tulsa, Okla, 87-89; Tatistcheff Gallery, Santa Monica, Calif, 89. *Teaching:* Vis prof, San Francisco Art Inst, Calif, 75, Univ Pa, 84; Philadelphia Col Art, Pa, 67-77; instr, Sch Visual Art, New York, 78-80. *Awards:* Nat Endowment Arts Fel, 72, 78; Guggenheim Award, 75. *Bibliog:* Stephen Prokopff (auth), Rafael Ferrer, An interview, Art & Artists, London, 4/72; Kenneth Baker (auth), New York: Rafael Ferrer, Whitney Museum, Artforum, 3/72; J L Dunham (auth), article, Artweek, Oakland, Calif, 11/74. *Mailing Add:* c/o Nancy Hoffman Gallery 429 West Broadway New York NY 10012

FERRIS, DANIEL B
GALLERY DIRECTOR, CURATOR
b Columbia, SC, Sept 10, 47. *Study:* Univ SC, BS, 69; Alliance Francaise, Paris, 73. *Collections Arranged:* Spirit of the Object, Humphrey Fine Arts, 92. *Pos:* Dir, Amos Eno Gallery, New York, 90-; cur, YWCA Gallery, Brooklyn, NY, 90-91. *Bibliog:* The Amos Eno Performance Arm, Downtown, 3/91; Plenty of Energy, The Villager, 2/28/91; Downtown Essentials, Best of the Week - Spirit of the Object; Downtown Express, 4/26/92. *Mem:* Asn Artist Run Galleries (bd dirs); Coalition Independent Artists (exec dir, 85-); BWAC, 91- *Specialty:* Contemporary. *Mailing Add:* 210 E 15th St #11A New York NY 10003

FERRIS, (CARLISLE) KEITH
ILLUSTRATOR, PAINTER
b Honolulu, Hawaii, May 14, 29. *Study:* Tex A&M Col; George Washington Univ; Corcoran Sch Art. *Comn:* Murals, Nat Air & Space Mus, Smithsonian Inst, Washington, DC, 76 & 81; Gen Electric; Fairchild Industs; Bantam Books; McGraw Hill; and others. *Exhib:* USAF Exhib, New York Soc Illusr, 61-78; USAF Hq, The Pentagon, Washington, DC; one-man shows, Aerospace Hall, Nat Air & Space Mus, Smithsonian Inst, Washington, DC, 69-70, New York Soc Illusr, 70 & 79, Air Force Mus, 83 & US Air Force Acad, 83. *Pos:* Art dir-prod mgr, Cassell Watkins Paul Art Studio, St Louis, 52-56; chmn, Air Force Art Comt, Soc Illusr, 68-70 & 79- *Awards:* Citation of Merit, Soc Illusr, 66; Arts & Lett Award, Air Force Asn, NJ, 77; Citation of Honor, Air Force Asn, 78. *Mem:* Graphic Artists Guild; NY Soc Illusr. *Media:* Oil. *Mailing Add:* 50 Moraine Rd Morris Plains NJ 07950

FERRITER, CLARE
PAINTER, COLLAGE ARTIST
b Dickinson, NDak, June 18, 13. *Study:* Mass Col Art, Boston; Yale Univ, BFA; Stanford Univ, MA. *Work:* Butler Inst Am Art, Youngstown, Ohio; Hartcourt, Brace, Jovanovich, Inc, New York; George Washington Univ; Massillon Mus, Ohio; Addison Gallery Am Art, Andover, Mass. *Comn:* Portrait of Miss H D Lamont, comn by Class of 1909 for Westover Sch, Middlebury, Conn, 59; portrait, Dr Vincent McKelvey, Friends US Geological Survey, 78. *Exhib:* One-man shows, Univ PR Mus, 62, Corcoran Gallery Art, Washington, DC, 63, Franz Bader Gallery, Washington, DC, 64 & 76 & Int Monetary Fund, Washington, DC, 73; Four Decades of Growth & Distinguished Mid-Atlantic Artists, Univ Delaware, 80. *Teaching:* Instr art, MacMurray Col, 36-38, Westover Sch, 40-42; lectr painting, Cath Univ Am, 66- *Awards:* Nat Asn Women Artists, 63 & 66; Baltimore Mus, 66; Soc Washington Artists, 64, 66 & 72. *Bibliog:* Barbara Martin Johnson (auth), Conversation with Clare Ferriter, Washington Rev, 4-5/79. *Mem:* Nat Asn Women Artists; Washington Watercolor Asn; Artists Equity Asn. *Media:* Oil, Acrylic; Metallic. *Publ:* Illusr, Manila lights and shadows (weekly page), Manila Sun Tribune Mag, 10/4/31-8/32; covers in Philippine Mag, 9/32-2/33. *Dealer:* Franz Bader Gallery 1701 Pennsylvania Ave Washington DC 20006. *Mailing Add:* 4722 Rodman St NW Washington DC 20016

FERRO, WALTER
PRINTMAKER, DESIGNER
b Brooklyn, NY. *Study:* Art Students League, 46-48; Brooklyn Mus Art Sch, color theory with John Ferren, 48-52. *Work:* Permanent print collection, Metrop Mus Art, New York; First Nat Bank, Chicago. *Exhib:* Audubon Artists, 53; Am Inst Graphic Artists, 56 & Soc Am Graphic Artists, New York, 59; United Nations Traveling Exhib, 66; one-man show, Kings Col, 67. *Awards:* Kenneth Hays Miller Mem Prize, Audubon Artists, 53; Kate W Arms Mem Award, Soc Am Graphic Artists, 59; Guggenheim Fel, 72. *Bibliog:* Norman Kent (auth), The woodcuts of Walter Ferro, Am Artist Mag, 1/62. *Media:* Woodcuts. *Publ:* Illusr, Beowulf, Random, 62; Hold April, McGraw, 62; UN calendar, UN, 66; The invisible pyramid, Scribner, 70; Another Kind of Autumn, Scribner, 77. *Mailing Add:* PO Box 304 Pound Ridge NY 10576

FESSLER, ANN HELENE
PHOTOGRAPHER
b Toledo, Ohio, Oct 2, 49. *Study:* Ohio State Univ, Columbus, BA, 72; Webster Col, St Louis, MA(media), 75; Univ Ariz, MFA(photog), 82. *Work:* Whitney Mus Am Art; Ctr Creative Photog; Mus Contemp Art, Chicago; Franklin Furnace Book Arch, New York; Swedish Arch Artists Books, Bjarred. *Comn:* MAPTAP, Maryland Arts Place, 85; billboards, Art Against Aids, New York, 90; roadside installation, She Rode Horses, Washington Proj Arts, DC. *Exhib:* Ctr Exploratory & Perceptual Arts, Buffalo, 82; Copycat Show, Franklin Furnace, New York, 82; Rape, Ohio State Univ, 85; Floating Values: A Survey of Gendered Investigations, Hallwalls, Buffalo, NY, 87; Family Stories, Newhouse Ctr Contemp Art, New York, 90; Book Arts in the USA, Ctr Book Arts, New York, 90. *Collections Arranged:* Expanding Committment: Diverse Approaches to Socially Concerned Photography, Meyerhoff Gallery, MD Inst Col Art, 86. *Teaching:* Instr photog & video, Webster Col, St Louis, 74-79; vis artist photog, Tyler Sch Art, 81-82; instr photog & books, Md Inst Col Art, 82- *Awards:* Artist's Fel, Md State Arts Coun, 85, 88 & 92; Artist's Fel, Nat Endowment Arts, 89; Grant, Art Matters Inc, NY, 90. *Bibliog:* Reviews, Afterimage, 2/83 & New Art Examiner, 4/86; Andy Grunburg (auth), article, NY Times, 90. *Mem:* Soc Photog Educ. *Media:* Appropriated Image & Text. *Publ:* Auth, Guide to Coloring Hair, Tyler Offset Press, 82; First Aid for the Wounded, 87, Life Saving & Water Safety, Visual Studies Workshop, 89; Art History Lesson, copublished with Nat Mus Am Art, Washington, DC, 91; Genetics Lesson, Nexus Press, Atlanta, 92. *Dealer:* Books: Printed Matter New York NY; Washington Proj Arts Washington DC. *Mailing Add:* Photog Md Inst Col Art 1300 Mt Royal Ave Baltimore MD 21217

FETCHKO, PETER J
MUSEUM DIRECTOR
Yonkers, NY, July 3, 43. *Study:* Westminster Col, Fulton, Mo, BA, 65; George Washington Univ, Washington, DC, MA, 72; Univ Paris, Sorbonne, 72. *Collections Arranged:* Stone Age New England (coauth, catalog), 75; Japan Day by Day (coauth, catalog), 77; Christian Art of an African Nation, Ethiopia (coauth, catalog), 78. *Pos:* Cur, Peabody Mus, Salem, 68-80, dir, 80- *Mem:* Japan Soc Boston; Tattoong Club Japan; Am Ceramic Circle. *Res:* New Guinea and Pacific material culture; Japanese crafts. *Publ:* Auth, Pacific Collections of the Peabody Mus, S Pac Bull, 74; Salem Trading Voyages to Japan During the Early Nineteenth Century, Peabody Mus, 86; ed, Salem: To the Farthest Part of the Rich East, Maritime America, Peter Neill, 88. *Mailing Add:* 42 Charter St Salem MA 01970

FETT, WILLIAM F
INSTRUCTOR, PAINTER
b Ann Arbor, Mich, Sept 22, 18. *Study:* Sch Art Inst, Chicago. *Work:* Mus Mod Art, New York; Mus Mod Art, Rome, Italy; Chicago Art Inst; Mus Mod Art, Mexico City; Weatherspoon Art Gallery, Univ NC, Greensboro; McNay Mus, San Antonio, Tex, 83; San Carlos Art Mus, Mexico City, Mex, 88. *Exhib:* Romantic Paintings in America, Mus Mod Art, New York, 43; one-man shows, Int Watercolor Show, Art Inst Chicago, 44, De Young Mus, San Francisco, 54 & Weatherspoon Art Gallery, Univ NC, Greensboro, 71; Seattle Art Mus, Wash, 45; Santa Barbara Mus Art, Calif, 45; Mex-Am Cult Inst, Mexico City, 65 & 92; Watercolor USA, Springfield Art Mus, Mo, 71; Texas Watercolor Soc, San Antonio, Tex, 82; Messing Gallery, St Louis, Mo, 92. *Teaching:* Prof drawing & painting, Art Sch, Washington Univ, St Louis, Mo, 46-81, prof emeritus, 81- *Awards:* Anna Louise Raymond Grad Student Award, Art Inst Chicago, 41-43; Fulbright Scholar to Italy, US Govt, 50-51. *Media:* Watercolor, Oil; Charcoal. *Publ:* Articles, View Mag, View Inc, New York, 43; Romantic Paintings in American, Mus Mod Art, New York, 44; article, Dyn Mag, Wolfgang Paalen, Mex, 45; article, Arts Mag, St Louis, 81. *Mailing Add:* Sur 69-A 217-2 Colonia Banjidal Delegacion Ixtapalapa 09450 Mexico

FETTING, RAINER
PAINTER
b Wilhelmshaven, WGer, Dec 31, 49. *Study:* Hochschule der Kunste, Berlin, Meisterschuler, 77; Columbia Univ, New York, 78-79. *Work:* Mus Gegenwartskunst, Basel, Switz; Portland Art Mus, Ore; Mus Contemp Art, Sydney, Australia; Musée des Beaux Arts, Toulon, France. *Exhib:* A New Spirit in Painting, Royal Acad Arts, London, Eng, 81; Image Innovations, Va Mus, Richmond, 83; An International Survey of Recent Paintings, Mus Mod Art, New York, 84; Origen y Vision, Museo de Arte Moderno, Mexico City, 84; States of War: New American Painting, Seattle Art Mus, Wash, 85; 1945-1985 Kunst in BRD, National Galerie Berlin, WGer, 85; one-man shows, Kunsthalle Basel, Switz & Mus Folkwang, Essen, WGer, 86. *Bibliog:* Christo Joachimides (auth), Zeitgeist, Katalog, 82; Giovanni Testori (auth), Rainer Fetting, Flash Art, Italy, 4/86; Jean Christopher Ammann (auth), Rainer Fetting, Kunsthalle Basel Katalog, 86. *Dealer:* Marlborough Gallery 40 W 57th St New York NY. *Mailing Add:* 601 E Ninth St New York NY 10009

FEUERHERM, KURT K
PAINTER
b Berlin, Ger, Mar 22, 25. *Study:* Albright Art Sch; Univ Buffalo, BFA; Cranbrook Acad Art, MFA; Yale Summer Sch, Norfolk, Conn, with NaumGabo, Peter Blume & Ben Shahn; Yale Univ, with Josef Albers, Stuart Davis & Abraham Rattner. *Work:* Cranbrook Art Mus, Bloomfield Hills, Mich; Mem Art Gallery, Rochester, NY; Albright-Knox Art Gallery, Buffalo, NY; Henry Gallery, Univ Wash, Seattle; Am Fedn Art. *Comn:* Ceramic abstract mural, Midtown Plaza, Rochester, NY, 64; Stations on the Cross, Our Lady of Mercy Church, Rochester, 64; St John's the Evangelist Church, Rochester, 65; Liberty Pole (consult designer), City of Rochester, 66. *Exhib:* American Painting Today, Metrop Mus Art, New York, 50; Cranbrook Painting Exhib, Bloomfield Hills, Mich, 52; Columbia Mus of Art Painting Biennial, SC, 57; Everson Mus Art, Syracuse, NY, 57-70; one-man show, Henry Gallery, Univ Wash, Seattle, 69; New York Crafts, Munson-Williams-Proctor Inst, Utica, NY, 61; four-man show, Mem Art Gallery, Univ Rochester Fac Show, 70; and others. *Pos:* Conservator, Intermuseum Lab, Oberlin, Ohio, 71-72. *Teaching:* Asst prof painting, Univ Rochester, NY, 60-71; assoc prof studio arts, Empire State Col, Rochester, 73-87. *Awards:* Purchase Awards (painting & watercolor), Cortland Art Mus, 53; Award of Merit, Columbia Painting Biennial, 57; Henri Projansky Award, Rochester Finger Lakes Exhib, 69. *Media:* Collage, Acrylic. *Dealer:* Oxford Gallery 267 Oxford St Rochester NY 14607; Malton Gallery 2709 Observatory Ave Cincinnati OH 45208. *Mailing Add:* 75 Rhinecliff Dr Rochester NY 14618

FEUERMAN, CAROL JEANNNE
SCULPTOR, PAINTER
b Hartford, Conn, Sept 21, 45. *Study:* Hofstra Univ, NY, 63; Temple Univ, 64; Sch Visual Arts, BFA, 67. *Work:* Forbes Mag & Malcolm Forbes Mag Collection, New York, NY; Tampa Mus Art, Fla; Ft Lauderdale Mus Art, Fla. *Comn:* Attitude (sculpture), Rouse & Assoc, Columbia, Md, 88; Absolut Vodka (3 sculptures), Carillon Importers Ltd, Teaneck, NJ, 89, 90 & 92; Frederick Weisman Art Found (4 sculptures), Los Angeles, Calif, 92 & 93; V and S, The Swedish Wine & Spirits Corp (2 sculptures), Stockholm, Sweden, 92; 1 sculpture comn by Ruth Baum, Englewood, NJ, 92-93. *Exhib:* Solo exhibs, Espace Quasar, Paris, France, 90, Laura Larkin Gallery, Del Mar, Calif, 90, Arnesan Gallery, Vail, Colo, 90, Jaffe Baker Gallery, Boca Raton, Fla, 91, Gallery Henoch, New York, 89 & 92, Hokin Gallery, Palm Beach, Fla, 92 & Va Beach Ctr Arts, Va, 93; Ft Lauderdale Mus Art, Fla, 92; Heroism, Peconic Gallery, Riverhead, NY, 92; New York City by Day, City by Night, Gallery Henoch, New York, 92; NAm Sculpture Exhib, The Foothills Art Ctr, Golden, Colo, 92; and others. *Awards:* Amelia Peabody Sculpture Award, 82; First Prize, US Nat Fine Arts Competition, Tallahassee, Fla, 84. *Bibliog:* Virginia Watson-Jones (auth), Contemporary American Sculptors, 86; Mario Perazzi (auth), Vera! Anzi finta, Sette-Corriere Della Sera, Milan, Italy, 89; Arthur Williams (auth), Sculpture--Technique-Form-Content, 89; Carol Jeanne Feuerman-World Fax Interview, Popolo, Japan, pp 175-76, 7/92. *Mem:* Int Asn Art, UNESCO; Nat Asn Women Artists. *Media:* Resin; Oil Paint. *Dealer:* Gallery Henoch 80 Wooster St New York NY 10012; Hokin Gallery 245 Worth Ave Palm Beach FL 33480. *Mailing Add:* 371 Sagamore Ave Mineola NY 11501

FEUERSTEIN, ROBERTA
DEALER
b Los Angeles, Calif, 1950. *Pos:* Dir-owner, Gallery West. *Specialty:* Contemporary paintings, sculpture and drawings. *Mailing Add:* c/o Gallery West 107 S Robertson Blvd Los Angeles CA 90048

FEW, JAMES CECIL, PSA
PAINTER
b Orangeburg, SC, Aug 24, 30. *Study:* Clemson Col, BS(elec eng), 53; Univ Chicago, MBA, 64; also workshops with Albert Handel, PSA, 88 & 90 & Ben Konis, PSA, 89. *Work:* USAF Art Collection, Washington, DC; Air Force Armament Mus Art Collection, Eglin AFB, Fla. *Exhib:* Pastel Soc Am Ann Open Exhib, Nat Arts Club, New York, 88, 90, 91 & 92; Knickerbocker Artists NY 39th Nat Open Exhib, 89 & Am Artists Prof League Grand Nat Exhib, 91, Salmagundi Club, New York; Allied Artists Am 76th & 78th Ann Exhib, Nat Arts Club, New York, 89 & 91; Pastel Soc West Coast Int Open Exhib, Sacramento Fine Arts Ctr, Calif, 90 & 92. *Awards:* Award Merit, Degas Pastel Soc 2nd Biennial Nat Exhib, Degas Pastel Soc, 88; Art Student's League-NY Award, Knickerbocker Artists 39th Nat Open Exhib, Art Student's League, 89; Best Show, Pastel Soc NFla 2nd All Pastel Exhib, Pastel Soc NFla, 91. *Mem:* Pastel Soc Am; Knickerbocker Artists, New York; Degas Pastel Soc; Am Soc Aviation Artists; Pastel Soc NFla (bd dirs 88-). *Media:* Pastel, Mixed Media. *Mailing Add:* 22 Kohler Dr Mary Esther FL 32569

FICHTER, HERBERT FRANCIS
PRINTMAKER, PAINTER
b Jamaica, Long Island, NY, Dec 25, 20. *Study:* Sch Art League Scholar, New York Sch Fine & Applied Arts, 39; Corcoran Sch Art, Washington, DC; spec instr with Hal Reed, 75-76. *Work:* Pennell Collection, Libr Cong, Washington, DC; J F Kennedy Libr, Mass; Life/Time Mag Collection, New York; Paper Mus, Los Angeles, Calif; Mercantile Money Mus, St Louis, Mo. *Comn:* Oil-Scotch motif, Vince Dundee, Scotch Mist Restaurant, LaCanada, Calif, 65; portrait, Walt Disney, Disney Corp, 68; Wells & Fargo, Wells Fargo Bank, 72; Gen Fremont, Freemont Fed Finance Corp, 73; three paintings for pub relations, comn by William Freelove for McDonalds, New Bern & Greenville, NC, 74-75. *Exhib:* One-man show, Intalgio Graphics, Smithsonian Inst, Washington, DC, 51; two-man show, Burbank Creative Arts Ctr, Calif, 51; Soc Am Etchers, Kennedy Gallery, New York, 52; Bi-Ann, Corcoran Gallery Art, Washington, DC, 53; Bi-Ann, Laguna Mus Art, Calif, 76; Nat Exhib, Fla Miniature Soc, Clearwater, 77; Nat Exhib, Soc Miniature Soc, Clinton, 78. *Pos:* Banknote Engraver, Bur of Engraving & Printing, Washington, DC, 41-54. *Teaching:* Instr in banknote engraving, Vignette Engraving, Jefferies Banknote Co, Los Angeles, 62-84. *Awards:* Purchase Award, Ann Pennell, Libr Cong, 51; Kate W Arms Mem, Kennedy Gallery, Soc Am Etchers, 52; First Graphics, Nat Exhib, Miniature Art Soc NJ, 78. *Bibliog:* Man of steel, article, Ticor Mag, 74; American Print Collection, John Hopkins Press, 80; articles in Artist's Market Mag, 80 & Laguna Mag, 87. *Mem:* San Gabriel Fine Arts Asn; NJ Miniature Soc, 80; Laguna Art-A-Fair Festival, Calif, 76-89. *Media:* Intaglio, Engraving through Mezzotint; Oils on Canvas & Panels. *Mailing Add:* Studio-5105 Tendilla Ave Woodland Hills CA 91364

FICHTER, ROBERT W
EDUCATOR
b Ft Myers, Fla, 1939. *Study:* Univ Fla, BFA(printmaking & painting), 63; Ind Univ, MFA, 66. *Work:* Int Mus Photog, George Eastman House, Rochester, NY; Pasadena Art Mus, Calif; Nat Gallery of Can, Ottawa; Mus Fine Arts, Boston, Mass; Princeton Univ, NJ; and others. *Exhib:* Contemp Photog from the Collections, Boston Mus Fine Arts, 74; The Art of Offset Printing, Sch Art Inst Chicago, 78; Northern Ky State Col, 81; Whitney Biennial, Whitney Mus Am Art, 81; Robert Freidus Gallery, New York, 81; Photography in California 1945-1984, San Francisco Mus Mod Art, Calif, 84; Extending the Perimeters of Twentieth-Century Photography, San Francisco Mus Mod Art, 85; Photography & Art: Interactions since 1946, Los Angeles Co Mus, Calif, 87; Capturing an Image: Collecting 150 Years of Photography, Mus Fine Arts, Boston, Mass, 89; The Cherished Image: Portraits from 150 Years of Photography, Nat Gallery Can, Ottawa, 89; Graphic Studio, Contemp Art From the Collaborative Workshop at the Univ S Fla, Nat Callery Art, Washington, DC, 91; one-person exhib, Photography & Other Questions, Int Mus Photog, Rochester, NY, 82 traveled to FSU Fine Arts Gallery, Tallahassee, Fla, 83, Frederick White Gallery, UCLA, 84, Mus Contemp Photog, Columbia Col, Chicago, Ill, 84, Mus Mod Art, San Francisco, Calif, 84, Univ NMex, Albuquerque, 84 & Brooklyn Mus, NY, 85 & New Work, Univ Gallery, Memphis State Univ, 89. *Teaching:* Prof art, Fla State Univ, 72- *Awards:* Fels, Nat Endowment Arts, 79 & 84; Fla Visual Arts, 81. *Mem:* Col Art Assoc Am; Soc Photog Educ. *Publ:* Auth, Robert Fichter, Photography and Other Questions (exhib catalog), Univ NMex Press & George Eastman House Mus; contribr, Graphics Studio, Univ S Fla, Tampa, 12/10/84; Tamarind Inst, Albuquerque, NMex, 11/9/87; Rolling Stone Press, Atlanta, Ga, 88-90; illus, James Huginin, (auth) A-X Cavation, Dept Art, Univ Colo, 88. *Mailing Add:* 612 W Eighth Ave Tallahassee FL 32303

FIDLER, SPENCER D
PRINTMAKER
b Detroit, Mich, Nov 20, 44. *Study:* Calif State Univ, Northridge, BA, 66; Univ Iowa, MA, 76 & MFA, 78. *Work:* Univ of Miss,; Univ of Iowa; Dulin Gallery, Tenn; Musee de Petit Format, Couvin, Belg. *Exhib:* 12th Int Print Biennale, Cracow, Poland; 5th Int Print Exhib, Taipei Nat Mus, Taiwan; Ljubljana Bienale, Yugoslavia, 87; 15th Int Independent Exhib of Prints, Yokahama, Japan, 91; 11th Impact Festival, Kyoto City Mus, Kyoto, Japan,

92; and others. *Teaching:* Prof printmaking, N Mex State Univ, Las Cruces, 78- *Awards:* First Prize, Westwood Art Asn Print Competition, 77; Purchase Award, Dulin Nat Print Competition. *Bibliog:* Clinton Adams (auth), Printmaking in New Mexico, Univ NMex Press, Albuquerque, 91. *Mem:* Col Art Asn; Boston Printmakers; Southern Graphics Coun. *Dealer:* Spencer Fidler Las Cruces NM. *Mailing Add:* Dept Art NMex State Univ Las Cruces NM 88003

FIELD, LYMAN
ADMINISTRATOR, COLLECTOR
b Kansas City, Mo, Oct 6, 14. *Study:* Univ Kans, AB, 36; Harvard Law Sch, LLB, 39. *Pos:* Founding mem, Mo State Coun on Arts, 65-75, chmn, 66-74; founding mem & 1st chmn, North Am Assembly of State & Prov Arts Agencies, 68-70; trustee & bd dir, Kansas City Art Inst, 69-74; mem bd dir, Findlay Galleries, Chicago, New York, Palm Beach, Fla & Paris, France, 72-76; participant, 46th Am Assembly on Art Mus, Arden House, Harriman, NY, 75; chmn, Thomas Hart Benton Homestead Mem Adv Comn of Mo, 75-, trustee, Benton Testamentary Trusts; trustee, Mo Repertory Theater; co-chmn, Mid-West Regional Assembly on Future of Performing Arts, 79. *Awards:* Mo Arts Award, 89. *Mem:* Samuel H Kress Found, New York (trustee, 65-); Mid-Am Arts Alliance, Mo (mem bd dir, 71-); Kansas City Soc of Western Art (mem bd dir, 75-); Soc Fellows Atkins-Nelson Gallery of Art, Kansas City, Mo. *Collection:* Thomas Hart Benton paintings & lithographs; Jansem, Kluge, Michel Henry & Ardissone paintings. *Mailing Add:* 600 E 11th St Kansas City MO 64106

FIELD, PHILIP SIDNEY
PAINTER, PRINTMAKER
b Brooklyn, NY, Sept 17, 42. *Study:* Art Students League, with Arnold Blanch; Yale Norfolk Summer Sch Music & Art, 62; Syracuse Univ, BFA, 63; RI Sch Design, with Michael Mazur, MFA, 65; Vienna Acad Fine Arts, Fulbright Grant, 65-67. *Work:* Hunterdon Art Ctr, Clinton, NJ; Syracuse Univ; Univ Dallas; Tulsa City-Co Libr, Okla. *Exhib:* Prints, Drawings & Crafts Ann, 74 & 76 & Fantastic Images & Imaginary Worlds, 75, Ark Arts Ctr; Boston Printmakers Ann, Boston Mus Fine Arts, 75; Nat Print Show, Hunterdon Art Ctr, 75; Southwestern Prints & Drawings, Dallas Mus Fine Arts, 75; Miami Graphics Biennale, Fla, 75; Third Print Invitational, Univ Dallas, 76; Dulin Nat Print & Drawing Competition, Dulin Gallery Art, Knoxville, Tenn, 76 & 77; Nat Print & Drawing Competition, Okla Art Ctr, Oklahoma City, 76 & 77; Texas Printmakers, N Tex State Univ, Denton, 81; Xochil Art Inst, Mission, Tex, 82; Kansas Eight Nat Small Painting, Drawing & Print Exhib, Fort Hayes State Univ, 83; Across Texas, Patrick Gallery, 84; Dia de los Muertos Exhib, Xochil Art Inst, Mission, Tex, 87 & 88; one man shows, Shunjyo Gallery, Tokyo, Japan, 78, Tex Women's Univ, Denton, Tex, 82, Pan Am Univ, Edinburg, Tex, 86 & 88, Robinson Galleries, Houston, Tex, 90. *Pos:* Critic, For Art's Sake, column, McAllen Monitor, 80-81. *Teaching:* Instr art studio, Juniata Col, Huntingdon, Pa, 69-70; from instr to assoc prof, Pan Am Univ, 71-90. *Awards:* Augusta Hazard Award, Lowe Art Ctr, Syracuse Univ, 63; Merit Award, 88, Best of Show, 89 & 91, McAllen Internat Mus, McAllen, Tex; Art Fac of STex, McAllen Int Mus, 88. *Bibliog:* Al Brunelle (auth), article, Art News, 5/73; Maurice Schmidt (auth), Reflections on art, 1/76 & Art, light and history 6/76, Corpus Christi Caller. *Mem:* Col Art Asn. *Media:* Intaglio; Oil. *Dealer:* Robinson Galleries 3733 Westheimer No 7 Houston TX 77027. *Mailing Add:* Dept Art Pan American Univ 1201 West Univ Drive Edinburg TX 78539

FIELD, RICHARD SAMPSON
CURATOR, HISTORIAN
b New York, NY, Aug 26, 31. *Study:* Harvard Univ, AB, AM & PhD. *Collections Arranged:* 15th Century Woodcuts & Metalcuts from the National Gallery of Art (with catalog), 65; Jasper Johns: Prints 1960-1970 (with catalog), 70 & Silkscreen: History of a Medium (with catalog), 71, Philadelphia Mus Art; The Fable of the Sick Lion: A Fifteenth Century Blockbook (with catalog), 74, Gabriel de Sanit-Aubin (with catalog), 75, Jasper Johns: Prints 1970-1977, 78, Prints Drawings and Paintings by Philip Pearlstein, 79 & The Prints of Armand Seguin (1869-1903), 80, Davison Art Ctr, Wesleyan Univ; Fifteenth Century Woodcuts, Metrop Mus Art, 77. *Pos:* Asst to dir, Fogg Art Mus, Cambridge, Mass, 61-62; asst cur of prints, Alverthorpe Gallery-Nat Gallery Art, 62-68 & Philadelphia Mus Art, 69-72; cur, Davison Art Ctr, Wesleyan Univ, Middletown, Conn, 72-79; cur prints, drawings & photographs & assoc dir, Art Gallery, Yale Univ, New Haven, Conn, 79- *Teaching:* Assoc prof art, Wesleyan Univ, 72-79. *Awards:* Fulbright Grant, France, 59-60; Finley Fel, Nat Gallery Art, 65-67. *Mem:* Print Coun Am (dir, 70-72). *Res:* Fifteenth century woodcuts; Gauguin; contemporary prints. *Publ:* Auth, Gauguin's Noa Noa suite, Burlington Mag, 68; auth, Woodcuts from Altomunster, Gutenberg-Jahrbuch, 69; auth, Gauguin's Monotypes, 73; auth, The Prints of Richard Hamilton, 73. *Mailing Add:* Off of Curator Yale Univ Art Gallery Box 2006 Yale Station New Haven CT 06520

FIELDS, FREDRICA H
STAINED GLASS ARTIST, CRAFTSMAN
b Haverford, Pa, Jan 10, 12. *Study:* Landscape painting with Frank Morley Fletcher, 30 & Frank Logan, 31; Wellesley Col, 30-32; Art Students League, with Nicolaides, 33; stained glass with Mrs Orin Skinner, 38-39 & with George Sotter, 51. *Work:* Washington Cathedral, Washington, DC; YWCA, Greenwich, Conn; Church Holy Comforter, Kenilworth, Ill; Corning Mus Glass, Corning, NY; Asn Res & Enlightenment Prayer & Meditation Ctr, Virginia Beach. *Exhib:* Nat Conf on Relig Arch, New York, 67; Greenwich Art Soc Ann Exhibs, Conn, 68-78; one-woman exhib, Artist's Mart, Washington, DC, 55; First Presby Church, Stamford, Conn, 76; Concordia Col, Bronxville, NY, 82; YMCA, Greenwich, Conn, 82; Gallery at Hastings-on-Hudson, New York, 90. *Teaching:* Instr stained glass, YWCA, Greenwich, 66-67 & pvt studio, 68-71. *Awards:* For stained glass, 4th & 6th Int Exhib of Ceramic Arts, Nat Collection of Fine Arts, 53 & 57; 9th & 11th Ann Area Exhib, Corcoran Gallery of Art, 55 & 56; work included in US Info Agency Traveling Exhib, 57; Second award, Int Competition, Prof Stained Glass Mag, 86, 90. *Mem:* Stained Glass Asn Am; Greenwich Art Soc. *Publ:* Contribr, Stained Glass Asn Am Quart, 58-75; The Complete Book of Creative Glass Art, 74; Step by Step Stained Glass, 74; Decorating Glass, 76; Stained Glass Asn Am Reference and Tech Manual, 88. *Mailing Add:* 561 Lake Ave Greenwich CT 06830

FIERO, GLORIA K
EDUCATOR, HISTORIAN
b New York, NY, May 19, 39. *Study:* Univ Miami, Coral Gables, AB, 60; Univ Calif, Berkeley, MA, 61; Fla State Univ, Tallahassee, PhD, 70. *Teaching:* Prof hist, Univ Southwestern La, 69- *Awards:* Woodrow Wilson Hon Fel, 60; Fulbright Fel to Belg, 66-67; Amoco Found Award Outstanding Teaching, 83. *Mem:* Col Art Asn Am; Southeastern Col Art Conf; Int Ctr Medieval Art; South-Central Renaissance Conf (pres, 85-86). *Res:* Late Medieval, northern Renaissance painting and manuscripts; early 20th century painting. *Publ:* Courtier and commoner: Two styles of fifteenth century manuscript illumination, Explorations Renaissance Cult, 77; Geertgen tot Sint Jans & the Dutch manuscript tradition, Oud Holland, 82; Death Ritual in Fifteenth Century Manuscript Illumination, J Medieval Hist, 84; Three Medieval Views of Women, Yal Univ Press, 89; The Humanistic Tradition, 6 vols, WCBrown & Benchmark, 92. *Mailing Add:* 155 N Southlawn Dr Lafayette LA 70503

FILIPOVIC, AUGUSTIN
SCULPTOR, PAINTER
b Davor, Yugoslavia, Jan 8, 31; Can citizen. *Study:* Acad Fine Art, Rome. *Work:* Art Gallery Ont, Toronto; Ft William Libr, Ont; Palazzo Braschi, Rome, Italy; The Inn on the Park, Toronto, Ont; Montreal Mus Fine Arts, Can. *Comn:* Reclining figure (bronze), Parkin & Assocs for Don Mills Post Off, 69; poster 25th anniversary, Can Opera Co, 73. *Exhib:* Mostra Arte Lazio, Rome, Italy, 55; Nat Gallery Art, Ottawa, Ont, 62; Gallery Moos, Toronto, 67 & 73; Gallery Agnes Lefort, Montreal, PQ, 68; Bertha Schaefer Gallery, New York, 71 & 73. *Teaching:* Resident sculptor, Univ Toronto Sch Archit, 62; sessional lectr, Brock Univ, 77-81 & Guelph Univ, 81. *Awards:* Second Prize, Mostra Arte Lazio, Rome, 52; Prize of the Mayor of Rome, via Margutta, Rome, 58; Prize in Centennial Competition, Niagara Falls, 66. *Mem:* Sculpture Soc Can; Royal Canadian Acad. *Media:* Bronze. *Mailing Add:* 77 Mowat No 13 Toronto ON M6K 3E3 Canada

FILIPOWSKI, RICHARD E
SCULPTOR, EDUCATOR
b Poland, May 29, 23; US citizen. *Study:* Inst Design, Ill Inst Technol, with L Moholy-Nagy, BA. *Work:* Addison Gallery Am Art, Andover, Mass; State St Bank & Trust Co & First Nat Bank, Boston; Boston Safe Deposit & Trust Co; Chase Manhattan Bank, New York. *Comn:* Sculptural ark, Temple B'rith Kodesh, Rochester, 62; sculptural cross, Trinity Lutheran, Chelmsford, Mass, 63; sculpture, Atlantic, Sheraton Corp, Prudential Ctr, Boston, 64; sculptural cross, Trinity Evangel Lutheran, Philadelphia, 65; sculpture, Echo, Revere Copper & Brass Corp, New York, 65. *Exhib:* Art for US Embassies, Inst Contemp Art, Boston, 66; Nat Exhib Art, Ogunquit, Maine, 67; one-man shows, Fitchburg Art Mus, Mass, 68 & State Univ Oneonta, NY, 69; Outdoor Sculpture Exhib, De Cordova Mus, Lincoln, Mass, 72; Mass Inst Technol, 84; Arch Am Art, Boston, Mass, 89 & 90; Art Career: Photos Sculpture Reviews & Exhibs, Archives Am Art Smithsonian, 89-90. *Pos:* Prof emer, Mass Inst Technol, 88. *Teaching:* Assoc prof visual design, Mass Inst Technol, 53- *Awards:* First Prize Sculpture, Boston Arts Festival, 58; Aleck & Ruth McLean Award, Nat Exhib Art, Ogunquit, 67. *Bibliog:* Katherine Kuh (auth), Abstract and surrealist American art, Art Inst Chicago, 48; Patricia Boyd Wilson (auth), The home forum, Christian Sci Monitor, 65; Phoebe Cutler (auth), Richard Filipowski's sculpture, Harvard Art Rev, 67. *Media:* All Media. *Mailing Add:* 10 Round Hill Rd Lexington MA 02173

FILKOSKY, JOSEFA
SCULPTOR, EDUCATOR
b Westmoreland City, Pa, June 15, 33. *Study:* Seton Hill Col, BA, 55; Carnegie-Mellon Univ, BFA, 63; Cranbrook Acad Art, MFA, 68; Art Inst Chicago, 68. *Comn:* Pipe Dream IX, Taubman Corp, Southfield; Pipe Dreams I & II, Oxford Merchandise Mart, Monroeville, Pa; Pipe Theme in Oranges II, Everson Mus, 76; Pipe Theme in Oranges IV, St Lawrence Univ, NY, 76; Spirals in Blue, Pittsburgh, Pa, 83. *Exhib:* One-man shows, The Art Image In All Media, NY, 70 & Bertha Schaefer Gallery, New York, 73; Sculpture in the Fields, Storm King Art Ctr, 74-76; Sculpture on Shoreline Sites, Roosevelt Island, New York, 79-80; Sculptors Guild, New York, 84-88; Ten Pennsylvania Sculptors, Southern Alleghenies Mus, Loretto, Pa, 86. *Teaching:* Prof art, Seton Hill Col, 56- *Awards:* Three Rivers Purchase Award, 72; Assoc Artists Pittsburgh Award, 76; Nat Grant, St Lawrence Univ, 76. *Bibliog:* Suzanne Benton (auth), Metal Sculpture, 75; Sandak Slide Set, Am Woman's Art, 74; M Rohinetto (auth), Object/Environment, 76. *Mem:* Asn Artists Pittsburgh; Sculptors Guild New York. *Media:* Aluminum, Steel Pipe. *Dealer:* Dorothea Silverman 500 E 83rd St New York NY 10028; Marcia Rosenthal 410 Schenley Rd Pittsburgh PA 15217. *Mailing Add:* Dept Art Seton Hill Col Greensburg PA 15601

FILLERUP, MEL
PAINTER
b Lovell, Wyo, Jan 28, 24. *Study:* Art Students League; study with Paul Bransom, Serge Bongart, William Reese, Conrad Schwiering & Robert Meyers. *Work:* Nat Cowboy Hall of Fame, Okla City. *Comn:* Husky dogs, Husky Oil Co; mural, Vis Ctr, Cody, Wyo. *Exhib:* Western States Show, Cody Country Art League, 65-75; Springville Art Mus Show, 70-75; C M Russell Auction, Great Falls, Mont; Wind River Artists Asn; New York Life Ann Calendar Competition; Nat Cowboy Hall of Fame, Wild Animal Art Exhib, 79; Western Rondezvous of Art, Bozeman, Mont. *Teaching:* Oil painting, North West Community Col, 74-75. *Awards:* Best of Show, Cody Country Art League Western Show, 91; Nick Eggenhoffer Award, 92; Peter Hassrick Award, Western Rondezvous of Art, 92. *Mem:* Am Indian & Cowboy Artists; Cody Country Artist Asn (pres, 68-70); Soc Animal Artists. *Media:* Oil, Watercolor. *Publ:* Articles, Southwest Art, 9/80 & Palette Talk, No 54; auth & illusr, Sidon: The Canal That Faith Built. *Mailing Add:* PO Box 938 Cody WY 82414

FILLIN-YEH, SUSAN
MUSEUM DIRECTOR
b New York, NY. *Study:* City Univ New York, PhD, 81. *Collections Arranged:* Charles Sheeler: American Interiors, The Technological Muse & American Art in the 1950's (auth, catalog), 87. *Pos:* Curator, Douglas F Cooley Mem Art Gallery, Reed Col, Portland, Ore, 91-92, dir, 92- *Teaching:* Asst prof, Yale Univ, New Haven, Conn, 82-89; adj prof, Hunter Col New York, 91. *Awards:* Ann Achievement Award, PhD Alumni Asn City Unvi New York, 92. *Mem:* Col Art Asn Am; Alliance of Independent Colleges Art. *Mailing Add:* D F Cooley Memorial Gallery Reed College 3203 SE Woodstock Blvd Portland OR 97202-8199

FILMUS, MICHAEL ROY
PAINTER
b New York, NY, May 12, 43. *Study:* Boston Univ, BA, 66; Art Students League. *Work:* Berkshire Mus, Pittsfield, Mass; Minneapolis Inst Art; Art Inst Chicago; Denver Art Mus; Hunter Mus Art, Chattanooga, Tenn. *Exhib:* Drawings USA, Minn Mus Art, 75; solo exhib, Hirschl & Adler Galleries, New York, 75, 77 & 79 & David Findlay Jr, New York, 84; Albrecht Mus Art, 76; 200 Years of American Art, Berkshire Mus, Pittsfield, Mass, 76; Flint Inst Arts, Mich, 77; Art of the State, Rose Art Mus, Waltham, Mass, 79; Contemporary Naturalism, Nassau Co Mus Fine Art, Roslyn Harbor, NY, 80; Welles Gallery, Lenox, Mass, 91. *Awards:* Purchase Prize, 40th Ann Midyear Show, Butler Inst Am Art, 76. *Bibliog:* John Arthur (auth), The temperament of nature: Recent paintings by Michael Filmus, Arts Mag, 4/84; Michael Brenson (auth), Michael Filmus, NY Times, 4/84. *Mem:* Life mem Art Students League. *Media:* Oil, Pastel. *Mailing Add:* 4 Fern Hill Rd Great Barrington MA 01230

FILMUS, STEPHEN I
PAINTER, PRINTMAKER
b New York, NY, Feb 4, 48. *Study:* Univ Pittsburgh, BA, 70; Columbia Univ, MA, 71; Art Students League, 72. *Work:* Ball State Mus, Muncie, Ind; Bank New Eng, Springfield, Mass; Berkshire Mus, Pittsfield, Mass. *Exhib:* Solo shows, Still-Lifes, Berkshire Mus, Pittsfield, Mass, 80 & 84, Welles Gallery, Lenox Mass, 89; Still Life: Five Visions, David Findlay Jr, New York, 84; Works on Paper, David Findlay Jr, New York, 85; 2 plus 4 Artists Working, Clark-Whitney Gallery, Lenox, Mass, 86; Welles Gallery, Lenox, Mass, 90. *Awards:* First Place, Works on Paper, Berkshire Art Mus, 79. *Bibliog:* Tess Panfil (auth), Still Lifes by Stephen Filmus, Berkshire Eagle, 7-17/84; Gerrit Henry (auth), Still Life: Five Visions, Arts Mag, 9/84; Charles Bonenti (auth), Filmus, Works on Paper, Arts Mag, 6/85. *Mem:* Artists Equity; Great Barrington Cultural Coun. *Media:* Oil on Canvas. *Mailing Add:* 4 Fern Hill Rd Great Barrington MA 01230

FILMUS, TULLY
PAINTER, LECTURER
b Otaki, Russia, Aug 29, 08; US citizen. *Study:* Pa Acad Fine Arts, Philadelphia; NY Univ; Barnes Found, Philadelphia; Art Students League; Cresson traveling scholar for study in Paris & Rome. *Work:* Metrop Mus Art & Whitney Mus Am Art, New York; Joslyn Art Mus, Omaha; Butler Inst of Art, Youngstown, Ohio; Univ of NC Permanent Collection; St Lawrence Univ Permanent Collection, Canton, NY; Permanent Collection, Nat Gallery, Washington, DC; and others. *Exhib:* Whitney Mus Am Art, 40-46; Art Inst Chicago, 41; Carnegie Inst Int, Pittsburgh, 41-46; Pa Acad Fine Arts, Philadelphia, 41-46; Corcoran Gallery Art, Washington, DC, 42; Yeshiva Univ Mus, NY, 77; one-man shows, ACA Gallery, New York, 63 & 71, The Berkshire Mus, Pittsfield, Mass, 73 & 80 & ACA Gallery, Rome, Italy, 74, Findlay Gallery, New York, 87, & Wells Gallery, Lenox, Mass, 89. *Teaching:* Instr painting & drawing, Am Artists Sch, New York, 36-38 & Cooper Union Art Sch, New York, 38-50. *Awards:* Pa Acad Fine Arts Fel, 48; Salmagundi Prize, Audubon Artists, 69. *Bibliog:* Dr Alfred Werner (auth), The painter Tully Filmus, World Publs, 63; Tully Filmus--selected drawings, Jewish Publ, 71. *Mem:* Artist Equity NY; Audubon Artists; Art Comn Nassau Co, NY. *Media:* Oil. *Dealer:* ACA Gallery 21 E 67th St New York NY 10021. *Mailing Add:* 4 Fern Hill Rd Great Barrington NY 01230

FINCH, RUTH WOODWARD
WRITER, PHOTOGRAPHER
b Rochester, NY, Feb 27, 16. *Study:* Bryn Mawr Col, BA(art hist), 37; Le Louvre, Paris, France; Photographic Workshop, New Canaan, Conn. *Exhib:* Arteder Show, Balboa, Spain, 82; Collection 83, 84, 85 & 86, Silvermine Guild Artists, Richardson Vicks Inc, Wilton, Conn; Salon des Nations Show, Centre Int d'Art Contemporain, Paris, France, 84; Brazil & Mexico Photogr, 85, New Canaan Soc Arts; Sculpture & Photogr Show, Silvermine Guild Artists, 85; Photogr Show, NC Soc Arts, 85-88; and others. *Awards:* Albert Jacobson Patron's Award, Silvermine Guild Artists, 72; Save the Children Award-Am Indian Sect, 83. *Mem:* Silvermine Guild Artists; Rowayton Arts Ctr, Conn; New Canaan Soc Arts, Conn; Int Ctr Photog, New York. *Interests:* American sculpture and work by American Indian artists. *Mailing Add:* 293 Laurel Rd New Canaan CT 06840-2707

FINCHER, JOHN H
PAINTER, ASSEMBLAGE ARTIST
b Hamilton, Tex, Aug 4, 41. *Study:* Hardin-Simmons Univ, Abileen, Tex Tech Col, BA, 64; Univ Okla, MFA, 66. *Work:* Dallas Mus Fine Arts; Univ Okla Mus Fine Arts; Wichita Mus Art; Albuquerque Mus, NMex; St Louis Art Mus; and others. *Exhib:* Second Western States Exhib, Corcoran Gallery, Washington, DC, 83; Col Springs Fine Arts Ctr, 86; Elaine Horwitch Gallery, 87; Albuquerque Mus, NMex, 88; J Cacciola, NY, 90; Elaine Horwitch, Santa Fe, 91; and others. *Teaching:* Assoc prof art, Wichita State Univ, 66-77. *Awards:* Wurlitzer Found Grant, Taos, NMex, 72. *Media:* Oil. *Publ:* Auth, articles in Art Space, Arts, Art News & Art in Am; plus various catalogs. *Mailing Add:* 611 Caminito Del Donaldo Santa Fe NM 87501

FINCK, FURMAN J
PAINTER, INSTRUCTOR
b Chester, Pa, Oct 10, 1900. *Study:* Pa Acad Fine Arts, dipl; Ecole des Beaux Arts & Acad Julian, Paris; Am Acad, Rome; Muhlenberg Col, DFA. *Work:* Mass Gen Hosp; Univ Calif, Riverside; Nat Portrait Gallery; Univ Bridgeport, Conn; Dartmouth House, London. *Comn:* Med faculty (portrait ser), Temple Univ, 44; med clinics (ser), Med Schs US, 45; portrait of President Truman, Nat Dem Club, New York, 50; portrait of President Eisenhower, Union League, Philadelphia, 54; deans schs pharm US (ser), Wyeth Labs, 60-64. *Exhib:* Pa Acad Fine Arts Ann; Carnegie Inst Int; Nat Acad Design Ann; Arnold Bernhard Arts & Humanities Ctr, 88; Portraits Inc Ann, Grand Cent Art Galleries; retrospective, Woodmere Art Gallery, Philadelphia. *Teaching:* Instr sci paint & painting, Cheltenham Art Ctr, Pa, 67; dean, du Cret Sch Arts, Plainfield, NJ, 68-; mem staff painting, Philadelphia Mus Art, 69-78; fac mem, Nat Acad, 83- *Awards:* Cresson European Traveling Scholar, Pa Acad Fine Arts, 24; First Altman Prize, Nat Acad Design, 55; Krindler Prize, Salmagundi Club Ann, 64. *Bibliog:* Henry Pitz (auth), Furman Finck, Am Artist Mag, 3/56; Martin Zipin (auth), Finck paints a portrait (film), produced by WFIL-TV. *Mem:* Salmagundi Club; Twenty Five Year Club of Temple Univ; Players; Artists' Fellowship, Inc (pres, 73-77); Dutch Treat. *Media:* All. *Publ:* Auth, The meaning of art in education, Columbia Univ Publ, 38; coauth, The Artist as Teacher, Appleton, 50; auth, The artist and the architect, Am Inst Architects J, 59; auth, Complete Guide to Portrait Painting, Watson-Guptill, 70. *Mailing Add:* 285 Central Park W New York NY 92634-3854

FINDLAY, DAVID B, JR
DEALER
b Kansas City, Mo, June 30, 33. *Study:* Cornell Univ, BME & MBA. *Pos:* Pres, David Findlay Jr Fine Art, currently. *Specialty:* American 19th and early 20th Century paintings and sculpture. *Mailing Add:* Cherokee Sta PO Box 20080 New York NY 10028-0060

FINDLAY, JAMES ALLEN
LIBRARIAN
b Saginaw, Mich, Aug 13, 43. *Study:* Wayne State Univ, BA, 70, MSLS, 72; Univ Calif, Los Angeles, 75. *Pos:* Reference & cataloging libr, Univ Calif, Los Angeles Art Libr, 75-79; Latin Am archivist, Mus Mod Art Libr, New York, 79-82; dir, RI Sch Design Libr, 82-87; dir, Fashion Inst Tech, New York City Libr, 87-89; head librn, The Wolfsonian Found, Miami Beach, Fla, 89- *Mem:* Art Libr Soc NAm; Col Art Asn; Am Libr Asn; Mus Computer Network. *Res:* Modern Latin American art; design; decorative arts; propaganda arts. *Interests:* Modern art; architecture; fashion; decorative arts; propaganda arts. *Publ:* Auth, Modern Art of Latin America: A Bibliography, Greenwood Press, 83; Cecil Beaton: A Bibliography, 88 & Tartan: A Bibliography, Fashion Inst Tech, 88. *Mailing Add:* 702 13th St No 305 Miami Beach FL 33139

FINE, JANE
PAINTER
b Forest Hills, NY, Sept 25, 58. *Study:* Harvard Univ, BA (magna cum laude), 80, Sch Mus Fine Arts, Boston, 81-83; Skowhegan Sch Painting & Sculpture, 89. *Work:* Brooklyn Union Gas Co, NY. *Exhib:* Selections 42, Drawing Ctr, New York, 88; Paint, PS 122 Gallery, New York, 89; Short Stories, Epoche Gallery, Brooklyn, 90; Who Laughs Last, MMC Gallery, Marymount Manhattan Col, New York, 90; White Room Solo Show, White Columns, New York, 92. *Awards:* Yaddo Artist in Residence, Saratoga Springs, NY, 90; Residency, Millay Colony Arts, Austerlitz, NY, 90; Fel, Fine ArtsWork Ctr, Provincetown, Mass, 92-93; and others. *Media:* Acrylic, Oil. *Mailing Add:* 179 Grand St Brooklyn NY 11211

FINE, JUD
SCULPTOR, EDUCATOR
b Los Angeles, Calif, Nov 20, 44. *Study:* Univ Calif, Santa Barbara, BA, 66; Cornell Univ, MFA, 70. *Work:* Minneapolis Inst Art; Los Angeles Co Art Mus & Mus Contemp Art, Los Angeles; Pasadena Mus Mod Art; Art Inst Chicago & Mus Contemp Art; Yale Univ Art Mus; Power Inst Fine Arts, Sydney, Australia; Guggenheim Mus, New York; Yale Univ Art Mus, New Haven, Conn; Lo Jolla Mus Contemp Art, Calif. *Comn:* Security Pac, Costa Mesa Gallery, Calif; Mem Garden Carnation Co, Glendale, Calif; Los Angeles Cent Libr, West Lawn. *Exhib:* Solo exhib, Ronald Feldman Gallery,

72, 73, 76, 78 & 81, Margo Leavin Gallery, Los Angeles, 77, 79, 81 & 84, Anderson Gallery, Va Commonwealth Univ, Richmond, 82, Thomas Segal Gallery, Boston, 83 & Los Angeles Munic Art Gallery, 85; Los Angeles County Mus, 72; 71st Am Exhib, Art Inst Chicago, 74; Inst Contemp Art, Boston, 74; Indianapolis Mus Art, 76; Santa Barbara Mus Art, 78; La Jolla Mus Contemp Art; Univ Calif Fine Arts Gallery, Irvine, 87; Laguna Beach Mus Art, Calif, 88; and others. *Teaching:* Prof art, Univ Southern Calif, 79- *Awards:* Contemp Art Coun New Talent Grant, Los Angeles Co Art Mus, 72; Laura Slobe Mem Award, Art Inst Chicago, 74; Individual Artist Fel, Nat Endowment Arts, 82; Grant, Calif State Arts Coun, Sculpture Comn, Exposition Park, Los Angeles, 83. *Bibliog:* Articles, Arts Mag, 9/74 & 3/75 & Artforum, 4/75; Arts Mag, 5/72, 10/73, 9/74 & 3/75; Robert McDonald (auth), Poles Remain as Theme in Sculptures by Fine, Los Angeles Times, 2/24/87. *Media:* Mixed. *Publ:* Auth, Or: An Introduction, 74 & Walk, 75, pvt publ. *Dealer:* Ronald Feldman Gallery New York NY 10013. *Mailing Add:* 1366 Appleton Way Venice CA 90291

FINE, RUTH E
CURATOR, PRINTMAKER
b Philadelphia, Pa, May 10, 41. *Study:* Skowhegan Sch Painting & Sculpture; Philadelphia Col Art, BFA, 62; Univ Pa, MFA, 64. *Work:* Philadelphia Mus Art; Nat Gallery Art, Washington, DC; Fleming Mus, Univ Vt, Burlington; Hunterian Art Gallery, Glasgow Univ, Scotland. *Collections Arranged:* Lessing J Rosenwald: Tribute to a Collector (auth, catalog), 82 & Gemini GEL: Art & Collaboration (auth, catalog), 84-, Nat Gallery Art, Washington, DC; Drawing Near: Whistler Etching from the Zelman Collection (auth, catalog), Los Angeles Co Mus Art, 84-; The 1980's: Prints from the collection of Joshua P Smith, Nat Gallery, 89; The Art of John Marin, Nat Gallery, 90. *Pos:* Cur, Lessing J Rosenwald's Collection, Alverthorpe Gallery, 72-80; cur modern prints & drawings, Nat Gallery Art, Washington, DC, 80- *Teaching:* Lectr, Philadelphia Col Art, 65-69, Beaver Col, 69-72 & Univ Vt, 76 & 77. *Awards:* Ingram Merrill Found Grant. *Mem:* Col Art Asn; Print Coun Am (mem bd dirs, 85-88). *Media:* Etching, Watercolor. *Res:* American and British graphic arts, 18th-20th centuries. *Publ:* Coauth, The Prints of Benton Spruance: A Catalogue Raisonné (with R Looney), Pa Press & Free Libr, Philadelphia, 86; contribr, In Honor of Paul Mellon: Collector & Benefactor, Nat Gallery Art, 86; ed, James McNeill Whistler: A Reevaluation, Nat Gallery, 87; coauth, The Drawings of Jasper Johns, Nat Gallery Art, 90. *Dealer:* Dolan Maxwell Gallery Philadelphia Pa. *Mailing Add:* c/o Nat Gallery Art Washington DC 20565

FINK, AARON
PAINTER, PRINTMAKER
b Boston, Mass, Mar 10, 55. *Study:* Skowhegan Sch Painting & Sculpture, 76; Md Inst Col Art, BFA, 77; Yale Univ Col Art, MFA, 79. *Work:* Mus Mod Art, New York; Metrop Mus Art, New York; Philadelphia Mus Art, Pa; Mus Fine Arts, Boston, Mass; Art Inst Chicago, Ill; New York Pub Libr; Prudential Life Insurance Co; Libr Congress, Washington, DC. *Exhib:* Solo exhibs, Galerie Barbara Farber, Amsterdam, Neth, Works on Paper, David Beitzel Gallery, New York, Rutgers Barclay Gallery, Santa Fe, NMex & Alpha Gallery, Boston, Mass, 91, Lisa Sette Gallery, Scottsdale, Ariz, 92; New Work, David Beitzel Gallery, New York, 91; Images from the Eighties: Part I, Samuel P Harn Mus Art, Univ Fla, Gainesville, 91-92; New Year, New Work, Galerie Barbara Farber, Amsterdam, Neth, 92; A Feast for the Eyes, Mus Mod Art, 92; The Art Collection of the Federal Reserve Board: Five Years of Accessions, Bd Gov Bldg, Washington, DC, 92. *Awards:* Fel, Nat Endowment Arts, 82 & 87; Fel, Mass Coun Arts & Humanities, 84. *Bibliog:* Lea Saslav (auth), Open Season, Boston, 10/91; Nancy Stapen (auth), Two Artists Who View Nature & Culture, Boston Globe, 11/21/91; Gary Susman (auth), Artists on Art, Boston Phoenix, 5/15/92; Lois Tarlow (auth), Profile: An Interview with Aaron Fink, Art New Eng, 3/89. *Media:* All. *Dealer:* David Beitzel 113 Greene St New York NY 10012; Alpha Gallery 121 Newburg St Boston MA 02116. *Mailing Add:* 63 Maverick Sq East Boston MA 02128

FINK, ALAN
ART DEALER
b Chicago, Ill, July 17, 25. *Study:* Univ Ill, BA. *Pos:* Dir, Alpha Gallery Inc. *Mem:* Art Dealers Asn Am; Boston Art Dealers Asn. *Specialty:* Twentieth century painting, sculpture and graphics; modern master prints. *Mailing Add:* c/o Alpha Gallery 121 Newbury St Boston MA 02116

FINK, HERBERT LEWIS
PAINTER, EDUCATOR
b Providence, RI, Sept 8, 21. *Study:* Carnegie Inst Technol, 41; RI Sch Design, BFA, 49; Yale Univ, MFA, 56; Art Students League; also with John Frazier, Gabor Peterdi, Arshile Gorky & Rico Lebrun. *Work:* Boston Mus Art; Art Inst Chicago; Baltimore Mus Art; Md Inst; Brown Univ; Corcoran Gallery, Washington, DC; Philadelphia Mus Art. *Comn:* Mural, RI Post Off Lobby, Providence, 59; metal sculpture, Sen Green Airport, 60; archit screen, Hartford Bank & Trust Bldg. *Exhib:* Philadelphia Mus Art; Merrill-Chase Galleries, 79; Farnsworth Mus, 82; Republic China, 86; State Ill Bldg, Chicago, 86; and others. *Pos:* Print ed, Int Graphic Arts Soc; trustee, Tiffany Found; trustee, Mitchell Found, Mt Vernon, Ill. *Teaching:* Instr painting & drawing, RI Sch Design, 51-61; instr, Yale Univ, 56-61; prof art & chmn dept, Southern Ill Univ, Carbondale, 61-83, distinguished prof, 83-; lectr, univs in Chancum, Chandu, Guanju, Julin & Sezvan Province, Cult Ministry, Peoples Repub China, 85. *Awards:* Purchase Prizes, Soc Am Graphic Artists, 59 & Libr Cong, 59; Guggenheim Fel, 65-66; Visual Artist of the Year, State of Ill, 86. *Mem:* Nat Acad of Design. *Publ:* Auth, Graphic Artist, Univ Southern Ill Press; book with 100 full page illus, China, 91. *Mailing Add:* R Rte One Box 712 Rockport ME 04856

FINK, JOANNA ELIZABETH
ART DEALER, GALLERY DIRECTOR
b Boston, Mass, Aug 8, 58. *Study:* Wellesley Col, Mass, 76-78; New York Univ, BA, 80; Inst Fine Arts, New York Univ, MA, 83. *Pos:* Admin asst & photogr, Dept Fine Arts, New York Univ, 80-82; res consult, art prog, Chase Manhattan Bank, New York, 83; assoc dir, Alpha Gallery, Inc, Boston, Mass, 83- *Teaching:* Teaching asst, art hist, New York Univ, 82. *Specialty:* Contemporary American painting, sculpture and works on paper; 20th century American and European works; modern master prints. *Publ:* Auth, Georg Baselitz: Selected Prints, 1963-1985 (exhib catalog), Alpha Gallery, Boston, 85. *Mailing Add:* Alpha Gallery, Inc 14 Newbury St Boston MA 02116

FINK, LARRY (LAURENCE B)
EDUCATOR, PHOTOGRAPHER
b Brooklyn, NY, Mar 11, 41. *Study:* With Lissette Model, 59; Coe Col; New Sch Soc Res. *Work:* Mus Mod Art, New York; Corcoran Gallery Art, Washington, DC; Mus Fine Arts, Boston; New Orleans Mus Art; Seattle Mus Art. *Exhib:* Broxton Gallery, Los Angeles, 76 & Case Solway Gallery, Cincinnati, 77; one-man shows, Light Gallery, New York, 77 & 80, Lehigh Univ, Bethlehem, Pa, 78, Sander Gallery, Washington, DC, 78-79, Mus of Mod Art, New York, 79 & Gallery Forum, Spain, 85; San Francisco Mus Art, 81; retrospectives, Harrison Gallery, 86 & Light Gallery, 86. *Teaching:* Instr, Parson Sch Design, 67-72, Kingsborough Community Col, City Univ New York, 69-73, Inst Contemp Photog, Lehigh Univ, 76, Int Ctr Photog, New York, 77; prof photog, Yale Sch Fine Arts, 77-78; prof, Cooper Union, 79; prof photog, Lehigh Univ, 84-87, Bard Univ, 87- *Awards:* Creative Artists Pub Serv Fel, 71-72 & 73-74; Guggenheim Fels, 76-77 & 79-80; Nat Endowment Arts Photog Fel, 78-79; Hazlett Award for Excellence in Art, Governor Pa, 85. *Dealer:* Lieberman & Saul Gallery New York NY; Light Gallery 724 Fifth Ave New York NY 10019. *Mailing Add:* PO Box 295 Martins Creek PA 18063

FINK, LOIS MARIE
HISTORIAN, CURATOR
b Michigan City, Ind, Dec 30, 27. *Study:* Capital Univ, BA, 51; Univ Chicago, MA, 55, PhD, 70; Capital Univ, Hon Dr Humanities, 82. *Collections Arranged:* Academy: The Academic Tradition in American Art (auth, catalog), Nat Collection Fine Arts, 75. *Pos:* Cur, Off Res & Fels, Nat Mus Am Art, 70- *Teaching:* Instr art hist & sociology, Lenoir Rhyne Col, 55-56; instr art hist & educ, Midland Col, 56-58; instr, Roosevelt Univ, 58-64, asst prof, 64-70. *Mem:* Col Art Asn; Am Studies Asn. *Res:* Nineteenth and early twentieth century American art; relationship of French art to American art. *Publ:* Auth, American artists in France, 1850-1870, Am Art J, 73; coauth, Academy: The Academic Tradition in American Art, Smithsonian, 75; auth, French art in the United States, 1850-1870, Gazette Beaux Arts, 78; American participation at the Paris salons, 1870-1900, Int Comt Hist Art 24th Cong, 82; contribr, Elizabeth Nourse, 1859-1938: A Salon Career, Smithsonian, 83; Am Art at the Nineteenth Cent Paris Salons, Cambridge Univ Press, 90. *Mailing Add:* Off of Research & Fellowship, Nat Mus Am Art Smithsonian Inst Washington DC 20560

FINK, RAY (RAYMOND RUSSELL)
SCULPTOR, EDUCATOR
b Long Beach, Calif, July 8, 22. *Study:* Art Inst Chicago, BAE, 52; Ill Inst Technol, Chicago, MSAE, 55. *Work:* Nev Southern Univ, Las Vegas. *Comn:* Steel sculpture & six woodcuts, 50 & steel sculpture, 51, US War Bonds, US State Dept; relief painting, Pittman & Moore, Chicago, 54; sculptural mural (in collab with Rip Woods), Nat Housing Indust, Phoenix, Ariz, 73 & Greyhoud Inc, Phoenix, 75. *Exhib:* US Steel's Iron in the Fire, Birmingham Mus Art, Ala, 54; one-man show, Am Univ, Washington, DC, 57; Int Sculpture, Contemp Art Mus, Houston, Tex, 57; Am Exhib, Art Inst Chicago, 57; Art USA 58, Madison Sq Garden, NY, 58; Seven State Regional Contemp Art Traveling Exhib, Fedn Rocky Mountain States Coun on the Arts & Humanities, 75; Ariz Comn Arts & Humanities Traveling Exhib, 77. *Teaching:* Instr metal sculpture, Art Inst Chicago, 53-55; instr sculpture, Inst Design, Chicago, 53-58; prof art, Ariz State Univ, Tempe, 58- *Awards:* First Prize, Momentum Mid-Continental, Momentum, 53; Walter M Campana Award, Chicago & Vicinity, Art Inst Chicago, 56; George Bright Mem Prize, Phoenix Art Mus, Ariz, 67. *Bibliog:* Watercolor Painting (videotape), KAET-TV, Ariz State Univ, 68. *Media:* Mixed Media. *Dealer:* Yares Gallery 3625 Bishop Lane Scottsdale AZ 85251. *Mailing Add:* Dept Art Ariz State Univ Tempe AZ 85287

FINKE, LEONDA FROELICH
SCULPTOR, MEDALIST
b Brooklyn, NY. *Work:* Norfolk Mus Arts & Sci, Va; Nassau Community Col; Port Washington Pub Libr; Plainview-Old Bethpage Pub Libr; Smithsonian Inst, Washington, DC; Nat Portrait Gallery Smithsonian; Brit Mus; Mus Foreign Art Sofia, Bulgaria. *Comn:* Soc Medalists, The Prodigal Son, 88; Three 6 ft figures, Women in the sun, Atlanta, Ga, 88; Virginia Woolf, British Art Medal Soc, 89; 7 ft figure bronze, pvt collection, Conn, 90; Max Som Medal, Otolaryngology Dept, Montefiore Hosp, NewYork, 92. *Exhib:* Images of Am, US Info Agency traveling exhib (bronze figure sculpture selected); New York Botanical Gardens, 81; Int Fedn Medalists, Stockholm, 85 & Brit Mus, London, 92; Port Hist Mus, Philadelphia, Pa, 87; Sculpture Garden, Stamford, Conn; and others. *Teaching:* Adj prof sculpture & drawing, Nassau Community Col, 70- *Awards:* Medal Honor, Nat Asn Women Artists, 80; Gold Medal, Nat Sculpture Soc, 89 & Maurice Hexter Award, 92; Alexettl Award, Nat Acad Design, 90. *Bibliog:* Watson Jones (auth), Contemp Am Women Sculptors; Stella Pandell Russel (auth), Art in the World. *Mem:* Nat

Asn Women Artists; Audubon Artists; New York Soc Women Artists; fel Nat Sculpture Soc; Am Medallic Sculptors Asn. *Media:* Miscellaneous Media; Ink, Silverpoint. *Dealer:* Fisher Galleries 1511 Connecticut Ave NW Washington DC 20036; Cast Iron Gallery 159 Mercer St New York NY 10012. *Mailing Add:* 10 The Locusts Roslyn NY 11576

FINKELSTEIN, HENRY D
PAINTER, EDUCATOR
b Bar Harbor, Maine, Sept 3, 58. *Study:* Cooper Union, with Reuben Kadish & Nicolas Marsicano, BFA 80; Yale Sch Art, with Lester F Johnson, MFA 83. *Exhib:* Solo exhib, Prince St Gallery, New York, 86 & 88; Young and the Beautiful, Ingber Gallery, New York, 87; Maine Painters, Parkerson Gallery, Houston, Tex, 89; Cranberry Island Artists, Maine Coast Artists, Rockport, 88; 163rd Ann Exhib, 88, 165th Ann Exhib, 90, Nat Acad Design. *Teaching:* Asst prof, Hartford Art Sch, 84-; vis asst prof, Pratt Inst, New York, 86-87. *Awards:* Fulbright Fel, Italy, 83-84; Julius Hallgarten Prize, Nat Acad Design, 87. *Bibliog:* Michael Brenson (auth), article, NY Times, 1/18/86; Edgar Allen Beane (auth), Cranberry Island Artists, Maine Times, 88. *Mailing Add:* 46 W 22nd St New York NY 10010

FINKELSTEIN, LOUIS
EDUCATOR, PAINTER
b New York, NY, Mar 24, 23. *Study:* Cooper Union; Art Students League; Brooklyn Mus Art Sch. *Work:* Nat Acad Design; Yale Univ; CIBA-GEIGY Corp. *Exhib:* Whitney Mus Ann; Pa Acad; Corcoran Biennial; Stable Ann; Nat Acad Design. *Teaching:* Prof art, Philadelphia Col Art, 58-62; Yale Univ, 62-64; Queens Col, City Univ New York, 64-, chmn dept, 64-69. *Awards:* Fulbright Fel, Italy, 56-58; Distinguished Teaching Award, Col Art Asn, 78; Nat Endowment Arts, 83. *Mem:* Col Art Asn Am (mem bd dir, 68-70); Int Asn Art Critics. *Media:* Oil. *Res:* Abstract expressionism; impressionism; art theory. *Publ:* Auth, Gotham news, 69 & Thoughts about painterly, 70, Art News; Seeing Stella, Artforum, 73; Al Held, Art in Am, 74; Paintings of Mercedes Matter, Modern Masters, 91. *Mailing Add:* 459 W Broadway New York NY 10012

FINKELSTEIN, MAX
SCULPTOR, PAINTER
b New York, NY, June 15, 15. *Study:* Los Angeles City Col; Sculpture Ctr, New York; Calif Sch Art, Los Angeles; Univ Calif, Los Angeles. *Work:* Krannert Art Mus, Univ Ill, Champaign; Hirshhorn Mus, Washington, DC; Univ Calif Mus, Berkeley; Santa Barbara Mus Art, Calif; Los Angeles Co Mus Mod Art; and others. *Exhib:* Highlights of the 1967-1968 Art Season, Larry Aldrich Mus Contemp Art, Ridgefield, Conn, 68; one-man shows, La Jolla Mus Art, Calif, 68 & Esther Robles Gallery, 70; Microcosm, Long Beach Mus Art, 69; Painting & Sculpture Today, Indianapolis Mus Art, Ind, 70; and many others. *Teaching:* Instr sculpture, Univ Judaism. *Awards:* Los Angeles Munic Gallery, 65; Long Beach Mus, 65 & 67; Krannert Mus, Univ Ill, Champaign, 67. *Bibliog:* Ray Faulkner & Edwin Ziegfield (auths), Art Today, Holt, 69. *Media:* Metal, Wood Construction. *Mailing Add:* 621 N Curon Ave Los Angeles CA 90036

FINKLER, ROBERT ALLAN
EDUCATOR, PAINTER
b Chicago, Ill, Nov 22, 36. *Study:* Ill Wesleyan Univ, with Rupert Rilgore & Fred Brian, BFA, 59; State Univ Iowa, with Byron Burford & Robert Knipschild, MFA, 62. *Work:* St Cloud State Col, Minn; Waldorf Col, Iowa; Wis State Univ, Oshkosh; Mankato State Univ; Gen Mills, Minn; West Point, New York. *Exhib:* Drawings USA, St Paul Art Ctr, Minn, 66; Minn Artists Biennial, Minneapolis Art Inst, 67 & 70; Akron Art Inst, Ohio, 70; Rochester Art Ctr, Minn, 77; Minn Artists Compt, 79, 81, 84 & 86; MAEP Minneapolis Inst Arts, 82; Artbanque (Minneapolis) Gallery, Minn, 86, 87 & 89. *Pos:* Art dept chairperson. *Teaching:* Prof art, Mankato State Univ, 61- *Awards:* Pres lectureship, Winter Holidays, Presidents Fund, Mankato State Univ, 77. *Mailing Add:* Dept of Art Mankato State Univ Mankato MN 56001

FINLEY, DONNY LAMENDA
PAINTER
b Goodwater, Ala, Oct 7, 51. *Study:* Jacksonville State Univ, BS, 75. *Work:* Birmingham Mus Fine Arts, Ala; Columbus Mus Arts & Sci, Ga; Fine Arts Mus of the South, Mobile, Ala; LaGrange Mus Fine Arts, Ga; Fayette Mus Fine Arts, Ala. *Comn:* Painting, Ala Cattleman's Asn, Talladega, 76. *Exhib:* Am Watercolor Soc, Nat Acad Design, New York, 78, 80 & 82; Donny Finley Watercolorist, Bot Hall, Cheekwood Mus Fine Arts, 78; Alabama Art, US Senate Bldg, 79; Watercolor USA, Springfield Art Mus, Mo, 80; Rocky Mountain Nat, Foothills Art Ctr, Golden, Colo, 81; Nat Watercolor Soc, Palm Springs Desert Mus, 83 & 84; Salmagundi Club, New York, 85; Nat Acad Design, 88. *Awards:* Larry Quackenbush Mem Award, Am Watercolor Soc, 80; Strathmore Award, Nat Watercolor Soc, 83; Charlotte Livingston Award, Salmagundi Club, New York, 85; Walter Biggs Mem Award, Nat Acad Design, New York, 90. *Bibliog:* Marda Kaiser Burton (auth), Just a country boy, Southwest Art, 79; Joyce Deaton (auth), Down home Donny, Birmingham Mag, 79; Nell Luter (auth), Donny Finley's Moments Captured, Royal Publ, 87. *Mem:* Am Watercolor Soc. *Media:* Watercolors, Egg Tempera. *Publ:* Contribr, The Tennessee Conservationist, Tenn Dept Conserv, 78, Southwest Art, Art Mag, 79 & Birmingham Mag, 79; illusr, A Catalogue of the South, Oxmoor House, 79; Watercolor page, Am Artist Mag, 81. *Dealer:* Finley Gallery 2242 Highland Ave Birmingham AL 35205. *Mailing Add:* c/o Bryant Galleries Mountain Brook Village 2419 Canterbury Rd Birmingham AL 35223

FINLEY, GERALD ERIC
HISTORIAN
b Munich, Ger, July 17, 31; Can citizen. *Study:* Univ Toronto, BA, MA; Johns Hopkins Univ, PhD. *Teaching:* Lectr art & archeol, Univ Toronto, 59-60; lectr art, Univ Sask, Regina, 62-63, actg dir, Norman Mackenzie Art Gallery, 62-63; from asst prof to prof art hist, Queen's Univ, 63- *Awards:* Gustav Bissing Rotating Fel, Johns Hopkins Univ, 61; Inst Advan Studies Humanities Fel, Edinburgh Univ, 79-80; Fel, Royal Soc of Can, 84. *Mem:* Royal Can Acad Art; Ont Soc Artists; fel Royal Soc Canada, 84. *Res:* British late eighteenth and early nineteenth centuries painting; landscape, especially J M W Turner; history of ideas. *Publ:* Auth, J M W Turner's Rome from the Vatican: A Palimpsest of History?, Zeitschrift fur Kunstgeschichte, 86; Turner and the steam revolution, Gazette des Beaux-Arts, 7-8/88; Love and Duty: J M W Turner and the Aeneas Legend, Zeitschrift fur Kunstgeschichte, 90; The Theatre of Light: J M W Turner's Vision of Medea and Regulus, Gazette des Beaux-Arts, 5-6/92; Pigment into Light: J M W Turner and Goethe's "Theory of Colours", European Romantic Review, summer 91; and others. *Mailing Add:* c/o Queen's Univ Dept Art Kingston ON K7L 3N6 Canada

FINN, DAVID
PHOTOGRAPHER
b New York, NY, Aug 30, 21. *Study:* City Col of Univ New York, BA. *Exhib:* Oceanic Sculptures, Metrop Mus of Art, New York, 74; Henry Moore Photographs, l'Orangerie, Paris, France, 77. *Collections Arranged:* Exploring Sculpture, Canova (auth, catalog), & Cellini, Andrew Crispo Gallery, New York; Henry Moore Sculpture and Environment (photographs), Fischer Fine Art Ltd, London, 77; Large Two Forms (auth, catalog), Fairweather-Hardin Gallery, Chicago; Henry Moore, Am Cult Ctr, Madrid. *Awards:* Herbert Adams Mem Medal, Nat Sculpture Soc. *Mem:* MacDowell Colony (mem bd); Artists for Environ Found (mem bd); Int Ctr of Photog (mem bd dir & trustees); Parsons Sch of Design (mem bd overseers). *Publ:* Auth, Sculpture at Storm King, 79 & New Rochelle, Portrait of a City, 80, Abbeville Press; auth, The Florence Baptistery Doors, Viking Press, 80; auth, Henry Moore at the British Museum, Brit Mus Publ Ltd, 81; Monumental Greek Bronze Sculpture, Abbeville Press, 83. *Mailing Add:* c/o Salvatore Ala Gallery 560 Broadway New York NY 10012

FINN, DAVID
SCULPTURE
b Urbana, Ill, 1952. *Exhib:* Solo exhibs, Newspaper Children, Overland Theatre, Mass Col Art, Boston, 82, Salvatore Ala Gallery, New York, 87, Third Eye Ctr, Glasgow, New Gallery, Bemis Found, Omaha, Nebr, 88, City Contemp Gallery, Kowloon, Hong Kong 89, Salvatore Ala Gallery, New York, 86, Mass Col Art, Boston, 87, Masked Figures, Scottish Arts Coun Traveling Gallery, Edinburgh, Scotland & Weatherspoon Art Gallery, Univ NC Greensboro, 90, Atrium Gallery, Univ Conn, Storrs, 91, Watermans Art Centre, London & Leeds City Art Gallery, 92; Art on Paper 1989, Weatherspoon Art Gallery, Univ NC, Greensboro, 90; Lost and Found, Sculpture Ctr, New York, 91; de'Persona, Oakland Mus Art, Calif, 91; Disjuntive, Valencia Community Col Gallery, Orlando, Fla, 91; Assemblage, Southern Ctr Contemp Art, Winston-Salem, NC, 92. *Bibliog:* Chuck Twardy (auth), VCC Show: Compelling Social Comment, Orlando Sentinel, 8/28/91; RECYCLED: Assemblage is stylish nod to modernity, Winston-Salem J, 3/29/91; Margaret Shearin (auth), From Trash to Art, 4/29/92 & More Art from the Everyday, 5/6/92, Style mag. *Mailing Add:* 2200 Faculty Dr Winston-Salem NC 27106

FINNEGAN, SHARYN MARIE
PAINTER
b New York, NY, Aug 16, 46. *Study:* Art Students League, New York; Acad de Belli Arti, Rome, Italy; Marymount Col, Tarrytown, NY, BFA; NY Univ, studied with Esteban Vicente, MA. *Exhib:* Report from Soho, Grey Art Gallery, New York, 75; Artists' Choice: Figurative Art in New York, Bowery Gallery, and four others, New York, 76; one-woman exhibs, Roswell Mus & Fine Arts Ctr, NMex, 77, Prince St Gallery, 74, 75, 77, 80, 86 & 89 & Interiors, One Penn Plaza, 86, New York; Painted Light, Queens Mus, 83. *Pos:* Gallery coordr, Prince St Gallery, New York, 74-75 & 77-79. *Teaching:* Instr art & art hist, Parsons Sch Design, New York. *Awards:* Artist-in-residence, Roswell Mus & Fine Arts Ctr, 76; Palisades Artist-in-Residence, NY, summer 79; Residency, MacDowell Colony, Peterborough, NH, 79. *Bibliog:* J Mellow (auth), Rev, New York Times, 1/74; P Frank (auth), Rev, Soho Weekly News, 1/74; J Dreiss (auth), Rev, Arts Mag, 4/74, 3/78 & 4/81; Ellen Lubel (auth), Views by Women Artists, NY Women's Caucus for Art, 82; and others. *Mem:* Women in the Arts, New York; Col Art Asn. *Media:* Oil, Gouache. *Publ:* Claire Moore, Women's Art Jrnl, Spring/Summer 81. *Dealer:* Prince St Gallery 121 Wooster St New York NY 10012. *Mailing Add:* 5550 Fieldston Rd No 9E Bronx NY 10471-2532

FIORE, JOSEPH A
PAINTER, INSTRUCTOR
b Cleveland, Ohio, Feb 3, 25. *Study:* Black Mountain Col, with Josef Albers, Ilya Bolotowsky & William De Kooning, 46-48; Calif Sch Fine Arts, 48-49. *Work:* Whitney Mus Am Art, Chase Manhattan Collection, New York; Corcoran Gallery, Washington, DC; Colby Mus, Waterville, Maine; State Mus Art, Raleigh, NC. *Exhib:* Whitney Mus Am Art Ann, 59; solo exhibs, Staempfli Gallery, 60, Schoelkopf Gallery, 65 & 69, Green Mountain Gallery, 73, John B Myers Gallery, 74 & Fischbach Gallery, 77 & 81; Six Maine Artists, Farnsworth Mus, Rockland, 83; Art at Black Mountain, Grey Gallery, New York Univ, 87. *Teaching:* Instr painting & drawing, Black Mountain Col, 49-56, chmn dept art, 51-56; instr painting, Philadelphia Col Art, 62-70 & Md Inst Col Art, 70-75; vis instr, Artists Environ Found, NJ, 72-83; instr

landscape painting, Nat Acad Design, NY, spring 79 & Parsons Summer Painting Prog, France, 80; resident critic, Vt Studio Sch, Johnson, 87. *Awards:* First Prize, Metrop Young Artists First Ann, Nat Arts Club, 58; Hassam-Speicher Fund Purchase Award, 81; Nettie M Jones Fel, Ctr Music, Drama & Art, Lake Placid, 83. *Bibliog:* Fairfield Porter (auth), The Oriental in American Art, Art in its Own Terms, Taplinger, 79; Mary E Harris (auth), The Arts at Black Mountain College, MIT Press, 87; Patrick E White (auth), The Black Mountain connection, Arts Journal, 6/87. *Mem:* Assoc mem, Nat Acad Design. *Media:* Oil, Watercolor. *Mailing Add:* 178 W 82nd St New York NY 10024

FIORE, ROSARIO RUSSELL
SCULPTOR
b New York, NY, Jan 5, 08. *Study:* Nat Acad Design; Beaux Arts Inst Fine Arts; Mech Inst. *Work:* Ft Dobbins, Ga; Home of Pres Suharto. *Comn:* Bronze sculptures, Interior Dept, Washington, DC, US Air Force, Ft Dobbins, Ga, Freeport Minerals Co, New York, White House, Washington, DC & Cornell Univ; heroic size bronze statue of Gen George C Marshall, Leesburg, Va; white bronze sculpture, Teamster Int Bldg, Washington, DC. *Exhib:* Grand Central Art Gallery & Archit League, New York; Montclair Exhib, NJ; Westchester Art Gallery, NY; Corcoran Art Gallery, Washington, DC. *Pos:* Visual info officer, US Army Exhibs, 42-47. *Teaching:* Instr sculpture, Jekyll Island Art Ctr, 69-70 & Glynn Art Ctr, St Simons, 70-72, Ga. *Awards:* Nat Acad Prize, 30; Anna V Huntington Award, Nat Acad, 31. *Mem:* Jekyll Art Ctr (vpres, 75); Ga Coun for Arts Panel; Nat Sculpture Soc. *Media:* All. *Publ:* Auth, Fundamentals of Clay Modeling, House of Little Books, 46. *Mailing Add:* 5 Nelson Lane Jekyll Island GA 31520

FIRESTEIN, CECILY BARTH
PRINTMAKER
b Brooklyn, NY, Apr 25, 33. *Study:* Art Students League, Adelphi Univ, BA, 53; with Hans Hofmann, New York, 54; New York Univ, cert advanced study, 58, MA, 55. *Work:* Corcoran Gallery Art, Washington, DC; Delaware Mus Art Wilmington; Lufthansa Airlines, WGer; Deutsche Bank, WGer; Newark Mus, NJ; Cincinnati Mus Art; Yale Univ Art Gallery, New Haven, Conn; Columbia Mus, SC; Rose Art Mus, Waltham, Mass; Skirball Mus, Los Angeles, Calif. *Comn:* Edition of rubbings & poster, Cathedral of St John the Divine, New York, 74 & 80; illustrations for handbook, The Central Synagogue, NY, 78 & 79; rubbing of monument, Tarrytown Historical Soc, NY, 79; art deco door, Miami Design Preservation League, Miami, Fla, 80; rubbing illusration for notepapers, South Street Seaport Mus, New York, 81. *Exhib:* One-woman shows, Phoenix Gallery, New York, 62-92, In Loving Memory, Mus City New York, 78, South Street Seaport Mus, New York, 81, Spanish Inst, New York, 83 Farleigh Dickenson Univ, 92; Galerie Meissner, Hamburg, Ger, 83; and many others. *Pos:* Printmaker & art consult, District 24, Valley Stream, NY, 53-60; arts coordr, Cent Synagogue NY, 75-78; Critic, Artspeak, 82-90. *Teaching:* Lectr, many univ, 72-82; instr/lectr rubbings, Cooper Hewitt Mus, NY, 80, South Street Seaport Mus, New York, 81 & Parsons Sch Design, New York, 83, Univ SC, 89, Ym, YMHA New York City, 90. *Awards:* Traveling Exhib Am Art, Am Fedn Arts, 68; Grant, Unique New York, Nat Coun Arts, 74; Artist-in-Residence, Bronx Co Hist Soc, 75-81; Kappa Delta Pi. *Bibliog:* Angela Taylor (auth), She teaches a modern form of an ancient art, New York Times, 76; Jerry Talmer (auth), Art among the headstones, New York Post, 78; Barbara B Buchholz, article, House & Garden Guides, 79. *Mem:* Life mem Art Students League; NY Soc Women Artists. *Publ:* Auth & illusr, Rubbing Craft, Quick Fox, NY, 77; Rub a Landmark, Nat Trust Hist Preserv, 78; Rubbing brass & stone, New World Book of Knowledge, Grolier, Inc, 80; The Art of making rubbings, Seaport Mag, 80; Reach Out and Touch Something, New York Daily News, 88. *Dealer:* Phoenix Gallery Inc 568 Broadway New York NY; Galerie Meissner Edition Lemsahler Dorfstrasse 51 Hamburg 65 WGer. *Mailing Add:* 8 E 96th St New York NY 10128

FIRESTONE, EVAN R
ADMINISTRATOR, HISTORIAN
b Richmond, Va, Nov 21, 40. *Study:* Kent State Univ, BA, 62; Univ Wis-Madison, MA, 65, PhD, 71. *Teaching:* From instr to assoc prof, Southeastern Mass Univ, 68-77, chmn, dept art hist, 73-77; prof & head, dept art, Western Carolina Univ, 77-83 & Univ Ga; prof & chmn, dept art & design, Iowa State Univ, 83-90. *Awards:* Throne-Aldrich Award, State Hist Soc Iowa, 92. *Res:* Nineteenth and twentieth century art, especially abstract expressionism and art since 1940. *Publ:* Auth, John Linnell: The eve of the deluge, Cleveland Mus Art Bull, Vol 62, 4/75; Herman Melville's Moby Dick and the abstract expressionists, Vol 55, No 7, 3/80, James Joyce and the first generation New York school, Vol 56, No 10, 6/82 & In praise of steel: Notes on some recent direct-metal sculpture, Vol 60, No 4, 4/86, Arts Mag; Incursions of modern art in the regionalist heartland, Palimpsest, Vol 72, No 3, fall 91; and many others. *Mailing Add:* Dept Art Univ Ga Athens GA 30602-4102

FIRESTONE, SUSAN PAUL
ASSEMBLAGE ARTIST, PAINTER
b Madison, Wis, Nov 13, 46. *Study:* Mary Baldwin Col, BA, 68; Am Univ, MA, 73; Pa Acad Fine Arts, 69-71; Skowhegan Sch, 72. *Work:* Corcoran Gallery Art, Nat Mus Women Arts, Peat Marwick & Riggs Nat Bank, Washington, DC. *Exhib:* Step by Step Collage, George Mason Univ, Fairfax, Va, 89; From Potomac to Anacostia, Washington Project Arts, Washington, DC, 89; Tools as Art, Heckilger Col, Nat Bldg Mus, Washington, DC, 89; Sculpture 89, Washington Sq, Washington, DC, 89; Int Sculpture Conference, 90; 24th Univ Del Open exhib, 90; Fairfax Coun Arts, Biennial, 90; Sculpture on the Grounds '92, Rockville Cultural Arts Comn; 17th National, Print Club of Albany; Spare Parts, Marine Midland Bank, New York; Diane Ferris Gallery, Vancouver, Can; Prints '92, Corcoran Gallery Art, Washington, DC. *Pos:* Acquisitions, Corcoran Gallery, 84; Collectors Comns, 85-90. *Awards:* Geico Award for Painting, Corcoran Sch Art, 78; First Prize, Washington Sq Lawyers, 89. *Mem:* Artist Equity; Art Table; Washington Sculptors Group. *Media:* Acrylic, Metal; Miscellaneous Media. *Mailing Add:* 2320 Wyoming Ave NW Washington DC 20008

FIRFIRES, NICHOLAS SAMUEL
PAINTER
b Santa Barbara, Calif, Nov 10, 17. *Study:* Los Angeles Art Ctr; Otis Art Inst, Los Angeles. *Work:* Riveredge Found Mus, Calgary, Can; Santa Barbara Hist Mus, Calif; Southwest Mus, Los Angeles; Univ Wyo Mus, Laramie. *Exhib:* Cowboy Artists Am, Cowboy Hall of Fame & Ariz Mus Art, 66-77; Western Art Show, San Antonio, Tex, 68-77; Stamford Art Found Exhib, Tex, 74-77; Trailside Galleries, Scottsdale, Ariz, 77; De Silva Gallery, Santa Barbara, Calif, 77. *Bibliog:* Ed Ainsworth (auth), The Cowboy in Art, World Publ Co, 68; Dorothy Harmsen (auth), Harmsen's Western Americana, Northland Press, 71; Royal B Hassrick (auth), Western Painting Today, Watson-Guptill, 75. *Media:* Oil, Watercolor. *Publ:* Illusr, The Vaquero, 64 & Conquering the Frontiers, 74. *Mailing Add:* 1330 Pepper Lane Santa Barbara CA 93108

FIRSTENBERG, JEAN
DIRECTOR
Study: Boston Univ, BS(summa cum laude), 58. *Pos:* Dir, Am Film Inst, 80-; dir, Trans-Lux Corp, currently; advisory boards, Big Sisters of LA, Will Rogers Inst & Scott Newman Found, currently; Trustee, Boston Univ. *Awards:* Alumni Award, Boston Univ, 82; Women in Film Crystal Award, Women in Film, Los Angeles, 90. *Mem:* Acad Motion Picture Arts & Sci; Women in Film; Women's Trusteeship for Betterment of Women. *Mailing Add:* American Film Inst Ctr for Advanced Film & Television Studies 2021 N Western Ave Los Angeles CA 90027

FISCH, ARLINE MARIE
JEWELER, EDUCATOR
b Brooklyn, NY. *Study:* Skidmore Col, BS(art); Univ Ill, Urbana, MA(art); Fulbright student grant to Denmark, 56-57; Fulbright res grant to Denmark, 66-67; Sch Arts & Crafts, Copenhagen, Denmark; also with Bernhard Hertz Guldvaerefabrik, Copenhagen. *Work:* Victoria & Albert Mus, London; Vatican Mus, Rome; Am Craft Mus New York; Royal Scottish Mus, Edinburgh; Schmuckmus, Pforzheim. *Exhib:* Schmuck-Objekte, Mus Bellerive, Zurich, Switz, 71; Goldsmith, 74, 76 & 79; Tokyo Int Jewelry Art Exhib, 77, 80 & 83; Mus Für Angewandt Kunst, Vienna, 82; Jewelry USA, 84; plus many solo exhibs. *Pos:* Trustee, Am Craft Coun, 72-75; bd dirs, Haystack Mt Sch Crafts, 73-82 & 91-; vpres, World Crafts Coun, 77-81; pres, SNAG, 82-85. *Teaching:* Instr design & weaving, Skidmore Col, 58-61; prof jewelry & weaving, San Diego State Univ, 61-; guest lectr design, Guldsmedshojskole, Copenhagen, Denmark, 67 & 71; vis lectr, Crafts Coun of Australia, 75; vis prof, Boston Univ, 75-76; Fulbright lectr, Inst Applied Arts, Vienna, Austria, 82. *Awards:* Gold Medal, Int Handicraft Fair, Munich, 71; Distinguished Alumni Award, Skidmore Col, 86; Living Treasure of Calif Declaration, 85. *Bibliog:* J Keefer Bell (auth), Metalsmith, summer 88; Dormer & Turner (auth), The New Jewellery, 85; Wendy Ramshaw (auth), American Craft, 4-5/86; and others. *Mem:* World Crafts Coun (dir, 74-76, vpres for N Am, 76-81); founding mem Soc N Am Goldsmiths (pres, 82-); fel Am Crafts Coun (Calif rep, southwest regional assembly, 69-72, craftsman-trustee, 72-75); Allied Craftsmen San Diego. *Publ:* Auth, Textile Techniques in Metal, Van Nostrand Reinhold, 75; Contemporary Dutch Jewelry, 4/91 & Ronald Pearson, Silversmith, 6/92, Am Craft. *Mailing Add:* 4316 Arcadia Dr San Diego CA 92103

FISCHER, HAL (HAROLD ALAN)
WRITER, CONSULTANT
b Kansas City, Mo, Dec 18, 50. *Study:* Univ Ill, Champaign-Urbana, BFA, 73; San Francisco State Univ, with Jack Welpott, MA, 76; Univ Calif, San Diego, with David Antin, MFA, 88. *Exhib:* Photo-Linguists, Santa Barbara Mus Art, Calif, 77; Camerawork Gallery, San Francisco, 78; Photographs and Words, San Francisco Mus Mod Art, 81; Photography in California, 1945-1980, San Francisco Mus Mod Art, 84. *Pos:* Contrib ed, Artweek, 77-83; reviewer, Artforum, 78-82; develop assoc, Fine Arts Mus, San Francisco, 82-84; develop consult, Timken Mus Art, 85-, Asian Art Museum, 88-, San Francisco; develop consult, Asian Art Mus, 88. *Teaching:* Lectr photog, Calif Col Arts & Crafts, Oakland, 78-80; instr, City Col San Francisco, 79-82. *Awards:* Art Critics Fel, 77, Photogr Fel, 80, Critic-in-Residence Grant, 81, Art Writers Fel, 84, Nat Endowment Arts. *Bibliog:* Joan Murray (auth), Reading the structure of a subculture, 8/13/77 & Judith Dunham (auth), Messages on the skyline, 10/6/79, Artweek; Jeff Perrone (auth), Hal Fischer, Artforum, 10/19/77. *Mem:* Int Asn Art Critics. *Res:* Contemporary photography and art. *Publ:* Auth, Gay Semiotics, 78; 18th Near Castro, 79; contribr, The Still Photograph: The Problematic Model, NFS Press, 81; auth, Don Worth: Photographs 1955-1985, Friends of Photog, 86. *Mailing Add:* Ten Lyon Street No 211 San Francisco CA 94117

FISCHER, HENRY GEORGE
HISTORIAN, CURATOR
b Philadelphia, Pa, May 10, 23. *Study:* Princeton Univ, BA, 45; Univ Pa, PhD, 55. *Pos:* Asst, Egyptian Sect, Univ Mus, Univ Pa, 49-56; from asst cur to cur, Dept Egyptian Art, Metrop Mus Art, New York, 58-70, Wallace cur Egyptology, 70-79, research cur, 79-91, cur emeri, 92- *Teaching:* Adj prof Egyptian art & lang, Inst Fine Arts, NY Univ, 62-79. *Mem:* Deutsches Archeologisches Inst; Egypt Explor Soc, London; Soc Francaise Egyptologie, Paris. *Res:* Palaeography; iconography; sculpture; minor arts of ancient Egypt.

Publ: Auth, Ancient Egyptian Representations of Turtles, 68, auth, Egyptian Studies II: The Orientation of Hieroglyphs, Part 1: Reversals, 77 & auth, Ancient Egyptian Calligraphy, 83, Metrop Mus Art; Dendera in the Third Millennium BC, J J Augustin, 69; coauth, Treasures of the Cairo Museum, Thames & Hudson, 70; L'e01criture et l'art de l'E01gypte ancienne, Presses Universitaires de France, 86. *Mailing Add:* RR 1 Box 389 Sherman CT 06784

FISCHER, JOHN
PAINTER, SCULPTOR
b Antwerp, Belg, Aug 11, 30; US citizen. *Study:* City Univ New York, 48-49. *Work:* Fond De Decoration Du Canton De Genève, Geneva, Switz; Univ Ky, Louisville; Everson Mus, Syracuse, NY. *Comn:* Decorative mural (20 ft), Keebler Co, Chicago, 69. *Exhib:* Jewelry by Contemp Artists, Mus Mod Art, New York, 67; The Baker's Art, Mus Contemp Crafts, New York, 68; solo shows, Everson Mus, Syracuse, 72, NY Cult Ctr, New York, 73 & Musée Cantonal, Lausanne, Switz, 87; one-man retrospective, Scholoss Hardenberg, Velbert, Ger, 83; Community Arts Special Events Festivals at various galleries, mus, parks & many other locations, 1960-70. *Media:* Oil, Computer; Bread. *Dealer:* Brö & Kase Galerie L'Anciene Laiterie Soral Geneva Switz. *Mailing Add:* 75 Warren St New York NY 10007

FISCHER, MILDRED (GERTRUDE)
DESIGNER, CRAFTSMAN
b Berkeley, Calif, Sept 15, 07. *Study:* Mt Holyoke Col, AB; Wiener Kunstgewerbe Schule; Art Inst Chicago; Cranbrook Acad Art; Wetterhoff Inst, Finland, cert in tapestry; tapestry with Martta Taipale, Finland & Else Halling, Oslo, Norway; papermaking with Eishiro Abe, Japan. *Work:* Mus Contemp Crafts, New York; Scripps-Howard Inc; Cincinnati Bell; Federated Dept Stores, Inc; Cincinnati Art Mus. *Exhib:* Woven Hall Hangings by Eleven Americans, circulated by Victoria & Albert Mus, London, 62-63; Ohio Designer Craftsmen, Ohio Fedn Arts, 79-85; Paper '84 Int Invitational, Creative Arts Wkshp, New Haven, Conn, 84; Contemporary Paperwork of the 80's, Hurlbutt Gallery, Greenwich Libr, Conn, 84; The Best of 1989, Columbus Cult Art Ctr; Miami Univ Art Mus; and others. *Teaching:* Asst prof art & head dept, Knox Col, 46-49 & Lindenwood Col, 52-55; assoc prof emer fine arts, Univ Cincinnati Col Design, Archit & Art, 55-72. *Awards:* Centennial Award in Fine Arts, Mt Holyoke Col Alumnae Asn, 72; Award, Cincinnati Art Mus Awards Exhib, 75; Achievement Award, 78 & Spec Merit Award, Best Show, 85, Ohio Designer Craftsmen; Award, Mid Am Col Art Asn, 89. *Bibliog:* B J Foreman (auth), The Fischer papers, Cincinnati Enquirer Sunday Mag, 6/25/78; James Duesing & Chris Lewis, A Legacy: Living Archives citing 4 Cincinnati artists, video, Cincinnati Hist Soc, 87. *Mem:* Ohio Designers-Craftsmen; Am Crafts Coun. *Media:* Handmade Paper; Monoprints. *Mailing Add:* 1002 Evergreen Ridge Dr Cincinnati OH 45215-5701

FISCHER, R M
SCULPTOR
b New York, NY, Mar 21, 47. *Study:* Long Island Univ, NY, BA, 71; San Francisco Art Inst, Calif, MFA, 73. *Work:* Whitney Mus Am Art; Dallas Mus Art; Cincinnati Art Mus; Tamayo Museo Mexico City; Mus Mod Art, NY. *Comn:* Double gateway to park, comn by MacArthur Park Proj, Los Angeles, Calif, 85; Rector Gate, Battery Park City, NY, 89; State House clock, Boston, Mass, 90; Brooklyn Balters Tunnel Clock, New York, 92. *Exhib:* One-man show, Contemp Arts Ctr, Cincinnati, Ohio, 81, Whitney Mus Am Art, 84, Musee de La Ville de Toulon, France, 84, Inst Contemp Art, Boston, Mass, 85; Whitney Mus Am Art, 83, 85 & 88; Chicago Sculpture Int, 85; Fundaca Bienal de Sao Paulo, Brasil, 85; Lafonet Mus, Tokyo, 85; High Style, Whitney Mus Am Art, 85; Modern Detour, Wiener Secession, Vienna, Austria, 90 & Sidney Janis Gallery, 91. *Teaching:* Instr, Sch Visual Arts, NY, 85 & 86 & Skowhegan Sch Painting & Sculpture, 87. *Awards:* Nat Endowment Arts, 81 & 86; Creative Artists Pub Serv Fel, 82; Tiffany Found, 83. *Bibliog:* Suzanne Stesin (auth), Home Furnishings, 82; Denise Domerque (auth) Artist Design Furniture, 85; Dan Cameron (auth), High-Tech Redux, Flash Art, summer 88. *Mem:* Found Community Artists. *Media:* All media. *Dealer:* Texas Gallery Houston TX; Donald Young Gallery Seattle Washington. *Mailing Add:* 12 Warren Street New York NY 10007

FISCHER, VICTOR
GALLERY DIRECTOR
US citizen. *Study:* Univ Calif, Berkeley; Calif Sch Fine Arts; Calif Col Arts & Crafts. *Collections Arranged:* Brook House Sculpture Invitational at Kaiser Ctr, Oakland, Sculptors of Brook House, Palo Alto Cult Ctr, California Sculpture Inside-Out, Brook House Gallery, 12th Int Sculpture Conf, Oakland, 82; Sculpture at Civic Ctr, Walnut Creek, Calif, 85; and others. *Pos:* Mem panel, Calif Arts Coun Advisory Panel, Art in Public Buildings Prog, 83-85; dir, Victor Fischer Galleries, Oakland, Calif, currently. *Mailing Add:* 1300 Clay St Suite 600 Oakland CA 94612

FISCHL, ERIC
PAINTER
b New York, NY, 1948. *Study:* Calif Inst Arts, Valencia, BFA, 72. *Work:* Metrop Mus Art & Dominique DeMenil, New York. *Exhib:* Kunsthalle, Mary Boone, New York; solo exhibs, Inst Contemp Art, London, 85, Whitney Mus, New York, 86, Univ Art Mus, Long Beach, Calif, 86 Galerie Michael Werner, Koln, WGer, 88, Walker Art Ctr, Minneapolis, Minn, 90, Cleveland Ctr Contemp Art, Ohio, 90 & Montgomery Mus Fine Arts, Ala, 92; Biennial, Whitney Mus, New York, 85 & 91; Mus Art, Ft Lauderdale, Fla, 86; Cincinnati Art Mus, Ohio, 86; Ludwig Mus, Koln, WGer, 86; Mus Contemp Art, Los Angeles, 86; Michael Kohn Gallery, Los Angeles, 86; Inst Contemp Arts, London, Eng, 87; Los Angeles Co Art Mus, 87; Sara Hilden Art Mus, Tampere, Finland, 88; Whitney Mus Art at Equitable Ctr, New York, 89; Inst Contemp Art, Philadelphia, Pa, 91; Aldrich Mus Contemp Art, Ridgefield, Conn, 92; and many others. *Bibliog:* Phoebe Hoban (auth), Artists on the beach, New York Mag, 7/1/91; Kristine McKenna (auth), Cozy Connection, Los Angeles Times, 2/2/92; Phyllis Braff (auth), On the ocean fair and or at seasides here and in Euorpe, New York Times, Long Island Weekly, 8/2/92. *Mailing Add:* c/c Mary Boone Gallery 417 W Broadway New York NY 10012

FISH, ALICE GROSS See Gross, Alice

FISH, GEORGE A
PAINTER
b Cornwall, Eng; US citizen. *Study:* Nat Acad Design; Art Students League; Grand Cent Sch Art. *Comn:* Calendar Art for Provident Mutual Insurance Co, Philadelphia, 72 & NY Life Insurance Co, 73. *Exhib:* Audubon Artists, Allied Artists Am & Am Watercolor Soc Shows, Nat Acad Galleries, New York; Nat Arts Club & Salmagundi Club, New York; and many others. *Awards:* Nell Broadman Scholar, Washington Sq Outdoor Art Exhib, 66; Purchase Award, Salmagundi Club, 67; Best in Show, Hudson Artists, 68; and many others. *Mem:* Salmagundi Club; Am Watercolor Soc; Allied Artists Am; life mem Ariz Watercolor Asn; Am Artists Prof League; plus others. *Media:* Watercolor. *Mailing Add:* San Ridge 12221 W Bell Rd Surprise AZ 85374

FISH, JANET I
PAINTER
b Boston, Mass, May 18, 38. *Study:* Smith Col, BA; Yale Sch Art & Archit MFA; Skowhegan Summer Sch. *Work:* Whitney Mus Am Art, New York; Dallas Mus Art, Tex; Metrop Mus Art, New York; Art Inst Chicago; Pa Acad Fine Arts; and others. *Exhib:* Art Inst Chicago, 72 & 74; Am Drawings 1963-1973, Whitney Mus Am Art, 73; Philadelphia Mus Art, 74; The Liberation, Corcoran Gallery, Washington, DC & US Info Agency Traveling Exhib, Europe, 76-77; Am 76 (traveling exhib), Brooklyn Mus, NY & US Dept Interior, 76-78; Eight Contemp Am Realists, Pa Acad Fine Arts & NC Mus Art, 77; Butler Inst Am Art, 79; At the Table, Taft Mus, Seattle, Wash, 89; 300 Years of Still Life, Michael Kohn Gallery, Los Angeles, Calif; Collector's Annual, Contemporary Art, Boca Raton Mus Art, Fla, 90; Aspects of Summer, Marianne Friedland Gallery, Toronto, Can, 90; Selections from the Glenn C James Collection, Spiva Art Mus, Joplin, Ohio; and others. *Pos:* Bd governors, Skowhegan Sch Painting & Sculpture; bd governors, Marie Walsh Sharpe Art Found. *Awards:* MacDowell Fel, 68, 69 & 72; Harris Award, Chicago Biennale, 74; Australia Coun Arts Grant, 75; Hubbard Mus Award, 91. *Bibliog:* Garret Henry (auth), Janet Fish, Burton Skina Publ. *Mem:* Artists Equity. *Media:* Oil, Watercolor. *Dealer:* Robert Miller 724 Fifth Ave New York NY 10019. *Mailing Add:* 101 Prince St New York NY 10012

FISH, RICHARD G
DESIGNER, PAINTER
b Philadelphia, Pa, Apr 7, 25. *Study:* Univ Pa, BA(appl arts); Philadelphia Mus Sch Art, with Azio Martinelli, dipl(advert design); Haverford Col. *Work:* Frito Lay Corp; Col Southwest Art, Dallas, Tex; Rocky Mountain Nat Park, Colo. *Comn:* Paintings, Dravo Corp, Pittsburgh, Pa, 69; Caleco, West Chester, Pa, 79-86. *Exhib:* One-man shows, Gross-McCleaf Gallery, Philadelphia, 75, 78 & 83; Del Art Mus, Wilmington, 68-70; Butler Inst Am Art, Youngstown, Ohio, 68, 70 & 74; Norfolk Mus Art, Va, 69; Philadelphia Mus Art, 69; Cummer Gallery Art, Jacksonville, Fla, 69; Munson Gallery, Santa Fe, NMex, 84, 89 & 90; and others. *Pos:* Freelance designer & owner, Richard Fish Assoc, Ardmore, 52- *Teaching:* artist-in-residence, Rocky Mountain Nat Park, Colo, 91-92. *Awards:* Gold Medal, Philadelphia Graphic Arts, 62-65 & 76; Gold Medal, Philadelphia Art Dirs, 65; Silver Medal, Pennational Arts Ann, State of Pa, 67. *Mem:* Print Club, Philadelphia. *Media:* Ink, Watercolor; Egg Tempera, Acrylic. *Publ:* Illusr, Life & Death of the Salt Marsh, Atlantic Little Brown, 69; One Day in Summer, Random House, 69; auth, The Artist in Scotland, Small World-Volkswagen of Am, 72; illusr, Pathways to Independence, Chatham Press, 75; Haym Salomon, Liberty's Son, Jewish Publ, 75; Return to Big Grass, Ducks Unlimited, 87. *Dealer:* Muson Gallery 225 Canyon Rd Sante Fe NM 87501. *Mailing Add:* 1733 Academy Lane Havertown PA 19083

FISHBURNE, ST JULIAN (LE ROY)
PAINTER
b Brooklyn, NY, Mar 2, 27. *Study:* Sch for Art Studies, 46-47; Contemp Art Sch, New York, 47-48. *Work:* Wilmington Art Mus, Del. *Exhib:* Ann exhibs, Nat Acad Design, New York, 55-82; 14th Ann Exhib, Audubon Artists, New York, 56; one-man show, Albany Inst History & Art, NY, 60 & 67; A Realistic View, Nat Arts Club, 61; Artists of the Upper Hudson, Albany Inst History & Art, New York, 63; 20 Representational Artists, State Univ New York at Albany, Buffalo & New Paltz, 69; Realism Now, Frank Caro Gallery, 89. *Teaching:* Instr drawing, Nat Acad Design, 79, floral painting, 90. *Awards:* Frank & Annie Shikler Prize, Nat Acad Design, 82. *Bibliog:* Elinor Lathrop Sears (auth), Pastel Painting, Watson/Guptill, 68; Drawings from the David Daniels Collection, Harvard, 68; Leonard Richmond & J Littlesons (coauths), Fundamentals of Pastel Painting, Watson/Guptill, 70. *Media:* Oil, Pastel. *Dealer:* Fer-Duc Inc P O Box 1303 Newburgh NY 12550. *Mailing Add:* 48 Jenkinstown Rd New Paltz NY 12561

FISHER, CAROLE GORNEY
PAINTER, SCULPTOR
b Minneapolis, Minn. *Study:* Minneapolis Col Art & Design, BFA, 64; Pa State Univ, MFA, 66. *Work:* Roanoke Fine Arts Ctr, Va. *Comn:* Print ed, Minn State Arts Coun, 70; sculpture, Univ Minn, Morris, 73. *Exhib:* Pa State

Univ, 72; Two Nations, Six Artists, Minn-Can, 74; Walker Art Ctr, Minneapolis, 74; Whitney Biennial Contemp Am Art, New York, 75; Woman as Viewer Exhib, Winnipeg Art Gallery, 75. *Pos:* Comnr, Minneapolis Art Comn, 75- *Teaching:* Instr printmaking & drawing, Minneapolis Col Art & Design, 68-69; artist in residence printmaking, Bemidji State Univ, 69-70; instr drawing, Col St Catherine, 73-82. *Bibliog:* Cindy Nemser (auth), Whitney Biennial, Changes, New York, 75; Amy Goldin (auth), The New Whitney Biennial, Art in Am, 5-6/75; Chris Kohlmann (auth), 1975 Whitney Biennial, Mid West Art, 5/75. *Mem:* Col Art Asn Am. *Media:* Miscellaneous. *Dealer:* One Hundred Eighteen: An Art Gallery 1007 Harmon Minneapolis MN 55400. *Mailing Add:* 2524 Stevens Ave S Apt 2 Minneapolis MN 55404

FISHER, JAMES DONALD
SCULPTOR, MUSEUM DIRECTOR
b Houghton, Mich, July 24, 38. *Study:* Corcoran Sch Art, with Richard Lahey, 56-61; George Washington Univ, 68-73, with H Irving Gates, BA, 71, MFA, 73. *Exhib:* Washington Area Exhib, Corcoran Gallery Art, Washington, DC, 67; Prince Georges Community Col, Largo, Md, 68. *Collections Arranged:* Dual Retrospective-Peter Hurd-Millard Sheets, Amarillo Art Ctr, 74, When You Say Cowboy-Survey of Western Art in Texas (with catalog), 74 & Elisabet Ney in Austin, 81. *Pos:* Technician Mus Hist & Technol, Smithsonian Inst, 60-68; dir, Amarillo Art Ctr, 73-77; dir, George Washington Carver Mus, Elizabeth Ney Mus & O Henry Mus, 77- *Teaching:* Grad teaching asst & asst prof lectr design & drawing, George Washington Univ, 71-73. *Mem:* Am Asn Mus. *Media:* Welded Steel, Vacuum-Formed Plastics. *Res:* 19th century industrial design and 20th century non-objective sculpture. *Publ:* Auth, Two Centuries of American Quilts and Coverlets, Amarillo Art Ctr, 76; coauth, Central Texas rural schs, Tex Heritage Mag, 87. *Mailing Add:* 1305 Bentwood Rd Austin TX 78722

FISHER, JOEL
SCULPTOR
b Salem, Ohio, June 6, 47. *Study:* Kenyon Col, AB(magna cum laude, phi beta kappa). *Work:* Mus Mod Art, New York; Stedelijk Mus Amsterdam; Victoria & Albert Mus, London, Eng; Tate Gallery, London; Ctr George Pompidou, Paris; Kunst Mus Bern, Switz. *Exhib:* One-man shows, Victoria & Albert Mus, London, 71, Stadt Mus Monchengladbach, 75, Mus Mod Art, Oxford, Eng, 77, Stedelijk Mus, Amsterdam, 78, Kunst Mus, Luzern, 84, Univ Art Mus Berkeley, 87, Diane Brown Gallery, 92, C Grimaidis Gallery, 92 & Int Bird Mus, South Hampton, NY, 92; Documenta V Kassel, 72; Representing Reality: Fragments from the Image Field, Crown Point Press, Oakland, Calif, 82; Between, John Weber Galllery, New York, 83; An International Survey of Contemporary Painting and Sculpture, Mus Mod Art, New York, 84; Spuren, Sculpturen and Monumente, Ihrer Prazisen Reise, Kunsthaus Zurich, 85; Structure to Remblance: 8 Sculptors, Albright Knox Gallery, Buffalo, 87; Four Am, Brooklyn Mus, 89. *Teaching:* Sch of Visual Arts, 89-90; Vt Studio Sch, 90; Parsons Sch of Design, 90-91; lectr, Boston Mus Sch; Royal Col Art, London; guest prof, Ecole des Beaux Arts, Paris, 91. *Awards:* Thomas J Watson Traveling Fel, 71; Prize, Wroclaw Drawing Triennale, 78; Nat Endowment Fel in Sculpture, 84; George A & Eliza Gardner Howard Found, 86-87. *Bibliog:* Simon Field (auth), Joel Fisher on Paper, Art & Artists, 1/72; Lisa Bear (auth), Strong as a Spider's Web, Avalanche, 12/74; Robin White (auth), View Mag, 81. *Mem:* Col Art Asn Am. *Publ:* Auth, Double Camouflage, Mansfield Fine Arts Ctr, 70; The Berliner Book, Berlin Kunstler Prog des DAAd, 73; Instances of Change, Bonomo Diffusione, Bari, Italy, 75; Dissolution, Stadt Mus Monchengladbach, 75; An Image in Blankness, Mus Mod Art, Oxford, 77. *Mailing Add:* 99 Commercial St Brooklyn NY 11222

FISHER, LEONARD EVERETT
PAINTER, ILLUSTRATOR
b Bronx, NY, June 24, 24. *Study:* With Moses Soyer, New York, 39; Art Students League, with Reginald Marsh, 41; Brooklyn Col, with Olindo Ricci & Serge Chermayeff, 41-42; Yale Univ Sch Fine Arts, BFA, 49, MFA, 50. *Work:* Butler Inst Am Art, Youngstown, Ohio; Libr of Cong, Washington, DC; Univ Ore, Eugene; Mt Holyoke Col, S Hadley, Mass; New Brit Mus Am Art, Conn. *Comn:* Am Bicentennial (four block eight cent commemorative postage stamps), 72, Legend of Sleepy Hollow (ten cent commemorative postage stamp), 74, Liberty Tree (thirteen cent embossed envelope), 75 & Skilled Hands for Independence (four block thirteen cent commemorative stamps), 77, US Postal Serv, Washington, DC. *Exhib:* Painters Panorama, Am Fedn Arts Sponsored Tour, 54-56; New Eng Painting Ann, Silvermine Guild Artists, 68, 69 & 71; Butler Inst Am Art, Youngstown, Ohio, 72; retrospective, New Brit Mus Am Art, Conn, 73 & Am Mus Illus, New York, 91; one-man shows, Rotunda, Free Libr Philadelphia, 76, Univ Hartford, Conn, 76, Gen Elec Corp, 76 & NY Hist Soc: 200 Yrs of Am Illus, 76; Soc Illustr Mus Am Illus, NY, 90-92. *Pos:* Illusr & auth, children's books for major publ, 54; deleg-at-large, White House Conf, Libraries & Info Serv, 79. *Teaching:* Dean studies, Whitney Sch Art, 51-53; instr art hist, painting, life drawing & bk illus, Paier Sch Art, 66-78, dean acad affairs, 77-81, dean emer, 82- *Awards:* Pulitzer Scholar Art, 50; Christopher Medal, New York, 81; Nat Jewish Book Award, New York, 81; Regina Medal, Cath Libr Asn, 91. *Bibliog:* Joan Hess Michel (auth), Leonard Everett Fisher, illustrator and painter, Am Artist, 9/66; Charles M Daugherty (ed), Six Artists Paint a Still Life, North Light, 77; Howard Munce (ed), Magic and Other Realism, Hastings House, 81. *Mem:* Soc of Illusr; Silvermine Guild Artists (bd dir 70-74); Authors Guild; PEN; Soc Children's Book Writers. *Media:* Acrylic, Soft Engraving. *Publ:* Auth & illusr, The Great Wall of China, Macmillan, 87; The White House, Holiday House, 89; Prince Henry the Navigator, Macmillan, 90; The Oregon Trail, Holiday House, 90; The ABC Exhibit, Macmillan, New York, 91; Tracks Across America, Holiday House, New York, 92; Galileo, Macmillan, New York, 92. *Mailing Add:* 7 Twin Bridge Acres Rd Westport CT 06880

FISHER, PHILIP C
PAINTER, ART DEALER
b Oil City, Pa, Nov 17, 30. *Study:* Graceland Col, 50; Univ of Nebr, 55; studied with Norman Rockwell, Stevan Dohanos, Albert Dorne & Al Capp, 58-61. *Work:* Sagendorf Int Dollhouse Mus. *Exhib:* Int Platform Asn Invitational Art Show, Hyatt Regency Hotel, Washington, DC, 86; The Great Colorado Showcase, Denver, 89. *Pos:* Cartoonist-illusr, 'Brenda Starr' syndicated comic strips, Chicago, Ill, 77-78; portrait artist, Omaha, Nebr & Denver, Colo, 80-88; art dealer, Fisher's Master Artists, Inc, Golden, Colo, 86-88. *Mem:* Am Portrait Soc; Int Platform Asn. *Media:* Oil on Linen. *Specialty:* Realist oils on canvas, portraiture, genre, landscapes, still lifes, seascapes, impressionism. *Publ:* An illustrated survey of leading contemporaries, Am Artists, Chicago, Ill, 89; An illustrated survey of the city's museums, galleries and leading Artists, New York Art Rev, 90. *Mailing Add:* 13325 W 15th Dr Applewood Golden CO 80401

FISHER, ROB (ROBERT NORMAN)
SCULPTOR, WRITER
b Cleveland, Ohio, May 28, 39. *Study:* Mass Inst Technol, with Gyorgy Kepes, BSc, 61; State Sch Design, Oslo, Norway, cert, 62; Univ Rome, Italy, cert, 63; Syracuse Univ, with Arthur Pulos, MS(indust design), 65. *Work:* Indianapolis Mus Art; Joslyn Art Mus, Omaha, Nebr; Apollo Plastics Collection, Chicago; Mus Art & Sci, Pa State Univ. *Comn:* A Page from the Book of skies, suspended sculpture, Medical Ctr, Saudi Arabia, 88-89; Environmental Sculpture; Osaka-Skyharp suspended sculpture, Osaka Hilton Int, Osaka, Japan, 86; Flying Fish (sculpture), Hammamatsu City Ctr, Japan, 90; Symphony of the Air (800' suspended sculpture), Scottsdale Fashion Sq Mall, Ariz, 90-91. *Exhib:* 14th Midwest Biennial, Joslyn Art Mus, Omaha, 69; Electra 83, Musee d'Art Modern, Paris, 83; One-man show, Computer-Aided-Environmental Sculpture, Recruite G-7 Gallery, Tokyo, Japan, 88; The Second Emerging Expression Biennial; The Artist and the Computer Bronx Mus Art, New York, 88; Creative Computers, USIA Traveling Exhib, 90; Computers & the Creative Process, Univ Ore Mus Art traveling show, 90; Infinite Illusions, Ripley Gallery, Smithsonian Inst, Washington, DC, 90; Computer Age Fine Art, Williams Gallery, Princeton, NJ, 92; NICAF Yokohama '92, Int Contemp Art Fair, Japan, 92. *Pos:* Res fel, Materials Res Lab, Pa State Univ, 82-; res affil, Ctr Advan Visual Studies, Mass Inst Technol, 83-; artist-in-residence, Col Engineering, Pa State Univ, 88; co-chmn, Computers & Sculpture Forum, Int Sculpture '92, Philadelphia, Pa, 92. *Teaching:* Dir, Visual Eng Lab, Penn State Univ, 89 & 90; invited lectr, Technology & Art, Japan & China 86, Nat Computer Graphics Asn, Calif, 87, 89 & 91, Inter Sculpture Symposium, Wash, DC, 90 & 2nd Int Symposium Electronic Art, Netherlands, 90; smithsonian studio arts lectr, Washington, Dc, 91; speaker, ACM-Siggraph, Los Vegas, Nev, 91; vis lectr, Taliesin West, Ariz, 92; artists in residence, Inst Studies in the Arts, Ariz State Univ, 92. *Awards:* Fulbright Fel to Norway in Design, 61-62; Third Award, Nat Sculpture Exhib, Southern Asn Sculpture, 69; Merit Award, Vietnam Vet Mem Competition, 81; Special Projects Fel Pa Coun Art, 86, 87 & 90; Fulbright Asn, 92. *Bibliog:* Richard Childers (auth), Infinite Illusions, 90; Lillian Schwartz (auth), the Computer Art Book, 92; television revs, CNN Science & Technology Report - Computer Sculpture, 89, Fandango, computer designed sculpture, 90; The Sculptor's Apprentice, Computer Graphics World, 8/91; High-Tech Sculpture, 3/92. *Mem:* Pa Coun on the Arts (spec proj panel, 84-87); Hist & Archit Rev Bd, Bellefonte, Pa, 76-86; Int Sculpture Asn, 87. *Media:* Metal, Plastic. *Publ:* Coauth, Understanding Visual Forms, Van Nostrand Reinhold, 76; Computer-aided sculpture, Leonardo, J Sci & Art, Pergamon Press, Oxford, Eng, 85; Escultura Asistida por Ordendor: Considerciones Visuales y Tecnicas, Telos, Spain, 86; Computer-aided Sculpture: Implications for the Design Professions, conf Proceedings, Nat Computer Graphics Asn, 87; Computers & Sculpture, Sculpture Mag, 91; producer & dir, The Computer: A New Tool for Sculptors (film), 92. *Mailing Add:* 228 N Allegheny St Bellefonte PA 16823

FISHER, SANDRA
PAINTER
b New York, NY, May 6, 47. *Study:* Chouinard Art Sch; Calif Inst Arts, BFA, 68. *Work:* British Mus & London Transport Mus, London, Eng; Graves Art Gallery, Sheffield, Eng; Nat Acad Design, New York; Metrop Mus Art. *Comn:* Portrait, Pembroke Col, Cambridge, Eng, 81; Poster, London Transport, Eng, 88; Portrait, Peterhouse, Cambridge, Eng, 90; Poster, London Transport, Eng, 91. *Exhib:* The Human Clay, Hayward Gallery, London, Eng, 76; The Open & Closed Book, Victoria & Albert Mus, London, Eng, 79; Representation Abroad, Hirshhorn Mus & Sculpture Garden, Washington, DC, 85; Die Spur des Anderen (Traces of Another Self), Heine Haus, Hamburg, Ger, 88; Summer Exhib, Royal Acad Arts, London, Eng, 92. *Pos:* Asst to dir, Gemini Graphics Editions Ltd, Los Angeles, Calif, 70-71. *Teaching:* Guest lectr art hist, Ruskin Sch Drawing, Oxford, Eng, 76-83; vis artist painting, Byam Shaw Sch Painting & Drawing, London, 83-84; guest lectr painting, St Martin's Sch Art, London, 86. *Bibliog:* Edward Lucie-Smith (auth), Sandra Fisher: A painter's progress, Art & Artists, 82; Joe Shannon (auth), Representation Abroad, Smithsonian Inst Press, 85; Marco Livingstone (auth), British Figurative Painters of the 80s II, Art Random, Japan, 89. *Media:* Oil. *Publ:* Illusr, Sappho, Coracle Press, London, 82 & Sonnets & Tableaux, 87. *Dealer:* Odette Gilbert Gallery 5 Cork St London W1X 1PB. *Mailing Add:* 80 Redcliffe Gardens London SW10 England United Kingdom

FISHER, SARAH LISBETH
CONSERVATOR
b Washington, DC, Nov 1, 45. *Study:* Wellesley Col, BA(art hist), 67; Florence, Italy, with pvt painting conservator, 67-68; Inst Technol Paintings,

Stuttgart, Ger, with Dr R Straub, 69-70; Swiss Inst Art Res, Zurich, Switz, with Dr T Brachert, cert in conserv, 72; with T Hermanes, Canton of Vaud, Switz, 69 & 70; Cent Inst Art Res, Amsterdam, Holland, with Dr J Mosk, 73; Inst Royal du Patrimoine Artistique, Brussels, Belg, with N Gortghebeur, cert in conserv, 75. *Pos:* Conservator & asst to the dir, Swiss Inst for Art Res, Zurich, Switz, 72-74; conservator, Intermus Lab, Oberlin, 75-77, Balboa Art Conserv Ctr, San Diego, Calif, 77-81 & Nat Gallery Art, Washington, DC, 81- *Teaching:* Instr painting conserv, Intermus Conserv Asn, Oberlin, Ohio, 75-77. *Mem:* Am Inst Conserv Hist & Artist Works; Int Inst Conserv Hist & Artistic Works; Western Asn Art Conserv; Washington Conserv Guild. *Publ:* Ed, Rubens' The finding of Erichthonius: Examination and treatment, Allen Mem Art Mus Bulletin, Oberlin Col, XXXVIII, No 1, 80-81. *Mailing Add:* Nat Gallery Art Fourth & Constitution Ave NW Washington DC 20565

FISHER, VERNON
CONCEPTUAL ARTIST
b Fort Worth, Tex. *Study:* Hardin-Simmons Univ, BA, 67; Univ Ill, MFA, 69. *Work:* Hershhorn/Smithsonian, Corcoran, Washington, DC; Guggenheim Mus & Mus Mod Art, New York; Albright-Knox, Buffalo. *Exhib:* Bronx Mus Arts, New York, 84; Hirshhorn Mus & Sculpture Garden, Washington, DC, 84; New Orleans Mus Art, La, 86; Brooklyn Mus, New York, 86; Walker Art Ctr, Minneapolis, Minn, 87; Los Angeles Co Mus Art, 87; Inst Contemp Arts, London, 87; solo exhib, Asher-Faure Gallery, Los Angeles, 86, Barbara Gladstone Gallery, New York, 87, Hiram Butler Gallery, Houston, Tex, 87, Lannan Mus, Lake Worth, Fla, 87, Fred Hoffman Gallery, Buffalo, NY, 89 & Hiram Butler Gallery, Houston, 90; Karsten Schubert Ltd, London, 89; Mus Fine Arts, Houston, 90; Asher-Faure Gallery, Los Angeles, 91; Rena Bransten Gallery, San Francisco, 92; and others. *Teaching:* Assoc prof art, Austin Col, Sherman, 69-78; prof art, NTex State Univ, 78- *Awards:* Visual Artist Award Grant, SECCA, 81, 88; Louis Comfort Tiffany Found Grant, 80-81, 84. *Bibliog:* John Habich (auth), Past/imperfect Proust marathon, Minneapolis Star & Tribune, 4/11/87; Colleen O'Conner (auth), High profile: Vernon Fisher, Dallas Morning News, 9/20/87; Gary Schwan (auth), Lannan's walls teach perspective, Palm Beach Post, 10/23/87. *Publ:* Ed, Five stories, No 2, winter-spring 79 & A childhood friend, No 4, summer 80, White Walls; The Paris Review, Paris Review Inc, Vol 23, No 80, summer 81; auth, Navigating By the Stars, Landfall Press, Chicago, 89; ed, Navigating by the stars, Neon, summer 92. *Mailing Add:* 1109 N Main Ft Worth TX 76106

FISHKO, BELLA
DEALER
b Russia; US citizen. *Study:* Hunter Col. *Pos:* Dir emer, Forum Gallery. *Mem:* Art Dealers Asn Am; Friends Whitney Mus Am Art; Mus Mod Art, New York; Benefactor, Metrop Mus Art. *Specialty:* American art of the 20th century, painting and sculpture. *Publ:* Contrib to var nat art mags. *Mailing Add:* 745 Fifth Ave, 5th floor New York NY 10151

FISKIN, JUDY
PHOTOGRAPHER, EDUCATOR
b Chicago, Ill, Apr 1, 45. *Study:* Pomona Col, with John Mason, BA, 66; Univ Calif, Berkeley, 66-67; Univ Calif, Los Angeles, MA(art hist), 69. *Work:* Bibliotheque Nat, Paris, France; Dallas Mus Fine Arts, Tex; Mus Contemp Art, La Jolla, Calif; Mus Fine Arts, Houston, Tex; Mus Contemp Art, Los Angeles. *Exhib:* Los Angeles in the 70's, Ft Worth Art Mus, Tex, 77; Group Material: Democracy, DIA Art Found, New York, 88; Typologies: Nine Contemporary Photographers, Newport Harbor Art Mus, Newport Beach, Calif, San Francisco Mus Mod Art, Akron Art Mus & Corcoran Gallery Art, Washington, DC, 91; Special Collections: The Photographic Order from Pop to Now, Int Ctr Photog, New York, 92; Judy Fiskin: Some Photographs, 1973-1992, Mus Contemp Art, Los Angeles, 92; solo shows, Desert Photographs, Castelli Graphics, New York, 76, Some Art, Curt Marcus Gallery, New York & Ashes-Faure Gallery, Los Angeles, 91. *Pos:* Co-dir, Womanspace Gallery, 73-74. *Teaching:* Instr photog, Calif Inst Arts, Valencia, 77-, assoc dean, 79-84. *Awards:* Nat Endowment Arts Grant, 80 & 90. *Bibliog:* Richard Armstrong (auth), Judy Fiskin's Photographs J S Calif Art Mag, 9-10/79; Robert L Pincus (auth), Judy Fiskin: some questions of aesthetics visions, winter 89; Terry R Myers (auth), Judy Fiskin, Arts, 4/91. *Mem:* Soc Photog Educ; Los Angeles Ctr Photog Studies. *Media:* Black & White. *Dealer:* Asher-Faure Gallery 612 N Almont Dr Los Angeles CA 90069. *Mailing Add:* c/o Calif Inst Arts 24700 McBean Parkway Valencia CA 91355

FITCH, GEORGE HOPPER
COLLECTOR, PATRON
b New York, NY, Nov 29, 09. *Study:* Yale Univ, BA, 32. *Pos:* Gov bd, Yale Univ Art Gallery; trustee emer, Fine Arts Mus San Francisco; comnr, Asian Art Mus, San Francisco, formerly. *Mem:* Mus Soc, De Young Mus & Calif Palace of Legion of Honor (chmn, 71-72); Art Comn City New York (vpres, 67-68); founder Art Collectors Club Am; fel Pierpont Morgan Libr (coun, 66-69); Munic Art Soc New York (dir, pres, 58-60); Am Fedn Arts (trustee, 53-74, first vpres, 55-64); Royal Oak Found (founding dir, 73-88, hon dir, 88-; Honorary (dir, 88-). *Interests:* Increasing art appreciation. *Collection:* Twentieth century American watercolors; East Indian miniatures; Melanesian dagger handles; African bobbins; photography. *Publ:* Auth, So You're Going to Heaven, 71. *Mailing Add:* 1960 Broadway San Francisco CA 94109

FITCH, STEVE (STEVEN RALPH)
PHOTOGRAPHER, INSTRUCTOR
b Tucson, Ariz, Aug 16, 49. *Study:* Univ Calif, Berkeley, BA, 71; San Francisco Art Inst, 77; Univ NMex, Albuquerque, MA, 78. *Work:* Mus Mod Art, New York; Mus Fine Arts, Boston; Fogg Art Mus; Oakland Mus; Houston Mus Fine Arts. *Exhib:* Light and Substance, Univ NMex Art Mus, Albuquerque, 73; solo exhib, Art Mus, Univ Calif, Berkeley, 75; Visitors to Arizona 1846 to 1980, Phoenix Art Mus, 80; The Aesthetics of Graffiti, 79 & Beyond Color, 80, San Francisco Mus Mod Art; Color as Form: History of Color Photography, George Eastman House, Rochester, NY, 82; Exposed & Developed: Photography Sponsored by Nat Endowment Arts, Smithsonian Inst, Nat Mus Am Art, 84; Marks & Measures: Linda Connor, Rick Dingus, Steve Fitch & Charles Roitz, Spencer Art Mus, Univ Kans, Lawrence, 85. *Teaching:* Instr, Assoc Students Univ Calif Studio, Berkeley, 71-77; teaching asst, Univ NMex, Albuquerque, 78-79; instr, Univ Colo, Boulder, 79-85; vis assoc prof, Univ Tex, San Antonio, fall 85; vis lectr, Princeton Univ, 86- *Awards:* Nat Endowment Arts Fel, 73, 75 & 81. *Bibliog:* Lois Fishman (auth), article, Creative Camera, 8/77; Jonathon Greene (auth), American Photography: A Critical History, Abrams, New York, 84; Rick Dingus (auth), article, Artspace Mag, spring 84. *Mem:* Soc Photog Educ. *Publ:* Auth, Diesels and Dinosaurs, Long Run Press, 76; contribr, photogs, Bombay Duck, 76, Creative Camera, 77 & Picture Mag, 79; Personal notes on teaching the history of photography, Exposure, 81. *Mailing Add:* Visual Arts Princeton Univ Princeton NJ 08544

FITERMAN, DOLLY
GALLERY DIRECTOR, COLLECTOR
b Minn. *Study:* Univ Minn; St Cloud Bus Col. *Pos:* Owner & dir, Dolly Fiterman Fine Arts; guest cur, Milton Avery Exhib, Boca Raton, Fla,. *Teaching:* Guest lectr, Univ Minn & Boca Raton Mus, Fla; lectr, Minneapolis Woman's Club. *Awards:* Eleanor Roosevelt Award, Women's Div, State of Israel, 85; App by Gov to Minn State Arts Bd, 91; Guest of USSR Cent Union of Artists at Tretyakov Mus, Moscow, 90. *Bibliog:* Daniel Farson (auth), Referenced in with Gilbert and George in Moscow, Minneapolis Star Tribune (cover story), 9/91; This Old Library, Minneapolis Skyway News, 9/91; Hello Dolly, St Paul Pioneer Press, 11/91. *Mem:* Minneapolis Inst Art; Univ Minn Art Mus; Walker Art Ctr, Minneapolis; Women's Asn Minn; Minn Opera Co. *Specialty:* Paintings; fine prints; sculpture--American and European. *Mailing Add:* Dolly Fiterman Fine Arts 100 University Ave SE Minneapolis MN 55414

FITZGERALD, ASTRID
PAINTER, PRINTMAKER
b Wil, Switz, July 28, 38; US citizen. *Study:* Col St Agnes, Fribourg, Switz, 55; Art Students League, New York, 62; Fashion Inst Technol, New York, 68; Pratt Graphics Ctr, New York, 72. *Work:* Aldrich Mus, Ridgefield, Conn; Wellesley Col, Mass; Marymount Col, Tarrytown, NY; Rockefeller Ctr Collection; Educ Mgt Ctr, Atlanta, Ga. *Comn:* Kindercare Corp, Montgomery, Ala; IBM, Boca Raton, Fla; Ashley Plaza Hotel, Tampa, Fla; Union Bank Switz, New York. *Exhib:* Albright-Knox Mus, Buffalo, NY, 73; Contemp Reflections, Aldrich Mus, 78; 57th Soc Am Graphic Artists Nat Exhib, Parsons Sch, NY, 79; Atlantic Gallery, New York, 80-81; Galerie Steinfels, Zurich, Switz; Jayne H Baum Gallery, New York, 82-83; Nohra Haime Gallery, New York, 85; Pietrasanta Fine Arts, New York, 86. *Awards:* Michael M Engel Mem Award, Nat Arts Club, New York, 73; Charles Levitt Award, Nat Asn Women Artists Ann, 78; Juror's Award, Fourth Ann Small Works Competition, NY Univ, 80. *Bibliog:* Roger Lipsey (auth), The Art of Astrid Fitzgerald-New Images, Old Faith, 85; Richard H Pichler (auth), Swiss Artist in New York, 85. *Media:* Pastel, Watercolor. *Publ:* Harmony by Design, Parabola, winter 91. *Dealer:* Art Options New York NY; Ellen Price New York NY. *Mailing Add:* 650 West End Ave New York NY 10025

FITZPATRICK, JOSEPH CYRIL
PAINTER, SCULPTOR
b Williamstown, Pa, Mar 14, 09. *Study:* Carnegie-Mellon Univ, Pittsburgh; Edinboro State Col, Pa, BS(art educ); Teachers Col, Columbia Univ, New York, MA; L'Ecole des Beaux Arts, Marseille, France. *Work:* Latrobe High Sch, Pa; Equitable Life Assurance Soc, New York. *Comn:* Oil paintings, Cats, Pittsburgh Playhouse Bd, 54, The Caliph, Univ Pittsburgh, 57 & Dejeuner, Pittsburgh Bd Pub Educ, 59; and many others. *Exhib:* Mountain Playhouse, Jennerstown, Pa, 53; Slippery Rock State Col, Pa, 68; Regional Art Exhib, Westmoreland Co Mus Art, Greensburg, Pa, 70-79; one-man show, Gallery Upstairs, Pittsburgh; many Assoc Artists Shows, Carnegie Mus, Pittsburgh. *Teaching:* Art supervisor & teacher, Pittsburgh Bd Pub Educ, now retired; art dir & teacher, Carnegie Inst. *Awards:* Man of the Yr in Art, Pittsburgh Jr CofC, 62; Teacher of the Yr, Allegheny Asn Lawyers' Wives, 70; Artist of the Yr, Arts & Crafts Ctr, Pittsburgh, 73. *Bibliog:* Sam Hood (auth), Fitzpatrick's world of art, 57 & George Swetnam (auth), Art in the Open, 60, Pittsburgh Press; Artist on the Spot (film), KDKA TV, Pittsburgh. *Mem:* Assoc Artists Pittsburgh; Pittsburgh Watercolor Soc (pres, 54-55); Pittsburgh Soc Sculptors; Nat Art Educ Asn; Nat Soc Arts & Lett. *Media:* Oil, Watercolor; Welded Steel. *Publ:* Auth, Knights armor, and teenagers, Carnegie Mag, 53; Art for the classroom, Pittsburgh Teachers Bulletin, 53. *Mailing Add:* 2707 Fifth Ave Pittsburgh PA 15213

FITZSIMONDS, CAROL STRAUSE
PRINTMAKER
b Richmond, Va, Mar 13, 51. *Study:* Hollins Col, Va, BA, 73; Art League Sch, Torpedo Factory Art Ctr, 84-85. *Work:* Libr Congress, Nat Mus Am Hist, Smithsonian Inst, Corcoran Mus Art & Nat Mus Women in Arts, Washington, DC; Heritage Plantation, Sandwich, Mass. *Exhib:* Boston Printmakers 40th N Am Print Exhib, Brockton Mus, Mass, 88; 38th Nat Exhib of Comtemp Realism, Acad Artists Asn, Springfield, Mass, 88; solo exhib, Prints & More Prints, Heritage Plantation, Sandwich, 89; 96th Ann Catharine Lorillard Wolfe Exhib, Nat Arts Club, New York, 92; Int Prints I

Competition, Int Monetary Fund Gallery, Washington, DC. *Pos:* Partner, Spectrum Gallery, Washington, DC, 85-87, Printmaker's Inc, Alexandria, Va, 86-87 & 92- & DeBlois Gallery, Newport, RI, 89-90. *Awards:* Hortene Fern Mem Award, 87; Leila Gardin Sawyer Award, 89; First Award in Graphics, Cape Cod Art Asn, 89. *Bibliog:* John Pantalone (auth), Artistic life of a traveling printmaker, Newport this Week, 5/4/89. *Mem:* Nat Asn Women Artists Inc; Catharine Lorillard Wolfe Art Club Inc; Newport Artist's Guild (pres, 89-90). *Media:* Aquatint Etching. *Publ:* Auth, Imagined journeys, J Print World, fall 89 & Eye Wash, 10/89. *Dealer:* Miriam Perlman Inc 474 N Lake Shore Dr Suite 5806 Chicago IL 60611. *Mailing Add:* 12332 Washington Brice Rd Fairfax VA 22033

FIX, JOHN ROBERT
SCULPTOR, SILVERSMITH
b Pittsburgh, Pa, Oct 31, 34. *Study:* Rochester Inst Technol, Sch Am Craftsmen, BFA; Conn Col, MAT; study with Lawrence G Copeland, Hans Christianson, William A McCloy & Frances Felten. *Comn:* Host box, Glenwood Lutheran Church, Minn, 57; chalice, St Andrew's Episcopal Church, New Kensington, Pa, 62; chalice, 68 & menorah, 71, Harkness Chapel, Conn Col, New London; altar set, St Paul's Episcopal Church, Westbrook, Conn, 79; plus many pvt comn in sculpture & metalsmithing. *Exhib:* Assoc Artists Pittsburgh Ann, Carnegie Mus, 57-80; New England Invitational, De Cordova Mus, Lincoln, Mass, 62; RI Arts Festival, Providence, 64; Soc Conn Craftsmen Traveling Show, 66; Three Rivers Arts Festival, Pittsburgh, 71, 73 & 74; 25th Anniversary Exhib, Brookfield Craft Ctr; one man show, Metal Works, Lyman Allyn Art Mus, New London, Conn, 1-3/90. *Teaching:* Metalsmithing, Norwich Art Sch, The Norwich Free Acad, Conn, 60-92 (retired), head art dept, 89-92; instr sculpture & art hist, Upward Bound, Conn Col, 69; dir young peoples art prog, Lyman Allyn Art Mus, New London, 74-82; jewelry workshops, Guilford Handcraft Ctr, Conn, Wesleyan Potters, Brookfield Craft Ctr, Conn. *Awards:* First Prize in Crafts, 58, Mrs Roy A Hunt Award, 61 & Jury Award for Distinction in Crafts, 68, Assoc Artists Pittsburgh Ann; Award for Excellence in Silver, Katheryn Forrest Trust Crafts Invitational, Slater Mus, Norwich, Conn, 86; Award in Sculpture, Mystic Art Asn, juried exhib, 86; Purchase Prize, Katheryn Forrest Trust, 89 & 92. *Bibliog:* John D Morris (auth), Creative Metal Sculpture, Bruce Pub Co, NY, 71; Shirley Charron (auth), Modern Pewter, Van Nostrand Reinhold Co, 73; Gold Smiths J, 79. *Mem:* Mystic Art Asn Inc (pres, 74); Assoc Artists Pittsburgh; Lyman-Allyn Art Mus (bd dir, 88-), New London, Conn. *Media:* Silver, Gold, Pewter. *Mailing Add:* 256 Elm St Stonington CT 06378

FLACH, VICTOR H
DESIGNER, WRITER
b Portland, Ore, May 31, 29. *Study:* Univ Ore, Sch Archit & Allied Arts, with Jack Wilkinson, BS & MFA; Univ Pittsburgh, Henry Clay Frick Fine Arts Dept, with Walter Read Hovey; also with R Buckminster Fuller, 53 & 59. *Comn:* Three-wall collage mural, with John Otto, Erb Mem Union, Univ Ore, 52; three-wall mural, Clearlake Sch, Eugene, Ore, 56; The Heritage Series Interview with American Painter Ben Shahn, PBS-TV, 65; two-wall, three-story mosaic tile mural, Sci Ctr, Univ Wyo, 67-68; The Arts in Practice, TV prog, with Richard Evans, UW-TV, 71. *Exhib:* One-man, group & traveling shows, incl: Portland Art Mus, 52, Denver Art Mus, 71, Contextualist Arts Gallery, 84-85 & Univ, Mus & Galleries from various cities across the US; 40 year Photo Retrospective, Black Hills State Univ, SDak, 89. *Pos:* Ed, In/sert: Active Anthology for the Creative, 55-62. *Teaching:* Prof painting, design & theory, Univ Wyo, 65- *Res:* Toward a comprehensive tetradic typologic systems programming as model for archetypal-prototypal iconographic and colorfielding structural morphology. *Publ:* Auth, Gloss of the Four Universal Forms, The Eyes' Mind, Anatomy of the Canvas: R Wells Paintings, Univ Pittsburgh; By These Presents: Richard Evans Retrospective, 76 & The Stage: Joseph Deadrick Drawings, Univ Wyo, 78; Indigenous Image, 79 & Contextualist Manifesto, 82; Displacings & Wayfarings, North Atlantic Bks, 2nd Ed, 88; Iconography of Wilkinson's Orientation Mural, Univ Oreg, 90; and many others. *Mailing Add:* Dept Art Univ Wyo Laramie WY 82071

FLACK, AUDREY L
PAINTER, PHOTOGRAPHER
b New York, NY, May 30, 31. *Study:* Cooper Union, grad, 51; Cranbrook Acad Art, Yale Univ, scholar & study with Josef Albers, 52; NY Univ, Inst Fine Arts, 53. *Work:* Whitney Mus Am Art, Mus Mod Art, Metrop Mus Art & Guggenheim Mus, New York; San Francisco Mus Fine Art, Calif; St Louis Mus, Mo; Nat Mus Women Arts, Smithsonian Inst, Washington, DC; Nat Mus Arts, Canberra, Australia. *Comn:* Family portrait comn by Oriole Farb, Dir, Riverside Mus & Stuart M Speiser Collection, Smithsonian Inst, Washington, DC; Civitas: Four Visions (Gateway to the City of Rock Hill), four bronze figures (13' ea), Rock Hill, SC, 91; 10-story-high monument to Catherine of Braganza (1638-1705), Princess of Portugal & Queen of England, Hunter's Point, Queens, NY, 92. *Exhib:* 22 Realists, Whitney Mus Am Art, 70; Whitney Mus Am Art, 72 & 78; Illusion & Reality, Australia Coun Traveling Exhib, 77-78; Nat Gallery Art, 80, Guggenheim Mus, 81 & Contemporary American Realism since 1960, Pa Acad Fine Arts, 81-83; Sacred Images in Secular Art, Whitney Mus Am Art, 86; solo exhibs, Saints & Other Angeles: The Religious Paintings of Audrey Flack, traveling exhibs, sponsored by Cooper Union, New York, 86-88, A Pantheon of Female Deities (catalog), Louis K Meisel Gallery, New York, 91; Classical Myth & Imagery in Contemp Art (catalog), Queens Mus, Flushing, NY, 88; In Sharp Focus: Super Realism (catalog), Nassau Co Mus Art, Roslyn, NY, 91; Six Takes on Photo-Realism, Whitney Mus Am Art at Champion, Stamford, Conn, 91-92; Photo-Realism: Revisited, Mus Art, Ft Lauderdale, Fla, 91-92; retrospective, Breaking the Rules, 1950-1990, traveling exhib, Wight Art Gallery, UCLA, Calif, Butler Inst Am Art, Youngstown, Ohio, Nat Mus Women Arts, Washington, DC, J B Speed Art Mus, Louisville, Ky, 92-93. *Teaching:* Pratt Inst, Brooklyn, NY, 65-71; prof anat, NY Univ, 68-71; Sch Visual Arts, NY, 71-74; Mellon prof anat, Cooper Union, 82. *Awards:* Albert Dorne Prof, Univ Bridgeport, 75; Nat Exhib Paintings Award of Merit, Butler Inst Am Art, 74; The Cooper Union Citation, 77 & St Gaudens Medal, 82, Cooper Union. *Bibliog:* Laurie S Hurwitz (auth), A Bevy of Goddesses: Paintings & Sculptures by Audrey Flack, Am Artist, 9/91; Amy Fine Collins & Bradley Collins (auth), Audrey Flack, Art Am, 11/91; Arthur C Danto, Books & the Arts: Our Holiday Lists, The Nation, 12/30/91; Carol Strickland (auth), Individualist-Idealist Breaks the Rules, NY Times, 9/27/92; Thalia Gouma-Peterson (auth), Breaking the Rules: Audrey Flack, a Retrospective 1950-1990, Harry N Abrams, Inc, New York, 92. *Media:* Oil, Bronze. *Publ:* Illusr, Tokyo Biennale (catalog), 74; Art in Am, 74; Vanitas (exhib catalog), L K Meisel Gallery, 78; auth, Audrey Flack on Painting, Harry N Abrams Inc, 81; Audrey Flack, Art and Soul, E P Dutton, 86; auth, Photorealism (vol I & II), Harry N Abrams Inc, 80 & 93. *Mailing Add:* c/o Louis K Meisel Gallery 141 Prince St New York NY 10024

FLAHAVIN, MARIAN JOAN
PAINTER
b Colton, Wash. *Study:* Holy Names Col, BA(art), 59; studied with John Howard Sanden & Daniel Greene. *Work:* Deaconess Hosp, Ronald MacDonald House, St Anne's Children's Home, Valley Gen Hosp, Spokane, Wash; Leanin' Tree Publs, Boulder, Colo. *Comn:* Plate/figurine series, comn by Goebel, Ger, 84; many portraits throughout US. *Exhib:* Northwest Pastel Soc, Seattle, 89; West Coast Pastel Soc, Sacramento, Calif, 89; Maryland Pastel Soc Ann, John-Hopkins Univ, Baltimore, 90; Catherine Lorillard Wolfe 94th Ann, Nat Arts Club, New York, 90; Salmagundi 14th Ann, New York, 91; and others. *Teaching:* Pastel, Corbin Arts Ctr. *Awards:* Best of Show/People's Choice, Northwest Pastel Soc Ann, 89; Merit/People's Choice, Md Ann, 90; Merit Award, Salmagundi Ann, 91. *Mem:* Pastel Soc Am (signature mem); Pastel Soc West Coast (signature mem); Northwest Pastel Soc (signature mem); Women Artists Am West (emeritus). *Media:* Pastel, Oil. *Publ:* Contribr, Southwest Art Mag, 82; Collectors Mart Mag, 84; Art Talk mag, 84; Midwest Art Mag, 85. *Mailing Add:* Rte 7 Schafer Rd Spokane WA 99206

FLAM, JACK D
HISTORIAN, EDUCATOR
b Paterson, NJ, Apr 2, 40. *Study:* Rutgers Univ, BA, 61; Columbia Univ, MA, 63; New York Univ, PhD, 69. *Collections Arranged:* Henri Matisse Paper Cut-Outs (auth, catalog), Nat Gallery, 77. *Pos:* Ed, The Documents of 20th Century Art, 81-; art critic, Wall Street J, 84- *Teaching:* Instr art hist, Rutgers Univ, 62-66; assoc prof art hist, Univ Fla, 66-70; prof art hist, Brooklyn Col & Grad Ctr, City Univ New York, 75-91; distinguished prof, City Univ New York, 91- *Awards:* Guggenheim Fel, 79-80; Nat Endowment Humanities Fel, 87-88; Charles Rufus Morey Award, Col Art Assoc, 88; and others. *Mem:* Int Asn Art Critics; Col Art Asn. *Res:* Currently working on a major critical study of Matisse and on a series of articles on early Modernist painting. *Publ:* Auth, Matisse on Art, Phaidon, 73 & Dutton, 78; coauth, Henri Matisse Paper Cut-Outs, Detroit Inst Arts & St Louis Art Mus, 77; Matisse, The Man & His Art, Cornell Univ Press, 86; Matisse, A Retrospective, Levin, 88; Motherwell, Rizzoli, 91. *Mailing Add:* 171 W 79th St New York NY 10024

FLANAGAN, BARRY
SCULPTOR
b Flintshire, North Wales, 1941. *Study:* Birmingham Col Art Crafts (fine art dept), 58; St Martin's Sch Art, 60 & 63. *Work:* Art Inst Chicago; Arts Coun Gt Brit; Mus Mid Art, New York; Nat Gallery Canada, Ottowa; San Francisco Mus Mod Art. *Exhib:* One-man exhib, Waddington Galleries, 80, 81, 83 & 85, Pace Gallery, New York, 83, Richard Gray Gallery, Chicago, 85; Inner Worlds, British Arts Coun Exhib, London, 82; British Drawings and Watercolour, Traveling exhib, People's Repub China, 82; Hayward Gallery, London, 82. *Bibliog:* Michael Compton (auth), Barry Flanagan: Recent Sculpture, The Pace Gallery, 83; William Feaver (auth), Alice doesn't live here, The Observer, 6/9/85; Sandra Miller (auth), On Barry Flanagan, No 2, Irish Arts Re 3, summer 86. *Media:* Bronze. *Mailing Add:* 505 LaGuardia Pl No 3C New York NY 10012

FLANAGAN, E MICHAEL
MUSEUM DIRECTOR, EDUCATOR
b Ft Bragg, NC, Dec 13, 48. *Study:* Kans State Univ, BFA, 74; Northern Ill Univ, MA, 77, MFA, 78. *Collections Arranged:* Peter Dean: Paintings and Stories, 92; Michiko Itatani: Recent Paintings, 92; Richard Haas: Architectural Drawings, Paintings and Prints, 92; UWM Art Mus, Milwaukee, Wis; and others. *Pos:* Cur & admin asst, Northern Ill Univ, 78-79, dir, Univ Galleries, 80-88; registr & cur exhibs, Midwest Mus Am Art, Elkhart, Ind, 79-80; dir, Univ Mus, Univ Wis, Milwaukee, 89-; dir, UWM Art Mus, Univ Wis-Milwaukee, 89- *Teaching:* Asst prof museology, Northern Ill Univ, DeKalb, 80-88; acad staff gallery studies, Univ Wis-Milwaukee, 89- *Mem:* Asn Corp Art Curators (secy, 85-87, vpres, 88-89, pres 90-91, chair, 92; DeKalb Arts Comn (chair, 86); wis Fedn Mus, 89-92; Midwest Mus Conf, 90-92; Asn Col & Univ Mus & Galleries, 92. *Publ:* Ethnographic Art from Faculty Collections, 89; Auth, Richard Haas: Architectural Drawings, Paintings and Prints, 92. *Mailing Add:* Univ Wis Art Mus PO Box 413 Milwaukee WI 53201

FLANAGAN, MICHAEL
PAINTER
b Buffalo, NY, Dec 24, 43. *Study:* Parsons Sch Design, 63-66; Yale Univ, 66-67. *Work:* Chicago Mus Contemp Art, Chicago, Ill; Ark Art Ctr, Little Rock; Hood Mus, Hanover, NH. *Exhib:* Grace Borgenicht Gallery, New York, 88; solo exhib, Sherry French, New York, 89, Wichita Art Mus, Kans, 89 & Nat Acad Sci, Washington, DC, 89; Sherry Finch Gallery, New York, 89; Three Romantic Realists, Fendrick Gallery, Washington, DC, 91; one-person exhib, The Chrysler Mus, Norfolk, Va, 92-93. *Teaching:* Instr painting, Sch Visual Arts, 90- *Awards:* Nat Endowment Arts Fel, 87; Yaddo Fel, 88. *Bibliog:* Vivien Raynor (auth), By Train and Plane and Oh Yes, the Car, NY Times, C20, 4/29/90; Kay Larson (auth), New History, New York, 62-63, 3/18/91; Jerry Tallmer (auth), One Track Mind, NY Post, 3/9/91. *Dealer:* PPOW Gallery 532 Broadway New York NY 10012. *Mailing Add:* 120 Hudson St New York NY 10013

FLANERY, GAIL
PAINTER, PRINTMAKER
b Cleveland, Ohio, May 7, 47. *Study:* Cooper Union, New York, BFA, 72. *Work:* Citicorp, Chemical Bank, Lehman Bros & Solomon Bros, New York; IBM Collection, Fla. *Exhib:* Kornblee Gallery, New York, 77; Tanglewood Gallery, New York, 78; Nat Drawing Show, Holman Gallery, State Col, Trenton, NJ, 79; Landscapes, 83 & Invitational, 86, Painting Space 122, New York; Contemp Am Landscapes, Hudson River Mus, Yonkers, NY & Tuscon Mus Art, Ariz, 84; K Caraccio Collection, Montgomery Col, Rockville, Md, 85. *Bibliog:* Rev, Arts Mag, 10/76; Today's landscape, NY Times, 2/84; Comtemporary American Landscapes, New Vistas, Hudson River Mus, 84. *Media:* Oil; Miscellaneous. *Dealer:* Orion Editions 270 Lafayette St New York NY 10012. *Mailing Add:* 511 Eighth St Brooklyn NY 11215

FLANNERY, THOMAS
CARTOONIST
b Carbondale, Pa, Dec 16, 19. *Study:* Pratt Inst, 39-40; Univ Scranton, 46-47. *Pos:* Staff cartoonist, Yank Mag, 43-45; polit cartoonist, Lowell Sun, Mass, 47-57, Baltimore Eve Sun, 57-73 & Baltimore Sun, 73- *Mem:* Am Soc Ed Cartoonists. *Mailing Add:* 911 Darthmouth Rd Baltimore MD 21212

FLATTMANN, ALAN RAYMOND
PAINTER, INSTRUCTOR
b New Orleans, La, Aug 6, 46. *Study:* John McCrady Art Sch, 64-66. *Work:* Okla Art Ctr, Oklahoma City; Lauren Rogers Mus Art, Laurel, Miss; Miss Mus Art, Jackson; New Orleans Art Asn; New Orleans Mus Art. *Comn:* Murals, Old Zion Baptist Church, New Orleans, 67 & Grace Episcopal Church, 72. *Exhib:* Solo exhibs, Lauren Rogers Mus Art, 70,75, 81 & Okla Arts Ctr, 79; Biena de Arte, Bogota Mus Art, Colombia, 72; Mainstreams, Hermann Fine Arts Ctr, Marietta, Ohio, 72, 75 & 76; Am Watercolor Soc Ann, Nat Acad Design, New York, 72 & 76; Pastel Soc Am, New York, 76-92; Columbus Club, New York, 81; Degas Pastel Soc, New Orleans, 83-92; Kans Pastel Soc, 84, 85, 86 & 88; Hermitage Found Mus Invitational, 86; Miss Mus Art Collection Exhib, 86; Soc des Pastellistes de France, Lille, France, 87. *Teaching:* Instr painting & drawing, John McCrady Art Sch, New Orleans, 67-82; pvt workshops in oil & pastel. *Awards:* Elizabeth T Greenshields Found Grant Award, 73; Award of Exceptional Merit, Degas Pastel Soc 2nd Biennial Nat Exhib, 88; Master Pastelist Designation, Pastel Soc Am, 91; and others. *Bibliog:* Keith C Marshall (auth), Alan Flattmann's reflections of the South, Am Artist, 7/79; Marda Burton (auth), No subject too common, Southwest Art, 9/80; Joyce Kelly (auth), The Poetic Realism of Alan Flattmann, ACM Publ Co, 80. *Mem:* Pastel Soc Am; Degas Pastel Soc; Hellenic Arts Soc. *Media:* Pastel & Oil. *Publ:* Auth, The Art of Pastel Painting, Waston Guptill, 87. *Dealer:* Bryant Galleries 2845 Lakeland Dr Jackson MS 39208 & 524 Royal St New Orleans LA 70130 & 2419 Canterbury Rd Birmingham AL 35223 & 99 West Paces Ferry Rd Atlanta GA 30305 & 2401 PGA Blvd Suite 186 Palm Beach Gardens FL 33410. *Mailing Add:* 20071 Brunning Rd Covington LA 70433

FLAVIN, DAN
ARTIST, WRITER
b New York, NY, Apr 1, 33. *Study:* Self-educated as artist; Cathedral Col Immaculate Conception, 47-52; studied art hist, Univ Md Exten, Repub Korea, 54-55; New Sch Social Res, 56; Columbia Univ, 57-59. *Work:* Mus Mod Art, Whitney Mus Am Art, Guggenheim Mus, Metrop Mus Art, New York; Philadelphia Art Mus. *Comn:* Courtyard & inner arcade, Kunstmuseum Basel, 75; several platforms of Grand Cent Station, New York, 76; ultra-violet & blue fluorescent light, Kroller-Muller Mus, Eindhoven, 77; entranceway & gallery skylights, Hudson River Mus, Yonkers, 79; north facade, Fed Bldg & US Courthouse, Anchorage, 80. *Exhib:* Solo exhibs, Galerie Thaddaeus Ropac, Salzburg, Austria, 87, Karsten Schubert Ltd, London, 88, Dia Art Found, Bridgehampton, NY, 88, Pat Hearn Gallery, New York, 88, Staatliche Kunsthalle, Baden, WGer, 89, Leo Castelli Gallery, 89 & Pace Gallery, New York, 92; Exhib for the Benefit of the Foundation for Contemp Performance Arts, Leo Castelli/Brooke Alexander, New York, 88; Coleccion Leo Castelli, Fundation Juan March, Madrid, Spain, 88; Langer Co, Fine Arts, New York, 89; Sculpture, Grob Gallery, London, 89; Margo Leavin Gallery, Los Angeles, Calif, 89; Repetition, Hirschl & Adler Mod, New York, 89; Sculpture: 1960's-1980's, Greenberg Gallery, St Louis, Mo, 89; Influences, Marisa Del Re Gallery, New York, 89; retrospective, Galerie Nächst St Stephan, Vienna, Austria, 90-91, David Weinberg Gallery, Santa Monica, Calif, 90-91, Fred Hoffman Gallery, Santa Monica, Calif, 90-91, Galerie Grasslin-Ehrhardt, Frankfurt, Ger, 90-91, Galerie Jean Bernier, Athens, Greece, 91, Mary Boone Gallery, New York, 91, Solomon R Guggenheim Mus, New York, 92; Arte Americana 1930-1970, Torino, Italy, 92; La Realidad Desautorizada, Galería Gamarra y Garrigues, Madrid, Spain, 92. *Teaching:* Lectr grad fac, Univ NC, Greensboro, spring 67; Albert Dorne vis prof, Univ Bridgeport, 73. *Awards:* William & Noma Copley Found Award, 64; Nat Found Arts & Humanities Award, 66; Skowhegan Medal for Sculpture, 76. *Bibliog:* Paul Taylor, Leo Castelli in His 85th Year: A Lion in Winter, NY Times, 2/16/92; Rose Slivka, From the Studio, East Hampton Star, 2/27/92; Berenice Reynaud, Donald Judd Regle ses Comptes, Beaux Arts, No 99, 3/92. *Mem:* Scenic Hudson Preserv Conf; Nat Trust Hist Preserv; Nat Audubon Soc. *Mailing Add:* Pace Gallery 32 E 57 St New York NY 10022

FLECKENSTEIN, OPAL R
PAINTER, CERAMIST
b Macksville, Kans, Nov 19, 11. *Study:* Eastern Wash State Col, BA & MA(educ); Univ Wash; Study with Guy Anderson, James Fitzgerald & Mark Tobey. *Work:* Cheney Cowles Mus, Wash. *Exhib:* Seattle Art Mus; one-man show, Watercolors & Oils, Seattle Art Mus; one-man retrospectives, Cheney Cowles Mus & Eastern Wash Univ, Cheney; Arts Centre S Hill Park, Bracknell, Berkshire, London, 81; All Hollows by the Tower, London, Eng, 83. *Teaching:* Assoc prof painting & humanities, Eastern Wash Univ, 49-75; guest instr art educ, Univ Sask, 57, 58 & 60; emer prof art, Int Prog, Guadalajara, Mex, 77-; workshops, Ore, Wash & BC, 77-79. *Awards:* Watercolor Purchase Prize, Seattle Art Mus, 50; Purchase Award, Cheney Cowles Mem Mus, Spokane, Wash, 76. *Media:* Oil, Watercolor. *Publ:* Prod 36 half hour TV progs, KSPS-PBS, Spokane, 71. *Mailing Add:* 3118 Ultra Spokane WA 99204

FLECKER, MAURICE NATHAN
PAINTER, EDUCATOR
b Brooklyn, NY, Feb 27, 40. *Study:* State Univ NY Col, New Paltz, with Ilya Bolotowsky, Gabriel Laderman, George Wexler & George Wardlaw, BS; Brooklyn Col, with Philip Pearlstein, Ad Reinhardt, Carl Holty & R J Wolff, MFA; Art Students League, painting scholar; New Sch Social Res; Brooklyn Mus, painting scholar; Pratt Inst. *Work:* Fed Savings Bank, State Univ NY Col, New Paltz; Brooklyn Mus. *Exhib:* One-man shows, Aegis Gallery, New York, 62, Icarus Gallery, New York, 66, Bank Gallery, New York, 69 & First Street Gallery, New York, 77; Wadsworth Atheneum, Hartford, Conn, 65; W V Smith Art Mus, Springfield, Mass, 65; Brooklyn Mus, New York, 68-75; Vered Gallery, East Hampton, 84; East End Arts Coun, New York, 86; Mill Pond Exhib, Haupaugeny, 88; Col Gallery, Selden, NY, 88. *Teaching:* Instr, Brooklyn Mus Art Sch, New York, 68-75; prof life drawing & sculpture, head art, music & philos, 72-82, Suffolk Co Community Col. *Bibliog:* Amei Wallach (auth), One road to realism, Newsday, 77; Maria Latona (auth), Inspiration from Life, Long Island Press, 77; Ellen Frisina (auth), Artist believes in taking time, Mid Island News, 10/18/79. *Mem:* Soho Ctr for Visual Arts; Col Art Asn. *Media:* Oil, Watercolor. *Mailing Add:* Suffolk Co Community Col Ammerman Seldon NY 11784

FLEISCHER, ROLAND EDWARD
HISTORIAN, EDUCATOR
b Baltimore, Md, Feb 12, 28. *Study:* Western Md Col, BA, 52; Johns Hopkins Univ, MA, 54, PhD, 64. *Teaching:* Assoc prof art hist, Univ Miami, Fla, 56-66; prof art hist, George Washington Univ, 66-74; prof art hist, Pa State Univ, 74- *Awards:* Fulbright Award, Univ Amsterdam, 54-55. *Mem:* Col Art Asn. *Res:* Colonial painting in America; Dutch painting of the 17th century. *Publ:* Auth, Ludolf de Jongh and the Early Work of Pieter de Hooch, Oud Holland, 78; co-ed & contribr, The Age of Rembrandt: Studies in Seventeenth Century Dutch Painting, In: Vol III, Papers in Art History from The Pennsylvania State University, Univ Park, Pa, 88; auth, Gustavus Hesselius: Face Painter to the Middle Colonies, NJ State Mus, Trenton, 88; Emblems & Colonial Am Painting, The Am Art J, Vol XX, No 3, 88; Ludolf de Jongh (1616-1679): Painter of Rotterdam, Davaco Publ, 89; and others. *Mailing Add:* Pa State Univ Main Campus University Park PA 16802

FLEISCHMAN, LAWRENCE ARTHUR
ART DEALER, PUBLISHER
b Detroit, Mich, Feb 14, 25. *Study:* Western Mil Acad, Alton, Ill; Purdue Univ, 42-43; Univ Detroit, BS, 48; St John's Univ, LHD, 78. *Pos:* Comn mem, Fine Arts Comt, US Info Agency, 57-59; pres, Detroit Inst Arts, 62-66; White House Comt Fine Arts, 62-66; pres, Detroit Arts Comn; ed, Am Art J, 69-; chmn & owner, Kennedy Galleries Inc, New York, currently. *Awards:* Papal Knight of the Order of St Sylvester, 78; Copley Medal, Nat Portrait Gallery, 78; Decorated Knight of the Order of San Silvestre Pope Paul XI, 78. *Mem:* Metrop Mus Art, New York (chmn, Philodoros Soc); Art Dealers' Asn Am (mem bd); Arch Am Art (pres, 59-66, dir, 67-); life mem Pa Hist Soc; life mem Pa Acad Fine Arts. *Specialty:* 18th, 19th and 20th century American art. *Collection:* American art and Roman and Greek antiquities. *Mailing Add:* Kennedy Galleries Inc 40 W 57th St New York NY 10019-4001

FLEISCHMAN, STEPHEN
MUSEUM DIRECTOR
b Newton, Mass, July 7, 54. *Study:* Univ Wis-Madison, BS(fine arts), 77; MA, 83. *Collections Arranged:* Co-curator, Highlights from the Permanent Collection, 91; Co-curator, Self-Portraits from the Permanent Collection, 92; Curator, Sculpture by Mark Lorenzi, 92; Curator, Jim Dine: Drawing from the Glyptothek (auth, catalog), 93. *Pos:* Spec asst dir, Walker Art Ctr, Minneapolis, 83-86, dir prog planning, 86-90; dir, Madison Art Ctr, Wis, 91- *Mem:* Am Asn Mus; Madison Comt Arts. *Mailing Add:* Madison Art Center 211 State St Madison WI 53703

FLEISCHNER, RICHARD HUGH
ENVIRONMENTAL ARTIST, SCULPTOR
b New York, NY, July 1, 44. *Study:* RI Sch Design, BFA, 66, MFA, 68. *Work:* Guggenheim Mus, New York; Whitney Mus Am Art, New York; Dallas Mus Art, Tex; Mus Art, RI Sch Design; Los Angeles Mus Contemp Art; Mus Contemp Art, San Diego. *Comn:* Mass Inst Technol, 85; MBTA, Arts on the Line, Cambridge, 85; Temple Univ, Philadelphia, 85; General Mills, Minneapolis, 85-87; Becton Dickinson Project, Franklin Lakes, NJ, 87; East Capital Plaza, St Paul, Minn, 91; and many others. *Exhib:* One-man exhibs, Univ Gallery, Univ Mass, Amherst, 77, Mus Art, RI Sch Design, Providence, 80, Max Protech Gallery, New York, 80 & 81, Philadelphia Col Art, 83, Univ RI, Kingston, 83, Portica Harcus Gallery, Boston, 86, McIntosh Drysdale Gallery, Washington, DC, 87; Drawings/Structures, Inst Contemp Art, Boston, 80; The Figurative Tradition, 80, Whitney Biennial, 81, New Am Art Museums, 82, Whitney Mus Am Art, New York; Form and Funtion--Proposals for Public Art for Philadelphia, Pa Acad Fine Arts, 82; Artist as Social Designer, Los Angeles Co Mus Art, 85; traveling exhib, Sitings, La Jolla Mus Contemp Art, Dallas Mus Art, High Mus Art, Atlanta, Ga, Tel Aviv Mus, Israel, 86; Individuals, A Selected History of Contemporary Art-1945-86, Mus Contemp Art, Los Angeles, 86-88; Vanguard Gallery, Philadelphia, Pa, 87; Works on Paper, Nina Freudenheim Gallery, Buffalo, NY, 88. *Teaching:* Asst prof art, Brown Univ, Providence, 70-74; vis guest lectr & critic, many schools & museums throughout US. *Awards:* Am Acad Art & Letts Grant, 74-75; Nat Endowment Arts Fel, 75-76 & 80-81; Gov's Award Art, RI Gov Edward Di Prete, 86. *Bibliog:* Calvin Tomkins (auth), Post to Neo--The Art World of the 1980's, Henry Holt & Co, 88; Robert Campbell (auth), Arts and crafts--Spirit pervades corporate offices, Architecture, 5/88; Bruce Serlen (auth), Whats new in corporate art, NY Times, 2/12/89. *Media:* Miscellaneous. *Mailing Add:* 224 Williams St Providence RI 02906

FLEISHER, PAT
PUBLISHER, DESIGNER
b Toronto, Ont. *Study:* Univ Toronto, BA; painting, Skowhegan, Maine; Ont Col Art; St Adele, Quebec; printmaking, York Univ, 71. *Work:* Palm Springs Desert Mus, Calif; Harbourfront Art Gallery, Toronto; Robert McLaughin Art Gallery, Oshawa. *Exhib:* Photos, Palm Springs Desert Mus, 79; Koffler Art Gallery, Toronto, 80;; Idee Gallery, Toronto, 81; Spaces Gallery, Cleveland, 81; Gallery One, Toronto, 80 & 82; Aaron Berman Gallery, New York; Arnold Gottlieb Gallery, Toronto, Ont; Roschar Gallery, Toronto, 89; Forsyth Gallery, Toronto, 89. *Collections Arranged:* Toronto Women Artists: Three Decades, 83; So; SW USA Art, juror, Jewish Community Ctr, Houston, 82. *Pos:* Founder-ed, Art Mag, 69-82; pres, Art Mag, Inc, 74-87; founder, Toronto Int Art Fair, 80; publ & ed, Art Post, 83-92; founder, Art Expo, Toronto, 83; founder, Discovery, 85; dir, 291 Gallery, Toronto, 89-92; pres, Fleisher Fine Arts Inc, 92- *Teaching:* Lectr & art guide, Toronto & New York galleries & studios, 71-; Toronto bd educ, Koffler Art Gallery. *Awards:* Merit Award, Art Mag, Soc Publ Designers New York, 75; Queen Elizabeth Silver Jubilee Medal, awarded by Jules Leger, Gov Gen of Can, 78; Ont Asn Art Galleries Design Award, 80. *Bibliog:* Joan Murray (auth), Pat Fleisher: Photoartist, Canadian Women's Studies, 81. *Mem:* Int Asn Art Critics (treas, Can Br); Can Periodical Pub Asn; Friends Can Mus Asn; Ont Periodicals Artistic Expression & Criticism. *Media:* Cibachrome and Colour Xerox Photography. *Publ:* Auth, Atlantic Provinces J, Art Mag 76; A Western pilgrimage, 77 & The mystery of the Maya, Art Mag, 79; The Woman as artist, Ave Mag, 83; Artist Rose Lindzon: A profile, City & Co Home Mag, 84; Botero review, Latin Am Art, USA, 90. *Mailing Add:* 15 McMurrich St Apt 706 Toronto ON M5R 3M6 Canada

FLEMING, FRANK
SCULPTOR
b Bear Creek, Ala, June 17, 40. *Study:* Univ Ala, BS, 62, MA, 69, MFA, 73. *Work:* City of Birmingham, Five Points South; Montgomery Mus Art, Ala; Nat Mus Am Art, Smithsonian Inst; Nelson Rockhill Mus, Kansas City, Mo; Utah Mus Fine Art, Salt Lake City. *Comn:* Wire wrapped bamboo hanging, AT&T, Atlanta, Ga, 79; The Magic Hoop, Montgomery Mus Art, Ala, 89; rabbit sculpture, 90, porcelain sculpture, 92, Birmingham Botanical Gardens, Ala; Five Points South Fountain, City of Birmingham, Ala, 91. *Exhib:* Contemporary Crafts of the Americas, Ft Collins, Colo, 75; American Porcelain, 81 & Animal Imagery, 81, Renwich Gallery, Smithsonian Inst; Art from Appalachia, Nat Mus Art, Washington, DC, 81; one-man shows, Birmingham Mus Art, Ala, 82 & Montgomery Mus Art, Ala, 83; Poetry of the Physical, Mus Am Crafts, New York, 86; Fourth Int Shoebox Sculpture Exhib, Univ Hawaii Art Gallery, 91. *Awards:* Harriet Murray Award, Birmingham Mus Art, 90; Ala State Arts Coun Fel, 90; Southern Arts Fedn Sculpture Fel, 91. *Bibliog:* R M N McAusland (auth), Frank Fleming's fantasy in porcelain, Am Artist, 4/79; Annette Hatton (auth), Frank Fleming, Ga Rev, summer 85; Janet Kopolos (auth), Frank Fleming, Am Ceramics, 4/2/85. *Mailing Add:* 1309 Saulter Rd Birmingham AL 35209

FLEMING, LEE
WRITER, CURATOR
b Philadelphia, Pa, Jan 26, 52. *Study:* Yale Col, BA, 72; Univ Toronto, MA, 74. *Exhib:* Strange (auth, catalog), Rockville Arts Place, Md, 91. *Collections Arranged:* Critics Picks, Md Art Pl, 92; Family Matters, Tartt Gallery, Washington, DC, 92. *Pos:* Sr ed, Mus & Arts Mag, formerly; Art & film ed, Washington Rev Arts, 79-89; Washington Correspond, Artnews, 83-88; visual arts commentator, Nat Pub Radio, 88-; sr ed, Garden Design Mag, currently. *Awards:* Washington, DC Comn Arts & Humanities Fel Lit & Criticism, 81 & 84; Ucross Found Residency Fel, 85; Larry Neal Writer's Award, 89. *Publ:* On metaphor, Washington Rev, 82; Biennial directions: Direction 1983, ARTNews & What's at issue is the issue, Artnews, 83; Art, Am Quart, 83; Manon Cleary (Gulbenkian Indth, Lisbon), 84. *Mailing Add:* 1924 Park Rd NW Washington DC 20010

FLEMING, RONALD LEE
DESIGNER, ADMINISTRATOR
b Los Angeles, Calif, May 13, 41. *Study:* Pomona Col, BA(cum laude), 63; Harvard Univ, MCP, 67. *Comn:* Developed art plans & strategies, Carriagetown & Flint, Mich; James Ctr, Richmond, Va; Bethesda Meridian, Prince Georges Co, Md; highway corridor megalithic landscape with sculptor William P Deimann, Radnor, Pa. *Exhib:* On Common Ground, 81; What So Proudly We Hailed: America's Threatened Cultural Landscapes, 90-92. *Pos:* First chmn, Cambridge Arts Coun, 75-79, Cambridge One Percent Pub Art Comn, 79-85; Pres, Townscape Inst, 79- *Awards:* Merit Award, Am Soc Landscape Architects, 80; Commendation Design Excellence, Dept Transportation-Nat Endowment Arts, 81. *Mem:* Founding mem Cambridge Arts Coun (chmn, 74-79); fel, Royal Soc Arts, London; Tavern Club, Boston; Century Asn, New York; Knickerbocker Club, New York. *Publ:* Ed, Censored Laughter, Boston Publ, 76; coauth, Place Makers, Creating Public Art that Tells You Where You Are, 81, second revised ed, 87; On Common Ground, Harvard Common Press, 82; auth, Facade Stories, Hastings House, 82; New Providence: A Changing Cityscape, Harcourt Brace Jovanivitch, 87. *Mailing Add:* 2 Hubbard Park Cambridge MA 02138

FLEMING, STEPHEN
PAINTER, CERAMIST
b Oxford, Pa, Apr 6, 50. *Study:* Royal Acad, London, certificate, painting, 74; Calif State Univ, Sacramento, BFA; Univ Calif-Davis, MFA, 85. *Work:* Roswell Mus & Art Ctr, NMex; Kemper Collection, Kansas City, Mo. *Exhib:* Apocalyptic Vision, Sioux City, Iowa, 90; Expo at Chicago Navy Pier, 91; Roswell Mus & Art Ctr, NMex, 92. *Teaching:* Asst prof painting, Kansas City Art Inst, 89. *Awards:* Nat Endowment Arts, 86; Grant, Roswell Mus & Art Ctr, 86-87 & 92. *Media:* All. *Dealer:* The Allrich Gallery San Francisco CA; Nancy Margolis Gallery Portland ME & New York NY. *Mailing Add:* c/o Kansas City Art Inst 4415 Warwick Blvd Kansas City MO 64111

FLEMING, THOMAS MICHAEL
SCULPTOR, PAINTER
b Philadelphia, Pa, May 12, 51. *Study:* Harrisburg Area Community Col, AA(with honors), 72; Pa State Univ, BFA(with honors), 75; Univ Minn, MFA, 78. *Work:* Musee des Arts, Lausanne, Switz; Int Glasmuseum, Ebeltoft, Denmark; Univ Minn Art Mus, Minneapolis; Corning Mus, New York; Ga State Univ, Urban Life Plaza, Atlanta, Ga. *Comn:* Ceramic sculpture, Wausau Insurance Cos, Wis, 83; sculpture, McDonald's Corp, Houston, Tex, 87. *Exhib:* Americans in Glass 1981, L Y Woodson, Wis & Cooper-Hewitt Mus, New York; Int Directions Glass, Art Mus W Australia, Perth, 82; Order/Chaos, Minn Mus Art, St Paul, 83; Directions IV, Milwaukee Art Mus, Wis, 84; Glass from USA & Japan, Mus Basel, Switz, 86; Expressions En Verre, Musee des Arts, Lausanne, Switz, 86. *Pos:* Co-founder & dir, SoHo Studio Ctr, New York, 87-; pres, Art Shoot, New York, 88-; artistic prog consult, Anglo-Am Workshops, New York, 88-89. *Teaching:* Assoc prof art, Univ Wis Ctr, Wausau, 78-; inst, Anglo-Am Workshops, London, Eng, 88. *Bibliog:* Robert Silberman (auth), Americans in Glass: A Requiem?, Art in Am, 3/85; Dan Klein (auth), Glass: A contemporary art, Rizzoli Int, 90; Olivier Royant (auth), Les Milliardaires Americans: Scope 90, Didier Hatier, 90. *Mem:* Int Sculpture Soc; Glass Art Soc; Nat Coun for Educ in Ceramic Arts. *Media:* Miscellaneous; Acrylic, Oil. *Publ:* coauth, Recyclable Ceramics, 78 Coun Educ Ceramic J, 87; Auth, Studio Molds--Three Approaches, 83, Interview with artist Ron Nagle, 87, Nat Coun Educ Ceramic J. *Mailing Add:* 518 S Seventh Ave Wausau WI 54401

FLEMINGER, SUSAN N
ADMINISTRATOR, EDUCATOR
b New York, NY, Nov 23, 41. *Study:* Hofstra Univ, BA, 65; Hunter Col, MA, 67. *Collections Arranged:* Assembled & arranged, Riding on a Blue Note, 89-92, Exchanges I, II & III, Artists Select Artists (3 yr exhib ser); and many others. *Pos:* Consult, NY Found Arts, NY State Coun Arts; freelance cur, Fordnam Univ/Lincoln Ctr, Brooklyn Mus/Community Gallery; educ dir, Yeshiva Univ Mus, New York, 78-80; dir, Visual Arts & Arts in Educ, Henry Street Settlement Arts Ctr, New York, 81-; arts ed, Prospect Press, Brooklyn, NY, 84-85. *Teaching:* Instr art hist, New York Community Col, Kingsborough Community Col, Stern Col Women, Art Ctr Northern NJ, Levittown Mem Art Sch, 61-78. *Awards:* Schools & Culture Award, NY Comn Cultural Affairs, 88; Very Special Arts Award from very Special Arts, 92; Training Prog for Early Childhood Teachers in Visual Arts, Nat Endowment Arts. *Mem:* Art Table; Nat Art Educ Asn; Nat Alternative Arts Orgns. *Publ:* Auth, Art Reviews, Prospect Press Newspaper, 82-85; Joseph Delaney: An Interview, Arts & Artists, 3/82; Laura Schechter, 86 & Bert Hasen (monogr), 87, Arts Mag; Emilio Cruz: Spilled Nightmares, Revelations & Reflections (catalog essay), Studio Mus Harlem, 87. *Mailing Add:* 571 Ninth St Brooklyn NY 11215

FLETCHER, LELAND VERNON
SCULPTOR, PAINTER
b Cumberland, Md, Sept 18, 46. *Study:* Univ Minn, BS, 72. *Work:* Victoria & Albert Mus, London, Eng; Minneapolis Inst Art, Minneapolis, Minn; Mus Ludwig, Cologne, Ger; Mus de Arte Mod, Barcelona, Spain; Mus de Arte Contemporanea, San Paulo, Brazil; Bradford Mus, Eng; Kunsthalle Hamburg, Ger. *Comn:* Art Zone Maubeuge (200' x 300' urban environmental sculpture) & Construction 1A:11 (16' x 10' x 10' painted steel sculpture), Ministry Cult & Ville de Maubeuge, France, 87. *Exhib:* 9th Int Brit Print Biennale, Victoria & Albert Mus, London, Eng, 86; Solo exhib, Constructed Shadows, Univ Art Gallery, Calif State Univ, Hayward, 89; Artists Books, Anchorage Mus Art, Alaska, 90; Cars in Art, Pensacola Mus Art, Fla, 90; 44th Salon des Realities Nouvelles, Grand Palais, Paris, France, 90; 2nd Int Biennial of Prints, Bharat

Bhavan, Bhopal, India, 91; and others. *Pos:* Fine art specialist, City of San Rafael, Calif, 77-78. *Awards:* Hon Mention, Minn State Fair Fine Arts Exhib, 70. *Bibliog:* Stephen Moore (auth), Leland Fletcher, Wordworks, Vol 3, No 2, 79; Carl Loeffler (auth), Performance Anthology, Contemp Arts Press, 80; Leland Fletcher, La Voix du Nord, 7/87. *Media:* Welded Metal, Miscellaneous Media. *Mailing Add:* 3288 Konocti Lane Soda Bay CA 95451

FLETCHER, VALERIE J
CURATOR, HISTORIAN
b Madison, Wis, Aug 26, 51. *Study:* Conn Col, BA, 73; Columbia Univ, MA, 77, MPh, 79. *Collections Arranged:* Josef Albers, 80, Barbara Hepworth, 81, Dreams & Nightmares: Utopian Visions in Modern Art (auth, catalog), 83-84, 20th Centruy Sculpture, 85-, Surrealist Art (auth, catalog), 86-87, Cubist Sculpture (auth, catalog), 87-88, & Alberto Giacometti 1901-66 (auth, catalog), 88-89, Hirshhorn Mus & Sculpture Garden-Smithsonian Inst, Washington, DC. *Pos:* Res asst, Metrop Mus Art, New York, 76-78; assoc cur sculpture, Hirshhorn Mus-Smithsonian Inst, 78- *Teaching:* Lectr, dept educ, Mus Mod Art, New York, 77-78; vis prof Utopian art, Continuing Educ, Georgetown Univ, 86. *Res:* 19th and 20th century painting and sculpture. *Publ:* Coauth, The Self and Others, Wildenstein Gallery, 1976; auth, Sunlight in 19th Century Art-The Fire of Life, Smithsonian Bks, 81; coauth, The Gustave & Marion Ring Collection, Smithsonian Inst, 85. *Mailing Add:* Dept Painting & Sculpture-Hirshhorn Mus & Sculpture Garden Independence Ave SW Washington DC 20560

FLEXNER, JAMES THOMAS
WRITER, HISTORIAN
b New York, NY, Jan 13, 08. *Study:* Lincoln Sch, Teacher's Col; Harvard Col, grad (magna cum laude), 29. *Awards:* Guggenheim Fel, 53 & 80; Nat Bk Award, 74; Pulitzer Prize, 74; Gold Medal For Eminence in Biography, Am Acad Arts & Letters, 88. *Mem:* Century Asn; Am Inst Arts & Lett (vpres lit, 83-85); Soc Am Historians (pres, 75-78); PEN Am Ctr (pres, 54-55). *Res:* American painting as an expression of American life. *Publ:* Auth, America's Old Masters, 39, rev ed, 79 & 92; American painting, First Flowers of Our Wilderness, 47, 69, 79 & 88; Pocket History of American Painting, 50; American Painting, The Light of Distant Skies, 54, 69, 79 & 88; American Painting, That Wilder Image, 62, 70, 79 & 88; and others. *Mailing Add:* 530 E 86th St New York NY 10028

FLICK, PAUL JOHN
COLLECTOR, PAINTER
b Rock Island, Ill, Feb 5, 43. *Study:* Univ Minn, BA & MFA(printing & printmaking); studied with Herman Cherry & Mario Valpe. *Work:* Univ Minn. *Exhib:* Group show, Minneapolis Inst Arts, 80 & 90. *Teaching:* Instr drawing & color, Bur Engraving, 72-83. *Mem:* Artist Equity Asn (pres, 76-77); Twin Cities Metrop Arts Alliance; Vietnam Vets Art Group. *Media:* Paintings, Assemblages. *Collection:* Primitive and African art. *Dealer:* Richard Halonen Fine Arts Ltd 89 S Tenth St Suite 210 Minneapolis MN 55403. *Mailing Add:* 4032 Lyndale Ave S Minneapolis MN 55409

FLICK, ROBBERT
PHOTOGRAPHER, EDUCATOR
b Amersfoort, Holland, Nov 15, 39; US citizen. *Study:* Univ BC, BA, 67; Univ Calif, Los Angeles, MA, 70, with Robert Heinecken & Robert Fichter, MFA, 71. *Work:* Ctr Creative Photog, Tucson, Ariz; Chicago Art Inst, Ill; Hallmark Collections, Kansas City, Mo; Mus Mod Art, New York; Oakland Mus Art, Calif; San Francisco Mus Mod Art. *Exhib:* Art Inst Chicago, Chicago Ill; Ctr Creative Photog, Tucson, Ariz; Fine Arts Gallery, Univ Calif, Davis; Fine Arts Gallery, Univ BC, Can; Frederick S Wight Art Gallery, Univ Calif, Los Angeles; Henry Art Gallery, Univ Wash, Seattle; Light Gallery, New York; Los Angeles Co Mus; Min Galllery, Tokyo; Musee d'Art, Mod de la Ville de Paris, France; Mus Mod Art, Lodz, Poland; Photo-Kina, Koln, WGer; Vancouver Art Gallery. *Teaching:* Prof art, Univ Ill, Champaign-Urbana, 71-76 & Univ Southern Calif, Los Angeles, 76- *Awards:* Nat Endowment Arts Survey Grant, 79; Nat Endowment Arts, Individual Artist Fel, 82 & 84; Nat Endowment Arts Individual Artist Grant, 83. *Bibliog:* Article, Afterimage, Vol 8, No 5, 12/80; article, Journal, Southern Calif Art Mag No 29; Berger, Searle & Wadden (coauths), Radical, Rational, Space, Time, Idea Networks in Photography, Henry Art Gallery, Univ Wash, Seattle, 82; Van Deren Coke (auth), Facets of Modernism: Photographs from the San Francisco Museum of Modern Art, Hudson Hills Press, NY, 86. *Mem:* Soc for Photog Educ; Col Art Asn. *Media:* Silverprint. *Publ:* Auth, Camera, Nos 2 & 10, C J Bucher Ltd, Lucerne, Switz, 72 & 81; Photographer's Choice, Addison House, Danbury, NH, 75; Robbert Flick, Selected Work: 1980-1981 (exhib catalog), Los Angeles Mun Art Gallery, Calif, 81; The Photographic Vision, Tele Course, Coast Community Col, Fountain Valley, Calif, CBS/Holt, Rinehart & Winston, 84; Robbert Flick, MIN Gallery, Tokyo, Japan, 87. *Dealer:* Photoman Inc 42 E 76th St New York NY 10021. *Mailing Add:* Dept Fine Arts, Univ S Calif Univ Park Los Angeles CA 90089

FLINT, JANET ALTIC
CURATOR, HISTORIAN
b Louisville, Ky, Aug 24, 35. *Study:* Louisville Art Ctr; Univ Louisville, BS(painting & art hist); Univ Minn, MA(art hist). *Collections Arranged:* And there was light, Studies by Abraham Rattner, 76; Jacob Kainen: Prints, A Retrospective, 77; Prints and Personalities; the American Theater's First Hundred Years, 79; Art for All: American Print Publishing Between the Wars, 81; Charles W Hawthorne: The Late Watercolors, 83. *Pos:* Assoc cur, Minneapolis Inst Arts, 59-66; asst cur & cur graphic arts, Nat Mus Am Art, Smithsonian Inst, 69-84; dir, dept Am prints, Hirschl-Adler Galleries, New York, 84- *Res:* American prints and drawings. *Publ:* Auth, George Miller and American Lithography, 76; New Ways with Paper, 78; The Print in the United States from the Eighteenth Century to the Present, 81; The Prints of Louis Lozowick: A Catalogue Raisonne, 82; Provincetown Printers: A Woodcut Tradition, 83. *Mailing Add:* Nat Mus Am Art 8G St NW Washington DC 20560

FLOETER, KENT
SCULPTOR
b Saginaw, Mich, Oct 22, 37. *Study:* Boston Univ, BFA; Yale Univ, MFA. *Work:* Prudential Life Insurance Collection, Newark, NJ; Etzold Collection, Stadtisches Mus, Monchengladbach, Ger; Ronald Lauder Collection, Estee Lauder Inc, New York; Mobil Oil Corp Collection, New York; Needham Harper Collection, Needham Harper Worldwide, New York. *Comn:* Al Paul Lefton Co Inc, Independence Mall, Philadelphia, Pa. *Exhib:* Biennial Exhib Contemp Am Art, Whitney Mus Am Art, New York, 75; Drawings Series Number 3, Painters-Sculptors USA, Stadtisches Mus, Schlob Morsbroich, Levenkusen, Ger, 75; Soho Downtown Manhattan, Akad der Kunst, Berlin, Ger, 76; Selections, La Mus Mod Art, Humlebaeck, Denmark, 76; Drawing selections, Wilkey Fine Arts, New York, 85; Group Exhib, Athena Fine Arts, New York, 89; Group Exhib, Wilkey Fine Arts, Seattle, 90; one-man exhib, Wilkey Fine Arts, Seattle, 91, 3 NY Artists, Wilkey Fine Arts, Seattle, Wash, 91. *Awards:* Fulbright Grant, Barcelona, Spain, 64-65; National Endowment Arts Artists Fel 80-81 & 83-84; middle states vis artists prog, New Arts Prog, Kutztown, Pa 87-88; Adolph & Esther Gottlieb Found Award, 92. *Bibliog:* Carl Baldwin (auth), article, 6/75 & Robert Pincus-Witten (auth), Entries, 3/76, Arts Mag; Lynn Smallwood (auth), Visual Arts, Seattle Weekly Mag, 5/91. *Publ:* Variations on a Theme: Embellished Elevation of the Carnegie Mansion, Cooper-Hewitt Mus, Smithsonian Inst Nat Mus Design, New York. *Mailing Add:* 1024 Adams St Hoboken NJ 07030

FLOMENHAFT, ELEANOR
MUSEUM DIRECTOR, HISTORIAN
b Brooklyn, NY, Aug 21, 33. *Study:* Hofstra Univ, Hempstead, NY, BA(art hist), 76; Queens Col, NY, MA(art hist), 84. *Collections Arranged:* British Watercolors and Drawings 1750-1910 (auth, catalog), 80 & CoBrA, 81, Emily Lowe Gallery, Hofstra Univ; The New Explosion: Paper Art (auth, catalog), Nat Traveling exhib, 82; Celebrating Contemporary American Black Artists (auth, catalog), 83; Adja Yunkers: A Twentieth Century Master (auth, catalog), 84; Transit: Russian Artists Between East & West (auth, catalog), 89; Faith Ringgold: 25-Year Survey (auth, catalog), 90. *Pos:* Cur art, Emily Lowe Gallery, Hofstra, 78-80; dir, Fine Arts Mus, Long Island, NY, 81-92. *Awards:* Pres Award, Long Island, 84; Women of Year, Hemstead Chamber of Commerce, 89; Pathfinder Award, Hempstead, 90. *Bibliog:* Phyllis Braff (auth), Many ideas meet in Yunkers' art, NY Times, 6/3/84; Karen Lipson (auth), Back in the USSR, a hit from Long Island, Newsday, 3/13/90; Betty Freudenheim (auth), An artist traces her life on quilts, New York Times, 5/27/90. *Mem:* Am Asn Mus; Art Table. *Res:* Art of the Cobra group 1948-1951; the abstract experimentalists of Europe; The Barcelona School, Post World War II; contemporary Russian art; contemporary American art. *Publ:* Auth, The Roots & Development of Cobra Art, Hempstead, NY, FAMLI, 85; Josep Guinovart, essay in catalog for retrospective exhib, Hempstead, NY, FAMLI, 87; Karel Appel, The Dupe of Being, ed by Roland Hagenberg NY: Ed Lafayette, 89, pp 243-259; Outside the USSR, essay in catalog, Transit: Russian Artists Between East & West, NY: Eduard Nakhamkin Fine Arts, 89; Interviewing Faith Ringgold: A Contemporary Heroine, essay in catalog for exhib, Hempstead, NY, FAMLI, 90. *Mailing Add:* 1294 Seawane Dr Hewlett NY 11557

FLOOD, RICHARD SIDNEY
WRITER, GALLERY DIRECTOR
b Philadelphia, Pa, Nov 10, 43. *Study:* St Joseph's Col, BA, 65; Univ Pa, Annenberg Sch Commun, MA, 67. *Collections Arranged:* PSI (Inst Art & Urban Resources), Figuratively Sculpting, 81; Franklin Furnace, The Page as Alternative Space: The Last Decade, 81; Memento Mori, Centro Cultural/Arte Contemporaneo, Mexico City, 86. *Pos:* Ed, Art Exchange, Philadelphia, Pa, 76-79; managing ed, Artforum, New York, 80, books ed, formerly; dir, Barbara Gladstone Gallery, New York, 85- *Res:* Contemporary art; particularly as it relates to popular culture. *Publ:* Contribr, Robert Gober, An Interview, The Print Collector's Newsletter, 4-5/90, 6-9; The Knickers' Effect, SHIFT, Vol 3, No 4, 90, 16-23; Down the Airshaft, Parkett, No 17, 88, 152-160; Go Fetch the New Yorker, Parkett, No 21, 89, 62-66; The Dog & the Suicide, Parkett, No 23, 90, 146-151. *Mailing Add:* c/o Barbara Gladstone Gallery 99 Greene St New York NY 10012

FLORA, JAMES ROYER
ILLUSTRATOR, PAINTER
b Bellefontaine, Ohio, Jan 25, 14. *Study:* Urbana Univ, Ohio, 31-33; Art Acad Cincinnati, 34-39; also study & asst to Carl Zimmerman (muralist) & Stanley William Hayter at Atelier 17. *Work:* Smithsonian Inst, Washington, DC; Container Corp Collection. *Exhib:* Equity Gallery, Stamford, Conn, 84; Saugatuck Gallery, Westport, Conn, 84-85; Mystic Maritime Gallery, Conn, 85-90; Lockwood-Mathews, Norwalk, Conn, 86; Andrea Ruoff Assocs, Ft Lee NJ, Publ of Serigraphs. *Pos:* Art dir, Columbia Records, Bridgeport, Conn, 42-50, Park East Mag, New York, 51-53 & Computer Design Mag, Littleton, Mass, 62-80. *Awards:* Bronze Medal Printing, Slivermine Guild, 83. *Bibliog:* Something About the Author, Gale Res, 88. *Media:* Ink, Acrylic. *Publ:* Auth & illusr, The Fabulous Firework Family, 55, The Day the Cow Sneezed, 57 & Leopold, the See-Through Crumbpicker, 61, Harcourt Brace; The Great Green Turkey Creek Monster, 76 & Grandpa's Ghost Stories, 78, Atheneum; and many others. *Dealer:* Mystic Maritime Gallery Mystic CT 06355; Portland Place Gallery 25 S Main St South Norwalk CT 06854. *Mailing Add:* St James Pl Rowayton CT 06853

FLORIN, SHARON JUNE
PAINTER
b Brooklyn, NY, Feb 16, 52. *Study:* Art Students League, with David Leffel, Issac Soyer, among others, 69-77; Adelphi Univ, BA, 73. *Exhib:* Nat Asn Women Artists Ann Exhib, 90; Hoyt Nat, Hoyt Inst Fine Arts, New Castle, Pa, 90; 55th Ann Nat Midyear Exhib, Butler Inst Am Art, Youngstown, Ohio, 91; 35th Chautauqua Nat Exhib Am Art, Chautauqua Inst, NY, 92; Her Artworks, South Bend Art Ctr, Ind, 92; 11th Sept Competition Exhib, Alexandria Mus Art, La, 92. *Awards:* Elizabeth Erlanger Mem Award, Nat Asn Women Artists, 90; Hon Mention, 55th Ann Nat Midyear Exhib, Butler Inst Am Art, Youngstown, Ohio; Elizabeth Stanton Blake Memorial Award, 103rd Ann Exhib Nat Asn Women Artists, 92. *Mem:* Women's Caucus Arts; Women Arts, Inc; Nat Asn Women Artists. *Media:* Oil. *Mailing Add:* 40-39 48th St Sunnyside NY 11104

FLOWER, MICHAEL LAVIN
ART DEALER, PHOTOGRAPHER
b Queens, NY, Aug 31, 58. *Study:* Simon's Rock Early Col, AA, 77; Dartington Col Art, UK, dipl, 78; Philadelphia Col Art, BFA, 80. *Work:* Mednick Gallery, Philadelphia Col Art. *Comn:* Balloon's at Lake Placid, Winter Olympic Games, comn by Dr Clayton Thomas, Brimfield, Mass, 80; The Mayans (photograph), comn by Gladys Carbo, Stockbridge, Mass, 81; Berkshire Landscapes (photograph), Arcadian Shop, Lenox, Mass, 83. *Exhib:* Year End, Fed Bldg, Philadelphia, 80; TV Veg, Main Gallery, Philadelphia Col Art, 80. *Collections Arranged:* City Reception, 84, Photo & Pencil, 84, China: The People and Landscape, 84, Photographic Silkscreens, 84 & Photographic Installations, 85, Chiaroscuro Gallery, Lenox, Mass. *Pos:* Supv dept photog, Moore Col Art, Philadelphia, 81; owner & dir, Chiaroscuro Gallery, Lenox, Mass, 83- *Teaching:* Substitute prof, experimental photog, Simon's Rock, Great Barrington, Mass, 86; internship dir, photog, Lenox Mem High Sch, Mass, 86; photo instr, Miss Ponters Sch Interim Prog, 87. *Specialty:* Fine art photography. *Mailing Add:* E Main St Stockbridge MA 01262

FLOWERS, THOMAS EARL
PAINTER, EDUCATOR
b Washington, DC, Feb 17, 28. *Study:* Furman Univ, BA; Univ Iowa, MFA. *Work:* Greenville Co Mus Art, SC; Columbia Mus Art, SC; Chase Manhattan Bank, New York; Vincent Price Enterprises, Chicago; Fed Reserve Bank Va, Charlotte, NC, Nations Bank. *Comn:* Mural, Vince Perome, Greenville, SC, 62; mural, Saad Rug Co, Greenville, 63; mace & medallion, Furman Univ, Greenville, 65; mural, City Hall, Greenville, SC. *Exhib:* Eighteenth Ann Guild SC Artists Exhib, 68; 11th Ann Southern Contemp Art Exhib, Mobile, Ala, 69; Best in Show, Springs Art Exhib, Lancaster, SC, 81; Atlanta Artists Club, Nat 1, Ga, 70; Southeastern Painter's Choice Exhib, Ga Col, Milledgeville, Ga, 71. *Pos:* Co-owner, Tate Gallery, Liberty, SC. *Teaching:* Asst prof art & chmn dept, Ottawa Univ, 56-58; instr sculpture, E Carolina Col, 58-59; assoc prof art & chmn dept, Furman Univ, 59-89; retired. *Awards:* Purchase Award, SC Arts Comn, 71; Second Award, Franklin Mint, 72; Art in Archit Award, SC Chap, Am Inst Architects, 77; Spartanburg Art Asn Bureau Award, 91. *Bibliog:* Jack A Morris (auth), Contemporary artists of South Carolina, Greenville Co Mus Art, 70; R Smeltzer (auth), article, Southern Living Mag, 12/70; M Hays (auth), article, Furman Univ Mag, spring 72. *Mem:* Guild SC Artists (pres, 61-62, bd dirs, 71-72); Greenville Artists Guild (pres, 72-73); Southeastern Col Art Asn; Am Craftsman's Coun. *Media:* Mixed. *Publ:* Illusr covers, Furman Univ Mag, winter 67, summer 68 & 5/69; illusr cover, Springs Cotton Mill Ann Report, 69; illusr, Images, Univ NC, Asheville, summer 69. *Dealer:* Hampton III Gallery Ltd 10 Gallery Ctr Greenville SC 29601. *Mailing Add:* 516 Belle Shoals Rd Pickens SC 29671

FLOYD, CARL LEO
SCULPTOR, ENVIRONMENTAL ARTIST
b Somerset, Ky, Oct 12, 36. *Study:* Kansas City Art Inst, BFA, 64; Cranbrook Acad Art, MFA, 67. *Work:* Praltown Park, Lexington, Ky; Vt Freeway, St Albans; Hogback Nature Park, Madison, Ohio; Mand Corning Prof, Holden Arboretum, Mentor, Ohio; Univ Vt Art Mus, Burlington. *Comn:* Steel & wood sculpture, Willoughby Fine Arts, Ohio, 72; Stone Earth, Inner City, Bad Kreuznach, WGer, 75; All People's Park, Lake Co Metrop Parks, 76-77; Earth-Stone, Cleveland Pub Libr, 79; One Acre Proj, Ohio Arts Coun, Madison, 80. *Exhib:* Contemp Sculpture, J B Speed Mus Art, Louisville, Ky, 68; Environ Sculpture, Dulin Gallery Art, Knoxville, Tenn, 69; 2nd Cincinnati Biennial, Cincinnati Art Mus, 69 & Biennial Awards Exhib, 70; Sculpture of New Era, Chicago Fed Plaza, 76; Sculpture on the Green, Columbus Arts Coun, Ohio, 79; Nature Environ, Minn State Univ, Bemidji, 79. *Teaching:* Instr sculpture & archit, Univ Ky, Lexington, 67-71; instr sculpture, Cleveland Inst Art, 71- *Mailing Add:* Dept Sculpture, Cleveland Inst Art 11141 East Blvd Cleveland OH 44106

FLUDD, REGINALD JOSEPH
PAINTER, CRAFTSMAN
b New York, NY, June 10, 38. *Study:* Ind Univ, BS(art); Queens Col, MS(art); study with Kenneth Campbell & Barse Miller; Art Inst Chicago; New York City Col. *Work:* Alcoa Aluminum Corp, New York; Norton Mus, Palm Beach, Fla; Nassau Community Col, Garden City, NY; Ocean City Cult Arts Ctr, NJ; Rose Art Mus, Brandeis Univ, Waltham, Mass; and others. *Exhib:* Am Drawing Biennial, Norfolk Mus, 71; Okla Art Ctr, Oklahoma City, 72; Aldrich Mus, Ridgefield, Conn, 74; New Britian Mus Contemp Art, Conn, 74; one-man show, Hecksher Mus, Huntington, NY, 75; and others. *Teaching:* Instr art, Syosset High Sch, NY, 64-; asst prof painting, Suffolk Community Col, 74-77. *Awards:* Best in Show, Bayshore CofC, 68 & Patchoque CofC, 70; Grand Prix, Locust Valley Art Show, Operation Democracy, 73. *Bibliog:* Laurie Anderson (auth), article in Art News, 1/72; Malcom Preston (auth), article in Newsday, 3/12/75; Jean Paris (auth), article in Long Island Press, 7/6/75. *Mem:* Nat Educ Asn; Nat Art Educ Asn; Huntington Art League. *Media:* Oil, Watercolor. *Mailing Add:* 24 W Sanders Greenlawn NY 11740

FLUEK, TOBY
PAINTER, GRAPHIC ARTIST
b Czernica, Poland, Feb 20, 26; US citizen. *Study:* Art Students League, with Robert Beverly Hale; also with Joe Hing Lowe & Irving Koenig. *Exhib:* Bronx Mus Arts Ann, NY, 72 & 74-76; Am Artists Prof League Grand Nat Exhib at Lever House, NY, 72-76, 78 & 79; Hudson Valley Art Asn Ann, White Plains, NY, 73, 75-84 & 86; Queensborough Community Col Art Gallery, New York, 85, 87 & 88; Rockland Ctr Holocaust Studies, Spring Valley, NY, 90; United Jewish Apeal Art Gallery, New York, 92. *Teaching:* Instr oil painting, Woodside Jewish Ctr, NY, 72. *Awards:* Best Show, Art League Nassau Co, 79; Prix du Roman Historique, Historical Novel Prize, 91; Chosen Best Book for Young Adults 1991 by Am Libr Asn, Young Adults Servs Div; and others. *Bibliog:* Lionel Klass (auth), The Past Remembered, The Jewish Press, 3/20/87, Jerusalem Times, Jewish Press Isreael, 3/27/87; Image Before My Eyes (doc film), Inst Jewish Res; Meryl Gordon (auth), Paint by Memories, NY Mag, 10/22/90; Rabbi Jack Riemer (auth), How Another Holocaust Book is So Special, Miami Jewish Tribune, 10/26/90. *Mem:* Am Artists Prof League; Hudson Valley Art Asn; Catharine Lorillard Wolfe Art Club. *Media:* Oil, Charcoal. *Publ:* Auth, Memories of My Life in a Polish Village 1930-49, Alfred A Knopf, 90. *Mailing Add:* 60-10 47th Ave Woodside NY 11377

FLUME, VIOLET SIGOLOFF
DEALER, RESTORER
b Huntington, WVa. *Study:* Trinity Univ, with Phillip Wilson. *Work:* Paintings & portraits in pvt collections, US & Mex. *Exhib:* San Antonio Art League, 64-70; one-woman shows, Southwestern Fine Arts Exhib, Univ Tex, 67, HemisFair, 68 & Trinity Univ, 68. *Pos:* Owner & dir, Wonderland Gallery, 66-72 & Wonderland Art Sch, 69-72; owner, Sigoloff Fine Art Galleries, 72- *Awards:* Watercolor & Miniature Award, Composers, Authors & Artists Exhib, New York, 65; San Antonio's Outstanding Woman in Art, San Antonio Express & Eve News, 67. *Mem:* Tex Fine Arts Asn; San Antonio Art League. *Media:* Oil. *Specialty:* Fine art, contemporary and antique paintings. *Mailing Add:* 2318 NW Military Hwy No 103 San Antonio TX 78231

FLYNN, PAT L
JEWELER, GOLDSMITH
b Edinboro, Pa, Oct 29, 54. *Study:* Edinboro State Col, 73-76; State Univ Col New York, New Paltz, BFA, 78. *Work:* Chicago Art Inst; Nordenfjeldske Kunstindustt Mus, Trondheim, Norway; also pvt collections of Mr & Mrs Ron Abramson, Mr & Mrs Malcolm Knapp & Robert Pfannebecker. *Exhib:* Am Craft Mus, 84 & 87; Jewelry Now, Virginia Mus, Richmond, 86-87; Silver in Service, Castle Gallery, New Rochelle, New York, 87; Goldsmithing, Louisiana State Univ, 88; 20th Century Decorative Art, Naval Pier, Chicago, 87, 88 & 89. *Pos:* Freelance jeweler, goldsmith & modelmaker, 82-85; owner, Flynn Studios, New Paltz, NY, 85- *Awards:* Nat Endowment Arts, 85 & 88; Christofle Prize, Philadelphia Craft Show, 87. *Mem:* Am Crafts Coun. *Dealer:* Susan Cummins Gallery 12 Miller Ave Mill Valley CA 94941; America House 466 Piermont Ave Piermont NY 10968. *Mailing Add:* 330 Old Ford Rd New Paltz NY 12561

FOGG, MONICA
PAINTER, EDUCATOR
b Belaire, Tex. *Study:* Washington Univ, 73; Principia Col, Elsah, Ill, BA, 74; St Cloud Univ, Minn, MA, 86. *Work:* General Mills & Honeywell, Minneapolis; Prudential Insurance Co Am, Plymouth, Minn; Principia Col, Elsah, Ill; Marathon Oil Co, Midland, Tex. *Comn:* Minn Protective Life, Eden Prairie, 75; Woodhill Country Club, Wayzata, 82; AMFAC-City Ctr, Minneapolis, 82; Univ Minn Hosp, 86. *Exhib:* Metamorphose-One, Minn Mus Art, St Paul, 76; Midwest Watercolor Ann, Tweed Mus, Duluth, Minn, 77 & 78; Northstar Soc Ann, Minneapolis, 77-83; Aqueous Open, Pittsburgh Watercolor Soc, Pa, 78; one-woman show, Expressive of Alaska, Artique, Anchorage, 81; Minn Artist Asn, Minneapolis, 82; Expressive Chroma on Paper, Kieale Gallery, St Cloud, Minn. *Teaching:* Instr, St Louis Watercolor Soc, 74, Northstar Watercolor Soc, 77, Univ Minn, 80-86, Edina Art Ctr, 80-81, Fogg Studio, 81-83, Art Ctr Minn, 83 & St Cloud State Univ, 84-86. *Awards:* Second Prize, Minn 77, State Arts Coun, 77; Award Excellence, Northstar Watercolor Soc Ann, 77, 80, 82 & 83; Award of Excellence, Minn Artists Asn, 82; and others. *Bibliog:* Fredric Appel (auth), Watercolor: When it's good, Minn Star & Tribune, 78; Cindy Rumsey (auth), Artist on the move (film), WCCO-TV, Minneapolis, 81; Warren Martin (auth), Watercolor-An Art (film), WTCN-TV, Minneapolis, 81. *Mem:* Minn Soc Fine Arts; Northstar Watercolor Soc (treas, 78-81 & bd mem, 78-81); Midwest Watercolor Soc; Twin Cities Watercolor Soc; Women's Caucus Arts. *Media:* Watercolor. *Mailing Add:* 5720 10th Ave S Minneapolis MN 55147

FOGG, REBECCA SNIDER
PRINTMAKER, PAINTER
b Washington, DC, Dec 16, 49. *Study:* Rochester Inst Technol, summer 72; RI Sch Design, BFA, 72. *Work:* Rochester Inst Technol, Henrietta, NY; Am Fed Savings & Loan, Sacramento, Calif; Resorts Unlimited, Atlantic City, NJ. *Comn:* Etching, Columbia Bank, Newark, NJ, 74; etchings with Michael Harris, Rickey's Calif Hyatt, Palo Alto, Calif, 83. *Exhib:* Printmakers Regional Exhib, Rochester Mem Art Gallery, 75; Kala Inst Printmakers, Hearst Mus, St Mary's Col, Moraga, Calif, 79; Biennial Exhib, Mus Munic de las Artes Graphicas, Maracaibo, Venezuela, 81. *Teaching:* Instr drawing

& graphic design, Genesee Community Col, Batavia, NY, 75-77; instr computer graphics & design, Ohlone Col, Fremont, Calif, 91- *Awards:* Community Prog Grant Award, Burlington in Transition, Mayor's Coun Arts, Burlington, Vt, 86. *Media:* Etching; Watercolor. *Dealer:* San Francisco Mus Mod Art Rental Gallery Bldg A Ft Mason San Francisco CA 94123. *Mailing Add:* 4701 San Leandro Suite 16 Oakland CA 94601

FOHR, JENNY
PAINTER, PRINTMAKER
b New York, NY. *Study:* Hunter Col, BA; Alfred Univ; Univ Colo, MA; City Col. *Work:* Norfolk Mus, Va; Long Beach Island Found Arts & Sci, NJ; Dr Wardell Pomeroy, New York; Oakland Mus, Calif; Charles Suter, Ciba-Geigy, New York. *Exhib:* One-man show, Chautauqua Art Asn Galleries, NY, 60 & Brooklyn Mus, 61; Nat Asn Women Artists, Chauteau de la Napoule, France, 65; Nat Asn Women Artists Traveling Show, India, 66; NJ State Mus, Trenton, 68; Am Color Print Soc Traveling Show, 72. *Teaching:* Asst instr sculpture, Brooklyn Mus, 49-51; instr art, Beekman Hill Sch, 69-81. *Awards:* Samuel Mann Award, Am Soc Contemp Artists, 71; May Granick Award, Nat Asn Women Artists, 75; Doris Kreindlr Award, 81; The Alvin & Co Award, 83. *Bibliog:* Article, New York News, 76. *Mem:* Am Soc Contemp Artists (pres, secy, bd dir); Nat Asn Women Artists (secy, jury chmn, dir); Painters & Sculptors Soc NJ (selection jury, bd); Am Color Print Soc; New York Soc Women Artists (dir, cat chmn). *Media:* Miscellaneous Media. *Mailing Add:* 165 E 32 St Apt 5E New York NY 10016

FOLDA, JAROSLAV (THAYER), III
HISTORIAN
b Baltimore, Md, July 25, 40. *Study:* Princeton Univ, AB, 62; Johns Hopkins Univ, PhD, 68. *Teaching:* From asst prof to prof medieval art, Univ NC, Chapel Hill, 68-78, prof, 78-, chmn, 83-87. *Awards:* Dumbarton Oaks Ctr Fel, 67-68; Jr Humanist Award, Nat Endowment Humanities, 74-75; Nat Endowment Humanities, 81-83; Guggenheim Fel, 88-89; Nat Humanities Ctr Fel, 88-89. *Mem:* Medieval Acad Am; Col Art Asn Am; Int Ctr Medieval Art; Soc for the Study of the Crusades and the Latin East; ASOR; US Nat Byzantine Comt. *Res:* Medieval art of the High and Late Middle Ages, especially Crusader art, 1099-1291. *Publ:* Auth, Crusader Manuscript Illumination at St Jean d'Acre, Princeton Univ Press, 76; contribr, K M Setton (ed), A History of the Crusaders, Vol 4, Univ Wis Press, 77; ed, Crusader art in the twelfth century, British Archeol Reports, Vol 152, 82; auth, Crusader frescoes at Crac des Chevaliers and Marqab castle, Dumbarton Oaks Papers, Vol 36, 82; The Nazareth Capitals and the Crusader Church of the Annunciation, CAA Monograph, 42, 86; and others. *Mailing Add:* Dept of Art, Hanes Art Ctr Univ of NC Chapel Hill NC 27599-3405

FOLEY, DOROTHY SWARTZ
PAINTER, GRAPHIC ARTIST
b Wall, Pa. *Study:* Art Students League, studied with Robert Brackman & Howard Trafton; Adelphi Univ, studied with Milton Goldstein. *Work:* Military Mus, NY State Capitol Bldg, Albany; Nat Baseball Hall Fame, Cooperstown, NY; Nat Basketball Hall Fame, Springfield, Mass. *Comn:* Painting, Cabrini Medical Ctr, New York, 89; portrait of George Seuffert, Comn by Claire Shulman borough pres of Queens, NY, 88. *Exhib:* One-woman show, Long Beach Mus Art, NY, 80; Orange Co Watercolor Exhib, Mus of the Trotter, Goshen, NY, 87; Metrop Mus Art, New York; Queens Mus, Flushing Meadow Park, NY; Nat League Am Pen Women, Nat Art Mus Sport, New York; Nassau Co Mus Fine Art, Roslyn, NY, 88. *Pos:* Artist & head graphic arts, US Military, 51-73. *Teaching:* Instr oil painting, Youth Ctr, Mitchel Air Force Base, NY, formerly; instr art, Alliance Queens Artists, NY, 86- *Awards:* Award of Excellence, Art League Nassau Co, Lever House, New York, 84; Award of Merit, Long Island Branch, Nat League Am Pen Women, 88; Best Oil Painting, Alliance Queens Artists, Lever House, New York, 88; Grumbocher Award, 86 & Award Excellence, 90, Long Island Br, Nat League Am Pen Women; and many others. *Bibliog:* Malcolm Preston (auth), Five different roads to realism, 5/18/84 & rev, 2/13/85, New York Newsday; Exhibition Spotlights: Contemporary Spiritual Artists, Paul VI Inst Arts, Washington, DC, 86. *Mem:* Art League Nassau Co; Hudson Valley Art Asn; Am Artists Prof League; Alliance Queens Artists; Nat League Am Pen Women. *Media:* Oil, Watercolor; Etching, Silkscreen. *Publ:* Illusr, Recipe Masterpieces, Wimmer Bros, 82. *Mailing Add:* 81-48 169th St Jamaica NY 11432

FOLEY, KATHY KELSEY
DIRECTOR, HISTORIAN
b Perth Amboy, NJ, Aug 24, 52. *Study:* Trinity Col, Hartford, Fall semester in Rome, 72-73; Vassar Col, AB(hist art), 74; Nat Gallery Art, Washington, DC, internship cert, Summer 74; Johns Hopkins Univ, MA(hist art), 75. *Collections Arranged:* Edward Weston's Gifts to His Sister (125 photographs), Dayton Art Inst, 78; Collaborations (auth, catalog), 80, Exploring Society Photographically, 81, Chinese Ceramics from Chicago Collections, 82, Discoveries from Kurdish Looms, 83 & Painting at Northwestern: Conger, Paschke & Valerio, 86, Mary & Leigh Block Gallery, Northwestern Univ; Birds in Art 1988, 88 & Delight for the Senses: Dutch & Flemish Still-life painting from Budapest, 89, Leigh Yawkey Woodson Art Mus, Wausau, Wis. *Pos:* Asst cur, Dayton Art Inst, Ohio, 75-76, cur, 76-79; dir, Mary & Leigh Block Gallery, Northwestern Univ, Evanston, 79-86; dir, Leigh Yawkey Woodson Art Mus, Wausau, Wis, 87- *Teaching:* Instr, Brooklyn Mus, NY Dept Educ, Summer 73; lectr, Dept Art Hist, Northwestern Univ, 80-86. *Mem:* Am Asn Mus; Col Art Asn; Int Coun Mus. *Publ:* Co-auth, Selected Checklist of the Collection of the Dayton Art Inst, 76, auth, Handbook of the American Collection of the Dayton Art Inst, 76 & Joseph Stella-Enigmatic Painter, Bulletin of Dayton Art Inst, 77, Dayton Art Inst. *Mailing Add:* c/o Leigh Yawkey Woodson Art Mus Franklin & 12th Sts Wausau WI 54401-5007

FOLEY, TIMOTHY ALBERT
ART DEALER
b New Orleans, La, May 11, 47. *Study:* Loyola Univ, New Orleans; Univ New Orleans, BA(anthrop), 71. *Awards:* Distinguished Alumni, Univ New Orleans, 91. *Specialty:* Quality contemp art as well as important 19th and 20th century art; Southern artists of the 19th and early 20th centuries. *Mailing Add:* 4119 Magazine St New Orleans LA 70115

FOLKUS, DAN (DANIEL ALAN FREDRICKSON)
DESIGNER, ILLUSTRATOR
b Rice Lake, Wis, Oct 1, 46. *Study:* Lawrence Univ, BA(philos & art), 68; assisted muralist Granville Bruce, Dallas, 72. *Work:* US Golf Asn, Golf House Mus, Far Hills, NJ; Kenosha Pub Mus, Wis; Charleston Mus, SC. *Comn:* 5th Avenue Murals, comn by Madame Alexander, New York, 92. *Exhib:* Permanent mural, Forbidden Planet, New York. *Pos:* Preparator, Dallas Mus, 72-74; freelance illusr, 74-78; cur exhibs, Kenosha Pub Mus, Wis, 78-79; chief exhibs planner-designer, Charleston Mus, SC, 79-80; asst film dir, WCBD-TV, SC, 80-81; pres, Visual Syntax, Collingswood, NJ, 82- *Awards:* Exhib Builders Asn Award, Dupont Print Show, 85. *Mem:* Am Asn Mus. *Media:* Latex Casting, Acrylic Painting. *Publ:* Illusr, Pests Control, auth, Dr E P Cheatum, Prestige Press, 73; Dust storms of Mars, Astronomy Mag, 77; Biologic Cardiac Assit, In: Assisted Circulation, Springer- Verhag, 88. *Mailing Add:* 465 Haddon Ave Collingswood NJ 08108

FOLSOM, FRED GORHAM, III
PAINTER, CONSERVATOR
b Washington, DC, July 31, 45. *Study:* Pratt Inst, NY, with Martha Erlebacher, 64-67; Sch Visual Arts, NY, 67; Corcoran Sch Art, Washington, DC, 69. *Work:* Immaculata Col, Washington, DC; Lyndon B Johnson Libr, Austin, Tex; Dimock Gallery, George Washington Univ; Hickory Mus Art, NC. *Comn:* James M Goode, Collection of American Self-Portraits. *Exhib:* Md Biennial Exhib, Baltimore Mus Art, 74 & 85; Crimes of Compassion, Chrysler Mus, Norfolk, Va, 81; Wash-Moscow Art Exchange, Tretya Kov-Gallery, Russia; The Washington Show, Corcoran Gallery Art, 85. *Pos:* Actor, Robert Wilson Theater Productions, New York, 66; conservator & owner, Art Restoration Ctr, Takoma Park, Md, 77-; juror, Dimock Gallery, George Washington Univ, 86. *Awards:* Works in Progress Grant, Md State Arts Coun, 81; Best of Show, Artscape '82, Mayor's Comn Arts, Baltimore, 82; Individual Grant Visual Arts, Nat Endowment Arts, 85. *Bibliog:* Nina Ffrench-Frazier (auth), Fred Folsom, Art Int, 1-2/81; David Tannous (auth), Washington, DC, Fred Folsom, Art in Am, 2/81; Benjamin Forgey (auth), Portrait of DC's art scene, Washington Post, 6/22/85; Gregory Wolfe (auth), Fred Folsom A Profile, IMAGE, 92. *Publ:* Cover illusr, The poet John Pauker, Art Int, 1/79. *Mailing Add:* 908 Hudson Ave Takoma Park MD 20912

FOLSOM, ROSE
CALLIGRAPHER, WRITER
b Madison, Wis, July 31, 53. *Study:* Pvt study with Sheila Waters, 74-75; Rochester Inst Technol, calligraphy master class with Hermann Zapf, 79-80. *Exhib:* Lettering Arts in the '80s, Northrop Gallery, Univ Minn, Minneapolis, 84; solo exhibs, Recent Calligraphic Works, 88 & Calligraphic Murals, 89, Foundry Gallery, Washington, DC; Scene in DC, Amos Eno Gallery, New York, 88; The Book as Art II, Nat Mus for Women in Arts, 89; Calligraphia USA/USSR, 90-93. *Pos:* Owner, Folsom Calligraphy Studio, 73-; Washington corresp, Calligraphy Rev Mag, Norman, Okla, 85- *Teaching:* Instr, Washington Calligraphers Guild, 78-; lectr hist calligraphy, Nat Mus Am Art, Renwick Gallery, 90, Smithsonian Inst, 92. *Bibliog:* Pamela Kessler (auth), Abstract colors & lamb chops, Washington Post, 4/22/88; Jane Snow (auth), Living treasures, Washingtonian Mag, 8/88; Michael Welzenbach (auth), Bare bones beauty, Washington Post, 10/7/89. *Mem:* Washington Calligraphers Guild. *Media:* Ink on Paper. *Publ:* Illusr, Calligraphy Today, Pentalic, 76; International Calligraphy Today, Watson-Guptill, 82; Copperplate manual reviews, Lettering Arts Bk Club, 84; Auth, The Calligraphers' Dictionary, Thames & Hudson, 90. *Mailing Add:* 908 Hudson Ave Takoma Park MD 20912

FONDAW, RON
SCULPTOR
b Paducah, Ky, Apr 25, 54. *Study:* Memphis Col Art, Tenn, BFA, 76; Univ Ill, Champaign, MFA, 78. *Work:* Renwick Gallery, Smithsonian Inst, Washington, DC; Columbus Mus Fine Art, Ohio; Tenn State Arts Comn, Nashville; John Michael Kohler Arts Ctr, Sheboygan, Wis; Richard & Joy Haft, Miami, Fla; Dr Carl Djerassi, Woodside, Calif; Martin Z Margulies, Grove Isle, Fla. *Comn:* Art in Public Places, Ghost Islands, Key Biscayne, Fla, 87; outdoor sculpture, Fragments, Southeastern Ctr Contemp Art, Winston-Salem, NC, 87; outdoor sculpture, NAOS, Coconut Grove, Fla, purchased by City of Miami, Coconut Grove Asn, 88; outdoor sculptures, Earth Structures, E Hampton Ctr Contemp Art, NY, 88; Now and Never, Socrates Sculpture Park, Long Island City, NY, 89; Ferro's Dream, Fla Int Univ, Miami, 90. *Exhib:* Am Ceramics Now, Everson Mus Art, Syracuse, NY, traveling juried exhib: Am Craft Mus, New York & Crocker Art Mus, Sacramento, Calif, 87; Am Ceramics Now, traveling, De Cordova & Dana Mus & park, Lincoln, Mass, Butler Inst Art, Youngstown, Ohio, Sheldon Mem Art Gallery, Univ Nebr-Lincoln, 89; Birmingham Mus Art, Ala, 89; The BMW Gallery, New York, 90; Twenty-Five in Miami, Miami Dade Comn Col, S Campus Gallery, Fla, 90; Abstraction, Eve Mannes Gallery, Atlanta, Ga, 90; Buildings with Clay, Hoffman Gallery, Ore Sch Art and Crafts, 90; 3, Sampson Gallery, Stetson Univ, Deland, Fla, 90; Art in Industry, John M Kohler Art Ctr, Sheboygan, Wis, 90; one-man exhibs, Of Iron and Earth, Atlantic Ctr for Arts, New Smyrna Beach, Fla, 89, Ron Fondaw, drawings, Nat Acad Sci, Washington, DC, 90; and others. *Teaching:* Vis instr art, Ohio Univ, 78; assoc

prof art, Univ Miami, Coral Gables, Fla, 79-; lectr, Ohio State Univ, 83, Univ Gainesville, Fla, 84, Chicago Art Inst, Ill, 86, Ft Lauderdale Mus Art, Fla, Ormond Mem Art Mus & Tokyo Nat Univ Fine Art, Japan, 87, Chautauqua Sch Art, NY, 88, Northern Ill Univ, Dekalb, & Chicago Art Inst, Ill 89 & Hollufgard Kulturcenter, Odense, Denmark, 90. *Awards:* Nat Endowment Art Fel, 88 & 89; Awards in Visual Arts 8, 89; New Forms, Fla, 90; Fla Arts Coun Fel, 92. *Bibliog:* Paula Harper (auth), Sculpture-Ron Fondaw, Am Ceramics, Vol 2, 4, 84; Helen Kohen (auth), Staring and shivering, Art News, 6/81; Susan Peterson (auth), The Art and Craft of Clay, Prentice Hall, 91. *Media:* Ceramics. *Mailing Add:* 6795 SW 59th St Miami FL 33143

FONDREN, HAROLD M
DEALER
b Canton, Ohio, Feb 5, 22. *Study:* Harvard Col, AB. *Pos:* Asst dir, Stable Gallery, 54-55; asst dir, Poindexter Gallery, 55- *Specialty:* Contemporary painting and sculpture. *Mailing Add:* 1150 Fifth Ave New York NY 10128

FONTAINE, E JOSEPH
PAINTER
b Springfield, Mass. *Study:* Tufts Univ, BA(magna cum laude), 51; Harvard Law Sch, LLB, 58; Fogg Mus Art, 82-83. *Work:* Springfield Mus Fine Arts; US Trust Co; Bank of New Eng; Liberty Mutual; Nat Fire Prevention Asn; Bank of Boston; Middlesex Savings Bank. *Exhib:* One-man shows, Mass Inst of Technol, 85, Crane Collection, 86; Copley Soc of Boston, 80-86 & 91; Brockton Art Mus, 85; Babson Col, 87-88; Springfield Mus Fine Arts, 90; Lily Pad Gallery, 92. *Awards:* First Prize, Brockton Art Mus, 84 & 85. *Media:* Oil; Pastels. *Mailing Add:* 73 Greylock Rd Wellesley Hills MA 02181

FONTANA, BILL PATRICK
ENVIRONMENTAL ARTIST, CONCEPTUAL ARTIST
b Cleveland, Ohio, April 25, 47. *Study:* John Carroll Univ, 65-68; New Sch Social Res, BA, 70. *Comn:* Flight Paths Out to Sea, Newport Harbor Art Mus, Newport Beach, Calif, 80; Oscillating Steel Grids, Contemp Art Ctr, Cincinnati, 80; Landscape Sculpture with Fog Horns, New Music Am, San Francisco, 81; Sound Sculpture with a Sequence of Level, 12th Int Sculpture Conf, Oakland, Calif, 82; Crossings Rochester Birds: 1983, Nat Shopping Ctrs, Rochester, NY, 83. *Exhib:* Sound Sculpture, Nat Gallery Victoria, Melbourne, Australia, 78; Space Between Sounds, San Francisco Mus Mod Art, 78; Fur Augen und Ohren, Akad Künste, West Berlin, 80; Ecouter par les Yeux, Mus Art Mod, Paris, 80; Soundings, Neuberger Mus, Purchase, NY, 81; Great East River Bridge, Brooklyn Mus, 83. *Teaching:* Guest artist, Berliner Künstlerprogramm, Deutscher Akad Austauschdienst, 83-84. *Bibliog:* The Art of Sound, CBS News, 9/19/82. *Media:* Sound Sculpture. *Publ:* Auth, The music of sound, Village Voice, 83; Brooklyn Bridge Sound Sculpture by Bill Fontana, Am Haus Berlin, 83. *Mailing Add:* c/o Gallery Panle Anglim 14 Geary St San Francisco CA 94108

FOOLERY, TOM
ASSEMBLAGE ARTIST, PAINTER
b Green Bay, Wis, Aug 29, 47. *Study:* Self-taught. *Work:* Pierotti Pavillion, San Francisco; and others. *Comn:* Murals, St Francis Mem Hosp, San Francisco, 79-81. *Exhib:* Humor in Art, Los Angeles Inst Contemp Art, 81; one-man shows, William Sawyer Gallery, San Francisco, 81 & Jacqueline Anhalt Gallery, Los Angeles, 82; Dobrick Gallery, Chicago, 83; Anxious Interiors, Laguna Beach Mus Art, Calif, & traveling, 84; Miniature Environments, Whitney Mus, New York, 89; Forty Years of California , traveling, Univ Calif, Los Angeles, 89-; Miniature Environments, Whitney Mus at Phillip Morris, 89; 40 Years of California Assemblage, Univ Calif Los Angeles, (traveling), 89. *Bibliog:* Frank Cabulski (auth), Art of control, Artweek, 2/21/81; Neal Menzies (auth), Carrot Commentaries, Artweek, 11/27/82. *Media:* All. *Dealer:* Dobrick Gallery, Chicago. *Mailing Add:* 435 Joost San Francisco CA 94127

FOOSANER, JUDITH
EDUCATOR, PAINTER
b Sacramento, Calif, Aug 10, 40. *Study:* Univ Calif, Berkeley, BA, 64 & MA, 68. *Work:* Newport Harbor Art Mus, Newport Beach, Calif; Everson Mus, Syracuse, NY; Albuquerque Mus, NMex. *Exhib:* Laguna Beach Mus, Calif, 67; Calif Palace Legion Honor, San Francisco, 69; Bellevue Art Mus, Wash, 76; M H DeYoung Mem Mus, San Francisco, 77; Oakland Mus, Calif, 81; Ark Arts Ctr, 90; Space Gallery, Los Angeles, Calif, 90. *Teaching:* Prof fine arts, Calif Col Arts & Crafts, Oakland, 70-82; vis asst prof art, Univ Calif, Berkeley, 75-77. *Media:* Oil. *Mailing Add:* c/o Space Gallery 6015 Santa Monica Blvd Los Angeles CA 90038

FOOSE, ROBERT JAMES
PAINTER, DESIGNER
b York, Pa, Oct 17, 38. *Study:* Univ Ky, AB, 63. *Work:* J B Speed Art Mus, Louisville, Ky; Owensboro Mus Art, Ky; Springfield Art Mus, Mo; New York Pub Libr; Libr of Cong, Washington, DC; and others. *Comn:* Bks & bk jackets, Univ Ky Press, 60-78 & bk illus, 78; portraits, UK Law Alumni Asn, Univ Ky, 79, 81 & 83; posters & catalogs, Univ Ky Art Mus, 88; State of the Art, Parkland Col, Ill, 89. *Exhib:* 600 Years of American Watercolor Painting, J B Speed Art Mus, 77; one-person show, Katholische Akademie Trier, WGer, 82; The Kentucky Tradition in American Landscape Painting, Owensboro Art Mus, Ky, 83, The Experienced Eye, 88; Kentucky Art, James Hunt Barker Galleries, New York, 83 & Univ Ky Art Mus, 85; Watercolor Now, Springfield Am Mus, Mo, 88; Realism Today, Evansville Art Mus, Ind, 89; and others. *Pos:* Founder & proprietor, Buttonwood Press, Lexington, Ky, 68-; art dir, Odyssey, Univ Ky Res Found, Lexington, 80- *Teaching:* Instr Europ Summer Acad Fine Art, Trier, WGer, 80-81; res artist, Blackhawk Sch Art, Colo, 86, 87, 88; assoc prof graphic design & painting & chmn Art dept, Univ Ky, currently. *Awards:* John Singer Sargent Award, Southern Watercolor Soc, 78 & 80; Grand Prize, Aqueous '79, Ky Watercolor Soc; First Place, Ky Watercolor Soc, 83. *Bibliog:* Am Artist, 10/87. *Mem:* Ky Guild Artists & Craftsmen (pres, 69-73); Ky Watercolor Soc; Southern Watercolor Soc; and others. *Media:* Watercolor; All Print Media. *Publ:* Illusr, Uncle Will of Wildwood, 74 & Bestiary, 75, Univ Ky; The Trembling Land, Halocon Press, 80; and others. *Dealer:* Gallery 3 213 Market St Roanoke VA 24011. *Mailing Add:* PO Box 22541 Lexington KY 40522-2541

FOOTE, HOWARD REED
ARTIST, PRINTMAKER
b Richmond, Ind, Dec 15, 36. *Study:* Toledo Mus Art, Ohio, 54-55; Sch of Mus Fine Arts, Boston, 55-57; San Francisco Art Inst, BFA, 60; Stanford Univ, MA, 70; additional study with Nathan Oliveira. *Work:* Achenbach Found, Palace of the Legion of Honor, San Francisco; City of Leeds, Eng; City of San Francisco; Stanford Univ. *Exhib:* Bay Area Printmakers Soc Fourth Nat Exhib, Oakland Mus, Calif, 58; 1970 Peace Exhib, Philadelphia Mus Art, 70; San Francisco Art Inst Centennial Exhib, Palace of the Legion of Honor, San Francisco, 71; Four Printmakers, San Francisco Mus Art, 71; 18th Nat Print Exhib, Brooklyn Mus, NY, 72; San Francisco Area Printmakers, Cincinnati Art Mus, Ohio, 73; Interstices, San Jose Art Mus, Calif & Cranbrook Acad Art Mus, Bloomfield Hills, Mich, 75. *Teaching:* Instr printmaking, Acad Art, San Francisco, 70- & Calif State Univ, Hayward, 71-72; instr printmaking, drawing & 3-D design, Col Notre Dame, Belmont, Calif, 75- *Publ:* Contribr, Ramparts Mag, 6/70; contribr, BYTE, 9/81. *Mailing Add:* 205 Park Ave Inverness CA 94937

FORBES, DONNA MARIE
MUSEUM DIRECTOR
b Albion, Nebr, Mar 19, 29. *Study:* Mont State Univ; Pratt Inst; Eastern Mont Col, BS(art educ), 52; Harvard Summer Inst in Arts Admin; Univ Calif, Berkeley, Mus Mgt Inst, 83. *Collections Arranged:* The Christmas Story, 78, The Cowboy, 78, Using Paper, 80, Chinese Robes: 1750-1900, 82 & The William Andrews Clark Collection: Treasures of a Copper King, 88, Yellowstone Art Ctr, Billings, Mont. *Pos:* Dir, Yellowstone Art Ctr, Billings, Mont, 74-; mem, Eastern Mont Col Found Bd, 74-79 & 82-, pres, 78; mem selection comt, Downtown Redevelopment Bd, Billings, Mont, 86; mem, Downtown Coordr Coun, Billings, Mont, 86. *Teaching:* Instr design & art educ, Eastern Mont Col, 52-53. *Mem:* Art Mus Asn; Am Asn Mus; Mont Art Gallery Dirs Asn (adv exec bd, 78-, pres, 80-82); Mountain-Plains Mus Asn; Am Fedn Arts (bd dirs, 87-). *Mailing Add:* 1116 Eighth St W Billings MT 59102

FORBES, JOHN ALLISON
HISTORIAN, PAINTER
b Evansburg, Alta, Sept 19, 22. *Study:* Univ Alta, BEd, 48, MEd, 51; Univ London, associateship, 56; Univ Iowa, MA, 67. *Collections Arranged:* Bart Pragnell-Watercolours, Univ Art Gallery, Edmonton, 67; J B Taylor-Memorial (auth, catalog), Edmonton Art Gallery, 73. *Teaching:* Assoc prof art educ, Univ Alta, 49-65, prof art hist, 65-85, prof emer, 85- *Mem:* Royal Soc Arts, London; Univs Art Asn Can. *Media:* Watercolor, Acrylics. *Res:* Western Canadian landscape painters; military art. *Publ:* Coauth, Mountain landscapes of J B Taylor, Can Alpine J, Vol 57, 74; auth, Douglas Haynes (exhib catalog), Glenbow Art Gallery, Calgary, 74; Robert Sinclair (exhib catalog), Aggregation Gallery, Toronto, 76. *Mailing Add:* 11523-77 Ave Edmonton AB T6G 0M2 Canada

FORCE, ROLAND WYNFIELD
MUSEUM DIRECTOR
b Omaha, Nebr, Dec 30, 24. *Study:* Stanford Univ, BA, 50, MA, 51, MA, 52 & PhD, 58; Hawaii Loa Col, Honolulu, DSc, 73. *Pos:* Assoc ethnology, Bishop Mus, 54-56, dir, 62-76; cur, Oceanic Archeol & Ethnology, Field Mus, 56-61; dir, Mus Am Indian, 77-90. *Teaching:* Actg instr, Stanford Univ, 52-54; lectr, Univ Chicago, Ill, 56-61. *Mem:* Am Asn Mus; Int Coun Mus. *Publ:* Coauth, Art and Artifacts of the 18th Century, Bishop Mus Press, 68; coauth, The Fuller Collection of Pacific Artifacts, Praeger, 71. *Mailing Add:* 161 Kalaiopua Pl Honolulu HI 96822

FORD, HARRY XAVIER
EDUCATOR, ADMINISTRATOR
b Seymour, Ind, Jan 12, 21. *Study:* John Herron Art Inst; Univ Calif Los Angeles, BA; Sacramento State Col, MA; Univ Calif Berkeley; Kansas City Art Inst, Hon DFA, 74. *Exhib:* Crocker Mus, 52; Stuttgart Amerikhaus, 56. *Pos:* Chmn dept teacher educ, Calif Col Arts & Crafts, 58-60, pres, 60-85; pres bd dir, World Print Coun, 85-87. *Teaching:* Art, Placer Union High Sch, 51-53 & Stuttgart Am High Sch, Ger, 53-58; prof emeritus & hon trustee, Osaka Univ Fine Arts, Naniwa Col, Osaka, Japan, 85. *Mem:* Nat Asn Schs Art; Union Independent Cols Art (chmn, 72-74); Alliance Independent Cols Art (bd mem). *Media:* Oil. *Mailing Add:* 1831 Sun Mountain Dr Santa Fe NM 87501

FORD, JOHN
PAINTER, SCULPTOR
b Washington, DC, Mar 2, 50. *Study:* Self-taught. *Work:* Oakland Mus Art; Prudential Insurance Co, Newark, NJ; Nashville Med Corp, Tenn; Sidney Lewis Collection, Richmond, Va. *Comn:* Trap sculpture, Kenmare Sq, New York. *Exhib:* Whitney Mus Am Art Biennial, 75; Aspects of Abstract, Crocker Art Mus, Sacramento, Calif, 79; Coastal Currents, Ctr Arts, Corpus Christi, Tex, 81; Sacramento Connection, Laguna Gloria Mus, Laguna Beach, Calif, 82; Jersey City Art Mus, NJ, 82; solo exhib, State Univ NY, Purchase,

82. *Teaching:* Lectr, Bakersfield State Univ, 77, Sacramento State Univ, 78 & C W Post Ctr, Long Island Univ, 83. *Awards:* Artists Fel, Nat Endowment Arts, 82. *Bibliog:* Thomas Albright (auth), Sleepers and spectacles, Art News, 9/79; Vivien Raynor (auth), article, NY Times, 82; Thomas Albright (auth), Art in the San Francisco Bay Area, Univ Calif Press, 85. *Media:* Acrylic, Oil; All Media. *Mailing Add:* 28 Overlook Terr Simsbury CT 06070

FORD, JOHN GILMORE
COLLECTOR
b Baltimore, Md. *Study:* Baltimore City Col, degree; Johns Hopkins Univ; Loyola Col; Md Inst Col Art, BFA. *Exhib:* Collection Indo-Asian art, Walters Art Gallery, Baltimore, 71. *Pos:* Nat vpres, Am Inst Interior Designers, 70- *Awards:* Citation of merit, Md Inst Col Art, 60. *Bibliog:* P Pal (auth), Indo-Asian art, 71, Walters Art Gallery, Apollo Mag & Connoisseur Mag. *Mem:* Am Fedn Arts; Asia Soc. *Collection:* Indian, Nepalese, Tibetan, Javanese, Chinese & Japanese bronzes, stone sculptures and paintings. *Mailing Add:* 2601 N Charles St Baltimore MD 21218

FORD, WALTON
PAINTER
b White Plains, NY, 60. *Study:* RI Sch Design, Providence, BFA, 82, Europ Honors Prog, Rome, Italy. *Exhib:* Solo shows, Bess Cutler Gallery, New York, 90, 91 & 93, Contemp Arts Ctr, Cincinnati, Ohio, 93; Ctr Bk Arts Exhib, Harper Collins, New York, 91; Galerie Schulze, Koln, Ger, 91; Marion Locks Gallery, Philadelphia, Pa, 92. *Awards:* Grant, Mid-Atlantic Arts Found, 90; Nat Endowment Arts Fel, 91; John Simon Guggenheim Mem Found Fel, 92. *Bibliog:* Richard Maschal (auth), Through the looking glass, Charlotte Observer, 7/21/91; Chris Redd (auth), In the looking glass: Contemporary narrative painting, Art Papers, 9-10/91; Jimmie Duvham (auth), To be a pilgrim: Walton Ford, Artforum, 1/92. *Mailing Add:* 119 Chambers St New York NY 10007

FOREMAN, LAURA
CONCEPTUAL ARTIST, SCULPTOR
b Los Angeles, Calif. *Study:* Parsons Sch Design, New York, ongoing studies since 1979. *Work:* Antwerp Mus, Belg; Storefront for Art & Archit, New York; Vermont Studio Colony, Vt. *Comn:* Time Coded Woman (art video), Channel 13 WNET-TV, New York, 78 & Brooklyn Acad Mus, 82; art video installation, New Sch Social Res, New York, 78; art holograms, Holographic Film Found, New York, 83; public art sculptor, 5 parks in New York City, JBR Found, 90. *Exhib:* The Doll Show, Hillwood Art Gallery, C W Post Col, NY, 86; The Ultimate Exhibition, traveling internationally, 87; Souyun Yi Gallery, NY, 89 &91; Barbara Krakow Gallery, Boston, 91; Cityarts Show, Brooklyn & Bronx Mus, 91-92; Kleinert Arts Ctr, Woodstock, 92. *Pos:* Consult, Nat Endowment Humanities, 70-75; judge, Television Emmy Awards, 79-81; visual arts juror, Ill Arts Coun, 85. *Teaching:* Dir, PolyArts, New Sch Social Res, New York, 79- *Awards:* ACT Found Fel, 88; Watershed Ctr Ceramic Arts, 91; Cummington Community Arts, 92. *Bibliog:* Georgia Dullea (auth), Artfully built nests await feathering, New York Times, 4/12/90; Leslie Garisto (auth), From Bauhaus to Birdhouse, Harper Collins, 2/92; Tucker J Coombe (auth), The Artists' Life, Artist's Mag, 4/92. *Mem:* Artists Talk on Art, New York. *Media:* Mixed Media. *Publ:* Auth, The Act, Performance Proj Publ, 86. *Dealer:* Souyun Yi Gallery 249 Centre St New York NY 10013. *Mailing Add:* 94 Chambers St New York NY 10007

FORESTA, MERRY
CURATOR
b Aug 3, 49. *Study:* Cornell Univ, BA(eng lit), 71, MA(art hist), 79. *Pos:* Asst cur, painting & sculpture, Nat Mus Am Art, Smithsonian Inst, Washington, DC, 78-82, assoc cur, 83-88, cur, 88- *Teaching:* Various lectrs, sumposia & conferences, 84-88. *Awards:* Smithsonian Res Opportunity Fund Recipient, spring 85; Smithsonian Workshop Grant, 2/86; Smithsonian Scholarly Studies Res Grant, 2/86, renewed 2/87. *Mem:* Nat Endowment Arts (overview panel & photog fel panel, 90); Minn State Coun Arts (fel panel, 90); Soc Photog Educ; Col Art Asn. *Publ:* Coauth (with Willis Hartshorn), Man Ray in Fashion, Int Ctr Photog, 9/90; contribr, Past Perfect Future: The Appalachia Photographs of Dick Arentz, in Dick Arentz, Huntington Mus Art, 12/90; Irving Penn: The Passion of Certainties, for Irving Penn: Master Images at the Smithsonian, Smithsonian Inst Press, 90; and others. *Mailing Add:* 146 12th St SE Washington DC 20003

FORESTER, RUSSELL
PAINTER, SCULPTOR
b Salmon, Idaho, May 21, 20. *Study:* Inst of Design, Chicago, 50. *Work:* Guggenheim Mus & McCrory Corp, New York; La Jolla Mus Contemp Art, Calif; Security Pac Bank & Cedars-Sinai Med Ctr, Los Angeles; Bank of Am, San Francisco; Zurich Insurance Co, Switz; Sheldon Mem Art Gallery, Lincoln, Nebr; Aerojet-Gen Corp, La Jolla, Calif; Flint Inst of Art, Mich. *Exhib:* Houston Mus Fine Art, Tex, 62; Nat Drawing Exhib, San Francisco Mus Art, 70; Santa Barbara Mus Art, Calif, 74; Phoenix Art Mus, Ariz, 75; Sheldon Mem Art Gallery, 76; San Diego Mus of Art, 76 & Drawing Show, 77 & 78; Everson Mus Art, Syracuse, NY, 77; New Acquisitions, Guggenheim Mus, 77; La Galerie, Paris, France, 77; La Jolla Mus of Contemp Art, 79, 81 & 83; Mod Art Ctr, Zurich, Switz, 88. *Bibliog:* Roland Anrig (auth), Art Int, 1/73; Melinda Wortz (auth), articles, Art News, 9/79 & 4/83; Betty Brown (auth), article, Arts Mag, 1/83; Numerous art catalogues. *Mem:* Grand chambellan, Chevaliers of the Tastevih; Artist in collection, life mem, Guggenheim Mus. *Media:* Mixed. *Mailing Add:* 2025 Soledad Ave La Jolla CA 92037

FORGE, ANDREW MURRAY
WRITER, PAINTER
b Hastingleigh, Kent, Eng, Nov 10, 23. *Study:* Camberwell Sch Art, London, 57-59, with William Coldstream & Kenneth Martin. *Work:* Tate Gallery, London; Arts Coun Gt Brit. *Exhib:* Retrospective, Bristol Mus, Eng, 64; Inst Contemp Arts, Boston, 75. *Pos:* Trustee, Tate Gallery, London, 64-72, Nat Gallery, London, 66-70, Am Acad Rome, 82-88. *Teaching:* Lectr painting, Slade Sch, London, 50-64; prof painting, Yale Sch Art, 75- *Awards:* Guggenheim Fel, 79-80. *Media:* Oil. *Res:* 19th and 20th century art. *Publ:* Auth, Soutine, 65; Rauschenberg, Abrams, 69; Monet, Abrams, 83. *Mailing Add:* c/o Ruggiere PO Box 1451 Canal St Sta New York NY 10013

FORMAN, ALICE
PAINTER
b New York, NY, June 1, 31. *Study:* Cornell Univ, with Kenneth Evett & Norman Daly, BA; Art Students League, with Morris Kantor. *Exhib:* Whitney Mus Am Art, 60; White Mus Art, Cornell Univ, 61; Phoenix Gallery, NY, 66, 68, 71, 74 & 75; Marist Col, 68 & 71; Butler Inst Exhib, 72; Kornblee Gallery, 77 & 79; American Still Life, Contemp Arts Mus, Houston, 83; and others. *Teaching:* Lectr, Marist Col, 77; vis asst prof painting & drawing, Vassar Col, 80-81. *Awards:* Nat Student Asn Regional Awards; Daniel Schnackenberg Merit Scholar, Art Students League. *Media:* Oil. *Dealer:* Kornblee Gallery 20 W 57th St New York NY 10019. *Mailing Add:* 8 Croft Rd Poughkeepsie NY 12603

FORMAN, KENNETH WARNER
PAINTER
b Landour, India, June 5, 25; US citizen. *Study:* Wittenberg Col, AB, BFA; Ohio State Univ, MA. *Work:* Wittenberg Col, Springfield, Ohio; Univ RI, Kingston; Conn Com on the Arts; Univ Zagazig, Cairo, Egypt; Off of the Treas, State Conn; Moldex Corp, Putnam, Chimerix Corp, Glastonbury, Conn. *Comn:* Seattle Art Mus, Wash, 62. *Exhib:* Nat Drawing Exhib, Ball State Teachers Col, Muncie, Ind, 65; 12th Biennial Exhib Contemp Am Prints, Brooklyn Mus, 65; 23rd Int Exhib Soc Printmakers, US Nat Mus, 66; Monotypes Today IV, Artworks Gallery, Hartford, Conn, 78; A Kademia Sztuk Piekynch, Krakow, Poland, 87; Legislative Off Bldg, State Conn, Hartford; Bradley Int Airport, Conn Comn Arts, 89; Four Decades (Retrospective), William Benton Mus Art, Univ Conn, Storrs, 92. *Teaching:* Instr media & techniques, painting, Am Archit & art hist, Univ Conn, 57-, prof art, 68-89, (retired). *Awards:* First Painting Award, Mystic Art Asn, Conn, 63; Hartford Art Festival Purchase Award, Hartford CofC, 72; Third Ann Prints Exhib Award, Shippee Gallery, NY, 86. *Media:* Oil, Watercolor. *Res:* Victorian architecture in England and New England; traditional media with synthetic media in painting. *Publ:* Auth, Understanding in the Arts, 59 & illusr, 61, Fine Arts Mag; illusr, spec ed, Penny Paper, 64; auth, Salvador Dali's moustache, Floating Opera, 67; auth, Connecticut Architecture During the Growth of the Nation, William Benton Mus of Art, Univ Conn, 76. *Mailing Add:* 1010 Warrenville Rd Mansfield Center CT 06250

FORMICOLA, JOHN JOSEPH
PAINTER, EDUCATOR
b Philadelphia, Pa, Dec 27, 41. *Study:* Fleischer Art Mem, 56-59; Pa Acad Fine Arts, cert(Cresson Award, Schiedt Award), 64. *Work:* Philadelphia Mus Art; Cleveland Mus Art, Ohio; Miami Mus Mod Art, Fla; Mus Art, Carnegie Inst, Pittsburgh; Prudential Insurance Co Am; Exxon Corp; Mus Philadelphia Civic Ctr; Noyes Mus, NJ. *Comn:* Brandywine Graphic Workshop, Philadelphia, 82. *Exhib:* Del Art Mus, Wilmington, 78; Contemporary Drawings, Philadelphia Mus Art & Pa Acad Fine Arts, 78; solo exhibs, Frank Marino Gallery, New York, 80 & Marian Locks Gallery, Philadelphia, 80 & 84; 20th Anniversary Del Biennial Exhib, Univ Del, Newark, 82; Decades of Design, Baltimore, 88; Images and Objects, Boston, 90. *Pos:* Owner & dir, Gallery Pane Vino, 65-68; dir, Marian Locks Gallery, Philadelphia, 68-73; designer & consult, Danhart-Heim Architects, 76-77; partnr-dir, Chew and Formicola Gallery, 83- *Teaching:* Instr design, Drexel Univ, Philadelphia, 70-; instr painting, Cleveland Inst Art, Ohio, 79-80. *Awards:* First Hallgarten Award, Nat Acad Design, 65. *Bibliog:* Frank Goodyear & Anne Percy (auth), Pa Academy Fine Arts, Contemp Drawing, 78; Patterson Sims (auth), The 20 Univ Del Biennial Exhib Introd 82. *Media:* Oil, Fabric. *Publ:* Images, Arts Mag, 69; John Canada (auth), New York times, 70; Lenore Malen (auth), Arts Mag, 9/80; Michael Stolback (auth), Arts Mag, 10/80. *Dealer:* Chew and Formicola Gallery, Philadelphia, PA. *Mailing Add:* 725 Carpenter St Philadelphia PA 19147

FORNAS, LEANDER
PRINTMAKER, INSTRUCTOR
b Gardner, Mass, June 18, 25. *Study:* Pratt Inst, cert, 50; Kunstgewerbeschule, Zurich, 51; Ateneum, Helsinki, 51-53; Univ Mass, MFA, 73 & currently, Doctorate candidate, 90. *Work:* Mus Mod Art, New York; Ateneum, Helsinki; Libr Cong; Rockefeller Collection; New York Pub Libr. *Comn:* Developed new glass engraving methods, Steuben Glass, New York, 55; graphic indust illus, portrait comns & misc design, Finland, 59-65; designed & instituted graphics facilities, Pratt Inst, NY, 58, Fine Arts Ctr, Univ RI, 66 & Holyoke Community Col, 72-75. *Exhib:* One-man shows, New Talent, Mus Mod Art, 55 & Sao Paulo Biennial Prints, 59; Curator's Choice, Print Club, Philadelphia, 56; Printmakers Soc Finland Traveling Exhib, US, Europe & Far East, 59-66. *Pos:* Dir, Design & Graphics Studio, Helsinki, 58-66; chmn art dept, Holyoke Community Col, 70-74. *Teaching:* Instr printmaking & drawing, Holyoke Community Col, 70- *Mem:* Printmakers Soc Finland (bd dirs, 59-61); Lit Soc Finland; Finno-Urgarian Soc Finland. *Media:* All Media. *Res:* Multicultural: North Eurasians (Siberia), Subarctic Cree, (Canada). *Mailing Add:* 2 Dudleyville Rd Leverett MA 01054

FORNELLI, JOSEPH
PAINTER, SCULPTOR
b Chicago, Ill, May 21, 43. *Study:* Art Inst, Chicago. *Work:* Cornell Univ, Ithaca, NY; Columbia Mus, SC; Jim Bridger Pub Sch System, Bridger, Mont; Park Ridge Pub Libr, Ill. *Comn:* Dell Publ for Pres Nixon, New York, 74; Encycl Britannica for Pope Paul VI, Chicago, 74; Columbus Hosp, Chicago, 76; Ducks Unlimited, Memphis, Tenn, 89; US Hist, Richmond, VA, 91. *Exhib:* Birds in Art, Leigh Yawkey Woodson Art Mus, 80, 82 & 92; Palette & Chisel Club, Chicago, 82; Denver Mus Natural Hist, 82; Nat Wildlife Fedn, Vienna, Va, 83; Acad Natural Sci Mus, Philadelphia, 83; Reflexes & Reflections, Vietnam Vet Arts Group, WPA Gallery, Senate Rotunda & US House Rep Rotunda, Washington, DC, LBJ Mus, Austin, Tex, 83 & Lincoln Ctr, Cork Gallery, New York, 84; Am Mus Fly Fishing, Manchester, Vt, 91; Southeastern Wildlife Expos, Charleston, SC; and others. *Pos:* Painter & sculptor, Richard Rush Studio, Chicago, 73-74; art dir, Monastery Hill Bindery, Chicago, 74-77; design coordr, Ducks Unlimited, Chicago, 79-83; bd dirs, Chicago Munic Art League, 79-; pres, Vietnam Veterans Arts Group, 81- *Awards:* Gold Medal, Chicago Munic Art League, 79; Award of Merit, Soc Animal Artists Denver Mus, 82; Blue Ribbon, Nat Wildlife Fedn, 83. *Bibliog:* Ann Keegan (auth), Art snares wild spirt, The Treasures of Vietnam, Chicago Tribune, 5/87; Art reflects Vietnam War, NY Times, 10/81; Joan Johnson (producer), Good Morning America, ABC TV, 10/81. *Mem:* Chicago Munic Art League; Chicago Artists Guild; Soc Animal Artists; assoc Am Watercolor Soc; Oil Painters Am; Vietnam Vet Arts Group. *Media:* Watercolor, Oil; Bronze, Stone. *Publ:* Illusr, Moving Along with Charlie Dickey, Charles Dickey, Winchester Press, 85; Fly Fishingest Gentleman, Keith Russel, Winchester Press, 86; The Wildfowler's Quest, George Reiger, Lyons Burford, 89; Steel Barbs, Wild Waters, Jerry Gibbs, Outdoor Life Books, 90; A Rough Shooting Dog, Charles Fergus, Lyons & Burford, 91. *Dealer:* Fornelli Studio 1017 S Prospect Park Ridge IL 60068. *Mailing Add:* 1017 South Prospect Park Ridge IL 60068

FORREST, CHRISTOPHER PATRICK
PRINTMAKER, PAINTER
b Trenton, NJ, Oct 2, 46. *Study:* Va Polytechnic Inst, BS, 68; NC State Univ, MS, 74. *Work:* Nat Acad Sci, Washington, DC; NJ State Mus, Trenton; Ferrum Col, Va; Metro-Goldwyn Mayer, Los Angeles; Bausch & Lomb, Rochester, NY. *Exhib:* Easton Waterfowl Festival, Md, 80-87; Soc Animal Artists Exhib, Acad Nat Sci, Philadelphia, 81; one-man shows, Golden Door, New Hope, Pa, 81, Town Plaza, Brea, Calif, 83 & Chabot Galleries, Campbell, Calif, 83 7 84; Soc Animal Artists Ann, Denver Mus Nat Hist, 82; Nat Wildlife Fedn Wildlife in Art Show, Vienna, Va, 83; Sterling Fine Arts Gallery, Laguna Beach, Calif, 84; Soc Am Artists Exhib, Cleveland Mus Natural Hist, 84; Hang Ups, Orange, Calif, 85. *Pos:* Gen production mgr, Evergreen Publ Inc, 80-81. *Bibliog:* Cathy Lyons Colletti (auth), All-enveloping moods, Southwest Art Mag, 81; article, The Artist-Chris Forrest, Prints Mag, 84; Judy Hughes (auth), Lasting Impressions Lithography, Wildlife Art News, 88. *Mem:* Soc Animal Artists; Buzzard Coun Am. *Media:* Lithography, Intaglio; Acrylic, Oil. *Publ:* Duck Unltd Mag, 78, Readers Digest, 82, Outdoors, 83, & Conservationist Mag, 84. *Dealer:* Hang Ups 1319 W Katella Ave Orange CA 92667; Primrose Press PO Box 302 New Hope PA 18938. *Mailing Add:* 6 Cranberry Ln Vincentown NJ 08088

FORREST, JAMES TAYLOR
MUSEUM DIRECTOR, EDUCATOR
b New Castle, Ind, Sept 22, 19. *Study:* Hanover Col, Ind; Ind Univ, Indianapolis; Univ Wis, BS, 48 & MS, 49. *Comn:* Art and artifacts for interior trapper room, Grand Teton Lodge, Jackson Lake, Wyo, 55. *Collections Arranged:* National Painting Exhibition, Gilcrease Inst, Tulsa, Okla, 59; Collector's Choice-European Art, Fine Arts Mus, Santa Fe, NMex, 61; Art of the American West, Fine Arts Mus, Santa Fe; Santa Fe Arts Festival, 81. *Pos:* Cur mus, Colo State Mus, Denver, 53-55; dir, Gilcrease Inst, 55-61, Mus NMex, Santa Fe, 61-64 & Univ Wyo Art Mus, 68-85; mem, Wyo Gov Coun Art in Pub Places; dir, Branford Brinton Mem Mus, Wyo, 64-89. *Teaching:* Instr Am hist, Tulsa Univ, 58-60; instr Am art, Sheridan Col, Wyo, 66-67; instr, Am art hist, Univ Wyo, Laramie, 68-85; retired, 85. *Awards:* Wyoming Governor Award for the Arts, 85. *Mem:* Am Asn Mus (secy, 79-82, nat coun mem, 83-86); Mountain-Plains Mus Conf (coun, 72-79, vpres, 79-80, pres, 81); Colo-Wyo Asn Mus (chmn, 73-); Wyo Coun Arts (coun, 67-81, chmn, 71-73). *Res:* Art and artists of the American 19th century. *Publ:* Contribr, Keepers of the Past, Clifford Lord, Chapel Hill, 65; auth, Hans Kleiber-Artist of the Big Horns, 67 & Bill Gollings-Ranahan Artist, 69, Bradford Brinton Mem Ranch Mus, Big Horn, Wyo; History of New Mexico, Teachers Press, Columbia, 72; Bill Gollings--The Man and His Art, Northland Press, 79. *Mailing Add:* 45 Cabezon Rd Placitas NM 87043

FORRESTALL, THOMAS DE VANY
SCULPTOR, PAINTER
b Middleton, NS, Mar 11, 36. *Study:* Mt Allison Univ, 54-58; Can Coun grant to travel & study in Europe, 58-59, sculpture grant, 67. *Work:* Can Coun; Winnipeg Art Gallery; Art Gallery Windsor; Confederation Mem Gallery; Nat Gallery, Hungary; and others. *Comn:* Kennedy & Churchill Mem, Prov NB, 64; steel sculpture, Atlantic Pavilion, Expo 67; welded relief mural, Centennial Bldg Fredericton, 68; two large welded steel sculptures, Can Govt, Fed Bldg, Antigonish, NS, 70; mural abstract for playhouse, Beaverbrook Can Found, Fredericton, 72. *Exhib:* One-man shows, Montreal Mus Fine Arts, 72, Nat Mus Art, Bulgaria, 80, Nat Gallery Art, Romania, 81, Nat Mus Art, Transylvania, Nat Mus Art, Hungary, 81 & Bayard Gallery, New York, 81; Can Cult Centre, Rome, Italy, 83; Habema Centre Tel Aviv, 84; Nat Mus Art Prague, 85; Nova Scotia Pavilion, Expo '86 Vancouver; and others. *Pos:* Asst cur, Beaverbrook Art Gallery, 59-60. *Awards:* Citation of Art Merit, Secy State, Commonwealth Mass, 72; Can Coun Lectr Tour Grants, 77-79; Queen's Jubilee Medal, 78. *Bibliog:* P Murphy (auth), Shaped paintings..., article, Art Mag, 78. *Mem:* Royal Can Acad Arts; St Vincent De Paul Soc; Order Can. *Media:* Tempera; Steel, Iron. *Publ:* Coauth, Shapes, 72. *Mailing Add:* c/o Forrestall Fine Arts Ltd 3 Albert St Dartmouth NS B2Y 3M1 Canada

FORRESTER, CHARLES HOWARD
SCULPTOR, EDUCATOR
b Jersey City, NJ, Sept 30, 28. *Study:* Univ Wash, BFA, 58; Univ Ore, MFA, 60. *Work:* Bundy Art Gallery, Waitsfield, Vt; Shakespeare Mem Theatre, Ashland, Ore; Medford Pub Parks, Ore; Western Ky Univ, Bowling Green. *Comn:* Two Figures, Mathews Co, Little Rock, Ark, 67; two sculptures (cast aluminum & cor-ten steel), PCA Bldg, Glasgow, KY, 74; Family Group, Bowling Green Hosp, Ky; sculpture (wood), Northern Telecom Bldg, Nashville, Tenn, 85; sculpture (wood), Dr Iwrin Eskind, 92. *Exhib:* Capitol Arts Ctr, Bowling Green, 87-89 & 90; Regional Sculptors Exhib, Vanderbuilt Univ, Nashville, Tenn, 85; Leu Gallery, 86, 40th & 41st Ann Mid-States Evansville Mus Art, 87, 88 & 92, Summer Lights Fes, Ambiance Gallery, 87, Montgomery Bell Ann Sculpture Exhib, 90 & Centennial Art Ctr, 90 & 91, Nashville, Tenn; The Nude, 88 & Sculpture Indoors and Out, 88, Lexington Art League; Water Tower Ann, Louisville, KY, 89;; and others. *Teaching:* Lectr sculpture, Salford Tech Col, Eng, 63-65; prof sculpture, Western Ky Univ, Bowling Green, 65- *Awards:* Citizens Nat Bank Purchase Award, Capitol Arts Ctr, Bowling Green, Ky, 81. *Bibliog:* Anon (auth), Some Younger Northwest Sculptors, NW Rev, 61; M Harold (ed), Prize-Winning Sculptures, Allied Publ Inc, 67. *Mem:* Southern Asn of Sculptors (vpres, 66-70). *Media:* Cast Metal, Fabricated Metal. *Dealer:* Katzman-Werthan Gallery 4309 Beekman Dr Nashville TN 37215. *Mailing Add:* PO Box 102 Col Heights PO Bowling Green KY 42101

FORRESTER, PATRICIA TOBACCO
PAINTER, PRINTMAKER
b Northampton, Mass, Sept 17, 40. *Study:* Yale Summer Sch Music & Art, 61; Smith Col, BA, 62; Yale Univ Sch Art, BFA, 63, MFA, 65. *Work:* Brooklyn Mus; San Antonio Mus Art; Achenbach Found, Legion Hon; Oakland Mus; Mem Art Gallery, Univ Rochester; and others. *Exhib:* Solo exhib, San Francisco Mus Art, 68, M H De Young Mem Mus, 77, Fischbach Gallery, New York, 85, 87 & 88, Fendrick Gallery, Washington, DC, 86, Reynolds/Minor Gallery, Richmond, Va, 87, Steven Scott Gallery, Baltimore, Md, 92; American Watercolors, Mitchell Mus & Cedar Rapids Art Ctr, Mt Vernon, Ill, 79; West Coast--Art for the Vice President's House, Washington, DC, 80; Real, Really Real, Super Real, San Antonio Mus Art, 81; Ten Plus Ten Plus Ten Washington Painters, Corcoran Gallery, 82; American Realism, Davidson Collection, Pa Acad Fine Arts, 83; Washington Watercolor, Corcoran Gallery, 84; E F Hutton Collection, Metropolitan Mus, Miami, FL, 86; Sierra Nevada Mus Art, Reno, Nev, 88; Atmospheres, Steven Scott Gallery, Baltimore, Md, 92. *Teaching:* Asst prof printmaking, Calif Col Arts & Crafts, 72-81; guest artist painting, Kent State Univ, 81, Art Inst Chicago, 82, New Orleans Acad Fine Art, 84. *Awards:* Guggenheim Fel Printmaking, 67; Yaddo Fel, 79 & 81; MacDowell Colony Fel, 80. *Bibliog:* John Arthur (auth), Realist Drawings & Watercolors, New York Graphic Soc, 80; Ann Gerocimos (auth), article, Am Artist, 11/83; Robert Merritt (auth), Watercolor: in a new light, Times-Dispatch, 11/21/8 7. *Media:* Watercolor. *Dealer:* Fischbach Gallery 24 W 57th St New York NY 10019; Fendrick Gallery 3059 M St NW Washington DC 20007. *Mailing Add:* 2220 20th St NW Washington DC 20009

FORSMAN, CHUCK (CHARLES STANLEY)
PAINTER, EDUCATOR
b Nampa, Idaho, May 5, 44. *Study:* Univ Calif, Davis, study with Wayne Theibaud & William Wiley, BA, 67; study with Gabriel Laderman, 70, MFA, 71; Skowhegan Sch Painting & Sculpture, Maine, 70. *Work:* Phoenix Art Mus, Ariz; Metrop Mus Art, New York; Yellowstone Art Ctr, Billings, Mont; Wichita Art Mus; Denver Art Mus. *Exhib:* One-man shows, Tibor De Nagy Gallery, New York, 73, 75, 77, 79, 81, 83, 85 & 88, Watson De Nagy Gallery, Houston, 76, Wichita Art Mus, 81, Yellowstone Art Ctr, 83, Denver Art Mus, Colo & Tucson Mus Art, 85; Whitney Mus Am Art, Stamford, Conn, 81; Hudson River Mus, Yonkers, NY, 84; Am Mus Natural Hist, New York, 85; Va Mus Fine Arts, Richmond, 90; and others. *Teaching:* Asst painting & sculpture, Univ Calif, Davis, 70-71; prof fine arts, Univ Colo, Boulder, 71- *Awards:* Nat Endowment Arts Grant, 79 & 85; Fac fel, Univ Colo, Boulder, 79 & 88; Mus Purchase, Am Acad Arts & Lett, 79. *Bibliog:* Gerrit Henry (auth), Art News, 11/83; Carter Radcliffe (auth), Art International; Richard Martin (auth), articles, Arts Mag. *Media:* Oil on Masonite. *Dealer:* Tibor de Nagy Gallery 41 W 57th St New York NY. *Mailing Add:* 511 Pleasant St Boulder CO 80302

FORSYTH, ILENE H(AERING)
EDUCATOR, HISTORIAN
b Detroit, Mich, Aug 21, 28. *Study:* Univ Mich, AB, 50; Columbia Univ, AM, 55, PhD, 60. *Teaching:* Lectr, Barnard Col, 56-58; instr, Columbia Univ, 59-61; asst prof, Univ Mich, Ann Arbor, 61-68, assoc prof, 68-74, prof, 74-84, Arthur F Thurnau prof, 84-; vis prof hist art, Harvard Univ, 80; Andrew W Mellon prof, Univ Pittsburgh, 81. *Awards:* Charles Rufus Morey Book Award, Col Art Asn, 74; Inst Advan Study Fel, 77. *Mem:* Int Ctr Medieval Art (dir, 70, vpres, 81-85); Acad Arts, Sci & Belles Lett, Dijon; Midwest Hist Soc (mem bd dirs, 79-81; Col Art Asn (mem bd dir, 80-84, mem exec comt, 82-84); Medieval Acad Am (mem bd adv, 85-). *Res:* Medieval art, especially Romanesque sculpture. *Publ:* Auth, Magi and majesty: Romanesque sculpture and liturgical drama, Col Art Asn Bulletin, 68; Throne of Wisdom, Princeton Univ Press, 72; Ganymede capital at Vezelay, Gesta, 76; Cockfighting in Burgundian Romanesque sculpture, Speculum, 78; Vita apostolica, Gesta, 86. *Mailing Add:* 5 Geddes Heights Ann Arbor MI 48104

FORSYTHE, DONALD JOHN
PRINTMAKER, EDUCATOR
b Pittsburgh, Pa, July 2, 55. *Study:* Ind Univ Pa, BS, 77; Rochester Inst Technol, MFA, 79. *Work:* Bank of NY, Wilmington, Del; Franklin Mint, Philadelphia, Pa; Graham Ctr Mus, Wheaton, Ill; Philadelphia Savings Fund Soc, Philadelphia, Pa; Rochester Inst Technol, NY. *Comn:* 6 choir windows, stained glass, Cathedral St Stephen, Harrisburg, Pa. *Exhib:* La Grange National VI, CUAA Gallery, Ga, 81; 6th NC Printing & Drawing Society Exhib, Charlotte, NC, 82; Tactile Vision, William Penn Mus, Harrisburg, Pa, 84; New Drawings, Dolan/Maxwell Gallery, Philadelphia, Pa, 85; Visions of the World, Shoemaker Mus, Juniata, Pa, 86; 44th Ann Juried Exhib, Woodmere Art Mus, Philadelphia, 86; Sacred Arts IX, Graham Ctr Mus, Wheaton, Ill, 87; Christian Imagery in Contemporary Art, Albany Inst Art, NY, 88; New American Talent, Laquana Gloria Art Mus, Austin, Tx, 89; Perspectives from Pennsylvania, Carnegie Mellon Univ Mus, Pittsburgh, Pa; Art of the State, William Penn Mus, Harrisburg, Pa. *Pos:* Dir, Louise Aughinbaugh Art Gallery, Messiah Col, 83-89; pres, Christians Visual Art, 91-93. *Teaching:* Assoc prof art, Messiah Col, Grantham, Pa, 81- *Mem:* Christians in the Visual Arts (mem bd, 85-); Int Soc Christian Artists. *Media:* Mixed Media. *Mailing Add:* 2709 Mill Rd Grantham PA 17027

FORT-BRESCIA, BERNARDO M
ARCHITECT
b Lima, Peru, Nov 19, 51. *Study:* Princeton Univ, BA(archit), 73; Harvard Univ, March, 75. *Comn:* Babylon, Pacific Developers, Miami, Fla, 77; Atlantis, Stonecrest Development, Miami, Fla, 78; The Palace, Helmsley Enterprises, Miami, Fla, 78; Imperial at Brickell, Harlon Group, Miami, Fla, 79; Overseas Tower, Overseas Finance Corp, Miami, Fla, 80. *Exhib:* New Americans, Inst Archit & Urban Studies, Rome, Italy, 79; Work of Arquitectonica, Cooper-Hewitt Mus, New York, 79, Pa State Univ, 80 & Univ Va, 81; and others. *Pos:* Principal, Arquitectonica, Coral Gables, Fla, 77- *Teaching:* Vis prof archit, Univ Miami, Coral Gables, Fla, 75-77. *Awards:* Citation, Progressive Archit Ann Design Awards, 78 & 80. *Bibliog:* Articles, Wall St J, 7/7/83, Archit Rec, 7/83, Global Archit Document 7, 8/83 & others. *Mem:* Am Inst Architects; Architectural Club of Miami (pres, 78-80). *Mailing Add:* Arquitectonica 2151 Lejeune Rd, Ste 300 Coral Gables FL 33134

FORTESS, KARL E
PAINTER, PRINTMAKER
b Antwerp, Belg, Oct 13, 07; US citizen. *Study:* Art Inst Chicago; Art Students League; Woodstock Sch Painting, with Yasuo Kuniyoshi. *Work:* De Cordova Mus, Lincoln, Mass; Mus Mod Art, New York; Wichita Art Mus, Kans; Nat Collection Fine Arts, Smithsonian Inst; Butler Inst Am Art, Youngstown, Ohio; Tamarind Inst Collection; Brooklyn Mus; Nat Mus Am Art; Jason Schoen pvt collection, Houston, Tex; plus many others. *Exhib:* Art Inst Chicago; Mus Mod Art, New York; Whitney Mus Am Art; Nat Inst Arts & Letters; Nat Acad Design; Carnegie Inst; Corcoran Gallery Art; Pa Acad Fine Arts; one-man shows, Sawkill Gallery, Woodstock, NY, Bucknell Univ, La Art Comn, Baton Rouge, Delgado Mus, Univ Ga, Krasner Gallery, New York & Petrucci Gallery, Saugerties, New York. *Pos:* Artist fed art projects, Works Proj Admin; contract with US Dept Health, Educ & Welfare for tape-recorded interviews with contemp Am artists (over 350 tapes). *Teaching:* Instr art, Art Students League, Brooklyn Mus Art Sch, La State Univ & Am Art Sch; vis artist, Ft Wright Col; from prof art to prof emer, Boston Univ Sch Arts. *Awards:* Nat Endowment Arts Grant; Adolph & Clara Obrig Award, 79; Audubon Artists Medal of Honor, 88. *Bibliog:* Holger Cahill (auth), New Horizons in American Art, 36; Ralph Pearson (auth), Modern Renaissance in American Art, 54; Arthur Zaidenberg (auth), Prints & How to Make Them, 64; Clinton Adams (auth), American Lithographers--1900-1963, 83; plus many others. *Mem:* Artists Equity Asn; Soc Am Graphic Artists; Art Students League; Am Asn Univ Prof; Brit Film Inst. *Media:* Oil. *Res:* Participated in making a pictorial record of the Territory of Alaska for the US Dept of Interior. *Publ:* Auth, On the nature of things or the things of nature, in: Art of the Artist (ed, Arthur Zaidenberg), Crown, 51; Comics as non-art, in: Funnies: An American Idiom (eds, David Manning White & Robert H Abel), Free Press, 63. *Mailing Add:* 311 Plochmann Rd Woodstock NY 12498

FORTUNATO, NANCY
PAINTER, ILLUSTRATOR
b Highland Park, Ill, Nov 29, 41. *Study:* Studied with Ed Betts, 80, Dong Kingman, 85; Zhejiang Inst Fine Arts, Hangzhou, China, 84. *Work:* Leigh Yawkey Woodson Art Mus, Wausau, Wis; Int Crane Found Mus, Baraboo, Wis; People of the Century Goldblatt Collection, Chicago; also pvt collections of Reverend Billy Graham & Winston Lord. *Exhib:* Birds in Art, Leigh Yawkey Woodson Art, Wausau, Wis, 82, 86, 87, 90, 91 & 92; Watercolor, Exhib Hall, Hangzhou, China, 84; 118th Ann Am Watercolor Soc, Canton Art Mus, Ohio, 85; Impressions in Nature, Elliott Mus, Stuart, Fla, 89; 19th Ann Watercolor Exhib, W Riverside Art Mus, Calif, 89; Soc Animal Artists, Cleveland Mus Nat Hist, Ohio, 91; Soc Animal Artists, Roger Tory Peterson Inst, Jamestown, NY, 92. *Awards:* Highly Commended, Artists in Watercolor, Saunders & Bockingford, London, 77; M Grunbacher Award, Int Soc Artists,80; Windsor & Newton Award, Cuyahoga 4 State Nat, 85; Ill State Fair, Prof Exhib, First Place, 91. *Bibliog:* James Auer (auth), Mountaintop gave artist new outlook on her art, Milwaukee J, 87; Pam & Ed Menaker (coauths), She doesn't paint inside the lines, N Shore Mag, 88. *Mem:* Midwest Watercolor Soc (bd mem, 89-); Am Soc Marine Artists; Catharine Lorillard Wolfe Art Club; Nat Asn Women Artists; Whiskey Painters Am; Soc Animal Artists; Int Soc Marine Artists; US Coast Guard Artist. *Publ:* Auth, So, You Want to Be an Artist, pvt publ, 80; Watercolor, My Way, Palette Talk, 82; Watercolor Tips, private publ, 82; North Light Mag, N Light Book, 82; illusr, Birdwatcher's Digest, W Thompson, 84, 86 & 87; US Lighthouse Log Mag, Lighthouse Soc, 85-92. *Mailing Add:* 249 N Marion St Palatine IL 60067

FOSTER, APRIL
PRINTMAKER, EDUCATOR
b Berwyn, Ill, Oct 9, 47. *Study:* Univ Ill, Champaign-Urbana, BFA, 70, MA(art educ; fel), 71; Tyler Sch Art, Temple Univ, MFA(printmaking; fel), 73. *Work:* Cincinnati Art Mus, Ohio; Boston Mus Fine Art, Mass; Univ Mich Art Mus; Dayton Art Inst, Ohio; Miami Univ Art Mus. *Exhib:* Cincinnati Selections, 84; solo exhib, Merida-Rapp Gallery, Louisville, Ky, 87, Prints & Sculpture, Univ Cincinnatti, 87, Prints & Drawings, Thomas More Col, 88; Col of Mt St Joseph, 88 & 90. *Teaching:* Asst printmaking, Temple Univ, 71-72, instr printmaking, summer 73; prof printmaking & drawing, Art Acad Cincinnati, 73- *Awards:* Award for Excellence in Teaching, Greater Cincinnati Consortium of Cols & Univs, 89. *Mem:* Col Art Asn; Women's Caucus Art; Nat Women's Studies Asn. *Media:* Lithography, Intaglio. *Mailing Add:* Art Acad Cincinnati, Dept of Fine Art and Found Eden Park Cincinnati OH 45202

FOSTER, DON
SCULPTOR
b London, Eng, Sept 3, 32; US citizen. *Study:* Nottingham Col Art, Eng, 49-53; Royal Col Art, London, Eng, 55-58. *Work:* Memphis Acad Arts, Tenn; Univ Houston, Tex; Tex A&M Univ; Ferreira Collection, Barcelona, Spain. *Comn:* Bronze Doors, City Southend-on-Sea, Eng, 65; mural, Shell Oil Singapore, 67; mosaic mural, Bank West Africa, Lagos, 68; neon wall relief, Hyatt Regency Hotel, Houston, Tex, 72. *Exhib:* Neon Works, Waco Art Mus, Tex, 78; 72 Hour Private View, Robinson Galleries, Houston, Tex, 78; PV Series 100, Am Embassy, Mexico City, 81; Off the Wall, San Antonio Mus Art, Tex, 81; Recent Mixed with Neon Works, McAllen Int Mus, Tex, 82; PV Series Robinson Galleries-Galeria Uno, Puerto Vallarta, Mex, 82; Networking, Robinson Galleries-Galeria Clave, Guadalajara, Mex, 84 & 86. *Teaching:* Tutor, Royal Col Art, London, Eng, 61-66; head fine art dept, Coventry Col Art, Eng, 66-70; guest lectr, Derby Col Art, Eng, 69; head design dept, Colchester Col Art, Eng, 70-72; guest lectr, Rice Univ, 71; vis artists, Mus Fine Arts, Houston, Tex, 75; guest artist, Edward Albee Found, 79. *Awards:* Traveling Scholarship, Royal Col, London, Eng, 59; First Prize, Fry-Drew Mural Co, 59. *Bibliog:* Art & Architecture, McGraw-Hill, 66; Plumb (auth), Houses Architects Live In, Viking Press, 77. *Media:* Mixed Media, Neon. *Mailing Add:* 2116 1/2 Strand Galveston TX 77550

FOSTER, DONALD ISLE
DEALER
b Seattle, Wash, July 9, 25. *Study:* Stanford Univ, BA, 47, MBA, 49. *Pos:* Owner, Foster-White Gallery, Seattle, 72- *Specialty:* Contemporary Northwest art. *Mailing Add:* 311 1/2 Occidental Ave S Seattle WA 98104

FOSTER, MAELEE THOMSON
EDUCATOR, PRINTMAKER
b Milford, Conn, Sept 19, 32. *Study:* Univ Bridgeport, BS(art educ), 64; Tyler Sch Art, Temple Univ, MFA, 69. *Work:* State Fla, State Senate Bldg, Tallahassee; Champion Paper Co, Stamford, Conn; Barnett Bank, Fla Artists Collection, Jacksonville; Trans-Co Company Public, Houston, Tex; Housatonic Community Col, Bridgeport, Conn. *Comn:* Collagraphs, Honeywell Int, Philadelphia, Pa, 69-74; cover & logo, Vupak Control System, Honeywell Int, Philadelphia, Pa; collage & cover designs, Technical Publ Co, Chicago, Ill, 71-72. *Exhib:* Nat Print Exhibs, 64-80; New England Annuals, 65-79; Six Printmakers, Philadelphia Art Alliance, Pa, 70; Prints USA: 1982 Traveling Exhib, Pratt Graphics Ctr, NY; Stonehenge Series, Bi-Ann Nat Photog Exhib, Southwestern La Univ, 84; solo exhibs, Crime in Alachua County, Copier Print Collages, Gainesville City Hall, Gainesville Sun, Col Law, Univ Fla, 85 & 85; Traveling Exhib, Italy, Int Soc of Copier Artists under auspices of Post Machina Group & Am Consulate in Florence, 86; Works-A Visual Arts Celebration, Iscagraphics Exhib, Edmonton, Alta, Can, 88; AIA Nat Photog Competition, St Louis, AIA Conv, Reno, Nev & Washington, DC, 89. *Pos:* Art dir, State Conn, Long Lane Sch, 64-67. *Teaching:* Instr drawing & design, Univ Bridgeport, Conn, 69-71; assoc prof graphic & design, Univ Fla, Col Archit, Gainesville, 71-92. *Awards:* John Kellem Award, Silvermine Ctr Arts, 70; First Prize, Barnum Arts Festival, Mus Art, Sci & Indust, Bridgeport, Conn, 71; Am Inst Architects Educ Honors, 89. *Bibliog:* Creative Spatial Exploration: Process Drawing, Representation J Graphic Educ, Vol 3, No 3, 86; Diane Greer (auth), A link to the profession, Fla Architect, 7-8/89. *Mem:* Archeol Inst Am; New Eng Antiquities Res Asn; Inst Study Am Cult; Artists Equity Nat Asn; Am Color Print Soc. *Media:* Collage, Collograph. *Res:* On site investigation of the prehistoric sites of Mesoamerica, South America, North America and Megalithic sites of Europe. *Publ:* Ed, An Introduction to Cards on the Table, concept drawings by the Architect, Richard England, MRSM Publ, Malta, Gt Brit, 81; auth, Creative Spatial Exploration: Process Drawing, Representation, J Graphic Educ, Vol 3, No 3, 86; Experiencing a Creative High, J Creative Behavior, Vol 26, No 1, 92; Megalithic Sites Reexamined as Spatial Systems, Power of Place, 91; An Anthology. *Dealer:* Gallery Contemporanea Jacksonville FL. *Mailing Add:* 4030 NW 19th Pl Gainesville FL 32605

FOSTER, MARY
ADMINISTRATOR, CURATOR
b Dunkirk, NY, Mar 18, 51. *Study:* Skidmore Col, BA, 73; Independent Study Prog for Curators, Whitney Mus, New York, cert, 73-74. *Collections Arranged:* Three: Calder, Nevelson, Smith, Whitney Mus Br, New York, 73 & Frank O'Hara, A Poet Among Painters, Whitney Mus Am Art, 73; Summer Dances in the Garden, Cooper Hewitt Mus, New York, 80; 10 Years of Film Fellowships: MOMA Salutes CAPS, Mus Mod Art, New York, 81. *Pos:* Curatorial asst, Solomon A Guggenheim Mus, New York, 74; dir artists activities & exhibs, Creative Artists Pub Serv Prog, NY, 74-83; exec dir,

Visual Artists & Galleries Asn, Inc, New York, formerly; corp art consult, Dumont Landis Fine Arts, Inc, NJ, 86-; exec dir, Children's Prog, Solomon A Guggenheim Mus, New York, currently. *Mailing Add:* Solomon R Guggenheim Mus 1071 Fifth Ave New York NY 10128

FOSTER, STEPHEN C
HISTORIAN, WRITER
b Princeton, Ill, Dec 3, 41. *Study:* Northern Ill Univ, BA; Univ Ill, MA; Univ Pa, PhD. *Pos:* Dir, Prog for Mod Studies, Univ Iowa, Iowa City. *Teaching:* Asst prof art hist, Bowdoin Col, Brunswick, Mass, 72-74, mem fac, Am Painting Summer Inst, 74 & 76; prof art hist & criticism, Univ Iowa, Iowa City, 74- *Awards:* Smithsonian Fel, 85; Taipei Fine Arts Mus Grant, 87; Getty Grant, 92; and others. *Mem:* Col Art Asn Am; Midwest Art Hist Soc; Midwest Col Art Asn Am. *Res:* Sociology of modern art with research emphasis in the areas of Dada and Abstract Expressionism; folk art. *Publ:* The Critics of Abstract Expressionism, 80, Dada/Dimensions, 84 & Events, Art & Art Events, 87, Univ Mich Res Press; Contrib ed, Lettrisme: Into the Present, exhib catalogue, Visible Lang, 83; Co-ed with Estera Milman, The Avent-Garde & the Text, Visible Lang, XXI, 3/4, 88; contrib ed, The World According to Dada, TFAM, 88. *Mailing Add:* Dept Art & Art Hist Univ Iowa Iowa City IA 55242

FOSTER, STEVEN DOUGLAS
PHOTOGRAPHER
b Piqua, Ohio, Sept 10, 45. *Study:* Nathan Lyons Home Workshop, Rochester, 64-66; Rochester Inst Technol, AAS, 65; Inst Design, Ill Inst Technol, BS, 68; Univ NMex, MFA, 72. *Work:* Art Inst Chicago; High Mus, Atlanta; Int Mus Photog at George Eastman House, Rochester; Visual Studies Workshop, Rochester; Univ NMex Art Mus; Mus Mod Art, New York. *Exhib:* Vision & Expressions, Int Mus Photog at George Eastman House, Rochester, 69; Artists in Ga, High Mus, Atlanta, 74; Wis Dirs II, Milwaukee Art Ctr, 78; Am Photog in the 70's, Art Inst Chicago, 79; Perception: Field of View, Los Angeles Ctr for Contemp Photog, 79. *Teaching:* Asst prof photog, Ga State Univ, Atlanta, 72-75; prof photog, Univ Wis-Milwaukee, 75- *Awards:* Wis Arts Bd Visual Arts Fel, 77; Wis Arts Bd Project Grant-in-Aid, 78; Grad Sch Res Grant, Univ Wis-Milwaukee, 79. *Mem:* Soc Photog Educ. *Media:* Black, White, Color and Silver Print. *Publ:* Contribr, Vision and Expression, 69 & The City: American Experience, 71, Horizon Press; The Print, Time/Life Libr, 71; Niine Contemporary Photographers, Ga State Univ, 75; Wisconsin Directions II, Milwaukee Art Ctr, 78; The Lake Series, Art Inst Chicago, 82. *Dealer:* Ehler Crudill Gallery Chicago; Michael Lord Gallery Milwaukee. *Mailing Add:* c/o Michael H Lard Gallery 420 E Wisconsin Ave Milwaukee WI 53202

FOTH, JOAN B
PAINTER, EDUCATOR
b July 13, 30. *Study:* Art Students League, 48, Barnard Col, BA, 52. *Work:* Wichita Art Mus, Kans; Mulvane Art Ctr, Topeka, Kans; Hallmark Collection, Kansas City, Mo; Mobil Oil Corp, New York; US Comptroller of the Currency Collection, Washington, DC. *Exhib:* American Watercolorists, Bucknell Univ, Lewisburg, Pa, 81; A Kansas Collection, Nat Mus Women Arts, Washington, DC, 87; Five Landscape Artists, Wichita Art Mus, Kans, 87; Boundless Realism, Rockwall Mus, Corning, NY, 87; Watercolor USA, Springfield Art Mus, Mo, 88. *Pos:* Docent for Oriental collections, Metrop Mus Art New York, 53; asst dir, Kans Hist Mus, 53-57. *Teaching:* Adj prof watercolor & drawing, Washburn Univ, Topeka, Kans, 63-83. *Bibliog:* Albert W Porter (auth), Expressive Watercolor Techniques, Davis Publ, 82; Joy Murphy (auth), Introducing Joan Foth, Southwest Art, 6/87; Donald B Doe (auth), Mountain Cantos - The Art of Joan Foth, 10 Year Retrospective, Catalogue, Mulvane Art Ctr, 91. *Media:* Watercolor. *Dealer:* Dewey Galleries Ltd 74 E San Francisco Santa Fe NM 87501. *Mailing Add:* PO Box 100 Chimayo NM 87522

FOULKES, LLYN
PAINTER
b Yakima, Wash, Nov 17, 34. *Study:* Univ Wash, 53-54; Cent Washington Col Educ, 54, Chouinard Art Inst, 57-59. *Work:* Whitney Mus Am Art, New York; Guggenheim Mus, New York; Mus Mod Art, New York; Art Inst, Chicago; Los Angeles County Mus Art, Calif; Oakland Mus Art, Calif; San Francisco Mus Mod Art, Calif. *Exhib:* Contemp Arts Forum, Santa Barbara, Calif, 86, Kent Fine Art, NY, 87 & 90, Hooks Epstein Gallery, Houston, Tex, 88, Gallery Paule Anglia, San Francisco, Calif, 88; solo exhibs, Kent Fine Arts, Forum, Zurich, 87, Hooks-Epstein Gallery, Houston, Tex, 88, Herter Art Gallery, Univ Mass, Amherst, 89, POP: The First Picture, Kent, NY, 90; LA Hot and Cool, Stux Gallery, NY, 88; Art of the 70's, Manny Silverman Gallery, Los Angeles, Calif, 88; American Pie, Bess Cutler Gallery, NY, 89; Real Allusions, The Whitney Mus Am Art, New York, 90; Helter Skelter, Mus Contemp Art, Los Angeles, 92. *Collections Arranged:* Cur, Imagination, Los Angeles Inst of Contemp Art, Calif. *Teaching:* Prof painting & drawing & artist in residence, Univ Calif, Los Angeles, 65-71; resident painter, Painting workshop, Art Ctr Sch, Los Angeles, 71-77; vis prof art, Univ Calif, Irvine, 81-82, Santa Barbara, 83-84; prof, Otis Art Inst, Los Angeles, 86-87. *Awards:* New Talent Purchase Grant, Los Angeles Co Mus Art, 64; Medal of France (first award for painting), 5th Paris Bienniale, Mus Mod Art, Paris, 67; Guggenheim Found fel, 77-78; Fel Grant, Nat Endowment Arts, 86. *Bibliog:* Hilary Dole Klein (auth), Time out: Sticking Up the one-man band, Santa Barbara News & Rev, 1/23/88; Mark Van Proyen (auth), Navigating the semiotic mire, Artweek, 8/20/88; Robert Taylor (auth), LA hot and cool: A Rewarding Exhibit, Boston Globe, 1/88; Peter Frank (auth), Forty Years of California Assemblage, Wright Gallery, Sculpture, 1-2/90; Peter Plagens (auth), Welcome to Manson High, Newsweek, 3/22/92. *Media:* Oil, Acrylic. *Dealer:* Asher/Faure 612 N Almont Dr Los Angeles CA 90069. *Mailing Add:* 2002 Tuna Canyon Topanga CA 90290

FOURCARD, INEZ GAREY
PAINTER
b Brooklyn, NY. *Study:* Pratt Inst, Brooklyn, NY; McNeese State Univ, Lake Charles, La, BFA, 63. *Work:* Bertrand Russell Peace Found, London, Eng; Gallery Ancient & Mod Art, Salsomaggiore, Italy. *Comn:* Landscape with Pond, New Emanuel Baptist Church, Lake Charles, La, 75; Jesus & The Nativity, Mt Pilgrim Baptist Church, Lake Charles, 83. *Exhib:* La State Art Comn, travelling exhib, 64; one-woman shows, Lynn Kottler Galleries, New York, 71 & Art Mus Southwest La, Lafayette, 72; Eminent Black Artist of Louisiana, Cent La Art Asn Inc, Alexandria, 76; Prominent Black Artists of Louisiana, La Black Legislators Caucus, State Capitol, 87; Black Heritage Festival, Civic Ctr, Lake Charles, La, 88; and others. *Awards:* Cash Award, First Prize, Mother & Son, La State Art Comn, 64; Gold Medal First Prize, The Connoisseur, Accad Italia dell Artie del Savro, 80; Statua della Vittoria, The Connoisseur, Centro Studie Ricerche Dalle Nazioni, 85. *Bibliog:* Herbert Lieberman (auth), Artist-USA, Artists Equity Asn, Inc, 70, 72 & 74; Bernadine Proctor (auth), Black Artist of Louisiana, 88. *Media:* Oil. *Publ:* Contribr, International Artist Directory, 75; The History of Contemporary Art, Int d'Arte Mod, 82. *Mailing Add:* 1414 St John St Lake Charles LA 70601

FOURNIER, ALEX
PAINTER
b Port Arthur, Tex, Aug, 31, 24. *Study:* Cass Tech, Detroit, 39; Art Student League, New York; Provincetown Sch with Henry Heusche, Nat Acad, 60. *Work:* New York Community Col; Tuffs Univ, Haynes underwear; Boardroom, several corps. *Comn:* Offical seal, Newark, NJ, 80. *Exhib:* Am Artist Prof League, New York, 71; Brooklyn Union Gas, show of work, NY, 92. *Pos:* Demas, Bergen Co Artist Guild, 82-92; Long Island Art Guild, currently; Major Clubs throughout NY State. *Awards:* Gold Medal, Am Artist Prof League, 71. *Bibliog:* Video tapes, Demos, San Slateo, 82-92. *Mem:* Pastel Soc Am. *Media:* Oil, Pastel. *Mailing Add:* 126 Front St Brooklyn NY 11201

FOWLE, GERALDINE ELIZABETH
HISTORIAN
b Grand Rapids, Mich, Jan 3, 29. *Study:* Am Univ, 53-58; Univ Mich, Ann Arbor, MA(art hist), 60, PhD(art hist), 70. *Pos:* Newslett ed, Midwest Art Hist Soc, 77-80 & Soc Archit Historians, 80- *Teaching:* Asst lectr English art, Univ Manchester, England, 63-66; vis instr Baroque art, Univ Pittsburgh, 67; assoc prof, Univ Mo, Kansas City, 67- *Mem:* Col Art Asn; Soc Archit Historians; Midwest Art Hist Soc; Mid-Am Col Art Asn (treas, 74-75). *Res:* Sebastien Bourdon, French artist of the 17th century. *Publ:* Contribr, Two pendants by Sebastien Bourdon, Bulletin, Boston Mus Fine Arts, 73; Sebastien Bourdon's acts of mercy, Hortus Imaginum, 74; The lady who got Tassi thrown into prison, Helicon Nine, 80; Crucifixion of St Peter, Mus Art, Univ Kans, 87. *Mailing Add:* Dept Art & Art Hist Univ Mo 5100 Rockhill Rd Kansas City MO 64110

FOWLER, ERIC NICHOLAS
ILLUSTRATOR, PAINTER
b Morristown, NJ, Feb 14, 54. *Study:* Syracuse Univ, NY, 72-74; Illusr Workshop (First Scholar award), 77; Pratt Inst, Brooklyn, NY, BFA(honors), 78; Syracuse Univ, NY, 72-74. *Work:* Pvt collection, Mrs Robert Black, Mill Valley, Calif & F Helmut Weymar, Princeton, NJ. *Exhib:* One-man shows, Studio 53, New York, 78-79 & Soc Illusr, New York, 86; Graphis Ann Show, Switz, 83-84; Diaz-Marciall Gallery, New York, 84; Art Dirs Club Ann, New York, 86; Joy Kreves, Frenchtown, NJ, 89; Larsen-Dulman, Newhope, PA, 89-91; and others. *Pos:* Illusr, Post Grad Med, McGraw-Hill, 77-86 & Travel & Leisure, Am Express, 78-85; book illus, Harper & Row, 87-91 & Viking/ Penguin 89-91. *Teaching:* Asst prof illus, Moore Col Art & Design, 86-91. *Awards:* Certificates Merit, Soc Illusr Ann Show 77, 82, 86, 89, 91 & Soc Publ Designers, 82 & 86; Print Regional Design Ann, 86 & 88; Distinguished Artist Grant, NJSCA, 90-91; and many others. *Mem:* Soc Illusr; Artworks, Trenton, NJ. *Media:* Colored Pencils, Mixed; Oils, Pastels. *Publ:* Illustr, The Joy of Stuffed Preppies, Holt, Reinhart, Winston, 82; The Directory of Illustrations vol 8, 92. *Mailing Add:* 417 Beatty St Trenton NJ 08611

FOWLER, FRANK EISON
ART DEALER, CONSULTANT
b Chattanooga, Tenn, June 2, 46. *Study:* Univ Ga, BBA, 69. *Comn:* Produced Inaugural Portfolio, 76 & Presidential Portfolio, 80, comn by Pres Jimmy Carter. *Pos:* Mem adv bd, John F Kennedy Ctr Performing Arts, formerly & Ga Mus Art, Athens, currently. *Mem:* Appraisers Asn Am; Int Soc Appraisers. *Res:* Represent Andrew Wyeth, Jamie Wyeth & estate of N C Wyeth. *Mailing Add:* 1213 Ft Stephenson Oval Lookout Mountain TN 37350

FOWLER, HARRIET WHITTEMORE
MUSEUM DIRECTOR
b Geneva, NY, Apr 6, 46. *Study:* Smith Col, 64-67; Cornell Univ, BA(cum laude), 77; PhD, 81. *Collections Arranged:* Horses (dir, video film), 88; New Deal Art: WPA Works at The University of Kentucky (auth, catalog), 85. *Pos:* Cur, Univ Ky Art Mus, 81-90 & dir, 90- *Awards:* Frances Sampson Fine Arts Prize, Cornell Univ, 77. *Mem:* Southeastern Mus Conf (state dir, 92-95); Ky Asn Mus (pres, 92-94); Ky Citizens Arts (bd mem, 89-); Lexington Arts & Cult Coun (pres comt, 90-); Phi Kappa Phi. *Publ:* Auth, A Bluegrass Blockbuster, Mus News, 83; Ann O'Hanlon's Kentucky mural, Ky Rev, Vol VIII, No 1, spring 88; A Handbook of the Permanent Collection, Univ Ky Art Mus, 91; contribr, The Kentucky Encyclopedia, Univ Press Ky, 92. *Mailing Add:* University of Kentucky Art Museum Rose and Euclid Sts Lexington KY 40506-0241

FOWLER, MARY JEAN
WEAVER
b Ames, Iowa, Feb 5, 34. *Study:* Iowa State Univ, Ames, BS(appl art), 56, MS, 57; Arrowmont Sch Arts & Crafts, Gatlinburg, Tenn; also various workshops under nationally known artists. *Comn:* 3 landscape blankets, Hilton Hotel, Bryan-College Station, Tex, 55; Flyers in the Breeze (hanging), First Nat Bank Quail Valley, Houston, 83; 3 woven landscape panels, First City Bank Forum NAm, San Antonio, 83; 6 woven landscape panels, First City Bank Gulf Gate, Houston, 84. *Exhib:* One-man shows, Archway Gallery, 81, Travels in Quiet Landscapes, 84 & Watkins, Carter & Hamilton Archit, 85, Houston, Tex; Dimension Houston, Houston Art League, Tex, 82; Instr Show, Convergence Fibers for Architectural Spaces, Southern Methodist Univ, Houston, 83 & Dallas, 84; Five Fiber Artists, Baylor Univ, Waco, Tex, 84; Concepts: Work and Wearables, Owatonna Arts Ctr, Minn, 85. *Pos:* Vchmn, Arrowmont Bd Govs, Arrowmont Sch Arts & Crafts, Gatlinburg, Tenn, 72-88. *Teaching:* Independent weaving consultant working with school systems on contract basis; instr, St John's Sch Art, Houston, Tex, 86, Arrowmont Sch Arts & Crafts, 90-92 & Rice Univ Summer Sch for high sch students, Houston, Tex, 91- *Awards:* Master chair in Primary Educ, 92, St John's Sch, Cullen Found, 92. *Mem:* Am Craft Coun; Handweavers Guild Am. *Mailing Add:* 1415 Hamlin Valley Dr Houston TX 77090

FOWLER, MEL
PRINTMAKER, PAINTER
b Chicago, Ill, July 29, 22. *Study:* Minneapolis Inst Art, (scholar), 39-40; Calif Sch Fine Art, with Ralph Stackpole. *Work:* Brit Mus, London; Klingspor Mus, Offenbach, Ger; Walker Mus, Minneapolis; Clark Libr, Univ Calif, Los Angeles; New York Pub Libr; Univ Iowa. *Comn:* Porcelain steel sculpture, M Mogenson, Burlingame, Calif, 58 & Kaiser Hosp, Oakland, 59; hammered bronze sculpture, F Rosenthal, San Francisco, 59; porcelain steel mural, M Wornum, San Francisco, 59; aluminum sculpture, Cris Caras, Los Angeles, 65. *Exhib:* San Francisco Annual, 42 & 43; Mondrianna, Ann Arbor Film Festival & Mus Mod Art, 70; Museo de Ponce, PR, 73; Westbeth Graphic Arts Workshop, Belles Artes, Mexico City, Mex, 73-74 & traveling exhib sponsored by NY State Coun Arts, 74-75; plus ten one-man shows. *Pos:* Pres, Westbeth Painters, New York, 72-73. *Mem:* Fedn Mod Painters & Sculptors, New York. *Publ:* Illusr, Home for the Night, 64; Lyric Poems, Franklin Watts Co Inc, 68 & Psychiatry: What It Is, 69; Row With Your Hair, 69; The King of Numbers (childrens' bk), Jarrow, 71; and many others. *Dealer:* Greenwich Village Art Gallery 315 Bleeker St New York NY 10014; Wenniger Graphics 164 Newbury St Boston Ma 02116. *Mailing Add:* Studio G-224 Westbeth 463 West St New York NY 10014

FOX, FLO
PHOTOGRAPHER, LECTURER
b Miami, Fla, Sept 26, 45. *Study:* With Lisette Model, 80-83 & Andre Kertesz, 85. *Work:* Focus Gallery, San Francisco; Brooklyn Mus, New York. *Comn:* Three-dimensional photography, Minn Mus Art, 86. *Exhib:* Asphalt Garden, Canon Gallery, Paris, 81, Camden Arts Ctr, Eng, 81, Focus Gallery, San Francisco, 83, Catskill Ctr Photog, Woodstock, NY, 86 & Janapa Gallery, 86; Auto-Focus Photography, Boston Mus Fine Art, 82 & Philadelphia Mus Art, 83. *Teaching:* Instr photog, Lighthouse for Blind, New York, 79-80, Village Nursing Home, 84 & YWCA, 85-86, New York. *Awards:* Cert Merit, Boston Mus Fine Art, 82 & Philadelphia Mus Art, 83. *Bibliog:* Georgia Dullea (auth), A camera does the seeing, New York Times, 4/80; Elizabeth Mehren (auth), Trades sight for insight, Los Angeles Times, 9/81; article in The Plain Dealer, Cleveland, Ohio, 6/85. *Mem:* Park West Camera Club. *Publ:* Photogr, The Picture Book of Greenwich Village, 85; The Human Animal, by Phil Donahue; Art of the Eye, Minn Mus Art, 86. *Mailing Add:* 135 W 23rd St No 607 New York NY 10011

FOX, HOWARD NEAL
CURATOR, CRITIC
b Atlantic City, NJ, Oct 4, 46. *Study:* Univ Md, BA, 68; Univ Wis, Madison, MA, 70. *Collections Arranged:* Directions: Survey of Contemporary American Art (auth, catalog), 79, Metaphor: New Projects by Vito Acconci, Siah Armajani, Alice Aycock, Lauren Ewing, Robert Morris & Dennis Oppenheim, (auth, catalog), 81-82, Content: A Contemporary Focus, 1974-1984 (auth catalog), 84 & New Romanticism: Sixteen Artists from Italy (auth catalog), 85, Hirshhorn Mus & Sculpture Garden, Washington, DC; Avant-Garde in the Eighties: A Viewpoint (auth catalog), Los Angelas Co Mus Art, 87; Tears of Steel: A Video Installation by Marie Jo Lafontaine, Los Angeles County Mus Art, 88; Robert Longo Retrospective (auth catalog) Los Angeles Co Mus Art, 89; A Primal Spirit: Ten Contemporary Japanese Sculptors (auth catalog) Los Angelas Co Mus Art, 90. *Pos:* Assoc cur exhibs, Hirshhorn Mus, Washington, DC, formerly; mem bd dirs, Washington Proj Arts, Washington, DC, 81-85; cur contemp art, Los Angeles Co Mus Art, currently. *Res:* Modern art and critical theory, art in public places. *Publ:* Auth, The thorny issues of temporary art, Mus News, 79; contribr, The New Imagery, Pluralist Decade, Inst Contemp Art, Philadelphia, 80; auth, Suzanne Caporael (catalog), Santa Barbara Mus Art, 86; Odd Nerdrum (catalog), Univ Art Mus, Calif State Univ, Long Beach, 88; and others. *Mailing Add:* Los Angeles County Mus Art 5905 Wilshire Blvd Los Angeles CA 90036

FOX, JOHN
PAINTER
b Montreal, PQ, July 26, 27. *Study:* Montreal Mus Fine Arts; Slade Sch, London, Eng. *Work:* Nat Gallery Can, Ottawa; Montreal Mus Fine Arts; Mus Que, PQ; Beaverbrook Art Gallery, Frederickton, NB; Art Gallery Greater Victoria, BC. *Teaching:* Assoc prof painting & drawing, Concordia Univ, 79- *Media:* Oil. *Mailing Add:* Art Dept, Concordia Univ 1455 deMaissoneuve W Montreal PQ H3G 1M8 Canada

FOX, JUDITH HOOS
CURATOR
b Oakland, Calif, June 13, 49. *Study:* Bryn Mawr Col, BA, 71; Univ Minn, MA, 74. *Collections Arranged:* One Century: Wellesley Families Collect (with catalog), 78 & Sitework (auth, catalog), 80, Wellesley Col Mus; Catherine Urguhart Warren Collection (auth, catalog), 83 & Furniture, Furnishings: Subject and Object (auth, catalog), 84, Mus Art, RI Sch Design; Boston Collects Today (auth, catalog), Mus Fine Arts, 86; The Multiple Object (auth, catalog), Fine Arts Planning Group, 87; S & Y Ombra: An Autobiography in Form, Beverly Pepper, MIT, 88; Erikson Ziegler: The Wellesley Method, Wellesley Col Mus, 90. *Pos:* Cur intern, Walker Art Ctr, Minneapolis, 73-74; cur, Inst Contemp Art, Boston, 74-75; asst dir, Wellesley Col Mus, Mass, 77-82; cur painting & sculpture, Mus Art, RI Sch Design, Providence, 82-84; adj cur, 20th century dept, Mus Fine Arts, Boston, independent cur, 84-88; cur, Wellesley Col Mus, currently. *Teaching:* Instr mus studies, Wellesley Col, 84. *Mem:* Art Table. *Publ:* Contribr, Naives and Visionaries, Walker Art Ctr, 74; The Railroad in the American Landscape: 1850-1950, Wellesley Col Mus, 81; Handbook of the Museum of Art, Rhode Island Sch of Design,86. *Mailing Add:* 21 Myrtle St Jamaica Plain Boston MA 02130

FOX, LINCOLN H
SCULPTOR
b Morrilton, Ark, June 14, 42. *Study:* Univ Tex, Austin, with Charles Umlaf, BFA, 66; Univ Dallas, with Heri Barscht, MA, 67; Univ Kans, Lawrence, with Elden Tefft, MFA, 68. *Work:* El Paso Art Mus; Mus Southwest, Midland, Tex; Land of the Four Seasons Collection, Lake of the Ozarks, Mo. *Comn:* Child of Prague, Cistercian Prep Sch, Irving, Tex; Turn of the Century Cable Tool Workers, Permian Basin Petroleum Mus, Midland, Tex, 76; wall relief, First Christian Church, Ruidoso, NMex, 82. *Exhib:* One-man show, Smithsonian Inst, 75, Fine Arts Mus Albuquerque, 78 & El Paso Art Mus, 79; Nat Acad Western Art Ann, Nat Cowboy Hall Fame, Oklahoma City, 75, 79 & 80; Nat Sculpture Soc Ann Exhib, Equitable Bldg, New York, 82 & 83; Nat Western Artists First Ann Exhib, Civic Ctr, Lubbock, Tex, 82 & 83; and others. *Teaching:* Instr sculpture, Univ Kans, Lawrence, 67-68; instr sculpture & drawing, Amarillo Col, 69-71. *Awards:* Purchase Award, 60th Ann Nat Competition Am Art, 70; Bronze Medal, Solon Borglum Mem Sculpture Exhib, Nat Cowboy Hall Fame, 75; Misner Award, 49th Ann Exhib Nat Sculpture Soc, 82. *Bibliog:* Morgan Catherine Merrill (auth), Lincoln Fox: Mood, media and idea, Southwest Art Mag, 5/80; Peggy & Harold Samuels (auths), Contemporary Western Artists, Southwest Art Publ, 82; article, Nat Sculpture Rev, summer 82. *Mem:* Nat Sculpture Soc; Nat Western Artist Asn. *Media:* Bronze, Stone; Pastel. *Dealer:* Christine's Gallery Sante Fe NM; Soderburg/Stevenson Sculpture Galleries 671 Hwy 179 Act 2 Sedona AZ 86336. *Mailing Add:* PO Box 276 Paonia CO 81428

FOX, MICHAEL DAVID
SCULPTOR, PROFESSOR
b Cortland, NY, Dec 29, 37. *Study:* State Univ NY Col, New Paltz, with Ilya Bolotowsky & Ken Green; State Univ NY Col, Buffalo, with Robert Davidson & George Stark, BS, 62, MS, 69; Brooklyn Mus Sch, with Tom Doyle, Rueben Tam & Toshio Odate, cert, 64. *Work:* State Univ Col NY, Buffalo, Cortland, Oswego & New Paltz; Brooklyn Mus; Morehead State Univ, Morehead, Ky; Pvt collecttions through out the world. *Exhib:* Finger Lakes Ann, Rochester Mem Art Gallery, 63-83; Ann Prof Exhib, Brooklyn Mus, 64; J B Speed Art Mus, Louisville, Ky, 65-67; Cent NY Ann, Everson Mus, Syracuse, 68-84; Artists Cent NY, Munson-Williams-Proctor Inst, Utica, 68-89; State Univ Ark Nat, Univ Gallery, 73; Cooperstown Art Mus Nat, NY, 81; State Univ NY Painters Invitational, Geneso, 88; solo exhibs, Elmira Col, 78, Oswego Art Guild 78 & 88, Univ Vermont, State Univ NY, Oswego & many others in New York, Toronto & Rome. *Pos:* Dir, Popular Image Gallery, Oswego, NY, 73-; proj dir, Nat Endowment Arts Grant, State Univ NY Col, Oswego, 78- *Teaching:* Teacher art, Rochester City Schs, NY, 62-65; instr, Morehead State Univ, Ky, 65-67; prof art, State Univ Col, Oswego, NY, 67- *Awards:* Sculpture Award, Ann Exhib, Brooklyn Mus, 64; Painting Awards, Finger Lakes Exhib, Rochester Mem Art Gallery, 78 & NY State Fair, Syracuse, 78-81 & 92. *Bibliog:* Sculpture (feature), CBS TV, 76, 78 & 80; Sculpture (feature), Can Nat Television, 79; PM Mag (feature), CBS TV, 81; and others. *Media:* Plastic, Polyester Resin. *Mailing Add:* 7 W End Ave Oswego NY 13126

FOX, PEARL
ART DEALER, COLLECTOR
b Philadelphia, Pa. *Study:* Philadelphia Normal Sch; Temple Univ; Univ Pa. *Pos:* Dir, Cheltenham Art Ctr, Pa, 45-46; owner, Pearl Fox Gallery, 48- *Teaching:* Teacher, Philadelphia Sch Syst, 30-42. *Mem:* Pa Acad Fine Arts. *Specialty:* Painting and sculpture. *Interests:* Subsidizing and aiding artists for the past thirty-five years. *Mailing Add:* Pearl Fox Gallery 103 Windsor Ave Philadelphia PA 19126

FOX, TERRY ALAN
CONCEPTUAL ARTIST, SCULPTOR
b Seattle, Wash, May 10, 43. *Study:* Self taught. *Work:* Univ Art Mus, Berkeley; Mus Modern Art, San Francisco; Kuntzmuseum, Luzern, Switz; Folkwang Mus, Essen, Ger; Mus Contemp Art, Vienna, Austria. *Comn:* Sculpture (stone), Podio del Mondo di Arte, Middelberg, Holland, 78. *Exhib:* Solo exhibs, Univ Art Mus (with catalog), Berkeley, 73, Everson Mus, Syracuse, 74, Long Beach Mus Art, 75, Kunstmuseum (with catalog), Luzern, Switz, 82, Folkwang Mus (with catalog), Essen, Ger, 82, DAAD Galerie, Berlin, Ger, 82 & Kunstraum, Munich, Ger, 85. *Pos:* Artist-in-residence, DAAD, Berlin, WGer, 82-83. *Publ:* Auth, Catch Phrases & Hobo Signs, Kunstraum, Munich, Ger, 85. *Dealer:* Ronald Feldman Fine Arts 31 Mercer St New York NY 10013. *Mailing Add:* 58 Rue Pierreuse Liege B-4000 Belgium

FRA, DAHLI-STERNE
PAINTER, SCULPTOR
b Stettin, Ger, Jan 3, 1895; US citizen. *Study:* Kaiserin Auguste Victoria Acad, BA; and with Albert Pels, Ludolf Liberts & Josef Shilhavy, US. *Work:* Oklahoma City Art Ctr; Evanston Mus Art; Fla Southern Col; Seton Hall Univ; Gracie Mansion, New York; plus others. *Exhib:* Nat Arts Club, 53-58; Allied Artists Am, 55; 50 Am Artists, 55-58; Col Mt St Vincent, New York; Allied Artists Am; Metrop Mus, New York, 80; and others. *Pos:* Art dir, Nat Coun Jewish Women. *Awards:* Citation, Okla Art Asn, 54; Award, Am Artists Prof League, 55; Gold Medal, Ogunquit Art Ctr, 57. *Mem:* Am Artists Prof League; Catharine Lorillard Wolfe Art Club; Artists Equity Asn; fel Royal Soc Arts, Eng; Nat Soc Arts & Lett (vpres, 71-72). *Media:* Oil; All. *Mailing Add:* 315 W 70th St New York NY 10023

FRABEL, HANS GODO
SCULPTOR
b Jena, EGer, June 9, 41. *Work:* Smithsonian Inst, White House & Nat Bldg Mus, Washington, DC; Wertheim Mus, WGer; Botanical Mus, Harvard Univ, Cambridge, Mass; Dusseldorf Mus, WGer; Headly-Whitney Mus, Lexington, Ky. *Comn:* Gift to Deng Xiaoping, comn by City Atlanta, Ga, 79; gift to people of Berlin, comn by VPres Rockefeller, Washington, DC; gift to Lord High Mayor, London, Delta Airlines, Atlanta, Ga, 79; gift to Pres Carter, Ga Democratic Party, Atlanta, Ga; Gardens for Peace, Moscow, 88; Queen Elizabeth II, 91. *Exhib:* Jr Art Gallery, Louisville, Ky, 75; New Glass, traveling, 79-; Contemp Glass Gallery, New York, 80; Westlake Gallery, White Plains, NY, 81; Glass Gallery, Bethesda, Md; Crystal Fox, Carmel, Calif; Global Gallery, Tampa, Fla; Foster-White, Seattle, 92. *Pos:* Bd, Ga Coun on Int Visitors. *Awards:* Phoenix Award, Atlanta Chamber of Commerce, Ga; Peoples Choice Best in Glass, Artists Soc Int, 87; Am Interfaith, Silver Award, 92. *Bibliog:* Sampling of contemporary picture, Cleveland Plain Dealer, 80; Creating art in glass, Dallas Times-Herald, 80; Frabel's glass meets the flame, Southern Living, 5/81. *Mem:* Glass Art Soc; Am Sci Glassblowers Soc. *Media:* Borosilicate Glass. *Dealer:* Frabel Gallery 231 Peachtree St NE Atlanta GA 30303; Frabel Gallery 3393 Peachtree Rd NE Atlanta GA 30326. *Mailing Add:* 695 Antone St, NW Atlanta GA 30318

FRACE, CHARLES LEWIS
PAINTER
b Mauch Chunk, Pa, Feb 18, 26. *Study:* Philadelphia Col Art, Pa. *Work:* Nat Wildlife Fedn, Washington, DC. *Comn:* Official portrait of Morris the Cat, 9-Lives Cat Food, 76; paintings for reprod of ltd ed prints, Frame House Gallery, 73-80 & Am Masters Found, 81- *Exhib:* one-man show, Cumberland Mus & Sci Ctr, Nashville, 78, 81 & 89 & Houston Mus Nat Sci, Tex, 60 original paintings, 91; Ann Orginal Art Showcase, Mississauga, Ont, Can, 89, 90 & 91; Royal Ont Mus, Ornitholology Gallery, Toronto, Can, 87; Northeastern Wildlife Expos, Albany, NY, 87, 88; Nat Mus Natural Hist, Smithsonian Inst, Washington, DC, 35 original paintings, The American Wildlife Image and Charles Frace, 92-93; and others. *Awards:* Spec Award of Merit, Denver Mus Natural Hist, Colo, 82; Inducted into publication's First Ann Hall of Fame (wildlife category), US Art Mag, 91; Spec Honored guest at official opening ceremonies, Nashville Zoo, Tenn, 91. *Mem:* Soc Animal Artists, New York. *Media:* Oil, Acrylic. *Publ:* Illusr, Last Chance on Earth, Chilton 5096, 66; illusr, The Life of the Jungle, McGraw-Hill, 70; illusr, Wonders of Island Life & Animals in Action, Readers Digest, 72; illusr, The Wolf, Coward, McCann, 73. *Mailing Add:* c/o AM Masters Found 10688 Haddington Houston TX 77043

FRACKMAN, NOEL
CRITIC, HISTORIAN
b New York, NY, May 27, 30. *Study:* Mt Holyoke Col, Sarah Williston Scholar, 48-50; Sarah Lawrence Col, BA, 52, MA, 53; Columbia Univ, 64-67; Inst Fine Arts, NY Univ, MA, 76, PhD, 87. *Pos:* Lectr, Aldrich Mus Contemp Art, Ridgefield, Conn, 67-75; partic, Art Critics Workshop, Am Fedn Arts, 68; lectr, Gallery Passport Ltd, New York, 68-; contrib ed, Arts Mag, New York, 68-; cur educ, Storm King Art Ctr, Mountainville, NY, 73-75. *Teaching:* Instr, Continuing Educ Div, State Univ NY, Purchase, 88-93. *Awards:* Mademoiselle First Prize, Col Publ Contest, 61. *Mem:* Int Asn Art Critics; Art Table. *Publ:* Auth, Super-chair, Art Voices, fall 66; The Stein family and the era of avant-garde collecting, 2/71 & The enticement of watercolor, 6/74, Arts Mag; Jump into the New York art world, Harper's Bazaar, 2/72; plus art rev in Scarsdale Inquirer, 62-67, Patent Trader, 62-71 & Arts Mag, current issues; John Storrs retrospective catalog, Whitney Mus Am Art, 86. *Mailing Add:* 3 Hadden Rd Scarsdale NY 10583

FRAENKEL, JEFFREY ANDREW
ART DEALER
b Shreveport, La, Jan 28, 55. *Study:* Antioch Col, BFA, 77. *Pos:* Pres, Fraenkel Gallery, San Francisco. *Mem:* Art Dealers Asn of Am; Asn Internat Photography Art Dealers. *Specialty:* 19th and 20th century photographs. *Publ:* Carleton E Watkins: Photographs 1861-1874, 89; The Insistent Object, 87; Photography in Spain in the Nineteenth Century, 83; The Kiss of Apollo: Photography & Sculptue 1845 to the Present. *Mailing Add:* 49 Geary St San Francisco CA 94108

FRAILEY, STEPHEN A
PHOTOGRAPHER
b Chicago, Ill, Sept 3, 57. *Study:* San Francisco Art Inst, 77; Bennington Col, BA, 79. *Work:* Fogg Art Mus, Harvard Univ, Boston, Mass; Polaroid Collection, Frankfurt, WGer; Chase Manhattan Bank, New York; Int Ctr Photog, New York; Mus Fine Arts, Houston. *Exhib:* Art & Advertising, Int Ctr Photog, New York, 87; Avant Garde in 80's, Los Angeles Mus, Calif, 87; Contemporary Diptychs, Whitney Mus/Equitable, New York, 87; Photographic Fabrications, Carpenter Ctr, Cambridge, 88; The Photography of Invention, Nat Mus Am Art, Washington, DC. *Pos:* Dir, Mary Boone Gallery, 80-85. *Teaching:* Instr photog, Sch Visual Arts, New York, 85- *Awards:* Macdowell Colony Fel, 88; Nat Endowment Arts, 88. *Bibliog:* Portfolio, The Paris Rev, spring 89; David Robbins (auth), Stephen Frailey, Arts Mag, 9/89; Portfolio, Art Forum, 10/90; and others. *Publ:* Auth, Context as Content, Ctr Quart, spring 86; Richard Avedon, Print Collector, 5/86; Ray Metzger, Art News, 9/87; and others. *Mailing Add:* 11 Charleton St New York NY 10014

FRALEY, DAVID K
PAINTER, EDUCATOR
b Novato, Calif, Aug 18, 52. *Study:* Wheaton Col, Ill, 70-71; Tex Tech, Lubbock, BArchit, 76; Tulane Univ, New Orleans, MArchit, 78. *Work:* Ga Arts Coun, Atlanta. *Comn:* Helping Hand (metal sculpture), Presbyterian Med Ctr, Lubbock, Tex, 76; painting diptych, comn by Marcia Ascanio, Dallas, Tex, 89; Gestural Wall (painting), comn by Gary Maurice Burk, New York, 90; Children's Hosp Chapel (painting), Cincinnati, 92. *Exhib:* Solo exhibs, Auburn Univ Gallery, Ala, 85, Galerie Simonne Stern, Atlanta, 89, Upstairs Tryon, NC, 90, Trinity Gallery, Atlanta, 91, Blue Spiral I, Asheville, NC, 92 & Prudential Insurance Co, Atlanta, 92; Spotlight on Georgia Artist's, Atlanta, 90-92; Vital Signs, Nexus Contemp Arts Ctr, Atlanta; Shrines, Emory Gallery, Atlanta; Taboo XMas, 91; As a Member of Taboo: Angry Love, 92; and others. *Teaching:* Instr 1st & 3rd year design, Tulane Univ, New Orleans, 76-78; instr color theory, Univ NC, Charlotte, 81-86; instr archit rendering, Auburn Univ, Ala, 85; instr drawing & archit rendering, Atlanta Col Art, 91. *Awards:* Individual Artist Grant, Ga; Artist-in-Residence Fel, Hambridge Ctr Creative Arts, 91; Coun Arts, 92. *Bibliog:* J W Cullum (auth), David Fraley and Mark Jordan, Art Papers, 7-8/89; Susan Dillon (auth), Profile of the artist, J Am Med Asn Ga, 4/90; Leigh Conner (auth), Artcare--A bid for life, Etcetera, 7/6/90; Art, aids and the homoerotic image, Southern Voice, 8/2/90. *Mem:* Atlanta-based artist group, Taboo. *Media:* Acrylic, Pastel. *Publ:* Auth & ed, Bulltide Manuscript, Tex Tech Univ, 76; auth & illusr, What is the Sound of One Bird Chirping & Why Don't We Shop a Different Store, 90, ZooCo Press; Art about a guy named Art, Celestine Press, 90; contribr, Will of the People, 91 & Big Brother, Weird Relatives, 92, Art/Line Press. *Dealer:* Trinity Gallery 249 Trinity Ave Atlanta GA 30303; Blue Spiral I 38 Biltmore Ave Asheville NC 28807. *Mailing Add:* PO Box 1123 Decatur GA 30031

FRAME, JOHN
SCULPTOR
b San Bernardino, Calif, Nov 27, 50. *Study:* San Diego State Univ, BA, 75; Claremont Grad Sch, MFA, 80. *Work:* California Collection, Crocker Ctr, Los Angeles, Calif; Collection of Los Angeles Community Redevelopment Agency. *Comn:* Monumental sculpture, Walnut Plaza, Pasadena, Calif, 85; sculptural tableau, Cedars Sinai Hosp, Los Angeles, Calif, 87. *Exhib:* Return of the Narrative, Palm Springs Desert Mus, Palm Springs, 84; Crime and Punishment, Triton Mus, Santa Clara, Calif, 84; Three Sculptors, ARCO Ctr Visual Art, Los Angeles, Calif, 84; Sprektrum Los Angeles, Galerie Hartje, Berlin, WGer, 85; Kindred Spirits, Los Angeles Munic Art Gallery, 86; Avante-Garde in the 80's, Los Angeles Co Mus, 87; solo exhib, Los Angeles Co Mus Art, 92. *Awards:* Visual Artists Grants, Nat Endowment Arts, 84 & 86; Young Talent Award, Los Angeles Co Mus Art, 85. *Bibliog:* Marlena Donohue (auth), Whimsical, probing narratives, Sculpture Mag, 87; K Zimmerer (auth), Fools and fallacies, Visions Mag, 87; Mac Mcleod (auth), Small sculptural dramas, Artweek, 87. *Media:* Wood. *Mailing Add:* 2421 S Santa Fe No 21 Los Angeles CA 90058

FRAME, ROBERT (AARON)
PAINTER
b San Fernando, Calif, July 31, 24. *Study:* With Henry Lee McFee & Millard Sheets, 47-50; Pomona Col, BA, 48; Claremont Col, MFA, 51. *Work:* Desert Art Mus, Palm Springs, Calif; State Calif, Sacramento; Nat Acad Design, New York; Munic Art Dept, City Los Angeles; Pasadena Art Mus, Calif. *Exhib:* Ill Biennial, Urbana, 58-65; American Painting, Richmond, Va, 65; De Young Mus, San Francisco; Los Angeles Co Mus; Univ Calif, Los Angeles; David Findlay Galleries, New York; and 38 one-man exhibs. *Awards:* Purchase Prizes, Pasadena Art Mus, 52, St Albans & Home Savings & Loan, Los Angeles, 68; Guggenheim Fel in Creative Painting, 57-58; First Prize, James D Phelan Awards, 65. *Bibliog:* Schaad (auth), Realm of Contemporary Still Life, Reinhold, 61; Mugniani (auth), Oil Painting, Van Nostrand, 69. *Mem:* Artists Equity. *Media:* Oil. *Publ:* Exploring Painting by Gerald F Brommer & Nancy Kinne, Davis Publications, Worcester, Mass. *Dealer:* Adelle M Gallery 3317 McKinney Ave Dallas TX; Dubins Gallery 11948 San Vicente Blvd Los Angeles CA 90049. *Mailing Add:* 2102 Edgewater Way Santa Barbara CA 93109

FRANCES, HARRIETTE ANTON
PAINTER, PRINTMAKER
b San Francisco, Calif. *Study:* San Francisco Sch Fine Arts, 42-45; San Francisco Art Inst, 63 & 65-66; James Weeks, Painting Instructor, Tamarind Inst, Univ of NMex, 88-90. *Work:* Fresno Art Ctr, Calif; Charles D Clark Collection, McAllen, Tex; Achenbach Found Graphic Arts; San Francisco Legion of Honor Fine Arts Mus. *Exhib:* James D Phelan Award Exhib, De Young Mus, San Francisco, 63 & Palace Legion of Honor, 65; Fifth Winter Invitational, Palace Legion of Honor, 64 & Calif Printmakers, 71; one-person shows, Calif Palace Legion of Honor, San Francisco, 68 & Western Asn Art Mus traveling one-man shows at mus & univ galleries throughout US, 68-70; New Sch Art Ctr, New York, 73; Bicentennial Exhib, Mus of Mod Art, San

Francisco, 76; Pacific Prints, Palo Alto, 90. *Teaching:* Instr life drawing, Exten, Univ Pac; instr lithography, Artists Proof Graphics Workshop, Larkspur, Calif; instr monotype, Col of Marin, Kentfield, Calif. *Awards:* Calif State Fair Award, 64; James D Phelan Award in Art, 65; First Place, San Francisco Women Artists, 74. *Bibliog:* George Christy (auth), Are you with it, Town & Country Mag, 67; Martin Fox (ed), A graphic artist depicts her LSD trip, Print Mag, 67; Joan Lisetor (auth), Reviving an ancient art, Independent J, 75. *Mem:* San Francisco Women Artists; Calif Soc of Printmakers; Marin Arts Coun. *Media:* Lithography, Acrylic. *Publ:* Contribr, Ramparts Mag, 66; contribr, Print Mag & Psychedelic Art, 67; Erotic Art of the Masters, 18th, 19th & 20th Centuries, Lyle Stewart Publ; contribr, The Spirit of Shamanism, Tarcher Publ, 90. *Mailing Add:* 105 Rice Lane Larkspur CA 94939

FRANCIS, BILL DEAN
DESIGNER, ADMINISTRATOR
b Salem, Ill, Oct 14, 29. *Study:* Ill State Univ, BS(art educ), 51; Univ Wis, MS(appl art), 52; Ind Univ, 56-63. *Comn:* Tapestry, Phillips Petrol Co, Phillips, Okla, 64 & Bank South Austin, Tex, 75. *Exhib:* Midwest Landscape Art Exhib, Ill State Fair, Springfield, 52; Exhib Momentum, Inst Design, Chicago, 53; 29th Ann Am Graphic Arts & Drawing Exhib, Wichita, Kans, 60; Tex Designer-Craftsman Exhib, Wichita Falls, 72; one-man exhib, Longview Mus, Tex, 73; Recent Realism, Clary-Miner Gallery Ltd, Buffalo, NY, 88. *Teaching:* Asst prof sec & elem art methods, Drake Univ, 58-60; assoc prof sec & elem art methods, Univ Tex, Austin, 64-74, prof art & educ, 74-, assoc dean, Col Fine Arts, 78- *Awards:* NAEA Distinguished Serv Award, 87; Best of Show, Tex Art Educ Asn, Electronic Gallery, Houston, 87; UT-CFA/Teaching Excellence, 88. *Mem:* Nat Art Educ Asn (Western Region, vpres, 82-84); Tex Art Educ Asn. *Media:* Pencil, Prismacolor. *Publ:* Auth, Getting to Know Art (TV ser), KLRN, Tex, 70; The Humanities in Retrospect, Kendall-Hunt, 74; Helping Children See Art and Make Art, Benson Publ Co, 82. *Mailing Add:* 1100 Yaupon Valley Rd Austin TX 78746

FRANCIS, JEAN THICKENS
ASSEMBLAGE ARTIST, PAINTER
b Laurel, Miss, Mar 15, 43. *Study:* Millsaps Col, 61-63; Memphis Art Acad, BFA(sculpture), 66. *Work:* South Central Bell, Miss; Deposit Guaranty Nat Bank, Tupelo & Jackson, Miss; First Nat Bank, Miss; Boyle Investment CO, Memphis Tenn; Int Paper Co, Memphis, Tenn. *Comn:* N Mississippi Women's Health Ctr, Tupelo; Peoples Bank and Trust, Tupelo; Community Federal Savings & Loan, Tupelo. *Exhib:* Mississippi River Crafts Exhib, Brooks Mem Art Gallery, 77; Papermakers & Paperusers, Southeastern Artists, Southeastern Ctr Contemp Art, Winston-Salem, NC, 80; one-person shows, The 500 lb Paper Project, Miss Mus Art, Jackson; Prints, Drawings & Crafts Show, Ark Art Ctr, Little Rock, 81; one-person shows, Artsite Invitational, New Orleans, La, 80, Open Gallery, Miss Mus Art, 81 & Jessie C Wilson Galleries, Anderson, Ind, 84; More Than Land or Sky: Art from Appalachia, Nat Mus Am Art, Smithsonian Inst & traveling, 81-84; The State of The Art: Mississippi, Contemp Art Ctr, New Orleans, La, 83; Papermakers Invitational, Western Carolina Univ, Cullowhee, NC, 85; Paper Art-New Directions, Texas Tech Univ Mus, Lubbock, Tex, 85; 100 Gloves: And Then Some, Univ Mus, Oxford, Miss, 85. *Pos:* self-employed artist, currently. *Teaching:* Instr art, Memphis City Sch, Tenn, 66-67; instr sculpture, Memphis Acad Art, Tenn, summer 74; vis artist, Jackson City Sch, Miss, 76; guest artist, papermaking, Nat Mus Am Art, 81, Miss Mus Art, Jackson, 81, Arrowmont Sch Arts & Crafts, Gatlinburg, Tenn, 84 & Itawamba Jr Col, Fulton, Miss, 85; instr, papermaking, Appalachia Ctr Crafts, Smithville, Tenn, 83; artist in residence, Tupelo City Sch, Miss, 83-84, Bellazio Study Ctr, Italy, 90. *Awards:* Grand Prize, 76 & Second Prize, 77, Miss Artist Competitive Exhib, Miss Art Asn; Merit Award, Greater New Orleans Int Art Exhib, 77; Grant, Rockefeller Found, 90. *Bibliog:* Articles, Art Voices South, 5/79, Cityscape, 81 & 82 & Art Papers, 7-8/82; Annette Cone-Skelton (auth), Southeastern artists today: a cross section, Contemp Art/SE, 78; Gary Witt (auth), Ke & Jean Francis of Tupelo, Mississippi: A union of opposites, Art Voices/South, 5/79; Stephen Flynn Young (auth), A visit with Jean Thickens Francis, Art Papers, 82. *Media:* Mixed Media. *Dealer:* Albers Fine Art Gallery 1027 Yates Rd Suite 101 Memphis TN 38119. *Mailing Add:* 512 Magnolia Dr Tupelo MS 38801

FRANCIS, MADISON KE, JR
SCULPTOR, PRINTMAKER
b Memphis, Tenn, Aug 19, 45. *Study:* Miss State Univ, Starkville; Memphis State Univ, Tenn; Memphis Acad Art, Tenn; Cleveland Inst Art, Ohio, BFA(sculpture), 69; Cape Sch Art, Provincetown, Mass, study painting with Henry Hensche. *Work:* Southeastern Ctr Contemp Art, Winston-Salem, NC; Mint Mus, Charlotte, NC; New Orleans Mus, La; Mus Fine Arts, Boston, Mass; Rose Mus, Brandeis Univ, Waltham, Mass. *Comn:* Steel sculpture, People's Bank, Tupelo, Miss, 73; sculpture, Itawamba Jr Col, 78; time capsule sculpture, North Miss Med Ctr, Tupelo. *Exhib:* Southern Exposure: Not a Regional Exhib, Alternative Mus, New York, 85; A Sense of Place: Contemp Southern Art, Minneapolis Col Art & Design Gallery, Minn, 86; Fact/Fiction/Fantasy: Recent Narrative Art in the Southeast, Traveling exhib, Ewing Gallery, Univ Tenn, Knoxville, 87; Southern Arts Fedn Touring Sculpture Exhib, Atlanta, Ga, 87- 89; Solo exhibs, Recent Works, Memphis Ctr Contemp Art, Tenn, 88, Recent Prints, Drawings & Sculpture, Marcia McCoy Gallery Contemp Art, Santa Fe, NMex, 89 & Reconstruction: Tornado Series, Clara Eagle Gallery, Murray State Univ, Ky, 89; Looking S: A different Dixie, Touring exhib, Birmingham Mus, Ala, 88; Freneticism, Valencia Community Col, Orlando, Fla, 88; The Blues Aesthetic: Black Cult & Modernism Touring Exhib, Washington Pro Arts, Washington, DC, 89; and others. *Teaching:* Instr, Cleveland Inst Art, 69-71; instr sculpture, Memphis Acad Art, summer 73; instr graphics, Penland Sch, NC, 78-79. *Awards:* SAF/NEQ Regional fel sculpture, Southern Arts Fedn, 87; Award for visual arts, Mississippi Inst Arts and Letters, 87; Rockefeller Found Grant, Bellagio Study Ctr, Italy, 90. *Bibliog:* Becky Hendrick (auth), El Paso/Las Cruces Letter, Art Space, winter 87-88; Jane Bedno (auth), Tornadoes in Beulah Land, Vol 2, No 3, winter 89; Stephen Flinn Young (auth), Post-southernism: The Southern Sensibility in Postmodern Sculpture, Southern Quarterly, Vol XXVIII, No 4, fall 89. *Media:* Miscellaneous Media; Intaglio, Silkscreen. *Dealer:* Galerie Simone Stern New Orleans La; Morgan Gallery Kansas City Mo. *Mailing Add:* 512 Magnolia Dr Tupelo MS 38801

FRANCIS, PETER See Cramer, Peter

FRANCIS, SAM
PAINTER
b San Mateo, Calif, June 25, 23. *Study:* Univ Calif, Berkeley, BA, 43, MA, 50; Atelier Fernand Leger, Paris; Univ Calif, Berkeley, Hon DFA, 69. *Work:* Guggenheim Mus, NY; Mus Mod Art; Albright Art Gallery; Kunsthaus, Zurich, Switz; Dayton Art Inst; Hirshhorn Mus & Sculpture Garden, Smithsonian Inst, Washington, DC; Dallas Mus Fine Arts, Tex; Los Angeles Co Mus Art, Calif; Musée D'Art Moderne, Paris, France; Nat Collection Fine Arts, Smithsonian Inst, Washington, DC; Nat Gallery Art, Washington, DC; St Louis Art Mus, Mo; San Francisco Mus Art, Calif; Seattle Mus Art; and others. *Comn:* Murals, Kunsthalle, Berne, Switz, 57, Sofu Sch Flower Arrangement, Tokyo, Japan, 57 & Chase Manhattan Bank, New York, 59, mural, Opera Nat, Theatre Royal de la Monnaie, Brussels, 86. *Exhib:* Retrospective, Albright-Knox Art Gallery, Buffalo, NY, 72; Katonah Mus Art, NY, 90; Nagoya City Art Mus, Japan, 90; one-man exhibs, New York & Smith Andersen Gallery, Palo Alto, 90, Galerie Jean Fournier, Paris, James Corcoran Gallery, Los Angeles, Angles Gallery, Los Angeles, Assoc Am Artists, New York (prints), Gagosian Gallery, New York, Centre Regional d'Art Contemporain Midi-Pyrenees, Toulouse-Labege, France, 91; forty yr retrospective, Galerie Kornfeld, Bern, 91. *Awards:* First Prize, Int Biennial Exhib Prints, Tokyo, 62; Dunn Int Prize, Tate Gallery, London, 63; Tamarind Fel, 63; and others. *Bibliog:* Werner Haftman (auth), Paintings in the Twentieth Century, Praeger, 60; Peter Selz (auth), Sam Francis, Abrams, 75; Michel Waldberg (auth), Sam Francis: Metaphysics of the Void, Philosophy of the Arts, Moos Book Publ, 86; and many others. *Publ:* Contribr, The New American Painting (exhib catalog), Mus Mod Art, NY, 28 & 59; auth, Bonnar, or be kind to yourself, human being (poem), Bijutsu Techo, Tokyo, 4/68; Book of Aphorisms, Los Angeles, 75, pvt publ; Jackson Pollock (exhib catalog), Centre Georges Pompidou, Musée Nat d'Art Moderne, Paris, 82. *Dealer:* André Emmerich Gallery New York NY; Jean Fournier Gallery Paris France. *Mailing Add:* c/o The Litho Shop 2058 Broadway Santa Monica CA 90404

FRANCIS, TOM
PAINTER
b Sheboygan, Wis, Mar 12, 51. *Study:* Univ Wis, BS, 73, MA, 75, MFA(Henry Vilas Fel), 76. *Work:* State Wis, Madison; Chase Manhattan Bank, New York; Omni Int, Atlanta; Europco Corp, Fla; Coca Cola Corp, Atlanta, Ga. *Comn:* Paintings, Made in Heaven (film), comn by Alan Rudolph, dir; Hyatt Corp, Aruba & Puerto Rico; Embassy Suites, Orlando, Fla. *Exhib:* Walker Art Ctr, 75; Columbia Mus, SC, 82; Atlanta in France, Paris, Toulouse France, 85; Volte del Sud, Rome, Italy, 85; Sandler/Hudson Gallery, Atlanta, 90; McIntosh Gallery, Atlanta, 92. *Teaching:* Chmn dept painting, Atlanta Col Art, 78- *Media:* All. *Mailing Add:* Dept Art Atlanta Col Art 1280 Peachtree NE Atlanta GA 30309

FRANCK, FREDERICK S
PAINTER, WRITER
b Maastricht, Holland, Apr 12, 09; US citizen. *Study:* Belg, Eng & US; Univ Pittsburgh, hon DFA, 63. *Work:* Whitney Mus Am Art & Mus Mod Art, New York; San Francisco Mus Art, Calif; Stedelijk Mus, Holland; Mus Nat France, Paris; Tokyo Nek Mus. *Comn:* Murals, Temple Beth-El, Elizabeth, NJ & Nat Mus Tokyo; stage designs for off-Broadway shows; drawings for New Yorker; Pacem in Terris (community artwork), Warwick, NY; sculptures, Cathedral St John the Divine, New York, Pa State Univ, Church of the Savior, Washington, DC & Omega Inst, Rhinebeck, NY, Wainwright House, Rye, NY, 91 & Fondacion Elpis, Buenos Aires, 91. *Exhib:* Group shows in Whitney Mus Am Art & Metrop Mus Art, New York, Corcoran Gallery Art, Washington, DC, Butler Inst Am Art, Youngstown, Ohio, Calif Palace Legion of Honor, San Francisco & shows in Paris, Amsterdam, Geneva, London, Brussels, Rome & Japan; Foster/White Gallery exhib, Seattle, Wash, 77; Puget Sound Univ exhib, Tacoma, Wash, 78; Lowenstein Gallery, Fordham Univ, 85; Singer Mem Mus, Holland, 86; collection of 100 drawings acquired by Univ Nymegen, Holland; plus many other group & one-man shows. *Teaching:* Over 250 workshops on "Seeing/drawing as Meditation" in US, Europe, Japan. *Awards:* Purchase Prizes, Carnegie Inst, Am Acad Arts & Lett & others; Living Arts Found Award, Maastricht Mus, Holland, 58; Medal of the Pontificate, Pope John, 63; plus others. *Mem:* Fel Int Inst Arts & Lett (dir); Soc Arts, Relig & Cult; Artists Equity Asn (hon dir, New York); Temple of Understanding. *Publ:* Auth, Art as 2 Way, a Return to the Spiritual Roots, 81, The Supreme Koan, Confessions on a Journey Inward, 82 & The Buddha Eye, 82, Crossroad Publ; Echoes from the Bottomless Well, Vintage, 85; Little Compendium That Which Matters & Life Drawing Life, Great Ocean Publ, 89; To Be Human Against All Odds, Asian Humanities Press, 91; My Days with Albert Schweitzer, Lyons & Burford, 25th Anniversary Ed, 91. *Mailing Add:* 96 Covered Bridge Rd Warwick NY 10990

FRANCO, BARBARA
MUSEOLOGIST
b New York, NY, Mar 16, 45. *Study:* Bryn Mawr Col, BA; Cooperstown Grad Progs, MA. *Collections Arranged:* White's Utica Pottery (catalog), 69-70 & Shaker Arts & Crafts (catalog), 70-71, Munson-Williams-Proctor Inst, Utica, NY; Masonic Symbols in American Decorative Arts (catalog), Mus of Our Nat Heritage, 75-76; Decorated Masonic Aprons (catalog), Mus of Our Nat Heritage, 80-81; Fraternally Yours (catalog), Mus Our Nat Heritage, 86. *Pos:* Cur decorative arts, Munson-Williams-Proctor Inst, 66-73; cur, Mus of Our Nat Heritage, 73-90; asst dir, Minnesota Hist Soc, 90- *Res:* Symbolism and history of Fraternal Organizations in America; American hooked rugs; American 19th-century decorative arts and cultural history. *Publ:* Auth, Stoneware made by the White Family in Utica, NY, 71 & New York City furniture bought for Fountain Elms, 73, Antiques; John Henry Belter; A Rococo Revival Cabinetmaker in the Limelight, Nineteenth Century, Vol 6 No 2, summer 80; A Treasury of Hooked Rugs, Country Living, 87; Masonic Imagery, Aspects of American Printmaking, 1800-1950, James F O'Gorman (ed), Syracuse Univ Press, 88. *Mailing Add:* 690 Cedar St St Paul MN 55101

FRANK, CHARLES WILLIAM, JR
WOOD CARVER, WRITER
b New Orleans, La, June 8, 22. *Study:* BChemEng. *Exhib:* New Orleans Mus Art, 75; Hillsborough Co Mus, Tampa, Fla, 76; Univ New Orleans Fine Arts Mus, 76; Huntsville Mus Art, Ala, 76-77; West Baton Rouge Hist Asn, 76; Nat Crafts Coun, Winston-Salem, NC, 77. *Pos:* Auth & contribr, NAm Decoys, 72-77; auth, La Duck Decoys, 75-79; La Out of Doors, 77-78 & Ward Found Mag; Anatomy of a Waterfowl, Pelican Publ, 81 & Wetland Heritage, 85. *Awards:* Best of Show, Catahoula Lake Wildfowl Festival, 75 & 76; First Place, La Wildfowl Carvers Exhib, 76; La Master Craftsman, 77. *Bibliog:* Article in La Conservationist, State of La, 73 & 75; Phillips Petroleum Co (auth), Louisiana's Wetland Heritage, The Decoy, 76. *Mem:* La Crafts Coun; La Wildfowl Carvers & Collectors; Int Wildlife Carvers; Nat Wood Carvers Asn. *Media:* Wood, Polychrome. *Collection:* Definitive collection of several thousand Louisiana and world wide duck decoys. *Publ:* Auth articles, Am Shotgunner, 76 & Southern Outdoors, 77. *Mailing Add:* 3112 Octavia New Orleans LA 70125

FRANK, DAVID
ADMINISTRATOR, EDUCATOR
b St Paul, Minn, Sept 13, 40. *Study:* Univ Minn, Duluth, with Glenn C Nelson, BS(art); Tulane Univ La, MFA. *Work:* Tweed Gallery, Duluth; Newcomb Art Sch Collection; Mid Tenn State Univ Collection, Murfreesboro; Miss Univ for Women, Columbus; Miss Dept Archives & Hist. *Comn:* Pohl Gym, Miss Univ for Women, Columbus & St Ignatius Catholic Church, Mobile, Ala. *Exhib:* Mid South Ceramics & Crafts Exhib, Tenn; 14th Ann Delta Art Exhib, Ark; Crafts Invitational, Univ of Ala; Invitational Exhib, Nat Endowment Arts; Miss River Crafts Exhib, Brooks Gallery, Memphis, Tenn; 13th Bi State Exhib, Meridian Mus Art, Miss. *Teaching:* Prof art, Miss Univ for Women, 65-, head, div fine arts & performing arts, currently. *Mem:* Craftsmen's Guild Miss; Am Craftsman's Coun. *Media:* Clay. *Mailing Add:* Dept of Art Miss Univ for Women Columbus MS 39701

FRANK, HELEN (GOODZEIT)
PAINTER, PRINTMAKER
b Jersey City, NJ, May 29, 30. *Study:* Tyler Sch Fine Arts, Temple Univ; Cooper Union; New Sch, with Abraham Rattner & Seymour Lipton, 48; Art Students League, with George Grosz, 50. *Work:* NJ State Mus, Trenton; Newark Public Libr Print Collection, NJ; Am Mus Immigration, New York; UNICEF; Libr Congress. *Comn:* Portfolio, Grant Union Co, NJ, 80-81. *Exhib:* NJ State Exhib, Montclair Mus, 63; Am Watercolor Soc, New York, 65; Pratt Graphic Int, New York, 75 & 77; Morris Mus, Morristown, NJ; NJ Watercolor Soc, Morristown; Rutgers Univ, NJ. *Teaching:* Artist-in-residence, Springfield Public Sch. *Mem:* Artists Equity. *Mailing Add:* 445 Meisel Ave Springfield NJ 07081

FRANK, PETER SOLOMON
CRITIC, CURATOR
b New York, NY, July 3, 50. *Study:* Columbia Col, BA(art hist), 72; Columbia Univ, MA(art hist), 74. *Collections Arranged:* Artists' books section of Documenta 6, Kassel, WGer, summer 77; Artists' Books USA Traveling Exhib, 78-80 & Mapped Art: Charts Routes Regions Traveling Exhib, 81-83, Independent Curators Inc; Young Fluxus, Artists Space, New York, 82; Indiana Influence-The Modern Legacy, Fort Wayne Mus Art, 84; To the Astonishing Horizon, Los Angeles Visual Arts, 85; Earsights: Visual Scores & Musical Images, Nexus Gallery, Philadelphia and Southern Alleghenies Mus, Johnstown, Pa, 85; Southern Abstraction, City Gallery of Contemp Art, Raleigh, NC, 87 & Contemp Arts Ctr, New Orleans, 88; Line and Image, Independent Curators, Inc, 88-90; The Theater of the Object, 1958-1972, Alternative Mus, NY, 89; Visual Poetry, Otis/Parsons Art Inst, Los Angeles, 90. *Pos:* Art critic, SoHo News, 73-76, Village Voice, 77-79 & Diversion Planner, 83-90; cur assoc, Independent Curators Inc, 74-81; assoc ed, Tracks, 74-78, Nat Arts Guide, 79-81 & Art Express, 80-81; cur, Exxon National Exhibition, 19 Emergent Americans, Guggenheim Mus, 81; contrib ed, Art Economist, 81-83; ed, Re Dact, 83-87; Am cur adv, Documenta 8, Kassel, WGer, 87; Art critic, Los Angeles Weekly, 88-; Ed, Visions, 90-; Los Angeles corresp Contemperanea, 88-90; contrib ed, Artspace, 90-; Gallery coordr, Long Beach City Col, Calif, 92. *Teaching:* Vis asst prof contemp arts, Pratt Inst, Brooklyn, NY, 75-76; adj assoc prof, Sch Arts, Columbia Univ, 78; adj lectr, Tyler Sch Art, Temple Univ, 83; lectr, Univ Calif, Irvine, 88-90; vis critic, Calif State Univ, Fullerton, 90-91. *Awards:* Nat Endowment Arts Grant, 78 & 81; Fluxus Research Fel, Royal Norwegian Minintry For Affairs, 87. *Bibliog:* Jacqueline Brody (auth), Peter Frank: A Case for Marginal Collectors, Print Collectors Newsletter, 6/78; Grace Glueck (auth), How emerging artists really emerge: Getting the biennials together, Art News, 5/81; Katherine Cook (auth), Talking Art: A Conversation with Peter Frank & Peter Selz, Artspace, summer, 91. *Mem:* Int Asn Art Critics; Poets & Writers; Col Arts Asn of Am; Int Künstlers Gremium. *Publ:* Something Else Press: An Annotated Bibliography (document text), MacPherson & Co, Kingston, NY, 83; New, Used & Improved: Art for the '80s, Abbeville Press, 87; Intermedia: Die Verschmelzung der Künste, Benteli Verlag, 87; Roller: The Paintings of Donald Roller Wilson, Chronicle Books, 88; Lawrence Gipe: Paintings, Karl Bornstein, 89. *Mailing Add:* PO Box 24A36 Los Angeles CA 90024-1036

FRANKEL, DEXTRA
EDUCATOR, GALLERY DIRECTOR
b Los Angeles, Calif, Nov 28, 24. *Study:* Long Beach State Col. *Work:* Philadelphia Free Libr; La Jolla Art Mus, Calif; St Paul Art Ctr, Minn; Pac View Mem Park, Corona Del Mar, Calif; Kennecott Copper Co, Salt Lake City, Utah; also in pvt collections. *Exhib:* Los Angeles Co Mus Art, 59, 62 & 66; Cincinnati Art Mus; Newport Harbor Art Mus, Newport Beach, Calif; Butler Inst Am Art, Youngstown, Ohio; Calif Palace of Legion of Honor, San Francisco; Denver Art Mus; Seattle Art Mus, Wash; Portland Art Mus, Ore; San Francisco Mus Art; H M deYoung Mus, San Francisco; Smithsonian Inst; and many others. *Collections Arranged:* Recorded Images/Dimensional Media, 67, Intersection of Line, 67, Frazer/Lipofsky/Richardson, 68, Transparency/Reflection, 68 & others, Art Gallery, Calif State Univ, Fullerton; and numerous others. *Pos:* Dir art gallery, cur & designer exhib, Calif State Univ, Fullerton, 67- *Teaching:* From asst prof to assoc prof art, Calif State Univ, Fullerton, 64-79, prof art, 79- *Awards:* 8 Nat Endowment for Arts grants, 75, 77-82; Design Award, Soc Typographic Arts Union Bank Hist Mus, 81. *Mem:* Am Asn Mus; Am Craft Coun; Art Mus Asn. *Publ:* Auth, article, Pasadena Mus, 65 & 68 & Crafts Horizons Mag, 73. *Mailing Add:* Art Gallery PO Box 34080 Fullerton CA 92634-9480

FRANKENBERG, ROBERT CLINTON
ILLUSTRATOR, PAINTER
b Mt Vernon, NY, Mar 19, 11. *Study:* Art Students League, New York, 28-29; study with William McNulty. *Work:* War Mus, Washington, DC; St Patrick's Cath Collection, New York; Univ Ore Libr; Kerlan Collection of Children's Lit, Univ Minn. *Comn:* Murals, Pa State Bldg & NC Bldg; stage sets & dioramas, Chase Brass & Copper Exhib, New York World's Fair, 39. *Exhib:* Six one-man shows in New York, 53-70. *Pos:* Artist, Jenter Exhib, NY & NJ, 33-40; artist, US Army Signal Corps, 40-45. *Teaching:* Instr figure drawing, Sch Visual Arts, New York, 47-, head drawing dept, 58-67. *Awards:* Jews in Am, 54 & Einstein, 56, Nat Filmstrip Award, Nat Jewish Coun for Audio Visual Aids; First Merit Award for Teaching, Alumni Asn, 76 & Teacher of the Year Award, 84, Sch Visual Arts. *Bibliog:* Nick Maglin (auth), On The Spot Drawing, Animals in Motion, Watson-Guptill Publ, 69; Anne Commire (ed), Something about the author, Gale Res Co. *Media:* Watercolor, Oil; Mixed Media. *Publ:* Illusr, Two Years Before the Mast, Doubleday, 49; The Christmas Book, 52 & The Easter Book, 54, Harcourt-Brace; Boston, Seabury, 67; Indians, Parents Mag Press, 68. *Dealer:* Hans Fybel Assoc 648 Kelton Ave Los Angeles CA 90024. *Mailing Add:* 601 E 20th St New York NY 10010

FRANKENTHALER, HELEN
PAINTER
b New York, NY, Dec 12, 28. *Study:* Horace Mann, Brearly & Dalton Sch: Bennington Col, Vt, BA, 49; Studied with Rufino Tamayo, Wallace Harrison, Paul Freeley & Hans Hoffman; nineteen hon degrees from US univs and cols, 69-92. *Work:* Brooklyn Mus, Cooper Hewitt Mus, New York Univ Art Collection, Solomon R Guggenheim Mus, Whitney Mus of Am Art, Metrop Mus Art & Mus Mod Art, New York; Art Inst Chicago; Cleveland Mus Art; Pasadena Art Mus, Calif; Nat Gallery Art, Wash, DC; Mus Fine Art, Boston; Carnegie Inst, Pittsburgh; Philadelphia Mus Art, Pa; Baltimore Mus Art, Md; San Francisco Mus Art; Seattle Art Mus; Butler Inst Am Art, Youngstown, Ohio; Milwaukee Art Inst, Wis; Walker Art Inst; plus many others. *Comn:* Shield (acrylic on canvas), First Wis Nat Bank, Milwaukee, 73; installation (7' x 17'), North Cent Bronx Hops, NY, 73-74; design for tapestry (10' x 45'), Fourth Nat Bank, Wichita, Kans, 73-74; Tapestry design (10' x 57'), Hong Kong Club, Hong Kong, 84. *Exhib:* New York Painting & Sculpture: 1940-1970, Metrop Mus Art, New York, 69-70; Retrospective, Whitney Mus Am Art, New York, 69 & Berggruen Gallery, San Francisco, Calif, 72; Albright-Knox Art Gallery, Buffalo, NY, 70; Abstract Painting in the 70's, Mus Fine Arts, Boston, 72; Block Prints, Whitney Mus Am Art, 82; From Munch to Johns: Modern Prints from the Collection, Fogg Art Mus, 83; Changes: The 1960's into the 1980's, Aldrich Mus Contemp Art, 83; American Print Renaissance 1958-1988, Selections from the Permanent Collection, Whitney Mus Am Art, Stamford, Conn, 88; Made In the Sixties, Painting and Sculpture from the Permanent Collection, Whitney Mus Am Art, New York, 88; Twentieth Century Paintings and Sculpture: Selections for the Tenth Anniversary of the East Building, Nat Gallery Art, Washington, DC, 88; The Gestural Impulse 1945-60, Whitney Mus Am Art, New York, 89; Projects and Portfolios; the 25th National Print Exhibition, Brooklyn Mus, 89; Baltimore Collects: Painting and Sculpture since 1960, Baltimore Mus Art, 90; The Unique Print, Mus Fine Arts, Boston, 90; one-woman exhibs, Rosa Esman Gallery, New York, 91, Asn Am Artists, New York, 92, Galerie Karin Fesel, Dusseldorf, Ger, 92, Knoedler & Co, New York, 92, Century Club, 93, Meredith Long, 93 & Nat Gallery Art, Washington, DC, 93; Color Block Prints of the 20th Century, Asn Am Artists, New York, 92; Les Heroes de la Peinture Americaine, Galerie Gerald Piltzer, Paris, France, 92; A Celebration of Abstraction, Gallery One, Toronto, Ont, 92; Innovation in

Collaborative Printmaking: Kenneth Tyler, 1963-1992, travelling exhib, Yokohama Mus Art, Marugame Inokuma- Genichiro Mus Contemp Art, Mus Mod Art, Wakayama, Tokushima Mod Art Mus & Hokkaido Obihiro Mus Art (with catalog),, 93; and many others. *Pos:* Trustee, Bennington Col, 67-; fel, Calhoun Col, Yale Univ, 68- *Teaching:* Instr contemp painting sem, Yale Univ, spring 70; instr contemp painting sem, Hunter Col, 70 & Princeton Univ, 71; lectr, Univ Ariz, Tuscon, 78, Graphics Art Coun New York, Nat Arts Club, 79, Duke Univ & Art Inst Chicago, 83 & 91, Lowe Art Mus, Miami, Fla, 84 & Fla Int Univ, Miami, 92; slide lect, Aspen Art Mus, Colo, 91; slide lect & questions & answers, Phillips Col & New York Pub Libr, 92; plus many other lectures & seminars. *Awards:* Bennington Col Alumni Award, 79; Conn Arts Award, Conn Comn Arts, 89; and others. *Bibliog:* Hilton Kramer (auth), Helen Frankenthaler's art in the 50's, New York Times, 6/7/81; Sister Wendy Beckett (auth), Concerning the Spirtual in Art, Modern Painters, 45-49, summer 89; John Russell (auth), What's at the Modern? All the new that endured, 8/25/89 & Barbara Gamarekian (auth), Frohnmayer approves environmental project, 2/4/91, NY Times; Horst Richter (auth), Malerei Unseres Jahrhunderts, DuMont Buchverlag Koln, Ger, 33, 91; plus many others. *Publ:* Auth, Letters to the editors, Print Collectors Newsletter, Vol 16, No 2, 5-6/85; Artist' Choice, Art & Antiques, 12/86; Did we spawn an arts monster?, NY Times, 7/17/89; Profile, Visual Arts, 89; Hans Namuth; an appreciation, 12/90; and others. *Dealer:* Andre Emmerich Gallery 41 E 57th St New York NY 10022. *Mailing Add:* 173 E 94th St New York NY 10028

FRANKFURTER, JACK
PAINTER, DESIGNER
b Vienna, Austria, Mar 25, 29; US citizen. *Study:* Cooper Union Sch Art, 50-51; Col City NY, BS, 51; Columbia Univ, BA, 52. *Work:* Springfield Mus Fine Arts, Mass; Wichita Art Mus, Kansas; Uaniv Cincinnati Art Mus, Ohio; Malcolm Forbes Collection, New York. *Exhib:* Allied Artists Am, Nat Acad Design, New York, 54 & 56; Am Artists Ann, Whitney Mus, New York, 55; X Quadriennale Di Roma, Galleria D'Arte Moderna, Rome, Italy, 77; Biennial Int, Biennale Di Lignano, Italy, 70. *Pos:* Designer, Tiffany & Co, New York, 56-57; stage designer, Bayriscues Schauspielhaus, München, Ger, 77-79. *Bibliog:* Sterling McIlhany (auth), American Artist in Rome, Am Artist, 6/61; Mario Praz (auth), Paintings of Frankfurter, Agraf Art Editions, 73; Antonio Porcella (auth), Frankfurter Galeria La D'Ora, Roma, 76. *Media:* Oil on Canvas. *Publ:* Contribr, numerous articles in NY Times, 60-71; cover art, Am Artist, 9/65 & 11/68; title page, Arts & Leisure, NY Times, 12/5/71; auth, article for UNICEF Art Calendar, 72; auth & cover art, Wichita, Wichita Chamber Commerce, 76. *Dealer:* Galleriea CA D'Ora Via Condotti 6A Roma Italy 00187. *Mailing Add:* 90 Park Terrace E New York NY 10034

FRANKLIN, CAROLE R
ART DEALER, PUBLISHER
b Chicago, Ill, Jan 8, 33. *Study:* Univ Calif, Los Angeles; studying art mktg with Calvin Goodman. *Pos:* Managing dir & owner, Designart (formerly Mirzelle Inc), Los Angeles, 79- *Mem:* Am Soc Interior Designers; Interior Business Designers. *Specialty:* Realistic and non-objective art. *Publ:* Auth, Paper sculpture, an important new medium, Decor, 4/84; The corporate art search, Interior Design, 9/84; Art trends of the corporate market, Art Bus News, 3/85. *Mailing Add:* 2700 S La Cienega Blvd Los Angeles CA 90034

FRANKLIN, DON (DONALD WAYNE FRANKLIN)
PAINTER
b Uniontown, Pa, Mar 16, 31. *Study:* Art Inst Pittsburgh, 49-50. *Work:* Locust Hill Gallery, Pittsford, NY; Six Nations Mus, Onchiota, NY; Akwesasne Mus, Hogansburg, NY; Strawberry Castle Gallery, Penfield, NY; Dick Moll's Gallery, Rochester, NY. *Exhib:* Arts for Greater Rochester, Nazareth Arts Ctr, Pittsford, NY, 89; solo exhib, 1570 Gallery, Rochester, NY, 90; Fine Art Showcase, Wilson Arts Ctr, Rochester, NY, 90-91 & Mem Art Gallery, Rochester, NY, 92. *Pos:* Art dir, Bausch & Lomb, 70-73 & creative dir, 77- *Teaching:* Instr art, Univ Rochester Mem Art Gallery, NY, 77-82. *Awards:* Award Excellence, Fine Art Showcase, WXXI Pub Television, 90; Award Excellence, Fine Art Showcase, Archit Inst Am, 91. *Mem:* Rochester Art Club (treas, 67-68). *Media:* Watercolor, Pastel. *Dealer:* B Weir Elegant Earth Enterprises PO Box 18451 Rochester NY 14618. *Mailing Add:* 160 Chelmsford Rd Rochester NY 14618

FRANKLIN, GILBERT ALFRED
SCULPTOR, EDUCATOR
b Birmingham, Eng, June 6, 19; US citizen. *Study:* RI Sch Design, BFA, 46; Nat Mus Mexico City; Am Acad Rome, fel, 49. *Work:* RI Sch Design Mus Art; Hopkins Ctr Gallery, Dartmouth Col, NH; Boston Mus Fine Arts; Vassar Col Art Gallery, Poughkeepsie, NY; NC State Col, Greensboro; and others. *Comn:* Lincoln Mem Statue, Harvey Trust Comt, Providence, RI; Harry S Truman Mem, Harry S Truman Statue Comn, Independence, Mo; Orpheus ascending fountain, comn by Mrs Murray S Danforth, Providence & Daybreak--S O Metcalf Mem;; Bronze Group, Providence Col; Twin Towers, Roselyn, VA, 86, among others. *Exhib:* De Young Mem Mus Ann Am Art, San Francisco, 46; Whitney Mus Ann, New York, 50; Ann Sculpture & Painting, Pa Acad, Philadelphia, 52, 54 & 56; Inst Contemp Art, Boston, 59; Sculpture, De Cordova Mus, Lincoln, Mass, 64; Hopkins Ctr Gallery Retrospective Exhib, Hanover, NH, 75; plus others. *Pos:* Sculptor-in-residence, Am Acad Rome, 64-65 & Dartmouth Col, spring 75; co-dir, Europ Honors Prog, Rome, 69-71; trustee, Am Acad Rome, 75-80. *Teaching:* Lectr sculpture, Harvard Univ, 50-52 & Yale Univ, 52-54; prof sculpture, RI Sch Design, 56-82, dean fine arts & design, 78-82, H M Danforth prof fine arts, 85-85, emer prof, 85- *Awards:* Prix de Rome, Am Acad Rome, 48; Grand Prize, Boston Arts Festival, 59; Providence Art Club Medal for Excellence in the Arts, 75. *Mem:* Providence Art Club; Nat Acad Design; Century Asn. *Media:* Bronze, Marble. *Dealer:* Cavalier Gallery Stamford CT; Helander Gallery Palm Beach FL. *Mailing Add:* c/o Long Point Gallery Inc 492 Commercial St Provincetown MA 02657

FRANKLIN, HANNAH
SCULPTOR, PAINTER
b Poland, June 20, 37; Can Citizen. *Study:* Montreal Mus Fine Art Sch, BA, 68; studied with Arthur Lismer. *Work:* Montreal Mus Art, Que; Musé d'Art Contemporian, Montreal; Musée du Quebec, Ont; Can Coun Art Bank, Ottowa; Cabinet du Quebec; Simon Fraser Univ, Vancouver, BC. *Comn:* Sculptures, Comn by Jacque Cortier, 84 & Vancouver Centenniel Comn, 86; St Jean Port Joli (sculpture), Mus Que, 84. *Exhib:* Small Sculpture Biennial, Budapest, Hungary, 71; Saidye Bronfman Ctr, Montreal, 73; Biennial, Basel, Switz, 74; Fête du Fleuve, Que, 84; 3 Sculptors & 12 Sculptors, Palais de Cong Montreal, 85. *Teaching:* Instr sculpture, Saidye Bronfman Ctr, Montreal, 74-76. *Awards:* First Prize Sculpture, Hadassah Wiz Exhib, 70, 72 & 74; Purchase Award Que Concour, Govt Que, 70. *Bibliog:* Guy Robert (auth), l'Art au Quebec, La Presse, 73; Art Actuel Quebec, Iconia, 83. *Mem:* Soc Sculptors Que (vpres, 72); Vancouver Sculptors Asn; Int Sculptors Asn. *Media:* Acrylic, Oil; Plastic. *Mailing Add:* 85 Holton Ave Montreal PQ H3Y 2G1 Canada

FRANKLIN, PATT
PAINTER, SCULPTOR
b 1941. *Study:* Pratt Inst, BFA, 62; Tulane Univ, MFA, 70. *Work:* Bowdoin Col Mus Art, Brunswick, Maine; Boston Libr Print & Drawing Collection & New England Medical Ctr Lobby Collection, Boston, Mass; Int Telephone & Telegraph, New York; Colby Col, Waterville, Maine; Gilette Corp, Boston; L L Bean, Maine. *Comn:* Painted murals, Doctors of Touro Hospital, New Orleans, La, 68. *Exhib:* Soup Tureens, Campbells Mus, Camden, NJ, 76-77 & Mus Contemp Craft, New York, 77; All New England Drawing, DeCordova Mus, Lincoln, Mass, 79-80; one-man show, State House, Augusta, Maine, 79-80, Lamont Gallery, Phillips/Exeter, NH, 81 & Bates Col, 83; Views, Impressions Gallery, Boston, Mass, 81; Wheelock Col, Boston, 84; Walt Kuhn Gallery, Cape Neddick, Maine; Varley & Stevens, Portsmouth, NH, 85; Univ South Maine, 86; Davis Gallery, Tucson, Ariz, 88; Congress Sq Gallery Portland, Maine, 87, 88 & 89; Merrimack Col, Andover, Mass, 90; Bowdon Mus Group Exhib, 92. *Teaching:* Prof drawing & ceramics, Univ South Maine, Gorham, 70-; instr ceramics, Mass Col Art, summer 73 & Haystack Sch Art & Crafts, Deer Isle, Maine, 77. *Awards:* Fellar Award, Silvermine Competition, 73. *Mem:* Am Craft Coun; Women's Caucus Art; Nat Coun Educ Ceramic Arts; Col Art Asn. *Media:* Watercolor, oils. *Mailing Add:* Box 94 Gorham ME 04038

FRANSIOLI, THOMAS ADRIAN
PAINTER, PRINTMAKER
b Seattle, Wash, Sept 15, 06. *Study:* Univ Pa, BArch, 30; Art Students League. *Work:* Currier Gal Art, Manchester, NH; Whitney Mus Am Art, New York; Seattle Art Mus, Wash; Dallas Mus Fine Arts, Tex; Farnsworth Mus, Rockland, Maine; Mus Fine Arts, Boston; Boston Pub Libr. *Comn:* Murals in dining rm, Aetna Life Bldg, Hartford, Conn, 62; four paintings of old New York, Univ Club, New York, 64; mural in stair hall, Princeton Club, New York, 66; mural in lobby, Brevoort East Hotel, New York, 67; painting of Brit Embassy, Washington, DC, comn by the Brit Ambassador to US, 75. *Exhib:* Boston Art Festival, 48-49; Whitney Mus Ann, New York, 48-52 & 58; Carnegie Inst, Pittsburgh, Pa, 49 & 52; Am Art Today, Metrop Mus Art, New York, 50; Maine & It's Role in American Art, Colby Col, Waterville, Maine & Whitney Mus Am Art, New York, 63. *Awards:* Purchase Prize, Boston Arts Festival, 52. *Media:* Oil, Watercolor. *Mailing Add:* 55 Dodges Row Wenham MA 01984

FRARY, MICHAEL
PAINTER, EDUCATOR
b Santa Monica, Calif, May 28, 18. *Study:* Univ Southern Calif, BA(archit), 40, MFA(painting), 41; Acad Grande Chaumiere, Paris, dipl, 50. *Work:* Nat Collection Fine Arts, Smithsonian Inst; Santa Barbara Mus, Calif; Butler Inst Am Art, Youngstown, Ohio; Dallas Mus Fine Art; McNay Art Inst, San Antonio, Tex. *Comn:* Murals, Brackenridge Hosp, Austin, Tex, 58 & Headliners Club, Austin, 62; tapestry, Hatfield Galleries, Los Angeles, 72; paint reclamation sites, US Dept of Interior, Colo & Wyo, 72; paint Psyche prize for best film Canada, San Antonio, Tex, 78. *Exhib:* Fifth Ann Exhib Southwest Am Art, Okla Art Ctr, Oklahoma City, 70; Water Reclamation, Nat Gallery Art, DC, 72; 24th Ann Mid-Yr, Butler Inst Am Art, Youngstown, Ohio; Ann Nat Watercolor Soc Exhib, Calif; Ann Tex Watercolor Exhibs, McNay Art Inst, San Antonio. *Teaching:* Instr painting, Chorinard Art Inst, Los Angeles, 47 & UCLA, 48-49; fac chmn painting, San Antonio Art Inst, 49-51; prof drawing & painting, Univ Tex, Austin, emer, 52-85. *Awards:* Over 180 Purchase Prizes and Awards. *Bibliog:* Dorothy Blodgett (auth), Michael Frary: Person and palette-quicksilver, Southwestern Art Mag, 12/70;; Michael Frary, artist-teacher, Southern Living, 6/71; Beulah Hodge (producer), People and Ideas, Michael Frary (color video cassette), KLRN, 77. *Mem:* Nat Watercolor Soc (treas, 47); hon life mem Southwestern Watercolor Soc; Tex Watercolor Soc; Watercolor USA Hon Soc. *Media:* Watercolor, Oil. *Publ:* Coauth, Impressions of the Big Thicket, Univ Tex Press, 73; auth, Impressions of the Texas Panhandle, 77; illusr, Stolen steers, 78; auth, Watercolors of the Rio Grand, 84; contribr, Texas Gulf Coast, 79 & Texas hill country, 81, Univ Tex A&M Press; and others. *Dealer:* Sol Del Rio Gallery San Antonio TX. *Mailing Add:* 3409 Spanish Oak Dr Austin TX 78731

FRASCONI, ANTONIO
GRAPHIC ARTIST, PAINTER
b Buenos Aires, Arg, Apr 28, 19, citizen of Uruguay. *Study:* Archit Acad, Montevideo, 36-37; Art Students League, 45; New Sch Social Res, 47. *Work:* Bibliotheque Nat, Paris, France; Mus Mod Art, New York; Metrop Mus Art; Casa Americas, Havana, Cuba; Univ Puerto Rico. *Comn:* Snow Flakes, Christmas ornaments, Metrop Mus Art, New York, 72. *Exhib:* solo exhib, Books & Posters of Antonio Frasconi, State Univ New York, 85; Univ Puerto Rico Mus, San Juan, 86; Repression, Exilio y Democracia-La Cultura Uruguaya Univ Md, 86; 1986 Biennial, Orgn Int Biennial Illus, Tokyo, Japan, 86; 196 Fiera del Libro, Bologna, Italy, 86; Museo d' Arte Contemporanea, Bologna, Italy, 86; Mus Contemp Art, New York, 86; Commission Arts Showcase Gallery, Conn, 87; over 100 Nat & Int exhibs. *Teaching:* Adj assoc prof, State Univ NY, Purchase, 73-77, assoc prof, 77-79, prof, 79-, distinguished teaching prof art, 86- *Awards:* Ralph Fabri Prize, Nat Acad Design, New York, 83; Purchase Award, Am Acad Inst Arts & Letters, 86; Distinguished Teaching Prof, State Univ New York, 86. *Bibliog:* Margit Varga (auth), Woodcuts by Antonio Frasconi, Am Artist, 10/74; Nat Hentoff & Charles Parkhurst (auth), Frasconi-Against the Grain, MacMillan, 75; Jane Sterett (auth), Interview with Antonio Frasconi, Print Rev 17, 83. *Media:* All. *Publ:* Illusr, The Salamander, Red Ozier Press, 82; Yentl the Yeshiva Boy, Farrar, Straus, 83; Monkey Puzzle and Other Poems, Atheneum, 84; Prima Che tu Dica Pronto, Plain Wrapper Press, 85; Sat at Midnight, Nadja, 86. *Dealer:* Terry Dintenfass Gallery 50 W 57th St New York NY 10019. *Mailing Add:* 26 Dock Rd South Norwalk CT 06854

FRASER, ANDREA R
CONCEPTUAL ARTIST, MUSEOLOGIST
b Billings, Mont, Sept 27, 65. *Study:* Sch Visual Arts, 82-83; Whitney Mus Am Art, independent study prog, 84-85. *Exhib:* Damaged Goods, New Mus Contemp Arts, New York, 86; solo exhibs & performances, Museum Highlights, Philadelphia Mus Art, 89, Welcome to the Wadsworth, Wadsworth Atheneum, Hartford, Conn, 91 & Aren't They Lovely? Univ Art Mus, Berkeley, Calif, 92; The Desire of the Museum, Whitney Mus, Fed Plaza, New York, 89; Dirty Data, Ludwig Forum, Aachen, Ger, 92. *Teaching:* Guest artist sculpture, Cooper Union, 90; part-time fac performance, Tyler Sch Art, 92. *Awards:* Fel, Art Matters Inc, 87 & 89; NY Found Arts, 91; Nat Endowment Arts, 91. *Media:* Performance, Installation. *Publ:* Auth, Woman 1/Madonna and Child 1506-1967, Andrea Frutsen, 84; In and out of Place, Art Am, 85; Individual Works, John Weber Gallery, 88; Notes in the museum's publicity, Lusitania, 90; Museum highlights: a gallery talk, October, 91. *Dealer:* Colin De Land American Fine Arts 40 Wooster St New York NY 10014. *Mailing Add:* 273 W Tenth St New York NY 10014

FRASER, MARY EDNA
DESIGNER, CRAFTSMAN
b Fayetteville, NC, Mar 20, 52. *Study:* E Carolina Univ, Greenville, NC, BS(textiles), 74; Univ Ga, Surface Design Southeast, 77, with Chungi Choo. *Work:* Smithsonian Inst, Nat Air & Space Mus, Washington, DC. *Comn:* three large batiks, Thomson Indust, Port Washington, NY, 86; two batiks, Charleston Int Airport, SC, 86; 70 yds batik sculpture, Charleston Int Airport, SC, 88; 15 yds batik sculpture, Symmes Libr, Greenville, SC; 5 batiks, SC Visitor Ctr, Charleston, 90; and others. *Exhib:* Solo exhibs, Islands from the Sky, Surroundings, New York, 82, Spoleto Festival USA, Charleston, 85, Islands from the Sky, Gibbes Mus Art, 89 & Nat Air & Space Mus, 94; Fourth Int Batik Exhib, Verbena Galleries, New York, 84; Batik Exhib, Donnell Libr, New York, 85; Earth Views, Nat Air & Space Mus, Washington, DC, 86; Contemp Batik Artists, Southern Ohio Mus, Portsmouth, 90. *Pos:* Design consult, City Charleston; lectr, AATCC Symp. *Teaching:* Instr batik, Textile Mus, Washington, DC, summer, 84. *Awards:* Third Place, Nat Air & Space Mus, 86. *Bibliog:* Islands from the Sky (video), batiks by Mary Edna Fraser. *Mem:* Textile Artists Guild; Surface Design Asn; Am Craft Coun. *Media:* Batik. *Publ:* Contribr, Artcraft, 80; Art with architecture in mind, Am Inst Architects, 2/91; Textile Designs: Ideas and Applications, PBC Int, 92. *Mailing Add:* PO Box 12250 Charleston SC 29422

FRATER, HAL
PAINTER
b New York, NY, Mar 3, 09. *Exhib:* Minnesota Mus, 80 & 82; Nat Acad Design; Brooklyn Mus; Allied Artists Am; Chrysler Mus, Provincetown, Mass; Seton Hall Univ; Permanent collection & exhib of 24 works, Thundering Seas Mus, Ore State Univ; and others. *Teaching:* Instr, Sch Art & Design & Educ Alliance, New York. *Awards:* Jane Peterson Award, Allied Artists, 59. *Mem:* Painters & Sculptors Soc NJ; Allied Artists Am; Soc Illusr; Artists Equity Asn; Audubon Artists. *Media:* Acrylic, Watercolor. *Mailing Add:* 215 Park Row New York NY 10038

FRAUCHIGER, FRITZ A
MUSEUM DIRECTOR, ADMINISTRATOR
b Oklahoma City, Okla, Sept 23, 41. *Study:* San Jose State Col, BA, 69; Calif State Univ, San Jose, MA, 72. *Collections Arranged:* Herbert Bayer: Photographic Works (contribr, catalog), 77; Anderson Collection of Indian Art, 78; Ed Ruscha: New Paintings (auth, catalog), 81; Larry Bell: New Work (auth, catalog), 83; Robert Graham: Studies for the Olympic Gateway (coauth, catalog), 84; ARCO Ctr Visual Art, 88; Masami Teraoka: Waves and Plaques, Contemp Mus, Honolulu, 90 & David Hockney: Some New Pictures. *Pos:* Cur asst, J Paul Getty Mus, Malibu, Calif, 73-74; asst cur-dir, ARCO Ctr Visual Art, Los Angeles, Calif, 76-84; dir, Contemp Arts Ctr, Honolulu, Hawaii, 86-90; exec dir, Palm Springs Desert Mus, Calif, 90- *Mem:* Am Asn Mus; Directors Asn Art Mus; Calif Asn Mus. *Publ:* Contribr, Textiles from Sumatra, 81 & ed, The Art of the Movie Miniature, 82, ARCO Ctr Art; Waves and Plaques: Masami Teraoka, Contemp Mus, Honolulu, 88. *Mailing Add:* PO Box 2288 Palm Springs CA 92263

FRAUGHTON, EDWARD JAMES
SCULPTOR
b Park City, Utah, Mar 22, 39. *Study:* Univ Utah, BFA, 62; studied under Dr Avard T Fairbanks & Justin Fairbanks. *Work:* Riveredge Found, Calgary, Can; Leanin' Tree Mus Western Art, Boulder, Colo; Valley Bank, Las Vegas, Nev; Nat Cowboy Hall of Fame & Western Heritage Ctr, Oklahoma City, Okla; Favell Mus Western Art, Klamath Falls, Ore. *Comn:* Mormon Battalion Monument, Sons of Utah Pioneers, Prisidio Park, San Diego, Calif, 69; Ben H Bohac (relief portrait), Talman Savings & Loan, Chicago, 70; All is Well, Family Monument, Sons of Utah Pioneers, Brigham Young Cemetery, Salt Lake City, 74; Truman O Angell Portrait, Church of Jesus Christ of Latter-day Saints, Salt Lake City, Utah, 77; Spirit of Wyo, 15 ft major monument, Capitol Grounds, Cheyenne, 80; Official Inaugural Medal, President Ronald Reagan. *Exhib:* Nat Acad Western Art, Oklahoma City; Nat Sculpture Soc, New York; Whitney Mus Western Art, Cody, Wyo; Bohemian Club, Bohemian Grove, Monte Rio, Calif; Nat Acad Design, New York; Artists of America, Denver. *Teaching:* Instr, Scottsdale Artist's Sch, 86. *Awards:* Lance Int Prize, Nat Sculpture Soc, 79; Artist of the West, San Dimas Festival of Western Arts, 81; The Tallix Foundry Prize, Spirit of Man, Nat Sculpture Soc, 81; and others. *Bibliog:* Pat Broder (auth), Bronzes of the American West, Abrams, 74; Peggy & Harold Samuels (auths), Contemporary Western Artists, Southwest Art Publ, 82; Profiles in American Art (film), Ken Meyer Prod. *Mem:* San Francisco Bohemian Club; Nat Sculpture Soc; Nat Acad Western Art. *Media:* Bronze & Stone Carving. *Mailing Add:* 10353 S 1300 West South Jordan UT 84065

FRAZE, DENNY T
COLLAGE ARTIST, EDUCATOR
b Weatherford, Tex, May 28, 40. *Study:* Univ Tex, Austin, BFA(studio, art hist), 62; Univ Colo, MFA(painting), 64, study with Luis Eades & Roland Reiss. *Work:* Univ Colo, Boulder; Dishman Art Gallery, Beaumont, Tex; Museo Internacional De Electro Grafica, Cuenca, Spain. *Comn:* Amarillo Art Ctr, Tex. *Exhib:* Over 150 exhibs including one-man shows, Odessa Col, 80, Mus Art, Norman, Okla, 83, Koenig Art Gallery, Seward, Nebr, 87, Tex Tech Mus, Lubbock, Tex, 87, Art Inst Permian Basin, Odessa, Tex, 89 & Meadows Gallery, Denton, Tex, 90; one-man retrospective, Amarillo Art Ctr; Nat Works on Paper Exhib, Tyler, Tex, 88; Amarillo Competition, Tex, 88; 23rd Bradley Nat Print & Drawing Exhib, Peoria, Ill, 91; Texas Art Celebration, Houston, 91-92; Dishman Competition, Beaumont, Tex, 92; and others. *Teaching:* Prof art & chmn dept, Amarillo Col, Tex, 65- *Awards:* Artists Award, 45th Competition, Abilene Mus Fine Arts, Tex, 89; Juror's Award, 24th Southwestern exhib, Yuma Art Ctr, Ariz, 90; Third Prize, Dishman Competition, Beaumont, Tex, 92; and others. *Mem:* Tex Asn Sch Art (pres, 70-72 & 86-88, bd mem, 70-74 & 83-86); hon mem Amarillo Fine Arts Asn; Tex Coun Arts Educ (bd mem, 70-72). *Media:* Collage, Drawing. *Mailing Add:* 2219 S Hayden Amarillo TX 79109

FRAZER, JAMES (NISBET), JR
MURALIST, PHOTOGRAPHER
b Atlanta, Ga, Oct 6, 49. *Study:* Amherst Col, BA(cum laude), 71; Ga State Univ, MFA, 73; also with Fairfield Porter. *Work:* High Mus Art, Atlanta; Corcoran Gallery; Chase Manhattan Bank; Addison Gallery of Am Art; J Paul Getty Mus. *Comn:* Southern Bell Telephone Co, 80; Veterans Admin Med Ctr, Atlanta, 83; Omni Int Hotel, Atlanta, 85. *Exhib:* South Am Travelling exhib, Arte EUA: El Sur, US Info Agency, 76-77; 35 Artists in the Southeast, High Mus Art, 76-78; Art Patron Art, Southeastern Ctr for Contemp Art, Winston-Salem, NC, 78; one-man shows, High Mus Art, Ga & Southeastern Ctr Contemp Art, Winston-Salem, NC, 81; Contemporary Panoramic Photography, Addison Gallery Am Art, Andover, Mass, 84; Iron Bridge Show, Appalachian Environ Art Ctr, Highlands, NC, 89-90. *Pos:* Pres, Nexus Inc, Atlanta, 73-74, men bd dir, 73-81. *Teaching:* Instr photog, Atlanta Col Art, Ga State Univ, 72-76 & Mercer Univ, 77-81. *Bibliog:* Peter Morrin (auth), Jim Frazer: Hand-Colored Photographs, High Mus Art, Atlanta, 81; Laura Lieberman (auth), Jim Frazer, Southern Accents, 5-6/88. *Media:* Hand-Colored Photographs. *Publ:* Contribr, The Southern Ethic, Inst for Southern Studies, 75; The Avant-Garde: 12 in Atlanta, High Mus Art, 79. *Dealer:* Heath Gallery 416 E Paces Ferry Rd Atlanta GA 30305. *Mailing Add:* 1010 Pearl Johnson Rd Ranger GA 30734

FRAZER, JOHN THATCHER
FILMMAKER, PAINTER
b Akron, Ohio, Apr 2, 32. *Study:* Univ Tex, BFA; Yale Univ, MFA; with Joseph Albers; Wesleyan Univ, Hon MA. *Work:* Davison Art Ctr, Wesleyan Univ, Middletown, Conn; Libr Cong, Washington, DC; Cullinan Collection, Houston Mus Fine Arts; Nicholson Mem Libr, Longview, Tex. *Exhib:* Tex Ann, Dallas Mus Fine Arts, 58; New Haven Arts Festival, Conn, 60; Boston Arts Festival, Mass, 61; Flaherty Film Festival, Lakeville, Conn, 66; Am Film Festival, New York, 68. *Teaching:* Prof art, motion pictures & drawing, Wesleyan Univ, 59- *Bibliog:* New talent, USA, Art in Am, 62; Bernard Chaet (auth), The Art of Drawing, Holt, 70. *Mem:* Am Asn Univ Prof; Col Art Asn Am; Am Film Inst. *Media:* Acrylic, Oil. *Interests:* Motion pictures. *Publ:* Auth, Documentary films & books on documentary films, Choice Mag, 69; Artificially Arranged Scenes, The Films of George Melies, G K Hall, 79. *Mailing Add:* Dept of Art Wesleyan Univ Middletown CT 06457-6038

FRAZIER, PAUL D
SCULPTOR, EDUCATOR
b Pickaway Co, Ohio, May 6, 22. *Study:* Ohio State Univ, BFA, 48; Cranbrook Acad Art, MFA, 49; Skowhegan Sch Painting & Sculpture, with Jose de Creeft, 49; L'Academie de la Grande Chaumiere, with Ossip Zadkine, 49-50. *Work:* Cranbrook Mus & Acad, Bloomfield Hills, Mich; Skowhegan

Sch Painting & Sculpture & Finch Col, New York; Munson-Williams-Proctor Inst, Utica, NY; Rochester Gallery Art, NY; Colgate Univ, Hamilton, NY. *Exhib:* Whitney Mus Am Art Annual, 54 & 56, Biannual, 62, 64 & 66, New York; one-man shows, Munson-Williams-Proctor Inst, Utica, NY, 57, St Augustine Art Ctr, Fla, 59, Fischbach Gallery, New York, 68 & 69, Queens Col, 68-69, Washington Art Asn, Washington, Conn, 85 & The Sculpture Ctr, New York, 86; Skowhegan Ann Exhib, Einhorn Auditorium, Lenox Hill Hosp, New York, 65 & 67 & Acad Design, New York, 68; Arts Forum Drawing Exhib, The Women's Col of Univ NC, Greensboro, 69; 25th Anniv Exhib, Skowhegan Sch Painting & Sculpture, Colby Col, Maine, 70; Sculpture in the Spring, Univ Conn, Storrs, 71; Drawing Exhib, Studio Sch, New York, 71; Sculptor's Guild Ann, Lever House, New York, 72; Washington Art Asn Ann, Washington, Conn, 78, 83 & 84; Greenwich House Mem Exhib, New York, 78. *Teaching:* Instr sculpture, ceramics & design, Univ Minn, Minneapolis, 50-53; instr, Munson-Wiliams-Proctor Inst, Utica, NY, 53-58, Skowhegan Sch Painting & Sculpture, Maine, 61, Greenwich House Pottery, New York, 62-64; lectr to assoc prof, Queens Col, 64-89. *Awards:* Purchase Prize, Cranbrook Alumni Exhib, 52; Purchase Awards, Munson-Williams-Proctor Inst, 54, 56 & 58 & Hon Mention, 55; First Prize, 22nd Ann, Cooperstwon, NY, 58; Purchase Prize, The Gallery, Ft Lauderdale, Fla, 60; Marine Midland Trust Co Purchase Award, Utica, NY, 62; Mark Rothko Found Grant, 75. *Bibliog:* Ralph Pomeroy (auth), Confirmed out-of-towner, Art Int, 10/28/68; Gregory Battcock (auth), Minimal Art, Dutton; Sam Hunter (auth), American Art in the 20th Century, Abrams; Review, Art in Am Mag, 4/86. *Mem:* Sculptor's Guild; Conn Union Visual Artists; Found for Community of Artists; Int Sculpture Ctr. *Media:* Wood, Metal. *Mailing Add:* RR 1 Box 921 Cold Brook NY 13324-9778

FRECKELTON, SONDRA
PAINTER
b Dearborn, Mich, 1936. *Study:* Art Inst Chicago. *Work:* Amerada Hess Corp, Reader's Digest Asn, Inc; Va Mus Fine Arts, Lewis Collection; Nat Mus Am Art, Washington, DC; Springfield Art Mus, Mo; Toledo Mus, Ohio. *Exhib:* One-woman shows, Tibor de Nagy Gallery, New York, 62, & 63, B C Holland Gallery, Chicago, 65, LoGuidice Gallery, Chicago, 70, Brook Alexander Gallery, New York, 76 & 79-81, Allan Frumkin Gallery, Chicago, 77, Fendrick Gallery, Washington, DC, 80, John Berggruen Gallery, San Francisco, 82 & Robert Schoelkopf Gallery, New York, 86, 88 & 90; Realism Today: Contemp Am Realism from 1960, travelling exhib in US & Europe, 81-82; Perspectives on Contemp Am Realism, Pa Acad Fine Arts & Art Inst, Chicago, 82-83; Am Realism, travelling exhib (with catalog), 85-87; Mod Am Realism: Sara Roby Found Collection, Nat Mus Am Art, Washington, DC, 87; The Graphic Muse: Prints by Contemp Am Women Artists, travelling exhib (with catalog), 87-88; Retrospective of Prints plus Watercolors, Univ Mich Mus Art, 90; Realist Watercolors, Palmer Mus Art, Penn State Univ, 90. *Teaching:* Vis artist & lect at many schs & univs; McAndless Distinguished Prof Chair, Eastern Mich Univ, Ypsicanti, Mich, 92. *Awards:* Ingram Merrill Grant; Bradford Print Prize. *Bibliog:* Janice Oresman (auth), Article, Arts Mag, 12/82; Paul Cummings (auth), article, Drawing Mag, 11/83; Thomas Bolt (auth), article, Arts Mag, 1/86. *Media:* Watercolor. *Publ:* Contribr, Realist Drawings and Watercolors, NY Graphic Soc, 81; Contribr, Dynamic Still Life in Watercolor, Watson Guptill, 83. *Dealer:* Maxwell Davidson Gallery 415 W Broadway New York NY; Brooks Alexander Gallery 476 Broome St New York NY 10013. *Mailing Add:* 67 Vestry St New York NY 10013

FREDELL, GAIL
CRAFTSMAN
b San Francisco, Calif, Aug 13, 51. *Study:* Univ Calif, Berkeley, AB, 74; Rochester Inst Technol, NY, MFA, 80. *Comn:* Sculpture, Fire-Storm Mem Gardens, Berkeley, Calif. *Exhib:* Appalachian Ctr Crafts, Smithville, Tenn, 84; Triton Mus Art, Santa Clara, Calif, 85; Elements Gallery, Greenwich, Conn, 86; Am Craft Mus, traveling tour, 87; Axis 20 Gallery, Atlanta, 89; Oakland Mus, 90; Univ Calif, Art Mus at Blackhawk, 92. *Teaching:* Instr furniture design, Univ Calif, Davis, 85, Penland Sch, Penland, NC, 86; vis lectr, San Diego State Univ, 87 & 90; instr, Calif Col of Arts & Crafts, Oakland, Calif, 80-88; vis lectr, Univ Calif, Berkeley, 90; guest instr, various workshops, 84- *Awards:* Nat Endowment Arts, 88. *Mailing Add:* 929 Grayson St Berkeley CA 94710

FREDENTHAL, RUTH ANN
PAINTER
b Detroit, Mich, Aug 20, 38. *Study:* Philadelphia Mus Col Art, 57; Yale-Norfolk Sch Art with Bernard Chaet, 58; Bennington Col with Paul Feeley, Tony Smith & Vincent Longo, BA, 60. *Work:* Chase Manhattan Bank, New York & Albany; Bennington Col, Vt; Aldrich Mus Contemp Art, Ridgefield, Conn; Fine Arts Center of Cheekwood, Nashville, Tenn; Brooklyn Mus, NY. *Exhib:* Collection in Process, Moore Col Art Gallery, Philadelphia, Pa, 77; Women Artists from New York, State Univ NY, Stony Brook, 78; In the Realm of the Monochromatic, Renaissance Soc, Univ Chicago, 79; 10 Year Retrospective, Clock Tower, New York, 80; Rigor, John Good Gallery, 87; Underknown in New York II, Leubsdorf Gallery, Hunter Col, New York, 88. *Awards:* Fulbright Fel Painting & Graphic Arts to Florence, Italy, US State Dept, 60-61. *Bibliog:* Ellen Lubell (auth), Ruth Ann Fredenthal at the Clocktower, Art Am, 1/81; Nina French-Frazier (auth), article, Art Int, 1/81; Stephen Westfall (auth) article, Art Am, 3/90. *Media:* Oil. *Dealer:* Stark Gallery 594 Broadway New York NY 10012. *Mailing Add:* 150 First Ave #501 New York NY 10009

FREDERICK, DELORAS ANN
PAINTER, INSTRUCTOR
b Fletcher, Okla, Jan 25, 42. *Study:* Central State Univ, 75; with Joseph Mugnaini, 79-80; with M Doug Walton, 79-80. *Work:* Presbyterian Hosp, Baptist Mem Hosp, Patrick Petroleum & CMI Corp, Oklahoma City, Okla; CCI Corp, Tulsa, Okla. *Exhib:* Artist Salon, Okla Mus Art, Oklahoma City, 75-80; Okla Territorial Mus, Guthrie, 78-80; Nat Small Painting Exhib, W F Mullaly Galleries, Birmingham, Mich, 78; The Miniature Painter, Sculptors & Gravers Soc, Art Club Washington, Washington, DC, 80; Ann Art Exhib, Mus Great Plains, Lawton, Okla, 80-81; and others. *Pos:* Instr watercolor, Art Supply Shop, Oklahoma City, Okla, 75-79; instr, Wkshps for Art Club in Okla, Oklahoma City, 77-81. *Teaching:* Instr water, Nichels Hills Elementary Sch, Oklahoma City, Okla, 81. *Awards:* Best of Show, Mid-Del Art Guild, 77, 79 & 80; Best Still Life Award, Founders Arts Club, Washington, DC, 80; Artist Holiday Award, Tri State Kans, 83. *Bibliog:* Deloras Frederick, Okla Art Gallery Mag, 80; Peggy Ridgeway (auth), Deloras Frederick, Art Voices, 81. *Mem:* Mid-Del Art Guild (1st vpres, 76-77); Oklahoma Watercolor (1st vpres, 77-78); Watercolor Oklahoma (1st vpres, 78-79); Oklahoma Art Guild (1st vpres, 79-80); Nat League Am Pen Women, Inc. *Media:* Watercolor, Acrylic. *Dealer:* House Gallery 5536 N Western Oklahoma City OK 73116; Studio Gallery 2020 E Eleventh Tulsa OK 74104. *Mailing Add:* 7301 NW 13 Oklahoma City OK 73127

FREDERICK, HELEN
PRINTMAKER
b Pottstown, Pa, 1945. *Study:* RI Sch Design, BFA, 67, MFA, 69. *Work:* Nat Mus, Stockholm, Sweden; Fogg Mus, Cambridge, Mass; Nat Mus Am Art, Washington, DC; Fogg Mus, Cambridge, Mass; USA Today Nat Hq, Arlington, Va. *Exhib:* Solo Exhibs, Recent Paperworks, George H Dalsheimer Gallery, Baltimore, Md, 84, Univ Ark, Fayetteville, Ark, 91 & Treading Water, David Adamson Gallery, 91; Montgomery Col, Takoma Park, Md, 85; Baltimore Mus Art, Md, 87; Gallery Contemp Art, Univ Colo, Colo Springs, 89; Object D'Art: Contemporary Screens, Va Mus Fine Art, Richmond, Va, 90. *Mem:* Fulbright Grant & Am Scandinavia fel, Munch Mus, Oslo, Norway, 73-74. *Mailing Add:* c/o David Adamson Gallery 406 7th St NW Washington DC 20004

FREDERICK, SARADELL ARD See Ard, Saradell (Saradell Ard Frederick)

FREDERICKS, BEVERLY MAGNUSON
PAINTER, RESTORER
b Colorado Springs, Colo, June 14, 28. *Study:* Colorado Springs Fine Arts Ctr, Archie Music, Boardman Robinson, Emerson Woelffer & Vaclav Vytacil, 46-54; Magnuson Antiques Restoration, Oscar & India Magnuson Co; Antelope Valley Col Calif, Paul Greenlee; Santa Monica Col Lucille Brown Green; UCLA; Emerson Ctr, Printmaking, Nancy Grenier, Calif; Kala Inst & Uno Grafico, Milan Italy, Geogio Upiglio, 85. *Work:* Nat Burn Ctr, Univ Tex, Galveston; Lawrence Welk Mus, Escondido, Calif; Univ Akron, Ohio; Bank of America, permanent collections, Calif; Toyota Corp, Mich; Home Savings Am. *Comn:* Rocky Mountains suite, Universal City Bank, Calif, 83; Turn of the Century Oils, 86 & Constable's England, 88, Las Vegas Hilton; monotype diptychs, Marriott Hotels, Los Angeles, New Orleans & Newport, 88; 1890's Figurative Series, TRW Corp, Calif, 89; oil spirit of freedom, Tianamen Square, Florence Jean Goodman, Calif, 89. *Exhib:* Los Angeles County Mus, 59; Ringling Mus Art, Fla, 59; Ambassador Col, Calif, 77 & 80; Riverside Mission Inn, Robertson, Calif, 82; Wilshire Miracle Mile, Warner, Calif, 82; retrospective, Am Inst Fine Arts, Calif, 88; Barton Galleries, Akron, Ohio; Newman Galleries, Beverly Hills, Calif. *Pos:* Restorer, selected works by Benton, Prendergast, Burkhardt, Kline, Kollwitz, Dixon, Kuntz, Cauduro, Stamos, Vicente. *Teaching:* Lectr, Monotype hist & technoc, Calif, 88 & Instr & Narrator Monotype, HRP Video (2 hrs), Calif, 90- *Awards:* Fel, Am Inst Fine Arts, Calif, 80; Hall of Fame, Palmer Alumni Asn, Colo, 85; The Ten Best Teachers on Tape, Elliot, Artists Mag, 91. *Bibliog:* Robin Longman (auth), American tonalist, Am Artist, 82; Dorene Parsons (auth), Moods of nature, The Pen Woman, 83; Les Krantz (auth), Calif Art Review, Am References, 88. *Mem:* Artists Equity Asn, Los Angeles; Am Inst for Conserv, Washington, DC; Am Inst Fine Arts, Calif (bd dir & treas, 78-85); Intern Inst for Conserv, London, Eng; Nat Mus Women Arts, Washington, DC. *Media:* Oils, Monotype. *Publ:* Contribr, Watercolor Monotypes, Watercolor, 88; prod/dir, Harvey Ray Fredericks, video, with companion book (auth) John Stafford Fredericks, The Art of Creating Monotypes, HR Productions, 90; auth, Mary Carroll Nelson; The Art of Creating Monotypes, Am Artist, 90; M Stephen Doherty, Watching Monotypes Being Made, Am Artist, 91; Kent Anderson (video) & David Baker (book), Creating Monotypes, Sch Arts Mag, 92. *Dealer:* Louis Newman Gallery 322 N Beverly Dr CA 90210. *Mailing Add:* 8227 Westlawn Ave Los Angeles CA 90045

FREDERICKS, MARSHALL MAYNARD
SCULPTOR
b Rock Island, Ill, Jan 31, 08. *Study:* John Huntington Polytech Inst, Cleveland; Cleveland Sch Art, grad, 30; Heimann Schule, Munich; Schwegerie Schule, Munich; Acad Scandinav, Paris; pvt studies in Copenhagen, Rome & London; Carl Milles Studio; Stockholm Cranbrook Acad Art, fel, Cranbrook Sch, Bloomfield Hills, Mich, 32-42; Kingswood Sch, Cranbrook, 32-42. *Work:* Detroit Inst Arts, Mich; Cranbrook Mus Art, Bloomfield Hills, Mich; Milwaukee Pub Mus, Wis; City New York; US Govt. *Comn:* Emigrants Monument, Stavanger, Norway; Milles Garden, Stockholm, Sweden; Ministry Foreign Affairs, Copenhagen, Denmark; Brookgreen Gardens; Man and the Expanding Universe Fountain, State Dept, Washington, DC; Fountain of Eternal Life-War Memorial, Cleveland, Ohio;

Foreign Ministry Copenhagen, Her Majesty Queen Margrethe II of Denmark; Freedom of the Human Spirit, Shain Pk, Birmingham, Mich, 86. *Exhib:* Carnegie Inst Nat, Pittsburgh, Pa; Philadelphia Int; Art Inst Chicago Nat; Detroit Art Inst; Whitney Mus Am Art Nat; Cleveland Mus Art; Mod Sculpture Int Exhib, Detroit; Int Sculpture Soc, Architectural League of NY; Mich Acad; Port of Hist Mus, Philadelphia; and others. *Teaching:* Instr sculpture, Cranbrook Sch, 32-38, Kingswood Sch, 32-42 & Cranbrook Acad Art, 32-42. *Awards:* Fine Arts Gold Medal, Am Inst Archit, 52; Gold Medal Hon, Mich Acad Sci, Arts & Lett, 53 & Archit League New York, 56; Henry Hering Medal; Herbert Adams Mem Medal & Medal 0f Honor, Nat Sculpture Soc. *Mem:* Academician Nat Acad Design; Pres Comt for Employment of Handicapped; Gov's State Capitol Comt; DIADEM Program for Int Exchange of Handicapped (co-founder, dir); Am Scand Found (trustee); People to People Program, Inc. *Mailing Add:* c/o Brookgreen Gardens 1931 Brookgreen Gardens Dr Murrells Inlet SC 29576

FREDMAN, FAIYA R
ENVIRONMENTAL ARTIST, PAINTER
b Columbus, Ohio, Sept 8, 25. *Study:* Calif State Univ, San Diego; Univ Calif, Los Angeles. *Work:* Cedars-Sinai, Los Angeles, Calif; Oakland Mus, Calif; Mus Photog Arts, San Diego; Key Corp, Portland, Ore; Luce-Forward, San Diego, Calif. *Exhib:* Solo shows, La Jolla Mus Contemp Art, 68, 74 & 81, Thomas Babeour Gallery, La Jolla, 81 Univ Calif, San Diego & Irvine, 84, Ruth Bachofner Gallery, Los Angeles, 85 & 88 & Univ Calif, Riverside, 85; Earth & Water, Women's Bldg, Los Angeles, 79; New Artists in New York, Alex Rosenberg Gallery, 79; Sao Paulo Mus Contemp Art, Brazil, 80; Mus Photog Arts, La Jolla, Calif, 88; Ruth Bachofner Gallery, Los Angeles, 90; Palomar Col Boehm Gallery, San Marcos, Calif, 90. *Teaching:* Instr, Exten, Univ Calif, San Diego, 77- *Awards:* US Dept Housing & Urban Develop Nat Community Art Competition Award, 73; First Prize, San Diego Pub TV Program, 78. *Bibliog:* Lucy Lippard (auth), Body, Nature & Ritual in Women's Art, Chrysalis Mag, 77; Jean Luc Bordeaux (auth), Unstretched surfaces Southern Calif, Los Angeles Inst of Contemp Art J, 11/77. *Media:* Mixed. *Publ:* Auth, Faiya Fredman Akroteri Series Catalog, Univ Calif, 84, Faiya Fredman Selected Works 1968-1989 (with catalog), Palomar Col Boehm Gallery, 90. *Dealer:* Margaret Lipworth Gallery Ctr 608 Banyan Trail Suite 113 Boca Raton FL 33431. *Mailing Add:* PO Box 2735 La Jolla CA 92038

FREDRICKSON, DANIEL ALAN See Folkus, Dan (Daniel Alan Fredrickson)

FREED, DAVID
PRINTMAKER, PAINTER
b Toledo, Ohio, May 23, 36. *Study:* Miami Univ; Univ Iowa; Royal Col Art, London. *Work:* Art Inst Chicago, Ill; Nat Collection Fine Arts, Washington, DC; Va Mus Fine Arts, Richmond; Victoria & Albert Mus, London; Mus Mod Art, New York; and others. *Exhib:* Photography in Printmaking, AAA Gallery, New York, 68-70; one-man shows, Franz Bader Gallery, Washington, DC, 68, 70, 73, 76 & 82 & Va Mus Fine Arts, Richmond; Albright-Knox Art Gallery, Buffalo, NY; Biennial Graphic Art, Moderna Galerija, Ljubljana, Yugoslavia; Il Bisonte, Florence, Italy, 89; among others. *Teaching:* Prof printmaking, Va Commonwealth Univ, 66-, prof, 78-; guest lectr etching, Cent Sch Art, London, 69. *Awards:* Fulbright grant, 63-64; Va Mus Fine Arts Fel, 83-84; Natie Marie Jones Fel, Lake Placid, NY, 83; and others. *Mailing Add:* 1825 W Grace Richmond VA 23220

FREED, DOUGLASS LYNN
PAINTER, EDUCATOR
b Garden City, Kans, Dec 24, 44. *Study:* Ft Hays Kans State Univ, BS, 67, MA, 68; Rotary Int Group Study Exchange to Italy, 78. *Work:* Univ Mo Mus Art & Archeol, Columbia; St Louis Art Mus; Steinburg Art Mus, Washington Univ, St Louis; Newark Mus, NJ; Emporia State Univ, Kans. *Comn:* KEO Bldg Corp, Sedalia, Mo, 91. *Exhib:* Visions, Mid Am Arts Alliance, 81 & traveling; Vorpal Gallery, New York, 81-84, 86 & 88; one-man shows, Vorpal Gallery, San Francisco, 82 & 90, Batz-Lawrence Gallery, Kansas City, 83, 85; Zola-Lieberman Gallery, Chicago, 85; Greenberg Gallery, St Louis, 85; St Louis Design Ctr, 86; Mus Art & Archeol, Univ Mo, 92, Elliot Smith Contemp Art, St Louis, 92; Leedy Voulilos Arts Ctr, Kans City, 93. *Collections Arranged:* Works on Paper, Mo State Coun on Arts (contribr, assembled 12 sites), 80-81; Mid America Art Alliance, 24 sites, 82-83; Missouri Painters, 12 sites, Mo Coun Arts, 85. *Teaching:* Chmn dept art, State Fair Community Col, Sedalia, Mo, 68- *Awards:* Creative Artists Grant, Mo State Coun on Arts, 90; Biannual Grant, Mo Art Coun, 84; Design Arts Grant, Nat Endowment Arts, 87. *Bibliog:* Patterson Sims (auth), catalog, Mo Artist's Exhib, 84; Nancy N Rice (auth), Doug Freed, New Art Examiner, 3/85; Jim White (auth), Douglas Freed, Abstract Painter, Dept Art Hist, Univ Mo, Columbia, 92. *Media:* Acrylic, Welded Steele. *Dealer:* Vorpal Gallery Soho New York NY; Vorpal Gallery San Francisco CA. *Mailing Add:* 1100 W Fourth Sedalia MO 65301

FREED, HERMINE
PHOTO ARTIST
b New York, NY, May 29, 40. *Study:* Cornell Univ, BA, 61; NY Univ, with Irving Sandler & Lawrence Alloway, MA, 67. *Work:* Chicago Art Inst; Donnell Libr, NY; Hartwick Col, Oneonta, NY; Calif Inst Arts, Valencia; Everson Mus, Syracuse, NY; and others. *Comn:* Videotape, Guild Hall, East Hampton, NY, 73; video portrait of pres Jill Ker Conway, Smith Col, Northampton, Mass; photo-mural, Pacific Enterprises, Los Angeles. *Exhib:* Video Art 1975, Corcoran Gallery, Washington, DC, 75; Projections, 75 & Art About Art, 78, Whitney Mus; Changing Channels, Boston Mus Fine Arts, 76; one-woman shows, Everson Mus, Syracuse, NY, 78, Columbia Univ, Avery Hall, 79, Stefanotti Gallery, NY, 80, Leo Castelli Gallery, New York, 81, Southern Light Gallery, Amarillo Col, Tex, 87 & Sherkat Gallery, New York, 87; What Does She Want?, 85 & Floating Values, 87, Artists Space, NY 85; Public Places, Private Spaces, Gallery Camino Real, Boca Raton, Fla, 86; Free Spirits, Elaine Benson Gallery, NY, 90; Univ Colo, Boulder, 92; Douglass Col, North Brunswick, NJ, 92; and others. *Pos:* Art rental cur, Inst Contemp Art, Boston, 63-65; asst cur, NY Univ Art Collection, 65-67. *Teaching:* Ideas in contemp art, NY Univ, 68-72; instr video & photo art workshop, Sch Visual Arts, New York, 72-; assoc prof, Univ Ill, Chicago, 76. *Awards:* Nat Endowment Arts Grant, 74; Creative Artists Pub Serv Grant, NY State Coun Arts, 78; Rockefeller Found Grant, 78; Aiko Bush (auth), Hermine Freed-The Photographer's Eye, Metropolis, 5/82; Bettina Gruber (auth), Video und Kunst, Berlin, 83. *Bibliog:* Grace Glueck (auth), Video is replacing canvas, New York Times, 75; Margot Jefferson (auth), Veni, vedi, video, Newsweek Mag, 75; Ronny Cohen (auth), Hermine Freed: Information please, Print Collector's Newsletter, 5-6/81. *Media:* Photography, Painting. *Publ:* Auth, Video and abstract expressionism, 12/74 & In time-of time, 6/75, Arts Mag; Where Did We Come From, Where Are We, Where Are We Going?, Harcourt, Brace, Jovanovich, 76; Collecting video, Print Collector's Newsletter; Naum June Paik at the Whitney, Art J, 82. *Mailing Add:* 60 Grammercy Park N New York NY 10010

FREEDBERG, SYDNEY JOSEPH
HISTORIAN, EDUCATOR
b Boston, Mass, Nov 11, 14. *Study:* Harvard Col, AB(summa cum laude); Harvard Univ, AM(Sachs Res Fel), 39, PhD, 40. *Pos:* Bd dirs, Col Art Asn Am, 62-66; nat vchmn, Comt to Rescue Italian Art, 66-71; dir, Save Venice, Inc, 71-89; chmn, Univ Mus Coun, 77-80; chief cur, Nat Gallery Art, Washington, DC, 83-88, Emeritus, 88- *Teaching:* Asst & tutor fine arts, Harvard Univ, 38-40; asst prof art, Wellesley Col, 46-49, assoc prof art, 50-54; vis lectr fine arts, Inst Mod Art, Boston, 47; assoc prof fine arts, Harvard Univ, 54-60, chmn dept, 59-63, prof, 60-79, Arthur Kingsley Porter prof fine arts, 79-83, prof emer, 83- *Awards:* Grand Officer, Order Star Italian Solidarity, 68; Grand Officer, Order Merit, Italy, 8; Nat Medal Arts, 88. *Mem:* Fel Am Acad of Arts & Sci. *Publ:* Auth, Parmigianino: His Works in Painting, 50, auth, Painting of the High Renaissance in Rome & Florence, Vols I & II, 61, auth, Andrea del Sarto, Vols I & II, 63, Harvard Univ; auth, Painting in Italy, 1500-1600, Penguin Bks, London & Baltimore, 71; Circa 1600, Harvard Univ, 83. *Mailing Add:* Office of Curator Nat Gallery of Art 4th St and Constitution Ave NW Washington DC 20565

FREEDMAN, DEBORAH S
PAINTER, PRINTMAKER
b New York, NY, May 1, 47. *Study:* Studied Art Students League, 67 & New York University, BS, 70. *Work:* New York Pub Libr; New York State Facilities Corp. *Comn:* Touch Sanitation Map New York, Ronald Feldman Gallery, 84; waterfall suite folding screen, comn by Jeff Winant, Short Hills, NJ, 89; monoprint etching, KOP Finnish Bank, New York, 90. *Exhib:* Alternative Imaging Systems, Everson Art Mus, Syracuse, NY, 79; Electro Works, Int Mus Photog, Rochester, NY, 79 & Cooper Hewitt Mus, New York, 80; Artists Books, Rutgers Univ, New Brunswick, NJ, 82; Abstract Energy Now, Islip Art Mus, NY, 86; Projects & Portfolios, Brooklyn Mus, NY, 89; Works on Paper '90, Long Island Univ, Brooklyn Campus, NY, 90; Garbage Out Front, Munic Arts Soc, New York, 90; Retakes, Canadian Coun Prints & Drawings, Toronto, 90. *Awards:* MacDowell Colony fel, 90. *Bibliog:* Video Portrait, interview, Asaaiti Broadcasting, Tokyo, 88; Jack Anderson, rev, That was fast, NY Times, 88; Jackie Brody (auth), Deborah Freedman-Monoprints, Print Collectors Newsletter, 89. *Media:* Monoprint etching. *Publ:* Contribr, The great goddess!, Heresies, 78; auth, Flue--a painter testifies to the glory of xerox, Franklin Furnace, 82. *Dealer:* Betsy Senior 55 Crosby St New York NY 10012. *Mailing Add:* 121 Wooster St New York NY 10012

FREEDMAN, JACQUELINE
PAINTER
Study: New Sch Social Res, New York, 65; Sch Visual Arts, 70. *Work:* Everson Mus Art, Syracuse, NY; Hudson River Mus; Queens Mus; Mus Mod Art, Art Lending Serv; Air France. *Exhib:* Solo shows, Painted: Over Pages, Ctr Book Arts, New York, 82, Founds Gallery, 82, Painted Photographs of Queen Streets & Neighborhoods, La Guardia Community Col, Long Island City, 85 & Recent Paintings, Flushing Gallery, Flushing Coun on Cult & Arts, NY, 87; group show, Art By The Book, Islip Mus, NY, 88; Queens Artists, Queens Mus, 89; Works on Paper, Queensboro Community Col, 90; Henri Gallery, Washington, DC; plus others. *Teaching:* Instr painting & drawing, Jamaica Arts Ctr, 75-85. *Awards:* Adolph & Esther Gottlieb Found Grant, 78; Nat Endwoment Arts Proj Grant, 80-81; Fel, Creative Arts Pub Serv, 82-83. *Mailing Add:* 41-06 Case St Elmhurst NY 11373

FREELAND, WILLIAM LEE
SCULPTOR, PAINTER
b Pittsburgh, Pa, June 16, 29. *Study:* Philadelphia Mus Sch Art; Hans Hofmann Sch, Provincetown, Mass. *Work:* Wilmington Mus & Soc Fine Arts, Del; Int Tel & Tel Collection, NY; Am Express; Pa Acad Fine Arts; Montclair Mus; Philadelphia Mus Art, 87. *Comn:* Sculpture, South St Develop Co, Philadelphia, Pa. *Exhib:* One-man shows, Touchstone Gallery (with catalog, 80), New York, 78 & 80, Dolan/Maxwell (with catalog), New York, 89; 25th Corcoran Biennial Exhib, Washington, DC, 57; Color Show, Birmingham Mus, Ala, 63; Artists Tribute to J F K, Swarthmore Col, 64; Nat Watercolor Show, Pa Acad Fine Arts, Philadelphia, 69; Drawing Show, Montclair Mus, Montclair, NJ, 78; From the Winston Malbin Collection Traveling Exhib (with catalog), 80; Pa Acad Fine Arts, 85; Oscarson Siegeltuch, New York,

86. *Teaching:* Prof emer fine arts, Moore Col Art, 69-90. *Awards:* Purchase Awards, Univ Del, 71 & 84; Hereward Lester Cooke Found Grant, 78 & 79; Pa State Grant, 87; Pollock-Krasner Found Grant, 89. *Bibliog:* David Bowman (auth), article, Arts Exchange, Marc, 4/78; Edgar Buonagurio (auth), article, Arts Mag, 5/78; John Russell (auth), article, New York Times, 10/24/80; Douglas Blau (auth), article, Flash Art, 2/81; Theodore F Wolf (auth), articles, Christian Sci Monitor, 3/24/81 & 1/16/84; Robert M Murdock (auth), The Sculpture of Bill Freeland, Peter Maxwell, 89. *Media:* Wood, Steel; Oil. *Dealer:* Dolan/Maxwell 2046 Rittenhouse Sq Philadelphia PA 19103. *Mailing Add:* Quarry Box 67D Rd 1 Malvern PA 19355

FREEMAN, DAVID L
PAINTER, GRAPHIC ARTIST
b Columbia, Mo, Nov 10, 37. *Study:* Univ Mo, BA & MA; State Univ Iowa, MFA; Penland Sch Crafts & Penland Weavers. *Work:* Mint Mus Art, Charlotte, NC; Minn Mus Art, St Paul; SC Nat Bank, Columbia; SC State Art Collection; NCNB Corp, Charlotte, NC; Dupont, Atlanta, Ga; US Teledsta, Atlanta, Ga; SC State Art Collection, Columbia; Fannie Mae, Atlanta, Ga; Bank Mecklenburg, Charlotte, NC. *Comn:* Painting, RJ Reynolds Inc, Winston, Salem, 85; painting, Swanston Fine Arts, Atlanta, Ga, 86; painting, GE/Electrical Distribution & Control, 90. *Exhib:* Eleventh Piedmont Painting & Sculptor Show, Mint Mus Art, NC, 71; three-man show, Mint Mus Art, NC, 78; two-man show, Greenville Co Mus Art, SC, 81, Asheville Mus Art, NC, 87; Three SC Painters, Waterworks Gallery, Salisbury, NC, 82; solo shows, High Point Theater Galleries, NC, 84 & Carlson Lobrano Gallery, Atlanta, Ga, 90; Columbia Col, SC, 87; SC Arts Comn Triennial, 92-93. *Teaching:* Asst prof studio art, Univ Wis, Madison, 63-70; prof studio art, Winthrop Univ, Rock Hill, SC, 70- *Awards:* Purchase Awards, Drawings USA, Minn Mus Art, St Paul & 8th Ann Piedmont Graphics Exhib, Mint Mus Art, 71; Spring Mills Exhib & Traveling Show Award, New York, 78. *Mem:* Nat Col Art Asn. *Media:* Acrylic. *Dealer:* Carlson-Labrono Gallery Atlanta GA. *Mailing Add:* 630 University Dr Rock Hill SC 29730

FREEMAN, GERTRUDE
COLLECTOR
b Newark, NJ, July 20, 27. *Study:* Newark Sch of Fine & Indust Arts, NJ; Univ Miami, Fla, BA(art hist). *Pos:* Consultant & purchasing agent for corporate collections, specializing in Contemporary prints, watercolors (works on paper) & sculpture; advisor & coordinator for art show for regional artists; artist representative for sculptor Enzo Gallo & painter Ivy Volpe; exclusive representative for multi-media artist Leon Gordon Miller & graphic artist Mark Freeman; collector of Modern & Contemporary 20th century art in all media, recent acquisitions: John Grauback, James Carlin, Matthew Geddes, David Maxwell. *Mailing Add:* 3192 Yattika Pl Longwood FL 32779

FREEMAN, JEFF(REY VAUGHN)
PAINTER, EDUCATOR
b Bismarck, NDak, Oct 19, 46. *Study:* Moorhead State Univ, Minn, BS(art), 70; Univ NDak, Grand Forks, MA(art), 72; Univ Wis-Madison, MFA(painting), 80. *Work:* Sheldon Mem Art Gallery, Lincoln, Nebr; Madison Art Ctr, Wis; SDat Art Mus, Brookings; Plains Art Mus, Moorhead, Minn; NDak Mus Art, Grand Forks. *Exhib:* Out of Bounds, Richards Hall Gallery, Univ Nebr, Lincoln, 89; Art For a New Century, SDak Art Mus, Brookings, 89; Midlands Invitational, Joslyn Art Mus, Omaha, Nebr, 90; Off the Wall, 91 & Midwest Visions: Constructed Realities, 89, Sheldon Mem Art Gallery, Lincoln, Nebr; SDak Sculpture Invitational, Lincoln Gallery, Northern State Univ, Aberdeen, 92; and others. *Teaching:* Assoc prof art, Univ SDak, Vermillion, 80-93. *Awards:* Visual arts fel (painting), SDak Arts Coun, 88-89; visual arts fel (painting), Arts Midwest/Nat Endowment Arts, 90-91; visual arts fel (painting), Nat Endowment Arts, 91-92. *Bibliog:* Patrick White (auth), The Painting as Artifact, Sioux City Art Ctr, Iowa, 86; Mason Riddle (auth), Jeff Freeman: Constructions, Univ SDak Art Galleries, Vermillion, 90. *Mem:* Col Art Asn Am; SDaks Arts. *Media:* Construction, Assemblage. *Dealer:* Thimmesh Gallery 25 N Fourth St Suite 201 Minneapolis MN 55401. *Mailing Add:* 900 W Main St Vermillion SD 57069

FREEMAN, KATHRYN
PAINTER, INSTRUCTOR
b Elmira, NY, Oct 28, 56. *Study:* Univ NH, BFA 79; Brooklyn Col, MFA, 81; Skowhegan Sch Painting & Sculpture, 81. *Work:* Chemical Bank, New York; Paul, Weiss, Rifkind, Wharton & Garrison, New York; and numerous pvt collections. *Exhib:* Solo exhibs, First Street Gallery, New York, 83, Rozbrat-Warsaw, Warsaw, Poland & Tatistcheff Gallery & Co, New York, 86; Bodies & Souls, Artist Choice Mus, New York, 83; The New American Scene, Squibb Gallery, Princeton, NJ, 85; New Talent-New York, Sioux City Ctr, Iowa, 86. *Teaching:* Instr design & color, Brooklyn Col, 82; instr painting, New York Acad Art, 82-84. *Awards:* Fel, Elizabeth Greenshields Found, 83. *Media:* Oil. *Mailing Add:* c/o Tatistcheff & Co 50 W 57th St New York NY 10019

FREEMAN, MALLORY BRUCE
DEALER, CURATOR
b Tulsa, Okla, Jan 9, 38. *Study:* Univ Tulsa, BA, 61. *Pos:* Dir, Tortue Gallery, Santa Monica, Calif, currently. *Teaching:* Guest lectr, Univ Southern Calif. *Specialty:* Contemporary art. *Publ:* Auth, catalogues for Tortue Gallery. *Mailing Add:* c/o Tortue Gallery 2917 Santa Monica Blvd Santa Monica CA 90404

FREEMAN, MARK
PAINTER, PRINTMAKER
b Austria, Sept 27, 08. *Study:* Columbia Col, BA; Columbia Univ, MArch; Sorbonne, Paris, dipl, Int Inst Educ Fel, 30; Nat Acad Design. *Work:* Libr Cong, Washington, DC; Philadelphia Mus Art, Pa; Mus Mod Art, NY; Hengelose Kunstzaal, Holland; Metrop Mus Art; British Mus, London; Corcoran Gallery; Whitney Mus; Brooklyn Mus; Mus City New York; Queens Mus; Mus Hist Am Art. *Exhib:* Int Biennial Color Lithography, Cincinnati Mus, 52-53; 80 Prints USA, State Dept Traveling Exhib, Europe & Africa, 54; Artists of the Region, Easthampton Guild Hall Mus, 56 & 66; Major Am Artists, Southampton Col, 68; Nat Inst Arts & Letts, 68 & 69; Sylvan Cole Gallery, 87. *Pos:* Ed-in-chief newsletter, NY Artists Equity Asn, 78-88, consult, 84-88. *Teaching:* Teaching asst, Graphic Arts, Teacher's Col, Columbia Univ, 33-34. *Awards:* Gold Medal, Nat Soc Artists in Casein, 64; Medal, Audubon Artists, 69; Today's Art Medal, 73; Fabri Medal of Merit, 86; Lotus Club Medal of Merit, 88. *Bibliog:* Gorman (auth), Texture prints of Mark Freeman, Today's Art, 78; Jerry Tallmer (auth), Penn is Stronger Than the Sword, NY Post. *Mem:* Nat Soc Artists in Casein & Acrylic (pres, 74-88); League Present Day Artists (pres, 75); Am Soc Contemp Artists (pres, 75-77); New York Artists Equity (vpres, 76-80 & 82-84); Artists Fellowship (bd trustees, 80-88). *Media:* Acrylic, Oil; Lithography. *Publ:* Auth, Reaching for the Sky, A Historic Record of NY Drawings. *Mailing Add:* 117 E 35th St New York NY 10016

FREEMAN, ROBERT
PAINTER
Study: Boston Univ, BFA, 71, MFA, 81. *Exhib:* Solo exhibs, Art in the Embassies Abroad, Smith & Mason Gallery, Washington, DC, 70, Nat Mus Afro-Am Artists, Roxbury, Mass, 81, Addison Gallery Am Art, Andover, Mass, 82, Wendall Street Gallery, Cambridge, Mass, 83, 86 & 87, Zenith Gallery, Washington, DC, 84, June Kelly Gallery, New York & Isobel Neal Gallery, Chicago, Ill, 89; Boston Collects: Contemporary Painting and Sculpture, 86 & Massachusetts Masters: Afro-American Artists, 88, Mus Fine Arts, Boston; Collected Visions, 87 & Spring Thaw, 88, Cambridge Art Asn; Faculty Exhib, Carpenter Ctr Visual Arts, Harvard Univ, Cambridge, Mass, 88; Selections: Six Contemporary African-American Artists, Williams Col Mus Art, Williamstown, Mass, 89. *Teaching:* artist-in-residence & painting inst, Noble & Greenough Sch, Dedham, Mass, 81-; instr & lectr, Harvard Univ, Cambridge, Mass, 88- *Bibliog:* Phyllis Koenig (auth), Robert Freeman, Art NEng, 12/83; Allan Gold (auth), Boston curator defends black artists' exhibition, NY Times, 1/26/88; Marty Carlock (auth), Electric Lady Land series energizes Clark Gallery exhibit, Lincoln J, 1/21/88. *Mailing Add:* c/o Clark Gallery PO Box 339 Lincoln Station Lincoln MA 01773

FREEMAN, ROBERT LEE
PAINTER, SCULPTOR
b Rincon Indian Reservation, Calif, Jan 14, 39. *Study:* Boston Univ, Mass, MA, BFA, 71, MA, MFA, 81. *Exhib:* Solo exhibs, Smith & Mason Gallery, Washington, DC, 70, Nat Mus Afro-Am Artists, Roxbury, Mass, 81, Chapel Gallery, W Newton, Mass, 82, Addison Gallery Am Art, Andover, Mass, 82, Wendell St Gallery, Cambridge, Mass, 83, 86 & 87, Clark Gallery, Lincoln Mass, 83, 86, 88 & 90, Zenith Gallery, Washington, DC, 84, Isabel Neal Gallery, Chicago, 89, June Kelly Gallery, New York, 89; Cambridge Art Asn, 71, 87 & 88, Carpenter Ctr Visual Arts, Harvard Univ, Cambridge, Mass, 88; Trenton State Mus, NJ, 71; Boston Univ, 72, Ginsburg-Hallowell, 83, Boston Collects: Contemp Painting & Sculpture, 86, Massachusetts Masters: Afro-Am Artists, Mus Fine Arts, Boston, Mass, 88; Guild Hall Art Mus, E Hampton, NY, 78; Parrish Art Mus, S Hampton, NY, 79 & 80; Salon Show, Clark Gallery, Lincoln, Mass, 83, 84, 86, 87 & 88; Crystal Britton Gallery, Atlanta, Ga, 85; June Kelly Gallery, New York, 87; Selections: Six Contemp African-Am Artists, Williams Col Mus Art, Williamstown, Mass, 89. *Teaching:* Art dir, Weston Pub Schs, Mass, 73-81; artist-in-residence & painting instr, Noble & Greenough Sch, Dedham, Mass, 81-; lectr/instr, Harvard Univ, Cambridge, Mass, 88- *Awards:* First Watercolor & First Graphics, Red Cloud Indian Art Nat, 74; Spec Award Misc, First Graphics & Second Prints, Nat Indian Exhib, Scottsdale, 75; Gold Medal drawing, Am Indian Cowboy Artists, 80; and others. *Bibliog:* Petty Peyton (auth), Portrait of the artist as a rising star, The Tab, 1/17/88; Marty Carlock (auth), Electric Lady Land, Lincoln J, 1/21/88; Allan Gold (auth), Boston Curator Defends Black Artists' Exhibition, New York Times, 1/26/88. *Media:* Pen & Ink; Oil. *Mailing Add:* c/o Wendell St Gallery 17 Wendell St Cambridge MA 02138

FREEMAN, ROLAND L
PHOTOGRAPHER
Pos: Freelance photog, currently. *Teaching:* Instr, doc photog, George Washington Univ; photog-in-residence/res assoc, Inst for the Arts & Humanities at Howard Univ, Smithsonian Inst Ctr Folklife Progs & Cult Studies. *Publ:* Auth, Something to Keep You Warm: The Roland Freeman Collection of Black American Quilts from the Mississippi Heartland, Miss Dept Arch & Hist, 79; Southern Roads/City Pavements: Photographs of Black Americans, Int Ctr Photog, New York, 81; Stand By Me: African American Expressive Culture in Philadelphia, Smithsonian Inst Off Folklife Progs, 89; The Arabbers of Baltimore, Tidewater Publ, Centreville, Md, 89; Margaret Walker's For My People: A Tribute, Photographs by Roland L Freeman, Univ Miss Press, Jackson, Miss, 92. *Mailing Add:* 117 Ingraham St Washington DC 20011

FREEMAN, TINA
PHOTOGRAPHER, CONSULTANT
b New Orleans, La, May 5, 51. *Study:* Art Ctr, Col Design, BFA, 72; Rochester Inst Technol, 78; also with Helmet Gernsheim & Beaumont

Newhall. *Work:* New Orleans Mus Art; Bibliot Nat, Paris. *Comn:* NEA Art in Pub Places, Pascagoula, Miss. *Exhib:* Solo exhibs, Cunningham-Ward Gallery, New York, 77, Galerie Simonne Stern, New Orleans, 78, 80 & 84, Newcomb Art Gallery, Tulane Univ, New Orleans, 83 & Southeastern Ctr Contemp Art, Winston-Salem, NC, 85, Univ Ore Mus Art, 88; Contemp Art Ctr, New Orleans, 79-86; Clouds and Trees, 84 & A Tribute, 85, Witkin Gallery, New York; A Sense of Place: Contemp Southern Art, Minneapolis Col Art & Design, Minn, 86; Arthur Roger Gallery, New Orleans, La, 92; and others. *Collections Arranged:* Paris After the Great War, 77; Diverse Images (auth, catalog), Photog Collection of New Orleans Mus Art, 78; Hard Times, Farm Security Administration Photography, 79; Women in Photography, 79; Deep Ocean Photography (with assistance from US Navy), 80; Lisette Model: A Retrospective (auth, catalog), Washington, DC, 81; New Acquisitions: New Directions in Black and White, 81; The Photographs of Mother St Croix (auth, catalog), 82 & Leslie Gill: A Classical Approach to Photography (auth, catalog), New Orleans Mus Art and traveling, 83- *Pos:* Assoc cur photog, New Orleans Mus Art, 77-79, sr cur, 79-, consultant, 82-85; vpres arts, Contemp Arts Ctr, New Orleans, 85-86. *Teaching:* Lectr, Free Univ, New Orleans, 80. *Bibliog:* John Lawrence (auth), monograph, Women Artists News, 80; Kathleen Moak (auth), The enduring appeal of portraits, Contemp Arts Southeast, 80; Eric Bookhardt (auth), Tina Freeman photographing artists, Uptown, 83; John Lawrence (auth), Tina Freeman: A sense of place and mortality, New Orleans Art Rev, 3-4/83. *Mem:* Soc for Photog Educ; Am Soc Mag Photogrs. *Publ:* Auth, Diverse Images, Amphoto, Garden City, 78; The Photographs of Mother St Croix, New Orleans Mus Art, 82; Leslie Gill: A Classical Approach to Photography, New Orleans Mus Art, 84; contribr, Arts Quart, New Orleans. *Mailing Add:* 1640 State St New Orleans LA 70118

FREEMAN-APPELBAUM, MARGERY
SCULPTOR
b Washington, DC. *Study:* Univ Md, BA(summa cum laude), 75, MFA(summa cum laude), 78. *Comn:* Fiber, hand made paper I, II, III & IV, Hyatt Regency Inc, Baltimore, Md, 81; IBM, Bethesda, Md, 85; Gannett Corp, Arlington, Va, 86; Trammel Crow, Woodholm Ctr, Md, 89; Evirons, Alexandria, Va, 90. *Exhib:* Corcoran Gallery, Washington, DC, 80; Baltimore Mus Arts, Md, 83; Musee Cantonal des Beaux-Arts, Lausanne, Switz, 85; David Adamson Gallery, Washington, DC, 87; Southeby's, NY, 87; Sande Webster Gallery, Philadelphia, Pa, 88; Anderson Gallery, Richmond, Va, 89; Catonsville Community Col, Baltimore, Md, 89; Washington Projs for the Arts, 89; Bergstrom-Mahler Mus, Neenah, Wis, 90; Del Ctr Contemp Arts, 91. *Pos:* Asst program dir, Div Performing Arts, Smithsonian Inst, Washington, DC, 75-76; visual arts prog dir, Arts Div, Md Nat Capital Park & Planning Comn, Riverdale, 78-86. *Teaching:* Prof, Montgomery Col, Takoma Park, Md, 88- *Awards:* Md State Fel, 79; Md Crafts Biennal Award, 83; Md Biennale Award, Baltimore Mus, 83; Visual Art Fel, Montgomery Co Arts Coun, 84; Third Place Award, Art Quest, 86; Juror's Award, 20th Anniversary Nat Biennial, Md Crafts Coun, Baltimore, 86; Montgomery Co, Art Fel, 90. *Bibliog:* Hans Lehrman (auth), Textile Sculptor, TextilKunst, 9/85; Kathleen McCann (auth), Architectural Imagery of Margery Freeman Applebaum, FiberArts, 2/86; Dr Larra Fattal (auth), Cover Arts, New York, 3/87. *Mem:* Artists Equity; Md State Arts Coun; Montgomery Co Arts Coun; Cultural Alliance Greater Washington. *Media:* Hand-Made Paper, Fiber. *Mailing Add:* 10320 Windsor View Dr Potomac MD 20854

FREILICHER, JANE
PAINTER, PRINTMAKER
b New York, NY, Nov 29, 24. *Study:* Brooklyn Col, BA, 47; Hans Hofmann Sch Fine Arts, 47; Columbia Univ, MA, 48. *Work:* Brooklyn Mus, NY; Metrop Mus Art & Mus Mod Art, New York; Brandeis Art Mus, Mass; NY Univ; Hirshhorn Mus, Washington, DC; and others. *Comn:* Book Cover, Homage to Frank O'Hara, Creative Arts Bk Co, Berkeley, Calif, 80; sets, The Heroes, Eye & Ear Theatre, New York, 81; lithograph, Self-Portrait in a Convex Mirror, Arion Press, San Francisco, 84. *Exhib:* Whitney Mus Am Art Ann, 55-; one-woman shows, John Bernard Myers Gallery, New York, 71, Fischbach Gallery, New York, biennial from 75-92, Utah Mus Fine Arts, 79 & Heath Gallery, Atlanta, Ga, 90; 30 Yrs of Am Printmaking, Brooklyn Mus, 76; Am 1976, Dept of Interior Traveling Show, 76; Poets and Painters, Denver Mus Art, 79; Twentieth Century Acquisitions, Metrop Mus Art, 79; Travelling Retrospective, Currier Gallery, NH, Parrish Art Mus, Southampton, NY, Contemporary Art Mus, Houston & Marian Koogler McNay Mus, San Antonio, Tex, 86-87; Painting Horizons, Parrish Art Mus, Southampton, NY, 89; American Panorama, Tibor de Nagy Gallery, NY, 92; Recent Works by Fischback Gallery Artists, Fischbach Gallery, NY, 92; Color as a Subject, Artists' Mus, NY, 92. *Teaching:* Vis critic & lectr, Univ Pa Grad Sch Fine Arts, 68, Skowhegan Sch Art, 68-88, Carnegie-Mellon Inst, 71, Mus Fine Arts, Boston; Parsons Sch Design, MFA Prog, 89 & 90; and others. *Awards:* Nat Endowment Arts Grant, 76; Saltus Gold Medal, Nat Acad Design Ann Exhib, 87; Eloise Spaeth Award for Distinguished Achievement in Painting, Guild Hall Mus, 91. *Bibliog:* Hilton Kramer (auth), Two Artists take Risks in the Realm of Beautiful, New York Observer, 4/25/88; John Ashbery (auth), Jane Freilicher--Reported Sightings, Viking, 89; Robert Rosenblum (auth), The Withering Greenbelt: Aspects of Landscape in Twentieth-Century Painting, Denatured Visions: Landscape and Culture in the Twentieth Century, Harry N Abrams, New York, 92. *Mem:* Nat Acad Design; Am Acad Inst Arts & Letts. *Media:* Oil. *Publ:* Illusr, Turandot & Other Poems, 53 & Paris Review (portfolio of drawings), 65; auth, Jane Freilicher: Paintings, Taplinger Publ, 86. *Dealer:* Fischbach Gallery 29 W 57th St New York NY. *Mailing Add:* 51 Fifth Ave New York NY 10003

FREIMARK, BOB (ROBERT)
PRINTMAKER, PAINTER
b Doster, Mich, Jan 27, 22. *Study:* Univ Toledo, BEd; Cranbrook Acad Art, MFA; independent study in Mex & Czech. *Work:* Nat Gallery, Prague, Czech; Smithsonian Inst & Libr Cong, Washington, DC; Los Angeles Co Mus, Calif; Brit Mus. *Comn:* Brenton Banks, Des Moines, 74; Kundalini Found, New York, 74; Impressions Workshop, Boston, 74-75; Am Micro Systs, Inc, Santa Clara, Calif, 75; tapestry, Olympic Games, Moscow, 80. *Exhib:* Drawings of 12 Countries, Art Inst Chicago, 52; Pa Acad Fine Art Painting Ann, 52-53; Brooklyn Mus Biennial Watercolor Exhib, 64; Mich State Univ, E Lansing, 80; Yosemite Nat Park, Calif, 85; Triton Mus Art, Santa Clara, Calif, 90; Strahov Kloster (Nat Palace), Praque, 91; Kunsthaus Ostbayern, Viechtach, Ger, 92. *Pos:* Guest artist, Joslyn Mem Mus, Omaha, Nebr, 61, Huntington Galleries, WVa, 63 & Riverside Art Ctr, Calif, 64; guest artist & lectr, Columbia Univ, 63; vis prof, Harvard Univ, 72-73. *Teaching:* Instr drawing, Toledo Mus Art, 52-55; instr painting, Ohio Univ, 56-59; resident artist, Des Moines Art Ctr, 59-63; prof graphics, San Jose State Col, 64-86. *Awards:* New Talent in USA Award, Art in Am, 57; Ford Found Grant, WVa, 65; Spec Creative Leave, Calif State Col Syst, 67. *Bibliog:* Chamberlain & Crockett (auth), Beyond Weaving, Watson-Guptill, 74; Roberta Loach (auth), In conversation with Robert Freimark, Visual Dialog, 76; Dan McGuire (auth), Kaleidoscope, TV video, KTEH, 79-8080. *Media:* Monotype, Lithography; Tapestry. *Res:* Mexican popular culture; rehabilitation through art; environmental planning for contemporary living; Art Protis tapestries. *Interests:* Graphics, film and video. *Dealer:* Walter Bischoff Galerie Stuttgart Germany; Percival Galleries Ltd Des Moines IA. *Mailing Add:* Rte 2 Box 539A Morgan Hill CA 95037

FREITAG, WOLFGANG MARTIN
LIBRARIAN, EDITOR
b Berlin, Ger, Oct 27, 24; US citizen. *Study:* Univ Freiburg, Ger, PhD; Simmons Col, Boston, MS(libr sci). *Pos:* Chief librn, Fine Arts Libr, Harvard Col Libr, Fogg Art Mus, 64-91. *Teaching:* Lectr bibliog & art historiography, Harvard Univ, 67-75, sr lectr, 75-91. *Awards:* Distinguished Serv Award, Art Libr Soc NAm, 90. *Mem:* Col Art Asn; charter mem Art Libr Soc NAm (pres, 80); Asn Col & Res Libr; Metrop Mus Art, New York; Syracuse Univ Sch Info Studies; and others. *Publ:* Auth, Tapping a serviceable reservoir: The selection of periodicals for art libraries, Art Libr J, 76; Early uses of photography in the history of art, Art J, 79; Monographs on Artists, Garland, NY, 85; Cooperative Collection Development, 87; Art Reproductions in the Library in The Documented Image, Syracuse UP, 87; and others. *Mailing Add:* Fogg Art Mus Cambridge MA 02138

FRENCH, RAY H
PRINTMAKER, PAINTER
b Terre Haute, Ind, May 16, 19. *Study:* John Herron Art Sch; Ind State Univ; Univ Colo; Univ Iowa, BFA & MFA; Accad Belle Arte, Florence, Italy; Hobart Sch Welding Technol, Troy, Ohio; also study with Mauricio Lansansky & James Lechay. *Work:* Mus Mod Art, New York; Pennell Collections, Libr Cong; Victoria & Albert Mus, London; Nat Mus Am Art; Bibliot Nat, Paris. *Exhib:* Soc Am Graphic Artists Ann Exhib, Nat Acad, 47; A New Direction in Intaglio, the Work of Lasansky and His Students, Walker Art Ctr, Milwaukee, 49-53; Young Am Printmakers, Mus of Mod Art, New York, 53; Ray H French, 25 Yrs of Printmaking, Sheldon Swope Art Gallery, Terre Haute, Ind, 70; Forerunners of the American Print Renaissance, Pratt Graphics Ctr, New York, 77. *Pos:* Cur, Univ Collection, DePauw Univ, Greencastle, Ind, 78-84, emer cur, 84- *Teaching:* Prof printmaking, DePauw Univ, Greencastle, Ind, 48-84, head dept art, 70-78, prof art, 84- *Awards:* Art Asn First Prize, Indianapolis Mus Art, 56; Joseph Pennell Purchase Award for Etching, Philadelphia Free Libr, 60; Mus Purchase Award, Pasadena Mus, 70. *Bibliog:* American Prints Libr Cong; Who's Who in America, 80 & 81; Who's Who in the World, 82 & 83. *Mem:* Soc Am Graphic Artists; Print & Drawing Soc, Indianapolis Mus Art; Ind Artists Club (pres, 62-63); Ind Soc Printmakers (pres, 53-54). *Media:* All. *Dealer:* Weintraub Gallery 992 Madison Ave New York NY 10021; Annex Galleries Santa Rosa Calif. *Mailing Add:* 106 E Seminary St Greencastle IN 46135

FRENCH, STEPHEN WARREN
PAINTER, ADMINISTRATOR
b Seattle, Wash, Sept 6, 34. *Study:* Univ Wash, BA, 56; MFA, 60. *Work:* San Francisco Mus Art, Calif; San Jose Mus Art, Calif; Johnson Wax Found, Racine, Wis; Univ Okla, Norman; Univ Wis, Madison. *Exhib:* Prints of the Sixties, Smithsonian Inst, Washington, DC, 65; Nat Print Exhib, Brooklyn Mus, New York, 65; Painters Behind Painter, Palace of Legion of Honor, San Francisco, Calif, 67; British Int Graphics Exhib, Bradford Mus, Eng, 69 & 71; two man exhib, San Francisco Mus, 70; three man shows, Redding Mus, 80 & San Jose Art Mus, 80, Calif. *Pos:* Adv bd, Inst Contemp Art, San Jose, 89-; pub art adv comt, City of San Jose, 90; comnr, Fine Arts Comn, San Jose, 90- *Teaching:* Asst prof painting & prints, Univ Wis, Madison, 61-66; prof, San Jose State Univ, 66-, assoc dean humanities & art, 90- *Awards:* Ford Found Purchase Award, Walker Biennial, Minn, 64; Art in Embassies Purchase Award, US Information Agency, 65-66; Am Graphics Award, Univ Pac, 69. *Mem:* Col Art Asn; Nat Conf Art Admin; Nat Asn Schs of Art & Design. *Media:* Acrylic, Silk Screen. *Mailing Add:* 512 S Fifth San Jose CA 95112

FRERICHS, RUTH COLCORD
PAINTER, LITHOGRAPHER
b White Plains, NY. *Study:* Conn Col, BA; Art Students League. *Work:* Thunderbird Bank, Phoenix, Ariz; First Nat Bank, Continental Bank, Valley Nat Bank, Ariz; permament collection, Mus State Univ Southeastern Mo; and others. *Exhib:* Watercolor West Nat Exhib, Riverside, Calif, 72; Southwestern Fedn Watercolor Exhib, Mus Albuquerque, 76; Nat Watercolor Soc Ann, 76; Scottsdale Watercolor Biennial, Ariz, 78; Conn Col Alumni Exhib, New London, 78; and others. *Mailing Add:* 321 E Pomona Rd Phoenix AZ 85020

FRETS, BARBARA J
PAINTER
b St Louis, Mo. *Study:* Stephes Col, Columbia, Mo, AA, 49; Univ Mo, Columbia, BS, 51, MA, 52. *Work:* Continental Insurance Corp, New York; Sheldon Mem Art Gallery Mus, Lincoln, Nebr; Yellow Freight & Transit System & Hallmark Cards Inc, Kansas City, Mo; Minnesota Mining Corp, Minneapolis. *Comn:* Kansas City Intersection, painting, Munic Arts Comn, Kansas City, Mo. *Exhib:* Mid Four, Nelson-Atkins Art Mus, Kansas City, Mo, 74-79 & 83-85; Joslyn Biennial, 78, 80, 82, 84 & 88 & Regionalism: Seven Views, 79, Joslyn Art Mus, Omaha, Nebr; Eyes on the Land, Sheldon Art Mus, Lincoln, Nebr, 81; Owensboro Mus Fine Arts Nat Exhib, Ky, 82; The Am Artists Mag Competition Winners, Grand Cent Galleries, New York, 85; The Kansas Collection, Mus Women Arts, Washington, DC, 87; Main Stream America, Butler Inst Art, Youngstown, Ohio, 87. *Teaching:* Instr painting, Johnson Co Community Col, Shawnee Mission, Kans, 78-80. *Awards:* Visual Arts Grants for Visions, 81, Mid Am Arts Alliance; First Award for Acrylics, Am Artist Mag, 85; Nat Endowment Arts Fel Award, Mid Am Art Alliance, 86. *Media:* Oil, Acrylic. *Dealer:* Douglas Drake 50 W 57 St New York NY 10019. *Mailing Add:* 1903 Bay Rd No 306 Vero Beach FL 32863

FREUDENHEIM, NINA
DEALER, COLLECTOR
Pos: Owner, Nina Freudenheim Gallery. *Specialty:* Contemporary, national and international art. *Collection:* Works by Pol Bury, Jules Olitski, Georges Noel, Lucas Samars, Fontana and many others. *Mailing Add:* 300 Delaware Ave Buffalo NY 14202

FREUDENHEIM, TOM LIPPMANN
MUSEUM ADMINISTRATOR
b Stuttgart, Ger, July 3, 37; US citizen. *Study:* Harvard Col, AB; NY Univ, MA; Univ Md, Hon DFA, 82. *Collections Arranged:* Pascin (with catalog), 66 & Arnaldo Pomodoro (with catalog), 70, Univ Art Mus, Berkeley, Calif; Alfred Leslie, Worcester, 84. *Pos:* Cur, Jewish Mus, New York, 62-65; asst dir, Univ Art Mus, Berkeley, 66-71; dir, Baltimore Mus Art, 71-78; dir, Mus Prog, Nat Endowment Arts, 78-82, Worcester Art Mus, 82-86; asst secy, Museums of the Smithsonian Inst, 86-92; asst secy, Arts & Humanities of the Smithsonian Inst, 92. *Mem:* Col Art Asn Am; Am Asn Mus; Am Fedn Arts (vpres); Nat Found Jewish Cult (vpres). *Publ:* Auth, Myer Myers, American Silversmith, 65; auth, Illuminated Hebrew Manuscripts, 65; auth, Persian Faience Mosaic Wall, Kunst Orients, 68; Holocaust art, 78; ed, American Museum Guide, 83. *Mailing Add:* Smithsonian Inst 1000 Jefferson Dr Washington DC 20560

FREUND, HARRY LOUIS
PAINTER, ILLUSTRATOR
b Clinton, Mo, Sept 16, 05. *Study:* Univ Mo, 23-25; St Louis Sch Fine Arts, Washington Univ, 25-29; D H Wuerpel Travel Scholar, 29; Colarossi Acad, Paris, 29-30; Carnegie Fel, 40; Princeton Univ, 40-41; Colorado Springs Fine Arts Ctr, 46-47; Carnegie-Stetson Grant, Mex, 53; Stetson Univ Grant, Cent Am, 59, DFA, 79. *Work:* IBM Corp; Libr Cong, Washington, DC; Seattle Art Mus, Wash; St Louis Sch Fine Arts; Mus Fine Arts, Little Rock, Ark; Springfield Art Mus, Mo; Mus Fine Arts, Deland, Fla; Mint Mus, Atlanta; Ralph Foster Mus, Mo. *Comn:* Mural, Deland Mem Hosp, Fla; libr murals, Bishop Col & Shaw Univ; Centennial Mural, Eureka Springs, Ark, 79; plus many others in pub & pvt collections. *Exhib:* Contemp Am Art Exhib, New York World's Fair; Nat Acad Design; Pa Acad Design; Carnegie Inst; Corcoran Gallery Art; plus many others in mus, schs & libraries in US & abroad. *Pos:* Free lance illusr, Crowell Publ & Ford Motor Co Publs; mural designer, State of Mo at Chicago World's Fair, 33; mural artist, sect fine arts, US Treas Dept, 34-40; visual aids dir, Eighth Serv Command, US Army, 45-46. *Teaching:* Resident artist, Hendrix Col, 39-41, head dept art, 41-46; founder dept art, Little Rock Jr Col, 40; founder & dir, Art Sch Ozarks, 7 yrs; lectr & faculty artist vis, Asn Am Cols, 5 seasons; head dept art, Stetson Univ, 49-59, resident artist, 59-67. *Awards:* Award Neighborhood Hist Alliance of Ark, 83; Senior Peacemaker of Ark, 84; Governor's Award, State of Ark, 92. *Bibliog:* Wall to Wall America, 82; A Fine Age, 84; Democratic Vistas, 84. *Mem:* Fla Artist Group (past pres); Nat Soc Mural Painters; Eureka Springs, Ark Guild of Artists & Craftspeople; Fla Craftsmen (past pres). *Media:* Oil, Acrylic. *Mailing Add:* 31 Steel St Eureka Springs AR 72632

FREUND, PEPSI
PAINTER
b New York, NY, Oct 17, 38. *Study:* Self taught. *Work:* Citibank & Chase Bank, New York. *Exhib:* Long Beach Mus, Long Island; Fine Arts Mus, Long Island; Guggenheim Mus, Long Island; one person shows, Elmont Libr, Oceanside Libr & W Hempstead Libr; Long Beach Celebrity Arts, Nat Art League. *Teaching:* Instr, various Nassau Co Schs. *Awards:* Gold & Silver Awards, Nat Art League; Bronze Award, Nassau Mus Fine Art. *Mem:* 30 Artists; Nat Asn Women Artists Am. *Media:* Collage, Watercolor. *Dealer:* Soundview Art Gallery 35 Chandler Sq Port Jefferson New York NY; Ariel Gallery 470 Broome St Soho, NY. *Mailing Add:* 37 Alhambra Dr Oceanside NY 11572-5425

FREUND, TIBOR
PAINTER, MURALIST
b Budapest, Hungary, Dec 29, 10; US citizen. *Study:* Fed Tech Univ, Zurich, dipl archit, 32; Vilmos Aba-Novak Art Sch, Budapest, 34; studies Oriental techniques of mosaics, Meshed, Iran, 40. *Work:* Mus Fine Arts, Budapest; James A Michener Collection, Univ Tex, Austin; Goucher Col, Md; Ravinia Art Festival Asn, Chicago, Ill; Ball State Univ, Muncie, Ind. *Comn:* First moving mural on ridged surface, Bd Educ, Pub Sch 111, New York, 63; first moving mural on flat surface, Bd Educ Sch 162, New York, 70. *Exhib:* Seven one-man shows, New York, 60-76; Am Fedn Arts Traveling Exhibs, 63-67, & 71-72; Abstract Art, Riverside Mus, New York, 65; An American Report on the Sixties, Denver Art Mus, Colo, 69; Painting & Sculpture Today, Indianapolis Mus Art, Ind, 70. *Awards:* First Prize, 19th Ann New Eng Exhib, Silvermine Guild, 68. *Bibliog:* John Canaday (auth), Tibor Freund, NY Times, 10/4/69; Peter Schjeldahl (auth), Fourth show in New York, 69 & Phyllis Derfner (auth), Sixth show in New York, 74, Art Int; and others. *Mem:* Nat Soc Mural Painters. *Media:* Acrylic. *Res:* Developed motion painting from a crude nineteenth century invention called three-sided picture. *Publ:* Auth, Motion in painting--a new art form, Am Artist Mag, 11/64. *Mailing Add:* 34-57 82nd St Jackson Heights NY 11372

FREUND, WILL FREDERICK
PAINTER, EDUCATOR
b Madison, Wis, Jan 20, 16. *Study:* Univ Wis, BS, MS; Univ Mo; Tiffany Found Fel, 40 & 49. *Work:* William Rockhill Nelson Gallery Art, Kansas City, Mo; Joslyn Mus Art, Omaha, Nebr; Okla Art Ctr, Oklahoma City; Mulvane Mus Art, Topeka, Kans; Univ Nebr Art Galleries, Lincoln; and others. *Exhib:* Mo Pavilion, New York World's Fair, 64; New Talent USA, Art in Am Mag, 65; Watercolor USA, Springfield Art Mus, Mo, 70 & 72; Evansville Mus Art, Ind; Denver Art Mus; Butler Inst Art; Nat Gallery Art, Washington, DC; and others. *Teaching:* Instr art, Stephens Col, 46-64; prof fine art, Southern Ill Univ, Edwardsville, 64-81. *Awards:* First Prize Watercolor, Ruth Renfro Award, St Louis City Art Mus, 63; Purchase Prize & Bronstein Award, Evansville Mus Art; First Prize Watercolor, Quincy's 24th Ann. *Bibliog:* Article, Prize winners, Life Mag, 9/12/55; A B Louchheim (auth), Prize $, Art News, 10/56; article, Will Freund, painter, potter, woodworker, boombass player, Wis Alumnus, 1/61. *Media:* Oil, Watercolor. *Mailing Add:* Box 182 Watersmeet MI 49969

FREUNDLICH, AUGUST L
ADMINISTRATOR, COLLECTOR
b Frankfurt, WGer, May 9, 24; US citizen. *Study:* Antioch Col, BA, 49, MA, 50; New York Univ, PhD, 60. *Pos:* Consult, Nat Found Advan Arts; pres & exec dir, R A Florsheim Art Fund. *Teaching:* Head art dept, Eastern Mich Univ, 54-58; chmn arts div, George Peabody Col, 58-64; dir & chmn art dept, Lowe Art Mus, Univ Miami, 64-70; dean Sch Art, Syracuse Univ, 70; dean, Col Visual & Performing Arts, 71-82; dean, Col Fine Arts, Univ SFla, 82-86 & prof fine arts 86-91. *Mem:* Int Coun Fine Art Deans; Col Art Asn; Am Asn Mus; and others. *Res:* Social commentary art, American & German; American graphics and sculpture. *Collection:* Self-portraits; 20th century prints. *Publ:* Auth, William Gropper, Ward, Richie Press, 63; Frank Kleinholz, Univ Miami, 66; Karl Schrag, 70 & 80; Richard Florsheim, A S Barnes, 76; auth, Federico Castellon, Syracuse Univ, 78; S Rosenblum, Nogorme Press, 89. *Mailing Add:* Timberlan Dr Lutz FL 33549

FREY, BARBARA LOUISE
CERAMIST, EDUCATOR
b Bloomington, Ind, Apr 28, 52. *Study:* Ind Univ, Bloomington, BFA, 76; Syracuse Univ, MFA, 78. *Work:* Columbia Col Art Collection, SC; Ark Art Ctr, Little Rock; Grant Arnold Print Collection, State Univ NY, Oswego. *Comn:* Ceramic tile mural, comn by Dr Karl F Frey, Harlingen, Tex, 85. *Exhib:* Texas Crafts: New Expressions, Dallas Mus Fine Arts, 81; A Tea Party, Ferrin Gallery, Northampton, Mass, 89 & 91-92; The Tea Party, Am Craft Mus, New York, 91; Teapot Invitational, Dorothy Weiss Gallery, San Francisco, 91; Rituals of Tea, Garth Clark Gallery, New York, 91; A Tea Party: A Group Exhibition of Teapots, Soc Arts & Crafts, Boston, 92; and many others. *Teaching:* Instr ceramics, State Univ NY, Oswego, 78-80; assoc prof, E Tex State Univ, Commerce, Tex, 80- *Awards:* Bankers Trust Co Award, 49th Cooperstown Art Asn Nat, 84; Merit Award, NCECA Juried Member's Exhib, 88; Ceramics Prize, 55th Cooperstown Art Asn Nat, 90; and others. *Mem:* Nat Coun Educ Ceramic Arts; Col Art Asn. *Media:* Ceramics. *Publ:* Contribr, Porcelain: Traditions and New Visions, Watson-Guptill, 81; Electric Kiln Ceramics, 81 & Ceramics: Mastering the Craft, 90, Chilton Bk Co. *Dealer:* Dorothy Weiss Gallery 256 Sutter St San Francisco CA 94108; Ferrin Gallery 179 Main St Northampton MA 01060. *Mailing Add:* 1513 Park St Commerce TX 75428

FREY, VIOLA
SCULPTOR, PAINTER
b Lodi, Calif, Aug 15, 33. *Study:* Delta Col, Stockton, Calif, AA; Calif Col Arts & Crafts, BFA; Tulane Univ, MFA. *Exhib:* Overglaze Imagery, Calif State Univ, Fullerton, 77; Soap Box Derby, San Francisco Mus Mod Art, 78; A Century of Ceramics in the US, Everson Mus Art, Syracuse, NY, 79, Renwick Mus, Washington, DC, 79 & Cooper-Hewitt Mus, New York, 79; Large Scale Ceramic Sculpture, Davis, Calif, 79; The Unpainted Portrait, Kohler Arts Ctr, Sheboygan, Wis, 79; and others. *Teaching:* Assoc prof ceramics, Calif Col Arts & Crafts, 65-, chmn dept ceramics, Noni Eccles Treadwell Ceramic Arts Ctr, currently. *Awards:* Nat Endowment Arts fel grant, 78. *Bibliog:* Wenger (auth), Currant, Art Mag, 8/75; Garth Clark (auth), Commentary and Review. *Mailing Add:* c/o Asher/Faure 612 N Almont Dr Los Angeles CA 90069

FRIBERG, ARNOLD
PAINTER, PUBLISHER
b Winnetka, Ill, Dec 21, 13. *Study:* Art Instr Schs; Chicago Acad Fine Arts; Am Acad Art, Chicago. *Work:* Tweed Mus, Duluth, Minn; Prince Wales Northern Heritage Ctr, Yellowknife, Can; Leaning Tree Mus, Boulder; Sheldon Mus, Lincoln, Nebr; Temple Square, Salt Lake City; Favell Mus, Ore. *Comn:* 100 Years of American Inter-collegiate Football (series of

paintings), Chevrolet Sports Art Collection, 69; The Northwest Mounted Police (series over 200 paintings), Northwest Paper Co, Tweed Mus, Duluth, Minn, 37-72; Winners and Losers (painting), comn by Steve Wynn, 76; life size portrait of Prince Charles with horse Centenial, comn by Govt Northwest Territories, Can, 79; Golden Nugget Casino, Las Vegas, Nev. *Exhib:* Ten Commandments Series, toured every continent, 57-58; Motion Picture Indust Exhib, New York World's Fair, 64-65; De Mille Dynasty Exhib, Los Angeles, 85-86; Expo-86, Vancouver, BC, Can. *Pos:* Chief artist-designer, Cecil B De Mille, 54-57. *Teaching:* Lectr vitality in relig painting, art as serv & Russell & Remington. *Awards:* Hon Best Artist of 1991 Western Heritate Art Show, Salt Lake City, 91. *Bibliog:* Vern Swanson (auth), Southwest Art Mag, 12/81; Ted Scharz (auth), Arnold Friberg, Northland Press, 84; Vicki Stavig (auth), Art of the West, 1/92. *Mem:* Life mem Royal Soc Arts, London; Chelsea Arts Club, London; Newcomen Soc, Philadelphia. *Publ:* Auth & illusr, The Ten Commandments, 57 & Arnold Friberg's Little Christmas Book, 58. *Dealer:* Friberg Fine Art Prints 4533 Highland Dr Salt Lake City UT 84117. *Mailing Add:* 4533 Highland Dr Salt Lake City UT 84117

FRICANO, TOM S
PAINTER, PRINTMAKER
b Chicago, Ill, Oct 28, 30. *Study:* Bradley Univ, BFA, 53; Univ Ill, Urbana, MFA, 56. *Work:* Libr Cong, Washington, DC; Philadelphia Mus; Art Inst Chicago; Los Angeles Co Mus Art; Seattle Art Mus; Utah Mus Fine Art; Brooklyn Mus Art, New York. *Exhib:* One-man shows, Harmon Fine Arts Ctr, Drake Univ, Des Moines, Iowa, 77, Fresno State Univ Gallery, Calif, 78, Pepperdine Univ, Malibu, Calif, 79, Univ NDak, Grand Forks, NDak, 80, Bibo Gallery Art, Peoria, Ill, 81, Arts Place II, Okla Arts Ctr, Oklahoma City, 83, A Survey: 25 Years of Printmaking, Fairweather Hardin Gallery, Chicago, Ill, 88; The Collograph, An Experience in Problem Solving (traveling), 89-90; Visiting Artists Print Collection, Univ Tex, Austin, 90; Three Faculty Artists, Calif State Univ, Northridge, 90; Photo Printmaking-A Partnership, Golden West Col, Huntington Beach, Calif, 90. *Teaching:* Instr painting & printmaking, Bradley Univ, Peoria, Ill, 58-63; prof painting & printmaking, Calif State Univ, Northridge, 63-; vis artist, Ohio State Univ, Columbus, 69, Univ Utah, 71, Univ Mont, Bozeman, & Art Inst Chicago, 75, Univ NDak, Grand Forks, Cranbrook Acad Art, Bloomfield Hills, Mich & Eastern Mich Univ, Ypsilanti, 80. *Awards:* Calif State Univ Found Res Grant, 66, 68, 74 & 78; Guggenheim Found Fel, 69 & 70; Fulbright Grant, Florence Italy, 60-61; Louis Comfort Tiffany Res Grant, 65. *Bibliog:* Lawrence C Goldschmidt (auth), Watercolor Bold and Free, NY/Pitman Publ, 80; John Ross & Claire Romano (coauths), The Complete Collagraph, Free Press, 80; Leonard Edmondson (auth), Etching, Van Nostrand Reinhold. *Mem:* Hon mem Los Angeles Printmaking Soc (vpres, 64-65). *Publ:* Auth, Thoughts Emerging, 91; Contemporary Flight, 91; It All Adds Up, 92. *Mailing Add:* 9820 Aldea Ave Northridge CA 91325

FRICK, ARTHUR CHARLES
PAINTER, EDUCATOR
b Milwaukee, Wis. *Study:* Univ Wis, Milwaukee, with R Von Neuman, E Ulbricht & H Thomas, BS(art educ), 48; Univ Wis, Madison, with F Logan, A Bhorad & Z Zingale, MS(art appl), 49; Ox-Bow, Saugatuck, Mich, with Franklin Watkins & E Rupprecht, 49-54; Escuela de Pintura y Escultura, Mexico City, with J Ruiz, 50-51. *Work:* Univ Wis Permanent Collection, Green Bay; Sioux City Art Mus, Iowa; Milwaukee Art Inst. *Comn:* Fountain sculpture, Irving Galleries, Milwaukee, 64; sculptures, Royal Palace, Govt of Kuwait, 67; relief sculpture, Am Univ Beirut, Lebanon, 73; mural, Arms, Perkins & Will Archit Co, Chicago, 74; painting, Austin Archit Design Corp, Des Plaines, Ill, 76. *Exhib:* Frederick Fursman Memorial Exhib, Art Inst Chicago, 50; Michigan Artist's Annual, Detroit Inst Arts, 51 & 55; Mid-America Annual, Kansas City Art Inst, 53 & 56; Int Biennial, Cincinnati Art Mus, Ohio, 54; St Louis and Vicinity Annual, City Art Mus, St Louis, Mo, 55, 56 & 57; Current Trends: Mid-Eastern Art, Gulbenkian, 66 & Rothman Found International, Musee Sursock, 67, Beirut, Lebanon; Watercolor USA, Springfield Art, Mus, Mo, 69. *Collections Arranged:* First Retrospective: Khalil Gibran, 58, First Retrospective: Boris Novikof, 64, Drawings of Henry Moore, 68, Modern Japanese Printmakers, 71 & Current Middle East Directions, 74, Am Univ Beirut Gallery. *Pos:* Dir, Pub Arts Progs, Duke Found, Beirut, 57-60; art consult, US Point Four, Indust Inst, Beirut, 57-62; art educ consult, UNESCO, Beirut, 59-74. *Teaching:* Mem fac lithography, Ox-Bow, Saugatuck, Mich, 49-56; prof painting, Am Univ Beirut, 57-76 (dept chmn, 57-67 & 74-76) & Univ Wis, Milwaukee, 72-73; chmn, Art Dept, Wartburg Col, 76- *Awards:* Hon Mention, Second Ann Nat Sculpture Exhib, Ball State Univ, 56; Hon Mention, Nat Print & Drawing Exhib, Ohio State Univ, 65; Hon Mention, 16th Regional Painting Exhib, Mac Nider Mus Art, 81. *Bibliog:* Madeline Grapes (dir), Conquest of Space (film), Univ Mich-Stephens Col, 56; Farid Moukheibir (auth), Propos sur l'art abstrait par Frick, La Revue du Liban, 66. *Mem:* Col Art Asn Am; Mid-Am Col Art Asn; Iowa Watercolor Soc; Midwest Art Hist Soc. *Media:* All. *Publ:* Auth, Graphic Arts Processes, US Dept State, 57. *Dealer:* Douglas-Baker Gallery Hyatt Regency 1300 Nicolet Mall Minneapolis MN; Bradley Galleries 2639 Downer Ave Milwaukee WI. *Mailing Add:* 212 Second Ave Waverly IA 50677

FRICK, JOAN
PAINTER, CONCEPTUAL ARTIST
b Toronto, Ont, Mar 11, 42. *Study:* Univ de Montreal: Ecole Beaux-Arts, 63. *Work:* Art Gallery Ont; Gallery Stratford, Ont; Can Coun Art Bank, Ottawa; Can Art Arch, Vancouver Art Gallery; Norman McKenzie Art Gallery, Regina, Sask. *Comn:* Art Gallery Peterborough, 87; Art Gallery Northumberland, 88; Art Gallery Hamilton, 88; Art Gallery Algoma, 92; Kiechener-Waterloo Art Gallery, 92. *Exhib:* Ontario Now, Art Gallery Hamilton, Ont & Kitchener, Waterloo Art Gallery, Ont, 76; Abstractions, Place Bonaventure, Montreal, Gallery-Stratford, Ont & Can Cult Ctrs, London & Paris, 76; Summer Show, Royal Acad, London, 77; Markings, Can Embassy, Washington, DC, Ga State Univ Art Gallery, Atlanta & Can Consulates, Chicago & Boston, 78-79; Future Traditions Ontario 81 Travelling Exhib, 80-82. *Awards:* Can Coun Proj Costs Grants, 72, 74, 86 & 87; Ont Arts Coun Grants, 82, 84, 85 & 88. *Bibliog:* John Bentley Mays (auth), Joan Frick's artistic vision isn't gun shy, Globe & Mail, 9/22/80; Cathy Arthur (auth), article, Artscanada, 12/80-1/81; Mark Frutkin (auth), Hidden lines of colour, Beau Joust, 12/14/82; David Burnett & Marilyn Shiff: Contemporary Canadian Art, Hurtig, 83. *Mem:* Visual Arts Ont; life hon mem, Art Gallery Ont; Mercer Union; Int Sculpture Ctr. *Media:* Miscellaneous Media. *Publ:* O A Publication of the Arts, Winter 76; Works by Offset, Artists in Books, 78. *Mailing Add:* 648 Richmond St W Toronto ON M6J 1C3 Canada

FRICK, ROBERT OLIVER
PAINTER, INSTRUCTOR
b Philadelphia, Pa, Feb 19, 20. *Study:* Pa Acad Fine Arts; also with Frank Benton Ashley Linton, Philadelphia; Daniel Garber, New Hope, Pa; Stanley Woodward, Rockport, Mass. *Work:* Pittsford, Vt Pub Libr; Chaffee Art Gallery; Southern Vt Art Asn private collection. *Exhib:* One-man shows, Chaffee Art Gallery, Chester Art Guild, Blue Hill Art Guild & Southern Vt Art Asn, 77-81 & 88, McNichols Gallery Fine Arts, Naples, Fla, 86, 87 & 88; Salmagundi Club, 72-74; Concord Art Asn, Mass, 73-74; Saxtons River Art Assoc, 81; Chester Art Asn 78, 79 & 87. *Pos:* Trustee, Chaffee Art Gallery, Rutland, Vt, 89-90 & Southern Vt Artists, Manchester, Vt, 80- *Teaching:* Instr oil & watercolor, Rutland Jr High, Vt, 68-80, Saxtons River Art Asn, 69- & Southern Vt Art Ctr, 71-87. *Awards:* Spring Oil Exhib Award, 85; American Artist Professional League, 91; Presidents Award, Fall Oil Exhib, 91. *Mem:* Allied Artists Am; Am Artists Prof League; Knickerbocker Artists; Copley Soc; Salmagundi Club; and others. *Media:* Oil, Watercolor. *Mailing Add:* PO Box 121 Pittsford VT 05763

FRID, TAGE P
DESIGNER
b Copenhagen, Denmark, May 30, 15; US citizen. *Study:* Copenhagen Tech Sch, Master craftsman with honors woodworking & furniture design, 34; Vedins Sch, Copenhagen, Denmark, 40; Sch Interior Design, Copehagen, Denmark, 44; RI Sch Design, hon DFA, 84. *Work:* Boston Mus Fine Arts; RI Sch Design; Renwick Gallery; Smithsonian Inst. *Comn:* Furniture, Libr & Assembly Hall, Rochester Inst Technol, NY, 52; designed & mass produced motel furniture, Howard Johnson's & Trreadway Inn motel chains, 56; furniture, Design Dept, Men's Dormitory & Mus Art, RI Sch Design, Providence, 63, 64, 67 & 69; design & execution, Cross & Altar, Lutheran Church, Rochester, NY, 68, altar, Baptist Church, Lincoln, RI, 73, cross, Episcopal Church, Mitchell, SDak, 74 & Wickford, RI, 75; display unit design, Main Showroom, Hallmark Cards, New York, 70. *Pos:* Various Cabinet Shops in Denmark, 34-36; designer & cabinetmaker, Govt Denmark, 36-46; interior designer, Reykjavik, Iceland, 46-48; partner, Donovan & Frid, a design & woodworking firm specializing in interiors & handmade furniture, 50-58; co-founder & owner, Shop One, 53-; co-founder, ESPAN, 65-68; consul, Mystic Seaport Mus, Conn, 69-81, Int Mint, Washington, DC, 72, new high rise, RI Hosp Trust Nat Bank, Providence, 73-74. *Teaching:* Assoc prof & dept head, Woodworking and Furniture Design, Sch Am Craftsmen, Rochester Inst Technol, NY, 48-62; prof & dept head, Woodworking and Furniture Design, RI Sch Design, Providence, 62-69, prof emer, 69-85; lectr throughout US, Can, & Alaska for several major univs, cols, art schs, craft ctrs & craft organizations. *Awards:* Fel distinguished achievement in Crafts, Am Crafts Coun, 80; Grant, Nat Endowment Arts, 90; Gov's Art Award, RI State Coun Arts, 92. *Media:* Furniture. *Publ:* Auth, Tage Frid Teaches Woodworking, Eng & Ger; contr ed, Fine Woodworking, 75- *Mailing Add:* 96 Daniel Dr North Kingstown RI 02852

FRIED, HOWARD LEE
SCULPTOR
b Cleveland, Ohio, June 14, 46. *Study:* Syracuse Univ, 64-67; San Francisco Art Inst, BFA, 68; Univ Calif, Davis, MFA, 70. *Work:* Cleveland Mus Art, Ohio; Syracuse Univ, NY; Univ Calif, Davis; Ft Worth Art Mus, Tex; San Francisco Mus Mod Art, Calif. *Comn:* Mural, Syracuse Univ, 66. *Exhib:* Looking West, Joslyn Art Mus, Omaha, Nebr, 70; The 80's, Univ Art Mus, Univ Calif, Berkeley, 70; Projection, Kunsthalle, Dusseldorf, Ger, 71 & Louisiana Mus, Denmark, 72; Documenta 5, Kassel, Ger, 72; and many others. *Teaching:* Instr sculpture, San Francisco Art Inst, 68-, chmn performance & video dept, 83- *Awards:* Augusta Hazard Award, Syracuse Univ, 66; Adeline Kent Award, San Francisco Artist's Comt, 71-72; Nat Endowment Arts Grant, 75. *Bibliog:* Grace Glueck (auth), New York: Big thump on the bass drum, Art in Am, 5-6/71; Brenda Richardson (auth), Howard Fried: Paradox of approach-avoidance, Arts Mag, 6/71; Steve Davis (auth), Howard Fried installation piece, Art Week, 3/25/72. *Publ:* Auth, Inside the harlequin, Flash Art, 71; auth, Studio relocation, Breakthroughs in Fiction, 72; auth, Cheshire cat 4, Avalanche. *Mailing Add:* 1101 Georgia St Vallejo CA 94590

FRIEDBERG, RACHEL (RAY)
PAINTER, DIRECTOR
b Brooklyn, NY, Jan 9, 29. *Study:* Art Students League, with Reginald Marsh; also with Leon Goldin & George Picken. *Work:* Newark Mus. *Exhib:* Enigmatic Image, Newark Mus, NJ, 84-85; Dunev Gallery, San Francisco, Calif, 86-92; Vered Gallery, New York, 86, 87, 88, 89 & 90; Guildhall Mus, New York, 86; Jersey City Mus, 87; Nassau Co Mus, 88; Judy Youens Gallery, Houston, Tex, 89, 90 & 91; Hal Katzen Gallery, New York, 90;

Avanti Galleries, New York, 91 & 92; Lieberman/Saul Gallery, New York, 92; Palo Alto Cult Ctr, Calif, 92. *Pos:* Dir, Edward Williams Gallery, Fairleigh Dickinson Univ, 74-, Becton Hall Gallery, 89- *Teaching:* Artist in residence, Fairleigh Dickinson Univ, 73- *Awards:* Northshore Competition First Prize, Mus Mod Art, 71; NJ Coun Arts Fel Painting, 83; First Prize, Guild Hall, 88, Mus Award, 89, 91 & 92. *Bibliog:* Vivian Raynor (auth), article, NY Times, 79, 85 & 87; Phyllis Braff (auth), article, NY Times, 86, 87, 88 & 90; Karen Lipson (auth), article, Newsday, 1/29/88 & 8/22/86; Patricia Johnson (auth), article, Houston Chronicle, 7/13/89. *Media:* Encaustic. *Publ:* Dona Meilach, (auth), Box Art Assemblage, 73; Kayliss, Sunstorm Art Mag, 11/87, 10/88; Jeremy Kramer, Hampton Mag, 8/88; Image Forecast, Nikkei Publications, Tokyo, Japan, 89. *Dealer:* Avanti Galleries 22 E 72nd St New York NY; Michael Dunev Gallery 77 Geary San Francisco Ca. *Mailing Add:* 408 W 14th St New York NY 10014

FRIEDBERG, RICHARD S
SCULPTOR, EDUCATOR
b Baltimore, Md, Aug 10, 43. *Study:* Antioch Col, BA, 65; Yale Univ, BFA & MFA(Graham Found Fel), 68. *Work:* Citicorp Bank, Chase Manhattan Bank, New York. *Comn:* Sculpture, Rutgers Univ, NJ, 70; sculpture, Mobil Corp, Va, 79. *Exhib:* Whitney Ann, 71 & Whitney Biennial, 73, Whitney Mus Am Art, New York; Munson-Williams Proctor Inst, New York, 77; Storm King Art Ctr, NY, 79; Prospect Mountain Sculpture Show, Lake George, NY, 79; Alexander Milliken Gallery, New York, 81. *Teaching:* Assoc prof fine art, Fairleigh Dickinson Univ, Rutherford, 70- *Awards:* Nat Endowment Arts Fel, 74. *Bibliog:* Ellen Schwartz (auth), Richard Friedberg, Art News, 78; Carter Ratcliff (auth), Richard Friedberg, Arts Mag, 79. *Mem:* Col Arts Asn. *Media:* Steel, Aluminum. *Mailing Add:* 62 Green St No 5 New York NY 10012

FRIEDLAENDER, BILGE
SCULPTOR, PHOTOGRAPHER
b Istanbul, Turkey. *Study:* Robert Col, Istanbul, Turkey, BA, 55; Acad Fine Arts, Istanbul, Turkey, dipl, 58; NY Univ, MA, 59. *Work:* E F Hutton, Chase Manhattan Bank, New York; Prudential Insurance Co, Boston; Houghton Libr, Harvard Univ; Newark Mus, NJ; Ministry Foreign Affairs of Turkey. *Exhib:* Drawings USA Traveling Show, Minn Mus Art, 75-76; Painting and Sculpture Today, Indianapolis Mus Art, 76; Purchase Show, 76 & Book-Objects, 77, Albright-Knox Mus; Paper as Medium, Smithsonian Inst Traveling Exhib, 78-80; Artists Books Traveling Exhib, New England Found Arts, 80; Drawings, Sculpture and Unique Books, Pa Acad Fine Arts, 81; New American Paperworks, World Print Coun, San Francisco, 82-86; Paperart-New Directions, Tex Tech Univ Mus, Lubbock, 85; Altered Sites: Fairmount Park, Philadelphia, 88; Fiber Chronicles, Moore Col Art, Philadelphia, 88; solo exhibs, Cedar Forest: Tooks and Offerings, Galeri B/M, Istanbul, Turkey, 89, Gilgamesh, Galeri Nev, Istanbul, Turkey, 89 & Illuminations for the Gilgamesh Epic, Print Club, Philadelphia, Pa, 90; Second Int Plastic Arts Istanbul Bienali, Turkey, 89; After 300 Years: A Natioanl Exhib of Handmade Paper Art, Univ Arts, Philadelphia, Pa, 90; Three Sculptors: Handmade Paper Forms, Luckenbach Mill Gallery, Bethlehem, Pa, 90. *Teaching:* Asst prof, Temple Univ, 80-81; Instr envir design, School Fine Arts, Univ PA, 83. *Awards:* Residency Grant at Pyramid Prints & Paperworks, Inc, Mid-Atlantic Arts Consortium. *Bibliog:* Allen Ellenzweig (auth), Solo show at Kornblee, Arts Mag, 4/76 & 11/77; Jane Farmer (auth), Prints and the art of the book in America, In: American Prints & Printmaking 1956-1981, 81; Marcia Moss (auth), Altered sites; Lale Filoglu (auth), Bilge Friedlaender in the Second Istanbul Biennial, Cumhuriyet, Istanbul, Turkey, 89; Margaret Irish, Bilge Friedlaender installation exhibited in the 2nd Int Istanbul Bienali, Pen in Ink, Univ Pa, 89. *Mem:* College Arts Asn. *Media:* Mixed media, installation sculpture. *Publ:* Illusr & contribr, War is a Boy Game, 81 & Amputee, 81, Esse Est Percipipress; contribr, Words, Images and Objects, self pub, 81. *Dealer:* Jessica Berwind Gallery 301 Cherry St Philadelphia PA 19106; Marsha Mateyka Gallery 2021 R St Washington DC 20009. *Mailing Add:* c/o Jessica Berwind Gallery 301 Cherry St 2nd Fl Philadelphia PA 19106

FRIEDLAND, SEYMOUR
PATRON, COLLECTOR
b New York, NY, Oct 8, 28; Can citizen. *Study:* Harvard Univ, PhD. *Pos:* Syndicated columnist, Financial Times News Serv; prof finance & econ, York Univ, Toronto, currently. *Interests:* Art as investment. *Collection:* More than 300 pieces of painting and sculpture; emphasis on native art, including American Indian, and nineteenth century Canadian watercolors. *Mailing Add:* 160 Frederick St Apt 707 Toronto ON M5A 4H9 Canada

FRIEDLANDER, LEE
PHOTOGRAPHER
b Aberdeen, Wash, July 14, 34. *Work:* Mus Mod Art, New York; Nat Gallery Can; Victoria & Albert Mus, London; Libr Congress; Nat Gallery Australia, Canberra; George Eastman House, Rochester, NY. *Exhib:* One-man exhibs, Seibu Mus, Tokyo, 87, Laurence Miller Gallery, New York, 88, Bombay Ctr Photog As An Art Form, India, 88, Seattle Art Mus, 89, Friends of Photog, San Francisco, 90, Victoria & Albert Mus, London, Eng, 91, Nudes, Mus Mod Art, New York, 91. *Awards:* MacDowell Colony Medal, 86; E Leitz Medal Excellence, 87; MacArthur Award, 90-95; MacDowell Medal, 86. *Bibliog:* Shiloh, 81 & Hirshhorn Museum Sculpture Garden, Haywire Press; Cherry Blossom Time in Japan, Gravures, Haywire Press, 86; 10 Nudes, Waywire Press, 91. *Publ:* Auth, Flowers and Trees, Haywire Press, 81; Factory Valleys, Callaway Ed, 82; Cray at Chippewa Falls, Cray Res Inc, 87; Like a One-Eyed Cat, Harry Abrahms, 89; Nudes, Jonathan Cape, London, 91. *Dealer:* Laurence Miller Gallery 138 Spring St New York NY 10012. *Mailing Add:* 44 S Mountain Rd New City NY 10956

FRIEDMAN, ALAN
SCULPTOR, DESIGNER
b Philadelphia, Pa, Sept 9, 44. *Study:* Rochester Inst Technol Sch Am Craftsman, BFA, 67; Univ Wis, Madison, MFA(sculpture), 69. *Work:* Univ Wis, Union Galleries, Madison, 69; Ind State Univ, Terre Haute, 72; Indianapolis Mus of Art, 77. *Comn:* Entrance doors (wood), St Paul's Univ Cath Church, Madison, 68; sculpture (plywood), Cunningham Mem Libr, Ind State Univ, Terre Haute, 73. *Exhib:* retrospective, Wis Directions, Milwaukee Art Ctr, 75; Indianapolis Mus Art Traveling Exhib & Mus Gallery Exhib, 75-76; New Handmade Furniture, Mus Contemp Crafts, New York, 79; Contradictions, Fendrick Gallery, DC, 79; Fine Arts Comt Visual Arts, Program of the XIII Olympic Winter Games, Lake Placid, NY, 80; Recent Art Furniture, Niagara Univ, 82; and others. *Pos:* Designer furniture, E A Roffman Co, New York, 72; A F Works, Mansfield Rd Studio, Hillsdale, New York, 78. *Teaching:* Vis asst prof art, Univ Wis, Madison, 69-70; assoc prof furniture design & sculpture, art dept, Ind State Univ, Terre Haute, 72-79; guest lectr, State Univ NY, New Paltz, 83; lectr, The Creative Process, NY Found Art Grant, Hudson River Mus, Yonkers, 89. *Awards:* Award, Indianapolis Mus Art, 75; Jurors Award, Marietta Col Crafts Nat Exhib, 75; Nat Endowment Arts Individual Fel Grant, 76-77. *Bibliog:* Thelma Newman (auth), Woodcraft, Chilton Bks, NY, 78; Nicholas Rookes (auth), Masters of Wood Sculpture, Watson-Guptill, NY, 80; Dona Meilach (auth), Woodworking, The New Wave, Crown, New York, 81. *Mem:* Am Crafts Coun. *Publ:* The Designer, NY, 80; Progressive Archit, 81; Archit Record, 81. *Mailing Add:* 61 Mansfield Rd Hillsdale NY 12529

FRIEDMAN, B H
WRITER
b New York, NY, July 27, 26. *Study:* Cornell Univ, BA, 48. *Pos:* Adv coun mem, Cornell Univ Arts Col & Herbert F Johnson Mus; trustee, Am Fedn Arts, 58-64; trustee, Whitney Mus Am Art, currently; dir, Fine Arts Work Ctr, Provincetown, Mass, 68-82. *Teaching:* Lectr Eng, Cornell Univ, 66-67. *Awards:* Fels, Coord Coun Lit Mag, 75; Nelson Algren Award, 83. *Mem:* Century Asn. *Publ:* Auth, Whispers, 72; auth, Jackson Pollock: Energy Made Visible (biog), 72; auth, Alfonso Ossorio (monogr), 73; auth, Museum, 74; auth, Almost a Life, 75; auth, Gertrude Vanderbilt Whitney (biog), 78; plus many others. *Mailing Add:* 439 E 51st St New York NY 10022

FRIEDMAN, BENNO
PHOTOGRAPHER
b New York, NY, Mar 28, 45. *Study:* Brandeis Univ, BA. *Work:* Mus Mod Art, New York; Boston Mus Fine Arts; Fogg Mus, Cambridge, Mass; George Eastman House, Rochester, NY; Vassar Col Mus, Poughkeepsie, NY; Australian Nat Gallery; Va Mus, Richmond; and the pvt collections of Belinda Rathbone, William Turnage, Frank Kolodny, Micky Ruskin & Claude Picasso. *Exhib:* 60's Continuum, George Eastman House, 72; Octave of Prayer, Mass Inst Technol, 72; Light & Lens, Hudson River Mus, 73; one-man show, Light Gallery, 73 & 75; Private Realities, Boston Mus Fine Arts, 74; Image & Surface, Visual Studies Workshop Gallery, Rochester, NY, 80; Photofusion, Pratt Manhattan Ctr Gallery, New York, 81; Contemporary Photography as Fantasy, Santa Barbara Mus Art, Calif, 82; Altered Photographs, Jane Baum Gallery, New York, 84; Photographic Alternatives, Hong Kong Arts Ctr, 84. *Teaching:* Instr, Col Art & Design, Minneapolis, Minn, 82, Sch Mus Fine Arts, Houston, 82, Smith Col, North Hampton, Mass, 83 & Anderson Ranch, Aspen, Colo, 83. *Awards:* Mass Coun Arts & Humanities; grant, Creative Artists Publ Serv, NY State. *Bibliog:* Jim Stone (ed), Darkroom Dynamics, 79; articles, Photoshow Mag, 80 & Popular Photography, 8/82. *Publ:* Contribr, Art in Am, 70 & Aspen Mag; Idea, NY Photogr, 74; plus others. *Dealer:* Charles Lowles Gallery 420 W Broadway New York NY. *Mailing Add:* RR 2, Box 44 Kellogg Rd Sheffield MA 01257

FRIEDMAN, DAN
CONCEPTUAL ARTIST, DESIGNER
b Cleveland, Ohio, July 18, 45. *Study:* Carnegie Inst Technol, Pittsburgh, BFA, 67; Hochschule Gestaltung, Ulm, Ger, 67-68; Allgemeine Gewerbeschule, Basel, Switz, 68-70. *Work:* Art Inst Chicago, Ill; Musee des Arts Decoratifs, Montreal, Can; Mus Mod Art, New York; Va Mus Fine Arts, Richmond; Gewerbemuseum, Basel, Switz. *Exhib:* The East Village Scene, Inst Contemp Art, Philadelphia, Pa, 84; Made in India, Mus Mod Art, New York, 85; New York Art Now, Laforet Mus, Tokyo, 85; Figuration Libre, Goya Mus, Custres, France, 85; Progetts D'Artista, Museo Alchimia, Milan, Italy, 86; The Modern Poster, Mus Mod Art, New York, 88; Rain of Talent, Am Craft Mus, New York, 89; Graphic Design Am, Walker Art Ctr, Minneapolis, 89. *Teaching:* Asst prof design, Yale Univ, 69-73; vis lectr, Philadelphia Col Art, 71-72; chmn design, State Univ New York Purchase, 72-75. *Bibliog:* Pierre Staudenmeyer (auth), Private Jokes, L'Atelier, Paris, 87; Deyan Sudjic (auth), A room in the life of Dan Friedman, Blueprint, London, 89; Carla Capalbo (auth), A design explosion, Vogue Decoration, 89. *Mem:* Am Inst Graphic Arts. *Publ:* Auth, A view: introductory education in typography, Visible Lang, 73; Life, style and advocacy, Am Inst Graphic Arts J, Vol 7, No 4, 90; co-ed, Artificial Nature, Deste Found, 90. *Dealer:* Gallery Neotu 162 Greene St New York NY 10012; 25 rue du Renard 75004 Paris France. *Mailing Add:* 2 Fifth Ave Suite 15 U New York NY 10011

FRIEDMAN, KEN
PAINTER, DESIGNER
b New London, Conn, Sept 19, 49. *Study:* San Francisco Stat Univ, BA, MA, 71; Grad Sch Human Behavior, US Int Univ, PhD, 76. *Work:* Mus Mod Art & Guggenheim Mus, New York; Tate Gallery, London, Eng; Henie Onstad Mus, Oslo, Norway; Mus Ludwig, Cologne, Ger. *Comn:* Omaha Flow Systems, Joslyn Art Mus, Nebr, 73; Sightings Proj, Western Mus Asn, 74-75;

The Acropolis of Tulsa, Univ Tulsa, Okla, 78; Flags Proj, Gran Pavese Found, Rotterdam, Holland, 87; Theories of Fluxus, Mudima Found, Milan, Itally, 89. *Exhib:* Fluxus & Happening, Kölnischer Kunstverien, Cologne, Ger, 70; Biennial of Paris, 71; NY Correspondence, Whitney Mus, New York, 71; Arte de Sistemas, Mus Mod Art, Buenos Aires, ARgentina, 71; Fluxus, Cranbrook Mus Art, Detroit, Mich, 81; Fluxus & Friends, Univ Iowa Mus Art, Iowa City, 87; Fluxus, Mus Mod Art, New York 89; Biennial of Venice, Italy, 90. *Awards:* Gov's Award, State of Idaho, 75; Mayor's Award, Tulsa, Okla, 78; King Olav V Fel, Am-Scandinavian Found, 88. *Dealer:* Emily Harvey Gallery 537 Broadway New York NY 10012. *Mailing Add:* c/o Emily Harvey Gallery 537 Broadway at Spring St 2nd F; New York NY 10012

FRIEDMAN, MARTIN
MUSEUM DIRECTOR
b Pittsburgh, Pa, Sept 23, 25. *Study:* Univ Pa; Univ Wash, BA, 47; Univ Calif, Los Angeles, MA, 49; Columbia Univ, 56-57; Belg-Am Found Grant, Brussels, 57-58; Univ Minn, Am Art Fel, 58-60; numerous honorary degrees, nationally & internationally. *Exhib:* Jean Dubuffet: Monuments, Simulacres, Practicables, 73; Nevelson: Wood Sculpture, 73; Naives & Visionaries, 74; Projected Images, 74; Oldenburg: Six Themes, 75; The River: Images of the Mississippi, 76; Noguchi's Imaginary Landscapes, 78; George Segal Sculptures, 78; Picasso: From the Future, Musee Picasso, Paris, 80; Hockney Paints the Stage, 83; Tokyo: Form and Spirit; Jan Dibbets, 87; Sculpture Inside Outside, 88. *Collections Arranged:* Scale and Environment: 10 Sculptors, 77. *Pos:* Fel, Brooklyn Mus, 56-57; sr cur, Walker Art Ctr, 58-60, dir, 61-; co-chmn mus panel, Nat Endowment Arts, 77-78; mem, Nat Coun Arts, 78-84. *Awards:* Ford Found Fel, 61-62; Intellectual Interchange Fel, 82. *Mem:* Am Fedn Arts; Nat Collection Fine Arts Comn; Asn Art Mus Dirs (pres, 78-79); Century Asn. *Publ:* Auth, Charles Sheeler, Watson-Guptill; Hockney Paints the Stage, Abbeville Press co-publ, 83; Tokyo: Form and Spirit, Harry N Abrams co-publ, 86; Jan Dibbets, 87 & Sculpture Inside Outside, 88, Rizzoli Int, co-publ; Sculpture Inside Outside, Rizzoli Int, co-publ, 88. *Mailing Add:* 125 E 12th St Penthouse D New York NY 10003

FRIEDMAN, MARVIN ROSS
DEALER
b Minneapolis, Minn. *Study:* Univ Miami, BA, 63, JD, 66. *Awards:* Guest cur, James Rosenquist Metrop Mus, Antoni Tapias Metrop Mus & Komar & Melamid Metrop Mus. *Bibliog:* Joan Kleinman (auth), The Art Market: Interview with Leading Dealers, Metrop Mus, 79; Tim Harris (auth), Great art dealers, Venture Mag, 9/83. *Specialty:* Major modern and contemporary pictures. *Publ:* Auth, Antoni Tapias (exhib catalog). *Mailing Add:* 2600 Douglas Rd Coral Gables FL 33134

FRIEDMAN, SABRA
PAINTER
b New York, NY. *Study:* New York Univ. *Work:* Bellevue Hospital; Islip Art Mus. *Exhib:* Primordial Elementaire, Caidoz Gallery, 83; Emblems of Imaginations, Islip Art Mus, 84; Affirmations of Life, Kenkeleba House; Chain Reaction, 55 Mercer St, 85; Queens Artists Salon, Flushing Gallery, 86; Second Ann Long Island City Open Studios, 87; Laguardia Community Col, 87. *Bibliog:* Margaret Betz (auth), New York reviews: Fourteen artists, ArtNews, 12/80. *Mailing Add:* 243 W 70 St, No 9A New York NY 10023

FRIEDMAN, SALLY CEILA
PAINTER
b New York, NY, Jan 21, 32. *Study:* Queens Col, City Univ New York, BS, 53, MA, 59; Ruskin Sch Art, Oxford Univ, England, 62-64; Art Students League, 65-70. *Work:* Mus Art & Sci, Daytona Beach, Fla; Okla Art Ctr; New Eng Ctr Contemp Art, Brooklyn, Conn; Berkshire Bank & Trust Co, Pittsfield, Mass; Mitsubishi Paper Int & Warwick, Welsh & Miller Inc, New York. *Exhib:* Works on Paper, Brooklyn Mus, 75; Butler Inst Am Art Ann, 75 & 76; Color Harmonious & Discordant, Marymount Manhattan Col, 83; Pratt Inst, 85; Donnell Libr Ctr, NY, 87 & 91; Queens Col, NY, 90; Long Island Univ, NY, 92; and others. *Pos:* Secy, Phoenix Gallery, New York, 80-81, pres, 82-83. *Teaching:* Elementary sch teacher, New York City, 85- *Awards:* Medal Hon, 75, Grumbacher Award, 80, Sara Winston Mem Prize, 82 & Erlanger-Seligson Mem Prize, 86, Nat Asn Women Artists. *Bibliog:* Art from Ports Far & Near, Art Speak, 87; Artist/teacher exhibits, Queens Tribune, 6/90; Artists stick to their guns, 6/90, Art values both the home and the exotic, 9/91 & Three solos of artists at their peak, 5/92, Art Speaks; and others. *Mem:* Nat Asn Women Artists; Women's Caucus Art; Art Students League. *Media:* Oil. *Publ:* Contribr, Art Now--color slides, Vol VI, No 3 & 4, 78. *Dealer:* Stone Hill Gallery Egremont MA; Dumont Landis Princeton NJ. *Mailing Add:* 160 Riverside Dr Apt 14A New York NY 10024

FRIEND, PATRICIA M
PAINTER
b Philadelphia, Pa, May 4, 31. *Study:* Goucher Col, BA, 54; Am Univ, MFA, 75; studied with Laura G Douglas. *Work:* Deke Perrerea Int Bank, New York; Fed Reserve Bank Richmond, Baltimore; Arent, Fox, Kintner, Plotkin & Kahn Col, Washington, DC; Squires, Sanders & Dempsey Col, Washington; C&P Tele Co, Exec Off, Arlington. *Comn:* Large oil painting, exec lobby, Am Physical Therapist Asn, Alexandria, 83; painting for advertising, Nat Security Bank, Washington, DC, 86; Delta Airlines. *Exhib:* One-woman shows, Emerson Gallery, McLean, Va, 67, Plum Gallery, Kensington, Md, 80, 82, 84 & 86 & Franz Bader Gallery, Washington, DC, 86, 89 & 91; Landscape in Art, Int Monetary Fund, Washington, 81; Painting: A Decade, Art Place, Rockville, Md, 90. *Pos:* Corresponding secy, Washington Soc Artists, 70-71; art in embassies prog, State Dept, 78-88; reproduction of work for 1991 calendar, Women Art. *Teaching:* Kensington Workshop (teacher & co-founder), 77-; Mt Vernon Col, Washington DC, 79-83; Pvt instr, currently. *Mem:* Wash Soc Artists (corp secy, 70-71); Artists Equity. *Dealer:* Franz Bader Gallery 1701 Pennsylvania Ave NW Washington DC 20006. *Mailing Add:* 7206 45th St Chevy Chase MD 20815

FRIESE, NANCY MARLENE
PRINTMAKER, PAINTER
b Fargo, NDak, Sept 1, 48. *Study:* Yale Univ Summer Sch Music & Art, with Louis Finkelstein Fel, summer, 76; Art Acad Cincinnati, studied with Stewart Goldman, April Foster, Diploma of Art, 77; Univ Calif, Berkeley, studied with Sylvia Lark, One Year Grad Sch, 77-78; Yale Univ Sch Art, studied with Gabor Peterdi, Gretna Campbell, MFA, 80. *Work:* NDak Mus Art, Grand Forks; Grunwald Ctr Graphic Arts, Univ Calif, Los Angeles; William Benton Mus Art, Storrs, Conn; Yale Univ Gallery Art, New Haven. *Exhib:* Painterly Landscape, Jersey City Mus, NJ, 81; Contemporary American Monoprints, Chrysler Mus Art, Norfolk, 85; National Drawing Exhibition, Everson Mus Art, Syracuse, 86; New York State Artists: Prints & Process, Herbert Johnson Mus Art, Ithaca, 87; Vision and Tradition, Morris Mus, Morristown, NJ, 87; Recent Work, NDak Mus Art, Grand Forks, 89-90; Cast Light: Acknowldeging the Shadow, Washington State Univ Mus, Pullman, 92; American Art in Miniature, Gilcrease Mus, Tulsa, 92; Tributes to the Taft, Taft Mus, Cincinnati, 92. *Pos:* Artist-in-Residence, Millay Colony for the Arts, Austerlitz, NY, 81; artist-in-residence, Artists for the Environ Found, Walpack, NJ, fall 81; artist-in-residence, Theodore Roosevelt Medora Found, NDak, summer 92. *Teaching:* Drawing, Bennington Col, VT, 80-81; asst prof, Printmaking, Univ Tulsa, 83-87; vis asst prof, Visual Art Dept, Princeton Univ, NJ, 86; head of printmaking dept assoc prof, RI Sch Design, Providence, 90- *Awards:* Visual Artists Fel/Painting, Nat Endowment Art, 91; Individual Artists Grant/Painting, Nat Endowment Arts, 87; Giverny Grant, Reader's Digest & Col Art Asn, 90. *Bibliog:* Norman Turner (auth, catalog), Painterly Landscape, Jersey City Mus, 81; Hearne Pardee (auth), Vision & Tradition, Morris Mus, Morristown, 87; Michael Jonew & Betty Collings (auth), Moving the Margin Catalog, Emily Davis Gallery, Akron, 90. *Mem:* Col Art Asn; Women's Caucus for Art; Calif Soc Printmakers; Los Angeles Soc Printmakers; Printmakers Network of Southern New England, (co-founder, 92). *Media:* Acrylic, Oil. *Publ:* Auth, The Poetic Etchings of Mary Nimmo Moran, Gilcrease Mus & Univ, Tulsa, 84; coauth, Prints of Thomas Moran, Gilcrease Mus, 86. *Dealer:* Toni Birckhead Gallery 342 W 4th St Cincinnati OH 45202. *Mailing Add:* 108 Narragansett St Cranston RI 02905-4202

FRIESZ, RAY LEE
CONCEPTUAL ARTIST, CURATOR
b Moberly, Mo, May 12, 30. *Study:* Biola Univ, 47; study under John McLaughlin (hard edge painter), 73-74. *Work:* Downey Mus Art, Calif; Laguna Beach Mus Art, Calif; Shearson Lehman Corp, Orange, Calif; Mod Mus Art, Santa Ana, Calif; Charles Whitchurch Gallery, Huntington Beach, Calif. *Comn:* Painting, comn by Dr Linus Pauling, twice Nobel Prize winner, Sierra Madre, Calif, 61; painting, comn by Mr & Mrs Jack Warner, Warner Bros, Palm Springs, Calif, 63; 70 paintings, comn by Thomas X Singer, Shearson Lehman Corp, Orange, Calif, 87. *Exhib:* New Talent Awards, Los Angeles Co Mus Art, Calif, 66; Long Beach Invitational, Long Beach Mus Art, Calif, 69; solo exhibs, Laguna Beach Mus Art, 73 & Downey Mus, Calif, 78; one-man retrospective, Biola Univ, La Mirada, Calif, 85; California Perspective, Mod Mus Art, Santa Ana, Calif, 91. *Collections Arranged:* Expressions of the Faith, Jerome Gastaldi (auth, catalog), Retrospective, Lori Zagon, Monumental Art, John Lyster & Major Works, Duncan Simcoe, Cross Contemp Artspace, 92. *Pos:* Artist & founder, Free Spirit, Costa Mesa, Calif, 74-77; founder & dir, Crosshatch, Los Angeles, 84-88; founder & cur, Cross Contemp Artspace, Capistrano Beach, Calif, 92- *Teaching:* Instr art, Southern Calif Col, Costa Mesa, 73-74. *Bibliog:* Henry Seldis (auth), Exhibition not to be missed, LA Times, 10/6/66; Dr Douglas Deaver (auth), Expressions of the faith, Visions Mag, 92; Duncan Simcoe (auth), Ray Friesz, Los Angeles Artcare, 92. *Media:* Acrylic. *Publ:* The Fine Art Index (NAm ed), Int Art Reference Inc, 92. *Dealer:* Charles Whitchurch Contemp Artists 5973 Enginger Dr Huntington Beach CA 92649. *Mailing Add:* 1046 Calle del Cerro No 240 San Clemente CA 92672

FRINTA, MOJMIR SVATOPLUK
HISTORIAN, EDUCATOR
b Prague, Czech, July 28, 22; US citizen. *Study:* Col Fine & Appl Arts, Prague; Karlova Univ, Prague, BA; Ecole des Beaux Arts, Paris, France; Ecole du Louvre, Paris; Univ Mich, MA, 53, PhD(hist art), 60. *Pos:* Sr restorer, Metrop Mus Art, New York, 55-63. *Teaching:* Prof art hist, State Univ NY, Albany, 63- *Awards:* Nat Endowment Humanities Grant, 77-78 & 82-84; Mellon Senior Fel, CASVA; Fulbright Fel Yugoslavia. *Mem:* Col Art Asn; Int Inst Conserv Art; Int Ctr Medieval Art. *Res:* Late medieval & Byzantine painting & sculpture; early Netherlandish painting; art technology. *Publ:* Auth, Master of the Gerona martyrology & Bohemian illumination, 64, auth, Investigation of the punched decoration of medieval Italian & non-Italian panel paintings, 65 & auth, The quest for a restorer's shop of beguiling invention: Restorations and forgeries in Italian panel paintings, 3/78, Art Bulletin; auth, Genius of Robert Campin, Mouton, 66; auth, The puzzling raised decoration in the paintings by Master Theodoric, Simiolus, 76. *Mailing Add:* Dept of Art State Univ NY Albany Albany NY 12222

FRITZLER, GERALD J
PAINTER
b Chicago, Ill, Aug 27, 53. *Study:* Am Acad Art, Chicago, AA(graphic art), 74, AA(fine art, scholar), 76. *Work:* Am Acad Art, Chicago; Am Western Art Collection, Peking; Rockwell Int, Pittsburgh, Pa; Pvt collection of Pres & Mrs

Reagan; Western Colo Ctr Arts, Grand Junction. *Exhib:* Art-USA Nat Exhib, Grand Junction, Colo, 87; Western Rendezvous Art, Helena, Mont, 87-90; Midwest Watercolor Soc Exhib, Greenbay, 88-90; Northwest Rendezvous Show, Park City, Utah, 92; Colo Watercolor Soc, Colo Hist Mus, 92. *Teaching:* Instr outdoor painting wkshp & figure painting, Western Colo Ctr Arts, 83-92; Jackson Hole Acad Art, 90; Western State Col, Gunnison, Colo, 90. *Awards:* Strathmore Paper Award, Watercolor Soc, 86; Colo Watermedia Award, Colo Watercolor Soc, 92. *Bibliog:* Gerald J Fritzler (auth), Preserving the Quality of Light, Am Artist, 1/90; Walter Gray & Dan Blanchard (auth), Gerald Fritzer, Southwest Art, 6/91; Peggy & Harold Samuels (auth), Contemporary Western Artists; and others. *Mem:* Colo Watercolor Soc; Rocky Mountain Nat Watermedia Soc; Nat Watercolor Soc; Midwest Watercolor Soc; Northwest Rendezvous Group. *Media:* Watercolor, Oil. *Dealer:* Grapevine Gallery Oklahoma City OK; Total Arts Gallery Taos NM. *Mailing Add:* PO Box 253 Mesa CO 81643

FROMAN, ANN
SCULPTOR
b New York, NY, Apr 7, 42. *Study:* Fashion Inst Technol, NY, AA, 61; Palace of Fontainebleau Sch Fine Art, France, cert, 61; Nat Acad Sch Fine Art, New York; Art Students League. *Work:* Congregation Emanu-El of New York; Butler Mus Art, Youngstown, Ohio; Richmond Libr, Wichita, Kans; Brooklyn Col, NY; Time Warner Inc, New York. *Comn:* Queen Esther (bronze), Temple Israel, Wilkes Barre, Pa, 79; Women of the Bible (bronze), Temple DeHirsch Sinai, Seattle, Washington, 80; Swirl (bronze), Bankers Trust Co & Footwear Asn of New York, 82; Holy Family, St Raphael Church, Livingston, NJ, 83; American Bounty (bronze), Culinary Inst Am, Hyde Park, NY, 83. *Exhib:* New York Artists, Brooklyn Mus, 71; one-woman shows, Berkshire Mus, Pittsfield, Mass, 77, Col Misericordia, Dallas, Pa, Bennington Mus, Vt, 81 & Judaica Mus, Phoenix, Ariz, 82; US Customs Mus, New York, 80; and others. *Awards:* Mortimer C Ritter Award, Fashion Inst Technol, 71; Watson Guptill Award, Nat Art Club, 76; First Prize Sculpture, Salmagundi Club, Am Soc Contemp Artists, 80. *Bibliog:* Gerry Raker (auth), Life is cast realistically in bronze, Poughkeepsie J, 12/7/80; Joe Frisino (auth), Women of the Bible in bronze, Seattle Post, 4/17/80; Richard Lessner (auth), Bronze dance from sculptor's mind, Ariz Repub, 1/30/82; Bobby Brennon (auth), Sculptor's talent gives life to statues, Sunday Independence, Wilkes Barre, PA, 6/5/88; Merle English (auth), Survival, honors those who suffer under oppression, 9/27/89. *Mem:* Am Soc Contemp Artists; Artists Equity Asn. *Media:* Bronze, Acrylic. *Dealer:* Froman Studios Anson Rd Stanfordville NY 12581. *Mailing Add:* S Anson Rd Box 173 RR 2 Stanfordville NY 12581

FROMBOLUTI, IONA
PAINTER
b New York, NY. *Study:* Boston Univ, Tanglewood, 71; Skowhegan Sch Painting & Sculpture, 72; Tyler Col Fine Art, BFA, 70-74. *Work:* Bryn Mawr Col, Pa; Harnsburg State Mus, Pa. *Exhib:* One-woman shows, Gross McCleaf Gallery, Philadelphia, Pa, 84, Prince Street Gallery, New York, HUB Gallery, Moravian Col, Bethlehem, Pa, 86, 89 & 92; Still Life, Theater of the Object, WCA, Marymount Col, New York, 90; Summer Still Life, IV, Pandion Gallery, Fisher's Island, NY, 91; 2-person exhib, President's Gallery, Pratt Inst, Brooklyn, NY, 92. *Teaching:* Vis instr, Pratt Inst, 90- *Awards:* Tobelaeh Wechsler Award, Cheltenham Art Found, 83; Drawing Award, Skowhegan Sch Paint & Sculpture, 73. *Bibliog:* Olga Zafferatos (auth), Painting the Still Life, Watson & Guptill, 85; William P Scott (auth), Iona Fromboluti, Am Artist, 86; Victoria Donnhoe, Philadelphia Inquirer, 88. *Media:* Oil. *Dealer:* Jane Haslem 2025 Hillyer Place Washington DC. *Mailing Add:* 43 Gr Jones St New York NY 10012

FROMBOLUTI, SIDEO
PAINTER
b Philadelphia, Pa, Oct 3, 20. *Study:* Tyler Col Fine Art, Philadelphia, Pa. *Work:* Philadelphia Mus Art, Pa; Mus Art, Carnegie Inst, Pittsburgh, Pa; The Nelson Rockefeller Collection; Corcoran Gallery, Washington, DC; Allentown Mus, PA; Allegheny Col Mus, Pa; Southern Ill Univ; Ciba-Geigy Corp, Ardsley, NY; First Nat Bank, Chicago; Boston Mutual Life Insurance Co, Mass Hyatt Hotel, NY; Fidelity Bank, Philadelphia, Pa. *Exhib:* Solo exhibs, Galerie Darthea Speyer, Paris, 70-74, Landmark Gallery, New York, 73, 75, 78, 80 & 82, Brownson Art Gallery, Purchase, NY, 83, Gross McCleaf Gallery, Philadelphia, 83, Maurice M Pine Libr, Fairlawn, NJ, 84 & Ingber Gallery, New York, 87; Visual R&D Corp Collections, Univ Tex, Austin, 73; Works by Women, Kresge Art Ctr, Mich State Univ, Lansing, 74; Art on Paper, Weatherspoon Gallery, Greensboro, NC, 75; Butler Inst Am Art, Youngstown, Ohio, 78; A Gray Day, Longpoint Gallery, Provincetown, Mass, 82; Images and Imagery, Pace Univ Art Gallery, New York, 84; Woman Artists, Paris, France, 84; Knowing what I like, John Myers, Kouros Gallery, New York, 87; Jerald Melberg Gallery, Charlotte, NC, 87; and others. *Awards:* Drawing Award, Acad Design Juried Exhib, New York, 84. *Bibliog:* Sandler (auth), article, Aujourd'hui; Oeri (auth), article, Quadrum; Kingsley (auth), article, Art Int. *Mem:* Century Club, New York. *Media:* Oil on Canvas. *Dealer:* Barbara Ingber Gallery 415 West Broadway New York NY 10012. *Mailing Add:* c/o American Scene Gallery 1463 Main St Sarasota FL 34236

FROMENTIN, CHRISTINE ANNE
PAINTER, GRAPHIC ARTIST
b New York, NY July 6, 53. *Study:* Elmira Col, NY, BFA, 75; New York Univ, MFA, 77, studied figurative painting with John Kacere, realism with Don Eddie & Idelle Webber. *Work:* Gelmart Indust, New York; Cole of Calif, Los Angeles; and many pvt collections. *Comn:* Paintings, Essilor Co Inc, Joinville, France, Gellis & Mellinger Inc, New York, Prisma-Sun Bow, Inc, Los Angeles & Logo-Paris, Inc, Novato, Calif, World Market Equities, Inc, New York. *Exhib:* Washington Square Galleries, New York, 77; Gallerie Liliane Francois, Paris, 79; Martin Molinary Galleries, New York, 82; Gallerie Jean Pierre Lavignes, Paris, 83; Yve Arman Gallery, New York, 84; Vered Gallery, East Hampton, NY, 85; De Marigny Gallery, New York, 86. *Pos:* Illusr, Joseph Bruck Artist's Rep, 84-85 & Joseph Mendola Inc, 85-86, New York; graphic designer, The Gap, New York, 89-90, Wathne Ltd, 90-91 & Polo Ralph Lauren, 91-92. *Awards:* Hample Ctr Scholar Prize, Contemp Paintings Exhib, Arnot Art Mus, 75. *Bibliog:* Josette Malèze (auth), Christine Fromentin: The myth of women, Paris-Scope, Le Matin & Vital Mag, Paris, 83; Toni Canger (auth), Christine Fromentin, NJ Art Forum, 82. *Media:* Oil on Linen. *Publ:* Illusr, Lee Iacocca, Time Mag, Switch, Signet Bks, Allesandro, Bantam Bks, 85, Dark Side, Berkley Bks & Point of Purchase, Smirnoff Liquors, 86. *Mailing Add:* 395 Broadway No 15A New York NY 10013

FRONTZ, LESLIE
PAINTER
b Cleveland, Ohio, Aug 23, 50. *Study:* Southern Ore State Col, BS(art), 81; Univ NC-Greensboro, MFA(studio arts), 86. *Exhib:* Adirondacks at Exhib Am Watercolors, Community Arts Ctr, Old Forge, NY, 86-87; Highlands Small Painting Nat Exhib, Ky Highlands Mus, Ashland, 87; Arts for the Parks, Wort Hotel, traveling show to Smithsonian, Jackson, Wyo, 87; Uncommon Ground, Loveland Mus Gallery, Colo, 90; Art on Paper 1992, MFA Gallery Circle, Annapolis, Md. *Teaching:* Instr oil painting, Davidson Co Community Col, Lexington, NC, 86-87; adj fac art hist, Front Range Community Col, Fort Collins, Colo, 89-90; instr drawing, 2-d design & art appreciation, Wash State Community Col, Marietta, Ohio, 91-92. *Awards:* Painting Competition Finalist, Artist's Mag, 91; Award Excellence, Watercolor Ohio, 92. *Bibliog:* Shelly Fling (auth), Private showings: Leslie Frontz, US Art, 12/89. *Mem:* Elected mem Ohio Watercolor Soc; elected mem Nat Asn Women Artists; Oil Painters Am. *Media:* Oils, Watercolor. *Dealer:* Compton Art Gallery 409 W Fisher St Greensboro NC 27401. *Mailing Add:* R R 1 Box 326 A Richmond OH 43944

FROST, STUART HOMER
EDUCATOR, PAINTER
b Arendtsville, Pa, Nov 22, 25. *Study:* Pa State Univ, BA; Brooklyn Mus Sch; Skowhegan Sch Painting & Sculpture. *Work:* Pa Acad Fine Arts, Philadelphia; Butler Art Inst, Youngstown, Ohio; Dulin Gallery Art, Knoxville, Tenn; Mus Art, Pa State Univ, University Park; Mansfield State Col, Pa. *Exhib:* Am Watercolors, Drawings & Prints, Metrop Mus Art, 62; Recent Drawings USA, Mus Mod Art, 64; Watercolor USA, 66; Butler Art Inst Mid-Yr Show, 75; 9th Dulin Nat Print & Drawing Competition, 75; Drawings from Four Decades, Stuart Frost Babcock Galleries, 88. *Teaching:* Emer prof art, Pa State Univ, University Park, currently. *Media:* Pen, Ink. *Dealer:* Babcock Galleries 725 Fifth Ave New York NY. *Mailing Add:* 139 E Hubler Rd State College PA 16801

FRUDAKIS, ANTHONY P
SCULPTOR
b Bellows Falls, Vt, July 30, 53. *Study:* Pa Acad Fine Arts, cert, 75. *Work:* Brookgreen Gardens Mus, SC. *Comn:* Summer (male & female runners), Tropicana Hotel & Casino, Atlantic City, NJ, 86; Otter Fountain (lifesize cold cast bronze), Bally Hotel & Casino, Atlantic City, NJ, 86; Mother & child (cold cast bronze), Atlantic City Day Nursery, Atlantic City, NJ, 88; Justice (bas relief), Cape May Ct House, NJ, 89; Dr Charles Drew (bust), Drew Ct, Atlantic City, NJ, 89; Jonah (monument), Ocean City Cult Ctr, NJ, 90. *Exhib:* Nat Sculpture Soc, New York, 76-89; Brookgreen Gardens Mus, SC, 83; Accent Gallery, Northfield, NJ, 88; Aaron's Gallery, Indianapolis, Ind, 88; Philadelphia Sketch Club, Pa, 88; Image of Women in Art, Renaissance Gallery, Philadelphia, Pa, 88; Corporate Art, Trammel & Crow, Philadelphia, Pa, 89; Five Artists, Gloucester Co Col, Deptford, NJ, 89; and others. *Teaching:* Instr sculpture, Frudakis Acad Fine Arts, Philadelphia, Pa, 74-77, Stockton State Col, Pomona, NJ, 77 & Fashion Inst Technol, New York, 81-82. *Awards:* Best Portrait, Lantz Award, 78 & 88, Gold Medal, 82, Gloria Medal, 83 & L Miselman Prize, 86, Nat Sculpture Soc, New York; First Prize for Sculpture, NJ State Art Show, 79; M B Hexter Award, Allied Artists Am, 82. *Mem:* Nat Sculpture Soc, New York; Assoc mem, Nat Acad Design. *Mailing Add:* 26 Westwood St Hillsdale MI 49242-1529

FRUDAKIS, EVANGELOS WILLIAM
SCULPTOR, INSTRUCTOR
b Rains, Utah, May 13, 21. *Study:* Greenwich Workshop, New York, 35-39; Beaux Arts Inst Design, New York, 40-41; Pa Acad Fine Arts, Cresson, Scheidt & Tiffany Scholar; Am Acad Rome, Italy, Prix de Rome Fel, 50-52. *Work:* Pa Acad Fine Arts, Philadelphia; Smithsonian Inst; Weizmann Inst, Israel; Nat Acad Fine Arts, New York; Airlie Found, Va; Woodmere Art Mus. *Comn:* Naiad Fountain, Philadelphia Civic Ctr, 82; The Signer, Independence Nat Hist Park, Philadelphia, 82; Icarus & Daedalus Fountain, Little Rock, Ark; Welcome Fountain, Philadelphia, Pa, 88; Minute Man, Washington, DC, 91; and others. *Exhib:* Nat Sculpture Soc Ann, 41-62; Pa Acad Fine Arts Ann, 41-62; Nat Acad Design Ann, 48-86; Philadelphia Mus Art, 59 & 62 & Twenty-three Sculptors Exhib, 72; one-man shows, Atlantic City Art Ctr, 56 & 61, Woodmere Art Mus, 57 & 62, Philadelphia Art Alliance, 58, Pa Acad Fine Arts, 62 & Briarcliff Col Mus Art, 74. *Teaching:* Instr, var art centers, NY, NJ & Pa, 41-63; instr, Nat Acad Design, Sch Fine Art, New York, 70-76, Old Church Cult Ctr, Demarest, NJ, 75-78; sr instr, Pa Acad Fine Arts, Philadelphia, 72; founder & instr, Frudakis Acad Fine Arts, Philadelphia, 76-90. *Awards:* Gold Medal, Nat Acad Design, 64, 84; Gold Medal, Nat Sculpture Soc, 72; Artists Fund Prize 75, 79 & 90; and

others. *Mem:* Fel Pa Acad Fine Arts; fel Am Acad Rome; fel Nat Sculpture Soc; academician Nat Acad Design; Allied Artists Am. *Media:* Bronze, Marble. *Res:* Statues of the Roman Forum; Michelangelo's Rondanini Pieta. *Mailing Add:* 10 S Oxford Ave Ventnor NJ 08406

FRUDAKIS, GERD HESNESS
SCULPTOR
b New York, NY, May 5, 52. *Study:* Fashion Inst Technol, New York, AA(fine arts), 75; Nat Acad Design, New York; Frudakis Acad Fine Arts, Philadelphia, Pa. *Work:* Fashion Inst Technol, New York. *Comn:* Filter Square Ram (bronze), Philadelphia, Pa, 81; Honey Bees (bronze), 82; Germinal (bronze grill), 86; Athletes (wall relief), 86; Scandinavian Relief (bronze), Ellis Island, 86. *Exhib:* Nat Sculpture Soc Ann, New York, 80, 81 & 82; Nat Acad Design Ann, New York, 80 & 81; Allied Artists Am Ann, New York, 80 & 81; Salmagundi Club, New York, 81; Shidoni Gallery, Santa Fe, NMex, 82. *Pos:* Studio asst to Evangelos Frudakis, Sculptor, 76-; adminr, Frudakis Acad, 76-90; Studio Asst to Erte, 86-89. *Teaching:* Instr sculpture & drawing, Frudakis Acad Fine Arts, Philadelphia, Pa, 76-80. *Awards:* Marguerite Hexter Prize, Allied Artists Am Ann Exhib, 80; Maurice Hexter Prize, Nat Sculpture Soc, 80; Rachel Leah Armour Prize, Allied Artists, 81. *Mem:* Allied Artists Am; Nat Sculpture Soc. *Media:* Bronze, Precious Metal. *Mailing Add:* 10 S Oxford Ave Ventnor NJ 08406

FRUDAKIS, ZENOS
SCULPTOR
b San Francisco, Calif, July 7, 51. *Study:* Pa Acad Fine Arts, Philadelphia, 73-76; Univ Pa, Philadelphia, BFA, 81, MFA, 83. *Work:* LBJ Libr, Tex, King Ctr, Philadelphia, Brookgreen Gardens, SC; two over life size bronze figures, Utsukushi-Ga-Hara Mus, Japan; Bronze portrait, Afro-Am Mus, Philadelphia. *Comn:* Portraits, Dilworth, Paxson, & Kalish, Philadelphia, 80-81; Boy & Elephant (life size fountain sculpture), Burlington Mall, NJ, 81; bronze portrait busts, Martin Luther King Jr, Samuel Evans, W Wilson Goode, Joseph E Coleman, & K Leroy Irvis, 84, Vance Henry Trimble, 86 & Douglas MacArthur, & Mr & Mrs Hillenbrand, 88; Joseph J Ruvane, Glaxo, Inc; Sir Paul Girolami, Glaxo Holdings, London, 90; Wolfhound & Wolf (life size bronze garden sculpture), pvt comn, Orlando, Fla; Maquette, Taylor, & Mathes, Atlanta; Dream to Fly (3 over life size figures), Rouse, & Assocs, NJ; Reaching & Flying (life-size bronze figures), Indianapolis Capital Ctr Plaza, 87; Coach Fritz Brennan (8 ft high bronze), Lower Merion High Sch, Philadelphia, Pa, 90. *Exhib:* Nat Sculpture Soc, 79-90; Allied Artists Am, New York, 80-81; Nat Acad Design, New York, 80, 84, 86 & 90; Pa Acad Fine Arts Fel Ann, 81; Inst Contemp Art, Philadelphia, 81-83; Rutgers Univ Fac Show, 84-86; Sculpture in the Park, Loveland, Colo, 87-88; Invited artist, Utsukushi-Ga-Hara Open Air Mus, Japan, 90. *Pos:* Mem bd dirs, Nat Sculpture Soc; mem, ed bd, Nat Sculpture Rev Mag. *Teaching:* Instr, Frudakis Acad, Philadelphia, 78-79; coadj prof sculpture & drawing, Rutgers Univ, 84-85; guest lectr anat & sculpture, Med Col Pa, Philadelphia, 86 & 87, Scottsdale Artist's Sch, Ariz, 90. *Awards:* John Spring Art Founder Award, Nat Sculpture Soc, 81, Gloria Medal, 81, Tallix Award, 82, President's Prize, 85, Silver Medal of Honor, 86; Liskin Award, Knickerbocker Artists, 85; Henry Hearing Art-in-Archit Award, 90; Hakone Open-Air Mus Award, Japan, 90. *Mem:* Fel Nat Sculpture Soc; Allied Artists Am; fel Pa Acad Fine Arts; Knickerbocker Artists; Col Art Asn Am; Am Artists Prof League. *Media:* Bronze. *Publ:* Drawing, Nat Sculpture Rev Mag, 86; The National Sculpture Society Celebrates the Figure, Dr Jean Henry, 87. *Dealer:* Cavalier Galleries Stamford CT; Portraits Inc 985 Park Ave New York NY 10028. *Mailing Add:* c/o Primarily Portraits The Studio 3 Lehman Lane Philadelphia PA 19144

FRUEH, JOANNA
CRITIC, EDUCATOR
b Chicago, Ill, Jan 18, 48. *Study:* Sarah Lawrence Col, BA, 70; Univ Chicago, MA, 71, PhD, 81. *Pos:* Dir, Artemisia Gallery & Fund, Chicago, 74-76. *Teaching:* Asst prof mod art, Oberlin Col, Ohio, 81-; asst prof contemp art & art criticism, Univ Ariz, Tucson, 83-85; assoc prof art and art hist, Univ Nev, Reno, 90- *Awards:* Susan Koppelman Award for Feminist Art Criticism: An Anthology, 89. *Bibliog:* Marla Schor (auth), Joana Frueh, High Performance, 72-73, Spring 89; Michele Rabkin (auth), Joanna Frueh, Heidi Lang, New Art Examiner, 60, 5/89; Elise LaRose (auth), Vampiric Strategies, Dialogue, 25-26, 9-10/90. *Mem:* Women's Caucus Art; Col Art Asn. *Res:* Contemporary art, with a special interest in women artists and feminist art theory. *Publ:* Auth, Chicago's emotional realists, Artforum, 78; auth, Brumas: A Rock Star's Passage to a Life Re-Vamped, Freshcut Press, 83; Has the Body Lost its Mind?, High Performance, 44-47, Summer 89; Hannah Wilke: A Retrospective, Thomas H Kochheiser (ed), Univ Mo Press, Columbia, 89; co-editor & contr, Feminist Art Criticism: An Anthology, 2nd printing, includes essay, Towards a Feminist Theory of Art Criticism, 153-165, Harper Collins, New York, 91. *Mailing Add:* 965 Gear St Reno NV 89503

FRUMKIN, ALLAN
DEALER
b Chicago, Ill, July 5, 26. *Study:* Univ Chicago. *Pos:* Dir, Frumkin/Adams Gallery, New York, 88-91, pres, currently. *Awards:* Prof Achievement Award, Alumni Asn, Univ Chicago, 81. *Mem:* Art Dealers Asn Am. *Specialty:* Contemporary American artists; 19th and 20th century drawings. *Mailing Add:* 50 W 57th St New York NY 10019

FRYBERGER, BETSY G
CURATOR
b Chicago, Ill, May 7, 35. *Study:* Bryn Mawr Col, BA, 56; Radcliffe Col, MA, 58. *Collections Arranged:* Gavarni: Prints (auth, catalog), Stanford Univ, 71, Toulouse-Lautrec: Prints and Drawings (auth, catalog), 72, Morris and Company (coauth, catalog), 75, Whistler: Themes and Variations (coauth, catalog), 78, Paul Klee: In Celebration of/50 Prints (coauth, catalog), 79 & Gwen John (coauth, catalog), 82. *Pos:* Asst cur prints & drawings, Art Inst Chicago, 60-67; cur prints & drawings, Stanford Univ Mus Art, 70- *Mem:* Print Coun Am (bd mem, 79-, vpres, 81-); Col Art Asn. *Mailing Add:* Stanford Univ Mus & Art Gallery Lomita Dr & Museum Way Stanford CA 94305

FUCHS, MARY THARSILLA
EDUCATOR, PAINTER
b Westphalia, Tex, Apr 19, 12. *Study:* Our Lady of the Lake Col, BA, 38; Columbia Univ, MA, 42; Univ Sch Handicrafts, 42; Art Inst Chicago, 45; Univ Tex, 49-51; with Buckley McGurrin, 50-54; NY Univ, 52; Pratt Graphics Ctr, 69. *Comn:* Twelve faceted glass windows, St Timothy Church, San Antonio, Tex, 71. *Exhib:* 7th & 8th Tex Gen, Witte Mus, San Antonio, 45 & 46; First Ann Tex Watercolor Soc, San Antonio, 50; San Antonio Press Club, 65. *Teaching:* Elem sch instr, St Joseph Acad, 32-37, high sch instr, 38-41; from instr to prof art, 42-86, Our Lady of the Lake Col, chmn dept, 42-72 & 76-90, prof emer, 86- *Media:* Watercolor, Oil. *Publ:* Designer, Toddler's Rosary, 54; auth, Rocky personalities, Sch Arts Mag, 3/57; Religion worksheets for beginners, Confraternity of Christian Doctrine, 62. *Mailing Add:* 411 SW 24th St San Antonio TX 78285

FUERST, SHIRLEY MILLER
SCULPTOR, PRINTMAKER
b Brooklyn, NY, June 3, 28. *Study:* Brooklyn Mus Art Sch, with Reuben Tam; Pratt Ctr Contemp Printmaking; Art Students League, with Roberto DeLamonica; Hunter Col, MFA, 71. *Work:* James A Michener Found Collection of Twentieth Century Am Art, Univ Tex, Austin; Exxon Corp, NJ; Allentown Art Mus, Pa. *Comn:* Translucent sculpture, comn by Marcia Frazier, Beverly Hills, Calif, 84. *Exhib:* Transparent/Translucent, Aljira, Newark, NJ, 87; Sculpture for a Dance Performance, St Marks Church-in-the-Bowery, NY, 87; Lite Works, The Gallery at Hastings-on-Hudson, New York, 90; Underwater Gardens, Steinhardt Conservatory Gallery, Brooklyn Botanic Garden, 90; Reef and Cloud Gardens, Broadway Windows, New York Univ, 91; and others. *Awards:* Oil Competition First Prize, Village Art Ctr, New York, 63; Merit Award with Distinction, Enjay Chem Co, NJ, 66; Eric Schwartz Graphics Award, Nat Asn Women Artists, 70. *Bibliog:* Sculpture for the Dance (videotape), Hudson River Mus, 73; John Gruen (auth), Shirley Fuerst, Soho Weekly News, 75; Conversation with an artist, Shirley Fuerst, Joy Goodman (videotape), Channel 31, 77. *Mem:* Women's Caucus for Art. *Media:* Plastic, Miscellaneous Media. *Publ:* Auth, Health hazards in art, Art Workers News, 75; videotape documentaries of women artists, 70 & Women Artists Newsletter, 76; ed, Feminism and ecology, Heresies, 80. *Mailing Add:* 266 Marlborough Rd Brooklyn NY 11226

FUHRMAN, ESTHER
SCULPTOR, JEWELER
b Pittsburgh, Pa, Feb 25, 39. *Study:* Pa State Univ, 56-57; Frick Dept Fine Arts, Univ Pittsburgh, BA, 60; also with Sabastiano Mineo & Hana Geber, New York. *Work:* Port New York Authority; World Trade Ctr, New York; Am Crafts Coun, New York; UAHC Architects Adv, New York; Deere & Co, Moline, Ill; and others. *Comn:* Gemstone & bronze memorial, Temple Sinai, Pittsburgh, 78; bronze memorial, Temple Keneseth Israel, Philadelphia, 79; pvt residential comns, New York, Philadelphia, Pittsburgh, Miami, NJ, Los Angeles, Paris, Sydney, 79-81; bronze figure, Scott Paper Co, Philadelphia, 81; and others. *Exhib:* Nat Asn Women Artists, New York; Sculptors League, New York; Equitable Life Assurance, New York; Lever House, New York; Jewelers of Am, Javits Ctr, New York; and others. *Teaching:* Lectr sculpture today, Sands Point Acad, Long Island, 71 & Kimberley Sch, NJ, 72; lectr studio secrets, Montclair Mus Art. *Bibliog:* Marilyn Goldstein (auth), Massive sculpture shapes her life, Newsday, 3/69; article, La Rev Mod, 3/72; Jewelers Circular Keystone 6/88; Modern Jeweler, 7/88; Accent Mag, 3/89; Accessories Mag, 3/4/5-89. *Mem:* Nat Asn Women Artists; Sculptors League (vpres, currently). *Media:* Bronze, Gold. *Dealer:* The Gallery 2105 Central Ave Barnegat Light NJ 08006; Lavon Art Gallery 184 Rte 9 S Freehold NJ 07728. *Mailing Add:* Riva Pointe 1022 Harbor Blvd Lincoln Harbor-Weehawken NJ 07087

FUJITA, KENJI
SCULPTOR
b New York, NY, 1955. *Study:* Bennington Col, BA. *Exhib:* Solo exhibs, Cable Gallery, New York, 85 & 86, Daniel Weinberg Gallery, Los Angeles, 87 & Jean Bernier, Athens, 89, Luhring Augustine, New York, 91 & 92; Wacoal Art Ctr, Tokyo, Japan, 85; Aldrich Mus, Ridgefield, Conn, 86; Aperto '88, Venice Biennale, 88; Schmidt/Markow Gallery 1709, St Louis, Mo, 90; Recent Acquisitions of Prints & Drawings by Contemp Artists, Brooklyn Mus, NY 92; Contemp Wood Sculpture, Brooklyn Mus, NY, 92. *Awards:* Nat Endowment Arts, 84 & 88 & 91; NY Found Arts Fel 87. *Bibliog:* Dan Cameron (auth), Kenji Fujita, Flash Art, 1-2/89; Marlena Donohue (auth), La Cienega Area, Los Angeles Times, 2/10/89; Joshua Decter (auth), Kenji Fujita, Arts, 4/92. *Mailing Add:* c/o Luhring Augustine Gallery 41 E 57th St New York NY 10022

FUKUHARA, HENRY
PAINTER, INSTRUCTOR
b Los Angeles, Calif, Apr 25, 13. *Study:* With Edgar A Whitney, 72; with Rex Brandt, 74; with Robert E Wood, 74; with Carl Molno, 76. *Work:* Heckscher Mus, Huntington, NY; Abilene Mus Fine Art, Tex; Nassau Community Col, Garden City, NY; Los Angeles Co Mus Art, Calif; Hiroshima Mod Mus Art, Japan. *Exhib:* One-man shows, Dowling Col, Oakdale, Long Island, 78 &

Friends World Col, Lloyds Neck, NY, 80; Elaine Benson Gallery, Bridgehampton, NY, 79; Nat Invitational Watercolor, Zaner Gallery, Rochester, NY, 81; Kawakami Gallery, Tokyo, Japan, 86; Setagaya Mus of Art, Tokyo, 87, 88, 89, 90, 91 & 92; and others. *Pos:* Watercolor instr, Venice High Sch, Calif, 92-93. *Teaching:* Instr painting workshops, Cutchogue, Long Island, 81-83, Mont Miniature Art Soc, 82, Islip Art Mus, NY, 82, Parrish Art Mus, Southampton, 83, Fullerton Col, Santa Monica Col & Palos Verdes Art Ctr, Calif, 88 & Yosemite Nat Park, Calif, 89 & 90. *Awards:* Purchase Award, Nassau Community Col, 76; Elise Brown Mem, Mamaroneck Art Guild, NY, 78; Best in Show Watercolor, Strathmore Paper Co, 79. *Bibliog:* Nancy Dustin Wall Moure (auth), Painting/Sculpture in Los Angeles, California 1900-1945, Los Angeles Co Mus Art; Helen A Harrison (auth), Paper is his palette for flowing colors, New York Times, 2/17/80; Frank Webb (auth), Watercolor energies, North Light, 83. *Mem:* Pittsburgh Watercolor Soc; Ala Watercolor Soc; Nat Watercolor Soc. *Media:* Watercolor, Acrylic. *Mailing Add:* 1214 Marine St Santa Monica CA 90405-5814

FUKUI, NOBU
PAINTER
b Tokyo, Japan, June 2, 42, US citizen. *Study:* Art Students League, 64-65. *Work:* Indianapolis Mus Art, Ind; Larry Aldrich Mus, Conn; Nat Mus Mod Art, Tokyo & Kyoto; Chase Manhattan Bank, New York; and others. *Exhib:* Japanese Artists in Europe & America, Nat Mus Mod Art, Tokyo, 65, 73 & 74; Painting & Sculpture Today, Indianapolis Mus Art, 70, 72 & 74; one-man shows, Daniel's Gallery, 65, Max Hutchinson Gallery, 70, 72, 73, 75 & 79 & Patricia Hamilton Gallery, 87 & 88, Marisa Del Re Gallery, New York, 89-90 & 93, Richard Green Gallery, Santa Monica, Calif, 90, Hokin Gallery, Fla, 92 & 93; Richard Greene Gallery, Santa Monica, Calif, 90; Camino Real Gallery, Fla, 91. *Bibliog:* Stuart Preston (auth), The bodybuilder: Nonobjecticity, The New York Times, 1/15/65; David Shirley (auth), Art downtown: Construction shifts, The New York Times, 1/15/72; Carter Ratcliff (auth), Notes on line, Art Am, 90. *Media:* Oil. *Dealer:* Marisa Del Re Gallery 41 East 57th St New York NY 10022. *Mailing Add:* 141 W 26th St New York NY 10001

FULLER, DIANA
ARTS COORDINATOR, CONSULTANT
b New York, NY, Jan 14, 31. *Study:* Sorbonne, art hist. *Pos:* Co-owner, Hansen Fuller Gallery, 64-77, Hansen Fuller Goldeen Gallery, 78-82, Fuller Goldeen Gallery, 82-87, Fuller Gross Gallery, 87-90; trustee, Headlands Ctr Arts, San Francisco Art Inst; co-founder, Bacva and 80 Langton St; pres, Performing Arts Workshop, formerly; founder & pres, Proj Sculpture Pub Site, 82-86; owner/dir, Creative Arts Enterprises, 90- *Specialty:* Contemporary art. *Mailing Add:* 844 Bay St San Francisco CA 94109

FULLER, EMILY RUTGERS
PAINTER
b New York, NY, Aug 9, 41. *Study:* Garland Jr Col, Boston, Mass, Assoc BD, 62; Mus Sch Fine Arts, Boston, Mass, 62-66; Tufts Univ, BS(art educ), 66; Art Students League, New York, study with Richard Mayhew, 68-69. *Work:* Mus Mod Art, Chase Manhattan Bank, New York; Aldrich Mus Contemp Art, Ridgefield, Conn; Prudential Ins Corp Am; Indianapolis Mus Art, Ind; City Bank NAm, New York; Miami Dade Pub Libr System, Fla; IBM Corp, New York; and others. *Exhib:* One-person shows 55 Mercer, New York, 72, 75, 78 & 79, Soho 20, New York, 77, Webb & Parsons, Bedford Village, NY, 77, Frank Marino Gallery, New York, 80, Cardet Gallery, Coral Gables, Fla, 81, New Materialism, Frauen Mus, Bonn, Ger, 85, Stanford Mus & Nature Ctr, Conn, 88, Maine Coast Artists, Rockport, 89, Foxhall Gallery, Washington, DC, 90 & Bergen Mus Art & Sci, Paramus, NJ, 92; Art in Transition: A Century of The Mus Sch, Mus Fine Arts, Boston, Mass, 77; Paper as Medium, Smithsonian Inst Travelling Exhib Serv, 78-79; Gifts of Drawings: European Acquisitions, American Acquisitions, Mus Mod Art, New York, 79; and other group & one-person shows. *Bibliog:* Susan Heinemann (auth), articles, Artforum, 4/75; Michael Florescu (auth), Emily Fuller, article in Arts Mag, 4/79; John Russell (auth), Art: New drawings at the Modern, New York Times, 8/10/79. *Mem:* NY Artists Equity. *Media:* Acyrlic, Pastels. *Publ:* Contribr, Emily Fuller pioneers in art, Garland Mag, Garland Jr Col, 74. *Mailing Add:* 644 Broadway New York NY 10012

FULLER, JEFFREY P
DEALER, GALLERY DIRECTOR
b Chicago, Ill, May 14, 50. *Study:* Univ Vienna, 70-71 & 73-74; Holy Cross Col, Mass, BA, 72. *Pos:* Dir, Jeffrey Fuller Fine Art, 79- *Mem:* Philadelphia Art Dealers Asn (treas, 82-83); Inst Contemp Art, Univ Pa; Philadelphia Art Alliance (bd mem, 82-); Swedish Am Hist Mus (art adv panel, 82-). *Specialty:* Twentieth century American and European art. *Mailing Add:* c/o Jeffrey Fuller Fine Art, Ltd 132 S 17 St Philadelphia PA 19103

FULLER, JOHN CHARLES
HISTORIAN, PHOTOGRAPHER
b Laconia, NH, Oct 7, 37. *Study:* Rochester Inst Technol, AAS; Syracuse Univ, AB & MA; Ohio Univ, PhD. *Work:* Eastman Kodak Co; Ohio Univ; State Univ NY, Oswego. *Exhib:* Contemp Photog Nat, Univ Nebr, Lincoln, 72; Invitational, Univ of the S, Sewanee, Tenn, 72; Two Photographers, Eckerd Col, Fla, 73 & Johnson State Col, Vt, 73; and others. *Teaching:* Teaching fel fine arts, Ohio Univ, Athens, 64-67; asst prof art, State Univ NY Col Oswego, 67-69, assoc prof, 70-80, prof, 80- *Awards:* Nat Endowment Humanities Seminars, Col Teacher Seminar, 76; Lightwork Res Grant, 85. *Bibliog:* Irving Desfor (auth), Camera News, AP Newsfeatures, 1/58; Jacob Deschin (auth), Ex-Navy Photographer, Army-Navy-Air Force Times 6/59; Ralph Miller (auth), Camera Column, NY World Telegram-Sun, 1/60. *Mem:* Col Art Asn Am; and others. *Res:* History of photography. *Publ:* Auth, An un-Victorian photograph, 70 & Atget and Man Ray in the context of surrealism, 76-77, Art J; Frederick H Evans as late Victorian, Afterimage, 76; The photo secession, Camera Work and New York, Royal Photo Soc J, 84; Seneca Ray Stoddard's photography, In: Vol II, No 3, History of Photography, 87. *Mailing Add:* Box 373 Fair Haven NY 13064

FULLER, MARY (MARY FULLER MCCHESNEY)
SCULPTOR, WRITER
b Wichita, Kans, Oct 20, 22. *Study:* Univ Calif, Berkeley, AA, 43. *Work:* Andrew Hill High Sch, San Jose, Calif; Children's Sculpture Garden, Community Ctr, Salinas, Calif; San Francisco Art Comn; Petaluma Pub Libr; San Francisco Gen Hosp; and others. *Comn:* Cushing Lions, Squaw Valley, 83; Earth, Air, Sea, San Francisco Art Comn, 86 & Los Angeles State Off Bldg, 87; Broadway Plaza, Walnut Creek, Calif, 92; Calabi-Whisenand Totem, Sebastopol, Calif, 92; Shakti, Pac Sch Healing Arts, Gualala, Calif, 92. *Exhib:* San Francisco Mus Art, 47-50 & 60; Gump's Gallery, San Francisco, 65; Calif State Univ, Sonoma, at Cotati, 71; Santa Rosa City Hall, Calif, 74 & 86; Fremont, Calif, 80; Lafayette, Calif, 82; Portland, Ore, 88; Carmel, Calif, 88. *Collections Arranged:* Period of Exploration (with catalog), Oakland Mus, 73. *Pos:* Researcher, Arch Am Art, 64-65; staff writer, Currant Mag, San Francisco, 75-76. *Awards:* First Prize Ceramic Sculpture, Pac Coast Ceramic Ann, 47 & 49; Merit Award, San Francisco Art Festival, 71; Nat Endowment Arts art critic grant, 75; and others. *Media:* Miscellaneous. *Publ:* Auth, articles in Art Digest, 54, Artforum, 62, 63, 70 & 71, Art in Am, 63 & 64 & Craft Horizons, 73, 76, 77 & 78; A Period of Exploration, 73. *Mailing Add:* 2955 Sonoma Mountain Rd Petaluma CA 94952

FULLER, SUE
SCULPTOR, PRINTMAKER
b Pittsburgh, Pa. *Study:* Carnegie Inst Technol, BA, 36; Columbia Univ Teachers Col, MA, 39; and with Hans Hofmann, S W Hayter & Josef Albers. *Work:* Metrop Mus Art & Whitney Mus Am Art, New York; Nat Collection Fine Arts, Smithsonian Inst, Washington, DC; Tate Gallery, London; Guggenheim Mus, New York; plus others. *Comn:* String Composition 52, comn by M Greef for bd rm, Com Investment 200; String Composition T-250, Emerson Crocker Mem for Gail Borden Pub Libr, Elgin, Ill, 72; String Composition T252, All Souls Unitarian Church, New York, 79; String Construction No 253, McNay Art Inst, San Antonio, 83. *Exhib:* First Biennial Sao Paulo, Brazil, 50; Abstract Art in America, Mus Mod Art, New York, 51; Edward Root Collection, Metrop Mus Art, New York, 53; Plastics USA, US Info Agency traveling exhib, USSR, 61; Responsive Eye, Mus Mod Art, New York, 65. *Teaching:* Instr mobile design, Mus Mod Art, New York, 45-47; guest artist, Univ Ga, 51-52; instr art, Columbia Univ Teachers Col, 52 & 58; instr two-dimensional design, Pratt Inst, 65-66. *Awards:* Carnegie Mellon Univ Alumni Merit Award, 74; Women's Caucus Art Hon Award, 86; Honoree, First Women Sculptors Conf, Cincinnatti, Ohio, 87. *Bibliog:* Rosalind Browne (auth), Sue Fuller: Threading transparency, Art Int, 1/20/72; David Shirey (auth), Esthetic magic of geometry, New York Times, 4/23/78; Harry A Broadd (auth), The String Constructions of Sue Fuller, Arts & Activities, 4/82. *Mem:* Soc Am Graphic Artists (vpres Soc Am Etchers, 46-51); Artists Equity Asn New York (vpres, 52-53); Sculptor's Guild. *Media:* Plastic, String. *Publ:* Auth, Mary Cassatt's use of soft-ground etching, Mag Art, 2/50; 20th century cat's cradle, Craft Horizons, 4/54; dir, String Composition (film), NY State Coun Arts, 70; co-dir (with film maker Maurice Amar), String Composition (video), 74. *Mailing Add:* PO Box 1580 Southampton NY 11968

FULLERTON, MARY See Faulconer, Mary (Fullerton)

FULTON, FRED FRANKLIN
PAINTER, HISTORIAN
b Leslie, Idaho, Sept 27, 20. *Study:* Univ Fla; Mt San Antonio Col; spec study with Manuelito Leal, Guanajuato, Mex. *Work:* State Capitol & Cult Inst, Chihuahua, Mex; City Hall, Juarez, Mex; Pub Libr Juarez, Mex; Mex Consul, Del Rio, Tex; Univ Guanajuato, Mex. *Comn:* Oil mural, Mexican Consul, Del Rio, Tex. *Exhib:* Cult Inst, Chihuahua, 72 & Mexicali, Mex, 74; Univ Guanajuato, 73; Museo Arte & Hist, Juarez, Mex. *Pos:* Critic, Univ Mexicali & Univ Guanajuato, Mex; rep, Us Cult Exchange to Mex, 73-74; mem bd dirs, Soc Am Military Engrs. *Teaching:* Pvt studio, San Miguel, NMex & El Paso, Tex. *Mem:* El Paso Tex Art Asn; Conserv, Exploration, Diving, Archeol, Mus Int. *Media:* All. *Res:* Coronado's expedition; Spanish in New Mexico 1600-1800. *Mailing Add:* 5121 Harlan Dr El Paso TX 79924

FULTON, HAMISH
CONCEPTUAL ARTIST
b London, Eng, 1946. *Study:* Hammersmith Col Art, London; St Martin's Sch Art, London; Royal Col Art, London. *Work:* Mus Mod Art, New York; Tate Gallery, London; Stedelijk Mus, Amsterdam; Van Abbemuseum, Eindhoven. *Exhib:* Solo exhibs, Stedelijk Mus, Amsterdam, 73, Kunst Mus, Basel, 75, Cent d'Art Contemp, Geneva, 78 & Gallery Beauborg, Cent Georges Pompidou, Paris, 81; ARS, 83, Helsinki, 83; As of Now, Walker Art Gallery, Liverpool, Eng, 83-84; A Contemporary Focus 74-84, Hirshhorn Mus, Washington, DC, 84; Second Nature, Common Ground, London, 85; Retrospective 1975-1985, Stedelijk Van Abbemuseum, Eindhoven & traveling, Europe, 85; The Real Picture, Queens Mus, NY, 86; and many others. *Bibliog:* Michael Auping (auth), Moral landscape, Art in Am, 2/83; Earthworks & beyond, Abbeville Press, 84; Robert Morgan (auth), The residue of vision, Arts Mag, 3/86. *Media:* Photography. *Publ:* Photogr, Nepal 1975, Van Abbemuseum, Eindhoven, 77; Roads and Paths, Schirmer Mosel, Munich; Twilight Horizons, CAPC, Bordeaux, France, 83; Coast to Coast Walks, Coracle, London, 85. *Mailing Add:* c/o John Weber Gallery 142 Greene Street New York NY 10012

FULTON, JACK E
PHOTOGRAPHER, EDUCATOR
b San Francisco, Calif, June 30, 39. *Work:* San Francisco Mus Mod Art, Calif; Bibliotech Nat, Paris, France; Oakland Mus, Calif. *Exhib:* 2 Saunters, Summer & Winter, Port Photog Fest, 89; Halsted Gallery West, San Francisco, Calif, 91; Suite Nevada, Nev Hist Soc, Las Vegas, 91. *Awards:* Art Fel, 80 & 92 & Publ Fel, 2 Saunters: Summer & Winter, 86, Nat Endowment Arts; Residency Award, Nev State Coun Arts, 91. *Mem:* Soc Photog Educ (Western regional conf coordr), 89; Friends Photog. *Mailing Add:* 109 Orange St San Rafael CA 94901

FUMAGALLI, BARBARA MERRILL
PRINTMAKER, PAINTER
b Kirkwood, Mo, Mar 15, 26. *Study:* Univ Iowa, Iowa City, BFA, 48, MFA, 50, with Mauricio Lasansky; Univ NMex, 80-81, with Garo Antreasian, John Sommers & Jim Kraft. *Work:* Mus of Mod Art, New York; Nelson A Rockefeller Collection, New York; Univ Ill, Urbana; Univ Iowa, Iowa City; Hamline Univ, St Paul, Minn; St John's Univ, Collegeville, Minn. *Exhib:* Walker Art Ctr, Minneapolis, Minn, 49, 56 & 63; Young Am Printmakers, Mus Mod Art, New York, 53; solo exhibs, Tweed Gallery, Univ Minn, 65 & 82, Concordia Col, Moorhead, Minn, 65, Suzanne Kohn Gallery, St Paul, 67, Hamline Univ, St Paul, 69 & 84, Paine Art Ctr & Arboretum, Oshkosh, Wis, 73 & St John's Univ, Minn, 84; Smithsonian Inst, traveling exhib, 66-68; NW Printmakers, Seattle Art Mus, Washington, 66-69; Drawing on Dance, Avery Fisher Hall, Lincoln Ctr, New York, 82; Univ Art Gallery, Baylor Univ, Waco, Tex, 90; Shore Art Gallery, Abilene Christian Univ, Abilene, Tex, 91; Multnomah County Libr, Portland, Ore, 91. *Teaching:* Instr, Univ Wis, Stout, 79 & 81. *Awards:* Post Facto Prize, City Art Mus, St Louis, Mo, 47; Purchase Prize, Univ Ill, 54; Best in Show, Arrowhead Art Exhib, 63. *Bibliog:* Donald M Anderson (auth), Elements of Design, Holt, Rinehart & Winston, 61. *Media:* Engraving, Serigraphy; Oil, Watercolor. *Publ:* Illusr, Swing Around the Sun, Lerner Publ, 65. *Mailing Add:* Rte 4 Box 282A Menomonie WI 54751

FUNDORA, THOMAS
PAINTER
b Havana, Cuba, March 7, 35; US citizen. *Study:* Candler Col (art), 58, Escuela San Alejandro (oil painting), 59, Wash Sch Art (drawing & oil), 61, Escuela de Arte Bologna (restoration), 65, Sch Art, Bologna, Italy (art restoration), 65. *Work:* Mama Leone's Art Gallery, New York; Spanish Pavillion, New York World's Fair; Record World Art Collection, New York; J Cayre Art Exhib, New York; Coleccion Arte Latinoamericano, Rio de Janeiro, Brazil. *Comn:* Gran Canal, Venice, Mama Leone's Restaurant, New York, 68; Plaza Catedral de La Habana, Ital Art Gallery, Miami, Fla, 90; Jose Marti, Fundacion Cubanoamericana, Miami, Fla, 90; Balseros, Garces Com Col, Miami, Fla, 91. *Exhib:* Bienal Latinoamericana, Instituto Arte Latino, Washington, DC, 68; Los 10 Grandes, Instituto de Puerto Rico, New York, 69; Bienal de Sao Paulo, Arte Latinoamericano, Brazil, 71; Int Art Exhib, Int Art Gallery, Miami, Fla, 89; European & Latin Masters, Martin's Art Gallery, Coral Gables, Fla, 90. *Awards:* Int Grand Prize, Mama Leone's Art Show, 66; Painter Year, Carteles Mag, 67; Second Prize, CCIA Art Show, 69. *Bibliog:* Don Galaor (auth), Fundora Pinta Milagros, Diario Las Americas, 10/65; Ramon Cotta (auth), Obra Pintor Cubano en NY, El Imparcial, Puerto Rico, 5/66; Efrain Hidalgo (auth), Cristo se Movio, Diario La Prensa, 11/68. *Mem:* Asn Pintores Latinoamericanos, NY; Circulo Pintores de Miami; Thomas Fund Art Ctr, Coral Gables. *Media:* Watercolor, Oil. *Mailing Add:* c/o Fundora Art Gallery 2771 Coral Way Miami FL 33145

FUNK, CHARLOTTE M
TAPESTRY ARTIST, WEAVER
b Milwaukee, Wis, Sept 27, 34. *Study:* Univ Wis-Whitewater, BS, 71; Ill State Univ, Normal, MS, 75, MFA, 76. *Comn:* Passage to the Sea: Land, Sand & Sea, Corpus Christi Nat Bank, Tex, 81; Wind in the West, Lubbock Munic Bldg, 86. *Exhib:* Seventh Int Biennial Tapestry, Lausanne, Switz, 76; Clay, Fiber, Metal--Women Artists, Bronx Mus Arts, New York, 78; Contemporary Tapestry, Pratt Inst, New York, 80-81; Fiber Structure Nat, 87; Nine in Texas, Houston, 89; Chicago Textile Arts Ctr, 90; solo show, Hueser Art Ctr, Bradley Univ, 90. *Teaching:* Instr textiles, Tex Tech Univ, Lubbock, 78-; instr, Arrowmont Sch Arts & Crafts, 81-88. *Awards:* Judges' Choice Award, Contemp Crafts Americas, Handweavers Guild Am, 75. *Bibliog:* article, Interweave Mag, winter 80-81; article, Hanowoven Mag, 11-12/85; Geometric Design in Weaving, Regensteiner, 86; Art Space, 1-2/90. *Mem:* Am Craftsmens Coun; Handweavers Guild Am. *Media:* Wool. *Mailing Add:* 2312 58th St Lubbock TX 79412

FUNK, ROBERT NORRIS
EDUCATOR, ADMINISTRATOR
b Yakima, Wash, Nov 10, 30. *Study:* Univ Ore, BA, 52, LLB, 55; Stanford Univ, PhD, 67. *Pos:* Pres, Cornish Col Arts, 85- *Mailing Add:* Cornish College of the Arts 710 E Roy St Seattle WA 98102

FUNK, ROGER L
EDUCATOR, DESIGNER
b White Hall, Ill, Sept 2, 34. *Study:* Univ Ill, BFA, 57; Syracuse Univ, MID(indust design), 64. *Pos:* Designer, Gen Elec Co, 57-63; pres, Midwest Design Inc, 81-86; pres, Funk & Assocs Design, Inc, 86- *Teaching:* Prof design, Mich State Univ, 65-81, 89-; prof & chmn dept design, Kansas City Art Inst, 81-86; dir, Sch design, Univ Cincinnati, 86-89. *Mem:* Indust Designers Soc Am (chmn educators comt, 84-86); Inter-Soc Color Coun. *Mailing Add:* 843 Lantern Hill Dr Lansing MI 48823

FUNK, VERNE J
CERAMIST, SCULPTOR
b Milwaukee, Wis, July 19, 32. *Study:* Univ Wis-Milwaukee, BS, MS & MFA. *Work:* Milwaukee Art Ctr; Mus Contemp Crafts, New York; Lannon Found, Palm Beach, Fla; Columbus Gallery Fine Arts, Ohio; Ariz State Univ, Tempe; and others. *Exhib:* Objects: USA; Clayworks, 20 Americans, Mus Contemp Crafts, New York, 71; solo exhibs, The Dance, W Tex Mus, 86; The Figure in Clay, Craft Alliance, 91 & Steppin' Out, Canton Art Inst, 92; Ceramics Now-1989, Downey Mus, Calif; Third Ceramic Nat Invitational, Canton Art Inst, 89. *Pos:* Pres, Wis Designer-Craftsmen, 64-66; chmn, Visual Arts II, Wis Arts Found & Coun, 67. *Teaching:* Instr, Carthage Col, 66-69 & Univ Wis-Whitewater, 69-73; guest artist ceramics, Calif State Univ, Fresno, 72; prof ceramics & dir art sch, Bradley Univ, Peoria, Ill, 73-77; assoc prof ceramics, Tex Tech Univ, Lubbock, 77-81 & prof, 81- *Bibliog:* Donald Key (auth), Prominent Wisconsin potters, Milwaukee J, 71; Elizabeth Sasser (auth), Verne Funk: The dance, Ceramics Mo, 1/87; Gene Kleinsmith (auth), Clay's the Way, Victor Valley Press, 2nd Ed, 88. *Mem:* Am Craftsmen's Coun; Tex Sculpture Symp. *Media:* Clay. *Publ:* Contribr, Hard Core Crafts; The Container Book; New Ceramics; History of American Ceramics: the Studio Potter; Objects: USA; and others. *Mailing Add:* 2312 58th St Lubbock TX 79412

FURMAN, (DR & MRS) ARTHUR F
COLLECTORS, PATRONS
Dr Furman, b Scranton, Pa; Mrs Furman, b Hazleton, Pa. *Study:* Dr Furman, Temple Univ, DMD; Mrs Furman, Pa State Univ, BA. *Pos:* Trustees, Furman Family Trust; pres & vpres, Found Visual Arts. *Interests:* Arranging and exhibiting items from collection in various institutions, museums, galleries and schools. *Collection:* American contemporary masters painting and sculpture; ancient Thai, Cambodian and Indian bronzes; Chinese incense burners, Oriental artifacts. *Mailing Add:* 12308 Loch Carron Circle Ft Washington MD 20744

FURMAN, DAVID STEPHEN
SCULPTOR, EDUCATOR
b Seattle, Wash, Aug 15, 45. *Study:* Univ Ore, BA(ceramics), 69; Univ Wash, MFA(ceramics & glassblowing), 72. *Work:* Univ Puget Sound Mus Art; Security Pac Nat Bank; Los Angeles Co Mus Art; Oakland Mus Art; Fulbright Comn, Lima, Peru; Marietta Col Art Mus; US Embassy, Lima, Peru; and others. *Exhib:* Clay (ceramic sculpture), Whitney Mus, 74; one-man shows, David Stuart Galleries, 74-75, Univ Ore, Eugene, Jacqueline Anhalt Gallery, Los Angeles, Tortue Gallery, Santa Monica, Elaine Horwitch Gallery, Santa Fe, 89, OK Harris Works of Art, New York, 90 & Margulies Taplin Gallery, Miami, 90; Small Scale in Contemporary Art, Chicago Art Inst, 75; Hard and Clear, Los Angeles Co Art Mus, 75; Seattle Art Mus; M H De Young Mem Mus; Everson Mus Art, 90; Taft Mus, Cincinnati, 90; Ctr Contemp Art, Santa Fe, 90. *Teaching:* Prof sculpture, Claremont Grad Sch, Pitzer Col, 73-, prof art & head, Studio Arts Prog; instr clay sculpture, Otis Art Inst, 75-; lectr, Univ Utah, Boston Univ, Ind State Univ, Univ Ga, Univ Washington, Univ Calif, Los Angeles & Irvine. *Awards:* Fac Dev Fel, Pitzer Col, 81-83; Craftsman's Fel, Nat Endowment for Arts, 75 & Interdisciplinary Fel, 86-87; Fulbright Fel, Peru, 79-80 & Fulbright Sr Artist Fel, Costa Rica, 90. *Bibliog:* C H Hertel (auth), David Furman-Biographical Narrative Sculpture, 74; W C Hunt (auth), David Furman-miniature environments, Ceramics Monthly, 1/75; article in Am Ceramics, 8/2/90. *Mem:* World Crafts Coun; Am Crafts Coun; Nat Coun Educ Ceramic Arts; Artists Equity. *Media:* Clay, Glaze. *Dealer:* Tortue Gallery Santa Monica CA. *Mailing Add:* Pitzer Col Art Dept 1150 Mills Ave Claremont CA 91711

FURR, JIM
PAINTER, PRINTMAKER
b Camden, Tenn, Aug 14, 39. *Study:* Univ Tenn, BFA; Tulane Univ, MFA; Tamarind Inst Lithography. *Work:* Montgomery Mus Fine Arts, Ala; Equitable Life Assurance Soc US, Bank Am Corp; Kans State Univ, Lawrence; R J Reynolds Corp; IBM Corp; and others. *Comn:* Colony Sq Hotel Corp, Atlanta, 78; Loew's Anatole Hotel Corp, Dallas, 79; Cannon Chapel, Emory Univ, Atlanta, 81; Marriott Marquis, Atlanta, 87. *Exhib:* Drawings, Mint Mus Art, NC, 79; one-person show, Tex A&I Univ, Kingsville, 74 & Montgomery Mus Fine Arts, 81; Southeast Seven IV, Southeastern Ctr Contemp Art, 81; Continuum III, Dulin Gallery Art, Knoxville, Tenn, 81; Red Clay Survey: Southeastern Biennial, Huntsville Mus, Ala, 90; Southern Abstraction: Contemp Arts Ctr, Raleigh, NC & traveling, 89; and many others. *Teaching:* Sabbatical replacement printmaking, Tulane Univ, New Orleans, La, 73-74; vis artist printmaking, Tex A&I Univ, Kingsville, 74-75; prof painting & drawing, Auburn Univ, Ala, 77- *Awards:* Southeastern Ctr Contemp Art/Nat Endowment Arts Grant, 80; Nat Endowment Arts Individual Artists Fel Grant, 81; Special Merit Award, Southeastern Exhib, Spartanburg, SC, 82. *Bibliog:* Mark Price (auth), Jim Furr, Artpapers, 3-4/81; Norman Pendergraft (auth), Southeastern Seven at SECCA, Art Voices, 7-8/81. *Media:* Oil; Charcoal, Oilstick. *Dealer:* Heath Gallery 416 E Paces Ferry Rd Atlanta GA 30305. *Mailing Add:* Dept Art Auburn Univ Auburn AL 36849

FUSCO, LAURIE S
HISTORIAN, EDUCATOR
b Boston, Mass, Oct 31, 41. *Study:* Wellesley Col, Mass, with John McAndrew & Curtis Shell, BA(art hist), 63; NY Univ Inst Fine Arts, with Colin Eisler, Ludwig Heydenreich, Craig Smyth, Richard Krautheimer & Charles Sterling, MA & PhD(art hist), 77. *Pos:* Sr lectr & head scholarly progs; J P Gerry Mus, 78- *Awards:* Fulbright-Hays Grant, 72-73; Samuel H Kress Res Grant, 74-75; Harvard Fel, Villa I Tatti, 83. *Mem:* Col Art Asn Am;

Art Historians of Southern Calif (secy-treas, 79-80). *Res:* Study of anatomy and movement by fifteenth century Italian artists; New documents for Lorenzo de Medici as a collector of antiquities. *Publ:* Auth, Antonio Pollaiuolo's use of the antique, J Courtauld & Warburg Inst, Vol 42, 257-263; auth, The use of sculptural models by painters in fifteenth century Italy, Art Bulletin, Vol 65, 175-194; auth, An unpublished Fra Filippo Lippi, J Paul Getty Mus J, vol 10, 1-16; auth, Pollaiuolo's Battle of the Nudes, In: M Natale, Scritti di storia dell'arte in onore di Federico Zeri, Vol 1, 196g, Milan, 84. *Mailing Add:* J Paul Getty Mus PO Box 2112 Santa Monica CA 90406

FUSCO, PETER RICHARD
CURATOR, HISTORIAN
b Englewood, NJ, Apr 24, 45. *Study:* Williams Col, BA, 67; NY Univ, MA, 71; Altingham Sch of Decorative Arts, 82. *Collections Arranged:* European Bronzes, 78; The Romantics to Rodin, French Nineteenth Century Sculpture (coauth, catalog), Los Angeles, 80. *Pos:* Cur Europ sculpture, Los Angeles Co Mus Art, 75-80, cur decorative arts & Europ sculpture, 81-84; cur, sculpture & works of art, J Paul Getty Mus, 84- *Teaching:* Instr baroque, Univ Southern Calif, 77. *Awards:* Chester Dale Fel, Metrop Mus Art, 70-72; David E Finley Fel, Nat Gallery Art, 72-75; Nat Endowment Arts Fel, 83. *Mem:* Decorative Arts Soc; Furniture Hist Soc. *Res:* European sculpture, Renaissance through the 19th century. *Publ:* Auth, L S Adam's bust of Neptune, 75, Falguiere, The Female Nude & La Resistance, 77, Los Angeles Co Mus Bull; Early eighteenth century sculpture in Rome, Art J, Vol 39, No 1, 79; The Romantics to Rodin: French Nineteenth Century Sculpture, 80; Annibale Fontana, Anthologia di belle arte, 84; handbook, Los Angeles Co Mus, 87. *Mailing Add:* J Paul Getty Mus PO Box 2112 Santa Monica CA 90406

FUSCO, YOLANDA
PAINTER, PRINTMAKER
b Benkovce, Czech, Oct 24, 22; US citizen. *Study:* Art Students League of New York, 40-45; Pratt Inst, Brooklyn, NY; studied with Ernest Fiene, Vaclao Vytlaci & Harry Sternberg. *Work:* Michael Waldorf Asn, Los Angeles, Calif; Donald Commors Asn, Duxbury, Mass; many private and corp collections. *Comn:* Portrait, comn Nassau County New York, 81; many portraits comn of various individuals. *Exhib:* Group shows, Columbia Univ, New York, 65, Heckscher Mus, Huntington, NY, 76; Farleigh Dickenson Univ, NJ, 80; Audubon Artist Nat, Nat Arts Club, New York, 81; Traveling watercolor exhib, Buller Inst of Am Art, Youngstown, OH, 82; one-woman shows, Daytona Art League Gallery, Daytona Beach, Fla, 92 & Adelbi Univ, New York, 91. *Pos:* dir, Washington County Mus. *Teaching:* Pvt art teacher, Adult Ed, 60-87. *Awards:* Sadie & Max Tesser Award, Audubon Artists, Nat Arts Club, New York, 81; R W Rall Award, Daytona Beach, Fla, 90. *Mem:* Nat Asn Women Artists; New York Artists Equity; Life mem, Art Students League; Monhegan Artists; Art League of Daytona Beach, Fla. *Media:* Watercolor, Oil; Lithography. *Publ:* Prize Winning Watercolors, Allied Publ, 62. *Mailing Add:* 48 Alden Ave Valley Stream NY 11580

FUSSINER, HOWARD
PAINTER
b New York, NY, May 25, 23. *Study:* Am Peoples Sch, 38-42; Art Students League, 46-47; Cooper Union, 47-49; Hans Hofmann Sch, 48; NY Univ, 49-52. *Work:* Everhart Mus, Scranton, Pa; Staten Island Inst Mus, New York; Slater Mus, Norwich, Conn; Mattatuck Mus, Waterbury, Conn; Hobart & William Smith Cols, Geneva, NY. *Comn:* Mural, NY Univ, 51-52. *Exhib:* Pa Acad Fine Arts Biennial, Philadelphia, 62; Boston Arts Festival, 63; Am Acad & Inst Arts & Lett Art Awards Show, 84; one-man show, Georgetown Univ, Washington DC, 88; Retrospective, Slater Mus, Norwich, Conn, 91; and others. *Teaching:* Instr humanities, Morehouse Col, 52-55; instr art, Colby Jr Col, 58-60; prof art, Southern Conn State Univ, 60-88, prof emer. *Awards:* Best in Show, New Haven Arts Festival, 64, Hartford Plaza 7, 64, Waterbury Arts Festival, 68 & Conn Artists, Slater Mus, 77. *Bibliog:* John Sell Cotman (auth), A modernist before hist time, Conn Rev, summer 90. *Media:* Oil, Watercolor. *Publ:* Auth, Organic integration in Cezanne's painting, summer 56 & Use of subject matter in recent art, spring 61, Art J. *Dealer:* Munson Gallery 33 Whitney Ave New Haven CT 06510. *Mailing Add:* 1 Everit St New Haven CT 06511

FYFE, JO SUZANNE (STORCH)
PAINTER, SCULPTOR
b Omak, Wash, May 8, 41. *Study:* Wash State Univ, BA(fine arts), 64, MFA, 68; Whitworth Col, Spokane, Wash & Eastern Wash State Univ, Cheney, grad studies. *Work:* Mt Vernon Sch Dist, Wash; Oak Harbor Sch Dist, Wash; Cashmere High Sch, Wash; Wash State Univ, Pullman; Gt Northwestern Bank, Spokane. *Comn:* Triptych-painting/mixed-media, Wash State Arts Comn, Cashmere, 84; sculpture, Spokane Art Comn, Spokane Fire House, 90. *Exhib:* 54th Annual, Seattle Art Mus Pavilion, 68; Gallery 76, Wenatchee, Wash, 76; 2nd Annual Women's Art, Ore State Univ, Corvallis, 79; Women in Art, Eastern Wash State Univ Art Gallery, Cheney, Wash, 81; Juried Show, Carnegie Art Ctr, Walla Walla, Wash, 83; Works on Paper, The Art Gallery, Longview, Wash, 86; Works of Heart, Cheney Cowles Mus, Spokane, Wash, 86-90; Western Art Show, Ellensburg & Spokane, Wash, 86-88; Works on Paper, Evergreen State Col, 87-89; Past Presence, A Circle of Women's Vision, Corvallis, Ore, 87; Art on the Green, Coeur D'Alene, Ind, 90; Art Walk, Sand Point, Ind, 90. *Teaching:* Part-time instr design, Wash State Univ Exten, Spokane, 64-72; instr art, design, & sculpture, Spokane Falls Community Col, 65-, chmn dept, 75-84, 88- *Awards:* Best of Show, Bicentennial Traveling Exhib, Allied Arts Ctr, 76; 1st Prize, acrylic, Clarkson Valley Ann, Lewis & Clark Art Asn, 81; Painting Award, Art on the Green, 90. *Bibliog:* Dodie Murphy Wagner (auth), Painting and sculpture said good combination, Pullman Herald, 83; other newspaper articles. *Mem:* Nat Computer Graphics Asn; Wash Community Col Humanities Asn, Cheney Cowles Mus, Spokane, Wash; Mus Native Am Cultures (bd oper comt). *Media:* Acrylic; Mixed Media, Wood. *Dealer:* Nica Art Gallery NE 125 Olson Pullman WA 99163; Holbrook Gallery Lewiston IN. *Mailing Add:* S 8017 Ramona Rd Spokane WA 99204

G

GABE, RON See Partz, Felix (Ron Gabe)

GABELER-BROOKS, JO
PAINTER
b Baton Rouge, La, Feb 14, 31. *Study:* Stephens Col, with John Pike, Ray Ellis, Fred Messersmith, Dong Kingman, Tony van Hasselt, Tom Hill, Millard Wells, Miles Batt, Al Brouillette, & Christopher Schink. *Work:* Elliott Mus, Stuart, Fla; Moody Found & Rosenberg Libr, Galveston, Tex; Transco Energy Co, Houston; Allied Bank of Seabrook, Tex. *Comn:* Nine Watercolors, Lily Pulitzer, Palm Beach, Fla, 65; Commemorative plaque, Corps Diplomatic, Vientiane, Laos, 68; Christmas cards, Am Womens Club, Vientiane, Laos, 68-71; Lao Silk Pavilion, Mme Tao Peng Sananakone, Vientiane, Laos, 70; watercolor, City of Galveston, 82, presented to City of Nigata, Japan. *Exhib:* Group shows with Florida Watercolor Society: Mus Arts & Sci, Daytona, 78, Brevard Art Ctr & Mus, Melbourne, 81, State Capitol, Tallahassee, 82 & Boca Raton Mus Art, 84; Watercolor Art Soc, Houston Pub Libr, 81; Galveston Art League, Rosenberg Libr, 83; Prof Artists Guild, Boca Raton Mus Art, 84-86; one-woman shows, Elliott Mus, Stuart, Fla, 86 & Scarborough House, Savannah, Ga, 88. *Awards:* President's Award, Fla Watercolor Soc, 81 & 82; Purchase Award, Galveston Art League, 82; Merit Award, Watercolor Art Soc Houston, 82 & Fla Watercolor Soc, 86. *Bibliog:* Eileen B Flaum (auth), Watercolorist-Jo Gabeler, Focus, 3/86. *Mem:* Salmagundi Club, New York; Fla Watercolor Soc; Galveston Art League (pres, 81-82); Prof Artists Guild; Landings Art Asn (pres 90). *Media:* Watercolor. *Dealer:* Red Piano Gallery Hilton Head Island SC. *Mailing Add:* 23 Delegal Road Savannah GA 31411-2616

GABIN, GEORGE JOSEPH
PAINTER, INSTRUCTOR
b Brooklyn, NY, Apr 16, 31. *Study:* Brooklyn Mus Art Sch; Art Students League, with Reginald Marsh, Ivan Olinsky & Will Barnett. *Work:* Bank Boston, Mass; Tenn Botanical Garden & Fine Arts Ctr, Cheekwood; Grunwald Ctr Graphic Arts, Los Angeles, Calif; Jane Voorhees Zimmerli Art Mus, New Brunswick, NJ; Brush Art Gallery, Canton, NY; and others. *Exhib:* Nat Acad Design, Allied Artists Am & Audubon Artists, 60-91; one man shows, Carl Seimbab Gallery, 63 & 67, Guild Boston Artists, 72, Doll & Richards Gallery, 75, Montserrat Col Art, 83, Edna Stebbins Gallery, Cambridge, Mass, 86, Pingree Sch, Hamilton, Mass, 90 & Chase Gallery, Boston, Mass, 91; Am Fedn Arts Nat Traveling Show, 64-65; Albright Mus, Buffalo, NY, 66; Wisteriahurst Mus, Holyoke, Mass, 83; Montserrat Col Art, Beverly, Mass, 90. *Teaching:* Instr illus & drawing, New Eng Sch Art, Boston, 63-70; instr drawing & painting, Montserrat Col Art, 70-, assoc prof, co-chmn, dept painting & drawing, founding fac; landscape painting, La Scoula del Verde, Trieste, Italy, 89- *Awards:* Grumbacher Gold Award, Holyoke Art Coun, 81; Stow Wengenroth Awart, Rockport Art Asn, 82; Ralph Fabri Medal Merit, Allied Artist Am, 83; and others. *Mem:* Allied Artists Am; Guild Boston Artists; Rockport Art Asn. *Media:* Oil. *Mailing Add:* Studio B554 One Fitchburg St Somerville MA 02143

GABLE, JOHN OGLESBY
PAINTER
b Frankfort, Ky, Mar 7, 44. *Study:* Univ Ky; Art Ctr Col Design, BS(indust design), 66. *Work:* Oxford Univ; Union Mutual; Charles S Payson collection; Wesleyan Univ; Bank New Eng. *Comn:* Watercolors, comn by Alan Bond, Australia, 83, Boston Classical Orch, 83, Dennis Conner, 87, Oxford Univ, 89, Northeastern Univ, 89. *Exhib:* 46th Nat Ann, Butler Inst Am Art, 82; 161st Ann Exhib, Nat Acad Design, New York, 86 & 88; Coe Kerr Gallery, New York, 82; one-man shows, Payson-Weisberg Gallery, New York, 83 & Barridoff Galleries, Portland, Maine; Portland Mus Art, Maine; Forum Gallery, New York, 86. *Awards:* Wurdemann Prize, Nat Watercolor Soc; William A Paton Prize, Nat Acad Design, NY; Artist Mag Award, Am Watercolor Soc. *Bibliog:* Alexander Bridge (auth), article, Am Artist, 83; Philip Isaacson (auth), article, Maine Sunday Telegram, 83. *Mem:* Nat Watercolor Soc. *Media:* Watercolor, Oil. *Dealer:* Barridoff Galleries 26 Free St Portland ME 04101; Forum Gallery 1018 Madison Ave New York NY. *Mailing Add:* 12 Oak Bluff Rd Kennebunkport ME 04043-1508

GABLIK, SUZI
PAINTER, WRITER
b New York, NY, Sept 26, 34. *Study:* Black Mountain Col, NC, summer 51; Hunter Col, BA, 55, with Robert Motherwell. *Exhib:* Solo exhibs, Alan Gallery, New York, 63 & 66, Landau-Alan Gallery, New York, 67, Henri Gallery, Washington, DC, 71, Terry Dintenfass, 72 & 78 & Hester Van Royen Gallery, London, 78; Photographic Image, Guggenheim Mus, New York, 66; Young & Fantastic, Inst Contemp Arts, London, 69; After Surrealism: Metaphor & Simile, Ringling Mus Art, Sarasota, Fla, 72; Women Choose Women, NY Cult Art Cts, 73; Menagerie, Mus Mod Art Lending Serv, 75. *Pos:* Vis artist & lectr, Univ Colo, Syracuse Univ, Yale Univ, Univ Wis, Boston Col, San Francisco Art Inst, Oberlin Col, Bard Col & Md Inst Art, 74-75.

Teaching: Vis prof fine arts, Univ South, Sewanee, Tenn, fall, 82 & 84, Univ Calif, Santa Barbara, spring, 85, 86 & 88, Va Tech, Blacksburg, fall, 89 & spring, 90. *Bibliog:* London Correspondent, article in Art in Am. *Mem:* Int Asn Art Critics. *Media:* Miscellaneous Media. *Publ:* Coauth, Pop Art Redefined, 69 & auth, Magritte, 70, New York Graphic Soc; auth, Progress in Art, Rizzoli, 77; Has Modernism Failed?, Thames & Hudson, 84; The Reenchantment of Art, Thames & Hudson, 91. *Dealer:* Terry Dintenfass Inc 50 W 57th St New York NY 10022. *Mailing Add:* 3271 Deer Run Rd Blacksburg VA 24060

GABRIEL, HANNELORE
GOLDSMITH
Study: Apprentice under Master Goldsmith-Essen, Ger, 4 yrs; Gewerblicke Unterrichtsanstalt, Essen, Ger. *Work:* Ft Lauderdale Mus of Fine Arts, Fla. *Comn:* Presentation piece, Cleveland Area Arts Coun, Ohio, 76. *Exhib:* Goldsmiths 77, Phoenix Art Mus, Ariz; Am Goldsmiths Now, Washington Univ, 78; Der Ring, Goldschmiedehaus, WGer, 78; Beaux Arts Designer Craftsmen, Columbus Mus Art, 79; Nat Invitational, Kipp Gallery, Ind Univ Pa, 87. *Pos:* Pvt classes, 74-75. *Teaching:* Instr, Oberlin Col, 75 & Penland Sch Crafts, 78- *Awards:* Horace Potter Mem Award, May Show, Cleveland Mus Art, 79; Purchase Award, Ohio Artists & Craftsmen Show, Massillon Mus Art, 80; Best of show--Metals, Oakbrook Invitational, Ill. *Bibliog:* Article, European jeweler, Ornament Mag. *Mem:* Am Crafts Coun; distinguished mem Soc NAm Goldsmiths; Ohio Designer-Craftsmen. *Res:* Traditional jewelry in the Nepalese culture area. *Publ:* Auth, articles on Himalayan jewelry in Ornament Mag; articles on Arts of Asia, Lapidary J. *Mailing Add:* 1469 Rosena Ave Madison OH 44057

GABRIELSON, WALTER OSCAR
PAINTER, SCULPTOR
b Orr, Minn, July 25, 35. *Study:* Univ Calif Los Angeles, BS, 58; Chouinard Art Inst, 61-63; Otis Art Inst, BFA, 63, MFA, 65. *Work:* Chase Manhattan Bank, New York; Crocker Bank, Los Angeles Co Mus Art, Cedars-Sinai Hosp & Capitol Group, Los Angeles; Hilton Hotel, Burbank, Calif. *Comn:* Burbank Airport Hilton Hotel, Los Angeles. *Exhib:* Newport Harbor Art Mus, Calif, 72 & 75; Six Calif Artists, Saskatoon, Sask Mus, Can, 78; Karl Bornstein Gallery, 81-82 & 84-85; Los Angeles Mus Art, 82; Car Show, Sherry Frumkin Gallery, Santa Monica, 92. *Pos:* Printer, Tamarind Lithography Workshop, 64-66; writer, Artweek, Art in Am, 74-79; vis artist, Univ Hawaii, 79, Claremont Grad Sch, 80, Wash State Univ, 84, Murray State Univ, Ky, 86; co-cur, Addictions, Santa Barbara Contemp Arts Forum, 91. *Teaching:* Asst prof, Calif State Univ, Northridge, 66-82. *Bibliog:* Article in Artnews, 4/83; article in Images & Issues, 5/6/83; article in Los Angeles Times, 12/10/83; and others. *Mem:* Los Angeles Inst Contemp Art (chmn jour comt, 74-75); Santa Barbara Contemp Arts Forum, 89-92. *Media:* Oil; Wood. *Publ:* Auth, 41 Airplanes, 70 & Pop Dawson, the Formative Years, 71, Dawson Aircraft; Why suck the mainstream if you don't live in New York, Art in Am, 1-2/74; Winged beauty, Air Progress, 11/75; The ironic Los Angeles artist, Los Angeles Inst Contemp Art J, 10-11/76; CAF Addictions Catalogue, 91. *Dealer:* Sherry Frumkin Gallery 1440 Ninth St Santa Monica CA 90401. *Mailing Add:* 375 Pine Ave #2 Goleta CA 93117

GACH, GEORGE
SCULPTURE, PAINTER
b Budapest, Hungary, Jan 27, 09; US citizen. *Study:* Hungarian Acad Fine Art, grad. *Work:* Hungarian Nat Gallery, Budapest; Nassau Community Col. *Comn:* Bas reliefs, Methodist Church, Dallas, Tex, 69-70; 24 bronze bas reliefs of Okla hist, Liberty Bank, Okla, 72. *Exhib:* Audubon Artists, Allied Artists, Nat Sculpture Soc; 30 one-man shows incl Hammer Galleries, New York, 75-77. *Teaching:* Prof Sculpture, Acad Fine Arts, Beirut, Lebanon, 47-52. *Awards:* Gold Medals, Hudson Valley Art Asn, NY, 59, Art League Long Island, NY, 62 & 67, Nat Sculpture Soc, NY, 70 & Nat Art League, NY, 77; L Bennet Award, 73 & Percival Deitsch Award, 74, Nat Sculpture Soc, NY; Silver Medal, Audubon Artist, New York, 83; and many others. *Mem:* Allied Artists Am; fel, Nat Sculpture Soc; Nat Art League; Hudson Valley Art Asn; Nassau Art League. *Media:* Bronze, Wood; Oil. *Dealer:* Jewel Spiegel Gallery Englewood ND; Vail Fine Art Gallery Vail CO. *Mailing Add:* 212 Willow Roslyn Heights NY 11577

GAGE, FRANCES M
SCULPTOR
b Windsor, Ont, Aug 22, 24. *Study:* Ont Col Art; Art Students League; Ecole Beaux-Arts, Paris, Royal Soc Can scholar. *Work:* Univ Western Ont Med Sch; Womens Col Hosp, Toronto; Univ Ottawa; McMaster Univ; Queens Univ, Ont. *Comn:* Fountain, Albright Gardens, London, Ont; figure & reliefs, Prov Inst Trades Bldg, London, Ont; memorial, Charles Lake Gundy, Mt Pleasant Cemetery, Toronto; Elmer Iseler, Roy Thompson Hall, Toronto; protrait head, Col Sam, R S McLaughlin, Royal Col Physicians & Surgeons Inst, Ottawa, Ont, 92; and others. *Exhib:* Royal Can Acad Art; Sculptors Soc Can; Ont Soc Art; FIDEM Exhib, Florence, Italy, 83, Colo, 86, Helsinki, 90 & London, 92. *Mem:* Royal Can Acad Art; Arts & Lett Club Can. *Mailing Add:* 60 Birch Ave Toronto ON M4V 1C8 Canada

GAGNIER, BRUCE
PAINTER, SCULPTOR
b Williamstown, Mass, Dec 18, 41. *Study:* Skowhegan with Isabel Bishop, Nicolas Carone, Peter Agostine & John Heliker. *Exhib:* Leslie Cecil Gallery, New York 86 & 88; Aspects of the Figure, Gaumann Cichinno Gallery, Ft Lauderdale, Fla, 89; M13 Gallery, New York, 92. *Pos:* Dean, NY Studio Sch, 79-87; chmn, Parsons MFA Prog, 90- *Media:* Oil; Clay. *Mailing Add:* 921 Fairview Lake Rd Newton NJ 07860

GAGNON, CHARLES
PAINTER, PHOTOGRAPHER
b Montreal, Que, May 23, 34. *Study:* Parsons Sch Design, 56-57; NY Univ, 57; New York Sch Design, 57-59. *Work:* Nat Gallery Can, Ottawa; Hirshhorn Mus, Smithsonian Inst, Washington, DC; Montreal Mus Fine Arts, Musee D'Art Contemp, Que; Art Gallery Ont, Toronto. *Comn:* Lester B Pearson Mem, Closed Competition, Can Government, Ottawa, Ont, 74-75. *Exhib:* 14 Canadians, Hirshhorn Mus, Smithsonian Inst, Washington, DC, 77; one-man shows, Montreal Mus Fine Arts, Que, 78, Nat Gallery Can, Ottawa, Ont, 79 & Art Gallery, Ont, Toronto, 80; Nat Award, Banff Ctr Arts, Alta, 81. *Teaching:* Assoc prof photog, Concordia Univ, Montreal, Que, 67-75; prof visual arts, Univ Ottawa, Ont, 75- *Bibliog:* Philip Fry (auth), Charles Gagnon, Montreal Mus Fine Arts, 78; Dore Ashton (auth), Charles Gagnon's point of view, Artscanada, 8-9/79; David Burnett (auth), Charles Gagnon--The Ambiguous Object, Vanguard & Vancouver Art Gallery, 79. *Media:* Oil. *Mailing Add:* Dept Visual Art Univ Ottawa Ottawa ON K1N 6N5 Canada

GAGNON, CHARLES EUGENE
SCULPTOR, CONSULTANT
b Minneapolis, Minn, Feb 24, 34. *Study:* Univ Minn, AA, 56, BS, 58 & MEd, 60; Minneapolis Sch Art, 59; with Berthold Schiwetz, Florence, Italy, 64-65; Jacques Lipchitz, 68. *Work:* numerous public and private collections throughout the US, Can, Japan, S Am, UK & Europe. *Comn:* Hubert H Humphrey (life size portrait), New Govt Ctr, Worthington, Minn, 79; Saint Francis and the Birds (heroic size sculpture), Vatican Collection, Rome Italy, 84; Vatican Collection, Rome, Italy, 84; 12 ft Peace Fountain, Rochester, Minn, 89; Emergence of Life, Chicago, Ill, 92; & others. *Exhib:* Nat Acad Galleries, New York, 62; Nat Arts Club, New York, 62; Walker Art Ctr Biennial, Minneapolis, 62; Minneapolis Art Inst, 63. *Teaching:* Instr sculpture, Univ Minn, Rochester, 72. *Awards:* One of ten students from US chosen to teach art in Europe, Univ Minn, 57-58; Purchase Award & Two-Man Show Award, Madison Ave Art Gallery, New York, 62; Mayor's Gold Medal Honor, Artistic Cult Achievement, 87. *Bibliog:* Kling (auth), The Sculpture of Charles E Gagnon, Preview, Collegeville, Minn, 68; Hardie (auth), Charles E Gagnon, Mohave, Kingman, Ariz, 73; Ehrbar (auth), A Ten-year Dance to the Music of Bronze, Kenyon Col, 83. *Media:* Bronze. *Res:* Figurative bronze sculpture; Working predominantly in the field of large architectural commissions. *Publ:* Contribr, An artist fulfilled, 71; Progeny, 73; Kenyon College, Its Third Half Century, 75; An Art Tour of Saint Mary's, 75; Voice of a New Age, 76. *Mailing Add:* PO Box 4 Rochester MN 55903

GAHAGAN, JAMES (EDWARD), JR
PAINTER, EDUCATOR
b New York, NY, Sept 20, 27. *Study:* Goddard Col, Plainfield, Vt, BA, 51; Hans Hofmann Sch Fine Art, New York, 52-58. *Work:* Provincetown Mus; Univ Calif Berkeley Mus; Metrop Mus Art, New York; Chrysler Mus, Norfolk, Va. *Exhib:* Festival of Two Worlds, Spoleto, Italy, 58; 10th Street Days Co-ops of the 50's, Ward-Nasse Landmark Galleries, New York, 77; Provincetown Painters 1890-1970, Everson Mus, Syracuse, NY, 77; Days Lumberyard Studios Provincetown 1914-71, Provincetown Mus, Mass, 81-86; Tirca Karlis, Provincetown, 81-86; and others. *Pos:* Pres, Artist Tenants Asn, New York, 60-62 & 65-66; co-ed, New York Element, 68-72; bd trustees, Printmaking Workshop, New York, 70-76; artists adv comt, Vt Studio Sch, 84. *Teaching:* Instr painting & drawing, Pratt Inst, Brooklyn, NY, 64-71; instr painting, Columbia Univ Grad Sch, NY, 68-71; dir & instr painting & drawing, James Gahagan Sch Fine Art, Woodbury, Vt, 69-70; prof & chmn painting & drawing aesthetics, Goddard Col, Plainfield, Vt, 71-79; instr, Lesley Col, Cambridge, Mass, 81; instr, Vt Col, 83-; instr, Vt Studio Sch, Johnson, Vt, 84-; instr, Int Artists Colony, Dunedin, New Zealand, 91 & 92. *Awards:* Prize, Cape Cod Art Asn, Mass, 57; Longview Fund Purchase Grant, 58; Adolph & Esther Gottlieb Found Grant, 84. *Bibliog:* Irving Sandler (auth), Thirteen Americans under thirty, Art News Mag, 58; Eileen Tolchin (auth), Action when enough people try, The Villager New York, 62; Gilbert Millstien (auth), New York: True North, Doubleday, 64. *Mem:* Art Resource Assoc, Woodbury, Vt (pres, 73-75, bd trustees, 73-79); Vt Coun Arts; and others. *Media:* Oil, Tempera. *Publ:* Illusr, Loaf of Earth, Spruce Mountain Press, 58; co-ed New York Element, 68-72; contribr, J Aesthetic Educ, Univ Ill Press, Urbana, 69; VizArt, 76-80. *Dealer:* Feingarten Gallery Los Angeles CA; Hells Kitchen Provincetown MA. *Mailing Add:* RFD 1 Box 116 East Calais VT 05650

GAINES, ALAN JAY
PRINTMAKER, PUBLISHER
b New York, NY, Aug 23, 42. *Study:* NY Univ, BS, 65; New Sch, Parsons Sch Design, with John Ross, 72-74. *Work:* South Street Seaport Mus, Mus Gallery, New York; and others. *Comn:* Historic American Ship, Franklin Mint, Pa, 75; Nantucket Whalers & New Bedford Whalers, 77 & Develop of Am Transportation, 78, Collector's Guild, New York; Gloucester Schooners (etching), Bk of Month Club & 260 Club, 77; marine etchings, 77 & two railroad etchings, 78, Graphics Guild, Div of Doubleday, New York; spec series five important & hist Am ships, Am Express, 78; America's Maritime Heritage (four etchings), Franklin Mint, Pa, 81; and others. *Exhib:* One-man shows, South Street Seaport Mus, 74, Oestreicher Gallery, New York, 74, Wiseman Gallery, Newport, RI, 76, Redwood Libr & Atheneum, Newport, RI, 79 & Providence Pub Libr, RI, 81. *Bibliog:* Joseph Patrick Henry (auth), Artist of the sea, The Franklin Mint Almanac, 7/75; article, RI Mag, 9/80. *Media:* Mixed. *Mailing Add:* 40 Franklin St Newport RI 02840

GAINES, WILLIAM ROBERT
HISTORIAN, PHOTOGRAPHER
b Madison, Va, Aug 12, 27. *Study:* Pa Mil Col; Va Commonwealth Univ, BFA; Columbia Univ, MFA; and with Renato Guttuso, Italy, 56-57. *Work:* Univ Va, Charlottesville; Va Polytech Inst & State Univ, Blacksburg; Retreat for the Sick, Richmond; Philip Morris Inc; First & Merchants Nat Bank; St Mary's Hosp, Richmond. *Exhib:* Five Va Artists Biennials, 49-63; Abingdon Sq Painters, New York, 53; Va Beach Boardwalk Exhib, 58; Va Commonwealth Univ, 64; one-man exhib, Tappahannock, Va, 72. *Collections Arranged:* Art Nouveau (with catalog); Francisco Goya: Portraits in Paintings, Prints & Drawings (with catalog), 72; Sculpture by Willi Gutmann, 72; 12 American Painters (with catalog), 74. *Pos:* Registr, Va Mus, 51-53, artmobile cur, 53-54, supvr educ, 54-56, 57-62, head progs div, 62-82; dir, Inst Contemp Art Va Mus, 80-82; interim dir, Anderson Gallery, Va Commonwealth Univ, 87. *Teaching:* Instr painting, drawing & art hist, Va Mus, Richmond, 54-56, 57 & 62; dir, Gov Sch Gifted, Mus Ctr, 73; instr, painting, drawing, art history, Rappahannock Community Col, Warsaw, Va, 82-87; instr, Va Commonwealth Univ, Richmond, 78-84. *Awards:* Best in Show Awards, Va Beach Boardwalk Exhib, 58 & Thalhimers Invitational, 63; James R Short Award, SEMC, 81; Distinguished Alumnus, Va Commonwealth Univ, Richmond, 91. *Mem:* Am Asn Mus; Coun Va Mus. *Media:* Acrylic. *Publ:* Auth, Art kits, Arts Va, Vol VI, No I; auth, Virginia Museum: Two pioneer programs, Mus News, Vol 50, No 2; producer, 12 American Painters (TV), 74 & Style & Expression: Encounter I (TV), 75. *Mailing Add:* PO Box 500 Grant FL 32949-0500

GAITHER, EDMUND B
MUSEUM DIRECTOR, HISTORIAN
b Great Falls, SC, Oct 6, 44. *Study:* Morehouse Col, BA, 66; Ga State Col; Brown Univ, MA, 68. *Collections Arranged:* Afro-Am Artists: New York & Boston (with catalogue), Jamaica Art Since the Thirties, Henry O Tanner, A Romantic Realist, Home Folks Africa, For Us, Abdias Do Nascimento: A Brazilian Brother, African Gods in Brazil, Our Elders, Crite & Dames, Ah Haiti, Glimpses of Voudou, Haiti-Haiti, Bannister & Duncanson, Twentieth Century Afro-Am Artists, Mus Fine Arts, Boston. *Pos:* Dir & cur, Mus Nat Ctr Afro-Am Artists, Boston, 69-; dir visual arts prog, Elma Lewis Sch Fine Arts, Boston, 69-; spec consult, Mus Fine Arts, Boston, 69- *Teaching:* Asst prof art hist, Boston Univ, 70-78; lectr art hist, Wellesley Col & Harvard Col, 71-76. *Bibliog:* An American Collector, Mus Art, RI Sch Design, Providence, 68; Robert H Glauber (auth), Black American Artists, Ill Bell Tel Co, 71; Leo Twiggs (auth), Opinion, Mus News, 5/72. *Mem:* Nat Conf Artists; Col Art Asn; Pan-African Conf of Artists; Boston Black Artists Asn. *Res:* Historical and critical discussion of Afro-American art. *Publ:* Contribr, A new criticism needed, New York Times, 5/70; ed, Affairs of Black Artists, 71; contribr, Artists Proofs, The Annual of Prints and Printmaking, NY Graphic Soc, 72; Afro-American Art, in: Negro Reference Book, Phelps-Stokes Found, New York, NY, 73; and numerous others. *Mailing Add:* c/o Mus Nat Ctr Afro Am Artist 300 Walnut Ave Boston MA 02119

GALE, PEGGY
WRITER, CURATOR
b Mackenzie, Guyana, May 18, 44; Can citizen. *Study:* Univ Toronto, 63-67; Univ degli Studi, Florence, Italy, 65-66; Univ Toronto, BA, 67. *Pos:* Educ officer, Art Gallery of Ont, Toronto, 67-74; asst film & video officer, Can Coun, Ottawa, 74-75; video dir, Art Metropole, Toronto, 75-79, spec proj coordr, 85-87; exec dir, A Space, 79-81; contrib ed, Candadian Art (mag), Toronto; guest cur Nat Gallery, Art Gallery Ont, Toronto & other Can and Int mus. *Teaching:* Instr, Nova Scotia Col Art & Design; lectr video & performance art, var schs, mus & galleries, 75- *Awards:* Canada Coun A Grant, 83. *Mem:* Int Asn Art Critics. *Res:* Media art, specializing in performance, video, installations, thematic assessment and development of critical language, 65- *Publ:* co-ed, Performance by Artists, 79 & Museums by Artists, 83, Art Metropole; auth, Earlier Askevold, In: David Askevold (catalog), Stedelijk van Abbemuseum, Eindhoven, 81; The Problem of Description in Video, Artextes E01ditions Payant, 86; Zu Performance und Mediakunst, In: Okanada (catalog), Akad der Künste, Berlin, 82; James Coleman: Call to Mind, Parachute, summer 91. *Mailing Add:* 176 Cottingham St Toronto ON M4V 1C5 Canada

GALE, WILLIAM HENRY
PAINTER, DESIGNER
b Yonkers, NY, May 3, 15. *Study:* Columbia Univ; Art Students League; Nat Acad Design; Cooper Union; spec study with John Pike & Charles Kinghan. *Work:* Springfield Fine Arts Mus, Mass; Jasper Rand Mus, Westfield, Mass; Vt Art Ctr, Manchester; Manhattan Savings Bank, New York; AT&T, New York; and others. *Comn:* Housatonic, NY, 70; Old Vt Landmarks, New York Life Ins Co, 72; AT&T, New York; Merrill Lynch; IBM; and others. *Exhib:* Worcester Mus Fine Arts, Mass, 74-75; Allied Artists New York, 78; Butler Mus, 82; Alburquerque Mus, NMex, 92; Brea Mus, Calif, 92; and others. *Pos:* Artist-designer, Ruth Ruthrauff & Ryan, New York, 35-40; art dir-designer, Batten Barton Durstine, Osborn, New York, 40-68. *Awards:* Quimby Award, Smithsonian Inst, 69; First Awards Mass Bicentennial, Springfield Fine Arts Mus, 75; Watercolor Award, Rockport Art Asn, 83; and others. *Bibliog:* Lee Sheridan (auth), New England painter, Springfield News, Mass, 63; Watercolorists, Festival of the Arts, Vt Art Ctr, 69. *Mem:* Am Watercolor Soc; Salmagundi Club; Rockport Art Asn; Acad Artists (vpres, 73-75); Hudson Valley Art Asn. *Media:* Watercolor, Oil. *Dealer:* Grand Central Art Gallery 40 Vanderbilt Ave New York NY 10017; Ellsworth Gallery 800 Hopmeadow Simsbury CT 06070. *Mailing Add:* 14 Hunting Lane Box 156 Wilbraham MA 01095

GALEN, ELAINE
PAINTER, SCULPTOR
b New York, NY, July 12, 28. *Study:* Philadelphia Mus Sch Art, dipl, 50; Univ Pa, BA, 51; Art Students League, 55-59; NY Univ, MA, 63; major study with Morris Kantor. *Work:* Neuberger Mus, Purchase, Ny; Univ Ariz Mus, Tucson; Philadelphia Mus Art; Mus Rigaud, France; Brooklyn Mus; Eastern Ill Univ; and others. *Exhib:* Whitney Mus Am Art Ann, New York, 61; Brooklyn Mus Int, 63 & 78; NJ State Arts Coun, 70; one-person show, Pa Acad Fine Arts, Peale House, 72; State Mus Ill, 74; Art Inst Chicago, 78; The Jewish Mus, 88; Soho 20, New York, 88, 90 & 92; Chautauqua Inst, NY, 87; Rathbone Gallery, Albany, NY, 88; Neuberger Mus, Purchase, NY, 92; plus numerous solo exhibs and others. *Pos:* Consult & lectr-teacher, Developing Art Progs, NJ Schs, 68-72, lectr-instr painting & drawing, 73 & asst prof, 84- *Teaching:* Lectr hist art, painting & drawing, NY Univ, 70-73, Prairie State Col, Chicago Heights, Ill, 74-, Lake Forest Col, 78-80, Manhattanville Col, 81-88, NY, Purchase, 81-; Columbia Univ, 84-90; assoc prof drawing & design, State Univ New York, Purchase, currently. *Awards:* Nat Print Award, Hunterdon Ctr, NJ, 70; Am Iron & Steel Inst Award for Design Excellence, 72; Ieorsheim Art Fund Grant, 92. *Bibliog:* Conversation with the Artist, Channel 19, NY State Coun Arts. *Mem:* Print Club, Philadelphia (artist mem); Col Art Asn Am; Women's Caucus Art. *Media:* Oil, Multi-Media. *Dealer:* Soho 20 Gallery 469 Broome St New York NY 10013. *Mailing Add:* RFD 1, Millwood Rd Mt Kisco NY 10549

GALINSKY, NORMAN
PAINTER, GRAPHIC ARTIST
b Charleston, WVa, Jan 28, 42. *Study:* Univ Cincinnati, BS, 64; Columbia Univ, with Philip Guston , Stamos, Malcolm Morley & Jack Tworkov, MFA, 73; Art Students League, printmaking workshop with Bob Blackburn. *Work:* Columbia Univ, New York; Mobil Oil Corp, New York; Four Seasons Hotel, Washington, DC; IBM, Armonk, NY; Pepsico, Purchase, NY. *Exhib:* Solo exhibs, Truman Gallery, New York, 78 & Katonah Gallery, NY, 79; Five on Paper, Spencer Mus, Univ Kans, Lawrence, 78; Small Works, 6th Ann Juried Show, Washington Sq Gallery, NY Univ, 82; Paperworks '80, Hudson River Mus, Yonkers, NY; The Abstract Vision, Cork Gallery, Lincoln Ctr, New York, 85; Constructions, Wooden Tent Gallery, Vineyard Haven, Mass, 90. *Pos:* Bd dirs, Rockland Ctr Arts, West Nyack, NY, 84- *Awards:* Contemp Artist Prize, Paperworks 80, Hudson River Mus, 80; NY Tele Award, Mt Aramah Exhib, Arden, NY, 86. *Bibliog:* Gordon Brown (auth), rev, Arts Mag, 9/78; Martin Filler (auth), Remodeled house-remodeled lives, House & Garden, 5/80; Steve Bush (auth), Salon West 3, Artspeak, 2/16/86. *Media:* Miscellaneous. *Dealer:* Orions Editions 270 Lafayette St New York NY 10012; Katonah Gallery 28 Bedford Rd Katonah NY 10536. *Mailing Add:* Lawrence Lane Palisades NY 10964

GALLAGHER, CAROLE
PHOTOGRAPHER, WRITER
b New York, NY, July 16, 50. *Study:* New Sch, with Philippe Halsman, 73; Hunter Col, City Univ New York, with Tony Smith, Robert Morris, Doug Ohlson & Rosalind Krauss, MA, 77. *Work:* Bibliot Nat, Paris; State Mus, Pazin, Yugoslavia. *Exhib:* Douglas Huebler Retrospective, Van Abbe Mus, Eindhoven, Holland, 79; All the Time, 79 & Greenhouse, 81, Leo Castelli Gallery; Surrealist Photography, Dept Cult, Vienna, 81; First Intl Atomic Photogr Guild Exhib, NY Open Art Ctr, 87; Utah '88: Photography, Utah Mus Fine Arts, Univ Utah, 88; one-man shows, Mus Contemp Photog, Chicago, 89, Int Ctr Photog, New York, 93; Int Atomic Photog Guild Exhib: Almaata, USSR, Trau to NGBK Gallery, Berlin, Kiel & Women's Mus, Bonn, Munich, Hannover, Frankfurt, Ulm, Ger; group show, Nuclear Matters, San Francisco Camerawork, 91. *Pos:* Dir Nuclear Towns Doc Proj, Utah State Hist Soc, 85-90. *Teaching:* Instr photog, Col New Rochelle, NY, 77-78 & Kingsborough Col, City Univ New York, 77-79 & Univ Utah Commun Dept, Salt Lake City, 88; vis prof, Univ Utah Art Dept, 88-89. *Awards:* Grants, The Ruth Mott Fund, Flint, Mich, 88 & 89 & The John D & Catherine T MacArthur Found, Chicago, 88; Utah Arts Coun Award, 88; Deer Creek Found, St Louis, 87. *Bibliog:* Paul Stimson (auth), Between the signs, Art in Am, 10/79; Rene Denizot & R Barry (auths), Il Est Temps--It's About Time, Yvon Lambert, Paris, 80; Carole Gallagher at Leo Castelli, Express, fall 81; Susan Lyman (auth), Fallout: picturing the downwind survivors, The Deseret News, 2/25/87; Judy Rollins (auth), Clouds of Creation, The Salt Lake Tribune, 6/19/88. *Publ:* Illusr, Muscles, 83 & Punch, 83, Avon; Nuclear Test's Legacy of Anger: Workers See Betrayal on Peril, The New York Times, 12/14/89; American Ground Zero: The Secret Nuclear War, Cambridge: MIT Press, 93. *Dealer:* Ronald Feldman Gallery 31 Mercer St New York NY 10013. *Mailing Add:* 79 Mercer St New York NY 10012-4430

GALLAGHER, CYNTHIA
PAINTER
Study: Philadelphia Col Art, BFA, 72; Queens Col, Flushing, NY, MFA, 74. *Work:* Metrop Mus Art, New York; First Nat Bank of Chicago; Shearson-Lehman American Express, New York; also pvt collections of James & Beth Rudin DeWoody, Curt Marcus & Robin Tewes and Mary Ryan & Bruce Liebowitz. *Exhib:* 118 Landmark Gallery, New York, 78; one-woman shows, 55 Mercer St, New York, 76 & 78, Grace Borgenicht Gallery, New York, 81, Luise Ross Gallery, New York, 88, Edward Thorden Gallery, Göteborg, Sweden, 89, Charles More Gallery, Philadelphia, 90 & 91 & Mary Ryan Gallery, New York, 92; Art on Paper, Weatherspoon Mus, Greensboro, NC, 82; Screen Print Images, NY Inst Technol, Old Westbury, NY, 85; Collectors Choice, Ark Art Ctr, Little Rock, 88; Parrish Art Mus Design Biennial, Southampton, Long Island, NY, 91. *Pos:* Graphics consult, New York State CAPS. *Teaching:* Instr, Queens Col, City Univ New York, 74-89; vis critic, New York Univ, 74-75; Philadelphia Col Art, Philadelphia, Pa, 76-77; instr,

NY Inst Technol, Old Westbury, NY, 76-88; Manhattan Community Col, City Univ New York, 77-78; Yale Univ, Summer Sch of Music & Art, Norfolk, Conn, 80; vis critic, Brandeis Univ Alumni Asn, New York, 84; guest lectr, Stanford Univ Alumni Asn, 85; life drawing, two-dimensional design, Fashion Inst Technol, New York, 88. *Awards:* Creative Artists Pub Serv Prog, 81; Nat Endowment Arts, 83 & 89; New York Found Arts, 89. *Bibliog:* Articles in NY Times, 1/18/87 & Philadelphia Inquirer, 4/13/90; Mary Cummings (auth), Southampton Press, 8/29/91; Edward Sosanski (auth), On galleries, Philadelphia Inquirer, 10/31/91. *Dealer:* Solo Gallery 578 Broadway 6th Fl New York NY 10012; Charles More Gallery 1630 Walnut St Philadelphia PA. *Mailing Add:* 178 Franklin St New York NY 10013

GALLAGHER, KATHLEEN ELLEN
PRINTMAKER, PAINTER
b New York, NY, Dec 18, 49. *Study:* Marymount Manhattan Col, New York, BA, 71; Herbert H Lehman Col, Grad Sch, New York, with Arun Bose, MA, 75. *Work:* Brooklyn Mus, Mus Mod Art & Pratt Graphics Ctr, New York; DeCordova Mus, Lincoln, Mass; Philadelphia Mus Art, Pa; Portland Mus, Ore. *Comn:* Etching editions, Lyndhurst, Tarrytown, NY & Drayton Hall, Charleston, SC, Nat Trust Hist Preserv-Christie's, London & New York, 82. *Exhib:* Contemp Prints of New York, Mus City New York, 81; Prints USA, Pratt Graphics Ctr, New York, 82; Archit in Contemp Print, Pratt Graphics Ctr, New York, 83; Grunwald Ctr, Univ Calif, Los Angeles, 86; New York Inspired: Past & Present, John Szokey Gallery, New York, 88; Lynd Ward Exhib, Saga, 92. *Teaching:* Instr watercolor, Elizabeth Seton Col, Yonkers, NY, 84-88; instr printmaking & painting, Col New Rochelle, NY, 86-; vis artist watercolor & printmaking, Westchester Coun Arts, NY, 86-; instr printmaking, Herbert H Lehman Col, 92. *Awards:* Stuart M Egnal Award, 55-65, Print Club, 80; Purchase Award, Prints USA, Pratt Graphics Ctr, New York, 82. *Mem:* Found Community Artists; Printmaking Workshop; Print Club Pa; Westchester Coun Arts; Soc Am Graphic Artists NY (Adv Coun); Nat Artists Equity. *Media:* Etching; Watercolor. *Dealer:* Szoke Koo Assocs New York NY. *Mailing Add:* 255 Drake Ave New Rochelle NY 10805

GALLANDER, CATHLEEN S
ART DEALER, REPRESENTATIVE
b San Antonio, Tex, Feb 4, 31. *Study:* Univ Tex, Austin, BA(hist); Harvard Univ, scholar art hist; Harvard Bus Sch, Inst Arts Admin. *Pos:* Dir, Art Mus of S Tex, Corpus Christi, 61-80 & Newport Harbor Art Mus, Calif, 80-83; panelist, Nat Endowment for the Arts; prt consult, currently. *Mem:* Col Art Asn Am; Am Asn Mus; Am Fedn Arts; Western Asn Art Mus; Art Cable. *Mailing Add:* 465 W Broadway New York NY 10012

GALLES, ARIE ALEXANDER
PAINTER, EDUCATOR
b Tashkent, USSR, Oct 29, 44; US citizen. *Study:* Temple Univ, BFA, 68; Univ Wis, MFA, 71. *Work:* NJ State Mus, Trenton. *Comn:* Charles Allen, New York; Edgar Kaiser Jr, Vancouver, Can. *Exhib:* Solo exhibs, O K Harris Gallery, New York, 77, 79 & 82, Zolla-Liberman Gallery Chicago, Ill, 79 & NJ State Mus, Trenton, 89; Abstract, Material, Pictorial, Illusionism, O K Harris West, Scottsdale, Ariz, 80; Contemp Painting, Del Mus, Wilmington, 80; Five Decades: Recent Works by Alumni of the Dept Art, Elvehjem Mus Art, Univ Wis, Madison, 80; Art of Fashion, Bernice Steinbaum Gallery, New York, 90; Painting: NJ Benjamin Gallery, William Paterson Col, Wayne, NJ, 92; and others. *Pos:* Dir, Madison Acad of Art & Morris Gallery, 77-80, Phyllis Rothman Gallery, Fairleigh Dickinson Univ, 88- *Teaching:* Prof art & chmn fine arts dept, Fairleigh Dickinson Univ, Madison, NJ, 72-81, assoc prof, 81-84, prof, 84- *Bibliog:* Article in Chicago Sun Times, 9/23/79; article in Phoenix Gazett, 12/27/80; Robert Paschal & Robert Anderson (auths), Advanced Air Brush The Techniques-Art of the Dot, Van Nostrand Rineholt, 84. *Media:* Flourescent Acrylic on aluminum Extrusions, Caran D Ache Oil Pastel. *Publ:* Auth, Air Brush Action, Mag, 10/88. *Dealer:* O K Harris 383 W Broadway New York NY; Zolla-Lieberman Gallery 356 W Huron Chicago IL 60610. *Mailing Add:* 81 Ridgedale Ave Madison NJ 07940

GALLI, STANLEY WALTER
PAINTER
b San Francisco, Calif. *Study:* Calif Sch Fine Arts, San Francisco; Art Ctr Sch, Los Angeles. *Work:* Air Force Mus, Colo; Baseball Hall of Fame Mus, Cooperstown, NY; Palm Springs Desert Mus; Hall Fame Soc Illusr, NY. *Comn:* Conserv series, Weyerhaeuser Co, Tacoma, Wash, 52-68; wildlife paintings, Calif Casualty Group Collection, San Mateo, 73-78. *Exhib:* One-man shows, Nut Tree Gallery, Calif, 76, Crocker Art Mus, Sacramento, Calif, 80, Robert Mondavi Winery, Calif, 81 & Charles & Emma Frye Art Mus, Seattle, 83; NY Hist Soc, 77; group show, Oakland Mus, Calif, 78, Gallery Imago, San Francisco, Calif, 88; two-man exhib, Palm Springs Desert Mus, Calif, 78; Calvin R Vander Woude Gallery, Palm Springs, Calif, 85; and others. *Pos:* Illusr, Saturday Evening Post, 50-68, McCalls Mag, 60-67, Reader's Digest Mag & Condensed Bks, 60-78 & US Postal Serv Stamp Design, 68-78. *Teaching:* San Francisco City Col Art Dept, Prof Practices for Adv Students, 68, 69, 71, 72 & 73. *Awards:* Silver Medal, Dillon Lauritzen Award, los Angeles Art Dir Club, 58; Best US Postage Stamp of Yr, Postal Commemorative Soc, 68, 72 & 78. *Bibliog:* 200 Years of American Illustration, Random House, 77; The Illustrator in America, Madison Sq Press, NY, 84; Outstanding American Illustrators Today, Graphic Sha Publ Co, Tokyo, 84. *Mem:* Soc Illusr New York & San Francisco. *Media:* Acrylic, Oil. *Mailing Add:* PO Box 66 Kentfield CA 94914

GALLO, ENZO D
SCULPTOR
b Italy, Oct 25, 27. *Study:* San Alejandro Univ Fine Arts, Havana, Cuba, MFA; Senatus Univ Verae Arademirus, BA; study with Jose Sicri & Ramos Blanco, sculptor & Augusto Valderama, painter, Havana. *Work:* Pagani Mus, Milan, Italy; Young Circle, Hollywood, Fla; Town of Padula, Italy; Art Mus the Amercias, Wash, DC; Port Everglades Park, Ft Lauderdale, Fla. *Comn:* Sculpture & mosaic murals, Hollywood Mem Gardens, Fla; mosaic murals, Am Savings & Loan, Miami Beach; sculpture, Doral Beach Club, Miami Beach; sculpture (bronze), Hallandale Pub Libr. *Exhib:* Metrop Mus, Miami, 75; one-man shows, Heller Bldg, 87, Omni Int, Miami, 78, West Palm Beach Art Gallery, 79, Inter-Am Art Gallery, Coral Gables, 80, Fedn of Cuban Teachers of Fine Arts, Miami, Fla, 86; Latin Am Artist of the Southeastern US, Lowe Art Mus, Miami, 78; First Ann Art Competition, Nova Univ, 79. *Teaching:* Prof sculpture, San Alejandro Inst Fine Arts, Havana, Cuba & Broward Adult Educ, 62-65. *Awards:* Selected by US Dept of HUD for Environ Art in Pub Places, 73; First Monumental Proj Assigned by Pres Reagan for Christopher Columbus Quincentenary, Port Everglades, Fla, 88; Medallion Design Accepted as the Off Medallion of Grand Regatta Columbus 1992 Quincentenary, Wash, DC, 89. *Bibliog:* John R Thompson (auth), Traveling Tribune Reporter Pays Visit to Sculptor in Exile, The Chicago Tribune, 69; Marian Vynne (auth), Italian Artist Works, The Miami News, 2/73; Thomas Lawrence (auth), Enzo Gallo Reduces Natural Data to Pure Forms, Manhattan Arts Mag, 9/91. *Mem:* Fla Sculpture Asn; Artist Equity Asn Fla (pres, 75-78); Am Fedn Arts; Fla Artist Group; Broward Art Guild. *Media:* Marble, Bronze. *Publ:* Auth, Columbus Rediscovered, The Miami Herald, 8/87; The Man of the Mountain, The El Nuero Miami Herald, 92. *Mailing Add:* 500 N Ansin Blvd Hallandale FL 33009

GALLO, FRANK
SCULPTOR, EDUCATOR
b Toledo, Ohio, Jan 13, 33. *Study:* Toledo Mus Sch Art, BFA, 54; Cranbrook Acad Art, 55; Univ Iowa, MFA, 59; Univ Ill, 85, sr scholar. *Work:* Mus Mod Art & Whitney Mus Am Art, New York; Art Inst Chicago; Los Angeles Mus Art; Cleveland Mus Art; plus others. *Comn:* Portrait, Daniel Pope Cook, Ill, 69; portraits, String Teachers of Am, 69-72; seven life-size concrete figures, Bicentennial Comn, Champaign, Ill, 76; stained glass wall, Harry Thoroue, 80; ed paper castings, Beethoven Found, 85. *Exhib:* Ann, Whitney Mus Am Art, 64-67, Young America, 65; Alliance on Art, Smithsonian Inst, Washington, DC, 68; Venice Biennale, 68; Works in Paper, Art Inst Chicago, 78; retrospective, Paine Art Ctr, Oshkosh, Wis, 83; and others. *Teaching:* Prof sculpture, Univ Ill, 60- *Awards:* Guggenheim Found Fel, 66; Best Illus of the Year, Soc Publ Designers, 79. *Bibliog:* Peter Plagent (auth), article, Schlock Elite, New York, 12/3/78; Frank Gallo, Famous Artists Ann I (catalog), NY Hastings House, 80; Frank H Goodyear (auth), Contemporary American Realism since 1960, Archives of American Art Series, Little Brown, Boston, 81. *Publ:* Illus, cover, Raquel Welch, Time Mag, 11/69, The faint, Playboy Mag, 1/78 & Illus 21, NY Hastings House, 80. *Mailing Add:* Dept Art Univ Ill Champaign IL 61820

GALLO, WILLIAM VICTOR
CARTOONIST, ILLUSTRATOR
b New York, NY, Dec 28, 22. *Study:* Columbia Exten Cartoonists & Illusr. *Work:* Baseball Hall Fame, Cooperstown, NY. *Exhib:* One-man show, Spectrum Art Gallery, New York, 80. *Pos:* With NY Daily News, 41-, sports cartoonist, 60- *Awards:* Page One Awards, NY Newspaper Guild, 65, 68-70, 72-73, 75, 77-81, 85-86; Best Sports Cartoonist, Nat Cartoonist Soc, 68, 69, 70, 72, 73, 78, 85 & 86; Outstanding Achievement, Alumni Soc Sch Visual Arts, 75; and others. *Mem:* Nat Cartoonists Soc; Soc Silurians; and others. *Mailing Add:* 1 Mayflower Dr Yonkers NY 10710

GALLOWAY, STEVE
CONCEPTUAL ARTIST
b Los Angeles, Calif, 52. *Study:* Calif Inst Arts, Valencia, BFA, 74. *Exhib:* solo exhibs, Los Angeles Inst Contemp Art, 82, Mus Contemp Art, Los Angeles, 85, monterey Peninsula Mus Art, Calif, 86, Acme Art, San Francisco, Calif, 87, James Corcoran Gallery, 87, 90 & 93 & Gallery Paule Anglim, San Francisco, Calif, 93; A California Collection, Circus Gallery, Los Angeles, Calif, 88; The Great Drawing Show, Michael Kohn Gallery, Los Angeles, Calif, 88; Selections from the Berkus Collection, Long Beach Mus Art, Calif, 88; Birds and Beasts, Pacific Bell, San Ramon, Calif, 88; Lost and Found in California: Four Decades of Assemblage Art, James Corcoran Gallery, Santa Monica, Calif, 88; 20 Artists/Los Angeles, City Gallery Contemp Art, Raleigh, NC, 88-89; Painting, Rosa Esman Gallery, New York, 90; Works on Paper, Ctr Contemp Art, Chicago, Ill, 90; Painting, Rosa Esman, New York, 91; Drawings, James Corcoran Gallery, Santa Monica, Calif, 92; Beyond Appearance, Armory Ctr Arts, Pasadena, Calif, 94. *Awards:* Fel, Nat Endowment Arts, 87. *Bibliog:* Susan Sanford Whitehead (auth), article, Visions, winter 87; Ben Marks (auth), Artweek, 2-3/90; Cathy Curtis (auth), LA Times, 2/23/90. *Dealer:* James Corcoran Gallery 1327 Fifth St Santa Monica CA 90401. *Mailing Add:* 238 Mills St Santa Monica CA 90405

GALUSZKA, FRANK RICHARD
PAINTER
b Newark, NJ, Jan 24, 47. *Study:* Syracuse Univ, 64-65; Tyler Sch Art, Philadelphia, BFA, 68; Tyler Sch Art-Rome Campus, MFA, 72. *Work:* LaSalle Univ Mus, Philadelphia; State Comt Cult & Art, Bucharest, Romania. *Comn:* Numerous private portrait commissions. *Exhib:* American Tradition and the Image of the Postmodern Man, Univ Va Art Mus, Charlottesville, 79; 62 by 12, The Drawing Ctr, New York, 80; New Drawing in America, The Drawing Ctr, New York, 82; Design in America, Galleria di Ca Pesaro,

Venice, 83; Philadelphia Painters, Southern Alleghenies Mus, Pittsburgh, 85; The Figure in the Landscape, Artists' Choice Mus, New York, 85; 161st Annual, Nat Acad Design, New York, 86. *Teaching:* Assoc prof, Philadelphia Col Art, 72- *Awards:* Fulbright Grant US Govt- Romanian Govt, 69-70; Tobleah Wechsler Award, Cheltenham Annual, 77. *Media:* Oil, Watercolor. *Dealer:* Sherry French Gallery New York NY; Charles More Gallery Philadelphia PA. *Mailing Add:* c/o More Gallery 1630 Walnut St Philadelphia PA 19103

GAMBLE, KATHRYN ELIZABETH
MUSEUM DIRECTOR
b Van Wert, Ohio, Aug 19, 15. *Study:* Oberlin Col, AB, 37; Dayton Art Inst, 38; Newark Mus, cert, 41; New York Univ Grad Sch Fine Arts, MA, 48. *Collections Arranged:* Montclair in Manhattan, exhib of permanent collection, 61; American Painting Collection (with catalog), Montclair Art Mus; Asher B Durand Retrospective, 71; A B Durand (with catalog). *Pos:* Dir, Montclair Art Mus, 52-79, emer dir, 80- *Teaching:* Supvr art, Covington Pub Schs, Ohio, 38-40. *Awards:* Pewter Pitcher Award in recognition of distinguished contrib of Kathryn E Gamble to public knowledge and preserv of NJ hist, 83. *Bibliog:* Past and Promise, Lives of New Jersey Women, Scarecrow Press, Metuchen, NJ, 90. *Res:* 2-Dimensional visual arts for the blind & sight impaired, with continuing work with color. *Mailing Add:* 887 Sonoma Ave Apt 17 Santa Rosa CA 95404

GAMMON, JUANITA-LA VERNE
PAINTER, EDUCATOR
b McLeansboro, Ill. *Study:* Univ Ill, BFA & MFA. *Work:* Work in many pvt collections. *Comn:* Many pvt comns. *Exhib:* Dream Mus, Champaign, Ill, 70; McKinley Found, Urbana, Ill, 70; Nat Acad Design, New York, 70-71; Univ Ill, 71; Parkland Col, 75, 79-88; and others. *Pos:* Judge, local, regional & nat art exhibs, 67-; art lectr & critic & consult curric design, 67-; supvr, Champaign Co Art Show, 69- & others. *Teaching:* Applied arts & visual arts dir, fine & applied arts dept, Parkland Col, Champaign, 67- *Awards:* Many prof hons & awards. *Mem:* Many prof orgns. *Media:* Acrylic, Oil. *Publ:* Ed, Parkland Intercom, Story Shop Book. *Mailing Add:* Commun Parkland Col 2400 W Bradley Ave Champaign IL 61821

GAMMON, REGINALD ADOLPHUS
EDUCATOR, PAINTER
b Philadelphia, Pa, Mar 31, 21. *Study:* Philadelphia Mus Col Art, cert; Tyler Sch Fine Art, Temple Univ, one yr. *Work:* Chase Manhattan Bank, Fine Arts Div, New York; Denison Col, Ohio; Endicott Bd Educ, NY; plus numerous pvt collections. *Exhib:* New Voices--15 New York Artists, Am Greetings Gallery, New York, 68; Afro-Am Artists Since 1950, Brooklyn Col, 68; 30 Contemp Black Artists, Minneapolis Inst Art, Minn (travel), 68-70; Afro-Am Artists, New York & Boston, Mus Fine Arts, Boston, 70; Blacks: USA: 1973, New York Cult Ctr, 73. *Pos:* Artist, Lifton, Gold & Asher Advert, New York, 55-64; artist-in-residence, New York Bd Educ, 67-69. *Teaching:* Assoc prof humanities, painting & drawing, Western Mich Univ, 70-82. *Awards:* Fac Res Fel & Grant, Western Mich Univ, 75. *Bibliog:* Eugene Redden (auth), Reggie (film), prod by Western Mich Univ, 71; Judith Wragge Chase (auth), Afro-American Art & Crafts, Van Nostrand Reinhold, 72; Barry Schwartz (auth), Humanism in 20th Century Art, Praeger, 74. *Mem:* Col Art Asn; fel MacDowell Colony. *Media:* Oil, Acrylic. *Mailing Add:* c/o Art Ctr of Battle Creek 265 E Emmett St Battle Creek MI 49017

GAMWELL, LYNN
CURATOR, HISTORIAN
b Chicago, Ill, June 24, 43. *Study:* Univ Ill, BA, 67; Claremont Grad Sch, MFA, 70; Univ Calif, Los Angeles, PhD, 77. *Collections Arranged:* West Coast Realism, 83 & Stephen deStaebler & The Figure, 88, Laguna Art Mus; Art About Museums, State Univ NY, Binghamton, 89; The Sigmund Freud Antiquities: Fragments from a Buried Past, Freud Mus, London, 89; A Century of Silence, State Univ NY, Binghamton, 92. *Pos:* Cur, Laguna Art Mus, Calif & Newport Harbor Art Mus, Calif; dir, Art Mus, State Univ NY, Binghamton. *Teaching:* Lectr art hist, Univ Calif, Los Angeles, 72-74; asst prof art hist, Saddleback Col, Mission Viejo, Calif, 84-87; assoc prof art hist, State Univ NY, Binghamton, 87-92. *Mem:* Col Art Asn; Art Table. *Res:* Contemporary art. *Publ:* Auth, Cubist Criticism: 1905-1952, UMI Res Press, 80; coauth, Inside/Out: Self Beyond Likeness, Newport Harbor, Calif, 81; ed, Stephen DeStaebler: The Figure, Chronicle Bks, San Francisco, 88; auth, Leveled art and elevated theory, Mus News, 90; ed contribr, Sigmund Freud and Art: His Personal Collection, Abrams, NY, 89. *Dealer:* State Univ New York Univ Art Mus Binghamton NY 13902. *Mailing Add:* 101 W 80th St New York NY 10024

GANDERT, MIGUEL ADRIAN
PHOTOGRAPHER, LECTURER
b Española, NMex, Jan 12, 56. *Study:* Univ NMex, BA, 77, MA, 83. *Work:* Mus Fine Arts, Santa Fe; Univ NMex Fine Arts Mus, Albuquerque; Millicent Rogers Mus, Taos, NMex; Albuquerque Mus, NMex; Spec Collections Libr, Univ NMex, Albuquerque. *Comn:* New Mexico (photog survey), Mus NMex, Santa Fe, 83. *Exhib:* Contemporary-American Photography, Galeria Licht, Oslo, Norway, 77-78; Boxers & Wrestlers, Blue Sky Gallery, Portland, Ore, 78; Let's Boogie at Okies, ASA Gallery, Univ NMex, Albuquerque, 80; Burque, Santa Fe Ctr Photogr, NMex, 84; The New Photographic Survey, Mus Fine Arts, Santa Fe, 85; Statements, NMex State Fair Gallery, Albuquerque, 85 & 86. *Teaching:* Instr photogr, Univ NMex, Albuquerque, 82-83. *Bibliog:* Kathy Livingston (auth), Riding low, Am Photogr, 4/84; Bart Ripp (auth), The south valley knows the photographer, Albuquerque Tribune, 8/12/85; Hal Rhodes (dir), The Illustrated Daily, 85 & Miguel Gandeft photographer-on assignment, KNME TV. *Mem:* Hispanic Cult Found. *Publ:* Auth, Appearances Within My Own Time or: A Formal Exploration of People Pretending to Be, Univ NMex, 83; coauth, The Essential Landscape, Univ NMex Press, 85; coauth, Flow of River, Hispanic Culture Found. *Dealer:* Andrew Smith Gallery 76 E San Francisco St Santa Fe NM 87501. *Mailing Add:* 1205 Lobo Pl NE Albuquerque NM 87106

GANEK, DOROTHY SKEADOS
PAINTER, SILVERSMITH
b Athens, Greece, Aug 8, 46; US Citizen. *Study:* New York Sch Interior Design, 65-68. *Work:* Schering Plough Corp, NJ; Hoffman La Roche Inc, Nutley, NJ; Cigna Corp; PSE & Gas Co, Warner Lambert Inc; Caldwell Banker; Kenwood Electronics; Kessler Institute, NEC. *Exhib:* Am Watercolor Soc Exhib, Nat Acad Galleries, 82, Canton Inst, Ohio, 85 & Salmagundi Club, New York, 86 & 88; Bergen Mus Arts & Sci 2nd & 3rd Juried Exhib, Paramus, NJ, 84 & 85; Nat Asn Women Artists Traveling Exhib, 88; Los Angeles Artcore Invitational, Nat Watercolor Soc, Calif, 88; Am Watercolor Soc, 82, 85, 86, 88, 89. *Pos:* Interior designer, Dorothy Ganek Interiors, 69-85. *Awards:* Silver Medal Honor, NJ Watercolor Soc; John Young Hunter Award, Am Watercolor Soc, 92; Cecil Shapiro Award, Nat Asn Women Artists, 91. *Mem:* Catherine Lorillard Wolf Arts Club; NJ Watercolor Soc; Allied Artists Am; Audubon Artists; Am Watercolor Soc; Am Artist, Leading Contemp. *Media:* Watermedia. *Publ:* Splash (watercolor book), 90; Goodlife Mag, 90. *Dealer:* Gallery 9 Chatham NJ; Art Forms Red Bank NJ. *Mailing Add:* 125 Rynda Rd South Orange NJ 07079

GANNON, LANIE E
CRAFTSMAN
Study: Memphis Col Art, BFA, 81; Appalachian Ctr for Crafts, with Wendy Maruyama & Trent Whitington, 83-86. *Exhib:* Cumberland Gallery, Nashville, Tenn, 83 & 86; New Talent Show, Convergence, New York, 84; Carr Gallery, Houston, Tex, 85; one-woman shows, Cumberland Gallery, Nashville, Tenn, 86 & 90, A Not So Still Life, Mobilia, Cambridge, Mass, 89, Bennett Gallery, Knoxville, Tenn, 92; Make it New: Computer Art of Middle Tennessee, Cheekwood Fine Art Ctr, Nashville, Tenn, 91; Gallery 500, Philadelphia, Pa, 91. *Teaching:* Adj instr sculpture/3-D design, Belmont Univ, Nashville, Tenn, 91-92. *Awards:* Visual Artists Fel Grant, Nat Endowment Arts, 88. *Bibliog:* Is it Furniture or Is it Art?, Nashville Mag, 10/84; Art Papers, review, 3-4/91; Show Review, New Art Examiner, 10/91. *Media:* Aluminum, Wood. *Mailing Add:* c/o Cumberland Gallery 4107 Hillsboro Circle Nashville TN 37215

GANS, LUCY C
SCULPTOR, EDUCATOR
b Plainfield, NJ, Nov 18, 49. *Study:* Art Students League, 70; Lake Erie Col, BFA, 71; Pratt Inst, with Calvin Albert & George McNeil, MFA, 74. *Work:* Lehigh Univ, Westtown Sch, Pa; ARA Services. *Exhib:* May Show, Cleveland Mus Art, 74; Drawings USA, Smithsonian Inst Traveling Exhib, 76-79; solo exhib, Westchester State Col, Pa, 79; For the Love of Drawing, Kemerer Mus, Bethlehem, Pa, 81; Del Biennial, Univ Del, Newark, 81 & 83; Installation of Drawings & Sculpture, Muse Gallery, Philadelphia, 83 & 85; Installation of Sculpture and Drawings, Lehigh Univ, 85; Allentown Art Mus, 86; Southern Vt Art Center, 86. *Collections Arranged:* Womens Caucus Art Nat Exhib (auth, catalog), 84. *Teaching:* Vis lectr sculpture & drawing, Lake Erie Col, Ohio, 74-75; instr sculpture, Univ SAla, 76-77; assoc prof sculpture, drawing & painting, Lehigh Univ, Pa, 81- *Mem:* Col Art Asn; Women's Caucus Art. *Dealer:* Muse Gallery 1915 Walnut St Philadelphia PA 19103. *Mailing Add:* Dept Art Lehigh Univ Ullman Bldg 17, 104 Chandler Bethlehem PA 18015

GANTZ, ANN CUSHING
PAINTER, INSTRUCTOR
b Dallas, Tex, Aug 27, 35. *Study:* Memphis Acad of Art; Southwestern Univ, Memphis; Newcomb Col Tulane Univ, New Orleans, La, BFA, 55. *Work:* Dallas Mus Fine Arts, Tex; Denver Mus, Colo; Smithsonian Inst, Washington, DC; Boston Mus, Mass; Los Angeles State Mus; Okla City Mus, Okla. *Comn:* Tex Instruments, Inc, 85; Landmark Ctr, 87; Southwest Med Sch, 88; KERA-TV, 88; Trammell Crow Co, 88. *Exhib:* Ann Exhib, Springfield Mus, Mass, 56 & 57; Painting Ann, Portland Mus, 56, 59 & 60; Oklahoma City Art Ctr, 56-58; Painting & Sculpture Ann, Nat Acad Design, New York, 57, 60; Norfolk Mus, Va, 58, 59; Printmaking Today, Brooklyn Mus, NY, 59; Ann Shows, Ark Art Ctr, Little Rock, 59, 60 & 61; Dallas Mus, Tex, 55-62; and others. *Pos:* Pres, Cushing Galleries Inc, 63-79; owner, Cushing Studio, 79- *Teaching:* Instr printmaking & painting, Dallas Mus Fine Arts Sch, 56-62; instr painting, printmaking & drawing, Cushing Galleries Sch Studio Art, 62-79, instr, Cushing Studio, 79- *Awards:* TFAA Artist of Year Award, 79; Oak Award, 81; McMurray Found Award, 83; Delta Kappa Award, 87. *Mem:* Dallas Print & Drawing Soc (pres, 58-60); YWCA Art Comt; Tex Printmakers (pres, 60-63); Dallas Art Gallery Asn (founder, 78). *Media:* Oil. *Mailing Add:* 4654 Edmondson Dallas TX 75209

GANZ, SYLVIA SQUIRES See Tykie (Sylvia Squires Ganz)

GANZARAIN, MIRENTXU
SCULPTOR, PAINTER
b Santiago, Chile, 57; US citizen. *Study:* Kans Univ, Lawrence, BA, 82, BFA, 84; Art Inst Chicago, MFA, 86. *Work:* Daryl Gerber, Chicago; D Gray Vogelmann, Chicago. *Exhib:* Superior St Gallery, Art Inst Chicago, 86; Advina! Latino Chicago Expressions, Mus Mod Art, Mexico City, Mex, also Mexican Fine Arts Ctr, Chicago, 88; Mus Sci & Indust, Chicago, 91; Amalgamations, Gallery 2, Art Inst Chicago, 91; Bi-State Exhib, Davenport Mus Art, Iowa, 92; Los Encuentros, Betty Rymer Gallery, Art Inst Chicago,

92. *Awards:* Spec Assistance Grant, Ill Arts Coun, 87 & 89; Finalist, Art Quest 88, Los Angeles, 88; First Prize, Mus Sci & Indust, Chicago, 91. *Mem:* Col Art Asn. *Media:* Mixed. *Mailing Add:* 1437 W Oakdale Ave Chicago IL 60657

GARABEDIAN, CHARLES
PAINTER
b Detroit, Mich, 1923. *Study:* UCLA, MA, 61. *Exhib:* Solo exhibs, L A Louver, Venice, 80, 83, 86, 88, 90 & 92, La Jolla Mus Contemp Art, Calif, 82, Holly Solomon Gallery, 82, Hirschl & Adler Mod, New York, 84 & 87, Gallery Paule Anglim, San Francisco, Calif, 85; Chas and Eddie Paint the Baja, Joseph Chowning Gallery, San Francisco, Calif, 90; Faces, Marc Richards Gallery, 90, LA When it Began, James Corcoran Gallery, Los Angeles, Calif, 91; Spirit of Our Time, Santa Barbara Contemp Arts Forum, Calif, 90. *Awards:* Nat Endowment Arts Fel, 77; Guggenheim Fel, 80. *Mailing Add:* c/o L A Louvre Inc 55 N Venice Blvd Venice CA 90291

GARBATY, MARIE-LOUISE
COLLECTOR, PATRON
b Berlin, Ger, Mar 9, 10; US citizen. *Study:* Univ Berlin. *Mem:* Am Fedn Arts; Renaissance Soc Am; China Inst Am; Carnegie Inst; fel perpetuity Metrop Mus Art, New York; life fel Mus Fine Arts, Boston; benefactor & life mem Chrysler Mus; hon mem Allentown Mus Art. *Interests:* Patron to many museums, universities & colleges nationally. *Collection:* Fifteenth and seventeenth century Dutch and Flemish paintings; decorative art of the Renaissance; antique Syrian glass; fifteenth to eighteenth century blue white China; antique oriental textiles; old English silver; antique English furniture; Egyptian antiquities. *Mailing Add:* 923 Fifth Ave New York NY 10021

GARBUTT, JANICE LOVOOS
PAINTER, WRITER
b Dubuque, Iowa. *Study:* Chouinard Art Inst. *Comn:* Mural, comn by Mr & Mrs Walter Frey, San Clemente, Calif. *Exhib:* Los Angeles Co Art Mus; Calif Art Club; solo exhibs, Circle Gallery, San Diego, Descanso Gardens, Carol Hard's Rancho Mirage Gallery & the Gallery, Palm Springs, Calif. *Teaching:* Instr fashion promotion, Chouinard Art Inst, 47-48. *Awards:* Award for Biography Frederick Whitaker, Southern Book Competition, 73; James A Marshall Award, Univ Mich, Ann Arbor, 80; Bookbinder's Award for Distinguished Bks, San Francisco, 83. *Mem:* Am Soc Composers, Authors & Publishers; Author's Guild; Dramatist's Guild Am. *Media:* All. *Publ:* Auth & illusr, Design is a Dandelion; co-auth, Making Pottery without a Wheel, Prentice Hall, in prep; many articles in Los Angeles Times, Am Artist, Westways, Christian Sci Monitor, Charm, Parade, Toledo Star News & Southwest Art; Antiques & Fine Arts. *Dealer:* ART Beasley Gallery 2802 Juan St San Diego CA 92110. *Mailing Add:* 3357-P Monte Hermoso Laguna Hills CA 92653

GARCHIK, MORTON LLOYD
PAINTER, PRINTMAKER
b Brooklyn, NY, June 25, 29. *Study:* Brooklyn Mus, painting with Max Beckmann & printmaking with Gabor Peterdi; Sch Visual Art, New York. *Work:* Minn Mus Art; Libr Cong. *Comn:* Book cover for Gimpel the Fool, Avon Paperback, 63. *Exhib:* One-man show, Union of Am Hebrew Congregations, 63; 7th Ann Contemp Am Printmakers Exhib, DePauw Univ, 65; Ohio Univ 7th Ann, 66; Seattle Art Mus Int Exhibs, 66 & 67; two-man show, Art Corner, Milburn, NJ, 75; Artists Equity, New York, 78. *Pos:* Art dir, Commun Channels, Inc, New York, 72-77. *Awards:* First Prize, Drawing, Sch Visual Arts, 55; Purchase Award, Olivet Col 5th Nat Print Exhib, 65. *Mem:* Artists Equity New York. *Media:* All. *Publ:* Auth, Art Fundamentals: Basics of Drawing, Painting, Sculpture & Printmaking, Stravon Educ Press; Creative Visual Thinking: How to Think Up Ideas Fast, Art Direction Bk Co; illusr, in: Harpers, Avon paperback, Farrar, Straus & Cudahy, Parents Mag Press. *Mailing Add:* 21-25 34th Ave Long Island City NY 11106

GARCIA, FRANK
GALLERY DIRECTOR, HISTORIAN
b Victoria las Tunas, Cuba, Feb 1, 24; US citizen. *Pos:* Dir, Galeria Cubana, Havana, 52-59; dir, Sardio Gallery, Caracas, Venezuela, 55-57; dir, Cisneros Gallery, New York, 65-; publ & dir, Noticias de Arte, 76- *Awards:* Cintas Fel, 64-65; Third Prize, 78, Second Prize, 79, Circulo de Escritores y Poetas Iberoamericanos; Cintas Fel, 86-87. *Bibliog:* G Chase (auth), Art in Latin America, Free Press, 70; D Bayon (auth), America Latina y sus Artes & Las Artes Plasticas en la America Latina; Maximo Gomez (auth), Caudillo o Dictador?, 86, Jose Marti y la Pintura Espanola, 87, Ediciones Universal; Vicente Garcia (auth), El Leon de Santa Rita, 89. *Mem:* Circulo Pan Americano de Cult; Seminars on the Acquisition of Latin American Libr Materials; Int Asn Art Critics. *Specialty:* Latin American art. *Publ:* Auth, Latin American painters in New York, 64; Maternity in Precolumbian art, 70; Jose Marti y las Artes Plasticas, 72; Santos of Puerto Rico and the Americas, Blaine Etheridge Bks, 79. *Mailing Add:* 172 E 89th St Apt 5-A New York NY 10028

GARCIA, OFELIA
ADMINISTRATOR, PRINTMAKER
b Havana, Cuba, Feb 12, 41; US citizen. *Study:* Escuela Nacional de Bellas Artes, Havana, Cuba, 58-60; Manhattanville Col, BA, 69; Tufts Univ & Boston Mus Sch, MFA(printmaking), 72. *Work:* Princeton Univ Graphic Arts Col; NJ State Mus, Trenton; Free Libr Philadelphia; Museo Grafico, Inst Puerto Rican Culture, San Juan; Barnard Col, New York. *Exhib:* Third Miami Graphics Biennial, Metrop Mus & Art Ctr, Fla, 77; 53rd Ann Juried Show, The Print Club, Philadelphia, 77; NJ State Mus, Trenton, 78; Barnard Col, New York, 79; solo shows at Colegio Universitario, Santurce, PR, 70, Cohen Arts Ctr, Tufts Univ, 72 & Duke Univ Gallery, 74; Five Hispanic Artists, Deshong Mus, Pa, 82; A Growing American Treasure, Pa Acad Fine Arts, William Penn Mus, 83. *Collections Arranged:* Invitational Print Exhib in honor of Lessin J Rosenwald (auth, catalog), Print Club, Philadelphia, Pa, 80; Contemp Prints from Lehigh Univ Collection (auth, catalog), Bethlehem, Pa, 80; Recent Gifts: Print at Univ Pa (auth, catalog), Grad Sch Fine Arts, 81; Printed by Women (auth, catlog), Philadelphia, Pa, 83; Int Mezzotint Comptetion, The Print Club & Pratt Graphic Ctr, New York, 84. *Pos:* Dir, The Print Club, Philadelphia, 78-85; critic, Pa Acad Fine Arts, 82-; pres, Atlanta Col Art, 86- *Teaching:* Asst prof printmaking & drawing, Newton Col Sacred Heart, 69-73, chmn dept, 70-73; asst prof, Boston Col, 75-76. *Awards:* First Prize, All-Sch Competition, Escuela de Bellas Artes, Havana, Cuba, 59; Am Bk Builders Scholar Prize, Boston Mus Sch, 69; Kent Fel, Danforth Found, 75-80. *Bibliog:* Ross Romano (auth), The Complete Collagraph, Macmillan, 80; articles in Philadelphia Inquirer, 8/79 & Print Collector's Newslett. *Mem:* Fel Soc Values Higher Educ; Woman's Caucus Art (pres, 84-86); Citizens Arts Pa; Col Art Asn Am (bd dirs, 86-90); Univ Ctr Ga (bd trustees). *Dealer:* The Print Club 1614 Latimer St Philadelphia PA 19103. *Mailing Add:* 1728 Delancey Pl Philadelphia PA 19103-6715

GARCIA, RUPERT (MARSHALL R)
PAINTER, EDUCATOR
b French Camp, Calif, Sept 29, 41. *Study:* San Francisco State Univ, with John Gutmann, BA, 68, with Richard MacLean & Robert Bechtle, MA, 70; Univ Calif, Berkeley, with Peter Selz, Herschel Chipp & T J Clark, MA, 81. *Work:* Nat Mus Am Art, Smithsonian Inst, Washington, DC; Oakland Mus, Calif; Univ Art Mus, Berkeley, Calif; San Francisco Mus Mod Art, Calif; The Mex Mus, San Francisco. *Comn:* Posters and Society (poster), San Francisco Mus Mod Art, 74; posters for Amnesty Int, San Francisco, 76; Mex Mus, San Francisco, 76; Nat Chicano Coun Higher Educ, Berkeley, Calif, 79; pastel painting, Ruben Libr, Sonoma State Univ, Rohnert Park, Calif, 79. *Exhib:* One-man show, Oakland Mus, 70, San Francisco Mus Mod Art, 78, Univ Art Gallery, State Univ NY, Binghamton, 81, Univ Art Mus, Berkeley, Calif, 84, Mex Mus, San Francisco, 86 & The Haggin Mus, Stockton, Calif, 88; Images of an Era: The Am Poster 45-75, Nat Collection Fine Arts, Smithsonian Inst & Corcoran Gallery Art, Washington, DC, 75; Raices Antiquas/Visones Nuevas, Tucson Mus Art, Ariz, 77; Prelude to the Fifth Sun, Univ Art Mus, Berkeley, Calif, 77; Mex-Am Artists San Francisco Bay Area, Mex Mus, 78; Das Andere Am, Staaliche Kunsthalle, Berlin, WGer, 83; The Human Condition, Mus Mod Art Biennial III, San Francisco, 84; Close Focus, Nat Mus Am Art, Washington, DC, 87; Committed to print, Mus Mod Art, New York, 88; Latin American Presence in US, Bronx Mus Arts, NY, 88; and others. *Collections Arranged:* Arte de la Revolucion Cubana: Silkscreens by Rene Mederos, Galeria de La Raza, San Francisco, 73; Realismo Chicano: Drawings by Juan Fuentes, Chicano Students Libr, Univ Calif, Berkeley, 76. *Pos:* Artist in residence, Calif Arts Coun, 86, Inst Cult Commun EW Ctr, Honolulu, Hawaii, 87. *Teaching:* Lectr silkscreen, printmaking, painting & drawing, San Francisco State Univ, 78, 79 & summer 81; lectr art hist Mex, Univ Calif, Berkeley, 79-81, lectr graphic design, 82-85; vis asst prof art hist Mex, Wash State Univ, Pullman, 84; vis artist, Ill State Univ, Bloomington, 88; assoc prof art, San Jose State Univ, 88- *Awards:* Printmaking, San Francisco Arts Comn, 86; Purple Globe Award, San Francisco State Univ, 86. *Bibliog:* Ramon Favela (auth), The Art of Rupert Garcia, The Mexican Mus, San Francisco, 86; Peter Selz, (auth), Rupert Garcia: The Moral Fervor of Painting and its Subjects, Arts, 4/87; Bill Berkson (auth), Rupert Garcia, The Haggin Mus, 88. *Media:* Oil, Pastel. *Res:* Art and culture of the Chicano and Mexican. *Publ:* Coauth, Recent Raza murals in the US, Radical Am, 78; auth, Politics of Popular Art, Chimearte, Los Angeles, 78; Murales Recientes de La Raza en Estado Unidos, Plural, Mex, 79; Mexican Movie Poster Art, Myth, Illusion, Deception, Galeria de la Raza, San Francisco, 79; Frida Kahlo, A Bibliography and Biographical Introduction, Univ of Calif, Berkeley, 83. *Dealer:* Iannetti-Lanzone Gallery 310 Grant Ave San Francisco CA 94108; Saxon-Lee Gallery 7525 Beverly Blvd Los Angeles 90036. *Mailing Add:* c/o Daniel Saxon Gallery 7525 Beverly Blvd Los Angeles CA 90036

GARDINER, HENRY GILBERT
ART DEALER, MUSEUM DIRECTOR
b Boston, Mass, Aug 27, 27. *Study:* Harvard Col, AB, 50; Harvard Univ, MA, 59. *Collections Arranged:* Color & Form, 1909-1914, & Cross & Sword, 76, San Diego Mus, 76. *Pos:* Cur paintings & sculpture, Philadelphia Mus Art, 60-69; dir, San Diego Mus Art, 69-79 & Mitchell Wolfson Mus, Miami, 83-84. *Teaching:* Prof mus studies, Univ Southern Calif, 81. *Specialty:* European and American art from 1850 to 1950, with emphasis on abstract painting 1900-1915. *Mailing Add:* PO Box 3121 Palm Beach FL 33480

GARDINER, T MICHAEL
PAINTER
b Seattle, Wash, Feb 5, 46. *Study:* St Thomas Seminary, BA, 69; Cornish Col Arts, 73; Univ Wash, teaching cert, 78. *Work:* Seattle Water Dept & City Light; SAFECO, Seattle; Nordstrom, Seattle; US West, Seattle. *Comn:* Painting on a City Bus, Art Project, Metro-Seattle, 92. *Exhib:* Seattle Art Mus, 75; one-man shows, Polly Friedlander Gallery, Seattle, 77, Manolides Gallery, 79-85, MIA Gallery, 88 & 90, Augen Gallery, Portland, 89 & Susan Cummins Gallery, Mill Valley, Calif, 89 & 91; Small Works National, Zaner Gallery, Rochester, NY, 85; Sea-First Bank Gallery, 91. *Teaching:* Vis artist, Painting, Drawing, Cent Wash Univ, Ellensburg, 91. *Awards:* Nat Endowment Arts, 89. *Media:* Acrylic, Mixed Media. *Mailing Add:* c/o MIA Gallery 314 Occidental Ave S Seattle WA 98104

GARDNER, ANDREW BRADFORD
PRINTMAKER, PAINTER
b Chicago, Ill, Nov 17, 37. *Study:* Antioch Col, BA, 61; Ohio State Univ, MA, 66; Escuela Cent Bellas Artes San Fernando, Madrid, Spain, 64. *Work:* Metrop Mus Art, New York; Johnson Wax Collection; Atlantic Richfield. *Exhib:* Door, Mus Contemp Crafts, New York, 68; Nat Print Exhibs, Brooklyn Mus, 68 & 72; New Talent in Printmaking-1969, Asn Am Artists Gallery, New York, 69; 2nd Biennale Int Estampe, Paris, France, 70; 4th Am Print Biennial, Santiago, Chile, 70. *Teaching:* Instr art & design, Rochester Inst Technol, 66-67; asst prof fine arts, Rutgers Univ, Newark, 67-76. *Media:* Silkscreen, Stencils; Spray Paint. *Publ:* Auth & illusr, The Artist's Silkscreen Manual, Grosset & Dunlap, New York, 76. *Mailing Add:* c/o Lewis Lehr PO Box 1008 Gracie Sq Sta New York NY 10028

GARDNER, ANN
CERAMIST
Study: Univ Ore, Portland & State Univ, Maude Kerns Art Ctr (ceramics & fine arts). *Work:* Am Craft Mus, New York; Nordstrom, Montgomery, Md; Saks Fifth Ave; City of Seattle; Detroit Inst Arts, Mich. *Exhib:* One-woman shows, Sculpture in Glass & Mixed Media, Esther Saks Gallery, Chicago, 87, William Traver Gallery, Seattle, Wash, 87, 88 & 89, Art Gym, Maryhurst Col, Portland, 87, Familiar Rhythyms, Linda Farris Gallery, Seattle, Wash, 92; group shows, Bellevue Art Mus, 88 & 91, Linda Ferris Gallery, Seattle, 88 & 91; Spirit of the West, traveling exhib, 92; Dreams & Sheilds, Salt Lake Art Ctr, Utah. *Teaching:* Artist in residence, Kohler Foundry, 84 & 86, Pilchuck Glass Sch, 85 & 87, Centrum Found, printmaking, 89; lectr, Univ Wash, Seattle, 90. *Awards:* Nat Endowment Arts Grant, 86. *Bibliog:* Linda Humphrey & Fred Albert (auths), The Northwest, 91; Ronnie Miller (auth), Out of the Fire, p 44-46, 91; Ann Gardner shows a tender side, Seattle PI, 2/91. *Mailing Add:* c/o Linda Farris Gallery 320 Second Ave Seattle WA 98104-2619

GARDNER, COLIN R
WRITER, CRITIC
b Isleworth, Middlesex, Eng, Oct 15, 52. *Study:* St John's Col, Cambridge, Eng, BA(hons), 75, MA(hons), 79; Univ Calif, Los Angeles, MA, 77, PhD Prog, 92- *Comn:* Territories of Art Series (radio drama), Nat Pub Radio, comn by Mus Contemp Art, Los Angeles, Calif, 86. *Exhib:* Group show, Robert Berman Gallery, Los Angeles, 87. *Pos:* Art critic & ed, California Mag, Los Angeles, 83-88; art critic (Los Angeles corresp), Art Forum, NY 85-92; art reviewer, Los Angeles Times, 85-87; contrib ed, Artweek, Oakland, 84-88; art critic, Los Angeles Herald Examiner, 88; ed, Visions Arts Quarterly, 88-89. *Teaching:* Vis lectr, art theory & aesthetics, Univ Calif, Los Angeles, 88-92, Otis/Parsons, 88, Sch Art Inst Chicago, 89; grad adv, Art Ctr Sch Design, Pasadena, 88-92. *Awards:* Univ Calif, Los Angeles Film & Television, 92-93. *Mem:* CAA; Nat Writers Union. *Res:* Elements of post-structural philosophy and their relations to contemporary art and film, specifically deconstruction, language of representation; immanence & contradiction in the films of Joseph Losey. *Publ:* Contribr, Wallace Berman, ICA Amsterdam & Hans Burkhardt: The War Paintings, Santa Susana Press, 85; Magill's History of the Cinema: Foreign Language Films, Salem Press, 86; auth, article on Douglas Huebler, Artforum, 11/88; auth, article on John Baldessari, Artforum, 12/89. *Mailing Add:* 1015 N Edinburgh Ave Apt 2 West Hollywood CA 90046

GARDNER, JOAN A
PAINTER, PRINTMAKER
b Joliet, Ill, May 3, 33. *Study:* Univ Ill, BFA & MFA(Kate Neal Kinley Mem fel), 55; Norfolk Summer Art Sch, Yale Univ, with Rico Lebrun & Gabor Peterdi, fel, 56. *Work:* Univ Ill; Am Fedn Art; Art Inst Chicago; Yale Univ; Lyman Allyn Mus, New London, Conn. *Exhib:* Yale Univ, 70; New Britain Mus Art, Conn, 73; 55 Mercer Gallery, New York, 74-80; Slater Mem Mus, Norwich, Conn, 77; traveling show, NY State & Akron Art Mus; retrospective, Lyman Allyn Mus, New London, Conn, 81. *Teaching:* Instr art, Southern Conn State Col, 65-77; asst prof, Univ New Haven, 78-81; assoc prof, Kent State Univ, 82- *Awards:* Fulbright-Hays Award, 74-75; Conn Comn Arts Grant, 79-80. *Mem:* Conn Acad Fine Arts; Women's Caucus on Art; Col Art Asn; Conn Women Artists; Spaces, Cleveland, Ohio. *Media:* Paintings, Collage. *Publ:* Coauth, Robot (film), 72; Rooms (bk of drawings), 79; If I Were, poetry-picture bk, 81; Cast of Characters (bk of drawings). *Dealer:* Mercer Gallery 55 Mercer St New York NY 10013. *Mailing Add:* 10 Silver Sands Rd East Haven CT 06512-4635

GARDNER, ROBERT EARL
PRINTMAKER, EDUCATOR
b Indianapolis, Ind, June 29, 19. *Study:* John Herron Art Sch, BFA, 48; Atelier 17, New York, 48-49; Cranbrook Acad Art, MFA, 52. *Work:* Carnegie Mus, Pittsburgh; Univ Okla Mus, Norman; Wichita Mus Art, Kans; Ohio Univ, Athens; Ga Comn Arts. *Exhib:* Pa Acad Fine Arts Exhibs; Brooklyn Mus Print Biennials; Libr Cong Print Exhibs; Northwest Printmakers Exhibs; Philadelphia Print Club Exhibs. *Pos:* Artisan-printer, Tamarind Lithography Workshop, Los Angeles, Calif, summer 62 & 63-64. *Teaching:* From assoc prof to prof printmaking, Carnegie-Mellon Univ, 53- *Awards:* Sixteen national & regional prizes & purchase awards. *Bibliog:* Michael Knigin & Murray Zimilis (authors), The technique of fine art lithography, Print Collectors Newslett, 9-10/70; Donald Saff & Deli Sacilotto (authors), Printmaking: History and process, Tamarind Papers, fall 78. *Media:* Intaglio, Lithography. *Mailing Add:* 5658 Forbes Ave Pittsburgh PA 15217

GARDNER, SHEILA
PAINTER
b Jersey City, NJ, Mar 31, 33. *Study:* Endicott Col, AA, 52; Art Students League, 54-57; New Sch, 56-59. *Work:* AT&T, Mobil Oil & Chemical Bank, New York; Portland Mus Art, Maine; Boise Art Mus, Idaho. *Comn:* Arthur Anderson, Boston, Mass, 87. *Exhib:* Contemporary Images: Watercolor, Allen Priebe Gallery, Univ Wis, Oshkosh, 83; Traveling Exhib, American Realism-20th Century Drawings & Watercolors, San Francisco Mus Mod Art, Calif, 85-86, De Cordova & Dana Mus, Lincoln, Mass, 86, Akron Art Mus, Ohio & A M Huntington Art Gallery, Univ Tex, Austin, 87; The Monumental Image: Watercolor USA, Springfield Art Mus, Mo, 86; Boise Art Mus, 88-90; Univ Idaho, Moscow, 90. *Teaching:* Workshops, Sun Valley Ctr Arts & Humanities, 85, 89 & 90; instr painting & drawing, Univ Maine, 86. *Bibliog:* Women Artists and American Watercolors, Abbeville Press, 88; John Arthur (auth), Spirit of Place, Bullfinch. *Media:* Oil, Watercolor. *Dealer:* Tatistcheff Gallery 50 W 57th St New York NY 10019. *Mailing Add:* PO Box 1529 Hailey ID 83333

GARDNER, SUSAN ROSS
PAINTER
b New York, NY, Oct 25, 41. *Study:* Brooklyn Mus, 59; Antioch Col, BA, 63; Ohio State Univ, MA, 66. *Work:* Metrop Mus Art, New York; Southern Ill Univ; Northern Ill Univ; Atlantic Richfield Corp; Woman's Interart Ctr; Art Embassies Prog, Washington, DC; and many others. *Comn:* Two wall murals, Pub Sch 94, Dept Cult Affairs Percent for Arts Prog, NY; Noah's Ark, St Peters Church, Citicorp, NY. *Exhib:* Seattle Art Mus, 71; De Cordova Mus, Lincoln, Mass, 71; Cook Gallery, Lincoln Ctr, 81; Brooklyn Mus, 72, 78, 79, 82 & 84; 55 Mercer St, New York, 82; one person shows, Webb & Parsons Gallery, Conn, 82, Twinning Gallery, New York, 83, LaGuardia Community Col, 84 & Saint Peter's, Citicorp, New York, 86; The Doll Show, Hillwood Art Gallery, CW Post Col, New York, 85; and many others. *Teaching:* Asst prof studio & art hist, Manhattan Community Col, New York, 66-70; assoc prof, head of Art Dept, Yeshiva Univ, 75- *Awards:* Purchase Award, Northern Ill Univ, 71. *Bibliog:* Wendy Schuman (interview), NY Times, 5/27/73; photo & article, Long Island Press, 4/27/73, East Hampton Star, 5/73 & Arts, 6/83. *Mem:* Col Art Asn Am. *Media:* Acrylic, Rhoplex, Metal. *Mailing Add:* 108 Wyckoff St Brooklyn NY 11201

GAREL, LEO
PAINTER
b New York, NY, Oct 8, 17. *Study:* Parsons Sch Art, NY; Art Students League, with George Grosz & Vaclav Vytlacil. *Work:* Norfolk Mus Arts & Sci; Chase Manhattan Bank Collection; Midland Bank Collection; NY Univ; Mus Taos Art. *Exhib:* Albany Inst Hist & Art, NY, 61; one-man show, Berkshire Mus, Pittsfield, Mass, 67; Pa Acad Fine Arts, Philadelphia, 69; Montclair Art Mus, NJ, 75; Zabriskie Gallery, New York; Image Gallery, Stockbridge, Mass. *Teaching:* Instr painting, Austen Riggs Ctr, Stockbridge, Mass, 59-75. *Awards:* First Prize in Watercolor, Albany Inst Hist & Art, 61. *Bibliog:* Mabel Dodge Luhan (auth), Taos and its Artists, 47; Joan M Erickson (auth), Activity, Recovery, Growth, 76 & Wisdom and the Senses, 88. *Media:* Watercolor, Gouache. *Mailing Add:* Box 331 Stockbridge MA 01262

GARET, JEDD
PAINTER
b Los Angeles, Calif, 1955. *Study:* RI Sch Design, Providence, 73-75, Sch Visual Arts, New York, BFA, 75-77. *Work:* Brooklyn Mus; Fogg Mus, Cambridge, Mass; Mus Mod Art, New York; Tate Gallery, London; Whitney Mus Am Art, New York. *Exhib:* Max Hutchinson Gallery, New York, 78; one-man shows, Felicity Samuel Gallery, London, 79, Galerie Bischofberger, Zurich, Switz, 80, Robert Miller Gallery, New York, 81, 83, 84, 89 & 91, John Berggruen Gallery, San Francisco, 82 & Origrafica Malmö, Malmö, Sweden, 88; 1981 Biennial Exhib, Whitney Mus Am Art, New York; Kunstmuseum Lucerne, Switz, 83-84; San Francisco Mus Mod Art, 84; 41st Venice Biennale, 84-85. *Bibliog:* Robert Mahoney (auth), Jedd Garet, Arts, 89; John Zinsser (auth), Jedd Garet at Robert Miller, Art in America, 9/89; Robert Pincus-Witter (auth), Jedd Garet, Twelvetrees Press, 84; Donald Kuspit (auth), Jedd Garet, Robert Miller Gallery, 89. *Media:* Acrylic. *Mailing Add:* c/o Robert Miller Gallery 41 E 57th St New York NY 10022

GAREY, PAT
DRAFTSMAN, PAINTER
b State College, Miss, Nov 11, 32. *Study:* Tex Woman's Univ, BS(costume design & fashion illus); Tex Tech Univ, Lubbock, MFA, with Jim Howze, Terry Morrow, Lynwood Kreneck, Hugh Gibbons, 2-Dimensional Studio & Minor Art Hist; Art Students League, 77; Villa Maria Ctr Arts, Perugia, Italy, 85. *Exhib:* 17th Ann Nat Exhib Prints & Drawings, Okla Art Ctr, 75; Santa Fe Festival of Arts, 79 & 80; Sangre Cristo Art Ctr, Pueblo, Colo, 79; one-woman shows, NMex Jr Col, Hobbs, 81 & Univ Tex Permian Basin, Odessa, 81, Dallas Mus Fine Art, Beaux Arts Ball Art Auction & Exhib, Dallas, Tex, 86-88 & 90; and many others. *Pos:* Artist in sch prog, HEW Emergency Sch Aid Proj, Hobbs, 74-; bd dir, Southwest Symphony, Hobbs, NMex, 88, 90. *Teaching:* Instr drawing & painting, Col Southwest, NMex, 67-70, instr art hist, 74; instr, Dossant Meadows Mus Art, Dallas, Tex, 90; summer workshops, Cloud Croft, NMex, 89, 91 & 92. *Awards:* Cash Award, Figure Study No 1, 72; First Prize Ceramics, 74 & First Prize Graphics, 75, Llano Estacado Art Asn. *Media:* Ink; Watercolor, Acrylic. *Dealer:* Beverly Gordon Gallery Dallas TX; El-Dor Gallery Alburqueque NM. *Mailing Add:* 315 E Alto Hobbs NM 88240

GARHART, MARTIN J
PRINTMAKER
b Deadwood, SDak, July 2, 46. *Study:* SDak State Univ, BA, 69; WVa Univ, MA, 70; Southern Ill Univ, Edwardsville, MFA, 72. *Work:* Libr Cong, Smithsonian Inst, Washington, DC; Cleveland Mus Art; Brit Mus, London; Calif Palace Legion of Honor, San Francisco. *Exhib:* Drawings USA, 72; Colorprint USA, 73; Bradley Print Show 15th Nat, 74; 2nd NH Int Print Competition, 74; Davidson Nat Print & Drawing Competition, 74. *Teaching:* From asst to assoc prof art, Kenyon Col, 72- *Awards:* Spec Purchase Award, Davidson Print & Drawing Competition, 74; Purchase Award, Bradley Print Show 15th Nat, 74; Jurors Award of Merit, 2nd NH Int. *Mem:* Col Art Asn Am; NH Graphic Soc. *Media:* Lithography. *Mailing Add:* Dept Art Kenyon Col Gambier OH 43022

GARMAN, ED
PAINTER, WRITER
b Bridgeport, Conn, July 4, 14. *Study:* Self-taught. *Work:* Sheldon Mem Art Gallery, Univ Nebr, Lincoln; Mus NMex, Santa Fe; Metrop Mus Art, New York; Salt Lake Art Ctr, Utah; Nat Mus Am Art, Washington, DC. *Exhib:* Painters & Sculptures of the Southwest Ann, Mus NMex, 41-44; Solomon Guggenheim Found 5th Ann, New York, 43; Lure of the West, Salt Lake Art Ctr, 70; Masterpieces from the Mus of NMex, Marion Koogler McNay Art Inst, San Antonio, Tex, 70. *Bibliog:* Marilyn Hagberg (auth), Hot Geometry of Ed Garman, San Diego Mag, 9/68; Tiska Blankenship (auth), Ed Garman: Ideal-Modern, Jonson Gallery, Univ NMex. *Mem:* Transcendental Painting Group. *Media:* Acrylic, Gouache. *Publ:* Auth, Art of Raymond Jonson, Painter, 75. *Dealer:* Michael Rosenfeld Gallery 1014 Madison Ave New York NY 10021. *Mailing Add:* PO Box 1013 Imperial Beach CA 92032

GARNETT, WILLIAM ASHFORD
PHOTOGRAPHER, EDUCATOR
b Chicago, Ill, Dec 27, 16. *Work:* Smithsonian Inst, Washington, DC; Mus Mod Art & Metrop Mus Art, New York; George Eastman House, Rochester. *Comn:* Photographic mural, Mus Mod Art & State Dept, US Pavillion, Osaka World's Fair; The Searching Eye (film), comn by Saul Bass & Eastman Kodak & From Here to There (film), comn by Saul Bass & United Airlines, NY World's Fair, 64-65; America Begins in New England (aerial essay), Life Mag, 67 & Splendors Where the Eagles Soar (aerial essay), 68. *Exhib:* William Garnett, Aerial Photography, Eastman House, Rochester; The Family of Man & Diogenes IV, Mus Mod Art; Photographer & the American Landscape & photography from mus collection, Mus Mod Art. *Teaching:* Prof design & photography, Univ Calif, Berkeley, 68-84. *Awards:* Ctr Advan Visual Studies Fel, Kepes, Mass Inst Technol, 67-68; Guggenheim Fel, 53, 56 & 75; Outstanding Achievement in Landscape Photog Award, Am Soc Mag Photogr, 83. *Bibliog:* Beaumont Newhall (auth), The History of Photography, Mus Mod Art; Peter Pollack (auth), The Pictorial History of Photography, Abrams; Walker Evans (auth), Over California, Fortune, 3/54. *Collection:* Aerial photography from US, Can, Mex, Japan, Hong Kong, Manila and Australia. *Publ:* Auth, The Extraordinary Landscape: Aerial Photographs of America, New York Graphic Soc, 82. *Mailing Add:* 1286 Congress Valley Rd Napa CA 94558

GARNSEY, CLARKE HENDERSON
HISTORIAN, EDUCATOR
b Joliet, Ill, Sept 22, 13. *Study:* Cleveland Inst Art, dipl, 47; Western Reserve Univ, BS(art educ), 47, MA(art hist), 48 & PhD(art hist), 62. *Comn:* Fourteen murals, Volusia Co Schs, Fla, 34-38 & series of etchings of historic locations, Eastern Fla, WPA Fed Art Proj; watercolors, Amarillo Col, Tex. *Exhib:* Daytona Beach Art League Ann Exhib, 34-42; Southern States Art League Ann Exhib, 35-38; Wichita Art Asn Exhib, Kans, 37-38; May Show, Cleveland Mus Art, 49 & 58; Nat Exhib Relig Art, Rochester, NY, 69. *Pos:* Chmn studio work, Amarillo Col, 49-63; chmn art hist, Wichita States Univ, 63-66. *Teaching:* Lectr, Cleveland Mus Art & Cleveland Inst, 57-59; prof art, Univ Tex, El Paso, 66-79, emer prof, 79- *Awards:* Numerous awards and mentions nationally. *Mem:* Col Art Asn Am; Soc Archit Hist; Tex Fine Arts Asn; Tex Asn Sch of Art; Rio Bravo Watercolorists. *Media:* Watercolor, Enamel. *Res:* Latin American colonial architecture with emphasis on Neo-Classicism. *Mailing Add:* 607 Linda Ave El Paso TX 79922

GAROIAN, CHARLES RICHARD
CONCEPTUAL ARTIST, EDUCATOR
b Fresno, Calif, Nov 7, 43. *Study:* Calif State Univ, Fresno, BA(visual art), 68, MA(visual art), with Allen Bertoldi, 69; Stanford Univ, with Elliot W Eisner, PhD(educ), 84. *Exhib:* San Francisco Mus Mod Art, Calif, 74; Esoteric Investigations, Zoller Gallery, Penn State Col, 88; Dada Again, S/Laughter, Painted Bride Art Ctr, Philadelphia, 90; Circumstancial Evidence, Birmingham Loft, Pittsburgh, 91; Flayed Ox, Paul Robeson Cult Ctr, Penn State Univ, 92; Butt of the Media in the Face of the Public, Cleveland Performance Art Festival & Ward-Nasse Gallery, New York, 92; and others. *Pos:* Educ dir, Palmer Mus Art, Penn State, 86-90, asst dir, 90-91. *Teaching:* Supervisor art educ, Stanford Teacher Educ Prog, Calif, 75-76; lectr art educ, Univ Washington, Seattle, summer 77; assoc prof art educ, Sch Visual Arts, Penn State, 91-; lectr performance art, Deep Creek Sch, Ariz State Univ Summer Inst, 92. *Awards:* Soc for Encouragement Contemp Art, San Francisco Mus Mod Art, 74; Mus Prog & Arts Educ Grant, Penn Coun Arts, 87, 88, 91 & 92; Creative Prog Award, Nat Univ Continuing Educ Asn, 89. *Bibliog:* Jan McCambridge (auth), Be True to Your School (play), High Performance, spring, 81; Judith Maloney (auth), The Farmer as Artist, Research Penn State, 12/87; Paul Blaum (auth), The lonely passion of Charles Garoian, Ararat Quarterly, spring 91. *Mem:* Nat Art Educ Asn; Col Art Asn. *Publ:* Coauth, Christo on art, education, and the running fence, Art Educ, 77; auth, Art history has meaning for high school students, Art Workers News, 82; Teaching critical thinking through art history in high school, Design for Arts Educ, 88; Art in crises: an attack on recent body metaphors, Penn State J Contemp Criticism, 92; Art history and the museum in the schools: a model for museum-school partnerships, J Visual Arts Res, 92. *Mailing Add:* Pa State Univ Palmer Mus Art University Park PA 16802

GARRARD, MARY DUBOSE
HISTORIAN, EDUCATOR
b Greenwood, Miss, July 25, 37. *Study:* Newcomb Col, BA, 58; Radcliffe Col, MA, 60; Johns Hopkins Univ, PhD, 70. *Teaching:* From asst prof to prof art hist, Am Univ, Washington, DC, 64- *Mem:* Women's Caucus for Art (pres, 74-76); Col Art Asn Am (bd dirs, 77-81); Am Asn Univ Prof. *Res:* Sculpture of Jacopo Sansovino; painting of Artemisia Gentileschi; other aspects of 16th century and 17th century Italian art; gender studies, 16th-20th century. *Publ:* Auth, Of men, women and art: some historical reflections, Art J, 76; Artemisia Gentileschi: The Image of the Female Hero in Italian Baroque Painting, Princeton Univ Press, 89; co-ed, Feminism and Art History: Questioning the Litany, Harper & Row, 82; auth, The liberal arts and Michelangelo's first project for the tomb of Julius II, Viator: Medieval & Renaissance Studies, 84; co-ed, The Expanding Discourse: Feminism and Art History, Harper Collins, 92. *Mailing Add:* Dept Art Am Univ Washington DC 20016

GARRETT, STEPHEN
MUSEUM DIRECTOR
b Ashtead, Surrey, Eng, Dec 26, 22. *Study:* Cambridge Univ, Eng, MA. *Pos:* Dir, J Paul Getty Mus, 73-83; dir, Long Beach Mus Art, 84-88 & Armand Hammer Mus, 90- *Teaching:* Lectr design, Cent Sch Arts & Crafts, London, 54-64; sr lectr archit, Polytech Cent, London, 64-72. *Mem:* Assoc Royal Inst Brit Architects; Asn Art Mus Dirs. *Mailing Add:* c/o Armand Hammer Mus of Art: Cultural Ctr 10899 Wilshire Blvd Los Angeles CA 90024

GARRETT, STUART GRAYSON
PAINTER, EDUCATOR
b Oklahoma City, Okla. *Study:* Cooper Union; Art Students League. *Work:* USN Hist Collection; Southern Vt Art Ctr; Factory Point Bank; Prudential Ins Co; Univ Md; NY Univ; Chrysler Mus, Norfolk, Va; Dubuque Art Asn, Iowa; plus pvt collections. *Exhib:* Nat Acad Design, New York; Am Watercolor Soc, New York; Am Artists Prof League, New York; Audubon Artists, New York; Mus Marine, Paris; Metrop Mus, New York; Nat Art Club, New York; Allied Artists Am. *Pos:* Art dir, Ad Press Ltd, 58-63. *Teaching:* Prof emer art, City Col New York, currently. *Awards:* Gold Medal, Am Artists Prof League, 59 & 60; Acad Artists Asn Awards, 59 & 78; Award, Am Watercolor Soc, 61, 63, 66 & 72; Salmagundi Club Awards, 62, 63, 65 & 67. *Mem:* Am Watercolor Soc; Nat Soc Painters Casein & Acrylic; Southern Vt Artists; Salmagundi Club; Knickerbocker Artists; Allied Artists Am. *Media:* Miscellaneous Media. *Mailing Add:* RD 1 Box 184 Salem NY 12865

GARRIGUES, SUZANNE
HISTORIAN
b New York, NY, May 15, 45. *Study:* Lindenwood Col, St Charles, Mo, BA(art), 67; Univ de las Am, Mex, MA(Latin Am art hist), 70; Johns Hopkins Univ, with Phoebe Stanton, MA(art hist), 75; Univ Md, with James B Lynch, PhD(art hist; grad fel), 83. *Pos:* Mem archeol team, Las Pilas, Morelos, Mex, 73 & Xochicalco, Morelos, 78; asst area supv, Joint Archeol Exped to Caesarea Maritima, Israel, summer 79. *Teaching:* Prof art hist, Md Inst, Col Art, 87. *Awards:* Fac grant-in-aid res, Morgan State Univ, 71, 72, 75 & 82. *Res:* Iconography of highland Olmec and lowland Izapa monumental art; Wifredo Lam and contemporary Cuban painting; modern Latin American art. *Publ:* Auth, Century Latin American Paintings, Drawings and Sculpture, Sotheby, Park Bernet, Inc, 5/84 & 11/84; Celtic Expressions: Sculpture by Patrick F McGuire, Loyola Col Art Gallery, Baltimore, 2/86; The National Museum of Anthropology in Mexico City, The Museum of Modern Art in Mexico City & The Gold Museum in Bogota Columbia, In: Art Museums of the World, Greenwood Press, 86; Art of the Fantastic: Latin America 1920-1987, Indianapolis Mus Art, 87; Wilfredo Lam (auth), Culture and Revolution in the Eternal Presence, Plastica del Caribe, Habana, 89. *Mailing Add:* Md Inst Col Art 1300 Mount Royal Ave Baltimore MD 21217

GARRISON, BARBARA
PRINTMAKER, ILLUSTRATOR
b London, Eng, Aug 22, 31. *Study:* Wellesley Col, Mass, BA, 53; Columbia Univ, MA, 56; Pratt Graphics Ctr. *Work:* New York Pub Libr Print Collection, Grey Gallery, NY Univ, New York; Butler Inst Am Art, Youngstown, Ohio; Ga Mus Art, Athens; Slater Mem Mus, Norwich, Conn. *Exhib:* Mini-Gravat International, Barcelona, Spain, 84; International Miniature Print, Seoul, Korea, 84; International Miniature Print, Pratt Graphics Ctr, New York, 84-85; Statue of Liberty Travelling Exhib, 86; Society Graphic Artists, New York, 86. *Teaching:* Instr art, Spence Sch, 63-69, Nightingale-Bamford Sch, 70-78, New York. *Mem:* Nat Asn Women Artists; Artists Equity New York; Graphic Artists Guild; Manhattan Graphics Ctr; Int Graphic Arts Found. *Media:* Etching. *Publ:* Illusr, The Sultan's Perfect Tree, Parents Mag Press, 77; Breakfast Books and Dreams, Frederick Warne, 81; Junior Great Books, Great Books Found, 86. *Mailing Add:* 12 E 87th St No 3C New York NY 10128

GARRISON, DAVID EARL
PAINTER, MURALIST
b Jacksonville, Ill, Mar 23, 40. *Study:* Am Acad Art, studied pastel with Daniel Green & watercolor with Irving Shapiro, 64-68; Anatomy with Bill

Parks; Iowa Wesleyan Col, BA, 87. *Work:* Video Warehouse Iowa; Hardee's Family Restaurants. *Comn:* Hist mural, Iowa Welcome Ctr; Hardees Retaurant Chain. *Exhib:* Pastel Soc France, 88-90; Hudson Valley Art Asn, Westchester Co Ctr, White Plains, NY, 87-90; Wichita Art Asn Nat Honors Show, 89-90; Nat Artists Prof League Exhib, New York, 87-90; Kans Pastel Soc, 88, 89 & 90; Pastel Soc Am, New York, 88. *Teaching:* Instr, Iowa Arts Coun, Des Moines, 79-90. *Awards:* W & J Nath Award in Oil, Wichita Art Asn, Kans, 88. *Mem:* Kans Pastel Soc; Midwest Pastel Soc; Hudson Valley Art Asn; Pastel Soc Am; Nat Artist Prof League. *Media:* Oil, Pastel. *Publ:* Contribr, Impressions, Southwest Art, 77. *Dealer:* Sue McVay Burlington IA 52601. *Mailing Add:* 831 S Garfield Burlington IA 52601

GARRISON, ELIZABETH JANE
PAINTER, JEWELER
b Elmira, NY, Feb 11, 52. *Study:* Ringling Sch Art & Design, BFA, 73; Mansfield Univ, 78; Fla State Univ, with William Harper, MS, 80. *Work:* Kunstgewerbe Mus, Berlin, Ger; Yale Univ Art Gallery, New Haven, Conn; Honolulu Acad Arts, Hawaii. *Exhib:* Contemporary Arts: An Expanding View, Monmouth Mus Art, Lincroft, NJ, 86; Modern Jewelry 1964-1986, Philadelphia Mus Art, Pa, 86; Infinite Riches: Jewelry Through the Ages, Mus Fine Arts, St Petersburg, Fla, 89; Schmuckezene '89, International Handwerkemesse, Munich, Ger; American Dreams, American Extremes, Het Kruithuis, Mus of Contemp Art, The Netherlands, 90; Everson Biennial, Everson Mus, Syracuse, NY, 92. *Awards:* Fla State Univ Fel, 80; Nat Endowment Arts Fel, 81 & 88. *Dealer:* State of the Art Gallery 120 W State St Ithaca NY 14850; Helen Drutt Gallery 1721 Walnut St Philadelphia PA 19103. *Mailing Add:* PO Box 6670 Ithaca NY 14851

GARRISON, EVE
PAINTER
b Boston, Mass, Apr 22, 08. *Study:* Art Inst Chicago, grad, 31; Wayne Univ; Lawrence Inst Technol; Lewis Inst Chicago. *Work:* Metrop Mus Art, Miami, Fla; Drian Gallery, London; Roosevelt Univ Rehabilitation Hosp, Union League Club, Chicago; Nat Mus Art, Warsaw, Poland; Gdanske Mus, 83-88; House Myrth Mus, Bulgaria, 87; and others. *Exhib:* Smithsonian Inst, 70-72; retrospectives, Ill Inst Technol, Chicago, 72 & Miami Mus Mod Art, 72; one-woman shows, Galerie Vallombreuse, Biarritz, France, 72, Spertus Mus, Chicago, 76, Atlante Galerie Salammbo, St Gervais, Paris, 87- & Salammbo LA, Geneve, 87-88. *Awards:* Awards for Old Colored Maid, Corcoran Mus, 34, Gold Medal for Figure & Bride & Groom, Union League Club, Chicago, 61. *Bibliog:* Dona Meilach (auth), Collage and found art, 65; Dale Dach (producer, dir), What is Art? (video), 89; Louise Dunn Yochim (auth), Harvest of Freedom, 89. *Mem:* Chicago Artists Coalition. *Media:* Oil, Casein. *Mailing Add:* PO Box 15338 Plantation FL 33318-5338

GARRISON, GENE K
PHOTOGRAPHER, PAINTER
Study: Ariz State Univ; Phoenix Col, AFA; Glendale Community Col; study with Bill Ahrendt, Jason Williamson & Helen del Grosso. *Exhib:* Art Barn ana Art Room, Cave Creek, Ariz; Conrad's Imagine & Es Posible, El Pedregal, N Scottsdale, Ariz. *Pos:* Cur, various art shows, Cactus Shadows Fine Arts Ctr, Cave Creek, Ariz, 90-91. *Publ:* Various articles on artists & art shows published in magazines such as Carefree Enterprise & Antiques World. *Mailing Add:* PO Box 536 Cave Creek AZ 85331

GARSTON, GERALD DREXLER
PAINTER
b Waterbury, Conn, May 3, 25. *Study:* Johns Hopkins Univ, BA, 51; Art Students League, 52, painting with Louis Bouche & printmaking with Harry Sternberg. *Work:* Rose Mus, Brandeis Univ; Los Angeles Co Mus; William Rockhill Nelson Gallery Art, Kansas City, Mo; Philadelphia Mus Art, Pa; Wadsworth Atheneum, Hartford, Conn. *Exhib:* Poindexter Gallery, New York, 62; A M Sachs Gallery, New York, 65; Susan Morse Hilles Collection, Mus Fine Arts, Boston, Mass, 66; Graham Gallery, New York, 67; Pucker-Safrai Gallery, Boston, 71, 74, 76, 78, 80, 82, 84, 86, 88 & 90; Freedman Gallery, Albright Col, Reading, Pa, 77; traveling exhib, Diamonds are Forever, State Mus, Albany, NY, 87. *Mem:* Phi Beta Kappa. *Media:* Oil. *Dealer:* Pucker-Safrai Gallery 171 Newbury St Boston MA 02116. *Mailing Add:* George Lamb Rd Leyden MA 01337

GARTEL, LAURENCE M
PHOTOGRAPHER, COMPUTER ARTIST
b New York, NY, June 5, 56. *Study:* Art Students League, with Knox Martin, 75; Sch Visual Arts, with Al Brunelle, George Trakas, Bill Beckley & Cora Kennedy, BFA, 77. *Work:* Bibliotheque Nationale, Paris; Polaroid Corp, Cambridge, Mass; Lending Collection, Mus Mod Art, New York; Universita Degli Studi Di Camerino, Italy. *Comn:* Absolut Gartel, Absolut Vodka. *Exhib:* Exchange of Information, Mus Mod Art, New York, 90; Mondo Miami,Virginia Miller Galleries, Coral Gables, Fla, 91; Cybernetic Romance, Fotogalerie Bordenao, Ger, 92; A Cybernetic Romance, Musneo01le Francais De La Photographie Paris, France, 92; Nuvo Japonica & Other Cybernetic Romances, Norton Gallery Art, West Palm Beach, Fla, 91; Nuvo Japonica & Other Cybernetic Romances, Ringling Sch Art, Sarasota, Fla, 92; and others. *Pos:* Cover artist video drawings, Computer Design Mag, Littleton, Mass, 81-82; Nikkei Computer Mag, Japan Cover Art, Tokyo, 82, 83, 84; special feature artist, Golf Illus Mag, 92. *Teaching:* Instr manipulating photog images, Creative Photog Workshop, Sch Visual Arts, New York, 78-83, instr computer art, Computer Graphics Workshop, 83-; lectr, Graphic Computer Communications, Boston, 82 & Computer Conf, Univ Ore, 84; lectr computer art, Bronx Community Col, NY & NY State Art Teachers' Asn, Monticello, 84 & Bronx Mus Art, NY, 85; instr computer graphics, Univ S Fla, 87, C W Post Col, 88-; Image Du Futur, Montreal, Que, 88; Westbrook Col, Maine, 89; Univ Southern Colo, 89; Murray State Univ, Ky, 90; Int Ctr Photog, NY, 90. *Awards:* Residency Grant, Experimental Television Ctr, Owego, 78-92; Poster Award, Art Director's Club, NJ, 85; Artist-in-Residency Grant, NY State Coun Arts, 85. *Bibliog:* End of artistic barbarians, Computerworld, Australia, 85; Mary Ann Marger (auth), Computer art, St Petersburg Times, Tampa, Fla, 87; Helen Harrison (auth), Mod Romance, Via Computer, New York Times, 10/88. *Media:* Computer Graphics. *Publ:* Co-auth & illusr, Messing up the signals, Camera 35, 12/81; auth & illusr, The incubation of electronic imaging, Photomethods, 82; illusr, Laurence Gartel video, fantasy or future?, Camera Weekly, England, 82; coauth & illusr, Fantasia Ben Calcolata, PM Mag, Italy, 83; auth, Laurence M Gartel: A Cybernetic Romance, Gibbs Smith, Utah, 89. *Dealer:* Corporate Art Directions NY. *Mailing Add:* 270-16B Grand Central Parkway Floral Park NY 11005

GARTEN, CLIFF
SCULPTOR
b Ridgewood, NJ, May 3, 54. *Study:* State Univ NY, BFA, 74; RI Sch Design, MFA, 78. *Work:* Everson Mus Art, Syracuse, NY. *Comn:* Ceramic Installation, Meyer, Scherer and Rockcastle Ltd Archit Offices, 88; Design & interpretive plan, Kellogg Mall Park, St Paul, Minn, 88-90; study garden, Brainerd Community Col, Minn, 91; entry plaza, Beaverton City Hall, Ore, 92. *Exhib:* Solo exhibs, Paired Vases, Minneapolis Col Art & Design, Minn, 85 & Situations, Thomson Gallery, Minneapolis, Minn, 86; Nat Endowment Arts Regional Fel Exhib, traveling exhib, 86; Poetry of the Physical, Am Craft Mus, New York, 86; Second Ann Monarch Tile Ceramic Competition, San Angelo Mus Fine Arts, Tex, 87; The Syracuse National: American Ceramics Now, Everson Mus Art, Syracuse, NY, 87; Quadriennale Int Faenza, La Ceramica Nell'Arredo Urbano, Faenza, Italy, 89. *Pos:* Mem bd dirs, Pub Art, St Paul, Minn, 87- *Teaching:* Teaching fel ceramics, RI Sch Design, Providence, RI, 75-78; assoc prof, Hamline Univ, St Paul, Minn, 78-87. *Awards:* Visual Artists Fel Grant, Nat Endowment Arts, 86; Third Ann Am Crafts Award, Meyer, Scherer and Rockcastle Archit Offices, 89; Visual Arts Travel Study Grant, Jerome Found, Saint Paul, Minn, 90. *Bibliog:* Grace Glueck (auth), Art: Using Ceramics to Adorn Architecture, New York Times, 7/12/85; Nancy Roth (auth), The Vessel in Context: Cliff Garten's Paired Vases, Am Ceramics, Vol 4, No 3, 85. *Publ:* The History of American Ceramics: 1607 to the Present, Harry N Abrams, Inc, New York, 88; American Ceramics, The Collection of the Everson Museum of Art, ed, Barbra Perry, Rizzoli, New York, 89. *Mailing Add:* 255 E Kellog Blvd Apt 506 St Paul MN 55101

GARVENS, ELLEN
PHOTOGRAPHER
b Omro, Wis. *Study:* Univ NMex, Albuquerque, MA, 82, MFA, 88. *Exhib:* Solo exhibs, Am Cult Ctr, Cameroon, W Africa, 80, New Ctr Contemp Arts, Santa Fe, NMex, 85 & Jayne H Baum Gallery, 87, 89 & 93; Elvehjem Mus Art, Madison, Wis, 82; Los Angeles Ctr Photog Studies, Calif, 86; Poetic Injury: The Surrealist Legacy in Postmodern Photography, Alternative Mus, New York, 87,; Haggerty Mus Art, Milwaukee, Wis; Herter Art Gallery, Univ Mass, 89; Cleveland Center Contemp Art, Ohio, 90; Constructed Spaces, Photographis Resource Ctr & Boston Arch Ctr, Boston Univ, 90; At One/At War with Nature, Pratt Manhattan Gallery, New York, 91; Schafler Gallery, Brooklyn, NY, 91; Spaces Gallery, Cleveland, Ohio, 92. *Teaching:* Asst prof art, Oberlin Col, Ohio, currently. *Awards:* Fulbright-Hayes Scholarship, 79; Visual Artists Fel Grant, Nat Endowment Arts, 86; H C Powers Grant, Oberlin Col, 90; B Wade & Jane B White Fel in the Humanities, Oberlin Col, 91. *Bibliog:* Andy Grundberg (auth), Critics' Choices, New York Times, 6/8/86; Robert Mahoney (auth), New York Press, 7/88; Robert Mahoney (auth), Arts Mag, 3/90. *Mem:* Soc Photogr Educ; Col Art Assoc. *Dealer:* Jane H Baum New York NY. *Mailing Add:* Dept Art Oberlin Col Oberlin OH 44074

GARVER, FANNY
ART DEALER
b Racine, Wis, Apr 3, 27. *Study:* Univ Wis, BA, 49, BLS, 50; Middlebury Col, Vt. *Collections Arranged:* Regional Artists of Wisconsin (auth, catalog), 77 & Nineteenth Century British Watercolour Drawings, Fanny Garver Gallery, Madison, Wis. *Pos:* Dir, Jane Haslem Gallery, 69-72; dir & pres, Fanny Garver Gallery, 72-; vpres, Garver Crafts, 85. *Mem:* Art Inst Chicago; Am Craft Coun; Madison Print Club (membership chmn); Milwaukee Art Ctr; Madison Art Ctr. *Specialty:* 19th century British, Wisconsin and regional artists; American fine arts crafts. *Publ:* Auth, Master Prints, 82 & Fanny Garver Collection of American Crafts, 85, Fanny Garver Gallery, Madison, Wis. *Mailing Add:* 230 State St Madison WI 53703

GARVER, THOMAS H
CONSULTANT, CURATOR
b Duluth, Minn, Jan 23, 34. *Study:* Barnes Found, Merion, Pa; Haverford Col, BA; Univ Minn, Mass, Mus Mgt Inst, Univ Calif, Berkeley, 79. *Collections Arranged:* Rose Art Mus, Brandeis Univ; Bruce Conner; Assemblages, Drawings & Films; 12 Photographers of the American Social Landscape, Newport Harbor Art Mus; Just Before the War: Urban America From 1935-1941 as seen by Photographers of the Farm Security Administration; Robert Rauschenberg in Black and White; Tom Wesselman: Early Still Lifes, 1962-64; Wood, Sculpture of Gabriel Kohn; Edward Hopper: 15 Paintings; Don Potts: My First Car; New Art of Vancouver; Reginald Marsh Retrospective; George Tooker Retrospective, Fine Arts Mus San Francisco, 74; New Photography: San Francisco and Bay Area, 74; Representations of America (co-organized with Henry Geldzabler, co-auth, catalog), traveling USSR, 77-78; Joseph Raffael, The California Years, 1969-78 (auth, catalog),

78 & Nathan Oliveira, 84, San Francisco Mus Mod Art; Sylvia Plimack Mangold, Madison Art Ctr, 82; Corp art collection, Rayovac corp, Madison, Wis, 85; Regarding Art: Artworks about Art, John Michael Kohler Arts Ctr, Sheboygan, Wis, 90; Mind and Beast: Contemporary Artists and the Animal Kingdom (auth, catalog), Leigh Yawkey Woodson Art Mus, Wausau, Wis, 92. *Pos:* Asst to dir, Krannert Art Mus, Univ Ill, 60-62; asst dir, Seattle World's Fair, 62 & Rose Art Mus, 62-68; dir, Newport Harbor Art Mus, Newport Beach, Calif, 68-72 & 77-80 & Madison Art Ctr, Wis, 80-87; consult art gallery design, Univ Chicago, Calif Inst Arts, 69 & ARCO Ctr Visual Arts, 73; cur exhibs, Fine Arts Mus San Francisco, 72-77; site visitor, Mus Accreditation Prog, Am Asn Mus. *Teaching:* Hist of art & museology, Calif State Univs, Long Beach & Fullerton, San Quentin Prison, through Col Marin, Kentfield & Univ Wis, Madison. *Mem:* Art Mus Asn (pres, 79-82, bd trustees, 79-84); assoc Int Inst Conserv Hist & Artistic Works. *Res:* Contemporary American art. *Publ:* Balboa & the fun zone, Art Am, 71; auth, Nathan Oliveira, Survey Exhib (catalog essay), San Francisco Mus Mod Art, 84; George Tooker, Clarkson N Potter, Inc, Publ, 85; George Tooker, Recent Paintings, 88, Marisa del Re Gallery, New York, 88; Mind and Beast: Contemporary Artists and the Animal Kingdom, Leigh Yawkey Woodson Art Mus, Wausau, Wis, 92. *Mailing Add:* 1962 Atwood Ave PO Box 3493 Madison WI 53704

GARVER, WALTER RAYMOND
PAINTER, WRITER
b Medina, NY, Aug 29, 27. *Study:* State Univ NY Buffalo, BFA, 55; also with Charles Burchfield, 50. *Work:* Butler Inst Am Art, Youngstown, Ohio; Minn Mus Art, St Paul; Cincinnati Univ; Indiana Univ Pa; Burchfield Art Ctr, Buffalo, NY. *Exhib:* Nat Acad Design Ann, New York, 56, 60, 70, 71 & 75; Chautauqua Nat Exhib, NY, 58-; one-man show, Albright-Knox Art Gallery, 72 & 90; Okla Art Ctr Ann, Oklahoma City, 81-83; Audubon Artists Ann, New York, 83-92; Am Watercolor Soc, 85 & 86; and many others. *Pos:* Contrib ed, Artist's Mag, 86- *Awards:* Medal Honor, Audubon Artists Ann Exhib, 83; Remy Award, Am Watercolor Soc Ann Exhib, 85; Ject-Key Award, 87; and others. *Mem:* Buffalo Soc Artists (pres, 64); Audubon Artists; Nat Watercolor Soc; Allied Artists Am; Knickerbocker Artists. *Media:* Oil, Watercolor. *Publ:* Numerous articles & reviews in The Artist's Mag. *Dealer:* Vern Stein Fine Arts 5747 Main St Williamsville NY 14221. *Mailing Add:* 4230 Tonawanda Creek Rd East Amherst NY 14051

GARWOOD, AUDREY
PAINTER, PRINTMAKER
b Toronto, Ont, July 7, 27. *Study:* Ont Col Art; Rijksacad, Amsterdam, scholar; Le Chaumiere, Paris. *Work:* London Gallery & Art Mus, Ont; McLaughlin Art Gallery, Oshawa, Ont; Burnaby Art Gallery, BC; Hamilton Art Gallery, Ont; Ont Art Gallery, Toronto. *Exhib:* Royal Can Acad; Ont Soc Artists; York Univ Hayward State, Calif; San Francisco Univ, Calif; Nat Gallery Showcase, Ottawa. *Teaching:* Life painting & printmaking, Central Tech, Toronto, 65-71;; Calif Col of Arts, Crafts, Advan Painting, Landscape painting, 76-78. *Awards:* Can Graphic Art Soc Award; Sterling Trust Award, Can Painters & Etchers; J Forester Award, Ont Soc Artists. *Mem:* Royal Can Acad Art; Ont Soc Art. *Media:* Oil, Watercolor. *Mailing Add:* 97 Dixon Ave Toronto ON M4C 1G1 Canada

GARY, DOROTHY HALES
COLLECTOR, WRITER
b San Francisco, Calif, Nov 21, 17. *Study:* Stanford Col. *Pos:* Owner, pvt gallery. *Specialty:* Abstract, contemporary art. *Collection:* Abstract art. *Publ:* Auth, Sun, Stones & Silence, Simon & Shuster, 63; coauth, Splendors of Asia, 65, coauth, Splendors of Byzantium, 67 & coauth, Moracco, Viking Press. *Mailing Add:* One E 66th St New York NY 10021

GARY, JAN (MRS WILLIAM D GORMAN)
PAINTER, PRINTMAKER
b Ft Worth, Tex, Feb 13, 25. *Study:* Art Ctr Sch, Los Angeles; San Antonio Art Inst, Tex; Art Students League. *Work:* Butler Inst Am Art, Youngstown, Ohio; Pensacola Art Ctr, Fla; Wis State Univ, Eau Claire; Brandeis Univ, Waltham, Mass; Rosenberg Libr, Galveston, Tex. *Exhib:* One-person show, Caldwell Col, NJ, 78; Am Acad Arts & Lett, 67-68; Four NJ Artists, Canton Art Inst, Ohio, 71; Cent Wyo Mus Art, Casper, 75; Charles & Emma Frye Mus Art, Seattle, Wash, 77; and others. *Pos:* Assoc dir, Old Bergen Art Guild, Bayonne, NJ, 62-90. *Awards:* Childe Hassam Fund Purchase Award, Am Acad Arts & Lett, 68; Dorothy F Seligson Mem Prize, Nat Asn Women Artists Ann, 75; David Soloway Mem Award, Allied Artists Am, 85. *Bibliog:* Henry Gasser (auth), article, Am Artist, 10/70. *Mem:* Nat Soc Painters Casein & Acrylic; Audubon Artists; Allied Artists Am. *Media:* Acrylic, Casein; Woodcut. *Mailing Add:* 43 W 33rd St Bayonne NJ 07002

GARZIO, ANGELO C
POTTER, CRAFTSMAN
b Campobasso, Italy, July, 22, 22. *Study:* Syracuse Univ, NY, BA, BS, 49; Univ Iowa, MA(art hist), 54, MFA(ceramics), 55. *Work:* Mus Contemp Crafts, NY; Wichita Art Asn; A Prieto Mem Collection, Mills Col, Oakland, Calif; Univ Art Mus, Hong Ik, Seoul, S Korea; Art Mus, Univ Benin, Benin City, Nigeria. *Exhib:* Biannual Nat Ceramic Exhib, Syracuse Mus Art, NY, 56, 58, 62, 64 & 66; Fiber-Clay-Metal Nat Craft Exhib, St Paul Art Mus, Minn, 57; Invitational Int Exhib, Brussel's World Fair Art Pavillion, Belg, 58-59; Smithsonian Inst, Washington, DC, 60, 62 & 63; Ceramic Arts USA, Int Mineral Corp Mus, Skokie, Ill, 66; 24th, 25th, 28th & 31st Int Ceramic Competition, Int Ceramic Mus, Faenza, Italy, 68, 69, 72 & 75; Sargadelos Gallery, Madrid, Spain, 89. *Teaching:* Prof ceramic art, Kans State Univ, 57-92; vis lectr & prof ceramic art, Hong Ik Univ, Seoul, Korea, 73-74; lectr & dept head, Dept Indus Design, Ahmadu Bello Univ, Nigeria, 77-78; lectr & prof ceramic art, Univ Misiones, Arg, 92. *Awards:* First Ceramic & Beaux Art Awards, Coral Gables Art Gallery, 57; Award of Excellence, 2nd Int Ceramics Exhib, Ostend, Belg, 59; Purchase Award, Wichita Art Asn, 62; Sr Fullbright Lectr Grant, 73, 77 & 92. *Bibliog:* Sandra B Ernst (auth), Angelo Garzio, Ceramics Monthly, Vol 29, No 1, 81; LuAnn F Culley (auth), Angelo Garzio: Life as the ultimate form, Kans Quart, Vol 14, No 4, 82; Antonio Vivas (auth), Angelo Garzio, Ceramica, Madrid, Spain, Vol 6, No 22, 85. *Mem:* Nat Conf Educ Ceramic Art; Kans Artist Craftsman Asn (vpres, 63-64). *Media:* Clay. *Publ:* Auth, German salt glazing, Craft Horizons, Vol 13, No 3, 63; Raku (portfolio feature article), Ceramics Monthly, Vol 15, No 6, 67; Kansang Mus Collection of Koryo Celadons, Korea J, Vo 14, No 7, 74; A Man & A Kiln: Mark Zamantakis, New Zealand Potter, Vol 26, No 1, 84; Antonio Prieto: In retrospect, Ceramica, Spain, Vol 6, No 23, 86. *Dealer:* Pewabic Pottery 10125 E Jefferson Detroit MI 48214; Clay Pidgeon Gallery Denver CO. *Mailing Add:* RR 4 Box 281A Manhattan KS 66502

GARZON-BLANCO, ARMANDO
DESIGNER, PAINTER
b Havana, Cuba, Feb 1, 41. *Study:* La State Univ, BA, 66, MA(design), 68, MA(art hist), 69, PhD(theatre-art), 76; Fulbright-Hays Res Grant, Spain, 72-73, La State Univ Coun on Res & Rodriguez-Acosta Fund Grants, Spain, 74. *Work:* Centroplex, Baton Rouge; Anglo-Am Mus & Univ Libr, La State Univ, Baton Rouge; Cath Student Ctr, Baton Rouge. *Comn:* Baptistry murals, St Paul Cath Church, Baton Rouge, 70; sanctuary & chapel, Christ the King Chapel, Baton Rouge, 73-75; altarpiece, St James Lutheran Church, Gonzales, La, 77. *Exhib:* Jay Broussard Mem Gallery, State La Dept Art, Hist & Cult Preserv, 72; US Cult Ctr of Am Embassy, Madrid, Spain, 73; Fundacion Rodriguez-Acosta Banco de Granada Gallery, Spain, 73. *Teaching:* From instr to prof design, painting & art hist, La State Univ, Baton Rouge, 68-77; prof design, painting & art hist & head art dept, Nicholls State Univ, Thibodaux, 77- *Awards:* Purchase Award, 2nd Ann Int La Watercolor Soc, 71. *Bibliog:* Miguel Rodriguez-Acosta Carlstrom (auth), Los artistas por el sureste espanol, Banco de Granada & Fundacion Rodriguez-Acosta, Spain, 73. *Mem:* La Watercolor Soc; SCent Renaissance Asn; Col Art Asn Am; Northeastern Mod Lang Asn; Nat Coun Art Adminr. *Media:* Watercolor, Mixed Media. *Res:* Interrelation of the theatre arts and visual arts; Spanish Jesuit theatrical practice in the 16th and 17th century; Afro-Cuban art. *Publ:* Auth, Note on the authorship of the Spanish Jesuit play of San Hermenegildo, Theatre Survey, 74; auth, The Tragedia de San Hermenegildo, Seville, 1590, Explorations in Renaissance Culture, 76; La Tragedia de San Hermenegildo en el teatro y en el arte, Estudios sobre literatura y arte dedicados al profesor, Emilio Orozco Diaz, II, Universidad de Granada, 79. *Mailing Add:* c/o Sacred Heart Sch Theology PO Box 429 Hales Corners WI 53130

GASPARRO, FRANK
SCULPTOR, INSTRUCTOR
b Philadelphia, Pa, Aug 26, 09. *Study:* Pa Acad Fine Arts; also with Charles Grafly. *Comn:* Designed reverse of Kennedy Half-Dollar, Am Numismatic Asn Medal, 69, obverse & reverse of President Richard M Nixon Medal, 69, obverse & reverse of Eisenhower Dollar & reverse of Lincoln Mem US One Cent; designed obverse & reverse of Susan B Anthony One Dollar, 79; Statue of Liberty Commemorative Medal Series, 86; reverse of Isabella & Columbus $2500 Proof Gold Coin, Bahamas, 87; also many medals for US mint. *Exhib:* Philadelphia Mus Art Sculpture Exhib, 40; Pa Acad Fine Arts, Philadelphia, 46; Medals at French Mint, Paris, 50; Spanish Int Medallic Art Exhib, Madrid, 52 & 68; Woman on the Medal, Int Medallic Exhib. *Pos:* Engraver, US Mint, Philadelphia, 42-65, chief engraver, 65-81. *Teaching:* Instr, Fleisher Art Sch, Philadelphia, 46-; instr, Pa Acad Fine Arts, 81- *Awards:* Order of Merit, Ital Repub (Cavaliere Ufficiale), 73; Citation for Super Performance of the US Treasury, 77; Percy Owenx Award Outstanding Artist, Pa, 79; plus others. *Mem:* Soc Medalists; Fr Soc of the Medal. *Media:* All. *Mailing Add:* 216 Westwood Park Dr Havertown PA 19083

GAST, CAROLYN BARTLETT (LUTZ)
ILLUSTRATOR, ILLUMINATOR
b Cambridge, Mass, Apr 30, 29. *Study:* Col Practical Arts & Lett, Boston Univ, BS(bk illus), 50. *Work:* Nat Mus Natural Hist, Smithsonian Inst & US Geol Surv, US Dept Interior, Washington, DC. *Exhib:* Seventeenth Area Exhib of Corcoran Gallery Art, Washington, DC, 65; Scientific Illus, Nat Mus of Natural Hist, Smithsonian Inst, 68; solo exhib & demonstration, Kotor, Yugoslavia, 70; Ann Exhibs of Asn of Med Illusr, 69-79; Nat Exhibs, Guild Natural Sci Illusr, 79 & 81-85; 30 Year Retrospective, Nat Mus Nat Hist, Smithsonian Inst, 84; solo shows, Tyler Gallery, NVa Community Col & Cosmos Club, Washington, DC, 85; invitational exhib, Guild Natural Sci Illusr, Nat Acad Sci, 85; Nat Exhib, Calligraphers Guild, Washington, DC, 86. *Pos:* Scientific illusr, US Geol Surv, Dept Interior, 52-56; scientific illusr, Nat Mus Natural Hist, Smithsonian Inst, 59-85. *Awards:* Honorable Mention in Sculpture, 17th Area Exhib Corcoran Gallery Art, Washington, DC, 65; First Place, Nat Exhibs, Guild Nat Sci Illusr, 79 & 82. *Mem:* Founding mem Guild of Natural Sci Illusr (vpres, 71-73, pres, 73-75); Col Art Asn Am. *Media:* Mixed. *Publ:* Illusr, Proceedings of the Us Nat Mus, 60-67; illusr, Proceedings of the Bio Soc of Washington, DC, 61-85; illusr, Smithsonian Contributions to Zoology, 67-85; illusr, Mary S Gardiner's The Biology of the Invertebrates, McGraw-Hill, 72; illusr, numerous scientific publications and journals, 59-85. *Mailing Add:* 5730 First St S Arlington VA 22204

GAST, DWIGHT V
WRITER, CRITIC
US citizen. *Study:* New Sch Social Res, New York, NY, BA, 79; Villa Schifanoia, Florence, Italy, 83. *Collections Arranged:* Critica ad arte, Palazzo

Lanfranco, Pisa, Italy, 83. *Pos:* Contrib ed, Art/World, New York, 79-82; ed, Italy Italy Mag, Rome, 83-84 & Diversion Mag, New York, 85-87; contrib ed, Art & Auction, New York, 88 & J Art, New York, 89- *Bibliog:* Article, Forma senza forma, in Comune de Modena, 82; Enzo Cucchi (auth), article, Solomon Guggenheim Found, New York, 86. *Mem:* Asn Int des Critiques d'Art Board; Nat Bk Critics Circle; Soc Am Travel Writers; NY Travel Writers. *Res:* Contemporary Italian and American painting and sculpture; historical Italian painting and sculpture. *Publ:* Contribr, Houghton Mifflin, 86; Birnbaum's Italy, 87-; Fodor's Rio, Penguin Italy, 88, Penguin New York, 89 & Penguin Portugal, 90, Viking Penguin; and others. *Mailing Add:* 265 Lafayette St No 25C New York NY 10012

GAST, MICHAEL CARL
PAINTER
b Chicago, Ill, June 11, 30. *Study:* Sch Art Inst Chicago, BFA, 52; Univ Am, Mex, MFA(cum laude), 60. *Exhib:* Washington Watercolor Asn 66th Ann Nat Exhib, Smithsonian Inst, 63 & Metrop Area Exhib, Howard Univ, Washington, DC, 70; Soc Washington Artists 70th & 71st Ann Exhib, Smithsonian Inst, 63 & 64; four-man show, Mickelson Gallery, Washington, DC, 66; Foundry Gallery, Washington, DC, 80; Downtown Gallery, Del Art Mus, Wilmington, Del, 80; Portraits, Gallery 10 Ltd, Washington, DC, 85; A Tribute to Isobel MacKinnon, Sch Art Inst Chicago Gallery, 85. *Pos:* Mus technician, div ceramics & glass, Nat Mus Hist & Technol, Smithsonian Inst, 61-64 & mus specialist, Nat Collection Fine Arts, 69-71. *Teaching:* Asst prof painting, George Washington Univ, 71. *Bibliog:* Andrea O Cohen (auth), article, Washington DC Gazette, 4/19/72. *Mem:* Artists Equity Asn (chap vpres, 73-77, nat secy-treas, 75-79, nat pres, 79-81); Col Art Asn Am. *Media:* Polymer, Oil. *Publ:* Contribr, Fed Art Patronage Notes, 77, Ceramics Monthly, 78 & Artists Equity Asn Nat Newsletter, 77-81. *Mailing Add:* 5730 First St S Arlington VA 22204

GASTALDI, JEROME
PAINTER, SCULPTOR
b Oakland, Calif, Mar 24, 45. *Study:* Orange Coast Col, 65. *Work:* South Bay Contemp Mus, Torrance, Calif; Art Inst Southern Calif, Laguna Beach; Riverside Mus, Calif; Nat Art Mus Sport, Indianapolis, Ind. *Exhib:* Venice Art Walk, Calif, 91 & 92; Celebration, Laguna Art Mus, Calif, 92; Question of Balance (auth, catalog), South Bay Contemp Mus, Torrance, Calif, 92; Expressions of the Faith (auth, catalog), Cross Contemp Art Space, Capo Beach, Calif, 92; Best of Laguna, Art Inst Southern Calif, Laguna Beach, Calif, 92; Images du Futur, Int Exhib, Montreal, Can, 92. *Media:* Mixed Media, Video. *Publ:* Gastaldi Light into Dark, 91, Fine Art Index, 92, N Dawn Shiba. *Dealer:* Charles Whitchurch Gallery 5973 Engineer Dr Huntington Beach CA 92694. *Mailing Add:* 1345 Coral Dr Laguna Beach CA 92651

GATES, HARRY IRVING
SCULPTOR, EDUCATOR
b Elgin, Ill, Dec 8, 34. *Study:* Univ Ill, BFA, 58, MFA, 60. *Work:* Chase Manhattan Bank, New York; Corcoran Gallery Art, Washington, DC; Int Art Prog Div, Nat Collection Fine Art, Washington, DC; Washington Co Mus Fine Arts, Hagerstown, Md; Baltimore Mus Fine Art, Md; Washington & Lee Univ, Va. *Exhib:* One-man show, Baltimore Mus Fine Art, 64; Small Sculpture Purchases for Int Art Prog, Nat Collection Fine Art, 69; New Sculpture, Corcoran Art, Washington, DC, 70; Five Maryland Artists, Md Arts Coun, 72-73; Sculpture Invitational, Rochester Inst Technol, 75; The Object as Poet, Renwick Gallery, Washington, DC & Mus Contemp Crafts, New York, 77; 18 year retrospective, Washington Co Mus Art, Md, 78; two-man exhib, Dimock Gallery, George Washington Univ, 79. *Teaching:* Asst prof sculpture, George Washington Univ, 64-78, assoc prof, 78- *Awards:* First Prize, 21st Ann Contemp Art, Palm Beach, Fla, 59; Artists Coun Award, 25th Ann Exhib for Sculpture, 61; Gov Prize, Md Ann, 70. *Mailing Add:* Dept Art George Washington Univ Washington DC 20052

GATES, JAY RODNEY
ADMINSTRATOR, CURATOR
b Kansas City, Mo, Nov 21, 45. *Study:* Col Wooster, Ohio, BA, 68; Univ Rochester, NY, MA, 70. *Exhib:* Mitthoefer Collection of African Sculpture, Col Wooster Mus, Ohio, 74; Prints & Drawings by Sculptors, Cleveland Mus Art, Ohio, 75; Tenn Quilts, Brooks Mem Art Gallery, Memphis, 79; Arts of Ancient Egypt: Treasures on Another Scale, Memphis & Washington, DC, 81. *Pos:* Asst cur art hist & educ, Cleveland Mus, 73-76; cur educ, St Louis Art Mus, 76; dir, Brooks Mem Art Gallery, Memphis, 79-81; asst dir & cur Am art, Nelson Gallery, Atkins Mus, 81-; dir, chief cur, Spencer Mus Art, Univ Kans, Lawrence, currently; dir, Seattle Art Mus. *Teaching:* Instr art hist, Col Wooster, Ohio, 71-73; instr art hist, Case Western Reserve Univ, Cleveland, 73-76; prof art hist, Univ Kans, 83-87. *Mem:* Am Asn Mus; Col Art Asn; Asn Art Mus Dirs. *Res:* Public education in art museums; American painting. *Publ:* Auth, Television from the galleries, Mus News, 75; co-auth, Teaching advanced placement art history in a museum, Art J, 75. *Mailing Add:* c/o Seattle Art Mus Volunteer Park Seattle WA 98112

GATES, JEFF S
PHOTOGRAPHER
Study: Mich State Univ, E Lansing, BA, 71; UCLA, Los Angeles, Calif, MFA, 75. *Exhib:* Cultural Participation, 88, City: Visions and Revisions, Dia Found, New York, 89; solo exhibs, Midtown Y, New York, 89, Baltimore Mus Art, Md, 92; Outcry: Artists Answer AIDS (auth catalog), Mus Contemp Art, Baltimore, Md, 91; Multi Media Grunderzeit: Computergraphics State of the Art, Univ Wuppertal, Ger, 92. *Bibliog:* Patrick Finnegan (auth), Baltimore, Contemporanea, summer 90; John Dorsey (auth), Power Plays: those who have it, those who don't, Baltimore Sun, Md, 3/12/92. *Mailing Add:* 1440 E Baltimore St, #2E Baltimore MD 21231

GATES, THOMAS PAUL
EDUCATOR, CURATOR
b Cleveland, Ohio, Aug 21, 41. *Study:* Western Reserve Univ, BA, 67; Univ Southern Calif, MA, 70; Univ NMex, MA, 73. *Collections Arranged:* Man: The Music Maker (auth, catalog), Maxwell Mus, 73; Artists Proof/The Multiple Image, survey of printmaking, 77; A Shade of Light, history of int illum, 78; Ceramic containers, ceramic vessels, 79; American Still Lifes, paintings & prints, 79. *Pos:* Educ coordinator, Fine Arts Mus San Francisco Downtown Ctr, 75-80, acting dir, 80; registrar, M H De Young Mus Art Sch, San Francisco, Calif, 80-, libr asst, currently; mus educ consult, Univ Art Mus Berkeley, Calif, 81. *Teaching:* Lectr art hist, M H De Young Mus Art Sch, San Francisco, Calif, 75-79, Chabot Col, Livermore, Calif, 76-77 & Foothill Col, Los Altos Hills, Calif, 75-79. *Awards:* Rockefeller Fel, Fine Arts Mus San Francisco, 73-74. *Mem:* Col Art Asn; Am Asn Mus; Soc Architectural Historians; Nat Trust Historic Preserv. *Publ:* Auth, Community Murals in San Francisco, De Young Mus Art Sch, 77; ed, The Work Show, Fine Arts Mus San Francisco Downtown Ctr, 78. *Mailing Add:* Dept Drama Calif State Univ Sacramento 600 Jr St Sacramento CA 95819

GATEWOOD, MAUD
PAINTER
b Yanceyville, NC, Jan 8, 34. *Study:* Univ NC, Greensboro, AB; Ohio State Univ, MA; Univ Vienna; Fulbright grant, 62-63; Acad Appl Arts, Vienna; Harvard Summer Sch. *Work:* Mint Mus Art, Charlotte, NC; Nat Collection of Fine Arts, Washington, DC; NC Mus Art, Raleigh; pvt collections. *Comn:* Glaxo Pharmaceuticals; Research Triangle, NC; Chase Manhattan Bank; Coca Cola; McDonald Corp; and others. *Exhib:* Painting in the South, Va Mus, 83; NC Mus Art, Raleigh, 83; Somerhill Gallery, Chapel Hill, NC; Hodges/Taylor Gallery, Charlotte, NC; Heath Gallery, Atlanta; and others. *Teaching:* Adj prof, Averett Col, Danville, Va. *Awards:* Am Acad Arts & Lett Award, 72; Nat Endowment Arts/South Eastern Ctr Contemp Art Southeastern Seven, 81. *Media:* Acrylic. *Dealer:* Heath Gallery 416 E Paces Ferry Rd Atlanta GA 30305; Hodges-Taylor Gallery 227 N Tryon St Charlotte NC 28202. *Mailing Add:* Box 726 Yanceyville NC 27379

GATLING, EVA INGERSOLL
CONSULTANT, HISTORIAN
b Mobile, Ala, Dec 28, 12. *Study:* Richmond Prof Inst, Col William & Mary, cert art, 35; Univ Ala, BA, 41; Yale Univ, MA, 44. *Collections Arranged:* Eliel Saarinsen Mem Exhib (with catalog), Cranbrook Acad Art, 51; Whence Pop, 65, Moran Family, 65 & Salute to Small Museums, 70 (with catalogs), Heckscher Mus; collections of Helen Torr, 72, Ibram Lassaw, 73, Stanley Twardowicz, 74 & Fairfield Porter, 74-75; George Grosz Works in Oil, Heckscher Mus, 77. *Pos:* Dir exhib & supvr art equip, Duke Univ, 45-49; cur, Mus Cranbrook Acad Art, 49-54; asst dir, Des Moines Art Ctr, 59-61; dir, Heckscher Mus, 62-77. *Awards:* Katherine Coffee Award, Northeast Mus Conf, 79. *Mem:* Soc Archit Historians. *Res:* American art, particularly after 1900; American architecture of the 19th and 20th centuries; Buddhist art. *Publ:* Contribr, Soc Art Historians J, 51; contribr, Art J, 55; contribr, Artibus Asiae, 57. *Mailing Add:* 3100 Shore Dr Apt 1219 Virginia Beach VA 23451

GATTO, PAUL ANTHONY
PAINTER, INSTRUCTOR
b Brooklyn, NY, Sept 19, 29. *Study:* Self taught fine artist. *Work:* Jennings Hall, S Oaks Hosp, Amityville, NY; Kramer Lane Sch, Bethpage, NY; Garden City Inn, NY; Manhasset High Sch, NY; Methodist Church Community Ctr, NY. *Comn:* The Visitation, The Annunciation, The Parable, The Ministry & The Shepherd, (oil panels) Maria Regina RC Church, Seaford, NY, 89- *Exhib:* Ninth Art Festival, Two Flags, Douglas, Ariz, 81; 61st Ann Nat Exhib, Ogunquit Art Ctr, Maine, 81; 59th Ann Nat Apr Salon, Springville Mus, Utah, 83; Pro Art Exhib, Utah Pageant Arts, American Fork, 83; Artists at Work, Nassau Co Mus Art, Roslyn, NY, 90; and others. *Pos:* Pres & bd trustees, Farmingdale Pub Libr, 77-; pres, Ital Cult Soc, 75-78; art damage appraiser, Royal, Home, Aetna & Utica Mutual Insurance, 70- *Teaching:* Lectr demonstr fine arts, painting, 67-; teacher fine arts, painting, Paul Gatto Gallery, Farmingdale, NY, 67-; teacher fine arts, painting, NY Inst Technol, Islip, 88- *Mem:* Hechscher Mus, Huntington, NY, Artists Regist, 82. *Media:* Oils, Watercolor. *Publ:* Illusr, Published prints, 11/76 & Times Square-New Years Day, 82, Paul A Gatto; poster, portrait Alexander, Fundraiser, Polish Gift Life Charity, 91. *Mailing Add:* Paul Gatto Gallery 300 Main St Farmingdale NY 11735

GATTO, ROSE MARIE
PAINTER
b Brooklyn, NY, Apr 11, 31. *Study:* Brooklyn Col, 49; Art Students League, 80. *Work:* Cranford Pub Libr, NJ, 80. *Exhib:* Summit Art Ctr, NJ, 83; Nat Asn Women Artists, 89-90. *Teaching:* Instr, Jane Law Gallery, 86-; Teen Festival Union Col, 86-89; Westfield Adult Sch, 87-88. *Awards:* First Place, NJ Watercolor Soc, 86. *Bibliog:* Three Generations of Artists, Daily J, 82. *Mem:* NJ Watercolor Soc (asst nat chmn, 89); Nat Asn Women Artists (record secy 89). *Media:* Watercolor, Mixed Media. *Mailing Add:* Seven Ramsgate Rd Cranford NJ 07016

GAUCHER, YVES
PRINTMAKER, PAINTER
b Montreal, Que, 34. *Study:* L'Ecole des Beaux Arts, Montreal, 54-56. *Work:* Mus Mod Art, New York; Libr of Cong, Washington, DC; Victoria & Albert Mus, London, Eng; Mus d'Art Contemp, Montreal; Nat Gallery of Can, Ottawa, Ont. *Exhib:* Contemp Painters as Printmakers, Mus Mod Art, New York, 64; Expo 70, Japan; Aspects of Can Art, Members Gallery, Albright-Knox Art Gallery, Buffalo, NY, 74; Thirteen Artists from Marlborough

Gallery, New York, 74; one-man shows, Mural Installation, Nova Corp, Calgary, Alberta, 82, Centre Cult Can, Bruxelles, Belgium, 83, Can House, London, England, 83, Centre Cult du Can, Paris, 83, Galerie Esperanza, Montreal, 86, Olga Korper Gallery, Toronto, 85, 86 & 88, 49th Parallel Centre Contemp Can Art, New York, 89; 15th Anniv show, Olga Korper Gallery, Toronto, 88; Waddington & Gorce Inc, Montreal, 88; Montreal Painting of 1960's, Americas Soc Art Gallery, New York, 89; Living Impressions, Art Gallery, Hamilton, Ont, 89; and others. *Teaching:* Asst prof fine arts, Sir George Williams Univ, Montreal, 63-69, assoc prof, 70-; prof, Concordia niv, Montreal, 66- *Awards:* First Prize, Nat Print Competition, Burnaby, BC, 61; Second Prize, Int Triennale of Colored Prints, Grenchen, Switz, 64; Grand Prize, Sandage 68, Montreal Mus Fine Arts, 68. *Bibliog:* Donald Brackett (auth), Yves Gaucher & Christopher Kier, Arts Report, 3/8/88; Perceiving painting through the pores, Now Mag, 3/10/88; Norman Theriault (auth), Art: Style over story, Forces, winter 88. *Publ:* Auth, Living Impressions (exhib catalog), Art Gallery Hamilton, Ont, 89. *Mailing Add:* Dept Art Concordia-U-G Williams 1455 De Maissoneuve W Montreal PQ H3G 1M8 Canada

GAUDARD, PIERRE
PHOTOGRAPHER, GRAPHIC ARTIST
b Marvelise (Doubs), France, Oct 6, 27, Can citizen. *Study:* Ecole Estienne, Paris, France. *Work:* Can Mus Contemp Photog, Ottawa, Ont; Musee Art Contemporain, Montreal, Que; Galerie FNAC, Paris, France; Bibliotheque Nationale, Paris, France; Winnipeg Art Galerie, Can; Can Coun Bank of Ottawa; Nat Art Galerie, Ottawa. *Exhib:* One-man shows, Les Prisons, Galerie de L'Image, Ottawa, 77, Musee d'Art Contemporain, Montreal, 80, Galerie Canon, Amsterdam, Holland, 80, Univers Carceral, Galerie FNAC Forum, Paris, 80, En France, Galerie de L'Image, Ottawa, 82, Place des Arts, Montreal, 83 & Exercises de Style, Galerie Dazibao, Montreal, 84; Exposure, Art Gallery Ont, Toronto, 75; Tendances Actuelles au Quebec, Musee d'Art Contemporain, Montreal, 78; 66-Photographes-Actuels, Palais des Beaux Arts, Brussels, Belg, 81; Photographie au Quebec, Galerie du Rip, Arles, France, 82; Photographie Actuelle au Quebec, Galerie Quebec, Paris, France, 82; Le Mois de la Photo Á Montréal, Maisons de la Culture, (invité d'honneur), 89; and others. *Teaching:* Photo workshop, Col Bois de Boulogne, Montreal, Can, 88- *Awards:* Medaille de la Fedn Int d'Art Photo-graphique, Montreal, 69; Carveth Award, Hamilton Camera Club, Can, 70; Medaille d'or ONF, Ottawa, Nat Film Bd, 72; Ministere des Affaires Cult du Que Grants, 82 & 86; and many others. *Bibliog:* Jacque Giraldeau (auth), La Toile d'Araignee, Films Nat Film Bd, Can, 79; Francois Caillat (auth), Pierre Gaudard, Zoom, Paris, 3/80; Serge Jonque (auth), Photo a l'Air Libre, Vie des Arts, 7/83. *Publ:* Coauth, Canada du Temps Qui Passe, ONF, 67; auth, Image-10-Les Ouvriers, Nat Film Bd, Ottawa, 72; coauth, Exposure, Art Gallery, Toronto, 75; Entre Amis, ONF, 76; auth, Les Prisons, OVO, 77. *Mailing Add:* 10255 Jeanne Manee Montreal PQ H3L 3B7 Canada

GAUDIERI, ALEXANDER V J
MUSEUM DIRECTOR
b Columbus, Ohio, Apr 23, 40. *Study:* Ohio State Univ; Univ Paris, Sorbonne; Colgate Univ; Barton Kyle Yount Scholar, Am Grad Sch of Int Com; Inst of Fine Arts, NY Univ, with Robert Rosenblum, Sir Francis Watson & James Parker. *Exhib:* Picasso: Meeting in Montreal, 85 & Miro: Works on Paper & in Bronze, 86, Montreal Mus Fine Arts. *Pos:* Dir, Telfair Acad Arts & Sci, 76-83 & Montreal Mus Fine Arts, 83- *Mem:* Asn Art Mus Dirs; Am Asn of Mus; Soc Archit Historians; and others. *Res:* European decorative arts--wood marquetry; development of geometric forms into curvilinear and floral motifs from circa 1715 to mid-century; French romantic painting--the horse paintings of Alfred de Dreux and the influence of Gericault on his oeuvre. *Collection:* Decorative arts including Georges II & III furniture, silver and porcelain. *Mailing Add:* 444 Central Park W, Apt 19A New York NY 10025-4359

GAUTHIER, NINON
CRITIC, HISTORIAN
b Verdun, Que, Nov 9, 43. *Study:* Univ de Montréal, BS, 67; MS, 68; Ecole des Hautes Etudes, 72-74. *Pos:* Asst dean, Fac Fine Arts, Univ du Qué à Montréal, 74-77; Dir, Centre d'étude et ed communication sur l'art, 89- *Awards:* Spec Collab Award, Nat Bus Writing Award, Toronto Press Club, Royal Bank of Can, 87; Cult Journalism Excellency Award, Can Conf Arts, Samuel & Saydie Bronfman Found, 89. *Mem:* Asn Art Critics Can (secy); Art Collectors Asn Que (dir); Centre d'étude et de communications sur l'art (pres). *Res:* Quebec art of fifties and sixties; history of Canadian and Contemporary art market; interraction between institutions, media and art market on artist's career and on art works prices. *Publ:* Coauth, Le marché de l'art et le statut de l'artiste, Ministère des affaires culturelles du Qué, 82; Le Mécénat privé au Québec: mythe ou réalité?, Possible, 85 & 86; auth, Vivre des arts visuels, Publs du Qué, 87; Code d'éthique des sculpteurs, Conseil de la sculpture du Qué, 90; coauth, Marcel Barbeau: le regard en fugue, CECA, 90. *Mailing Add:* 1637 Amherst Montreal PQ H2L 3L4 Canada

GAUTHIER, SUZANNE ANITA
PAINTER
b Saint-Boniface, Man, Aug 12, 48. *Study:* Univ Man, Winnipeg, BFA(hons), 69. *Work:* Can Coun Art Bank & Mus of Man, Ottawa; Winnipeg Art Gallery, Man; Collection Prêt d'Oeuvres d'Art, Mus Québec; Bemis Foundation, Omaha; Musée D'Art Contemporaine, Collection Lavalin, Montréal. *Exhib:* Palazza Della Esposizioni, Faenza, Italy, 85-86; 37th Salon de la Jeune Peinture, Grand Palais, Paris, 86; Jane Corkin Gallery, Toronto, 88; Exten Print & Drawing Coun of Can, Toronto, 90; Subject/Matter, Art Gallery NS, 92; and others. *Teaching:* Lectr printmaking, Sch Art, Univ Man, 77-79; asst prof painting, NS Col Art & Design, 88-92. *Awards:* B Grant, Can Coun, 87; Soutien Aux Artistes, Ministér des Affaires, Culturelles, Que, 88; Travel Grant, Can Coun, 89. *Bibliog:* Françoise Legris-Berggman (auth), L'ouevre polymorphe de Suzanne Gauthier, Vie des Arts, 88; Bernard Mulaire (auth), Chien, Les Editions du Blé, 85; Gérard Xuriguera (auth), Le dessin, le pastel, l'aquarelle dans l'art, Éditions Mayer, Paris, 87. *Mem:* Can Artists Representation/Front des Artistes Canadiens. *Media:* Encaustic Painting; Photography. *Publ:* Illusr, Canadian Artists in Exhibition, 1973-1974, Roundstone Coun, 74; Le Nu, La Lumiére et Les Ombres, Les Editions du Blé, 75; coauth & illusr, Vortex, Les Editions du Blé, 85; Figures Nomades, Migrant Images, Les Ed Ink, Inc, 89. *Mailing Add:* 5654 Harris St, Apt 2 Halifax NS B3K 1H2 Canada

GAUVIN, CLAUDE E
PAINTER
b Bathurst, NB, June 14, 39. *Study:* Ecole Beaux Arts Montreal, dipl, 60; Univ Que, Montreal, BA(spec educ), 74; Tyler Art Sch, 76. *Work:* Banque Art NB, Fredericton; Consolidated Bathurst, Montreal; Univ Moncton, NB. *Exhib:* Solo exhib, Radio-Can, Moncton, NB, 80 & Rothmans Gallery, Moncton, NB, 83; Collections, Art Bank NB, Dieppe, 81; Univ Maine, 82; Art Collections, Univ Moncton, NB, 83. *Teaching:* Instr art, Montreal Sch Design, 60-63 & Philadelphia Sch Bd, 74-77; prof painting, Univ Moncton, NB, 78- *Awards:* Constance Carlston Award, Univ Maine, 82. *Bibliog:* Bernard Levy (auth), Le plaisir de l'objet, Vie Arts, 80. *Mem:* Can Art Rep, Fedn Artistes Can (secy, 81, exec secy, 82-83). *Mailing Add:* Bureau Bourgeois, CP 47 Grande-Digue NB E0A 1S0 Canada

GAUVREAU, ROBERT GEORGE
PHOTOGRAPHER, EDUCATOR
b Renton, Wash, Aug 14, 48. *Study:* Cent Wash State Univ, BA, 70; Ariz State Univ, Tempe, MFA, 73. *Work:* Coos Art Mus, Coos Bay, Ore. *Exhib:* Phoenix Art Mus, Ariz, 73; Spectrum Gallery, Tucson, 76; Creative Eye Gallery, Sonoma, Calif, 76; Cent Wash State Univ, Ellensburg, 77; Coos Bay Mus, Ore, 78; and others. *Teaching:* Lectr photog, State Univ NY, New Paltz, 73-74; instr photog, Modesto Jr Col, Calif, 74- *Mem:* Soc Photog Educ. *Media:* Color. *Mailing Add:* 1425 Glenhaven Dr Modesto CA 95355

GAVALAS, ALEXANDER BEARY
PAINTER
b Limerick, Ireland, Jan 6, 45; US citizen. *Study:* Sch Art & Design, dipl, 63; Manhattanville Col, 69- *Work:* Tweed Mus Art, Duluth, Minn; and others. *Exhib:* One-man shows, Tweed Mus Art, Minn, 80, Western Ill Univ Libr Gallery, 81, Ft Wayne Mus Art, Ind, 82, Marycrest Col Eberdt Art Gallery, Iowa, 82, Arnot Art Mus, New York, 82 & Queens Col Art Ctr/Paul Klapper Libr, New York, 83. *Teaching:* Instr art & music, St Catherine of Alexandria, Brooklyn, NY, 84-86. *Awards:* Commemorative Award, Men of Achievement, IBC, 85. *Bibliog:* Matt Santoro (auth), At peace with his environment, Queens Ledger, 80; Alan Garfield (auth), Alexander Beary Gavalas Recent Paintings & Drawings, Krasl Art Ctr, 80; Idealism, serenity mark Gavalas' landscapes, Ft Wayne Sentinel, 4/82. *Mem:* Int Platform Asn. *Media:* Oil, Pen & Ink. *Publ:* Auth, articles, Irish Echo, 82 & 83; articles, New York Daily News, 82; articles, Western Queens Gazette, 82. *Mailing Add:* 65 Horton St Malverne NY 11565

GAWARECKI, CAROLYN ANN See Grosse, C(arolyn Ann Gawarecki)

GAY, BETSY (ELIZABETH DERSHUCK GAY)
PAINTER, INSTRUCTOR
b Philadelphia, Pa, Nov 27, 27. *Study:* Sweet Briar Col, Va, BA, 49; Nat Acad Fine Arts, New York, 56; studied with Edgar A Whitney, Charles Reid, Frank Webb, Gerald Brommer, Virginia Cobb, Nita Engle & others. *Work:* George B Markle Gallery, Penn State Univ Gallery, Pardee Collection Church Gallery, Hazelton, Pa; Sweet Briar Col Gallery, Va; Pelham Art Ctr Gallery, NY. *Comn:* Painting, Eleventh Hole, Whippoorwill Club, Armonk, NY, 72; painting, Creation, Art Comt Church Collection, Hazleton, Pa, 75; painting, Summer Delights, Bedford Gourmet, NY, 90. *Exhib:* Hudson Valley Art Assn, White Plains, NY, 75; Knickerbocker Artists, New York, 76; Nat Arts Club, New York, 78; Nat Asn Women Artists, Ber Community Mus, Bergen, NJ, 82. *Teaching:* Instr water media, Northcastle Adult Educ, Armonk, NY, 77-82, Pelham Art Ctr, NY, 78- & Briarcliff Continuous Educ, New York, 79-83. *Awards:* First Prize, Beaux Arts Harrison, 74; First Prize, Pound Ridge Art Show, 77; First Prize, New Rochelle Art Asn, 78. *Bibliog:* Les Krantz (auth), Am Artists-Survey of Leading Contemporaries, 90; Les Krantz (auth), The New York Art Review, 91. *Mem:* Knickerbocker Artists, New York; Nat Asn Women Artists; Catherine Lorrilard Wolfe Art Club, New York; Mamaroneck Artists Guild. *Media:* Watercolor. *Mailing Add:* 37 Round Hill Rd Armonk NY 10504

GAY, ELIZABETH DERSHUCK See Gay, Betsy (Elizabeth Dershuck Gay)

GAYAS-JUNGWIRTH, I(RENE)
PAINTER, DESIGNER
b McKees Rocks, Pa. *Study:* Cass Tech, Detroit, 31; Marygrove Col, BA(art & philos), 35; Wayne State Univ, 37; Mich State Univ; also studied abroad. *Work:* Detroit Inst Arts; Marquette Univ Art Collection; Marygrove Col Art Collection; CSSP Seminary Collection, Ann Arbor; St Joseph's Provincial House, Emmitsburg, Md; and many church & pvt collections-esp clergymen. *Comn:* Stations of Cross (with Leonard D Jungwirth), Churches, Detroit, 55-62; crown in gold, topaz & diamonds, St Mary's Church, Detroit, 57-58; crucifixion (with Leonard D Jungwirth), St John's Church, East Lansing, 60; stained glass windows, YMCA-Children's Chapel & large window, Baptist

Church, 60-63, Lansing; mural painting, Dept Hort, Mich State Univ, 67. *Exhib:* Michigan Artists, Detroit Art Inst, 43-63; two-person exhib (husband-wife show with Leonard D Jungwirth), Flint Art Inst, 51; Int Ecclesiastical Show, 55-62; Butler Inst Am Art, Youngstown, Ohio; Art 76, Int Armory, Washington, DC; retrospective, Benjamin Gallery, Hagerstown, Md, 75, East Lansing Peoples Church, Mich State Univ Art Dept, 80-82. *Pos:* pvt lessons (adults); speaker to many groups. *Teaching:* Instr art, Detroit Public Sch (36-41); Detroit Art Inst. *Awards:* Painting of Child, Detroit Inst Arts, 43; Prize, Spring Nocturne, Butler Art Inst, 52; Whitcomb & Mus Purchase Award for Nocturne with Female Figure & Peacocks, Detroit Inst Arts, 57. *Bibliog:* Many interviews in newspapers, on radio & TV. *Media:* Oil with Tempera, Watercolor; Ink, Blockprints. *Mailing Add:* 1872 Fulmer St Ann Arbor MI 48103

GAYDOS, TIM (TIMOTHY JOHN)
PAINTER
b New York, NY, Dec 6, 41. *Study:* Univ Calif, Berkeley, 59-61; Accademia Di Belli Arti Di Brera, Milano, Italy, 62-63. *Work:* Rutgers Univ, New Brunswick & Newark, NJ; Vets Admin Hosp, Paramus, NJ. *Comn:* Painting of Richard Wagner (composer), Bloomfield Libr, NJ, 84. *Exhib:* NJ Biennial, NJ State Mus, Trenton, 83 & Newark Mus, 85; Pastel Invitational, Hermitage Mus, Norfolk, Va, 85 & 87; solo exhib, Montclair Art Mus, NJ, 88-89; 165th Ann, Nat Acad Design, New York, 90; NJ Arts Ann, Noyes Mus, Oceanville, NJ, 92. *Pos:* Freelance bk jacket illusr & designer, 63- *Teaching:* Portraits, Montclair Art Mus Sch, NJ, 76-88 & 92-93. *Awards:* Bd Dirs Award, 88 & Nat Arts Club Award Excellence, 90, Pastel Soc Am Ann, New York; Silver Medal Pastel, Knickerbocker Artists Ann, New York, 89. *Bibliog:* Eileen Watkins (auth), rev, 6/27/76 & Artist draws on compassion, 1/18/89, Newark Star Ledger; Robert Filanzetti (auth), Art Comments on Social Scene, Herald News, 5/12/85. *Mem:* Pastel Soc Am (master pastellist); Nat Soc Painters in Casein & Acrylic. *Media:* Pastel, Acrylic. *Publ:* Contribr, Pastel Interpretations, North Light, 93. *Mailing Add:* 11 Fair St Paterson NJ 07501

GAYLORD, FRANK CHALFANT, II
SCULPTOR, DESIGNER
b Clarksburg, WVa, Mar 9, 25. *Study:* Carnegie Inst Technol Col Fine Arts; Tyler Sch Fine Arts, Temple Univ, BFA. *Comn:* Firemen Mem (granite), Nyack, NY; Pioneer Family (granite), Akron, Ohio; Arthur Fiedler (granite portrait), Boston Univ Libr, 82; William Penn (granite figure), Pen Treaty Park, Philadelphia, 82; William Shakespeare (granite portrait), Old Globe Theater, San Diego, 83; Nat Korean War Mem on the Mall, Washington, DC, 93. *Exhib:* Nat Sculpture Soc Ann Exhib, 65, 79 & 90. *Bibliog:* Article, The memorial sculpture of Frank Gaylord, Stone Am Mag, 4/82; The Stone Whistle (film), Barre Granite Asn. *Mem:* Assoc Nat Sculpture Soc; Fel, Nat Sculpture Soc. *Media:* All Media. *Publ:* Auth, Why Christ? & A portrait of Hector, 68, Monumental News Rev. *Mailing Add:* PO Box 464 Barre VT 05641

GEALT, ADELHEID MEDICUS
MUSEUM DIRECTOR, HISTORIAN
b Munich, Ger, May 29, 46; US citizen. *Study:* Ind Univ, PhD, 79. *Collections Arranged:* Italian Portrait Drawings, 1400-1800 from North American Collections Traveling Exhib (auth, catalog), 83. *Pos:* Cur, Ind Univ Art Mus, Bloomington, 76-, dir, 89- *Awards:* Nat Endowment Arts Cur Grant, 80; Nat Endowment Arts Planning & Implementation Grant, 81; Am Philos Soc Grant, 81; Nat Endowment Humanities Grant, 85. *Mem:* Ind Arts Comn(adv panelist, 89-). *Res:* Primarily Italian painting and drawing from 1300-1800. *Publ:* Some Thoughts on the Minneapolis Nardo di Cione, Minn Inst Arts Bulletin, 10/81; The Uffizi lamentation, In: Gazette Beau-Arts, 4/83; auth, Looking at Art, A Visitor's Guide to Art Museums, R R Bowker, 83; The Punchinello Drawings of Domenico Teipolo, Braziller, 86; coauth, Art of the Western world, Summit Bks, 89. *Mailing Add:* Ind Univ Art Mus Bloomington IN 47405

GEAR, JOSEPHINE
HISTORIAN, GALLERY DIRECTOR
b London, Eng, Nov 24, 38. *Study:* The English equivalent of a degree in museology; the dipl of Mus Asn Gt Brit, 65; Woodrow Wilson Dissertation fel, 73-74, Inst Fine Arts, NY Univ, scholar award, 75-76, PhD, 76; study with Bob Rosenblum & Gert Schiff. *Pos:* Dir, Univ Art Gallery, State Univ NY, Binghamton, 79- *Teaching:* Asst prof art hist, Briarcliff Col, NY, 75-77; asst prof art hist, State Univ NY, Binghamton, 79- *Mem:* Mus Asn Gt Brit; Col Art Asn Am (co-chmn Marxist caucus, 78). *Publ:* auth, Master or Servant?, A Study of Selected English Painters and Their Patrons of the Late 18th and Early 19th centuries, Garland, 77; coauth, The 70's Alternative View of Design: Danger from the Drawing Boards?, Contemp Art/SE, 77; auth, Trapped Women: The Work of Two Sister Designers, Margaret and Frances Macdonald, Heresies, 78; auth, Some alternative spaces in New York and Los Angeles, Studio Int, 80; and others. *Mailing Add:* 298 State St Brooklyn NY 11201

GEBHARD, DAVID
MUSEUM DIRECTOR, HISTORIAN
b Cannon Falls, Minn, July 21, 27. *Study:* Univ Minn, BA, MA & PhD. *Collections Arranged:* Walker Art Ctr, 53; Purcell & Elmslie, Architects, 69; The Enigma of Ralph A Blakelock 1847-1919, 69, Charles Demuth, 71, Art Galleries, Univ Calif, Santa Barbara; Indian Art of the Northern Plains, 74; 200 Years of American Architectural Drawings (coauth, catalog), 77-78; The Architecture of Gregory Ain (auth, catalog), 80; Joseph Hoffmann, Design Classic (auth, catalog), 82; Santa Barbara, The Creation of a New Spain in America, (auth, catalog), 82; Lutah Maria Riggs, 90. *Pos:* Dir, Roswell Mus & Art Ctr, 55-60; dir, Univ Calif Santa Barbara Art Mus, 61-80; cur, Archit Drawing Collection, Univ Calif, Santa Barbara, 80- *Teaching:* Instr art hist, Univ NMex, 53-55; prof art hist, Univ Calif, Santa Barbara, 61- *Mem:* Soc Archit Historians (pres, 80-83); Nat Archit Accrediting Bd. *Res:* 19th and 20th century architecture; architecture of California; rock art of North America. *Publ:* Coauth, S & J C Newsom Victorian Architectural Imagery in California, 79; California Crazy, 80; Tulsa Art Deco, 80; Home Sweet Home, American Domestic Vernacular, 83; A Guide to Architecture in Los Angeles, 83; Legacy of Minneapolis, Preservation amid Change, 83; High Style, Twentieth Century American Design, Whitney Mus Am Art, New York, 85; An Arcadian Landscape, The California Gardens of A E Hanson, 1920-1932, 85; Santa Barbara, El Pueblo Viejo, 86; Romanza: California Architecture of Frank Lloyd Wright, 88. *Mailing Add:* 895 E Mountain Dr Santa Barbara CA 93108

GEBHARDT, ROLAND
SCULPTOR, DESIGNER
b Paramaribo, Suriname, Sept 24, 39; US citizen. *Study:* Art Acad Hamburg, Ger, with Theo Ortner; Kuntsgewerbeschule, Zurich, Swiss; also apprenticeship in stained glass, Marburg, Ger. *Work:* Art Acad, Hamburg; Brandeis Univ; Storm King Art Ctr, Mountainville, NY; City of Ludwigshafen, Ger; Neuberger Mus, Purchase, NY. *Exhib:* One-man sculpture & painting exhib, Hudson River Mus, 71, Gallery 84, New York, 73 & Robert Freidus Gallery, 78; 20th Century Sculpture in Westchester Collection, Yonkers, NY, 72; Carlton Gallery, New York, 74 & 77; Storm King Art Ctr, 75 & 76; The Minimal Tradition, Aldrich Mus, Ridgefield, Conn, 79; Pumpkins, Art Et Industry, New York, 82; Eight one-day exhibs, Kunstmuseum, Dusseldorf, Fed Repub Ger, 82. *Awards:* Annual Prize, Art Acad Hamburg, 62. *Bibliog:* Fred Salaff (auth), Roland Gebhardt--Sculptor (film), 72; Arlene Krebs (dir), Liniar Void (video), 78. *Media:* Metal, Stone; Fiberglass, Concrete. *Publ:* Auth, Fresh Sculpture, 81. *Mailing Add:* 67 Vestry St New York NY 10013

GECHTOFF, SONIA
PAINTER
b Philadelphia, Pa, Sept 25, 26. *Study:* Philadelphia Mus Col Art, BFA, 50; Ford Found Fel, Tamarind Lithography Workshop, 63. *Work:* Guggenheim Mus, Mus of Mod Art & Metropolitan Mus Art, New York; Baltimore Mus of Art; San Francisco Mus Mod Art. *Exhib:* Am Painters, US Pavilion, Brussels Fair, Belg, 58; First Paris Bienale, France, 59; Sao Paulo Bienale, Brazil, 61; Calif Painting: Mod Era, San Francisco Mus of Art, 76 & Nat Collection of Fine Arts, Washington, DC, 76-77; Drawing Acquisition Shows, Mus of Mod Art, New York, 77 & Extraordinary Women & Am Drawn & Matched, 76-77; solo show, Gruenebaum Gallery, New York, 79, 80, 82, 83, 85 & 87 & Kraushaar Gallery, New York, 90 & 92; New Dimensions in Drawing, 1950-1980, Aldrich Mus Contemp Art, Conn, 81; American Women-American Art, Stamford Mus, Conn, 85; Art on Paper: Weatherspoon Guild, NC, 87; 56th Nat Midyear Exhib, Butler Inst Art, Youngstown, Oh, 92. *Teaching:* lectr art, Queens Col, 70-74; assoc prof art, Univ NMex, 74-75; Artist-in-residence, Skidmore Col, NY, 88, 89 & 90; vis artist, Chicago Art Inst, 89; Artist-in-residence, Adelphi Univ, New York, 91. *Awards:* Purchase Award, San Francisco Mus Art, 57; Drawing Prize, Four Corners States Bienale, Phoenix Art Mus, 75; Gottleib Found Grant, 87, Mid-Atlantic Nat Endowment Arts Grant, 88. *Bibliog:* Hilton Kramer (auth), Triumphant new work, 5/20/79 & Sonia Gechtoff's abstract drawing at its best, 10/31/80, NY Times; James Mellow (auth), Sonia Gechtoff: A different kind of knowledge, Arts Mag, 2/82; Michael Brenson (auth), Sonia Gechtoff's New Direction, NY Times, 11/25/83; John Loughery (auth), Sonia Gechtoff: The Theatre of the Visible Kraushaar Galleries Catalogue, 5/92. *Mem:* Archives Am Art. *Media:* Acrylic, Oil. *Dealer:* Kraushaar Galleries 724 Fifth Ave New York NY 10019. *Mailing Add:* 463 West St Apt 936 New York NY 10014

GECK, FRANCIS JOSEPH
EDUCATOR, DESIGNER
b Detroit, Mich, Dec 20, 1900. *Study:* New York Sch Fine & Appl Art & Paris Atelier, France, dipl; Syracuse Univ, MFA, 46. *Exhib:* Washington Watercolor Club 54th Ann, Smithsonian Inst, Washington, DC, 50; Pavilion of American Interiors, New York World's Fair, 65; Boulder Nat Bank, Colo, 66; Village Theatre Lobby, Boulder, 67-74; Manufacturers Hanover Trust Gallery, New York, 71; and others. *Pos:* Interior architect & designer, William Wright Co, Detroit, 27-30; interior architect & consult, T Eaton Co, Toronto, 30; dir, Sherwood Art Gallery, Boulder, 37-40; dir exhib, Boulder Hist Soc, 44-58 & Pioneer Mus, Boulder, 58-80; cur exhib, Univ Colo, 47-57; design consult, Mullins Plastics, 69-72. *Teaching:* Instr interior design, New York Sch Fine & Appl Art, Paris Atelier, France, 24-27; prof interior design, Univ Colo, Boulder, 30-69, prof emer, 69- *Awards:* Gold Medal Winner, Grand Nat Show, Am Artists Prof League, 53; Tommaso Campanella Silver Medal, Acad Int Léttre-Arti-Scienze, 70; and others. *Mem:* Boulder Artists Guild; Boulder Hist Soc; Am Inst Interior Designers; Interior Design Educ Coun; Am Soc Interior Designers. *Publ:* The Period of Henry IV, 86; The Period of Gothic, 88; Fundamentals of Interior Design and Decoration, 89; The Louis XIII Period, 89; The Louis XIV Period, 90; and others. *Mailing Add:* 18360 Martin Rd Roseville MI 48066-4805

GEDEON, LUCINDA HEYEL
CURATOR, ADMINISTRATOR
b Port Chester, NY, Oct 13, 47. *Study:* Calif State Univ, Long Beach, BA(art hist), 81; Univ Calif, Los Angeles, MA(art hist), 81, UCLA, PhD(art hist), 89. *Collections Arranged:* The Graphic Art of Henri Matisse (auth, catalog), 80

& Tamarind: From Los Angeles to Albuquerque (auth, catalog), 84, Univ Calif, Los Angeles; Artists Select: Contemporary Perspectives by Afro-American Artists (auth, catalog), Univ Art Mus, Ariz State Univ, 86; Sculpture in glass & works on paper (auth, catalog), Univ Art Mus, Ariz State Univ, 87; Fiber Concept (auth, catalog), Univ Art Mus, Ariz State Univ, 89. *Pos:* Asst dir, Grunwald Ctr Graphic Arts, Univ Calif, Los Angeles, 81-83, actg dir & cur, 83-85; chief cur, Univ Art Mus, Ariz State Univ, Tempe, 85- *Awards:* Afro-Am Studies Fel & Edward A Dickson Hist Art Fel, Univ Calif, Los Angeles, 84; Col Fine Arts Research Grant, Ariz State Univ, Tempe, 90; Arts Exhib Grant, Ariz Comn, 90-91. *Mem:* Am Asn Mus; Cent Ariz Mus Asn; Col Art Asn; Mus Asn Ariz (bd mem); Tempe Arts Comn (vice-chmn, 87-89, chmn 89-90). *Res:* History of American and African-American art; history of prints. *Publ:* Auth, The Art of Leonard Lehrer, Lamspringe, WGer, 86; ed, Visual Arts Research Institute: A Catalogue Raisonne, Ariz State Univ, 86; auth, Tony Delap and the Floating Lady: the Artist/Magician as Magician/Artist, Ariz Stat Univ, 88; ed, Meeting Ground: Basketry Traditions and Sculptured Forms (exhib catalog), 90 & Collaborations and Connections: 20th Century Collaborative Bookworks (exhib catalog), 90, Ariz State Univ. *Mailing Add:* Neuberger Mus State Univ NY-Purchase 735 Anderson Hill Rd Purchase NY 10577-1400

GEE, HELEN
ART CONSULTANT, CURATOR
US citizen. *Collections Arranged:* Guest cur, Stieglitz & the Photo-Secession, NJ State Mus, 78; Bank Tokyo, New York; Indust Bank Japan, New York; Photography of the Fifties (catalog), Ctr Creative Photog, Tucson; curated 78 exhibs, 54-88. *Pos:* Owner & dir, Limelight Gallery. *Teaching:* Parsons Sch Design, 80- *Interests:* 19th and 20th century painting, sculpture and photography. *Publ:* Photography of the Fifties: An American Perspective, Univ Arizona Press, 83. *Mailing Add:* 263 W 11th St New York NY 10014

GEE, LI-LAN See Li Lan

GEERLINGS, GERALD KENNETH
GRAPHIC ARTIST, ARCHITECT
b Milwaukee, Wis, Apr 18, 1897. *Study:* Univ Pa, BA(archit), 21, MA(archit), 22; Royal Col Art, London, two yrs. *Work:* Victoria & Albert Mus, London; Metrop Mus Art, New York; Libr Cong & Nat Collection Fine Arts, Washington, DC; Chicago Art Inst; plus others. *Exhib:* Royal Acad, London; Paris Int Exhib; New York Worlds Fair, 39; Nat Acad Design, New York; Philadelphia Acad Fine Arts; plus others. *Awards:* Gold Medal for Best Black & White of the Year, Philadelphia Acad Fine Arts, 31; First Prize for Best Etching, Chicago Worlds Fair, 33; Nat Arts Club Award, New York. *Bibliog:* Joseph S Czestochowski (auth, catalog), raisonné, Cedar Rapids Mus Art, 84. *Mem:* Soc Am Graphic Artists; Am Inst Architects; Pastel Soc Am. *Media:* Pencil; Pastels. *Publ:* Auth & illusr, Metal Crafts in Architecture, 29 & 72, Wrought Iron in Architecture, 29 & 72 & Color Schemes of Adam Ceilings, 28, Scribners; Paris along the Seine, French Inst & Cedar Rapids Mus Art, 87. *Dealer:* Am Assoc Artists 20 W 57th St New York NY 10019. *Mailing Add:* 26 Gower Rd New Canaan CT 06840

GEESLIN, LEE GADDIS
PAINTER, EDUCATOR
b Goldthwaite, Tex, June 28, 20. *Study:* Univ Tex; New Orleans Art & Crafts; Art Inst Chicago, BFA & MFA. *Exhib:* Annually with local & regional shows of the Southwest; one-man shows, Brownsville, San Angelo, Houston, Corpus Christi, Brady, Lufkin, Dallas & Texarkana, Tex, also Shreveport, La, 63- *Pos:* Dean, Col Fine Arts, Sam Houston State Univ. *Teaching:* Prof art, Sam Houston State Univ, retired. *Mem:* Tex Watercolor Soc; Tex Fine Arts Soc; Tex Art Educ Asn; Am Asn Univ Prof; Col Art Asn Am. *Media:* Oil, Watercolor. *Mailing Add:* 6112 Kirby Dr Houston TX 77005

GEFFERT, HARRY
SCULPTOR
b Live Oak, Tex, Apr 11, 34. *Study:* SW Tex Univ, San Marcos, Tex, BA; NMex Highlands, Las Vegas, NMex, MA. *Exhib:* Dallas Mus Fine Arts, Tex, 90; Betty Moody Gallery, Houston, Tex, 92. *Pos:* Owner, Green Mountain Fine Arts Foundry, Ft Worth, Tex, 84- *Teaching:* Assoc prof sculpture, Tex Christian Univ, Ft Worth, 60-87. *Awards:* Grant, Nat Endowment Arts, 90. *Media:* Bronze. *Dealer:* Betty Moody 2815 Colquitt Houston TX 77098. *Mailing Add:* Rte 1, Box 13A2 Crowley TX 76036

GEFTER, JUDITH MICHELMAN
PHOTOGRAPHER
b Gloversville, NY. *Study:* Pratt Inst, cert; NY Univ; Univ Fla; Fla State Univ; also with William E Parker & Wilson Hicks Conf, Univ Miami. *Work:* Mint Mus, Charlotte, NC; Jacksonville Art Mus, Fla; Tampa Art Inst, Fla; Southern Bell Collection, 85; Barnett Bank, 90. *Comn:* Two wood carvings, comn by Mem Hosp, Jacksonville, Fla, 84; sculpture, Art-in-Public Places, Housing Urban Develop, 85. *Exhib:* Am Soc Mag Photogr Traveling Show, 62-63; one-woman shows, Pratt Inst, 66 & 67, Breast & Face, Steiglitz Gallery, New York, 75, Phillips Gallery, Jacksonville Univ, Fla, 77, Univ Fla, 78 & Computography, Neikrug Gallery, New York, 92; retrospect, Jacksonville Art Mus, 70; There is No Female Camera Traveling Show, Neikrug Gallery, New York, 75 & Univ NFla, 81; Fabulous Photographs, Cummer Mus, Jacksonville, Fla, 92. *Teaching:* Adj prof photogr, Fine Arts Dept, Univ NFla, 80-81; Kodak, Guest Artist, Ctr Creative Imaging, Camden, Maine, 92. *Awards:* Best Ann Report (2 yrs), Koger Co, Mead Paper Co, 79-80; Best Cover (photograph) Ann Reports, J Cato Ann Report Dept Cato Inst, 85. *Bibliog:* Elizabeth Kaufman (auth), My life & my art, Arts Assembler, 11/75; portfolio, Charter Issue Kalliope, A Tour of Women's Art, winter 79; Challenge of Freelance Photography (audio-visual prog), Media Loft Inc, 80 & Jacksonville Mag, 10/85. *Mem:* Am Soc Mag Photogr; Soc Photogr Commun (pres, NFla chap, 65-70); Nat Soc Lit & Arts. *Media:* Computer Art, Photography. *Publ:* Illusr, Jacksonville Calendar Diary Bicentennial Ed, 76; contribr, Longman Dict Mass Media & Communication, 82. *Mailing Add:* 1725 Clemson Rd Jacksonville FL 32217

GEHR, MARY (RAY)
PRINTMAKER, PAINTER
b Chicago, Ill. *Study:* Smith Col; Art Inst Chicago, with Paul Wieghardt; Inst Design of Ill Inst Technol, with Misch Kohn. *Work:* Art Inst Chicago; Philadelphia Mus; Libr Cong, Washington, DC; Nelson Rockefeller Collection; Free Libr, Philadelphia. *Comn:* Golden Santorini (intaglio-edition of 210 etchings printed by Leterio Calapai), Int Graphic Arts Soc, 67. *Exhib:* Chicago & Vicinity Exhibs & Soc Contemp Am Art, Art Inst Chicago; Brooklyn Mus Nat Print Exhib; Boston Printmakers, Mass; Print Club, Philadelphia; 54 one-man shows in US & Europe, 57-; 21 Views of China, Chicago Cult Ctr, 79; one-person retrospective, Univ Ill, Chicago, 86. *Pos:* Mem artists adv comt, Art Rental & Sales Gallery, Art Inst Chicago, 64-83. *Teaching:* Lectr China, Art Inst Chicago, 79, 81 & 82. *Awards:* Print Fair Award, Philadelphia; First Purchase Award, Artist Guild Chicago; Award for Graphics, Old Orchard Festival, Chicago. *Bibliog:* John Fink (auth), The Greece of Mary Gehr, Chicago Tribune Mag, 67; T J Carbol (ed), The printmaker in Illinois, Ill Art Educ Asn, 71-72; plus many articles in local papers. *Mem:* Arts Club Chicago; Alumnae of Art Inst Chicago; Am Ctr Design. *Media:* Intaglio, Batik; Oil, Acrylics. *Publ:* Illusr, designer & art ed, Exploring the World of Archaeology, 66; designer & art ed, Exploring the World of Pottery, 67. *Mailing Add:* 1829 N Orleans Chicago IL 60614

GEHRY, FRANK O(WEN)
ARCHITECT
b Toronto, Ont, Feb 28, 29; US citizen. *Study:* Univ Southern Calif Col Fine Arts, 49-51, Col Archit, BArch, 54; Harvard Univ Grad Sch Design, 56-57. *Work:* Mus Mod Art, Metrop Mus Art, New York; Los Angeles Mus Contemp Art; Philadelphia Mus Art. *Comn:* Cabrillo Marine Mus, City Los Angeles, San Pedro, Calif, 79; Loyola Law Sch, Loyola Marymount Univ, 81; Calif Aerospace Mus, State Calif, Los Angeles, 83; Frances Howard Goldwyn Regional Branch Libr, comn by Samuel Goldwyn Jr, Los Angeles, 83. *Exhib:* Chicago Tribune Late Entries, Inst Contemp Art, Chicago, 80; La Presenza del Passato, Biennale Venezia, Italy, 80; Documenta VII, Kasel, Ger, 82; Shape and Environment, Whitney Mus Am Art, 82; Ten New Buildings, Inst Contemp Art, London, 83; California Counterpoint, Nat Acad Design, New York, 83. *Teaching:* Vis critic, Rice Univ, 76, Univ Calif, Los Angeles, 79, Yale, 82, 85, 87, 88 & 89 & Harvard, 84. *Awards:* William Bishop Chair, 79 & Charlotte Davenport Prof Archit, 82, Yale Univ; Arnold W Brunner Mem Prize Archit, Am Acad & Inst Arts & Lett, 83. *Bibliog:* Beyond Utopia, Michael Blackwood Productions, 83; Joseph Morgenstern (auth), The Gehry style, New York Times Mag, 5/16/83; Lindsay Stamm Schapiro (auth), A minimalist architecture of allusion, Progressive Archit, 6/83. *Mem:* Am Inst Archit. *Publ:* Auth, Frank Gehry: Buildings and Projects, Rizzoli, New York, 85. *Dealer:* Fred Hoffman Gallery 912 Colorado Ave Santa Monica CA 90401. *Mailing Add:* Frank Gehry & Assoc 1520-B Cloverfield Blvd Santa Monica CA 90404

GEIGER, EDITH ROGERS
PAINTER
b New Haven, Conn, July 13, 12. *Study:* Smith Col, BA, 34; Art Students League, 34-35; Yale Univ, with Joseph Albers. *Work:* Wadsworth Atheneum, Hartford; Tryon Art Mus, Smith Col; Springfield Art Mus, Mass; Art Mus, Ann Arbor, Mich; Bridgeport Univ Art Collection. *Exhib:* Brooklyn Mus 21st Int Watercolor Biennial; Detroit Nat Watercolor Exhib; Boston Art Festival; Providence Festival, RI; solo exhibs, Bodley Gallery, New York, 56, Ruth White Gallery, New York, 59 & 62, Naples Art Gallery, Fla, 69 & 70. *Awards:* Best in Show Awards, New Haven Festival Arts, 57 & 62; Woman's Award, Am Watercolor Soc, 62; Nat Asn Women Artists Award, 63. *Mem:* Am Watercolor Soc. *Media:* Mixed Media. *Mailing Add:* 2750 Gulf Shore Blvd N Naples FL 33940

GEIGER, PHILLIP NEIL
PAINTER, DRAFTSMAN
b Ft Lauderdale, Fla, Feb 26, 56. *Study:* Wash Univ, BFA, 78; Yale Univ, MFA, 80. *Work:* Chemical Bank, New York, NY; Gen Foods, Minneapolis, Minn; CSX Corp, Richmond, Va; Stevens Co, Little Rock, Ark. *Exhib:* Solo exhibs, More Gallery, Philadelphia, 82 & 83, Swarthmore Col, 87 & Tatistcheff & Co, New York, 86, 88 & 90, Hollins Col, 89; Bodies & Souls, Artists' Choice Mus, New York, 83; Drawings, drawings, drawings, Forum Gallery, New York, 84; Painterly Realism, Fontbonne Col, St Louis, 84; Contemp Narrative Figure Painting (with catalog), Payne Gallery, Moravian Col, Bethlehem, Pa, 86; American Art Today: The Figure in Landscape, Art Mus at Ft Lauderdale Int Univ, Miami, 86; Landscape Painting (with catalog), Gibbes Mus Art, Charleston. *Teaching:* Asst prof art, Colo State Univ, Ft Collins, 80-83 & Univ Va, Charlottesville, 83. *Bibliog:* Kay Larson (auth), New Fares '86, New York Mag, 3/86; Michael Kimmelman (auth), New York Times, 2/26/88; Ronnie Cohen (auth), Art Forum, 5/90. *Media:* Oil. *Dealer:* Peter Tatistcheff 50 W 57th St New York NY 10019. *Mailing Add:* Dept Art Univ Va Charlottesville VA 22903

GEIS, MILTON ARTHUR
PAINTER, DESIGNER
b Milwaukee, Wis, Jan 31, 26. *Study:* Univ Florence, Italy, 45; Columbia Univ, 45; Layton Sch of Art, dipl, 50; Webster Univ, BFA, 83; Syracuse Univ,

NY, MFA, 86. *Work:* Milwaukee Art Ctr, Milwaukee Art Inst; Zadok-Gimbel, Univ Wis Collection; Tex Tech Univ Mus; Hallmark Corp Collection 91. *Comn:* Large Painting, Adminco Inc Corp Ctr, 90. *Exhib:* Vicinity Ann, Art inst Chicago, 54; Regional Ann, St Louis Artists Guild, Mo, 74-87; Butler Inst Am Art, 78, 80-81, 83 & 84; Nat Soc Painters in Casein & Acrylic, 78, 80, 83 & 90; Allied Artists Am, 79; Knickerbocker Artists, 79 & 83; Am Watercolor Soc, 81 & 83; Watercolor USA, 82, 84, 85, 87 & 91; Nat Watercolor Soc, 82 & 84; and many others. *Pos:* Art dir, WBAY-TV, Green Bay, Wis, 52-56, WXIX-TV, Milwaukee, Wis, 56-60; dir design, KMOX-TV, St Louis, Mo, 60-85. *Teaching:* Instr design & graphics, Maryville Col, 88- *Awards:* Jean Despujols Award & Meadows Mus Purchase Award, 54th Ann Shreveport Nat, 76; Grumbacher Award, Nat Arts Club 80th Ann, 80; Strathmore Award, Nat Watercolor Soc 62nd Ann, 82; Watercolor USA Award, Springfield Art Mus, 85 & 91; Silver Medal of Honor, Audubon Artists, 91. *Bibliog:* American Artist Watercolor, 1/86 & 10/87. *Mem:* Audubon Artists Am; Nat Watercolor Soc; St Louis Artists Guild: Watercolor USA Honor Soc. *Media:* Oil, Watercolor. *Publ:* Auth, article, Watercolor 86, 1/86. *Mailing Add:* 8978 Lindenhurst Dr St Louis MO 63126

GEISERT, ARTHUR FREDERICK
PRINTMAKER, ILLUSTRATOR
b Dallas, Tex, Sept 20, 41. *Study:* Concordia Teachers' Col, Seward, Nebr, BS, 63; Univ Calif, Davis, MA, 65; Chouinard Art Inst, Los Angeles; Otis Art Inst, Los Angeles; Art Inst Chicago. *Work:* Mus Art, Lodz, Poland; Freeport Art Mus, Ill; First Nat Bank Chicago; Standard Oil of Ind, Chicago; Calif Col Arts & Crafts, Oakland. *Exhib:* One-man shows, Ill Art Council Gallery, Chicago, 79, Foxley Leach Gallery, Washington, DC, 86, Boston Pub Libr, 86 & The Print Club, Philadelphia, 86; West 79, The Law, Minn Mus Art, St Paul, 79; 5th Univ Dallas Nat Print Invitational, Univ Dallas, 79. *Teaching:* From instr to asst prof art, Concordia Col, River Forest, Ill, 65-70; asst prof art, Concordia Col, Seward, Nebr, 70-71. *Awards:* Fel, Ill Arts Council, 86. *Mem:* Chicago Artists Coalition; Artists Equity Asn Inc; Boston Printmakers; The Print Club, Philadelphia; Los Angeles Printmaking Soc. *Media:* Etching. *Publ:* Auth & illust, Pa's Balloon & Other Pig Tales, 84, Pigs from A to Z, 86 & The Ark, 89, Oink, 91 & Aesop & Co, 91, Houghton Mifflin Co, Boston. *Mailing Add:* PO Box 3 Galena IL 61036

GEISSBUHLER, ARNOLD
SCULPTOR
b Delemont, Switz, Aug 9, 1897; US citizen. *Study:* Apprentice with Otto Munch, Zurich, Switz, 14-19; Acad Julian, Paris, France, 19-20; Acad Grande Chaumiere, with Bourdelle, 20-25. *Work:* Art Mus, Bern, Switz; Mus Jurassien, Delemont, Switz; Fogg Art Mus, Harvard Univ; Farnsworth Mus, Wellesley Col; Chester Dale Collection, Nat Gallery Art, Washington, DC. *Comn:* Somloire (stone war mem), Town of Somloire, Maine-Loire, France, 24; plaques & reliefs in wood, Foxboro Post Off, Mass, 40; plus many pvt comn. *Exhib:* One-man show, Delemont, 24 & 28; Philadelphia Sculpture Int Show, Pa, 40; Sculpture in US, Metrop Mus, New York, 51; Art in USA, Madison Garden, New York, 58; New Eng Painting & Sculpture Show, Boston, 71; plus many others. *Teaching:* Instr drawing & sculpture techniques, New York Sch Design, 29-30; instr drawing & sculpture techniques, Stuart Sch Design, Boston, 36-42; instr drawing & sculpture techniques, Wellesley Col, 37-58. *Awards:* Bronze Medal for Figure, Acad Julian, Paris, 19; Outstanding Award, Art USA, 58; Cambridge Centennial Award, Cambridge Art Asn. *Bibliog:* Dorothy Lefferts Moore (auth), Arnold Geissbuhler, The Arts, 2/29; Arnold Geissbuhler, Retrospective (exhib catalog), St John's Col Press, 87. *Mem:* Sculptor's Guild, New York. *Media:* Bronze, Ceramic. *Mailing Add:* Scargo Pines Box 202 Dennis MA 02638

GEIST, SIDNEY
SCULPTOR, CRITIC
b Paterson, NJ, Apr 11, 14. *Study:* St Stephen's Col; Art Students League; Acad Grande Chaumiere, Paris. *Work:* Bard Col, Annandale-on-Hudson, NY. *Exhib:* Salon Jeune Sculpture, Paris, 50; one-man shows, Paris, 50, New York, 51, 57, 60, Bard Col, 69 & New York, 74, 76, 78, 83 & 88, Gallery Tsubaki, Tokoyo, 92 & Takamiya Gallery, Osaka, 92; Pittsburgh Int, 58; Silvermine Guild, New Canaan, Conn, 60; Am Ann, Chicago Art Inst, 62; Baltimore Mus Art, 69; Anita Shapolsky Gallery, New York, 91; retrospective, New York Studio Sch, 92. *Pos:* Dir, New York Studio Sch, 64-66; guest cur, Brancusi Retrospective, Guggenheim Mus, 69. *Teaching:* Instr sculpture, Pratt Inst, 61-65; instr sculpture, New York Studio Sch, 64-87; instr sculpture, Vassar Col, 67-81; instr sculpture, Vt Studio Sch, summer 87; instr sculpture, Int Sch Art, Todi, summer 89; artist-in-residence, Carving Studio, Vt, summer 91; Int Sch Art, Montecastello di Vibio, summer, 92. *Awards:* Olivetti Award, Silvermine Guild, Conn, 60; Guggenheim Fel, 75-76. *Bibliog:* Thomas B Hess (auth), US sculpture: Some recent directions, Portfolio, 59. *Mem:* Col Art Asn Am. *Media:* Wood, Stone. *Publ:* Auth, Brancusi: A Study of the Sculpture, Grossman, 68; auth, Constantin Brancusi: A Retrospective Exhibition, Guggenheim Mus, 69; Brancusi: Sculpture and Drawings, Abrams, 75; auth, Brancusi: The Kiss, Harpers, 78; Interpreting Cézanne, Cambridge, Harvard Univ Press, 88; Auth, Sculpture from Seven Decades in Japan, Edobori Gallery (exhib catalog), Osaka, 92. *Mailing Add:* PO Box 58 New York NY 10101

GEKIERE, MADELEINE
PAINTER, FILMMAKER
b Zurich, Switz; US citizen. *Study:* Art Students League, with Kantor; Brooklyn Mus Art Sch, with Tamayo; NY Univ, with Sam Adler. *Work:* Worcester Art Mus, Mass; Fogg Mus Art, Cambridge, Mass; NY Univ Collection; Brooklyn Mus, NY; Currier Gallery of Art, Manchester, NH; and others. *Exhib:* Univ Ga, 67; Western Carolina Univ, 72; NY Univ Loeb Ctr; many one-man shows in New York, Babcock Galleries, film showings, Millenium & Artists Space, The Collective for Living Cinema, NY & 2nd Int Women's Film Festival, Donell Branch New York Pub Libr. *Teaching:* Asst prof painting, NY Univ, 58-67; prof painting, City Col New York, 67-90; vis prof painting, Univ Ga, 67. *Awards:* Best Ill Bk of Year, New York Times, 57, 59 & 63; Audubon Medal of Honor, 69; Childe Hassam Purchase Prize, Soc Art & Lett, 73. *Mem:* Artists Equity Asn. *Media:* Ink, Oil. *Publ:* Auth & illusr, Who Gave Us, 53; illusr, Switch on the Night, 57; auth & illusr, The Princess & the Frilly Lilly, 60; illusr, The Reason for the Pelican, 60; illusr, John J Plenty and Fiddler Dan, 63. *Mailing Add:* 427 W 21st St New York NY 10011

GELBER, SAMUEL
PAINTER, EDUCATOR
b Brooklyn, NY, Mar 14, 29. *Study:* Brooklyn Col, BA; NY Univ, MA. *Work:* Brooklyn Mus, NY; Purchase Mus, NY. *Comn:* Painting, Bellevue Hosp, 86. *Exhib:* Brooklyn Mus Biennial, 56; one-man shows, Green Mountain Gallery, New York, 72, 74, 76 & 79, A Sense of Place, Wichita Art Mus, Kans, 73, Springfield Art Mus, Mo, 74 & Joslyn Art Mus, Nebr, 74; Artist's Choice--Figurative Art in New York, 76; and others. *Teaching:* Instr drawing, Pratt Inst, Brooklyn, 62-65; prof painting & drawing, Brooklyn Col, 62-, chmn, 88. *Awards:* Crane & Co Award for Painting, Berkshire Mus, 66. *Bibliog:* Lee Wallin (auth), New Realism 70, St Cloud State Col, 70; Alan Gussow (auth), A Sense of Place--the Artist and the American Land, Friends of Earth, 72; Sanford Sintz Shannan (auth), An interview with Philip Pearlstein, Art in Am, 9/81. *Media:* Oil, Lithography. *Mailing Add:* 215 W 98th St New York NY 10025

GELDERMANN HAILS, BARBARA
PAINTER, PUBLISHER
b New York, NY. *Study:* Cath Univ Am, Washington, DC, BA, 65. *Work:* Bank of Baltimore Corp Collection, Md; Gannet Publ Corp Collection, Washington, DC; Montgomery Co Contemp Art Collection, Rockville, Md; Sandy Spring Mus, Olney, Md. *Comn:* The Bridge, pastel painting, Suburban Hosp, Bethesda, Md, 86. *Exhib:* Nat Biennial Exhib, Nat League Am Penwomen, Washington, DC, 79; 10th Ann Pastel Exhib, Pastel Soc Am, New York, 82; 6th Ann Open Exhib, Salmagundi Club, New York, 83; 41st Ann, Audubon Artists, New York, 83; 48th Ann Midyear Nat, Butler Inst Am Art, Youngstown, Ohio, 84; Art on Paper 1984, Md Fedn Art, Annapolis, 84; Soc des Pastellistes de France, Palais Rameau, Lille, 87; Art Expo NY, Jacobs Javitz Conv Ctr, 88-92. *Pos:* Publ, Dimensional Aesthetics, Olney, Md, 85- *Awards:* Outstanding artist, Nat League Am Penwomen, 83; Individual grant, Montgomery Co Arts Coun, 86. *Bibliog:* Painting in Pastel, Katchen, North Light Books, 91. *Mem:* Pastel Soc Am; Md Pastel Soc; Artists Equity. *Media:* Pastel on Ground Glass Board. *Publ:* Auth, several articles in Artist Mag & Am Artist, 79-88. *Dealer:* McBride Art Gallery 117 Main St Annapolis Md 21401. *Mailing Add:* 3904 Ashland Brooke Way Olney MD 20832

GELINAS, ROBERT WILLIAM
PAINTER, EDUCATOR
b Springfield, Mass, Mar 1, 31. *Study:* Univ Conn; Univ Ala, BFA & MFA; also with Lawrence Calgagno & Tatsuiko Heima. *Work:* Kelley Fitzpatrick Mus, Montgomery, Ala; Mead Corp Collection, Atlanta, Ga; Fla House of Rep, Tallahassee; Mus Fine Arts, Little Rock, Ark. *Comn:* Chapel sculpture, Wesley Found Student Ctr, Memphis, 60. *Exhib:* Art USA, 58, New York, 58; 26th & 27th Corcoran Biennials, Washington, DC, 59 & 61; Painting of the Yr Ann, Mead Corp, Atlanta, 61; Bon Marche Nat Gallery Exhib, Seattle, Wash, 63; Fla Showcase, Rockefeller Ctr, New York, 64; Soc of Four Arts Exhibs, Palm Beach, Fla, 66, 72, 77, 78 & 79. *Pos:* Art dir, Tuscaloosa News, Ala, 55-57; artist in residence, Maitland Res Ctr, 65; artist in residence, Upham Studio, Naples, 66-69. *Teaching:* Guest artist instr, Allisons Wells Art Colony Workshops, Canton, Miss, 58-62; asst prof art, Memphis State Univ, 58-63; from assoc prof to prof art, Univ SFla, 63- *Awards:* First Purchase Prize, Mid South Ann, 61; 18th Ann Purchase Exhib Prize, Carrol Reese Mus, 67; Best of Show, Gulf Coast Art Exhib, Bellaire, Fla, 78. *Bibliog:* Benbow (auth), All out war, St Petersburg Times, 8/65; Gelinas the modern master, Tampa Tribune, 66. *Media:* Acrylic. *Dealer:* Virginia Miller Galleries Coconut Grove Miami FL 33133. *Mailing Add:* c/o Jacksonville Univ Alexander Brest Gallery & Mus 2800 University Blvd N Jacksonville FL 32211

GELLATLY, MICHAEL
PAINTER
Study: Paire Sch Art, 72-73. *Exhib:* Solo exhibs, Groadway Gallery, New Haven, Conn, 79, Carlson Gallery, Univ Bridgeport, Conn, 85 & Gracie Mansion Gallery, New York, 87; Nine Connecticut Painters, 86 & Connecticut Sculpture, 90, Real Art Ways, Hartford; Nine Sculptors, Silo Gallery, New Milford, Conn, 89; Art for the Airways, Carlson Gallery, Univ Bridgeport, Conn, 90; Litchfield Co Arts Festival, Bachelier-Cardonsky Gallery, Kent, Con, 90; Artspace, New Haven, Conn, 91; Lyman Allyn Art Mus, New London, Conn, 92. *Awards:* Nat Endowment Arts Fel, 87. *Bibliog:* C W Vrtacek (auth), A New Preston ARtist's Lifesize 'Visual Ramblings', Litchfield Co Times, 12/13/85; Frank Merkling (auth), Soho at the Silo, Modern Living, 9/88. *Mailing Add:* 29 Cream Hill Rd West Cornwall CT 06796

GELLER, ESTHER (ESTHER GELLER SHAPERO)
PAINTER, PRINTMAKER
b Boston, Mass, Oct 26, 21. *Study:* Mus Fine Arts Sch, Boston, dipl; also with Karl Zerbe. *Work:* Mus Fine Arts, Boston; Addison Gallery Am Art, Andover, Mass; Brandeis Univ; Walters Gallery, Regis Col; St Mark's Sch

Gallery, Southboro, Mass. *Exhib:* Art Inst Chicago Ann; Boston Art Festivals; US Info Serv Circulating Exhibs in the US & Far East; one-man show, Am Acad Art Gallery, Rome, 71, Newton Art Ctr, 78, Artworks at the Wayne, 79 & Stonehill Col, 86; Pastel Show, Regis Col, 84; and others. *Teaching:* Instr painting & drawing, Sch Mus Fine Arts, Boston, 43, Boris Mirski Art Sch, 46-48, Natick Art Asn Sch, 55-61 & Wayland Art Asn, 83. *Awards:* Cabot Fel, 49; Fels, MacDowell Colony, Yaddo & Am Acad, 50-71. *Bibliog:* Pratt & Fizell (auth), Encaustic, Lear Publ, 49; Bern Chaet (auth), Artists at Work, Webb, 60; B Hayes (auth), The Layman's Guide to Modern Art; R Lister (auth), Drawing with Pastel; and others. *Media:* Watercolor, Encaustic. *Dealer:* Geller Studio 5 Summer St Natick Mass 01760. *Mailing Add:* 9 Russell Circle Natick MA 01760

GELLER, MATTHEW
SCULPTOR
b New York, NY, Sept 28, 54. *Study:* Conn Col, BA, 76; Univ Del, MFA, 78. *Work:* Mus Mod Art, Whitney Mus Am Art, Franklin Furnace, New York; Stedelijk Van Abbemuseum, Einhoven, Moderna Musset, Stockholm. *Exhib:* The Times Square Show, Collaborative Proj Inc, 80, Mus Mod Art, 82, 87 & 88, Int Ctr for Photog, New York, 89; Mus Mod Art, Jerusalem, 81; Long Beach Mus, 82, La Jolla Mus, Calif, 87; Inst Contemp Art, Boston, 84; Laforet Mus, New Orleans, 84; Your Television, Your Home, New Mus Contemp Art, New York, 90. *Pos:* VPres, Collaborative Proj Inc, New York, 81-82; co-dir, Line Asn, New York, 81-83; consult, Visual Arts, Nat Endowment for the Arts, 84, 85; co-chair media panel, NY State Coun on the Arts, 86-88. *Teaching:* Sch of Visual Arts, New York, 83-84, 86-90, Univ Calif, San Diego, 87, Princeton Univ, 88, William Col, Williamstown, Mass, 90. *Awards:* Nat Endowment Arts Fel Visual Arts, 85, 87 & 89; NY Found Arts Fel, 88; Rome Prize, Am Acad in Rome, 91-92. *Bibliog:* Articles in Village Voice, NY Times, Artnews, Art in American, 90 & 91. *Media:* Mixed Media, Installation. *Mailing Add:* 4 White St New York NY 10013

GELLERT, VANCE F
PHOTOGRAPHER
Study: Univ Minn, PhD(pharmacology), 75; Va Commonwealth Univ, MFA (photog), 84. *Work:* Mus Art, Princeton, NJ; Ctr Creative Photog, Univ Ariz, Tucson; Dains Bosworth Inc, Minneapolis, Minn; Mus Fine Arts, Houston, Tex; Minn Mus Art, St Paul; Univ Ore, Eugene. *Exhib:* One-man shows, Perimeter Gallery, Minneapolis, Minn, 90 & pARTs Alternative Artspace, Minneapolis, Minn, 91; Minn Artists, Minn State Fair, St Paul, 91; Artists Respond to War, pARTs Alternative Artspace, Minneapolis, Minn, 91; FITC/McKnight Fel Exhib, Film in the Cities, St Paul, Minn, 92; Flesh & Blood, Friends Photog, San Francisco, Calif, 92; and others. *Pos:* Art com photogr, Richmond, Va, 83-84; bd dir, Eye Gallery, San Francisco, 87-88. *Teaching:* Instr photog, Va Commonwealth Univ, 82-83 & Film in the Cities, St Paul, Minn, 89; instr, Calif Col Arts & Crafts, 85-86, Univ Calif, Berkeley, 86-87, Friends of Photog Workshop, San Francisco, 88; guest lectr art, Univ Calif, Davis, 88; lectr photog, Minn Col Arts & Design, 89-90; co-founder & dir, pARTs Gallery Photog Arts, Minneapolis, Minn, 89- *Awards:* Individual Visual Artist Grant, Nat Endowment Arts, 88; McKnight Found Fel, 91. *Bibliog:* Cynthia Freeland (auth), Family/Extensions (cover), Spot, fall 87; Pamela Allara & Anne Tucker (auths), Cross Currents/Cross Country, Views/San Francisco Camerawork, fall 88; Alice Rose George, Abigail Heymen & Ethan Hoffman, (auths), Flesh and Blood: Photographers' Images of Their Own Families, Milan, Sfera/Garzanti, 92. *Publ:* Auth, Carl Vision: The Human Condition, Darkroom Photog, cover, 11/85; The Photoreview, fall 85; Carl Vision, Portland, Blue Sky Press, 87; A Portrait is Not a Likeness, Ctr Creative Photog, Archive 29, 91; Readings, Harpers, 10/92; and others. *Dealer:* 2800 Lyndale Ave S Minneapolis MN. *Mailing Add:* 1808 Irving Ave S Minneapolis MN 55403

GELLIS, SANDY L
SCULPTOR
b New York, NY. *Study:* Sch of Visual Arts; City Col of New York; New Sch for Social Res, FTT (AAS). *Work:* Humanities Birches, C W Post Univ; Brooklyn Mus, New York; Prudential Insur Co Am, Newark, NJ; J P Morgan & Co, New York. *Comn:* Viewing Mounds, Stephlen Farms, Pine Plains, NY, 90; Environment, Pub Libr Plaza, Bronz, NY, 92. *Exhib:* solo exhibs, Environ Point of Departure, 55 Mercer, New York, 77, 78 & 80, Studies for Dump Sites, New York Experimental Glass Workshop, Gallery, New York, 85, Earth, Air and Water Studies, Storefront for Art & Archit, New York, 89 & Gallery Three Zero (with catalog), 92; Tropical Rainforest, Sundered Ground, New York, 89; Projects and Portfolios, 25th Nat Print Biennial, Brooklyn Mus, NY, 89; Political Landscapes, Hillwood Art Mus, CW Post Univ, Greenvale, NY, 90; Garbage Out Front: A New Era of Public Design, Munic Art Soc, New York, 90; Summer Exhib, Gallery Three Zero, New York, 91; Presswork: The Art of 100 Women Printmakers (travelling), Nat Mus Women Arts, Washington, DC, 91. *Teaching:* Instr, Sch Visual Arts, NY, 79-89 & Fashion Instr Technol, 80-83. *Awards:* Grants, Sculpture, 79-80 & 81-82 & Drawing & Printmaking, 87-88, Nat Endowment Arts; MacDowell Fel, Sculpture, 79. *Bibliog:* Gretchen Faust (auth), New York in review, Arts Mag, Vol 64, No 4, 12/4/89; Susan Tallman (auth), The other biennial, Arts Mag, Vol 64, No 7, 2/7/90; Phyllis Braff (auth), Fate of the world as a theme, NY Times, 4/8/90. *Media:* Environment. *Publ:* Auth, Intericon 1986 (exhib catalogs, 1 & 2), Charlottenborg, Denmark, 86; Glass (exhib catalog), Soc Arts Crafts, Pittsburgh, Pa, 89; Projects and Portfolios, 25th Nat Print Biennial (exhib catalog), Brooklyn Mus, NY, 89; Political Landscapes (exhib catalog), Hillwood Art Mus, Greenvale, NY, 90; and numerous other exhib catalogs. *Dealer:* Actual Art Foundation Seven Worth St New York NY; Luise Ross Gallery New York NY. *Mailing Add:* 39 Bond St New York NY 10012

GELTMAN, LILY
COLLAGE ARTIST, PAINTER
b New York, NY, Nov 25, 03. *Study:* Hunter Col, New York, BA, 25, La Grande Chavmieré, Paris. *Work:* Butler Inst Am Art, Youngstown, Ohio; Smithsonian Inst, Washington, DC; Woodstock Hist Soc, NY. *Exhib:* Collectors Am Art, New York, 63; Salon Int de la Femme, Cannes, France, 69; London Art Mus, Ont, Can, 69; Woodstock Art Asn, NY 77-87; one-person show, Woodstock, NY, 87; and others. *Teaching:* Instr art, S J Tilden High Sch, Brooklyn, NY, 39-58. *Awards:* Watercolor Award, Nat Asn Women Artists, 49 & 54; Oil Award, Am Soc Contemp Artists, 74, 80 & 81; Don Gottschalk Award, Woodstock Art Asn, 88. *Mem:* Nat Asn Women Artists (chairwoman, Watercolor Comt, 67-80 & Nom Comt, 78-80); Am Soc Contemp Artists; Artists Equity Asn; Woodstock Art Asn. *Media:* Watercolor, Oil. *Mailing Add:* 299 W 12th St New York NY 10014

GELTNER, DANITA SUE
SCULPTOR, PAINTER
b Atlanta, Ga, May 19, 52. *Study:* Studied at Sorbonne, Paris, France, certificat Francaise, 73; Univ Pittsburgh, BA, 76; Md Inst Col Art; MFA, 78. *Work:* K & B Found, New Orleans, La; Verlain Found, New Orleans, La; Prudential Collection, Newark, NJ. *Comn:* Window installation, Charles Jordan Shoes, Trump Tower, New York, 92. *Exhib:* Art Mart Gallery, New York, 85 & 86; PPOW Gallery, New York, 87; Grace Borgenicht Gallery, New York, 88; UP Gallery, Pittsburgh, Pa, 91; Mendelson Gallery, Pittsburgh, Pa, 92. *Awards:* Art Matters Inc, Found Grant, New York, 86 & 88; Committee Award, Biennial Exhib, Fine Arts Mus S, 87. *Bibliog:* Michael Brenson (auth), Danita Geltner, NY Times, 2/7/86; Elizabeth Hess (auth), Faux foe, Village Voice, 6/30/87; Kate Linker (auth), Review, Art Forum, 10/87. *Mem:* Orgn Independent Artists, New York; Artists in Residence, New York; Artists Equity, New York; White Columns, New York (secy bd dirs, 90-92); Ringside, New York. *Mailing Add:* 80 Warren St No 19 New York NY 10007-1029

GENAUER, EMILY
CRITIC, WRITER
b New York, NY. *Study:* Hunter Col, grad; Sch Jour, Columbia Univ, BLit; Nat Acad. *Pos:* Staff writer & art feature writer, New York World, 29-31; art critic & ed, New York World-Tel, 32-49; art critic, New York Herald Tribune, 49-66; art critic & ed, New York World Jour Tribune, 66-67; art commentator, Educ TV, New York, 67-77; art critic-columnist, Newsday Syndicate, 67-76; adv bd, Sch Jour, Columbia Univ. *Awards:* New York Newspaper Women's Club Award for Outstanding Column in Any Field, 49, 56, 58, 60 & 69; Columbia Univ Jour Alumni Award, 60; Pulitzer Prize, Distinguished Critic in Journalism, 75. *Mem:* Nat Coun Humanities; Int Asn Art Critics; New York Newspaper Women's Club. *Publ:* Auth, Toulouse-Lautrec (monogr), 53, Biography of Chagall, 57, Hommage a l'Ecole de Paris, 62, Biography of Tamayo 74, Metrop Mus Art, New York; Chagall at the Met, 71; and others. *Mailing Add:* 243 E 49th St New York NY 10017

GENERAL IDEA, See Bronson, A A (Michael Wayne Tims)

GENERAL IDEA, See Partz, Felix (Ron Gabe)

GENERAL IDEA, See Zontal, Jorge (Jorge Saia)

GENIUSZ, ROBERT MYLES
PRINTMAKER, FILMMAKER
b Milwaukee, Wis, Aug 30, 48. *Study:* Sch Fine Arts, Univ Wis, Milwaukee, BFA, 74, MFA, 76. *Work:* Kohler Art Ctr, Sheboygan, Wis; Sheboygan Pub Schs, Wis; Performing Art Ctr, Theatre Sch, Milwaukee. *Comn:* Puppet Theatre, Kohler Art Ctr, Sheboygan, Wis, 76. *Exhib:* Strange Tales, Kohler Art Ctr, Sheboygan, Wis, 76; Ann Beloit & Vicinity, Wright Arts Ctr, Beloit, Wis, 76, 77 & 79; Artists/Toys, Milwaukee Art Ctr, 77 & 79; Toys Designed by Artists, Ark Arts Ctr, Little Rock, 78 & 27th Ann Delta Invitational, 79; Form, Fun & Fantasy, Mt Mary Col, Milwaukee 78; one-man show, Printed Worlds, Oshkosh Pub Mus, Wis, 79; Wisconsin Artists, Cudahay Gallery, Milwaukee Art Mus, 83; International Paper Conference, Kyoto, Japan, 83; and others. *Teaching:* Instr 3-D, 2D & drawing, Univ WisParkside, Kenosha, Jan, 78; instr filmaking, Univ Wis-Milwaukee, Sept, 79; artist in residence filmaking, Performing Art Ctr, Milwaukee, Wis, 79-80, Milwaukee Public Schs, 81-83. *Awards:* Nat Endowment Arts Grant, Artist-in-Residence Prog, 76-77 & 79-84. *Bibliog:* Evelyn Terry Bridges (auth), Wisconsin artists make toys, Milwaukee, Vol 4, No 12, 12/79. *Mem:* Col Art Asn Am; Artists Equity Asn. *Mailing Add:* 997 Granville Rd Cedarburg WI 53012-9379

GENKIN, JONATHAN
PAINTER
b New York, NY, 57. *Exhib:* Solo exhibs, Damon Brandt Gallery, New York, 86-89, Galeria Bonk, Cologne, Ger, 87 & Daniel Newburg Gallery, New York, 89; Glastnost, Galeria Bonk, Cologne, Ger, 87; From the Monochrome and Beyond, Univ Maine, Orono, 88; The Colour Alone: The Monochrome Experiment, Mus St Pierre, Lyon, France, 88. *Awards:* Nat Endowment Arts Fel, 87. *Mailing Add:* 134 Broadway Brooklyn NY 11211

GENN, NANCY
PAINTER, SCULPTOR
b San Francisco, Calif. *Study:* San Francisco Art Inst, Calif; Univ Calif, Berkeley. *Work:* Albright-Knox Art Gallery, Buffalo, NY; San Francisco Mus Mod Art; Aldrich Mus, Ridgefield, Conn; Cincinnati Art Mus, Ohio; Mus Mod Art, Brooklyn Mus, New York; Nat Mus Am Art, Smithsonian Inst, Libr Congress, Washington, DC; Los Angeles Co Mus Art, Calif; Univ Art Mus,

Univ Calif, Berkeley. *Comn:* Bronze lectern & five bronze sculptures for chancel table, First Unitarian Church, Berkeley, Calif, 61 & 64; bronze fountain, Cowell Col, Univ Calif, Santa Cruz, 66; bronze menorah, Temple Beth Am, Los Altos Hills, Calif, 68; 17 murals in ceramic glazed tile & two bronze fountain sculptures, Sterling Vineyards, Caligosta, Calif, 72 & 73; bronze fountain sculpture, Expo 74, Spokane, Wash, 74; pair of mixed media paintings on paper, IBM, San Jose, Calif. *Exhib:* Solo shows, M H De Young Mem Mus, San Francisco, 55 & 63, San Francisco Mus Art, 61, New Worlds, Oakland Art Mus, 71, Los Angeles Inst Contemp Art, 76, Harcourts Gallery, San Francisco, 91, Brendan Walter Gallery, Los Angeles, Calif, 92; Twentieth Century Drawings, Stanford Univ, Palo Alto, Calif, 55; Winter Invitational, Calif Palace Legion Hon, San Francisco, 60-63; Contemporary Reflections, Aldrich Mus, Ridgefield, Conn, 72-73; Works on Paper, Mus Mod Art, New York, 76; Paper as Medium Smithsonian Inst Traveling Exhib, 78-80; Making Paper, Am Craft Mus, NY, 82-84; Paper as Image, Arts Coun Gt Brit, 83-84; Paper Works: Seven Perspectives, Tampa Mus, Fla, 86; First Int-Biennale Paper Art, Leopold-Hoesch Mus, Duren, WGer, 86; plus others. *Awards:* Purchase Award Painting, State of Calif, 57; Honor Award for Design Excellence, US Dept Housing & Urban Develop, 68; US-Japan Creative Arts Fel, 78-79. *Media:* Working in handformed and embossed paper in multiple layers. *Mailing Add:* 1515 La Loma Ave Berkeley CA 94708

GENOVESE, RICHARD
PHOTOGRAPHER, COLLAGE ARTIST
b New York, NY, May 31, 47. *Study:* Long Island Univ, BA, 78; study with Judith Murray, Martin Ries & Jerome Zimmerman. *Work:* Bayville Hist Mus, NY. *Comn:* Binder for book, comn by Dr J H Matthews, Lake Placid, NY, 74; Masque, Fine Arts Mus Long Island, Hempstead, NY, 86. *Exhib:* Watergate, Fyns Stifts Kunstmuseum, Odense, Denmark, 74; Surrealism & Contemporary Painting, Oswego Univ, NY, 84; one-man show, Masques, Discovery Gallery, Glen Cove, NY, 85; Alternative Spaces, Islip Art Mus, NY, 86; 3-D, Then & Now, Bayville Hist Mus, NY, 90. *Bibliog:* Wesles Sidon (auth), Masques, WCWP-FM Radio, 2/85; Ray Jason (auth), Frissons, Post Haste, 6/87. *Dealer:* Sikkema Gallery 155 Spring St New York NY 10012. *Mailing Add:* 76 Pine St Freeport NY 11520

GENTILE, GLORIA IRENE
DESIGNER, SCULPTOR
b New York, NY. *Study:* Cooper Union, New York, 47-50; Yale Univ, 51-54, BFA & MFA; study with Josef Albers, Will Barnet, Abraham Rattner, Nicholas Marscicano, Stuart Davis, Buckminster Fuller, Philip Johnson, Frederick Kiesler, Louis Kahn, Frank Lloyd Wright & Alvin Lustig. *Exhib:* One-person shows, Harbrace Gallery, 67, Aleksandra Kierekieska Gallery, 68, Art Dir Club Gallery, 68, Young & Rubican Gallery, New York, 68 & Ogilvy & Mather Inc Gallery, 68; Sculpture Happening, Mus Mod Art, 72. *Pos:* Founder & dir, Gentile Studio Graphics, 75- *Teaching:* Instr concepts & promotion, Sch Visual Arts, New York, 68-74 & Parsons Sch Design, 72-; instr promotional design, Cooper Union, 74-; Queens Col, 78-79; instr, Fashion Inst Technology, 80-81 & Pratt Inst, 82-83. *Awards:* Graphic Design Desi Award. *Bibliog:* Article in New Worlds of Reading, Harcourt Brace Jovanovich, 69. *Media:* Articulated Bronze, Ball Joints. *Mailing Add:* 333 E 46th St No 108 New York NY 10017

GENTRY, AUGUSTUS (CALLAHAN), JR
PAINTER, PRINTMAKER
b Tyler, Tex, Feb 5, 27. *Study:* Tyler Jr Col, AA, 48; Univ Tex, with Boyer Gonzales, Ralph White & Seymour Fogel, BFA, 52. *Work:* Am Nat Life Collection, Galveston, Tex; Shell Oil Collection, Houston; Repub Nat Bank, Dallas; First City Bank & InterFirst Bank, Tyler, Tex; Spring Valley Collection, Dallas. *Comn:* McKittrick Canyon (16 pieces), comn by Donors of McKittrick Canyon Nat Park, Houston, 70. *Exhib:* New York Int, 70; Southwest Watercolor Soc 100 Best Ann, 73 & 74; Midwest Wildlife Art Show, Kansas City, Mo, 74-75; Outdoors in Ga, Nat Wildlife Show, 76-77 & 79-82. *Teaching:* Grad asst sculpture, Univ Tex, Austin, 52-53; instr art, Tyler Independent Sch Dist, 53-59; instr watercolor, Tyler Jr Col, 70-73; artist-in-residence, Univ Tex, Tyler, 80-, instr overseas grad studies in watercolor, 83. *Awards:* Tex State Artist, 73; Signature Mem Award, Southwest Watercolor Soc, 74. *Bibliog:* Wilkins (auth), The local gentry, Chronicles, Smith Co Hist Soc, 70. *Mem:* Southwest Watercolor Soc; Graphics Soc. *Media:* Watercolor; Etching. *Publ:* Illusr, Chronicles of Smith Co, Tex, 70 & 71. *Mailing Add:* 922 S Bois D Arc Tyler TX 75701-1507

GENTRY, HERBERT
PAINTER, GRAPHIC ARTIST
b Pittsburgh, Pa, July 17, 19. *Study:* NY Univ, 40-42; Acad Grande Chaumiere, Paris, 46-49, Ecole des Hautes Etudes, Paris, 47-49. *Work:* Stedlijk Mus, Amsterdam, Neth; Moderna Museet, Stockholm, Sweden; Metrop Mus Art, New York; Nat Mus Am Art, Washington, DC; Carnegie Inst Art, Pittsburgh, Pa; Bronx Mus; Mus Mod Art, New York; Nat Galerie Oslo; Biblioteque Nationale, Paris; and others. *Exhib:* One-man shows, Galerie Andre Zarre, New York, 74, Royal Art Acad, Stockholm, Sweden, 75, Amos Anderson Mus, Helsinki, Finland, 76, Gallery Glaub, Cologne, Germany, 81, Gallery Goovier Fine Arts, Amsterdam, 85 & Maison Francaise, New York Univ, 86; and many other group & one-man shows. *Teaching:* Vis instr, Montclair State Col, 80 & 82 vis specialist; vis prof, Rutgers Univ, Newark, NJ, 86. *Media:* Acrylic, Gouache. *Dealer:* Peder Olin Galleri Futura Karlaplan 14 Stockholm Sweden; Alitash Kebede Fine Arts 1310 N Alta Vista Los Angeles CA. *Mailing Add:* 222 West 23rd St New York NY 10011

GENTRY, WARREN MILLER
INSTRUCTOR, PAINTER
b Manville, Wyo, Oct 3, 21. *Study:* Ariz State Univ, BA, 50, MA, 55; Univ Calif, Berkeley, with Frank Lobdell, 64. *Work:* Munic Collection, Orange, France. *Exhib:* Ariz State Fair Fine Arts Exhib, 49-63; 1st Ariz Ann, Phoenix, 59; Fresh Paint Show, M H De Young Mus, 59; Old Phoenix Art Mus. *Pos:* Founding chmn dept art, 63-68, Glendale Col & founding dir, Art Collection, 63-69; co-owner & founder, The Gentry Gallery, Scottsdale, Ariz. *Teaching:* Prof art hist & painting, Glendale Community Col, 63-; retired, 90. *Awards:* Valley Bank Purchase Award, 1st Ariz Ann, 59. *Mem:* Scottsdale Beautification Com (first chmn). *Media:* Oil, Watercolor. *Mailing Add:* PO Box 4082 Scottsdale AZ 85261

GEORGE, RAYMOND ELLIS
PRINTMAKER, EDUCATOR
b Cedar Falls, Iowa, Sept 13, 33. *Study:* Univ Northern Iowa, BA, 55, MA, 62. *Work:* Smithsonian Inst, Washington, DC; The Dupont Corp; Victoria & Albert Mus, London, Eng; Libr Cong, Washington, DC; New York Pub Libr. *Comn:* Ceramic mural, Dubuque Pub Schs, Iowa, 60. *Exhib:* Contemporary American Prints, State Univ NY Col Oneonta, 69; Nat Drawing Exhib, Ark Art Ctr, 88; one-man show, Printworks Gallery, Chicago, Ill, 87-88; Am Miniature Printmakers Exhib, San Diego, Calif, 88; 11th Nat Print Invitational, Univ Dallas, 89; American Portfolio II, Printmaking Coun NJ, 89. *Teaching:* Prof art, Ill State Univ, Normal, 71-; artist in residence, Munson Williams Proctor Inst, Sch Art, Utica, NY. *Awards:* Purchase Awards, Eight-State Print Exhib, J B Speed Art Mus, 74, 83 & Nat Drawing Exhib, Southern Ill Univ, Carbondale, 75; Visual Artist Award, Nat Endowment Arts, 85. *Mem:* Boston Printmakers; Col Art Asn. *Media:* Intaglio, Drawing. *Publ:* Auth, Graphite Lithography, Tamerind Tech Papers, 77; Chicago Art Rev, 89. *Mailing Add:* 1907 Garling Dr Bloomington IL 61701

GEORGE, RICHARD ALLAN
PAINTER
b Chicago, Ill, Nov 28, 35. *Study:* State Univ NY Buffalo, with Larry Calcagno, BFA; Art Students League, with Frank Reilly; Miami Univ, Ohio, with Edwin Fulwider, MFA. *Work:* Allen Mem Art Mus, Oberlin, Ohio; Chase Manhattan Bank, New York; Cincinnati Bell, Ohio. *Comn:* Painting, Ohio State Off Tower, Columbus, 74; four paintings, First Nat Bank, Hamilton, Ohio, 77-78; painting, Southwestern Ohio Steel Co, Hamilton. *Exhib:* Ann Mid-Year Show, Butler Inst Am Art, Youngstown, Ohio, 72, 78, 81, 86 & 88; Biennial Contemp Art, Whitney Mus Am Art, New York, 75; one-man show, Sheldon Swope Art Mus, Terre Haute, Ind, 89, Sazama Gallery, Chicago, 90; Chicago Art Fair and Solway Gallery, 81-86; Choices: Twenty Painters from the Midwest, Minneapolis Col Art & Desgin, 87. *Teaching:* Instr drawing & painting, Middletown Fine Arts Ctr, Ohio, 71- *Awards:* Best of Show, 73 & Award for Painting, 79, 84-85 & 87-88, Ohio State Fair; First Award for Painting, Art League Regional, Indianapolis, 82 & 85; Cash Award for Painting, Exhib 280, Huntington Galleries, WVa; Arts Midwest Regional Visual Arts Fel Award, Nat Endowment for the Arts, 86-87; Individual Artists Fel, Ohio Arts Coun, 86-87. *Mem:* Art Students League; Nat Col Art Asn. *Media:* Acrylic, Oil. *Dealer:* Carl Solway Gallery 314 W Fourth St Cincinnati OH 45202; Sazama Gallery Chicago Ill. *Mailing Add:* 4440 W Elkton Rd Hamilton OH 45011

GEORGE, SYLVIA JAMES
PORTRAIT PAINTER, ILLUSTRATOR
b Syracuse, NY, Oct 13, 21. *Study:* Pratt Inst, 44; Am Univ, 53; pvt study with Robert Gates, 53, John H Sanden 77-78 & Daniel Greene, 82. *Work:* John F Kennedy Libr, Boston, Mass; Howard High Sch, Ellicott City, Md; DuFief Elementary Sch, Gaithersburg, Md; St Louis Church, Clarksville, Md; Howard Community Col, Columbia, Md; S Bauman, Elkridge Hist Soc. *Comn:* Portrait, Adele Simpson, New York, 44; etched silver plates, pvt comn, Charles Jubb, Crownsville, Md, 69-79; B & O Railroad, Ellicott City, Md, 69; Martin Luther King, Gallery G, Columbia, Md, 73; four murals, Nat Ctr Community Asn, Washington, DC, 78; two portraits, Belgian dignitaries. *Exhib:* Solo exhib, Howard Community Col, Columbia, Md, 73; Artists Equity Show, Turner Bldg, Johns Hopkins Univ, Baltimore, 75-84; Baltimore Watercolor Soc Show, Turner Bldg, Johns Hopkins, 76; Slayton House Gallery, Columbia, Md, 70-88; Life of Baltimore Gallery, Baltimore, 84; Corcoran Gallery, Washington, DC, 85; Faces: A Look Within, Shenandoah Col, Winchester, Va, 85; 100th Anniversary of the Automobile, Daimler-Benz, Stuttgard, WGer, 85. *Pos:* Chmn registry, Howard County Arts Coun, Md, 79-80; vpres, Visual Arts Alliance, 80-82; dir publicity, Md Pastel Soc, 86; chmn, art selection comt, Slayton House, Columbia, Md, currently; pres, SJG Art Studio/Gallery, currently. *Teaching:* Art asst, drawing & painting, Palotti High Sch, Md, 80-82; artist-in-residence, Oakland Mills High Sch, Md, 82. *Awards:* Dey Brothers Award, 36; First Prize, Johns Hopkins Univ-APL Art Competition, 79. *Bibliog:* Virginia Leach (auth), The Howard County News, Attractions, 11/81; Jack Dillinger (auth), Art notes, Columbia Flier, 1/85 & 6/85; Les Krantz Am Artists; Mary Carter Smith (auth), Town Child, 80. *Mem:* Artists Equity; Md Pastel Soc; New Art Ctr; Nat Mus Women Arts; Md Soc Portrait Painters; Portrait Club New York; Visual Arts Alliance; Col Art Asn. *Media:* Oil, Watercolor. *Publ:* Illusr, covers, Guard Mag, Johnson Studios, 76-78. *Mailing Add:* SJG Art Studio/Gallery 8600 Foundry St Savage MD 20763

GEORGE, THOMAS
PAINTER, DRAFTSMAN
b New York, NY, July 1, 18. *Study:* Dartmouth Col, BA, 40; Art Students League; Acad Grand Chaumiere, Paris; Ist Statale Arte, Florence, Italy. *Work:* Guggenheim Mus, Mus Mod Art, Whitney Mus & Brooklyn Mus, New

York; San Francisco Mus; Mus Am Art, Washington, DC; Tate Gallery, London, Eng; Mus Fine Arts, Housto; Nat Gallery, Oslo, Norway; Bridgestone Mus, Tokyo; and many others. *Comn:* Tapestry, Slatkin Art Gallery, New York, 68; poster/print, US Olympic Comt & Kennedy Galleries, New York, 74; Dodge Found, 87. *Exhib:* Whitney Mus Am Art Ann, 60-62 & 65; Princeton Univ Art Mus, 75; Nat Collection Fine Arts, 77; Betty Parsons Gallery, 68, 70, 72, 74, 76, 78 & 81; Maxwell Davidson, New York, 83 & 85; Retrospective, NJ State Mus, 87, Galleri Riis, Oslo, 90, Snyder Fine Art, New York, 90, 91. *Teaching:* Vis artist, Univ Tex, 78; artist-in-residence, Dartmouth Col, 79. *Awards:* Award, NJ State Mus, 72; Pres Medal for Life Achievement, Dartmouth Col, 91; Princeton Arts Coun Award, 92. *Mem:* Fel Edward MacDowell Colony. *Media:* Oil, Ink; Pastel. *Publ:* Illusr, A Line of Poetry, A Row of Trees, Jargon, 65; illusr, Kweilin's An American artist in China, 76; illusr, The Norway Series, Capellen, Oslo, 80. *Dealer:* Snyder Fine Art New York NY; Riis Gallery Oslo Norway. *Mailing Add:* 20 Greenhouse Dr Princeton NJ 08540

GEORGES, PAUL G
PAINTER
b Portland, Ore, June 15, 23. *Study:* Univ Ore, study with Jack Wilkinson 46; study with Hans Hoffman, New York and Provincetown, 47 & Fernand Leger, Paris, 49-52. *Work:* Mus Modern Art, Whitney Mus, New York; Hirschorn Collection, Smithsonian Inst, Corcoran Art Collection, Washington, DC; Richmond Mus, Sydney & Frances Lewis Wing, Va. *Exhib:* Rose Art Mus, Brandeis Univ, Waltham, Mass, 81; Mead Art Mus, Amherst, Mass, 85; Greenville Co Mus Art, SC, 85; Slow Art, PS 1 Mus, Long Island City, New York, 92, O'Reilly Galleries, New York, 92. *Teaching:* Retired prof painting, Brandeis Univ, Waltham, Mass. *Awards:* Ranger Purchase Award, Nat Acad Design, 85; Hassam Purchase Award, Inst Arts & Letts, 90; Individual Support Grant, Adolph & Esther Gottlieb Found, 92. *Bibliog:* Carter Ratcliff (auth), Paul Georges, A C M J, fall 83; Jed Perl (auth), Autumn Alphabet, The New Criterion, No 7, 3/89; Lisa Liebman (auth), Art, The New Yorker, 8/17/92. *Mem:* Nat Acad Design (assoc, 79-83, academician, 83-). *Media:* Oil. *Dealer:* Salander-O'Reilly Galleries 20 E 79th St New York NY 10021; Charles More Gallery 1630 Walnut St Philadelphia PA 19103. *Mailing Add:* 85 Walker St New York NY 10013

GEPPONI, ANGELO
PAINTER, EDUCATOR
b Tuscany, Italy, Feb 3, 11, US citizen. *Study:* Nat Acad Design, Tiffany Fel, 41; Art Students League, 47; New York Univ, BS, 50, MA(cum laude), 51; Mus Mod Art, Victor D'Amico, Hon Dr, 60; Northern Ill Univ, Dr Jack Arends (art tour), Hon Dr, 66; Crative Art Studies, Lucca, Italy, John DelMonte (prof), Hon Dr, 72. *Work:* NJ State Mus, Trenton; Bergen Mus Art & Sci, Paramus; Kent State Univ, Ohio; Teaneck Pub Libr, NJ. *Exhib:* Outdoor Art Show, Brooklyn Mus, New York, 68; Allied Artists, New York, 70; solo exhib, Fort Lee Pub Libr, NJ, 84; Am Artists Prof League, New York, 85; Hudson Valley Art Asn, Yonkers, NY, 89; Outdoor Art Show, Bergen Mus Arts & Sci, Paramus, NJ, 90. *Teaching:* Art, Cliffside Park High Sch, 51-76. *Awards:* Silver Medal, NY Int Art Show, 70; First Prize, Hudson Art Exhib, Hudson Art Asn, 78; Honorable Mention, Am Artists League, 82. *Mem:* Am Artists Prof League; Hudson Valley Art Asn. *Media:* Oil. *Mailing Add:* 702 SW 15th St Boynton Beach FL 33426

GERACI, LUCIAN ARTHUR
PAINTER, DEALER
b New Haven, Conn, Mar 13, 23. *Study:* Wesleyan Univ, Middletown, Conn, BA, 48; Skowhegan Sch Painting & Sculpture, Maine, scholar, 48; Beaux Arts Acad, Paris, cert, 49; Acad Julian, Paris, cert, 48-49; Ital Acad, Rome, certs, 50; RI Sch Design, BFA, 53. *Work:* Acad Julian, Paris; Accad Belli Arti, Rome; Armstrong Cork Company, Lancaster, Pa; Abraham Sharpe Found, New York; Conn Gen Life Insurance Co, Hartford. *Exhib:* Allied Artists, New York, 69; Nat Art Club, New York, 70-71; Knickerbocker Artists, New York, 76 & 77; Butler Art Inst, Ohio, 76 & 78; Salmagundi Club, New York, 70-92; Rockport Art Asn, Mass, 74-92; North Shore Arts Asn, 84-92. *Pos:* Owner, Art Gallery 123, Lancaster, Pa, 58-59; designer & stylist, Hygeine Co, New York, Maartex, Cannon Mills, New York, Armstrong Cork, Pa, 55-70; pres & owner, Geraci Galleries Ltd, Rockport, Mass, 78-92. *Awards:* Prix-Ann Concours, Acad Julian, Paris, 48; Ann Knickerbocker Artists, Delta Brush Company, NY, 77; Pres Award, Salmagundi Club, New York, 78. *Bibliog:* Lucian Geraci's Art Ctr, Gloucester D Times, Mass, 5/23/78; Kasha Gula (auth), Lucian Geraci's gallery--A work of art itself, Rockport Horizon, Mass, 6/16/78; Virginia Bohlin (auth), Where the art is, Boston Globe, 7/7/78. *Mem:* Salmagundi Art Club; Rockport Art Asn; North Shore Arts Asn. *Media:* Oil, Watercolor. *Specialty:* Cape Ann deceased master paintings, Realist and modern eastern seaboard contemporary artists; large selection of woodblock prints by Winslow Homer and Gustave Dore. *Mailing Add:* Geraci Galleries & Art Ctr Ltd Six South Street Rockport MA 01966

GERAN, JOSEPH, JR
SCULPTOR, DESIGNER
b 1945. *Study:* San Francisco City Col, AA, 66; Calif State Univ, San Francisco, BA, 70; Calif Col Arts & Crafts, MFA, 73. *Comn:* Prints of movie stars, Oakland Mus, 74; Bronze bust of Dr Martin Luther King Jr, RI State, 87. *Exhib:* Los Angeles Co Mus, Los Angeles, 74; RI Sch Design, 75; Southeastern Mass Univ, 75; Bryant Col, 75; Univ Vt, 75; San Francisco Mus Art, 76; Ctr Art & Culture of Bedford Stuyvesant, 88; plus numerous group & one-man shows. *Pos:* Corp vpres, Col Inc, 70-71; processing chmn, FESTAC 74, 73-74; freelance jewelry designer. *Teaching:* Instr, EOC Summer Youth Prog, 69; lectr, Calif State Univ, San Francisco, 69-71; art consult & sch aide, Galileo High Sch, San Francisco, 70; instr, Booker T Washington Community Ctr, San Francisco, 71; asst prof painting, drawing & sculpture & co-dir ethnic studies div, Calif Col Arts & Crafts, 70-74; adj fac mem, Antioch Col West, 74; dean third world prog, RI Sch Design, 74-; prof art, Community Col RI, 81-; instr, The Jewelry Inst, 85-86. *Awards:* Guy F Atkinson Found Award, 69-71; Ill State Univ Sculpture Award, 73; Distinguished Serv Award, Congressman Ron Dellums, 75. *Mem:* Nat Conf Artists; San Francisco Art Comn Screening Comt. *Media:* Bronze, Wood; Multi. *Publ:* Cover design, Black Art, Black Cult, issue, J Black Poetry, 72; photog of art work, Yardbird Reader, 73; cover design, Blacks on Paper, Brown Univ, fall 75. *Mailing Add:* 19 Academy Ave Providence RI 02908

GERBARG, DARCY
PAINTER
b Baltimore, Md, May 20, 49. *Study:* NY Studio Sch Drawing, Painting & Sculpture, 73-74, Univ Pa, BA, 76. *Work:* Siemens Mus, Ger; Insurance Co N Am; Polaroid Corp; Sierra Fed. *Exhib:* SIGGRAPH Ann Art Show, US & Int tours, 81-87; Electra, Mus Art Mod de la Ville de Paris, France, 83; Bronx Museum Art, 85, Computers & Art, IBM Mus Sci & Art, 87-89, New York; Siemans Mus, Munchen, Ger, 85; CADRE Exhib, San Jose Mus Art, Calif, 86; artware, Kunst und Elektronik, Landesmuseum Volk und Wirtschaft, Dusseldorf, WGer, 87; one-woman show, Fine Arts Mus Long Island, 89; Everson Mus, Syracuse, NY; Smithsonian Inst, Washington, DC, 90. *Teaching:* adj fac, Tisch Sch Arts, NY Univ, 81-84; artist residence Courant Inst Mathematics, Robotics & Manufacturing Res Lab, NY Univ, 88-, founding dir MFA prog computer art, Inst Computers Arts, Sch Visual Arts, NY, 84-88; lectr, Computer Graphics Ctr, Pratt, NY. *Bibliog:* Digital Portfolio Computer Graphics World, 83; Dale Petersen (auth), Genisis II: Creation & recreation with Computers, Reston, 85; Computer Graphics: Village Voice, 88. *Mem:* Spec Interest Groups Graphics Siggraph Nat (art show chmn, 81); Nat Computer Graphics Asn Arts (bd dir), 85-89. *Media:* Acrylic. *Publ:* Ed, Siggraph 82 Art Show (exhib catalog), Acme Printers, 82; auth, Digital Imaging: Paint Systems, Computer Graphics World, 8/83; contrib, Computers as Artist's Tool, Springer-Verlag, 86; auth Anniversary Spec: Reflections on a Goldan Decade: Pennwell Publ Co, 12/87. *Mailing Add:* PO Box 413, Old Chelsea Station New York NY 10113

GERBRACHT, BOB (ROBERT THOMAS)
PAINTER, INSTRUCTOR
b Erie, Pa, June 23, 24. *Study:* With Joseph Plavcan, 38-42; Yale Sch Fine Arts, with Rudolph Zallinger, Deane Keller & Josef Albers, BFA, 51; Univ Southern Calif, with Jules Heller, MFA, 52. *Work:* Triton Mus Art, Santa Clara, Calif; City of Sunnyvale, Calif, 90. *Comn:* Stations of the Cross (oil painting) & Creche (sculpture), Queen Apostles Church, San Jose, Calif, 63; portraits, notably, Mrs Bruce Jenner and children, Malibu, Calif, 80 & 82; Rev Jack La Rocca, Los Altos, Calif, 88; Rev Cecil Williams, Glide Mem Methodist Church, San Francisco, 90; Historical Portraits Competition Comn Award to paint John Hendy, City of Sunnyvale, Calif, 90; and others. *Exhib:* One-man shows, Fisher Art Gallery, Univ Southern Calif, 51, Laudau Gallery, Los Angeles, 52, Images West Gallery & Montalvo, Saritoga, Calif, 72, San Jose Art Ctr, 79 & 83, Montalvo, 82, Discovery Gallery, La Tarentella, Cupertino, Calif, 84 & Commonwealth Club, Calif, 92; 2nd Ann Open Exhib, Salmagundi Club, New York, 79; San Jose Mus Art, 50th Ann Celebration Exhib of San Jose Art League, 88; San Jose Art League World Without War Exhib, 88; Pastel Soc Am Ann Nat Exhib, New York, 79, 88, 90, 91 & 92; Bedford Biennial, Regional Ctr Arts, Walnut Creek, Calif, 91; Grand Exhib, Akron Soc Artists, Cuyahoga, Ohio, 91; 78th Ann, Allied Artists Am, New York, 91; 6th Ann Open Exhib, Pastel Soc West Coast, Sacramento, Calif, 92; and many others. *Pos:* Vpres, Images West Gallery, Saratoga, Calif, 72. *Teaching:* Instr art, Col Notre Dame, Calif, 58-60 & San Jose City Col, 68-71; founder & instr, Nat Ann Portrait & Figure Painting Workshops, Univ Calif, Santa Cruz & Asilomar, Pacific Grove, Calif, 80-; nat sem portrait & figure painting, Calif, Nev, NMex, Tex, Vt, Mex & NY. *Awards:* Best of Show, 2nd Ann Nat Open Exhib, Sacramento, 88 & Degas Pastel Soc Award, 92, Pastel Soc W Coast; Honorable Mention, Grand Exhib Akron Soc Artists, 91; Paul Puzinas Mem Award, 70th Ann Allied Artists Am, 91. *Bibliog:* Nat art Competition winners, Am Artist Mag, 7/85; Cathy Kosier (auth), Best of show, US ART, 12/88; Private showings, US ART, 9/89. *Mem:* San Jose Art League; Soc Western Artists (trustee, 87-88); Pastel Soc West Coast; Pastel Soc Am; Oil Painters Am. *Media:* Pastel, Oil. *Publ:* Auth, Drawing what you see, Am Artist Mag, 82; Let go and look, Profile Mag Am Portrait Soc, spring 84; Tips on painting the head & figure, Am Artist Mag, 9/92. *Mailing Add:* 1301 Blue Oak Court Pinole CA 94564

GERDES, INGEBORG
PHOTOGRAPHER
b Merseburg, Ger, July 20, 38. *Study:* San Francisco Art Inst, MFA, 70. *Work:* Bibliot Nat, Paris, France; Fogg Mus Art, Harvard Univ; Washington Art Consortium, Whatcom Mus; San Francisco Mus Mod Art; Stanford Mus Art, Palo Alto, Calif; and others. *Exhib:* Women of Photography: An Historic Survey, San Francisco Mus Mod Art, 75; one-woman shows, Galerie Spectrum, Hannover, Ger, 76, Blue Sky Gallery, Portland, Ore, 76, Focus Gallery, San Francisco, 78 & Alaska State Mus, Juneau, 79; Henry Art Gallery, Univ Wash, Seattle, 81; and others. *Teaching:* San Francisco Art Inst, 78; Univ Calif, Santa Cruz, 81-86. *Awards:* Nat Endowment Arts Photogr Fel, 75 & 77, Photog Survey Grant, 78; Seattle Arts Comn Grant, 80. *Publ:* Contribr, Camera, Lucerne, Switz, 75; Latent Image, 78; Camera Mainichi, Japan, 80; and others. *Mailing Add:* 3025 21st St No 7 San Francisco CA 94110

GERDTS, ABIGAIL BOOTH
HISTORIAN, CURATOR
b New Milford, Conn, June 20, 37. *Study:* Radcliffe Col, AB(fine arts), 60; Syracuse Univ, Sch Art, 62-63. *Collections Arranged:* Spec exhib, Charles Sheeler (auth, catalog), Nat Collection Fine Arts, Smithsonian Inst, 68; The Working American (auth, catalog), Dist 1199 & Smithsonian Inst Travelling Exhib Serv, 79. *Pos:* Mem secy, Corcoran Gallery Art, Washington, DC, 59-61; res asst painting dept, Mus Fine Arts, Boston, 61-62; asst cur exhib, Nat Collection Fine Arts, 64-70, coordr bicentennial inventory Am paintings, 70-77, coordr 19th century exhibs index, 77-78; spec asst to dir, Nat Acad Design, New York, 80-87, cur paintings & sculpture, 88-89; dir, Winslow Homer Catalogue Raisonne, City Univ New York Grad Center, 90- *Mem:* Am Asn Mus. *Publ:* Auth, The Working American, Sites, 79; Winslow Homer in Monochrome, Knoedler Galleries, 86; An American Collection: Paintings and Sculpture, Nat Acad Design, 89. *Mailing Add:* 1120 Park Ave New York NY 10128

GERDTS, WILLIAM H
HISTORIAN, EDUCATOR
b Jersey City, NJ, Jan 18, 29. *Study:* Amherst Col, BA, 49, LHD, 92; Harvard Univ, MA, 50, PhD, 66. *Collections Arranged:* Thomas Birch (auth, catalog), 66; and many others. *Pos:* Dir, Myers House, Norfolk, Va, 53-54; cur painting & sculpture, Newark Mus, NJ, 54-66; dir gallery, Univ Md, 66-69; assoc with Coe Kerr Gallery, New York, 69-71. *Teaching:* Assoc prof, Univ Md, 66-69; assoc prof art, Brooklyn Col, 71-74, prof, 74-85; prof, Grad Ctr, City Univ New York, 85-; lectr Am art in mus, cols, univs & adult schs. *Publ:* Auth, Painting and Sculpture in New Jersey, Rutgers Univ, 65; American Still-Life Painting, Praeger, 71; American Neo-Classical Sculpture: The Marble Resurrection, Viking, 73; The Art of Henry Inman, Nat Portrait Gallery, Smithsonian Inst, Washington, DC, 87; American Impressionism, 84 & Art Across America: Regional Painting in America Through 1920, 3 vols, 90, Abbeville Press. *Mailing Add:* Dept Art Hist City Univ New York 33 West 42nd St New York NY 10036

GERENDAY, LACI ANTHONY DE
SCULPTOR
b Budapest, Hungary, Aug 17, 11. *Study:* SDak Sch Mines; Ursinus Col; Univ Shrivenham, Eng; Nat Acad Design; Beaux Arts Inst, New York. *Work:* Salle d'Honneur, Mus Africa, Algiers; Adm Farragut Medal, NY Univ Hall of Fame Mus. *Comn:* Wood reliefs, Fed Govt, Tell City, Ind, 39 & Aberdeen, SDak, 41; bronze relief, St Francis of Assisi Sch, Torrington, Conn, 65; medal, Soc Medalists, 81; self-portrait, Nat Acad Design, 82; medal, Brookgreen Gardens, SC, 86. *Exhib:* Pa Mus, Philadelphia; Gold Medal Exhib, Archit League, New York; Boston Mus; Mus Mod Art Nat Sculpture Soc Ann; Allied Artists Ann; two-man show, Art Ctr, Old Lyme, Conn; and others. *Teaching:* Instr sculpture, Lyme Acad Fine Arts, 80- *Awards:* Ellen Speyer Award, Nat Acad Desigh, 47, 63 & 91; Lindsey Morris Mem Award, Nat Sculpture Soc 55, 81 & 88; Bennet Prize, 63, Roman Bronze Foundry Award, 80, Bedi-Makky Foundry Prize, 83, Nat Sculpture Soc; Silver Medal Honor, 77, Wendel Clinedinst Award, 82, Allied artists Am. *Mem:* Nat Arts Club; Nat Acad Design; Am Medallic Sculpture Asn; fel Nat Sculpture Soc; Allied Artists Am. *Media:* Wood, Clay. *Mailing Add:* 2 Mill Pond Lane Old Lyme CT 06371

GERHOLD, WILLIAM HENRY
PAINTER, EDUCATOR
b Ashtabula, Ohio, Mar 30, 29. *Study:* Oberlin Col, with Jeanne Miles, BA; Ohio State Univ, MA. *Work:* Army-Navy Club, Charleston, WVa; Marietta Col, Ohio; Marshall Univ, WVa; WVa Univ, Morgantown. *Exhib:* Butler Midyear, Youngstown, Ohio; Appalachian Corridors II, Charleston; Perspectives, Cincinnati, Ohio, 70; Forest Festival, Elkins, WVa; Ohio State Fairs. *Teaching:* Assoc prof educ, Antioch Col, 57-58; assoc prof art, Marietta Col, 62- *Awards:* First Prize Watercolor, Appalachian Arts & Crafts Fair, 70; Best Prof & Best WVa Landscape, Forest Festival, 71-75. *Mem:* Cent Ohio Watercolor Soc; Am Artists Prof League; WVa Artists & Craftsmen Guild; Allied Artists; Am Watercolor Soc. *Publ:* Auth & illusr, Trinity Rev, 58; WVa Mag, 73 & 74. *Dealer:* Bonfoeys 1710 Euclid Ave Cleveland OH 44115. *Mailing Add:* Dept Art Marietta Col Marietta OH 45750

GERIN-LAJOIE, GUY
ARCHITECT
b Montreal, PQ, May 6, 28. *Study:* McGill Univ, Montreal, BArch. *Exhib:* Physical Educ & Univ Ctr, Univ Ottawa, Ont; Sci Res Lab, Igloolik, NW Territories; New Montreal Int Air Terminal Bldg; Girls' Residence, Univ Montreal, Que; Off Bldg, Phase IV, Govt Can, Quebec; and many others. *Awards:* Award Nat Housing Design Coun, 62; Massey Medals, Quebec Pavilion, Expo 67, Montreal, 70; Ann Award, Can Archit Yearbk, Povungnituk Sch & Housing Proj, 73. *Mem:* Ont Asn Archit; Royal Acad Arts; Nat Design Coun; fel Royal Archit Inst Can; Royal Can Acad Arts. *Mailing Add:* 133 dela Commune W Rm 300 Montreal PQ H2Y 2C7 Canada

GERLACH, CHRISTOPHER S
PAINTER
b Wareham, Mass, Dec 8, 52. *Study:* Lake Forest Col, Ill Univ Calif, BA, 74; Calif State Univ, San Diego, MA, 77; Oxford Univ, 79; Royal Acad London, 79. *Work:* Oxford Univ, England; Buckingham Palace, London; Calif State Univ, San Diego. *Exhib:* Exhibition XI, Fine Arts Mus, San Antonio, Tex, 83; Contemp Art, La Jolla Mus, Calif, 85; Art & the Law, traveling, 87-88; Utopian Visions, Mus Mod Art, New York, 88; American Beach Paintings, Tampa Mus, Fla, 89. *Teaching:* Instr, Calif State Univ, San Diego, 75-77. *Awards:* Bank Am Award, Eggerton Coghill Landscape, Oxford Univ, 69. *Bibliog:* Abigail Wender (auth), Venice--Painting by CG, Diversion, 9/87; Jan Jennings (auth), A World in Oils--Ranch & Coast, 4/90. *Media:* Oil. *Dealer:* William Sawyer Gallery 3045 Clay St San Francisco Calif 94115. *Mailing Add:* c/o Fischbach Gallery 24 W 57th St New York NY 10019

GERMANO, THOMAS
PAINTER, PRINTMAKER
b New York, NY, Nov 11, 63. *Study:* Cornell Univ, Scholar, BFA, 85; Yale Univ, Scholar, MFA, 89. *Work:* Arthur Anderson & Co, Int Hqtrs, St Paul, Ill & Melville, NY; Acad Arts, Moscow, Russia; Yale Univ Art Mus, New Haven, Conn; Cape Cod Retreat House, Mass. *Exhib:* Solo exhib, Hofstra Mus, Hempstead, NY, 87; First Time in New York, New Renaissance Gallery, New York, 90; Works on Paper, Maya's Room Art Gallery, 89 & Five Painters, Yale Sch Art & Archit, 89, New Haven, Conn; First Street Gallery, New York, 90; Am Labor Mus, Haledon, NJ, 92; Michael Ingbar Gallery, New York, NY, 92. *Teaching:* Adj instr art & art hist, C W Post Col, Westbury, NY,Suffolk Community Col, Garden City, NY & Suffolk Community Col, Selden, NY, currently. *Awards:* Traveling Grant to Russia, Int Res & Exchanges Bd, 89. *Media:* Oil. *Mailing Add:* 100 Clark St Apt 11 Brooklyn NY 11201

GERNHARDT, HENRY KENDALL
SCULPTOR, CERAMIST
b Salem, Conn, Aug 3, 32. *Study:* Norwich Art Sch, Conn; Sch Am Craftsmen, Rochester Inst Technol, NY, with Frans Wildenhain; Sch Art, Syracuse Univ, NY, BA & MFA; Sch Appl Arts, Helsinki, Finland, study with Kyllikki Salmenhaara, Fulbright Scholar. *Work:* Everson Mus Art, Syracuse, NY; Syracuse Univ; DePauw Univ, Greencastle, Ind; Chrysler Mus, Provincetown, Mass; Univ SDak, Vermillion. *Comn:* Pottery, Imperial House, New York, 60; tile mosaic, Syracuse Univ, 63; vase, State Univ NY, Cortland, 67; baptismal font, Lynnwood Reformed Church, Guilderland, NY, 69; sculpture, comn by Alexander E Holstein, Syracuse, 72. *Exhib:* Ceramic Nat, Everson Mus Art, 54-72; Int Trade Fair, Posen, Poland, 58; Contemp Crafts Exhib, Skidmore Col, Saratoga Springs, NY, 62, 71 & 75; Int Ceramic Exhib, Silvermine Guild Artists, New Canaan, Conn, 64; 22nd Ceramic Ann, Scripps Col, Claremont, Calif, 66. *Teaching:* Prof ceramics, Sch Visual & Performing Arts, Syracuse Univ, 60- & Sch Am Craftsmen, summer 71. *Awards:* Merle Alling Sculpture Award, Rochester Finger Lakes Exhib, Mem Art Gallery, 63 & 71; O Hommel Prize for Pottery, Ceramic Nat, Everson Mus, 68; 1st, 2nd & 3rd Awards, NY State Expos, Syracuse, 71. *Bibliog:* Lewenstein & Cooper (auth), New Ceramics, Van Nostrand Reinhold, 74; Rick Hirsch (auth), Raku, Watson Guptill, 75; article, Craft Horizons, 75. *Mem:* Nat Coun Advan Ceramic Arts; Am Crafts Coun; New York Craftsmen. *Media:* Clay, Glaze. *Mailing Add:* Dept Art Syracuse Univ Syracuse NY 13210

GERSH, BILL
PAINTER, SCULPTOR
b Charleston, SC, July 15, 43. *Study:* State Univ New York, New Paltz, BS, 64; with Ilya Bolotowsky & Manuel Bromberg. *Work:* State Univ NY, New Paltz; Denver Art Mus, Colo. *Comn:* Steel Fountain, Delmar Corp, Lafayette, La, 89. *Exhib:* New Gallery, Houston, Tex, 86, 87 & 88; Tally Richard Gallery Contemp Art, 87 & 88; New Directions Gallery, Taos, 90 & 91; Lumina Gallery, Taos, 92 & 93; Copeland/Rutherford, Santa Fe, 92; and others. *Teaching:* Vis artist, Univ Maine, 89 & Univ Utah, 91. *Awards:* Sante Fe Coun Arts Grant, 83. *Bibliog:* Steve Parks (auth), Interview, Art Lines, 80; William Peterson (auth), Smoke rings, Shinto shrines, Artnews, 80; articles in Taos Review, 89 & 90. *Mem:* Taos Artist Assn; Magic Tortoise Found. *Media:* Acrylic, Metal Welded. *Mailing Add:* PO Box 44 San Christobal NM 87564

GERSOVITZ, SARAH VALERIE
PAINTER, PRINTMAKER
b Montreal, Que. *Study:* McDonald Col; Montreal Mus Fine Arts; Concordia Univ, MA. *Work:* Am Embassy, Ottawa; Libr Cong, Washington, DC; New York Pub Libr; Nat Gallery SAustralia; Israel Mus; Universitat Kaiserslattern, WGer; and many Can Mus, Univ & Embassies. *Exhib:* One-man shows, Montreal Mus Fine Arts, 62 & 65, Confederation Art Gallery, 76 & London Art Gallery, 82; Biennales Graphic Art, Ljubljana, Yugoslavia, 79 & 75; Drawing Exhib, Miro Mus, Barcelona, Spain, 79, 82 & 86; Bienal de Arte Valparaiso, Chile, 83, 85, 87, 89 & 91; Int Print Biennale, Taipei, Taiwan, 84 & 86; and many others in USA, France, Spain, Venezuela, Peru, Switz, Italy, Norway, Bulgaria, Korea, Ger, Brazil, Eng, Colombia, Czech, Hungary & Hong Kong. *Pos:* Critic, Artsatlantic. *Teaching:* Instr painting & drawing, Saidye Bronfman Ctr, Montreal, 72-85; Visual Arts Ctr; and others. *Awards:* Purchase Awards, Mus du Que, 66, Nat Gallery S Australia, 67, Dawson Col, 74, Thomas More Inst, 77 & l'Universite de Sherbrooke; First Prize, Concours Graphique, Univ Sherbrooke, 79 & Graphics, 89 biennale, Gabrovo, Bulgaria; Travel Award, House of Humor & Satire, Gabrovo, Bulgaria, 85 & 91. *Bibliog:* Guy Robert (auth), L'Art au Quebec depuis 1940; G Daigneault (auth), La Gravure au Quebec, Printworld; and others. *Mem:* Royal Can Acad Arts (coun mem). *Media:* Acrylic, Oil; Silkscreen. *Publ:* Illusr, cover, Figures in a Landscape, Oberon, 67; illusr cover, Feminin Pluriel, Masculin Singulier, 80; and others. *Dealer:* Dominion Gallery 1438 Sherbrooke St W Montreal Que H3G 1K4. *Mailing Add:* 4360 Montrose Ave Montreal PQ H3Y 2B1 Canada

GERST, HILDE W
DEALER
US citizen. *Study:* Ploner Acad, Italy. *Pos:* Owner, Hilde Gerst Gallery, New York. *Mem:* Am Asn Mus; Nat Soc Lit & Arts; Nat Mus Women Arts. *Specialty:* French painting from Impressionist to contemporary; sculpture. *Mailing Add:* c/o Hilde Gerst Gallery 685 Madison Ave New York NY 10021

GERSTEIN, DAVID STEVEN
FILMMAKER
b Cleveland, Ohio, Sept 23, 51. *Study:* Antioch Col, BA, 74; Art Inst Chicago; San Francisco Art Inst. *Exhib:* One-man shows, NAME to Name Gallery, Chicago, 76 & Canyon Cinematheque, San Francisco, 78, 80 & 82; High Mus Art, Atlanta, Ga, 79; Anthology Film Archive, New York, 81; Newberger Mus, Purchase, NY, 81; Arsenal Cinema, Berlin; Austrian Film Mus, Vicuna; and others. *Pos:* Bd dirs, Canyon Cinema Coop, San Francisco, 77-82, Found Art Cinema, 83- *Awards:* 3rd Place, San Francisco Art Inst Film Festival, 77; Ann Arbor Film Festival, 78; Hon Mention, Athens Int Film Festival, 78. *Bibliog:* Linda Dackman (auth), Kino-Frisco, Cinema News, Found Art Cinema, 77. *Publ:* Auth, Films of Joel Singer, 77, auth, A modest confutation, 78 & ed, Cinemanews. *Dealer:* Canyon Cinema Coop 2325 3rd St 338 San Francisco CA 94133. *Mailing Add:* San Francisco Cinema Tech 480 Potrero Ave San Francisco CA 94110

GERZSO, GUNTHER
PAINTER, GRAPHIC ARTIST
b Mexico City, Mex, June 17, 15. *Study:* German Sch, Mexico City, 34; self-taught. *Work:* Alvar Carrillo Gil Collection, Mus Mod Art, Mexico City. *Exhib:* FIAC Art Contemporain, Grand Palais, Paris, 78; Tamayo, Merida y Gerzso, First Ann Exhib, Inst Fine Arts, Mexico, 80; El Arbol Florido, traveling, 81-82; FIAC 82 Retrospective, Paris, 82; Mus du Petit Palais, 82; solo exhib, Mary-Ann Martin Fine Art, NY, 84 & Galeria de Arte Mex, DF, 90; Imagen de Mex, Frankfort, Vienna, & Dallas, 87-88. *Awards:* Nat Prize Fine Arts, Mexico, 78; Guggenheim Fel, 73. *Bibliog:* L Cardoza y Aragon (auth), Gunther Gerzso, Nat Univ Mex, 72; Octavio Paz (auth), Gerzso: Centella Glacial, Visual Arts, Mus Mod Art, Mexico City, spring 74; Gerzso, Merida, Tamayo, Instituto Nacional de Bellas Artes, Mexico, 79; John Golding & Octavio Paz (auths), Gerzso, Editions Griffon Neuchatel, 83. *Media:* Oil, Acrylic; Metal, Cast. *Mailing Add:* c/o George Belcher Gallery 340 Townsend Suite 407 San Francisco CA 94107

GESKE, NORMAN ALBERT
MUSEUM DIRECTOR, EDUCATOR
b Sioux City, Iowa, Oct 31, 15. *Study:* Univ Minn, BA; NY Univ Inst Fine Arts, MA; Doane Col, hon DFA, 69. *Collections Arranged:* Ernst Barlach (first Am mus exhib), 55; American Participation, 34th Venice Biennale, 68; American Sculpture, 70; Ralph Albert Blakelock (auth, catalog), 75. *Pos:* Asst dir, Univ Nebr Art Galleries, 50-53, actg dir, 53-56, dir, 56-83, dir emer, 83. *Teaching:* Prof, Univ Nebr-Lincoln. *Awards:* Gov Art Award, 78; Distinguished Service Award, Kearney State Col, 80; Mayor's Art Award, Lincoln, 87. *Mem:* Hon mem Asn Art Mus Dirs. *Res:* Nebraska Blakelock inventory. *Publ:* Auth, The Figurative Tradition in Recent American Art, 68; auth, Rudy Pozzatti, American Printmaker, 71; Ralph Albert Blakelock 1847-1919, 75; Light & Color, Images from New Mexico, 81; The American Painting Collection of the Sheldon Memorial Art Gallery, Univ Nebr Press, 88. *Mailing Add:* 128 N 13th St No 408 Lincoln NE 68508

GETLER, HELEN
ART DEALER, CONSULTANT
b New York, NY, May 30, 25. *Study:* Bryn Mawr Col, BA, 45. *Pos:* Co-dir, Getler/Pall Gallery, New York, currently. *Specialty:* Contemporary artists; works on paper, prints, paintings and drawings. *Mailing Add:* c/o Helen Getler Gallery 303 E 37th New York NY 10016

GETTY, NILDA FERNANDEZ
EDUCATOR, SILVERSMITH
b Buenos Aires, Arg, June 2, 36; US citizen. *Study:* Archit at Buenos Aires Univ, Univ NC, Raleigh & Univ Pa; Stetson Univ, Deland, Fla, BFA(art); Univ South Fla, Tampa; Univ Ga, MFA(metalsmithing & printmaking). *Work:* Deland Mus, Fla; Univ South Fla; Denver Art Mus; Minn Mus of Art, St Paul; Colo State Univ. *Comn:* St Luke's Chalice, St Luke's Episcopal Church; eleven copper emblems, Larimer Co High Sch. *Exhib:* Goldsmiths Invitational (travelling exhib), Minn Mus Art, St Paul, 74; Metals Invitational, Fullerton Gallery, Calif, 75; two-person show, Gryphon Gallery, Denver, 75 & 77; Sheldon Mem Art Gallery, Lincoln, Nebr, 76; NAm Goldsmith Invitational, Phoenix Mus, Ariz, 76-77; Metals Invitational, Henry Gallery, Seattle, Wash, 77; solo exhib, Minn Mus Art, St Paul, 74; and others. *Teaching:* From instr to prof metalsmithing, Colo State Univ, Ft Collins, 70- *Bibliog:* Donald Willcox (auth), Body Jewelry: International Perspectives, Regnery, 73; Philip Morton (auth), Contemporary Jewelry, Holt, Rinehart & Winston, 2nd ed 76. *Mem:* Soc NAm Goldsmiths; Am Crafts Coun; World Crafts Coun. *Media:* Silver, Gold. *Publ:* Auth, Contemporary Crafts of the Americas, Regnery, 75; auth, articles, Contemporary Crafts, 75 & Ceramics Mo, 75; auth, Crafts in the Americas, Crafts Horizons, 74. *Mailing Add:* Dept Art Colo State Univ Ft Collins CO 80523

GHENT, HENRI
CRITIC, WRITER
b Birmingham, Ala, June 23, 26. *Study:* US Armed Forces Inst, Honolulu, Hawaii, 45-46; New Eng Conservatory, Boston, 47-51; Marian Anderson scholar, 51 & 52; Georges Longy Sch, Cambridge, 51-53; Martha Baird Rockefeller grant, 57; Univ Paris, 58-60; also pvt study in Ger & Eng; Vogelstein Found Fel, 78; Yaddo Found Fel, 79. *Collections Arranged:* The Invisible Americans: Black Artists of the 1930's, 69; 10 Afro-American Artists, Mt Holyoke Col, 69; 15 International Artists, Community Gallery, Brooklyn Mus, 69, Allusions, 2nd Anniversary Exhib, 70 & Native North American Art: Mixed Media Works by Contemporary American Indian Artists, 72; Afro-American Artists: Since 1950, Brooklyn Col, 69; 8 Afro-American Artists (catalog), Rath Mus, Geneva, Switz, 71; 1972 All-Ohio Painting & Sculpture Biennial, Art Inst, Dayton, 72. *Pos:* Consult, Nat Endowment Arts, Minn Mus Art, St Paul, Dayton Art Inst, Mt Holyoke Col, Rath Mus, Geneva & Mus d'Art Haitien, Port-au-Prince, Haiti; with Allen Univ; dir, Community Gallery, Brooklyn Mus, 68-72; corresp, Le Monde de la Musique, Paris, France, 83- *Teaching:* Vis lectr, Col Finger Lakes Series, 70-71 & Dayton Art Inst, Ohio; Queens Col, NY, 74; lectr, Teachers Col, Columbia Univ, 75-80. *Awards:* Ford Found Res-Travel Grant, 74-75; Crane Found Res-Travel Grant, 81-82; Cottonwood Found Grant, 83. *Bibliog:* Articles in Boston Sunday Globe, 12/7/75, Village Voice, 7/19/76, Los Angeles Times, 10/10/76, Artforum, New York Times, Cleveland Plain Dealer,; plus others. *Mem:* Smithsonian Assocs; Int Soc Educ Through Art; African-American Inst; Nat Art Educ Asn; Nat Soc Lit & Arts. *Interests:* Eclectic art with emphasis on contemporary painting, sculpture and graphics. *Collection:* Contemporary painting, sculpture & graphics. *Publ:* Auth, White is not superior, NY Times, 12/8/68; Black creativity in quest of an audience, Art in Am, 5-6/70; The second generation, Art Gallery Mag, 6/74; Spanish art in transition, Art Int, 10/15/75; contribr, Le Monde de la Musique, Danser Mag, Paris; and others. *Mailing Add:* 310 E 75th St Apt 1-F New York NY 10021

GHIKAS, PANOS GEORGE
PAINTER, EDUCATOR
b Malden, Mass. *Study:* Yale Univ Sch Fine Arts, BFA, 43, MFA, 47; Akad der Bildenden Kunste, Stuttgart, Ger, with Willi Baumeister, 53-54. *Work:* Wadsworth Atheneum, Hartford, Conn; Walker Art Mus, Bowdoin Col; New Britain Mus Am Art, Conn; Colby Col; Art Mus, Waterville, Maine; and others. *Exhib:* Abstract & Surrealist Show, Chicago Art Inst, 47; 2nd Int Salon des Realites Nouvelles, Paris, France, 48; Annual of American Painting, Whitney Mus Am Art, 49; American Painting Annual, Univ Ill, 50; Worcester Mus Biennial Contemp Am Painting, 52. *Pos:* Asst conservator, Yale Univ Art Gallery, 57-59. *Teaching:* Vis artist design, Carpenter Ctr, Harvard Univ, 64-66; vis prof drawing, Bowdoin Col, 70-71; prof painting, RI Sch Design, Providence, 71-82 & Mass Col Art, 72- *Awards:* Fulbright Fel, 53; MacDowell Colony Fel, 67; Blanche E Colman Found Grant, 69. *Bibliog:* Chaet (auth), Artists at Work, Webb, 61. *Media:* Egg Tempera. *Publ:* Illusr, Tales of Christophilos, 54; illusr, Again Christophilos, 56; illusr, The Golden Bird, 57; illusr, The Golden Sword, 60. *Mailing Add:* Mass Col Art Boston MA 02115

GHIKAS, PATIENCE HALEY See Haley, Patience E (Patience E Haley Ghikas)

GIACALONE, VITO
PAINTER, HISTORIAN
b Newark, NJ. *Study:* Montclair State Col, BA, 60; Univ Iowa, MA, 65, MFA, 66. *Work:* Mus Univ Iowa; Guggenheim Mus; Metrop Mus Art; Smithsonian Nat Mus Am Art; Brit Mus; Prudential Insurance Co; Mus Mod Art Study Collection; New York Public Libr; Brooklyn Mus Print Collection; Princeton Univ Libr Graphic Arts Collection. *Exhib:* Provincetown Art Asn & Mus, Mass, 69 & 80; Newark Mus, NJ, 69; NY State Mus, 69; Westbeth Gallery, NY, 70, solo exhib, 71-72 & 79-83; Orgn Independent Artists Exhib, PS 1 Galleries & traveling, 78-79; Guild Hall Mus, East Hampton, NY, 82-88 & 90; Howe Gallery, Kean Col, NJ, 85, 86, 87 & 90; Fine Arts Mus Long Island, NY, 86; NJ State Mus, Trenton, 87; Albright Knox, Buffalo, NY, 87; Philadelphia Mus Art, 88; solo exhibs, Anita Shapolsky Gallery, New York, 84, Benton Gallery, Southampton, NY, 90. *Collections Arranged:* Chu Ta, Selected Paintings and Calligraphy (auth, catalog), Vassar Col Art Gallery, 72-73 & New York Cult Ctr, 73; Style & Theme in Japanese Art: from the 13th to the 20th Centuries (auth, catalog), 88, Power of the Brush: Calligraphic Painting by Wang Fang-yu (auth, catalog), 89, James Howe Gallery, Kean Col, NJ; The Eccentric Painters of China (auth, catalog), China House Gallery, China Inst Am, New York, 90. *Teaching:* Prof painting, Kean Col NJ, 66-; artist in residence, Univ Ill, Urbana, 75-; lectr Chinese painting, China Inst Am, New York, 78-80 & 90, Inst Asian Studies, New York, 82-89; vis artist, Columbia Col, Mo, 84; instr, Detroit Art Inst, 85. *Awards:* Painting Fels, MacDowell COlony, NH, 84 & 85 & Va Ctr Creative Arts, 86 & 87. *Bibliog:* John Canaday (auth), article, New York Times, 71; Suzanne Frank (auth), article, Arts Mag, 72; Karen Lipson (auth), article, Newsday, 86. *Mem:* China Inst Am; Am Abstract Artists. *Media:* All Media. *Res:* Chinese eccentric painting of the 17th and 18th centuries. *Publ:* Auth, Chu Ta (1626-1705): Toward an understanding of his art, 75, Wen Cheng Ming exhibition, 76, Eight dynasties of Chinese painting, 81 & The John M Crawford Jr Collection of calligraphy and painting in the Metropolitan Museum of Art, Part 1, 85, Part 2, 86, Oriental Art Mag; Style and Theme in Japanese Art: from the 13th to the 20th centuries, 88; Power of the Brush: calligraphic paintings by Wang Fang-Yu, 89; The Eccentric Painters of China, 90. *Dealer:* Anita Shapolsky Gallery 99 Spring St New York NY 10013; Benton Gallery Southhampton NY 11937. *Mailing Add:* 463 West St B938 New York NY 10014

GIALANELLA, DONALD G
VIDEO ARTIST, SCULPTOR
b Plainfield, NJ, June 9, 56. *Study:* Montclair State Col, 74-77, The Cooper Union, BFA, 79, with Jim Dine, Milton Glazer & Louise Bourgeois. *Comn:* The Fire Unleashed, graphics, ABC Documentary Unit, 85; 25th anniversary, opening animation, Wide World of Sports, 86; Superbowl XIX, opening animation, ABC Sports, 87; Good Morning America, opening animation, 87 & 90; Loving, Opening Animation, 90; and others. *Pos:* Art dir, ABC News, New York, 84-86, ABC Sports/Entertainment, 86- *Teaching:* Lectr, Montclair State Col, State Univ New York, Long Island. *Awards:* Advert Design Award, Calif Publ Asn, 82; Award of Excellence, Broadcast Designers

Asn, 84; Nat Emmy Award, Monday Night Football, New York, 90; and others. *Bibliog:* Computer manipulation of news, Computer Pictures, 1/85; Computer graphics on television, Computer Graphics World, 4/85; The changing face of news graphics, Technol Rev, 3/87. *Mem:* Broadcast Designers Asn. *Media:* Three dimensional computer generated imagery. *Publ:* Auth, Electronic wizardry, computer graphics at ABC, Capitol Cities/ABC, 86. *Mailing Add:* 9 Essex Ave Maplewood NJ 07040

GIAMBERTONE, PAUL
SCULPTOR
b Italy; US citizen. *Study:* Beaux Arts Inst Design, New York, with Gaetano Cecere; Educ Alliance, New York, with Chaim Gross. *Work:* Safad Mus, Israel; Philothea Mus, London, Ont. *Exhib:* NJ Soc Painters & Sculptors, Jersey City Mus, 59 & 60; Am Soc Contemp Artists, Nat Arts Club, New York, 76-79; Salmagundi Club, 81; Gallery 54, New York, 87; Westbeth Gallery, New York, 88; Broome St Gallery, 91. *Awards:* Ivan R Laskins Award for Sculpture, 70; First Prize Sculpture, Am Soc Contemp Artists, 82. *Bibliog:* Dorothy Hale (auth), article, Parkeast, 11/77; Palmer Poroner (auth), article, Artspeak, 3/80, 4/85 & 4/88. *Mem:* Artists Equity Asn New York; League Present Day Artists (dir, 60-); Am Soc Contemp Artists (dir, 73-); Sculptors League, Contemp Artists Guild. *Media:* Welded and Cast Bronze. *Dealer:* Art for Indust 663 Fifth Ave New York NY 10022; Brownstone Gallery 76 Seventh Ave Brooklyn NY 11217. *Mailing Add:* 400 E 20th St New York NY 10009

GIAMPIETRO, ISABEL (ISABEL A GIAMPIETRO KNOLL)
SCULPTOR, DESIGNER
b Marsicovetere, Potenza, Italy; US citizen. *Study:* Scuola Dell'Arte Della Medaglia, with G Romagnoli, dipl, 50; Fine Arts Acad, Rome, Italy, with Calori, Rivosecchi & Fazzini, dipl, 51; Konstfachskolan, Stockholm, Sweden, glass with S E Skawonius, cert, 56; Manhattanville Col of the Sacred Heart, BA (humanities). *Work:* Smithsonian Inst; Corning Glass Mus; Metrop Mus Art; Mitchell Wolfson Jr collection of decorative arts, Fla; and other mus in Europe and pvt collections. *Comn:* Seal of State of Va (bas-relief), Jr CofC, Oklahoma City, 52; portrait of George Washington (bronze relief), George Washington Masonic Nat Mem, Alexandria, Va, 82. *Exhib:* Triennale, Stedelijk Mus, Amsterdam, Holland, 57; two-person exhib, Leerdam New Glass, Utrecht Mus, Holland, 57; Expos Int, Brussels, Belgium, 58; Glass 1959, Metrop Mus Art, New York; Corcoran Gallery, Washington, DC; and others. *Awards:* Nominee of the Gold Medal, Triennale XI, 57; Grand Prix, Expo, Brussels, Belgium, 58; Environmental Design Grant, Nat Endowment Arts, 78. *Bibliog:* Renzo Marchelli (auth), Portrait of an artist, Negozi e Vetrine, 57; The Metropolitan Museum of Art: Glass 1959, Corning Mus, 59; Geoffrey Beard (auth), International Modern Glass, Charles Scribner's & Sons, 76. *Mem:* Am Medallic Sculpture Asn; Federation Internationalle des Editeurs de Medailles. *Media:* Bronze, Glass. *Mailing Add:* 300 E 40th St Apt 31H New York NY 10016

GIANAKOS, CRISTOS
SCULPTOR, ENVIRONMENTAL ARTIST
b New York NY, Jan 4, 34. *Study:* Sch Visual Arts, cert. *Work:* Mus Mod Art, New York; Moderna Museet & Nat Mus, Stockholm; Nassau Co Mus Fine Arts; Smithsonian Inst; and others. *Comn:* Gemini (steel sculpture), City Malmö, Sweden. *Exhib:* Mus Mod Art, New York, 71; PS 1, Queens, NY, 78; Los Angeles Inst Contemp Art, 80; Brooklyn Mus, NY, 89; one-man exhibs, Nassau Co Mus Fine Arts (with catalog), New York, Hal Bromm Gallery, New York, 79 & 81, Galerie Nordenhake, Stockholm, Sweden, 85 & Siegeltuch Gallery, New York, 86 & 88, Univ Gallery, Univ Mass, Amherst, 89 & Stark Gallery, NY, 90 & 92; and others. *Teaching:* Instr Sch Visual Arts, 65- *Awards:* Nat Endowment Arts Award, 80; Adolph & Ester Gottlieb Grant, 89; Pollack-Krasner Found Grant. *Bibliog:* Images of an Era: The American Poster 1945-1975, Smithsonian Inst, 75; Peter Frank (auth), Where is New York, Art News, 80; Sarah McFadden (auth), Going places, part II: The outside story, Art Am, 80; Gianakos-4 Scandanavian Exhibitions (catalog), 85-86; Stephen Westfall (auth), Rev, Art Am, 87 & 89. *Media:* Mixed. *Dealer:* Stark Gallery 594 Broadway New York NY 10012; Betsy Senior Contemporary Prints 375 W Broadway New York NY 10012. *Mailing Add:* 93 Mercer St New York NY 10012

GIANAKOS, STEVE
SCULPTOR, PAINTER
b New York, NY, 38. *Study:* Pratt Inst, Brooklyn, NY, 64. *Work:* Guggenheim Mus, New York; Chase Manhattan Bank; Contemp Arts Mus, Houston, Tex; Univ Mus, Berkeley; Edward R Downe Collection. *Exhib:* One-man exhibs, Fischbach Gallery, New York, 68, Alesandra Gallery, New York, 76, Droll-Kolbert Gallery, New York, 77 & 79, Texas Gallery, Houston, 80 & 82, Barbara Gladstone Gallery, New York, 83 & Barbara Toll Fine Arts, 84, 85, 90 & 91; Theodoron Awards Exhib, Guggenheim Mus, New York, 77; Contemp Greek-Am Artists, Brooklyn Mus, NY, 77; Contemp Arts Mus, Houston, Tex, 79; Art in Pursuit of a Smile, Muhlenberg Col, Allentown, Pa, 81; Sports, Gen Electric Co, Mus Mod Art, 82; Greenville Co Mus Art, SC, 85; Whitney Mus Am Art, New York, 86; New York State Mus, 87; Milwaukee Arts Mus, Wis, 90; Annina Nosei Gallery, New York, 91; Home for Contemp Theatre & Art, New York, 91; Charles Cowles Gallery, New York, 91. *Teaching:* Vis Artist Prog, Univ Colo Boulder, Dept Fine Arts, 77, NTex State Univ, Denton, 83 & Memphis Acad Arts, 83. *Awards:* Theodoron Award, Guggenheim Mus, 77; Grant, Nat Endowment Arts, 77. *Bibliog:* Marty Berry (auth), Innocence and Experience: Poetry Becomes Art, Greenville News, 10/17/85; Eleanor Neartney (auth), Steve Gianakos at Barbara Toll, Vol 76, No 5, Art in Am, 5/89; Tom Sokolowski (auth), The art of the melting pot, Greece's Weekly, p 8-11, 6/15/92. *Mailing Add:* c/o Barbara Toll Fine Arts 146 Green St New York NY 10012

GIANLORENZI, NONA ELENA
PAINTER, ART DEALER
b Virginia, Minn, July 20, 39. *Study:* Queens Col, 61-65, studied color with John Ferron & Herb Aach; New Sch Social Res, 62-67, studied sculpture with T Doyle & C Guinnivar, painting with A Savelli; Brooklyn Col, 67-68, studied painting with H Holtzman & Carl Holty; studied sculpture with Lee Bonticou, 89; studied color & portraiture with Lois Dodd, 91; studied mod & contemp art hist with Mona Hadler, 92. *Work:* Brooklyn Col. *Exhib:* 9th Street Survival Show; Black Velvet Erotic Arts Show, 81; Projective-Kinetic Traveling Exhib, 86; Asage Gallery, New York; Outdoor Sculpture Exhib, 92. *Pos:* Asst dir, Am Art Gallery, New York, 61-67; dir, ASAGE Art Gallery, New York, 77-88; dir, Art Space Inc New York, 89-92. *Teaching:* Art teacher, Charles Borromeo, Brooklyn & Mt Carmel & St Francis Sch Deaf, Queens, 68-71. *Awards:* Work Study Grant, St Scholastica, Duluth, Minn; Art Studio Scholar, New Sch Soc Res; Ford Found Fel, Brooklyn Col. *Bibliog:* Grace Glueck (auth), No More Raw Eggs at the Whitney, New York Times, 2/13/72. *Media:* Acrylic; Wood, Metal Detritus. *Specialty:* Three-dimensional art existing in real space with movement, light and/or sound (kinetic); contemporary art masters, side by side with works by emerging artists. *Publ:* Auth, The Art Market, Jackie Fine Arts, 79; Don Jacobson: Kinetic Art (exhib catalogs), ASAGE Gallery, 81 & 84; Position paper (for an emerging gallery), ASAGE Gallery, 82; coauth, Yudel Kyler: Cool Surrealism (exhib catalog), 85 & Gerald Lindahl and the Creation of Psychological Space (exhib catalog), 86, ASAGE Gallery; Grace Glveck (auth), No More Raw Eggs at the Whithey, NY Times, 2/13/72. *Dealer:* Am State of the Art Gallery Exchange 162 W 4th St New York NY 10014; Art Space Inc 415 Rugby Rd Brooklyn NY 11226. *Mailing Add:* 415 Rugby Rd Brooklyn NY 11226

GIBALA, LOUISE
PAINTER
b Allegheny, Pa, May 2, 1897. *Study:* Art Students League, New York, 27-30; Nat Acad Design, 30-31; Nat Art League, 50-60; Dimitri Romanovsky 61-66; Edgar A Whitney, 52-70. *Work:* Dutch Reformed Church, Flushing, NY; Christ Lutheran Church, Long Island, NY. *Exhib:* New York City Open Competition, Metrop Mus, 50; Ann Open Competition, Nat Art League, 55-90; Flower Painting Exhib, Parrish Mus, Southampton, NY, 64; Catharine Lorillard Wolfe Mem Exhib, Nat Acad Design, 67; 14th Ann Golden Age Art Exhib, World Trade Ctr Gallery, New York, 78; Non-Mem Exhib, Salmagundi Club, 81. *Collections Arranged:* Artists Exhib for 60 Years and Over, 56-78. *Teaching:* Instr landscapes & still life, Nat Art League, 48-70. *Awards:* Gold Medal for wash drawing, 68 & Claude Parsons Mem Award, 76, Am Artists Prof League; Gold Trophy, 14th Ann New York City Art Exhib, 78. *Mem:* Nat Art League (pres, 51-53 & 63-65); Catharine Lorillard Wolfe Art Club (dir, 81-82); Am Artists Prof League; Hudson Valley Art Asn; Burr Artists. *Media:* Oil, Watercolor. *Publ:* Auth, Art clubs of America: Art League of Long Island, Artist Mag, 57. *Mailing Add:* 251-24 51st Ave Flushing NY 11362

GIBBONS, HUGH (JAMES)
PAINTER, EDUCATOR
b Scranton, Pa, Oct 26, 37. *Study:* Pa State Univ, with Elaine de Kooning & Robert Mallary, BA(painting), 59, MA(painting), 61. *Work:* WTex Mus, Lubbock; Bucknell Univ Collection. *Exhib:* Eight Texas Realist Painters, Plano, Tex, 87; Seeing It All, Univ Tex, San Antonio, 88; Summer Faculty, Arrowmont Sch, Gatlinburg, Tenn, 89; Painting from NY, TX, CA, Laguna Gloria Mus, Austin, Tex, 89; one-man shows, Univ Tex, Permian Basin, Odessa, Tex, 90 & Charleston Heights Gallery, Las Vegas, Nev, 90; TVAA Citation, Dallas, 91. *Teaching:* Prof painting & drawing & MFA coordr, Tex Tech Univ, 63- *Media:* Oil, Pencil. *Mailing Add:* Dept Art Tex Tech Univ Lubbock TX 79409

GIBBS, BARBARA
MUSEUM DIRECTOR
b Newton, Mass, Feb 15, 50. *Study:* Brown Univ, AB (fine arts, magna cum laude), 72, Univ Calif, Los Angeles, Grad Sch Mgt, MBA (arts mgt), 79. *Pos:* Deputy dir, Portland Art Asn, Ore, 79-83; dir, Crocker Art Mus, Sacramento, Calif, 83- *Mem:* Asn Art Mus Dir; Am Asn Mus. *Mailing Add:* 216 O St Sacramento CA 95814

GIBBS, TOM
SCULPTOR
b Dubuque, Iowa, Sept 17, 42. *Study:* Loras Col, BA(art); Univ Iowa, with Olivier Strabelle, MA(sculpture) & MFA; also with Walter Arno, Ger. *Work:* Tweed Mus, Univ Minn, Duluth, 89. *Comn:* four large scale steel sculptures, City of Dubuque, Iowa, 75-76; Western Electric Corp, 80; Esterville Public Libr, 81; Univ Dubuque, 88; Morningside Col, Sioux City, Iowa, 89. *Exhib:* Sculpture in the Landscape, Paine Art Ctr, 88; Univ Minn, Duluth, 88; Riverwalk Outdoor Invitational, Chicago, 89; Sculpture Tour 91, Walters State Col, Tenn; Ala Bienniel, Univ Ala, Tuscaloosa, 93; and others. *Teaching:* Instr art, Clarke Col, 68-69; asst prof sculpture, Ariz State Univ, 70-72. *Awards:* Honorable Mention, Nat Vietnam War Memorial Design Compt, Washington, DC, 81; Nominee, Second Ann Awards in the Visual Arts, 82; Creative Artists Planning Proj Task Force, Iowa, Art Coun, 88-90; Gov's Award for Service to Arts, 89. *Bibliog:* Articles, Chicago Sun Times, 6/29/80 & 5/23/82 & Art News, 11/80; Joan Jeremy Hewes (auth), Worksteads, Tom Gibbs, Sculptor, pp 24-29 & 120, Doubleday, NY, 81. *Mem:* Int Sculpture Ctr. *Media:* Welded & Cast Metal. *Publ:* Auth, Field hearings on the reauthorization of the National Foundation for the Arts on Humanities Act J pp 412-421. *Dealer:* Nina Owen Gallery Ltd 120 N Lake Shore St Chicago IL 60610; Molly-Rose Gallery 5400 SW 99th Terr Coral Gables FL. *Mailing Add:* 1333 Kaufmann Dubuque IA 52001

GIBBS, Y GALE
PAINTER, SCULPTOR
b Oklahoma City, Okla, Dec 7, 46. *Study:* Cameron Univ, BFA, 88; Univ NTex, grad studies, 90; workshops with James Surls, Dave Hickey & Jack Mims. *Work:* Cameron Univ, Lawton, Okla. *Comn:* Sculpture, Eisenhow High Sch, Lawton, Okla; sculpture, comn by Mr & Mrs Tom D'spain, Duncan, Okla; sculpture, comn by Keith Bishop, Oklahoma City; sculpture, comn by Dr Jack Bowman, Lawton, Okla; drawing, comn by Mr & Mrs Bob Ott, Duncan, Okla. *Exhib:* 22nd Bradley Nat, Bradley Univ, Peoria, 89; solo exhibs, Ill Central Col, Peoria, 89, Ritual Rhetoric & Resolution, La State Univ, Shreveport, 92; 28th Beaux Arts Ball, Dallas Mus, 92; Masur Mas, La, 91; Longview Mus & Arts Ctr, Tex, 91. *Pos:* Secy, Wave, Denton, Tex, 92. *Teaching:* Fel design, Univ NTex, Denton, 89-90. *Awards:* Third Place, For Love or Money, Cameron Unv, 86; First Place, Clary-Miner Gallery Nat, 89; Third Place, 24th Ann Del Mar Nat, Leisure Time, 90. *Bibliog:* Gibbs work exhibited in New York, Lawton Constitution, 87; Richard Huntington (auth), Woodcuts, pencils, paint, Buffalo News, 4/21/89; Lori Baker (auth), Gibbs bares abstract messages, College Harbinger, 89. *Mem:* Tex Sculpture Asn, Dallas. *Media:* Oil on Canvas. *Mailing Add:* 3108 Oxford Ct Plano TX 75075

GIBRAN, KAHLIL GEORGE
SCULPTOR
b Boston, Mass, Nov 29, 22. *Study:* Boston Mus Sch, 40-43, painting with Karl Zerbe. *Work:* Chrysler Collection, Va Mus, Norfolk; Pa Acad Fine Art, Philadelphia; Cheekwood Art Ctr, Nashville, Tenn; Elmira Col, NY; Brockton Fine Arts Ctr, Mass; Swope Gallery, Ind; Rockhill Nelson Gallery, Kans. *Comn:* Bronze wall mural, Forsythe Dental, Boston, 71; bronze plaque of Judge Francis Ford, Fed Ct House, Boston & poet Kahlil Gibran, Copley Sq, Boston, 77; madonna (bronze figure), Jamaica Plain, Mass, 81; silver medallion of Elliot Norton, Boston Theatre Dist Asn, 83; Port Gibran Kahlil Gibran, Worcester State Col, 87. *Exhib:* Whitney Mus Am Art Ann, 56; Int, Trieste, Italy, 66; New Eng Artists, Provincetown Art Asn & Cyclorama, Boston, 71; one-man show of bronze sculpture, Cambridge Art Asn, 77; Cambridge Art Asn, Mass, 80; Boston Atheneum, 81; Boston Arts Festival, 85; Esthetix Gallery, 89; La Posada, Santa Fe, 89. *Teaching:* Wellesley Col, 58 & Boston Mus Sch. *Awards:* George Wiedner Medal, Pa Acad Fine Arts, 58; John S Guggenheim Fel, 59-60; Nat Inst Arts & Lett Award & Fel, 61. *Bibliog:* Gregory MacDonald (auth), Kahlil Gibran a Boston sculptor, Boston Globe Mag, 67; Nathan Hale (auth), Welded Sculpture, Watson-Guptill, 68; Donald Irving (auth), Sculpture Material and Process, Van Nostrand Reinhold, 70. *Mem:* Nat Sculpture Soc; New Eng Sculpture Soc; Cambridge Art Asn (vpres, 68); Provincetown Art Asn. *Media:* Steel, Bronze. *Publ:* Auth, Sculpture in process, Nat Sculpture Rev, 70; Sculpture Kahlil Gibran, 72; coauth, Kahlil Gibran--His Life and World, New York Graphic Soc, 74. *Mailing Add:* 160 W Canton St Boston MA 02118

GIBSON, BENEDICT S
PAINTER, EDUCATOR
b Grand Rapids, Mich, Sept 21, 46. *Study:* Kendall Sch Design, dipl, 67; Aquinas Col, BA, 70; Univ Nebr, MFA, 73. *Work:* Albright-Knox Art Gallery, Buffalo, NY; Butler Inst Am Art, Youngstown, Ohio; Mem Art Gallery, Rochester, NY; Rutgers Univ, New Brunswick, NJ; Flint Inst Arts, Mich; and others. *Exhib:* 34th Western NY Exhib, Albright-Knox Art Gallery, 74; Midwest Invitational II, Springfield Art Mus, Mo, 74; Reo-Realist Exhib, Col St Catherine, St Paul, Minn, 74; Mich Surv, San Jose Art Gallery, Calif & Cranbrook Acad, Bloomfield Hills, Mich, 75 & 76; 41st Midyear Show, Butler Inst Am Art, Youngstown, Ohio, 77; Nat Drawing, Rutgers State Univ, NJ, Camden, 77; Hassam & Speicher Fund Exhib, Am Acad & Inst Arts, New York, 78; and others. *Collections Arranged:* Drawing Invitational (cataloged), 76; First Decade, Charles B Burchfield Ctr Col, 76; Penney Collection (cataloged), State Univ NY Upstate Med Ctr, 77; Three Painters, Millersville State Col, 77; Tenth Anniversary Exhibition, Kenan Ctr, Lockport, NY, 77. *Teaching:* Asst prof art, Damaen Col, Buffalo, NY, 73-76; assoc prof art, Edinboro State Col, Pa, 76- *Awards:* First Prize, Birge Co, Inc, 74, Chautauqua Inst, 74 & Edinboro State Col, 77; Best of Show, Ann Spring Show, Erie Art Ctr, 80; and others. *Bibliog:* Nancy Tobin Willig (auth), Gibson's Show: Superrealism with a plus, Buffalo Courier-Express, 74; Jean Reeves (auth), Gibson's craftsmanship produces mystery, illusion, 74 & Hal Crowther (auth), Gibson Art dominates 4-man show, 75, Buffalo Evening News. *Mem:* Patteran Artists Asn, Buffalo, NY; Col Art Asn Am. *Media:* Acrylic, Oil. *Mailing Add:* Dept Art Edinboro Univ Edinboro PA 16444

GIBSON, EDWARD G
PHOTOGRAPHER
Study: Ariz State Univ, BFA, 73; Univ Colo, MFA, 79. *Exhib:* Nelson Atkins Art Mus, Kansas City, Mo, 75; Spark Gallery, Denver, Colo, 81; Yellowstone Art Ctr, Billings, Mont, 86-89, invitational; Franklin Furnace, New York, NY, 86; solo exhibs, Northcutt Gallery, Billings, Mont, 86 & Brunswick Contemp Arts Ctr, Missoula, Mont, 88; Hockaday Ctr Arts, Kalispell, Mont, 90; Montana Reflections, Mont Hist Soc, Helena, 91; Cermony of Innocence, Mont Asn Gallery Dirs, 92. *Awards:* Can Coun Grant, 79; Nat Endowment Arts, 88. *Mailing Add:* 406 S 31st Billings MT 59101

GIBSON, GEORGE
PAINTER, ADMINISTRATOR
b Edinburgh, Scotland, Oct 16, 04; US citizen. *Study:* Edinburgh Col Art; Glasgow Sch Art, Scotland; W E Glover Scenic Studios, Glasgow; Chouinard Sch Art, Los Angeles; also with F Tolles Chamberlain, Pasadena, Calif. *Work:* Calif Nat Watercolor Soc Collection, Los Angeles Co Mus Art; Home Savings & Loan, Los Angeles; Laguna Beach Mus Art, Calif; Fresno Mus Art, Calif; Santa Paula Chamber of Commerce, Calif. *Comn:* US Navy Combat Art Collection. *Exhib:* Calif Nat Watercolor Soc Ann, 47-71; Am Watercolor Soc Ann, 49-72; Nat Acad Design, New York, 54-58; Phoenix Art Mus, Ariz, 72. *Pos:* Supvr scenic art prod, MGM Studios, Culver City, Calif, 34-69. *Awards:* Calif Nat Watercolor Soc 32nd Ann Award, 51; Nat Acad Design 134th Ann Watercolor Award, 59; Verda Karen McCracken Young Award, Am Watercolor Soc 105th Ann, 72. *Bibliog:* V Heutschy (auth), From any angle, 10/54 & Ron Ross (auth), Cameraman's comments, 12/54, Int Photogr; G Gibson (auth), Scenic art in motion picture industry, Soc Motion Picture & TV Eng J, 10/62. *Mem:* Assoc Nat Acad Design; Am Watercolor Soc; life mem Nat Watercolor Soc (secy, 47, 1st vpres, 49, pres, 51). *Media:* Watercolor. *Publ:* Contribr, The California Style, Am Artist, 5/68 & 9/69; Changing Times/Changing Styles, 85; Antiques & Fine Arts, 7/88; Calif Romantics, 3/87. *Dealer:* Stary-Sheets Gallery 14988 Sand Canyon Ave Suite I-5 Irvine CA 92718. *Mailing Add:* 1449 Santa Maria Ave Los Osos CA 93402

GIBSON, JAMES D
EDUCATOR, CARTOONIST
b Milbank, SDak, Dec 13, 38. *Study:* Ill Wesleyan Univ, BFA; Ohio Univ, BFA. *Work:* State Univ NY Col, Fredonia; Univ NDak. *Comn:* Videotape animation, St Mary's Col, Notre Dame, Ind. *Exhib:* Artists of Montana, Senate Off Bldg, Washington, DC, 65; Hawaiian Nat Print Competition, 71; 12th Midwest Biennial, Joslyn Art Mus, Omaha, Nebr, 72; Emerging Expressions, Bronx Mus Arts, 88; Artiste Computer Art Symp, Marycrest Col; SIG Graph, Computer Art Show, Dallas, 86. *Teaching:* Instr art, Eastern Mont Col, 65-67; prof art, Northern State Univ, SDak, 67-, chmn dept art, 67-78. *Awards:* Purchase Awards, Paintings, 68, SDak Works on Paper, 71-72, & videotape, 89, SDak Mem Art Ctr; Project Grant, SDak Arts Coun, 90. *Mem:* Nat Asn Sch Art (bd dirs, 71-72). *Media:* Computers, Ink. *Publ:* Illusr, Motive Mag, Methodist Church, 68-70; auth, Campus Call, Catholic Church, 68; illusr, Composites, Indust Press, New York. *Mailing Add:* Dept Art Northern State Col Aberdeen SD 57401

GIBSON, JOHN STUART
PAINTER, PRINTMAKER
b Northampton, Mass, Oct 14, 58. *Study:* RI Sch Design, BFA, 80; Yale Sch Art, MFA, 82. *Work:* New York Pub Libr; Acklin Mus, Charlotte, NC; Univ Mass, Amherst. *Exhib:* Beyond Realism, Southern Alleghenies Mus, Loretto, Pa, 92. *Teaching:* Instr, art, Smith Col, Northampton, Mass, 85-92. *Media:* Oil. *Mailing Add:* c/o Allan Stone 47 E 86th St New York NY 10028

GIBSON, RALPH H
PHOTOGRAPHER
b Jan 16, 39. *Study:* US Navy, studied photog, 56-60; San Francisco Art Inst, 60- 61; Univ Md, DFA(hon). *Work:* Mus Mod Art & Metrop Mus Art, New York; Int Mus Photog, George Eastman House, Rochester, NY; Fogg Art Mus, Cambridge, Mass; Corcoran Mus; Bibliotheque National, Paris, France; plus many others. *Exhib:* One-man exhibs, Int Mus Photog, George Eastman House, 73, Galerie Agathe Gaillare, Paris, France, 75, 77, 82 & 85, Baltimore Mus Art, 76, Mus Mod Art, Oxford, Eng, 77, Centre Georges Pompidou, 82, Seattle Art Mus, 83, Consejo Argentino De Fotografía, Buenos Aires, 85, Bouwfonds Hovelaken, Holland, 85 & many others; Photog for Collectors, Mus Mod Art, New York, 75, Rooms, 77, Mirrors and Windows, 78 & Penthouse, 80; Counterparts: Form and Emotion in Photog, Metrop Mus Art, New York, 82; Prototypes, Whitney Mus Am Art, New York, 83; Exposed and Developed, Nat Endowment Arts, Nat Mus Art, Washington, DC, 84; Aquisitions Recents, Mus Mod Art, Paris, 84; Das Aktfoto 1840-1985, Kunsthaus, Munich, WGermany, 85; L'Autoportrait a L'Age de la Phtoog, Mus Cantonal, Lausanne, Switz, 85; plus numerous others throughout the world. *Teaching:* Lectr at var places including Ont Col of Art, Toronto, Sun Valley Ctr for the Arts, Idaho, Int Festival at Arles, France, Ansel Adams Gallery, Yosemite Valley, Calif & Tyler Sch of Art, Temple Univ, Philadelphia, Pa, 75 & Cranbrook Acad, Detroit, Mich, Inst of Contemp Art, London, Eng, Sydney Acad of Art Australia, Mus Fine Art, Houston, Tex & Frei Univ, Amsterdam, Neth, 77. *Awards:* Nat Endowment for the Arts Grant, 73, 75 & 86; Creative Artists Pub Serv Grant, NY State Coun of the Arts, 77; John Simon Guggenheim Fel, 85; Officer de L' Ordre des Arts et des Lettres, France, 86; Leica Medal of Excellence Award, 88. *Bibliog:* Encyclopedie International des Photographes de 1839 a Nos Jours, Camera Obscura, Geneva, 85; Popular Photography, Vol 92, No 7, 85; International Museum of Photography Encyclopedia of Photography, 84; plus many other books and serials, 67-86. *Mem:* Arts Club Chicago. *Publ:* Archive 24, Ralph Gibson: Early Work, 88; Center for Creative Photograph, Ariz, 88; Tropism, 30 year Aperture Retrospet, 87; L'Histoire de France, Aperture, 91. *Dealer:* Leo Castelli 420 West Broadway, New York NY 10013. *Mailing Add:* 331 W Broadway New York NY 10013

GIBSON, WALTER SAMUEL
EDUCATOR, WRITER
b Columbus, Ohio, Mar 31, 32. *Study:* Ohio State Univ, BFA, 57, MA, 60; res at Kunsthistorisch Inst Rijksuniversiteit, Utrecht, 60-61 & 64-66; Harvard Univ, PhD, 69. *Pos:* Murphy Lectureship, Univ Kans & Nelson-Atkins Mus Art, Kansas City, Mo, 88. *Teaching:* Asst prof art, Case Western Reserve Univ, Cleveland, 66-71, chmn dept & assoc prof, 71-79, Andrew W Mellon prof humanities, 78-; Clark vis prof art hist, Williams Col, 89. *Mem:* Col Art Asn Am; Int Ctr Medieval Art; Midwest Art Hist Soc; Renaissance Soc Am; Medieval Acad Am; Am Asn Netherlandic Studies; Historians Netherlandish Art; Soc Emblem Studies. *Res:* Dutch and Flemish art of the 15th and 16th century; iconography. *Publ:* Auth, Hieronymus Bosch, Praeger, 73; Bruegel, Oxford Univ Press, 77; The Paintings of Cornelis Engebrechtsz, Garland, 77; Hieronymus Bosch: An Annotated Bibliography, G K Hall, 83; Mirror of the Earth: The World Landscape in Sixteenth-Century Flemish Painting, Princeton, 89; numerous articles in American & European journals. *Mailing Add:* Dept Art Case Western Reserve Univ Cleveland OH 44106

GIFFORD, J NEBRASKA
PAINTER, SCULPTOR
b Omaha, Nebr, Nov 25, 39. *Study:* Bennington Col, BA; Atelier 17, Paris, with S W Hayter. *Work:* Owens-Corning Fiberglas Collection, Toledo, Ohio; NY Univ; Joslyn Art Mus, Omaha, Nebr; Sheldon Mus, Lincoln, Nebr; Libr Congress, Readers Digest Collection. *Comn:* Acrylic painting, indoor wall, Omaha Community Playhouse, 61; oil & enamel painting, outdoor wall, Old Market, Omaha, 69; sculpture, Bovinitron and Little Moo, Omaha Pub Libr, 90. *Exhib:* One-person shows, Louis K Meisel Gallery, 74, 55 Mercer Gallery, New York, 76, Univ Nebr, Omaha, 77, Anatomy of Romance, John Nichols Gallery, 86 & Gallery 72, Omaha, 90 & Small painting, Zodiac Gallery, Omaha, 90; Blockbusters, Univ Kans, 86; Prints by Women, Assoc Am Artists Gallery, NY, 86; Noah's Art, Cent Park, New York, 89; Summer Prints, Susan Teller Gallery, New York, 90; and others. *Pos:* Columnist, Gallery Mag & Art Initiatives; exhib dir, John Nichols Gallery, 85; dealer, Susan Teller Gallery. *Awards:* Pratt Inst Prize, 83; Philadelphia Print Club's Benton Spruance Award, 86; Nat Print Exhib, Trenton, NJ, 88 & 91; and others. *Mem:* Int Soc Copier Artists. *Media:* Oil, Ceramic; Woodcut, Metal. *Publ:* Ed, Int Soc Copier Artists Newsletter; article, New York Mag, 6/6/83; article, NY Times, 7/8/83. *Dealer:* Susan Teller Gallery 568 Bway New York NY 10012. *Mailing Add:* Four Great Jones St New York NY 10012

GIFFUNI, FLORA BALDINI
PAINTER, LECTURER
b Naples, Italy; US citizen. *Study:* New York Univ, BFA, 42; Teachers Col, Columbia Univ, MFA, 45. *Work:* Univ Hawaii; Medgar Evers Col, New York; Cabrini Col, Pa; New York City Hall. *Exhib:* Nat Art League, Douglaston, NY, 71; Pastel Soc Am, Nat Arts Club, New York, 72-88; Am Artist Prof League, Grand Cent Gallery, New York, 77; Salmagundi Open, Salmagundi Club, New York, 78-84; Knickerbocker Artists, Salmagundi Club, 80-81; Allied Artists, Nat Arts Club, New York, 88. *Awards:* Best in Show, Catharine Lorillard Wolfe Art Club, Nat Acad, New York, 70, Am Artists Prof League, 77 & Nat Arts Club, 82. *Mem:* Pastel Soc, Nat Arts Club; founder Pastel Soc Am (pres, 72-88); hon mem Salmagundi Club. *Media:* Pastel. *Res:* History of pastels. *Mailing Add:* 180-16 Dalny Rd Jamaica NY 11432

GIGLIOTTI, JOANNE MARIE
ADMINISTRATOR, PAINTER
b Pittsburgh, Pa, June 12, 45. *Study:* Carnegie-Mellon Univ, BFA, 67; Penn State Univ, MA, 78. *Work:* Westinghouse Collection, Pittsburgh, Pa; Penn State Univ, University Park, Pa; Nat Mus Women Arts, Washington, DC; Gettysburg Col, Pa. *Exhib:* Carnegie Mus Art, Pittsburgh, Pa, 68 & 71; Beautiful Batik, Arts & Sci Ctr, Nashua, NH, 74, Battle Creek Art Ctr, Mich, 75, Brigham City Mus Art, Brigham City, Utah, 75, Arnut Mus Art, Elmira, NY, 75, Abilene Fine Arts Mus, Tex, 76, Bronx Libr, Manhattan Branch, 76, Fayette Art Mus, Ala, 76. *Pos:* Dir, Hub Arts & Craft Ctr, Penn State Univ, 78-80; founder & dir, Fine Arts Connection, Washington, DC, 80-87; dir, Studio Arts Dept, Resident Assoc Prog, dir, Discover Graphics, Smithsonian Inst, Washington, DC, 87-; head, Smithsonian Inst Women's Coun, 92-. *Teaching:* Instr, Batik-silkscreen-color-design, Smithsonian Inst - Resident Assoc Prog, 83-87; Art application, Am Univ, 84-86. *Awards:* Westinghouse Purchase Award, 3 Rivers Art Co, Westinghouse, 67; Best in Category (mixed media), Big Bends Nat Art Competition, Tallahassee, 68; Selected to represent 5 state region, Nat Conf Col Unions Inter. *Mem:* Phi Kappa Phi, Nat Interdisciplinary Hon Soc, 78; Am Asn Mus, 80; Women in Mus Network (pres, 87); Nat Computer Graphics Asn (pres, 86-). *Media:* Miscellaneous Media. *Publ:* Coauth, Time-Life Art Ser, Time-Life Publ, 88; auth, The Business of Art, Prentice-Hall, 89. *Mailing Add:* 69 Bralan Court Gaithersburg MD 20877

GILBERT, ALBERT EARL
PAINTER, ILLUSTRATOR
b Chicago, Ill, Aug 22, 39. *Work:* Am Mus Natural Hist, New York; Carnegie Mus, Pittsburgh; Ill State Mus, Springfield; Nat Audubon Soc, New York; du Pont Collection, Del Mus Natural Hist, Wilmington; Princeton Univ. *Comn:* Paintings of Am wildlife & plants, Nat Wildlife Fedn, Washington, DC, 67-74; Audubon bird proj (20 color plates of Am birds), Franklin Mint, Pa, 75. *Exhib:* Wildlife in Art, Brandywine River Mus, Chadds Ford, Pa, 73; SAm Birds, Am Mus Natural Hist, New York, 73; one-man show, Wildlife Portraits, Incurable Collector Gallery, New York, 74; Animals in Art, Royal Ont Mus, Toronto, 75; Bird Art Exhib, Leigh Yawkey Woodson Art Mus, Wausau, Wis, 77; and others. *Awards:* Winner, Fed Duck Stamp Competition, 78-79. *Bibliog:* B J Lancaster (auth), Gilbert's birds, Cornell Univ Lab of Ornithology Bulletin, 75; The artist--Al Gilbert, Prints Mag, spring, 79. *Mem:* Soc Animal Artists; Ridgefield Guild Artists. *Media:* Opaque Watercolors, Acrylics. *Publ:* Illusr, The Audubon Illustrated Handbook of American Birds, 68, The Red Book--Wildlife in Danger, 68, Curassows and Related Birds, 73 & Birds of New York State, 74; auth, My studio is the jungle, Int Wildlife Mag, 9-10/76; and others. *Dealer:* Blakeslee Gallery 350 Royal Poinciana Palm Beach Fl 33480; Steep Rock Wildlife Art Box 107 Bridgewater CT 06752. *Mailing Add:* PO Box 107 Bridgewater CT 06752

GILBERT, ARNOLD MARTIN
COLLECTOR, PHOTOGRAPHER
b New York, NY, Mar 28, 21. *Study:* Univ of Chicago. *Work:* Mus Contemp Art, Chicago; Mus Mod Art, New York; Victoria & Albert Mus, London; Nat Mus Mod Art, Kyoto, Japan. *Exhib:* One-man shows, Univ Wis, Milwaukee, 77 & 78, Monterey Peninsula Mus Art, 79, Gilbert Gallery, Chicago, Ill, 79 & 80, Prairie State Col, Chicago Heights, Ill, 81 & Photo Gallery Int, Tokyo, Japan, 84 & 87; Lensless Photog Show, IBM Gallery, New York, NY, 84; John Michael Kohler Art Ctr, Sheboygen, Wis, 85. *Teaching:* Prof photog, Governors State Univ, Park Forest S, Ill, 74-82. *Mem:* Friends of Photog. *Collection:* Modern 20th century photography. *Mailing Add:* 1100 N Lake Shore Dr Chicago IL 60611

GILBERT, CREIGHTON EDDY
HISTORIAN, WRITER
b Durham, NC, June 6, 24. *Study:* NY Univ, with Walter Friedlaender, Richard Offner, Lionello Venturi, Erwin Panofsky, Meyer Schapiro & Richard Krautheimer, BA, 42, PhD, 55; Adelphi Univ, Hon DHL, 90. *Pos:* Cur, Ringling Mus, Sarasota, Fla, 59-61; ed in chief, Art Bulletin, 80-85. *Teaching:* Jr posts, Emory Univ, Univ Louisville, Ind Univ, Bloomington, 46-58; from assoc prof to Sidney & Ellen Wien prof hist art, Brandeis Univ, 61-69; prof hist art, Queens Col, 69-77; vis prof, Univ Leiden, Netherlands, 74-75; Robert Sterling Clark vis prof, Williams Col, 76; Jacob Gould Schurman prof hist of art, Cornell Univ, 77-81; prof, Yale Univ, 81-; Vis Zacks prof, Univ Jerusalem, 85. *Awards:* Fulbright Sr Lectr, Univ Rome, 51-52; Mather Award for Best Art Criticism of Year, Col Art Asn Am, 64; Fel, Netherlands Inst Advan Study, 72-73. *Bibliog:* Interviews Rotterdam Courant-Handelsblad, 2/75 & Giornale Dell' Arte, Turin, 11/88. *Mem:* Fel Am Acad Arts & Sci; Col Art Asn Am; For Mem, Ateneo Veneto. *Publ:* Transl, Complete Poems & Selected Letters of Michelangelo, 63, Mod Libr Ed, 65, Vintage, 70, 3rd Revised Ed, Princeton, 80; auth, Change in Piero della Francesca, Augustin, 68; ed, Italian Art 1400-1500, Sources and Documents, Prentice-Hall, 79, Italian ed, IRSA, 88, rev ed, Northwestern Univ Press, 92; auth, The Works of Girolamo Savoldo, Garland, 86; Poets Seeing Artists' Work, Olschki, 91. *Mailing Add:* Dept Art Hist Yale Univ New Haven CT 06520

GILBERT, HELEN ODELL
PAINTER, PRINTMAKER
b Calif. *Study:* Mills Col, Oakland, Calif, AB, 43; Cent Sch Art, London, 60; Univ Calif, Berkeley; with J Frielander, Paris, Univ Hawaii, MFA, 68; Pratt Graphics, New York. *Work:* Mus Mod Art, New York; Simon Gassenheim Mus, New York; Metrop Mus Art; Brit Mus; Bibliot Nat, Paris. *Comn:* Environ Wall Relief Paintings, Kaiser Outpatient Clinic, Honolulu; Environ Installations, King Kalakaua Ctr, Japan Travel Bureau, First Hawiian Bank, Honolulu, HI. *Exhib:* L'Estampe Aujourd'hui, Bibliot Nat, Paris, 78; Soc Am Graphic Artists, New York, 79, 83 & 87; Dusseldorf, Basel & Koln Art Fairs, 80, 81,83, 84 & 86; Meissner Gallery, Hamburg, 84; La Strutture Dela Visualita, Musei Civisi Da Varese, Varese, Italy, 84; Exhib Am Abstract Artists Asn, City Gallery New York, 87; Contemp Art Mus, Honolulu, 89; Karen Fesel Galerie, Dusseldorf, 90; and others. *Teaching:* Prof art, Univ Hawaii, 65-; vis exchange prof, Parsons Sch, New York, 78-79; vis prof, Pratt Inst, 83. *Awards:* Res Grant, Univ Hawaii, 69 & 70; Study & Res Grant, Pratt Graphics, Ford Found, 79; Purchase Awards State Found Cult & Arts, Hawaii, 78, 81, 83 & 86; Study & Res Grant, Pratt Graphics, Ford Found, 79; Honolulu Printmakers Merit Award, 83, 84, 85 & 87. *Bibliog:* Virginia Watson-Jones (auth), Contemporary Women Sculptors, Ornyx Press, 86; Hans Heinz Holz (auth), Le Strutture Delia Visualita, Edizioni Milano, 85. *Mem:* Am Abstract Artists Asn; Honolulu Printmakers Asn; Nat Arts Club; Hawaii Artists League; Soc Am Graphic Artists. *Dealer:* Artloft 1021 Auahi St Bldg 4 Honolulu HI 98614; Sande Webster Gallery 2018 Locust St Philadelphia PA 19103. *Mailing Add:* Dept Art-Art 311 Univ Hawaii at Manoa 2500 Campus Rd Honolulu HI 96822

GILBERT, HERB
PAINTER
b Brooklyn, NY, Oct 30, 29. *Study:* Art Career Sch, 48-51; Brooklyn Mus Art Sch, with Reuben Tam, 55-58; Pratt Inst with Walter Murch, Reuben Nakian & George McNiel, 56-57; Univ Calif, 73. *Work:* Mus NMex, Santa Fe; Motorola Corp, Phoenix, Ariz; Am Republic Insurance Co, Des Moines, Iowa; Salt River Proj, Phoenix, Ariz; Bahai Nat Ctr, Wilmette, Ill; Univ Ariz Mus Art. *Exhib:* Own Your Own Regional, Denver Art Mus, 64; Southwest Fine Arts Biennial, Mus NMex, 74; Invitational, Cochise Col, Douglas, Ariz, 77; Birds Eye View Gallery, Newport Beach, Calif, 78; Cochise Fine Arts, Bisbee, Ariz, 79, 82 & 84; Lambert-Miller Gallery, Phoenix, Ariz, 81; Ariz Biennial, TMA, Tucson, Ariz, 82; Dinnerware Gallery, Tucson, Ariz, 82; Galeria Mesa-Chroma-Zone, Mesa, Ariz, 88; Davis Gallery Tucson, Ariz, 89, 90 & 92; Univ Ariz Mus Art, 89. *Teaching:* Instr graphics & drawing, Inst Am Indian Arts, Santa Fe, 71-75, chmn dept commun design, 74-75. *Awards:* Three Distinctive Merit Awards, Two Gold Medals & Eight Honor Awards, Art Dirs Club Denver, 59-69. *Bibliog:* Interview: Six Bisbee Artists, Artspace, winter 79; Michael Cadieux (auth), Herb Gilbert, Artspace, summer 83. *Media:* Acrylic. *Publ:* Contribr, Impressions of Arizona (painting), Art Am, 4/81. *Mailing Add:* PO Box 1294 Bisbee AZ 85603

GILBERT, LIONEL
PAINTER, INSTRUCTOR
b Newark, NJ, May 29, 12. *Study:* Newark Sch Fine & Indust Art, grad, 33; Acad Grande Chaumiere, Paris, 33; with Suzanne Valadon, Paris, 34; Chicago Sch Design, with Maholy-Nagy, 41; NY Univ, with Sam Adler, 55. *Work:* Joslyn Mus Art, Omaha, Nebr; Slater Mus, Conn; Eureka Col Collection; Silver Springs Acad, Colo; Newark Mus, NJ; also in many pvt & corp collections. *Exhib:* One-man shows, Gallery Contemp Art, Toronto, 58, New Sch Social Res, New York, 66 & Alonzo Gallery, New York, 68, 70, 71, 73, 75, 76 & 80; Childe Hassom Fund Exhib, Acad Arts & Lett, 69; Nat Acad Design; and others. *Teaching:* Instr drawing & painting, YMHA, New York, 67-; instr drawing & painting, NY Univ, 68-69; instr painting, Summit Art Ctr, NJ, 75- *Awards:* Certificate of Merit, Nat Acad Design, 75; Carlsen Award, Nat Acad Design, 86. *Media:* Oil. *Mailing Add:* 244 West 74th St New York NY 10023

GILBERT, SHARON
COLLAGE ARTIST, SCULPTOR
b Brooklyn, NY, Feb 15, 44. *Study:* Skowhegan Sch, 65; Cooper Union, BFA, 66. *Work:* Bibliotheque National of France, Paris; Mus Mod Art Libr Book Collection, Whitney Mus Libr, Franklin Furnace, Brooklyn Mus Libr, New York; Archiv Sohm, Staatsgalerie of Stuttgart, Ger; Univ Pittsburgh Libr, Pa; Int Electrographic Mus, Cueenca, Spain. *Exhib:* Committed to Print, Mus Modern Art (with catalog), New York, 88; Reading the Personal, Women's Building, Los Angeles, Calif, 89; Book Arts in the USA, USIA & Ctr for Bk Arts, Touring Africa, 90-92; Neverland, Long Island Univ, New York & Barrett House, Poughkeepsie, NY, 90; Completing the Circle: Artists' Books on the Environment, Minn Ctr Bk Arts, 92; By Any Means Necessary/ Photocopier Artist Books and the Politics of Accessible Printing Technologies, Printed Matter, New York, 92; and others. *Awards:* Carl Schurz Haus, Feiburg im Br, Ger, 80; Womens' Studio Workshop, Rosendale, NY, 82; New York Found Arts, 89. *Bibliog:* Lucy Lippard (auth), Conspicious Consumption: New Artists Books, 85; Joan Lyons (ed), Artists Books: A Critical Anthology & Sourcebook, Visual Studies Workshop Press, Rochester, NY, illus, page 52. *Mem:* Women's Caucus for Art (NY Chapt adv bd, 79-83); Artists Equity; Orgn Independent Artists. *Publ:* Contribr, illusr, page 23, Book Arts USA, Ctr Bk Arts & US Info Agency, 90; A Nuclear Atlas, Women's Studio Workshop, Rosendale, NY, 82. *Mailing Add:* 323 Atlantic Ave Brooklyn NY 11201

GILBERT-ROLFE, JEREMY
PAINTER
b Tunbridge Wells, Kent, Eng, Aug 4, 45. *Study:* Tunbridge Wells Sch Art, NDD, 65; London Univ, ATC, 67; Fla State Univ, MFA, 70. *Work:* Getty Study Ctr, Santa Monica; Commodities Corp, NJ; Chase Manhattan, New York. *Exhib:* Drawings by Painters, Long Beach Mus, Calif, 82; Melancholia, Anne Plumb, New York, 87; Formal, Dart Gallery, Chicago, 88; Marc Richards Gallery, 89; one-man shows, Anne Plumb Gallery, New York, 90, Genovese Gallery, Boston, 90. *Awards:* Nat Endowment Arts, 74, 80 & 89. *Bibliog:* John Russell (auth), NY Times, 2/11/77, 6/6/80. *Mailing Add:* c/o Genovese Gallery 535 Albany St Boston MA 02118

GILBERTSON, CHARLOTTE
PAINTER, LECTURER
b Boston, Mass. *Study:* Boston Univ, BA; Art Students League; Pratt Inst, New York; studied with Fernand Leger, Paris. *Exhib:* E A T Show, Brooklyn Mus, New York, 68-69; Erik Nord Gallery, Nantucket, 75; Bodley Gallery, 75 & 77; Irving Galleries, Palm Beach, Fla, 77; Pace Univ Mus & St Peters Col Mus, 78; Galeria Bryna, Palm Beach, 80 & 81; plus many others. *Pos:* Dir, Iolas Gallery, New York, 62-74 & Galeria Bryna, Palm Beach, 79-80; free lance lecturer, 80- *Mem:* Visual Arts Galleries Asn; Am Fedn Arts; Int Women's Writing Guild; life mem, Art Students League; Palm Beach Co Coun Arts. *Media:* Acrylic, Mixed Media. *Mailing Add:* Old Sch House Rd Harwich Port MA 02646

GILBOY, MARGARETTA
EDUCATOR, PAINTER
b Philadelphia, Pa, Aug 10, 43. *Study:* Philadelphia Col Art, BFA, 65; Univ Colo, Boulder, MFA, 81. *Work:* Univ Colo, Boulder; City of Boulder, Colo. *Comn:* Pub Libr, Boulder, Colo, 85; mural, Philadelphia Anti-Grafitti Network, 91. *Exhib:* Biennial, Joslyn Art Mus, Omaha, Nebr, 68; 5th Colo Ann, Denver Art Mus, 79; Colo Women Arts, Arvada Ctr Arts & Humanities, 79; Nat Painting Show, Washington & Jefferson Col, Washington, Pa, 80; Portraits, Philadelphia Col Art, Pa, 80; Colo Biennial, Colo Springs Art Ctr, 81. *Pos:* Vis artist, Anderson Ranch Art Ctr. *Teaching:* Instr painting, Univ Colo, Boulder, 76-77 & 80-; lectr drawing & painting, Pa Acad Fine Arts, 86- *Awards:* Award for Creative Work, Univ Colo, 81; Teaching Excellence Award, 81 & Eugene Kayden Colo Arts Award, 83, Univ Colo; Yaddo Fel, 86. *Bibliog:* Eve Medoff (auth), Realism plus, Am Artist Mag, 3/79; Richard Torchia (auth), Margaretta Gilboy (catalog essay), Marian Locks Gallery, 90. *Mem:* Col Art Asn. *Media:* Oil, Watercolor. *Dealer:* FAN Gallery 311 Cherry St Philadelphia PA 19106. *Mailing Add:* 401 Green Lane Philadelphia PA 19128

GILCHRIEST, LORENZO
CONSTRUCTIONIST, EDUCATOR
b Thomasville, Ga, Mar 21, 38. *Study:* Newark Sch Fine & Indust Arts, 57-58; Newark State Col, BA, 62; Pratt Inst, MS, 67; Md Inst, MFA, 75. *Work:* Newark State Col; Fairleigh Dickinson Univ. *Exhib:* Some Negro Artists, Fairleigh Dickinson Univ, 65; one-man shows, Univ Md, 70 & Morgan State Univ, 79; Md Regional, Baltimore Mus Art, 71; Black Art, Towson State Col, 75; three solo & many group shows, Argus Gallery. *Pos:* Assoc art dir, Sen Robert Kennedy Proj, Bedford Stuyvesant Youth in Action, Brooklyn, NY, 65-67. *Teaching:* Asst prof art, Towson State Col, 67-; guest prof sculpture, Cornell Univ, summers 72 & 73; teacher constructions, painting & drawing, Baltimore Mus Art, 73-74; guest prof print workshop, Morgan State Univ, summer 77. *Awards:* Afro American Slide Depository for Afro Americans, Samuel Kress Found, 71; Fel Int Arts Sem, Fairleigh Dickinson Univ, 62. *Bibliog:* Barbara Gold (auth), Blackmarks, Black art, Sun Paper Art Sect, 6/75. *Mailing Add:* 1013 Woodbourne Ave Baltimore MD 21212

GILCHRIST, ELIZABETH BRENDA
EDITOR
b Coulsdon, Eng; US citizen. *Study:* Smith Col, BA(art hist); Art Students League. *Pos:* Asst, Durlacher Brothers Art Gallery, New York, 54-57; art admin asst, Brussels World's Fair, Belg & New York, 57-58; fund raiser, Mus Mod Art, New York, 59-62; reporter, Show Mag, New York, NY, 62-64; staff writer, Am Heritage Publ Co, 64; sr art ed, Praeger Publ, New York, 65-75; ed publ, Cooper-Hewitt Mus, Nat Mus of Design, Smithsonian Inst, New York, 76-81; mem adv coun for continuing educ prog, Mus Collaborative Inc, 77-78, publ consult, 81- *Mem:* Drawing Soc (mem bd dirs, 60-81, mem exec comt, currently); Soc Archit Historians; Col Art Asn; Am Asn Mus; Victorian Soc Am. *Publ:* Translr, Jacques Lassaigne's Marc Chagall: The Ceiling of the Paris Opera, 66; ed, American Art & Artists series, Praeger, 71-75; gen ed, The Smithsonian Illustrated Library of Antiques, Cooper-Hewitt Mus, 76-81. *Mailing Add:* 175 W 93rd St New York NY 10025

GILDEN, ANITA
LIBRARIAN
b Bronx, New York, June 30, 38. *Study:* State Univ NY, Buffalo, BA(art history), 74, MLS, 79. *Pos:* Asst Librn, Albright-Knox Art Gallery, Buffalo, NY 79-81; librn, Baltimore Mus Art, Md, 81-89; head librn, Philadelphia Mus Art, Pa, 89- *Mem:* Art Libr Soc NAm (secy 89-91). *Mailing Add:* Philadelphia Mus Art Libr PO Box 7646 Philadelphia PA 19101

GILDZEN, ALEX
WRITER, COLLECTOR
b Monterey, Calif, April 25, 43. *Study:* Wagner Col, with Kenneth Koch, 63; Kent State Univ, BA, 65, MA, 66. *Collections Arranged:* The Photographer's Art: An Exhibition of Prints and Books on Photography, 81; The Art of P Craig Russell, 92. *Pos:* Assoc cur, Spec Collections, Libr, Kent State Univ, 77-85, acting cur, Mus, 82-83, cur, Spec Collections, 85-; ed, Dress: J Costume Soc Am, 82-84. *Teaching:* Prof, Libr Admin, Kent State Univ, 85- *Awards:* Exhib Catalog Award, Comt Rare Bk Section, Ala. *Bibliog:* Roberta Berke (auth), Bounds Out of Bounds, Oxford Univ Press, 81. *Mem:* Costume Soc Am (region III pres, 82-83). *Res:* Film and theater history; modern sculpture. *Collection:* Contemporary sculpture, drawings, prints and photographs. *Publ:* Ed, Six Poems-Seven Prints, Kent State Univ Libr, 71; auth, Haber's shattered landscapes: Studies in nature and time, (exhib catalog), Kent State Univ, 77; Partially buried woodshed: A Robert Smithson log, 78 & Ira Joel Haber: Poolside reflections on coming out of the box, 82, Arts Mag; The Avalanche of Time: Selected poems 1964-1984, 86; Joseph Chaikin: A Bio-bibliography, 92; A Gathering of Poets, 92. *Mailing Add:* 1129 Morris Rd Kent OH 44240

GILES, NEWELL WALTON, JR
PAINTER
b Flushing, NY, June 20, 28. *Study:* Wesleyan Univ, BA(art hist); New York-Phoenix Sch Design; also studied watercolor with Herb Olsen, Westport, Conn. *Comn:* Watercolor renderings, Stanwich Presby Church, Greenwich, Conn, 69 & main lobby, Innis Arden Golf Club, Old Greenwich, Conn, 71; Pan Ocean Oil Corp, New York, 72; and var pvt comns. *Exhib:* Greenwich Art Soc Ann Show, Greenwich Libr, 66-70; Hudson Valley Art Asn Ann Show, White Plains, NY, 66-77; Am Watercolor Soc Ann Show, New York, 68; Hammond Mus Exhib Contemp Am Art, North Salem, NY, 68; Am Artists Prof League Regional Show, New York, 72-77. *Pos:* Art dir, J M Mathes Inc, New York, 55-63; art & prod dir, J J Lane Inc, Advert, New York, 63-78; sr art dir advert, Kohler Co, Riverside, Conn, 78- *Teaching:* Pvt instr watercolor, 70-71. *Awards:* Puck Award for Newspaper Advert, New York J-Am, 60; First Prize for Watercolors, Greenwich Art Soc, 68 & Old Greenwich Art Soc, 70, 72, 75 & 77. *Bibliog:* Article, La Rev Mod, 69. *Mem:* Assoc Am Watercolor Soc; Am Artists Prof League; Hudson Valley Art Asn; Greenwich Art Soc; Old Greenwich Art Soc. *Media:* Watercolor, Oil. *Mailing Add:* 26 Mimosa Dr Cos Cob CT 06807

GILHOOLY, DAVID JAMES, III
SCULPTOR
b Auburn, Calif, Apr 15, 43. *Study:* Univ Calif, Davis, BA, 65, MA, 67. *Work:* Whitney Mus; Philadelphia Mus Art, Pa; Bronfman Collection Can Art, Nat Gallery, Ottawa, Ont; Albright-Knox Art Gallery, Buffalo, NY; San Francisco Mus Mod Art; Whitney Mus Am Art; and others. *Comn:* Seattle's Own Ark, Woodland Park Zoo, Wash, 79; Breadwall, Govt Can Bldg, Calgary, Alta; and others. *Exhib:* Funk Show, Inst Contemp Art, Boston, 67; Realism '70, Montreal Mus Art & Art Gallery, Ont, 70; Whitney Mus Am Art, 70, 74, 71 & 82; Matrix Gallery, Wadsworth Atheneuem, Hartford, Conn, 76; Painting & Sculpture: the Mod Era, San Francisco Mus Art & Nat Collection Fine Art, Washington, DC, 77; Mus Contemp Craft, New York, 78; E B Crocker Art Mus, Sacramento, Calif, 81; Ceramic Sculpture: Six Artists, Whitney Mus Am Art, 81 & San Francisco Mus Mod Art, 82; Frederick Weissman Found Collection, Palm Springs Desert Art Mus, Calif, 84; Thirty Ceramic Sculptors, Natsoulas Gallery, Davie, Calif, 88; The Third Nat Ceramic Invitational, Canton Art Inst, Ohio, 89; var exhibs at major mus incl Whitney Mus, Los Angeles Co Mus Art, Philadelphia Mus Art & San Francisco Mus Art; and others. *Teaching:* Instr drawings & watercolor, San Jose State Col, 67-69; instr ceramics & sculpture, Univ Sask, Regina, 69-71; instr ceramic sculpture, York Univ, 71-75 & 76-77; instr ceramics & drawing, Univ Calif, Davis, 75-76. *Bibliog:* Charlotte Sprieght (auth), Hands in Clay, Alfred, 79; Charlotte Sprieght (auth), Images in Clay, Harper & Row, 83; T Albright (auth), Art in the San Francisco Bay Area, Univ Calif Press, 85; and others. *Mem:* Royal Can Acad. *Media:* Plastics, Clay. *Publ:* Contribr Gazette Beaux Arts, 1/78; Art Int, 1/78; Artscanada (cover), 79-80; Instructor (cover), 5/79; Images and Issues, Los Angeles, summer 81; and others. *Mailing Add:* c/o Smith Anderson Gallery 200 Homer Palo Alto CA 94301

GILKEY, GORDON WAVERLY
CURATOR, EDUCATOR
b Linn Co, Ore, Mar 10, 12. *Study:* Albany Col, BA, 33; Univ Ore, MFA, 36; Lewis & Clark Col, Hon DA, 57. *Work:* Metrop Mus Art, New York; Libr Cong, Washington, DC; Brit Mus, London; Bibliot Nat, Paris; San Francisco

Art Mus; plus others. *Comn:* Etchings, Univ Ore Libr Construct, 36; etchings, New York World's Fair, 1939; etchings, Charles Scribner's Sons, 38-39. *Exhib:* Northwest Printmakers Int, 50-72; Soc Am Graphic Artists, New York, 52-80; Expos Int Gravure, Ljubljana, Yugoslavia, 65-73; Biennale Int Gravure, Cracow, Poland, 68-70 & 74; Expos in Dessins Originaux, Rijeka, Yugoslavia. *Pos:* Head, US War Dept Spec Staff Art Proj, Europe, 46-47; dir, Int Exchange Print Exhibs, US Prints Exhibs, US Prints in Europe & Africa, 56 & 65; importer contemp prints, 56-65, 69-72 & 75; trustee & chmn art comt, Portland Art Mus, 61-67, cur prints & drawings, 78-88; chmn, Gov Planning Coun Arts & Humanities Ore, 65-67; emer & hon cur prints & drawings, Portland Art Mus, 88; spec asst pres, Portland Art Mus, 88- *Teaching:* Instr art & studio, Stephens Col, 39-42; prof art hist & studio & head dept, Ore State Univ, 47-64, dean, Sch Humanities & Social Sci, 63-73, Col Liberal Arts, 73-77; prof, Pacific Northwest Col Art, 78- *Awards:* Off Order Palms Acad, Repub France, 69; King Carl XVI Gustaf's Gold Medal Art, Sweden, 77; Chevalier, Nat Order Legion Hon, France, 78. *Mem:* Soc Am Graphic Artists; Col Art Asn Am; Calif Soc Printmakers; Print Coun Am. *Media:* Printmaker. *Res:* History of printmaking. *Collection:* Historical and contemporary prints. *Publ:* Auth, Etching Showing Construction Progress of the University of Oregon Library, 36; Etchings: New York World's Fair, 39; numerous articles on printmaking. *Mailing Add:* Oregon Art Inst 1219 SW Park Ave Portland OR 97205

GILKEY, RICHARD CHARLES
PAINTER, SCULPTOR
b Bellingham, Wash, Dec 20, 25. *Study:* Self-taught with guidance of Mark Tobey, Morris Graves & Guy Anderson. *Work:* Seattle Art Mus; Whatcom Mus Hist & Art, Bellingham, Wash; Port Seattle; Skagit Co Admin Bldg, Mt Vernon, Wash; Bellevue Art Mus, Wash; Osaka Found Cult, Osaka, Japan. *Comn:* Oil paintings, Western Wash Univ, 70, Peoples Nat Bank, Seattle, 74, Williams, Lanza, Kastner & Gibbs, Seattle, 76 & Pay N Save Corp, Seattle, 78; Northwest Hosp, Seattle, Wash, 86. *Exhib:* Grantee Exhib, Acad Art Gallery, New York, 58; solo exhibs, Seattle Art Mus, 60 & Bellevue Art Mus, Wash, 80; Artists West of the Mississippi, Seattle Art Mus Pavillion, 63; Exhibition of American Painters, Kobe Mus, Japan, 66; Washington Artists, Expo 70, Osaka, Japan, 70; Northwest Traditions, Seattle Art Mus, 79; Pacific Northwest Artists and Japan, Nat Mus Art, Osaka, Japan, 82; Seattle Art Mus, 83. *Awards:* Purchase Prize, Bellevue Art Mus, Bellevue, Wash, 87; Grand Prize, Osaka Trienovale, Japan, 90; Gov Award, Wash State Art Comn, 90. *Bibliog:* Paul V Thomas (auth), Richard Gilkey artist, Seattle Times, 63; Robert C Arnold (auth), Traveling through Richard Gilkey's landscape, Argus, 78; John S Robinson (auth), Richard Gilkey's darker vision, Seattle Weekly, 89. *Media:* Oil; Stone. *Mailing Add:* 2278 Mann Rd Mt Vernon WA 98273

GILL, GENE
PAINTER, PRINTMAKER
b Memphis, Tenn, June 18, 33. *Study:* Memphis State Univ; Chicago Art Inst, Ill; Chouinard Art Inst, Los Angeles, BFA. *Work:* Los Angeles Co Mus, Los Angeles; Palm Springs Desert Mus, Calif; Atlantic Richfield Corp, Los Angeles; Home Savings, Los Angeles; Northrop Corp, Los Angeles. *Exhib:* All Calif Print Exhibs, Los Angeles, 69-71; 9th Ann Southern Calif Exhib, Long Beach Mus Art, 71; Laguna Beach Art Mus Exhib Ten, Calif, 71; Dimensional Prints, Los Angeles Co Mus Art, 73; Laguna Beach Art Mus, 77; Los Angeles Printmakers 1960-1980, Los Angeles Co Mus Art, 81; one-man shows, Comara Gallery, 70-71 & 74. *Awards:* Purchase Award, Home Savings, 69; Purchase Award, Westside Jewish Community Ctr, 70; Jurors Award, Laguna Beach Art Mus, 70. *Bibliog:* Gatto, Porter & Selleck (auths), Exploring Visual Design, 78; George Magnan (auth), Today's Art, 79; Gerald F Brommer (auth), Discovering Art History, 81. *Media:* Acrylic, Oil; Serigraphy, Silkscreen. *Mailing Add:* 2430 Cascadia Dr Glendale CA 91206

GILLEN, JOHN
SCULPTOR
b Uniontown, Pa, 1947. *Study:* Univ Calif, Los Angeles, 64-68, BA, Univ Calif, Berkeley, 72-74, MA. *Exhib:* One-man exhibs, Davis Art Ctr, Calif, 72, The Clocktower, New York, 80, Wall Constructions, Paul Klein Gallery, Chicago, 87, Wall Sculptures, Laurie Rubin Gallery, New York, 87, New Work, Burnett Miller Gallery, Los Angeles, 88 & Concept Gallery, Pittsburgh, Pa, 92; Los Angeles Munic Art Gallery, 84; Abstraction: Painting & Sculpture, Angles Gallery, Santa Monica, Calif, 86; Selections from the Berkus Collection, Long Beach Mus Art, Calif, 88; and many others. *Teaching:* Asst prof studio arts, Univ Pittsburgh, 88- *Awards:* Eisner Prize for Creative Achievement in the Arts, Univ Calif, Berkeley, 74; Creative Artists Pub Serv Grant, NY State Coun Arts, 78; Artists Fel, Nat Endowment Arts, 80, 84 & 86; Artists Spaces, Nat Endowment Arts, 80-81. *Bibliog:* Peter Frank (auth), Art, Village Voice, 5/78; Tiffany Bell (auth), John Gillen, Arts Mag, 9/78; Joan Quinn (auth), L A, Art & Auction, 11/86; Deborah Gimelson, It's all relative, Art & Auction, 3/87. *Dealer:* Concept Art Gallery Pittsburgh PA. *Mailing Add:* c/o Studio Arts Dept Univ Pittsburgh Frick Fine Arts Bldg Pittsburgh PA 15260

GILLESPIE, DOROTHY MURIEL
PAINTER, SCULPTOR
b Roanoke, Va, June 29, 20. *Study:* Md Inst Col Art, Baltimore; Art Students League; Atelier 17, New York, with Stanley William Hayter; Caldwell Col, NJ, Hon DFA, 76; Niagara Univ, NY, Hon Doctor Pedagogy, 90. *Work:* Guggenheim Mus & NY Univ; Mus Art, Ft Lauderdale, Fla; Birmingham Mus Art; NC Mus Art, Raleigh; Newark Mus Art; Fort Wayne Mus Art; Lafayette Mus, Ind; Brooklyn Mus; Castellani Mus, Buffalo, NY; Virginia Mus Fine Arts, Richmond; Yale Univ Art Gallery, Conn. *Comn:* City Wall, City Walls Inc, New York, 75; Venetian Gardens (frieze), Housing & Urban Develop Proj, North Miami, Fla, 79; fountain sculpture, US Mission to UN, New York, 81; sculptural wall environment, Univ Ark Conf Ctr, Little Rock, 83; Summerscape (sculptural set), Cleveland Ballet, 83; posters, Lincoln Ctr/List Art Posters, New York, 84 & 89; Ft Lauderdale Airport, Fla, 89; USA Culinary Team (sculptural centerpiece), 90. *Exhib:* Solo exhibs, Del Art Mus, Wilmington, 83, Mus Art, Ft Lauderdale, Fla, 83, Wash Co Mus, Hagerstown, Md, 83 & Squibb World Hq, Princeton, NJ, 83; Huntsville Mus, Ala, 85; Asn Am Artists, New York, 86; Alcan, Artluminum, Montreal, 89. *Collections Arranged:* Women Artists Paint Women Artists, Virginia Miller Gallery, 78; Artist Choice, Clayworks Gallery, New York, 79; PCA: Invites, Philadelphia Col Art, 83; traveling show, Art in Fashion/Fashion in Art, 87-89; Fordham Univ at Lincoln Ctr, New York, 90. *Pos:* Co-coordr, Women's Interart Ctr, 73-76; dir, Art & Community Inst, New Sch Social Res, New York, 77-83; vis artist, Radford Univ, VA, 81-83; vis fel, Woodrow Wilson, 86-92. *Teaching:* Instr, Human Relations Ctr, New Sch Social Res, 72-83. *Awards:* Gov Ark Travelers Award, 83; Distinguished Alumni Award, Md Inst Art, 83; Allied Professions Award, Va Soc, Richmond, 86; Women of Distinction Award, Birmingham-Southern Col, Ala, 87; Grant Award, Alice Baber Art Fund, 90. *Bibliog:* David L Shirey (auth), article, 1/13/83 & Phyllis Braff (auth), Spirit of dance captured, 3/13/83, New York Times. *Mem:* Col Art Asn; Southeastern Conf Art Cols. *Media:* Painted Sculpture. *Publ:* Contribr, Professionalism & the woman artist, Womens Studies & Arts, 79 & Feminist Collage, 79; contribr, Overcoming barriers: The woman artist in the South, Southern Quart, 79. *Dealer:* Associated American Artists 20 W 57th St New York NY 10019. *Mailing Add:* 549 West 52nd St New York NY 10019

GILLESPIE, GREGORY JOSEPH
PAINTER
b Roselle Park, NJ, Nov 29, 36. *Study:* Cooper Union Art Sch; San Francisco Art Inst, MFA. *Work:* Whitney Mus Am Art & Metrop Mus Art, New York; NJ State Mus, Trenton; Hirshhorn Collection; Nat Mus Am Art, Wash, DC; Va Mus Fine Arts, Richmond; and many others. *Exhib:* Ann, 66, 68 & 72 & Biennial, 73, Whitney Mus Am Art; Smith Col Mus Art, 71; Univ Ga, 71 & 78; Nat Acad Design, 72; Forum Gallery, New York, 75; Retrospective Exhib, Hirshhorn Mus, Washington, DC & Ga Mus Art, Univ Ga, Athens, 78; Univ Bridgeport, 80; Fitchburg Art Mus, Mass, 89; San Diego Mus Contemp Art, La Jolla, Calif, 91; Ways to See, Inst Contemp Art, Boston, 92; solo exhib, Forum Gallery, New York, 76, 77, 79, 82, 84, 86 & 89, Duke Univ Art Mus, Durham, NC, 86, J Rosenthal Fine Arts, Chicago, 88, Cooper Union, New York, 89, Nielsen Gallery, Boston, 90 & 92, Forum Gallery, 91 & 92 & Harcourts Mod & Contemp, San Francisco, 92. *Awards:* Am Acad Rome Award, 65-68; Fulbright Fel, 67; Nat Inst Arts & Lett Award, 69. *Bibliog:* Gregory Gillespie (paintings Italy, 1962-70), Forum Gallery, 71. *Mem:* Nat Acad Design. *Media:* Oil, Acrylic. *Mailing Add:* c/o Forum Gallery 1018 Madison Ave New York NY 10021

GILLIAM, SAM
PAINTER
b Tupelo, Miss, 1933. *Study:* Univ Louisville, Ky, BA, 52-55, MA, 58-61, LHD, 80; Northwestern Univ, LHD, 90. *Work:* Mus African Art, Phillips Collection, Nat Collection Fine Arts, Corcoran Gallery Art & Howard Univ, Washington, DC; Mus Mod Art & Metrop Mus Art, New York; Carnegie Inst, Pittsburgh, Pa; Walker Art Ctr, Minneapolis, Minn; Art Inst Chicago, Ill; Princeton Univ, Rutgers Univ, New Brunswick, NJ; Madison Art Ctr, Wis; Baltimore Mus Art, Md. *Comn:* Union Labor Life Ins Co, Washington, DC, 85; Washington Convention Ctr, Washington, DC, 85; A New River Rising, Broward Co Govt Ctr, Ft Lauderdale, Fla, 87; Solar Canopy, York Col, Queens, NY, 88; CAAM Hues, Calif Afro-Am Mus, Los Angeles, 89. *Exhib:* Art Ctr Annual, J B Speed Mus, Louisville, Ky, 61; Tribute to Martin Luther King, 68, Works on Paper, 70, Cut- Bend-Spindle-Fold, 74 & Handmade Paper, 76, Mus Mod Art, New York; Ann Exhib of Contemp Am Painting, Whitney Mus Am Art, New York, 69; Gilliam-Krebs-McGowan, 69, 34th Biennial of Contemp Am Painting, 75 & 10 plus 10 plus 10, 82, Corcoran Gallery Art, Washington, DC; 69th Am Exhib (with catalog), 70 & 72nd Am Exhib (with catalog), 76, Art Inst Chicago; Works for New Spaces (with catalog), Walker Arts Ctr, Minneapolis, 71; Kid Stuff? (with catalog), Albright-Knox Art Gallery, Buffalo, NY, 71; Works for Spaces: Antonakos, Bladen, Gilliam, Irwin & Rockburne (with catalog), San Francisco Mus Art, 73; 30 Years of American Printmaking (with catalog), Brooklyn Mus, 76; Arts on the Line: Art for Public Transit Spaces, Hayden Gallery, MIT, Cambridge, Mass, 80; Am Abstraction Now, 82 & Painting in the South, 84, Va Mus Fine Art, Richmond; solo exhibs, Davis/McClain Gallery, Houston, Tex, 86, Alice Simsar Gallery, Ann Arbor, Mich, 86, G H Dalsheimer Gallery, Baltimore, Md, 86, Carl Solway Gallery, Cincinnati, Ohio, 87, Klein Gallery, Chicago, 87 & 88, Robert Kidd Gallery, Birmingham, Mich, 87 & Iannetti-Lanzone Gallery, San Francisco, 88, Frederick Gallery, New York, 91, Gallery Simone Stern, New Orleans, 91 & Smith Andersen Gallery, Palo Alto, Calif, 92; The Experienced Eye, Ownesboro Mus Fine Art, Ky, 88; Looking South: A Different Dixie, Birmingham Mus Art, Ala, 88; African Am Art From the Collection, Philadelphia Mus Art, Pa, 90. *Teaching:* Instr, art, Pub Sch System, Washington, DC, 58-67; Corcoan Sch Art, Washington, DC, 64-67; Md Art Inst, Baltimore, 67-82; prof painting, Univ Md, 82-85; prof art, Carnegie Mellon Univ, 85-89. *Awards:* Individual Artist Grants, 67 & 89, Workshop Activities Grant, 73-75, Nat Endowment Arts; President's Award, Md Col Art & Design, 87; Order of Merit Award, Univ Louisville Alumni Asn, 87. *Bibliog:* John Beardsley (auth), Modern Painters at the Corcoran: Sam Gilliam, Corcoran Gallery Art, 83; Gerrit Henry (auth), A Metaphor for Human Being: New Paintings by Sam Gilliam, Arts Mag, 2/85; Jane Addams Allen (auth), Letting Go, Art in Am, 1/86. *Mem:* Washington Proj Arts (bd dirs, 80-85); Col Art Asn (art comt, bd dir, 85-88); Anacostia Community Orgn (pub art work comt, adv bd, 87-88). *Mailing Add:* 1752 Lamont NW Washington DC 20010

GILLING, LUCILLE
PRINTMAKER
b Hamilton, Mo. *Study:* Kansas City Art Inst; New York Sch Fine & Appl Arts in Paris, France, Eng & Italy, dipl; Queens Univ. *Work:* Nat Libr Can, Ottawa; Montreal Mus Fine Art; Victoria & Albert Mus, London, Eng; Ohio State Univ; Wayne State Univ. *Exhib:* Soc Can Painters, Etchers & Engravers, Toronto, Ont, 56-; one-man shows, Pascall Gallery, Toronto, 66, Sobot Gallery, Toronto, 69 & Marjorie Kauffmann Graphics, 72; Can Fine Art Gallery, Toronto, 74; plus others. *Awards:* Sterling Trust Award, 59; Anaconda Award of Merit, 68. *Mem:* Toronto Heliconian Club (exec coun, 71-75). *Media:* Etching. *Publ:* Portfolios of etchings, The Canterbury Tales, 66 & Don Quixote, 69, original signed etchings Ed 100. *Dealer:* Campbell Tomi Gallery 210 Gerrard St E Toronto Ont Can. *Mailing Add:* 602 Melita Cres Apt 723 Toronto ON M6G 3Z2 Canada

GILLINGWATER, DENIS CLAUDE
SCULPTOR, EDUCATOR
b Glendale, Calif, Feb 15, 46. *Study:* Univ Cincinnati, BFA, 68, MFA, 70. *Exhib:* Eighth West Biennial, Western Colo Ctr Arts, 74; Southwest & Rocky Mountain States Exhib, Scottsdale Fine Arts Comn, 75; solo exhib, Scottsdale Ctr Arts, 78; Ariz Sculpture, Northern Ariz Univ Art Gallery, Flagstaff, 80 & 81; Four Corners State Biannual, Phoenix Art Mus, 81; and others. *Teaching:* Asst prof intermedia, Ariz State Univ, 73-78, assoc prof, 78- *Awards:* Nat Endowment Arts Artist-in-Residence, Mesa, Ariz, 73; Acquisitions, Phoenix Art Mus, 77 & Scottsdale Ctr Arts, 75; and others. *Mailing Add:* Dept Art Ariz State Univ Tempe AZ 85287

GILLMAN, BARBARA SEITLIN
DEALER
b Miami, Fla, Jan 14, 37. *Study:* H Sophie Newcomb Col, 55; Univ Miami, with Dr Virgil Barker, BA(Am art), 58. *Collections Arranged:* Israel 25, contemp Israeli art (auth, catalog), Bacardi Bldg, City of Miami, 79. *Pos:* Panelist, State Fla Grant Panel. *Specialty:* Contemporary original art, paintings and sculpture; Regional artists. *Mailing Add:* c/o Barbara Gillman Gallery 270 NE 39th St Miami FL 33137

GILMARTIN, F THOMAS
PAINTER, ADMINISTRATOR
b Palmer, Mass, Aug 6, 40. *Study:* Worcester Art Mus Sch, grad; Goddard Col, BA; Penland Sch Crafts, NC; AGFA Tecknikum, Munich, WGer. *Exhib:* Appalachian Crafts/Thirteen States, traveling exhib, 79. *Pos:* Dir, Arts & Crafts Ctr, Ft Knox, Ky, 63-65; prog supvr, Arts & Crafts Ctr, Ft Eustis, Va, 68-70; civilian supvr, US Army Artist Team, Thailand, 70-71; dir, Asheville Art Mus, NC, 73-77; dir, Ga Coun Arts & Humanities Crafts Prog, 77-79; co-owner, Abtin Ltd, 79- *Teaching:* Instr exhib design & printmaking, Asheville Art Mus, NC, 73-77. *Res:* Researched and authored, Contemporary Art History of the Eastern Cherokee Indians. *Mailing Add:* 12 Winthrop St Palmer MA 01069

GILMOR, JANE E
SCULPTOR, EDUCATOR
b Ames, Iowa, June 23, 47. *Study:* Iowa State Univ, Ames, BS(textiles), 69; Univ Iowa, Iowa City, MA(paint), 76 & MFA(painting), 77. *Work:* Hoover State Office Bldg, Des Moines, Iowa; Sioux City Art Mus, Iowa; Mus Contemp Crafts Libr, New York; Augustana Col, Rock Island, Ill; Ragsdale Found, Lake Forest, Ill; and others. *Comn:* Davenport Mus Art. *Exhib:* 27th-36th Ann Iowa Artists, Des Moines Art Ctr, 75-90; La Grange Nat VII & VIII, Atlanta, 82-83; TFAA Nat, Austin, Tex, 82-83; NAME Gallery, Chicago, 84; Bernice Steinbaum Gallery, New York , 86; Minn Mus Art, Minneapolis, 86; Nat Sculpture Exhib, Cincinnati, 88; Artemesia, Chicago, 89; AIR Gallery, New York, 89, 90 & 92. *Teaching:* Prof art painting & drawing, Mount Mercy Col Cedar Rapids, Iowa, 74-; guest artist-lectr, Univ Iowa, Iowa City, 81-89; guest artist, Columbia Col, Mo, 83; Univ Ga, Cortona, Italy program, 87. *Awards:* Sculpture Award, Des Moines Art Ctr Ann, 90; Va Ctr Arts Fel, 92; Tyrone Guthrie Ctr Fel, Newbless, Ireland, 92. *Bibliog:* Lucy Lippard (auth), Overlay: Contemporary Artists and the Art of Prehistory, Pantheon Books, 83; David McWacken (auth), rev, Chicago Tribune, 10/20/89; A Williams (auth), Sculpture Technique Form Content, pg 50, Davis Pub, 90; Gloria Orenstein (auth), The Reflowering of The Goddess, Perganon, 90. *Media:* All Media. *Mailing Add:* Art Dept Mt Mercy Col Cedar Rapids IA 52402

GILMORE, ROGER
ADMINISTRATOR, CONSULTANT
b Philadelphia, Pa, Oct 11, 32. *Study:* Dartmouth Col, AB; Univ Chicago Divinity Sch, grad study. *Pos:* Dean, Sch Art Inst Chicago, 65-87, provost, 87-89; pres, Ox Bow Summer Sch Art, 87-89; pres, Portland Sch Art, Maine, 89. *Mem:* Soc Archit Historians; Nat Art Educ Asn; Col Art Asn; Nat Trust Hist Preserv; fel & life mem Nat Asn Schs Art & Design (pres, 87-). *Publ:* Ed, Over a Century: A History of the School of the Art Inst of Chicago, 82. *Mailing Add:* 145 Greely Rd Cumberland Center ME 04021-9303

GILPIN, HENRY EDMUND
PHOTOGRAPHER, INSTRUCTOR
b Cleveland, Ohio, Nov 10, 22. *Study:* Los Angeles City Col, 46-48; Univ Calif, Los Angeles, 49-50; Cleveland Inst Art, 51; Ansel Adams Yosemite Workshop, 59. *Work:* Monterey Peninsula Mus Art, Calif; Amon Carter Mus, Ft Worth, Tex; Utah State Univ Gallery, Logan; Currier Gallery, Manchester, NH; State Univ Calif, Long Beach; The Nat Mus Mod Art, Kyoto, Japan. *Exhib:* Friends of Photog, Carmel, Calif, 72; Rockford Art Asn, Ill, 72; Sam Houston State Univ, 74; Art & Sci Mus, Nashua, NH, 78; Photo Gallery Int, Tokyo, Japan, 81; Expo 90, Osaka, Japan. *Teaching:* Instr photog, Monterey Peninsula Col, 64-, Ansel Adams Yosemite Workshop, 67-73 & 81-82 & Friends of Photog, Carmel, 69-86; Univ Calif, Santa Cruz, 86- *Mem:* Friends of Photog (trustee, 69-79); Photog Ctr of Monterey Peninsula (trustee, 88-). *Dealer:* Susan Spiritis Gallery 522 Old Newport Blvd Newport Beach CA 92663; Josephus Daniels Gallery Su Vencino Ct Delores near 6th Carmel CA 93921. *Mailing Add:* 1353 Jacks Rd Monterey CA 93940

GILSON, GILES
SCULPTOR, DESIGNER
b Philadelphia, Pa, July 19, 42. *Study:* Self-taught. *Work:* Metrop Mus Art, New York; Wood Turning Ctr, Philadelphia, Pa; Schenectady Mus, NY; Ariz State Univ, Mus Art, Tempe; The Cousins Collection, Atlanta, Ga. *Comn:* Wall sculpture, Lewis Collection, Richmond, Va, 81 & 82; Story Piece, Lipton Collection, Los Angeles, 84; Library Table, Hunter-Stieble Collection, New York, 86. *Exhib:* 20th Century Decorative Arts, Metrop Mus Art, New York, 81; Turned Objects, Greenville Co Mus Art, SC, 82; Art of Woodturning, Am Craft Mus, New York, 83; Nat Wood Invitational, Craft Alliance, St Louis, Mo, 83; Polished Perfection, The Renwick, Washington, DC, 86; Int Turned Object Show, Port of Hist Mus, Pa, 88. *Pos:* Consult artist & technician, Creative Advantage, Schenectady, NY, 78-; consult artist, Gen Elec Co, Schenectady, NY, 82; tech consult, Steinberger Sound, Newburgh, NY, 85. *Teaching:* Instr, State Univ NY, New Paltz, 84-87. *Awards:* Spec Award, NAm Turned Object Show, 81; Best Dimensional Display, Upstate NY Ad Club, 85; Artist-in-Residency, Mid-Atlantic Found Arts, 88. *Bibliog:* Dale Nish (auth), Artistic Woodturning, Brigham Young Univ Press, 80; Donna Meilach (auth), Woodworking: The New Wave, Crown, 81; Edward Jacobson (auth), The Art of the Turned Wood Bowl, E P Dutton, 85; articles in Crafts UK, Fine Woodworking Mag, Holzaelgenbien- Germany, & American Craft; Design Book II, Taunton Press; Albert Locolf (auth), A Gallery of Turned Objects; Lathe Turned Objects, Wood Turning Ctr. *Mem:* Am Craft Coun; Am Asn Woodturners. *Media:* Wood, Metal. *Publ:* Auth, Working with designers, Craft Report, 79; Making machinery, Fine Woodworking, 80; Router rail, Techniques 4, Taubton Press, 82; Polychromatic turning, Turning Points, 88; introd, Works of the Lathe: Old and New Faces, 88. *Mailing Add:* 766 Albany Schenectady NY 12307

GIMBLETT, MAX(WELL)
PAINTER, CERAMIST
b Auckland, NZ, Dec 5, 35; US & NZ citizen. *Study:* Ont Col Art, Toronto, 64; San Francisco Art Inst, 65. *Work:* Marion Koogler McNay Art Inst, San Antonio, Laguna Gloria Art Mus, Austin; San Francisco Mus Mod Art, Achenbach Found, San Francisco; Pa Acad Fine Arts, Philadelphia; Prudential Insurance Co of Am, Newark, NJ; Power Gallery of Contemp Art, Sydney, Australia, Art Gallery New South Wales, Univ New South Wales; Kunsthall Malmo, Malmo, Sweden, 85; Gallery of Queensland, Brisbane, Australia; Nat Art Gallery, NZ. *Comn:* ceramic sculpture, Auckland Art Gallery, NZ. *Exhib:* Modernism Gallery, San Francisco, 80, 83 & 85; Genovese Gallery, Boston, Mass, 87 & 89; Color-Four Painters, Oscarsson Hood Gallery, New York & Galerie Nordenhake, Malmo, Sweden, 82; Seven Painters/The Eighties, Auckland City Art Gallery, NZ, 83; Auckland City Art Gallery, NZ, 84; Artis Gallery, Auckland, New Zealand, 86, 88, 89 & 90; White Columns New York, NY, 88; R C Erpf Gallery, New York, 85, 86. *Teaching:* Vis artist printmaking, Ind Univ, Bloomington, 79; vis assoc prof, Pratt Inst, Brooklyn, 79-89; vis lectr, Univ Canterbury, Christchurch, NZ, 81; vis assoc prof, Int Honors Program in Japan, India & Kenya; vis artist, City Art Inst, Sydney, Australia, 86. *Awards:* Grant, Queen Elizabeth II Arts Coun NZ, 80, 86; Painting Fel, Nat Endowment Arts, Washington, DC, 89. *Bibliog:* Stephen Henry Madoff (auth), Science & Attention Max Ginblett's Island, Art Mag, 84; Stephen Westfall (auth), Max Gimblett at R C Erdf, Art in Am, 85; Vivien Raynor (auth), article, New York Times, 86. *Mem:* Asia Soc; Japan Soc; Nat Art Gallery. *Media:* Oil, Acrylic Polymer. *Publ:* Contribr, In the presence, Art NZ, 80; Max Gimblett and Wystan Curnow, Modernism, San Francisco, 82; Spirit Tracks, Pratt Manhattan Gallery, NY, 86; Sightings & Drawing with Color, Pratt Inst & Instituto de Estudios Norte Americanos, 88; Wystan Curnow, Objects of Alchemy, Artis Gallery, Auckland, NZ, 90. *Dealer:* Genouese Gallery 535 Albany St Boston MA 02118; Artis Gallery 280 Parnell Rd Auckland NZ. *Mailing Add:* 231 Bowery New York NY 10002

GINNEVER, CHARLES
SCULPTOR
b San Mateo, Calif, Aug 28, 31. *Study:* With Zadkine & Hayter, Europe, 53-55; Calif Sch Fine Arts, San Francisco, BFA, 57; Cornell Univ, MFA, 59. *Work:* Wadsworth Atheneum, Hartford, Conn; Hirshhorn Mus, DC; Storm King Art Ctr, Mountainville, NY; Univ Mich, Ann Arbor; State Univ NY, Albany; Walker Art Ctr, Minn; Metrop Mus Art, New York. *Exhib:* One-man shows, Dag Hammarskjold Plaza Sculpture Garden, New York, 73, Max Hutchinson Gallery, 78-79 & 86, Long Beach Mus Art, 78, Construct, Chicago, 79 & 81, Storm King Art Ctr, 80, Marlborough Gallery, New York, 83, Fuller-Goldeen Gallery, San Francisco, 84 & 86, & Dorothy Goldeen Gallery, Santa Monica, 87 & 90; Am Acad & Inst Arts & Lett, New York, 85; Anchorage Mus Hist & Art, Alaska, 87; Seattle Art Mus, Wash, 87; Palo Alto Cult Ctr, Calif, 88; Gerald Peters Gallery, Santa Fe, NMex, 90-91; and others. *Teaching:* Instr, Cornell Univ, 57-59, Pratt Inst, 63, New Sch Soc Res, 64, Brooklyn Mus Sch, 64-65, Newark Sch Fine & Indust Art, 65, Dayton Art Inst, 66, Aspen Sch Contemp Art, Colo, 66, Orange Co Community Col, NJ, 66 & Windham Col, 67-75; vis artist, Univ Calif, Berkeley, spring semester, 89. *Awards:* Guggenheim Fel, 74; Nat Endowment Arts Grant, 75; Hewlett-Packard Corp, Calif, 85. *Media:* Steel. *Mailing Add:* PO Box 411 Putney VT 05346

GINSBURG, ESTELLE
PAINTER, SCULPTOR
b St Louis, Mo, Mar 27, 24. *Study:* Univ Mo; Brooklyn Mus Art Sch; Cornell Univ. *Work:* C W Post Col, NY; Univ Mass, Amherst; pvt collections in Europe, SAm & US. *Exhib:* Ball State Univ, Muncie, Ind, 73; solo exhibs, Cent Hall Gallery, New York, 75, 77-79, Fine Arts Mus Nassau Co, NY, 77 & Royal Acad, Stockholm, Sweden, 79; Invitational, York Col, Pa, 77; Brentano Gallery, New York, 79, 81 & 82. *Pos:* Art lectr mus collections, North Shore Community Arts Ctr, New York, NY, 70-73; Instr, Five Towns Music & Art Found, New York, 73-83, Nassau Off Cult Develop, 74-77 & Art Resources Ltd, New York, 79-80. *Awards:* Mixed Media Award, Heckscher Mus, NY, 72; Sculpture Award, North Shore Art Exhib, 74; Painting Award, Port Washington Libr, 75. *Bibliog:* Malcum Preston (auth), rev, Newsday, NY, 76-79; Jeanne Paris (auth), rev, Long Island Press, 77 & 78; articles, New York Times, 79, 86 & 87. *Mem:* Cent Hall Artists, NY; Prof Artists Asn NY (mem chmn, 74-76). *Media:* Wood, Paint; Mixed Media, Silkscreen,. *Publ:* J Digby (auth), Collage Handbook, Thames & Hudson. *Mailing Add:* 370 Longacre Ave Woodmere NY 11598

GINSBURG, MAX
PAINTER, ILLUSTRATOR
b Paris, France, Aug 7, 31. *Study:* Syracuse Univ, BFA; Nat Acad Design; City Col New York, MA. *Work:* New York Cult Ctr; Martin Luther King Labor Ctr. *Exhib:* Allied Artists Am, 56-72; Am Vet Soc Artists, 61-72; Audubon Artists, 62-72; Harbor Gallery, Cold Spring Harbor, 66, 68, 69, 71 & 72; Reyn Gallery, 80; Grand Central Gallery, 80-81; Soc Illurs, 79-83 & 85. *Teaching:* Instr painting & illus, Sch Visual Arts, New York, currently. *Awards:* Prize, 61 & Gold Medal, 62 & 65, Am Vet Soc Artists; Allied Artists Am, 61 & 72; Nat Art Club, 63; Gold Medal, Soc Illusrs, 83. *Mem:* Allied Artists Am; Audubon Artists; Am Vet Soc Artists; Artists Equity Asn; Soc Illusrs. *Media:* Oil. *Mailing Add:* Sch Visual Arts 209 E 23rd St New York NY 10010

GINZBURG, YANKEL (JACOB)
PAINTER, SCULPTOR
b Alma-Ata, USSR, Mar 23, 45; US citizen. *Study:* Inst Art Israel, dipl, 61. *Work:* Israel Mus, Jerusalem; Hirshhorn Mus; Bat-Yam Mus, Israel; Skirball Mus, Los Angeles; Tel Aviv Mus, Israel. *Comn:* A Hope Fulfilled is a Source of Life (mural), comn by B'nai B'rith, Jerusalem, 73; Freedom Road (tapestry), comn by Janus; Hands & Hearts (monumental mural), Washington, DC, 79; Bicentennial Poster, comn by Pres Reagan, Air & Space Mus, Washington, DC, 83; comn to design 3 graphics commemorating the Bicentennial of the Constitution, 85; Invisible Hands (monumental sculpture), Tampa, Fla, 86. *Exhib:* One-man shows, Washington Gallery Art, 69, Martin Lawrence Galleries, Los Angeles, Calif, 79, 82 & 83, Arthur Charles Galleries, Washington, DC, 82 & 83, Hallowell Gallery, Philadelphia, 83, Dyansen Gallery, San Francisco, Carmel, Beverly Hills & San Diego, Calif, New Orleans, La, New York, Boston, Tokyo, Japan, 89, Bronte Contemp Arts, Boston, 92 & many others; Janus Gallery, Washington, DC, 74 & 77; Int Art Fair, Cologne, Ger, 75; Int Art Show, Dusseldorf, Ger, 76; Guildhall Galleries, Chicago, Ill, 77; Mod Masters of Israel Show, Philadelphia Mus Art Civic Ctr, 78; Works on Paper, Skiball Mus, Los Angeles, Calif, 78; Washington Light Show, Washington, DC, 80; Gallery Hawaii, 80; Gallery Virgin Islands, St Thomas, 80. *Awards:* Silver Medal, Rome Biennale, 62; First Prize, Bat-Yam Mus Art Competition, Israel, 65; First Israeli artists to exhib in Cairo, Egypt as guest of Anwar Sadat, 79 & invited by Soviet Union to exhib in Moscow, 90; Humanitarian Award First Class, hon by Pres Yeltsin & Supreme Soviet of the Russian Fedn, 92. *Bibliog:* Eli Nisan (producer), The Art of Yankel Ginzburg (film), 79; The Art of Yankel Ginzburg, Alef Editions, 85; Ginzburg: The Russian Collection, Russian Academy of the Arts, 92. *Media:* Acrylic, Serigraph. *Publ:* Art book, Soc of Art Collectors, 75; Treasures of the Sea, 79. *Mailing Add:* 5810 Connecticut Ave Chevy Chase MD 20815

GINZEL, ANDREW See Jones & Ginzel,

GINZEL, ROLAND
PAINTER, PRINTMAKER
b Lincoln, Ill, 1921. *Study:* Art Inst Chicago, BFA; State Univ Iowa, MFA; Slade Sch, London. *Work:* Univ Southern Calif; Univ Mich; Ill Bell Tel Co; Art Inst Chicago; US Embassy, Warsaw, Poland; and others. *Exhib:* Art Inst Chicago, 69; Madison, Wis, 69; Notre Dame Univ, 69; one-man show, Phyllis Kind Gallery, 69; Whitney Mus Am Art Biennial, New York, 75. *Teaching:* Prof printmaking, Univ Chicago, 57-58; prof prints & painting, Univ Ill, Chicago Circle, 58-69; instr painting, Univ Wis, 60; instr art, Saugatuck Summer Sch, 61-62. *Awards:* Print & Drawing Prize, 67 & Campana Prize, 69, Art Inst Chicago; Fulbright Fel to Rome, 62. *Mailing Add:* PO Box 1045 Stockbridge MA 01262-1045

GIOBBI, EDWARD GIOACHINO
PAINTER, SCULPTOR
b Waterbury, Conn, July 18, 26. *Work:* Boston Mus Fine Arts; Whitney Mus Am Art, New York; Hirshhorn Mus; Art Inst Chicago; Albright-Knox Gallery. *Exhib:* One-man exhibs, Neuberger Mus, 77 & Gruenebaum Gallery, New York, 78 & 79; Young America, Whitney Mus Am Art, 60; Recent Figure USA, Mus Mod Art, New York, 60; 40 Painters under 40, Whitney Mus Am Art, 62; and others. *Teaching:* Artist-in-residence, Memphis Acad, Tenn, 59-60 & Dartmouth Col, 72. *Awards:* Emily Lowe Award, 49; Ford Found Artist-in-Residence Prog, 66; Guggenheim Fel, 72. *Media:* Oil; Mixed. *Mailing Add:* c/o Irving Galleries 332 Worth Ave Palm Beach FL 33480

GIOELLO, DEBBIE
PAINTER, DESIGNER
b Jan 1, 35. *Study:* Univ State NY, 68; Oswego State Univ, BS,70; H Lehman Col MA, 72. *Work:* Hudson River Mus, Yonkers, NY; Queens Cult Ctr, NY; Fashion Inst Tech, New York; State Office Building, Albany, NY. *Exhib:* Hudson River Mus, Yonkers, NY; Bronx Mus Arts, NY; Bruce Mus, Greenwich, Conn; Nat Asn Women Artists, New York; Dickinson State Univ, NDak. *Teaching:* Prof design, Fashion Inst Tech, 68-, chairperson fashion design dept, 89- *Awards:* Award, Mamaroveck Int, 74; Award Silvermine Guild, 75. *Mem:* Artists Equity Asn; Nat Asn Women Artists; Fashion Group Inc. *Media:* Watercolor; Graphics. *Publ:* Coauth, Fashion Production Terms, Fairchild Publ, 79; auth, Profiling Fabrics, 80, Designer Stylist Handbook, Vol I & II and Figures, 80, & Understanding Fabrics, 82, Fairchild Publ; contribr, Random House Dictionary-Fashion & Textile Area, Random House, 83-85. *Mailing Add:* 237 Van Cortland Pk Ave Yonkers NY 10705

GIORDANO, GREG JOE
PAINTER, PHOTOGRAPHER
b New York, NY, Nov 27, 60. *Study:* Sch Visual Arts; Robert Bateman Master Class, Wausau, Wis, 86. *Exhib:* 1984 Winter Olympic Games, Int Olympic Comt Hq, Saravejo, Yugoslavia, 84; National Art Exhib Alaskan Wildlife, Anchorage, 84 & 85; Group Miniature Exhib, Wild Wings Gallery, San Francisco, Calif, 85; Federal Duck Stamp Competition, Easton Waterfowl Festival, 85 & 86; Trailside Galleries. *Teaching:* Scottsdale Artists Sch. *Awards:* Finalist, Fed Duck Stamp Competition, 84 & 85; People's Choice Award-Best in Show, Alaskan Art Exhib, 85. *Bibliog:* Leonard Lang (auth), Artist vignette, Wildlife Art News, 9/85. *Media:* Gouache. *Publ:* Field & Stream Mag. *Mailing Add:* 76 Tally Ho Rd Ridgefield CT 06877-2818

GIORNO, JOHN
CONCEPTUAL ARTIST, PRINTMAKER
b New York, NY, Dec 4, 36. *Study:* Columbia Univ, BA, 58. *Work:* Mus Mod Art, New York. *Comn:* Innovated Dial-A-Poem, 68. *Exhib:* Performance, Beacon Theatre, Ritz & Palladium, New York. *Pos:* Founder & Pres, Giorno Poetry Systems Inst Inc, 65- *Media:* CD Video, Silkscreen. *Publ:* Balling Buddha, Kulchur Press, 70; Cancer in my Left Ball, Something Else Press, 73; Shit, Piss, Blood, Pus, & Brains, Painted Bride Press, 77; Grasping at Emptiness, Kulcur Press, 85; You Got to Burn to Shine, Serpents Tail Press, 92. *Mailing Add:* 222 Bowery New York NY 10012

GIOVANNI
PAINTER, PRINTMAKER
b Laurence, Mass, March 13, 49. *Study:* Vesper George Art Sch, 69-70; Art Inst Boston, 70-71; Boston Univ Sch Fine & Appl Arts, BFA, 87; Boston Univ Col of Lib Arts (scholarship Renaissance study, Padera, Italy), 87-88. *Work:* Alamo Rent-A-Car headquarters, Ft Lauderdale; Nat Portrait Gallery, Washington, DC; Mus Fine Arts, Boston, Mass; Fogg Mus, Cambridge, Mass; The White House, George Bush Libr Collection, Washington, DC; Pres George Bush Libr, Houston, Tex. *Comn:* Portrait, M I T Hist Collection, Boston, Mass, 89; various canvases, Westwood Int, Caleo, Peru, 89; mural, Boston Redevelopment Authority City Hall, Padua, Italy, 89; American Flag, Bass Energy Corp, Fairlawn, Ohio, 91; The American Spirit, Republican Nat Conv, Houston, Tex, 92. *Exhib:* Gallery of the Southwest, Taos, NM, 88-89; Dallas Design Center, 89; Ergane Gallery, New York, 91-92; one-man show, Francesco Anderson Gallery, Boston, 89-90, Pierce Galleries Inc, Hingham, Mass, 91-92, Boston Design Ctr, 91, Gallery at 4 India, Nantucket, 92; one-man retrospective, Bridgewater State Col, Bridgewater, Mass, 91. *Pos:* Owner, Giovanni Studios, Boston, Mass, 88- *Bibliog:* Patricia Jobe Pierce (auth), Giovanni DeCunto, Nantucket Beacon, 8/7/91; Patricia Jobe Pierce (auth), Italian-American painter makes an impact, Boston Post Gazette, 5/15/92; Patricia Jobe Pierce (auth), The leather district goes "pop" with art of Giovanni, Improper Bostonian, 5/27/92. *Media:* Acrylic, Oil, Lithography. *Mailing Add:* c/o Pierce Galleries Inc 721 Main St Rte 228 Hingham MA 02043

GIPE, LAWRENCE
PAINTER
b Baltimore, Md, 1962. *Study:* Va Commonwealth Univ, BFA, 84; Otis Art Inst Parsons Sch Design, MFA, 86. *Exhib:* The Last Juried Show, Va Mus Fine Art, Richmond, Va, 83; Otis/Parsons North Gallery, Los Angeles, Calif, 85; one-man shows Karl Bornstein Gallery, Santa Monica, 86, 87 & 90, Claremont Col, 87, Laguna Art Mus, Laguna Beach, Calif, 88, Galerie Six Friedich, Munich, Amerika Haus, Berlin & Hartje Gallery, Frankfurt, Ger, 89, Shea & Beker, New York, 90, Shea & Bornstein Gallery, Santa Monica, 91; Richard/Bennett Gallery, Los Angeles, 87; Barbara Fendrick Gallery, New York & Washington, DC, 89; Katonah Mus, Katonah, NY, 90; We Interrupt Your Regularly Scheduled Programming, White Columns, New York, 92; How Is It, Tony Shafrazi Gallery, New York, 92. *Pos:* Writer & critic, 85-; bd dirs, Found Art Resources, Los Angeles, 86-87; co-cur, Natural Sources, Angel's Gate Cultural Ctr, San Pedro, Calif, 87; cur, Cultural Fetish, Pasadena City Col Gallery, 89; vis artist, Art Ctr Pasadena, 89. *Awards:* Fel, Nat Endowment Arts, 89. *Bibliog:* Peter Frank (auth), Lawrence Gipe, Artspace, Jan/Feb, 90; James Lewis (auth), Lawrence Gipe, Artforum, 1/91; Paul Gardner (auth), Do Titles Really Matter, Artnews, pg 92-97, 2/92. *Mailing Add:* c/o Karl Bovnstein Gallery 1658 1/2 Tenth St Santa Monica CA 90404

GIPS, C L TERRY
PHOTOGRAPHER, EDUCATOR
b Oneida, NY, Mar 4, 45. *Study:* Cornell Univ, BS, 67; Yale Sch Art & Architecture, MArch, 71. *Work:* Nat Mus Am Art, Washington, DC; Picker Gallery, Colgate Univ, Hamilton, NY; State Vermont, Montpelier; Nat Mus Women in Arts, Washington, DC. *Exhib:* One-person shows, 112 Workshop, New York, 77, Light Work Gallery, Syracuse, NY, 89 & Tweed Mus Art, Duluth, Minn, 90; Annual Invitational Photography Exhib, Atrium Gallery, Conn, 83; Printed by Women, Port of History Mus, Philadelphia, 83; Selected Photographs 86, Philadelphia Print Club, Pa, 86; AIR Gallery, New York, 88; American Artists, Deutsch-Amerikanisches Inst, Regensberg, WGer, 88. *Pos:* VPres Bd trustees, VT Coun Arts, 83-84; actg dir, Univ Md, 92-93. *Teaching:* Core fac Fine Art, Goddard Col, Plainfield Vt, 76-80; adj fac art & photog, Univ Vt, Burlington, 80-84; asst prof photog, Univ Maryland, 84-89, assoc prof photog, 90- *Awards:* New York State Council Exhib Grant, 74; Nat Endowment Arts artist's Fel, 86; Creative and Performing Arts Grant, Univ Md, 90. *Mem:* Col Art Asn; Soc Photog Ed; Womens Caucus Art (Chair, Nat Honor Awards Committee 84-86). *Publ:* Auth, Alice Austen, At Views, 83; ed, contribr, National Honor Awards, 84-85 (exhib catalog) Womens Caucus for Art, 85, 86; Auth, A New Goddess of Memory, SPOT, 88; Guest ed, Computers & Art, Art J, 90. *Mailing Add:* 9408 Thornhill Rd Silver Spring MD 20901-4834

GIRARD, BILL
SCULPTOR
b Reno, Nev, May 12, 36. *Study:* San Diego State Univ, BS, 58; Ariz State Univ, 64; Scripps Univ, Calif, 66. *Comn:* Portrait with eagle, pvt comn, Albuquerque, NMex, 83; miniature Indian pow-wow dancers, Franklin Mint, Pa, 91; two life-size champion show dogs, pvt comn, Hillsborough, Calif, 92; earthenware Indian, Ray Tracey Gallery, Santa Fe, NMex, 92. *Exhib:* Sculpture in the Park, Loveland, Colo, 87-92; Southwest Art in the Wine Country, Sharpsteen Mus, Calistoga, Calif, 90-92; Mountain Oyster 23rd Ann Show, Tucson, Ariz, 91092; Western Regional Art Show & Sale, Cheyenne, Wyo, 92; AICA Western Art Exhib, San Dimas, Calif, 92; Cantingy Sculpture Invitational, Chicago, 93; and others. *Awards:* Best of Show, US Air Force Competition, KAFB, 83; Best of Show, Heritage Am Show, Heritage Am Mus, 88; Peoples' Choice Award, Southwest Art in the Wine Country, Art West Mag, 91. *Bibliog:* Weems Galleries, Profile Mag, 9/86; Katherine Newman (auth), Bill Girard, 91 & Vicki Stavig (auth), Girard Studio, 92, Art West. *Mem:* NMex Sculpture Guild; Albuquerque United Artists; Albuquerque Arts Alliance. *Media:* Bronze. *Publ:* Auth, Artistic News, Artistic Galleries, 92. *Mailing Add:* 1628 Sagebrush Trail SE Albuquerque NM 87123

GIRARD, (CHARLES) JACK
PAINTER, EDUCATOR
b Ft Knox, Ky, May 15, 51. *Study:* ECarolina Univ, BFA, 73, MFA, 76; Univ SC, 73. *Work:* SC Mus Comn, Columbia; Berea Col, Ky; Appalachian State Univ; Coca-Cola Bottling Co, Atlanta; Cent Bank & Trust Co, Ky. *Comn:* Drawings in collab with writer Jo Carson, Lexington Alzheimers Asn, 90. *Exhib:* Greater Lafayette Mus Art, Ind, 90; Univ Tenn/Chattanooga, 90; Carnegie Art Ctr, Covington, Ky, 91; Univ Ky Art Mus, Lexington, 91; Alice Lloyd Col, Pippa Passes, Ky, 92; and others. *Pos:* Asst, Walker Gallery, Columbia, SC, 76-78. *Teaching:* Vis artist, Carteret Tech Col, 78-79; instr art, Berea Col, 79-80; asst prof art, Centre Col, Ky, 80-81 & assoc prof art, Transylvania Univ, 81- *Awards:* Jones Develop Grant, 87, 90 & 92; Lexington Arts & Cult Coun Grant, 90. *Bibliog:* Steve Lyon (auth), Keeping tabs on the masquerade, J Seamus, 10/86. *Mem:* Am Asn Univ Prof; Col Art Asn Am; Found Art: Theory & Educ. *Media:* All Media. *Publ:* Coauth (with Ann Kilkelly), Confinement and isolation in the art of Edward Kienholz, Med Heritage J, 1-2/86; Censorship in Colleges, Ky Eng Bull, Vol 41, No 2, winter 92. *Mailing Add:* 348 Merino St Lexington KY 40508-2528

GIRAUDIER, ANTONIO
PAINTER, WRITER
b Havana, Cuba, Sept 28, 26; US citizen. *Work:* Harvard Univ Libr; Am Poets Fel Soc, Charleston, Ill; Greenville Mus Art, SC; Maryhill Mus Fine Arts, Wash; Trinity Episcopal Church, Boston; also in pvt Am & foreign collections. *Exhib:* Congress Arts & Communications, IBC Gallery, Hyatt-Regency, Cambridge, Mass, 79 & Krasuaplosky, Amsterdam, Holland, 80; solo exhibs, Jefferson Market Libr, New York, 80, NY Poster Forum, Am Asn Univ Women, 80-81 & ECHA, New York, 89; Artwork, Nat Arts Club, Gregg Gallery, 86; Asn of Consults & Critics of Art, Royal Trust Tower, 89; Palacio Viana Cordoba, Spain, 92; and others. *Pos:* Ed, Art & Poetry Mag, 78-81. *Awards:* Academician of Italy with Gold Medal, 80; Master of Painting, H C Accademia Italia, 82; Grand Prize of the Nations, Italy, 83. *Bibliog:* Reviews, Arts Mag, 12/71-1/72; review, The Inner Loom, 72; art work reproduced in many publ, US & abroad. *Media:* Acrylic, Mixed Media. *Publ:* Auth, 127 definitive works in English, French & Spanish; contribr, many books & periodicals, US & abroad. *Mailing Add:* 215 E 68th St New York NY 10021

GIRO, R (R GIRONDA)
ARCHITECT, SCULPTOR
b Brooklyn, NY, Dec 3, 36. *Study:* Pratt Inst, BFA; Nat Acad Design; Metropolitan Col, BS, 72; Art Students League. *Comn:* Sculptures, stainless steel, Kenneth Richardson, 69; stainless steel, Selma Wallace Assoc, 72; bronze, George T Rossi, 72; sculpture, Joseph S Sample, Billings, Mont; and others. *Exhib:* Silvermine Guild, New Canaan, Conn, 63; Nat Acad Design Galleries, 72-75; Brooklyn Mus Show, 73-75; Caravan House, New York, 74; Eric Galleries, 75-88; Giró Galleries. *Awards:* First Prize, Brooklyn Mus, 73 & 75. *Mem:* Nat Acad Design; Am Inst Archit. *Media:* Carved Brass, Welded Stainless Steel. *Mailing Add:* 305 Degraw St Brooklyn NY 11231

GIRONDA, R See Giro, R (R Gironda)

GITLIN, MICHAEL
SCULPTOR, DRAFTSMAN
b Capetown, SAfrica, April 23, 43. *Study:* Hebrew Univ Jerusalem, BA, 67; Bezalel Acad Art, Jerusalem, dipl, 67; Pratt Inst, MFA, 72. *Work:* Guggenheim Mus; Stedelijk Mus, Amsterdam; Lenbachhaus, Munich; Israel Mus, Jerusalem; Wilhelm Lehmbruck Mus, Duisburg, WGer. *Comn:* Sculpture (Cor Ten steel), Schmela Gallery, Düsseldorf, 76; Adam's Gate (mahogany), Jerusalem Found, Israel, 83; Sequence, Tel Aviv Mus, Israel, 84. *Exhib:* One-man shows, Israel Mus (with catalog), Jerusalem, 77, ICC (with catalog), Antwerp, Belg, 80, Exit Art (with catalog), New York, 85, Kunstraum Munich (with catalog), 86, Kunstverein (with catalog), Bonn, WGer, 88, Carnegie-Mellon Art Gallery (catalog), 90 & Muhka Mus (with catalog), Antwerp, 91; Documenta 6, Kassel, WGer, 77; Israel Mus, Jerusalem, Here & Now, 82; Kunstverein, Frankfurt About Drawing, 85; Kunsthalle, Dusseldorf, Skulptursein, 86; Drawings from the Eighties, Carnegie-Mellon Univ Art Gallery. *Teaching:* Instr art, Parsons Sch Design, 79-84; prof, Columbia Univ, NY, 87 & Univ Calif, Davis, 88. *Awards:* Fel, Nat Endowment Arts, 84-85 & 85-86; Guggenheim Fel, 87-88; Augustus St Gaudens Mem Fel, 88. *Bibliog:* Stephen Westfall (auth), Humanizing Sculpture (text in Kunstraum exhib catalog), Munich, 86; Annelie Pohlen (auth), From Seeing to Feeling (text in Bonner Kunstverein exhib catalog), Bonn, 88; Maig Damianovic (auth), Silence and Reprieve (text in Muhka Mus catalog), Antwerp, 91. *Media:* Wood, Mixed Media. *Dealer:* Erik Stark 594 Broadway New York NY 10012. *Mailing Add:* 280 Lafayette St New York NY 10012

GJERTSON, STEPHEN ARTHUR
PAINTER, WRITER
b Minneapolis, Minn, May 21, 49. *Study:* Univ Minn, 67-70; Sch Assoc Arts, St Paul, 70-71; Atelier Lack, Minneapolis, Minn, 71-75. *Work:* Col St Benedict, St Joseph, Minn; Christ Col Irvine, Calif; Montclair Art Mus. *Comn:* Triptych, Nokomis Heights Lutheran Church, Minneapolis, Minn, 79-86. *Exhib:* Classical Realism-The Other 20th Century, travelling exhib, 82-83; Classical Realist Conf & Exhib, Heritage Art Gallery, Alexandria, Va, 86, 88 & 92; 63rd & 64th Nat Apr Salons, Springville Mus Art, Utah, 87 & 88. *Teaching:* Atelier Lack, 73-88; Atelier N, 84-; Atelier LeSueur, 91- *Awards:* Grant, Elizabeth T Greenshields Found, 73-75; Juror's Award, 63rd Nat Apr Salon, Springville Mus Art, 87; Cash Award, 64th Nat Apr Salon, Friend Grand Central Art Galleries, 88. *Bibliog:* Stephen Gjertson (auth), Am Artist, 10/83; Carole Katchen (auth), Creating a Joyous Beauty, Painting Faces & Figures, Watson-Guptill, 86; Annette LeSueur (auth), Nature's Light and Life-The Work of Stephen Gjertson, Am Soc Classical Realism, 92. *Mem:* Full Guild Mem, Am Soc Classical Realism. *Media:* Oil. *Publ:* Auth, The Necessity of Excellence, Realism in Revolution/Taylor, 85; Hippolyte Flandrin-A Personal Appreciation, Classical Realism Quarterly, summer 88; contribr, Classical Realism Quarterly, Atelier Lack, Inc. *Dealer:* LeSueur Assocs 3565 Deephaven Ave Deephaven MN 55391. *Mailing Add:* 3855 Colfax Ave N Minneapolis MN 55412

GLADSTONE, BARBARA
DEALER, HISTORIAN
b Philadelphia, Pa. *Study:* Univ Pa; Hofstra Univ, BA, 68, MA, 70. *Pos:* Owner & dir, Barbara Gladstone Gallery, New York, currently. *Teaching:* Instr art hist & mod archit, Hofstra Univ, 71-75. *Mem:* Art Dealers Asn Am. *Specialty:* Contemporary painting, sculpture and photography; publisher of contemporary American prints and photographs. *Mailing Add:* Barbara Gladstone Gallery 99 Greene St New York NY 10012

GLADSTONE, M J
PUBLISHER
b New York, NY, May 4, 23. *Study:* Harvard Univ, SB(anthrop), 44, MA(fine arts), 46. *Pos:* Ed, Print & Print Collector's Quart, 50-53, Merriam-Webster Dictionary, 53-55, Collector's Quart Report, 62-63; assoc dir publ, Mus Mod Art, New York, 63-64; consult, NY State Coun Arts, 67-73; dir, Mus Am Folk Art, New York, 69-70, Publ Ctr Cult Resources, New York, 73-88, ed-in-chief, 88-89, publ, 89-; ed, Furthermore Press, Germantown, NY, 91- *Publ:* Contribr, Britannica Encycl Am Art, 73; auth, A Carrot for a Nose, Scribner, 74; contribr, How to Know American Folk Art, Dutton, 77. *Mailing Add:* Box 355 Germantown NY 12526

GLANCY, MICHAEL
SCULPTOR
b Detroit, Mich, Feb 11, 50. *Study:* Univ Denver, BFA(ceramics), 73; RI Sch Design, BFA(sculpture), 77, MFA(sculpture), 80. *Work:* Metrop Mus Art, New York; Victoria & Albert Mus, London, England; Nat Mus Am Hist, Smithsonian Inst, Washington, DC; Philadelphia Mus Art, Philadelphia, Pa; Hokkaido Mus Mod Art, Sapporo, Japan; Chrysler Mus, Norfolk, Va; The High Mus, Atlanta, Ga; Detroit Inst Art, Mich; Carnegie Inst Mus Art, Pittsburgh, Pa; Corning Mus Glass, Corning, NY; Los Angeles County Mus Art, Los Angeles, Calif; Musee Arts De'coratifs, Paris, France. *Comn:* Sculpture (large scale), New York. *Exhib:* Oakland Mus, Oakland, Calif, 86; Matrix Transformed, Heller Gallery, New York, 86; New Art Forms, Navy Pier, Chicago, Ill, 86-90; Darmstadt Mus, Darmstadt, WGer, 87; World Glass Now, Hokkaido Mus Art, Sappora, Japan, 85 & 88; New Works in Glass & Metal, Habatat Galleries, Detroit, Mich, 88; Newport Art Mus, RI, 88; Heller Gallery, New York, 89. *Pos:* Artist & Artist in Residence. *Teaching:* Assoc fac, Metals Prog, RI Sch Design, 82-88; instr, Pilchuck Glass Ctr, Seattle, Wash, 82-88. *Awards:* Nat Endowment Arts Fel 86; Mass Coun Arts Fel, 87. *Bibliog:* Sculptural glass, Am Art Glass Quart, fall, 83; Elegant glass made by masters, New York Times, 12/13/84; Breaking into glass, Esquire, 2/85. *Mem:* Gas Soc, Corning, NY. *Publ:* Auth, Shadow & Substance, Glancy, Heller & Hampson, 89. *Dealer:* Heller Gallery 71 Greene St New York, Ny 10012; Habatat Galleries 32255 Northwestern Highway, Farmington Hills, MI 48018. *Mailing Add:* 85 Carpenter St Rehoboth MA 02679

GLANTZMAN, JUDY
PAINTER
b Long Island, NY, May 24, 56. *Study:* RI Sch Design, BFA(Silver Medal: Outstanding Student), 78. *Work:* Franklin Furnace, New Sch Social Res, Grey Art Gallery, Chase Manhattan Bank, New York; Can Imperial Bank; Equitable Bank, New York; Bell Savings Bank, Pa. *Exhib:* Solo exhibs, Civilian Warfare, 83 & 84, Gracie Mansion, 85, New York & Paris Green Gallery, La Jolla, Calif, 86, St Mary's Col, Md & Hudson River Mus, 90; Portraits-East Village, PS 1, Long Island City, NY, 84; Women of Influence, Amerika Haus, Berlin, Ger, 84; Santa Barbara Mus, Calif, 85; Saidye Bronfman Center, Montreal, 85; Ackland Art Mus, Chapel Hill, NC. *Teaching:* Mem fac, part time, Parsons Sch Design, New York; 2-D Design, Sch Visual Arts; RI Sch Design, Providence, 82-83. *Awards:* Silver Award, Royal Soc Arts, London, 78; Artist on Location; NY found Arts, 87. *Bibliog:* Donald Kuspit (auth), Climbing, Art Forum, 4/84; Walter Robinson & Carlo McCormick (auths), Slouching towards Avenue D, Art in Am, summer 84; David Bourbon (auth), Sitting pretty, Vogue, 11/85; John Russell (auth), Art: New paintings, New York Times, 1/25/85; Robert Pincus-Witten (auth), The new irascibles, Arts, 9/85; Edward Sozanski (auth), article, Philadelphia Enquirer, 9/87; Elisa Turner (auth), article, Miami Herald, 11/88. *Mem:* CAA. *Media:* Oil on Canvas. *Dealer:* Carol Getz Gallery Miami FL & Da Entlang Germany. *Mailing Add:* 214 E 2nd St New York NY 10009

GLANZ, ANDREA E
ADMINISTRATOR, CURATOR
b New York, NY, Oct 14, 52. *Study:* Cornell Univ, BS(human develop & expressive arts); Stanford Univ, MA(art educ). *Pos:* Grad asst, Stanford Univ Mus Art, Calif, 74-75; cur educ, Triton Mus Art, Santa Clara, Calif, 75-77, dir, 77-78; from asst cur to cur, San Jose Mus Art, Calif, 78-79; asst dir, Continuing Prof Educ, Mus Collab, New York, 79-80, dir, 80-85. *Teaching:* Instr, West Valley Community Col, Saratoga, Calif, 76. *Mem:* Am Asn Mus; Mus Educators Roundtable; Col Art Asn; Nat Trust for Hist Preserv. *Publ:* Coauth, A Catalog of Paintings by Theodore Wores in the Collection of the Triton Museum of Art, 76 & Two Hundred Years of Santa Clara Valley Architecture: A Stylistic Survey, 76, Triton Mus Art; auth, The Role of Museum Management Training in Developing Effective Museum Managers & In Search of Excellence: The American Museum Experience, Scottish Mus Coun, Edinburgh, 85. *Mailing Add:* 90 Jane St Hartsdale NY 10530-1927

GLASCO, JOSEPH M
PAINTER, SCULPTOR
b Pauls Valley, Okla, Jan 19, 25. *Study:* Univ Tex, 41-42; study with Rico Lebrun, 46; study in Mexico City, 47; Art Students League, New York, 48. *Work:* Metrop Mus Art & Mus Mod Art, New York; Hirshhorn Mus & Sculpture Garden, Washington, DC; Whitney Mus Am Art, New York; Princeton Univ Mus, NJ. *Exhib:* One-man shows, Perls Gallery, New York, 51, Catherine Viviano Gallery, New York, 52, 55, 58, 60, 63, 67 & 70 & Gimpel & Weitzenhoffer Gallery, 79; 15 Americans, Mus Mod Art, New York; The New Decade, Whitney Mus Am Art; Metrop Mus Art, New York; Solomon R Guggenheim Mus; Art Inst Chicago; Corcoran Gallery Art; Dallas Mus Fine Arts; Los Angeles Co Mus Fine Arts. *Collections Arranged:* 15 Americans, Mus Mod Art, New York; The New Decade, Thirty-five American Painters & Sculptors, Whitney Mus Am Art, New York. *Mem:* Nat Soc Lit & Arts. *Mailing Add:* c/o Meredith Long & Co 2323 San Felipe Houston TX 77019

GLASER, BRUCE
HISTORIAN, EDUCATOR
b Brooklyn, NY, Sept 25, 33. *Study:* Columbia Col, BA; Columbia Univ, MA. *Pos:* Dir, Howard Wise Gallery, New York, 60-61; dir, Gallery of Israeli Art, Am-Israel Cult Found, New York, 65-68; exec dir, Art Ctr Northern NJ, Tenafly, 68-70. *Teaching:* Instr art hist, Pratt Inst, 61-62; instr, Hunter Col, 62-65; prof art hist, Univ Bridgeport, 70-, chmn dept, 70-77, dean, Col Fine Arts, 77-81. *Awards:* Mem Found for Jewish Cult Fel, 70-72; Summer Inst, Nat Endowment Humanities, Chicago, 84; Vis Scholar, Coun for Humanities, 86. *Mem:* Col Art Asn Am; Int Coun Mus; Am Asn Mus. *Res:* Modern and contemporary art; Israeli art. *Publ:* Ed & coauth, Oldenburg, Lichtenstein, Warhol: A discussion, Artforum, 2/66; coauth, Questions to Stella & Judd, Art News, 9/66; ed & coauth, An interview with Ad Reinhardt, Art Int, 12/66; ed & coauth, Modern art and the critics, Art J, winter 70-71; auth, Robert Natkin, Arts, 6/78. *Mailing Add:* 78 Gaybowers Rd Fairfield CT 06430-2011

GLASER, DAVID
PAINTER, SCULPTOR
b Brooklyn, NY, Sept 29, 19. *Study:* Art Students League, scholar; NY Sch Indust Art; NY Sch Contemp Art, with Philip Evergood; Brooklyn Mus Art Sch, with Moses Soyer, Xavier Gonzales & Edwin Dickinson. *Comn:* Poster ser for US Army, 43-44; Created (Giggy F Useless) World War II cartoon character, USA, 42-46. *Exhib:* Nat Arts Club, 59; Art Directions, 59; City Ctr, New York, 60; Allied Artists Am, 60-71; three-man exhib, Heckscher Mus, Huntington, 64; Hofstra Univ; Adelphi Univ; Islip Mus, 83; Levittown Libr, 86. *Pos:* Inventor, art dir & designer, Mosamics Co pres, 46-48; art dir, 54-60; dir & designer, Studio Concepts, 60-; pres, Allied Artists Am, 85. *Teaching:* Instr, Art Ctr Island Jewish Sch, 59. *Awards:* Grand Prize, Redesign of Levitt House, 67 & Printing Indust New York, 73 & 77; Monadnock Mills Graphic Excellence Award, 75; Cert of Merit, Vet Soc Am Artists, 79; Desi Graphics Award, 80 & 82; Inst Elec & Electronics Engrs Award, 83. *Mem:* Allied Artists Am; Huntington Township Art League. *Media:* Mixed Media; Copper, Illumination. *Res:* Experimental silk screen production for industry; developed Process Mosaic Reproduction; new approaches in advertising and media including all communication skills; architectural sculpture using copper, plastics or electricity; pictorial Map Entire Am Revolution. *Publ:* Illusr for Popular Sci, Popular Mechanics & Electronics Illustrated, 61-65; auth & illusr, My Mother Died Dancing. *Mailing Add:* 33 Downhill Lane Wantagh NY 11793

GLASER, MILTON
DESIGNER, ILLUSTRATOR
b New York, NY, June 26, 29. *Study:* Cooper Union Art Sch, 51; Acad Fine Arts, Bologna, Italy, with Giorgio Morandi, Fulbright Scholar, 52-53; Minneapolis Inst Art, Hon DFA; Moore Col Art, Hon Degree; Philadelphia Mus Sch, Hon Degree; Sch Visual Arts, Hon Degree; State Univ Col, Buffalo, Hon Degree, 87. *Work:* Mus Mod Art, New York; Israel Mus, Jerusalem; Nat Archives, Smithsonian Inst, Washington, DC. *Comn:* Mural, Fed Off Bldg, Indianapolis, 74; permanent exhib, Port Authority NY, World Trade Ctr, 75; mural, Astor Place Subway Station, New York, 85. *Exhib:* Push Pin Decorative Arts Show, The Louvre, Paris, 70; one-man show, Portland Visual Arts Ctr, Maine, 75, Mus Mod Art, New York, 75 & Wichita State Univ, 75; Pompidou Cult Ctr, Beaubourg, Paris, 77; Mus Mod Art, Liege, Belgium, 82; Houghton Gallery at The Cooper Union, New York, 84; Hammer Gallery, NY, 86; Museo Bellas de Artes of Buenos Aires, Argentina, 87; Galleria d'Arte Maderna, Bologna, Italy; Universidad Cent Mus, Barcelona, Spain; Errepidue Evento, Vicenza, Italy; Sch Visual Arts, New York. *Pos:* Pres, Push Pin Studios, New York, 54-74; chmn bd & design dir, New York Mag, 68-77; pres, Milton Glaser Inc Design Studio, 74-; vpres & design dir, Village Voice, 75-77. *Teaching:* Instr design prog, Sch Visual Arts, New York, 61- *Awards:* Gold Medal, Am Inst Graphics Arts, 72; Gold Medal, Soc Illusr, 78; Art Dirs Club Hall of Fame, 79. *Bibliog:* Linda Moss (auth), Milton Glaser at 58, Crains' NY Businessman, 7/13/87; Gael Greene (auth), Over the rainbow, the renaissance of a New York classic, NY Mag, 2/88; Ruth Reichl (auth), Heaven's plate Metrop Home, 6/88. *Mem:* Int Graphic Alliance; Am Inst Graphic Arts (co-chmn, 73); Art Dir Club; Int Design Conf (pres), Aspen; Soc Arts London. *Publ:* Illusr, Cats and Bats and Things With Wings, 65; Fish in the Sky, 71; Don Juan, 72; Graphic Design, 73; Milton Glaser Poster Book, 77. *Mailing Add:* 207 E 32nd St New York NY 10016

GLASGOW, VAUGHN LESLIE
CURATOR, HISTORIAN
b Apr 23, 44; US citizen. *Study:* La State Univ, BA; Borso di Studii, Centro Int Studii Archit A Palladio, Vicenza, Italy, cert, 68; Pa State Univ, MA(Nat Defense Act Title IV Grant), 70; Inst Mus Mgt, Univ Calif, Berkeley, fel, 79; Int Partnership Among Mus, La Rochelle, France, fel, 81. *Exhib:* Solo exhib, Rocks of Ages, Central Conn State Univ, New Britain, 92. *Collections Arranged:* Permanent Collection, Anglo-Am Art Mus, La State Univ, 66-67; G P A Healy: Famous Figures and La Patrons (coauth, catalog), 76; Savoir Faire: The French Taste in Louisiana, 77; Played With Immense Success, 79; L'Amour de Maman: The Acadian Textile Heritage (auth, catalog), 80; The Sun King: Louis XIV and the New World (auth, catalog), 84; The Old State Capital, Baton Rouge, 88; and others. *Pos:* Reader youth grants, Nat Endowment Humanities, Washington, DC, 71-76; arts mgr, State Arts Coun, New Orleans, La, 73-75; chief cur, La State Mus, New Orleans, 75-83, assoc dir, 83-86; dir, spec projs, La State Mus, New Orleans, 86- *Teaching:* Instr art hist & admin asst, Pa State Univ, 70-71; asst prof art hist, Middle Tenn State Univ, 72-73; lectr art hist, Tulane Univ, 74-79; lectr arts mgt, St Mary's Dominican Col, 81-82. *Awards:* Chevalier de Palmes Académiques, French Govt, 84; Chevalier des Arts et des Lettres, France Govt, 86; Am Asn State Local Hist Award, 92. *Mem:* Am Asn Mus; Int Coun Mus (exhib exchange comt); La Asn Mus; Am Asn State & Local Hist (awards comt); Southeastern Mus Conf. *Res:* European post-Renaissance period; Louisiana studies; architectural history; post-revolutionary French painting. *Publ:* Auth, The Sun King: Louis XIV & the New World (with S Reinhardt, R Macdonald & P Lemoine), LMF, New Orleans, 84; Planning a Traveling Exhibition: American Asn State & Local Hist Technical Report No 10; A Social History of the American Alligabar, St Martin's Press, NY, 91; and others. *Mailing Add:* La State Mus 751 Chartres St Box 2448 New Orleans LA 70176

GLASHAUSSER, SUELLEN
SCULPTOR
b New York, NY, Mar 17, 45. *Study:* Manhattanville Col, BA, 65; Sorbonne, degre superieur, 67; Univ Calif, Berkeley, MA, 69. *Exhib:* One-person show, State Mus, Trenton, NJ, 73 & 87; First Biennial of NJ Artists, Newark Mus, Newark, NJ, 77; 12th Biennale Internationale de la Tapisserie, Lausanne, Switz, 81 & 85; Manifestation Internationale des Livres d'Artistes, Galerie NRA, Paris, 82 & 84; Bookworks, Gallery Miyazaki, Osaka, Japan, 83; Boucles et Noeudes, Maison de la Culture, Namur, Belg, 83; Visual Books, Metrop Mus Art, New York, 85; Textilkunstler der 12th internationalen Biennale, Maya Behn Gallery, Zurich, 85; Postscriptum-librifibra (with catalog), Studio E, Rome, Italy, 86. *Teaching:* Instr fine arts, Middlesex County Col, NJ, 70-71; vis lectr, Livingston Col, Rutgers Univ, 71-75; asst prof, Montclair State Col, NJ, 74- *Awards:* Hon Mention, El Paso Designer Craftsmen, El Paso Mus, Tex, 77; First Prize Fiber, First Ann Statewide Exhib, Artists League Cent NJ, 78; Purchase Award, Rutgers Univ, Camden NJ, 90. *Bibliog:* Barbara Meise (auth), Pages of revelations, Artbuilders, Inc, 86. *Publ:* Auth, reviews, Craft Horizons, 6/75, 8/77 & 12/78; coauth, Plaiting, Watson-Guptill, 76; auth, Belgisch Kreatief Ambracht, Drukkerij ESIM, 6-7/82. *Mailing Add:* 202 S Second Ave Highland Park NJ 08904

GLASIER, ALICE GENEVA See Kloss, Gene (Alice Geneva Glasier)

GLASS, DOROTHY F
HISTORIAN
b New York, NY. *Study:* Vassar Col, BA, 64; Johns Hopkins Univ, PhD, 68. *Teaching:* Asst prof medieval art, Boston Univ, 69-74; assoc prof, State Univ NY, Buffalo, 74-81, prof, 81-, chair, 87-89. *Awards:* Rome Prize, Am Acad Rome, 85-86; Fulbright Fel, Western European Regional, 89-90; Jane & Morgan Whitney Senior Fel, Metrop Mus Art, 91-93. *Mem:* Medieval Acad Am; Col Art Asn; Int Ctr Medieval Art (bd dirs, 80-83, domestic adv & publ comt, 87-90); Soc Fels, Am Acad Rome; Int Ctr Medieval Art (ed Newsletter), 92-95. *Publ:* Auth, Romanesque sculpture in Campania: a problem of method, Art Bulletin, 74; auth, The archivolt sculpture at Sessa Aurunca, Art Bulletin, 69; auth, Italian Romanesque Sculpture: An Annotated Bibliography, Boston, G K Hall & Co, 83; Pseudo-Augustine, Prophets & Pulpits in Romanesque Campania, Dumbarton Oaks Papers 41, 87; Romanesque Sculpture in Campania: Patrons, Programs and Style, Pa State Press, 91. *Mailing Add:* Dept Art Hist-Rm 601 Clemens Hall State Univ NY-North Campus Buffalo NY 14260

GLASS, MICHAEL L
DESIGNER, EDUCATOR
b New York, NY, Dec 21, 45. *Study:* Clark Univ, Mass, BA, 68; Yale Univ, BFA, 69, MFA, 71. *Exhib:* Inst Graphic Arts & Art Dirs Club New York, 72-83; 32nd, 33rd & 34th Chicago Book Clinic, 81-83; Asn Art Museums, 82; The 100 Show, 83 & Ill Show, 83, Soc Typographic Arts. *Pos:* Malcolm Greer Designers Inc, Providene, RI, 71-77; Michael Glass Design Inc, Chicago, Ill, 77-; consult, Unimark Int, Chicago, 78 & Goldsmith, Yamasaki, Specht Inc, Chicago, 79. *Teaching:* Assoc prof visual commun, RI Sch Design, 73-77, Inst Design, Ill Inst Technol, 78-80 & Univ Ill, Chicago, 80- *Awards:* Six Am Corp Identity Awards, Station Chicago '86; Am Corp Identity Awards, 86 & 88; Am Inst Graphic Arts Ann, 89. *Bibliog:* Bryan Fuermann (auth), On Chicago, Beaux Arts, 10/83. *Mem:* Soc Typographic Arts (bd mem, 80-82); Am Inst Graphic Arts; Art Dirs Club New York; Am Ctr Design, Chicago; Chicago 27 Designers. *Publ:* Articles in Idea Mag, (Tokyo, Japan), Progressive Archit Mag & L'Architecture Aujourd'hui Mag. *Mailing Add:* 213 W Institute Place Suite 702 Chicago IL 60610

GLASS, WENDY D
DEALER, COLLECTOR
b New York, NY, Aug 28, 25. *Study:* Bard Col, study of art hist with Stefan Hirsch. *Collections Arranged:* Temple Shaaray Tefila, New York; Temple Israel, New Rochelle, NY; Temple Soc Advan of Judaism, White Plains, NY; Waldamar Cancer Res Found, Hilton Hotel, New York, 65. *Pos:* Dir & owner, Glass Art Gallery, 60- *Mem:* Appraisers Asn Am. *Specialty:* Figurative art; American paintings and graphics, 20th Century; Japanese Ukiyo-e prints. *Interests:* Impressionistic graphics; South American graphics. *Collection:* Max Weber, Pascin, Chaim Gross, Raphael Soyer & Benny Andrews; contemporary 20th century painters; Ukiyo-e masters of the 19th century. *Mailing Add:* 315 Central Park W Apt 8W New York NY 10025

GLASSER, NORMA PENCHANSKY
SCULPTOR
b New York, NY, March 6, 41. *Study:* Leslie Col, BS, 62; Eastern Mich Univ, MFA, 74. *Work:* Marietta Col, Ohio; La Grange Col, Ga; Saginaw Valley State Col, Mich; Boone Sculpture Garden, San Marino, Calif; Pac Enterprises, Los Angeles, Calif; Ind-Purdue Univ, Ft Wayne, Ind. *Comn:* Women Waiting, comn by Charles Givens, Oklahoma City, 84; Summer Garden, Ind Univ-Purdue Univ, Ft Wayne, Ind, 91. *Exhib:* 56th Ann Nat Exhib, Springville Mus, Utah, 80; 16th Ann Drawing & Small Sculpture Exhib, Del Mar Col, Corpus Christi, Tex, 82; Nat Sculpture Soc Exhib, Equitable Gallery, New York, 83; Mich Outdoor Sculpture II, Southfield Civic Ctr, 89; Taubman Gallery, Ann Arbor, Mich, 91; Power Ctr Performing Arts, Ann Arbor, Mich, 92. *Pos:* Staff, Ann Arbor Street Art Fair, 87- *Teaching:* Instr sculpture-drawing, Ann Arbor Art Asn, 73-; guest lectr, Univ Mich, 85 Ann Arbor Publ Schs, 86. *Awards:* Purchase Award, Mainstreams '76 (national); Medal of Honor, Nat Asn Women Artists, 86; Silver Medal Best of Show, Scarab Club Exhib, 88; First Place, Annie Achievement Award, Visual Arts Three Demensional, Washtenaw Coun Art, Ann Arbor, Mich, 91; Shidon Bronze Gallery, Tesuque, NMex. *Mem:* Ann Arbor Art Asn (bd mem, 82-87); Nat Asn Women Artists; Mich Guild Artists & Craftsmen. *Media:* Bronze. *Publ:* Contribr, Heroic Sculpture, Western Art Digest, 86. *Dealer:* Lizardi/Harp Gallery W Colorado Blvd Pasadena CA. *Mailing Add:* 776 Watersedge Dr Ann Arbor MI 48105

GLASSON, LLOYD
SCULPTOR, EDUCATOR
b Chicago, Ill, Jan 31, 31. *Study:* Art Inst of Chicago, BFA, 57; Tulane Univ, MFA, 59. *Work:* New Brit Mus Am Art, Conn; George Walter Vincent Smith Mus, Springfield, Mass; Wichita Art Mus; Forma Viva Sculpture Garden, Slovenija, Yugoslavia. *Comn:* Finial angels atop soldiers & sailors mem arch, DeVane Mem, Yale Univ, Conn, 68; Shapiro Mem & Herbert Portraits, Karen Horney Clin, New York, 67; Fox Mem & Patterson Mem, Univ Conn Med Ctr, Farmington; Church of St Helena, Whitefield, Conn. *Exhib:* One-man shows, Dorsky Gallery, New York, 66 & 74, Trinity Col, 77 & Saltbox Gallery, 85, Hartford, Conn; Univ NH, Durham, 76; Manchester Community Col, 90; Central Conn State Univ, 91. *Pos:* Exhib designer, Newark Mus, NJ, 60-61. *Teaching:* Prof sculpture & drawing, Univ Hartford, West Hartford, Conn, 64- *Awards:* First Prizes, Art Asn Regional, Delgado Mus, New Orleans, 59; Gold Medal, Nat Sculpture Soc, 85 & Nat Acad Design, 86; James E & Francis W Bent Award for Creativity, 89. *Bibliog:* Jolene Goldenthal (auth), Adventurous Revivalist, Hartford Courant, 4/77; Anthony Padovano (auth), The process of sculpture, 81. *Mem:* Sculptors Guild; Nat Acad Design; Nat Sculpture Soc; Am Medallic Sculpture Asn. *Media:* Bronze, Ceramic. *Mailing Add:* Wilcox Hill Rd Portland CT 06480

GLATT, LINNEA
SCULPTOR
b Bismarck, NDak, Sept 8, 1949. *Study:* Moorhead State Univ, Minn, BS, 71; Univ Dallas, Irving, Tex, MA, 72. *Work:* Expose, Acknowledge, Reconcile, Dallas Mus Art, 89; Mimi's Garden, Dallas Arboretum, collaboration, 88; Waste Mgt Facility, City of Phoenix, 89-92. *Comn:* Harrow, Lubben Plaza, Dallas, Tex, 92; Passage Inacheve, Buffalo Bayou, Houston, Tex, 90. *Exhib:* Univ Colorado Art Galleries, Boulder, 87-88; Aspen Art Mus, Colorado, 87-88; Tex Women Exhib Nat Mus Women Art's, Wash, DC, 88; Archer M Huntington Art Gallery, Austin, Tex, 90; Circum-stance, Blue Star Art Space, San Antonio, Tex, 90. *Pos:* Bd dirs, Tex Sculpture Assoc, 86-87; Dallas Mus Awards to Artist Committee, 88-91. *Teaching:* Instr art, Richland Col, Dallas, Tex, 74-84; art, Southern Methodist Univ, Dallas, Tex, 85-88. *Awards:* Fel, Nat Endowment Arts, 86; Individual art grant, Art Matters Inc, New York, 89; Anne Giles Kimbrought Fund Grant, Dallas Mus Art, Tex, 92. *Bibliog:* Watson-Jones (auth), Contemporary American Women Sculptors, Oryx Press, 86; Laurel Jones (auth), 50 Texas Artists: A Critical Selection of Painters and Sculptors Working in Texas, Cronical Books, 86; Charles Dee Mitchell (auth), Linnea Glatt & Francis Merritt Thompson, Art Forum, 120, summer 91. *Mem:* Founding mem, D W Galllery, 75- *Media:* Miscellaneous Media. *Mailing Add:* 2412 Hardwick Dallas TX 75208

GLENDINNING, PETER
PHOTOGRAPHER
b New York, NY, Sept 23, 51. *Study:* Syracuse Univ, BFA, 76, MFA, 78. *Work:* Int Mus Photog, Rochester, NY; Everson Mus Art & Light Work, Syracuse, NY; Tweed Mus Art; Murray State Univ, Ky; Unicolor Corp; Ctr Creative Photography, Tucson, Ariz. *Comn:* Official portrait, Gov John Engler, State of Mich; Photog, State Capitol Restoration Proj, Lansing, Mich. *Exhib:* Everson Mus Art, Syracuse, NY, 79; one-person shows, Lightsong Gallery, Tucson, 80, CEPA Gallery, Buffalo, NY, 81, Foto Gallery, New York, 82 & Lowe Art Gallery, Syracuse Univ, 84; Fugitive Color, Slusser Gallery, Ann Arbor, Mich, 82; Proj Art Ctr, Cambridge, Mass, 82; Contemporary Photography as Phantasy, Santa Barbara Mus Art, 82; Main Street Gallery, Nantucket, Mass, 90. *Pos:* Dir, Light Fantastic Gallery, Mich State Univ, East Lansing, 78-; portrait photogr for corp & advert, 84- *Teaching:* Prof dept art & head photog, Mich State Univ, 78- *Awards:* Ford Found Grant, 78; Res Grant, Mich State Univ, 81; Unicolor Artist Support Grant, 82; Individual Artist Grant, Mich Arts Coun, 89-90. *Mem:* Soc Photog Educ; Friends of Photog; Ctr Creative Photog. *Media:* Color. *Publ:* Contribr, Fugitive Color (exhib catalog), Univ Mich, 82;; Color Photography: History, Theory and Darkroom Technique, Prentice-Hall, 85; Michigan Quilts: 150 Years of a Textile Tradition, Mich State Univ Mus, 88. *Mailing Add:* c/o Art Dept Mich State Univ East Lansing MI 48824

GLENN, CONSTANCE WHITE
MUSEUM DIRECTOR, WRITER
b Topeka, Kans, Oct 4, 33. *Study:* Univ Kans, BFA; Univ Mo, Kansas City; Calif State Univ, Long Beach, MA. *Collections Arranged:* Lucas Samaras: Photo-Transformations (catalog), 75; Roy Lichtenstein: Ceramic Sculpture (catalog), 77; George Segal: Pastels 1957-1965 (catalog), 78; Jim Dine Figure Drawings: 1974-1979 (catalog), 79; Frederick Sommer at Seventy-Five (catalog), 80; Apropos Robinson Jeffers: Robert Motherwell-Renate Ponsold (catalog), 81; Robert Longo (catalog), 86; Eric Fischl: Scenes Before the Eye (catalog), 86; Imagenes Liricas: New Spanish Visions (catalog), 90; James Rosenquist: Time Dust (catalog raisonné), 93. *Pos:* Co-dir, Jack Glenn Gallery, 70-73; prof & dir, Mus Studies Cert Prog, Univ Art Mus, Calif State Univ, Long Beach, 73-; chmn south Calif adv bd, Arch Am Art, 78-90; art consult, Archit Digest, 80-88; publ & ed, Artexpress, 88-; contrib ed, Angeles Mag, 88-90 & Antiques & Fine Art, 90- *Awards:* Distinquished Scholarly & Creative Achievement Award, Calif State Univ Long Beach; Outstanding Contribr to the Field, Calif Mus Photog, 86; Arts Admin of the Year, Long Beach Pub Corp Arts, 89. *Mem:* Am Asn Mus; Assoc Art Mus Dir; Col Art Asn; Southern Calif Bd Arch Am Art; Adv Comn Pub Art, Long Beach (vice chair). *Res:* American art since 1945. *Collection:* Contemporary American art & American photography. *Publ:* Auth, Jim Dine Drawings, 85, Roy Lichtenstein: Landscape Sketches, 86, Lucas Samaras: Doodles, Sketches and Plans, 87, Wayne Thiebaud: Private Drawings, 88 & Robert Motherwell: The Daedalus Sketches, 88, Harry N Abrams; ed, Imagenes Liricas: New Spanish Visions, 90; James Rosenquist: Time Dust, The Complete Graphics 1962-1992, Rizzoli, 93. *Mailing Add:* Univ Art Mus, Calif State Univ 1250 Bellflower Blvd Long Beach CA 90804

GLESMANN, SYLVIA MARIA
PAINTER
b Bavaria, Ger, June 8, 23; US citizen. *Study:* Acad Fine Arts, Nurnberg, Ger; Acad Fine Arts, Munich, Ger, 44. *Work:* Ortho Diagnostics, Bridgewater, NJ. *Comn:* Many pvt comns. *Exhib:* K Keane, Mason Gallery, New York, 81; NJ WC Soc, Morris Mus, Morristown, NJ, 80; Summer Selections, Nabisco Brands, East Hanover, NJ, 84; Salmagundi Club Gallery, New York, 88-89; Nat Asn Women Artists, New York, 91-92; and many others. *Pos:* Pres, Raritan Valley Arts Asn, NJ, 76-78 & Am Artists Prof League (NJ chapter), 88-91. *Awards:* Many awards from 70-92. *Bibliog:* Les Krantz (auth), NY Art Review, 89. *Mem:* Nat Asn Women Artists, New York; Salmagundi Club, New York; Am Artist Prof League (NJ chapter); Raritan Valley Arts Asn; Nat Mus Women Arts, Washington, DC (charter member). *Media:* Egg Tempera, Watercolor. *Publ:* Auth, She is Hearts and Flowers, 78, From the Heart, 89, Showcase, 90, Messenger Gazette; Heart in Home, Courrier News, 89; On the Towns, Star Ledger, 91. *Mailing Add:* 36 Twin Oaks Rd Bridgewater NJ 08807

GLEZER, NECHEMIA
ART DEALER, COLLECTOR
b Vilno, Lithuania, 1910; US citizen. *Study:* Acad Fine Arts, Vilno; Stefana Batorego Univ, Vilno; Brera Acad Fine Arts, Milan, with Aldo Carpi. *Collections Arranged:* Fourteen Italian Artists, sponsored by Italian Ambassador to USA, Veerhoff Gallery, Washington, DC, 60; French Artists, C W Post Col, Long Island Univ, NY, 61; I Pailes, Maison Francaise, NY Univ, sponsored by French Cult Attache to USA, 63; Ferruccio Steffanutti, Vatican Pavilion, New York World's Fair, 64-65; Trento Longaretti, Casa Italiana, Columbia Univ, New York, 67; I Pailes, Maison Francaise, Columbia Univ, 72 & I Pailes Exhib, Yeshiva Univ Mus, New York, NY, 75. *Pos:* Pres, Nechemia Glezer Gallery, New York, 53- *Awards:* Award for Cult Enrichment, Fr Cult Attache, 63; Award for Introducing Italian Artists to USA, Ital Consul Gen, 69; Academician, Accad Tiberina di Rome, 72. *Bibliog:* Elspeth Flynn (auth), Southeby at Glezer Gallery, Brit Info Serv, 2/5/63; Mr Glezer from NY visits Museum at Casteleone, La Notte, Milan, 5/24/64; Mario Pescara (auth), Collection of Nechemia Glezer, Am Rev Art & Sci, 4/69. *Res:* Macchiaioli; Italian nineteenth century artists. *Specialty:* School of Paris artists; contemporary Italian artists. *Interests:* Bringing contemporary French and Italian art to the attention of the American public. *Mailing Add:* 760 West End Ave New York NY 10025

GLICK, JOHN P
CERAMIST
b Detroit, Mich, July 1, 38. *Study:* Wayne State Univ, BFA, 60; Cranbrook Acad, MFA, 62. *Work:* Everson Mus Art; Cranbrook Art Acad Mus; Renwick Gallery, Nat Mus Am Art, Smithsonian Inst, Wash, DC; Detroit Inst Arts. *Exhib:* Edmonton, Atla, Can, 73; Everson Mus Art, Syracuse, NY, 79 & 89; Craftsman Potters Asn Gallery, London, Eng, solo exhib, 85; Detroit Inst Arts, Mich, 88; Nat Mus Ceramic Art, Baltimore, MD, 89; solo exhib, Fosdick-Nelson Gallery, Sch Art & Design, Alfred Univ, Alfred, NY, 90; Am Craft Mus, New York, 92. *Awards:* Mich Found Arts, 77; Nat Endowment Arts, 77 & 88. *Mem:* Am Craft Coun; Mich Potters Assoc. *Dealer:* Habatat Shaw Northwest Hwy Farmington Hills MI 48336. *Mailing Add:* 30435 W Ten Mile Rd Farmington Hills MI 48336

GLICK, PAULA FLORENCE
ART DEALER, WRITER
b Baltimore, Md. *Study:* Am Univ; George Washington Univ, BA & MA; Columbia Univ. *Pos:* Assoc dir, Capricorn Galleries, 64-87, co-dir, 87- *Teaching:* Instr art hist, Cath Univ, 85. *Mem:* Col Art Asn Am; Soc Archit Hist; Asn Independent Historians of Art. *Res:* Paul Sample; 1939-40 World's Fair; James J Mapes; architecture of Michelangelo. *Interests:* Italian Renaissance and Baroque; American Art of the 1930's & 1940's; American contemporary realists. *Collection:* Contemporary American realists from 1900 to 1940. *Publ:* Coauth, Paul Sample: Painter of the American Scene, Hood Mus Art, Dartmouth Col. *Mailing Add:* 9536 Lawnsberry Terr Silver Spring MD 20901

GLICKMAN, ARTHUR
SCULPTOR
b New York, NY, Apr 29, 23. *Study:* With Issac Soyer, 53; Nat Acad Design, with Jeon DMarco & Envangelo Frudakis, 64-68; New Sch Social Research, with Bruno Luccesi, 69. *Work:* Bergen Community Mus, Paramus, NJ. *Comn:* Bird in Flight, IBM, NJ, 74; Freedom Series, comn by Roger Williams Mint, Providence, RI, 76. *Exhib:* Allied Artists Am, Nat Acad Gallery, New York, 70, 74, 78, 80, 81, 84 & 85; Nat Acad Design, Nat Acad Gallery, New York, 75; Nat Sculpture Soc, Equitable Life Assurance Soc, New York, 76; Newark Mus, NJ, 76; Sculptors Asn NJ, Madison Square Garden, New York, 76. *Awards:* First Prize in Sculpture, Bergen Co Artists Asn, 65 & West New York, NJ, 66; Second Prize in Sculpture, Washington Square, New York, 70; Assoc Members Award, Allied Artists Am, 84. *Mem:* Allied Artists Am (vpres, 85, pres, 86); Sculptors Asn NJ. *Media:* Bonded Bronze on Plexiglass. *Dealer:* Zantmon Gallery Carmel Ca 93921. *Mailing Add:* 538 Rutland Ave Teaneck NJ 07666

GLIER, MIKE
DRAFTSMAN, MURALIST
b Fort Thomas, Ky, Aug 26, 53. *Study:* Williams Col, BA, 76; Hunter Col, with Robert Morris, MA, 79. *Work:* Addison Gallery Am Art, Andover, Mass; Norton Gallery, West Palm Beach, Fla; Hartford Atheneum, Conn; Albright-Knos Mus, Buffalo, NY. *Comn:* BAM-Next Wave, set design comn by Tim Miller, Brooklyn, NY, 84; Walls, Norton Gallery Art, West Palm Beach, 86; Green (wall drawings), comn by Wave Hill, Bronx, NY, 89. *Exhib:* Biennial, Whitney Mus, New York, 83; Hair Breadth: New Wall Drawings (with catalog), La Jolla Mus Contemp Art, Calif, 84; Sydney Biennial, Art Gallery New South Wales, Australia, 84; South Africa Drawings, Washington Project for Arts, Washington, DC, 86; Committed to Print, Mus Mod Art, New York, 88. *Pos:* Adv bd mem, Printed Matter Inc, 83; artist adv bd, New Mus, New York, 89; vis comt, Williams Col Mus Art, 90. *Awards:* Nat Endowment Art Fel, 81. *Bibliog:* Sally Yard (auth), The shadow of the bomb, Arts Mag, 4/84; Robin Carson (auth), Untamed visitiation, Garden Design, winter 89; Elizabeth Hess (auth), The equalizer, Village Voice, 6/21/89. *Media:* Mixed Media. *Publ:* Auth, The 1979 dime store figurine, Art Forum, 80; White Male Power, Senators, Game Show Hosts, National Monuments, pvt publ, 82; Patience observation & investigation, Art Forum, 82; Working Watteau, Art Forum, 4/88; Satisfaction, Hallwalls, San Jose Mus Art, 89. *Dealer:* Barbara Gladstone 99 Greene St New York NY 10012. *Mailing Add:* c/o Barbara Gladstone Gallery 99 Greene St New York NY 10012

GLIMCHER, ARNOLD B
DEALER, WRITER
b Mar 12, 38; US citizen. *Pos:* Dir, Pace Gallery, New York, 63- *Specialty:* Twentieth-century art. *Publ:* Auth, Jean Dubuffet--Simulacres (catalog), 70 & Ernest Trova--Recent Sculpture (catalog), 71, Pace Ed; Louise Nevelson, Praeger, 72; Louise Nevelson, E P Dutton & Co, Inc, 76; coauth (with Paul Vitz), Modern Art and Modern Science: The Parallel Analysis of Vision, Praeger, 83. *Mailing Add:* Pace Gallery 32 E 57th St New York NY 10022

GLOBUS, DOROTHY TWINING
CURATOR
Study: Swarthmore Col, Pa, BA(art hist, magna cum laude). *Collections Arranged:* Immovable Objects I: Lower Manhattan From Battery Park to Bridge (auth, catalog), New York, 74; MAN transFORMS, 76; More than Meets the Eye (design & coordr), 77, Ornament in the 20th Century, 78, Gardens of Delight, Cooper-Hewitt Mus Decorative Arts & Design. *Pos:* Asst to dir, Wilcox Gallery, Swarthmore Col, Pa, 67-69; apprentice design & prod, Off of Exhib, Smithsonian Inst, Washington, DC, summer 68, exhib specialist res, design & coordr for spec exhib, DRUGS, 70-72, exhib specialist res & design on assignment to James S Ward Inc, New York, Smithsonian Inst, 72-73; exhib coordr, Cooper-Hewitt Mus Decorative Arts & Design, New York, 73- *Mailing Add:* Cooper-Hewitt Mus Smithsonian Inst Nat Mus of Design 2 E 91st St New York NY 10128

GLORIG, OSTOR
PAINTER, CRAFTSMAN
b New York, NY, Feb 14, 19. *Study:* Am Art Sch, New York, with Robert Brackman, Raphael Soyer & Gordon Samstag, four yr cert. *Work:* Mark Twain Portrait, Mark Twain Libr & Mem, Hartford, Conn. *Exhib:* One-man shows, Lynn Kottler Galleries, 56, 59, 61, 64 & 72, Clarksville Gallery, 65 & Col Mt St Vincent, 67; Nat Soc Arts & Lett Empire State Chap Showing, 69 & 79. *Awards:* Interior Design Cover Award, 51; Grumbacher Merit Award, 61. *Bibliog:* Elaine Israel (auth), From diamond to canvas, Long Island Star-J, 5/9/67. *Mem:* Life fel Royal Soc Arts Eng; life mem Nat Soc Arts & Lett; hon mem Kappa Pi. *Media:* Oil. *Dealer:* Lynn Kottler Galleries 3 E 65th St New York NY 10021. *Mailing Add:* 21-56 47th St Astoria NY 11105

GLOVER, ROBERT
SCULPTOR, CERAMIST
b Upland, Calif, May 20, 36. *Study:* Los Angeles County Art Inst, with Peter Voulkos & Helen Watson, MFA, 60. *Work:* Security Pacific Bank, First Bank of Los Angeles & Bella Lewitsky Dance Found, Los Angeles; Fluor Corp, Irvine, Calif; Everson Mus Fine Arts, New York; Oakland Mus Art, Calif. *Exhib:* Drawing Exhib, San Francisco Mus Art, 57; Ceramics National, Everson Mus Fine Arts, Syracuse, NY, 60; Design 11, Pasadena Art Mus, Calif, 71; Sculpture Invitational, San Diego Mus Art, 73; duo exhib, Munic Gallery, Los Angeles, 79; Dualism, Otis-Parsons Exhib Ctr, Los Angeles, 82. *Teaching:* Asst prof ceramics, Otis Art Inst, 62-79; instr color & design, Otis-Parson Sch Design, 79-, instr ceramics, 92. *Awards:* Ford Found Fac Grant, 78. *Bibliog:* Peter Clothier (auth), Remembrances of things past, Los Angeles Weekly, Vol 8, No 5, 12/27/84; Kristine McKenna (auth), Galleries, Los Angeles Times, 12/13/85; Mac McCloud (auth), Metamorphosis of form, Artweek, Vol 16, 12/21/85. *Mem:* Los Angeles Contemp Exhibs. *Media:* Clay, Mixed Media. *Dealer:* Space Gallery 6015 Santa Monica Blvd Los Angeles CA 90038. *Mailing Add:* 9830 Portola Dr Beverly Hills CA 90210

GLOVSKY, ALAN
SCULPTOR, ENVIRONMENTAL ARTIST
Study: Dartmouth Coll, NH, BA, 73, Goldsmith's Col, Univ London, diploma of Advanced Study in Fine Art, 77, Tyler Sch Art, Philadelphia, Pa, MFA, 79. *Exhib:* Stillwater/Agua Blanca, 22 Wooster Gallery, New York, 85; If You Don't Have a Partner, Thorpe Intermedia Ctr, Sparkill, NY, 86; Face Gazing At Things Far, Hands Alone, Tossan-Tossan Gallery, New York, 87; BACA Downtown, Brooklyn, NY, 87-90; Geography of Judgement, Ihara Ludens Gallery, 90 & 91, An Exact Address, PS 122 Gallery, New York, 91. *Awards:* Nat Endow Arts Fel, 82, 84; Individual Artists Grant, NYSCA, 85, 87 & 89; MacDowell Colony Fel, 80, 82, 87 & 91. *Bibliog:* Mel Gussow (auth), Identity Loss in Imperceptible Mutabilities, New York Times, 9/20/89; David Hirsh (auth), Other Worlds, New York Native (interview), 10/7/91; photo, Alternative Galleries, Art in America (ann issue), 8/92. *Mailing Add:* 377 Hoyt St Brooklyn NY 11231

GLUCK, HEIDI
PAINTER, EDUCATOR
b Brooklyn, NY, Dec 30, 44. *Study:* Bennington Col, with D Smith, T Smith, Caro, Londo, Stroud & P Feely, BA, 66; Hunter Col, New York, with E Goosen, T Smith, R Humphrey & R Morris, 66-70. *Work:* Guggenheim Mus, New York; Israel Mus, Jerusalem; State Univ Ohio, Columbus; Picker Art Gallery, Colgate Univ, Hamilton, NY; Bennington Col, Vt. *Exhib:* Sensible Exploration, Univ Gallery Fine Art, Ohio State Univ, Columbus, 70; A Painting Show, PSI Projects Studios One, Inst Art & Urban Resources, NY, 77; A Brooklyn Portfolio, Brooklyn Mus, NY, 80; Contemp Drawings & Watercolors, Mem Art Gallery, Univ Rochester, 80; Creative Artists Public Service Program Grantees, Brooklyn Mus, NY, 81; 19 Artists-Emergent Am, Guggenheim Mus, New York, 81. *Teaching:* Vis artist painting, Princeton Univ, 80-82. *Awards:* Creative Artists Public Service Program Grant, 78-79. *Bibliog:* Robert Pincus-Witten (auth), Entries: Glück, Stephen, Acconci, Arts Mag, 3/78; Donald B Kuspit (auth), Heidi Glück, Arts Mag, 6/79; Donald B Kuspit (auth), Stops & starts in seventies art and criticism, Arts Mag, 3/81. *Media:* Oil, Acrylic. *Mailing Add:* 414-416 2nd St Jersey City NJ 07302

GLUHMAN, JOSEPH WALTER
HISTORIAN, GRAPHIC ARTIST
b Corpus Christi, Tex, July 21, 34. *Study:* Johns Hopkins Univ, AB, 55; Western Reserve Univ, MA, 62; Fulbright fel, Ger, 68; Harvard Univ, PhD, 70. *Work:* Owensboro Mus Fine Art, Ky; Merrill Lynch, Louisville, Ky; Meridian Mus Art, Miss; Ala Power Co, Birmingham; Fine Arts Mus of the South, Mobile, Ala. *Exhib:* Drawing USA, Minn Mus Art, St Paul, 71; 23rd-27th & 29th Nat Drawing-Sculpture, Ball State Univ, Muncie, Ind, 77-81 & 83; 4th Nat Potsdam Drawing, State Univ NY, Potsdam, 79; Photo-regional, 82 & Eight State Graphics, 85, J B Speed Art Mus, Louisville, Ky; Southeastern Photogr, Greenville Art Mus, SC, 83; Nat Drawings, Trenton State Col, NJ, 83; Greater Mid-West Int Photo Show, Warrensburg, Mo, 86; 20th, 22nd & 23rd Nat-Drawing Sculpture, Del Mar Col, Corpus Christi, Tex, 86, 88 & 89; The Kentuckians, Nat Arts Club, New York, 87; Halpert Biennial, Boone, NC; Midwest Photogr VI, Univ Wis/Green Bay, 90-92. *Collections Arranged:* Lyonel Feininger: Nature Notes (auth, catalog), Watson Gallery, Norton, Mass, 70; Italian Drawings from Janos Scholz Collection (auth, catalog), 71 & Drawings '74 National Exhibition (auth, catalog), 74; Kazimieras Zoromskis: Recent Paintings (auth, catalog), Van Wickle Gallery, Easton Pa, 77; Regional Artists I: Tennessee, Ivan Wilson Gallery, Bowling Green, 79; and others. *Teaching:* Prof & head, Dept Art, Auburn Univ, 87- *Awards:* Nat Watercolor Soc Award, 14th Ann Del Mar Show, 80; 12th & 13th Ann Owensboro Photog Award, 83, 84 & 87; 18th Ann Owensboro Guild Merit Award, 83; Photog Award, Nat Parkersburg Art Ctr, 85; Citizens Nat Bank Purchase Award, Ky, 87; and others. *Mem:* Col Art Asn; Southeastern Col Art Conf. *Media:* Drawing, Photography. *Res:* Nineteenth and twentieth century German painting. *Mailing Add:* 2095 S Evergreen Dr Auburn AL 36830

GLUHMAN, MARGARET A
GRAPHIC ARTIST, PHOTOGRAPHER
b Bethel Park, Pa. *Study:* Univ Pittsburgh; Cleveland Inst Art. *Work:* Rutgers Univ Art Mus; Meidinger Corp, Louisville, Ky; Owensboro Mus Fine Art; Eastman Pharmaceutical, Pa; and others. *Exhib:* Nat Drawing & Sculpture Exhib, Ball State Univ, 74, 79, 81 & 82; Mid-States Exhib, Evansville Art Mus, 78, 80, 81 & 83; Nat Drawing & Sculpture Exhib, Del Mar Col, 79-81; Mid-Am Nat, Owensboro Art Mus, Ky, 80 & 82; Kentucky Artists, Barker Gallery, New York, 83; Landscape 84, Contemp Arts Ctr, Cincinnati, Ohio; Rutgers Univ Nat, 85-86; J B Speed Art Mus, 86; Sixth Biennial Paper/Clay, Memphis, Tenn, 87; Headley-Whitney Mus, Lexington, Ky, 88; 19th Nat Works on Paper, Minot, NDak, 89; La Grange Nat XIV, XVI, XVII, Photogr, Ga, 89, 91, 92. *Collections Arranged:* New Works Series I-XXV, 81-87; Collectors & Collections (auth, catalog), 85; Mid-South Monotypes (auth, catalog), 86-87; New Works/New Alabamians (auth, catalog), 90-91. *Pos:* Exhib coordr, Capitol Arts Ctr, Bowling Green, Ky, 81-87. *Media:* Paper. *Mailing Add:* 2095 Evergreen Dr S Auburn AL 36830-6934

GLUSKA, AHARON
PAINTER
Study: AVNI Inst Fine Arts, Israel, 73-76; Academie Ecole des Beaux Arts, Paris, 76-77. *Work:* Albright Knox Mus; Brooklyn Mus; Tel Aviv Mus; Cornell Univ Mus; Jerusalem Mus. *Exhib:* One-man shows, Bertha Urdang Gallery, New York, 83, 86 & 88, Jessica Berwind Gallery, Philadelphia, 86, E L Stark Gallery, New York, 87 & 88, Tiro Gallery, Copenhagen, Denmark, 87, Shoshana Wayne Gallery, Los Angeles, 90; Phoenix Gallery Invitational, New York, 85; Robeson Ctr Gallery, Newark, NJ, 86; Siegeltuch Gallery, New York, 87 & 88; Shoshana Wayne Gallery, Los Angeles, 89; Recall Show, C S Schulte Gallery, South Orange, NJ, 91; E M Donahue Gallery, New York, 92; 3 Points of You, Estok & Lanza Fine Art, New York, 92. *Awards:* Pollock-Krasner Found Grant, 89; Nat Endowment Arts Grant, 89. *Mailing Add:* 535 Broadway New York NY 10012

GLYDE, HENRY GEORGE
PAINTER, EDUCATOR
b Luton, Eng, June 18, 06. *Study:* Hastings Sch Art & Sci; Royal Col Art, London, hons; Can Arts Coun, sr fel, 58-59; Univ Alta, LLD, 82. *Work:* Edmonton Art Gallery; Nat Gallery Can; Glenbow Found, Calgary; Alta Col Art; Univ Alta; plus others. *Comn:* Mural, Student Union Bldg, Univ Alta; mural, Medicine Nat Libr, Alta; murals, Univ Alta Libr; bas relief design, City Hall, Edmonton, Alta; bas relief design, Victoria High Sch, Edmonton, Alta. *Exhib:* Royal Brit Artists; Royal Acad, London; Can Group Painters; Can Soc Graphic Art; Royal Can Acad; plus others. *Teaching:* Instr, Borough Polytech, London; instr, Croydon Sch Art; instr, High Wycombe Sch Art; head art dept, Prov Inst Technol & Art, Alta; emer prof fine arts, Univ Alta & Banff Sch Fine Arts. *Awards:* Univ Alta Nat Award, 66. *Mem:* Royal Can Acad Arts. *Media:* Egg Tempera, Oils, Watercolors. *Mailing Add:* 1280 Hampshire Rd Victoria BC V8S 4T2 Canada

GOAD, ANNE LAINE
ART DEALER
b Nashville, Tenn. *Study:* David Lipscomb Univ, Nashville, Tenn, BA(magna cum laude), 67. *Bibliog:* Lisa Whitfill (auth), Artist's friend joins creativity clients, Brentwood J, 87; Laura Millard (auth), Anna Jaap: painting for pleasure, Nashville Bus & Lifestyles, 5/91; Pat Swingley (auth), Italian charm, Tennessean, 5/92. *Mem:* Visual Artists Alliance Nashville. *Specialty:* Original paintings featuring mid-south regional artists since 1984. *Mailing Add:* Anne Laine Goad Art Inc PO Box 2165 Brentwood TN 37024

GOBUZAS, ALDONA M
ART DEALER, COLLECTOR
b Brooklyn, NY. *Study:* Notre Dame Col, St John's Univ, BA. *Specialty:* Contemporary American art. *Collection:* Contemporary paintings, sculpture, drawings, etchings. *Mailing Add:* Galerie Aldonna 215 E 79th St New York NY 10021

GODDARD, DONALD
EDITOR, WRITER
b Cortland, NY, Apr 16, 34. *Study:* Princeton Univ, BA, 56. *Pos:* Writer & ed, McGraw-Hill Book Co, New York, 66-69; managing ed, Art News Mag, New York, 74-78, contrib ed, 78- 90; ed, Harry N Abrams Inc, 79-82 & New York Zoological Soc, 82- *Publ:* Auth, Mark di Suvero: An epic reach, 76 & Rothko's journey into the unknown, 79, Art News Mag; Harry Jackson, Harry N Abrams Inc, 81; Sound-Art, Sound Art Found, 83; Am painting, 90; and others. *Mailing Add:* 62 Greene St New York NY 10012

GODDARD, VIVIAN
PAINTER
b San Francisco, Calif. *Study:* San Francisco Inst Fine Arts: Art Students League, New York; Stanford Univ; Art League San Francisco; Robert Brackman Summer Sch, Noank & Madison, Conn; Otis Art Inst, Los Angeles; Acad Grande Chaumiere, Paris; Simi Studio, Florence, Italy. *Work:* Pioneer Mus & Hagan Gallery, Stockton, Calif; Hall Justice, San Francisco; City Sacramento, Calif; Stanislaus State Col. *Comn:* Portraits, Richard Cragin, Dr Alexander Capurso, Otto Kruger, Mrs Bernard McFayden & Mrs E Mannux; and many others. *Exhib:* One-man shows, La Galeria, NH & San Francisco, Pioneer Mus, Hagan Gallery, Sacramento, Stanislaus State Col, Barrios Gallery, Rosecrucian Mus, San Jose, Calif; Soc Western Artists, De Young Mus, San Francisco, 68-70; and others. *Teaching:* Instr pvt studio, 69-71. *Awards:* First Award Graphics, Crocker Mus, 67; Oil Portrait Award, Soc Western Artists, 67; Portrait Award, Mother Lode Nat, 70; Ayling Award. *Mem:* Life mem, Art Students League. *Media:* Oil, Pastel. *Dealer:* Portraits Inc 41 E 57th St New York NY 10022; Kertesz Gallery 521 Sutter St San Francisco CA 94108. *Mailing Add:* Metropolitan Club 640 Sutter St San Francisco CA 94102

GODFREY, ROBERT
PAINTER, CRITIC
b Mt Holly, NJ, Apr 17, 41. *Study:* Philadelphia Col Art, BFA, 66; Royal Acad Fine Arts, Copenhagen, post grad, 66-67; Ind Univ, MFA, 69. *Work:* Ind Univ Art Mus, Bloomington; Butler Inst Am Art; Asheville Art Mus. *Exhib:* Solo exhibs, Blue Mountain Gallery, New York, 79, 81 & 82, Butler Ints Am Art, Youngstown, Ohio, 83 & 92, site specific installatiion, NC Mus Art, 88, St John's Mus, NC, 91; Figure in Recent American Painting, traveling exhib, Pa & NY, 74-75; Am Figure Drawing, traveling exhib, Pa & Australia, 76; Neo-Expressionism, SECCA, NC, 89; plus many others. *Pos:* Dir, Artists' Choice Mus, New York, 79-80, ed, 80-82; art critic, Asheville Citizen Times, 85-89; ed, CRITS: Discourses on the Visual Arts, 88- *Teaching:* Vis artist, Univ Pa, Philadelphia, 79-82; prof art, painting, drawing & art hist, Westminster Col, New Wilmington, Pa, 82-85; head art dept, Western Carolina Univ, Cullowhee, NC, 85- *Awards:* Drawing Award, Philadelphia Col Art, 66; Fulbright-Hays scholar, Denmark, 66-67; Buhl Found grant, 78. *Bibliog:* William Kelly (auth), Robert Godfrey (monograph), Arts Mag, 80; James Ashbrook Perkins (auth), Presentational Immediacy (monograph), Butler Inst Am Art, 83; Chris Redd (auth), Robert Godfrey's Psycological Neo- Expressionism (monograph), Arts J, 88. *Mem:* Int Asn Art Critics. *Media:* Oil. *Publ:* Auth, Have museums slighted certain types of art--particularly figurative art?, Am Artists Mag, 79; About sentimentality, 83 & A lesson in still life painting, 84, Artists' Choice Mus J. *Dealer:* Blue Mountain Gallery 121 Wooster St New York NY 10012; Art Gallery Ltd 502 Pollock St Newbern NC 28560. *Mailing Add:* PO Box 5 Downtown Station Asheville NC 28802

GODFREY, WINNIE (WINIFRED M)
PAINTER, INSTRUCTOR
b Philadelphia, Pa, Nov 21, 44. *Study:* Marycrest Col, Iowa, 61-63; Art Inst Chicago, 62; Univ Wis, Madison, BS, 66, MFA, 70. *Work:* Ill State Mus, Springfield; Portland Mus, Ore; Borg-Warner Art Collection, Kemper Insurance Art Collection, Chicago; Rochester Art Ctr, Minn. *Comn:* Oil painting, State Ill, Danville, 83; oil painting, Oakton Community Col, Ill, 86; oil painting, Marshall Fields, Ill. *Exhib:* Two-person show, Art Inst Chicago Sales Gallery, 81; solo exhib, Chicago Botanic Garden, Glencoe, Ill, 86, Rahrwest Art Mus, Manitowoc, Wis, 88; Hot House, John Michael Kohler Art Ctr, Sheboygan, Wis, 89; 20th Century Flower Painting, Mus Art, Ft Lauderdale, Fla, 91; Headley-Whitney Mus, Lexington, Ky, 91; and others. *Teaching:* Artist-in-residence drawing & painting, Rochester Art Ctr, Minn, 70; vis lectr drawing, Univ Ill, Chicago, 75-76; instr portraits, Evanston Art Ctr, Ill, 80-85. *Awards:* First Prize, Milwaukee Lakefront, Milwaukee Art Ctr, 75 & 78; Best of Show, Arthur Baer Mem Competition, Beverly Art Ctr, 83; Award of Excellence, Flora Exhib, Chicago Botanic Garden, Glencoe, Ill, 86, 88. *Bibliog:* Richard Waller (auth), article, New York Gallery Guide, 5/82; Jim Hatfield (producer), Two on two, CBS, 84. *Mem:* Artists Equity; Chicago Artists Coalition; North Shore Art League. *Media:* Oil. *Publ:* Auth, article, New Art Examiner, 81; article, In: Gallery Guide, Art Now Inc, 82; contribr, The New York Art Review, Macmillan, 82; Illustrators 23, Madison Sq Press, 83; Artists Mag, F & W Publ, 86 & 91. *Dealer:* Winifred Godfrey 2647 N Orchard Chicago IL 60614. *Mailing Add:* 2647 N Orchard St Chicago IL 60614

GODSEY, GLENN
EDUCATOR, PAINTER
b Amarillo, Tex, June 1, 37. *Study:* Okla State Univ; Univ Tulsa, BA & MA; and with Alexandre Hogue. *Work:* Springfield Art Mus, Mo; Okla State Art Collection, Okla Arts & Humanities Coun, Oklahoma City; Gilcrease Mus, Tulsa. *Comn:* Portrait, Univ Tulsa; portraits, Oral Roberts Univ, The Union Depot & Gilcrease Mus, Tulsa. *Exhib:* One-man shows, Philbrook Art Ctr, Tulsa, 71, Amarillo Art Ctr, 85 & Univ Tulsa, 85; Traveling Exhib of Okla Art,

Washington, DC, 76; Saltillo, Mex, 77; two-man show, Univ Tulsa, 78; Am Watercolor, Taipei Fine Arts Mus, Taiwan, 85; Aquarelles Americaines, Tours, France, 86. *Teaching:* Assoc prof painting, Univ Tulsa, 67- *Awards:* Watercolor USA Purchase Award, SMo Mus Asn, 74; Okla Artist Ann Award, 72 & 74. *Bibliog:* Rev Blakey (auth), Delineating the mysterious, Univ Tulsa Mag; Maurice DeVinna (auth), Music & the arts, Tulsa World Mag, 71; Bill Donaldson (auth), Showcase, Tulsa Tribune, 71. *Mem:* Watercolor USA Hon Soc. *Media:* Acrylic, Watercolor. *Publ:* Auth, Hip generation, Univ Tulsa Mag, 68; illusr, Okla State Univ Lit Quart, Nimrod, Tulsa Mag & Univ Tulsa Mag. *Mailing Add:* Phillips Hall Rm 102 Sch Art Univ Tulsa Tulsa OK 74104

GODWIN, JUDITH
PAINTER
b Suffolk, Va. *Study:* Mary Baldwin Col, Staunton, Va; Va Commonwealth Univ, BFA; Art Students League, with Vaclav Vytlacil, Will Barnet & Harry Sternberg; Hans Hofmann Sch, Provincetown, Mass & New York; Va Commonwealth Univ, Hon DFA. *Work:* Metrop Mus, New York; Milwaukee Art Ctr, Wis; San Francisco Mus Mod Art; Nat Mus Art, Osaka, Japan; Chase Manhattan Collection, New York; Nat Mus Wales, Cardiff; Ulrich Mus, Wichita, Kans; Va Mus, Richmond; Newark Mus, NJ; Yale Univ; Utah Mus, Salt Lake City; Herbert F Johnson Mus, Cornell Univ. *Comn:* Painter's Themes (fabric design), Bloomcraft Inc, New York, 76. *Exhib:* One-person shows, Ingber Gallery, New York, 77, 79, 81-82, 84 & 90, Womensbank, Richmond, Va, 81, Loonam Gallery, Bridgehampton, NY, 82, Phoenix II Gallery, Washington, DC, 83, Mukai Gallery, Tokyo, Japan, & Lockwood-Mathews Mansion Mus, Norwalk, Conn, 85; Anderson Gallery, Va Commonwealth Univ, Richmond, 79 & 82; Am Fedn Art Traveling exhib, Hans Hoffman as Teacher, 79 & 82; Marisa del Re Gallery, New York, 83 & 90; Kenkeleba Gallery, New York, 85; retrospective, Northern Mich Univ, Va Polytech Inst & Northern Va Community Col, Alexandria. *Awards:* Popular Prize, Leache Mem Exhib, Norfolk, 51. *Bibliog:* Joyce E Davis (auth), Judith Godwin, Art Voices S, 5-6/79; Natalie Edgar (auth), Judith Goodwin, Arts Mag, 5/81; Cynthia Nadelman (auth), Judith Godwin, Art News, 81. *Mem:* Am Fedn Arts; Col Art Asn; Women's Caucus Art. *Media:* Oil, Acrylic. *Mailing Add:* c/o Davis 247 W 13th St New York NY 10011

GODWIN, LAWRENCE
PAINTER, SCULPTOR
b Ala, Nov 20, 34. *Study:* Auburn Univ, Ala, BASC, 53-57. *Comn:* Sculpture, murals & monument, Ala State Univ Campus; monument, Powered Flight, Maxwell AFB, Ala, 85; portrait, Pea River Historical Soc, Enterprise Ala, 86. *Exhib:* One-man shows, Art Acres Gallery, 59-61, Sculpture, Montgomery Mus Fine Arts, Ala, 72; Gov Gallery, Ala State Capitol, 66; Birmingham Festival Art, Ala, 72; Green Garden Gallery, Montgomery, Ala, 83. *Pos:* Artist-in-Sch, Nat Endowment Arts Off Educ, 73. *Teaching:* Instr painting, drawing & sculpture, Fort Rucker, Army Aviation Sch, Art Acres Gallery. *Bibliog:* Bennett Schiff (auth), Artist-in-School, Nat Endowment Arts, 73; Emma Lila Fundaburk (auth), Art in Public Places, Bowling Green Univ. *Mailing Add:* RFD 1 Brundige AL 36010

GOEDICKE, JEAN
PAINTER, CONSULTANT
b DePass, Wyo, Sept 24, 08. *Study:* Taos Sch Art, NMex, with Emil Bisttram; Casper Col, with Ed Gothberg, AA; Univ Wyo, with James M Boyle & Richard Evans, BA & MA(with hon); also with Robert E Wood & Bud Shackelford, Calif, Mario Cooper, Dale Meyers & Edgar Whitney, NY & Milford Zornes, Utah; workshops with Virginia Cobb, NMex, Jeanne Dobie, Pa, Carole Barnes, Colo Jane Burnham, Calif. *Work:* Wyo State Art Gallery, Cheyenne; Wyo State Capitol, Cheyenne; Casper Counseling Center; Nicholsen Art Mus, Casper; St James Episcopal Church, Riverton, Wyo; Casper Col. *Exhib:* Wyo Traveling Art Exhib, 57-74; Univ Fed de Goias, Brazil, 69; eight state regional watercolor exhib, Fedn Rocky Mountain States, Inc, 69-71; Invitational, Nicolaysen Art Mus, Casper, Wyo, 79-90; Juried regional and nat exhibs, Mont, Nebr, Ky & Wyo, 80-87; and others. *Teaching:* Instr watercolor & drawing, Mobile Art Symp, Wyo Coun Arts, 67-79, Friends of Artists, 75- *Awards:* Wyo Artist of the Year, Wyo Artists Asn, 86; Wyo Writers Award, 89 & 91. *Bibliog:* Peggy Simson Curry (auth), A Tool Box & a Talent, In Wyoming, summer 70; Jean Mead (auth), Wyoming in Profile, 82. *Mem:* Casper Artists Guild (pres, 40-65); Wyo Artists Asn (pres, 66-67); Scotch & Watercolor Soc, Wyo, 74-; Wyo Watercolor Soc, 84- *Media:* Transparent Watercolor. *Publ:* Contribr, This Is Wyoming--Listen, 77. *Dealer:* West Wind Gallery 1040 W 15th Casper WY 82604; Wild Goose Gallery 211 W 19th Cheyenne WY 82001. *Mailing Add:* 2125 S Coffman Casper WY 82601

GOEDIKE, SHIRL
PAINTER
b Los Angeles, Calif, 1923. *Study:* Univ Calif, Los Angeles; Art Ctr Sch, Los Angeles. *Work:* Los Angeles Co Mus Art; Louvre, Paris; Palm Springs Mus; Birmingham Mus Art, Ala; Hirshhorn Mus, Washington, DC; and others. *Exhib:* Los Angeles Co Mus, 55-56; Stanford Univ, 56; one-man shows, Palace Legion of Honor, San Francisco, Calif, 59 & Elysee Palace, Paris, 83; Santa Barbara Biennial, Santa Barbara Mus & Nat Tour, 59; 26th Biennial, Corcoran Gallery Art, Washington, DC; Pasadena Art Mus, Calif; Whitney Mus Ann, 60; Pasadena Art Mus, Calif; Palm Springs Mus, Calif, 76. *Bibliog:* Alfred Frankenstein (auth), articles, San Francisco Chronicle, 59, 60 & 62; Henry Seldis (auth), articles, Los Angeles Times, 72; Alfred Frankenstein (auth), Shirl Goedike (monogr), Hammer Publ, 78. *Media:* Oil, Watercolor. *Mailing Add:* c/o Joan Ankrum Gallery 327 N Orange Dr Los Angeles CA 90036

GOEHLICH, JOHN RONALD
EDUCATOR, ADMINISTRATOR
b Chicago, Ill, Sept 29, 34. *Study:* Bard Col, with Louis Schanker, BA, 56. *Pos:* Art dir, Doyle Dane Bernbach Inc, New York, 57-64. *Teaching:* Dean admis, Sch Visual Arts, New York, 66-68; head dept commun design, Ray Col Design, Chicago, 69- *Awards:* Cert Merit, Art Dirs Club, New York, 63 & 64. *Mem:* Am Ctr Design. *Mailing Add:* 1749 North Wells, Apt 717 Chicago IL 60614

GOELL, ABBY JANE
PAINTER, ASSEMBLAGE ARTIST
b New York, NY. *Study:* Art Students League, with Harry Sternberg & Charles Alston; Syracuse Univ, BA; NY Sch Interior Design, Cert; Columbia Univ, with Robert Motherwell, Stephen Greene & John Heliker, MFA(painting), 65; Attingham Park, Shropshire, UK, 63; Pratt Graphic Ctr, 65. *Work:* Mus Mod Art, New York; Yale Univ Art Gallery; Chase Manhattan Bank Collection, New York; Kresge Art Ctr, Mich; Altantic Richfield Oil Co; Neuberger Mus, Purchase, NY; Print Collection, New York Pub Libr; Smith Col Art Mus; Princeton Univ Art Gallery, Grafisches Cabinet, Munich. *Comn:* Original print, Pratt Graphics Ctr, 75. *Exhib:* One-person show, Automation House, 73; Grey Gallery & Study Ctr, NY Univ, 77; Am Acad Arts & Letters, 77; Childe Hassam Purchase Prize Exhib, 77; US Mission, Havana, Cuba, 79-81; Sculpture Ctr, NY, 81; TAGA-PRATT Exhib, Caracas, 82; Silvermine, Conn Ann, 81-82; John Szoke Gallery, New York, 88-89; Southeastern Ohio Cult Ctr, 92. *Pos:* Publ, Arcadia Press, New York. *Teaching:* Instr art hist, Hunter Col, 67; lectr, Lab Inst Merchandising, 67-70. *Awards:* Yaddo Fel, Saratoga Springs, NY, 68; Va Ctr Creative Arts Fel, Sweet Briar, 81. *Mem:* Life Mem, Art Students League; Women's Caucus Art; sr mem Am Soc Appraisers; Victorian Soc in Am; panelist, Am Arbitration Assoc; The Coffee House, New York. *Media:* Acrylic; Collage, Serigraph, Lithograph. *Publ:* Ed, English Silver 1675-1825, Ensko & Wenham, revised ed, 80. *Mailing Add:* 37 Washington Sq W New York NY 10011

GOERTZ, AUGUSTUS FREDERICK, III
PAINTER, PHOTOGRAPHER
b Greenwich Village, New York, NY, Aug 15, 48. *Study:* High Sch of Music & Art, New York; Carnegie-Mellon Univ, Pittsburgh, Pa; San Francisco Art Inst, BFA; also with Tom Akawie, Jay Defeo, Augustus Goertz Sr, Wally Hedrick, Bruce Nauman & Jim Rienekin. *Work:* San Francisco Art Inst; Chicago Art Inst; Aldrich Mus Contemp Art, Ridgefield, Conn; Huntington Bank of Ohio; Hyatt Collection, New York; Aetna Casualty & Insurance, Harrison, NY; Siemens Electronics: Shersan Lehman, Chubb Avatav Brokerage. *Exhib:* Selections from The Collection, Aldrich Mus of Contemp Art, 78; Arte Fiera, Bologna, Italy, 78; Todd Capp Gallery, New York; Ruth Bachoffner, Los Angeles; one-man shows, New York Law Sch, 77 & Sarah Rentschler Gallery, 78-85; Are You Experienced, Univ Brussels, Belgium, 81; Somers Gallery, Somerstown, NY; Todd Capp 85-86; The Gallery, Bond St, New York, 90; New-Persona, New York, 90; Patricia Correa, Los Angeles; Robin Rice Photo, New York. *Collections Arranged:* Contemporary Reflections, Aldrich Mus of Contemp Art, Ridgefield, Conn, 73; Encounter, Warren Benedek Gallery, New York, 73. *Pos:* Dir, Art Time Found, New York; consultant, Downtown Ventures, New York; corresp, Viva Mag, Germany, Maire-Claire Mag, German edition. *Awards:* Spec Achievement Award, New York Taxi Drivers, Robert Scull, 65; Honor Student Award, San Francisco Art Inst, 67. *Bibliog:* J Wiessman (auth), article, Art News, 75; Ellen Stern (auth), article, NY Mag, 78; Eleanor Blan (auth), article, NY Times, 80; Ellen Handy (auth), article, Arts Mag, 87. *Mem:* Orgn of Independent Artists; New York WPA Artists Inc; San Francisco Art Inst Alumni Asn. *Media:* Oil, Acrylic; Photo Emulsion. *Publ:* Contribr, New York Art Review, 89; photographs, Viva Magazine, Ger & Bilden Suntag, Ger. *Dealer:* Patricia Correia 1355 Abbot Kinney Blvd Venice Los Angeles CA; Romy Barron 95 Horatio St New York NY 10014. *Mailing Add:* 319 Greenwich St New York NY 10013

GOETZ, MARY ANNA
PAINTER, INSTRUCTOR
b Oklahoma City, Okla, Oct 7, 46. *Study:* Okla city Univ, BA, 68; Cape Sch Art, Provincetown, Mass, 69-70; NY Acad Art, New York, 81-82. *Work:* Meyers Gallery State Univ NY, Plattsburgh; Union Pac, Union League Club, White & Case, New York. *Comn:* Landscape of golf course, PGA World Hall of Fame, Pinehurst, NC. *Exhib:* Allied Artists Am, Acad Arts & Letters, New York, 74; Collector's Choice, Miss Mus Art, Jackson, 86, 87 & 88; solo exhibs, Grand Cent Art Galleries, New York, 91, Newman Galleries, Philadelphia, 86; Ann Nat Salon, Springfield Mus Art, Utah, 86 & 87; Brooklyn Bounty: Natural Splendor & Domestic Opulence, Mus Borough Brooklyn, NY, 85. *Pos:* Bd mem, Nat Asn Women Artists, 89- *Teaching:* Instr, landscape & still life painting, Woodstock Sch Art, 91- *Bibliog:* Stephen Dougherty (auth), Survey of Outdoor Painters, Am Artist, 10/88; Joan D'Arcy (auth), The Richly Diverse Art of Mary Anna Goetz, Santa Fe Focus, 7/92. *Mem:* Nat Arts Club; Salmagundi Club (jury of awards); Nat Asn Women Artists (newsletter ed); Artists Fel; Woodstock Artists Asn. *Media:* Oil. *Publ:* Auth, Robert Shultz: In Memoriam, Portraiture, It's Two Irresistable Forces: Artist & Subject, The Illuminator, 79; Painting Landscapes in Oil, North Light, 91; Impact of Brush Strokes, Am Artist, 92. *Dealer:* James Cox Gallery 26 Elwyn Lane Woodstock NY 12498. *Mailing Add:* 70 Mill Hill Rd Woodstock NY 12498

GOETZ, PETER HENRY
PAINTER, LECTURER
b Slavgorod, Russia, Sept 8, 17; Can citizen. *Study:* Waterloo Col, 45; Doon Sch Fine Art, with F H Varley; study watercolor in Japan. *Work:* Queen Elizabeth Collection, Windsor Castle, Eng; London Pub Libr & Art Mus, Ont; Sarnia Pub Libr & Art Mus, Ont; Kitchener Waterloo Art Gallery; Univ Waterloo, Ont; Arnot Art Mus, Elmira, NY; 45 paintings, New City Hall, Waterloo, Ont. *Comn:* Series of twelve paintings from around the world, Waterloo Co Health Bldg, 65; painting of Parliament bldgs, Nat Club, Toronto, 67; Peace Tower, comn by Sen John B Aird, Toronto, 69; painting of Budapest, CFTO-TV, Toronto, 69; View of Prague, Toronto Stock Exchange, 69. *Exhib:* Royal Can Acad; Ont Soc Artists; Can Soc Painters Watercolour; Nat Gallery Ottawa; Am Watercolor Soc, New York, 72. *Teaching:* Lectured and demonstrated adult education classes throughout Ontario for Department of Education. *Awards:* Watercolor Prize, Western Ont Exhib; First Prize, Brampton Ann Exhib; Purchase Award, Image 76, Ont Soc Artists, 76; Grand Prize, Que Nat Exhib. *Mem:* Ont Soc Artists; Canada Soc Painters Watercolour; Soc Can Artists; Centro Studi & Scambi Int, Rome; fel Int Inst Arts & Lett; Am Fedn Art. *Media:* Watercolor. *Mailing Add:* 784 Avondale Ave Kitchener ON N2M 2W8 Canada

GOETZL, THOMAS MAXWELL
LECTURER, EDUCATOR
b Chicago, Ill, May 31, 43. *Study:* Univ Calif, Berkeley, AB(psychology), 65 & Boalt Hall Sch of Law, JD, 69. *Pos:* Mem bd dirs, Calif Lawyers Arts, currently; assoc mem, Nat Conf State Legislatures, Arts Tourism and Cult Resources Comt, currently. *Teaching:* Prof Art Law, Golden Gate Univ, Sch of Law, San Francisco, Calif, 72- *Mem:* Artists Equity Asn; Calif Lawyers Arts; Calif State Bar. *Publ:* Copyright & the Visual Artists Display Right, A New Doctrinal Analysis, 9 Colum VLA J L & Arts, 84; Kennedy Proposal to Amend the Copyright Law; In Support of the Resale Royalty, 7 Cardozo A & E L J 249, 89; Visual Arts and the Public: A Legislative Agenda for the 1990's, 12 Hast Comm/Ent L J 403, 90. *Mailing Add:* Dept Law Golden Gate Univ 536 Mission St San Francisco CA 94105

GOFF, THOMAS JEFFERSON
SCULPTOR, MEDALIST
b Bristol, RI, Dec 22, 07. *Study:* RI Sch Design, study under Louise A Atkins, Hugo O E Carlborg & William A Heath, BFA, 30. *Work:* US Naval Mus, Washington, DC; Smithsonian Inst, Washington, DC; Newport News Mus, Va; US Naval War Col Mus, Newport, RI; RI Hist Soc Mus, Providence. *Comn:* Armed servs insignia, Craven & Whitaker Co, Providence, 40-45; Bryant Col bronze seal, pres Bryant Col, Providence & Smithfield, RI, 62; Gordon Col bronze seal, Seal Comt, Wrentham, Mass, 71; Univ RI bronze podium seal, Foundry-Auburn Brass Foundry, Cranston, RI, 69; Jackson State Col bronze seal, Herff-Jones Co, Indianapolis, Ind, 70. *Exhib:* Nat Sculpture Soc Exhib, 49 & 62; Bristol Art Mus, 65; Int Exhib by Uno A Erre, Arezzo, Italy, 69; Int Exhib, Arezzo, Italy, 70. *Awards:* Steel Engraving, RI Sch Design, New Eng Jewelers & Silversmiths Asn, 34; Lunar 1969 Landing Award, Uno A Erre, Arezzo, Italy, 70. *Bibliog:* Wayne Worchester (auth), Designs ship's insignia, Providence J Co, 66; K Nelson (auth), Ship's insignia, an art, The Newport Navalog, 67; Rose Derosiers (auth), Heraldic art, Bulletin RI Sch Design, 12/73. *Mem:* Soc Medalists, Danbury, Conn; Orders & Medals Soc Am; Naval League, US Naval Inst; Am Medallic Sculpture Asn. *Media:* Wax, Modeling Clay; Bronze, Die Steel. *Dealer:* Block Artists' Material Co 129 Dyer St Providence RI 02901; Manufacturers Supply Co 171 Chestnut St Providence RI 02901. *Mailing Add:* 1227 Hope St Bristol RI 02809

GOFFMAN, JUDY
ART DEALER, GALLERY OWNER
Study: Univ Penna, BA, 63, Grad Sch Educ, MS, 64. *Collections Arranged:* Norman Rockwell: An American Tradition, Greenville Co Mus, Greenville, SC, 85-86; A Celebration of American Illustration 1920-1950, C-TEC Corp, Wilkes-Barre, Pa, 87; Norman Rockwell: The Great American Storyteller, Miss Mus Art, Jackson, 88-89; American Illustrators 1880-1950, Parkersburg Art Ctr, Parkersburg WVa, 89; Norman Rockwell In Italy, Cortina d'Ampezzo & Rome, 90; Norman Rockwell in Japan, Tokyo, Osaka, Nagoya, 92. *Pos:* Guest cur for var travel exhibs of Am illstrs: guest lectr at Miss Mus Art; guest lectr ar Miss Mus Art & Lotos Club. *Mem:* Norman Rockwell Mus (Nat Steering Comt); Univ Pa Club of NY; Pa Soc. *Specialty:* Norman Rockwell, Paintings, drawings & watercolors by important American illustrators of the Golden Age (1890-1950); 19th Century American genre & landscape; early 20th century American Moderns, WPA, Ash-Can & American Impressionists. *Collection:* Golden Age of Great American illustrators, including Norman Rockwell, Maxfield Parrish, NC Wyeth, JC Leyendecker & Howard Chandler Christy. *Publ:* Auth, American Illustrators, Vol 1-5, 1979-84; Norman Rockwell: An American Tradition, 86; Norman Rockwell: The Great American Storyteller, Judy Goffman Fine Art, 88; contribr, Currier's Price Guide to American Artists, 1645-1945 at Auction, 87; auth, Artists as Illustrators: An International Directory with Signatures & Monograms, 1800 to the Present, 89. *Mailing Add:* Am Illustrators Gallery 18 E 77th St New York NY 10021

GOGORZA, PATRICIA (GAHAGAN) DE
SCULPTOR, PRINTMAKER
b Detroit, Mich, Mar 17, 36. *Study:* Smith Col, BA, 58; S W Hayter's Atelier 17, Paris, France, 58-60; Goddard Col, Plainfield, Vt, MA, 75. *Work:* Collection Ville de Paris (Louvre), France; Victoria & Albert Mus, London, Eng; Boston Mus Fine Arts; Provincetown Art Asn Mus, Mass; Bard Col, Annandale-on-Hudson, NY. *Comn:* Tobias & the Angel, granite, Kerson, at Worcester, Vt 87; Sun/Moon Cycle, granite, Johnson State Col, Vt; large marble sculpture, Riverbirds, Marble St Sculpture Park, W Rutland. *Exhib:* Salon des Realites Nouvelles, Mus Art Mod, Paris, France, 58-61 & Paris Biennale, 61; Vt Artists, Bundy Mus, Waitsfield, Vt, 67 & 76; Manhattan Counterpoints, Lever House, New York, 67; Arts Festival, White Mountain Art Festival, Jefferson, NJ, 78; Solo exhibs, First Branch Gallery, Chelsea, Vt, 78, Wood Art Gallery, Montpelier, Vt, 81, Bundy Mus, Waitsfield, Vt, 82 & retrospective, 58-88, Wood Art Gallery, 88; The Garage Gallery, Montpelier & Dibden Gallery, Johnson, Vt, 84; Moonbrook Gallery, Rutland, Vt & AVA Gallery, Hanover, NH, 85; Women's Caucus Arts Northeast Regional, Burlington, Vt, 85; Seven Vermont Artists, Helen Day Art Ctr, Stowe, Vt, 86; Currents in Stone, Barre Sculpture Studios, Barre, Vt, 88; Hillyer Art Gallery, Northampton, Mass, 89; Krystal Art Gallery, Waitsfield, Vt, 89; Sculpture Fest, Woodstock, Vt, 91 & 92; Beside Myself Gallery, Arlington, Vt, 92; Shelburne Farms, Vt, 92. *Pos:* Bd mem, Printmaking Workshop, New York, 70-74, Carving Studio, W Rutland, Va, 90-92. *Teaching:* Asst prof print & sculpture, Bard Col, 66-69; instr sculpture, Goddard Col, 77-79; instr drawing, Univ Vt, 80-81; instr, Johnson State Col External Degree Prog, 82-86 & Vt Col MA prog, 82-90; vis artist, Vt Studio Sch, Johnson, 85-90, instr, 89; Vt Col External Degree Prog, 87 & 88; vis artist, Carving Studio, WRutland, Vt, 88-90; Brattleboro Artists' Seminar, Vt, 89-90; Vt Col MFA Prog, 92. *Awards:* First Prize Sculpture, Norwich Ann, Vt, 78 & 86; First Prize, All Vt Juried Show, Bundy Mus, Waitsfield, Vt, 82. *Bibliog:* V Watson-Jones (auth), Contemporary Women Sculptors, Oryx Press, Phoenix, Ariz, 85. *Mem:* Soc Am Graphic Artists; Provincetown Art Asn; Vt Women's Caucus Art; Vt Coun Arts (bd mem, 89-92); Carving Studio (bd mem, 90-92). *Media:* Wood, Stone; Color Etching, Copper. *Mailing Add:* Box 116 RFD East Calais VT 05650

GOHEEN, ELLEN ROZANNE
HISTORIAN, CURATOR
b New York, NY, Mar 30, 44. *Study:* Univ Kans, Lawrence, BA & MA. *Collections Arranged:* Masters of 20th Century Photography, 73, American Impressionism, 74, Friends of Art Retrospective, 76, Joseph Cornell, 77, Jasper Johns in Kansas City 1967-1977, 78, Thomas Hart Benton An American Original, 89 & The Drawings of Ralph Barton, 91, Nelson Gallery-Atkins Mus, Kansas City, Mo. *Pos:* From asst cur to assoc cur Europ painting & sculpture, Nelson Gallery-Atkins Mus, 70-75, 20th century art, 75-81, sr lectr, 81-85; coordr, Thomas Hart Benton Proj, 85-89, admin spec exhib & collections mgt, 89- *Awards:* Sir George Trevelyan Scholar, Attingham Park Summer Sch, Shropshire, Eng, 73. *Mem:* Archaeol Inst Am (pres, Kans Chap, 74-77); Nat Trust Hist Preserv; Royal Oak Found. *Res:* Twentieth century American and European art, European and American architecture. *Publ:* Contrib, Christo: Wrapped Walk Ways, 79, The Collections of the Nelson-Atkins Mus Art, Abrams, 88; Warren Rosser, Turn and Turn About Kansas City Art Inst, 89. *Mailing Add:* 6135 Overhill Rd Shawnee Mission KS 66208

GOHLKE, FRANK WILLIAM
PHOTOGRAPHER
b Wichita Falls, Tex, Apr 3, 42. *Study:* Univ Tex, Austin, BA, 64; Yale Univ, New Haven, Conn, MA, 66; pvt study with Paul Caponigro, 67-68. *Work:* Nat Gallery Can, Ottawa, Ont; Australian Nat Gallery, Canberra; Bibliothéque Nationale, Paris, France; Mus Mod Art, New York; Cleveland Mus Art, Ohio. *Comn:* American Images (photo works), comn by AT&T, Washington, DC, 79; photog murals, Tulsa Int Airport, Okla, 81 & 88; Tex Sesquicentennial (photog survey), comn by Tex Hist Found, Austin, 84. *Exhib:* Solo exhibs, Int Mus Photog, George Eastman House, Rochester, NY, 74, Amon Carter Mus Western Art, Ft Worth Tex, 75, Mt St Helens: Work in Progress, Mus Mod Art, 83, Landscapes from the Middle of the World, Mus Contemp Photography, Chicago, 88; New Topographics: Photographs of a Man-Altered Landscape, Int Mus Photogr, George Eastman House, Rochester, NY, 74; Mirrors & Windows: Am Photography since 1960, Mus Mod Art, New York, 78; An Open Land: Photographs of the Midwest 1852-1982, Art Inst Chicago, Ill, 83; Landscapes from the Middle of the World, Mus of Contemp Photog, Chicago, 88. *Teaching:* Vis lectr, Colo Col, Colorado Springs, 87-88. *Awards:* Guggenheim Fel, 75 & 84; Photogr Fel, Nat Endowment Arts, 77 & 86; Artists Fel, Bush Found, St Paul, Minn, 78. *Bibliog:* Andy Grundberg (auth), Reflecting the supremacy of nature, NY Times, 3/28/82; Owen Edwards (auth), In the valley of the shadow, Am Photogr, 1/83; Robert Silberman (auth), Our town: Tulsa murals, Art Am, 7/85. *Publ:* Landscapes from the Middle of the World (exhib catalog), Friends of Photography, 88; Measure of Emptiness: Grain Elevators in the American Lanscapes (monograph, with a concluding essay by John C Hudson), John Hopkins Univ Press, 92. *Mailing Add:* 65 Cross St Ashland MA 01721-1301

GOIN, PETER
PHOTOGRAPHER, VIDEO ARTIST
b Madison, Wis. *Study:* Hamline Univ, BA, 73; Univ Iowa, MA, MFA, 60. *Work:* Nat Mus Am Art, Washington, DC; Los Angeles Co Mus Art; San Francisco Mus Mod Art; Amon Carter Mus, Ft Worth, Tex; Minneapolis Inst Art, Minn. *Exhib:* Picturing California, Oakland Mus Art, 89; Baltimore Mus Art, Md, 91, Phoenix Mus At, Ariz, 92, Mint Mus Art, Charlotte, NC, 92 & Seattle Mus Hist & Indust, Wash, 92; Between Home and Heaven, Nat Mus Am Art, Washington, DC, 91; Wasteland, Fotographie Biennale, Rotterdam, 92; New Orleans Triennial, New Orleans Mus, La, 92. *Teaching:* Assoc prof art, Univ Nev, 84- *Awards:* Nat Endowment Arts Fels, 82 & 90; Nathan Cummings Grant, 92. *Publ:* Auth, Tracing the Line: A Photographic Survey of the Mexican American Border, 87; Nuclear Landscapes, Johns Hopkins Univ Press, 91; Stopping Time: A Rephotographic Survey of Lake Tahoe, Univ NMex Press, 92; ed, Arid Waters, Univ Nev Press, 92. *Mailing Add:* 815 Humbolt St Reno NV 89509

GOING, JO
VISUAL ARTIST
b Jan 6, 47. *Study:* Newton Col, Mass, BA, 68; Parsons Sch Design, New York, 68-69; Univ Calif, San Diego, MFA, 69. *Work:* Art Bank Purchase, Alaska State Coun Arts; The Price Collection, Univ Calif, San Diego. *Exhib:* Solo-exhibs, Univ RI, Kingston, Fairbanks Arts Asn, Alaska, 87, Alaska State Mus, Juneau, 87 & Mandeville Gallery, Univ Calif, San Diego, 89; Anchorage Mus Fine Arts, Alaska, 88; Maine Coast Graphics, Camden, Maine; Harvard Univ, Cambridge, Mass; Museo Italoamericano, San Francisco, 91. *Pos:* Artist-in-residence, Univ RI, 81, Alaska State Coun Arts, 82-, Mont Arts Coun & Idaho Comn Arts, 90; art dir, Boston Now Mag; staff artist, Boston After Dark Newspaper. *Teaching:* Painting, oil & water color, drawing, 3-D design, Windhover Sch Arts, Rockport, Mass; drawing, Little Compton Art Asn; painting, RI Col, Providence; Univ RI, Kingston, summer 81; lectr painting, Univ Alaska, Fairbanks, summer 84 & 91; painting, Univ Alaska, Nenana, fall 86; teacher training workshops, Alaskan Arts Educ, 86; painting workshop, Cent Wyo Col, Riverton, 87; drawing, Univ Calif, San Diego, 88-89, primitive art hist, 88-89; Univ Calif, Craft Ctr, San Diego, 86-88. *Awards:* Individual Fel, Art Matters, 91; Nat Endowment Arts Individual Painting Fel, 89; Pollock-Krasner Found grant, 90. *Publ:* Illusr, children's bk, Houghton Mifflin Publ Co, Boston, Mass; broadside, Fairbanks Art Asn, 86; The Owl and the Mask of the Dreamer, Greywolf Publ Co, 88; Maine Houses, Iowa Publ Co, 88; Rain Country, Mad River Press, Richmond, Mass, 90. *Mailing Add:* PO Box 81267 College AK 99708

GOINGS, RALPH
PAINTER
b Corning, Calif, May 9, 28. *Study:* Calif Col Arts & Crafts, Oakland, BFA, 53; Calif State Univ, Sacramento, MFA, 65. *Work:* Mus Mod Art, Solomon R Guggenheim Mus, New York; Mus Contemp Art, Chicago; Whitney Mus Am Art, New York; Sheldon Art Mus; and many private colls. *Exhib:* One-man exhibs, OK Harris, 70, 73, 77, 80, 83, 85, 88 & 91, Mus Mod Art, 77, New York; Urban Aesthetics, Queens Mus, 76; Contemp Images in Watercolor, Akron Art Inst, Ohio, 76; Perspective 1976, Albright Col, 76; Illusion and Reality, Canberra, 77; Mus Fine Arts, Boston, MA, 86-87; Tampa Mus Art, FL, 87-88; Butler Inst Am Art, Youngstown, Ohio, 90; Gallery Henoeh, New York, 90; Boca Raton Mus Art, Fla, 92; Cheekwood Fine Arts Ctr, Nashville, 92; and others. *Pos:* Chmn art dept, La Sierra High Sch, Carmichael, Calif, 59-70. *Teaching:* Instr, Del Norte High Sch, Crescent City, Calif, 55-59, Calif State Univ, Sacramento, 71 & Univ Calif, Davis, 72. *Bibliog:* Linda Chase (auth), Ralph Goings, (essay), Harry N Abrams Publ, Inc, 88; John L Ward (auth), American Realist Painting 1945-1980, UMI Research Press, 89; Richard Kalina (auth), Freeze Frame, Art in Am, 3/92; Ruth Bass (auth), Don Celender/OK Harris, Artnews, 3/92; Ronnie Greenspan, Reviews, Florida: The Articulated Thumbprint, 7-8/92. *Media:* Oil, Watercolor. *Mailing Add:* c/o O K Harris Works of Art 383 W Broadway New York NY 10012

GOLBIN, ANDREE
PAINTER, ILLUSTRATOR
b Leipzig, Ger, June 4, 23; US citizen. *Study:* Art Students League; Parsons Sch Design; Hans Hofmann Sch Art; New Sch Social Res, Printmaking Workshop. *Work:* Indust Bank Japan; Wako Securities Co, Tokyo, Japan; Eastman Kodak; Klopman Mills; Corcoran Gallery Art, Washington, DC; World Trade Ctr, New York. *Exhib:* Los Angeles Co Mus Art Ann, 49-50; solo exhibs, Camino Gallery, 56 & 58, Roko Gallery, 64, Grand Central Moderns Gallery, 64 & 65, Contemp Arts Gallery, New York Univ, 71 & Grace Gallery, New York City Tech Col, 88; group exhib, Women Choose Women, New York Cult Ctr, 73; Works on Paper, Brooklyn Mus, 75; Noah Goldowsky Gallery, 76; Marymount Manhattan Col, 83; Kenkeleba Gallery, 85; Hudson Guild Gallery, 89. *Pos:* Prom art dir, Mademoiselle Mag, 50-52. *Teaching:* Instr graphic design, Kean Col, NJ, 79-80 & Fashion Inst Technol, 80-81; instr drawing, Parsons Sch Design, 79-; instr graphic design, New York City Tech Col, 82- *Awards:* Ann Cole Phillips Award, Nat Asn Women Artists, 53; Int Women's Year Award, 76. *Bibliog:* Reviews in Art News, Arts Dig, New York Times, Art Forum, 3/73, Nation, 6/25/73; article, Artspeak, 2/16/88. *Mem:* Artists Equity Asn New York; Woman's Caucus for Art; Fedn Mod Painters & Sculptors. *Media:* Acrylic, Oil; Watercolor. *Publ:* Illusr, New York Sunday Times gardening section, 74-75 & children's books publ by Lothrop, Lee & Shepard Co, 74, Rand McNally, Grossett & Dunlap. *Mailing Add:* 521 East 14th St Apt 9B New York NY 10009

GOLD, ALBERT
PAINTER, EDUCATOR
b Philadelphia, Pa, Oct 31, 16. *Study:* Philadelphia Mus Sch Indust Art, dipl, 39. *Work:* Libr Cong & Smithsonian Inst, Washington, DC; New Brit Mus Am Art, Conn; Fogg Mus, Harvard Univ, Boston, Mass; Forbes Col, New York. *Comn:* Murals, Bur Agr, Philadelphia, 51 & Pew House, Haverford, 68, Pa; five fund raising prints, Wills Eye Hosp, Philadelphia, Pa, 84. *Exhib:* The Artist in America, New York World's Fair, 39; Annual, 40 & Gimbel Pa Collection, 47, Pa Acad Fine Arts, Philadelphia; Directions in American Painting, Carnegie Inst, Pittsburgh, Pa, 41; Artists for Victory, Metrop Mus Art, New York, 42; The Artist at War, The Pentagon, Washington, DC, 43; Nat Acad Design Ann, New York, 46-; Artists Equity Ann, Philadelphia Mus Art, 60- *Collections Arranged:* American War Artist, Nat Gallery, London, Eng, 44 & Musée Galleria, Paris, France, 45; Am Watercolor Painters (with catalog), Burlington Acad, London, 62; Three Pennsyvania Painters (with catalog), Lehigh Univ, 70; Regional Painters (with catalog), Univ Del, Newark; Retrospective, D Wigmore Gallery, New York, 4-5/91. *Pos:* War artist, US Army, Europ Theater, 43-45; chmn painting, Philadelphia Art Alliance, 50-65. *Teaching:* Prof & chmn dept illus, Philadelphia Col Art, Pa, 46-82, prof emer, currenty. *Awards:* Prix de Rome, Nat Acad Design, New York, 42; Tiffany Found Grants, 47 & 48; Smith Grant, Woodmere Mus, Chestnut Hill, Pa, 68. *Bibliog:* Henry C Pitz (auth), Albert Gold, Am Artist, 56; James Jones (auth), WW II, Grosset & Dunlap, 75. *Mem:* Philadelphia Watercolor Soc; Am Watercolor Soc; Am Asn Univ Profs. *Media:* Oil, Watercolor. *Publ:* Contribr, The Commodore-Abrahams, 54, The Court Factor-Abrahams, 64 & The Captive Rabbi-Freehof, 63, Jewish Publ Soc, Our Philadelphia-Brookhouser, 59 & This Was Our War-Brookhouser, 61, Macmillan Publ; Articles, Step-By-Step Graphics, 88-91. *Dealer:* D Wigmore Fine Arts 22 E 76th St New York NY 10021. *Mailing Add:* 6814 McCallum St Philadelphia PA 19119

GOLD, FAY HELFAND
PAINTER
b Brooklyn, NY, Oct 15, 07. *Study:* Master Inst United Arts, New York, 29. *Work:* Evansville Mus Art, Ind; Libr Performing Arts, Lincoln Ctr, New York. *Exhib:* One-woman shows, Norlyst Gallery, 46 Roko Gallery 49 & 51, Partita Gallery, Southampton, NY, 56, Village Art Ctr, 64 & John J Myers Gallery, New York, 64, Special shows, Hudson Park, Countee Cullen & Ottendorfer Branches of the New York Pub Libr Galleries; Orlando Art Assn, Fla, 64; Columbia Mus Art, SC, 64; Davenport Munic Art Gallery, Iowa, 65; Moore Col Art, Pa, 65; Arnot Art Gallery, NY, 65; Baldwin-Wallace Col, Ohio, 65; Brooks Mem Gallery, 65. *Awards:* Popular Prize, Munic Art Ctr, 39; First Prize, Village Art Ctr Drawing Competition, New York, 64; John J Karpnick Prize, Audubon Artists, 64; Fel, Yaddo, 49; Ms Gold's papers are in the Collection of the Archives of American Art, Smithsonian Inst, Washington, DC & at 1285 Ave of Americas, New York; First Prize, one-woman show, Am Watercolor Soc, 64, 65, 67 & 68. *Mem:* Art Students League (life mem); Artists Equity Asn; Am Watercolor Soc. *Media:* Oil, Watercolor. *Mailing Add:* Times Square Station Box 256 New York NY 10108

GOLD, MARTHA B
SCULPTOR
b New York, NY, Sept 20, 38. *Study:* Univ Rochester; Barnard Col, Columbia Univ, BA; Columbia Univ, MA; Nat Acad Sch Fine Arts, cert; Art Students League. *Exhib:* NAm Sculpture Ann, Foothills Art Ctr, Golden, Colo, 80, 83 & 88; Allied Artists Am, Am Acad Inst Arts & Letts, 80, Audubon Artists Ann, Nat Arts Club, 81 & Nat Sculpture Soc Ann, Equitable Life Insurance Bldg, 81, New York; Philadelphia Tricentennial, 82; solo shows, Ward-Nasse Gallery, 87, 89 & 90. *Teaching:* Privately. *Awards:* Mem Award, Audubon Artists, 79; Youth Award, Nat Sculpture Soc, 79 & 80; Gold Medal Honor, Allied Artists Am, 80 & 83; Foondry Award, NAm Sculpture Exhib. *Bibliog:* Article, Nat Sculpture Rev, 80, Sculpture Mag, 87, Manhattan Arts, 87, NY Art Review, 89, Arte el dia, Argentina, 89. *Mem:* Allied Artists Am; Nat Asn Women Artists; Artists Equity. *Media:* Bronze, Clay. *Dealer:* Ward-nasse Gallery, Prince St New York NY. *Mailing Add:* 315 E 91st St New York NY 10128

GOLD, SHARON CECILE
PAINTER, EDUCATOR
b Bronx, NY, Feb 28, 49. *Study:* Hunter Col, City Univ of NY, 68; Columbia Univ, 69-70; Pratt Inst, BFA, 76. *Work:* McCrory Corp, Chase Manhattan Bank, Norsearch Indust & Chemical Bank, New York; Prudential Insurance Co Am, NJ; Best Products, Inc, Va; Rose Art Mus, Brandeis Univ, Mass; Southeast Bank, Fla; Everson Mus, Syracuse, NY. *Comn:* Painting on aluminum & fiberglass, Humbolt-Hospital Station, Niagara Frontier Transportation Authority, Buffalo, NY, 82-84. *Exhib:* Works on Paper, Mus Mod Art, Art Lending Serv, New York, 81; solo exhibs, Galerie Michael Storrer, Zurich, Switz, 81, John Davis Gallery, Akron, Ohio, 86, Stephen Rosenberg Gallery, New York, 87, 89, 91; Tyler & Penrose Galleries, Tyler Sch Art, Philadelphia, 83; Summer Show, GH Dalsheimer Gallery, Baltimore, Md, 88; four person Group exhib, Stephen Rosenberg Gallery, New York, 88; Painting Beyond the Death of Painting, Kuznetsky Most Exhib Hall, Moscow, USSR, 89; The Image of Abstract Painting in the 80's, Rose Art Mus, Brandeis Univ, Waltham, Mass, 90; and many others. *Pos:* Assoc ed, Re-View Mag, New York, 77- *Teaching:* lectr, Princeton Univ, 79-80; NY Univ, 83; vis assoc prof, Univ Tex, San Antonio, 80 & Syracuse Univ, 80-81; vis prof, Va Commonwealth Univ, 82; adj prof, NY Univ, 83; assoc prof painting & drawing, Syracuse Univ, 85- *Awards:* MacDowell Colony Fel; Nat Endowment Arts Painting Fel, 81-82. *Bibliog:* Joseph Masheck (auth), Sharon Gold, Arts Mag, 10/87; Stephen Westfall (auth), Review, Art in America, 1/88; and others. *Mem:* Distinguished Artist Award Lifetime Achievement; Col Art Asn Comt (chair, 89). *Media:* Acrylic, Oil. *Publ:* Contribr, reviews in Artforum, 77; auth, Statement, Re-View Mag, 79; The Texas Paintings-Modernism: Forms and Concepts, Univ Tex Press (in prep); auth, Statement, Forum, 89. *Mailing Add:* 10 Leonard St New York NY 10013

GOLDBERG, ARNOLD HERBERT
PAINTER, PRINTMAKER
b Brooklyn, NY, May 16, 33. *Study:* Univ Wis, BS(appl arts), 55; Pratt Inst, BArch, 59; Univ Houston, painting, 70-72. *Exhib:* Twelfth Midwest Biennial, Joselyn Mus, Omaha, Nebr, 72; 17th Ann Delta Art Exhib, Ark Art Ctr, 74; 16th Ann Eight State Exhib, Okla Art Ctr, 74; 52nd Exhib, Shreveport Art Guild, 74; Corpus Christi Art Found Ann Exhib, Art Mus STex, 75; Corpus Christi Art Found Ann Exhib, Art Mus STex, 77. *Teaching:* Instr desktop publ, Houston Community Col, 87- *Awards:* Dimension VI Award, Art League Houston, 71; Eighth Jury Award Art Exhib, Jewish Community Ctr, Houston, 72; Corpus Christi Art Found Grant, Art Mus STex, 75 & 77. *Media:* Acrylic; Silkscreen. *Mailing Add:* 425 White Wing Lane Houston TX 77079

GOLDBERG, GLENN
PAINTER
b Bronx, NY, Aug 31, 53. *Study:* Queens Col, MFA. *Work:* Mus Mod Art, New York; The Brooklyn Mus; Metrop Mus Art, New York; Mus Contemp Art, Los Angeles; Nat Gallery Art, Wash, DC. *Exhib:* One-man shows, Willard Gallery, New York, 85, Dart Gallery, Chicago, Ill, 86, Albany Mus Art, Albany, Ga, 89; Brandeis Univ, Mass, 86; Indianapolis Mus Art, Ind, 86; M Knoedler & Co Gallery, New York, 87; Ronald Greenberg Gallery, St Louis, 88; retrospectives, Green Gallery (with catalog), St Louis, Mo, 90, Hill Gallery, Birmingham, Mich, 90, Knoedler & Co Inc, New York, 91 & 92, David Beitzel Gallery, New York, 92; Play Between Fear and Desire, Germans Van Eck Gallery, New York, 92; Paper Houses, David Beitzel Gallery, New York, 92; Numbers, Angles Gallery, Santa Monica, Calif, 92. *Awards:* Guggenheim Fel, 88-89; Nat Endowment Arts, 89. *Bibliog:* Alisa Tager (auth), Glenn Goldberg at Knoedler, Art in Am, 4/92; Gerard Haggerty (auth), Glenn Goldberg, Cover, 15, 4/92; Alan G Artner (auth), Goldberg Returns with Vibrant Works, Chicago Tribune, sect 7, 5/92. *Mailing Add:* c/o Knoedler & Co 19 E 70th St New York NY 10021

GOLDBERG, JIM
PHOTOGRAPHER
Study: Western Wash Univ, BA, 75; San Francisco Art Inst, MFA (photography), 79. *Work:* Akron Art Mus, Ohio; Baltimore Mus Mod Art, Md; Boston Mus Fine Arts, Mass; Hallmak Collection, Kansas City, Mo; High Mus Art, Atlanta, Ga; Libr of Congress, Washington, DC. *Comn:* Photographs (16), Neville Manor Nursing Home, comn by Cambridge Arts Coun, Mass, 87. *Exhib:* Photographs (with catalog), 79, Form-Freud and Feeling, 83, Bay Area Collects, 83, Photography in California (traveling, with catalog), 84 & Extending the Perimeters of 20th Century Photography (with catalog), 85, San Francisco Mus Mod Art, Calif; Selection 3 (with catalog), Polariod Gallery, Photokina 86, Cologne, WGer; Un Si Grand Age (traveling, with catalog), Palais de Tokyo, Paris, France, 88; Portraits, Purdue Univ, Ind, 88; The Other Side of the Dream, Phillips Exeter Acad, NH, 88; Recent Acquisitions, Nat Mus Am Art, Smithsonian Inst, Washington, DC, 88; Photography International, Vigo, Spain, 90; Art in the Anchorage, 90, Shoot Back Exhib, 91, New York. *Teaching:* Asst prof, Univ Mass, Boston, 84-85; vis instr, Univ Calif, San Francisco, 88-90, undergrad instr, 89 & 90; undergrad instr, Calif Col Arts & Crafts, Oakland, 89. *Awards:* Guggenheim Award, 85; NEA Photog Fel, 90. *Bibliog:* Carol Rafferty (auth), Policies of Neglect, San Francisco Focus Mag, 12/88; Louise Steinman (auth), Jim Goldberg - Capp St Project, Artscribe, 9-10/89; Paul Richards (auth), article, Washington Post, 10/90. *Mailing Add:* 1007 Haight St #3 San Francisco CA 94117

GOLDBERG, JUDITH
ART DEALER
b New York, NY, Feb 22, 47. *Study:* City Col New York, BA, 71. *Pos:* Owner, Judith Goldberg Gallery, currently. *Specialty:* 19th and 20th century prints & drawings. *Mailing Add:* c/o Judith Goldberg Gallery 52 E 76 St New York NY 10021

GOLDBERG, MICHAEL
PAINTER
b New York, NY, Dec 24, 24. *Study:* Art Students League, 38-42; City Col New York, 40-42; Hans Hofmann Sch Art, 41-42 & 48-50; Art Students League, with Jose de Creeft, 46; City Col New York, 46-47; studied with Hans Hofmann. *Work:* Baltimore Mus Art, MD; Albright-Knox Gallery, Solomon R Guggenheim Mus, Whitney Mus Art, NY; Walker Art Ctr, Minneapolis, MN; Nat Gallery Art & Hirshorn Mus & Sculpture Garden, Washington, DC; Hirshhorn Mus & Sculpture Garden, Washington, DC; Tel Aviv Mus, Israel; Wadsworth Atheneum, Hartford, Conn; and many others; Mus Mod Art, Jerusalem; Mus Mod Art, Tokyo. *Exhib:* Smithsonian Inst, 66; Mus Mod Art, New York, 68; Corcoran Biennial, 69; Review-Preview, Vanderwoude Tananbaum, NY, 84, 86, 87 & 90; Action-Precision: The New Direction in New York, 1955-60, traveling exhib, Newport Harbor Art Mus, Calif, Worcester Art Mus, Mass, Grey Art Gallery, New York, Contemp Arts Ctr, Cincinnati, Ohio & Archer M Huntington Gallery, Univ Tex, Austin, 84-86; Paintings as Landscape traveling exhib, 85, solo exhibs, Caludia Nastuzzo, Salo, 88, Galerie Peccolo, Livorno, 88 & 90, Stacke, Copenhagen, 88 & 89, Turchetto/Plurima, Milan, 90 & 91, Plumira, Udine, 90, Galerie Weinberger, Copenhagan, 90 & 92 & Vanderwoude Tannebaum, New York, 90; Art from Two Continents, Bruce Helander Gallery, Palm Beach, Fla, 86; L A Louver, Venice, Calif, 86; Drawings, Janet Steinberg Gallery, San Francisco, Calif, 86; Bass Mus Art, Miami Beach, Fla, 87; The Art of Abstract Painting, Gallery Camino Real, Boca Raton, Fla, 87; Bette Stoller Gallery, New York, 87; Vanderwoude Tananbaum Gallery, New York, 87, 89 & 91; Lennon, Weinberg Inc, New York, 90 & 91; Manny Silverman Gallery, Los Angeles, Calif, 91. *Teaching:* Instr art, Univ Calif, Berkeley, 61-62; Yale Univ, 67; Univ Minn, 68, Sch Visual Arts, New York, 79- *Bibliog:* Irving Sandler (auth), The New York School: The Painters & Sculptors of the Fifties, Harper & Row, 78; John Johnston (auth), Michael Goldberg's new paintings, Artforum, summer 79; V Tatransky (auth), Arts Mag (rev), 5/79. *Publ:* Auth, The canvas plane, or onwards and upwards, It Is, spring 58. *Dealer:* Lennon-Weinberg Gallery 580 Broadway New York NY 10012. *Mailing Add:* 222 Bowery New York NY 10012

GOLDBERG, ROSELEE
HISTORIAN, CURATOR
b Durban, SAfrica; UK citizen. *Study:* Rand Univ, BFA, 68; Courtauld Inst Art, London, with John Golding, MA(art hist), 70. *Collections Arranged:* Record as Artwork, Royal Col Art Gallery, 73; Piero Manzoni, Royal Col Art Gallery, 74; IMPORTS (int performance series), Kitchen Ctr, 78 & 79; Mus Mod Art performance series, 90. *Pos:* Dir, Royal Col Art Gallery, London, 72-75; cur, The Kitchen Ctr, New York, 78-80. *Teaching:* Lectr performance hist, Archit Asn London, 77-78, Sch Visual Arts, New York, 79-82 & New York Univ, 88. *Awards:* Publ Award, Arts Coun Gt Brit, 75; Nat Endowment for Arts Art Critic's grant, 79. *Mem:* Int Asn Art Critics; Col Art Asn; Nat Union Journalists, UK. *Res:* Thesis on Oskar Schlemmer and performance at the Bauhaus; specialist in history of performance art and related contemporary media. *Publ:* Ed & contribr, special issue, Studio Int on Archit-Art, 75 & Performance Studio Int, 76; contribr, Oskar Schlemmer's performance art, Artforum, 77; contribr, Performance: a Hidden History, In: Battcock's Anthology, Dutton, 80; auth, Performance Art: Form Futurism to the Present (rev ed), Abrams, 88. *Mailing Add:* 327 E 18th St New York NY 10003-2802

GOLDEEN, DOROTHY A
DEALER, CONSULTANT
b San Francisco, Calif, Nov 12, 48. *Study:* Univ Calif, Berkeley, BA Sculpture & design, 72. *Pos:* Dir, Hansen Fuller Gallery, 72-79; vpres, Hansen Fuller Goldeen Gallery, 79-82; principle, Fuller Goldeen Gallery, 82-87; pres, Dorothy Goldeen Gallery, Santa Monica, 87- *Teaching:* Instr, Contemp Art Gallery, Col Marin, 75; frequent lectr for mus & univs. *Mem:* San Francisco Art Dealers Asn (prog dir assoc); Santa Monica-Venice Art Dealers Assoc (vpres 87-88, pres, 88, 90-); Cur Coun, Mus Contemp Art, Los Angeles, 90- *Specialty:* Contemporary painting, sculpture and works on paper. *Publ:* Auth, California Gold, US Embassy (traveling exhib catalog), beginning Brussels, 75; Joan Brown, Univ Adron, Ohio (traveling exhib catalog); American Eight, Interspace Corp NJ (traveling exhib catalog), 80; and others; American Eight (catalog essay), Interpace Corp, NJ, 80. *Mailing Add:* 1547 Ninth St Santa Monica CA 90410

GOLDEN, EUNICE
PAINTER, FILMMAKER
b New York, NY. *Study:* Univ Wis; Brooklyn Col, MFA; New Sch Social Res; Art Students League; Empire State Col, BFA. *Work:* Hudson River Mus, Yonkers, NY; New York City Dept Parks & Recreation; Bronx Community Col, NY. *Comn:* Portrait of Poet Leon Herald, comn by Leon Herald, 71; murals, Dept of Parks & Recreation, New York, Dept of Cult Affairs, New York & Bronx Mus of Art; Bronx Community Col. *Exhib:* Alan Stone Gallery, New York, 73; 148th Nat Acad Design Ann, New York, 73; Soho 20 Gallery, New York, 73 & 81; Works on Paper, Brooklyn Mus, NY, 75; Nothing But Nudes, Downtown Whitney, 77; film exhib, Gemeente Mus, The Hague, Holland, 79; Grey Art Gallery, New York, 81; Artists Space, New York, 83; Long Beach Mus, Calif, 85; Hudson Ctr Galleries, 86. *Pos:* Dir, Walk-On Community Art Proj, Dobbs Ferry, NY, 68; dir, Westbeth Gallery I, New York, 80-82, Mus Mod Art, 89. *Teaching:* Lectr erotic art, New Sch Social Res, 73; instr mural painting, Guggenheim Mus Prog, New York, summer 75; instr painting, Pratt Inst, 80-81; artist-in-residence, Univ SDak, 76 & Cooper Union, 84. *Awards:* Purchase Award, Hudson River Mus, 63; One of Outstanding Women, NY State Women's Unit Exec Chamber, Albany, 68; MacDowell Colony Fel, 69 & 71; Award, Archives Am Art, Smithsonian Inst, Washington, DC. *Bibliog:* Lucy Lippard (auth), From the Center, Feminist Essays on Women's Art, Dutton, 76 & Art in Am, 11/81; Carter Ratcliff (auth), Art Int, 3/77; Lucy Lippard (auth), Overlay, Random House, 83. *Mem:* fel MacDowell Colony; Col Art Asn Am; Women's Caucus Art. *Media:* Oil, Acrylic. *Publ:* Illusr, Ms Mag, 75; auth, article, Art Workers News, New York, 76; coauth, article, An Anti-Catalog, 77; auth, The male nude in womens art, Heresies, spring 81; and others. *Mailing Add:* 463 West St Apt 332B New York NY 10014

GOLDEN, JUDITH
PHOTOGRAPHER
b Chicago, Ill, Nov 29, 34. *Study:* Art Inst Chicago, BFA, 73; Univ Calif, Davis, MFA(Regents Graduate Fel), 75; Moore Col Art, Philadelphia, Hon PhD, 90. *Work:* San Francisco Mus Mod Art, Calif; Oakland Mus, Calif; Ctr Creative Photog, Tucson, Ariz; Fogg Mus, Cambridge, Mass; Mus Mod Art, New York; Mus Photog Art, San Diego, Calif; Art Inst Chicago; Tokyo Metrop Mus Photog, Japan. *Exhib:* One-person shows, Sch Art Inst Chicago, 77, San Francisco Mus Mod Art, Calif, 81, Ctr Creative Photog, Tucson, Ariz, 83, Univ Oregon, Eugene, 84, Mus Photog Art, San Diego, 86, Tucson Mus Art, Ariz, 87 & Mus Contemp Photog, Chicago, 88; Group exib, Contemp Photog, Fogg Mus, Cambridge, Mass, 77; Silver & Ink, Oakland Mus, Calif, 78; Attitudes-Photog in the 70's, Santa Barbara Mus Art, Calif, 79; Erweiterte Fotografe, Wiener Int Biennale, 81; Photographer as Printmaker, Arts Coun Gt Brit, 81; Autoportraits Photographiques, Ctr Georges Pompidou, Paris, France, 81; Extending the Perimeters of 20th Century Photography & Photography Facets of Modernism, 86, San Francisco Mus Mod Art; Ariz Biennial, Tucson Mus Art, 84, 86 & 88; Phoenix Biennial, Phoenix Art Mus, 85; Self Portrait Photography 1840-1985, Nat Portrait Gallery, London, Eng, 86; Photography and Art, Los Angeles Co Mus Art, Calif, 87; Univ Hawaii, Symbol & Surrogate, 89; Nature & Culture, Ansel Adams Ctr, San Francisco, 89; Selections 5: From the Polaroid Collection, Traveled Europe/US, 90-94; Self Portraits of Contemporary Women: Exploring the Self, Tokyo Metrop Mus Photog, 91. *Pos:* Bd mem, Los Angeles Ctr Photog Studies, Calif, 77-79; bd mem, Camera Work, San Francisco, Calif, 81. *Teaching:* Vis lectr photog, Univ Calif, Los Angeles, 75-79 & Univ Calif, Davis, 80; assoc prof photog, Univ Ariz, Tucson, 81-89, Prof, 89- *Awards:* Nat Endowment Arts Individual Photogrs Fel, 79; Photog Fel, Ariz Comn on the Arts, 84; Individual Artists' Fel, Tucson/Pima Arts Coun, 87. *Bibliog:* Serious Masquerades, Time-Life Ann, 78; Joyce Tennyson Cohen (auth) Insights: Self Portraits by Women Artists, Davis Goldine, 78; Connections: An Invitational Portfolio of Images

and Statements by Twenty-Eight Women, Exposure, fall 81; Van Deren Coke (coauth with Diana du Pont), Photography: Facets of Modernism, Hudson River Press, NY, 86; Claire V C Peeps (auth), Cycles: A Decade of Photographs by Judith Golden, Friends of Photog, 88. *Mem:* Soc Photog Educ; Women,s Caucus Arts; Friends of Photog; Camera Work. *Media:* Collage. *Dealer:* Etherton Stern Gallery Tucson AZ. *Mailing Add:* 4108 W Camino Nuestro Tucson AZ 85745

GOLDEN, LIBBY
PRINTMAKER, PAINTER
b New York, NY. *Study:* Cooper Union Art Sch, dipl, 34; Hunter Col, NY Univ & Art Students League, 34-42; Pratt Graphic Arts Inst, 58-60. *Work:* Philadelphia Mus Art; Detroit Inst Arts; Grand Rapids Mus Art; Colby Col Mus Art, Mass; US State Dept. *Comn:* Ctr Beethoven Studies, San Jose Univ, 85. *Exhib:* Silvermine Guild, Conn, 66-68; Boston Printmakers, Boston Mus Fine Arts, Mass, 66-69; Northwest Printmakers, Seattle Mus Art & Portland Mus Art, 68 & 69; Audubon Artists, New York, 70 & 71; Colorprint, USA, Lubbock, Tex, 71; Retrospective Exhib, Scottsdale Center Arts, Ariz, 82; one-woman show, Preston Burke Gallery, Detroit, Mich, 88; and others. *Awards:* Print Prizes, Mich State Fair, 65-69 & Nat Acad Design, New York, 69; Purchase Prize, Mich Painters & Printmakers & Colorprint USA. *Media:* Serigraphy, Silkscreen; All. *Mailing Add:* 7527 N Del Norte Dr Scottsdale AZ 85258

GOLDEN, MORTON J
ADMINISTRATOR, DIRECTOR
b Brooklyn, NY, Apr 11, 29. *Study:* Univ Southern Calif, BS, 52. *Pos:* Dep dir admin, Los Angeles Co Mus Art, 72-82; dir, Palm Springs Desert Mus, Calif, 82-89; dept dir, Mus Fine Arts, Boston, 89- *Awards:* Honor of the Republic, Treasures of the Tutankhamun-Govt of Egypt, 79; Calif Asn Mus (chair, 79, 80, 81 & 82. *Mailing Add:* 582 Beacon St Newton Center MA 02159

GOLDEN, ROLLAND HARVE
PAINTER, PRINTMAKER
b New Orleans, La, Nov 8, 31. *Study:* John McCrady Art Sch, study with John McCrady. *Work:* Pushkin Mus, USSR; Masur Mus; New Orleans Mus Art; Miss Mus Art; St John's Mus; Springfield Mus Art. *Comn:* Fifty watercolors, La State Hwy Dept, Baton Rouge, 59-60; four watercolors, comn by Gov John McKeithen, La, 65; mural, Furash & Co, 88. *Exhib:* Seven Am Watercolor Soc Exhibs, New York, 65-78; Watercolor USA, Springfield, 66-90; Butler Inst Am Art, Youngstown, Ohio, 67-78; Nat Arts Club, New York, 68 & 72-90; Nat Soc Painters in Casein & Acrylics, New York, 72-88; one-man show touring USSR, Moscow, Kiev, Leningrad and Odessa & over 100 one-man shows in USA. *Pos:* vpres, Watercolor USA Honor Soc. *Awards:* Nine Awards, Nat Arts Club, New York, 79-90; Five Awards including Thomas Hart Benton, Watercolor USA; Five Awards, Rocky Mountain Nat Watercolor Soc, 78-90. *Bibliog:* Don Lee Keith (auth), Golden boy of watercolor, Delta Rev Mag, 68 & World of Rolland Golden, Royal Publ Co, 70; Jim Keyser (auth), Rolland Golden's Southland, WDSU TV, 73; Mel Leavitt (auth), First Person, 86. *Mem:* Nat Watercolor Soc; Nat Soc Painters Casein & Acrylics; Allied Artists Am; Watercolor USA Hon Soc (vpres); hon mem La Watercolor; Rocky Mt Nat Watermedia. *Media:* Watercolor, Oil; Lithography. *Publ:* Contribr, Transparent watercolor-ideas and techniques, 73, Southwest Art Mag, 5/7 & Art Voices South, 3-4/79 & 7-8/79; article in Louisiana Life Mag, 9/82; article in Miss Mag, 5/86; auth, Palette Talk Mag, 5-6/87 & 9-10/88; articles in Int Fine Art Collector Mag, 9/91 & Am Artist Mag, Watercolor, fall 91; and others. *Dealer:* Bryant Galleries 524 Royal St New Orleans LA; Bryant Galleries 2845 Lake-Land Dr Jackson MS. *Mailing Add:* 78207 Woods Hole Lane Folsom LA 70437

GOLDFIELD, EDWARD L
DEALER, COLLECTOR
b Philadelphia, Pa, Dec 3, 30. *Pos:* Pres, Goldfield Galleries, Ltd, currently. *Mem:* Art Dealers Asn Southern Calif. *Specialty:* 19th and early 20th century American impressionists, ash can, Western paintings and sculpture. *Publ:* contribr, The West as Art, Palm Springs Desert Mus, 82; contribr, California: The State of Landscape 1872-1981, Newport Harbor Art Mus & Santa Barbara Mus Art, 81; contribr, Plein Air Painters of California, The Southland, Westphalia Publ, 82; contribr, Americans in Brittany & Normandy 1860-1910, Amon Carter Mus, Phoenix Art Mus & Nat Mus Am Art, 83; publ, Edgar Payne, pvt publ, 87. *Mailing Add:* Goldfield Gallery 8380 Melrose Ave Los Angeles CA 90069

GOLDFINE, BEATRICE
PAINTER, SCULPTOR
b Philadelphia, Pa, Aug 17, 23. *Study:* Studied with Jimmy Leuders, Roy Nuse & Will Barnett, 69-74; also pvt instr with Morris Blackburn, 75-80; Pa Acad Fine Arts, 5 yr cert art, 80. *Work:* Blue Cross, Philadelphia, Harrisburg, Norristown; Bell Atlantic, Philadelphia; Merck Sharp & Dohme, West Point, Pa; Philadelphia Co Med Soc; E I DuPont. *Comn:* Bust, Sir Winston Churchilll, Technion-Israel Inst Technol, Haif, 82; bust, Golda Meier, New York, 84. *Exhib:* 71st Ann, Allied Artists Am, New York, 84; Philadelphia Watercolor Club, Art Inst, Pa, 86; Forms to Figure With, Glassboro State Col, NJ, 89; one-woman show, Nudes & Other Landscapes, Joy Berman Gallery, Philadephia, Pa, 90; Cheltenham Sch Fine Arts Ann, Philadelphia, Pa, 91; Fel, travel show, Pa Acad Fine Arts, Philadelphia & Pittsburgh, 91 & 92. *Awards:* First Prize, Woodmere Art Mus, 79; Bok Award, Harrisburg Mus, 84; First Prize Pastel, Philadelphia Sketch Club, 85. *Bibliog:* Dr Burton Wasserman (auth), Art Matters, 87; Guide to Manhattan's Outdoor Sculpture, Art Comn & Munic Art Soc, 88; Palmer Poroner (auth), Art Speak, Monthly Gallery Rev, NY, 91. *Mem:* Pastel Soc Am, New York; fel Pa Acad Fine Art; Philadelphia Watercolor Club; Friends Bezaiel Acad Arts & Design (bd dirs); Philadelphia Art Alliance. *Media:* All; Clay. *Dealer:* Joy Berman Gallery 2201 Pennsylvania Blvd Philadelphia PA 19130. *Mailing Add:* Sale Dept Philadelphia Mus Art Philadelphia PA 19126

GOLDFINGER, ELIOT
SCULPTOR
b New York, NY, Aug 14, 50. *Study:* Pratt Inst, BFA, 74; Nat Acad Sch, New York, 77-78. *Work:* Am Mus Natural Hist; Metrop Opera House; Mus City of New York; Tel Aviv Cult Ctr, Israel. *Comn:* Bust of Mayor John Lindsay, 78, Mayor Abe Beame, 79, Mayor Robert Wagner, 80 & Mayor Ed Koch, Mus City New York, 81; Bust Leonid Brezhnev, comn by Newsweek for cover, 4/12/82; Bust of Judge Henry Friendly, comn by US Court of Appeals, New York, 89. *Exhib:* Ann Exhib, Allied Artists Am, New York, 78, 80 & 82-86; Ann Exhib, Nat Acad Design, New York, 79 & 86; Mem Exhibs, Salmagundi Club, New York, 79-81; Ann Exhib, Nat Sculpture Soc, New York, 80-91. *Pos:* Staff artist, Am Mus Natural Hist, New York, 74-79. *Teaching:* Instr human & animal anat, NY Acad Art, 83-86; instr human anat, Art Students League, New York, 88-90. *Awards:* Gloria Medal, 80 & Meiselman Prize, 84, Nat Sculpture Soc; Dr H Debellis Prize, Salmagundi Club, 81; Allied Artists Mem Award, 85. *Bibliog:* John David Klein, Apple Polishers (film), WOR-TV News, 81; Sculpture in the News, Sculpture Review, 81; Interview, Sculpture Rev, 1st quarter, 92. *Mem:* Nat Sculpture Soc. *Media:* Plastillene, Bronze. *Res:* Human anatomy for artists, research from life & from cadavers; anatomy of the horse; comparative anatomy for artists. *Publ:* Auth, A sculptural approach to a three-dimensional subject, Catasus J Soc Animal Artists, spring 86; Human Anatomy for Artists, Oxford Univ Press, 91. *Mailing Add:* 37 Rolling Way New Rochelle NY 10804-2405

GOLDIN, LEON
PAINTER
b Chicago, Ill, Jan 16, 23. *Study:* Art Inst Chicago, BFA, 48; Univ Iowa, MFA, 50. *Work:* Brooklyn Mus, NY; Va Mus Fine Arts, Richmond; City Mus St Louis, Mo; Pa Acad Fine Arts, Philadelphia; Munson-Williams-Proctor Inst, Utica, NY. *Exhib:* American Painting at Mid-Century, Metrop Mus Art, New York, 51; American Drawings, Mus Mod Art, New York, 56; Corcoran Gallery Art Biennial, Washington, DC, 62; Carnegie Inst Int, Pittsburgh, Pa, 64; Pa Acad Fine Arts Ann, 66. *Teaching:* Instr painting & drawing, Calif Col Arts & Crafts, 50-55; instr painting & drawing, Cooper Union, 61-64; from assoc prof to prof painting, Columbia Univ, 64-, chmn dept, 73-75 & 77-80. *Awards:* Guggenheim Fel, 59; Award in Painting, Nat Inst Arts & Lett, 68; Nat Endowment Arts Grant, 80; and others. *Mem:* Nat Acad Design. *Media:* Oil, Gouache. *Dealer:* Kraushaar Galleries 724 Fifth Ave New York NY 10019. *Mailing Add:* 438 W 116th St New York NY 10027

GOLDIN, NAN R
PHOTOGRAPHER
b Washington, DC, 53. *Study:* Boston Mus Fine Arts, BA/BFA, 77. *Work:* Folkwang Mus, Essen, Ger; Victoria & Albert Mus, London; Bayley Art Mus, Univ Va Art Gallery; First Bank, Minneapolis; George Eastman House, Rochester; Princeton Art Mus, NJ; and others. *Exhib:* Solo shows, Mus 20th Century Art, Vienna, Orangerie, Munich & DADD Galerie, Berlin, 92 & Pace/MacGill Gallery, New York, 93; Wewerka & Weiss Galerie, Berlin, 92; Galerie du Jeu de Paume, Paris, 92; Kunstverein Hamburg, 92. *Awards:* Mother Jones Doc Photog Award, 90; Nat Endowment Arts Grant, Washington, DC, 90; Louis Comfort Tiffany Found Award, 91. *Publ:* Contribr, Cookie Mueller (catalog), Pace/MacGill Gallery, New York, 91; The Other Side 1972-1992, Scalo Verlag, 92. *Mailing Add:* 334 Bowery New York NY 10012

GOLDMAN, JUDITH
WRITER, CRITIC
b Chicago, Ill. *Study:* Bard Col, Annandale-on-Hudson, NY, printmaking with Louis Schanker, BA(Lit), 64; Inst Design Ill Inst Technol, printmaking with Misch Kohn, 64. *Pos:* Managing ed, Artist's Proof, Pratt Graphics, New York, 67-69; ed, Print Collector's Newslett, New York, 70-72; managing ed, Artnews, New York, 73-75, contrib ed, 75-; adj cur, Print Collection, Whitney Mus Am Art, 76-92. *Teaching:* Adj instr graphics, Hunter Col, New York, 74-75; asst prof criticism, Pratt Inst, 76-78. *Awards:* Nat Endowment Arts Grant Criticism, 78. *Res:* Twentieth century graphics, painting and photography: biography. *Publ:* Auth, Jasper Johns Prints: 1977-81, 81; Jasper Johns: 17 Monotypes, United Art Ed, 82; Frank Stella, Fourteen Prints, Princeton, 83; James Rosenquist, Viking, 85; James Rosenquist: The Early Pictures, Rizzoli, 92; and others. *Mailing Add:* 525 West End Ave New York NY 10024

GOLDMAN, LESTER
PAINTER
b Philadelphia, Pa, Aug 15, 42. *Study:* Philadelphia Col Art, BFA, 64; Indiana Univ, MFA, 66. *Work:* Univ Maine; Ind Univ; Kans City Art Inst; Albrecht Mem Gallery; H & R Block; Kemper Insurance Co; State Hist Soc; Nelson Gallery Art; Mutual Benefit Life Insurance Co; IBM; Realex Corp; Continental, Twentieth Century Corp. *Exhib:* One-man shows, Pane-Vino Gallery, Philadelphia, 68, Walter Kelly Gallery, Chicago, 75, Unitarian Church, Kansas City, Mo, 80 & Contemp Art Ctr, Kansas City, Mo, 89; Works on Paper, Ind Univ, 87 & Athena on Broadway, Kansas City, Mo, 90; Leedy-Voulkos Gallery, Kansas City, Mo, 88; Portrait, Blue Dolphin, 92; Midland Invitational installation, Joslyn Art Mus, 92. *Pos:* Lectr, Joslyn Art Mus, 92. *Teaching:* Teaching asst, Indiana Univ, 65-66; prof painting, Kansas City Art Inst, 66-; vis fac, Alliance of Independent Col Art, NY Studio prog,

85; vis artist, Studio Sch, New York, summer 88; Vermont Studio Sch, summer 89. *Awards:* Andrew W Mellon Fac Develop Grants, 84, 87, 88 & 92; Nat Endowment Arts, 86 & 89; Alliance Independent Col of Art Grant, 86. *Bibliog:* Rick Hellman (auth), Multi-media artist offers variations on a theme, Chronicle, Kansas City, 89; Lily Pruizo (auth), Yard Full of Art, Kansas City Star, 90; Sybil Zimmerman (auth), A Festival of Lights, Kansas City Chronicle, 90. *Dealer:* Leedy-Voulkos Gallery 1919 Wyandotte Kansas City MO 64108. *Mailing Add:* 37 W 57 Kansas City MO 64113

GOLDMAN, MATT
CONCEPTUAL ARTIST, KINETIC ARTIST
b New York, NY, May 2, 61. *Study:* Clark Univ, BA(econ), 83, MBA, 84. *Work:* New Mus Contemp Art (performance), New York; Milwaukee Art Mus (performance), Wis; Contemp Art Ctr New Orleans (performance), Fla. *Awards:* Obie, Tubes, Village Voice, 91; Drama Desk, Tubes, 92; Lucille Lortel Found Award, Tubes, 92. *Bibliog:* Alisa Soloman (auth), Pissing on propriety, Village Voice, 1/15/91; Vicki Goldberg (auth), Hi tech meets God with Blue Man Group, NY Times, 1/17/91; Thomas M Disch (auth), Blue Man Group: Tubes, Nation, 1/20/92. *Media:* Performance. *Mailing Add:* 575 West End Ave New York NY 10024

GOLDMAN, RACHEL BOK
COLLECTOR, PATRON
b Philadelphia, Pa, Mar 28, 37. *Study:* Univ Pa, BA(hist art). *Work:* Donated paintings & prints: Philadelphia Mus Art, LaSalle Col/Baldwin Sch, & Benedictine Col of Lisle, Ill. *Pos:* Chmn bd dir, Arts Exchange Mag, 77-79; exhib selection comt, Morris Gallery, Pa Acad Fine Arts, 79-82; co-chmn, Friends Philadelphia Mus Art, 82-83; co-founder, Samuel Yellin Found; bd dir, Art Resources in Teaching; exhib selection comt, Soc Contemp Art, Art Inst Chicago, 88-90. *Mem:* Friends Philadelphia Mus Art; Pa Acad Fine Arts; Chicago Art Inst; Mus Contemp Art, Chicago. *Collection:* Living Philadelphia, Chicago, Southwest & Mid-Coast Maine Painters, watercolorists and printmakers. *Mailing Add:* 1411 N State Pkwy Chicago IL 60610

GOLDNER, JANET
SCULPTOR
b Washington, DC, June 6, 52. *Study:* Asgard Sch, Hurup Thy, Denmark, 71; Penland Sch, NC, 72; Antioch Col, BA, 74; NY Univ, MA, 81. *Work:* Terry Gallery, Sudbury, Mass; Rockrose Develop Corp, New York; and many other private collections. *Comn:* Sculpture, Millay Colony Arts, Austerlitz, NY, 81; sculpture, comn by Claire & Lester Goldner, Bethesda, Md, 81 & 82; sculpture, comn by Robert Mitchell, Ridgefield, Conn, 82. *Exhib:* Solo exhibs, Stamford Mus, Conn, 78 & 80, Washington Sq East Galleries, New York, 79 & 80 Prehistoric Sites: Phoenix Gallery, New York, 83, Jewish Community Ctr, Stamford, Conn, 84, Hamilton Gallery, Elmira Col, NY, 84, Women's Studio Workshop, Rosendale, NY, 85 & Soho 20 Gallery, 89 & 91; Art Over AIDS, CSPS, Cedar Rapids, Iowa, 92; NYNEX Corp Hq, New York, 92; Soho Gallery, New York, 92; Art in the Anchorage, Creative Time, New York, 92; and others. *Pos:* Dir, S African Women Artists in Resistance, 88-; dir, Until That Last Breath: Women with Aids, NY, 88-89; cur, South African Mail: Messages from Inside, Soho Gallery, 90 & toured 90-92. *Teaching:* Lectr, Elmira Col, NY, 84, Cornell Col, Mt Vernon, Iowa, 85 & UN Women's Conf, Nairobi, Kenya, 85; vis artist lect series, Cortona, Italy, 87; panel moderator, Nat Conf, Women's Caucus Art, New York, 90 & 92 & Studio Mus Harlem, New York, 92; slide lect, Univ Arts, Philadelphia, Pa, Homeless Servs Network, Yonkers, NY, Franklin & Marshall Col, Lancaster, Pa, Univ Iowa, Iowa City, Mt Mercy Col, Cedar Rapids, Iowa, Univ Ga, Athens, Ga Southern Univ, Statesboro & Soho 20 Gallery, NY. *Awards:* Yaddo Fel, Saratoga Springs, NY, 82; Va Ctr Creative Arts, Fel, 82 & 88; Visual Artists Exchange Award, NY Feminist Art Inst, New York, 83; and others. *Bibliog:* Arlene Raven (auth), rev, Village Voice, New York, 2/20/90; Helen Harris (auth), rev, NY Times, 2/17/91; Froposta N2: Il Cibo Nell'Arte (catalog), Circolo Culturali Il Gabbiano, La Spezia, Italy, 91. *Mem:* Women's Caucus Art; Int Sculpture Ctr; Col Art Asn; Nat Women's Studies Asn; Women's Action Coalition, 92. *Media:* Welded Metal, Cast Metal. *Publ:* Contribr, Heresies, Vol II, No 4, 80 & Women Artists News, Vol VIII, No 4, 83; auth, South African Mail: Messages from Inside (essay, catalog), 90; Artists on the Home Front (essay, catalog), 91. *Mailing Add:* 52 Warren St New York NY 10007

GOLDRING, ELIZABETH
WRITER, ENVIRONMENTAL ARTIST
b Forest City, Iowa, Feb 13, 45. *Study:* Smith Col, BA, 67; Harvard Univ, MEd, 77. *Exhib:* Artransition (coordr), Mass Inst Technol, Cambridge, 75; Inst Contemp Art, Boston, 76; Centerbeam (coordr), Documenta 6, Kassel, Ger, 77 & Smithsonian Inst, DC, 78; Int Biennial Exhib Graphic & Visual Art (doc), Secession, Vienna, Austria, 79; International Alarm (with Otto Piene), Munich, 83; Coyote for Desert Sun/Desert Moon (CAVS artists) Lone Pine, CA, 86; Eye/Sight (with Vin Grabill) for LightsOrot, Yeshiva Univ Mus, New York, 87; Eye/Sight (with Vin Grabill) & International Alarm (with Otto Piene) for Otto Piene and CAVS, Kunstrevien, Karlsruhe, Fed Repub Ger, 88. *Pos:* Elem educ specialist, Nat Collection Fine Arts, Smithsonian Inst, 71-72; exhib developer, Childrens Mus, Boston, 73-75; exhib & proj dir, Ctr Advan Visual Studies, Mass Inst Technol, 78- *Teaching:* Lectr, Art & Environment, CAVS/MIT, 75- *Awards:* Grant, Diabetes Res & Educ Found, 87. *Res:* Sky Art; Visual Language. *Publ:* Contribr, You are Here (exhib catalog), Mass Inst Technol, 76; ed, CAVS Report on Elemental Sculpture in Public-Predominantly Urban-Places, Nat Endowment Arts & Ctr Advan Visual Studies, Mass Inst Technol, 78; auth, Sky Art-Art That Flies, Flying Colors, Braniff, 79; ed & contribr, Centerbeam, Ctr Advan Visual Studies, Mass Inst Technol, 80; Laser Treatment: Poems and Two Stories, Blue Giant Press, Boston, 83; The Sky Art Conference, Lightworks, No 17, 85; The Sky Art Manifesto, (coauth with Otto Piene and Lowry Burgess), CAVS/MIT, 86; auth, Desert Sun/Desert Moon and the Sky Art Manifesto, Leonardo, Vol 20, No 4, 12/88; The Inner Eye from the Inside Out, 88. *Mailing Add:* Ctr for Advan Visual Studies Mass Inst Technol 77 Massachusetts Ave Cambridge MA 02139

GOLDRING, NANCY DEBORAH
EDUCATOR, PHOTOGRAPHER
b Oak Ridge, Tenn, Jan 25, 45. *Study:* Smith Col, BA(art hist); Univ Florence, with Nina Gregori (Fulbright Fel), 67-68; NY Univ, MFA(graphics, NDEA Fel & Grad Teaching Fel), 69-70. *Work:* Herzliya Mus, Israel; Padiglione d'Art Contemporanea, Milan, Italy; Polaroid Corp; IBM; pvt collections; NYNEX; Citibank, New York; and others. *Comn:* Set design for Ode, Nat Choreography Proj, Nat Endowment Arts & Exxon, 85; set design for Ode with Ze' Eva Cohen & dancers, Joyce Theater, New York, 87. *Exhib:* Inside Spaces, Mus Mod Art, 83; solo exhibs, Univ Calif Berkeley, San Francisco, 88, Drury Col, Springfield, Mo, 88, Jayne H Baum Gallery, New York, 90, Meridian Gallery, San Francisco, 91, Instituto d'Arte Dosso, Ferrara, Italy, 91, Eliot Smith Gallery, 92 & Arts for Transit, Grand Cent Sta, New York, 92; Fac Grants Exhib, Montclair State Col, 91; The Frame: Multiplied and Extended, Pac Security, Los Angeles, 92; Points of View, Champion Corp, Stamford, Conn, 92; Concrete Poetry, Columbia Univ Arch, NY, 92; and others. *Pos:* Co-founding dir, SITE, New York, 69-72 & Chamber, New York, 76- *Teaching:* Assoc prof drawing, Montclair State Col, NJ, 72-; vis prof contemp art, RI Sch Design, Providence, 74-75; vis prof, Haverford Col, Pa, 78; lectr contemp art, Univ Bridgeport, Conn, 80 & 81; lectr, Univ Calif, Berkeley, 88, Univ Houston, 90, Meridian Gallery, San Francisco, 91, Trinity Col, Conn, 91 & Elliot Smith Gallery, 92. *Awards:* NY State Coun on Arts, 70-73, 77-79 & 86-87; Research Grant, Montclair State Col, 82-89 Alumni Grant, 86-87; Polaroid 20 x 24 Camera, 86-89; and others. *Bibliog:* Caisare Giatti (auth), La Mostra di Nancy Goldring, La Gazzetta di Ferrara, 8/26/91; Antonio Caggiano (auth), Questa e' l'America, Carlino di Ferrara, 9/4/91; Robert Duffy (auth), Coming home, St Louis Post Dispatch, 3/15/92; and others. *Media:* Pencil, Gouache. *Publ:* Contribr, Fleurs de Verite, cover design, Eds Ouverture, Switz, 87; auth, rev, Deconstructive architecture, 7/88 & George Ranelli: buildings & projects, 3/89, Bldg Design, London; rev, Identity, Arts Mag, 3/89; contribr, Generatoin of place, Offramp, Univ SCalif, Vol 1, No 3, fall 90; Imagining Egypt, Avant Garde: J Archit & Aesthetics, Univ Colo, Denver, 7/91; and others. *Mailing Add:* 463 West St A1112 New York NY 10014

GOLDSCHMIDT, LUCIEN
DEALER
b Brussels, Belg, Mar 3, 12. *Pos:* Pres, Lucien Goldschmidt, Inc. *Teaching:* Lectr prints & illus books, Harvard, NYPL, SUNY Purchase & Minn Mus Fine Arts. *Mem:* Art Dealers Asn Am. *Specialty:* Continental European art, circa 1500-1950, mainly prints and drawings. *Publ:* Coauth, Unpublished Correspondence of Henri de Toulouse-Lautrec, 69 & The Truthful Lens, 80. *Mailing Add:* 285 Riverside Dr New York NY 10025

GOLDSLEGER, CHERYL
PAINTER, DRAFTSMAN
b Philadelphia, Pa, Dec 16, 51. *Study:* Tyler Sch Art, Rome, 71; Philadelphia Col Art, BFA, 73; Washington Univ, MFA, 75. *Work:* Herbert F Johnson Mus, Ithaca, NY; Chase Manhattan Bank, Brooklyn Mus; Lannan Found, Los Angeles, Calif; Albright-Knox Gallery, Buffalo, NY; Tel Aviv Mus, Israel. *Exhib:* Works on Paper, Dayton Art Inst, 80; Members Gallery Exhib, Albright-Knox Gallery, 81; New Gallery Contemp Art, Cleveland, 82; Connections, Inst Contemp Art, Philadelphia, 83; solo exhibs, High Mus Art, Atlanta, 85, Southeastern Ctr Contemp Art, Winston-Salem, 85, E Carolina Univ, Greenville, 86, New Work/New York, Inst Art, Sydney, Australia, 86 & 1986 Triennial, New Orleans Mus Art, La, 86; Am Acad & Inst Arts & Letters, New York, 87; 41st Biennale of Contemp Am Paintings, Corcoran Gallery, Washington, DC, 89. *Teaching:* Asst prof painting, Western Carolina Univ, 75-77; instr art, Univ Ga, Athens, 78-87; lectr drawing, Ga Southern Col, 81; vis artist, E Carolina Univ, Greenville, NC, 86; chmn art dept, Piedmont Col, Demorest, Ga, 88- *Awards:* Grants, Pa Coun Arts, 81, Ohio Arts Coun, 82 & Nat Endowment Arts, 82 & 92; Coun Arts Award, Ga, 83; Southeastern Ctr Contemp Art Fel, 86. *Bibliog:* Gerrit Henry (auth), article, Art News, 2/82; Evan Firestone (auth), Cheryl Goldsleger, Arts Mag, 11/84; Patricia C Phillips (auth), Cheryl Goldsleger at Bertha Urdang, Gallery Art Forum, 1/85; Donald Kuspit (auth), Cheryl Golds Leger, Art in Am, 3/85; Carla Schulz-Hoffman (auth), Rooms Devoid of People, Filled with Shadows, Comments on the Work of Cheryl Goldsjeger, catalog essay, Bertha Urdang Gallery, 1/89. *Mem:* Col Art Asn. *Media:* Oil. *Dealer:* Bertha Urdang Gallery 23 E 74th St New York NY 10021. *Mailing Add:* 170 Greenwood Dr Athens GA 30606

GOLDSMITH, BARBARA
WRITER, CRITIC
b New York, NY, May 18, 31. *Study:* Wellesley Col, BA, 53; Pace Univ, Hon DLit, 81; Syracuse Univ, Hon DLett, 81. *Pos:* Ed, New York Mag, 66-74; sr ed, Harper's Bazaar, 70-74; Vanity Fair, 87- *Awards:* Nat Arch Award, 91; Lit Market Pl Publ Award, 92; Penn Paper-Pres & Access Award, 92. *Mem:* Whitney Mus Am Art; Mus Mod Art, New York; Mus City New York (pres coun, 70-); New York Coun on Arts. *Publ:* Auth, articles New York Mag, Esquire, Vanity Fair & Harpers; The Straw Man, 75; Little Gloria, Happy at Last, 80; Johnson v Johnson, 87. *Mailing Add:* Morton L Janklow Assocs 598 Madison Ave New York NY 10022

GOLDSMITH, BENEDICT ISAAC
GALLERY DIRECTOR, EDUCATOR
b New York, NY, Aug 1, 16. *Study:* NY Univ, BS, 40; Art Students League, New York & Woodstock, NY, with Arnold Blanch; Teachers Col, Columbia Univ, MA, 50; Inst Del'Arte, Florence, Italy, 64. *Collections Arranged:* Potsdam Prints (with catalog), 63-74; Robert Mallary, 68; Sculpture, NY Six, 69; New Realism, 71; Women in Art, 72, New Realism, Revisited, 74; Potsdam Plastics, 75; African Sculpture Selections, Anspach Collection, 75; Maine Coast Artists Open, 79; Artists as Teachers, 79; Associates Selects, 79; Off the Wall, 80; & Painters, 80; Richard Derby Tucker Mem Retrospective, 80. *Pos:* Gallery dir, State Univ NY Col Potsdam, 65-78; exhib dir, Maine Coast Artists, 79-82. *Teaching:* Prof art, State Univ NY Col Potsdam, 50-78. *Mem:* Gallery Asn NY (exec comt, 75); Asn Exhib & Gallery Dirs, NY (pres, 68-69). *Mailing Add:* 45 Lakeview Terrace Rockland ME 04841

GOLDSMITH, CAROLINE LERNER
ADMINISTRATOR, CONSULTANT
B New York, NY. *Study:* cornell Univ, BA; Art Students League; Parsons Sch Design. *Pos:* Pres, Gallery Passport Ltd, 60-67; sr vpres, Arts & Communications Counselors, 66-; exec dir, Art Table Inc, 81- *Mem:* Col Art Asn; Am Asn Mus; Int Council Mus; Am Fed Art. *Mailing Add:* 301 E 57th St 3rd fl New York NY 10022

GOLDSMITH, ELSA M
PAINTER, GRAPHIC ARTIST
b New York, NY, Jan 26, 20. *Study:* Parsons Sch Fine & Appl Art, scholar award, BA; NY Univ; Pratt Graphic Ctr, (lithography); etching with Ruth Leaf; painting with Betty Holiday. *Exhib:* Am Drawing Biennial, Norfolk Mus, Va, 71; Palazzo Vechio, Florence, Italy, 72; Brooklyn Mus, NY, 75; M J Greene Gallery, Bridgehampton, New York, 81; Cayuga Mus, NY, 83; Syosset Libr, NY, 83; and others; East Meadow Library Retrospective, 90; Les Malamut Art Gallery NJ, 90. *Pos:* Advert artist, Newsweek Mag, New York, 40-41; indust designer, Belle Kogan Assoc, New York, 41-48; freelance artist, Book & Magazine Illustrating, New York, 42- *Teaching:* Teacher, Elsa Goldsmith's Studio, 50-74 & North Shore Commun Ctr, 71-73, Great Neck, NY; teacher painting, Adult Educ, Sewanhake High Sch, Floral Manor, NY, 72-74. *Awards:* Int Gold Medal of Honor, Cannes, 69; Susan Kahn Award, Nat Asn Women Artists, New York, 74; Doris Krindel Award, 80; and others. *Bibliog:* Community Leaders Am 11th Ed. *Mem:* Nat Asn Women Artists; Int Art Asn; Women in the Arts, Inc (bd mem & bicentennial chmn, 74-76); North Shore Community Art Ctr (bd dir & art coordr, 73-, vp; UN Int Womens Year Arts Festival (bd mem, 75-76). *Media:* Drawing. *Publ:* Southern Quart, Vol XVII, No 2, 79; Feature, North Shore, Mag, 83. *Mailing Add:* 52 Ruxton Rd Great Neck NY 11023

GOLDSMITH, LAWRENCE CHARLES
PAINTER, INSTRUCTOR
b New York, NY, Nov 22, 16. *Study:* Yale Univ Sch Fine Arts; Brooklyn Mus Art Sch, with Reuben Tam; Art Students League. *Work:* Lamont Gallery, Phillips Exeter Acad, NH; Univ Maine, Orono; Loma Linda Univ, Riverside, Calif. *Exhib:* One-man shows, Watercolors, Lamont Gallery, Phillips Exeter Acad, NH, 72 & Univ Maine, Orono, 80; San Diego Watercolor Soc Gallery, Calif, 79 & 85; Watercolors, Frenso Arts Ctr, Calif, 80; Georgia Watercolor Soc, 81; and others. *Teaching:* Guest instr watercolor, Art Students League, 65-69; lectr art, Queens Col, New York, 68-70; instr painting, Univ Vt Continuing Educ, 77- *Awards:* Winsor & Newton Award, 69. *Bibliog:* Susan E Meyer (auth), 40 Watercolorists and How They Work, Watson-Guptill Publ, 76; Edward Betts (auth), Creative Seascape Painting, Watson-Guptill, 81; Nita Leland (auth), Exploring Color, North Light Publ, 85. *Mem:* Am Watercolor Soc; Artists Equity. *Media:* Oil, Watercolor. *Publ:* Auth, Watercolor page, American Artist, 75 & auth, Watercolor Bold and Free, 80, Watson-Guptill Publ. *Dealer:* Gallery Two Woodstock VT 05091. *Mailing Add:* RD 2 Fairfax VT 05454

GOLDSTEIN, CARL
HISTORIAN, SCULPTOR
b New York, NY, June 24, 38. *Study:* Brooklyn Col, BA, 60; Columbia Univ, MA, 62, PhD, 66. *Exhib:* Brooklyn Artists, Brooklyn Mus, 56; NC Sculpture, Weatherspoon Gallery, Greensboro, 79; Custom & Culture II, Custom House, New York, 79; NC Sculpture Invitational, Green Hill Gallery, Greensboro, 80; one-man show, Durham Art Guild, NC, 80 & Weatherspoon Gallery, Greensboro, 82. *Teaching:* Instr art hist, Wheaton Col, Norton, Mass, 66; asst prof, Brown Univ, 66-71; prof, Univ NC, Greensboro, 71- *Awards:* Grants, Am Philosophical Soc, 77 & 82. *Bibliog:* W Zimmer (auth), articles, Arts Mag, 1/77 & 5/77. *Mem:* Col Art Asn Am. *Media:* Wood. *Res:* Baroque art; twentieth century sculpture; history of academies of art. *Publ:* Auth, Studies in seventeenth century French art theory and ceiling painting, Art Bulletin, 65; Observations on the role of Rome, Art Quart, 70; The erotic Baroque of Lachaise, Art Int, 74; Towards a definition of academic art, Art Bulletin, 75; Visual Fact Over Verbal Fiction, A Study of the Carracci and the Criticism, Theory and Practice of Painting in Renaissance and Baroque Italy, Cambridge Univ Press, 88. *Mailing Add:* 801 Greenwood Greensboro NC 27410

GOLDSTEIN, CHARLES BARRY
ART DEALER, APPRAISER
b New York, NY. *Study:* Ohio Univ, Athens, BBA, 67; Am Univ, Washington, DC, MPA, 75; Ind Univ Int Soc Appraisers, CAPP Diploma, 91. *Pos:* Art dealer, Charles Barry Int, Rockville, Md, 75-, art appraiser, 79- , court qualified expert witness & trial consult, 92-; arts comnr, City of Rockville, Md, 91- *Teaching:* Lectr & forums art & appraisals, Int Soc Appraisers, Hoffman Estates, Ill Nat Confs, 89- *Mem:* Certified mem, Int Soc Appraisers, (nat fine arts comt, 90-). *Mailing Add:* c/o Charles Barry International 8 Hardwicke Place Rockville MD 20850

GOLDSTEIN, DANIEL JOSHUA
PRINTMAKER, SCULPTOR
b Mt Vernon, NY, June 19, 50. *Study:* Brandeis Univ; Univ Calif, Santa Cruz, BA; St Martin's Col, London, Eng, post-grad study. *Work:* Brooklyn Mus, NY; Chicago Art Inst; Achenbach Found, San Francisco, Calif; Oakland Mus of Art, Calif; Carnegie Inst; and others. *Exhib:* Achenbach Found, 72; Prints Calif, Oakland Mus Art, 75; Nat Print Exhib, Brooklyn Mus, NY, 76 & 80; one-man shows, Getler-Pall Gallery, New York, 77, ADI Gallery, San Francisco, 77 & Brooklyn Mus, 83; New Talent in Printmaking, AAA Gallery, New York, 77; Calif Palace Legion Honor, San Francisco; 12th Nat Print Exhib, Silvermine Guild Artists, New Canaan, Conn, 78; RI Sch Design Mus, 79. *Dealer:* Fischbach Gallery 29 W 57th St New York NY 10019. *Mailing Add:* 224 Guerrero San Francisco CA 94103

GOLDSTEIN, FERN
PAINTER, DESIGNER
b Chicago, Ill, Jan 26, 35. *Study:* Univ Ill, Urbana, 54; Art Inst Chicago, 66. *Work:* Mus Contemp Art Gift Shop (handcrafted jewelry), Chicago; Edward Sherbyn Gallery, Chicago. *Comn:* Sterling Silver Jewelry, comn by Mrs Goldsmith, Chicago; Sterling Silver Jewelry, comn by Mrs Sher, Chicago; Sterling Silver Jewelry, comn by Mrs Miller, Chicago; and many others. *Exhib:* Fine Art, Evanston Women's Club, Ill; Tactile Show for the Blind, Light House for the Blind, CHicago, Ill; Sterling Silver Jewelry, Evanston Art Ctr, Ill; Fine Art, Highland Park Art Festival, Ill; Fine Art, Howard Western Art Festival, Chicago; paintings & prints, Art Inst Chicago; numerous one woman shows, Northtown Libr, Chicago. *Pos:* Colorist & Designer, Chatham Fabrics, Chicago; make up artist, Adrien Arpel Cosmetics, Chicago; founder art dept for Learning Disabled, Asn Talmud Torahs. *Teaching:* Drawing & painting, Fine Art Studio, Chicago. *Awards:* Int Woman Yr(in recognition of contributions to art), Cambridge, Eng, 91-92; Prize for Banned in Coston at Univ of Ill Homecoming. *Mem:* Life mem Art Inst Chicago & Textile Soc Art Inst; Chicago Artists Coalistion. *Media:* Ink, Gouache; Colored Pencil. *Mailing Add:* 3270 N Lake Shore Dr, Apt 14C Chicago IL 60657

GOLDSTEIN, GLADYS
PAINTER, COLLAGE ARTIST
b Newark, Ohio. *Study:* Md Inst Art; Art Students League; Columbia Univ, New York; Pa State Univ, University Park; study with Hobson Pittman. *Work:* Baltimore Mus Art, Md; Pa State Univ; Univ Ariz; Goucher Col, Baltimore; Univ Md; Fed Reserve Bank; and others. *Exhib:* One-man shows, Baltimore Mus Art, Goucher Col, Duveen-Graham Gallery, New York, Galerie Philadelphie, Paris, IFA Gallery, Washington, DC, Western Md Col, Newark Gallery, Del, Richter Gallery, Weisbaden, Ger, 65-75. *Pos:* Co-chmn art festival, City Baltimore, 71-74; art comt, Mayor's Ball, 73-74; exec comt, Mayor's Adv Comt for Arts & Cult, 74- *Teaching:* Instr painting, Md Inst Col Art, 60-65; instr art, Col Notre Dame, Md, 65-85. *Awards:* Third Award, Md Art Today, H K & Co, 72; First Award, 25th Ann of Israel, JCC, 74; Awards, Baltimore Mus Art & Pa State Univ. *Media:* Oil; Paperwork, Acrylic. *Mailing Add:* 2002 South Rd Baltimore MD 21209

GOLDSTEIN, HOWARD
PAINTER, EDUCATOR
b New York, NY, Feb 10, 33. *Study:* Albright Art Sch, cert; State Univ NY, Col Buffalo, BS; NY Univ, MA; Columbia Univ, EdD. *Work:* NJ State Mus, Trenton; Morris Mus Arts & Sci, Morristown, NJ; YMCA, New York; Univ Frankfurt, WGer; Imperial Chem Industs, US, Wilmington, Del. *Exhib:* 154th Ann Nat Exhib, Pa Acad Fine Arts, Philadelphia, 59 & 65; Ann NJ State Exhib, Newark Mus, 61, 64, 66, 68 & 77; Art from NJ, NJ State Mus, Trenton, 66-73; 32nd Ann Nat Painting Exhib, Butler Inst Am Art, Youngstown, Ohio, 67; Nat Show, Chautauqua Exhib Am Art, NY, 68 & 69; Ann New Eng Exhib, Silvermine Guild Artists, New Canaan, Conn, 70, 72 & 73; one-person exhib, Westbroadway Gallery, New York, 73, 74, 76, 77, & 79; Summit Art Ctr, NJ, 81 & 83; Tenth Anniversary Exhib, Barron Arts Ctr, 88. *Collections Arranged:* Geometric Art: An Exhib of Paintings & Constructions by 14 Contemp NJ Artists, NJ State Mus, 67; Westbroadway Gallery Group, Rundetarn Mus, Copenhagen, Denmark, 73; one-man exhib, NJ State Mus, 74; Viewpoint 76, Morris Mus Arts & Sci, Morristown, NJ, 76; Retrospective Exhib, Trenton City Mus, 89; one-man show, Mercer Med Ctr, Trenton, NJ, 90; 50th Anniv Exhib Assoc Artists of NJ, Hunterdon Art Ctr, 90. *Pos:* Exec dir, Comn to study the arts in New Jersey, 64-66; Comnr, Mercer Co Cult & Heritage Comn, 71. *Teaching:* Prof painting, Trenton State Col, NJ, 60-, chmn art dept, 80- *Awards:* Emily Lowe Award, Emily Lowe Found Competition, 60; Videorecord Corp Am Award, 23rd New Eng Exhib, 72; Purchase Award, Art from NJ, State of NJ, 73. *Mem:* Assoc Artists NJ; Nat Art Educ Asn. *Media:* Acrylic. *Mailing Add:* 49 Rockleigh Dr Trenton NJ 08628

GOLDSTEIN, JACK
FILMMAKER, CONCEPTUAL ARTIST
b Montreal, Que, Sept 27, 45. *Study:* Chouinard Art Sch, Los Angeles, BFA, 70; Calif Inst of the Arts, MFA, 72. *Work:* Mus of Mod Art, Geneva, Switz; Brooklyn Mus, NY. *Exhib:* Twenty-four Young Los Angeles Artists, Los Angeles Co Mus of Art, Calif, 70; one-man shows, Nigel Greenwood Gallery, London, England, 71, Francoise Lambert Gallery, Milan, Italy, 74, Kabinette für Aktuelle Kunst Bremerhaven, Ger, 76, Centre d'Art Contemporain, Cite Univ, Geneva, Switz, 77, The Kitchen Ctr for Video & Music, New York, NY, 78, Umgang Mit der Stadtische Gallerie, Riedenburg, Wger, 84, Whitney Mus Am Art, New York, 85 & Josh Baer Gallrey, 86, Mus Contemp Arts, Los Angeles, Calif, 89; Haley's Comet, Light Gallery, NY, 85; Summer Group Show, Metro Pictures, New York, 85; Nocturne: Portraying the Night, Kemper Gallery, Kansas City Art Inst, 87; Chicago Int Art Expo, Dart

Gallery, 88. *Awards:* Can Coun Arts grant, 73-74; production grant, NY State Coun on the Arts, 77; Nat Endowment for the Arts Fel, 79-80. *Bibliog:* Carlo McCormick (auth), review, Art Forum, 11/86; Richard Huntington (auth), Buffalo Evening News, Review, 10/5/86; Rosetta Brooks (auth), Space Fictions, Flash Art, 1/87. *Mailing Add:* c/o Dart Gallery Inc 712 N Carpenter Chicago IL 60622

GOLDSTEIN, JULIUS
PAINTER, INSTRUCTOR
b New York, NY, Mar 17, 18. *Study:* Brooklyn Mus Art Sch, with Rufino Tamayo & John Ferren, 46-47; Art Students League; travel & study in Europe, 48, 54, 66 & 67; England, 75. *Exhib:* Speed Art Mus Ann, Louisville, Ky, 57; Brooklyn Mus Int Watercolor Show, 61 & 63; Butler Inst Am Art Ann, Youngstown, Ohio, 66; Nat Inst Arts & Lett Contemp Painting & Sculpture, 70; Childe Hassam Fund Exhib, Am Acad Arts & Lett, 70; one-man exhib, Christ Hosp Col Art Ctr, Horsham, Sussex, Eng, 80. *Teaching:* From asst prof drawing & painting to assoc prof art, Hunter Col, 61- *Awards:* Yaddo Found Fel, Saratoga Springs, NY, 64-66. *Media:* Oil, Watercolor. *Mailing Add:* Hunter Col CUNY 695 Park Ave New York NY 10021

GOLDSTEIN, MILTON
PRINTMAKER, PAINTER
b Holyoke, Mass, Nov 14, 14. *Study:* Art Students League, 46-49; also with Harry Sternberg, Morris Kantor & Will Barnet; Guggenheim Fel, 50. *Work:* Philadelphia Mus Art; Metrop Mus Art, New York; Mus Mod Art, New York; Smithsonian Nat Mus, Washington, DC; Brooklyn Mus, NY. *Comn:* Collection of etchings for Europe & US (200 ed), Int Graphic Arts Soc, New York, 52; collection of etchings (150 ed), 54. *Exhib:* Libr Cong, Washington, DC, 48; Smithsonian Inst, Washington, DC, 55; Outstanding Prints Produced in America, Brooks Mem Mus, Memphis, Tenn, 59; Am Printmakers in Italy, sponsored by Boston Pub Libr, 60; Masters Engraving Show, Queens Col, New York, 64; 30 Yrs of Am Printmaking, Brooklyn Mus, 77; Merchant Marine Acad Mus, Kings Point, NY, 89. *Teaching:* Prof printmaking emer, Adelphi Univ, 53-85. *Awards:* First Prize & Purchase Award, New York State Fair, NY, 50; First Prize & Purchase Award, Philadelphia Mus, 52; First Prize & Purchase Award, Philadelphia Print Club, Pa, 52; First Prize & Purchase Award, Nat Print Show, Western NMex Univ, 71. *Bibliog:* Carl Zigrosser (auth), Fine Prints, Crown, 60; Jules Heller (auth), Printmaking Today, Holt, 60. *Mem:* Soc Am Graphic Artists (coun, 72); fel Royal Soc Arts, London; Am Color Print Soc; Kappa Pi; Print Club. *Media:* Miscellaneous; All Media. *Publ:* Auth, How to Make an Etching (film), Almanac Films, 51; A new color etching process, Everyday Art; Reprint, Design Mag, 55. *Mailing Add:* 56-16 219th St Bayside NY 11364

GOLDSTEIN, NATHAN
PAINTER, WRITER
b Chicago, Ill, Mar 26, 27. *Study:* Art Inst of Chicago, BFA, MFA, with Louis Ritman; Art Students League, with Julian Levi. *Pos:* Chmn, Found Prog of Study, Art Inst of Boston, 73- *Bibliog:* Gerald Monroe (auth), Technical drawing: The personal approach of Nathan Goldstein, Drawing, 5-6/80 & Am Artist, 2/82. *Media:* Oil, Pen and Ink. *Publ:* Auth, The Art of Responsive Drawing, 73, 2nd ed, 77, 3rd ed, 84, 4th ed, 92, Figure Drawing: The Structure, Anatomy and Expressive Design of Human Form, 76, 81 & 92, Painting: Visual and Technical Fundamentals, 79, 100 American and European Drawings: A Portfolio, 82 & A Drawing Handbook, Themes, Tools and Techniques, 86, Prentice-Hall; Design and Composition: The Forming of Order, Prentice-Hall, Simon & Schuster, 89. *Mailing Add:* c/o Art Inst Boston 700 Beacon St Boston MA 02215

GOLDSTEIN, SHELDON (SHELLY)
PAINTER
b St Louis, Mo, 1951. *Study:* Univ Mo; studied with James Harmon, St Louis & Val Dunnett, London. *Work:* Off Secy Interior, Washington, DC. *Comn:* Landscapes, portraits & still-lifes, Italy, Ireland & US. *Exhib:* Solo exhibs, Monaco Art Ctr, Monte Carlo, Monaco, 86, The Crane Collection, Boston, Mass, 88, Hotel de Paris, Monte Carlo, Monaco, 89, Kertesz Gallery, San Francisco, 89, US Info Servs, Milan, Italy, 89, The Region Tuscany, Laterina (Arezzo), Italy, 90; group exhibs, Jefferson Mem Mus, St Louis, Mo, 87. *Bibliog:* Victoria Fowler (auth), Sheldon Goldstein: Paintings 1980- 1989 (monogr), 89; Victoria Fowler (auth), Sheldon Goldstein: Un Pittore in Toscana, The Region of Tuscany (catalog), 90. *Dealer:* Kertesz Gallery 521 Sutter St San Francisco CA 94102; Max Bollag Gallery Werdmuhlestrasse 9 Zurich Switzerland. *Mailing Add:* The Crane Collection, c/o Amy Meserve 218 Newbury St Boston MA 02116

GOLDSZER, BATH-SHEBA
PAINTER, GRAPHIC ARTIST
b Warsaw, Poland, Jan 26, 32; US citizen. *Study:* Hertzeliah Teachers Sem, BA(educ), 56; Art Students League, with Gustav Rehberger; also with Joe Hing Lowe & Ludmila Morosova. *Work:* Many pvt collections, US, Israel, Poland & Argentina. *Exhib:* Hudson Valley Art Asn, Westchester Co Ctr; Catherine Lorillard Wolfe Arts Club, Nat Arts Club Gallery; Am Artists Prof League, Salmagundi Club, New York; Chung-Cheng Art Gallery, Sun Yat Sen Hall, St John Univ; and others. *Awards:* First Prize in Oil, Nat Art League, 74 & 82, Queensboro Soc Arts, 74-77 & Art League Nassau Co, 78 & 79; 7 first prizes in oil and numerous others. *Bibliog:* Jack Besterman (auth), Big Six Art League, Chapel & Pension News, 2/72, An accomplished artist, 2/73 & Coop art scene, 4/74 & 5/79, Towers Reporter. *Mem:* Life fel Am Artists Prof League; Hudson Valley Art Asn; Catherine Lorillard Wolfe Arts Club; Nat Art League; Art League Nassau Co; and others. *Media:* Oil. *Mailing Add:* 46-10 61st St Apt 2H Woodside NY 11377

GOLER, ROBERT
CURATOR, HISTORIAN
b Cleveland, Ohio, Aug 20, 56. *Study:* Yale Univ, AB, 79; Univ Wyoming-Western Am Studies Inst, Cert, 80; Case Western Reserve Univ, MA, 84. *Collections Arranged:* 20th Century Images of George Washington (with catalog), 83; Pageant of Independence, Harry A Ogden Collection, 85; Capital City: New York After the Revolution (with catolog), 86; Kovler Family Installation, 88; Say It Ain't So Joe: The 1919 Black Sox Scandal; A City Comes of Age: Chicago in the 1890s (with catalog), 90. *Pos:* Researcher & asst cur, Western Reserve Hist Soc, 79-80; cur of collections, Fraunces Tavern Mus, New York, 81-88, actg dir, 86-88; cur, decorative & indust arts, Chicago Hist Soc, 88- *Teaching:* Lectr Am Hist, New Sch for Social Res, New York, 86. *Awards:* Lawrence Redway Award, Med Soc State NY, 88. *Bibliog:* Audrey Davis (auth), review, Technol & Cult, 87; Edward Pershey (auth), The Healing Arts, Hist News, 86; Richard Lindberg (auth), review, J Sport Hist, 90; James Grossman (auth), review, Public Hist, 91. *Mem:* Am Asn Mus; Soc Indust Archeol; Soc Hist Technology; Am Hist Asn. *Res:* Analysis of material culture & cultural history of early America; history of city of Chicago, with particular emphasis on 1880-1920 era. *Publ:* Auth, The marriage of Aescepalus and Clio: Recent bibliography in the health sciences of early America, Trends in Hist, 88; Black Sox Chicago History, 89; ed, Federal New York: A Symposium, 90; auth, A City Comes of Age: Chicago in the 1890's 90; contribr, Encyclopedia of New York City, in prep. *Mailing Add:* Chicago Hist Soc Clark St at N Ave Chicago IL 60614-6099

GOLEY, MARY ANNE
HISTORIAN, DIRECTOR
b Washington, DC, July 1, 45. *Study:* Univ Md, asst to Dr William H Gerdts, BA, 67; Oberlin Col, 70-71; Case Western Reserve Univ, with Wolfgang Steckow & Karal Ann Marling, MA, 73; Cleveland Mus Art, cert, 75. *Collections Arranged:* John White Alexander: 1856-1915 (auth, catalog), Nat Mus Am Art, 76-77; The Hague School and Its American Legacy (auth, catalog), Fed Reserve Bd & Norton Gallery, West Palm Beach, Fla, 82; also permanent collections of Fed Reserve Bd, 75 & Fed Reserve Banks, Miami, 79, Jacksonville, 86 & Dallas, 92; The Office as Art: Furnishings & Fixtures, Arlington Arts Ctr, 86; Paintings of Edward Steichen, 88 & Samuel Halpert, 91, Fed Reserve Bd. *Pos:* Asst registrar, Nat Mus Am Art, 68-71; dir, Fine Arts Prog, Fed Reserve Bd, 75- *Awards:* Lady of the House of Orange-Nassau, Queen of Neth, 82; House of Nassau, Grand Duke of Luxembourg, 88. *Mem:* Am Asn Mus; Asn Prof Art Advisors; Arlington Arts Ctr (bd pres, 87-90); Archives Am Art. *Res:* Late 19th century American artists in the context of their European influences; J W Alexander & Childe Hassam. *Publ:* Auth, Gerald Murphy: Toward an Understanding of his Art and Inspiration (exhib catalog), Fed Reserve Bd, 83; Panel for Music Room by John White Alexander, Detroit Inst Arts Bull, 89. *Mailing Add:* Fed Reserve Syst Fine Arts Prog 20 & Constitution Ave NW (Stop 56) Washington DC 20551

GOLUB, LEON
PAINTER
b Chicago, Ill, Jan 23, 22. *Study:* Univ Chicago, BA(hist art), 42; Art Inst Chicago Sch, BFA, 49, MFA, 50; Acad Fine Arts, Hon Mention, 61, Sch Art Inst Chicago, DFA, 82 & Swarthmore Col, 86. *Work:* Mus Mod Art, New York; Art Inst Chicago; Nat Collection Fine Arts, Smithsonian Inst; Brooklyn Mus, New York; Malmö Konsthall, Swed; and others. *Exhib:* One-Man Shows, Hayden Gallery, Mass Inst Technol, 70, San Francisco Art Inst, 76, Fawbush Gallery, 88, Galerie Neuendorf, 88; Retrospective Traveling Exhib, New Mus Contemp Art, New York, 84, La Jolla Mus Contemp Art, Calif, Mus Contemp Art, Chicago, Montreal Mus Fine Arts, Corcoran Gallery, Washington, DC & Mus Fine Arts, Boston, 85 & 86; The Saatchi Collection, London, Eng, 88; Leon Golub/Nancy Spero, Orchard Gallery, Derry, Northern Ireland, 87; Galerie Darthea Speyer, Paris, France, 87 & 90; Committed to Print, Mus Mod Art, New York, 88; Prospect 89, Kunstverein, Frankfurt, Ger, 89; Eli Broad Family Found, Los Angeles, Calif, 89; Josh Baer Gallery, New York, 90 & 92; The Decade Show, Mus Contemp Hispanic Art, New York, 90; 1968 - Concrete Utopia in Art & Soc, Stadtische Kunsthalle Dusseldorf, Ger & Mus Furgestaltung, Zurich, Switz, 90; Worldwide, Grand Lobby installation, Brooklyn Mus, New York, 91; Parallel Visions: Modern Artists & Outsider Art, Los Angeles Co Mus Art, 92 (256) Musée D'Art Contemporaine de Montréal, Que, 92. *Teaching:* Prof art, Mason Gross Sch Arts, Rutgers Univ, 70-91. *Awards:* Ford Found Grant, 60, Cassandra Found Grant, 67 & Guggenheim Found Grant, 68; Christian & Mary Lindback Found Award, 82; Skowhegan Medal for Painting, 88. *Bibliog:* Donald Kuspit (auth), Leon Golub: Existential-Activist Painter, Rutgers Univ Press, NJ, 85; Gerald Marzorati (auth), A Painter of Darkness: Leon Golub and Our Times, Viking, 90; Jo-Anne Isaak (auth), Who Wears the Pants in the House of Being, Arts Mag, 1/92. *Media:* Acrylic. *Publ:* Auth, Bombs & helicopters, the art of Nancy Spero, Caterpillar I, 67; Utopia/antiutopia, Art Criticism, 5/72; 2D/3D, Artforum, 3/73; What works, Art Criticism, 2/79; Split Infinities, Artforum, pgs 118-120, 1/90. *Dealer:* Josh Baer Gallery 476 Broome St New York NY 10013; Rhona Hoffman Gallery 215 W Superior Chicago IL 60610. *Mailing Add:* 530 La Guardia Pl New York NY 10012

GOLUBIC, THEODORE
SCULPTOR, DESIGNER
b Lorain, Ohio, Dec 9, 28. *Study:* Miami Univ, BFA; Art Students League, with Jon Corbino; Univ Notre Dame, asst to Ivan Mestrovic, MFA. *Comn:* Crypt Relief Series, Rock of Ages Corp, Barre, Vt, 65-67; Equinoctial Point (4-dimensional, sun/spectral), comn by Diane Dudley, Litchfield, Ill, 67; Nativity (limestone heroic relief), Cathedral Church of Nativity, Dubuque, Iowa, 68; Spectra-Cube (sun/time environ), comn by Josephine Davis, Escondido, Calif, 83; Infant Christ (bas relief, mahogany), Univ San Diego,

87. *Exhib:* 155th Ann Exhibit, Pa Acad Fine Arts, Philadelphia, 61; 13th Ann Drawing & Small Sculpture Show, Ball State Univ, Muncie, Ind, 63; 34th Ann Exhib, Nat Sculpture Soc, New York, 67; Art for 1970, Southern Calif Expo, Del Mar, 70; one-man show, Roswell Mus in conjunction with Sunspot Observatory, NMex, 72; Infant King bas relief, Mahogany, Univ San Diego, Calif, 87; Expressions of Faith V, Grand Canyon Univ, Phoenix, Ariz, 91; and others. *Pos:* Sculpture consult, Rock of Ages Corp, 65-67; artist in residence, Roswell Mus & Art Ctr, NMex, 71-72. *Teaching:* Guest instr sculpture, Univ Notre Dame, summer 59; guest instr, Art Sch Air, Educ TV & ABC-TV, Elkhart, Ind, 62-63; featured artist/lectr, 28th Ann Conf Workshop, Am Soc Aesthetics, 70. *Bibliog:* Hatch (auth), article, West Art, 11/70; article, Roswell Mus & Art Ctr Bulletin, fall 71 & spring 72; Community Arts Program, US Dept Housing & Urban Develop, 73. *Mem:* Int Sculpture Ctr; Artists Equity Asn. *Media:* All; Sun-Time, Diffractives. *Publ:* Guest ed, 3/67, contribr cover & auth, In art there is victory, 4/67, Am Art Stone. *Mailing Add:* 3321 W Orchid Lane Phoenix AZ 85021

GOMEZ, MIRTA & EDUARDO DELVALIE
PHOTOGRAPHER
Mirta Gomez: b Havana, Cuba, Dec 20, 53. *Study:* Mirta Gomez: Fla Int Univ, BFA, 76; Brooklyn Col, MFA, 81. *Work:* Mus Mod Art, New York; New Orleans Mus Art, La; Brooklyn Mus, New York. *Exhib:* Viva Nada, Blue Sky Gallery, Portland, Ore, 91; Contemp Southern Photog, New Orleans Tri-Annual Exhib, 92. *Teaching:* Assoc prof photog, Fla Int Univ, 83- *Awards:* Individual Artist Fel Photog, Nat Endowment Arts, 76 & 90; Photog Fel, NY State Coun Arts, 78; Photog Fel, Fla Arts Coun, 87. *Mailing Add:* 1600 SW 12th St Miami FL 33135

GOMEZ-QUIROZ, JUAN MANUEL
PAINTER, PRINTMAKER
b Santiago, Chile, Feb 20, 39; US citizen. *Study:* RI Sch Design, Fulbright Fel, 62-63; Yale Univ, Fulbright Fel, 63-64; Pratt Graphic Art Ctr, 64-66. *Work:* Guggenheim Mus; Metrop Mus Art, New York; Mass Inst Technol; Boston Mus Fine Arts; Mus Mod Art, New York; plus many others. *Exhib:* One-man shows, Schubert Gallery, Marbella, Spain, 77, Kornblee Gallery, New York, 78, Sutton Gallery, New York, 80-86, Held- Koupernikoff Gallery, Boston, 82, Omar Rayo Mus, Rodalnillo, Columbia, 84 & Todd Capp Gallery, New York, 88; DeArmas Gallery, Miami, Fla, 80 & 83; Art Consult Gallery, Boston, 85 & 86; Subject Women & Sacred Secrets, Todd Capp Gallery, New York, 86; The Contemporary Master Printmakers from Latin America, Hostos Art Gallery, Community Col, New York, 86; Exhib 88, NJ Ctr Visual Arts, Summit, 88; The Latin American Spirit: Art and Artists in the United States 1920-1970, Bronx Mus Art, New York, 88; ST LIFER, Art Exchange, NJ & NY, 89; The Dead Blimpee Show II, New York, 89; IX Biennal Int DeArte, Valparaiso, Chile, 89. *Teaching:* Lectr studio art, Univ Calif, Santa Barbara, 67-68; lectr, Summit Art Ctr, Summit, NJ, 72-77; Escuela de Bellas Artes, Lima, Peru, 75; NJ Ctr Visual Art, 87; Fla Inst Technol & Printmaker Workshop, 88. *Awards:* Grand Prize, IV Biennial Printmaking, San Juan, PR, 79; Prize Bienal Maracaibo Venezuela, 82; Hispanic Achievers Feria Mundial Hispana, New York, 85. *Bibliog:* David Shirley (auth), article in NY Sunday Times, 78; Joseph Merkel (auth), The flexibility of sculpture, Artspeak, 86; article in IBM Nachrichten, 6/89, Ger. *Media:* Oil, Acrylic; Intaglio. *Mailing Add:* 44 Grand St Apt 2 New York NY 10013

GONGORA, LEONEL
PAINTER, EDUCATOR
b Cartago, Colombia. *Study:* Wash Univ. *Work:* Pub Libr, Mus Mod Art, New York; Wash Univ Permanent Collection, St Louis, Mo; Staatsgalerie Mus, Stuttgart, Ger; Mus Mod Art, Bogota, Colombia. *Comn:* Paintings, comn by Fernando Gamboa for Mex Pavilion, Expo 67, Montreal, PQ & Expo 70, Osaka, Japan; lithographs, Lublin, Inc, New York, 69, Bank St Atelier, New York, 70 & Aquarius Press, New York, 71. *Exhib:* Confrontacion 66, Mus Bellas Artes, Mexico City, 66; Am Acad Arts & Lett, New York, 69; 1st Pan-Am Graphics Biennial, Mus Latertulia, Cali, Colombia, 71; 4th Int Miniature Print Exhib, AAA Gallery, New York, 71; 3rd Brit Int Print Biennale, Bradform Mus, Eng, 72. *Teaching:* Instr painting & drawing, People's Art Ctr, St Louis, Mo, 56-59; prof painting & drawing, Iberoamericano Univ, Mex, 60-61; prof painting & drawing, Univ Mass, Amherst, 63-74. *Awards:* First Prize in Drawing, Nat Mus, Bogota, 64; Nat Acad Arts & Lett Award in Painting, New York, 68; Tenth Nat Arte Prize in Lithography, Mus Latertulia, 70. *Bibliog:* Toby Joysmith (auth), Two painter poets, The News, Mexico City, 8/69; Roberto Paramo (auth), Gongora, el erotismo en persona, El, Mexico City, 10/71; Anna Mayo (auth), Never on Good Friday, Village Voice, New York, 11/71. *Publ:* Illusr, Mass Rev, 67; illusr, Minn Rev, 69; illusr, The intricate land, New Rivers Press, 70; illusr, Poemas podridos, Villa Miseria Press, 72; contribr, Requirements of yesterday and today, Spectrum, 72. *Mailing Add:* 2 Bray Ct Pelham MA 00102

GONZALES, CARLOTTA (MRS RICHARD LAHEY)
PAINTER, SCULPTOR
b Wilmington, NC, Apr 3, 10. *Study:* Pa Acad Fine Arts; Nat Acad Design; Art Students League; Corcoran Sch Art; Ogunquit Sch Art. *Work:* Am Battle Monuments Mem, Honolulu; Francis Bangs Collection, Ogunquit Mus Art, Maine; Print Collection, Corcoran Gallery Art, Washington, DC; and others. *Comn:* The Heavens Above (star charts), 41, state seals, 45 & flags of America, 47, Nat Geographic Soc, Washington, DC; mural (battle maps), Am Battle Monuments Comns, 60; and others. *Exhib:* Nat Acad Design, New York, 30; Corcoran Gallery Art Biennial, Washington, DC, 36-38; Goucher Col, Towson, Md, 43; Montclair Art Mus, NJ, 46; Baltimore Mus, Md, 56. *Pos:* Staff artist, Nat Geographic Soc, 41-47. *Teaching:* Instr sculpture, Goucher Col, 35-37, Corcoran Sch Art, 35-45; instr pvt classes, 55-71. *Awards:* Sculpture, Nat Acad Design, 30. *Mem:* Ogunquit Mus Art. *Media:* Oil, Stone. *Publ:* Coauth, Life of Rembrandt & Life of Picasso, Stravon. *Mailing Add:* 9530 Clark Crossing Rd Vienna VA 22180

GONZALEZ, ARTHUR PADILLA
SCULPTOR
b Sacramento, Calif, July 22, 54. *Study:* Calif State Univ, Sacramento, BA, 77, MA, 79; Univ Calif at Davis, MFA, 81. *Work:* Prudential Ins Art Collection, New York; Am Express Art Collection, New York; Rutgers College Art Collection, NJ. *Comn:* Sculptures, Metrop Transit Authority, Tuckahoe, Crestwood, & Fleetwood, NY, 88; wall mounted bronze sculptures, Sid Singer, New York, 76 & 77. *Exhib:* Daniel Jacobs Collection, DeCordova Mus, Lincoln, Mass, 84; Recent Ceramic Sculpture, Univ Mus, Albuquerque NMex, 85; Palo Alto Cult Ctr, Calif, 85 & 89; Contemporary American Ceramics: Twenty Artists, Newport Harbor Art Mus, Calif, 85; Romanticism and Cynicism in Contemporary Art, Haggerty Mus Art, Milwaukee, 86; What's New: American Ceramics Since 1980, J B Speed Art Mus, Louisville, 87; The Eloquent Object, Philbrook Art Ctr, Tulsa, 87; Imprimature, Greenville Co Mus Art, SC, 88; Solo exhib, Sharpe Gallery, New York, 84-86 & 88, Himoultz/Solomon Gallery, Sacramento, CA, 86, 87 & 90, Allrich Gallery, San Francisco, CA, 87, Robert Kidd Gallery, Bermingham, MI, 88, Susan Cummins Gallery, Mill Valley, CA, 90, CCAC Downtown Oakland Gallery, Davis, CA, 90, and many others; Walter/McBean Gallery, San Francisco Art Int, CA, 89; Everson Mus Art, Syracuse, NY, 90; Nat Mus Ceramic Art, Baltimore, MD, 90; Fortress, Savona, Italy, 90. *Teaching:* Asst prof, beginning sculpture, Univ Calif, Davis, 85; asst prof adv seminar, Univ Calif, Berkeley, 88. *Awards:* Nat Endowment Arts, 82, 84, 86 & 90. *Bibliog:* Michael Cone (auth), Arthur Gonzalez, Flash Art, 6/7/86; Jamie Brunson (auth), Personal Narratives Recorded, Artweek, 6/2/87; Elizabeth Hess (auth), Just Desserts, Village Voice, 7/7/88; Jamie Brunson (auth), Fresh Starts, Art Week, 3/90, vol 21, No 8, p 10-11. *Mem:* New Mus Contemp Art; San Francisco Mus Mod Art. *Media:* Clay, Bronze; Metal Cast. *Publ:* American Ceramics 1876 to the present, Abbeville Press, 87; The Eloquent Object, Wash Press, 87; The History of American Ceramic: from Pipkins and Bean Pots to Contemporary Forms 1607 to the Present, Harry N Abrams Inc, 88; American Craft Art: a collector's guide, Gibbs M Smith, 88; auth, Encyclopedia of Ceramics, Japan Art Publ Co Ltd, 90. *Mailing Add:* 3038 Texas St Oakland CA 94602

GONZALEZ, JOSE GAMALIEL
ADMINISTRATOR, DESIGNER
b Iturbide, Nuevo Leon, Mex, Apr 20, 33. *Study:* Chicago Acad Fine Arts; Univ Chicago; Am Acad Art, Chicago, dipl; Art Inst Chicago, BFA; Instituto Allende, San Miguel, Mex, study with Jaime Pinto; Univ Notre Dame, MFA candidate. *Collections Arranged:* Hispanic Festival of the Arts, Mus Sci & Indust, Chicago, 74-78; Mexposicion I-25 Paintings from Bellas Artes in Mexico, 76 & Mexposicion II-Agustin Casasola-1910 Mexican Revolution (photog), 77, Univ Ill, Chicago Circle; Anisinabe Waki Aztlan, Truman Col, Chicago, 77; La Mujer-Mexican Women of Mexico plus Midwest Latinas, Cult Ctr Chicago Pub Libr, 78; Raices y Visiones, Mus Contemp Art Chicago, 79. *Pos:* Art dir, Revista Chicano Riquena, Ind Univ NW, 73-80; art dir, Foxlady Mag, Chicago, 75-76; visual consult, Ill Arts Coun, 76-79 & Nat Endowment Arts, Washington, DC, 78-79; nominator, Chicago Art Awards, 78- *Teaching:* Instr mural painting, Ind Univ NW, Gary, 74; instr Mex crafts, Columbia Col, Chicago, 78- *Mem:* Chicago Artists Coalition; Movimiento Artistico Chicano (dir, 78-). *Media:* Acrylic, Mixed Media. *Publ:* Contribr, 450 Years of Chicago History, Albuquerque, NMex, 76; contribr, We Americans, 75 & Gallery, 76, Scott Foresman. *Mailing Add:* 1900 S Carpenter St First Fl Chicago IL 60608

GONZALEZ, JUAN J
PAINTER
b Camaguey, Cuba, Jan 12, 45; US citizen. *Study:* Univ Miami, BFA, 69, MFA, 72. *Work:* Carnegie Inst, Pittsburgh, Pa; Indianapolis Mus Art; Vassar Col Art Gallery; Hirshhorn Mus & Sculpture Garden; Art Inst Chicago, Ill. *Exhib:* Whitney Mus Ann Exhib, 72; one man exhibs, Allen Stone Gallery, New York, 72, Corcoran & Corcoran, Miami, Fla, 73, Nancy Hoffman Gallery, New York, 75, 78, 82, 85, 88 & 91, Tomasulo Gallery, Union Col, Cranford, NJ, 78, Frances Wolfson Art Gallery, Miami-Dade Community Col, Fla, 80-81, Ctr Inter-Am Relations, New York, 81, Cleveland Ctr Contemp Art, Ohio, 88, Meadows Mus, Dallas, Tex, 91-92; Focus on Realism, Mus Mod Art, San Francisco, 85; Preview, Nancy Hoffman Gallery, New York, 92; An Ode to Gardens and Flowers, Nassau Co Mus Art, Roslyn Harbor, NY, 92; The Figure in the Twentieth Century, New York Acad Design, 92; Drawing Exhibition, univ Fla, 92; The Purloined Image, Flint Inst Arts, Mich, 93-94. *Teaching:* Instr painting & drawing, Sch Visual Arts, 77- *Awards:* Cintas Fel Award, 74 & 76; Creative Artist Prog, 77; Nat Endowment Arts, 80, 85 & 91. *Bibliog:* Gert Schiff (auth), Images of Horror & Fantasy, Abahams, 78; Nina French-Fraise (auth), article, 79 & Roney Cohen (auth), article, 83, Arts Mag; John Arthur (auth), Realist Drawings & Watercolors & A Martin (auth), American Realism, 20th Century Drawings & Watercolors. *Mem:* New York Found Arts (bd govs, 84-87). *Mailing Add:* c/o Nancy Hoffman Gallery 429 W Broadway New York NY 10012

GONZALEZ, MAURICIO MARTINEZ
ADMINISTRATOR, GALLERY DIRECTOR
b Mexico City, Mexico, Sept 30, 45. *Study:* Univ Tex at Arlington, BFA, 73; Univ of Americas, MA, 76; Fla State Univ, PhD, 88. *Exhib:* Rio Azul: City of the Storm God, traveling exhib, Univ Tex San Antonio Art Teaching Gallery, Tex, 89, Denver Mus Nat Hist, Colo, 90, Nat Geographic Soc Explorers Hall, Washington, DC, 90, Nat Hist Mus Los Angeles, Calif, 90, Museo Nac de Arqueologia Etnologia, Guatemala City, 91. *Pos:* Gallery dir, Univ Tex, San Antonio, 82-; asst dean, Col Fine Art & Humanities, Univ Tex, San Antonio, 88-; asst v-pres, Off of Multicultural Student Develop, Univ Toledo, Ohio, 90- *Awards:* Fel Nat Endowment Art, 79; Award for minority

mus prof, Smithsonian, 88; Grant, USIA, 89. *Mem:* Am Fed Arts; Am Asn Mus. *Publ:* Coauth, The Museum as a field setting for Teacher Education, J of Mus Educ, 87; InterAmerican Cultural Development, Fla State Univ, Ctr Arts Admn, 88. *Mailing Add:* Off Multicultural Studies Univ Toledo Toledo OH 43606-3390

GONZALEZ, PATRICIA
PAINTER
b Cartagena, Colombia, Apr 3, 58. *Study:* Central Sch Art & Design, London, 76-77; Wimbledon Sch Art BFA, 77-80; Glassell Sch Art, Houston, Tex, 82-83. *Exhib:* One person exhibs, Graham Gallery, Houston, 84, 85, 86, 87 & 91, Perspectives, Contemp Arts Mus, Houston, 89, Mus Southeast Tex, Beaumont, 90; Corcoran Gallery Art, 87-88; Los Angeles County Mus, 2-4/89; Brooklyn Mus, 6-9/89; NW X SW: Painted Fictions (traveling catalog), Palm Springs Desert Mus, Calif, 90; Collage, Women and Their Work, Austin, Tex, 90; Woman Choose Women, Women and Their Work, Austin, Tex, 90; Summit 1990 Exhibition, Rice Univ, Houston, Tex, 90. *Teaching:* Painting Selection Panel, Nat Endowment for the Arts, 89; asst prof, Univ Tex, Austin, 89-90; CACH Visual Arts Panel, 90; vis asst prof, Univ Houston, 86-87 & 90-92. *Awards:* Grumbacher Award, 84; Dallas Mus Award, Anne Giles Kimbrough Fund, 85; Purchase Award, Synergy, 86; Nat Endowment Arts Fel, 87. *Bibliog:* Betty Ann Brown (auth), Exposures: Women and their Art, 89; Don Bacigalupi (auth), Houston, Contemporanea, 89; Rev, Houston Post, 5/10/89. *Publ:* Houston Chronicle, 3/2/91; Houston Post, 3/11/91; World Artists: 1980-1990, 90; Exposures: Women Artists and Their Work, New Sage Press, 90; Explorations: The Visual Arts Since 1945, Icon Ed, 91. *Dealer:* Moody Gallery Houston TX; Sette Gallery Scottsdale AZ. *Mailing Add:* 1801 Columbia Houston TX 77008

GONZALEZ, RONALD
SCULPTURE
b Johnson City, NY, 1952. *Study:* State Univ NY, Binghampton, BA, 82. *Exhib:* Everson Mus Art, Syracuse, NY, 84; one-man shows, Univ Art Gallery, SUNY Binghampton, 85, Arnot Art Mus, Elmira, NY, 86, Fine Arts Gallery, State Univ NY Oneonta, NY, 87, SPACES, Cleveland, 88, Rahr West Art Mus, Manitonoc, Wis, 89, Allan Stone Gallery, New York, 89, INTAR Gallery, New York, 90; Tempe Arts Ctr, Tempe, Ariz, 89; Sally Hawkins Gallery, New York, 90. *Awards:* Sculpture Grant, Pollock Krasner Found, 86. *Bibliog:* On galleries, Philadelphia Inquirer, 1/14/89. *Dealer:* Fredric Snitzer Opus Art Studio Coral Gables Fla. *Mailing Add:* 232 Clinton St Binghamton NY 13905

GONZALEZ, XAVIER
PAINTER, SCULPTOR
b Almeria, Spain, Feb 15, 1898; US citizen. *Study:* Art Inst Chicago, 21-23. *Work:* Whitney Mus Am Art & Metrop Mus Art, New York; New Orleans Mus Art; Witte Mus, San Antonio, Tex; Mus Fine Arts, Seattle; plus others. *Exhib:* Grand Central Moderns, New York, 51-53; Pa Acad Fine Arts, Philadelphia; Carnegie Inst, Pittsburgh; Brooklyn Mus, NY; retrospective, Witte Mus, San Antonio, 68; plus many others. *Teaching:* Instr art, San Antonio, 24; prof, Newcomb Col, Tulane Univ, 30; instr, Brooklyn Mus, 45; lectr, Nat Col Asn, 46; Western Reserve Univ, 53-54; Summer Sch Art, Wellfleet, Mass; lectr, Metrop Mus Art, New York; instr, Art Students League. *Awards:* Am Acad Arts & Lett Grant; Guggenheim Fel, 47; Ford Found Grant, 65; Gold Medal & the 79 Artist Ann Award, Nat Art Club of New York, 78; plus others. *Mem:* Am Nat Acad; Nat Asn Mural Painters (pres, 68). *Publ:* Auth, Notes About Painting, 55. *Mailing Add:* 222 Central Park S New York NY 10019

GONZALEZ-TORNERO, SERGIO
PAINTER, PRINTMAKER
b Santiago, Chile, May 22, 27. *Study:* Slade Sch, London, England; Atelier 17, Paris, with S W Hayter. *Work:* Metrop Mus Art, New York; Mus Mod Art, New York; Libr Cong, Washington, DC; Mus Fine Arts, Santiago, Chile; Smithsonian Inst, Washington, DC. *Exhib:* High Mus, Atlanta, Ga, 64; Printers & Sculptors as Printmakers, Mus Mod Art, New York, 64; Int Bienale of Prints, Krakow, Poland, 66; Int Bienal of Prints, Epinal, France, 71; Painting & Sculpture Exhib, Silvermine, Conn, 73; Gruenebaum Gallery, New York, 75; Intar Gallery, New York, 84; Int Biennial of Contemp Drawings, Rijeka, Yugoslavia, 88. *Teaching:* Vis artist, Concordia Univ, Montreal. *Awards:* Vera List Award for Printmaking, 83; NY State Coun Arts Fel, 87. *Bibliog:* S W Hayter (auth), About Prints, 62 & New Ways of Gravure, 66, Oxford Univ Press; Fritz Eichenberg (auth), The Art of the Print, Abrams, 76. *Mem:* Soc of Am Graphic Artists; Boston Printmakers; Philadelphia Print Club. *Media:* Oil, Intaglio. *Mailing Add:* Highridge Rd Mahopac NY 10541

GONZALEZ-TORRES, FELIX
PAINTER
Study: Whitney Mus Independent Study Prog, 81 & 83; Pratt Inst, Brooklyn, NY, BFA, 83; Int Ctr Photography, NY Univ, MFA, 87. *Exhib:* Solo shows, Luhring Augustine Hetzler, Los Angeles, 91, Billboard Proj, Mus Mod Art, New York, Andrea Rosen Gallery, New York, Galerie Peter Pakesch, Vienna, Austria, Magasin 3, Stockholm Konshall, Sweden, 92; Fudacao Cult Curitiba/Museu da Gravuva, Brazil, 92; Le Consortium, Dijon, France, 92; Tramway, Glasgow, Scotland, 92; and others. *Teaching:* Adj art instr, New York Univ, 89, prof, 92; CALARTS, Los Angeles, 90. *Awards:* Lannan Found Grant, 90; Gordon Matta-Clark Found Award, 91; Deutscher Akademischer Austauschdienst Fel Art-in-residence Prog, Berlin Ger, 92. *Bibliog:* David Bonetti (auth), rev, Healing, San Francisco Examiner, D11, 5/29/92; Nicolas Bouvriaud (auth), Catalogue briefs: 'not quiet', Jennifer Flay, Paris, Flash Art, 154, summer 92; Vince Aletti (auth), Voice choices, Village Voice, 70, 9/8/92. *Mailing Add:* c/o Andrea Rosen Gallery 130 Prince St, 3rd Fl New York NY 10012

GOO, BENJAMIN
SCULPTOR, PAINTER
b Honolulu, Hawaii, July 12, 22. *Study:* State Univ Iowa, BFA, 53; Cranbrook Acad Art, MFA, 54; Brera Acad Fine Art, Sch of Marino Marini, Milan, Italy, 54-55. *Work:* Phoenix Art Mus, Ariz; Ariz State Univ Art Collection, Tempe; Tucson Mus Art, Tucson, Ariz; Art Mus, Univ Ariz, Tucson; Utah State Univ Harrison Mus, Logan. *Comn:* Two non-objective white marble sculptures, Phoenix Civic Plaza, 71; bronze sculpture, Centennial Hall, Mesa, Ariz, 80; stainless steel sculpture, City Hall, Tempe, Ariz; copper & wood wall sculpture, Madison Square Lobby, Phoenix, Ariz. *Exhib:* 155th Ann Exhib Am Painting & Sculpture, Pa Acad Fine Arts & Detroit Inst Art, 60; 24th Ann Drawing, Print & Sculpture Exhib, San Francisco Mus Art, Calif, 61; Creative Casting: Exhibit of Art in Bronze, Mus Contemp Crafts, New York, 63; 73rd Western Ann, Denver Art Mus, 71; Fed Int Medaille, Palazzo Medici Riccardi, Florence, 83. *Teaching:* Prof art, Ariz State Univ, 55-83, emer prof, 83-; Nat Endowment for the Arts artist in residence, Mesa, Ariz, 72-73; artist in residence, Roswell Mus & Art Ctr, NMex, 75-76. *Awards:* First Ann Southwestern States Purchase Award, Roswell Mus & Art Ctr, 62; 4th Southwestern Invitational Purchase Award, Yuma Art Ctr, 69; 21st Ann Tucson Festival Art Exhib Award, Tucson Art Ctr, 71. *Media:* Metals, Stone. *Publ:* Auth, Education and the craftsman, 1-2/62 & auth, Dick Seeger: Artist craftsman in plastics, 7-8/62, Creative Crafts Mag. *Dealer:* Suzanne Brown Galleries 7160 Main St Scottsdale AZ 85251. *Mailing Add:* 3225 N Winstel Blvd Tucson AZ 85716-1430

GOOD, LEONARD
PAINTER
b Chickasha, Okla, June 25, 07. *Study:* Univ Okla, BFA, 27; Art Students League, with Nicolaides, 30; Univ Iowa, with Jean Charlot, 40. *Work:* Des Moines Art Ctr, Iowa; Milwaukee Art Ctr, Wis; Okla City Art Ctr; Urasenke Found, Kyoto, Japan; City Hall, Kofu, Japan. *Comn:* Portrait, Okla Hist Soc, Oklahoma City, 39; two portraits, Univ Okla, Norman, 49-50; three portraits, Drake Univ, 54-60; portrait, Iowa Hist Mus, Des Moines, 62; series of Iowa scenes for Sun features, Des Moines Register, 65. *Exhib:* First & Second Nat Exhibs Am Art, Metrop Mus Art, New York, 36 & 37; Am Painters in Paris Exhib, Palais des Congres, France, 75-76; one-man retrospective, Okla Mus Art, 80; Cent Col, Pella, Iowa, 85; Leslie Powell Found, Lawton, Okla, 87; one-man retrospective, Univ Okla Mus Art, 93; and others. *Collections Arranged:* Assembled permanent collection of paintings for Preferred Risk Life Insurance Co Home Off Bldg, Des Moines, 69. *Pos:* Vis artist in residence, Iowa State Univ, 60-61; artist-in-residence, Nat Endowment Arts & Iowa Arts Coun, Shenandoah, Iowa, 70-71; Cent Col, Pella, Iowa, 84; trustee, Mabee-Gerrer Mus Art, Shawnee, Okla, 86- *Teaching:* Prof painting & drawing, Univ Okla, 30-50; prof drawing & painting, Univ Wis, 50-52; prof art hist, Drake Univ, 52-77, head dept art, 52-68, emer prof art hist, 77- *Awards:* Purchase Prize for New Mexico Town (painting), Springville Mus Art, Utah, 74; Fourth Ann Nat Exhib Small Paintings, NMex, 74; First Prize, Iowa State Fair, 54, 62 & 74; plus others. *Bibliog:* An Artist in the School (video), Iowa State Arts Coun, 70. *Mem:* Delta Phi Delta (nat vpres, 54-58, nat pres, 58-60). *Media:* Multimedia. *Publ:* Illusr, A Certain Young Widow, Univ Okla Press, 30; illusr, instructional manuals for US Air Force, Tinker Field, Okla, 43-44; Marquis Who's Who in Am, 34-; Marquis Who's Who in the World, 74; Chronicles of Okla, Okla Hist Soc, 92. *Dealer:* Percival Galleries Sixth & Walnut Des Moines IA 50309. *Mailing Add:* PO Box 2181 Chickasha OK 73023

GOODACRE, GLENNA
SCULPTOR
b Lubbock, Tex, Aug 28, 39. *Study:* Colo Col, BA; Art Students League. *Work:* Tex Tech Mus, Lubbock; Presby Hosp, Denver, Colo; Brigham Young Univ Art Gallery, Provo, Utah; Cleveland Clinic Children's Hosp, Ohio; Denver Mus Natural Hist, Colo; Montgomery Mus Fine Arts, Ala; Sea World, San Antonio. *Comn:* Dr Harvie Pruitt, Lubbock Christian Col, 82; Patrick Haggerty, Tex Instruments, 82; Eric Sloan, 83; Erik Jonsson & Cecil Green, Tex Instruments, 83; William B Travis, Sea World, San Antonio, Tex, 88; Washington Monument to Women Vietnam Vets. *Exhib:* Solo exhib, Read-Stremmel Gallery, San Antonio, Tex, 88; Fifth Ann Sculpture Park, Loveland, Colo, 88; Eighth Ann Artists Am Show, Colo Heritage Ctr, Denver, 88; Twentieth Anniversary Invitational Exhib, NAm Sculpture Exhib, Foothills Art Ctr, Golden, Colo, 88; Borderlands, Second Ann Exhib, Americana Mus, El Paso, Tex, 88; Fifty-fifth Ann Exhib, Nat Sculpture Soc, New York, 88; two-person show, O'Brien's Art Emporium, Scottsdale, Ariz, 88; Artists Choice Show, Nat Acad Western Art, Oklahoma City, 88; American Art in Miniature, Thomas Gilcrease Mus, Tulsa, Okla, 88. *Teaching:* Scottsdale Artists Sch. *Awards:* Johnson Atelier Award, Audubon Artists, 83; Joyce & Elliot Liskin Award, Pen & Brush, 83; Leonard J Meiselman Award, Nat Sculpture Soc, 83. *Mem:* Allied Artists of Am; fel, Nat Sculpture Soc; Catharine Lorillard Wolfe Art Club; fel, Nat Acad Western Art. *Media:* Bronze. *Publ:* Illusr, bronze relief for jacket, The Flamboyant Judge, 73 & Trank Tenny Johnson, 75; illusr, silver relief for jacket, Robbing Banks was My Business, 74. *Mailing Add:* Knox Gallery 1632 Market St Denver CO 80202

GOODBRED, RAY EDWARD
INSTRUCTOR, PAINTER
b Brooklyn, NY, Dec 7, 29. *Study:* Art Students League, with Robert Brackman, 48-51; Nat Acad Sch Fine Arts, with Ogden Pleissner, 50-51; New York Univ, 53-56. *Work:* Gibbes Mus Art, Charleston, SC; Fine Arts Theatre, Virginia Weslayan Univ, Norfolk; City Hall Gallery, Charleston, SC; Art Students League Collection, New York; The Pentagon, Washington, DC. *Comn:* Portrait, Mus of Art, Raleigh, NC, 83; Home Federal of Charleston,

SC, 74; Finley-Wagner-Kumble Collection, New York, 80; Sch Architecture Clemson Univ, SC, 85; Integon Corp, Winston-Salem, NC, 85. *Exhib:* One-man exhib, Gibbes Mus Art, Charleston, SC; Ann exhib, Riverside Mus, New York; Ann exhib, Augusta Richmond Cty Mus, SC; Allied Artists Am, Nat Acad Design, New York, 70-79; Pastel Soc Am, Copley Soc, Boston, Mass & Nat Art Club, New York; South Carolina Artists, Columbia Mus Art, SC. *Teaching:* Instr, portraiture, Hastie Sch Art, Charleston, SC, 70-74; painting & drawing, Art Students League, New York, 75-81; French Inst, New York, 77-79. *Awards:* Trump Award, Pastel Soc Am, 78; First Prize, Salmagundi Club, 78; Medal of Merit, Knickerbocker Artists Am, 79. *Bibliog:* Jack Morris (auth), South Carolina Contemporary Artists, Greenville Mus Art, 75; Joe Singer (auth), Painting Women's Portraits & Painting Men's Portraits, Watson Guptill Publ, 77. *Mem:* Salmagundi Club; Pastel Soc Am; Charleston Artists Guild (bd dir). *Media:* Oil, Pastel. *Publ:* Illustr, Omni Mag, Omni Int, 6-12/79. *Dealer:* Portraits Incorporated 985 Park Ave New York NY 10028. *Mailing Add:* 85 Montagu St Charleston SC 29401

GOODE, JOE
PAINTER
b Oklahoma City, Okla, Mar 23, 37. *Study:* Chouinard Art Inst. *Work:* Mus Mod Art & Whitney Mus Am Art, New York; Pasadena Art Mus, Calif; Los Angeles Co Mus Art; Victoria & Albert Mus, London; Ft Worth Art Mus, Tex. *Exhib:* Solo exhibs, Contemp Arts Mus, Houston, 73, St Mary's Col, Los Angeles, 77, Arco Ctr Visual Art, 82, Asher/Faure Gallery, Los Angeles, 84, James Corcoran Gallery, Santa Monica, Calif, 86, 89 & 90, Pence Gallery, Santa Monica, Calif, 87 & Compass Ross Gallery, Chicago, Ill, 89; American Pop Art, Whitney Mus Am Art, 74; Chicago Art Inst, 74; California Painting and Sculpture: The Modern Era, San Francisco Mus Art, 76; Black and White Art Colors, Scripps Col, 78; American Painting in the Seventies, Albright-Knox Art Gallery, 78; Aspects of Abstract, Crocker Mus, 78; Art Park, LA/Brazil Projects 90, Los Angeles, Calif, 90; Takada Fine Arts, San Francisco, Calif, 91; Los Angeles Co Mus Art, Calif, 92. *Awards:* Copley Found; Nat Endowment Arts. *Bibliog:* T Henry (auth), Introduction (exhib catalog), Oklahoma City Art Mus, 89; Nora Halpern Brougher (auth), Looking Through the Work of Joe Goode (exhib catalog), James Corcoran Gallery, Santa Monica, Calif, 90. *Media:* Wood; Oil. *Mailing Add:* PO Box 10372 Marina Del Rey CA 90291

GOODELMAN, RUTH
SCULPTOR
b Johnstown, Pa, Sept 28, 14. *Study:* Traphagen Sch Design, 32; Columbia Univ, 33; Art Students League, 34. *Exhib:* Contemp Emerging Artists, Loris Ledis Gallery, New York, 85; Visual Individualists United, Lever House, New York, 88; Nat Asn Women Artists, New York, 88 & 90; Stone Sculpture Soc NY, Blue Hill Cult Ctr, Pearl River, NY, 88; Nat Asn Women Artists, Interchurch Ctr, New York, 89; Small Works, Marbella Gallery, New York, 89; Stone Sculpture Soc, Crystal Pavillion, New York, 89. *Pos:* Fashion Designer, Ben Shaw, Sam Friedlander, Harry Rentner, Frank Starr, Richard Cole & Jr Sophisticates, 34-66. *Teaching:* Prof draping, Fashion Inst Technol, 66-68; prof sketching, Parsons Sch Design, 68-70. *Awards:* Medal of Honor, 85 & 88 & Geffrey Childs Willis Mem Award, Nat Asn Women Artists, 90. *Mem:* Nat Asn Women Artists (publicity, 88-89); Stone Sculpture Soc NY; NY Artist Equity Asn. *Media:* Stone, All Media. *Mailing Add:* 24 E 11 St New York NY 10003

GOODINE, LINDA ADELE
PHOTOGRAPHER, SCULPTOR
b Watkins Glen, NY, July 29, 58. *Study:* Univ Rochester, NY, 80; Ithaca Col, NY, MS, 81; Fla State Univ, Tallahassee, MFA, 83. *Work:* Light Work, Menschel Gallery, Syracuse Univ, NY; Frederick R Weisman Collection, Los Angeles, Calif; Aaron Siskind Found; Int Sch Photog, Arles, France. *Exhib:* Personal Icon, Los Angeles Ctr Photog Studies, Calif, 86; The Manipulated Environment, Houston Ctr Photog, Tex, 87; Looking South: A Different Dixie, Birmingham Mus Art, Ala, 88; Vernon Fisher & Linda Adele Goodine, Pensacola Mus Art, Fla, 89; New Southern Photography, Burden Gallery, New York, 89-92; traveling shows, Selections from Weisman Collection, Frederick Weisman Found, Los Angeles & Linda Adele Goodine, Southeastern Ctr for Contemp Art, Winston-Salem, NC; Montgomery Bienial, Indianapolis Mus Art, 92; Cibachromes 1982-1992, Linda Adele Goodine, Ind State Mus, 92. *Teaching:* Artist in residence, photog, Lightwork Community Darkrooms, Syracuse, NY, 86; instr 3-D, Delgado Community Col, New Orleans, La, 88-89; vis artist & asst prof, Herron Sch Art, Indianapolis, Ind, currently. *Awards:* Nat Endowment Arts, Rockefeller Found, 90; Southern Arts Fedn, 91; Aaron Siskind Found Grant. *Bibliog:* Marcia E Vetrocq (auth), Linda Adele Goodine at Res Nova, Art in Am, 88; Jay Murphy (auth), Linda A Goodine & Vernon Fisher, Art papers, 89; Donald Kuspit Art papers, summer 92. *Mem:* Col Art Asn. *Publ:* Illusr, Exploring Color Photography, Wm C Brown, 89; Louisiana Artist's Pages: Love in the Ruins, Contemp Art Ctr, 89; article for Aperture, No 115, Aperture Found, 89; article for Red Bass, No 13, 89; North of Wakulla: An Anhinga Anthology Anhinga, Press, 90. *Dealer:* A Gallery for Fine Photography Royal St New Orleans LA. *Mailing Add:* PO Box 70525 New Orleans LA 70172

GOODMAN, BENJAMIN
PATRON
b Memphis, Tenn, Jan 18, 04. *Study:* Princeton Univ, AB, 24; Harvard Univ, LLB, 27; Memphis Acad Arts, Hon Doc Humanities, 78. *Pos:* Trustee & former pres, Memphis Acad Arts; chmn, Memphis Munic Art Comn, 60-76. *Mailing Add:* 115 S Rose Rd Memphis TN 38117

GOODMAN, BERTRAM
PAINTER
b New York, NY, Sept 21, 04. *Study:* Sch Am Sculpture, 23-24; Art Students League, 25. *Work:* Brooklyn Mus; Libr Cong; Abbott Labs, Chicago; Butler Art Inst, Youngstown, Ohio; Metrop Mus Art, New York; and others. *Exhib:* Mus Mod Art, New York; Whitney Mus Am Art; Carnegie Art Inst; Metrop Mus Art, New York; Nat Acad Fine Arts. *Awards:* First Prize Watercolor, Screen Publicists Guild, 46; Purchase Prize, Abraham Lincoln Gallery, 47; Jo & Emily Lowe Prize, 56. *Mem:* Artists Equity Asn (dir, 55-56); Brooklyn Soc Artists; Am Soc Graphic Artists. *Mailing Add:* 22 W 56th St New York NY 10019

GOODMAN, CALVIN JEROME
CONSULTANT, COLLECTOR
b Chicago, Ill, Mar 1, 22. *Study:* Harvard Univ, AB(hon), 49. *Pos:* Mgt consult to artists & art dealers, 60-; vpres, Tamarind Lithography Workshop, 59-74; nat consult, Artists Equity Asn, 74-76. *Teaching:* Instr bus methods for artists & artisans, Tamarind Lithography Workshop, 61-71; instr prof practices, Calif Inst Arts, 67-71; instr prof practices, Otis Art Inst, 68-71; lectr, seminar & workshops in marketing art for San Francisco Art Inst, Scripps Grad Sch of Art, Pratt Inst, & Ltd Ed Expo, Charlotte, NC, among others. *Bibliog:* Antreasian & Adams (auth), The Tamarind Book of Lithography, Abrams, 71; The booming art market, Los Angeles Mag, 1/82; B Fredericks (auth), The Art of Creating Monotypes, HR Productions, 90. *Res:* Fine art market; operations of specialized schools of art and music; original print market; making/marketing monotypes; paper specialties & reproduction prints market. *Publ:* Auth, Art Marketing Handbook, GeeTeeBee, 6th ed, 91; Wilson Hurley's color theory and practice, 5/86 & The art of Beverly Doolittle, 12/88, Am Artist; Thomas Hart Benton, 12/89 & 1/90 & How to Price Artworks, 6/91, Am Artist; and others. *Mailing Add:* 11901 Sunset Blvd Suite 102 Los Angeles CA 90049

GOODMAN, FLORENCE JEANNE
WRITER, COLLECTOR
b Detroit, Mich, Nov 28, 22. *Study:* Wayne State Univ, BA, 54; Univ Calif, Los Angeles, MA, 57. *Teaching:* Prof English, Pierce Col, Woodland Hills, Calif, 58-87. *Res:* Has written extensively on contemporary art and the art market. *Collection:* Contemporary US art. *Publ:* Auth, Assemblages and collages, 76, Martin Green, blending of Eastern and Western art, 76 & The work and thought of JW Grossman, 79, Southwest Art; ed, Art Marketing Handbook, 6th ed, Gee Tee Bee, 91; auth, Selling art, Am Artist, 88; What's the Good Word?, Am Artist, 89; Style and Individual Talent, Am Artist, 90. *Mailing Add:* 11901 Sunset Blvd Apt 102 Los Angeles CA 90049

GOODMAN, HELEN
HISTORIAN, CRITIC
b Detroit, Mich, May 18, 39. *Study:* Univ Mich, BA, 60; Wayne State Univ, MA, 66; New York Univ, PhD, 75. *Collections Arranged:* Art Rose O'Neill, Brandywine River Mus, Chadds Ford, Pa, 89. *Teaching:* Asst prof art hist, Stern Col Women, New York, 66-72; asst prof, Fashion Inst Technol, New York, 68- *Awards:* Research Found Grant, State Univ NY, 83; Nat Endowment Humanities Grant, 85, 89 & 91; John Sloan Mem Found Grant; Swann Found Caricature & Cartoon Grant, 85. *Mem:* Col Art Asn; Asn Hist Am Art. *Res:* American late 19th and early 20th century art. *Publ:* Auth, Robert Henri, teacher, 79, Alice Barber Stephens, illustrator, 84 & The plastic club, 85, Arts Mag; essay, In: America's Great Women Illustrators: 1850-1950 (exhib catalog), Madison Sq Press, 85; Women illustrators of the golden age of Am illustration, Woman's Art J, spring/summer 87; Emily Sartain: her career, Arts Mag, 5/87; The Art of Rose O'Neill, Brandywine Riv Mus, Chadds Ford, Pa, 89. *Mailing Add:* c/o Fashion Inst Technol 227 W 27th St New York NY 10001

GOODMAN, JAMES NEIL
DEALER, COLLECTOR
b Rochester, NY, Apr 11, 29. *Pos:* Dir, James Goodman Gallery. *Specialty:* Modern American and European masters, including Calder, Cornell, de Kooning, Klee, Leger, Lichtenstein, Matisse, Moore, Picasso and Tanguy. *Mailing Add:* c/o James Goodman Gallery 41 E 57th St New York NY 10022

GOODMAN, JANIS G
DRAFTSMAN, PAINTER
b New York, NY, Oct 21, 51. *Study:* Queens Col, NY, BA, 72; study at Pratt Graphics Ctr, 72; Corcoran Sch Art, George Washington Univ, MFA, 75. *Work:* Hirshhorn Mus, Washington, DC; Dulin Gallery Art, Knoxville, Tenn; Int Bus Machines, Raleigh, NC; Northern Telecom, Nashville, Tenn; Shearson Lehman Am Express, Bethesda, Md. *Exhib:* Solo exhib, Hom Gallery, Washington, DC, 83; Corcoran Gallery Art, Washington, DC, 80; Drawing 1900 to Present, Forum Gallery, New York, 81 & 84; Hudson River Mus, Yonkers, NY, 84; Chrysler Mus, Norfolk, Va, 84; Washington Views, Barbara Fendrick Gallery, Washington, DC, 85; National Drawing 85, Trenton State Col, NJ, 85; New Year Celebration, Sue Rankin Gallery, London, Eng, 86. *Teaching:* Instr drawing, Smithsonian Inst, 77-86, Corcoran Sch Art, 82-; instr color theory, Parsons Sch Design, New York, 85- *Awards:* Honorarium, Founding Women, Washington Women's Art Ctr, 80; Washington, DC Comn Arts Grant, 81; Montpelier Cult Award, Md State Drawing, 83. *Bibliog:* Lee Fleming (auth), Young artists on the way up, Washington Mag, 81; Benjamin Forgey (auth), Exhibition of gray, Washington Star, 83; Jane Addams Allen (auth), Giant step for Washington artist, Washington Times, 83. *Media:* Pencil. *Dealer:* Cumberland Gallery 4107 Hillsboro Circle Nashville TN 37215; Reynolds-Minor Gallery 1514 West Main St Richmond VA 23220. *Mailing Add:* c/o Virginia Miller Galleries 169 Madeira Ave Coral Gables FL 33134

GOODMAN, KEN(NETH HUNT)
PAINTER
b New York, NY, Oct 22, 50. *Study:* RI Sch Design, BFA, 72. *Work:* Dannheisser Found, New York; Hunter Mus Art, Chattanooga, Tenn; Huntington Art Gallery, Austin, Tex. *Exhib:* Gold Show, Mus Mod Art, New York, 79; Urban Kisses, Inst Contemp Art, London, Eng, 82; Body Language, Mass Inst Technol, Boston, 83; State of War: New European and American Paintings, Seattle Art Mus, Wash, 85; Public and Private: American Prints Today, Brooklyn Mus, New York, 86. *Bibliog:* Anna Wintour (auth), Interiors: Romantic classics, New York Mag, 82; Walter Winsheild (auth), Ken Goodman, East Village Eye, 84; Dan Cameron (auth), Report from the front, Arts, 86. *Media:* Oil on Canvas. *Mailing Add:* 130 Barrows New York NY 10012

GOODMAN, MARIAN
DEALER, PUBLISHER
b New York, NY, June 15, 28. *Study:* Columbia Univ Grad Sch Art Hist, BA. *Pos:* Dir publ, Multiples Inc, 65-, pres, 74-; dir, Marian Goodman Gallery, currently. *Mem:* Art Dealers Asn. *Specialty:* Publishing limited editions and sometimes books, records, etc by prominent contemporary artists such as Lewitt, Oldenburg, Warhol, Baldessor, Artswager and many others. *Mailing Add:* Multiples Inc 24 W 57th St New York NY 10019

GOODMAN, MARK
PHOTOGRAPHER
b Boston, Mass, May 19, 46. *Study:* Boston Univ, BA, 70; also with Minor White, 70 & Bruce Davidson, 71. *Work:* Mus Mod Art, New York; Mus Fine Arts, Boston; Mus Art, Univ Okla, Norman; Spencer Mus Art, Univ Kans, Lawrence; George Eastman House, Rochester, NY. *Exhib:* Recent Acquisitions, Mus Mod Art, New York, 78-79; solo exhib, George Eastman House, Rochester, NY, 80-81; American Children, Mus Mod Art, New York, 81; Vassar Col Art Gallery, 81; Contemporary Photographers IX, George Eastman House, Rochester, NY, 82; New American Photographs, Calif State Col Art Gallery, San Bernardino, 82; Capital Improvements, Austin Hist Ctr, Tex, 86; and others. *Teaching:* Artist in residence photog, Apeiron Workshops Inc, Millerton, NY, 72-76; asst prof, Univ Tex, Austin, 80-86, assoc prof, 86-*Awards:* Nat Endowment Arts Fel, 73; Guggenheim Fel, 77. *Bibliog:* Julia Scully & Andy Grundberg (auth), Currents: American photography today, Mod Photog, Vol 44, No 2, 80; James Kaufmann (auth), Works of love: The photographs of Mark Goodman, Exposure, Vol 20, No 1, 82. *Publ:* Contribr, Photographs of Millerton, NY, 1971-1975, Aperture, Vol 19, No 4, 75; Kansas Album, Addison House, 77; Photographing Children, Time-Life Books, 83. *Mailing Add:* PO Box 889 Bastrop TX 78602

GOODMAN, SIDNEY
PAINTER
b Philadelphia, Pa, Jan 19, 36. *Study:* Philadelphia Col Art, 58. *Work:* Art Inst Chicago; Libr Cong, Washington, DC; Whitney Mus Am Art, Mus Mod Art, New York; Hirshhorn Collection; Metrop Mus Art, New York; and others. *Exhib:* One man exhibs, Terry Dintenfass Inc, New York, 51, RI Col, 79, Col William & Mary, 79, Boston Univ Art Gallery, Mass, 82, Inst Contemp Art, Va Mus, 82 & Wichita Mus, Kans, 84; The Figure in Recent American Painting Traveling Exhib, 74-75; Three Centuries American Art, Philadelphia Mus Art, 76; American 1976 Bicentennial Exhib, US Dept Interior, Washington, DC, 76; Eight Contemporary American Realists, Pa Acad Fine Arts, 77; Contemporary Drawing: Philadelphia II, Philadelphia Mus Art, 79; 20th Century Drawings, 79-81 & 20th Century American Drawing & Context, 85-86, Whitney Mus Am Art, New York; retrospective traveling exhibs, Mus Art, Pa State Univ, Philadelphia, 80, Columbia Mus Art, Ohio, 81 & Del Art Mus, Wilmington, 81; The Elements-Arch Angel, Philadelphia Mus, 85; 20th Century Drawing & Watercolor American Realism, Glenn C Janss Collection, San Francisco Mus Art, Calif, 86. *Teaching:* Instr drawing & painting, Philadelphia Col Art, 60-78; instr, Tyler Sch, Philadelphia, 77 & Pa Acad Fine Arts, 78- *Awards:* Guggenheim Fel, 64; Philadelphia Print Club Purchase Award, 65; Nat Endowment Arts Grant, 74; and others. *Mailing Add:* c/o Terry Dintenfass 50 W 57th St New York NY 10019

GOODNOUGH, ROBERT
PAINTER
b Cortland, NY, Oct 23. *Study:* Syracuse Univ, Hiram Gell fel, 40, BFA; NY Univ, MA; New Sch Social Res; Ozenfant Sch Art; Hans Hofmann Sch Fine Arts. *Work:* Albright-Knox Art Gallery, Buffalo, NY; Solomon R Guggenheim Mus, Mus Mod Art & Metrop Mus Art, New York; Wadsworth Atheneum, Hartford, Conn; plus others. *Exhib:* One-man shows, Univ Minn, Univ Notre Dame, Arts Club Chicago, 64, Andie Emmerich Gallery, 82 & Tibor de Nagy Gallery, New York, 85; Cayuga Mus Hist & Art, Auburn, NY, 69, Albright-Knox Art Gallery, Buffalo, NY, 69 & Syracuse Univ, 72; Nat Inst Arts & Lett, 64; New American Painting & Sculpture, Mus Mod Art, 69; Univ Ill, 69; Indianapolis Mus Art, 69; Venice Biennial, 70; Am Acad Arts & Lett, 71; plus many other group & one-man shows. *Pos:* Art critic, Art News, 50-57; secy, Documents of Mod Art, 51; Am Acad Arts Gallery, currently. *Teaching:* Instr painting, Cornell Univ, NY Univ & Fieldston Sch, New York. *Awards:* Ada Garrett Award, Art Inst Chicago, 61; Ford Found Purchase Prize, 63. *Media:* All. *Mailing Add:* 68 Allison Lane Thornwood NY 10594

GOODNOW, FRANK A
PAINTER, EDUCATOR
b Evanston, Ill, Dec 14, 23. *Study:* Northwestern Univ, Evanston; Art Inst Chicago, BFA; Anna L Raymond Traveling Fel, 48; also with Boris Anisfeld & Fernand Leger, Paris, 50. *Work:* Philadelphia Mus Art; NY State Univ; Univ Rochester; Everson Mus Art, Syracuse; Syracuse Univ. *Exhib:* Pa Acad Fine Arts, 53, 57 & 65; Whitney Mus Am Art, 55; one-man shows, Schuman Gallery, Rochester, 65, 69, 71 & 72; Lubin House Gallery, New York, 76; Abstract Tradition, Munson-Williams-Proctor Inst, Utica, NY, 79; Hanover Gallery, Syracuse, NY, 79, 83 & 86; Chapman Art Ctr, Cazenovia Col, Cazenovia, NY, 88; Gallery Metro, Syracuse, NY, 92; and others. *Teaching:* Prof painting, Syracuse Univ, NY, 50-88. *Awards:* B Forman Award, Rochester Mem Gallery, 69; First Prize, Cooperstown Nat Show, 71 & NY State Fair, 81; Ford Found Grant, 77, 79 & 80. *Dealer:* Oxford Gallery 267 Oxford St Rochester NY 14607. *Mailing Add:* 214 Dawley Rd Fayetteville NY 13066

GOODRICH, JAMES W
ADMINISTRATOR, COLLECTOR
b Burlington, Iowa, Oct 31, 39. *Study:* Central Mo State Univ, BS, 62; Univ Mo, MA, 64, PhD, 74. *Collections Arranged:* Mo Decoys, Mo State Mus, 89. *Pos:* Exec dir, State Hist Soc Mo, 85- *Res:* Folk-art research on Missouri-made waterfowl decoys; Missouri artists. *Interests:* Missouri art, folk art. *Collection:* Missouri Decoys, Missouri Artists. *Publ:* Auth, Robert Ormsby Sweeny: Some Civil War Sketches, Mo Hist Review, 83; Ben Yeargan of Missouri: "Working" Decoy Carver, 1984 Ann Am Decoys, 84; Factory Decoys, Mo Conservationist, 86; Roy Shoop's Canadas, Decoy Hunter, 90; John Francis: Missouri Decoy Carver, Decoy Mag, 92. *Mailing Add:* State Historical Society of Missouri 1020 Lowry St Columbia MO 65201

GOODRIDGE, LAWRENCE WAYNE
PAINTER, SCULPTOR
b Cincinnati, Ohio, Mar 18, 41. *Study:* Univ Cincinnati, BFA(with hon), 63; Univ Cincinnati & Art Acad Cincinnati, MFA, 67. *Exhib:* All-Ohio Painting & Sculpture Exhib, Dayton Art Inst, 67; Mid-States Art Exhib, Evansville Mus Arts & Sci, Ind, 70; one-man show & Louisville Biennial, J B Speed Art Mus, Ky, 71; 17th Ann Drawing & Sculpture Show, Ball State Univ, Muncie, Ind, 71. *Pos:* Toy designer, Kenner Prod Co, 63-65. *Teaching:* Instr found design & color theory, Art Acad Cincinnati, 69-, co-dean, 72- *Awards:* Second Prize, Eastern Fine Paper Graphic Design, 65. *Publ:* Auth & illusr, European diary, 70 & Truck stop, 71, Cincinnati Mag. *Dealer:* Richard Feigen Gallery 226 E Ontario St Chicago IL 60611. *Mailing Add:* 29 Kathryn Ave Florence KY 41042

GOODSTEIN-SHAPIRO, F
PAINTER, HISTORIAN
b New York, NY, July 22, 31. *Study:* Cooper Union, 50-51; City Col New York, BS(art educ), 52; Hans Hofmann Sch Fine Arts, 56-57; Univ Minn, MA(art hist), 73. *Work:* Boynthon Gallery, Sydney, Australia; Martin Luther King Collection, Atlanta, Ga; Augsburg Col Collection, Minneapolis; Univ Minn Mus. *Exhib:* Am Watercolor Soc, Smithsonian Inst, Washington, DC, 63; Los Angeles Co Mus Art, 69; Hamline Univ, St Paul, Minn, 76; Peter M David Gallery, 83, 90-92; Artbanque, Minneapolis, Minn, 85, 86, 88 & 89; Col St Catherine, St Paul, Minn, 88; Sen Paul Wellstone Off, Minneapolis, 92; and others. *Pos:* Art prog dir, Emanuel-Midtown Y Community Ctr, 63-65; secy & pub rels dir, Aspects Gallery, New York, 64-66; dir, Artists Against War Exhib, New York, 67-68. *Teaching:* Instr art hist, Lakewood State Jr Col, 71- *Awards:* STA Award for Excellence, Art Inst Chicago, 54. *Bibliog:* New voices, Village Voice, 3/64; Artist paints death, Australian, 9/30/69; Shades of whispering glades, Sydney Morning-Herald, 9/30/69. *Mem:* Col Art Asn Am; Am Inst Archaeol; Exp Art & Technol. *Media:* Oil, Charcoal. *Publ:* Auth, Lumen room, Technol & Environ, 70. *Dealer:* MC Gallery 400 First Ave N Minneapolis MN. *Mailing Add:* 8066 Ruth St NE Minneapolis MN 55432

GOODWILL, MARGARET
PAINTER, DESIGNER
b Los Angeles, Calif, Sept 27, 50. *Study:* Carnegie Mellon Inst, cert, 66; Univ Calif, Santa Barbara, 68-70; Calif Col Arts & Crafts, Oakland, BFA (cum laude), 72. *Work:* Arco Gallery-Southwest Mus, Los Angeles; Calif Col Arts & Crafts, Oakland; Oakland Mus Collectors Gallery, Calif; Triple Crown Hall-Hilton Resort Hotel, Plesanton, Calif; Tamarack Beach Resort, Carlsbad, Calif. *Comn:* For Those Who Care (prog design with James Erickson), KRON TV Channel 2, San Francisco, 83; triptych, comn by D Padys, San Francisco, 86; Wave Waikiki (mural, 30' x 90'), Honolulu, Hawaii, 91; mag cover, Southern Poverty Law Ctr, Montgomery, Ala, 91; catalog cover, Benjamin Cummings Publ, Calif, 91; and others. *Exhib:* Contemporary Icons, Hewlett Packard Hq, Palo Alto, Calif, 90; Functional Fantasy, Transamerica Pyramid, San Francisco, 90; Stanford Ctr Integrated Systems, Calif, 91; Computer Artboards Show, Pac Bell Hqs, Concord, Calif, Microsoft & Tandem Hq, Calif, 92; and others. *Pos:* Graphic artist, City Arts, Oakland, 70-71; creative art dir, Am Analysis Corp, San Francisco, 74-76; dir, Lone Wolf Gallery, 82-84. *Awards:* First Prize, Ossining Woman's Club Competition & Poughkeepsie Art Ctr, 68; Merit Award, Delta Art Show, 71. *Bibliog:* Ken Wong (auth), Palm Trees: The Passing Show, San Francisco Examiner, 11/8/85. *Media:* Acrylic on Canvas, Oil Pastel on Handmade Paper. *Publ:* Illusr, 3 Stately Palms (poster) & Stately Dately Palms (poster), publ by Bruce McGaw, 86-92; Palm Parade (poster), publ by Portal, 92; Greeting cards, calendars, gift bags, etc, publ by Island Heritage; shower curtains, publ by The Springs; plus 18 other posters, 1986-92 calendars & t-shirts. *Mailing Add:* 68-511 Crozier Dr Watalua HI 96791-9304

GOODWIN, GUY
PAINTER
b Birmingham, Ala, June 19, 40. *Study:* Univ Ala; Auburn Univ, BFA, 63; Univ Ill, MFA, 65. *Work:* Patrick Lannen Mus, Palm Beach, Fla; Chase Manhattan Bank, New York. *Exhib:* One-person shows, Area X Gallery, New

York, 84 & Dolan-Maxwell Gallery (with catalog), Philadelphia, Pa, 86; Abstract Issues (with catalog), D Hood, S French & Tibor Denage Galleries, New York, 85; Drawing with Respect to Painting II, NY Studio Sch Gallery, 86. *Teaching:* Vis artist painting, Wayne State Univ, Detroit, Mich, 78 & Art Inst Chicago, Ill, 80; instr painting & drawing, Bennington Col, Vt, 80- *Awards:* Nat Endowment Arts, 74 & 80; Creative Artists Pub Serv, 76. *Bibliog:* Michael Brenson (auth), Drawing with respect to painting, NY Times, 5/2/86; Tiffany Bell (auth), Drawing with respect to painting, 6/86 & Margaret Berensen (auth), Guy Goodwin, 10/86, Arts Mag; Edward Suzanski (auth), rev, Philadelphia Inquirer, 9/25/86. *Media:* Oil, Watercolor. *Dealer:* Dolan-Maxwell 1701 Walnut St Philadelphia Pa 19103. *Mailing Add:* 105 Franklin St New York NY 10013

GOODWIN, LOUIS PAYNE
CARTOONIST
b Flintville, Tenn, Oct 9, 22. *Study:* Ark Polytech Col, 41-42; Univ Chattanooga, BA, 48; Ohio State Univ, 74. *Pos:* Advert & ed cartoonist, Dispatch Printing Co, Columbus, 52-62; ed cartoonist, Columbus Eve Dispatch, 62-87. *Awards:* Cartoon Award, Freedoms Found, 62-69, 71, 73 & 79; Cartoonists Award, Hwy Safety Found, 66. *Mailing Add:* 5158 Woodside Dr Columbus OH 43229

GOODYEAR, FRANK H, JR
ADMINISTRATOR, HISTORIAN
b New York, NY, Jan 5, 44. *Study:* Yale Univ, BA, 66; Univ Del, Winterthur Prog, MA, 69. *Collections Arranged:* Pennsylvania Academicians (with catalog), Pa Acad of Fine Arts, 73, The Beneficent Connoisseurs, Gibson, Harrison (with catalog), 74 & In This Academy: The Pennsylvania Academy of the Fine Arts, 1805-1976 (with catalog), 76; Thomas Doughty: An American Pioneer in Landscape Painting, 1793-1856 (with catalog), Pa Acad, Corcoran Gallery of Art & Albany Inst, 73-74; American Paintings in the Rhode Island Historical Society, 74; Cecilia Beaux (1855-1942): Portrait of an Artist (with catalog), Pa Acad & Indianapolis Mus of Art, 74-75; American Art: 1750-1800 Towards Independence, Yale Univ Art Gallery, 76; Eight Contemporary American Realists: Philip Pearlstein, Alfred Leslie, Stephen Posen, Janet Fish, Duane Hanson, Joseph Raffael, Neil Welliver & Sidney Goodman, 77; Seven on the Figure (with catalog), Pa Acad Fine Arts, 79; A Man of Genius: The Art of Washington Allston, Pa Acad Fine Arts & Mus Fine Arts, Boston, 80; Contemporary American Realism since 1960 (with catalog), Pa Acad Fine Arts, 81. *Pos:* Cur, RI Hist Soc, 69-72; cur & ed exhib catalogs, Pa Acad Fine Arts, 72-82, pres, 83-; actg cur, Am Painting & Sculpture, Yale Univ Art Gallery, 74-75. *Teaching:* Guest lectr, Univ Tex, Austin, 91. *Mem:* Am Asn Mus (mem, Legislative Comt, currently); Fairmount Park Art Asn (dir, currently); Conserv Ctr Art & Hist Artifacts (dir); Yale Univ Coun Comt on the Art Gallery & Brit Art Ctr (chmn). *Publ:* Auth, Welliver, Rizzoli Int Publ Inc, 85. *Mailing Add:* Pa Acad Fine Arts Broad & Cherry Sts Philadelphia PA 19102

GOODYEAR, JOHN L
SCULPTOR, PAINTER
b Los Angeles, Calif, Oct 22, 30. *Study:* Univ Mich, BD, 52, MD, 54. *Work:* Guggenheim Mus, Whitney Mus Am Art, Metrop Mus Art & Mus Mod Art, New York; Bibliot Nat, Paris; Brit Mus, London. *Comn:* State NJ, 81 & 90; IBM, Raleigh, NC, 81; Jewish Ctr, Princeton, NJ, 84. *Exhib:* Responsive Eye, Mus Mod Art, New York, 65; solo exhibs, Amel Gallery, New York, 66, Mass Inst Technol Ctr Advan Visual Studies, Cambridge, 76, Pyramid Gallery, New York, 89 & Snyder Fine Arts, New York, 92; Whitney Mus Am Art Ann, New York, 66 & 68; Smithsonian Inst, Washington, DC, 67-68; Albright-Knox Art Gallery, Buffalo, NY, 68; Boston Mus Fine Arts, 71; Mus Mod Art, New York, 72; City Gallery, New York, 87; Deutsch-Amerikanische Inst, Tubigen, WGer, 89; and others. *Teaching:* Instr, Univ Mich, Grand Rapids, 56-62 & Univ Mass, Amherst, 62-64; prof design, Mason Gross Sch Art, Rutgers Univ, 64-, chmn dept visual arts, 87-89. *Awards:* Graham Found Fel, 62 & 70; Ctr Advan Visual Studies Fel, Mass Inst Technol, 70-71. *Bibliog:* Vivien Raynor (auth), Goodyear's transmutation of Zen at the Princeton Gallery, New York Times, 6/7/87. *Mem:* Am Abstract Artists. *Media:* Mixed. *Mailing Add:* RD 2 Lambertville NJ 08530

GOOSSEN, EUGENE COONS
WRITER, EDUCATOR
b Gloversville, NY, Aug 6, 20. *Study:* Hamilton Col; Corcoran Sch Fine Arts; Sorbonne, Paris, cert; New Sch Social Res, BA. *Collections Arranged:* Kenneth Noland, Morris Louis & First Barnett Newman Retrospective, Bennington Col, Vt, 58-61; Eight Young Artists, Hudson River Mus, NY, 64; The Art of the Real, Mus Mod Art, New York, Grand Palais, Paris, Kunsthalle, Zurich, Switz & Tate Gallery, London, Eng, 68-69; Helen Frankenthaler, Whitney Mus Am Art, New York, Whitechapel Gallery, London, Herrenhausen, Hanover & Kongresshalle, Berlin, Ger, 69; Ellsworth Kelly, Mus Mod Art, New York, 73. *Pos:* Art critic, Monterey Peninsula Herald, 48-58; dir exhibs, Bennington Col, 58-61. *Teaching:* Prof art, Bennington Col, 58-61; prof art & chmn dept, Hunter Col, 61-82, prof art hist, 82-91. *Awards:* Frank Jewett Mather Citation for Excellence in Art Criticism, 58; Guggenheim Fel, 70; City Univ New York Res Grant, 72. *Bibliog:* Article, Time Mag, 4/7/67; Michael Murphy (auth), The Art of the Real (film), US Info Agency, 68. *Mem:* Int Art Critics Asn; Am Asn Univ Prof; Col Art Asn Am. *Publ:* Auth, Ellsworth Kelly, 58; auth, Stuart Davis, 59; auth, The Art of the Real, Eng, Fr & Ger ed, 68-69; auth, Helen Frankenthaler, 69; coauth, Encyclopaedia of American Art, Chanticleer Press, 72. *Mailing Add:* RD 1 Buskirk NY 12028

GORCHOV, RON
PAINTER
b Chicago, Ill, Apr 5, 30. *Study:* Art Inst Chicago, 47-50; Univ Ill, 50-51. *Work:* Whitney Mus Am Art, New York; Mus Mod Art, New York; Metrop Mus of Art, New York; Guggenhiem Mus, New York; Detroit Inst of Arts; Chicago Art Inst. *Teaching:* Assoc prof art, Hunter Col, presently. *Media:* Oil on Canvas, Watercolor. *Dealer:* Jack Tilton Gallery New York. *Mailing Add:* 461 Broome St New York NY 10013

GORDIN, MISHA
PHOTOGRAPHER, VIDEO ARTIST
b Rija Latvia, Russia, Mar 12, 46. *Study:* Self taught in art; Aviation Inst, Russia, MEng, 72. *Work:* Nat Mus Mod Art, Georges Pompidou Ctr, Paris, France; Art Inst Chicago; Detroit Inst Art; Int Mus Photog at George Eastman House, Rochester, NY; Toledo Mus Art, Ohio. *Exhib:* Habatat Galleries, Fla, 86; Shout, Detroit Inst Art, Mich, 87, Mus Photographic Arts, San Diego, Ca, 89 & Mark Masuoka Gallery, Las Vegas, Nev, 90; Klein Art Works, Chicago, Ill, 91; Bentley Tomlinson Gallery, Scottsdale, Ariz, 92; Dennos Mus Ctr, Traverse City, Mich, 92. *Awards:* Fel, Nat Endowment Arts, 86; Creative Artist Grant, Mich Coun Arts, 85; Mich Arts Award, Art Found Mich, 87. *Bibliog:* C Reeve & M Sward (auth), The New Photography, Spectrum Publ, 89; Afterimage, Vol 15, Visual Studies, 1/88. *Mailing Add:* 2913 Roundtree Dr Troy MI 48083

GORDIN, SIDNEY
SCULPTOR, EDUCATOR
b Cheliabinsk, Russia, Oct 24, 18. *Study:* Cooper Union, New York, 37-41, with Morris Kantor, Carol Harrison & Leo Katz. *Work:* Art Inst Chicago; Newark Mus, NJ; Walter T Chrysler Mus Art at Norfolk, Va; Southern Ill Univ; Whitney Mus Am Art, New York; and others. *Comn:* Sculpture, Temple Israel, Tulsa, Okla, 59 & Envoy Towers, New York, 60; sculpture, Davies Symphony Hall, San Francisco, Calif. *Exhib:* Metrop Mus Art, New York, 51; Whitney Ann, 52-57; Mus Mod Art, New York; Art Inst Chicago; Pa Acad Fine Arts, 54 & 55; Brooklyn Mus, NY; Newark Mus; San Francisco Mus Art, Calif; Oakland Art Mus, Calif; Philbrook Art Ctr, Tulsa, Okla, 60; one-man shows, New Sch Social Res, 57 & de Young Mem Mus, San Francisco, 57. *Teaching:* Instr, Pratt Inst, 53-58, Brooklyn Col, 55-58, New Sch for Social Res, 56-58, Sarah Lawrence Col, 57-58 & Univ Calif, Berkeley, 58- *Mailing Add:* 903 Camilia St Berkeley CA 94710

GORDLEY, MARILYN CLASSE
PAINTER
b St Louis, Mo, Aug 4, 29. *Study:* Washington Univ, BFA; Univ Okla, MFA; Ohio State Univ. *Work:* Greenville Mus Art, NC; Spring Mills, Lancaster, SC; Univ Okla; NC Nat Bank, Greenville. *Comn:* Portraits of Gov Kerr Scott, Arthur Tyler, Henry Belk, Elmer Browning & Weldell Smiley, ECarolina Univ, 64-74. *Exhib:* Cent South Exhib, Nashville, Tenn, 69; Nat Drawing Exhib, Southern Ill Univ, Carbondale, 75; Miss Mus Art, Jackson, 78; Fayetteville Mus Art, NC, 79; Southern Exposure, Hanson Gallery, New Orleans, 80; Now & Then, Mus York Co, Rockhill, SC, 90; Arlington Hall, Greenville, NC, 90; and others. *Teaching:* Assoc prof drawing & painting, ECarolina Univ, 64- *Awards:* 18th Irene Leache Award, Norfolk Mus, 66; Spring Mills First Prize, 67; Cent South Exhib Award, 69. *Mem:* Am Asn Univ Women; Col Art Asn Am; NC Artists Asn. *Media:* Oil. *Mailing Add:* Dept Art East Carolina Univ Greenville NC 27834

GORDLEY, METZ TRANBARGER (TRAN)
PAINTER
b Cedar Rapids, Iowa, May 24, 32. *Study:* Wash Univ, BFA; Univ Okla, MFA; Ohio State Univ; Univ NC, Chapel Hill. *Work:* Greenville Mus Art, NC; NC Nat Bank Collection, Charlotte; NC State Soc Print & Drawings, Raleigh; Univ Okla, Norman. *Comn:* Aycock portrait for E Carolina Univ. *Exhib:* 21st Ann Drawing & Small Sculpture Show, Ball State Univ Art Gallery, 75; Biennial Exhib Piedmont Painting & Sculpture, Mint Mus, Charlotte, NC, 75; two-person shows, High Point Exhib Ctr, NC, 77, Mark Twain S Co Bank, St Louis, Mo, 78, Fayetteville Mus, NC, 79, Greenville Mus Art, 82, Bank of the Arts, New Bern, 84 & Arlington Hall, Greenville, 85 & 90; one-man shows, Mint Mus, Charlotte, 78; Razor Gallery, NY, 79; 44th Ann, Butler Inst Am Art, Youngstown, Ohio, 80; Art on Paper, Weatherspoon Gallery, Greensboro, NC, 88; 30th Irene Leache Mem , Chrysler Mus, Norfolk, Va, 90; Judge Gallery, Durham, NC, 90. *Teaching:* Prof painting, ECarolina Univ, 59- *Awards:* First Prize, NC Print & Drawing Soc, 66; Second Prize for Watercolor & Second Prize for Oil, Kinston Art Show, 68; Merit Award, Wake Visual Arts Asn, Raleigh, 86. *Bibliog:* Emily Farnham (auth), Behind a Laughing Mask, Charles Demuth; SECAC Review, Vol V, No 2, 4/72; Philip Fehl, The Classical Monument, SECAC, Vol VII, No 1, spring 74; Lucy Lippard, Overlay: Contemporary Art and Art of Prehistory, SECAC, Vol XI, No 1, spring 86. *Mem:* Southeastern Col Art Asn; Col Art Asn. *Media:* Oil. *Mailing Add:* Dept Art East Carolina Univ Greenville NC 27834

GORDON, ALBERT F
ART DEALER
b Antwerp, Belg, June 18, 34; US citizen. *Study:* Sorbonne, Univ Paris; Columbia Univ, MA, 60. *Collections Arranged:* Aspects of the Doubled Image in African Art (auth, catalog), 76; Beauty and the Beast: A Study in Contrasts (auth, catalog), 77; Ekon Society Puppets: Sculptures for Social Criticism (auth, catalog), 77. *Pos:* Pres, Tribal Arts Galleries, Inc, New York, 68- *Bibliog:* Terry Trucco (auth), Primitive art, Art News, 4/81. *Mem:* Am Appraisers Asn; Explorers Club. *Specialty:* African art. *Publ:* The Tribal Bead, Tribal Arts Gallery Publ Inc, 74. *Mailing Add:* c/o Tribal Arts Gallery 35 E Ninth New York NY 10003

GORDON, JOHN S
SCULPTOR, EDUCATOR
b Milwaukee, Wis, Nov 16, 46. *Study:* Antioch Col, BA, 70; Claremont Grad Sch, MFA, 73. *Work:* Prudential Insurance Co. *Exhib:* Whitney Mus Am Art, Biennial Contemp Am Art, New York, 75; one-man show, Los Angeles Louver Gallery, Venice, Calif, 77, Artists Space, New York, 79; USC Atelier, Santa Monica, 88; Shidoni Contemp Gallery, Santa Fe, NMex, 91. *Pos:* Consult, Community Redevelopment Agency, Los Angeles, 84; Southern Calif Rapid Transit District Metro Rail Art-in-Transit Comt, 85-90; mem, Mayor's Task Force Arts, 87-88; consult, Los Angeles Co Transportation Comn, 90-91; bd trustees, Santa Fe Chamber Music Festival, 92- *Teaching:* Instr ceramics, Mt St Mary's Col, Los Angeles, 73; assoc prof sculpture & ceramics, Univ Southern Calif, 73-; vis asst prof, Claremont Grad Sch, fall 79; dean, Sch Fine Art, Univ Southern Calif, 81-87; acad vpres, Calif Col Arts & Crafts, 88; assoc prof, Sch Fine Arts, Univ Southern Calif, 89-91; dean fine arts & cult studies, Inst Am Indian Arts, 91- *Awards:* Nat Endowment Arts Grant, 76; Mayor's Cert Appreciation, City of Los Angeles, 84. *Bibliog:* Susan C Larsen (auth), John S Gordon, Arts Mag, 3/77; Peter Frank (auth), On the trail of the emergent American, The Nat Gallery Guide, 1/81; Margaret Lazzari (auth), Delving into minor works, Artweek, 2/6/88. *Mem:* Col Art Asn Am; Int Coun Fine Arts Deans. *Media:* Mixed Media. *Publ:* How about some art in next year's Los Angeles festival, Los Angeles Herald Examiner, 10/6/87; References to Political Climate, Fragility of Human Emotions, Santa Fe New Mex, 10/11/91; New Mexico: Growing Internationalism, Art News, 4/92; Authenticity and the Curatorial Dilema, The Mag, 7/92. *Mailing Add:* PO Box 4157 Santa Fe NM 87502-4157

GORDON, JOSEPHINE
PAINTER
b Walla-Walla, Wash. *Study:* Univ Guadalajara, with Maria Medina; Ariz State Univ, with Dr Harry Wood; Sedona Art Ctr, Ariz, with Nassan Abiskhairoun; also with A E Park, William Kimura & Wassily Sommer, Anchorage, Alaska; and with Perry Acher, Seattle, Wash. *Work:* Bank of North Anchorage & Miller Construction Co, Anchorage; Alaska Seafood Corp, Homer; Alaska Sales & Serv, Alaska Pioneer Home & Alaska Community Col; and many pvt collections. *Exhib:* All Alaska Exhib, 70 & 71; Artists of Alaska Traveling Show, 73-75; one-woman show, Artique Ltd, 73-75; Ariz State Univ, 73; Univ Guadalajara, Mex, 74. *Teaching:* Private classes. *Bibliog:* Lael Morgan (auth), Jo Gordon, painter, Alaska J, fall 75. *Mem:* Alaska Artist Guild. *Media:* Watercolor, Acrylic. *Mailing Add:* 1521 McHugh Lane Anchorage AK 99501

GORDON, JOY L
MUSEUM DIRECTOR, EDUCATOR
b New York, NY, Jan 31, 33. *Study:* NY Univ, BA, 57, MA, 72. *Collections Arranged:* Contemporary Latino Americano Art, 72; Prints from the NYU Art Collection, Hudson River Mus, Yonkers, 73; Paintings & Sculpture from the NYU Art Collection, Art Gallery, Univ Notre Dame, 73; William Benton Mus Art, Univ Conn, 73; Contemporary Asian & Middle Eastern Art from the Grey Foundation Collection, 75; Report from Soho, 75; Aspects of Am Realism, 76; Prints & Techniques (with catalog), 76; Drawing & Collage (with catalog), 76; Contemp Israeli Crafts, 77; Am Impressionist Painting, 77; Am Still Life Paintings, 19th & 20th Centuries, 78; Containers, Mass Crafts, 79; Art in Process, 79; Directions in Realism: Boston, 80; American Artists in Dusseldorf, 82 & On the Threshold of Modern Design, The Arts & Crafts Movement, 84, Danfort Mus. *Pos:* Asst cur educ, cur & researcher pvt collections, NY Univ Art Collection, 72-74; cur, Grey Art Gallery & Study Ctr, NY Univ, 74-77; dir, Danforth Mus, Framingham, Mass, 77-88 & Guild Hall, East Hampton, NY, 88- *Teaching:* Adminr mus studies, New York Univ, 72-77 & Framingham State Col, 78-88. *Mem:* Col Art Asn; Am Asn Mus; New Eng Mus Assoc; Art Table; Mass Cultural Alliance (trustee). *Mailing Add:* 185 Massachusetts St East Hampton NY 11937

GORDON, MARTIN
DEALER, COLLECTOR
b New York, NY, Aug 15, 39. *Study:* Rochester Inst Technol, BS. *Pos:* Pres & publ, Martin Gordon Inc; Gordon's Print Price Ann Inc; Elegant Hay Hart Ink Inc. *Mem:* Print Dealers Asn Am; Art Dealers Asn Am; Graphic Arts Coun NY; Int Fine Print Dealers Asn (pres, 89-90). *Specialty:* Mid-19th through mid-20th century original prints. *Publ:* Gordon's Print Price Ann, 78-93. *Mailing Add:* Martin Gordon Inc 1840 Eighth St S Naples FL 33940

GORDON, P(ATRICK) S(COTT)
PAINTER
b Claremore, Okla, Oct 24, 53. *Study:* Univ Tulsa, BFA, 74, grad studies, 74-75. *Work:* Philbrook Art Mus, Tulsa, Okla; McNay Art Inst, San Antonio, Tex; Boise Mus, Idaho; City of Tulsa Performing Arts Ctr, Okla. *Comn:* Painting, Tulsa Opera Co, Okla, 79; large scale painting, City of Tulsa, Okla, 89. *Exhib:* Collector's Gallery XV, Marion McNay Art Inst, San Antonio, Tex, 81; Still Life/Interiors, Contemp Arts Ctr, New Orleans, La, 82; Focus on Realism, Boise Gallery Art, Idaho, 84; American Realism: Twentieth Century Drawings and Watercolors, San Francisco Mus Mod Art, Calif, 85; Permanent Collection: Philbrook Mus Art, Tulsa, Okla, 88; Realist Watercolors, Palmer Mus Art, Philadelphia, Pa, 90. *Pos:* Bd mem, Arts and Humanities Coun, 77-85; comt mem, Arts in Public Places Comt, 87-90; bd dir, Philbrook Art Mus, 89-90. *Awards:* Nat Endowment for Art, 79; Outstanding Alumnus, Univ Tulsa, 89. *Bibliog:* John Arthur (auth), American realist drawings & watercolors, NY Graphic Soc, 80; Dr Alvin Martin (auth), American realism: 20th Century drawings & watercolors, Abrams, 85; Judith Bumpus (auth), International Flower Painters Since 1945, Phaidon Press, London, 86. *Media:* Watercolor. *Dealer:* Fischbach Gallery 24 57th St New York NY 10019. *Mailing Add:* c/o Tower Park Gallery 4709 N Prospect Rd Peoria Heights IL 61614

GORDON, RUSSELL TALBERT
PAINTER
b Philadelphia, Pa, June 3, 36. *Study:* Temple Univ, Tyler Sch, BFA, 62; Univ Wis, MS, 66, MFA, 67. *Work:* Philadelphia Mus Art; Oakland Mus; Cincinnati Mus Art; Can Coun, Ottawa; Walker Art Ctr, Minneapolis. *Comn:* Philadelphia Print Club. *Exhib:* Printmakers Invitational, Oakland Mus, 70; Poetic Fantasies, San Francisco Mus Art, 71; Extraordinary Realities, Whitney Mus Am Art, 73; Afro-American Abstraction, Los Angeles Munic Art Gallery, 82; Selected Works by Five Twentieth Century American Artists, Hastings Gallery Art, Univ Calif, San Francisco, 82; Two Artists, The Chevron Gallery, San Francisco, Calif, 83; one-person exhibs, Miami Dade Pub Libr, Fla & Waddington Gallery, Montreal, 83; and many others. *Teaching:* Asst beginning drawing, Univ Wis, 65-67; asst prof printmaking & grad sem, Univ Utah, Salt lake City, 67-69; asst prof, Univ Calif, Berkeley, 69 & 72. *Awards:* Fac Res Grant, Limited Ed Bk, Univ Utah, 69; George Marshall Fel, Vikingsberg Kunst Mus, Am Scandinavian Found, 72; Nat Endowment Arts Grant for Painting, 81. *Bibliog:* The Artists Proof Vol XI, Pratt Graphics Ctr, 71; Edward Atkinson (auth), Black dimensions in contemporary American art, New Am Libr, 71; Leonard Edmonson (auth), Etching, Van Nostrand Reinhold Co, 73. *Publ:* Auth, Images & Impressions, Printmaking Dept, Univ Utah, 69. *Mailing Add:* Dept Art & Painting, Concordia Univ 1455 De Maisonneuve Blvd W, Room PS-VA 309 Montreal PQ H3G 1M8 Canada

GORDON, TINA
SCULPTOR
b New York, NY. *Study:* Goddard Col, BA, 71, Nat Acad with Chaim Gross & Bruno Lucchesi, 83 & New Sch Soc Res, 73-80. *Work:* New York State Mental Health, Wards Island. *Comn:* Manhattan Psychiatric Ctr, New York. *Exhib:* Washington Square Outdoor Art Exhib, 77-84; Allied Artists, New York, 77, 78 & 82-87; Nat Acad Art, New York, 77 & 78; Nat Art Club, New York, 78, 79 & 88; Am Soc Contemp Artists, 81, 82 & 83; and others. *Teaching:* Instr, Nassau Community Col, 69-72 & East River Montessori Sch, NY, 73-76; Art therapist, Manhattan Psychiatric Inst, 76- *Awards:* Roman Bronze Award, Knickerbocker Artists, 81; Elliot Lisken Award in Sculpture, Salmagundi Club, New York, 84, 86 & 89; Pen & Brush Award, 90. *Mem:* Salmagundi Art Club; Nat Asn Women Artists; Allied Artists Am; Knickerbocker Artists; Am Asn Prof Artists. *Media:* Bronze, Welded Metal. *Publ:* The New Sch for Social Research, SRP Review, 88 & 89. *Mailing Add:* 24 Fifth Ave New York NY 10011

GORDON, VIOLET
ILLUSTRATOR, WRITER
b Buffalo, NY, May 22, 07. *Study:* Albright Fine Arts Acad, with Urqhart Wilcox, Harry Jacobs, Mildred Green & Franc Root McCreery, grad (with hons); Univ Buffalo, with Dr Charles LeClair, Dorothy Shay, Harvey Beverman & Catherine Koenig. *Work:* Grosvenour Libr, Buffalo, NY; State Univ NY Buffalo. *Exhib:* San Francisco Worlds Fair, 35; Buffalo Soc Artists, Albright Knox Art Gallery, 63; one-man shows, Roycroft-Elbert Hubbard Mus, East Aurora, NY, 66 & 81 & Lincoln Room, Wilcox Mansion, 75; Cork Gallery, Lincoln Ctr, 81 & 82; Carnegie Ctr, 91. *Pos:* Fashion illusr, Buffalo Eve Times & News, 29-33; designer, Ed Muth Co, 30-35. *Teaching:* Instr art & critic teacher, var grade schs, high schs & univs, 30-68; instr art, Fosdick Masten Sr High Sch, 55-68; assoc teacher art, Univ Buffalo, 65. *Awards:* Outstanding Achievement Award, Assoc Arts Orgn, 73. *Bibliog:* Betty Ott (auth), About V Gordon, Courier-Express Newspaper, 73; Natalie Fiedler (auth), And who thought up Peter Rabbit?, Ariz Repub, 74. *Mem:* Nat League Am Pen Women; Buffalo Soc Artists. *Media:* Oil, Conte Crayon. *Publ:* Contribr & illusr, Col Humor Mag, 29-32; contribr, Sch Arts Mag & Arts & Activities Mag; yearbk ed, Herald, 64-67; auth & illusr, Who's Who at the Zoo, 72; recorded, Libr Cong, 75. *Dealer:* Bonnie Flickinger 31 Nottingham Terr Buffalo NY 14216. *Mailing Add:* 891 Amherst Buffalo NY 14216

GORE, DAVID ALAN
PAINTER, CONSERVATOR
b Ann Arbor, Mich, June 6, 47. *Study:* Tyler Sch Art, Philadelphia, BFA, 68; Acad Fine Art, with Joseph Amerotica, 72; Philadelphia Mus Art, with Theodore Segal, 72-74. *Comn:* Eight conservation murals, Bucks Co Community Col, 78; Empire & Flute Player (murals), comn by Wilbur Pierce, 85; Pompeian Room, comn by Dr James Sullivan, 85; sculpture, comn by Dr R Shafto, 91. *Exhib:* Chestnut Hill Ann Art Show, Pa, 85; British & Australian Embassy, 85; Very Victorian, Del State Mus, Dover, 88-89; Mixed Media by David Gore, Widener Univ Mus, Chester, Pa, 90. *Pos:* Chief Conservator, Bureau of Mus Del, 74-; chief conservator, Henry M Flagler Mus, 75-80; chief conservator, Widener Univ Mus, 87- *Teaching:* Instr painting, drawing & design, Bucks Co Community Col, Pa, 71-73. *Awards:* French Int Poster Contest, Paris, 63; Nat Designers Award, 68. *Bibliog:* Kim Sargent (auth), Flagler Museum Celebrates, Palm Beach Daily News, 80; Art Carey (auth), Restoring Masterpieces, Philadelphia Inquire, 81; Rita Beyer (auth), David Gore Works Shown at Schwartz Gallery, Chestnut Hill Local, 92. *Media:* Oil. *Mailing Add:* 44 E 24th St Chester PA 19013

GORE, JEFFERSON ANDERSON
CURATOR
b Selma, Ala, April 25, 43. *Study:* Harvard Col, BA(visual studies), 65; Skowhegan Sch Painting & Sculpture, 66; Grad Sch Fine Arts, Univ Pa, MFA(sculpture), 70. *Collections Arranged:* Sesquicentennial of Railroad in the Arts (auth, catalog), 79; Exquisite Nomads: Seashells Real and in Art (auth, catalog), 80; Season of Mists (auth, catalog), 81; Spacetoys: Fifty Years of Fantasy, 82; Painted Light (auth, catalog), 83; Mushroom Magic: The R Gordon Wasson Collection of Mycological Art. *Pos:* Cur fine arts, Reading

Pub Mus, Pa, 78- *Teaching:* Asst sculpture, Grad Sch Fine Arts, Univ Pa, 68-70; instr, Albright Col, Pa, 70-74. *Mem:* Citizens Arts in Pa; Philadelphia Art Alliance. *Res:* Cross-cultural influences between Europe and Asia in art and philosophy. *Mailing Add:* Reading Pub Mus Art Gallery 500 Museum Rd Reading PA 19611

GORE, KEN (KENNETH LEON)
PAINTER
b Elvira, Ill, Oct 2, 11. *Study:* Meinzinger Art Sch, Detroit, 40-42; with George Rich, 40-45 & Aldro T Hibbard, 49. *Work:* Rockport Art Asn, Cape Ann, Mass. *Exhib:* Guild Boston Artists, 60-83; Hudson Valley Art Asn, White Plains, NY, 63-86; Nat Acad Design Invitational, New York, 76; solo exhib, Frye Mus, Seattle, 77; Salmagundi Club Ann, New York, 79-82; Baker Gallery Lubbock, TX; Copley Soc, Boston, Mass. *Teaching:* Instr, co-dir, Meinzinger Art Sch, 42-48. *Awards:* Mary F Salvia Mem Award, Salmagundi Club, New York, 79; Catherine McGovern Mem Award, Hudson Valley Art Asn, 83; Marguerite Pearson Gold Medal, Rockport Art Asn, Mass, 83; Gold Medal, Salmagundi, Club, 84. *Mem:* Guild Boston Artists (vpres, 70-80); Am Artists Prof League; Allied Artists Am; North Shore Arts Asn; Rockport Art Asn (pres, formerly). *Media:* Oil. *Publ:* Auth, article, Am Artist, 2/76. *Dealer:* Baker Gallery Lubbock TX; Gallery Southwest Taos NM. *Mailing Add:* 186 E Main St Gloucester MA 01930

GORE, SAMUEL MARSHALL
PAINTER, SCULPTOR
b Coolidge, Tex, Nov 24, 27. *Study:* Atlanta Col Art, BFA; Miss Col, BA; Univ Ala, MA; Ill State Univ, EdD. *Work:* Hull Gallery, Hinds Community Col, Raymond, Miss; Ill State Univ; Miss Univ Women; Aven Galleries, Miss Col; Miss Mus Art. *Comn:* Mural, Van Winkle Methodist Church, Jackson, Miss, 74; portrait bust (bronze), US Sen John Stennis, Miss Wing, Civil Air Patrol, 74 & William Faulkner, Sta WJTV, Howard Lett, Jackson, Miss, 74; Bronze Nurse, Miss Baptist Hosp, 88; Bronze Working Man, Miss Mus Agr & Forestry. *Exhib:* One-man shows, Miss Art Asn, 57 & House Admin Off Suite, US Capitol Bldg, 75; Nat Oils Show & Mem show, Miss Art Asn, Jackson 58; Sears Traveling Show, 63. *Teaching:* Prof drawing, painting & sculpture & head art dept, Miss Col, 51- *Bibliog:* Ruth Campbell (producer), Conversation with Sam Gore (video tape), Miss Educ TV, 11/75. *Mem:* Miss Art Educ Asn (secy, 61, vpres, 62, pres 63); Nat Art Educ Asn; Southeastern Art Educ Asn; Med-Art USA (bd dir); Christians in Visual Arts. *Media:* Oil, Watercolor; Terra Cotta, Bronze. *Publ:* Illusr, Mississippi Game and Fish, 58-59; Freshwater species of Mississippi, 59. *Mailing Add:* Art Dept Miss Col Clinton MS 39058

GORE, TOM
PHOTOGRAPHER, EDUCATOR
b Victoria, BC, Aug 7, 46. *Study:* Univ Victoria. *Work:* Prov Collection, Parliament Bldgs, Victoria; Vancouver Art Gallery, BC; Univ Victoria, BC; City Seattle. *Comn:* Illusr, Earth Meditations, Mike Doyle, 70 & Vancouver Island Poetry Soft Press, 74. *Exhib:* Art Gallery Greater Victoria, 71, 75, 82, 86 & 87; one-man shows, Open Space Gallery, Victoria, BC, 76, Mind's Eye Gallery, Idaho, 79 & Gallery 666, 90; group show, Spokane Art Mus, 79; Works in Progress, Mind's Eye Gallery, Idaho, 79; Sask Cult Exchange, 86 & 87; Escuela Artos Aplicadas, Ibiza, Spain, 88; and others. *Collections Arranged:* Victoria & Victoria Five, Secession Gallery; Polaroid Collaboratory, 78 & The Stereo Show, 80, Open Space; Latitudes and Parallels, Winnipeg Gallery, 81. *Pos:* Ed art mag, Tryste, 66-68; com photogr, 69-71; cur photog, Open Space, Victoria, 75-84; ed, Rhino Press, 79-; consult, Winnipeg Art Gallery, 81-; photo ed, Raddled Moon, 86- *Teaching:* Lectr photog, Univ Victoria, 77-; instr photog, Camosun Col, Victoria, BC, 73-78. *Awards:* Hon Mention, BC Photogr Show, Simon Fraser Art Gallery, 73; First Prize, Vancouver Island Juried Show, Art Gallery of Greater Victoria, 74; Can Coun Grants, 77, 78 & 90; Dept Communications Grant, 90. *Bibliog:* Glen Howarth (auth), Bio-article, Victoria Press, 70; Carolyn Leier (auth), Bio-article, Arts W, 76; Contemporary Personage, Padua, Italy, 80; Photographic Artists & Innovators, 84. *Mem:* Open Space Arts Soc (pres, 78-); Soc for Photog Educ, NW Region (chmn, 78-81); Victoria Civil Liberties Asn (pres, 88-); Can Federation of Rights & Liberties (bd, 92-). *Media:* Collage and photography. *Res:* Criticism of photography; John Thomson biography; the photograph as theatre; evolution of photographic landscape. *Publ:* Contemporary Photography in British Columbia, Ryerson, 79; auth, In perspective: Vancouver art, Arts W, 1/79; Collecting the paradoxical magic mirror, Photo Communique, PI, 5/79; Portfolio, Camera Mainichi, Tokyo, 10/81 & 3/83; George Craven's Objects and Images, New York, 88; Portfolio, Camera Canada, Toronto, 84; An Admirable View, Rhino Press, Victoria, 86; Robert Hirsch's Photographic Possibilities, New York, 90; Building Consensus, Democrat, 92. *Mailing Add:* 102-1709 Mackenzie Victoria BC V8N 1A6 Canada

GOREE, GARY PAUL
INSTRUCTOR, PAINTER
b Jackson, Miss, Apr 8, 51. *Study:* Southwestern Okla State Univ, BFA, 72; Tex Tech Univ, MA(educ), 80. *Exhib:* Greater Fall River Nat, Mass, 78; Nat Cape Coral Ann, Fla, 79; Okla Art Ann, Tulsa, 80; Okla 81, Univ Okla, Norman, 81. *Pos:* Art supervisor, Tulsa pub schs, 82-86, fine arts coordr, 86- *Teaching:* Instr art, Lewis & Clark Jr High, Tulsa, 73-81; teaching asst art, Tex Tech Univ, 77; instr watercolor, Tulsa Jr Col, Okla, 74-; vis prof art, Tex Tech Univ, 85-88. *Awards:* Okla Art Educr of Yr, 83; Nat Western Region Art Supervisor of Yr, 87. *Mem:* Nat Art Educ Asn; Okla Art Educ Asn; Southwestern Art Asn; Okla Art Guild; Tulsa Artist Guild. *Media:* Watercolor. *Publ:* Coauth, Found Object Design in Jewelry, 76, Weaving, Soft Sculpture & Natural Dyes, 77 & Plans, Projects and Processes, 80, Tulsa Pub Schs. *Dealer:* Margo Shorney 6616 N Olie Oklahoma City OK 74128. *Mailing Add:* 1541 S Florence Ave Tulsa OK 74104-5208

GORELICK, SHIRLEY
PAINTER, PRINTMAKER
b Brooklyn, NY, Jan 24, 24. *Study:* Brooklyn Col, BA; Teachers Col, Columbia Univ, MA. *Work:* Norfolk Mus, Va; Brooklyn Mus; Post Col; Housatonic Mus, Conn; Aldrich Mus, Ridgefield, Conn; and others. *Exhib:* 3rd Ann Contemporary Reflections, Aldrich Mus, Ridgefield, Conn, 74; 19th Nat Print Exhib, Brooklyn Mus, NY, 74; solo shows, Angelski Gallery, New York, 61, Cent Hall Gallery, Port Washington, NY, 74, 76 & 78, Soho 20 Gallery, New York, 75, 77, 79, 82, 84 & 86 & Art Gallery, State Univ NY Stony Brook, 79; Nothing but Nudes, Whitney Mus of Am Art, New York, 77; Hassam Fund Exhib, Am Acad-Inst Arts & Letters, New York, 78; 43rd Nat Midyear Show, Butler Inst Am Art, Youngstown, Ohio, 79; Contemporary Naturalism, Nassau Co Mus, Roslyn, New York, 80; and many others. *Teaching:* Instr painting, NShore Community Arts Ctr, Great Neck, NY, 61-79; instr drawing, Nassau Co Off Cult Develop, 73-74. *Awards:* RI Arts Festival Award, 64; Purchase Award, Nassau Community Col, 72; Creative Artists Pub Serv Fel-Painting, NY State Coun on the Arts, 75-76. *Bibliog:* Yvette Sencer (auth), article, Arts Mag, 79; Jeanne Paris (auth), article, Newsday, 80; David Shirey (auth), NY Times, 80. *Mem:* Women's Interart Ctr, New York; Woman's Caucus Art; Prof Artist Guild (vpres, 71-75); Central Hall Artists (treas, 74-78); and others. *Media:* Acrylic; All. *Dealer:* Soho 20 Gallery 469 Broome St New York NY 10013. *Mailing Add:* Three Mirrielees Circle Great Neck NY 11021

GORENIUC, MIRCEA C PAUL
SCULPTOR
b Bucharest, Romania, Dec 12, 42. *Study:* San Francisco State Univ, BA, 76; San Jose Univ, Calif, MA, 75, MFA, 78. *Work:* Palo Alto, San Jose, Concord, Los Altos & Los Gatos, Calif. *Comn:* Space Dance for Peace, Wolfe-Sesnon & Buttery, San Jose, Calif, 82, Syntex Corp, Palo Alto, 83, City of Los Gatos, 87; Homage to the Challenger, Lyncoln Park, Los Altos, Calif, 86; Rock and Roll for Peace, City of Concord, Calif, 90. *Exhib:* One-person shows, Twelfth Int Sculpture Conference, Oakland Calif, 82 & Centre Int d'Art Contemporain, Paris, France, 85. *Pos:* VPres, IAA/UNESCO US chap, W Coast. *Teaching:* Instr sculpture, West Valley Col, Saratoga, Calif, 80-82. *Awards:* Most Controversial Pub Sculpture, Sunnyvale, Calif, Metro News, 89; Phi Kappa Phi, First Prize & People's Choice Concord 1 percent Art in Pub Places Prog, 91. *Bibliog:* Art reviews in San Jose mercury news, Oakland Tribune, Palo Alto News, Los Gatos Times, Contra Costa Times, Metro News. *Mem:* Int Art Asn, USA Chapter (vpres 87-91); Artist Equity Asn; Calif Confederation for the Arts. *Media:* Cast Metals, Granite. *Mailing Add:* 100 Wood Rd Los Gatos CA 95030-6704

GORMAN, R C
PAINTER, DEALER
b Chinle, Ariz, July 26, 33. *Study:* Northern Ariz Univ, with Jack Salter & Ellery Gibson; Mexico City Col. *Work:* Heard Mus, Phoenix, Ariz; Philbrook Art Ctr, Tulsa, Okla; Northern Ariz Univ, Flagstaff; Gonzaga Univ, Spokane, Wash; Santa Fe Fine Arts Mus, NMex; and the pvt collections of Elizabeth Taylor, Lee Marvin, Gregory Peck, Barry Goldwater, Andy Warhol, Walter & Jean Mondale, Corbin Bernson. *Comn:* Dance of the Hohokam Masked Figures, St Luke's Hosp, Phoenix, 71. *Exhib:* Muirhead Gallery, Costa Mesa, Calif, 78; Art Wagon Gallery, Scottsdale, Ariz, 78; Munic Mus, St Paul de Vence, France, 79; Navajo Turquoise Gallery, Paris, France, 80; Marjorie Kauffman Graphics Gallery, Houston, Tex, 80; solo exhibs, Impressions II Gallery, Tucson, Ariz, 81 & 83, Gallery Hawaii, Maui, 82, American West Gallery, Chicago, 83, 84 & 91, Galeria Capistrano, San Juan Capistrano, Calif, 83 & 91, Galerie Calumet, Heidelberg, Ger, 86 & Navajo Gallery, Taos, NMex, 86; Old Jail Found, Albany, Tex, 82; Arts NMex, Continental Tour, 84. *Collections Arranged:* US Indian Arts & Crafts Bd, Washington, DC, 68. *Pos:* Owner, Navajo Gallery, Taos, currently. *Awards:* Grand Award, Am Indian Art Exhib, Oakland, 66; First Award, Scottsdale Nat Indian Exhib, 67; First Award, Heard Mus Guild Exhib, Phoenix, 68; Humanitarian Award Fine Art, Harvard Univ, 86. *Bibliog:* Robert A Ewing (auth), An Indian artist & hist art-this is Gorman, NMex Mag, 71; Phil Valdez (auth), R C Gorman: The Picasso of American Indian Artists, Colo Mountain Journal, 5/25/83; Tricia Hurst (auth), R C Gorman: The saga continues, Taos Lifestyle 8/86; Jim Clark & M J Miller (auths), The One, The Only R C Gorman, Fine Arts Collector, 8/91; Susan Gaines (auth), Under the Magic Mountain, US Art, 4/92. *Mem:* Taos Art Asn. *Media:* Acrylic, Oil, Pastel. *Specialty:* Southwest art; Indian painters. *Interests:* Modern Indian painters. *Collection:* F Scholder, Tavlos, Pletka, C Counter, C Bissell, C Lovato, C Cannon, Kin-ya-onny Beyeh & Bob Hoasous. *Publ:* Contribr, 23 contemporary Indian artists, Art in Am, 72; contribr, American deserts, Nat Geog Mag, 72. *Dealer:* Jamison Galleries 111 E San Francisco Santa Fe NM 87501; Mary Livingston Gallery II 1211 N Broadway Santa Ana CA 92701. *Mailing Add:* Navajo Gallery PO Box 1756 Taos NM 87571

GORMAN, WILLIAM D
PAINTER, GRAPHIC ARTIST
b Jersey City, NJ, June 27, 25. *Study:* Newark Sch Fine & Indust Arts, NJ. *Work:* Newark Mus; Butler Inst Am Art, Youngstown, Ohio; Montclair Art Mus, NJ; Colorado Springs Fine Art Ctr; US Dept State, Washington, DC. *Exhib:* One-man shows, Philadelphia Art Alliance, 65 & Acad Ctr, State NJ Dept Educ, 86; US Dept State Art in Embassies Prog, Europe, Africa & Orient, 67-75; NJ Artists, Newark Mus, 68; US Watercolor Invitational; Seven American Watercolorists, Davenport Mus, Iowa, 73; Int Waters, Canada/US/UK, 91-93; plus others. *Pos:* Dir, Old Bergen Art Guild, Bayonne, NJ, 62- *Teaching:* Art programs & critiques. *Awards:* Strathmore Award, Allied Artists Am, 85; Mary Lou FitzGerald Award, Allied Artists Am, 91; Mary S Litt Medal, Am Watercolor Soc, 92; plus others. *Bibliog:*

Henry Gasser (auth), article in Am Artist, 10/70. *Mem:* Audubon Artists; Am Watercolor Soc (1st vpres, 81-86 & pres, 86-); Allied Artists Am (past pres); Nat Soc Painters Casein & Acrylic; NJ Water Color Soc (past pres); and others. *Media:* Casein Tempera; Pen & Ink. *Publ:* Auth, articles in Today's Art Mag & Am Artist. *Mailing Add:* 43 W 33rd St Bayonne NJ 07002

GORNEY, JAY PHILIP
GALLERIST
b Brooklyn, NY, Sept 26, 52. *Study:* Oberlin Col, with Ellen H Johnson, BA(art hist), 73; Whitney Mus Independent Study Prog, fall 72. *Collections Arranged:* New Biomorphism and Automatism, Hamilton Gallery, 83; Post Style, Wolff Gallery, 85; and many other collections in US & abroad. *Pos:* Pres, Jay Gorney Mod Art, New York, currently. *Bibliog:* Articles in New York Mag 6/25/90 & Flash Art Int, No 154, 10/90. *Res:* Contemporary painting, drawing and sculpture. *Publ:* Auth, Oberlin's tribute to Ellen Johnson, Art News, 4/75; Review of drawing today in New York, Col Art J, winter 76/77; article, East Village galleries, Washington Post, 2/85. *Mailing Add:* 100 Greene St New York NY 10012

GORNIK, APRIL
PAINTER
b Cleveland, Ohio, April 20, 53. *Study:* Cleveland Inst Art, 71-75; NS Col Art & Design, FBA, 76. *Work:* NS Art Bank, Halifax; Chase Manhattan Permanent Collection, London, Eng. *Exhib:* One-person exhibs, Univ Colo Art Galleries, Boulder, 82, New Gallery Contemp Art, Cleveland, Ohio, 84, Texas Gallery, Houston, 84, Galerie Springer, Berlin, 85, Sable-Castelli Gallery, Toronto, Can, 85 & 88, Univ Art Mus, Calif State Univ, Long Beach, 88 & Edward Thorp Gallery, New York, 90 & 92; Public and Private: American Prints Today, 24th Nat Print Exhib, Brooklyn Mus, New York, 86; Spectrum, Natural Settings, Corcoran Gallery Art, Washington, DC, 86; A View of Nature, Aldrich Mus Contemp Art, Ridgefield, Conn, 87; The New Romantic Landscape, Whitney Mus Am Art, Stamford, Conn, 87; Nocturnal Visions in Contemporary Painting, Whitney Mus Am Art at Equitable Ctr, New York, 89; Biennial Exhib, Whitney Mus Am Art, New York, 89; Harmony & Discord: American Landscape Today, Va Mus Fine Arts, Richmond, 90; Art on Paper, Weatherspoon Art Gallery, Univ NC, Greensboro, 91; Romance and Irony in Recent American Art, Parrish Art Mus, Southampton, NY, 91; Selective Vision, Transamerica Pyramid Lobby, San Francisco, 92; Gallery Group, Edward Thorp Gallery, New York, 92; Four Friends, Aldrich Mus Contemp Art, Ridgefield, Conn, 92; and others. *Bibliog:* Kristine MdKenna (auth), The allure of the dark side, Los Angeles Times, 5/20/90; John Yau (auth), rev, Artforum, 9/90; Robert C Edelman (auth), Le Paysage dans la Peinture, Art Press, 3/91; and others. *Media:* Oil. *Mailing Add:* c/o Edward Thorp Gallery 103 Prince St New York NY 10012

GORNY, A-P (ANTHONY-PETER)
CONCEPTUAL ARTIST, ILLUMINATOR
b Buffalo, NY, May 3, 50. *Study:* Univ Siena & Inst del'Arte, Italy, 70-71, State Univ NY, Buffalo, BFA, 72; Sch Art, Yale Univ, MFA, 74. *Work:* Solomon R Guggenheim Mus, New York; Victoria & Albert Mus, London, UK; Albright-Knox Art Gallery, Buffalo; Philadelphia Mus Art; Brooklyn Mus, NY; Los Angeles Co Mus; Cleveland Mus Art, Ohio. *Comn:* Print image, Bookworks--Int Paper Conf, Philadelphia, 82; print ed, Philadelphia Chamber Orchestra, Pa, 85; print ed, Philadelphia Mus Art Friends, 88; Print Club of Rochester Mem Art Gallery, NY, 91. *Exhib:* Impressions: Experimental Prints, Va Mus Fine Arts, Inst Contemp Art, Richmond, 84; The Sympathy of All Things, Pa Acad Fine Arts Mus, Philadelphia, 84; Prints Ensvite, Caramoor Ctr Music & Art, Katonah, NY & Pratt Graphics Manhattan Ctr Gallery, New York, 85; New Horizons in American Art 1985, Nat Exxon Exhib, 85 & Emerging Artists 1978-1986: Selections from the Exxon Series, 86, Solomon R Guggenheim Mus, New York; American Graphic Arts: Watercolors, Drawings and Prints, Pa Acad Fine Arts, Philadelphia, 86; Made in Philadelphia 7, Inst Contemp Art, Univ Pa, Philadelphia, 87. *Pos:* Cur, Quiet Mus, Philadelphia, 78- *Teaching:* Assoc prof prints-photog-drawing, Tyler Sch Art, Temple Univ, Philadelphia, 74-81; fac, prints, Fleisher Art Mem, Philadelphia Mus Art, 86-; assoc prof photog & performance art, Univ Arts, Philadelphia, 89-; fac, Bryn Mawr Col, Pa, 92. *Awards:* Individual Artists Fel Grant, Nat Endowment Arts, 89-90; Int Arts Grant, Pa Coun Arts, 91; Pew Charitable Trusts Proj Grant, 91; and others. *Bibliog:* Barry Walker (auth), American Artist as Printmaker, Brooklyn Mus, 83; Lisa Dennison (auth), New Horizons in Art 1985: Nat Exxon Exhib, Guggenheim Found, 85; Janet Kardon & Judith Tannenbaum (auths), Made in Philadelphia 7, Inst Contemp Art, Univ, Pa, 87. *Mem:* Am Col Art Asn; Friends of Penland; Citizens for Am Way; Asn Independent Scholars; Inst Contemp Art Friends, Philadelphia, Pa. *Media:* Mixed Media. *Publ:* Auth, It's Another Thing All Together, Falcon Press, 78; Re: Pages Contemporary Bookworks, NEng Found Arts, 80; contribr, New American Photographs, Calif State Col, San Bernadino, 82; Emerging Artists 1978-1986, Selections from the Exxon Series, Guggenheim Found, 86; Searching Out the Best: 1978-1988, Pa Acad Fine Arts, 88. *Dealer:* Dolan/Maxwell Gallery 1701 Walnut St Philadelphia PA 191062. *Mailing Add:* 102 N Second St Philadelphia PA 19106

GOROVE, MARGARET JOAN
ADMINISTRATOR, EDUCATOR
b New York, NY, Aug 30, 35. *Study:* Art Students League, with Sternberg, 53-59; Manhattanville Col, BA, 57; Univ Miss, MFA, 68. *Work:* Univ Museums, Oxford, Miss; Wood Gallery, Hattiesburg, Miss; and pvt collections in NY, Miss, Ala, Tenn, Washington, DC, Va. *Exhib:* Solo exhib, Kottler Gallery, New York, 69; Who's Who in Traditional Am Art, Stanford Wright Gallery, New York, 70, 73 & 75; Mid-South Competition, Brooks Mus, Memphis, 72; Teachers Touch, Miss Mus Art, Jackson, 78; Miss Juried Artists Exhib, C W Woods Gallery, Univ Southern Miss, 86. *Pos:* Coordr humanities sessions, Int Astronautical Fedn, 78-83; Artists Series, 81-84; chmn, minority fac recruitment, Univ Miss, 84-88, Fin Comn Fac Senate, 89-92; accreditation comn, Nat Asn Sch Art & Design, 86-91, futures comt, 88-92, vpres & pres elect, 91-; dir, Bryant Galleries, 78- *Teaching:* Prof art, Univ Miss, 69-, chairperson dept art, 76- *Awards:* Grand Prize, Miss Juried Competition, 86. *Mem:* Southeastern Col Art Conf (pres, 81, bd dires, 90-92); Miss Inst Arts & Lett (bd dirs, 81-84); Nat Asn Schs Art & Design (accrediting comn, 84-89, futures comt, 88-90, vpres, 91-93 & pres, 93-96); Col Arts Asn; Nat Coun Arts Adminrs. *Media:* Mixed. *Res:* Interdisciplinary aspects of art, especially as it relates to developments in space technology. *Publ:* Auth, Impact of the Computer on Society: A Personal View from the World of Art, Chap V, Society and the Computer: Some Humanistic Perspectives, Univ Press Miss, 79; Emerging trends: Humanities & technology, Proceedings Int Astronautical Fedn, 35th ann meeting, Lausanne, Switz, 84 & Malaga, Spain, 89; coauth, Futures Work, Nat Asn Sch Art & Design, 90-92; Sourcebook & Supplements, 90-92. *Mailing Add:* Dept Art Univ Miss University MS 38677

GORSKI, DANIEL ALEXANDER
PAINTER, SCULPTOR
b Cleveland, Ohio, Oct 26, 39. *Study:* Cleveland Inst Art, dipl, 61; Yale Univ Sch Art & Archit, with Jack Tworkow & Al Held, BFA, 62 & MFA, 64. *Work:* Yale Univ. *Exhib:* Primary Structures, Jewish Mus, New York, 66; Cool Art, Larry Aldrich Mus, Ridgefield, Conn, 68; Hanging and Leaning, Emily Lowe Gallery, Hofstra Univ, 70; 26 x 26, Vassar Col Art Gallery, 71; Md Biennial Exhib, Baltimore Mus of Art, 76; Sculpture Outdoors, Temple Univ, Ambler, Pa, 77-80; Elements Style Artscape, Baltimore, Md, 86; Themes and Variations: Cubism, Artscape, Baltimore, Md, 87. *Teaching:* Artist/adminr, Glassell Sch Art; instr & dir, Mus Fine Art, Houston, Tex. *Awards:* Mr & Mrs Jules Horelick Award, Baltimore Mus of Art, 76; Ford Found Grant, Shelter Inst, summer 79; A Mellon Grant, 84; AICA Grant, 85; City Arts Grant, 87. *Bibliog:* L Lippard (auth), Recent sculpture as escape, 2/66 & Escalation in Washington, 1/68, Art Int; U Kalterman (auth), The New Sculpture, Praeger, 68. *Dealer:* Franz Bader Gallery Washington DC. *Mailing Add:* 4134 Blue Bonnet Blvd Houston TX 77025

GORSKI, RICHARD KENNY
EDUCATOR, GRAPHIC ARTIST
b Green Bay, Wis, Apr 20, 23. *Study:* Northern Ill Univ, De Kalb, 62-65; Univ Wis, Milwaukee & Madison, MS(art educ), 50. *Work:* Milwaukee Pub Schs collection of Wis Artists. *Exhib:* Wisconsin Painters & Sculptors, Wis Union Gallery, Madison, 39, 47, 49 & 53-56; Milwaukee Art Inst, 40, 46, 47, 49, 50, 53, 55-57 & 60; Walker Art Inst, 47 & 49. *Pos:* Cur & dir, Rahr Civic Ctr & Mus, Manitowoc, Wis, 50-53; illusr & designer, John Higgs Studios, Milwaukee, Wis, 56-57; art dir, United Educators Publ Inc, Lake Bluff, Ill, 60-61; dept head, art & design, Northern Mich Univ, Marquette, 65-75. *Teaching:* Instr art educ, Nat Col of Educ, Evanston, Ill, 57-60; assoc prof art educ, Northeastern Ill Univ, Chicago, 61-65; prof graphic design, visual commun, Northern Mich Univ, Marquette, 65- *Awards:* Journal Purchase Award, Wis Painters Ann, Milwaukee J Pub Schs Collection, 57; Special Merit Award, Wis Gimbels Salon, Gimbels Inc, 50. *Mem:* Graphic Design Educators Asn. *Res:* Structural basis of visual communication. *Publ:* Auth, Color; an article in United Educators Encycl & auth, Painting; an article in The Wonderland of Knowledge Encycl, United Educ Publ, 60. *Mailing Add:* 1502 N Garfield Ave Marquette MI 49855

GOSSAGE, JOHN RALPH
PHOTOGRAPHER
b New York, NY, Mar 15, 46. *Study:* Waldon Sch, 67-69. *Work:* Mus Mod Art, New York; Houston Mus Fine Art; San Francisco Mus Art; Philadelphia Mus Art; George Eastman House, Rochester, NY. *Comn:* Nation's Capitol in Photographs, Corcoran Gallery, 76; Photography in America, AT&T, New York, 78; Photography and the City, Seattle Art Comn, 79. *Exhib:* 14 American Photographers, Baltimore Mus & travelling, 75; solo exhibs, Castelli Gallery, New York, 76 & Lunn Gallery, Washington, DC, 80; 10th Biennale Paris, Mus Mod Art, France, 77; Contemporary Photographic Works, Houston Mus Fine Arts, 77; Gardens, Werkstalt Photog, Berlin, 78; Photography & Sense of Order, Inst Contemp Art, Philadelphia, 81; History of Portrait Photography, Mus Art, Bonn, Ger, 82. *Pos:* Vpres, Columbia Arts Inc, 82- *Teaching:* Assoc prof photog & art, Univ Md, 77- *Awards:* Grants, Stern Fund, 74 & Nat Endowment Arts, 74 & 78. *Bibliog:* Renato Dansse (auth), American Images, McGraw Hill, 79. *Publ:* Auth, Gardens, Castelli Graphics, 78; The Pond, Aperture Publ, 84. *Dealer:* Castelli Uptown 4 E 77 St New York NY 10021. *Mailing Add:* c/o Jones Troyer Fitzpatrick 1614 20th St NW Washington DC 20009

GOTO, JOSEPH
SCULPTOR
b Hilo, Hawaii, Jan 7, 20. *Study:* Art Inst Chicago; Roosevelt Univ. *Work:* Art Inst Chicago; Detroit Mus; Mus Mod Art, New York. *Comn:* Mus Art, Carnegie Inst, Pittsburgh, Pa. *Exhib:* Art Inst Chicago; Rhode Island Sch Design Mus Art, Providence; Whitney Mus Am Art, New York; Retrospective, RI Sch Design, 72; solo exhibs, Honolulu Acad, 73, Contemp Arts Ctr Hawaii, Honolulu, 73 & Zabriskie Gallery, 73; Canton Art Inst, Canton, Ohio; Lincoln Ctr, New York; John Herron Mus Art, Indianapolis, Ind; Undine Project Mus, Undine, Italy. *Teaching:* Prof Sculpture, Carnegie Mellon Univ, 58 & Brandeis Univ, 70; asst prof art, Univ Mich, 59-63, RI Sch Design, 63-65 & Richmond Prof Inst; lectr, Univ Ill, 65. *Awards:* Graham Found Fel, 57; John Hay Whitney Fel; Guggenheim Fel, 69; The Palmer Prize for Sculpture; The Blair Prize for Sculpture; Grant sculpture, Pollock-Krasner Found Inc, 86. *Mailing Add:* 17 Sixth St Providence RI 02906

GOTTLIEB, CARLA
EDUCATOR, HISTORIAN
b Cernauti, Bukovina, July 16, 12; US citizen. *Study:* Oltea Doamna, Cernauti, BA, 29; Carolina Univ, Cernauti, MA, 34, PhD 36; Columbia Univ, with Rensselaer Lee, Meyer Schapiro & Charles de Tolnay, PhD, 51. *Pos:* Interviewer fels, Am Asn Univ Women, 56-60; consult, F L Schwarz Col, NY & Paris, 65-70, S J Lefrak Col, NY, 67-73. *Teaching:* Asst, Bryn Mawr Col, 54-56; fac mem hist art, New Sch Soc Res, 56-60; vis prof, Sarah Lawrence Col, 58-59, Carleton Univ, Ottawa, 72; chmn dept, Ripon Col, 60-62; assoc prof, Univ Ill, Urbana-Champaign, 62-64. *Awards:* Am Philos Soc, 53 & 54; Am Coun Learned Soc, 60; Universidad Nacional Autonoma de Medico, 77. *Bibliog:* Lexikon der christlichen Ikonographie, Herder, 68; Woerterbuch der Symbolik, Kroner, 83 & 85; L S Katz & B Katz (auth), Writer's Choice: A Library of Rediscovery, Reston, 83. *Mem:* Am Asn Retired Persons; Nat Retired Teachers Asn; Gray Panthers. *Res:* Modern and contemporary history of art; Greek architecture; symbolic and expressive meaning of motifs; art history and law; the window; death. *Publ:* Auth, The Escape through the Window: A Figura for Christ's Victory over Death, Dumont, 73; Beyond Modern Art, E P Dutton, 76, 81, 83 & 86; Self-Portraiture in Post Modern Art, Dumont, 80; The Window as a Symbol: From Divinity to Doubt, Boian, 93; Self-Portraiture: From Ancient Egypt to World War II, Boian, 93. *Mailing Add:* 246 West End Ave 10B New York NY 10023

GOTTSCHALK, FRITZ
DESIGNER, LECTURER
b Zurich, Switz, Dec 30, 37. *Study:* Kunstgewerbeschule, Zurich, Switz, dipl; Art Inst Orell Fussli, Zurich, dipl; Allgemeine Gewerbeschule, Basel, Switz, post-grad dipl, with E Ruder & A Hofmann. *Exhib:* The Visual Image of the Montreal Mus, Montreal Mus Fine Arts, Que, Can, 68; Swiss Design, Mus du Louvre, Paris, France, 71; Alliance Graphique Internationale: 107 Int Designers, Milan, Italy, 74; The Work of Gottschalk & Ash Ltd, Ryder Gallery, sponsored by Container Corp of Am, Chicago, 76. *Pos:* Designer art & design dir, Gottschalk & Ash Int, Meilen, Zurich, Switz, 77-; dir design & quality control off, Organizing Comt of 1976 Olympic Games, 74-76. *Awards:* Award of Excellence, Swiss Contemp Design, Dept of Interior, Swiss Govt, 62; two Awards of Excellence, Soc Publ Designers, New York, 70; Bronze Medal, Foire Int du Livre, Leipzig, EGer, 77. *Bibliog:* Adrian Gatrail (auth), The Image Makers, The Gazette, Can, 70; Bill Bantey (auth), Gottschalk & Ash Ltd, Graphis, Switz, Vol 148 (1972); Midori Imatake (auth), Gottschalk & Ash Ltd, Idea (Japan), Vol 115 (1973). *Mem:* Que Soc Graphic Artists; Royal Can Acad; Asn of Swiss Graphic Artists; Alliance Graphique Inter; Graphic Designers Can. *Media:* Graphic Design, Books and Corporate Images. *Publ:* Auth & illusr, article, Idea, Seibundo Shinkosha Publ Co, Japan, Vol 115, 72; ed, article, Revue Suisse de l'Imprimerie, Zollikofer AG, Switz, 74; illusr & contribr, article, Communication Arts, Coyne & Blanchard, Inc, 75; ed, article, Graphis, Vol 185, 77. *Mailing Add:* Sonnhaldenstrasse 3 Zurich Switzerland

GOTTSCHALK, MAX JULES
DESIGNER, INSTRUCTOR
b St Louis, Mo, Dec 14, 09. *Study:* Painting, drawing & design with father, Max Gottschalk, also with Edmond Wurpel, Charles Quest, Fred Conway, E Ludwig, Goetsh, Hudson & Mylonas; Wash Univ, BA. *Work:* Agnese Udinotti, Scottsdale, Ariz; Robert Graham, New York; Dr Louis Gottschalk, Corona del Mar; Jeffrey Boehm, Ariz; Stan Schuman, Tucson. *Comn:* Nat indigenous product form, Newfoundland Comn Govt, 39-42; Scott Paper Towel Holder, Gerald C Johnson Assocs, New York, 44-48; new modular chassis systs, Hughes Aircraft, Tucson, Ariz, 52-60; first open frozen food refrigeration, electronic checkout, Hussmann Ligonier Co, St Louis; work on lunar escape vehicle, air cushion vehicle, Bell Aerosysts, Niagara Falls, NY; New Air Distribution Systems, Krueger Manufacturing, Tucson, 70-80; New Furniture Designs, Tucson, 70-89; New Chassis Systems, Burr Brown, Tucson, 75-79. *Exhib:* St Louis Artist Guild, 35 & St Louis Art Mus, 36, Mo; St John's, Nfld, 40-42; Mus Mod Art, New York, 48-50; Int Canvas Exhib, Tokyo, 75; Pima Col, Rosequist Wohlheim Gallery, Tucson; Udinotti Gallery, Los Angeles & San Francisco, Calif & Scottsdale, Ariz; and others. *Pos:* Pres Imagineering & vpres, Max Gottschalk Inc, currently; consult, Max's Enterprises & Max Rax. *Teaching:* Instr design, drawing & perception & chmn art & design dept, Pima Community Col, Tucson, 70-91, instr functional design, interior decoration & graphics & chmn design, decorating & drafting dept, 75, chmn, applied design dept, 81. *Mem:* Life mem Soc Audio Engineers. *Media:* Line drawings; contemporary and functional; products for industry. *Dealer:* Agnese Udinotti Scottsdale AZ; The Contemporary Craftsman 112 Don Gaspar Santa Fe NM. *Mailing Add:* 5620 N Campbell Tucson AZ 85718

GOUGH, GEORGIA BELLE
CRAFTSMAN, EDUCATOR
b Oklahoma City, Okla, Dec 21, 20. *Study:* Central State Univ, Okla, BS, 41; Univ NTex, MS, 45; with Carlton Ball, 48; with Daniel Rhodes, 54; Univ Okla, PhD, 60. *Work:* Campbell Mem Collection, Am Craft Mus, New York. *Comn:* Wall hanging, comn by Greater Denton Arts Coun, Festival Hall Ctr Visual Arts. *Exhib:* Syracuse Mus, NY, 51 & 56; Wichita Decorative Arts & Crafts, Wichita Mus, Kans, 50, 51 & 53; Miami Nat Ceramic Exhib, Fla, 56; Dallas Craft Market, Tex, 81 & 82; Handmade in Tex, 87; A Decade of Dallas Crafts, 88. *Teaching:* Prof ceramics, NTex State Univ, 47-75, prof emeritus art dept, currently. *Awards:* Third Place, Tex Fine Arts Asn, 53. *Mem:* Am Craft Coun (trustee, 76-80); Nat Coun Educ Ceramic Arts (secy, 70-73); Am Ceramic Soc Design Sect Southwest Region (pres & secy); World Crafts Coun (US delegate, 78 & 80); hon mem, Tex Designer-Craftsmen. *Publ:* Auth, Use of native clays in high-grade pottery, Ceramic Industry, 53; Computer data processing system calculations of glaze formulae, Am Ceramic Soc Bulletin, 65. *Mailing Add:* 1813 Willowwood N T Station Denton TX 76201

GOUGH, ROBERT ALAN
PAINTER
b Quebec, PQ, Aug 13, 31; US citizen. *Study:* Am Acad Art, Chicago, with William H Mosby & J Allen St John. *Work:* Am Fedn Arts; Butler Inst Am Art; Univ Nebr; Sheldon Swope Art Gallery; Marietta Col. *Exhib:* Painting & Sculpture Today, Herron Mus Art, 66; one-man shows, Gilman Galleries, Chicago, 67 & 69; 35 Years in Retrospect, Butler Inst Am Art, 71; Mainstreams, Marietta Col, 74, 75 & 77; Art from Appalachia Traveling Exhib, Smithsonian Inst, 81-; and others. *Awards:* Henry Ward Ranger Purchase Prize, Nat Acad Design, 62; Judges Award, Marietta Nat, 78; Ohioana Libr Asn Citation, 81. *Bibliog:* Documentary, WBNS-TV, Columbus, Ohio, 70. *Media:* Oil, Pencil. *Dealer:* Foster Harmon Galleries Am Art 1415 Main St Sarasota FL 33577; Harmon Gallery 1258 Third St S Naples FL 33940. *Mailing Add:* 220 Brookside Dr Chillicothe OH 45601

GOULD, JOHN HOWARD
PAINTER, FILMMAKER
b Toronto, Ont, Aug 14, 29. *Study:* Ont Col Art, AOCA, 52; Acad Julian, Paris, 52. *Work:* Nat Gallery Can; Montreal Mus Fine Arts; Beaverbrook Mus, Fredericton, NB; and others in pvt collections. *Comn:* Portrait of Alan Jarvis, Head of Nat Gallery Can, Ottawa, 62; Pikangikum (drawn film of Indians), Nat Film Bd Can, 67; performance drawings of Marcel Marceau, City Ctr, New York, 71. *Exhib:* Canadian Surrealism Today, touring exhib, 64; Focus on Drawing, Int Drawing Survey, 65 & The Work of Art, 79, Art Gallery Toronto; retrospectives, Univ Toronto, 65, The Drawn Image, traveling, 79 & Stratford Festival, 92; Can rep, Films on Art Category, Venice Biennale, 66; Flint Inst Arts Survey Exhib, 66. *Teaching:* Instr life drawing, Ont Col Art, Toronto, currently. *Awards:* Greenshield Award Figurative Painting, Spain, 60; Can Coun Grants, Drawn Film of Peru, 67 & Drawn Film of Japan, 70. *Bibliog:* John Griffin (dir), John Gould on Drawing (film), Gesture Productions, 72; incl in The Nude in Canadian Painting, New Press, Can, 72; The Drawn Image, Roberts Gallery, 79. *Mem:* Royal Can Acad. *Dealer:* Roberts Gallery 641 Yonge St Toronto ON M4Y 1Z9 Can. *Mailing Add:* Moonstone 100 McCaul St Toronto ON L0K 1N0 Canada

GOULD, KAREN KEEL
WRITER, CONSULTANT
b Austin, Tex, Sept 26, 46. *Study:* Univ Tex, Austin, BS, 68, MA, 70, PhD, 75. *Teaching:* Vis asst prof art hist, Univ Ore, 80; Mellon Fel, Duke Univ, 80-81; lectr hist, Univ Tex, Austin, 81-89. *Mem:* Col Art Asn; Int Ctr Medieval Art (mem adv bd, 81-83); Southeastern Medieval Asn (mem exec coun, 81-83); Medieval Acad Am; Bibliographical Soc Am. *Res:* Manuscript illumination; history of manuscripts & printed books. *Publ:* The Psalter and Hours of Yolande of Soissons, Medieval Acad, 78; Sequences De Sanctis Reliquiis as Sainte-Chapelle Inventories, Medieval Studies, 81; Terms for book production in a Latin-English nominale, Papers of the Bibliographical Soc Am; The Recovery of a Fifteenth-Century Book of Hours, HRC 2, Scriptorium, 89; Jean Pucelle and Northern Gothic Art, Art Bull, 92. *Mailing Add:* 2602 La Ronde Austin TX 78731

GOULD, PHILIP
HISTORIAN, EDUCATOR
b New York, NY, Oct 17, 22. *Study:* NY Univ, BA, 49; L'Univ Paris, Dr Univ, 53. *Collections Arranged:* Traditional Anatolian Kilims (coauth, catalog), 86, Artists from China - New Expressionism, 87, Sarah Lawrence Col Art Gallery. *Teaching:* Instr art hist, Columbia Univ, 54-59, lectr, 56-62; prof, Sarah Lawrence Col, 59-92 (ret); vis prof, Fordham Univ, spring 68, Pratt Inst, fall 73 & Col Chinese Cult, Taipei, Taiwan, 75-76. *Awards:* Sapirstein lect, Cooper-Hewitt Mus, Smithsonian Inst, 87; UN Develop Prog, Sr Tech Adv, Beijing Teacher's Col, PRC, 89; Elected Assoc Mem, Columbia Univ Sem: Traditional China, 92-95. *Bibliog:* Nick Natanson (auth), The craft of teaching, Sarah Lawrence Col Bulletin, spring 83. *Mem:* Soc Archit Historians; Am Soc Aesthet. *Res:* Chinese art in general and comparative occidental and Oriental iconography in particular. *Publ:* Contribr, Encycl Am, 58; New Cath Encycl, 64; auth, Exhibition of Chinese Painting, Ming & Ch'ing (catalog), 73 & Exhibition of Chinese Folk & Provincial Ceramics (catalog), 76, Sarah Lawrence Col; contribr, Acad Am Encycl, 80; auth, Jan van Eyck's Arnolfini Wedding Portrait: The mirror image, In: Iris, Notes Hist Art, Vol 2, 12/83. *Mailing Add:* 15 Claremont Ave New York NY 10027

GOULD, STEPHEN
SCULPTOR, COLLECTOR
b New York, NY, Dec 25, 09. *Study:* New Sch Social Res, with Manola Pascal; Geneva Theological Col, Hon DFA, 69, World Univ, Hon DFA, 71. *Work:* Newark Mus, NJ; Morris Mus Fine Art, NJ; Miami Mus Mod Art, Fla; Washington Co Mus Fine Arts, Hagerstown, Md; Allen R Hite Art Inst, Univ Louisville. *Exhib:* Nat Exhib Prof Artists, New York, 65; New Sch Social Res, 67; Nat Soc Arts & Lett, Seamans Bank, NY, 69; Nat Coun Jewish Women, South Orange, NJ, 71; Salmagundi Club, 75; Nat Soc Arts & Letters Exhib, Metrop Mus Art, New York, 79. *Pos:* Art lectr, Bermuda Club, Tamarac, Fla, 74-; Arts & Cult Comt, City Lauderhill, Fla, 88-; Arts & Cult Comt, City of Lauderhill, Fla. *Awards:* Award of Month for Heart of Humanity, Washington Co Mus Art, 70; First Prize for I Protest (bronze sculpture), Soc l'Ecole Francais, 71-72; First Prize for We are the Clay & Thou Lord our Potter, De Bellis, Salmagundi Club, 75. *Bibliog:* M Pescara (auth), Sculptor-Stephen Gould, Am Rev Art & Sci, 69. *Mem:* Royal Soc Arts; Nat Soc Arts & Lett. *Media:* Clay. *Collection:* Oils, French impressionist and post impressionist; prints, lithographs, watercolors, numismatics, glass; violin and bow collection; depicting human events rather than art objects. *Mailing Add:* 7400 Radice Ct Lauderhill FL 33319-6604

GOULDS, PETER J
DEALER, DESIGNER
b London, Eng, Oct 5, 48. *Study:* Walthamstow Sch Art, Eng, 65-67; Coventry Sch Art, Eng, 67-70; Sch Advan Studies, Manchester Polytech, Shell Fel, 72. *Pos:* Owner, LA Louver Gallery, Venice, Calif, 76- *Teaching:* Lectr commun design, Leeds Polytech, Yorkshire, Eng, 72; vis lectr video workshop & design, Univ Calif, Los Angeles, 72-75; vis lectr, Calif Inst Arts, 75-76. *Awards:* Leverhulme Award, Uni-Lever Trust, 71; Univ Res Grants, Univ Calif, 72-74. *Specialty:* Contemporary American and European painting & sculpture. *Mailing Add:* c/o LA Louver Gallery 55 N Venice Blvd Venice CA 90291

GOULET, CLAUDE
EDUCATOR, PAINTER
b Montreal, Que, June 5, 25. *Study:* Univ Montreal, LScBioChem, 48. *Work:* Mus Montreal, Que; Mus Que, Montreal; Nat Gallery Can, Ottawa; Cult Art Ctr Can, Paris; Contemp Art Mus, Montreal; Calgary Allied Art Ctr, Can. *Exhib:* Third Int Exhib, Cagnes-sur-Mer, France, 71; Can Cult Ctr, Paris, 71-87; Zwarte Panter Gallery, Anvers, Belg, 72; Neuilly-sur-Seine, Paris, 74; Galerie G Wolf, Deauville, France, 75. *Teaching:* Instr art environment, Univ Que, 75-90. *Awards:* Can Art Coun Grant, 70; Min Cult Affairs Grant, Prov Que, 71; Nat Prize, 3rd Int Festival, Cagnes-sur-Mer, France, 71. *Bibliog:* Articles, Vie Des Arts, 77; 16 Painters of Quebec in Their Environment. *Mem:* Royal Can Acad; Asn Prof Artists, Que (vpres, 65-69); Can Soc Artists. *Media:* Oil, Acrylic. *Mailing Add:* 15160 Notre-Dame Est Pointe Aux Trembles PQ H1A 1W6 Canada

GOULET, LORRIE
SCULPTOR, PAINTER
b Riverdale, NY, Aug 17, 25. *Study:* Inwood Potteries Studios, New York, 32-36, with Amiee Voorhees; Black Mountain Col, drawing & painting with Josef Albers; sculpture with Jose de Creeft, 43-44. *Work:* Sarah Roby Found; Joseph H Hirshhorn Mus & Sculpture Garden, Washington, DC; NJ State Mus; Nat Mus Women in the Arts, DC; Ball State Univ Art Gallery. *Comn:* Ceramic relief, New York Pub Libr, Grand Concourse, Bronx, 58; ceramic relief, Nurses' Residence & Sch, Bronx Munic Hosp, 61; stainless steel relief, 48th Precinct Police & Fire Sta, Bronx, 71. *Exhib:* Dimensions 69, Temple Emeth, NJ, 69; Outdoor Sculpture Show, Van Saun Park, NJ, 71; one-artist shows, Contemporaries Gallery, New York, 59, 62, 66 & 68, Kennedy Galleries, New York, 71, 73-75, 78, 80 & 83-86 & Retrospective, Carolyn Hill Gallery, 88; Summit Art Ctr, NJ, 78; Nat Arts Club, New York, 78; plus many other group & one-man shows. *Pos:* Guest demonstr, Around the Corner, New York Dept Educ, CBS-TV, 64-65. *Teaching:* Instr sculpture-var media & staff mem, Mus Mod Art, New York, 57-64; sculpture staff mem, Scarsdale Studio Workshop, 59-61 & New Sch Social Res, 61-75; staff instr sculpture, Art Students League, New York, 81. *Awards:* First Sculpture Prize, Norton Gallery, 49 & 50 & Westchester Art Soc, 64; Soltan Engel Mem Award, Audubon Artists, 67. *Mem:* Sculptors Guild; Audubon Artists; founding mem Visual Artists & Galleries Asn; Nat Comt Art Educ; Nat Sculpture Soc; Nat Acad Design. *Media:* Stone, Wood; Acrylic. *Publ:* Contribr, 20th century sculptors look at their work, The Palette; auth article on greenstone, In: Slate & Soft Stones, 71. *Dealer:* Carolyn Hill Gallery 109 Sprint St New York NY 10012. *Mailing Add:* 241 W 20th St New York NY 10011

GOUMA-PETERSON, THALIA
EDUCATOR, HISTORIAN
b Athens, Greece, Nov 21, 33; US citizen. *Study:* Mills Col, BA(art), 54, MA(art hist), 57; Univ Wis, PhD(art hist), 63. *Pos:* Cur, Sculpture Outdoors, 82, Faith Ringgold Retrospective, 85; dir, Col of Wooster Art Mus, 85-; pres, Byzantine Studies Conf, 89-90; bd dir, Col Art Asn Am, 90-91. *Teaching:* Instr art hist, Univ Wis, 58 & Oberlin Col, 60-61; from asst prof to assoc prof, Col Wooster, 68-76, prof, 76- *Awards:* Fulbright Scholar; Nat Endowment Art Grant; Ohio Arts Coun Grant. *Mem:* Women's Caucus for Art (vpres, 82-84); Col Art Asn; Medieval Acad Am; Int Ctr of Medieval Art; Nat Comt Byzantine Studies (gov bd conf, 85-86). *Publ:* Piero della Francesca's Flagellation: An Historical Interpretation, Storia dell' Arte, Vol 28 (1976): 219-233; ed & coauth, Miriam Schapiro: A Retrospective 1953-1980, Col Wooster, 80; auth, Christ as Ministrant and the Priest as Ministrant Christ in a Palaeologan Program of 1303, Dumbarton Oaks Papers, 80; Art and social change, Art J, Vol 43 (1983): 202-208; Audrey Flack, Vol 58 (1983): 136-141 & Faith Ringgold's Narrative Quilts, 1/87, 64-69, Arts Mag; The Feminist Critique of Art History, Art Bull, Vol 69, 326- 357, 87; The Icon as Cultural Presence after 1453, Icon, 48-64, 68. *Mailing Add:* Art Dept Col of Wooster Wooster OH 44691

GOUREVITCH, JACQUELINE
PAINTER
b Paris, France, Oct 28, 33; US citizen. *Study:* Black Mountain Col, NC, 50; Art Students League, 52; Univ Chicago, BA, 54; Art Inst Chicago, 54-55. *Work:* Chase Manhattan Bank; Am Acad of Arts & Lett, New York; Univ NMex, Albuquerque; Wesleyan Univ, Middletown, Conn; Univ Art Mus, Berkeley, Calif; De Cordova Mus, Lincoln, Mass; Tamarind Inst, Albuquerque, NMex; Charles A Wustum Mus, Racine, Wisc. *Comn:* Conn Comn Arts, Western Conn State Univ, Danbury, 83. *Exhib:* One-woman shows, Tibor de Nagy Gallery, New York, 71, 72 & 73, Painting & Sculpture Today, Indianapolis Mus Art, 72, Wesleyan Univ, Conn, 74, 77 & 83, Wadsworth Atheneum, Hartford, Conn, 75 & Condeso-Lawler Gallery, New York, 80, 82 & 84; De Cordova Mus, Lincoln, Mass, 71 & 78; Whitney Mus Art Ann, 73; Galerie Marina Dinkler, Berlin, 88; Conn Gallery, Marlborough; Bruce Mus, Conn, 89; Maxwell Davidson, New York, 90. *Teaching:* lectr, Hartford Art Sch, Univ Hartford, 73-78; vis artist, Univ Calif, Berkeley, 74, Vassar Col, 77, Univ Houston, 78 & Yale Univ, 82; artist in residence, Wesleyan Univ, 78-88; Cooper Union, 89- *Awards:* Purchase Award, Am Acad Arts & Letts, New York, 73; grants, Nat Endowment Arts, 76 & Conn Comn Arts, 76. *Bibliog:* Andea Miller-Keller (auth), Notes on Notations Exhibition, Wadsworth Atheneum, 75; article, Art New England, 11/80; interview in Art New England, 11/80; John Paoletti (auth), Activated and tenacious: The art of Jacqueline Gourevitch, Arts Mag, 11/82. *Mem:* Col Art Asn; Women's Caucus for Art. *Media:* Oil. *Publ:* Auth, article, Art Now: New York, fall 71. *Mailing Add:* 120 Duane St New York NY 10007

GOUTMAN, DOLYA
EDUCATOR, PAINTER
b May 5, 18; US citizen. *Study:* Art Inst Chicago, BFA; Univ Pa, MFA. *Work:* Pa Acad Fine Arts; Phoenix Art Mus; Dallas Mus Art; Butler Inst Am Art; White House, Washington, DC. *Exhib:* Calgary Allied Arts Ctr; Univ BC; Univ Man; Massillon Mus, Ohio; Washington Co Mus Fine Arts, Md. *Teaching:* Head painting dept, Moore Col Art, formerly, prof, formerly. *Media:* Oil, Acrylic. *Mailing Add:* 314 Williams Rd Rosemont PA 19010

GOVAN, FRANCIS HAWKS
EDUCATOR, PAINTER
b Marianna, Ark, Dec 19, 16. *Study:* Hendrix Col, BA; Art Inst South, Memphis; Univ Wis; Layton Sch Art; Columbia Univ, MA; San Miguel, Mex. *Work:* Ark Art Ctr; Choo Gakuin Univ, Japan. *Exhib:* Am Watercolor Exhib, France, 53-55; one-man shows, Feigl Gallery, New York, 54-56; retrospective, Brooks Mem Art Gallery, Memphis, 57 & 66; Kunst Am, 57-58; Art in the Embassies & Smithsonian Inst, 67-68. *Pos:* Instr & occup therapist, Rockland State Hosp, Orangeburg, NY, 52-54; freelance artist, New York, 54-55; educ dir, Brooks Mem Art Gallery, 55-56; cur exhibs, Memphis State Univ, 57-67. *Teaching:* Instr art & creative dramatics, Milwaukee Univ Sch, 43-45; assoc prof art, Hendrix Col, 45-52; prof art, Memphis State Univ, 56-82; retired. *Awards:* First Prize in Watercolor, Memphis Biennial, 46; Carnegie Found Grants Res Art Pottery Clays, 49 & Mus Fine Art, 50. *Media:* Oil, Watercolor. *Publ:* Illusr, Arkansas pioneer days, Ark Gazette Sun Suppl, 48-49; auth, Art--what is it?, 59 & My last duchess, 65, Educ Quest. *Mailing Add:* 540 Hawthorne Memphis TN 38112

GOWANS, ALAN
HISTORIAN, LECTURER
b Toronto, Ont, Nov 30, 23; US citizen. *Study:* Univ Toronto, BA, 45, MA, 46; Princeton Univ, MFA, 48, PhD, 50. *Pos:* Dir, Univ Mus, Univ Vt, Burlington, 53-56. *Teaching:* Asst prof art hist, Rutgers Univ, 48-53; assoc prof early Am art, Univ Del, Newark, 56-66; prof archit hist, Univ Victoria, BC, 66-88. *Awards:* Hitchcock Award, Soc Archit Historians, 66. *Bibliog:* Don Thomson (producer), The Critical Eye, 11 progs, TV-Ont, 83-84. *Mem:* Soc Archit Historians (pres, 70-74). *Res:* Social function in modernism, architectural history and popular commercial arts. *Publ:* Auth, Images of American Living: Four Centuries of Architecture & Furniture in the US, Lippincott, 64, reprint, Harper & Row, 80; The Comfortable House: Surburban Architecture 1890-1930, MIT Cambridge, 86; Styles and Types of North American Architecture: Social Function and Cultural Expression, Harper Collins, 92; An Elevated State of Christian Civilization: American Mission Churches in Hawaii, HI State Hist Preservation Off, 92; World Civilizations: A History in Architecture, 94. *Mailing Add:* 524-2020 F St NW Washington DC 20006

GRABEL, SUSAN
SCULPTOR, CERAMIST
b Brooklyn, NY, June 5, 42. *Study:* Brooklyn Mus Art Sch, with Joseph Konzal & Tom Doyle, 61-65; Brooklyn Col, NY, Ba, 63. *Comn:* Ceramic mural, Staten Island Children's Mus, 91. *Exhib:* Witness of the Time, Urban Inst Contemp Arts, Grand Rapids, Mich, 89; Clayworks, Queensborough Community Col, Bayside, NY, 89; Women in the Visual Arts, 1990, Erector Sq Gallery, New Haven, Conn; Mayday, M'Aidez the Tallahassee Gallery, Fla, 90; one-women shows, Wagner Col Gallery, 90, Giving Shelter, Bauhaus, Baltimore, Md, 91, Women: Diversity & Vision, Art Lab Gallery, Sing Harbor Cult Ctr, Staten Island, NY, 92; and others. *Bibliog:* Grace Glueck (auth), Art: Sculptured figures of 70's at Pratt Gallery, 80 & Michael Brenson (auth), Portraits: Form & concept, 84, New York Times; William Zimmer (auth), Mansion and former factory offer varied views of women, NY Time, 90; Michael J Fressola (auth), Sculpture with a Cause, Staten Island Advance, 90; and others. *Mem:* Women's Caucus Art (pres, New York chapter, 92-94); Taking Art Heart. *Media:* Clay, Wood. *Publ:* Art as Activism issue, Woman of Power Mag, spring 87. *Mailing Add:* 257 Oakland Ave Staten Island NY 10310

GRADO, ANGELO JOHN
PAINTER, INSTRUCTOR
b New York, NY, Feb 17, 22. *Study:* Art Students League, with Robert Brackman; Nat Acad Design, with Robert Philipp & Frank Reilly. *Exhib:* Am Watercolor Soc Exhibs, 58-71; Allied Artists Am Exhibs, 61-78; Nat Acad Design, New York, 63; Am Artists Prof League, New York, 63-90; Hudson Valley Art Asn, 69-88; 14 one-man exhibs. *Teaching:* Pvt classes, Nat Art League. *Awards:* Salmagundi Club Prize, 69; Eleven Am Artists Prof League Awards, 69-81 & 83-85; Hudson Valley Art Asn Awards, 69, 70, 72 & 84-85; 20 Nat Awards. *Bibliog:* Billi Boros (auth), New talent, Art Times Mag, 64. *Mem:* Am Watercolor Soc; Am Artists Prof League (pres emer, 78-88); Hudson Valley Art Asn; Pastel Soc Am; Fine Arts Fedn New York. *Media:* Oil, Pastel. *Publ:* Auth, Mastering the Craft of Painting, Watson-Guptill Publ. *Dealer:* Harbor Gallery 24 W 57th St New York NY 10019; Alterman Art Gallery 2504 Cedar Springs Dallas TX 75201. *Mailing Add:* 641 46th St Brooklyn NY 11220

GRADY, RUBY MCLAIN
PAINTER, SCULPTOR
b Bedford Co, Va, Jan 11, 44. *Study:* Corcoran Sch Art, Washington, DC, with Richard Lahey; Md Univ, with Pietro Lazzari. *Work:* Am Fine Art Exhibs, Washington, DC; NASA Gemini Collection, Washington, DC; Imprimerie Arte Galerie Maeght, Paris, France; West Collection, St Paul, Minn. *Exhib:* Va Mus Art, Richmond; Washington Sq Sculpture Exhib, Pub Art Trust, Washington, DC, 84; Solo exhibs, Jack Rasmussen Gallery, DC, 79, Roanoke Fine Art Mus, Va, 80 & VVKR Atrium, Int Architect Firm, Alexandria, Va, 84; Chrysler Mus Biennial, 86; West Art and the Law (travel exhib), USA & Canada, 88-89; Shared Visions, IBM Gallery Sci & Art, New York, 90; Art in Public Places Sculpture, Rockville, Md, 92. *Pos:* Art illusr, FBI, Washington, DC, 56-59; exhib coord for 3 Washington, DC restaurants, 61-73; currently free-lance photographer. *Awards:* Annapolis Fine Arts Exhib Award for Metal Sculpture, 74; Washington Artist Photog Exhib, Corcoran Gallery, Washington, DC, 77; Two Purchase Awards, West Collection, St Paul, Minn, 82-87. *Bibliog:* Frank Getlein (introd), Ruby Grady, booklet, Brooks Johnson, 72; Allen Smith (dir), Solo Exhibit in Washington (film), WTTG-TV, 72; article, Am Bar Asn J, Chicago, 82. *Media:* Steel, Acrylic. *Publ:* Contribr, Nat Community Arts Prog Publ, Govt Printing Off, 70, & Art and the Law National Exhibition Book, West Publ, 82, 83 & 86; The West Collection, West Publ Co, St Paul, Minn, 87. *Mailing Add:* Potowmack Bay Studio 431 Broadcreek Dr Ft Washington MD 20744

GRAESE, JUDY (JUDITH ANN)
PAINTER, PRINTMAKER
b Loveland, Colo, Nov 8, 40. *Study:* Augustana Col, 58-59; Univ Colo, Boulder, 65-67. *Work:* Nat City Bank, Denver, Colo; Rose Medical Ctr, Denver, Colo; Kent-Denver Day Sch, Colo; Enid Libr, Okla. *Comn:* Ink on stone, comn for Murray Louis, 78 & woodetching, comn for Hanya Holm, 81, by Colo Contemp Dance; ink on stone, Kent-Denver Country Day Sch, Colo, 83; watercolor, Estes Park Music Festival, 85, Children's Hospital, Denver, 89, 90. *Exhib:* One-man shows, Two-Twenty Two Gallery, El Paso, Tex, 71-72 & 73, Artisan, Princeton, NJ, 72 & 74 & Bishop's Antiques & Gallery, Scottsdale, Ariz, 73-92; Adobé Patio, Mesilla, NMex, 85; Beeches' Gallery, Carmel, Calif, 88, 91; Savageau Gallery, Denver, 89, 90 & 91. *Pos:* Designer, display dept, May D&F, 67-69. *Teaching:* Instr contemp dance, Kent-Denver Day Sch, Colo, 68-87, 92, visual & performing arts, 88- *Bibliog:* Robert Downing (auth), Ad Lib, Denver Post Roundup Sect, 2/2/75; Betty Harvey (auth), Judy Graese, Artists of the Rockies, 5/75; Marie Torrisi (auth), Colo Monthly Mag, 85. *Media:* Watercolor; Wood. *Publ:* Illusr, The Song of Francis, Northland Press, 73; The Treasure is the Rose, Pantheon Press, 73; Art prints, Woodhill Press, 83, Colo Music Festival, 85. *Mailing Add:* 2055 S Franklin Denver CO 80210

GRAFELMAN, GLENN ALLEN
PAINTER
b Minneapolis, Minn, Oct 9, 58. *Study:* Minneapolis Col Art & Design, BFA, 80; Univ Calif, Berkeley, MA, 85; Sch Visual Arts, NY Univ, MFA, 87. *Work:* Minneapolis Inst Art, Minn; Farnsworth Mus, Rockland, Maine; E B Crocker Art Mus, Sacramento, Calif. *Exhib:* National Art Show, Las Vegas, Nev, 84; Discovery '84, Simard Gallery, Los Angeles, Calif; Inaugural Exhib, Thomas Barry Fine Arts, Minneapolis, Minn, 84; Dorothy Weiss Gallery, San Francisco, Calif, 86 & 88; Landscape/Mindscape, Carlo Lamagna Gallery, New York, 90; White Columns, New York, 90. *Pos:* Printmaker, Vermillion Editions Ltd, Minneapolis, Minn, 77-80. *Teaching:* Instr color theory, Montserrat Col Art, Beverly, Mass, 87-; instr principles of art, Univ Southern Maine, Portland, 88-89; instr drawing, Univ NH, Durham, 88-89. *Bibliog:* Christopher French (auth), Southern exposure exhibition, Artweek, 11/85; Kathy Ann Jones (auth), Grafelman at University of Southern Maine, Art New Eng, 6/88; Ed Beem (auth), Connections & spaces in between, Maine Times, 11/10/89. *Media:* Oil. *Dealer:* Akin Gallery 164 Kneeland Boston MA 02111. *Mailing Add:* 135 E 17th St No 4C New York NY 10003

GRAFTON, RICK (FREDERICK WELLINGTON)
PAINTER
b Middletown, Conn, May 3, 52. *Study:* Calif Col Arts & Crafts, BFA(high distinction), 76. *Work:* Metrop Mus Art, Chase Manhattan Bank, New York; Art Inst Chicago; Arco Ctr Visual Art, Los Angeles; Bank Am, San Francisco, Calif. *Comn:* Meridian Building (watercolor), comn by J Lee, San Francisco, 83. *Exhib:* Solo exhib, Grapestake Gallery, San Francisco, 80 & 83, Galleria del Cavallino, Venice, Italy, 81 & San Jose Mus Art, 82; Bay Area Works on Paper, Seoul-San Francisco Exchange, USIS Gallery, SKorea, 83; Dealers Choice, San Francisco-Los Angeles, Kirk de Gooyer Gallery, Los Angeles, 83; Light & Heavy Light, Mem Union Art Gallery, Univ Calif, Davis, 85; Discreet Power: Reductive Issues in Contemporary Painting, Rockford Art Mus, Rockford, Ill, 88; Waterworks, Sierra Nevada Mus Art, Reno, Nev, 88. *Teaching:* Instr watercolor, Assoc Students Univ Calif, Berkeley. *Awards:* Watercolor Award, Calif State Expo, 78. *Mem:* Emeryville Artists Coop. *Media:* Watercolor on Paper, Acrylic and Oil on Canvas and Panel. *Mailing Add:* 1420 45 St #30 Emeryville CA 94608

GRAHAM, BOB
PAINTER, MURALIST
b Canton, Tex, Jan 1, 47. *Study:* N Tex State Univ, 66-69; Cape Sch, with Henry Hensche, 71-82. *Work:* New Orleans Mus Art, La. *Comn:* Portrait Alton Oschner, Oschner Found, New Orleans, La, 85; portrait Frank Barker, Nichols State Univ, Thibbodeau, La, 86; Life of Moses (mural) Jerry Katz & Jewish Community Ctr, New Orleans, 87; portraits First Parrish Judges (4) Jefferson Parrish, Metarie, La, 90; History of Kenner (mural) Kenner, La City Coun, 91. *Exhib:* Kansas Pastel Society, Wichita, 85; Seldom Seen Figures, New Orleans Hist Soc, 88; Allied Artist, Nation Arts Club, New York, 89; Texas & Neighbors, Irving, 89; American Realism Competition, Parkersburg Art Ctr, WVa, 90. *Awards:* Best of Show, Salmagundi Open, New York, 87; Best Painting in Any Medium, Am Artist Prof League, New York, 88; Best Printing in Any Medium, Knickerbocker Artists, New York, 90. *Bibliog:* Satoru Fugii (auth), Outstanding American Illustrators- Graphic-Sha Japan, 84; Stephen Doherty (auth) Southern Plantation, Am Artist, 1/89. *Mem:* Master pastellist, Pastel Soc Am; founder Degas Pastel Soc. *Media:* Oil, Pastel. *Mailing Add:* 319 Magazine St New Orleans LA 70130

GRAHAM, DANIEL H
CONCEPTUAL ARTIST, ENVIRONMENTAL ARTIST
b Urbana, Ill, Mar 31, 42. *Work:* Tate Gallery, London; Stadisches Mus, Monchengladbach, Ger; Allen Art Mus, Oberlin, Ohio; Van Abbemuseum, Eindhoven; Art Inst Chicago; Mod Museet, Stockholm. *Comn:* Argonne Nat Labs, Ill; Laumier Sculpture Park, St Louis, Mo; Nexus, Atlanta, Ga. *Exhib:* Information, Mus Mod Art, New York, 70; Documenta VI, Kassel, Ger, 76; Basel Kunsthalle, Swits, 77; Van Abbemuseum, Eindhoven, 77; Documenta VII, Kassel, Ger, 72; Berne Kunsthalle, Switz. *Teaching:* NS Col Art & Design, Halifax, summer 81; Hamburg Hochschnk, 87-88. *Awards:* Nat Endowment Arts Visual Arts Grant, 80; Creative Artists Pub Serv Grant, 81; Showgen Award. *Publ:* Auth, Performance, 70; Films, 77; Buildings and Signs, 80; Theatre, 82; Pavilions, 83; and others. *Mailing Add:* c/o Marian Goodman Gallery 24 W 57th St New York NY 10019

GRAHAM, DOUGLAS J M
MUSEUM DIRECTOR, COLLECTOR
b Gt Brit; US citizen. *Study:* Piarist Col, BA(humanities), 54; NY Inst Finance, MA, 61. *Pos:* Founder & dir, Turner Mus, Denver, Colo, 72- *Teaching:* Lectr on the work of Turner & Moran, currently. *Awards:* Founder's Award, Turner Mus, 74; Award for Excellence, Cambridge, Gt Brit, 75 & 85. *Bibliog:* Gerald Frank (auth), Douglas Grahams Dream, The Local, 89; Gerald W Bracey (auth), A Turner for the Better, Travel & Leisure, 91; David Alan (auth), Turners Cosmic Optimism Shines in Denver Mus, Colo Daily, 91. *Mem:* Turner Soc, London (vpres, 78-). *Media:* Watercolor, Original Etchings & Engravings. *Collection:* Turner and Moran; most varied and extensive Turner works outside England. *Publ:* Auth, Duerer and Domjan, Graham Collection, NY, 72; Turner and Moran, 77 & auth, Turner's Hand: The Master Touch, 78, Turner Mus; Turner on Paper, In: Joseph Mallord William Turner, Dixon Gallery & Gardens, Memphis, Tenn, 79; auth, Love Beginnings (poems, illus), privately publ, 80; Turner's Cosmic Optimism, 90 & Turner's Angels, 91, Turner Museum. *Mailing Add:* Turner Mus 773 Downing St Denver CO 80218

GRAHAM, K M
PAINTER, PRINTMAKER
b Hamilton, Ont, Sept 13, 13. *Study:* Univ Toronto, BA. *Work:* Art Gallery Ont; Art Bank Can, Ottawa; Edmonton Art Gallery, Alta; MacDonald Stewart Centre, Guelph, Ont; J Barnike Gallery Hart House, Toronto, Ont; Nat Gallery, Can; Art Gallery of Hamilton, Ont; plus others. *Exhib:* Art Gallery of Ont, Toronto, 74; Montreal Mus of Fine Arts, Que, 76; Hirshhorn Mus, Washington, DC, 77; Art Gallery of Hamilton, Ont, 77; Norman MacKenzie Art Gallery, Regina, Sask, 77; Edmonton Art Gallery, Alta, 77; Watson de Nagy Gallery, Houston, Tex, 77; Galerie Wentzel, Hamburg, WGer, 77; Canada House, London; Cult Ctr, Paris; Am Artists Assoc, New York; David Mirvish Gallery, Toronto; Klonaridis Inc, Toronto. *Awards:* Can Coun Travel Award, 73-74 & 79; Hon Fel, Trinity Col, Univ Toronto, 88. *Bibliog:* Karen Wilkin (auth), The late blooming vitality of Toronto Art, Artnews, 2/80; Ingrid Jenner, KM Graham 1970-85(catalogue), Macdonald Stewart Art Ctr, Guelph, Ont; Lora Carney (auth), Brick #39: The Art of K M Graham, 90; and others. *Mem:* Royal Can Acad of Arts. *Media:* Acrylic, Canvas; Dry Points, Lithographs. *Dealer:* Douglas Udell Gallery of Edmonton Vancouver BC. *Mailing Add:* 26 Boswell Ave Toronto ON M5R 1M4 Canada

GRAHAM, LANIER
CURATOR
b Shawnee, Okla, Mar 6, 40. *Study:* Kenyon Col, 58-60; Am Univ, 61-63; Columbia Univ, 63-66, MA, 66; NY Univ Inst Fine Arts, 66-67. *Work:* Multiple, Mus Mod Art, New York & Mus Arts Decoratifs, Paris. *Collections Arranged:* Ansel Adams, Photog of Nature, 82, Nature Symbolized: Bookbindings, 82, The Image of Nature in Modern Art, 83, Headlands Ctr for the Arts, Sausalito; Faces & Figures: Modern Master Prints, 85, Prints of the Surrealists, 86, The Spontaneous Gesture: Prints & Books of the Abstract Expressionist Era, 87, Australian Nat Gallery; Nature Studies: Photographs by Modern Masters, 89, Vincent van Gogh: Painter Printmaker Collector (auth, catalog), 90, Frederick Sommer: Master Photographer, 90, Bravo: Mexico's Master Photographer, 91, Silent Cities: Atget & the Urban Landscape, 91, Edward Weston: Still-Life Photographs, 91, Impossible Realities: Marcel Duchamp & the Surrealist Tradition (auth, catalog), 91-92, Norton Simon Mus, Pasadena, Calif. *Pos:* Assoc cur, Mus Mod Art, New York, 65-70; deputy dir, Collections, Exhib & Publ & chief cur, Fine Arts Museums of San Francisco, 70-76; dir cur, Cult Resource Mgt Ctr, 76-83 & Australian Nat Gallery, 84-87; cur, Norton Simon Mus Art, Pasadena, 87-91; dir/cur, Inst Aesthetic Develop, Antioch, Calif, 91- *Teaching:* Univ Calif, Berkeley, John F Kennedy Univ, Lone Mountain Col, San Francisco State Univ, San Jose State Univ & Diable Valley Col. *Mem:* Col Art Asn Am (local chmn nat conv, 72); World Print Coun; Am Asn Mus, Int Coun Mus; Prints of de Kooning, a catalogue Raisonne, Editions Lebon, 90. *Media:* Prints, Illustrated Books. *Res:* Symbolism ancient to modern and contemporary. *Collection:* Prints & Illustrated Books, Renaissance to Modern. *Publ:* Three

Centuries of American Painting, 71 & 77 & Three Centuries of French Art from the Norton Simon Collections, 73 & 76, Fine Arts Mus San Francisco; ed, The Rainbow Book, Fine Arts Mus San Francisco-Shambhala, 75 & Vintage-Random House, 79; The Spontaneous Gesture: Prints & Books of the Abstract Expressionist Era, Australian Nat Gallery, 87 & Univ Wash Press, 89. *Mailing Add:* Inst Aesthetic Develop Rivertown Sta PO Box 1516 Antioch CA 94509

GRAHAM, LOIS (M GORD)
PAINTER
b Kewanee, Ill, Aug 27, 30. *Study:* Knox Col, BA(magna cum laude), 52; Washington Univ, with Paul Burlin; also with Jack Tworkov, Nathan Oliviera & Lothar Schall. *Work:* City Seattle Portable Works Collection, Wash; City Bellevue City Hall Collection, Wash; Santa Barbara Mus Art; Seattle Art Mus; Northwest Special Collection, Seattle Arts Comn. *Comn:* Mural, Knox Col, Galesburg, Ill, 51; Bellevue, Wash, 75; painting, pvt collection, Seattle, Wash, 79; mural, Seattle Opera House, 86. *Exhib:* Seattle Art Mus, 58, 80-81 & 84; Seattle Pac Univ, 79-81; solo show, Foster White Gallery, Seattle, 81, 82 & 84; Bellevue Art Mus, Wash, 82, 83 & 85; E R Squibb Galleries, Princeton, NJ, 82; Portland Ctr Visual Arts, 82; and others. *Awards:* Honors Award, Seattle Arts Comn, 84. *Bibliog:* Mathew Kangas (auth), Lois Graham at Foster/White, Art Am, 12/81 & Lois Graham: A Decade in Review, 85, Bellevue Art Mus; Betty Brown (auth), Southern California, Lois Graham at Kirk deGooyer, Arts, 2/83. *Mem:* King County Arts Comn. *Media:* Oil, Monotype. *Dealer:* Harris Gallery 1100 Bissonnet Houston TX 77005. *Mailing Add:* c/o Foster/White Gallery 311 1/2 Occidental S Seattle WA 98104

GRAHAM, ROBERT
SCULPTOR
b Mexico City, Mex, Aug 38; US citizen. *Study:* San Jose State Col, 61-63; San Francisco Art Inst, 63-64. *Work:* Whitney Mus Am Art & Mus Mod Art, New York; Hirshhorn Mus & Sculpture Garden; Los Angeles Co Mus; Dallas Mus Fine Art, Tex; Kunstmuseum, Cologne, Ger. *Comn:* Fed Reserve Bank San Francisco, Calif, 83; San Jose Fed Bldg, Calif, 84; Los Angeles Olympic Organizing Comt, 84; Joe Louis Mem, Detroit, Mich; Duke Ellington Mem, Central Park, Manhattan, 92; and others. *Exhib:* Galerie Neuendorf, Hamburg, WGer, 79; one-man shows, Walker Art Ctr, traveling, 81 & Los Angeles Co Mus Art, Calif, 88; Dorothy Rosenthal Gallery, 81; Sch Visual Arts, New York, 81; Robert Miller Gallery, New York, 82, 89, 90 & 92; Whitney Mus Am Art, 83, 84, 86, 88 & 89; Mus Fine Arts, traveling, Houston, Tex, 87-89; Contemp Arts Ctr, New Orleans, La, 90. *Bibliog:* Maurice Tuchman (auth), Robert Graham: The Duke Ellington Mem in Progress, Los Angeles Co Mus Art, 89; John McEwen, Robert Graham Statues, Frankfurt: Galerie Neuendorf; Twenty-one Figures by Robert Graham, New York: Robert Miller Gallery. *Media:* Miscellaneous media. *Mailing Add:* c/o Robert Miller Gallery 41 E 57th St New York NY 10022

GRAHAM, ROBERT C, JR
ART DEALER
b New York, NY, Sept 6, 41. *Study:* Middlebury Col, BA, 63. *Pos:* Chmn & dir, Graham Gallery, New York, 63-92. *Mem:* Art Dealers Asn Am. *Specialty:* American painting and sculpture. *Mailing Add:* Graham Gallery 1014 Madison Ave New York NY 10021

GRAHAM, ROBERT CLAVERHOUSE, SR
DEALER, COLLECTOR
b New York, NY, Apr 28, 13. *Study:* Yale Univ, BFA, 36; NY Univ, 38-39. *Pos:* Dir, Graham Gallery. *Specialty:* Nineteenth and twentieth century American art. *Collection:* American and Oriental art. *Mailing Add:* Graham Gallery 1014 Madison Ave New York NY 10021

GRAHAM, ROBERT MACDONALD, JR
PAINTER
b New Rochelle, NY, Nov 1, 19. *Study:* Kansas City Art Inst, Mo, with Thomas H Benton, dipl, 41; Hoger Inst voor Schone Kunsten, Antwerp, Belg, with Jules van Vlasslaer, cert, 49. *Work:* War Art Collection, Pentagon, Washington, DC; Witte Mus, San Antonio, Tex; Tex Fine Arts, Austin; Topeka Art Mus, Kans; Butler Inst Am Art, Youngstown, Ohio; Inland Steel Co, Chicago; Georgetown Univ, Washington DC. *Exhib:* 53rd Nat Ann, Art Inst Chicago, 41; Univ Ill Nat Contemp Am Painting, Champaign, Ill, 48; Audubon Nat Ann Contemp Am Art, New York, 50; Dallas Mus Invitational, 52 & 53; Delgado Mus Invitational, New Orleans, La, 54; 38th Midyear Show, Butler Inst Am Art, Youngstown, Ohio, 74; Benedictine Art Awards Nat, New York, 75; 30th Ann Nat Soc Painters Casein & Acrylic, Nat Arts Club, New York, 83-88; W Churchill Mem Fulton, 85; Mainstream America, 87; Collection Phil Desind, Butler Inst, Youngstown; H S Truman Libr, Independence, 88. *Teaching:* Instr painting & drawing, Univ Tex, Austin, 51-55; teaching assoc painting & drawing, Univ Mo, Kansas City, 58-75. *Awards:* Purchase Prize, Topeka Art Mus, 56; Purchase Prize, Butler Inst Am Art, 74; Pres Citation Merit, 30th Ann Nat Soc Painters Casein & Acrylic Exhib, 83; M J Kaplan Award, NSPCA, New York, 87; John J Newman Medal, NSPCA, New York, 91. *Mem:* Nat Soc Painters Casein & Acrylic, New York. *Media:* Multi. *Publ:* Auth, An Artist's View of the Thomas Wolfe Memorial at Asheville, NC, Capricorn Galleries, 87-89. *Dealer:* Capricorn Gallery 4849 Rugby Ave Bethesda MD 20814. *Mailing Add:* 26405 150 Hwy Greenwood MO 64034

GRAHAM, WALTER
PAINTER, SCULPTOR
b Toledo, Ill, Nov 17, 03. *Study:* Chicago Acad Fine Arts; Chicago Art Inst; plus pvt instruction. *Work:* Cent Wash Mus, Wenatchee; Douglas Co Mus, Waterville, Wash; Favell Mus, Klamath Falls, Ore. *Comn:* Murals & wildlife paintings for ocean-going ships, State of Alaska, 69-72; murals & paintings, Rocky Reach Dam, Wenatchee, 60; fountain sculpture, Lincoln Savings, Spokane, Wash, 70; Mural, Central Washington Airport, East Wenatchee, 92. *Exhib:* Ann Western Art Exhib, Russell Mus, Great Falls, Mont, 73-74; NW Indian & Western Art Show, Ridpath Hotel, Spokane, 74-75; Artists of the Old West, Oldfield Gallery-Tacoma Inn, Wash, 75; Soc Animal Artists Exhib, Columbus Gallery of Fine Art, Ohio, 76; Mem Show, Palette & Chisel Acad, Chicago & Art Inst of Chicago; solo exhib, Frye Mus, Seattle, 86; Allied Arts Ann, 87-88; and others. *Pos:* Owner, Nugent Graham Studios, Chicago, 39-50; mem, Wash State Art Comn, 60-62; pres, Cent Wash Mus, 60-65. *Awards:* First Prizes, Chicago Galleries, 37, 38 & 42; Gold Medal, Palette & Chisel Acad, Chicago, 40; First Prize, Allied Arts Ann, 87. *Bibliog:* Royal B Hassick (auth), Western Painting Today, Watson-Guptill, 75. *Media:* Oil, Watercolor; Bronze. *Mailing Add:* 201 S Eliott Wenatchee WA 98801

GRAHAM, WILLIAM ANDREW
DEALER, COLLECTOR
b Leon, Iowa, Dec 13, 39. *Study:* Univ Iowa, BA, 62; studied lithography under Ferdnand Mourlot, 69-74; photography in Paris, with Man Ray, 69-74; Studio Salon, with Jean Helion, 69-71 & Charles Lapicque, 69-76. *Collections Arranged:* Leopold Survage: Retrospective (auth, catalog), Vestart, New York, 69; Justino Alvez: Paintings (auth, catalog), Documenta, Paris, 77; Figurative Painting: Six in America and Europe (auth, catalog), Graham Gallery, 81; Allen Jones: Print Retrospective, Sewall Art Gallery, 81; Sharon Kopriva: Sculpture & Paintings (catalog), 89. *Pos:* Dir & Europ buyer, Vestart, New York, 69-70; dir & co-owner, Galerie Balanci Graham, Paris, 72-77; coordr & asst dir, Sewall Art Gallery, Rice Univ, Houston, 80; dir, Graham Gallery, Houston, 81- *Teaching:* Pvt lectr collecting, Paris, 70-77; vis lectr, Rice Univ, Houston, 81- *Bibliog:* Michael Ennis (auth), Domain, (article), Texas Monthly, 87; Bonnie Gannelhoff (auth), Art Powerhouses, Mag of the Houston Post, Houston Post, 88. *Mem:* Houston Art Dealers Asn, Tex. *Specialty:* Contemporary Americans and Europeans. *Collection:* 20th century American and European. *Mailing Add:* 1431 W Alabama Houston TX 77006

GRAINGER, NESSA POSNER
PAINTER, COLLAGE ARTIST
b Atlantic City, NJ. *Study:* Philadelphia Mus Sch Art, BA; Tyler Sch Fine Arts;, Pa Acad Fine Arts. *Work:* Bergen Mus, Oradel, NJ; Chubb Corp, Basking Ridge, NJ; McDonalds Corp, Paterson, NJ; Mutual Benefit Life, NJ; Sea-Land Corp, NJ; First Fidelity Bank, Headquarters, NJ. *Exhib:* Photography/Collage, Hunterdon Art Ctr, Clinton, NJ, 88; NJ Watercolor Soc 50th Anniversary, Montclair Art Mus, NJ, 88; one-man shows, Douglas Col for Women, NJ, 90, The Interchurch Ctr, NY, 92, Elliot Mus, Stuart, Fla, 93; Nat Acad Design, New York, 92; Allied Artists Am, Nat Arts Club, New York, 92. *Awards:* Medal of Honor, Nat Asn Women Artists, 76; M Grumbacher Gold Medallion, Catharine Lorillard Wolfe Art Club, 82; NJ Watercolor Soc Silver Medal, 85; Audubon Artists of America, Silver Medal, 89. *Bibliog:* Dorothy Hall (auth), Parkeast, Art & Artists, 11/87; Who's Who of Women; Who's Who in the East. *Mem:* NJ Watercolor Soc (pres, 83-84); Audubon Artists Am (vpres 87-92); Nat Asn Women Artists (pres, 89-91); Allied Artists Am; Am Soc Contemp Artists; Knickerbacher Artists. *Media:* Watercolor. *Mailing Add:* Old Turn Pike 212 Old Turnpike Rd Califon NJ 07830

GRALNICK, LISA
JEWELER
b New York, 1956. *Study:* Kent State Univ, BFA, 77; State Univ NY, New Paltz, MFA, 80. *Work:* Am Craft Mus, New York; Stedijk Mus, Amsterdam; Schenectady Mus, NY. *Exhib:* Solo exhibs, Sculpture to Wear, Los Angeles, Calif & VO Galerie, Washington, DC, 87, Galerie RA, Amsterdam, Neth, 88, CDK Gallery, New York, 89, Susan Cummins Gallery, Mill Vallery, Calif, 90, Jewelerswerk Galerie, Washington, DC, 91 & Helen Drutt Gallery, Philadelphia, Pa, 92; Craft Today USA, Am Craft Mus, 89; Body Art, Security Pac Corp, 90; For the Tabletop, Galerie RA, Amsterdam, 91; Schmuckszene 92, Int Handwerksmesse, Munich, Ger, 92; Design Visions: The Second Perth International Crafts Triennial, Art Gallery Western Australia, Perth Cult Ctr, 92. *Teaching:* Vis prof, head enamelling dept, Kent State Univ, 80-81; vis prof, head jewelry dept, NS Col Art & Design, Halifax, 82-83; instr, jewelry, 92nd St, New York, 86-91; fac, Parsons Sch Design, New York, 91- *Awards:* Fel, Nat Endowment Arts, 88 & 92; Fel, New York Found Arts, 91; Award Excellence, Mobil Corp, 91. *Bibliog:* Alice Sprintzen (auth), Art Enamelling, 83; Peter Dormer & Ralph Turner (auths), New Jewelry: Trends & Traditions, 85; Roger Kuhn (auth), The Jewelry of Lisa Gralnick, Metalsmith, summer, 92. *Mailing Add:* c/o Box 238 Rosendale NY 12472

GRAMBERG, LILIANA
PAINTER, PRINTMAKER
b Treviso, Italy; US citizen. *Study:* Univ Rome, with Laurea; Escuela Nac Bellas Artes, Madrid; Ecole Nat Super Beaux Arts, Paris, Atelier Gravure, with Bersier; Atelier 17, Paris, with Hayter; Calif Col Arts & Crafts, MFA. *Work:* Mus Art Mod Ville Paris; Brit Mus, London; Nat Mus Am Art; Galleria Nazionale Arte Moderna, Rome; Albertina Mus Vienna; Nat Gallery of Art, Washington, DC; Australian Nat Gallery, Canberra; Libr Congress; and other museums in US & abroad. *Exhib:* 23 one-man shows, including Smithsonian Inst, Washington, DC, Folkwang Mus, Essen, Ger, Biblioteca Nac, Madrid, Galeria Arte Moderna, Lisbon; Kunstnerforbundet, Oslo; Univ

Chile, Santiago; Univ Kent, Canterbury; Libr Congress; Pa Acad Fine Arts; Seoul Int Print Biennale, 83; Galleria Cartesius, Trieste, Italy; Centro Internazionale per la Grafica, Venice, Italy. *Awards:* Treadwell Award, Nat Asn Women Artists, 63; Silver Medal, Asn Incisori Italia, 64. *Bibliog:* Margarita Nelken (auth), El grabado de Liliana Gramberg, Arte (Mex), 3/59; Cajide (auth), Tecnica y poesia de los grabados de Liliana Gramberg, Artes (Spain), 2/61; Uomini, androidi o manichini Gazzetta Ticinese, C N Trovato (Italy), 86; Carmelo Nino Trovato (auth), Rassegna Antologica delle Incisioni di Liliana Gramberg, Gazzetta Ticinese n108, 86. *Mailing Add:* 6322 32nd St NW Washington DC 20015

GRANDEE, JOE RUIZ
PAINTER, GALLERY DIRECTOR
b Dallas, Tex, Nov 19, 29. *Study:* Aunspaugh Art Sch, Dallas. *Work:* White House, Washington, DC; Xavier Univ Mus, Cincinnati, Ohio; Mont State Hist Soc Mus, Great Falls; Marine Corps Mus, Quantico, Va; Univ Tex, Arlington. *Comn:* Twenty Mules of Death Valley, US Borax Co, Hollywood, Calif, 65; Linda Bird & Chuck Robb Off Portrait, comn by Lyndon B Johnson family & friends, 67; portrait of Johnny Carson, comn by Rudy Tellez, Assoc Producer NBC, New York, 67; portrait of Robert Taylor, comn by US Borax Co for Robert Taylor, Hollywood, 68; portrait of Leander H McNelly, Texas Ranger, East Wing of White House, Washington, DC, 72. *Exhib:* Custer Exhib, Amon Carter Mus Western Art, Ft Worth, Tex, 68; one-man shows, Norton Art Gallery Mus, Shreveport, La, 71, El Paso Mus Fine Arts, Tex, 72 & Tex Ranger Mus Show, Waco, Tex, 72 & US Capitol, 74; and many others. *Pos:* Owner, Joe Grandee Gallery & Mus of Old West, currently. *Awards:* First Official Artist of Texas, Tex Legis & Gov, 71; Franklin Mint Gold Medal Western Art for Pursuit and Attack, 74; and others. *Bibliog:* Wayne Gard (auth), Joe Grandee--painter of the old west, Am Artist Mag, 67; Grandee Paintings (TV film), US Borax Co, 68; Joy Schultz (auth), The West Still Lives: Grandee, Heritage, 70. *Media:* Oil, Ink. *Specialty:* Paintings, drawings and sculpture works of Joe Ruiz Grandee and displays of historical artifacts. *Publ:* Illusr, Indian Wars of Texas, 65, Pictorial History of The Texas Rangers, 69, The Grand Duke Alexis in the USA, 72 & The Life of Jim Baker (mountain man), 1818-1898, 72; contribr, Cowboy Series, In: Time-Life Bks, 72. *Dealer:* Gene McDaniel PO Box 433 Midland TX 79701; Bob Hoff PO Box 231 Houston TX 77001. *Mailing Add:* Joe Grandee Gallery & Mus Old West 606 S Center St Arlington TX 76010

GRANLUND, PAUL THEODORE
SCULPTOR
b Minneapolis, Minn, Oct 6, 25. *Study:* Gustavus Adolphus Col, BA, 52; Univ Minn; Cranbrook Acad Art, George A Booth scholar, 53, MFA, 54; Gustavus Adolphus Col, LHD, 71. *Work:* Walker Art Ctr, Minneapolis Inst Art, Minn; Cranbrook Acad Art; Va Mus Fine Arts; Sheldon Mem Mus Art Gallery, Lincoln, Nebr; and others. *Comn:* Sculpture, Gustavus Adolphus Col & Lutheran Church of the Good Shepherd, Minneapolis; 21 pub sculptures, Minneapolis & St Paul. *Exhib:* One-man shows, Calif Palace Legion Honor, 62, Univ Nebr, 64 & Washington Univ, 65; La State Univ, 64; Art of Two Cities, Minneapolis Sch Art, 65; and others. *Teaching:* Cranbrook Acad Art, 54; Minneapolis Col Art & Design, 55-57 & 59-71; sculptor-in-residence, Gustavus Adolphus Col, 71- *Awards:* Fulbright Fel, 54; Guggenheim Fels, 57 & 58. *Publ:* Auth, Granlund: The Sculptor and His Work, Kathryn Christenson & Kelvin W Miller (eds), Gustavus Adolphus Col, 78. *Mailing Add:* c/o C G Rein Galleries 3523 W 70th St Edina MN 55435

GRANSTAFF, WILLIAM BOYD
PAINTER, ILLUSTRATOR
b Paducah, Ky, May 17, 25. *Study:* Kansas City Art Inst, with Ross Braught & Ed Lanning, grad; Am Acad Art, with William Mosby & Bill Fleming. *Comn:* Mural, Cadet Club, Garden City, Kans, 45; Old Homeplace, B J Farless, Princeton, Ky, 70; Vietnam (painting), comn by Nat Am Legion, 75 & Korea (painting), 78; 1st Bank & Trust, Princeton, Ky. *Exhib:* Mid-S, Nashville, Tenn, 53; one-man show, Planters Bank, Hopkinsville, Ky, 72. *Pos:* Mem, Art Dirs Club, Nashville, 55-58. *Teaching:* Instr illus, Famous Artist Sch, 59-61. *Awards:* Brackman Blue Ribbon, Nashville, 53. *Bibliog:* Meet your instructors, Famous Artist Mag, 61. *Mem:* Audubon Soc. *Media:* Oil, Watercolor. *Publ:* Illusr, What's in a Word, Abingdon, 65; The Way Out, Moody, 70; Golden Treasury of Bible Stories, Southern, 71; illusr, Man-US & Americas, 72 & illusr, Americans All, 72, Benefic. *Dealer:* Heritage Gallery Rosemont Gardens Lexington KY 40503. *Mailing Add:* Old Eddyville Rd Rt VI Box 7 Princeton KY 42445

GRANT, ART
CONCEPTUAL ARTIST, EDUCATOR
b San Francisco, Calif, June 22, 27. *Study:* San Francisco City Col, AA, 45-48; San Francisco State Univ, BA, 54-55; San Francisco Art Inst, 55. *Work:* San Francisco Mus Mod Art; Oakland Art Mus; City Sausalito, Calif; Fresno Art Mus; Univ Utah Mus. *Comn:* Murals, Coleman Sch, San Rafael, Calif, 74, Martin Luther King Sch, Sausalito, Univ Calif Exten, San Francisco & Liberty Sch, Petaluma, Calif, 75, Steffan Manor Sch, Vallejo, Calif, 76. *Exhib:* San Francisco Art Inst Show, De Young Mus, 62; Three Projective Sculptors, Oakland Art Mus, 63; Kinetic Forces, 65, Holiday Show, 65, 66 & 83 & Aesthetics of Graffiti, 78, San Francisco Mus Mod Art; Edible Art Show, Univ Calif Art Mus, Berkeley, 81 & 82; Found and Assembled, Matthews Gallery, Ariz State Univ, 82; Dinosaur Festival, Calif Acad Sci, San Francisco, 85; Fire Ant Festival , Marshall, Texas, 88. *Teaching:* Assoc prof art, Lincoln Univ, Calif, 63-66 & 77-; instr art & art educ, Univ Calif Exten, San Francisco, 64-77 & Sonoma State Univ Exten, Rohnert Park, Calif, 68-79; instr art & art educ, San Francisco State Univ Exten, 64-69. *Awards:* Sculpture Prize, 77th Ann Painting & Sculpture Show, San Francisco Art Asn, 58, San Francisco Art Festival, 60 & 77 & Sausalito Art Festival, 62 & 63; Art Grant Day proclaimed by mayor, San Francisco, 88. *Bibliog:* Sarah Grissom (auth), article, Arts, 5/58; Mary Fuller (auth), article, Art in Am, No 3, 64; Americana, Time Mag, 3/5/79; People Mag, 3/14/88. *Mem:* Nat Soc Mural Painters. *Media:* Junk, Food, Ice. *Publ:* Coauth, Sculpture from Junk, Van Nostrand Reinhold, 67. *Dealer:* Natsoulas/Novelozo Gallery 132 E St Davis CA 95616; Claudia Chapline Gallery 3445 Shoreline Hwy Stinson Beach CA 94970. *Mailing Add:* 154 Ethel Ave Mill Valley CA 94941

GRASHOW, JAMES BRUCE
SCULPTOR, PRINTMAKER
b Brooklyn, NY, Jan 16, 42. *Study:* Pratt Inst, BFA, 62, MFA, 65. *Work:* Mus Mod Art, Pub Libr, New York; Greenville Mus, SC; Libr Cong; Iron Range Mus, Minn. *Comn:* Ballet stage sets, San Francisco Ballet Co, 76 & Nat Ballet Cuba, Havana, 78; Book of the Month Club, 86. *Exhib:* A City, Am Inst Architect, Washington, DC, 65; Made with Paper, 67 & Tombstones & Monuments, 67, Mus Contemp Crafts, New York; Human Concern, Personal Torment, Whitney Mus, 69; Hudson River Mus, NY, 72; Univ Conn, Storrs, 79; Ctr Arts, State Univ NY, Purchase, 82; Aldridge, Ridgefield, Conn, 85. *Teaching:* Assoc prof painting & figure drawing, Pratt Inst, 68-81; prof sculpting, Fairfield Univ, 90- *Awards:* Fulbright Travel Grant, 63; Ital Govt Grant, 63; Tiffany Award Graphics, 65. *Bibliog:* Steven Heller (auth), article, Graphis, 81; Chauncey Howell (producer), Live at Five, NBC-TV, 82; Jane Cottingham (auth), article, Am Artist Mag, 5/82. *Media:* Fabric Mache; Woodcut. *Publ:* Illusr, Making Vegetables Grow, 75 & Twelve Moons Make a Year, 80, Knopf; illusr, New York Times Mag, 83. *Dealer:* Allan Stone Gallery 48 E 86th St New York NY. *Mailing Add:* 14 Diamond Hill Rd West Redding CT 06896

GRASS, PATTY PATTERSON
PAINTER
b Oklahoma City, Okla. *Study:* Univ Okla, BFA; Ecole Beaux-Arts, Fontainebleau, France; Taos Sch Art; Art Students League; Okla State Univ; additional study with Emil Bisttram, Robert E Woods, Milford Zarnes, George Post, Edgar Whitney & Millard Sheets. *Exhib:* One-woman show, Univ Okla Health Sci Ctr, 76; Mass Inst Technol; Oklahoma City Art Ctr; Art Students League; Okla Mus Art. *Teaching:* Instr art, Oklahoma City Schs & Oklahoma City Univ, 34-81. *Awards:* First Prize, Watercolor Okla, 75; Spec Award, Okla Art Guild, 75; Four Certs of Award for 100 Best Painters, Southwestern Watercolor Soc, Dallas, Tex, 71-80; and others. *Mem:* Okla Art Asn; Okla Watercolor Asn; Watercolor Okla; Southwestern Watercolor Soc; and others. *Mailing Add:* 2506 NW 66th St Oklahoma City OK 73116

GRASSI, MARCO
CONSERVATOR, RESTORER
b Florence, Italy, July 7, 34; US citizen. *Study:* Princeton Univ, BA(art hist), 56; apprenticeships at: Gabinetto del Restauro, Uffizi, Florence, 59-60; Istituto Centrale del Restauro, Rome, 60-62; & Schweitzerisches Institut für Kunstwissenschaft, 62. *Pos:* Vis conservator, Thyssen-Bornemisza Collection, Villa Favorita, Lugano, Switz. *Awards:* Ital Legion of Merit. *Mem:* Am Inst Conserv Hist & Artistic Works; Int Inst Conserv Hist & Artistic Works; fel Pierpont Morgan Libr. *Mailing Add:* 599 Broadway New York NY 10012

GRASSO, DORIS (TEN-EYCK)
PAINTER, SCULPTOR
b Fremont, NY, May 3, 14. *Study:* Educ Alliance, New York, with Moses Soyer, Alex Dobkin & John Hovannes; N Hudson Arts Sch, with Fabian Zaccone; Rutherford Art Sch, with Lucille Hobbie. *Work:* Paul Whitener Mem Collection, NC Mus Art; George B Burr Collection, New York; Jersey City Mus Art; Staten Island Pub Schs Collection, NY; Women's Club Collection, Lynhurst, NJ. *Exhib:* Knickerbocker Artists Int, New York, 63-65; Painters & Sculptors Soc NJ Nat, 65-72; Nat Casein Soc, New York, 68; Acad Artists Regional, NJ, 68-71; Am Artists Prof League Nat, New York, 69-70. *Teaching:* Instr art, YWCA, Bayonne, NJ, 50-55, Doris Grasso Sch Fine Arts, 52-62 & Bayonne's Woman's Club Eve Dept, 65-68; instr, Doris Ten-Eyck Grasso Gallery & Studio, Gloucester, Mass, currently. *Awards:* Pauline Wick Award for Oils, Am Artists Prof League, 68; Golden Lady Award, Nat Women of Achievement (Art), Amita, Inc, 69; First Award for Sculpture, State Fedn Women's Clubs, 70; and others. *Mem:* Fel Am Artists Prof League (pres, NJ Chap, nat dir, 60-62); Painters & Sculptors Soc NJ (bd dirs & secy, 62-65); Burr Artists (pub rels, 66-68); Assoc Rockport Artists; fel Int Arts & Lett, Ger & Switz; and others. *Media:* Oil, Watercolor. *Mailing Add:* 15 Langsford St Lanesville Cape Ann Gloucester MA 01930

GRASSO, JACK
PAINTER
b White Plains, NY, Jan 15, 27. *Study:* Study with Herb Olsen & Alex Ross, 67. *Work:* Univ Colo Sch Bus, Boulder; US Coast Guard traveling exhib, New York; YMCA, Stamford, Conn. *Exhib:* Allied Artists Show, Mus Fine Arts, Boston, 75; Hudson Valley Art Asn, White Plains, NY, 75-82; Conn Watercolor Soc, Hartford, 75-82; Lever House, New York, 82; Mystic International, Maritime Gallery, Mystic, Conn, 83-85; Orleans Art Gallery, Mass. *Pos:* Coast Guard & Navy combat artist, New York, 80. *Teaching:* Instr watercolor, East Ridge Jr High Sch, Ridgefield, Conn, 82- *Awards:* Mem award, Hudson Valley Art Asn, 75 & 82, Lever House Award, 82. *Media:* Watercolor. *Dealer:* Isabel Trimper 119 Riverside Ave Westport CT. *Mailing Add:* 37 Griffith Lane Ridgefield CT 06877-4401

GRASSO, SALVATORE FORTUNATO
PAINTER, CONCEPTUAL ARTIST
b Boston, Mass, April 27, 45. *Study:* Art Inst Boston, cert, 66. *Work:* DeCordova Mus, Lincoln, Mass; Suffolk Univ; Tom Nicholas Gallery, Rockport, Mass; Guild Boston Artist; Novo Labs, Holland. *Exhib:* Nat Acrylic & Casein Exhib, Nat Acad Design, New York, 78; New England Watercolor Soc Exhib, 78-82; Nat Acad Design Exhib, New York, 79; DeCordova Mus Exhib, Lincoln, Mass, 79; Hudson River Artist Nat Exhib, 80. *Awards:* Rockport Art Asn Awards, 77-82; Frank & Annie Shikler Award, Nat Acad Design Ann Exhib, 79; Purchase Prize, DeCordova Mus, 79; and others. *Media:* Acrylic, Egg Tempera. *Publ:* Am Artist; Pallett Talk. *Mailing Add:* 46 Langsford St Gloucester MA 01930

GRAUBARD, ANN WOLFE See Wolfe, Ann (Ann Wolfe Graubard)

GRAUER, GLADYS
PAINTER
b Cincinnati, Ohio, Aug 15, 23. *Study:* Art Inst Chicago, 41-45; Rutgers Univ, 80-84. *Work:* Newark Mus. *Exhib:* Emerging & Established, Newark Mus & Jersey City Mus, NJ, 81; Annual, Trenton City Mus, NJ, 83; one-woman show, The Invincibles, Courtney Gallery, Jersey City, 85; Nat Conference of Artists, Senegal Nat Mus, Dakar, Africa, 85; Progressions: Cultural Legacy, Clocktower, New York, 86; Tracking the Trends, Pavilion Gallery, Mt Holly, NJ, 86; Celebration, Morristown Mus, NJ, 86. *Teaching:* Instr advert design, Essex Co Voc Tech, Newark, NJ, (retired); instr painting, Newark Mus, NJ, currently. *Awards:* State Art Leaders, Robeson Gallery, Rutgers Univ, 82; First Prize Watercolor, James St Commons, 83; Mixed Media Fel, NJ State Coun Arts, 85. *Bibliog:* NJ Black Artists (tv), Channel 13, 2/3/82; Deborah Stapleton (auth), Black women artists: Images in the river, Graphica, 4/18/82; Edna Bailey (auth), Artists paintings a depiction of blacks, Newark Star Ledger, 1/13/86. *Mem:* Women's Caucus Art; Art Inst Chicago Alumni Asn; Black Woman Visual Perspective (pres, 73-75); Nat Conf Artists, NJ (pres, 82-85). *Media:* Mixed Media. *Dealer:* Russell A Murray 65 Fernwood Rd Maplewood NJ 07040. *Mailing Add:* 352 Seymour Ave Newark NJ 07112

GRAUER, SHERRY
PAINTER, SCULPTOR
b Toronto, Ont, Feb 20, 39. *Study:* Wellesley Col, 56-59; Ecole Louvre, Paris; Calif Sch Fine Art, BFA(hon), 64. *Work:* Vancouver Art Gallery; Mus Art Contemp, Montreal; Ont Heritage Fund; Can Coun Art Bank; Nat Gallery Can, Ottawa. *Comn:* Relief mural, Worldwide Int Travel, Vancouver, 69; ceiling panels (steel & fiberglass), DPW, Fed Bldg, Powell River, BC, 76; banners, City Vancouver, 76; Brave Birdmen (steel mesh ceiling sculpture), Ministry Transport, Cornwall, Ont, 80; relief sculpture, Cygnus, stainless steel mesh & chromed sheet steel, WESGAR Corp, Vancouver, BC, 90. *Exhib:* People in the Park, Rothmans Gallery, Stratford, Ont, 69; Art From Canada's West Coast, Vancouver Art Gallery, 71; Some Canadian Women Artists, Nat Gallery Can, 75; Current Pursuits, Vancouver Art Gallery, 76; retrospective, Surrey Art Gallery, 80; New Vancouver Art Gallery Inaugural Exhib, 83. *Pos:* Bd mem, hon secy, Van Art Gallery, 76-77; mem found bd, Arts, Sci & Technol Ctr, Vancouver, 80. *Bibliog:* Joan Lowndes (auth), Modalities of West Coast sculpture, Artscanada, Vol XXXI, No 2, 74; Ted Lindberg (auth), article, Sherry Grauer, Vanguard, 11/85; Jill Pollack (auth), monogr, On Certain Paths, 87. *Mem:* Royal Can Acad Art. *Media:* Oil, Acrylic; Canvas, Steel Mesh. *Dealer:* Bau-Xi Gallery 3045 Granville St Vancouver V6H 3J9; Bau-Xi Gallery 340 Dundas St W Toronto M5T 1G5. *Mailing Add:* 106-8828 Heather St Vancouver BC V6P 3S8 Canada

GRAUPE-PILLARD, GRACE
PAINTER, INSTRUCTOR
b New York, NY. *Study:* City Univ NY, BA, 63; Art Students League, George Bridgman Scholar, with Marshal Glasier and Julien Levi, 64-68. *Work:* Coca Cola Corp, Atlanta, Ga; Zimmerli Art Mus, NJ; Newark Pub Libr; Morris Mus, NJ; Bell-Atlantic, Washington, DC; and many others. *Comn:* Wall mural, Shearson Lehman Hutton, New York; Peat Marwick Main, NJ; AT&T, NJ. *Exhib:* One-woman shows, Hal Bromm Gallery, 86, 87 & 89, Real Art Ways, Hartford, Conn, 86, Millsaps Col, Jackson, Miss, 86, Sally Hawkins Gallery, New York, 90, Port Authority Bus Terminal, New York, 92, NJ State Mus, Trenton, 93 & NJ Ctr Visual Arts, Summit, 93; The Drawing Ctr, New York, 81 & 82; Painting & Sculpture Today, Indianapolis Mus, 86; Soho, East Village & Tribeca, Maier Mus, Randolph-Malon Col, Lynchburg, Va, 86; East Village, Fashion Inst Technol, New York, 86; Floating Values, Hallwalls, Buffalo, NY, 87; Drawing Show, Lyman Allyn Mus, Conn, 88; Columnar, Hudson River Mus, NY, 88; 100 Drawings by women, Traveling show, Hillwood Gallery, Long Island Univ, 89-90. *Teaching:* Instr painting & drawing, Monmouth Co Parks, 76- *Awards:* NJ State Coun Grant, 82-83; Nat Endowment Arts, 85-86; Ctr Innovative Printmaking, Rutgers Univ, NJ, 91. *Bibliog:* Jude Schwendenwien (auth), Art Forum Mag, summer 89; Judith Van Wagner (auth), Lines of Vision, Book-Hudson Hills Press, 89; Edward Waisnis (auth), Cover Mag, 5/90; Vivien Raynor (auth) revs, New York Times, 2/3/91 & 4/5/92; The Davis Visuals, Fantasy & Illusion, Worcester, Mass, 91. *Media:* Pastels. *Dealer:* Hal Bromm Gallery 90 W Broadway New York NY 10007. *Mailing Add:* PO Box 1032 Freehold NJ 07728

GRAUSMAN, PHILIP
SCULPTOR
b New York, NY, July 16, 35. *Study:* Syracuse Univ, BA(cum laude), 57; Skowhegan Sch Painting & Sculpture, summers 56 & 57; Cranbrook Acad Art, MFA, 59; Art Students League, with Jose de Creeft, 59. *Work:* Brooklyn Mus; Pa State Univ; Wadsworth Atheneum, Hartford; Univ Mich; Univ Conn, Storrs; and others. *Comn:* Graham Gund Assoc, Boston, 87. *Exhib:* Hartford Arts Festival, Wadsworth Atheneum, 74; A Mus Menagerie, Mus Mod Art, New York, 76; Am Drawing Exhib, Fine Arts Mus San Diego, 77; Drawing USA 78, St Paul Art Ctr, Minn, 78; one-man shows, Wash Art Asn, 78 & 81 & Wichita Mus Art, 88; Bethune Gallery, State Univ NY, Buffalo, 83; Robert Schoelkopf Gallery, New York, 83; Cleveland Mus Contemp Art, Ohio, 84; Marilyn Pearl Gallery, 86; Pratt Inst, Brooklyn, NY, 88; Likeness and Beyond: Portraits from Africa & the World, Ctr African Art, New York, also Kimball Mus, 90-91; Sculptors Draw the Nude, Luise Ross Gallery, New York, 90; Paris-New York-Kent Gallery, Kent, Conn, 91; Subterranean Devotion, Bachelier-Cardonsky Gallery, Kent, Conn, 91. *Pos:* Artist in residence, Dartmouth Col, 72. *Teaching:* Instr design, Cooper Union, 65-67; instr design & drawing, Pratt Inst, 65-69; vis asst prof, Yale Univ, 73-76, critic archit drawing, Grad Sch Archit, 74- *Awards:* Rome Prize Fel, 62-65; Solon H Borgliem Award, Silvermine Exhib, 80; Dessie Greer Prize, Nat Acad Design, 81, Gold Medal, 88. *Bibliog:* Hilton Kramer (auth), New York Times, 10-5/79; Michael Brenson (auth), New York Times, 11-20/87; Vivien Raynor (auth), Sculpture Metals from Aluminum to Zinc, at the Mattatuck, New York Times, 6-19/88. *Mem:* Nat Acad Design; Fel Am Acad Rome. *Media:* Cast Metal. *Dealer:* Babcock Gallery 724 Fifth Ave New York NY 10019. *Mailing Add:* c/o Babcock Gallery 724 Fifth Ave New York NY 10019

GRAVES, BRADFORD
SCULPTOR, EDUCATOR
b Dallas, Tex, July 26, 39. *Study:* Sch of Visual Arts; New Sch for Social Res, with Seymour Lipton; Goddard Col, BA & MA. *Work:* NJ State Mus, Trenton; Corcoran Gallery, Washington, DC; Weatherspoon Art Gallery, Univ NC, Greensboro; Sheldon Mem Art Gallery, Lincoln, Nebr; Chase Manhattan Bank; City of Aberdeen, Scotland, 88. *Comn:* Hwy sculpture, Adirondak Northway-Interstate 87, NY, 71, Vt Sculptor's Symposium, Interstate 89, 71 & Interstate 80, Nebr, 76; Scottish Sculpture Trust, 83. *Exhib:* Sculpture in the Fields, Storm King Art Ctr, Mountainville, NY, 74; First West Side Sculpture Exhib, New York, 76; one-man shows, NJ State Mus, Trenton, 76 & Georgetown Univ, Washington, DC, 86; Whitney Counterweight, New York, 77; Forms in Focus, Co-op City, 77; Scotttish Open Four, Scotland, 87; Connemara Sculpture Park, Tex, 87; and others. *Teaching:* Asst prof sculpture, Fairleigh Dickinson Univ, Madison, NJ, 69-; instr sculpture, Parsons Sch Design, New York, 74-80. *Awards:* Creative Artists Pub Serv Award, Hwy Sculpture, Vt, 71; Nat Endowment Arts Artist Fel, 80. *Bibliog:* Josh Cohn (auth), Between School and Castelli, Art in Am, 73; Barbara Rose (auth), Nebraska Highway Sculpture, Vogue, 76; Nancy Grove (auth), Interpretations, Southwest Arts, 85. *Media:* Stone sculpture and stone earthworks. *Publ:* Auth, John Coltrane, Doubleday & Co, New York, 73; auth, William Bronk--Poet, Occurrence Number 7, Philadelphia, 77; auth, John Taggart, In: Peace on Earth, Turtle Island Found, 81. *Dealer:* Peter Rose Gallery 200 E 58th St New York NY. *Mailing Add:* c/o Schmidt-Dean Gallery 1636 Walnut St Philadelphia PA 19103

GRAVES, KA (KATHLEEN ROSE)
PAINTER, SCULPTOR
b Detroit, Mich. *Study:* Am Col Paris, AA, 74; Ariz State Univ, BFA, 76, MFA, 79, PhD studies, 87-88. *Work:* Rutgers Univ; Scottsdale Ctr Arts, Ariz; Continental Can; Ariz State Art Collections. *Comn:* Drawings, Mesa Mus, Ariz, 80; set & costume design, Lyric Opera Theatre, 86; Musica Dolce, Costume Des & Construct, 87. *Exhib:* Nat Drawing Exhib, Rutgers Univ, 77; Four Corners States Biennial, Phoenix Art Mus, 79; Mother, Daughter & Wholly Beastie, Scottsdale Ctr Arts, Ariz, 82; Arizona's Finest, Ctr Arts, Tempe, 83; Personal Mythologies, The Hearst Art Ctr, Moraga, Calif, 90. *Teaching:* Adj instr painting & drawing, Grand Canyon Col, Ariz, 83-85; instr, life drawing, Glendale Community Col, Ariz, 86-87; assoc prof, Ariz State Univ, 86 & 92. *Bibliog:* Barbara H Perlman (auth), Phoenix: A Sun Palace, Art News, 12/81; Carol Donnell-Kotrozo (auth), The mythic core, Art Week, 6/5/82; Kiana Dicker (auth), Physical Graffiti Scottsdale Daily Progress, 7/5/90. *Media:* Mixed Media. *Dealer:* Elaine Horwitch Galleries Scottsdale AZ; Winged Horse Gallery Las Vegas NV. *Mailing Add:* 921 W Lynwood Phoenix AZ 85007

GRAVES, KENNETH ROBERT
PHOTOGRAPHER
b Portland, Ore, June 27, 42. *Study:* San Francisco Art Inst, with Jerry Burchard & John Collier Jr, BFA, 70, MFA, 71. *Work:* San Francisco Mus Art; Nat Libr, Paris; Ann Bremer Mem Libr, San Francisco Art Inst; Mus Mod Art, New York; George Eastman House, Rochester, NY; Erie Art Mus, Pa. *Exhib:* Three Photographers, San Francisco Mus Art, 71; New Photography in the Bay Area, M H De Young Mus, 73; Exchange DFW-SFO, Ft Worth Art Mus & San Francisco Mus Art, 75; Color as Form, George Eastman House & Corcoran Gallery, 82; solo exhibs, Blue Sky Gallery, Portland, 82 & 85, Portico Gallery, Philadelphia, 83. *Pos:* Photogr, Jeroboam Inc, San Francisco, 71- *Teaching:* Instr photog, San Francisco Art Inst & Photog Film Ctr West, Berkeley; assoc prof, Pa State Univ, 77- *Awards:* Nat Endowment Arts Fel, 76; Purchase Award, Alternatives, 83; First Award, Pa Festival Arts, 83-85. *Bibliog:* Joan Murray (auth), interview, Artweek, 1/22/72; Time-Life Photog, 75; Popular Photog Ann, 82. *Publ:* Coauth, American Snapshots, Scrimshaw Press, 77. *Dealer:* Portico Gallery 902 Spruce Philadelphia PA 19107. *Mailing Add:* Dept Art Pa State Univ University Park PA 16802

GRAVES, MICHAEL
ARCHITECT, EDUCATOR
b Indianapolis, Ind, July 9, 34. *Study:* Univ Cincinnati, BSArch, 58; Harvard Univ, March, 59; Am Acad in Rome(fel), Prix de Rome, 60-62. *Work:* Mus Mod Art, Metro Mus, Smithsonian Inst, Cooper-Hewitt, Brooklyn Mus, New

York; Berlin Mus, Ger; Deutsches Architekturmuseum, Frankfurt, Ger. *Comn:* Crown Am Corp Office Bldg, 86; Walt Disney World Swan & Dolphin Hotels, 87; Hotel New York, EuroDisneyland, France, 89; Denver Cent Libr, 90; Astridplein Hotel, Antwerp, Belg, 92. *Exhib:* One-man shows, Johnstown Art Mus, Pa, Syracuse Univ Sch Archit, Syracuse, NY, 90, Marini Marino Mus, Florence, Italy, 91, Mikimoto Hall, Tokyo, Japan, 92, Cheekwood Fine Arts Ctr, Nashville, Tenn; retrospective, 25 Years in Princeton, Princeton Arts Coun, Kirby Art Ctr, Lawrenceville Sch, NJ, 89. *Pos:* Dir visual studies prof, Princeton Univ, 70-72; architect-in-residence, Am Acad in Rome, Italy, 79. *Teaching:* Lectr archit, Princeton Univ, 62-67, assoc prof, 67-72, prof, 72-; vis prof archit, Univ Tex, Austin, 74, Univ Calif, Los Angeles, 77, Univ Houston, Tex, 78 & Univ NC, Charlotte, 79; architect-in-residence, Am Acad Rome, Italy, 79; Prof, Princeton Univ, 72. *Awards:* Am Inst Archit Honor Awards, 75, 79, 82, 83, 85, 87, 90 & 92; Progressive Archit Design Awards, 70, 76, 77, 78, 79, 80, 83 & 89; many others including, NJ Soc Archit, Interiors Mag, Progressive Archit Mag, PA Furniture Design, Inst Bus Design; and others. *Bibliog:* Five Architects, Oxford Univ, 72; Michael Graves, Academy Editions, 79; Michael Graves Buildings and Projects: 1966-1981, Rizzoli, 83; Kings of Infinite Space: Michael Graves and Frank Lloyd Wright, Academy Editions, 84; Michael Graves Buildings and Projects: 1982-1989, Princeton Archit Press, 90. *Mem:* fel Edward MacDowell Colony; Fel Am Inst Archit; Trustee Am Acad Rome; Dir Inst Archit & Urbanism. *Media:* Pencil, Colored Pencil; Acrylic Paint. *Publ:* Auth, Thought Models, Sch Design, NC State Univ, 78; auth, Value of color, Archit Rec, 80; contribr, Catalogue Venice Biennale, 80; contribr, Speaking a New Classicism, Smith Col Mus Art, 81; auth, Le Corbusier's drawn references, In: Introduction to Le Corbusier Drawings, Acad Ed, London, 81; A Case for Figurative Architecture, Rizzoli, 82; Ritual, The Princeton Journal, 84. *Dealer:* Max Protetch Gallery 37 W 57th St New York NY 10019; John Nichols Printmakers 83 Grand St New York NY 10013. *Mailing Add:* 341 Nassau St Princeton NJ 08540

GRAVES, MORRIS
PAINTER
b Fox Valley, Ore, Aug 28, 10. *Work:* Seattle Art Mus; Phillips Mem Gallery, Mus Mod Art, Whitney Mus Am Art & Metrop Mus Art, New York. *Exhib:* One-man shows, Morris Graves: A Vision of the Inner Eye Touring Retrospective, Phillips Collection, Washington, DC, 83-84; Art Mus Santa Cruz, Calif, 84; Los Angeles Co Mus Art, Mus Contemp Art, Chicago; Nat Gallery Art, Washington, DC, Cleveland Mus Art, Whitney Mus Am Art, Stamford, Conn; Wight Art Gallery, UCLA, Calif, Nat Gallery Mod Art, New Delhi, 88; Nat Acad Design, 74. *Awards:* Guggenheim Found fel, 46; Blair Prize, Art Inst Chicago, 48; Windsor Award, Duke & Duchess of Windsor, 57. *Bibliog:* Katherine Kuh (auth), The Artist's Voice, Harper & Row, 60; The Drawings of Morris Graves, NY Graphic Soc, 74; Morris Graves: Vision of the Inner Eye, Phillips Collection & George Braziller Inc, 83. *Mem:* Hon mem Am Watercolor Soc. *Media:* Tempera, Oil. *Mailing Add:* c/o Schmidt Bingham Gallery 41 W 57th St New York NY 10019

GRAVES, NANCY STEVENSON
PAINTER, SCULPTOR
b Pittsfield, Mass, Dec 23, 40. *Study:* Vassar Col, BA, 61, fel, 71; Yale Univ Sch Art & Archit, BFA, 62 & MFA, 64. *Work:* Whitney Mus Am Art, Mus Mod Art, Metrop Mus Art, New York; Nat Gallery, Ottawa, Ont; Albright-Knox Art Gallery, Buffalo, NY; Chicago Art Inst; Wallrat-Richartz Mus-Ludwig Collection, Cologne, Ger; Mus Mod Art, Vienna, Austria; Corcoran Gallery Art, Washington, DC; Walker Art Ctr, Minneapolis, Minn. *Exhib:* Solo exhibs, A Survey 1969/80, Albright-Knox Gallery, Clash of Cultures: New Paintings on Paper and Sculpture, Gerald Peters Gallery, Santa Fe, NMex, travelling to the Gerald Peters Gallery, Dallas, Tex, 90, Heland Wetterling Gallery (catalog), Gothenburg, Sweden, 91, Paradigm and Paradox (catalog), Locks Gallery, Philadelphia, Pa, 91, Energy Fields Transfixed: Recent Works by Nancy Graves, Meredith Long & Co, Houston, Tex, 91, Skin Series, Knoedler & Co, New York, 91 & Alchemy of Time, Irving Galleries, Palm Beach, Fla, 92; 45th Ann Midyear Show, Butler Inst Am Art, Youngstown, Ohio, 81; A Private Vision: Contemporary Art From The Graham Gund Collection, 82, 70's into 80's: Printmaking Now, 86 & Boston Collects: Contemporary Painting & Sculpture, 87, Mus of Fine Arts, Boston, Mass; Biennial Exhib, 83 & Vital Signs: Organic Abstraction from the Permanent Collection, 88, Whitney Mus Am Art, New York; Prints from Tyler Graphics, Walker Art Ctr, Minneapolis, Minn, 85; Primitives in 20th Century Art: Affinity of the Tribal & the Modern, Mus Mod Art, New York, 85; Six in Bronze (traveling), 85 & Public & Private: Am Prints Today, 86, Brooklyn Mus, NY; Structure to Resemblance: Work by Eight American Sculptors (with catalog), Albright-Knox Art Gallery, Buffalo, NY, 87; Arte Americana Anni Sessanta dal Ludwig Museum de Colonia, Galleria d'Arte Moderna di Ca'Pesaro, Venice, Italy, 87; A View of a Workshop: Selections from Tyler Graphics 1974-1987, Katonah Gallery, NY, 87; BIG little Sculpture, Williams Col Mus Art, Williamstown, Mass, 88 & New Britain Mus Am Art, Conn, 89; The World of Art today (with catalog), Milwaukee Art Mus, Wis, 88; The Feminine Touch, Thomas Fine Arts, Pasadena, Calif, 88; Contemporary American Art, Ho-Am Gallery, Seoul, Korea & Seed Hall, Seibu Mus, Tokyo, Japan, 88; First Impressions (catalog), Walker Art Ctr, Minneapolis, Minn, 89; The Experience of Landscape (catalog), Whitney Mus Am Art Downtown at Fed Reserve Plaza, New York, 89; Painted Forms: Recent Metal Sculptures, Whitney Mus Am Art at Philip Morris, New York, 90; Baltimore Collects: Painting and Sculpture Since 1960, Baltimore Mus Art, Md, 90; Process to Presence: Issues in Sculpture 1960-1990, in conjunction with the 14th Int Sculpture Conf, Locks Gallery, Philadelphia, Pa, 92. *Awards:* Nat Endowment Arts Grant, 72; Award Am Art, Pa Acad Fine Arts, 87; Spirit Achievement Award, Albert Einstein Col Med, 88. *Bibliog:* Bonnie Barrett Stretch (auth), Nancy Graves: Knoedler, ARTnews, 1/92; Jan Sjostrom (auth), The Alchemy of Time, Palm Beach Daily News, 2/9/92; Gary Schwan (auth), Gallery honors Graves for multicultural works, Palm Beach Post, 2/21/92. *Mem:* Col Art Asn (bd dir, currently); Am Acad Inst Art & Lett, New York. *Publ:* Auth, Festival of Women's Film (film), Cologne WGer, 73; An Evening of Films by Nancy Graves, Millenium Film Workshop Cineprobe, Mus Mod Art, 74; Sculpture of the 60's (film), Whitney Mus Downtown, New York Artists Space, New York. *Dealer:* M Knoedler & Co 19 E 70th St New York NY 10021. *Mailing Add:* 69 Wooster St New York NY 10012

GRAVES, ROBERT EDWARD
PAINTER, INSTRUCTOR
b Spokane, Wash, Feb 2, 29. *Study:* Whitworth Col, Spokane, BA, 52; study with Alden Mason,60-62; Univ Wash, Seattle, MFA, 62; also with Gandy Brodie, 68 & Elaine de Kooning, 79. *Work:* Seattle Art Mus, Evergreen State Col & Bremerton Housing Authority, Wash; Portland Art Mus, Ore; State Univ NY, Potsdam. *Exhib:* Northwest Ann, Seattle Art Mus, Wash, 57; Printmakers of Washington, Seattle Art Mus, Mod Art Pavilion, 78; one-man shows, Seattle Art Mus, 79 & 85, Kerns Gallery, Pa, 81, Warehouse Gallery, Yakima, Wash, 84 & Adam East Mus & Art Ctr, Moses Lake, Wash, 92; Governor's Invitational, State Capitol Mus, Olympia, Wash, 81 & 83; Littman Gallery, Portland, Ore; NW Printmakers Open, 89; Paper in Particular, Univ Mo & Columbia Art League Gallery, 90; Collagraphs, traveling exhib, Wash, 90-92; and others. *Pos:* Dir, Gallery 76, Wenatchee, Wash, 76-78. *Teaching:* Instr fine art, Wenatchee Valley Col, 62-; lectr art & printmaking, Leicester Polytechnic, England, 70-71. *Awards:* K B Baker Mem Award, 43rd Ann, Seattle Art Mus, 57; First Award, Nat Printmaking Exhib, State Univ NY, Potsdam, 61; Printmaking Award, Edmonds Arts Festival, Old Nat Bank, 80. *Bibliog:* Robert Graves, Monotypes & Prints, The Alliance, Everette, Wash, 12/89. *Mem:* Northwest Print Coun, Portland; Wash State Art Educ Asn (pres, 64-66). *Media:* Oil, Printmaking. *Mailing Add:* 1401 Sunset Hwy East Wenatchee WA 98801

GRAY, CLEVE
PAINTER, SCULPTOR
b New York, NY, Sept 22, 18. *Study:* Princeton Univ, BA, 40. *Work:* Guggenheim Mus & Whitney Mus Am Art, New York; Phillips Collection, Wash, DC; Albright-Knox Gallery, Buffalo, NY; Univ Art Gallery, Berkeley, Calif. *Comn:* Wall paintings, Neuberger Mus, 73; Hartford Transportation Ctr, Conn, 88. *Exhib:* Honolulu Mus Art, Hawaii, 71; Albright-Knox Gallery, 77; Columbus Gallery Fine Art, Ohio, 77; Krannert Art Mus, Urbana, Ill, 77; Brooklyn Mus, NY, 87. *Awards:* Purchase Award, Univ Ill, 51; Ford Found Award, 61; Conn Arts Award, 87. *Bibliog:* Daniel Robbins (auth), Cleve Gray, Art Int, 3/64; Thomas Hess (auth), Cleve Gray 1967-1977, Albright Knox Art Gallery, 77; David Shirey (auth), article, New York Times, 6/12/79. *Mem:* Century Asn, New York. *Media:* All. *Publ:* Ed, David Smith, 68; John Marin, 70; Hans Richter, 71. *Dealer:* Irving Galleries 332 Worth Ave Palm Beach FL 33480; Berry-Hill Gallery New York NY. *Mailing Add:* Cornwall Bridge CT 06754

GRAY, DON
PAINTER, CRITIC
b San Francisco, Calif, June 16, 35. *Study:* Ariz State Univ, Tempe, BA, 57; Univ Iowa, Iowa City, MA, 62. *Work:* Pepsico, NYNEX, Conde Nast & Kidder Peabody, New York, NY; Soc Hill Sheraton, Pa. *Exhib:* Art Students' League, New York, 82 & 84; CG Rein Galleries, Sante Fe, NMex, 87 & Scottsdale, Ariz, 88; Midtown Galleries, New York, 88; Western Images Gallery, New York, 89; and others. *Pos:* Art critic, Applause Mag, 70-71, New York Arts J, 75-79, Times-Herald Record, Middletown, NY, 82-86, Sunstorm Arts Mag, Long Island, NY, 82-84 & Art World Mag, New York, 82-; producer & moderator, Artist & Critic, Manhattan Cable TV Show, 75-. *Bibliog:* Phyllis Braff (auth), article, New York Times, 1/83; Theodore F Wolff (auth), article, Christian Sci/Monitor, 4/84; Ruth Bass (auth), article, Art News, 5/86. *Mem:* Col Art Assoc, New York; St Painters Group, New York; Silvermine Guild Artists, New Canaan, Conn. *Media:* Acrylic, Pastel. *Publ:* Auth, Reassessing the New York School, 8/82 & Contemporary art, video games and ET, 3/83, Sunstorm Arts Mag; Alfred Kubin's Leviathan, 4/83, Stanley Spencer: Visionary sexuality, 5/83 & Tom Benton's choice, 3/85, Art World; auth, John Constable: The mating of flesh and spirit, Sunstorm Arts Mag, 7/83. *Mailing Add:* c/o Univ Portland Buckley Ctr Gallery 5000 N Wilamette Blvd Portland OR 97203

GRAY, ELISE N
SCULPTOR
b Burkesville, Ky, Mar 9, 36. *Study:* Western Ky Univ, BS, 58; Univ Tenn, MS, 59; Arrowmount Sch Crafts, 59; study with Phyllis Hammond & Barbara Bisgyer, 72-77; Parsons Sch Design, 82. *Work:* IBM Corp, Burlington, Vt; AcQuest Capital Corp, New York; Am Fed Bank, Greenville, SC; AT&T Corp, Somerset, NJ; United Jersey Bank, Woodbury, NJ. *Comn:* Clay wall relief, Fla Nat Bank, Jacksonville, 86; wall sculpture, IBM Corp, Gaithersburg, Md, 87; wall sculpture, Fla educ dept, Tallahassee, Fla, 89. *Exhib:* Solo exhib, 14 Sculptors Gallery, New York, 79, 82, 84, 86, & 89; Art of Northeast, Exhib of Painting & Sculpture, Silvermine Guild of Artists, NY, 79, 82 & 83; Works in Clay-Elise Gray, Hudson River Mus, Yonkers, 83; Schick Art Gallery, Skidmore Col, 88. *Pos:* Co-founder, vpres & pres, Artisans Co-op, Westchester, NY, 73-77; chairperson exhibs publicity, 14 Sculptors Gallery, 78-89. *Teaching:* Field fac adv, archit ceramics, Vt Col Norwich Univ, 86-88; artist in residence, Macon Pub Sch, currently. *Awards:* Sculpture Award, Mamaroneck Artist Guild, 78 & Glickenhouse Found Award, 81; Pollock-Krasner Found Grant, 90-91. *Bibliog:* David Shirey (auth), Art View,

NY Times, 6/10/79; Robbie Ehrlic (auth), Elise Gray at 14 Sculptors, Arts Mag, 9/79; Rosalind Schneider (dir), Elise Gray-Fragments and Formations (video), Film Workshop of Westchester, 84. *Mem:* Am Crafts Coun; New York Artists Equity; Sculptors Int-Int Sculpture Ctr. *Media:* Clay. *Dealer:* Artspace Atlanta GA. *Mailing Add:* 1483 Oglethorpe St Macon GA 31201

GRAY, JIM
PAINTER, SCULPTOR
b Middleton, Tenn, June 4, 32. *Work:* Carnegie Libr, Regar Mus, Anniston, Ala; Brooklyn Navy Yard; 40 paintings, Loyal Am Life Ins Co, Mobile, Ala; City-Co Bldg, Knoxville, Tenn; Winsor & Newton, Secaucus, NJ; 16 paintings, Hiberhia Nat Bank, New Orleans; 6 paintings, Am Embassy, Oman. *Comn:* Design & sculpture for Bicentennial Medal, Sevier Co, Tenn; Gen John Sevier (2 bronze busts), Capitol Bldg, Nashville, & Knoxville, Tenn; Dr Robert F Thomas (mem painting), Sevierville, Tenn; Teaching Christ (bronze), Church St Methodist, Knoxville, Tenn; Dolly Parton (over lifesize bronze), Sevierville, Tenn; The Strike (heroic size bronze), Dallas, Tex, 87; bronze bear family, Riverhouse Park, Gatlinburg, Tenn. *Exhib:* Whiting Mus, Fairhope, Ala, 70, 73, 75 & 92; Watercolor USA, Springfield, Mo, 70; Realist Invitational, Gallery Contemp Art, Winston-Salem, NC, 71; Am Soc Marine Artists Ann, Grand Cent Gallery, New York, 80 & Peabody Mus, Salem, Mass, 81; 400 Years of Seafaring, Fine Arts Mus, Mobile, Ala, 82; Mystic Maritime Mus, 86-90; Mariners Mus, Newport News, Va 87; Md Hist Soc, Baltimore, 89; Retrospective, Arrowmont, Gatlinburg, Tenn, 89. *Teaching:* Instr painting, Buckhorn Art Workshop Ann, Gatlinburg, Tenn; instr watercolor, Atlanta Artist Club, Ga, 69-; lectr art & humanities, Univ Tenn, Knoxville, 70-71. *Awards:* Best in Show & Permanent Trophy, Azalea Trail Arts Festival, 57, 58 & 59; Best of Show, Hammel-Adams Glass, Mobile, 62 & 63; Paul VI Award, Paul VI Inst Arts, Washington, DC, 87; Art in Embassies Program, Washington, Dc. *Bibliog:* video, PBS, Knoxville; Am Artists Mag, 4/77. *Mem:* Am Soc Marine Artists (bd dirs, 83- , vpres, 88-92); Salmagundi Club; and others. *Media:* Watercolor, Oil; Clay, Bronze. *Publ:* Nat Geographic, 10/68; prints, Painting in Alkyds, Contemp Marine Art, 88. *Dealer:* Greenbriar Inc PO Box 1320 Pigeon Forge TN 37863. *Mailing Add:* 2405 Alcoa Hwy Knoxville TN 37920

GRAY, LARRY
PAINTER
b Columbia, Tenn, Sept 19, 44. *Study:* Univ Ga, with Lamar Dodd, BFA, 67; Yale Univ, with Jack Tworkov, Al Held & Bernard Chaet, MFA, 69. *Work:* Mus Mod Art, New York; Chicago Art Inst; Brooklyn Mus; Seattle Art Mus; Achenbach Found, Calif Palace Legion of Honor, San Francisco; Laguna Mus, Laguna Beach, Calif. *Comn:* Oil painting, comn by His Majesty, the King of Saudi Arabia, 79. *Exhib:* New Works, Stanford Univ, Palo Alto, 73; one-man shows, ADI Gallery, San Francisco, 77-78, Foster/White Gallery, Seattle, 77-79, 81, 83, 84 & 89, Mirage Gallery, Santa Monica, Calif, 79, Getler-Pall, New York, 80, Karl Bornstein Gallery, Santa Monica, 80, 82, 84, 85, 87 & 89, Adelle M Gallery, Dallas, Tex, 86, Philip Dash, New York, 87 & Harlene/Allen, San Francisco, 87; Am Painters, Tokyo Cent Mus Arts, Japan, 78; New Acquisitions, Brooklyn Mus, 79. *Teaching:* Assoc prof painting, Humboldt State Univ, 69-77. *Bibliog:* Robert McDonald (auth), Larry Gray's atmospheric paintings, 77, Landscapes sensitively interpreted, 78 & Landscape: macro and micro, 79, Artweek; Gerrit Henry (auth), Larry Gray at Phillip Dash, Art News, 2/88. *Media:* Dry Pigment and Pastel; Oil on Linen. *Mailing Add:* c/o Foster/White Gallery 3112 Occidental S Seattle WA 98104

GRAY, MARIE ELISE
PAINTER
b Bremanger, Norway, Oct 7, 14; US citizen. *Study:* Derbyshire Sch Fine Art, 64-65; Cornish Sch Allied Art, 66-70; Olympic Col, 71; and with Rex Brandt, Sergei Bongart, Warren Brandon, Raymond Brose, Richard Yip, Maxine Masterfield, Christopher Schink & Al Brouchette. *Work:* Frye Art Mus, Boeing Co & US Steel Co, Seattle; Univ Ore; AMFAC Inc, San Francisco; Dean Witter & Assoc; and numerous pvt collections throughout US, Japan, Guatemala & Scandinavia. *Comn:* Painting for retired vpres, Pac Lutheran Univ; five paintings, comn by William Dahlberg, DDS, 80; two paintings, Transglobe Travel, 81; 30 paintings for private collection in Norway; painting for crab fishing Co, Seattle, 90. *Exhib:* Solo exhibs, Freemanson Gallery, 65-71, Frye Art Mus, 72 & 79-80, Goodyears Gallery, Edmonds, 75, Matheson Gallery, Seattle, 76, Charles Wright Acad, Tacoma, 78, Stillwater Gallery, Seattle, 82 & 89 & Northwest Artists Gallery, Univ Village, Seattle, 84; Wash State Art Biennial, Nat League Am Pen Women, Unitarian Gallery, Seattle, 83; Nat League Am Pen Women Exhib, Kitridge Gallery, Tacoma, Wash, 87; Western Painters Spring Exhib, 87 & Northwest Watercolor Exhib, 87 & 88, Bellevue, Wash; NW Signature, Intermec Corp, Arts Coun Snohomish Coun, Everett, Wash, 90. *Pos:* Pres, Co-art Art Asn; exhib chmn, NW Watercolor Exhib, 72; state art chmn, Nat League Am Pen Women, 72-75 & 80-81. *Teaching:* Instr art, YWCA, 68, Wash Athletic Club, Women's Univ Club, 73, Seattle & Sandpoint Golf & Country Club, 75-77. *Awards:* Honor Award, Women Painters of Washington Exhib, Peter Kirk Gallery, Kirkland, Wash, 87; Second Award, Co-arts Ann, Seattle, Wash, 88; D D Jeneen Mem Award, Women Painters of Wash, 89; and others. *Bibliog:* Critic's choice, Seattle Times, 9/16/76 & 77. *Mem:* Northwest Watercolor Soc; Nat League Am Pen Women; Women Painters Wash; Olympic Art Asn. *Media:* Multi, Watercolor. *Dealer:* Kirsten Gallery 5320 Roosevelt Way NE Seattle WA 98105; Stillwater Gallery 1900 N Northlake Way #145 Mariner's Sq Seattle WA. *Mailing Add:* 7723 30th Ave NE Seattle WA 98115

GRAY, RICHARD
DEALER
b Chicago, Ill, Dec 30, 28. *Pos:* Owner & dir, Richard Gray Gallery; chmn bd governors, Smart Mus Art, Univ Chicago. *Mem:* Art Dealers Asn Am (dir & vpres); Chicago Art Dealers Asn (former pres); Col Art Asn Am; Am Asn Mus. *Specialty:* Paintings, sculpture, drawings and prints by established European and American Modern Masters and the avant garde. *Mailing Add:* Gallery 620 N Michigan Ave Chicago IL 60611

GRAY, ROBERT HUGH
PAINTER, EDUCATOR
b Dallas, Tex, Sept 22, 31. *Study:* Yale Univ, BFA(painting), 59, MFA(painting), 61. *Pos:* Dean, Visual Arts Div, State Univ NY Col, Purchase, 75-79 & Col Fine Arts, Univ Calif, Los Angeles, 80-87. *Teaching:* Instr design & visual commun, Cooper Union, New York, 60-66; instr drawing, painting & design & dean, Silvermine Col Art, Conn, 66-71; prof painting & head dept art, Pa State Univ, State Col, 72-75; prof painting & drawings, Univ Calif Los Angeles, 87-90; prof art & chmn dept art & art professions, New York Univ, 90-91,; dean fine arts dept, Univ Conn, 91- *Awards:* Outstanding Educator Award, 73; Order of Chavalier of Letters & Arts, France, 87. *Mem:* Nat Coun Art Adminrs; Col Art Asn; Am Asn Higher Educ; Confederation Calif Arts. *Media:* Oil, New Media. *Mailing Add:* Fine Arts Dept Univ Conn 875 Coventry Rd Storrs CT 06269-1128

GRAY, ROBERT WARD
ADMINISTRATOR
b Tallahassee, Fla, June 26, 16. *Study:* Univ Fla; Tri-State Col; Grad Sch Am Craftsmen, with Herbert H Sanders. *Collections Arranged:* Co-dir, New Eng Craft Exhib, 55. *Pos:* In charge pottery shop & coordr craft prog, Old Sturbridge Village, 49-51; dir, Worchester Craft Ctr, 51-61; dir, Southern Highland Handicraft Guild, 61-80, dir emer, 80; dir, Development, 80-84; Craft Mgt Consult, 84- *Mem:* Fel Am Crafts Coun, 80. *Mailing Add:* 17 Botany Court Asheville NC 28805

GRAY, THOMAS ALEXANDER
CONSULTANT, COLLECTOR
b Winston-Salem, NC, Feb 7, 48. *Study:* Duke Univ, BA(hist art), 70; Am Cult Winterthur Prog, Univ Del, MA, 74; Summer Inst Arts Admin, Harvard Univ, 74. *Pos:* Dir, Mus early Southern Decorative Arts, Winston-Salem, 76-79; consult, Graylyn Conf Ctr, Wake Forest Univ, 81- *Awards:* Ruth C Cannon Award, Hist Preserv Found NC, 83. *Mem:* Hist Preservation Soc NC Inc (pres exec comt, 76-78); Hist Preservation Fund NC Inc (bd, 76-, vpres, 79-, pres, 80-82); Stagville Preservation Ctr, Durham, NC (bd, 77-84); Piedmont Craftsmen Inc (bd, 85-); Old Salem Inc (develop dir, 74-76, bd, 81-, exec comt, 82-). *Mailing Add:* 10 West St Winston-Salem NC 27101

GRAZDA, ED
PHOTOGRAPHER
b New York, NY, Mar 27, 47. *Study:* RI Sch Design, BFA, 69. *Work:* Mus Mod Art, New York; Mus Fine Art, Houston, Tex; New Orleans Mus Fine Art. *Awards:* Nat Endowment Arts Grant, 86; NY Found Arts, 86. *Bibliog:* Creative Camera, 8/75; Camera, 5/74 & 7/78; Granta, Eng (issue 21), 87. *Mem:* Col Art Asn. *Publ:* Auth, Afganistan 1980-1989, Parkett/Der Alltag, Zurich & New York, 90. *Mailing Add:* 17 Bleecker St New York NY 10012

GRAZIANI, SANTE
PAINTER, MURALIST
b Cleveland, Ohio, Mar 11, 20. *Study:* Cleveland Sch Art, 38-41; Sch Fine Arts, Yale Univ, BFA, 43, MFA, 48. *Work:* Brooklyn Mus; Mus Mod Art, New York; Philadelphia Mus; Corcoran Gallery Art, Washington, DC; Dallas Mus Fine Arts, Tex; and others. *Comn:* Murals, Bluffton Post Off, Ohio, 41, Columbus Junction Post Off, Iowa, 42, Holyoke Pub Libr, Mass, 49-51, Am Battle Monument, Henri-Chapelle, Belg, 55-58 & Mayo Clin, Rochester, Minn, 69; and others. *Exhib:* One-man shows, Babcock Galleries, New York, nine times, 62-71, Kanegis Gallery, Boston, 64-70, Allentown Art Mus, 70, Fairweather-Hardin Gallery, Chicago, three times, 70-76, Inst Arts & Sci, Manchester, NH, 81; retrospective, Springfield Mus, Mass, 77; and others. *Pos:* Officer in charge arts & crafts, USA, Pac Theatre Operations, 45-46. *Teaching:* Instr drawing & painting, Sch Fine Arts, Yale Univ, 46-51; dean; head, Worcester Art Mus Sch, 51-72, dean, 72-81, dean emer, 81-; acad dean, Paier Col Art, 82-, dean, 89- *Awards:* Pulitzer Scholar, 42; Boston Art Dirs Club Award, 54; Spec Drawing Award, Norfolk Mus, 61; and others. *Mailing Add:* 6 Prospect Ct Hamden CT 06517

GREAR, JAMES MALCOLM
DESIGNER, EDUCATOR
b Mill Springs, Ky, June 12, 31. *Study:* Art Acad Cincinnati, Ohio, 58, cert. *Work:* Cooper-Hewitt, New York. *Comn:* Henri Matisse Catalogue, Detroit Inst Art, Mich, 77; HHS Seal, Dept Health & Human Serv, Washington, DC, 80; Vet Admin 50th Anniversary 15-cent Commemorative Stamp, US Postal Serv, Washington, DC; Presby Church (USA) Seal/Symbol, 85; US Inst of Peace Seal, 88; Merrimack Valley Textile Mus, N Andover, Mass, Permanent Exhib, 68. *Exhib:* New Eng Designers, Addison Gallery Contemp Art, Andover, Mass, 64; Commun by Design, Inst Contemp Art, Boston, 64; Malcolm Grear Designers Exhib, List Art Bldg, Brown Univ, 73, AIGA, NY, 74, Calif Col Arts & Crafts, Jorgensen Gallery Univ Conn, 75 & others; Biennale of Graphic Design Brno 74, Czech; Environmental Design: Signing & Graphics, AIGA, NY, 77; Color, Whitney Mus Am Art, New York. *Pos:* Designer/consult publ, RI Sch Design, 63- & Guggenheim Mus, New York, 69-; design consult, Comt to Rescue Italian Art, 67-68; nat design chmn, Nat Asn Partners of the Americas, 70-; designer/Sci Am Libr Ser, 82-87;

designer/Worth Publ, 69-; design consult, RI Tall Ships 76, 75-76 & Mayo Clinic Foun, 83- *Teaching:* Prof graphic design, RI Sch Design, 61-87; prof, Helen M Danforth, 88. *Awards:* Am Inst Graphic Arts Ann Award, 50 Best Bks Publ in US, 68, 70, 71, 74 & 77; Gov's Arts Award, RI State Coun Arts, 69; Art Libr Soc NAm Award, Henri Matisse: Paper Cut-Outs, 77. *Bibliog:* Walter Diethelm (auth), Signs/Signet/Symbol, ABC Ed, Zurich, 70; Albert Giacometti (auth), Solomon R Guggenheim Mus, NY, 74; article, Idea Mag, Japan, 75; Am Trademarks, Vol I, II; Eames Morrison (auth), Power of Ten, Sci An Libr, 81; Aaron Siskind (auth), Pleasures and Terrors, NY Graph Soc, 82. *Mem:* Am Inst Graphics Art, New York; Providence Art Club. *Publ:* Auth, Curtis: Biology, Worth Publ, 68;. *Mailing Add:* Dept Design RI Sch Design 2 College St Providence RI 02903

GREAVER, HANNE
PRINTMAKER, PAINTER
b Copenhagen, Denmark, Aug 1, 33. *Study:* Kunsthaandvaerkerskolen, Copenhagen. *Work:* Beloit Col, Wis; Univ Ga; Univ Maine, Orono; Mich State Univ; Univ Nebr. *Exhib:* Univ Maine, Orono, 70; Five Women Printmakers, Kalamazoo Inst Arts, Mich, 69; Boston Printmakers, 76; Mich Printmakers, 77; Northwest Print Coun Inaugural Exhib, 82. *Awards:* Purchase Award, Boston Printmakers, 76. *Mem:* Northwest Print Coun. *Media:* Lithography, Oil. *Mailing Add:* Box 120 Cannon Beach OR 97110

GREAVER, HARRY
PAINTER, PRINTMAKER
b Los Angeles, Calif, Oct 30, 29. *Study:* Univ Kans, BFA & MFA. *Work:* Amherst Col, Mass; Univ Maine, Orono; New York Pub Libr; Norfolk Mus Arts & Sci, Va; Univ Utah Mus Fine Arts. *Exhib:* Drawings USA, St Paul, Minn, 63; Drawing & Small Sculpture Show, Ball State Univ, Ind, 68; 2nd Nat Print Show, San Diego, Calif, 71; Drawings by Living American Artists, Univ Utah Mus Fine Arts, 72-73; 10 Year Print Retrospective, Cannon Beach Gallery, 89. *Collections Arranged:* Paintings by American Masters, Kalamazoo Inst Arts, Mich, 66, Western Art, 67, The Surrealist, 71 & Reginald Marsh, 74; Harvey Breverman, 76. *Pos:* Dir, Kalamazoo Inst Arts, 66-78; dir, Greaver Gallery, 78- *Teaching:* Assoc prof art, Univ Maine, Orono, 55-66. *Awards:* Purchase Awards, Norfolk Mus, 63 & 64. *Media:* Watercolor; Lithographs. *Mailing Add:* Box 120 Cannon Beach OR 97110

GREAVES, JAMES L
CONSERVATOR, RESTORER
b Middletown, Conn, Jan 25, 43. *Study:* Col William & Mary, BS; Inst Fine Arts, NY Univ, MA(art hist), 70, dipl(art conserv), 70. *Pos:* Conserv intern, Los Angeles Co Mus Art, 68-70, conservator, 70; chief conservator, Detroit Inst Arts, 70-76; conservator, Los Angeles Co Mus Art, 77-, actg head conservator, 79-80, senior paintings conservator, 80-85; consult conservator, Huntington Libr, Art Gallery & Botanical Gardens, 79-; pvt conservator, 85- *Teaching:* Instr, Calif State Univ, Fullerton, 80-87; vis lectr, Univ Calif, Los Angeles, 81-85. *Mem:* Fel Int Inst Conserv Hist & Artistic Works; fel Am Inst Conserv; Western Asn Art Conservators (pres, 78-79). *Publ:* Coauth, New findings on Caravaggio's technique in the Detroit Magdalen, Burlington Mag, 74. *Mailing Add:* 1018 Pacific St Apt D Santa Monica CA 90405

GRECO, ANTHONY JOSEPH
PAINTER, ADMINISTRATOR
b Cleveland, Ohio, Apr 24, 37. *Study:* Cleveland Inst Art, with Louis Bosa, BFA, 60; Kent State Univ, with Joseph O'Sickey, MFA, 66. *Work:* Omni Int Inc, Atlanta, Ga; Coca-Cola USA, Atlanta, Ga; Ga State Art Comn; Chase Manhattan Bank; Nationsbank, Charlotte, NC. *Comn:* Urban Walls Atlanta, one of six inner-city walls. *Exhib:* Butler Inst Am Art Ann; one-man shows, Armstrong State Col, Savannah, Ga, 76 & Javo Gallery, Atlanta, 78; Works on Paper, Kohler Arts Ctr, Sheboygan, Wis, 77; Aug Selection Atlanta Artists, Fay Gold Gallery, Atlanta, Ga, 81 & Unnatural Landscape, 88; Birmingham Biennial, Birmingham Mus Art, Ala, 87; Eighth Ann Auburn Works Paper, Auburn Univ, Ala, 87; Unnatural Landscape, Fay Gold Gallery, Atlanta, 88; Group Show McIntosh Gallery, Atlanta, 91 & 92; and others. *Teaching:* Chmn drawing dept, Atlanta Col Art, 66-75, chmn div advanced studio & asst to pres, 74-76, acad dean, 76-82; vis instr drawing & painting, Univ Wis-Madison, summer 70; prof painting & drawing, currently. *Awards:* Purchase Award, Butler Inst Am Art Midyear, 60; Southern Arts Fedn/Nat Endowment Arts Fel, 88; Gallery Affiliation, McIntosh Gallery, Atlanta. *Media:* Miscellaneous media. *Mailing Add:* Dept Drawing & Painting 1280 Peachtree St NE Atlanta GA 30309

GREELEY, CHARLES MATTHEW
PAINTER, SCULPTOR
b Teaneck, NJ, Sept 11, 41. *Study:* New York Sch Visual Arts, with George Ortman. *Work:* NMex Mus Fine Arts, Santa Fe; Mus Contemp Art, Houston, Tex; Longview Mus, Tex; Mus of Mod Art, San Francisco, Calif; Albuquerque Mus, NMex; and others. *Exhib:* Seven Year Retrospective, Capricorn Asunder Gallery, San Francisco, 71; two-person show, Contemp Arts Mus, Houston, Tex, 79; Ceramic Show, Glorieta Gallery, NMex, 79; Mariposa Gallery, Albuquerque, NMex, 81; one-person show, Elaine Horwitch Gallery, Santa Fe, 88; and others. *Pos:* Screening judge, San Francisco Art Festival, 71. *Teaching:* Instr painting & ceramics, Glorieta Pass Inst, Glorieta, NMex, 73-77. *Awards:* Cash Award, Weatherhead Found, NY, 74; Purchase Prize, Longview Mus Competition, Tex, 75; First Prize Cash Award, Southwest Biennial Weatherhead Found, NY, 76; and others. *Bibliog:* Tom Albright (auth), The Visionaries, Rolling Stone Mag, 71; Dr Roland Fischer (auth), The art of madness & the madness of art: an altered state experience, Md Psychiat Res Ctr, 72; Charlotte Moss (auth), Art in the Southwest, Art News, 8/77. *Media:* Acrylic, Watercolor; Wood. *Publ:* Contribr, Visions of Elsewhere, San Francisco Art Inst, 71. *Dealer:* Kathryn Fleck Gallery 610 Hyman Ave Aspen CO 81611. *Mailing Add:* Box 42 Glorieta NM 87535

GREEN, ART
PAINTER, EDUCATOR
b Frankfort, Ind, May 13, 41; Can citizen. *Study:* Art Inst Chicago, BFA, 65. *Work:* Art Inst Chicago; Nat Gallery Can, Ottawa; Pa Acad Fine Arts, Philadelphia; Mus Mod Kunst, Vienna, Austria; Mus Contemp Art, Chicago. *Exhib:* Five-man group, The Hairy Who, Chicago, 66-68; Personal Torment-Human Response, Whitney Mus Am Art, New York, 69 & Extraordinary Realities, 73; three-man show, Darthea Speyer Gallery, Paris, France, 70; two-man show, Pa Acad Fine Arts, Philadelphia, 74; Can Canvas, Time Mag Travel Show, 75-76; Ann, San Francisco Art Inst, 77; Who Chicago Traveling Show, Sunderland Arts Ctr, Eng, 79; one-man shows, Phyllis Kind Galleries, 74-86. *Teaching:* Asst prof painting, NS Col Art, Halifax, 69-71; assoc prof painting, Univ Waterloo, Ont, 77-, chmn fine arts dept, 88-91. *Awards:* Cassandra Award, Cassandra Found, Chicago, 70; Can Coun Arts Bursary, 71-73 & 76-77; Distinguished Teach Award, Univ Waterloo, 90. *Bibliog:* A Adrian (auth), rev in Art in Am, 7-8/74; T Gruber (auth), Arts Mag, 5/77; E Lucie-Smith (auth), American Art Now, William Morrow, New York, 85. *Media:* Oil. *Dealer:* Phyllis Kind Gallery 313 W Superior St Chicago IL 60610; Phyllis Kind Gallery 136 Greene St New York 10012. *Mailing Add:* 5 Elizabeth St Stratford ON N5A 4Z1 Canada

GREEN, DAVID OLIVER
SCULPTOR, EDUCATOR
b Enid, Okla, June 29, 08. *Study:* Am Acad Art; Nat Acad Art. *Work:* Los Angeles Co Mus Natural Hist. *Comn:* Dragonfly Fountain, Welton Beckett Asn, Hillsdale Shopping Ctr, San Mateo, Calif, 55; five figure group, Lytton Savings & Loan Asn, Hollywood, 60; children's sculpture, Women's Club for Bruggemeyer Mem Libr, Monterey Park, Calif, 68; Owl Tree (wall relief), dedicated to daughters of Maurice Fletcher & Tree of Life (fountain), Guyer Mem, Altadena Libr, Calif, 69. *Exhib:* Los Angeles Co Mus Art Ann, 61; Southern Calif Expos, San Diego Fair, Del Mar, 66; Citrus Col Invitational, Glendora, Calif, 68; 17th Ann All Calif Exhib, Laguna Beach Art Gallery, Calif, 71; Retrospective Exhib, Sculpture & Calligraphy, Walla Walla Col, Wash, 79; Lyons Gallery, Redlands, Calif, 85; San Bernardino Co Mus, Redlands, Calif, 85; and others. *Teaching:* Asst prof sculpture, Otis Art Inst, 47-73 & Scripps Col, 66; instr, Pasadena Art Mus, Calif, 56-59; instr calligraphy, Pasadena City Col, 74-76. *Awards:* First Prize for Sculpture, Laguna Beach Art Asn, 62 & 67; First Prize for Sculpture, Pasadena Soc Artists, 71, 75, 87 & 89. *Bibliog:* Jarvis Barlow (auth), David Green, Pasadena Independent, 7/13/47; Bev Johnson (auth), Owls, cats & bats, Los Angeles Times Sun Sect, 3/13/60; Peg Powell (auth), A way with animals, Independent Star-News, 12/15/63. *Mem:* Int Inst Arts & Lett; Pasadena Soc Artists; Soc Italic Handwriting (Western Am Br); Soc Calligraphy, Los Angeles. *Media:* Stone, Wood. *Mailing Add:* 176 W Jaxine Dr Altadena CA 91001

GREEN, DENISE G
PAINTER
b Melbourne, Australia, Apr 7, 46; US citizen. *Study:* Ecole Nat Superieure des Beaux Arts; Sorbonne Univ, Paris, BA, 69; Hunter Col, New York, MFA, 76. *Exhib:* Young Am Artists: 1978 Exxon National, Solomon R Guggenheim Mus, New York, 78; New Image Painting, Whitney Mus Am Art, New York, 78; Surfaces/Textures, Mus Mod Art, New York, 81; solo exhib, Ado Gallery, Bonheiden, Belgium, 82 & Gallery A Sydney, Australia, 83, Christine Abrahams Gallery, Melbourne, Australia, 85, 86, 87, 88, 89 & 90, Roslyn Oxley Gallery, Sydney, Australia, 85, 86, 88, 89 & 92, M13 Gallery, New York, 86, Althea Viafora Gallery, Brussels, Belg, 86, 87 & 88, Albert Baronian Gallery, Melbourne, Australia, 86, Anand Sarabhai Studio, Ahmedabad, India, 86, Gallery Contemp Art, Ahmedabad, India, 87, Univ Gallery, Melbourne Univ, Australia, 88; Contemporary Still Lifes Traveling Exhib, Mus Mod Art, New York, 82; Expatriate New York Works on Paper, City Art Inst, Paddington, Australia, 83; Premio Internazionale Biella per l'incisione 1983, Italy, 83; Extra-Critical Role, Gabrielle Bryers Gallery, New York, 83; Emerging Artists 1978-1986, Solomon R Guggenheim Mus, New York, 87; Seventeen Years at the Barn, Rosa Esman Gallery, New York, 88; No Trends, Nahan Contemp Gallery, New York, 90; Geometric Perspectives, Mus Mod Art, Art Lending Serv, New York, 91; Slow Art, Painting in New York Now, PS 1 Mus, Long Island City, New York, 92; and others. *Teaching:* Instr painting, Roger Willams Col, 72; instr studio & art hist, Fairleigh Dickinson Univ, 72-74; instr, Pratt Inst, 74; artist in residence, Ill State Univ, 76 & Art Inst Chicago, 77; instr, summer prog art, State Univ NY, Fredonia, 77; artist in residence, Va Commonwealth Univ, 81, Tyler Col Art, Temple Univ, 82 & Calif Inst Arts, 83. *Awards:* Ingram Merrill Found Grant, 72 & 73; Visual Arts Bd Grant, 74 & Traveling Grant, 77, Australian Coun Arts. *Bibliog:* Judy Cotton (auth), Denise Green, Australia Vogue, 9/87; Robert Smith (auth), Art: Exxon Show at Guggenheim, NY Times, 9/4/87; John Stringer (auth), Denise Green in Perth, Delaney Galleries (catalog), 91. *Publ:* Ed, Heresies, 2nd issue, 77. *Mailing Add:* 13 Laight New York NY 10013

GREEN, GEORGE D
PAINTER
b Portland, Ore, June 24, 43. *Work:* Guggenheim Mus, New York; Art Inst Chicago; Denver Art Mus; Detroit Inst Arts; Los Angeles Co Mus Art. *Comn:* AT&T Bldg, New York; Home Box Office Bldg, New York; Bulova Bldg, New York. *Exhib:* Solo exhibs, Triangle Gallery, San Francisco, 77, Louis Mus Am Art, Meisel Gallery, 78 & 79, 81-83 & 85-88, 90, 91-92, Hokin/Kaufman Gallery, Chicago, 81, 83 & 85-86, Hokin Gallery, Palm Beach, 81, 82, 84 & 86, Lavignes/Bastille, Paris; Abstract Painting Redefined, Danforth Mus, Munson Williams Proctor Inst; Reality of Illusion, Denver Mus, Oakland Mus, Alain Blondel, Paris; Phillip Johnson Art Ctr, Allentown, Pa, 86; Art Now Gallery, Gottenburg, Sweden, 87-88; Art Mus, Univ Ore,

Eugene, 87. *Teaching:* Instr, Univ Tex, Austin, 68-71; instr painting, State Univ NY, Potsdam 71-78; vis artist, Portland Art Mus, Ore, 77. *Bibliog:* Joe Jackobs (auth), The reality of artifice, Arts Mag, 2/83; Robert Atkins (auth), article, Archit Digest, 4/83; Edward Lucie-Smith (auth), American Art Now, 85. *Dealer:* Louis K Meisel Gallery 141 Prince St New York NY 10012. *Mailing Add:* c/o Louis K Meisel Gallery 141 Prince St New York NY 10012

GREEN, JONATHAN (WILLIAM)
MUSEUM DIRECTOR, PHOTGRAPHER
b Troy, NY, Sept 26, 39. *Study:* Mass Inst Technol, 58-60; Brandeis Univ, BA, 63; Harvard Univ, MA, 67. *Work:* Moderna Museet, Stockholm, Sweden; Mus Fine Art, Boston; Mus Art, Houston; Ctr Creative Photog, Tucson, Ariz; Int Ctr Photog, New York. *Comn:* Subway murals MTA, Cambridge Seven Architects, Boston, 66; mural, Cambridge Seven Architects, Rochester, NY, 69; photo projs, Architectural Record Mag, 70-75; phot projs, Baumeister, 71-74; Am Images photo proj, Bell System (AT&T), 79. *Exhib:* Four Contemporary Photographers, Fogg Art Mus, Harvard, Cambridge, Mass, 74; solo exhibs, Hayden Gallery, Mass Inst Technol, 76, Carl Seimbad Gallery, Boston, 76 & Art Mus, Ind Univ, Bloomington, 85; Tuseu Och En Bild, Moderna Museet, Stockholm, Sweden, 78; American Images, Corcoran Gallery, 80; Miami Color, Bass Mus Art, Fla, 86; two-person exhib, Emily Davis, Univ Akron, Ohio, 89; and many other group shows. *Pos:* Ed, assoc, Aperture Quart, New York, 74-76; dir, Univ Gallery & founding dir Wexner Ctr Arts & Ohio State Univ, Columbus, Ohio, 81-90; dir, Calif Mus Photog, Univ Calif, Riverside, 90- *Teaching:* Assoc prof photog, Mass Inst Technol, Cambridge, 68-76; prof photog, Ohio State Univ, Colombus, Ohio, 76-90; prof photog & art hist, Univ Calif Riverside, 90- *Awards:* Nat Endowment Arts Photogrs Fel, 78; Bell System (AT&T) Photog, Fel, 79. *Bibliog:* Hilton Kramer (auth), Camera work, NY Times Bk Rev, 4/21/74; Joan Murray (auth), American photography, Art Week, 9/84; James Hugunin (auth), American Photograpy, Exposure: 23 1, spring, 85. *Publ:* Auth, Camera Work: A Critical Anthology, 73 & The Snapshot, 74, Aperture; contribr, American Images: New Work by 20 Contemporary Photographers, McGraw Hill, 79; A Center for the Visual Arts: The OSU Competition, Rizzoli, 84; auth, American Photography: A Cultural History, Abrams, 84 & 92. *Mailing Add:* 1984 Bonne Brae Riverside CA 92506

GREEN, MARTIN LEONARD
PAINTER, PRINTMAKER
b Monterey Park, Calif, Oct 4, 36. *Study:* Brandt-Dike Sch Painting, 53-54; Pomona Col, Calif, 54-58; Mexico City Univ Americas, 57; Orange Coast Col, Calif, 75-76. *Work:* Los Angeles Co Mus of Art; Gruenwald Ctr for the Graphic Arts, Univ Calif, Los Angeles; Calif Palace Legion Honor; Standard Oil of Ind Arts Collections, Chicago; Fogg Mus Art, Harvard Univ; and others. *Comn:* Panels, Kapalua Bay Hotel, Maui, Hawaii, 77-78; Tobu-Ginza Hotel, Tokyo; Boca Raton Hotel, Fla; King Fahd, Saudi Arabia; and others. *Exhib:* All-Calif Show, Laguna Beach Mus of Art, 75; Contemp Monotypes, Santa Barbara Mus of Art, Calif, 76; Brand V, Brand Libr Art Gallery, Glendale, Calif, 76; New Am Monotypes, Smithsonian Inst Travelling Exhib, 78-80; Los Angeles Mus Sci & Indust; and others. *Pos:* Lectr monotype hist & demonstr technique, Los Angeles Co Mus of Art, Santa Barbara Mus of Art & Glendale Col. *Bibliog:* Florence Goodman (auth), A blending of eastern & western philosophies and art, SW Art, 4/76; Brendan Gill (auth), The Dream Come True, Lippincott & Crowell, 80; Calvin J Goodman (auth), Monotype: A singular art form, 81 & Martin Green-Monotypes and cliches-verre, 82, Am Artist. *Mem:* Los Angeles Printmaking Soc. *Media:* Monotype, Oil. *Dealer:* Louis Newman Galleries 322 N Beverly Dr Beverly Hills CA 90210. *Mailing Add:* c/o Art Angles Gallery 3411 E Chapman Orange CA 92669

GREEN, NANCY ELIZABETH
CURATOR, WRITER
Pittsfield, Mass, Apr 27, 55. *Study:* Conn Col, BA, 77; Sotheby Parke-Bernet Decorative Arts Prog, 79; Clark Inst Art Inst, Williams Col, MA, 84. *Collections Arranged:* Six in Bronze (with catalog), 84; The Modern Art of the Print: Selections from the Collection of Lois & Michael Torf (with catalog), 84; American Modernism: Precisionist Works on Paper (auth, catalog), 86-87; Bryan Hunt: Falls and Figures, (with catalog), 88-89; Arthur Wesley Dow & His Influence (auth, catalog), 90-91; Nature's Changing Legacy: The Photographs of Robert Glenn Ketchum, (auth, brochure), 92-93. *Pos:* Expert print dept, Christies East, New York, 80-82; curatorial asst, Williams Col Mus Art, 82-85; assoc cur prints & photographs, H F Johnson Mus, Ithaca, NY, 85-89, cur, 89- *Teaching:* Cornell Adult Univ, 88-89, 91 & 93. *Awards:* Moe Prize for scholarly research (Arthur Wesley Dow and his Influence) given by the NY State Hist Asn. *Mem:* Olive Press Adv Bd; Print Coun Am; Williamstown Regional Art Conserv Laboratory (mem bd). *Mailing Add:* Herbert F Johnson Mus Cornell Univ Ithaca NY 14853

GREEN, ROGER J
CRITIC, HISTORIAN
b New York, NY, Nov 16, 44. *Study:* Cornell Univ, BA, 67; Tulane Univ, MA, 72; Univ Chicago, PhD, 87. *Pos:* Critic art & archit, Times-Picayune, New Orleans, La, 78-92 & Booth News Service, Lansing, Mich, 92-; corresp, Berlin, Art News Mag, 91. *Res:* Art and Architecture in Europe, particularly Berlin, 1920-1940. *Publ:* Auth, Max Papart, Rizzoli, 84; contribr, Berlin/New York, Rizzoli, 91. *Mailing Add:* c/o Booth News Serv 217 Sycamore N Lansing MI 48933

GREEN, TOM
INSTRUCTOR, SCULPTOR
b Newark, NJ, May 27, 42. *Study:* Univ Md, BA, 67, MA(painting), 69. *Exhib:* New Sculpture: Baltimore-Washington-Richmond, Corcoran Gallery Art, Washington, DC, 70; Washington Sculpture, Philadelphia Art Alliance, 73; one-man show, Corcoran Gallery Art, 73; Whitney Biennial, Whitney Mus Art, New York, 75; North, East, West, South & Middle, Traveling Drawing Show, 75. *Pos:* Chair Fine Arts Dept, Corcoran Sch Art, currently. *Teaching:* Asst prof sculpture & drawing, Corcoran Sch Art, 69- *Bibliog:* Susan Sollins (auth), Washington report, Arts Mag, 9/73; David Tannous (auth), Tom Green: Words and images, Woodwind Mag, 12/11/73; Ben Forgey (auth), Washington: Pyramid shapes, Grenoble and theatrics, Art News, 1/74. *Mailing Add:* Dept Fine Arts Corcoran Sch Art 500 17th St NW Washington DC 20006

GREEN, WILDER
ARTS ADMINISTRATOR, ARCHITECT
b Paris, France, Apr 17, 27; US citizen. *Study:* Yale Col, 45-47; Ill Inst Technol & Design Inst, Chicago, 47-48; Yale Univ Sch Archit, BArch, 52. *Pos:* Asst dir & cur, Dept Archit & Design, Mus Mod Art, New York, 57-61, coordr planning for bldg prog, 61-63, coordr prog, 63-67, dir exhib prog, 67-69, dep to actg dir, 69-70, dir exhib prog, 70-71; pres, Cunningham Dance Found, 69-72; dir, Am Fedn Arts, 71-87;; spec consult & cur, Metrop Mus Art, 87-89;; pvt art consult & archit, 89- *Teaching:* Asst prof, Yale Sch Archit, 56-57; Hunter Col, 67-68. *Awards:* Am Craft Mus (acquisitions comt). *Mem:* Munic Art Soc New York; The Century Asn; MacDowell Colony (trustee, 81); Americas Soc (chmn arts adv comt, 87); Drawing Soc (trustee, mem exec comt, 62-). *Mailing Add:* 20 E 74th St New York NY 10021

GREENAMYER, GEORGE MOSSMAN
SCULPTOR, EDUCATOR
b Cleveland, Ohio, July 13, 39. *Study:* Philadelphia Col Art, BFA; Univ Kans, MFA; Ctr Advan Visual Studies (res fel); Mass Inst Technol, Cambridge. *Work:* De Cordova Mus, Lincoln, Mass; Brockton Art Mus, Mass; Duxbury Art Complex, Mass; Boston Univ. *Comn:* Steel sculpture, Am Elec Power Co, Columbus, Ohio, 83; Dadeland Rapid Transit Sta, Miami, Fl, 84; North Shore Comm Col, Lynn, Mass, 87; Public Safety Bldg, Wilmington, Del, 88; Libr, Univ Wis, Milwaukee, Wis, 89. *Exhib:* Lanmeir Int Sculpture Park, St Louis, Mo, 81; Queens Mus, Flushing, NY, 81; Public Sculpture in Columbus, Univ Gallery Fine Art, 84; Public Art Process, Miami, Fla, 86; Chesterwood, Stockbridge, Mass, 87; Caroline Freeland Park, Memesda, Md, 89; Univ Power Plant, Univ Alaska, Fairbanks, 90; Applied Sci Bldg, Iowa State Univ, Ames, Iowa, 90. *Teaching:* Prof sculpture, Mass Col Art, Boston, 81- *Awards:* Artists Fel Grant, Artists Found, Boston, Mass & Tiffany Grant, New York, NY, 77. *Bibliog:* John Baker (auth), review, Art in Am, 1/82; Peter Koenig (auth), article, South Shore Mag, summer 88; John Chandler (auth), article, Sculpture mag, 3-4/88; Christine Temin (auth), picture & review, 80 & Robert Taylor (auth), picture & review, 80, Boston Globe. *Mem:* Boston Visual Artists Union; Artist Blacksmiths NAm. *Media:* Steel. *Publ:* Auth, articles in numerous magazines. *Dealer:* Barbara Gillman Gallery Miami FL; Joy Horwich Gallery Chicago, IL. *Mailing Add:* Dept Art Mass Col Art 621 Huntington Ave Boston MA 02115

GREENBAUM, MARTY
PAINTER, SCULPTOR
b New York, NY, Mar 3, 34. *Study:* Univ Ariz, Tucson, BA, 56. *Work:* Picker Art Gallery, Colgate Univ, Hamilton, NY; Chrysler Mus at Norfolk, Va; The Print Club, Philadelphia, Pa; J Patrick Lannan Found, Los Angeles, CA; The Norman Fisher Collection, Jacksonville Art Mus, Jacksonville, Fla. *Comn:* Unique Book, comm by J Patrick Lannan Found, Los Angeles, CA, 68; Sept Calendar (centerfold), Changes Mag, New York, 71; eds of prints, Shenanigan Press at Jones Rd Print Shop, Barneveld, Wis, 74; Cajun Book, Comn by James McDonell, NY, 85. *Exhib:* Personal Torment & Human Concern, Whitney Mus Am Art, New York, 69; 4th Ann Contemp Reflections, Aldrich Mus Contemp Art, Ridgefield, Conn, 75; 20th Nat Print Exhib, Brooklyn Mus, NY, 76; The Object as Poet, Renwick Gallery, Smithsonian Inst, Washington, DC, 76-77; New Ways with Paper, Nat Collection of Fine Arts, Smithsonian Inst, 77; Solo exhib, Picker Art Gallery, Colgate Univ, 77; Paper as Medium, Smithsonian Inst Traveling Exhib, 78-80; Playground, installation, Inst for Contemporary Art, PS 1, Long Island City, Queens NY, 78; Artists' Books, Georges Pompidou Ctr, Paris, France, 85; Four Artists, Allan Stone Gallery, NY, 86; Fetishism Contemporary & Primative, Allan Stone Gallery, NY, 92. *Teaching:* Art, PS 63, New York, 88-90. *Awards:* The Inst for Art & Urban Resources Inc, 83; Creative Artists Public Service Prog, NY, 72, 75; Nat Endowment Arts Grant; The Inst for Contemp Art, 83. *Bibliog:* Dorothea Baer (producer), Marty & Lulu's Playground, Independent Film, 65; David Bourdon (auth), Marty Greenbaum, Village Voice, 65. *Mem:* Ctr Bk Arts. *Publ:* Human Concern/Personal Torment, Whitney Mus, 69; 30 Years of American Printmaking, The Brooklyn Mus, 77; The Object As Poet, Smithsonian Institution Press, 77; Paper as Medium Smithsonian Institution Traveling Exhibition Service, 78; RE: Pages, An Exhibition of Contemporary Americak Bookworks, Hera Educational Foundation, 81. *Dealer:* Galerie Caroline Corre 14 rue Guénégaud Paris France; Allan Stone Gallery 48 E 86th St New York NY. *Mailing Add:* 505 Court St #6D Brooklyn NY 11231

GREENBERG, BLUE (BLUMA KAFKA)
EDUCATOR, CRITIC
b Portsmouth, Va, Oct 13, 26. *Study:* Duke Univ, AB, 47; Univ NC, Chapel Hill, MA, 78; Univ Ital Stranieri, Perugia, Italy, 79. *Pos:* Art critic, Durham Herald, NC, 75- *Teaching:* Instr art hist, Meredith Col, NC, 76-; lectr, Wesleyan Col, NC. *Awards:* Am Found Fel, Reynolda House, Winston-Salem, 82; First Place, NC Press Club Award, 85; Communicator of year, NC Press Club, 90. *Mem:* Col Art Asn; Am Asn Univ Prof; Nat Fedn Press Women; NC Press Club. *Res:* Role of regional artists as independent voices against the force of international art trends, especially in the South. *Publ:*

Auth, North Carolina's Center Gallery, Art Voices, 80; Embellished visions, Darkroom, 81; Southern Painting Exhibition, Am Artist, 12/83; Vito Acconchi: the state of the art 1985, Arts, summer 85; Finery: An Exhibit of Wearable Art, Fiber Arts Mag; Regular Weekly Art Critical Column, Durham Herald. *Mailing Add:* Dept Art Meredith Col 3800 Hillsborough Raleigh NC 27607

GREENBERG, GLORIA
PAINTER, DESIGNER
b New York, NY, Mar 4, 32. *Study:* Cooper Union Art Sch, cert, 52; Yale-Norfolk Art Sch, painting with Nicholas Marsicano, scholar, 52; Brooklyn Mus Art Sch, printmaking with Gabor Peterdo, scholar, 53. *Work:* Kennedy Airport; Int Business Machines Corp; Bankers Trust, Los Angeles. *Exhib:* Brooklyn Mus Print Ann, 53; Soc Beaux Arts Dordogne, France, 59; eight one-woman shows, Mercer Gallery, New York, 70-80; Report from Soho, Grey Art Gallery, New York,75; Women in the Arts: Artists Choice, traveling exhib, 77; Women Invite Women, Warm, Minneapolis, Minn, 77; 15th Ann Drawing Show, Delmar Col, Corpus Christi, Tex, 80. *Pos:* Art consult & bk designer, Jr Bks Div, Harper & Row, 65-79. *Teaching:* Instr, Mid Westchester YWCA, Scarsdale, NY, 81; instr, Henry Street Settlement, 80-81, JASA, 81-83. *Awards:* Medal of Honor, Soc Beaux Arts Dordogne, France, 59. *Media:* Acrylic, Oil; Paper Works with Ink. *Publ:* Co-auth & illusr, Away We Go, 63 & Strange Plants & Animals, Harvey House, 64. *Mailing Add:* c/o 55 Mercer Gallery 55 Mercer St New York NY 10013

GREENBERG, IRWIN
PAINTER, INSTRUCTOR
b Brooklyn, NY, Apr 5, 22. *Study:* Art Students League; NY Univ, BS(art educ); study with Yasuo Kuniyoshi, Will Barnet, Hale Woodruff & Paul Gerchik. *Exhib:* Soldier Art, Nat Gallery, Washington, DC, 45; Mus Fine Arts, Boston, 45; Brooklyn Mus, 48; Springfield Mus, Mass, 60; Heckscher Mus, New York, 62; Birmingham Mus, Ala, 70-71; Grand Central Galleries, New York, 84-92; Kendall Gallery, Mass, 87-92; Milbrook Gallery, New York, 89-92; Wyckoff Gallery, NJ, 92; Taggart Art Gallery, Wyo, 92; and others. *Pos:* teacher painting & illusr, High Sch Art & Design, 68-65 & Sch Visual Arts, 86-90, New York. *Teaching:* Instr life drawing, Baruch Col, City Col New York, 53-54. *Awards:* Purchase Award, Watercolor USA, 92; First Prize, Fine Arts League, Colo, 92; Second Prize, Nat Arts League, Long Island, 92; and many others. *Mem:* Am Watercolor Soc. *Media:* Oil, Watercolor. *Publ:* Auth, Much depends on attitude, Am Artist Mag, 69; Max Ginsburg-Above ground & underground, Am Artist Mag, 70; contribr, Arts and Man, Scholastic Pub & Nat Gallery Art, 75-76; Splash 2, 92; Contribr, Irwin Greenberg, Working with body color, Watercolor, 92; and others. *Dealer:* Grand Cent Art Galleries 24 W 57th St New York NY 10019. *Mailing Add:* 17 W 67th St New York NY 10023

GREENBERG, RONALD K
DEALER, COLLECTOR
b St Louis, Mo, July 17, 37. *Study:* Washington Univ, St Louis, Mo. *Mem:* Art Dealers Asn Am. *Specialty:* Contemporary American art. *Collection:* Works by Lichenstein, Warhol, Stella, Kelly, Motherwell, Frankenthaler, Judd, Serra, Chamberlain and Rauschenberg. *Mailing Add:* The Greenberg Gallery 44 Maryland Plaza St Louis MO 63108

GREENBLATT, ARTHUR E
EDUCATOR, ADMINISTRATOR
b Baltimore, Md, Jan 16, 42. *Study:* Md Int Col Art, BFA, 63; Towson State Univ, 70. *Pos:* Assoc dir, Union of Independent Col Art, Kansas City, Mo, 74-75; acad dean, Ctr Creative Studies, Col Art & Design, Detroit, Mich, 78-79; pres, Monserrat Col Art, Beverly, Mass, 89- *Teaching:* Inst art educ, Md Inst Col Art, 70-74 & 75-78. *Mem:* Nat Asn Schs Art & Design (chmn ethics comt, 89-); Art Col Exchange (secy, 89-91); Nat Coun Art Adminrs (chmn, 84-86); Asn Independent Cols Art & Design (secy, 92-). *Publ:* Contribr, New Directions for Experintial Learning, Jossey-Bass, 81; Arts, liberal education & the undergraduate curriculum, Working Group on Arts in Higher Educ, 85. *Mailing Add:* Montserrat Col Art Box 26, Dunham Rd Beverly MA 01915

GREENE , CHRIS (CHRISTINE E GREENE) PSA
CARTOONIST, PAINTER
b Chelm, Poland, March 29, 45; US citizen. *Study:* Newark Sch Fine & Industrial Arts, cert 62-65; Moore Col Art, Philadelphia, BFA, 68; Art Students League, 70-71, pvt studio classes with Joe Hing Lowe, 74-75, pvt studio classes with John Howard Sanden, 76-77. *Work:* Northport High Sch, NY. *Comn:* Numerous portraits, caricatures & caricature portraits in NY, NJ, Ariz & Fla, 75-92. *Exhib:* Ann Art Show, Nassau Co Mus, Roslyn, NY, 77-78; Huntington Township Art League 25th Ann, Hecksher Mus, NY, 80; Pastel Soc Am Ann Mem Show, Salamagundi Club, New York, 81; Nat Soc Painters in Casein & Acrylic, Nat Arts Club, New York, 83; Kans Pastel Soc 1st Ann Nat Juried Show, Wichita Art Asn, 84. *Pos:* Portrait painter, independent, Hyannis, Mass, 68-69; textile designer, Schwartz & Liebman Textiles, New York, 70-76; Caricatures by Chris Green, indepdndent business, 82- *Awards:* First Prize, Huntington Township Art League Ann, 80; Grumbacher Art Award, Independent Art Soc Ann, Grumbacher Art Supplies, 81; Award of Excellence, Channel 21 Art Show, 82. *Bibliog:* Helen A Harrison (auth), Health building scores, New York Times, 10/4/79; Art around town, Glen Cove Weekender, 11/15/80; Art revs, Sunstorm, 7/15/84. *Mem:* Pastel Soc Am; Nat Cartoonists Soc; Am Soc Portrait Artists. *Dealer:* Norman Mack 12 Kodiak Dr Woodbury NY 11797. *Mailing Add:* 17 Edward Lane Syosset NY

GREENE, ETHEL MAUD
PAINTER
b Malden, Mass, Nov 11, 12. *Study:* Boston Univ Sch Art; Sch Boston Mus; Mass Col Art. *Work:* Calif Western Univ, San Diego Mus Art & Fine Arts Collectors, Inc, San Diego; Southwestern Col, Chula Vista, Calif; La Salle Col, Philadelphia. *Exhib:* Artists of Los Angeles & Vicinity, Los Angeles Co Mus, 50, 52 & 55; two-person show, San Diego Mus Art, 61 & 79; solo shows, Feingarten Gallery, Los Angeles, 70, Ariz State Univ, Tempe, 72 & Taylor Gallery, Taos, NMex, 80; Newspace Gallery, Los Angeles, 78; Mathis Cult Ctr, Escondido, Calif, 88; Calhoun Gallery, San Diego, 90; San Diego Art Inst, 91; Citizens Gallery, Yokohama, Japan, 92. *Awards:* San Diego Co Expos Awards, 48, 54, 63, 72, 78 & 81; La Jolla Mus Ann Award, 58; Two Californias Award, Calif Western Univ, 63; Small Image, Spanish Village San Diego, 92. *Bibliog:* Marilyn Hagberg (auth), The visual puns of Ethel Greene, San Diego Mag, 7/70; Susan Vreeland (auth), Ethel Greene: Idea woman, Hill Courier, 10/84; Phyllis Van Doren (auth), Profile: Ethel Greene, San Diego Home/Garden Mag, 6/86 & 9/90; Mark-Elliott Lugo (auth), Surrealism in Spring Valley, San Diego Mag, 11/91. *Mem:* San Diego Art Guild (pres, 56); Artists Equity. *Media:* Acrylic. *Publ:* Illusr, A Dog Called Bum, 60 & 81. *Mailing Add:* 2940 Helix St Spring Valley CA 92077

GREENE, LOUISE WEAVER
TAPESTRY ARTIST, WEAVER
b Lancaster, Pa, May 7, 53. *Study:* Haystack Mountain Sch Crafts, 75; Univ Md, BA(art hist), 92. *Work:* Gannett Co Inc/USA Today, Wash, DC; Fed Home Loan Mortgage Corp, Washington, DC; Bell Canada, Wash, DC. *Comn:* Woven Tapestry, Gateway Int, Baltimore, Md, 86; Woven Tapestry, Gannett Co Inc/USA Today, Wash, DC, 86; Woven Tapestry, Tyson Corp, Springdale, Ark, 87; Woven Tapestry, Int Point, Wash, DC, 88. *Exhib:* For the Floor, Am Craft Mus, New York, 85; Contemporary Crafts, Del Art Mus, Wilmington, Del, 85; Fiber Wall Works, Meredith Gallery, Baltimore, Md, 87; Fiber: State of the Art, Atlanta Financial Ctr, Atlanta, Ga, 88; Light Line & Plane, Scheuer Tapestry Gallery, New York, 88; Peripheral Perspectives, Soc Arts & Crafts, Boston, Mass, 89; Mixed Media Invitational, Miriam Perlman Gallery, Chicago, Ill, 89. *Awards:* Judges Choice Award, Wash Craft Show, Renwick Gallery, Smithsonian Inst, Wash, DC, 85. *Bibliog:* Nell Znamierowski (auth), For the Floor, Am Craft Mag, 85; Lisa Hammel (auth), Handmade Rugs at Craft, NY Times, 85; Carol Lawrence (ed), Fiberarts Design Book III, 87. *Mem:* Smithsonian Assoc, Wash, DC; Am Craft Coun, New York; Am Tapestry Alliance; James Renwick Alliance Renwick Gallery. *Media:* Woven tapestry, fiber. *Publ:* Contrib, Fiberarts Design Book II, & Fiberarts Design Book III, Lark Books, 83 & 87. *Mailing Add:* 2304 Ashboro Dr Chevy Chase MD 20815

GREENE, STEPHEN
PAINTER
b New York, NY, Sept 19, 17. *Study:* Art Students League; State Univ Iowa, BFA, 42, MA, 45; also with Philip Guston. *Work:* Whitney Mus Am Art, Guggenheim Mus & Metrop Mus Art, New York; Tate Gallery, London; Corcoran Gallery Art, Washington, DC; Mus Fine Arts, Houston; Zimmerli Art Gallery, Rutgers Univ. *Exhib:* The New Decade, Whitney Mus Am Art, 55; Abstract Expressionists & Imagists, Guggenheim Mus, 61; Internatinale Der Zeichnung, Darmstadt, Ger, 64; L'Art Vivant aux Etats-Unis, Fondation Maeght, France, 71; St Louis Art Mus, 89; Marilyn Pearl, 89; Ruth Bachofner Gallery, Santa Monica, Calif, 89; Meredith Long Gallery, Houston, Tex, 89. *Teaching:* Artist in residence, Princeton Univ, 56-59; instr painting & drawing, Art Students League, 59-65; from asst prof to prof painting & drawing, Tyler Sch Art, Temple Univ, 68-85; instr painting, Art Students League, 85- *Awards:* Prix de Rome, Am Acad Rome, 49; Coun Arts & Lett Grant, 66; Inst Arts & Lett Award, 67. *Bibliog:* H W Janson (auth), Stephen Greene, Mag Art, 48; Michael Fried (auth), The goals of Stephen Greene, Arts Mag, 4-5/63; Barbara Rose (auth), Stephen Greene, Art Int, 4/63. *Mem:* Tiffaney Fdn (bd trustees); Nat Acad Design. *Media:* Oil. *Dealer:* Marilyn Pearl Gallery 420 West Broadway New York NY 10012. *Mailing Add:* 408A Storms Rd Valley Cottage NY 10989

GREENE-MERCIER, MARIE ZOE
SCULPTOR, DRAFTSMAN
b Madison, Wis, Mar 31, 11. *Study:* Radcliffe Col, Harvard Univ, AB(fine arts), 33; New Bauhaus, Chicago, with Moholy-Nagy, Archipenko & Gyorgy Kepes, 37-38. *Work:* Mus des Sables, Barcares, France; Ca Pesaro, Mus Mod Art, Venice, Italy; Cronkhite Grad Ctr, Radcliffe Col, Cambridge, Mass; Bauhaus-Arch Mus, West Berlin; Oberhessisches Mus, Giessen, WGer; Randolph-Macon Col, Ashland, Va. *Comn:* Portrait in bronze of Rudolph Ganz, Ganz Hall, Roosevelt Univ, Chicago, 52; monumental chancellery cross, First Baptist Church, Chicago, 67; monumental steel sculpture, French Govt, Barcares, 71 & Arras, 74; monumental steel sculpture, Hamburg, WGer, 74. *Exhib:* 39 shows, including 40 Yr Retrospective, Amerika Haus, W Berlin, 77 & Musee de Poche Gallery, Paris, 78; Bad Homburg, Summer Festival & Am Haus, Stuttgart, Ger, 79; Alliance Francaise, Washington, DC, 80; Group Dialogue Grand Palais Paris, France, 90; Galerie Loehr, Frankfurt, Ger, 91; and many others. *Awards:* First Prize Composition, 68 & First Prize Mod Sculpture, 69, Semaines Int Femme, Cannes, France; First Prize Sculpture, Festival SGermain Pres, Paris, 75; Mary Mildred Sullivan Award, Randolph Macon Col, Ashland, Va, 85. *Bibliog:* Frank Elgar (auth), Greene-Mercier, Musee de Poche, Paris, 78; Lloyd Engelbrecht (auth), Art Int, spring 78. *Mem:* Artists Equity Asn (pres, Chicago Chap, 59-62); Arts Club Chicago; Renaissance Soc Univ Chicago (life mem, 85); Amis de Bourdelle, Paris. *Media:* All. *Publ:* Auth, Trieste, 101 Disegni, 69, Salzburg, 101 Zeichnungen,

70 & Venezia, 101 Disegni, 70, Ed Libr, Italo Svevo, Trieste; auth, The role of materials in my sculpture, Leonardo, Vol 15, No 1; Reminiscences, 50 years, Harvard Crimson, 6/4/83; Autobiography in prep, 92. *Dealer:* Ruth Volid Gallery Inc 225 W Illinois Chicago IL 60610. *Mailing Add:* 1232 E 57th St Chicago IL 60637

GREENFIELD, AMY
FILMMAKER, VIDEO ARTIST
b Boston, Mass, July 8, 40. *Study:* Radcliffe Col, with Anne Sexton & William Alfred, BA(hon), 62. *Work:* Lincoln Ctr Dance Collection, Mus Holography, New York. *Comn:* Resoled (film), 71 & For God While Sleeping (film), 71, Visual Learning Corp; One-O-One (film), comn by Douglas Dunn, New York, 76; Four Solos for Four Women (videotape), Artists TV Proj, New York, 80. *Exhib:* Solo exhibs, Womens Avant-Garde Film Festival, Whitney Mus Am Art, 72, New Videodance, Anthology Film Arch, New York, 77, 80 & 83, The Wave: Film & Holography, Hayward Gallery, London, 79 & Dance-Film-Video, Mus Mod Art, New York, 83; Two Channel Video, Whitney Mus Am Art, 78; London Film Festival, Nat Film Theatre, 82; Edinburgh Film Festival, Edinburgh Arts Festival, Scotland, 82. *Teaching:* Instr film, Tufts Univ, 72-74; vis asst prof, Univ RI, 77-78 & Montclair State Col, 78-79. *Awards:* Nat Endowment Arts Grants, 75, 78, 81 & 84; Rockefeller Found Grant, 80. *Bibliog:* Robert Haller (auth), article, Millennium Film J, 80; Deborah Jowitt (auth), Prisoners of the lens, Village Voice, 80; John Gruen (auth), Dance visions, Dancemag, 83. *Media:* Film, Video. *Publ:* Auth, Verticle roll, Film Libr Quart, 78; auth, The Big Apple: First in video, 80 & The case of the vanishing videotape, 81, Am Film; auth, Video and film and video, Video Roma, 82; auth, Filmdance space, time, energy, Film Dance, 83. *Dealer:* Filmmakers Coop 175 Lexington Ave New York NY 10016. *Mailing Add:* 135 St Pauls Ave Staten Island NY 10301

GREENFIELD, JOAN BEATRICE
PAINTER, ENAMELIST
b Bronx, NY, Apr 15, 31. *Study:* Adelphi Univ, New York, BA, art history, 5/78, MA, studio arts, 5/81; Nat Acad Design, Audrey Flack, 90. *Work:* Adelphi Univ, New York; Buffalo Children's Hosp, New York; Helentex Inc, New York; Rubin & Kimche law offices, Jerusalem, Israel. *Comn:* Portraits, comn by H Cytryn, Woodmere, New York, 87 & 88, P Henry, Franklin Square, New York, 84; enamels, comn by M Partem, Jerusalem, Israel, 88. *Exhib:* Solo exhib, R Harley Gallery, Adelphi Univ, New York, 82; group shows, Mus Philos, New York, 82, Figures, Nabisco Brands Gallery, NJ, 86, Salute Women's History Month, Paper Mill Playhouse Renee Foosaner Art Gallery, NJ, 87, Nat Asn Women Artist Fall Collection, Monmouth Mus Fine Arts, NJ, 87, Celebration 89, The Interchurch Ctr, New York, 89, Small works, Marbella Gallery, New York, 89, Roper Gallery, Frostburg State Univ, Md, 90, Hampton Square Gallery, West Hampton, NY, 91, Galarie des Hampton, 92, Fire House Gallery, Nassau Community Col, Garden City, NY, 92. *Pos:* Coordr, special events 78-81, Alumni Exhib, 80-83, Adelphi Univ, Traveling painting Nat Asn Women Artists, New York, 84-90. *Awards:* Greenblatt Mem, Nat Asn Women Artists, Forest Elec-P Rebhum, 4/84; New Concept, Nat Asn Women Artists, anonymous, 4/89. *Mem:* Kappa Pi; Nat Asn Women Artists (exec bd, 84-92); NY Artist Equity; Women's Caucus for Art; NY Found Community Artists. *Media:* Acrylic, Oil. *Mailing Add:* 876 Central Ave Woodmere NY 11598

GREENFIELD-SANDERS, TIMOTHY
PHOTOGRAPHER
b Feb 16, 52; US citizen. *Study:* Columbia Col, Columbia Univ, BA(art hist), 74; Am Film Inst, with Slavko Vorkapich, MFA(film fel), 77. *Work:* Mus Mod Art, Metrop Mus Art, Int Center Photog, New York; Australian Nat Gallery; Nat Portrait Gallery, Washington, DC. *Exhib:* One-man shows, Leo Castelli Gallery, New York, 87, Mary Boone Gallery, New York, 88, Zeit-Foto, Tokyo, Japan, 88, Greene Gallery, Fla, 89, Marimura Art Mus, Tokyo, Japan, 90, Mus Mod & Contemp Art, Trento, 91, Mod Art Mus, Ft Worth, Tex, 91. *Awards:* Fine Arts Photogr, Am Photogr Mag, 83. *Bibliog:* Hilton Kramer (auth), NY Artist of 50's in 80's, New York Times, 3/27/81; Robert Schwalberg (auth), Portfolio, Camera Arts Mag, 3/82; Dore Ashton (auth), Avenue, 11/82. *Media:* Black & White, Color Polaroid. *Publ:* Contribr, Barrons, 81-86 & Vogue, 83-86; auth, Downtown in the fifties, 81 & Art of the Real, 83, Horizon; Clarkson Potter, Artnews, 83; The New Irascibles, Arts Mag, 9/85. *Dealer:* James Danziger Gallery 415 W Broadway New York NY 10012. *Mailing Add:* 135 E 2nd St New York NY 10009

GREENLEAF, KEN (KENNETH LEE)
SCULPTOR, ART CRITIC
b Damariscotta, Maine, Aug 10, 45. *Work:* New Sch Social Res, Whitney Mus Am Art, New York; Houston Mus Fine Arts, Tex; Mint Mus Art, Charlotte, NC; Portland Mus Fine Art, Maine; Colby Col Mus. *Exhib:* Contemp American Art, Whitney Mus Biennial, 73; one-man shows, Tibor de Nagy Galleries, New York, 73-74, 76, 78, 80 & 81, Kelly Gallery, Chicago, 74, B R Konblatt Gallery, Baltimore, Md, 77, Barridoff Galleries, Portland, Maine, 80, Sculptors Guild, New York, 85, John Davis Gallery, 87 & 88, Ten Americans, Carnegie, Pittsburgh, Pa, 88, Hudson River Mus, 89, Eric Stark Gallery, 90 & 92 & Gleason Fine Art, Boothbay Harbor, Maine, 92; Opening Invitational, Stark Gallery, New York, 90; Beyond Geometry, Maine Coast Artists, Rockpoint, 91; Contemporary Sculpture at Chesterwood-1992, Stockbridge, Mass, 92. *Pos:* Art critic, Maine Sunday Telegram, 91- *Teaching:* Sculpture instr, Unity Col, Maine, 92; artist-in-residence, sculpture instr, Round Top Ctr Arts, Damariscotta, Maine, 92. *Bibliog:* Margot Brown McWilliams (auth), rev, Maine Sunday Telegram, 5/30/92. *Media:* Various. *Dealer:* Stark Gallery, 594 Broadway, Suite 301, New York, NY 10012; Gleason Fine Art, 15 Oak St, Boothbay Harbor, ME 04538. *Mailing Add:* PO Box 82 Nobleboro ME 04555

GREENLEAF, VIRGINIA
PAINTER
b Chicago, Ill. *Study:* Yale Univ Sch Fine Arts; Am Univ; also with Ivan Olinsky, Robert Brackman & Gene Davis. *Work:* Dept State. *Exhib:* Phillips Collection, Washington, DC, 71; one-person shows, Studio Gallery, Washington, DC, 71-76, Main St Gallery Ann, Nantucket, 71-92, Parsons Dreyfuss Gallery, New York, Gallery 124, New York, 83 & Main St Gallery, Boston; Mus Fine Arts, Brazil; Haller Gallery, New York; Cooley Gallery, Old Lyme, Conn. *Mem:* Artists Equity Asn. *Media:* Acrylic. *Dealer:* Main St Gallery Nantucket MA 02554. *Mailing Add:* PO Box 931 Old Lyme CT 06371

GREENLY, COLIN
ENVIRONMENTAL ARTIST, PAINTER
b London, Eng, Jan 21, 28; US citizen. *Study:* Harvard Univ, AB, 48; Columbia Univ Sch Painting & Sculpture, with Oronzio Maldarelli & Peppino Mangravite; Am Univ Grad Sch Fine Arts. *Work:* Mus Mod Art, New York; Corcoran Gallery Art, Washington, DC; Herbert F Johnson Mus, Ithaca, NY; Philadelphia Mus Art; Albright-Knox Art Gallery, Buffalo; and others. *Comn:* Wall painting, Everson Mus, Syracuse, NY, 71; participatory murals, NY State Off Bldg, Utica, 73 & Creative Artists Pub Serv Prog, 75; Restoration and Adaption: The Hulse Barn. *Exhib:* Young American Printmakers, Mus Mod Art, New York, 53; one-man exhib, Corcoran Gallery Art, 68 & Finch Col Mus, 74; Contemporary American Painting & Sculpture, Krannert Art Mus, Ill, 69 & 74; Images, Mus Mod Art, New York, 73; John Weber Gallery, New York, 75; Whitney Mus Am Art, New York, 78; and others. *Pos:* Vis artist, Cent Mich Univ, 72; artist in residence, Everson Mus, Syracuse, NY, 72 & Cazenovia Col, 72; Nat Endowment Arts & Humanities artist in residence, Finch Col, 74. *Teaching:* Dana prof art, Colgate Univ, 72-73. *Awards:* Nat Endowment Arts & Humanities Grant for Sculpture, 67; Creative Artists Pub Serv Prog Grant for Intangible Sculpture, New York, 72; Creative Artists Pub Serv Fel, 78. *Bibliog:* James Harithas (auth), Colin Greenly, Libr Cong No 68-19952, Corcoran Gallery Art, 1/68; Thomas W Leavitt (auth), Colin Greenly: intangible sculpture, Libr Cong No 72-9042, Andrew Dickson Mus Art, Cornell Univ, 72; Dore Ashton (auth), New York, article, In: Coloquio Artes, 10/74. *Media:* Acrylic, Intangible Art. *Publ:* Auth, A changing image of change, A J for Artists, winter, 86. *Mailing Add:* RD # 1 Box 545 Campbell Hall NY 10916

GREENSPAN, (MR & MRS) GEORGE
COLLECTORS
Mr Greenspan, b New York, NY, May 17, 1900. *Collection:* Comprehensive collection of impressionist and post-impressionist drawings; contemporary American paintings. *Mailing Add:* 885 Park Ave # 9C New York NY 10021

GREENSTONE, MARION
PAINTER
b New York, NY, Mar 30, 25. *Study:* Brooklyn Col, BA(cum laude), 46; Columbia Univ Teachers Col, MA, 47; Cooper Union, dipl(fine arts), 54. *Work:* Art Gallery London, Ont; Queens Col, Kingston, Ont; Exxon Corp, New York. *Comn:* Mural, comn by Bernard Rothzeid & Fine Arts Comn, New York, 76. *Exhib:* Brooklyn Mus Ann Print Show, 53; Whitney Mus Ann, 53; Pittsburgh Int, 55; Can Nat Exhib, 58; Ohio Univ Prints & Drawings Exhib, 63; one-women shows, Long Island Univ, New York, 70 & 76, Sixth Estate Gallery, New York, 76 & 77, Cusano Gallery, South Norwalk, Conn, 85, Owl Gallery, Long Island, 86, Plandome Gallery, NY, 90, Manhasset Libr Gallery, New York, 92; Works on Paper, Brooklyn Mus, 75; Mus Hudson Highlands, 83. *Teaching:* From adj assoc prof art to prof painting & design, Pratt Inst, 68-92. *Awards:* Fulbright Award, 54-56; Montreal Mus Spring Show Award, 60; Baxter Found Award, 61. *Media:* Oil on Canvas. *Mailing Add:* 790 Carrol St Brooklyn NY 11215

GREENWALD, ALICE (ALICE MARIAN GREENWALD-WARD)
LECTURER
b Oceanside, NY, Jan 2, 52. *Study:* Univ Exeter, Devon, Eng, with Theo Brown, 71-72; Sarah Lawrence Col, Bronxville, NY, BA(anthrop & Lit), 73; Univ Chicago Divinity Sch, Ill, AM(hist relig), 75. *Collections Arranged:* Los Angeles Collects: Works on Paper and Graphic Art from Israel, 78-79; The Five Sense Show, 78; The Custom Cut: Jewish Papercuts, Past & Present, 79; Jewish Marriage Contracts: A Celebration in Art, 79; Bill Aron: Portraits of Life, The Elderly Jews of Venice, Calif, 79-80, The Realm of Torah, 81, Between Holy & Profane: Xerography by Dina Dar, 81, Huc Skirball Mus, Hebrew Union Col, Los Angeles, Calif; The Tallis as a Metaphor of Community: Fiber Sculptures by Laurie Gross, 82 & Odyssey of Freedom: The Canvas Diary of a Soviet Jewish Emigre (paintings & works on paper by Tanya Kornfield), 83, The American Jewish Experience, 89, Mus Am Jewish Hist, Philadelphia. *Pos:* Dir, Mus Am Jewish Hist, Philadelphia, Pa, 81-86; consulting cur, US Holocaust Mem Mus, Washington, DC, 86-90, special consult, 89-; tech adv, The Pew Charitable Trusts, Philadelphia, 87. *Teaching:* Mus educator Jewish art, Hebrew Union Col, Los Angeles, Calif, 75-81. *Awards:* Nat Endowment Arts Fel Mus Prof, 81. *Mem:* Am Asn Mus; Int Coun Mus; Coun Am Jewish Mus. *Res:* All areas of Jewish art, emphasis on European ritual art and near eastern archaeology. *Publ:* Auth, The Mizrach: Compass of the heart, Hadassah Mag, 10/79; auth, The masonic Mizrach: Jewish ritual art as a reflection of cultural assimilation, J Jewish Art, Vol 10, 83; The American Jewish Experience (exhib cat), 89. *Mailing Add:* 42 Nassau Pl Princeton Junction NJ 08550

GREER, JANE RUTH
SCULPTOR
b New York, NY, Jan 28, 41. *Study:* New York Univ, BFA; Art Students League, with John Hovanes. *Work:* Chrysler Mus, Norfolk, Va; Grey Art Gallery, New York Univ, New York, NY; SE Bank of Fla, Miami. *Comn:* Murals, Holiday Inn, Ft Lee, NJ, 86. *Exhib:* Drawing & Collage, Grey Art Gallery, New York Univ, 77; First Anniversary Exhib, 78 & Works on Paper, 82, Drawing Ctr. *Media:* Wood, Paper. *Dealer:* Jane Kahan Gallery 922 Madison Ave New York NY 10021. *Mailing Add:* 81 Wooster St New York NY 10012

GREER, JOHN SYDNEY
SCULPTOR
b Amherst, NS, Can, June 28, 44. *Study:* NS Col Art, dipl(bursary), 62-64; Montreal Mus Sch Art & Design, dipl(hon sculpture; scholar), 66; Vancouver Sch Art, dipl, 67. *Work:* Nat Gallery, Ottawa; Can Coun Art Bank; Art Gallery Ont; Art Bank, Providence of Nova Scotia; Art Gallery NS; Dalhousie Art Gallery, Halifax. *Comn:* Y D Klein (lithograph), NS Col Art & Design, 74; Olympic poster proposal, Artist's Athletics Coalition, 75; silkscreen ed, Can Coun Art Bank, Grand Western Screen Shop, Winnipeg, 77; The Forks (Winnipeg), Parks, Can, 88. *Exhib:* Solo exhibs, Sculptured Objective, 68-81, Traveling Exhib, Art Gallery NS, 49th Parallel, New York, Mus d'Art Contemp, Montreal & others, 81-83, Dalhousie Art Gallery, Halifax, 87, Ottawa Sch Art Gallery, 87, Southern Alberta Art Gallery, Lethbridge, 90, St Mary's Univ Art Gallery, Halifax, 90; Art Contemporain 1990 Savoir-Vivre, Ctr Int Art Contemporian, Montreal, 90; Embodied Viewer, Glenbow Mus, 91; and others. *Teaching:* Assoc prof sculpture, NS Col Art & Design, currently. *Awards:* Can Coun Grant, 85, 88 & 90; Victor Martyn Lynch-Staunton Award, Can Coun, 88. *Bibliog:* Gemey Kelly (auth), review, Vanguard, 82; Ron Shuebrook (auth), review, Vanguard, 9-10/87; Robert Pope (auth), review, Arts Atlantic 29, summer/fall 87. *Mem:* Eye Level Gallery, Halifax (vchmn, 75-); Can Artist Representation, Provincial, Nat. *Media:* Stone, Cast Metal. *Publ:* Auth, Sceptical Spectacles, Dalhousie Art Gallery, 74; Waterrings, Dalhousie Art Gallery, 76; Onion Skin Maker Your Eyes Water, Coach House Press, 81; John Greer Sculptural Objective (exhib catalog), Art Gallery NS, 81; Reconciliation (exhib catalog), 90. *Mailing Add:* 5673 Woodill St Halifax NS B3K 1H1 Canada

GREER, WALTER (MARION)
PAINTER
b Ware Shoals, SC, Aug 11, 20. *Study:* The Citadel, BS, 42; Clemson Univ, BS, 47; Atlanta Sch Art, 59 & 60; Nat Acad Design, New York, with Robert Phillipp; also with Ben Shute, Atlanta, 62 & study abroad. *Work:* Telfair Acad Arts & Sci, Savannah, Ga; SC State Collection, Columbia Mus Art; paintings, Sea Pines Plantation Co, Hilton Head Island, SC; Greenville Mus Art, SC; C & S Collection, Atlanta & Greenville, SC; and others. *Comn:* Oil landscape, Gov Mansion, Columbia, 67; three paintings, Phipps Land Co, Hilton Head Island & New York, 70; portrait of pres, Emory Univ, 71; triptych, Simmons Collection, Atlanta, Ga; ltd ed print for Marriott Hotels, 81. *Exhib:* Mead Paper Show, Atlanta, Ga, 60; Hunter Ann, Chattanooga, Tenn, 62; SC Invitational, Columbia, 69; one-man shows, Columbia Mus Art, 73 & Telfair Acad Arts & Sci, 74, 76 & 82; Guild SC Artists, 81. *Teaching:* Instr pvt classes, 63-66, 78 & 81; instr spec art classes, USMC, Parris Island, SC, 64-65 & Savannah Art Asn Sch, 66. *Awards:* Savannah Arts Festival Award for Rivers, 66; SC Arts Coun Purchase Award for Pond, 69; SC Archit Award for Pond (Grey Phase), 71. *Bibliog:* Virginia Ball (auth), The man that got away, Atlanta Mag, 65; articles & 28 covers, Islander Mag; Jack Morris & Robert Smeltz (auth), Contemporary artists of South Carolina, 70. *Mem:* Guild SC Artists; hon life mem Beaufort Art Asn. *Media:* Oil, Acrylic. *Publ:* Cover and profile, Southern World Mag, 79 & 80; article, Southern Accents Mag, 82. *Dealer:* Tatler Gallery Hilton Head Island SC 29928. *Mailing Add:* One Indian Hill Lane Hilton Head Island SC 29928

GREER, WESLEY DWAINE
EDUCATOR, CRAFTSMAN
b Weyburn, Sask, Nov 25, 37; US citizen. *Study:* Univ BC, BEd, MEd; Stanford Univ, PhD. *Exhib:* Artists Equity Salute to the Bicentennial, Calif Mus Sci & Indust, 80; On the Face of It: 23 Los Angeles Artists, Calif State Univ, Dominguez Hills, 86. *Pos:* Dir, Getty Improving Visual Arts Educ Proj, Los Angeles, 82- *Teaching:* Prof art, Univ Ariz, 82- *Awards:* Art Educ Year, Nat Art Educ Asn, 88. *Mem:* Nat Art Educ Asn; Am Crafts Coun; Am Soc Aesthetics. *Res:* Art curriculum and staff development in public schools. *Publ:* Auth, Discipline based art education: Approaching art as a subject of study, Studies in Art Educ, 84; Hospers on Creativity, J Aesthetic Educ, 86; Structure for DBAE, Studies in Art Educ, 87. *Mailing Add:* 1240 W San Lucas Dr Tucson AZ 85704

GREEVES, R V (RICHARD VERNON)
SCULPTOR
b St Louis, Mo, Feb 24, 35. *Work:* Nat Cowboy Hall of Fame, Oklahoma City; Genesee Country Mus, Rochester, NY; Indianapolis Art Mus, Ind; Liberty Hall, Nat Trust Found, Elizabeth, NJ. *Comn:* Story Teller (bronze sculpture), Sheridan Publ Libr, Wyo, 77; The Cock (bronze sculpture), Bartlesville Civic Ctr, Okla, 82; The Unknown (bronze monument), Whitney Gallery of Western Art, Cody, Wyo, 84. *Exhib:* One-man shows, Wyo State Art Mus, Cheyenne, 71, Kennedy Galleries, New York, NY, 73, Barclays Int Bank, Chicago, Ill, 76, Wyo State Capitol Bldg, Cheyenne, 82 & Nicolaysen Art Mus, Casper, Wyo, 82-83; Nat Acad Western Art Show, Nat Cowboy Hall of Fame, 75-90; Peking Exhib Am Western Art, Beijing Exhib Palace, China, 81; 3M Western Art Show, Art Ctr Minn, St Paul, 83-84. *Pos:* Mem, Arts Ctr adv comt, Cent Wyo Col, Riverton, 85-86. *Awards:* Gold Medal, 76 & 79 & Prix de West, 77, Nat Acad Western Art, Nat Cowboy Hall of Fame. *Bibliog:* Will Carson (auth), A Genuine Greeves, Western Horseman, 6/71; Dean Krakel II (auth), My Life's Work, Southwest Art, 7-8/75; John Running (auth), The Unknown: A Monument by R V Greeves, 86. *Mem:* Nat Acad Western Art (mem exec comt, 82). *Media:* Bronze. *Publ:* Contribr, Bronzes of the American West by Broder, Abrams, Inc, 74; Contemporary Western Artists, Southwest Art, 82; Sculpture Review, Nat Sculpture Soc, 82 & 86; Art West Mag, 83; Four Centuries of Sporting Art by Schmitt, Genesee Country Mus, 84. *Mailing Add:* 53 N Fork Rd PO Box 428 Ft Washakie WY 82514

GREGOIRE, MATHIEU A
SCULPTOR
b New York, NY, Sept 3, 53. *Study:* Univ Chicago, 71-73; Portland State Univ, BA, 79-80. *Work:* Lannan Found, Los Angeles, Calif; City of Portland, Ore. *Exhib:* Solo exhibs: Hood/Slot/Section, Boehm Gallery, Palomar Col, San Marcos, Calif, 87, Dietrich Jenny Gallery, San Diego, Calif, 88, Mattress Factory (with catalog), Pittsburgh, Pa, 88, Sculpture, Laguna Mus South Coast Plaza, Costa Mesa, Calif, 89 & Winghouse, (with catalog), Artpark, Lewiston, NY, 89; group shows, Abstract Expressions: Recent Sculpture (with catalog), Lake Worth, Fla, 87 & Sculpture Arenas: Burden, Capps, Giegerich, Gregoire, Honda, Lere (with catalog), Mandeville Gallery, Univ Calif San Diego, La Jolla, Calif, 87; San Turner Gallery, Los Angeles, Calif, 91 & 92; Misplacement: Revision, Univ San Diego, 92. *Pos:* Consult, Stuart Collection, Univ Calif, San Diego. *Awards:* Grant, Metro Arts Comn, 82; Tiffany Award, Louis Comfort Tiffany Found, 89; Nat Endowment Art, 88 & 90. *Bibliog:* Michael McManus (auth), The application of rationality, Artweek, 4/87; Robert Pincus (auth), Minimalist sculptor furnishes Art that mimics furniture, San Diego Union, 3/16/89; Victoria Reed (auth), Gregoire Worth a Deeper Look, Los Angeles Times, 3/92. *Media:* Mixed Media. *Mailing Add:* PO Box 3 San Diego CA 92112

GREGOR, HAROLD LAURENCE
PAINTER, EDUCATOR
b Detroit, Mich, Sept 10, 29. *Study:* Wayne State Univ, BSEd, 51; Mich State Univ, MS(ceramics, painting), 53; Detroit Soc Arts & Crafts, 55-57, with John Foster; Ohio State Univ, PhD(painting, art hist), 60; and with Hoyt Sherman. *Work:* Filipacci Collection, Paris, France; Xerox Collection, Stamford, Conn; Springfield Art Mus, Mo; Rose Art Mus, Brandeis Univ; State of Ill Bldg, Chicago; Borg-Warner Collection, Chicago; Chicago Bd of Trade. *Comn:* Two murals, State Ill New Main Libr, Springfield, Ill, 91. *Exhib:* Solo exhibs, Nancy Lurie Gallery, 74-83, Tibor De Nagy Gallery, New York, 77-91, Richard Gray Gallery, Chicago, 83, 85 & 88 & traveling; Land, Sky, Water, Spokane World's Fair, 74; Contemp Am Realism Since 1960, Pa Acad Fine Arts, Philadelphia, 81; Watercolor, USA, Springfield Art Mus, Mo, 84 & 85; Contemp Midwest Landscapes, Ind Mus Art, Indianapolis, 86; Choices: 20 Painters from Midwest, traveling; exhib, Minn Col Art & Design, 87; retrospective, (with catalog), Lakeview Mus Arts & Sci, Peoria, Ill, 87-88. *Teaching:* Asst prof painting & art hist, San Diego State Univ, 60-63; asst prof painting, Purdue Univ, 63-66; assoc prof painting & art hist, Chapman Col, 66-70; prof painting & art hist, Ill State Univ, Normal, 70-88, distinguished prof, 88- *Awards:* Nat Endowment Arts Grant, 73 & 86; Outstanding Teacher & Researcher, Ill State Univ, 85 & 86; Watercolor USA Purchase Award, 84, 85 & 89. *Bibliog:* Robert Cross (auth), Cultivating art down on the farm, Chicago Tribune, 12/15/85; B Goldman-Shein, Harold Gregor, Am Artist Mag, 11/86; J Arthur (auth), Spirit of Place, 89. *Mem:* Watercolor Honor Soc. *Media:* Watercolor, Acrylic. *Publ:* Coauth (with K Gregor), Discovering a lost technique, 7/87 & The techniques of a flatscape, 12/86, The Artists Mag. *Dealer:* Richard Gray Gallery 620 N Michigan Chicago IL 60611; Sherry French Gallery 24 W 57th St New York NY 10019. *Mailing Add:* 107 West Market St Bloomington IL 61701

GREGOROPOULOS, JOHN
PAINTER
b Athens, Greece, Dec 16, 21; US citizen. *Study:* In Athens; Univ Conn, BA. *Work:* Minn Mus Art, St Paul; Ball State Found, Muncie, Ind; Slater Mus, Norwich, Conn; De Cordova Mus, Lincoln, Mass; Berkshire Mus, Pittsfield, Mass. *Exhib:* Whitney Mus Am Art Ann, 54 & Art USA, New York, 58; Pan Helleml Salon, Athens, 57-63; 1st Biennale Christlicher Kunst Gegenwart, Salzburg, 58; Drawings USA, Minn Mus Art, 71. *Teaching:* Prof emer, Univ Conn, 53-84. *Awards:* Small Drawings & Sculpture Purchase Award, Ball State Teachers Col, 55; Grumbacher Award, Chautauqua Art Asn 2nd Nat, 59; Drawings USA, St Paul Art Ctr, 63. *Bibliog:* F Walkey (auth), John Gregoropoulos, Art in Am, 2/55; John Gregoropoulos, Zygos, Athens, 57; Art & the new patron, WEDN-TV, 68. *Publ:* Auth, Change in art, Nea Estia, Athens, 57. *Mailing Add:* 644 Wormwood Hill Rd Storrs CT 06268

GREGORY, BRUCE
PAINTER, INSTRUCTOR
b Anadarko, Okla, June 27, 17. *Study:* Art Students League; Colorado Springs Art Ctr; and with Fernand Leger. *Comn:* Murals, UN, New York, 52 & Franklin D Roosevelt Sch, New York, 56; map murals, Civil Defense Hq, New York, 57. *Exhib:* Terry Art Inst, Miami, Fla, 51; Pa Acad Art, Philadelphia, 52; Art USA, New York, 58; Butler Art Inst Ann, 66; Fla State Fair, 66; Four Arts Soc, Palm Beach, Fla, 84, 86, 90 & 91. *Pos:* Color & design consult, Harrison & Abramovitz, New York, 52-56; prof serv contractor, Fine Arts Evan, Gen Serv Admin, 73. *Teaching:* Instr painting, Union Col, 56-57; instr painting, John Herron Art Inst, Ind, 60-61; instr painting, color & design, Ringling Sch Art, Sarasota, Fla, 61-84. *Awards:* Best of Show, Fla Artists Group, 83; Kenneth Stewart Mem Award, Artists Group, 84 & Hilton Leech Mem Award, 85. *Bibliog:* Aline Louchhien (auth), UN murals, 9/7/52 & Kathleen Teltsch (auth), US painter does UN Coats-of-Arms, 4/30/53, NY

Times; Gorden Brown (auth), Bruce Gregory, Arts Mag, 66. *Mem:* Sarasota Art Asn; Fla Artists Group. *Media:* Oil, Acrylic. *Publ:* Auth, Leger's atelier, UN murals, Col Art J, 62; contribr, New International Encyclopedia of Art, 67. *Mailing Add:* 2115 Lee Lane Sarasota FL 33581

GREGORY, JOAN
EDUCATOR, PAINTER
b Montgomery, Ala, Apr 1, 30. *Study:* Univ Montevallo, AB, 52; Peabody Col, MA, 53, EdD, 66; Inst Allende, San Miguel Allende, Mex. *Work:* NC Nat Bank; La State Art Comn; Springs Mills, Lancaster, SC; US Park Serv, Gatlinburg, Tenn. *Exhib:* Huntington Galleries, 56-61; one-woman shows, 63 & 13th Dixie Art Ann, Montgomery Mus Fine Arts; Southeastern Painting Show, Gallery Contemp Art, Winston-Salem, NC, 71 & 79; Ann NC Artists Exhib & Traveling Show, 71-72. *Teaching:* Instr art, Marshall Univ, 55-61; chmn dept art, Bloomsburg State Col, 63-64; prof art, Univ NC, Greensboro, 64-90, head dept, 74-85. *Awards:* Purchase Awards, Dillard Collection, Weatherspoon Gallery, Univ NC, Greensboro, 66 & Springs Art Show, Lancaster, SC, 72; Merit Award, NC/Va Art Educators, Southeastern Ctr Contemp Art, 75. *Mem:* Nat Art Educ Asn (mem states assembly, 71-73); NC Art Educ Asn (pres, 71-75); Southeastern Col Art Conf (bd dirs, 74-78, secy-treas, 81-); Assoc Artists NC (bd dirs, 69-71). *Media:* Collage. *Mailing Add:* Dept of Art Univ of NC Greensboro NC 27412

GREGORY, STAN(LEY WAYNE)
PAINTER, PRINTMAKER
b Tallahassee, Fla, Sept 22, 48. *Study:* Fla Southern Col, BA, 70; Univ South Fla, MFA, 80; asst to Mel Bochner, 80. *Work:* Brooklyn Mus Art, NY; Chase Manhattan Bank, New York; Cigna Found & Mus, Philadelphia; Solomon R Guggenheim Mus, New York; Herbert Johnson Mus, Cornell Univ, Ithaca, NY. *Comn:* Mural Cityscapes, City of Tampa, Fla, 82; Roadworks (hand painted bill-board), Barnett Bank, Jacksonville, Fla, 83. *Exhib:* Ringling Mus Art, Sarasota, Fla, 79; New Floridians, 79 & Florida Painting, 82, Jacksonville Art Mus, Fla; Florida Printers, Univ Cent Fla, Orlando, 80; New Acquisitions, Herbert Johnson Mus, Ithaca, NY, 84; Two-Dimensional Key West, East Martello Mus, Fla, 85; South Fla Collection, Art Mus, Univ SFla, Tampa, 90. *Pos:* Printmaker, Palm Press, Ltd, Tampa, Fla, 80-84; dir, Fla Ctr Contemp Art, Tampa, 84-85; registr, E Nakhamicin Fine Arts, New York, 86-90; preparator, Mus Mod Art, New York. *Teaching:* Instr painting color theory, Univ South Fla, 80-82. *Bibliog:* Charles Benbow (auth), Experiment a rich art experience, St Petersburg Times, 10/21/84; Gerrit Henry (auth), article, Art News, 11/84; Theodore F Wolff (auth), A true heir to the modernist tradition, Christian Sci Monitor, 9/8/85. *Media:* Acrylic, Oil; Etching. *Publ:* The New York Art Review, 4th Ed, Chicago, 89. *Mailing Add:* c/o Mus Mod Art, Register Office 11 W 53rd St New York NY 10019

GREGORY-GOODRUM, ELLNA KAY
PAINTER, PRINTMAKER
b Houston, Tex, Oct 3, 43. *Study:* Univ Okla, BFA, 65; NTex State Univ, MFA, 79. *Work:* Rockwell Int, Brown Found & Consult & Atlantic Richfield, Dallas, Tex; Ford-Renaissance Ctr, Detroit. *Exhib:* 29th Tex Watercolor Soc, McNay Art Inst, San Antonio, 78; Pastel Soc Am, Nat Arts Club, New York, 79; Watercolor Invitational, Birmingham Mus Art, Ala, 79; Nat Watercolor Soc, 85, 87 & 88; Women & Watercolor, Transco Energy Ctr, Houston, 88; Rocky Mountain Nat Water Media, Foothills Art Ctr, 86 & 88; Watercolor USA, Springfield Art Mus, 88; and others. *Teaching:* Instr art, Richland Col, 80- *Awards:* Best Abstract Award, 79 & Mixed Media Award, Pastel Soc Am, 87; Red Sable Award, Southern Watercolor Soc, 79; Southwestern Watercolor Soc Award, 79, 83, 85 & 88; Nat Watercolor Award, Okla, 88. *Bibliog:* Articles in Park E Publ, New York, 79 & Dallas Morning News, 79. *Mem:* Col Art Asn; Pastel Soc Am; Tex Watercolor Soc; Southwestern Watercolor Soc; Nat Watercolor Soc. *Media:* Watercolor. *Publ:* Auth, Watercolor '89, Am Artist. *Mailing Add:* 7214 Lane Park Dr Dallas TX 75225

GRELLE, MARTIN GLEN
PAINTER
b Clifton, Tex, Sept 17, 54. *Study:* Art Instruction Schs, 72; McLennan Community Col, 75. *Comn:* Bosque landscape, Bosque Co Mus, Clifton, Tex, 74; football mural, Cub Stadium, Clifton, Tex, 76; Bosque Autumn (painting), comn by King Olav IV of Norway, 82; mural, Trinity Lutheran Church, Clifton, Tex, 82; Misty Morning Gather (oil mural), Western Savings Asn, Gatesville, Tex, 86. *Exhib:* Am Indian & Cowboy Artists Ann, Sandmas Calif, 77-83; Western Heritage, Houston, Tex, 79, 81 & 84-85; Stamford Art Found, Tex, 79-86; Tex Art Gallery Preview, Dallas, 80-82; First Ann Student Exhib, Cowboy Artists of Am, Kerrville, Tex, 84; one-man shows, Tex Art Gallery, Dallas, Tex, 86 & 88, Overland Trail Gallery, Scottsdale, Ariz, 89, 90, 91, 92. *Awards:* Bronze Medal, Am Indian Cowboy Artists Exhib, 77; Gold Medal, Am Indian Cowboy Artists Exhib, 79; Silver Award for oil & Artist's Award, Tex Ranger Hall of Fame Show, 85. *Bibliog:* Article, Art West Mag, 1-2/83, 9-10/90; article, Southwest Art Mag, 3/86; Western Art Digest Mag, 1-2/87. *Media:* Oil, Arcylics. *Dealer:* Overland Trail Fine Art Gallery 7155 Main St Scottsdale AZ 85251. *Mailing Add:* Rte, 2 Box 113B Clifton TX 76634-9615

GRENELL, BARBARA
TAPESTRY ARTIST, WEAVER
b Paterson, NJ, July 30, 44. *Study:* Philadelphia Col Art, BFA with Honors, 66, apprenticed with Mary Frank, New York, 66-69. *Work:* Libr Congress, Washington, DC; Fine Arts Mus of the South, Montgomery, Ala; Sawtooth Ctr Vis Arts, Winston-Salem, NC; Duke Univ, Durham, NC. *Comn:* tapestry, IBM, Research Triangle Park, NC, 91; tapestry, Asn Am Med Cols, Washington, DC, 91; tapestry, Mills Distributing, Salinas, Calif, 92; dimensional tapestry, Southern Bell Tel, Atlanta, Ga, 92; dimensional tapestry, Chesapeake & Potomac Tel, Richmond, Va, 92; and others. *Exhib:* Winter Olympics Art Exhib, US Olympic Comt, Lake Placid, NY, 80; Southeast Invitational, Fine Arts Mus South, Montgomery, Ala, 81; Ann Invitational, Southeast Ctr Contemp Art, Winston-Salem, NC, 82; From the Loom and the Wheel, St John's Mus Art, Wilmington, NC, 82; Three From Nature, Dana Gallery-Agnes Scott Coll, Decatur, Ga, 87; Grenell-Koop Exhib, Belk Gallery West, Cullowhee, NC, 87; solo exhibs, Woven landscapes & gouaches, Asheville Art Mus, NC, 90, The Wool Council, New York, 91 & Focus, Blue Spiral Gallery, Asheville, NC, 92. *Teaching:* Vis Scholar Weaving/Dyeing, Penland Sch, NC, 75-78 & 81. *Awards:* Vis Arts Fel, Nat Endowment Arts, 74; Purchase Award, NC Fiber Arts Exhib, Burlington Indust, 84; Purchase Award, NC Fiber Competition, Arts Coun, Winston-Salem, 85; Visual Artist, Individual Proj Grant, NC State Arts Coun, 91-92. *Mem:* NC Volunteer Lawyers for the Arts (Bd Dir, 82-84); Piedmont Craftsmen (v pres, 82-86). *Media:* Fiber. *Mailing Add:* 1132 Hall's Chapel Rd Burnsville NC 28714

GRENON, GREGORY
PAINTER
Study: Ctr Creative Studies, Detroit, Mich, 70; Wayne State Univ, Detroit, 72. *Work:* Seattle Art Mus, Wash; Portland Art Mus, Ore; Harsh Investment, Portland, Ore; Met Arts Comn, Portland, Ore; Claremont Hotel, Oakland, Calif. *Exhib:* One-man shows, Women as a Second Language, Jamison/Thomas Gallery, Portland, Ore, 90, Women on Women in Women, William Traver Gallery, Seattle, Wash, 90, Simple Views, Esther Saks Gallery, Chicago, 90, It's Against the Rules, 90 & Line, Color, Emotion, 91, Jamison/Thomas Gallery, Moments, Gasperi Gallery, New Orleans, 91, About Relationships, William Traver Gallery, Seattle, Wash, 92; Jamison/Thomas Gallery, New York, 89, 90 & 91, Portland, Ore, 90; Ore Art Inst, 90; Portland Art Mus, Ore Art Inst, 91. *Awards:* Individual Fel Award, Ore Arts Comn, 84-85; Fel Grant, Nat Endowment Arts, 91. *Dealer:* William Traver Gallery 110 Union St 2nd Floor Seattle WA 98101. *Mailing Add:* 4931 NE 33rd St Portland OR 97211

GRESSEL, MICHAEL L
SCULPTOR
b Wurzburg, Ger, Sept 20, 02; US citizen. *Study:* Art Sch, Bavaria, with Arthur Schleglmünig; Beaux Art Inst Design, New York. *Work:* Bruckner Mus, Albion, Mich; Metrop Mus Art & Nat Theater & Acad, New York; Nat Theater, Washington, DC; County Trust Co, Mount Kisco, NY. *Comn:* bust, Charles Durning, Calif; portraits, George Meany & Walter Reuter, AFL Bldg, Washington, DC; sculpture for No Castle Libr, Hist Smith's Tavern, Armonk, NY; high relief of John Peter Zenger for Bill of Rights Mus, Mt Vernon, NY; bust of Gen von Steuben for the Pentagon, Washington, DC; and others. *Exhib:* Hudson Valley Art Asn Ann, White Plains, 46-72; Valhalla High Sch, NY, 49; Allied Artists Am, Nat Acad Design, 71; Nat Sculpture Soc, New York, 72; Armonk Libr & Hist Soc Armonk, NY. *Awards:* Mrs John Newington Award for Madonna, 63 & Gold Medal, 65; Gold Medal, Hudson Valley Art Exhib, 72; Lance Int Miniature Price, 86. *Mem:* Hudson Valley Art Asn (dir, 52-); Nat Sculpture Soc. *Media:* All Media. *Mailing Add:* Gressel Pl Armonk NY 10504

GRESSER, SEYMOUR GERALD
SCULPTOR
b Baltimore, Md, May 9, 26. *Study:* Maryland Univ, BS, 46, MA 72; Inst Contemp Art, 48-50; special study with William Taylor, 49-52. *Work:* St John the Divine Gallery, New York; Fairfield Col, Hartford, Conn; Pierson Col (Yale Univ) New Haven, Conn. *Exhib:* New Works, Fordham Univ, New York, 75; Third Ann Invitational, Eminent Artists/Art Bark, Washington, DC, 80; Religious Art, Sweetbriar Col, Va, 85; Blood Rites/Birth Rites, Duke Univ, Durham, NC, 86; New Sculptures, Montpelier Art Mus, Laurel, Md, 88. *Teaching:* Instr sculpture, Antioch Col (Columbia Campus) 79-81; residency, Colgate Univ, Hamilton, NY, 89, Thomas Jefferson Sch, Frederick, Md, 90. *Media:* Stone, Wood. *Mailing Add:* 1015 Ruatan St Silver Spring MD 20903

GREY, ALEX V
PAINTER, SCULPTOR
b Columbus, Ohio, Nov 29, 53. *Study:* Columbus Col Art & Design, 71-73; Boston Mus Sch, 74-75. *Work:* Mus Contemp Art-San Diego, La Jolla, Calif; Brooklyn Mus Fine Arts, NY; Kronnert Art Mus, Champaign, Ill; Islip Art Mus, NY. *Exhib:* Salon des Independants, Grand Palais, Paris, France, 80; solo exhibs, The Beast, PS1, Long Island, NY, 82 & Sacred Mirrors, Ill State Univ-Univ Galleries, Normal, 93; Sao Paolo Biennial, Sao Paolo Mus, Brazil, 85; Disarming Images, Univ Calif Mus Art, Santa Barbara, 85; Choices, New Mus, New York, 86; Revelations, Aspen Art Mus, Colo, 89; Sacred Mirrors, Univ Colo Mus, Boulder, 90. *Teaching:* Prof anatomy of artists, New York Univ, 87- *Bibliog:* Lewis MacAdams (auth), It Started out with Death, High Performance, spring 82; Carlo McCormick (auth), Through Darkness to Light, Sacred Mirrors/Inner Traditions, 90; John Strausbough (auth), X-ray Visions, New York Press, 4/7/92. *Media:* Oil, Acrylic; Bronze. *Publ:* Coauth, Art in Transformation: Interview with artist Alex Grey, New Frontier Mag, 89; auth, Sacred Mirrors, Inner Traditions, 90; The Life and Art of Alex and Allyson Grey, Tantra Mag, 92; Commencement Address: The Mission of Art, Boston Mus Sch News, 92; Visions of Body and Soul, Caduceus Mag, 92. *Dealer:* Carl Solway 314 W 4th St Cincinnati OH 45202. *Mailing Add:* 725 Union St Brooklyn NY 11215

GRIBIN, LIZ
PAINTER
b London, Eng, Mar 3, 34; US citizen. *Study:* Art Students League; Mus Mod Art; Boston Univ, BFA, 56; studied with David Aronson, Margit Beck & Paul Wood. *Work:* Emily Lowe Gallert, Hofstra Univ. *Exhib:* Solo shows, Great Neck House, NY, 83, Plandome Gallery, NY, 88, Art Upstairs, E Williston, NY, 89, Gallery Emanuel, Great Neck, NY, 90-91; Guild Hall Mus, E Hampton, NY, 88-90 & Elaine Benson Gallery, BridgeHampton, NY, 89; Chelsea Ctr, Muttontown, NY, 90; Kirkpatrick Art Ctr, Oklahoma City, Okla, 90; 92nd & 93rd Ann Mem Exhib, Nat Arts Club, 90-91; 35th & 37th Ann Exhib, Heckscher Mus, 90 & 92; 159th Ann Exhib, Nat Acad Design. *Pos:* Dir, Gallery Emanuel, Great Neck, NY, 88- *Teaching:* Lectr, Long Island Art Leagues & Nassau Co Fine Arts Ctr, currently; Studio Classes Great Neck & Brookville, NY. *Awards:* Grumbacher Award, 82, First Prize, 85, 88-91, Burt Lipper Award, 91, Founders Award, 92, Mahasset Art Asn; Doris Klein Award, 84, Susan Kahn Award, 86, Medal of hon, 88, 100 Years 100 Works, 89, Audrey Hope Shirk Mem Award, 90, Nat Asn Women Artists; First Prize, 88 & 91, Best show, 90, Artists Network Great Neck; Best of Show, Nassau Co Mus Fine Arts, 92. *Mem:* Nat Asn Women Artists; Audubon Artists; Nat Arts Club; Knickerbocker Artists; Nat Soc Painters in Casein & Acrylics. *Media:* Acrylic, Oil. *Mailing Add:* 16 Pine Tree Dr Great Neck NY 11024

GRIEDER, TERENCE
HISTORIAN
b Cedar Rapids, Iowa, Sept 2, 31. *Study:* Univ Colo, BA, 53; Univ Wis, MS(appl art), 56; Univ Pa, MA(art hist), 60, PhD(art hist), 61. *Teaching:* Instr art, Univ Wis, Milwaukee, 56-57 & Conn Col, New London, 60-61; from asst prof to prof art, Univ Tex, Austin, 61- *Awards:* US Govt Smith-Mundt Fel to Guatemala, 59-60; Am Coun Learned Soc Foreign Area Fel, 65-67. *Mem:* Col Art Asn; Soc Am Archaeol. *Res:* Archaeological study of the history of pre-Colombian art, emphasizing the Andean highlands of Peru. *Publ:* Coauth, Art of Latin America Since Independence, 66; auth, Art & Archaeology of Pashash, 78; Orgins of Pre-Columbian Art, 82; La Galgada, Peru: A Preceramic Culture in Transition, 88; Artist and Audience, 90. *Mailing Add:* 2603 Maria Anna Rd Austin TX 78703

GRIEFEN, JOHN ADAMS
PAINTER
b Worcester, Mass, Nov 24, 42. *Study:* Williams Col, BA, 66; Art Inst Chicago; Bennington Col; Hunter Col, 66-68. *Work:* Hirshhorn Mus & Sculpture Garden; Boston Mus Fine Arts; Whitney Mus Am Art & Mus Mod Art, New York; Brooklyn Mus; Metrop Mus Art, New York. *Comn:* Painting, Gerald Hines Interest, Framingham, Mass. *Exhib:* Lyrical Abstraction, Whiney Mus Am Art, New York, 71; NS Print Show, Mus Mod Art, New York, 74; Recent Aquisitions, Hirshhorn Mus & Sculpture Garden, DC, 77; Recent Aquisitions Contemp Art, Boston Mus Fine Arts, 77; solo exhibs, Martha Jackson Gallery, New York, Frank Walters Gallery, Sidney, Australia, 79, Moos Gallery, Toronto, Can, 81, Salander O' Reilly Galleries, 81-82 & 84-85 & Edmonton Art Gallery, Can, 84; and others. *Teaching:* Instr painting, Bennington Col, 67-68; pvt lessons, New York, 72-; instr sculpture, Great Neck Pub Schs, NY, 76- *Bibliog:* Larry Aldrich (auth), Lyrical Abstraction, Whitney Mus Am Art, 70; William Zimmer (auth), John Griefen, 76 & Earl Powell (auth), John Griefen, 78, Arts Mag; plus others. *Media:* Acrylics. *Publ:* Auth, Appreciating art, Update Mag, 85. *Dealer:* Salander-O'Reilly Galleries Inc 20 E 79th St New York NY 10021. *Mailing Add:* 57 Laight St New York NY 10013

GRIER, MARGOT EDMANDS
LIBRARIAN, ADMINISTRATOR
b Washington, DC, May 15, 46. *Study:* Old Dominion Univ, with Parker Lesley, BA(magna cum laude), 71; Univ Md, MLS, 72. *Pos:* Serials librn, Nat Gallery Art, Washington, DC, 73-; automation coord, Nat Gallery Art, Washington, DC, 87-90; adminr,Educ Division Nat Gallery Art, Washington, DC, 90- *Awards:* Hermitage Found Award, Norfolk, Va, 69 & 70. *Mem:* Art Libraries Soc North Am; Wasington Art Libr Resources Comt; Embroiderers' Guild Am. *Res:* Integrated museum online access systems. *Interests:* 20th century Mexican; contemporary; small press art magazines, textile history. *Publ:* Auth, Old St Paul's, Kent Co, Md, St Pauls Episcopal Church, 71; contribr, ARLIS/NA Newsletter, Art Libr Soc, 79-80; co-ed, Art Serials Union List, 81; contribr, Art Doc, 83-; ed, National Gallery of Art Serials, Nat Gallery Art, 83; contribr auth, Gemini GEL Art and Collaboration, Ruth Fine, Nat Gallery Art & New York, Abbeville Press, 84. *Mailing Add:* c/o Nat Gallery Art Washington DC 20565

GRIESEDIECK, ELLEN
PAINTER, PRINTMAKER
b Jan 26, 48. *Study:* Univ Colo, BFA, 70. *Comn:* Four paintings, Gen Motors, New York, 80; five paintings, Times Mirror Publs, New York, 82. *Exhib:* Royal Orleans, New Orleans, 78; Spectrum Olympics, Spectrum Gallery, New York, 79; Seagram's Special Exhib, New York, 80; solo exhibs, Gallery Henoch, New Yorkk, 85, 89 & Tour de France, Galerie de Poche, Paris, 90. *Bibliog:* Richard Martin (auth), Ellen Griesedieck, Arts Mag, 85. *Media:* Oil, Mixed Media; All Media. *Publ:* Illusr, Summer, Addison/Wesley, 90. *Dealer:* Marcel Fleiss Galerie De Poche 3 Rue Bonaparte Paris France 75006; George Henoch Shechtman Gallery Henoch 80 Wooster St New YOrk NY 10012. *Mailing Add:* c/o Gallery Henoch 80 Wooster St New York NY 10012

GRIFFIN, CHRIS A
SCULPTOR
b Boston, Mass. *Study:* Col of New Rochelle, NY, BFA, 72; Columbia Univ, MA, 73. *Work:* Pictogram Gallery, New York, NY; ISCIP Mus, New York; Everson Mus, Syracuse, NY; Prudential Insurance, Newark, NJ; Phillip Morris, New York, NY. *Exhib:* Lines of Vision, Long Island Univ, NY, 89; Words & Images, Henry Street Settlement, New York, 89; Issues of Identity, Dowling Col, NY, 92; Sculptors Drawings, E Hampton Ctr Contemp Art, NY; Geometric Sculpture, Tribeca 148 Gallery, New York; and others. *Teaching:* Assoc prof sculpture, State Univ NY, Old Westbury, 78- *Awards:* Sculptor Grant Award, NY State Found for Arts, 85; Artist in Residence Grant, Experimental Glass Workshop, New York, 89. *Bibliog:* Ann Kroncnburg (auth), Chris Griffin, Women Artists News, spring 85. *Media:* Mixed Media. *Mailing Add:* 230 W 105th St Apt 3D New York NY 10025

GRIFFITH, ROBERTA
EDUCATOR, CERAMIST
b Hillsdale, Mich, May 14, 37. *Study:* Chouinard Art Inst, BFA, 60; Southern Ill Univ, Carbondale, MFA, 62; Massana Sch, Barcelona, Spain with Llorens Artigas, 62-64. *Work:* Yager Mus, Hartwick Col, Oneonta, NY; Mus Ceramics, Barcelona, Spain; Roberson Ctr Arts & Sci, Binghamton, NY; Gallery State Univ New York, Albany, NY; Inst de Estudias Norte-Americanos & Escuela Massana, Barcelona, Spain; pvt collections in the US, Spain, Mex, Ger, Eng & Japan. *Exhib:* Solo exhibs, Aleneo, Madrid, Spain, 64, Camerote Granados Gallery, Barcelona, Spain, 74, Chautauqua Art Asn Galleries, NY, 79, Mus Ceramics, Barcelona, Spain, 81, Munson-Williams Proctor Inst, Sch Art Gallery, Utica, NY, 82 & 88, Ctr Galleries, Albany, NY, 84, Endicott Col Gallery, Beverly, Mass, 85 & Foreman Gallery, Hartwick Col, Oneonta, NY, 89; Ceramic Int, Faenza, Italy, 70, 74, 81 & 83; Ceramic Invitational, Stockholm, Sweden, 72; Fundacion Miro, Barcelona, Spain, 81, 82 & 84; Channel 13 Television Art Auction, New York, 83 & 84; 41st Ceramic Int, Mus Ceramics, Faenza, Italy, 83; 13th Chunichi Int Exhib Ceramic Arts, Nagoya, Japan, 85; Cooperstown Nat, NY, 87, 88, 89,90, 91 & 92; Munson-Williams Proctor Inst, Utica, NY, 88; Arlene McDaniel Galleries 7th Nat Invitational Sculpture Show, W Hartford, Conn, 89; Winfisky Gallery, Salem State Col, Mass, 92; and many others. *Pos:* Ceramic designer, Design Technics, Stroudsburg, PA, 65-66. *Teaching:* Arkell Hall Prof Art (Endowed Chair), ceramics, drawing, painting, Hartwick Col, Oneonta, NY, 66-, chmn art dept, 75-91, chmn Humanities, 88-89. *Awards:* Fulbright-Hays Grant, 5 major exhib, United States Govt, 62- 64; First Prize in Drawing, Hudson-Mohawk Regional First Albany Corp, Albany, NY, 79; First Prize ceramic sculpture, 54th Cooperstown Nat Exhib, 89; Nat Endowment for the Humanities Summer Inst, Ancient Mesoamerican Civilizations, Univ Pittsburgh, 91. *Bibliog:* article, New York Art Rev, 89; Richard Zakin (auth), Ceramic Processes, 90; Leon Nigrosh (auth), Clay Sculpture, 91. *Mem:* Upper Catskill Community Coun Arts (UCCCA), (sec, 74-78; vpres, 78-79; pres, 79-81); Nat Coun Educ Ceramic Arts; Col Art Asn; Am Crafts Coun; Artist-Craftsmen New York, Inc. *Publ:* Auth, Art, NCECA in Atlanta, Am Craft, 83; Spanish Ceramics, NCECA Newsletter, 84; NCECA Conference Turns Boston into Clay City, Crafts Report, 84; Cahokia; Ramey Incised Pottery, NCECA Journal, 85; Artigas and Miro, Studio Potter, 85. *Dealer:* The Gallery 248 Main St Oneonta NY 13820; Arlene McDaniel Galleries 10 Phelps Lane Simsburg CT 06070. *Mailing Add:* 32 Main St Otego NY 13825

GRIFFITHS, WILLIAM PERRY
EDUCATOR, JEWELER
b Traverse City, Mich, Sept 20, 37. *Study:* Western Mich Univ, BS, 61; Univ Wis, MFA, 68. *Work:* Mus Contemp Crafts, New York. *Comn:* Silver pendant, comn by Robert Arneson, Davis, Calif, 68; gold & silver pendants, comn by Don Reitz, Marshall, Wis, 85; silver ring, comn by Jack Youngerman, New York, 86; silver chancellor's chain, Univ Wis Ctr System, Madison, 87. *Exhib:* Objects USA (contribr, catalog), Smithsonian-World, Washington, DC, 69; Wisconsin Directions, 75 & All that Glitters: Personal Ornaments, 86, Milwaukee Art Mus, Wis. *Teaching:* Assoc prof art, Univ Wis Ctr, Fond du Lac, 68- *Media:* Silver & Gold, Precious Stones. *Mailing Add:* 67 N Lincoln Ave Fond du Lac WI 54935

GRIGORIADIS, MARY
PAINTER
b Jersey City, NJ, June 23, 42. *Study:* Barnard Col, BA, 63; Columbia Univ, MA, 65. *Work:* Chase Manhattan Bank, Athens & Piraeus, Greece; First Nat Bank Chicago; Nat Mus Am Art, Washington, DC; Va Mus Fine Art, Richmond; Allen Memorial Art Mus, Oberlin, Ohio; and others. *Comn:* Art work, Metropo Transit Authority. *Exhib:* One-woman shows, AIR Gallery, New York, 72, 75, 78, 82, 84, 86 & 89, O K Harris Gallery, New York, 76, Gallery K, Washington, DC, 78, Helen Shilien Gallery, Boston, 78, 81 & 83 & Barnard Col, 88; Biennial Contemp Am Art, Whitney Mus Am Art, 73; Small Works, Albright-Knox Mus Art, 76-77; Pattern Painting, PS I, New York, 77; The Brooklyn Mus, 77; Va Mus Fine Art, 90; Islamic Allusions, Alternative Mus, New York, 80; Aldrich Mus Contemp Art, Conn, 81; Lunds Konsthall, Sweden, 82; and others. *Pos:* Founding mem, AIR Gallery, exec comt, 83-86. *Awards:* NY Found for Arts, 89. *Bibliog:* Hayden Herrera, reviews, Art in Am, 3-4/77; Joan Marter (auth), Mary Grigoriadis, Arts Mag, 11/84; C Robins (auth), The Pluralist Era, 1968-1981, Harper & Row, New York, 84. *Media:* Oil, Pastel. *Dealer:* AIR Gallery 63 Crosby St New York NY 10012; Helen Shlien Gallery 14 Newbury St Boston MA. *Mailing Add:* 382 Central Park W New York NY 10025

GRIGSBY, JEFFERSON EUGENE, JR
EDUCATOR, PAINTER
b Greensboro, NC, Oct 17, 18. *Study:* Morehouse Col, with Hale Woodruff & Nancy Prophet, BA, 38; Am Artists Sch, with M Hebald, H Harrari & J Groth, 39; Ohio State Univ, with Prof Hopkins & R Fanning, MA, 40; Ecole Beaux Arts, Marseilles, 45; NY Univ, PhD, 63; Philadelphia Col Art, Hon DFA, 65. *Work:* Tex Southern Univ, Houston; Mint Mus, Charlotte, NC; Nat Mus Ghana, Cape Castle; Richmond Pub Schs, Va; Ariz State Univ; Glendale Community Col; Valley Nat Bank; Bank Am. *Exhib:* Am Negro Expos, Tanner Art Galleries, Chicago, 40; Baltimore Mus, 40; Ariz Ann, Phoenix Mus, 64; one-man show, Centennial Celebration, Morehouse Col, 67; Dimensions in Black, La Jolla Mus, Calif, 70; Dallas City Hall, 81; Ariz State Univ, 86; Benedict Col, 87. *Pos:* Head dept art, Carver High Sch, 46-54 & Phoenix Union High Sch, Ariz, 54-66. *Teaching:* Artist-in-residence, Johnson C Smith Univ, 40-41; prof art educ & drawing, Ariz State Univ, 66-88, distinguished res scholar, 82-83, prof emer, 88. *Awards:* Medallion of Merit, Nat Gallery Art, 66; Nat Art Educ Asn Educator of the Year, 88; Ariz Gov Award, 89. *Mem:* Fel Nat Art Educ Asn (vpres, 72-74); Black Orgn Arts; Ariz Artists Guild; Consortium of Black Orgns for the Arts; Nat Conf Artists; Artists of the Black Community, Ariz; Nat Found for the Arts (visual arts panel, 81-84); NAEA Comt on Minority Concerns. *Media:* Acrylic, Serigraph. *Res:* African art, its history, materials used and style. *Publ:* Auth, Ba Kuba art, In: Africa Seen by American Negroes, 58; Encounters (exhib catalog), J C Smith Univ Exhib, 68; Art & Ethnics, William C Brown Co; ed, Sch Arts Mag, 10/79. *Mailing Add:* Dept Art Ariz State Univ 1117 N 9th St Phoenix AZ 85006-2734

GRILLO, ESTHER ANGELA
SCULPTOR, PRINTMAKER
b Rome, Italy, Jan 28, 54; US citizen. *Study:* Queens Col, NY, study with Tom Doyle, 72-74; Brooklyn Col, BA(cum laude), 77, study with Terris & D'Archangelo & MFA, 81, study with Bontecou, Samuels & Mehlmen. *Work:* Brooklyn Col Print Collection, New York; Palmer Mus, Pa State Univ. *Comn:* Wall relief (38'), MTA/Creative Stations. *Exhib:* A Gender Show, Group Material, New York, 81; The Wild Art Show, PS 1, New York, 82; Earth Transformed by Fire, Rotunda Gallery, New York, 84; Beginnings & Endings, Mus Borough Brooklyn, NY, 84; Long Island Artists, Islip Art Mus, East Islip, NY, 85; Holocaust Memorial Art Exhib, Queensborough Community Col, NY, 85; Masters of War, Ammo Gallery, Brooklyn, NY, 85; Taking Liberties: Transcendence and Transgression, Pace Univ Art Gallery, Civic Ctr Campus, Pace Plaza, New York, 86; solo exhibs, Narrative Sculpture: Collage and Prints, 14 Sculptors Gallery, NY, 86, Meltdown, Palmer Mus, Pa State Univ, 88 & Esther A Grillo: Installation, Sculpture, Collage, Prints, 14 Sculptors Gallery, Soho, New York, 88; Queens Mus Juried Ann, Queens, New York, 87; and others. *Awards:* Exhibition Award, B J Spoke Gallery, New York, 83. *Bibliog:* Susan Koslow (auth), Esther A Grillo, Arts Mag, 86; David S Martin (auth), Exhib, events meant to raise nuclear awareness, Centre Daily Times, Assoc Press, 1/14/88; Fatal vision, The Palm Beach Post, Meltdown on display, Express-News, Tex & Nuclear art show to feature Meltdown, Cape Coral Press (all from Assoc Press, 1/11/88). *Mem:* Womens Caucus Art; Col Art Asn. *Media:* Mixed. *Publ:* Contribr, Words-Pictures--Collaborative Work of Women Artists, Womens Caucus Art, 82; Sculpting clay, Nigros H, 92. *Dealer:* 14 Sculptors Gallery 164 Mercer St New York NY 10012. *Mailing Add:* 158-06 95th St Howard Beach NY 11414

GRIMES, MARGARET W
PAINTER, EDUCATOR
b New Bern, NC. *Study:* Gov State Univ, BA, 74, MA, 75; Notre Dame Univ, with Alice Neel, 77; Univ Pa, with Neil Welliver, MFA, 80. *Work:* Pittsburgh Plate Glass Co; Conn Insurance Group NAm; Christian Sci Church Ctr, Boston; US Tobacco Co; Bellevue Hosp Ctr, New York; Atlantic Fed Bank, NJ; Ethan Allen Co, Conn. *Comn:* Print, New York Graphic Soc, 85; Calendar Reproduction, Cairo, Calendar Images, 88. *Exhib:* Int Womens Art Festival, Walker Art Inst, 76; Woodmere Mus 37th Ann Exhib, Philadelphia, 77; Works on Paper, Provincetown Art Mus, Pa, 78; one-person exhibs, Green Mountain Gallery, New York, 79 & Blue Mountain Gallery, New York, 80, 82, 87, 90 & 92, Fischbach Gallery, NY, 86, Columbus Mus Art, Ohio, 87, Newport Art Mus, RI, 88; Painted Light Traveling Exhib, Reading Mus, Pa, Queens Mus, New York, 83; Women Painters Today, Rahr-West Mus, Manitowac, Wis, 83; Fischbach Gallery, NY, 86; Katherina Rich Perlow, NY, 88; Univ Pa, 92. *Teaching:* Instr drawing & design, Thornton Community Col, Chicago, 74-79; prof painting & drawing, Western Conn State Univ, 80- *Awards:* Res Grant, Conn State Univ, 85 & 90; Henry Barnard Found Distinguished Lecturship Award, 90; Distinguished Prof, West Conn State Univ, 92. *Bibliog:* Helen Thomas (auth), article, 5/79 & Robert Godfrey (auth), article, 11/80, Arts Mag; John Priggs (auth), Fractals: Art and Science of Nature, Simon & Schuster, 92. *Mem:* Col Art Asn; Am Asn Univ Prof. *Media:* Oil. *Publ:* Co-ed, New Art Asn Newsletter, 71. *Mailing Add:* 25 Taunton Lake Rd Newtown CT 06470

GRIMLEY, OLIVER FETTEROLF
PAINTER, SCULPTOR
b Norristown, Pa, June 30, 20. *Study:* Pa Acad Fine Arts, William Emlen Clesson traveling scholar, 47, Henry J Scheidt traveling scholar, 50; Univ Pa, BFA & MFA. *Work:* Woodmere Art Galleries, Mus Art, Pa Acad Fine Arts, Philadelphia; Libr Cong, Washington, DC. *Comn:* Murals, Commonwealth Fed Savings & Loan, Norristown, 63, Continental Bank & Trust, 65 & Am Bank, Lafayette Hills, Pa, 72; papier-mache eagle, comn by Leonard Tose, Vet Stadium, Philadelphia, 71. *Exhib:* Whitney Mus Am Art, Libr Cong & Metrop Mus, 52-57; Pa Acad Fine Arts Watercolor Shows, 58-63; Philadelphia Mus Art. *Teaching:* Instr drawing, Hussian Sch Art, 60- & Pa Acad Fine Arts, 65- *Awards:* Ralph Pallen Coleman Prize for Illus, 73; First Prize for Sculpture, Regional Coun Community Arts Ctr, 74; J W Zimmerman Mem Prize for Work of Distinction, 79. *Bibliog:* Henry Pitz (auth), article, Am Artist, 71. *Mem:* Philadelphia Watercolor Club. *Media:* Pen & Ink, Watercolor; Miscellaneous. *Publ:* Auth, article, Am Artist, 50. *Mailing Add:* Dept Art Hussian Sch Art 1010 Arch St Philadelphia PA 19107

GRIMM, LUCILLE DAVIS
PAINTER
b Nashville, Tenn, Aug 20, 29. *Study:* George Peabody Col Teachers, Vanderbilt Univ, Nashville, BA, 51. *Work:* Fairfield Univ, Conn; Town Collection, Fairfield, Conn; Humana Woman's Hosp, Tampa, Fla; Vanderbilt Univ, Nashville, Tenn; Yale New Haven Hosp, New Haven, Conn. *Comn:* Painting, Richard Bower, Pres, Mo Electrochem, St Louis, 82; paintings, Mariott Hotels, Los Angeles & San Francisco, 85, Hanover, NJ, 86; Gallery Downtown, Ft Worth, Tex, 86; paintings, Financial Fed Bank, Hartford, Conn, 86, Holiday Inn, Windsor Locks, The Art Works, Old Lyme, Conn; Signature Gallery, Avon, Conn. *Exhib:* Three-woman show, Ctr for Financial Studies, Fairfield Univ, 85; 32nd New Eng Exhib, Silvermine Ctr Arts, New Canaan, Conn, 81; Watercolor Hon Soc, Springfield Art Mus, Mo, 87; one-woman show, New Eng Ctr, Univ NH, Durham, 81; Slater Mus, Norwich, Conn, 86 & 88; San Diego Watercolor Soc, Calif, 85; Shippee Gallery, New York, 85; and others. *Teaching:* Teacher art, Milford Area Sr High Sch, NH, 75-78. *Awards:* Purchase Award, New Haven Paint & Clay Club, Conn, 85; Best of Show, New Eng Watercolor Soc, 87; Hon Mention, Conn Watercolor Soc, 87; Purchase Award, New Haven Paint & Clay Club, New Haven, Conn, 85. *Bibliog:* Shirley Gonzales (auth), articles, New Haven Register, Conn, 81, 86, 87, 88. *Mem:* New Eng Watercolor Soc; The Watercolor USA Honor Soc, Springfield, Mo; Conn Women Artists; Conn Watercolor Soc; New Haven Paint & Clay Club, Conn. *Media:* Watercolor, Mixed. *Dealer:* Munson Gallery 33 Whitney Ave New Haven CT 06511; Greene Art Gallery Guilford Conn 06437. *Mailing Add:* Box 554 5 Oak Ridge Dr Clinton CT 06413

GRIMM, RAYMOND MAX
SCULPTOR, POTTER
b St Louis, Mo, June 20, 24. *Study:* Wash Univ Sch Fine Arts, BFA, 53; Southern Ill Univ, with F Carlton Ball in pottery, MS, 55. *Work:* Univ Ore Mus Art, Eugene; Contemp Crafts Gallery, & Fountain Gallery Art, Portland, Ore; Salem Civic Ctr, Ore. *Comn:* Design of 60ft x 12ft rock mosaic, Our Lady Queen of Peace Church, Portland, 65; ceramic plaque, 13ft x 3ft, Salishan Lodge, Gleneden, Ore, 65; brick mosaic, 60ft x 9ft, Mountain Park Recreation Ctr, Lake Oswego, Ore, 70; seven brick sculptures, Ore State Veterinary Teaching Hosp, Corvallis, 79; Weather Machine, Pioneer Courthouse Square, Portland, 88. *Exhib:* One-man show, Contemp Crafts Gallery, Portland, 57-59, 63 & 75; Fiber, Clay & Metal, St Paul Art Mus, Minn, 66; Int Exhib Ceramic Art, City Mus, Faenze, Italy, 66; Craft Alliance Gallery, St Louis, 67; Pauling Gallery, Portland Community Col, 89; and others. *Teaching:* Prof emer art, ceramics & glass, Portland State Univ, 56- *Awards:* Jr League Award, St Louis Art Mus, 56; Harold Hirsch Award, Ore Ceramics Studio, 64; Merit Award, Mus Contemp Crafts, New York, 66. *Bibliog:* Catherine Jones (auth), Jere and Raymond Grimm, Creative Crafts Mag, 63; Polly Rothenberg (auth), The Complete Book of Ceramics, Crown Publ, 72; Lamar Harrington (auth), Ceramics in the Pacific Northwest, Univ Wash, 79. *Mem:* Am Craftsmen's Coun (state rep, 58-61). *Media:* Ceramics. *Mailing Add:* Dept Art Portland State Univ PO Box 751 Portland OR 97207

GRIMMER, MINEKO
SCULPTOR
Feb 3, 49. *Study:* Iwate Univ, Morioka, Japan, BA, 72; Otis Art Inst, Parsons Sch Design, Los Angeles, Calif, BFA, 79, MFA, 81. *Work:* Security Pacific Bank; Fresno Art Museum; Norton Computing Co. *Exhib:* Traditions Transformed, Oakland Mus, Calif, 85; solo exhibs, Laguna Beach Mus Art, Costa Mesa, Calif, 85, Triton Mus Art, Santa Clara, Calif, 86, St Louis Gallery Contemp Art, Mo, 88 & Kala Inst Gallery, Berkeley, Calif, 88, Intermittent Composition, Ruth Siegel Gallery, New York, 88, Audible Sculpture, Cheney Cowles Museum, Spokane, WA, 89, Eternal/Ephemeral, Koplin Gallery, Los Angeles, 90, Sculpture, Music, Dance, Seibu Studio 200, Tokyo, 90; Elements: Four Installations, Whitney Mus Am Art at Equitable Ctr, New York, 87; New Work Japan, Danforth Mus Art, Framingham, Mass, 88. *Awards:* Fel, Nat Endowment Arts, 87; Fel, California Arts Council, 88; Grant Saison Foundation, 90. *Bibliog:* Merle Shipper (auth), Artists the critics are watching--Mineko Grimmer, Artnews, 5/86; Mary MacNaughton (auth), Sound and silence: the sculpture of Mineko Grimmer, Arts Mag, 11/87; Marge Bulmer (auth), Mineko Grimmer, Artscene, 3/88. *Media:* Natural Materials. *Publ:* Jim Jenkins & Dave Quick (coauth), "Motion/Motion Kinetic Art", Gibbs Smith, 89, Kathleen Stoughton (auth), "Mineko Grimmer, Palisade", 90. *Mailing Add:* 10747 Wilshire Blvd #504 Los Angeles CA 90024

GRINER, NED H
EDUCATOR, CRAFTSMAN
b Tipton, Ind, Dec 14, 28. *Study:* Ball State Teachers Col, BS; State Univ Iowa, MA; Ind Univ, MFA; Pa State Univ, DEd. *Work:* Evansville Mus Art & Ball State Univ Art Gallery, Muncie, Ind. *Exhib:* Midstates Craft Exhib, 66-67; Jewelry Exhib, Purdue Univ, 67; Indianapolis Mus Art, 75; Ind Univ Mus Art, Bloomington, 76; Ind State Mus, Indianapolis, 77; Ft Wayne Art Mus, Ind, 78. *Teaching:* Asst prof art, Ark State Col, 54-60; asst, Pa State Univ, 60-61; prof, Ball State Univ, 61-, head dept, 70- *Mem:* Nat & Ind Art Educ Asns; Col Art Asn Am; Ind Artist Craftsmen (pres, 66-68); Nat Coun Art Adminr. *Media:* Silver, Bronze, Brass. *Publ:* Auth, article, Quartet Mag, Vol 2, No 10; contrib, Art--search & self discovery, 68; auth, Side by Side with

Coarser Plants: The Muncie Art Movement, 1885-1985, Ball State Univ, 85; Gas Society, Minnetrista Cultural Found Inc, 91; J Ottis Adams: A Sense of Place, Minnetrista Cultural Found Inc, 92. *Mailing Add:* Dept of Art Ball State Univ Muncie IN 47306

GRIPPE, FLORENCE (BERG)
PAINTER, INSTRUCTOR
b New York, NY, Jan 6, 12. *Study:* Educ Alliance, 32-34; Works Proj Admin Art Courses, 34-38; pottery with William Soini, 39-41. *Work:* Rose Art Mus, Brandeis Univ. *Comn:* Portraits comn by Doris Brewer Cohen, Lexington, Mass, 69, Signora Attilio Roveda, Locarno, Switz, 70, Dr Luis Martinez & Julio Farinos Castillo, Valencia, Spain, 70 & Jose Marina Galvao Telles, Lisbon, Portugal, 71. *Exhib:* Brooklyn Mus, 51; Lower East Side Independent Artists 3rd Ann Exhib, 58; Guild Hall, Easthampton, Long Island, 75 & 87; Provincetown Art Asn & Mus, Mass, 78; Himmelfarb Gallery, Long Island, 80-81; Burnside Gallery, Long Island, 81 & 83; and others. *Pos:* Mem screening comt 78-79 competition sponsored Fulbright-Hayes Comn for grants for grad study abroad. *Teaching:* Instr drawing, painting, sculpture & puppetry, United Art Workshops, Brooklyn Neighborhood Houses, NY, 47-54; instr design & pottery, Brooklyn Mus Art Sch, 51-57. *Bibliog:* S Sheridan (auth), Native handicrafts, NY Times Mag, 7/52; article in Daily Transcript, Boston, 7/19/79; article in Peconic Bay Shopper, Long Island, 10/81; and others. *Media:* All. *Publ:* Auth, With the brush, Ceramic Age, 3/56; coauth, Art news from Boston, Art News, 61-63. *Mailing Add:* 28100 Main Rd Orient NY 11957

GRIPPE, PETER
PRINTMAKER, SCULPTOR
b Buffalo, NY, Aug 8, 12. *Study:* Albright-Knox Art Sch, 23-25; Art Inst Buffalo, with Edwin Dickinson, 29-35; sculpture with Wm Enrich & life drawing with Edwin Dickenson; Atelier 17, New York, with William Stanley Hayter, 44-48. *Work:* Albright-Knox Art Gallery, Buffalo, NY; Mus Mod Art, Metrop Mus Art & Whitney Mus Am Art, New York; Washington Univ, St Louis, Mo; Newark Mus, NJ; and others. *Comn:* Two sculpture murals, comn by James B Bell & Assoc, PR Info Ctr, New York, 58; sculpture, Theodore Shapiro Forum, Brandeis Univ, 63; portrait of Composer Irving Fine, Brandeis Univ, 64; sculpture, Sci Bldg lobby, Simmons Col, Boston, 69; portrait, Marver H Bernstein, pres Brandeis Univ, 80; and others. *Exhib:* Painting, Drawing & Sculpture, Am Acad Rome, Italy, 65; Sculptors Guild, New York, 67; The New American Painting & Sculpture: The First Generation, Mus Mod Art, New York, 69; Boston Now, Inst Contemp Art, Boston, 69; Whitney Mus Am Art, 80; Zabriskie Gallery, New York, 83; 14th Boston Arts Festival, 85; Flying Tigers: Painting and Sculpture in New York, 1939-1946, Cantor Art Gallery, Worcester, Mass, 85 & Parrish Gallery, Southampton, NY, 86; Monument to Hiroshima, Cantor Art Gallery, Worcester, Mass, 86; Sid Deutsch Gallery, 87 & 91. *Teaching:* Federal Arts Project, New York, 39-42; Black Mountain Col, NC, summer 48; instr design, Pratt Inst, 49-50, Smith Col, 50-51; dir printmaking, Atelier 17, New York, 51-54; prof fine arts, Brandeis Univ, 53-80. *Awards:* Contemp Watercolors, Drawings & Prints Award, Metrop Mus Art, 52; Boston Arts Festival Award, Art Comn Boston, 55; Guggenheim Fel for Sculpture, 64. *Bibliog:* On sculpture, It Is, autumn 65; W V Anderson (auth), The city of Peter Grippe, Connection, 66; Monument to Hiroshima, Cantor Art Gallery, Worcester, Mass, 86; E Lawrence (auth), Abstract Expressionism, Albright-Knox Art Gallery, 87. *Publ:* Contribr, Credo (Iconograph), 46; producer, ed & contribr, Twenty-one etchings & poems, Morris Gallery, New York, 58; contribr, Enter Mephistopheles with images, Art News, Vol 59, No 6; Contemporary American Painting & Sculpture, Univ Ill, 61; auth, Mots Trouvees (collage-poems), Nordness Gallery, New York, 63. *Dealer:* Sid Deutsch Gallery 29 West 57th St New York NY. *Mailing Add:* 28100 Main Rd Orient NY 11957

GRIPPI, SALVATORE WILLIAM
PAINTER, EDUCATOR
b Buffalo, NY, Sept 30, 21. *Study:* Mus Mod Art Sch, 44-45; Art Students League, 45-48; Atelier 17, 51-53; Inst Statale Arte, Florence, Italy, Fulbright Scholar, 53-55. *Work:* Whitney Mus Am Art & Metrop Mus Art, New York; Joseph Hirshhorn Collection, Washington, DC; St Lawrence Univ; Everson Mus, Syracuse, NY. *Exhib:* Biennials, Corcoran Gallery Art, 59 & 63; Whitney Mus Am Art Ann, 60; Walker Art Ctr, 60; Recent Painting USA, The Figure, Mus Mod Art, New York & throughout US, 62; Calif Palace Legion of Honor, 65; Drawing Invitational, Long Beach Mus, Calif, 66 & traveling exhib, Western Asn of Mus, 66-68; Selected American Painters, Phoenix Art Mus, Ariz, 67; Elvehjem Art Ctr, Univ Wis, 77 & traveling; Brooklyn Mus, NY, 78; Everson Mus, Syracuse, NY, 78; Krasner Gallery, New York, 79 & 81; others in New York, Los Angeles & Milwaukee. *Teaching:* Instr painting, drawing & 2-D design, Cooper Union Art Sch, 56-59; instr, Sch Visual Arts, 61-62; assoc prof art, Pomona Col & Claremont Grad Sch, 62-68; prof art, Ithaca Col, 68- *Bibliog:* Brian O'Dougherty (auth), Variety of exhibitions, New York Times, 3/22/62; Larry Campbell (auth), article, Art News, 10/64; Henry J Seldis (auth), Art walk: A critical guide to the galleries, Los Angeles Times, 5/29/70; and many others. *Mem:* Life mem Art Students League (treas, 61-62, bd control, 61-64); Col Art Asn Am. *Publ:* Auth, Visual impressions of Italy, Inst Int Educ Bull, 56; Turntable kaleidoscope, Mus Mod Art, 56, 57 & 59; contribr, Twenty-one Etchings & Poems, 58. *Mailing Add:* 423 E Seneca St Ithaca NY 14850

GRISSOM, EUGENE EDWARD
EDUCATOR, HISTORIAN
b Melvern, Kans, May 15, 22. *Study:* Philippine Univ, 45; Kans State Teachers Col, Emporia, BS, 48; State Univ Iowa, with M Lasansky, MFA, 51. *Work:* Univ Iowa, Iowa City; Univ Louisville, Ky. *Teaching:* Instr art educ, Kans State Teachers Col, summer 51; instr art, Univ Ky, 51-53; from asst prof to prof art, Univ Fla, 53-, chmn dept, 62-78, prof emeritus, 87. *Res:* Drawing workshops of the early 15th century in Italy; Antonio Pollaivolo, Florence engraver of the late 1400's; drawing marks & certain contemporary music notation systems. *Mailing Add:* Dept Art Univ Fla Gainesville FL 32611

GRISSOM, FREDA GILL
PAINTER, GOLDSMITH
b Groom, Tex. *Study:* WTex State Univ, Canyon, BS; Univ Tex, Austin; also watercolor workshop. *Work:* Montgomery Mus Fine Arts, Ala. *Exhib:* Ann Dixie Exhib, Montgomery Mus Fine Arts, 68; Nat Art Roundup, Las Vegas, Nev, 68; Greater New Orleans Nat, 71; 9th Grand Prix Int, Cannes, France, 73; Galerie Rene Borel, Deauville, France, 73. *Pos:* Co-chmn, Nat Sun Carnival Art Exhib, El Paso, Tex, 65-71. *Awards:* Purchase Award, Montgomery Mus Fine Arts, 68; Second Prize, Greater New Orleans Nat Exhib, 71; Medaille de la Ville de Cannes, First Prize, Watercolor, 9th Grand Prix Int, Cote D'Azur, 73. *Mem:* El Paso Art Asn, Inc (dir, 64-65); El Paso Mus Art; Black Range Art Asn; Tex Watercolor Soc. *Media:* Transparent Watercolor, Acrylic, Oil; Gold, Silver. *Mailing Add:* Rte 1 Box 321G Anthony TX 88021

GROAT, HALL PIERCE
PAINTER, MURALIST
b Syracuse, NY, Dec 31, 32. *Study:* Syracuse Univ, BFA, also Grad Sch Painting; Josef Albers. *Work:* Lincoln Everson Mus Art, Syracuse, NY; Philatelic Mus, Geneva, Switz; Syracuse Univ & Norstar Bank, NY; Skaneatelles Savings Bank, NY; Merrill Ctr, Bangor, Maine; Portrait of John Mulroy, Republican Collection, John Mulroy Civic Ctr, Syracuse, NY. *Comn:* Hist mural, Merrill Trust Co, Bangor, Maine, 75; hist mural (five panels), Fleet Bank, 77; hist mural, Skaneateles, NY, 79; mural, Miller Brewing Co, Fulton, NY, 80; mural, Bristol-Myers Squibb, 81; mural, Mutual of New York; North Med Ctr, Syracus, NY. *Exhib:* Rochester Finger Lakes Exhib, Rochester Mem Art Gallery, NY, 59 & 63; Springfield Nat, Mass, 62; Everson Mus Regional, Syracuse, 64 & 70; Cooperstown Nat, NY, 67-83; Butler Inst Am Art, Youngstown, Ohio, 68. *Teaching:* Instr advan painting, Berkshire Mus. *Awards:* UN Philatelic Award; Berkshire Mus Purchase Award, Berkshire Art Asn, Pittsfield, 62; First Prize, Cent NY Art Open, 81; Int Award for UN stamp; and others. *Bibliog:* 32nd annual midyear show--Butler, La Rev Mod, 2/68;; Review of selected artist, Art Rev, fall 68; An Artist and His Work (film), WCNY, Syracuse, NY. *Mem:* Sarasota Art Asn; Nat Soc Mural Painters. *Media:* Acrylic, Oil; Watercolor. *Mailing Add:* 8364 Vassar Dr Manlius NY 13104

GROAT, HALL PIERCE, II
MURALIST, PAINTER
b Cazenovia, NY, June 3, 67. *Study:* State Univ NY, Binghamton, BA, art & art hist; studied with Angelo Ippolito, Brooklyn Col, MFA; studied with Lennart Andersobn, John Walker. *Work:* Munson-Williams Proctor Inst, Utica, NY; State Univ New York, Binghamton, NY; Bristol Myers, Syracuse, NY; Contell Cellular, Vestal, NY; also pvt collections of Mrs Herman Grauer, Mrs Joseph Takefaman, Mr Lawrence Prunhuber, Mr Stuart Grauer, Dr Frederick Schwartz & Fred Perry, London, England, and others. *Comn:* Security Mutual, 90. *Exhib:* One-man Exhibs, Everson Mus Art, 80, Norstar Bank, 87 & Am Heart Asn, 87 & Westbeth Gallery, New York, 92; Old Queens Gallery, Highland Park, NJ, 88; Hist Images, Chapman Art Gallery, Cazenovia Col, 89; Binghamton Art Ctr, State Univ New York, 89; Tryringham Art Ctr, Mass, 92; and others. *Awards:* A guide to the up and coming, People Mag, 8/13/79. *Bibliog:* documentary film, Hall Groat, A Man and His Art, WCNY, Channel 24, Liverpool, NY; Lookout, a guide to the up in coming, People Mag, 8/79. *Mem:* Nat Soc Mural Painters; Assoc Artists Syracuse; Cooperstown Art Asn. *Media:* Oil; Sculpture. *Publ:* Intro, Hall Groat II, Everson Mus. *Mailing Add:* Hall Groat Art Studio 8364 Vassar Dr Manlius NY 13104

GRODSKY, SHEILA TAYLOR
PAINTER, COLLAGE ARTIST
b Newark, NJ, May 7, 33. *Study:* Douglass Col, BA(art ed), 54; Md Inst Art, 68-69; also studied with Nicholas Reale, Gerald Brommer, W Carl Burger & Paul St Denis. *Exhib:* Am Watercolor Soc Ann Juried Exhib, New York, 87; Nat Watercolor Soc, Ann Invitational, Boulder, Colo, 88; NJ Watercolor Soc Ann, East Hanover, 85-89; Baltimore Watercolor Soc Mid-Atlantic Ann Juried Exhib, Md, 91-92; Salmagundi Club Ann, New York, 92. *Pos:* Bd mem, Sussex Co Arts Coun, 75-80. *Teaching:* Instr art, Dover High Sch, NJ, 54-56; instr watercolor, Livingston Art Asn, NJ, 90-91. *Awards:* Forbes Mag, Salmagundi Club Ann, Malcolm Forbes, 85; Nicholas Reale Mem, NJ Watercolor Soc, Reale Family, 85; Nina Johnson Mem, NJ Watercolor Soc, Avery Johnson Family, 89. *Mem:* NJ Watercolor Soc; Pastel Soc Am; Catharine Lorillard Wolfe Art Club Inc (bd dir, 89-); assoc mem Nat Watercolor Soc; assoc mem Am Watercolor Soc. *Media:* Watercolor, Pastel. *Mailing Add:* RD 5 Box 5928 Newton NJ 07860

GROEDEL, BURT JAY
PAINTER, SCULPTOR
b New York, NY, Oct 14, 37. *Study:* Pratt Inst, BFA, 59; Art Students League, 60. *Work:* Pvt collections of Drs Lynn & Lawrence Levine, Cherry Hill, NJ, Michel Grandsard, Antwerp, Belgium, Marjorie Dorman, Mr & Mrs Robert Swersky, Mr & Mrs Sam Flax and Jane Wessman. *Comn:* Tapestries, Edward Fields, Inc. *Exhib:* Chiaroscuro Gallery, Chicago, Ill, 87-88; Lillian Heidenberg Gallery, New York, 88; Lillian Heidenberg, New York, 91-92; Vorpal Gallery, 91-92; Viridian Gallery, 92; and many others. *Bibliog:* Eleanor Ettinger, publisher of lithographs in limited edition, 80- *Media:*

Acrylic & oil on Canvas. *Publ:* Illusr, Am Rugs & Carpets, 78; Art in Am, 81; Art News; Archit Digest Mag; Interior Design Mag. *Dealer:* Straus Gallery 201 East 16th St New York NY 10003; Eleanor Ettinger 155 Sixth Ave New York NY 10013. *Mailing Add:* 200 E 15th St New York NY 10003

GROELL, THEOPHIL
PAINTER, INSTRUCTOR
b Pittsburgh, Pa, Feb 11, 32. *Study:* Carnegie Inst Technol, BFA, 53. *Work:* Randolph-Macon Women's Col, Lynchburg, Va; Weatherspoon Art Gallery, Univ NC, Greensboro; also pvt collections of Rita Rich Fraud, Margot Gordon; Glenn C Janss, Ben Johnson, Sydney Lewis, Loring, Short & Harmon, Philip Lowe; Metrop Life, Peat, Marwick; Edmund Pillsbury, Steven Robinson, Simpson & Thatcher, Steven's Inc, L L Bean; and many others. *Exhib:* Personal Things, Hopper House, Nyack, NY, 76; Fortieth Ann Midyear Show, Butler Inst Am Art, Youngstown, Ohio, 76; Figure as Form: Am Painting 1930-1976, St Petersburg, Fla, 76; Ann Exhib, Randolph Macon Col for Women, Lynchburg, Va, 76; The Opposite Sex A Realistic Viewpoint, Univ Mo, Kans City, 79; Contemp Am Realism Since 1960 (auth, catalaog), Pa Acad Fine Arts, World Tour, 81; Am Realism, 20th Century Drawings & Watercolors (auth, catalog), Glenn C Janss Col, San Francisco Mus Mod Art, Nat Tour, 85; Realism Today, Am Drawings from the Rita Rich Col (auth, catalog), Nat Acad of Design, 87 & 88. *Bibliog:* Cindy Nemser (auth), Representational painting in 1971, Arts Mag, 12-1/72. *Media:* Oil. *Publ:* Auth, Realism Today, Am Drawings from the Rita Rich Col, 87. *Dealer:* Elena Kubler Gallery Portland & Dear Isle ME. *Mailing Add:* PO Box 432 Deer Isle ME 04627

GROGAN, KEVIN
MUSEUM DIRECTOR
b Washington, DC, Oct 4, 48. *Study:* Franklin & Marshall Col; Am Univ, grad. *Collections Arranged:* Red Grooms: The Graphic Work; Karl Struss: A Retrospective View of His Photography; The American Scene, 1900-1950; Glamour Defined: The Photography of George Hurrell; Louise Dahl-Wolfe: A Retrospective. *Pos:* Asst cur, Phillips Collection, DC, 71-79; dir, Fine Arts Ctr at Cheekwood, Nashville, Tenn, 80- *Teaching:* adj assoc prof, Dept Fine Arts, Vanderbilt Univ, 82- *Awards:* Gordon Holl Outstanding Arts Adminr, 87; Brotherhood-Sisterhood Award, Nat Conf Christians & Jews, 89; Award of Merit, Tenn Asn Mus, 90. *Mem:* Am Asn Mus; Int Mus Coun of Nashville; Tenn Asn Mus; Southeast Mus Conf; Cosmos Club; Int Coun Mus. *Res:* American art of the late 19th and early 20th centuries; American collectors of the same period. *Publ:* The Phillips Collection, Univ Chicago Press, 76; The Phillips Collection in the Making: 1920-30, Smithsonian Inst, 79; Karl Struss: A Retrospective (exhib catalog), 80; ed & auth foreword, Red Grooms: A Catalogue Raissone of his Graphic Work, 81, rev ed, 85; Art in the Embassy, Paris, 86. *Mailing Add:* Knoxville Ctr Art, World's Fair Park 410 Tenth St Knoxville TN 37916

GROM, BOGDAN
SCULPTOR, PAINTER
b Devincina, Sgonico-Trieste, Italy, Aug 26, 18; US citizen. *Study:* Fine Arts Acad, Perugia, Italy, with Gerardo Dottori, Aldo Pascucci, 44; Fine Arts Acad, Venice, Italy, with Guido Cadorin, Armando Pizzinato, Arturo Martini, 44; Fine Arts Acad, Munich, Germany, with Joseph Oberberger, 52. *Work:* Solomon R Guggenheim Mus, New York; Nat Mus Art, Osaka, Japan; Cincinnati Art Mus, Ohio; NJ State Mus, Trenton; Galleria Nazionale D'Arte Moderna, Rome. *Comn:* Sculpture & murals, Winston-Muss Corp, Phoenix, Ariz, 62; glass windows & sculpture, St Vartan Armenian Cathedral, New York, 68; bronze sculpture, New York City Art Comn, Staten Island, 73; stained windows & sculpture, JCC, White Plains, NY, 86; sculpture, Hekemian Co, Hackensack, NJ, 90. *Exhib:* Grom, Opere di Arredo Urbano, 1959-1979, Sala Comunale D'Arte, Trieste, Italy, 79; Art Expo, New York Coliseum, New York, 81; Int Biennial of Graphic Art, Mod Art Mus, Ljubljana, Yugoslavia, 85; Arazzi Mitteleuropei, Palazzo Venezia, Rome, Italy, 87; Int Biennial of Graphic Art, RYU Contemp Art, Kawasaki, Japan, 89. *Pos:* Bd mem, North Jersey Art Ctr, Tenefly, 76-78; cur, North Salem Gallery Ltd, New York, 80-84. *Teaching:* Prof art & art hist, State Gymnasium, Yugoslavia 45-47; State Teachers Prep Sch & Gymnas, Trieste, Italy, 47-53; vis instr art, Pratt Inst, New York, 60. *Awards:* Am Inst Archit, 85; For Achievement in Art Teaching, European Recovery Plan. *Bibliog:* Aurelia Gruber Benco (auth), article, Galleria d'Arte La Fontanella (catalog), 56; Susan B Hirschfeld (auth), article, Yugoslavia Cult Ctr (catalog), 89. *Mem:* Col Art Asn; Am Medallic Sculpture As; Int Sculpture Ctr; Sculptors Asn NJ (pres, 76-78). *Publ:* Illustr, Tom Sawyer, 47 & Huckelberry Finn, 48, Mladinska Knjiga; auth, Slovene Ornaments, private publ, 49; Trieste and its Karst, private publ, 57; illustr, There is No Such Animal, T B Lippincott, 58. *Mailing Add:* 416 Cumberland St Englewood NJ 07631

GRONBORG, ERIK
SCULPTOR, CERAMIST
b Copenhagen, Denmark, Nov 12, 31; US citizen. *Study:* Univ Calif, Berkeley, BA, 62, MA, 63. *Work:* Oakland Art Mus, Calif; Everson Mus Art, Syracuse, NY; Am Crafts Mus, New York; Univ Art Collections, Ariz State Univ, Tempe; Contemp Crafts Asn, Portland, Ore. *Exhib:* One-man shows, Mus Mod Art, Paris, France, 65 & Mus Contemp Crafts, New York, 69; Ceramics '70, Everson Mus Art, Syracuse, NY, 70; World Crafts Coun, Int Exhib, Toronto, Can, 74; Americana, San Francisco Mus Art, 76; Philadelphia Crafts Show, Philadelphia Mus Art, 78; American Porcelain, Renwick Gallery, Smithsonian Inst, 80; Art in Clay, 1950-1980, Municipal Art Gallery, Los Angeles, 84. *Teaching:* Asst prof ceramics & sculpture, Reed Col, Portland, Ore, 65-69; assoc prof, San Diego State Univ, Calif, 73-75; prof ceramics & sculpture, Mira Costa Col, Oceanside, Calif, 75- *Awards:* Grand Prix, Mus Mod Art, Paris, 63; Nat Endowment Arts Craftsman Grant, 73; Award, Victoria & Albert Mus, London, 73. *Bibliog:* Kent Hall (auth), Erik Gronborg: the history of the present, Univ Portland Rev, 66; Ida Rigby (auth), Erik Gronborg's accessible art, Artweek, 2/3/79; Judi Nicolaidis (auth), Erik Gronborg: Portrait in Clay (video), Nicolaidis, 79. *Mem:* Am Crafts Coun (state rep, 71-73). *Media:* Wood, Ceramics. *Publ:* Auth, The new generation of ceramic artists, Craft Horizons, 69; auth, Man and art in the urban environment, Nat Park & Conserv Mag, 72; auth, Address to World Crafts Council Conference, Mexico, Ceramic Rev, 77; contribr, Ceramic Art, Comment and Review, 1882-1977, Dutton, 78. *Mailing Add:* 424 Dell Ct Solana Beach CA 92075

GRONK
PAINTER
b Los Angeles, Calif, 1954. *Exhib:* Cultural Currents, San Diego Mus Art, Calif, 88; solo exhibs, Gronk, Molly Barnes Gallery, Los Angeles, 84, The Titanic & other Tragedies at Sea, Galeria Ocaso, Los Angeles, 85, The Rescue Party, Saxon-Lee Gallery, 86-89, 50 Drawings, Daniel Saxon Gallery, Los Angeles, 91, Hotel Tormenta, Galerie Claude Samuel, Paris, France, 92, Fascinating Slippers/Pantunflas, San Jose Mus Art, Calif (originated by Mex Mus), San Francisco, 92 & Fascinating Slippers/Pantunflas Fascinantes, Daniel Saxon Gallery, Los Angeles, 92; Chicano & Latino: Parallels and Divergence (catalog), Daniel Saxon Gallery, Los Angeles, 91, El Paso Mus Art, Tex, 92 & Kimberly Gallery, Washington, DC, 92; Of Nature & the Human Spirit, Part II, Daniel Saxon Gallery, Los Angeles, 91; Myth & Magic in the Americas: The Eighties (catalog), Contemp Art, Monterrey, Mex, 91. *Awards:* Artist of Year, Mex Am Fine Art Asn, 77; Visual Artist Fel, Nat Endowment for Art, 83. *Bibliog:* Susan Kandel (auth), LA in Review, Arts Mag, 12/91; Suvan Geer (auth), Los Angeles Times, Calendar sect, 3/20/91; Leigh Ann Clifton (auth), Gronk at SJMA, Artweek, 4/9/92. *Mailing Add:* Daniel Saxon Gallery 7525 Beverly Boulevard Los Angeles CA 90036

GROOMBRIDGE, WALTER STANLEY
PAINTER, EDUCATOR
b London, Eng, Oct 7, 13. *Study:* Study with John Gould, 57-65; Bethlehem Art Sch, NY, 59-65; Tequest Sch Art, Fla, 74-86. *Work:* Loew Mus, Univ Miami; Tequesta Found Inc, Fla; Royal Tunbridge Wells, Kent, Eng. *Comn:* Perry Como (watercolor), comn by Mrs Perry Como, Fla, 74-75; watercolor, Rybovich Bros, Palm Beach, Fla, 75; watercolor, Harriman Estate, Harriman, NY, 78; Tim Horton Children's Camp, Nova Scotia, Can. *Exhib:* Trotters Hall Fame, Goshen, NY, 65; Four Arts Show, Palm Beach, Fla, 73; Loew Mus, Univ Miami, 74; Tequesta Sch Art, Fla, 76-86; Palm Beach Watercolor Soc, Fla, 82-86; Florida Watercolor Soc, var shows, 83-85. *Teaching:* Instr watercolor, Lake Worth Art League, 73-90, Tequesta Sch Art, 73-90 & Lost Tree Village, North Palm Beach, Fla, 80-83. *Awards:* Best of Show, Tequesta Sch Art, 75; Best of Show, Palm Beach Watercolor Soc, 83, Grumbacher Award, 84. *Bibliog:* Many local articles. *Mem:* Palm Beach Watercolor Soc; Fla Watercolor Soc; Schunnemunk Art League, NY (pres, 65). *Media:* Watercolor. *Mailing Add:* 2555 PGA Blvd No 168 Palm Beach Gardens FL 33410

GROOMS, RED
PAINTER, SCULPTOR
b Nashville, Tenn, June, 37. *Study:* Sch Art Inst, Chicago, 55; George Peabody Col for Teachers, 56; New Sch Soc Res, 56; Hans Hoffman Sch Fine Arts, 57. *Work:* Allen Mem Art Mus, Oberlin, Ohio; Ark Art Ctr, Little Rock; Art Inst, Chicago; Brooklyn Mus, NY; Chrysler Mus, Norfolk, Va; Cleveland Mus Art, Ohio; Del Art Mus, Wilmington; Denver Art Mus, Colo; Everson Mus Art of Syracuse & Onondago Co, NY; Hirshhorn Mus & Sculpture Garden, Washington, DC; Mint Mus, Charlotte, NC. *Comn:* sets for Kenneth Koch's Red Robins, 78; Way Down East, Univ Northern Ky, 79; The Shoot Out, New Height Orgn, Denver, 82; sets for Kenwood Elmsley's City Junket, 80; Tuts Fever (with Lysiane Luong), Am Mus Moving Image, New York. *Exhib:* One-man exhibs, tibor de Nagy Gallery, New York, 66 & 70, Ruckus Manhattan, 76 & Recent Works, 81, 84 & 87, Marlborough Gallery, New York, Galerie Rober d'Amecourt, Paris, 77, Discount Store, Southern Univ NY Purchase, 78, Work From the 60s, Colo State Univ, 80, Lowe Art Mus, Univ Miami, Fla, 80, Benjamin Mangel Gallery, Philadelphia, Pa, 82, Muscarelle Mus Art, Col William & Mary, Williamsburg, Va, 86, Retrospective 1956-84, Pa Acad Fine Arts & Stanton Gallery, Denver, Retrospective, Whitney Mus Am Art, New York, 87; Whitney Mus Am Art, 73 & 78; Twenty Americans, Art Inst Chicago, 66; Mus Mod Art, New York, 66; Madison Art Ctr, Univ Wis, 77-78; Late Twentieth Century Art, Va Commonwealth Univ, traveling, 78-79; plus many others. *Teaching:* Vis artist, Syracuse Univ, 80, Southern Ill Univ, 80 & Colo State Univ, 81; Albert Dorne Prof, Univ Bridgeport, 82. *Awards:* Lower Manhattan Cult Coun Award, 82; Pres Award, RI Sch Design, 85; Gold Medal of Honor, Nat Arts Club, 86; Governor's Award in the Arts, Tenn, 86; Mayor's Award of Hon for Art & Cult, New York, 88. *Bibliog:* William Olander & Mark Gottlieb (auths), Welcome to Cleveland, New Gallery Contemp Art, 82; Carter Ratcliff & Carrie Rickey (auths), Red Grooms' Philadelphia Cornucopia, Inst Contemp Art, Univ Pa, 82; Jean Frumkin (auth), The Early Sixties: Red Grooms (catalog), Frumkin Gallery, 82; and others. *Publ:* Illustr, Rembrandt Take a Walk, Crown Publ Inc, 86. *Mailing Add:* 85 Walker St New York NY 10013

GROOT, CANDICE BETH
CERAMIST
b Berwyn, Ill, Mar 4, 54. *Study:* Gustavus Adolphus Col, BA, 76; Tex Tech Univ, with Verne Funk, MFA, 80. *Work:* Contemp Mus NMex, Santa Fe. *Exhib:* 9th Marietta Col Crafts Nat, Ohio, 80; Clay Work/New Work, D W Gallery, Dallas, Tex, 80; Clay Workers Guild, Ill, 81; Small Work Nat, Zaner

Gallery, Rochester, NY, 81; Westwood Clay Nat, Calif, 81. *Teaching:* Asst prof ceramics, Gustavus Adolphus Col, St Peter, Minn, 81- *Awards:* Purchase Prize, Southwest Fine Arts Biennial, Hill Gallery, 78; Juror's Awards, Tex Col Art Show, 78 & Midland Col, 78. *Mem:* Am Crafts Coun; Nat Coun Educ Ceramic Arts. *Media:* Clay, Paper. *Mailing Add:* 9516 Harding Ave Evanston IL 60203

GROOVER, JAN
PHOTOGRAPHER
b Plainfield, NJ, Apr 24, 43. *Study:* Pratt Inst, BFA(painting), 65; Ohio State Univ, MA(art educ), 70. *Work:* Metrop Mus Art, Mus Mod Art, Whitney Mus Am Art, New York; Baltimore Mus Art, Md; Mus Fine Art, Minneapolis, Minn. *Exhib:* One-man exhibs, Corcoran Gallery Art, 76, Baltimore Mus Art, Md, 77, Akron Art Inst, 79, Milwaukee Art Mus, 80, Neuberger Mus, Purchase, NY, 82, Daniel Wolf Gallery, New York, 83, Baltimore Mus Art, 84, Texas Gallery, Houston, 85, Cleveland Mus Art, 86, Betsy Rosenfield Gallery, Chicago, 91, Robert Miller Gallery, New York, 92; Whitney Mus Am Art, New York, 78; Counter Parts, Metrop Mus Art, New York, 82; NJ State Mus, Trenton; retrospective, Mus Mod Art, New York, 87; Flora Photographia, traveling, 92; and many others. *Pos:* Asst prof, Art Sch, Univ Hartford, Conn, 70-73; adj fac, State Univ, NY, Purchase, 79- *Awards:* Photog Grant, Nat Endowment Arts, 78 & 90; Guggenheim Mem Found Grant, 79; Artists Fel, Nat Endowment Arts, 90. *Bibliog:* Ben Lifson (auth), Still life runs deep, Village Voice, 80; Constance Sullivan, Pure Invention: The Tabletop Still Life, Photographs by Jan Groover, Photographers at Work, A Smithsonian Ser, Smithsonian Inst, 90; Jan Groover, Art Forum, p 130, 3/91. *Publ:* Auth, Jan Groover: Color Photographs, Milwaukee Art Mus, 80; The New Color Photography, Abbeville Press, 81; Counterparts: Form & Emotion in Photographs, Metrop Mus Art, 82; Jan Groover, Photographs, Neuberger Mus, 83. *Dealer:* Robert Miller Gallery 41 E 57th New York NY 10022. *Mailing Add:* 189 Bowery New York NY 10002

GROPPER, CATHY
PAINTER, SCULPTOR
b Cleveland, Ohio, June 3, 49. *Study:* New York Univ, BS, 76; Columbia Univ, MA, 78 under Larry Rivers, Elaine de Kooning, Jane Wilson & Milton Resnick. *Work:* Mrs Harvey Meyerhoff Collection, Baltimore, Md & New York; Lillian Berkman, New York; Nathan Goldman Collection, Palm Beach, Fla & New York; Greek Embassy; George S Kaufman Collection. *Comn:* Pierette's Lament, 78, Nate & Me, 82, Nathan Cummings, New York; sculpture, Schermerhorn Inc, Chicago. *Exhib:* Lawrence Alloway, Hecksher Mus, Huntington, NY, 78; solo exhibs, Am Merchant Marine Mus, Kings Point, NY, 79 & Weintraub Gallery, New York, 86; group show, Hungers 1990's: Not by Bread Alone, Carson Co Sq House Mus, Panhandle, Old Jail Art Ctr, Abilene, Mus Mod Art, Santa Fe, Amon Carter Mus, Fort Worth , Tex & Denver Art Ctr, Colo 90-92; Helen Drutt Gallery, New York, 92; Cavalier Sculpture Garden, Stamford, Conn, 92-93. *Pos:* Dir, Artists Exchange, television interviews & documentaries, Conn & NY, 79-; Orgn Independent Artists, New York, 90- *Teaching:* Exec coun, Teachers Col Columbia Univ, 82- *Awards:* First Award, Mid-Western States Col Art Competition, Univ Wis, Madison, 66. *Bibliog:* Lynn Seeney (auth), India theme, Art World, 5-6/85; Amy Penn (auth), Brushing up on young talent, NY Post, 11/8/85; Les Krantz (auth), NY art rev, Am References, 88. *Mem:* Artists Equity; Visual Artists & Galleries Asn; Orgn Independent Artists (dir, 90-). *Dealer:* Jonathan Poole Gallery Oxfordshire Eng; Helen Drutt Gallery 724 Fifth Ave New York NY 10019. *Mailing Add:* 301 E 79th St New York NY 10021

GROSCH, LAURA
PAINTER, PRINTMAKER
b Worcester, Mass, Apr 1, 45. *Study:* Wellesley Col, Mass, BA(art hist), 63-67; Univ Pa, Philadelphia, BFA(painting), 68; study with Gertrude Whiting, James Rayen, Sigmund Abeles, Neil Welliver. *Work:* Libr Cong & Smithsonian Inst, Washington, DC; New York Pub Libr & Brooklyn Mus, NY; Boston Mus Fine Arts & Boston Pub Libr, Mass; Calif Palace Legion Honor, San Francisco; Victoria & Albert Mus & British Mus, London, Eng; Kohler Art Ctr, Sheboygan, Wis; Carnegie Mellon Univ, Pittsburgh, Pa; Univ of Calif, Riverside,; Newark Pub Libr & Rutgers Univ, New Brunswick, NJ; Free Libr Philadelphia, Pa; Greenville Co Mus Art, Greenville, SC; Honolulu Acad Arts, Honolulu, Hawaii; Madison Arts Ctr, Madison, Wis; and others. *Exhib:* 30 Years of American Printmaking (with catalog), Brooklyn Mus, NY, 76; solo exhibs, Hodges Taylor Gallery, Charlotte, NC, 83, Color Lithographs, Jerald Melberg Gallery, Charlotte, NC, 84, Eden Now, Davidson Col Art Gallery, NC, 85, Gilliam/Peden Gallery, Raleigh, NC, 86 & Greenville Mus Art & Greenville Co Mus Art, NC, 87; USA-Portrait of the South, Palazzo Venezia, Rome Italy, 84; Printmaking 85, The Tallahassee Invitational, Fla State Univ, 85; North Carolina Invitational, Hickory Mus Art, 86; The Printed Image: More Than Meets the Eye, Greenhill Ctr NC Art, 86; Collaborative American Printimaking, Syracuse Univ, NY, 87; Chinese Year of the Dragon, Hodges Taylor Gallery, Charlotte, NC, 89; Herbs, Christa Faut Gallery, Davidson, NC, 90; Artists in the Garden, Peden Gallery II, Raleigh, NC, 91; The Light Factory Photo Arts Ctr, Charlotte, NC, 92. *Bibliog:* Larry David Perkins (auth), Collaborative American Printmaking (exhib catalog), Lowe Art Gallery, Syracuse Univ, 87. *Media:* Acrylic; Hand-made Litho. *Publ:* The True Essentials of a Feast, Libr Cong, 87. *Dealer:* Hodges Taylor Gallery 227 N Tryon St Charlotte NC 28202; Christa Faut Gallery PO Box 891 Davidson NC 28036. *Mailing Add:* 497 S Main St PO Box 10 Davidson NC 28036

GROSS, ALICE
SCULPTOR
b New York, NY. *Study:* With Ruth Yates. *Work:* Berkshire Mus, Pittsfield, Mass. *Exhib:* Eastern States Exhib, Springfield, Mass, 64; Audubon Artists, Nat Acad Design, New York, 68 & Allied Artists Am, 69; Knickerbocker Artists, Nat Arts Club, New York, 71; New Rochelle Art Asn, Col New Rochelle, 71. *Awards:* Award for Duo, Allied Artists Am, 69; Award for Rhythm, Knickerbocker Artists, 70; Award for Who's the Fairest of Them All, Beaux Arts of Westchester, 71. *Mem:* Silvermine Guild Artists; Audubon Artists; Allied Artists Am; Knickerbocker Artists. *Media:* Multimedia. *Mailing Add:* 16 Sutton Pl New York NY 10022

GROSS, CHARLES MERRILL
PAINTER, ASSEMBLAGE ARTIST
b Cullman, Ala, Sept 18, 35. *Study:* Atlanta Col Art, BFA; Univ Guanajuato, Mex, MFA. *Work:* Jackson State Univ, Miss; Univ Southern Miss; Marion Military Inst, Ala; Miss Delta Jr Col; Judson Col. *Exhib:* Mid-South Exhib, Brooks Mem Art Gallery, Memphis, Tenn, 69, 70 & 72; Nat Arts & Crafts Exhib, Jackson, Miss, 69 & 71; Delta Art Exhib, Ark Arts Ctr, Little Rock, 69-71, 74-75 & 78; Regional Sculpture Exhib, Carroll Reece Mus, Jackson City, Tenn, 72; Monroe Nat Ann Art Exhib, Masur Mus Art, La, 73; plus others. *Teaching:* Instr drawing, painting & sculpture, Miss Col, 68-69; asst prof art, Univ Miss, 69-73, assoc prof art, 73-80, prof art, 80- *Awards:* Merit Awards, 14th Mid-South Exhib, Seventh Ann Southeastern Competition, Rome, Ga & Fifth Nat Arts & Crafts Exhib, Jackson. *Mem:* Nat Art Educ Asn; Southern Asn Sculptors (regional vpres, 72-76). *Media:* Acrylic, Mixed Media. *Mailing Add:* 300 Longest Rd Oxford MS 38655

GROSS, EARL
PAINTER, LECTURER
b Sept 11, 1899; US citizen. *Study:* Westminster Col; Carnegie-Mellon Univ. *Work:* New Britain Mus Am Art; Atlanta Art Inst, Ga; Reading Mus, Pa; Ill State Mus; Art Inst Chicago; and others. *Exhib:* Two-man show, Art Inst Chicago, 50; Paintings of Past Decade, Metrop Mus, 52; one-man show, Butler Art Mus, 52 & Albuquerque Mus, 90; Am Watercolor Soc, New York, 58; Frank Oehlschlaeger Galleries, Chicago & Sarasota, Fla. *Pos:* Off combat artist, US Air Force, Far East, formerly; pres, Stevens-Gross Studios, Chicago, 26-62. *Teaching:* Prof painting, Longboat Key Art Ctr, Fla, New Orleans Acad Art & Highland Park Art Ctr, formerly; instr, Chicago Acad Fine Art, Ill & Am Acad, Chicago, formerly. *Awards:* Second Prize, Denver Mus, Colo & Cosmopolitan Mag Competition; First Prize, Chicago Artists Guild. *Bibliog:* Norman Kent (auth), Sea scapes & landscapes & Wendell Blake (auth), Acrylic watercolor painting, Watson Guptill. *Mem:* Am Watercolor Soc, Philadelphia & Washington, DC; Arts Club Chicago; Artist Guild Chicago; hon mem Chicago Art Dir Club. *Media:* Watercolor, Oil. *Publ:* Auth, Watercolor Series, 47, Illustrators Page, 51, Robert Addison, 58 & Polymer colors in depth, 67, Am Artist Mag; also articles in Art News & Chicago Tribune. *Dealer:* Oehlschlaeger Galleries 107 E Oak St Chicago IL 60611; Frank Oehlschlaeger Gallery 28 Blvd of the Presidents St Armands Key Sarasota FL 33578. *Mailing Add:* 10501 Laqrina de Oro NE Apr 104 Albuquerque NM 87111

GROSS, ELISSA FRANCES
CONSULTANT, LECTURER
b Wheeling, WVa, Mar 24, 54. *Study:* Chatham Col, 72-74; Case Western Reserve Univ, Cleveland, BA, 76; Univ Chicago, MA, 77. *Pos:* Artists rep, Arts & Humanities Div, WVa Dept Cult & Hist, Charleston, 78-81; cultural arts dir, Memphis Jewish Community Ctr, 81-85; dir artists-in-educ prog, Ark Arts Coun, Little Rock, 85-87; invited consult, Nat Endowment Arts-Nat Assembly State Arts Agencies, 85 & 86, Gov's HIPPY Comt, Nat Parent Teacher Asn Conf, Little Rock, 86 & Getty Ctr Educ Round Table Meeting, Chicago, 86; exec dir, Quapaw Quarter Asn, Hist Pres Org, 89-91. *Teaching:* Art Appreciation, Univ Ark, Little Rock, 92; facilitator (long-range planning), Ark Craft Guild. *Bibliog:* Dale Carpenter (dir), The Eyes of the Beholder (film), Ark Educ TV Network, 7/86. *Media:* Arts Administration; Development. *Mailing Add:* 4 Eastwood Ct Little Rock AR 72211

GROSS, JULIE
PAINTER
Study: Pratt Inst, Brooklyn, NY, BFA(painting, graphics), 65; Hunter Col, New York, MA(painting, art hist), 74. *Work:* Chase Manhattan Bank; Cyrk, Oklahoma City; Prudential Life Insurance Co; AT&T Corp; Yaddo, Saratoga Springs. *Exhib:* Solo shows, State Univ NY, Rockland Community Col, Suffern, 76, Frank Marino Gallery, New York, 79, Stephen Rosenberg Gallery, New York, 85 & 89, City Univ New York, Kingsborough Community Col, 93; Nahan Contemp Gallery, New York, 90; Jessica Berwind Gallery, Philadelphia, 91; Eastern Mont Col, Billings, 92. *Teaching:* Painting, drawing & art hist survey, Fairleigh Dickinson Univ, Rutherford, NJ, 72-75; vis instr, Kutztown State Col, Pa, 75 & CUNY/Manhattan Col, 78-79; vis asst prof, Pratt/Manhattan, 75-81 & 86-90; instr, SUNY/Rockland Community Col, Suffern, NY, 75-76, Ramapo Col, Wayne, NJ, 76-77, Bloomfield Col, NJ, 77; master teacher painting, SUNY/Fredonia, NY, 76-79; instr painting, Metrop Mus Art, 81, RI Sch Design, 81-83; vis instr, Hunter Col, New York, 83-85, Parsons Sch Design, 81-; basic design, Fashion Inst Technol, 89- *Awards:* New Sch, Fac Develop Fund Grant, 89; Nat Endowment Arts Grant, Painting, 91-92; MacDowell Colony Residence, 92. *Bibliog:* Stephen Westfall (auth), rev, Art Am, 1/88; Judith Page (auth), Ground Works (catalog essay), Valencia Community Col, 89; Peggy Cyphers (auth), rev, Arts Mag, 12/90. *Publ:* Coauth, Women and textiles in five cultures, Heresies, New York, No 4, 78; auth, Substenance, Appearances, New York, No 3, 79. *Mailing Add:* 166 W 22nd St New York NY 10011

GROSS, MARILYN A
PAINTER, PRINTMAKER
b Rolla, Mo, Jan 23, 37. *Study:* St Louis Univ, BS, 58. *Work:* Schiff, Hardin & Waite Corp, Chicago, Ill; Com Nat Bank Corp Collection, Peoria, Ill. *Exhib:* 48th Nat Watercolor Exhib, Fine Arts Mus South, 89; Collection 90, Ft Wayne Mus Art, 90; Artforms 90, Greater Lafayette Mus Art, 90; Aqueous 91, Owensboro Mus Fine Art, 91; Fine Arts Inst 26th Ann, San Bernadino Mus, 91. *Awards:* Eileen Zeber Experimental Award, N Coast Col Soc, 88; Traveling Exhib Award, Ky Watercolor Soc, 91; Nominated as Woman of the Year, Am Biog Inst, Raleigh, NC, 91 & 92. *Bibliog:* Jeanne Derbeck (auth), Art notes, S Bend Tribune, 10/84; Who's Who Am Women, Marquis, 88 & 93; The Chicago Art Review: A Survey of the City's Museum, Galleries and Leading Artists, Am References, 89. *Mem:* Assoc mem Am Watercolor Soc; assoc mem Nat Watercolor Soc; assoc mem Midwest Watercolor Soc; signature mem, Ala Watercolor Soc; assoc mem Ky Watercolor Soc. *Media:* Watercolor; Mixed Media. *Publ:* Auth, The President's Book, E Re Nata Club, 71; Gift of Love, Peter Herring, 75; Studio Log--, Creative Systems, 88. *Dealer:* Global Gallery II Tampa FL; Metro 1 Gallery Egg Harbour WI. *Mailing Add:* 54 Sunset Dr Streator IL 61364

GROSS, RAINER
PAINTER
b Cologne, Ger, Apr 23, 51. *Study:* Art Acad Col, 71-73. *Work:* Bell Atlantic, Arlington, Va; Chase Manhattan Bank, New York; Hirschhorn Mus, Washington, DC; Kunsthalle, Emden, Ger; Ludwig Collection, Aachen, Ger; Mus Folkwang, Essen, Ger. *Exhib:* New York Now, Kestner Gesellschaft, Hannover, Ger, 82-83; solo exhibs, Musé Cantonal des Beaux Arts, Lausanne, Switz, 84, Kunsthalle Emden (traveling), Ger, Kunstverein Salzburg (traveling), Austria, 89, Mus Gesenkirschen (traveling), Ger, 91, Anderson Gallery, Richmond, Va, 93, Mus S Fla, Univ Tampa, 93 & Folkwang Mus, Essen, Ger, 93. *Bibliog:* Gerhard Finckel (auth, catalog), Breast Exam, Kunsthalle Emden, 89; Noel Frackman (auth, catalog), Without Words, Ruth Siegel Gallery, New York, 91. *Media:* Oil, Acrylic. *Publ:* Auth, Une Collection s'Anime, Le Musee Cantonal des Beaux-Arts, 84; Ut Poesis Pictura, S D Sauerbier, 86; Without Words, Ruth Siegel Gallery, 91. *Dealer:* Gallery Moos Toronto Can; Gallery Oz Paris France. *Mailing Add:* 122 Second Ave New York NY 10003

GROSS, SANDRA LERNER See Lerner, Sandra

GROSSBERG, JAKE
EDUCATOR, SCULPTOR
b Luban, Poland, Feb 13, 32; US citizen. *Study:* Columbia Univ, MA; Brooklyn Col, MFA. *Work:* Riverside Mus Collection, Columbia Univ, New York; Rose Art Mus, Brandeis Univ, Boston; Chrysler Mus, Provincetown, Mass; Stanford Mus Collection, Conn. *Comn:* Steel sculpture, Northern Ill Univ, DeKalb, 68. *Exhib:* Brooklyn Mus, New York, 58-60; Riverside Mus, New York, 60-67; Chrysler Mus, Provincetown, Mass, 62; Mus Mod Art, New York, 66; Philadelphia Art Alliance, 67; Central City Park, Atlanta, Ga, 76; Grey Art Gallery, New York Univ, 78. *Pos:* Dir, Milton Avery Grad Sch, Annondale-on-Hudson, NY, 80-83. *Teaching:* Prof fine arts, Bard Col, Annondale, NY, 69- *Media:* Steel. *Mailing Add:* c/o Genovese Gallery South 195 South St Boston MA 02111

GROSSE, C(AROLYN ANN GAWARECKI)
PAINTER, INSTRUCTOR
b Rahway, NJ, Oct 30, 31. *Study:* Douglass Col, BA, 53; Univ Calif, Berkeley; Univ Colo. *Work:* COMSAT, Washington, DC; Indust Col Armed Forces, Ft McNair, Washington, DC; CIGNA Corp, Washington, DC; James River Corp, Richmond, Va; Georgetown Univ; Texaco; Md Casualty Co. *Comn:* pvt comn by, Nancy Dickerson, Merrywood, Va. *Exhib:* One-person shows, Atlantic Gallery, Georgetown, Washington, DC, 78-81, & 91 & Art League Gallery, Alexandria, Va, 88; Children's Hosp, Washington, DC, 90; McBride Gallery, Annapolis, Md, 91; 20th Century Gallery, Williamsburg, Va, 92; Va Watercolor Soc State Show, 80-92; Nat Watercolor Soc, Brea, Calif, 87 & 89 (award); Rocky Mt Nat, Golden, Colo, 89; Aqueous 90, Murray, Ky; Allied Artists Am, New York, 90; 22nd La Nat Watercolor, New Orleans, 92; Knickerbocker Artists, New York, 92. *Pos:* Exhibits artist, Mus Nat Hist, Smithsonian Inst, 56-57; partic, Art in Embassies Prog, US State Dept. *Teaching:* Instr watercolor, City of Falls Church, 66-; instr watercolor workshops, Md, WVa, Eng, Acapulco, Mex & Ireland, currently. *Awards:* Awards, Mid-Atlantic Regional Baltimore Watercolor Soc, 82, 83 & 85; award, Va Watercolor Soc State Show, 87, 88, 89, 92; award, Nat Watercolor Soc 89 Traveling Show, 88; award, 2nd place, Louisiana 22nd Int, New Orleans. *Mem:* Assoc mem Am Watercolor Soc; Va Watercolor Soc & Art League; Washington Watercolor Soc; Southern Watercolor Soc; Potomac Valley Watercolorists (pres, 74-77). *Media:* Watercolor, Casein. *Publ:* Northlight, 3/79; Art Voices South, 7-8/80; Cover Hill Rag Congressional Guide, 1/85, 1/89, 4/89 & 1/90; Texture Watercolor with Casein, Artist's Mag, 1/91. *Dealer:* Atlantic Gallery Washington DC; Art League Gallery Alexandria VA. *Mailing Add:* 7018 Vagabond Dr Falls Church VA 22042

GROSSMAN, BARBARA
PAINTER, EDUCATOR
b New York, NY, Nov 10, 43. *Study:* Yale Sch Music & Art, 64; Cooper Union, BFA, 65; Fulbright Grant, Academie der Kunst, Munich, Ger, 67-68. *Work:* Corcoran Collection, Washington, DC; Bryn Mawr Col Lib, Pa; Weatherspoon Art Gallery, Univ NC, Greensboro. *Exhib:* Solo shows, Bowery Gallery, New York, 73, 77, 81, 85, 88 & 92, Mattatuck Mus, Waterbury, Conn, 79 & Lyman Allyn Mus, New London, Conn, 79; Paesagio Gallery, Hartford, Conn, 91; Connecticut Painters, Wadsworth Antheneum, Hartford, Conn, 83; Ann Exhibs, Nat Acad Design, New York, 86, 90 & 92; Fulbright Alumni Art Show, Smithsonian Inst, Washington, DC, 86; Drawing Invitational, Ind Univ, Bloomington, 87; Figure Invitational, Col William & Mary, Williamsburg, Va, 87; Quest, New York Studio Sch, 89. *Pos:* Applied arts adv comt, Tunxis Community Col, 79-85; chmn exhib comt, Wash Art Asn, 88- *Teaching:* Adj prof, drawing, Western Conn State Univ, Danbury, 81-; instr, painting & drawing, New York Studio Sch, 89-91; adj prof, painting, Hartford Art Sch, Univ Hartford, Conn, 92- *Awards:* Conn Comn Arts, 78-79; Ingram Merrill Found Award Painting, 82-83. *Bibliog:* Bill Scott (auth), rev, ARTS, 88; Ken Leslie (auth), Oil Pastels, Watson-Guptil, 91; Lawrence Campbell (auth), rev, Art Am, 10/92. *Media:* Oil Paint, Charcoal. *Dealer:* Bowery Gallery 121 Wooster St New York NY 10012. *Mailing Add:* 2338 Litchfield Rd Watertown CT 06795

GROSSMAN, MAURICE KENNETH
EDUCATOR, CERAMIC ARTIST
b Detroit, Mich, Sept 16, 27. *Study:* Wayne State Univ, Detroit, with J Foster, BS(art educ), 50; Alfred Univ, NY, with Dan Rhodes, 51; Ohio State Univ, Columbus, with Paul Bogatay, MFA(ceramics), 53. *Work:* Detroit Mus Art; Phoenix Mus Art; El Paso Mus; Utah State Mus, Salt Lake City; Albuquerque Mus Art, NMex; Tucson Mus of Art, Ariz. *Exhib:* Ceramic Nat, Everson Mus Art, Syracuse, 50-68; Clay Invitational, Smithsonian Inst, DC, 53 & 59; Designer-Craftsmen of the West, De Young Mus, San Francisco, 57; Western Artists, Denver Art Mus, 57; Krannert Mus Design, 64; Southwest Craftsmen, Santa Fe, NMex, 65; Crafts Invitational, Ark Art Ctr, Little Rock, 66; Eighth Ariz Ann, Phoenix Art Mus, 66; Objects Are, Mus Contemp Crafts, New York, 68; Westwood Clay Nat, Otis Art Gallery, Los Angeles, 80; Int Invitational, Arabia & Finland, 84. *Teaching:* Instr ceramics, Western Wash Col, Bellingham, 53-54; prof ceramics, Univ Ariz, Tucson, 55-88, prof emer, 88- *Awards:* Craft Fel, Nat Endowment Arts, 44; Fac Recognition Award, Tucson Trade Bureau, 68; Creative Teaching Award, Univ Ariz Found, 78; and many others; Fulbright Fel, Japan, 54-55. *Bibliog:* Polly Rothman (auth), The Complete Book of Ceramics, Crown Publ, 72; John Conrad (auth), Contemporary Ceramic Techniques, Prentice Hall, 79. *Mem:* Am Crafts Coun (southwest area rep, 63-66), Ariz Designer-Craftsmen (pres, 60); Nat Coun Educ for Ceramic Arts (regional rep, 72); Tucson Art Ctr (bd dirs, 68, adv 88); World Crafts Coun. *Media:* Ceramics. *Publ:* Auth, American ceramics, Tanko Mag, Kyoto, Japan, 56; auth, Clay in the Hand, an American in Japan, Inst of Int Educ, 56. *Dealer:* Wright Designs Assocs Foothills Ctr Tucson AZ 85741; Mind's Eye Gallery 4200 N Marshall Way Scottsdale AZ 85251. *Mailing Add:* Dept of Art Univ of Ariz Tucson AZ 85721

GROSSMAN, MORTON
PAINTER
b 1926. *Study:* Art Students League, scholar, 44-47; Queens Col, NY, BA(hons), 48; Louis Comfort Tiffany Found fel, 49-50. *Work:* Cleveland Mus Art; Norfolk Mus Art, Va; Ball State Univ, Ind; Birmingham Mus Art, Ala; SS United States; plus many pvt collections. *Exhib:* Whitney Mus Am Art; Dallas Mus Fine Arts; Baltimore Mus Art; Walker Art Ctr; Seattle Art Mus; Boston Mus Fine Art; San Francisco Mus of Art; Corcoran Gallery of Art; Okla Art Ctr; Inst Contemp Art, Boston; one-man shows, Albright-Knox Art Gallery, Miami Beach Art Ctr, Parnsworth Art Mus, Maine, Canton Art Inst, Ohio, San Joaquin Mus, Calif, Grand Central Moderns Gallery, New York; plus many others. *Teaching:* At Queens Col, NY, 55-56, State Univ NY Col Buffalo, 56-60, Cleveland Inst Art, 61-64, Univ Md, 64-69 & Tyler Sch Art, Temple Univ, summers 67 & 68; prof painting, Kent State Univ, 69- *Awards:* Dana Medal Pa Acad Fine Arts, 59; Grand Award & Gold Medal, Am Watercolor Soc, 60; Arches Award, Watercolor USA, Springfield Art Mus, 69. *Media:* Acrylic, Watercolor. *Mailing Add:* Dept Art 305 E Art Kent State Univ Kent OH 44242

GROSSMAN, NANCY
PAINTER, SCULPTOR
b New York, NY, Apr 28, 40. *Study:* Pratt Inst. *Work:* Whitney Mus Am Art, Metrop Mus Art, New York; Princeton Univ Art Mus; Univ Mus, Berkeley, Calif; Dallas Mus Fine Arts; Israel Mus, Jerusalem; Phoenix Art Mus, Ariz; Nat Mus Am Art, Smithsonian Inst, Washington, DC; Va Mus Fine Art, Richmond. *Exhib:* Corcoran Gallery Art Biennial Exhib, Washington, DC, 63; Whitney Mus Am Art Sculpture Ann, 68 & Whitney Biennial, 73; Recent Figure Sculpture, Fogg Art Mus, Harvard Univ, 72; Perceiving Modern Sculpture, Grey Art Gallery, NY Univ, 80; bronze, Hamilton Gallery, 80; Drawing Acquisitions, Whitney Mus Am Art, 81; Figuratively Sculpting, PS1, 81; The Americans: The Collage, Contemp Arts Mus, Houston, 82; The Sculptor as Draftsman, Whitney Mus Am Art, 83; Terminal New York, 83, Exit Art, 91, Sculpture Ctr, 91, Hillwood Art Mus, Brookville, 91. *Teaching:* Instr sculpture, Boston Fine Arts Sch, 85; instr drawing, Cooper Union, 89. *Awards:* Commencement Honoree, Mass Col Art, 74; Sculpture Award, Nat Endow Arts, 85; NY Found Arts Fel, Sculpture, 91. *Bibliog:* Cindy Nemser (auth), Art Talk, Conversations with 12 Women Artists, Scribners, 75; Charlotte Streifer Rubenstein (auth), American Women Artists, Avon, 82; Arlene Raven (auth), Nancy Grossman, Hillwood Art Mus, 91. *Mailing Add:* 105 Eldridge St New York NY 10002

GROSSMAN, SHELDON
MUSEUM CURATOR, HISTORIAN
b New York, NY, Aug 30, 40. *Study:* Hunter Col, BA, 62; NY Univ Inst Fine Arts, MA, 66. *Pos:* Cur, Northern & Later Ital Paintings, Nat Gallery Art, Washington, DC, formerly. *Awards:* Fulbright-Hays Travel Grant, 66; Ital Govt Study Grant, 66; Chester Dale Fel, Nat Gallery Art, 67-69. *Res:* Problems in Florentine painting in the late fifteenth and early sixteenth century; analysis of problems of style; archival research. *Publ:* Auth, National

Gallery of Art report and studies in the history of art, 68; auth, Mitteilungen des kunst-historischen institutes in Florenz, 69; auth, Master drawings, 72; auth, National Gallery of Art, Studies in the History of Art, 74; auth, Stadel-Jahrbach, 79. *Mailing Add:* 2312 Tunlaw Rd NW Washington DC 20007

GROSVENOR, ROBERT
SCULPTOR
b New York, NY, 1937. *Study:* Ecole des Beaux Arts, Dijon, France, 56; Ecole Superieure des Arts Decoratifs, Paris, 57-59; Univ di Perugia, Italy, 58. *Work:* Whitney Mus, New York; Storm King Art Ctr, Mountainville, NY; Mus Mod Art, New York; Hirshorn Mus, Washington, DC; Walker Art Ctr, Minneapolis. *Exhib:* Sculpture for the 60's, Los Angeles Co Mus, 67; Plus by Minus, Albright-Knox Art Gallery, Buffalo, NY, 68; Sculpture Ann, Whitney Mus Am Art, New York, 68, Biennial Exhib Am Painting & Sculpture, 73 & 200 Yrs Am Sculpture, 76; 14 Sculptors: the Industrial Edge, Walker Art Ctr, Minneapolis, 69; Works on Paper, 31st Ann Exhib, Soc Contemp Art, Art Inst Chicago, 71; NY State Mus, Albany, 77; one-man shows, Inst Art & Urban Resources, PS 1 Long Island City, NY, 84, Centre d'Art Contemporair du Domaine de Kerguehennec a Bignan, Locmine, France 89, Margo Leavin Gallery, Los Angeles, 90, Paula Cooper, New York, 91, Kunsthalle, Bern, 92, Galeria Max Hetzler, Cologne, 92; Private Images: Photographs by Sculptors, Los Angeles Co Mus Art, Contemp Art Galleries, Lytton Halls, 77-78; Drawings for Outdoor Sculpture: 1946-1977, Amherst Col, Mass, Univ Calif, Santa Barbara & Mass Inst Technol, 78; Minimal Tradition, 79 & postMINIMALism, 82, Aldrich Mus Contmep Art; Hayden Gallery, Cambridge, MA, 85; Musee Nat d'Art Moderne, Paris 87; Galerie Rolf Ricke, Koln, 88; Foundation Deutsch, Belmont-Sur-Lausanne, 90-91; Then & Now, Philippe Staib Gallery, New York, 92; and many others. *Awards:* Guggenheim Fel, 69; Nat Endowment Arts & Humanities Grant, 70; Nat Acad Arts & Lett Grant, 72. *Bibliog:* Jeremy Gilbert Rolfe (auth), Robert Grosvenor: Specific Clarity, Art in Am, 3-4/76; John Russel (auth), Critics Choice: Galleries, NY Times, 4/21/78; Deborah Perlberg (auth), Reviews in New York, Artforum, summer 78; Donald Kupsit (auth), Robert Grosvenor, Artforum, summer 84; John Russell (auth), Robert Grosvenor, NY Times, 4/18/86. *Mailing Add:* c/o Paula Cooper Gallery 155 Wooster New York NY 10012

GROTZ, DOROTHY ROGERS
PAINTER
b Philadelphia, Pa. *Study:* Univ Berlin, 29; Columbia Univ, MS, 45; Art Students League, 47. *Work:* Rochester Univ Mus Art; Santa Barbara Mus Fine Arts; Norfolk Mus Arts & Sci; Evansville Mus Arts & Sci; Univ Minn. *Comn:* Metrop Mus Art, New York. *Exhib:* Avery Libr, Columbia Univ, 50, Van Diemen Lilienfeld Gallery, 62-67 & Bodley Gallery, New York, 72; Univ Wis, 67; Salon Des Nations, Paris, France; Kendall Gallery, Wellfleet, Mass, 85. *Bibliog:* Archives of Am Art, Smithsonian Inst, Washington, DC. *Mem:* Artists Equity. *Media:* Oil. *Publ:* Auth rev in Archit Forum, 69 & Leonardo, 72-82. *Dealer:* Kendall Gallery Wellfleet Mass. *Mailing Add:* 7 St Lukes Pl New York NY 10014

GROVE, EDWARD RYNEAL
MEDALIST, PAINTER
b Martinsburg, WVa, Aug 14, 12. *Study:* Nat Sch Art, Washington, DC, 33; Corcoran Sch Art, Washington, DC, with Schuler & Weisz, 34-40; also with Robert Brackman, Noank, Conn, 46. *Work:* Metrop Mus Art; Smithsonian Inst; Imperial Palace, Tokyo; Portsmouth Royal Naval Mus, England; Mus Medallic Art, Poland. *Comn:* Communion Saints mural, Church Holy Comforter, Drexel Hill, Pa, 58; Cong gold medal for Bob Hope, 63; alphabet medal, Soc Medalists, 73; An American Eagle (bronze Bicentennial monument), Palm Beach, Fla, 76; Am Express goldpiece, 82. *Exhib:* Watercolor Ann, Pa Acad Fine Arts, Philadelphia, 54; 2nd Philadelphia Arts Festival, Philadelphia Mus Art, 62; Nat Sculpture Soc, Lever House, New York, 67, 69 & 71; Florida Creates Traveling Exhib, 73-74; 19 th Congress FIDEM, Florence, Italy, 83. *Pos:* Secy, treas & pres, Steel & Copper Engravers League, Philadelphia, 50-62; sculptor-engraver, US Mint, Philadelphia, 62-65; official sculptor-engraver, Order St John of Jerusalem, Knights of Malta Hq, Shickshinny, Pa, 67- *Teaching:* Instr drawing & portraiture, Flagler Art Ctr, West Palm Beach, 72-73. *Awards:* Sculptor Yr Gold Medal, Am Numismatic Asn, 69; Louis Bennett Mem Prize, Nat Sculpture Soc, 71; J Sanford Saltus Award, Am Numismatic Soc, 85. *Bibliog:* T W Becker (auth), Edward R Grove, commitment to America, Franklin Mint Almanac, 11/69; V Culver (auth), The four best, Coins Mag, 6/70; C W Hill (auth), Edward Grove, man of many talents, Coin Monthly, Eng, 3/76. *Mem:* Artists Equity Asn (nat first vpres, 65-67); fel Nat Sculpture Soc; Fedn Int de la Medaille; Am Numismatic Asn; Am Medallic Sculpture Asn. *Media:* Clay, Bronze & Silver; Oil, Watercolor. *Publ:* Contribr, Design Handbook, Nat Philatelic Mus, 54; co-auth & illusr, The Communion of Saints (brochure), Church of the Holy Comforter, 58; illusr, Our Christian Heritage, Morehouse-Gorham, 59; auth & illusr, Assignment: Malta, Coin World, 65; The making of a medal, Am Artist Mag, 1/72, reprinted, Numismatist, 7/78. *Mailing Add:* Sea-Lake Studio 3215 S Flagler Dr West Palm Beach FL 33405

GROVE, JEAN DONNER
SCULPTOR
b Washington, DC, May 15, 12. *Study:* Hill Sch Sculpture; Corcoran Sch Art; Cath Univ Am; Wilson Teachers Col, BS, 39; Cornell Univ; Philadelphia Mus Art; travel study in Europe; also with Clara Hill, Hans Schuler, Heinz Warneke & Fritz Janschka. *Work:* Rosenwald Collection, Philadelphia, Pa; Fine Arts Comn, City Hall, Philadelphia; Port of Hist Mus, Penn's Landing, Philadelphia, Pa. *Comn:* Many portrait comn, 40-; The Communion of Saints (mural with E R Grove), Church of the Holy Comforter, Drexel Hill, 52-58; garden figures, fountains & other works in pvt collections, New York, Washington, DC, Philadelphia, NJ, NC, Calif & WVa; Am Express goldpiece, 82; bronze mem portrait plaque, comn chambers, Palm Beach County Govt Ctr, West Palm Beach, Fla, 86. *Exhib:* Corcoran Gallery of Art, 43-47; Pa Acad Fine Arts Ann, Philadelphia, 47, 48 & 51, Regional, 53; Philadelphia Mus Art Regional Art Festivals, 55, 59 & 62; Nat Sculpture Soc Ann, 57, 74-78 & 83-90; Civic Ctr Mus, Philadelphia, 68; Flager Art Ctr, West Palm Beach, 73; Norton Gallery of Art, West Palm Beach, Fla, 74 & 81; Nat Acad Design, 78, 81, 83, 85, 87 & 89; plus others. *Awards:* Competition Prize, Artists Equity Asn Philadelphia, 60; Tallix Foundry Award, Nat Sculpture Soc Bicentennial Exhib, New York, 76; Acad of Italy with Gold Medal, 79; plus others. *Bibliog:* E Williams (auth), The mural, Today Mag, 11/58; H H Reinhold (auth), Third dimensional encounters, Palm Beach illus, 2/82 & Grove team designs, Coin World, 2/2/83. *Mem:* Nat Sculpture Soc; Artists Equity Asn (dir, Philadelphia Chap, 64-66); Soc Four Arts, Palm Beach, Fla; assoc Nat Acad Design, New York; Fedn Int de Medaille; and others. *Media:* Stone, Bronze. *Mailing Add:* Sea Lake Studio 3215 S Flagler Dr West Palm Beach FL 33405

GROVE, SAMUEL HAROLD
ADMINISTRATOR, HISTORIAN
b Joliet, Ill, Mar 8, 25. *Study:* Northeastern Ill Univ, BA, 74; Art Inst Chicago; Washington Univ, St Louis, Mo, Miami Univ, Oxford, Ohio. *Collections Arranged:* Shang Dynasty to Ching Dynasty, 75; Catlin Plains Indian Portraits, 75; Retrospective Exhibit, Clark Hulings, 78; Baroque European Painting, Amodeo Collection, 78; Contemporary Egyptian Art and Artifacts, 82; Masterworks Taos Founds, 84; Merrill Mahaffey, 87, Grace Spaulding John, 88 & Wilson Hurley, 89. *Pos:* Sr sci illusr, Field Mus Natural Hist, Chicago, 68-75; dir, Mus Southwest, Midland, Tex, 75-79 & Mus Art Am West, Houston, 83-; dir cult exchange projs, Res Art, Houston, 90. *Teaching:* Instr sci illus, Field Mus Natural Hist, Chicago, 68-75; instr art hist, Glassell Sch Art, Mus Fine Arts, Houston, 79- & Univ Houston, 79-83. *Bibliog:* Articles, Houston Post, 79 & Southwest Art Mag, 10/83. *Mem:* Fel Explorers Club, New York; Savage Club. *Res:* Rock art of the inner Sahara; Tassilli plateau expeditions 1974 and 1982. *Mailing Add:* 2200 S Gessner Rd, #1001 Houston TX 77063

GROVES, NAOMI JACKSON
WRITER, PAINTER
b Montreal, Que. *Study:* Rannows Art Sch, Copenhagen; Sir George Williams Col, McGill Univ, BA & MA; Heidelberg Univ; Univ Berlin; Univ Munich; Radcliffe Col, AM & PhD; McMaster Univ, DLitt, 72, Carleton Univ, DLitt, 90. *Work:* Nat Gallery Canada, Ottawa; McMaster Univ Collection, Hamilton, Ont; McLaughlin Art Gallery, Oshawa, Ont. *Exhib:* One-man shows, Radcliffe Col, Wheaton Col, McMaster Univ & Montreal Mus Fine Arts. *Pos:* Asst to dir, Nat Gallery Can, 42-43, consult, 63-64. *Teaching:* Lectr, Ernst Barlach as Sculptor, as Dramatist & Barlach in America, 64; The Group of Seven, Another Look, Nat Gallery Can, 69; McGill Univ, Wheaton Col, Carleton Col; assoc prof in charge fine arts, McMaster Univ. *Awards:* Gov Gen Gold Medal, McGill Univ, 33; Can Fedn Univ Women Traveling Fel, 36-37. *Mem:* Canadian Artists Representation; hon life mem E Barlach Soc, Hamburg. *Media:* Oil, Wood. *Publ:* Auth, Ernst Barlach-Leben im Werk, 72; Ernst Barlach-Life in Work, 81; Greenland Caper 1941, Northward J, 83; translr, The Sky Hangs Low, 86, One Summer in Quebec, 1925, 88, Lapland Diary, 89, Penumbra Press; Works by A Y Jackson from the 30's at Carleton Univ, Carleton Univ Press, 90; A Y Jackson, dessins, un été au Québec. *Mailing Add:* 2896 Highfield Crescent, Naomi Jackson Groves, Roussan Editeur Inc, Pointe-Claire, Qué, 91 Ottawa ON K2B 6G5 Canada

GROWDON, MARCIA COHN
ADMINISTRATOR, HISTORIAN
b San Francisco, Calif, Dec 17, 45. *Study:* Stanford Univ, BA, 67, PhD, 76; Univ Mich, BA, 68. *Collections Arranged:* Treasures of the Middle Ages (auth, catalog), 78, The New York School 1940-1960 (ed, catalog), 79, Computers and the Visual Arts: Research & Drawings of H Cohen (auth, catalog), 79, Artists in the American Desert, Nat Tour (auth, catalog), 80-81 & Sierra Nevada Museum Biennial: The Best of Nevada's Contemporary Art (auth, catalog), 86, Sierra Nevada Mus Art. *Pos:* Cur, Sierra Nevada Mus Art, Reno, 78-81, dir, 81-87; vice chmn, C I T Y 2000, Reno Arts Comn, 90- *Awards:* Samuel Kress Found Fel & Travel Grants, 68-70; Travel Award, Nevada State Coun on the Arts, 86. *Mem:* Am Asn Mus; Col Art Asn Am. *Res:* 19th and 20th century art, particularly in the Far West. *Mailing Add:* 10004 Forest St Reno NV 89509

GRUBB, DAVID
PAINTER, PRINTMAKER
b Ind. *Study:* Skowhegan Sch Art, 68; Ind Univ, BFA, 70; Queen's Col, MFA, 72. *Work:* Del Art Mus, Wilmington; Rutgers Univ Print Collection, New Brunswick; Ind Univ Permanent Collection, Bloomington; and others. *Exhib:* New Images, Queens Mus, New York, 75; Figurative Art, Green Mountain Gallery, New York, 76; First Eleven Years, Godwin-Ternbach Mus, New York, 82; Monotypes-Prints, Montgomery Col, Rockville, Md, 85; Contemporary Prints, Meredith Gallery, Baltimore, Md, 87. *Mem:* New York Artist's Equity. *Media:* Oil on Canvas, Gouaches. *Dealer:* Orion Editions 270 Lafayette St New York NY 10012. *Mailing Add:* 747 Union St #4 Brooklyn NY 11215

GRUBER, AARONEL DEROY
PAINTER, SCULPTOR
b Pittsburgh, Pa. *Study:* Carnegie Inst Technol. *Work:* Smithsonian Inst; Rose Art Mus, Brandeis Univ; Butler Inst Am Art; De Cordova Mus, Lincoln,

Mass; Aldrich Mus Contemp Art; Frederick R Weisman Found Art, Los Angeles; Westinghouse Elec Corp Collection; Kawamura Mem Mus Mod Art, Sakura, Japan; Carnegie Mus Art. *Comn:* Steelcityscape (steel sculpture, 21 ft), Fort Duquesne Park, Pittsburgh, 77; plexiglas sculpture, Westinghouse, Pittsburgh, Pa; 32 ft cor-ten sculpture, Gen Mills Corp, Minneapolis, 71; two sculptures, comn by DeBartolo, Melbourne Mall, Fla; Par Progress, Grand Cent Mall, Parkersburg, WVa; Blue Cross Blue Shield, Pittsburgh, Pa. *Exhib:* solo show, Carnegie Mus Art, 77; Twenty-Five Pennsylvania Women, Southern Alleghenies Mus Art, 79; A Look Back-A Look Forward, Aldrich Mus Continuing Art, 82; Butler Inst Am Art, Youngstown, Ohio, 88; World Expo '88, Brisbane, Australia, 88; Photo Forum, 91-92; Rated "X" Show, Neikrug Gallery, 92; and others. *Awards:* Int Award, Women in Photog, traveling US, Europe & Far East, 89-90; Natural World Photog Competition Prize, Carnegie Mus, 88; Purchase Award, 100 Friends Art, 92; and others. *Bibliog:* Donald Miller (auth), Arts Mag, 5/78; Virginia Watson-Jones, Contemporary American Women Sculptors, Oryx Press, 88; Donald Miller (auth), Artists will create, Pittsburgh Post Gazette, 9/3/88. *Mem:* Western Pa Soc Sculptors (pres, 74-78); Group A (pres, 79-85); Assoc Artists of Pittsburgh (bd dirs, 67-69); PhotoImagers Guild; Nat Mus Women in Arts; Silver Eye, Pittsburgh Ctr Arts (bd mem, 74-85); Women Photog. *Media:* Oil; Steel, Aluminum. *Dealer:* Photo Forum. *Mailing Add:* 2409 Marbury Rd Pittsburgh PA 15221

GRUBER, J RICHARD
MUSEUM DIRECTOR, HISTORIAN
b Louisville, Ky, Mar 30, 48. *Study:* Xavier Univ, BA(Eng), 71; Univ Colo, MA(cum laude), 80; Univ Kans, MPH, 82, PhD, 87. *Collections Arranged:* Memphis in Memphis, 83, Sheffield Silver: The Kirby Collection, Australian Art in Our Time & Kentucky Shaker Furniture, 84, Memphis: 1948-1958 (with catalog), 86, Memphis Brooks Mus Art, Tenn; In Plain View: The Collages of Irwin Kremen (catalog), 87; George Wardlaw: Transitions (catalog), 88. *Pos:* Cur of collections, Memphis Brooks Mus Art, Tenn, 83-85, interim dir, 84-85, dir, 85- *Teaching:* Lectr art hist, Univ Colo, Colorado Springs, 79-81. *Awards:* Smithsonian Res Fel, Nat Mus Art, 82-83; Kress Found Fel, Kans, 82-83. *Mem:* Asn Art Mus Dirs; Am Asn Mus; Am Inst Archit; Col Art Asn. *Res:* Nineteenth and twentieth century American art and architecture, emphasis on Thomas Hart Benton and regionalism. *Mailing Add:* Wichita Art Mus 619 Stackman Dr Wichita KS 67203

GRUCZA, LEO (VICTOR)
PAINTER, EDUCATOR
b Erie, Pa, Jan 3, 35. *Study:* Cleveland Inst Art, dipl, 57; Tulane Univ, MFA, 61, with George Rickey & others. *Work:* Ill State Mus, Springfield; Krannert Art Mus, Univ Ill, Champaign; Ill State Univ, Normal. *Exhib:* Corcoran Biennial Exhib, Washington, DC, 63; Art Inst Chicago, 80-81 & 84; Univ Malaya, 82; Ill Arts Consortium Traveling Show, 82-83; Zriny Gallery, Chicago, 83; Am Acad & Inst Arts & Letters, 83; Nihon Univ, Tokyo, 83; Viridian Gallery, New York, 85; one-man shows, Zriny Gallery, Chicago, 84, Artemisia Gallery, Chicago, 86, Renner Gallery, Blackburn Col, Carlinville, Ill, 87 & ARC Gallery, Chicago, 88. *Teaching:* Asst prof painting, Univ Ill, Champaign, 66-70, assoc prof painting, 70-84, prof, 85- *Awards:* First Prize-Painting, Ann Exhib, Delgado Mus, New Orleans, 61; Tiffany Found Grant, New York, 61; Nat Endowment Arts Grants, 82 & 83; Governor's Purchase Award, State of Ill Prof Exhib, Springfield, 82; Yaddo Fel, Hand-Hollow Found, East Chatham, NY, 83. *Media:* Oil. *Mailing Add:* 2204 Blackthorn Champaign IL 61821

GRUEN, JOHN
CRITIC, WRITER
b Enghien-les-Bains, France, Sept 12, 26; US citizen. *Study:* City Col New York; Univ Iowa, BA & MA. *Pos:* Critic of music & art, New York Herald Tribune, 62-68; art critic, New York Mag, 69-73; art critic, Soho Weekly News, 74-; contribr ed, Art News, 76-; sr ed, Dance Mag, 79- *Teaching:* Lectr, Metrop Mus Art, 79- *Publ:* Auth, Close-Up Viking Press, 69, The Private World of Leonard Bernstein, 69, The Party's Over Now, 73, The Private World of Ballet, 75 & Erik Bruhn: Danseur Noble, 79; The World's Greatest Ballets, Harry N Abrams, 82; People Who Dance, Princeton Bks, 88; The Artist Observed, A Cappella Bks, 91; Keith Haring, The Authorized Biography, Prentice Hall/Simon & Schuster, 91; and others. *Mailing Add:* 317 W 83rd St New York NY 10024

GRUEN, SHIRLEY SCHANEN
PAINTER, MOSAIC ARTIST
b Port Washington, Wis, Dec 2, 23. *Study:* Univ Wis, Madison, BS, (art educ) 45; Art Ctr Sch, Los Angeles, Calif, 46; Cardinal Stritch/col, Milwaukee, 72-88. *Work:* West Bend Fine Arts Gallery, Wis; Milwaukee Art Comn, Wis. *Comn:* paintings, Colonial Bank, Wis, 73; mural, Gruen, Schmidt, Knosel & Co, Glendale, Wis, 77; painting, Colonial Bank, Port Washington, Wis, 83; paintings, Port Washington State Bank, Wis, 87; paintings, Port Washington Savings and Loan, Wis, 88. *Exhib:* Chataugua Am Art, Chataugua, NY, 70-71; Springville Art Exhib, Springville, Mus Art, Utah, 74, 83, 85; Wisconsin Invitational, Rahr West Mus Art, Manitowoc, 80 & 81; Nat Soc Painters in Casein, 84 & Nat Arts Club 89th Annual, 88, Nat Arts Club, New York. *Teaching:* Instr watercolor & portrait, Milwaukee Area Tech Col, Wis, 70-74. *Awards:* Purchase Award, Art and Law, West Pub Co, St Paul, Minn, 80; purchase award, Response 83, Milwaukee Arts Comn, 83; oil pastel award, Salmagundi Club, Oil Pastel Assoc, New York, 88. *Bibliog:* En Provence, La Revue Moderne, 9/72; West 80-Art and Law, Am Bar Asn Journal, 7/80; Sally Prince Davis (auth), Selling Your Art, North Light Books, Spring 89. *Mem:* Wis Painters and Sculptors; Wis Watercolor Soc. *Media:* Acrylic, Watercolor. *Mailing Add:* 303 N Franklin Port Washington WI 53074

GRUNDBERG, ANDY (JOHN ANDREW)
CRITIC, EDITOR
b Bryn Mawr, Pa, June 25, 47. *Study:* Cornell Univ, BA, 69; Univ NC, Greensboro, MFA, 71. *Pos:* Picture ed, Mod Photog, 74-; photog critic, Soho Weekly News, 79-81 & NY Times, 81-; dir, the Friends Photog, San Francisco, 92- *Teaching:* Vis critic, RI Sch Design, Providence, 85; instr art hist, Sch Visual Arts, New York, 86- & instr grad photog prog 88-91; vis instr grad photog prog, San Francisco Art Inst, 92. *Awards:* Reva & David Logan Found Grant, Photog Resource Ctr, 85; Leica Medal Excellence ("Educator of the Year"), 88; Manufacturers Hanover Art/World Awrd, 89. *Bibliog:* Grundberg's Goof-Proof Photography Guide, Fireside, 89; Mike and Doug Starn, Harry N Abrams Inc, 90; Crisis of the Real: Writings on Photography, 1974-1989, Aperture, 90. *Mem:* Soc Photog Educ (bd dirs, 83-). *Res:* Twentieth century American photography, with emphasis on contemporary practice and theory. *Publ:* Contribr, The Camera Viewed, Dutton, 79; contribr, Reading into Photography, Univ NMex Press, 82. *Mailing Add:* c/o Ansel Adams Ctr 250 Fourth St San Francisco CA 94103

GRUPP, CARL ALF
PAINTER, PRINTMAKER
b Moorhead, Minn, Sept 11, 39. *Study:* Minneapolis Col Art & Design, BFA, 64; Vrije Acad, Netherlands, Vanderlip Scholar, 65; Ind Univ, MFA(with hons), 69; and with Rudy Pozzatti, Urban Couch, Marvin Lowe, William Bailey & James McGarrell. *Work:* Minneapolis Inst Art & Univ Minn Gallery, Minneapolis; Am Embassy, London; Chicago Art Inst; SDak Mem Art Ctr, Brookings. *Exhib:* Joslyn Art Mus 12th Biennial, Omaha, Nebr, 72; Pratt Graphic Art Exhib, New York, 72-73; Am Printmakers, Ind Univ, US Info Agency Tour Eng, 73; Drawings USA, Minn Mus Art, St Paul, 75; Boston Printmakers, 81; plus many others. *Teaching:* Asst lithography, Minneapolis Col Art & Design, 64-65; asst intaglio printmaking, Ind Univ, Bloomington, 68-69; asst prof art, Augustana Col, 69-81, prof art, 88- *Awards:* Gustave Krollman Award for Draftsmanship, Minneapolis Col Art & Design, 63; Purchase Awards, SDak Mem Art Ctr, 73 & Silvermine Guild, New Canaan, Conn; Individual SDak State Arts Coun Grant, 88. *Bibliog:* Spotted talents in America, Frasconi, Grupp, Tendensen, 11/65; Craig Volk (auth), Art of Carl Grupp (video tape), KUSD-TV, Univ SDak, 3/75. *Media:* Oil. *Dealer:* Miriam Perlman Inc 505 N Lake Shore Dr Chicago IL 60611; Gallery 306 3105 Phillips Sioux Falls SD 57105. *Mailing Add:* 1614 S Phillips Ave Sioux Falls SD 57105

GRUPPE, CHARLES
PAINTER
b New York, NY, July 1, 28. *Study:* Yale Univ; Nat Univ Mex; Columbia Univ, BFA, 54, MFA(Brevoort Fel), 55; Huntington Hartford Found, Pacific Palisades, 56; Fulbright Fel, Italy, 57. *Comn:* Paintings, Am Pres Lines, Coolidge, Jackson & Wilson, 65; Yale Divinity Sch, New Haven, Conn, 65; Dolly O'Brien Estate, Palm Beach, 64; First Nat Bank, New Haven, 65; apt complexes, Palm Beach, 72-73. *Exhib:* Silvermine Guild Artists, New Canaan, Conn, 65 & 77; Provincetown Art Asn, 65 & 77 & Rockport Art Asn, Mass, 70 & 77; Butler Mus Am Art, Youngstown, Ohio, 72 & 75; Lord & Taylor, New York, 75; Witte Mus, San Antonio, Tex. *Teaching:* Workshop instr, Marco Island, Fla & Greenwich, Conn, 87-89. *Awards:* Art & the Law Nat Competition Award, 83; Hudson Valley Award, 86; Silvermine Guild Award, 87. *Media:* Oil. *Mailing Add:* PO Box 841 Old Lyme CT 06371

GRUSHKIN, PHILIP
DESIGNER, CALLIGRAPHER
b New York, NY, June 1, 21. *Study:* Cooper Union Art Sch, BFA. *Exhib:* Calligraphy, Grolier Club, 58; Art Dirs Club, 60; Int Calligraphy & Lettering, Brown Univ, 61; and many others. *Pos:* Cartographer, US Geol Survey, 42-43 & Off Strategic Serv, USA, 43-45; designer, World Publ Co, 55-56; designer, Harry N Abrams, Inc, 57-59, art dir, 59-, vpres, 60-69; pres, Philip Grushkin Inc, Englewood, NJ, 69- *Teaching:* Instr lettering, calligraphy & illus, Cooper Union Art Sch, 46-68; dir bk design workshop, Radcliffe Col Publ Procedures & Harvard Summer Sch, Cambridge, Mass, 66-79; adj asst prof graphic design, NY Univ, 66-78. *Awards:* Cert of Excellence, Print for Com Exhib, Am Inst Graphic Arts, 50; and others. *Mem:* Grolier Club, NY; Am Printing Hist Asn; Typophiles, NY. *Publ:* Publ & calligrapher, Aesop's Fables, 46; publ, Christmas Carols, 48; contribr, Bouquet for Bruce Rogers, 50; contribr, Calligraphics, 55; and others. *Mailing Add:* 86 E Linden Ave Englewood NJ 07631

GRUSKIN, MARY JOSEPHINE
CONSULTANT, COLLECTOR
b Trani, Italy; US citizen. *Study:* Cooper Union, NY Sch Design. *Pos:* Emer dir, Midtown Galleries, currently. *Bibliog:* Art Times, 5/90. *Mem:* Metrop Mus Drawing Soc. *Specialty:* Contemporary American artists. *Publ:* Auth, article, Art & Auction, 12/85. *Mailing Add:* 200 E 57th St New York NY 10022

GRUVER, MARY EMMETT
PAINTER, PRINTMAKER
b Leavenworth, Kans, Nov 9, 12. *Study:* Univ Calif, Berkeley, BA(fine arts), 34, studied landscape painting with Robert Rishell, portrait with Peter Blos. *Work:* Main Lobby, Martinez Vets Hosp, Calif. *Exhib:* Calif State Fair-Exhib, Fairgrounds, Sacramento, Calif, 65 & 67; Jack London Sq Art Festival, 14th Ann Outdoor, Oakland, Calif, 68; Santa Cruz Statewide Exhib, Santa Cruz League Bldg, Calif, 70-71; San Francisco 26th Art Festival, Civic Ctr Plaza, 72; Soc Western Artists, 31st Ann Hall of Flowers, San Francisco, 78; and others. *Teaching:* Instr art, State Calif, Adult Educ, 61-75. *Awards:* First & Second Representational Oil, Livermore Art Asn 9th Ann, 65; First Pastel

Portrait, Santa Cruz Art Ann, 70-71; First Watercolor & Purchase Award, Placerville Art Ann, 76. *Mem:* Signature mem, Pastel Soc Am, New York; signature mem, Pastel Soc West Coast; signature mem, Soc Western Artists. *Media:* Watercolor, Pastel; Lino Prints. *Mailing Add:* 5471 Gold Hill Rd Placerville CA 95667

GRYGUTIS, BARBARA
SCULPTOR, ENVIRONMENTAL ARTIST
b Hartford, Conn, Nov 7, 46. *Study:* Univ Ariz, BFA, 68, MFA, 71. *Work:* Tucson Mus Art, Ariz; Research Corp, New York & Tucson, Ariz; Schirmer Collection, Dusseldorf, WGer; The Lannan Found, Palm Beach, Fla; Mus Folk Art & Craft, Los Angeles, Calif. *Comn:* Temple, Scudder Park Proj, Tempe, Ariz, 88; Cruising San Mateo I, II, III, Albuquerque, NMex, 91; Real Tools, Gateway, St Paul Tech Col, Minn, 91-92; Martin Luther King Jr Mem, Columbia, Mo, 92; Gardens of Absolutes, Col Eng, Ohio State Univ, Columbus, 93. *Exhib:* Am Crafts at the White House, Renwick Gallery, Smithsonian Inst, Washington, DC, 76; Mus Contemp Crafts, New York, 76; Everson Mus Art, Syracuse, NY, 76; Landscape, New Views, Herbert Johnson Mus, Cornell Univ, Ithaca, NY, 78; Women Artists: Clay, Fiber, Metal, Bronx Mus, NY, 78; The Parker Collection for the Vice-President's House, Washington, DC, 78; Southwest Sculpture, Scottsdale Ctr Arts, Ariz, 86 (group), 88 (individual); Ceramics in the Urban Setting, 2nd Int Quadriennal Competition, Faenza, Italy, 89. *Pos:* Artist-in-residence, Tucson Sch Dist 1, 73 & Haystack Mountain Sch Crafts, Deer Isle, Maine, 78. *Teaching:* Master Artist Workshop, Art in Pub Places, Tucson Mus Art Tucson, Ariz, 86. *Awards:* Nat Endowment Arts, 75 & 87; Second Prize, Ceramics in the Urban Setting, The Second Int Quadriennal Competition, Faenza, Italy, 88; The Albuquerque Conserv Asn Award of Merit: For Contrib to the Urban Quality of Albuquerque, 91. *Bibliog:* Chevy Art Cruises Into Town, Albuquerque Jour, NMex 6/6/91; Work Ethic was Inspiration for New St Paul Sculpture, Union Advocate, Vol 95, No 10, 10/7/91; Data Book/Int Contemp Art Fair, Int Sculpture Ctr, Yokohama, 3/92; Jan Sheridan (auth), PIece by Piece, The Ariz Repub, 86. *Media:* Environmental. *Dealer:* Radix 1429 N First St Phoenix AZ 85004. *Mailing Add:* 273 N Main Tucson AZ 85701

GUADAGNOLI, NELLO T
DEALER
b Walsenburg, Colo, Dec 16, 29. *Pos:* Owner & dir, Kiva Gallery. *Specialty:* Paintings by Indian artists of the Southwest. *Mailing Add:* c/o Kiva Gallery 202 W Hwy 66 Gallup NM 87301

GUALTIERI, JOSEPH P
MUSEUM DIRECTOR, PAINTER
b Royalton, Ill, Dec 25, 16. *Study:* Norwich Art Sch, Conn, dipl; Sch Art Inst Chicago, Ill, dipl. *Work:* Pa Acad Fine Arts, Philadelphia; Wadsworth Atheneum, Hartford, Conn; RI Sch Design Mus Fine Arts, Providence; Lyman Allyn Mus, New London, Conn; Slater Mem Mus, Norwich, Conn. *Comn:* Wall mural, New London Co Mutual Ins Co, Norwich, Conn; portrait, Gov John Dempsey, State of Conn. *Exhib:* Chicago Art Inst, Ill, 41; Pa Acad Fine Arts, Philadelphia, 48 & 51; Whitney Mus Am Art, New York, 52; Corcoran Gallery Art, Washington, DC; Nat Acad Design, New York; Albany Inst Hist & Art, NY; Wadsworth Atheneum, Hartford, Conn; Calif Palace of the Legion of Honor, Lincoln Park, San Francisco. *Collections Arranged:* Retrospective, Converse Art Gallery, Slater Mus, 92. *Pos:* Dir, Slater Mem Mus, Norwich, Conn, 62- *Teaching:* Instr art, oil painting, figure & portrait, The Norwich Free Acad, Conn, 43-79. *Awards:* First Prize & Logan Medal, Chicago Art Inst, 41; Purchase Prize, Pa Acad of Fine Arts, 48 & 51; Conn Artists Eastern States Expo Award, 51. *Mem:* Conn Acad Fine Arts Asn; Am Asn Mus; New Eng Conf, Am Asn Mus. *Media:* Oil, Mixed. *Mailing Add:* 60 Warren St Norwich CT 06360

GUASTELLA, C DENNIS
PAINTER, INSTRUCTOR
b Detroit, Mich, July 8, 47. *Study:* Macomb Co Community Col, 67; Wayne State Univ, BFA, 72; Eastern Mich Univ, MFA, 75. *Work:* Sheldon Mem Art Galleries, Univ Nebr, Lincoln; NDak Univ, Grand Forks; SDak Mem Art Ctr, Brookings. *Exhib:* Northwest Biennial III, SDak Mem Art Ctr, Brookings, 76; Biennial, Joslyn Art Mus, Omaha, Nebr, 76, 78 & 80; one-man shows, Sheldon Mem Art Galleries, Univ Nebr, Lincoln, 76 & Univ Mich, Slusser Gallery, Ann Arbor, 81; Mich Artists 80/81, Detroit Inst Arts & Flint Inst Arts, 81; and others. *Teaching:* Asst prof art, SDak State Univ, Brookings, 75-80; instr visual arts, Washtenaw Community Col, Ann Arbor, Mich, 80- *Awards:* Purchase Award, Rutgers Univ, Camden, NJ, 75; Best of Show/ Purchase Award, 16th Joslyn Biennial, Joslyn Art Mus, Omaha, Nebr, 80. *Bibliog:* Interview, Detroit Artist Monthly, 11/77; Mike Odom (auth), Exhibit Reflexs 80's Mood, Uno Gateway, Univ Nebr, 1/23/81; Robert Igelhardt (auth), Close examination, distance needed to appreciate works, Ann Arbor News, 8/9/81. *Mem:* Col Art Asn; Midwest Col Art Asn. *Media:* Acrylic, String. *Mailing Add:* Dept Com Art Washtenaw Community Col 4800 E Huron River Dr Bldg TI 214 Ann Arbor MI 48106

GUBERMAN, SIDNEY THOMAS
PAINTER, SCULPTOR
b Greenville, SC, Aug 24, 36. *Study:* Princeton Univ, with Stephen Greene, BA, 58; Univ Pa, with Robert Venturi, MA(archit), 67. *Work:* Nat Mus Am Art, Corcoran Gallery Art, Washington, DC; High Mus Art, Atlanta; Princeton Univ Art Mus; Birmingham Mus Art; and others. *Comn:* Coke USA, 89, McMaster-Carr Atlanta, 90. *Exhib:* One-man show, Greenville Co Mus, SC, 76, Princeton Univ Art Mus, 83, Southeastern Ctr Contemp Art, 84 & McKissick Mus, Univ SC, Columbia, 87; William Seitz Mem, Princeton Univ Art Mus, NJ, 77; Artists in Ga, High Mus, Atlanta, 80, 82 & 85; Small Sculpture, Del Mar Col, Corpus Christi, Tex, 81 & 83; Birmingham Biennial, 83; Atlanta in France, Paris, & Toulouse, 85; Ten Years of Visual Arts at Princeton, 85; Galerie von der Milwe, Aachen, Ger, 90; Susan Conway Carroll Gallery, Washington, DC, 91; Looking South, A Different Dixie, 22 Artists, Four Southern museums; Hodges-Taylor Gallery, Charlotte, NC, 90, 93. *Pos:* Exhib dir, Govt Services Savings & Loan, 76-79. *Teaching:* Prof painting, l'Ecole Cantonale Beaux Arts, Lausanne, Switz, 71-73; asst prof drawing, l'Ecole Polytech Fedn Lausanne, Switz, 73-75; vis lectr painting, Princeton Univ, NJ, 81-82; vis prof painting, Univ SC, Columbia, 86-87; vis artist, Atlanta Col Art, 89, 91. *Awards:* Individual Artist's Grant, Nat Endowment Arts, 80-81; Guggenheim Found Fel for Painting, 88-89. *Bibliog:* Benjamin Forgey (auth), An exhilarating abstract painter, Washington Star, 10/78; Mary Swift (auth), Sidney Guberman, Art Voices South, 4/80; Iris Welch (auth), Sidney Guberman, Art Papers, 8/82; Artists New Work Exhibs Maturity & Consistancy, Atlanta Constitution, 88. *Mem:* College Art Asn. *Media:* Oil, Acrylic; Steel, Wood. *Publ:* Auth, Frank Stella's polar coordinate series, Art Papers, 2/82; Sensation, Art Papers, 5-6/84. *Dealer:* McIntosh Gallery 587 Virginia Ave Atlanta GA 30306; Hodges-Taylor Gallery 227 Tryon St Charlotte NC 28202. *Mailing Add:* c/o Gallery 75 1174-C Zonolite Pl Atlanta GA 30306

GUCCIONE, JUANITA
PAINTER
b Chelsea, Mass. *Exhib:* One person exhibs, Recent Paintings and Watercolors, Colony Arts Ctr, Woodstock, NY, 78, Galerie Liliane Francois, Paris, France, 86; La Galerie Mouffe, Paris, France, 76; Metrop Painters and Sculptors, Manufacturers Hanover Trust Bldg, New York, 78; 46th Ann Exhib, Metrop Painters and Sculptors, New York, 83. *Awards:* Gold Medal, Academia Italia, Calvatone, Italy, 79; Golden Flame of the World Parliament, Academia Italia, Calvatone, Italy, 86. *Bibliog:* Raymond F Pier & Lila K Piper (co-auths), Cosmic Art, Hawthorn Books, New York, 75; Anniversary for Guccione, Ulster Co Gazette, 77. *Media:* Oil, acrylic. *Mailing Add:* 60 Sutton Place South Apt 14KNO New York NY 10022

GUENTHER, PETER W
HISTORIAN, EDUCATOR
b Dresden, Ger, Mar 29, 20; US citizen. *Study:* Univ Breslau; Acad Fine Arts, Stuttgart, Ger; Univ Tex, Austin, MA & PhD. *Collections Arranged:* Edward Munch (auth, catalog), Sarah Campbell Blaffer Gallery, Univ Houston, New Orleans, San Antonio & Dallas; German Expressionism, Toward a New Humanism (auth, catalog), Sarah Campbell Blaffer Gallery, Univ Houston. *Teaching:* Prof art, Univ Houston, 62-, chmn dept art, 62-72, prof emer, 90. *Awards:* Teaching Excellence Award, Univ Houston, 70; Master Teacher Award, Col Humanities & Fine Arts, Univ Houston, 82. *Mem:* Col Art Asn Am; Tex Asn Sch Arts (pres, 71-73); S Cent Renaissance Conf (pres, 73); S Cent Mod Lang Asn; Mid-Am Art Hist Asn. *Res:* Northern Renaissance; iconography; German expressionism. *Publ:* Auth, A Survey of Artist Groups: Their Rise, Rhetoric and Demise, German Expressionism, 1915-1925, The Second Generation, Los Angeles Co Mus Art, 88; Renaissance and mannerism north of the Alps, In: Encycl World Art, suppl Vol 18; An Introduction to the German Expressionist Movement, German Expressionist Prints and Drawings, The Robert Gore Rifkind Ctr for German Expressionist Studies, Los Angeles Co Mus Art, 89. *Mailing Add:* 10013 Hazelhurst Houston TX 77080

GUERIN, JOHN WILLIAM
PAINTER, EDUCATOR
b Houghton, Mich, Aug 29, 20. *Study:* Am Acad Art, Chicago; Art Students League; Escuela Bellas Artes, San Miguel, Mex; Colorado Springs Fine Arts Ctr. *Work:* Dallas Mus Fine Arts; Chrysler Mus, Provincetown, Mass; Joslyn Art Mus, Omaha, Nebr; Colorado Springs Fine Arts Ctr; Houston Mus Fine Arts; and others. *Exhib:* One-man shows, Kraushaar Gallery, New York, 59, 63 & 68; Galeria Realities, Taos, NMex, 60; Corcoran Gallery Art, 61; Whitney Mus Am Art, New York; retrospective, Ft Worth Art Ctr, 64; and others. *Teaching:* Instr painting, Dallas Mus Fine Arts, 50-52; prof art, Univ Tex, Austin, 53-80, prof emer, 80-; artist in residence, Skowhegan Sch Painting & Sculpture, 60. *Awards:* Am Acad Arts & Lett Grant, 59; Univ Tex Res Inst Grant, 60 & 66; Ford Found Grant, 79; and others. *Mem:* Tex Fine Arts Asn; Art Students League (life mem); assoc elect Nat Acad Design. *Media:* All. *Dealer:* Carlin Galleries 710 Montgomery St Ft Worth TX 76107. *Mailing Add:* 3400 Stoneridge Rd Austin TX 78746

GUERRERO, RAUL
PAINTER, SCULPTOR
b Brawley, Calif, 45. *Study:* Chouinard Art Sch, Los Angeles, BFA. *Work:* Phoenix Art Mus, Ariz; Long Beach Mus Art, Calif; La Jolla Mus Contemp Art, Calif; Security Pacific Bank, Los Angeles; Scripps Clinic, La Jolla. *Exhib:* Solo exhibs, Cirrus Gallery, Los Angeles, 74, Long Beach Mus Art, Calif, 77, Contemp Arts Forum, Santa Barbara & Los Angeles Inst Contemp Art, 82, Barbara Braathen Gallery, New York, 84, Boehm Gallery, Palomar Col, San Marcos, Calif, 86 & Saxon-Lee Gallery, Los Angeles, 87 & 88; Raul Guerrero & Doug Metzler, Santa Monica, Calif, 77; 2nd Ann Tokyo Video Festival, Tokyo, Japan, 79; A San Diego Exhib: 42 Emerging Artists, La Jolla Mus Contemp Art, 85; 1987 Phoenix Biennial, Phoenix Art Mus, Ariz, 87; From the Back Room, Saxon Lee Gallery, Los Angeles, 88, 89 & 90; and many other solo & group exhibs. *Awards:* Photography fel, Nat Endowment Arts, 79. *Bibliog:* Melinda Wortz (auth), Psychological manipulations, Artnews, 5/77; Hunter Drohojowska (auth), Raul Guerrero, Los Angeles Inst Contemp Art, Flash Art Int, 3/83; Christopher Knight (auth), Guerrero's art comes close to B-movie mysticism, 6/2/85, Exhibit of works by Raul Guerrero borders on

being retrospective, 10/5/86 & Phoenix joins major leagues in art, 8/25/87, Los Angeles Herald Examiner; Judith Spiegel (auth), Nostalgia: The world flattened, Artweek, 4/30/88; and many others. *Mailing Add:* Daniel Saxon Gallery 7525 Beverly Blvd San Diego CA 90036

GUICHET, MELODY
PAINTER
b Hammond, La, Nov 18, 49. *Study:* La State Univ, BFA, 71; Tyler Sch Art, Temple Univ, Philadelphia, MFA, 73. *Work:* Am Inst Arts & Lett, New York; New Orleans Mus Art; Ark Arts Ctr, Little Rock; Birmingham Mus, Ala. *Comn:* Eight sculptures, LaFayette Airport, La. *Exhib:* Ten years Southeast Seven, Southeastern Ctr Contemp Art, Winston-Salem, NC, 87; Fact, Fiction, Fantasy, Recent narrative art in the Southeast, Univ Tenn, Knoxville (travel), 87; Melody Guichet, Peter Halley, R M Fischer & Arthur Roger Gallery, New Orleans, La, 88; A Tribute to Excellence, Masur Mus Art, Monroe, La, 89; Chicago Int New Art Forms Exposition, Navy Pier, 90. *Pos:* Slide cur, Tyler Sch Art, Temple Univ, Philadelphia, 73. *Teaching:* Prof painting, La State Univ, 74-90. *Awards:* Southeast Ctr Contemp Arts Seven, 78; Artists Grant, La, 82; Nat Endowment Arts Fel, 86. *Bibliog:* Sam McMillan (auth), Melody Guichet: The crayola colors of dreams, Arts J, NC, Vol 5, No 3, 79; interview with artist, Way Out Art, KLSY TV, program, Lafayette, La, 82. *Media:* Oil. *Dealer:* Arthur Roger Gallery 432 Julia St New Orleans LA 70119. *Mailing Add:* 4716 Sweetbriar Baton Rouge LA 70808

GUIDA, DOMINICK
PAINTER
b New York, NY, June 24, 46. *Study:* Calif Inst Arts, with Edward Reep & Emerson Woelffer, BFA, 68. *Work:* Chemical Bank & Goldman Sachs & Co, New York; Conn Bank & Trust Co, Norwalk; Continental Corp, Sascataway, NJ; Cologne Life Reinsurance Corp, Stamford, Conn. *Comn:* Painting on wood relief structure, Edward Albee Found, New York, 78. *Exhib:* Biennial Exhib, Whitney Mus Am Art, New York, 75; New Spiritual Abstraction of the 1980's, Nora Haime Gallery, New York, 84; Painting & Sculpture Today 1984 (with catalog), Indianapolis Mus Art, Ind, 84; The Gang of 12 from New York in Italy (with catalog), Galleria Centro Mascarella, Bologna & Museo Civico, Siracusa, Italy, 86; Alumni Invitational Exhibition, Calif Inst of the Arts, Valencia, Calif, 88; Indianapolis Collects, Herron Art Gallery, Indianapolis, In, 90; and others. *Bibliog:* Amei Wallach (auth), Artworks of Albee's Barn, Newsday, Long Island, NY, 6/82. *Mem:* Painting Space. *Media:* Oil, Watercolor. *Mailing Add:* PO Box 1441 New York NY 10009

GUILMAIN, JACQUES
HISTORIAN, EDUCATOR
b Brussels, Belg, Oct 15, 26; US citizen. *Study:* Queens Col, City Univ New York, BS, 48; Columbia Univ, MA, 52, univ fel, 57, PhD, 58, and with Meyer Schapiro. *Teaching:* Vis asst prof hist art, Stanford Univ, 58-59; vis asst prof, Univ Calif, Riverside, 59-60; instr, Queens Col, 60-63; from asst prof to prof art hist, State Univ NY Stony Brook, 63-, chmn art dept, 70-76; vis prof, Columbia Univ, 68 & 70. *Awards:* Am Philosophical Soc Grant, 60; State Univ NY Res Found Grant, 64-79; and others. *Mem:* Col Art Asn Am; Int Ctr Medieval Art; Medieval Acad Am. *Res:* Early Medieval ornaments; Mozarabic manuscript illumination; Carolingian manuscript illumination; early Medieval metalwork. *Publ:* Contribr, American Watercolors, Drawings & Prints, 1952, Metrop Mus Art, New York; auth, Zoomorphic decoration and the problem of the sources of Mozarabic illumination, XXXV, 60, Illuminations of the Second Bible of Charles the Bald, XLI 66, The Geometry of the Cross- Carpet Pages in the Lindisfarne Gospels, LXII, 87, Speculum; Enigmatic beasts of the Lindau Gospels lower cover, Gesta, X, 71; On the chronological development and classification of decorated initials in Latin manuscripts of 10th century Spain, LXIII 81, Bulletin, John Rylands Univ Libr, Manchester; and others. *Mailing Add:* PO Box 2363 Setauket NY 11733

GULLY, ANTHONY LACY
HISTORIAN, ADMINISTRATOR
b Orange, Calif, Feb 28, 38. *Study:* Univ Calif, Riverside, BA; Univ Calif, Berkeley, MA; Stanford Univ, PhD; with Jean Boggs, Jean Bony, Walter Horn, Lorenz Eitner & Albert Elsen. *Teaching:* Instr 17th-18th century art hist, Pomona Col, Claremont, Calif, 65-66; asst prof 19th-20th century art hist, Calif State Univ, Los Angeles, 66-68; assoc prof 18th-19th century art hist, Ariz State Univ, Tempe, 72-83, asst dean col fine arts, 81-, chair grad humanities prog, 83-84; vis prof, Stanford Univ, 81. *Awards:* Nat Defense Educ Act Award, Stanford Univ, 68-71; Mabel McLeod Fel, Rowlandson Study, London, Stanford Univ, 71-72; Nat Endowment Humanities Award, Yale Univ, 76; and others. *Bibliog:* J Hayes (auth), Rowlandson, Phaidon Art Bks, 72; R Paulsen (auth), Rowlandson: New interpretation, Yale Univ, 72; R Wark (auth), Rowlandson drawings in Huntington Libr, 75. *Mem:* Col Art Asn; Mid-Am Col Art Asn; Rocky Mountain Conf on Brit Studies (pres, 78-79); Nat Conf Brit Studies; Pacific Conf on Brit Studies. *Res:* Nineteenth century British art; John Sell Cotman, 1782-1842. *Publ:* Auth, Book reviews on eighteenth century art and aesthetics, Current Bibliog: 18th Century, 76; auth, Mr B and the cherubim: William Blake's descriptive catalog, 78, An unpublished sketchbook by Rowlandson, 79 & Milton's unholy trinity, 81, Phoebus; auth, Source of Goya's May 3, 1808, In: Studies in Iconography, 83. *Mailing Add:* Sch Art Ariz State Univ Tempe AZ 85287

GUMMELT, SAMUEL
PAINTER
b Waco, Tex, Aug 28, 44. *Study:* NTex State Univ, BA, 68; Southern Methodist Univ, MFA, 71. *Work:* Dallas Mus Fine Arts; Am Tel & Tel, Chicago; Ft Worth Art Mus. *Exhib:* Proj South/Southwest, 71 & Focus: Sam Gummelt, 79, Ft Worth Art Mus; Interchange, Dallas Mus Fine Art, 72 & Walker Art Ctr, Minneapolis, 73; Exchange, Ft Worth Art Mus, 75 & San Francisco Mus Mod Art, 76; Recent Works on Paper by Contemp Am Artists, Madison Art Ctr, Wis, 77; Projects: Sam Gummelt, Art Mus STex, Corpus Christi, 78; Am Drawing in Black & White 1970-1980, Brooklyn Mus, NY, 80. *Awards:* Purchase Awards, 4th Ann Prints & Drawing Exhib, Ark Art Ctr, 70, 35th Tarrant Co Ann, Ft Worth Art Ctr, 73 & Tex Invitational, Beaumont Art Mus, 78; Nat Endowment Arts Fel, 82 & 85. *Bibliog:* Jan Butterfield (auth), The young Texans: The phenomenon of interstitial art on America's last frontier, Arts Mag, 73; Jozanne Rabyor (auth), article, Art in Am, 74; Susan Platt (auth), Reviews: Houston, Art Forum, 79. *Media:* Oil, Wax on Canvas. *Dealer:* Janie C Lee Gallery 1209 Berthea Houston TX 77006; Eugene Binder Gallery 2701 Canton Dallas TX 75226. *Mailing Add:* Gerald Peters Gallery 2913 Fairmount Dallas TX 75201

GUMMER, DON
SCULPTOR
b Louisville, Ky, 1946. *Study:* John Herron Art Inst, Indianapolis, 64-66; Sch Mus Fine Arts, Boston, 66-70; Yale Univ Sch Fine Arts, New Haven, BFA, 71, MFA, 73. *Work:* McCrory Corp & Chase Manhattan Bank Collection, New York; HHK Found Contemp Art, Milwaukee; Commodities Corp, Princeton, NJ; Joseph E Seagram Co Collection, New York; Chemical Bank, New York. *Comn:* Interpretations 79, comn by Castle Clinton/Manhattan Cult Coun, Battery Park, NY, 79; outdoor installations, Dag Hammerskjold Plaza, 80 & Joseph E Seagram & Sons, 82, New York. *Exhib:* Eight Sculptors, Albright-Knox Art Gallery, Buffalo, NY, 79; Current/New York, Joe & Emily Lowe Art Gallery, Syracuse Univ, NY, 80; one-man shows, Sperone Westwater Fischer, New York, 77, 79, 82, 84, 86 & 88, Akron Art Mus, Ohio, 80, Daniel Weinberg Gallery, Santa Monica, Calif, 92; New Visions, Aldrich Mus Contemp Art, Ridgefield, Conn, 81; Artists Return to Artists Space, NY, 81; Chicago Arts Club, 82; Invitational Exhib, Berkshire Mus, Pittsfield Mus, 82; Concept in Construction: 1910-1980, traveling, Tyler Mus Art, Tex, Alberta Col Art Gallery, Calgary, Anchorage Hist & Fine Arts Mus, Long Beach Mus Art, Calif, Palm Springs Desert Mus & Neuberger Mus, Purchase, NY, 83-85; Evansville Mus Arts & Science, Ind, 87; Am Academy & Inst Arts & Letters, 88; Blum Helman Gallery & German van Eck Gallery, New York, 90. *Awards:* Grant, Nat Endowment Arts, 76; Grant, Tiffany Found, 78; Grant, Creative Artists Pub Serv Prog, 79. *Bibliog:* Grace Glueck (auth), A critic's guide to the outdoor sculpture show, New York Times, 6/11/82; Jeffrey Hoqrefe (auth), New York, New York: Arts, Washington Post, 4/10/84; Linda L Cathcart (auth), A Decade of New Art, New York, 84; Vlvien Raynor (auth), The New York Times, Sunday, 2/10/85; John Russell (auth), New York Times, 5/20/88, p c23. *Media:* Wood, Stone. *Mailing Add:* c/o Sperone Westwater Fischer 142 Greene St New York NY 10012

GUMPEL, HUGH
PAINTER
b New York, NY, Feb 3, 26. *Study:* Columbia Univ; Art Students League; Grande Chaumiere, Paris, France. *Work:* Nat Acad Design, New York; Norfolk Mus, Va; Hagerstown Mus, Md; Univ Wash, Seattle; Art Inst Zanesville, Ohio. *Comn:* Mural, State of NY Pub Works Admin Bldg, 63. *Exhib:* Royal Soc Painters, London, Eng, 67; Mex Art Inst, Mexico City, 68; Art Mus, Ontario, Can, 72; Nat Acad Anns, 60-89; Am Watercolor Soc Anns, 53-78. *Teaching:* Instr painting, Nat Acad Sch Fine Arts, 59-; instr watercolor, State Univ New York, Purchase, Westchester Art Workshop. *Awards:* Gold Medal of Honor, Am Watercolor Soc, 59; Willlam A Paton Prize, Nat Acad, 73 & 78. *Bibliog:* Norman Kent (ed), Seascapes & Landscapes in Watercolor, pp 97-102, New York, 56; The Ranger Fund, Am Artist, p 50, 10/58; Ralph Fabri (auth), 147th Ann Nat Acad Design, Today's Art, p 7, 12/72. *Mem:* Nat Acad Design; Am Watercolor Soc. *Media:* Watercolor, Acrylic. *Mailing Add:* c/o Nat Acad Fine Arts 5 E 89th St New York NY 10028

GUMPERT, GUNTHER
PAINTER
b Krefeld, Ger, Apr 17, 19; US citizen. *Study:* Sch Fine Arts Krefeld; Sch Fine Arts, Wuppertal. *Work:* Metrop Mus Art, New York; Denver Art Mus, Colo; Phillips Collection, Washington DC; Victoria & Albert Mus, London; Albertina, Vienna, Austria; and others. *Comn:* Mural, Inter-Am Develop Bank, Washington, DC, 68. *Exhib:* Kaiser-Wilhelm Mus, 48, 49 & 52; Salon Realites Nouvelles, Paris, 58-60 & 62; Int Exhib Abstr Art, Pistoia, 61; Int Exhib Contemp Art, London, 62; Salon Mai, Paris, 62; one-man shows, USA, Latin Am & Eur, 53-90. *Bibliog:* Jean Grenier (auth), Gumpert, Preuves, Paris, 60; Victor Summa (auth), Gumpert & The Evolution of His Art (film), Educ TV Asn, 63; Willy Huppert (auth), Gunther Gumpert, Kunst-und Kunstgewerbe Verein, Pforzheim, 64. *Media:* All. *Dealer:* Franz Bader Gallery 1500 K St NW Washington DC 20005; Foster Harmon Galleries Am Art 1415 Main St Sarasota FL. *Mailing Add:* 3752 McKinley St NW Washington DC 20015

GUNASINGHE, SIRI
EDUCATOR, HISTORIAN
b Ruanwella, Sri Lanka, Feb 20, 25. *Study:* Univ Ceylon, BA, 48; Univ Paris, PhD, 55. *Teaching:* Instr sanskrit, Univ Ceylon, 48-70; prof, Univ Victoria, BC, 70- *Awards:* Sr Specialist, Univ Hawaii, 68; Fel, Can Coun Leave, 78; Smithsonian Travel, 87. *Res:* History of Buddhist and Hindu art in India, Sri Lanka and Southeast Asia. *Publ:* Auth, La Technique de la Peinture Indienne, Univ Press France, 56; Masks of Ceylon, Dept Cult Affairs, 63 & Album of Buddhist Paintings from Sri Lanka, Nat Mus, 78, Colombo. *Mailing Add:* Dept Art & History Univ Victoria Victoria BC V8W 2Y2 Canada

GUND, AGNES
COLLECTOR, ADMINISTRATOR
b Aug 13, 38. *Study:* Conn Col, BA, 60; Boston Univ Grad Sch, hist, 60-63; Harvard Univ, Fogg Mus, AM(art hist), 80. *Pos:* Trustee, Cleveland Inst Art, 68-72, Hirshorn Mus, Washington, DC, 87-91, Brown Univ, Providence, RI, 89-, Andy Warhol Found, New York, 90-; bd pres, Mus Mod Art, New York, 72-; bd pres, Studio Sch, New York, 77-91. *Awards:* Gov's Award, Gov Mario Cuomo; Mayor's Award, Mayor Edward Koch. *Collection:* Collection covers work produced from 1940-1992. *Publ:* Contribr, Mary Miss Catalogue for Fogg Mus, Harvard, 80; The New Democracy, Blueprints to Change Washington, Citizens Transition Proj, 92. *Mailing Add:* 765 Park Ave No 14B New York NY 10021

GUNDERMAN, KAREN M
CERAMIST
b New York, NY, Feb 15, 51. *Study:* Syracuse Univ, BFA, 73; Univ Mich, MFA, 75. *Exhib:* Solo exhibs, List Art Ctr, Hamilton Col, Clinton, NY, 77, Lawrence Col, Appleton, Wis, 79, Sinclair Galleries, Coe Col, Cedar Rapids, Iowa, 79, Centro-Cult Peruano-Noretamericano, Lima, Peru, 86, Bradley Galleries, Milwaukee, Wis, 87, Esther Saks Gallery, Chicago, Ill, 88 & Munson Gallery, Santa Fe, NMex, 90; Lill St Gallery, Chicago, Ill, 85; US Embassy, Lima, Peru, 87 & 88; San Angelo Mus Fine Arts, Tex, 89; Joan Robey Gallery, Denver, Colo, 90; and others. *Teaching:* Asst prof art, Col Wooster, 76-77; assoc prof art, Univ Wis-Milwaukee, 78- *Awards:* Visual Artists Fel, Nat Endowment Arts, 88; Ctr Latin Am Res Grant, 89. *Mem:* Nat Coun Educ Ceramic Arts; Col Art Assoc; Ctr Latin Am, Univ Wis-Milwaukee; Nat Fulbright Alumni Asn. *Mailing Add:* c/o Esther Saks Gallery 311 W Superior St Chicago IL 60610

GUNDERSHEIMER, HERMAN (SAMUEL)
HISTORIAN, EDUCATOR
b Wurzburg, Ger, Apr 25, 03; US citizen. *Study:* Univ Munich; Univ Wurzburg; Univ Berlin; Univ Leipzig, PhD, 26. *Pos:* Cur, Mus Ulm/Danube, Kunstgewerbe Mus, Frankfurt, Ger, 27-33; dir, Rothschild Mus, Frankfurt, 33-39. *Teaching:* From asst prof to prof art hist, Temple Univ, 41-70, prof & dir Temple Abroad, Tyler Sch Art, Rome, Italy, 70-73; guest prof, Univ Tel-Aviv, Israel, 73-74; guest prof, LaSalle Col, Philadelphia, 75-86, prof emer, 70- *Awards:* Lindbach Award for excellent teaching. *Bibliog:* Herman Gundersheimer, Ceremonial Art. *Mem:* Col Art Asn Am; hon mem Cambridge Art Soc, England; Renaissance Soc Am; Pa Acad Arts; Print Club. *Res:* Renaissance & Baroque art; Jewish ceremonial art. *Collection:* American furniture, Piranesi & contemporary graphics. *Publ:* Contribr to journals-magazines & contrib ed to encyclopedias. *Mailing Add:* 2 Franklin Town Blvd Apt 2403 Philadelphia PA 19103

GUNDERSON, BARRY L
SCULPTOR
b Baird, Tex, Feb 9, 45. *Study:* Augsburg Col, Minneapolis, BA; Univ NDak, Grand Forks; Univ Colo, Boulder, MFA. *Work:* Ball State Univ, Muncie, Ind; Minot State Col, NDak; Normandale Jr Col, Minneapolis; Augsburg Col, Minneapolis. *Comn:* Large outdoor sculptures, Downtown Plaza, Portsmouth, 79, EOTC, Pendleton, Ore, 86, Porirua, Wellington, New Zealand, 90 & Franklin Park Conservatory, Columbus, Ohio, 92. *Exhib:* 5 Ohio Sculptors, Contemp Arts Ctr, Cincinnati, 80; Sculpture Outside in Cleveland, Edgewater Part, Cleveland, 81; Ohio Sculptors II, Taft Mus, Cincinnati, 86; Art for Urban Gardens, Ohio Designer Craftsmen Gallery, Columbus, 89. *Teaching:* Prof sculpture, Kenyon Col, 74- *Mem:* Col Art Asn. *Media:* Welded, Painted Aluminum. *Mailing Add:* Dept Art Kenyon Col Gambier OH 43022

GUNDERSON, KAREN
PAINTER
b Racine, Wis, Aug 14, 43. *Study:* Wis State Univ, Whitewater, BEd, 66, Univ Iowa, Iowa City, MA & MFA, 68. *Work:* Wustum Art Mus, Racine & Milwaukee Art. *Comn:* Paintings, comn by Mr & Mrs Leonard Gordon, New York & Dr & Mrs Clinton Levin, New Bedford, Mass, 88. *Exhib:* Solo exhibs, Wustum Art Mus, Racine, 69 & 85, Wis & Cedar Rapids Art Ctr, Iowa, 69, Minneapolis Inst Art, Minn, 71 & Hopkins Hall Gallery, Ohio State Univ, Columbus, 72. *Teaching:* Adj asst prof perception, Sch Arts,New York Univ, 73-76; vis artist paintng, Chicago Art Inst, 77 & Hoffberger, Md Art Inst, Baltimore, 86. *Awards:* Distinguished Alumni Award, Univ Wis, Whitewater, 85. *Bibliog:* Theodore F Wolff (auth), She meets challenges that go back to Kline and Pollock, Christian Sci Monitor, 84; Carter Ratcliff (auth), Karen Gunderson (catalog), Perimeter Press, 85; Linell Smith (auth), Painting pictures in the clouds: Karen Gunderson puts life in cumulus, Baltimore Evening Sun, 87. *Media:* Acrylic, Oil, Miscellaneous Media. *Dealer:* Gremillion & Co 2930 Revere St Houston TX 77098. *Mailing Add:* 26 Beaver St New York NY 10004

GUNDLEFINGER, JOHN ANDRE
PAINTER, COLLAGE ARTIST
b St Die, France, Oct 3, 37; US citizen. *Study:* Sch of Visual Arts, New York; NY Univ. *Work:* Chase Manhattan Bank, New York; Sara Roby Found; Int Bus Machines; Am Tel & Tel Co; Mus Fine Arts, Caracas, Venezuela. *Exhib:* One-man show, Sneed-Hillman Gallery, Rockford, Ill, 77; Am Drawing 1970-73, Yale Univ Art Gallery, 73; Galerie Stevenson et Palluel, Paris, France, 76; Weatherspoon Art Gallery, Univ NC, Greensboro, 77; Nightfall, Del River Valley, A M Sachs Gallery, New York, 81; and others. *Teaching:* Instr painting & drawing, Sch of Visual Arts, New York, 63- & Parsons Sch of Design, New York, 71- *Bibliog:* John Bernard Myers (auth), The Gouaches of John Gundelfinger, Sachs Gallery Publ, 75 & Recent Paintings--John Gundelfinger, Sachs Gallery & Art Inst Mag, Fall 77. *Media:* Oil, Gouache. *Mailing Add:* c/o Katharina Rich Perlow Gallery 560 Broadway 3rd floor New York NY 10012

GUNN, ELLEN
PAINTER, PRINTMAKER
b Rockville Center, NY, Jan 8, 51. *Study:* Parsons Sch Design, BFA, 73; Sch Visual Arts, 74; Kala Inst, Berkeley, Calif, 80; Calif Col Arts & Crafts, studied with Charles Gill, 81-82. *Work:* San Francisco Mus Mod Art, Calif. *Comn:* Paintings, Inn Keeper Asn, San Francisco, 85; paintings & fabric design, Read House Hotel, Chatanooga, Tenn, 86 & Sheraton O'Hare, Chicago, Ill, 90; paintings & monotypes, Kaiser Hosp, Santa Rosa, Calif, 87; paintings & menu design, Phoenix Sheraton, 88, 89. *Exhib:* Art Expo, New York, 90. *Awards:* 1st Place, Sr Student Competition, Parsons Sch Design, 73; Dean's Hon List & Grad Cum Laude, Parsons Sch Design. *Media:* All. *Publ:* Auth, Fiber Arts Design Book II, Lark Books, 83; The Goodfellows Review of Crafts, 83; California Living, San Francisco Chronicle, 84; Vogue Mag, 74; Good Housekeeping Mag, 73. *Dealer:* Winn Art Group 6015 Sixth Ave South Seattle WA 98108. *Mailing Add:* 40 Stratford Rd Kensington CA 94707

GUNN, PAUL JAMES
PAINTER, EDUCATOR
b Guys Mills, Pa, June 21, 22. *Study:* Edinboro State Teachers Col, BS, 47; Calif Col Arts & Crafts, MFA, 48; wood block printing with Hideo Hagiwara, Tokyo, Japan, 61-62. *Work:* Portland Art Mus; Seattle Art Mus; Am Info Serv, Athens, Greece; Bibliot Nat, Paris, France; Victoria & Albert Mus, London, Eng. *Exhib:* Int Bordighera Biennial, Italy; Bay Printmakers Second Ann, Oakland Art Mus, Calif; Ann Northwest Artists, Seattle Art Mus; Western Artists Ann, Denver Art Mus; Ore Artists Ann, Portland Art Mus. *Pos:* Resident dir, Japan Studies Prog, Ore Study Ctr, Waseda Univ, Japan, 72-74 & 83-84. *Teaching:* Prof painting & printmaking, Ore State Univ, 48-, chmn dept art, 64-72. *Media:* Oil. *Mailing Add:* 609 NW 32nd Corvallis OR 97330

GUNSHOR, RUTH
PAINTER
b Brooklyn, NY. *Study:* Brooklyn Col, 51-53; Brooklyn Mus Art Sch, with Reuban Tam, Louis Finklestein & Fred Farr, merit scholar, 54-57; Educ Alliance Art Sch, with Alex Dopkin, merit scholar, 57-59. *Exhib:* Riverside Mus, New York, 62; Brooklyn Mus, NY, 69, 71-72, 74 & 80; Nat Acad Design, New York, 71-78; Nat Arts Club, New York, 74, 76, 78, 79 & 88; Saginaw Art Mus, Mich, 76; Cayuga Mus, Auburn, NY, 77, 80 & 83; and others. *Teaching:* Instr fine arts, Adult Educ, New York City Bd Educ, 68-77. *Awards:* Jean Magid Leeman Mem Prize, 80; Gehner Watercolor Prize, 81; Ralph Mayer Mem Prize, Nat Asn Women Artists, 83. *Bibliog:* Dorothy Hall (auth), articles in Art and Artists, 3/73, 4/79 & 11/82 & 5/88. *Mem:* Nat Asn Women Artists (bd dirs, 76-90); New York Soc Women Artists (bd dirs, 78-90); Am Soc Contemp Artists (bd dirs, 79-82); Contemp Artists Guild (vpres, 81-90); Prof Artist Guild, Boca Mus Art. *Media:* Acrylic, Watercolor. *Mailing Add:* Prescott K 202 Deerfield Beach FL 33442

GUNTER, FRANK ELLIOTT
PAINTER, EDUCATOR
b Jasper, Ala, May 8, 34. *Study:* Univ Ala, BFA; Fla State Univ, MA. *Work:* Sheldon Swope Gallery, Terre Haute, Ind; Evansville Mus Arts & Sci & Mead Johnson Corp, Evansville, Ind; Ill State Mus, Springfield; Birmingham Mus Art, Ala; Krannert Art Mus, Univ Ill, Champaign; Chase Manhattan Bank, Chicago; Ill Acad Mathematics & Science, Aurora. *Comn:* Painting, Rochester State Bank, Ill, 74; painting of facade, Bank of Ind, Merrillville, 75; Dental Col, Southern Ill Univ, Alton. *Exhib:* Cult Ctr for Am Embassy, Paris, 71; Mus Art, Besancon, France, 72; Am Libr, Brussels, Belg, 73; Maison Descartes, Amsterdam, 73; Varieties of Visual Reality, Northern Ariz State Univ, 75; Am Exhib, Krannert Art Mus, Univ Ill, Urbana, 77. *Teaching:* Instr art, Birmingham Pub Schs, Ala, 56-58; asst prof art, Murray State Univ, 60-62; prof art emeritus, Univ Ill, Urbana-Champaign, 62-91. *Awards:* Second Award for Painting, Soc Four Arts, 73; Purchase Awards, Wabash Valley Ann, Terre Haute, 74 & Union League Club, Chicago, 74. *Bibliog:* Stephen Spector (auth), Super realists, Archit Dig, 11/12/74; G A Rodetis (auth), Varieties of visual reality, Northern Ariz Univ Art Gallery 1-3/75; Henry Adams (auth), A Tribute, Nelson Gallery, 84; Katherine Manthone (auth), The Other Shore: River Landscapes, 90; Eunice Agar (auth), Am Artists Mag, p 41-45, 8/92. *Mem:* Am Ceramics Circle. *Media:* Acrylic on Canvas. *Dealer:* Capricorn Gallery Bethesda MD. *Mailing Add:* 211 W Second St Madison IN 47250-3722

GUNTHER, CHARLES F
PRINTMAKER, CONSULTANT
b Poughkeepsie, NY, Apr 7, 33. *Study:* Williams Col, Williamstown, Mass, BA(art hist), 55; Univ Colo, Boulder, MFA(graphics & painting), 58. *Work:* Dallas Mus Fine Arts, Tex. *Exhib:* Nat Exhib Prints, Bay Printmakers Soc, 57; Ann Drawing & Small Sculpture, Ball State Art Gallery, Munie, Ind, 57; Exhib Oils, Missouri Valley, Mulvane Art Ctr, Topeka, Kans, 58; Soc Washington Printmakers, Smithsonian Inst, Washington, DC, 58; Midwest Biennial, Joslyn Art Mus, Omaha, Nebr, 58; Ohio Printmakers, Dayton Art Inst, 61; 5th Nat Exhib Contemp Art, Okla Art Ctr, Oklahoma City, 65; Nat Black & White Exhib, Kans State Univ, Manhattan, 66. *Teaching:* Instr introd art, Univ Toledo, Toledo Mus Art, 58-59, supvr art educ, 59-66, asst dir-educ, 66-85, dean adult educ, 85-89. *Media:* Woodcuts. *Publ:* Contribr Landscapes of Fancy and Freedom, 60, 1900-The American Scene, 64 & Nature and Her Moods, Mus News, Toledo Mus Art; auth, How glass; is made, 72 & Children and art, 73, Mus News, Toledo Mus Art. *Mailing Add:* 3011 Hopewell Pl Toledo OH 43606

GURBACS, JOHN JOSEPH
PAINTER, RESTORER
b Budapest, Hungary, Oct 31, 47; US citizen. *Study:* Miami-Dade Junior Col, AA, 68; Fla State Univ, BFA, 70; Univ SFla, 72-75, with Bruce March & Paul Sarkisian. *Work:* Fla State House of Reps & Fla Senate, Tallahassee; Univ Cent Fla, Orlando; Southern Bell, Jacksonville, Fla; Tampa Elec & Barnett Bank, Tampa. *Exhib:* American Painting, Soc Four Arts, Palm Beach, Fla, 75; Critic's Choice, 80 & Jim Rosenquist Invitational, 82, Artist Alliance Gallery, Tampa; Mus Choice, Loch Haven Art Ctr, Orlando, 81; New Talent Exhib, Barbara Gillman Gallery, Miami, Fla, 82; Triennial & Gasparilla's Best, Tampa Mus Fla, 85; Four Painters, Fla Ctr Contemp Art, 87; Fantasy Landscapes, Tampa Mus W, 87; Southern Arts Fed/Nat Endowment Arts Regional Fel Awards Exhib, Atlanta Sch Art, 87 & Ruth Eckerd Hall, Clearwater, Fla, 88; Scarfone Gallery, Univ Tampa, 88. *Pos:* Self-employed designer & artist, specializing in wall design & lettering, 77-86; exhib asst, Tampa Mus, 81-82; proj painter, Tampa Theater Restoration Proj, 81-84. *Awards:* Merit Award, Gulf Coast Art Ctr, 78; Individual Artist Fel, Fla Arts Coun, 85; Regional Fel Award, Southern Arts Fedn & Nat Endowment Arts, 86. *Bibliog:* Joanne Rodriquez (auth), Critic's Choice Exhibition, Tampa Tribune, 80; Robert Martin (auth), John Gurbacs exhibition, Tampa Times, 81; Audrey Lawler (auth), Local residents receive state grants, Carrollwood News, 85. *Media:* Acrylic, Oil. *Dealer:* Joan Hodgell Gallery 46 S Palm Ave Sarasota FL 33577. *Mailing Add:* 12711 North Blvd Tampa FL 33612

GURNEY, GEORGE
CURATOR, HISTORIAN
b Sharon, Conn, Nov 26, 39. *Study:* Brown Univ, BA, 62; Univ Pa, MA, 65; Univ Del, PhD, 78. *Collections Arranged:* Nineteenth Century Sculpture (auth, catalog), Nat Gallery Art, 74; Sculpture and the Federal Triangle, Nat Collection Fine Arts, 79; Elizabeth Catlett, 90. *Pos:* Guest cur, Nat Mus Am Art, Washington, DC, 77-82, assoc cur sculpture, 85- *Teaching:* Teaching asst art hist, Univ Pa, Philadelphia, 64-65; instr art hist, Univ Hartford, Conn, 65-66 & Sweet Briar Col, Va, 66-69. *Awards:* Nat Gallery Art Samuel H Kress Fel, 73-74; Nat Mus Am Art Smithsonian Res Fel, 74-75; Herbert Adams Memorial Medal, Nat Sculpture Soc, 87. *Mem:* Col Art Asn Am; Soc Archit Historians; Nat Sculpture Soc. *Res:* Nineteenth and twentieth century American sculpture; Archit Sculpture at World's Columbian Exposition, 1893. *Publ:* Contribr, Sculpture of a City: Philadelphia's Treasures in Bronze and Stone, Walker & Co, 74; Sculpture and the Federal Triangle, Nat Sculpture Rev, 79; Cast and Recast: The Sculpture of Frederic Remington, Smithsonian Press, 81; Sculpture and the Federal Triangle, Smithsonian Press, 85. *Mailing Add:* 2023 N Taylor St Arlington VA 22207

GURNEY, SUSAN ROTHWELL
LIBRARIAN
b Rockville Centre, NY, Nov 19, 51. *Study:* Conn Col, BA(art hist), 74; Univ Md, MLS, 80. *Pos:* Reference librn, Nat Mus Am Art/Nat Portrait Gallery Libr, Smithsonian Inst, 80-81, acting librn, 81-82, asst librn, 82- *Mem:* Art Libr Soc NAm (chap treas, 81); Col Art Asn. *Res:* Art serials and little magazines. *Interests:* American art. *Publ:* Auth, Bibliography of little magazines in the visual arts in the USA, Art Libr J, 81; coauth, Art Serials; Union List, Washington Art Libr Resources Comt, 81. *Mailing Add:* Smithsonian Inst Horticultural Libr Arts & Industry 900 Jefferson Dr SW Room 2282 Washington DC 20560

GURSOY, AHMET
PAINTER
b Turkey, Mar 5, 29; US citizen. *Study:* Tech Univ Istanbul, Turkey, 47-52; Ill Inst Technol, 54-56; Art Students League, 58-63. *Work:* Chase Manhattan Bank; Cornell Univ; St Lawrence Univ; Grey Gallery, NY Univ; Ulrich Mus, Wichita, Kans. *Exhib:* Wells Col, Aurora, NY, 77; Niagara Arts Ctr, Niagara Falls, NY, 77; Mohawk Valley Community Col, Utica, NY, 77; Nassau Community Col, Garden City, NY, 77; Hyden Collection, Glen Falls, NY, 77; and many others. *Awards:* Painting Prize, 21st Ann New Eng Exhib, Silvermine, Conn, 70. *Bibliog:* Grace Glueck (auth), article, New York Times, 68; C Giuliano (auth), article, 68 & Gordon Brown (auth), article, 70, Arts Mag. *Mem:* Fedn Mod Painters & Sculptors (pres, 75-); Silvermine Guild Artists; Music for People (treas, 71-72). *Media:* Oil. *Publ:* Auth, Convergence of Engineering & Art, 70. *Mailing Add:* 490 Bellwood Ave North Tarrytown NY 10591

GUSELLA, ERNEST
VIDEO ARTIST
b Calgary, Alta, Can, Sept 13, 41. *Study:* Alberta Col Art, dipl; Art Student League; San Francisco Art Inst, BFA & MFA. *Work:* Pompidou Ctr, Paris; Palais Des Beaux-Arts, Brussels; Mus Mod Art, New York; Tokyo Univ; Neuer Berliner Kunstverein, Berlin. *Exhib:* Spiral Gallery, Tokyo, 87; Alfred Univ, NY, 89; State Univ NY, Buffalo, 89; Contemp Arts, Santa Fe, 89; Lewbachhaus, Munich, 90. *Teaching:* Guest prof, State Univ NY, Buffalo, 84-86; guest artist, Allgemeine Geweres Chule, Basel, 90 & Univ Appl Art, Vienna, 90. *Awards:* Guggenheim Found Fel, 82-83; Canada Coun Grant, 85-86 & 90 & Checkerboard Grant, 87; Checkerboard Grant, 87. *Bibliog:* The 2nd Link, Banff, 83; Dis/Patches: The Learning Channel, 84; Review, Port Washington News, 85. *Mem:* Col Art Asn. *Media:* Video, Performance. *Publ:* Contribr, Kunst Und Video Book, Dumont Buchverlag, Koln, 83; Clip, Klapp, Bum, Dumont-Koln, 86. *Dealer:* Scan Gallery Tokyo Japan; The Tape Connection Rome Italy. *Mailing Add:* 118 Forsyth St 4th fl New York NY 10002

GUSSOW, ALAN
PAINTER, SCULPTOR
b Bronx, NY, May 8, 31. *Study:* Middlebury Col, BA, 52; Cooper Union, 52-53; Atelier 17 Graphic Workshop, 52-53. *Work:* Portland Mus Fine Art, Maine; Guild Hall, Easthampton, NY; Sheldon Mem Art Gallery, Lincoln, Nebr; Corcoran Gallery Art, Washington, DC; Va Mus Fine Art, Richmond. *Exhib:* Paintings of the Delaware Water Gap, Corcoran Art Gallery, Washington, DC, 75; Eight Sensibilities, Thorpe-Intermedia Gallery, Sparkhill, NY, 82; Common Ground, Gallery Am Indian Community House, New York, 83; Sea Strand Project, Dir, Huntington, New York, 83; The New Response: Contempt painters of the Hudson River, Albany Inst Hist & Art, 85; The World is Round: Contemp panoramas, travelling exhib, 88. *Pos:* Consult arts, Nat Park Serv, US Dept Interior, 70- *Teaching:* Vis prof, Iowa State Univ, Ames, 84 & Middlebury Col, Vt, 86; artist-in-residence, Am Acad Rome, Italy, 86-87; vis artist & sr lectr, Univ Calif, Santa Cruz, 75 & 82, Regents prof, 90, adj prof art & environ studies, 92. *Awards:* Prix de Rome in Painting, Am Acad Rome, Italy, 53-55; Award in Art, Am Acad & Inst Arts & Lett, 77. *Bibliog:* Diane Cochrane (auth), Alan Gussow revives the Hudson River School, Am Artist, 3/73; P Mainardi (auth), Alan Gussow: A Sense of Place, Art News, 11/75; M Sawin (auth), Alan Gussow, 4/80 & Alan Gussow: Objects of Power, Arts Mag, 3/84. *Mem:* Friends of the Earth, (bd dirs); Art pub places comt, Rockland County, NY. *Media:* Oil, Pastel; Wood. *Publ:* Auth, A sense of place: The artist and the American land, Saturday Rev Press, 72; The Use of Artists as Artists in the Struggle for Population Control, Population, Environment & People, McGraw, 72; We Are What We See, In: Encycl of Ecol & Pollution, North Am Publ, 72; The traumas and relief of leaving a gallery, Artworkers News, 2/81; A land we know but have not valued: Visions of new beauty in the Hudson River Valley (catalog essay), Albany Inst Hist & Art, 86. *Mailing Add:* 121 New York Ave Congers NY 10920

GUSSOW, ROY
SCULPTOR, ENVIRONMENTAL ARTIST
b Brooklyn, NY, Nov 12, 18. *Study:* With Archipenko, Chicago & Woodstock, NY, 46-47; Inst Design, Chicago, BS, 48, with Moholy-Nagy. *Work:* Whitney Mus Am Art, Mus Mod Art, Brooklyn Mus & Guggenheim Mus, New York; NC Mus Art, Raleigh. *Comn:* Stainless steel sculpture, Xerox Corp, Rochester, NY, 69; Stainless steel sculpture, New York Family Ctr Bldg, New York, 72; sculpture, Combustion Engine Corp, Stamford, Conn, 76; sculpture, City Reading, Pa, 78; sculpture, City Harrisburg, Pa, 83; and others. *Exhib:* Sculpture 1951, Metrop Mus Art, New York, 51; Pa Acad, Philadelphia, 51-59; NC Artists, NC Mus Art, Raleigh, 52-61; Whitney Mus Am Art, 56 & 62-68; solo show, Borgenicht Gallery, 64, 71, 73, 77, 80 & 87; Nat Gold Medal Exhib Bldg Arts, Archit League, New York, 62 & 65. *Teaching:* Instr design & sculpture, Bradley Univ, 48-49 & Colorado Springs Fine Arts Ctr, Colo, 49-51; prof design & sculpture, Univ NC Sch Design, 51-62; adj prof sculpture, Pratt Inst Sch Archit, 62-68, Columbia Univ Sch Art, 81-85; vis critic, Grad Sch Art, Univ Pa, 91-92. *Awards:* Purchase Awards, Ford Found, 60 & 62; First Prize, New York Family Ct Sculpture Competition, 72. *Mem:* Sculptors Guild (bd dirs, 67-, pres, 76-80); NY Artists Equity Asn (bd dirs, 77-, vpres, 80-82 & pres, 85-87); Fine Arts Fedn, NY (bd dirs, 87, vpres, 92). *Media:* Stainless Steel, Bronze. *Dealer:* Grace Borgenicht Gallery 724 Fifth Ave New York NY 10019. *Mailing Add:* 4040 24th St Long Island City NY 11101

GUSSOW, SUE FERGUSON
PAINTER, EDUCATOR
b Brooklyn, NY, Aug 2, 35. *Study:* Cooper Union, with Stefano Cusumano & Bob Gwathmey, dipl, 56; Columbia Univ, BS, 60; Tulane Univ, MFA, 64. *Work:* Cooper-Hewitt Mus, New York; Minn Mus Art, St Paul; Seattle Art Mus; Dallas Mus Fine Arts; New Orleans Mus Art; and others. *Comn:* Portrait, Judge William O'Hara, Criminal Courts Bldg, New Orleans, 69. *Exhib:* Print Biennial, Brooklyn Mus, 64; Drawings in St Paul, Minn Mus Art, 71-72; Benson Gallery, Bridgehampton, NY, 86; Benton Gallery, Southampton, NY, 87; Ctr Contemp Art, East Hampton, NY, 88; Marcelle Fine Arts, Southampton, NY, 89 & 90; Palace of Journalists, St Petersburg, Russia; and others. *Teaching:* Prof drawing, Cooper Union, 70- *Awards:* Solo Exhib Award, Artists of La, New Orleans Mus Art, 65; Purchase Prize, Drawings USA, Minn Mus Art, 66; Pamela Djerassi Vis Artist Grant, Stanford Univ, 82-83; and others. *Bibliog:* Ann Glenn Crowe (auth), A French Heritage, Art Week, 7/2/83; Cassandra Langer (auth), Mother & Child in Art, Random House, 92; Sue Ferguson Gussow (ed), Trees, The Coope Union, 85. *Media:* Oil, Pastel. *Mailing Add:* PO Box 1609 Amagansett NY 11930

GUSTAFSON, PIER
ASSEMBLAGE ARTIST
Study: Gustavus Adolphus Col, BS, 78; Univ Wis, MFA (painting), 82. *Work:* Mus Fine Arts, Boston, Mass; Minneapolis Inst Art, Minneapolis, Minn; Bank Boston, Boston, Mass; Pfeizer Chemical, New York. *Exhib:* Solo exhibs, Paper Constructions, 84, Installation: Suite in Sonata Form, 85 & Drapery Studies, 88, Gallery NAGA, Boston, Mass, Carnegie Gallery, Univ Maine, Orono, Maine, 86, Univ Gallery, Clark Univ, Worcester, Mass, 88 & Clark Gallery, Lincoln, Mass, 92; Recent Painting & Sculpture 1944-1984, Mus Fine Arts, Boston, Mass, 85; All that Jazz, Boston Visual Artists Union, Boston, Mass, 86; 50th Anniversary, Inst Contemp Art, Boston, Mass, 86; Affixion: Collage, Assemblage, Construction, Danforth Mus Art, Framington, Mass, 88; City Place Gallery, Artists Found, Boston, Mass, 90. *Awards:* Mass Artists Fel, 83 & 86; Nat Endowment Arts Fel, 86. *Bibliog:* David Bonetti (auth), Boston Phoenix, 11/88; Tom Grabosky (auth), Bay Windows, 11/17/88; Christine Temin (auth), Boston Globe, 11/17/88. *Mailing Add:* c/o Gallery NAGA 67 Newbury St Boston MA 02116

GUSTIN, CHRISTOPHER
CERAMIST
b Chicago, Ill. *Study:* Kansas City Art Inst, Mo, BFA (ceramics), 75; NY State Col Ceramics, Alfred, MFA (ceramics), 77. *Work:* Everson Mus Art, Syracuse, NY; Los Angeles Co Mus Art, Calif; RI Sch Design Art Mus, Providence; Victoria & Albert Mus, London, Eng; Ore State Univ, Corvallis; Kalamazoo Inst Arts, Mich; Rayovac Corp, Madison, Wis; Bank Boston, New Bedford, Conn. *Exhib:* Craft Today: Poetry of the Physical, Am Crafts Mus, New York, 86; 27th Ceramic Nat Exhib: Am Ceramics Now, Everson Mus Art, Syracuse, NY, 87; solo exhibs, Mc Gallery, Minneapolis, Minn, 87, Pro Art, St Louis, Mo, 88 & 89, Kalamazoo Inst Arts, Mich, 88, Miami Univ, Oxford, Ohio, 88 & Garth Clark Gallery, New York, 88, 90 & 91,; The Ceramic Nat, Southern Ill Univ Edwardsville, 88; Fourth Ann Monarch Tile Nat Ceramic Competition, San Angelo Mus Fine Arts, Tex, 89; The Eccentric Teapot, Garth Gallery, Los Angeles & New York, 89; Ceramica No A R Co, Museo do Azuleju, Lisbon, Port, 89; American Ceramics, Gallery Koyanagi, Tokyo, Japan, 90; Tea Pots, Swidler Gallery, Royal Oak, Mich, 90; Shigaraki Mus Ceramic Art, Japan, 92. *Pos:* Pres, bd dirs, Watershed Ctr Ceramic Arts, N Edgecomb, Maine, 87-90, adv bd, 90- *Teaching:* Instr crafts, Parsons Sch Design, New York, 78-80; asst prof, Boston Univ, Mass, 80-85; assoc prof ceramics, Swain Sch Design, New Bedford, Mass, 85-88 & Col Visual & Performing Arts, Univ Mass, Dartmouth, N Dartmouth, 88-; lectr, Centro de Arte e Comunicacáo Visual, Lisbon, Portugal, 92. *Awards:* Visual Artists Fel Grant, Nat Endowment Arts, 86; Crafts Fel, Mass Artists Found, 87; Purchase Awards, Everson Mus Art 87 & Southern Ill Univ Edwardsville, 88. *Bibliog:* The Book of Cups, Abbeville Press, 90; Clay Today; Contemporary Ceramists and Their Work, Chronicle Bks, San Francisco, 90; Susan Peterson (auth), The Craft and Art of Clay, Prentice Hall, NJ, 91. *Dealer:* Garth Clark Gallery 24 W 57 St New York NY 10019; Objects Gallery 341 W Superior Chicago, IL 60610. *Mailing Add:* 231 Horseneck Rd South Dartmouth MA 02748

GUTHMAN, LEO S
COLLECTOR
b Chicago, Ill. *Mem:* Gov life mem Art Inst Chicago; Soc Contemp Art, Chicago (dir); Art Collectors Club, New York; Art Club Chicago; Nat Collectors Comt, Nat Gallery Art, DC; and others. *Collection:* Contemporary painting, especially by Americans; international sculpture. *Mailing Add:* 1040 N Lake Shore Dr Apt 24-C Chicago IL 60611

GUTKIN, PETER
SCULPTOR, DESIGNER
b Brooklyn, NY, 1944. *Study:* Tyler Sch Art, Temple Univ, BFA, 66; San Francisco Art Inst, MFA, 68. *Work:* Temple Univ, Philadelphia; Oakland Mus, Calif; Best Products; Portland Mus Art, Ore; San Francisco Mus Mod Art; and others. *Comn:* NASA/Ames Res Ctr, 87. *Exhib:* Contemp Am Sculpture Ann, Whitney Mus Art, New York, 68 & Contemp Am Painting & Sculpture Biennial, 73; one-man shows, San Francisco Mus Art, 72, San Francisco Art Inst, 84 & Modernism 90, San Francisco; Contemporary American Painting & Sculpture, Krannert Art Mus, Champaign, Ill, 74; Menace, Mus Contemp Art, Chicago, 75; Sculpture in California 1975-1980, San Diego Mus Art, Calif, 80; American Pop Culture Today, Laforet Mus, Tokyo, Japan, 87; and others. *Teaching:* Instr, Aspen Sch Contemp Art, Colo, 66 & Univ Calif, Berkeley, 72-74, San Francisco Art Inst, 78, Calif Col of Arts & Crafts, 82. *Awards:* Nat Endowment Humanities & Art Award, 66; Purchase Prize, San Francisco Art Festival, 72; Nat Endowment Arts Fel, 82 & 84; Product Design Award, Resources Coun, 86. *Bibliog:* Article, Compressed constructions, spiderweb sculptures, Art News, 12/77; Howard Junker (auth), San Francisco, Peter Gutkin at 170 Capp St, Art Am, 5/80; Jerome Tarshis (auth), San Francisco, Peter Gutkin at the San Francisco Art Inst, Art in Am Mag, 10/84; Lois Wagner Green (auth), Site specific, Peter Gutkin takes a furniture commission full circle in residential designs for a San Francisco art patron, Interior Design Mag, 5/86. *Media:* Wood; Miscellaneous. *Publ:* Thomas Albright (auth), Art in the San Francisco Bay Area, Chronicle Publ; Denise Domerque (auth), Artists Design Furniture, Abrams Publ. *Mailing Add:* 170 Capp San Francisco CA 94110

GUTMANN, JOHN
EDUCATOR, PHOTOGRAPHER
b Breslau, Ger, May 28, 05. *Study:* State Acad Arts & Crafts, Breslau, BA; Inst Higher Educ Berlin, MA. *Work:* Boston Mus Fine Arts; Amon Carter Mus; Mus Mod Art, New York; San Francisco Mus Art; Nat Gallery, Canberra; Metrop Mus Art, New York; Houston Mus Fine Arts; and others. *Exhib:* San Francisco Mus Art; M H De Young Mem Mus Art, 38, 41 & 47; one-man shows, Light Gallery, New York, 74, As I Saw It, San Francisco Mus of Mod Art, 76, Castelli Gallery, New York, 79, 81 & 85 & Fraenkel Gallery, San Francisco, 80, 83, 85 & 88, Art Gallery Ont, 85; traveling exhib, 99 photographs, Am 34-54, Spain, 89-90; Beyond the Document, San Francisco Mus Art; Nymoma, Oberlin Col Art Gallery, Lacma, 89-91. *Teaching:* Prof art, Calif State Univ, San Francisco, 38-73, prof emer, 73- *Awards:* Guggenheim Fel, 78. *Mem:* Col Art Asn Am. *Publ:* Contribr, Life, Time, Asia, Sat Eve Post & other national and international magazines; producer & photographer of two documentary films on China, 50; auth, The Restless Decade Photographs of the Thirties, New York, 84; catalogue "Gutmann," Toronto, 85, 99 photographs, Am 34-54, Spain, 89. *Dealer:* Castelli Gallery New York NY. *Mailing Add:* c/o Fraenkel Gallery 49 Geary St San Francisco CA 94108

GUTMANN, JOSEPH
ART HISTORIAN, LECTURER
b Würzburg, Bavaria, Ger, Aug 17, 23; US citizen. *Study:* Temple Univ, BS, 49; NY Univ, with C R Morey, MA, 52; Hebrew Union Col, PhD, 60; Hebrew Union Col, DD, 84. *Teaching:* Assoc prof art hist, Hebrew Union Col, 60-69; prof emer art hist, Wayne State Univ, 69-89; prof, Univ Mich, 85, Spertus Col, 89 & Univ Windsor, Can, 90- *Awards:* Wayne State Univ Bd Gov Fac Recognition Award, 80; Gershenson Distinguished Fac Fel, 86-88. *Publ:* Hebrew Manuscript Painting, G Braziller, 78; Ancient Synagogues, 81 & The Dura-Europos Synagogue, 92, Scholars Press; The Jewish Sanctuary, E J Brill, 83; The Jewish Life Cycle, E J Brill, 87; Sacred Images, Variorum, 89. *Mailing Add:* 13151 Winchester Huntington Woods MI 48070

GUTZEIT, FRED
PAINTER, EDUCATOR
b Cleveland, Ohio. *Study:* Yale Norfolk Summer Sch, 61; Cleveland Inst Art, Mary C Paige Traveling Scholar, 62; Hunter Col, MA, 79. *Work:* Aldrich Mus, Ridgefield, Conn; Alternative Mus, New York; Fashion Moda; Cleveland Art Asn. *Exhib:* Biennial, Butler Inst Am Art, 65; Contemporary Images in Watercolor, Akron Art Inst, 76; solo exhibs, NY State Artist Series, Herbert F Johnson Mus, Cornell Univ, 77 & Distinguished Alumnus, Cleveland Inst Art, 77; Personal Visions, Places/Spaces, Bronx Mus Arts, 78; May Show, Cleveland Mus Art, 82; A Look Back, A Look Forward, Aldrich Mus, 82. *Teaching:* Instr painting, Philadelphia Col Art, 79-82, Brooklyn Mus Art Sch, 81-84 & Cleveland Inst Art, Lacoste, France, 84 & 85; vis assoc prof, Pratt Inst, 86- *Bibliog:* Patricia Eakins (auth), Fred Gutzeit: An organic approach to images, Am Artist Mag, 10/75 & article, Arts Mag, 4/77. *Media:* Acrylic, Watercolor. *Mailing Add:* 264 Bowery New York NY 10013

GUZAK, KAREN W
PAINTER, PRINTMAKER
b Cambridge, Mass, May 21, 39. *Study:* Univ Colo, BS, 61; Cornish Inst Arts, BFA, 76. *Work:* Brooklyn Mus, NY; Portland Art Mus, Ore; Whatcom Co Art Mus, Bellingham, Wash; New York Pub Libr Print Collection, NY; City of Seattle, Wash. *Comn:* Lithographs, Sheraton Hotel, Seattle, Wash, 84; painting, Physicians Surgical Ctr, Everett, Wash, 86; lithographs, Providence Hosp, Anchorage, Alaska, 87; painting, Spieker Partners, Bellevue, Wash, 88; wall sculpture, Southern Ore State Col, Ashland, 91. *Exhib:* 22nd Ann Print Show, Brooklyn Mus, NY, 81; Seattle Artists, San Francisco Mus Mod Art, Calif, 83; Seattle Style, Mus de Carcassonne, France, 87; Emerging Expressions, Bronx Mus Arts, NY, 87; Contemporary Survey, Cheney Cowles Mus, Spokane, Wash, 88; Northwest Watercolors, Bellevue Art Mus, Wash, 88; Siggraph Nat Computer Art Show, Boston, Mass, 89; Laura Russo Gallery, Portland, Ore, 91; Foster White Gallery, Seattle, Wash, 91; Boston Printmakers, 43rd Print Exhib, De Cordova Mus, Mass, 91; American Print Survey, Baylor Univ, 91. *Pos:* Art comnr, King Co Arts Comn, 81-86, Metro Transit Tunnel Art Comt, 85-90; developer, proj mgr & pres, Sunny Arms Artists' Coop, Seattle, Wash, 88-90. *Teaching:* instr, Univ Ore Workshop, High Tech/Low Tech, 89. *Bibliog:* Mery Lynn McCorkle (auth), Profile: Karen Guzak, AIP Newsletter, spring, 87; Marson Kennedy, The Karen Guzak Video, 87; Deloris Tarzan Ament (auth), Karen Guzak's exhib, Seattle Times, 12/20/87. *Mem:* Ctr Contemp Art (bd dirs, 87); Northwest Print Coun (bd dirs, 84-88); On the Boards (bd dirs, 87-90). *Dealer:* Davidson Galleries & Foster White Gallery 313 Occidental Ave S Seattle WA 98104. *Mailing Add:* Studio 5A 707 S Snoqualmie Seattle WA 98108

GUZEVICH-SOMMERS, KRESZENZ (CYNTHIA)
PAINTER, INSTRUCTOR
b Munich, Ger, May 24, 23; US citizen. *Study:* Acad Art, Munich; also with Frank Gervasi, Paul Strisik, Louis Krupp, Helen Van Wyk, Ramon Froman & Ken Gore. *Work:* First Nat Bank, Las Cruces, NMex; Truth or Consequences Mus, NMex. *Exhib:* El Paso Mus Art Exhib, Tex; Grand Nat Exhib, New York; Southwest Intercult Exhib, El Paso; Artists Equity Show, Albuquerque, NMex; Truth or Consequences Hist Mus. *Teaching:* Instr painting, workshops in var states & pvt studio, 65- *Awards:* Artist of Year & Best in Show Award, Black Range Artists, 68; Best in Show Award, NMex Art League, 69. *Mem:* Am Artists Prof League; El Paso Mus Art Asn; Artists Equity Asn; Accademia Italia Delle Arti e Del Lavoro. *Media:* Oil. *Mailing Add:* 1635 Country Club Circle Las Cruces NM 88001

GUZMAN-FORBES, ROBERT
PAINTER, ILLUSTRATOR
b New York, NY, July 11, 29. *Study:* Univ Va, with John Canaday, BFA; Art Instr Inst, scholar; Sch Visual Arts, with Al Werner & Burne Hogarth, cert. *Work:* Univ Va Mus Fine Arts, Charlottesville; Conn Humane Soc, Newington; Baltimore City Ct House, Md. *Comn:* Animal portrait, comn by Mrs Anthony Biddle Duke, Jr, New York, 69; portrait of Alan H Murrell, attorney, 72 & Solomon Liss, Judge, 73, Saints & Sinners of Baltimore; Harris T Whittemore II, comn by Harris T Whittemore III, Middlebury, Conn, 75; animal portrait, comn by Kenneth E Keating, Simsbury, Conn, 79; DeRoy C Thomas, West Hartford, Conn, 89. *Exhib:* Old State House, Hartford, Conn, 80; Art Ctr, Old Lyme, Conn, 81; Saltbox Gallery, West Hartford, Conn, 81; Ethel Walker Sch Gallery, Simsbury, Conn, 81; Hartford Civic Ctr, Conn, 81; Conn Acad Fine Arts, Hartford, 84; Mus Am Political Life, Univ Hartford, West Hartford, Conn, 90. *Pos:* Freelance art dir, adv & educ, currently. *Teaching:* Pvt study at home in studio-residence. *Awards:* People's Choice Award, Animals in Art Exhib, Old State House, Hartford & Conn Humane Soc Centennial, Conn, 81. *Bibliog:* K Cassidy (auth), The fine art of Robert G Forbes, Twin Circle Cath Newspaper, 71; article in Christian Sci Monitor; Mary E Renn (auth), Animal art, My Weekly Reader, Xerox Educ Group, 75. *Mem:* Danbury Mint, Norwalk, Conn, 90. *Media:* Pastel, Watercolor. *Publ:* Contribr, Catmopolitan, Pocket Books, New York, 87. *Dealer:* Arts Universal Res Assocs Inc 275 Steele Rd West Hartford CT. *Mailing Add:* 23 Latimer Lane Simsbury CT 06070

GYERMEK, STEPHEN A
EDUCATOR
b Budapest, Hungary, Nov 9, 30. *Study:* Rijks Akad voor Beeldende Kunsten, Amsterdam, Holland, with Heinrich Campendonk; Academia de Bellas Artes Madrid, Spain; Univ Okla. *Comn:* Murals, Convent at Madrid, Spain, 55 & US Embassy, Spain, 55; stained glass windows, St Gregory's Abbey, Shawnee, Okla & St Benedict Church, Ada, Okla. *Exhib:* Amsterdam, 52-53; Madrid, 54; Okla Art Ctr, 60. *Collections Arranged:* Archaeology, Europe, Near & Far East, Egypt; American Indians & Central & South American Ethnology; Paintings from the Italian Renaissance; 19th Century American Paintings; plus others. *Pos:* Dir, Gerrer Mus & Art Gallery, Shawnee, Okla, 57-62; actg dir, Stovall Mus Sci & Hist, Univ Okla, 62-65; dir, Pioneer Mus & Haggin Art Galleries, Stockton, Calif, 65-70. *Teaching:* Lectr painting methods & religious art; asst prof art hist & art, Univ Okla; instr art hist, San Joaquin Delta Col, 67- *Awards:* Prizes & Van Alabbe Award, Amsterdam, Holland, 52. *Mailing Add:* Dept Art San Joaquin Delta Col 5151 Pacific Ave Stockton CA 95207

GYRA, FRANCIS JOSEPH, JR
INSTRUCTOR, PAINTER
b Newport, RI, Feb 23, 14. *Study:* RI Sch Design, dipl, hon BFA, 90; Parsons Sch Design, Paris, cert advert illus & X Ital Res Sch; Brighton Col Arts & Crafts, Sussex, Eng; Froebel Inst, Roehampton, Eng; Univ Hawaii; McNeese State Col; Keene State Col, BS. *Work:* Providence Art Mus, RI; Tenn Fine Arts Ctr, Nashville. *Exhib:* Int Watercolor Exhib, Art Inst Chicago, 38 & 40; First Int Ann, Marietta Col, Ohio, 69; First Art Ann, Northern New Eng, Canaan, NH, 69; Stratton Arts Festival, Vt, 70; Eighth Exhib Vt Artists, Norwich Univ, 71. *Pos:* Chmn, Vt Educ Asn Prog, 52; adv art & art educ, Aquinas Jr Col, Nashville, 66- *Teaching:* Supv, Woodstock Union & Dist Schs, Vt, 49-69; dir art workshops, Vt State Dept Educ, 54-70; art educator, Woodstock Sch Dist, 69-84; retired. *Awards:* Recognition Reward, Nat Endowment Arts, 80; Vt State Teacher of Yr, 83; New Eng Art Educ Conf Award, Vt, 83. *Mem:* Woodstock Design Review Bd; life fel Int Inst Arts & Lett. *Media:* Oil, Varnish. *Publ:* Coauth, Vermont Art Guide for the Classroom Teacher K-6, 69. *Mailing Add:* 6 Linden Hill PO Box 540 VT 05091

H

HAACK, CYNTHIA R
PAINTER, PRINTMAKER
b Eagle Bend, Minn. *Study:* St Cloud State Univ, Minn, AE, 53; Univ Wyo, Laramie, 54; Idaho State Col, Pocatello, 57-58. *Work:* Wachovia Bank; Nationsbank; Glaxo Pharmaceuticals. *Exhib:* Ann Small Painting Exhib, Albany Inst Hist & Art, 69; Tidewater Artists Biennial, Chrysler Mus, Norfolk, Va, 70-74; Invitational, Winston-Salem Arts & Sci Gallery, NC, 79; RSVP Ann Show, Pittsburgh, 86-88; NC Watercolor Soc, 90 & 91; and others. *Teaching:* Private lessons, 61-66; instr painting, Rawls Mus, Courtland, Va, 72-73; private lessons painting, 61-66. *Awards:* First Place, Southside Artists, Rawls Mus, 73-74; Merit Award, GCA, 90-91; ArtFest of Matthews Purchase Award, 90-92; and others. *Bibliog:* Staff, Southside scenes, Daily Press Newspaper, 73; Barclay Sheaks (auth), Landscape illusion, 73; Lynn Bonney (auth), Travels inspire art, Emporia Gazette, 81. *Mem:* Charlotte Art League (74-93); Guild of Charlotte Artists (74-93); NC Watercolor Soc (90-93); and others. *Media:* Acrylic. *Dealer:* Seaside Art Gallery PO Box 1 Nags Head NC 27959. *Mailing Add:* 9400 Marshbrooke Rd Charlotte NC 28105

HAACKE, HANS CHRISTOPH
SCULPTOR, CONCEPTUAL ARTIST
b Cologne, Ger, Aug 12, 36. *Study:* Staatl Werkakademie, Kassel, Ger, MFA; Atelier 17, Paris, with S W Hayter; Tyler Sch Art, Philadelphia; Hon DFA, Oberlin Col, 91. *Work:* Centre Georges Pompidou, Paris; Tate Gallery, London; Mod Museet, Stockholm; Art Gallery Ont, Toronto; Nat Gallery Can, Ottawa; Tate Gallery, London, Eng; Centre Georges Pompidou, Paris. *Exhib:* Avant garde in 80's, Los Angeles Co Mus Art, 87; Committed to Print, Mus Mod Art, 88; Image World, Art & Media Culture, Whitney Mus, 89; Endlichkeit der Freiheit, Berlin, 90; Argus Ange, Munich, 91; Inheritance & Transformation, Irish Mus Mod Art, Dublin, 91; Pour la Suite du Monde, Musé d'art Contemporain, Montreal, 92; Territorium Artis, Bundes Kunsthalle Bonn, 92; and others. *Teaching:* Prof art, Cooper Union, 67- *Awards:* Guggenheim Fel, 73; Nat Endowment Arts Fel, 78; Distinguished Artist Award for Lifetime Achievement, Col Art Asn, 91. *Bibliog:* Jack Burnham (auth), Hans Haacke's cancelled show at the Guggenheim, Artforum, 5/71; Douglas Crimp, Yve-Alain Bois, Rosalind Krauss (interview), October, Vol 30, fall 84; Benjamin Buchlon (auth), Hans Haacke: memory and instrumental reason, Art Am, 2/88. *Media:* All. *Publ:* Auth, Framing and Being Framed, NS Col Art & Design Press & New York Univ Press, 75; Working conditions, Artforum, summer 81; Museums, Managers of consciousness, Art in Am, 84; In the Vice, Art J, fall, 91. *Mailing Add:* c/o John Weber Gallery 142 Greene St New York NY 10012

HAAR, FRANCIS
PHOTOGRAPHER, FILMMAKER
b Csernatfalu, Hungary, July 19, 08; US citizen. *Study:* Nat Acad Decorative Arts, Budapest, Hungary, Master Photog. *Work:* Victoria-Albert Mus, London; Mus Mod Art, New York; Honolulu Acad Arts. *Comn:* The Arts of Japan (film), US Info Agency, Tokyo, Japan, 53; Ukiyoe, Japanese Print (film), Art Inst Chicago, 59; Hoolaulea (dance film), Honolulu Acad Arts, 60; Japan's Cultural History, Fuji TV Co, Tokyo, 64. *Exhib:* Art Inst Chicago, 56; Ind Univ, Bloomington, 61; one-man shows, Honolulu Acad Arts, 70 & Contemp Arts Ctr, Honolulu, 71. *Teaching:* Lectr photog, summer courses, Univ Hawaii, 62-64. *Awards:* Golden Eagle Award for Pineapple Country Hawaii, 63 & Hawaii's Asian Heritage, 66, Coun Int Nontheatrical Events, Washington, DC; Golden Eagle Award for Pineapple Country Hawaii, 63 & Hawaii's Asian Heritage, 66, Coun Int Nontheatrical Events, Washington, DC; designated Living Treasure of Hawaii, 84. *Mem:* Painters & Sculptors League; Honolulu Printmakers; Honolulu Acad Arts; Asn Hawaiian Artists. *Publ:* Auth, Around Mount Fuji, 41, Benlido Publ Co, Kyoto, Japan; auth, The Best of Old Japan, 49, coauth, Japanese Theatre in Highlights, 51 & Geisha of Pontocho, 53, C Tuttle Publ Co, Tokyo; coauth, Artists of Hawaii, Vols I & II, Univ Hawaii, 74; coauth (with C Black), Iolani Luahine; auth, A Zen Life: DT Suzuki Remembered, Wreatherhill Co, Tokyo-NY, 80. *Mailing Add:* 4236 Carnation Pl Honolulu HI 96816

HAAR, TOM
PHOTOGRAPHER, FILMAKER
b Tokyo, Japan, June 2, 41; US citizen. *Study:* San Francisco State Col, BA, 64; Univ Hawaii, MFA, 67; Alexei Bradovitch Design Lab, scholar, 68; Int Ctr Photog Advan Workshop, scholar, 75. *Work:* Hawaii State Found Cult & Arts, Contemp Mus. *Exhib:* solo exhibs, Green Collections Gallery, Tokyo, 80, Capen Gallery, State Univ NY, Buffalo, 81, Hamanoya Gallery, Tokyo, 81, Space Art Gallery, Seoul, Korea, 83, Amono Gallery Osaka, Japan, 83, Univ Tsukuba Gallery, Japan, 84 & Nagase Photo Salon, Tokyo, Japan, 86; Three Photographers: Tom Hoor, Lisa Kanemoto and Aaron Dygart, Honolulu Acad Arts, Graphic Gallery, 87; The Second Ann Flora Ho'omaluhia, Ho'omaluhia, Hawaii, 87; Koa Gallery, Kapiolani Community Col, 88; On/Off Paper - An Alumni Exhib, Univ Hawaii Art Gallery, 88; traveling exhibs, Artist of Hawaii, Honolulu Acad Arts, 88, Our Elders, Ourselves: Hawaii 1890-1990, funded by Hawaii Comt Humanities, 90, Budapest Art Gallery, Hungary, 91, Gallery Saka, Tokyo, Japan, 91 & Image XVIII, Amfac Plaza Exhib Rm, 92; and others. *Teaching:* Instr photog, Haystack Mountain Sch Crafts, Maine, 73 & 80; instr photog, Univ Hawaii, 74; vis prof photog, Seoul Inst Arts, Korea, 83 & Univ Tsukuba, Japan, 84-86; lectr photog, Kapiolani Community Col, Hawaii, 87-90. *Awards:* Grants, Japan Found & Ishibashi Found, 79, Univ Tsukuba Proj Grant, 84 & Asian Cult Coun Proj Grant, 85. *Publ:* Auth, Color Communication (film), Univ Hawaii, 67; asst dir, Artists of Hawaii (film), Honolulu, 9/75; producer & dir, Festival at Mizumi (film), Japan, 79; dir & camera, PLPL (film), Miami, 82; ed & chief planner, Photo Newsletter (article), Gallery Min, Tokyo, 86-87. *Mailing Add:* 1650 St Louis Dr Honolulu HI 96816

HAAS, RICHARD JOHN
PRINTMAKER, MURALIST
b Spring Green, Wis, Aug 29, 36. *Study:* Univ Wis, Milwaukee, BA, 59; Univ Minn, MFA, 64. *Work:* Mus Mod Art, Metrop Mus Art & Whitney Mus Am Art, New York; Yale Univ Art Gallery, New Haven, Conn; Walker Art Ctr, Minneapolis; St Louis Mus Art, Mo; Brooklyn Mus Art, NY. *Comn:* Murals, Edison Brothers Stores, Inc, St Louis, Mo, 84; murals, Fountainbleau Hilton Hotel, Miami Beach, Fla, 86; murals, Tarrant Co Civil Courthouse Annex, Fort Worth, Tex, 88; murals, Sovereign Hotel Bldg, Ore Hist Soc, Portland, 89; murals, Home Savings of Am, Pasadena Tower, Calif, 90. *Exhib:* Norton Gallery & Sch Art, West Palm Beach, Fla, 77; Galerie Biedermann, Munich, Ger, 78; San Francisco Mus Mod Art, Calif, 80; Rhona Hoffman Gallery, Chicago, 83, 90; Currents, 27, St Louis Mus Art, 84; Robert Martin Gallery, White Plains, NY, 86; Williams Col Mus Art, Williamstown, Mass, 87; Nat Acad Design, New York, 87; Hudson River Mus, New York, 88, Col Art Gallery. *Pos:* New York City Art Comn, 76-79; bd mem, Pub Art Fund, 80- & Preservation League, NY, 83-; bd governors, Skowhegan Bd Art, 80-; bd trustees, Hudson River Mus, 89-; adv bd, Billboard Mus Mod Art, 90- *Teaching:* Instr art, Univ Minn, 63-64; asst prof art, Mich State Univ, 64-68; instr printmaking, Bennington Col, 68-80; fac fine arts, Sch Visual Arts, 77-81. *Awards:* Medal Honor, Am Inst Archit, 77; Nat Endowment Arts Printmaking Grant, 78; Guggenheim Fel, 83; Doris C Freedman Award, 89. *Bibliog:* David Dillon (auth), Creating a whole new building solely with paint, Architecture, 11/88; Paul Goldberger (auth), The healing murals of Richard Haas, New York Times, 1/10/89; Amalie R Rothschild (auth), Painting the Town - The Illusionistic Murals of Richard Haas (film), 90. *Mem:* Archit League (vpres, 78-); Century Club. *Media:* Intaglio; Watercolor. *Publ:* Auth, An Architecture of Illusion, Rizzoli Publ, New York, 81. *Dealer:* Brooke Alexander 24 E 78th St New York NY 10021; Rhona Hoffman Gallery 215 West Superior Chicago IL 60610. *Mailing Add:* 361 W 36th St No 5A New York NY 10018

HABENICHT, WENDA
SCULPTOR
b Elkhart, Ind, June 7, 56. *Study:* Beloit Col, Wis, BA, 74-79; New York Studio Sch Drawing, Painting & Sculpture, 79; Columbia Univ, New York, MFA, 81. *Work:* Va Ctr Creative Arts, Sweet Briar; Long Island Univ, CW Post Campus, Brookville, NY. *Comn:* Site specific sculpture, Red River Revel Arts, Shreveport, La, 85; site specific sculpture, Oper Greenthumb, New York, 87. *Exhib:* The Ways of Wood, Queens Col, NY, 84; Sculpture: The Language of Scale, Bruce Mus, Greenwich, Conn, 85; The Chair Fair, Int Design Ctr, Long Island, NY, 86; Outdoor Sculpture, Connemara Conserv Found, Allen Tex, 86; The Engaging Object, The Clocktower, Inst Arts & Urban Resources, New York, 86; 10th Ann Sculpture Exhib, Snug Harbor Cult Ctr, Staten Island, NY, 87; Artists Choose Artists, Socrates Sculpture Park, Long Island, 87; Dream Retreat-City of Tilted Towers, Toronto Sculpture Garden, Can, 89. *Bibliog:* Michael Benson (auth), City as sculpture

garden, New York Times, 87; Tiffany Bell (auth), Insight on Site (exhib catalog), Hillwood Art Gallery, Long Island Univ, 88; Connie Hitzeroth (auth), Habenichts inviting retreat, Now, Toronto, 89. *Mem:* Int Sculpture Ctr, Washington, DC. *Media:* Wood, Miscellaneous Media. *Mailing Add:* RD1, Box 203 Worchester NY 12197

HABER, IRA JOEL
SCULPTOR, WRITER
b Brooklyn, NY, Feb 24, 47. *Work:* NY Univ Art Collection; Nueu Gallerie, Ludwig Collection, Aachen, Ger; Guggenheim Mus, New York; Hirshhorn Mus, Washington, DC; Albright-Knox Art Gallery, Buffalo, NY. *Exhib:* Information, Mus Mod Art, New York, 70; Whitney Mus Ann Sculpture Exhib, New York, 70; three one-man shows, Fischbach Gallery, New York, 71-74; Whitney Mus Contemp Art Biennial, 73; retrospective, Kent State Univ Art Gallery, 77, State Univ NY, Stony Brook, 81 & Philadelphia Art Alliance, 84; Tableaux Constructions, Univ Calif, Santa Barbara, 77; Pam Adler Gallery, New York, 78-80 & 82; Eight Sculptors, Albright-Knox Art Gallery; 1979 Street Sights, Inst Contemp Art, Philadelphia, 80; 55 Mercer St Gallery, 91. *Teaching:* Instr sculpture, Fordham Univ, 71-74; assoc prof, State Univ NY Stony Brook, 81; vis lectr, Univ Calif, San Diego, 82-84, Ohio State Univ, Columbus, 84. *Awards:* Creative Artists Pub Serv Grant, 74-75 & 76-77; Nat Endowment Arts Fel, 74-75, 77-78 & 83-84; Pollack-Krasner Fel, 86. *Bibliog:* Corrinne Robins (auth), Ira Joel Haber, Arts Mag, 11/77; Robert Berlind (auth), Ira Joel Haber at Pam Adler, Art in Am, 12/79; April Kingsley (auth), article, 9/80, Alex Gildzen (auth), article, 5/82 & William Schwedler (auth), article, 4/83, Arts Mag. *Media:* Mixed. *Publ:* Auth, Radio City Music Hall, 69; Five stories of the Music Hall, St Marks Poetry Proj, 73; Some thoughts on camouflage by John Perreault, Serif-Lit Quart, Kent State Univ, 74; M E Thelen Gallery Piece, Tri-Quarterly, 75; Some reasons why I do what I do, Appearances, Vol 1, 77. *Mailing Add:* 105 W 27th St New York NY 10001

HABERGRITZ, GEORGE JOSEPH
PAINTER, SCULPTOR
b New York, NY, June 16, 09. *Study:* Nat Acad Design; Cooper Union, grad; Acad Grande Chaumiere. *Work:* Butler Mus, Youngstown, Ohio; Wilberforce Univ, Ohio; Purdue Univ, Ind; Safad Mus, Israel; Jewish Mus, London. *Exhib:* Va Biennial, Richmond, 40; Am Watercolor Soc Ann, 47-49; Nat Asn Painters Casein, 47-74; Nat Acad Design Drawing & Painting Ann, 48-51; Univ Mont; Okla State Mus; Evansville Mus, Ind; Detroit Gallery of Fine Arts; Gallery Meindel & El Callejon Gallery, Bogota, Colombia, 74-77. *Pos:* Dir, Sch Continuing Art Educ, 68- *Teaching:* Lectr artist in Africa, SPac & India, 57-; instr painting, Art Students League, 60-64 & Friend Sch Art, 65-69; instr new media, Workshop Prof Artists, 67- *Awards:* Gold Medal for Drawing, Nat Acad Design, 38; Grumbacher Awards, Nat Soc Painters Casein, 68, 70, 72 & 74. *Bibliog:* G Klotz (auth), Two American artists, Galerie Klotz, Stuttgart, 67. *Mem:* Nat Soc Painters Casein (pres, 63-64). *Mailing Add:* 32 Morton St New York NY 10014

HACK, PHILLIP S & PATRICIA Y
COLLECTORS
Mr Hack, b Ill, Dec 8, 16; Mrs Hack, b Los Angeles, Calif, Dec 21, 26. *Study:* Univ Ariz; Stanford Univ; Oxford Univ; Ariz State Univ; Wabash Col; Purdue Univ. *Collection:* Contemporary paintings, sculpture, prints and drawings. *Mailing Add:* 7370 E Krall Scottsdale AZ 85250

HACKENBROCH, YVONNE ALIX
CURATOR, WRITER
b Frankfurt, Ger, Apr 27, 12; US citizen. *Study:* Univ Frankfurt, 32-33; Univ Rome, 33-34; Univ Munich, PhD(summa cum laude), 36. *Pos:* Asst dept Brit & medieval antiq, Brit Mus, London, 36-45; cur, Lee Fareham Collection, Univ Toronto, 45-49; cur, Irwin Untermyer Collection & cur, Western European Arts, Metrop Mus Art, 49- *Awards:* Ford Found Grant, 63; Fel Soc Antiquaries, London, 87; Verdienst Kreuz Am Bande Boron, 88. *Res:* Decorative arts. *Publ:* Auth, seven catalogues of the Irwin Untermyer Collection; contribr, Connoisseur & other mag; Bull, Metrop Mus Art; Renaissance Jewellery, London, 79; Reinhold Vasters Journal, Metrop Mus Art, New York, 86; Jewels of Anna Maria Luisa de Medici, ruseo digli Argenti catalog, Florence, 89. *Mailing Add:* Flat 4 31 Hyde Park Gardens London W2 2ND England United Kingdom

HACKETT, DWIGHT VERNON
PUBLISHER, DIRECTOR
b Modesto, Calif, Mar 21, 45. *Study:* San Francisco Art Inst, Calif. *Pos:* Manager, bronze casting, Nambe Mills Inc, Santa Fe, NMex, 71-80; dir, Art Foundry Inc (d/b/a/ Art Foundry Editions), Santa Fe, NMex, 80- *Media:* Cast Metal. *Mailing Add:* PO Box 8107 Santa Fe NM 87504-8107

HACKETT, MICKEY
PAINTER, EDUCATOR
b Louisville, Ky. *Study:* Univ Louisville, Univ Tex, 48. *Work:* Brown-Williamson Corp, Brown Forman Distilleries, Univ Louisville, Ky; Philip Morris Corp; Ala Power Co; and others. *Comn:* Convention cover, Ky Bankers Asn, 81, 83 & 85. *Exhib:* Ky W C Soc; Aqueous, Catherine Lorillard-Wolfe, Nat Arts Club, New York, 80-82; Patron's Gala, Okla; J B Speed Mus; Watermedia 83, Mont; Milford Fine Arts Ctr; and many others. *Pos:* Interior designer, George Fetter Co, Louisville, 65-69. *Teaching:* Instr adult educ, Jefferson Co Bd Educ, Ky, 76-; instr watercolor tech, Jefferson Community Col, Univ Ky, 78-82; instr, var workshops for artists, currently. *Awards:* Purchase Awards, Metrop Life Insurance Co, 85, Beacon Insurance Co, 88, Ind Chautauqua Arts, 89, Bank One, Ohio, 90, Magna Bank, Ill, Olan Mills & Otterbein Col, Ohio. *Mem:* Am Soc Artists; Ky Watercolor Soc (found mem); Mini Art Societies, Washington, DC, Fla, NJ & Mont; Nat Soc Painters, Sculptors & Gravers, Washington, DC; and others. *Media:* Watercolor, Acrylic. *Publ:* Limited Edition Prints & Posters, 92. *Mailing Add:* 1901 Woodfield Rd Louisville KY 40220

HACKLER, MITSUNO ISHII See Reedy, Mitsuno Ishii (Mitsuno Ishii Hackler)

HACKLIN, ALLAN DAVE
PAINTER, SCULPTOR
b New York, NY, Feb 11, 43. *Study:* Pratt Inst. *Work:* Whitney Mus Am Art, New York; Dallas Mus Fine Arts; Allen Mus, Oberlin, Ohio; Mus Fine Arts, Houston; NC Mus Art; Aldrich Mus Am Art. *Exhib:* Whitney Mus Am Art, 67; Meredith Long Gallery, 86 & 87; solo exhib, Meadows Mus, 87. *Pos:* Dir, Glassell Sch Art, Mus Fine Arts, Houston, 82-88. *Teaching:* Instr painting, Pratt Inst, 69-70; instr painting, Calif Inst Arts, 70-77; vis prof, Cooper Union, 77-80; vis prof, RI Sch Design, 79-82, chmn, Painting Dept, 80-82; Meadows Prof, Southern Methodist Univ, 87, chmn, Visual Arts Dept, 89- *Awards:* Nat Endowment Arts, 75, 80 & 84. *Publ:* Auth, article, Artforum, 67. *Mailing Add:* Sch of the Arts Columbia Univ 617 Dodge Hall 116th St & Broadway New York NY 10027

HADEN, EUNICE (BARNARD)
PAINTER, ILLUSTRATOR
b Washington, DC, Oct 21, 01. *Study:* Oberlin Col, BA; Abbott Sch Art, with Hugo Inden; also with Eliot O'Hara. *Comn:* Boookplate designs for individuals. *Exhib:* Ann Int Exhib, Miniature Painters, Sculptors & Gravers Soc, 39-91; Nat Collection Fine Arts, 53-56; Area Show, Corcoran Gallery Art, 55-56; Burr Gallery, New York, 59 & 60; solo exhib, Payne Gallery, Washington, DC, 64; Gallery on the Landing, Ft Wayne, Ind, 77; Art Contemp, Bathesda, Md, 81; and others. *Awards:* Awards, Arts Club Washington, 56, 59, 64 & 66; Miniature Painters, Sculptors & Gravers Soc Awards, 66, 68, 78, 79 & 86; Second Prize, Nat League Am Pen Women, 81 & 83. *Mem:* Minature Painter, Sculptors & Gravers Soc (pres, 60-64, recorder, 82-83); Arts Club Washington (chmn, 61-62, bd gov, 64-68); Order Descendants Colonial Gov (nat treas, 80-83); Nat League Am Pen Women; 50 yr mem Nat Soc Daughters Am Revolution. *Media:* Watercolor; Ink. *Publ:* Auth & ed, DAR Patriot Index, first Vol, 67, suppl, 69 & 82, Vol II, 80, Vol III, 86; auth & ed, Am Clan Gregor Soc Yearbks, 68-79 & 81-83. *Mailing Add:* 5112 Connecticut Ave NW Washington DC 20008

HADFIELD, TED LEE
SCULPTOR
b Flint, Mich, May 8, 50. *Study:* Mott Community Col, AA, 70; Colo State Univ, BFA, 78; Cranbrook Acad Art, MFA, 80. *Work:* Mott Community Col; Colo State Univ Art Gallery; Ingles & Assoc Design Firm; Uniprop Corp. *Comn:* Chair design, Artists Interpret Utility. *Exhib:* Marietta Nat, 79; Westwood Clay Nat, Otis Parsons Gallery, Los Angeles, 80; Variations in Clay, GMB Gallery, Birmingham, Mich, 82; Michigan Artists 80-82, Detroit Inst Art, 82; Cranbrook Ceramics 1950-1980, Cranbrook Mus, 83; Drawing with Space, Midland Mus, Mich, 84; New Vistas in Clay, Pewabic Pottery, Detroit, 84; Update, Detroit Artists, Mich, 86. *Pos:* Co-owner, Artpack Servs Co Art Installations, 81- *Awards:* Mich Coun Arts Grant, 84-85. *Bibliog:* Michigan artists, article in Detroit News, 7/81; Artists studio, Detroit Free Press, 8/86. *Media:* Mixed. *Mailing Add:* c/o Feigenson Preston Gallery 796 N Woodard Birmingham MI 48009

HADZI, DIMITRI
SCULPTOR, PRINTMAKER
b New York, NY, Mar 21, 21. *Study:* Cooper Union, cert, 50; Brooklyn Mus Art Sch, 48-50; Polytechnion, Athens, Greece, 50-51; Harvard Univ, hon MA, 77; Lawrence Univ, Hon DFA, 87. *Work:* Mus Mod Art, Guggenheim Mus & Whitney Mus Am Art, New York; Fogg Art Mus, Harvard Univ, Cambridge, Mass; Hirshhorn Mus, Washington, DC. *Comn:* Arcturus, Fed Reserve Bank Bldg, Minneapolis, 71-72; basalt & granite intarsia, Johnson Wax, Racine, Wis, 78-79; Bishop's Triad, Dallas Ctr, Tex, 79-80; Propylaea (granite fountain), Owens-Illinois Co, Toledo, Ohio, 80-81; Copley Place (stone foundation), Boston, 82-83; Harvard Sq, Cambridge, Mass, 85. *Exhib:* Recent Sculpture USA, Mus Mod Art, New York, 59; Pittsburgh Int, Carnegie Inst, Pa, 61 & 64; Venice Biennale, American Pavilion, 62; Richard Gray Gallery, Chicago, 71, Mekler Gallery, Los Angeles, 78 & Gruenebaum Gallery, New York, 78, 82 & 84; Joseph H Hirshhorn Collection, Guggenheim Mus, New York, 62 & Art in Am Since World War II, 79; Middleheim Park, Antwerp, Holland, 71; Obelisco Gallery, Rome, 74; Sculptors, Boston Athenaeum, 82; The Unique Print, Mus Fine Arts, Boston, 90. *Teaching:* Artist in residence, Dartmouth Col, summer 69; Int Sculpture Symposium, Univ Ore, Eugene, 74; prof emeritus, Dept Visual & Environment Studies, Harvard Univ. *Awards:* Fulbright Fel, 50; Guggenheim Fel, 57; St Gaudens Medal, The Cooper Union, 89. *Bibliog:* Albert Elsen (auth), Sculpture with a memory, Art News, 9/78; Joseph Masheck (auth), Dimitri Hadzi's Omphalos for Harvard Square, Arts Mag, 5/86; Gerald Nordland (auth), Dimitri Hadzi at Harvard, Exhib Catalog, Cambridge, Mass, 89. *Mem:* Am Acad Arts & Sci, 78; Am Acad & Inst Arts & Lett, 83. *Media:* Bronze, Stone. *Publ:* Illusr, Hellas, 71; The Venetian Vespers, Godine Press, 79. *Dealer:* Kouros Gallery 23 E 73 New York NY 10021; Richard Gray Gallery 620 N Michigan Chicago IL 60611. *Mailing Add:* c/o Levinson Kane Gallery 14 Newbury St Boston MA 02116

HAERER, CAROL
PAINTER
b Salina, Kans, Jan 23, 33. *Study:* Doane Col; Univ Nebr, BFA; Art Inst Chicago; Univ Calif, Berkeley, MA. *Work:* Whitney Mus Am Art, Guggenheim Mus & Brooklyn Mus, NY; Oakland Art Mus, Calif; Sheldon Mem Art Galleries, Lincoln, Nebr; Univ Kansas, Lawrence; and others. *Comn:* Mural, First City Bank-Westheimer, Houston, Tex, 80. *Exhib:* San Francisco Art Mus, 60; Whitney Mus Am Art Ann, New York, 70 & 72; Critics' Choice, Syracuse Univ Mus, NY, 77 & Munson-Williams-Proctor Inst, Utica, NY, 78; Ford & Haerer, Usdan Gallery, Bennington Col, Vt, 78; Recent Acquisitions, Brooklyn Mus, 78; Oscarsson-Hood Gallery, New York, 81 & 83; Invitational Exhib, Bershire Mus, Pittsfield, Mass, 81; Artists Space, New York, 90; Piccolo Spoleto, Charleston, SC, 92; and others. *Pos:* Dir, Hand-Hollow Artist's Found, 84; cur, Cross-Over: Artists in Two Mediums, Bennington Col, Vt, 85. *Teaching:* Dir & instr painting, Bennington Col Summer Workshops, 76-80 & Bennington Col, 73, 75, 77, 83 & 86; instr drawing & painting, Univ Vt, Burlington, 80, Vt Studio Sch, Johnson, 85, Fordham Univ, New York, 86-, Art Inst Chicago, 92. *Awards:* Yaddo Residency, 82; Grant, Nat Endowment Arts, 85; Guggenheim Fel, 88. *Bibliog:* Artist's Pages, New Art Examiner, 3/86; John Yau (auth), article, Artists Space Cat, 90; John Yau (auth), Painting Self-Evident: Evolutions in Abstraction (catalogue), 92; and others. *Media:* Oil, Acrylic. *Dealer:* Pelavin Editions 13 Jay St New York NY 10013. *Mailing Add:* Rte 2 Box 63B Hoosick Falls NY 12090

HAESSLE, JEAN-MARIE GEORGES
PAINTER
b Alsace, France, Sept 12, 39. *Study:* Ecole Nat des Beaux Arts, Paris; Ecole de la Grande Chaumiere, Paris. *Work:* Albright-Knox Art Gallery, Buffalo, NY; Bibliot Nat, Paris, France; Nat Art Mus, China; Southern Ill Univ, Edwardsville. *Exhib:* Lucien Durand Galerie, Paris, 87-88; Salon de Montrouge, Paris, France, 88; Jade Galerie, Colmar, France, 89; Athisma Galerie Lyon, France, 91; Navara Gallery, New York, 92; and others. *Bibliog:* Laurie Anderson (auth), reviews in Art News, 72; April Kingsley (auth), New York newsletter, Art Int, 73; Vivian Raynor (auth), review in Art in Am, 74. *Media:* Acrylic, Oil. *Mailing Add:* 112 Spring St New York NY 10012

HAFF, BARBARA J E
PAINTER, INSTRUCTOR
b New York, NY. *Study:* With A Haff; Art Student's League, with Sydney Dickinson, Dan Greene & Mario Cooper. *Work:* Wall Street Transcript & Ackerman Realty Co, New York. *Exhib:* Pastel Soc Am, Nat Arts Club; Allied Artists Am, Nat Acad/Nat Arts Club, New York; Salmagundi Club Ann, New York; Knickerbocker Artists, Nat Arts Club/Salmagundi, New York; Hermitage Found Mus, Norfolk, Va, 83. *Teaching:* Pastel painting, Pastel Soc Am, Nat Arts Club, 82-83. *Awards:* Gold Medal Hon, Wall Street Transcript; Grumbacher Gold Medal Hon, 84 & IBM Award, 85, C L Wolfe Art Asn. *Mem:* Pastel Soc Am (recording secy, 81-); Allied Artists Am (dir watercolor 91-); Knickerbocker Artists; C L Wolfe Art Asn; life mem Art Student's League NY. *Media:* Pastel, Watercolor. *Mailing Add:* 23-38 31 Rd Astoria NY 11106

HAFIF, MARCIA
PAINTER, EDUCATOR
b Pomona, Calif, Aug 15, 29. *Study:* Pomona Col, BA(art), 50; Claremont Grad Sch; Univ Calif, Irvine, MFA, 71. *Work:* Albright-Knox Art Gallery, Buffalo, NY; Am Medical Asn; Clemens-Sels Mus, Neuss, Ger; Chase Manhattan Bank; Mass Inst Technol. *Comn:* Ohio Red (clay mural), Wright State Univ, Ohio, 77; painting, Sheldon Solow, NY, 80. *Exhib:* Abstract Painting: 1960-69, PSI Mus, 83; 50th Anniversary of American Abstract Artists, Bronx Mus, 86; La Couleur Seule: L'Experience Monochrome, Musee St Pierre, Lyon, France, 88; Marcia Hafif, Inventory PSI Mus, 90; Red Colors, Kunsthalle, Winterthur Switz & Wamás, 92; and others. *Teaching:* Instr painting & color, Sch Visual Arts, New York, 74-76; instr, Sarah Lawrence Col, 78-80; vis asst prof, Hunter Col, 82 & 85-; vis artist, Univ Calif, Irvine, 83; adj assoc prof & coordr painting & drawing dept, New York Univ, 85-87; lectr, Princeton Univ, 89. *Awards:* Creative Artists Pub Serv Prog Grant, 76; Nat Endowment Arts, 80-81 & 90. *Bibliog:* Marisa Volpi (auth), Marcia Hafif, Data, 74; Carter Ratcliff (auth), Mostly monochrome, Art Am, 4/81; Lilly Wei (ed), Talking abstract (interview), Art in Am, 7/87. *Mem:* Am Abstract Artists; Artist's Eqinty. *Media:* All traditional paint media. *Publ:* Auth, Robert Ryman: Another response, Art in Am, 9/79; Getting on with painting, Art Am, 4/81; Plain painting, Artistes, Paris, 7/84; Monochrome and Beyond (catalogue essay), Univ Maire, 88; True Colors, Art in Am, 6/89. *Mailing Add:* 112 Mercer St New York NY 10012

HAGAN, FREDERICK
PRINTMAKER, PAINTER
b Toronto, Ont, May 21, 18. *Study:* Ont Col Art; Art Students League; also with George Miller, New York. *Work:* Nat Gallery Art, Ottawa, Ont; Art Gallery Hamilton, Ont; Grimsby Pub Art Gallery, Ont; McIntosh Gallery, London, Ont; MacDonald Stewart Art Ctr, Ont; Art Gallery Ontario, Toronto; Laurentian Univ Mus Art Ctr, Sudbury, Ont. *Comn:* Mural, Oakville Centennial Libr; Canada Post Corp, Ottawa. *Exhib:* Ont Soc Artists; Can Soc Painters Watercolour; Can Group Painters; Nat Gallery Can; Libr of Cong; plus others. *Teaching:* Res artist, Pickering Col, Newmarket, Ont, 42-46; instr drawing & printmaking, Ont Col Art, 46-83. *Bibliog:* Kenneth McNaught (auth, introd), Exploration, An Introduction, Poole Hall Press, 89; Roger Bordford Mason (auth, 14 interviews), Beat of a different drum, Print & Drawing Coun Can, 7-8/90; Susan Shantz (auth), Stations of the Cross, Univ Western Ont, 91. *Mem:* Ont Soc Artists; Ont Soc Artists; Print & Drawing Coun Can; and others. *Media:* Drawing, Oil; Lithography, Watercolor. *Publ:* The Mind & the Hand, Hagan, Grimsby Pub Libr & Art Gallery, 76. *Dealer:* Madison Gallery 80 Sparina Ave Toronto ON; Madison Gallery 334 Dundas St W Toronto ON M5T 1G5. *Mailing Add:* 53 Lundy's Ave Newmarket ON L3Y 3R9 Canada

HAGAN, JAMES GARRISON
SCULPTOR, INSTRUCTOR
b Pittsburgh, Pa, July 11, 36. *Study:* Carnegie-Mellon Univ, BFA; Iowa State Univ; Univ Pittsburgh, MA. *Work:* Column 5, Nat Gallery Art, Washinton, DC; Column 8, Princeton Univ, NJ; Barrier, Newark Mus. *Exhib:* One-man show, Zabriskie Gallery, 75; Nine Sculptures, Nassau Co Mus, NY, 76; Wood Works, Wadsworth Atheneum, Hartford, Conn, 77; Wood, Nassau Co Mus, NY, 77. *Teaching:* Prof sculpture, Univ Va, Charlottesville, 63- *Media:* Wood, Composites. *Dealer:* Zabriskie Gallery New York NY 10019. *Mailing Add:* Art Dept Univ Va Charlottesville VA 22903

HAGE, RAYMOND JOSEPH
ART DEALER, COLLECTOR
b Huntington, WVa, Nov 28, 43. *Study:* Univ Ky; Marshall Univ, BBA, 66; Colgate Darden Grad Bus Sch, Univ Va, TEP, 71. *Pos:* Pres & chief exec officer, Am Benefit Corp, currently; trustee, Huntington Galleries, formerly. *Collection:* American & European prints. *Publ:* Printsource. *Mailing Add:* 401 11th St Huntington WV 25701

HAGEMAN, CHARLES LEE
EDUCATOR, JEWELER
b Clay Center, Kans, June 22, 35. *Study:* Univ of Kans, BFA, 57, MFA, 67. *Work:* Ill State Univ, Visual Arts Ctr, Normal, Ill; Univ of Mo, Columbia. *Comn:* Univ Mace, Pres Chain of Office & 6 Board of Regent's Medallions, comn by Pres of Northwest Mo State Univ, Maryville, 77. *Exhib:* Juried Craft Exhib, Ark Arts Ctr, Little Rock, 73 & J P Speed Art Mus, Louisville, Ky, 74; Invitational Craft Exhib, Albrecht Mus, St Joseph, Mo, 75; Prof Jewelry Exhib, Univ of Mo, Columbia, 76; Mid-Am Metalcrafts, Kans City Pub Libr, Mo, 77. *Collections Arranged:* Mo Craftsman Exhib, Olive DeLuce Gallery, Maryville, Mo, 73. *Teaching:* Assoc prof of jewelry & metals & chmn dept art, Northwest Mo State Univ, Maryville, 67-; instr summer jewelry workshop, NMex State Univ, Las Cruces, 74- *Awards:* Best in Metals, Designer-Craftsman Show, Kans, 67; Metals Award, Springfield Art Mus, 69; Best in Metals, Mo Craftsman Exhib, 70. *Mem:* Mo Craft Coun; Am Craft Coun; Soc of NAm Goldsmiths. *Media:* Pewter & Gold. *Mailing Add:* 722 W Second St Maryville MO 64468

HAGER, HELLMUT W
HISTORIAN
b Berlin, Ger, Mar 27, 26. *Study:* Univ Bonn, PhD, 59. *Collections Arranged:* Architectural Fantasy and Reality, Mus Art, Pa State Univ, 81-82. *Pos:* Asst to dir, Bibliot Hertziana, Rome, 59-63. *Teaching:* Prof art hist, Pa State Univ, 71-, dept head, 72- *Awards:* Named Distinguished Professor, 90. *Mem:* Col Art Asn Am; Soc Archit Historians; Am Soc 18th Century Studies; Am Inst Archeol. *Res:* Baroque architecture in Italy and Germany. *Publ:* Auth, Filippo Juvarra e il concorso di modelli del 1715 bandito da Clemente XI per la nuova sacrestia di S Pietro, 70; coauth, Carlo Fontana: The Drawings at Windsor Castle, 77; Editor (co-editor Susan S Munshower), Projects and Monuments in Period of Roman Baroque, Vol I, 84 & Light on the Eternal City-Observations and Discoveries in Art and Architecture of Rome, Vol II, In: Papers in Art History, Pennsylvania State Univ, 84 & 87. *Mailing Add:* 318 E Prospect Ave State College PA 16801

HAGERSTRAND, MARTIN ALAN
MUSEUM DIRECTOR, ADMINISTRATOR
b Chicago, Ill, Nov 10, 11. *Study:* Metrop Theological Sem; Univ Richmond; Univ Va Exten; Univ Kans; US Army Command & Gen Staff Col; US Dept Defense Armed Forces Staff Col. *Collections Arranged:* Sponsored & administered numerous spec exhibs; Trail Of Tears Art Show, 66-82, Cherokee Nat Hist Soc & Cherokee Nat Mus since 69. *Pos:* Exec vpres, Cherokee Nat Hist Soc, Tahlequah, Okla, 63-82, dir, 63-82 & ed, The Columns, 67-82; producer, Trail of Tears Drama, Theatre at TSA-LA-GI, Tahlequah, 69-82; dir, Cherokee Nat Mus, Tahlequah, 74-82; bd dirs, Okla Arts Inst, 76-; pres, Okla Summer Arts Inst, 76-78; chmn, Hist Sites Comt, Okla Hist Soc, 83, bd dirs, 83-; chmn, Hist Ft Gibson Comn, 79-90; chmn, State Capital Preservation Comn, 81-90 & Honey Springs Battlefield Park Comn, 86-90; pres, Okla Hist Soc, 90- *Teaching:* Fac, US Army Command & Gen Staff Col, 58-60; adj instr, Nebr State Univ, 70-77. *Awards:* Arts & Tourism Award, Okla Arts & Humanities Coun & State Dept of Tourism & Recreation, 72; Governor's Arts Award, 81; Bd Serv Award, Okla Arts Inst, 90. *Bibliog:* Numerous newspaper articles. *Mem:* Nat Trust for Hist Preserv; Western Hist Asn; Cherokee Nat Hist Soc; Okla Hist Soc (pres 90-); Okla Arts Inst. *Interests:* Indian art. *Publ:* Ed, The Columns, CNHS, 67-82. *Mailing Add:* 720 W Shawnee Tahlequah OK 74464

HAGIN, NANCY
PAINTER
b Elizabeth, NJ, June 19, 40. *Study:* Carnegie-Mellon Univ; BFA, 62; Yale Univ, MFA, 64. *Work:* Mus Fine Arts, Boston, Mass; Butler Inst Am Art, Youngstown, Ohio; Utah Mus Fine Arts, Salt Lake City; New Britain Mus Am Art, Conn. *Exhib:* Contemporary Naturalism: Work of the 1970's, Nassau Co Mus, NY, 80; Eight Women-Still Life, New Britain Mus Am Art, Conn, 82; Plimpton Collection of Realistic Art, Rose Art Mus, Brandeis Univ, Mass, 82; American Realism: 20th Century Drawings & Watercolors, Mus Mod Art, San Francisco, Calif, 85; Four Artists Collaborating, Tatistcheff

Gallery, New York, 87. *Teaching:* Adj asst prof fine arts, Fashion Inst Technol, New York, 74- *Awards:* Fulbright Grant, 66; Creative Artists Pub Serv Grant, 75; Nat Endowment Arts Grant, 82 & 91. *Bibliog:* Marjorie Miller (auth), rev, Arts Mag, 82; Elaine King (auth), Celebrations of the Familiar (exhib catalog), Carnegie-Mellon Univ, 82; Gerrit Henry (auth), Hagin (exhib catalog), Lafayette Col, 86; John Arthur (auth), Hagin Exhibition Announcement Essay, 89. *Mem:* MacDowell Art Colony (colonist bd, 85-88); Nat Acad Design, 92. *Media:* Acrylic, Watercolor. *Dealer:* Fischbach Gallery 24 W 57th St New York NY 10019; Alpha Gallery Boston MA. *Mailing Add:* 55 W 28th St New York NY 10001

HAGMAN, JEAN CASSELS
MUSEUM DIRECTOR, ART HISTORIAN
b Des Moines, Iowa, Sept 17, 47. *Study:* Mich State Univ, BA, 69; Wayne State Univ, MA, Mus Mgt Inst, 90. *Collections Arranged:* Jordan Shepard, Stained Glass, 73, Samuel Kirk, Silver, 74, Navajo Rugs, 75 & Our Heritage in Weaving, 76, Grand Rapids Art Mus, Mich. *Pos:* Educ dir, Grand Rapids Art Mus, 70-78; Flint Inst Arts, Mich, 78-81; Philbrook Art Ctr, Tulsa, Okla, 81-84; independent consult, Tulsa, 84-87; dir, Mus Southwest, Midland, Tex, 87- *Teaching:* Instr, Midland Col, 89. *Mem:* Am Asn Mus. *Res:* Mid 19th to early 20th century American art; Southwestern art; Museum education. *Publ:* Auth, Mus Volunteers; The Fourth Dimension, Mus Info Serv, 85; The Museum Trustee: An Orientation, Mus Info Serv, 85. *Mailing Add:* Museum of the Southwest 1705 W Missouri Ave Midland TX 79701-6516

HAGUE, RAOUL
SCULPTOR
b Constantinople, Istanbul, Mar 28, 05; US citizen. *Study:* Iowa State Col, 21; Beaux Arts Inst Design, New York, 26-27; Art Students League, 27-28; Courtauld Inst London, Guggenheim Fel, 50-51. *Work:* Albright-Knox Art Gallery, Buffalo, NY; Whitney Mus Am Art, Metrop Mus Art, Mus Mod Art, New York; Art Inst Chicago; Mus Mod Art, San Francisco; Nat Gallery Art, Washington, DC; and many others. *Comn:* Xavier Fourcade, 80, 82-83 & 87;. *Exhib:* Mus Mod Art, 33 & 56; Curt Valentin Gallery, 45; Whitney Mus Am Art, 45-48, 52, 57, 58 & 89-90; one-man shows, Egan Gallery, New York, 62, Wash Gallery Mod Art, 64, Xavier Fourcade Gallery, New York, 79 & 87, Arts Club, Chicago, 83, Susanne Hilberry Gallery, Birmingham, Mich, 86, Lennon Weinberg Inc, New York, 88 & 91, Galerie Alfred Kren, Cologne, 90; Xavier Fourcade, 80, 82-83 & 87; Crey Art Gallery & Study Ctr, NY Univ, 81; Lennon Weinberg Inc, New York, 89, 90 & 91; 10 Sculptors of the New York School (with catalog), Manny Silverman Gallery, Los Angeles, 91. *Awards:* Ford Found Grant, 61; Am Arts & Letts, 73; Mark Rothro, 72. *Bibliog:* Art/World, Apr/May, 87; Marian Attarian (auth), The Language of Wood, Ararat, winter, 88; George Bacon (auth), Around the Galleries: New York, The Art Newspaper, No 12, 12/91. *Dealer:* Lennon Weinberg Gallery 580 Broadway New York NY 10012. *Mailing Add:* RD 2 Box 656 Maverick Rd Woodstock NY 12498

HAHN, BETTY
PHOTOGRAPHER, EDUCATOR
b Chicago, Ill, Oct 11, 40. *Study:* Ind Univ, BA, 63, MFA, 66 with Henry Holmes Smith. *Work:* Mus Mod Art, New York; Smithsonian Inst; Nat Gallery Can, Ottawa; Art Inst Chicago; San Francisco Mus Mod Art; and others. *Exhib:* Festival du Photographie, Arles, France, 75; Am Family Portraits 1730-1976, Philadelphia Mus Art, 76; Nat Gallery Can, Ottawa, 80; Smithsonian Inst, 80 & 81; Ctr Creative Photog, 81; Int Mus Photog George Eastman House, 81; San Francisco Mus Mod Art, 81 & 85; Musee d'Art Moderne de la Ville de Paris, France, 81; Houston Ctr Photog, Tex, 82; Hong Kong Arts Ctr, 82; Amerika Haus, Hanover, Berlin, Frankfurt, Heidelburg, Koln & Munich, Ger, 85. *Collections Arranged:* Spanish Photography Today, Univ NMex, 85. *Pos:* Consult, NY Graphics Soc, Boston, Mass, & Visual Arts Referral Serv Creative Pub Serv, NY, 77; guest artist, Tamarind Inst, Albuquerque, NMex, 78; adv, Art Students Asn Gallery & Conceptions Southwest (mag), Univ NMex, 81; consult ed, Univ NMex Press, 84. *Teaching:* Asst prof photog, Rochester Inst of Technol, NY, 69-76; assoc prof photog, Univ NMex, 76-86; lectr, numerous univs; prof photog, Univ NMex, 86- *Awards:* Creative Artists Pub Serv Prog Grant, New York State Coun, 75; Res Grant, Univ NMex, 77; Nat Endowment Arts Grants, 78 & 83; Polaroid Grant, 79 & 88. *Bibliog:* James N Miho (auth), More than real, Commun Arts, 72; R Sobieszek (auth), Photographer: Betty Hahn, Czech Photo, 74 & Russian Photo Rev, 74. *Mem:* Soc Photog Educ (bd dirs, 80). *Publ:* Auth, Speaking with a Genuine Voice: Henry Holmes Smith, IMAGE Eastman House, 73; contribr of chap on Gum Bichromate Printing, In: Darkroom, Lustrum Press, New York, 77; ed, Contemporary Spanish Photography, Univ NMex Press, Albuquerque, 87. *Dealer:* Witkin Gallery 41 E 57th St New York NY 10022; Andrew Smith Gallery 76 E San Francisco Santa Fe NM 87501. *Mailing Add:* 1511 Kit Carson Ave SW Univ of NMex Albuquerque NM 87104

HAHN, MAURICE & ROSLYN
DEALERS
US citizen. *Study:* Mr Hahn, Northwestern Univ, BS(bus); Mrs Hahn, Univ Pa, BA, grad studies in art hist; Temple Univ, Tyler Sch of Art. *Collections Arranged:* Benton Spruance, Retrospective, William Penn Mus, Harrisburg, Pa, 77; Benton Spruance Traveling Exhib, (coauth, catalog), with Dr Ricardo Viera, Lehigh Univ, 77-78; Alfred Bendiner, The Philadelphia Years, William Penn Mus, Harrisburg, 78; 17th, 18th and 19th Century Japanese Woodblock Prints, Longwood Gardens, Kennett Square, PA, 82. *Pos:* Dir, Hahn Gallery, Philadelphia. *Mem:* Philadelphia Print Club; Prints in Progress (Mrs Hahn, bd mem, 70-77); Philadelphia Art Dealers Asn; Friends of Artists Equity (Mrs Hahn, bd mem). *Mailing Add:* c/o The Hahn Gallery 8439 Germantown Ave Philadelphia PA 19118

HAHN, STEPHEN
DEALER
b Feb 1, 21; US citizen. *Study:* Sorbmne, Paris, LHD. *Pos:* Owner, Stephen Hahn Art Dealer, New York, currently. *Mem:* Art Dealers Asn Am (bd dirs, past pres). *Specialty:* French paintings, Nineteenth and Twentieth Century European Works of Art. *Mailing Add:* 9 E 79th New York NY 10021

HALABY, SAMIA ASAAD
PAINTER, EDUCATOR
b Jerusalem, Palestine, Dec 12, 36; US citizen. *Study:* Mich State Univ, with Abraham Rattner & Borris Margo, MA, 60; Ind Univ, with James McGarrell, MFA, 63. *Work:* Solomon R Guggenheim Mus, New York; Nat Mus Women in Arts, Washington, DC; Inst du Monde Arab, Paris, France; Mead Art Mus, Amherst, Mass; Art Inst Chicago; and others. *Comn:* Lithograph, Cleveland Mus Print Club, 74. *Exhib:* Nine Conn Artists, Wadsworth Atheneum, 74; Recent Acquisitions, Solomon R Guggenheim Mus, 75; solo exhibs, Marilyn Pearl Gallery, 78 , Galeria Palace, Granada, Spain, 86 & Tossan-Tossan Gallery, 86, New York; Kunstnernes Hus, Oslo, Norway, 81; Housatonic Mus, Bridgeport, Conn, 83; Tercero Bienal de la habana, Havana, Cuba, 89; and others. *Pos:* Artist in residence, Tamarind Lithography Workshop, 72. *Teaching:* Assoc prof painting & drawing, Ind Univ, Bloomington, 69-72 & Yale Univ, New Haven, 72-82; vis prof, Univ Hawaii, Honolulu, 85-86; instr, Cooper Union for Advancement Sci & Art, New York, 89-92. *Awards:* Creative Artists Pub Serv Prog Grant Painting, 79. *Bibliog:* Art is a living thing, Ind Univ Alumni News, 10/80; Art and liberation: Samia Halaby speaks, Aurora, spring 82; Jonathan Goodman (auth), Samia Halaby Arts Mag, 5/88. *Media:* Oil, Acrylic; Computer. *Publ:* Nature, Reality & Abstract Picturing, Leonardo, 10/87; Pictures in Computer Medium, Proceedings, 9th Symp of Small Computers in the Arts, 89; On Art and Politics, Arab Studies Quart, spring/summer 89. *Mailing Add:* 103 Franklin St New York NY 10013

HALAHMY, ODED
SCULPTOR
b Baghdad, Iraq, Oct 10, 38; US citizen. *Study:* Bat Yam Sch Fine Art, BA, 65; St Martin's Sch Fine Art, MA, 68. *Work:* Guggenheim Mus, Jewish Mus & Chase Manhattan Bank, New York; Aldrich Mus Contemp Art, Ridgefield, Conn; Herbert Johnson Mus Art, Ithaca, NY. *Comn:* Succah (abstract sculpture), Hebrew Union Col, Jerusalem, 79; Family (abstract sculpture), pvt comn, Palm Beach, Fla, 81; Blue Party (abstract sculpture), Aldrich Mus Contemp Art, Ridgefield, Conn, 82. *Exhib:* Solo exhibs, Herbert Johnson Mus Art, Ithaca, NY, 74 & Aldrich Mus Contemp Art, Conn, 82-83; Montreal Mus Fine Art, 68; Tel Aviv Mus, 70; American International Sculpture Symposium, New York, 74; Louis K Meisel Gallery, 88 & 90. *Teaching:* Instr art, Ont Col Art, Toronto, 69-70 & Parsons Sch Design, New York, 75-77; vis artist, Cooper Union Art Sch, 71, New York Univ, 71 & New Sch Social Res, 74, New York. *Awards:* Peter Samuel Found Fel, London, 67-68; Am-Israel Cult Found, New York, 75. *Bibliog:* Noel Frackman (auth), article, in: Arts Mag, 5/74; Gerrit Henry (auth), article, New York Times, 12/79; article, New York Times, 4/3/83. *Mem:* Am Int Sculpture Symposium. *Media:* Bronze, Wood. *Mailing Add:* c/o Louis K Meisel 141 Prince St New York NY 10012

HALASZ, PIRI
HISTORIAN, CRITIC
b New York, NY, April 5, 35. *Study:* Barnard Col, BA, 56; Columbia Univ, MA, 76, PhD, 82. *Collections Arranged:* The Expressionist Vision: A Central Theme in New York in the 1940s, Hillwood Art Gallery, C W Post Ctr, Long Island Univ, 83-84. *Pos:* Contrib ed, Time Mag, 63-69, writer art sect, 67-69. *Teaching:* Adj art hist, C W Post Ctr, Long Island Univ, 76-77, adj prof, 85-86, coordr art, Westchester Campus, 85-86; adj prof, Molloy Col, 85-86; asst prof, Bethany Col, WVa, 90- *Mem:* Int Asn Art Critics. *Res:* Twentieth century European and American art, especially in New York in the 1940s. *Publ:* Auth, Figuration in the 40s: The other expressionism, Art in Am, 82; Growing up progressive, Virginia Quart Rev, 90; Paris 1889 (exhib rev), Art J, fall 90. *Mailing Add:* PO Box 296 Bethany WV 26032

HALBACH, DAVID ALLEN
PAINTER
b Santa Barbara, Calif, Jan 12, 31. *Study:* Chouinard Art Inst, cert grad; with Rex Brandt, Edward Reep & Robert Uecker. *Work:* Permanent Collection, Bank Calif, San Francisco, San Jose & Seattle, Wash, also Buffalo Bill Mus, Cody, Wyo; Favell Mus Western Art, Klamath Falls, Ore; Cowboy Artists Am Mus, Kerrville, Tex. *Exhib:* Cowboy Hall of Fame, Oklahoma City, 75-79 & 81; Western Heritage Show, Houston, Tex, 78-81, 83 & 84, European tour, 83-; Biltmore Celebrity Show, Los Angeles, Calif, 81-84; Governor's Invitational, Cheyenne, Wyo, 81-84; Cowboy Artists of America, Phoenix Art Mus, Phoenix, Ariz. *Pos:* Illusr, US Navy, 52-54; with Walt Disney Studio, Burbank, 54-55; illusr & art ed, Cannon Elec Co, Los Angeles, 55-59; art dir, Mowinckle Advert, Los Angeles, 59-63. *Teaching:* Art teacher (adult educ), San Gabriel, Whittier & Covina High Schs, Calif, 65-73. *Awards:* Silver Medalist, Nat Acad-Cowboy Hall of Fame, 75; Gold Medal, Water Solubles, Cowboy Artists Am Show, 88-90; First Place, Art Parks Region II, 89; Mus Western Heritage Award, 90. *Mem:* Cowboy Artists Am. *Media:* Watercolor. *Publ:* Illusr, Orange County Illustrated, 75 & Southwest Art, 78; 1988 Cowboy Artists of America, Art W Mag, 11-12/88. *Dealer:* Buffalo Trails Scottsdale AZ; Settler's West Tucson AZ. *Mailing Add:* Iyokut Trail PO Box 338 Graeagle CA 96103

HALBROOK, ANNE-MIEKE PLATT
LIBRARIAN
b Dordrecht, Neth. *Study:* Rijksuniversiteit, Utrecht, Neth, Kandidaats, 66; Univ Mich, Ann Arbor, MLS, 72. *Pos:* Librn, Getty Ctr Hist Art & Humanities, 79-90 & Head Res Servs Collection Mgt, 90- *Mem:* Art Libr Soc North Am; Art Librns Asn. *Interests:* Western European art and archeology. *Mailing Add:* Getty Ctr Hist Art & Humanities 401 Wilshire Blvd No 400 Santa Monica CA 90401

HALBROOK, RITA ROBERTSHAW
PAPERMAKER, PAINTER
b Greenville, Miss, May 22, 30. *Study:* Miss Art Colony, with Ida Kohlmeyer, 77; Delta State Univ, BFA, 82. *Work:* Delta State Univ; William Carey Col, Miss; Pike Co Hosp, McComb, Miss; Northern Electric Co Laurel, Miss; Deposit Guaranty Nat Bank, Jackson, Miss. *Comn:* October (abstract landscape), Holmes Co Bank, Lexington, Miss, 70; stained canvas, Fed Land Bank, New Orleans, 77; Vestments, All Saints Cath Church, Belzoni, Miss, 78; cast paper prints, Delta Processors, Indianola, Miss, 85; paper sculptures, Northeast Miss Med Ctr Women's Hosp, 86; cast paper, comn by Am Legislative Exchange Coun for Vpres Dan Quale. *Exhib:* Mid-South Exhib, 66 & 67 & Artist Registry Show, 70, Brooks Men Mus; Miss Arts Festival, St Andrews Cath Gallery, Jackson, 70; Belzoni Group, Univ Fla, Gainesville, 71; Miss Gallery, Miss Mus Art, Jackson, 80-81; Wall Series, Cottanlandia Mus, Greenwood, Miss & Meridian Mus Art, Miss, 83; regional telecast, Miss Educ TV Studios; Nat League Am Pen women Bienniel, Washington, DC, 88; Miss Gov Mansion Invitational, 89-90; Miss Craftsmens Guild Invitational, 89. *Awards:* Best in Show, Miss Art Colony, Crosstie Festival, 71 & Cottonlandia Competition, 83 & 90; First & Second Award, Miss Art Colony, 85; Best in Show, Miss Pen Women Statewide Competition, 88. *Bibliog:* Porioer (auth), Mississippi Artists, Univ Southern Miss Press, 78; Louis Dollahide (auth), Of Arts and Artists, Univ Miss Press, 81. *Mem:* Miss Art Colony (mem bd dirs, 80-88); Miss Delta Br, Nat Pen Women; Craftsmen's Guild Miss. *Media:* Mixed Acrylic; Handmade Paper. *Dealer:* Gulf South Gallery Acton Ave McComb MS 39648; Brown's Gallery 620 Foundren Pl Jackson MS 39206. *Mailing Add:* PO Box 694 Belzoni MS 39038

HALBROOKS, DARRYL WAYNE
PAINTER, EDUCATOR
b Evansville, Ind, May 3, 48. *Study:* Univ Evansville, Ind; Murray State Univ, Ky; Southern Ill Univ. *Work:* Brooks Mem Art Gallery, Memphis, Tenn; Huntington Gallery, WVa; Evansville Mus Arts & Sci, Ind; Atlantic Richfield Corp; Millikin Univ; and others. *Exhib:* Dulin Nat Print & Drawing Exhib, Dulin Gallery, Knoxville, Tenn, 76; Exhib 280, 78 & 79; Watercolor USA, 79; one-man shows, Joy Horwich Gallery, Chicago, 79-81; Appalachian Nat, 80; and others. *Teaching:* Assoc prof painting, Eastern Ky Univ, Richmond, 72- *Awards:* Purchase Award, 72 Mid-S Exhib, Brooks Mem Art Gallery, Memphis, Tenn, 72-86, prof, 86-; Purchase Award, Appalachian Corridors & Exhib 280, Huntington, WVa, 74 & 77; Contemporary American Painting, Palm Beach, Fla, 81; and others. *Bibliog:* Marion Garmel (auth), Works on Paper, Indianapolis News, 5/74; article, Arts Mag, 5/77; article, New Art Examiner, Chicago, 10/81; and others. *Media:* Acrylic, Lithography, Film. *Dealer:* Joy Horwich Gallery 226 E Ontario Chicago 60611. *Mailing Add:* Art Dept 309 Campbell Eastern KY Univ Richmond KY 40475

HALE, NATHAN CABOT
SCULPTOR, WRITER
b Los Angeles, Calif, July 5, 25. *Study:* Chouinard Art Inst, Los Angeles; Art Students League; Empire State Col, BS; Union Grad Sch, PhD. *Work:* Bronze madonna, St Anthony of Padua, East Northport, NY; bronze reliefs, Rose Assoc Bldg, Bronx, NY; also in mus & pvt collections. *Exhib:* Many group & one-man shows since 1947. *Pos:* Dir, Ages Man Found, 68-, sculptor, Cycle Life Chapel Sculpture Proj, 68-; sr ed, Art/World, 85- *Teaching:* Mem fac, Pratt Inst, Brooklyn, 63-64; instr anat & drawing, Art Students League, 66-72, instr & lectr anat, 85- *Mem:* Art Students League; Audubon Artists. *Publ:* Auth, Welded Sculpture, 69, Embrace of Life--the Sculpture of Gustav Vigelund, 70 & Abstraction in Art & Nature, 72; Birth of a Family, Doubleday, 79; also contribr to archit & art mags. *Mailing Add:* RR1 Box 5 Amenia NY 12501

HALEGUA, ALFREDO
SCULPTOR
b Montevideo, Uruguay, May 4, 30; US citizen. *Study:* Sch Bldg Design, Montevideo, Uruguay, 47; Sch Plastic Arts, Montevideo, BFA, 50; MFA 52. *Work:* Nat Gallery Art, Washington, DC; Baltimore Mus Art, Md; Ringling Mus Art, Sarasota, Fla; Denver Art Mus, Colo; Daytona Beach Mus Arts & Sci, Fla. *Comn:* Sculpture, 70 & 77, City of Baltimore, Md; Obelisk, City of Salisbury, Md, 70; sculpture, Dade County, Miami, Fla, 82; Fountains, City of Charlotte, NC, 89. *Exhib:* One-man show: Baltimore Mus, Md, 63 & 68; Int Exhib Contemp Sculpture, Rodin Mus, Paris, France, 66; Halegua-Monumental Sculpture, Baltimore Mus Art, Md, 68; Contemp Am Artists, Baltimore Mus Art, Md, 70; Halegua-Recent Sculpture, Mint Mus Art, Charlotte, NC, 81; Int Biennial Contemp Art, Mus Contemp Art, Montevideo, Uruguay, 81; Five Int Artists in DC, Robert Brown Contemp Art, Washington, 82; Halegua-Public Sculpture & Proj, Mus Mod Art Latin Am, Washington, DC, 88-89; Washington Int Sculpture Art in Atrium, Washington, DC, 90. *Teaching:* Prof sculpture, Am Univ, Washington, DC, 64-65. *Awards:* Gold Metal, Nat Salon Fine Arts, Montevideo, Uruguay, 58; Research grant traveling exhib, Govt Uruguay, 59. *Bibliog:* Paul Richard (auth), Mood of elegance in H's, Washington Post, 7/28/68; Doug Davis (auth), Washington Letter, Arts Mag, 12/69 & 1/70. *Mem:* Int Sculpture Ctr. *Media:* Metals. *Publ:* Auth, Style and Content in Modern & Contemporary Art, Fine Arts Soc, 58; The role of art criticism, El Bien Publico, 2/8/59; Current trends in American Art, 9/12/63 & Models for integration of Sculpture & Architecture, 7/15/68, El Dia; The Magic Line-The Drawings of Pedro Figari, Monumental Sculptures, 88. *Mailing Add:* 2601 30th St NW Washington DC 20008

HALEMAN, LAURA RAND
SCULPTOR, CRAFTSMAN
b New York, NY, Mar 3, 46. *Study:* New York Univ, BS (summa cum laude), 68; Sch Visual Arts, Columbia Univ, 83; New Sch Social Res, 83; studio of Minoru Niizuma, 84. *Work:* Citibank Corp, New York; First Long Island Investors Corp, Jericho, NY; Sid Jacobson YMHA & YWHA, Roslyn, NY; Duralee Fabrics Corp, New York; All County Abstract Corp, Carle Pl, NY; Nubest & Co, Manhasset, NY. *Comn:* Lawrence Jr High Sch Lobby, Cedarhurst, NY, 81; Long Island Hall of Fame: New York Islanders; Gen Aerospace Materials Corp, 88. *Exhib:* Nassau Co Mus Fine Art, Roslyn, 83, 84 & 91; Fine Arts Mus Long Island, 85 & 91; Heckscher Mus, Huntington, NY, 85; CAPA Rotational Arts Exhib, 85-; Lever House, New York, 86-92; Crystal Pavillion, New York, 88 & 92; Blue Hill Cult Ctr, 88 & 92. *Collections Arranged:* Four Women Artists, 84 & 19 Artists, 85, Great Neck Libr Gallery, Hempstead Harbor Artists Asn, NY. *Pos:* Dir & prin owner, The Sculpture Workshop, Brookville, NY, 80-; artist-in-residence, Lawrence Jr High Sch, 81. *Teaching:* Instr cult arts develop prog, Jericho Pub Sch, 82-83; lectr on the art of stone carving, Sculpture Assoc Art Group, currently; instr sculpture seminars, Studio Tours Art Soc & Long Island Pub Sch Syst, currently. *Awards:* First Prize Sculpture, Suburban Art League; Hon Mention, Nassau Co Mus Fine Arts; Sculpture Award, Independent Art League Invitational Open; and others. *Mem:* Stone Sculpture Soc NY; Art Deco Soc NY (bd mem, 84); Hempstead Harbor Artists Asn (bd mem, 84-); Independent Art Soc; Huntington Twp Art League; Suburban Art League. *Media:* Sandstone, Marble. *Mailing Add:* 30 Ormond Pk Rd Brookville NY 11545

HALEY, GAIL E
ILLUSTRATOR, COLLECTOR
b Charlotte, NC, Nov 4, 39. *Study:* Richmond Prof Inst Va, 59-60. *Work:* Kerlan Collection, Univ Minn, Minneapolis; DeGrummond Collection, Univ Southern Miss, Hattiesburg; Collection of Culture of Childhood, Appalachian State Univ, Boone, NC. *Teaching:* Instr writing & illus for children (artist-in-residence), Appalachian State Univ, 80- *Awards:* Caldecott Medal Best Illus Children's Book USA, 71; Kate Greenaway Medal Best Illus Children's Book England, 76; Kodai Tosho Award, Japan Best Book, 80; The Kerlan Award, Univ of Minn, 89. *Bibliog:* David Considine (auth), Toys, technology & teaching, Top of the News, summer 85 & An integrated approach to visual literacy and children's books, Sch Libr J, 9/86; Susan Austin (auth), Author illustrator profile, Library Talk, 11-12/89. *Mem:* Puppeteers Am; Int Visual Literacy Asn. *Collection:* Antique and contemporary children's games, toys, books, dolls and puppets from Europe and the US. *Publ:* The Post Office Cat, 76, Go Away, Stay Away, 77 & the Green Man, 78, Scribner's; Birdsong, 84 & Jack and the Bean Tree, 86, Crown; auth, From the Ananse Stories to the Jack Tales: My Work with Folklores, Children's Literature Quart, fall 86; Jack and the Fire Dragon, 88, A Sea Tale, 90 & Puss in Boots, 91, Dutton; Of Mermaids, Myths and Meaning: A Sea Tale, The New Advocate, winter 90. *Mailing Add:* PO Box 1023 Blowing Rock NC 28605

HALEY, PATIENCE E (PATIENCE E HALEY GHIKAS)
PAINTER, CONSERVATOR
b Boston, Mass. *Study:* Oberlin Col, AB. *Work:* Addison Gallery Am Art, Andover, Mass; Smith Col Mus Art, Northampton, Mass; Ctr Arts, Wesleyan Univ, Middletown, Conn; Mus Art Ogunquit, Maine; Mus of Art, Lehigh Univ, Pa. *Comn:* History of Manchester, Conn (mural), Manchester Savings Bank; restoration of Faulkner murals, Columbia Univ, New York. *Exhib:* One-woman shows, George Walter Vincent Smith Mus, Springfield, Mass, 60, DeCordova Mus, Lincoln, Mass, 57 & Radcliffe Inst, Cambridge, Mass, 71; New England Drawings, Lyman Allyn Mus, Conn, 57; Highlights of Am Hist, Addison Gallery, Andover, Mass, 58. *Pos:* Asst painting conserv, Dept Painting Restoration, Boston Mus, Mass, 73- *Teaching:* Art instr, Abbot Acad, Andover, Mass, 56-59. *Awards:* Painting Scholar, Bunting Inst, Radcliffe Col, 69-71; Three-time Painting Fel, Yaddo Found & Macdowell Found; Gold Medal, New Eng Watercolor Soc, 79. *Bibliog:* Edward Betts (auth), Master Class in Watercolor, Watson-Guptill Publ, 75. *Mem:* New Eng Watercolor Soc; Ogunquit Art Asn, Maine; Radcliffe Inst Fels, Inc. *Media:* Watercolor; Ink. *Mailing Add:* 30 Ipswich St Boston MA 02215

HALEY, PRISCILLA J
PAINTER, PRINTMAKER
b Boston, Mass, June 22, 26. *Study:* Oberlin Col, Ohio, BA(fine arts), 48; Brooklyn Mus Art Sch, 52-53; with Kienbusch, Rogalski, 54. *Work:* Libr Congress, Washington, DC; Addison Gallery, Andover, Mass; Nat Acad Galleries, New York; Brooklyn Mus, NY; Philadelphia Mus Art, Pa. *Exhib:* Print Ann, Philadelphia Mus Art, Pa, 57; Print Show, Inst Contemp Art, Boston, Mass, 58; Print Ann, Libr Congress, Washington, DC, 60; Print Ann, Brooklyn Mus, NY, 60; Print Ann, Farnsworth Mus, Rockland, Maine, 63; Worcester Print Show, Worcester Art Mus, Mass, 64; New England Artists, DeCordova Mus, Lincoln, Mass, 65; Soc Am Graphic Artists Print Show, Kennedy Galleries, New York, 76; Isliptown Art Gallery, Islip, NY, 77. *Awards:* Tiffany Found Grant, 59; Graphics Award, Providence RI Art Asn, 79; First Prize Watercolor, Babylon Arts Coun, NY, 92. *Mem:* Soc Am Graphic Artists. *Media:* Watercolor; Etching, Intaglio. *Publ:* Contribr, The Print, Adele Lewis Publ, 59; illusr, The Island, P J Haley, 60. *Mailing Add:* 133 Livingston Ave Babylon NY 11702

HALEY, SALLY (SALLY FULTON HALEY RUSSO)
PAINTER
b Bridgeport, Conn, June 29, 08. *Study:* Yale Univ Sch Fine Arts, BFA, 31; studies with Prof Maxon, Munich, Ger, 33. *Work:* Portland Art Mus & City of Portland, Ore; State of Ore & Willamette Univ, Salem; Univ Wash, Seattle; Fed Reserve Bank, San Francisco; AT&T, New York. *Comn:* US Post Office, Works Progress Admin, McConnelsville, Ohio, 39. *Exhib:* Solo exhibs, Portland Art Mus, 60, Fountain Gallery Art, Portland, 62, 72, 77, 80, 81, 84 & 85, Governor's Office, Ore State Capitol, 76, Bush Barn, Salem, Ore, 84 & Wentz Gallery, Pac Northwest Col Art, Portland, 84; San Francisco Mus Art, 49; Reality and Fantasy, 1900-1954, Walker Art Ctr, Minneapolis, 54; Seattle Invitational, Seattle Ctr Art Pavilion, Wash, 76; Women's Building, Los Angeles, Calif, 77; Hubbard Mus, Ruidoso Downs, NMex, 90; Laura Russo Gallery, Portland, Ore, 90. *Awards:* Gov Awards Poster, State of Ore, 82; Oregon Governors Award for Arts, 89; Women's Achievement Award for Artistic Excellence, YWCA, 88. *Bibliog:* Ellen Nichols (ed), Northwest Originals, InUNISON Publ, Portland, Ore, 89; Barbara Melosh (auth), Engendering Culture: Manhood and Womanhood in New Deal Public Art and Theatre, Smithsonian Inst Press, Washington, DC, 91. *Mem:* Portland Art Mus. *Media:* Acrylic, Egg Tempera. *Dealer:* Laura Russo Gallery 805 NW 21st Portland OR. *Mailing Add:* 3227 NW Thurman Portland OR 97210

HALFF, ROBERT H
COLLECTOR
b San Antonio, Tex, Dec 1, 08. *Study:* Wharton Sch, Univ Pa, grad; New Sch Social Res; NY Univ; Univ Calif, Los Angeles Exten. *Work:* Chamberlain sculpture, Mus Contemp Art; pvt collections of Cornell, de Suvero, Joe Shapiro, Serra, Hepworth, Jasper Johns, Roy Lichtenstein, David Smith, de Kooning, Oldenburg, Puryear and others. *Pos:* Chmn spec proj & hon chairperson acquisitions comt, Mod & Contemp Art Coun, Los Angeles Co Mus Art; founding mem, Mus Contemp Art, Los Angeles; trustee & acquisitions comt, Los Angeles Co Mus Art. *Collection:* American contemporary & European art. *Publ:* Arts & Antiques Mag, 87 & 88; Top 100 Americas' Collectors, 91-92; Art News Top 200 Collectors in the world 91-92. *Mailing Add:* 1659 Waynecrest Dr Beverly Hills CA 90210

HALKIN, THEODORE
SCULPTOR, PAINTER
b Chicago, Ill, Mar 2, 24. *Study:* Art Inst Chicago, BFA, 50; Southern Ill Univ, MS(art), 52. *Work:* Art Inst Chicago; ButD; Smithsonian Mus, Washington, DC; Mus Contemp Art, Chicago. *Exhib:* 25th Biennial Contemp Am Oil Painting, Corcoran Gallery Art, Washington, DC, 57; Am Painting & Sculpture Ann, Pa Acad Fine Arts & Detroit Inst Arts, 58; one-man shows, Allan Frumkin Galleries, New York, 60-67, Chicago, 61, Phyllis Kind Gallery, Chicago, 68-76 & Jan Cicero Gallery, Chicago, 83, 84, 86, 87, 90 & 92; Chicago Images Show, Mus Contemp Art, Chicago, 72; Chicago Int Art Expos, Jan Cicero Gallery, Chicago, 86-89; Group shows, Jan Cicero Gallery, Chicago, 90-92. *Teaching:* From assoc prof art to wells prof, Art Inst Chicago, currently. *Awards:* 21st Ann Midyear Show Purchase Prize, Butler Inst Am Art, 56; Chicago & Vicinity Show First Prize for Sculpture, Art Inst Chicago, 65; Cass Andran Award, 72. *Bibliog:* Alan Artner (auth), Theodore Halkin, Chicago Tribune, 1/24/86; Michael Bonesteel (auth), New life to old form, Evanston Review, 2/86; James Yood (auth), Chicago draws, New Art Examiner, 12/86. *Mailing Add:* c/o Jan Cicero Gallery 221 W Erie Chicago IL 60610

HALKO, JOE
SCULPTOR, PAINTER
b Great Falls, Mont, Aug 11, 40. *Study:* Col Great Falls, Mont. *Work:* Leigh Yawkey Woodson Mus, Wis; C M Russell Mus, Great Falls, Mont. *Comn:* Mural, comn by C A Rumford, Great Falls Sporting Goods, Mont, 70; centennial sculpture, Great Falls Gas Co, Mont; large outdoor Can geese sculpture, State of Mont Percent for Arts & Mont Fish, Wildlife & Parks Dept, 87. *Exhib:* C M Russell Mus Art Show & Auction, Great Falls, 73, 75 & 77-92; Soc Animal Artists, Sportsmans Edge, New York, Cowboy Hall of Fame, Okla, 78; one-man show, C M Russell Mus Art, Great Falls, Mont, 82; NWR Show, Park City, Utah, 92; Western Rendezvous of Art, Helena, Mont, 80-92; and others. *Awards:* Best Sculpture, C M Russell Auction, 79 & 82; Western Rendezvous of Art Award Merit, 79, 81 & 91; Award, Western Heritage, Billings, Mont, 84-85. *Bibliog:* Article, Artwest Mag, 81; article, Southwest Art, 1/88; article, Art of the West, 91; and others. *Mem:* Soc Animal Artists; Northwest Rendezvous Group. *Media:* Wax, Clay; Oil. *Publ:* Illusr, A Century in the Foothills 1876 to 1976, Fairfield Times, 76. *Dealer:* Wilcox Gallery Jackson WY; Dodson Gallery Oklahoma City OK. *Mailing Add:* 2573 Old US Hwy 91 Cascade MT 59421

HALL, CARL ALBIN
PAINTER, INSTRUCTOR
b Washington, DC, Sept 17, 21. *Study:* Meinzinger Art Sch, Detroit, Mich, with Carlos Lopez. *Work:* Whitney Mus Am Art, New York; Boston Mus Art, Mass; Springfield Art Inst, Mass; Swope Art Gallery, Terre Haute, Ind. *Exhib:* 66th Ann Western, Denver Art Mus, 60; 18th Artists West Miss, Colorado Springs, 61; Drawings USA, St Paul Gallery, Minn & Traveling Show, 61; Century 21, Seattle, Wash, 62; The West, 80 Contemporaries, Univ Ariz, 66; Bicentennial Exhib, Ore, 76-77; Ore Art Heritage Exhib, Ore Hist Soc, 90; Ancient Forests, Ore, 90. *Teaching:* Artist in residence, Willamette Univ, 48-72, assoc prof, 78- *Awards:* Nat Inst Arts & Lett Grant, 49; Newberry Prize, Detroit Inst Art, 49. *Bibliog:* Collection of drawings, Northwest Rev, 63; article in Alaska J, Vol 7, 77; Neglected generation: American realist painters 1930-1948, Wichita Art Mus, 5-6/81. *Publ:* Auth, Voyage of the eye, Malahat Rev, 10/81. *Mailing Add:* 4626 Pettyjohn Rd S Salem OR 97302

HALL, JOHN (SCOTT)
PAINTER, EDUCATOR
b Edmonton, Alta, Jan 17, 43. *Study:* Alta Col of Art, dipl(fine arts); Inst Allende, Mex. *Work:* Nat Gallery Can; Montreal Mus Fine Arts; Can Coun Art Bank, Ottawa; Glenbow Mus, Calgary; Art Gallery Ont, Toronto. *Comn:* Cineplex-Odeon, New York, 88; Royal Bank Can, 89. *Exhib:* Alta Realists, Edmonton Art Gallery, 75; Realism in Can, Norman MacKenzie Art Gallery, Univ Regina, 78; solo exhibs, Nat Gallery Can, 79, Imitations of Life: John Hall's Still Life Portraits, Agnes Etherington Art Ctr, Queen's Univ, Kingston, Ont, 89, Glenbow Mus, Calgary, Alta, 89, Kitchener Waterloo Art Gallery, Ont, 90, Art Gallery NS, Halifax, 90, Mem Univ Art Gallery, St John's Nfld, 90, Trail of Evidence, Museo de Arte Moderno, Mexico City, 93 & Glenbow Mus, 93; PS1, New York, 80; Mendel Gallery, Saskatoon, Calgary; Wynick/Tuck Gallery, Toronto, 80-; Southern Alta Art Gallery, Lethbridge, 82; and others. *Collections Arranged:* The Rose Museum, A Major Survey of the Rose Motif in Western Culture Traveling Exhib, 73-74. *Teaching:* Vis instr painting & design, Ohio Wesleyan Univ, 69-70; instr painting & design, Alta Col of Art, Calgary, 70-71; asst prof painting & drawing, Univ Calgary, 71-81, assoc prof, 81- *Awards:* Proj grant, 73, travel grants, 75 & 77 & sr grant, 79, Can Coun. *Bibliog:* Dennis Ried (auth), The Death and Rebirth of Painting, A Concise History of Canadian Painting, pp 354-6, Oxford Univ Press, 88; Nancy Tousley (auth), Imitations of Life: John Hall's Still Life Portraits, 89; David Burnett (auth), Masterpieces of Canadian Art from the National Gallery of Canada, pp 220-1, Hurtig, 90. *Mem:* Royal Can Acad; Can Artists Representation; Alta Soc Artists (pres, 67-68). *Media:* Acrylic. *Dealer:* Wynick/Tuck Gallery 80 Spadina Ave Toronto Ont Canada M5V 2J3. *Mailing Add:* Univ Calgary Dept Art 2400 University Dr NW Calgary AB T2N 1N4 Canada

HALL, JOHN A
PAINTER, EDUCATOR
b Toronto, Ont, Oct 10, 14. *Study:* Ont Col Art. *Work:* Art Gallery Ont; Nat Gallery, Ottawa; Robert McLaughlin Gallery, Oshawa. *Comn:* Murals in porcelain enamel on steel panels, Delhi, Port Colborne & Simcoe, Ont & Expo '67, Montreal, Que. *Exhib:* Can Group Painters; Ont Soc Artists; Royal Can Acad; New York World's Fair, 39; Rio, 44 & 46; and others. *Teaching:* Instr, Art Gallery Toronto; instr painting, Ont Dept Educ, summer courses; assoc prof drawing & painting, Dept Archit, Univ Toronto, retired. *Awards:* Can Arts Coun Sr Artists' Award, 63. *Mem:* Hon mem Ont Asn Archit; Ont Soc Artists. *Media:* Oil, Watercolor. *Mailing Add:* Glencroft RRD 2 Newmarket ON L3Y 4V9 Canada

HALL, LEE
ADMINISTRATOR, PAINTER
b Lexington, NC, Dec 15, 34. *Study:* Univ NC, Greensboro, BFA; NY Univ, scholar, 65, AM & PhD; Warburg Inst, Univ London; Univ NC, Greenboro, DFA, 66. *Work:* Hudson River Mus; Montclair Art Mus; Drew Univ, NJ; Greenville Mus, SC; Citicorp; and others. *Exhib:* One-woman shows, Ruth White Gallery, 68, Drew Univ, 74 & Betty Parsons Gallery, 75, 77, 78, 80 & 82; RI Sch Design, 75; Phoenix Gallery, Washington, DC, 83; Elliot Smith Gallery, St Louis. *Pos:* Chmn dept art, Drew Univ, Madison, NJ, 65-74; consult, Nat Endowment for Humanities, 69-75; dean visual arts, State Univ NY, Purchase, 74-75; pres, RI Sch Design, 75-83; sr vpres & dir, Acad Educ Develop, 84- *Awards:* Am Philos Soc Grant, 65 & 68. *Mem:* Col Art Asn Am. *Media:* Watercolor, Oil. *Res:* History and theory of symbolism in 19th and 20th century art. *Publ:* Auth, Women artists in the academic world, Art & Sexual Polit, 73; Ruth Vollmer's sculpture (catalog), Everson Mus, Syracuse, 74; Art & sullen craft of portraiture, Craft Horizons, 74. *Mailing Add:* c/o Acad Educ Develop 100 Fifth Ave New York NY 10011

HALL, MICHAEL DAVID
SCULPTOR, EDUCATOR
b Upland, Calif, May 20, 41. *Study:* Western Wash State Col, 58-60; Univ NC, BA, 62; Univ Iowa, 62; Univ Wash, MFA(sculpture), 64. *Work:* Princeton Univ Art Mus, NJ; Jacksonville Art Mus, Fla; Univ Iowa Art Mus, Iowa City; J B Speed Art Mus, Louisville, Ky; Wright State Univ; and others. *Exhib:* Whitney Mus Am Art Ann Sculpture Exhib, New York, 68 & 73; American Sculpture, Sheldon Mem Art Gallery, Univ Nebr, Lincoln, 70; Hammarskjold Plaza, New York, 72; Sculpture Off the Pedestal, Grand Rapids, Mich, 73; Three Installations, Detroit Inst Arts, 77; Scale & Environment, Walker Art Ctr, Minneapolis, 77; Los Angeles Inst Contemp Art, 80; Nassau Co Mus, Roslyn, NY, 83; and others. *Teaching:* Instr ceramics & sculpture, Univ Colo, Boulder, 65-66; assoc prof sculpture, Univ Ky, 66-70; resident sculptor, Cranbrook Acad Art, 70- *Awards:* Guggenheim Found Fel, 73; Nat Endowment Art Fel, 74; Mich Found Arts Fel, 78. *Bibliog:* Articles, Arts Mag, 11/77, 2/78 & 6/79. *Mem:* Mus Am Folk Art; NY State Hist Asn; Visual Arts Div; Mich Coun Arts; Col Art Asn. *Media:* Steel, Aluminum. *Publ:* Auth, Icons of John Perates, Cincinnati Art Mus, 74; The Artist as Collector, Brooklyn Mus, 76; The Isolate Artist in America, Transmitters, Philadelphia Col Art, 81; The Hemphill Perspective, The Hemphill Collection, Milwaukee Art Mus, 81. *Dealer:* Hill Gallery 163 Townsend Birmingham MI 48011. *Mailing Add:* 1125 Sherman, #25 Royal Oak MI 48067

HALL, REX EARL
PAINTER, EDUCATOR
b Asbury, Mo, Feb 3, 24. *Study:* Washburn Univ, AB; Kansas City Art Inst; Univ Wichita, MFA. *Work:* Wichita Art Mus; Wichita State Univ. *Exhib:* Kans Ann, 56-63; Kans Biennial, 59-64; one-man shows, Birger Sandzen Gallery, 63, Kansas City Pub Libr, Mo, 63 & Wichita Art Mus, 64; and others. *Teaching:* Prof art, Kans State Teachers Col, 60-68; prof art & chmn dept,

Emporia Kans State Col, 69-86. *Awards:* Wichita Air Capital Award, 57 & 58; Living with Art, Wichita, 60; Designer-Craftsmen Show Award, Lawrence, Kans, 62. *Mem:* Kans Fedn Art (vpres, 62); Kans Art Educ Asn; Col Art Asn Am; founder Index Art Group; Wichita Art Guild (vpres, 58-); plus others. *Publ:* Auth, A profile, Kans Art Educ Asn J, 61; three booklets for Kans Art Educ Asn, 64-65. *Mailing Add:* 28 Union St Emporia KS 66801

HALL, ROBERT L
MUSEOLOGIST, PAINTER
b Miami, Fla. *Study:* Fisk Univ, BS(art); George Washington Univ, MAT(mus educ), 75. *Work:* Fisk Univ Mus Art; Carroll Reece Mus, ETenn State Univ. *Comn:* Mural, Miami-Dade Community Col, Cult Arts Ctr, Miami, 73. *Exhib:* Lowe Art Mus, Univ Miami, 70; Zale Mus, Bishop Col, Tex, 78; Black Artists South, Huntsville Mus Art, Ala, 79; Recent Works, Van Vechten Art Gallery, Fisk Univ, 82; Carroll Reece Mus, ETenn State Univ, 84. *Collections Arranged:* Lev Mills Prints (auth, catalog), 78; Betty Blayton (auth, catalog), 79; Recent Acquisitions (auth, catalog), Fisk Univ Mus Art, 80; Portraits by Carl Van Vechten Traveling Show (auth, catalog), 80; Anderson, Hyman and Wood (auth, catalog), 81; Gathered Visions, 90. *Pos:* Cur collections & educ, Fisk Univ Mus Art, 73-84; educ spec, Anacostia Mus, Smithsonian Inst. *Teaching:* Instr, Fisk Univ, 76-79. *Bibliog:* 250 Yrs of Afro-American Art: An Annotated Biography, Lynn Moody (auth), TT Bowker, 81. *Mem:* Am Asn Mus; African Am Mus Asn. *Media:* Acrylic, Oil. *Publ:* Gathered Visions: Selected Works by African American Women Artists, 92. *Mailing Add:* Anacostia Mus Smithsonian Inst Educ Dept 1901 Fort Pl SE Washington DC 20020

HALL, SUSAN
PAINTER, PRINTMAKER
b Point Reyes Station, Calif, Mar 19, 43. *Study:* Calif Col Arts & Crafts, Oakland, 62-65; Univ Calif, Berkeley, MA, 67. *Work:* Whitney Mus, New York; Brooklyn Mus, NY; Carnegie Inst, Pittsburgh, Pa; San Francisco Mus Art. *Exhib:* San Francisco Mus Art Ann, 66; one-woman shows, San Francisco Mus Art, 67, Whitney Mus, 72, Nancy Hoffman Gallery, New York, 73 & 75, Hamilton Gallery, 78-79 & 81 & Dart Gallery, Chicago, 81; Twenty-six Contemp Women Artists, Aldrich Mus Contemp Art, Ridgefield, Conn, 71; Ovsey Gallery, 81, 82, 84, 87, & 89; Back to the USA, traveling Ger & Switz, 83; Printmaking-the 70's into the 80's, Mus Fine Arts, Boston; American Realism, San Francisco Mus Art, 85; Trabia Macafee, New York, 87-89. *Teaching:* Instr, Univ of Calif, Berkeley, 67-70, Sarah Lawrence Col, Bronxville, NY, 72-75 & Sch Visual Arts, 81- *Awards:* Nat Endowment Arts Award, 79 & 88; Krosner Pollock Found, 86. *Bibliog:* William Zimmer (auth), article, New York Times-Westchester, 4/84; John R Clarke (auth), Image, technique & spirituality in Susan Hall's new work, Arts Magazine, 6/88; Christine Liotta (auth), Review Art News, 3/90. *Media:* Acrylic, Oil; Etching, Lithography. *Mailing Add:* 10 White St New York NY 10013

HALLAM, BEVERLY (LINNEY)
PAINTER, PHOTOGRAPHER
b Lynn, Mass, Nov 22, 23. *Study:* Mass Col Art, BSEd, 45; Cranbrook Acad Art, 48; Syracuse Univ, MFA, 51-53. *Work:* Fogg Art Mus, Harvard Univ; Addison Gallery Am Art; Corcoran Gallery, Washington, DC; Everson Mus, Syracuse, NY; Worcester Art Mus, Mass; Nat Mus Women Arts. *Exhib:* Fairweather Hardin, Chicago, 65-75; one-person retrospective, Addison Gallery Am Art, 71; Bowdoin Col Mus Art, Maine, 75, 81, 84 & 92; Portland Mus Art, Maine, 83, 84 & 92; solo exhibs, Midtown Galleries, New York, 88, Francesca Anderson Galleries, Boston, 88, Hobe Sound Galleries N, Portland, Maine, 88, Sheldon Swope Mus, Terre Haut, Ind, 90, Art Mus Southeast Tex, Beaumont, 90, Bergen Mus Art & Sci, Paramus, NJ, 90, Polk Mus Art, Lakeland, Fla, 91; one-man retrospective travelling exhib, Evansville Mus Arts & Science, Ind, 90; World Expo-92, Seville, Spain. *Teaching:* Chmn art dept, Lasell Jr Col, 45-49; assoc prof painting & teacher educ, Mass Col Art, 49-62; lectr & demonstr, Use of Polyvinyl Acetate (Acrylic) as Painting Medium, throughout Eastern US, 52- *Awards:* Blanche E Colman Found Award, 60; New Eng Watercolor Soc, 60, 62 & 64; Deborah Morton Award, Westbrook Col, Maine, 90. *Bibliog:* John Whitney Payson (auth), The Floral image, Midtown Galleries, 88; Edgar Allen Beem (auth), Maine Art Now, 90; John Whitney Payson (auth, catalog), Beverly Hallam: The Flower Paintings (video), Evansville Mus Arts & Sci, 90; Beverly Hallam (auth), Painting Acrylics with Airbrush, Watercolor 92, fall, 92. *Mem:* New England Watercolor Soc; Ogunquit Art Asn (pres, 64); Barn Gallery Assoc (bd dir, 70-). *Media:* Acrylic on Canvas. *Dealer:* Midtown Payson Galleries 745 Fifth Ave New York NY 10151; Hobe Sound Galleries 58 Maine St Brunswick ME 04011. *Mailing Add:* Surf Point Studio 30 Surf Point Rd York ME 03909

HALLAM, JOHN S
HISTORIAN, ADMINISTRATOR
b Seattle, Wash, Oct 10, 47. *Study:* Seattle Univ, BA, 70; Univ Wash, MA, 74, PhD, 80. *Pos:* Chmn dept art, Pacific Lutheran Univ, 90-92. *Teaching:* Assoc prof art hist, Pacific Lutheran Univ, 90-92. *Mem:* Col Art Asn; Am Soc 18th Century Studies. *Res:* 18th & 19th century Europ & Am Art, urban, imagery, still-life, genre painting & sculpture. *Publ:* Auth, Charles Willson Peale and Hogart's Line of Beauty, Mag Antiques, 86; Meaning & Manner in Chardin's La bonne Education, Bulletin Mus Fine Art, Houston, 86; 18th Century American Townscape and the Face of Colonialism, Smithsonian Studies in Am Art, 91. *Mailing Add:* Pacific Lutheran University Dept of Art Ingram Hall Tacoma WA 98447

HALLENBECK, POMONA JUANITA
PAINTER, PRINTMAKER
b Roswell, NMex, Nov 12, 38. *Study:* Eastern NMex Univ, AA, 65; Sch Visual Arts; Pan Am Sch Art; Arts Students League; Mario Cooper, John Groth & David Stone Martin. *Work:* Eastern NMex Univ, NMex Hist Soc Mus, Roswell, NMex; Union Theological Sem, Levi-Strauss Co, New York, NY; Rochester Mus Fine Art, NY; Blue Cross & Blue Shield, Tulsa, Okla; Ghost Ranch Conference Ctr, Santa Fe, NMex; Cotton, Inc, New York; Mountain Bell Tel & Tel Co, NMex; Jack Leib Filmakers, Chicago. *Comn:* Watercolor, Jack Tar Enterprises, Galveston, Tex, 65; banners & posters, UN Action Against Apartheid, New York, 74; fabric designs, Wamsutta, Huckapoo, Burlington & JC Penny, New York, 74; Cotton Inc, 86; Lady J Designs (painting on silk), 88, book covers for Wink Trilogy, Augsburg Fortress', Minneapolis, Minn, 92; Southwest Expressions, Chicago; Ghost Ranch & Friends (book cover), Santa Fe, NMex, 92. *Exhib:* Paris in the Spring, Raymond Duncan Gallery, 80 & Surindependent's Salon, 81; Wiggins Gallery Shows Pomona, Wiggins Gallery, Ruidoso, NMex, 86; Finishing Touches, Trunk Show, Roswell, MNex, 88; Compadre Conference, Ghost Ranch, NMex; Southwest Expressions, Chicago. *Pos:* Designer window decor, Highland Mall, Austin, Tex, 77; Co-ordination, Ghost Ranch Calendar Project, Santa Fe, NMex, 92. *Teaching:* artist & teacher watercolor & papermaking, Austin Community Col & Roswell Mus, 85; developer of 3 yr academic course in watercolor for NMex Military Inst '84, workshops (W/C, Papermaking, Wearable Art) Carrizo Art School Ruidoso, NMex, 86, 87 & 88; workshops, Ghost Ranch, NMex, 84-92; instr, Elderhostel programs, 86-92; artist in residence, Ghost Ranch, Santa Fe, 92. *Awards:* Purchase Award, Am Artist Exhib, 75; Best of Show, Japhet's of Houston, 79; Bronze Medallion, Prix d'Paris Exhib, Raymond Duncan Gallery, Paris, France, 81. *Bibliog:* NMex videos, silk printing & book covers for educational channels. *Mem:* Soc Illusrs; Surindependents Salon of France; NMex Watercolor Soc; Taos Fine Arts Asn. *Media:* Watercolor; Fiberart, Silk. *Publ:* Illusr, Scott Foresman Math, Scott Foresman, 75; Charles Dickens' Anthology, Crown Publ, 76; illusr bk covers, Julian of Norwich, Nachman of Bratslav & Pseudo Dionysius, Paulist Press, 77; Naming the Powers, Unmasking the Powers Engaging the Powers, Augsburg Fortress. *Dealer:* LeClaire's, Ruidoso, NM; Artisans Austin TX. *Mailing Add:* 3737 East Grand Plains Rd, Roswell NM 88201

HALLER, EMANUEL
PAINTER, PRINTMAKER
b Newark, NJ, Sept 7, 27. *Study:* Newark Sch Fine & Industrial Art, cert, 49. *Work:* Monmouth Col, West Long Branch, NJ; Rosenwald Collection, Nat Gallery Art, Washington, DC; AT&T, Bedminster, NJ; Baseball Hall of Fame, Cooperstown, NY; Football Hall of Fame, Canton, Ohio; and others. *Comn:* Painting, Bound Brook Bd Educ, NJ, 90. *Exhib:* NJ Ann, NJ State Mus, Trenton; NJ Ann, Newark Mus, 77; one-man show, NJ State Mus, Trenton, 85, Mortimer Gallery, NJ, 89, Swain's Galleries, Plainfield, NJ, 89 & Johnson & Johnson World Hq, New Brunswick, NJ, 90; Boston Mus Fine Arts; Philadelphia Mus Art; Seattle Art Mus; Wadsworth Athaneum, Hartford, Conn. *Pos:* Art critic, The Sunday Courier News, Bridgewater, NJ, 87. *Teaching:* Instr, Newark Mus, NJ, currently. *Awards:* State of NJ Visual Arts Fel Grant, 85. *Bibliog:* Charles H Waterhouse (auth), The Detail of Life: Drawings and Prints of Emanuel Haller. *Mem:* Printmaking Coun NJ (bd dirs); Somerset Art Asn, Far Hills, NJ. *Media:* All. *Publ:* Auth & illusr, article on travel drawings, Am Artist Mag, 70; illusr, All the Strange Hours, Scribners, 75. *Mailing Add:* 121 Greenbrook Rd North Plainfield NJ 07060

HALLEY, PETER
PAINTER
b New York, NY, Sept 24, 53. *Study:* Yale Univ, New Haven, Conn, BA; Univ New Orleans, MFA. *Work:* Guggenheim Mus, New York; Wright State Univ, Dayton; Carnegie Mus Art, Pittsburgh; San Francisco Mus Modern Art, Calif; Addison Gallery Am Art, Andover, Mass; Whitney Mus. *Comn:* Painting for bd rm, Chase Manhattan Bank, New York, 89. *Exhib:* Biennial, Whitney Mus, New York, 87; Viewpoints: Postwar painting & sculpture, Guggenheim Mus, New York, 88; Binational: Am Art of the late 80's, Mus Fine Arts, Boston, 88; Carnegie International, Carnegie Mus Art, Pittsburgh, 88; Ten plus Ten: Contemporary Soviet and American Painters, Ft Worth Mus, Tex, 89; Abstraction in Question, Ringling Mus Art, Sarasota, Fla, 89; Projects & Portfolios, Brooklyn Mus, New York, 89; Word as Image: American Art 1960-1990, Milwaukee, Wis, 90; Touring Europ Retrospective, Switz, France, Spain & Amsterdam, 91-92. *Teaching:* Instr painting & sculpture, Sch Visual Arts, New York, 89- *Bibliog:* Mark Stevens (auth), Neo-Geo Art's Computer Hum, Newsweek, 11/87; Roberta Smith (auth), Minimalism's Slow Fire, New York Times, 12/89; Jeanne Siegel, Art Talk Da Capo Press, NY, 89. *Media:* Acrylic, Oil. *Publ:* Auth, Collected Essays 1981-1987, Bruno Bischofberger, 88. *Dealer:* Gagosian Gallery 136 Wooster St New York NY 10012. *Mailing Add:* 12 Harrison St New York NY 10013

HALLIDAY, NANCY R
ILLUSTRATOR, INSTRUCTOR
b Chicago, Ill, Mar 30, 36. *Study:* Mich State Univ, East Lansing, 54-56 & 58-61; Art Sch Soc Arts & Crafts, Mich, 56-57; Univ Okla, Norman, BSc, 62, Northeastern Ill Univ, Chicago, MA, 88. *Work:* Fla State Mus, Gainesville; Nat Mus Natural Hist, Smithsonian Inst; Hunt Inst Botanical Documentation, Pittsburgh, Pa; Visual Arts Gallery, Pensacola Jr Col, Fla. *Comn:* Watercolor poster, Rare Animal Relief Effort, Inc, New York, 81; eight stamp paintings, Nat Wildlife Fedn, Washington, DC, 82, 83, 85, 89 & 92; oil landscape, Nat Hist Soc Barrington, Ill, 87; five watercolor illustrations, Scott, Foresman & Co, Glenview, Ill, 88; 29 watercolor plates, Hawaiian fauna & flora, Western Publ Co. *Exhib:* Perfectly Beautiful: Art in

Science, Smithsonian Inst, 78; Acad Natural Sci, Philadelphia, 81-82; Denver Mus Natural Hist, 82; two-person show, Macon, Ga, 82; Wildlife in Art, Nat Wildlife Fedn, Vienna, Va, 83; Wondrous Wildlife, Cincinnati Zoo, 83; Ann Bird Art Exhib, Leigh Yawkey Woodson Art Mus, Wausau, Wis, 83; Nature Interpreted, Cincinnati Mus Natural Hist, 84; Sixth Int Exhib Botanical Art & Illustration, Hunt Inst Botanical Doc, Pittsburgh, 88; and others. *Pos:* Lectr & asst exhib preparator, Mus Mich State Univ, East Lansing, 57-60; asst, Mus Northern Ariz, Flagstaff, summer 63; artist, Nat Mus Natural Hist, Smithsonian Inst, 66-70; illusr, dept natural sci, Fla State Mus, Gainesville, 73-81; artist-naturalist, Forest Preserve Dist Cook Co, Ill, 89- *Teaching:* Instr, animal illus, Univ Fla, Gainesville, 77, 78 & 82; artist-in-education, Ryerson Conserv Area, Deerfield, Ill, 86; instr, biol illus, Univ Ill, Chicago, 85-86; artist-in-residence, Rockford Art Mus, Ill, 91. *Awards:* First Prize Color Wildlife, Guild Natural Sci Illusr Show, Hunt Inst Botanical Doc, Pa, 79; Second Prize for Watercolor, Wildlife in Art Show, Nat Wildlife Fedn, 83. *Mem:* Soc Animal Artists; Guild of Natural Sci Illusr; Nature Artists' Guild of the Morton Arboretum. *Media:* Watercolor; Pen & Ink. *Res:* History of biological illustration. *Publ:* Illusr, Behavioral ecology of the Yucatan jay, Wilson Bulletin, 76; Hybridization in Calypte hummingbirds, Auk, 78; auth, Bird illustration, In: Guild Handbook of Biological Illustration (ed, Elaine R S Hodges), Van Nostrand Reinhold, 88; illusr, Scratchboard for Illustration, Ruth Lozner, Watson- Guptill, NY, 90; auth, To see distinctly: the art of Joseph Wolf, J Natural Sci Illusr, 91. *Mailing Add:* 1156 Pine St Apt 4 Glenview IL 60025

HALLMAN, GARY LEE
PHOTOGRAPHER
b St Paul, Minn, Aug 7, 40. *Study:* Univ Minn, Minneapolis, BA, 66, MFA, 71. *Work:* Mus Mod Art, New York; Int Mus Photog, Rochester; Nat Gallery Can, Toronto; Fogg Art Mus, Harvard Univ; Princeton Univ Art Mus. *Comn:* Photo murals, Dayton-Hudson Corp, Minneapolis, 70. *Exhib:* 60's Continuum, Int Mus Photog, 72; Fight of the Image, Contemporary American Drawings, Paintings & Photographs, Mus Turin, Italy, 73; one-man shows, Int Mus Photog, George Eastman House, 74 & Light Gallery, New York, 75; Fourteen American Photographers, Baltimore Mus, 75. *Teaching:* Vis artist, Southampton Col, summer 72 & 73; asst prof photog, Univ Minn, Minneapolis, 70-76, assoc prof photog, 76-; vis adj prof photog, RI Sch Design, 77. *Awards:* Grad Sch Univ Minn Res Grant, 73 & 76; Nat Endowment Arts Photog Fel Grant, 75; Bush Found Fel for Artists, 76. *Bibliog:* E W Peterson (auth), The photography of Gary Hallman, Image, 9/75. *Mem:* Soc Photog Educ. *Dealer:* Light Gallery 724 Fifth Ave New York NY 10019. *Mailing Add:* 2932 Pierce St NE Minneapolis MN 55418

HALLMAN, H THEODORE, JR
CRAFTSMAN, DESIGNER
b Bucks Co, Pa, Dec 23, 33. *Study:* Tyler Sch, Temple Univ, Sen scholar, BFA & BSEd; Fontainebleau Fine Arts, Pew scholar, cert, with Jacques Villon; Cranbrook Acad Art, West scholar, MFA(painting) & MFA(textile design); Bundestextilschule, Austria, cert; Univ Calif, Berkeley, PhD(educ); master classes philos & symbolic image with Kenneth G Mills, Toronto. *Work:* Chicago Art Inst; Victoria & Albert Mus, London; Metrop Mus Art, New York; Philadelphia Mus Art, Pa; Brooklyn Mus; Addison Gallery of Am Art, Andover, Mass; and others. *Comn:* Translucent tapestry, Nieman Marcus, Dallas; room, St John's Church, Allentown, Pa; Am Chem Soc, Washington, DC. *Exhib:* Am Wallhangings, Victoria & Albert Mus, London, 62; Three Centuries of Am Art, Philadelphia Mus Art, 76; The Art Fabric-Mainstream, Am Fedn Arts, 82; one-man shows, Fashion Inst Technol Gallery, New York, 83, Brooklyn Mus Art, 84, Gallery 21, Tokyo, Fuji Gallery, Osaka & Kyoto, Am Ctr, Kyoto, 85 & Hamilton Art Gallery, Can, 86; Fiber Revolution, Milwaukee Art Mus Invitational, 86; Talkative Textiles, Trans-Am Gallery, San Francisco & travelling in the US; Opening Show & Represented by Okun Gallery, Sante Fe, NMex; and others. *Pos:* Consult, ILO Textiles, Jamaica, summer 68; textile designer, var co. *Teaching:* Instr, Haystack Sch, Maine & Penland Sch Crafts, summers 58-69; prof textiles & chmn dept, Moore Col Art, 65-70; assoc prof textile design, San Jose State Univ, 72-75; lectr & workshop leader, US, Can & Eng (incl San Antonio, Vancouver, Ottawa & Mich, 77-78); head textiles, Ont Col Art, Toronto, 79-; guest lectr, World Craft Conf, Mex, 76. *Awards:* Tiffany Found Grant, 62; Textile Prize, Int Kunsthandwerk Expos, Stuttgart, 67; Fel Am Craft Coun, 88. *Bibliog:* Bevlin (auth), Design Through Discovery, Holt Reinhart Winston, 63; Neuman (auth), Plastics as an Art Form, Chilten, 68; Regensteiner (auth), Art of Weaving, 70, Willcox (auth), Techniques of Rya Knotting, 71 & Constantine/Larsen (auth), The Art Fabric-Mainstream, Van Nostrand Reinhold; Irene Waller (auth), Textile Sculptures, Studio Vista, 77; among others. *Mem:* Philadelphia Coun Prof Craftsmen; Ont Craft Coun; hon mem Zurich, Int Soc Arts & Lett; Nat Soc Lit & Arts; Toronto Textile Mus (adv bd), Can. *Media:* Weaving, Textile Designing. *Mailing Add:* 60 Ruddington Dr No 1604 Willowdale ON M2K 2J9 Canada

HALLMAN, TED See Hallman, H Theodore

HALLMARK, DONALD PARKER
MUSEUM DIRECTOR, LECTURER
b McPherson, Kans, Feb 16, 45. *Study:* Univ Ill, BFA(art hist), 67; Univ Iowa, MA(art hist), 70; St Louis Univ, PhD, 80. *Collections Arranged:* Richard W Bock Sculpture Collection (with catalog), Greenville Col, 75; Frank Lloyd Wright Decorative Arts Collection, Dana House, 81-88, Post Restoration Reopening of the Collection, 90. *Pos:* Cur & dir, Richard W Bock Sculpture Collection, Greenville Col, 72-81; supt, hist site, Dana House, Springfield, Ill, 81-; auth, SITE Brochures, 81-92. *Teaching:* Assoc prof art & fine arts, Greenville Col, 70-81, chmn dept art, 75-81, prof, 81-; lectr, Springfield Art Asn, 81-, Sangamon State Univ, 82-, Art Inst of Chicago, High Mus, Atlanta, Ga, Gamble House, Pasadena, Calif, Currier Gallery, Manchester, NH. *Awards:* Kress Found Res Grant, Univ Iowa, 69; Shell Found Fac Improv Grant, 72-73; Nat Endowment Arts & Am Asn Mus Cur Seminar Scholar, 75 & 80; Nat Trust Honor Award for Preservation of Dana House. *Bibliog:* W R Hasbrouck (auth), Editors note, Prairie Sch Rev, Vol VIII, No 1, 71; H Allen Brooks (auth), Prairie Sch, Univ Toronto, 72; D Hoffmann, Frank Lloyd Wright: Architecture & Nature, Dutton, 86; Narcisco Menocal (auth), Taliesin--and Flower in the Crannied Wall, Taliesin Studies, Vol I, 74. *Mem:* Am Asn Mus; Col Art Asn. *Res:* Late 19th and early 20th century sculpture and architecture with emphasis on the Chicago School, 1880-1915. *Publ:* Auth, Richard W Bock, Sculptor, Prairie Sch Rev, 71; Chicago's prairie sculptor, R W Bock, 82; The Studio Collaborations, Decorative Arts Soc Newsletter, 12/88; illusr, Frank Lloyd Wright's Dana-Thomas House, Ill Hist J, summer 89, rev ed 92. *Mailing Add:* 505 W Sheridan Rd Petersburg IL 62675

HALPERN, NATHAN L
COLLECTOR
b Sioux City, Iowa, Oct 22, 14. *Study:* Otis Art Inst, Los Angeles; Univ Southern Calif, BA, 36; Harvard Univ Law Sch, LLB(cum laude), 39. *Pos:* Pres, TNT Commun Inc. *Mem:* Hon trustee, Int Ctr Photog. *Collection:* French impressionist and post-impressionist art; Chinese bronzes and ceramics; Southeast Asian art. *Mailing Add:* 993 Fifth Ave New York NY 10028

HALPERN, NORA R
DIRECTOR, CURATOR
b New York, NY, Dec 5, 60. *Study:* Helena Rubenstein Fel, Whitney Mus Am Art Independent Study Prog, 82; Univ Calif, Los Angeles, BFA, 83, MFA, 90. *Collections Arranged:* Frames of Reference, Whitney Mus, Downtown Branch, 82; Jeune Californie, Am Ctr, Paris, 86; Fauxto graphy, Art Ctr Col Design, 89; Dynaton, Before & Beyond, Lee Mullican, Gordon Onslow-Ford, Wolfgang Paalen, Pepperdine Univ, 92. *Pos:* Cur Collections, Frederick Weisman Co, Frederick R Weisman Art Found & F Weisman Personal Collection, Los Angeles, 83-90; dir, Frederick R Weisman Mus Art, Pepperdine Univ, Malibu, CA, 92- *Teaching:* Adj prof art hist, Pepperdine Univ, Malibu, CA, 92- *Mem:* Los Angeles Inst Contemp Art (bd mem 83-87); Art Table. *Publ:* Auth & ed, Frames of Reference, Whitney Mus, NY, 82; FR Weisman Found Art, Volume II, 85, Selections from FR Weisman Collection, 87, Art & Architecture & Society, Vols I & II, 90, Weisman Found; ed, Art Fairs: Plans and Process, 89; ed, Conservation & Contemporary Art, 90; ed, Support for The Arts in Unsupportive Times, 90; ed, Dynaton, Before & Beyond: Lee Mullican, Gordon Onslow-Ford, Wolfgang Paalen, Pepperdine Univ, 92. *Mailing Add:* Frederick R Weisman Mus Art, Pepperdine Univ 24255 Pacific Coast Hwy Malibu CA 90263

HALSEY, BRIAN ELLIOTT
PAINTER, CONSULTANT
b Kendallville, Ind, July 16, 42. *Study:* Wheaton Col, Ill, with W Karl Steele, BA, 64; Trinity Col, Deerfield, Ill, MA, 67; Fla State Univ, with Gunar Bosch, PhD, 72. *Work:* Nat Gallery Art, Washington, DC; Metrop Mus Art, New York; Nat Mus Art, Kyoto, Japan; Los Angeles Co Mus Art, Calif; Detroit Inst Arts, Mich. *Comn:* Progressive suite (12 pieces), Northern Bell Labs, Ann Arbor, Mich, 83; progressive suite (11 pieces), Lazard-Frere, Rockefeller Ctr, New York, 85; Progressive Suite (10 pieces) Williams Int, Walled Lake, Mich, 87. *Exhib:* 38th Mid-Year Show, Butler Inst Art, Youngstown, Ohio, 74; 5th Int, Pratt Graphic Ctr, New York, 75; Biennial Int, Print Club Galleries, Philadelphia, Pa, 75; Soc Am Graphic Artists, 77-; 3rd Int Exhib, Nat Arts Club, New York, 77; Los Angeles Printmaking Soc, 79- *Pos:* Dir, Fine Art Serv, Ann Arbor, Mich. *Teaching:* Assoc prof art & art hist, Spring Arbor Col, Mich, 67-76. *Awards:* US Steel Fel, US Steel Found, 69-71; Grand Galleria, 3rd Ann Nat, 74; Nat Acad Design, 150th Ann Exhib, 75. *Bibliog:* Nicholas Roukes (auth), Acrylics Bold & New, Chap 9, Watson-Guptill, 85. *Mem:* Soc Am Graphic Artists; Los Angeles Printmaking Soc. *Media:* Acrylic; Screen Printing. *Res:* Christ-theme in contemporary art; Freudian studies. *Publ:* Auth, Paul Tillich on Religion and Art, Lexington Quart, 74; Freud on the nature of art, Am J Art Therapy, 77, illusr, Series of Mathematical Texts (6 Covers), Brooks-Cole, 80-82; Michigan Bar J, cover, 85; illusr, Economics, Arnold, West Publ, 89. *Dealer:* Fine Art Serv 91 Enterprise Dr Suite I Ann Arbor MI 48103. *Mailing Add:* 2513 Meade Ct Ann Arbor MI 48105

HALSEY, WILLIAM MELTON
PAINTER, SCULPTOR
b Charleston, SC, Mar 13, 15. *Study:* Univ SC; Sch Boston Mus Fine Arts, with Alexandre Iacovleff & Karl Zerbe, Paige Traveling Fel, 39-41; Univ Mex. *Work:* Baltimore Mus Art, Md; SC Arts Comn State Collection, Columbia; Mint Mus Art, Charlotte, NC; Gibbes Mus, Charleston; Greenville Co Mus Art, SC; Nat Mus Am Art, Smithsonian Inst, Washington, DC; SC State Mus, Columbia. *Comn:* Frescoes, Berkshire Mus Art, Pittsfield, Mass, 39; murals, Beth Elohim Synagogue, Charleston, 50 & Baltimore Hebrew Congregation Temple, 52; Container Corp Am; Ford Motor Co; and many portrait comn in pub bldgs. *Exhib:* Contemp Artists SC, Columbia Mus, Florence Mus, Greenville Mus & Gibbes Art Gallery; retrospective, four SC Mus, 72-73; Art in Transition, Boston Mus Fine Arts, 77; Spoleto Festival USA, 82; Painting in the South, Va Mus, 83; Volti del Sud, Palazzo Venezia, Rome, 84; South Eastern Ctr Contemp Art, Winston-Salem, 88; Gibbes Mus, 89; SC State Mus, 89; Piccolo Spoleto, Charleston, 91-92. *Teaching:* Asst prof painting & drawing, Col Charleston, 65-75; instr painting & drawing, Newberry Col, 68-70; artist-in-residence, Col Charleston, 76-83. *Awards:* Res Grant, SC

State Art Comn, 74-75; SC Comt Humanities Grant, 82; Col Charleston Grant, 82. *Bibliog:* Jack Morris (auth), Contemporary Artists of South Carolina, 70 & William M Halsey: Retrospective (monogr), 72, Greenville Co Mus Art. *Media:* Oil. *Publ:* Coauth, A Travel Sketch Book, 71; auth, Maya Journal, 77. *Mailing Add:* 26 Archdale St Charleston SC 29401

HALVORSEN, ELSPETH COLETTE (ELSPETH HALVORSEN-VEVERS)
ASSEMBLAGE ARTIST, SCULPTOR
b Staten Island, New York, Feb 23, 29. *Study:* New Sch Social Res, New York, 48-51; Art Students League, 48-52; Univ NC, Greensboro, NC, 63-64; Purdue Univ, WLafayette, Ind, BA, 64-71. *Work:* Provincetown Art Asn & Mus, Provincetown, Mass; Greater Lafayette Art Mus, Lafayette, Ind; Purdue Univ, Permanent Collection, WLafayette, Ind; Sculpture Ctr, New York. *Exhib:* One-woman shows, Provincetown Group Gallery, Mass, 79-82, 86, Visual Images Gallery, Wellfleet, Mass, 84,85, Lookmasters Gallery, Provincetown, Mass, 87 & Phoenix Gallery, 88; Box Constructions-Installation, Women's Art Registry, Minneapolis, Minn, 82; Mostra Exhib I, Univ Ga, Cortona, Italy, 84 & Mostra Exhib II, Athens, Ga, 85; retrospective exhib, Mass, 85; Looking at Earth Exhib, Nat Air & Space Mus, Smithsonian Inst, Washington, DC, 86-87; Rising Tide Gallery, Provincetown, Mass, 89, 90, 91 & 92; Wohlfarth Gallery, Washington, DC, 92. *Teaching:* Teacher ceramic sculpture, Lafayette Art Mus, Inc, 79-82; Instr sculpture, Truro Ctr Arts, Mass, 81-92; Provincetown Art Assoc & Mus, Mass, 87. *Awards:* Emily Lowe, Ward Eggleston Gallery, 51; Honor mention, Sculpture Show, Lafayette Art Ctr, 75; Installation Grant, Womens Art Registry, Minneapolis, Minn, 82. *Mem:* Provincetown Art Asn. *Media:* Miscellaneous Media. *Dealer:* Rising Tide Gallery 494 Commercial St Provincetown MA 02657; Wohlfarth Galleries 3418 Ninth St NE Washington DC 20017. *Mailing Add:* 250 Bradford St Provincetown MA 02657

HAMADY, WALTER SAMUEL
COLLAGE ARTIST
b Flint, Mich, Sept 13, 40. *Study:* Wayne State Univ, BFA, 64; Cranbrook Acad Art, MFA, 66. *Work:* Libr Congress; Lenin Libr, Moscow; New York Public Libr; Victoria & Albert Mus, London; Whitney Mus Art, New York. *Exhib:* Book Arts in the USA (catalog), traveling, 90-92; Americans in Print, Gutenberg Mus, Mainz, Ger, 89; Int Book Design Exhib, Leipzig, Ger, 89; Walter Hamady: 25 Years (catalog), Wustum Mus, Racine, 91; Art of Breathing, Marvin Sackner Archieve, Miami, 92. *Pos:* Proprietor, The Perishable Press Limited, 64- *Teaching:* Prof drawing, bk illus, collage & artists books, Univ Wis-Madison, 66- *Awards:* Wis Alumni Res Found Grants & Awards, 66-70 & 72-92; John Simon Guggenheim Fel, 69; Nat Endowment Arts Grant, 76, 78, 80. *Bibliog:* Walter Hamady: Handmade Books, Collage and Sculpture (monogr with essays by Toby Olson & Buzz Spector), Wustum Mus Art, Racine, Wis, 91; Janice T Paine (auth), The word on books and boxes, Milwaukee Sentinel, 4/5/91; Mary Lydon (auth), The book as trojan horse of art: Walter Hamady, perishable press limited and gabberjabbs 1-6, Visible Language, Vol 25, No 2/3, 92. *Mem:* Printing Hist Soc; Wis Phenological Soc; Am Typecasting Fel; Schwitters Soc. *Media:* Collage, Books. *Publ:* Auth, Breaking the Bindings/Am Book Art Now (exhib catalog), Elvehjem Mus Art, Madison, Wis, 83; Objects in Transition: Contemporary Book Art (exhib catalog), Temari Center, Honolulu, 84; Two Decades of Hamady and The Perishable Press Ltd: An Anecdotally Annotated Check-list for an Exhibition at Gallery 210, Univ of Mo, 84; Designing Literature, printing and the DP of the U, Fine Print, Vol 14 No 3, 7/88; Neopostmodrinism or Dieser Rasen Ist Kein Hundeklo or Gabberjabb Number 6, Perishable Press Ltd, 88. *Mailing Add:* The Perishable Press Ltd Postbox 7 Mt Horeb WI 53572

HAMAGUCHI, YOZO
PRINTMAKER
b Wakayama-ken, Japan, Apr 5, 09. *Study:* Sch Fine Arts, Tokyo, 28-30; independent study, painting & engraving, Paris, 30-39. *Work:* Nat Mus Mod Art, Tokyo; Mus Mod Art, New York; Victoria & Albert Mus, London; Libr Cong & Nat Gallery, Washington, DC; Cleveland Mus Art. *Exhib:* One-man exhibs, Paris, Turin, Sao Paulo, New York & others, 58-72 & Cleveland Mus Art, Ohio, 73, San Francisco, 83; and others. *Awards:* 1st Int Prize, Sao Paulo Biennale, 57; Grand Prizes, Ljubljana Int Print Biennale, 61 & 72; Purchase Prize, Warsaw Nat Mus, 66 & 72. *Bibliog:* Hamaguchi (exhib catalog), Vorpal Gallery, 88. *Mem:* Acad Fiorentina Della Arti del Disegno. *Mailing Add:* c/o Vorpal Gallery 393 Grove St San Francisco CA 94102

HAMANN, MARILYN D
EDUCATOR, PAINTER
b Los Angeles, Calif, Nov 24, 45. *Study:* Univ Calif, Berkeley, BA, 67, with Robert Hudson & Jim Melchert, MA, 70. *Work:* Univ Ky Art Mus, Lexington; Citizen's Fidelity Bank & Trust Co & Liberty Nat Bank, Louisville, Ky; Cincinnati Bell Info Systems; Cent Bank & Trust Co, Lexington. *Exhib:* Whitney Mus Am Art, New York, 73; Everson Mus Art, New York, 74; Contemp Art Ctr, Cincinnati, 74; New Orleans Mus Art, 75; Oakland Mus Art, Calif, 75; J B Speed Art Mus, Louisville, Ky, 74, 77, 81 & 82; Southeastern Ctr Contemp Art, Winston-Salem, NC, 81; Franklin Furnace, New York, 82; Archive Small Press & Communs Space, Antwerp, Belg, 82. *Teaching:* Assoc prof, Univ Ky, Lexington, 80- *Awards:* Al Smith Fel, Ky Arts Coun, 86; Ky Found Women Grant, 87; Award of Merit, Huntington Mus Art, 88. *Bibliog:* Diane Heilenman (auth), article, Louisville Courier-J, 77; Jacqueline Rapp (auth), article, New Art Examiner, 78; Guy Mendes (producer), Kentucky Now, Ky Educ Television, 79. *Mem:* Artists Equity. *Media:* Acrylic, Video. *Publ:* Int Soc Copier Artists Quart, Vol 1, No 1 & 3, New York, 82 & 83. *Dealer:* Triangle Gallery 522 W Short St Lexington KY 40508. *Mailing Add:* Art Dept Office 218 Reynolds Bldg No 1 Univ Ky Lexington KY 40506-0101

HAMAR, DIANA KATHLEEN
PAINTER
b Toledo, Ore. *Study:* Inst Am Univs, Aix-En-Provence, France; Univ Wash, Seattle, BFA, 78, MFA, 85. *Work:* Alaska State Mus, Juneau; Univ Alaska Mus, Fairbanks; Alaska State Coun Arts, Anchorage Mus Hist & Art, Anchorage. *Exhib:* Solo exhibs, Anchorage Mus Hist & Art, 90, Alaska State Mus, Juneau, 91, Gallery Parsons Paris Sch Design, France, 92 & Visual Arts Ctr Alaska, Anchorage, 92; Juneau Artists, Peterhof Benois Mus, St Petersburg, Russia, 92. *Awards:* Individual Artist Fel, Alaska State Coun Arts, 88; Visual Artist Fel Painting, 91-92 & US/France Artist Exchange Residency, 92, Nat Endowment Arts. *Media:* Oil on Canvas, Oil on Collaged Paper. *Mailing Add:* PO Box 21128 Juneau AK 99802

HAMBLEN, DR KAREN A
EDUCATOR, WRITER
Study: Univ Oregon, BS (art educ), 74, MS, 77, PhD, 81. *Pos:* Co-ed, Green Hills Press Publ, 75-81; ed reviewer, Bulletin of Caucus on Social Theory & Art Educ, 85-86, assoc ed, 87-88; ed bd mem, Studies in Art Educ, 86-88, co-ed, 89-91, senior ed, 91-; contrib ed, Arts Educ Rev of Books, 87-; ed reviewer, J on Social Theory and Art Educ, 89 & 90. *Teaching:* Visiting asst prof, art educ dept, Univ Ore, 81-82; asst prof, art dept, Calif State Univ-Long Beach, 82-85; assoc prof, Sch Art, La State Univ, Baton Rouge, 85-88, dept curric & instr, 88-90, prof, 90- *Awards:* Manuel Barkan Mem Award, Scholarly merit of published work, 85; Mary Rouse Mem Award, Women's Caucus of Nat Art Educ Asn, 87; La Endowment for Humanities, 88. *Publ:* Contribr, Implementing art criticism in the classroom, No 5, Trends in Art Educ, 87, 36-88; Testing in art: A critical theory perspective, Viewpoints: Dialogue in Art Educ, 88, 31-42; contribr, Rethinking roles: Art education, sexism, and DBAE, Vol 89, No 4, 88, 43-47 & Knowedge, skills and creativity: What balance? (essay), Vol 90, No 5, 89, 25-26, Design for Arts in Educ; Research in Art Educ as a form of Consumer Protection, Studies in Art Education, Vol 31, No 1, 37-45, 89; Local Art Knowledge, Australian Art Education, Vol 14, No 3, 22-29, 90. *Mailing Add:* Dept Curric & Instr Peabody Hall La State Univ Baton Rouge LA 70803

HAMBLETON, RICHARD A
PAINTER
b Seattle, Wash, June 23, 54. *Study:* San Francisco Art Inst, Calif, BA, 74. *Exhib:* Venice Biennial, Italy, 84-86; Salvatore Ala Gallery, Milano, Italy, 84 & New York, 85; Piezo Electric Gallery, New York, 85; Mus Contemp Art, Costa Rica, 85; Zellermayer Gallery, Berlin, Ger, 85; Diane Brown Gallery, New York, 87. *Dealer:* Milford Gallery 560 Broadway New York NY. *Mailing Add:* 199 Chrystie St 2nd & 3rd floor New York NY 10002

HAMBURGER, SYDNEY K
SCULPTOR, CURATOR
b New York, NY, Feb 2, 35. *Study:* Md Inst Col Art, 72; Towson State Univ, BS(sculpture), 72, MEd(art educ & sculpture), 73; Magdalen Col, Oxford Univ, Eng, 77. *Work:* Acad Arts, Easton, Md; MacDowell Colony, Peterborough, NH; Borough of Manhattan Community Col, New York; Helen Wurlitzer Found, Taos, NMex; Chesapeake Col, Wye Mills, Md; and others. *Exhib:* Solo shows, Washington Co Mus Fine Arts, Hagerstown, Md, 87, Marymount Manhattan Col, New York, 87, Gallery 10, Ltd, Washington, DC, 90 & 14 Sculptors Gallery, New York, 91; Curators as Artists, Acad Arts Sculpture Field, Shidoni Gallery, Tesuque, NMex, 88; Phillip Bareiss Gallery, Taos, NMex, 90, 91 & 92; Mill St Gallery, Aspen, Colo, 92; Sculpture Park, Col Sante Fe, NMex, 92; Washington Sculptor's Group Juried Exhib, Washington, DC, 92; and others. *Pos:* Cur, Acad Arts, Easton, 82-85. *Teaching:* Grad asst, Towson State Univ, 72-73, adj fac, 73-79; pvt students, sculpture & ceramics, 73-77; instr, Jewish Community Ctr, Baltimore, 74-77; instr, Manpower Prog, 76-79; adj fac, Essex Community Col, Md, 77-78 & Anne Arundel Community Col, Arnold, Md, 78-81; vis artist, Md Inst Col Art, 86. *Awards:* Sculpture Award, Acad Arts, 69, Annapolis Fine Arts Festival, 69 & Ctr Club Ann Invitational, Baltimore, 72; Outdoor Sculpture Award, Baltimore Arts Festival, 78; and others. *Mem:* Col Arts Asn; Artist Equity Asn; Washington Sculptors Group; Womens Caucus Arts; Sculptors Guild, New York. *Media:* Wood, Metal. *Dealer:* Shidoni Contemp Gallery Bishops Lodge Rd Tesuque NM 87574. *Mailing Add:* PO Box 250 Tesuque NM 87574

HAMER, CHARLES JAMES
PAINTER
b Elmira, NY, Jan 5, 31. *Study:* Rochester Inst Technol, with Ralph Avery & Hans Barschel, BS(art & design), 56. *Work:* Lake St Presby Church, Elmira, NY; also pvt collections. *Exhib:* Salmagundi Club Ann Non-Mem, New York, 79-81; 155th Ann, Nat Acad Design, New York, 80; Nat Arts Club Ann, New York, 80-81; Allied Artists Asn, World Trade Ctr, New York, 81; and others. *Awards:* 1st Prize Watercolor, US Postal Serv, New York, 78; and others. *Mem:* Nat Acad Design; Allied Artists Am Asn. *Media:* Watercolor. *Publ:* Illusr, Newsprint application of Webb offset colour, Penrose Ann, Hasting House, 59. *Mailing Add:* 133 E 35th St New York NY 10016

HAMES, CARL MARTIN
DEALER
b Birmingham, Ala, July 12, 38. *Study:* Birmingham Southern Col, BA, 58; Samford Univ, Birmingham, MA, 71, MSEd, 80, with Cornelia Rivers & Gene Smith. *Collections Arranged:* Collection of Altamont Sch, Town Hall Gallery, Birmingham; Doris Wainwright Kennedy in Private Collections, Birmingham Southern Col, 79; Paintings by Gerald Davis, Town Hall Gallery, 80; Recent Followers of Edith Frohock, 83; Recent Work by the Art Faculty the Univ of Ala, 85-; and others. *Pos:* Dir, Town Hall Gallery, Birmingham, 65-; mem

adv bd, Ala Alliance for Arts in Educ; comt chmn, Imagination Celebration, 81- *Teaching:* Instr art/sci, Birmingham Pub Sch, 62-64; teacher art & organizer art dept, Birmingham Univ Sch, 64-75; asst headmaster, Altamont Sch, 75-81, dean students, 81-90, headmaster, 91- *Awards:* Silver Bowl Award for Art, Birmingham Festival of Arts. *Mem:* Birmingham Arts Mus Art Educ Coun; Birmingham Mus Art; and others. *Specialty:* Alabama and southeastern artists. *Collection:* Prints by 20th century European and American masters; sculptures, paintings and contemporary photographs. *Publ:* Auth, A Patient and Discerning Eye: An Appreciation of Silvia Pizitz, Birmingham Mus Art, 80; auth introd, Rosalie Pettus Price Retrospective (catalog), Birmingham Mus Art; contribr, Ida Kohlmeyer Nat Retrospective (catalog). *Mailing Add:* 3963 Montclair Rd Birmingham AL 35213

HAMILL, TIM J
PAINTER, PRINTMAKER
b Clinton, Iowa, Dec 2, 42. *Study:* Univ Wis, 60-62; L'Ecole Nat Superieure Beaux-Arts, Paris, 62-63; Boston Univ Sch Fine Arts, BFA, 65, MFA, 68; Akademie Bildenden Künste, Munich, 65-66. *Work:* Boston Mus Fine Arts & Boston Pub Libr, Mass; DeCordova Mus, Lincoln, Mass; Minn Mus Art, St Paul; Worcester Mus, Mass; and many others. *Comn:* 11 paintings & 2 prints, Royal Palace, Riyadh, Saudi Arabia, 80. *Exhib:* One-man exhibs, Brockton Art Ctr, Mass, 69, Milton Acad, Mass, 71-80 & Gallery Naga, Boston, 78-83 & 85; Boston Printmakers, Rose Art Mus, Waltham, Mass, 70 & 72; DeCordova Mus, Lincoln, Mass, 73, 77, 80 & 82; Photography in Printmaking, Boston Mus Fine Arts, Mass, 75; Artists in Residence, Inst Contemp Art, Boston, 75; Art Complex Mus, Duxbury, Mass, 76-81; and many others. *Pos:* Founding mem, Boston Visual Artists Union, 72-, mem exec bd, 72-75. *Teaching:* Instr painting & drawing, Boston Univ, 68-71; instr painting & drawing, Milton Acad, Mass, 71-81. *Mem:* Boston Printmakers (exec bd). *Media:* Oil, Acrylic; Silkscreen, Lithography. *Dealer:* Gallery Naga 67 Newbury St Boston MA 02116. *Mailing Add:* 345 Centre St Milton MA 02186

HAMILTON, FRANK MOSS
PAINTER, ARCHITECT
b Kansas City, Mo, June 26, 30. *Study:* With Eliot O'Hara; Stanford Univ, 2 years; Univ Kans, BA(archit), 54. *Work:* Favell Mus, Klamath Falls, Ore; Leanin' Tree Gallery, Boulder, Colo; Walter Bimson's Valley Nat Bank Collection. *Exhib:* Laguna Beach Festival of Arts, Calif, 49-68; Orange Co Fair, 51; Laguna Art Asn Gallery; Nat Orange Show, Pomona; Gold Medal Western Competition, Franklin Mint Yearly Western Show, 74. *Teaching:* Pvt art classes, 49-88. *Awards:* First Awards, Laguna Beach Art Festival, 63-65; First Prizes, Lake San Marcos Art Festival, 66 & 68; Third Place, Franklin Mint Bicentennial Medal Design, 72. *Media:* Watercolor, Oil. *Publ:* Illusr, Orange Co Illus Mag, Calif, 66, 69 & Jerome Arizona Cookbook, 72. *Mailing Add:* 22467 N 27th Ave No 14 Phoenix AZ 85027

HAMILTON, GEORGE EARL
PAINTER, EDUCATOR
b Pittsfield, Mass, Oct 10, 34. *Study:* Int Christian Univ, 56-58; with Dr Samine Tuyoda, Japan, 58-60. *Work:* Frye Art Mus, Seattle; Univ Wash; Kaiser Found & First Nat Bank, Portland, Ore; Royal Bank Can; Ore State Univ. *Exhib:* One-man shows, Am Watercolor Soc, New York, 75 & 76, North Western Watercolor Soc, Seattle, 75-79, Mus Art, Casper, Wyo, 76, Frye Art Mus, Seattle, 76 & 81, Portland Art Mus, 77 & Univ Mus Art, Eugene, Ore, 77-79. *Teaching:* Instr watercolor, Univ Wash, 76- & Univ Idaho, 79-81. *Awards:* Am Watercolor Soc Award, 76; Ore Agriculture Purchase Award; SE Washington Silver Medal; 1st, 2nd, & 3rd prize, Beverly Hills Affaire in Garoew; Award of Excellence, Saratoga Rotorary Show. *Mem:* Ore Watercolor Soc; Northwest Watercolor Soc. *Media:* Watercolor, Collage. *Dealer:* Hamilton Fine Arts Salem Ore. *Mailing Add:* 6050 Fircrest St Salem OR 97306

HAMILTON, JUAN B
SCULPTOR
Dallas, Tex, Dec 22, 45. *Study:* City Col New York; New York Univ; Hastings Col, Nebr, BA(art), 68; Claremont Grad Sch, MFA prog. *Work:* Metrop Mus Art, New York; Art Inst Chicago; Albright-Knox Art Gallery, Buffalo, NY; Mus Fine Arts, Mus NMex, Santa Fe; Jacksonville Art Mus, Fla. *Exhib:* Robert Miller Gallery, New York, NY, 78, 81 & 83; Janie C Lee Gallery, Houston, Tex, 80; Janus Gallery, Los Angeles, Calif, 83; Mus NMex, Santa Fe, 83. *Collections Arranged:* Georgia O'Keeffe: A Portrait by Alfred Stieglitz (coauth, catalog), Metrop Mus Art, New York, 78; Alfred Stieglitz (coauth, catalog), Nat Gallery Art, Washington, DC, 83. *Awards:* Am Bk Award for Alfred Steiglitz: Photographs and Writings. *Bibliog:* Barbara Rose (auth), The Sculpture of Juan Hamilton, Arts Mag, 79; Robert Knafo (auth), Juan Hamilton at Robert Miller, Art in Am, 81; Barnaby Conrad III (auth), Rising stars, Horizon Mag, 82. *Dealer:* Robert Miller Gallery 41 E 57th St New York NY 10022. *Mailing Add:* Gerald Peters Gallery 439 Camino del Monte Sol PO Box 908 Santa Fe NM 87504

HAMILTON, PATRICIA ROSE
DEALER
b Upper Darby, Pa, Oct 21, 48. *Study:* Temple Univ, BA, 70; Rutgers Univ, MA(art hist), 71. *Collections Arranged:* Ten Americans, Masters of Watercolor (with catalogue), 74, Edward Hicks, A Gentle Spirit (with catalogue), 75 & Malta: A Totemic World, 75, Andrew Crispo Gallery; Outdoor Sculpture 1974 (with catalogue), Merriewold West Gallery, Far Hills, NJ, 74. *Pos:* Curatorial asst, Whitney Mus Am Art, New York, 71-73; sr ed, Art in Am, New York, 73-74; cur exhibs, Andrew Crispo Gallery, New York, 74-75; dir, Hamilton Gallery Contemp Art, 77-84, artist agent, 84-90; dir, West Coast Opers, Salander O'Reilly Gallery, Los Angeles, 90- *Bibliog:* Laura de Coppet & Alan Janes (auth), The Art Dealers, Clarkson N Potter Books, 84. *Mem:* ArTable, New York & Los Angeles. *Specialty:* 20th century art. *Mailing Add:* c/o Salander O'Reilly Gallery 456 N Camden Dr Beverly Hills CA 90210

HAMILTON, W PAUL C
EDUCATOR, HISTORIAN
b Toronto, Ont, Mar 13, 38. *Study:* Williams Col, BA, 59; Univ Toronto, MA, 64; Johns Hopkins Univ, PhD(Fel), 73. *Pos:* Coordr educ English, Educ Serv, Nat Gallery Can, Ottawa, 73-76. *Teaching:* Asst prof, Univ Sask, Saskatoon, 70-78, assoc prof, 78-84, head dept, 81-84, prof, 85- *Awards:* Grant, Italian Govt, 65-66; Can Coun Doctoral Fel, 68-69; Soc Sci & Humanities Res Coun Can Grant, 87-89. *Publ:* Auth, Andrea del Minga's Assunta in S Felicita, Kunsthistorisches Inst, 70; coauth, Grandmaison, Henderson, Kenderdine, Univ Sask, 79; auth, Disegni di Bernardino Poccetti, Olschki, 80; The Palazzo dei Camerlenghi in Venice, J Soc Archit Historians, 83. *Mailing Add:* Dept Art & Art Hist Univ Sask Saskatoon SK S7N 0W0 Canada

HAMLET, SUSAN H
EDUCATOR, JEWELER
b Evanston, Ill, 1954. *Study:* Mount Holyoke Col, BA, 76; Sch Am Craftsmen, Rochester Inst Technol, MFA, 78. *Work:* AT&T Dallas; Ark Art Ctr, Little Rock; Mus Mod Art, Kyoto, Japan; State Arts Collection, Okla; Bank One Ctr, Cleveland, Ohio. *Exhib:* One-person shows, Helen Drutt Gallery, Philadelphia, 83-85, Fergus-Jean Gallery, Columbus, Ohio, 87; Objects in Metal, Penn State Univ, 88; Today's Artisan, Newport Art Mus, 88; Craft Today USA, Paris, France, 89; Silver: New Forms & Expressions, Fortunoff, New York, 89 & 91; Jewelries/Epiphanies, Boton, Mass, 91; On Scale, Bennett Siegel Gallery, NY, 92. *Teaching:* Vis asst prof art, Okla State Univ, 79-80, asst prof, 81-86, assoc prof, 87-88; assoc prof metals, Swain Sch Design, 86-87; asst prof design, Southeastern Mass Univ, 88-92; assoc prof design, Univ Mass, Dartmouth, 92. *Awards:* Nat Endowment Arts, 79 & 88. *Mem:* Soc NAm Goldsmiths. *Dealer:* Helen Drutt Gallery Philadelphia & New York; Fergus-Jean Gallery 694 N High St Columbus Ohio 43215. *Mailing Add:* 75 Thomas St New Bedford MA 02740

HAMLETT, DALE EDWARD
EDUCATOR, PAINTER
b Memphis, Mo, Aug 15, 21. *Study:* Northeast Mo State Univ, BS(cum laude), 44; Am Acad Art, with William Mosby; Acad Appl Art, Chicago; Chicago Art Inst, with Charles Wilamoski; Univ NMex, with Ralph Douglass & Elaine de Kooning, MA(painting), 63; also with Robert Wood, Millard Sheets, George Post, Edgar Whitney, Morris Shubin, Charles Reid & Milford Zornes. *Work:* Univ NMex; State Fair Mus, Albuquerque; NMex Inst Mining & Technol; Eastern NMex Univ; Geronimo Mus, NMex. *Comn:* drawings of 18 founders of Sigma Tau Gamma, Warrensburg, Mo, 71; painting, KOA Campgrounds, Las Vegas, NMex, 75; portrait for Omar Naimi, Portales, NMex, 88; Double Portrait, Eastern NMex Univ Libr, 90; protrait, comn by for Dr Edward L Miller, Portales NMex, 90. *Exhib:* Sun Carnival, El Paso Mus Art, Tex, 80; 23rd Grand Prix Int de Peinture, Deauville, France, 73; Gran Premio della Citta Eterna Palazzo delle Esposizioni, Rome, Italy, 73; 14th Ann Artists Salon, Nat Show, Okla Mus Art, Oklahoma City, 75; Tucson Mus Art, 77; Western Fedn Watercolor Soc, San Diego, Calif, 90. *Pos:* Package designer, Montgomery Ward & Co, Chicago, Ill, 47-51; commercial artist, Ward Hicks Advert Agency, Albuquerque, NMex, 51-64; artist-in-residence, NMex Inst Mining & Technol, Socorro, NMex, 64-69. *Teaching:* Instr art, NMex Inst Mining & Technol, 65-69, teaching drawing, painting, figure study & art hist; prof art, Eastern NMex Univ, Portales, 69-87, teaching painting, figure drawing, drawing, color & design. *Awards:* First in Watercolor, Int Exhib Painting, Val de Isere, France, 72; Second Award in Watercolor, Panama City Art Asn, Nat Show, Fla, 79; Best of Show, Watercolor, Mus SW, Nat Show, Midland, Tex, 85; Best of Show, Black Canyon Painters, Hotchkiss, Colo, 80; Purchase Prize, Cent States Exposition, Pratt, Kans, 80; Award, 2nd NMex Watercolor Soc Show; First in watercolor, 14th Ann Nat, La Junta, Colo, 82. *Bibliog:* Artist Paints in Living Color, Nemo Scope, 82; Three Artists/Three Styles (painting demonstrations), KENW Educational Television, 84; Jean Burrough's (auth), article in one-man show, Portales News Tribune Newspaper, 12/84. *Mem:* charter mem, NMex Watercolor Soc; NMex Art League; Pintores Art Asn; La Escalara Art Guild; Llano Estacado Art Asn; NMex Art League; and others. *Media:* Watercolor, Oil. *Res:* Cataloging the graphic work of Frederic Remington. *Mailing Add:* 2104 S Ave H Portales NM 88130

HAMLIN, LOUISE
PAINTER, PRINTMAKER
b Litchfield, Conn, June 26, 49. *Study:* Univ Pa, BFA, 72; NY Studio Sch. *Exhib:* One woman shows, Blue Mt Gallery, New York, 84, 86, 89 & 92; plus many others. *Teaching:* Asst prof, Dartmouth Col, 90. *Awards:* Ingren Merrill Found Grant, 85; NY Found Arts Fel, 86; Djerassi Found Residency Award, 88. *Bibliog:* Greg Masters (auth), Louise Hamlin, Arts, summer 85; Painting on Location, American Artists, 10/88; Eric Holzman (auth), Louise Hamlin, cover, 1/90. *Media:* Sand. *Publ:* Auth of art reviews in Arts, 9/82, 3/85, 5/85, cover, 2/87, M/E/A/N/I/N/G, 5/89. *Dealer:* Blue Mountain Gallery 121 Worcester St New York NY 10012. *Mailing Add:* Dept Studio Art Dartmouth Col Hinman Box 6081 Hanover NH 03755

HAMMER, ALFRED EMIL
PAINTER, EDUCATOR
b New Haven, Conn, Jan 11, 25. *Study:* RI Sch Design, BFA; Yale Univ, BFA & MFA; and with John R Frazier, Josef Albers, Willem DeKooning, Stuart

Davis, Abraham Rattner, Alvin Lustig & John Howard Benson. *Work:* Nat JC Mus, Israel; Cleveland Art Asn; RI Sch Design; Portland Art Mus; Conn Bank & Trust; Bank New Eng. *Exhib:* Boston Art Festival, Mass, 58; Newport Ann, RI, 59; Four Americans, La State Univ, 62; one-man shows, Melnychenko Gallery, Winnipeg, 80, Univ Man, Winnipeg, 80 & Greene Gallery, Conn, 84; and others. *Pos:* Dean, Cleveland Inst Arts, 69-74; mem bd dirs, Hartford Arts Coun, 82-86. *Teaching:* Painting, drawing, design & calligraphy, RI Sch Design, 53-69, chmn div grad studies, 63-65; vis prof painting, Minneapolis Col Art, 67; vis lectr design & painting, Case Western Reserve Univ, 70; dir & prof sch art, Univ Man, 74-81; dir, Pac Northwest Col Art, 81; dean & prof, Hartford Art Sch, Univ Hartford, 82-86. *Awards:* First Prize, RI Artists Ann, 53, Providence Art Club Ann, 54-56, Newport Ann, 60; Temple Bethel Ann for Acrylic Award, Hartford, 86; Wintonbury Art League Open, Watercolor, 87. *Media:* Oil, Watercolor. *Publ:* Auth, Prize Winning Painting Allied Pub, 60. *Mailing Add:* 165 Tunxis Ave Bloomfield CT 06002

HAMMER, ELIZABETH B
PAINTER
b Washington, DC. *Study:* Univ Kans, Lawrence; Nat Art Sch, Washington, DC; Univ Md, Col Park, BA. *Work:* Nat Mus Women Arts, Wash, DC. *Exhib:* An Am Album, Md Col Art & Design, Md & Kenya, 86; Black Mountain Col, 87; Nat Mus Women Arts, Wash, DC, 91; Montgomery Col, Rockville, Md, 91; NVCC, Fairfax, Va, 92; and others. *Pos:* Illustr, US Govt, currently. *Teaching:* Instr 7th grade art, Rabat Am Sch, Morocco. *Awards:* Phi Kappa Phi Art Award, 81; Finalist, 34th Grand Prix Int de Deauville, France, 83; Art Citation, Montgomery Co Delegate, 86. *Bibliog:* Annuaire National Des Beaux-Arts, 91-92. *Mem:* Past Societaire, Salon des Artistes Independants, Paris; Nat Hon Soc. *Media:* Acrylic. *Res:* Hist of Am Art Schs; Hist of Fr Art. *Mailing Add:* 12312 Espalier Place Potomac MD 20854

HAMMERBECK, WANDA LEE
PHOTOGRAPHER
b Lincoln, Nebr, Mar 24, 45. *Study:* Univ NC, Chapel Hill, BA, 67, MA, 71; San Francisco Art Inst, MFA, 77. *Work:* Mus Mod Art, New York; Fogg Mus, Harvard Univ, Cambridge, Mass; RI Sch Design, Providence; Univ Calif, Los Angeles; Ctr for Creative Photog, Tucson, Ariz. *Exhib:* One-woman shows, Photographs by Wanda Hammerbeck, San Francisco Mus Mod Art, 78 & O K Harris, New York, 79; Object Illusion & Reality, Calif State Univ, Fullerton, 79; Images Considered, Visual Studies Workshop, Rochester, NY, 80; In Color, Ten California Photographers, Oakland Mus, Calif, 83; Cleveland Inst Art, Ohio, 85; Western Space, Burden Gallery, New York, 85; Solo exhibs, Schienbaum & Russek Gallery, Santa Fe & Etherton Gallery, Tucson, 86. *Collections Arranged:* California Views (auth, catalog), 79; Text and Context (auth, catalog), 79. *Awards:* Nat Endowment Arts Photogr Fels, 79 & 80 & Serv to the Field Award, 80; Guest artist, Ansel Adams Workshop, 86. *Bibliog:* Article, in: Untitled, Friends of Photog. *Mem:* Soc for Photog Educ; Friends of Photog. *Publ:* Auth, Depositions, 78 & contribr, Problematic Photography, 80, NFS Press. *Dealer:* Lumina Gallery 263 W 19th St No 905 New York NY 10011. *Mailing Add:* c/o Lumina Gallery 251 W 19th St No 73 New York NY 10011

HAMMERMAN, PAT JO
PRINTMAKER, PAINTER
b New York, NY, Oct 15, 53. *Study:* Queens Col, BA, 75; Hunter Col, MA, 78. *Work:* Grand Rapids Mus, Mich; Brooklyn Mus; Lockhaven Art Ctr, Orlando, Fla; Amarillo Art Ctr, Tex; Firehouse Gallery, Nassau Community Col, NY. *Comn:* Mural, Queensborough Community Col, 70; three-panel mural, Panell, Kerr, Foster, New York, 83; Deloitte, Haskins & Sells, Princeton, NJ, 87; Four Seasons Hotel, Newport, Calif, 87; Bankers Trust, New York, 88. *Exhib:* Print Biennial, Brooklyn Mus, 81; Handmade Paper Books, Am Craft Mus, New York, 82; International Impact, Kyoto Munic Mus, Japan, 82; New American Graphics, Alaska State Mus, Juneau, 83; Queens Mus, Flushing, NY, 85; American Prints, Cairo Mus, Egypt, 85; and others. *Teaching:* Asst prof fine art, Queensborough Community Col, 80- *Awards:* First Prizes, Firehouse Gallery, Nassau Community Col, 79, 26th Ann, Parrish Mus, 79. *Bibliog:* John Fremont (auth), Paperworks, Am Craft Mag, 8/82; Ronnie Cohen (auth), Papermaking, Art News, 10/83; Ronnie Cohen (auth), New editions, Art News, 10/84; Helen Harrison (auth), Paper: medium with a message, New York Times, 3/27/88. *Mem:* Col Art Asn. *Media:* All; Acrylic, Oil. *Res:* Etching; Acrylic, Oil. *Dealer:* John Szoke 164 Mercer St New York NY 10012. *Mailing Add:* 91-06 104th St Richmond Hill NY 11418

HAMMERSLEY, FREDERICK
PAINTER
b Salt Lake City, Utah, Jan 5, 19. *Study:* Univ Idaho Southern Br, Pocatello, 36-38; Chouinard Art Sch, Los Angeles, 40-42 & 46-47; Ecole des Beaux Arts, Paris, France, 45; Jepson Art Inst, Los Angeles, 47-50. *Work:* Los Angeles Co Mus Art & La Jolla Art Mus; Butler Inst Am Art, Youngstown, Ohio; Corcoran Gallery Art; San Francisco Mus Mod Art; Oakland Art Mus, Calif; Univ Art Mus, Berkely, Calif; Univ Nebr, Lincoln; Univ NMex, Albuquerque; Mus NMex Albuquerque; Mus Fine Art, Santa Fe, NMex. *Exhib:* Geometric Abstraction America, Whitney Mus Am Art, New York, 62; Responsive Eye, Mus Mod Art, New York, 65; one-man shows, Univ NMex, Albuquerque, 69 & 75, L A Louver Gallery, Venice, Calif, 78 & 81 & Modernism Gallery, San Francisco, 87 & 90; 35th Biennial, Corcoran Gallery, 77; California: Five Footnotes to Modern Art History, 77 & Private Images: Photographs by Painters, 77, Los Angeles Co Art Mus, Los Angeles; The Alcove Show, Mus Fine Arts, Sante Fe, NMex, 89-90; Paris, Berlin & Albuquerque, Photog Show, Calif State Univ, Northridge, 89-90; Turning the Tide: Early Los Angeles Modernists 1920-1956, travel to 6 mus, Calif, Utah, Tex, 90-92; Drawings & Paintings, Then & Now, Owings-Dewey Fine Art, Santa Fe, NMex, 92; and others. *Pos:* Guest artist, Tamarind Inst, Albuquerque, NMex, 73, 88 & 91. *Teaching:* Instr, Jepson Art Sch, Los Angeles, 48-51; lectr painting, drawing & design, Pomona Col, 53-62; instr, Pasadena Art Mus, 56-61; instr painting, drawing & design, Chouinard Art Inst, 64-68; vis assoc prof painting & drawing, Univ NMex, 68-71. *Awards:* Purchase Awards for Painting, Butler Inst Am Art, 61 & Los Angeles All City Ann, 64-66; Guggenheim Fel Painting, 73-74; Nat Endowment Arts Award Painting, 75 & 77. *Bibliog:* Jules Langsner (auth), Four abstract classicists, Los Angeles Co Mus Art, 59; Lawrence Alloway (auth), West Coast hard edge, Inst Contemp Art, London, 60; Michel Seuphor (auth), Abstract Painting, Abrams, 62. *Publ:* Contribr, Classicism or hard-edge?, 60 & Los Angeles letter, 2/61, Art Int; auth, My first experience with computer drawings, 10/69 & My geometrical paintings, 4/70, Leonardo Mag; contribr & illus, Visual Art, Mathematics and Computers, Pergamon Press, 79. *Dealer:* Modernism 685 Market St San Francisco CA 94105; Owings-Dewey Fine Art Santa Fe NM. *Mailing Add:* 608 Carlisle SE Albuquerque NM 87106

HAMMETT, POLLY HORTON
PAINTER, INSTRUCTOR
b Oklahoma City, Okla, Jan 31, 30. *Study:* Univ Okla, 48-50; Union Col, BA, 78; study with Richard V Goetz & Eugene Bavinger. *Work:* Albuquerque Mus Art; Houston Neurosensory Ctr; Women's Hosp-Houston; Houston Power & Lighting; Methodist Hospital, Houston, Tex; Hill Country Arts Found, Tex; Kerr Mus, Okla; II Houston Center, Tex; Hutchins Sealy Nat Bank, Galveston, Tex. *Exhib:* Am Watercolor Soc Ann, Nat Acad Galleries, 76, 77, 80 & 82; Watercolor, Southwest Two, Tucson Mus Art, 76 & 82; Nat Watercolor Soc 56th Ann, Laguna Beach Mus Art, Calif, 76; two-artist exhib, Foothills Art Ctr, Colo, 74-76; Western Federation Watercolor Socs, 81; Nat & Am Watercolor Soc Traveling Exhib, 82; Tweed Mus; Frye Mus; Univ Wisc; Williamette Univ; Stetson Univ; Foothills Art Ctr, Golden, Colo. *Pos:* Dir educ, Art League of Houston, Tex, 86-88; gallery dir, Nine Fine Artisans, 79-82. *Teaching:* Lectr & Instr watercolor sem, Okla Arts Coun, 73; instr painting workshops, Colo, Okla, Tex, La, Calif, Ark, Ariz, SC & NMex; originator workshop, The Art Experience, Tex Inst Child Psychiat, Houston, 74 & 75 & Houston Univ, Sch Continuing Educ Drug Abuse Prog, 76-77; instr, Art League of Houston 80-90 & Hill Country Arts Found, 83-84. *Awards:* Juror's Selection for Purchase, Eight-State Exhib Painting & Sculpture, Okla Art Ctr, 72; Mus Purchase Award & Merit Award Watercolor, Southwest One, Albuquerque Art Mus, 76; First Award, Southwestern Watercolor Soc, Dallas, Tex, 81; Graphics Award, Okla Mus Art. *Bibliog:* Lynn Haggard (auth), Artist's paintings test limits, Times Record News; Mimi Crossley (auth), Houston Post. *Mem:* Nat Watercolor Soc; Am Art Therapist Asn; Am Watercolor Soc; Art League Houston (bd dirs); Women's Caucus Art (adv bd). *Media:* Mixed Water Media. *Mailing Add:* 351 N Post Oak Lane Houston TX 77024

HAMMOCK, VIRGIL GENE
CRITIC, PAINTER
b Long Beach, Calif, Aug 5, 38; Can citizen. *Study:* San Francisco Art Inst, BFA, 65, with James Weeks; Ind Univ, MFA, 67, with James McGarrell. *Work:* Ind Univ, Bloomington; Univ Alta, Edmonton; Art Bank Collection, Can Coun, Ottawa, Ont; Univ Man, Winnipeg; Mt Allison Univ, Sackville. *Exhib:* The 84th Ann, San Francisco Mus Art, Calif, 65; Young Alta Painters, Alta Col Art, Calgary, 68; West-71, Edmonton Art Gallery, 71; Olympic Exhib, Montreal, 75; one-man shows, Owens Art Gallery, Sackville, NB, 73 & Drawings, Dalhousie Art Gallery, Halifax, NS, 77; two one-man shows, Struts Gallery, Sackville, NB, 85 & 87. *Pos:* Dir exhibs, Univ Alta, 68-70 & Univ Man 70-73; actg dir, Owens Art Gallery, Mt Allison Univ, 88-89. *Teaching:* Instr design & drawing, Univ Alta, Edmonton, 67-68, asst prof drawing & art hist, 68-70; assoc prof art criticism, Univ Man, Winnipeg, 70-75; prof & head, Dept Art, Mt Allison Univ, 75-90; prof Fine Art, Dept Art, Mt Allison Univ, 90- *Awards:* Phelan Award, Trustees James D Phelan Awards Lit & Art, 65. *Bibliog:* Cameron (auth), Virgil Hammock, la Nostalgie du Romantisme, Vie des Arts, summer, 78; B Sanderson (auth), Virgil Hammock: Studio pictures, Arts Atlantic 31, spring/summer 88. *Mem:* Univs Art Asn Can (pres, 73-79); Int Asn Art Critics, Can Sect (pres, 76-79 & 86-). *Media:* Oil, Pencil. *Res:* Contemporary Canadian painting. *Publ:* Jean-Paul Riopelle at the Beaubourg, Vol 13, Artmagazine, 82; The 49th Parallel: An Opinion, No 28, Artpost, spring, 88; Critical Word About Critical Words About Art, Arts Atlantic No 35, fall 89; Take Me Out to the Ballgame: Michael Snow's The Audience, Art Post 35/36, winter/spring 90; An Art Critic Visits the Soviet Union, Arts Atlantic 37, spring/summer 90. *Mailing Add:* c/o Mt Allison Univ Art Dept Sackville NB E0A 3C0 Canada

HAMMOND, GALE THOMAS
PRINTMAKER, EDUCATOR
b Lumberton, NC, Sept 27, 39. *Study:* Chicago Acad Fine Arts, com art dipl; ECarolina Univ, 62-64, BS & MAEd; Univ NC, Greensboro; Atelier 17, Paris, with S W Hayter, 77. *Work:* High Mus, Atlanta; NC Mus Art, Raleigh; Del Mar Col, Corpus Christi; Univ NC Sch Pub Health, Chapel Hill; Metrop Mus Art; Mint Mus; Italian Embassy, Washington, DC; Frans Masereel Ctr, Belg; and others. *Exhib:* Colorprint USA, Lubbock, Tex, 72; Ann Exhib, Davidson Col, NC, 73; Boston Printmakers, Mass, 75-; New American Graphics, Madison Art Ctr, Wis, 75; Netherlands & Russian Exchange Exhibs of the Southern Graphics Coun; Taipei Mus, Repub of China, 88-90; Trento, Italy Humor Exhib, 92; Budafest Hungary Cartoon Festival, 90. *Pos:* Mem, SC Governors Award Prog, The Penland Sch. *Teaching:* Assoc prof drawing & printmaking, Univ Ga, Athens, 70-; Western Carolina, Greensboro Col. *Awards:* Etching Award, Southeastern Ctr Contem Art, NC, 68; Drawing

Award, Ga Arts Comn, Atlanta, 71; Etching Award, Southeastern Printmakers; Sea Grant, Ossabaw Island Proj. *Mem:* Southeastern Graphics Coun (pres, 74-76); Boston Printmakers; Print Consortium. *Media:* Etching, Multimedia. *Mailing Add:* Dept Art Univ Ga Athens GA 30602

HAMMOND, HARMONY
PAINTER, SCULPTOR
b Chicago, Ill, Feb 8, 44. *Study:* Univ Minn, BA, 67. *Work:* Chicago Art Inst, Chicago, Ill; Brooklyn Mus, NY; Wadsworth Atheneum, Hartford, Conn; Gen Mills Corp, Minn; Metrop Mus Art, Brooklyn Mus Art, NY; Walker Art Ctr; Denver Art Mus; Mus Fine Arts, Santa Fe, NMex. *Comn:* Rendez-vous, Int Sculpture, Que, Can. *Exhib:* International Feminist Art, Haags Gementemuseum, The Hague, 80; retrospective, Glen Hanson Gallery, Minneapolis, 81; one-person shows, Lerner Heller Gallery, 79 & 82, Luise Ross Gallery, 84, Bernice Steinbaum Gallery Ltd, 86, New York, Jenson Gallery, Mus Univ NMex, Albuquerque, 87, Trabia Macafee Gallery, New York, Linda Durham Gallery, Santa Fe, NMex, 88 & UneasyJuxtapositions, Ctr Contemp Art, Santa Fe, NMex, 92; Luxuriance, Am Ctr, Paris, 83; The American Artist as Printmaker, Brooklyn Mus, 83; Requisition Clandestine, Conseil de Textiles, Montreal, 86; Lines of Vision: Drawings by Contemporary Women, Hillwood Art Gallery & traveling, NY, 89; Abstraction--Plant to Plane, Cleveland State Univ, 90; Painting Divergences, NMex State Univ, Las Cruces, 89; Bad Girls, Aljira, Neward, NJ, 89; 20th Anniversary Visiting Artist Exhib, Univ Colo, Boulder, 92; Mus NMex Fine Arts, Santa Fe & Univ NMex Mus & traveling. *Teaching:* Instr & visiting artist painting, Art Inst Chicago, 73; asst prof drawing & painting & vis artist, Tyler Sch Fine Art, Philadelphia, 77; asst prof, Univ NMex, Albuquerque, 78; vis lectr, Univ Va, Charlottesville, 80 & Univ NC, Chapel Hill, 81-82; vis artist & instr, Mason Gross Sch Art, New Brunswick, NJ 82; prof, Univ Ariz, Tucson, 88-; Anderson Ranch, Snowmass, Colo, 90; Int Art Workshop, Dunedin, NZ, 92. *Awards:* Nat Endowment Arts, 79-80 & 83-84; Creative Artists PubServ Grant, 82; John S Guggenheim Mem Found Fel, 91; Pollock Krasner Fel, 89-90. *Bibliog:* Judith Van Wagner (auth), Harmony Hammond's painted spirits, Arts Mag, 1/86; Len Kleckner & Malin Wilson (auths), Harmony Hammond: Radiant Spirits, Mus Univ NMex, 87; Thalia Vouma-Peterson & Patricia Matthews (coauths), The Feminist Critique of Art History, Art Bulletin, 87; Arlene Raven (auth), Crossing Over: Feminism & Art of Social Change, UMI Press, 88; Elizabeth Hess (auth), Sanctuary, Village Voice, 5/24/88; Judy Siegel (auth), Mutiny & the Mainstream, Talk That Changed Art, Midmarch Arts Press, 92; Neery Melkonian (auth, interview), The Mag, 10/92. *Mem:* Col Art Asn; Women's Caucus Art. *Media:* Oil, Acrylic; Mixed Media. *Publ:* Auth, Wrappings: Essays on feminism, art & martial arts, Time & Space Ltd Press, 83; Frida Kahlo, 13th Moon, spring 84; Hearing & Seeing, Heresies, spring 84; The arts of the North American Indian: native traditions in evolution, Artspace, fall 87; Historias: Women Tinsmiths of New Mexico, Heresies, 89. *Dealer:* Etherton-Stern Gallery 135 S Sixth Ave Tucson AZ 85701; Klein Gallery, Chicago, IL. *Mailing Add:* 129 W 22nd St New York NY 10011

HAMMOND, JANE
PRINTMAKER, PAINTER
b Bridgeport, Conn, 1950. *Study:* Mt Holyoke Col, BA, 72; Ariz State Univ, 73-74; Univ Wis, Madison, MFA, 77. *Work:* Albright-Knox Art Gallery; Bibliotiec Nationale, Paris, France; Mus Arte Contemporaneo, Mexico City, Mexico; Mus Fine Arts, Boston; New York Pub Libr. *Exhib:* Invitational, Stux Gallery, New York, NY, 87; Brooklyn Mus, NY, 89; Nat Art Libr, Victoria & Albert Mus, London, Eng, 90; Milwaukee Art Mus, Wis & travelling, 90; solo exhibs, Nina Freudheim Gallery, Buffalo, NY, 87, Exit Art, New York, 89, Wetterling, Goteborg, Sweden, 90 & Cincinnati Art Mus, 93; Zolla-Lieberman Gallery, Chicago, 90; Feigenson-Preston, Detroit, 91; fiction/non-fiction, New York, 91-93; Wetterling Gallery, Stockholm, 92; Transepoca Gallery, Milan, 92. *Teaching:* Md Inst Col Art, 80-90. *Awards:* Nat Endowment Arts, 89; Louis Comfort Tiffany Award, 89; Nat Endowment, Tiffany; CAPS, NY Found Arts. *Bibliog:* John Ashbery (auth), Jane Hammond New Paintings, (catalog), Wetterling Gallery; Elizabeth Hess (auth), Fly on the Wall, Village Voice, 2/90; Terry R Myers (auth), Review, Flash Art, summer 90; Ellen Handy (auth), The Pearls and the String, Jane Hammonds--, Arts Mag, 47-51, 9/90. *Dealer:* Fiction/Nonfiction New York. *Mailing Add:* 148 Spring St New York NY 10012

HAMMOND, LESLIE KING
HISTORIAN, WRITER
b Bronx, NY, Aug 4, 44. *Study:* Queens Col, with Louis Finkelstein, Herb Aach, Paul Frazer, Marvin Belick & Harold Bruder, BA, 69; Johns Hopkins Univ, MA, 73, PhD, 75. *Collections Arranged:* 3400 on State, Baltimore Mus Art, 73; Baltimore Black Arts Calendar Retrospect, 1973-1978, Morris Mechanic Gallery, 78; Montage of Dreams Deferred (auth, catalog), Baltimore Mus Art, 79-80; Three Episodes in Black American Art, Harmon Found, Bronx & Queens Mus, 80; Celebrations: Myth & Ritual in African-American Art (auth, catalog), Studio Mus Harlem, 82; Reconstructed Elements, Artscape, 83, Lyric Theatre, 83; The Intuitive Eye-The Art of Self Taught Baltimore Artists (auth, catalog), Md Art Place, 85; 18 Visions/Divisions, Eubie Blake Cult Ctr & Mus, 88; Art as a Verb-The Evolving Continum (coauth, catalog), Md Inst Col Art, 88; Black Printmakers and the WPA (auth, catalog), Lehman Gallery Art, Lehman College, Bronx, NY, 89; Hale Woodruff Biennial, Studio Mus Harlem, New York, 89. *Pos:* Actg dir, Cult Arts, Youth in Action, Bedford, Stuyvesant, NY, 66; chmn art dept, Performing Art Workshops, Queens, NY, 67-69; guest cur & mem bd dir, Morris Mechanic Gallery, formerly; coordr, Philip Morris Scholar for Artosts in Visual Arts, 85-, dean grad studies, 76- *Teaching:* Lectr art hist, Md Inst Col Art, 73-, dean grad studies, 76-; doctoral supvr, Dept African Studies & Res, Howard Univ, 77-82; instr, Corcoran Sch Art, 82. *Awards:* New York City SEEK Grant, 66-69; Horizon Fel, 69-73; Kress Found Fel, 74. *Mem:* Nat Conf Artists. *Res:* Ninteenth and twentieth century Afro-American art; African Art; women artists; self-taught artists. *Publ:* Contribr, National Landmarks Registry, Dept Interior, 75; auth, Impact of roots on American society, African Directions, Fall 1977; auth, African-American aesthetics, Aura of the Arts, 2/78; Search for an aesthetic identity, the art and politics of the Black artist in the 1960's, In: Selected Essays: Art and Artists from the Harlem Renaissance to the 1980's, Nat Black Arts Festival, Inc, 88. *Mailing Add:* Md Inst Col Art 1300 W Mount Royal Ave Baltimore MD 21217

HAMMOND, PHYLLIS BAKER
SCULPTOR
b Elizabeth, NJ, Apr 13, 30. *Study:* Sch Mus Fine Arts, Boston, Mass, 60; Kyoto City Col Fine Arts, Japan, 62; Tufts Univ, BS, 64. *Work:* Mem Hall Libr, Andover, Mass; Am Savings Bank, White Plains, NY; Schmeltzer, Aptaker & Shepard, Washington, DC; Conn State Univ, New Haven; Noyes Mus, Oceanville, NJ. *Comn:* Unitarian Fellowship, Mount Kisco, NY, 84; Guest Quarters Hotel, Bethesda, Md, 86; Center point, Fairoaks, Md, 87; William Shakespeare Award, Shakespeare Theater at the Folgers, Washington, DC, 87; Art in Public Places, Hartford, Conn, 90. *Exhib:* Clay Sculpture, Hudson River Mus, NY, 76; Art in Transition, Boston Mus, 77; Clay Sculpture, Pinder Gallery, New York, 86; Architectural Ceramics, Franz Badar Gallery, Washington, DC, 87; Clay Transformations, Rockland Ctr Arts Nyack, Flushing, NY, 87; Sculptures as Public Art, Art Gallery, Washington, DC, 89; Contemporary Sculpture, Chesterwood, Stockbridge, Mass, 89; New Bronzes, Elaine Benson Gallery, Bridehampton, NY, 89; Recent Sculpture, Greene St Gallery, New York, 90. *Collections Arranged:* Renaissance Festival, Westchester Coun Art, NY, 75 & 77. *Teaching:* Adj asst prof, Col New Rochelle Graduate Sch, 81; ceramic sculpture, Mendocino Art Ctr, Calif, 81, 82 & 86. *Awards:* Clarissa Bartlett Traveling Fel, Boston Mus, 60; Second Prize, Mamaroneck Artist Guild, 73; Grant for Apprentice, National Endowment Arts, 76. *Bibliog:* Patricia Malarcher (auth), Clay that qualifies as sculpture, New York Times, 4/7/85; Roslyn Tunis (auth), Ancient Inspiration/Contemporary Interpretation (catalog, rev), Robertson Ctr Arts Sci, 85; Lauretta Dimmick & Jonathan Fairbanks (coauths), Contemporary Sculpture at Chesterwood (catalog, rev), 89. *Mem:* Artist-Craftsman New York; Nat Coun Apprenticeship; Int Laison; Visual Arts Affiliates of Westchester (vpres, 79-81). *Media:* Clay, Bronze. *Dealer:* Kendell Gallery Wellfleet MA; Pindar 127 Greene St New York NY 10012. *Mailing Add:* 285 Scarborough Rd Briarcliff Manor NY 10510

HAMMOND, RED
PAINTER
b Niagara Falls, NY, Sept 26, 47. *Study:* Univ Buffalo, BFA, 70. *Comn:* Installation/enviroment, Dreyfus Corp, New York, 90. *Exhib:* Solo exhib, Exit Art, New York, 89; Why War Show, BYA Gallery, New York, 91; JFK Show, BYA Gallery, New York, 92; Abstraction Art, Art in General, New York, 92. *Pos:* Vis artist, Univ Maine, 90 & Univ Southern Maine, Portland, 91. *Awards:* Nat Endowment Arts Fel, 87 & 88. *Mailing Add:* 54 Franklin St New York NY 10013

HAMMONS, DAVID
PAINTER
b Springfield, Ill, 1943. *Study:* Los Angeles Trade Technical City Col, Calif, 64-65; Chouinard Art Inst, Los Angeles, 66-68; Otis Art Inst Parson's Sch Design, Los Angeles, 68-72. *Exhib:* Solo exhibs, The Window, New Mus Contemp Art, 80, Higher Goals, pub installation, Harlem, 82, Just Above Midtown, New York, 86, Exit Art, 89, Jack Tilton Gallery, 90; retrospective, Contemp Art, PS1, Long Island, 90 & ICA, Philadelphia & San Diego Mus Contemp Art, 91; Heimat, Wewerka & Weiss Galerie, Berlin, 91; Places with a Past, Spoleto Festival, Charleston, SC, 91; Dislocations, Mus Mod Art, New York, 91; Carnegie International, Carnegie Inst, Pittsburgh, Pa, 92; Documenta, Kassel, Ger, 92. *Awards:* Nat Endowment Arts Fel, NY State Coun Arts, 82; John Simon Guggenheim Mem Found, 83-84; DAAD, Berlin, 92. *Bibliog:* Maurice Berger (auth), Interview with David Hammons, Art in Am, 9/90; Michael Brenson (auth), New Curator at Modern Challenges Convention, 12/28/90 & Visual Arts Join Spoleto Festival USA, NY Times, 5/27/91; Dan Cameron (auth), Good-Bye to All That?, Art & Auction, 1/91. *Mailing Add:* PO Box 2754 New York NY 10027

HAMPSON, FERDINAND CHARLES
ART DEALER, CURATOR
b Detroit, Mich, June 26, 47. *Study:* Wayne State Univ, dipl, 71. *Collections Arranged:* Emergence Art in Glass (auth, catalog), Bowling Green Univ & Kent State Univ, 81-82; Glass: Artist and Influence Traveling Exhib (auth, catalog), 81-82; Kyohe: Fujita Blown Glass (auth, catalog), Leigh Yawkey Woodson Mus & Burgstrom Mus, 81-82; Four Artists Four Views (auth, catalog), Jesse Besser Mus, 82; The Fine Art of Contemporary American Glass (auth, catalog), Columbus Col Art & Design, 83; Contemp Czechoslovakian Glass Art (catalog), Boca Raton Mus Art, 85; Bildwerke in Glass 25 Jahre New Glass in Amerika (catalog), Hessisches Landesmuseum Darmstadt, 87; Cristalomancia Arte Contemporaneo en Vidrio (catalog), Museo Rufino Tamayo & Marco Museo de Arte Contemporaneo, Mex, 92; Glass: 1962 to 1992 and Beyond (catalog), Morris Mus, 92. *Pos:* Dir, Habatat Galleries, 71- *Bibliog:* Mack Talaba (auth), Art craft--glass has come a long way, Artcraft, 8/80; Janet Koplos (auth), Habatat Gallery, Am Craft, 9/80; Maureen Michelson (auth), Inside Habatat, Glass Studio, 4/81. *Mem:* Glass Art Soc; Detroit Art Dealers Asn (vpres, 76, pres, 78-80); Am Craft Coun; Mich Glass Month (chmn, 80-83). *Res:* Written history of contemporary glass. *Specialty:* Contemporary glass art. *Publ:* Auth, article, Glass Art J, 81;

auth, article, Nues Glas, Verlagsanstalt Handweek, 81; Glass: State of the Art, 84; Glass: State of the Art II, 87; The Annual Invitational Exhibition 1973-1992: A Tradition in the Evolution of Glass, 92. *Mailing Add:* 32255 NW Hwy Suite 45 Farmington Hills MI 48334

HAMPTON, AMBROSE GONZALES, JR
COLLECTOR
b Statesburg, SC, July 24, 26. *Pos:* Mem, SC State Mus Comn, 73-78; pres, Columbia Mus Art, 75-77 & mem acquisitions comt, 87-; mem collection comt, Gibbes Art Mus, Charleston, SC, 89. *Collection:* Chiefly contemporary oils, graphics and sculpture, with emphasis on South Carolina artists. *Mailing Add:* 937 Sugar Mill Rd Chapin SC 29036

HAMPTON, GRACE
ADMINISTRATOR, CRAFTSMAN
b Courtland, Ala, Oct 23, 37. *Study:* Art Inst Chicago & Univ Chicago, BAE, 61; Ill State Univ, MSEd, 68; Ariz State Univ, PhD(art educ), 76. *Exhib:* Traveling Crafts Show, State Ill Off Pub Instruction, Chicago, 72; Arizona Women, Tucson Art Mus, 75; Second World Festival of Black and African Arts and Culture, Lagos, Nigeria, 77. *Collections Arranged:* Dimension and Directions: Black Artists of the South (auth, catalog), Miss Mus Art, Jackson, 80. *Pos:* Asst dir expansion arts prog, Nat Endowment Arts, Washington, DC, 83-85; mem adv bd, Getty Inst for Educators on Visual Arts , 83-84, fac mem, 85-88; dir, Sch Visual Arts, Pa State Univ & vice provost. *Teaching:* Asst prof art educ, Univ Ore, Eugene, 76-78; fac mem art & chairperson dept, Jackson State Univ, 78-83; fac mem, Sch Visual Arts, Pa State Univ, 85- *Awards:* Nat Endowment Arts Expansion Arts Prog Fel, 78; Inst Educ Mgt, Harvard, 90. *Bibliog:* Linderman & Herberholz (auths), Developing Artistic and Perceptual Awareness, 74 & Herberholz (auth), Early Childhood Art, 74, W C Brown; Lanier (auth), Studio Potter, 82, The Art We See, 82 & The Visual Arts & The Elementary Child, 83. *Mem:* Nat Art Educ Asn; Nat Conf Artists; Col Art Asn; Pa Art Educ Soc (bd dir & futures Comt); Nat Asn Sch Art & Design, AERA. *Media:* Copper. *Publ:* Auth, Hayden House Program: Community involvement in the arts, Sch Arts, 79; auth, book reviews for J Negro Hist & Studies in Art Educ. *Mailing Add:* Pa State Univ Off of Pres 201 Old Main University Park PA 16802

HAMPTON, JOHN W
PAINTER, SCULPTOR
b New York, NY, 1918. *Work:* The Cow Punchers, Cowboy Hall Fame, Oklahoma City. *Awards:* First Prize, World Telegram Artist Contest, 35; Gold Medal/Sculpture, Cowboy Artist of Am Show, 77, 79-81. *Mem:* Founder Cowboy Artists Am. *Publ:* Illusr in Ariz Hwys & Western Horseman & other mags & books. *Mailing Add:* 7525 E Arlington Rd Scottsdale AZ 85250

HAMPTON, PHILLIP JEWEL
PAINTER, EDUCATOR
b Kansas City, Mo, Apr 23, 22. *Study:* Citrus Jr Col, Glendora, Calif; Kans State Univ; Drake Univ; Kansas City Art Inst, BFA, 51, MFA, 52; Univ Mo-Kansas City. *Work:* Tuskegee Inst, Ala; Ga Southern Col, Statesboro, Ga; New Atlanta Life Bldg, Ga; Obata Design, St Louis, Mo; Governor's Mansion, Ill. *Exhib:* Mid-Am Ann, Nelson Gallery, Kansas City & Art Mus, St Louis, 74; Huntsville Mus, Ala, 74; J B Speed Mus, Louisville, Ky, 82; Evansville Mus, Ind, 88; Mitchell Mus, Mt Vernon, Ill, 89. *Teaching:* Assoc prof art & dir, Savannah State Col, 52-69; assoc prof painting & design, Southern Ill Univ, Edwardsville, 69-78, prof, 78-, coordr ethnic & spec studies workshop, 71-72. *Awards:* Dr Scheinfurth Purchase Award, Mitchell Mus, Mt Vernon, Ill, 85; Lida & Jay Herndon Smith Fund Prize, St Artists' Guild, 88; Gov Award, Ill Purchase Award for exec mansion, 90. *Mem:* St Louis Artists Coalition. *Media:* Acrylic, Watercolor. *Res:* Investigating synthetic media; water-media techniques; an essence of form. *Publ:* Auth & designer, 3rd World Drawings 1979 (catalog), Soc Ethnic & Spec Studies Exhib, Los Angeles, 79; and others. *Dealer:* Marie Park Private Dealer 6254 Park Lane Dallas TX. *Mailing Add:* 832 Holyoake Rd Edwardsville IL 62025

HAMROL, LLOYD
SCULPTOR
b San Francisco, Calif, Sept 25, 37. *Study:* Univ of Calif, Los Angeles, BA, 59, MA, 63. *Work:* Laguna Art Mus, Calif; Los Angeles Co Mus Art, Calif; Smithsonian Inst, Washington DC. *Comn:* Univ NMex, Albuquerque, 80; Gallaudet Col, Washington DC, 82; Univ Iowa, Iowa City, 83; City of Monterey, Calif, 85; City Carlsbad, Calif, 89. *Exhib:* Ann Sculpture & Prints, Whitney Mus Am Art, New York, 66; Am Sculpture of the Sixties, Los Angeles Co Mus Art, 67; Four Los Angeles Sculptors, Mus Contemp Art, Chicago, 73; Los Angeles in the Seventies, Ft Worth Art Mus, Tex, 77; one-man shows, La Jolla Mus Art, Calif, 68, Pomona Col, Calif, 69 & Calif State Univ, Fullerton, 70; Sculpture in California 1975-1980, San Diego Mus Art, Calif, 80; The Museum as Site: Sixteen Projects, Los Angeles Co Mus Art, 81; Lloyd Hamrol: Works, Projects, Proposals, Los Angeles Munic Art Gallery, 86; and others. *Teaching:* Fac, Calif Inst Arts, Valencia, 70-74; lectr sculpture, Univ Calif, San Diego, 77-78 & Los Angeles, 78-79. *Awards:* Indiviual Artist's Fel Grant, Nat Endowment Arts, 74, 80 & 90. *Bibliog:* Ruth Iskin (auth), Public art as identity reinforcement: An interview with Lloyd Hamrol, Los Angeles Inst Contemp Art J, 1/76; Merle Schipper (auth), Public sculpture and the urban community: Recent work by Lloyd Hamrol, Journal: A Contemp Art Mag, 9-10/81. *Mem:* Int Sculpture Ctr. *Media:* Mixed. *Mailing Add:* P O Box 861025 Los Angeles CA 90086

HAMWI, RICHARD ALEXANDER
PAINTER, EDUCATOR
b Brooklyn, NY, June 11, 47. *Study:* Queens Col, BA(cum laude); Univ NMex, MA; Univ Calif, MFA; Pa State Univ, PhD; also with William Dole, Leonard Lehrer, Harry Nadler, James Brooks, Louis Finkelstein & John Ferren. *Work:* Phillips Mus; Queens Col; Nat Mus Am Art; Vassar Col; Ark Art Ctr; Art Mus, Univ Ky. *Exhib:* Parsons-Dreyfuss Gallery, New York, 79; Staempfli Gallery, 81; Phillips Collection, Washington, DC, 82; solo shows, Queens Col, 82, Mus Art, Pa State Univ, 82, Univ Indianapolis, Ind 90; Mus Art, Univ Ky, 90. *Teaching:* Asst, Univ NMex, 72-73, Univ Calif, 73-74; instr, Pa State Univ, 77-87; assoc prof, Cumberland Col, 87- *Awards:* Purchase Award, Ball State Univ, 79; Mem Award, Chautauqua Nat Exhib, 81; Yaddo Fel, 83; Djerassi Found Fel, 87. *Mem:* Col Art Asn Am; Nat Art Ed Assoc. *Media:* Ink, Watercolor. *Publ:* Thoughtnotes on the Teaching of Art, J Ky Art Educ Asn, 90. *Dealer:* Prince St Gallery 121 Wooster St New York NY 10012. *Mailing Add:* Cumberland Coll Williamsburg KY 40769

HANCHEY, JANET LYNN
PAINTER
b DeRidder, La, Oct 30, 56. *Study:* La State Univ, BFA, 78; Parsons Sch of Design, MFA, 81. *Work:* Swanston Fine Arts, Atlanta. *Comn:* Two 4'x 6' oils, Educational Mgt Corp, Pittsburgh, Pa, 84; Mr & Mrs D Trump, New York, 88; Mr & Mrs B Krasnoff, Atlanta, Ga, 88; Mrs Sammons, Grove Park Inn, Asheville, NC, 88; Bradley Mus, Columbus, Ga; IBM Corp, Atlanta, Ga; Marriott Corp, Los Angeles, Calif. *Exhib:* Parsons Sch Design. *Teaching:* Lectr, Md Inst Col of Art, Baltimore, 88 & Parsons Sch Design, New York, 82- *Media:* Oil Pigment, Dry Pastel-conte-charcoal. *Dealer:* Tom Swanston-Gail Foster Swanston 177 Harris St NW Atlanta Ga 30303. *Mailing Add:* 50Lexington Ave, Studio 226 New York NY 10010

HANCOCK, WALKER (KIRTLAND)
SCULPTOR
b St Louis, Mo, June 28, 01. *Study:* St Louis Sch Fine Arts; Washington Univ, 18-20, Hon DFA, 42; Univ Wis, 20; Pa Acad Fine Arts, 21-25; Am Acad Rome, fel, 28; Yale Univ, LHD, 86. *Work:* Pa Acad Fine Arts; Indianapolis Mus Art; Mus Fine Arts, Boston; Nat Portrait Gallery; Nat Mus Am Art; Nat Gallery Art; and many others. *Comn:* Eisenhower Inaugural Medals; Pa Railroad War Mem; statue of Douglas MacArthur, US Mil Acad; statue of John Paul Jones, Fairmount Park, Philadelphia; statue of James Madison, Libr of Cong, Madison Bldg; plus many other medals, monuments & portrait busts throughout US & abroad. *Exhib:* National & international museums & galleries. *Pos:* Resident sculptor, Am Acad Rome, 56-57 & 62-63; sculptor in charge, Stone Mountain Mem, Ga, 64. *Teaching:* Head sculpture dept, Pa Acad Fine Arts, 29-68. *Awards:* Widener Gold Medal, 25 & Medal Honor, 53, Pa Acad Fine Arts; Medal Honor, Nat Sculpture Soc, 81; Nat Medal of Arts, 89. *Bibliog:* The Sculpture of Walker Hancock, Cap Ann Hist Asn, 89. *Mem:* Nat Acad Design; fel Nat Sculpture Soc; Architectural League; Franklin Fel Royal Soc Arts; Nat Mus Am Art Comn; plus others. *Media:* Bronze, Stone. *Mailing Add:* Lanesville Box 133 Gloucester MA 01930

HAND, JOHN OLIVER
HISTORIAN, CURATOR
b New York, NY, Aug 17, 41. *Study:* Denison Univ, AB, 63; Univ Chicago, MA(art hist), 67; Princeton Univ, MFA(art hist), 71, PhD(art hist), 78. *Pos:* Docent, Nat Gallery Art, 65-69, cur, Northern European Painting, 73-84; cur, Northern Renaissance Painting, 84- *Teaching:* Teacher art & art hist, Denison Univ, 63 & Princeton Univ, 71. *Awards:* Samuel H Kress Found Fel, 71-72; Belg Am Educ Found Fel, 72-73. *Mem:* Historians Netherlandish Art. *Res:* Northern Renaissance painting; 15th and 16th century Northern Renaissance painting; Joos Van Cleve. *Publ:* Auth, Joos Van Cleve and the Saint Jerome in the Norton Gallery and School of Art, Norton Gallery, 72; Joos Van Cleve: The Early & Mature Paintings, Princeton Univ, 78; co-auth, The Collections of the National Gallery of Art Systematic Catalog, Early Netherlandish Painting, Wash, 86; essay, The 16th Century and catalogue entries in The Age of Bruegel, Netherlandish Drawings of the 16th Century (catalog), Nat Gallery Art, Washington, DC; The Pierpoint Morgan Library, New York, 86-87. *Mailing Add:* Nat Gallery Art Washington DC 20565

HANDELL, ALBERT GEORGE
PAINTER
b Brooklyn, NY, Feb 13, 37. *Study:* Art Students League; La Grande Chaumiere, Paris. *Work:* Bates Col; Brooklyn Mus Art, NY; Schenectady Mus Art, NY; Salt Lake City Mus Fine Arts; Art Students League. *Exhib:* One-man show Schenectady Art Mus New York, Berkshire Mus, Pittsfield MA; ACA Gallery, New York, 66 & Eileen Kuhlik Gallery, New York, 72; Harbor Galary Cold Spring, Harbor NY; Ventana Gallery, Santa Fe, NMex, 87-92; two-man show, Total Arts Gallery, Taos NM, 89. *Teaching:* Instr, Albert Handell Nation-wide Painting Workshops, 84- *Awards:* John F & Anna Lee Stacy Scholar Fund, 62-65; Ranger Fund Purchase Prize, Audubon Artist, 68; Elizabeth T Greenshields Mem Found, 72; Master Pastelist, 84, Pastel Hall of Fame, 87, Pastel Soc Am; over 50 awards, 58- *Bibliog:* Heather-Meredith-Owens (auth), The inner univers of Albert Handell, Am Artist Mag, 4/71; Joe Singer (auth), Pastel Portraits, Watson-Guptill; Leslie Trainer (auth), Pastel landscapes of Albert Handell, Am Artist Mag, 12/82; and others; Joy Murphy (auth), Albert Handell, Enraptured, Southwest Art Mag, 4/86; and others. *Mem:* Allied Artist Am; Salmagundi Club; Art Students League; Pastel Soc Am. *Media:* Pastels, Oil. *Publ:* Coauth (with Leslie Trainor Handell), Oil Painting Workshop, 80 & Pastel Painting Workshop, 81, Watson-Guptill; (with Leslie Trainor Handell), Intuitive Composition; A Creative Approach to Realistic Painting, Watson-Guptill. *Dealer:* Connie Axton, The Ventana Gallery, Santa Fe NM. *Mailing Add:* PO Box 8629 Santa Fe NM 87501

HANDLER, AUDREY
GLASS BLOWER, EDUCATOR
b Philadelphia, Pa, Dec 9, 34. *Study:* Tyler Sch Fine Arts, Temple Univ, Philadelphia, 52-54; Art Students League, New York, summer 55; Boston Univ Sch Fine & Appl Arts, BFA, 56, study with David Aronson; Univ Ill, Champaign, 62; sr res fel, Royal Col Art, London, Eng, 67-68; Univ Wis-Madison, MS, 67, MFA, 70, study with Harvey Littleton. *Work:* Corning Mus Glass, NY; Lannan Found, Palm Beach, Fla; Royal Col Art, London, Eng; Lobmeyr Mus, Vienna, Austria;; Hastings Col Glass Collections, Nebr; Ronald Abramson Glass Collection, Washington, DC; and others. *Exhib:* Nat Collection Fine Art, Renwick Gallery, Smithsonian Inst, Washington, DC, 73; Am Glass Now, San Francisco Mus Art, Calif, 74; Toledo Mus, 79; Renwick Gallery, 80; Metrop Mus Art, 80-81,; Calif Palace Legion Honor, 81,; Victoria & Albert Mus, London, 81,; Musee des Arts Decoratifs, Paris, & Japan, 82; Glasmuseum, Ebeltoft, 86; Hokkaido Mus Modern Art, Sapporo, Japan, 88; and others. *Teaching:* Instr glass, Penland Sch Crafts, NC, 71-83 & Haystack Mountain Sch Crafts, Deer Isle, Maine, 73; instr commercial art dept, Madison Area Tech Col, Wis, 73- *Awards:* Juror's Awards, 46th & 59th Wis Designer Craftsmen Shows, Milwaukee, 66 & 71 & Madison Artists Exhib, Madison Art Ctr, Wis, 70; Master Craftsmen Apprenticeship Prog Grant, Nat Endowment Arts, 77-78 & 80-81. *Bibliog:* Paula Orth (auth), Blown Glass, Milwaukee Sentinel, 72; Terri Gabriell (auth), Instructor Makes, Hunterdon Co Dem, Flemington, NJ, 72; S K Oberbeck (auth), Glass menagerie, Newsweek, 4/73. *Mem:* Glass Art Soc, Inc (mem bd, 76-78); Nat Coun on the Educ of Ceramic Arts; Am Crafts Coun; World Crafts Coun; Wis Designer Craftsmen Coun. *Media:* Blown Glass, Silver & Gold Figures. *Mailing Add:* 105 S Rock Rd Madison WI 53705

HANDVILLE, ROBERT T
PAINTER, ILLUSTRATOR
b Paterson, NJ, Mar 23, 24. *Study:* Pratt Inst, cert, 48; Brooklyn Mus Art Sch; also painting with Rubentam, 60-64. *Work:* J F Kennedy White House Collection; UNICEF; Univ Denver; Syracuse Univ; Univ Okla; and others. *Comn:* Design of Yellowstone Nat Park Commemorative US Postage Stamp, Presidential Citizens Adv Stamp Coun, 71-72; design of Alfred Verville Air Mail Commemorative US Postage Stamp, 81. *Exhib:* 200 Yrs Am Watercolor Painting, Metrop Mus Art, New York, 66; Exhib Olympic Games, Mus Acuarela, Inst Arte Mex, 68; New Eng Silvermine Guild, Conn, 70; Butler Inst Am Art, Youngstown, Ohio; Smithsonian Inst, Washington, DC; Champions of Am Sport Show, Nat Portrait Gallery, Washington DC, 81. *Teaching:* Mem fac, Fashion Inst of Technol, State Univ NY. *Awards:* 27th New England Exhib Am Can Co Award, Silvermine Guild Artists; Mary Pleissner Mem Award, 81; Speyer Prize, Nat Acad Design 157th Ann Exhib, 82. *Mem:* Am Watercolor Soc (dir, 73-75); Soc Illusrs; elect Nat Acad Design. *Media:* Watercolor, Acrylic; Ink, Oil. *Mailing Add:* 1 Barrows Rd East Falmouth MA 02536-5411

HANES, JAMES (ALBERT)
PAINTER
b Louisville, Ky, Feb 5, 24. *Study:* Philadelphia Sch Indust Art; US Army Univ, France; Pa Acad Fine Arts; Barnes Found, Pa. *Work:* Pa Acad Fine Arts, Philadelphia; Univ Tampa, Fla; Yale Univ, New Haven, Conn; La Salle Col, Philadelphia; Nat Acad Design, New York. *Exhib:* Palazzo Venezia, Rome, Italy, 52; Palazzo Esposizione, Rome, 53; Nat Inst Arts & Lett, New York, 56; Univ Pittsburgh, 72; Peale House Galleries of Pa Acad Fine Arts, 79; Goldsmith Gallery, Memphis, Tenn, 80. *Pos:* Art ed, Four Quarters, 70- *Teaching:* Instr painting, Pa Acad Fine Arts, 80-81; asst prof painting & artist in residence, La Salle Col, 65-92. *Awards:* Cresson, Thuron & Lambert Awards, Pa Acad Fine Arts, 49; Tiffany First Award, 50; Prix de Rome, Am Acad in Rome, 51-54. *Bibliog:* Valerio Mariani (auth), Un pittore Americano, Idea, 8/16/53. *Mem:* Am Acad in Rome; fel Pa Acad Fine Arts. *Media:* Oil. *Mailing Add:* 415 W Stafford St Philadelphia PA 19144

HANKEY, ROBERT E
EDUCATOR, ADMINISTRATOR
b Fargo, NDak, June 24, 31. *Study:* Quincy Col, Ill, BA, 57; Cath Theological Union, Chicago, MA, 61; Cath Univ Am, BA(studio art), 61, Loyola Univ Chicago, MEd, 71. *Pos:* Ed & illusr, Troubadour Mag, Franciscan Press, 59-61; dean of students, Minneapolis Col Art & Design, 70-80; freelance designer, 80-84; acad dean, Col Assoc Arts, St Paul, 84- & pres, 87- *Teaching:* Prof art & design, Col Associated Arts, 84- *Mem:* Nat Asn Schs of Art & Design; Minn Indian Consortium Higher Educ (dir, 80-); Am Inst Graphic Arts; Int Coun Design Schs. *Res:* Computer art, electronic media and phenomenology. *Publ:* Auth, Cybernetics, Duns Scotus Philos Rev, 57; Art and Theology, Duns Scotus Theology Rev, 61; Phenomenon of Art, Corcoran Art Gallery, 71. *Mailing Add:* Col Associated Arts 344 Summit Ave St Paul MN 55102

HANKS, DAVID ALLEN
CURATOR, WRITER
b St Louis, Mo, Dec 13, 40. *Study:* Washington Univ, St Louis, AB & MA. *Collections Arranged:* American Art of the Colonies and Early Republic (auth, catalog), Art Inst Chicago, 71; The Arts and Crafts Movement in America, 1876-1916 (contribr, catalog), 73; The Decorative Designs of Frank Lloyd Wright, Renwick Gallery, Smithsonian Inst, 77-78; Innovative Furniture in America, Smithsonian Inst, 81. *Pos:* Asst cur, Art Inst of Chicago, 69-74; cur, Philadelphia Mus of Art, 74-77; guest cur, Smithsonian Inst, 77- *Mem:* Decorative Arts Chap Soc Archit Hist (pres, 74-77); Philadelphia Chap Victorian Soc (pres 75-77). *Res:* American furniture of the 19th and 20th century. *Publ:* Auth, Isaac E Scott: Reform Furniture in Chicago, Chicago Sch of Archit Found, 74; co-auth, Daniel Pabst, Philadelphia Mus of Art, 77. *Mailing Add:* 800 Fifth Ave New York NY 10021

HANLEN, JOHN (GARRETT)
PAINTER, INSTRUCTOR
b Winfield, Kans, Jan 1, 22. *Study:* Pa Acad Fine Arts, three traveling fels; independent study with George Harding, muralist; Barnes Found, Merion, Pa. *Work:* Pa Acad Fine Arts, Moore Col Art, Philadelphia; Libr Cong, Washington, DC; War Dept of Combat Art, Washington, DC; Woodmere Gallery Art, Chestnut Hill, Pa. *Comn:* Mural, egg tempera (collaborated with George Harding), comn by Montgomery Co, John James Audubon Shrine, Mill Grove, Pa, 54-56. *Exhib:* Pa Acad Fine Arts Ann, Philadelphia, 48-; Philadelphia Mus Art, 55; Detroit Inst Art, 59; one-man shows, Pa Acad Fine Arts, Peale House Gallery, 65 & Woodmere Gallery Art, Chestnut Hill, Pa, 73; Am Drawing 1968, Moore Col Art, 68; Pa 71, William Penn Mem Mus, Harrisburg, 71 & 83. *Pos:* Mem bd, Fine Arts Com, Woodmere Gallery Art, 75-85; mem bd, fel of Pa Acad Fine Arts, 76. *Teaching:* Advan critic painting & drawing, Pa Acad Fine Arts, Philadelphia, 53-86; prof painting & drawing, Moore Col Art, Philadelphia, 54-84. *Awards:* First Award for Painting, Louis Comfort Tiffany Found, 50; first award, Edwin Austin Abbey fel for Mural Decoration, 51; Pa Acad Fine Arts Fel, Percy M Owens Award, Distinguished Artist, Pa, 86. *Mem:* Life mem Pa Acad Fine Arts Fel. *Media:* Roplex with Dry Color, White, Gold & Silver Mylar. *Dealer:* Sydelle Puchek 7304 Sharpless Rd Melrose Park PA 19126. *Mailing Add:* Logan Square E No 2004 2 Franklin Town Blvd Philadelphia PA 19103

HANLEY, JACK
PAINTER, GALLERY DIRECTOR
b New York, NY, Jan 8, 52. *Study:* State Univ NY, BFA, 74; Univ Calif, Berkeley, MA, 80, MFA, 82. *Work:* Prudential, New York; Michener, Austin, Tex; Mus Southern Tex, Corpus Christi. *Exhib:* Skowhegan, Leo Castelli Gallery, 85; Tex Artists, San Francisco Mus, San Francisco, 86; solo exhib, Ohio State Univ, Columbus, 86; Four Tex Painters, Hal Bromm Gallery, New York, 88; Tex Triennial (travelling exhib), Contemp Art Mus, Houston, Tex. *Pos:* Owner & cur, Trans-Avant Garde Gallery, 85-90, Jack Hanley Gallery, San Francisco, Calif, 90- *Teaching:* Vis lectr fine arts, Princeton Univ; asst prof fine arts, Univ Tex, 84-90. *Awards:* Visual Artist Fel, Nat Endowment Arts, 87. *Mem:* Col Art Asn. *Media:* Acrylic. *Dealer:* Barry Whistler Gallery 2909-A Canton St Dallas TX 75226. *Mailing Add:* 2210 Jackson St San Francisco CA 94115

HANNA, ANNETTE ADRIAN
PAINTER, INSTRUCTOR
b New York, NY. *Study:* Traphagen Inst Fashion Illus; Art Students League, studied with Greene, Sanden & Passantino, 79-80; pvt study with J H Sanden & Burton Silverman, 82-91. *Work:* Am Broadcasting Co, New York; US Coast Guard, Washington, DC; Schering Plough Corp, Madison, NJ. *Comn:* Portrait, US Navy, Washington, DC, 79; portrait, Hilton Hotels, Parsippany, NJ, 82; portrait, Riker, Danzig, Scherer, Hyland, Morristown, NJ, 84; portrait, State Senator Ret, Convent Station, NJ, 86; portrait, Judge Court of Appeals, Ret, New York, 87. *Exhib:* Grand Nat AAPL, 81-91 & Nat Open Juried Ann, 90-91, Salmagundi Club, New York; Hudson Valley Art Asn, Westchester Co Community Ctr, White Plains, NY, 88-90; Portraits of the Northeast, Creative Workshops, New Haven, Conn, 89; Art Showcase, Schering Plough Corp, Madison, NJ, 89; Pastels Only Nat Arts Club, New York, 91. *Pos:* Sem admin & adv coun, Nat Portrait Sems, New York 80-83; bd mem, Morris Co Art Asn, Morristown, NJ, 84-86; bd mem & pres, Blackwell St Ctr Arts, Dover, NJ, 89- *Teaching:* Fac mem, portrait, Nat Portrait Home Study, 85-87; painting, portrait, still life, landscape, oil & pastel, Morris Co Art Asn, Morristown, NJ, 89-; instr oil, pastel & portrait landscape, Int Workshops, Italy, Panama, 92. *Awards:* Portrait & Figure Award, Am Art Prof League, NJ, 81, 82, 84-87; Gold Medal Oil, Hudson Valley Art Asn, 88; Gold Medal Pastel, Am Art Prof League, NY, 90. *Bibliog:* Anne Corcoran (auth), Dover gallery, 8/91 & Janet Adamec (auth), Portrait artist, 3/92, Star Ledger, Newark, NJ. *Mem:* Pastel So Am, New York; Hudson Valley Art Asn, New York; Am Artist Prof Leage NY & NJ; Arts Coun Morris Area, NJ (visual art chmn, 82 & 92); Morris Co Art Asn, Morristown, NJ (bd, 84-86). *Media:* Oil, Pastel. *Dealer:* Blackwell St Ctr Arts 32-34 W Blackwell St Dover NJ 07801. *Mailing Add:* RD 4, Box 11 Boonton NJ 07005

HANNA, PAUL DEAN, JR
PAINTER, PRINTMAKER
b Alice, Tex. *Study:* Austin Col, BA; Chouinard Art Inst; Tex Christian Univ, MFA. *Work:* Tex Tech Mus, Lubbock; Pace Collection, San Antonio; Bell Reproduction Collection, Ft Worth; Lubbock Art Asn, Tex; First Nat Bank, Hobbs, NMex. *Comn:* Six glass engraved windows & four stained glass windows, Covenant Presbyterian Church, Lubbock, Tex, 77- *Exhib:* Two-man show, Witte Mus, San Antonio, 68; Northwest Printmakers' Int, Seattle & Portland, 69; Southwestern Exhib Painting & Sculpture, Dallas, 71; Printmaking Now, Nat Print Exhib, 73; Longview Painting Exhib, 74; Tex Tech Univ, Lubbock, 77, 87 & 88. *Teaching:* Prof painting & drawing, Tex Tech Univ, 69- *Awards:* Eight State Painting & Sculpture Award, Okla Art Ctr, 66 & 80; Longview Painting Award, 74; Juror's Award, 23rd Ann, Okla Art Ctr, 80; Grant, Nat Endowment Arts, 82. *Bibliog:* Gene Mittler & JAmes Howze (auths), Creating and Understanding Drawings, Glencoe Publ Co, 89. *Mem:* Tex Watercolor Soc; Tex Asn Schs Art (past pres). *Media:* Acrylic, Oil; Woodcut, Silkscreen. *Mailing Add:* 2831 24th St Lubbock TX 79410

HANNAH, DUNCAN (RATHBUN)
PAINTER
b Minneapolis, Minn, Aug 21, 52. *Study:* Minneapolis Col Art & Design, 70; Bard Col, 71-73; Parsons Sch Design, BFA, 75. *Work:* Republic Bank Houston; Chase Manhattan Bank, New York; Chemical Bank, New York;

Minneapolis Inst Art; Metrop Mus Art, New York. *Exhib:* New Talent, Albright-Knox Mus, 81; New Still Life, Mus Mod Art, New York, 82; Art Aid, Sothebys, New York, 86; Art Against AIDs, 87 & solo exhib, Phyllis Kind Gallery, New York, 88 & 89; solo exhibs, Jon Oulman Gallery, Minneapolis, Minn, 88, 90 & 92, Charles Cowles Gallery, New York, 89 & 91 & Tatistcheff & Co, New York & Los Angeles, Calif, 91; Metrop Mus Art, Philbrook Mus Art, Tulsa, Okla, Ctr Fine Arts, Miami, Fla, Joslyn Art Mus, Omaha, Nebr, Tampa Mus Art, Fla, Greenville Co Mus Art, SC, Madison Art Ctr, Wis, Grand Rapids Art Mus, Mich, 91-92; Art for Childrens Survival, Unicef, Sothebys, NY, 91; and others. *Teaching:* Instr visual essay, Sch Visual Arts, New York, 89-91. *Bibliog:* The Figure in 20th Century American Art, Metrop Mus Art, 85; Barry Blinderman (interviewer), Duncan Hannah: Mythic Times, Univ Galleries Ill State Univ, 90; Robert Rosenblum (intro), The Landscape in Twentieth Century Art: Selections from the Metropolitan Museum of Art, Rizzoli, NY. *Media:* Oil on Canvas. *Mailing Add:* Charles Cowles Gallery 420 W Broadway New York NY 10012

HANNAH, JOHN JUNIOR
PRINTMAKER, EDUCATOR
b Buffalo, NY, Mar 23, 23. *Study:* Univ Buffalo, BFA; Univ Ill, with Lee Chesney, MFA, 55; Albright Art Sch, with Letterio Calapai; Neth Royal Acad Painting & Sculpture, Fulbright grant, 60-61; Pratt Graphic Art Ctr, 67; also Birgit Skiold Workshop, London. *Work:* Northwest Printmakers, Seattle Mus Art, Wash; Okla Printmakers Collection, Oklahoma City; 3-M Collection, Tweed Gallery, Duluth, Minn; Bradley Univ Collection, Peoria, Ill; Joslyn Art Mus, Omaha, Nebr; and others. *Comn:* Tourist, Friends of Art, Kans State Univ, 67. *Exhib:* 1st Int Print Exhib, Hilo, Hawaii, 76; Three Decades of Am Printmaking, Brooklyn Mus, NY, 77; Nat Color Blend Print Exhib, Univ Miss, 77; 44th Ann Miniature Printers Sculptors & Gravers, Washington, DC, 77; Six Printmakers, Loyola Univ, Los Angeles, 77; and others. *Teaching:* Instr drawing, Ohio State Univ, Columbus, 56; assoc prof printmaking, Kans State Univ, Manhattan, 57-68; prof printmaking & drawing, Calif State Univ, Northridge, 69-; retired. *Awards:* Calif Art Coun Artist Grant, 78. *Mem:* Los Angeles Printmaking Soc (bd mem, 70-); Artists Econ Action (bd mem, 73-74). *Media:* Etching, Serigraphy. *Publ:* Contribr, Etching, Van Nostrand, 73; American Printmakers, 74 & California Graphics, 74, Graphis Group Arcadia, 74. *Mailing Add:* 665 Haverford Pacific Palisades CA 90272

HANNAY, JANNEKA (JANN)
PAINTER
b Orange, NJ, Aug 16, 33. *Study:* Miami Univ, Oxford, Ohio, BFA, 55; Kean Col, MA, 73; NJ Ctr Visual Arts, with Voy Fangor, 76-78; Art Students League, 80-81; Pratt Inst, MPS, NY, 89. *Work:* Shearing Plough Collection, Morristown, NJ; Schoor & De Palma Collection, NJ; Pub Serv Elec & Gas Collection. *Exhib:* Invitational, Lever House, New York, 80 & Kean Col, 81; NJ Ctr Visual Arts, Stricoff Gallery, 87; Vorpal Gallery, 88 & 91. *Pos:* Vpres, Summit Art Ctr Mus, 72-74, trustee, 72-80; Chmn art dept, Kent Place Sch, 75-83; cur, Teaching Gallery, 77-83; registered art therapist, Carrier Found, 86-90. *Awards:* Best in Show, NJ Ctr Visual Arts. *Bibliog:* Hedy O'Beil (auth), article, 78 & Addison Parks (auth), New artists, 80, Arts Mag; Diana Freedman (auth), article, Artspeak, 87; Dennis Wepman (auth), Sunspeak (article), 88. *Mem:* Artists Equity, NY; Women's Caucus Art, NY. *Media:* Oil on Canvas. *Dealer:* Vorpal Gallery 411 Broadway New York NY 10012. *Mailing Add:* 15 Gerard Court New Providence NJ 07974

HANNIBAL, JOSEPH HARRY
EDUCATOR, PAINTER
b Brooklyn, NY, May 4, 45. *Study:* Austin Peay State Univ, Clarksville, Tenn, BS, 68; Univ Tenn, Knoxville, MFA, 72. *Work:* Austin Peay State Univ; Univ Wis, Stout. *Exhib:* one-man show, 118 Gallery, Minneapolis, 80; Austin Peay, State Univ, 81; Los Angeles City Col, 82; Ontario Mus Art & History, Calif, 83; Laguna Beach Sch Art, 83; Distinguished Artist Exhib, The Chancellary, Long Beach, Calif, 86. *Teaching:* Head, Printmaking Area, Dept Art, Univ Wis-Stout, Menomonie, 72-81; head lithography dept, Cent Col Art & Design, London, Eng, 75-76; chmn art dept, Calif State Polytech Univ, Pomona, 81-85, head painting area, 85- *Awards:* Gold Medal, Italy, 81; Purchase Award, 12th Nat Drawing Exhib, Minot, NDak, 82; Cash Award, Multicultural Art Inst, San Diego, 82. *Mem:* Col Art Asn; Los Angeles Printmaking Soc. *Dealer:* 118 Gallery 1007 Harmon Pl Minneapolis MN 55403. *Mailing Add:* Dept Art Calif State Polytech 3801 W Temple Ave Pomona CA 91768

HANSELL, FREYA
PAINTER
b Detroit, Mich. *Study:* Wayne State Univ, BFA, 70; Northwestern Univ, MFA, 72; Sch Art Inst of Chicago, 72-74. *Work:* Contemp Art Ctr, Hawaii; Mus Contemp Art, Chicago; Chase Manhattan, New York; Best Collection, Va; Tishman Speyer, New York. *Exhib:* A View of Nature, The Aldrich Mus, Ridgefield, Conn, 86; The New Romantic Landscape, Whitney Mus Am Art, Stamford, Conn, 87; Nocturnes, Whitney Mus Am Art, New York, 89; USA/USSR Exchange Exhib, Kuznetsky Most Exhib Hall, Moscow, 89; solo exhibs: Artists Space, New York, 80, Marianne Deson Gallery, Chicago, 81, Public Image Gallery, New York, 84, Piezo Electric Gallery, New York, 84, 86 (with catalog) & 87; Lorence-Monk Gallery, New York, 91; Burning in Hell, Franklin Furnace, New York, 91; PS 1, New York, 92; Paris-Montenay, 92; Penine Hart Gallery, New York, 92. *Teaching:* Instr, Bard Col, 81-82; Parsons Sch Design, 85-90; Sch Visual Arts, 86-89; State Univ NY, Purchase, 91. *Awards:* Nat Endowment Arts, 89-90. *Bibliog:* Michael Brenson (auth), 12/9/88 & Grace Glueck (auth), 9/10/89, NY Times; Art in America, 3/89. *Mem:* Women's Action Coalition (WAC). *Publ:* Auth, Beyond Boundaries, Van Der Marck, 87. *Mailing Add:* 70 Fulton St New York NY 10038

HANSEN, FRANCES FRAKES
EDUCATOR, PAINTER
b Harrisburg, Mo. *Study:* Univ Denver, BFA; Art Inst Chicago; Univ Northern Colo, MA; Univ Southern Calif; Univ Denver; Ecoles Art Am, Fontainebleau, France. *Exhib:* Denver Art Mus, 45, 49, 50-60, 62 & 68; Joslyn Mus Biennial, Omaha, Nebr 46, 49, 50, 52, 53 & 67; Gilpin Co Ann, Central City, Colo, 48-51, 53-58, 60, 61, 69 & 72; William Rockhill Nelson Mus, Kansas City, Mo, 50; Mus NMex Ann Regional, Santa Fe, 57 & 59; Colorado Springs Fine Arts Ctr, 61; Colo State Univ Centennial Exhib, 70; Mex Consulate, Denver, 80; and others. *Pos:* Researcher & display designer, Am Indian, Denver Mus Natural Hist, 73-78, 90-; artist-mem ed bd & illusr, Denver Botanic Gardens, 77- *Teaching:* Prof art, Colo Women's Col, 45-73; lectr, Am Indian Art. *Awards:* Painting Prize for Oils, Canyon Pastoral, Colo State Fair Prof Show, 65; Colo Women's Col Faculty Res Grant, 69; Painting Prize for Acrylic, Lights, Univ Northern Colo Centennial Exhib, 70; and others. *Mem:* Delta Phi Delta (Art Inst Chicago Chap); Am Asn Univ Prof; Nat Audubon Soc; and others. *Media:* Acrylic, Watercolor. *Publ:* Auth, Native arts in America, US Cult Bull, 66; illusr, Song of the Ghost Trains, Denver Symphony Guild, 81. *Mailing Add:* 700 Pontiac St Denver CO 80220

HANSEN, GAYLEN CAPENER
PAINTER, EDUCATOR
b Garland, Utah, Sept 21, 21. *Study:* Otis Art Inst, 39-40; Art Barn Sch Fine Arts, 40-44; Art Ctr, Sale Lake City, 40-44; Univ Utah, 43-44 & 45-46; Utah State Agricultural Col, BS, 52; Univ Southern Calif, Los Angeles, MFA, 53. *Work:* Wash State Univ, Pullman; Seattle Arts Comn; Utah State Permanent Collection, Salt Lake City. *Comn:* Painting on canvas, Art in Archit Prog, Moscow, Idaho, 80. *Exhib:* Solo exhibs, Monique Knowlton Gallery, New York, 80, 81 & 83, Boise Gallery Art, Idaho, 85, Galerie Redman, Berlin, Ger, 85 & 87, Greg Kucera Gallery Art, Seattle, Wash, 87, Whatcom Mus Hist & Art, Bellingham, Calif, 88, Yellowstone Art Ctr, Billings, Mt, 88 & Arts Club Chicago, 90; retrospectives, Seattle Art Mus, Wash & Univ Art Mus, Pullman, Wash, 85 & Mus Art, Pa State Univ, Portland Ctr Visual Arts, Ore & San Jose Mus Art, Calif, 86; 38th Corcoran Biennial Exhib Am Painting - 2nd Western States Exhib, Washington, DC, traveling, 83; 5 Amerikanische Kunstler, Galerie Redmann, Berlin, Ger, 84; Second Western Biennial, Brooklyn Mus, NY, 85; Beyond the Real, Prichard Art Gallery, Moscow, Idaho, 86; Folk Images: The Animal Kingdome, Hippodrome Gallery, Long Beach, Calif, 87; Masters of the Inalnd Northwest, Cheney Cowles Mus, Spokane, Wash, 88; Northwest x Southwest Exploring Painted Fictions, Palm Springs Desert Mus, Calif, 90. *Teaching:* Instr painting & drawing, Univ Tex, Austin, 47-52; prof art, Wash State Univ, Pullman, 57-84. *Awards:* Purchase Prize, Utah State Fair Exhib, 44; First Prize, Fifth Ann Oil Exhib, Woessner Gallery, Seattle, 58; Second Prize, Northwest Watercolor Ann, Seattle Art Mus, 60. *Bibliog:* Lissa August (auth), Westtern Artists Strut Their Stuff, People Weekly, 3/83; Grace Glueck (auth), Two Biennials: One Looking East & the Other West, NY Times, 3/27/83; Matthew Kangas (auth), Little Romances/Little Fictions, Vanguard, 5/84; Dieterich Kinderman (auth), Don't Mistake Gaylen Hansen's Art for Primitive, Idaho Statesman, 5/85. *Media:* Oil on Canvas. *Mailing Add:* Koplin Gallery 1438 Ninth St Santa Monica CA 90401

HANSEN, HAROLD JOHN
EDUCATOR, PAINTER
b Chicago, Ill, June 18, 42. *Study:* Univ Ill, BFA, 64; Univ Mich, MFA, 66. *Work:* SC State Art Collection; SC Florence Mus Art; Univ South; Univ Pac; Carroll Reese Mus, E Tenn State Univ. *Exhib:* Drawings USA Travelling Show, 73; Potsdam Drawings, Univ New York Potsdam, 79. *Teaching:* Instr art, Kendall Sch Design, Grand Rapids, Mich, 66-69; asst prof art, Ferris State Col, Big Rapids, Mich, 69-70; from asst prof art to assoc prof, Univ SC, 70-86, chmn, Div Art Studio, 75-82, assoc head dept art, 75-90 & prof, 86- *Awards:* First Prize for Graphics, 15th Annual Springs Mills Art Exhibition, Lancaster, SC, 73; First Prize, Caroliniana Watercolor Competition, Columbia, SC, 81; Grand Prize, SC State Fair, Columbia, 87. *Media:* Encaustic, Watercolor. *Res:* Technical investigation of the encaustic to improve working characteristics and hardness. *Publ:* Auth, A method for modern encaustic painting, Southeastern Col Art Asn Rev, spring 76; The development of new vehicle recipies for encaustic paints, Leonardo, 77. *Dealer:* Portfolio Gallery 2007 Devine St Columbia SC 29205. *Mailing Add:* 1314 Brentwood Dr Columbia SC 29206

HANSEN, JAMES LEE
SCULPTOR
b Tacoma, Wash, June 13, 25. *Study:* Portland Art Mus Sch. *Work:* San Francisco Art Mus; Seattle Art Mus; Portland Art Mus, Ore; Univ Ore Mus Art, Eugene. *Comn:* The Guardian, Clark Col, Vancouver, Wash, 77; Talos 2, Civic Transit Mall, Portland, Ore, 78; The Crescent Probe, Civic Ctr Fountain, Salem, Ore, 78; Stempost, Stadium Plaza, Wash State Univ, Pullman, 80; The Oasis, Bur Land Mgt Bldg, Medford, Ore, 80; The Shaman, State Capitol Campus, Olympia, Wash; Autumn Rider (cast bronze), Gresham, Ore. *Exhib:* Whitney Mus Am Art Ann, 53; Artists Environ, Amon Carter Mus, Ft Worth, Tex, 62; one-man shows, Fountain Gallery, Portland, 69, 77-81 & 84, Portland Art Mus, 71, Friedlander Gallery, Seattle, 73 & 77, Hodges/Banks Gallery, Seattle, Wash, 83 & 85 & Abante Gallery Art, Portland, Ore, 86 & 88; Art of the Pacific Northwest, 1930 to Present, Nat Col Fine Art, Smithsonian Inst, Washington, DC, 74; An American Tradition: Abstraction, Henry Gallery, Seattle, Wash, 81-82; Hodges/Banks Gallery, Seattle, 83. *Pos:* Founder & 1st pres, Alliance of NW Sculptors, 77-80. *Teaching:* Prof sculpture, Portland State Univ, 64-90. *Awards:* Norman Davis Award for Neo Shang, Seattle Art Mus, 58; Am Trust Co Award, 56 & Award for Ritual, 60, San Francisco Art Mus; Nat Ann, Award for Huntress, 52. *Bibliog:* William Davenport (auth), Art treasures in the West, Lane, 10/66;

J A Schinneller (auth), Art/search & self discovery, Int Textbk, 12/67. *Publ:* New Totems & Old Gods, Surgo Publ, 90. *Dealer:* Abante Gallery 204 SW Yamhill Portland OR 97204. *Mailing Add:* 28219 NE 63rd Ct Battle Ground WA 98604

HANSEN, ROBERT
EDUCATOR, PAINTER
b Osceola, Nebr, Jan 1, 24. *Study:* Univ Nebr, AB, BFA, 48; Escuela Univ Bellas Artes, San Miguel Allende, Mex, MFA, 49; also with Alfredo Zalce, Morelia, Mex, 52-53. *Work:* Mus Mod Art & Whitney Mus Am Art, New York; Los Angeles Co Mus Art; San Diego Gallery Fine Arts; Long Beach Mus Art. *Exhib:* Carnegie Int, Pittsburgh, Pa, 61 & 63; Painting USA: Figure, 62 & Tamarind: Homage to Lithography, 69, Mus Mod Art, New York; retrospectives, Long Beach Mus Art, Calif, 67 & Los Angeles Munic Gallery, 73; New Vein, organized & mounted in mus of nat capitols in Europe & SAm, Smithsonian Inst, 68-70; and numerous solo exhibs. *Teaching:* Prof art, Occidental Col, 56-87, emer prof, 87- *Awards:* Guggenheim Fel, 61; Fulbright Sr Grant, 61; Tamarind Fel, 65. *Media:* Lacquer. *Publ:* Auth, This curving world: Hyperbolic linear perspective, J Aesthetics & Art Criticism, winter 73; transl, Curvilinear Perspective, Flocon and Barre, Univ Calif Press, 87. *Mailing Add:* 1498 Santa Ynez Carpinteria CA 93013

HANSEN, SARAH EVELETH (CAMPBELL)
ART DEALER, GALLERY DIRECTOR
b Attleboro, Mass, June 15, 17. *Study:* Wellesley Col, BA, 39; Boston Univ, MA, 41. *Pos:* Dir, Sarah Eveleth Antiques, Washington, DC or Bethesda, Md, 69-; from co-dir to dir, The Glass Gallery, Bethesda, Md, 72- *Mem:* Glass Art Soc. *Specialty:* Contemporary glass, including mixed media pieces, in which glass is being used as an art medium for individual expression. *Mailing Add:* The Glass Gallery 4720 Hampden Ln Bethesda MD 20814

HANSON, ANNE COFFIN
HISTORIAN
b Kinston, NC, Dec 12, 21. *Study:* Univ Southern Calif, BFA(painting), 43; Univ NC, Chapel Hill, MACA(painting), 51; Bryn Mawr Col, PhD(art hist), 62. *Pos:* Dir, Int Study Ctr, Mus Mod Art, 68-69, consult, 69-70; acting dir, Yale Univ Art Gallery, 85-87. *Teaching:* Instr drawing & painting, Albright Art Sch, Univ Buffalo, 55-58; asst prof art hist, Swarthmore Col, 63-64 & Bryn Mawr Col, 64-68; adj assoc prof, NY Univ, 69-70; prof art hist, Yale Univ, 70-78, dept chmn, 74-78, John Hay Whitney prof, 78-92; Robert Sterling Clark vis prof art hist, Williams Col Grad Prog, Clark Art Inst, fall 90; John Hay Whitney prof emer, 92- *Awards:* Nat Endowment for Humanities fel, 67-68; Inst for Advanced Study, Princeton, 83; Distinguished Alumna Award, Univ NC, 89; Distinguished Teaching of Art Award, Col Art Asn, 90. *Mem:* Nat Comt, Comt Int de l'Hist de l'Art; Col Art Asn Am (bd dirs, 69-73 & 79-83, pres, 72-74); Yale Univ Press (bd gov, 77-92); Swann Found Caricature & Cartoon (adv bd, 80-); Hillstead Mus, (bd gov, 88-). *Res:* Nineteenth century French painting, particularly the work of Edouard Manet; 15th century Italian sculpture, particularly the work of Jacopo della Quercia; problems in perspective and perception; Italian Futurism. *Publ:* Articles & reviews in Art Bulletin, Burlington Mag, and others, 60-; auth, Jacopo della Quercia's Fonte Gaia, Clarendon Press, Oxford, 65; Edouard Manet: 1832-1883, Philadelphia Mus Art, 66; Manet and the Modern Tradition, Yale Univ Press, London, 77; The Futurist Imagination, Yale Art Gallery, 83. *Mailing Add:* 28 Lincoln St New Haven CT 06511

HANSON, DUANE
SCULPTOR, EDUCATOR
b Alexandria, Minn, Jan 17, 25. *Study:* Macalester Col, BA; Univ Minn; Cranbrook Acad Art, MFA; DHL Nova Univ, Ft Lauderdale, 79. *Work:* Whitney Mus; Wadsworth Atheneum, Hartford; Norton Gallery, West Palm Beach; Milwaukee Art Mus; Nelson Gallery, Kansas City, Mo; Orlando Airport; Va Mus, Richmond; Ludwig Collection, Aachen, Cologne, Ger. *Comn:* Businessman, for Melvin Kaufman, New York, 71; Dockman, Yellow Trucking Co, Kansas City, 79; Ft Lauderdale Airport, 90. *Exhib:* Norton Gallery, West Palm Beach, Fla, 81; Cranbrook Acad Art, 85; solo exhibs, World Design Expos, Nagoya, Japan, 89, Contemp Art Mus, Honolulu, 89, Real People: Life-like Sculptures, Traveling Show, 89-90, Cranbrook Acad Art, Bloomfield Hills, Mich, 90, Philbrook Art Ctr, Tulsa, Okla, 90, Pa Acad Art, Philadelphia, 90 & David Winston Bell Gallery, Brown Univ, Providence, RI, 90; Josef-Haubrich-Kunsthalle, Cologne, Kunstuevein Hamberg, Haus am Waldsee, Berlin, Ger, 91; Hebonder Gallery, Palm Beach, Fla, 92; Galerie Neuendorf, Frankfurt, Ger, 92; Kunst Haus Wien, Vienna, Austria, 92; and others. *Teaching:* Asst prof art, Miami-Dade Jr Col, Miami, Fla, 65-69; adj prof art, Univ Miami, Fla, 79- *Awards:* Blair Award, Art Inst Chicago, 74; Ger Acad Exchange Serv Grant, West Berlin, 74; Ambassador Arts, Fla, 83; Fla Prize, NY Times Regional Newspapers, 85. *Bibliog:* Varnedoe (auth), Duane Hanson retrospective and recent work, Art News, 1/75; John Canaday (auth), What is Art?, Knopf, 80; Chistine Lindey (auth), Superrealist Sculpture & Painting, Morrow, 80; Harry Adams (auth), Duane Hanson, Varnedoe Essay, 85. *Mem:* Ft Lauderdale Art, Mus Art in Pub Places, Broward Co (bd mem). *Media:* Mixed Media, Polyvinyl-acetate. *Publ:* Duane Hanson Edition Cantz, Ger, 92. *Dealer:* Hans Neuendorf Beethovenstrasse 71 Frankfurt/Main Ger. *Mailing Add:* 6109 SW 55th Ct Davie FL 33314

HANSON, J B
SCULPTOR, WEAVER
b Gadsden, Ala, Oct 23, 46. *Study:* Md Inst, Col Art, 72-76. *Work:* Univ Md, College Park; Washington Co Mus Fine Art; Cloisters Children's Mus, Baltimore; Centre Int de la Tapisserie Ancienne et Moderne, Lusanne, Switzerland. *Comn:* 6 banners depicting the History of the Govans Community, City Baltimore, Md, 79, tapestry for Medfield Recreation Ctr, 79; mural, Mallory Ctr, Inst Arts, Inc, 81. *Exhib:* Maryland Ann, Baltimore Mus Art, 72; Maryland Biennial, Baltimore Mus Art, 74; Miniatures, West Tex Mus Art, Lubbock, 76; 11th Int Sculpture Symp, Studio Gallery, Washington, DC, 80; American Clay 1981, Meredith Contemp Art, Md, 81; Fine Art Auction Exhib, Metrop Mus, Fla, 81; Art of Ceramics, Atheneum Mus, Va, 81. *Awards:* Sculpture Award, Baltimore Mus Art, 74; Sculpture Award, Md Crafts Coun, 78. *Bibliog:* David Tannous (auth), Baltimore art scene, Smithsonian Assoc Mag, 79; Thomas Haulk (auth), reviews, Craft Horizon Mag, 79; Elisabeth Stevens (auth), Pots full of wit: sculptor shows he has a way with animals, Baltimore Sun, 80. *Mem:* Artist Equity Asn (pres, 80-81, nat ECoast vpres, 81-83); Md Crafts Coun (pres, 76). *Media:* Clay; Fibers. *Mailing Add:* 622 Homestead St Baltimore MD 21218

HANSON, JO
SCULPTOR
b Carbondale, Ill. *Study:* San Francisco State Univ, MA(sculpture), 73. *Work:* San Francisco Mus Mod Art; Mills Col, Oakland, Calif; Oakland Mus Art; Herbert F Johnson Mus, Cornell Univ; Rochester Inst Technol Libr. *Exhib:* Corcoran Gallery Art, DC, 74; San Francisco Mus Mod Art, 76 & Pa Acad Fine Arts, Philadelphia, 77; San Francisco Mus Mod Art & San Francisco City Hall, 80, Illegal Sights-Sites, Int Sculpture Conf, San Francisco, 82; Mus Contemp Art, Univ Sau Paulo, Brazil, 80; Pratt Manhattan Ctr Gallery, New York, 81; Rochester Inst Technol, 83; Chance and Change, A Century of the Avant-Garde, Auckland City Gallery, New Zealand, 85; Garbage Out Front, Municipal Art Soc, New York, 90. *Pos:* Art comnr, City of San Francisco, 83-89; Art Programs Consultant, Sanitary Fill Co, SAn Francisco. *Awards:* Nat Endowment Arts Grant, 77 & 79; Citations, San Francisco Bd Supervisors, 80 & Mayor, 89; Lifetime Achievement Award, Northern Calif Regional Womens Caucus Art, 92. *Bibliog:* Thelma R Newman (auth), Innovative Printmaking, Crown Publ Inc, NY, 77; Suzanne Lacy (auth), Broomsticks and banners, Artweek, 5/80; Virginia Watson-Jones (auth), Contemporary American Women Sculptors, Oryx Press, Phoenix, 86. *Mem:* Artists Equity Asn; Women's Caucus Art; Col Art Asn. *Media:* Multimedia. *Publ:* Auth, Artists Taxes, the Hands on Guide, Vortex Press, San Francisco, 87; The View From A Public Agency, Beyond Power Catalog, Southern Exposure Gallery & Women's Caucus for Art, SAn Francisco, 87; Eleanor Dickinson the Crucifixtion Series, Women Artists News, Spring-Summer, 89; Rachel Rosenthal: Pangaean Dreams, Women Artists News winter, 91. *Mailing Add:* 201 Buchanan San Francisco CA 94102

HANSON, JUDY See Cooke, Judy

HANSON, PHILIP HOLTON
PAINTER, LECTURER
b Chicago, Ill, Jan 8, 43. *Study:* Univ Chicago, BA, 65; Art Inst Chicago, MFA, 69. *Work:* Mus des 20 Jahrhunderts, Vienna, Austria; Mus Contemp Art, Chicago; Krannert Mus, Champaign, Ill. *Exhib:* Extraordinary Realities, Whitney Mus, 73; Madison Art Ctr, 77; Contemp Chicago Painters, Univ North Iowa Gallery Art, 78; Fabrications, Univ Miami, Lowe Art Mus, 80; Some Recent Art from Chicago, Ackland Art Mus, Univ NC, Chapel Hill, 80; Who Chicago, London, Edinburgh and traveling, 80; Six Chicago Artists, Pace Gallery, NY, 82; one-man show, Phyllis Kind Gallery, Chicago, 82, Hyde Park Art Ctr, 85. *Teaching:* Assoc prof, Sch Art Inst Chicago, 72- *Awards:* Casandra Grant, 73; Nat Endowment Arts Grant, 78 & 83. *Dealer:* Phyllis Kind Gallery 313 W Superior Chicago IL. *Mailing Add:* Sch Art Inst Chicago Columbus Dr & Jackson St Chicago IL 60603

HAOZOUS, BOB
SCULPTOR
b Los Angeles, Calif, Apr 1, 43. *Study:* Utah State Univ, 61-62; Calif Col Arts & Crafts, BFA, 71. *Work:* Albuquerque Mus, NMex; Heard Mus, Phoenix, Ariz; Joslyn Mus Art, Omaha, Nebr; Philbrook Art Ctr, Tulsa, Okla; Southwest Mus, Los Angeles. *Comn:* Mahogany relief wall mural, Daybreak Star Art Ctr, Seattle, Wash, 78; ann award bronze, Busn Comt Arts, New York, 83; sculpture for permanent collection, Heard Mus, Phoenix, Ariz, 83; monumental outdoor sculpture, City of Philadelphia, 88; 5 paired monumental sculptures, City of Phoenix, Ariz, 90. *Exhib:* One-man shows, Taylor Mus, Colorado Springs, 87, Wheelwright Mus, Santa Fe, NMex, 88 & Dartmouth Col, Hanover, NH, 89; Muerte/Amor, UNAM, Galeria Aristos, Mexico City, Mex, 90; Recent Major Work, Nev State Mus, Las Vegas, 92; The Vanishing White Man, Scotsdale Ctr Arts, Ariz, 92. *Pos:* Artist-in-residence, Dartmouth Col, Hanover, NH, 89. *Bibliog:* Rosalind Constable (auth), Six Artists, Horizon, 82; Lucy Lippard (auth), New Art in Multicultural America, Pantheon Bks, 90; Robin Cembalilst (auth), Pride & prejudice, Artnews, 92. *Media:* Steel. *Dealer:* Rettig y Martinez Gallery 901 W San Mateo Santa Fe NM 87501. *Mailing Add:* PO Box 8526 Santa Fe NM 87504

HAPGOOD, SUSAN T
CURATOR, CRITIC
b Riverhead, NY, Oct 18, 57. *Study:* Univ Rochester, BA, 79; Inst Fine Arts, NY Univ, MA, 85. *Collections Arranged:* Recent Acquisitions, 85, Homage to Louise Nevelson (auth, brochure), 86 & The Early Years: Non-Objective Paintings from the Permanent Collection, (auth, brochure), 88, Guggenheim Mus; Five Attitudes, Hallwalls, 91; New Mus Contemp Art, 92. *Pos:* Archivist, Sperone Westwater Gallery, New York, 79-82, asst to dir, formerly; coordr, Art Quest, New Mus Contemp Art, New York, 83-84; cur coordr, Solomon R Guggenheim Mus, New York, 85-89, cur asst, formerly. *Teaching:* Instr art hist, Sch Visual Arts, 88. *Mem:* Col Art Asn. *Res:* Contemporary American art. *Publ:* Auth, Irrationally in the age of

technology, 83, Lucas Samaras, 84 & Neil Jenney, 85, Flash Art Mag; Richard Artschwager, Ashley Bickerton & Blinky Palermo, Tema Celeste Mag, 88; Remaking Art History, 90 & Whitney Mus: How American Is It?, Art Am, 91. *Mailing Add:* 326 W 22nd St New York NY 10011

HARA, KEIKO
PAINTER, PRINTMAKER
Japanese citizen. *Study:* Miss State Univ Women, BFA(painting), 74; Univ Wis, Milwaukee, MS(printmaking), 75; Cranbrook Acad Art, MFA(printmaking), 76. *Work:* Milwaukee Art Mus, Wis; Art Inst Chicago; Johnson Wax Coun House; Detroit Inst Art; Muskegon Mus Art, Mich; King Co Art Comn. *Comn:* Lithography, Perimeter Press, Racine, Wis, 81. *Exhib:* Maru, Miyuki Gallery, Tokyo, Japan, 68; 30th Am Printmakers Invitational, 76 & 20th Nat Print Exhib, 76, Brooklyn Mus; one-person shows, Westum Mus Fine Art, Racine, Wis, 81 & Calerie in Den Vierlanden, Hamburg, WGer, 81-82; solo exhibs, Perimeter Gallery, Chicago, 82-92; Nat Prints & Photos by Women, Philadelphia Landing Mus, 83; Works on paper & canvas, Washington State Capital Mus, 91. *Pos:* Assoc prof, Whitman Col, 85- *Teaching:* Instr printmaking, Carthage Col, 79-80 & Univ Wis, River Falls, 80-85. *Awards:* First Prize, Mich Prints & Drawing, Detroit Inst Arts, 76. *Bibliog:* Article, Print Newsletter, 82; Printed By Women, US, 83; Visions, summer 92. *Publ:* Contemporary Screens, Art Mus Asn Am, 86; Work on Paper and Canvas: Multi Cultural Perspectives, Olympia, Wash, 90; Collaboration in Print: Stwart & Stwart Prints, Mich, 91; Allan Artner, Chicago Tribune, 92. *Dealer:* Perimeter Gallery 750 N Orleans Chicago IL 60610; Brendan Walter Gallery 1001 Colorado Ave at Tenth Santa Monica CA 90401. *Mailing Add:* Dept Art Whitman Col Walla Walla WA 99362

HARARI, HANANIAH
PAINTER
b Rochester, NY, Aug 29, 12. *Study:* Syracuse Univ Col Fine Arts; Fontainebleau Ecole Fresque, France; also with Fernand Leger, Andre Lhote & Marcel Gromaire, Paris. *Work:* Metropolitan Mus Art, Whitney Mus, New York; Yale Univ Art Gallery; Brooklyn Mus; Philadelphia Mus Art; Nat Mus Am Art, Smithsonian Inst, Washington, DC; and others. *Exhib:* Whitney Mus Am Art Painting Ann, 42-47; American Realists & Magic Realists, Mus Mod Art, New York, 43; Pa Acad Fine Arts Ann, 46 & 49; Am Abstract Artists, Art Mus, Univ NMex, Albuquerque, 77; Decade of Transition 40-50, Whitney Mus, 81; American Abstract Prints, Metrop Mus Art, 86; American Cubism: 1909-1949, Sid Deutsch Gallery, 92; and others. *Teaching:* Instr painting, New Sch Social Res, 74, Sch Visual Arts, New York, 74-90 & Art Students League, 84- *Awards:* Medal Award, Art Dir Club, Chicago, 50; Binney & Smith Award, 87; Art Students League Award, Audubon Artists, 91, 92. *Bibliog:* Clement Greenberg (auth), article, Nation, 1/43; Doris Brian (auth), Who's who, Art News, 1/43; Virginia M Mecklenburg (auth), American Abstraction 1930-1945, Smithsonian Inst Press, 97-101, 85. *Mem:* Artists Equity Asn NY; Audubon Artists. *Media:* All Media. *Dealer:* Michael Rosenfeld Gallery 50 W 57 St New York NY 10019. *Mailing Add:* 34 Prospect Pl Croton-on-Hudson NY 10520

HARBART, GERTRUDE FELTON
PAINTER, INSTRUCTOR
b Michigan City, Ind, Dec 25, 08. *Study:* Univ Calif; Univ Ill; Art Inst Chicago; Art Students League, NY; and with Aaron Bohard, Charles Birchfield & Hans Hofmann. *Work:* Purdue Univ; Ind Univ; Ind State Univ; South Bend Art Inst; Indianapolis Mus Art; St Mary's College, S Bend. *Comn:* In many private collections. *Exhib:* Art Inst Chicago; Corcoran Biennial, Washington, DC; Butler Inst Am Art, Youngstown, Ohio; Indianapolis Mus Art; Michiana Biennial, South Bend; S Ariz Watercolor Guild. *Teaching:* Instr art, South Bend Art, Dunes Art Found & Michigan City Art League; Pima Col, Tucson, Ariz, 79-80; pvt classes, one week acrylic workshops, 85-86; Community Ctr Art, Michigan City Workshops, 92. *Awards:* Northern Ind Art Patrons Award, Hammond Art Ctr, 70; First Award, Sarasota Art Asn, 74, Southern Ariz Watercolor Guild, 89-91 & Southwest Fourstate Competition, 85. *Mem:* Ind Artists; Southern Ariz Watercolor Guild; Am Pen Women. *Media:* Acrylic, Watercolor. *Publ:* Auth, Basics of Design & Design with Transparent Watercolor, Art News, 6/55 & Sch Arts, 60; two Art Workbooks I & II. *Mailing Add:* 5578 N LaCasita Dr Tucson AZ 85718-5310

HARBUTT, CHARLES
PHOTOGRAPHER
b Camden, NJ, July 29, 35. *Study:* Marquette Univ, BS, 56. *Work:* Mus Mod Art, New York; Art Inst Chicago; Smithsonian Inst; Bibliotheque Nat, Paris; George Eastman House, Rochester, NY. *Exhib:* Photography as a Fine Art, Metrop Mus, New York, 60; Photography in the 20th Century, Eastman House, Rochester, NY, 67; Sao Paulo Biennale, Nat Collection Art, Washington, DC, 70; Photography in America, Whitney Mus Am Art, New York, 76; Photography, Beauborg Mus, Paris, 77; Tusen Och en Bild, Mod Mus, Stockholm, Sweden, 78; Mirrors and Windows, Mus Mod Art, New York, 78; one-man exhib, Univ Salford, Eng, 80; Bibliotheque Nat, Paris, 86. *Teaching:* Vis artist photog, Art Inst Chicago, 75, RI Sch Design, 76 & Mass Inst Technol, 79. *Awards:* Best Photog Book, Arles Festival, 74. *Bibliog:* Andy Grundberg (auth), Sympathetic Explorations, Plains Art Mus, 78; A Grundberg & J Scully (auth), Currents, Mod Photog, 79. *Publ:* Ed & contribr, American in Crisis, Holt Rinehart, 69; auth, Travelog, MIT Press, 73; contribr, Sympathetic Explorations: Kertesz/Harbutt, Plains Art Mus, 78; contribr, I Grandi Photografi: Charles Harbutt, Editoriale Fabbri, 82; auth, Progreso, Actuality Inc, 86. *Dealer:* Actuality Inc 1 Fifth Ave New York NY 10003. *Mailing Add:* One Fifth Ave #16-G New York NY 10003

HARCUS, PORTIA GWEN
DEALER, CONSULTANT
b Brockton, Mass. *Study:* Wheaton Col, BA. *Pos:* Dir, Harcus Krakow Gallery, 64-82; dir & pres, Harcus Gallery, 82- *Mem:* Art Dealers Asn Am; Asn Int Photog Art Dealers; Art Table Inc; Confederation Int Negociants Oeuvres D'Art. *Specialty:* Contemporary painting, sculpture, grahics and major 20th century works. *Mailing Add:* 6 Melrose St Boston MA 02116-5510

HARDEN, MARVIN
PAINTER, EDUCATOR
b Austin, Tex. *Study:* Univ Calif, Los Angeles, BA(fine arts) & MA(creative painting); Los Angeles City Col. *Work:* Whitney Mus Am Art & Mus Mod Art, New York; Home Saving & Loan Asn, Los Angeles; Mus, Univ Calif, Berkeley; New York Pub Libr Spencer Collection. *Exhib:* 19 one-man shows incl, Whitney Mus Am Art, New York, 72, Irving Blum Gallery, Los Angeles, 72, James Corcoran Gallery, 78, Newport Harbor Art Mus, 79 & Los Angeles Munic Art Gallery, 82; and many other group exhibs. *Pos:* Co-founder, Los Angeles Inst Comtemp Art, 73, exhib comt mem, 73-74; bd dirs, Images & Issues, 80-86. *Teaching:* Instr drawing, Univ Calif, Los Angeles, 64-68; instr drawing, Los Angeles Harbor Col, 65-68; prof painting & drawing, Calif State Univ, Northridge, 68- *Awards:* Nat Endowment Arts Fel, 72; Guggenheim Found Fel, 83; Exceptional Merit Serv Award, Calif State Univ, Northridge, 84; Awards in the Visual Arts, 83. *Media:* Mixed. *Dealer:* Jan Turner Gallery 9006 Melrose Ave Los Angeles CA 90069; Cirrus Editions Ltd 542 S Alameda Los Angeles CA 90013. *Mailing Add:* Painting Dept Calif State Univ Northridge 18111 Nordhoff St Northridge CA 91330

HARDER, RODNEY
PAINTER
Study: Fresno Pac Col, Calif, BFA, 73; Calif State Univ, Fresno, MA, 75. *Work:* Citibank, New York; IBM, New York; Can Imperial Bank, New York; Baltimore City Health Dept, Md; Fresno Art Mus, Calif; many pvt collections throughout US. *Exhib:* Solo shows, Gallery 25, Fresno, Calif, 82, Fresno Art Mus, Calif, 83 & 89, Farleigh Dickinson Univ, Hackensack, NJ, 87 & Peoples Place Gallery, Intercourse, Pa, 88; Gallery Ellipse, Arlington, Va, 91; Gallery M, Fresno, Calif, 91; Sweet Briar Col, Va, 91. *Teaching:* Prof art, Fresno Pac Col, Calif, 74-83; art instr, Fresno Art Mus, Calif, 80-83 & Calif State Univ, Fresno, 81-83; art instr/coordr, Col Sch, New York, 84-; adj art instr, New York Sch Visual Arts, 86. *Awards:* Nat Endowment Arts Fel, painting, 90 & 91; Hellenic Study Tour/Greece & Egypt, 90; Study Grant, St Johns Col, Oxford Univ, 91. *Mailing Add:* 71 W Broadway New York NY 10013

HARDER, ROLF PETER
GRAPHIC DESIGNER, PAINTER
b Hamburg, Ger, July 10, 29; Can citizen. *Study:* Hamburg Acad Fine Arts, 48-52. *Exhib:* Design Collaborative Int Travelling Exhib, 70-72; Biennale of Graphic Design, Brno, 70, 74, 78, 80, 82, 84 & 90; Experimental Graphic Design, Venice Biennale, 72; group exhibs, Can, USA, Europe, South Am, Japan, Russia & Korea. *Teaching:* Guest lectr, graphic design. *Awards:* Symbol Competition First Prize, Can Asn Retarded Children, 64; Spec Prize, 4th Biennale Graphic Design, Brno, 70; Spec Prize, Int Poster Competition, Moscow, 87. *Bibliog:* Theodore Hilten (auth), Rolf Harder, 9/64 & Hans Kuh (auth), Design Collaborative, 9/70, Gebrauchsgraphic, Munich; Peter Bartl, Novum, Munich, 87; Rose Deneve, Print, New York, 90. *Mem:* Royal Can Acad Arts; Alliance Graphique Int; Am Inst Graphic Arts; Int Ctr Typographic Arts; fel Soc Graphic Designers Can; Union Club, St John, New Brunswick. *Publ:* Auth, Introd, Can Sect, World History of the Poster, Paris. *Mailing Add:* Rolf Harder & Assoc 1638 Sherbrooke W Montreal PQ H3H 1C9 Canada

HARDIN, SHIRLEY G (MRS LOUIS S)
ART DEALER, CONSULTANT
b La Grange, Ill, May 13, 20. *Study:* Art Inst Chicago; with Maurice Saulo, Paris. *Pos:* Co-dir & owner, Fairweather-Hardin Gallery, Chicago, 47-91. *Mem:* Art Dealers Asn Am; Chicago Art Dealers Asn (co-founder). *Mailing Add:* 101 E Ontario St Chicago IL 60611

HARDING, ANN
PAINTER
b Minneapolis, Minn, Mar 16, 42. *Study:* Univ Minn, with Walter Quirt, BA, 66; Univ Cincinnati, MFA, 71. *Work:* Lutheran Brotherhood, Minneapolis; Alabama Power Company, Birmingham; Sterling Drug Corp, Philapelphia, Pa; Ochsner Med Found, New Orleans, La; Rhone-Poulenc Rorer Corp, Philadelphia, Pa; and others. *Exhib:* 20th Exhib Southwest Prints & Drawings, Dallas Mus Fine Arts, 75; one-person exhibs, Friends Gallery, Minneapolis Inst Fine Arts, 81, West Baton Rouge Mus, Port Allen, La, 83 & Still-Zinsel Contemp Fine Art, New Orleans, La, 91; Nat Ann Midyear Show, Butler Inst Am Art, 81 & 82; Biennial Piedmont Painting & Sculpture, Mint Mus, 81 & 83; Louisiana Women in Contemporary Art Traveling Exhib Invitational, 83-84; Hoyt Nat Painting Show, Hoyt Inst Fine Art, 83 & 85; Tampa Triennial, Tampa Mus, Fla, 85; Nat Art Festival, Atlanta, 89; and others. *Teaching:* Instr painting & drawing, La State Univ, 73-76, from asst prof to assoc prof, 76-86, prof, 86- *Awards:* Purchase Award, 35th Ann, La State Art Exhib, 80; SECCA Artist Fel, 81; Visual Arts Fel, La State Arts Coun, 85. *Media:* Oil on Canvas, Acrylic on Paper. *Mailing Add:* 2114 North Blvd Baton Rouge LA 70806

HARDING, NOEL ROBERT
VIDEO ARTIST, ENVIRONMENTAL ARTIST
b London, Eng, Dec 21, 45. *Work:* Art Gallery of Ont, Toronto; Nat Gallery of Can, Ottawa, Ont; Univ Guelph, Can; Kitchen Gallery, New York; Vehicule, Montreal. *Exhib:* Minneapolis Col Art & Design & Walker Art Ctr, Minneapolis, Minn, 72; Nat Gallery of Can, 77; Mus Mod Art, New York, 78; one-man videotape, Alta Col Art & Design, Calgary, 76, Ctr Georges Pompidou, Paris, France, 77 & Acme Gallery, London, 79; group exhib, videotapes, Washington Proj for the Arts, DC, 79 & Faculty Show, Univ Guelph, 79; and others. *Teaching:* Instr fine art video, Univ Guelph, 74-77; instr independent 74-77, instr independent study utilizing video, 72-76, instr sr independent study utilizing any/all of film slide & video, 76 & instr experiments in art performance, 77; instr creative film/video, Photo Electric Arts Dept, Ont Col Art, 77; instr creative film video, Univ Guelph & Ont Col Art, 77-; plus many lectr in Can. *Awards:* Can Coun Arts Grant, 76 & 78-79, Travel Grant, 77 & Proj Grant, 78; Ont Arts Coun Grant, 77 & 79. *Bibliog:* Art Perry (auth), Noel Harding: once upon the idea of two, Vancouver in Rev, 1/78; Peggy Gale (auth), Temporal realities & Eric Cameron (auth), Video as painting, Parachute, spring 78. *Media:* Videotape, Film, Live Video. *Dealer:* Videotape: c/o Art Metropole 217 Richmond St W Toronto ON M5V 1W2; Installations/Sculpture: John Gibson Gallery 392 W Broadway New York NY 10012. *Mailing Add:* 2154 Dundas St W Toronto ON M6R 1X3 Canada

HARDING, TIM
DESIGNER
Work: Minn Hist Soc. *Comn:* Hyatt Regency Hotels, Minneapolis & Los Angeles, 82. *Exhib:* Arango Int Design Competition, Metrop Mus Art, Miami, 80; Art to Wear, Am Craft Mus, New York, (and touring US), 84; Handmade Clothing: 10 American Artists, Brit Crafts Ctr, London, Eng, 85; Poetry of the Physical, Am Craft Mus, 86. *Awards:* Arts Midwest Artist Fel Grant, 85; Visual Artist Fel, Nat Endowment Arts, 86. *Bibliog:* Linda Dyett (auth), article, Am Craft Mag, 10-11/83. *Media:* Art Garments. *Mailing Add:* c/o Julie: Artisan's Gallery 687 Madison Ave New York NY 10021

HARDY, DAVID WHITTAKER, III
PAINTER, INSTRUCTOR
b Dallas, Tex, Oct 5, 29. *Study:* Austin Col; Southern Methodist Univ; Univ Colo; Laney Col; Am Acad; Art Students League; Sch Visual Art; Calif Col Arts & Crafts; and with Ramon Froman, William Moseby, Joseph Van Der Brock, Robert Beverly Hale & Frank Mason. *Work:* Hall of Justice, Hayward, Calif. *Comn:* Pvt collections in US & abroad. *Exhib:* One-man shows, North Park, Dallas, 64, Pantechnicon Gallery, San Francisco, 70 & Arden Van Wijk Gallery, Saratoga, Calif, 84; Hemisfair Art, Witte Mem Mus, San Antonio, 68; Soc Western Artists, M H De Young Mus, San Francisco, 70; San Francisco Ann, 71; Audubon Artists, Nat Acad, New York, 73; and others. *Pos:* Guest, Wurlitzer Found, Taos, NMex, 65; owner, 13th Street Crafts Garden, Oakland, 73-76; training prog, Fine Arts, Mus San Francisco, 82 & 86. *Teaching:* Pvt art classes, 60-; instr art, Mendocino Art Ctr, Calif, 73-74 & Calif Col Arts & Crafts, Oakland, 79-86; guest lectr, Univ Calif, Berkeley, 81, 82 & Docent training prog, Fine Arts Mus, San Francisco, 82, 86. *Awards:* First Place Painting, Alameda Co Fair 73 & Valley Artists Asn, 73. *Bibliog:* Daniel M Mendelowitz and Duane A Wakeham (coauth), A Guide to Drawing, 4th ed, Holt, Rinehart and Winston Inc, 88. *Mem:* Berkeley Art Festival Guild (pres, 72-77); Soc Western Artists; Lillian Paley Ctr Visual Arts (bd trustees, 74-78). *Media:* Oil, Pastel. *Res:* Old master Baroque painting techniques. *Specialty:* Florals, still lifes, portraits, landscapes and figure paintings. *Dealer:* Alma Gilbert Galleries 1419 Burlingame Ave Burlingame CA 94010; Cottage Gallery at Carmel PO Box 335 Carmel CA 39321. *Mailing Add:* 4220 Balfour Ave Oakland CA 94610

HARDY, (CLARION) DEWITT
PAINTER, ADMINISTRATOR
b St Louis, Mo, June 25, 40. *Study:* Syracuse Univ, 58-62. *Work:* Bowdoin Col Mus Art, Brunswick, Maine; Cleveland Mus Art; British Mus; Joseph Hirshorn Found; Calif Palace Legion Hon, San Francisco. *Exhib:* Four New England Artists, Kalamazoo Inst Art, 63; one-man shows, Frank Rehn Gallery, New York, 66-71 & Robert Schodkopt Gallery, NY 81-83; Butler Inst Am Art, 69-70; Art on Paper, Weatherspoon Art Gallery, Univ NC, Greensboro, 81. *Collections Arranged:* Young American Draughtsmen, Mus Art Ogunquit, 69. *Pos:* Assoc dir, Mus Art Ogunquit, 64-77. *Awards:* First Prize for Drawing, Summit Art Ctr, NJ, 65; Purchase Award, Butler Inst Am Art, 69. *Bibliog:* Watercolors by Dewitt Hardy, NY Times, 2/20/81; The watercolor page: Dewitt Hardy, Am Artists, 11/81. *Media:* Watercolor. *Dealer:* Gerald Peters Gallery Camino del Monte Sol Santa Fe NM. *Mailing Add:* Oak Woods Rd North Berwick ME 03906

HARDY, JOHN
PAINTER
b Tours, France; US citizen. *Study:* Ga State Univ, BFA, 69. *Work:* Brooklyn Mus, NY; Nat Mus Am Art & Art in Embassies, US State Dept, Washington, DC; Mint Mus, Charlotte, NC; Mus Art, Univ of Iowa; Grey Art Gallery, NY Univ; High Mus Art, Atlanta, Ga. *Exhib:* Brooklyn Mus, New York, 80; Armstrong Gallery, New York, 84; traveling retrospective, Lamar Dodd Art Ctr, La Grange, Ga, 85-87; Ga Mus, Athens, 87; McIntosh Gallery, Atlanta, 89; Ratner Gallery, Chicago, 91. *Teaching:* Chmn visual arts, Sch Archit, Ga Tech, 69-75; vis artist painting, Rice Univ, Houston & La State Univ, Baton Rouge, 79; adj fac painting, NY Univ, 80-82; masters workshop, Huntington Mus, WVa. *Awards:* Nat Endowment Arts Grant, Huntington Mus, WVa, 87. *Bibliog:* Ann Weinstein (auth), article, Roanoke Times & World News, 10/7/87; Carol Graham Beck (auth), article, Art Papers, 90; Alan G Arther (auth), rev, Chicago Tribune, 91. *Mailing Add:* 130 W 26th St New York NY 10001

HARDY, ROBERT
GALLERY DIRECTOR, CERAMIST
b Millville, NJ, Aug 2, 38. *Study:* Calif State Univ, Long Beach, BA, MA; Univ Calif, Irvine; Scripps Grad Sch, Claremont, Calif. *Comn:* Numerous comns for interior designers in bas-relief ceramic sculptures. *Exhib:* Los Angeles Mus Sci & Indust, 62; Craftsmen USA, Lytton Gallery, Los Angeles Co Art Mus, Los Angeles, 66; Mus Contemp Crafts, New York, 66 & Ravinia Festival, Chicago, 67; Saginaw Art Mus, Mich, 68; Grand Rapids Art Mus, Mich, 68; Columbia Mus Art, SC, 68; Laguna Mus Art, Calif, 74. *Collections Arranged:* Religious Expressions in Art, 75, National Basketry Exhibition, 76, California Indian Basketry: An Artistic Overview (ed, catalogue), 76, June Wayne: Weaver of Tapestries, Painter & Printmaker, 77 & Year of the Horse: 4676, 78, Fine Arts Gallery, Cypress Col. *Pos:* Gallery dir, Fine Arts Gallery, Cypress Col, 66-92. *Teaching:* Prof interior design, Cypress Col, 66- *Awards:* Merit Award, Craftsmen USA, Lytton Gallery, 66. *Mailing Add:* c/o Cypress Col Fine Arts Gallery 9200 Valley View Cypress CA 90630

HARDY, THOMAS (AUSTIN)
SCULPTOR
b Redmond, Ore, Nov 30, 21. *Study:* Ore State Univ, 38-40; Univ Ore, BA, 42, with Archipenko, summer 51, MFA, 52. *Work:* Whitney Mus Am Art, New York; Seattle Art Mus, Wash; San Francisco Mus Art; Neuberger Mus, New York; Portland Art Mus, Ore; Santa Barbara Mus Calif; Springfield, Mo. *Comn:* Diving Birds, Fed Bldg, Juneau, Alaska, 64; Duck Fountain, Univ Ore, Eugene, 64; Flight, Dorothy Chandler Music Ctr, Los Angeles, Calif, 65; wall sculpture, State Dept Agr, Salem, Ore, 68; Bear, Univ Calif, Berkeley, 80. *Exhib:* 3rd Biennial, Sao Paulo, Brazil, 55; Am Watercolors, Drawings & Prints, Metrop Mus Art, 56; Mus Mod Art Sculpture Exhib, 63; Whitney Mus Am Art Sculpture Ann, 64; Exhib Cand Grants, Am Inst Arts & Lett, 68. *Pos:* Mem, Portland Art Mus & Friends Mus Art, Univ Ore. *Teaching:* Lectr, Univ Calif, Berkeley, 56-58; instr, Calif Sch Fine Arts, San Francisco, 56-58; assoc prof sculpture, Tulane Univ, La, 58-59; artist-in-residence, Reed Col, 60-61; vis prof sculpture, Univ Wyo, 75-76. *Awards:* Color Lithography Award, Soc Am Graphic Artists, 52; Seattle Art Mus Northwest Ann Sculpture Award, 55; Distinguished Serv Award, Univ Ore, 64; Ore State Gov Ann Art Award, 86; Webfoot Award, Univ Ore, 87. *Bibliog:* H Wurdemann (auth), Recent art of the West Coast, Art Am, 2/55; Metal sculptures by Tom Hardy, Am Artist, 4/55; L Jones (auth), Tom Hardy: Sculptor-craftsman, Creative Crafts, 7/62. *Mem:* Contemp Crafts Asn; Portland Ctr Visual Arts; Metrop Arts Comn (comnr, 81-85); Portland Rev Comn (comnr, 86). *Media:* Welded Bronze, Aquatint. *Dealer:* Kraushaar Galleries 724 Fifth Ave New York NY 10019. *Mailing Add:* 1023 N Killingsworth Portland OR 97217

HARE, DAVID
SCULPTOR
b New York, NY, Mar 10, 17. *Study:* Studied in New York, Ariz & Colo. *Work:* Metrop Mus Art, Mus Mod Art, Whitney Mus Am Art & Guggenheim Mus, New York; Los Angeles Co Mus Art; Brooklyn Mus, NY; San Francisco Mus Art; Mus Art, Carnegie Inst, Pittsburgh; plus others. *Comn:* Sculpture for New York City, States of RI, Mass & Ill. *Exhib:* One-man shows, Delgado Mus Art, New Orleans, 65, Philadelphia Mus Art, 69, Guggenheim Mus, 77, Hamilton Gallery, New York, 79 & 80 & Gruenbaum Gallery, New York, 85 & 87; Dada, Surrealism and Their Heritage, 68 & The New American Painting and Sculpture, 69, Mus Mod Art, New York; Whitney Mus Am Art, 76; Nat Gallery Am Art, 76; Albright-Knox Art Gallery, 78; Contemp Arts Mus, Houston, 81 & 82; Mus Fine Art, Houston, 82. *Pos:* Co-ed, VVV, surrealist mag (with Andre Breton, Marcel Duchamp & Max Ernst). *Teaching:* Lectr extensively; guest critic & lectr, Md Inst Col of Art, 83; Binghampton Univ, New York, 84- *Bibliog:* Hilton Kramer (auth), David Hare: A painter of the human psyche, NY Times, 9/30/77; Harold Rosenberg (auth), An American Surrealist, New Yorker, 10/24/77; Katharine Kuh (auth), David Hare; American Surrealist, Saturday Rev, 10/24/77. *Dealer:* Stemphley 415 W Broadway New York NY. *Mailing Add:* P O Box 241 Victor ID 83455

HARI, KENNETH
PAINTER, PRINTMAKER
b Perth Amboy, NJ, Mar 31, 47. *Study:* Newark Sch Fine & Indust Arts, dipl, 66; Md Inst Art, BFA, 68; also with Leon Franks & John Delmonte, Yale Univ, New York Univ. *Work:* Mus Mod Art, Barcelona, Spain; Baltimore Mus, Md; Nat Portrait Galleries, London, Eng & Washington, DC; Vatican, Rome, Italy; Brooklyn Mus; Liv Collection Peking, China. *Comn:* Portraits, W H Auden & M Moore, New York, 69, Pablo Casals, comn by Mrs Pablo Casals, Vt, 70, Salvador Dali, New York, 72, Ernest Hemingway, Hemingway House, Cuba, Michael York, & Aaron Copland, 82; Paul Robeson, for Paul Robeson Ctr, Rutgers Univ, 79; Douglas Fairbanks Jr, Nat Portrait Gallery, London, Eng, 92. *Exhib:* Union Col, 69; Monmouth Col, 70; Newark Mus, 71; Trenton State Mus, 72; Va Polytechnic Inst, 74; solo exhibs, Centenery Col, NJ & Tennesser Williams Portraits, Pargot Gallery, NJ, 91; Tenn State Mus. *Pos:* Dir, NJ Art Festival, 64-69. *Awards:* Pulaski Award, Kusciuszko Found, 63; Felice Found Award, 69; Trenton State Mus Award, 72. *Bibliog:* Art in the Hamptons, 69 & feature story, 73, NY Times; M Lenson (auth), Portrait of Casals, Newark News, 71; D Brown (auth), Poetess an artist, Home News, 72. *Media:* Oil, Graphite. *Publ:* Illusr, Vermont, 72, Folk Singer, 72 & Time for Peace, 72, H S Graphics; Abraham, 74, Marcel Marceau, 75, The Prophet, 92, Beatrice, 92, Moses, 92, Harmony, 92 & Portrait of 5, 92; and others. *Dealer:* Eastman & John Watson Art Galleries Box 243 Keasby NJ 08832 Tel: 201-442-8031; Eastman & International Galleries c/o Xiaoyi Liu Box 243 Keasbey NJ 08832. *Mailing Add:* 228 Sherman St Perth Amboy NJ 08861

HARJO, BENJAMIN, JR
PAINTER, PRINTMAKER
b Clovis, NMex, Sept 19, 45. *Study:* Inst Am Indian Arts, cert, 66; Okla State Univ, BFA, 74. *Work:* Inst Am Indian Arts, Santa Fe; McFarlin Libr Indian Collection, Univ Tulsa & Tulsa City Co Libr; US Embassy, Mogadiscio, Somalia; Mus Northern Ariz. *Exhib:* Young American Indian Artist, Riverside Mus, New York, 65-66; Nat Indian Arts Exhib, Heard Mus, Phoenix, Ariz, 66; Philbrook 30th Ann Am Indian Arts Exhib, Tulsa, 75; Ann Competition, 5 Tribes Mus, Muskogee, Okla, 76 & 80; Southern Plains Indian Mus, Anadarko, Okla, 80; Trail of Tears Ann, Cherokee Mus, Tahlequah, Okla, 81; Native Am Ctr Living Arts, Niagara Falls, NY, 81. *Pos:* Cult recreational coordr, Tulsa Indian Youth Coun, 74-76. *Teaching:* Jr gallery instr Indian cult, Philbrook Art Ctr, Tulsa, 76-77. *Awards:* Grand award, 1st place painting & 2nd place graphics awards, Red Earth Festival; Best of division, 1st place painting-minature, 2nd place painting & 1st place graphics award, 67th ann Indian Market; 1st place painting, Masters Show, Five Tribes Mus, 88; First Place, 69 Ann Indian Market, Santa Fe, 90; Woody Crumbo Mem Award; Second Prize, Red Earth, 90. *Bibliog:* Peggy Ridgeway (auth), Benjamin Harjo Jr, Art Voice S, 81; Rennard Steickland (auth), Indians of Oklahoma, Okla Press, 81; Southwest Art Mag, 3/88; Southern Living Mag, 10/88. *Mem:* Am Indian Cowboy Artist, San Dimas, Calif; Master Artist Five Civilized Tribes, Muskogee, Okla. *Media:* Gouache, Acrylic; Etching, Woodblock. *Mailing Add:* 1516 Northwest 35th Oklahoma City OK 73118

HARKEY, RONALD P See Rophar,

HARKINS, DENNIS RICHTER
ADMINISTRATOR, PHOTOGRAPHER
b Nelsonville, Ohio, July 20, 50. *Study:* Ohio Univ, BFA, 72, MA(int affairs), 73. *Collections Arranged:* African Art (with catalog), Ohio Univ, Alden Libr, 73. *Pos:* Educ chmn, Prof Photogr Guild Fla, 78-79 & bd dirs, 79. *Teaching:* Dir photog, Art Inst Ft Lauderdale, 74-81; vpres & dir educ, Art Inst Atlanta, 81- *Awards:* Cert Prof Photogr, 79; Lecture Award, Fla Prof Photogr Conf. *Mem:* Prof Photogr Am; Kodak Educ Adv Coun, Nat. *Mailing Add:* Photog Art Inst Atlanta 3376 Peachtree NE Atlanta GA 30326

HARKINS, GEORGE C, JR
PAINTER
b Philadelphia, Pa, June 15, 34. *Study:* Philadelphia Col Art, BFA, 56; Univ Ariz, MFA, 69. *Work:* Charleston Mus Fine Art, SC; Montgomery Mus Fine Art, Ala. *Exhib:* Am Watercolor Soc Ann Exhib, Nat Acad Design, New York, 79; Am Realism: 20th Century Watercolors & Drawings, San Francisco Mus Mod Art, 85; Mus Choice, Orlando Mus, Fla, 86; Selections from E F Hutton Collection, Metrop Mus, Coral Gables, Fla, 86; Watercolor USA, Monumental Image, Springfield Art Mus, Mo, 86; The Face of the Land, S Alleghenies Mus Art, Loretto, Pa, 88; Realism Today: Am Drawings from the Rita Rich Collection, Nat Acad Design, New York, 88; Watercolor: Contemp Currents, Riverside Art Mus, Calif, 89. *Bibliog:* Alvin Martin (auth), American Realism: 20th Century Drawings & Watercolors, H N Abrams, 86; Steven Doherty (auth), George Harkins, Am Artist, 5/89; John Arthur (auth), Spirit of Place, Bullfinch Press, Little Brown Co, 89. *Media:* Watercolor. *Dealer:* Peter Tatistcheff 50 W 57th St New York NY 10019. *Mailing Add:* 137 Duane St New York NY 10013

HARKNESS, MADDEN
PAINTER
b Montclair, NJ, July 21, 48. *Study:* Calif Col Arts Crafts, MFA, 85; Boston Mus Sch, Tufs Univ, BS, 72. *Work:* Everson Mus, Syracuse, NY; Fresno Art Mus, Calif. *Exhib:* One-man show, Forum 88, Hamburg, Ger, 88; On the Horizon: Emerging in California, Fresno Art Mus, Calif, 87; Figurative Dimensions, Univ Art Gallery, Calif State Univ, Dominquez Hills, Calif, 88; Madden Harkness, Southern Calif Art Inst, Laguna Beach, 89 & Pepperdine Univ (catalog), Malibu, Calif, 90; The Figure, Tatistcheff Gallery, Santa Monica, Calif, 91; Addictions (catalog), Santa Barbara Contemp Arts Forum, Calif, 91; and others. *Awards:* Purchase Award, Everson Mus, 88; Julia Morgan Mem, Riverside Art Mus, 87; vis artist, Am Acad in Rome, Italy, 90; Artist-in-Residence, Ragdale Found, 87. *Bibliog:* Colin Gardener (auth), The Galleries, Los Angeles Times, 12/18/87; Betth Ann Brown & Arlene Raven (auths), Exposures; Women and Their Art, 89; David Pagel (auth), When Reason Dreams-Madden, Harkness, Vol II, No 3, Visions, 88. *Media:* Mixed Media, Oil. *Dealer:* Sylvia White Santa Monica CA; Roy Boyd Chicago IL. *Mailing Add:* 333 E 79th St Apt 21M New York NY 10021

HARLAN, ROMA CHRISTINE
PAINTER
b Warsaw, Ind, June 23, 12. *Study:* Art Inst Chicago, Daughters Ind Scholar; Purdue Univ, Lafayette; and with Ralph Clarkson, Francis Chapin, Constantine Pougialis & Marie Goth. *Work:* portrait, Rev Thomas Stone, Nat Presbyterian Church, Washington, DC; portraits, US Supreme Court, Fed Courthouse, Securities & Exchange Comn, US Capitol, Nat Guard, Washington, DC; and others. *Comn:* Portraits: Rear Adm Albert Cushing Read, pioneer aviator, Sen Kenneth Spicer Wherry, minority leader, US Senate, Rev Peter Marshall, chaplain, US Senate, Maj Gen Edward Martin, gov Pennsylvania & US sen, Maj Gen Ellard A Walsh, Adjutant Gen, Minn, Maj Gen Charles H Grahl, Adjutant Gen, Iowa, Col Mildred Irene Clark, Chief Army Nurse Corps; plus many others. *Exhib:* One-man exhibs, Lake Shore Club, Chicago, Purdue Univ, Lafayette, Ind, Arts Club, George Washington Univ, Washington, DC & Arts Club of Washington, DC; Hoosier Salon Ind; All Ill Soc Fine Arts; pvt exhib, Sen Capehart, US Capitol, Washington, DC; and others. *Bibliog:* Eleanor Jewett (auth), article, Chicago Tribune; Florence Berryman (auth), article, Washington Eve Star, 67; John T McCutcheon (auth), article, Chicago Tribune; and others. *Mem:* Arts Club, Washington, DC; Washington Forum Club; DC Fedn Women's Clubs. *Media:* Oil, Pastel. *Publ:* Auth, Rembrandt, Cong Rec, 57. *Mailing Add:* 1600 S Joyce St A-1607 Arlington VA 22202

HARLOW, ANN
MUSEUM DIRECTOR, CURATOR
b Glen Cove, NY, June 15, 51. *Study:* Stanford Univ, BA, 73; Univ Calif, Berkeley, MA, 77. *Pos:* Cur asst, Oakland Mus, Calif, 77-78; asst dir, Mills Col Art Gallery, Oakland, Calif, 80-82; dir, Hearst Art Gallery, St Mary's Col, Moraga, Calif, 82. *Mem:* Asn Col & Univ Mus & Galleries (pres 88-90). *Publ:* Co-auth, The Color Woodcut in America, 1895-1945 (exhib catalog), 84; auth, The MA Circle: Budapest and Vienna, 1916-1925 (exhib catalog), 85; Bicoastal artists in the 1870's (exhib catalog), Art Calif, 7/92. *Mailing Add:* St Mary's Col of Calif Hearst Art Gallery St Mary's Rd PO Box 5110 Moraga CA 94575

HARMAN, MARYANN WHITTEMORE
PAINTER
b Roanoke, Va, Sept 13, 35. *Study:* Univ Va, Mary Washington Col, BA; Va Polytech Inst & State Univ, MA. *Work:* Minn Mining & Mfg Corp, Minneapolis; Philip Morris Corp, Richmond, Va; Hunter Mus, Chattanooga, Tenn; Gen Motors, Detroit; Boston Mus Fine Arts; and others. *Exhib:* Irene Leach Mem Exhib, Chrysler Mus, Norfolk, 67-72 & 90; Butler Inst Art Nat Show, Youngstown, Ohio, 69 & 72; one-person shows, Andre Emmerich Gallery, New York, 76 & 78, Allen Rubiner Gallery, Detroit, 77, 79 & 90, Meredith Long Gallery, New York, 80; Haber-Theodore Gallery, New York, 81, 82 & 84; Osuna Gallery, Washington DC, 82, 84 & 87; Wade Gallery, Los Angeles, Calif, 86-87, 89 & 91; Ulysses Gallery, New York, 90. *Pos:* Artist-in-residence, Emma Lake Workshop, Univ Saskatechewan, Can. *Teaching:* Assoc prof painting & drawing, Va Polytech Inst & State Univ, 64-81, prof, 81- *Awards:* Purchase Awards, Hunter Mus, 74; Cert of Distinction, Va Mus Fine Arts, 74; Purchase Award, Mint Mus, 83. *Bibliog:* Barclay Sheaks (auth), Painting Natural Environment, 74 & Painting with Oils, 77, Davis; Marsha Miro (auth), rev, Detroit Free Press, 12/78; Edgar Buonagurio (auth), rev, Arts Mag, 5/80, 81, 82 & 84; articles, Los Angeles Times & Hollywood Press, 86. *Mem:* Col Art Asn Am; Southeastern Col Art Asn; Va Mus Fine Arts; Am Fedn Arts. *Media:* Acrylic, Oil. *Mailing Add:* 602 Landsdowne Dr Blacksburg VA 24060

HARMON, BARBARA SAYRE
PAINTER, BOOK ARTIST
b Yerington, Nev, Aug 8, 27. *Study:* Bisttram Sch Fine Art, painting & drawing; etching with Lawton Parker; Black Mountain Col, bookbinding with Johanna Jalowitz. *Work:* Harwood Found, Univ NMex; Stanford Univ Libr, Univ NMex; Univ NMex Libr. *Comn:* Numerous private commissions for fantasy and portrait paintings. *Exhib:* Continuous exhibitions in southwestern galleries since 1963. *Bibliog:* Mary Carrol Nelson (auth), Barbara Harmon: magic & mastery, Am Artist Mag, 5/75; Kelly Malore Cribbs (auth), The tumpfee wood world of Barbara Harmon, Santa Fe Mag, 7/79; Tricia Hurst (auth), All things are possible, NMex Mag, 81. *Media:* Watercolor; Lithography. *Publ:* Auth & illusr, Tabbigail's Garden, 67, The Little People's Counting Book, 68, Monday's Mouse, 70, This Little Pixie, 69, The Tumpfee Wood Acorn Book, 77 & Thimbly Hill, 80, The Children's Gallery Press & The Baker Co. *Mailing Add:* 234 Los Cruces Rd Box 6584 Taos NM 87571

HARMON, CLIFF FRANKLIN
PAINTER
b Los Angeles, Calif, June 26, 23. *Study:* Bisttram Sch Fine Art, Los Angeles, Calif & Taos, NMex, with Emil Bisttram, 46-48; Black Mountain Col, NC, with Joe Fiore, 49-50; Taos Valley Art Sch, with Louis Ribak, 50-52. *Work:* Mus NMex, Santa Fe; Okla Art Ctr, Oklahoma City; Mus of Taos Art, Harwood Found, NMex. *Exhib:* NMex & Southwest Biennials, NMex Mus, 66, 70-72, Watercolor NMex, 74; 11th Midwest Biennial, Joslyn Art Mus, Omaha, Nebr, 70; 1st Four Corners Biennial, Phoenix Art Mus, Ariz, 71; Bertrand Russell Centenary Art Exhib, Rotunda Gallery, London, Eng, 72. *Awards:* First Premium for Abstract Painting, NMex State Fair, 68; Hon Mention, NMex Mus & Phoenix Art Mus, 71. *Mem:* Taos Art Asn (first vpres, 68-69, pres, 78-79). *Media:* Oil, Watercolor. *Dealer:* The Torreon Gallery Taos NM 87571. *Mailing Add:* 234 Las Cruces Rd PO Box 202 Taos NM 87571

HARMON, DAVID EDWARD
PAINTER, EDUCATOR
b St Louis, Mo, May 30, 53. *Study:* Webster Univ, St Louis, Mo, BFA, 77; Penn State Univ, MFA, 82. *Work:* Gibson Gallery, State Univ NY, Potsdam; Univ Mo St Louis; Univ Southern Miss, Woods Gallery, Hattiesburg; Liverpool Inst Higher Ed, UK; Univ Scranton, Pa. *Comn:* Painting, Crane Sch Music, Potsdam, NY, 86-87. *Exhib:* Missouri Photog Competition, City Art Mus, St Louis, 76; 14th Ann W & J Nat Paint Show, Olin Ctr Gallery, Washington, Pa, 82; competitive exhib, Miss Mus Art, Jackson, 83; 51st Ann Art Exhib, Cooperstown Art Mus, NY, 86; 30th Ann Nat Draw/Print Show, Univ NDak, Grand Forks, 87; 49th Ann juried exhib, Munson-Williams-Proctor Inst, Utica, NY, 87; Christ Imagery in Contemp Art, Albany Inst Art/Hist, NY, 88; South Bend Reg Mus Art, Inc, 92-93. *Pos:* Art dir, Bethel Col, 90-; ed bd mem, Collegiate Press, Alta Loma, Calif, 92. *Teaching:* vis prof gallery art hist, Univ S Miss, 82-83; vis prof paint draw design, Univ Ariz, Tucson, 84-85; prof art paint draw design, State Univ NY, Potsdam, 85-89; vis prof, Keystone Jr Col, La Plume, Pa, 89-90; art dir & prof art, Bethel Col, Mishawaka, Ind, 90- *Awards:* Purchase Award, Mo Photog, Univ Mo, St Louis, 76 & 5th Miss Annual, Univ Miss, 83; First Place, Sacred Arts Nat

Show, Wherton Col, 90. *Bibliog:* Jonas Kover (auth), Harmon Collection tugs at emotion, Utica Observer Dispatch, NY, 11/7/86; Blair Schiller (auth), Group shows explore reality and dreams, Art Speak, 12/89; Carol Kotlarczyk (auth), Artist brings out intensity in soft colors, Daily Herald, 9/7/91. *Mem:* Col Art Assoc, New York; Southeastern Col Art Asn; Christians in Visual Arts. *Media:* Oil, Pastel; Paper. *Publ:* Illus, Samuel Beckett and His Critics, Cassandra Press, 88; contribr, Contemp Southwest Art, Gibson Gallery, 88. *Dealer:* Ariel Gallery 76 Greene St New York NY 10012. *Mailing Add:* 513 Smith St Mishawaka IN 46544

HARMON, FOSTER
DEALER, DIRECTOR
b Judsonia, Ark, Nov 5, 12. *Study:* Ind Univ; Ohio Univ; State Univ Iowa, BA, 35, MFA, 36. *Pos:* Pub relations dir, Ringling Mus Art, Sarasota, Fla, 58-59; dir, Oehlschlaeger Galleries, Sarasota, 61-70; bd trustees, Ringling Sch Art & Design; bd dirs, Asolo State Theatre, Sarasota Opera Asn & Van Wezel Performing Arts Ctr Found; founder & dir, Harmon Gallery, Naples, Fla, 64-78; owner-dir, Foster Harmon Galleries of Am Art, Sarasota, Fla. *Teaching:* Instr drama & dir univ theatre prod, Ind Univ, Bloomington, 36-42. *Awards:* Award of Merit for Long Serv & Contrib to Art, Ohio Univ, 70. *Mem:* Am Fedn Arts; Fla Cultural Action Alliance; Ringling Mus Art; Sarasota Art Asn (pres, 59-60); Fla Artists Group; Archives of Am Art, Smithsonian Assocs. *Specialty:* Paintings, drawings and sculpture by major American artists of the 20th century. *Collection:* American art. *Mailing Add:* 1415 Main St Sarasota FL 34236

HARMON, JAMES RODERICK
DESIGNER, GLASS BLOWER
b Warsaw, NY, Nov 18, 52. *Study:* RI Sch Design with Dale Chihulu, BFA, 75; Ill State Univ with Joel Myers, MFA, 78. *Work:* Corning Mus Glass, NY; Lobmyer Collection, Vienna, Austria; Honolulu Acad Arts, Hawaii; New Orleans Mus Fine Arts, La; Toledo Mus Arts, Ohio. *Comn:* Neon wall installation, Miami Restaurant Corp, Fla, 87; neon sculpture, Hardy Holzman Pfeiffer, New York, 88; neon installation, Heller Gallery, New York; Glass Wall, Mobil Corp, Fairfax, Va, 89. *Exhib:* New Glass, Corning Mus, NY, 80; Americans in Glass, Cooper-Hewitt, New York, 81; World Glass Now, Hokkaido Mus Mod Art, Sapporo, Japan, 82; Art and/or Glass, Nippon Ctr, Tokyo; Contemp Am Glass, Kulturhusset, Stockholm, 85; New York/ Montreal Grand Prix Des Metiers D'Art, Montreal, 87; Glass America, Heller Gallery, New York, 87; Memories of a New Light, Clara Scremin, Paris, 87; traveling show, Art that Works: The Decorative Arts of the Mint Mus, Charlotte, NC & De Cordova & Dana Mus, Lincoln, Mass, and others, 90-92. *Pos:* Bd Dir, Empire State Crafts Alliance, 85-88; affil artist Chmn, NY Experimental Glass, 86-88, head hot shop, 90- *Teaching:* Instr glass sculpture, Univ Hawaii 81-82; instr glass sculpture, RI Sch Design 87-88; instr 3-D product design, Parson Design, 90-91. *Awards:* Masters Fel, Nat Endowment Arts, 79; Artist in Residence, Artpark, 83; Grant, Pyramid Arts Ctr, New York, 87. *Mem:* Experimental Glass Workshop (bd dirs, 88-); Found Comn Artists. *Media:* Glass, neon; Mixed. *Publ:* Contribr, Product Design II, PBC Int, 87; Metropolis, 86; La Ceramic et Du Vere, 87; Masterpieces of American Glass, Crown Pub, 89; Contemporary Glass; A World Survey from Corning Mus Glass, Harry N Abrams, 89. *Mailing Add:* 31 Second Ave New York NY 10003

HARMON, LILY
PAINTER, WRITER
b New Haven, Conn, Nov 19, 12. *Study:* Yale Sch Art; Acad Colarossi, Paris; Art Students League. *Work:* Whitney Mus; Butler Art Inst, Youngstown, Ohio; Newark Art Mus, NJ; Tel Aviv Mus, Israel; Hirshhorn Mus, Washington, DC. *Comn:* Mural, Port Chester Jewish Ctr, NY, 50. *Exhib:* Metrop Mus Art, New York, 43; Carnegie Inst, Pittsburgh, 44-49; Univ Ill, 49; 20 one-man shows, Int Salon, Palace Fine Arts, Mexico City, 44-73; 50 Year Retrospective, Wichita Art Mus, 81; Butler Art Inst Am Art, 82; Provincetown Art Asn & Mus, 83. *Teaching:* Instr oil painting, Nat Acad Design, New York, 74- *Awards:* La Tausca Art Award, 47; Hallmark Art Award, 49; Pearl Safir Award, Silvermine Guild, 54; plus others. *Bibliog:* A Lily for a Lily, Limited Ed Club, 75; Art in boxes, Norman Laliberte, 75; Contemporary American Painting 1945 (catalog), Wichita Art Mus, 81. *Mem:* Provincetown Art Asn; Artists Equity; Nat Acad Design; Author's Guild Inc. *Publ:* Illusr, Jean Paul Sartre's Dirty Hands, 67, Kafka's Castle, 67 & Thomas Mann's Buddenbrooks, 67, Japan Publ; Guy de Mauppasant's Short Stories, Franklin Libr, 77; auth, Freehand autobiography, Simon & Shuster, 81; and others. *Mailing Add:* 151 Central Park W New York NY 10023

HARMS, ELIZABETH
PAINTER
b Milwaukee, Wis, May 26, 24. *Study:* Art Inst Chicago, BFA & MFA. *Work:* Newark Mus, NJ; Jersey City Mus; Zimmerli Art Mus, Rutgers Univ, New Brunswick, NJ; AT&T; Time/Life, New York; Deloitte, Haskins & Sells, Stamford, Conn; and others. *Exhib:* Art Inst Chicago Ann, 61-64 & 66; one-man shows, Mus Art, Carnegie Inst, 69, Mercer Gallery, New York, 80 & Condeso-Lawler, New York, 82-86 & 90; Contemp Images in Watercolor Touring Show, 76; Eight Painters, Jersey City Mus, 80; Selected Women Painters, Castle Gallery, Col New Rochelle, 82; Contemp Syntax, Rutgers Univ, Newark, NJ, 88; and others. *Awards:* Third Prize Nat Watercolor exhib, Smithsonian Inst, 63; Armstrong Prize, Art Inst Chicago, 63; Tiffany Found Grant for Painting, 77. *Bibliog:* Hilton Kramer (auth), Art: More from Dubuffet feast, NY Times, 9/27/75; David Shirey (auth), Unsensational art in a municipal office, NY Times, 11/11/79; William Zimmer (auth), Harms at Condeso-Lawler, Art Gallery Scene, 10/30/82; Robert Richman (auth), Mostly minimal, Arts & Antiques, 2/91; Gerrit Henry (auth), Elizabeth Harms, Art News, 5/91. *Media:* Oil, Pastel. *Dealer:* Condeso-Lawler 76 Green St New York NY. *Mailing Add:* PO Box 245 Jeffersonville NY 12748

HARNETT, MR & MRS JOEL WILLIAM
COLLECTORS
Mr Harnett, b New York, NY, Dec 3, 25. *Study:* Mr Harnett, Univ Richmond, BA; New Sch Social Res; Mrs Harnett, Brooklyn Col, BA; New Sch Social Res. *Pos:* Joel Harnett, vpres, LOOK Mag, 50-69; chmn, Media Horizons, Inc, 69-88; publ & chmn, Phoenix Home & Garden; Lila Harnett, publ, Bus Atomics Report, 53-63; cult reporter, NY State newspapers, 64-74; fine arts ed, Cue Mag, 75-80; consult ed, Phoenix Home & Garden, 80-88, assoc publ, 88-, publ, Scottsdale Scene. *Mem:* Art Table Inc; Mrs Harnett, mem, NY State Coun Arts, 83-89. *Collection:* Works by Hopper, Burchfield, Marsh, Greene, Warhol, Anuszkiewcz, Seley, Tooker, Pearlstein, Lamis, Fletcher Benton, Audobon, Catlin, Beal & Birmelin, Allan Houser, Fritz Scholder, and Dennis Numkena. *Mailing Add:* 4523 E Clearwater Pkwy Scottsdale AZ 85253

HARNICK, SYLVIA
PAINTER
b New York, NY. *Study:* Brooklyn Col, BA, 54; C W Post with Robert Yasuda, 87-89. *Work:* Fine Arts Mus Long Island, Hempstead, NY; Queensborough Community Col Art Gallery, Bayside, NY. *Exhib:* 34th Ann Long Island Artists Exhib, Heckscher Mus, Huntington, NY, 88; Nat Ddrawing Asn, Hermitage Mus, Norfolk, Va, 88; Art of the Northeast USA, Silvermine Guild Arts, New Canaan, Conn, 90; Drawings, Gallery North, Setauket, NY, 91; 10th Ann Juried Exhib, Fine Arts Mus Long Island, Hempstead, NY, 91; 36th Nat Biennial, Sumner Art Mus, Washington, DC, 92; Earthly Visions, Nassau Co Mus Art, Roslyn, NY, 92; Landscape Observed-Landscape Transformed, Islip Art Mus, E Islip, NY, 92. *Pos:* Membership Chairperson, Discovery Gallery, 91- *Awards:* Purchase Prize, Works on Paper, Queensborough Community Col, 90; First Prize, One person show Tenth Ann juried Exhib, Fine Arts Mus Long Island, 91; Best in Show, Earthly Visions, Nassau Co Mus Art, 92. *Bibliog:* Helen Harrison (auth), When Abstraction Prevails, NY Times, 11/26/89; Phyllis Braff (auth), Exploring Abstract Polarities of Warm and Cool, NY Times, 1/13/91; interview, TV Channel 44, Art Scene on Long Island, Shirley Romaine, 6/2/92. *Mem:* Nat Asn Women Artists (mem jury, 92-94); Nat Drawing Asn; Nat League Am Pen Women; Hempstead Harbor Artist Asn (membership chairperson, 91-); Long Island Network Women Artists. *Media:* Acrylic. *Mailing Add:* Four Parkside Dr Great Neck NY 11021

HAROOTUNIAN, CLAIRE M
SCULPTOR, EDUCATOR
b Philadelphia, Pa, Feb 7, 30. *Study:* Univ Pa, BA, 52; Univ Del, MEd, 64; Syracuse Univ, MFA (sculpture), 79. *Work:* Munson-Williams Proctor Inst, Utica, NY; Cazenovia Col, NY; Va Ctr Creative Arts, Sweetbriar. *Exhib:* Cooperstown Art Gallery, NY, 80; Outside New York City, Lowe Art Gallery, Syracuse, NY, 82; View from Upstate, AIR Gallery, New York, 82; solo exhibs, Everson Mus, Syracuse, NY, 83 & Ben Mangel Gallery, Philadelphia, 84; Ransburg Art Gallery, Indianapolis, Ind, 84; Arco Art Fair, Madrid, 92. *Teaching:* Instr sculpture, Everson Mus Art, Syracuse, 79-80; adj prof sculpture, Syracuse Univ, 80-88. *Awards:* Fel, Va Ctr Creative Arts, 83-85 & 88; Yaddo Fel, Saratoga Springs, NY, 83; Fel, Int Workshop, San Pere, Barcelona, Spain, 88. *Media:* Cast Metal, Forged Metal. *Mailing Add:* 602 Jamesville Ave Syracuse NY 13210

HARPER, ELEANOR O'NEIL
PAINTER
b Newburyport, Mass, Dec 23, 19. *Study:* Radcliffe Col, AB(fine arts); Sch Practical Art, Boston. *Exhib:* Catharine Lorillard Wolfe Art Club Exhib, Nat Arts Club, New York, 72-73; Nat Exhib, Mus Fine Arts, Springfield, Mass, 75; Butler Mus, Ohio, 77-78; Guild Boston Artists; Hudson Valley Art Asn, 80-81; Allied Artists Am Ann Exhib, Nat Arts Club, New York, 83. *Pos:* Copywriter, Filene's, Boston, 42-43; dir advert, Br Shop, 43-45. *Awards:* Carl R Matson Mem Award, Rockport Art Asn, 80; Morton Donald Catok Mem Award, Academic Artists Asn, 80; Margaret Fitzhugh Brown Mem Award, NShore Arts Asn, 83; 12 painting awards, 84-92; and others. *Mem:* Rockport Art Asn; Copley Soc; Guild Boston Artists; Academic Artists Asn. *Media:* Oil, Watercolor. *Mailing Add:* Penzance Rd Rockport MA 01966

HARPER, WILLIAM
JEWELER, PAINTER
b Bucyrus, Ohio, June 17, 44. *Study:* Western Reserve Univ, BS, 66, MS, 67; Cleveland Inst Art, cert, 67. *Work:* Vatican Mus; Detroit Inst Art; Metrop Mus, New York; Mus Fine Art, Boston; Cleveland Mus Art. *Comn:* Collar and Jewel of Office of the President, Yale Univ, 82. *Exhib:* Goldsmith, 74 & solo exhib, 77-78, Renwick Gallery; Goldsmiths Hall, London, 78; Craft Art & Religion, Vatican Mus, 78; one-man show, Kennedy Galleries, NY, 81 & 82, Ruth Siegel Ltd, New York, 87; Masterworks of American Jewelry, Victoria & Albert Mus, London, 85; The Eloquent Object, Philbrook Mus, Tulsa & traveling, 87-89; William Harper: Artist As Alchemist Orlando Mus Art & Traveling, 89-91. *Teaching:* Vis artist enamels, Kent State Univ, 70-73; from assoc prof to prof metals & enamels, Fla State Univ, 73-91; vis prof, Parsons Sch Design, New York, 79 & Cleveland Inst Art, 84-85. *Awards:* Craftsman's Res Fel, Nat Endowment Arts, 74-75 & 78-79; Fla Artist Fel, 80-81 & 85-86; Individual Artists Grant, Nat Endowment Arts, 90-91. *Bibliog:* Penelope Hunter-Stiebel (auth), William Harper talismans for our time, Am Crafts, 8-9/81; Tom Manhart (auth), William Harper: Artist as Alchemist Orlando Museum of Art (catalog), 11/89. *Mem:* Soc NAm Goldsmiths; Am Crafts Coun. *Publ:* Contribr, The Art of Cloisonne, Lowe Art Mus, Coral Gables, Fla, 72; auth, Step by Step Enameling, Western, 73; auth, The magic of cloisonne: William Harper, Craft Horizons, 6/77. *Mailing Add:* 3516 Trillium Ct Tallahassee FL 32312

HARRIES, MAGS (MARGARET L)
SCULPTOR
b Barry, SWales, Gt Brit, April 6, 45. *Study:* Leicester Col Art & Design, England, dipl, 67; Univ Southern Ill, MFA, 70. *Work:* Boston Mus Fine Arts; Univ Southern Ill; Nat Mus Wales; Rose Art Mus, Brandeis Univ, Waltham, Mass. *Comn:* Asaroton 1976, City Boston, 76; Bellingham Square (bronze artifacts), City Chelsea, Mass, 78; Glove Cycle (bronze narrative), Mass Bay Transit Authority, Boston, 79-83; Three Gardens (topiary sculpture), DeCordova Mus, Lincoln, Mass, 81-82; Gateway (wood table), City Cambridge, Mass, 83; Wall Cycle to Ocotillo (concrete & steel sculpture), City of Phoeniz, Ariz, 92; Topiary (a 20 yr project) (aluminum & boxwood), City of New York Parks Dept, 92. *Exhib:* Collectors Collect Contemporary, Inst Contemp Art, Boston, 78; Impressions in Clay, Everson Mus, 79; Directions in Realism, Danforth Mus, Framingham, Mass, 81; Cast Illusions, Wellesley Col Mus, 82; solo exhib, DeCordova Mus, Lincoln, Mass, 82; Sculptural Objects & Installations, Rose Art Mus, Brandeis Univ, Waltham, Mass, 86; Know No Bounds, Installation & Performance, Mass Bay Transit Authority, 86; Art for the Public: New Collab, Dayton Art Inst, Ohio, 88; The Man from City Hall, Boston, 88 & 89; Border Gardens Installation, San Diego Mus Contemp Art, La Jolla, Calif, 90; River Runes, Art Park, Lewiston, NY, 90. *Teaching:* Instr sculpture, Sch Mus Fine Arts, Boston, 78- *Awards:* Bicentennial Sculpture Comn, City Boston, 76; Bunting Fel, Radcliffe Col, 77-78; Design Excellence Pub Art, Nat Endowment Arts & US Dept Transportation, 81. *Bibliog:* Sculpture in the Subways, Smithsonian Mag, 4/87; Comn, Sculpture, 11-12/88; Socially Interactive Art, Art New Eng, 90. *Mailing Add:* Fine Arts Dept Sch Mus Fine Arts 230 The Fenway Boston MA 02115

HARRINGTON, BRYAN RULISON
PAINTER, COLLAGE ARTIST
b San Francisco, Calif, Apr 18, 53. *Study:* Univ Calif, Santa Cruz, BA, 75. *Work:* Vanderbilt Univ, Nashville, Tenn; Hunter Mus Art, Chattanooga, Tenn; Amoco Oil Corp & Chemical Bank, New York; Northern Telecom, Nashville, Tenn. *Comn:* Acrylic mural, Univ Calif, Santa Cruz, 75; three large oil paintings for lobby, Col Eight, Univ Calif, Santa Cruz, 76. *Exhib:* Tenn Fine Arts Ctr, Nashville, 82; Beyond Words, San Jose Inst Contemp Art, Calif, 82; Alexandria Visual Arts Competition, La, 82; Wesleyan Second Int Exhib Print & Drawing, Macon, Ga, 83; Dusseldorf Art Fair, WGer, 84; Basel Art Expo, Kunst Hall, Switz, 85; Crocker-Kinsley Mus, Sacramento, Calif, 85. *Pos:* Arts coordr, Univ Calif, Santa Cruz, 75-78, gallery dir, 76-78. *Awards:* Show Prize, Alexandria Visual Arts Ctr Competition, 82; Prize Winner, San Jose Inst Contemp Art, 82; Prize Winner, Cupertine Art Asn, Calif, 82. *Bibliog:* Clara Hieronymos (auth), Art works highlight Northern Telecom Building, 10/85 & Mystery-laden work at Comberland Gallery, 11/85, The Tennessean. *Media:* Gouache, Oil. *Dealer:* Carol Stein 2213 Bandywood Dr Nashville TN 37215. *Mailing Add:* c/o Cumberland Gallery 4107 Hilsboro Circle Nashville TN 37215

HARRINGTON, CHESTEE MARIE
PAINTER, SCULPTOR
b New Iberia, La, Dec 5, 41. *Study:* Art Students League, New York, with Sidney Simon & Michael Pelletieri, 84; Woodstock Sch Art, with Richard McDaniel, 85; Shidon, Bronze Foundry, with Tommy Hicks, 86. *Work:* Art Ctr SW La, Lafayette, La; Mc Ilhenny Collection, La State Univ, Baton Rouge; La State Mus, New Orleans. *Comn:* mural, wood polychromatic bas relief, Cameron State Bank, Sulphur, La, 89; bronze bust, Bouliguy Plaza, New Iberia, La, 76; Wood Polychromatic bas relief, St Landry Bank, Opelousas, La, 81; Lead Relic Tricentennial, Dept Cult, Baton Rouge La, 83; Womans Hosp Wood Polychromatic bas relief, Baton Rouge, La, 87. *Exhib:* One woman shows, Art Ctr SW La, Lafayette, La, 68-75, Masur Mus, Monroe, La, 76, Zigler Mus, Jennings, La 77 & Meet the Artist, McNeese State Univ, Lake Charles, La, 84; group shows, French Louisiana Bicentennial, Fr Radio Network, Paris, Fr, 75 & Legacy in Progress, La State Univ, Alexandria, La, 85; Tricentennial Celebration, La State Mus, New Orleans, La, 84; We're Saving a Place for You, Shadows on the Teche, Nat Trust. *Teaching:* Instr, basic drawing, Iberia Parish Park Serv, 66-68. *Bibliog:* Mary Champagne (auth), Chestee Harrington, Sunday Advocate, 11/28/71; Morris Raphael (auth) Battle in the Bayou Country, Harlo Press, 75; Kenneth Nahan (auth) Chestee Harrington Biog, Nahan Galleries, 75. *Mem:* Nat Artist Equity. *Media:* Wood, Bronze. *Publ:* Illusr, Battle in the Bayou Country, Harlo Press, 75; So you want to invest in art, Baton Rouge Mag, 82. *Mailing Add:* Hc69 Box 435cv Jacock Rd St Francisville LA 70775

HARRINGTON, LAMAR
CURATOR, DIRECTOR
b Iowa, Nov 2, 17. *Study:* Iowa State Col, 35-36; Cornish Sch Fine Arts, Seattle, 45-50; Univ Wash, BA, 79. *Collections Arranged:* Art and Machines: Light, Motion and Sound, 69; Claes Oldenburg Icebag, 71; More Art for Public Places, 71; New Works from the Walker, 71; Kenneth Callahan: A Universal Voyage, 73; Adventures in Photography, 75; Another Side to Art: Ceramic Sculpture in the Northwest, 79; Washington Craft Forms: Creators and Collectors, 82; Historical Survey of Crafts in the Northwest, 83. *Pos:* Staff mem, Henry Gallery, Univ Wash, 56-75, assoc dir, 72-75; cur, Arch of Northwest Art, Univ Wash, 75-77; panel mem visual arts, Nat Endowment for the Arts, 76-78; bd trustees, Pilchuck Sch, Seattle, Wash, 81-88; dir & chief cur, Bellevue Art Mus, Bellevue, Wash, 85-; cur, Wyoming Arts Coun, Third Wyoming Biennial, 88-89; res cur/mgr, Bellevue Art Mus, Frank Lloyd Wright: In the Realm of Ideas, Nat Traveling exhib, 89; cur, Bellevue Art Mus, James W Washington, Jr: The Spirit in the Stone, 89; cur, Bellevue Art Mus, Eternal Laughter: A Sixty-Year Retrospective by George Tsutakawa, 90. *Awards:* Gov's Writer's Award, Wash State Comn, 80; Hon Fel, Am Crafts Coun, 87; Wash State Gov's Arts Award, 88. *Mem:* Western Asn Art Mus (bd trustees, vpres, 73, pres, 74 & 75); Pac Northwest Arts & Crafts Asn (life mem bd trustees, pres, 57 & 58); Pottery NW (bd trustees, vpres, 76 & 77); Pilchuck Int Coun, Pilchuck Sch, 88-; Santa Fe Chamber Music Adv Bd, 85- *Res:* Contemporary American art and handcrafts; American design of late nineteenth and twentieth centuries. *Publ:* Contribr, 74th Western Annual (exhib catalog), Denver Art Mus, 73; auth, Ceramics in the Pacific Northwest: A History, Univ Wash Press, 79; Washington Craft Forms: An Historical Perspective, State Capitol Mus, Olympia, Wash, 82; The making of a modernist metalworker, J Archives Am Art, 10/83; Robert Sperry, the Growing of a Taproot, Bellevle Art Mus, 85. *Mailing Add:* 511 Galer St Seattle WA 98109

HARRINGTON, WILLIAM CHARLES
SCULPTOR
b Chicago, Ill, June 20, 42. *Study:* Hartford Art Sch; Univ Ill, with Roger Majorowicz & Frank & Julio Gallo, BFA; Univ Hartford with Ted Behl & Lloyd Glasson, MFA. *Work:* Nat Archives, Washington, DC. *Comn:* 15 ft concrete & steel, Cabot, Cabot & Forbes, Seattle, Wash, 75; 4 ft wood relief, Amalgamated Spirits & Provisions, Ames, Iowa, 75 & Cedar Rapids, Iowa, 76; carved compos, Cabot, Cabot & Forbes, Bellevue, Wash, 84. *Exhib:* Pull up a Chair, Luckenbach Mill Gallery, Bethlehem, Pa, 90; Sculpture Court Installation, Radford Univ, Va, 92-93; Dream House, Peninsula Arts Ctr, Newport News, Va, 92; Burlington Sculpture Garden Exhib, Pemberton, NJ, 91-92, 92-93; Construction Site, Toys & Art, Dairy Barn, Athens, Ohio, 92; and others. *Pos:* Workshop asst, George Rickey, East Chatham, NY, 65; mem, Combat Artists Team Vietnam, 68-69. *Teaching:* Asst prof sculpture & drawing, Ind State Univ, Terre Haute, 70-72; asst prof sculpture, Iowa State Univ, 74-78. *Mem:* Tri-State Sculptors. *Media:* Wood, Welded Steel. *Mailing Add:* RR 1 Box 407-A Crozet VA 22932

HARRIS, ALFRED PETER
PAINTER, ADMINISTRATOR
b Toronto, Ont, Apr 4, 32. *Study:* Ont Col Art, Toronto, hon dipl; Brock Univ, St Catharines, Ont, LLD, 85. *Work:* Sir George Williams Univ, Montreal; Bronfman Collection, Montreal Mus Fine Art; Brascan Collection, Toronto; Can Coun Art Bank; Northern & Cent Gas Co. *Exhib:* Mem Gallery, Albright-Knox Gallery, Buffalo, 62; four-man exhib, London Pub Libr & Art Mus, 63-65; two-man exhibs, Dorothy Cameron Gallery, 64-65; two-man show, Roberts Gallery, Toronto, 70; Ann Exhib Contemp Can Art, Hamilton, 70-72. *Collections Arranged:* J W Morrice, J Chambers Retrospective & William Kurelec Retrospective, 66; Baker, Boyle & Hollenback, 67; John Newman, 68; Soul of Niagara, 69; John Boyle, Ed Fantinel, 70; Harvey Breverman & Niagara Now, 71. *Pos:* Dir, Rodman Hall Arts Ctr, 59-; pres, Ont Asn Art Galleries, 70-71. *Teaching:* Art instr, Ont Col Art, 59-60; instr gen art, Ridley Col, St Catharines, 63-65; spec lectr mod art, Brock Univ, 66. *Bibliog:* Harry Malcomson (auth), Artist, Toronto Life, 69. *Mem:* Can Soc Graphic Art; Ont Soc Artists; Ontario Arts Coun. *Media:* Oil. *Publ:* Contribr, Nude in Canadian Art, 72. *Dealer:* Roberts Gallery 641 Yonge St Toronto ON Can. *Mailing Add:* 901-165 Ontario St St Catharines ON L2R 5K4 Canada

HARRIS, ANN SUTHERLAND
HISTORIAN, ADMINISTRATOR
b Cambridge, Eng, Nov 4, 37. *Study:* Courtauld Inst Art, Univ London, BA(hon, first class), 61, PhD, 65; Eastern Mich Univ, Hon DA, 81; Atlanta College of Art, LHD. *Collections Arranged:* Women Artist 1550-1950 (coauth, catalog), Los Angeles Co Mus Art, Los Angeles, 76-77; Univ Art Mus, Univ Tex, Austin, 77; Mus Art, Carnegie Inst Int, Pittsburgh, 77; Brooklyn Mus, 77. *Pos:* Chmn acad affairs, Metrop Mus Art, New York, 77-80. *Teaching:* Asst prof art hist & archeol, Columbia Univ, 66-71; vis lectr, Yale Univ, 72-73; asst prof art hist, Hunter Col, New York, 71-73; assoc prof, State Univ NY, Albany, 73-77; vis assoc prof, Inst Fine Arts, NY Univ, 74-75; adj prof, Juilliard Sch, 78-; Mellon prof, Univ Pittsburgh, spring 84 & prof art hist, 84. *Awards:* Woman of Year, Mademoiselle Mag, 77. *Mem:* Col Art Asn Am (mem bd dir, 75-79); Women's Caucus for Art (pres & founder mem, 71-74, mem exec adv bd, 74-80). *Res:* Italian and French, 16th & 17th century painting and drawing; contemporary women artists. *Publ:* Coauth, Die Zeichnungen von Andrea Sacchi & Carlo Maratta, Kataloge des Kunstmuseums, Düsseldorf, III, Düsseldorf, 67; ed, Selected Drawings of Gian Lorenzo Bernini, Dover Publ, 77; auth, Andrea Sacchi, Complete Edition of the Paintings, Phaidon, Oxford, 77. *Mailing Add:* c/o Univ Pittsburgh Dept Artistry Pittsburgh PA 15260

HARRIS, CHARNEY ANITA
PAINTER, SCULPTOR
b Chicago, Ill. *Study:* Univ Arts, Philadelphia; Philadelphia Mus Art, with Hobson Pittman, 64-68; New Sch Social Res, with Henry Pearson, 70-73; private study with Will Barnet, 74. *Work:* Philadelphia Mus Art; Allentown Art Mus, Pa; Hobson Pitman Mus House, Bryn Maur, Pa. *Comn:* Universal Domain, Hudson River Mus, Yonkers, NY, 85 & Moore Col Art, Philidelphia, 86. *Exhib:* 3D Invitational Show, Carnegie-Mellon Univ Mus, Pittsburgh, 80; Pertaining to Philadelphia, Philadelphia Mus Art, 81; West/Art and the Law Traveling Exhib, 85; Artists Xmas Show, Cleveland Ctr Contemp Art, 86; Important Pennsylvania Women Artists, Shippenburg Univ Mus, 87; Honoring Hobson Pittman, Woodmere Art Mus, Philadelphia, 89. *Awards:* Painting Prize, New York Sch Social Res, 70; Painting Prize, Pennsylvania Gallery Fine Arts. *Bibliog:* Victoria Donohoe (auth), article, Philadelphia Inquirer, 82 & 88; article in the Washington Post, 84; Aimee Young Jackson (auth), article, Kalliope, 89. *Mem:* Artists Equity Asn Inc; Am Fedn Arts. *Media:* Oil; Wood. *Dealer:* Mangel Gallery 1714 Rittenhouse Sq Philadelphia PA 19103. *Mailing Add:* 2 Sunnyside Lane Yardley PA 19067

HARRIS, CONLEY
PAINTER, PRINTMAKER
b Kans, July 7, 43. *Study:* Univ Kans, BFA, 65; Univ Wis, MFA, 68. *Work:* Fogg Art Mus, Harvard Univ, Cambridge, Mass; Boston Mus Fine Art; DeCordova Mus, Lincoln, Mass; Wichita Art Mus, Kans; Citi-Corp Bank, New York; and others. *Comn:* Oil painting, Chubb Insurance Co, 85; Oil painting, Gannett Co, 87. *Exhib:* Made in Boston, Fogg Art Mus, Harvard Univ, Cambridge, Mass, 80; Am Drawings, Smithsonian tour, 83-85; Figuration on Paper, Boston Mus Fine Arts, 83; one-person shows, Cutler-Stavaridis Gallery, Boston, 82, Barridoff Galleries, Portland, Maine, 83, Univ NH, Durham, 88, Levinson-Kane Gallery, Boston, 90, Thomas Segal Gallery, Boston, Mass, 85 & DeCordova Mus, Lincoln, 85; Visions of Landscape, Virginia Miller Gallery, 88; New Prints, EES Studio, Estampe du Rhin, Strasbourg, France, 90; Barbara Greene Gallery, Miami, Fla, 91; Rugg Rd Papers Gallery, Boston, Mass, 92; and others. *Teaching:* Vis artist drawing, Boston Univ, Mass, 69-70; assoc prof drawing & painting, Univ NH, Durham, 70-88; Art New England Workshops, Bennington Col, 84, 85, 87, 88 & 90. *Awards:* Wurlitzer Found Residence Grant, Taos, NMex, 75; Purchase Prize, Am Drawing, Portsmouth, Va, 76; Mass Artist Found Fel, 86. *Bibliog:* Robert Taylor (auth), article, Boston Globe, 3/24/76; Pamela Allara (auth), The Boston art party, Art News Mag, 11/80; Nancy Stapen (auth), article, Art New Eng, 12/80; Christine Temin (auth), review, 7/5/84 & Robert Taylor (auth), review, 2/85, Boston Globe; Anne Neely (auth), review, Art New Eng, 6/85; Margo Clark (auth), article, Art New Eng, 5/88. *Media:* Oil, Watercolor; Monotype. *Mailing Add:* 68 Waltham St No 4 Boston MA 02118

HARRIS, DAVID JACK
PAINTER, MURALIST
b San Mateo, Calif, Jan 6, 48. *Study:* San Francisco State Univ, BA, 72, MA, 75. *Work:* San Francisco State Univ, Bain & Co, Pacific Bell & Int Red Cross, San Francisco; Stanford Univ, Palo Alto, Calif; Litton Industs, Mountain View, Calif; N Cent Wash Mus, Wenatchee, Wash; Matur Augo Mus, Ridgecrest, Calif. *Comn:* Wells Fargo Bank, Los Altos, Calif; Easton Aluminum, Van Nuys, Calif; Am Airlines, Miami, Columbus, Bogota & Lima, Peru; Lawrey's, Beverly Hills, Calif; Sheraton Grande, Los Angeles; and others. *Exhib:* Fine Arts Mus, San Francisco, 68-70; San Mateo County Mus, Calif, 70; California Artists, Palace Fine Arts, San Francisco, 75; solo exhib, Hewlett Packard Gallery, Palo Alto, Calif, 86, California Concepts, N Cent Wash Mus, Wash, Coastal Arts League Mus, San Mateo, Calif, 88 & Matur Augo Mus, Ridgecrest, 92. *Pos:* Dir, Galerie de Tours, San Francisco, 71-72; pres, 1870 Gallery & Studio, Belmont, Calif, 86-87; UP Coastal Arts League Mus, 90- *Teaching:* Instr painting & art hist, Chabot Col, Hayward, Calif, 76-81. *Awards:* Best of Show, Univ Santa Clara, Calif, 75; First Place, Bay Area Artists Group, San Francisco County, 78; First Place, San Mateo County Artist Show, 80. *Bibliog:* Mary Helen McAllister (auth), David Harris, N County Publ, 84; Mark Stevens (auth), David Harris: A World in Motion, Valley Mag, San Clemente, Calif, 89. *Mem:* Int Soc Interior Designers; 1870 Gallery & Studios; Coastal Arts League, San Mateo, Calif; Col Art Asn. *Media:* Oil, Acrylic. *Publ:* Auth, California Concepts brochure, N Cent Wash Mus Publ. *Dealer:* A Gallery 73-580 El Paseo Palm Desert CA 92260. *Mailing Add:* 1870 Ralston Ave Belmont CA 94002

HARRIS, DOLORES ASHLEY
DESIGNER, EDUCATOR
b Tuskegee, Ala. *Study:* Tuskegee Inst, with Mathilda Schwalbach, BS, 51; Univ Wis, Madison, MS, 56; Sophia Univ, Tokyo, cert(art & cult), 65; Arrowmont Sch Arts & Crafts, with Meda Parker Johnson, 71; Penland Sch Arts & Crafts, summer 72; Univ Oslo, Norway (int div), summer 73; Haystack Sch Arts, Maine, summer 74; Educators Africa/African Am Inst, New York, summer 75; Russ Winter Sem, 78; Fulbright-Hayes Res/Study Abroad: Senegal, Cameroon & Liberia, 85. *Work:* Meharry Hubbard Hosp & Tenn State Mus, Nashville; Fisk Univ Mus. *Exhib:* Art Fibers and Fabrics, Univ Ctr Art Gallery, Cookeville, Tenn, 74; The Early Eighties, Tenn State Mus, Nashville, 81; Womans Perspective, Schenectady Mus, NY, 82-83; Wearable Art, Nashville Artist Guild Gallery, 83; Artist Guild Exhib, Cheekwood Fine Arts Mus, Nashville, 83; Arts Mus, Washington, DC, 85; Vertical File, Women in the Arts Nat Conf Artists, Philadelphia, 86; Van Vechten Gallery, Fisk Univ, Nashville, 87; Austin Peay Univ, 88; J B Speed Mus, Louisville, Ky. *Teaching:* Asst prof design, Prairie View Col, 64-66; prof, Tenn State Univ, Nashville, 67-; guest lectr, Murray State Univ, summer 73. *Awards:* Excellence in Teaching, Tenn State Univ, 74; Hanging Arts Award, Arts Jamboree, Fla State Univ, 80; Progression Award, Early 80s, Tenn State Mus, 82. *Bibliog:* Clara Hieronymous (auth), A time to live and a time to dye, 71 & Art is unifying factor, 75, Nashville Tennessean; Caroline McNeilly (auth), Three figures, Nashville Banner, 81. *Mem:* Nashville Artist Guild; Nat Conf Artists; Cheekwood, Tenn Botanical Gardens Fine Arts (bd trustees, 92-94); Children's Creative Workshop (bd trustees); Women Arts, Wash. *Media:* Textiles. *Publ:* Contribr, Contemporary Batik and Tie-Dye, Crown Publ, 73; Educators to Africa 75, Approaches to the Study of West Africa, Sch Educ, Howard Univ & African Am Inst, 75; The American Artist Today in Black, Vol 1, RNM Publ, 82. *Mailing Add:* PO Box 320 Tenn State Univ Nashville TN 37203

HARRIS, DOROTHY D
EDUCATOR, PAINTER
b Columbus, Ga, Aug, 19, 35. *Study:* Univ Colo, with Mark Rothko, BFA, 57; Columbia Univ, Teachers Col, MA, 60 Ed D, 84. *Work:* Jersey City State Col. *Comn:* Block Drug Co. *Exhib:* 51st Ann Opening Show, Birmingham Mus, 59; St Louis Art Mus, Mo, 61; solo exhibs, Viridian Gallery, New York, 87 & 92, Montclair Mus, NJ, 89; Mussavi, New York, 88; Nabisco Gallery, 88; Chang Won Univ, Korea, 90; Columbus Mus (group), Ga, 90; Korean Cult Ctr, New York, 90; and others. *Pos:* Bd dirs, Nat Asn Schs Art & Design, 86-; cur, Lever House Group Show, New York, 92; adv coun, Hudson Repertory Dance Theatre; bd trustees, Thomas A Edison Film Consortium. *Teaching:* Prof painting, Jersey City State Col, 62-, chmn dept art, 82-; dean, Sch Arts & Scis, Jersey City, 92. *Awards:* Second Prize Watercolor, 12th Ann Juried Exhib, Summit Art Ctr, NJ, 76; Cert Appreciation, Jersey City Cult Arts Comn, 85. *Mem:* Hudson Co Cult & Heritage Coun (adv coun, 84-85); Nat Asn Sch Art & Design (bd dirs, 85-); Hudson Repertory Dance Theatre (adv bd, 85-). *Media:* Oil. *Mailing Add:* Jersey City State Col Jersey City NJ 07305

HARRIS, ELLEN SCHWARTZ
ADMINISTRATOR, MUSEOLOGIST
b Washington, DC, Nov 3, 49. *Study:* Yale Univ, BA(A Conger Goodyear Award & Marshall-Allison Fel), 71; Inst Fine Arts, NY Univ, MA, 79; Yale Sch Mgmt, MPPM, 86. *Collections Arranged:* Images of Experience (auth, catalog), 82, The Art of Notation (auth, catalog), 82, Partitions, 82, The Destroyed Print (auth, catalog), 82, Exceptions, 83, Bridges (auth, catalog), 83, Contemporary Third World Architecture (auth, catalog), 83 & Beauties & Beasts, 84, Pratt Inst; and others. *Pos:* Paris corresp, Art Int Mag, Lugano, Switz, 71-72; admin asst, Hirshhorn Mus & Sculpture Garden, 76; ed, Harry N Abrams, New York, 76-79; contrib ed, Art News Mag, New York, 77-86; dir exhibs, Pratt Inst, Manhattan & Brooklyn, 79-84; chmn bd trustees, Rotunda Gallery, Brooklyn Borough Hall, 81-84; treas, Franklin Furnace, 87-; deputy dir finance & auxiliary activities, Mus Mod Art, New York, 89-92; dir, Montclair Art Mus, 92- *Teaching:* Vis asst prof, Pratt Inst, 81-84. *Mem:* Am Asn Mus; Art Table. *Publ:* Ed, The Mechanism of Meaning (Arakawa/Gins), Harry N Abrams, 79; auth, Vito Acconci, 81, Artists the critics are watching, 81, At the Whitney and the Guggenheim: No surprises, 81, Dennis Oppenheim, 82 & others, Art News. *Mailing Add:* c/o Montclair Mus Three S Mountain Ave Montclair NJ 07042

HARRIS, GLORIANE
PAINTER, EDUCATOR
b Santa Monica, Calif, Jan 7, 47. *Study:* Art Ctr Col Design, Los Angeles, 64; Univ Southern Calif, 64-66; El Camino Col, 65; Los Angeles City Col, 66; Otis Art Inst of Los Angeles Co, 66, BFA, MFA(fel), 70; Los Angeles Trade Tech Col, 78. *Exhib:* New Talent, New Work, Los Angeles Co Mus Art, Calif, 71; Video Los Angeles, Palais de Beaux Artes, Brussels, Belg, 77; Painting Show, Mount San Antonio Col, Walnut, Calif, 78; Painting, Newport Harbor Art Mus, Calif, 79; Hang Eight: Artists from Southern California (with catalog), Foundations Gallery, New York, 82; Self-Portrait Invitational, Am Gallery, Los Angeles, 82; solo exhibs, Sea Sections, AAA/Michael Salerno Gallery, 84, Metro Rail Transit Consult Visual Arts, Los Angeles, 84 & Culver Nat Bank, Culver City, Calif, 84-85. *Pos:* Co-organizer, Experiments in Art & Technol, 68-71; co-organizer & founding mem, Los Angeles Inst Contemp Art, 73-75; tech asst, Documenta, Kassel, Ger, 77; art dir, Vintage Image, 81-83; freelance production graphic artist & photo retoucher, 83-; graphic artist, Mark Taper Forum, 84-85; art dir, Lone Eagle Publ, 85-; asst art dir, Bon Appetit Mag, Knapp Commun Corp, 85-90. *Teaching:* Lectr painting, drawing & design, Cerritos Col, Calif, 70-72; lectr painting & drawing, W Los Angeles Col, Culver City, Calif, 71-74; lectr design & drawing, El Camino Col, Torrance, Calif, 74-78; lectr photo retouching, Otis Art Inst of Parsons, Los Angeles, Calif, 80-81. *Bibliog:* William Wilson (auth), article in Los Angeles Times, 6/14/74; Ronald Steen (auth), Gloriane Harris and Steven Semeyer, Artweek, 9/27/75; Peter Frank (auth), Unslick in Los Angeles, Art in Am, 9-10/78; Juri Koll (dir), Oil and Water--A Portrait of Gloriane Harris (film), 83. *Mem:* Artists Equity. *Media:* Oil, Watercolor. *Mailing Add:* 7740 Redlands St M2074 Playa Del Rey CA 90293

HARRIS, HARVEY SHERMAN
PAINTER, EDUCATOR
b Hartford, Conn, Aug 31, 15. *Study:* Hartford Art Sch, dipl; Kansas City Art Inst, with Thomas Hart Benton & John de Martelly; Yale Univ, with Josef Albers & Willem de Kooning, BFA & MFA. *Work:* Speed Mus, Louisville, Ky; Southern Ill Univ Mitchell Gallery, Carbondale; State Univ NY Oswego Libr Art; La State Univ Libr Art, Baton Rouge; La State Div of the Arts, Baton Rouge Centroplex. *Comn:* Illustrations for Look Homeward, Angel, 45; sets/costumes, Rockefeller Fund Louisville Symphony & Opera, 56 & 57. *Exhib:* Drawings, USA, Mus Mod Art, New York, 55; Pa Acad Nat Watercolor & Drawing Biennial, 58 & 59; Butler Inst Am Art Nat Mid-Year Show, Youngstown, Ohio, 64; Norfolk Mus 21st Am Drawing Biennial & Smithsonian Inst Traveling Drawing Show, 65; Avanti Gallery, New York, 75; and others. *Teaching:* Lectr basic studio graphic design, Louisville Art Ctr & Univ Louisville, 54-57; asst prof drawing & art hist, State Univ NY Oswego, 57-60; assoc prof, Southern Ill Univ, Carbondale, 60-67; prof painting & drawing, La State Univ, Baton Rouge, 67-82, prof emer, 82- *Awards:* Hon Mention, Conn Artist-Teachers, Yale Art Gallery, 49; Robert B Tunstall Prize, Norfolk Mus 21st Am Drawing Biennial, 65. *Bibliog:* Ann Price (auth), Harvey Harris, Cataloguing a Lifetime of Artwork, Baton Rouge Morning Advocate, 1/24/88. *Mem:* Artists Equity. *Media:* All Media. *Dealer:* Michael Stone Collection 1055 Thomas Jefferson St NW Washington DC 20007. *Mailing Add:* 2209 Glendale Ave Baton Rouge LA 70808

HARRIS, LEON A, JR
COLLECTOR, PATRON
b New York, NY, June 20, 26. *Study:* Harvard Col. *Collection:* Paintings, drawings and prints. *Publ:* Auth, The great picture robbery, Young France, The fine art of political wit & Only to God: the life of Godfrey Lowell Cabot; articles in NY Times, New York Mag, Town & Country, Harper's Bazaar, Esquire, Good Housekeeping, McCalls & Encycl Americana. *Mailing Add:* 4512 Fairfax Dallas TX 47205

HARRIS, LILY MARJORIE
ART DEALER, ADMINISTRATOR
b Rochester, NY, Nov 12, 56. *Study:* Syracuse Univ, BFA(textile design), 78; Victoria & Albert Mus, London, 78; Rochester Inst Technol, MS, 81. *Pos:* Restorer, Metrop Mus Art, New York, 78-79; colorist, Thomas Strahan Co, Chelsea, Mass, 79; asst dir, George Frederic Gallery, Rochester, NY, 82-83; admin asst, Thomas Burke Woodworkers, Rochester, NY, 84-85; dir-owner, Galerie Oboussier, Nantucket, Mass, 84-86; asst dir, Main St Gallery, Nantucket, 86- *Teaching:* Instr, Mem Art Gallery, Rochester, 80; workshop instr, Nantucket Island Sch Design & Arts, 81. *Mem:* Am Asn Mus. *Specialty:* Contemporary art, fine crafts, and photography. *Mailing Add:* PO Box 532 Nantucket MA 02554

HARRIS, PAUL
SCULPTOR
b Orlando, Fla, Nov 5, 25. *Study:* With Joy Karen Winslow, Orlando; Univ NMex; New Sch Social Res, with Johannes Molzahn; Hans Hofmann Sch. *Work:* Los Angeles Co Mus Art; Mus Mod Art, New York; Univ NMex; Yale Univ; San Francisco Mus Mod Art; Neue Galerie der Stadt Aachen. *Exhib:* Sculpture USA, 59 & Hans Hofmann & His Students, 64-65, Mus Mod Art, New York; Sculpture of the Sixties, Los Angeles Co Mus & Sao Paulo Biennial, 67; Crocker Art Gallery Asn, Sacramento, 68; Soft Art, NJ Mus, 69; New Vein Show, Vienna, Cologne, Belgrade, Baden-Baden, Geneva, Brussels & Milan, 69-70; solo exhibs, San Francisco Mus Art, 72, Univ Calif, Santa Barbara, 72, Univ NMex, 73 & Ark Art Ctr, Little Rock, 74 & Galerie Redmann, Berlin, 90, 91 & 92. *Teaching:* Instr art, Univ NMex, Knox Col, BWI, New Paltz State Col, Calif Art Inst, Cath Univ Chile, NY Univ & Univ Calif Berkeley; prof art, Calif Col Arts & Crafts, retired. *Awards:* Neallie Sullivan Award, 67; Tamarind Fel, 69-70; Resident MacDowell Colony, 77; Longview Found Grant, 78; Guggenheim Fel, 79. *Media:* Bronze, Cloth. *Publ:* Contribr, Art News & Art in Am; illusr, Dorothy Schmidt's Torso, 74 & Pas d' Une, 79. *Mailing Add:* Box 930 Bolinas CA 94924

HARRIS, PAUL ROGERS
CURATOR, DIRECTOR
b Dallas, Tex, Jan 2, 33. *Study:* NTex State Univ, BA, 54, MA, 56; NY Univ, 65-67; Inst Arts Admin, Harvard Univ, cert, 78. *Collections Arranged:* Emerging Texas Photographers (with catalog), 80, Hearts & Flowers (with catalog), 82, James Dowell: Paintings (with catalog), 83; Inaugural Exhibition, Gateway Gallery, Dallas Mus Fine Art, 84; Handmade in Texas, Craft Guild Dallas, 87; City Life: Views of the City, Zoomorphism: Animals in Art & A Decade of Dallas Crafts, 1949-1959, 88; Houses of God: Charles De Bus, 89; Texas Printmakers: 1940-1965, 90; Mystery and Intrigue, Peregrine Gallery, Dallas, 91; Metal and Mettle: Art and Spirit, Ida Green Gallery, Austin Col, Sherman, Tex, 92; Landscape Remembered: Paintings by Mary Vernon, Wichita Falls Mus & Art Ctr, Tex, 93. *Pos:* Coordr educ servs, Mus Mod Art, New York, 66-70; dir, The Art Ctr, Waco, Tex, 74-86; chmn visual arts & archit adv panel, Tex Comn on the Arts, 80-83; exec dir, Craft Guild Dallas, 86-88; mem, Arts Adv Comt, Mus African-Am Life & Culture, Dallas, 90- *Teaching:* Supvr art, Children's House, Dallas Mus Contemp Arts, Tex, 60-65; head dept art educ, Southern Methodist Univ, Dallas, Tex, 70-74; instr art, El Centro Col, Dallas, 92 & Navarro Col, Corsicana, Tes, 92- *Awards:* Alumni Hon, NTex State Univ, 85; Twentieth Anniversary Celebration, Art Ctr, Waco, 92. *Bibliog:* Janet Kutner (auth), Texas small museums discovering each other, Art News, 2/77; Charlotte Moser (auth), Texas museums: Gambling for big change, Art News, 12/79; Janet Kutner (auth), A celebration of city life, Dallas Morning News. *Mem:* Am Asn Mus; Nat Art Educ Asn; Tex Arts Alliance (bd dir, 80-86); Am Crafts Coun. *Publ:* Auth, Gillian Bradshaw-Smith: Soft Sculptures & Drawings, 76, Richard Hunt: Sculpture, Drawings, Prints, 78, Pedro Friedeberg, 78 & many others. *Mailing Add:* 7211 Concord Ave Dallas TX 75235-4414

HARRIS, PAUL STEWART
CURATOR, MUSEUM DIRECTOR
b Orange, Mass, Mar 7, 06. *Study:* Antioch Col, BS; Harvard Col, SB(hist art); New York Univ Grad Sch Fine Arts. *Collections Arranged:* Assisted in installation of The Cloisters and medieval gallery displays, Metrop Mus Art, New York; numerous exhibs, Des Moines Asn Fine Arts, Iowa & J B Speed Art Mus, Louisville, Ky, 33-62. *Pos:* Curatorial asst & asst cur, Metrop Mus Art, New York, 33-38; dir & secy, Des Moines Asn Fine Arts, 38-40; sr cur, Minneapolis Inst Arts, 41, 46; dir & cur, J B Speed Art Mus, 46-62; dep dir, H F du Pont Winterthur Mus, 62-67; dir collections, Henry Ford Mus & Greenfield Village, Mich, 67-71. *Teaching:* Lectr Am Art, Univ Minn, 46. *Mem:* Am Asn Mus; Col Art Asn Am; Early Am Indust Asn. *Res:* Mediaeval European art, American art, European decorative arts and paintings, and modern art. *Publ:* Auth, Fourteen seasons of art accessions, J B Speed Art Mus, 60; also var articles in mus bulletins, 34-64. *Mailing Add:* RFD Chesham Marlborough NH 03455

HARRIS, ROBERT GEORGE
PAINTER, ILLUSTRATOR
b Kansas City, Mo, Sept 9, 11. *Study:* Kansas City Art Inst, with Monte Crews; Grand Cent Sch Art, with Harvey Dunn; Art Students League, with George Bridgeman. *Work:* Portraits, Phoenix Jr Col, Dept of Justice, Washington, DC, Seabury Western Theol Sem, Chicago, Ill, Wabash Col, Crawfordsville, Ind & Franciscan Renewal Ctr, Scottsdale, Ariz; also in many pvt collections in US. *Exhib:* Soc Illusr; Art Dirs Club, 43-46; New Rochelle Art Asn, 49; Westport Artists, 50; one-man show of portraits, Phoenix Art Mus, 62. *Mem:* Soc Illusr; Phoenix Fine Art Asn; Phoenix Art Mus. *Media:* Oil. *Publ:* Illusr, McCall's, 39-60, Sat Eve Post, 39-61, Good Housekeeping, 40-60, Ladies' Home J, 40-61 & other nat mags. *Mailing Add:* PO Box 1124 Carefree AZ 85377

HARRIS, TRACY
PAINTER
b Lawton, Okla, Aug 24, 58. *Study:* Southern Methodist Univ, BFA, 80, MFA, 83. *Work:* Mus Fine Art, Houston, Tex; Longview Mus, Tex. *Exhib:* Affinities, Univ Tex, Arlington, 88; First Tex Triennial, Contemp Arts Mus, Houston, 88; Lawnview Mus Art, Tex, 90; Graham Gallery, Houston, Tex, 91; Univ Tex, Arlington, 92. *Pos:* Mem Outreach comt, Dallas Mus Art, 87-92. *Awards:* Visual Artist Fel, Nat Endowment Arts, 87; Hugo Neuhaus Award, 88; Nat Endowment Arts, 89; and others. *Media:* Miscellaneous Media. *Dealer:* McMurty Gallery 3508 Lake St Houston TX 77098; Gerald Peters 2913 Fairmont Dallas TX. *Mailing Add:* PO Box 1210 Wainscott NY 11975

HARRIS, WILLIAM WADSWORTH, II
PAINTER, COLLAGE ARTIST
b Hamden, Conn. *Study:* Yale Univ, BA; Univ Mich, MA; also with Richard Wilt, Deane Keller & Jerry Farnsworth. *Work:* Galerie Moos, Geneva, Switz; Toledo Mus Fine Arts, Ohio; Yale Univ Collection; Mattatuck Mus Arts & City Nat Bank, Waterbury, Conn; Northwestern Conn Col, Winsted; and in pvt collections in Europe, Mid East & US. *Exhib:* Ringling Mus Art, Sarasota, Fla, 61; Galerie Georges Moos, Geneva, Switz, 64-69; Hub Gallery, Pa State Univ, State College, 73; Conn Soc Fine Arts, Wadsworth Atheneum, Hartford, 74; Am Painters in Paris Exhib, France, 75-76; Berkshire Mus Fine Arts, Pittsfield, Mass, 77; Munson Gallery, New Haven, Conn, 80-83. *Awards:* Top Award, Conn Artists 23rd Ann, Slater Mus, Norwich, 66; Top Awards, Waterbury Arts Festival, Conn, 67 & 68; Winsted Award, 75 & Top Purchase Award, 79, Northwest Conn Art Asn. *Bibliog:* Prize Winning Art, Bk 7, Allied Publ, 67. *Mem:* New Haven Paint & Clay Club (bd dirs, 67-69); New Haven Festival Arts (bd dirs, 71-73); Conn Acad Fine Arts. *Media:* Oil on Canvas, Collage in Mixed Media. *Dealer:* Munson Gallery 33 Whitney Ave New Haven CT 06511. *Mailing Add:* 156 Chestnut Hill Rd Killingworth CT 06417

HARRISON, CAROLE
SCULPTOR
b Chicago, Ill, Oct 30, 33. *Study:* Cranbrook Acad Art, BFA, 55, MFA, 56; Cent Sch Art, London, with Robert Adams, Fulbright Scholar, 58. *Work:* Hackley Art Mus, Muskegon, Mich; Springfield Mus Art, Ill; Kalamazoo Inst Art; Cranbrook Mus Art; Fine Arts Complex, Western Mich Univ. *Comn:* Unity and Growth (brass & copper), City Oak Park, Ill, 66; Seated Figure (cast brass), Kalamazoo Art Inst, 69; Fountain (welded brass); Three Figures (welded brass), 72 & Motif (welded brass & copper), Western Mich Univ, 82; Friends Meet (welded brass), Cottey Coll, Nevada, Mo, 84. *Exhib:* Second Biennial Am Painting & Sculpture, Detroit Art Inst & Pa Acad Fine Arts, 59; New Horizons in Sculpture, McCormick Pl, Chicago, 61; Painting & Sculpture Today, Herron Mus Art, Indianapolis, 67; solo exhib, Women & Landscape, Kalamazoo Inst Arts, 76; Nat Acad Design Exhib, New York, 82 & 92. *Teaching:* Assoc prof sculpture, Western Mich Univ, 60-74 & State Univ NY, Fredonia, 75-78. *Awards:* Tiffany Found Fel, 60; First Prize, New Horizons in Sculpture, McCormick Pl, Chicago, 61; 161st Ann Artists Fund Prize, Nat Acad of Design, 86. *Bibliog:* Cesta Peekstok (producer), Art and Architecture in Kalamazoo (video), Western Mich Univ, 76; Marcia Wood (auth), Sculpture, Carole Harrison, Kalamazoo Col, 77; Cesta Peekstok (producer), Art is All Around Us (video), Western Mich Univ, 80; Virginia N Jones (auth), Contemporary American Women Sculptors, Oryx Press, 86. *Mem:* New York Artists Equity; Nat Asn Women Artists; Sculptors Guild. *Media:* Metal, Wood. *Publ:* Auth, Building three figures, Western Mich Univ Press, 73. *Mailing Add:* Box 19555 Kalamazoo MI 49019

HARRISON, HELEN AMY
MUSEUM DIRECTOR, CRITIC
b Richmond Hill, NY, Dec 4, 43. *Study:* Adelphi Univ, Garden City, NY, AB(art), 65; Brooklyn Mus Art Sch, Max Beckmann Mem scholar in sculpture, 65-66; Hornsey Col Art, London, Eng, 66-67; Case Western Reserve Univ, Cleveland, MA(art hist), 75. *Collections Arranged:* Seven American Women: The Depression Decade (co-auth, catalog), 76; David Burliuk: Years of Transition, 1910-1931 (auth, catalog), 78; Dawn of a New Day: the 1939/40 New York World's Fair (auth, catalog), 80; Lithographs of George Bellows, 82; Larry Rivers: Performing for the Family (auth, catalog), 83; Robert Gwathmey, 84; Jimmy Ernst: A Survey, 1942-1983, 85; Crosscurrents: East Hampton and Provincetown (coauth, catalog), 86; American Masters, 87; Ibram Lassaw: A Retrospective Survey, 1929-1988 (auth, catalog), 88; En Plein Air (coauth, catalog), 89; East Hampton Avant-Garde (auth, catalog), 90; Alfonso Ossorio: The Victorias Drawings, 1950, 91; Betty Parsons: Paintings on Paper, 92. *Pos:* Cur, Parrish Art Mus, Southampton, NY, 77-78; art critic, NY Times, Long Island Weekly, 78-; guest cur, Queens Mus, Flushing, NY, 79-81; exec dir, Pub Art Preserv Comt, 81-82; cur, Guild Hall Mus, East Hampton, NY, 82-90; dir, Pollock-Krasner House Study Ctr, East Hampton, NY, 90. *Teaching:* Instr, Sch Visual Arts, 85 & 86 & State Univ NY, Stony Brook, 92. *Awards:* Acad of Distinction, Adelphi Univ Alumni Asn, 86; Media Awards, Press Club of Long Island, 86, 87. *Mem:* Int Asn Art Critics, Am Section; Am Studies Asn. *Res:* Federal art patronage projects of the New Deal era, especially mural painting; the 1939/40 New York World's Fair; contemporary American Art. *Publ:* Auth, Dawn of a New Day: The New York World's Fair, 1939-1940, NY Univ Press, 80; Larry Rivers, Harper & Row, 84; contribr, The Figurative Fifties (exhib catalog), Newport Harbor Art Mus, 88; contribr, Remembering the future, Queens Mus, Rizzoli, 89; On the floor (essay), Long Island Hist J, 91; and others. *Mailing Add:* RD 3 Box 487 Sag Harbor NY 11963

HARRISON, HELEN MAYER (MRS NEWTON HARRISON)
ENVIRONMENTAL ARTIST, CONCEPTUAL ARTIST
b New York, NY. *Study:* Queens Col, BA; Cornell Univ; NY Univ, MA, 53. *Work:* Brooklyn Mus; Mus Mod Art, New York; Chase Manhattan Bank; Metromedia Inc; Washington Univ Gallery Art, St Louis; and others. *Comn:* Pasadena Parts 1 & 2, Pasadena Civic & Art Orgn; Yarkon River, Tel Aviv Found, Israel; Intersection: Pico-Seagate, Santa Monica, Calif; San Diego Landfill, Calif; Disappearing Path, Newport, Calif. *Exhib:* Maps, Mus Mod Art, Penthouse Gallery, New York, 77; Lagoon Cycle, Johnson Mus, Cornell Univ, 85 & Los Angeles Co Mus Art, 87; Mus Revolution, Zagreb, 90; Palmer Mus & Zolar Gallery, Penn State Univ, 90; Nagoya Bienale, Japan, 91; Washington Univ Gallery Art, St Louis, 91; Fragile Ecologies, Queens Mus, NY, 92; and others. *Pos:* Consult, Presidential Task Force on Educ, Nat Endowment Arts, 79; mem, Pub Art Adv Bd, San Diego, 83-88. *Teaching:* Prof visual arts, Univ Calif, San Diego, 81-, chmn visual arts dept, 83. *Awards:* DAAD Fel, Berlin, 88 & 89; 2nd Prize, Nagoyo Bienale, 91; Vesta Award, Women's Bldg, La, 89; and others. *Bibliog:* Robin Cembalest (auth), Ecological Art Explosion, Art News, Vol 90, No 6, 91; Arlene Raven (auth), Main Stream, Village Voice, 4/9/91; Craig Adcock (auth), Conversational drift: Helen Mayer Harrison & Newton Harrison, Art J, Vol 51, No 2, 92; and others. *Media:* Mixed. *Publ:* Illusr, San Diego as the center of the world, Los Angeles Inst Contemp Art J, 2/75; illusr, One full work and part of another, 12/77-1/78 & Great Lakes Meditations, summer 79, New Wilderness Lett, New York; auth, The Book of the Grab, In: Dialogue, Discourse, Research, Santa Barbara Mus Art, 79; The Book of the Seven Lagoons, Limited Eds Artists Bk, 85; A Lattice or a Serpentine, Seattle Arts Lett, 92. *Dealer:* Ronald Feldman Fine Arts 31 Mercer St New York NY 10013. *Mailing Add:* PO Box 446 Del Mar CA 92014

HARRISON, JIMMIE
JEWELER, CRAFTSMAN
b Shiprock, NMex, Feb 4, 52. *Study:* Univ NMex, 71-73; Acad Arts, Paris, France, 76. *Work:* Heard Mus, Phoenix, Ariz; Wheelwright Mus, Santa Fe, NMex; Northern Ariz Mus, Flagstaf,; Squash Blossoms, Vail, Colo. *Comn:* Gold buckle, watchband & bolo tie, Toh-Atin Gallery, Durango, Colo, 84. *Exhib:* All Navajo Show, Northern Ariz Mus, Flagstaff, 81, 87 & 88; Santa Fe Indian Market, NMex, 84, 85, 87 & 88; Indian Arts & Crafts Asn, Denver, Colo, 84 & 88; Gallup Ceremonials, Red Rock State Park, Gallup, NMex, 87 & 88; Northern Pueblo Show, San Idelfonso, NMex, 88; Heard Mus, Phoenix, Ariz, 88; Palm Springs Indian Art Show, Palm Springs, Calif, 88; Gallery of Functional Art, Santa Monica, Calif, 88. *Awards:* Best of Show, All Navajo Show, Northern Ariz Mus, 81; Best of Show, Navajo Nation Fair, 81; Best in Class & Design, Northern Pueblo Show. *Bibliog:* Article, Aspen Times, 2/84; Off hours, Farmington Daily Times, Farmington, NMex, 4/86. *Mem:* Indian Arts & Crafts Asn; Am Crafts Coun & Enterprises. *Media:* Gold, Silver. *Dealer:* Christophers Enterprises PO Box 25621 Albuquerque NM 87125. *Mailing Add:* c/o Christophers Enterprises PO Box 25621 Albuquerque NM 87125

HARRISON, JOSEPH ROBERT, JR
COLLECTOR, PATRON
b Chicago, Ill, June 20, 18. *Study:* Wabash Col, AB; Univ Chicago Law Sch. *Pos:* Pres bd trustees, Metrop Mus & Art Ctr, Miami, Fla, 74-77, chmn bd trustees, 76-79; mem, Metrop Dade Co Coun Arts & Sci, 76-78. *Mem:* Am Asn Mus (trustees comt). *Interests:* Museums, art education, sculpture. *Collection:* Late Cubist paintings and watercolors; late 19th century watercolors and drawings. *Mailing Add:* 3120 Munroe Dr Miami FL 33133

HARRISON, NEWTON A
ENVIRONMENTAL ARTIST, CONCEPTUAL ARTIST
b New York, NY, Oct 20, 32. *Study:* Yale Univ Sch Art & Archit, BFA & MFA; Pa Acad Fine Arts, cert. *Work:* Los Angeles County Mus, Calif; Brooklyn Mus & Mus Mod Art, New York; Mus Photog Art, San Diego, Calif; Washington Univ Gallery Art, St Louis; and others. *Comn:* Baltimore Promenade, Md Inst, 81; Pasadena Parts 1 & 2, Pasadena Civic & Art Orgns; Santa Barbara Sites, City of Santa Barbara: The Yarkon River, Tel Aviv Found, Israel; Intersection: Pico-Seagate, Santa Monica, Calif; Disappearing Path, Newport, Calif; San Diego Landfill, Calif. *Exhib:* Art & Technology, Los Angeles Co Mus Art, 71; Earth, Air, Fire, Water: Elements of Art, Boston Mus Fine Art, Mass, 71; Maps, Mus Mod Art, Penthouse Gallery, New York, 77; Mus Revolution, Zagreb, 90; Palmer Mus & Zolar Gallery, Penn State Univ, 90; Nagoya Bienal, Japan, 91; Washington Univ Gallery Art, St Louis, 92; Fragile Ecologies, Queens Mus, NY, 92; and others. *Pos:* Chmn Policy Panel, Nat Endowment Arts, Vis Arts Sect, 77-79; founding mem, Stewart Found Sculpture Gardens, 82-87. *Teaching:* Asst prof art, Univ NMex, 65-67; assoc prof art, Univ Calif, San Diego, 67-77, prof & chmn dept, 73-76, prof, 75- *Awards:* Nat Endowment Arts Grant, 75; DAAD Fel, Berlin, 88& 89; 2nd Prize, Nagoya Bienal, 91; and others. *Bibliog:* Madeleine Burnside (auth), Helen Mayer Harrison and Newton Harrison, New York Rev Arts News, 4/78; Kim Levin (auth), Helen and Newton Harrison: New grounds for art, Vol 52, No 6 & Peter Selz (auth), Helen and Newton Harrison: Art as survival instructions, Vol 52, No 6, Arts Mag; and others. *Publ:* Illusr, San Diego as the center of the world, Los Angeles Inst Contemp Art J, 2/75; illusr, One full work and part of another, 12/77-1/78 & Great Lakes meditations, summer 79, New Wilderness Lett, New York; auth, The book of the crab, In: Dialogue, Discourse, Research, Santa Barbara Mus Art, 79; The Book of Seven Lagoons, limited edition artists book, 85; A Lattice or a Serpentine, Seattle Arts Comn Lett, 92. *Dealer:* Ronald Feldman Fine Arts 31 Mercer St New York NY 10013. *Mailing Add:* PO Box 446 Del Mar CA 92014

HARRISON, TONY
PAINTER, EDUCATOR
b Gt Brit, Aug 18, 31; US citizen. *Study:* Northern Polytech Eng; Chelsea Sch Art, London; Cent Sch Arts & Crafts, London. *Work:* Aldrich Mus Contemp Art, Ridgefield, Conn; Achenbach Found, Calif Palace Legion Honor, San Francisco; Arts Coun Gt Brit, London; Royal Collection, Stockholm, Sweden; Nat Gallery S Australia; and many others. *Exhib:* One-man shows, San Francisco Mus Art, 64, Bertha Shaefer Gallery, New York, 68-69, 72 & 74 & Soho Ctr for Visual Artists, New York, 77; Third Int Biennial Print Exhib, Taiwan, 87; Nat Inst Arts & Lett, New York, 73; Wood, Anita Shapolsky Gallery, New York, 90; and others. *Pos:* Printmaking Workshop, New York, 74-75. *Teaching:* Instr drawing & printmaking, Columbia Univ, 71-; sr lectr painting, NY Univ, 72. *Awards:* Fel, NJ State Coun Arts, 87; Nat Endowment Arts Grant, 75; Creative Artists Pub Serv Grant, 76. *Bibliog:* Robert Erskine (producer), Artists proof (film), St Georges Gallery, 57; Collectors Choice, produced on ITV, London, 62. *Media:* Acrylic, Mezzotint. *Mailing Add:* 106 Hopkins Ave Jersey City NJ 07306

HARROUN, DOROTHY SUMNER
PAINTER, INSTRUCTOR
b El Paso, Tex, Nov 29, 35. *Study:* With Roderick Mead, 44-53; Univ NMex, BFA; Univ Paris, France(Fulbright Scholar), 57; Univ Colo, MFA, 60; with Peter Hurd, 63. *Work:* Univ Colo Fine Arts Mus, Boulder; Mus Fine Arts, Carlsbad, NMex; Nat Conf Women (albums), Nat Mus Women in Arts, Washington, DC. *Comn:* Mural of Sandia Mountains, comn by Jon ver Ploegh, Albuquerque, 77. *Exhib:* Am Watercolor Soc 112th Ann, New York, 79; 19th Ann Nat Art Show, Coos Art Mus, Coos Bay, Ore, 80; Images of Albuquerque, Albuquerque Mus, 82; Ga Watercolor Soc Exhib, Atlanta, 83; 12th Annual International Biographical Centrés Arts' Congress, Budapest, Hungary, 85; Focus International, American Women in Art, United Nations World Conference on Women, Nairobi, Kenya, 85; Church Farm House Mus, London, Eng, 88; St John's Col, Santa Fe, 91. *Pos:* Art dir, Wood-Reich Advert Agency, Boulder, Colo, 60-61. *Teaching:* Instr, Univ Colo, 61-62, San Francisco State Col, 63-65, Art Ctr Sch, Albuquerque, 75-79, Sanado Group, Sandia Base, Albuquerque, 78-80 & Univ NMex, 80-81. *Awards:* First Place Painting, Ouray Nat Show, Colo, 78; First Prize Watercolor, Carlsbad Area Art Asn, Carlsbad Fine Arts Mus, 80 & Black Canyon Nat Art Show, Hotchkiss, Colo, 80. *Mem:* Nat League Am Penwomen (pres Albuquerque branch, 82-84); NMex Watercolor Soc (pres 85-86); Artists Equity Asn (pres Albuquerque chapter & mem nat bd, 77-79); Albuquerque United Artists (mem bd, 78-80); Am Asn Univ Women (State Cultural chmn, 80-84); Univ NMex Fine Arts' Alumi Bd (pres, 89-91. *Media:* Tempera, Watercolor. *Publ:* Auth & illusr, Take Time to Play and Listen, Chapman Press, 63; auth & illusr, Phun-y Physics, Living Vine Press, 75; illusr, Mini Walks on the Mesa, 89. *Mailing Add:* 1365 Thunder Ridge Santa Fe NM 87501

HART, ALLEN M
PAINTER, ADMINISTRATOR
b New York, NY, June 12, 25. *Study:* Art Students League, with Anne Goldthwaite, Frank Vincent Dumond & Jean Liberte; Brooklyn Mus Art Sch, with Vincent Candell; Morelia, Mex with Alfredo Zolée. *Work:* Butler Inst Am Art, Youngstown, Ohio; Univ Mass, Amherst; Slater Mem Mus, Norwalk, Conn; Children's Aid Soc, New York; Union Am Hebrew Congregations. *Exhib:* Solo shows, Visual Arts Ctr, 70, Boiborik Gallery, 76, NJ Cult Arts Ctr, 78 & Broome Street Gallery, 92; Cober Gallery, 66-70; Joseph & Betty Harlem Gallery; Lerner Heller Gallery, 73; Visual Arts Ctr, 74-90;; Flat Rockbrook's Wildlife Exhib, 92; Multimedia Arts Gallery, 92; and others. *Teaching:* Instr painting, Samuel Field YMHA & YWHA, Little Neck, NY, 62-68; dir painting, Visual Arts Ctr, 68-; dean visual arts, Union Am Hebrew Congregations, 70-, resident artist, 72-; art consult, Bd Coop Educ Serv, 71-; art consult, Children's Aid Soc, NY, Painting instr Adult Dept. *Bibliog:* NY illustrated, NBC-TV, 70. *Mem:* Life mem Art Students League; Artists Equity Asn. *Media:* Oil, Mixed Media. *Publ:* Auth, articles, Lower Manhattan Twp, 2/20/71 & Herald, 5/1/71. *Mailing Add:* 34 Jackson Rd Valley Stream NY 11581

HART, BETTY MILLER
PAINTER, GRAPHIC ARTIST
b East Orange, NJ, Apr 15, 18. *Study:* Van Deering Perrine; Syracuse Univ Sch Fine Arts; Newark Col Eng. *Work:* Monmouth Col; Henry Chaucey Conf Ctr, Princeton; Monmouth Med Ctr. *Comn:* Panoramic view of Mobile, Ala & oil field, comn by Everet Eaves, Shreveport, La, 65; self portrait, comn by James Elder, Washington, DC; landscape, Philip Desind Collection, Silver Spring, Md, 75. *Exhib:* Pa Acad Fine Arts, 69; Philadelphia Mus Art, 70; one-person show, Capricorn Galleries, Bethesda, Md, 75, 78, 83 & 93; 36th Ann Nat Exhib of Audubon Artists, Nat Acad Design, New York, 78; Second Biennial NJ Artists, NJ State Mus-Newark, Trenton, 79; Nat Drawing 79, Stedman Arts & Sci, NJ, 79; Nat exhib, Boulder Ctr Visual Arts, Colo, 82;; Nat Open Exhib, Am Artist Prof League, Salmagundi Club, New York, 85; Mainstream USA, Butler Inst Art, Youngstown, Ohio, 87. *Awards:* First Place Drawings, Arts Coun Suburban Essex, 80; Drawing Award, Salmagundi Club, New York, 81; Cert of Merit, Catherine Lorillard Wolfe Art Club, Inc, 85; Grumbacher Award, Eighth State Exhib, Ocean County Guild, NJ, 88. *Bibliog:* Feature, New York Sunday News, 61; Michael Lenson (auth), Realm of art, Newark Sunday News, 67; Florence Lonsford (auth), Spot light on Kappa artists, Key of Kappa Kappa Gamma, Vol 91 No 4. *Mem:* Guild Creative Art (pres, 70-71); Arts Club, Washington, DC. *Media:* Oil, Pastel; Pencil, Ink. *Dealer:* Capricorn Galleries 4849 Rugby Ave Bethesda MD 20014. *Mailing Add:* Sea Colony 30 Bristol Dr Palm Coast FL 32137

HART, CLAUDIA
PRINTMAKER
b New York, NY, 55. *Study:* New York Univ, BA(art hist), 78; Columbia Univ, MS(archit), 83. *Exhib:* One-woman shows, Pat Hearn Gallery, New York, 88 & 90, Barbara Krakow Gallery, Boston, 89, Greenberg Gallery, St Louis, 90, Structures, Deson-Saunders Gallery, Chicago, 90, Tanit Gallery, Munich, Ger, 91; group exhib, White Columns, New York, 87; Scott Hanson Gallery, New York, 88; Rhona Hoffman Gallery, Chicago, 88; Thaddeus Ropac Gallery (with catalog), Salzburg, 89; Terrain Gallery, San Francisco, 90. *Awards:* Nat Endowment Arts, 89. *Bibliog:* Joshua Decter (auth), New Yorker, 3/5/90. *Mailing Add:* c/o Barbara Krakow Gallery Ten Newbury St Boston MA 02116

HART, JOHN LEWIS
CARTOONIST
b Endicott, NY, Feb 18, 31. *Pos:* Comic strip BC nat syndicated, 58- & The Wizard of Id, 64- *Awards:* Outstanding Cartoonist of Year, 68; Yellow Kid Award, Int Cong Comics for Best Cartoonist, Lucca, Italy; France's Highest Award Best Cartoonist of Year, 71. *Mem:* Nat Comics Coun; Nat Cartoonists Soc. *Publ:* The Peasants are Revolting, Remember the Golden Rule & There's a Fly in my Swill; The Wonderous Wizard of Id; The Wizard's Back; plus others. *Mailing Add:* Nat Cartoonist Soc 157 W 57th St New York NY 10019

HART, ROBERT GORDON
ADMINISTRATOR
b San Francisco, Calif, Dec 28, 21. *Pos:* Ed, Brooklyn Mus, NY, 59-61; gen mgr, Indian Arts & Crafts Bd, US Dept of Interior, 61-; pres, The Crafts Report Educational Fund, 90. *Mem:* Am Asn of Mus; Conseil Int des Musees; Foxfire Nat Bd; Am Crafts Coun; World Crafts Coun; Fed Interagency Crafts Comt (chmn, 74-). *Mailing Add:* 916 25th St NW Washington DC 20037

HARTAL, PAUL
PAINTER, WRITER
b Szeged, Hungary, April 25, 36; Can citizen. *Study:* Hebrew Univ Jerusalem, BA, 64, dipl, 66; Concordia Univ, Montreal, MA, 77; Univ Delle Arti, Salsomaggiore, Italy, Hon Dipl, 82; Columbia Pacific Univ, San Rafael, Calif, PhD, 86. *Work:* Mus Fine Arts, Montreal; Nat Gallery, Ottawa; Guggenheim Mus; Israel Mus, Jerusalem; Galleria Naz Arte, Rome; Musee du Quebec; Seoul Int Fine Art Ctr, Korea. *Comn:* Art Montreal (TV), 80; Olympic Project (graphs), Seoul, Korea, 86. *Exhib:* Festival Int Peinture, St Germain Pres, Paris, 78; Lyrical Conceptualism, Acad Raymond Duncan, Paris, 78; Concrete Poetry, Vehicule Art, Montreal, 80; solo exhib, Painted Melodies, J Yahouda Meir, Montreal, 83; retrospective, Psycho-Soc, Univ Lausanne, Montreux, Switz, 83; Osaka Mail Art, Japan, 85; Artistamp, Davidson Galleries, Seattle, Wash, 89; Visions of Space, Switz, 90; Ward-Nasse Gallery, New York, 92; Message Earth, Arte-Studio, Bergamo, Italy, 90-92. *Pos:* Dir, Ctr Art, Sci & Technol, 87-; consult, McGill's Teacher Training Prog, currently. *Awards:* Prix Paris, Acad Raymond Duncan, 78; Rubens, Antwerpen, Asn Belgo-Hispanica, 78; Selected Olympic Artist, Seoul, Korea, 88. *Bibliog:* Roger Delneufcourt (auth), Les expositions, Nouveau J, Paris, 6/24/78; Tom Konyves (auth), Poetry corner, Montreal Star, 7/21/79; Kara Szathmary (auth), Cosmic Symbiosis, Artist/USA, 7th ed, 82 History of International Art, Academia Italia, 84. *Mem:* Int Soc Artists; Graphic Soc; Les Surindependants, Paris,; founding mem Lyrical Conceptualist Soc (dir, 77-); Orbiting Unification Ring Satellite Project, Switz. *Res:* Interdisciplinary aspects of the relationship of art & space exploration. *Publ:* Auth, A History of Architecture, R Mass, Jerusalem, 72; Statement, Art in Am, 11-12/76; contribr, Artists/USA, 76-; auth, Painted Melodies, 83 & Black and white, 84, Lyrical Conceptualist Soc, Montreal; The Brush and the Compass, Univ Press Am, 88. *Mailing Add:* Box 1012 St Laurent Montreal PQ H4L 4W3 Canada

HARTE, JOHN
PAINTER
b Omaha, Nebr, June 11, 27. *Study:* Univ Wyo, Laramie, BA, 55; Univ Calif, Berkeley, study with Glen Wessels; Calif Col Arts & Crafts, Oakland, study with Jason Schoener. *Work:* Chevron USA, Richmond, Calif; Virginia Realty & Develop Co, Richmond, Va; Southern Distributors Inc, Washington, DC; Oakland Mus, Calif; Riverside Art Mus, Calif; Mono Lake Visitor Ctr, Lee Vining, Calif; Mrs Leonard Firestone, Rancho Mirage, Calif; and others. *Exhib:* Mesa Verde Nat Park Chapin Mesa Mus, Colo, 86; Los Angeles Audubon Soc, Calif, 87; Chevron Corp, San Francisco, Calif & Concord, Calif, 88; Barbara Sinatra Prof & Celebrity Auction, Rancho Mirage, Calif, 90; Spectrum Contemporary Fine Art, Palm Desert, Calif, 91; and others. *Awards:* Gold Star Merit Award, Marin Soc Artists, 71; Gold Ribbon, Chevron USA, San Francisco, 77. *Bibliog:* Calif Art Rev, 89, 91. *Media:* Watercolor. *Dealer:* Albertson-Peterson Gallery Inc 329 Park Ave S Winter Park FL 32789. *Mailing Add:* PO Box 2628 Palm Springs CA 92263

HARTELL, JOHN
PAINTER
b Brooklyn, NY, Jan 30, 02. *Study:* Cornell Univ, BArch; Royal Acad Fine Arts, Stockholm, Sweden. *Work:* Herbert F Johnson Mus Art, Cornell Univ; Brooklyn Mus; Munson-Williams-Proctor Inst, Utica, NY; Univ Nebr, Lincoln; Wake Forest Univ; and others. *Exhib:* four exhibs, Whitney Mus Am Art, 45-56; Munson-Williams-Proctor Inst, Utica, NY, 48-58; Chicago Art Inst, Ill, 51; Pa Acad Fine Arts, Philadelphia, 53; Mus Fine Arts, Houston, 55 & Dallas, 57; Walker Art Ctr, Minneapolis, Min, 58; Mus Art Indianapolis, 70; Lehigh Univ, 71; Butler Inst Am Art, Youngstown, Ohio, 77; Ins Arts & Lett, New York, 91; and others. *Teaching:* Prof archit & art, Cornell Univ, 30-68, chmn dept art, 39-59, emer prof archit & art, 68- *Bibliog:* Rosamund Frost (auth), Hartell: builder in paint, Art News, 10/15/45; Verlaine Boyd (auth), John Hartell, Arts, 10/80; Ray Matthew (auth), John Hartell, Art World, 4/83. *Media:* Oil; Watercolor. *Dealer:* Kraushaar Galleries 724 Fifth Ave New York NY 10019. *Mailing Add:* 319 The Parkway Ithaca NY 14850

HARTER, JOHN BURTON
CURATOR, PAINTER
b Jackson, Miss, Oct 7, 40. *Study:* Hanover Col, Univ Louisville, BA(art hist); Univ Vienna; Univ Pa; grad archaeol, Hebrew Univ, Jerusalem; La State Univ, MA(studio art); Williamsburg Seminar. *Collections Arranged:* Louisiana Folk & Native Art, 75, Louisiana Portrait Gallery (coauth, catalog), 77 & Louisiana Landscape, 81, La State Mus. *Pos:* Cur paintings & graphics, La State Mus, 67-83. *Mem:* Am Asn Mus. *Media:* Oil, Acrylic. *Mailing Add:* Louisiana State Mus 751 Charles St New Orleans LA 70116

HARTFORD, JANE DAVIS
TEXTILE ARTIST, CRAFTSMAN
b Erick, Okla, Aug 21, 27. *Study:* Univ Okla, Norman, BFA, 49; Univ Louisville, Ky, MA, 60; Parson's Sch Design; Univ Ill, art hist; Univ Hawaii, graphics with Jean Charlot; weaving with Lou Tate, Theo Moorman, Sallie O'Sullivan, Irene Waller, Mary Jane Leland & Jon Eric Riis. *Comn:* Ceremonial basket, Mrs LeRoy W Horne, Tulsa, Okla, 78; tapestry, Mr & Mrs Leonard Good, Chickasha, Okla, 82; eucharistic vestments, Zion Lutheran Church, Salt Lake City, Utah, 86 & 89. *Exhib:* Art for Worship Spaces, Salt Lake City, Utah, 85; Small Expressions, Amherst, Mass, 85 & Calif, 87; Liturgical Weaving Convergence, Toronto, Can, 86; Conference of S Calif Handweavers, Riverside, 91; Fabrics of Faith, Nat Cathedral, Washington, DC, 92. *Pos:* Bd dirs, Handweavers Guild Am Inc, 80-88, pres, 83-85, chmn bd, 85-88; bd dirs, Intermountain Weavers Conf, 79-83. *Teaching:* Utah Handweavers Conf, Logan, 82; Midwest Weavers Conf, Denver, Colo, 86; Conference S Calif Handweavers, Riverside, Calif, 91. *Awards:* Merit Award, Southwest Crafts Biennial, NMex Art Mus, 75; Fiber Award, Utah Arts Coun Exhib, 80; Cash Award, Intermountain Weavers Conf Exhib, 83; First Prize (cash award), Containers, Branigan Cult Ctr, Las Cruces, NMex, 90; HGA Award, Las Jejedoras Guild Exhibit, Fuller Lodge Art Ctr, Los Alamos, NMex, 91. *Mem:* Hon life mem, M M Atwater Weavers Guild (pres, 74-75); Cross Country Weavers; Las Tejedoras de Santa Fe y Los Alamos, NMex (vpres 90-92); Las Aranas Spinners & Weavers Guild, Albuquerque, NMex; Midwest Weavers Conf. *Media:* Handweaving, Surface Design. *Publ:* Auth, Fashion Ballet, winter 74, auth, Sheep to shawl, spring 77, & coauth, Flight into fantasy, fall, 80, Shuttle, Spindle & Dyepot. *Mailing Add:* 500 Washington Ave Santa Fe NM 87501

HARTGEN, VINCENT ANDREW
EDUCATOR, PAINTER
b Reading, Pa, Jan 10, 14. *Study:* Sch Fine Arts, Univ Pa, BFA & MFA, Univ Maine, Hon DFA, 87. *Work:* Mus Fine Arts, Boston; Wadsworth Atheneum, Hartford, Conn; Sheldon Swope Art Gallery, Terre Haute, Ind; Walker Art Ctr, Minneapolis, Minn; Wichita Art Mus, Kans. *Exhib:* One-man shows, Md Inst, Baltimore, Md; Kalamazoo Art Inst; Brooks Mem Art Mus, Memphis, Tenn; Chase Gallery, NY; Fla Gulf Coast Art Ctr, Clearwater; Kings Col, Wilkes-Barre, Pa & others; Artists of Maine, Am Fedn Arts Traveling Exhib, 64-66; Embassies Art Prog, Dept State, Washington, DC, 66-70; 200 Yrs Watercolor Painting Am, Metrop Mus Art, 67; Landscape I, De Cordova Mus, Lincoln, Mass, 70. *Collections Arranged:* Contemp Schs, USA, Contemp Churches, USA, 56-57, Ceramics & Dinnerware, 68 & Boxes, Sacks & Bags, 71, Univ Maine Art Gallery. *Pos:* Trustee, Haystack Sch Crafts, 50-55; comnr, Maine State Comn Arts & Humanities, 65-70; dir art gallery & collection, Univ Maine, Orono, 46-82, emer cur, 82- *Teaching:* Prof art, Univ Maine, Orono, 46-62, Huddilston prof, 62-82, emer prof, 82- *Awards:* Creative Aquarelle Award, 65 & Silver Medal, 74, Audubon Artists; Maine State Gov Art Award; Maine Bicentennial Prize; Black Bear Award, Univ Maine; Distinguished Prof Award, Emer Prof, Univ Maine; Hon exhib: Hartgen at 75 Founder and Futurist, Univ Maine Art Mus, 89. *Bibliog:* H J Seligmann (auth), Vincent Hartgen artist & teacher, Downeast Mag, 60; Ralph Fabri (auth), Watercolorist for all seasons, Today's Art, 65; Norman Kent (auth), 100 Techniques of Watercolor Painting, 70. *Mem:* Am Asn Univ Prof; Audubon Artists; Am Watercolor Soc; hon mem Can Soc Painter-Etchers & Engravers. *Media:* Watercolor, Drawing. *Publ:* Auth, Watercolor, Pen & Brush, 54; Defending the middle ground of the semi-abstract, Am Artist, 67 & Maine Alumnus, 75. *Mailing Add:* 109 Forest Ave Orono ME 04473

HARTIGAN, GRACE
PAINTER
b Newark, NJ, Mar 28, 22. *Study:* Pvt art classes with Isaac Lane Muse; Moore Col, Philadelphia, Hon DFA; Md Inst Art, Baltimore, Hon DFA; Goucher Col, Hon DFA; Towson State Univ, Hon DFA. *Work:* Whitney Mus Am Art & Metrop Mus Art, New York; Walker Art Ctr, Minneapolis, Minn; Art Inst Chicago, Ill; Albright-Knox Art Gallery, Buffalo, NY; plus many others. *Exhib:* Tibor De Nagy Gallery, 51-57; Carnegie Int, 61; American Vanguard, US Info Agency, Austria, Eng, Ger & Yugoslavia, 61-62; Martha Jackson Gallery, 62-70; A Decade of New Talent, Am Fedn Arts Exhib, 64-65; solo exhibs, Univ Chicago, 67 & Gertrude Kasle Gallery, Detroit, 68; Gruenebaum Gallery, New York, 84 & 86; and others. *Teaching:* Dir, Md Inst Grad Sch Painting, 65- *Awards:* Mademoiselle Mag Merit Award for Art, 57. *Bibliog:* Dr Robert Mattison (auth),Grace Hartigan, A Painters World (monogr), Hudson Hills Press. *Media:* Oil, Watercolor. *Dealer:* ACA Galleries 41 E 57th St New York NY 10022. *Mailing Add:* 1701 1/2 Eastern Ave Baltimore MD 21231

HARTIGAN, LYNDA ROSCOE
CURATOR, HISTORIAN
b Scranton, Pa, Aug 26, 50. *Study:* Bucknell Univ, Lewisburg, Pa, BA(art hist, cum laude), 72; George Washington Univ, DC, MA(art hist), 75. *Collections Arranged:* James Hampton: The Throne of the Third Heaven for Naives and

Visionaries (contribr, catalog), Walker Art Ctr, 74; Joseph Cornell: An Exploration of Sources, 82 & Sharing Traditions: Five Black Artists in 19th Century Am (auth, catalog), 85-, Nat Mus Am Art. *Pos:* Curatorial asst, 20th Century Painting & Sculpture Dept, Nat Mus Am Art, Smithsonian Inst, Washington, DC, 74-76, asst cur, 76-86, cur, Joseph Cornell Study Ctr, 78-; assoc curator, 86- *Teaching:* Vis art critic, Md Inst, Col Art, Baltimore, 85. *Awards:* Grad internship, Nat Collection Fine Arts, Smithsonian Inst, DC, 73-74; Nat Endowment Humanities Res Grant, 76-78; Smithsonian Inst Scholarly Studies & Special Exhib Grants, 86-89. *Bibliog:* Peggy Thomson (auth), Museum People, Prentice-Hall, 77. *Mem:* Col Art Asn; Art Table; Am Folklore Soc. *Res:* 20th century American art, especially sculpture 1930s to present, with major research conducted on Joseph Cornell; American folk art; Afro-American art. *Publ:* Contribr, Joseph Cornell: A Biography (monograph), Mus Mod Art, New York, 80; Yuri Schwebler: His Art and the Studio (exhib catalog), Hudson River Mus, Yonkers, NY, 81; Sited Toward the Future: Proposals for Public Sculpture (exhib catalog), Arlington Arts Ctr, Va, 84; auth, Made with Passion: Hemphill Folk Art Collection , Smithsonian Inst Press, 90. *Mailing Add:* Nat Mus Am Art Eighth & G Sts NW Washington DC 20560

HARTLEY, PAUL JEROME
PAINTER, EDUCATOR
b Charlotte, NC, Dec 30, 43. *Study:* NTex State Univ, BA; ECarolina Univ, MFA. *Work:* Burroughs Welcome, Inc; Southeastern Ctr Contemp Art; Rausch Indust Collection; NC Art Soc, Raleigh; Greenville Mus Art. *Teaching:* Prof, ECarolina Univ, 75- *Media:* All. *Dealer:* Artefino Gallery Charlotte NC. *Mailing Add:* Sch Art ECarolina Univ Greenville NC 27834

HARTLEY, W DOUGLAS
SCULPTOR, EDUCATOR
b Indianapolis, Ind, Nov 24, 21. *Study:* Ind Univ, Bloomington, BS, 48, MFA, 49; Kansas City Art Inst, MFA, 51; NY Univ, PhD, 71. *Comn:* Pres Frank H Sparks, Wabash Col Union, Crawfordsville, Ind, 58; Madonna & Child (sculpture), St Matthew's Episcopalian Church, Bloomington, Ill, 59; Jesse W Fell (bronze bust), City Hall, Normal, Ill, 76; Ambassador Adlai E Stevenson III, Adlai Stevenson Lect Comt, Bloomington, Ill, 78; Gen Chuck Yeager (bronze bust), Marshall Univ, WVa. *Teaching:* Asst instr sculpture, Kansas City Art Inst, 50-51; prof art hist, Ill State Univ, 54-89; retired, 89. *Media:* Bronze, Stone. *Publ:* Auth & illusr, Indian drawings of the Cimarron Country, Ford Times, 6/53; The head I almost lost, Reader's Digest, 7/57; The Search for Henry Cross: An Adventure in Biography, Ind Hist Soc, 66; co-ed, Readings in the Humanities, Xerox Corp, 76; auth, Things Invisible to See: An Introduction to Art Appreciation, Advocate Publ, 79. *Mailing Add:* 1001 S Fell Ave Normal IL 61761

HARTMAN, JOANNE A
PAINTER, EDUCATOR
b Brooklyn, NY, Nov 15, 31. *Study:* Brooklyn Col, City Univ New York, BA, 52; Queens Col, City Univ New York, MFA, 75. *Exhib:* Solo exhibs, Ingber Gallery, New York, 81 & Nassau Co Mus Fine Arts, Roslyn, NY, 88; 55 Mercer, New York, 87; June Kelly Gallery, New York, 87; Fed Hall, New York, 90; Islip Art Mus, NY, 90; Gallery North, Setauket, NY, 91. *Teaching:* Adj assoc prof art, Suffolk Community Col, Selden, NY, 75- & NY Inst Technol, Westbury, NY, 82- *Awards:* Va Ctr Creative Arts, 87-88 & 90; Ragdale Found, 89. *Bibliog:* Phyllis Braff (auth), Diverse paths at Nassau Museum, NY Times, 1/88; Karin Lipson (auth), Visual and mental images, Newsday, 1/88; Betty Booker (auth), Colony gives artists time for creativity, Richmond Times Dispatch, 7/88. *Mem:* Col Art Asn; Nat Drawing Asn. *Media:* Acrylic, Mixed Media. *Dealer:* June Kelly 591 Broadway New York NY 10012. *Mailing Add:* 111 Eighth Ave Suite 1004A New York NY 10011

HARTMAN, ROBERT LEROY
PHOTOGRAPHER, EDUCATOR
b Sharon, Pa, Dec 17, 26. *Study:* Univ Ariz, BFA & MA; Colo Springs Fine Arts Ctr, with Vaclav Vytlacil & Emerson Woelffer; Brooklyn Mus Art Sch. *Work:* Nat Collection Fine Arts, Smithsonian Inst, Washington, DC; Colo Springs Fine Arts Ctr; Oakland Mus Art, Calif; Achenbach Found Graphic Arts, San Francisco; Henry Gallery, Univ Wash; Istituto D'Arte Dosso Dossi, Ferrara, Italy, 89; Expo '90 Photomuseum, Osaka, Japan. *Exhib:* Santa Barbara Mus Art, 73; Whitney Mus Biennial, New York, 73; photog, San Jose Mus Art, 83; Bluxome Gallery, San Francisco, 84 & 86; Univ Art Mus, Berkeley, 86; Triangle Gallery, San Francisco, 92; and others. *Teaching:* Instr art, Tex Technol Col, 55-58; asst prof art, Univ Nev, Reno, 58-61; from assoc prof to prof art, Univ Calif, Berkeley, 61-, prof emer, 91- *Awards:* Emanuel Walter Fund First Prize, 85th Ann San Francisco Art Inst, 67; Hon mention, 4th Int Young Artists Exhib Am-Japan, 67; Award, Snap! Photography '85, San Francisco Arts Comn Gallery. *Bibliog:* Peter Nabokov (auth), Flight patterns--photographs by Robert Hartman, Camera Arts, 1/83. *Media:* Photography, Oil. *Dealer:* Triangle Gallery 165 Post St San Francisco CA 94108. *Mailing Add:* 1265 Mountain Blvd Oakland CA 94611

HARTSHORN, WILLIS E
PHOTOGRAPHER, CURATOR
b Fairfield, Conn, Sept 9, 50. *Study:* Univ Rochester, NY, BA, 73; Pratt Inst, Brooklyn, NY, 75; Visual Studies Workshop, Rochester, NY, MFA, 81. *Work:* Visual Studies Workshop Arch, Rochester, NY. *Exhib:* Contemp Still Life Photography Traveling Exhib, 82-84; one-man show, Mass Inst Technol, 83; Washington Projects Arts, Washington, DC, 83; The Bond Gallery, New York, 86; Lieberman & Saul Gallery, New York, 88; White Columns, New York, 88; and others. *Pos:* Assoc dir exhibs, Int Ctr Photog, 82-85, dir, 86-89, deputy dir progs, 90. *Teaching:* Instr photog, Int Ctr Photog, New York, 79-; teaching asst photog, Sch Visual Arts, New York, 79. *Awards:* Resource Access Develop Proj, State Univ NY, 79; Materials Grant, Polaroid Corp, 79; Major Fel in Photog, Nat Endowment Arts, 81 & 86. *Media:* Black & White. *Publ:* Auth, Printletter, Zurich, Switz, 80; coauth (with John Esten), Man Ray/Bazaar Years, Rizzoli, NY, 88; auth, Man Ray: Fashion, ICP, New York, 90; coauth, Czech Modernism, Mus Fine Arts, Houston, 90. *Mailing Add:* 98 Luquer St Brooklyn NY 11231

HARTWELL, PATRICIA LOCHRIDGE
ADMINISTRATOR
b Austin, Tex, Sept 22, 16. *Study:* Wellesley Col, BA; Columbia Univ, MS; Ariz State Univ; Univ Hawaii. *Collections Arranged:* Lew & Mathilde Davis, 72; Naive Art, Scottsdale & Honolulu, 72 & 73; Fibers '74, Dorothy Fratt Retrospective, 74; continuing exhibs, Civic Ctr Gallery, Scottsdale, Ariz & Arts Coun Gallery, Prince Kuhio Fed Bldg, Honolulu, Hawaii, 69- *Pos:* Dir, UN Children's Greeting Card Fund, 56-62; exec dir, Scottsdale Fine Arts Comn, 69-75 & Hawaii Coun for Cult & the Arts, 76-79; dir, Arts Coun Hawaii, 80-; ed, Artreach (bimonthly), 85-91. *Teaching:* Adj lectr, Univ Hawaii, Manoa, 83- *Awards:* Ford Found Study Arts Grant, 75. *Res:* Mainstreams in contemporary European, Middle European and American naive art. *Mailing Add:* 44-003 Aumoana Pl Kaneohe HI 96744

HARTWIG, HEINIE
PAINTER
b Santa Clara County, Calif, Feb 3, 39. *Study:* Self taught. *Work:* Monterey Inst Foreign Studies, Calif; Brigham Young Univ, Provo, Utah; Mills College, Oakland, Calif; Robert Louis Stevenson School, Monterey, Calif. *Teaching:* Instr art, pvt studio. *Awards:* First Place, Triton Mus, Santa Clara, Calif, 71; First Place Oil, First Place Popular & Best of Show, Twain Harte Art Show, 81. *Media:* Oil. *Mailing Add:* 349 Duchess Ct Copperopolis CA 95228

HARVEST, JUDITH R
CONCEPTUAL ARTIST, PAINTER
b Miami, Fla. *Study:* Barry Univ, Miami, Fla, BFA(cum laude), 73; Tyler Sch Art, Temple Univ, Rome, Italy, 73; New York Studio Sch, with Robert Storr, Ross Bleckner & Peter Agostini, 85; Sch Visual Arts, Urbino, Italy, with Enzo Cucchi & Kounellis, MFA, 87. *Work:* Aldrich Mus Contemp Art, Ridgefield, Conn; Art Forum, Galerie Thomas, Munich, Ger. *Comn:* Campbell Soup Painting, comn by Dorrance Family, Paradise Valley, Ariz, 92. *Exhib:* Recent Acquisitions, Aldrich Mus Contemp Art, Ridgefield, Conn, 88; Judith's Harvest, Artforum, Galerie Thomas, Munich, Ger, 88; Il Soffio Di Eolo, Isole Eolie, Salina, Sicily, 90; Small Works, 80 Wash Square East, New York, 91; Art from Italy, Harvest, Pistoietto, Paladino and Baj, Greene Gallery, Bal Harbour, Fla, 91; Modern Times Through the Concerned Eye, Katonah Mus, NY, 92; National Showcase Exhib, Alternative Mus, New York, 92. *Awards:* Honorable Mention, Small Works, New York, Brooke Alexander, 91. *Bibliog:* Andrea Pagnes (auth), Judith Harvest, Veranda del Arsenale, Venice, Flash Art, summer 90; Stuart Morgan (ed), Judith Harvest 1990, Artscribe, 5/90; Isa Vercelloni (ed), The seasons of Judith, Casa Vogue, 10/90. *Media:* Oil on Linen, Motorized Sculptures. *Publ:* Auth, Il Soffo Di Eolo, Mazzotta, Milano, 90; Where have all the suicides gone?, Pig Mag, Erik Oppenhiem, 92; auth & illusr, Safe Art, Spark, Romar & Melamio's Sch Bayonne, 92. *Dealer:* Bugno & Samueli Campo San Fantin 1966/A Venice Italy 30124. *Mailing Add:* 230 Central Park S New York NY 10019

HARVEY, (WILLIAM) ANDRÉ
SCULPTOR
b Hollywood, Fla, Oct 9, 41. *Study:* Univ Va, BA; additional study with Michael Anasse, Valauris, France & Charles Parks, Hockessin, Del. *Work:* Del Art Mus, Wilmington; Hunter Mus, Chattanooga; Greenville Mus Art, SC; Brandywine River Mus, Chadds Ford, Pa; Int Ctr Wildlife Art, Nature Art, United Kingdom. *Comn:* Sculpture, De Bartold Corp, Youngstown, Ohio, 89 & 90; Meijer Corp, Grand Rapids, Mich. *Exhib:* Hunter Mus, Chattanooga, Tenn, 77; Greenville Art Mus, SC, 80; Gibbes Art Gallery, Charleston, SC, 83; NSS, Port Hist Mus, Philadelphia, Pa, 89; Brandywine River Mus, Chadds Ford, Pa, 91; and others. *Awards:* Joel Meissner Award, 80 & Tallix Foundry Award, 89, Nat Sculpture Soc. *Bibliog:* Lisa Lyons (auth), Andre Harvey, Art Voices S, 5-6/80; John Caldwell (auth), Andre Harvey, Southern Accents, fall 82; Forbes FYI; and others. *Mem:* Nat Sculpture Soc; Artists Equity; Int Ctr Wildlife Art, Nature Art, Gloucester, United Kingdom. *Media:* Bronze. *Dealer:* Frank Fowler 1213 Ft Stephenson Oval Lookout Mountain TN 37350. *Mailing Add:* Box 8 Rockland DE 19732

HARVEY, DERMOT
KINETIC ARTIST, SCULPTOR
b Amersham, Eng, June 26, 41. *Study:* Univ Dublin, Trinity Col, MA; Univ London, MPhil. *Work:* Okla Art Ctr. *Comn:* Muse Aurora (liquid projections exhib operated by viewer), Brooklyn Children's Mus, 70; portable, multi-image aurora, Okla Art Ctr, 73; liquid projection exhib, Arnot Mus, Elmira, NY, 75; portable muse aurora, Continuum Mus, Ft Lauderdale, Fla, 76. *Exhib:* 24 Hour Technicolor Dream, Alexandra Palace, London, 67; Alliance of Light Artists, Fillmore East, New York, 69; Liquid Projections, Montreux Television Festival, Switz, 69; Projected Environments, New York Avant Garde Festival, 72, 74 & 75; Light Works, Intermedia Found, Garnerville, NY, 75. *Pos:* Dir theater of light prog, Intermedia Found, 74-; spec effects lighting for revue, Hot Stuff, Wailea Town Ctr, Maui, Hawaii, 80. *Teaching:* Instr kinetic & light art, Rockland Community Col, Suffern, NY, 75-77. *Awards:* Creative Artists Pub Serv Grant, NY Cult Coun, 71. *Bibliog:* Martha Geacintov (auth), He practices his art in the light side, 3/5/74 & Michael Hitzig (auth), Theater of light, 5/4/75, Journal News; Carol Lawson (auth), Film night with a Gothic twist, NY Times, 6/18/76. *Mailing Add:* 17 Church St Garnerville NY 10923

HARVEY, DONALD
PAINTER, PRINTMAKER
b Walthamstow, Eng, June 14, 30; Can citizen. *Study:* West Sussex Col Art, nat dipl painting; Brighton Col Art Eng, art teachers dipl. *Work:* Nat Gallery Can, Ottawa; Montreal Mus Fine Arts; Charlottetown Confedn Gallery, PEI; Seattle Art Mus, Wash; Albright-Knox Mus, Buffalo, NY. *Comn:* Large mural, BC Provincial Govt, Nelson, BC, 75. *Exhib:* Brit Print Biennial, Bradford, Eng, 68; Int Print Exhib, Seattle, 69; Art Gallery Greater Victoria, 79; Kyles Art Gallery, Victoria, 80; Can Nat Exhib, Toronto, 80; and others. *Teaching:* Prof painting, Univ Victoria, 61- *Awards:* Sadie & Samuel Bronfmann Purchase Prize, Montreal Mus, 63; First Prize, Vancouver Island Show, Art Gallery Gt Victoria, 64-66 & 69; First Prize, Exhib Can Art, Vancouver Art Gallery, 64. *Bibliog:* Tony Emery (auth), Canadian art today, Artscanada, 65. *Mem:* Royal Can Acad Arts. *Dealer:* Paul Kuhn Fine Arts Gallery Calgary AB Canada; North Park Gallery Store St Victoria BC Canada. *Mailing Add:* 1025 Joan Crescent Victoria BC V8S 3L3 Canada

HARVEY, DONALD GILBERT
SCULPTOR, INSTRUCTOR
b Louisville, Ky, June 25, 47. *Study:* Dixie Col, 65; Utah State Univ, BFA, 69; Univ Hawaii, MFA, 71. *Work:* Honolulu Acad Arts, Hawaii; State Found Cult & Arts, Honolulu; Utah State Univ; Honolulu Community Col; Honolulu Int Airport; and others. *Exhib:* Hawaii Craftsman, 69-70; Artist of Hawaii, 70; Easter Art Festival, Honolulu, 70-71; one-man show, Contemp Art Ctr Pac, 72; Artist Hawaii, Honolulu Acad Arts, 83. *Teaching:* Lectr art, Univ Hawaii, 70-71; instr art, Kamehameha High Sch, 71- *Awards:* Honolulu Acad Arts Purchase Award, 70; Purchase Award, Contemp Art Ctr, Hawaii, 78; Juror's Award of Excellence, Easter Art Festival, 79. *Bibliog:* Nicholas Roukes (auth), Masters of Wood Sculpture, Watson-Guptill. *Mem:* Hawaii Painters & Sculptors League; Nat Art Educ Asn. *Media:* Mixed Media. *Mailing Add:* Sch Art Univ Akron Akron OH 44325

HARVEY, ROBERT MARTIN
PAINTER
b Lexington, NC, Sept 16, 24. *Study:* Ringling Sch Art, with Elmer Harmes & Georgia Warren; San Francisco Art Inst, with Nathan Oliveira & Sonia Gechtoff. *Work:* Corcoran Gallery Art & Hirshhorn Collection, Washington, DC; Wichita Art Mus, Kans; Fine Arts Mus of the South, Mobile, Ala; Stanford Univ Mus, Calif; Crown-Zellerbach Found, San Francisco; and others. *Exhib:* American Painting, Va Mus Fine Arts, Richmond, 66; Butler Inst Am Art, Youngstown, Ohio, 66; Univ Ill, 67 & 69; Phoenix Art Mus; Centro Cult de Los Estados Unidos, Madrid, 77; Malacke Gallery, Malaga, Kresler Dos, Madrid, 79; and others. *Awards:* Award of Merit, San Francisco Art Festival, 63; Western Wash State Col Purchase Prize, 65; Mead Painting of the Year, 67; and others. *Mailing Add:* c/o Gump's Gallery 250 Post St San Francisco CA 94108

HARWOOD-BAUMEL, BERNICE
PAINTER, PRINTMAKER
b Brooklyn, NY. *Study:* 5 Towns Music & Art Asn, NY, with Jacob Lawrence, 57-58; Hofstra Univ, Hempstead, NY, with Pearl Fine, BS(Art Educ), 68-73; Ruth Leaf Studio, Douglastown, NY, 80-85; Pratt Graphics Ctr, New York, 85-86; Studio Camnitzer, Valdottavo, Italy, with David Finkbeiner, 85. *Work:* Am Stock Exchange, New York; IBM, Bethlehem, Pa; Chase Manhattan Bank, New York; Nassau Co Mus Fine Art, Roslyn, NY; Arthur Andersen & Co, St Louis, Mo. *Exhib:* Solo exhib, Etchings & Monoprints, Calkins, Gallery, Hofstra, NY, 85; Nat Asn Women Artists Traveling Print, Greenville Mus Art, NC, 86, Albrecht Mus Art, St Joseph, Mo, 86, & Corcoran Sch Art, Washington, DC, 87; Works on Paper, Monmouth Mus, NJ, 87 & Bergen Community Mus, Paramus, NJ, 87; Long Island Artists, Nassau Co Mus, Roslyn, NY, 88; Body Conscious, Elaine Benson Gallery, Bridgehampton, NY, 89; Mari Gallery, Westchester, NY, 90. *Pos:* Nassau Co Mus Fine Arts (bd adv 81-88); Graphic Eye Gallery, Port Washington, NY (pres, 86-88); Nat Asn Women Artists (juror graphics, 88-90). *Teaching:* Artist in residence, Monoprints, Syosset High Sch, NY, 86. *Awards:* Second Prize, Emily Lowe Gallery, Hofstra Univ, 83; Leila Sawyer Award, Ann Exhib, Nat Asn Women Artists, 83; Award Excellence, Long Beach Mus, Long Beach Art Asn, 85. *Bibliog:* Interview with Artist, Art In the World Radio Program Nassau Community College. *Mem:* Artists Equity Asn, NY; Nat Asn Women Artists (juror, 88-90); Long Beach Art League; Nat Mus Women in the Arts (charter mem). *Media:* Etchings, Monoprints. *Mailing Add:* 835 Fiske St Woodmere NY 11598

HASEGAWA, NORIKO
PAINTER
b Toyama Prefecture, Japan; US citizen. *Study:* Toyama Univ, Japan, BS(pharmacy), 56 & PhD(pharmacy), 71; private intsr Ikebana, MA(design), 65. *Work:* Nat Mus Women Art, Washington, DC; San Francisco Art Comn, Calif; Redwood City Pub Libr, Calif; Marriott Suite Hotel, Reston, Va; Kaiser Permanente, Vallejo, Calif. *Comn:* Painting of Koi, Redwood City Pub Libr, Calif, 88. *Exhib:* Rocky Mountian Watermedia Exhib, Foothill Art Ctr, Golden, Colo, 89; one women shows, Watercolors, Student Union Art Gallery, San Francisco, Calif, 88 & Stanford Fac Club, Palo Alto, Calif, 90; Allied artists Am Ann, Nat Arts Club, New York, 90; East Meets West (2 artists), Exhib Gallery, Marin Co Ctr, San Rafael, Calif, 91; Biennial Watercolor Exhib, Triton Mus Art, Santa Clara, Calif, 92. *Awards:* David & Elsie Ject-Key Mem Award, Audubon Artists Exhib, Audubon Artists Inc, 87; medal honor, Katherine Lorilart Wolf Art Club Ann, The Club, 88; best show, Marin Art Guild, The Guild, 88. *Bibliog:* John Schwartz (auth), East meets west, Am Artists Mag, Spring, 90. *Mem:* Watercolor West; Midwest Watercolor Soc; West Coast Watercolor Soc; Audubon Artists Inc; Nat Asn Women Artists. *Media:* Watercolor. *Mailing Add:* 3105 Burkhart Lane Sebastopol CA 95472

HASELTINE, JAMES LEWIS
PRINTMAKER, PAINTER
b Portland, Ore, Nov 7, 24. *Study:* Portland Mus Art Sch, Ore, 47 & 49; Art Inst Chicago, 47-48; Brooklyn Mus Sch, 50-51. *Work:* Portland Art Mus, Ore; Oakland Art Mus, Calif; Mus Art, Univ Ore; Fine Art Mus, Univ Utah. *Exhib:* Libr Cong, Washington, DC, 51; Brooklyn Mus, NY, 51-52; Portland Art Mus, Ore, 51-58; Seattle Art Mus, Wash, 52, 53, 57 & 59; San Francisco Mus Art, Calif, 53-54; Evergreen State Col, 82; Phillips Gallery, Salt Lake City, Utah, 84. *Pos:* Dir, Salt Lake Art Ctr, Utah, 61-67; exec dir, Wash State Arts Comn, Olympia, 67-80. *Teaching:* Vis lectr art hist, Univ Utah, 64-65. *Awards:* Purchase Prize, Portland Art Mus, 53; best monogr, Mormon Hist Asn, 65. *Mem:* Western Asn Art Mus (pres, 64-66); British Am Arts Asn (bd mem, 80-83); Nat Assembly State & Prov Arts Agencies (exec comt, 68-70); Nat Endowment Arts (mus panel, 70-72 & visual arts policy panel, 77-79). *Media:* Oil; Woodcut, Drawing. *Publ:* Auth, 100 Years of Utah Painting, 65; contribr, Mus News, 65; Utah Hist Quart, Dialogue & American West, 66. *Mailing Add:* 3820 Sunset Beach Dr NW Olympia WA 98502

HASELTINE, MAURY (MARGARET WILSON)
PAINTER, CONSULTANT
b Portland, Ore, May 7, 25. *Study:* Reed Col; Pac Northwest Col Art, Portland; Eastern NMex Univ. *Work:* Salt Lake Art Ctr, Utah; Mus Art, Univ Ore, Eugene; State Capital Mus, Evergreen State Col, Olympia, Wash; Nora Eccles Harrison Art Mus, Logan, Utah. *Comn:* Assemblage collage mural, Donald Lloyd, Assoc Grocers Off, Salt Lake City, 65; Plexiglass collage, Columbian Optical Co, Seattle, Wash, 74; M D paintings, office of Jack M Crabs, Olympia, Wash. *Exhib:* Governor's Invitational, State Capitol Mus, Olympia, Wash, 79 & 81; Univ Puget Sound, Tacoma, Wash, 84; Pacific Northwest Col Art, 84, Reed Col, Portland, Ore, 86; Northwest Ann, Ctr Contemp Art, Seattle, Wash, 89; Northwest Cubism, Tacoma Art Mus, 91; and others. *Teaching:* Instr oil painting, Salt Lake Art Ctr, 64-65; instr oil & acrylic painting, Creative Activities Ctr, State Capitol Mus, Olympia, Wash, 67-79. *Awards:* Southwest Fiesta Biennial Prize, Santa Fe, NMex, 66; 8th Utah Biennial Salt Lake Art Ctr Award, 66; 3rd Ann Painting & Sculpture Award, Tacoma Art Mus, 73. *Bibliog:* Prize-Winning Graphics, Allied Publ, 66. *Mem:* NW Print Coun, Portland, Ore; Arts Olympia, Wash. *Media:* Acrylic, Collage. *Publ:* Contribr, Forms Upon the Frontier, Utah State Univ, 69; contribr, The Art of Collage (by Gerald F Brommer), Davis Publ. *Dealer:* Marianne Partlow Gallery Olympia WA 98501. *Mailing Add:* 3820 Sunset Beach Dr NW Olympia WA 98502

HASEN, BURT STANLEY
PAINTER, PRINTMAKER
b New York, NY, Dec 19, 21. *Study:* Art Students League, 40, 42 & 46, with Morris Kantor; Hans Hoffmann Sch Fine Arts, 47-48; Acad Grande Chaumiere, Paris, 48-50, with Ossipe Zadkine; Accad Belle Arti, Rome, 59-60. *Work:* Walker Art Ctr, Minneapolis; Princeton Univ; Ciba-Geigy Collection; CCNY, New York; State Univ, Buffalo, NY; Albright Col, Pa; and others. *Comn:* Mural, YMHA & YWHA, New York, 47. *Exhib:* One-person shows: Landmark Gallery, New York, 76, Martin Sumers Gallery, New York, 78, Galerie T'Pandje, Belgium, 81, Landmark Gallery, New York, 81, Anita Shapolsky Gallery, New York, 86, 87 & 92 & Manhattanville Col, NY 87; Philadelphia Mus Art, Pa, 88; Anita Shapolsky Gallery, New York, 89; Albright Col, Reading, Pa, 92; Albright Knox Mus, Buffalo, 92; Rider Col, NJ, 92; Islip Mus, Islip, NY 92; Cleveland Art Inst, 92; and others. *Teaching:* Prof painting & drawing, Sch Visual Arts, 53-92; visting prof painting, Col Art & Design, Minneapolis, 66. *Awards:* Purchase Prize, Emily Lowe Found, 54; Fulbright Grant to Italy, 59-60; New York Found Arts, 90. *Bibliog:* Eric Protter (auth), Artists on Art, Grosset & Dunlap, 64; Susan Fleminger (auth), Arts, 86; Fred McDarrah (auth), The Artists World in Pictures, 89; and others. *Mem:* Fulbright Asn. *Media:* Oil, Acrylic. *Publ:* Illusr, Contes del'Inattendu, 59, De la Terre a la Lune, 61, Voltaire, 61, Moliere, 61, Lavoisier, Fourier, Faraday, 85 & Beyond the "Furies" by Paul Oppenheimer, 85. *Dealer:* Anita Shapolsky Gallery 99 Spring St New York NY 10012. *Mailing Add:* 7 Dutch St New York NY 10038

HASKELL, BARBARA
CURATOR
b San Diego, Calif, Nov 13, 46. *Study:* Univ Calif, Los Angeles, BA(philos & art hist), 69. *Collections Arranged:* Claes Oldenburg: Object into Monuments (with book), 71; Arthur Dove (author, catalog), 74; H C Westerman (auth, catalog), Whitney Biennial, 77, 79, 81, & 83; Marsden Hartley (auth, catalog), 80; Milton Avery (auth, catalog), 82; Charles Demuth (auth, catalog), 87; Donald Judd (auth, catalog), 89; BLAM! The Explosion of Pop, Minimalism and Performance (auth, catalog), 84 & Ralston Crawford (auth, catalog), 85, Whitney Mus Am Art; Burgoyne Diller (auth, catalog), 90; Agnes Martin Retrospective (auth, catlog), 92-93. *Pos:* Cur painting & sculpture, Pasadena Mus Mod Art, 72-74, dir exhib & collections, 74; cur painting & sculpture, Whitney Mus Am Art, New York, 75- *Awards:* Woman of the Year, Mademoiselle Award, 73; Leadership Among Professional Women, Los Angeles Soroptimist, 73. *Publ:* Marsden Hartley, NY Univ Press, 80; Milton Avery, Harper & Row, 82; BLAM! The Explosion of Pop, Minimalism and Performance 1958-64, 84; Burgoyne Diller, 90; Charles Demuth, Harry N Abrams Inc Publs, New York, 87; and others. *Mailing Add:* Whitney Mus 945 Madison Ave New York NY 10021

HASKELL, JANE
ENVIRONMENTAL ARTIST, PAINTER
b Cedarhurst, NY, Nov 24, 23. *Study:* Skidmore Col, Saratoga Springs, NY, BS, 44; Univ Pittsburgh, Pa, MA, 61. *Work:* Carnegie Mus Art, Pittsburgh, Pa; Mead Art Mus, Amherst, Mass; Milwaukee Art Mus, Wis; Mus Neon Art,

Los Angeles, Calif; Westmoreland Co Mus Art, Greensburg, Pa. *Comn:* Rivers of Light (neon, alumunum & glass block 5000 sq ft), Steel Plaza Subway Sta, Port Authority Transit, Pittsburgh, Pa, 85; Tree of Knowledge (neon 12' x 18'), William Pitt Student Union, Univ Pittsburgh, Pa, 87; Neon & Geometric (painted wooden forms), YMCA, Pittsburgh, Pa & Everbright Elec Signs Inc, Greenfield, Wis, 88; Windows of Light (nion), Massport, Boston, Mass, 90. *Exhib:* One-woman shows, Mus Art Carnegie Inst, Pittsburgh, Pa, 64, Color & Light Environment, Allegheny Col, Meadville, Pa, 85, Drawings & Neon Constructions, Assoc Artists Pittsburgh Ctr Arts, Pa, 87, Construction with Light & Installation with Light, AIR Gallery, New York, 88 & 90, Window Series, Concept Art Gallery, Pittsburgh, 91 & AIR Gallery, New York, 92; Winterlude, Westmoreland Mus Art, Greensburg, Pa, 90; Recent Abstract Works, Ctr Gallery, Pittburgh Ctr Arts, Pa, 92. *Teaching:* Instr art hist, Duquesne Univ, Pittsburgh, Pa, 68-78. *Awards:* AAP Juror's Award, Assoc Artists Pittsburgh, Susan & Morton Gurrentz, 82; Nat Torchtip Award, Soc Sculptors, Pittsburgh, Pa, Nat Torchtip Co Inc, 86; Pittsburgh Highlights Award, Three Rivers Art Festival, Pa, 87. *Bibliog:* Vilma Barr (auth), Best of Neon, Allworth Press/Rockport Pubs, 82. *Mem:* Soc Sculptors; Assoc Artists Pittsburgh; Artists Equity; Pittsburg Ctr Arts (bd trustees, 91-). *Media:* Neon, Fluorescent Light. *Mailing Add:* 146 Beechmont Rd Pittsburgh PA 15206

HASKIN, DONALD MARCUS
EDUCATOR, SCULPTOR
b St Paul, Minn, July 28, 20. *Study:* Univ Minn, study with Tovish, BA; Cranbrook Acad Art, MFA. *Comn:* Bronze figure & stainless steel fountain, 72, City Tucson; sculpture, Univ Ariz, 73; portrait, Tucson Boys Choir; portrait, McKale Ctr, Univ Ariz. *Exhib:* Contemp Crafts Mus, New York, 61; San Francisco Mus Art, 62; Preview '65, Alamo Gallery, Benicia, Calif, 65; Southwestern Invitational, Yuma Art Asn, 72-75; Tucson Mus Art, 75. *Teaching:* Lectr sculpture, Univ Calif, Berkeley, 63-65; prof sculpture, Univ Ariz, Tucson, 65-82, prof emer, 82; retired. *Awards:* First Prize, Minn State Fair, 58; Purchase Award, City of Benicia, 65; Purchase Prize Award, Yuma Art Asn, 72. *Media:* Metal, Cast. *Mailing Add:* 3242 N Kelvin Tucson AZ 85716

HASLEM, JANE N
DEALER
b Knoxville, Tenn, Dec 26, 34. *Study:* DePauw Univ, BA; Ind State Univ; Grad Studies Art Hist, Univ Md, 90- *Collections Arranged:* Var nat & int exhibs. *Pos:* Dir, Jane Haslem Gallery, Chapel Hill, NC, 60-65, Madison, Wis, 65-71 & Washington, DC, 69-71; pres, Haslem Fine Arts, Inc, Jane Haslem Gallery, Washington, DC, 71- *Teaching:* Instr art, Mecklenburg Co, NC, 58-59; resident assoc prog, Smithsonian Inst. *Mem:* Washington Print Club; Art Dealers Asn Washington DC (found mem & bd dirs, 81-89); Int Fine Print Dealers Asn. *Specialty:* Contemporary American paintings, prints; publisher of art catalogues. *Publ:* Auth Jane Haslem Gallery Newsletter, 72-; American Drawings/Realism Idealism, 86; David Hollowell, 86; Larry Day Paintings: 1958-1988, 88; Gabor Peterdi: Pacific and Other Recent Works, 90. *Mailing Add:* 2025 Hillyer Pl NW Washington DC 20009

HA-SO-DE (NARCISO ABEYTA)
ILLUSTRATOR, PAINTER
b Canyoncito, NMex, Dec 18, 18. *Study:* Santa Fe Indian Sch, with Dorothy Dunn Kramer, 35-39; Am Indian Art Inst Am; Somerset Art Sch, Pa, 41-42; Univ NMex, with Johnson & Haas, BFA, 53. *Work:* Am Indian Art Dietrich Collection; Phil Brook Mus, Tulsa, Okla. *Comn:* Navajo Antelope Hunt (mural), Maisel Store Entrance, Albuquerque, NMex, 35. *Exhib:* Painting & Reproduction Exhib, Paris, France by Paul Coze, 35; Philbrook Mus, 35-53; Scottsdale Nat Indian Art Coun, 67-74; NMex Art & Crafts Fair, Albuquerque, 74; NMex State Fair, 75. *Teaching:* Instr silversmithing, Santa Fe Indian Sch, 47-48. *Awards:* Poster Antelope Hunt & Scholar, Indian Golden Gate Int Exposition Courts, San Francisco, summer 39; First Prize, for: Faun Hunt, NMex State Fair, 75. *Bibliog:* Jeanne O Snodgrass (auth), American Indian Painters, Heye Found, 68; J J Brody (auth), Indian Painters & White Patrons, Univ NMex, 75; Doris Monthan (auth), article, Am Indian Art Mag; article, New York Art Rev, fall 88. *Mem:* NMex Teacher-Counr Orgn. *Media:* Shiva Casein. *Res:* Early explorers in Ft Wingate; Navajo sand paintings, mythology and history. *Publ:* Illusr, Dorothy Dunn's American Indian Painting, Univ NMex Press, 68; Robert Ashton & Jozefa Stuart's Images of American Indian Art, Walker & Co; Arthur Silberman's 100 Years of Native American Painting, Okla Mus Art, 78; Jamake Highwater's The Sweet Grass Lives On, 81. *Dealer:* Kiva Gallery 202 W 66th Gallup NM 87301. *Mailing Add:* 102 Viro Circle Gallup NM 87301

HASSRICK, PETER H
MUSEUM DIRECTOR, HISTORIAN
b Philadelphia, Pa, Apr 27, 41. *Study:* Univ Colo, BA(hist & classics); Harvard Univ(classics); Univ Denver, MA(art hist). *Collections Arranged:* Albert Bierstadt, 72, Frederic Remington (auth, catalog), 73 & Peter Rindisbacher, 70, Amon Carter Mus, Ft Worth, Tex; The Rocky Mountains, Buffalo Bill Hist Ctr, Cody, Wyo, 83; Treasures of the Old West, 84; Am Frontier Life, 87; Frederic Remington: The Masterworks, 88. *Pos:* Cur collections, Amon Carter Mus, Ft Worth, Tex, 69-75; dir, Buffalo Bill Hist Ctr, Cody, Wyo, 76- *Teaching:* Adj prof hist, Univ Wyo, Laramie, 80- *Mem:* Wyo Coun on the Arts (vchmn, 76-85); Nat Endowment Arts Mus (oversight panel, 91-). *Res:* Nineteenth and early twentieth century artists of the American West. *Publ:* Auth, The Way West: Art of Frontier America, 77 & Treasures of the Old West, 84, Harry N Abrams Inc; coauth (with Patricia Trenton), The Rocky Mountains: A Vision for Artists of the Nineteenth Century, Univ Okla Press, 83; auth, Drawings of the North American Indian, Doubleday, 84; coauth, American Frontier Life, Abbeyville, 87; coauth, Frederic Remington: The Masterworks, Harry N Abrams Inc, 88; auth, Charles M Russell, Harry N Abrams, Inc, 89. *Mailing Add:* Box 1000 Cody WY 82414

HASTENTEUFEL, DIETER
SCULPTOR, PAINTER
b Krefeld, Ger, 39; Can citizen. *Study:* Sch Applied Arts, Gelsenkirchen, Ger, 58-60; Werkkunstschule, Krefeld, 61; Werkkunstschule, Wuerzburg, 64; Acad Fine Art, Stuttgart, Ger, dipl, 68. *Work:* Art Gallery Ont; Art Gallery Hamilton; Art Gallery Peterborough, Ont; Sculpture Park, Liberty Hill, Tex; Can Coun Art Bank. *Exhib:* solo exhibs, Art Gallery Windsor, 83, Burlington Cult Ctr, 83, Kitchener-Waterloo Art Gallery, 83, New Art Gallery Toronto, 85, Ed Video Media Arts, Guelph, 91, White Water Gallery, North Bay, 91, Koffler Gallery, Toronto, Ont, 92; Hamilton Art Gallery, Ont, 82; Art Gallery Ont, 85; Cold City Gallery, Toronto, Ont, 87; Ed Video, Guelph, Ont, 88; Workscene Gallery, Toronto, Ont, 92; and others. *Teaching:* Sheridan Col, Brampton, 72 Dundas Valley Sch Art, 72-80, Manitou-Wabing Sports & Art Ctr, Parry Sound, 81-92, Mohawk Col, Hamilton, Artsake Inc, Ont; Vis artist in numerous schools. *Awards:* Grants, Can Coun, 76, 79, 82 90-91, Ont Art coun, 76-78, 80-82, 85, 90 & 92, CAIS, 83-92. *Bibliog:* Joy Ilakanson Colby (auth), article, Detroit News, 4/24/83; John Bentley Mays (auth), The Globe & Mail, 12/85; Kate Taylor (auth), Art About, Globe & Mail, Can, 5/15/92. *Mailing Add:* Nine Davies Ave Toronto ON M4M 2A6 Canada

HASWELL, HOLLEE
CURATOR, LIBRARIAN
b Albany, NY, May 4, 48. *Study:* Russell Sage Col, Troy, NY, BA; Simmons Col, Boston, Mass, MLS. *Work:* Russell Sage Col. *Collections Arranged:* Eisenhower at Columbia, 90. *Pos:* Art & music librn, Forbes Libr, Northampton, Mass, 73-78; librn, Worcester Art Mus, Mass, 78-81; librn, Sleepy Hollow Restorations, Tarrytown, NY, 81-87; cur, Columbiana, Distinctive Collection, Office of the Secretary, Columbia Univ, New York. *Mem:* Am Libr Asn; Art Libr Soc NAm; Soc Am Archivists. *Interests:* Development of resource collections to serve researcher and artist alike. *Mailing Add:* Cur Columbiana Columbia Univ 210 Low Mem Libr New York NY 10027

HATCH, CONNIE
PHOTOGRAPHER
Study: Univ Tex Austin, BFA, 73; San Francisco Art Inst, MFA, 79. *Exhib:* Who Counts?, Randolph St Gallery, Chicago, Ill, 90; Spectacular Women, Film Cities, St Paul, Minn, 90; After the Fact, Mills Col Art Gallery, Oakland, Calif, 90; Picture Plane to Object, Brea Cult Ctr, Calif, 91; In and Around: Selections from the Permanent Collection, Univ Art Mus, State Univ NY, Binghampton, 91; Sightlines, Newport Harbor Art Mus, Calif, 91; We interrupt your regularly scheduled programming, White Columns Gallery, New York, 92. *Teaching:* Fac, Calif Inst Arts, Valencia, 83-92; vis lectr photog, Univ Calif, Los Angeles, 91-92. *Awards:* Calif Arts Fac Develop Grant, 85-90; Charlene Engelhard Found Award, 88; Visual Artists' Fel, New Genre, Nat Endowment Arts, 91. *Bibliog:* David Trend (auth), Connie Hatch at Mills Col, Art Am, 5/91; H Pakasaar, Brian Wallis, William Wood (auths), Camera Lucida: What is not Seen, Camera Lucida, Banff Centre, Alta, Can, 91; Daniel Veneciano (auth), Power rips, Artweek, 12/26/91. *Publ:* Contrib, Form Follows Finance, Obscura, LACPS, summer 89; The DeSublimation of Romance: Consider the Difference, Spec Issue Sexuality, Wedge, winter 84; Serving the Status-Quo, Blasted Allegories: An Anthology of Writings by Contemp Artists, 87; Small Miracle, red, New Langton Arts: The First 15 Years, San Francisco, 90; After the Fact, Exposure, Boulder, Colo, 90. *Mailing Add:* c/o Roy Boyd Gallery 1547 Tenth St Santa Monica CA 90401

HATCH, JOHN DAVIS
CONSULTANT, HISTORIAN
b Oakland, Calif, June 14, 07. *Study:* Univ Calif, 26-28; Harvard Univ, 32; Princeton Univ, 38, Yale Univ, 40; St Johns, Santa Fe, NMex, 90. *Collections Arranged:* Traveling Exhibs for Carnegie Corp, 36-37; American Drawings, 42; Thomas Cole, 43; Pioneer exhib, Negro Artist Comes of Age, 45; Painting in Canada, 46. *Pos:* Exec secy, Seattle Art Inst, 28-29, dir, 29-31; vpres, Western Asn Art Mus, 30-31; asst dir, Isabella Stewart Gardner Mus, 32-35; dir, US art projs, New Eng States, 33-34; ed, Parnassus, 37-39; founder, Am Art Depository, 38 & Am Drawing Ann, 40; dir, Albany Inst Hist & Art, 40-48; ed, Albany Co Hist Asn Rec, 41-48; ed, Early Am Indust Chronicle, 42-49, pres, 46-47; dir, Norfolk Mus Art & Sci, 50-60. *Teaching:* Vis prof, Univ Ore, 48-49; Univ Calif, summer 49; coordr adv & actg chmn fine arts div, Spelman Col, 64-70; vis prof, Univ Mass, summer 71. *Mem:* Master Drawing Asn (trustee, founder, 62); Am Drawing Soc; Berkshire Co Hist Soc; Col Art Asn Am; MacDowell Colonist. *Interests:* Life of John Vanderlyn, and a study of American drawings and draughtsmen. *Publ:* Masterpieces and Details, J S Gardner Mus, 35; The Major Artist Comes of Age, 45; Painting in Canada, 46. *Mailing Add:* 640 Camino Lejo Santa Fe NM 87501

HATCH, JOHN W
PAINTER, EDUCATOR
b Saugus, Mass, Nov 1, 19. *Study:* Mass Col Art; Sch Fine Arts, Yale Univ, BFA & MFA. *Work:* De Cordova & Dana Mus, Lincoln, Mass; Currier Gallery Art, Manchester, NH; Portland Mus Art, Maine; Addison Gallery Am Art, Andover, Mass; Pa Acad Art, Philadelphia; and others. *Comn:* Mural, Army Map Serv Bldg, Washington, DC; mural, Profile Bank, Rochester, NH; mural, Kingsbury Hall, Univ NH; mem window, Student Union, Univ NH; hist mural, Ledges, Durham, NH; and others. *Exhib:* US Info Agency Exhib, Russia, 61; Centennial Exhib of Land Grant Cols, Kansas City, Mo, 62; De Cordova & Dana Mus, 62 & 64; Boston Mus Fine Arts, 67-69; Addison Gallery Am Art; and others. *Teaching:* Prof art, Univ NH, formerly; retired. *Awards:* City Manchester Award, NH, 64; NH Art Asn Award, 82; Portland Mus Art Festivals Award; and others. *Mem:* NH Art Asn (pres, 58-60); Artist's Equity. *Media:* Acrylic, Watercolor. *Mailing Add:* 28 Mill Rd Durham NH 03824

HATCH, (MR & MRS) MARSHALL
COLLECTORS
Mr Hatch, b Seattle, Wash, Aug 26, 18; Mrs Hatch, b Seattle, Wash, July 7, 18. *Study:* Mr & Mrs Hatch, Univ Wash. *Pos:* Mr Hatch, pres, Seattle Art Mus, formerly. *Collection:* Morris Graves, Mark Tobey, other Northwest artists, The Eight (Ashcan Group), Mexican paintings and ethnic art. *Mailing Add:* 1301 Spring St No 19 G & J Seattle WA 98104

HATCH, MARY
PAINTER
b Saginaw, Mich, Dec 12, 35. *Study:* Skidmore Col, 51-53; Western Mich Univ, MA(painting), 72; studied with Harvey Breverman, 74-77. *Work:* St Johns Univ, New York; Southwestern Mich Col, Kalamazoo Inst Arts, Mich, Art Ctr Battle Creek, Mich; Upjohn Co; Michigan Comn Art in Public Places. *Exhib:* West 81 Art and the Law, Minn Mus Art, 81; one-person exhibs, CPL Cult Ctr, Chicago, 82, Gilman-Gruen Galleries, Chicago, 92; New Talent--New Visions, Zolla/Lieberman Gallery, Chicago, 83; Kouroi & Korai, Kouros Gallery, New York, 84; Constructing A Modern World, Mich Coun Arts, Detroit, 90. *Awards:* Susan Kahn Prize, 83 & Charles Horman Mem Award, 85, Nat Asn Women Artists; Mich Coun Arts Grant, 85-86 & 88-89. *Bibliog:* Ben Mitchell (auth), To Get Hold of the Invisible, Passages North, Win 87; Western Michigan Presents, Western Mich Univ, Vol 3, No 3; Andy Argy (auth), New Art examiner, Chicago, 89. *Mem:* Chicago Artists Coalition; Orgn Independent Artists, New York. *Media:* Oil. *Mailing Add:* 6917 Willson Dr 2007 Pauline Ct Kalamazoo MI 49009

HATCH, W A S
PAINTER, EDUCATOR
b Bridgeport, Conn, Mar 19, 48. *Study:* Syracuse Univ, BFA, 70; Pratt Inst, MFA, 72. *Work:* City Col New York; Kemper Collection, Chicago, Ill; US Info Agency Embassy Collection; Univ Leeds; San Diego Mus; and others. *Comn:* Spec ed prints, Pratt Graphic Ctr, New York, 73. *Exhib:* Brooklyn Mus 19th Nat Print Exhib, 74-75; 5th Int Drawing Show, Mus Mod Art, Riejka, Yugoslavia, 76; World Print Competition, 77; Am Printmakers, Venice, 77; Sande Webster Gallery, Philadelphia, Pa, 75, 77 & 84; New Talent in Printmaking Show, Assoc Am Artists, New York, 77; 6th Brit Int Print Biennale, 79; Handmade Paper, Silver Cloud Gallery, Chicago, 81; Delaware Art Mus, 85 & 91; and many others. *Pos:* Cur, The Making of Print, OCCA, Del, 90. *Teaching:* Asst prof printmaking, Bradley Univ, 73-79; instr drawing, Columbia Col, 79-80; adj prof, Widener Univ, 82- *Awards:* Purchase Award, Los Angeles 2nd Nat Print Exhib, 74; Merit Award, Boston Printmakers 26th Ann Exhib, 74; Purchase Award, Eastern Regional Drawing Exhib, 83. *Bibliog:* The European Graphic Biennale, Print Rev, 77. *Mem:* Del Ctr Contemp Arts (vpres, 82-83). *Media:* Intaglio, Watercolor. *Dealer:* Sande Webster Gallery 2018 Locust St Philadelphia PA 19103. *Mailing Add:* 2100 Kentmere Pkwy Wilmington DE 19806

HATCHER, (L) BROWER
SCULPTOR
Study: Vanderbilt Univ, Nashville, Tenn, 61-63; Pratt Inst, Brooklyn, NY, BA(indust design), 67; St Martins Sch Art, grad studies sculpture, London, Eng, 67-69. *Work:* Adirondack Guide Monument, NY State Coun Arts, Lake George, 84. *Comn:* 100' structure, Southern Pac Gas Ctr, Calif Redevelopment Authority, Los Angeles; Herberger Theater Ctr, Phoenix Arts Comn, 92; 11' dome, State Off Bldg, Largo Regional Serv Ctr, Fla, 92; landscae & garden design with curved pergola & 8' come, Lloyd Nolan Hosp, Birmingham, Ala, 92; Thomas Jefferson Park, Dept Cult Affairs, New York, 93; and others. *Exhib:* Sculpture Inside Outside, Walker Art Ctr, Minn, 88-89; Houston Mus Fine Arts, Tex, 89; solo shows, Vaughn & Vaughn, Minneapolis, Minn, 89, Ctr Int Contemp Art, New York, 91, Paul Cava Gallery, Philadelphia, Pa, 91, Margaret Lipworth Fine Arts Gallery, Boca Raton, Fla, 91, Nancy Drysdale Gallery, Washington, DC, 92, Heath Gallery, Atlanta, Ga, 92 & Eve Mannes Gallery, Atlanta, Ga, 92; Sculpture Commerce Square, IBM Ctr, Philadelphia, Pa, 90; Roanoke Mus Fine Arts, Va, 90; Gateway Ctr, Prudential Art Prog, Newark, NJ, 90; Paul Cava Gallery, Philadelphia, Pa, 90; and others. *Teaching:* Fac sculpture, Bennington Col Art, 72-85; vis artist & lects, many col & univs, 70-91, including Walker Art Ctr, 89 & RI Sch Design, Providence, 91; sculpture, St Martins Sch Art, London, Eng, 69-72; vis prof, State Univ NY, Plattsburg, 88-89. *Awards:* Nat Endowment Arts Fels, 74, 80 & 90; Guggenheim Fel, 85; New York Found Arts Fel, 91. *Bibliog:* Irving Sandler (auth), Brower Hatcher Structures (catalog), Ctr Int Contemp Art, New York, 91; Carol Vogel (auth), The art market, NY Times, 2/14/92; Janet Wilson (auth), Sculpture of new dimensions, Wash Post, 2/22/92. *Mailing Add:* Diamond Point Rd Diamond Point NY 12824

HATCHETT, DUAYNE
SCULPTOR, PAINTER
b Shawnee, Okla, May 12, 25. *Study:* Univ Mo; Univ Okla, BFA & MFA. *Work:* Whitney Mus Am Art; Rochester Mem Mus, NY; Ft Worth Art Mus, Tex; Carnegie Inst, Pittsburgh, Pa; Albright-Knox Gallery, Buffalo, NY; Pittsburgh Univ, Pa. *Exhib:* Solo exhibs, Photograph & Sculpture, Flint Art Inst, Mich, 80, Rockefeller Art Ctr, Fredonia, NY, 82, Kirkpatrick Ctr, Okla City, 87, Chautauqua Art Asn Galleries, NY, 87 & Concept Gallery, Pittsburgh, Pa, 90; Public Works, Smithsonian Gallery, Washington, DC, 80; Sculptors Drawings: 1910-1980, Whitney Mus, New York, 81; Outside New York City: From Drawings to Sculpture, Syracuse Univ, NY, 82; The Sculptor as Draftsman, Whitney Mus, New York, 83; The Wayward Muse, Albright Knox Art Gallery, Buffalo, NY, 87; The Eloquent Object, traveling show, 87-89; Western NY Invitational, Albright Knox Art Gallery, Buffalo, 89. *Pos:* Comt chmn, Coun for Int Exchange of Scholars, Washington, DC. *Teaching:* Assoc prof sculpture, Ohio State Univ, 64-68; prof art, State Univ NY Buffalo, 68- *Mem:* Nat Sculpture Soc. *Media:* Metal. *Mailing Add:* c/o Barbara Schuller Gallery 345 Franklin St Buffalo NY 14202

HATFIELD, DAVID UNDERHILL
PAINTER
b Plainfield, NJ, July 16, 40. *Study:* Miami Univ, BFA, 62; Sch Visual Arts, 63; Art Students League, 64. *Exhib:* Nat Acad Design Ann, New York, 70, 73 & 84; Nat Arts Club Ann, New York, 69-72, 75 & 76; Am Artists Prof League Grand Nat, New York, 71-77; one man shows, Nat Arts Club, 76, Christopher Gallery, New York, 81 & Southern Vt Art Ctr, 86. *Awards:* Elizabeth T Greenshields Mem Found Grant, 73 & 74; Figure Award, Rockport Art Asn, 82, 88; Jane Petersen Prize, Salmagundi Club Ann, 85; Margaret Fitzhugh Browne Award, Northshore Arts Asn, 86; Emile A Gruppe Award, Northshore Arts Asn, 90; Wm Meyerowitz Award, Rockport Art Asn, 90. *Bibliog:* C Movalli (auth), article, Am Artist Mag, 12/81. *Mem:* North Shore Arts Asn; Allied Artists Am; Rockport Art Asn; Southern Vt Artists Inc; and others. *Media:* Oil. *Publ:* Illusr, Prevention Mag, 1/82. *Dealer:* Grand Central Art Galleries 24 W 57th St New York NY 10019; Gallery Henoch 80 Wooster St New York NY 10012. *Mailing Add:* 9 River St Hoosick Falls NY 12090

HATFIELD, DONALD GENE
PAINTER, EDUCATOR
b Detroit, Mich, May 23, 32. *Study:* Northwestern Mich Col, AA; Mich State Univ, BA & MA; Univ Wis, MFA. *Work:* Jacksonville State Univ, Ala; Tuskegee Inst, Ala; Brandt Corp, New Orleans; South Cent Bell, Birmingham; Southern Servs, Birmingham; and others. *Exhib:* Ala Art League, Mongomery, 81; Columbia Col, Mo, 83; Del Mar Col, 83; Ala Works on Paper, Auburn, Ala, 83; Competition for Spoleto, Marble Arch Gallery, Charleston, SC, 83; and others. *Teaching:* Elem art supvr, Auburndale Elem Sch Syst, Wis; instr jr & sr high art classes, Auburndale High Sch, 62-64; asst prof art, Auburn Univ, 64-71, assoc prof art, 71-81, prof art, 81-; part time instr hist archit & art, Tuskegee Inst, 68-69. *Mem:* Ala Art League (first vpres, 69-70, pres, 70-72); Opelika Arts Asn (bd trustees, 71-73). *Media:* Watercolor. *Mailing Add:* 550 Forest Park Circle Auburn AL 36830

HATGIL, PAUL
EDUCATOR, PAINTER
b Manchester, NH, Feb 18, 21. *Study:* Mass Col Art, BFA; Columbia Univ, MFA; Harvard Univ, summer 50. *Work:* Fed Aviation Agency, Balboa, CZ; Litton Industs; Ft Worth Nat Bank; Mitchell Energy Corp; Tandy Corp; Univ Tex, Performing Arts Ctr, Austin. *Comn:* St Paul's Lutheran Church, Austin, Tex; Univ Tex Bus & Admin Bldg, Austin; Our Saviour's Lutheran Church, Victoria, Tex; Design Assocs Bldg, Dallas, Tex; Rio Bldg, Austin; plus others. *Exhib:* 4th-6th Int Invitational, Smithsonian Inst, Washington, DC; Int Invitational, Gulf-Caribbean Exhib, Houston, Tex; Philbrook Art Ctr Int, Tulsa, Okla; US World's Fair Pavilion, NY; Hemisphere 1969, Tex Pavilion, San Antonio, Tex; US Senate, St Petersburg, Jacksonville & Fla Mus. *Teaching:* Instr, Columbia Univ; instr, San Antonio Art Inst; instr, Tex Fine Arts Asn, Austin; prof art, Univ Tex, Austin, 51-; retired. *Awards:* Univ Tex Res Inst Grants, 64 & 65. *Mem:* Am Craftsmen Coun; Col Art Asn Am. *Media:* Encaustic Painting. *Publ:* Auth, articles in, Ceramic Monthly, Sch Arts, Tex Trends Art Educ, La Rev Mod, Ceramic Age & Hellenic Chronicle. *Mailing Add:* 2203 Onion Creek Pkwy Austin TX 78747

HATKE, WALTER JOSEPH
PAINTER, EDUCATOR
b Topeka, Kans, Jan 11, 48. *Study:* 1st painting asst to Jack Beal, 69 & 72-73; DePauw Univ, BA, 71; asst to Alexander Calder, 74-76; Univ Iowa, Iowa City, MA, 81, MFA, 82. *Work:* Chase Manhattan Bank & Chemical Bank, New York; Metrop Mus Art, New York; Sheldon Mem Art Gallery; Smith Col Mus Art, Northampton, Mass; Art Inst Chicago. *Comn:* Mobile sets, Nat Tribute to Alexander Calder, Socrate, New York, 77. *Exhib:* Solo exhibs, Wilcox Gallery, Swathmore Col, 84, Emison Gallery, DePauw Univ, 86, Robert Schoelkopf Gallery, NY, 89 & Babcock Galleries, NY, 92 & 93; group exhibs, American Realism traveling exhib, San Francisco Mus Mod Art, 86-87, Narrative Paintings & Sculpture, Nassau Co Mus Art, NY, 91, New Horizons in Am Realism, Flint Inst Arts, Mich, travel 91-92 & Major Works, John Pence Gallery, San Francisco, 92; Am Drawings, Nat Acad of Design, NY, Travel 87-88. *Collections Arranged:* 1992 Mohawk (juror), Hudson Art Exhib, Albany Inst Art, Schenectady Mus & Planetarium, Univ Art Mus, State Univ NY-Albany. *Pos:* Asst to dir, Perls Galleries, New York, 73-77; vis artist/critic/lectr, Am Univ, Washington, DC, Dartmouth Col, Hanover, NH, Kansas City Art Inst, Smith Col, Northampton, Mass & Swarthmore Col, Pa. *Teaching:* asst prof, Pa State Univ, 82-86; assoc prof, Union Col, Schenectady, NY, 87- *Awards:* Ingram Merrill Grant, 81; Nat Endowment Arts Fel, 85; Pa State Univ Res Initiation Grant, 85; Union Col Humanities Develop Grants, 87, 88 & 89. *Bibliog:* John Russell (auth), The many faces of naturalism, New York Times, 8/11/80; Donald Lambert (auth), article, Am Artist, 10/82; PBS (dir), The Sheldon Mus Art (film), 89. *Media:* Oil, Watercolor. *Dealer:* Babcock Galleries 724 Fifth Ave New York NY 10019. *Mailing Add:* 1513 Lenox Rd Schenectady NY 12308

HAUFT, AMY
SCULPTOR
b Cincinnati, Ohio. *Study:* Univ Calif, Santa Cruz, BA, 80; Skowhegan Sch Painting & Sculpture, 81; Art Inst , Chicago, MFA, 83. *Comn:* Outdoor installation, Art Awareness, Lexington, NY, 87; outdoor installation, Art Park, Lewiston, NY, 88. *Exhib:* A Descent into the Maelström, Univ Southern Calif, Atelier Gallery, Los Angeles, 88; The Irony of Geology, New Mus, New York, 89; You Are Here, Contemp Arts Forum, Santa Barbara, Calif, 90; Working in Brooklyn-Installations, Brooklyn Mus, NY, 90; A Reasonable Facsimile, Ctr Arts, Wesleyan Univ, Middletown, Conn, 90; If This is True--, Berland/Hall Gallery, New York, 91; and others. *Teaching:* Vis

instr installation sculpture, Calif Arts, Los Angeles, 88; vis lectr sculpture, Princeton Univ, 89; asst prof sculpture, Tyler Sch Art, Philadelphia, 89- *Awards:* Grant, Art Matters, Inc, 88-89; Granti Flintridge Found, 89; Grant-in-Aid-of-Research, Tyler Sch Art, 92; and others. *Bibliog:* Charlotta Kotik (ed), Working in Brooklyn- Installations (exhib catalog), Brooklyn Mus, 90; Jan Avgikos (auth), Green Piece, Art Forum, 91; Robet Mahoney (auth), Amy Hauft at Berland/Hall, Flash Art, 91. *Mem:* Col Art Asn. *Media:* Installation Sculpture. *Dealer:* Patrick Owens & Amy Lipton 67 Prince St New York NY 10012. *Mailing Add:* 1155 Manhattan Ave Brooklyn NY 11222

HAUG, DONALD RAYMOND
PAINTER
b Detroit, Mich, May 12, 25. *Study:* Mich State Univ, 46-47; Albright Art Sch, dipl, 52 & 53; State Univ NY, BS, 56, MS, 60; Univ Chicago, John Hay Whitney Found Fel, 62-63. *Work:* Butler Inst Am Art; Ball State Univ Art Gallery; Charles Burchfield Art Ctr; Charles R Penney Collection of Western NY, Burchfield Art Ctr. *Exhib:* Butler Inst Am Art Ann Midyear Show, 56-79; Chautauqua Art Asn Nat Jury Show, NY, 59, 66 & 72-74; Cooperstown Art Asn Nat Ann, NY, 71-72 & 73-75; Drawing & Small Sculpture Ann, Ball State Univ, 72-75; Smithsonian Inst Traveling Show, 76-78; Third Nat Drawing Exhib, Emporia State Univ, 79; The Wayward Muse: A historial survey of painting in Buffalo Albright-Knox Art Gallery Buffalo, NY, 87; The Unique Object Centenary Anniversary of the Buffalo Society of Artists, Burchfield Art Ctr, Buffalo, NY, 91. *Pos:* Dir, Chautauqua Art Asn Galleries, NY, currently. *Awards:* Purchase Award, Butler Inst Am Art, 70 & Drawing & Small Sculpture Show, Ball State Univ, 74; Manufacturers & Traders Trust Co Award, 39th Western NY Show, Albright-Knox Art Gallery, Buffalo, 82; plus others. *Mem:* Buffalo Soc Artists. *Media:* Oil. *Publ:* Illusr, Techniques of Trompe L'oeil Illusionism, F & W Publ Inc, 7/86. *Mailing Add:* 9267 W Lane Angola NY 14006

HAUGHEY, JAMES M
PAINTER, CALLIGRAPHER
b Courtland, Kans, July 8, 14. *Study:* Univ Kans Sch Fine Art, 32-34; with Leroy Greene, 43-53. *Work:* Mont Inst Arts Permanent Collection & Yellowstone Art Ctr, Billings, Mont; Mont Hist Soc Mus, Helena. *Exhib:* Am Watercolor Soc Ann Exhib, Nat Acad Galleries, New York 61-80; Allied Artists Am, 63; Am Artists Prof League, various galleries, New York, 71-82; Rocky Mountain Watercolor Painters, 13 western states, 75; retrospective, Yellowstone Art Ctr, 80 & Watercolor West, 85. *Pos:* Pres, Yellowstone Art Ctr Found, 64-65 & Mont Inst Arts Found, 65-66. *Awards:* First Award Watercolor, Hockaday Ctr Arts, 73; Coun Am Artists Socs Award, Am Artists Prof League, 81; Governor's Award for Arts, 81. *Bibliog:* Dale A Burk (auth), The Element of Chance: James Haughey, New Interpretations, Western Life Publ, 69; Jeanne Rhodes (auth), James Haughey, The Arts in Mont, Mont Press Publ Co, 77; Weldon Blake (auth), James Haughey, Acrylic Watercolor Painting, Watson-Guptill. *Mem:* Am Watercolor Soc (vpres, 78-81); fel Am Artists Prof League; Kans Watercolor Soc (hon mem, 71); life mem, Northwest Watercolor Soc; hon mem Mont Watercolor Soc; and others. *Media:* Watercolor, Acrylic. *Publ:* Auth, Calligraphy: The gracile art, 67 & The arts in our society, 73, Mont Arts, Mont Inst Arts; The watercolor page, Am Artist, 80; The arts and the lawyer, Kansas Law Review, 81. *Mailing Add:* 2205 Tree Lane Billings MT 59102

HAUPTMAN, SUSAN
ILLUSTRATOR
b Detroit, Mich, 47. *Study:* Carnegie Inst Technol, Pittsburgh, Pa, 65-66; Univ Mich, Ann Arbor, BFA, 68; Wayne State Univ, Detroit, Mich, MFA, 70. *Work:* Corcoran Gallery Art, Washington, DC; Detroit Inst Art; Minn Mus Art, St Paul; Norton Gallery Art, West Palm Beach, Fla; Oakland Mus, Calif. *Exhib:* Solo exhibs, Jeremy Stone Gallery, San Francisco, 84 & 89, Triton Mus Art, Santa Clara, Calif, 84, Allan Stone Gallery, New York, 84 & 88, Corcoran Gallery Art, Washington, DC, 90, Tatistcheff Gallery, Santa Monica, Calif, 92, Norton Gallery Art, West Palm Beach, Fla, 92; Campbell-Thiebaud Gallery, 90, Recent Acquisitions of the Achenbach Foundation for Graphic Arts, Palace Legion Hon, San Francisco, Calif, 92; The Essential Image, Calif Col Arts & Crafts, Oakland, 90; Allan Stone Gallery, 90, 43rd Ann Acad-Inst Purchase Exhib, Am Acad & Inst Arts & Letts, New York, 91; Still Life: Paintings & Drawings, 91, Under the Influence: Mentors/Teachers/Colleagues, Tatistcheff Gallery, Santa Monica, Calif, 92; In Thine Own Image, San Jose Inst Contemp Art, Calif, 91; Freehand Drawing Loosely Defined, Euphrat Gallery, DeAnza Col, Cupertino, Calif, 91; (Basically) Black & White, Riverside Art Mus, Calif, 92; The Female Nude in Western Art, Ind Univ Art Mus, Bloomington, 92. *Awards:* Nat Endowment Arts Fel Drawing, 85 & 91; Art Matters Inc Grant, 89; Visual Artist Fel, Calif Arts Coun, 90. *Bibliog:* Jan Sjostrom (auth), Inner limits, Palm Beach Daily News, 5/4/92; Gary Schwan (auth), Art review, Palm Beach Post, 5/8/92; Helen L Kohen (auth), Art review, Miami Herald, 5/10/92k. *Dealer:* Tatistcheff Gallery 1547 Tenth St Santa Monica CA 90401. *Mailing Add:* 2501 Ocean Front Walk Venice CA 90291

HAUSEY, ROBERT MICHAEL
PAINTER
b Baton Rouge, La, Nov 25, 49. *Study:* La State Univ, BFA, 71; Univ Pa, MFA, 74; Skowhegan Sch Painting & Sculpture, 75. *Work:* La State Univ & City Nat Bank, Baton Rouge; West Baton Rouge Art Mus, Port Allen, La; Louisiana Nat Bank, Baton Rouge. *Exhib:* Robert Hausey & Chris Guarusco, Galerie Simonne Stern, New Orleans, La, 87; Landscape, Seascape, Cityscape, Contemp Art Ctr, New Orleans, 86; Southern Discomfort, Mint Mus, Charlotte, NC, 86; Southern Exposure, Alternative Mus, New York, 86; New Orleans Acad Art miniatures, 89; Cult Activities Ctr, Temple, Tex, 90; one-person shows, Arthur Roger Gallery, New Orleans, 91, Sylvia Schmitt Gallery, New Orleans, 92, Zigler Mus, Jennings, La, 92 & Cason Gallery, Baton Rouge, 93; and others. *Teaching:* Instr painting, Univ Tex, San Antonio, 76 & Sam Houston State Univ, 76-77; assoc prof, La State Univ, 77-90, prof, 90- *Awards:* Merit Award, Birmingham Biennial, Birmingham Mus, 81; Jean Despuljols Award, Meadows Mus Biennial, 82; Nat Endowment Arts-Southeasten Ctr Contemp Arts Fel, 83-84. *Media:* Oil on Canvas, Watercolor. *Dealer:* Simms Fine Art 827 Girod St New Orleans La 70113. *Mailing Add:* 9498 Hooper Rd Baton Rouge LA 70818

HAUSMAN, FRED S
SCULPTOR, DESIGNER
b Bingen on Rhine, Ger, Apr 27, 21; US citizen. *Study:* Pratt Inst; New Sch Social Res, with Stuart Davis. *Work:* Emily Lowe Collection, Univ Miami; Mus Mod Art, Bogota, Colombia; Evansville Mus; Rutgers Univ; Fordham Univ. *Exhib:* NY Univ, 66; Contemporary Art USA, Norfolk Mus, 67; Columbia Univ, 68; Black & White Show, Smithsonian Inst, 69-70; 2nd Biennial, Medellin, Colombia, 70. *Media:* Acrylic. *Dealer:* Bodley Gallery 1063 Madison Ave New York NY 10028. *Mailing Add:* 100 Pembroke Dr Stamford CT 06903

HAUSMAN, JEROME JOSEPH
EDUCATOR
b New York, NY, May 4, 25. *Study:* Pratt Inst, 42-43; Cornell Univ, AB, 46; Columbia Univ, 47-48; Art Students League, 48; NY Univ, MA, 51, EdD, 54. *Pos:* Mem arts & humanities panel, US Off Educ, 64-70; ed bd, J Aesthetic Educ, 68-80; consult, John D Rockefeller III Fund, 69-75; pres, Minn Alliance Arts Educ, 77-79; bd dirs, Arts, Educ & Americans, 79; bd trustees, Minn Mus Art, 79-82. *Teaching:* Instr art, Elizabeth Pub Schs, NJ, 49-53; assoc prof, Sch Fine & Appl Arts, Ohio State Univ, 53-68, actg dir, 58-59, dir, 59-68; vis lectr, Sch Art, Syracuse Univ, 57; vis prof art educ, Pa State Univ, 58; prof div creative arts, NY Univ, 68-75; pres & prof, Minneapolis Col Art & Design, 75-82; acad vpres, Mass Col Art, 82-85, prof art, 85-; dir Ctr Curric Planning & Evaluation, Urban Gateways, Chicago, 86- *Awards:* Art Educator Award, Nat Art Educ Asn, 86. *Mem:* Distinguished fel Nat Art Educ Asn, 84-; Nat Comn Art Educ (chmn); Am Soc Aesthetics; Western Arts Asn; Inst Study Art Educ. *Publ:* Ed, Research in Art Education (yearbk), Nat Art Educ Asn, 59; contribr, articles in prof journals; ed, Arts and the Schools, McGraw-Hill, 80; Art Education J Nat Art Educ Asn, 89. *Mailing Add:* 1501 Hinman Apt 4A Evanston IL 60201

HAUSRATH, JOAN W
WEAVER, EDUCATOR
b Detroit, Mich, May 29, 42. *Study:* Bowling Green State Univ, Ohio, BS(educ), 64, with Philip Wigg, MFA, 66; Ohio State Univ, MA(art hist), 70. *Work:* Teradyne Inc, Nashua, NH; Nat Fire Prevention Agency, Quincy, Mass; Bowling Green State Univ, Ohio; Iceland Air, Reykjavik. *Comn:* Fiber panel, Spaulding & Slye, Burlington, Mass; Sheraton Hotel, Tulsa, Okla; Magner-Harris, Atlanta, Ga. *Exhib:* Marietta Col Craft Nat, G M Hermann Art Ctr, Ohio, 80 & 81; solo exhibs, Signature Gallery, Boston, 82, Bridgewater State Col, 89, Massachusetts Arts, Boston Ctr Arts, 90; American Crafts in Iceland, Kjarvalsstadir Mus, Reykjavik, 83. *Collections Arranged:* New England Fiber Arts, Newport Mus, RI, 85. *Teaching:* Instr art hist, Ohio State Univ, Columbus, 70-71; prof art, Bridgewater State Col, Mass, 71-, co-dir art gallery, 76-77, 80-81, 83-84 & 90-91; craft instr weaving, Summer Workshops, Eastern Conn State Col, Willimantic, 79-81. *Awards:* Mass Artists Found Fel Crafts, 83. *Bibliog:* Roger Dunn (auth), The Ikats of Joan Hausrath, a painterly approach to weaving, Fiberarts Mag, 11-12/81. *Mem:* Mass Asn Crafts; Boston Soc Arts & Crafts; Boston Weavers' Guild. *Media:* Fiber. *Mailing Add:* Dept Art Bridgewater State Col Bridgewater MA 02324

HAUT, CLAIRE (JOAN)
PAINTER, GRAPHIC ARTIST
US citizen. *Study:* Augustana Col; Am Acad Art, Chicago; Sch Design, Chicago, Lazlo Moholy-Nagy scholarship; Inst Design; also with Hin Bredendieck, John Kearney & Gyorgy Kepes. *Work:* Libr Cong, Washington, DC. *Comn:* Screen, woven and printed drapes, rug and upholstery, Teachers Rm & Home Econ Rm, Saarinens Crow Island Sch, Winnetka, Ill, 40; libr traveling display throughout S & Cent Am, Am Libr Asn, 40; and pvt comn. *Exhib:* One-man shows, Jonson Gallery, Univ NMex, 79, Artichoke Gallery, 80 & Balloon People, Go-Shoppe, 80 & 81, Albuquerque; Traveling Exhib, Works Progress Admin Crafts, Chicago Art Inst, Mus Mod Art, New York, Corcoran Mus, San Francisco Mus, Carnegie Inst, Mus St Louis & Toledo Mus; Contemp NMex Fine Art Invitational, Sweeney Ctr & Santa Fe Festival of Arts, 79; 18th Ann Nat Artists Salon, Okla Mus Art, 79; 20th Nat Sun Carnival Exhib, El Paso Mus, 78-79; Carlsbad Fine Arts Mus, NMex, 82; Fiesta Encantada Exhib, Albuquerque Mus, 82; Watercolor & Area Show, Albuquerque, 82; and others. *Pos:* Artist-designer, Experimental Design Workshop, Ill Art Project, Chicago, 39-42; art ed, Cudahy Packing Co, Chicago, 43-45; illusr, Sandia Labs, Albuquerque, 58-74. *Awards:* Pop Art Exhib First Prize, NMex Art League, 64; First Prize for Graphics, NMex State Fair Prof Artists Exhib, 67; First Purchase Prize for Crafts & Sculpture, Llano Estacado, 71; and others. *Mem:* Artists Equity (secy-treas, 73 & pres, 76, Albuquerque Chap); Albuquerque Designer Craftsmen; Nat League Am Pen Women (pres, Manzanita Br, 70-72, state chmn, Biennial Exhib, 75-76); NMex Art League. *Media:* Acrylic, Watercolor. *Mailing Add:* 9836 McKnight NE Albuquerque NM 87112

HAVEL, JOSEPH G
SCULPTOR
b Minneapolis, Minn, Aug 20, 54. *Study:* Univ Minn, BFA, 76; Pa State Univ, MFA, 79. *Work:* Mus Fine Art, Houston; Dallas Mus Art; The Barrett Collection, Dallas. *Exhib:* Solo exhibs, A Century of Texas, Sculpture, Huntington Gallery, Austin, 89, Barry Whistler Gallery, Dallas, Tex, 91, Davis/McClain Gallery, Houston, Tex, 92, Linda Farris Gallery, Seattle, Wash, 92. *Teaching:* Assoc dir, Glassell Sch Art, Houston. *Awards:* Nat Endowment Visual Arts Fel, 86; Otis & Velma Dozier Travel Grant, Dallas Mus Art, 91. *Bibliog:* Joan Davidow (auth), Balancing act, Detour Mag, 3/90; Elizabeth McBride (auth), Multiples, Art News, 5/90; Don Bacigulup (auth), Houston Contemp Mag, 9/89; Susan Chadwick (auth), Sculpting with poetic license, Houston Post, 7/89; Patricia Johnson (auth), Introductions gains strength, Houston Post, 7/89. *Media:* Miscellaneous. *Mailing Add:* Humanities Dept Austin Col Sherman TX 75090

HAVELOCK, CHRISTINE MITCHELL
HISTORIAN, EDUCATOR
b Cochrane, Ont, June 2, 24; US citizen. *Study:* Univ Toronto, AB; Radcliffe Col, AM; Harvard Univ, PhD(Charles Eliot Norton Fel), 58. *Pos:* Chairperson art, M C Mellon, 85-90. *Teaching:* Prof art hist, Vassar Col, 53-90, cur classical collection, currently. *Awards:* Am Asn Univ Women Fel, 58-59; Radcliffe Grad Medal, 87. *Mem:* Col Art Asn Am; Archeol Inst Am. *Res:* Greek sculpture of Hellenistic period. *Publ:* Auth, Hellenistic Art, W W Norton, rev ed 81. *Mailing Add:* Vassar Col Poughkeepsie NY 12601

HAVENS, JAN
SCULPTOR, PRINTMAKER
b Norfolk, Va, May 7, 48. *Study:* Atlantic Christian Col, BS, 70; Peabody Col Vanderbilt Univ, Nashville, Tenn, MA, 73. *Work:* Tenn Botanical Garden & Fine Arts Ctr, Nashville; Dirkson Senate Office Bldg, Washington, DC; Appalachian Cult Ctr, Boone, NC; Radio City Music Hall Golden Jubilee, New York; Hanes Collection, Winston-Salem, NC. *Comn:* Sculpture, Radio City Music Hall, New York, comn by, Governor Alexander, Nashville, Tenn, 81. *Exhib:* Solo exhibs, Tenn Botanical Garden & Fine Art Ctr, Nashville, 81, Southeastern Ctr Contemp Art, Winston-Salem, NC, 83, Zimmerman/Saturn Gallery, Nashville, Tenn, 91; Greenwood Gallery, Washington, DC, 81; The Animal Image: Contemporary Objects and the Beast, Renwick Gallery, Smithsonian Inst, Washington, DC, 81; Bloomingdale's, New York, 84; Creatures in Craft, Hand Workshop, Richmond, Va & Piedmont Craftsman, Winston-Salem, NC, 86; Cong Art Caucus Exhibit, Metro Arts Comn, 87 & 91, Concepts in clay & glass, Vanderbilt Univ, Nashville, Tenn, 90; Mountain Birds, Appalachian Cult Ctr, Appalachian State Univ, Boone, NC, 88; Animalia, Farmington Valley Arts Ctr, Avon, Conn, 91. *Bibliog:* Sandy Seawright (auth), Clay fantasies by Jan Havens, Artcraft Mag, 80; Clara Hieronymus (auth), Artist to show clay creations, Tennessean, 2/3/80; Leon Nigrosh (auth), Low Fire: Other Ways to Work in Clay, 80; Virginia Watson-Jones (auth), Contemporary American Women Sculptors, Oryx Press, 86; The Crafts Report, 1/87. *Mem:* Am Craft Coun; Tenn Artist-Craftsmen's Asn; Southern Highland Guild; Piedmont Craftsmen; Carolina Designer Craftsmen. *Media:* Clay; Etching. *Mailing Add:* 1121 Graybar Ln Nashville TN 37204

HAVERSAT, LILLIAN KERR
CONSULTANT, CURATOR
b New York, NY, Jan 12, 38. *Study:* Famous Artist Sch, cert com art; Trinity Col, Vt, BA, 83; also with David K Merrill & Patricia Reynolds. *Collections Arranged:* Schoonover, The Illustrator as Artist, 81 & Quilts: A Survey of Time, 82, Red Mill Gallery, Vt; Vermont Artists, Fleming Mus, Vt, 83; Patricia Reynolds Retrospect, Wood Gallery, Norwich Univ, Vt, 88. *Pos:* Owner, Monk's House Art Serv & Gallery, Jericho, Vt, 74-; consult, Vt Educ Television Arts Auction, 75-78, state coordr, 75-76 & 88-89; consult, Lake Champlain CofC Regional Exhib, 77-79, coordr, 79; dir, Red Mill Gallery, Jericho, Vt, 81-85; marketing mgr, Fleming Mus, Burlington, Vt, 85-88; art supt, Champlain Valley Exposition, 83-; consult, Kerr Enterprises, Boston, 87. *Awards:* Grants, Vt Coun Arts, 81-83 & 86; Merit Award, Nat League Am Penwomen, 89-90. *Mem:* Founding mem Essex Vt Art League; founder Jericho Historical Soc Art Coun; Nat Pen Women, Vt Press, 85-86; Am Asn Mus; Fel Soc Antiquities, Scotland. *Specialty:* Contemporary American art; contemporary and antique prints, sculpture, pottery; New England representative for David K Merrill. *Publ:* Auth, Artfully Speaking, 74; ed, Northern Vt Artists Newsletter, 78-83; contribr, Jottings from Jericho, 77-83; Patricia Reynolds (monograph), 90. *Mailing Add:* 20 Loon Lane Warren ME 04864

HAVERTY, GRACE LIGAMMARI
PAINTER
b Brooklyn, NY. *Study:* Am Acad Art, Chicago; Col Du Page, Glen Ellen, Ill, 70-89. *Work:* Du Page Libr System, Geneva, Ill; Sandburg Sch, Wheaton, Ill. *Comn:* Cathy (portrait), comn by Devereux Family, Winfield, 81; 3 vegetable pastels, Margaret Babcock Assoc, Glen Ellyn, 89; landscape, IMC Fertilizer Inc, North Brook, 90. *Exhib:* Invitational Exhibit of Master Pastelist Award Winners, Ann Pastel Soc Am, 88; Signature & Assoc Members of Pastel Soc, Ray Vogue Col Design, Schaumburg, Ill, 88; Pastel 89, 90 & 92, Nat Art Club, New York, 89-92; Four Drawers Look at Same Model, Univ Ill, Champaign & Beverly Art Ctr, Ill, 90; two-person exhib, North Central Col, Naperville, Ill, 91. *Awards:* First Place, 90 & Honorable Mention, 92, All Mem All Media Exhib, Palette & Chisel, Chicago, Ill; Scottsdale Art Sch Scholarship, 91; Merit Award, The Best & Brightest Art Exhib, Scottsdale, Ariz, 91 & 92. *Bibliog:* O'Toole & Triner (auths), Profile of an Artist, DuPage Arts Life, Ill Benedictine Col, 92. *Mem:* Pastel Soc Am; Allied Artist Am; Palette & Chisel. *Media:* Pastel. *Publ:* Illusr, New Philharmonic, Col DuPage Prog, 89-90 & 90-91; coauth, Four Ways to Activate Your Drawing, Artists Mag, 6/89. *Mailing Add:* 27 W 244 Carrell St Winfield IL 60190

HAWES, LOUIS
HISTORIAN
b Rochester, NY, Feb 25, 31. *Teaching:* From instr to asst prof, Columbia Univ, 58-68; assoc prof, Indiana Univ, Bloomington, 68-73, prof, 73-; resident fel, Yale Ctr Brit Art, 78-79; sr fel, Ctr Advan Study Visual Arts, Nat Gallery, Washington, DC, fall 85. *Awards:* Fulbright Fel to Eng, 57-58. *Mem:* Col Art Asn; Midwest Art Hist Soc; Victorian Soc; Turner Soc. *Res:* Later 18th and 19th century European and American painting; romantic landscape painting. *Publ:* Auth, The American Scene: Landscape & Genre Painting 1820-1900, Ind Univ Art Mus, 70; Turner's fighting temeraire, Art Quart 35, 72; Constable's Stonehenge, Victoria & Albert Mus, 75; Constable's Hadleigh Castle & British Romantic ruin painting, Art Bulletin 65, 83; Presences of Nature: British Romantic Landscape 1789-1830, New Haven, 82. *Mailing Add:* Fine Arts Ind Univ at Bloomington Bloomington IN 47405

HAWKES, ELIZABETH H
CURATOR, CONSULTANT
b Wilmington, Del, Aug 12, 43. *Study:* Mary Washington Col, BA, 65; Univ Del, MA, 69. *Collections Arranged:* American Painting and Sculpture (auth, catalog), 75; Bertha Corson Day Bates (auth, catalog), 78; City Life Illustrated (auth, catalog), 80; New York: New Work (auth, catalog), 86; Howard Pyle: The Artist & his Legacy (contribr, cat), 87; John Sloan: Spectator of Life (coauth, cat), 88. *Pos:* Asst cur, Del Art Mus, 69-79, cur, John Sloan Collection, 77-90, actg cur mus, 80-81, assoc cur, 81-90, Independent cur, 90-. *Mem:* Asn Am Mus; Mid-Atlantic Assoc Mus. *Publ:* Contribr, Artists in Wilmington: 1890-1940, 80, The Students of Howard Pyle, 80, William Glackens: Book & Magazine Illustrations, 88 & John Sloan's Illustrations, 92, Del Art Mus. *Mailing Add:* 715 N Creek Rd West Chester PA 19380

HAWKINS, BARBARA
PAINTER
b Columbia, Mo, Feb 1, 47. *Study:* Univ Mo, Columbia, BA, 71, MA(teaching asst), 74. *Exhib:* Nat Painting Show, Butler Inst Am Art, Youngstown, Ohio, 80; Watercolor USA, Springfield Art Mus, Mo, 80; Ky Watercolor Soc Nat Ann, Art Ctr, Louisville, 80; Nat Watercolor Soc Ann, Laguna Beach Art Mus, Calif, 81; Kansas Three, Washburn Univ, 83; Mid-Four, Nelson Art Mus, Kansas City, Mo, 83. *Awards:* Top Cash Award, Kans Watercolor Soc Tri-State Ann, 81; Third Prize, Washburn Univ, 83; Lithography Grant, Kans Art Comn, 83. *Mem:* Nat Watercolor Soc. *Media:* Charcoal, Watercolor. *Publ:* Contribr, Literature and Graphics from US Small Press 1965-1977, Spirit That Moves Us Press, 81. *Mailing Add:* c/o Kellas Gallery 7 E 7th St Lawrence KS 66044

HAWKINS, MYRTLE H
PAINTER, WRITER
b Merrit, BC. *Study:* Harnell Col, AA; San Jose State Univ; Univ Calif; WValley Col; also with Marshall Merrit, Maynard Stewart & Thomas Leighton. *Work:* Nat Easter Seal Soc, Chicago. *Comn:* Portrait, Rev John Foster, First Congregational Church, San Jose, Calif, 70; portrait, Rose Shenson, Triton Mus, Santa Clara, Calif, 71. *Exhib:* De Saisset Gallery, Santa Clara, 68; Hartnell Col, 69; one-man shows, Triton Mus Art, 71 & Rosicrucian Mus Art, San Jose, 73 & 77; Am Artist Prof League Nat Exhib, Lever House, New York, 71. *Pos:* Judge & juror of many art shows. *Teaching:* Instr painting, Calif State Dept Vocational Rehab, San Jose & Palo Alto, 69-71; also pvt painting lessons. *Awards:* First Place, Nat Easter Seal Soc, Chicago, 65; Gold Seal Award, de Saisset Art Gallery, 66; Best of Show, St Mark's Art Ann, Santa Clara, 68. *Bibliog:* Article, Rosicrucian Digest, 11/73; article, Grit, 8/28/77; Directory of American Portrait Artists, 8/85; Little Known Women: Twenty Extraordinary Achievers, 10/87. *Mem:* Nat Mus Women Arts; Triton Mus Art. *Media:* Pastel, Oil. *Publ:* Illusr, The Adventures of Mimi, Books I & II, 66; auth, Art as Therapy, Recreation and Rehabilitation for the Handicapped, 74. *Mailing Add:* 646 Bucher Ave Santa Clara CA 95051

HAWKINS, THOMAS WILSON, JR
PAINTER, INSTRUCTOR
b Los Angeles, Calif, May 15, 41. *Study:* Calif State Univ, Long Beach, BA(design) & MA(drawing, painting); Calif State Univ, Los Angeles, art hist, design & ceramics. *Work:* Overholt & Overholt Law Off, Los Angeles; Home Savings & Loan Art Collection; Dr Ambler Collection, Palos Verdes, Calif; Whittier Art Asn, Calif. *Exhib:* Southern Calif Expos, Del Mar, 67-77; Inland Exhibs, 68-77; Butler Inst Am Art, Youngstown, Ohio, 70; DaVinci Open Art Competition, New York, 70; Bertrand Russell Centenary Art Exhib, London & Nottingham, Eng, 73; and others. *Teaching:* Instr drawing & design & introd to art, Rio Hondo Col, Whittier, Calif, 67-; instr art, drawing & art hist, Long Beach City Col, 67-72; instr painting, Golden West Col, Huntington Beach, Calif, 72-78. *Awards:* Best Painting, Art in All Media, Southern Calif Expos, 67, Third Prize, 70; Second Award, Inland Exhib, San Bernardino Art Asn, 71 & 73; Purchase Award 25th All City Los Angeles Art, Barnsdall, 77. *Mem:* Los Angeles Art Asn; Whittier Art Asn; Art Teachers Asn; Calif Teachers Asn; Nat Educ Asn. *Media:* Acrylic, Oil. *Mailing Add:* 414 Fairview Ave Arcadia CA 91007

HAWTHORNE, JACK GARDNER
EDUCATOR, PAINTER
b Philadelphia, Pa, May 8, 21. *Study:* Philadelphia Col Art, BA, 43, DFA, 59; Univ Pa, MSEd, 56, MFA, 58. *Teaching:* Dir art educ, Pub Schs, Pa & NJ, 43-50; instr drawing, Philadelphia Col Art, 43-53, dean & registr, 57-60; guest lectr, Villanova Univ, 59; asst prof educ, Beaver Col, 60-63; assoc prof art, West Chester Univ, 65-86, chmn art dept, 73-74 & 77-78, emer prof, 87-. *Awards:* Award in Drawing, Pa Acad Fine Arts, 39; City of Philadelphia

Scholar, 39. *Mem:* Nat Trust Hist Preserv; Am Asn Univ Profs; life mem Nat Educ Asn; Friends of St George, Windsor Castle; Scotch-Irish Soc, USA. *Media:* Watercolor. *Publ:* Contribr, Course of study in art educ, Commonwealth Pa, 51. *Mailing Add:* 620 S High St, Suite B West Chester PA 19382

HAXTON, DAVID
COMPUTER ANIMATOR, PHOTOGRAPHER
b Indianapolis, Ind, Jan 6, 43. *Study:* Univ South Fla, BA, 65; Univ Mich, MFA, 67. *Work:* Whitney Mus Am Art, New York; Denver Art Mus; Mus Mod Art, New York; Australian Mus Art. *Exhib:* Two-man show, Whitney Mus Am Art, New York, 78 & Biennial Exhib, 79; Cineprobe, Mus Mod Art, New York, 78; Photography in the 70's, Art Inst Chicago, 79; Attitudes, Santa Barbara Art Mus, Calif, 79; Concept Narrative Doc, Mus Contemp Art, Chicago, 79; one-man show, Sonnabend Gallery, New York, 79 & 83; Whitney Biennial Exhib, 79 & 83; Recent Color, San Francisco Mus Art, 83; Rosa Esman Gallery, NY, 86; Siggraph Film & Video Show, 88; Nat Computer Graphics Asn Video Show, 89; Nat Computer Graphics Asn Video Theater, 90. *Teaching:* Instr art, San Diego State Univ, 69-72; computer graphics, William Paterson Col, Wayne, NJ, 74- *Awards:* NY State Coun on Arts Grant, 77; Nat Endowment for the Arts Individual Artist's Grants, 78-79; Gold Plaque Award, Chicago Int Film Festival, 89; First Prize Computer Animation, Montreal Int Film Festival, 89. *Bibliog:* Sally Euclaire (auth), The new color, Abbyville, 81; article, The art of photography, Time-Life, 81; David Shapiro (auth), Inner city, Camera Arts, 1-2/82. *Media:* Computer Animation. *Mailing Add:* 139 Spring St New York NY 10012

HAY, A JOHN
HISTORIAN, EDUCATOR
b Penang, Malaysia, May 9, 38; Brit citizen. *Study:* Exeter Col, Oxford Univ, BA, 61; Princeton Univ, PhD, 78. *Teaching:* Asst prof Asian art hist, Univ Denver, 76-77; from asst prof Chinese art hist to assoc prof, Harvard Univ, 77-84; assoc prof, Inst Fine Arts, NY Univ, 84- *Res:* Chinese art, especially painting. *Publ:* Auth, The human body as a microcosmic source of macrocosmic values in calligraphy, Bush, Theories of Arts in China, 83; Values and history of Chinese painting I and II, RES 6, 83-84; Surface and the Chinese painter, Archives of Asian Art, 85; Kernels of Energy, Bones of Earth: The Rock in Chinese Art, China Inst, NY, 85. *Mailing Add:* Inst Fine Arts New York Univ One E 78th St New York NY 10021

HAY, DICK
SCULPTOR, EDUCATOR
b Cincinnati, Ohio, Nov 19, 42. *Study:* Ohio Univ, BFA; NY State Col Ceramics, Alfred Univ, MFA. *Work:* Pushkin Mus, Moscow, Russia; Butler Inst Am Art, Youngstown, Ohio; Latuia Art Mus, Riga; Sea of Japan, Kanazawa-shi, Japan; Northern Ariz Univ, Flagstaff. *Exhib:* Sensible Cup Int Exhib, Sea of Japan Expos, 73; Contemp Ceramic Sculpture, Univ NC, Chapel Hill, 77; Nat Clay, Univ Hartford, Conn, 81; The Art of Ceramics, Paducah Gallery, Ky, 89; Maj Artists, Ctr for the Arts, Phoenix, Ariz, 91; American Exhibition, Latuia Art Mus, Riga, 91; and over two hundred others. *Teaching:* Prof art/ceramics, Ind State Univ, Terre Haute, 66-; guest lectr, Univ Del, 72, Ariz State Univ, 83, Sheridan Col Appl Arts, Toronto, Ont, 74, La State Univ, 76, Univ Miami, 76, Col Santa Fe, 77, Princeton Univ, 79, Ga State Univ, 83, NDak State Univ, 85, Alfred Univ, 86 & Buffalo State Univ, 90, and over one hundred others. *Awards:* Nat Coun Educ Ceramic Arts Fel; Distinguished Teaching Award, Ind State Univ. *Mem:* Nat Coun Educ Ceramic Arts (pres, 78-80). *Media:* Clay. *Dealer:* Martha Schneider Gallery Inc Chicago IL; Signature Gallery Boston MA. *Mailing Add:* Dept of Art Ind State Univ Terre Haute IN 47809

HAY, GEORGE AUSTIN
PAINTER, FILMMAKER
b Johnstown, Pa, Dec 25, 15. *Study:* Pa Acad Fine Arts; Art Students League; Nat Acad; Univ Rochester; Univ Pittsburgh, BS & MLitt; Columbia Univ, MA; also with Robert Brackman & Dong Kingman. *Work:* Pub Libr, Metrop Mus Art, New York; Dept Army; Libr Cong, Washington, DC; numerous pvt collections. *Exhib:* Duncan Galleries, New York, 73; Manufacturers Hanover Trust, 73; Bicentennial Exhib of Am Painters in Paris, 76; Watergate Gallery, Washington, DC, 81; Salon des Nations, Paris, 83. *Awards:* Documentary award, Int Film Festival, Zagreb, Yugoslavia, 75; Academy Gold Medal, Accademia Italia, 80; Pictorial Award, Smithsonian Inst, 82. *Mem:* Am Artists Prof League; Allied Artists Am; Nat Soc Arts & Lett; Nat Acad Television Arts & Sci; Washington Film Coun (bd dir). *Media:* Oil, Miscellaneous media. *Publ:* Auth & illusr, Seven Hops to Australia, 45; Life About the Universe (television prog), Nat Coun of Churches, 65; The Performing Arts Experience, 69; auth & dir, Visit to the Museum of Modern Art (film), 72; dir, Highways of History (film depicting 100 oil paintings), 76. *Dealer:* Arts Club Galleries 2017 Eye St NW Washington DC 20006. *Mailing Add:* 2022 Columbia Rd NW Washington DC 20009

HAY, IKE
SCULPTOR, EDUCATOR
b Atlanta, Ga, Apr 28, 44. *Study:* Univ Ga, BFA & MFA. *Work:* Indianapolis Mus Art; New Orleans Mus Art; Mint Mus Art, Charlotte, NC; Chancellor's off, Pa Univ System, Harrisburg; State Mus Pa, Harrisburg; and others. *Comn:* Hines Industrial Develop Corp, Tulsa, 83; Reading Redevlopment Authority Ctr Park Place, Reading, Pa, 86; Harrisburg/Dauphin Co, 86; Rouse & Assoc, Univ Place, Tampa, Fla, 88; Environmental Compliance Servs Corp, Exton, Pa, 92. *Exhib:* High Mus Art, 69; one-man shows, New Orleans Mus Art, 69 & Franklin & Marshall Col, 81; Nat Sculpture 73 traveling show, 73; Pa State Mus, Harrisburg, Pa, 79; PSEA, State Mus Pa, 84; Invitational, Messah Col, Grantham, Pa, currently. *Pos:* Nat Endowment artist in residence, Decatur, 74-75. *Teaching:* Asst prof sculpture, Purdue Univ, West Lafayette, 69-74; asst prof sculpture, Millersville Univ, Pa, 75-81, assoc prof, 81- *Awards:* Rosenblatt Scholarship, Univ Ga, 68; Grant in Aid, Arts Festival Atlanta, 68; Fac Grant, Purdue Univ, 70. *Bibliog:* John Spofforth (auth), The Ike Hay workshop, Ala-Arts, Ala State Arts Coun, 74. *Mem:* Am Asn Univ Prof. *Media:* Steel, Bronze. *Mailing Add:* 3200 Blue Rock Rd Lancaster PA 17603

HAYASHI, MASUMI
PHOTOGRAPHER, EDUCATOR
b Rivers, Ariz, Sept 3, 45. *Study:* Fla State Univ, BA, 75, MFA, 7; Sheridan Col, certificate in computer graphics, 85. *Work:* St Petersburg Fine Arts Mus, Fla; Jacksonville Fine Arts Mus, Fla; George Eastman House, Rochester, NY; Cleveland Mus Art, Ohio. *Exhib:* Southeastern Graphics Invitational, Mint Mus Art, 82; Women's Art, Miles Apart, Berman Gallery, New York, 82; Collage and Assemblage, Miss Mus Art, Jackson, 82; Unrestricted Color, Handwerter Gallery, Ithaca, NY, 83; History of Stereo Photography, Boston Mus Sci, 83; Color, On the Edge, Mather Gallery, Cleveland, 84; Newspeak, BC Space, Laguna Beach, Calif, 84; Life Forms, Simulated, Andrew Grant Gallery, Edinburgh Col Art, Scotland, 85; Stereo Photography Exhib, Gallery 44, Toronto, 85; Taking Liberties, Mus Art, New York, 86. *Pos:* Gallery cur, Univ Central Fla, 81-82; gallery dir, Miami-Dade Community Col, summer 82; artist-in-residence, Koehler Art Ctr, Sheboygan, Wis. *Teaching:* Adj instr photog, Univ Central Fla, 80-82; vis instr, Loyola Marymount Univ, 83; asst prof, Cleveland State Univ, 82-, dir, 83-85. *Awards:* Fla Fine Arts Coun Fel, 80; Res & Creative Activities Grant, Cleveland State Univ, 83 & 85. *Mem:* Los Angeles Ctr Photog Studies; Spec Interest Group on Computer Graphics; Soc Photog Educ. *Media:* Photography, Computer Graphics. *Publ:* Contribr, Photo Images in Art: Design, Process and Materials, 79. *Dealer:* Kate Tabor Fine Art Co Cleveland OH 44115. *Mailing Add:* c/o Corcoran Fine Arts 2341 Roxborro Rd Cleveland OH 44106

HAYDON, HAROLD (EMERSON)
PAINTER, EDUCATOR
b Ft William, Ont, Apr 22, 09; US citizen. *Study:* Univ Chicago, PhB, 30, MA, 31; Sch Art Inst Chicago, 32-33. *Work:* Pickering Col, Newmarket, Ont. *Comn:* Wool ark cover, Temple Beth Am, Chicago, Ill, 58, now in Temple Sholom, Chicago; glass mosaic murals, Beth El, Gary, Ind, 59-60, now in Beth Israel, Hammond, Ind; St Cletus Roman Cath Church, La Grange, Ill, 63, Temple Beth Am, Chicago, 68; mosaic & stained glass murals, Sonia Shankman Orthogenic Sch, Univ Chicago, 66-77, porcelain enamel on steel mural, 77; stained glass windows, Rockefeller Mem Chapel and Surgery Brain Res Inst, Univ Chicago, 72-79; wool Ark curtain, Niles Township Jewish Congregation, Skokie, Ill, 76. *Exhib:* Seven Exhibs Artists Chicago & Vicinity, 37-67 & 58th Ann Am Painting--Abstr & Surrealist Art, 47, Art Inst Chicago; Options, Mus Contemp Art, Chicago, 68; 50-Year Retrospective, Univ Ill Chicago, 82. *Pos:* Pres, Renaissance Soc Univ Chicago, 56-65 & 74-75; art critic, Chicago Sun-Times, 63-85. *Teaching:* From instr art to asst prof, George Williams Col, 34-44; from instr art to prof, Univ Chicago, 44-75, emer prof, 75-; dir, Midway Studios, Univ Chicago, 63-75; vis lectr murals, Sch of Art Inst of Chicago, 75-81; adj prof fine arts, Ind Univ NW, 76-82. *Awards:* Excellence in Teaching Prize, Univ Chicago, 45; Alumni Citation for Public Service, Univ Chicago, 78. *Mem:* Artists Equity Asn, Chicago Chap (pres, 50-52, 55-57); Chicago Soc Artists (pres, 59-61); Nat Soc Mural Painters; hon life mem Artists Guild Chicago; Renaissance Soc (pres, 56-67, Univ Chicago, 74-75). *Media:* Oil, Mosaic, Porcelain Enamel, Stained Glass. *Publ:* Auth, Great Art Treasures in America's Small Museums, 67. *Mailing Add:* 5009 Greenwood Ave Chicago IL 60615

HAYES, DAVID VINCENT
SCULPTOR
b Hartford, Conn, Mar 15, 31. *Study:* Univ Notre Dame, AB; Ind Univ, sculpture with David Smith, MFA. *Work:* Mus Mod Art, Brooklyn Mus, Guggenheim Mus, New York; Mus Arts Decoratif, Paris; Mus Fine Arts, Houston. *Comn:* Ceramics, walls, De Porceleyne Fles, Delft, Holland, 67, Lee Kolker, Stanfordville, NY, 70 & Elmira Col, 71, mural, Great Southwest Corp, Atlanta, Ga, 68 & relief, comn by David Anderson, Ardsley, NY, 69. *Exhib:* Salon Mai, Mus Art Mod, Paris, 66; Jewelry 71, Art Gallery Ont, 71; State Univ NY, Albany, 78, Dartmouth Col, NH, 78, Amherst Col, Mass, 79, Nassau Co Mus, Port Washington, NY, 79 & Univ Conn, Storrs, 79; and others. *Teaching:* Vis artist, Carpenter Art Ctr, Harvard Univ, 72. *Awards:* Fulbright Res Grant, 61; Guggenheim Found Fel, 61; Nat Inst Arts & Lett Award, 64. *Media:* Metal, Ceramics. *Dealer:* David Anderson Gallery 521 West 57th St New York NY 10019. *Mailing Add:* c/o Anderson Gallery Martha Jackson Pl New York NY 14214

HAYES, GERALD
PAINTER, PHOTOGRAPHER
b Los Angeles, Calif, April 9, 40. *Study:* Auburn Univ, BVA, 62; Univ Ill, MFA, 66. *Work:* Addison Gallery, Amherst, Mass; Art Ctr Am, Englishtown, NJ; AT&T, Liberty Corner, NJ. *Exhib:* Elements of Art, Mus Fine Art, Boston, 71; Dark-Light, Univ Calif Art Mus, Santa Barbara, 80; Abstract Painting, New York City, Hofstra Univ Gallery, 81; Art Abstrait, Univ Lavel, Que, 82; Tondos & Squares, Harm Bouckaert Gallery, New York, 82; Newcastle Salutes New York, Polytech Art Gallery, Eng, 83; Small Scale Abstraction, Grace Borbenicht Gallery, 86; Calkins Gallery, Hofstra Univ, New York, 90; Stockton State Col, Pomona, NJ, 90. *Teaching:* Prof grad art, Pratt Inst, 71-83, chmn painting & drawing, 83-85, asst chmn fine arts, 92; vis prof painting, Parsons Sch Design, 81-83. *Bibliog:* Virginia Gunter (auth), Gerald Hayes: The creativity of the psychological eye, Artforum, 5/73; Robert Pincus-Witten (auth), Entries: Styles of artists and critics, Arts Mag, 11/79; Saul Ostrow (auth), Gerald Hayes, Tema Celeste, Contemp Art Rev, 3-4/91. *Mem:* Col Art Asn, New York. *Mailing Add:* 126 Chambers St New York NY 10007

HAYES, LAURA M
DEALER, HISTORIAN
b Birmingham, Ala, Nov 28, 27. *Study:* Univ Wyo. *Pos:* Head photog section, Wyo State Art Gallery, 65-74, art registrar, 67-71, curator art, 71-79; owner, Wild Goose Gallery, Cheyenne, Wyo. *Mem:* Wyo Press Women; Wyo Artist Asn; Nat Fedn Press Women; and others. *Media:* Watercolor. *Specialty:* Original Works of Art & Limited Edition prints. *Mailing Add:* PO Box 2561 Cheyenne WY 82003

HAYES, RANDY (RANDOLPH ALAN)
PAINTER
b Jackson, Miss, June 11, 44. *Study:* Southwestern Univ, Memphis, Tenn, 62-65; Memphis Acad Arts, BFA(Ford Found Grant), 68; Univ Ore, Eugene, 68. *Work:* Laguna Beach Mus Art, Calif; Seattle Art Mus; City Seattle One Percent for Art; Wash State One Percent for Art, Olympia. *Comn:* Murals, Seattle Ctr, 83 & State of Wash, Monroe, 83. *Exhib:* Outside New York: Seattle, The New Mus, New York, 83 & Seattle Art Mus, 83; West Coast Realism, Laguna Beach Mus Art, Calif, 83; solo exhibs, Manolides Gallery, Seattle, 83 & Linda Farris Gallery, Seattle, 84; Setting the Stage, Los Angeles Co Mus Art; Scapes, Univ Calif Art Mus, Santa Barbara; Linda Farris Gallery, Seattle, Wash, 86. *Awards:* WGBH New TV Workshop Grant, Boston, 75. *Bibliog:* Suzanne Muchnic (auth), What's wrong with West Coast realism, Los Angeles Times, 6/22/83; Regina Hackett (auth), Seattle artists come home in New York show, Seattle Post-Intelligencer, 10/20/83; Lynn Smallwood (auth), Seattle art from New York City, The Weekly, 10/26/83; Bruce Guenther (auth), 50 Northwest Artists, Chronicle Bks, 83; Lynn Smallwood (auth), Randy Hayes, Art News, 5/1/86. *Media:* Pastels, Oils. *Mailing Add:* 83 Columbia St Seattle WA 98104

HAYES, TUA
PAINTER
b Anniston, Ala. *Study:* Converse Col, BA; Columbia Univ Teacher's Col; also with Henry Lee McFee. *Work:* Del Art Mus, Wilmington; Wilmington Trust Co; Univ Del; Blount Collection; Converse Col, Spartanburg, SC; and others. *Exhib:* Philadelphia Pro-Show, Pa, 67; Nat Acad Design, New York, 70; Baltimore Mus Regional Show, Md; Am Drawings 1976, Portsmouth, Va; Distinguished Mid-Atlantic Artists, Univ Del, 80; Del Ctr Contmep Art, 83; and other group and one-man shows. *Awards:* First Prize for Drawing, Del Art Mus, 67; Second Prize, Asn Community Art Ctrs, Philadelphia, 82; First Prize, Hercules Expo, 82. *Mem:* Philadelphia Art Alliance; Studio Group, Inc (pres, 54-56); Del Art Mus (bd dirs, 62-80); Hilton Head Art League; Delaware Ctr Contemp Arts. *Media:* Oil, Watercolor. *Dealer:* Carspecken-Scott Gallery 1707 N Lincoln St Wilmington DE 19806. *Mailing Add:* 115 Bellant Circle Wilmington DE 19807

HAY-MESSICK, VELMA
PAINTER
b Bloomington, Ill. *Study:* Watercolor with Dong Kingman, 44; Chouinard Art Inst, 47, 48 & 50; Otis Art Inst, 49. *Work:* Seton Hall Univ, Newark, NJ; City of Hope, Duarte, Calif; Grumbacher Artists' Palettes, New York. *Exhib:* Nat League Am Pen Women Southwest Regional, Albuquerque, NMex, 71; Long Beach Community Theatre Gallery, 75; Exhibs, Nat League Am Pen Women, 76 & 77; Messick-Hay Studio Gallery, Apple Valley, Calif, currently; Scottish Cult, Scotland & Colonial Scots Immigrants, 17th century, Guild St Margaret of Scotland, 80; and others. *Pos:* Dir, Messick-Hay Studio Gallery, 52- *Awards:* Key Award, Seton Hall Univ, 58; Second Oils, Calif State Exhib, Nat League Am Pen Women, 71. *Bibliog:* John Oglesby (auth), Lively arts, Sacramento Bee, 57; Vera Williams (auth), Art is a way of life, Southland Mag, 66; Geraldine H Wheeler (ed), Profile, Ben Messick & Velma Hay-Messick, Athelings Mag, 75. *Mem:* Nat League Am Pen Women. *Media:* Oil. *Publ:* Auth, Art spirit in XVII century America, Pen Woman, 6/73; auth, XVII century art, Guild St Margaret of Scotland Mag, 78. *Mailing Add:* 16627 Zenda No B Victorville CA 92392

HAYNES, DOUGLAS H
PAINTER, EDUCATOR
b Regina, Sask, Jan 1, 36. *Study:* Provincial Inst Technol & Art, Calgary, Alta, with R Spickett; Royal Acad Fine & Appl Arts, The Hague, Holland. *Work:* Edmonton Art Gallery, Alta; Confederation Art Gallery, Charlottetown, PEI; London Pub Mus & Art Gallery, Ont; Univ Calgary, Alta. *Comn:* Edmonton City Hall. *Exhib:* Fifth Biennial Exhib Can Art, London, Eng & Ottawa, Can, 63 & Sixth Biennial Exhib, Ottawa, 65; All Alberta '70, Edmonton, 70; West '71 Exhib, Edmonton, 71; Royal Can Acad Arts 91st Ann, Montreal, 71; Nat Can Touring Exhib, 91-92. *Pos:* Art adv, Govt Alta, 67-70. *Teaching:* From assoc prof to prof art & design & chair dept, Univ Alta, 70- *Awards:* Govt of Neth Scholar, 60; All Alta First Prize, Jacox Gallery, 65; Can Coun Sr Award, Can Govt, 67. *Bibliog:* N Yates (auth), Three from Edmonton, Arts Can, 10/69; K Wilkin (auth), Western Canada, a survey, Art in Am, 5-6/72. *Mem:* Assoc Royal Can Acad Arts; Univ Art Asn Can. *Media:* Acrylic, Mixed. *Dealer:* Kathleen Laverty Gallery Edmonton AB Canada. *Mailing Add:* 14312 Ravine Dr Edmonton AB T5M 3M3 Canada

HAYNES, GEORGE EDWARD
PAINTER, ILLUSTRATOR
b Hinton, WVa, Apr 29, 10. *Study:* Phoenix Art Inst, New York; Lockwood Sch Art, Kalamazoo, Mich; Art Inst Pittsburgh. *Work:* United Va Bank, Richmond; Country Club of Va, Richmond; Media General, Richmond; Northminster Baptist Church, Richmond. *Comn:* First Day Docking in America & First Clipper Built in United States Shipyard, Officers Mess, Norfolk Naval Shipyard, 60; mural, Merrimac Restaurant, Portsmouth, 65. *Exhib:* Irene Leach Mem, 64, Norfolk Mus, Tidewater Artists Ann, 65; Hunter Gallery Ann, Chattanooga, Tenn, 64; Va Mus Fine Art, 65; Watercolor USA, Springfield Art Mus, Mo, 72. *Pos:* Dir-owner, Portsmouth Artists Guild, Va, 38-66. *Awards:* Grumbacher Award, Norfolk Mus, 65; Best in Show, Portsmouth Jaycees, 66; Purchase Prizes, Petersburg Arts Festival, 72-74. *Mem:* Tidewater Artist Asn, Norfolk (pres, 63-64); James River Art League, Richmond (gallery dir, 68-). *Media:* Oil, Watercolor. *Dealer:* Art Cove 9030 W Broad St Richmond VA 23229. *Mailing Add:* 1521 Avondale Ave Richmond VA 23227

HAYNES, NANCY
PAINTER
b Conn, 47. *Work:* Brooklyn Mus; Hood Mus, Dartmouth, NH; Denver Art Mus; Gemeentemuseum, Holland; Mus Fine Arts, Houston, Tex; Addison Gallery Am Art, Phillips Acad, Andover. *Exhib:* Solo exhibs, PS 1 Project Room, Long Island City, NY, 84, Haags Gemeentermseum, The Hague, Holland, 85, Plus-Kern Gallery, Brussels, Belg, 85, John Gibson Gallery, NY, 85 & 86, Julian Pretto, NY, 87, John Good Gallery, NY, 89, 90, 91 & 92, Monoprints, Pamela Auchincloss, NY, 90, Chrysler Mus Art, Norfolk, Va, 92; Contemporary Fresco, Stark Gallery, NY, 90; Unique Works on Paper, Mem Art Gallery, Univ Rochester, NY, 90; A Question of Paint, Hallwalls Contemp Art Ctr, Buffalo, NY, 90; Artists for Amnesty, BlumHelman Gallery, NY, 90 & Germans Van Eck Gallery, NY, 90; Am Abstraction at the Addison, Addison Gallery Am art, Phillips Acad, Andover, 91; Singular & Plural, Recent Accessions, Drawing & Prints 1945-1991, Mus Fine Arts, Houston, 92. *Teaching:* Adj Lectr, Hunter Col, New York, 86-88; vis lectr, Brandeis, Univ, Waltham, Mass, 88-89; lectr, Carpenter Ctr, Harvard Univ, 92. *Awards:* Fel, Nat Endowment Arts, 87 & 90; New York Found Arts, 87. *Bibliog:* David Carrier (auth), Afterlight: Exhibiting abstract painting on the era of its belatedness, Acts Mag, 3/92; Carol Rand (auth), Forces of light, dark comes forth through Haynes' pure painting, Virginian-Pilot & the Ledger Star, 4/26/92; Abstraction as aporetical incident, Tema Celeste, 4-5/92. *Mailing Add:* c/o John Good Gallery 532 Broadway New York NY 10012

HAYNES, R (RICHARD THOMAS)
PAINTER, ILLUSTRATOR
b Rome, Ga, Feb 17, 34. *Study:* Auburn Univ, BS, 56; painting with James Harmon, 60; watercolor with Zoltan Szabo, 75. *Work:* Univ Pac, Stockton, Calif; Colby Col, Waterville, Maine; Mo Hist Soc Print Collection, St Louis. *Exhib:* NMex Int, Portales, 76; St Louis Artists Guild, Webster Groves, 77; Southern Watercolor Soc, Columbus Art Mus, Ga, 78; Pittsburgh Aqueous 78, Pa; Ark Wildlife Fedn, Pine Bluff, 78 & 79; and others. *Awards:* First Place, St Louis Co Div Parks, 75; Second Place, NMex Int, 76. *Bibliog:* Member of the issue, North Light Mag, 81. *Mem:* Southern Watercolor Soc; Acad Professional Artists. *Media:* Egg Tempera, Watercolor. *Dealer:* Aldridge Fine Arts I & II 104 Romero NW Albuquerque NM 87104. *Mailing Add:* c/o Essex Fine Art Gallery 13 S Fullerton Ave Montclair NJ 07042

HAYNIE, HUGH
CARTOONIST
b Reedville, Va, Feb 6, 27. *Study:* Col William & Mary, AB, 50; Univ Louisville, LHD, 68. *Pos:* Cartoonist, Richmond Times/Dispatch, Va, 50-53, Greensboro Daily News, NC, 53-55 & 56-58, Atlanta J, 55-56, with Louisville Courier J, 58- *Awards:* Headliner Award, 66; Freedoms Found Award, 66-70. *Mem:* Soc Alumni Col William & Mary (past dir); Filson Club, Louisville, Ky; Windmill Pt, Va. *Publ:* Hugh Haynie: Perspective, 74. *Mailing Add:* Courier-Journal 525 W Broadway Louisville KY 40202

HAYNIE, RON
PAINTER, EDUCATOR
b Farmville, Va, Dec 31, 45. *Study:* Am Univ, BA, 68, MFA, 69. *Work:* George Mason Univ, Fairfax, Va; Watkins Collection, Am Univ, Washington, DC; Northern Va Community Col, Annandale, Va; WVa Wesleyan Col, Buckhannon; Rehoboth Art League, Del. *Exhib:* 19th Area Exhib, Corcoran Gallery Art, Washington, DC, 74; Areawide Juried Exhib, Arlington Arts Ctr, Va, 85; New on View, Strathmore Hall Arts Ctr, Rockville, Md, 88; I Am: Self Portraits, Dundalk Community Col, Baltimore, Md, 90; Past as Prologue, Greater Reston Arts Ctr, Va, 91. *Pos:* Dir, Watkins Collection, Am Univ, Washington, DC, 90- *Teaching:* Instr painting & drawing, Dumbarton Col, Washington, DC, 69-73; instr painting & drawing, Trinity Col, Washington, DC, 74- 77; assoc prof painting & drawing, Am Univ, Washington, DC, 80- *Awards:* Purchase Award, 1975 Area Exhib, Fairfax Coun Arts, 75. *Bibliog:* Joanne Lewis (auth), Reviews column, Wash Post, 87; Marci Nadler (auth), From the beach series, Eye Wash, 91; Roberta Morgan (auth), Two solitary visions, Rockville Gazette, Md, 91. *Mem:* Wash Proj Arts; Arlington Arts Ctr; Phillips Collection; Coalition Wash Artists. *Media:* Acrylics. *Mailing Add:* 4811 Hutchins Place NW Washington DC 20007

HAYWARD, JAMES
PAINTER
b San Francisco, Calif, Sept 22, 43. *Study:* San Diego State Univ, BA; Univ Calif, Los Angeles; Univ Wash, Seattle, MFA. *Work:* Los Angeles Co Mus Art; San Francisco Mus Mod Art. *Exhib:* New Abstract Painting in Los Angeles, Los Angeles Co Mus Art, 76; Less is More, Sidney Janis Gallery, New York, 77; three-person exhib, Los Angeles Inst Contemp Art, 79; Contemporary Los Angeles Artists, Nagoya City Mus, Japan, 82; Changing Trends--Content & Style, Laguna Beach Mus Art, 82 & Los Angeles Inst Contemp Art, 83; Black on Black, Santa Barbara Contemp Arts Forum, 83; Young Talent 1963-1983, Los Angeles Co Mus Art, 83; Awards in the Visual Arts 10, Hirshhorn Mus, Washington, DC, 91. *Teaching:* Instr painting, Univ Calif, Berkeley, 83, Univ Calif Santa Barbara 85, Univ Southern Calif, 87, Univ Calif Los Angeles, 92. *Awards:* Japan-US Friendship Comn Fel, 81-82;

Guggenheim Fel, 83-84; Awards in the Visual Arts 10, Hirshhorn Mus. *Bibliog:* Jeremy Gilbert-Rolfe (auth), Abstract painting and the historical object: considerations on the new paintings of James Hayward, Arts, 4/87; Buzz Spector (auth), James Hayward: The Space Behind the Gesture, Visions (cover), spring 89. *Media:* Acrylic, Oil. *Dealer:* Modernism 685 Market St San Francisco CA 94105; M13 72 Greene St New York NY 10012. *Mailing Add:* 12241 Broadway Rd Moorpark CA 93021

HAYWARD, JANE
HISTORIAN, CURATOR
b Orange, Conn, Aug 13, 18. *Study:* Pa Acad Fine Arts, Philadelphia, 36-42; Cresson scholar, 40, 42; Sch Fine Arts, Univ Pa, BFA, 52, MA, 54; Yale Univ, Fel, 57-58, PhD, 58; Stonehill Col, Hor Dr Art, 80. *Collections Arranged:* Medieval Art from Private Collections (with catalog), 68-69; The Year 1200 (with catalog), 70; Ecclesiastical Vestments of the Middle Ages, 70; Stained Glass Windows of the Middle Ages & the Renaissance, 71-72; Cloisters Apocalypse Exhib, 73; The Secular Spirit: Life & Art at the End of the Middle Ages (with catalog), 75; Radiance and Reflection, Pitcairn Col (with catalog), 82. *Pos:* Tech illusr, Am Viscose Corp, Philadelphia, 45-54; res asst, Art Gallery, Yale Univ, 58-61; cur, Lyman Allyn Mus, New London, 61-65; cur, The Cloisters, Metrop Mus Art, New York, 69- *Teaching:* Lectr art hist, Yale Univ, 61; asst prof art hist, Conn Col, New London, 64-67; adj assoc prof art hist, Columbia Univ, 71-76, adj prof, 76- *Awards:* Am Coun Learned Socs Fel, 66-67; Int Ctr Medieval Art Fel, 87. *Mem:* Col Art Asn; Int Ctr Medieval Art. *Res:* Medieval stained glass. *Publ:* Auth, Stained glass windows from Boppard-am-Rhein, Metrop Mus Art J, 69; Cistercian glazed cloisters, Gesta, Vol XII, 73; The choir windows of Saint-Serge, Gesta, Vol XV, 76; Stained glass before 1700 in American collections, Studies Hist Art, Vol 15, 85, Vol 23, 87, Vol 28, 89. *Mailing Add:* The Cloisters Ft Tryon Park New York NY 10040

HAYWARD, PETER
PAINTER, SCULPTOR
b Keene, NH, Nov 8, 05. *Study:* Middlebury Col, 21-23. *Work:* USN Combat Art Collection, Washington, DC; State Found Cult & Arts, Hawaii; and others. *Comn:* Destroyers on Maneuvers, San Diego to Pearl Harbor, 60, Proteus, Guam, 66, Apollo 8 Splashdown & Recovery, 68 & Apollo 15 Splashdown & Recovery, Navy Art Coop & Liaison Comt, 72; Reader's Digest covers, Jan & Apr, 78; 12 menu covers, United Airlines. *Exhib:* Washington Sq Outdoor Art Show (Hors de Concours), New York, 56-63; Salmagundi Fall Show, New York, 60-70; Four Easter Art Festivals, Honolulu, Hawaii, 63-71; Nat Acad Design Shows, New York, 66, 68 & 70; Artists of Hawaii, Honolulu Acad, 68-70. *Teaching:* Instr sculpture, Riverdale Country Sch for Girls, 46-56; instr oil painting, pvt studio, New York summers & Honolulu winters, 62-67. *Awards:* Proctor Prize in Portrait Sculpture, Nat Acad Design, 48-49; Grand Prize All Media, Washington Sq Outdoor Art Show, 56-58. *Mem:* Salmagundi Club; Asn Honolulu Artists; Windward Artists Guild (pres, 69-70); Lahaina Art Asn. *Media:* Oil, Bronze, Clay. *Dealer:* Grand Central Galleries 40 Vanderbilt Ave New York NY 10017; Royal Hawaiian Gallery 2259 Kalakaua Ave Honolulu HI 96815. *Mailing Add:* c/o Artworks Fine Art 15 Potter Dr Old Greenwich CT 06870

HAZEN, JOSEPH H
COLLECTOR
b Kingston, NY. *Mem:* Int Coun Mus Mod Art; Vis Comt Fogg Art Mus; Metrop Mus Art; Acquisitions Comt Nat Gallery; Chmn Emer Am Friends Israel Mus. *Collection:* Late nineteenth and early twentieth century paintings. *Mailing Add:* 645 Madison Ave New York NY 10022

HAZLEHURST, FRANKLIN HAMILTON
HISTORIAN, EDUCATOR
b Spartanburg, SC, Nov 6, 25. *Study:* Princeton Univ, BA, 49, MFA, 52, PhD, 56. *Teaching:* Instr art hist, Princeton Univ, 54-56; lectr art hist, Frick Collection, New York, 56-57; from asst to assoc prof, Univ Ga, 57-63; prof & chmn dept fine arts, Vanderbilt Univ, 67-91. *Awards:* Fulbright Fel, 53-54; Am Coun Learned Soc Grant in Aid, 67; Madison Sarratt Prize, Vanderbilt Univ, 70; Alice Davis Hitchcock Award, Soc Archit Hist, 82. *Mem:* Am Archaeol Soc; Col Art Asn Am; Southeastern Col Art Asn (pres, 73-74); French Soc Hist Art; Soc Archit Historians. *Res:* Seventeenth and 18th century French art, especially landscape architecture. *Publ:* Auth, Artistic origins of David's oath of the Horatii, Art Bulletin, 60; auth, Jacques Boyceau and the French Formal Garden, 66; auth, Additional sources for the Medici Cycle, Bulletin Musees Royal Beaux Arts Belg, 67; ed, French Formal Garden, Third Colloquium Landscape Archit, Dumbarton Oaks, 74; auth, Gardens of Illusion: The Genius of Andre Le Nostre, 80; and others. *Mailing Add:* Dept Fine Arts Vanderbilt Univ Nashville TN 37240

HAZLEWOOD, CARL E
CURATOR, PAINTER
b Georgetown, Guyana, SAm, Apr 28, 50; US citizen. *Study:* Brooklyn Mus Sch (scholarship), 71 & 73-74; Skowhegan Sch Painting & Sculpture (scholarship), 73; Pratt Inst, New York, BFA(with honors), 75; Hunter Col City Univ New York, MA, 77. *Work:* Dept of the Treasury, State NJ, Trenton; Nat Collection Fine Arts, Georgetown, Guyana; Booker Brothers & McConnel & Co Ltd, London, Eng; State Legislative Bldgs, Albany, NY; Borough Manhattan Community Col, City Univ New York. *Comn:* Many portraits in Am & abroad, 67-72. *Exhib:* Artists Select: Contemporary Perspectives by Afro-Am Artists, Ariz State Univ Mus, Tempe, 86; Vital Abstractions, William Carlos Williams Ctr Arts, Rutherford, NJ, 87; Four Artists, Newark Mus, NJ, 90; Monochrome, Inst Contemp Art, Clocktower Gallery, New York, 90; Generated Realities, Middleton-McMillan Gallery, Charlotte, NC, 91; Drawings from Beginning to End, Ben Shahn Galleries, William Patterson Col, Wayne, NJ, 92. *Collections Arranged:* Revelations (paintings; auth, catalog), Hallwalls, NY, 87; Nexus, Transformation/Transfiguration (auth, catalog), PS 122, 3 Artists of Diverse Cultures, 89; Environmental Explorations (auth, catalog), Three Part Ser, 90-91; Selections (auth, catalog), NY & NJ Artists, Multi Media Work, 90; Essential Structures (auth, catalog), 3 Installations, NJ, 92. *Pos:* Cur, Hazelewood Fine Arts, Brooklyn, NY, 77-; co-founder & artistic dir, Aljira, Ctr Contemp Art, Newark, NJ, 84- *Teaching:* Instr painting, Newark Mus Art, NJ, 91; adj prof art hist, Jersey City State Col, NJ, 91- *Awards:* Edward Arthur Mellinger Found Scholar; Max Beckmann Int Award for Advanced Study; Anco-wood Found Award/Rosalie Retrash Schmidt Mem Award Exhib Grants-Artist Space. *Bibliog:* Lyn Moody Igoe (coauth with James Igoe), 250 Years of Afro-American Art: An Annotated Bibliography, R R Bowker, NY & London, Eng, 81; Joseph E Young (coauth with Barbara Cortright), Phoenix letter, Artspace Mag, 8/86; Vivian Raynor (auth), Art: Drawing from beginning to end, NY Sunday Times, 4/92. *Mem:* Newark Arts Coun; Nat Asn Artists Orgn; NY State Arts Coun Visual Arts Panel. *Media:* Multi Media. *Publ:* Auth, Newark Boasts Long History of Public Art, Newark Arts Coun, 88; illusr (cover), The Signal Network Int Lit, Art Ideas, Signal, 89. *Mailing Add:* Hazelwood Fine Art 499 Lincoln Pl No 4N Brooklyn NY 11238

HAZLITT, DON
PAINTER
b Stockton, Calif, Jan 6, 48. *Study:* San Joaquin Delta Col, AA, 69; Sonoma State Col, BA(art), 71; Calif State Univ, Sacramento, MA(art), 73. *Work:* Musee de Toulon, France; Yale Univ Art Gallery, New Haven, Conn; Vogel Collection, Nat Gallery Art, Washington, DC; Univ Calif Art Gallery, Berkley; Legion of Honour, De Young Mus, San Francisco, Calif; Oakland Mus, Calif; and others. *Exhib:* Crocker-Kingsley Art Ann, crocker Art Mus, Sacramento, Calif, 73-74; Whitney Biennial Contemp Art, New York, 75; Contemp Reflections, Aldrich Mus Contemp Art, Ridgefield, Conn, 75; 15 Contemp New York Artists, Univ Denver, 75; one-man shows, Brabara Gladstone Gallery, 80-81 & Gallery, 83-85 & 87, New York, Mus Toulon, France, 82, Halle Sud, 86 & Galerie Pierre Huber, 87, Geneva & Galerie Vorstadt, 87, Basel, Switz. *Teaching:* Instr, Corpus Christi State Univ, Tex, 81 & Columbia Univ, New York, 82-93. *Awards:* Gold Key Award Art, Scholastic Mag, 67; August Ben-Day Award Art, Alpha Rho Tau, Delta Col, 69; Int Achievement Award, Stockton Arts Comn, 82. *Bibliog:* John Fitzgibbons (auth), article, Arts Mag, 2/80; Susan Larsen (auth), Artists to watch, Artnews, 5/81; Gerrit Henry (auth), article, Art Am, 83; John Russell (auth), rev, NY Times, 4/6/84. *Media:* All. *Dealer:* Pierre Huber Gallerie Geneva Switz. *Mailing Add:* 182 Nevins St Brooklyn NY 11217

HEAD, CECIL FRANKLIN
PAINTER
b Boone Co, Ind, July 1, 06. *Study:* John Herron Sch Art, Indianapolis, Ind, 25-29; special study with Paul Hodley, Clifton Wheeler & Frank Schoonover. *Work:* Hist Soc Johnson Co Mus, Franklin; Indianapolis Mus Art, Ind; Childrens Mus Indianapolis; Ind State Mus, Indianapolis; Franklin Pub Libr. *Exhib:* Ann Exhib, Carnegie Inst Fine Art, Pittsburgh, Pa, 41; Tealist Show, Evansville Mus Art & Sci, Ind, 87; Joslyn 20th Ann Exhib, Jolsyn Art Mus, Omaha, Nebr, 88; First Biannual, Va Mus Art, Richmond, 88; 48th Ann Exhib, Sheldon Swope Art Mus, Terre Houte, Ind, 92; Herron Students & Instructors Early Generation, Indianapolis Mus Art, Ind 92. *Awards:* Third Prize, Ind Bi-centennial, Franklin Mint, 76; Second Prize, pastel, Channel 20 Tv Sta, 87; Best of Show, Ind Heritage Art Show, 92. *Bibliog:* Flora Lauter (auth), Ind artists to 40's, Samuel R Guard Inc, Spencer, Ind, 41. *Mem:* Ind Artists Club; Hoosier Salon; Southside Art League; Ind Heritage Arts Inc. *Media:* Oil. *Mailing Add:* RR 1, Box 235 Whiteland IN 46181

HEAD, GEORGE BRUCE
PAINTER, DESIGNER
b St Boniface, Man, Feb 14, 31. *Study:* Univ Man, Dipl(fine art), 53. *Work:* Nat Gallery Can; Pub Libr, Art Mus, London; Montreal Mus Art; Can Coun Art Bank. *Comn:* Oil on panels, Manitoba Teachers Col, 59; cast concrete sculpture, City of Winnipeg Underground Concourse, 78; mural, Woodsworth Bldg, Manitoba Govt. *Exhib:* Nat Gallery, Australian Art Tour, 67-68; Tenth Winnipeg Art Gallery Biennial, 70; Montreal Spring Exhib; Nat Gallery Can Biennial; one-man show, Winnipeg Art Gallery, 73, Univ Winnipeg, 88 & Univ Manitoba, 89. *Awards:* Purchase Prizes, Winnipeg Show, Winnipeg Art Gallery & 20th Western Ont Exhib; Benson & Hedges Art Wall Design Award, 72. *Bibliog:* H Ochi (auth), article, Ideas Mag; W Hertig (auth), Graphics Annual, Graphic Press; article, Art Director Ann; and others. *Mem:* Royal Can Acad. *Media:* Acrylic. *Mailing Add:* 19 Woodlawn Ave Winnipeg MB R2M 2P3 Canada

HEAD, ROBERT WILLIAM
PAINTER, EDUCATOR
b Springfield, Ill, Aug 6, 41. *Study:* MacMurray Col, BA(art educ), 63, with Sidman & Foresterling; Kent State Univ, MFA, 65, with Shock, Morrow, Petersham & Short; Colo Outward Bound Sch, 71. *Work:* J B Speed Art Mus, Louisville, Ky; Mint Mus, Charlotte, NC; Del Mar Col, Corpus Christi, Tex; MacMurray Col, Jacksonville, Ill; Massillon Mus, Ohio. *Exhib:* Ball State Univ Nat Drawing Show, Muncie, Ind; Bucknell Nat Drawing Exhib, Lewisburg, Pa; Mainstreams Int Painting Exhib, Marietta, Ohio; Brooks Mem Gallery Show, Memphis, Tenn; Weatherspoon Ann Drawing Exhib, Univ NC; solo shows, J B Speed Mus, Louisville, Ky, Univ Mass, Amhurst, Yeiser Art Ctr, Paducah, Ky, Capitol Arts Ctr, Bowling Green, Ky, Sangamon State Univ, Springfield, Ill, Concord Col, Athens, WVa. *Teaching:* Prof drawing & painting, Murray State Univ, 65-; assoc prof drawing & introd art, World

Campus Afloat, Chapman Col, spring 70 & 72; vis prof, Univ Alaska, Fairbanks, fall 86. *Awards:* Merit Award for Excellence in Teaching, Murray State Univ, 70; Purchase Award, Mid-States Exhib, Evansville Mus; Distinguished Professor, Murray State Univ. *Mem:* Nat Art Educ Asn; Wilderness Soc; Ky Ornith Soc. *Media:* All. *Mailing Add:* Murray State Univ Dept Art Box 2438 Univ Sta Murray KY 42071

HEADLEY, DAVID ALLEN
PAINTER
b Washington, Pa, Dec 11, 46. *Study:* Washington & Jefferson Col, BA, 68. *Work:* Corcoran Gallery Am Art, Washington, DC. *Exhib:* Eastern Mich Univ, Ypsilanti, Mich, 67; Butler Inst Art, Youngstown, Ohio, 67 & 68; Detroit Inst Art, 72; Corcoran Gallery, Washington, DC, 76 & 77; Health, Educ & Welfare Bldg, Washington, DC, 79-80; Manhattan Ctr Gallery, New York, 83; Pratt Inst Gallery, New York, 83; and others. *Awards:* First Prizes, Washington & Jefferson Arts Festival, 65 & 66 & Morgantown Art Asn, WVa, 66 & 67. *Bibliog:* John Deckert (auth), David Headley, Arts Mag, 9/81. *Mailing Add:* c/o Martha Tepper Contemporary 120 Forest Ave West Newton MA 02165

HEALY, ANNE LAURA
SCULPTOR, EDUCATOR
b New York, NY, Oct 1, 39. *Study:* Queens Col, New York, BA, 62. *Work:* Chemical Bank, NY; New York Cult Ctr; Allen Art Mus, Oberlin, Ohio; City Univ Grad Ctr, New York; Mich State Univ, East Lansing; and others. *Comn:* Washington State, 85; City of Oakland, 85; Stanford Univ, 89-90; Art Inst Southern Calif, 89. *Exhib:* individual exhib, AIR Gallery, New York, 72, 74, 78, 81 & 83, Matrix Gallery, Sacramento, Calif, 82, Public Art Fund, New York, 83, Douglas Col, Rutgers Univ, New Brunswick, NJ, 84, Festival Lake, Okla, Calif, 85, San Francisco Mus Mod Art Rental Gallery, 88; Mus Contemp Crafts, New York, 72; Sculpture Outdoors, Nassau Co Mus Fine Arts, Roslyn, NY, 75; Int Women's Year, Bronx Mus, New York, 75; South East Tex Mus, Corpus Christi, 77, Baruch Col, New York, 78, Candidates for Grants, Am Acad & Inst of Arts & Lett, 79 & Hofstra Univ, Hempstead, NY, 80; New Directions in Drawing, 1950-80; A Women's Place, Kingsborough Community Col, Brooklyn, NY, 82; KQED Art Auction Invitational, Fuller-Golden Gallery, San Francisco, Calif, 85; Am Heart, San Francisco Art Inst, Calif, 86. *Pos:* Bd mem, bd dirs, head curatorial comt, San Francisco Arts Comm Gallery, Calif, 85-89; bd trustees, San Francisco Art Inst, Calif, 85-88; Art Comnr for Sculpture City of San Francisco, Head, Visual Art Comt, Mem, Civil Design Comt, 89-; pres, San Francisco Art Comn, 92- *Teaching:* Instr sculpture, St Ann's Sch, Brooklyn; vis artist, Mich State Univ, East Lansing, 73 & Broward Col, Ft Lauderdale, Fla, 76; vis artist-in-residence, Univ Cincinnati, 76; adj asst prof, Baruch Col, City Univ New York, 76-; guest lectr, Sch Visual Arts, New York, 77, Bard Col & Univ Iowa, 78 & Univ Northern Iowa, 79; vis prof sculpture, Univ Iowa, Iowa City, 79,; asst prof, Univ Calif, Berkeley, 81-85, assoc prof, 85-, chair of Art Dept, 90- *Awards:* Award for Sculpture, Asn Am Univ Women, 76-77; Am Acad & Inst Arts & Lett, 79-80; Macdowell Colony, 80. *Bibliog:* Ellen Lubbell (auth), Healy's double header, Soho Weekly News, 10/18/78; Corinne Robins (auth), Anne Healey: ten years of temporal sculpture, Arts, 10/78; The great goddess, Heresies 5th Issue, spring 78. *Mem:* Col Art Asn; Women's Caucus Art Asn. *Media:* Sculpture, Drawing. *Dealer:* AIR Gallery 63 Crosby St New York NY 10012. *Mailing Add:* Dept Art Hist Univ Calif Berkeley CA 94720

HEALY, DEBORAH ANN
ILLUSTRATOR, EDUCATOR
b Newark, NJ. *Study:* Col New Rochelle, BA; Montclair State Col, MA, 76; Syracuse Univ, with Isadore Selzer, James McMullen, Doug Johnson & others, MFA, 79. *Work:* Danish Pub Television; Swedish Pub Television; Italian Pub Television; Vanderbilt Univ; US Army. *Comn:* Films, animated Women, 80, Owl & Pussycat, Little Birds, 81 & Three Love Poems; paintings & illus for Harper & Row, Doubleday, Glazen Advert, Douglas Group, Monsanto, Donald Sacks, Inc, United Nations, Yankee, New Eng, Living, Simon & Schuster, Bantam, New Am Libr, Philadelphia Mag, Enquirer & others. *Exhib:* Film Festival, Morris Mus Arts & Sci, Morristown, NJ, 76; Artist in Am Series, Fairleigh Dickenson Col, Madison, NJ, 76; Annecy Int Film Festival, Paris, France, 77; Zagreb Int Animation Festival, Yugoslavia, 78; Sinking Creek Winners' Invitational, Chicago Art Inst, 78; Invitational, Montclair Art Mus, NJ, 79; Painting Exhib Soc Illustr, 85; paintings of Turkey in Pentagon, Airforce Artist, 89; Earth Island proj, UN, 90. *Teaching:* Prof & pres illustration dept, Moore Col Art, Philadelphia, Pa, 86-present; lectr, Parsons Sch Design, 82- & Kean Col, 85; hist illusr, Rochester Inst Technol & Second Ann Graphic Design Symposium. *Awards:* Fels, New Jersey Coun Arts; First Prize-Best in Show, Stockton State Spring Film Festival, NJ, 78; Nat Mag Nomination, Philadelphia Mag, 88; Film grant, NJ State Coun Arts, 81-82; and others. *Bibliog:* Interview, Edison Black Maria Film Fest, NJ Independent Filmmakers, NJ Cablevision, 5/29 & 6/15/85. *Mem:* Art Dirs Club NJ; Art Ctr of NJ; Col Art Asn; Graphic Artists Guild; Soc Illustrators; Presidext. *Media:* Film, Oil. *Publ:* Illusr, Elizabeth and The Water Troll, The Little Old Man and His Dream, Waiting For You, Desserts, Harper & Row, 87-89. *Dealer:* Clapp & Tuttle Gallery CT. *Mailing Add:* 72 Watchung Ave Upper Montclair NJ 07043

HEALY, JULIA SCHMITT
PAINTER, EDUCATOR
b Elmhurst, Ill, Mar 28, 47. *Study:* Univ Chicago, 66-70; Yale Univ Summer Sch, 69, with Mel Bochner, Bob Mangold & Bob Moskowitz; Art Inst of Chicago, BFA, 70, MFA, 72. *Work:* Can Coun Art Bank, Ottawa, Ont; NS Art Bank, Halifax; Confederation Art Gallery, Charlottetown, PEI; Mount St Vincent Univ Art Gallery, Halifax; Dept of Educ, Prov of NS, Halifax. *Comn:* Halifax Diary (print), Dept Pub Works, NS, 75; Staten Island Children's Mus, 89-91. *Exhib:* Art Inst Chicago, 72 & 76; solo exhibs, Owens Art Gallery, Mt Allison Univ, Sackville, NB, 77 & Susan Whitney Gallery, Regina, Sask, 81 & 83; Young Contemporaries (traveling exhib), London Art Gallery, Ont, 76-78; Atlantic J (traveling exhib), Nat Gallery of Can, 76-77; Drawing Centre, New York, 80 & 82; The Cutting Edge, Fine Arts Mus Long Island, NY, 89; Newhouse Center for Contemp Art, 87, Mus of Staten Island, 89; Artists Space, 89, 90 & 91. *Collections Arranged:* Intercourse (co-cur with Ray Johnson), Wabash Transit Gallery, Chicago, 71; Grassroots-Nova Scotian Folk Art, Eye Level Gallery, Halifax, 75. *Pos:* Dir, Eye Level Gallery, 75-76. *Teaching:* Instr visual art, Ocean Co Col, Toms River, NJ, 79-82; asst prof, Pratt Inst, Brooklyn, NY, 91-, dir, Saturday School, 92- *Awards:* Can Coun Arts grant, 76-77 & 77-78; Purchase Award, Staten Island Mus, 86; Staten Island Coun Arts Grant, 87 & 91. *Bibliog:* Ron Shuebrook (auth), The Atlantic Provinces: Letter, Artscanada, 3/75; Marilyn Smith (auth), Some Nova Scotian Women Artists, 12/75 & Ron Shuebrook (auth), Some Major Nova Scotian Painters, 10-11/76, Art Mag; Vivian Raynor (auth), Eccentric vision, Humorous touches, NY Times, 8/27/89; John Perreault (auth), Dispatches from the Front, 1989, Artmakers Staten Island Advance, 90- *Mem:* Col Art Asn; Found Commun of Artists; Chancellors Art Adv Bd, 91- *Media:* Mixed Media. *Publ:* Ed, Recent Work: Julia Schmitt Healy, Dalhousie Art Gallery, 76. *Dealer:* Susan Whitney Gallery 2220 Lorne St Regina SK Can. *Mailing Add:* 294 Edgewater St Staten Island NY 10305

HEARD, LILLIAN
PAINTER
b Bainbridge, Ga, Feb 7, 65. *Study:* Univ Ga, BFA, 88; Art Inst Chicago, MFA, 91. *Exhib:* Solo exhib, Grit Gallery, Athens, Ga, 89 & Betsy Rosenfield Gallery, Chicago, 91 & 93; Window to the Imagination, Gallery Z, Sch Art Inst Chicago, 90; Gigantic Women, Miniature Work, Gallery Z, Sch Art Inst Chicago, 90; New Work, Betsy Rosenfield Gallery, Chicago Art Expo, 91; Face to Face: Self Portraits by Chicago Artists, Chicago Cult Ctr, 92; Art Fair/Seattle, Betsy Rosenfield Gallery, 92; From America's Studio: Drawing New Conclusions, Betty Rymer Gallery, Sch Art Inst Chicago, 92; May 1992, Betsy Rosenfield Gallery, Chicago Int Art Expo, 92; and others. *Teaching:* Asst, Art Inst Chicago, 90. *Awards:* Visual Arts Fel Award, Arts Midwest, Nat Endowment Arts Regional, 92. *Bibliog:* John Mehlferber (auth), Lillian Heard, Art Papers, 7/90; Elisabeth Condon (auth), Peggy Shaw, Lillian Heard, New Art Examiner, 5/91; Giselle Atterberry (auth), Mystery Ties Artists Together at Parkland Show, Champaign-Urbana News Gazette, 3/92. *Media:* Oil on Copper. *Mailing Add:* c/o Betsy Rosenfield Gallery 212 W Superior St Chicago IL 60610

HEARN, M F (MILLARD FILLMORE), JR
ADMINISTRATOR, HISTORIAN
b Lincoln, Ala, Aug 18, 38. *Study:* Auburn Univ, Ala, BA, 60; Ind Univ, MA(hist), 64, MA(art hist), 66, PhD, 69; Univ Calif, Berkeley, study with Jean Bony, 65-66; Courtauld Inst Art, 66-67. *Teaching:* From instr to prof medieval art & archit, Univ Pittsburgh, 67-, actg chmn fine arts dept, 73-74, chmn, 74-78, dir archit studies prog, 81- *Awards:* Grant, NEH Summer Inst, 84; Grant, NEH Summer Stipend, 90; Grant, CASVA, Paul Mellon Vis Senior Fel, 92. *Mem:* Soc Architectural Historians; Int Ctr Medieval Art; Brit Archeol Asn. *Res:* Twelfth-century architecture of England and Northern France; Romanesque sculpture; Frank Lloyd Wright. *Publ:* Auth, The Rectangular Ambulatory in English Medieval Architecture, J Soc Archit Historians, Vol 30, 71; Romsey Abbey: A Progenitor of the English National Tradition in Medieval Architecture, GESTA, Vol 14, 75; Romanesque Sculpture: The Revival of Momental Stone Sculpture in the Eleventh and Twelfth Centuries, Ithaca and Oxford, 81; Ripon Minster: The Beginning of the Gothic Style in Northern England, Philadelphia, 83; The Architectural Theory of Viollet-le-Duc: Readings and commentary, Cambridge, Mass, 90. *Mailing Add:* Univ Pittsburgh 104 Frick Fine Arts Bldg Pittsburgh PA 15260

HEARTNEY, ELEANOR
CRITIC
b Des Moines, Iowa, Aug 5, 54. *Study:* Univ Chicago, BA, 76, MA, 80. *Pos:* Ed Assoc, Art News, currently; contrib ed, Art Am, New Art Examiner, currently. *Awards:* Frank Jewitt Mather Award for Distinguished Art Criticism, 92. *Mem:* Int Asn Art Critics; Adv Committee-Independent Curs. *Publ:* Auth, David Salle: Impersonal effects, Art Am, 6/88; A necessary transgression: pornography & posmodernism, New Art Examiner, 11/88; auth, April Gorniks Stormy weather, Art News, 5/89; auth, Mirror Vision: Alfredo Jaar, Contemporania, 6/89; auth, The whole earth show part II, Art Am, 7/89. *Mailing Add:* 313 E Sixth St New York NY 10003

HEATH, DAVE (DAVID MARTIN HEATH)
EDUCATOR, PHOTOGRAPHER
b Philadelphia, Pa, June 27, 31. *Study:* Philadelphia Col Art, 54-55; New Sch, with W Eugene Smith, 59 & 61. *Work:* Nat Gallery Can, Ottawa; Nat Film Bd Can; Mus Mod Art, New York; Int Mus Photog, George Eastman House, Rochester, NY; Minneapolis Inst Art. *Comn:* Collab with Robert Frank, Robert Heinecken & John Wood, William Johnson & Susan Cohen (dirs), 83-85. *Exhib:* A Dialogue with Solitude, Eastman House, Rochester & Art Inst Chicago, 64; Nat Gallery Can, 67, 74 & 81; Photography in America, Whitney Mus Art, New York, 74; Mirrors & Windows: Am Photog since 1960, Mus Mod Art, New York, 78; Songs of Innocence, Harbourfront Gallery, Toronto, 81; Le plaisir de voir, la passion du regard, Light Impressions Spectrum Gallery, Rochester, 88; Lesley Walker, a collaborative portrayal, Artscourt, Ottawa, 89. *Pos:* Artist in residence, Univ Minn, Minneapolis, 65 & Int Ctr Photog, NY, 78. *Teaching:* Instr photog, Sch Dayton Art Inst, 65-67; asst prof photog, Moore Col Art, Philadelphia, 67-70;

prof photog, Ryerson Polytech Inst, 70-; adj fac, Visual Studies Workshop, 76-77. *Awards:* Guggenheim Found Fel, 63 & 64. *Bibliog:* Charles Hagen (auth), Le grand ALBUM ordinaire, Afterimage Visual Studies Workshop, 2/74; James Borcoman (auth), David Heath: a dialogue with solitude, J 34, Nat Gallery of Can, 10/79; Michael Torosian (auth & ed), David Heath, Extempore, Reflections on Art & Personal History, Lumiere Press, Toronto, 88. *Media:* Slide, Sound, Chromogenic Print. *Publ:* Contribr, Contemporary Photographer, Vol 5, No 1; auth, A Dialogue with Solitude, Community Press, 65; contribr, Photography in the 20th Century, 67; contribr, Photography in America, 75; contribr, Mirrors and Windows, 78. *Dealer:* The Collected Image 806 Montroe St Evanston IL 60202. *Mailing Add:* 120 Wolfrey Ave Toronto ON M4K 1L3 Canada

HEATH, DAVID C
DEALER
b Atlanta, Ga, June 6, 40. *Study:* Vanderbilt Univ; Univ Vienna; Columbia Univ. *Pos:* Pres, Heath Gallery, DC Heath & Assoc & Adv on Int Sculpture Inc, currently. *Specialty:* 20th century American & large scale sculpture. *Mailing Add:* c/o Heath Gallery 416 East Paces Ferry Rd NE Atlanta GA 30305

HEATH, DAVID MARTIN See Heath, Dave (David Martin Heath)

HEATH, SAMUEL K
MUSEUM DIRECTOR
b Exeter, NH, Sept 10, 54. *Study:* Yale Univ, BA(art hist), 76; Columbia Univ, Dept Art Hist, MA, 83, MPhilos, 83. *Pos:* Staff lectr, Nat Gallery Art, Washington, DC, 76-78; curatorial intern, Boston Mus Fine Arts, 80-81; proj dir inventory & catalog colonial paintings, Cuzco, Peru, Int Found Art Res, NY, 83-85; lectr spec exhibs, Dept Pub Progs, Metrop Mus Art, 83-90; prog specialist Spain & Latin Am, World Monument Fund, NY, 88-90; cur Span Art, Meadows Mus, Southern Methodist Univ, Dallas, Tex, 90-92, dir, 92- *Teaching:* Instr art hist, Phillips Exeter Acad, NH, summers 76-79, Sch Visual Arts, NY, 85 & Southern Methodist Univ, Dallas, Tex, 90- *Mem:* Int Coun Mus; Am Asn Mus; Tex Mus Asn; Art Mus Asn; Asn Art Mus Dirs. *Mailing Add:* Meadows Mus Owen Art Ctr Southern Methodist Univ Dallas TX 75275

HEATON, JANET N
PAINTER, GALLERY DIRECTOR
b Miami, Fla, May 27, 36. *Study:* Fla State Univ. *Work:* State House, Nairobi, Kenya; Leigh Yawkey Woodson Art Mus, Wausau, Wis. *Comn:* PGA National, Palm Beach Gardens, Fla. *Exhib:* Birds in Art, 88, 91 & 92 & Wildlife the Artists View, 89, Leigh Yawkey Woodson Art Mus, Wausau, Wis; SAA Ann Exhib, Witte Mus, San Antonio, 92; Birds In Art, Travel Exhib, Am RMus Natural Hist, New York, 92; Art & The Animal, SAA Va Mus Natural Hist, Martinsville, 92; Birds In Art Travel Exhib, The Ward Mus of Wildfowl Art, Salisbury, Md, 92; SAA '93, traveling exhib. *Awards:* Winslow Homer Award & Liquitex Award, Fla Watercolor Soc, 90; Merit Award, Fla Watercolor Soc, 92. *Mem:* Signature Mem Soc Animal Artists; Signature Mem Pastel Soc Am; Signature Mem Fla Watercolor Soc; Catharine Lorillard Wolfe Art Club Inc; Outdoor Writers Asn Am. *Media:* Pastel, Watercolor. *Publ:* Contribr, Wildlife Art, The Female Perspective, Sports Afield, 86; A Painting Safari Through Southern Africa, Am Artist, 88; Artists of Florida, Mountain Products of Tex, Vol II, 90-92; African Wildlife In Art, Clive Holloway Bks, London, Eng, 91; The Killers of Old Africa, Outdoor Life, 91. *Dealer:* J N Bartfield Gallery 30 W 57th St New York NY 10019. *Mailing Add:* 1169 Old Dixie Hwy No 5 Lake Park FL 33403

HEBALD, MILTON ELTING
SCULPTOR, PRINTMAKER
b New York, NY, May 24, 17. *Study:* Art Students League, with Ann Goldwaithe, 27-28; Nat Acad Design, with Gordon Samstag, 31-32; Master Inst United Arts, 31-34; Beaux-Arts Inst Design, 32-35; Nat Acad Design, 32-33. *Work:* Whitney Mus Am Art; Philadelphia Mus Art; Tel-Aviv Mus, Israel; Va Mus Fine Arts; Joyce Mus, Dublin, Ireland; Shakespeare Monument, Oslo, Norway, 76; and many others. *Comn:* Bronze frieze, Pan-Am Terminal, Kennedy Airport, NY; Ackland Mem, Univ NC; James Joyce Monument, Zurich, Switz, 66; Tempest Group Bronze, Cent Park, New York, 72; Bronze Olympiads (2), YMCA, Los Angeles, 86; and many others. *Exhib:* Va Mus Fine Arts, 67; solo exhibs, Yares Gallery, Scottsdale, Ariz, 76-78, Harmon Gallery, Naples, Fla, 78, Randall Galleries, New York, 78, Byck Gallery, Louisville, Ky, 78 & Cheekwood, Nashville, Tenn, 78; and others. *Teaching:* Instr, Brooklyn Mus Sch Art, 46-51, Cooper Union, 46-53, Univ Minn, 49, Skowegan Sch Painting & Sculpture, 50-52 & Long Beach State Univ, Calif, 68. *Awards:* Second Prize, Pa Acad Fine Arts, 51; First Prize New York City Dept Pub Works, E Bronx TB Hosp, 52; Prix de Rome, 55-58; and others. *Bibliog:* Martha C Cheney (auth), Modern Art in America, McGraw-Hill, 39; C Ludwig Brumme (auth), Contemporary American Sculpture, Crown, 48; Frank Getlein (auth), Milton Hebald, Viking, 71. *Mem:* Fel Am Acad in Rome; Asn Am Group; Cosmos Club, Washington, DC. *Media:* Bronze, Wood; Lithography. *Publ:* Illusr, An Alphabestiary, Ciardi Lithograph 34, Touchstone Press, Lippincott Co, NY, 66; Sounds & Shapes, Univ Soc, 70. *Mailing Add:* Via Santo Celso 22 Bracciano 00062 Italy

HEBERLING, GLEN AUSTIN
PAINTER, ILLUSTRATOR
b Ambridge, Pa, Nov 18, 15. *Study:* Ad Art Studio Sch, Pittsburgh, Pa, 36; Art Inst Pittsburgh (scholar), 36-38; Art Students League, New York, 46-48 & 51. *Work:* Old Economy Pa State Hist Mus, Ambridge, Pa; Ladycliff Col & West Point Credit Union, Highland Falls, NY; Norstar Bank Hq, Newburgh, NY; WPoint Mus, NY. *Comn:* World War II Mem Mural, Highland Falls High Sch, 50; five paintings, Marine Midland Bank, Highland Falls, 67; and many pvt comns. *Exhib:* Am Watercolor Soc, Nat Acad Galleries, NY, 44-46; Butler Inst Am Art, Youngstown, Ohio, 45; US Army Arts Contest Nat, Nat Gallery Art, Washington, DC, 45; ACA Gallery, New York, 46; Boston Mus Fine Arts, 49; Kennedy Gallery, New York, 50; Artists of the Upper Hudson, Albany Inst Art & Hist, NY, 62; Garrison Art Ctr, Garrison, NY, 91-92; and others. *Pos:* Illusr, US Military Acad, West Point, NY, 58-71. *Teaching:* Instr & lectr, Ladycliff Col, 61-71, Garrison Art Ctr, NY, 76, Mt St Mary Col, Newburgh, NY, 76. *Awards:* Arts Coun Orange Co, NY Awards, 81 & 83; Norstar Bank Purchase Award, Orange Co, NY Watercolor Soc, 86; Nat Times Herald Record Prize, 88 & Alice Beal VS Mem Award, 89, Coun Am Artist's Award, 91 Northeast Watercolor Soc. *Bibliog:* News of the Highlands (article), Highland Falls, NY, 87; Evening News (article), Newburgh, NY, 87. *Mem:* Orange Co Watercolor Soc, NY, 75-86; Northeast Watercolor Soc, 87-; Garrison NY Art Ctr, 91- *Media:* Oil, Watercolor. *Publ:* Illusr, Handbook on Physical Education, 44; En Busco de Oro Negro, 59; Assembly, Asn Grads, West Point, 66; Kepler & Discovery of His Planetary Laws, 69; Engineering Fundamentals, 70. *Mailing Add:* 58 Church St Highland Falls NY 10928

HECHT, IRENE
PAINTER
b New York, NY, Dec, 1, 49. *Study:* Case Western Reserve Univ, BA, 71; Art Student League with Everett Raymond Kinstler, Burt Silverman & Aaron Shikler & David Levine. *Work:* Portraits of Isaac Stern, Martin Bookspan & Zubin Mehta, Nat Arts Club, Prof Eugene P Wigner, Princeton Univ. *Comn:* Portraits, Louis Nizer, 82, Arthur Krim, 83 & Charles Scribner IV, 86, New York; portrait, Nobel Laureate Nuclear Physicist Prof Eugene P Wigner. *Teaching:* Instr portrait painting, Delaware Art Mus, 84-87. *Mem:* Nat Arts Club; Artists Fel; Lotus Club. *Media:* Oil. *Mailing Add:* 2400 Baynard Blvd Wilmington DE 19802

HECKSCHER, WILLIAM SEBASTIAN
HISTORIAN, PAINTER
b Hamburg, Ger, Dec 14, 04; Can citizen. *Study:* Univ Hamburg, PhD, 35; NY Univ; Oxford Univ; McGill Univ, Montreal, DLett, 81, McGill Univ, Hon PhD, 84. *Work:* Drawings, Kunsthalle, Hamburg, Ger. *Exhib:* One-man show, Allied Arts Gallery, Durham, NC, 67. *Pos:* Consult, Dept Rare Bks, Princeton Univ Libr, 76- *Teaching:* Univ Man, Sask, State Univ Iowa, 47-55; chmn & dir, Iconological Inst, Univ Utrecht, 55-66; chmn dept art, Duke Univ, 66-69, Benjamen N Duke prof & dir, Art Mus, 70-; Samuel H Kress prof in residence, Nat Gallery Art, Washington, DC, 79-80; lectr, Col de France, Paris, 80-81. *Awards:* Festschrift, Netherlands Yearbook Hist Art, 64; W S Heckscher, Art and Literature, (ill), Durham NC, 85; Carey Award, Soc Indexers, London, 87; The Verbal and the Visual Essays in honor of William S Heckscher, (ill), New York, 90. *Bibliog:* Eric Koch (auth), Deemed Suspect, Toronto, Ont, 80; Elizabeth Sears (auth), The Life and Work of William S Heckscher, Zeitschrift fu Kunstgeschichte vol 53, p 107-133, i, 90. *Mem:* Fel Folger Shakespeare Libr; Benjamin Franklin Fel Royal Soc Arts, London; corresp mem Soc Indexers London; Inst Advan Study, Princeton, NJ; res fel Herzog August Bibliothek, Wolfenbuttel, Ger, 81; Int Soc for Emblem Studies, Glasgow-Montreal (pres, 88). *Publ:* Auth, books, exhibition catalogues, articles in the field of art history, iconology, history of anatomy, index making & emblematics; illusr books. *Mailing Add:* 32 Wilton St Princeton NJ 08540

HEDBERG, GREGORY SCOTT
ART DEALER, GALLERY DIRECTOR
b Minneapolis, Minn, May 2, 46. *Study:* Princeton Univ, BA, 68; Inst Fine Arts, NY Univ, MA, 71, PhD, 80. *Collections Arranged:* Picasso, Braque, Leger (coauth, catalog), 75; Charles Biederman: A Retrospective (auth, catalog), 76; Millet's Gleaners (auth, catalog), 78; Victorian High Renaissance (auth, catalog), Manchester City Art Galleries, Minneapolis Inst Arts & Brooklyn Mus, 78-79; Leger's Le Grand Dejeuner (auth, catalog), 80; German Realism of the Twenties: The Artist as Social Critic (auth, catalog), Minneapolis & Chicago, 80; The Tremaine Collection (auth, catalog), Hartford, 84; J Pierpont Morgan, Collector (coauth, catalog), travelling exhib, 87; Soviet Art from the Academy, NY Acad Art, 88. *Pos:* Lectr, Frick Collection, New York, 71-74; cur paintings, Minneapolis Inst Arts, 74-81; chief cur, 81-86, asst dir, 86-87, Wadsworth Atheneum, Hartford, Conn; dir, NY Acad Art, 87-92; dir European art, Hirschl & Adler Gallery, New York. *Res:* Fifteenth century painting in Rome. *Publ:* Auth, The Farnese Courtyard Windows and the Porta Pia: Michelangelo's creative process, Marsyas, 71; auth, The Jerome Hill bequest: Delacroix's Fanatics of Tangiers and Corot's Silenus, 76 & In favor of Nicola di Maestro Antonio d'Ancona, 77, Minneapolis Inst Arts Bulletin. *Mailing Add:* 336 E 69th St New York NY 10021

HEDDEN-SELLMAN, ZELDA
PAINTER, INSTRUCTOR
b Farmington, Ill. *Study:* Bradley Univ, BS & MA; Ohio Univ; Harvard Univ; Western Reserve Univ; also with Ben Shahn, Arnold Blanch & Gladys Rockmore Davis. *Work:* Manias Manor, Peoria, Ill; Expos Bldg, Springfield, Ill; Spoon River Col, Canton, Ill. *Exhib:* Old Northwest Territory Show, Springfield, 52; Ohio Valley Watercolor Show, Athens, 53; Ill State Mus, Springfield, 59; three-man show, Kottler Gallery, New York, 72; one-man show, Western Ill Univ, 79 & 81. *Pos:* Dir, Peoria Art Ctr Sch, 54-56. *Teaching:* Instr art, Ind State Univ, Terre Haute, 53-54; instr art, Ill Cent Col, Peoria, 69-71 & 88-; instr art, Spoon River Col, 66-74; instr, Bradley Univ, 76-86. *Awards:* Cent Ill Artists Award. *Media:* Acrylic, Watercolor. *Publ:* Auth, Treasures in the Snow, 64. *Dealer:* Upstairs Gallery Lakeview Ctr for Arts & Sci 1125 W Lake Ave Peoria IL 61614. *Mailing Add:* 241 Timberland Metamora IL 61548

HEDMAN, TERI JO
PRINTMAKER, PAINTER
b St Paul, Minn, Oct 10, 44. *Study:* Univ Minn, BS(design); also with Paul Hapke, Toshi Yoshido, Pat Austin & Marge Horton. *Exhib:* All Alaska Exhib, 72, 74, 75 & 78; one-man show, Univ Minn, 67 & Artique Ltd, 73-80. *Pos:* Designer-draftsman, Minneapolis Housing Authority, 68-70; interior designer, Tiptons Interiors, Anchorage, 70-71. *Teaching:* Traveling instr printmaking, Naknek, Bethel & Nome, Alaska, 73. *Awards:* Print Award, All Alaska Juried Exhib, 78; Purchase Award, State Art Bank, State Print Competition, 79. *Mem:* Alaska Artists Guild (prof chmn, 72, funding chmn, 73, vpres, 74, pres, 75, mem bd, 76, vpres, 80); Anchorage Arts Coun (visual arts adv comt, 75). *Mailing Add:* 2219 Saint Elias Dr Anchorage AK 99517

HEDRICK, WALLY BILL
PAINTER, SCULPTOR
b Pasadena, Calif, July 21, 28. *Study:* Otis Art Inst, 46-47; Calif Sch Fine Arts, BFA, 55; Calif Col Arts & Crafts; San Francisco State Col, MA, 58. *Work:* Mus Mod Art, New York; Aldridge Mus Contemp Art, Ridgefield, Conn; San Francisco Mus Mod Art; Los Angeles Co Mus Art; Smithsonian Inst, Washington, DC. *Exhib:* 16 Americans, Mus Mod Art, New York, 59; Places, San Francisco Mus Art, 62; solo exhibs, San Francisco Art Inst, 67 & 85, Sonoma State Col, Rohnert Park, Calif, 68 & Gallery Paule Anglim, San Francisco, 82 & 84; Poets of the Cities, Dallas Mus Art, 74; Chicago Int Art Expos, 84; American Art Now! Paintings in the 1980's, Columbus Mus Arts & Sci, Columbus, Ga, 84; 2nd Newport Biennial-The Bay Area, Newport Harbor Art Mus, Newport Beach, Calif, 86; The Spiritual in Art: Abstract Painting 1890-1985, Los Angeles Co Mus Art, Mus Contemp Art, Chicago & Haags Gemeentemuseum, The Hague, Belg, 86-87; The Painted Word, Richmond Art Ctr, Calif, 90; The Urban Mileu, Gallery Paule Anglin, 92. *Teaching:* Instr painting & drawing, San Francisco Art Inst, 64-70 & San Jose State Univ, 72-73; instr painting & sculpture, Indian Valley Col, 74-87 & Univ Calif, Davis, 84-86. *Awards:* Purchase Award, Los Angeles Co Mus, Los Angeles, 53; Purchase Award, San Francisco Art Comn, 58 & 76 & San Francisco Mus Mod Art, 76; Nat Endowment Arts, 68 & 82; Adline Kent Award, San Francisco Art Asn, 85. *Bibliog:* Jerome Tarshis (auth), Wally Hedrick at San Francisco Art Institute, Art Am, 7/85; Mark Van Proyen, Atypical prototypes: the art of Wally Medrick, Artweek, 4/27/85; Leah Goldman (auth), A view to the north, Artweek, 11/8/86. *Media:* Oil, Welded Metal. *Dealer:* Gallery Paule Anglim 14 Geary St San Francisco CA 94108. *Mailing Add:* Box 302 Bodega CA 94922

HEDSTROM, ANA LISA
CRAFTSMAN
b Ind. *Study:* Mills Col, BA, 65; Kyota Art Col, Japan, 66-67. *Comn:* Miniature hangings, US Govt Bldg, ICS, Islambad, Pakistan. *Exhib:* Renwick Gallery, Smithsonian Inst, Washington, DC, 78; Metrop Mus Philippines, Manila, Philippines, 80; Am Craft Mus, New York, 83-84, int tour, 84-85; Brit Crafts Ctr, London, Eng, 85. *Awards:* Nat Endowment Arts, 82. *Mailing Add:* c/o Julie: Artisans' Gallery 687 Madison Ave New York NY 10021

HEE, HON-CHEW
PAINTER, INSTRUCTOR
b Kahului, Hawaii, Jan 24, 06. *Study:* Calif Sch Fine Arts, dipl, 32; Art Students League, 48-49; Andre L'hote & Fernand Leger, Paris, 49-51. *Work:* Honolulu Acad Arts; Tennent Art Found Art Gallery, Honolulu; State of Hawaii Found Cult & Arts. *Comn:* Concrete mural, Hawaiian Holiday Bldg, Honolulu, 62; carved redwood mural, Honolulu Community Church, 65; enamel on metal murals, Manoa Libr, 78; enamel on metal mural, Hilo Hosp, 85; marble bas relief mural, Mililani Libr, comn by State of Hawaii, 86. *Exhib:* 11th Ann Exhib, Artist Hawaii, Honolulu, 66; Nat Ann Exhib, El Paso Mus Art, Tex, 72; Taiwan Nat Hist Mus, 73; one-man show, Honolulu Acad Arts. *Collections Arranged:* Int show, Solon de l'Art Libre, Paris, 50. *Pos:* Dir, Tennent Art Found Gallery, 67- *Teaching:* Lectr watercolor, Univ Hawaii, Honolulu, 60-70; prof watercolor, Taiwan Normal Univ, Taipei, 71-72, prof serigraph, 72-73. *Awards:* Serigraphy for Text Book, Dr Sun Yet Sen Grant, Taiwan, 71; Artist of the Year, Hawaii Sertoma Club, 81; Gold Plaque for Serigrapher of Taiwan, 83; Oscar D'Italia Award for Masters of the World, 85. *Bibliog:* Demonstration of watercolor, Pau Hana Year, Univ TV Sta, 73; Haar & Neogy (auths), Artists of Hawaii, Univ Hawaii, 74. *Mem:* Hawaii Watercolor Soc (founder & pres, 61). *Publ:* Ed, Serigraphy Text, 71; auth, Thirty Serigraphs, 73; auth, Water Color, 75; ed & illusr, White Serpent, 78; auth, Yin Yang, 82. *Mailing Add:* 45-650 Kapunahala Rd Kaneohe HI 96744

HEEKS, WILLY
PAINTER
b Providence, RI, Apr 28, 51. *Study:* Univ RI, BFA, 73; Whitney Mus Am Art Independent Study Prog, 73. *Work:* Brooklyn Mus Art; Corcoran Gallery Art, Washington, DC; Mus Fine Arts, Boston, Mass; Mus Mod Art, New York. *Exhib:* Solo exhibs, Inaugural Exhibition, 85, McNeil Gallery, 86 & 88, Univ RI, Kingston, 86, David Reitzel Gallery, New York, 87, 88 & 90, Galerie Barbara Farber, Amsterdam, 87, 89 & 92, Rena Bransten Gallery, San Francisco, 89, Works on paper, Trans Avant Garde Gallery, Austin, Tex, 89 & Nielson Gallery, Boston, Mass, 92; Apocalypse & Resurrection, Amfar Benefit, Gallery Three Zero, New York, 92; Focus, 13th Ann Chicago Int Art Expo, 92; In the Spirit of Landscape, Nielsen Gallery, Boston, Mass, 92; Paper Houses, David Beitzel Gallery, New York, 92; Elga Wimmer Gallery, New York, 92. *Awards:* Artists Fel, Nat Endowment Arts, 78, 87 & 89; Louis Comfort Tiffany Award, 85; Painting Award,Am Acad & Inst Arts & Let, 89. *Bibliog:* Thea Figee (auth), Heeks; Paul Depondt (auth), Modern Drippings Met Slierten en Cirkels, de Volkskrant, 3/5/92; Kay Larson (auth), Better Light Than Never, New York, 3/9/92. *Mailing Add:* c/o David Beizel Gallery 102 Prince St New York NY 10012

HEFLIN, TOM PAT
PAINTER, DESIGNER
b Monticello, Ark, July 18, 34. *Study:* Northeast La State Col; Chicago Art Inst. *Work:* Marietta Col; Burpee Art Mus, First Nat Bank, & First Fed Savings, Rockford, Ill; Hill, Sherman, Meroni, Gross & Simpson Law Off, Chicago. *Exhib:* Chicago Art Inst, 71-73; House of Cong, Washington, DC, 72; Butler Inst Am Art, Youngstown, Ohio, 73; New Horizons in Art, Chicago, 75; Am Watercolor Soc, New York, 75. *Teaching:* Instr painting, Burpee Art Mus, 69-71 & Rock Valley Col, 70- *Awards:* First Prize Medal, Nat Soc Painters Casein & Acrylic; First Prize, Ark Nationwide Bicentennial Medal Design, Franklin Mint; First Prize in Painting, Mainstreams 72, Ohio. *Bibliog:* Article, Famous Artists Mag, 70. *Mem:* Nat Soc Painters in Casein & Acrylic; Rockford Art Asn; Fishy Whale Litho Workshop, Milwaukee. *Media:* Oil, Acrylic. *Publ:* Auth, Quiet Places, 77. *Dealer:* Gateway Gallery LaJolla CA; Heflin Gallery Rockford IL. *Mailing Add:* 1162 S Weldon Rd Rockford IL 61102

HEFNER, HARRY SIMON
PAINTER, EDUCATOR
b Kalamazoo, Mich, Nov 20, 11. *Study:* Western Mich Univ, BA, 36; Columbia Univ, MA, 39. *Work:* Kalamazoo Col; South Bend Art Ctr; Albion Col; Western Mich Univ. *Exhib:* Detroit Inst Arts, 63-64; Kalamazoo Inst Arts, 63-66; Grand Rapids Inst Arts, Mich, 64-65; South Bend Inst Arts, Ind, 64-66; Battle Creek Inst Arts, 66; plus others. *Teaching:* Instr, Muskegon Pub Schs, Mich, 37-38, Cranbrook Boys Sch, summers 37-39 & Skidmore Col, 39; mem fac, Western Mich Univ, 40-77, prof watercolor & design, 56-77, head dept art, 63-66, emer prof, 77-; teacher, Harvard Univ, summer 41 & Univ Vt, summers 54-56; retired. *Media:* Watercolor. *Mailing Add:* 1700 Bronson Way No 147 Kalamazoo MI 49009-1008

HEIDEL, FREDERICK (H)
PAINTER, EDUCATOR
b Corvallis, Ore, Dec 29, 15. *Study:* Univ Ore, with Andrew Vincent, David McCosh & Lance Hart, BS; Art Inst Chicago, with Boris Anisfeld & Francis Chapin, BFA & MFA(Anna Louise Raymond Foreign Traveling Fel). *Work:* World Bk Art Collection, Chicago; Portland Art Mus, Ore; Hazeltine Collection, Mus Art, Eugene, Ore; Eastern Ore Col, La Grande, Ore; Kaiser Found, Portland. *Comn:* Mural, Lane Co Comn, Lane Co Courthouse, Eugene, 58; fused glass wall, comn by Sally Stafford, Eugene, 70; fused glass panel, Brock Dixon House, Forest Grove, Ore, 70; laminated glass construction, Portland State Univ, Sci I Bldg, 71; laminated glass window, comn by Mr & Mrs Marvin Witt, Portland. *Exhib:* Drawing & Watercolor Exhib, Metrop Mus Art, New York, 51; Sao Paulo 3rd Biennial, Brazil, 56; 2nd Pac Coast Biennial, WCoast, 57; Vancouver, BC, 58; The West: 80 Contemporaries, 67. *Teaching:* Instr painting, Long Beach City Col, 46-49; instr painting, Univ Ore, 49-53; prof painting, Portland State Univ, 51-, head dept art & archit, 55-82, emer prof, 82. *Awards:* Painting Award, San Francisco Mus Art, 48; Chapelbrook Found Fel, 67. *Bibliog:* Rachel Griffin (auth), Painting & Sculpture of the Pacific Northwest, Portland Art Mus, 59; Nancy McCauley (auth), article, Artweek, Vol 13, No 15. *Mem:* Portland Art Asn; Col Art Asn Am; Art Ore. *Mailing Add:* Foster White Gallery 3112 Occidental S Seattle WA 98101

HEIFERMAN, MARVIN
CURATOR, PUBLISHER
b New York, NY, 1948. *Study:* Brooklyn Col, BA, 68; Columbia Univ: Sch Arts, Film Div; Sch Visual Arts, New York; Brooklyn Mus Art Sch. *Collections Arranged:* The Family of Man, 1955-1984, PS 1, Long Island City, NY; Still Life, Whitney Mus Am Art, Newport Harbor Art Mus & Minneapolis Inst Arts, 83-85; The Real Big Picture, Queens Mus, 86; Image World, Whitney Mus Am Art, 89; The Indomitable Spirit, Int Ctr Photog, New York, 90. *Pos:* Asst dir, Light Gallery, New York, 72-74; dir photog, Castelli Graphics, New York, 75- *Teaching:* MFA prog photog, Sch Visual Arts, 91- *Mem:* Photographers & Friends United Against AIDS, 89- *Publ:* Still Life, Callaway Eds, 83; Image World, Whitney Mus, 89; I'm So Happy, Vintage Bks, 90; My Day, Chronicle Bks, 93; Talking Pictures, Chronicle Bks, 94. *Mailing Add:* 1024 Ave Americas New York NY 10018

HEILOMS, MAY
PAINTER
US citizen. *Study:* Hunter Col; Art Students League. *Work:* Philadelphia Mus, Pa; Norfolk Mus, Va; Samuel Fleisher Art Found, Philadelphia; Bat Yam Mus, Israel; Kenny Int Art Found. *Exhib:* Pa Acad Fine Arts, Philadelphia; Denver Mus, Colo; Corcoran Gallery, Washington, DC; Okla Mus, Oklahoma City; Butler Inst Am Art, Youngstown, Ohio; one-man shows, Bennett Col, 61, Silvermine Guild, Conn, Cent State Mus, Okla, Cortland Art Ctr, New York, Hudson Gallery & Mus Fine Arts, Mexico City; also in Portugal, Italy, Greece, Belg, Israel, Can, Mex & Arg. *Pos:* Adv, Ford Found Prog in Humanities, 58-59. *Teaching:* Instr fine art, City Col New York, 60-62; instr indust & fine art, Fashion Inst Technol, 63-65. *Awards:* Ann Prizes for Oil, Painters & Sculptors Soc NJ, 50-75; Elizabeth Morse Genios Mem Watercolor Prize, Nat Asn Women Artists, 60; Windsor Newton Award for Oil, Am Soc Contemp Artists, 80, Simmons Prize, 84 & Art Award, 85; Allied Artist-Emily Lowe Prize for Oil, 83; Stefan Hirsh Award for oil, 87, Emily Lowe Award for oil, 88, Silver Medal of Honor for oil, 90, Audubon Artists. *Bibliog:* Archives Am Art, Smithsonian Inst. *Mem:* Fel Royal Acad Arts, London, Eng; Audubon Artists (vpres, 56-58); Nat Soc Painters Casein & Acrylic (dir, 65-); NY Soc Women Artists (dir & chmn mem comt, 72-75); Am Soc Contemp Artists (mem comt); Painters & Sculptures Soc of NJ. *Mailing Add:* 340 W 28th St New York NY 10001

HEIMDAL, GEORG
PAINTER, INSTRUCTOR
b Pocatello, Idaho, Aug 6, 43. *Study:* San Francisco State Univ, BA, 66; Univ Calif Davis, MA, 68; Claremont Grad Sch, res fel, 78-79; Wash State Univ, MFA, 80. *Work:* Eastern Wash State Hist Soc, Spokane; Ohio State Univ, Columbus Mus Art, Huntington Bank, Columbus, Ohio; McDonald's Corp, Dayton, & Westerville, Ohio. *Exhib:* Nat Drawing Ann, San Francisco Mus Art, 70; Northwest Ann, Seattle Mus Art, 75; solo exhibs, Wash State Univ, 80, Traver-Sutton Gallery, 82, Hank Baum Gallery, San Francisco, 80, 81, 83 & 85, Belmont Gallery, Columbus, Ohio, 86, Ala State Univ, Montgomery, 87, Ind State Univ, Terre Haute, 88 & Roberta Kuhn Gallery, Columbus, Ohio, 89. *Pos:* Dir studio humanities, Ohio State Univ, Columbus, 80-89, chmn grad studies, 89-90. *Teaching:* Instr drawing, Spokane Falls Community Col, Wash, 69-80; assoc prof, Ohio State Univ, Columbus, 80- *Awards:* Painting Award, Spokane Ann, Fremont Lane S, 73; Purchase Award, Columbus Mus Art, 85; Nat Endowment Humanities/Mellon Found Grant, 79; GCAC Individual Artists Fel, 87. *Bibliog:* Allegra Berrian (auth), Bringing art to life, Spokesman-Rev, 74; Ron Glowan (auth), Painters from the other side, Artweek, 77; Terry Barrett (auth), Trouble in the house, Columbus Art, 84; Jeanne Fryer Kohles (auth), Georg Heimdal, New Art Examiner, 3/89; Terry Barrett (auth), New Works, New Directions, Dialogue Mag, 89. *Media:* Multi. *Publ:* Auth, New Generation Drawings (exhib catalog), 74 & Northwest Eccentric Art (exhib catalog), 76, Eastern Wash Hist Soc; Reflections on a decade, Dialogue Mag, 11/88. *Mailing Add:* 25 Crestview Rd Columbus OH 43202

HEIN, JOHN
CRAFTSMAN
b Albany, NY, July 21, 55. *Study:* Temple Univ, Philadelphia, AB, 77. *Exhib:* American Craft at the Armory, Seventh Regiment Armory, New York, 90; one-man show, Newark Mus, NJ, 92; Comtemporary Furniture Makers of the American Northeast, Gallery at Bristol-Myers Squibb, Princeton, NJ, 91; Meredith Gallery, Baltimore, Md, 91 & 92; NJ Arts Annual: Crafts, Morris Mus, Morristown, 91; and others. *Teaching:* Lectr, Works in Wood, NJ Designer Craftsmen Gallery, New Brunswick, 89. *Awards:* NJ State Coun Arts Individual Fel, 88; Nat Endowment Arts Visual Artists Fel, 90; NICHE Award Winner, wood, functional category, NICHE Mag, Baltimore, Md, 92. *Bibliog:* Bill Kraus (auth), Contemporary Crafts for the Home, Kraus Sikes Inc, New York, 90; Toni Fountain Sikes (ed), Creative Designs in Furniture, Kraus Sikes Inc, Madison, Wis, 91; Wendy Rosen (publ), Profiles, Who's Who in American Crafts, Baltimore, Md, 92. *Mem:* Am Craft Coun; Am Soc Furniture Artists; NJ Designer Craftsmen. *Media:* Wood. *Mailing Add:* 87 Woodland Ave Trenton NJ 08638-2520

HEIN, MAX
GRAPHIC ARTIST, EDUCATOR
b Lincoln, Nebr, Dec 27, 43. *Study:* San Diego State Univ, AB, 66; Univ Calif, Los Angeles, MA, 68, MFA, 69. *Work:* Int Mus Photog, George Eastman House, Rochester, NY; Frederick S Wight Galleries, Univ Calif, Los Angeles; Newport Harbor Mus Art, Calif; Bradford City Art Gallery, Yorkshire, Eng; DeAnza Col Art Gallery, Calif; plus others. *Exhib:* Four Printmakers: Benson, Foote, Hein & Quandt, San Francisco Mus Art, 71; 3rd Brit Int Print Bienniale, Bradford City Art Gallery, Yorkshire, Eng, 72; Recent Photog, NS Col Art & Design, Halifax, 72; San Francisco Bay Area Printmakers, Cincinnati Art Mus, Ohio, 73; 8th Nat Print & Drawing Competition, Dulin Gallery Art, Knoxville, Tenn, 74-75; Smithsonian Traveling Exhib, Nat Collection Fine Art, Washington DC. *Teaching:* Instr silkscreen printmaking, Univ Calif, Los Angeles Exten, 68-69; instr art, Santa Rose Jr Col, Calif, 69-; vis artist silkscreen printmaking, Visual Studies Workshop, Rochester, NY, summer 75. *Awards:* Guest Ed Award, 6th Ann Los Angeles Printmaking Soc Exhib, 69; Purchase Award, 3rd Brit Int Print Biennale, 72 & Bay Area Print Exhib, DeAnza Col Gallery, 75. *Bibliog:* Alfred Frankenstein (auth), Photo Image in Printmaking, San Francisco Chronicle, 11/71; Carole Schuck (auth), Max Hein Prints, 9/72 & Gerry Payne (auth), Geometric Dynamics, 11/75, Art Week. *Mem:* The Graphics Soc. *Media:* Silkscreen, Mixed Media. *Publ:* Illusr, Half a Century, Nat Football League, 70. *Dealer:* Allrich Gallery 251 Post St San Francisco CA 94108. *Mailing Add:* Dept Art Santa Rosa Jr Col 1501 Mendocino Ave Santa Rosa CA 95401

HEINE, HARRY
PAINTER
b Edmonton, Alta, July 24, 28. *Work:* Wash State Arts Comn; Govt British Columbia; Captain Cook Mus, Eng; Nat Maritime Mus, Eng; Mystic Seaport Mus, Conn; and others. *Comn:* Facade-relief mural, Royal Can Legion, Edmonton, Alta, 68; murals, Syncrude & Vegreville, Can, Ft Saskatchewan, Alta, Chemainus, BC. *Exhib:* Royal Soc Marine Artists, Guildhall & Mall Galleries, London, Eng, 79-86; Fedn Can Artists, 79-86; Watercolor West Ann, Riverside, Calif, 80; Earls Court, London, Eng, 81-86; Mystic Int & Mystic Invitational, 83-86, Mystic Seaport Mus, Conn; and others. *Teaching:* Guest lectr, Fedn Can Artists & Capilano Col, Vancouver. *Awards:* Purchase Award, Mystic Seaport Mus, 83; Mystic Int Exhib Award, 85. *Bibliog:* Francis Dayee (auth), Five artists and the sea, Sea, 80; articles, Western Living Mag, 84 & Beautiful BC Mag, 85; and others. *Mem:* Royal Soc Marine Artists; Fedn Can Artists (past vpres); Northwest Watercolor Soc (past vpres); Can Soc Marine Artists (past vpres). *Media:* Watercolor. *Publ:* Illusr, Sound Heritage, Prov Arch, BC, 78; illusr, Beautiful British Columbia, Govt BC, 78; Curve of time, 79 & Frances Barkley, 80, Grays Publ; Pacific salmon, Dept Fisheries & Oceans, Can, 79; and others. *Dealer:* Matzke Runnings Gallery 413 1st Ave S Seattle WA 98104; Mystic Seaport Mus Maritime Gallery Mystic CT 06355. *Mailing Add:* 7059 Brentwood Brentwood Bay BC V0S 1A0 Canada

HEINE-BAUX, MANFRED
PAINTER, PRINTMAKER
b Munich, Ger, Dec 24, 40, nat Canadian. *Study:* Acad Fine Arts, Munich, PhD(art hist), 64. *Work:* Mercedes-Benz, Stuttgart, Ger; BMW Munich, Toronto; Price Waterhouse; Univ Toronto; Univ Kyoto. *Comn:* Portrait, King Faisal, Saudi Arabia, 74; Siemens Calendar, 92. *Exhib:* First exhibitions in Germany, 67-75; Thompson Gallery, New York, NY, 74; Living Arts Biennale, Johannesburg, S Africa, 76; Le Grand Palais, Paris, 77; solo exhibs, Carimor Gallery, New York, 85 & 86; retrospective, BMW Gallery, Toronto, 89; Art Guild of Can, 90. *Teaching:* Asst prof, Acad Fine Arts, Munich, 64-66. *Awards:* First Place Painting, Living Arts Biennale; First Place Etching, Living Arts Biennale, Best Show, Deaborn, 92. *Mem:* Soc Coun Artists; Am Soc Artists. *Media:* Acrylic; Aquatint-etchings. *Dealer:* Art Guild of Canada 6 hl Queenskon Rd Cambridge ON N3H 3K2; The Hahn Gallery 8439 Germantown Ave Philadelphia PA 19118. *Mailing Add:* 641 Queenston Rd Cambridge ON N3H 3K2 Canada

HEINECKEN, ROBERT FRIEDLI
PHOTOGRAPHER
b Denver, Colo, Oct 29, 31. *Study:* Univ Calif, MA, 60. *Work:* Mus Mod Art, New York; Int Mus Photog, Rochester, NY; Fogg Art Mus, Harvard Univ; Pasadena Art Mus; San Francisco Mus Art. *Exhib:* Persistence of Vision, George Eastman House, Rochester, 67; one-man shows, Robert Heinecken, Witkin Gallery, New York, 70, Light Gallery, New York, 73 & Int Mus of Photog, George Eastman House, Rochester, NY, 76; Photography into Sculpture, Mus Mod Art, New York, 70; Photography in America, Whitney Mus, New York, 74. *Teaching:* Prof art & photog, Univ Calif, Los Angeles, 60-91; vis prof art & photog, Art Inst Chicago, 70; vis prof art & photog, Harvard Univ, 72. *Awards:* Guggenheim Mem Fel, 75; Nat Endowment Arts Grants, 77, 81 & 86. *Bibliog:* Carl Belz (auth), Robert Heinecken, Camera, Bucher Ltd, Luzerne, Switz, 1/68; Fred Parker (auth), Robert Heinecken, Untitled Number 5, Friends of Photog, 73; Andy Grundberg (auth), Robert Heinecken-Asking provocative questions, New York Times, 6/81; and others. *Mem:* Soc Photog Educ. *Publ:* Contribr, Contemp Photogr, Vol 5, No 4; contribr, Untitled Number 7 & 8, Friends of Photog, 74. *Dealer:* Pace/MacGill New York NY; Fahey/Klein Los Angeles CA. *Mailing Add:* Univ Calif Los Angeles Dept of Art 405 Hilgard Ave Los Angeles CA 90024

HEINEMANN, PETER
PAINTER, INSTRUCTOR
b Denver, Colo, Apr 22, 31. *Study:* Black Mountain Col, 1 yr, with Joseph Albers, 48-49. *Comn:* Multi-figure oil mural, New York Coun Arts, 71-72. *Exhib:* Nat Inst Arts & Lett, New York, 60, 61 & biennially 70, 71 & 72; Heckscher Mus, Huntington, NY, 79; Nat Acad Design, 81 & 82; Gallery 120, New York, 83; Visual Arts Mus, 83; Schlesinger Boisante Gallery, New York, 85; Schlesinger Boisante Gallery, 87; and others. *Teaching:* Instr painting & drawing, Sch Visual Arts, New York, 60- *Awards:* Creative Artists Pub Serv Grants, 71-72, 74-75 & 77-78; Childe Hassam Purchase Award, 72; Nat Endowment Arts, 83-84; NY Found Arts Grant, 86. *Media:* Oil. *Mailing Add:* c/o Schlesinger Gallery 24 E 73rd St New York NY 10021

HEINICKE, JANET L HART
PAINTER, EDUCATOR
b Richmond, Ind. *Study:* Wittenberg Univ, BS(art educ, cum laude), 52; Univ Wis-Madison, MS(art educ), 56, study with Colescott & Meeker; Northern Ill Univ, EdD, 76, MFA(painting), 77, Syracuse Univ, 92. *Work:* Richmond Art Asn, Ind; Kankakee Community Col, Ill; Simpson Col, Indianola, Iowa; Wausau Medical Group, Wis; Iowa Lakes Community Col, Estherville, Iowa; We-toast Corp, Chicago, Ill; Artists of Iowa Collection, Nat Bank Waterloo; Hy Vee Corp, Chariton, Iowa. *Comn:* Painting, Caterpillar Corp, Peoria, Ill, 80. *Exhib:* Solo exhibs, Western Ill Univ, Macomb, 83 & Cedar Rapids Mus Art, Iowa, 84; Iowa Printmakers Invitational, Iowa Arts Coun, traveling Iowa, 85; Margaret Harwell Art Mus, Poplar Bluffs, Mo, 88; Stauropol City Mus, Stauropol Krai, Russia, 92; Iowa State Univ, Ames, 93; and others. *Pos:* Art dept prog coordr, Kankakee Community Col, Ill, 77-81. *Teaching:* Asst prof art, Judson Col, Elgin, Ill, 69-74; chmn art dept, Simpson Col, Indianola, Iowa, 81-, prof, currently. *Awards:* Lontz Watercolor Prize, Richmond Art Asn, Ind, 60, Joseph Hill Merit Award, 78; Best in Show, Landscape Painters Midwest, Tower Park Gallery, Peoria, Ill, 79. *Mem:* Iowa Arts Coun; Ill Arts Coun; Col Art Asn; Chicago Artists Coalition; Mid-Am Col Art Asn; Nat Coun Art Adminrs. *Media:* Acrylic, Watercolor. *Dealer:* Olesen-Larson Gallery West Des Moines IA. *Mailing Add:* 1302 W Boston Ave Indianola IA 50125

HEINZ, SUSAN
ADMINISTRATOR
Study: Brown Univ, BA; Harvard Univ, MA; Univ Calif, Los Angeles, MA(film hist & criticism). *Pos:* Educ coordr, Jr Arts Ctr, Los Angeles Munic Arts Dept, 68-73; mem, Los Angeles Munic Arts Comn, 73-78; exec dir, Palos Verdes Art Ctr & Mus, Rancho Palos Verdes, 74-78; mem, Mayor's Citizen's Adv Comt Arts, Los Angeles; dir, Corp Progs, Asia Soc, New York, 78-; mem bd dirs, Cult Assistance Ctr, New York, 79-83. *Awards:* Am Film Inst Scholar, 72-73; Smithsonian Inst Grant (res in India), 74; Phi Beta Kappa. *Mailing Add:* 311 E 72nd St New York NY 10021

HEINZEN, MARYANN
PAINTER, ASSEMBLAGE ARTIST
b Bronx, NY, July 30, 52. *Study:* Art Students League, 86, with Mario Cooper & Joseph Rossi; Nat Art League, Douglaston, NY, with Ed Whitney; Pvt instr, 6 yrs with Yukio Tashiro. *Work:* DuPont Pharmaceuticals, Endo Bldg, Garden City, NY. *Exhib:* Salmagundi Club Exhib, New York, 83, 88 & 91;

Nat Arts Club Exhib, New York, 88; Nassau Co Mus Art, Vaali, 88 & Artists at Work, 91; The Expert Eye, Wunsch Gallery, Coun Arts, Long Island, 90. *Pos:* Pres, Nat Art League, Douglaston, NY, 90-92, vpres, 92-; demonstr, Nat Art League, Floral Park, Flushing Art League, NY & Tri County Artists. *Teaching:* Teacher watercolor, East Islip Adult Educ, 89; guest instr, Valley Stream HS Art Class, 88 & 90; instr watercolor, Nat Art League, Douglaston, 91-92. *Awards:* Award of Excellence, Tri Co Exhib, Tri Co Art League, 90; First Prize, Rockville Ctr Guild Arts, 90; Award of Excellence, Indep Art Soc, Long Island, 90. *Mem:* Nat Asn Women Artists; Coast Guard Artists (mem chmn 88-90, pres 90-92 & vpres, 92-); Nat Art League; Nassau Co Art League; Tri Co Artists. *Media:* Watercolor. *Publ:* Contribr, The Artists Guide to Showing & Selling Your Work, North Lights Books, 89; summer & fall issues of continuing educ; Queens Borough Community Col, 92. *Dealer:* Chandler-Edwards Gallery Port Washington NY; Owl 57 Gallery Woodmere NY. *Mailing Add:* 28 Firwood Rd Port Washington NY 11050

HEIPP, RICHARD CHRISTIAN
PAINTER, INSTRUCTOR
b Cleveland, Ohio, June 23, 52. *Study:* Ceveland Inst Art, BFA(Agnes Gund Scholar), 76; Univ Wash, Seattle, MFA, 79. *Work:* Seattle Art Mus, Seattle, Wash; Jacksonville Art Mus, Jacksonville, Fla; Art in State Bldgs, State Fla; Shriners Children's Hosp, Tampa, Fl; Miami Univ, Oxford, Ohio; Albion Col, Mich; Polk Mus, Lakeland FL. *Comn:* Paintings, Citrus Res Ctr, Lake Alfred, Fla, 87; State Fire Col, Art in State Bldg Prog, Marion Co, Fla, 89; Hurston Regional Serv Ctr, Orlando, Fla, 90; Student Recreation Ctr, Fla State Univ, Tallahassee, 91. *Exhib:* One-person exhibs, Seattle Pac Univ, Wash, 80, Huntingdon Col, Montgomery, Ala, 83, Ctr Contemp Art, Univ Ky, Lexington, 84, The Barn Gallery, Middle Tenn State Univ, Murfreesboro, 87, Fine Art Gallery, Stetson Univ, Deland, Fla, 92, Savannah Col Art & Design, Savanna, Ga, 92; May Show, Cleveland Mus Art, Ohio, 75-77; Florida Creates, Jacksonville Art Mus, 87; All Florida-Bi-Annual, Polk Mus Art, Lakeland, Fla, 89; All Florida Exhib, Boca Raton Mus Art, Fla, 91. *Teaching:* Vis instr drawing, Univ Puget Sound, 79-80; assoc prof painting, Univ Fla, Gainesville, 80- *Awards:* Ford Found Travel Grant, Univ Wash, 79; Fla Individual Artist Fel, State of Fla, 83 & 89; Res Develop Award, DSR, Univ Fla, 82, 87 & 92. *Media:* Airbrush, Mixed. *Mailing Add:* 4420 NW 21st St Gainesville FL 32605

HEISE, MYRON ROBERT
PAINTER
b Bancroft, Nebr, June 30, 34. *Study:* Univ Omaha; Art Students League; Pratt Ctr Contemp Printmaking, New York; Acad Fine Arts, Florence, Italy; also with Arthur Lee, Robert Brackman, Marshall Glaisier & Frank Mason. *Work:* Mus City New York, NYNEX Corp & Peat, Marwick Main & Co, New York; Creighton Univ, Omaha, Nebr; John G Neihardt Found, Bancroft, Nebr. *Comn:* Mural, Manhattan Lab Mus,80; two murals, NYNEX Corp, New York, 84. *Exhib:* one-man exhibs, Capricorn Gallery, Bethesda, Md, 80, Wayne State Col, Nebr, 81, Norfolk Arts Ctr, Nebr, 81, Neihart Ctr, Bancroft, Nebr, 81 & 82, Creighton Univ, Omaha, Nebr, 85, Dana Col, Blair, Nebr, 86 & Noho Gallery, New York, 89; Street Painters, Art Students League, NY, 80, 83 & 90; Street Painters, Lever House Gallery, NY, 82, 87 & 90; Street Painters, Lincoln Ctr Cork Gallery, New York, 84-90; Artists Choice, The First Eight Years, Artist's Choice Mus, New York, 84; Street Painters, Summit Art Ctr, NJ, 84; Street Painters, NY Inst Technol, 85; New York City Works, 1 Penn Plaza, 88; and many others. *Pos:* Assoc art ed, Time Capsule Mag, currently. *Teaching:* Teacher painting & drawing, New Sch Social Res, 77-78, Educ Alliance Art Sch, 78-84 & Sch Body-Mind Centering, 78-83; numerous workshops 81, 82 & 89. *Awards:* Nat Endowment artist-in-residence Grant, St Mary's Creative Arts Forum, 80; artist-in-residence, Neihardt Found, Bancroft, Nebr, 81-86; and others. *Bibliog:* Judy Johnson (auth), The New York street painter who also does Main Street, Mag Midlands, 10/83; article, Myron Heise does demonstration painting, Norfolk News, 8/85; article, Myron heise celebrates hometown, Sioux City J, 8/85; Night visions of Myron Heise, Art World, 5/89; Artist and Critic, Channel C, Cable TV, New York, 4/89. *Mem:* Alliance Figurative Artists (founding mem, 69-, chmn, 76-78); Artists Equity, New York; Audubon Artists, New York. *Media:* Oil, Etching. *Publ:* Auth, Introducing the street painters, Time Capsule, fall 81; and others. *Dealer:* Carol Schwartz Gallery Chestnut Hill Ave Bethlehem Pike Philadelphia PA 19118. *Mailing Add:* 102 Forsyth St New York NY 10002

HEISER, SCOTT THOMAS
PHOTOGRAPHER
b Wilmington, Del, Mar 12, 49. *Study:* RI Sch Design, Providence, studied photography with Harry Callahan, BFA, 71. *Work:* Mus City New York, New York Pub Libr, Main Branch & Lincoln Ctr Theater Collection Branch; Centro Int de la Fotografia, Mexico City. *Exhib:* Silhouettes of Style, Hudson River Mus, Yonkers, NY, 82; Faces Photographed, Grey Art Gallery, NY Univ, 82; Travelling Exhib, French Cultural Serv, New York, 85-87; Next from New York, Tokyo Design Space, Tokyo, Japan, 86. *Bibliog:* Owen Edwards (auth), The Last Tribe of 7th Avenue, Am Photographer, 82; François Caillat (auth), Scott Heiser, Zoom, 82; Mark Holborn (auth), Scott Heiser, Creative Camera, 82. *Media:* Black & White. *Publ:* Illusr, Top dogs, 82 & auth, Euro-collections, 86, Interview Mag; The Gallery of World Photography, Schueisha Publ Co, 83; Her honky-tonk heart, Vogue, 86; The Fashion Quartet '86, The Fashion Found, 86. *Mailing Add:* 15 W 29th St New York NY 10001

HEISKELL, DIANA
PAINTER
b Paris, France; US citizen. *Work:* Santa Barbara Mus Art, Calif; Slater Mus, Norwich, Conn; S Vermont Art Ctr, Manchester. *Exhib:* Whitney Mus Am Art Ann, 2 yrs; Chicago Art Inst; Boston Arts Festival; De Cordova & Dana Mus, Lincoln, Mass; Southern Vt Art Ctr, Manchester; and others. *Awards:* Hon Mention, Berkshire Art Asn; Grumbacher Prize, Southern Vt Art Ctr. *Mem:* Southern Vt Art Asn (trustee); Berkshire Art Asn. *Media:* Oil, Watercolor. *Mailing Add:* RFD 4 Box 375 West Brattleboro VT 05301

HELANDER, BRUCE PAUL
PAINTER, DEALER
b Great Bend, Kans, Jan 27, 47. *Study:* RI Sch Design, Providence, BFA(illus), MFA(painting); Univ Kans, Lawrence, cert; RI Col, Providence. *Work:* Rochester Airport, Minn;; RI Sch Design;; Albany Mus Art, Ga;; Portland Mus, Ore; Mus Art, Ft Lauderdale, Fla; Hudson River mus, Yonkers; Textron Corp; Norton Mus Art, W Palm Beach, Fla; Metrop Mus, New York; Butler Art Inst, Youngstown, Ohio. *Comn:* Animated film, Perpetual Motion Pictures, New York, for Ohio Bell Systs, 71; Exhib Poster, Exec Comt, RI State Coun Arts, 72. *Exhib:* Solo exhibs, Gallery Parr, New York, 86, Tilghman Gallery, Boca Raton, Fla, 87, Kastoriano-Shasham Gallery, New York, 87, J P Natkin Gallery, New York, 87, Shippee Gallery, New York, 88, Carlo Lamagna Gallery, New York, 90 & Virginia Lynch Gallery, Tiverton, RI, 90; Frank Bernarducci Gallery, New York, 87; 36th All Fla Ann; Boca Raton Mus Art, 87; Tribute to Andy Warhol, Joy Moss gallery, Miami, Fla, 87; Small Works, Artifacts, Miami, Fla, 88; Fourth Anniversary Exhib, Artifacts, Miami, Fla; The Armory Show, Shippee Gallery, New York, 89; New Work-New York, O K Harris S, Miami, Fla, 89; Ruth Siegel Gallery, New York; Carl Schlosberg Gallery, Los Angeles; O K Harris Gallery, New York; Metro Pictures, New York. *Pos:* Asst dir admis, RI Sch Design, 70-72, dir summer sessions & exten sch, 72-, actg assoc provost, 76, provost & vpres acad affairs, 77; spec asst to coordr, Fed Graphics Improv Prog, Nat Endowment Arts, Washington, DC, 73-; adv, Inst Am Indian Art, 75-; publ, Art Express Mag, 79-81; dir, Helander Gallery, Palm Beach, Fla, 83-; vpres, Worth Ave Asn, Palm Beach, Fla, 85- *Teaching:* Lectr design, RI Sch Design, 71-, mem, Fine Arts Workshop, summer 76; lectr painting, Inst Am Indian Art, Santa Fe, NMex, 75-; vis artist, Art Park, Lewiston, NY, 75-, N Miami Mus, 85 & Vero Beach Mus, 86; instr, Northwood Inst, West Palm Beach, Fla, 87; vis artist & lectr, Boca Raton Mus Art, Fla, 90, Norton Mus Art, W Palm Beach, Fla, 90 & Pilchuck Sch, Standwood, Wash. *Awards:* Purchase Prize, Providence Art Club, 71; Chmns Grant, 73 & Fel, 74, Nat Endowment Arts. *Bibliog:* Richard Johnson (auth), Mixed crew, NY Post, 11/18/89; Nancy Grove (auth), In the galleries, Arts Antiques, New York, 5/90; Jed Perl (auth), Successes, New Criterion, New York, 5/90. *Mem:* Appraiser's Asn Am; Providence Athenaeum; Am Asn Univ Adminr; Col Art Asn Am; Provincetown Art Asn; Nat Art Educ Asnrtory Theatre. *Media:* Collage. *Publ:* reviews, Art Express Mag, 80 & 81; Auth, Roadside Architecture, Art Express Mag, Providence, RI, May-June, 82; Contribr, The Real Thing (exhib catalog), N Miami Mus, Fla, 85; Auth, Public art lift-off, the Lannan collection and public sculpture, Arts Mag, W Palm Beach, Fla, 86. *Mailing Add:* c/o Helander Gallery 210 Worth Ave Palm Beach FL 33480

HELD, AL
PAINTER
b New York, NY, Oct 12, 28. *Study:* Art Students League; Acad Grande Chaumiere, Paris. *Work:* Albright-Knox Gallery, Buffalo; High Mus Art, Atlanta; Milwaukee Art Center, WI; Mus Mod Art, Whitney Mus Art, Metrop Mus Art, New York; San Francisco Mus Mod Art; William Hayes Ackland Mem Art Center, Chapel Hill, NC; and others. *Comn:* Two murals, Social Security Admin Mid-Atlantic Prog Ctr, Philadelphia, Pa; mural, Southland Ctr, Dallas, Tex; Mural, Akron Govt Bldg, OH, 85. *Exhib:* Systemic Painting, Guggenheim Mus, 66; Documenta IV, Kassel, Ger, 68; one-man shows, San Francisco Mus Art, 90, Corcoran Gallery Art, Andre Emmerich Gallery, New York, 67, 78, 70, 72, 73, 75, 76, 78, 79, 80, 82, 84-90 & Switz, Marianne Friedland Gallery, Toronto, Can, 89, John Berggruen Gallery, San Francisco, CA, 89; Retrospective, Whitney Mus Am Art, New York; Pratt Manhattan Gallery, New York, 89; Rupelle & Norman Schaffer Gallery, Pratt Inst, Brooklyn, 89. *Teaching:* Prof art, Yale Univ, 62-80. *Awards:* Logan Medal, Art Inst Chicago, 64; Guggenheim Found Fel, 66; Painting Medal, Jack I & Lillian L Poser Brandeis University Creative Arts Award, 83. *Bibliog:* Jerry Tallmen (auth), Journey to a Geometric Work, New York Post, 3/10/89, p 39; Jack Flam (auth), Making the Gallery Rounds, Wall Street J, 3/22/89, p 66-7; Deborah Solomon (auth), Al Held's Catskill Pastoral, Archit Digest, 6/89, p 170-173 & 223. *Media:* Acrylic on Canvas. *Dealer:* Donald Morris Gallery 105 Townsend Birmingham MI 48011. *Mailing Add:* c/o Andre Emmerich Gallery 41 E 57th St New York NY 10022

HELD, (JON) JONATHAN, JR
LIBRARIAN, CONCEPTUAL ARTIST
b New York, NY, April 2, 47. *Study:* Utica Col, Syracuse Univ, BA, 69, Sch Info Sci, MLS, 71; Studied with Prof Emer Antje Lemke. *Work:* Jean Brown Collection, Getty Ctr Humanities, Santa Monica, Calif; Mus Mod Art Libr, New York; Admin Ctr, Wellen, Belg; Art Unidentified, Nishinomiya, Japan. *Comn:* Stanley Marsh III, Amarillo, Tex. *Exhib:* Alternative Philately, Local Hist Mus, Eysk, Russia, 90; La Posta in Gioco, Uffizi Nat Gallery, Florence, Italy, 90; Rubber Stamps of John Held Jr, Beverly Hills Pub Libr, Calif, 91; Estampillas y Matasellos de Artistas, Fundación Centro de Artest Visuales, La Plata, Arg, 91; Networking Fresco, Stamp Art Gallery, San Francisco, Calif, 92. *Collections Arranged:* Mail Art About Mail Art, Richard Col, Dallas, 84; Int Artist Cooperation: Mail Art Shows 1970-1985, Dallas Pub

Libr, 85; Mail Art from the Collection of John Held Jr, Glassell Sch Art, Houston Mus Art, Tex, 86; Henning Mittendorf, Rubber Stamp Gallery, Dallas, 91; Destination Dallas: Envelope Art from Around the World, Dallas City Hall, 91; Fax Congress and International Networker Culture, Dallas Pub Libr, 92. *Pos:* Video librn, Mid-York Libr System, Utica, NY, 76-81; art librn, Dallas Pub Libr, 81- *Teaching:* Mentor video art, Empire State Col, 80-81; Art Camp, Arlington Mus Art, Tex, 92. *Awards:* Tartu (Estonia) Artist Soc Vis Artist Fel, 90. *Bibliog:* Mike Crane (auth), Correspondence Art, Art Com Press, 84; Daniel Plunkett (auth), John Held, ND, 85; Alan Sondheim (auth), Interview with John Held Jr, Dallas Arts Rev, 90; Robin James (ed), Cassette Mythos, Automedia Press, 92; Joan Stahl (auth), Book Reviews: Contemporary Art, Art Documentation, summer 92; Clive Phillpot (auth), Mail Art Review, Art Libr J, 92. *Mem:* Art Libr N Am Soc. *Media:* Mail Art, Performance. *Interests:* Currently researching a bibliography of Internationl Networker Culture. *Publ:* Networking the Nineties, Factsheet Five, 4/90; Mind the Gap: Bridging Art and Life, Lightworks, 90; The Question of Mail Art, Umbrella, 5/91; Mail Art Archives, Artpapers, 5-6/91; Rubber Stamps and Libraries, Whole Library Handbook, ALA Books, 91; Mail Art: An Annotated Bibliog, Scarecrow Press, 92. *Dealer:* Moderen Realism Gallery 1903 McMillan Ave Dallas TX 75206. *Mailing Add:* 1901 McMillan Dallas TX 75206

HELD, JULIUS S
EDUCATOR, WRITER
b Mosbach, Ger, Apr 15, 05; US citizen. *Study:* Univ Heidelberg, 23; Hon degree, 86; Univ Berlin, 23-24, 27-28; Univ Vienna, 25-26, 29; Univ Freiburg, PhD, 30; Williams Col, DHL, 72; Columbia Univ, hon DLitt, 77; Dickinson Col, DFA, 83. *Pos:* Asst, Staatliche Mus, Berlin, 31-33; mem ed bd, Art Bull, 42-& Art Quart, 59-74; consult, Mus Arte Ponce, PR, 59-; mem, Inst Advan Study, Princeton Univ, 67. *Teaching:* Lectr, NY Univ, 35-41; lectr art, Barnard Col, Columbia Univ, 37-44, asst prof, 44-50, assoc prof, 50-54, prof, 54-70, chmn dept art hist, 67-70, emer prof, 70-; vis lectr, Bryn Mawr Col, 43-44; vis prof, New Sch Social Res, 46-47 & Yale Univ, 54 & 58; Robert Sterling Clark prof art, Williams Col, 69 & 74; Andrew W Mellon prof, Univ Pittsburgh, 72-73. *Awards:* Hon Fel, The Pierpont Morgan Libr, NY, 86; Fel, Vt Acad Arts & Sci, 90; Corresponding Fel, Brit Acad, 92; and others. *Mem:* Col Art Asn Am (dir, 59-64, hon dir, 75, mem ed bd); Mediaeval Acad Am; Renaissance Soc Am; Deutscher Verein Fur Kunstwissenschaft. *Res:* Flemish and Dutch art. *Publ:* Auth, Rubens, Selected Drawings, Phaidon, 59; Rembrandt Aristotle & other Rembrandt Essays 69 & Rubens and His Circle, 8, Princeton; coauth, 17th & 18th century art: Baroque & Rococo, 72, Abrams; auth, The Oil Sketches of Peter Paul Rubens, Princeton, 80. *Mailing Add:* 81 Monument Ave Bennington VT 05201

HELD, PHILIP
PAINTER, PHOTOGRAPHER
b New York, NY, June 2, 20. *Study:* Art Students League, 38-42 & 46, with Kuniyoshi, Fiene, Blanch, Lee & Vytlacil; Sch Art Studies, New York, with Moses Soyer, 47-48; Columbia Univ Teachers Col, serigraphy with Arthur Young, 49. *Work:* Berkshire Mus, Pittsfield, Mass; Univ Mass, Amherst; Philadelphia Mus Lending Collection; Art Students League Collection; Ringling Mus, Sarasota Fla; and others. *Exhib:* Pa Acad Fine Arts, 62; Philadelphia Mus, 66; Harmon Gallery, Naples, Fla, 80; Sixteen solo exhibs in NY, Mass, SC & Fla; Pleiades Gallery, NY State Coun Arts, 81-82; Southwest Fla Artscape, 89, 90 & 91; Lee Co Alliance Arts, Frizell Gallery, 92; and others. *Pos:* Exhib juror, Manatee & Sarasota Co, 77-; photogr, Sarasota County Sch Bd Pub Info Off, Fla, 83-; and others. *Teaching:* Instr Fine Arts, Scarborough Sch, NY, 47-52, Fieldston Sch, Riverdale, NY, 52-62, chmn dept, 62-71; instr & coordr Fine Arts Prog, Booker-Bay Haven Sch, Sarasota, Fla, 71-78; instr, Visual & Performing Arts Ctr, Sarasota Co, 79-83; retired. *Awards:* H Kleinert Found Grant, 66; Sarasota Art Asn Figure Exhib Award, 75, Realism Award, 77, Photo Award, 81; Photo Awards, Art League of Manatee Co, 84 & 85; and others. *Bibliog:* Gordon Brown (auth), Art voices 1964-65, Art Voices, 65; article, St Petersburg Times, 3/12/82. *Mem:* Life mem Art Students League; Woodstock Artists Asn; Am Fed Musicians Local 721; Fla Artists Group; Art League Manatee Co, Fla. *Media:* Oil. *Dealer:* Art Resource Inc 65 Bleeker St New York NY 10012. *Mailing Add:* 325 Island Circle Siesta Key Sarasota FL 34242

HELDER, DAVID ERNEST
PAINTER, SCULPTOR
b Seattle, Wash, Feb 4, 47. *Study:* Calif Col Arts & Crafts, BA, 69, MFA, 71; Stanford Univ, MA, 75. *Work:* Oakland Mus, Calif. *Exhib:* Galex 23 Nat Juried Exhib, Galesburg Civic Art Ctr, Ill, 89; The Surrealist Salon, RayKo Ctr, San Francisco, 91; The Summer Salon, Helio Gallery, New York, 91; Macro/micro Int Exhib, Helio Gallery, New York, 91; and others. *Pos:* Aesthetic ed consult, Isaacson Inst, Berkeley, Calif, 72-74 & Univ Minneapolis, 88-; Aesthetic Ed Consult, Univ of Minneapolis,88- *Awards:* Westmorland Award, 88; Cert of Excellence Int Art Comp, Westmorland Art and Heritage Festival, 88. *Bibliog:* Charles Shere (auth), Mind in the matter, Oakland Tribune, 5/74; Bob Harrison (auth), Artist makes it easy to see, San Francisco Visitors News, 2/81; Diane L Saiget (auth), David Helder's magic doors, City Arts, 2/81. *Media:* Acrylic, Oil; All Media. *Dealer:* Michael Bell 140 Page St No 1 San Francisco Calif 94102. *Mailing Add:* 636 Stanyan St San Francisco CA 94117

HELDT, CARL RANDALL
EDUCATOR, PAINTER
b Stanford, Ill, Sept 8, 25. *Study:* Wittenburg Col, Springfield, Ohio, 43-44; Univ Ill, Urbana, BFA, 53; Ariz State Univ, Tempe, 60-61. *Work:* Valley Nat Bank Collection & Phoenix Col, Ariz; Col Southwestern Utah. *Comn:* Murals, Kahler Hotel, Rochester, Minn, 54; watercolors, Ford Motor Co, Deerborn, Mich, 63; oil paintings, cards, toys, Hallmark Cards, Kansas City 68-73; mural, Campus Christian Ctr, Tucson, Ariz, 70; murals, New Libr Univ Ariz, Tucson, 74-75. *Exhib:* Southwestern Invitational, Yuma Art Ctr, Ariz, 67-75; Cedar City Invitational, Utah, 67-76; 5 Ariz Artists, Rocky Mountain, 68; 12th Nat Prints & Drawings, Oklahoma Art Ctr, 70; 4 Corners Biennial, Phoenix Mus, Ariz, 71; 22nd Ann NY Soc Illustrators; plus others. *Pos:* Med illusr, Univ Ill, Urbana, 49-53; art dir, Our Wonderful Encycl, Champaign, Ill, 53-55. *Teaching:* Instr graphic design, Univ Ill, Urbana, 55-60; prof graphic design, Univ Ariz, 61- *Awards:* Phoenix Art Dirs Club, 68; Purchase Award, Cedar City Invitational; Col Southwestern Utah, 75. *Media:* Oil, Acrylic. *Publ:* Illusr, New York Times, 62; illusr, Ford Times Mag, 63; contribr, Arizona Alumnus, Univ Ariz, 65; contribr, Crown Ctr News, Hallmark Cards, 69; contribr, Star-Citizen, 79; and others. *Dealer:* Gekas-Nichols Gallery 6538 East Tanque Verde Rd Tucson AZ; Elaine Horwitch Gallery 4200 North Marshall Way Scottsdale AZ 85251. *Mailing Add:* 320 S Country Club Rd Tucson AZ 85716

HELFOND, RIVA
PAINTER, PRINTMAKER
b Brooklyn, NY. *Study:* Art Students League, with William Von Schlegell, Harry Sternberg, Yasuo Kuniyoshi, Morris Kantor & Alexander Brook; Sch Indust Arts, New York. *Work:* Mus Mod Art, New York; Libr Cong, Washington, DC; Los Angeles Mus; Newark Mus Fine Art; Springfield Mus Fine Art, Mass. *Exhib:* Carnegie Inst, Pittsburgh, 54; one-man show, Gallerie Collette Allendy, Paris, 57; Art USA, New York, 58 & 59; Corcoran Gallery Art, Washington, DC, 60; Newark Triennials, Newark Mus Fine Art, 64 & 67; Bethesda Art Gallery, Md, 83; Tamasulo Gallery, Cranford, Wis, 86; Ellen Sragow Gallery, NY, 88-; and others. *Teaching:* Instr graphics, NY Univ, 65-67; instr painting & art appreciation, Union Col, Cranford, NJ. *Awards:* Mus Mod Art, NY; Penell Purchase Prizes, Libr Congress; Prize for Painting, Audubon Artists, 83; and many more. *Mem:* Audubon Artists; Soc Am Graphic Artists (mem coun bd); Assoc Artists NJ (pres, 66-70); Artists Equity Asn NY; Artists Equity Asn NJ (treas, 62-). *Media:* Oil; Etching, Lithography. *Dealer:* Frank Fidele Fine Arts 42 East 57th St New York NY 10022. *Mailing Add:* 919 Knollwood Ct Plainfield NJ 07062

HELIKER, JOHN EDWARD
PAINTER, EDUCATOR
b Yonkers, NY, 1909. *Study:* Art Students League, 27-29; Colby Col, hon DFA. *Work:* Mus Mod Art, Whitney Mus Am Art, Metrop Mus Art, New York; Cleveland Mus Art, Ohio; Philadelphia Mus Art. *Exhib:* Am Painting Today, Metrop Mus Art, 50; Nature in Abstraction, 58, Art of the United States 1670-1966, Whitney Mus Am Art, 66; retrospective exhib, Whitney Mus Am Art, 68; one-man exhibs, Drew Univ, Madison, NJ, 71, Saint-Gaudens Nat Historical Site, Cornish, NH, 72, Edmonton Art Gallery, Alta, 74 & Kramshpor Gallery, 89; Windows and Doors, Heckscher Mus, Huntington, NY, 72; Centennial, Art Students League, 75; America 1976, US Dept Interior, 76. *Pos:* Vpres, Am Acad Arts & Lett, 72-74. *Teaching:* Prof painting, Columbia Univ, 47-74; instr, Art Students League, 75-, Parsons Sch Design, & New York Studio Sch, currently. *Awards:* First W A Clark Prize, Corcoran Gallery Art, 41; Prix de Rome, 48; Award of Merit Medal, Am Acad Arts & Lett, 67. *Bibliog:* J I H Baur (auth), New decade, 55 & L Goodrich (auth), John Heliker, 68, Whitney Mus Am Art; W Nordness (auth), Art USA now, Viking, 62. *Mem:* Nat Inst Arts & Lett. *Media:* Oil, Watercolor. *Dealer:* Kraushaar Galleries 724 Fifth Ave New York NY 10019. *Mailing Add:* c/o Kraushaar Galleries 724 Fifth Ave New York NY 10019

HELIOFF, ANNE GRAILE (MRS BENJAMIN HIRSCHBERG)
PAINTER, COLLAGE ARTIST
b Liverpool, Eng; US citizen. *Study:* Art Students League; Homer Boss & Kuniyoshi; Hans Hofmann Sch. *Work:* Archives Am Art; Smithsonian Mus; Whatcom Mus; Woodstock New York Hist Soc. *Exhib:* Paintings of the Year, 46, Pepsi Cola Nat; Pa Acad Fine Arts, Philadelphia; Dedication Exhibition, Nat Gallery Art, Washington, DC; Art USA Traveling Exhib; American Exhibition, Palazzo Uecchio, Florence, Italy & Mus Naples, Italy, 72; Bicentennial Expo Six Am Painters, Annemasse & Cluses, France; Philadelphia Mus; Berkshire Mus; solo exhibs, Capricorn Gallery, 64, 66, 69 & Phoenix Gallery, New York, 71, 73, 76, 82, 83 & 85; Woodstock Artists Asn, 88; Milch Gallery, New York; Albany Mus Art & Sci. *Pos:* Mem, US Deleg to 5th Cong, Int Asn Artists, Tokyo, 66; dir exhib, Dedication New York City Lighthouse, Tricentennial; 50 Years of Woodstock Art, YMHA Series, Kaufmann, New York. *Teaching:* Lectr, Y Kuniyoshi Summer Sch, Woodstock, New York, 42-44. *Awards:* Silver Medal, Albany NY Mus Art & Sci; Oil Awards, Am Soc Contemp Artists, Riverside Mus, 62 & Berkshire Mus; Three Cert of Merit, Am Soc Contemp Artists, 70; and others. *Bibliog:* C Offin (auth) article, Pictures exhib, 11/76; N Frachtman (auth) article, Arts Mag, 1/77; William Pellicone, 82 & Palmer Poroner, Artspeak, 85; Gordon Brown, Arts, 82; Dorothy Hall, Park East, 85; and others. *Mem:* Am Soc Contemp Artists; New York Soc Women Artists; life mem Woodstock Artists Asn. *Media:* Acrylic, Oil. *Mailing Add:* 340 W 28th St New York NY 10001

HELLER (MRS EDWARD W GREENBERG), GOLDIE
COLLECTOR, CONSULTANT
b Salem, Mass. *Study:* Mass Col Art. *Exhib:* Andy Warhol Gold Shoe, Andy Warhol: A Retrospective, 89. *Pos:* Art dir, vpres. *Mem:* Mus Mod Art. *Collection:* Braque, Roualt, Henry Botkin, Ralph Rosenborg, Byron Browne, Noel Rockmore, Andy Warhol, Francisco Larez, Jose de Creeft, John Ross, June Rogoff, Joseph Bolegard, Clare Romano, Erwin Wending, and others. *Mailing Add:* 440 E 56th St New York NY 10022

HELLER, BEN
DEALER, COLLECTOR
b New York, NY, Oct 16, 25. *Study:* Bard Col, BA. *Pos:* Benefactor, Metrop Mus Art, New York; past trustee or bd mem, Int Coun of Mus Mod Art, Friends of Whitney Mus Am Art & Jewish Mus. *Collection:* Contemporary American painting and ancient, Eastern and primitive arts. *Mailing Add:* 14 Webber Rd Sharon CT 06064

HELLER, DOROTHY
PAINTER
b New York, NY. *Study:* With Hans Hofmann. *Work:* Metrop Mus Art, New York; Univ Calif Art Mus, Berkeley; Smithsonian Inst-Archives; Wadsworth Atheneum, Hartford, Conn; Allen Mem Art Mus, Oberlin, Ohio; Johnson Mus at Cornell Univ, Ithaca, NY; and others. *Exhib:* Solo exhibs, Poindexter Gallery, NY, 56-57, Easthampton Gallery, NY, 63, Betty Parsons Gallery, NY, 72, 76 & 78, Libr, NJ, 75, Cathedral St John Divine, NY, 76, Univ Pa, Philadelphia, 76 & St Pete's Church, NY 79; Whitney Mus Ann, New York, 57; Carnegie Int, Pittsburgh, 59; Mus Mod Art Traveling Show, 63; Wadsworth Atheneum, Hartford, Conn, 64; Betty Parsons Gallery, NY, 72-91; Albright-Knox Gallery, Buffalo, NY, 74; Univ Calif Art Mus, Berkeley, 74; Otis Art Inst, Los Angeles, 79; Metrop Mus Art, New York, 79; Brooklyn Col Art Gallery, NY, 90; and others. *Teaching:* Lectr, Smithsonian Inst, Washington, DC & Carnegie Endowment Ctr, NY. *Awards:* Int Women's Year Award, 76. *Bibliog:* Simone Auger (auth), La Presse, Montreal, Can, 63; Diana Loercher (auth), Christian Sci Monitor, 10/22/76; Theodore Wolff (auth), Christian Sci Monitor, 5/22/79. *Media:* Acrylic on Paper & Canvas. *Mailing Add:* 8 W 13th St New York NY 10011

HELLER, JULES
PRINTMAKER, WRITER
b New York, NY, Nov 16, 19. *Study:* Ariz State Univ, BA, 39; Columbia Univ, MA, 40; Univ Southern Calif, PhD, 48; York Univ, Can, DLitt, 85. *Work:* Libr Cong, Washington, DC; Allan R Hite Inst, Univ Louisville; Tamarind Inst, Univ NMex; Toronto Dom Centre; Can Coun Art Bank, York Univ. *Comn:* Ariz Repub, Phoenix, 82; Herberger Theatre, Phoenix, 83; The Phoenician, Phoenix, 87. *Exhib:* Pa Acad Fine Arts Ann, 59 & 63; Martha Jackson Gallery, New York, 76; Smith Andersen Gallery, Calif, 84 & 93; Amerika Haus, Hannover, Ger, 85; Lisa Sette Gallery, Scottsdale, 89; Ariz State Univ, Tempe, 92; and others. *Pos:* Dir sch arts, Pa State Univ, University Park, 61-63 & founding dean, Col Arts & Archit, 63-68; founding dean, fac fine arts, York Univ, 68-72; dean, Col Fine Arts, Ariz State Univ, Tempe, 76-85. *Teaching:* Prof printmaking & art hist, Univ Southern Calif, 46-61; prof fine arts, York Univ, 72-76; prof art, Ariz State Univ, Tempe, 76-85, prof art, 76-90. *Awards:* Can Coun Grant, 75; Fulbright Fel Argentina, 90. *Bibliog:* Rudy Turk, introduction (catalog), Jules Heller, A Printmakers Monotypes, Ariz State Univ, 83. *Mem:* Col Art Asn Am; Int Coun of Fine Arts Deans; Authors League; Int Asn Paper Historians. *Media:* Graphics, Computer Art. *Publ:* Contribr & illus, Estampas de la revolucion Mexicana, 48; Prints by California Artists, 54; Dictionary of Art, McGraw, 69; auth, Printmaking Today, rev ed, 72; auth, Papermaking, 5/78. *Mailing Add:* 6838 E Cheney Rd Scottsdale AZ 85253

HELLER, PAMELA
SCULPTOR
b Cleveland, Ohio, Apr 28, 54. *Study:* Cleveland Inst Art, BFA, 79. *Comn:* Model of Monticello, Thomas Jefferson Mem Found, Charlottesville, Va, 86; Am Indian Artifacts, Childrens Mus, New York, 88. *Exhib:* May Show, Cleveland Mus Art, Ohio, 84; Invitational, Craig Cornelius Galley, New York, 86; Invitational, Studio F, Rome, Italy, 88; Alignments, E Hampton Ctr, NY, 88; Percussion, Lawrence Oliver Gallery, Phila, Pa, 88; solo exhibs, Momentum, Cleveland Ctr Contemp Art, Ohio, 88, Percussion, Lawrence Oliver Gallery, Philadelphia, Pa, 88, Dust, Sculpture Space, Utica, NY, 91; Small & Stellon, Ruth Siyel Gallery, New York, 89; China, PS1, Long Island, NY, 90; Fiumara D'Arte, Galleria Dei Banchi Nuovi, Rome, Italy; Art Meets Science & Spirituality, Mus Fodor, Amsterdam, Holland, 90; Art on the Block, Cleveland Ctr Contemp Art, Ohio, 91; Paper & Nature, Int Biennale der Papierkunst, Keopold-Hoesch Mus, Duren, Ger, 91. *Pos:* Consul, Thomas Jefferson Mem Found, 86; consul, James Polshek Architects, 88; consul, Childrens Mus, 88. *Awards:* Nat Endowment Arts Fel, 86 & 87; Artists Space Spec Proj Grant, 86; Sculpture Space Proj Grant, Utica, NY, 91. *Bibliog:* Helen Cullinan (auth), Momentum, The Cleveland Plain Dealer, Ohio, 8/14/88; Alignment, East Hampton Star, 8/88; Rose Slivka (auth), From the Studio, Southhampton Press, Southhampton, NY, 9/88. *Mem:* NY Artists Equity Assn. *Media:* Mixed Media. *Publ:* Contribr, Terminal New York & Opinion, Express News, 84; contribr, In Suspension, Womens Quarterly Review, 88; contribr, Alignments, Southhampton Press, 88; contribr, Alignments, East Hampton Star, 88; Fiumara D'Arte (catalog), Rome, Italy, 89. *Mailing Add:* 112 Sixth Ave Brooklyn NY 11217

HELLER, REINHOLD AUGUST
HISTORIAN
b Fulda, Ger, July 22, 40; US citizen. *Study:* St Joseph's Col, Philadelphia, BS, 63; Ind Univ, Bloomington, MA, 66, PhD, 68, with Albert Elsen, John Jacobus & Sven Loevgren. *Pos:* Guest cur, Nat Gallery, Washington, DC, 78-79. *Teaching:* Prof art hist, Univ Pittsburgh, 68-78 & Univ Chicago, 78-. *Awards:* Foreign Area Prog Fel, 66-68; Guggenheim Found Fel, 73-74; d'Harnoncourt Fel, Mus Mod Art, New York, 70. *Mem:* Col Art Asn; Mod Lang Asn; Ger Studies Asn. *Res:* Art criticism; Symbolism; Expressionism; German Romanticism; German art of the 1920's. *Publ:* Auth, Art of Wilhelm Lehmbruck, Nat Gallery, Washington, DC, 72; Munch: The Scream, Viking, 73; Hildegard Auer: A Yearning for Art, Belserverlag, 87; Brücke: German Expressionist prints in the Granvil and Marcia Specks Collection, Block Gallery, Northwestern Univ, Evanston, Ill, 88; Art in Germany 1909-1936: From Expressionism to Resistance, The Marvin and Janet Fishman Collection, Prestel-Verlag, 90. *Mailing Add:* Art Dept Univ Chicago 5540 S Greenwood Chicago IL 60637

HELLER, SUSANNA
PAINTER
b New York, NY, 1956. *Study:* Nova Scotia Col Art & Design, BFA, 74-77, NY Univ, hist of art with Robert Rosenblum, 76. *Work:* Air Canada Corp; Canadian Art Bank, Ottawa; Concordia Univ Art Gallery, Montreal; Osler, Hoskin & Harcourt, Toronto; Toronto Dominion Bank. *Exhib:* Solo exhibs, Embassy Cult House, London, Ont, 85, Anna Leonowens Gallery, Halifax, Nova Scotia, 85, Galerie Paul Andriesse, Amsterdam, Netherlands, 86, Grunwald & Watterson, Toronto, Ont, 87, Tomoko Ligouri Gallery, New York, 88, Mt St Vincent Univ Art Gallery, Halifax, NS, 89, Grunwald Gallery, Toronto, 89; Contemporary Landscapes, Watercolors Visual Arts Ctr, Salisbury, NC, 88; Gallery Artists, Tomoko Gallery, New York, 89; 49th Parallel, New York, 86; Chicago Int Art Expo, Ill, 90. *Awards:* Project Cost Grants, 78 & 83, Arts Grant 'B', 80, 85 & 86, Canada Council; Fel, Millay Colony Residence, 82; Fel, Leighton Art Colony, Banff, Alta, 86; John Simon Guggenheim Mem Found Fel, 88. *Bibliog:* John Clark (auth), No Apologies, Vanguard, Vancouver, 2-3/89; Robert Berlind (auth), review, Art in Am, 2/89. *Mailing Add:* c/o Tomoko Liguori 93 Grand St New York NY 10013

HELMAN, EVE
COLLAGE ARTIST, PAINTER
b New York, NY. *Study:* Hunter Col, BA; Columbia Univ, MA; Am Artists Sch; Brooklyn Mus Art Sch; studied with Anton Refregier, Nicholas Marsicano & Charles Seide. *Work:* Monhegan Mus, Monhegan Island, Mass; Rutgers Univ, Newark, NJ; Dewey Ballantine Law Firm Collection. *Exhib:* Nat Assoc Women Artists, Tel-Aviv Mus, Israel, 84; Judaica, Ancient & Modern, Union Am Hebrew Congregations, NY, 86; Figurative Artists, Lehman Col, New York, 87; Soc of Landscape & Figurative Artists, Lever House, New York , 89; Ann Exhib, Nat Acad Design, New York, 90. *Pos:* Chmn awards, Nat Asn Women Artists, New York, 79-; Am Soc Contemp Artists (mem chmn, 83-88 & secy 90), NY. *Awards:* Top Award, Knickerbocker Artists, 71; Award for innovative art, Nat Asn Women Artists, 82; Elsie Ject Key Award, Nat Asn Women Artists, 87. *Mem:* Hunter Col Alumni Hall of Fame; Nat Asn Women Artists (chmn awards, 79-); Am Soc Contemp Artists (chmn mem, 83-88); NY Artists Equity. *Media:* Paper, Oil. *Mailing Add:* 30 W 60 St 10P New York NY 10023

HELMAN, PHOEBE
SCULPTOR, PAINTER
b New York, NY, Oct 29, 29. *Study:* Wash Univ, with Paul Burlin, BFA; Art Students League; also with Raphael Soyer. *Work:* Hampton Inst Mus, Va; Ciba-Geigy, Ardsley, NY; Fox, Flynn & Melamed, New York; Friedlich, Fearon & Strohmeier, New York; Guggenheim Mus, New York; NY Psychoanalytic Inst. *Comn:* Steel wall piece, comn by Milan Stoeger, New York, 73; steel wall piece, comn by Muriel Mannings, New York, 73; City of Raleigh, NC, 78. *Exhib:* One-woman shows, Sculpture Now Inc, New York, 78, Max Hutchinson Gallery, 78, Wright State Univ Gallery, 79 & Spoleto Festival Col, 92; Sculptors Drawings, Touchstone Gallery, New York, 79; Work on Paper--Four Artists, Upstairs Gallery, Ithaca, 79; Andre Zarre, New York, 81; SUNY Cortland, NY, 87; Islip Mus, NY, 87; Russel Sage, New York, 88; Painting After the Death of Painting, Moscow, USSR, 89; The Question of Drawing, Miami-Dade, Miami, 89-90; Painting, Charleston, SC, 92. *Teaching:* Adj prof art, Pratt Inst, 72-; vis critic, Syracuse Univ, 85-86; vis critic, Skowhegan Sch Painting, 89. *Awards:* Creative Artists Pub Serv Grant, 75; Guggenheim Fel, 79; Nat Endowment Arts Grant Visual Arts Prog, 83-84; NY Found Arts Grant, 86. *Bibliog:* Carol Spence (auth), Beyond the edges of the paper, Ithaca Times, 10/79; C Robins (auth), American urban art triumphant; Cohn, Held, Helman, Stella, Arts, 5/82; Karin Upson (auth), Recent Work on the Avant-Garde Side, Newsday, 7/3/87; and others. *Media:* Laminite & Wood; Steel. *Dealer:* Sculpture Now Inc & Max Hutchinson Gallery 142 Greene St New York NY 10012. *Mailing Add:* 217 E 23rd St New York NY 10010

HELSMOORTEL, ROBERT
SCULPTOR, PAINTER
b Antwerp, Belg; US citizen. *Study:* Acad Royale Belgium, 46; Inst Superieur, Belgium, 48. *Work:* Chicago Art Inst, Ill; Yale Univ, New Haven, Conn; Royal Collection, Brussels, Belgium; Carnegie Mus, Pittsburgh, Pa. *Comn:* Sculpture (metal), Place Ville Marie, Montreal, 62; bas relief (metal), Alcan, London, Eng, 67; sculptures & bas relief, Forte Plaza, Miami, Fla, 73; sculpture, La Mer Bldg, Naples, Fla, 78; bas relief, Am Telephone & Telegraph Co, Ft Lauderdale, Fla, 79. *Exhib:* One-man shows, Palazzo Strozzi, Florence, Italy, 55, the Parrish Mus, Southampton, NY, 67 & The Nova-Scotia Mus Fine Arts, Halifax, Can, 69; Art in Architecture, Mus City London, Eng, 69; The Harmon Gallery, Naples, Fla, 80; The Antwerp Gallery, Belgium, 80. *Awards:* First Prize Painting & Prize Als Ickkan, Belgium State, 48. *Bibliog:* Louis G Redstone (auth), Art in Architectue, McGraw Hill, 68; Margaret O Robinette (auth), Outdoor Sculpture, Whitney Libr of Design, 76. *Mem:* Artists Equity Asn, Washington, DC; Artists Equity Asn, New York; P Bench Council Arts. *Media:* Oil; Steel, Bronze. *Dealer:* Helsmoortel Gallery. *Mailing Add:* PO Box 851 Palm Beach FL 33480

HELZER, RICHARD BRIAN
METALSMITH, SCULPTOR
b Hastings, Nebr, Aug 27, 43. *Study:* Kearney State Col, Nebr, BA, 65; Univ Kans, MFA, 69. *Work:* C M Russell Mus, Great Falls, Mont. *Comn:* Altar serv, St Elizabeth's Episcopal Church, Nebr, 69 & Hope Lutheran Church, Kans, 70; alter cross, Univ Kans Chapel, Lawrence, 70 & Sacred Heart Cath Church, Butte, Mont, 86. *Exhib:* Hist of Gold & Silversmithing in Am, Lowe Art Mus, Univ Miami, Coral Gables, Fla, 75; NW Invitational Silversmiths, Seattle Art Mus, Wash, 76; US Off Info Goldsmiths Exhib, Melbourne, Australia, 76; NW Designer-Craftsman, Henry Gallery, Seattle, Wash, 77; 3rd Profile of US Jewelry, Tex Tech Univ, Lubbock, 77; Goldsmiths 77, Phoenix Art Mus, Ariz, 77; Metal-non Metal, Synopsis Gallery, Chicago, 80; North Am Goldsmiths European Exhib (traveling); San Francisco Mus Mod Art, 89; and others. *Pos:* Guest Cur, Metalsmithing Invitational, Yellowstone Art Ctr, Billings, Mont, 81; vis artist, E Carolina Univ, 89. *Teaching:* Teaching asst, Univ Kans, Lawrence, 68-69, instr metalsmithing, 69-70; asst prof art, Mont State Univ, Bozeman, 70-74, assoc prof, 75-80, prof, 80- *Awards:* Nat Endowment Arts Fel, 76; Western State Found fel, 77. *Bibliog:* Articles, in: Craft Horizons, 12/78; Jewelry Making, revised ed, Bavin Publ, 80. *Mem:* Soc NAm Goldsmiths; Am Crafts Coun. *Media:* Multi-Metals, Wood. *Dealer:* Chiaroscuro Gallery 750 N Orleans Chicago IL 60610. *Mailing Add:* 52 Hitching Post Rd Bozeman MT 59715

HEMMERDINGER, WILLIAM JOHN, III
PAINTER, CRITIC
b Burbank, Calif, July 7, 51. *Study:* Col Desert, Calif, AA, 72; Univ Calif, Riverside, BA, 73; Claremont Grad Sch, MFA, 75, PhD, 79. *Work:* Smithsonian Inst; Tate Gallery, London; Barbara Hepworth Mus, Cornwall, Eng; Fed Reserve Bank San Francisco. *Comn:* Stouffers Esmeralda Resort, Indian Wells, Calif, 89; Ruth J Cooper Mem, Living Desert Reserve, Palm Desert, Calif, 90; McWhirter Fountain & Passing Rain Bronze Fountain, Rancho Mirage, Calif, 92. *Exhib:* Solo Exhibs, Cirrus Eds, Ltd, Los Angeles, 82 & 84; Nat Acad Design, NY; Nagasaki Mus Art, Japan, 81; Act IV: Mixed-Media, Los Angeles Co Mus Art, 77; Ten Contemp Watercolor Painters, Scripps Col, Claremont, Calif; Calif Collage, Baum-Silverman Gallery, Los Angeles, 79; A Southern Calif Collection, Cirrus Eds, Ltd; Am Watercolor Soc, New York; and others; Boyusan Citizen's Hall, Pusan, Korea; Olympic Arts Festival, Seoul, Korea; and others. *Pos:* Cur, Calif Mus Photog, Univ Calif, Riverside, 73-74; William & Catherine Hemmerdinger Gallery, Palm Desert, Calif, 84- *Teaching:* Instr art, Col Desert, Calif, 74-84; lectr, Calif State Univ, Long Beach, 79-80, Otis Art Inst, Parsons Sch Design, Los Angeles, 79-81, Univ Calif, Riverside, 82-85, Calif Inst Arts, Valencia, Calif, 89 & Pomona Col, Claremont, Calif, 90- *Awards:* Award for Drawing, Nat Watercolor Soc, 74; Nat Watercolor Soc, 79. *Bibliog:* Marlena Donohue, (auth), The Galleries Downtown, Los Angeles Times; Katherine Holland (auth), The Art Collection, Fed Reserve Bank San Francisco; Robert Perine (auth), The California Romantics, Artras Press. *Mem:* Nat Watercolor Soc (4th vpres, 81-82); Col Art Asn. *Media:* Watercolor, Acrylic. *Res:* Contemporary art, education, aesthetics and new materials. *Publ:* Auth, Ansel Adams: The Museum Set (exhib catalog), Galleries of Claremont Cols & Barican Ctr, London, 87; auth, Elaine Lustig Cohen/Raimund Girke, Arts Mag, 81; Lowell Nesbitt (exhib catalog), Louis Newman Galleries, Los Angeles, 87; Matsumi Kanemitsu (exhib catalog), Japanese Am Community Cult Ctr, Los Angeles, 88; Katherine Chang-Liu (exhib catalog), Louis Newman Galleries, Beverly Hills, 88; Chinese Artists (exhib catalog), Macao Mus. *Dealer:* William & Catherine Hemmerdinger Gallery Palm Desert CA. *Mailing Add:* c/o Hemmerdinger Gallery 42240 Greenway Palm Desert CA 92260

HEMPHILL, HERBERT WAIDE, JR
CURATOR, LECTURER
b Atlantic City, NJ, Jan 21, 29. *Study:* Bard Col, Annandale-on-Hudson, NY. *Work:* Mus Am Folk Art, New York; Nat Mus Am Art, Smithsonian Inst, Wash, DC. *Collections Arranged:* Hunt for the Whale; Plenty of Pennsylvania; Occult; Tattoo!; Macrame: Hail to the Chief; Fabric of the State (with catalog), 73; Commerce in Wood; 20th Century American Folk Art, 74; Collector's Choice; America Expresses Herself, The Hemphill Collection, New Children's Mus, Indianapolis, Ind, 76; Missing Pieces--George Folk Art, 76; Japan Celebrates America's Bicentennial--The Hemphill Collection, Tokyo & Osaka, Japan, 76; Milwaukee Mus Art, Mus & Tour Am Mus. *Pos:* Founder, Mus Am Folk Art, 58, cur, 61-72, emer bd mem, currently; guest cur, Brooklyn Mus, 76-, Abby Aldrich Rockefeller Folk Art Collection, 80 & Sotherby Parke Bernet Mus Am Folk Art, 87. *Teaching:* Guest lectr, NY Univ, Smithsonian Inst, Univ Vt, Libr Cong, Univ NC & Univ Ga. *Awards:* James Smithson Soc Medal, Smithsonian Inst, 87. *Bibliog:* Robert Bishop, Mary Black, Tom Armstrong, Louis Jones, et al (auth), The H W Hemphill Collection of 18th, 19th & 20th Century American Folk Art, Heritage Plantation Mus; Michael Hall (auth), The Hemphill Collection of 20th Century American Folk Art, Contemp Arts Ctr, Cincinnati, 73; 18th, 19th & 20th century American folk art. *Publ:* Co-auth, Metal of the State, 74; coauth, with Julia Weissman, 20th Century American Folk Art & Artists, 74. *Mailing Add:* 108 E 30th St New York NY 10016

HEMPLER, ORVAL F
PAINTER, SCULPTOR
b Almena, Kans, Jan 9, 15. *Study:* Univ Colo, BFA, 38; Colorado Springs Arts Acad, 38; Frank Alva Parsons scholar, Paris, France, 38-39; Ital traveling & painting scholar, 39; Univ Iowa, with Jean Charlot, MA, 41. *Work:* Los Angeles Co Mus Mod Art & Litton Mus Visual Arts, Los Angeles; Univ Kans Mus Art, Manhattan; Colorado Springs Fine Arts Acad, Colo; Denver Mus Art. *Comn:* Tropical Jungle Cyclorama Mural, Baker Furniture Co, Chicago, 44. *Exhib:* New York Watercolor Soc, Mus Mod Art, New York, 42; print show, Wichita Mus Art, Kans, 43; invitational, Los Angeles Co Mus Mod Art, 50; serigraph show, Fine Arts Ctr, Sacramento, Calif, 78; watercolor show, Philadelphia Mus, 79; plus others. *Collections Arranged:* Sculptured Paintings (cataloged), St Johns Gallery, Santa Monica, Calif, 63. *Pos:* Designer, Carson Pirie Scott, Chicago, 42-45; artist designer, Lamps of Calif, Los Angeles, 46-65. *Teaching:* Instr watercolor, Univ NH, Durham, 40-42; instr, Los Angeles Unified Schs, 65-68. *Awards:* Sweepstakes, Kans State Fair Asn, 37; Best Am Painter in Europe, Paris, 38-39; Best of Show, Westwood Art Asn, 75. *Bibliog:* Art Seidenbaum (auth), Art and the market place, Los Angeles Times, 10/63; Caroll Heiss (auth), Artist returns to Colorado, Denver Post, 75; Michael Donohue (commentator), The art of Orval Hempler, videotape, 78. *Mem:* Delta Phi Delta (secy & publ); Univ Calif, Los Angeles Art Coun (jury bd). *Media:* Watercolor; Sculptured Paintings. *Publ:* Illusr, The Palette, Hayes, 38; auth, Designers West, Art Alliance Corp, 63; contribr, Kans Mag, Univ Kans, 75. *Dealer:* Mary Browne 401 E Main St Norton KS 67654. *Mailing Add:* 2302 Second St Santa Monica CA 90405

HENDERSHOT, J L
PRINTMAKER, EDUCATOR
b Cleveland, Ohio, Nov 3, 41. *Study:* Cleveland Inst Art, with H C Cassill, Louis Bosa & Julian Stanczak; Syracuse Univ, NY, with George Vander Sluis & Donald Cortesse. *Work:* Rochester Mus Art, NY; Pennell Fund, Libr Cong. *Comn:* Drawing, Alumni Asn, St John's Univ, Collegeville, Minn, 73; drawing for gift, Spira Dance Co, Portland, Ore, 74; print, St Cloud State Col, 75; 50th Anniversary lithographs (50 ed), Minn Mus; lithographs ed, Assoc Am Artist. *Exhib:* One-man shows, RI Sch Design, Providence, 75, Assoc Am Artists Gallery, New York, 76, Red River Art Ctr Mus, Moorehead, Minn, 76 & Uptown Gallery, New York, 77; 7th Nat Biennial Drawing US Show, St Paul, Minn, 75; and others. *Pos:* Art gallery dir, St John's Univ, 75- *Teaching:* Asst instr drawing & printmaking, Syracuse Univ, 68-70; asst prof drawing & printmaking, St John's Univ, 71- *Awards:* Philadelphia Print Club Purchase Award, Philadelphia Mus Art, 68; Univ NDak Purchase Award, 15th Nat Print & Drawing Exhib, 72; Minn Mus Art Purchase Award, 7th Nat Biennial Drawing US Show, 75. *Mem:* Graphic Soc, Hollis, NH; Boston Printmakers; Pratt Graphics Print Club, New York. *Media:* Intaglio, Lithography. *Mailing Add:* 169 Riverside Dr Saint Cloud MN 56304

HENDERSON, JACK W
PAINTER, INSTRUCTOR
b Kenosha, Wis, Mar 12, 31. *Study:* Kansas City Art Inst, BFA & MFA, 47-52; Ecole des Beaux Arts, Paris, 52-53; Art Students League, 55-58; also with Edward Laning, Louis Bouche & Robert Beverly Hale. *Work:* Nat Acad Design, New York; Smithsonian Inst; Am Acad Rome, Italy; Nat Portrait Gallery, England; Curtis Inst Mus; and others. *Comn:* Murals in pvt collections, Rome & New York. *Exhib:* Pa Acad Fine Arts, 59 & 61; one-man shows, Nat Acad Design, 68 & Ranger Fund Exhib, 74; Am Watercolor Soc Ann, New York, 69-70; plus others. *Teaching:* Prof drawing, Moore Col Art, 67-; instr life drawing & painting, Art Students League, 75- *Awards:* Pulitzer Traveling Fel, 55; Abbey Fel for Mural Painting, Am Acad Rome, 63-65; Ranger Fund Purchase Award, Nat Acad Design, 74; plus others. *Mem:* Nat Acad Design; Am Watercolor Soc; Nat Soc Mural Painters; Art Students League; Artists Equity. *Media:* All Media. *Mailing Add:* Dept Art Students League 215 W 57th St New York NY 10019

HENDERSON, LINDA DALRYMPLE
HISTORIAN, EDUCATOR
b Warren, Pa, Jan 22, 48. *Study:* Dickinson Col, BA, 69; Yale Univ, MA, MPhil, 72, PhD, 75. *Pos:* Assoc cur mod art, Mus Fine Arts, Houston, 74-76, cur, 76-77. *Teaching:* Asst prof, Univ Tex, Austin, 78-84, assoc prof, 84-91, prof, 91- *Awards:* Teaching Excellence Award, Univ Tex, 81; Vasari Award, Dallas Mus Art, 85; Guggenheim Fel, 88-89. *Mem:* Col Art Asn; Soc for Sci & Lit. *Res:* Twentieth century European and American art, including its interaction with geometry, science and mysticism/occultism. *Publ:* Auth, A new facet of cubism: The fourth dimension and non-Euclidean geometry reinterpreted, Art Quart, 71; The Fourth Dimension and Non-Euclidean Geometry in Modern Art, Princeton Univ Press, 83; Mysticism, Romanticism, and the Fourth Dimension, In: The Spiritual in Art: Abstract Painting 1890-1986, Los Angeles Co Mus, 86; Mysticism as 'the tie that binds': the case of Edward Carpenter and modernism, Art J, 87; X-rays and the quest for invisible reality in the art of Kupka, Duchamp and the cubists, Art J, 88. *Mailing Add:* Art Dept Univ Tex Austin TX 78712

HENDERSON, MIKE
PAINTER, FILMMAKER
Study: San Francisco Art Inst, BFA, 69, MFA, 70. *Work:* Crocker Art Mus, Sacramento; Honolulu Acad Arts; Oakland Mus; San Francisco Mus Mod Art. *Exhib:* San Francisco Mus Mod Art, 70, 76 & 78; Whitney Mus, New York, 70 & 71; solo exhibs, San Francisco Mus Mod Art, Calif, 80, Loeb Galerie, Bern, Switz, 85, Natsoulas Novelozo Gallery, David, Calif, 87, Fuller Gross Gallery, San Francisco, Calif, 89, Marcia McCoy Gallery, Santa Fe, NMex, 89, Adeline Kent Award Exhib, Walter/McBean Gallery, San Francisco, Calif, 90 & Recent Paintings, Haines Gallery, San Francisco, Calif, 91 & 92; 6 East Bay Artists, Mills Col Art Gallery, Oakland, Calif, 89; Oakland Artists '90, Oakland Mus, Calif, 90; Why Painting, Susan Cummins Gallery, Mill Valley, Calif, 92; From the Studio: Recent Paintings & Sculpture by 20 California Artists, Oakland Mus, Calif, 92; and others. *Teaching:* Instr art, Univ Calif, Davis, 70- *Awards:* Guggenheim Fel, 73; Nat Endowment Arts, 78 & 89; Adeline Kent Award, 90; Distinguished Alumni Award, San Francisco Art Inst, 90. *Bibliog:* Kenneth Baker (auth), An abstract painter who skirts a fine visual line, San Francisco Chronicle, 5/23/91; David Bonetti

(auth), Mike Henderson, San Francisco Examiner, 5/17/91; Mark Van Proyen (auth), Extending abstraction, Visions Art Quart, p 25-27, fall 91; and others. *Dealer:* Haines Gallery 49 Geary St 5th Floor San Francisco CA 94108. *Mailing Add:* Univ Calif-Davis Davis CA 95616

HENDERSON, ROBBIN LEGERE
PAINTER, CURATOR
b Stockton, Calif, April 19, 42. *Study:* Reed Col, 59-61; Univ Calif, Berkeley, BA, 63; San Francisco Art Inst, 68-70. *Exhib:* Solo exhib, Mills Col Gallery, 76, Floating Mus, 77, Southern Exposure Gallery, San Francisco, 78 & 85 & Intersection Gallery, San Francisco, 82; 13 Artists from California, Bologna Festival, Italy, 77; Art for Giving & Collecting, 78, San Francisco Mus Mod Art; 14 Proposals for Battery Hill 129, Clorox World Hq, Oakland, 82; San Francisco Exchange Show, Fashion Moda, New York, 82; San Francisco Art Inst Ann, 84; Alternative Mus, 84; Mission Cult Ctr, 85. *Collections Arranged:* Alice Neel, Paintings from 1920-1974, Am Can Gallery, 74; Ethnic Notions: Black Images in the White Mind, 82 & Mothers Gifts to their Children, 84, (with catalogs), Berkeley Art Ctr. *Pos:* Dir, Southern Exposure Gallery, San Francisco, 74-77; cur, Intersection Gallery, San Francisco, 77-79; cur & exec dir, Berkeley Art Ctr, 79-85; artist-in-residence, Calif Arts Coun, 83-86. *Bibliog:* Thomas Albright (auth), The underground is looking up, San Francisco Chronicle, 4/18/78 & Forty Years of Bay Area Art, Univ Calif Press, 84; Robert MacDonald (auth), Images of women, Artweek, 4/79; Charles Shere (auth), article, Oakland Tribune, 8/30/82. *Mem:* Northern Calif Gallery Asn. *Media:* Oil on Canvas, Mixed Media. *Mailing Add:* 2310 Ninth St Berkeley CA 94710

HENDERSON, VICTOR
PAINTER, MURALIST
b Cuyahoga Falls, Ohio, Nov 30, 39. *Study:* San Francisco State Col, BA, 63. *Work:* Newport Harbor Mus, Newport Beach, Calif; Chicago Art Inst; M H De Young Mem Mus, San Francisco. *Comn:* Beverly Hills Sidhartha, Michael Huit, Los Angeles, 69-70; Venice in the Snow, Jerry Rosen, Los Angeles, 70; Isle of Calif, Jordy Hormel, Los Angeles, 70-72; Hippy Knowhow, French Govt, Paris, 71; Ghost Town, Ed Janss, Thousand Oaks, Calif, 72-73 (all the above murals were executed under the name Los Angeles Fine Arts Squad); Breakers Mural, comn by Arco Co, Santa Barbara, Calif, 78-79; Biltmore Hotel, Los Angeles, 85. *Exhib:* LA 8, Los Angeles Co Mus Art, Calif, 76; 100-plus, Los Angeles Inst Contemp Art, 77; Illusion & Reality, Australian Nat Gallery, Canbera, and six other Australian galleries & mus, 77; Victor Henderson Takes a Walk, Newport Harbour Art Mus, 78; one-person shows, Ulrike Cantor Gallery, Los Angeles, 81 & Los Angeles Co Mus, Calif, 83; Artists Space, New York, 83; and others. *Pos:* Co-founder, Los Angeles Fine Art Squad, Calif, 69-73. *Teaching:* Lectr drawing, Univ Calif, Los Angeles, 75-77; Otis Art Inst, Los Angeles, 80-83 & Univ Calif, Irvine, 84-85. *Awards:* Nat Endowment Arts Painting Fel, 83-84. *Bibliog:* T H Garver (auth), Artforum, Vol 9, 71; Peter Plagens (auth), Sunshine Muse, Praeger, NY, 73; Eva Cookcroft (auth), Towards a People Art, E P Dutton & Co, NY, 76; Volger Barthelmeh (auth), Street Murals, Alfred A Knopt, 82; Edward Lucie-Smith (auth), American Art Now, William Marrow, 85. *Publ:* Auth, Mega Murals & Big Art, Running Press, Philadelphia, 77. *Mailing Add:* 571 S Arizona Ave East Los Angeles CA 90022

HENDRICKS, BARKLEY LEONNARD
PAINTER
b Philadelphia, Pa, Apr 16, 45. *Study:* Pa Acad Fine Arts, 63-67, William Cresson European Traveling scholar, 66; Yale Univ Sch Fine Art, 70-72. *Work:* Philadelphia Mus Art; Pa Acad Fine Arts, Philadelphia; Cornell Univ; Wichita State Univ, Kans; Nat Gallery, Washington, DC. *Exhib:* Fel Exhib, Pa Acad Fine Arts, 67-72; Nat Acad Design Ann, New York, 70-71 & 74-75; Contemp Black Artists, Whitney Mus Am Art, New York, 71; Childe Hassam Fund Exhib, Am Acad Arts & Lett, 71 & 75; Nat Inst Arts & Lett Ann, 71-72. *Teaching:* Instr painting & drawing, Pa Acad Fine Arts, 71-72; asst in painting, Yale Univ, 71-72; asst prof painting & drawing, Conn Col, 72-81, prof, 81-88. *Awards:* Julius Hallgarten Second Prize, Nat Acad Design, 71; Richard & Hilda Rosenthal Award, Nat Inst Arts & Lett, 72. *Media:* Oil, Acrylic. *Mailing Add:* Box 5462 Conn Col 270 Monegan Ave New London CT 06320

HENDRICKS, DAVID CHARLES
PAINTER, VISUAL ARTIST
b Hammond, Ind, Mar 25, 48. *Study:* Skowhegan Summer Sch Painting & Sculpture, Maine, 69, Univ Ill, BFA, 70; Ox-Bow Summer Sch Painting, Saugatuck, Mich, 70. *Work:* Brooklyn Mus, NYNEX & Reader's Digest, New York; Hirshhorn Mus & Sculpture Garden, Washington, DC; NC Nat Bank; AT&T; Haynes & Boone, Dallas, Tex; Nat Health Insurance Underwriters, Dallas, Tex; and others. *Exhib:* One-man shows, Monique Knowlton Gallery, 77, Fischbach Gallery, NY, 84, 87, 88 & 90, Keene State Col, NH, 89; Davidson Nat Print and Drawing Show, Davidson Col, NC, 76; Childe Hassam Foundation Show, Am Acad & Lett, NY, 76; Queensboro Community Col, Bayside, NY, 77; Wave Hill Ctr for Environ Studies, Riverdale, NY, 79; Portsmouth Community Arts Ctr, Va, 82; Greenville County Mus Art, SC, 85; William Sawyer Gallery, San Francisco, Calif, 85; travelling exhib, San Francisco Mus Mod Art, De Cordova & Dana Mus & Park, Lincoln, Mass, Archer M Huntington Art Gallery, Austin Tex, Mary & Leigh Block Gallery, Evanston, Ill, Arkon Art Mus, Ohio, Madison Art Ctr, Wis; 50th Nat Midyear exhib, Butler Inst Am Art, Ohio, 86; Face of the Land, Southern Alleghenies Mus Art, Loretto, Pa, 88; Art on Paper 1988, Weatherspoon Art Gallery, 88; Drawn from Life: Contemp Interpretive Landscape, Sewall Art Gallery, Tex, 88; Utopian Visions, Art Adv Serv Mus Mod Art, New York, 88; Water, Pfizer Inc, Art Adv Service Mus of Mod Art, 89. *Awards:* Mary C McLellan Scholar, 70; MacDowell Colony Fel, Peterborough, NH, 71, 72, 74, 75, 79, 80, 83, 85 & 86; Fel, Ossabow Island Proj Found, Ga, 76; Davidson Nat Print & Drawing Show Purchase Award, Davidson Col, NC, 76; Fel, Yaddo Corp, Saratoga Springs, NY, 77, 81 & 82; Nat Endowment for the Arts, Visual Arts Fel, 77 & 80. *Bibliog:* John Russell (auth), Invigorating breezes of the fall season, NY Times, Arts & Leisure, 10/2/76; Lenore Malen (auth), David Henricks, Arts Mag, 2/77. *Media:* Pencil, Graphite; Oil. *Dealer:* Fischbach Gallery 24 W 57th St New York NY 10019. *Mailing Add:* c/o Fishbach Gallery 24 W 57th St New York NY 10019

HENDRICKS, EDWARD LEE
SCULPTOR, KINETIC ARTIST
b Charleston, WVa, Nov 9, 52. *Study:* Birmingham Southern Col, BFA, 74; Univ NC, Chapel Hill, MFA, 76. *Work:* Hunter Mus Art, Chattanooga, Tenn; Mint Mus Art, Charlotte, NC; New Orleans Mus Art; Phoenix Art Mus, Ariz; Birmingham Mus Art, Ala. *Comn:* Sculpture, Birmingham Bd Educ, 76; sculpture, Birmingham Realty Co, 85; sculpture, Birmingham Mus Art, 86; sculpture, Am Republic Insurance, Des Moines, 86; sculpture, Datran Ctr, Coral Gables, Fla; sculpture, Turco Develop Co, St Louis, 89. *Exhib:* One-man shows, Southeastern Ctr Contemp Art, 80, 84, Alexander F Milliken Inc, New York, 80, 82, 84 & 89, Montgomery Mus Fine Arts, Ala, 81, Osuma Gallery, Washington, DC, 81 & 83, O K Harris West, Scottsdale, Ariz, 81, 83 & 84, Birmingham Mus Art, 81 &84, Hunter Mus Art, 82, Eric Makler Gallery, Philadelphia, 82 & 83 & Davis McClain Gallery, Houston, 85, 87 & Ardew Gallery, Boston, 87; Elaine Horwitch, Palm Spring, Calif, 88 & 90. *Awards:* Second Award, Nat Sculpture, 75; Juror's Award, Birmingham Art Asn, 79; Southeast Artists Fel, Southeastern Ctr Contemp Art, 83. *Bibliog:* Bob Yoskowitz (auth), articles, Arts Mag, 80 & 81; Carol Donnel-Kotrozo (auth), article, Art Express, 82; Vivien Raynor (rev), article, NY Times, 10/5/84. *Media:* Metal. *Dealer:* Alexander F Milliken Inc 98 Prince St New York NY 10012. *Mailing Add:* c/o Eve Mannes Gallery 116 Bennett Suite A Atlanta GA 30309

HENDRICKS, GEOFFREY
PAINTER, ENVIRONMENTAL ARTIST
b Littleton, NH, July 30, 31. *Study:* Amherst Col, BA, 53; Norfolk Art Sch, Yale Univ, scholar, summer 53; Cooper Union Art Sch, 53-56; Columbia Univ, MA, 62. *Work:* NJ State Mus, Trenton; Mus Mod Art & Metrop Mus Art, New York; Lehmbruck Mus, Duisburg, WGer; Mus Moderner Kunst, Vienna, Austria; Nordjyllands Kunstmuseum, Aalborg, Denmark. *Exhib:* Alternatives in Retrospect, New Mus, New York, 81; 1962 Wiesbaden Fluxus 1982, Mus, Wiesbaden, Ger; Fluxus, Etc, Neuberger Mus, Purchase, NY, 83; NJ State Mus, Trenton, 84; Neue Galerie-Samlung Ludwig, Aachen, Ger, 84; and many other group & one-man shows. *Teaching:* From assoc prof art, Douglass Col, Rutgers Univ to prof art & grad dir, Mason Gross Sch Arts, Rutgers Univ, 56-; instr art, New York Fine Arts Winter Term Prog of Earlham Col, Richmond, Ind, 65-69. *Awards:* MacDowell Colony Fel, 55; Nat Endowment Arts Fel, 76-77; Deutscher Akad Austauschdienst, Berliner Kunstler Prog, 83; Barkenhoff Stiftung, Found Fel, Worpswede, Ger, 85-86. *Bibliog:* Ichiro Haryu (ed), Art as action & concept, Art Now, 72; Gerd Winkler (auth), Wolken und Gitarren, Kunstforum Int, 2/74; Geoffrey Hendricks, Flash Art, 2/76; and others. *Mem:* Col Art Asn Am; Am Asn Univ Prof; Fluxus. *Media:* Acrylic, Intermedia. *Publ:* Auth, Ring Piece, Something Else Press, 73; Between Two Points/Fra Due Poli, Edizioni Pari & Dispari, 75; A Sheep's Skeleton & Rocks, Unpublished Ed, New York, 77; Five Found Photos, Printed Ed, 79; La Capra, Edizioni Morra, Napoli, 79; Ed, A Search for Accidental Significance for Brian Buczak, Money for Food Press, New York, 87. *Dealer:* Galerie Baecker St Apern Strasse 21 D5000 Koln 1 WGer. *Mailing Add:* 486 Greenwich St New York NY 10013

HENDRICKS, JAMES (POWELL)
SCULPTOR, PAINTER
b Little Rock, Ark, Aug 7, 38. *Study:* Univ Ark, Fayetteville, BA, 63; Univ Iowa, MFA, 64. *Work:* Mus Fine Arts, Springfield, Mass; Smithsonian Inst, Washington, DC; Ark Arts Ctr, Little Rock; Hudson River Mus, Yonkers, NY; Mus fine Arts, Boston. *Comn:* Painting, Apollo 14 Launch, Nat Gallery Art & NASA, 71; painting (cover), Time Mag, 8/9/71. *Exhib:* One-man shows, Smithsonian Inst Nat Air & Space Mus, 69, Hudson River Mus, Yonkers, 70; State Univ NY; Helen Shlien Gallery, Boston, 80, 82 & 84; IV Int Bien de Arte Medellin, Colombia, S Am, 81; Tyler Art Gallery, 83; Portland Sch Art & Baxter Gallery, 85; Mus Fine Arts, Springfield, Mass, 86; Space Art Gallery, Seoul, Korea, 86; Slater-Price Fine Arts, New York, 89 & 90. *Pos:* Vis artist, Portland Sch Art, ME, 85 & Seoul Inst Arts, Korea, 86. *Teaching:* Grad instr drawing, State Univ Iowa, 63-64; instr art, Mt Holyoke Col, 64-65; from asst prof to assoc prof painting & drawing, Univ Mass, Amherst, 72-79, dir grad progs in art, 72-, prof art, 79- *Awards:* Painting Awards, Soc Four Arts, 68 & Silvermine Guild Artists, 69; Ark Traveler Award, 71. *Bibliog:* Robert Ackermann (auth), article, Arts Mag, 9-10/74 & Art in Am, 3-4/76; Nancy Stapen (auth), article, Artforum, 1/83; and others. *Media:* Acrylic, Wood; Bronze, Mixed Media. *Publ:* Illusr cover, Time, 71. *Dealer:* Joy Moos Gallery Miami FL. *Mailing Add:* Dept of Art Univ of Mass Amherst MA 01003

HENDRIX, CONNIE (CONNIE SANDAGE MANUS)
PAINTER, INSTRUCTOR
b Mt Ayr, Iowa, May 30, 42. *Study:* Drake Univ, Des Moines, BFA, 64; Memphis State Univ; special study with Jason Williamson, Irving Shapiro, Murray Wentworth, Lee Weiss, Ed Betz & Charles Reid. *Work:* Foothills Art Ctr, Golden, Colo; Ponca City Fine Arts Ctr, Okla; Tenn Arts Comn, State of Tenn, Nashville; State of Iowa, Wallace Agriculture Bldg, Des Moines; Nat

Bank Commerce, Memphis, Tenn. *Comn:* Six watercolors of vegetables (with Julie Wells), United Foods, Bells, Tenn, 76; three watercolors of Olympics for limited ed wall covering (with Tom Welsh), Welsh Forest Products, Memphis, Tenn, 79-80; three watercolors for poster, Opera memphis, Tenn, 88. *Exhib:* Rocky Mountain Nat Watermedia Exhib; Southern Watercolor Soc, NTex State Univ Art Gallery, Denton; Georgia Watercolor Soc; Columbus Mus Arts & Sci & Cheekwood Fine Arts Ctr, Nashville, Tenn, 76-79; Allied Artists Am Ann Exhib, Nat Arts Club, New York, 81. *Collections Arranged:* Nat Bank Commerce (auth, catalog), Commerce Sq Invitational, Memphis, Tenn, 73; Bicentennial Salute to Memphis, Nat Bank Commerce Salutes, 76. *Pos:* Artist, Look Mag, Des Moines, Iowa, 60-64; sr art dir, Ward Archer & Assocs Advert, Memphis, 69-79; creative dir, designer & illusr, Connie Hendrix & Assocs, Memphis, 79- *Teaching:* Memphis City Sch System, Tenn, 66-69; instr watercolor, Univ Tenn Student Alumni Educ Ctr, Adult Educ Prog, 73-; Memphis State Univ Continuing Educ, 75-; and various workshops in midsouth area. *Awards:* First Place Purchase Award, 11th Tenn All-State, First Am Nat Bank, 71; Top Cash Award, Watercolor Div, 8th Cent South Art Exhib, Commerce Union Bank, 73; Nat Bank of Commerce Award, Tenn Watercolor Soc Ann, 73, 74, 76, 78, 81, 83 & 87. *Mem:* Tenn Watercolor Soc (regional dir, 71-73, corresp secy, 72, vpres, 74 & pres, 75-76); assoc mem Am Watercolor Soc; assoc mem Allied Artists Am; Art Dirs' Club Memphis (secy, 70 & 71, vpres, 72 & pres, 73); charter mem Memphis Watercolor Soc; Memphis Soc Visual Commun; charter mem Southern Watercolor Soc (secy, 75-76); Memphis Ad Fed (dir, 89, 90, 91 & 92). *Media:* Watercolor. *Publ:* Auth, article, Northlight Mag, 5-6/75; Bicentennial Salute to Memphis (film), Cablecom/Educ TV, 76. *Dealer:* Elkanah Gallery, Jackson, TN; Classic Antiquities Ltd Gallery Los Angeles CA. *Mailing Add:* 43 Union No 3 Memphis TN 38103

HENES, DONNA
ENVIRONMENTAL ARTIST, SCULPTOR
b Cleveland, Ohio, Sept 19, 45. *Study:* Ohio State Univ; City Col New York, BS, 70, MS, 72. *Comn:* Pub participatory event, Bicentennial Comn, New York, 76; Vernal Equinox Celebration, Port Authority NY & NJ, New York, 80-90; web installation, Indianapolis Mus, 83; installation, Maine Monument, New York Cult Affairs Dept, 83; seasonal pub celebrations, Lower Manhattan Cult Coun, 83; Olympia Ticker Tape Parade, New York City Mayor's Off, 84; Holiday Lighting Installation, Rosendale, NY, 86 & 87, Bay Shore, NY, 88. *Exhib:* Women in American Architecture, Brooklyn Mus & traveling, 77; Hilosphia, Spain, 82; Sculpture Tricentennial, Philadelphia Arts Alliance, 82; solo shows, Washington Proj Arts, 82 & Indianapolis Mus Art, 83; At Home, Newport Harbor Mus, Calif, 83; Artist Books Biennial, Ctr Arte & Communicacion, Buenos Aires, 83; Latitudes of Time, New York City Gallery, 85; Streets, Gardens & Altars, Cent Hall Gallery, 86; Public Visions-Public Monuments, Soho 20 Gallery, 86; Ritual in the 20 Century, Islip Mus Art, 87; Completing the Circle, Minn Ctr Bk Art & Nat Tour, 92-93; The Meeting of the Holy Pictures, Panstwowe Mus Ethograficzne, Warsaw, Poland, 91. *Pos:* Writer, celestially auspicious occasions, nationally syndicated column, currently. *Teaching:* Minneapolis Col Art & Design, 87, 89; The Cooper Union, 92. *Awards:* NY Found Arts Fel, 86. *Bibliog:* Lucy Lippard (auth), Overlay, Pantheon Books, 82; Eggs on end, New Yorker, 83; Moira Roth (auth), The Amazing Decade, Astro Art, 83; Artists' Books: A Critical Anthology, Visual Studies Workshop, 85; Annie Gottlieb (auth), Do You Believe in Magic?, 87. *Mem:* Founding mem Ctr Celebration (bd dirs, 80-). *Media:* Ritual Celebration, Environmental Transformation. *Publ:* Contribr, The Politics of Women's Spirituality, Doubleday, 81; auth, Dressing Our Wounds in Warm Clothes, Astro Artz, 82; ed, Celebration News, 86. *Mailing Add:* 279 Sterling Pl No 4A Brooklyn NY 11238

HENKLE, JAMES LEE
SCULPTOR, DESIGNER
b Cedar Rapids, Iowa, Mar 13, 27. *Study:* Univ Nebr, BA; Pratt Inst, cert(indust design). *Work:* Univ Okla Art Mus, Norman; Okla State Art Collection, Okla Arts & Humanities Coun, Okalahoma City; Ark Art Ctr, Little Rock. *Comn:* Sculpture mural, Numerical Anal Res Ctr, Norman, 63 & Tulsa Pub Libr, Tulsa Hist Soc, Okla, 65; sculpture, Norman Pub Libr, 75th Anniversary Comt, 66; wall sculpture, Dale Hall, Univ Okla; communion table, First Presby Church, Norman, 88; Furniture Designs, Mabee-Gerrer Mus Art, Shawnee Okla, 90. *Exhib:* Eight State Art Exhib, Oklahoma City Art Ctr, 61; one-man sculpture exhib, Univ Okla Mus Art, 68 & Philbrook Art Ctr, Tulsa, 70; Okla State Univ, 79; Okla Designer Craftsman Exhibs, 76-81; Vision Makers, Kilpatrick Ctr, Oklahoma City, 88; Philbrook Art Ctr, Tulsa, Okla, 88. *Pos:* Designer, Dave Chapman Design Firm, 52-53. *Teaching:* Prof art, Univ Okla, 53-; prof art, emer, 90. *Awards:* Purchase Prize Sculpture, Okla Art Ctr, 65; Purchase Prize Painting, Springfield Art Mus; Purchase Award Crafts, Eighth Ann Print, Drawing & Crafts Exhib, Ark Arts Ctr, 75. *Publ:* Contribr, Fine Woodworking Biennial Design Book (Vol 1, 2, 3 & 4), Taunton Press. *Mailing Add:* Sch Art Univ Okla Norman OK 73069

HENLE, FRITZ
PHOTOGRAPHER, FILMMAKER
b Dormund, Ger, June 9, 09; US citizen. *Study:* Univ Heidelberg, 30; Univ Munich, 30; Sch Photog, Munich, Ger, dipl(photog), 31. *Work:* Mus Mod Art, Int Ctr Photog, New York; Ctr Creative Photog, Tucson; George Eastman House, Rochester, NY; Univ Tex Photog Collection; Mus Ludwig, Cologne; and many others. *Comn:* Alcoa; United Airlines; Viking Press. *Exhib:* Solo exhibs, Caribbean (traveling exhib), Smithsonian Inst, Washington, DC, 54, retrospective, Art Mus, Allentown, Pa, 77, New York Cult Ctr, 77, Michener Gallery, Univ Tex, Austin, 79, Color Photographs, Trinity Univ, San Antonio, Tex, 79, 50 year retrospective, Witkin Gallery, New York, 80, Theme In Variations & American Impressions, 1936-86 (traveling exhib), Amerika-Haus, Heidelberg & many cities, Ger, 86, San Juan, Pablo Casals, 91, Frauen, Studio Du Mont, Photo Xiner, 92; APA Int Exhib Photog, Tokyo, Japan, 78; Body Electric: Color, Squibb Inst, Princeton, NJ, 80; Germany: The New Vision, Fraenkel Gallery San Francisco, 81; The Henle Family, Reichhold Ctr Arts, St Thomas, VI, 83; Sammlung Gruber, Mus Ludwig, Cologne, 84. *Pos:* Photogr, Life, 37-42, Harpers Bazaar, 45-52, City Serv Oil Co, 52-59 & free-lance, 60-; and many others. *Awards:* Merit Award Photog, Popular Photog, eight times, 48-60; VI Coun Arts Grants; Nat Endowment Arts Photogr Fel. *Bibliog:* Article, Foto Mag, Munich, 3/80; Grace Glueck (auth), Art: Fritz Henle, Witkin Gallery, New York Times, 5/2/80; Grace Naismith (auth), Who, what, where, Overseas Press Club Bulletin, 5/15/80. *Mem:* Life mem VI Acad Arts & Lett; founding mem Am Soc Mag Photogr; Overseas Press Club Am; St Croix Environmental Asn; Deutsche Gesecceschart tus Photog. *Publ:* Illusr, Holiday in Europe, 63; A New Guide to Rollei Photography, 65; The American Virgin Islands, 71; Casals, 75; The Rolliflex SL66 and SLX Way, 75; and many others. *Mailing Add:* PO Box 723 Christiansted, St Croix VI 00821

HENNESSEY, WILLIAM JOHN
MUSEUM DIRECTOR
b Summit, NJ, July 15, 48. *Study:* Wesleyan Univ, BA, 70; Ford Found fel, Worcester Art Mus, 71-73; Columbia Univ, PhD, 78. *Collections Arranged:* The American Portrait: From Stuart to Sargent (auth, catalog), Worcester Art Mus, 73; Artists Look at Art (auth, catalog), 78 & Permanent Collection, 78, Spencer Art Mus, Univ Kans; Hudson Valley People, Vassar Col Art Gallery, 82; Russel Wright: American Designer, Gallery Asn NY State & MIT Press, 83; Thomas S Noble, Univ Ky Art Mus, 88. *Pos:* Res assoc, Solomon R Guggenheim Mus, 73-74; cur, Spencer Art Mus, Univ Kans, 75-79; dir, Vassar Col Art Gallery, 79-82; dir, Univ Ky Art Mus, 82-90; dir, Univ Mich Mus Art, 90. *Teaching:* Instr, Brooklyn Col & Sch Visual Arts, 73-75; asst prof, Univ Kans, 75-79; asst prof, Vassar Col, 79-82; adj prof art, Univ Ky; assoc prof, Univ Mich. *Mem:* Col Art Asn; Soc Archit Historians; Asn Art Mus Dirs. *Res:* 19th & 20th Century architecture & design. *Publ:* Auth, A Handbook of the Worcester Art Museum, 73; Friedrich Overbeck's Drawing of Elijah, Regist Spencer Mus, spring 77; Frank Lloyd Wright and the design of the Guggenheim Museum, Arts Mag, 4/78; series of 24 articles for the World Book Encyclopedia. *Mailing Add:* Mus Art Univ Mich Ann Arbor MI 48109

HENNESY, GERALD CRAFT
PAINTER, PUBLISHER
b Washington, DC, June 11, 21. *Study:* Corcoran Sch Art; George Washington Univ; Am Univ; Univ Md; also with C Gordon Harris. *Work:* Nat Hq Am Legion & Nat Hq Daughters Am Revolution, Washington, DC; Md State Exec Mansion, Annapolis; US House Rep Off Bldg, Washington, DC. *Comn:* Paintings, Gibson Bldg, Fairfax, Va, 74, United Va Bank, Richmond, 75, Hq Blue Cross & Blue Shield Asn, 82 & Nat Hq Fed Deposit Insurance Corp, 83, Washington, DC. *Exhib:* Corcoran Gallery Art, Washington, DC; Am Art League, Smithsonian Inst, Washington, DC, 62 & 64; Baltimore Mus Art Regional, 63; New York World's Fair, 65; Allied Artists of Am, New York, 75 & 76; one-man show, Pla Gallery, McLean, Va, 67; and many others. *Pos:* Advert artist, Washington Times Herald, Washington, DC, 41-42. *Awards:* First Prize, Gilham Show, 66; Watercolor Medal, Landscape Club, 74. *Mem:* Washington Soc Landscape Painters (treas, 73-77, 87-); Artists Equity Asn; Fairfax Co Coun Arts. *Media:* Oil, Watercolor. *Dealer:* Venable Neslage Galleries 1803 Connecticut Ave NW Washington DC 20009. *Mailing Add:* 6811 White Rock Rd Clifton VA 22024

HENNING, EDWARD BURK
CURATOR, HISTORIAN
b Cleveland, Ohio, Oct 23, 22. *Study:* Cleveland Inst Art, cert(painting); Western Reserve Univ, BS, MA; Acad Julian, Paris. *Collections Arranged:* Paths of Abstract Art (with catalog), 60; Fifty Years of Modern Art: 1916-1966 (with catalog), 66; Landscapes Interior and Exterior: Avery, Rothko and Schueler (with catalog), 75; The Spirit of Surrealism (with catalog), 79; and others. *Pos:* Asst cur educ, Cleveland Mus Art, 55-56, assoc cur educ, 56-59, asst to dir, 59-70, cur mod art, 63-75, chief cur mod art, 75-85, res cur, 85- *Teaching:* Adj prof mod art, Case Western Reserve Univ, 68- *Mem:* Col Art Asn; Am Asn Mus; Am Soc Aesthetics; Int Coun Mus. *Res:* Impressionism to present, especially Cezanne, cubism, dadaism and surrealism; abstract-expressionism, color-field painting and conceptualism. *Publ:* Auth, Patronage and Style in the Arts: A Suggestion Concerning Their Relations, 60; contribr, On Understanding Art Museums, 75. *Mailing Add:* Cleveland Mus Art 11150 East Blvd Cleveland OH 44106

HENRICH, BIFF
PHOTOGRAPHER
b Erie, Pa, Oct 2, 53. *Study:* Hiram Col, BA, 75; Visual Studies Workshop, 76; State Univ NY, Buffalo, MFA, 78. *Work:* Albright-Knox Art Gallery; Los Angeles Co Art; Castellani Art Mus; Burchfield Art Ctr. *Exhib:* In Western NY, Albright-Knox Art Gallery, 79, 81, 83, 85, 87, 89, 91; New Photography, Contemp Art Mus, Houston, 81; Grand Galop, Artist Space, New York, 83; Burchfield Art Ctr, Buffalo, 88; Linda Cathcart Gallery, Santa Monica, Calif, 90 & 92; Light Work, Syracuse, 91; Tex Gallery, Houston, 92; and others. *Pos:* Dir, CEPA Gallery, Buffalo, 78-82, pres bd dirs, 78-87. *Teaching:* Tutor & mentor photog, Empire State Col, 78-80; vis lectr, State Univ NY, Buffalo, 80 & 83. *Awards:* Nat Endowment Arts Fel, 79 & 82; NY State Coun Arts Sponsored Proj, 83. *Dealer:* Linda Cathcart Gallery 945 Colorado Santa Monica CA. *Mailing Add:* PO 111 Buffalo NY 14222

HENRICKSON, MARTHA (KLEIN)
CONCEPTUAL ARTIST, PHOTOGRAPHER
b Brooklyn, NY, Feb 20, 42. *Study:* Arts Students League, 64. *Work:* Can Coun Art Bank & Can Mus Contemp Photog, Ottawa; Metrop Toronto Publ Libr & Art Gallery, Toronto; IBM; Coca Cola; Prudential Life. *Comn:* Zucchini, Art Gallery Ont, Toronto, 74; Zucchini Preparation (28 courses), Artpark, Lewiston, NY, 75; Toronto Sesquicentennial, Toronto Photogrs Workshop, 85. *Exhib:* 85th Ann San Francisco, San Francisco Mus Art, Calif, 66; Grass in Art & Architecture, Los Angeles Co Mus, travelling exhib, Calif, 76; Plant Shadows, TPW Gallery, Toronto, Ont, 84; Thomas & Martha Henrickson, Art Gallery Hamilton, Ont, 85; Canada in Amsterdam, de Meervart, Holland, 86; In Focus, Art Gallery Ont, Toronto, 87; solo exhib, Jane Corkin Gallery, 91. *Teaching:* Instr photogr, Ryerson Polytech Inst, 78-87. *Awards:* Explorations Prize, Can Coun, 76; Photog Prize, Plant Shadows, 84 & Exhib Asst Award, Martha Henrickson, 85, Ont Arts Coun. *Bibliog:* Scott Lauder (auth), Hard edge to Zucchini, Can Forum, 6/77; Michael Mitchell (auth), Martha & Thomas Henrickson, Photocommunique, winter 84. *Mem:* Toronto Photogr Workshop. *Media:* Mixed; Hand Colored Silver Prints. *Publ:* Coauth & illusr, The Organic Zucchini, 76 & Awakenings, Arterial, Toronto, 77. *Dealer:* Jane Corkin Gallery 179 John St Toronto ON M5T 1X4 Can. *Mailing Add:* 187 Glenmanor Way Thornhill ON L4J 3A3 Canada

HENRICKSON, PAUL ROBERT
PAINTER, WRITER
b Boston, Mass. *Study:* RI Sch Design, BFA; Boston State Col, ME; Univ Minn, PhD; Clark Univ; Statens Kunst Akademiet, Oslo; Statens Kunst Industriskole, Oslo. *Work:* Mus of NMex, Santa Fe; Statens Kunst Industriskole. *Comn:* Crash (canvas panel), in pvt collection, NDak; four part canvas panel, pvt collection, New York. *Exhib:* One-man exhibs, Am & Mex Mus. *Pos:* Exec dir, Insular Arts Coun, Gov Guam, 65-68; free lance art critic, Santa Fe Reporter, NMex & Art Voices/South, Palm Beach, Fla; producer, Santa Fe Int Scandinavian Film Festival, 84. *Teaching:* Prof & head div fine arts, Univ Gaum, 64-68; prof res art, Univ Northern Iowa, 68-72. *Res:* Psychology of art. *Publ:* Auth, Two Primitive Micronesian Art Forms, 68; Lying, Dogmatic and Creative Persons, 70; The Perceptive and Silenced Minorities, 72; auth, The Word for Cross is Cryptic, 77. *Mailing Add:* PO Box 3731 Santa Fe NM 87501-0731

HENRICKSON, THOMAS
CONCEPTUAL ARTIST, PHOTOGRAPHER
b New York, NY, Apr 22, 44. *Study:* Pratt Inst, New York, with R Lindner, BFA, 65. *Work:* Can Coun Art Bank & Nat Gallery Can, Ottawa, Ont; Metro Toronto Pub Libr; de Meervaart, Amsterdam. *Comn:* Zucchini presentation, Art Gallery Ont, Toronto, 74 & Artpark, Lewiston, NY, 75; photo proj documentary, Toronto Photogr Workshop, 84. *Exhib:* Tor Documentary Proj, Gallery Harbourfront, Toronto, 842; Seeing People-Seeing Space, Photog Gallery, London & Bradford, Eng, 84; Thomas & Martha Henrickson, Art Gallery Hamilton, Ont, 85; Canada in Amsterdam, de Meervaart, Amsterdam, 86; Memorable Meals, Dazibao Gallery, Montreal, 87; and others. *Teaching:* Prof photog, color & graphics & 3D design, Ryerson Polytech Inst, Sch Interior Design, Sch Film & Photog, Toronto, 69- *Awards:* Award, Can Coun, 71-89; Award, Ont Arts Coun, 82. *Bibliog:* Scott Lauder (auth), Hard-edge to zucchini, Can Forum, 6/77; Isaac Applebaum (auth), Memorable meals, Impressions, 80; Michael Mitchell (auth), Martha-Thomas Henrickson, Photocommunique, winter 84. *Mem:* Toronto Photogr Workshop (exhib comt, 82-86); Visual Arts Toronto, Ont. *Media:* Mixed. *Publ:* Coauth & illusr, The Organic Zucchini, 76 & Awakenings, 77, Arterial, Toronto. *Mailing Add:* 187 Glenmanor Way Thornhill ON L4J 3A3 Canada

HENRY, GERRIT VAN KEUREN
CRITIC
b Baldwin, NY, May 30, 50. *Study:* Columbia Col, Columbia Univ, BA, 72. *Collections Arranged:* Work by Joe Brainard, Sch Visual Arts, 72; Contemporary Nudes, One Penn Plaza, New York, 88. *Pos:* New York corresp, Art Int, 70-72; art critic, New Republic, 73-74; assoc ed, Artnews, New York, 73-75, contr ed, 85-; sr ed, Print Collector's Newsletter, 79- 84. *Teaching:* Adj asst prof art hist, C W Post Col, Greenvale, NY, 72-74; instr, Sch Visual Arts, 89- *Awards:* Art Critics' Fel, Nat Endowment Arts, 72. *Bibliog:* Lawrence Alloway (auth), The renewal of realist criticism, Art in Am, 81. *Res:* Mid-20th century American painterly realism. *Publ:* Auth, two articles, In: Super Realism, Dutton, 75; auth, Interview with Jack Levine, Artnews, 79; auth, Painterly realism and the modern landscape, Art in Am, 81; Donald Sultan: Tar and tulips, Art News, 87; Janet Fish, Burton Skira, Geneva, 87. *Mailing Add:* 265 W 90th St No 7 New York NY 10024

HENRY, JEAN
PAINTER, INSTRUCTOR
b Oakland, Calif. *Study:* Art Acad, Amsterdam, Holland; Am Univ Berlin; Md Inst, Baltimore; Western Reserve Univ. *Work:* Triton Mus Art, San Jose, Calif; Chamber of Commerce, San Francisco; Schwartz Hall, Presidio, Calif; Kaiser Hosp, San Francisco; Letterman Hosp, San Francisco. *Comn:* Portrait of Sen Graham, Capitol Bldg, Frankfurt, Ky, 72; portrait, Dr Arthur Sammis, 80; portrait, Eubie Blake (famous jazz pianist & composer), 80; Turk Murphy (famous jazz musician), 80. *Exhib:* Soc Western Artists, De Young Mus, 68; De Saisset Gallery, Santa Clara, Calif, 69; one-man show, Triton Mus Art, 70; Marin Art & Garden Show, 71; Rosicrucian Mus Invitational Show, 71; impressionist painting at semi-ann exhibs, Vel Oyana Gallery, Tokyo, Japan & Mihan Gallery, Nagoya, Japan. *Pos:* Owner, art gallery, Burlingame, Calif; Jean Henry Sch Art, San Francisco, currently. *Teaching:* Instr portrait painting, Md Inst, Johns Hopkins Univ, 58-60; owner & instr painting, Jean Henry Sch Art, San Francisco, 69- *Awards:* First Award, De Young Mus, 68; First Award, Antioch Outdoor Festival, 69; First Award for Portrait, De Saisset Gallery Ann, 70. *Mem:* Soc Western Artists. *Media:* Oil, Acrylic. *Mailing Add:* Jean Henry Sch Arts 2636 Ocean Ave San Francisco CA 94132

HENRY, JEAN
MUSEUM DIRECTOR, CURATOR
Study: Fla Atlantic Univ, BA, 71; Univ Miami, MA, 73; Fla State Univ, PhD(hist & criticism of art), 78; Mellon Post-Doctoral Fel, Yale Univ, 82-83; Western New Eng Inst Psychoanalysis, 82-83, Bryn Mawr Col, Miss, 92. *Collections Arranged:* Drexel's Great Sch of Am Illus (ed, catalog), 84-85; Frank E Schoonover at Drexel: Illus and the Am Tradition 1892-1903 (co-ed, catalog), 86; Nat Sculpture Soc Celebrates the Figure (ed, catalog), 87. *Pos:* Dir & cur, Drexel Univ Art Mus, 83-92; exec bd, Mus Coun of Philadelphia and the Del Valley, 85-87; guest cur, Nat Sculpture Soc, 87. *Teaching:* Adj assoc prof, Drexel Univ, 83-92; assoc prof & chair, dept art, Univ New Haven, 79-83. *Awards:* Col Art Asn travel grant, 79. *Mem:* Col Art Asn; Soc of Archit Historians; Am Asn of Mus; Victorian Soc; World Affairs Coun. *Publ:* essay in John Frazee, Sculptor (exhib catalog), Smithsonian Nat Portrait Gallery, 86; auth, Sculpture Entries Since 1970 (exhib catalog), Pa Acad Fine Arts, 90. *Mailing Add:* 1810 Rittenhouse Sq Apt 803 Philadelphia PA 19103

HENRY, JOHN RAYMOND
SCULPTOR
b Lexington, Ky, Aug 11, 43. *Study:* Univ Ky; Univ Wash; Univ Chicago; Art Inst Chicago, BFA; Edward L Reyerson fel, 69. *Work:* British Mus; Smithsonian Inst, Washington, DC; Dade Co Art in Pub Places, Miami, Fla; Dallas Mus Art, Tex; Hunter Mus Art, Chattanooga, Tenn. *Comn:* Illinois Landscape (sculpture), Nat Endowment Arts, Works of Art Pub Places, Nathan Manilow Sculpture Park, Govs State Univ, Univ Park, Ill, 74; Bridgeport (sculpture), State Ill, 82; Anchorage (sculpture), Anchorage Int Airport, Alaska, 85; Alachua (sculpture), Fla Art State Bldgs, Fla Arts Coun, Univ Fla, Gainesville; Dance of the Sun (sculpture), Sonje Mus Contemp Art, Kyongju City, Korea, 91. *Exhib:* Art Inst Chicago, 68; Eight American Sculptors, Chicago, 68; Ill State Mus, Springfield, 69, 79 & 84; Sculpture off the Pedestal, Grand Rapids Art Mus, Mich, 73; one man shows, Ill State Mus, Springfield, 73, Riverside Park, New York, 75; Heavy Mettle, Mus Art, Ft Lauderdale, Fla, 86; retrospectives, Evolution in Scale, 88-89, Art Mus STex, Corpus Christi, Mus Art, Ft Lauderdale, Mus Fine Arts, St Petersburg, Fla, Hunter Mus Art, Chattanooga, Tenn & Ctr for the Arts, Vero Beach, Fla, 91; Konkrete Multiples II, Galerie L'Indee, Zoetermeer, Neth, 91; Florida Artist Collections, Polk Mus Art, Lakeland, Fla, 92; Made in Florida, Univ SFla Art Mus, Tampa, additional venues in Marseille, France; Geneva, Switz; Hasselet, Belg; Barcelona, Spain; & many others. *Pos:* Bd Trustees, Nat Found Advancement Arts, 91-93. *Teaching:* Vis prof, Univ Iowa, 69; artist in residence, Univ Wis-Green Bay, 69-70; vis prof, Univ Chicago, 70-71; vis lectr, Art Inst Chicago, 78. *Awards:* Edward L Ryerson Fel, Art Inst Chicago, 69; Individual Artists Grant, Nat Endowment Arts, 75; Fla Individual Artists Fel, 90. *Bibliog:* Dennis Adrian (auth), Masterpieces of Recent Chicago Art, Chicago Pub Libr Cult Ctr, Ill, 77; James L Reidy (auth), Chicago Sculpture, Univ Ill Press, Urbana, Chicago, London, 81; Claudia Sabin & Philip Yenawine (auths), Evolution in scale: The Sculpture of John Henry 1967-1988, Design Found, Chicago, Ill, 88. *Mem:* Int Sculpture Ctr, Washington, DC; Chicago Artists Coalition; Nat Found Advancement Arts, Miami, FL. *Media:* Metal, Stone. *Dealer:* Stein Bartlow Gallery 620 Michigan Ave Chicago IL 60611; Jaffee Baker Gallery 608 Banyan Trail Boca Raton FL 33431. *Mailing Add:* PO Box 68 Parkers Lake KY 42634

HENRY, ROBERT
PAINTER, EDUCATOR
b Brooklyn, NY, Aug 3, 33. *Study:* Hans Hofmann Sch Fine Art, New York & Provincetown, Mass; Brooklyn Col, with Ad Reinhardt & Kurt Seligmann, BA. *Exhib:* One-man shows, Green Mountain Gallery & Ingber Gallery, New York; Contemporary Figurative Painting, Suffolk Co Mus, Stony Brook, NY, 71; Hudson River Mus, Yonkers, NY, 71. *Teaching:* From asst prof to prof art, Brooklyn Col, 60- *Bibliog:* L Campbell (auth), Stop, look & look & look, Art News, 2/72; April Kingsley (auth), The interiorized image, Soho Weekly News, 2/5/76; Susan Koslow (auth), Robert Henry, Arts, 80. *Media:* Oil, Watercolor. *Publ:* Auth, Horizontally oriented rotating kinetic painting, Leonardo, 69. *Dealer:* Ingber Gallery 415 W Broadway New York NY 10012. *Mailing Add:* c/o Berta Walker Gallery 208 Bradford St Box 261 Provincetown MA 02657

HENRY, SARA CORRINGTON
HISTORIAN, CRITIC
b Teaneck, NJ, Sept 24, 42. *Study:* Denison Univ, BFA; NY Univ, with Robert Goldwater, BA(art hist); Univ Calif, Berkeley, with Peter Selz & Herschel B Chipp, PhD. *Teaching:* Lectr art hist, Goucher Col, Towson, Md, 70-71; vis instr, Ohio State Univ, Columbus, 71-72; instr, Carnegie-Mellon Univ, Pittsburgh, 73-76; assoc prof, Drew Univ, 76- *Mem:* Col Art Asn; Women's Caucus for Art. *Res:* Paul Klee; abstract expressionism; contemporary art. *Publ:* Contribr, New Catholic Encyclopedia, McGraw-Hill, 66; contribr, Selection 1968, Univ Art Mus, Univ Calif, Berkeley, 68-69; coauth, The Political Art of Duncan MacPherson, Can Dimension, 3-4/70; auth, Form-creating energies: Paul Klee & physics, Arts Mag, 9/77; auth, Klee's Kleinwelt & creation, Print Rev, fall 77. *Mailing Add:* Dept Art BC Drew Univ Madison NJ 07940

HENSCHE, HENRY
PAINTER, INSTRUCTOR
b Chicago, Ill, Feb 20, 01. *Study:* Charles W Hawthorne's Cape Cod Sch Art; Art Inst Chicago; Nat Acad Design; Art Students League; Beaux Arts Inst Design New York. *Work:* Fort Wayne Art Inst, Ind; Chrysler Collection, Norfolk; Mint Mus, NC; Harvard Club, New York; Oklahoma City Mus. *Exhib:* Pittsburgh Int, Nat Acad Design, New York, Chicago Am, Philadelphia Ann & Corcoran Biennial, Washington, DC, 22-33. *Teaching:* Instr oils & watercolors, Cape Cod Sch Art, 28- *Awards:* Hallgarten Prize, Nat Acad Design, 30. *Mem:* Boston Guild Artist; Provincetown Art Asn. *Media:* Oil. *Dealer:* Grand Central Art Gallery 27 W 57th New York NY 10019. *Mailing Add:* Box 806 Gray LA 70359

HENSELMANN, CASPAR
SCULPTOR
b Mannheim, Ger, Mar 13, 33; US citizen. *Study:* Univ Ill Col Med, dipl Med-Art, 55; Art Inst Chicago, BFA, 56; Northwestern Univ, 50-52; Columbia Univ, 61-62. *Work:* Lehmbruck Mus, Duisburg, Ger. *Comn:* glass lobby piece (oil, air), Marshall-Ilsley Bank, Milwaukee, 71; Union Bank Switzerland, New York, 83; SMS Eng, Pittsburg, Pa, 89; Deutsche Bank, New York, 90; Julius Bear Bank, New York, 92. *Exhib:* Cult Coun Found, NY, 79; one-man shows, Sculpture Now, New York, 79 Wilhelm Lehmbruck Mus, 82, Benson Gallery, Bridgehampton, NY, 83 & 87 & Nina Owen Gallery, Chicago, 86, Sandra Gerina Gallery, 89, Dorothea Van Der Koelen, Mainz, Ger, 89, Walter Bischoff Gallery, Stuttgart, Ger, 90; Kunstuerein Bielefeld, Ger, 91; Int Sculpture Symposium, Luxhaven, Ger, 91; Bill Bage Gallery, New York, 92. *Teaching:* Instr, St Cloud State Col, 75; asst prof, C W Post Ctr, Long Island Univ, 76-77, Univ NC, Chapel Hill, 83, Hofstra Univ, Hempstead, NY. *Awards:* Tiffany Award, 62; Ford Found Artist in Residence, Am Fedn Arts, 65; Nat Endowment Arts Award, 79, Grant, 84. *Bibliog:* Articles in: The Village Voice, 74 & 79 & The Soho News, 76, 77, 78 & 79. *Mailing Add:* 21 Bond St New York NY 10012

HENSLEY, JACKSON MOREY
PAINTER
b Portales, NMex, Sept 6, 40. *Study:* Nat Acad Design, 59-61. *Work:* Mus NMex, Santa Fe; Springfield Mus Art, Ohio; Desert Caballeros Mus, Wickenburg, Ariz; Arabian Horse Trust Mus, Denver, Colo; Los Angeles Natural Hist Mus, Calif. *Exhib:* Nat Acad Fine Arts, New York; Nat Arts Club; Salmagundi Club, New York; over 200 other exhibits. *Awards:* Dr Ralph Weiler Award, Nat Acad, 60; Arthur T Hill Mem, Salmagundi Club, New York, 63; Mary Hingman Carter Award, Nat Arts Club, 63. *Bibliog:* Peggy & Harold Samuels (auth), Contemporary Western Artist, 82. *Media:* Watercolor, Oil. *Publ:* Illusr, Rockies Mag & Landscape Printers Am. *Dealer:* Seth Gallery Santa Fe NM; Thompson Gallery New York NY. *Mailing Add:* Rt 2 Box 286 Santa Fe NM 87505

HEPPER, CAROL
SCULPTOR
b McLaughlin, SDak, Oct 23, 53. *Study:* SDak State Univ, Brookings, BS, 75. *Work:* Solomon R Guggenheim Mus & Dannheisser Found, New York; SDak Mem Art Ctr, Brookings; Walker Art Ctr, Minneapolis, Minn; Metrop Mus, New York; Newark Mus, NJ. *Exhib:* Project Studios One, Queens, NY, 82; New Perspectives in American Art (with catalog), Guggenheim Mus, 83; The Sculptural Membrane (with catalog), The Sculpture Ctr, New York, 86; America: Art and the West (with catalog), Art Gallery of Western Australia, Perth, 86 & Art Gallery of New South Wales, Sidney, 87; solo exhibs, Dahl Fine Arts Ctr (with catalog), Rapid City, SDak, 87, Hill Gallery, Birmingham, Mich, 88 & Rosa Esman Gallery, New York, 88; group show, Natural Inflections: Inside/Outside, Sculpture Ctr, New York, 87; Innovations in Sculpture, 1985-1988, Aldrich Mus Art, Ridgefield, Conn, 88; 100 Drawings by Women, Hillwood Art Gallery, Long Island Univ, 89. *Teaching:* Instr drawing, Standing Rock Sioux Indian Community Col, Fort Yates, NDak, 80-82 & Sch Visual Arts, New York, 84; vis fac sculpture, Md Art Inst, Baltimore, & RI Sch Design, 88, State Univ NY, Purchase, 89 & Princeton Univ, NJ, 90. *Awards:* Djerassi Found Fel, 88; NY Found, 89; Nat Endowment Arts, 90; and others. *Bibliog:* Cynthia Nadelman (auth), New American sculpture, 1/84 & Gabo's Progeny, 12/87, Art News; Michael Brenson (auth), Sculpture breaks the mold of minimalism, NY Times, 11/23/86; Diane Waldman (auth), Emerging artists 1978-86: Selections from the Exxon Series & Deborah Pearlburg (auth), New York: Day by day, 9/88, Art News. *Media:* All. *Mailing Add:* 9 E Broadway New York NY 10038

HERA
SCULPTOR, ENVIRONMENTAL ARTIST
b New Orleans, La, Sept 28, 40. *Study:* Mt Holyoke Col; Sch Art Inst Chicago; Univ Dallas, Tex, BA, 70; Southern Methodist Univ, MFA, 74. *Work:* Okla Arts Ctr, Oklahoma City; Longview Mus, Tex; Rose Art Mus, Brandeis Univ, Waltham, Mass; Mount Holyoke Col Art Mus; Tampa Mus Art. *Comn:* Spirit House, Laumeier Sculpture Park, St Louis, Mo, 86; Singing Rock Sitting Place, The Arboretum, Fairmont Park, Philadelphia, 88; Orbital Connector, Gov Smith Houses, Manhattan, 89; Tower as Inland Lighthouse, Marion St Transit Pkwy, Tampa, Fla, 90; Community Based Design Pilot, Philadelphia Art Comn, 91-92. *Exhib:* One-woman shows, Lifeways, Inst Contemp Art, Boston, 76, Butcher Shop, Brooks Jackson Gallery Iolas, New York, 79; Family Room, Contemp Art Ctr, New Orleans, La & Nexus Gallery, Philadelphia, 81; Dream Feast, Alternative Mus, New York, 81; Niagara-Knossos-Carranza Connector, Artpark, 82. *Pos:* Procession designer, First Night, Inc, Boston, 77-78; consult, Women's Slide Arch, Schlesinger Libr Hist Women Am, Radcliffe Col, 77-80; vis artist, Sch Mus Fine Arts, Boston, 78; artist-in-residence, Palisades Interstate Park Com, Bear Mountain, NY, 81; major proj artist, Artpark, 82; vis artist, Gerrit Rietveld Acad, Amdterdam, 85; design team, Marion St Transit Pkwy, Tampa, Fla, 88. *Teaching:* Artist-in-residence painting, drawing & sculpture, Fed Correctional Inst, Nat Endowment for Arts Pilot Prog, Tallahassee, Fla, 75-76; instr, Framingham State Col, Mass, 77-78, & Cooper Union, 91-92. *Awards:* Dept Cult Affairs New York Award, 83 & 87; NY State Coun Arts Award, 83; Unity Day Citation from David Dinkins, New York, 88. *Bibliog:* Ronald Fleming & Renata Von Tscharner (auths), Placemakers, Hastings House, NY, 81 & 87; Lucy Lippard (auth), Overlay, Pantheon, 83; George McCue (auth), Sculpture St Louis, Hudson Hills Press, NY, 88. *Mem:* Col Art Asn; Women's Caucus Art. *Media:* Steel, Wood; Plants. *Mailing Add:* 32 W 20th St New York NY 10011

HERARD, MARVIN T
SCULPTOR, EDUCATOR
b Puyallup, Wash, July 4, 29. *Study:* Burnley Sch Art, Seattle; Seattle Univ; Univ Wash, BA; Cranbrook Acad Art, MFA; Acad Fine Arts, Florence, Italy; Fonderia Artistica Florentina, Italy. *Comn:* Sculpture, Renton Pub Libr; Lemieux Libr, Seattle Univ. *Exhib:* Palazzo Venezia, Rome, 62; Seattle Art Mus, 65-67; Gov Exhib, State Capitol Mus, 67-69; Henry Gallery, Univ Wash, 68; Cheney Cowles Mus, Spokane, Wash, 69; and others. *Teaching:* Instr, Seattle Pub Schs, 56-58; teaching fel sculpture, Cranbrook Acad Arts, 59-60; from assoc prof to prof art & chmn fine arts dept, Seattle Univ, 60-; instr painting, Pius XII Inst Art, Florence, Italy, 62. *Awards:* Am Craftsmen Award, Henry Gallery, 61 & 65; Spokane Pac Northwest Exhib, 63, 64 & 66; Seattle Art Mus, 65; and others. *Mem:* Nat Art Educ Asn; Am Asn Univ Prof. *Mailing Add:* Fine Arts Seattle Univ Broadway & Madison Seattle WA 98122-4460

HERBERT, APRIL H
SCULPTOR
b New York, NY, Apr 30, 34. *Study:* Empire State Col, State Univ New York, BA, 67; welding workshop with Jean Woodham, 83. *Comn:* Steel sculptures & jewelry, pvt collectors, New York & Conn, 86-89. *Exhib:* In Celebration, A Room of One's Own, Somerstown Gallery, New York, 85-89; 39th & 43rd Art of the Northeast, Silvermine Guild, Conn, 88 & 92; Ridgefield Guild of Artists, Conn, 89-91; Faber-Birren Color Show, Stamford Mus & Nature Ctr, Conn, 90; Modern Times through the Concerned Eye, Katonah Mus Art, 92. *Awards:* Silvermine second prize, Amidar Award, Silvermine Guild Art, Conn, 88; Fred Kraus Mem Award, Stamford Art Asn, 90. *Mem:* Katonah Mus Artists Asn; Stamford Art Asn (bd dirs, 87-90); Ridgefield Guild Artists; Pound Ridge Art Guild. *Media:* Welded Steel. *Publ:* Auth, The Tailgate Cookbook, Funk & Wagnalls, 69. *Dealer:* Leander Pope-Somerstown Gallery Rte 100 Somers New York NY 10589. *Mailing Add:* RD2 Box 245 Pound Ridge NY 10576

HERBERT, JAMES ARTHUR
PAINTER, FILMMAKER
b Boston, Mass, Feb 13, 38. *Study:* Dartmouth Col, AB(art hist, magna cum laude); Univ Colo, MFA; also with Clyfford Still, Kenzo Okada & Stan Brakhage. *Work:* Whitney Mus Am Art, New York; Mus Mod Art, New York; Walker Art Ctr; Royal Film Arch Belgium; Centre Beaubourg, Paris, France. *Comn:* film, Libr Congress, 83; Kennedy Ctr, 84. *Exhib:* One-man shows, Walker Art Ctr, 73 & 82, Cineprobe: An evening with James Herbert, Mus Mod Art, 70-77, High Mus Art, 75, Kennedy Ctr, 81 & Mus Mod Art, 81 & 88; Whitney Mus Am Art, 74 75 & 83; Libr Congress, 83; Los Angeles County Mus, 88; Corcoran Biennial, Corcoran Mus, Washington, DC, 89; New Orleans Mus Fine Arts, 89; Telluride Film Festival, Colo, 89; Painting Beyond the Death of Painting, Kuznetsky Most Exhib Hall, Moscow, USSR, 89; Westdeutsche Kurzfilmtage, Oberhausen, Ger, 90 & 92; NY Film Festival, Lincoln Ctr, 92; Melbourne Int Film Festival, Australia, 92; Toronto Int Film Festival, 92; European Media Art Festival, Osnabrück, Ger, 92; Instituto de Estudios Norte Americanos, Barcelona, Spain, 92. *Teaching:* Resident artist, Yale Summer Sch Art & Music, Norfolk, Conn, 65; prof painting, Univ Ga, 62-, Res Prof, 92- *Awards:* Guggenheim Mem Found Fel, 71; Nat Endowment Arts Grant, 75, 78, 81 & 82; Louis Comfort Tiffany Found Award, 80; Awards in the Visual Arts 7, Rockefeller Found, 88; Guggenheim Mem Found Fel, 89; Adolph & Esther Gottlieb Found, 92. *Bibliog:* David Curtis (auth), The informal vision, in Experimental Cinema, Dell, 71; Roger Greenspun (auth), Quick-who are David Rimmer & James Herbert?, NY Times Sunday Ed, 10/8/72; Larry Kardish (auth), Of Light and Texture, Andrew Noren/James Herbert, Mus Mod Art, 81; Larry Kardish (auth), Afterimages, Ga Rev, spring 89. *Publ:* Stills, Photographs by James Herbert, Twelvetrees Press, Santa Fe, NMex, 92. *Mailing Add:* 243 Dearing St Athens GA 30605

HERBERT, PINKNEY
PAINTER, EDUCATOR
b Charlotte, NC, April 23, 54. *Study:* Rhodes Col Art, BA, 77; Univ Ga, Independant Study, 79; Memphis State Univ, MFA, 82. *Work:* NYNEX Corp, White Plains, NY; Prudential-Bach, New York; Arthur Anderson Assoc, Chicago, Ill; Ark Art Ctr Found, Little Rock. *Exhib:* Alternative Mus, New York, 87; solo exhib, Caro Lamagna Gallery, New York, 88, Univ Ark, Little Rock, 91, City Gallery Contemp Art, Raleigh, NC, 92; First Street Gallery, New York, 88; Unrealism, Fayerweather Gallery, Univ Va, Charlottesville, 88; Alice Bingham Gallery, Memphis, Tenn, 88; John Davis Gallery, New York, 88; Ledis/Flam Gallery, Brooklyn, NY, 89; MCCA, Memphis, Tenn, 90; In Touch with Art, Brooks Mus Art, Memphis, 91. *Teaching:* Instr art dept, Memphis State Univ, 89-91; vis artist, Univ Tenn, Knoxville, 92. *Awards:* Artist in Residence, NC Arts Coun, 82; Artist Grant, Artists Space, 85; Nat Endowment Arts Fel, 87; Va Ctr Creative Arts Fel,

Sweet Briar, 90 & 91; Art Fel, Tenn Arts Comn, 91. *Bibliog:* Rose CS Sliva (auth), From the Studio, East Hampton Star, 8/14/86; Megan Marlatt (auth), Pinkney Herbert at Carlo Lamagna Gallery, Number IV, spring 88; Fredric Koepell (auth), MCCA Sequel, Memphis Commercial Appeal, 7/27/90. *Mem:* Col Art Asn. *Media:* Oil, Drawing. *Mailing Add:* 639 Marshall Memphis TN 38103

HERBERT, ROBERT L
HISTORIAN, EDUCATOR
b Worcester, Mass, Apr 21, 29. *Study:* Wesleyan Univ, BA, 52; Inst Art & Archeol & Ecole du Louvre, Paris, Fulbright Scholar, 51-52; Yale Univ, MA, 54, PhD, 57; Am Coun Learned Soc Grant, 60; Morse fel, London, Eng, 60-61; sr fac fel, Paris, 68-69; Guggenheim fel, Paris & New Haven, Conn, 71-72. *Collections Arranged:* Barbizon Revisited (auth, catalog), Mus Fine Arts, Boston, Mass, Toledo Mus Art, Ohio,Cleveland Mus Art, Ohio, Calif Palace Legion Honor, 62-63; Neo-Impressionism (auth, catalog), Solomon R Guggenheim Mus, New York, 68; Retrospective, J F Millet (auth, catalog), Reunion des musees nationaux, Paris, Arts Coun, London, 75-76; Millet's Gleaners, Minneapolis Inst Arts, Minn, 78; Leger's Le Grand Dejeuner (auth, catalog), Minneapolis Inst Arts, Minn, Detroit Inst Arts, Mich, 80; Seurat, Reunion des musees nationaux, Paris, Metrop Mus, New York, 91 (in progress). *Pos:* Chmn, Sessions Mod Art, Col Art Asn, 65, 71, 81 & 85. *Teaching:* Asst instr hist of art, Yale Univ, 54-55, actg instr, 55-56, instr & mem comt hist, arts & lett, 56-60, from asst prof to prof hist art, 60-74, Robert Lehman prof hist of art, 74-, dir undergrad studies, 62-64, actg chmn, 65-66, chmn, 66-68; Slade prof, Oxford Univ, 78. *Awards:* Fel Am Acad Arts & Sciences, 78; Distinguished Teaching of Art History Award, Col Art Asn, 82; Rockerfeller Found Humanities Fel, 86. *Bibliog:* A note on four Millet drawings, Bulletin, Yale Univ Art Gallery, spring 87; Dorney's intaglio prints (catalog), Bertrand Dorny Gravures, Paris (La Hune) 87; Impressionism, originality, and laissez-faire, Radical Hist Rev 38, spring 87. *Res:* 19th and 20th century French art. *Publ:* Auth, Impressionism, Art, Leisure, and Parisian Society, Yale Univ Press, London, 88; co-ed, The Societe Anonyme and the Dreier Bequest at Yale University: A Catalogue Raisonne, Eleanor S Apter & Elise K Kenney, Yale Univ Press, New Haven, 84; auth, David, Voltaire, Brutus and the French Revolution, Penguin, London & Viking, New York, 72. *Mailing Add:* Dept of Art Mount Holyoke Col South Hadley MA 01075

HERFIELD, PHYLLIS
PAINTER
b Dec 6, 47. *Study:* Art Students League, 65; Tyler Sch Art, Rome, 67-68; Temple Univ, BFA, 69; Nat Acad Design, 79-80. *Work:* Malcolm Forbes Collection; Hunter Col; Brooklyn Acad Music. *Comn:* Prints, Orion Gallery; portraits, Salander O'Reilly Galleries & Portraits Inc. *Exhib:* Mus Mod Art, Paris, 75; Kathryn Markell Gallery, NY, 76; Inst Contemp Art, Philadelphia, 77; Spectrum Gallery, NY, 77 & 78; Nat Arts Club, 80; Nat Acad Design, 84; Butler Inst, Youngstown, Ohio, 85; Gallery Parr, NY, 85; Valentin Tatransky Gallery, NY, 86; Parkerson Gallery, Houston, Tex, 87; Hanson Gallery, Los Angeles, Calif, 88. *Awards:* Julius Hallgarten Prize, Nat Acad Design, 81. *Bibliog:* Reviews, Print Collectors Newslett, 5-6/77 & 5-6/78; Hilton Kramer (auth), rev, NY Times, 3/5/81; article, Christian Science Monitor, 3/81; Valentin Tatransky (auth), article, Arts Mag, 10/85; Diversions, 2/89 & Femme Mag, 1/89. *Media:* Oil. *Publ:* Illusr, NY Times, Esquire, Psychology Today; and many others. *Dealer:* Salander O'Reilly Gallery 22 E 80th St New York NY 10021; Portraits Inc 985 Park Ave New York NY 10028. *Mailing Add:* c/o Helander Gallery 415 W Broadway New York NY 10012

HERIC, JOHN F
SCULPTOR
b Reno, Nev, Feb 28, 42. *Study:* Ariz State Univ, with Ben Goo, BFA; Southern Ill Univ, Carbondale, with Milt Sullivan, MFA, 65. *Work:* City of Scottsdale, Ariz; Grossmont Col; Ariz State Univ; Mus Northern Ariz, Flagstaff; Mesa Community Col, Ariz. *Comn:* Steel sculpture, Ridgewood High Sch, 64; courtyard, Sopori Sch, Sahaurita Sch Dist, Ariz, 71. *Exhib:* St Paul Mus Art, Minn, 65; one-man shows, Univ Wis-Milwaukee, 66, Grossmont Col, 69 & Elaine Horwitch Gallery, Scottsdale, 74; Southwestern Invitational, Yuma, Ariz, 69-74. *Pos:* Vis artist, Grossmont Col, 74-75. *Teaching:* Instr sculpture, Wis State Univ-Platteville, 65-67; vis lectr sculpture, Ariz State Univ, 67-69; from lectr sculpture to assoc prof art, Univ Ariz, 69- *Awards:* Best of Show, Ariz Designer Craftsmen, 68; First Award Sculpture, Ariz Ann, 68; Purchase Award, Southwestern Invitational, 71, 72 & 74. *Media:* Stone, Plastics. *Dealer:* Elaine Horwitch Gallery 4200 N Marshall Way Scottsdale AZ 85251. *Mailing Add:* Dept Art Univ Ariz Tucson AZ 85721

HERMAN, ALAN DAVID
DESIGNER, GRAPHIC ARTIST
b Kew Gardens, NY, Mar 8, 47. *Study:* Pratt Inst Sch Art & Design, Ida D Haskell scholarship & BFA(cum laude), 69. *Comn:* Consumer advert promotion, Carrier Air Conditioning Co, Southern Calif, 73-; med insurance commun & marketing prog, Johnson & Higgins, Los Angeles, 76-; international design programs, Xerox Corp, 80- *Exhib:* 1972 Exhibit of Best Advertising & Editorial Art in the West, 72; IAM Graphics Exhib, New York, 74; Indust Graphics Int, San Jose, Calif, 77; AIGA Packaging Exhib, Chicago, 80; Creativity 80 Show, New York. *Pos:* Pres & creative dir, Alan Herman & Assoc, Inc, Los Angeles, 70- *Awards:* Top Package of the Yr, Print Mag, 76; IGI Distinctive Merit, 77; AIGA Graphic Design USA Award, 79. *Mem:* Art Dir Club Los Angeles; Los Angeles Co Mus Art. *Mailing Add:* c/o Alan Herman & Assoc 1313 Foothill Blvd La Canada CA 91011

HERMAN, KATHERINE BELLE
ART DEALER, COLLECTOR
b Houston, Tex, June 13, 63. *Study:* Univ Calif, San Diego, BA, 85, studied with Allen Kaprow, Eleanor Antin, J P Gorin, Fred Lonidier, Phil Steinmetz & Herb Schiller; New York Univ, MA, 92, studied with Andrew J Svedlow & RoseLee Goldberg. *Pos:* Mus educator, Mus City New York, 89-90; assoc, Corp Art Directions, New York, 90-91; assoc, Young Gallery, Los Gatos, Calif, 91- *Mailing Add:* Young Gallery 307 N Santa Cruz Ave Los Gatos CA 95030

HERMAN, LLOYD ELDRED
MUSEUM DIRECTOR
b Corvallis, Ore, Mar 19, 36. *Study:* Ore State Univ, 54-56; Univ Ore, 58-59; Am Univ, Washington, DC, BA lib arts, 59-60. *Pos:* Prog mgr, Off Dir-Gen Mus, Smithsonian Inst, 66-71; dir, Renwick Gallery, 71-86; cur, mus consult, auth, Am craft & design topics, 86-; consult dir, Cartwright Gallery, Vancouver, BC, Can, 88-90, curatorial consult, 90-92; acting cur, Can Craft Mus, Vancouver, BC, 92. *Awards:* Potomac Chap Am Soc Interior Designers Award, 79; Decoration, Order of Leopold II King of Belgians, 79; Decoration, Order of Danebrog, Chevalier, Queen of Denmark, 82. *Mem:* Hon fel, Am Craft Coun; Pittsburg Ctr for Arts. *Interests:* Twentieth century crafts and industrial design. *Publ:* Auth, introduction, The Woven and Graphic Art of Anni Albers, Smithsonian Inst Press, Washington, DC, 85; introduction, Material Evidence: New Color Techniques in Handmade Furniture, Smithsonian Inst Traveling Exhib Serv, Washington, DC, 85; The Art of the Turned Wood Bowl (essay), E P Dutton, NY, 85; foreward, Northwest Ceramics Today, Boise State Univ, Idaho, 87; foreword, Contemporary American Craft Art: A Collector's Guide, Peregrine Smith Bks, Salt Lake City, Utah, 87; Art that Works: The Decorative Arts of the Eighties, Crafted in America, Univ Wash Press, Seattle, 90; Brilliant Stories: American Narrative Jewelry, US Information Agency, 92. *Mailing Add:* 1537 Glen Cove Lane Bellingham WA 98226

HERMAN, ROGER
PAINTER, PRINTMAKER
b Saarbruchen, Saarland, Nov 21, 47, Ger citizen. *Study:* Kunstakademie Karlsruhe, MFA, 79. *Work:* Walker Art Ctr, Minneapolis; Los Angeles Co Mus, Calif; San Francisco Mus Art; Denver Art Mus; Newport Harbor Art Mus. *Exhib:* One-man show, La Jolla Mus, 83; III Bienale, San Francisco Mus, 84; Painters Who Print, Walker Art Ctr, Minneapolis, 84; Inst for Contemp Art, Philadelphia, 84; Larry Gagosian Gallery, Los Angeles, 85, 86. *Awards:* New Talent Award, Los Angeles Co Mus, 83; Nat Endowment Art, 83 & 89. *Media:* All; Woodcuts. *Dealer:* Ace Gallery 5514 Wilshire Blvd Los Angeles CA. *Mailing Add:* 729 Academy Rd Los Angeles CA 90012

HERMAN, VIC
PAINTER, WRITER
b Fall River, Mass. *Study:* Yale Puppeteers, Los Angeles, Calif, with Harry Burnett; Art Students League, with George Bridgeman; New York Com Illus Sch, with Lu Kimmel; Columbia Univ, with Ed Johnson; Mount Sinai Hospital New York, with Dr Samuel Penchansky. *Work:* Four US White House Presidential Collections; Syracuse Univ, NY; Columbia Univ, New York; Rutgers Univ, New Brunswick, NJ; Mus Cartoon Art, Port Chester, NY; and others. *Exhib:* Many Faces of Mexico Int Traveling Exhib, co-sponsored by US Info Serv & Govt Mex, 60-; San Diego Combo Exhibs, 80-86; Ohio State Univ Festival Cartoon Art, 83, 86 & 88; one-man shows, San Francisco Int Art Expo, 81, San Diego City Hall, 84 & 88, US Int Univ, San Diego, 85 & Southern Calif Expo, Del Mar Fair, 86, 90, 91 & 92; Del Mar Fair, 90, 91 & 92. *Pos:* Asst art dir, Warner Bros Studios, New York, 40-43; artist-field corresp, Yank Mag & Stars and Stripes, 43-46; pres & prod chief, Vic Herman Prod, 47-72; staff illusr & corresp, Hearst Features, New York Times, Readers Digest, Holt, Rinehart & Winston & Golden Books, New York & Mex, 50- *Teaching:* Bd Educ Los Angeles & San Diego, 65- *Awards:* Children's Book Coun Showcase Award, 76; Best Children's Book of the Year Award, Printing Industries Am, 78 & Independence Star, Mo, 80; Pres Lett Commendations, 82, 86 & 90; and others. *Bibliog:* Speaking of Pictures-Vic Herman and Winnie The Wac, Life Mag, 3/45; Sally Cass (auth), US artist portrays the Mexican feeling, Mexico City News, 68; Frederic Whitaker (auth), Vic Herman, ambassador with a brush, Am Artist Mag, 74; Herbert Johnson (auth), Vic Herman goes where the action is, Los Angeles Examiner, 79. *Mem:* Soc Illusr New York; Am Soc Training Dirs; Soc Children's Book Writers Calif; Nat Cartoonists Soc; Southern Calif Cartoonists Soc; San Diego Press Club; and others. *Media:* Mixed Media. *Publ:* Auth & illusr, Winnie the Wac, McKay, 45; auth & illusr, My Days Are Made of Butterflies, 70, Sunday in Zamora Park, Holt, Rinehart & Winston, 72; illusr, God and Mr Gomez, Readers Digest Condensed Books, 75; auth & illusr, Juanito's Railroad in the Sky, Golden Books, 76; auth of over 52 books; cartoons & paintings in numerous national magazines. *Mailing Add:* 25 South Lane Del Mar CA 92014

HERMANN, M(ILDRED) L
PAINTER
b Brooklyn, NY. *Study:* Artists in Am Sch Painting, with Leo Manso & Jerry Okimoto, 68-74. *Work:* Norton Gallery & Mus, West Palm Beach, Fla; Fine Arts Mus Long Island, Hempstead, NY; The Bond Buyer, NY; YMCA, NY. *Exhib:* Childe Hassam Purchase Fund Exhib, Am Acad & Inst Arts & Lett, New York, 78; Collage and Assemblage, Miss Mus Art, Jackson, 81 & Tampa Mus, Fla, 82; 36th Art Northeast USA, Silvermine Guild Artists, New Canaan, Conn, 85; Butler Inst Am Art, Youngstown, Ohio, 86; Sixth Juried Show, Fine Arts Mus Long Island, 85; Tex Fine Arts Asn, Austin, Tex; Gloria Lagona Mus. *Pos:* Juror, Works on Canvas, Nat Asn women Artists, NY,

84-86. *Awards:* Childe Hassam Purchase Award, 78; Four Winners Exhib, Fine Arts Mus, Long Island, Hempstead, NY 88; Juror's Choice Award, Tex Fine Arts Asn, Austin, 89. *Bibliog:* Addison Parks (auth), Free style--Viridian, Arts Mag, 5/80; Helen A Harrison (auth), Beyond the conventional, NY Times, 8/14; Margaret Moorman (auth), Themes in mixed media, Newsday, 3/25/88. *Mem:* Nat Asn Women Artists; Audubon Artists; Artists Involvement Art; Artists Guild, Norton Gallery & Sch Art. *Media:* Collage, Mixed Media, & Acrylic. *Publ:* Collage & Assemblage, Miss Mus Art, catalogue no 41, 81; New York, Texas, California: New Art (catalog), Tex Fine Arts Asn, 89, 10. *Dealer:* Viridian Gallery 24 W 57th St New York NY 10019. *Mailing Add:* 55 Salem Rd Roslyn Heights NY 11577

HERNANDEZ, ANTHONY LOUIS
PHOTOGRAPHER
b Los Angeles, Calif, July 7, 47. *Study:* E Los Angeles Col, 66-70; Ctr Eye, Aspen, Colo, 69, with Lee Friedlander. *Work:* Univ Calif, Davis; Mus Mod Art, New York; Bibliot Nat, Paris, France; Int Mus Photog, George Eastman House, Rochester, NY. *Comn:* Photographs, Corcoran Gallery Art, Washington, DC, 76. *Exhib:* Calif Photogr, Pasadena Art Mus & Oakland Mus Art, Calif, 70; The Crowded Vacancy, Pasadena Art Mus & San Francisco Mus Art, Calif, 71; The Nation's Capital in Photographs, Corcoran Gallery of Art, 76; Unposed Portrait, Whitney Mus Am Art, New York, 77; Contemp Am Photog Works, Mus Fine Arts, Houston, Tex, 77. *Awards:* Ferguston Grant, Friends Photog, Carmel, Calif, 72; Nat Endowment Arts Photog Fel, 75 & 78. *Bibliog:* Douglas Davis (auth), Sweeping up American, Newsweek, 7/12/76. *Mailing Add:* 255 1/2 S Carondelet Los Angeles CA 90057

HERNANDEZ, JO FARB
MUSEUM DIRECTOR, CURATOR
b Chicago, Ill, Nov 20, 52. *Study:* Univ Wis-Madison, BA, 74; Univ Calif, Los Angeles, MA, 75; Univ Calif, Berkeley; Mus Mgt Inst, 81. *Collections Arranged:* Made in Japan: Noritake Art Deco Porcelains, 82; Mexican Indian Dance Masks (auth, catalog), 82; Art of the Cuna, 82; Jewish Marriage Contracts, 83; Harriete Estel Berman: A Family of Appliances You Can Believe In (auth, catalog), 83; New Work/New Looks, 83; Day of the Dead: Tradition and Change in Contemporary Mexico (coauth, catalog); Crime and Punishment: Reflections of Violence in Contemporary Art (auth, catalog); Henrietta Shore: Retrospective (ed, catalog), 85; The Monterey Photog tradition: The Weston Years (ed, catalog), 85; Adat: Tribal Imagery/ Ancestral Law, 86; The Artist and Myth (auth, brochure), 87; The Art of Eating, 88; Colors & Impressions: The Early Work of E Charlton Fortune (ed, catalog), 89; Lorser Feitelson: Exploration of the Figure, 1919-1929 (auth, brochure), 90; Chipping Award at the Layers: The Puzzle of Tramp Art, 91; The Quiet Eye: Pottery of Shoji Hanada & Bernard Leach (ed, catalog), 91; Painted Tintypes, 92. *Pos:* Curatorial asst, Mus Cult Hist, Los Angeles, 74-75; cur/educ asst, Dallas Mus Fine Arts, 76-77; dir, Triton Mus Art, Santa Clara, Calif, 77-85 & Monterey Peninsula Mus Art, 85- *Teaching:* Adj prof, ETex State Univ, 77, John F Kennedy Univ, 79 & San Jose State Univ, 79-80. *Awards:* Trewartha Award, Univ Wis, 74; Ralph C Altman Award, Mus Cult Hist, 75; Rockefeller Fel, 76-77. *Mem:* Non-Profit Gallery Asn, 179-83 (vpres, 79-80); Calif Asn Mus (bd dirs, 85- , vpres, 87-91, pres, 91-92); Western Mus Conf (bd dirs, 89-91 , exec comt, 89-91, prog chmn, 90); Calif Folklore Soc. *Publ:* Ed, The Expressive Sculpture of Alvin Light, 90; auth, Lorser Feitelson: Exploration of the Figure 1919-1929 (brochure), 90; Two Sides of the Same Reality, The World and I, 90; The Language of Stone: Alan Shepp, 91; Anders Aldrin (brochure), 92. *Mailing Add:* c/o Monterey Peninsula Mus Art 559 Pacific Monterey CA 93940

HERNANDEZ, JOHN
PAINTER
b San Antonio, Tex, 52. *Study:* Our Lady Lake Univ, San Antonio, Tex, BA, 75; N Tex State Univ, Denton, MFA, 80. *Work:* Dallas Mus Art, Tex; Tyler Mus Art, Tex; Groninger Mus, Holland; Barrett Collection, Dallas, Tex; Frito-Lay Collection, Plano, Tex. *Exhib:* Solo shows, Plus-Kern Gallery, Brussels, Belg, 89, Edith Baker Gallery, Dallas, Tex, 90, Pilot Point, San Antonio, Tex, 90, Encounters 1 Gallery, Dallas Mus Art, Tex, 92 & Moody Gallery, Houston, Tex, 92; Galveston Arts Ctr, Tex, 91; Gray Matters Gallery, Dallas, Tex, 91; Washington Proj Arts, Washington, DC, 92; and others. *Teaching:* Lectr, Plus Kern Gallery, Brussels, Belg, 88, DW Gallery, Dallas, Tex, 88, San Antonio Art Inst, Tex, 90, Lindsborg Col, Kans, 90 & Emporia State Univ, Kans, 90. *Awards:* Mid-Am Arts Alliance Grant, 88; Nat Endowment Arts Artists Grant, 89. *Bibliog:* Susan Chadwick (auth), Ideas don't separate Northwest, Southwest artists, Houston Post, D-1, 11/21/90; Janet Kutner (auth), Rooms with a view, Dallas Morning News, C1, 9, 2/29/92; Janet Tyson (auth), Close encounters of the artistically disparate kind, Ft Worth Star Telegram, 3/19/92; and others. *Mailing Add:* c/o Moody Gallery 2815 Colquitt Houston TX 77098

HERNANDEZ, SAM (SAMUEL RUDOLPH)
SCULPTOR, EDUCATOR
b Hayward, Calif, Jan 23, 48. *Study:* Calif State Univ, Hayward, BA, 70; Ariz State Univ; Univ Wis-Madison, MFA, 74; Univ Sonora, Hermosillo, Mex, Hon Degree, 72. *Work:* New Orleans Mus Art, La; Oakland Mus, Calif; Contemp Mus, Honolulu; Mexican Mus, San Francisco; Mus Contemp Art, Skopje, Yugoslavia. *Exhib:* Phelan Award Exhib, San Francisco Mus Art, 79; Animal Image, Renwick Gallery, Smithsonian Inst, Washington, DC, 81; Three Sculptors, Arco Ctr Visual Art, Los Angeles, 84; Contemp Wood Sculpture, Crocker Art Mus, Sacramento, 84; solo exhibs, San Jose Mus Art, 84 & Rena Bransten Gallery, 88; Works in Wood, Monterey Peninsula Mus Art, Calif, 85; Poetry of the Physical, Am Craft Mus, New York, 86; Contemporary Screens, Contemp Art Ctr, Cincinnati, 86; Eloquent Object, Philbrook Mus Art, Tulsa, 87; and others. *Collections Arranged:* The Day of the Dead: Tradition and Change in Contemporary Mexico (coauth, catalog), Triton Mus Art, 79. *Pos:* Mem adv bd, Triton Mus Art, 81-85. *Teaching:* Instr sculpture, E Tex State Univ, Commerce, 74-77; asst prof, Univ Santa Clara, Calif, 77-83, chmn art dept, 80-88, assoc prof sculpture, 83-; vis prof sculpture, Univ Wis-Madison, summer 80. *Awards:* Phelan Award Sculpture, San Francisco Found, 78; Nat Endowment Arts Fel, 84; Sr Fulbright Scholar, 86. *Bibliog:* Mark Levy (auth), The spirit of primitivism, Artweek, 4/28/84; Mark Van Proyen (auth), A synthesis of exuberant forms, Artweek, 5/28/85; Judith Dunham (auth), A faculty for art, Santa Clara Univ, 88. *Mem:* Col Art Asn; Int Sculpture Asn; Nat Coun Educ Ceramic Arts; Calif Folklore Soc. *Media:* Wood. *Publ:* Auth, Day of the Dead: Tradition and Change in Contemporary Mexico, Triton Mus Art, 79; coauth, Mexican Indian Saisset Mus, Univ Santa Clara, Calif, 82. *Mailing Add:* Art Dept Santa Clara Univ Santa Clara CA 95053

HERNANDEZ-CRUZ, LUIS
PAINTER, SCULPTOR
b San Juan, PR. *Study:* Univ PR, BA; Am Univ, MA. *Work:* Chase Manhattan Bank, New York; Ponce Mus Art, PR; Mus Mod Art Latin Am, Washington, DC; Univ PR Mus; Mus Contemp Art, Seoul, Korea; and others. *Comn:* Murals, PR Med Ctr, 64 & 65; glass walls, Fine Arts Ctr, Santurce, PR, 80-81; and others. *Exhib:* Arte Actual de America y Espana, Madrid, Spain, 63; Esso Salon of Young Artists, Washington, DC, 64; 2nd Biennial, Coltejer-Medellin, Colombia, 70; Sao Paulo Biennial Brazil, 75; III Int Triennial Graphic Art, Jyvaskyla, Finland, 81; Virginia Miller Gallery, Miami, 83; Eco-Art, Rio de Janeiro, 92. *Teaching:* Prof painting, Univ PR, Rio Piedras, 68, dir dept fine arts, 75-78. *Awards:* First Prize in Painting, Inst PR Cult, 63; First Prize, Esso Art Contest, 64; Nat Prize, 2nd Biennial Latin Am Prints, 72; Gold Medal, Acad Soc, Arts, Sci & Letters Paris, France, 91. *Bibliog:* Pintores Puertorriquenos de Luis Hernandez-Cruz, Ed Artisticas de PR, 67; Marta Traba (auth), El abstracto que se salva, Artes Visuales, 71; Olympiad of Art, Seoul, Korea, Ante Glibota, 88. *Media:* Acrylic, Silkscreen; Wood. *Mailing Add:* Patricia St No 6 Susan Ct Guaynabo PR 00966

HERO, PETER DECOURCY
ADMINISTRATOR, HISTORIAN
b Washington, DC, Sept 10, 42. *Study:* Williams Col, Williamstown, Mass, with George Heard Hamilton & Whitney Stoddard, BA, 64, MA(art hist), 75; Stanford Univ, Calif, MBA, 66. *Collections Arranged:* The Elegant Academics (contribr, catalog), Clark Art Inst, Williamstown, Mass & Wadsworth Atheneum, Hartford, Conn, 75; Folk Art of the Oregon Country, Univ Ore Art Mus, Ore Hist Soc, Renwick Gallery, 80; On-Site New England, Public Art in Perspective (curator), traveling exhib, open at Bank of Boston, 89. *Pos:* Exec dir, Ore Arts Comn, 75-85; pres, Portland Sch of Art, Maine, 85-89; pres, Santa Clara Found, San Jose, Calif, 89- *Teaching:* Arts adminr, Lewis & Clark Col, Portland State Univ Grad MPA Program, 82-86. *Awards:* Kress Found Fel, 6/75. *Mem:* Western States Arts Found (bd chmn, 83-85); Art Mus Asn (bd dir, 79-81); Nat Assembly State Arts Agencies (bd dirs, 77-81, chmn bd, 79-81); Nat Endowment Arts; Maine Independent Col Asn (bd dirs, 86-); Art Col Exchange (chmn bd, 88-89); Non profit Develop Ctr, (bd dirs, 89-); Arts Coun Santa Clara Co (bd dirs, 89-). *Res:* Influence of Japanese prints upon evolution of perspective and space in Edgar Degas' work; cultural economics and public policy in the arts; non-profit organization management; public and private partnerships to promote cultural development. *Publ:* Contribr, New legislation can integrate art and architecture, Western States Arts Found, 76; Marketing the arts, Study Ctr Cult Policy & Arts, Univ Calif, Los Angeles Grad Sch Mgt, 78; Cultural Development with Non-appropriated Funds, Assoc for Cult Econ, Akron, Ohio, 86; Des Modes de Financement Culturel public, French Ministry of Culture, Paris, 88; Community Foundation and Cultural Pluralism, J of Cult Econ, Akron, Ohio, 90. *Mailing Add:* Santa Clara Found 960 W Hedding St San Jose CA 95126

HERRERA, CARMEN
PAINTER
b Havana, Cuba, May 31, 15; US citizen. *Study:* Studio Federico Edelman, Havana; Marymount Col; Paris, France; Sch Archit, Havana; Art Students League. *Work:* Havana Mus; Cintas Collection. *Exhib:* Art Cubain Contemporain, Mus Mod Art, Paris, 51; Ctr Interam Rels, 68 & 75; Inst Int Educ, 80-81; Buecker & Harpsichords, 81; solo exhibs, Rastovski Gallery, New York, 87 & 88; Outside Cuba, Jane Vorheeszimerli Art Mus, Rutgers, State Univ NJ, 87; The Latin American Spirit: Art & Artists in the United States, 1920-1970, Bronx Mus Arts, New York; Duo Geo; Two Geometric Artists, Carmen Herrera & Ernesto Briel, Jadite Galleries, New York, 92. *Awards:* Cintas Found Fel, 66 & 68; Creative Artists Pub Serv, 77-78. *Bibliog:* William Zimmer (auth), NY Times, NJ ed, 4/19/87; Stephen Westfall (auth), Art in Am, 3/89; Don Bacigalupi (auth), Contemporanea, 6/89. *Mem:* Women in Arts. *Mailing Add:* 37 E 19th St New York NY 10003

HERRING, JAN (JANET MANTEL)
PAINTER, WRITER
b Havre, Mont, May 17, 23. *Study:* Northern State Teachers Col; also painting with Frederic Taubes. *Work:* Grumbacher Collection, New York; Lubbock Art Ctr, Tex; Univ Idaho, Pocatello; Roswell Mus, NMex. *Exhib:* One-woman shows, El Paso Mus Art, Santa Fe Mus Art, Tulsa Art Ctr, Roswell Mus & Brigham Young Univ. *Teaching:* Pvt instr. *Bibliog:* F Taubes (auth), article, Am Artist Mag, 55; articles, La Rev Mod, 61 & House Beautiful, 64. *Publ:* Auth, The Painters Composition Handbook, 71 & The Painter's Complete Portrait and Figure Handbook, 77, Poor-Henry Publ Co. *Mailing Add:* Box 156 Clint TX 79836

HERRING, WILLIAM ARTHUR
PAINTER
b El Paso, Tex, Feb 18, 48. *Study:* Tex A&M Univ, BA, 71; spec studies with Jan Herring, 72-82 & Charles Reid, 80-83. *Work:* San Angelo Mus Fine Art, Tex; El Paso Mus Fine Art, Tex; Tex A&M Univ, College Station; Eastern NMex Univ, Portales; US Air Defense Mus, Fort Bliss, Tex. *Comn:* Watercolor, horse racing, Ruidoso Racetrack Jockey Club, NMex, 87; watercolor, dancer, viva El Paso Production Co, 90; rodeo drawing, Coors World Finals Rodeo, El Paso, Tex, 90; watercolor, prints of three cultures, El Paso Legislative Days, 90; pastel landscape, El Paso Symphony Orchestra, 91. *Exhib:* Solo exhib, Centenial Mus, El Paso, Tex, 86; 75th Allied Artists of Am, Nat Arts Club, New York, 88; Borderlands Exhib, Americana Mus, El Paso, Tex, 89; 1992 Knickerbocker Artists, Salmagundi Club, New York, 92; Sierra Med Ctr 25th Exhib, El Paso Mus Art, 92; and others. *Teaching:* Guest instr landscape, Parsons Sch Design, New York, 91. *Awards:* William Hollingsworth Award, Miss Watercolor Soc Exhib, 87; Gold Medal for Watercolor, El Paso Mus Art, Melvin Simon & Assocs, 88; Bd Dirs Award, Pastel Soc Am, New York, 90. *Bibliog:* William Herring, artist, Santa Fean Mag, 5/87; Museum shows off top paintings, Accent Mag, El Paso Herald Post, 6/87; Cover artist, Southwest Guide Mag, 4/88. *Mem:* Knickerbocker Artists, New York (pres, currently); Pastel Soc Am, New York; Am Artists Prof League, New York; Acad Artists Am, Mass; Niagara Frontier Watercolor Soc, New York. *Media:* Pastel, Watercolor. *Dealer:* Joan Cawley Gallery 133 W San Francisco Santa Fe NMex 87501. *Mailing Add:* 276 Herring Rd Box 223 Clint TX 79836

HERRITT, LINDA S
SCULPTOR
b Columbus, Ohio, June 20, 50. *Study:* Ohio State Univ, BFA, 78; Univ Mont, MFA, 80. *Exhib:* Decor/Decorum, Art Inst, San Francisco, Calif, 90; Wash Proj Art, Washington, Dc, 91; Altering the Familiar, Spaces, Cleveland, Ohio, 92. *Teaching:* Assoc prof painting, Univ Colo, 82- *Awards:* Sculpture Fel, Nat Endowment Arts, 90 & 91. *Mem:* Col Art Asn; Women's Caucus Art. *Mailing Add:* 3980 19 St Boulder CO 80304

HERRMANN, JOHN J, JR
CURATOR
b Chicago, Ill, Mar 16, 37. *Study:* Yale Col, BA, 59; Inst Fine Arts, NY Univ, MA, 64, PhD, 73. *Collections Arranged:* Pompeii AD 79 (coauth, catalog), 78, Roman and Classical and Hellenistic Greek Galleries, 79, The Excavations of Assos Revisited, 79, The Search for Alexander (coauth, catalog), 81, The Gods Delight (auth, catalog), 88 & Human Figure in Early Greek Art, 88, Mus Fine Arts, Boston; In the Shadow of the Acropolis: Popular and Private Art from 4th Century Athens (auth, catalog), Brockton Art Mus, 84. *Pos:* Fel, Comt Rescue of Italian Art, 69-70; asst cur, Mus Fine Arts, Boston, 76-85, assoc cur, 85- *Mem:* Archeol Inst Am; Col Art Asn. *Publ:* Auth, Ravenna, Corinth & Constantinople: The Case of an Impost Block at Fenway Court, Isabella Stewart Gardner Mus, Boston, 89; Thasos & the Ancient Marble Trade, Marble, J Paul Getty Mus, 90; Rearranged Hair, J Mus Fine Arts, Boston, 91; Exportation of Dolomitic Marble from Thasos, Univ Leuven, 92; Carrieres et Sculpture en Marbre a L'epogue Romaine et Tardive, Dossiers d'archeologie, 92; and others. *Mailing Add:* c/o Mus Fine Arts 465 Huntington Ave Boston MA 02115

HERSCHLER, DAVID ELIJAH
SCULPTOR, PAINTER
b Brooklyn, NY, Mar 1, 40. *Study:* Acad Belli Arte, Perugia, Italy, 60; Univ Rome, 60; Cornell Univ, BArch, 62; Claremont Grad Sch, MFA, 67. *Work:* Joseph H Hirshhorn Found, Washington, DC; La Jolla Mus Art, Calif; Storm King Art Ctr, Mountainville, NY; Palm Springs Mus, Calif; Israel Mus, Jerusalem; Hartford Life Insurance; Daimle-Benz Corp; General Motors. *Comn:* Sculptures, comn by Mr & Mrs N S Walbridge, La Jolla, 70, Sigmund Edelstone, Chicago, 71, Mr & Mrs J W Constance, Santa Barbara, 72, Mr & Mrs Marvin Smalley, Beverly Hills, 72 & Storm King Art Ctr, 72. *Exhib:* One-man shows, La Jolla Mus, 72, Santa Barbara Mus, 74, Palm Springs Mus, 77, Aspen Inst, 85, NASA-Kennedy Space Ctr, 86 & Westment Col, 90. *Awards:* United States Info Serv Golden Eagle Award; Specialty Steel Committee of United States Award; Nat Space Club Award. *Media:* Stainless Steel, Gold. *Mailing Add:* PO Box 5859 Santa Barbara CA 93108

HERSEY, GEORGE LEONARD
HISTORIAN, EDUCATOR
b Cambridge, Mass, Aug 30, 27. *Study:* Harvard Univ, BA, 51; Yale Univ, MFA, 54, MA, 61, PhD, 64; Fulbright scholar & Am Philos Soc fel, Italy, 62. *Pos:* Co-ed, Architectura, 71-; ed, Yale Publ in Hist of Art, 74-; mem, Conn State Comn Capitol Restoration, 77-79; contribr, Pre-Raphaelite Review, 81- *Teaching:* Instr art, Bucknell Univ, Lewisburg, Pa, 54-55, asst prof, 54-59, actg chmn dept, 58-59; instr hist art, Yale Univ, New Haven, Conn, 63-65, asst prof 65-68, assoc prof, 68-74, prof, 74- *Awards:* Morse Fel, 66; Schepp Fel & Vogelstein Fel, Florence, Italy, 72 & 80. *Mem:* Soc Archit Historians (dir, 71-73); Renaissance Soc Am; Col Art Asn; Victorian Soc US & Gt Brit. *Publ:* Auth, Pythagorean Palaces: Magic and Architecture in the Italian Renaissance, 75; Architecture, Poetry and Number in The Royal Palace at Caserta, 83; contribr, Storia dell'Arte Italiana, 83; auth, The Lost Meaning of Classical Architecture, 87; Possible Palladian Villas (with Richard Freedman), 92; High Renaissance Art in St Peter's & the Vatican, 93. *Mailing Add:* Dept Hist Art Yale Univ 180 York St New Haven CT 06520

HERSHEY, NONA
PRINTMAKER, PAINTING
b New York, NY, Oct 31, 46. *Study:* Tyler Sch Art, BFA, 67; Tyler Sch Art in Rome, MFA, 69; Instituto Statale d'Arte di Urbino, dipl, 79. *Work:* Libr Congress, DC; Metrop Mus Art, New York; Minn Mus Art, St Paul; Pa Acad Fine Arts, Philadelphia; Calcografia Nazionale, Rome, Italy. *Exhib:* New Talent in Printmaking, Asn Am Artists, New York, 75; 14th Int Biennial Graphic Art, Ljubljana, Yugoslavia; Prints USA 82, Pratt Graphics Ctr, New York, 82; one-man shows, Galleria Il Ponte, Rome, 82 & 85 & Mary Ryan Gallery, New York, 83 & 87; Great American Prints, Dolan-Maxwell Gallery, Philadelphia, 85; 24th Nat Exhib, Brooklyn Mus, NY, 86; 12th Int Print Biennial, Krakow, Yugoslavia, 88; and many others including over 60 group exhibitions and 13 solo shows. *Teaching:* Asst prof printmaking, Daemen Col, Buffalo, NY, 72-73 & Temple Abroad, Rome, Italy, 79- *Awards:* Special Purchase Award, Davidson Nat Print Competition, Davidson Col, NC, 73 & 75; J R Marsh Mem, 17th Nat Print Exhib, Hunterdon Art Ctr, 73; Special Purchase Award, 13th Lario Int Exhib, Cadorago, Italy; Purchase Award, 8th Ann Eastern US Print & Drawing Exhib, Charlotte, NC, 85; and others. *Bibliog:* Enzo Billardello (auth), Art a Roma, Nona Hershey, Corriere della Sera, 85; Marisa Volpi Orlandini (auth), Nona Hershey, Artisti Contemporanei, Interviste, 85; Ruth Bass (auth), New editions, Artnews, 86. *Mem:* Printmaking Coun NJ. *Media:* All Media. *Dealer:* Assoc Am Artists 20 W 57th St New York NY 10019; Mary Ryan Gallery 452 Columbus Ave New York NY 10024. *Mailing Add:* c/o Mary Ryan Gallery 24 W 57th St New York NY 10019

HERSHMAN, LYNN LESTER
PHOTOGRAPHER, VIDEO ARTIST
b June 17, 41. *Study:* Case Western Reserve Univ, BS, 63; Calif State Univ, San Francisco, MA, 72; Calif Col Arts & Crafts, Univ Calif, Los Angeles; Ohio Univ; Otis Art Inst; Cleveland Inst Art. *Work:* Nat Collection Fine Arts, Smithsonian Inst; Cleveland Inst Art; City of San Francisco Collection Art; Calif State Cols Collection Art; Richmond Art Ctr; plus other pub & pvt collections. *Comn:* Art poster, San Francisco Mus, 69; cover for Robopaths, Penguin Books, 72. *Exhib:* Butler Inst Am Art, Youngstown, Ohio; Ball State Univ Painting Exhib; Nat Sculpture Exhib, San Diego Mus Art, 72; Nat Gallery, Adelaide, Australia, 77; Contemp Art Mus, Houston, 78; Musee National d'Art Moderne, Centre National d'Art et de Culture George Pompidou, Paris, 79; San Francisco Mus Mod Art, 80; Inst Contemp Art, London, Eng, 89 & 90, Fresno Mus Art & Long Beach Mus Art, Calif, 90; Whitney Mus Am Art, New York, 86 & 89; Robert Koch Gallery, San Francisco, 88; Berlin Film Festival, Ger, 88; San Francisco Mus Mod Art, Calif, 89; Intl Ctr Photography, New York, 90; solo retrospective, Inst Contemp Art, London, 91; Festival Internacional De Video, Vigo, Spain, 91; Inst Contemp Art, Boston, 91; and many others. *Pos:* Corresp ed, Artweek, 71-73; coordr, Insights, San Francisco Mus Art, 72-74; gallery curator, Walnut Creek Civic Art Ctr, Calif, 74-76; assoc coordr, Christo's Running Fence Project, 74-76; invited artist, Int Inst Experimental Printmaking, Santa Cruz, Calif, 75. *Teaching:* Instr, Cleveland Mus Art, 62-63; vis asst prof drawing, Calif Col Arts & Crafts, 72-73, assoc prof, 74; instr, Melville Col, Scotland, 73; dir, Inter-Arts Ctr, San Francisco State Univ, 85- *Awards:* First Prize, Marin Video Festival, 86, 87 & 88; Award, San Francisco Int Film/Video Festival, 87; Jonas Mekas Award for Documentary, Humboldt State, 91. *Bibliog:* Christine Tamblyn (auth), article, Arts J, 9/90; Tori Dent (auth), cover feature, Arts Mag, 11/90; Penelope Rollins (auth), article, Vogue, 1/91; plus many others. *Publ:* Auth, Harold Paris, the Berkeley Years, Artweek, Vol 3, No 21; auth, Edinburgh as Oz, Vol 186, No 959 & Interview with Dennis Oppenheim, 11/73, Studio Int; coauth, Toward light and space, City Mag, Vol 1, No 7; auth, Forming a Sculptured/Drama in Manhattan, Marginal Arts & Stefanotty Gallery, 75; How I became a Video Artist (ed, Arthur Asa Berger), Longman Press, London, Eng, 88; and others. *Dealer:* Robert Koch Gallery 210 Post St San Francisco CA 94108. *Mailing Add:* 1935 Filbert St San Francisco CA 94123

HERTZ, RICHARD A
EDUCATOR, CRITIC
b La Crosse, Wis, Aug 19, 40. *Study:* Univ Calif, Los Angeles, BA, 62; Univ Calif, Santa Barbara, MA, 64; Univ Pittsburgh, PhD, 67. *Teaching:* Asst prof philos, Calif Inst Technol, 68-74; instr art theory, Calif Inst Arts, 74-79; chmn acad studies & grad prog, Art Ctr Col Design, 79- *Mem:* Col Art Asn, Mus Contemp Art, Los Angeles. *Res:* Twentieth century art theory and criticism. *Publ:* Auth, Philosophical foundations of modern art, Brit J Aesthet, summer 78; ed, J Los Angeles Inst Contemp Art, summer 82; auth, A critique of authoritarian rhetoric, Real Life Mag, summer 82; ed, Theories of Contemporary Art, Prentice-Hall, 85, 2nd ed, 93-; ed, with Norman Klein, Twentieth Century Art Theory: Urbanism, Politics and Mass Culture, Prentice-Hall, 90. *Mailing Add:* 1700 Lida St PO Box 7197 Pasadena CA 91109

HERTZBERG, ROSE
PAINTER, COLLAGE ARTIST
b Passaic, NJ, Dec 17, 12. *Study:* With Ben Benn; Hans Hofmann Art Sch; Art Students League, with Vaclav Vytlacil & Will Barnet; New York Graphics Workshop; Rockland Community Col; Fairleigh Dickinson Univ Art Seminars. *Work:* Edward Williams Col, Hackensack, NJ; Rockland Community Col, Suffern, NY; Bloomfield Col; Broadway Bank & Trust Co, Paterson, NJ; Hackensack Pub Libr & Ramsey Pub Libr, NJ; plus numerous pvt collections. *Comn:* Numerous pvt commissions. *Exhib:* Am Watercolor Soc, 66-68; Painters & Sculptors Soc NJ, Jersey City, 69-83; Nat Asn Women Artists, 71-89; one-woman shows, Bergen Community Mus, NJ, 75 & 77, Spring St Gallery, New York, Centro des Artes, Mijas, Spain, Sisti Gallery,

Buffalo, NY, Fullerton Gallery, Monclair, NJ & Rockland Ctr Arts, Hertzl Inst, NY; and others. *Teaching:* Instr, Fairlawn, NJ, 60-63 & Mahwah, 63; lectr, Hertzl Inst, NY. *Awards:* Invitational Winner, Cannes, France, 69; Painters & Sculptors Soc, 71 & 76; Putnam Mem Awards, 71 & 77; Medal of Honor, Watercolor, 79; Bertha P Greenblatt Mem Award, 83; and others. *Bibliog:* Alfred Wermer (auth), catalog, Hertzl Inst, NY, 68. *Mem:* Life mem Art Students League; Nat Asn Women Artists; Mod Artists Guild; Artist Affil NJ; Altrusa Int. *Media:* Oil, Watercolor; Paper. *Mailing Add:* 27 Buckingham Dr Ramsey NJ 07446

HERTZMAN, GAY MAHAFFY
ADMINISTRATOR, HISTORIAN
b West Liberty, Iowa, Jan 22, 31. *Study:* Univ Iowa, Iowa City, BA, 60; Univ NC, Chapel Hill, MS(libr sci), 65, MA(art hist), 69. *Pos:* Registr-librn, NC Mus Art, Raleigh, 61-64; actg cur, Wm Hayes Ackland Art Ctr, Univ NC, Chapel Hill, 67-69; asst cur & cur European painting, NC Mus Art, 71-75, head collections res & publ, 75-79, chief cur, 80-81, asst dir, 81- *Res:* Western European art. *Mailing Add:* 6308 Lakeway Dr Raleigh NC 27612

HERZBERG, THOMAS
PRINTMAKER, ILLUSTRATOR
b Chicago, Ill. *Study:* Northeastern Ill Univ, BA, 75; Art Inst Chicago, 76-77; Northern Ill Univ, MFA, 79. *Work:* Van Straaten Gallery, Chicago; De Cordova Mus, Lincoln, Mass; Terrance Gallery, Palenville, NY; Metrop Mus & Art Ctr, Coral Gables, Fla; Silvermine Guild Artists. *Exhib:* Chicago and Vicinity Show, Art Inst Chicago, 78 & 84; Boston Printmakers, De Cordova Mus, Lincoln, Mass, 78, 79 & 82; Int Mini Print Show, Pratt Graphic Ctr, New York, 79, 81 & 83; 13th Nat Print Exhib, Silvermine Guild Artists, New Canaan, Conn, 80; Miami Int Print Biennial, Metrop Mus & Art Ctr, Coral Gables, Fla, 80 & 82; 26th Nat Print Exhib, Hunterdon Art Ctr, Clinton, NJ, 82; Eighth Nat Print Invitational, Univ Dallas, 83; Tenth Soc Newspaper Design; Am Soc Illusrs 28th Ann Exhib. *Pos:* Illusr, Chicago Mag, Advertising Age, Playboy Mag, 81-, World Bk Am Bar Asn, 83-, Chicago Tribune, 85 & Washington Post. *Teaching:* Instr photog, Oak Park River Forest High Sch, 76-77; asst printmaking, Northern Ill Univ, 78-79, instr, 81-82. *Awards:* Best of Show, Third Ann Ill Regional Print Show, 80 & Award Excellence, New Horizons in Art, 80-82, North Shore Art League; Weston Press & Gallery Award, Eighth Int Miniature Print Exhib, Pratt Graphic Ctr, 81. *Bibliog:* Articles in Print Rev 13, 81, Chicago Midwest Flash, spring 85 & Illusr 28, 86. *Mem:* Chicago Artists Coalition. *Media:* Etching, Wood Engraving. *Mailing Add:* 4128 W Eddy St Chicago IL 60641

HESS, JOYCE
LIBRARIAN
b Shreveport, La. *Study:* Tex Christian Univ, Ft Worth, BA, 66; Univ Tex, Austin, MLS, 69. *Pos:* Art libr, Univ Tex, Austin, 67-85; retired. *Interests:* Painting. *Mailing Add:* 908 Red Bud Trail Austin TX 78746

HESS, SCOTT
PAINTER
b Baltimore, Md, 55. *Study:* Univ Wis, Madison, BSA, 77; Acad Fine Arts, Vienna, Austria, 79-83. *Work:* Fresno Art Mus, Calif; Smithsonian Inst, Washington, DC; Univ Wis, Madison; Los Angeles Co Mus Art, Calif; Prudential Insurance Co Am, Newark, NJ. *Exhib:* One person exhibs, Ovsey Gallery, Los Angeles, 90 & 92, Fresno Art Mus (with catalog), Calif, 91; Ovsey Gallery, Los Angeles, Calif, 91; Addictions (with catalog), Contemp Arts Forum, Santa Barbara, Calif, 91; Five Hundred Years Since Columbus (with catalog), Triton Mus, Santa Clara, Calif, 92; Corollaries of Apprehension, Calif Col Arts & Crafts, Oakland, 92; From the Studio: Recent Painting & Sculpture by Twenty California Artists, Oakland Mus, 92. *Awards:* Western States Arts Fedn Award, 90; Getty Fel Award, 91; Nat Endowment Arts Award, 91. *Bibliog:* Christopher Young (auth), Horizons in American realism, Flint Inst Art, Mich, 5/91; Suzanne Muchnic (auth), Artists get real In Santa Barbara, LA Times, 11/2/91; Walter Gabrielson & Ed Wortz (auths), Addictions (catalog), Calif Art Forum, Santa Barbara, 11/91. *Dealer:* Ovsey Gallery 170 S LaBrea Los Angeles CA 90036. *Mailing Add:* 1830 Lake Shore Ave Los Angeles CA 90026

HESS, STANLEY WILLIAM
LIBRARIAN
b Bremerton, Wash, July 9, 39. *Study:* Olympic Community Col, 58-60; Univ Wash, BA, 64 & grad work, 67-71; Case Western Reserve Univ, MSLS, 76. *Pos:* Supvr, Photog & Slide Libr, Seattle Art Mus, Wash, 64-73; assoc librn photographs & slides, Cleveland Mus Art, 73-80; head librn, Spencer Art Reference Libr, Nelson-Atkins Mus Art, Kansas City, 80-91. *Awards:* Pi Beta Mus, 76. *Mem:* Art Libr Soc NAm, (Central Plains, secy-treas, 86-87, vchmn-chmn, 90-91); Spec Libr Asn (picture div, pres elect & pres, 78-79); Kansas City Metrop Libr Network (mem, 80-91, secy, 85-86). *Interests:* Publishing, lecturing and teaching about the visual resources in the fine arts, information resources. *Publ:* Auth, Annotated Bibliography of Slide Library Literature, Sch Info Studies, Syracuse Univ, 2/78; coauth, with A Hoffberg, et al, Directory of Art Libraries, Neal-Schuman Publ, 5/78; contribr, Picture Librarianship, Libr Asn, London, 81; and others. *Mailing Add:* 14841 Olympic View Loop Rd NW Silverdale WA 98383

HESTON, JOAN
PAINTER, INSTRUCTOR
b Hartford, Conn. *Study:* Pratt Inst, three yr cert; Art Students League, with Robert Brackman; Stamford Mus, 73; Silvermine Guild Art, 73-74; Studio II, 75-76; with Charles Reid, 76-78. *Exhib:* Nat Acad Design, New York, NY; Am Watercolor Soc Traveling Exhib; Nat Acad Arts & Lett, New York; Wadsworth Atheneum, Hartford, Conn; Frye Mus, Seattle, Wash; Tweed Mus, Duluth, Minn; Salmagundi Club, New York; Loveland Mus, Colo; Stamford Mus, Conn; Grants Pass Mus, Ore; and many others. *Teaching:* Instr oils & watercolor, Silvermine Guild of Arts, 86-; Int workshops, The Oil Painters Solution Bk, 90. *Awards:* Gold Medal, Catharine Lorillard Wolfe Art Club, 81 & 83; Silver Medal, Allied Artists Am, 85 & Knickerbocker Artists, 86; and many others. *Bibliog:* Jolene Goldenthal (auth), Show at Atheneum, The Hartford Courant, 6/29/75; Muriel Brooks (auth), Art scene, New York Sunday News, 12/26/76; Public interest, Channel 13, 12/81 & 12/82; Letter from the editor, Artist's Mag, 9/85. *Mem:* Allied Artists Am (pres, 84 & hon lifetime pres); Silvermine Guild; Audubon Artists; Nat Arts Club; Catharine Lorillard Wolfe Art Club (mem, bd dirs, 82); Knickerbocker Artists. *Media:* Oil, Watercolor. *Publ:* Contribr, Painting Flowers in Watercolor, 80, Light: How to See It, How to Paint It, 88, The Watercolor Painter Solution Book, 88 & Tonal Values, 88, North Light Bks; auth, Concept and design in oil painting, Artist Mag, 9/85. *Mailing Add:* 29 Hemlock Dr Stamford CT 06902

HEUSSER, ELEANORE ELIZABETH (ELEANORE HEUSSER FERHOLT) PAINTER
b North Haledon, NJ. *Study:* Cooper Union, dipl; Columbia Univ Sch Painting & Sculpture, fel, 45-46; Innsbruck Univ, Fulbright Fel, 52-55. *Work:* Newark Mus; Lending Libr Mus Mod Art, New York. *Exhib:* Kunsthistorisches Inst, Innsbruck, Austria, 54; Konzerthaus Gallery, Vienna, Austria, 54; Fulbright Grantees Show, Duveen-Graham Gallery & mus throughout US, 57-58; Pa Acad Fine Arts Ann, Philadelphia, 59 & 65; NJ Artists Biennial, NJ State Mus, Trenton, 72 & 79. *Pos:* Juror, Fulbright Painting Fel, 85-87; juror, Fulbright Collaborative Res Grant, 87. *Teaching:* Instr fundamentals art, Columbia Univ Sch Painting & Sculpture, 46-52; instr drawing, City Col New York, 60-62; pvt instr painting, New York, 60-72 & North Haledon, NJ, 72- *Awards:* Private Grant Study in Mex, provided by George Grebe, 43. *Bibliog:* M Finkelstein (auth), Artist in the Alps, Inst Int Educ News Bulletin, 6/55; article, Revue Mod, 10/72. *Media:* Ink, Oil. *Mailing Add:* 60 Roosevelt Ave North Haledon NJ 07508

HEWITT, DUNCAN ADAMS
SCULPTOR, EDUCATOR
b New York, NY, April 5, 49. *Study:* Colby Col, BA, 71; Univ Pa, MFA, 75. *Comn:* Bronze, stone & earthwork installation, Univ Maine, Augusta. *Exhib:* Philadelphia Mus Art, 72; Inst Contemp Art, Philadelphia, 73-75; Payson Gallery Art, Portland, Maine, 81; Maine Artists Invitational, Bowdoin Col Mus Art, 83; one-person exhib, Baxter Gallery, Portland Sch Art, Maine, 85; Perspectives, three person show, Portland Mus Art, 89; Contemp Sculpture at Chesterwood, Stockbridge, Mass, 91. *Teaching:* Asst prof art, Univ Southern Maine, 76-92, assoc prof, 82-, chairperson dept, 82-; vis artist, Colby Col, fall 82 & Portland Sch Art, spring 83, chairperson, spring 92. *Mem:* Visual Arts Panel; Maine State Comn Arts & Humanities. *Media:* Steel, Wood. *Mailing Add:* Dept Art Univ Southern ME 37 College Ave Gorham ME 04038

HEWITT, THURMAN H
PAINTER, DESIGNER
b Broken Bow, Nebr, Aug 28, 19. *Study:* Univ Tex, 36-37; Rudolph Schaeffer Sch Design, (scholarship), 37-41; Univ Houston, BFA, 47-49. *Exhib:* New Designers, Mus Contemp Art, Houston, Tex, 52. *Pos:* Chief color consult, Emporium, San Francisco, 40-41; chief designer, Frank Sharp Construct, Houston, 47-51; head designer, Houston House, Tex, 51-58. *Teaching:* Guest instr color/design, Univ Houston, 50-52; workshop teacher color/design, Asilomar Conf Ctr, Carmel, 82-88. *Bibliog:* Thurman Hewitt (auth), Handweaving in Mexico (film), 50 & Handweaving in Guatemala (film), 54; Best New Design, Archit Forum, 52. *Mem:* Contemp Handweavers Tex (pres, 50-52); San Diego Watercolor Soc; Southwestern Watercolor Soc. *Media:* Watercolor, Textiles. *Publ:* Contribr, New Textiles (photo & mention), INTERIORS Mag, 56; New Home Designs, Better Homes & Gardens Mag, 58; A Unique Art School (Life Mag), Time-Life Inc, 69; auth, article San Diego Union-Tribune, Copley Press, 88. *Mailing Add:* 1221 Willow St San Diego CA 92106-2538

HEYMAN, LAWRENCE MURRAY
PAINTER, PRINTMAKER
b Washington, DC, June 30, 32. *Study:* Tyler Sch Fine Arts, Temple Univ, BFA, 54, BS(educ), 55; Atelier 17, Paris, experimental printmaking with S W Hayter, 60-63, 69-70; Am Univ, MFA, 72. *Work:* Brooklyn Mus; Bibliotheque Nat, Paris, France; Brooks Mem Mus, Memphis, Tenn; Portland Art Mus, Ore; Free Libr Philadelphia; Mus City New York. *Comn:* Print eds, Assoc Am Artists, New York, 64, 68 & 69 & Antares Eds d'Art, Paris, France, 70, 71 & 72; cover painting for History of American West, US Info Agency, for Vent d'Ouest Book Collection, Paris, France, 65; prints, Judith Selkowitz Fine Arts, New York, 78. *Exhib:* Northwest Printmakers Int, Seattle Mus Fine Arts, 62-65; Audubon Artists Ann, Nat Acad Design, New York, 76; Realites Nouvelles, Parc Floral, Paris, 76 & 78; Le Trait, Cite des Arts, Paris, 77; World Print Competition '77, San Francisco Art Mus, 77; Atelier 17 Retrospective, Brooklyn Art Mus, 77-78 & Elvehjem Art Ctr, Minn, 77-78; L'Estampe Aujourd hui 73/78, Bibliotheque Nat, Paris, 79; solo exhibs, Mus City New York, 84, Nat Inst Health, Bethesda, Maryland, 89-90; The Capital Image Today, Plum Gallery, Kensington, Md, 85 & 89; New England Artists, Newport Art Mus, Newport, RI, 88. *Pos:* Critic/Evaluator printmaking books, Choice Mag, Middletown, Conn, 77-79. *Teaching:* Instr printmaking, RI Sch Design, 67-69, asst prof, 72-79 & dir print prog, 76-79; lectr printmaking, Am Univ, Washington DC, 71-72. *Awards:* Providence Art Club prizes, Open Print Show, 74 & 76; Purchase Award, Le Trait, Bibliotheque Nat, Paris, 77; Nominated & Finalist National Art Medal, Nat

Endow Arts, 87. *Bibliog:* Dale Jacquette (auth), Lawrence Heyman's paintings of street life, RI Rev, 1/81; Jo Ann Lewis (auth), Heyman paintings at Plum, The Washington Post, 10/86; Les Krantz (auth), Artist Profile: Lawrence Heyman, New York Art Rev, 3rd ed, 88. *Media:* Oils, Watercolor; Intaglio. *Mailing Add:* 182 Raleigh Ave Pawtucket RI 02860

HEYMAN, STEVEN
PAINTER
b Los Angeles, Calif, Sept 22, 52. *Study:* Univ Calif, Los Angeles, BA, 76; Art Inst Chicago, MFA, 80. *Work:* Mus Contemp Art, Chicago; Coca-Cola Corp; Prudential Insurance Co Am, Newark, NJ; also many private collections. *Exhib:* Painting and Sculpture of 1980-82: Fellowship Winners, Art Inst Chicago, 83; Chicago: Some Other Traditions, Madison Art Ctr, Wis (toured US & Can), 83-86; Illinois Abstract, Springfield Ard Asn, Ill, 84-85; Chicago Artists in the European Tradition, Mus Contemp Art, Chicago, 89; solo exhibs, Fay Gold Gallery, Atlanta, 89, Galerie Rohrbach, Obernburg, Ger, 90, Lichthof Gallery, State Acad Pictorial Art, Karlsruhe, Ger, 92; Buy Low, Prairie St Gallery, Chicago, 91; The Passover Haggadah, Cheekwood Arts Ctr, Nashville, Tenn, 91; Books from the Pardes Rimonim Press, Italian Cult Inst, Chicago, 91; The Landscape in Art: New Traditions & Extended Meanings, Rockford Art Mus, Ill, 91; The Layaway Show, Flat Iron Bldg Gallery, Chicago, 92. *Pos:* Illus, Passover Haggadah for the Pardes Rimonim Press, Woodmere, New York, 88-89; co-cur, Goethe Inst, Chicago, 92. *Awards:* Fel, Nat Endowment Arts, 87; John Quincy Adams Fel, 80; Skowhegan Scholarship, 80. *Bibliog:* Micheel Bonesteel (auth), Chicago, Art Am, 6/89; articles, Chicago Tribune, 1/22/87, 2/22/89. *Dealer:* Zolla/Lieberman Gallery Inc 230 West Huron Chicago Ill 60610. *Mailing Add:* c/o Zolla/Lieberman Gallery 356 W Huron St Chicago IL 60610

HEYMAN, THERESE THAU
CURATOR, HISTORIAN
b New York, NY. *Study:* Smith Col, BA; Yale Univ, MA(art hist), 58. *Exhib:* Picturing California: 100 Yrs of Photographic Genius. *Collections Arranged:* California Prints, Prints of Calif; Monotypes in California, 72-73; Mirror of California (auth, catalog), Daquerreotypes in Calif, 72-74; Looking at Lange Today, Dorothea Lange Collection, 77-78. *Pos:* Cur catalog, Yale Univ Art Gallery, summers 56 & 57, cur Am prints & catalog, 61-62; educ asst Am art, Smithsonian Inst, 58-59; sr cur, Oakland Mus, Calif, 69- *Mem:* Col Art Asn; Women's Caucus Arts; Alameda Art Comn. *Res:* Prints and photographs in art and history of the West; American graphics. *Publ:* Auth, An American Exodus, Yale Press, 69; auth, Celebrating Collections, Sites, 78; auth, New California Views, Landweber Artists, 79; auth, Edward Weston: Beneficial to Bohemia, Friends of Photography; Picturing California: A Century of Photographic Genius, Chronicle Press, San Francisco, Calif, 89. *Mailing Add:* 785 San Luis Rd Berkeley CA 94707

HEYWOOD, J C
PRINTMAKER
b Toronto, Ont, Can, June 6, 41. *Study:* Ont Col Art, assoc degree, 63; Atelier 17, Paris, France, with Hayter, 67-69. *Work:* Nat Gallery Can; Victoria & Albert Mus, London; Mus Mod Art, Paris; Art Gallery of Ont; Brooklyn Mus; Metrop Mus Art, New York. *Exhib:* Brit Int Print Biennale, 68, 74, 76, 79, 84 & 86; Int Print Biennale, Krakow, Poland, 70-88; Ninth-Seventeenth Int Biennale of Graphic Art, Ljubljana, Yugoslavia, 71-89; World Print Four, San Francisco, Calif, 83; and many others, including 64 one-man shows in Can & Europe. *Teaching:* Prof, drawing & painting, Univ Guelph, 73-74; prof, printmaking & painting, Queen's Univ at Kingston, 74- *Awards:* Graphex Award, Art Gallery of Brantford, 75, 78, 79 & 81; Prize, Int Print Biennale, Krakow, 80; World Print Ed Award, San Francisco, 83; and many others in USA and Can. *Bibliog:* Printvoice, Univ of Alta Press, 84. *Mem:* Royal Can Acad; Ont Soc Artists; Print & Drawing Coun of Can. *Media:* Etching, Silkscreen. *Dealer:* Mira Godard Gallery 22 Hazelton Ave Toronto ON Can. *Mailing Add:* Dept Art Queen's Univ Kingston ON K7L 3N6 Canada

HIBEL, EDNA
PAINTER, LITHOGRAPHER
b Boston, Mass, Jan 13, 17. *Study:* With Gregory Michael, 30-34; also with Eliot O'Hara, 35-36; Boston Mus Fine Arts Sch, with Alexander Yakovlev & Karl Zerbe, Ruth B Sturtevant Traveling Fel, 35-39. *Work:* Mus Fine Arts, Boston; Philatelic Mus, Palais Nations, Geneva, Switz; Columbus Mus Arts & Crafts, Ga; Harvard Univ; Hibel Mus Art, Palm Beach; Lomonosov Porcelain Mus, St Petersburg, Russ. *Comn:* Mother Earth (oil on cameo paper), Ltd Ed Art Print & UN First Day Cover, World Fedn UN Asn, 83; United Nations Postal Admin Commemorative Stamp, 86. *Exhib:* Nat Mus Women Arts, Washington, DC, 89; Exhib Hall Russian Union Artists, Leningrad, 90; Mus Soviet Union Acad Art, Leningrad, USSR, 90; Northern Indiana Arts Asn, Munster, 90; Grenchen Mus Art, Switz, 92; and many others. *Pos:* Dir art & design, Edna Hibel Studio, 72- *Teaching:* Pvt masterclasses, Brookline, Mass, 60-63. *Awards:* Presented to Queen Elizabeth II, 76; Medal of Honor, King Baudouin, Belgium, 82; Medal of Honor & Citation, Pope John Paul II, 83. *Bibliog:* Paintings of Edna Hibel, 74, Hibel Lithographs, 76 & Edna Hibel: The World I Love (film), 76, JAR Publ; Kay Pedrik (auth), Edna Hibel: An Album and Biography, Tradition Inks, 85; Hibel's Russian Palette (film), Hibel Mus Art, 90. *Mem:* Fel Royal Soc Arts, London; Fel, World Acad Art & Sci; World Cult Coun, Juror. *Media:* Oil, Gold Leaf. *Publ:* Auth, Edna Hibel Demonstrates the Art of Lithography, 72, Hibel on Porcelain, 78 & The Sundial Ticking, 78, JAR Publ; Hibel Museum of Art Date Book, Hibel Mus Art, 81; Fay Burg's Lake Kezar Cookbook with a Gallery of Paintings by Edna Hibel, JAR Publ, 82. *Dealer:* Edna Hibel Studio Box 9967 Riviera Beach FL 33404. *Mailing Add:* 1530 W 53rd St Mangonia Park FL 33407

HICKEY, ROSE VAN VRANKEN See Van Vranken, Rose (Rose Van Vranken Hickey)

HICKS, LEON NATHANIEL
PRINTMAKER
b Deerfield, Fla, Dec 25, 33. *Study:* Kans State Univ, BS; State Univ Iowa, with Mauricio Lasansky, MA & MFA; Stanford Univ, study with Albert Elsen; La Romita Sch Art, Italy; Atlanta Univ, Ga. *Work:* Charleston Art Gallery at Sunrise, WVa; Tuskegee Inst, Ala; Oakland Art Mus, Calif; Libr Cong; Albrecht Art Mus, St Joseph, Mo. *Exhib:* St Mary's Col, Notre Dame, Ind, 80; The Studio Mus In Harlem: Impressions/Expressions: Black American Graphics, Washington DC, 80; Smithsonian Inst: Black Am Graphics Traveling Exhib, 80-83; Midwest Mus Am Art Exhib: Black Expression, Elkhart, Ind, 81. *Pos:* Chmn bd & exec vpres, Hicks Etchprint, Inc, Philadelphia, Pa. *Teaching:* Instr art, Concord Col, Athens, WVa, 65-67; asst prof art, Lincoln Univ, Jefferson City, Mo, 67; asst prof printmaking, drawing & hist, Lehigh Univ, Bethlehem, Pa, 70-74; assoc prof printmaking, drawing & hist, Webster Univ, St Louis, Mo, 74- *Awards:* Second Prize, Atlanta Univ, 65; First Prize, Tuskegee Inst, Ninth Ann Beaux Arts Guild Exhib, 68; Arts and Humanities Commission winner, St Louis Edition Portfolio, 81. *Bibliog:* Black Artists on Art, Samella S Lewis & Ruth G Waddy, 70; Directions in Afro-American Art, Herbert F Johnson Mus Art, Cornell Univ, Ithaca, NY, 74; Art: African-American, Samella Lewis, 78. *Mem:* Assoc Brandywine Graphic Workshop, Philadelphia, Pa. *Media:* Drawing, Engraving, Etching, Photo-etching. *Dealer:* Smith Mason Art Gallery 1207 Rhode Island NW Washington DC 20005. *Mailing Add:* 7791 Charing Square Ln St Louis MO 63119

HICKS, SHEILA
TAPESTRY ARTIST, PUBLISHER
b Hastings, Nebr, July 24, 34. *Study:* Yale Univ, BFA, 57, MFA, 59; RI Sch Design, Hon Dr, 85. *Work:* Mus Mod Art & Metrop Mus, New York; Stedelijk Mus, Amsterdam; Mus des Arts Decoratifs, Paris; Victoria & Albert Mus, London; Mus Mod Art, Tokyo & Kyoto, Japan. *Comn:* 7 wall Panels, Mecca, Saudia Arabia, 71; stage curtain, Fiat Tour, Paris, 74; auditorium tapestry, Dresdner Bank, Frankfurt, 79; textile sculpture, Embarcadero Ctr, San Francisco, 81; Fuji City Cultural Ctr, Tokyo, 92. *Exhib:* One-person show, Art Inst Chicago, 62 & Stedelijk Mus, 74; Grand Palais, Paris, 78,79 & 84; Milwaukee Art Mus, 86; Am Crafts Mus, 86, 87 & 88; Belfast Festival, 88; Matsuya-Ginza, Tokyo, Japan, 90; Seoul Art Ctr & Sonjeme; and others. *Pos:* Chief ed, Am Fabrics & Fashions, 80-83; trustee, Textile Mus, Washington, DC, currently; dir, Atelier, Paris, currently. *Teaching:* Instr, The Hague, 78, Middlebury Col, Vt, 79 & Fontainbleau, 81-88. *Awards:* Gold Medal for Craftsmanship, Am Inst Architects, 74; Hon fel Royal Acad Art, Hague, 75; Fel, Am Crafts Coun, 83; Silver Medal, Academie de Architecture, Paris, 86. *Bibliog:* M Levi-Strauss, Sheila Hicks Studio Vista, London, 74; B Diamondstein (auth), Handmade in America, Abrams, NY, 83; article, Cimaise, Paris, No 158; B Freudeheim (auth), article, NY times, 4/86. *Mem:* Yale Club, New York; Centre Int d'Estudes des Textiles Anciens, France; Art Table, New York. *Dealer:* The Merrin Gallery 724 Fifth Ave New York NY; Cora de Vries Kaizergracht 516 1017 Amsterdam The Netherlands. *Mailing Add:* 3 Bis Cour de Rohan Paris 75006 France

HIDE, PETER NICHOLAS
SCULPTOR, EDUCATOR
b Carshalton, Surrey, Eng, Dec 15, 44. *Study:* Croydon Col Art, 61-64; St Martin's Sch Art, 64-67. *Work:* Tate Gallery, London, Eng; Mus Fine Art; Univ Calif; Arts Coun Gt Brit, London; Can Coun Art Bank, Ottawa; City of Barcelona; Univ Alta. *Comn:* Sculpture for travelling show, Arts Coun Gt Brit, 69; Sculpture, cast iron & concrete, Peter Stuyvesant Found, Southampton, Eng, 72; steel sculptures, Commonwealth Games Comt, Edmonton, Alta, 78 & City of Red Deer, Alta, 81; Stainless steel sculpture, Campeaux Corp, Edmonton, 84. *Exhib:* The Condition of Sculpture, Hayward Gallery, London, Eng, 75; Silver Jubilee Exhib, Battersea Park, London, 76; solo exhibs, Serpentine Gallery, London, 76, Sculpture Made in USA, Clayworks Gallery, New York, 84, Peter Hide in Canada, Edmonton Art Gallery, Alta, 86, Recent Sculptures, Mira Godard Gallery, Toronto, 88 & Andre Emmerich Gallery, New York, 90. *Pos:* Artist/advisor, Triangle Workshop, NY & Hardingham Sculpture Workshop. *Teaching:* Lectr sculpture, Norwich Sch Art, Norfolk, Eng, 68-74; lectr, St Martins Sch Art, London, 71-78; prof, Univ Alta, Edmonton, 77- *Bibliog:* Terry Fenton (auth), Peter Hide & the monolith, Vanguard Mag & Peter Hide in Canada (catalog), Edmonton Art Gallery, 86. *Media:* Steel. *Dealer:* Kathleen Laverty Gallery 12323-104 Av Edmonton Alta; Andre Emmerich Gallery 41 E 57th St New York NY 10022. *Mailing Add:* c/o Univ Alberta Fine Arts Bldg, Room 1-10 Edmonton AB T6G 2E1 Canada

HIGA (YOSHIHARU)
PRINTMAKER, PHOTOGRAPHER
b Okinawa, Japan, Jan 15, 38. *Study:* Tama Art Univ, Tokyo, BFA; Art Students League; Pratt Graphic Ctr, New York. *Work:* Mus Mod Art, New York; Brooklyn Mus; Philadelphia Mus; Los Angeles Co Mus; and others. *Exhib:* Contemp Japanese Art Exhib, Mus Tokyo, 64; 50th Ann Exhib, Soc Am Graphic Artists, 69; New Talent Printmaker, Assoc Am Artists, New York, 70; Int Engraving Biennial, Buenos Aires, Arg, 70; Am Graphics Artists traveling show to tour the East, US Info Agency, 70. *Teaching:* Asst prof fine arts, Southampton Col, Long Island Univ, currently. *Awards:* Best Print in Show, 50th Ann Exhib, Soc Am Graphic Artists, 69; Mus Purchase Awards, Int Print Exhib, Seattle Art Mus, Wash, 70 & Nat Print Exhib, Boston. *Bibliog:* Original art, hot off the presses, Life, 6/23/70; Famous Artist Annual, A Treasury of Contemporary Art, Famous Art Sch, 70. *Mailing Add:* 138 Wakeman Rd Hampton Bays NY 11946

HIGBY, (DONALD) WAYNE
PAINTER, SCULPTOR
b Colorado Springs, Colo, May 12, 43. *Study:* Univ Colo, BFA, 66; Univ Mich, MFA, 68. *Work:* Philadelphia Mus Art; Mus Contemp Crafts, New York; Brooklyn Mus, Am Craft Mus & Metrop Mus Art, New York; Minneapolis Mus Art, Wis; Everson Mus Art, Syracuse. *Exhib:* One-man shows, Joslyn Art Mus, 69, Mus Contemp Crafts, 73, Helen Drutt Gallery, New York, 88 & 90; Ceramic Echoes, Nelson-Atkins Mus Art, Kansas City, Mo, 82; International Ceramic, Taipei Fine Arts Mus, Taiwan, Republic of China, 85; The Eloquent Object, Philbrook Mus Art, Tulsa, Okla, 87; Power over the City: American Studio Potters, Detroit Inst Arts, Mich, 88; East-West Contemp Ceramics Exhib, Seoul Olympic Arts Festival, South Korea, 88; Power Over the Clay: American Studio Potters, Detroit Inst Arts, Mich, 88; Everson Mus Art, Syracuse, NY, 89; Am Craft Mus, New York, 90; Kanazawa Ishibtawa Pref, Japan. *Pos:* Chmn, Div Ceramic Art, New York State Col Ceramics, Alfred Univ, 84-; juror, Young Am: Clay/Glass, Am Crafts Coun, 78; adv, Task Force Individual Artist, New York State Coun Arts, 80-82; bd dirs, Haystack Mountain Sch Crafts, Deer Isle, Maine, 83. *Teaching:* Asst prof ceramic art, RI Sch Design, 70-73; prof ceramic art, NY State Col Ceramics, Alfred Univ, 73- *Awards:* Nat Merit Awards, Am Crafts Coun 66; Nat Endowment Arts Fels, 73-74, 77-78 & 88-89; Howard Found Fel, 86-87; NY Found Arts Fel, 85-86 & 89-90; Individual Artist Grant, NY Found Arts, 85 & 89. *Bibliog:* Susan Wechsler (auth), Low Fire Ceramics, Watson-Guptill, New York, 81; B Diamonstein (auth), Handmade in American, H Abrams, 83; The Eloquent Object, Philbrook Mus Art, Univ Wash Press, 87. *Mem:* Am Crafts Coun; Empire State Craftsmen; NCECA. *Media:* Clay, Glaze, Fire. *Publ:* Contribr, Craft Horizons, ed by Rose Slivka, Am Crafts Coun, 70; contribr, Creative Landscape Containers, by Jane Holtz Kay, Christian Sci Monitor, 73; contribr, High Crafts (collecting boom), by Monica Meenan, Town & Country, 77; contribr, Ceramic Art, Comment and Review, 78 & Century of Ceramics in The United States, 79, by Garth Clark, E P Dutton; Ann Jarmusch (auth), Feature article, Am Craft, 4/81. *Dealer:* Helen Drutt Gallery Philadelphia PA 19106; Helen Pruitt Gallery 1625 Spruce St Philadelphia PA 19103. *Mailing Add:* RR One Box 261 Alfred Station NY 14802

HIGGINS, DICK
PAINTER, PRINTMAKER
b Cambridge, Eng, Mar 15, 38; US citizen. *Study:* Yale Univ, 55-57; Columbia Univ, BS(Eng), 60; NY Univ, AM(Eng), 77; additional study with John Cage & Henry Cowell. *Work:* Berlinische Galerie, Berlin; Gallery Mod Art, Wien, Austria; Sonja Henie-Niels Onstad Foundation, Oslo-Hovikodden, Norway; Museu de Arte Contemporanea, Sáo Paulo, Brazil; Mus Mod Art, Lobenhavn, Denmark; and many other public & pvt collections. *Exhib:* One-man shows, La Mamelle, San Francisco, Calif, 77, Studio Morra, Naples, Italy, 77, Galerie Inge Baecker, Bochum, WGer, 78 & 82, Micro Gallery, Sacramento, 79, Franklin Furnace & C Space, New York, 79, Brown Paintings, Emily Harvey Gallery, New York, 90, Gallery Fine Art, Berry Col, Rome, Ga, 91, Blue Cosmologies, Galerie Schüppenhauer, Köln, Ger & Galerie Blau, Seeheim, Ger, 91; Bookworks, Mus Mod Art, New YorK, 77; Neo-da da at Masc, Mid-Hudson Arts & Sci Ctr, Poughkeepsie, NY, 90; Fluxus SPQR, Galeria Fontana Borghese, Roma, Italy, 90; Ubi Fluxus Ibi Motus, Biennale de Venezia, Italy, 90; Imagination/Texture/Text, Gallery at Hunter Mountain, NY, 92; and others. *Teaching:* Prof, Graphics Workshop, Calif Inst Arts, 70-71; dir, Vis Artists Prog & instr, Univ Wis, Milwaukee, 77; research assoc, State Univ NY, Purchase, 83-; vis prof art, Williams Col, 87. *Awards:* Purchase Col Found: Grants (for pattern poetry projects), 84-86 & 88; Bill C Davis Drama Award, 88; Grant, Visual Arts Prog, NY State Coun Arts, 89. *Bibliog:* Carolyn Bennett (auth), Fluxus Ruckus, Woodstock Times, 8/17/89; Bruce Altshuler (auth), Fluxus Redux, Arts Mag, 9/89; Michael Duff (auth), Performance Art Publishers: a Sampling, Small Press, 12/89; and others. *Media:* Acrylic on Canvas; Photo Silkscreen. *Publ:* Auth, The Journey, Left Hand Books, 91; The Autobiography of the Moon, with a translations of the Hsin-Hsin-Ming by George Brecht, Generator, 92; Happytime the Medicine Man, Geneva, Switz, J J Agius, 93; Life Flowers, Woodbine Press, 93; Bodies Electric: Arches, Station Hill Press, 93; and others. *Dealer:* Emily Harvey Artworks 537 Broadway New York NY 10012; Solway Gallery Cincinnati OH. *Mailing Add:* Station Hill Rd PO Box 27 Barrytown NY 12507

HIGGINS, (GEORGE) EDWARD
SCULPTOR
b Gaffney, SC, Nov 13, 30. *Study:* Univ NC, BA, 54. *Work:* Mus Mod Art, Guggenheim Mus, Whitney Mus Am Art, New York; Albright-Knox Art Gallery, Buffalo, NY; Dallas Mus Fine Arts; and others. *Comn:* Sculpture, Cameron Bldg, New York, 62 & NY State Theatre, Lincoln Ctr for Performing Arts, New York, 64. *Exhib:* New York World's Fair, 64-65; Contemporary American Sculpture, Selection 1, Whitney Mus Am Art, 66; Flint Inst Art, Mich, 66; Documenta IV, Kassel, Ger, 68; Duke Univ, 69. *Teaching:* Instr sculpture, Parsons Sch Design, 61-62; Philadelphia Mus Sch, 63; Cornell Univ, 67; Univ Wis , 68; Univ Ky, 70. *Awards:* Louis C Tiffany Grant, 62; Purchase Prize, Flint Inst Art, 66. *Bibliog:* Harriet Janis & Rubi Blesh (auth), Collage: Personalities--Concepts--Techniques, Chilton, 62; Sam Hunter (ed), New Art Around the World: Painting & Sculpture, Abrams, 66; Eduard Trier (auth), Form & Space: Sculpture in the 20th Century, Praeger, 68. *Media:* All. *Mailing Add:* 7315 Henley Rd Sanford NC 27330

HIGGINS, EDWARD FERDINAND III See Doo Da Post (Edward Ferdinand Higgins III),

HIGGINS, EDWARD KOELLING
CERAMIST, JEWELER
b Milwaukee, Wis, Apr 30, 26. *Study:* Univ Wis, Milwaukee, BS(art educ), MS(ceramics); Univ Wis-La Crosse; Northwestern Univ. *Work:* Mus of Contemp Crafts, New York; Theo Portney Gallery, New York; many pvt collections. *Exhib:* Mississippi River Art Festival, Jackson, Miss, 67-; Southern Tier Art & Craft Exhib, Corning Mus, NY, 69-; Crafts-1970, Inst of Contemp Art, Boston, 70; Appalachian Corridors Exhib, Charleston Art Gallery, WVa, 70-; Harrisburg Festival of the Arts, Harrisburg Art Gallery, Pa, 70; Cooperstown NY Festival of the Arts, 70. *Collections Arranged:* Fantasy in Silver, Akron Art Inst, Ohio; Jewelers, USA, Calif State Col at Fullerton; Am Evolution in Art, Chambers Gallery, Pa State Univ; Box Exhib, Kohler Art Ctr; Celebration 20, Mus of Contemp Crafts, New York; Forms in Metal, Montgomery Mus of Fine Arts, Fine Arts Mus at Mobile, Ala, Philbrook Art Ctr, Tulsa, Okla, Va Mus of Fine Arts, Richmond & Huntsville Mus of Art, Ala; 100 Artists Celebrate 200 Yrs, Fairtree Gallery, New York; Xerox-Fun & Fantasy Exhib, Xerox Hall, Rochester, NY. *Teaching:* Asst prof jewelry, Mansfield State Col, Pa, 69-70; assoc prof jewelry, ceramics & photog, Mercyhurst Col, 71-82. *Awards:* Sculpture Award & Merit Award for Metal, Mississippi River Art Festival, Jackson Art Gallery; Silver Award, Appalachian Corridors Exhib, Charlestown Art Gallery. *Bibliog:* Dona Meilach (auth), Box Art Assemblages, Crown, 76; Jewelry: The Fine Art of Adornment Fabrication Method & Jewelry: The Fine Art of Adornment Casting Method (filmstrips), Warner Educ Productions; Casting, Bovin Publ. *Media:* Silver & clay. *Publ:* Contribr, Body Jewelry, Regnery, 73; contribr, Box Art Assemblages, 76 & Career Opportunities in Crafts, 77, Crown. *Mailing Add:* Fearrington Post Box 166 Pittsboro NC 27312

HIGGINS, MARY LOU
CERAMIST, PAINTER
b Milwaukee, Wis, June 27, 26. *Study:* Univ Wis-Milwaukee, BS(art educ), MS(weaving). *Work:* Mint Mus, Charlotte, NC; Newark Mus, NJ; Northern Telecom Res, Glaxco Res, Triangle Park, NC; High Mus, Atlanta, Ga. *Comn:* 10 stoneware goblets, comn by Ctr Women Policy Studies to be given to recipients of Wise Women Awards, Washington, DC. *Exhib:* One-woman shows, Sol Del Rio, San Antonio, Tex, 77-80 & Shelia Nussbaum Gallery, NJ, 85 & 88; Nothern Telecom Juried Sculpture, Ceramic, NC, 85-88; NC Mus His Juries Ceramics & Painted Wood Chest; Biennial '88 Ceramics, Mint Mus, Charlotte, NC; Carlynn Gallery, New York; Auction Benefit, Bewitched by Craft, Am Craft Mus, New York 88 & 89; North Carolina Clay, invitational, Visual Arts Ctr, NC State Univ, Raleigh, 92. *Teaching:* Instr art educ & fiber & fabrics, Mansfield State Col, 69-71; asst prof ceramics, fiber & fabrics & art educ, Mercyhurst Col, 71-74. *Awards:* Sculpture Purchase Award, Northern Telecom, 85; Purchase Award, 4th Ann Exhib NC Sculpture, Northern Telecom, 85; Mint Mus Biennial Purchase Award, Sculptural Vessel, Charlotte, NC, 88. *Bibliog:* Nancy Tilly (auth), Carolina original, NC Homes & Gardens, 12/90; Harriet Gamble (auth), Mary Lou Higgins, Arts & Activities, 92. *Mem:* Am Craft Council. *Publ:* Contribr, Basketry, 44, A New Look at Crochet, 75 & Wearable Crafts, 76, Crown; Inventive Fiber Crafts, Prentice-Hall, 77; Career Opportunities in Crafts, Crown, 77. *Dealer:* Somerhill Gallery 3 Eastgate E Franlin St Chapel Hill NC 27514; Sheila Nussbaum Gallery 341 Millburn Ave Millburn NJ 07041. *Mailing Add:* Fearrington PO Box 166 Pittsboro NC 27312

HIGH, STEVEN S
MUSEUM DIRECTOR, CURATOR
b Twin Falls, Idaho, June 17, 56. *Study:* Univ Utah, Salt Lake City, 74-76; Antioch Col, Yellow Springs, Ohio, BA, 79; Williams Col, Williamstown, Mass, MA, 85. *Collections Arranged:* Young German Painters, 86; Antoni Tapies: Graphic Work, 88; Abstraction Contemporary Photography, 89; Nightmare Works: Tibor Hajas, 90; Alfredo Jaar: Geography-War, 91. *Pos:* Researcher, San Francisco Mus Mod Art, Calif, 79-80; preparator/asst cur, MIT Mus, Cambridge, Mass, 80-82; dir, Baxter Gallery, Portland Sch Art, Maine, 85-88 & Anderson Gallery, Va Commonwealth Univ, Richmond 88- *Teaching:* Instr art hist, Portland Sch Art, Maine 85-88; asst prof art, Va Commonwealth Univ, Richmond, 88- *Mem:* Am Asn Mus; Va Mus Asn; Asn Col & Univ Mus & Galleries; Richmond Arts Coun (bd mem, 89-). *Publ:* Auth, Antoni Tapies: Graphic Work 1947-1987, Baxter Gallery, Portland, Maine, 88; Young German painters, Art Criticism, spring, 88; contribr, Clemens Weiss: Towards Knowledge, Neurer Achener Kunstverein, 90; Nightmare Works: Tibor Hajas (catalog), Anderson Gallery, 90; Alfredo Jaar: Geography equals War, Va Mus & Anderson Gallery, 91. *Mailing Add:* 3804 Kensington Ave Richmond VA 23221

HIGH, TIMOTHY GRIFFIN
STUDIO ARTIST, EDUCATOR
b Memphis, Tenn, Mar 10, 49. *Study:* Tex Tech Univ, BFA(printmaking & drawing), 73; Univ Wis-Madison, MA(printmaking), 75, MFA(printmaking & art hist), 76. *Work:* Chicago Art Inst; Grunwald Ctr Graphic Arts, Univ Calif, Los Angeles; Brooklyn Mus Fine Art, NY; Archer Huntington Gallery, Univ Tex, Austin; Milwaukee Art Mus, Wis; Boston Mus Fine Art; Fogg Mus, Harvard Univ; Metrop Mus Fine Art, New York. *Comn:* Point of Departure (portfolio), Univ Wis, 84. *Exhib:* 4th-10th Ann Colorprint USA Nat Competition, Tex Tech Univ, Lubbock, 73-83; Texas Realism, Austin, Tex, 86; Seventh & Eighth Brit Biennale, 79 & 82; solo exhib, Branigan Cult Ctr, Las Cruces, NMex, 89; Pepperdine Gallery Art, Los Angeles, Calif, 89; Baylor Univ Gallery, Waco, Tex, 89; Metrop Ctr Visual Arts, Denver, Colo, 91; Creative Spirit I, Austin, Tex, 92. *Teaching:* Vis artist & lectr, Univ Tex, Austin, 76, assoc prof serigraphy-printmaking, papermaking, drawing & design, 82-90. *Awards:* Nat Endowment Arts, Individual Fel, works on paper category, 89; Ford Found Travel Enrichment Grant to Peru & Ecuador;

Juror's Purchase Awards, 5th Int Nat Media Exhib, Dickerson, NDak, 75, Boston Print, De Cordova Mus. *Bibliog:* Arthur Williams (auth), Sculpture, Form and Content, 89; Terrence Greider (auth), Artist & Audience, 90; E C Cunningham (auth), Printmaking: A Primary Form of Expression, 92. *Mem:* Boston Printmakers; Austin Visual Arts Asn; Tex Fine Arts Asn; Austin Christian Arts Fel; Christians in Visual Arts Asn. *Media:* Prismacolor, Enamel Drawing; Serigraphy, Papermaking. *Publ:* Contribr, New American Graphics--1975, Univ Wis-Madison, 75; Terrence Greider (auth), Artist & Audience, 90. *Mailing Add:* c/o Dept of Art Univ of Tex Austin TX 78712

HIGHSTEIN, JENE
SCULPTOR
b Baltimore, Md, 42. *Study:* Univ Md, BA, 63; Univ Chicago, 63-65; New York Studio Sch, 66; Royal Acad Sch, London, dipl, 70. *Work:* Victoria & Albert Mus, London; Musee de la Ville de Paris, France; La Jolla Mus Contemp Art, Calif; Rose Art Mus, Brandeis Univ, Mass; Guggenheim Mus, New York; and many pvt collections. *Comn:* Granite carvings, City Hall Park, Lincoln, Nebr, 83; granite carvings, General Mills Corp, 89; granite carvings, Walker Arts Ctr, 89; concrete sculptures and Park, Rutgers Univ, 90. *Exhib:* One-man exhibs, Univ Art Mus, Berkeley, Calif, 79, Renaissance Soc, Univ Chicago, 80, Ugo Ferranti Gallery, Rome, Italy, 81, Oscarsson Hood Gallery, New York, 82, Miami-Dade Community Col, 83, Anders Tornberg Gallery, Lund, Sweden, 84, Mattress Factory, Pittsburgh, 85 & Flow Ace Gallery, Los Angeles, 86; Iron Cast, Pratt Inst Galleries, New York, 83; An International Survey of Recent Painting and Sculpture, Mus Mod Art, New York, 84; Sculptor's Drawings, Diane Brown Gallery, New York, 85; Inside/Outside, Walker Arts Ctr, Minn, 89. *Teaching:* Instr, Sch Visual Arts, 73, Parsons Sch Design, 83 & New York Univ, 84-85, NY; vis artist, Yale Univ, 74-75, C W Post Col, Old Westbury, NY, 75 & 79, Emily Carr Col, Vancouver, BC, 80, Rutgers Univ, Camden, NJ, 82 & Miami-Dade Community Col, Fla, 83; artist-in-residence, Sarah Lawrence Col, Bronxville, NY, 76. *Awards:* Sculpture Awards, Creative Artists Pub Serv Prog, 79 & Nat Endowment Arts, 84; Guggenheim Fel, 85. *Bibliog:* Linda Forshey (auth), Jene Highstein, La Jolla Mus, Calif, 87; Jean Feinberg (auth), Jene Highstein at Wave Hill, Wave Hill, 89; Jene Highstein (auth), Gallery/Landscape Santa Barbara, Contemp Arts Forum, 91. *Media:* All Media. *Mailing Add:* 145 Chambers St New York NY 10007

HIGHTOWER, JOHN B
ADMINISTRATOR, MUSEUM DIRECTOR
b Atlanta, Ga, May 23, 33. *Study:* Yale Univ, BA, 55; Calif Col Arts & Crafts, hon DFA, 75. *Pos:* Asst to pub, Am Heritage Publ Co, 61-63; exec asst, NY State Coun on the Arts, 63-64, exec dir, 64-70, mem, 70-76; cult adv, Rockefeller Mission to Latin Am, 69; Am rep, United Nations Educ, Sci & Cult Orgn Conf on Performing Arts, Canberra, Australia, 69; dir, Mus Mod Art, New York, 70-72; pres, Assoc Councils of the Arts, 72-74 & S St Seaport, 77-83; founder & chmn, Advocates for the Arts, 74-77; vchmn & dir, The Maritime Ctr, 83-84, exec dir, 84-89; dir planning & develop for arts, Univ of Va, 89- *Teaching:* Instr arts mgt, Wharton Sch of Bus, New Sch, Yale Grad Sch Drama, 75-77. *Awards:* NY State Award, 70. *Mem:* Buffalo Acad Fine Arts; and others. *Mailing Add:* RR 3 Box 163 Charlottesville VA 22901

HIGHWATER, JAMAKE
CRITIC, LECTURER
b Mont, Feb 14, 42. *Study:* Spec study in comparative lit, music, dance, cult anthrop & art hist; Minn Col Art & Design, Hon DFA, 86. *Pos:* Consult, Task Panel on the Individual Artist & Lit Panel, Ny State Coun Arts, 75-80; mem art task panel, Pres Carter's Comn on Mental Health, 77-79; pres cult coun, Am Indian Community House, New York, 77-79; nominator, Awards in the Visual Arts, WNET-NY, 80-84; writer & narrator, Native Americans (8 part series), The Primal Mind & Native Land, PBS; moderator, Aspen Inst Seminar, Indian America: Past, Present and Future, 81-84; exec bd, PEN, Am Ctr, 83-85; art critic, Christian Science Monitor, 88. *Teaching:* Lectr for Fox Chase Agency, Philadelphia; appointed lectr, NY Univ, Continuing Educ, 76-80; adjunct asst prof, Grad Sch Archit, Columbia Univ, 84-85; gen dir, Native Arts Festival, Houston, 86 & Festival Mythos, Philadelphia, 91; nat adv comt, Pew Fels Arts, 90-92; bd, Am Poetry Ctr, 91. *Awards:* Virginia McCormich Scully Literary Award, 83; Best film of the Yr, Nat Educ Film Festival, 84; Finalist, Am Film Festival, 84. *Mem:* Author's Guild; Indian Arts & Crafts Found, NMex; Dramatists Guild; PEN Int. *Res:* Concerned with all aspects of art, crafts and culture. *Publ:* Writer, host & co-producer, The Primal Mind (documentary film), PBS, 84; Native Land (documentary film), PBS, 86; auth, Arts of the Indian Americas, Harper & Row, 83; The Primal Mind, Harper & Row, 81; Song from the Earth: North American Indian Painting, New York Graphic Society, 76; The Sweet Grass Lives On: Fifty Contemporary North American Artists, Harper & Row, 80; Shadow Show: An Autobiographical Insinuation, Harper & Row, 86. *Mailing Add:* Native Land Found 1201 Larrabee St, Suite 202 Los Angeles CA 90069

HILDEBRAND, JUNE MARIANNE
PRINTMAKER, ILLUSTRATOR
b Eureka, Calif, Nov 2, 30. *Study:* Calif Col Arts & Crafts; Art Students League, scholar; Queens Col, BFA; Hochschule Bildende Kunste Berlin; Hunter Col, MA; Pratt Graphic Ctr. *Work:* Philadelphia Mus Art, Pa; Univ Wis-Madison; New York Pub Libr; Everson Mus Art; Univ Minn; Hunt Inst, Carnegie Mellon Univ. *Exhib:* Pratt Int Miniature Print Exhib, 66 & 68; Oneonta State Univ, 67; Montclair State Col, 68; Gotham Bk Mart, New York, 69; Pratt Inst, 79; and others. *Media:* Linoleum, Silkscreen. *Publ:* Illusr, Eight Poems by Michael Benedikt, Assoc Am Artists, 65; contribr, graphics, Artists Proof Mag, 66 & 67; Wild Fruits and Flowers, 80 & A Book of Flowers, 82, Claremount Press; Four Poems by Kirby Congdon, Ctr Book Arts, 86. *Dealer:* Associated American Artists 663 5th Ave New York NY 10022. *Mailing Add:* PO Box 177 Cooper Station New York NY 10003

HILDEBRANDT, WILLIAM ALBERT
PAINTER, SCULPTOR
b Philadelphia, Pa, Oct 1, 17. *Study:* Tyler Sch Art, Temple Univ, BFA, 38, BSEd, 39 & MFA, 44; Philadelphia Col Art, cert advert design; with Franklin Watkins & Boris Blai. *Work:* Glen-Croft Baptist Church, Folcroft, Pa; Sch Dist Philadelphia; Temple Univ, Philadelphia. *Comn:* Created design for medal presented to Lieutenant Colonel Guion S Bluford, astronaut, Philadelphia Sch Dist, 83. *Exhib:* Nat Drawing Soc Eastern Cent Regional Drawing Exhib, Philadelphia Mus Art, 65 & 70; Am Drawing Biennial, Norfolk Mus Arts & Sci, Va, 67; Avanti Gallery, New York, 69; Pennsylvania 71, William Penn Mem Mus, Harrisburg, Pa, 71; West '79 & West '84 Art and the Law, Minn Mus Art, St Paul, 79 & 84; Expressions, Philadelphia Civic Ctr Mus, 79; solo shows, Temple Univ, 46 & 87, Radnor High Sch, 61, Widener Col, Chester, 65, Springfield Township Libr, 69, Philadelphia Art Alliance, 62 & 73 & Del Co Community Col, Media, 85, Darlington Fine Arts Ctr, Wawa, Pa, 88; and others. *Pos:* Art consultant & tech illustr, Franklin Inst Labs for Res & Develop, 44-52; art ed, Winston Publ Co (textbook div), 52-54; Illusr, Off Instrnl Publ & Mat, Sch Dist Philadelphia, 67-70. *Teaching:* Supervisor art educ, Sharon Hills Pub Schs, 39-44, Upper Darby Pub Schs, 44-52 & Philadelphia Pub Schs, 54-84, emer; retired. *Awards:* Four Chaplains Legion of Honor Citation, 77; First Prize for Drawing, Villanova Univ Ann, 86 & 88; First Prize for Drawing, 88, Mixed Media, 89, 90 & 92, Pa Sr Arts Festival, Harrisburg. *Mem:* Temple Univ Gen Alumni Asn; Philadelphia Art Teachers Asn (pres, 50-52); Tyler Sch Art Alumni Asn (founding pres & bd dirs, 46); hon life mem, Temple Univ Gen Alumni Asn; Del Co Poets Coop; Abington Cult Ctr (evaluation comt, 63). *Media:* Oil; Miscellaneous Media. *Publ:* Illusr, The Keystone State, Arthur Graef (auth), 53 & Minnesota's Government, Joseph Kise (auth), 53, Winston, Humanities Curriculum, 68 & Echoes from Mount Olympus, 70; auth, Art in the middle years, Off Curric & Instr, Sch Dist Philadelphia, 80; A Few Lines from Desert Shield (poem entered in the Cong Rec 1st session), 102nd Cong, 91. *Mailing Add:* 417 Turner Rd Media PA 19063

HILDRETH, JOSEPH ALAN
PRINTMAKER, PAINTER
b Bowling Green, Ky, Sept 2, 47. *Study:* Western Ky Univ, BFA, 69; Pratt Inst, with Walter Rogalski, MFA, 71. *Work:* Mint Mus, Charlotte, NC; Erie Fine Arts Ctr, Pa; State Univ NY Col, Potsdam. *Exhib:* Eight Upstate, Artists' Space Gallery, New York, NY, 74; Nat Print Exhib, Second St Gallery, Charlottesville, Va, 76; 16th Bradley Nat Print Exhib, Bradley Univ, Peoria, Ill, 77; New York Landscape, Plaza Gallery, Albany, 81; 11th Nat Print & Drawing Exhib, Minot State Col, NDak, 82; and many others. *Pos:* Chmn art dept, State Univ NY, Potsdam, 86- *Teaching:* Assoc prof printmaking, State Univ NY Col Potsdam, 71- *Awards:* Carnegie Found Grant, 81; NY State Coun Arts Grant, 82. *Media:* Mixed. *Publ:* Auth, Contemporary Realism (catalog essay), 82. *Mailing Add:* Pierpoint Ave Dept Art State Univ Potsdam Potsdam NY 13676

HILGEMAN, LIESE
CURATOR, GALLERY DIRECTOR
b Waukesha, Wis, March 19, 61. *Study:* Vanderbilt Univ, BA(fine arts, cum laude), 82; Boston Univ, MA(art hist), 86. *Collections Arranged:* Palisades Gallery Series, (13 one-person exhibs, catalog) 88-90; Omnibus '91 (10 mid-career artists), 91; Selections from the Robert J Shiffler Collection, 92; Adrian Piper and Carl Pope (two-person show, catalog), Herron Gallery, 92; Jon Tower (one-person show, catalog), Herron Gallery, 92. *Pos:* Cur exhibs, Hudson River Mus, Yonkers, 88-90 & guest cur, Palisades Gallery, 90-91; dir/cur, Herron Gallery, Indianapolis Ctr Contemp Arts, 90- *Res:* Contemporary art & the history of photography. *Publ:* Coauth & ed, The sphinx and the lotus, Hudson River Mus, 90; auth & ed, Problems & Solutions: Surveying the Art of Jon Tower, Herron Gallery, 91. *Mailing Add:* Indianapolis Center for Contemporary Art Herron Gallery 1701 N Pennsylvania Indianapolis IN 46202

HILL, CHARLES CHRISTOPHER
COLLAGE ARTIST, PAINTER
b Greensburg, Pa, Mar 4, 48. *Study:* E Los Angeles Col, AA(art), 68; Univ Calif, Irvine, BA, 70, MFA 73. *Work:* Gugenheim Mus, New York,; Metrop Mus Art, New York,; Mus Nat d'Art Moderne, Ctr George Pompidou, Paris; Los Angeles Co Mus Art, Calif; Honolulu Acad Art, Hawaii. *Comn:* Painting, Northrup, El Segundo, Calif, 80; Drawings, Hilton Hotels, Narita, Japan 87. *Exhib:* Market St Prog, Oakland Mus Art, Calif 73; Los Angeles Artists, Mus Mod Art, New York, 76; Eighth Int Painting Festival, Cagnessur Mer, France, 77; Matter-Meaning-Memory, Honolulu Acad Art, Hawaii, 80; One-person exhibs, Cirrus Gallery, Los Angeles, 80, 82-84 & 87-88, Simon Lowinsky Gallery, San Francisco, 81, Galerie Maurer, Zurich, 81 & 82, Baudoin Lebon, Paris, 82 & 85, Van Straaten Gallery, Chicago, 83, DBR Gallery, Cleveland, 84, Galleria del Cavallino, Venice, 85 & Ctr d'Action Culturelle de St-Brieuc, France, 87. *Teaching:* Vis instr, Art Ctr Col Design, 78-79; Univ Calif, Los Angeles, 80-81. *Awards:* Young Talent Award, Los Angeles Co Mus Art, 76; Grant, Slides, Nat Endowment Arts, 76; Special Mention, Modern Trends, City of Cagnes sur Mer, France, 76. *Bibliog:* Deborah Irmas (auth), Charles Hill, Carte d'Arte, Messina, Italy, 11/87; Gilbert Lascault (auth), Le Bamboo, Bambouserie de Prafrance, 8/88; Constance Glenn (auth), New Venice vernacular, Angeles Mag, 11/88. *Media:* Watercolor & Paper. *Dealer:* Cirrus Gallery 520 S Alameda Los Angeles CA 90291. *Mailing Add:* 1158 Palms Blvd Venice CA 90291

HILL, CLINTON J
PAINTER, SCULPTOR
b Payette, Idaho, Mar 8, 22. *Study:* Univ Ore, BS, 47; Brooklyn Mus Art Sch, 49-51; Acad Grande Chaumiere, Paris, 51; Inst Arte Statale, Florence, Italy, 51-52. *Work:* Mus Mod Art, New York; Philadelphia Mus Art; Metrop Mus, New York; Albright-Knox Gallery, Buffalo, NY; Worcester Art Mus, Mass; plus others. *Exhib:* Solo exhibs, Zabriskie Gallery, New York, 55-75, Gallerie Darthea Speyer, Paris, 73-75, Marilyn Pearl Gallery, 79-93, Montclair Art Mus, NJ, 81 & Alice Simsar Gallery, Ann Arbor, Mich, 85-93; Prints from Blocks, Mus Mod Art, New York, 83; Int Paper Biennale, Leopold Huesch Mus, Duren, Fed Repub Ger; Galleria Blu, Milano, 84; Centro Culturale, Villa Borzino, Borzino, Italy, 87; Paperworks & Constructions, Worcester Art Mus, Mass, 92. *Teaching:* Prof emer, Queens Col, City Univ New York, 68-87. *Awards:* Caps Grant, 74-75; Fac Res Grant, City Univ New York, 75 & 79; Nat Endowment Arts, 76-77 & 80-81. *Bibliog:* Harriet Janis & Rudi Blesh (auth), Collage: Personalities, Concepts, Techniques, Chilton, 62; Leo Steinberg (auth), Other Criteria, Oxford Univ, 72; Jeremy Gilbert-Rolfe (auth), article, Artforum, 12/73 & 9/79; Gerrit Henry (auth), The permitting medium, Art Int, summer 74. *Mem:* Am Abstract Artists Asn. *Media:* Handmade Paper, Oil. *Dealer:* Marilyn Pearl Gallery 29 W 57th St New York NY 10019; Alice Simsar Gallery 301 N Main St Ann Arbor MI 48104. *Mailing Add:* 178 Prince St New York NY 10012

HILL, DRAPER
EDITORIAL CARTOONIST, HISTORIAN
b Boston, Mass, July 1, 35. *Study:* Harvard Col, BA(magna cum laude), 57; Slade Sch Fine Arts, London, Eng, 60-63. *Work:* Wiggin Gallery, Boston Pub Libr; Univ Va; Lyndon B Johnson Libr, Austin; Nat Gallery Can, Ottawa; Worcester Art Mus, Mass. *Exhib:* Int Salon de Caricature, Montreal, PQ, 66-86; Editorial Art of Draper Hill, Brooks Mem Art Gallery, Memphis, 75; Image of America in Caricature and Cartoon, Amon Carter Mus, Ft Worth, 75; American Presidency in Political Cartoons, Univ Art Mus, Berkeley, 75-76; one man retrospective, Political Asylum, Art Gallery of Windsor, Ontario, Can, 85-86; and others. *Collections Arranged:* Cartoon and Caricature from Hogarth to Hoffnung, 62 & James Gillray 1756-1815, 67, Arts Coun Gt Brit; exhib on hist caricature, Boston Pub Libr, 64, 66 & 70. *Pos:* Ed cartoonist, Worcester Telegram, Mass, 64-71, Com Appeal, Memphis, Tenn, 71-76 & Detroit News, 76-; contrib ed, Eighteenth Century Life, Williamsburg, Va, 80-88. *Teaching:* Instr life drawing, Sch Worcester Art Mus, 67-71; lectr, Amon Carter Mus, Fort Worth, Tex, 75 & Yale Ctr for British Art, New Haven, Conn, 84. *Awards:* Guggenheim Fel, 83-84. *Bibliog:* Lydel Sims (auth), article, Cartoonist Profiles, 3/75; Guy Northrop (auth), The Editorial Art of Draper Hill, Brooks Gallery, Memphis, 75; Alan Westin (auth), Getting Angry Six Times a Week, Beacon Press, Boston, 79. *Mem:* Asn Am Ed Cartoonists (vpres & dir, 70-75, pres, 75-76). *Collection:* Caricature and cartooning, with particular emphasis on eighteenth and nineteenth century English satire. *Publ:* Auth, Mr Gillray, The Caricaturist, London, 65 & Fashionable Contrasts, London, 66; Illingworth on Target, 70; co-illusr, The Decline and Fall of the Gibbon, 74; auth, The Satirical Etchings of James Gillray, 76; three collections of cartoons about Detroit's Mayor Coleman Young, 77, 82 & 86; auth, Cartoons and Caricatures, Vol III, Time-Life Encycl of Collectibles, 78; and others. *Mailing Add:* Detroit News 615 W Lafayette Blvd Detroit MI 48231

HILL, ED
DEALER, COLLECTOR
b El Paso, Tex, June 23, 37. *Study:* Univ Tex, El Paso, BA(Eng lit), 62. *Pos:* Dir, Ed Hill Editions, El Paso, Tx, currently. *Specialty:* Original prints by American, European & Japanese Artists. *Collection:* Mezzotints by Anne Dykmans (Belgium); published first etchings & aquatints by Fritz Scholdet; agent for Chicano artists Gaspar Enriquez. *Mailing Add:* 4141 Pinnacle St El Paso TX 79902

HILL, GARY
VIDEO ARTIST
b Santa Monica, Calif, Apr 4, 51. *Study:* Art Students League, Woodstock, 69. *Exhib:* Solo exhibs, Mus Mod Art, New York, 80 & 90, Whitney Mus Am Art, New York, 83, Galerie des Archives, Paris, 90 & 91, Galerie Huset-Glyptotek Mus, Copenhagen & YYZ Artist's Outlet, Toronto, 90, OCO Espace d'art contemporain, Paris, 91; retrospectives, Am Ctr, Paris, 83, Whitney Mus Am Art, New York, 86, St Gervais, Geneva, 2nd Seminar on Int Video, 87, ELAC Art Contemporain, Lyon, France, 88; Biennial Exhibition, Whitney Mus Am Art, 91; Metropolis, Martin-Gropius-Bau, Berlin, 91; Topographie 2, Wiener Festwochen, Vienna, 91; Artec 91, Int Biennale, Nagoya, 91; Doubletake: Collective memory & current art, Hayward Gallery, London & Japan Video & Television Festival, 92. *Pos:* Founder & dir, Open Studio Video, Barrytown, NY, 77-79. *Teaching:* Vis assoc prof, Ctr Media, State Univ NY, Buffalo, 79-80; vis prof art, Bard Col, Annandale-on-Hudson, NY, 83; art fac, Cornish Col Arts, Seattle, Wash, 85-91. *Awards:* US Exchange Fel, Japan, 84-85; Nat Endowment Arts France US Exchange Fel, Ctr Georges Pompidou, 88; Guggenheim Fel, 90. *Bibliog:* Jacinto Lageira (auth), Une Verbalisation du Regard, Parachute, 4-11, 4-6/91; Corinne Pencenat (auth), L'Experience Limite de Gary Hill, Beaux Arts, 113, 91; Ann-Sargent Wooster (auth), The Heart of Darkness (film & video), Arts Mag, 10/91. *Publ:* Auth, Primarily Speaking, 1981-83, Whitney Mus Am Art, 83; Primarily Speaking, Communications, 88; And if the Right Hand did not know What the Left Hand is Doing, Illuminating Video, 90; Unspeakable Images, Camera Obscura, 91. *Mailing Add:* c/o Donald Young Gallery 2107 Third Ave Seattle WA 98121

HILL, J TWEED
PAINTER, GRAPHIC ARTIST
b Boston, Mass. *Study:* Taubes Pierce Sch Art, Provincetown, Mass, 59-60; with Steven Trefonides, Boston, Marguerite Pearson & Wayne Morrell, Rockport, Mass & Roger Curtis, Gloucester, Mass. *Exhib:* North Shore Arts Asn, Gloucester, 66-81; Jordan Marsh Annual Exhibit of New England Artists, 67; Newburyport Art Asn Show, 71-77; Butler Art Inst Show, Youngstown, Ohio, 72; Grand National Show, Am Artists Prof League, New York, 75-76 & 79-81; Cayuga Mus Hist & Art, 81-82. *Pos:* Dir & owner, Pigeon Cove Gallery, Rockport, Mass, 68-71; mem & co-operator, Harbor Gallery, Rockport, 73- *Awards:* Third Prize for Oils, Newburyport Art Asn, 75 & First Prize, 77; Kiwanis Club Silver Bowl Award for Most Popular Painting, 76 & 77, Best in Show, 78. *Mem:* North Shore Arts Asn (mem bd dir, 73-87); Newburyport Art Asn; Salmagundi Club; Am Artists Prof League. *Media:* Oil, Pen & Ink. *Dealer:* Harbor Gallery Main St Rockport MA 01966. *Mailing Add:* 3 Pidgeon Hill Rockport MA 01966

HILL, JAMES BERRY
DEALER
b New York, NY, June 24, 45. *Study:* Cornell Univ, AB, 67. *Collections Arranged:* Coggins Collection, Selections from the Robert P Coggins Collection of American Painting, 76. *Pos:* Co-dir, Berry-Hill Galleries, Inc, 67- *Awards:* Presidential Appointment (2 terms), Cult Property Adv Comt, Washington, DC. *Mem:* Nat Arts Club; Appraisers Asn Am; Artists Fel; Art Dealers Asn Am. *Specialty:* American art of the nineteenth and early twentieth century; China trade paintings. *Mailing Add:* Berry-Hill Galleries 11 E 70th St New York NY 10021

HILL, JOAN (CHEA-SE-QUAH)
PAINTER, ILLUSTRATOR
b Muskogee, Okla, Dec 19. *Study:* Northeastern State Col, BA, 52; Famous Artists Course, 53-; spec study Indian art, with Dick West, 58-63; pvt study with int artists, 58-72; extensive air-travel-study on T H Hewitt Painting Workshops, 65-78, with Dong Kingman, Millard Sheets, Robert E Wood, Rex Brandt & George Post. *Work:* Heard Mus, Phoenix; Mus Am Indian, Heye Found, New York; Fine Arts Mus NMex, Santa Fe; Philbrook Art Ctr Mus, Tulsa, Okla; US Ctr Military Hist, Smithsonian Inst, Washington, DC. *Comn:* Mural-type oil paintings of Cherokee Nation through Dept Interior, Tahlequah, Okla, 67; portrait (gouache) for book, Sam Houston with the Cherokees, comn by Rennard Strickland & Jack Gregory Collection, Tulsa, 67; portrait & illus for book poetry, Five Civilized Tribes Mus, Muskogee, 68; oil painting, USA Ctr Mil Hist for Bicentennial Collection, Washington, DC, 75; mural, Seattle Arts Comn, 77. *Exhib:* Five Ann Center Arts Indian America, Dept Interior, 64, 67-70; American Embassies Overseas, Dept Interior Traveling Exhib, 65-66; America Discovers Indian Art, Smithsonian Inst, Washington, DC, 67; solo exhib, Circulating via Photographs, For Lang Inst, Beijing, People's Repub China, 79; Night of the First Americans, under the patronage of Pres & Mrs Reagan, Kennedy Ctr Performing Arts, Washington, DC, 82; Contemp NAm Indian Art, Nat Mus Natural Hist, Smithsonian Inst, Washington, DC, 82-83; Southeast Am Indian Art Show, Marietta-Cobb Fine Arts Ctr, Marietta, Ga, 88; and others. *Pos:* Career day art consult, Am Asn Univ Women, 62-63; mem bd dirs, Youth & Art Adv Bd, Oklahomans for Indian Opportunity, Norman, Okla, 73-82. *Teaching:* Instr art, Tulsa Secondary Pub Schs, 52-56; instr art & adult art educ, Muskogee Art Guild, 59-60. *Awards:* First Award, 66, 68, 71 & 75 & Waite Phillips Special Artists Trophy for Career Achievement, Philbrook Art Ctr Mus, 73; Walter Bimson Grand Award, Scottsdale Nat Indian Arts Exhib, Ariz, 68; Outstanding Achievement in Art, Commemorative Medal, Royal Mint, London, Eng, 74; Oscar D'Italia 1985, Acad Italia, Cremona, Italy, 85; and many others. *Bibliog:* Nat Comt on Indian Work (film & brochure), Exec Coun of Episcopal Church, New York, 72; Jamake Highwater (auth), Song From the Earth--American Indian Painting, NY Graphic Soc, 76; History of Art, Elementary, Holt, Rinehart & Winston, 89. *Mem:* Nat League Am Pen Women; Southwestern Art Asn; Muskogee Art Students Guild (art dir & publicity dir, 58-64); Intercontinental Biog Asn. *Media:* Oil, Gouache; Collage, Acrylic. *Publ:* Illusr, Life en Espanol, Time-Life Int, Mex, 69; contribr & illusr, The American Way, Am Airlines, 72; illusr, The Cherokee People, Indian Tribal Series, Phoenix, 73; Gateway Lit Ser, Scot, Foresman & Co, 84; auth & illusr, Indian Art, A Form of Visual Prayer, The Creative Woman, Governors State Univ, 87. *Mailing Add:* 3110 Red Bird Lane Muskogee OK 74403

HILL, JOHN CONNER
ART DEALER, DESIGNER
b Philadelphia, Pa, Feb 17, 45. *Study:* Pratt Inst, BID, 68; Cosanti Found, Paradise Valley, Ariz, with Paolo Soleri, 72-76. *Exhib:* Ariz Photog Biennial, Phoenix Art Mus, 69; Southwest Biennial, Int Folk Art Mus, Santa Fe, NMex, 70, NMex Biennial, 71; Tucson Festival Crafts Exhib, Tucson Mus, Ariz, 77; Ariz Textile Exhib, Matthews Ctr, Ariz State Univ, Tempe, 77. *Pos:* Bronze sculpture casting, Cosanti Found, 74-76; publ-owner, Kokopelli Press, Phoenix, 76-; Gallery owner, Scottsdale, 89. *Teaching:* Instr art, Rough Rock Demonstration Sch, Navajo Nation, Ariz, 68-70. *Awards:* Third Award, Ariz Textile Exhib, Scottsdale Ctr for the Arts, 76. *Mem:* Charter mem Antique Tribal Art Dealers Asn. *Specialty:* Early American Indian art, American folk art. *Dealer:* John C Hill Gallery 6990 E Main St Scottsdale AZ 85251. *Mailing Add:* 6990 E Main St Scottsdale AZ 85251

HILL, MEGAN LLOYD See Romero, Megan H

HILL, PETER
PAINTER, EDUCATOR
b Detroit, Mich, Nov 29, 33. *Study:* Albion Col, AB, 56; Cranbrook Acad Art, Bloomfield Hills, Mich, MFA, 58. *Work:* Joslyn Art Mus, Omaha, Nebr; Sheldon Mem Gallery, Lincoln, Nebr; Springfield Art Mus, Mo; Sioux City Art Ctr, Iowa; Spiva Art Gallery, Joplin, Mo. *Exhib:* Springfield Art Mus Ann, Mo, 70 & 74; Midwest Biennial, Joslyn Art Mus, 72, 74, 78, 82 & 84; Colo-Nebr Exchange Exhib, Denver, 73; one-man show, Sheldon Mem Art Gallery, Lincoln, Nebr, 78; American Art, Pillsbury Co, Minneapolis, 81; Watercolor Now, Springfield Art Mus, Mo, 87; and others. *Teaching:* From instr to chmn dept, Univ Nebr, Omaha, 58- *Awards:* Ann Exhib Purchase Awards, Springfield Art Mus, 63 & 74; Best Painting, Joslyn Mus, 78 & 82; Purchase Award, Nat Competitive Exhib, Peru State Col, Nebr, 89. *Mem:* Watercolor USA Honor Soc. *Media:* Acrylic, Oil. *Dealer:* Gallery 72 37th & Leavenworth Omaha NE 68102; Anderson-O'Brien Gallery 87th & Pacific Omaha NE 68114. *Mailing Add:* 11734 Shirley St Omaha NE 68144

HILL, RICHARD WAYNE
PAINTER, PHOTOGRAPHER
b Buffalo, NY, Aug 7, 50. *Study:* Art Inst of Chicago, 68-71; State Univ NY, Buffalo, 77-80. *Work:* Native Am Ctr for the Living Arts, Niagara Falls, NY; Arts & Crafts Bd, Dept of Interior, Washington, DC; Woodland Indian Cult & Educ Ctr, Brantford, Ont; Int Ctr of Photog, New York. *Comn:* Watercolor series, Farmer's Mus, Cooperstown, NY, 71; photog, Everson Mus, Syracuse, 72; drawings series, Buffalo Courier Express, NY, 74; photog, Smithsonian Inst, Washington, DC, 75-76. *Exhib:* Iroquois Confederacy Arts & Crafts Exhib, Everson Mus, Syracuse, NY, 72; one-man show, Paintings by Richard Hill, Buffalo Mus of Sci, NY, 73; Exhib of Iroquois Art, Dortmund, Ger, 76; 32nd Am Indian Artists Exhib, Philbrook Art Ctr, Tulsa, Okla, 77; Spirit of the Earth, Castilani Gallery, New York, 80; John F Kenndy Ctr, 82; and others. *Pos:* Photogr, Woodland Indian Cult & Educ Ctr, Brantford, Ont, 72-73; res asst, Buffalo & Erie Co Hist Soc, Buffalo, 73-76; treas, Native Am Ctr for the Living Arts, Niagara Falls, 75-; mem bd, Int Native-Am Coun of Arts, 75-77; mem expansion arts adv panel, Nat Endowment for the Arts, 77; mus adv panel, Nat Endowment Humanities. *Teaching:* Instr art & photog, Buffalo NAm Indian Cult Ctr, 74-76; lectr Indian art, State Univ NY, Buffalo, 75- *Awards:* Am the Beautiful Fund grant, NY, 74; Creative Artist Pub Serv grant, NY, 76. *Bibliog:* Susan Greenwood (auth), Indian mind, 74, Rebecca Irving (auth), Indian art, 75, Niagara Falls Gazette; Anthony Bannon (auth), CAPS winners, Buffalo Evening News, 77. *Media:* Watercolor, Graphite; Black & White Photog. *Publ:* Illusr (series on local hist), Buffalo Courier Express, 74; illusr, 1975 Festival of american Folklife, Smithsonian Inst Prog, 75; auth, On returning cultural objects, Mus News, 77. *Mailing Add:* 1100 Richards Ave Santa Fe NM 87505

HILL, ROBIN
SCULPTOR
b Houston, Tex, Apr 14, 55. *Study:* Kansas City Art Inst, Mo, BFA, 77. *Work:* Long Island Univ, C W Post Campus, Hillwood Art Gallery, Greenvale, NY; The Metro Companies, Atlanta, Ga; Bingham, Dana, Gould, Attys, Boston, Mass; Champion Int, Rosenthal & Rosenthal, New York; Prudential Insurance Co, Newark, NJ. *Exhib:* Selections, Artists Space, New York, 86; solo exhibits, Lang & O'Hara Gallery, New York, 87, 89 & 91, Brooklyn Union Gas, Lobby Installation, Brooklyn, NY, 92; Material & Abstraction, Kunsthaus, Aarau, Switz & Musëe des Beaux Arts, Lausanne, Switz, 88 & City Gallery, New York, 89; The Inst Contemp Art, PS 2 Mus, 90, Socrates Sculpture Park, Long Island City, 90 & 92; Wax & Lead, Stephen Wirtz Gallery, San Francisco, Calif, 90; White Columns, Benfit Exhib, 91, Organization of Independent Artists, Benefit Exhib, M-13 Gallery, New York, 91. *Teaching:* Vis artist in residence, Middlebury Col, Vt, 89; vis artist, Parsons Sch Design, New York, 91, State Univ Ark, Jonesboro, 91, State Univ New York, Albany, 91; fac, sculpture dept, Parsons Sch Design, New York, 92. *Awards:* Pollack-Krasner Found Fel, 86-90; fel, Nat Endowment Arts, 86; NY Found Arts, 87 & 91. *Bibliog:* Peggy Cyphers (auth), Sculptural works by Robin Hill, Arts Mag, 9/91; George Melrod (auth), Robin Hill at Lang & O'Hara Gallery, Artnews, 9/91; Michael Kimmelman (auth), Six Sculptors, New York Times, 7/31/92. *Mem:* NY Artists Equity. *Media:* Mixed Media. *Dealer:* Lang & O'Hara Gallery 568 Broadway Suite 1007 New York NY 10012. *Mailing Add:* 18 Eckford St Brooklyn NY 11222

HILL, ROBYN LESLEY
PAINTER, DESIGNER
b Sydney, New South Wales, Australia, Apr 28, 42. *Study:* Nat Art Sch, Sydney, Australia, ASTC, 62; studied with Edward Betts, Nita Engle & Fred Leach in USA. *Work:* Key West Mus, Fla; Springfield Mus Art, Utah; Palm Springs Desert Mus, Calif; Nat Arts Club, New York; Canton Art Inst, Ohio; Massillon Mus Invitational, Ohio. *Exhib:* Am Watercolor Soc Traveling Exhib, Salmagundi Club, New York; Nat Watercolor Soc Traveling Exhib, Palm Springs Desert Mus, Calif; Catherine Lorillard Wolfe Nat Exhib, Nat Arts Club, New York; Watercolor USA, Springfield Art Mus, Mo; solo exhib, Moments in Nature, Wagner Gallery, Sydney, Australia; Massilou Mus Invitational, Ohio, 87; Adirondacks Nat Show, NY. *Pos:* Art dir, Am Greetings, (1st woman in marketing) Cleveland; sr prog dir, Those Characters from Cleveland, Ohio. *Teaching:* Art Mistress, Sydney Church of Eng Girls Grammar Sch, Redlands, Sydney, Australia, 62-65. *Awards:* Humana Award, Blue Grass Biennial, Humana Inc; Southern Ohio Bank Award, Ohio Watercolor Soc; Springfield Art Mus Award, Watercolor USA. *Mem:* Watercolor USA; Nat Watercolor Soc; Ohio Watercolor Soc; N Coast Collage Soc; Nat Mus Women in Arts. *Media:* Watercolor, Watermedia. *Publ:* Artists directory, Portfolio 83, Cleaveland, Ohio; article, Palette Talk, No 75 Grumbacher. *Dealer:* A Gallery West 20370 Center Ridge Rd Rocky River OH 44116. *Mailing Add:* 2770 Wildflower Dr Rocky River OH 44116

HILL, WILLIAM MANSFIELD
HISTORIAN, MUSEUM DIRECTOR
b Middlesbrough, England, Dec 4, 25. *Study:* Calif State Univ, San Jose, BA, 49; Univ Calif, Berkeley, MA; Univ Calif, Los Angeles, post grad study with Walter Horn & James Ackerman. *Collections Arranged:* Southern California Regional Print & Drawing Annuals, 73-78 & Four Santa Monica Artists: Stanton MacDonald Wright, John Altoon, Sam Francis, Richard Diebenkorn, 75, Santa Monica Col; and others. *Pos:* Sr cur, Los Angeles Co Mus of Art, Los Angeles, 64-65; assoc dir arts & humanities, Univ Exten, Univ of Calif, Los Angeles, 68-71; dir, Art Gallery, Santa Monica Col, Calif, 73- *Teaching:* Lectr art hist, Otis Art Inst, Los Angeles, 58-71; chmn dept of art & assoc prof art hist, Calif State Univ, Northridge, 65-68. *Awards:* Four Creative Prog Awards, Nat Univ Exten Asn, 68-69. *Bibliog:* Walter W Horn (auth), Medieval origins of the bay system, Soc of Archit Hist J, 58. *Mem:* Western Asn of Art Mus; Col Art Asn. *Res:* Architecture of Constantine; Cathedral of St Pierre; Angouleme; history of 19th and 20th century art history and city planning. *Publ:* Contribr, Handbook, Los Angeles Co Mus of Art, 64. *Mailing Add:* Santa Monica Col 1900 Pico Blvd Santa Monica CA 90405

HILLER, BETTY R
CONSULTANT, APPRAISER
b El Paso, Tex, Sept 25, 25. *Study:* Univ Tex, El Paso; Univ NMex; Univ Southern Calif, BFA, 45; Univ Nebr, Omaha; Creighton Univ. *Pos:* ed arts, Spectrum Page, Sun Newspaper, 68-69; gallery dir, Creighton Univ, Omaha, 68-70; original developer, Children's Mus of Omaha, 75, first mus pres, 77-78; gallery dir, Univ Nebr, Omaha, 76; dir & mgr gallery, Univ Nebr, Omaha, 76-78. *Bibliog:* George Shane (auth), Lubetkin Gallery, Des Moines Register, 62; Elizabeth Flynn (auth), Betty Hiller, painter & gallery director, 76, Omaha World Herald; Beth Weiver (auth), Rancho Bernardo J; Jimmy Thornton (auth), San Diego Union. *Mem:* San Diego Mus Art (trustee); sr mem Am Soc Appraisers; Int Soc Appraisers; Balboa Art Conserv Ctr (trustee). *Mailing Add:* 11937 Bajada Rd San Diego CA 92128

HILLIS, RICHARD K
PAINTER, PRINTMAKER
b Cincinnati, Ohio, Oct 3, 36. *Study:* Ohio Univ, BFA, 60, MFA, 62, Carnegie Mellon Univ, DA (Dr Arts), 73. *Work:* Muscarelle Mus Art, Col William & Mary, Williamsburg, Va; Hoyt Inst Fine Arts, New Castle, Pa; Ark Art Ctr, Little Rock, Ark; Glendale Publ Libr, Ariz; Southwest Airlines. *Exhib:* 49th Ann Midyear Exhib, Butler Inst Am Art, Youngstown, Ohio, 84; Art USA Exhib, Western Colo Ctr Arts, Grand Junction, 86; 64th April Salon, Springville Art Mus, Utah, 88; Am Drawing Biennial, Muscarelle Mus Art, Va, 88; Los Angeles Nat Watercolor Exhib, 91; 35th Chataqua Nat, 92; and many others. *Teaching:* Asst prof art, Kent State Univ, Ohio, 69-73; assoc prof, Tex Tech Univ, Lubbock, 73-74; prof, Glendale Col, Ariz, 82-88. *Awards:* First prize, painting, Two Flags Int Art Exhib, Douglas Art Asn, 87; Award of Excellence, Ariz Aqueuus, 89. *Media:* Oil. *Publ:* Auth, Visual Aspects of Drama, Oriental Arts, London, 69; numerous articles in Design Mag, 70-81; Line Shape & Contrast, Sch Arts Mag, 88; Hooked on Colored Pencils, Sch Arts, 91. *Mailing Add:* 6741 W Cholla Peoria AZ 85345

HILLMAN, ARTHUR STANLEY
GRAPHIC ARTIST, EDUCATOR
b Brooklyn, NY, Feb 21, 45. *Study:* Philadelphia Col Art, with Jerome Kaplan & Benton Spruance, BFA; Univ Mass, Amherst, MFA. *Work:* Libr Congress, Washington, DC; Northern Ill Univ. *Exhib:* 21st & 22nd Nat Exhibs, Libr Cong, Washington, DC, 69 & 71; Prize Winning Am Prints, 69 & 4th Int Miniature Print Exhib, 71, Pratt Graphics Ctr, New York; one-man shows, Philadelphia Art Alliance, 70, Williams Col Mus Art, 76, Simon's Rock Col 83, 84, 90 & 92, & Chiaroscuro Gallery, 84; 29th Nat Print Exhib, Hunterdon Art Ctr, NJ, 85; 16th Nat Works on Paper, Minot State Col, NDak, 86; Northern Nat, Nicolet Col, 89. *Teaching:* Instr & asst prof printmaking & chmn dept, Mass Col Art, Boston, 68-74; prof graphic arts, design & photog, Simon's Rock Col, Great Barrington, Mass, 74-, chmn arts div, 81-84 & 89-92, chmn visual arts prog, 87-89. *Awards:* Univ Mass Fel, 67; Pennell Fund Purchase Award, Libr Cong, 69; Northern Ill Univ Purchase Award, 70. *Mem:* Col Art Asn Am; Philadelphia Print Club; Photog Resource Ctr, Boston Univ; Housatonic Craft Artists' Guild. *Mailing Add:* Dept Art Simons Rock of Bard Col Great Barrington MA 01230

HILLS, PATRICIA
HISTORIAN, CURATOR
b Baraboo, Wis, Jan 31, 36. *Study:* Stanford Univ, BA, 57; Hunter Col, City Univ New York, MA, 68; NY Univ Inst Fine Arts, PhD, 73. *Collections Arranged:* Eastman Johnson (auth, catalog), Clarkson-Potter, 72; The American Frontier: Images and Myths (cur, auth, catalog), 73, Turn-of-the-Century America: Paintings, Graphics, Photographs (auth, catalog), 77 & The Figurative Tradition and the Whitney Museum (coauth, catalog), 80, Whitney Mus Am Art; The Painter's America: Rural and Urban Life, 1810-1910 (cur, auth, catalog), Praeger, 74; John Singer Sargent (cur, auth, catalog), 86. *Pos:* Assoc cur, Whitney Mus Am Art, 72-74, adjunct cur, 74- *Teaching:* Assoc prof, York Col, City Univ New York, 74-78; assoc prof Am painting, Boston Univ, 78-88, prof, 88- *Awards:* Guggenhaim, 82-83; Mid-Career Award, Women's Caucus for Art, 87; W E B DuBois Inst, Harvard Univ, 91-92. *Mem:* Col Art Asn; Women's Caucus for Art; Arch Am Art; Am Studies Asn. *Res:* American painting from Civil War to present, particularly figurative painting; art & politics. *Publ:* Alice Neel, Abrams, 83. *Mailing Add:* Dept Art Hist Boston Univ Boston MA 02215

HILLSMITH, FANNIE
PAINTER, ASSEMBLAGE ARTIST
b Boston, Mass, Mar 13, 11. *Study:* Boston Mus Fine Arts Sch; Art Students League, with Alexander Brook, Kuniyoshi, Zorach & Sloan; Atelier 17, with Stanley Hayter. *Work:* Mus Mod Art, New York; Boston Mus Fine Arts; Currier Gallery Art, Manchester, NH; Fogg Mus Art, Cambridge, Mass; Metrop Mus Art, New York; and others. *Exhib:* Boston Arts Festival, 50-54 & 56-61; Cornell Univ, 64; one-man retrospective, Brockton Mus, Mass, 71, Bristol Mus, RI, 72 & Currier Gallery Art, Manchester, 87; Brattleboro Mus, 74; group show, American Cubism, Sidney Deutsch Gallery, NY, 92. *Teaching:* Vis critic, Black Mountain Col, 45 & Cornell Univ, 63-64. *Awards:* Alumni Traveling Scholar, Boston Mus Fine Arts Sch, 58; Tour Gallery Award, 64; Berkshire Mus Award, 64; and others. *Publ:* Auth & illusr, The Ups and Downs of Needlepoint, Barnes, 76. *Dealer:* Susan Taller Gallery 568 Broadway Rm 405A New York NY 10012; Graham Gallery 1014 Madison Ave New York NY 10021. *Mailing Add:* Wedgwood 21 Gilson Rd Jaffrey NH 03452

HILSON, DOUGLAS
PAINTER, EDUCATOR
b Flint, Mich, Dec 7, 41. *Study:* Cranbrook Acad Art, Bloomfield Hills, Mich, BFA; Univ Wash, MFA. *Work:* Indianapolis Mus Art; Ill Art Mus, Springfield, DeWaters Art Inst, Flint, Mich; Decatur Art Mus, Ill; Western Mich Univ Art Mus, Kalamazoo. *Exhib:* From NY to Newcastle Traveling Exhib, 83-84; one-person shows, Bernice Steinbaum Gallery, New York, 83 & 85; Innagural Exhib, Triaba Gallery, New York, 88; New Still Life, Borgenicht Gallery, New York, 90; and others. *Pos:* Dir, Calkins Art Gallery, Hofstra Univ, Hempstead, NY. *Teaching:* Prof painting & dir grad painting prog, Univ Ill, Champaign, 65-; vis prof, Pratt Inst, 81-; prof art, Hofstra Univ, 86- *Awards:* First Prize, Nat Works Art on Paper, 76; Purchase Award, 29th Ill Invitational, Ill Art Mus Permanent Collection, 76; Ctr Advanced Study, 73-74. *Media:* Oil, Acrylic; Graphite. *Mailing Add:* 407 Greewich St New York NY 10013

HILTS, ALVIN
SCULPTOR
b Newmarket, Ont, Apr 2, 08. *Study:* In Mex & Can. *Work:* Churches, Kirkland Lake, Welland & Newmarket; also in schs. *Comn:* Memorial, Newmarket, 36; Univ Guelph, 61; Univ Lennoxville, 70; also pvt comn, Vancouver, Toronto, Ottawa, Oshawa & St Louis. *Exhib:* Sculpture Soc, 31-72; Royal Can Acad; Ont Soc Artists. *Mem:* Sculpture Soc Can (pres, 57, 58 & 61). *Media:* Wood, Stone. *Mailing Add:* 605 Oshawa Blvd N Oshawa ON L1G 5T8 Canada

HILTY, THOMAS R
GRAPHIC ARTIST, PAINTER
b Gary, Ind, May 29, 43. *Study:* Ind Univ; Western State Col, Colo, BFA, 65; Univ NMex; Bowling Green State Univ, MFA, 68. *Work:* Dayton Art Inst, Ohio; Toledo Mus Art, Ohio; Omni Marketing Inc, Chicago; IBM Corp; Toledo Trust Corp. *Comn:* Frames of Reference, Boston New TV Wrokshop, 79-80; Musical Arts Ctr, Bowling Green State Univ, 80; J Barrett Galleries, Toledo, 82; R Valicenti Design, Chicago, 83; Riverside Hosp, Toledo, 86. *Exhib:* Ankrum Gallery, Los Angeles, 83; US Nat Fine Arts Competition & Int Exhib, 84; 20th Cent Am Drawing, Chicago, 84; Rosenthal Gallery, Chicago, 84 & 86; and others. *Teaching:* Prof art, drawing & painting, Bowling Green State Univ, 68-, dir, Sch Art, 86- *Awards:* Purchase Awards, All Ohio Exhib, Ohio Arts Coun, 72, All Ohio Exhib, Dayton Art Inst, 76, 80 & 81 & Toledo Area Artists Exhib, Toledo Mus, 80, 81, 82, 84 & 85. *Bibliog:* Louise Bruner (auth), Thomas Hilty, Am Artist, 80. *Media:* Graphite, Charcoal, Pastels. *Publ:* Auth, article, Art News, 6/83. *Dealer:* J Rosenthal Fine Arts Ltd 212 W Superior St Suite 200 Chicago IL 60610; Robert L Kidd Assoc Inc 107 Townsend St Birmingham MI 48011. *Mailing Add:* 21 Parkwood Dr Bowling Green OH 43402

HIMMELFARB, JOHN DAVID
PAINTER, GRAPHIC ARTIST
b Chicago, Ill, June 3, 46. *Study:* Harvard Univ, BA, 68, MAT, 70. *Work:* Art Inst Chicago; Nat Mus Am Art, Smithsonian Inst, Washington, DC; Musee Nat d'Art Moderne Centre George Pompidou, Paris, France; Cleveland Art Mus, Ohio; Brooklyn Mus. *Comn:* Ceramic tile mural, Omaha Pub Schs, Nebr, 92. *Exhib:* 19th Ann Print Exhib, 76, American Drawings in Black and White--1970-1980, 80, Monumental Drawings--20 Contemporary Americans, 86, Brooklyn Mus, NY; Works on Paper, 78, Prizewinners Revisited, 79, Prints and Multiples, 81, 81st Chicago and Vicinity Show, 85, Art Inst Chicago; solo exhibs, Terry Dintenfass Gallery, New York, 79, 83, 86, 89 & 91, Huntington Mus Art, WVa, 90; Nat Drawing Invitational, Ark Art Ctr, Little Rock, 88; Prints from Landfall Press, San Antonio Art Inst, 89; Meetings in the Garden: The Art of John Himmelfarb, Kalamazoo Inst Art, 89, Miami Univ Art Mus, Oxford, Ohio, 90, Madison Art Ctr, 90, Ark Art Ctr, Little Rock, 90; Two Generations Chicago--The Influence of Family, Evanston Art Ctr, Ill, 90; and others. *Teaching:* Vis artist, Southern Ill Univ, Carbondale, 86 & 88, Ill State Univ, 86 & 91, Univ Chicago, 86 & Whitman Col, Walla Walla, Washington, 87. *Awards:* Nat Endowment for the Arts, 82 & 85; Pollock-Krasner Found, 86; Ill Arts Coun, 86. *Bibliog:* L G Hoffman (auth), The Artist as Translator (catalog), Davenport, Iowa, 1/86; Frederick Ted Castle (auth), John Himmelfarb at Terry Dintenfass, Art in Am, 12/87; Michael Bonesteel & Helen Sheridan (coauths), Meetings in the Garden--the Art of John Himmelfarb (catalog, essays), Kalamazoo Inst Art, 90. *Media:* Oil. *Publ:* Lumber Street Meeting, Landfall Press, 88. *Dealer:* Terry Dintenfass 50 W 57th St New York NY. *Mailing Add:* 2400 S Oakley 2R Chicago IL 60608

HINDES, CHUCK (CHARLES AUSTIN)
CERAMIST, EDUCATOR
b Muskegon, Mich, May 30, 42. *Study:* Univ Ill, Urbana-Champaign, BFA(crafts), 66; RI Sch Design, MFA(ceramics), 68. *Work:* St Louis Mus Art; Everson Mus Art. *Exhib:* Teapots, De Pauw Univ, Greencastle, Ind, 91; Redefining Clay, St Louis, Mo, 91; Contemporary Views: Teapots, Pro-Art Gallery, St Louis, Mo, 92; Teapot Exhibition, Octagon Art Ctr, Ames, 92; One on One, group exhib, Northwest Craft Ctr, Seattle, Wash, 92; and others. *Teaching:* Instr ceramics, Univ Fla, Gainesville, 69-72; adj prof, RI Sch Design, 72-73; from asst prof to prof, Univ Iowa, Iowa City, 73- *Awards:* Purchase Award, Nat Exhib Ceramic Sculpture & Jewelry, Brigham Young Univ, 76; First Prize Ceramics, 32nd Ann Iowa Artists Exhib, Des Moines Art Ctr, 80; Hon Mention Int Ceramics Festival, Mino, Japan; Hon Mention, The Dripless Spout: Innovative Teapots, Arrowmont Sch, 88. *Mem:* Nat Coun Educ Ceramic Arts. *Publ:* Auth, Saggar firing, Studio Potter, 79. *Mailing Add:* 728 E Fairchild Iowa City IA 52240

HINES, JESSICA
PHOTOGRAPHER
b St Louis, Mo, Nov 4, 58. *Study:* St Louis Community Col, Meremec, AA, 80, Washington Univ, St Louis, BFA, 82; Univ Ill, Champaign-Urbana, MFA, 84. *Work:* Erie Art Mus, Pa. *Exhib:* Alternatives, Ohio Univ, Athens, 84; Photonational, Erie Art Ctr, Pa, 84; Light Sensitive, Univ Fla, Gainesville, 84; After Her Own Image, Fine Art Ctr, Salem Col, Winston-Salem, NC, 85; Dream Series, Elgin Community Col, Ill, 85, Duke Univ, NC, 85-86, Women's Study Workshop, Rosendale, 86; Second Annual Photo Salon, Nexus Contemp Art Ctr, Atlanta, 86; Atlanta 2nd Ann Photo Salon, 86 & Artists in Georgia, 88, Nexus Contemp Art Ctr; Fantasy Landscapes, Tampa Mus Art, Fla, 87; St Louis Community Col, Meramec Gallery, Mo, 88; solo exhib, Ark State Univ Gallery, Jonesboro, 88. *Teaching:* Instr photog, Univ Ill, 83-84; asst prof photog, Ga Southern Col, 84- *Mem:* Soc Photog Educ. *Mailing Add:* 28 N Easy St Statesboro GA 30458

HINKHOUSE, FOREST MELICK
CONSULTANT
b West Liberty, Iowa, July 7, 25. *Study:* Coe Col, AB; Univ Mex; Fogg Art Mus, Harvard Univ; NY Univ Inst Fine Arts, MA; Univ Madrid, PhD; Eureka Col, DHL, 83. *Collections Arranged:* Industrial Gouaches of John Hultberg, 57; Paintings & Portraits by Frank Mason, 58; Contemporary Arizona Painting, 58; Festival of Arts, 58; One Hundred Years of French Painting 1860-1960, 61; English Landscape Painting, 61. *Pos:* Pub relations, Int House Asn, New York; art critic, Buffalo Eve News, Ariz Repub & Phoenix Gazette; founding dir, Phoenix Art Mus & Phoenix Fine Arts Asn, 57-67; co-founder, Hinkhouse Gallery, Coe Col, 65; consult & adv, Phoenix Art Mus, 67-; consult, Calif Art Comn, 68-; co-founder, Hinkhouse Collection, Melick Libr, Eureka Col, 69; mem bd trustees, Coe Col, Cedar Rapids, Iowa; founder, Hinkhouse Gallery Art, Stephens Col, Columbia, Mo; founder, Forest Melick Hinkhouse Collection, Lakeview Mus Arts & Sci, Peoria, 86. *Teaching:* Asst prof art, Albright Art Sch, Univ Buffalo, 56-57; guest lectr, Prudential Lines, 77. *Mem:* Claustro Extraordinario, Madrid; Col Art Asn Am; Am Asn Mus. *Publ:* Auth, Catalogue of the Collections of the Phoenix Art Museum; contribr, articles in Oregonian, 75- *Mailing Add:* 1815 Jones St Russian Hill San Francisco CA 94109

HINMAN, CHARLES B
PAINTER, SCULPTOR
b Syracuse, NY, Dec 29, 32. *Study:* Syracuse Univ, BFA, 55; Art Students League, with Morris Kantor. *Work:* Mus Mod Art, New York; Whitney Mus Am Art, New York; Los Angeles Co Mus; Hirshhorn Mus, Smithsonian Inst, Washington, DC; Mus Mod Art, Nagaoka, Japan; Louisiana Mus, Humlebaek, Denmark; and many others. *Comn:* Red Vista, 3-D painting, Continental Group, Stamford, Conn, 81; Excelsior, 3-D painting, Southeast Bank, Miami, Fla, 83; Adretto, 3-D painting, Europ Am Bank, Huntington, NY, 85; Aviary, suspended 3-D painting, Greenway Plaza, Hempstead, NY, 86; Zephyr, stainless steel sculpture, Burton Resnick, New York, 87. *Exhib:* Smithsonian Inst, Washington, DC, 68; Honolulu Acad Arts, Hawaii, 68; Mus Mod Art, New York, 69; Whitney Mus Am Art, New York, 69; Aldrich Mus Contemp Art, Ridgefield, Conn, 71, 75 & 77; solo exhibs, Irving Galleries, Milwaukee, 77, Palm Beach, 77-87, Donald Morris Gallery, Birmingham, Mich, 79, Galleri Bellman, New York, 83, Virginia Lust Gallery, New York, 89, Douglas Drake Gallery, New York, 90; Laguna Gloria Mus, Austin, Tex; Mus of Art, Ft Lauderdale, Fla, 80-81; Hickory Mus, NC, 90-92. *Pos:* Artist in residence, Aspen Inst, Colo, 66. *Teaching:* Instr painting, Cornell Univ, New York, 67-68, Syracuse Univ, 71, Pratt Inst, Brooklyn, 75, Sch Visual Arts, New York, 76, Cooper Union, New York, currently. *Awards:* Int Prize Exhib, Torcuato di Tella, Buenos Aires, 57; First Prize, Mus Contemp Art, Nagoako, Japan, 65; Grant, Nat Endowment Arts, 80; and others. *Media:* Acrylic, Pigment on Fabric; Metals, Wood. *Dealer:* Hinman Studios 231 Bowery New York NY 10002. *Mailing Add:* 231 Bowery New York NY 10002

HINSON, TOM EVERETT
CURATOR, HISTORIAN
b Henderson, Tex, Oct 25, 44. *Study:* Univ Tex, Austin, BA(art hist), BS(archit studies); Case Western Reserve Univ, Cleveland, Ohio, MA(art hist). *Pos:* Mus fel, Toledo Mus Art, Ohio, 70-71; Asst cur, Dept Mod Art, Cleveland Mus Art, Ohio, 73-77, assoc cur, 78-81, cur contemp art, 82- *Mem:* Am Asn Mus. *Res:* Contemporary and modern art; 19th and 20th century photography; 20th century architecture. *Mailing Add:* c/o Cleveland Mus of Art 11150 E Blvd Cleveland OH 44106

HIOS, THEO
PAINTER, GRAPHIC ARTIST
b Sparta, Greece, Feb 2, 08; US citizen. *Study:* Am Artists Sch; Art Students League; Pratt Inst; Nat Univ Athens. *Work:* Carnegie Inst, Pittsburgh; Nat Collection Fine Art, Washington, DC; Guild Hall Mus, Easthampton, NY; Parrish Art Mus, Southampton, NY; Nat Pinokothiki Mus, Athens, Greece; plus others. *Exhib:* Brooklyn Mus, 58; one-man retrospective, Harpur Col, 61; Nat Exhib, Pa Acad Fine Arts, 62; one-man shows, Watermill Mus-Retrospective 87, Goat Alley Gallery, 87, Benton Gallery, 87 & 88, Clayton & Liberatore Gallery, 90; solo exhib, Pinakothiki Mus, Sparta, Greece, 89; Long Island Univ, Southampton, NY, 90; and others. *Teaching:* Instr painting & drawing, City Col New York, 58-61; instr painting & drawing, Dalton Sch, 62-73; instr painting & drawing, New Sch Social Res, 62- *Awards:* First Prize, New Eng Exhib, Silvermine Guild Artists, 48; Purchase Awards, Guild Hall Mus, 69 & Parish Art Mus, 70; Adolph & Esther Gottlieb Found Grant $10, 000, 81; and others. *Bibliog:* Articles, Southampton Press, 87, 88 & 90; Article, NY Times, 90; Theo Hios, 52 Years of Painting, 87; and others. *Mem:* Fedn Mod Painters & Sculptors (vpres, 57-62 & 66-75); Audubon Artists. *Media:* Oil, Acrylic; Pastel, Watercolor. *Publ:* Auth, Theu Hias 52 Years of Painting, 87. *Mailing Add:* 136 W 95th St New York NY 10025

HIRONDELLE, ANNE E
CERAMIST
Study: Univ Puget Sound, BA, 66; Stanford Univ, MA, 67; Factory Visual Art, Ceramics Prog, 73-74; Univ Wash, BFA prog, 74-76. *Work:* Ariz State Univ; Howard & Gwen Laurie Smits Collection, Los Angeles Co Mus Art; JMB Realty Co, Chicago; Nora Eccles Harrison Mus Art, Utah State Univ; Pacific Lutheran Univ; also pvt collections of Sanford M Besser, Daniel Jacobs, Jack Lenor Larsen & others. *Exhib:* Solo-exhibs, Foster/White Gallery, Seattle, Wash, 89 & 92, Garth Clark Gallery, Kansas City, Mo, 90, New York, 92, The Works Gallery, Philadelphia, Pa, 91, Maveety Gallery, Salishan, Ore, 91, The Hard and the Spirit, Joanne Rapp Gallery, Scottsdale, Ariz, 91 & Schneider-Bluhm-Loeb Gallery, Chicago, Ill, 92; Teapot Invitational, Pro Art Gallery, St Louis, Mo, 92; 100 Cups, invitational, Pro Art Gallery, St Louis, Mo, 92; Spirit of the West, curated travelling exhib, Idaho, Ore & Wash, 92; Built, Thrown and Touched: Contemporary Clay Works, 2-3 yr travelling exhib, Media Gallery/Enterprises, Garnett, Kans, 92; and others. *Pos:* Var workshops, lect & artist-in-residences, 78-92. *Awards:* Visual Arts Fel, Nat Endowment Arts, 88; $1000 First Place Award, Cedar Creek Nat Teapot Show, 89; First Place Award, Women in Washington: The First Century, 89. *Bibliog:* Martha Drexler Lynn (auth), Clay Today, Contemporary Ceramists and Their Work, Los Angeles Co Mus Art, Chronicle Bks, San Francisco, 90; Northwest Originals - Washington Women and Their Art, MatriMedia Inc, Portland, Ore; Edward J Sozanski (auth), on Galleries, Philadelphia Inquirer, 6/91; and others. *Publ:* Auth, Deliberations, Ceramics Monthly, summer 86; Teapot as Metaphor, Ceramics Rev, July/88. *Mailing Add:* c/o Foster/White Gallery 311 1/2 Occidental Ave S Seattle WA 98104

HIRSCH, GILAH YELIN
PAINTER, WRITER
b Montreal, PQ, Aug 24, 44. *Study:* McGill Univ; Hebrew Univ; Sir George Williams Univ; Boston Univ; San Francisco State Univ; Univ Calif, Berkeley, BA, 67; Univ Calif, Los Angeles, MFA, 70. *Work:* Security Pac Banks, Calif State Univ & Greenberg & Glusken, Los Angeles; City of Santa Monica Art Bank, Calif; Nat Endowment Arts, Washington, DC; Charles Wustum Mus Fine Arts, Racine, Wis. *Exhib:* Whitney Mus Am Art, New York, 72; Pasadena Mus, Calif, 73; Los Angeles Inst Contemp Art, Calif, 74; Suffolk Mus, New York, 74; Neue Geselshaft, Berlin, Ger, 77; solo exhibs, Space, Los Angeles, Calif, 81, Reed Whipple Cultural Ctr, Las Vegas, 84, Turnbull Lutjeans Kogan, Costa Mesa, Calif, 84, Alligator, San Francisco, 88, Merging One, Santa Monica, Calif, 88-89, SPARC, Venice, Calif, 88-89 & Univ Calif, Irvine, 90, 91, 92 & 93; Univ Calif, Irvine, 83; Univ Calif, Los Angeles, 84; Orange County Ctr Arts, Calif, 87; Loyola Marymount Univ, Los Angeles, Calif, 88; Santa Barbara Contemp Arts Forum, Calif, 91. *Collections Arranged:* Metamagic (auth, catalog), Calif State Univ, Dominguez Hills, 78. *Teaching:* Prof art, Calif State Univ, Dominguez Hills, 73-; fac tutors, Int Col, 80- *Awards:* Dorland Mountain Colony Fel, 81 & 83; Award, Banff Ctr for the Arts, 85; Nat Endowment Arts Fel, 85; Rockefeller Bellasio Grant, 92. *Bibliog:* Articles in over 75 international newspapers, journals & magazines. *Mem:* Artists Equity. *Media:* Oil, Acrylic. *Publ:* Auth, Joan of art seminars, Artweek, 72; Emily Carr, Feminist Art J, 76; The Pararational, Visionary and Mystical Pespective, Calif State Univ, Dominguez Hills, 77; Emily Carr, Women's Studies, 78; Persistence of time and memory: The art of Ruth Weisberg, Womans Art J, winter 85; The illusion of potential: The delusion of the creative person in relationships, The Quest, autumn 92. *Mailing Add:* Dept Art Calif State Univ Dominguez Hills 1000 E Victoria Ave Carson CA 90747

HIRSCHFELD, ALBERT
GRAPHIC ARTIST
b St Louis, Mo, June 21, 03. *Study:* Nat Acad Design, New York; Julien's, Paris; London Co Coun; Art Students League; Hartford Univ, hon DFA. *Work:* Whitney Mus Am Art, Mus Mod Art, Metrop Mus Art, New York; Brooklyn Mus Art, NY; William Hayes Fogg Mus, Boston. *Comn:* History of Cinema, Fifth Ave Playhouse, New York, 45; Personalities, Eden Roc Hotel, Miami, Fla, 55; American Theatre, Brussels World's Fair, 59. *Exhib:* One-man shows, Staten Island Mus, NY, 61, Hammer Gallery, New York, 67, Mus Performing Arts, Lincoln Ctr, New York, 68, Margo Feiden Gallery, New York, 72-74 & Seibu Gallery, Tokyo, Japan, 75; Gallery 18, London, Eng, 77; Fogg Mus & Posey Libr, Harvard Univ, Cambridge, Mass, 83; Gracie Mansion, New York, 83. *Pos:* Theatre caricaturist, New York Times, 23- *Awards:* Nat Soc Arts & Lett, 81; Special Tony Award, 84; Theater Hall of Fame, 89; and others. *Mem:* The Players Club. *Media:* Ink. *Publ:* Auth, The World of Hirschfeld, Abrams, 71; Kabuki, Goodstadt, 76; The Entertainers, Elm Tree, London, 77; Hirschfeld by Hirschfeld, Dodd, Mead, 79; Art & Recollections from 8 Decades, Scribners, 91; and others. *Mailing Add:* 122 E 95th St New York NY 10028

HIRSCHFIELD, JIM
SCULPTOR, ARCHITECT
Study: Kan City Art Inst, Mo, BFA, 73-76; Univ Ore, Eugene, MFA, 76-78. *Comn:* Connomara Found, Dallas, Tex; Mass Coun Arts, Bunker Hill Col, Charlestown, Mass; Wash State Arts Comn, Glenn Terrell Mall, Design Team, Pullman; Duke Med Ctr, Durham, NC; Pub Art Works, San Rafael, Calif. *Exhib:* Solo exhibs, Wake Forest Univ, Winston-Salem, NC, 90, Nexus Contemp Arts Ctr, Atlanta, Ga, 91, Sarratt Gallery, Vanderbilt Univ, Nashville, Tenn, 91, Walker's Point Ctr Arts, Milwaukee, Wis, 92, Kala Inst, Berkeley, Calif, 92; Atlanta Col Art, 90, The Bathhouse Exhib, Arts Festival, Atlanta, Ga, 91; Weatherspoon Gallery, Greensboro, NC, 90; Sculptor Tour, Univ Tenn, Knoxville, 92. *Teaching:* Asst prof, Univ NC, Chapel Hill, 88- *Awards:* Nat Endowment Arts, 80, 86, 89 & 90; Publ Grant, 91 & Res Grant, 92, Univ NC; NC Arts Coun Fel, La Napoule, France, 91. *Bibliog:* Jim Hirschfield Observatory, Wake Forest Univ, Winston-Salem, 91; 38th Arts Festival Atlanta, Ga, 91; Public Art Proposals, Int Contemp Art Fair, Yokohama, 92. *Mailing Add:* 410 Franklin E Chapel Hill NC 27514

HIRSH, ANNETTE MARIE
SILVERSMITH, GOLDSMITH
b Milwaukee, Wis, Oct 20, 21. *Study:* Milwaukee State Teachers Col, 39-41; Milwaukee Area Tech Col, 53-57;. *Work:* Milwaukee Art Mus, Baron Mus Judaica, Milwaukee, Wis; Madagascar Nat Mus; Israeli Embassy, Washington, DC. *Comn:* Silver spice-box, North Shore Congregation Israel, Glencoe, Ill, 70; silver kiddush cup, Shalom Temple, Sun City, Ariz, 76; silver rimonim & torah pointer, Congregation Emanuel, Chicago, Ill, 81; breast-plate (silver & semi-precious stones), Sinai Temple, Champaign, Ill, 85; Holecaust Mem (brass & wood), Milwaukee Jewish Home, 90. *Exhib:* Biennial Painting & Sculpture, Walker Art Inst, Minneapolis, Minn, 47; Small Sculpture, Ball State Col, Muncie, Ind, 65, 67 & 68; Religious Art, Cranbrook Acad, Bloomfield Hills, Mich, 66; Mississippi River Craft Show, Brooks Mem Art Gallery, Memphis, Tenn, 69; Chicago and Vicinity Biennial, Chicago Art Inst, 77; Chicago Area Jewish Artists, Spertus Mus, Chicago, 85; Contemp Artifacts, Nat Mus Am Jewish Hist, 87, 88, 89, 90 & 91. *Collections Arranged:* Old Testament, 72 & Exodus, 74, Milwaukee Jewish Community Ctr. *Pos:* Illusr, Boston Store, Milwaukee, Wis, 42-44 & Goldblatt's Dept Store, Chicago, Ill, 44-46; mus chmn & cur, Baron Judaica Mus, Milwaukee, 70- *Teaching:* Teacher drawing & watercolor, Milwaukee Area Tech Col, Wis, 68- *Awards:* Purchase Award, Wis Designer Crafts Exhib, Milwaukee Art Mus, 64; Sculpture Award, Wright Art Ctr, Beloit, Wis, 66; Purchase Award, Mizel Mus Judaica, Denver, Colo, 86. *Bibliog:* Bob Orvis (auth), Point of view, Milwaukee Mag, 2/78; James Auer (auth), Hebrew imagery, an updating, Milwaukee J, 4/5/81; Rachel Heimovics (auth), The Chicago Jewish Source Book, 81; James Auer (auth), Dual Show, Milwaukee Jour, 11/19/89. *Mem:* Wis Designer Crafts Coun (treas, 60-66); Soc NAm Goldsmiths. *Media:* Metal Jewelry; Small Sculpture, Judaica Objects. *Mailing Add:* 4124 N Ardmore Ave Milwaukee WI 53211

HIRSHFIELD, PEARL
PAINTER, SCULPTOR
US citizen. *Study:* Sch of the Art Inst Chicago, BA, 79; Northwestern Univ, Columbia Col. *Work:* The Peace Mus, Chicago, Ill; many pvt collections; Franklin Furnace Mus Archives, New York. *Exhib:* Whirlpool Found traveling exhib, 86; Nat Sculpture Conf/Works by Women, Cincinnati, Ohio, 87; Nat Holocaust Mem Competition, Scarsdale, NY, 88; Gimme Shelter, nat traveling exhib, Peace Mus, Chicago, Ill, 88; Nuclear War Game Plan, Hiroshima, Japan, 89; Art Forms, 90, 18th Biennial Competition, Mus Art, Lafayette, Ind, 90; Nat Invitational, Franklin Furnace Mus, New York, 91; Int exhib, Palais de Congres, Montreux, Switz, 92. *Pos:* Film coordr, Peace Productions, Inc, 83; art adv & consult, Gallery Workshop, Evanston, Ill. *Awards:* Technical Assistance Grant, 83, Sculpture Grant, 84, Fel Award-Visual Arts, 86, Ill Arts Coun; Whirlpool Found Sculpture Competition Prize, 86; Bill of Rights Award for art work by Citizens Alert Orgn, 91. *Mem:* Assoc mem, Int Soc for Arts, Sci & Technol; Nat Women's Caucus for Art; Chicago Artists Coalition. *Media:* All Media. *Publ:* Auth, Limited Edition Portfolio of 13 Major Artists, Ctr Constitutional Rights, New York, 72; Conspiracy, The Artist as Witness, Godine Press; Sculptural Constructions Involving Water Dynamics, Leonardo, Pergamon Press, Vol 18, Issue 3. *Mailing Add:* 1333 Ridge Ave Evanston IL 60201

HITCH, JEAN LEASON
PAINTER
b Sydney, Australia, Oct 18, 18; US citizen. *Study:* Melbourne Tech Art Training Sch, Australia; Leason Sch Painting; Wayman Adams Sch Painting, Adirondacks, NY. *Work:* Dr Hall, Cape Cod Community Col; Co Sheriff Gerry Bowes, Barnstable Co Ct House, Cape Cod; Dr Irving Bartlett, Cape Cod Community Col, 92. *Comn:* Buccaneer, Mass Maritime Acad, 82. *Exhib:* Allied Artists Am, Am Artist Prof League & Catharine Lorillard Wolfe Art Club, New York; Hudson Valley Art Asn, White Plains, NY; Audubon Artists, New York. *Pos:* Art cur, Staten Island Inst Arts & Sci, 45-51; dir & owner, Dennis Common Fine Art Gallery. *Teaching:* Instr painting, Cape Cod Art Asn, currently. *Awards:* Anna Hyatt Huntington Horse-Head Award, 72; Bronze Medal, Cape Cod Art Asn, 77; Margaret Dole Portrait Award, 91. *Mem:* Cape Cod Art Asn; Allied Artists Am; Catharine Lorillard Wolfe Art Club; Hudson Valley Art Asn; Am Artist Prof League. *Media:* Oil. *Mailing Add:* 51 Gordon Lane Yarmouth Port MA 02675

HITCH, ROBERT A
PAINTER
b Brooklyn, NY, May 12, 20. *Study:* Art Career Sch, New York; also painting with Wilford S Conrow, Percy Leason, Douglas Grant & Marshall Joyce. *Work:* Hickory Art Mus, NC; Tamassee DAR Sch, SC. *Exhib:* Allied Artists Am & Am Artists Prof League, New York; Hudson Valley Art Asn, White Plains, NY; Staten Island Mus Arts & Sci, NY; Nat Arts Club, New York. *Teaching:* Instr painting, Cape Cod Art Asn. *Awards:* Henry Ward Ranger Prize, Nat Acad Design, 54; Grand Nat Award, Am Artists Prof League, 54; Best Cape Cod Scene, Cape Cod Art Asn & Best Oil Painting, 85. *Mem:* Allied Artists Am (pub rels, 69-); Cape Cod Art Asn; Copley Soc of Boston; Hudson Valley Art Asn; Am Artists Prof League. *Media:* Oil. *Mailing Add:* 51 Gordon Lane Yarmouth Port MA 02675

HITCH, STEWART
PAINTER
b Lincoln, Neb, Feb 26, 40. *Study:* Univ Neb, BFA, 64, MFA, 68. *Work:* Aldrich Mus Contemp Art, Ridgefield, Conn; Ewing Mus Art, Normal, Ill; Cornell Univ, Ithaca, NY; Brooklyn Mus, NY; Nat Gallery Art, Washington, DC. *Exhib:* Aldrich Mus, Ridgefield, Conn, 73; New Acquisitions, Ewing Mus, Normal, Ill, 74; American Painting: The 80's, Grey Gallery, NY Univ, 79, Am Ctr, Paris, 80 & Mus Contemp Art, Houston, 80; Painting Up Front, Cornell Univ Mus, Ithaca, NY, 81; Surface & Texture, Mus Mod Art, New York, 81; one-man show, Jack Shainman Gallery, 86; group show, Jack Shainman Gallery, 87; Ruth Siegle Contemp Art, New York, 90. *Teaching:* Artist in residence, Fla Int Univ, Miami, 73; vis artist, Syracuse Univ, 83-86, NY Univ, 87; substitute, NY Univ, 88 & Cooper Union, 89. *Awards:* Nat Endowment Arts Award, 87; Adolph & Esther Godley Found Award, 92. *Bibliog:* Anita Feldman (auth), Space & subjectivity, Art Forum, 10/79; Hilton Kramer (auth), Neo-Modernists, New York Times, 10/23/79; Ted Bonin (auth), Stewart Hitch: New paintings, Arts Mag, 2/83. *Media:* Oil, Acrylic. *Dealer:* Ruth Siegel New York NY. *Mailing Add:* 85 Mercer St New York NY 10012

HITNER, CHUCK
PAINTER, EDUCATOR
b Nashville, Tenn, Sept 10, 43. *Study:* Mid Tenn State Univ, with David LeDoux, BS(art), 67; Southern Ill Univ, Carbondale, MFA(painting & drawing), 68. *Work:* Chrysler Mus, Norfolk, Va; Southern Ill Univ, Carbondale; Allersmaborg, Ezinge, Neth; Tucson Mus Art, Ariz. *Exhib:* Calif State Poly-Tech Univ, Pomona, Calif, 81; Triton Mus Art, Santa Clara, Calif, 84; Mus Art, Univ Ariz, Tucson, 87; Univ Ctr Gallery, Univ Mont, Missoula, 88; Traditions 3 Thousand Gallery, New York, 88; Pentonville Gallery, London, Eng, 88; Allersmaborg, Ezinge (Gr), Neth, 88; Roland Gibson Gallery, State Univ NY, Potsdam, 88; Selections 45, Drawing Ctr, New York, 89. *Teaching:* Asst prof painting & drawing, Eastern Ky Univ, 69-72; assoc prof painting & drawing, Univ Ariz, 72-82, prof, 82-; prof, Univ Ariz, Tucson, 82- *Bibliog:* Donald Kuspit, Chuck Hitner: Recent Work (catalog), Mus Art, Univ Ariz, Tuscon, Ariz, 87; Robert Quinn, Frantic images from a calm hand, Artspace Mag, 85; Marcia Tucker, 20 Arizona artists (catalog), Phoenix Art Mus, 78. *Media:* Drawing, Painting. *Mailing Add:* 3839 E Calle Ensenada Tucson AZ 85716

HLAVINA, RASTO R(ASTISLAV)
SCULPTOR
b Topolcany, Slovakia, June 5, 43; Can citizen. *Study:* Art Col, Bratislava, with A Drexler & L Korkos, dipl(sculpture), 62; Nat Conservation & Restoration Inst, Pelhrimov, with Vaclav Vanek, 66; Cult DFA, W Univ Ariz, 88. *Work:* Hakone Open-Air Mus; Utsukushi-Ga-Hara Open-Air Mus; Slovak Nat Gallery. *Comn:* Restorations: Altarpiece Dobra Voda, 64-65, Loreta, Royal Summer Palace, Prague, 65 & Monastery Libr Cistercian Abbey, Vyssi Brod, 65-66, Nat Heritage Inst, Prague; sculpture, Melody, Prov Gov, Japan, 88. *Exhib:* Look, Pub Art Gallery Sarnia, Ont, 82; Synthesis: Idea and Form, Multicult Mus & Gallery, Toronto, 82; New Artists, New York, 82; Artists of Czechoslovak Origin, Univ Pittsburgh, 82; CKOC Arts Hamilton, Art Gallery Hamilton, 82-83; Int Juried Art Competition/Exhib, by IJAC, New York, 85; First & Second Rodin Grand Prize Exhib, Hakone Open-Air Mus, 86-87. *Pos:* Conservator & restorer fine arts, Nat Conservation & Restoration Inst Fine Arts, Pelhrimov, Czech, 64-66; art dir, MIER Nat Enterprise, Topolcany, Czech, 67-68. *Awards:* Merit Distinction, Expo Brno, 67; Award, Outstanding Achievement in Sculpture, IJAC, New York, 85; Superior Prize, 1st Rodin Grand Prize Exhib, Hakone Open-Air Mus, 86; Superior Prize, 2nd Rodin Grand Prize Exhib, Hakone Open-Air Mus, 88. *Bibliog:* Jenny Bergin (auth), Sculptor takes your all, Ottawa Citizen, 10/28/72; Nancy Baele (auth), Perseverance pays off, Citizen, 11/26/81; Margarat Virany (auth), Aylmer sculptor starts art movement, Aylmer Bulletin, 12/17/81; Celina Bell (auth), Area artists to exhibit with best in New York, Citizen, 8/23/85. *Media:* All. *Publ:* Auth, Legacy of Vinland: The Multiple Sculpture, pvt publ, 81; Introduction, Multiple Sculpture and the Multiple Art, ABIRA Digest, Spring, 88; Collection of postal cards Les Artistes et Matres du XXe siecle (Artists & Masters of XXth Century), Inclusion in The Golden Book for Art Collectors and Art Lovers, Arts et Images du Monde, Paris, France; Inclusion in The Golden Book for Art Collectors and Art Lovers, Arts et Images du Monde, Paris, France. *Mailing Add:* 1769 Rte 148 Luskville Pontiac PQ J0X 2G0 Canada

HO, FRANCIS T
PHOTOGRAPHER, EDUCATOR
b Honolulu, Hawaii, Aug 29, 38. *Study:* Yale Univ, BFA, 61; Rochester Inst Technol, MFA, 67. *Work:* Nikon Camera Co, New York; Canon Photo Gallery, Amsterdam; Photo Gallery Int, Tokyo; Silver Image Gallery, Seattle. *Comn:* Photograph, Seattle Arts Comn, 83. *Exhib:* Focus Gallery, San Francisco, 73; A Temporary Possession: The Human Image in 20th Century Photography, Wash State Univ Mus Art, 76; solo exhibs, Canon Photo Gallery, Amsterdam, 77 & Photo Gallery Int, Tokyo, 80; Fantastic Photography in the USA, Mus Fundacio Miro, Barcelona, 78, Hall Palais Beaux Arts, Brussels, 78 & Mus Mod Art, Mexico City, 79. *Teaching:* Prof photog & graphic design, Wash State Univ, 67-; exchange prof graphic design, Nihon Univ, Tokyo, 79-80. *Awards:* Cert Excellence, Exhib Communication Graphics, Am Inst Graphic Arts, 74-75; Merit Award, The One Show, New York Art Dirs Club, 75; Award Excellence, 16th Ann Exhib, Communication Arts Mag, 75. *Bibliog:* Drukkerij Rosbeek (auth), Hose Valley, Hoensbroek, Neth, 76; Attilio Columbo (auth), Fantastic Photographs, Random House & Gordon Frazer, 79; Yaomi Yoshikawa (auth), article, Commercial Photo, Japan, 80; Tokumi Sawamoto (auth), article, Camera Mainichi, Tokyo, 2/80. *Mem:* Friends Photog. *Mailing Add:* 1045 NE Duncan Lane Pullman WA 99163

HOADLEY, THOMAS A
CERAMIST
Study: Skowhegan Sch Painting & Sculpture, Maine, 70; Amherst Col, Mass, BA(cum laude), 71; Apprentice to Malcolm Wright, Marlboro, Vt, 74; Ill State Univ, Normal, MS(ceramics), 77. *Exhib:* One-man shows, Jackie Chalkley Gallery, Washington, DC, 81 & 83, Clay Pot, Brooklyn, 82, 83 & 84, Venture Gallery, Lathrup Village, Mich, 83 & 85, Elaine Potter Gallery, San Francisco, Calif & Swan Gallery, Philadlephia, Pa, 84, Lawrence Gallery, Portland, Ore, 87 & Mendelson Gallery, Washington Depot, Conn, 88 & 91; Porcelain Invitational, Holsten Galleries, Palm Beach, Fla, 81; Clay Invitational, DBR Gallery, Cleveland, Ohio, 83; Malcolm Wright & Apprentices, Benchmarks Gallery, Washington, DC, 85; Int Ceramics Festival, Mino, Japan, 86; Art that Works: Decorative Arts of the Eighties, Crafted in America, Mint Mus Art, Charlotte, NC, 90. *Awards:* Franklin Mint Ceramics Award, Philadelphia Craft Show, 88; Award Excellence, Wash Craft Show, 89; Visual Artists Fel, Nat Endowment Arts, 90 & 92. *Bibliog:* Donald E Frith (auth), Moldmaking for Ceramics, Chilton Bk Co, 85; Paula Deitz (auth), American pottery, NY Times Mag-Home Design, 4/13/86; Peter Lane (auth), Ceramic Form, Design & Decoration, Rizzoli, New York, 88. *Mailing Add:* Box 372 Lanesborough MA 01237

HOARE, TYLER JAMES
SCULPTOR, PRINTMAKER
b Joplin, Mo, June 5, 40. *Study:* Univ Colo, 59; Sculpture Ctr, New York, 60; Univ Kans, BFA, 63; Calif Col Arts & Crafts, Oakland, 66; Univ Arti, Italia, Hon Dipl Merit. *Work:* US Info Agency, Washington, DC; State Univ NY Albany; Oakland Mus, Calif; Calif Col Arts & Crafts; and many pvt collections. *Exhib:* One-man shows, John Bolles Gallery, San Francisco, Calif, 69, 71 & 74, Camberwell Sch Art, London, Eng, 71, Cent Sch Art & Design, London, 74, Purdue Univ, Gallery 1, West Lafayette, Ind, 76 & Geotrope Gallery, Berkeley, Calif, 81; 22nd Nat Print Exhib, Libr Cong, Washington, DC, 71; Xerographic Art, Xerox Corp, New York; Int Mail Art, Guanajuato, Mex, 81; The Centre Documentazione Organizzazione, Parma, Italy, 82; Works by California Cookbook Artists, San Francisco Mus Mod Art, 82 & Artists, in the Spotlight, 84; Whitney Mus Am Art Libr, 83; Gracie Mansion Gallery, New York, 83; Contemporary Suprealism Slide Lecture, San Francisco Art Inst, Calif, 84; plus many others. *Pos:* Guest cur, Magic Machine, Ctr Gallery, Univ Calif, San Francisco, 73 & The Trading Company, 74 & Ctr Visual Arts Catalog, Oakland, 82. *Teaching:* Guest lectr, San Francisco Art Inst, 72, San Francisco State Univ, 72-75, Oakland Mus, Calif, 74, Calif State Univ, Hayward, 74 & 79, Col of San Mateo, 75, Mo Southern State Col, 79, Univ Wyo, Laramie, 79, Colo State Univ, 79, Solano Community, Suisun City, Calif, 83 & Calif Col Arts & Crafts, 84; instr, Univ Calif, Berkeley, 73-74. *Awards:* 2nd Ann Graphic Exhib, Olive Hyde Art Ctr, 72; Focuserie Award, Nat Photog Exhib, Erie, Pa, 74; Master of Painting Honoris Causa, Accademia Italia; plus many others. *Bibliog:* Thelma Newman (auth), Innovative Printmaking, Crown Publ, Inc, NY; article, Spotlight on Sculpture, Tyler James Hoare, Ctr Visual Arts, 82; Nicholas Roukes (auth), Art Synectics, Juniro Arts Publ, Calgary, 84; and many others. *Mem:* Nat Soc Lit & Arts; Metal Arts Guild, San Francisco; Richmond Art Ctr, Calif; Fel Int Biographical Asn Ctr Visual Arts; Pro Arts, Oakland, Calif. *Media:* Wood, Metal. *Mailing Add:* 30 Menlo Pl Berkeley CA 94707

HOBBIE, LUCILLE
PAINTER, PRINTMAKER
b Boonton, NJ, June 14, 15. *Study:* Self-taught. *Work:* Colonial Williamsburg, Va; Seeing Eye, Morristown, NJ; Prudential Life, Newark; Nabisco World Hq, Hanover, NJ; A T & T, New York; and others. *Comn:* Drawings of bicentennial historic sites, Jersey Cent Power & Light Co; portfolio of drawings, Koehler Estate, 82-83. *Exhib:* NJ Watercolor Soc Ann, 50-85; Audubon Soc Ann, 53-72; Am Watercolor Soc Ann, Nat Acad Design Gallery, 56; 50 Artists, NJ State Mus, Trenton, 56; AANJ, City Mus, Trenton, NJ. *Pos:* Admin asst, Newark Sch Fine & Indust Art, 63-75. *Awards:* First Prize Award for Lithography, 51 & First Award for Watercolor, 52 & 62, NJ State Exhib; Agnes Noyes Award, NJ Watercolor Soc, 56 & 63. *Mem:* NJ Watercolor Soc (pres, 50-52, mem bd, 81-86 & 92); Asn Artists NJ (bd dirs, 70-72 & 86); NJ Printmaking Coun; Hon mem, NJ Watercolor Soc, 84- *Media:* Watercolor; Graphics. *Publ:* Illusr, A Calendar for Dinah, 69; Ecliptecs, 70; Mansion Magic, 79; On the Green, 1890's, 84; Historic Morris Co Lithographs 80-86 & 86-92. *Dealer:* Best Portfolios Bernardsville NJ 07924; Thomas Vokes Gallery Morristown NJ 07960. *Mailing Add:* 226 Talmadge Rd Mendham NJ 07945

HOBBS, (CARL) FREDRIC
SCULPTOR, FILMMAKER
b Philadelphia, Pa, Dec 30, 31. *Study:* Cornell Univ, BA; Acad San Fernando Belles Artes, Madrid, Spain. *Work:* Mus Mod Art, New York; Metrop Mus Art, New York; Finch Col Mus, New York; San Francisco Mus Mod Art, San Francisco Fine Arts Mus; Oakland Mus Art; Johnson Mus, Cornell Univ, Ithaca, NY. *Exhib:* Biennial Exhib Am Art, Pa Acad Fine Arts, Philadelphia, 64; Nat Fine Arts Collection, Smithsonian Inst, Washington, DC, 64; The Highway Traveling Exhib, Inst Contemp Art, Philadelphia, 70; one-man shows, Calif Palace Legion of Honor, San Francisco & Mus Sci & Indust, Los Angeles, 76; San Francisco Mus of Mod Art, 80. *Pos:* Chmn bd, CED, Virginia City Restoration Corp. *Bibliog:* John W McCoubrey (auth), Art & the road, Highway, 70; Thomas Albright (auth), Visuals, Rolling Stone Mag, 71; plus others. *Media:* Steel Supported Fiberglass, Latex Acrylic. *Publ:* Coauth, The Richest Place on Earth, Houghton-Mifflin, 78; auth, An American Paradise, Calif Living Bks, 80 & 82; Eat your house: ART ECO guide to self sufficiency, Mayfield, 80; feature articles, City Mag, San Francisco Mag; writer, dir & producer, feature films & TV-Expo short features. *Mailing Add:* 2847 Clay St No 2 San Francisco CA 94115-1716

HOBBS, GERALD S
DEALER, PUBLISHER
b New York, NY, Nov 5, 41. *Pos:* Publ, Am Artist Mag, 73, The Artist Mag, 76, Art & Antiques: The Am Mag for Connoisseurs & Collectors, 78-, Interiors Mag, 78, Residential Interiors Mag, 78 & Int Soc Artists. *Mem:* Nat Arts Club; Salmagundi Club; Nat Art Material Trade Asn; Artists' Fel. *Specialty:* Publisher of The American Artist Collection (unlimited edition prints). *Mailing Add:* 33 Thornbury Rd Scarsdale NY 10583

HOBBS, JACK ARTHUR
EDUCATOR, WRITER
b Lincoln, Nebr, Dec 26, 30. *Study:* Univ Iowa, BA, 52, MA, 56, PhD, 71. *Exhib:* 14th & 17th Nat Exhibs Prints, Libr Cong, Washington, DC, 56 & 59 & Invitational Traveling Show, 59-61; Art in the Embassies Prog, Dept of State, Washington, DC, 69. *Pos:* Publ ed, Studies in Art Educ, 85-87; Editorial Board, Studies in Art Educ, 89-93. *Teaching:* Prof art appreciation & art educ, Ill State Univ, 70- *Bibliog:* Robert Hiedemann (auth), bk rev in Art Educ J, Vol 29, 1/76; Howard Conant (auth), bk rev in Leonardo, spring 77; Georgia C Collins (auth), bk rev in Studies in Art Educ, Vol 27, 3/86. *Mem:* Nat Art Educ Asn. *Publ:* Auth, An Aesthetic Model for Art Education, Univ Mich, Ann Arbor Microfilms, 71; Art in Context, Harcourt Brace Jovanovich, 75, 2nd ed, 80, 3rd ed, 85 & 4th ed, 91; Arts, Civilization and Ideas, Prentice-Hall, 89, rev ed, 92; The Visual Experience, Davis Publ, Inc, 90; Arts in Civilization: Prehistoric culture to the twentieth century, Bloomsbury Books, London, 92. *Mailing Add:* Dept Art-Ctr Visual Arts 202D Ill State Univ Normal IL 61761

HOBBS, JOE FERRELL
ADMINISTRATOR, SCULPTOR
b Deport, Tex, June 30, 34. *Study:* Univ Tex, BFA, 57; Univ Southern Calif, MFA, 60. *Work:* Mus Fine Arts, Houston, Tex; Ft Worth Art Ctr Mus, Tex; Mus Fine Arts, Dallas, Tex. *Comn:* With John Alberty, belt buckle, Ft Worth Art Ctr Mus, 75 & brand, Art Park, Lewiston, NY, 77. *Exhib:* Ft Worth Art Ctr Mus, 75; Art Park, NY, 77. *Pos:* Dir, Sch Art, Univ Okla, Norman, 66- *Teaching:* From instr to prof art, Univ Okla, Norman, 66- *Bibliog:* Jan Butterfield (auth), article, Arts Mag, 75; Don Lipski (auth), article, Crisscross Art Commun, 76; article, Currant Mag, 76. *Mailing Add:* PO Box 452 Hemphill TX 75948

HOBBS, ROBERT CARLETON
MUSEUM DIRECTOR, HISTORIAN
b Brookings, SDak, Dec 6, 46. *Study:* Univ Tenn, Knoxville, BA, 69; Nat Defense Educ Act grant fel, 71-74; Samual H Kress fel, 74-75; Helena Rubinstein fel, 75; Univ NC, Chapel Hill, PhD, 75. *Pos:* Cur, Mint Mus Art, 69-71; adj cur, Cornell Univ, Herbert F Johnson Mus, 76-; sr cur & chmn curatorial div, Tehran Mus Contemp Art, 78; dir, Univ Iowa Mus Art, formerly. *Teaching:* Lectr mod art, Yale Univ, 75-76; assoc prof mod art, Cornell Univ, Ithaca, NY, 76-83. *Mem:* Am Asn Mus; Col Art Asn; Int Asn Art Critics. *Res:* Currently under contract to edit writings of Robert Motherwell for documents of 20th century art series. *Publ:* Auth, Elliott Daingerfield Retrospective Catalogue, Mint Mus, 71; coauth, Abstract Expressionism: The Formative Years, Whitney Mus & Cornell Univ Press, 78; auth, Robert Motherwell, Stadtische Kunsthalle, Dusseldorf, 76; auth, Michelle Stuart, Comt Visual Arts, MIT, 77; Auth, Robert Smithson: Sculpture, Col Art J, fall 82; auth, Tony Smith, Pace Gallery, 83; and others. *Mailing Add:* Sch Arts & Hist Va Commonwealth Univ 922 W Franklin Box 2519 Richmond VA 23284

HOBBS, ROBERT DEAN
PRINTMAKER, CONSULTANT
b Merkel, Tex, Apr 21, 28. *Study:* WTex State Univ, Canyon, with Emillio Caballero, BA; Northern Colo State Univ, Greeley, with Richard Ellinger, MA; Pa State Univ, State Col, with Will Barnett, DEd. *Work:* WTex State Univ, Canyon; Colo State Col, Greeley; Viktor Lowenfiel Mem Collection, Pa State Univ, State College; Smithsonian Inst, Washington, DC. *Exhib:* Solo exhibs, John Sloan Gallery, Lock Haven State Col, Pa, 78 & 80, Nat Art Educ Bldg, Reston, Va, 78, West Broadway Gallery, New York, 80 & Haas Gallery, Bloomsburg State Col, Pa, 81. *Teaching:* Art teacher in pub sch, Midland, Tex, 54-58; instr art, WTex State Univ, 58-63, assoc prof art, 67-71; grad asst, Pa State Univ, 65-67; prof art & chmn art dept, Clarion Univ Pa, 71-88; retired, summer 88. *Mem:* Nat Art Educ Asn; Pa Art Teacher Asn, Harrisburg. *Media:* Serigraphy, Silkscreen. *Dealer:* West Broadway Gallery 431 West Broadway New York NY 10012. *Mailing Add:* 8005 Classic Ave NE Albuquerque NM 87109

HOBGOOD, E WADE
ADMINISTRATOR, DESIGNER
b Wilson, NC, June 28, 53. *Study:* ECarolina Univ, Greenville, NC, BFA, 75, MFA, 77. *Work:* R J Reynolds, Winston-Salem, NC; Orthopedic Hosp of Charlotte, NC; Governor's Office, Little Rock, Ark; ECarolina Univ, Greenville, NC; Winthrop Univ, Rock Hill, NC. *Exhib:* NCarolina Photographers Invitational, High Point Mus Art, NC, 80; Western Carolina Univ Invitational, Black Mountain, NC, 81; solo exhib, Limestone Col, Gaffney, SC, 85; Southern Vision's , traveling exhib, 87; Art Fac Exhib, Stephen F Austin State Univ, Nacogdoches, Tex, 92; and others. *Pos:* Chmn dept art & design, Winthrop Univ, Rock Hill, SC, 84-89; assoc dean, Sch Visual & Performing Arts, 88-92; dean, Col Fine Arts, Stephen F Austin State Univ, Nacogdoches, Tex, 92- *Teaching:* Asst prof design & photog, Ark State Univ, Jonesboro, 77-78; asst to assoc prof, Western Carolina Univ, 78-84. *Awards:* Higher Educ Art Educator of Year, SC Art Educ Asn, 89; Art Educator of Year, SC Art Educ Asn, 90. *Mem:* Graphic Design Educ Asn Inc (treas, bd dir, 86-90); Arts in Basic Curriculum, Nat Endowment Arts (proj dir, 87-92); Am Ctr for Design; Col Art Asn. *Mailing Add:* 2504 Carole St Nacogdoches TX 75961

HOCHHAUSER, MARILYN HELSENROTT
PAINTER, EDUCATOR
b Chicago, Ill, April 18, 28. *Study:* C W Post Ctr, Long Island Univ, BA(art educ; magna cum laude), 73, MA(painting; scholar), 75; New York Univ, Mus Studies, 86-88. *Work:* Language Plus, Alma, Que; Ore Art Inst, Portland. *Exhib:* Muscarelle Mus Art, 88; Col William & Mary, Williamsburg, VA, 88; Sculpture & Abstract, San Francisco State Univ, 90; Columbia Col, Mo, 91; Perth Galleries, Australia, 92; and others. *Pos:* Prof Art, Trenton State Col, 80-85. *Teaching:* Art Lectr, Adult Educ, Roslyn & Merrick, NY, 71-79; prof, Trenton State Col, 80-85; instr, Santa Barbara Mus Art, 89-90 & City Col Art, 90. *Bibliog:* Lelac-Jean Papier (auth), article, Alma, PQ Canada, 2/82; C Laforge (auth), New York Daily News, 9/83; Joan Shepard (auth), article New York Post, 9/83. *Mem:* Women in Arts. *Mailing Add:* 1409 Las Canoas Lane Santa Barbara CA 93105

HOCHMAN, KITTY
PRINTMAKER
b Brooklyn, NY. *Study:* Hans Hofmann Sch Painting with E Eisgraw, 75; Art Am Sch with Nicholas Carone, 80; printmaking with Ruth Leaf Atelier, 80- *Work:* Orion Pictures & Dupont, New York; Sandos Pharmaceutical, Int Serv Systems & Clairol, NJ. *Exhib:* Nat Asn Women Artist Traveling Show, Roanoke Mus Fine Arts, Va, 84; 8th Int Miniatures, Pratt Graphic Ctr, New York, 85; Soc Am Graphic Artists, New York, 85; Int Miniature, Space Gallery, Seoul, Korea, 85; Larger Print Invitational, Midge Karr Art Ctr, Glen Cove, NY, 90; and others. *Pos:* Dir, Prints Etc, New York, 87- *Teaching:* Instr, Clearview Community Coun, 70-75, pvt lessons, 80-; adult educ, Forest Hills High Sch, NY. *Awards:* Edith Raskin Mem Award, 82; Janet Turner Graphic Award, 84; Printing Special Award, Nassau Mus, 88. *Bibliog:* Phyllis Braff (critic), NY Times, 83; Helen Harrison (critic), NY Times, 83; Malcolm Preston (critic), New York Newsday, 84. *Mem:* Nat Asn Women Artists (juror, 88-90); Artists Equity; Audubon Artists; Philadelphia Print Club. *Media:* Etching, Monoprint. *Publ:* Auth, Space, art architecture and environment, Korean Publ, 82; Brides Mag, 83; Monotypes, New York Newsday, 83; Graphics everywhere, NY Times, 84; Works on paper, NY Times, 85. *Dealer:* Skidmore Assoc 645 Snowden Lane Princeton NJ 08540. *Mailing Add:* 15-17 163 St Whitestone NY 11357

HOCHSTETLER, T MAX
PAINTER, EDUCATOR
b Terre Haute, Ind, May 13, 41. *Study:* Univ Evansville, BA, 64; Southern Ill Univ, MFA, 67. *Work:* Owensboro Art Mus; Tenn State Mus & Cheekwood Fine Arts Ctr, Nashville; Evansville Mus Arts & Sci; Tenn Valley Authority. *Comn:* First Am Tapestries, First Am Nat Bank, Nashville, 75; Nashville murals, 76-77 & Centennial murals, 80-81, Opryland Hotel, Nashville; Cheatham County Paintings, Dominion Bank of Ashland City, Tenn, 82; Public Square Clarksville (mural); First Am Bank, Clarksville, Tenn, 83; Hist Broadcasting mural, the Nashville Network (TNN), Nashville, 85. *Exhib:* Ind Artists Exhib, Evansville Mus, 75; Tenn Bicentennial Exhib, State Mus, Nashville, 76; Mid-Am Art Exhib, Owensboro Mus Art, Ky, 79; Tenn Artists, Doyle Fine Arts Ctr, Western Ky Univ, Bowling Green, 79; Choice Painting Invitational, Ctr Contemp Art, Univ Ky, 82; Ten in Tennessee, Dulin Gallery Art, Knoxville, 86. *Teaching:* Chmn & prof painting & drawing, Austin Peay State Univ, 67- *Awards:* Second Place Award, City of Owensboro, 74; Patrons Purchase Award, Evansville Mus, 75; Mus Purchase Award, Owensboro Mus, 79. *Mem:* Tenn Watercolor Soc; Col Art Asn; Southeastern Col Art Asn. *Media:* Acrylic, Watercolor. *Mailing Add:* Austin Peay State Univ Clarksville TN 37044

HOCKNEY, DAVID
DESIGNER, PHOTOGRAPHER
b Bradford, Yorkshire, Eng, July 9, 37. *Study:* Bradford Col Art, 57; Royal Col Art, 62, hon doctor Univ Aberdeen, 88. *Exhib:* One-man shows, Kasmin Gallery, 63-89, Mus Mod Art, New York, 64, Stedelijk Mus, Amsterdam, Nether, 66, Metrop Mus Art, 88, Tate Gallery, London, 88 and many other solo shows. *Pos:* Lectr, Univ Iowa, 64, Univ Colo, 65, Univ Calif-Los Angeles, 66, Univ Calif-Berkeley, 67; designer, sets for Magic Flute, 78, Parade Triple Bill, Stravinsky Triple Bill, Metrop Opera House, 80-81, and others. *Awards:* Guiness Award & First Prize for etching, 61; Gold Medal, Royal Col Art, 62; Kodak Photog Book Award for Cameraworks, 84. *Publ:* Illustr, Six Fairy Tales of the Brothers Grimm, 69; The Blue Guitar, 77; Hockney's Alphabet, 91; and others. *Mailing Add:* 7508 Santa Monica Blvd W Los Angeles CA 90046-6407

HODES, BARNEY
ADMINISTRATOR
b Mar 11, 43. *Study:* Columbia Col, AB, 64; Brooklyn Mus Art Sch, 64-66; Univ NC, MFA, 68. *Exhib:* NC Mus Art; Brooklyn Mus, Brooklyn Mus Art Sch; one-man show, Weatherspoon Gallery; Artists & Friends, First St Gallery, 81; Numeroff Gallery; and others. *Pos:* Co-dir, New York Acad Art, formerly. *Teaching:* Lectr, Fairleigh Dickinson Univ, Teaneck, NJ, 70-72; instr, Brooklyn Mus Sch Art, 70-81; instr, Brooklyn Col, 73-76; assoc prof, St John's Univ, 77- *Mailing Add:* Art Students League 215 W 57th St New York NY 10019

HODGE, DOROTHY W (SCOTTIE)
GALLERY DIRECTOR, ASSENBLAGE ARTIST
b Darlington, SC, Oct 21, 40. *Study:* Winthrop Col, Rock Hill, SC, BA, 62; Furman Univ, Greenville, SC, MA, 73; Greenville Co Mus Art Sch, 74-75. *Work:* Garfield Inc, Greenville, SC; Greenville Hosp System, SC. *Exhib:* Charlotte Open Exhib, NC, 80 & 81; Tempo Gallery, SC, 80, 83 & 93; Curators Choice Exhib, Greenville Mus, SC, 81; Francis Marion Col, SC, 83. *Pos:* Founder & dir, Tempo Gallery, Greenville, SC, 75-; co-founder, SC Watercolor Soc, 77; pres, Greenville Artists Guild, 78-79. *Teaching:* Lectr, Prof Presentation of Art Works on Paper, Art-Gallery Relationships & Selecting Original Art for Home Interiors. *Awards:* Curators Choice Award, Greenville Mus, SC, 80; Special Recognition Award, SC Watercolor Soc, 88. *Bibliog:* Article, in: The Greenville Woman Mag, 3/86. *Mem:* SC Watercolor Soc (bd mem, 81-87 & 91-); Upstate Visual Arts, Greenville, SC (founding bd mem, 90); Greenville Art Asn (bd mem, 78-79); co-founder SC Watercolor Soc (bd mem, 81-87); Greenville Metrop Arts Council. *Specialty:* Original artworks by local, regional artists only. *Publ:* Auth, How to Mat and Frame Your Art Works on Paper, 85, rev 92; article, Don't Kill the Artists' Market, SC Watercolor Soc, 2/92; article, Shipping Artwork to Juried Shows, SC Watercolor Soc, 6/92. *Mailing Add:* c/o Tempo Gallery 125 W Stone Ave Greenville SC 29609

HODGE, R GAREY
PAINTER, INSTRUCTOR
b Moweaqua, Ill, July 27, 37. *Study:* Eastern Ill Univ, BS, 61, MA(painting), 73; Harvard Univ Summer Sch, with William Georgenes. *Exhib:* Tri-State Exhib, Evansville Mus, Ind, 59; Miss Valley Exhib, Ill State Mus, Springfield, 64; Ill Bell Tel Exhib, Chicago, 67; River Roads Exhib, St Louis, 69, 70 & 72; 5th Int Biennial Sport Fine Arts, La Pinacoteca, Barcelona, Spain, 75; Western Ill Univ, 78. *Teaching:* Instr painting, graphics & design, Springfield High Sch, 62- *Awards:* Runner Up, New York World's Fair Sculpture Design, Int Fair Consults, 63; Second in Painting, Northside Art Asn, St Louis, 69; Grand Prize, US Hockey Hall of Fame, 76. *Mem:* Artists Equity; Ill State Mus Soc; Springfield Art Asn; Visual Artists & Gallery Asn. *Media:* Acrylic, Graphite. *Mailing Add:* 2413 Raleigh Rd Springfield IL 62704

HODGELL, ROBERT OVERMAN
PRINTMAKER, SCULPTOR
b Mankato, Kans, July 14, 22. *Study:* Univ Wis, BS & MA; Dartmouth Col; Univ Iowa; Univ Ill; Univ Michoacana, Mex; also with John Steuart Curry. *Work:* Joslyn Art Mus; Dartmouth Col; Libr Cong, Washington, DC; Ringling Mus Art, Sarasota, Fla; Metrop Mus Art; and others. *Pos:* Asst art dir & illus, Our Wonderful World, Champaign, Ill, 53-56; art dir, ed & commun serv, Exten Div, Univ Wis-Madison, 57-59; bk illusr for UNESCO in Pakistan, 60; co-owner, Joan Hodgell Gallery, Sarasota, Fla, 77-88. *Teaching:* Artist in residence & instr, Des Moines Art Ctr, 49-53; assoc prof art, Eckerd Col, 61-67, artist in residence, 67-77, adj art instr, 81-; instr, Ringling Sch of Art, 77-; art instr, New Col, Univ SFla, Sarasota, 80. *Awards:* Artist of the Year, Pinellas Co, Fla Art Coun, 91-92. *Mem:* Nat Acad Design. *Media:* Lino-Cut. *Mailing Add:* PO Box 20463 Bradenton FL 34203-0463

HODGKINS, ROSALIND SELMA
PAINTER
b Farmington, Maine, May 25, 42. *Study:* Univ SFla; Pratt Inst, BFA; Art Students League. *Work:* Southern Ill Univ, Carbondale; Bronx Mus Fine Arts, NY; Hewitt Sch, New York; Prudential Insurance Co. *Exhib:* One-woman shows, Warren Benedek Gallery, New York 72 & 73 & James Yu Gallery, New York, 76; Kensington Arts Asn, Toronto, Ont, 75; PS 1 Pattern Painting Show, New York, 77; O1A Art in Pub Places Show, New York, 77; Soho Ctr Visual Arts Show, New York, 81; 55 Mercer Gallery, New York, 86. *Awards:* MacDowell Colony Fel, 77-78. *Media:* Oil. *Mailing Add:* 325 W 16th St New York NY 10011

HODLEY, JANE See Dixon, Jenny (Jane Hodley)

HOENER, ARTHUR
PAINTER
b Brooklyn, NY, June 4, 29. *Study:* Cooper Union, New York, cert, 53; Yale Univ, BFA, 56, MFA, 58. *Work:* Art for Embassies Prog, Smithsonian Inst, Washington, DC; Invest Wellington Collection, DeCordova Mus, Lincoln, Mass; Arthur D Little Corp, Cambridge, Mass. *Comn:* Poly dimensional painted wall hanging, Gen Cinema Corp, Boston, 68. *Exhib:* Twenty-Ninth Biennial, Corcoran Art Mus, DC, 59; Wood Sculpture, Soc Arts & Crafts, Boston, 63; Good Design, Mus Fine Arts, Boston, 64; Multiplicity, Inst Contemp Art, Boston, 66; Structured Art, 69 & 77 & New England Drawing Competition, 79, De Cordova Mus, Lincoln, Mass; Mass Open, 81 & Illusions of Light, 81, Worcester Art Mus, Mass. *Collections Arranged:* New England Art Today, Paintings & Sculpture, Northeastern Univ, Boston, 63 & 65. *Pos:* Moderator & producer, Studio Talks, WGBH-FM, Boston, 63-67. *Teaching:* Prof graphic design, Mass Col Art, Boston, 60-70; prof art & design, Hampshire Col, Amherst, Mass, 70-84; prof art & design, Univ Conn, 84- *Awards:* First Prize Drawing, Springfield Art League, George Walter Vincent Smith Art Mus, Springfield, Mass, 77; Drawing Prize, Mass Open, Worcester Art Mus, 77; Outstanding Achievement, Wistariahurst Mus, Holyoke, Mass, 81; Bowater Inc Award, The Thirty-Sixth Art of the Northeast USA, Silvermine Guild Arts, New Canaan, Conn; and others. *Bibliog:* Bernard Chaet (auth), Artists at Work, Webb Bks, 60; Thelma Newman (auth), Plastics as an Art Form, Chilton Co, 64; Paul Zelanski & Pat Fisher (auth), The Art of Seeing, Prentice-Hall, 88. *Mem:* New England Contemp Artists Inc (chmn, 63-67); Silvermine Guild Arts. *Mailing Add:* 289 Elm St Northampton MA 01060

HOFER, EVELYN
PHOTOGRAPHER
b Marburg, Ger; Brit citizen. *Study:* Switz. *Work:* Metrop Mus Art, New York; Smith Col Mus Art, Northampton, Mass; Univ Colo Libr, Boulder. *Exhib:* Manhattan Now, New York Hist Soc, 74; Witkin Gallery, 77. *Media:* Four by Five Camera. *Publ:* Coauth, The Stones of Florence, 59, London Perceived, 63, The Presence of Spain, 64 & New York Proclaimed, 65, Harcourt, Brace, Jovanovich; coauth, Dublin, A Portrait, Harper & Row, 67; Emerson in Italy, Henry Holt, 87. *Dealer:* Witkin Gallery 41 E 57th St New York NY 10022. *Mailing Add:* 55 Bethune St New York NY 10014

HOFER, INGRID (INGEBORG)
PAINTER, INSTRUCTOR
b New York, NY. *Study:* Meisterschule Fuer Mode, Hamburg, Ger, BA, 48; Univ Hamburg; Traphagen Sch Design, New York, 51; with A Odefey, Goettingen, Ger, Albert Bross, Jr, John R Grabach, Adolf Konrad & Nicholas Reale. *Work:* Fairleigh Dickinson Univ, NJ; First Nat Bank Barrington, Ill; Good Shepherd Hosp, Ill; Lumus Co, NJ; Dana Corp, Ohio. *Comn:* Many pvt comns in Ger, Switz & US, 56- *Exhib:* Hudson Valley Art Asn, White Plains, NY, 70 & 71; Catharine Lorillard Wolfe Art Club, Nat Acad Design, New York, 70, 71, 77 & 85; Am Artist Prof League Grand Nat, Lever House, New York, 70-75 & 78-81; Am Watercolor Soc, 73; Mich Art Inst, Founders Gallery, 73-76; Rocky Mountain Nat Watercolor Exhib, Colo, 75; Tweed Mus; Scarab Club, Detroit, 75-78; Union League, Chicago, 81; Winter Sojourn, Edison Plaza, Toledo, 87; Women Alive, Toledo, Ohio, 86 & 87; and others. *Teaching:* Instr mixed media, Acad Artists, Trailside Mus, Mountainside, NJ, 68-70; instr, Grosse Pointe War Mem, Mich, 74-78, Country Side Art Ctr, Arlington Heights, Ill, 81-83 & Toledo Artists Club, 83-; Lourdes Col, Sylvania, Ohio, 88- *Awards:* Award for Lily Lever House, Am Artists Prof League, 72; Am Watercolor Soc Traveling Show Award, 73; Purchase Award, Union League, Ill, 81; and others. *Mem:* Fel Am Artists Prof League; Catharine Lorillard Wolfe Art Club; Midwest Watercolor Soc; NJ Watercolor Soc; assoc Am Watercolor Soc; Northwest Ohio Watercolor Soc. *Media:* Watercolor, Graphics. *Dealer:* Nathan's Art Gallery West Patterson NJ 07013; Seagate Art Gallery Toledo OH. *Mailing Add:* 9775 Carnoustie Rd Perrysburg OH 43551

HOFF, MARGO
PAINTER, COLLAGE ARTIST
b Tulsa, Okla. *Study:* Tulsa Univ; Art Inst Chicago; Pratt Graphics Ctr; St Marys Col, Notre Dame, hon DFA, 69; Drew Univ, hon DFA, 86. *Work:* Whitney Mus Am Art, New York; Brooklyn Mus, NY; Art Inst Chicago; Krannert Mus, Univ Ill; Rosenwald Found Collection; Metrop Mus, NY, 82-86. *Comn:* Wall design, Home Fed Bank, Chicago, 66; Mirror to Man (mural), Mayo Clinic, Rochester, Minn, 68; stage set & costumes for Murray Louis Dance Co, 69; portrait of S Madeleva, St Marys Col, Notre Dame, 70; two murals, New Govt Bldg, Plattsburgh, NY, 77-79; Wall Hanging: Peat, Marwick, Mitchel, Washington, DC. *Exhib:* One-man shows, Banfer Gallery, New York, 64, 66 & 68, Fairweather Hardin Gallery, 64-79, 81, 83, 86, Bednarz Gallery, Los Angeles, 67 & Babcock Gallery, New Y ork, 74; Hadler Rodriguez Galleries, 78 & 79; Betty Parsons Gallery, New York, 81-82. *Teaching:* Teaching Grant, Duke Foun, Am Univ, Beirut, 56-57; artist in residence, Univ Southern Ill, 66-67; artist in residence, St Marys Col, Notre Dame, 69-70, 78, 82, & 84; teaching grant, Goretti Sch, Fort Portal, Uganda, E Africa, 71; Col St Maria, Sao Paulo, Brasil; AIR, Rhode Island Sch Design, 80. *Publ:* Illusr, Christmas House, Coachhouse, 65; illusr, 4 Seasons & 5 Senses, 66 & Christmas Cupboard, 67, Funk & Wagnall. *Mailing Add:* 114 W 14th St New York NY 10011

HOFFBERG, JUDITH A
PUBLISHER, CURATOR
b Hartford, Conn, May 19, 34. *Study:* Univ Calif, Los Angeles, BA, MA & MLS; Ital Govt grant, study of Leonardo da Vinci. *Pos:* Dir, Umbrella Assoc, 78-; bd dir, Franklin Furnace, 76-77; exec dir, Assoc Art Publ, 78-79; cur, Umbrella Show, Univ Calif, Riverside, 79; co-cur, Traction Gallery, Los Angeles, 81; cur, Editions & Additions, Int Bookworks, IDEA, Norhtlight Gallery, Tempe, Ariz, 85, traveled to Sacramento & Univ Calif, Riverside, 86; cur, Undercover: The Book as Format, Fresno, 87; cur, Art from the Page: Booksworks, Salem, Ore, Salem Art Asn, traveled to Tex Women's Univ, Denton, 87; cur, a Book of His Own: Men's Visual Diaries, Woodland Pattern, Milwaukee, Wis, 87 & Univ Calif Los Angeles Art Libr, 90; A Book in Hand, Arvada Ctr for Arts, Colo, 89; Books from the Edge of the Pacific, Univ Calif, Santa Barbara, 90-91; Boundless Vision: Contemporary Bookworks, San Antonio Art Inst, 91; Ringling Sch Art Gallery, Sarasota, 92, New Zealand, 93- *Teaching:* Lectr on artist's books worldwide; lectr, Univ Calif, Santa Barbara, 90. *Awards:* British Coun grant, 83; Fulbright Grant, New Zealand, 84; Fluxus Res Fel, Sonja Henie & Onstad Fdn, Oslo, Norway. *Mem:* Soc Archit Historians (mem bd dirs, 79-82); Int Coun Mus; Honorary life mem, Art Libr Soc of NAm, Art Libr Soc of United Kingdom; Int Asn

of Art Critics, Am Sect; Nat Writer's Union. *Publ:* Auth, Introductions to various books in field of book arts, Correspondence Art; The medium is the message, Press/Art, Long Beach Pres-Telegram, 4/23/87; Sandra Schwimmer: Bookworks (exhib catalog), Riverside Art Mus, 87; interview: Piotr Rypson, Warsaw in High Performance, 10/88; review, Edie Danieli Ellis at Orlando Gallery, Artscene, 1/90. *Mailing Add:* Po Box 40100 Pasadena CA 91104

HOFFELD, JEFFREY M
ART DEALER
b Brooklyn, NY, Dec 3, 45. *Study:* Brooklyn Col, BA, 66; Columbia Univ, MPhil, 73; New York Univ, MA, 86. *Pos:* Asst cur, Medieval art & The Cloisters, Metrop Mus Art, New York, 67-73; dir, Neuberger Mus, State Univ NY, Purchase, 74-77; vpres & partner, Pace Gallery, New York, 78-83; pres, Jeffrey Hoffeld & Co, Inc, 83-; sr vpres, Hir Sch & Adley Galleries, New York, 86-87. *Teaching:* Asst prof art, Brooklyn Col, NY, 68-73, State Univ NY, Purchase, 73-77; assoc prof english, New York Univ, 86. *Awards:* Nat Endowment Arts Grant, 75-76. *Res:* Medieval and contemporary art. *Specialty:* European and American 20th century art. *Publ:* Coauth, The Cloisters Apocalypse, Metrop Mus Art, New York, 70. *Mailing Add:* 279 Central Park W No 9B New York NY 10024

HOFFMAN, CAROL MAREE
DIRECTOR, PUBLISHER
b Denver, Colo, Sept 5, 44. *Study:* Cornell Univ, Ithaca, NY, BA, 66; Columbia Univ, New York, 67; Community Col Denver, assoc degree, 78. *Work:* Mus Folk Art, Santa Fe, NMex. *Comn:* Wallpiece, Mountain Bell, Denver, Colo, 78; Marietta Nat Crafts/Sculpture Show, Ohio, 77; Threads Unlimited, Foothills Art Ctr, Golden, Colo, 77; Object '79, W Colo Ctr Arts, Grand Junction, 79. *Pos:* Publ mag & exec dir, Craft Range, 74-80; publ, New Denver Arts Publ. *Mem:* Colo Artist Craftsmen (bd mem, 74-80); Am Crafts Coun; Metrop Denver Arts Alliance (mem bd dirs, 81-84). *Media:* Assemblage; Found objects. *Mailing Add:* 4109 Columbia Pike Franklin TN 37064

HOFFMAN, ELAINE JANET
PAINTER
b Oak Park, Ill. *Study:* Averett Col; Portland Art Mus; Northwest Watercolor Sch, with Irving Shapiro; Maryhurst Educ Ctr, BA, 78; also with Charles Mulvey, Perry Acker, George Hamilton & Phil Austin. *Work:* US Interstate Bank; Boise Cascade Paper Co; Payless Drug Store; Beloit Corp; Willamette Indust. *Exhib:* Artists of Ore, Portland Art Mus, 70; Am Artists Prof League, New York, 71; Am Artists Prof League, New York, 71; Prof Ore Artists Invitational, Coos Bay, Ore, 72-74; George Fox Col Invitational Newberg, Ore, 72-75; one man shows, Courtyard Gallery, 79 & Art Adventures, 80-81, Hoffman Studios, 84-90, Portland. *Pos:* Bd dirs, Lake Oswego Art Guild, Ore, 65-68; pres, Lake Area Artist & Lake Oswego Art Develop, 89. *Teaching:* Pvt classes in watercolor landscapes, 65-81; instr, Portland Community Col, 75-81. *Awards:* Purchase Award, Coos Bay Mus, 73; First Award, Lake Oswego Art Festival, Ore, 78 & 82; Best of Show, Ciackahas Fair, 91. *Mem:* Fel Am Artists Prof League; Ore Watercolor Soc; Lake Area Artists (pres, 67-68, 71-72 & 75-76); Watercolor Critique Group, Ore Art Inst. *Media:* Watercolor. *Dealer:* Hoffman Studios Lake Oswego. *Mailing Add:* 16695 Glenwood Ct Lake Oswego OR 97034

HOFFMAN, ERIC
PAINTER, PRINTMAKER
b Santa Cruz, Calif, July 16, 52. *Study:* Cabrillo Col, Aptos, Calif, AA, 72; San Jose State Univ, BA, (painting), 75, & MFA (painting), 78. *Work:* Am Express; Monterey Peninsula Mus Art, Calif; San Jose Mus Art; E F Hutton, New York; Bumper Develop Corp, Ltd, Calgary; Price-Waterhouse; Merril, Skidmore, Owens, New York. *Comn:* Large scale 2-part panel painting, Bumper Develop Corp Ltd, Calgary, Alta, 81; 2-part panel painting, Juan Montoya Design, New York, 83; 3-part enviro piece, Emerald Fund, San Francisco, Calif, 84; 3-part panel, Battenberg, Fillhardt & Wright, San Jose, Calif, 84; series of 28 monogotypes, Arts Coun, Santa Clara Co, 86. *Exhib:* Oakland Mus, Calif, 81; Chain Reaction, San Francisco Arts Comt, Calif, 85; Scratching the Surface, San Jose Mus Art, Calif, 85; San Jose Inst Contemp Art, Calif, 86; Metrop Mus Art, Miami, Fla, 86; Miller-Brown Gallery, San Francisco, 86; Expressive Surfaces, Beverly Gordon Gallery, Dallas, Tex, 88; Twining Gallery, New York, 88; Maison du Culture, Grenoble, France, 88. *Pos:* Asst preparator, San Jose Mus Art, Calif, 76-79. *Teaching:* Guest lectr expressive drawing, Calif Polytech Univ; grad seminar ceramics & pictorial arts, San Jose State Unvi, 85; instr, color-design, Cabrillo Col. *Awards:* Du Credit Commercial de France Award, 85; Du Ministere de al Culture, Paris, France, 85; De la Villa de Granonle, France, 85. *Bibliog:* Article, Arts Mag, 82; Sally Robertson (auth), Art in San Jose, Art Week, 76; Catalog, E F Hutton Collection, 86. *Mem:* San Jose Inst Contemp Art. *Media:* Miscellaneous. *Dealer:* Twining Gallery 568 Broadway Suite 107 New York NY 10012; Katia LaCoste Gallery 227 N First St San Jose CA 95062. *Mailing Add:* c/o Katia LaCoste Gallery 227 N First St San Jose CA 96113

HOFFMAN, HELEN BACON
PAINTER
b San Antonio, Tex, July 14, 30. *Study:* Ogontz Col, Philadelphia; Parsons Sch Design. *Work:* NAm-Mex Inst Cult Relations, Mexico City, Mex; Wichita Art Asn, Kans. *Exhib:* One-man shows, North Star Gallery, San Antonio, Tex, 66-80, Grand Cent Art Galleries, New York, 69-80 & Veerhoff Galleries, Washington, DC, 64, 74 & 78; Musselman River Walk Gallery, San Antonio, 81 & 82 & Houston, 82 & 83. *Awards:* First Place Award, Catherine Lorillard Wolfe Art Club Show, 73; First Place Painting, Salmagundi Club, 74; Kalikow Award Excellence, Pastel Soc Am, 82. *Mem:* Artists Equity Asn; Soc Washington Artists; Pastel Soc Am; Nat Arts Club; Catherine Lorillard Wolfe Art Club; and others. *Media:* Pastel, Oil. *Dealer:* Veerhoff Galleries 1604 17th St NW Washington DC 20009; Grand Central Art Galleries 24 W 57th St New York NY 10019. *Mailing Add:* c/o Veerhoff Galleries 1604 17th St NW Washington DC 20009

HOFFMAN, MANDY LIPPMAN
CONSULTANT, WRITER
b Baltimore, Md, Sept 23, 56. *Study:* George Washington Univ, BA, 78; Parson's Sch Design, AAS, 81. *Collections Arranged:* Baltimore Off of KPMG/Peat Marwick (law off of Melnicove, Weiner, Smouse & Garbis); Artist Designed Furniture, Norton Gallery Art, W Palm Beach, Fla, 86. *Pos:* Dir, Meredith Gallery, Baltimore, Md, 81-87; self-employed consultant, 88-*Teaching:* Instr, Md Inst Art, Baltimore, 83, Visit the Artist, Jewish Community Ctr, Washington, DC, 89, Contemp Art in Washington, Smithsonian, 90. *Mem:* James Renwick Alliance (bd mem), 90. *Collection:* Contemporary American crafts, prints and paintings (1970 to present). *Publ:* Auth, The new art furniture: functional creativity, Home Mag, 11/90. *Mailing Add:* c/o Meredith Gallery 805 N Charles St Baltimore MD 21201

HOFFMAN, MARILYN FRIEDMAN
DIRECTOR
Study: Brown Univ, Providence, RI, BA(hon; art hist), 67, MA(art hist), 71. *Pos:* Cur asst, Educ Dept, Mus Art, RI Sch Design, 67-68; gallery asst, Adelson Galleries, Inc, Boston, 68-69 & 70-71; grad asst, Educ Dept, Metrop Mus Art, New York, 69; adj lectr, Dept Pub Educ, Mus Fine Arts, Boston, 70-71; cur, Brockton Art Mus-Fuller Mem, Mass, 71-73, actg dir, 73-74, dir, 74-84; cur, Currier Gallery Art, Manchester, NH, 84-88, dir, 88- *Teaching:* Teaching asst, Brown Univ, 69-70. *Mem:* Am Asn Mus; Col Art Asn Am; New Eng Mus Asn (secy, treas); NH Large Cult Orgn (chair, 91). *Publ:* Auth, Pssst, Airbrush Painting (catalog), 72, The Good Things in Life/19th Century American Still Life (catalog), 73 & Unstretched Paintings (catalog), 73, Brockton Art Ctr-Fuller Mem; Museum Loans at Brockton, Art J, Vol 32, 73. *Mailing Add:* The Currier Gallery Art 192 Orange St Manchester NH 03104

HOFFMAN, MARTIN
PAINTER, ILLUSTRATOR
b St Augustine, Fla, Nov 1, 35. *Study:* Univ Miami, 55; Fla State Univ, 56. *Work:* Miami Mus Mod Art; Va Mus Fine Arts, Richmond; Indianapolis Mus Art; J B Speed Mus, Louisville, Ky. *Comn:* numerous paintings & illus, Playboy Mag, 66-92; NASA Space Shuttle Program, 82-92; Basile, Milan, 80-82; Hakehodo Agency, Tokyo, 85; Toyo Cinema, Japan, 86; and others. *Exhib:* Mus Mod Art, New York, 64-67; Air & Space Mus, Smithsonian Inst, 82-83; Johnson Space Ctr, Univ Houston, 83; Retrospectives, Miami Mus Mod Art, 61, 65 & 67; The Educated Eye, State Mus, Albany, NY, 84; The Epic New York Paintings, Stetson Univ, 90; Intimate Works, R Thames Fine Art, Ormond, Fla, 91; The Realist Painting, Ormond Mem Mus, 91; and others. *Pos:* Art dir, munerous Miami advert agencies, 57-70; designer-illusr, Graphic Arts, Inc, 60-70. *Teaching:* Instr grad painting & drawing, Univ Miami, 69-71 & Casements Cult Ctr, 91-92. *Awards:* Art Dir Awards, Miami Art Dirs Club, 59-70; Illus Awards, Chicago Advert Club, 71-79; Elegance for the Eighties, Best Serv Illusr, Playboy, 79; and others. *Bibliog:* Griffin Smith (auth), article in Tropic Mag, 9/71; article, Illus Japan, No 18, 10/82; Diane Copelon (auth), article, Ormond Beach Observer, 8/26/90; John Wirt (auth), article, Daytona Beach News-J, 5/26/91; Chuck Twardy (auth), article, Orlando Sentinel, 6/2/91; and others. *Publ:* Illusr, Playboy, 67-92; Art Direction, 4/72; NY Times & Artforum, 74; Fortune, 74; and others. *Dealer:* OK Harris Gallery 383 W Broadway New York NY 10012; Advert Rep: Frank & Jeff Lavaty 50 E 50th St New York NY 10022. *Mailing Add:* 1229 Ruger Pl Daytona Beach FL 32118

HOFFMAN, MICHAEL E
EDITOR, CURATOR
b New York, NY, July 5, 42. *Study:* St Lawrence Univ, BA, 64; also adv studies with Minor White, Mass Inst Technol. *Collections Arranged:* Paul Strand: Retrospective, Clarence John Laughlin: The Personal Eye & French Primitive Photography, Philadelphia Mus Art; August Sander: Photographs of an Epoch; The Face of China; Tibet: The Sacred Realm; Minor White: Retrospective; 40 exhibs at Philadelphia Mus Art, with many traveling in US, Canada & abroad, 69- *Pos:* Ed & publ, exec dir, Aperture Found Inc, 64-; exec dir, cur, Alfred Stieglitz Ctr, Philadelphia Mus Art. *Awards:* Pi Delta Epsilon. *Mem:* Soc Photog Educ. *Publ:* Editor of over 350 publications in fine arts & photog, 64- *Mailing Add:* RD 2 Box 85 Pine Plains NY 12567

HOFFMAN, NANCY
DEALER
b New York, NY, Feb 23, 44. *Study:* Wellesley Col, 62-64; Barnard Col, Columbia Univ, BA(art hist), 66. *Pos:* Asst registrar, Asia House Gallery, New York, 64-69; dir, French & Co Contemp Gallery, New York, 69-72 & Nancy Hoffman Gallery, New York, 72- *Specialty:* Contemporary art: paintings, drawings, sculpture and graphics. *Mailing Add:* Nancy Hoffman Gallery 429 W Broadway New York NY 10012

HOFFMAN, NEIL JAMES
ADMINISTRATOR, EDUCATOR
b Buffalo, NY, Sept 2, 38. *Study:* State Univ NY Buffalo, BS, 60, MS, 67. *Pos:* Dir, Prog Artisanry, Boston Univ, 74-79; dean & chief admin officer, Otis Art Inst Parsons Sch Design, 79-83; pres, Sch Art Inst Chicago, 83-85; pres, Calif Col Arts & Crafts, 85- *Teaching:* Art & chmn unified art dept, Grand Island Pub Schs, NY, 61-68; assoc prof design & art educ & assoc dean col fine & appl arts, Rochester Inst Technol, 68-74. *Mailing Add:* 5212 Broadway Oakland CA 94618

HOFFMAN, RICHARD PETER
PAINTER, PHOTOGRAPHER
b Allentown, Pa, Jan 10, 11. *Study:* Mercersburg Acad, grad, 29; Parsons Sch Design, grad, 33. *Work:* Butler Inst Am Art, Youngstown, Ohio; Maravian Col, Bethlehem, Pa; Pa Power & Light Co, Allentown; Call-Chronicle Newspapers, Allentown; Liberty High Sch, Bethlehem, Pa. *Exhib:* One-man shows, Woodmere Art Gallery, 70, Allentown Art Mus, Pa, 72-77, Kemmerer Mus, Bethlehem, Pa, 73, Meirhans Art Gallery, Quakertown & New Britain Mus Am Art, Conn, 75; and many others. *Awards:* Gertrude Rowan Capolino Prize, Woodmere Art Gallery, Philadelphia, 52; Grumbacher Prize for Casein, Knickerbocker Artists, 55; Com Mus Civic Ctr Award, Philadelphia, 65. *Mem:* Philadelphia Watercolor Soc; Lehigh Art Alliance. *Publ:* Auth, articles, Am Artist, 11/48 & La Rev Mod, 3/53; A Pennsylvania German Precisionist: The Art of Richard Peter Hoffman, The Pa German Soc, 90. *Mailing Add:* 1035 N 30th St Allentown PA 18104

HOFFMAN, WILLIAM A
CERAMIST, EDUCATOR
b Roswell, NMex, May 4, 20. *Study:* Eastern NMex Univ, Portales, AA, 40; Art Inst Chicago, EdB, 49, EdM, 50; Univ Southern Calif, Los Angeles, 51; State Univ NY, Col Ceramics, Alfred, MFA, 53. *Work:* Roswell Mus, NMex; St Mary's Col, South Bend, Ind; Kessel Ceramic Collection, Whitewater, Wis; and many pvt collections. *Exhib:* One-man shows, St Mary's Col, South Bend, Ind, 69, Chicago Publ Libr, 67, Lewis Towers Galleries, Loyola Univ, Chicago, 73, Triton Col, River Grove, Ill, 74, Pot Shop, Evanston, Ill, 75, Nina Owen Gallery, 86, Marmion Acad, Aurora, Ill, 88 & Valparaiso Univ, Ind, 89; Ceramics and Fibres, Chicago State Univ Gallery, 77; Univ Wis, Whitewater, 86; Union Gallery, Mankato State Univ, Minn, 78; Fairweather-Hardin Gallery, 81, 84 & 87; and other one-man shows. *Collections Arranged:* Japanese Prints Exhib, Northwestern State Col, Natchitoches, La, 50; Tower League of Young Adults Exhib, New York, 55. *Teaching:* Instr design, ceramics & figure drawing, La State Univ, Baton Rouge, 57-58; instr design, pottery & sculpture, Art Inst Chicago, 58-70; instr pottery, Loyola Univ, Chicago, 70-83. *Bibliog:* Joshua Kind (auth), rev, New Art Examiner; American Artists, 85 & 90, NY Art Review, 87, Chicago Artists, 89, Les Krantz. *Mem:* Am Crafts Coun, New York; Chicago Artists Coalition; Arts Club Chicago. *Media:* Clay. *Dealer:* Nina Owen Gallery Suite 520 620 N Michigan Ave Chicago IL 60610. *Mailing Add:* 1925 N Hudson Chicago IL 60614

HOFFMAN, WILLIAM MCKINLEY, JR
PAINTER, EDUCATOR
b Blairsville, Pa, Jan 25, 34. *Study:* Pa Acad Fine Arts & Univ Pa, BFA, 62; Tyler Sch Art, Temple Univ, MFA, 67. *Work:* NJ State Mus, Trenton; Stedman Art Gallery, Rutgers Univ, Camden, NJ; Camden Co Cult & Heritage, NJ; Thomas Jefferson Univ, Philadelphia; City Camden, NJ. *Comn:* Portrait paintings, Sch of Law, Rutgers, Camden, 86 & 88; landscape painting, Marriott Corp, 87; cityscape, Copper Hosp Univ Med Ctr, 92. *Exhib:* 139th Ann Exhib, Nat Acad Design, New York, 64; Eastern Regional Drawing Soc Show, Philadelphia Mus Art, 65; 55th Ann, Allied Artists Am, Nat Acad Design, New York, 68; 164th Ann, Pa Acad Fine Arts, Philadelphia, 69; 34th & 35th Ann, Butler Institute Am Art, Youngstown, Ohio, 69 & 70; Earth Art 1 & 2, Philadelphia Civic Ctr Mus, 73 & 79; Art from NJ IX & X, 74 & 75 & Visual Arts Fel Winners Exhib, 80, NJ State Mus, Trenton; Peale House Gallery, Pa Acad Fine Arts, Philadelphia, 83. *Teaching:* Instr to assoc prof, Rutgers Univ, Camden Col Arts & Sci, NJ, 67-, chmn, Dept Art, 67-76, 79-82 & 92-95. *Awards:* Purchase Award, Earth Art 3, Touche, Ross & Co, Philadelphia, 79; Artists Fel, NJ State Coun Arts, 80 & 84; Purchase Award, City of Camden, NJ, 88; and others. *Bibliog:* Piri Halasz (auth), State artists display skills, New York Times, 7/6/75; Robert Baxter (auth), Romantic realist, Courier Post, NJ, 10/30/81; Judy Baeher (auth), Preserving Camden's history on canvas, Philadelphia Inquirer, 4/7/91. *Mem:* Artists Equity Asn; fel Pa Acad Fine Arts; Col Art Asn. *Media:* Oil, Casein. *Mailing Add:* 167 Elm Ave Woodlynne NJ 08107

HOFFMANN, GARY DAVID
PAINTER, SCULPTOR
b Detroit, Mich, June 6, 47. *Study:* Ctr for Creative Studies, 66-69; Atelier Lack, 71-74; R H Ives, Gammell Studios, 74-76. *Work:* Old Kent Bank, Owosso, Mich; Ill Hist Soc, Ill. *Exhib:* Nat Exhib, Acad Artists Asn, Springfield, Mass, 75; Nat Open, Allied Artists Am, New York, 80; Grand Nat, Am Artists Prof League, New York, 80; Fall Show, Copley Soc, Boston, 87. *Awards:* F T Greenshields Grant, Greenshields Found, 72 & 75; Gold Medal, Springville Mus Art, 81. *Bibliog:* James Thorton (auth), Gary Hoffman, Midwest Art Mag, 8/85. *Mem:* Copley Soc of Boston; Guild of Boston Artists; Am Artists' Prof League; Pastel Soc Am. *Media:* Oil, Pastel. *Publ:* Contribr, Edmund Tarbell and the Boston School, Patricia Pierce, 77; The Boston School Continued, Hammer Gallery, 85; coauth, Realism in Revolution, Taylor Publ, 85; auth, Boston school artists in Nantucket, The Inquirer & Mirror, 88. *Dealer:* Guild of Boston Artists 162 Newbury St Boston MA 02116. *Mailing Add:* 301 Ipswich St Boston MA 02215

HOFFMANN, LEESA L
PAINTER
b St Paul, Minn, Aug 31, 47. *Study:* Richard Jack Atelier, Minneapolis & Atelier Hoffman, Detroit; Atelier Hoffman, Detroit, Mich. *Work:* The Gallery, Cable, Wis; The Copley Soc, Boston, Mass; Robert Wilson Gallery, Nantucket, Mass; Heritage Art Gallery, Va. *Exhib:* Annual Show, Springville Mus Art, Utah, 82; Am Artists Prof League Ann, New York; Copley Soc Ann Show, Boston, Mass; Heritage Gallery of Art, Alexandria, Va; Salmagundi Club, New York; Classical Realist Show, Alexandria, Va. *Teaching:* Nantucket Artists Asn. *Awards:* Gold Medal, Am Artists Prof League, 79 & The Newington Award; First Place, Elizabeth Morris Genius Award, Pastel Soc Am, 80; Silver Medal, Springville Mus Art, 81; First Place for Landscape, Pastel Soc of W Coast, Sacramento, Calif; First Place, Copley Soc, Boston. *Bibliog:* Andy Driscoll (auth), Painter of light, Highland Newspaper, 84. *Mem:* Am Artists Prof League; Copley Soc Boston; Pastel Soc Am; The West Coast Pastel Soc; Soc Classical Realism; Nantucket Artists Asn. *Media:* Oil, Pastel. *Publ:* Auth, essay, In: Realism in Revolution, Taylor Publ, 85. *Dealer:* The Gallery Cable WI 54821; The Copely Soc 158 Newbury St Boston Mass. *Mailing Add:* 30 Ipswich St Boston MA 02215

HOFMANN, DOUGLAS WILLIAM
PAINTER, PRINTMAKER
b Baltimore, Md, Feb 13, 45. *Study:* Md Inst Col Art, BFA(cum laude), studied with Joseph Sheppard, 64-68. *Work:* Del Art Mus, Wilmington; Joslyn Art Mus, Omaha; Marquette Univ Fine Art Collection, Milwaukee; Nat Mem Mus & Archives, Washington, DC; Nassau County Mus, NY. *Comn:* Painted stained glass panels, Baltimore City Schs, Md, 70. *Exhib:* Peale Mus, Baltimore, 70; Md Biennial, Baltimore Mus Art, 71 & 73; Realism in Maryland, Washington Co Mus, Hagerstown, Md, 72; Allied Artists Am, 74 & Audubon Artists Ann, 76, Nat Acad, New York; Ann Mid-Yr Exhib, Butler Inst, Youngstowm, Ohio, 74-75; Cherry Creek Gallery, Denver, 78; one-man show, Jack Gallery, New York, 79, 81 & 84; 30th Nat Print Exhib, Hunterdon Art Ctr, Clinton, NJ, 86. *Teaching:* Instr painting, Md Inst, Baltimore, 74-75. *Awards:* Best Traditional Painting, Md Biennial, Baltimore Mus, 71; Best in Show, Realism in Maryland, Washington Co Mus, 72; Grant, Stacey Scholar Fund, 75. *Bibliog:* Jack Solomon (auth), Douglas Hofmann, Circle Fine Art Corp, 81; Will Grant (auth), Old and established, Artspeak, 6/2/81; Jerry Tallmer (auth), Mr Vermeer say hello to this here Mr Hofmann, New York Post, 10/31/81. *Media:* Oil; Lithography. *Dealer:* Jack Gallery 138 Prince St New York NY 10012. *Mailing Add:* c/o Charles Barry Int Eight Hardwicke Pl Rockville MD 20850

HOFMANN, KAY
SCULPTOR
b Green Bay, Wis, Dec 3, 32. *Study:* Art Inst Chicago(Ryerson Fel), grad, 55; studied at Acad de Grande Chaumiere, Paris, with Ossip Zadkine, 55-56. *Work:* Borg Warner, Chicago. *Comn:* Marble sculpture, Continental Plaza Hotel, Chicago, 70; two wood carvings, comn by Hugh Hefner, Los Angeles, 77; marble portrait, Gonstead Med Ctr, Mt Horeb, Wis, 81; alabaster sculpture, Arthur Anderson Assocs, Chicago, 84-90. *Exhib:* Solo exhibs, Art Inst Chicago, 78 & Rahr-West Mus, Manitowoc, Ill, 85; 30th Illinois Invitational, Ill State Mus, Springfield, 78; 37th & 40th Indiana Salon Shows, Northern Ind Arts Assoc, Munster, Ind, 79 & 83; Lakeview Mus, Peoria, Ill, 79; Foothills Art Ctr, Golden, Colo, 83. *Teaching:* Instr sculpture, N Shore Art League, Winnetka, Ill, 58-83; instr stone carving, Suburban Fine Arts Ctr, Highland Park, Ill, 59-90 & Blackhawk Mountain Sch Art, Colo, summers, 83-90. *Awards:* Best of Show, 29th Ann Open Spectrum, Libertyville Art Ctr, 83 & Arthur Baer Competition, 85. *Bibliog:* Elaine Snyderman (producer), Viewpoints/Kay Hofmann, Cable TV, 86; Michael Bonesteel (auth), Caught in the Coils, Pioneer Press, 86; Arthur Williams (auth), Sculpture: Technique, Form, Content, 89. *Mem:* N Shore Art League; Suburban Fine Arts Ctr. *Media:* Stone, Wood. *Dealer:* Mindscape 1506 Sherman Evanston IL 60201. *Mailing Add:* 1531 N Bell Chicago IL 60622

HOFSTED, JOLYON GENE
SCULPTOR, EDUCATOR
b San Antonio, Tex, Oct 21, 42. *Study:* Calif Col Arts & Crafts, Oakland; Brooklyn Mus Art Sch, NY. *Work:* Mus Mod Art, Kyoto, Japan; Brooklyn Mus & Mus Contemp Crafts, New York; Queens Mus, NY; Sea of Japan Expos Secretariat, Kanazawa-shi; Newark Mus, NJ; and others. *Exhib:* Retrospective, 11 years, Brooklyn, NY, 73; Clay Attitudes, Queens Mus, New York, 79-80; Eighth Chunichi Int Exhib Ceramics Arts, Nagoya, Japan, 80; Ulster Co Coun Arts Gallery, Kingston, NY, 85; Contemporary American Ceramics, Brooklyn Mus, NY, 86; Dome Gallery, New York, 90 & 92; and others. *Pos:* Dir, Brooklyn Mus Art Sch, 70-73. *Teaching:* Instr art, Brooklyn Mus Art Sch, 63-71; assoc prof art, Queens Col, City Univ New York, 66-, deputy chmn art dept, 85-88; instr ceramics, Haystack Mountain Sch Crafts, Maine, 66 & 68. *Awards:* Del Art Mus, 66; Res Award, PSC-City Univ NY, 85, 88, 90 & 92; NY Award, Works on/of Paper, 86; and others. *Mem:* Ulster Co Coun for Arts (vchmn, 74-76). *Media:* Clay. *Publ:* Auth, Ceramics, Western Publ Co, 67; auth, Pottery, Pan Bks, London, 74; contribr, Craft Encyclopedia, Time-Life Publ, 75; auth movie, Textures, Clay Works, 78; contribr, Encyclopedia of Crafts, Scribners, New York, 80. *Mailing Add:* Box 66 Shady NY 12479

HOGARTH, BURNE
ARTIST, ILLUSTRATOR
b Chicago, Ill, Dec 25, 11. *Study:* Art Inst Chicago, 25-27; Chicago Acad Fine Arts, 26-29; studio classes with Todros Geller, 27-31; Crane Col, 28-30; Univ Chicago, 30-32; Northwestern Univ, 31-32 & 37-38; Columbia Univ, 56-57. *Work:* Mus Bandes Dessinees, Paris, France; Pavilion Humour, Terre des Hommes, Montreal, Can; Graham Gallery, Inc, New York; Escola Pan-Am de Arte, Sao Paulo, Brazil; Mus Cartoon Art, Portchester, NY. *Exhib:* One-man shows, Societe Francaise Photographie, Paris, 66, Bibliotheque Municipals, Palais de Longchamps, Marseille, 85; Bandes Dessinees et figuration Narrative, Louvre, Paris, 67; Exposicao de Quadrinhos, Museu de Arte, San Paulo, 70; 75 Years of Comics, New York Cultural Ctr, 71; The Comics, Kennedy Cultural Ctr, Washington, DC, 72; Four Masters of Narrative Art, Graham Gallery, Inc, New York, 77; Smithsonian Traveling Exhib, Gallery Kari Katury, Warsaw, Poland, 89-90. *Pos:* Illusr, Tarzan

Sunday comic page, 37-50; pres, Pendragon Press, New York, 75; bd mem, Mus Cartoon Art, Portchester, NY, 77-79. *Teaching:* Founder, vpres, coordr curriculum & instr, Sch Visual Arts, Inc, New York, 47-70; instr anat, Parsons Sch Design, New York, 76-81; instr, Nat, Otis-Parsons Sch, Los Angeles, 81-83; instr analytical drawing, Art Ctr Col Design, Pasadena, 83- *Awards:* Best Illus Cartoonist, Nat Cartoonists Soc, 74, 75 & 76; Cartoonist of Yr, Pavilion Humour, Montreal, Can, 75; Caran D'Alhe Lifetime Award, illus, Lucca, Italy, 84; Lavriers D'or (Golden Palms) Award, Cesar Soc, Paris, 85. *Bibliog:* Francis Lacassin (auth), Tarzan, ou le Chevalier Crispe, Union Gen Ed, Paris, 71; Walter James Miller (auth), Burne Hogarth and the art of pictorial fiction, In: Jungle Tales of Tarzan, Watson-Guptill, 76; Maurice Horn (auth), World Encyclopedia of Comics, Chelsea House, New York, 76; and others. *Mem:* Nat Art Educ Asn; Am Soc Aesthet; Nat Cartoonists Soc (pres, 77-79); Int Asn Aesthetics, 89. *Media:* Oil. *Publ:* Auth-illusr, Dynamic Anatomy, 58, Dynamic Figure Drawing, 65, Drawing the Human Head, 68, Drawing Dynamic Hands, 77 & Dynamic Light and Shade, 81, Watson-Guptill, New York. *Dealer:* Richard Pryor Collector's Press Box 1009 Carmel Valley CA 93924. *Mailing Add:* 6026 W Lindenhurst Ave Los Angeles CA 90036

HOGBIN, STEPHEN
SCULPTOR
b Tolworth Surrey, United Kingdom. *Study:* Kingston Col Art, United Kingdom, NDD; Royal Col Art, United Kingdom, Des RCA. *Work:* Art Bank Can Coun, Ottawa, Ont; Australia Coun, Sydney; Melbourne State Col, Australia; Can Mus Civilization, Ottawa; Mendel Art Gallery, Sask; Tom Thomson Mem Art Gallery, Ont; and others. *Comn:* Sculpture, Melbourne State Col, Australia; entrance & screen, Metrop Toronto Libr Can, 77 & 89; murals, Queens Park, 80 & CIL Inc, Toronto, 81; installation, Cambridge Gallery, Ont; and others. *Exhib:* Chairs, Art Gallery Ont, Toronto, 75; Art of Woodturning, Am Craft Mus, New York, 83; Painted Reliefs Traveling Exhib (catalog), 89; Re; Turning (catalog), 90, John B Aird Gallery, Toronto; McMaster Univ, Hamilton, 92; Progress of Walking: The Body in Public Art, Can Ctr Arts at Owen Sound, 92; and others. *Pos:* Artist-in-residence, Melbourne State Col, Australia Coun, 75-76. *Teaching:* Instr wood, Sheridan Sch Design, Port Credit, Ont, Can, 68-71; Col Educ, Univ Toronto, 71-72; instr sculpture, Georgian Col, Barrie, Ont, 85-87; lectures & workshops, Royal Col Art, UK, RI Sch Design, USA, Melbourne State Col, Australia; and others. *Awards:* Ont Arts Council Awards, 83-86; Sculpture Award, Tom Thomson Gallery, 80 & 81; John Mather Award, 85. *Bibliog:* D L McKinley (auth), The forms of Stephen Hogbin, Craft Horizons, 4/74; Jeanne Parkin (auth), Art in Architecture, 82; Helen Duffy (auth), Stephen Hogbin, Ont Craft, spring 84. *Mem:* Ont Crafts Coun (dir, 77-78); Can Crafts Coun (vpres, 73-74); Can Artists Representation; Visual Arts Ont; Royal Can Acad. *Media:* Multimedia. *Publ:* Auth, Turning full circle, 79 & Variable-arm milling machine, No 53, 85, Fine Woodworking; Wood Turning, Van Nostrand Reinhold, 80. *Mailing Add:* 753 Third Ave E Owen Sound ON N4K 2K4 Canada

HOGE, ROBERT WILSON
MUSEUM DIRECTOR, EDUCATOR
b Wilmington, Del, Jan 5, 47. *Study:* Univ Colo, BA(anthrop), 69; Univ Chicago. *Collections Arranged:* Thematic Exhibitions in Art & Sci, 76-81, Sanford Mus & Planetarium; Exhibits of Coins, Paper Money, Tokens & Medals, 81-90, Mus Am Numismatic Asn. *Pos:* Asst dir, Sanford Mus & Planetarium, Cherokee, Iowa, 76, actg dir, 76 & dir, 76-81; instr anthrop, Buena Vista Col, Storm Lake, Iowa, Fall 76; cur, Mus Am Numismatic Asn, 81- *Teaching:* Anthrop, Buena Vista Col, Storm Lake, Iowa, 76; instr sems, Am Numismatic Assoc, 82- *Awards:* Outstanding Young Men of Am, 81. *Mem:* Am Numismatic Soc; Int Coun Mus; Colo-Wyo Asn Mus; Am Asn Mus. *Res:* American archaeology, historical studies; Old World archaeology; numismatics. *Publ:* Ed, Northwest Chapter Newsletter, Iowa Archaeol Soc, Sanford Mus; Museum, Column, Tha Numismatist, 83- *Mailing Add:* Am Numismatic Asn 818 N Cascade Ave Colorado Springs CO 80903

HOGLE, ANN MEILSTRUP
PAINTER
b San Francisco, Calif, Sept 23, 27. *Study:* Univ Ore; Portland Mus Sch; Calif Col Arts & Crafts, BFA, MFA, 79. *Work:* Neuberger Collection, New York; Kemper Group, Long Grove, Ill; St Francis Mem Hosp & Security Pac Bank, San Francisco; Int Bus Machines; Merril Lynch; and others. *Exhib:* Artists of Oregon, Portland Mus, 63 & 70; Phelan Awards, Calif Palace Legion Hon, San Francisco, 65; solo exhibs, Stanford Univ, Calif, 66, Janus Gallery, Los Angeles, 75, Ritz Gallery, Point Reyes, Calif, 79 & William Sawyer Gallery, San Francisco, 82, 85 & 87; Syntex, Palo Alto, 89; and others. *Bibliog:* Helga Epstein (auth), Ann Hogle: Painting toward consciousness, Am Artist, 79; Allison Campbell (auth), US Art 1990 Pvt Showings. *Media:* Oil. *Dealer:* William Sawyer Gallery 3045 Clay St San Francisco CA. *Mailing Add:* 45 Meadow Rd Woodside CA 94062

HOGUE, ALEXANDRE
PAINTER, LITHOGRAPHER
b Memphis, Mo, Feb 22, 1898. *Work:* Mus Nat Art Mod, Paris; Nat Mus Am Art, Washington, DC; Dallas Mus Art, Tex; Okla Art Ctr, Oklahoma City; Univ Ariz Mus Art & Phoenix Art Mus, Ariz; Springfield Mus Art, Mo; Carl Millesvag, Lidingo, Sweden; and others. *Exhib:* Int Exhib, Jeu de Paume, Paris, 38; Carnegie Inst Int Exhibs, 38 & 39; Tate Gallery, London, Eng, 46; Whitney Mus Am Art, New York; Wilderness, Corcoran Gallery Art, DC, 71; Hayward Gallery Art, London, 77; Berlin Acad Arts, 80 & Hamburg Kunstverein, 81, Ger; Haus Der Kunst, Munich, Ger, 83; one-man comprehensive, Philbrook Art Ctr, 84. *Teaching:* Instr life drawing & painting, Taos, Tex State Col Women, summers 31-42; prof art & head dept, Univ Tulsa, 45-68, emer prof, 69- *Awards:* Purchase Award, 9th Southwest Prints & Drawings, Dallas Mus Fine Art, 59; Grand Awards, Philbrook Art Ctr, Tulsa, Okla, 61 & 75; Purchase Award, Springfield Mus Art, Mo, 65. *Bibliog:* John Bauer (auth), Revolution & Tradition in Modern American Art, 51; Nouvelles acquisitions, La Revue Du Louvre, 61; Ralph K Andrist (ed), History of the 20's and 30's, Am Heritage, 70; Lea Rossen de Long (auth), Nature's forms nature's forces, Archives Am Art, Wash. *Media:* Oil, Watercolor; Lithography. *Publ:* Illusr, Spirit and Vison: Images of Ranchos de Taos Church, Mus of NMex, 87; Art in New Mexico, 1900-1945, Nat Mus Am Art. *Dealer:* Geoffry Cline Gallery 2519 E 67th St Tulsa OK 74136. *Mailing Add:* 4052 E 23rd St Tulsa OK 74114

HOI, SAMUEL CHUEN-TSUNG
EDUCATOR, ADMINISTRATOR
b Hong Kong, Mar 25, 58; US citizen. *Study:* Columbia Col, NY, AB, 80; Columbia Sch Law, NY, JD, 83; Parsons Sch Design, NY, AAS, 86. *Pos:* Dir AAS degree prog, Parsons Sch Design, NY 87-88; dir, Parsons Sch Design, Paris, 88-91; dean, Corcoran Sch Art, Washington, DC 91- *Mem:* Alliance Independent Sch Art & Design. *Mailing Add:* c/o Corcoran Sch Art 500 17th St NW Washington DC 20006-4899

HOIE, CLAUS
PAINTER, ETCHER
b Stavanger, Norway, Nov 3, 11; US citizen. *Study:* Pratt Inst; Art Students League; Ecole Beaux Arts, Paris. *Work:* Brooklyn Mus, NY; Norfolk Mus, Va; Butler Inst Am Art, Youngstown, Ohio; Okla Mus Art; Guild Hall Mus, East Hampton, NY; South St Seaport Mus, New York. *Exhib:* Am Watercolor Soc Ann, New York, 60-80; Brooklyn Mus Watercolor Biennial, 63; Mus Watercolor Painting, Mexico City, Mex, 68 & 89; Pa Acad Fine Arts Ann, 69; Childe Hassam Award Exhib, Nat Inst Arts & Lett, 73; one-man shows, Akershus Castle Mus, Oslo, Norway, 82, South St Seaport Mus, New York, 92; and others. *Awards:* Gold Medal of Honor, Am Watercolor Soc, 62; Award for Painting, Nat Inst Arts & Lett, 75; Award of Merit, Nat Acad Design, 81; Obrig Prize, Nat Acad Design, 85. *Mem:* Nat Acad Design; Am Watercolor Soc (vpres, 60-62); Nat Arts Club, Audubon Soc. *Media:* Watercolor, Graphics. *Publ:* Auth, Technique of watercolor, Am Artist Mag, 57; auth, My views on watercolor painting, North Light Mag, 70. *Mailing Add:* 20 W 12th St New York NY 10011

HOIE, HELEN HUNT
PAINTER, COLLAGE ARTIST
b Leetsdale, Pa. *Study:* Carnegie-Mellon Univ, BA; Univ Vt, with Kenneth Shopen, 45; with Alexander Russo, 68, New Sch Social Res, with Henry Pearson, 69. *Work:* Stephen's Collection, Little Rock, Ark; Centre Col of Kentucky, Danville; Parrish Art Mus, Southampton, NY; Nat Mus Women in the Arts, Washington, DC; Guild Hall Mus, East Hampton, NY. *Exhib:* Parrish Mus Art, Southampton, NY, 90; Guild Hall Mus, East Hampton, 72-73, 75, 85-86; one-man shows, Babcock Galleries, New York, 74-77 & 80-81, New York Univ, 76, Vered Gallery, E Hampton, 82, 84-92 & Forum Gallery, New York, 84-86; Women Artists, Brooklyn Mus, NY, 75; Ann Exhib, Butler Inst Am Art, Youngstown, Ohio, 75; Ranger Fund Exhib, Nat Acad Design, New York, 78 & 86; Selections from the East Hampton Guild Hall Collection, Ft Lauderdale, Pensacola & Miss Mus, 79; Stavanger Mus, Norway, 83; Elaine Benson Gallery, Bridgehampton, 72-83; Bergen Mus Art & Sci, Paramus, NJ, 85; Nat Arts Club, 91. *Awards:* First Prize Abstract Painting, Guild Hall Mus, 70; Individual Exhib Award for Ten Yr Retrospective, Parrish Mus Art, 77; Gold Medal - First Prize, Nat Soc Painters Acrylic & Casein, 78; Cert of Merit, 163rd Ann Exhib, Nat Acad Design, 88. *Bibliog:* Ellen Russotto (auth), Helen Hole: Atmospheres & Intervals; John & Joan Digby (coauth), The Collage Handbook, 85. *Mem:* Women Arts; Artists Equity; Audubon Soc; Nat Soc Painters Acrylic & Casein; Jimmy Ernst Art Alliance. *Media:* Acrylic on Canvas. *Dealer:* Forum Gallery 1018 Madison Ave New York NY 10021; Vered Gallery 68 Park Pl East Hampton NY 11937. *Mailing Add:* 20 W 12th St New York NY 10011

HOKANSON, HANS
SCULPTOR, COLLAGE ARTIST
b Malmoe, Swed, Aug 22, 25. *Study:* Studied drawing with Prof Warshaw, Los Angeles, 53; studied drawing at the Art Students League, New York, 61-63. *Work:* Brooklyn Mus, Metrop Mus Art & Port Authority of New York and New Jersey, New York; Malmoe Mus, Swed; Hirshhorn Mus and Sculpture Garden, Washington, DC. *Comn:* Altar, Zen Community of New York. *Exhib:* Los Angeles County Mus Annual, 54; Long Island Univ, Southampton, NY, 67; American Drawing 1970-1973, Yale Univ, 73; Solo exhibs, Wood Sculpture, Guild Hall Mus, East Hampton, NY, 80 & Collages, Malmoe Mus, Swed, 86; Poets and Artists Collaborating, Guild Hall Mus, East Hampton, NY, 82; Inaugural Exhibition, Herbert H Lehman Collection, New York, 85. *Pos:* Mus technician, Mus Primitive Art, New York, 56-61. *Teaching:* Adj prof sculpture, Long Island Univ, Southampton, NY, 78. *Awards:* First Purchase Prize, Long Island Univ Invitational, Southampton, NY, 67-; First Purchase Prize, Membership Exhibition, Guild Hall Mus, East Hampton, NY, 80; General Prize, Pollock-Krasner Found, Inc, 86. *Bibliog:* Hilton Kramer (auth), reviews, New York Times, 65-76; Stella Rosemarch (auth), The wood works of Hans Hokanson, Craft Horizons, 72; Michael Brenson (auth), reviews, New York Times, 82-84. *Media:* Wood. *Dealer:* The Grace Borgenicht Gallery Inc 724 Fifth Ave New York NY 10019. *Mailing Add:* PO Box 996 East Hampton NY 11937

HOLABIRD, JEAN
PAINTER, PRINTMAKER
b Boston, Mass, Dec 3, 46. *Study:* Art Students League, New York, 65-69; Inst Allende, Mexico, summers 65-69; Bennington Col, Vt, BA, 69. *Work:* Prudential Life Insurance Co, Newark, NJ; First Nat City Bank, Chicago; Staatmuseum, West Berlin, Ger; Ragdale Found, Lake Forest, Ill; Metrop Mus Art, New York. *Comn:* Drawings, Bennington Rev, Vt, 69-70; cover illus, World Mag, New York, 80; cover, Hanging Loose Mag, New York, 81; and others. *Exhib:* Camden Coun Arts, London, England, 73; Two Painters, Saray Y Rentschler Gallery, New York, 78; one-woman show, Nathan A Bernstein Ltd, New York, 80; Hand-colored Etchings, Sarah Y Rentschler Gallery, New York, 82; Usdan Gallery, Vt, 84; Neo Persona, New York, 88, 90 & 91. *Teaching:* Instr painting, Inst Allende, San Miguel Allende, Mexico, summer 68; guest lectr, Parsons Sch Design, Pratt Inst, Cooper Union, New York, 75 & Sch Visual Arts, 79; artist-in-residence, Ragdale Found, 81. *Awards:* Cert Merit, Vt Coun Arts, 69; and others. *Bibliog:* Palmer Hasty (auth), A collaboration, Villager, 3/82; Bob Mahoney (auth), Arts Mag, 5/88; Greg Masters (auth), Interview Cover Mag, 5/91. *Mem:* Artists Equity Asn. *Media:* Watercolor, Oil. *Mailing Add:* 81 Warren St New York NY 10007

HOLBROOK, PETER GREENE
PAINTER, PRINTMAKER
b New York, NY, Apr 13, 40. *Study:* Dartmouth Col, BA(Marcus Heiman Award), 61; Brooklyn Mus, with Reuben Tam, cert(Beckman fel), 63. *Work:* Nat Collection Fine Arts, Washington, DC; Brooklyn Mus, NY; Art Inst Chicago; Springfield Art Mus, Mo; Mus of Southwest, Midland, Tex; Boise Art Mus, Idaho. *Exhib:* Chicago and Vicinity, Art Inst Chicago, 65 & 67-69; solo exhib, Indianapolis Mus Art, 70; Koffler Found Collection, Smithsonian Inst, 79; Realism, Walnut Creek Civic Arts Gallery, Calif, 80; Contemporary American Watercolor, Univ Wis-Madison, 82; Davidson Collection, Pa Acad Fine Arts, Philadelphia, 82; Invitational Watercolor Exhib, Hamline Univ, St Paul, Minn, 83; Watercolor USA Invitational, Springfield Art Mus, Mo, 86; The Big Picture, Riverside Art Mus, Calif, 90. *Teaching:* Lectr painting, Univ Ill, Chicago Circle, 68-70 & Calif State Univ, Hayward, 70-71. *Awards:* Wild, Bartels & Clark Prizes, Chicago and Vicinity, Art Inst Chicago, 65, 67 & 68; Walter H Stevens Award, Watercolor USA, Springfield Art Mus, 81; Raffael Prize for Watercolor, Humboldt Cult Ctr, Eureka, Calif, 81. *Bibliog:* Barbara Whipple (auth), Peter Holbrook, Am Artist Mag, 3/84; John Arthur (auth), Spirit of Place, Bullfinch Press, 89; Peter Holbrook, The Living Landscape, The World I Mag, 6/92. *Media:* Watercolor, Acrylic. *Publ:* Auth, article, 11/67 & The Chicago saga of Carolee Schneemann, 3/68, Art Scene Mag. *Mailing Add:* 5719 Briceland-Thorn Rd Redway CA 95560

HOLBROOK, VIVIAN NICHOLAS
PAINTER, ADMINISTRATOR
b Mount Vernon, NY, Mar 31, 13. *Study:* Yale Univ, BFA. *Work:* Univ Ga. *Exhib:* Butler Inst Am Art Ann, Youngstown, Ohio, 52; Ball State Univ Ann, 72; Ten Yr Retrospective, Fla Southern Col, Lakeland, 76; Prof Women Artist of Fla, Lowe Art Mus, Univ Miami & Women's Hemispheric Cong, 76; four-man show, Ctr Mod Art, Micanopy, Fla, 77; West 80, Art and the Law, Minn Mus Art, 80-81; American Drawings III, Va Arts Ctr, Portsmouth, 81; 27th Ann Drawing & Sculpture Show, Ball State Univ, Ind, 81; Gouache Paintings & Drawings, Santa Fe Community Col, Gainesville, Fla, 86; 20-year retrospective show, Thomas Ctr Gallery, Gainesville, Fla, 86. *Pos:* Dir, Ctr Mod Art, Micanopy, Fla, 69-; designer exhibs, Fla State Mus, summer 70. *Teaching:* Instr painting & drawing, Colby Jr Col, New London, NH, 36-39; interim instr painting & drawing, Univ Fla, 42-44; instr painting, Ctr Mod Art, Micanopy, Fla, 69-70. *Awards:* Second Award, Harry Rich Competition, Miami, 57; Top Award, Soc Four Arts, 58, Atwater Kent Award, 66. *Media:* Oil, Ink. *Mailing Add:* 1710 SW 35th Pl Gainesville FL 32608

HOLCOMB, GRANT
MUSEUM DIRECTOR, EDUCATOR
b San Bernardino, Calif, Sept 30, 44. *Study:* Univ Calif, Los Angeles, AB, 67; Univ Delaware, MA, PhD, 72. *Pos:* Dir, Mt Holyoke Col, South Hadley, Mass, 72-79; assoc dir, Timken Art Gallery, San Diego, Calif, 82-85; dir, Mem Art Gallery, Rochester, NY, currently. *Teaching:* Asst prof, Mt Holyoke Col, South Hadley, Mass 72-79 & State Univ, NY, Stony Brook, 79-81. *Awards:* Kress fel, Nat Gallery Art, 71. *Mem:* Asn Art Mus Dirs (chmn mus oper); Asn Art Mus; Col Art Asn. *Publ:* Auth, The Forgotton Legacy of Jerome Myers, Am Art J, 5/77; John Sloan in Santa Fe, Am Art J, 5/78; John Sloan, The Gloucester Years, Mus Fine Arts, Springfield, 80; John Sloan, The Wake of the Ferry, Timken Art Gallery, 84; Joyce Treiman, Friends & Strangers, Univ Southern Calif, 88. *Mailing Add:* 202 Clovercrest Dr Rochester NY 14618

HOLCOMBE, ANNA CALLUORI
CERAMIST, GALLERY DIRECTOR
b Newark, NJ, Sept 15, 52. *Study:* Montclair State Col, NJ, BA, 70; La State Univ, MFA, 74. *Work:* Int Mus Ceramics, Faenza, Italy; and others. *Exhib:* Solo exhib, Washington Univ, St Louis, 81 & Mem Art Gallery, Rochester, NY, 91; two-person show, Nazareth Col Art Gallery, Rochester, NY, 86; Rochester Fingerlakes, Memorial Art Gallery, Rochester, NY, 86; Craft Art 1988, Buchfield Art Ctr, Buffalo, NY. *Collections Arranged:* Ceramics Invitational, 80, Functional Ceramics with a Decorative Approach, 81 & Retrospective: Fred Brian, 84, Ill Wesleyan Univ, Bloomington; National Council Education Ceramic Arts Show (auth, catalog), traveling, 83-86 & 91; New Approaches to Figurative Art & Retrospective: Jack Wolsky, 86, Tower Fine Arts Gallery, Brockport, NY; Off the Pedestal, On the Walls, Village Gate Art Ctr, Rochester, NY. *Pos:* Dir, Tower Fine Arts Gallery, State Univ NY, Brockport, currently. *Teaching:* Asst prof art, Ill Wesleyan Univ, Bloomington, 79-84; assoc prof art & gallery dir, State Univ NY, Brockport, 84- *Awards:* Gold Medal, 46th Int Exhibit Ceramics, Italy, 89. *Bibliog:* Vicki Lewin (auth), Anna Calluori Holcombe, Ceramics Monthly, summer 86; Richard Zakin (auth), Ceramics, Mastering the Craft, Chilton Bk Co, 90. *Mem:* Nat Coun Educ Ceramics Arts (pres-elect 92-94, dir exhibs, 83-86 & presently, pres, 92-94); Empire State Crafts Alliance, NY (bd mem); Am Crafts Coun; Col Art Asn; Arts Greater Rochester. *Publ:* Auth, Master of Fine Arts and Careers, Nat Coun Art Adminrs Ceramics Art J, 80. *Mailing Add:* 192 Evergreen Rd Brockport NY 14420

HOLCOMBE, R GORDON, JR
COLLECTOR, PATRON
b Lake Charles, La, Oct 28, 13. *Study:* Vanderbilt Univ; Tulane Univ, BS, Sch Med, MD. *Pos:* Past pres, Art Assocs Lake Charles. *Collection:* Paintings, including works by Bernard, Derain, Buffet, Levier & Courbet; early 19th century American paintings. *Mailing Add:* 3624 Lake Lake Charles LA 70605

HOLDEN, DONALD
ARTIST, WRITER
b Los Angeles, Calif, Apr 22, 31. *Study:* Parsons Sch Design, New York, 46-47; Art Students League, 48; Columbia Univ, BA, 51; Ohio State Univ, MA, 52; Portland Sch Art, LLD, 86. *Work:* New Britain Mus Am Art; Ga Mus Art; Wichita Art Mus; Springfield Art Mus, Mo; Corcoran Gallery; Fine Arts Mus San Francisco; Metrop Mus Art; Victoria & Albert Mus; Yale Univ Art Gallery; and others. *Exhib:* Solo exhibs, Manhattanville Col, 83, Century Asn, 84 & Susan Conway Gallery, 90 & 92. *Pos:* Dir pr, Philadelphia Col Art, 53-55; dir, pr & personnel, Henry Dreyfuss Assocs, New York, 56-60; assoc mgr pr, Metrop Mus Art, New York, 60-61; art consult, Fortune Mag, 62; ed dir, Watson-Guptill Publ, 63-79, ed consult, 79-88; ed dir, Am Artist Mag, 71-75. *Teaching:* Instr painting & drawing, Scottsdale Artists Sch, Ariz, 85-86. *Mem:* Authors Guild; Nat Art Educ Asn; New York Artists Equity Asn; Artists Fel; Century Asn. *Media:* Aquamedia, drawing. *Publ:* Auth, Whistler Landscapes and Seascapes, 69; Creative Color for the Oil Painter, 83; The Complete Acrylic Painting Book, 89; The Complete Oil Painting Book, 89; The Complete Watercolor Book, 89; and many others. *Dealer:* Susan Conway Gallery 1058 Thomas Jefferson St NW Washington DC 20007; Holloway Howard 59 Grant Ave San Francisco CA 94108. *Mailing Add:* 128 Deertrack Ln Irvington NY 10533

HOLDEN, RUTH EGRI
PAINTER
b New York, NY, April 23, 11. *Study:* Nat Acad Design, New York, 26; Art Students League, New York, 32; Master Inst Roerich Mus, scholar, 34. *Work:* Del Art Mus, Univ Del, Wilmington; Du Pont Co; Blue Cross & Blue Shield Del; pvt collections of Greta Garbo & William Smith. *Comn:* Painting, Works Proj Admin, Lincoln Hosp, Bronx, 38. *Exhib:* Lynch Scene, Mus Mod Art, New York, 41; Corcoran Gallery Art, 43; NJ State Mus, 50; Girl With Bird, Isaac Delgado Muss, New Orleans, 57; solo exhib, Philadelphia Art Alliance, 75, Ware Gallery, Arden, Del, 81 & Univ Del. *Bibliog:* Articles, Del Today Mag, 76 & Am Artist, 12/77; Twenty Figure Painters and How They Work, Watson-Guptill, 79. *Media:* Acrylic, Pen and Ink. *Mailing Add:* c/o Peter Holden 19312 E Eldorado Dr Aurora CO 80013

HOLDER, KENNETH ALLEN
PAINTER, EDUCATOR
b Heald, Tex, Sept 11, 36. *Study:* Tex Christian Univ, BFA(com art), 59; Art Inst Chicago, MFA(painting), 65. *Work:* Ill State Mus, Springfield; Cultural Activities Ctr, Temple, Tx; Ratir/West Mus, Manitowoc, Wis; Mazur Mus, Monroe, La; Univ Chicago, Ill. *Comn:* Fresno City Col, Calif, 73; Va Commonwealth Univ, 73; Cent Mich Univ, 75; all in collab with Harold Gregor. *Exhib:* Watercolor USA, Springfield, Mo, 77, 80, 81, 82, 85, 87 & 88; Chicago Vicinity Show, Art Inst Chicago, 73; The Chicago Connection, Crocker Gallery, Sacramento, Calif; one-man shows, Nancy Lurie Gallery, Chicago, 75 & Zolla/Lieberman Gallery, Chicago, 82 & Conduit gallery, dallas, 85, 87 & 90. *Teaching:* Asst prof drawing & painting, Western Ill Univ, 65-69; prof drawing & painting, Ill State Univ, 69- *Awards:* NEA Artist Fel, 87. *Bibliog:* Henry Glover (auth), Artist (video), Ill State Univ, 72; "Ken Holder's Autobiographical Art," American Artist, 9/86. *Mem:* Charter mem, Watercolor USA Honor Soc. *Media:* Acrylic; Mixed Media. *Publ:* Ken Holder (auth, catalog for one-man, travelling show), 84-85. *Mailing Add:* 104 Streitzer Ave Bloomington IL 61701

HOLDER, TOM
PAINTER
b Kansas City, Mo, Jan 21, 40. *Study:* San Diego State Univ, BA; Univ Wash, MFA. *Work:* Metromedia Collection, Los Angeles; ITT, Los Angeles, Calif; San Diego Fine Arts Gallery, Calif; Valley Bank, Las Vegas & Reno, Nev; Las Vegas Art Mus, Nev. *Comn:* Mural, Seattle-Tacoma Int Airport, 73; exterior wall mural, Seattle Steam Corp Plant, Seattle Arts Comn, 75; exterior wall mural, CETA Bldg, Las Vegas, Nev, 79; painting, State Capitol Bldg, Nev, 81. *Exhib:* Univ Mass, Amherst, 91; Pensacola Art Mus, Fla, 91; Brenau Col, Gainesville, Ga, 91; Brendan Walter Gallery, Santa Monica, Calif, 92; Northern Ariz Univ Art Mus, Flagstaff, 92. *Pos:* Founding dir, Nev Inst Contemp Art, 85-91. *Teaching:* Instr painting, Univ Wash, 67-69; prof painting, Univ Nev, Las Vegas, 71- *Awards:* Charles Vanda Award for Creative Excellence, 92; Visual Arts Fel, Nev State Coun of the Arts, 92-93. *Bibliog:* James P Rupp (auth), Art in Seattle's public places, Univ of Wash Press, Seattle, 92. *Dealer:* William Traver Gallery 110 Union St Seattle WA 98101; Brendan Walter Gallery 1001 Colorado Ave Santa Monica CA 90401. *Mailing Add:* Dept Art Univ Nev Las Vegas 4505 Maryland Pkwy Las Vegas NV 89154

HOLEN, NORMAN DEAN
SCULPTOR, EDUCATOR
b Cavalier, NDak, Sept 16, 37. *Study:* Concordia Col, BA, 59; State Univ Iowa, MFA, 62; Univ Minn, Minneapolis, 72. *Work:* 3M Co, Minneapolis, Minn; Univ Lutheran Church of Hope, Minneapolis; Augsburg Col, Minneapolis; Civic Plaza, Richfield, Minn; and others. *Comn:* Half life size bronze figure, St Bridget's Catholic Church, Cavalier, NDak, 74; brazed steel bas relief, Luther Theological Seminary, St Paul, Minn, 77; half life size terra cotta figures, Vinge Lutheran Church, Wilmar, Minn, 80; 7 figure composition, St Phillip the Deacon Lutheran Church, Plymouth, Minn, 85; Brazed steel sculpture & baptismal font, St Paul, Minn, 86. *Exhib:* One-man show, Minneapolis Inst Art, 68; Nat Gallery, Washington, DC, 69; Nat sculpture Soc, 77, 80-86; Allied Artists Am, New York, 80, 82, 83 & 85; Port of Hist Mus, Philadelphia, Penn, 87. *Teaching:* Prof art, drawing, sculpture & ceramics, Augsburg Col, 64- *Awards:* Rachel Leah Armour Award, 80 & 82 & In Memorium Award, 83, Allied Artists Am; Bronze Medal, 80 & Joel Meisner Award, 83, Nat Sculpture Soc; Alumni Achievement Award, Concordia Col, Moorhead, Minn, 85. *Bibliog:* Article, Norman Holen's Work on Display in Philadelphia, Cavalier Chronical, 11/3/87; Jennifer Bowles (auth), Sculpture honors Christensen, Echo, 10/13/89; Lynn Flemming (auth), Artists Outddor Gallery, Richfield Sun, 11/7/89. *Mem:* Allied Artists Am; Nat Sculpture Soc; Minn Sculptors Soc. *Media:* Welded Steel, Terra Cotta. *Publ:* Auth, Upper midwest art: Minnesota, North Dakota, South Dakota, Rev of the Arts, 77; Preserving your self expression, Artists Market, 79; Soft core sculpture, Arts & Activities, 5/84; Origin of three dimensional art, Int Sculpture Mag, 85; Sculpture the Human form in terra cotta, Am Artists, 11/86. *Mailing Add:* 7332 12th Ave S Minneapolis MN 55423

HOLLADAY, HARLAN H
HISTORIAN, PAINTER
b Greenville, Mo, Dec 10, 25. *Study:* SE Mo State Col, BS(educ); Wash Univ, St Louis Mo; State Univ Iowa, MA; Cornell Univ, PhD. *Work:* Munson-Williams Proctor Inst, Utica, NY; St Lawrence Univ Collection, Canton, NY; Des Moines Art Ctr, Iowa; SE Mo State Univ Collection; Springfield Art Mus, Mo. *Exhib:* Corcoran Gallery Art Biennial, Washington, DC, 51; Whitney Mus Am Art, New York, 52; Pa Acad Fine Arts, Philadelphia, 52, 53 & 59; 61st Nat Watercolor Ann, Washington, DC, 58; and others. *Teaching:* Art teacher, Poplar Bluff Pub Schs, Mo, 51-53 & Des Moines, Iowa, 53-55; from instr to asst prof drawing & painting, Univ Nev, Reno, 55-58; prof fine arts, St Lawrence Univ, 61-, head dept, 65-71, L M & G L Flint prof, 67-, prof emer, 91; prof art & artist in residence, Am Col Switz, 68-69. *Awards:* Hon Mention, 61st Nat Watercolor Ann, Washington, DC, 58; Reynolds Awards, Cooperstown Art Asn, 67; First Prize Painting, NY State Fair, Syracuse, 74; plus others. *Mem:* Col Art Asn Am; Soc Archit Historians; Cooperstown Art Asn; St Lawrence Co Hist Asn. *Media:* Oil, Acrylic. *Res:* 15th century art, especially Italian painters; mosaics & studies related to Venice. *Publ:* Auth, Art in the liberal arts curriculum, 64 & auth, The value of a teaching collection, 70, St Lawrence Bull; auth, Catalogue for the McGinnis Collection, St Lawrence Univ, 70. *Mailing Add:* Dept of Fine Arts St Lawrence Univ Canton NY 13617

HOLLADAY, WILHELMINA COLE
COLLECTOR, PATRON
b Elmira, NY. *Study:* Elmira Col, BA, 44; Univ Paris; Univ Va; Dr Humanities Moore Col Art, Dr, 88, Mt Vernon Col, DHL, 88, Elmira Col, Dr Humanities, 89. *Pos:* Dir, Holladay Corp, Interior Design, Washington DC, 72-84; pres, The Holladay Found, Washington DC, 80-84; pres & chmn bd, Nat Mus Women in the Arts, 81- *Awards:* Woman Distinction, Coun Independent Col, 87; Women Achievers Award, Int Alliance, 91; Woman That Makes a Difference, Int Womens' Forum, 91. *Mem:* Corcoran Gallery, Washington DC (trustee); Am Asn Mus; Am Federation Art; Mus Mod Art; Women's Caucus Art; Nat Women's Economic Alliance (bd). *Interests:* Contribution of women to history through art from Renaissance to present. *Collection:* Women's art from the Renaissance to contemporary period. *Mailing Add:* 3215 R Street NW Washington DC 20007

HOLLAND, HARRY CHARLES
COMPUTER ARTIST, PAINTER
b Childress, Tex, Jan 2, 37. *Study:* Univ Tex, Austin, 55-57; Sch of Art Inst Chicago, BFA, 62; Carnegie Inst Technol, MFA, 63. *Work:* Dravo Corp Collection, Pittsburgh. *Comn:* Mural, Urban Design Asn Bldg, Pa Coun Arts, Pittsburgh, 76; interior mural, Plaza, Reiber Construction, Pittsburgh, 80. *Exhib:* Solo exhibs, Carnegie Inst Mus Art, Pittsburgh, Pa, 75, Univ Mo, 76 & Sordoni Gallery, Wilkes Col, Wilkes-Barr, Pa, 79; Electra 83, Mus Mod Art, Paris, France, 83; Art Computacion, Mus Provincial De Belles Artes, Cordoba, Arg, 87; CRASH, Write Mus Art, Beloit, Wis, 89; SIGGRAPH 82, 83 & 89 Traveling Exhib; Inst de Estudios Norteamericanos, Barcelona, Spain, 90; Univ de Salamanca, Spain, 90; Adelaide Festival Ctr, Australia, 90. *Pos:* Act dir, The Ctr Art & Technol, Pittsburgh, 87-88. *Teaching:* Prof painting & computer graphics, Carnegie Mellon Univ, Pittsburgh, 63- *Awards:* Allegheny Found & Purchase Award, Assoc Artists, 76; Hornbostle Teaching Award, Carnegie Mellon Univ, 82; Pittsburgh Artist Year, Pittsburgh Ctr Arts, 91. *Mem:* SIG Graph Computers Graphics Asn; Assoc Artists Pittsburgh; Asn Computing Machinery. *Media:* Computer, Acrylic. *Publ:* Auth, Is Alechinsky Worth $50,000?, Pittsburgh Mag, 10/77. *Mailing Add:* 1140 Murray Hill Ave Pittsburgh PA 15217

HOLLAND, HILLMAN RANDALL
ART DEALER
b Athens, Ala, Apr 17, 50. *Study:* Auburn Univ, BA, 73; Ga State Univ, BS, 75; Atlanta Law Sch, JD, 76; Parsons in Paris, cert, 80; Attingham Summer Sch, Eng, cert, 82; Winterthur Summer Inst, Del, cert, 83. *Pos:* Dir, Hillman Holland Gallery, 83-; Trustee, Atlanta Col Art; Trustee Nexus Contemp Arts Ctr; & Trustee Decorative Arts, High Mus Art, Atlanta. *Specialty:* International avant-garde art, Arnulf Rainer, Milan Kunc, Tishan Hsu, Barbara Kruger, Tim Head, Pat Courtney, Thomas Nozowski, Francesco Clemente & Mimmo Paladino. *Mailing Add:* 2575 Peachtree Rd NE Atlanta GA 30305

HOLLAND, TOM
PAINTER
b Seattle, Wash, 1936. *Study:* Willamette Univ, 54-56; Univ Calif, Santa Barbara & Berkeley, 57-59. *Work:* Whitney Mus Am Art, New York; St Louis City Mus; San Francisco Mus Art; Mus Mod Art, New York; Art Inst Chicago; plus many others. *Exhib:* Kid Stuff, Albright-Knox Art Gallery, Buffalo, NY, 71, Working in Calif, 72; New Options in Painting, Walker Art Ctr, Minneapolis, 72; California Prints, Mus Mod Art, New York, 72; Calif Printmakers, Whitney Mus Am Art, 73, New Aquisitions, 78; Corcoran Biennial, Washington, DC, 75; one-man shows, San Francisco Art Inst, 79, Blum-Helman Gallery, New York, 79 & Watson-De Nagy, Houston, 79; Felicity Samuel Gallery, London, 80; James Corcoran Gallery, Los Angeles, Calif, 80, 82 & 84-88; Charles Cowles Gallery, New York, 81-86, 88-90; Berggruen Gallery, San Francisco, 87-89 & 91. *Teaching:* Instr art, San Francisco Art Inst, 61-68 & 72-80, Univ Calif, Los Angeles, 68-69, Berkeley, 78-79 & Cornish Inst, Seattle, 78. *Awards:* Fulbright Grant, Santiago, Chile, 59-60; Nat Endowment Arts Sculpture Grant, 75-76; Guggenheim Fel, 79. *Media:* All. *Dealer:* John Berggruen Gallery 228 Grant Ave San Francisco CA 94108; Charles Cowles Gallery 420 W Broadway New York NY 10012. *Mailing Add:* 28 Roble Rd Berkeley CA 94705

HOLLEN-BOLMGREN, DONNA
PAINTER, PAPERMAKER
b Willmar, Minn, May 28, 35. *Study:* Univ Minn, BS(art educ), 57; Univ Pittsburgh, 58; Carnegie-Mellon Univ, 59. *Work:* Blount Inc; Westinghouse; Alcoa; McDonalds; Zanesville Art Ctr, Ohio; many corp & pvt collections. *Comn:* Vista Int Hotel, Pittsburgh. *Exhib:* Gallery Upstairs, Pittsburgh Ctr for Arts, 70, 76 & 82; William Penn Mus, Harrisburg, Pa, 71-73; Ogleby Mus, Wheeling, WVa, 72; Butler Inst Am Art Mid-Year Nat, Ohio, 73 & 81; 10 year retrospective, Allegheny Co Courthouse Gallerie, 85; Chatauqua Nat Painting, Gallery 6, 89; and others. *Teaching:* Instr design, Pittsburgh Ctr for Arts, 70-, instr painting & papermaking, 73- *Awards:* Excellence in Contemp Art, William Penn Mus; Assoc Artist, Pittsburgh, Carnegie Mus Art, 87; Frank Ross Award, Pittsburgh Craftsmen's Guild, 91-92; and others. *Mem:* Assoc Artists of Pittsburgh (pres, 74-); Craftsmen's Guild; Artists Equity; Int Asn Papermakers & Artists; Friends of Dard Hunter Mus. *Media:* Pure Pigment; Handmade Paper Pulp. *Dealer:* Gallery G 211 Ninth St Pittsburgh PA 15222; Artsouth Philadelphia PA. *Mailing Add:* 5703 Kentucky Ave Pittsburgh PA 15232

HOLLERBACH, SERGE
PAINTER, INSTRUCTOR
b Pushkin, Russia, Nov 1, 23; US citizen. *Study:* Acad Fine Arts, Munich, Ger, 46-49; Art Students League, with Ernst Fiene, 50; Am Art Sch, with Gordon Samstag, 51. *Work:* St Paul Gallery Art, Minn; Bridgeport Mus Art, Sci & Indust, Conn; Ga Mus Art, Athens; Seton Hall Univ Art Gallery; Norfolk Mus Art & Scis, Va. *Exhib:* Am Watercolor Soc Ann Exhib; Nat Acad Design Ann Exhib; Drawings USA, St Paul, Minn; 200 Years of Watercolor Painting in America, Metrop Mus Art, New York; Am Acad Arts & Lett, New York. *Teaching:* Instr painting, Nat Acad Sch Fine Arts, New York. *Awards:* Adolph & Clara Obrig Prize, Nat Acad Design, 71, 75 & 81; Gold Medal, Allied Artists Am, 76; Gold Medal, Am Watercolor Soc, 83. *Bibliog:* Aleksis Rannit (auth), Arts Mag, 1/81; Scott Elliot (auth), Portrait of an artist, Artists' Mag, 6/86. *Mem:* Am Watercolor Soc (vpres, 79); Audubon Artists; Allied Artists; Nat Soc Painters in Casein & Acrylics; Nat Acad Design. *Media:* Acrylic, Watercolor. *Publ:* Auth, Composing in Acrylics, Watson-Guptill Publ, 88. *Dealer:* Newman & Saunders Galleries Wayne PA. *Mailing Add:* 304 W 75th St New York NY 10023

HOLLIDAY, JUDITH
LIBRARIAN
b Butler, Pa, Mar 16, 38. *Study:* Col Wooster, BA, 60; Columbia Univ, MSLS, 61. *Pos:* Head librn, Fine Arts Libr, Cornell Univ, 70-; pub ed, Soc Arch Hist Newletter, 79- *Mem:* Art Libr Soc NAm; Soc Archit Historians. *Interests:* Nineteenth century American architectural periodicals. *Mailing Add:* 215 N Cayuga St Apt 113 Ithaca NY 14850

HOLLINGSHEAD, JOE EDGAR
PAINTER, SCULPTOR
b Amarillo, Tex, Dec 18, 46. *Work:* Nat Cowboy Hall Fame, Oklahoma City, Okla; Nat Mus Am Art, Washington, DC; Nat Mus Southwest, Midland, Tex. *Exhib:* Phippen Memorial, Phoenix, Ariz, 82; Western Regional, Old West Mus, Cheyenne, Wyo, 83; Art LXXIV, Amarillo Rotary, Tex, 84; West Texas Boys Ranch Annual, San Angelo, Tex, 84. *Media:* Oil; Bronze. *Mailing Add:* HC Rte Box T33D Big Spring TX 79720

HOLLINGSWORTH, ALVIN CARL
PAINTER, INSTRUCTOR
b New York, NY, Feb 25, 30. *Study:* City Univ New York, BA, 56, MA, 59; Art Students League, with Kunioshi, Ralph Fabri & Dr Bernard Myers, 50-52. *Work:* Chase Manhattan Bank, New York; Brooklyn Mus Permanent Collection, NY; IBM Collection, White Plains, NY; Williams Col Art Collection; Johnson Publ Permanent Art Collection, Chicago; plus others.

Comn: Don Quixote limited ed lithographs, Orig Lithographs Inc, 67; Don Quixote murals, Don Quixote Apts, Bronx, NY, 69; mural, Rutgers Univ, New Brunswick, NJ, 70. *Exhib:* Emily Lowe Award Exhib, 63; Traveling Exhib Black Painters America, Univ Calif, Los Angeles, 66; 15 New Voices, Hallmark Gallery, New York & traveling, 69; Am Black Painters, Whitney Mus Am Art, New York, 71; one-person shows, The Women, Interfaith Coun of Churches, 78, Reflections of the Prophet, Pa State Univ, 78 & others. *Pos:* Consult art & art coordr, Harlem Freedom Sch, Off Econ Opportunity, 66-67; dir, Lincoln Inst Gallery, Lincoln Inst Psycho-Ther, 66-68; supvr art, Proj Turn-On, New York, 68-69. *Teaching:* Instr graphics, High Sch Art & Design, 61-70; instr painting, Art Students League, 69-75; asst prof painting, Hostos Community Col, 71-77, assoc prof, 77-, prof visual & performing arts, currently. *Awards:* Emily Lowe Art Competition Award, 63; Whitney Found Award, 64; Award of Distinction, Smith Mason Gallery, 71. *Bibliog:* Cedric Dover (auth), American Negro Art, 61; Samella Lewis (auth), Black Artist on Art, pvt publ, 71. *Media:* Acrylic, Collage. *Res:* Aesthetic use of fluorescent materials in the fine arts. *Publ:* Auth & illusr, I'd like the Goo-gen-heim, Regnery, 69; coauth, Art of Acrylic Painting, Grumbacher, 69; illusr, The Sniper, McGraw, 69; illusr, Black Out Loud, Macmillan, 70; illusr, Journey, Scholastic, 70. *Dealer:* Lee Nordness Gallery 252 W 38th St New York NY 10021; Harbor Gallery 43 Main St Cold Spring Harbor NY 11724. *Mailing Add:* Dept of Visual-Performing Arts Hostos Community Col 475 Grand Concourse Bronx NY 10451

HOLLIS, DOUGLAS
SCULPTOR
b Ann Arbor, Mich, Apr 21, 48. *Study:* Univ Mich, BFA, 70. *Work:* Nat Oceanic & Atmospheric Admin, Seattle, Wash; San Francisco Exploratium, Calif. *Exhib:* Rain Column, Rincon Ctr, San Francisco, Calif; Listening Vessels, Univ NC, Raleigh. *Awards:* Art Fel, Nat Endowment Arts, 80 & 86; Art Fel, Calif Arts Coun, 87; Ann Artists Awards, Oakland Mus, 90. *Dealer:* Max Protetch 560 Broadway New York NY 10012. *Mailing Add:* PO Box 411105 San Francisco CA 94141

HOLLISTER, PAUL
WRITER, PAINTER
b New York, NY. *Study:* Harvard Col, BS, 41. *Work:* Boston Mus Fine Arts; Mont Mus, Helena. *Exhib.* Eighteen solo exhibits; Parsons Sch Design, Small Works I & II, 89, 90. *Pos:* Ed, glass historian, lectr, critic. *Teaching:* Adj assoc prof, Masters prog in Decorative Arts, Cooper-Hewitt Mus, Parsons Sch Design, 84-; adj prof, Bard Col, 93. *Mem:* Nat Early Am Glass Club; Glass Circle, London; Int Asn Hist Glass, Amsterdam, Neth; Nat Artists Equity Asn; Int Asn for Hist of Glass. *Media:* Pastel, Oil. *Res:* Millefiore glass, hist of window glass. *Publ:* Auth, Glass Paperweights of the New York Hist Soc, Potter, 74; The glazing of the Crystal Palace, Corning J Glass Studies, 74; Papers in Annals of the Int Asn for Hist of Glass, 77, 79, 85, 88 & 91; Flowers Which Clothe the Meadows, Corning Mus Glass, 78; Muranese Millefiori revival of the nineteenth century, Corning, Jour Glass Studies, 83; The Dodwell Bowls, 85 & American Studio Glass Studies, 88, Annales; Louis XIV's Glass Table, Annales, 91; 175 articles & reviews, NY Times, Am Craft, Antiques, Neues Glas & many others. *Mailing Add:* 200 E 66th St Apt B-1206 New York NY 10021

HOLLISTER, VALERIE (DUTTON)
PAINTER
b Oakland, Calif, Dec 29, 39. *Study:* Stanford Univ, AB, 61 & MA, 65; San Francisco Art Inst, 63; Col Art Study Abroad, Paris, 64-65. *Work:* Stanford Univ Mus; Madison Art Ctr, Wis; Williams Col; Woodrow Wilson Sch-Princeton Univ. *Comn:* Winter Light (outdoor mural), Swarthmore Col, 88. *Exhib:* Biennial Contemp Am Painting & Area Show, Corcoran Gallery Art, Washington, DC, 67; Whitney Mus Ann Contemp Am Painting, 67-68; one-woman shows, Madison Art Ctr, Wis, 68, Swarthmore Col, Pa, 72, 77, 82 & 90 Westbroadway Gallery, New York, 73 & Selected Paintings Since 1965, Washington Proj for the Arts, Washington, DC, 78; and other one-woman & group shows. *Publ:* Coauth, Toward A History of Women's Traditional Arts, Heresies, winter 78. *Mailing Add:* 1 Whittier Pl Swarthmore PA 19081

HOLM, BILL
HISTORIAN, PAINTER
b Roundup, Mont, Mar 24, 25. *Study:* Univ Wash, BA, 49, MFA, 51. *Work:* Alaska State Mus. *Exhib:* Burke Mus, 92. *Collections Arranged:* Arts of the Raven (with Doris Shadbolt, Bill Reid & Wilson Duff), Vancouver Art Gallery, 67; Crossroads of Continents, Smithsonian Inst, 88; Crooked Beak of Heaven, Henry Art Gallery, Univ Wash, Seattle; Smoky-Top (auth, catalog), Pac Sci Ctr, 83; The Box of Daylight (auth, catalog), Seattle Art Mus, 83. *Pos:* Cur, Northwest Coast Indian art, Thomas Burke Mem Wash State Mus, Univ Wash, Seattle, 68-85, cur emer, 85- *Teaching:* Prof Northwest Coast Indian art, Univ Wash, Seattle, 68-85. *Awards:* Governor's Art Award, 76 501 Governor's Writers Award, 66, 77, 81, 84 & 87; Honor Award, Native Am Art Studies Asn, 91. *Mem:* Native Am Art Studies Asn. *Media:* Acrylic. *Res:* All aspects of Northwest Coast Indian art, with concentration on form and style and relation to ceremonialism. *Publ:* Auth, Northwest Coast Indian Art: An Analysis of Form, 65; auth, Crooked Beak of Heaven, 72, Univ Wash Press; coauth (with Bill Reid), Indian Art of the Northwest Coast, Univ Wash Press, 76; The Art and Times of Willie Seaweed, Univ Wash Press, 83; auth, Spirit and Ancestor, Univ Wash Press, 87. *Mailing Add:* 1027 NW 190th St Seattle WA 98177

HOLM, MILTON W
PAINTER
b Rochester, NY. *Study:* With Edward S Siebert, Rochester. *Work:* Mem Art Gallery, Rochester, NY; Rochester Inst Technol; Univ Rochester; Greenville Pub Libr, SC. *Exhib:* Mem Art Gallery, Rochester, NY, 24-82; Nat Acad Design Ann, New York, 35-73; Allied Artists Am, New York, 38-71 & 77; Currier Art Gallery, Manchester, NH, 40; Cincinnati Art Gallery, 45. *Awards:* Ranger Purchase Award, Nat Acad Design, 40; James Hogarth Dennis Award, Mem Art Gallery, 58-62; Rochester Art Club Award, 69-82. *Bibliog:* C Movalli (auth), article, Am Artist, 11/78. *Mem:* Allied Artists Am; Rochester Art Club (pres, 57-59); Genesee Group (pres); Rockport Art Asn, Mass. *Media:* Oil. *Dealer:* Oxford Gallery 267 Oxford St Rochester NY 14607. *Mailing Add:* 30 Hathaway Rd Rochester NY 14617

HOLMAN, ARTHUR (STEARNS)
PAINTER
b Bartlesville, Okla, Oct 25, 26. *Study:* Univ NMex, BFA, 51; Hans Hofmann Sch Art, Provincetown, Mass, 51; Calif Sch Fine Arts, San Francisco, 53. *Work:* San Francisco Mus Art; Oakland Mus, Calif; Achenbach Collection, Fine Arts Mus San Francisco; Eureka Col; Mills Col. *Exhib:* One-man shows, Esther Robles Gallery, Los Angeles, 60, M H De Young Mem Mus, San Francisco, 63, William Sawyer Gallery, San Francisco, 71, 73, 74 & 76, David Cole Gallery, Inverness, Calif, 80, Gumps Gallery, San Francisco, 87 & Braunstein/Quay Gallery, San Francisco, 92; Fifty California Artists, Whitney Mus Am Art, New York, 62; Calif Painting & Sculpture: The Mod Era, San Francisco Mus, 76; Smithsonian Inst, Washington, DC, 77; Bay Area Regionalists, Hall of Flowers, San Francisco, 85 & 86; 20th Century Landscape Drawings, De Young Mus, San Francisco, 89; Jan Holloway Gallery, San Francisco, 89. *Awards:* Purchase Award, Invitational Show, Stanford Univ, 62; Public Vote Prize, Bay Area Art, First Savings Bank of San Francisco, 64. *Media:* Oil. *Mailing Add:* Box 72 Lagunitas CA 94938

HOLMES, DAVID BRYAN
PAINTER, PRINTMAKER
b London, Eng, Aug 8, 36; Can citizen. *Study:* Twickenham Tech Col, Eng; Harrow Sch Art, London; Queen's Univ, Ont; Art Students League, with Robert Beverley Hale; London Sch Art & Design, Eng. *Work:* Willistead Art Gallery, Windsor, Ont; Rice Univ, Houston; US Steel Corp. *Comn:* Many pvt comn in Europe & NAm. *Exhib:* Country Scenes in Quebec, City of Montreal, PQ, 69; one-man shows, Galerie Gauvreau, Montreal, 69 & 70, Wally F Findlay Galleries, Inc, New York, 74-75, 78, 80, 82, 85, 87, 89 & 92, Chicago, 77, 85 & 93 & Palm Beach, Fla, 79, 84, 86 & 91; and others. *Teaching:* Art master, St Lawrence Col Appl Arts & Technol, Kingston, Ont, 68-74. *Awards:* Ann Nat Spring Exhib, Queen's Univ, Ont, 67, 69 & 71; Award for Country Scenes in Quebec, City of Montreal, 69. *Mem:* Int Soc Artists, New York; Print & Drawing Coun Can; Soc Can Artists; Art Students League. *Media:* Tempera, Oil; Etching. *Dealer:* Wally F Findlay Galleries Int 17 E 57th St New York NY 10022. *Mailing Add:* RR 3 Odessa ON K0H 2H0 Canada

HOLMES, DAVID VALENTINE
SCULPTOR, PAINTER
b Newark, NY, Nov 27, 45. *Study:* Temple Abroad Tyler Sch, Rome, Italy, 66-67; Tyler Sch Art, Temple Univ, Philadelphia, Pa, BFA(cum laude), 68; Univ Wis, Madison, MFA, 72. *Work:* Milwaukee Art Mus, Wis; Kohler Arts Ctr, Sheboygan, Wis; Madison Art Ctr, Wis; Kent State Univ. *Exhib:* Chicago & Vicinity, Chicago Art Inst, Ill, 75; one-man shows, Madison Art Ctr, Kohler Arts Ctr, Wis, 72 & 77 & Ringling Sch Art, 91; Harmonious Craft, Am Craft Mus, New York & Renwick Gallery, Smithsonian Inst, Washington, DC, 79; two-artist exhib, Milwaukee Art Mus, Wis, 80; Animal Images, Renwick Gallery, Smithsonian, Washington, DC, 81; Renwick Souvenir Show, Smithsonian Inst, 82; Traveling one-man show, Ind State Univ, Kent State Univ & Northwestern Univ, 83; Midwest Int Exhib, Cent Mo State & Maastricht, Holland, 87; Traveling Exhib (Alchemic Emporium), 91-93: Swope Art Mus, Terre Haute, Ind; MacNider Mus, Mason City, Iowa; Fed Reserve Bank, Kansas City, Mo; Southeast Ark Arts Ctr, Pine Bluff, Ark, Edison Community Col, Ft Meyers, Fla, Bergstrom-Mahler Mus, Neenph, Wis, Muscatine Art Ctr, Muscatine, Iowa. *Teaching:* Resident artist, Madison Public Schools, Wis, 72-74; asst prof drawing & design, Univ Wis, Milwaukee, 74-76; prof drawing & design, Univ Wis-Parkside, Kenosha, 77- *Awards:* Nat Endowment Arts Fel, US Government, 76-77. *Mem:* Col Arts Asn Am. *Media:* Wood; Acrylic. *Mailing Add:* 1428 S Wisconsin Ave Racine WI 53403

HOLMES, LARRY W
PAINTER, EDUCATOR
b Kansas City, Kans, Nov 12, 42. *Study:* Pittsburg State Univ, Kans, BFA, 64, MS, 65; Cranbrook Acad Art, with George Ortman, MFA, 73. *Work:* Cranbrook Acad Art, Bloomfield Hills, Mich; Pittsburg State Univ, Kans; City of Newark, Del; City of Parsons, Kans; St Lawrence Univ, Canton, NY; McDonald's Corp, Glencoe, Ill. *Exhib:* Solo exhibs, Del Art Mus, Wilmington, 84, Univ Fla, Gainesville, 86, Rosenfeld Gallery, Philadelphia, 86, Greenville Mus Art, NC, 87 & Littlejohn-Smith Gallery, New York, 88; Dog Days of August, Littlejohn-Smith Gallery, New York, 86; The Nature of the Beast, Hudson River Mus, NY, 89; A XX Century Bestiary, Renee Fotouhi Fine Art, New York, 90; Pastels: Big and Otherwise, Asheville Mus Art, NC, 92. *Teaching:* Prof painting, Univ Del, Newark, 73, chmn dept art, 82-92. *Awards:* Yaddo Fel, Yaddo Corp, Saratoga Springs, NY, 80. *Bibliog:* Ann Jarmusch (auth), Larry Holmes at Arch St Gallery, Art News, summer 79; Carrie de Santis Tull (auth), Larry Holmes at Delaware Art Mus, New Art Examiner, 1/85; Victoria Donohue (auth), Larry Holmes at Rosenfeld, Philadelphia Inquirer, 6/21/86; Frank Thomson (auth), Catalogue for Pastels: Big and Otherwise, Asheville Mus Art. *Mem:* Col Art Asn. *Media:* Pastel, Oil. *Dealer:* Littlejohn-Sternau Gallery 41 East 57th St New York NY 10022. *Mailing Add:* 13 Rocky Glen Rd Oxford PA 19363

HOLMES, WENDY (DIANA H NOYES)
PHOTOGRAPHER
b New York, NY, Oct 21, 46. *Study:* Mass Inst Technol. *Work:* Bibliot Nat, Paris; NJ State Mus, Trenton; Addison Gallery Art, Andover, Mass; Vassar Gallery, Poughkeepsie, NY; Toledo Mus of Art, Ohio; State Univ Art Mus, New Paltz. *Exhib:* Peters Valley Exhib, Newark Mus, NJ, 80; NJ State Mus, Trenton, 80 & 86; Upstate Exhib, NY State Mus, Albany, 82; Paul Mellon Arts Ctr, Wallingford, Conn, 82; Catskill Ctr Photog, Woodstock, NY, 84 & 86. *Collections Arranged:* Seven Photographers: The Delaware Valley (auth, catalog), Peters Valley, NJ, NJ State Mus & Nexus, Atlanta, Ga, 76-78. *Pos:* Staff photogr, Wave Hill Environ Ctr, Bronx, NY, 70-73. *Teaching:* Instr photog, Peters Valley Photog Workshop, Layton, NJ, 75-83, Int Ctr Photog, New York, 79-81 & Catskill Ctr Photog, Woodstock, NY, 86. *Awards:* Survey Grant for Seven Photographers Exhib, Nat Endowment Arts, 76; Fel, NJ State Coun Arts, 79; Photogr Fund Award, Catskill Ctr Photog, 84. *Bibliog:* Article, New York Times, 7/22/79. *Publ:* Auth & illusr, Hudson City: The Living River, Wave Hill Ctr, 72; coauth, Brother Can You Spare a Dime, Paddington Press, 75. *Mailing Add:* 119 Woodbine St Providence RI 02906

HOLMES, WILLARD
GALLERY DIRECTOR
Mailing Add: Vancouver Art Gallery 750 Hornby St Vancouver BC V6Z 2H7

HOLO, SELMA R
MUSEOLOGIST, MUSEUM DIRECTOR
b Chicago, Ill, May 21, 43. *Study:* Northwestern Univ, BA, 65; Hunter Col, City Univ NY, MA, 72; Univ Calif, Santa Barbara, PhD, 80. *Work:* Norton Simon Mus, Pasadena, Calif; Getty Mus, Malibu, Calif; Fisher Gallery, Univ Southern Calif, Los Angeles; Milwaukee Art Mus. *Pos:* Cur acquisitions, Norton Simon Mus, 77-81; dir, Fisher Gallery, Univ Southern Calif, 81- *Teaching:* Instr art hist, Art Ctr Col Design, Pasadena, 73-77. *Awards:* La Napoule Distinguished Scholar Fel, 88; Tokyo Fuji Mus Fine Arts Award, 90. *Bibliog:* Eric Young (auth), Los Disparates, Burlington Mag, 2/77; various reviews in Los Angeles newspapers. *Mem:* Am Asn Mus; Col Art Asn; Int Coun Mus. *Res:* Goya. *Publ:* Auth, Despreciar los Insultos: A New Goya Acquisition, 83 & An Unsuspected Poseur in a Goya Drawing, 85, J Paul Getty Mus J; Joseph Alsop's The rare art traditions, Art News, 83; Training Future Curators to buy Art, Mus Studies J, 85; Interns Ins & Outs, Mus News, 89. *Mailing Add:* c/o Fischer Gallery Univ of South Calif University Park 823 Expos Los Angeles CA 90089-0292

HOLOUN, HAROLD DEAN
PAINTER, SCULPTOR
b Ord, Nebr, Oct 16, 39. *Study:* Hastings Col, Nebr, BA, 61; Univ Wyo, Laramie, MA, 62. *Work:* Sheldon Mem Gallery, Univ Nebr, Lincoln; Nebr Art, Kearney; Nebr Wesleyan Univ, Lincoln. *Comn:* Portrait, Baker Univ, Baldwin, Kans, 75; two portraits, Liberty Glass Corp, Sapulpa, Okla, 79; painting-sculpture, City of Grand Island, Nebr, 81. *Exhib:* Painting-Sculpture Today, Indianapolis Mus Art, Ind, 78; Visions 81, Mid-Am Arts Alliance Touring Exhib, Kansas City, 80-81; Sheldon Mem Gallery, Lincoln, Nebr, 81; Art and Artists in Nebraska, Sheldon Mem Gallery, Lincoln, Nebr, 82; Twelve Midwest Realists, Sioux City Art Ctr, Iowa, 82; Reflectons Exhib, Elder Gallery, Lincoln, Nebr, 83; MJF Gallenigi, Kansas City, Mo, 85. *Awards:* Juror's Award, Reflections Exhib, Elder Gallery, 83. *Media:* Oil, Alkyd; Bronze, Photography. *Dealer:* Pickaro Galleries Inc 7108 N Western Oklahoma City OK 73116. *Mailing Add:* 219 E 17th St Grand Island NE 68801

HOLSCH, ROBERT FRED
SCULPTOR
b Rosebud, Tex, Aug 10, 52. *Study:* Univ Tex, Austin, BFA, 70; Tex A&I Univ, BFA, 75; North Tex State Univ, MFA, 78. *Work:* Renaissance Ctr, Detroit, Mich; Rockwell Enterprises, Dallas, Tex; and other pvt collections. *Comn:* Sculpture, EnCom Graphics, Houston, Tex, 80. *Exhib:* One-man shows, Adelle M Fine Art Gallery, Dallas, 80 & O'Kane Gallery, Houston, 81; Nat Small Sculpture & Drawing Exhib, Los Angeles, Calif, 81; Le Salon de Nation, Paris, 83; DuBose Gallery, Houston, 84; and others. *Teaching:* Asst instr sculpture, Tex A&I Univ, 74-75 & North Tex State Univ, 77-78. *Awards:* Honors Award, Tex A&I Univ, 75. *Bibliog:* Harry Reed (auth), Artist profile, Art Voices, 9/81. *Media:* Wood, Marble. *Dealer:* DuBose Gallery Houston TX 77098; Adelle M Fine Art 3317 McKinney Ave Dallas TX 75204. *Mailing Add:* 9318 Carvel Lane Houston TX 77036

HOLSCHUH, (GEORGE) FRED
SCULPTOR, ARCHITECT
b Beerfelden, Ger, Nov 19, 02; US citizen. *Study:* Indust art & archit dipl; Pa Acad Fine Arts; Univ Pa; also with Bauhaus founder, Walter Gropius. *Work:* Süddeutsches Mus, Darmstadt, Ger; Addisson Gallery, New York; Brookgreen Garden, SC; City Hall, Tallahassee; Hilmar & Kristin Skagfield Collection, Bruce & Mary Jo Weale Collection & Barnett Bank, Tallahassee, Fla; Edgewater Estate Collection, Md; Brinson McGowan Collection, Haiti. *Comn:* St Francis Monument, Yugoslav Order of St Francis, Washington, DC, 36; Murrell Dobbins Mem, Bd Educ, Philadelphia, 38; bronze sculptures (collabr with Bass Studio, Philadelphia), Penn Mutual Life Insurance Bldg, 39; copper sculpture, Irene Edmond Mem, Tallahassee, Fla, 67 & 10th anniversary figure, Garden Le Moyne Art Found, 72. *Exhib:* Pa Acad Fine Arts, Philadelphia, 36; Nat Acad Design, New York, 37; Int Sculpture Outdoor Show, Parkway Mus, Philadelphia, 39; Regional Sculpture Show, Smithsonian Inst, Washington, DC, 40. *Teaching:* Prof design & art hist & head dept art, Cedar Crest Col, Allentown, 36-38; prof humanities & sculpture, Fla State Univ, 46-72, emer prof, 72- *Awards:* Stimson Prize in Sculpture, Pa Acad Fine Arts, 35 & Europ Traveling Scholars, 35 & 36; Regional First Prize, Southern Sculptors Nat Show, 66. *Mem:* Asn Southern Sculptors (bd dirs, 63-65); Am Asn Univ Prof. *Media:* Wood, Copper. *Dealer:* Harmon Gallery 1258 Third St Naples FL 33940. *Mailing Add:* 2007 W Randolph Circle Tallahassee FL 32312

HOLSTE, THOMAS JAMES
PAINTER, EDUCATOR
b Evanston, Ill, Jan 12, 43. *Study:* Calif State Univ, Fullerton, study with Vic Smith, BA, 67, MA, 68; Claremont Grad Sch, study with Guy Williams & Mowry Baden, MFA, 70. *Work:* La Jolla Mus Contemp Art, Calif; Chase Manhattan Bank, New York; Solomon R Guggenheim Mus, New York; Security Pac Nat Bank; Int Tel & Tel, New York. *Exhib:* The Market St Prog, Los Angeles Co Mus Art, Los Angeles, 72; one-man show, Newspace Gallery, Los Angeles, 73-88; Aber, Buchanan, Holste, Newport Harbor Art Mus, Newport Beach, Calif, 76; Mind Set: An Ongoing Involvement with the Rational Tradition, John Weber Gallery, New York, 79; Four Artists, Otis Art Inst Parsons Sch Design, Los Angeles, 79; Emergent Americans, Guggenheim Mus, New York, 81; Alice Aycock, Tom Holste, Michael Singer, Fort Worth Art Mus, Tex, 81; Concepts in Construction: 1910-1980 Traveling Exhib, 83-; and others. *Teaching:* Prof painting, Calif State Univ, Fullerton, 69- *Awards:* Individual Artists Fel Grant, Nat Endowment Arts, 80. *Bibliog:* Peter Frank (auth), Review--Tom Holste, Artforum, 2/78 & Unslick in LA, Art Am, 9-10/78. *Media:* Mixed. *Dealer:* Newspace Gallery 5241 Melrose Ave Los Angeles CA 90038. *Mailing Add:* 17201 Harding Cyn Rd Modjeska Cyn CA 92676-9801

HOLT, LOUISE
GALLERY DIRECTOR
b Kingston, Tenn, Nov 12, 24. *Study:* Univ Nebr-Lincoln, BA, 87. *Pos:* Dir, Haymarket Art Gallery, 90- *Mem:* Metrop Mus Art, NA; charter mem, Nat Mus Women in Arts; assoc mem, Nat Soc Painters in Casin & Acrylic. *Specialty:* Promote new and student artists in the region and facilitate education of visual arts in the community. *Mailing Add:* Haymarket Art Gallery 119 S Ninth St Lincoln NE 68508

HOLT, MARTHA A
CERAMIST, SCULPTOR
b Chatham, NJ, Apr, 15, 45. *Study:* Univ Miami, Fla, BS, 67; Norfolk Mus Sch, 67-68; Penland Sch Crafts, 68-69; Cranbrook Acad Art, MFA, 71. *Work:* Ga Power & Light Co, Atlanta; Peat Marwich Co, Pittsburgh, Pa; W Forest High Sch, Tionesta, Pa; Erie Art Mus, Pa. *Exhib:* Solo exhibs, Portnoy Gallery, New York, 77, 79, 80 & 82, Erie Art Mus, Pa, 83, Pittsburgh Ctr Arts, Pa, 83 & Belk Art Gallery, W Carolina Univ, NC, 85, Lill Street Gallery, Chicago, 86 & The Clay Place, Pittsburgh, 87 & 89, Canton Art Inst, 89. *Pos:* Dir, Allegheny Col Galleries, 76-83. *Teaching:* Instr ceramics, Penland Sch Crafts, 86, 87, 89 & 91; conducts workshops nationally. *Awards:* Visual Arts Fel Grants, Pa Coun Arts, 80 & 86; Vis Artist, Penland Sch, 87-88. *Bibliog:* Susan Wechsler (auth), Low-Fire Ceramics, Watson Guptill, 81; Charlotte Speight(auth), Ceramic Sculpture, Harper & Row, 83; Richard Zakin (auth), Ceramics, Mastering the Craft, Chilton Bk Co, 90. *Mem:* Int Sculpture Ctr; Artists Equity Asn. *Media:* Clay. *Publ:* Coauth, New Relationships, private publ, 80. *Dealer:* The Clay Place 5416 Walnut St Pittsburgh PA 15232. *Mailing Add:* Box 636 Tionesta PA 16353

HOLT, NANCY LOUISE
SCULPTOR, FILMMAKER
b Worcester, Mass, Apr 5, 38. *Study:* Tufts Univ, BS, 56-60. *Comn:* Landscape Sculptures, Art park, Lewiston, NY, 74, Western Wash Univ, 78, Wellesley Col, Mass, 80, Miami Univ, Ohio, 80, Laguna Gloria Art Mus, Austin, 81, Arlington Co, Va & Gallaudet Col, Washington, DC, 84; Southern Conn Univ, New Haven, 85; Univ SE Mass, Dartmouth, 91. *Exhib:* New Am Filmaker's Series, Whitney Mus Am Art, New York, 75 & 77; Art in Landscape Traveling exhib, Independent Cur, Washington, DC, 76; Whitney Biennial, 77, 79 & 81; Probing the Earth: Contemp Land Proj, Hirshhorn Mus, Washington, DC, 77; 11th Int Sculpture Conf, Washington DC, 80; Archit Sculpture, Los Angeles Inst Contemp Art, 80; Artists' Gardens and Parks, Hayden Gallery, Mass Inst Technol, 81; City Site Sculpture, Toronto, 82; Independent Artists Open Air Sculpture Exhib, Marlay Park, Dublin, Ireland, 83; Content: A Contemp Focus, Hirshhorn Mus, Washington, 84; Artist as Social Designer, Los Angeles Co Mus, Calif, 85; Standing Ground: Sculpture by American Women, Contemp Arts Ctr, Cincinnati, Ohio, 87; Making Their Mark, Cincinnati Art Mus, New Orleans Mus Art, Denver Art Mus, Pa Acad Fine Arts, 89; Consumer Tools: Personal Visions, Mus Mod Art, New York, 91; Fragile Ecologies: Artists' Interpretations & Solutions, Queens Mus, Flushing, NY, Smithsonian Inst Traveling Exhibs, 91; Strata, Tampere Art Mus & Contemp Mus Art, Helsinki, Finland, 92. *Awards:* Creative Artists Pub Serv Grant, 75 & 78; Nat Endowment Arts Fels, 75, 78, 85 & 88; Guggenheim Fel, 78. *Bibliog:* Norma Broude (auth), Alternative Monuments, Art Am, 2/91; Altti Kuusamo (auth), Nancy Holt--Pipes and Tracks, Strata (catalog), Tampere Art Mus & Mus Contemp Art, Helsinki, Finland, 2/92; Alan Hess (auth), Technology exposed, Landscape Archit, 5/92. *Publ:* Auth, Pine barrens, Avalanche, summer 75; Some notes on video works, In: Video Art, Harcourt Brace Jovanovich, 76; Sun Tunnels, Artforum, 4/77; Stone enclosure: rock rings, Arts, 6/79; Ransacked, Printed Matter, 80; Time Outs, Visual Studies Workshop Press 85. *Mailing Add:* 166 Bank St New York NY 10014

HOLTZ, ITSHAK JACK
PAINTER, PRINTMAKER
b Skernewiz, Poland, Dec 14, 25; US citizen. *Study:* Bezalel Acad Art, Jerusalem; Art Students League; Nat Acad Design, New York. *Exhib:* Karlebach Gallery, Fair Lawn, NJ, 65-85; Audubon Artists of New York, 66; Tyringham Galleries, Mass, 66-86; Allied Artists Am, New York, 72; Nat Acad Design, 77; Yeshiva Univ Mus, New York, 83 & 92; Jewish Community Ctr on the Palisades, 90; YMWA, Washington Township, NJ, 91. *Awards:* Gold Medal, Academia Italia, 83; Bd Dir Award, NY Art's Interaction, 89-90. *Bibliog:* Articles in Art Rev Mag, 5/66 & La Rev Mod, 6/66. *Mem:* Art Students League; Academia Italia delle Arti; Artists Equity Asn New York. *Media:* Oil, Felt Pen & Ink; Lithography. *Mailing Add:* 118 E 28th St New York NY 10016

HOLVERSON, JOHN
DEALER, CURATOR
b Marshfield, Wis, June 14, 46. *Study:* Univ Iowa, 65-66; MacMurray Col, Jacksonville, Ill, BA, 67; Univ Iowa, Iowa City, MA, 71; Attingham Summer Sch, 82. *Collections Arranged:* Images of Women Photog Exhib (auth, catalog), 77; The Revolutionary McLellans, 77; Miss Mary Cassatt: Impressionist from Pennsylvania, 79; James Brooks: Paintings and Works on Paper 1946-1982, 83; Winslow Homer: The Charles Shipman Payson Collection, 83; Maine Light: Temperas by Andrew Wyeth, 83; Gaston Lachaise: Sculpture & Drawings (auth, catalog), 84; Jamie Wyeth: An American View, 84; 1985 Maine Biennial; John Marin in Maine, 85. *Pos:* Summer intern, Art Inst Chicago, 68-69; grad asst, Mus Art, Univ Iowa, 68-69, head grad asst, 69-70; cur, Portland Mus Art, Maine, 70-73, cur collections, 73-81, actg dir, 73-75, dir, 75-87. *Teaching:* Asst dept art, MacMurray Col, Jacksonville, Ill, 63-67. *Mem:* Am Asn Mus; Asn Art Mus Dirs; Soc Preserv New England Antiq; Nat Trust for State & Local Hist Soc; Col Art Asn. *Publ:* Auth, Rene Dubois and the cathedrals of the future, Greater Portland Landmarks Observer, fall 73; Fire buckets and bags in Portland, 1783, Antiques, 3/74. *Mailing Add:* 292 Spring St Portland ME 04102

HOLVEY, SAMUEL BOYER
SCULPTOR, DESIGNER
b Wilkes Barre, Pa, July 20, 35. *Study:* Syracuse Univ, BFA, 57; Am Univ, MA, 69. *Comn:* Bas-relief mural, Wyo Valley Country Club, Wilkes Barre, 62. *Exhib:* Corcoran Gallery Area Show, Washington, DC, 68; Greater Washington Area Show, 72; 2nd Ann Washington Area Sculpture Show, 74; The Am Genius, Corcoran Gallery, 76. *Pos:* Designer, William Fertig Interiors, Kingston, Pa, 57-58, 63-64; art dir, WFM-TV, Eatontown, NJ, 60-61; designer display exhibs, The Displayers Inc, New York World's Fair Pavilions, 61-63; designer, Robert Kayton Assocs, New York, 62; pres, Holvey Asn Inc, 87-93. *Teaching:* Assoc prof graphic design, Corcoran Sch Art, DC, 78-93; asst prof design, Univ Md, College Park, 67-78. *Mem:* Art Dirs Club Metrop Washington, 72-88; Graphic Design Educators Asn, 86-93. *Media:* Metal Direct Construction, Lumia. *Mailing Add:* 5100 Elm St Bethesda MD 20814

HOLZER, JENNY
CONCEPTUAL ARTIST
b Gallipolis, Ohio, July 29, 50. *Study:* Ohio Univ, BFA, 72; RI Sch Design, MFA, 77; Whitney Mus Independent Study Prog, fel, 77. *Work:* Van Abbe Mus, Eindhoven, Neth; Mus Contemp Art, Chicago; Tate Gallery, London; Mus Mod Art Lending Serv, New York. *Comn:* Project Grand Central, Remy Martin, New York, 80; posters, Nouveau Mus, Lyon, France, 82; sign, City Amsterdam, 82; spectacolor board, Pub Art Fund, New York, 82; Urban Art Works Proj, City Seattle, 83. *Exhib:* 1983 Biennial Exhibition (catalog), Whitney Mus Am Art, NY, 83; The Human Condition Biennial III (catalog), San Francisco Mus Art, 84; 1985 Biennial Exhibition (catalog), Whitney Mus Am Art, NY, 85; Currents 7: Words in Action, Milwaukee Art Ctr, 85; Dissent: The Issue of Modern Art in Boston, The Expressionist Challenge (catalog), Inst Contemp Art, Boston, 85; In Other Words (catalog), Corcoran Gallery Art, Washington, DC, 86; Committed to Print: An Exhibition of Recent American Printed Art with Social and Political Themes (catalog) Mus Mod Art, NY, 88; 1988: The World of Art Today, Milwaukee Art Mus, 88; Modes of Address: Language in Art Since 1960, Whitney Mus Am Art Downtown Fed Plaza, NY, 88; solo exhibs, Brooklyn Mus, NY, 88; Signs/ Under a Rock (catalog), Inst Contemp Art, London, 88; Ydessa Hendeles Art Found, Toronto, 89; Laments 1988-89 (catalog), Dia Art Found, NY, 89; Benches, Doris C Freidman Plaza, NY, 89; 44th Venice Biennale (catalog), American Pavilion, Venice, 90; First Impressions: Early Prints by Forty-Six Contemporary Artists, Walker Art Ctr, Minneapolis, 89; Image World-Art and Media Culture (catalog), Whitney Mus Am Art, NY, 89; Timespan (catalog), Fundacio Caixa de Pensions, Barcelona, 90; Culture and Commentary - An Eighties Perspective, Hirshhorn Mus & Sculpture Garden, Washington, DC, 90; Energies (catalog), Stedelijk Mus, Amsterdam, 90; Affinities--The Gerald S Elliot Collection (catalog), Art Inst Chicago, 90; Positions of Art in the 20th Century, Wiesbaden Mus, WGer, 90. *Awards:* Blair Award, 79th Americans Show, Art Inst Chicago, 82. *Bibliog:* Time Span (portfolio), Fundacio Caixa de Pensions, Barcelona, 90; Hiroko Tanaka (auth), Art is Beautiful: Interviews with New York Artists, Kawade Shobo Shinsha, Tokyo, 90, 98-115; Susan R Suleiman (auth), Subversive Intent: Sender, Politics and the Avant-Garde, Howard Univ Press, Cambridge, 90. *Mem:* Collaborative Proj, New York. *Media:* Multi-Media. *Publ:* Coauth, Position papers, Art Forum, 80; contribr, Hotel, 80 & coauth, Eating Through Living, 81, Tanam Press; coauth, Eating Friends, Top Stories, 81; auth, Truisms and Essays, Press NS Col Art & Design, 83. *Mailing Add:* c/o Barbara Gladstone Gallery 99 Greene St New York NY 10012

HOLZMAN, ERIC
PAINTER
b Bronx, NY, Nov 9, 49. *Study:* Tyler Sch Art, BFA, 71; Yale Univ, MFA, 73. *Exhib:* Tuthill Gallery, New York, 81; Queens Mus, New York, 83; One Penn Plaza, 85; Tatischeff Gallery, New York, 86; Union Square Gallery, New York, 87; Nancy Bratten Gallery, New York, 88; East Hampton Ctr Contemp Art, 90. *Teaching:* Vis critic & lectr, Pace Col, 90. *Awards:* Nat Endowment Arts, 89. *Mailing Add:* 121 Wooster New York NY 10012

HOMAR, LORENZO
PRINTMAKER, PAINTER
b Puerta de Tierra, PR, Sept 10, 13. *Study:* Pratt Inst, 40-42; Brooklyn Mus, with Peterdi, Tamayo & Osver, 46-50; Inter-Am Univ PR, hon DFA. *Work:* Libr Cong, Washington, DC; Mus Mod Art & Metrop Mus Art, New York; Klingspor Mus, Offenbach, WGer; Children Art Mus, Rutgers Univ, NJ. *Comn:* Tile murals of olympic swimming pool, Dept Parks, San Juan, 67-68; ceramic mural of pub sch, Dept Educ, San Juan, 71; portfolio, Blanco-Casals-Homar, Galeria Colibri, San Juan, 71; portfolio six Colombian artists, Mus de Arte Mod, Cali, Colombia, 75. *Exhib:* Poster Biennale, Warsaw, 70 & 74; Havana Exhib Prints, Cuba, 72; Norwegian Int Print Biennale, 74; Ljubljana, Yugoslavia Biennale; Comprehensive Exhib 1942-83, Princeton Univ, 83, collection now permanently at the Graphics Collection Firestone Library, Princeton Univ; and others. *Collections Arranged:* First San Juan Print Biennale; Retrospective Exhib, Mus Int PR Cult, San Juan, 70; retrospective--45 yrs as an artist, Mus de Arte de Ponce, PR. *Pos:* Jewelry designer, Cartier Inc, New York, 38-50; dir graphic workshop, Div Community Educ, 50-56; dir graphic workshop, Inst PR Cult, 58-72. *Teaching:* Master printing silk-screen, Inter-Am Univ PR, summer 72; instr, Cali, Colombia, 72; instr, Sch Plastic Arts, Inst PR Cult, presently. *Awards:* Guggenheim Fel, 57. *Bibliog:* Lorenzo Homar & Fritz Eichenberg (auth), Posters in Puerto Rico, Artist Proof, Vol 6, No 9-10; Jose Gomez Sicre (auth), Six Puerto Rican Artists (film), Pan-Am Union, 68; Marta Traba (auth), Proposed Polemics on Puerto Rican Art, Libr Int Rio Piedras, PR, 71. *Media:* Silk-Screen, Woodcut. *Publ:* ITC's Modern Calligraphy Today, New York; Contemporary Calligraphy, Eng. *Mailing Add:* c/o Galeria Palomas 207 Cristo St Old San Juan PR 00901

HOMER, WILLIAM INNES
HISTORIAN, EDUCATOR
b Merion, Pa, Nov 8, 29. *Study:* Princeton Univ, BA; Harvard Univ, MA & PhD. *Pos:* Cur, Mus Art, Ogunquit, Maine, 55-58; actg asst dir, Princeton Univ Art Mus, 56-57. *Teaching:* Asst prof art & archaeol, Princeton Univ, 61-64; assoc prof art hist, Cornell Univ, 64-66; prof art hist, Univ Del, 66-, chmn art hist dept, 66-81, 86- *Awards:* Am Coun Learned Soc Fel, 64-65; Guggenheim Fel, 72-73; Nat Endowment Humanities Fel, 80-81. *Mem:* Col Art Asn; Royal Photog Soc; Royal Soc Arts; Nat Arts Club; Cosmos Club. *Publ:* Auth, Robert Henri & His Circle, 69; Alfred Stieglitz & the American Avant-Garde, 77; Alfred Stieglitz and the Photo-Secession, 83; Albert Pinkham Ryder: Painter of Dreams, 89; Thomas Eakins: His Life and Art, 92. *Mailing Add:* Dept Art Hist Univ Del Newark DE 19716

HOMITZKY, PETER
PAINTER
b Berlin, Ger, Dec 7, 42; US citizen. *Study:* Art Students League, with F Reilly, J Leberte, J Hirsh, 59-63; San Francisco Art Inst, 65-66. *Work:* Wichita Mus Art, Kans; San Francisco Mus Art; Prudential Ins Co, Newark, NJ; Newark Mus, NJ; NJ State Mus, Trenton, NJ; Rutgers Univ; Jank Voorhis Zimmerli Mus. *Exhib:* One-man shows, Roko Gallery, New York, 74 & State Mus, Trenton, NJ, 77; Alonzo Galleries, New York, 76-77; Educ Testing Serv, Princeton, NJ, 82; Sid Deutsch Galley, New York, 83; Jersey City Mus, 84; Robeson Gallery, Rutgers Univ, Newark, 84; Frank Caro Gallery, New York, 89; Art Awareness, Lexington, NY, 89. *Teaching:* Instr painting, Art Students League, New York, currently. *Awards:* Purchase Awards, First NJ Biannual, Newark Mus, 77 & NJ State Mus; Aidekman Found, Newark Mus, 78; Harry Devlin Visual Arts Award, NJ State Coun Arts, 81 & 82; NJSCA Fel, 82. *Bibliog:* Diane Cochrane (auth), Industrial American landscapes of Peter Homitzky, Am Artist, 5/74; Susan Myer (ed), 20 Landscape Painters, Watson-Guptill, 77; Hilton Kramer (auth), article, New York Times, 12/9/77. *Media:* Oil, Pastel. *Dealer:* Frank Caro Gallery 41 E 57th St New York NY. *Mailing Add:* 227 Grand St Hoboken NJ 07030

HOMMA, KAZUFUMI
PAINTER
b Matudo-City, Japan, Apr 21, 43. *Study:* Tokyo Contemp Art Sch, 66-68; Brooklyn Mus Art Sch, 68-71. *Work:* Chase Bank Int & Home Insurance, New York, NY. *Comn:* Acrylic on canvas, Repub Bank, Houston, Tex. *Exhib:* Surugadi Gallery, Tokyo, Japan, 68; Brooklyn Mus Community Gallery, NY, 75; Brooklyn '81, Brooklyn Mus, 81; one-man shows, Limbo Lounge, 84 & Hal Bromm Gallery, 84 & 88, New York. *Collections Arranged:* Mixed Bag (auth, catalog), Alternative Mus, 82. *Media:* Acrylic. *Dealer:* Hal Bromm Gallery 90 W Broadway New York NY 10007. *Mailing Add:* 437 16th St Brooklyn NY 11215

HOMPSON, DAVI DET (DAVID ELBRIDGE THOMPSON)
PAINTER
b Sharon, Pa, Aug 7, 39. *Study:* Anderson Col, BA; Indiana Univ, MFA. *Work:* Virginia Mus Fine Arts; Moma Libr; Jean Brown Archives-Getty Ctr Art; Franklin Furnace Archives; The New Mus, New York. *Exhib:* Art by Telephone Show, Chicago Mus Contemp Art, 69; one-man shows, Alexandre Iolas Gallery, New York, 70, Apple Gallery, New York, 71-73; Franklin Furnace, New York, 78; Alternatives in Retrospect, New Mus, New York, 81; Va Mus Fine Arts, 90; Henri Gallery, Washington, DC, 92. *Teaching:* Asst

prof vis commun, Herron Sch Art, Ind Univ, 67-69; guest artist sculpture, Va Commonwealth Univ, 72-74; guest artist graphic design, RI Sch Design, summers 75-79; guest artist found, Kansas City Art Inst, 79-80. *Bibliog:* George Cruger (ed), Arts in Virginia, Va Mus Art, 74; Clive Phillpot (ed), article, Art J, 82; Harriet Runkle (auth), article art papers, 90. *Media:* Encaustic. *Publ:* Auth, S553 Study Manual, 69; auth, Blue Light Containment, 69; coauth, Word and Image Equations, 75; auth, 15, Hook, 80. *Dealer:* Bound & Unbound 351 W 30th New York NY 10001; Herri Gallery 1500 21st St Washington DC 20036. *Mailing Add:* 3409 Hawthorne Ave Richmond VA 23222

HONDA, MARGARET
PAINTER
b San Diego, Calif, 1961. *Study:* Univ Calif, San Diego, BA, 84; Univ Del, MA, 89. *Exhib:* A San Diego Exhibition: Forty-two Emerging Artists, La Jolla Mus, Contemp Art, 85; Newcomers, Munic Art Gallery, Los Angeles, 87; Neofest V, Sushi, San Diego, 84; Sculpture Arenas: Burden, Capps, Giegerich, Gregoire, Honda, Lere, Mandeville Gallery, Univ Calif, 87; Abstract Expressions, Lannan Mus, Fort Worth, Fla, 88; From the Back Room, Saxon-Lee Gallery, 88; solo shows, Anuska Galerie, San Diego, 86, Grossmont Col Art Gallery, El Cajon, Calif, 87 & Saxon-Lee Gallery, Los Angeles, 88. *Teaching:* Vis artist, Calif Polytechnic State Univ, San Luis Obispo, 84. *Awards:* San Diego Artist's Fel, Nat Endowment for Arts, 86. *Bibliog:* Christopher Knight (auth), Dueling exhibits celebrate emerging artists in San Diego, Los Angeles Herald Examiner, 4/14/85; Robert L Pincus (auth), Honda Plays it unsafe with powerful sculpture, San Diego Union, 3/6/86; Suzanne Muchnic (auth), Newcomers: A familiar story, Los Angeles Times, 10/17/87. *Mailing Add:* PO Box 1663 Solana Beach CA 92075

HONIG, ELEANOR D
PAINTER, PRINTMAKER
b New York, NY. *Study:* Fashion Inst Technol & Design, NY, Apparel Design Prof Fashion Degree; Queens Col, NY, BA, 67; CW Post Univ, Greenvale, NY, MA, 72. *Work:* Islip Art Mus, Long Island, NY. *Comn:* Mural, Boces Cult Arts, Syosset, NY, 79. *Exhib:* Artists in the Permanent Collection, Islip Art Mus, NY, 91; Nat Asn Women Artists Travelling Exhib, Richmond Art Mus, Ind, 91-92 & Mus Southwest, Midland, Tex, 91-92; Parrish Art Mus XXIII Exhib, South Hampton, NY, 92; Artists Invitational Exhib, Fine Arts Mus Long Island, Hempstead, NY, 92. *Pos:* Artist-in-residence, Boces Cult Arts, Syosset, NY, 79-81; package designer, Cher-Ami Natural Sweet Treats, New York, 79-84; fashion designer, clothing indust & freelance, New York. *Teaching:* Secondary supervisor art, Oyster Bay-East Norwich Cent Schs, Oyster Bay, NY, 67-79; artist-vis instr, Boces Cult Arts Ctr, Syosset, NY, 79-81; adj prof, Art Dept, Nassau Community Col, Garden City, NY, 80-92. *Awards:* Medal Honor & Elizabeth Stanton Blake Award Excellence, Nat Asn Women Artists Exhib, New York, 91; First Prize, Wunsch Art Ctr - The Expert Eye, N Shore Coun Arts, 92. *Bibliog:* Thomas Cassese (auth), Artists of a different kind, Newsday, Long Island, NY, 6/30/91; Dr Stella Russell (auth, interview), Art in the World - Pastels, WHPC-FM (radio), 83 & 87; Eleanor Honig - Lecture Biography, Art a la Carte, Heckscher Mus, 84 & 87 & Lecture Biography, Aspect Int Language Sch, C W Post Col, NY, 91. *Mem:* Nat Asn Women Artists, New York (exec bd, 86-92); Pastel Soc Am, New York; Hempstead Harbor Artists Asn, Glen Cove, NY (exec bd & vpres, 82-92); Nat Drawing Asn. *Media:* Oil, Mixed. *Mailing Add:* 25 Hightop Lane Jericho NY 11753

HONIG, MERVIN
PAINTER, PAINTING CONSERVATOR
b New York, NY, Dec 25, 20. *Study:* Art with Francis Criss, 39-41, Amadee Ozenfant, 46 & Hans Hofmann, 47-50; Brooklyn Mus, conservation with Caroline & Sheldon Keck, 56-58, Brooklyn Col, BA, 73. *Work:* Okla Mus Art, Oklahoma City; Nat Acad Design & Metrop Mus Art, New York; Hofstra Mus, Hempstead, NY; Siena Heights Col. *Exhib:* Portrait of America, Metrop Mus Art, New York, 44 & Carnegie Inst Fine Arts, 45; Whitney Mus Am Art Artists Ann, 49; Brooklyn & Long Island Artists, Brooklyn Mus, 60; Wadsworth Atheneum Artists Ann, 65; one man shows, Nat Art Mus Sport, Madison Sq Garden, NY, 77, Bergen Mus Arts & Sci, NJ, 84, William Benton Mus Art, Storrs, Conn, 85 & Bronx Mus Arts, 86, Country Art Gallery, Locust Valley, New York, 90; Nat Acad Design, Ann Exhib, 78 & 79; Los Angeles Co Mus; The Queens Mus; The William Rockhill Nelson Gallery; The Butler Inst Am Art; and others. *Pos:* Trustee, Nat Art Mus Sport, New Haven, Conn, currently; conserv consult, Hofstra Mus, Hempstead, NY, 78 & Guild Hall Mus, East Hampton, 82- *Teaching:* Lectr conserv painting, Hofstra Univ, 72-; fac mem conserv painting, New Sch, 77-83; Art Students League, 89. *Awards:* Gold Medal for Best in Show, Am Vet Soc Artists, 66; Samuel Morton Mem Award, Audubon Artists, 83; First Prize, oil painting, Silvermine Guild Artists, Conn, 88. *Bibliog:* Amy Pett (auth), Beneath suburban exterior are two dedicated artists, Pt Washington News, 70; Cover story, Palette Talk, 80; demonstr, Conservation of Paintings, Channel 21-TV, 77. *Mem:* Audubon Artists; Nat Acad Design; Nat Arts Club, NY; fel Am Inst Conserv Artistic & Hist Works; Allied Artists Am (vpres, formerly). *Media:* Oil on Canvas. *Publ:* The problem of fungus infestation of a framed pastel portrait, 71 & Polyurethane foam in the process of a transfer, 10/14/73, Bull Am Group, Int Inst Conserv Hist & Artists Works. *Mailing Add:* 64 Jane Ct Westbury NY 11590

HONJO, MASAKO
PAINTER
b Gi Fu Pref, Japan, May 3, 48. *Study:* Art Student League, 82. *Exhib:* Nat Asn Women Artists Traveling Painting Exhib USA, Monmouth Mus, NJ, 87, Hiddenite Art Mus, NC, 88 & Nicolaysen Art Mus, Casper, Wyo, 88; 100 Years/100 Works, Nat Asn Women Artists, Islip Mus, East Islip, NY, 89, Fine Art Mus of the S, Mobile, Ala, 89, Chattanooga Regional Hist Mus, Tenn, 89, Longview Mus Art, Tex, 89 & Kirkpatrick Art Ctr, Oklahoma City, 90. *Awards:* Zluta & Joseph Akston Found Award, 88. *Bibliog:* David Howard (auth), David Howard art seen, Visual Studies, 90. *Mem:* Nat Asn Women Artists (oil juror, 88-89); Hudson River Contemp Artists; Am Soc Contemp Artists. *Media:* Oil. *Dealer:* Gallery 84 50 W 57th St New York NY 10019. *Mailing Add:* 923 Fifth Ave New York NY 10021

HOOD, DOROTHY
PAINTER
b Bryan, Tex. *Study:* RI Sch Design, grad, Hon DFA; Art Students League. *Work:* Mus Mod Art, New York; Whitney Mus Am Art, New York; Brooklyn Mus, NY; Everson Mus, Syracuse, NY; Menil Found, Houston; and others. *Comn:* Sets, Royal Hunt of the Sun, Royal Ont Mus, Toronto; Allen's Landing, Houston Ballet, 78. *Exhib:* One-man shows, Mus Fine Art, Houston, 76, Meredith Long Contemporaries, NY, 78 & 80 & Wallace Wentworth Gallery, Washington, DC, 85 & 88; Retrospective, Everson Mus, 72; Exhib New Work in Clay, V Everson Mus & Edmonton Art Gallery, 78; A Sense of Spirit, Paolo Soleri-Arcosanti, 81; The Americans: Collage, Contemp Arts Mus, Houston, 82; Rutgers Univ, 82; Salzburg Kutsverein, Villach, Austria, 83; American Women Artists Works on Paper, United Nations Conf, Kenya, Africa, 85; The Comet Show, Bard Col, NY & The Light Gallery, New York, 85; Fresh Paint, Mus Fine Arts, Houston & PS 1, New York; Maier Mus, Lynchberg, Va, 88; and others. *Pos:* Set designer, Houston Ballet, Allen's Landing, 75; ed, Bull Mus Art & Archeol, Univ Mich, currently. *Awards:* Childe Hassam Fund Award, Am Acad Arts & Lett, 73 & 74; Mayors Award, Outstanding Contribution to the Visual Arts, Houston, 83; Achievment Ann Award, Nat Women's Caucus for Art, 88. *Bibliog:* Philippe de Montebello (auth), Dorothy Hood, Haiti, a surrealist abstraction, Mus Fine Arts Bull, 71; Carl Colby (dir), The Color of Life, Dorothy Hood (documentary), 85; Robert Hobbs (auth), Dorothy Hood's Collages Catalog, Wallace Wentworth Gallery, DC, 88. *Media:* Oil, Collage. *Publ:* Auth, Sighting the invisible frontier, Art J, summer 80. *Dealer:* Meredith Long Houston Galleries 2323 San Felipe Houston TX 77019; J Rosenthall Gallery, Chicago. *Mailing Add:* 819 Highland Houston TX 77009

HOOD, GARY ALLEN
CURATOR, PRINTMAKER
b Wichita, Kans, Oct 22, 43. *Study:* Wichita State Univ, BAE, 67, MA, 72, MFA(printmaking), 75; Walker Art Ctr, Minneapolis, 72-73; Minneapolis Inst Arts (Ford Found Grant), 72-73. *Work:* Philbrook Art Ctr, Tulsa, Okla; Wichita State Univ, Kans. *Exhib:* Eight State Exhib Painting & Sculpture, Okla Art Ctr, Oklahoma City, 71; Midwest Regional Exhib, Tulsa Pub Libr, Okla, 73; Western Ann Exhib of Works on Paper, Western Ill Univ, 74; Nat Exhib of Images on Paper, Springfield Art Asn, Ill, 74; Am Indian Ann Nat Exhib, Philbrook Art Ctr, 75 & 76; Kans Regional, Kans State Capitol, Topeka, 77; and others. *Collections Arranged:* Eisenhower Paintings, Kans Arts Comn, 89. *Pos:* Asst, Walker Art Ctr & Minneapolis Inst Arts, 72; asst cur, Edwin A Ulrich Mus Art, Wichita State Univ, 73-76, sr cur, 76-89; consult, Mobile Art Gallery, Kans Cult Art Comn, 74-76, Kans Art, 76 & Indian Ctr, Wichita, 79-81 & 89; cur art, Mus Southwest, Midland, Tex, 90- *Teaching:* Lectr, Am Indian art, Walker Art Ctr & Minneapolis Inst Arts, 72; guest lectr, Minn Asn State Colleges, 72, Wichita State Univ, 71-90, Univ Santa Clara Sem, Wichita, 73; instr, Midland Col, Tex, 90- *Awards:* Ford Found Grant, 72 & 73-74 & Grad Fel Grant, 73-74; Int Kings Grant, 73; Graphics award, Philbrook, 76; Art Res Study Grant, Kans Art Comn, 89. *Mem:* Am Asn Mus; Am Fed Arts; Nat Art Educ Asn. *Media:* Intaglio, Mixed. *Res:* Realism to abstraction to nonobjectivism; tradition, change & influences in American-Indian art; 20th century sculpture, contemporary American art; art of the Southwest. *Publ:* Twentieth Century Sculpture, 87; Majesty in Motion, Paintings of Frederick Waugh, 88; The Paintings of Dwight D Eisenhower, 89. *Dealer:* Joan Cawley Gallery, Scottsdale, Santa Fe, Kansas City. *Mailing Add:* c/o Museum of the Southwest 1705 W Missouri Ave Midland TX 79701-6516

HOOD, GRAHAM STANLEY
MUSEUM DIRECTOR, WRITER
b Stratford-on-Avon, Eng, Nov 6, 36; US citizen. *Study:* Keble Col, Oxford Univ, MA(mod hist); Courtauld Inst Art, London Univ. *Work:* Detroit Inst Art; Colonial Williamsburg Found, Va. *Pos:* Cur Europ decorative arts, Wadsworth Atheneum, Hartford, Conn, 61-64; assoc cur, Garvan Collection, Yale Univ Art Gallery, New Haven, 64-68; cur Am art, Detroit Inst Art, 68-71; vpres, Carlisle H Humelsine & cur, Colonial Williamsburg Found, 71. *Teaching:* Adj prof hist art, Wayne State Univ; lectr hist art, Col William & Mary, Williamsburg, Va, 74- *Mem:* Asn Art Mus Dirs; Am Antiquarian Soc. *Publ:* Auth, American Silver, a History of Style, 1650-1900, Praeger Publ, 71; coauth, The Garvan Collection of American Silver at Yale, Yale Univ Art Gallery, 71; auth, Bonnin and Morris of Philadelphia: The First American Porcelain Factory, Univ NC Press, 72; co-auth, The Williamsburg Collection of Antique Furnishings, 73 & auth, Charles Bridges and William Dering: Two Virginia Painters, 1735-1750, 78, Colonial Williamsburg Found; The Governor's Palace in Williamsburg: A Cultural Study, Colonial Williamsburg Found & Univ NC Press. *Mailing Add:* Colonial Williamsburg Found Williamsburg VA 23185

HOOD, MARY BRYAN
MUSEUM DIRECTOR, ADMINISTRATOR
b Central City, Ky, July 5, 38. *Study:* Ky Wesleyan Col, dipl(theatre), 60, dipl(art & art hist), 74. *Collections Arranged:* The American Artist Looks at the American Soldier: 1915-1975, 80; The Kentucky Tradition in American

Landscape Painting (coauth, catalog), 83; Kentucky Expatriates: In Major American Museum Collections (auth, catalog), 84; The Art of the Native American: The Southwest 19th Century to the Present (auth, catalog), 85; Christianity and the the Visual Arts: Kentucky Collections (auth, catalog), 86; The Kentuckians (auth, catalog), 87; The Experienced Eye (auth, catalog), 88; Contemplating the American Watercolor: The Transco Collection, 89; Kentucky Spirit: The Naive Tradition, 91. *Pos:* Exec dir, Owensboro Arts Comn, Ky, 73-77; founding dir, Owensboro Mus Fine Art, Ky, 77- *Mem:* Ky Arts Comn (mem bd, 77-78); Am Asn Mus; Ky Citizens for the Arts (exec bd, 84-); Ky Bicentennial Steering Comt (mem, 90-92); Year of American Craft, Ky Comt, 91-93. *Res:* Regional art with emphasis on art and artists with Kentucky connections. *Mailing Add:* 432 Maple Ave Owensboro KY 42301

HOOD, (THOMAS) RICHARD
PRINTMAKER, DESIGNER
b Philadelphia, Pa. *Study:* Univ Pa Sch Fine Arts; Philadelphia Mus Sch Art, BFA, 53. *Work:* Philadelphia Mus Art; Yale Univ Mus; Mus Mod Art, New York; Nat Portrait Gallery, Libr Cong, Washington, DC. *Exhib:* New Horizons, Mus Mod Art, New York, 36; Am Art Today, New York World's Fair, 39; Art Dirs Ann, Philadelphia, 52-72; Fabulous Decade, Smithsonian Inst, 64; Color Prints of Americas, NJ State Mus, Trenton & tour to mus in Hawaii, Alaska & nine cities in Japan, 70. *Pos:* Assoc dir advert design, Philadelphia Col Art, 57-60, dir exhibs, 67-; design consult, 67- *Teaching:* From instr to prof, Philadelphia Col Art, 51-82. *Awards:* Franklin Gold Medal, Printing Industs Philadelphia, 59, 69 & 70; Nat Graphic Arts Design Award, 68 & 70; Andy Award of Merit, 73. *Bibliog:* Gertrude Benson (auth), Tradition versus innovation, Pa Traveler, 5/59; Sam Gamburg (auth), Professor Hood and award winning invitation, Centennial News, spring 71; Victoria Donohoe (auth), Dick Hood's timeless, abstract, balancing act, Philadelphia Inquirer, 2/25/72. *Mem:* Philadelphia Art Alliance (chmn, 77, bd dirs, 79); Print Club Philadelphia; Am Color Print Soc (pres, 56-); fel Int Inst Arts & Lett; Wisdom Hall of Fame. *Mailing Add:* c/o Marianne Vadorsky 3535 Sunnyside Ave Philadelphia PA 19129

HOOD, WALTER KELLY
HISTORIAN, PAINTER
b Catawba Co, NC, Aug 19, 28. *Study:* Antioch Col, 48-49; Pa Acad Fine Arts, 49-53; Am Acad Rome, 53-55; Univ Pa, BFA, 57; Univ Hawaii, MFA, 61; Northwestern Univ, PhD(art hist), 66; mural studies with George Harding & Jean Charlot. *Work:* Pa Acad Fine Arts, Philadelphia; Fred T Foard Sch, Vale, NC; Corriher-Linn-Black Libr, Salisbury, NC. *Comn:* Six egg tempera murals, Christ's Life, Death & Resurrection, St Peter's Episcopal Church, Glenside, Pa, 57-58; three frescoes, Bd Regist for Engrs, Architects & Land Surveyors, Honolulu, 61; egg tempera mural, Chapel Hill, NC, residence, 87; egg tempera mural, History of Rowan County, Salisbury Mall, NC, 90. *Exhib:* III Mostra de Pittura Americana, Bordighera, Italy, 55; one-man exhib of mural designs, Archit League New York, 56; 152nd Ann Exhib, Pa Acad Fine Arts, 57; 1974 Grand Nat Exhib, Am Artists Prof League, Lever House, New York, 74. *Awards:* Cresson European Traveling Award, Pa Acad Fine Arts, 52 & Schiedt Foreign Traveling Award, 53; Abbey Mural Fel, Am Acad Rome, 53-54. *Bibliog:* Frederick Williams (auth), To the Glory of God: Glimpse of a Man (biog film), 70. *Mem:* Nat Soc Mural Painters; fel Am Acad Rome. *Media:* Fresco, Egg Tempera. *Res:* Definitive study of the art life of George Harding. *Publ:* Auth, Estival Imaginings, 85, Gossamer Days, 86, Thoughts in Monochrome, 87, Springtide Cadences, 88 & Permutations, 89, pvt publs. *Mailing Add:* 2508 W Innes St Salisbury NC 28144

HOOKHAM, ELEANOR KING See King, Eleanor (Eleanor King Hookham)

HOOKS, CHARLES VERNON
DEALER, COLLECTOR
b Houston, Tex, Aug 8, 30. *Study:* Univ Tex, 48; Univ Houston, 51. *Pos:* Pres, Hooks-Epstein Galleries, Houston. *Mem:* Houston Art Dealers Asn (pres, founder). *Specialty:* Late 19th century and 20th century representational American, European and Latin paintings; sculpture; works on paper; publisher and distributor of original graphics. *Collection:* Works on paper of 20th century American and European masters and sculpture from the 1950s. *Mailing Add:* 4726 Yoakum Blvd Houston TX 77006

HOOKS, EARL J
EDUCATOR, SCULPTOR
b Baltimore, Md, Aug 2, 27. *Study:* Howard Univ, BAE; Cath Univ; Rochester Inst of Technol, NY, cert. *Work:* DePauw Univ, Greencastle, Ind; Harmon Found, New York; City of Gary, Ind; State of Tenn Arts Comn. *Comn:* Ceramic sculpture, State Gift to Gov Ray Blanton, Tanzania, 77. *Exhib:* Howard Univ Invitational, 61; 21st Syracuse Biennial Traveling Exhib, Smithsonian Inst, 61-62; Int Minerals & Chemicals, Skokie, Ill, 66; three-man show, Art Inst Chicago, 67; Ball State Mus, Muncie, Ind, 69; Two Centuries of Black Am Art, Los Angeles Co Mus Art, 76; Dallas Mus Fine Arts, 77; High Mus, Atlanta, 77; Brooklyn Mus, 77. *Teaching:* Instr ceramics & drawing, Shaw Univ, Raleigh, NC, 53-54; instr & art consult, Gary Pub Schs, Ind, 59-68; instr ceramics & drawing, Ind Univ, Gary, 64-67; assoc prof sculpture & ceramics & chmn dept art, Fisk Univ, 68- *Awards:* Second Prize, Arts & Crafts, John Herron Art Sch, 59; Purchase Prize, Dedication of Art Bldg, Howard Univ, 60; Cert of Honor, Int Festival of Lagos, Nigerian Govt, 77. *Bibliog:* Cedric Dover (auth), American Negro Art, 60; Elton Fax (auth), Seventeen Black Artists, Dodd-Mead, 71; Bruno Bak (auth), The Rites of Color and Form, Fisk Univ, 74. *Media:* Ceramics. *Publ:* Coauth, Extended Services in Museum Science Training, 72 & Ben Jones (catalog), 77, Fisk Univ. *Mailing Add:* 935 18th Ave N Nashville TN 37208

HOOKS, GERI
DEALER, COLLECTOR
b Houston, Tex, Apr 24, 35. *Study:* Stephens Col, AA, 53; Tex Univ, 53-54. *Pos:* Owner & dir, Hooks-Epstein Galleries Inc, currently. *Mem:* Houston Art Dealers Asn (founder). *Specialty:* Late 19th century and 20th century representational American, European and Latin paintings, sculpture and works on paper. *Collection:* Sculpture and works on paper. *Mailing Add:* 4726 Yoakum Blvd Houston TX 77006

HOOPER, JACK MEREDITH
PAINTER, PRINTMAKER
b Los Angeles, Calif, Aug 26, 28. *Study:* Los Angeles City Col, AA(art), 51; Col Am, Mexico City, asst to Siqueiros, BA(art; cum laude), 52; Acad Julian, Paris, with Chaplin Midi & Pierre Jerome, 54; Univ Calif, Los Angeles, MA(art), 56. *Work:* Lannan Found, Fla; Stanford Univ Mus; Long Beach Mus; Univ Calif, Los Angeles & Santa Cruz. *Exhib:* The Artist's Environment--The West Coast, Oakland Art Mus, Amon Carter Mus, Ft Worth & Univ Calif, Los Angeles Galleries, 62; Fifty Calif Artists, Whitney Mus Am Art, Albright Art Gallery & Walker Art Ctr, 62-63; Art Across America, San Francisco Mus Mod Art & Knoedlers Galleries, New York, 65-66; retrospective, Smith & Cowell Gallery, Santa Cruz & Univ Santa Cruz, 75; Sixth Hawaii Nat Print Exhib, Honolulu Acad Art, 82. *Pos:* Dir, Sculptural Walls, Los Angeles, 62-66. *Teaching:* Asst prof art, Univ Calif, Los Angeles, 57-62; vis prof, Univ Colo, Boulder, 62; prof, chmn dept & dir art galleries, Mt St Marys Col, 63-69; prof, Univ Calif, Santa Cruz, 76. *Awards:* New Talent in America--Top 100 in Nation, Art in Am, 57; Los Angeles Ann Award Painting, 59; Purchase Award, Long Beach Mus Art, 65. *Bibliog:* Jack Hooper, Univ Calif, Santa Cruz, 75. *Mem:* World Print Coun. *Mailing Add:* c/o Gallery 30 311-315 Primrose Rd Burlingame CA 94101

HOOTON, BRUCE DUFF
EDITOR, PUBLISHER
b Waukegan, Ill, Dec 11, 28. *Study:* Southwestern Col, 46-50; Memphis Acad Arts, 48-50; Harvard Univ, scholar, 51-52. *Collections Arranged:* Sculptors Guild Bryant Park Exhibition, in association with New York Cultural Affairs, 67; Niezvestny (modern Russian sculpture), Sculptors Guild, New York, 68; Drawing Society Regional Drawing Exhib (8 museums), Am Fedn Arts, 70-72; Venice Biennale, Castelli Gallery, 73; Benito Retrospective, New York Cult Ctr, 74. *Pos:* Ed & auth, Drawing Mag, 57-60, pres & founder, Drawing Soc, 59; art critic, ed & reviewer, New York Herald Tribune, 62-65; head New York off, Archives Am Art, 65-66; ed, Art News, 68-69; assoc, Lee Ault & Co, 71-; ed & pub, Art World Newspaper, New York; dir, Manufacturers Hanover/Art World Awards; dir, Nassau Co Mus Art. *Mem:* Drawing Soc (vpres, 75); NY State Coun Arts. *Specialty:* Twentieth century paintings, sculpture and drawings; French and European masters; South American masters; young masters. *Publ:* Ed, Drawings of Edwin Dickinson, Yale Univ, 60; Mother & Child in Modern Art, Duell, Sloan & Pearce, 64; American Paintings in Reynolda House, Reynolda House, 70. *Mailing Add:* 55 Wheatley Rd Glen Head NY 11545

HOOVER, FRANCIS LOUIS
COLLECTOR, JEWELER
b Sherman, Tex, Mar 12, 13. *Study:* NTex State Univ, BS, 33; Columbia Univ, MA, 35; Art Students League, 40-41; New Sch Social Res, 40-41; NY Univ, DEd, 41. *Exhib:* Biennial exhibs, Am Child Art, 55, 57, 59 & 61. *Pos:* Dir, LaSalle Art Gallery, 33-36; ed, Arts & Activities Mag, 52-67; dir, Fairway Gallery, 62-67; pres, Quadradic Soc, 90-91. *Teaching:* Art dir, Carden Pvt Sch, New York, 34-36; asst prof art, NTex State Univ, 36-40; asst prof art, Eastern Ill State Univ, 41-44; prof art & chmn dept, Ill State Univ, 44-73, dir, Univ Mus, 72-73. *Awards:* Merit Award Ed Excellence, Indust Mkt 6th Ann, 54; Distinguished Prof Art, Ill State Univ, 72; Distinguished Fel, Nat Art Educ Asn, 86. *Mem:* Appraisers Asn Am; Am Soc Appraisers; Int Platform Asn; Art Educ Found (bd dirs, 56-66); Delta Phi Delta. *Collection:* Art of the Cuna Indians; pre-Columbian ceramics and jade; primitive arts of Africa and Oceania; folk arts of Middle America; works are in permanent collections of Philadelphia Museum of Art, Cleveland Museum of Art, Art Institute of Chicago, Field Museum of Natural History, Harvard Univ, Peabody Museum, Smithsonian Inst and others. *Publ:* Auth, Guide for Teaching Art Activities in the Classroom, 56; Art Activities for the Very Young, 62; Young Printmakers I, 63 & II, 64; Young Sculptures, 67; African Art, 74. *Mailing Add:* 3450 3rd Ave No 405 San Diego CA 92103

HOOVER, JOHN JAY
SCULPTOR
b Cordova, Alaska, Oct 13, 19. *Study:* Derbyshire Sch of Fine Arts, Seattle, Wash. *Work:* Bur Indian Affairs, Washington, DC; Seattle Art Mus, Wash; Gulf Paper Co; Heard Mus, Phoenix, Ariz; King Co & Seattle Art Comn. *Comn:* Mural, Tyonek Tribe, Anchorage, Alaska, 64; mobile, James Bialac, Ariz, 76; mural, City Light Co, Seattle, 77. *Exhib:* Sculpture I & Sculpture II, Heard Mus, Phoenix, Ariz, 73 & 74; one-man shows, Whatcom Co Mus, Bellingham, Wash & Mus of Plains Indians, Browning, Mont, 75; Sculpture Invitational, Heard Mus, Phoenix, Ariz, 77. *Teaching:* Artist-in-residence sculpture, Inst of Am Indian Art, Santa Fe, NMex, 72 & DOD Sch Syst, Japan, Taiwan & the Philippines, 74; instr, Northern Ariz Univ, Flagstaff, 79. *Awards:* First Prize/Sculpture, Cent Wash State Col, 73, Philbrook Art Ctr, Tulsa, Okla, 74 & Heard Mus, Phoenix, Ariz, 75. *Media:* Wood, Cast Metal. *Publ:* This Song Remers Jane B Katz, HM Co; Aleut & Eskimo Art, Dorothy J Ray, Washington; Aleut Art, Lydia T Black & Aleutian/Pribilof; Sweet Grass Lives On Highwater, Lippincott & Crowell. *Dealer:* Gallery Wall Santa Fe NM & Phoenix AZ; Stonington Gallery 2030 First Ave Seattle WA. *Mailing Add:* E 841 W Stadium Grapeview WA 98546

HOPKINS, B(ERNICE ELIZABETH)
PAINTER
b Marinette, Wis, Mar 7, 26. *Study:* Maryvill Col, Tenn. *Work:* Edna Carston Gallery, Univ Wis, Stevens Point; Visual Arts Ctr NW Fla, Panama City; City of Tallahassee, FL. *Exhib:* Pastel Soc Am, Nat Arts Club, NY, 84 & 87, Hermitage Mus, Norfolk, Va 84, Monmouth Mus, Lincraft, NJ, 85 & Harmon Meek Gallery, Naples, Fla, 91-92; Degas Pastel Soc, World Trade Bldg Gallery, New Orleans, La, 87; Societe des Pastellists de France, Lille, France, 88; Pastel Soc West Coast, Sacramento Fine Arts Ctr, Carmichael, Calif, 88. *Awards:* Still Life, Pastel Soc Am, Philip M Lahn, 84; Still Life, Pastel Soc Am, David Rosenthal, 87; Still Life, Pastel Soc Am, Morilla-Conson-Talens, 89; Master Pastelist Status, Pastel Soc Am, NY, 88. *Mem:* Pastel Soc Am; Pastel Soc N Fla; Visual Arts Ctr NW Fla (secy, 86-88). *Media:* Pastel. *Dealer:* The Gallery of Art 36 Beach Dr W Panama City FL 32401. *Mailing Add:* 121 Rose Coral Dr Panama City Beach FL 32408

HOPKINS, BUDD
PAINTER, SCULPTOR
b Wheeling, WVa, June 15, 31. *Study:* Oberlin Col, BA, 53; Columbia Univ, with Meyer Schapiro, 53-54. *Work:* Brooklyn Mus, NY; Whitney Mus Am Art, Guggenheim Mus Art, Metrop Mus Art, Mus Mod Art, New York; San Francisco Mus Art; Corcoran Gallery Art, Libr Cong, Washington, DC; Houston Mus Fine Arts, Tex; Philadelphia Mus Art, Pa; Walker Art Ctr, Minneapolis, Minn; Mass Inst Technol; and others. *Comn:* Oil painting, WVa State Humanities Coun, 72. *Exhib:* Solo exhibs, Poindexter Galerie, New York, 56-63, 66, 67 & 71, Galerie Liatowitsch, Basel, Switz, 74, Long Point Gallery, Provincetown, Mass, 82, 85 & 91, Jan Cicero Gallery, Chicago, 85, Marilyn Pearl Gallery (with catalog), New York, 85 & 88 & Drew Univ, Oakland, NJ, 90; Two Decades of American Painting, Solomon R Guggenheim Mus, NY, 75; Recent Acquisitions, Solomon R Guggenheim Mus, 87; Postwar Geometrical Painting, Marilyn Pearl Gallery, 91; Corporations Collection, Morris Mus, NJ, 91; American Abstract Artists, Valletta, Malta & Ottawa Mus, Can, 91; Gallery Group, Longpoint Gallery, Provincetown, 92; and others. *Teaching:* Docent, Mus Mod Art, summers 55-56; docent, Whitney Mus Am Art, 57-60; instr, Pratt Inst, Provincetown, summer 75; instr, RI Sch Design, Provincetown, summer 75. *Awards:* Guggenheim Fel, 75; Nat Endowment Arts Award, 79; Special Project Grant, NY State Coun Arts, 82. *Bibliog:* Brian O'Doherty (auth), Budd Hopkins, master of a movement manque, Object & Idea, 67; April Kingsley (auth), Energy and order--the paintings of Budd Hopkins, Art Int, 4/73; Peter Frank (auth), Budd Hopkins: The works on paper, Kresge Art Ctr Bull, 4/74; Carter Ratcliffe (auth), The distractions of theme, Art in Am, 9-10/78; Robert Motherwell (auth), catalogue, Marilyn Pearl Gallery, 88. *Mem:* Provincetown Art Asn (hon vpres, 68-70 & 77-79); Am Abstract Artists, 85-88. *Media:* Acrylic, Oil; Wood. *Publ:* Auth, First person singular, Art Gallery Mag, 4/72; Budd Hopkins on Budd Hopkins, Art in Am, 7-8/73; contribr, Roundtable on painting, 9/75, Richard Diebenkorn & Franz Kline, 79, Artforum; auth, de Kooning's Drawings, Drawing, 3-4/84; The collages of Fritz Bultman, Provincetown Arts, 6/86; and others. *Dealer:* Marilyn Pearl Gallery 420 W Broadway New York NY 10012. *Mailing Add:* 246 W 16th St New York NY 10011

HOPKINS, HENRY TYLER
MUSEUM DIRECTOR, EDUCATOR
b Idaho Falls, Idaho, Aug 14, 28. *Study:* Art Inst Chicago, BAE & MAE; Univ Calif, Los Angeles; Calif Col Arts & Crafts, Hon PhD, 84; San Francisco Art Inst, Hon PhD, 86. *Collections Arranged:* 30 California Artists, 61; Reuben Nakian, 62; Josef Albers: White Line Squares (with catalog), 66; Robert Rauschenberg: Selections, 69; Milton Resnick: Large Paintings (with catalog), 71; Irwin-Wheeler, 72; Joe Goode: Work Until Now (with catalog), 73; Clyfford Still (with catalog), 75; Painting & Sculpture in California: The Modern Era (with catalog), 76; Philip Guston (with catalog), 80; Expressionism & German Intuition, 83; The Human Condition, 84; Lita Albuquerque, 89. *Pos:* Head educ, Los Angeles Co Mus Art, Los Angeles, 61-65, cur exhib, 65-68; dir, Ft Worth Art Mus, Tex, 68-74; dir, San Francisco Mus Mod Art, 74-86; dir, Frederick R Weisman Found, 86-91; chmn, art dept & dir, F S Wight Gallery, Univ Calif Los Angeles, 91- *Teaching:* Instr art hist & theory, Univ Calif, Los Angeles Exten, 58-68; instr art hist, Tex Christian Univ, 68-73; vis prof, Univ Calif, Los Angeles, 90 & prof, 91. *Awards:* Order of Leopold II, Knight. *Mem:* Nat Endowment Arts (chmn mus policy panel, 79-83); Nat Endowment Humanities (panelist, 76-77); Art Mus Asn Am (trustee, 75-77, pres, 78); Asn Art Mus Dir (vpres, 84, pres, 85); Int Exhibs Comt. *Res:* Twentieth century art of California; modern art. *Publ:* Contribr, Art in Am, Art News & Artforum Mag, 61-75; auth, Modern & contemporary art, Artnews; auth, Clyfford Still, 76, Fifty California Artists, 84, California Painters, 89. *Mailing Add:* Frederick R Weisman Art Found 10350 Santa Monica Blvd Suite 160 Los Angeles CA 90025

HOPKINS, KENNETH R
MUSEUM DIRECTOR, RESTORER
b Springfield, Mass, Aug 24, 22. *Study:* Pratt Inst; Univ Vt; Parsons Sch of Design; NY Univ, BS; Univ Wis, MS. *Pos:* Art dir, Univ Wis, Madison, 48-50; cur exhib, State Hist Soc Wis, Madison, 50-52; art dir, Old Sturbridge Village, Mass, 52-56; cur, Buffalo & Erie Co Hist Co, Buffalo, NY, 56-60; hist preservationist, Bethelehm Steel Co, Pa, 60-62; dir, Explorers Hall, Nat Geog Soc, Washington, DC, 62-65; dir, State Capitol Mus, 65-82; retired; woodcarver and restorer, currently. *Mailing Add:* 3001 Monte Vista Olympia WA 98501

HOPKINS, PETER
PAINTER, WRITER
b New York, NY, Dec 18, 11. *Study:* Art Students League. *Work:* Mus City of New York. *Comn:* Scenic design, Theatre Guild, New York, 49-50; mural, comn by Gino di Grandi, 55; portrait, Nancy Lybolte, 89; panorama New York, comn by Dr G F Schwartz, 91; portrait of Elizabeth Davidson, 92. *Exhib:* Artists Equity, Whitney Mus Am Art, 51, Contemp Painting, 52; Jr League of Buffalo, NY, 60; Women's Club of Westport, NY, 61; Am Mural Painters Asn, 76; Distinguished Mid-Atlantic Artists, Univ Del, 80; Window on Wonder City, Mus City New York, 89; and many others. *Pos:* Supvr libr, NY Univ, 53; asst dir, Mortimer Brandt Gallery, 53-58; art consult, Nabisco Co, 76; writer, essays, Christian Sci Monitor, 74-79. *Teaching:* Instr drawing & painting, Moore Inst Art, Sci & Indust, 49-50; Newark Acad Art, 50; Cartoonists & Illusr Sch, New York, 51; instr art, New York-Phoenix Schs Design, 61-77, chmn dept fine art & dean of men; asst prof art hist, Pratt Inst, 75-77; lectr, Art Students League, 75-85. *Awards:* Art Grant, Am Acad Arts & Lett, 50; Art Grant, Nat Inst Arts & Lett, 50. *Bibliog:* The artist & the Copa girls, See, 52; C B (auth), Art exhibition notes, New York Herald Tribune, 1/25/58; article in The USA Hist Art, 75. *Mem:* Life mem Art Students League; World Federalist Asn; Nat Space Soc. *Media:* Oil, Chinese Ink. *Publ:* Contribr, Population and Geonomics, NY-Phoenix Sch Design, 70; The Rubens workshop secret, 7/12/73, What do you hear, 9/27/73, Draw me, 3/25/74 & The water hole crowd, 6/6/78, CS Monitor. *Dealer:* Schwaeber Fine Arts 30 Beechwood Way Briarcliff Manor NY 10510. *Mailing Add:* 36 Horatio St Apt 5A New York NY 10014

HOPKINS, TERRI
CURATOR, ADMINISTRATOR
b Tenn, 49. *Study:* Oberlin Col, BA(art hist), 71; Univ Chicago, MA(art hist), 72. *Collections Arranged:* Approximately 60 exhibs, 80- *Pos:* Dir art gym, Marylhurst Col, 80- *Publ:* Auth, Paul Sutinen: Five Works 1982-1987, 87, Barbara Thomas: Paintings, 89, Fernanda D'Agostino: Offering, 89, Barbara Fealy's Gardens, 90 & Unabandoned Abstraction, 91, Marylhurst Col. *Mailing Add:* Marylhurst College Gallery of Art Marylhurst OR 97036

HOPKINSON, HAROLD I
PAINTER, COLLECTOR
b Salt Lake City, Utah, Aug 8, 18. *Study:* Univ Wyo, BA & MA; Art Ctr Sch, Los Angeles; Brigham Young Univ; also with Paul Bransom, O Conrad Schwiering & Robert W Meyers. *Work:* Church of Jesus Christ of Latter Day Saints, Historical Ctr, Salt Lake City; USAF Acad, Colorado Springs, Colo; Marriott Hotel, Salt Lake City; Hotel Utah, Salt Lake; Cult Ctr Am Embassy Prague; Embassy USA, Guatemala. *Comn:* Mural & four paintings, Col Bus Admin, Ariz State Univ, 71; mural, Blue Cross & Blue Shield, 81; five murals, Cody Latter Day Saints Visitors Ctr, Wyo, 82, 89 & 90. *Exhib:* Whitney Gallery Western Art, 72; C M Russell Gallery & Mus, Great Falls, 73-74; Mormon Temple, St George, Utah, 89; Mormon Temple, Mesa, Ariz, 90. *Pos:* Contribr & illusr, Nat Fedn State High Sch Asn, 63-70. *Awards:* First Place, Western Art Show, Cheyenne Frontier Days, 86; First Place & Purchase Award, Wyo Cowboy Spectacular, 86; Purchase Prize, Ellensburg Western Art Asn, 87. *Bibliog:* Lucille N Patrick (auth), Hopkinson, Wyoming Artist, Western Horseman, 68; Royal B Hassrick (auth), Western Painting Today, Watson-Guptill, 75; South West Art Mag, 76. *Mem:* Life mem Nat Cowboy Hall of Fame & Western Heritage Ctr. *Media:* Oil. *Collection:* Paintings by Ken Riley, Robert Meyers, Harley Brown, Edward Grigware, James Bama, Ron Crook, Newman Myrah and others; historical paintings and studies of river life during 1840's on Mississippi from St Paul to St Louis. *Publ:* Contribr, Western Horseman, 68-74, Wyoming the Proud Land, 70 & Westerner, 74; illusr, Wyoming, Wild & Wooley, 83. *Mailing Add:* Box 175 Byron WY 82412

HOPPER, FRANK J
PAINTER, MURALIST
b Evansville, Ind, Oct 15, 24. *Study:* Ind Univ, BFA; Art Inst Chicago; Am Acad Art, Chicago. *Work:* Famous Am Series, Historic Mus, Washington, DC. *Comn:* 200 paintings, Archdiocese of Chicago, 67; mural, St Peter & Paul, Bradenton, Fla, 89; mural & 14 stations of the cross, St Mary Star of the Sea Catholic Church, Longboat Key, Fla, 78; mag covers, Yachting; portraits, Pres Nixon, Pres Reagan & Pres Bush, White House; The Story of Israel, Technion. *Teaching:* Instr, Art Inst & Am Acad, formerly. *Awards:* Gold Medal, Accademia Italia; Posey Found Scholarship evaluations. *Bibliog:* Time study of mural production (film), NBC doc. *Mem:* Am Portrait Soc; Artist Watercolor Soc; Int Soc Marine Painters; Artist Guild, Chicago; Mensa, Chevaliers du Tastevin. *Media:* Acrylic, Oil. *Publ:* Illusr, co-auth, ed or contribr to various publ including Chicago publs & newspapers, Western Publ Co, Chicago Tribune, Art Inst Chicago & books for Chicago Area Sch TV. *Mailing Add:* PO Box 1806 Sarasota FL 34230

HOPPER INC, See Hopper, Frank J

HOPPES, LOWELL E
CARTOONIST
b Alliance, Ohio, July 1, 13. *Pos:* Freelance cartooning for 60 yrs. *Publ:* Created over 39,000 cartoons in Colliers, Post, American, Esquire, New Yorker, Farm Journal, Parade, Family Weekly, King Features Syndicate, New Woman & others worldwide; cartoons for advertisers in numerous fields (including trade/technical publications). *Mailing Add:* 642 Calle del Otono Sarasota FL 34242

HOPTNER, RICHARD
SCULPTOR
b Philadelphia, Pa, Apr 3, 21. *Study:* Univ Pa, 51-57; Cranbrook Acad Art, scholar, 60. *Work:* Philadelphia Civic Ctr Mus. *Comn:* St Malachy Roman Cath Church, Philadelphia, Pa, 87; Episcopalian Diocese Hq, Harrisburg, Pa, 88; Mt Calvary Episcopal Church, Camp Hill, Pa, 88. *Exhib:* Philadelphia Mus Art, 61; Pa Acad Fine Arts, 69; Haverford Col, 74; Gallerie Illien, Atlanta, Ga; one-man show, Greenville Co Mus Art, Greenville, SC, 79; Allentown Mus Fine Arts, Pa, 83; Lutheran Theological Sem, Philadelphia, 84; LaSalle Univ, Philadelphia, 85; Rosemont Col, Rosemont, Pa, 86. *Teaching:* Instr 3-D design, Univ Pa, 68-70. *Awards:* Sculpture Grant, Louis Comfort Tiffany Found, 64. *Bibliog:* New forms-new materials (film), Pa Acad Fine Arts, 69; Sculpture at St Joseph College, WCAU TV, 69. *Media:* Teakwood, Rare Woods. *Publ:* Auth, Anti-art/anti-life, Great Speckled Bird, Atlanta, Ga, 70; Masters of Wood Sculpture, Watson-Guptill; Wood: The New Wave, Crown Publ. *Dealer:* Hahn Gallery 8439 Germantown Ave Philadelphia Pa 19118. *Mailing Add:* 250 Harvey St Philadelphia PA 19144

HORIUCHI, PAUL C
COLLAGE ARTIST
b Kawaguchiko, Yamanashiken, Japan, April 12, 06; US citizen. *Study:* Self taught; Honorary doctorates from Univ Puget Sound, Tacoma, Wash, 65, St Martin's Col, Olympia, Wash, 79 & Seattle Univ, 88. *Work:* Seattle Art Mus, Wash; San Francisco Mus, Calif; Santa Barbara Mus, Calif; Brandeis Univ Mus, Waltham, Mass; Mus Art, Munson-Williams Proctor Inst, Utica, NY. *Comn:* Free standing mural, Seattle Worlds Fair, 62. *Exhib:* Solo exhibs, Seattle Art Mus, 58, Retrospective, Univ Ore, 69 & Tacoma Art Mus, 87-88; Carnegie Art Int, Pittsburgh, Pa, 61-64; Art Since 1950, Seattle Worlds Fair, 62; Berlin Art Festival, Ger, 65; Art Across America, Rockford, Ill, 65; Contemp Am Paintings & Sculpture, Univ Ill, Champaign, 65; Nat Mus Art, Tokyo, Osaka, Kyoto, Japan, 70. *Awards:* Purchase Award, Ford Found, 60. *Dealer:* Woodside Braseth Gallery 1101 Howell Seattle Wash 98101. *Mailing Add:* 9773 Arrowsmith Av S Seattle WA 98118

HORMUTH, JO
SCULPTOR, PRINTMAKER
b Grand Rapids, Mich, 1955. *Study:* Slade Sch Art, London, 78; Grand Valley State Col, Allendale, Mich, BFA, 81; Art Inst Chicago, MFA, 83. *Work:* Art Inst Chicago; Cranbrook Acad Art; MacArthur Found. *Exhib:* Group Show, Sch Gallery, Art Inst Chicago, 85; What Price Beauty; Looking at Labor, Randolph St Gallery, Chicago, 91; Home Sweet Home, Columbia Col Art Gallery, Chicago, 92; Buy/Low, Prairie Ave Gallery, Chicago, 91; Valentine's Day Auction, NAME Gallery, Chicago, 92; Forecast, Zolla/Lieberman Gallery, Chicago, 92. *Bibliog:* Carol Vogel (auth), Visions of Home Sweet Home, NY Times, 2/14/91; Alan Artner (auth), Installations: Things to Catch the Eye and Ear, Chicago Tribune, 7/24/92; Mandy Morrison (auth), The Harder They Drum, The Reader, 8/14/92. *Media:* Mixed. *Mailing Add:* 1742 W Haddon Chicago IL 60622

HORN, BRUCE
PAINTER, EDUCATOR
b Circleville, Ohio, June 30, 46. *Study:* Miami Univ, BFA; Ohio State Univ, MFA; Arnot Mus, New York with Clyde Aspevig; Fechin Inst, NMex with Gregg Kreutz. *Work:* Bradley Univ, Ill; Tyler Sch Art, Philadelphia; Philadelphia Mus Art; Univ Ariz; Clemson Univ, SC; and others. *Exhib:* Fifth Hawaii Nat Print Exhib, Honolulu Acad Arts, 79; one-man show, Univ Ariz, 82; Tenth Int Print Biennale, Cracow, Poland, 84; Ninth Nat Painting Exhib, Wichita, Kans, 89; Fiftieth Nat Competition, Lake Worth, Fla, 91. *Pos:* Package designer, Diamond Nat Paper Co, Middletown, Ohio, summer 68; art dir, Eighth Ann Flagstaff Summer Festival, Ariz, 74. *Teaching:* Assoc prof painting, Blackburn Col, Carlinville, Ill, 70-72 & Northern Ariz Univ, 72- *Awards:* Res Grants, Northern Ariz Univ, 76, 87; Purchase Awards, Trenton State Col, NJ, 80; Honolulu Academy of Arts, Hawaii, 80; Purchase Award, Int Exhib Prints, Wesleyan Col, Macon, 83. *Mem:* Am Color Print Soc; Los Angeles Printmaking Soc; Print Consortium; Mid-Am Col Art Asn; Col Art Assoc Am. *Media:* Oil, Miscellaneous Media. *Mailing Add:* Dept Art Northern Ariz Univ Flagstaff Flagstaff AZ 86011

HORN, MILTON
SCULPTOR
b Russia, Sept 1, 06; US citizen. *Study:* With Henry H Kitson, Boston; Beaux Arts Inst Design, New York; Olivet Col, Mich, Hon DFA, 76. *Work:* Brookgreen Gardens, SC; Nat Mus Fine Arts, Washington, DC; Olivet Col; Smithsonian Inst Div Numismatics; Nat Acad Design, New York. *Comn:* Chicago Raising From the Lake (Bronze 12ft X 14ft) Comn by The Dept Pub Works, Chicago, 54; eight marble reliefs, WVa Univ Med Ctr, 54-59; symbolic bronze on facade & holy ark in sanctuary, B'nai Israel Temple, Charleston, WVa, 59-60; Hymn to Water (bronze), Central Water Filtration Plant, Chicago, 65; bronze, Nat Bank Commerce, Charleston, WVa, 68-69. *Exhib:* American Art Today, New York World's Fair, 39 & 40; Third Int Exhib Sculpture, Philadelphia Mus Fine Arts, 49; American Sculpture--1951, Metrop Mus, New York, 51; Chicago & Vicinity Exhib, Art Inst Chicago, 52; Nat Inst Arts & Lett, New York, 53, 55 & 77; one-man retrospective, Spertus Mus Judaica, Chicago, 89. *Teaching:* Artist in residence & prof art, Olivet Col, 39-49. *Awards:* Am Photogrs Award, 83; Nat Citation Honor, Nat Conf, Am Inst Architects, Washington, DC, 57; Henry Hering Mem Medal, Nat Sculpture Soc, New York, 72. *Bibliog:* Avram Kampf (auth), Contemporary Synagogue Art, Union Am Hebrew Congregations, 61; Cecil Roth (ed), History of Jewish Art, 61 & 71 & Louis Redstone (auth), Art in Architecture, 68, McGraw-Hill; Spurtus Mus Judaica, (illus catalog) Chicago, 89. *Mem:* Founding mem Sculptors Guild; nat academician Col Art Asn Am; fel Nat Sculpture Soc. *Media:* Bronze, Wood. *Publ:* Contribr, Proceedings of Teachers Seminar, Col Schs Archit, Aspen, Colo, 57; contribr, The Christian Century, 2/59; contribr, Indland Architect, 65; contribr, Nat Sculpture Rev, 72. *Mailing Add:* 1932 N Lincoln Ave Chicago IL 60614

HORN, ROBERT NELSON
PAINTER, DESIGNER
b Alton, Ill, Oct 02, 47. *Study:* Southern Ill Univ, Carbondale, BA, 69; Art Inst Chicago, independent study art hist with Dr Joshua Kind, 71. *Work:* Mitchell Gallery, Southern Ill Univ, Carbondale; Moss Thorns Gallery of Art, Fort Hays State Univ, Kans. *Comn:* Sculpture of Edgar Miller, Carl St Studios, Chicago, 89. *Exhib:* Alternative Spaces, Mus Contemp Art, Chicago, Ill, 84; American Realism, Parkersburg Art Ctr, WVa, 89; 14th Nat Small Painting, Drawing & Print Exhib, Fort Hays State Univ, Kans, 89; Hoyt Nat Drawing & Painting Show, Hoyt Inst Fine Arts, New Castle, Pa, 89; 22nd Bradley Nat, Bradley Univ, Peoria, Ill, 89; Artists View the Human Form International Competition, Clary-Miner Gallery, Buffalo, NY, 89; The Chicago Show, Art Inst & Mus Contemp Art, Chicago, Ill, 90. *Pos:* Dir, NAB Gallery, Chicago, 74-, inst drawing workshops, 85-; artist in residence, Carl St Studios, Chicago, 86- *Awards:* Purchase Prize, 14th Nat Small Painting Exhib, Fort Hays St Univ, 89; Artist Grant, Chicago Dept Cult Affairs, 89; Pauline Palmer Prize, Art Inst Chicago, 90. *Bibliog:* Joseph Omblets (auth), Te Chicago Kan Het Wel, Het Laaste Nieuws, Belgian, 80; Joshua Kind (auth), Six Artists, New Art Examiner, 82; Les Krantz (auth), American Artists An Illustrated Survey, Am References, 90. *Media:* Oil. *Mailing Add:* 1433 W Wolfram St Chicago IL 60657

HORN, RONI
SCULPTOR
b New York, NY, 55. *Study:* RI Sch Design, BFA, 74; Yale Univ Sch Art, MFA, 78. *Work:* Toledo Mus Art, Toledo, Ohio; Harfa, Chinati Found, Presidio Co, Tex. *Comn:* Collection of Eric Mosel, comn by Doln Mühle. *Exhib:* Kunstforum Lenbachaus State Mus, Munich, Ger 83; Glyptothek Mus, Munich, Ger 83; Neuberger Mus, State Univ NY, Purchase, 86; Detroit Inst Arts, Mich, 88; Similia/Dissimilia, Castelli Gallery, NY & Kunstalle, Dusseldorf, Ger. *Awards:* Nat Endowment Arts Fel, 84 & 86; AVA Awards in the Visual Arts, 88. *Bibliog:* H Kern (auth), Roni Kern 1977-1980, Kunstraum, Munich, Ger, 80; Rainer Crone (auth), Similia/Dissimilia, Rizzoli Bks, 87; Jeremy Gilbert-Rolfe (auth), Nonrepresentation in 1988, Arts Mag, 5/88. *Mailing Add:* c/o Susanne Hilberry Gallery 555 S Woodward Birmingham MI 48009

HORNADAY, RICHARD HOYT
PAINTER, EDUCATOR
b Joplin, Mo, Aug 15, 27. *Study:* Iowa State Univ, BFA & MFA; Art Inst Chicago. *Work:* Iowa State Univ Collection, Iowa City; Turner Print Gallery, Calif State Univ, Chico; Shasta Col Collection, Redding, Calif. *Exhib:* Ruthermore Gallery, San Francisco, 58 & 64; Recent Painting, USA, The Figure (with catalog), Mus Mod Art, New York, 65; 23rd Am Drawing Biennial, Norfolk Mus, Va, 69; Nat Small Painting Exhib, Univ of the Pac, Stockton, Calif, 70; Fifty Years of Crocker-Kingsley (with catalog), Crocker Art Gallery, Sacramento, 75; Nat Drawing & Painting Exhib, Southeastern Mass Univ, 81; 30-Year Retrospective Survey(with catalog), Redding Mus & Art Ctr, Calif, 83; relief print, Manhattan Kans Nat, 84; Watercolor Gallery, Berkeley, Calif, 85; Rosicrucian Egyptian Mus, Iman, 86; Brand XVIII-XIX, Brand Libr Art Galleries, Glendale, Calif, 88-89; Blue Heron Fine Arts, Chico, Calif, 90; Himovitz-Miller Payilions Gallery, Sacramento, 92. *Pos:* Grad adv, Calif State Univ, Chico, 68-72, prof grad studies, 68, chmn dept art, 72-80, prof emer, 88. *Teaching:* Instr drawing & painting, Shasta Col, 56-63; prof drawing & painting, Calif State Univ, Chico, 81- *Bibliog:* Alfred Frankenstein (auth), Ruthermore Gallery--Richard Hornaday, San Francisco Chronicle, 62; Annual Guide, Art in Am, 84-85; Calif Art Review, Am References, Chicago, 89. *Media:* Watercolor, Graphite. *Dealer:* James Snidle Fine Arts 835 Main St Chico CA 95928. *Mailing Add:* Dept Art Calif State Univ Chico CA 95929

HORNAK, IAN JOHN
PAINTER
b Philadelphia, Pa, Jan 9, 44. *Study:* Univ Mich; Wayne State Univ, BFA, MFA. *Work:* Corcoran Gallery Art, Washington, DC; Indianapolis Mus Art, Ind; Canton Art Inst, Ohio; Owens Corning Fiberglass Corp, Toledo, Ohio; Albrecht Art Mus, St Joseph, Mo. *Exhib:* Tibor de Nagy Gallery, New York, 71-75; The Realist Revival, Am Fedn Arts Traveling Exhib, 72-73; one-man shows, Gertrude Kasle Gallery, Detroit, 74, Fischbach Gallery, New York, 77, 79 & 81, A J Wood Gallery, Philadelphia, 79 & Marie Selby Mus Art, Sarasota, Fla, 80; Armstrong Gallery, New York, 85; Katherina Rich Perlow Gallery, New York, 88, 89 & 91. *Teaching:* Instr drawing, Wayne State Univ, Detroit, Mich, 65-67 Henry Ford Col, Dearborn, Mich, 66- *Awards:* NY Found Arts Grant, 89. *Mem:* Jimmy Ernst Artist's Alliance East Hampton. *Media:* Acrylic, Oil. *Dealer:* Katherina Rich Perlow Gallery 560 Broadway New York NY 10012. *Mailing Add:* PO Box 1371 East Hampton NY 11937

HORNE, (ARTHUR EDWARD) CLEEVE
PAINTER, SCULPTOR
b Jamaica, BWI, Jan 9, 12. *Study:* Ont Col Art, AOCA; also with D Dick, Eng & Europe. *Work:* Nat Gallery Can. *Comn:* Alexander Bell Mem, Brantford, Ont; War Mem, Law Soc Upper Can; Shakespeare Mem; Stratford, Ont; and others. *Exhib:* Nat Gallery Can; Royal Can Acad Arts, 28-; Sculptors' Soc Can, 35-; Ont Soc Artists, 39. *Pos:* Art adv, Ont Hydro-Elec Power Comn, St Lawrence Seaway Power House Proj, 57-58; art consult, Imperial Oil Bldg, Toronto; art consult, Can Imperial Bank Com, 61-63; mem art consult comt,

York Univ, 63-; art consult, Queen's Park Proj, Ont Govt, 66-69. *Awards:* Allied Arts Medals, Royal Archit Inst Can, 63, Royal Can Acad of Arts & Silver Jubilee; Fel OSA, 82; Fel, Ont Col Art, 84; Order Ont, 87. *Mem:* Ont Soc Artist (pres, 49-51); Arts & Lett Club (pres, 55-57); Royal Can Acad Arts. *Media:* All. *Mailing Add:* 181 Balmoral Ave Toronto ON M4V 1J8 Canada

HORNUNG, CLARENCE PEARSON
DESIGNER, WRITER
b New York, NY, June 12, 1899. *Study:* Cooper Union, Baccalaureate Award; Art Students League; City Col New York, BS(Townsend Harris Medal), 20. *Work:* New York Pub Libr; Springfield Mus, Mass; Newark Pub Libr, NJ; NY State Mus, Albany; Nat Gallery Art, Washington, DC. *Comn:* Graphic, advertising & industrial design for: Coca-Cola Co, Encyl Britannica, Int Bus Machines, Richfield Oil Co & Seagram Distilling Corp. *Exhib:* Over 60 exhibs fin US & abroad, in libr & mus incl Yale Univ, Adelphi Univ, Newark Pub Libr, Springfield Mus & NY State Mus, Albany, NY. *Mem:* Am Inst Graphic Artists; Typophiles. *Publ:* Gallery of the Am Automobile, Collectors' Prints, 65; Treasury of American Design, 2 vols, Harry Abrams, 76; The Way It Was: New York, 1850-1890, Schocken Bks, 77; The American Eagle in Art and Design, Dover Publ, 78; The Way It Was in the USA, Abbeville Press, 78; and many others. *Mailing Add:* 66 Allen Rd Rockville Centre NY 11570

HORNUNG, GERTRUDE SEYMOUR
LECTURER, COLLECTOR
b Boston, Mass. *Study:* Wellesley Col, AB; Case Western Reserve Univ, MA & PhD(visual arts), 49. *Pos:* Founder & chmn, Jr Coun, Cleveland, 41-42; deleg, White House Conf Educ, Washington, DC, 55; pres, Adult Educ Coun Greater Cleveland, 56-58; founder & chmn, Greater Cleveland Educ TV Comt, 58-60; trustee, Cleveland Area Arts Coun, 75-79; consult to dir-gen, Mus Iran, 75; deleg, Int Coun Mus Cont, USSR, 77 & London, Eng, 83; founder & pres, Decorative Arts Trust, Cleveland Circle, 87-88. *Teaching:* Lectr art hist, Cleveland Mus Art, 37-45, supvr, 45-60; free lance writer & lectr, 60-; lectr, John Carroll Univ, 72-81, Dublin, Ireland, Rome, Italy & Tehran, Iran, 74-75, Honolulu, 74-93 & Bangkok, Thailand, 78. *Awards:* Ital Ministry Foreign Affairs Res Grant, 62. *Mem:* Cleveland Mus Art; Asia Soc; Japan Soc; Am Arts Coun; Honolulu Acad Arts; and others. *Res:* History of Italian art; art of the South Seas, especially Polynesia & Melanesia; contemporary American art; interrelations arts of East and West; art of Ancient Iran, Oriental Art. *Collection:* Contemporary Italian, Chinese, Japanese and American paintings, prints and ceramics. *Publ:* Auth & ed, Cultural Directory of Greater Cleveland, 47; contribr, articles on art history and education in art museums, var mags & journals, 50-88; ed Univ Hawaii Educ Jour, 88. *Mailing Add:* 13801 Shaker Blvd Cleveland OH 44120

HOROWITZ, BENJAMIN
ADMINISTRATOR, DEALER
b New York, NY, Mar 13, 12. *Study:* Jamaica Teachers Col, cert; City Col New York, BA; NY Univ. *Pos:* Pres, Art Dealers Asn Southern Calif, 70-80, chmn appraisal comt; dir, Heritage Gallery. *Mem:* Los Angeles Co Mus Print Coun; Univ Calif, Los Angeles Print Coun; Calif Confederation Arts; Nat Mus Woman Arts. *Res:* American art. *Specialty:* American artists; international prints. *Publ:* Images of Dignity-Drawings of Charles White, 67. *Mailing Add:* 718 N La Cienega Blvd Los Angeles CA 90069

HOROWITZ, (MR & MRS) RAYMOND J
COLLECTOR
b US citizen. *Study:* Mr Horowitz, Columbia Univ, AB, 36 & LLB, 39; Mrs Horowitz, NY Univ, AB, 36; Columbia Univ, MA, 37. *Bibliog:* John K Howat & Dianne H Pilgrim (auth), American Impressionist and Realist Paintings and Drawings from the Collection of Mr and Mrs Raymond J Horowitz, Metrop Mus Art, 4-6/73. *Collection:* American turn of the century Realist and Impressionist paintings, watercolors and drawings. *Mailing Add:* 930 Fifth Ave New York NY 10021

HORRELL, JEFFREY L
LIBRARIAN
b Carbondale, Ill, Sept 19, 52. *Study:* Miami Univ, Oxford, Ohio, BA, 75; Univ Mich, AMLS, 76, MA(art hist), 78. *Pos:* Archivist, Mus Art, Univ Mich, 76-78; libr internship, Nat Gallery Art, Washington, DC, 77; asst art librn, Art & Arch, Libr, Univ Mich, 78-80; art librn, Sherman Art Libr, Dartmouth Col, 80-86; asst librn, Personnel, Budget & Planning, Syracuse Univ Libr, New York, 86-92; librn, Fine Arts Libr, Havard Univ. *Awards:* Coun Libr Resources Acad Libr Mgt Intern, 86-87. *Mem:* Art Libr Soc NAm (treas, 82-84, vpres & pres elect, 86-88); Col Art Asn; Am Libr Asn. *Res:* Development of automated database on art works produced in Florence and Siena in the 13th and 14th centuries. *Interests:* Art documentation and access. *Publ:* Auth, The picturesque: Literature of the English landscape garden, Dartmouth Col Libr Bull, 83; contribr, Treasures of the Hood Museum of Art, Hudson Hills Press, 85; Second international conference on automatic processing of art history and data documents, Art Doc, 85. *Mailing Add:* 246 Brattle St Cambridge MA 02138

HORVAY, MARTHA J
PAINTER
b Schenectady, NY, Jan 7, 49. *Study:* Univ Mich, Ann Arbor, BS(design), 71, Univ Louisville, MA, 74, Temple Univ, Tyler Sch Art, MFA, 80. *Work:* Sheldon Memorial Gallery Art & Sculpture Garden, Lincoln, Nebr; Springfield, Ill Art Asn; Del Mar Col, Corpus Christi, Tex. *Exhib:* 34th Small Drawing & Sculpture, Ball State Univ, Muncie, Ind, 88; 2-person exhib, Quincy Col Art Gallery, Ill, 89; 33rd Chautauqua Nat, Chautauqua Art Asn Gallery, NY, 90; Midlands Invitational 1990, Joslyn Art Mus, Omaha, Nebr; New American Talent, Laguna Gloria Art Mus, Auston, Tex; solo show, A Personal Geometry, Sheldon Memorial Gallery Art, Lincoln, Nebr, 92. *Teaching:* Vis asst prof drawing found, Univ Tex San Antonio, 81-82; temporary instr drawing design, Kans State Univ, Manhattan, Kans, 82-83; assoc prof drawing painting found, Univ Nebr Lincoln, 83- *Awards:* Juror's Award, 49th Ann Competition, Sioux City Art Ctr, Iowa, 90; Artist's Fel Award, Nebr Arts Coun, 91; Individual Artist's Fel Award, Mid-Am Arts Alliance, 92. *Bibliog:* Kyle MacMillan (auth), Unusual work explores space, volume, time, Omaha World-Herald, 7/24/91; Daphne Anderson Deeds (auth), A Personal Geometry, Sheldon Memorial Gallery Art, 92; Joel Geyer (producer), Is It Art? (film), Nebr Educ TV, fall 92. *Mem:* Col Art Asn NAm. *Media:* Acrylic. *Dealer:* Haydon Gallery 335 N 8th St Lincoln NE 68508. *Mailing Add:* 4433 Pawnee St Lincoln NE 68506

HORVITZ, SUZANNE JOAN
PAINTER, PRINTMAKER
b Philadelphia, Pa. *Study:* Philadelphia Col Art, BFA, MA, 72; Columbia Univ, doctorate, 77. *Work:* Jean Brown Archives, Shaker Seed House, Tyringham, Mass; Deshong Mus, Widner Univ, Chester, Pa; Va Commonwealth Univ, Richmond; Pittsburgh Ctr Arts. *Exhib:* one-woman exhibs, Nexus Found Today's Art, Philadelphia, 77-80, Univ City Sci Ctr, Philadelphia, 80, ABF Gallery, Hamburg, Ger, 80 & Asinelli Gallery, Bologna, Italy, 81; Southern Alleghenies Mus, Loretto, Pa, 79; Unpainted Portrait, Kohler Art Found, Sheboygan, Wis, 79; and others. *Collections Arranged:* Toronto Philadelphia Exchange, ACT Gallery, Toronto, 78; 800 Miles From Home, Name Gallery, Chicago, 79; Xerox Art, Univ City Sci Ctr, Philadelphia, 80; Sexus at Nexus, Found Today's Art, 80; Words and Images (auth, catalog), Philadelphia Art Alliance, traveling, 81. *Pos:* Chmn & trustee, Found Today's Art/Nexus, Philadelphia, 75-; co-dir & pres, Synapse, Visual Art Press, Philadelphia, 80- *Teaching:* Instr, Corcoran Art Sch, Washington, DC, 61-64; instr, Fleisher Art Mem/Philadelphia Art Mus, 67-79; instr, Pa Acad Fine Arts, 80-81. *Awards:* Advan Painting Award, 69 & Samuel Heller Award, 70, Fleisher Art Mem, Philadelphia; Blumenthal Award, Cheltenham Art Ctr Ann, Pa, 77. *Bibliog:* Joel Colton (auth), Hot water review, New York, 77; Patrick Firpo (auth), Copyart, Richard Marek, New York, 78; Burton Wasserman (auth), In touch with tomorrow, Sch Arts Mag, 12/79. *Mem:* Philadelphia Art Alliance (vpres, 79-); Artists Equity Asn; Women's Caucus Arts. *Media:* Acrylic, Watercolor; Electrography. *Publ:* Auth, Graffetti and boxed assemblages, Sch Art Mag, 74; auth, Xerox art: Counterpoint, Philadelphia Print Club, 80; auth, Rope Trick, 80, auth, Thou Hast Ravished My Heart, 81 & auth, Sick of Love, 81, Synapse Press. *Dealer:* Benjamin Mangel Gallery 1604 Locust St Philadelphia PA 19103. *Mailing Add:* c/o Benjamin Mangel Gallery 1714 Rittenhouse Sq Philadelphia PA 19103

HORWITZ, CHANNA
PAINTER, GRAPHIC ARTIST
b Los Angeles, Calif, May 21, 32. *Study:* Art Ctr Sch Design, 50-52; Calif State Univ, Northridge, 60-63; Calif Inst Arts, BFA, 72. *Work:* Los Angeles County Mus Art, Calif; Atlantic Richfield Company, Los Angeles, Calif; Security Pacific, Los Angeles; Nat Gallery Art, Washington, DC. *Comn:* Volt Industs, Orange Co, Calif; Ramada Renesaunce Hotel, Long Beach, Calif; Grand Champion Hotel, Indian Well, Calif. *Exhib:* Three Directions, Newport Harbor Art Mus, Calif, 76; Prints & Drawings, Los Angeles County Mus Art, Calif, 84; Undercover, Fresno Art Ctr & Mus, Calif, 87; solo exhib, Los Angeles Munic Art Gallery, Barnsdall, Calif, 88; paintings, The Drawing Room, Malinda Wyatt, Tucson, 90; and others. *Awards:* James D Phelan Award, 63; Winner's Circle, Los Angeles, Calif, 65; Artist Fel, Nat Endowment Arts, 78. *Bibliog:* Lucy Lippard (auth), 3 Directions (catalog), 76; Dr Susan C Larsen (auth), The Poetry of Systems (catalog), 78 & New Editions, Art News, 3/19/79. *Mem:* Los Angeles Artists Equity Asn. *Media:* Acrylic, Oil. *Publ:* Auth, My statement, 76; auth, Sun & Moon-A Quarterly Statement by Artist, Howard Fox, 76. *Dealer:* Malinda Wyatt 801 Fuller Los Angeles CA 90046. *Mailing Add:* 1742 S Barrington #4 Los Angeles CA 90025

HOTVEDT, KRIS J
PRINTMAKER, PAINTER
b Wautoma, Wis, 1943. *Study:* Layton Sch Art, Milwaukee, Wis, 61-64; San Francisco Art Inst, BFA, 65; Inst Allende, Mex, with D Kortlang, MFA, 67. *Work:* Mus NMex; Univ Sonora, Mex; Huntington Art Alliance, Calif; Ariz State Univ Mem Union Collection; Westat Inc, Rockville, Md; Farmers & Merchants Bank, Menomonee Falls, Wis; St Vincent's Hosp, Santa Fe. *Comn:* Scandinavian Film Festival Poster, Santa Fe, 84. *Exhib:* One-woman exhib, Ore Univ Mus, 74-76; La Bodega, Santa Fe, 83; Lincoln Ctr, Ft Collins, Colo, 85; Waxlander Gallery, Santa Fe, 86 & 89; City Gallery, Sacramento, Calif, 86; Euro Am Gallery, Santa Fe, 92. *Pos:* Art ed, Pembroke Mag, 72- *Teaching:* Instr painting & printmaking, Pembroke State Univ, 67-69; art instr, St Johns Col, NMex, 69-80. *Awards:* NMex Arts Comn Grant, Art in Pub Places, 77-78. *Bibliog:* Article, Art Voices South, 7-8/80. *Media:* Woodcut; Mixed Media. *Publ:* Auth, Southwest Art, 74 & 90; Society for Common Insights, 77 & 78; Int Grafik, 77; Katapult-Pembroke, 77; Fry Breads, Feast Days & Sheeps, Sunstone Press, 87; Coyote Stars the Tree, Vista Grande Design, 88. *Dealer:* Euro-American Gallery 325 Aztec St Santa Fe NM 87501. *Mailing Add:* 2307 Calle Brocha Santa Fe NM 87505

HOUGH, JENNINE
PAINTER
b Charlotte, NC, Mar 17, 48. *Study:* Univ NC, Chapel Hill, BA, 70; Univ NC, Greensboro, MFA with cert, 73; Skowhegan Sch Painting & Sculpture, Maine, summer 74. *Work:* High Mus Art & Ga Arts Coun, Atlanta; Columbus Mus Art, Ga; Miss Mus Art, Jackson; Gibbes Art Mus, Charleston, SC; State

of Georgia, Fine Arts Mus, South Mobile, Ala; and others. *Comn:* Dekalb County Libr System, Dunwooday, Ga, 91. *Exhib:* One-woman shows, Columbus Mus Fine Arts, Ga, 77, Trinity Gallery, Atlanta, 90, 91 & 92, Jane Haslem Gallery, Washington, 91, Marita Gilliam Gallery, Raleigh, 91; Southeastern Competition, Southeastern Ctr Contemp Arts, Winston-Salem, NC, 77 & 79 & Realist Ann-Landscape, 79 & 88; Southern Realism, Miss Mus Art, 79; New in New York, Monique Knowlton Gallery, 81. *Teaching:* Eve prog, Emory Univ, 79-84; Atlanta Col Art, 86-87. *Awards:* Fel, MacDowell Colony, Peterborough, NH, 76; Best of Show, LaGrange Nat III & IV, LaGrange, Ga, 77 & 80; Nat Endowment Arts & Southeastern Ctr Contemp Arts Fel Grant, 80; Archives Nat Mus Women Arts, 90. *Bibliog:* Southern realism reviewed, Art Voices Southeast, 12/79; Southern Realism, Art in Am, 12/80; Southern Accents, Honoring American Artists, 87. *Media:* Acrylic, Watercolor. *Dealer:* Trinity Gallery Atlanta; Marita Gilliam Gallery Raleigh. *Mailing Add:* 265 Brighton Rd NE Atlanta GA 30309

HOUGHTON, BARBARA JEAN
PHOTOGRAPHER, VIDEO ARTIST
b Chicago, Ill, Nov 2, 47. *Study:* Univ Ill, Chicago, BA(art), 71; Sch Art Inst Chicago, MFA(photog), 73, also grad study with Shigeko Kubota. *Work:* Art Inst Chicago; Atlantic Richfield Corp, Denver & Houston; Chase Manhattan Bank, New York; Am Oil Co, Denver; Ctr Creative Photog, Univ Ariz, Tucson. *Exhib:* 74th Chicago & Vicinity Show, Art Inst Chicago, 73; Lensless Photography, Franklin Inst, Philadelphia, 82; Colorado; State of the Arts, Denver Art Mus, 82; New Epiphanies, Ohio Found Arts & traveling, 83; Unsportsmanlike Conduct, Sebastian-Moore Gallery, Denver & Univ Conn, 83 & 84; Photograms, John Michael Kohler Art Ctr, Sheboygan, Wis, 85; The Art of Tattoo, City of Denver, 85; I Always Cheat at Croquet, Ctr Idea Art, Denver, 86. *Teaching:* Asst prof art & photog, Metrop State Col, Denver, 74- *Awards:* Nat Endowment Arts Photog Grant, 78; Grant, Mayor's Comn Cult Affairs, City of Denver, 85; Interdisciplinary Grant, Nat Endowment Arts/ Rockefeller Found, 86. *Bibliog:* Andy Grundberg (auth), From this land, Mod Photog, 6/79; William Peterson (auth), 4/81 & Jane Fudge (auth), summer 84, Photography Notes, Artspace. *Mem:* Nat Educ Asn; Soc Photog Educ. *Dealer:* Martin Gallery 2427 18th St Washington DC. *Mailing Add:* c/o Art Dept Northern Ky Univ Highland Heights KY 41076-1448

HOUK, EDWYNN L
ART DEALER, GALLERY DIRECTOR
b Knoxville, Tenn, Mar 13, 52. *Study:* Ctr Creative Studies, Detroit, BA, 74. *Pos:* Dir, Halstead 831 Gallery, 75-78, Edwynn Houk Gallery, Chicago, currently. *Teaching:* Instr art hist, Wayne State Univ & Ctr Creative Studies, Detroit, 75-76. *Mem:* Art Inst Chicago; Chicago Art Dealers Asn. *Specialty:* 20th century vintage prints, especially those from the period of 1917-1939. *Publ:* Ed, Atget's Vision, 81, Arthur Siegel: Retrospective, 82, Andre Kertesz: Vintage Photographs, 85 & Bill Brandt: Vintage Photographs, 85, Exhib Catalogs, Houk Gallery, Chicago. *Mailing Add:* Edwynn Houk Gallery 200 W Superior Chicago IL 60610

HOUK, PAMELA P
CURATOR
b Dayton, Ohio, Jan 8, 35. *Study:* Skowhegan Sch Painting & Sculpture, Maine, 54; Sch Dayton Art Inst, Ohio, 55-65; Cincinnati Art Acad, Ohio, 61-63; Wright State Univ, Dayton, Ohio, BS, 71, MA, 81. *Work:* Bradford Col, Haverhill, Mass; Cincinnati Mus Art, Ohio. *Collections Arranged:* Bookforms (auth, catalog), Artists' Books, 78; Patterns Plus (auth, catalog), Patterns and Systems, 79; Japanese House (auth, catalog), Household Objects of Edo Period, 79; Woodworks II: Folk Traditions in Ohio and Kentucky (auth, catalog), 81; Cloth Forms (auth, catalog), Fabric Constructions, 82; Inside Self, Someone Else (auth, catalog), The Alter Ego as Self Portrait, 83; Lines of Art Nouveau (auth, catalog), Aspects and Sources of International Art Nouveau Movement, 83-84; Ink Under Pressure (auth, catalog), 84; Clay (auth, catalog), 85; Thomas Macaulay: Sculptural Views on Perceptual Ambiguity, 1968-1986 (coauth, catalog), Dayton Art Inst, Ohio, 86; Art for the Public: New Collaborations (coauth, catalogue), 88; Art that Flies (book, coauth), Sky Art, 90; Fit to Print, Basic Printmaking Processes in 500 years of Master Prints, 92; Inside Japanese Space, Japanese Aesthetic Concepts Related to Space, 93. *Pos:* Dir, Living Arts Ctr Gallery, Dayton, Ohio, 72-76; cur, Experiencenter Gallery, Dayton Art Inst, Ohio, 76- *Mem:* Am Asn Mus. *Mailing Add:* 310 W Schantz Ave Dayton OH 45409

HOULIHAN, PATRICK T
MUSEUM DIRECTOR
b New Haven, Conn, June 22, 42. *Study:* Georgetown Univ, BS, 64; Univ Minn, MA, 69; Univ Wis, PhD, 72, Occidental Col, DSc, 86. *Pos:* Dir, Heard Mus, Phoenix, Ariz, 72-80 & Southwest Mus, Los Angeles, Calif, 81-; asst comr-dir, NY State Mus, Albany, 80-81. *Mem:* Am Asn Mus. *Specialty:* American Indian art museology. *Mailing Add:* c/o Millicent Rogers Mus PO Box A Taos NM 87571

HOUSE, SUDA KAY
PHOTOGRAPHER, EDUCATOR
b Du Quoin, Ill, Jan 31, 51. *Study:* Univ Southern Calif, BFA, 73; Calif State Univ, Fullerton, MA, 76. *Work:* Polaroid Corp, Boston; Los Angeles Co Mus Art; Mus Photog Arts, San Diego; Creative Ctr Photog, Univ Ariz; Minneapolis Inst Arts. *Exhib:* Attitudes: Photography in the 1970s, Santa Barbara Mus Art, 79; Uniquely Photographic, Honolulu Acad Art, 79; Electro Works, George Eastman House, Rochester, NY, 81; Photographer as Printmaker, Arts Coun Gt Brit, London, 82; Eight from San Diego, San Diego Mus Art, 82; Polaroid: The Big Picture, Mus Photog Arts, San Diego, 83. *Teaching:* Guest instr photog, Univ Calif, Los Angeles Exten, 77; instr, East Los Angeles Col, 78-79; prof, Grossmont Col, 79- *Awards:* Nat Endowment Arts Emerging Photogr Fel, 80. *Mem:* Los Angeles Ctr Photog Studies (trustee, 74-81, pres, 75-78); Soc Photog Educ (chmn western region, 81-82). *Publ:* Auth, Artistic photographic processes, Amphoto, 81. *Dealer:* Quint Gallery 664 Ninth Ave San Diego CA 92101. *Mailing Add:* Dept Commun Arts & Sci Grossmont Col 8800 Grossmont El Cajon CA 92020

HOUSER, ALLAN C
SCULPTOR, PAINTER
b Apache, Okla, June 30, 14. *Study:* Chilocco Indian Sch, Okla; Santa Fe Indian Sch, NMex, spec study with Dorothy Dunn; mural techniques with Olle Nordmark, Okla; Utah State Univ, Logan; St Michael's Col, Santa Fe. *Work:* Heard Mus, Phoenix, Ariz; Philbrook Art Ctr, Tulsa, Okla; Mus Northern Ariz, Flagstaff; Denver Art Mus, Colo; Univ of Okla, Oklahoma City; and others. *Comn:* Murals, Dept of Interior, Washington, DC; dioramas, Southern Plains Indian Mus, Anadarko, Okla; medals, Soc Medalists; portrait of Stewart Udall, Dept Interior, Washington, DC. *Exhib:* Contemp Indian Painters, Nat Gallery Art, Washington, DC, 53; Art Inst Chicago, 53; Gov's Gallery, State Capital, Santa Fe, 77; Jamison Gallery, Santa Fe, 77; Sacred Circles Art Exhib, Kansas City, Mo, 77; Am Indian & Cowboy Exhib, San Dimas, Calif, 78; Wagner Gallery, Austin, Tex, 78. *Teaching:* Instr art, Intermountain Indian Sch, Brigham City, Utah; head, Dept Sculpture, Inst of Am Indian Arts, Santa Fe; slide lect, Lake Forest Col, Chicago, Ill, 78; slide lect & sem, Thomas Burke Mem State Mus, Univ of Wash, Seattle, 78; artist-in-residence, Dartmouth Col, Hanover, NH, 79. *Awards:* Gold Medal in Bronze, Silver Medal in Stone & Silver Medal in Other Metal, Heard Mus Sculpture I Show, 73; Best of Show & First Place in Sculpture, Am Indian & Cowboy Show, San Dimas, Calif, 78. *Bibliog:* Allan Houser, Working Sculptor (film), In: Am Indian Artists 1976 (TV series), Pub Broadcasting System, KAET TV, 76. *Mailing Add:* 1020 Camino Carlos Rey NM 87505

HOUSER, CAROLINE MAE
HISTORIAN
b Walla Walla, Wash. *Study:* Mills Col, BA; San Francisco Art Inst; Harvard Univ, AM, PhD; Am Sch Classical Studies, Athens, Greece. *Teaching:* Asst prof art hist, Univ Tex, Austin, 75-78; Mellon Fel art hist, Harvard Univ, Cambridge, Mass, 78-79; asst prof art hist, Smith Col, Mass, 79- *Awards:* Andrew W Mellon Fel. *Mem:* Archaeol Inst of Am; Col Art Asn; Am Sch Classical Studies (managing comt). *Res:* Greek sculpture, especially monumental work in bronze. *Publ:* Auth, Is it from the Parthenon, Am J Archaeol, 72; auth, Dionysos and his circle, 79; auth, The Riace Marina bronze statues, classical or classicizing?, Source, 82; auth, Greek Monumental Bronze Sculpture, Vendome, 83. *Mailing Add:* Art Dept Smith Col Northampton MA 01063

HOUSER, JIM
PAINTER, EDUCATOR
b Dade City, Fla, Nov 12, 28. *Study:* Ringling Sch Art; Fla Southern Col, BS; Art Inst Chicago; Univ Fla, MFA; Johns Hopkins Univ. *Work:* Univ Notre Dame; Cornell Univ; NY Univ; Soc Four Arts Collection, Palm Beach, Fla; Syracuse Univ Art Collection; and others. *Exhib:* One-man shows, Grand Cent Mod, New York, 67 & Lehigh Univ, Bethlehem, 68; Mainstreams USA, Ohio, 68; David Findlay Galleries, New York, 76-84; Yellow Banks 50th Art Exhib, Owensboro, Ky, 89; Ft Lauderdale Mus Art Invitational Exhib, 91; & others. *Teaching:* Asst prof painting, Ky Wesleyan Col, 54-60; instr painting, Palm Beach Jr Col, 60-, chmn dept, 64-70. *Awards:* Akston Award, Soc Four Arts, 77; Merit Award, 16th Hortt Competition, Ft Lauderdale Mus Arts, 74; Philip Hulitar Award, Soc Four Arts, Palm Beach, 82; Atwater/Kent Award, Soc of the Four Arts, 89. *Bibliog:* Article, Arts Mag, 81. *Media:* Acrylic. *Publ:* Auth, Color for the Artist, Palm Beach Jr Col, 75; Perspective, video, Palm Beach Jr Col, 86; Perspective Drawing, video, Palm Beach Jr Col, 90. *Dealer:* Gallery Camino Real 399 Camino Gardens Blvd Boca Raton FL 33432. *Mailing Add:* 693 Jog Rd West Palm Beach FL 33415

HOUSEWRIGHT, ARTEMIS SKEVAKIS
PAINTER, SCULPTOR
b Tampa, Fla, July 18, 27. *Study:* Fla State Univ, Tallahassee, BA, 49, MA, 52. *Work:* Tallahassee Democrat Bldg, Fla; Gulf Life Insurance Bldg, Jacksonville, Fla; Washington Federal Bldg, Hollywood, Fla; Tallahassee Community Col, Admin Bldg, Fla; Student Union Bldg, LSU, Baton Rouge, La. *Comn:* Mural, Municiple Airport, City of Tallahassee, 61; painting, US Forestry Dept, Tallahassee, 62; Am Nat Bank, Winter Haven, Fla, 65; murals, Old Westbury Gardens, LI, NY, 69; oil/mixed media mural & archit decoration, Ceresville Mansion, Md, 90. *Exhib:* 21st Annual Mid-Year Show, Butler Inst Am Art, Youngstown, Ohio, 56, 57 & 60; two-person exhib, Jacksonville Mus Art, Fla, 58, Florida State Art Gallery, Tallahassee, 59; Invitational Paul Miller exhib, Jacksonville Art Mus, 61; one-man show: Cosmos Club, Washington, DC, 81; 66 Artists of the Southeast, Delgado Mus, New Orleans, La, 66. *Awards:* Purchase Award, Soc Four-Arts, Palm Beach, Fla, 55, 56 & 57; Purchase Award, Tampa Art Inst, 57; Purchase Award, Mississippi Art Asn, 57. *Mem:* Artists Equity. *Media:* Oil; cement & shell mosaic. *Mailing Add:* 147 Fairview Frederick MD 21701

HOUSKEEPER, BARBARA
SCULPTOR, PAINTER
b Ft Wayne, Ind, Aug 25, 22. *Study:* Knox Col, Ill; RI Sch Design; Art Inst Chicago; workshops with Marcia Tucker & Alan Kaprow. *Work:* Ill Bell & Tel, Chicago; Gould Found, Rolling Meadows, Ill; Kemper Ins Co, Long Grove; Phillips Corp, New York. *Comn:* Large sculpture, Exec Off Condecor Mfg, Mundelein, Ill, 72; sculpture, Kemper Ins Co, Long Grove, Ill, 74; Mem Sculpture, Am Bar Asn, Chicago, 75; Michael Reese Hosp, 81. *Exhib:*

One-artist shows, Zaks Gallery, Chicago, 78, Artemesia Coop Gallery, Chicago, 79, Name Gallery, Chicago, 79, Kohler Art Ctr, Sheybogan, Wis, 80 & Montalvo Ctr Arts, Saratoga, Calif, 82; San Jose State Univ Gallery, Calif, 81; Klein Gallery, Chicago, 83. *Teaching:* Oxbow Summer Sch Art, Saugatuck, Mich, 72-75, dir, 73-74; teacher advan critique, North Shore Art League, Winnetka, Ill, 73-78; instr, Columbia Col, Chicago, 77-79; vis artist, Countryside Art Ctr, Arlington Heights, Ill, 80, 82-84 & 86, Fine Arts Ctr, Highland Park, Ill, 81 & North Shore Art League, Winnetka, Ill, 83; instr, private studio, El Granada, Calif, 80-89. *Bibliog:* To Chicago with love from Half Moon Bay, New Art Examiner, 7/79. *Mem:* Soc Arts Am, San Francisco. *Publ:* Auth, Carrie Ricky, Art Am, 79; Spectacle of light, New Art Examiner, 10/80; Dorothy Burchart, San Jose Mercury, 9/3/81. *Mailing Add:* 930 Columbus St El Granada CA 94018

HOUSMAN, RUSSELL F
PAINTER, EDUCATOR
b Buffalo, NY, Jan 13, 28. *Study:* Albright Art Sch, Buffalo, dipl; State Univ NY Col Buffalo, BS; NY Univ, MA & PhD; also with Hale Woodruff & Revington Arthur. *Work:* Anderson Col; Butler Art Inst; Chautauqua Art Ctr; Dayton Art Inst; Decatur City Art Ctr; Forum Gallery, New York; L Goodyear Collection; Legislative Collection, Albany, NY; Col of Ozarks; Kirkland Art Ctr. *Comn:* Mural, USA, Kans Munic Auditorium, 52; painting, L Goodyear Collection, 57; Discovery Ctr, Human Resources Ctr, 72. *Exhib:* Retrospectives, Albany Inst Hist & Art & Nassau Community Col; solo exhibs, Silvermine Guild Art, Conn, Country Art Gallery, Locust Valley, NY & Nassau Community Col; one-man shows, Silvermine Guild Art, Albany Inst Hist & Art, Wellons Gallery, New York, retrospectives, Albany Inst; plus others. *Pos:* Dir, Decatur City Art Ctr, 59-61; art consult, Human Resources Ctr, Albertson, NY, 61-, Mind Inc, currently, Planners Industry & Educ, currently, Aging in America, currently. *Teaching:* Prof art, Adelphi Univ, 56-59; prof art & chmn dept, Milliken Univ, 59-61; prof art, Nassau Community Col, 63-, dir, Firehouse Gallery, 63-70; lectr, Nassau Co Mus Fine Arts, currently. *Awards:* Purchase Award, State Univ NY, 68; Prizes, Silvermine Art Guild & Chautauqua Art Ctr; Nat Endowment Arts; NY State Coun Arts. *Bibliog:* Viscardi (auth), The School, Eriksson, 64; 21 Paint in Hyplar, Grumbacher, 68; Watson (auth), The Artist as a Cook, Country Art Gallery, 72. *Mem:* Am Fedn Art; Silvermine Art Guild; NY State Art Teachers (ed, 69); Long Island Art Teachers. *Publ:* Auth, Psychological Warfare Capabilities & Vulnerabilities as Found in Soviet Art, 54; The Design of an Art Room, 55; Utilization of Artist Personnel in Psychological Warfare, 63; Telephone Assisted Teaching Devices, 69; Core Humanities Curriculum for Disabled Children, 70. *Dealer:* Country Art Gallery Locust Valley NY; Wellons Gallery New York NY. *Mailing Add:* 307 Steamboat Rd Kings Point NY 11024

HOUSTON, BRUCE
SCULPTOR, ASSEMBLAGE ARTIST
b Iowa City, Iowa, Jan 23, 37. *Study:* Univ Nebr, Lincoln, BA, 59; Art Ctr Col Design, Los Angeles, 61-62; Univ Calif Los Angeles, MA(graphic design), 65; Univ Iowa, MFA(painting), 74. *Work:* Univ Art Mus, Albuquerque. *Comn:* Outdoor Sculpture, Progressive Corp, Cleveland, Ohio. *Exhib:* One-man shows, Allan Stone Galleries, New York, 82 & 85, 90, Claremont Grad Sch, Calif, 82, Jan Baum Gallery, Los Angeles, 84, 85 & 87, Calif & Gracie Mansion Gallery, New York, 85, 87 & 89 Beach Mus Art, 88, Tory Folliard Gallery, Milwaukee, Wisc, 89, Hokin-Kaufman Gallery, Chicago, Ill, 89; Return of the Narrative, Palm Springs Desert Mus, Calif, 84; Fantastic, Henry Gallery, Univ Wash, Seattle, 85; Contemp S Calif Art, Univ Santa Barbara, 86; Taipei Fine Arts Mus, Taiwan, 87; Des Moines Art Ctr, 87; Lost & Found in Calif! Four Decades of Assemblage Art, James Corcoran Gallery, Santa Monica, Calif, 88; Forty Years of Calif Assemblage, Frederick Wight Gallery, UCLA, Los Ageles, San Jose Mus Art, Fresco Art Mus & Joslyn Art Mus, Omaha, Nebr, 89; Calif Surrealism, Bronx River Art Gallery, Bronx, NY, 89. *Teaching:* Slide lectr in many cols & univs throughout Calif, 79- *Awards:* Best in Show, Davenport Art Mus, 72. *Bibliog:* Suzanne Muchnic (auth), Bruce Houston assemblages, Art Voices S, 1/80. *Dealer:* Allan Stone Galleries 48 E 86th St New York NY; Greenie Mension Gallery 532 Broadway New York NY 10012. *Mailing Add:* 17102 Sanborn St PO Box 16 North Palm Springs CA 92258

HOUSTON, JAMES A
DESIGNER, SCULPTOR
b Toronto, Ont, June 12, 21. *Study:* Ont Col Art, Toronto, 39-40, hon fel, 81; Ecole Grande Chaumiere, Paris, studied life drawing, 47-48; Unichi Hiratsuka, Tokyo, studied printmaking, 58-59; Carleton Univ, Ottawa, DLitt, 72, RI Sch Design, Providence, DFA, 75. *Work:* Nat Mus Can, Ottawa; Corning Mus Glass, NY; St Petersburg Mus Art, Fla; Glenbow-Alberta Mus, Calgary; Montreal Mus Fine Arts. *Comn:* Angel Raphael, Steuben glass, Kennedy Found, Washington, DC, 65; Beaver Dam, Steuben glass, Beaverbrook Mus, Moncton, NB, 66; The White Dawn (film), Paramount Pictures, Los Angeles, 73; Aurora Borealis (70 foot translucent sculpture), Glenbow Mus, Calgary, Alta, 75; The Hand and the Eye (film), Can Broadcasting Corp, Toronto, 82. *Exhib:* Montreal Mus Fine Arts, 51; Winnipeg Art Gallery, Man, 69; Animals in Art, Royal Ont Mus, Toronto, 75; Contemporary Glass, Corning Mus Glass, NY, 79. *Pos:* Assoc dir design, Steuben Glass, New York, 62-; mem & chmn, Can Eskimo Arts Coun, Ottawa, 62-79, Am Indian Art Ctr, New York, 65-72. *Awards:* Award, Am Indian & Eskimo Cult Found, Dept Interior, Washington, DC, 66; Order of Can, 74; Inuit Kuavati Award Merit, Eskimo Cooperatives, Ottawa, Ont, 79. *Bibliog:* John Ayre (auth), James Houston, the neglected hero, Saturday Night, Toronto, 5/74; Charles Taylor (auth), Six Journeys, House Anansi, Toronto, 77; Barbara Etlin (auth), James Houston, En Route, Southam Press, 2/85. *Mem:* Century Asn, New York; fel Royal Soc Arts, London; Pratt Graphics Ctr, New York (bd adv, 65-); Mus Anthrop, Brown Univ (bd governors, 72-); Alaska Indian Arts (bd dirs, 77-). *Media:* Pen, Glass; Engraving. *Publ:* Auth, Canadian Eskimo Art, Queens Printer, 55; Eskimo Prints, Barre, 67; coauth, Sculpture Inuit, Univ Toronto Press, 72. *Dealer:* Yaneff Gallery 119 Isabella St Toronto ON M4Y 1P2 Canada. *Mailing Add:* 24 Main Street Stonington CT 06378

HOUSTON, JOHN STEWART See Stewart, John (John Stewart Houston)

HOUSTON, MARY ETTA (KING)
PAINTER, SCULPTOR
b Oklahoma City, Okla, Dec 8, 12. *Study:* Tex Christian Univ, Ft Worth, BFA(art), 65; Claremont Grad Sch, Calif, design with mosaic artist Jean Ames, MA(art), 69; St John Damascus Acad Sacred Art (iconography), Ligonier, Pa, 91. *Work:* Nat Women Arts, Washington, DC; Elmhurst Art Mus, Ill; Hist Mus & Libr, Decatur, Tex; Cross Gallery, Ft Worth. *Comn:* Sculpture (bronze horse), comn by atty Rusty Duncan, Decatur & Denton, Tex, 75; wall mural (oil), comn by Mrs Jerry Koneckny, Decatur, 76; logo (trademark US #1267638), Houston & Sons Res, Dan Diego, Calif, 84; children's altar, St John's Episcopal Church, Chula Vista, Calif, 86; icons, comn by Rev & Mrs W H Beste, Mineral Wells, Tex, 92; and others. *Exhib:* One-woman show, First Nat Bank, Rhome, Tex, 78; Int Art Show, Southwestern Col, Chula Vista, Calif, 84; Chula Vista Pub Libr, 91 & 92; Signature Gallery, 92; Chula Vista Multi-Cult Arts Festival, 92; and others. *Pos:* Guest lectr, Wise Co Art Asn, Tex, 79-80; juror, Sr Citizens Art, San Diego, Calif, 84-86; cult comt, Am Asn Univ Women, Chula Vista, Calif, 84-88; cult chair, Delta Kappa Gamma Int Educ Asn, Eta Nu Chap, 90-93. *Teaching:* Fac drawing, San Bernardino Valley Col, Calif, 66-69; fac oil painting, Riverside Art Ctr, Calif, 68-69; fac painting & sculpture, Cooke Co Col, Gainesville, Tex, 72-74. *Awards:* Gold Medal Award, Sons Am Revolution, 87; Winner Nat Art Contest, Daughters Am Revolution, Washington, DC, 87 & 88; Mayor's Proclamation, contributions Quincentennial Christopher Columbus Celebration, Chula Vista, 92; and others. *Bibliog:* Ken Roselle (auth), Housewife artist, Wise Co Messenger, Decatur, 73; Arlene Eagan (auth), Moving realism aside, 85 & Sculptors work, 12/91, Star News, Chula Vista. *Mem:* Am Asn Univ Women, Chula Vista (art & cult chair). *Media:* Oil; Clay, Wood. *Dealer:* Signature Gallery 3693 Fifth Ave San Diego CA 92103. *Mailing Add:* 518 Jasmine St Chula Vista CA 91911

HOVING, THOMAS
CONSULTANT, EDITOR
b New York, NY, Jan 15, 31. *Study:* Princeton Univ, BA(summa cum laude), 53, Grad Sch Art & Archaeol, Nat Coun Humanities Fel, 55, Grad Sch Fine Arts, MFA(Kienbusch & Haring Fel), 58, PhD(art hist), 59; five honorary doctorates. *Collections Arranged:* Initiated and developed series of art exchanges between museums of France, Soviet Union and the US; arranged Tutankhamun Tour of US, 76-79. *Pos:* Curatorial asst, Dept Medieval Art & The Cloisters, Metrop Mus Art, 59-60, asst cur, 60-63, assoc cur, 63-65, cur, 65-66, dir, 67-77; admin, Recreation & Cult Affairs, New York, 66-67; ed-in-chief, Connoisseur Mag, 81-91. *Awards:* Distinguished Achievement Award, Advert Club Am, 66; NY Univ Creative Leadership in Educ Award, 75; Woodrow Wilson Award, Princeton Univ, 77. *Mem:* Int Ctr Medieval Art (mem bd dir). *Publ:* Auth, The Bury St Edmunds Cross, 64 & Italian Romanesque Sculpture, 65, Metrop Mus Art Bull; Tutankhamun, The Untold Story, 78; King of the Confessors, 81; Masterpiece, 86; Discovery, 89; Making the Mummies Dance--Inside the Metropolitan Museum of Art, 93. *Mailing Add:* 150 E 73rd St New York NY 10021

HOVSEPIAN, LEON
PAINTER, DESIGNER
b Bloomsburg, Pa, Nov 20, 15. *Study:* Worcester Art Mus Sch, cert; Yale Univ, Alice Kimball traveling fel, BFA, 42; Fogg Mus. *Work:* Worcester Art Mus, Mass; Fitchburg Art Mus, Mass; Fine Arts Collection, Washington, DC; Springfield Mus, Mass; Mus Mod Art, Yerevan, Armenia, USSR. *Comn:* Mosaics, Oblate Fathers Retreat House, Willimantic, 61; stained glass, Holy Cross Col, Worcester, 65; portraits, Leiceister Jr Col, Mass, 68-69; fresco mural, Church of the Annunciation, Washington, DC, 74; portrait, Judge Morris N Gould, Worcester, Mass; design of Archeveque Chapel, Papeet, Tahiti, 83; resurrection mural, St Joseph's Cemetery, Chelmsford, Mass, 84; and others. *Exhib:* Art Inst Chicago, 41; Albright Art Gallery, 46; Nat Gallery Art, 47; RI Sch Design, 48; Worcester Art Mus Am Biennial, 48; By the People For the People--New Eng, De Cordova Mus, Lincoln, Mass, 77; one-man exhib, Armenian Libr & Mus Am Inc, Watertown, Mass, 91; traveling exhib, Looking past the painting--Underlying Structure, Fitchburg Art Mus, Mass, 92-93. *Pos:* Dir, Boylston Summer Art Sch, Mass, 41-; fac, Clark Univ Sch Worcester Art Mus, formerly. *Teaching:* Instr art, Bancroft Sch, 36-38; prof, Woman's Col, New Haven, 38-40; instr, Worcester Art Mus Sch, 40-, instr, Pub Educ Div, 41-56. *Awards:* St Wulstan Soc Art Award, 38-40; Painting Prize, Fitchburg Art Mus; Ford Found Grant to exhib in Armenia, USSR. *Bibliog:* Adlow (auth), Stuart Gallery, Christian Sci Monitor, 46; Sandrof (auth), Artist in his studio, Feature Parade, 53; Browne (auth), Leon Hovsepian, Art News, 11/66. *Publ:* Illusr, Worcester Federal, Past--Present--Future, 52; illusr, Androck, 58. *Dealer:* Triart Studios 90 Pocasset Ave Worcester MA 01606. *Mailing Add:* 96 Squantum St Worcester MA 01606

HOWARD, (HELEN) BARBARA
PAINTER, PRINTMAKER
b Long Branch, Ont, Mar 10, 26. *Study:* Western Tech & Commun Sch, Toronto; Ont Col Art, Toronto, AOCA, 51; St Martins Sch Art, London, 54.

Work: Nat Gallery Can; Art Gallery Ont; Brit Mus, London; Bodleian Libr, Oxford, England; Libr Cong; Nat Libr of Can. *Exhib:* Can Soc Graphic Arts, 58-60 & 63; Can Watercolours, Drawings and Prints, Nat Gallery, Can, 66; solo-exhib, Wells Gallery, Ottawa, 66, 82 & 84 & Prince Arthur Galleries, Toronto, 80 & 82, O'Keefe Ctr, Toronto, 86; Douglas Duncan Collection, Windsor, London, Hamilton, 67; Drawings and Sculpture, Art Gallery, Ont, 76. *Bibliog:* Passionate Spirits; A History of the Royal Canadian Academy of Arts, 1880-1980, Clarke, Irwin, Toronto, 80; Profile of Barbara Howard, City & Country Home, Toronto, 4/84 & Equinox Mag, 87. *Mem:* Royal Can Acad Arts (mem coun, 80-82); hon life mem Art Gallery of Ont; Arts and Letters Club of Toronto. *Media:* Oil; Wood Engraving, Black and White Graphic. *Publ:* Illusr, Turns and Other Poems, Anson-Cartwright Ed, 75; The Promise of Light, Anson-Cartwright Ed, 80; Selected Poems: Exile Ed, 84; illusr, Man in Love, Porcupine's Quill, Inc, 85; Hiram and Jenny, Porcupine's Quill, Inc, 88. *Dealer:* Contemp Fine Arts Serv Inc 413 Dundas St E Toronto ON M5A 2A9. *Mailing Add:* 226 Roslin Ave Toronto ON M4N 1Z6 Canada

HOWARD, CECIL RAY
PAINTER, SCULPTOR
b Wichita, Kans, Jan 25, 37. *Study:* Kans State Teachers Col, BS; Wichita State Univ, MFA. *Work:* Amarillo Col Gallery, Tex; Wichita State Univ; Glendale Community Col, Ariz; Emporia Kans State Col. *Comn:* Collage mural, Western NMex Univ, 69; tympanum ceramic sculpture, Church Good Shepherd, Silver City, 71. *Exhib:* One-man shows, Marion Koogler McNay Gallery, San Antonio, Tex, 60 & Wichita Art Mus, 67; Mid-America Show, Nelson Gallery, Atkins Mus, Kansas City, Mo, 62; Mainstreams '68 Int Exhib, Marietta, Ohio, 68; Int Designer-Craftsmen Exhib, El Paso Art Mus, Tex, 69; Installations '78, Mus NMex, Santa Fe; Armory Sculpture Show, Santa Fe, 79; Santa Fe Mus Int Folk Art; Tucson Art Mus, Ariz. *Pos:* Dir, McCray Gallery, Western NMex Univ, 63- *Teaching:* Assoc prof painting & sculpture, Western NMex Univ, 63- *Awards:* Purchase Awards, Wichita Art Mus, 60 & 62; Juror's Award for Distinction, Mainstreams '68 Int Exhib, 68; First Place Award in Ceramics, El Paso Art Mus, 69. *Mem:* NMex Potters' Asn. *Media:* Collage, Assemblage. *Publ:* Illusr, Voyage to America, Univ Nebr, 67; contribr, Donna Meilach's Collage on Construction, Crown. *Dealer:* Mariposa Gallery Old Town Albuquerque NM 87104. *Mailing Add:* Rt 10, Box 540 Glenwood NM 88039

HOWARD, DAN F
PAINTER, EDUCATOR
b Iowa City, Iowa, Aug 4, 31. *Study:* Univ Iowa, BA, 53, MFA, 58. *Work:* Joe & Emily Lowe Art Mus, Miami, Fla; Blanden Mem Art Mus, Ft Dodge, Iowa; Chautauqua Inst, Ny; Sioux City Art Ctr, Iowa; Sheldon Mem Art Gallery, Univ Nebr, Lincoln. *Exhib:* Chautauqua Nat Exhib Am Art, NY, 78, 80, 83 & 86; West/Art & Law Nat Exhib, Minn Mus Art, St Paul, 79 & 82; Contemp Am Painting Exhib, Soc Fine Arts, Palm Beach, Fla, 79, 83, 84, 85, 86 & 89; Tex Fine Arts Nat Exhib, Laguna Gloria Art Mus, Austin, 82, 83 & 84; Butler Midyear Show, Butler Inst Am Art, Youngstown, Ohio, 83 & 84; travelling retrospective, 83-84; solo exhibs, Wichita Art Asn Galleries, Kans, 88, New Gallery, Houston, Tex, 89; Joy Horwich Gallery, Chicago, Ill, 90 & Vorpal Gallery, New York, 91. *Teaching:* From instr to assoc prof painting & drawing, Ark State Univ, 58-71, chmn div art, 65-71, dir art gallery, 67-71; prof painting & drawing & head dept art, Kans State Univ, 71-74; prof art, Univ Nebr, Lincoln, 74-, chmn dept, 74-83. *Awards:* First Prize, Atwater Kent Award, Contemp Am Painting Exhib, Palm Beach, Fla, 83; Butler Institute Top Award, Nat Midyear Show, Youngstown, Ohio, 84; Chautauqua Inst Top Award, Chautauqua Nat Exhib, Chautauqua, New York, 86; $4000 Top Purchase, Mid-Four Ann Juried Exhib, Hallmark Found Collection, Kansas City, 87; First Award, Fla Nat Exhib, Tallahassee, 88; Hulitar Award, Contem Am Painting Exhib, Palm Beach, Fla, 89. *Bibliog:* In View of the Law, West Publishing Co, St Paul, Minn, 79; Dan Howard: A Retrospective: A Selection of Paintings from 1968-1982, Blanden Mem Art Mus/Sioux City Art Ctr; Born in Iowa: The Homecoming Exhib, Iowa Arts Coun, 86. *Mem:* Col Art Asn Am; Am Fedn Arts; Mid-Am Col Art Asn (vpres, 75, pres, 76, bd dir, 75-79); Nebr Art Asn (bd trustees, 74-83). *Media:* Oil Painting, Drawing. *Dealer:* Vorpal Galleries 411 W Broadway New York NY 10012; Joy Horwich Gallery 226 E Ontario Chicago IL 60611. *Mailing Add:* 2110 Heritage Pines Ct Lincoln NE 68506

HOWARD, DAVID
PHOTOGRAPHER, PAINTER
b Brooklyn, NY. *Study:* Ohio Univ; San Francisco Art Inst, MFA, 74; addn study with Ansel Adams, Duane Michaels & Jerry Ulesman. *Work:* Mus Mod Art, Whitney Mus Am Art, New York; San Francisco Mus Mod Art; Oakland Mus, Calif; de Saisset Art Gallery & Mus, Santa Clara, Calif; San Francisco Art Inst; Hirshorn Mus, Smithsonian Inst; and others. *Exhib:* One-person shows, Third Eye Gallery, New York, Chicago Film Festival, 86, Marc Richards Gallery, Los Angeles, 87, EZ TV, Los Angeles, 87 & 88, G Ray Hawkins Gallery, 88, Hirshhorn Mus/Smithsonian Inst, Washington, DC & Philadelphia Mus Art, 90; 10th & 13th Int Festivals of Contemp Art, Royan, France, 73 & 76; 34th Int Salon of Japan, Tokyo, 74; Whitney Mus Art, New York, 85; Video Refuses, San Francisco, 86; Hadley Martin Gallery, San Francisco, 87; San Francisco Pub Libr System, 87; Cal State Univ, Northridge, 88; Chandler Gallery, Seattle, 91; and many other major museums. *Pos:* Vis artist art hist, San Francisco City Col, 73; dir photog, San Francisco Ctr Visual Studies, 74-, photog instr, 73-78. *Teaching:* Vis instr, City Col San Francisco. *Awards:* Purchase Award, 27th San Francisco Art Festival, City of San Francisco, 73. *Bibliog:* K Baker (auth), San Francisco Chronicle, 3/14/86 & 4/24/86; Cableview, San Francisco, 87; TV broadcast on Los Angeles Art Scene, 2/86 & East Village 3/87, Channel 37, San Francisco Art Scene #1, 3/87 & 3/88, Channel 3 & Art Scene, San Francisco, Channel 6, 3/88. *Publ:* Illusr, Artweek, 73; illusr, Wester D Kemp (auth), Photography for Visual Communicators, Prentice-Hall, 73; illusr, San Francisco Chronicle, 75; auth & illusr, Realities, 76 & Perspectives, 77, San Francisco Ctr for Visual Studies; dir & producer, New York's East Village Art Scene, 85. *Mailing Add:* c/o Visual Studies 49 Rivoli St San Francisco CA 94117

HOWARD, HUMBERT L
PAINTER
b Philadelphia, Pa, July 12, 15. *Study:* Univ Pa; Howard Univ Sch Fine Arts; Int Acad Arts & Lett, Rome, Italy, hon degree. *Work:* Howard Univ; Civic Ctr Mus, Pa Acad Fine Arts, Philadelphia; Philadelphia Mus Art; Libr Cong; Stanley Bernstein Collection; Smithsonian Inst. *Exhib:* Grabar Gallery, 68; Howard Univ; Int Acad Arts & Lett, 70; William Penn Mem Mus Exhib, 71 & 77; Gross McCleaf Gallery, Philadelphia, 77 & 79; and others. *Teaching:* Fac mem, Allens Lane Art Ctr, Philadelphia, formerly. *Awards:* Silver Medal for Painting, Int Acad Arts & Lett, Rome, 70. *Mem:* Pyramid Club; Artists Equity Asn; Peale Club; Philadelphia Art Alliance; Pa Coun Arts. *Mailing Add:* 3411 Hamilton St Philadelphia PA 19106

HOWARD, LINDA
SCULPTOR
b Evanston, Ill, Oct, 22, 34. *Study:* Univ Colo; Northwestern Univ; Chicago Art Inst, 53-55; Univ Denver, BA, 57; Hunter Col, New York, MA, 71; City Col New York, archit, 82. *Work:* K & B Plaza, Virlane Found, New Orleans, La; Allstate Insurance Corp, Bush Corporate Ctr, Columbus, Ohio; Zig-Zag, Col City Tampa, Fla Council, Spain, 82. *Comn:* Space Wave (aluminum), Barclays Bank, Miami, 90; Up/Over Around (5' x 15' x 8' aluminum), Tropicanna Corp, Bradenton, Fla, 90; Wall Wave (12' x 6' x 6' aluminum), Gen Servs, Miami, Fla, 91; Archway (12' x 18' x 9' aluminum), Fla Int Univ, Miami, 91; Centerpeace (aluminum), Bradley Univ, Peoria, Ill, 91. *Exhib:* One-woman exhibs, Silvermine Guild, Conn, 71 Sculpture Now Gallery, New York, 75 & 78, Northwestern Univ, Evanston, Ill, 78, Construct Gallery, Chicago, Ill, 80, Max Hutchinson Gallery, Houston, Tex, 80 & New York, 81, Heath Gallery, Atlanta, Ga, 88 & Mus Art, Ft Lauderdale, Fla, 93; New Reflections, Aldrich Mus, Ridgefield, Conn, 73; Penthouse Show, Mus Mod Art, New York; 100 Years, 100 Artists, Chicago Art Inst, 80; Sculpture, The Language of Scale, Bruce Mus, Greenwich, Conn, 85; American Women, American Art, Stamford Mus, Conn, 85; Park Sculpture, Whitney Mus, 86 & Stamford Mus, Conn, 86 & 87; Contemporary Sculpture, Univ Fla, Gainesville, 87; Artpark, Art Mus, Fla Int Univ, Miami; Paris Art International, France, 82; Sculpture, The Language of Scale, Bruce Mus, Greenwich, Conn, 85; American Women, American Art, Stamford Mus & Nature Ctr, Stamford, Conn, 85; Continuity and Change, The Gallery, Ringling Art Sch, Sarasota, Fla; Sculpture Fields, Kenosa Lake, NY; Contemporary Sculpture from Florida Collections, Univ Gallery, Univ Fla, Gainesville, 87. *Pos:* Vis artist, Alfred Univ, New York, Bennett Col, Milbrook, NY & Colgate Univ, Hamilton, NY, 73, Potsdam State Univ, NY, 75, San Jose State Univ, Calif & Northwestern Univ, Evanston, Ill, 78; designer-model studio, Skidmore, Owings & Merrill Archits, New York, 84-85; vis artist master print prog & sculpture, Bradley Univ, Peoria, Ill, 91. *Teaching:* Asst prof sculpture, Hunter Col, New York, 69-72 & Lehman Col, New York, 73-76; assoc prof, New York Univ, 76-77 & Hunter Col, 77-82; adj assoc prof, Univ S Fla, Tampa, 85; adj prof, Manatee Community Col, Bradenton, Fla, 89. *Awards:* NJ Cult Coun; City Univ New York Fac Res Grant, 74 & 75; Creative Artists Pub Serv Grant, NY State, 75. *Bibliog:* Doc films, Linda Howard, Sculpture, 76, Constructions Sculpture, 76 & 500 Mile Sculpture Garden, 76, Nebr Educ TV; and others. *Dealer:* David Heath Atlanta GA; Barbara Gilman Miami FL. *Mailing Add:* 527 72nd St Holmes Beach FL 34217

HOWARD, ROBERT A
SCULPTOR, EDUCATOR
b Sapulpa, Okla, Apr 5, 22. *Study:* Phillips Univ; Univ Tulsa; with Ossip Zadkine, Paris, France. *Work:* NC Mus Art, Raleigh; Ackland Art Ctr & NC Nat Bank, Chapel Hill, NC. *Comn:* Monumental sculpture, Fed Bldg, Louisville, Ky, 76. *Exhib:* 153rd Ann Exhib, Pa Acad Fine Arts, Philadelphia, 58; Art 65--Young American Sculpture, New York World's Fair, 65; Sculpture of the Sixties, Los Angeles Co Mus, 67; Ann Contemp Sculpture, Whitney Mus Art, New York, 68, 70 & 72; Contemp Am Painting & Sculpture, Univ Ill, 69. *Teaching:* Prof sculpture, Univ NC, 51-72 & 74-88 & Univ Southern Calif, 72-73. *Awards:* Coop Prog in Humanities, Duke Univ, Univ NC & Ford Found, 65 & Univ NC, 71; Nat Endowment for the Arts, 72. *Bibliog:* La Review Modern, Paris, 58; Robert A Howard Welded Sculpture, Reflections, Vol 1, No 3, 61; Donald W Thalaker, The Place of Art in the World of Architecture. *Media:* Multimedia. *Publ:* Auth, Space as form, Col Art J, 51; Howard on Higgins, Reflections, Vol 2, No 1, 62; Three Dimensional Sculptural Unities, Genesis of Knowledge, 63. *Mailing Add:* 1201 Hillview Rd Chapel Hill NC 27514

HOWARTH, SHIRLEY REIFF
PUBLISHER, HISTORIAN
b Ft Benning, Ga, Oct 1, 44. *Study:* Dickinson Col, Carlisle, Pa, BA(art hist); Pa State Univ, University Park, MA(art hist). *Collections Arranged:* Recent Sculpture: Steven Urry, Hackley Art Mus, Muskegon, Mich, 76; C Paul Jennewein (auth, catalog), Tampa Mus, Fla. *Pos:* Asst cur, William Penn Mem Mus, Harrisburg, Pa, 69-74, cur prints, Pa Collection Fine Arts, 74-75; dir, Hackley Art Mus, Muskegon, Mich, 75-79; dir, Tampa Mus, Fla, 79-80; publ, dir & ed, Int Art Alliance, Largo, Fla, 80-; dir & ed, Humanities Exchange, Largo Fl, 80-; publ & ed, Artworld Europe, 90- *Teaching:* Adj prof, St Leo Col, Fla, 80-87. *Mem:* Am Asn Mus; Col Art Asn; Int Coun Mus; Southeast

Mus Conf. *Res:* Primarily in fields of Medieval and Northern Renaissance art; history of prints and photography. *Publ:* Auth, Care of Works of Art on Paper and Care, Display and Storage of Photographs, Pa Hist & Mus Comn, 73; auth, European Paintings, Muskegon Mus Art, 81; ed, Int Directory of Corporate Art Collections, Artnews & Int Art Alliance, 82, 83, 84, 86, 88 & 90; auth, Marcel Breuer: Concrete and The Cross, Hackley Art Mus, 79. *Mailing Add:* PO Box 1500 Largo FL 34649

HOWAT, JOHN KEITH
CURATOR, HISTORIAN
b Denver, Colo, Apr 12, 37. *Study:* Harvard Univ, BA, 59, MA, 62. *Collections Arranged:* David Smith, Hyde Collection, 64; John F Kensett (with catalog), Am Fedn Art, 68; 19th Century America: Paintings & Sculpture (with catalog), 70, American Paintings & Sculpture, 71, Heritage of American Art: Paintings from the Collection, 75 & A Bicentennial Treasury: American Masterpieces from the Metropolitan, 76, Am Wing, Metrop Mus Art, 80; John Frederick Kensett (with catalog), 85; American Paradise: The World of the Hudson River School (with catalog), 87. *Pos:* Cur, Hyde Collection, 62-64; asst cur Am painting, Metrop Mus Art, 67-68, assoc cur, 68-70, cur Am painting & sculpture, 70-81, chmn, Dept Am Art, 81. *Awards:* Ford Found Fel, 65; Chester Dale Fel, Metrop Mus Art, 65-67. *Mem:* Arch Am Art. *Res:* American paintings of 18th and 19th centuries, especially the Hudson River School. *Publ:* Auth, Hudson River & Its Painters, 72. *Mailing Add:* Dept Am Art Metrop Mus Art New York NY 10028

HOWE, NELSON S
DESIGNER, ASSEMBLAGE ARTIST
b Lansing, Mich, Nov 5, 35. *Study:* Univ Mich, BA, 57, MA, 61. *Work:* New Orleans Mus Fine Arts, La; Libr Collections, Mus Mod Art, Finch Col Mus Art & Chase Manhattan Bank Collection, New York; Univ Calif, Berkeley; and others. *Comn:* Wall I (fabric wall), comn by Mr & Mrs Keith Waldrop, Providence, RI, 68; Fur Music (installation unit), Mus Contemp Crafts, New York, 71; Fur Score (fur wall), New Orleans Mus Fine Arts, 72. *Exhib:* One-man show, Little Gallery, Minneapolis Inst Art, Minn, 67; Fur & Feathers Show, Mus Contemp Crafts, 71; Experimental Sound, ICES Festival, London, Eng, 72; Mus Mod Art, New York; and other group & one-man shows. *Pos:* Pres & founding artist mem, bd dirs, Participation Proj Found, 73- *Awards:* 50 Best Books of the Yr Award, Am Inst Graphic Arts, 69; Intermedia Found Grant for Lab Serv, 72. *Bibliog:* Rose De Neve (auth), Art - notation - art, Print Mag, Vol 25, No 1; Source: Music Avant Garde, No 9, 72; and others. *Publ:* Illusr, To the Sincere Reader, 68 & Body Image, 70 & co-auth, Job Art, 71, Wittenborn; illusr & auth, Daily translating systems, Circle Press (London), 71; contribr, Harpers' Mag Wraparound Sect, 5/73; and others. *Mailing Add:* 637 Carlton Ave Brooklyn NY 11238

HOWE, OSCAR
PAINTER, EDUCATOR
b Joe Creek, SDak, May 13, 15. *Study:* Dakota Wesleyan Univ, BA, 52; Univ Okla, MFA, 54. *Work:* Denver Art Mus; Joslyn Art Mus, Omaha, Nebr; Mus NMex, Santa Fe; Philbrook Art Ctr, Tulsa, Okla; Smithsonian Inst, New York Br; and others. *Comn:* Murals, Mitchell Libr, SDak, 40, Nebraska City, Nebr, City of Mobridge, SDak & Hillside, Ill, 56. *Exhib:* Mus Mod Art, New York, 36; Collectors Choice Exhib, Denver Art Mus, 63; one-man shows, Philbrook Art Ctr, Tulsa, 64, Joslyn Art Mus, 67 & Heard Mus, Phoenix, 71. *Pos:* Dir art, Pierre High Sch, SDak, 53-57. *Teaching:* Artist in residence, Dak Wesleyan Univ, 48-52; from prof art to prof emer & artist in residence, Univ SDak, 57-82; US State Dept lectr, SAsia & Near East, 71. *Awards:* Dorothy Field Award, Denver Art Mus, 52; Mary Benjamin Rogers Award, Mus NMex, 58; Waite Phillips Trophy, Philbrook Art Ctr, Tulsa, 66. *Bibliog:* Robert Pennington (auth), Oscar Howe, Artist of the Sioux, Dakota Territory Cent Co, 61; Panorama for Pakistan, US Info Serv, 71; John Milton (auth), Oscar Howe, The Story of an American Indian, Dillon, 72. *Mem:* Delta Phi Delta; fel Int Inst Arts & Lett. *Media:* Casein. *Mailing Add:* Col of Fine Arts Univ Gallery Univ of SDak Vermillion SD 57069

HOWELL, CLAUDE FLYNN
PAINTER, EDUCATOR
b Wilmington, NC, Mar 17, 15. *Study:* With Charles Rosen, Woodstock, NY, Bernard Karfiol & Jon Corbino; Wake Forest Univ, DHL, 75. *Work:* Weatherspoon Gallery, Univ NC; Wachouia Bank, Winston-Salem, NC; NC Mus Art, Raleigh; IBM Corp, New York; and others. *Comn:* Illus, John F Blair Publ Co, Winston-Salem, 58; mosaics, NC Dept Arch & Hist, Mus Old Brunswick, 65 & State Ports Maritime Bldg, Wilmington, 66. *Exhib:* Am Watercolors 1952, Metrop Mus Art, New York; Fifth Ann Painting Yr, Atlanta Art Asn Galleries, Ga, 59; Piedmont Purchase Award Show, Mint Mus Art, Charlotte, 63; retrospective, NC Mus Art, 75; St John's Mus Art, 81; OMS, Greenhill Ctr NC Art, Greensboro, 92. *Teaching:* Assoc prof painting & art hist & chmn dept art, Univ NC, Wilmington, 58-80. *Awards:* Rosenwald Found Fel, 48; Purchase Awards, NC Mus Art, 54 & NC Award, 85. *Bibliog:* Senta Bier (auth), Notes on a North Carolina artist, Longview J, 71; and others. *Mem:* NC Art Soc; St John's Mopa, NC Arts Coun. *Publ:* Illusr, Hatterasman, 58, Exploring the Seacoast of North Carolina, 70 & Beachcombers Handbook of Seafood Cookery, 71; auth, A Balkan Sketchbook, 77; illusr, The Tessie C Price, 79. *Mailing Add:* 44 Carolina Art 420 Market St PO Box 214 Wilmington NC 28402

HOWELL, ELIZABETH (MITCH) COON
PAINTER, GALLERY OWNER
b Hartselle, Ala, Feb 27, 32. *Study:* Birmingham Southern Col, BA; Famous Artists Sch; also with Edgar Whitney, Zoltan Szabo & Charles Reid. *Work:* Birmingham Mus Art, Ala; Montclaire Gallery, Birmingham; Firt Nat Bank, Decatur, Ala; Citizens Bank, Hartselle, Ala; Parkway Med Ctr, Decatur, Ala. *Comn:* illus & cover for cook bk, Decatur Jr Serv League, Inc, 72; portraits of vpres Dan Quayle & Gov Guy Hunt by USX. *Exhib:* Williamsburg Art Exhib, Va, 70; Charleston Art Exhib, SC, 70; Int Platform Asn Art Exhib, Washington, DC, 71; Ala Watercolor Soc Nat Exhib, 80; and others. *Pos:* Dept head, Hubert Mitchell Industs, Inc, Hartselle, 49-55; owner, Howell-Baxter Gallery, Hartselle, Ala, 83- *Teaching:* Head dept fine art, Morgan Co High Sch, 64-66. *Awards:* Hannah Elliott Award, Lovemans of Birmingham, 69. *Bibliog:* France-Amerique, Courrier Etats-Unis, New York, 69; Huida G Lawrence (auth), article, Park East News, New York, 69; article, Aufbau, New York, 69. *Mem:* Life mem Kappa Pi (pres col chap, 53-54); founding mem Decatur Arts Coun; Decatur Art Guild (founder, actg pres, publ chmn & vpres, 67-); Ala Watercolor Soc; Birmingham Art Asn. *Media:* Watercolor, Acrylic. *Publ:* Illusr, Emmanuel-God With Us, 67 & Cotton Country Cooking, 72. *Dealer:* Mitch Howell Gallery 601 Barkley St SW St Hartselle AL 35640. *Mailing Add:* 601 Berkeley Ave SW Hartselle AL 35640

HOWER, ROBERT K
PHOTOGRAPHER
b Boston, Mass, 47. *Study:* Middlebury Col, BA(Am lit), 64; studied with Len Gittleman, Harvard; studied with Minor White, Mass Inst Technol. *Comn:* Photog, Flat Iron Bldg, pvt comn, New York, 83; photog oil indust, Polaroid, Houston, 81. *Exhib:* Water Tower Art Asn, Louisville, 85; Images, Cincinnati, 86; Zephyr Gallery, Louisville, 89; solo shows, J B Speed Mus, Louisville, 89, Cheekwood Fine Arts Ctr, Nashville, 91, Photog Arch, Univ Louisville & Galerie Hertz, Louisville, 92. *Pos:* Co-founder, Quadrant, Jeffersonville, Ind, 86- *Teaching:* Photog, Wright State Univ, 74-78. *Awards:* Residency, Light Work, Syracuse, NY, 81; Ohio Arts Coun Individual Artist's Fel, 83 & 85; Nat Endowment Arts Individual Artist's Grant, 90-91. *Bibliog:* Stern Mag, 3/86; Ohio Mag, 1/87, 2/87, 11/87, 1/88 & 11/90; Am Photogr, 10/89. *Mailing Add:* 2119 Highland Ave Louisville KY 40204

HOWES, ROYCE BUCKNAM
PAINTER
b Mt Clemens, Mich, Sep 20, 50. *Study:* RI Sch of Design, BFA, 73; Skowhegan Sch of Painting & Sculpture, 74; Tyler Sch Art, MFA, 77. *Work:* Metrop Mus Art, New York; Univ Tenn, Knoxville; Kans State Univ, Manhattan. *Bibliog:* Wayne Toepp (auth), The Image Combines of Royce Howes, Arts Mag, 1/88. *Media:* Oil. *Dealer:* Grace Borgenicht Gallery 724 Fifth Ave New York NY. *Mailing Add:* HC 2 Box 94 Margaretville NY 12455-9632

HOWETT, JOHN
HISTORIAN, CRITIC
b Kokomo, Ind, Aug 7, 26. *Study:* John Herron Inst, BFA; Univ Chicago, MA, 62, PhD, 68. *Collections Arranged:* Kress Study Collection Notre Dame (auth, catalog), 62; Renaissance Illuminations (auth, catalog), High Mus Art, Atlanta, 74; Twelve in Atlanta (auth, catalog), 79. *Teaching:* Asst prof & cur collections, Univ Notre Dame, 61-66; assoc prof Renaissance & Mod art, Emory Univ, 66-80, prof, 80-, chairperson dept hist art, 73- *Awards:* Emory Teaching Award, 82. *Mem:* Col Art Asn; Southeastern Art Conf. *Res:* Italian and Northern Renaissance painting and sculpture; contemporary art and culture. *Publ:* Auth, Two panels by the master of the St George Codex in the Cloisters, Metrop Mus J, Vol 11, 85-102; Boondocks Bohemias: A case for the regional avant-garde, Contemp Art/SE, Vol 1, 77; coauth, Martin Emanuel, High Mus Art, 80; Carl Andre, Heath Gallery Art, 83; Woodcuts by Albrecht Durer, Emory Univ Mus, 86. *Mailing Add:* Art Hist Dept Emory Univ Atlanta GA 30322

HOWLAND, RICHARD HUBBARD
ARCHITECTURAL HISTORIAN
b Providence, RI, Aug 23, 10. *Study:* Brown Univ, AB, 31; Harvard Univ, AM, 33; Johns Hopkins Univ, PhD, 46; Brown Univ, Hon DArts, 62. *Pos:* Fel Agora Athens, Greece, 36-38; chief pictorial rec sect, OSS, 43-44; pres, Nat Trust Hist Preserv, 56-60; chmn dept civil hist, Smithsonian Inst, 60-67, spec asst to secy, 68-85; founding mem, Am Comt Int Comn Hist Sites & Monuments; trustee, Sotterley Fund & Evergreen Found. *Teaching:* Instr, Wellesley Col, 39-42; organizer dept hist art, Johns Hopkins Univ, 47, chmn dept, 47-56. *Awards:* Athenaeum of Philadelphia Fel; Royal Soc of Arts Fel, London. *Mem:* Fel US Int Coun Monuments & Sites; Soc Archit Historians; Irish Georgian Soc (trustee); Archaeol Inst Am; Am Sch Classical Studies, Athens (trustee). *Publ:* Coauth, Architecture of Baltimore, 54; auth, Greek Lamps & Their Survivals, 58 & 66. *Mailing Add:* 3900 Cathedral Ave Washington DC 20016

HOWLETT, CAROLYN SVRLUGA
EDUCATOR, PAINTER
b Berwyn, Ill, Jan 13, 14. *Study:* Art Inst Chicago, BAE, 37, MAE, 52; Northwestern Univ, MA, 53. *Comn:* Stained glass windows, State Ill Host House, Chicago World's Fair, 33. *Exhib:* Art Inst Chicago Ann, 45, 46, 52 & 55; Am Fedn Arts Print Show, 48; Assoc Am Artists Galleries, Chicago, 50; Arts Club Chicago Ann Exhib, 53-89; two-man shows, Chicago Press Club, 66, 68, 73, 74 & 81; retrospective, Morton Col, 83. *Pos:* Tech consult, Arts & Skills Prog, Am Red Cross, 42-45; head dept art educ & Jr Sch, Art Inst Chicago, 43-63, assoc dean & educ consult, 63-68; dir, Gallery Studio, Nat Hist Landmark, Coonley Estate, 70-; lectr, Travel Dept, Chicago Coun Foreign Relations, 74-78. *Teaching:* Instr art educ, Oak Park & Libertyville Pub Schs, 34-37; instr design & crafts, Art Inst Chicago, 37-70, prof art educ, 52-70, emer prof, 70-; lectr fine art & crafts, Univ Ill Exten, 67-73. *Awards:* Gen Excellence Award, 32 & Conf Club Pres Award, 33 & 34, Art Inst Chicago, Ill; Outstanding Serv Award, Ill Art Educ Asn, 76; Special

Recognition Award, 81 & Distinguished Fel Award, 86, Nat Art Educ Asn. *Mem:* Around Chicago Art Educ Asn (pres, 38-39); Nat Art Educ Asn; Ill Art Educ Asn (pres, 62-63); Arts Club Chicago. *Media:* Acrylic. *Publ:* Contribr, Arts & Activities, Sch Arts, House Beautiful & Design, 42-70; auth, The need for art, Related Arts Serv Bull, 49; contribr, World Bk Encycl & Childcraft Encycl, 49-59; auth, Art in Craftmaking, Van Nostrand Reinhold, 74. *Mailing Add:* Gallery Studio 336 Coonley Rd Riverside IL 60546

HOWLETT, D(ONALD) ROGER
ART DEALER, HISTORIAN
b Syracuse, NY, Mar 27, 45. *Study:* Hamilton Col, NY, BA, 66; State Univ NY, Cooperstown, grad prog, MA, 67; Yale Univ, PhD prog, art hist. *Collections Arranged:* George Luks (auth, catalog), 73-74 & Molly Luce: Eight Decades of the American Scene (auth, catalog), 83, Childs Gallery, Boston. *Pos:* Vpres, Childs Gallery, Boston, 73-83, pres, Boston & New York, 83- *Mem:* Am Asn Mus; Emerson Gallery, Hamilton Col, NY (bd adv); St Botolph Club; Boston Athenaeum. *Res:* 19th and 20th century American artists, including Molly Luce, I M Gaugengigl, Laura Hills, Donald De Lue and George Luks. *Specialty:* American and European paintings, prints and drawings, 16th to mid 20th centuries; 19th and 20th century realist sculpture; Japanese prints and China Trade paintings. *Publ:* Auth, Legal requirement of appraisal of architectural drawings, Mass Copar, 86; The Sculpture of Donald De Lue: Gods, Prophets, and Heroes, David R Godine, 90; American Figurative Sculpture of the Thirties: A Rebirth in Bronze, The Journal of Decorative and Propaganda Arts, No 16, 90; Willaim Partridge Burpee: American Marine Impressionist, Northeast Univ Press, 91. *Mailing Add:* Childs Gallery 169 Newbury St Boston MA 02116

HOWZE, JAMES DEAN
DRAFTSMAN, EDUCATOR
b Lubbock, Tex, Apr 8, 30. *Study:* Austin Col, BA; Art Ctr Col Design; Univ Mich, MS. *Work:* Del Mar Col, Corpus Christi; Hobbs Pub Schs, NMex; San Antonio Col; San Diego State Univ, Calif. *Exhib:* Two Smithsonian Inst Travelling Exhibs, US & Can, 79-82; Nat Drawing & Small Sculpture Show, Ball State Univ, 79-80; American Drawing II & III, Portsmouth, Va, 79 & 81; Nat Small Works Exhib, Schoharie Co, New York, 83; Toys Designed by Artists, 12th Ann Exhib, Ark Arts Ctr, Little Rock, 84; Nat Drawing Asn, Hermitage Found Mus, Norfolk, 88, CW Post Ctr, Long Island Univ, NY, 89 & Md Inst Col Art, Baltimore, 92; and others. *Teaching:* Assoc prof, Dept Archit & Allied Arts, Tex Tech Univ, 58-68, prof studio art, Dept Art, 68-92, dir core curric, 79-87, assoc chmn, 88-91, prof emer, 92. *Awards:* Cash Awards, Nat Drawing & Small Sculpture Exhib, Del Mar Col, 70, 74, 78 & 81; Best in Exhib, Nat Mensa Mem Exhib, 71; Silver Award, Wichita Art Dir Club, 76; Purchase Prize, Nat Miniature Print Exhib, San Diego State Univ, 88. *Mem:* Hon mem Dallas-Ft Worth Soc Visual Commun; Tex Faculty Asn; Nat Drawing Asn; Tex Asn Schs Art. *Media:* Charcoal Pencil; Mixed Media. *Publ:* Contribr, cartoons & humorous verse, Sports Car Graphic, 65-66; designer & illusr, var advert publ; poet & illusr, Images from the High Plains, Staked Plains Press, Canyon, Tex, 79; drawing, Cheatham, Cheatham & Haler, Design Concepts and Applications, Prentice Hall, p 86, 83; drawing, Frank M Young, Visual Studies, Prentice-Hall, p 86, 85; auth & illusr, Creating and Understanding Drawings, Mittler & Howze, Glencoe, 89. *Mailing Add:* Dept Art Tex Tech Univ Lubbock TX 79409

HOY, HAROLD H
SCULPTOR
b Spokane, Wash, May 16, 41. *Study:* Central Wash Univ, BA, 65; Univ Oregon, MFA(painting), 67, MFA(sculpture), 69. *Exhib:* Solo exhibs: Univ Oregon Art Mus, Eugene, 79, William Sawyer Gallery, San Francisco, Calif, 79, Blackfish Gallery, Portland, Ore, 81 & Univ Northern Iowa, Cedar-Falls, 89; The Animal Image, Smithsonian Mus, Washington, DC, 81; Animals, Celebration, Communion, San Jose Mus, Calif, 81; Orgon Biennial Exhib, Portland Art Mus, Ore, 81. *Teaching:* Instr art, Lane Community Col, 70- *Awards:* Fel Oregon Arts Comn, 71 & 77. *Bibliog:* Jean Cutler (auth), Sculpture of the Pacific Northwest: A Photographic Essay, Univ Ore Press; Thelma R Newman (auth), Encyclopedia of Woodworking, Crown Publ; 2nd Biennial Book, Fine Woodworking Mag. *Mem:* Col Art Asn. *Media:* All. *Dealer:* New Zone Gallery 411 High St Eugene OR 97401; Quartersaw Gallery 528 NW 12th Ave Portland OR. *Mailing Add:* Lane Community College Art Gallery 4000 E 30th Ave Eugene OR 97405

HOYAL, DOROTHY
PAINTER, PRINTMAKER
b Beaver, Ore, July 15, 18. *Study:* Frank Wiggins Sch Art, 36-37; Pasadena Col, 45-47; study with Frederick Taubes, George Cherapov & David Friend, 63-68. *Work:* State of Calif Interpretive Ctr, Lancaster; NASA Edwards AFB, Calif; Antelope Valley Col, Lancaster, Calif. *Comn:* Mission Collection, San Juan Capistrano Bank Am, Calif, 82. *Exhib:* Aquarius III, San Luis Obispo Art Ctr, Calif, 80; Desert West, 81 & 85 & Women in the Arts, 82, Antelope Valley Col Gallery, Lancaster, Calif; Fine Arts-30, San Bernadino Co Mus Art, 84 & 85; All Media Exhib, Lancaster Mus, Calif, 86; Am Prints From Currier & Ives to Andy Warhol, Lancaster Mus, Calif, 87. *Pos:* Instr painting & drawing, Cabrini Acad, Burbank, Calif, 49-59; painting instr, var seminars & wkshps of artists' associations, 60-90. *Bibliog:* Art Marketing Handbook, GeeTeeBee, 86; Julia Ayres (auth), Making Watercolor Monotypes, Am Artist Publ, 88; Julia Ayres (auth), Monotype-Mediums and Methods for Painterly Printmaking, Watson Guptill Publ, 91. *Media:* Watercolor; Monotype. *Publ:* Auth, Taking oneself seriously as an artist, Am Artist, 6/86. *Dealer:* Art Angles Gallery 3411 East Chapman Ave Orange CA 92669. *Mailing Add:* PO Box 3216 Quartz Hill CA 93536

HOYT, ELLEN
PAINTER
b Brooklyn, NY, Nov 8, 33. *Study:* Pratt Inst, 53; Brooklyn Mus & Mus Nat Hist, 65-75 & 83; with Ed Whitney, Frank Webb, Jankowski DeStefano & Ernest Chrichlow. *Work:* Gateway Nat Recreation Area, New York; Austrian Lender Bank; Stuhr Mus Prarie, NB; Griplock Corp. *Comn:* Painting, Sierra Club for Gateway Nat Park, New York, 82; British Consulate Gen, 92. *Exhib:* Metrop Mus Art, New York, NY, 79; Brooklyn Mus, NY, 80; Nat Watercolor Show, Salmagundi Club, 80, Nat Arts Club, 81 & 82 & Knickerbocker Club, 82, New York; Stuhr Mus, Grand Island, Nebr, 83; Lever House, New York, 85; Nat Tour, 88; Fed Bldg New York, 89; Pam Am Bldg, New York, 91; Metrotech, Brooklyn, 92. *Pos:* Instr, consult auth & juror, Nat Contemp Expos Artists Archievement, Fed Bldg, NYC, 87. *Teaching:* Instr art, Kingsway Acad, 70-75, Studio Dragonette, 77-80 & Unger Studios, 83-90; Hemlock Farms Art Soc, 88-92; Brand Studio, 91-93. *Awards:* Best in Show, Brooklyn Mus, 80; Travel Award, Washington Sq Outdoor Art Exhib, 81; Pilots Club Award, 83, 4th prize 87 & Landscape Award, 90. *Bibliog:* Emanuel Stromm (auth), Profile of an artist, Courier, 82; Eve Wilen (auth), New Exciting Approach, NY Artists Equity, 82. *Mem:* Artists Equity, New York; Visual Individualist; Brooklyn Watercolor Soc (secy, 79-86); Am Artist Prof League; Assoc Am Watercolor Soc. *Media:* Watercolor. *Publ:* Auth, Flare Printing, 75; Mariner, Flare Printing, 75; Never on Sunday Cookbook, Peerless Press, 70; NY Art Review, 88, 89; Sierha Club Periodical, 88-92. *Mailing Add:* 1551 E 29th St Brooklyn NY 11229

HOYT, FRANCES WESTON
PAINTER
b Elizabeth, NJ, Nov 15, 08. *Study:* Art Students League with Frank Vincent Dumond, 31-35. *Work:* Bloomfield Art League, NJ; Montclair Womans Club, NJ; Smith Col Mus, North Hampton, Mass. *Comn:* Two large dioramas in a nature ctr in Pa; triptych for use in the service by the Chaplain Corps of the US Armed Forces during WW II; many pvt comns. *Exhib:* Hudson Valley Art Asn, White Plains, NY, 60-; Am Artists Prof League, Grand Central Galleries, New York, 77; Allied Artists of Am, 80; Landscape Paintings, Montshire Mus, Hanover, NH, 86; Landscapes, Audubon Gallery, Concord, NH, 88; Libr Arts Ctr, Newport, NH, 89 & 92; Students of Frank Vincent Dumond, Cooley Gallery, Old Lyme, Conn, 90. *Pos:* Dir, Hudson Valley Art Asn, 77- *Teaching:* Pvt instr, Studio, 35- *Awards:* First Prize, Nat Arts Club, 41 & Women Painters of the West, 45; Gold Medal at the Grand Nat Exhib of the Am Artists Prof League, 74; Highest Honor, HVAA, 90. *Bibliog:* Frances Weston Hoyt (videos), Kearsarge Valley Mag, 90 & 92. *Mem:* Fel, Am Artists Prof League; Artists Fel; Salmagundi; Copley Soc; Allied Artists Am. *Media:* Oil. *Mailing Add:* 51 Hilltop Pl New London NH 03257

HSIAO, CHIN
PAINTER, SCULPTOR
b Shanghai, China, 1935. *Study:* Taipei Normal Col, BA; with Li Chun-Sen, Taipei, Taiwan. *Work:* Mus Mod Art & Metrop Mus Art, New York; Nat Gallery Mod Art, Rome, Italy; Philadelphia Mus Art; Detroit Inst Art; Musee de Arte Moderno, Barcelona; Art Gallery of Ont. *Comn:* Mural, Mr S Marchetta, Messina, Sicily, 71. *Exhib:* Carnegie Inst, Pittsburgh, 61; Int Malerei 1960/61, W Eschenbach, 61; Art Contemporain, Grand Palais, Paris, 63; 7th Biennial, Sao Paulo, Brazil, 63; 4th Salon Galeries-Pilotes, Lausanne, Switz & Paris, 70; Quadriennale Naz di Roma, 77. *Pos:* Prof artistic anat, Urbino Fine Arts Acad, Italy, 83-84; prof decoration, Turin Fine Arts Acad, Italy, 84-85; prof printmaking, Milan Fine Arts Acad, Italy, 85-90. *Teaching:* Instr art, Southampton Col, Long Island Univ, 69; prof visual commun, Inst Europ Design, Milan, Italy, 71-72; vis artist, La State Univ, Baton Rouge, 72- *Awards:* City of Capo d'Orlando, Italy Prize, 70; Gold Medal, Norwey Print Biennial, 84; First Achievement Award Contemp Painting, Li Chun-Shen Found, Taipei, 89. *Bibliog:* K Leonhard (auth), Hsiao Chin, 63 & Hsiao Chin, 65, V Scheiwiller; W Schonenberger (auth), Hsiao, Prearo, 72; La Via Di Hsiao, Nuova Foglio, 78, Hsiao, Vanessa, 79. *Media:* Acrylic, Ink. *Publ:* retrospective, print portfolio, Milan, 63; Oh! Che Vertigine, poems & prints, Milan, 66; Un processo di penetrazione, lithograph collection, Milan, 72; Ch'an, prints portfolio, Milan, 77; Hsiao Chin, Monography, Mazzotta ed, Milan, 88; and others. *Dealer:* Giorgio Marconi 15 Via Tadino Milan Italy. *Mailing Add:* Via G Modena 35 Milano 20129 Italy

HU, CHI CHUNG
PAINTER
b Chekiang, China, Jan 27, 27. *Study:* Self-taught. *Exhib:* Bienal Sao Paulo, Mus Art Modern, Brazil, 59, 61, 63 & 67; Fifth Moon Group Exhib, Honolulu Acad Arts, 71, Taft Mus, Cincinnati, 71 & Arts Club Chicago, 74; Contemp Chinese Paintings & Prints, Denver Art Mus, 73; Pittsburgh Int Exhib, Mus Art, Carnegie Inst, Pa, 67; Now Current Show, Smithsonian Mus, Washington, DC, 68; Sangre de Cristo Arts & Conf Ctr, Pueblo, Colo, 83; one-man shows, Fine Arts Gallery, San Diego, 73, Nat Mus Hist, Taipei, Taiwan, 86, Ming Ren Art Gallery, Taiwan, 89, Gauguin Gallery, Taiwan, 90 & Contemp Gallery, Taiwan; and others. *Bibliog:* The Imagery of Hu, Chi-Chung, Heritage Press, 62; Hu, Paintings by the Contemporary Artist, Nat Taiwan Arts Ctr, 67; Five Chinese Artists, Nat Mus Hist, 70. *Media:* Oil. *Dealer:* Zantman Art Gallery Box 5818 Carmel CA 93921. *Mailing Add:* PO Box 1039 Carmel CA 93921

HU, MARY LEE
EDUCATOR, JEWELER
b Lakewood, Ohio, Apr 13, 43. *Study:* Miami Univ, Oxford, Ohio, 61-63; Sch for Am Craftsmen, Rochester Inst Technol, with Hans Christensen; Cranbrook Acad Art, Bloomfield Hills, Mich, BFA, 65, with Richard Thomas; Southern Ill Univ, MFA, 67, with Brent Kington. *Work:* Goldsmith Hall,

London, Eng; Mus Contemp Crafts, New York; Renwick Gallery, Washington, DC; Yale Univ Art Gallery, New Haven, Conn; Art Inst Chicago; Victoria & Albert Mus, London. *Exhib:* Rings & Rattlesnakes, Goldsmiths Hall, London, 78; 4th Int Jewelry Art Exhib, Mikimoto, Tokyo, 79; Goldsmith '78, Schmuck Mus, Pfortzheim, Ger & touring 8 Europ countries, 79-80; Silver in Am Life, Carnegie Inst, Pittsburgh & touring US, 79-81; Good as Gold, Renwick Gallery & touring US & S Am, 81-84; Jewelry USA, Am Craft Mus, New York & touring US, 84-85; Am Jewelry Now, Am Craft Mus & touring Asia, 85-87; Craft Today: Poetry of the Physical, touring US, 86-88; Korean Am Contemp Metalwork Exhib, Seoul, Korea, 88; Craft Today USA, Touring Europe, 89-92; and many others. *Teaching:* Vis artist metalsmithing, Univ Iowa, Iowa City, fall 75; lectr, Univ Wis, Madison, 76-77; asst prof, Mich State Univ, East Lansing, 77-80; assoc prof metal design, Univ Wash, Seattle, 80-85, prof, 85- *Awards:* Nat Endowment Arts Craftmen's Fel, 76, 84 & 92; Purchase Award, Beaux Arts Designer/Crafts, 75; Alumni Achievement Award, Southern Ill Univ, Carbondale, 88. *Bibliog:* Carolyn Benesh (auth), Mary Lee Hu, Ornament, spring 83; Karen Du Priest (auth), Craft into art: Mary Lee Hu takes gold & silver jewelry in a new direction, Connoisseur, 10/86; Annette Mahler (auth), Mary Lee Hu: The purpose and persistence of wire, Metalsmith, winter 89. *Mem:* Soc North Am Goldsmiths (vpres, 76-77, pres, 77-80); Am Crafts Coun (craftsman trustee, 80-84); World Crafts Coun; Northwest Designer Craftsmen; Seattle Metals Guild. *Media:* Silver, Gold Wire. *Publ:* Contribr, Body Jewelry--International Perspectives, Henry Regnery, 73; Wire Art, Crown, 75; Textile Techniques in Metal, Van Nostrand Reinhold, 75; Jewelry Concepts & Technology, Doubleday, 82; Artists at Work, Alaska NW Bks, 90; Contemporary American Jewelry Design, Van Nostrand Reinhold, 91. *Dealer:* The Merrin Gallery 724 Fifth Ave New York NY. *Mailing Add:* Dept Art Univ Washington Seattle WA 98105

HUBBARD, JOHN
PAINTER
b Ridgefield, Conn, Feb 26, 31. *Study:* Harvard Univ, Cambridge, Mass, AB, 53; Art Students League, New York, study with Morris Kantor, 56-58; study painting with Hans Hofmann, Provincetown, Mass. *Work:* Tate Gallery, London, England; Scottish Nat Gallery of Mod Art, Edinborough; Arts Coun of Great Brit, London; Arts Coun of Northern Ireland, Belfast; Australian Nat Gallery, Melbourne; and others. *Comn:* Midsummer, 83 & Sylvia, 85, Royal Opera House, Covent Garden, London. *Exhib:* From Brit 75, Taidemuseo & Alvar Aalto Mus, Helsinki, 75; Brit Colour (S Am tour), Brit Coun, 78-79; one-man shows, Fischer Fine Art, London, 79 & 81 & Warwick Arts Trust, London, 81; Mus Mod Art, Oxford, 85; Yale Ctr Brit Art, 86. *Pos:* Member, Coun of Mgt, SPACE/AIR, London, 71-75; collaborator, Mark Rothko Mem Portfolio, London, 73; chmn, Art Panel, Southwest Arts, Exeter, Devon, 73-75; mem, Arts Panel, Arts Coun of Great Brit, London, 73-78; consult, J Sainsbury Ltd, 79-81. *Teaching:* Vis painting instr, Camberwell Sch Art, London, 63-65. *Bibliog:* Hubbard's Search, Art Int, 78-79; article, Times, London, 2/81; Jeff Dunlop (dir), film, London Weekend Television, 3/81. *Dealer:* Fischer Fine Art 30 King St London SWI Eng. *Mailing Add:* Chilcombe Dorset DT6 4PN England United Kingdom

HUBBARD, ROBERT
SCULPTOR, WRITER
b New York, NY, Mar 27, 28. *Study:* Lafayette Col, BA, 50; RI Sch Design, BFA, 61. *Work:* Ingalls Hosp, Harvey, Ill; Lafayette Col, Easton, Pa; Mus Am Art, Smithsonian Inst, Washington, DC. *Comn:* Pair Figures, comn by J Postell, 75 & Wind Figure, comn by R Warner, 85, Chicago; dance figures, Woods Group, Sharon, Conn, 80; Triad, Ingalls Hosp, Harvey, Ill, 82. *Exhib:* RI Sch Design, Providence, 61; Whitney Mus, New York, 66 & 72; De Cordova Mus, Lincoln, Mass, 80. *Teaching:* Instr design-sculpture-photog, Regina Col, Newport, RI, 70-74; sculpture dept chmn, Swain Sch Design, New Bedford, Mass, 74-77; instr design & sculpture, Evanston Art Ctr, Ill, 80-88. *Awards:* First Prize, Newport Art Asn, 68 & 69; First Prize, Providence Art Club, 69; Howard Fel, 69. *Media:* Stone, Steel. *Mailing Add:* 1076 N Paulina St, No 2RR Chicago IL 60622-3861

HUBENTHAL, KARL SAMUEL
CARTOONIST, PAINTER
b Beemer, Nebr, May 1, 17. *Study:* Chouinard Art Inst, Los Angeles. *Work:* Syracuse Univ; Truman Mem Libr; Eisenhower Mem Libr; Lyndon B Johnson Libr; Ohio State Univ Graphic Arts Res Libr. *Exhib:* Am Ed Cartoonists Traveling Exhib, US, Mexico, Can & Eng, 62-77; Los Angeles Co Mus, 69 & 73; Madison Sq Garden Gallery Sport, 71; Univ Southern Calif, 75; Calif State Univ, Northridge, 77; private galleries, Washington, DC, NY, Los Angeles, San Francisco, 78-81; Phippen Mus Western Art, Prescott, Ariz, 92; and others. *Pos:* Political cartoonist, Hearst Newspapers, 55-83. *Teaching:* Instr, Calif State Univ; instr, Orange Coast Col. *Awards:* Nation's Best Ed Cartoonist, Nat Cartoonist Soc, 62, 67, 70 & 72; Helms Athletic Found Medal Contrib Sport in Art, 64; Nation's Best Sports Cartoonist, Nat Cartoonists Soc, 71, 79, 80 & 82. *Bibliog:* Articles, Cartoonist Profiles, 11/76 & 9/82. *Mem:* Marine Corps Newsmens Asn; Nat Cartoonists Soc (dir, 63-69); Los Angeles Soc Illusr (pres, 58-59); Asn Am Ed Cartoonists (pres, 63-64). *Media:* Pen and Ink, Oil, Watercolor. *Publ:* Contribr, Comic Art in America, Simon & Schuster; contribr, The World Encyclopedia of Cartoons, Chelsea House; contribr, How to Draw: Tips from the Top Cartoonists, Donnor Publishing; contribr, Cartooning, Regnery; contrib, The 70's: Best Political Cartoons of the Decade, McGraw-Hill. *Mailing Add:* 5536A Via La Mesa Laguna Hills CA 92653

HUBERT, EDGAR F & ANNE M
CURATOR, COLLECTOR
US citizens. *Study:* Mr Hubert, Northeastern Univ, Boston, BS; Mrs Hubert, Boston Mus Fine Art, spec studies, with Claude Croney & King Coffin. *Exhib:* James Fitzgerald 1898-1971, Hopkins Ctr, Dartmouth Col, Hanover, NJ, 75, Mead Gallery, Amherst Col, Mass, 76, Ctr Visual Arts, Antioch Col, Columbia, Md, 77, Danforth Mus, Framingham, Mass, 77, Monterey Peninsula Mus Art, Calif, 79 & 85, Mass Col Art, Boston, 80, Farnsworth Mus, Rockland, Maine, 84, DeCordova Mus, Lincoln, Mass, 85, Portland Mus Art, Maine, 92 & Plattsburgh Art Mus, NY, 92. *Pos:* Curators, James Fitzgerald Collection, James Fitzgerald Mem Studio, Monhegan, Maine, 71- *Mem:* Hon Charter Mem, Steinbeck Ctr Found; Portland Mus Art; Boston Mus Fine Arts; Farnsworth Libr & Art Mus. *Collection:* Twentieth century watercolors, oils and prints. *Publ:* Auth, Legacy of beauty, Kent Collector, 76; auth, Recollections of the Artist, Fitzgerald Mem Studio, 77. *Mailing Add:* One Rocky Brook Rd Dover MA 02030

HUBLER, JULIUS
PRINTMAKER, PAINTER
b Granite City, Ill, Dec 11, 19. *Study:* SE Mo State Univ, BS, 42; Columbia Univ, MA, EdD, 51; also studied with Hans A Mueller & Arthur Young & Philip Guston. *Work:* B Spruance Collection, Philadelphia Mus Art, Pa; Nat Acad Design & Adolph Dehn Collection, New York Public Libr, New York; J Von Wicht Collection, Brooklyn Mus Art; Everson Mus Art, Syracuse, NY. *Exhib:* Nat Acad Design, New York, 56-89; Libr Cong, Washington, DC, 58-; US Print Exhib, Smithsonian Inst, Washington, DC, 62; US Info Agency Print Exhib, traveling, 65-68; traveling exhib, 67, 50 Years Am Prints, Asn Am Artists Gallery, New York, 69 & Nat Traveling Exhib, 77-79, Soc Am Graphic Artists; Int Print Exhib, Taipei Mus Fine Arts, Repub of China, 83-89 & 92; one-man shows, Lyrical Images, Albright-Knox, 91 & Rodman Hall Nat Exib Ctr Can, St Catharines, Ont, 91. *Teaching:* Instr, City Col New York, 46-48; prof, State Univ NY Buffalo, 48-82. *Awards:* Warren Mack Mem Award, Soc Am Graphic Artists, 62; Samuel F B Morse Medal, 152nd Ann Exhib, Nat Acad Design, 77; anonymous prize, 155th Ann Exhib, Nat Acad Design, 80; Leo Meissner Prize, Nat Acad Design, 89. *Mem:* Soc Am Graphic Artists; Assoc Nat Acad Design. *Media:* Collage, Relief. *Publ:* Auth, J Print World, Lynd Ward, 89. *Mailing Add:* 9855 Hollingson Rd Clarence NY 14031

HUCHEL, FREDERICK M
HISTORIAN, CONSULTANT
b Brigham City, Utah, Aug 28, 47. *Study:* Weber State Col, Odgen; Brigham Young Univ, Provo, Utah, Charles James Painting Sch. *Work:* Brigham City Mus-Gallery, Utah; religious art, Minerva Teichert, 79. *Collections Arranged:* Minerva Kohlhepp Teichert, Brigham City Mus-Gallery, 77 & 79; Beersheba Collection, 78; Ella Peacock, 79. *Pos:* Dir, Brigham City Mus-Gallery, 77-82; Pvt Consult, 82- *Bibliog:* Robert S Olpin (auth), Dictionary of Utah Art, Salt Lake Art Ctr, 80; Vern G Swancon, Robert S Olpin & William C Seifrit (auths), Utah Art, p 208, Peregrine Smith Books, Layton, Utah, 91. *Mem:* Western Asn Art Mus; Utah Mus Asn; Utah State Hist Soc. *Res:* Utah and Mormon art and artists; Prehistoric and native American art of the Great Basin; Utah & Morman history architecture; Book and paper marbling; Faux finish golding, marbelizing, graining, illumination. *Specialty:* Varied types of mostly representational art. *Publ:* Research Notebook, Box Elder News J, 8 1; Promontory Utah and Vicinity, Golden Spike Assoc, 86; The Box Elder Flouring Mill, Vol 56, No 1, Utah Historical Quart, winter 88. *Mailing Add:* 13 N Second E Brigham City UT 84302

HUCHTHAUSEN, DAVID RICHARD
SCULPTOR, EDUCATOR
b Wisconsin Rapids, Wis, 1951. *Study:* Univ Wis, BS, study with Harvey K Littleton; Ill State Univ, MFA, study with Joel Philip Myers; Vienna Univ of Applied Arts (Fulbright scholar). *Work:* Hokkaido Mus Art, Saporro, Japan; Smithsonian Inst; Metrop Mus Art, New York; Musee du Verre, Liege, Belg; Art Mus, Dusseldorf, Ger; Mus Fine Arts, Lausanne, Switz; Corning Mus of Glass, Corning, New York; High Mus Art, Atlanta; Los Angeles Co Mus Art; and many others. *Comn:* Sculpture, Hospital Corp Am, 85. *Exhib:* Lake Superior Int Crafts Exhib, Tweed Mus, Duluth, Minn, 75-77; Mod Glass of Europe, Am, Japan, Ger Mus Tour, 76; Mod Glass & Porcelain of Austria, Lugano Mus, Switz, 78; New Glass, Corning Mus Traveling Exhib, 79-81; Glass of Vienna, Mus, Zurich & Frankfurt; Glass from America, Glass Mus, Ger Tour, 79-80; Huntsville Mus, Ala, 81; Morris Mus, Morristown, NJ, 82; A Decade Apart, Boise Mus Art, Idaho, 84; International Glass, KulturHuset Stockholm, Sweden, 85; Inaugural Exhib, Int Glass Mus, Ebeltoft, Denmark, 86; solo exhibs, Habatat Galleries, 75-88, St Louis Art Mus, Missouri, 85 & Mus Contemp Photogr, Chicago, 85; Poetry of the Physical, Am Craft Mus Tour 86-88; Eloquent Object, Philbrook Mus, Tulsa, Okla Tour 87-89. *Pos:* Consult, Woodson Art Mus, Wausau, Wis, 77-; vis artist, J & L Lobmeyr, Vienna, 77-78; design dir, Milropa Studios, New York, 79-80. *Teaching:* Instr glass, Ill State Univ, Normal, 76-77; lectr glass, Royal Col Art, London, 78; assoc prof, Tenn Tech Univ, 80- *Awards:* Newberry Award, Univ Wis, 73; Elizabeth Stein Fel, Ill State Univ, 76; Nat Endowment Arts Grant, 82. *Bibliog:* Cover article, Neues Glas, Eng/Ger ed, 9/83; Sidney Goldstein (auth), Huchthausen, solo exhib catalog, St Louis Mus Art, 84; Robert Silverman (auth), cover article, Am Craft, 9/87. *Mem:* Am Craft Coun; Glass Art Soc. *Media:* Glass, Light. *Publ:* Auth, Americans in Glass, Marathon Press, 81 & 84. *Mailing Add:* c/o Univ of Okla Mus of Art 410 W Boyd St Norman OK 73019

HUDSON
CONCEPTUAL ARTIST, ART DEALER
b New Haven, Conn, Oct 4, 50. *Study:* Philadelphia Col Art, 68-69; Southern Conn State Col, BS(art educ), 69-72; Col Art, Univ Cincinatti, MFA(painting), 77. *Comn:* Poodle Theater, Ohio Arts Coun, Columbus, 80; Greek & French Arts, Allen Art Mus, Oberlin, Ohio, 81; Uncle Sam's States, Cincinnati Art Mus, Ohio, 81; No More Magic, Artists Space, New York, 82; Sex Pot, NAME Gallery, Chicago, 86. *Exhib:* No More Magic, Artists Space, New York, 82; Sophisticated Boom Boom, Los Angeles, Contemp Exhib, 85; Sex Pot, NAME Gallery, Chicago, 86; Deep Kissing, Contemp Arts Ctr, Cincinnati, 86. *Collections Arranged:* Out Art (auth, catalog), 81; Zap that Zit: City Sures (auth, catalog), 82; Promises, Promises, 86. *Pos:* Pres, Cincinnati Artists Group Effort, 80-82; dir live events, Randolph Street Gallery, Chicago, 82-84; pres, Nat Asn Artists' orgns, 85-88. *Awards:* Ohio Arts Coun Fel, 80 & 82; Nat Endowment Arts Fel, 83-84; Ill Arts Coun Fel, 84. *Bibliog:* William Olander (auth), Hudson, Arts Mag, 82; Richard Pollack (auth), Sophisticated Boom Boom, Reader Mag, Chicago, 85; Robert C Morgan, Hudson-Brendon de Vallance, High Performance Mag, 86. *Mem:* Nat Asn Artists' Orgns (vpres, 84-85, pres, 85-87). *Media:* Performance. *Specialty:* Post-conceptual & post-pop. *Publ:* Ed, Artists' Pulp, Cincinnati Artists Group Effort, 80-81. *Mailing Add:* c/o Feature 484 Broome St New York NY 10013

HUDSON, JACQUELINE
PAINTER, GRAPHIC ARTIST
b Cambridge, Mass. *Study:* Sch Nat Acad; Art Students League, with Jean Liberte, Will Barnet & Michael Ponce de Leon; Columbia Univ. *Work:* Libr Cong (Pennell Purchase), Washington, DC. *Exhib:* Am Watercolor Soc, New York; Pa Acad Fine Arts, Philadelphia; Allentown Art Mus, Pa, 74; Bowdoin Col Mus Art, Brunswick, Maine, 75; Rockport Art Asn, Mass, 87 & 90; one-man shows, Maine Art Gallery, Wiscasset, 77 & 85 & Moulton Union, Bowdoin Col, Brunswick, Maine, 79; Galerie Salambo, Paris, 88; and others. *Awards:* Donna Miller Mem Prize, 80; Third Graphic Prize, Butler Inst Am Art, Youngstown, Ohio, 83; Thelma Karr Graphic Prize, 86, Bronze Medal of Honor, 89, Rockport Art Asn, Excellence in Graphics Prize, 92; and others. *Mem:* Nat Asn Women Artists; Rockport Art Asn; Monhegan Assocs Inc, Maine (trustee, 60-63, chmn Monhegan Mus comt, 62-65). *Media:* Oil, Watercolor; Lithography. *Mailing Add:* Monhegan Island ME 04852

HUDSON, JON BARLOW
SCULPTOR, ENVIRONMENTAL ARTIST
b Billings, Mont, Dec 17, 45. *Study:* Calif Inst Arts, with Allen Kaprow, Paul Brach, Lloyd Hamroll & Judy Chicago, BFA, 71, MFA, 72; Stuttgart State Art Acad, West Germany, with Rudolph Hoflehner, 69; Dayton Art Inst, with Charles Ginnever, Bob Koepnick, Ann Tabatchnick & Kimber Smith, BFA, 75. *Work:* State of Queensland, Brisbane, Australia; City of Brisbane, Australia; Anchorage Mus Hist Art, Alaska; BP/Standard Oil Co, Cleveland, Ohio; Green Co Pub Libr, Yellow Springs, Ohio. *Comn:* Shiva: Shiwana (sculpture), Nat Radio Astronomy Observatory, Socorro, NMex, 80; Fire in the Hole! (sculpture), Eppley Field Int Airport, Omaha, Nebr, 86; Morning Star (sculpture), Brisbane, Australia, 88; Paradigm & Morning Star (sculptures), World Expo, Brisbane, Australia, 88; Sublime Portal: Pl (sculpture), Mulia Tower, Jakarta, Indonesia, 91; Rivers of Time Sculpture, Royal Abjar Hotel, Dunbai, United Arib Emerites, 92. *Exhib:* Amos Eno Gallery, New York, 89; one-person show, Construct Gallery, Phoenix, Ariz, 89-90, Gallery 10, Washington, DC, 90 & Nina Owen Ltd, Chicago, Ill, 91; Malton Gallery, Cincinnati, Ohio, 90. *Teaching:* Vis sculptor, Stephens Col, Columbia, Mo, 75-76; adj instr sculpture, Wright State Univ, Dayton, Ohio, 76-77; asst prof sculpture, Antioch Univ, Yellow Springs, Ohio, 80. *Awards:* Projs Grant, 78 & Prof Develop Award, 85, Ohio Arts Coun; Lusk Mem Fel, IIE, Italy, 82-83; Art in Public Places Plan Grant, Ohio Arts Coun, 91. *Bibliog:* Johan DeRoey (auth), Geometry of mysticism, KNACK, Brussels, Belgium, 2/80; B Lealman & E Robinson (auths), Exploration into Experience, Knowing and Unknowing, Manchester Col, 81; Baile Oakes (auth), Sculpture expo in Australia, Sculpture, 5-6/89. *Mem:* Int Sculpture Ctr, Washington, DC. *Media:* All. *Publ:* Auth, Pluralistic Vocabulary of Spiritual Unity, Studia Mystica, Calif State Univ, Sacramento, 80. *Mailing Add:* 325 N Walnut PO Box 710 Yellow Springs OH 45387

HUDSON, RALPH MAGEE
HISTORIAN, EDUCATOR
b Fields, Ohio, Dec 18, 07. *Study:* Ohio State Univ, BA & BS, 30, MA, 31; Univ Ala, Advanced Inst Art Appreciation Ohio State Univ, 66, EdD, 65. *Work:* Univ Ark, Fayetteville; Mus Fine Arts, Little Rock, Ark. *Exhib:* Grumbacher Aquarelle Travel Exhib, 38; one-man show, Hendrix Col, Conway, Ark, 40-41, Episcopal Church Gallery, Huntsville, Ala, 89; Meridian Art Asn, Miss, 46-50; Miss State Col Women, Columbus, 46-68; Miss Univ for Women, 84; water colors & photographs, Episcopal Church Gallery, Huntsville, Ala, 90, 91. *Pos:* Guest cur, Huntsville Mus Art, Black Artists/South Exhib, 79; dir art tour, Holland, Belgium & France, summer 84; co-dir art tour, Spain, 87, Great Britain, 88. *Teaching:* Instr art & actg head dept, Morehead State Col, 31-36; head dept art, Univ Ark, Fayetteville, 36-46; prof art & chmn dept, Miss State Col Women, 46-69; prof art & chmn dept, Univ Ala, Huntsville, 69-73, lectr, 74-79; vis prof art hist, Inst Allende, Mex, 74; prof emer art, Miss Univ Women, 84. *Awards:* Univ Ala & Nat Endowment Humanities Res Grants Afro-Am Art; Distinguished Serv Award, Southeastern Col Art Conf, 74; Ralph M Hudson Art Scholarship established, Miss Univ Women, 83. *Mem:* Southeastern Col Art Conf (pres, 66-67, treas, 71-73); Nat Art Educ Asn; Kappa Pi (int historian, 48-74, int first vpres, 74-); Ala Art Educ Asn; Huntsville Mus Art. *Media:* Watercolor, Photography. *Res:* Nineteenth century American art, architecture and furnishings; Afro-American art. *Publ:* Art in Arkansas, Ark Hist Quarterly, 44; ed, Ida Kohlmeyer, 68; auth, Afro-American art: A bibliography, Nat Art Educ Asn, 70; auth, Afro-American Art (slide sets with lecture scripts), Nat Endowment Humanities, 72-75; auth, Black Artists/South (exhib catalog), Huntsville Mus Art, 79; coauth, African American arts and the ancestral African heritage, Art Teacher, 4/80. *Mailing Add:* 7102 Criner Rd SE Huntsville AL 35802

HUDSON, ROBERT H
PAINTER, SCULPTOR
b Salt Lake City, Utah, Sept 8, 38. *Study:* San Francisco Art Inst, BFA, 62, MFA, 63. *Work:* Los Angeles Co Mus; San Francisco Mus Art; Stedelijk Mus, Neth; Oakland Mus Art, Calif. *Comn:* Fed Bldg, Anchorage, Alaska. *Exhib:* Five Whitney Mus Am Art Ann, New York, 64-72; Los Angeles Co Mus Art, 67; Philadelphia Mus Art, 67; Art Inst Chicago, 67; Walker Art Ctr, Minneapolis, 69; Retrospective, Moore Col of Art, 77. *Teaching:* Instr, San Francisco Art Inst, 64-65, chmn sculpture & ceramic dept, 65-66; asst prof art, Univ Calif, Berkeley, 66-73; asst prof art, San Francisco Art Inst, 76-78. *Awards:* Purchase Prize, San Jose State Col, 64; Nealie Sullivan Award, San Francisco, 65; Guggenheim Found Fel, 76; plus others. *Bibliog:* Peter Selz (auth), Funk, Univ Calif, 67; Maurice Tuchman (auth), American Sculpture of the Sixties, Los Angeles Co Mus Art, 67; Graham Beal (auth), Robert Hudson, A Survey, San Francisco Mus Mod Art, 85. *Dealer:* John Berggruen Gallery 228 Grant Ave San Francisco CA; Dorothy Goldeen Gallery Santa Monica CA. *Mailing Add:* 392 Eucalyprus Cotati CA 94931

HUEBLER, DOUGLAS
CONCEPTUAL ARTIST
b Ann Arbor, Mich, 1924. *Study:* Univ Mich, Ann Arbor, MFA; Cleveland Sch Art, Ohio; Acad Julian, Paris, France. *Work:* Nat Gallery, Australia, Canberra; Van Abbemuseum, Eindhoven, The Neth; Nat Gallery of Can, Ottawa; Mus Mod Art, New York; Stedelijk Mus, Amsterdam, Neth; Israel Mus, Jerusalem; Tate Gallery, London, Eng; Musee St Pierre, Lyon, France; and others. *Exhib:* One-man shows, Galerie Yvon, Lambert, Paris, 75, Galeria Akumulatory II, Poznan, Poland, 76, Leo Castelli Gallery, 78 & Van Abbemuseum, Eindhoven, 79, Los Angeles Co Mus Art, Calif, 78, Dittmar Mem Gallery, Northwestern Univ, Ill, 80; Palazzo Ducale, Genova, Italy, 79; Mus Contemporary Art, Los Angeles, 84; La Jolla Mus Contemp Art, Calif, 5/27-8/7/88; Musee St Pierre, Lyon, 89; Kuhlenschmidt Gallery, Los Angeles, 90; Holly Solomon, New York, 90; Lia Rumma, Naples, 90; Sperone Westwater, New York, 90. *Pos:* Dean, Calarts Sch Art & Design, Calif Inst Arts, formerly. *Teaching:* Instr, Harvard Univ, Cambridge, Mass, vis prof formerly; instr studio art & printmaking, Calif Inst Arts. *Bibliog:* Colin Gardner (auth), article, Artforum, 11/88; Robert Morgan (auth), article, Arts, 2/89; Ann Lloyd (auth), article, Flash Art, 10/90. *Publ:* Auth, Untitled, Xereox-Book, New York, 68; auth, Durata/Duration, Turin, 70; auth, Statements plus Location Pieces 1, 2, VH 101/3, Paris, autumn 70; auth, Trois Travaux, VH 101/6, Paris, 72. *Dealer:* Holly Solomon 724 Fifth Ave New York 10019; Richard Kuhlenschmidt Gallery 1634 17th St St Santa Monica CA 90404. *Mailing Add:* Box 102 Truro MA 02666

HUEBNER, SISTER ROSEMARITA
EDUCATOR, SILVERSMITH
b Neenah, Wis, Jan 21, 32. *Study:* Mount Mary Col, Milwaukee, Wis, BA, 61; Univ Wis, Madison, MS(art), 65, MFA, 67. *Work:* Univ Wis, Madison; Mount Mary Col, Milwaukee; Contemp Craft Collection, Greenville Co Mus, SC. *Comn:* Diamond studded gold ciborium, Sch Sisters of Notre Dame, Generalate, Rome, Italy, 79; Ciborium, candlesticks, Sanctuary Lamp & stained glass windows, Notre Dame Congregation, Milwaukee, 86. *Exhib:* Contemporary Crafts, Greenville Mus, SC, 77; Invitational Jewelry & Metalsmithing, Univ Wis, River Falls, 78; Three Women in the Arts, Bergstrom Art Ctr, Neenah, Wis, 78; Silver in American Life, Milwaukee Art Mus, Wis, 80; Silver Today in Wisconsin, Milwaukee Art Mus, Col of Design, Ames Iowa & North Co Mus Art, Park Rapids, Minn, 83. *Pos:* Wis Art Adv Bd, Milwaukee Art Mus, 78-80; States Assembly Rep, Nat Art Educ Asn, 85-; counr, Sch Sisters of Notre Dame, currently. *Teaching:* Prof art metal, Mount Mary Col, Milwaukee, Wis, 65-, chmn art dept, 69-73 & 81-87. *Awards:* Scholastic Honors Art Awards, Regional Adv Bd, Wis, 69-; Awards, Milwaukee Area Teachers of Art Exhib, 69, 77 & 83; Special Presidents' Award, Wisconsin Art Educ Asn, 81; Art Educ Award, City Milwaukee, 88. *Bibliog:* Verna Curtis (auth), New Dimensions in Wisconsin Art, Exclusively Yours, 80; James Auer (auth), A New Mold of Old Metal, Milwaukee J, 80; Rosalie Goldstein (auth), Silver Today in Wisconsin, Milwaukee Art Mus, 82. *Mem:* Wis Designer Crafts Coun (pres-elect & pres, 78-80); Am Crafts Coun (North Central rep, 73-76); Wis Art Educ Asn (mem bd, 76-80, vpres, 84-, pres, 87-); Nat Art Educ Asn(mem States Assembly, Wis Rep). *Media:* Enamels, Silversmithing. *Publ:* Coauth, Future of Art Education, Wis J Art Educ News, 78; To be a teacher, Wis Art Educ News, 79; editorials for Wisconsin Designer Craftsmen Newsletter, 78-79 & Wisconsin Art Educ J, 84-87. *Mailing Add:* 1233 N Marshall St Milwaukee WI 53202

HUEMER, CHRISTINA GERTRUDE
LIBRARIAN
b Orange, NJ, May 24, 47. *Study:* Mt Holyoke Col, BA, 69; Columbia Univ, MS, 70; Cornell Univ, MA, 75. *Pos:* Asst art librn, Cornell Univ, Ithaca, NY, 70-75; indexer, Art Index, H W Wilson Co, Bronx, NY, 75-76; art librn, Oberlin Col, 76-80; deputy librn, Avery Library, Columbia Univ, 80-85; librn, ICCROM, 85-87 & Am Acad Rome, 92-; ed, RILA/BHA, 88-92. *Teaching:* Instr, Sch Libr Serv, Columbia Univ, New York, 83. *Mailing Add:* via Felice Cavallotti 74 Rome Italy

HUETER, JAMES WARREN
SCULPTOR, PAINTER
b San Francisco, Calif, 1925. *Study:* Pomona Col, BA; Claremont Grad Sch, MFA, with Henry Lee McFee, Albert Stewart & Millard Sheets. *Work:* Scripps Col, Claremont, Calif; Univ Calif, Davis, Calif; Long Beach State Col; Pomona Col, Claremont, Calif; Security Pacific Nat Bank, Los Angeles, Calif; Carnation Co, Calif. *Exhib:* San Gabriel Valley Artists, Pasadena Art Mus, 50-56 & 58; Artists Los Angeles & Vicinity, Los Angeles Co Mus, 52 & 54-59; Denver Mus Art Ann, 54 & 59; Butler Inst Am Art Midyear Ann, 55, 57-59 & 62; Long Beach Mus Art Drawing Exhib, 60; Southern Calif 100, Laguna Beach Mus, 77; one-man shows, Pasadena Art Mus, 55 & Mt San Antonio Col, Walnut, Calif, 77; 38th Corcoran Biennial Am Painting, Washington, DC, 83; Univ Calif, Davis, Calif, 86. *Teaching:* Instr sculpture, Pomona Col, 59-60; instr drawing, Claremont Grad Sch, summer 63; lectr art, Pitzer Col, 72. *Awards:* First Prize for Sculpture, Los Angeles Co Mus, 55; First Prize for Painting, Frye Mus, Seattle, 57; Nat Design Award Drawing, Boulder Ctr Visual Arts, Colo, 82. *Bibliog:* A Segunda (auth), Reviews, Vol 1, No 8 & Delores Yonker (auth), James Hueter, Vol 2, No 2, Artforum; Fidel Danieli (auth), Rev, Artscene, 86. *Media:* Wood, Oil. *Dealer:* Tobev C Moss Gallery 7321 Beverly Blvd Los Angeles CA 90036. *Mailing Add:* 190 E Radcliffe Dr Claremont CA 91711

HUFF, HOWARD LEE
EDUCATOR, PHOTOGRAPHER
b Kansas City, Mo, July 18, 41. *Study:* Col Idaho, BA; Univ Idaho, MFA. *Work:* J R Simplot Co, Boise; Boise Cascade Co, Boise; State of Ore Permanent Collection, Salem; Boise Gallery Art. *Comn:* Photographs (five 16in x 20in), Boise Cascade Corp, 71; photomurals (three 6ft x 12ft), Simplot Co, 76-78; six photographs, Boise City Hall Permanent Collection, 79; six photographs, Ore-Ida Permanent Collection, 79. *Exhib:* La Grange Nat Competition III, Ga, 77; Photog 78, Colby, Kans, 78; 4th Ann Coos Bay Regional Photo Competition, Ore, 78; two-man show, Univ Mo, Columbia, 78; Photospiva, Joplin, Mo, 81. *Teaching:* Prof photog, Boise State Univ, 65- *Awards:* Judges Merit Award, 41st Ann Exhib for Idaho Arts, Boise Art Asn, 76; Best of Show, Image 2000; Honorable Mention, Photospiva, Joplin, Mo, 81. *Media:* Photography. *Mailing Add:* c/o Ochi Gallery 1322 Main St Boise ID 83702

HUFF, LAURA WEAVER
PRINTMAKER, INSTRUCTOR
b Mt Vernon, NY, Dec 24, 30. *Study:* Syracuse Univ, NY; Univ Del, Newark, BA, 64; painting with James Twitty, Corcoran Sch Art, 65-67; George Washington Univ, Washington, DC, MFA, 68. *Work:* Libr Congress Collection of Fine Prints; Am Embassy, Jakarta, Indonesia; Corcoran Gallery of Art, Washington, DC; Nat Mus, Women in the Arts, Washington, DC; Nat Mus Am Hist, Graphic Arts, Smithsonian Inst, Washington, DC. *Comn:* 200 silkscreen posters, Amelia Earhart's Lockhead Vega, 85, comn by Carol Heiderman, 200 posters, The Tin Goose, Nostalgic Aviators, Los Angeles, Calif, 87. *Exhib:* Grabados, USA, Museo de Arte Mod de Buenos Aires, Argentina, 87; Montgomery County Juried Art, Exhib Prints and Sculpture, Strathmore Hall Arts Ctr, Bethesda, Md, 88 & 90; Washington Printmakers, DB&C Gallery, Brussels, Belg, 88; Maryland Printmakers in Action, 90, Recent Works, Loyola Col, Baltimore, Md, 91; one-person shows, Washington Printmakers Gallery, 86 & 89, Am Asn Advan Sci, Washington, DC, 86 & 89, River Road Unitarian Church, Bethesda, Md, 92; Not Simply Black & White, Frostburg State Univ, Md, 91; Chautaqua Artists' Show, Glen Echo Gallery, Md, 91. *Pos:* Illusr, Project LIFE, Washington, DC, 71-73; graphics specialist, Hazeltine Corp, McLean, Va, 79-80. *Teaching:* Lectr painting, Howard Community Col, Columbia, Md, 70-71; instr screen printing, Graphics Workshop, Glen Echo Park, Md, 74-76, Chautauqua artist/ instr, 91-; lectr screen printing, NVa Community Col, Alexandria, 76; instr screen printing, Art League Sch, Alexandria, 85; drawing & painting for sr adults continuing educ, Montgomery Col, Germantown, Md, 89-91; Arts for the Aging, Bethesda, Md, 89- *Bibliog:* Colleen Caprara, (auth), Laura Huff-Designing with Nature's Beauty, The World & I 6/86; JoAnn Goslin (auth), Making a Mark in Silkscreens, Potomac Life, 9/90. *Mem:* Washington Area Printmakers; Southern Graphics Coun; Art League, Alexandria, Va; Torpedo Factory Artists' Asn, Alexandria, Va; Md Printmakers. *Media:* Screenprinting, Miscellaneous Media. *Publ:* Illusr, Copycat Sam, Human Sci Press, New York, 82. *Mailing Add:* 11636 Brandy Hall Ln North Potomac MD 20878

HUFF, ROBERT
SCULPTOR, PAINTER
b Kalamazoo, Mich, Jan 4, 45. *Study:* Univ SFla, BA, 66, MFA, 68. *Work:* Ringling Mus Art, Sarasota, Fla; Mus Art, Ft Lauderdale, Fla; Erie Art Ctr, Pa. *Comn:* Sculptures, Dade Co Art in Pub Places, Miami, 77 & 81; paintings, Broward Co Art in Pub Places, 91; paintings, Palm Beach Art in PubPlaces, 92. *Exhib:* Chicago Int Art Expos, Lakeside Gallery, Ill, 91 & 92; SFla Invitational: George Bolge Selects, Mus Art, Ft Lauderdale, 91; Chicago Int New Art Forms Expos, Lakeside Gallery, Ill, 91; 41st Ann All Fla Juried Exhib, Boca Mus, Boca Raton, 92; Sculpture for Sculptors, New Gallery, Univ Miami, Fla, 92; and others. *Teaching:* Prof sculpture, Miami Dade Community Col, 68-, chmn dept, 78-; vis artist, Soviet Artists Union & Lakeside Studios, USSR, 89; vis artist sculpture, Univ Miami, 90. *Awards:* Fla Fine Arts Fel, Fla Arts Coun, 78 & 80; Channel 2 Juried Exhib Award, Miami, Fla, 80; Honorable Mention, Fla Nat, Fla State Univ, 88. *Bibliog:* Robert Sindelir (auth), Art corner, Ideas, 78; Elisa Turner (auth), Artists the critics are watching, Art News, 86; Leslie Judd Ahlander (auth), Miami art scene, Miami News, 87. *Media:* Miscellaneous Media. *Mailing Add:* 7231 SW 61st St Miami FL 33143

HUGGINS, VICTOR, JR
PAINTER, PRINTMAKER
b Durham, NC, July 23, 36. *Study:* Univ NC, Chapel Hill, AB & MA. *Work:* Ackland Art Ctr, Univ NC, Chapel Hill; B Carroll Reece Mus, ETenn State Univ; Brooks Mem Gallery Art, Memphis, Tenn; Vanderbilt Univ; Weatherspoon Art Gallery, Univ NC, Greensboro. *Comn:* Mural, Colonial Williamsburg Found, Durham, NC, 84. *Exhib:* One-man shows, Jane Haslem Gallery, Washington, DC, 71, 20th Century Gallery, Williamsburg, Va, 71, B Carroll Reece Mus, Johnson City, Tenn, 72 & Somerhill Gallery, Durham, NC, 85; group show, Nat Mus Am Art, Washington, DC, 81. *Teaching:* Asst prof art, Vanderbilt Univ, 68-69; prof, Va Polytech Inst & State Univ, currently. *Awards:* First Purchase Awards, NC Nat Bank, 67, Springs Art Contest, Springs Mills, 67 & Ann Southern Contemp Painting Exhib, 68. *Media:* Acrylic. *Mailing Add:* 401 Clay St SW Blacksburg VA 24060

HUGHES, BEVERLY
DESIGNER, WEAVER
b Belcrossing, NC, Feb 24, 49. *Study:* Barn Studio, Millville, NJ, studied with Pat Witt, 71-74; Acad Fine Arts, studied with Morris Blackburn, 74; Moore Col Art, Philadelphia, Pa, BFA, 76, Moore Col Art, Art Ed Cert, 90. *Work:* Fidelity Bank, Philadelphia, Pa; Afro-Am Cult Mus, woven mask, permanent collection, 89; Arco Chemical Corp, raffia mask, permanent collection, 91; United Bank, Philadelphia, Pa. *Exhib:* Group show, The Nexus, Animal Magic, Philadelphia, 91; Group show, Ctr Arts Southern NJ, Marlton, 92; The Connoisseurship of African-American Art, African-American Studies Ctr, Smithsonian Inst, Washington, DC, 92; Liberty House Crafts, New York, 92; Group show, Gallery 50, Bridgeton, NJ, 92; and other. *Pos:* Owner-designer, Winterwood Designs, Philadelphia, Pa, 85- *Teaching:* Instr art textiles, Moore Col Art, Philadelphia, Pa, 76; art teacher, Philadelphia Sch Dist, 86-91; Moore Col Art Saturday classes, Phildelphia, Pa, 90. *Awards:* First Prize, Expressions 80, Afro Am Cult Mus, 80. *Bibliog:* Edward J Sozanski, rev masks, Philadelphia Inquirer, 9/9/91. *Mailing Add:* 4832 Sansom St Philadelphia PA 19139

HUGHES, EDWARD JOHN
PAINTER
b North Vancouver, BC, Feb 17, 13. *Study:* Vancouver Sch Art. *Work:* Nat Gallery Can, Ottawa; Art Gallery Ont, Toronto; Vancouver Art Gallery; Montreal Mus Fine Art; Gtr Victoria Art Gallery. *Exhib:* Retrospective, Vancouver Art Gallery, 67 & Surrey Art Gallery, 83; Art Gallery of Greater Victoria, 83; Edmonton Art Gallery, 83; Nat Gallery Can, 83; Glenbow Mus Calgary, 83; and others. *Pos:* War artist, Can Army, 40-42, off war artist, 42-46. *Awards:* Emily Carr Scholar, Lawren Harris, 47; Can Coun Fels & Awards, 58, 63 & 67, Short Term Grant, 70. *Bibliog:* Doris Shadbolt (auth), E J Hughes, Can Art Mag, spring 53; Anthony Robertson (auth), E J Hughes, Vanguard Mag, 12/81; Patricia Salmon & Leslie Black (auths), E J Hughes, Raincoast Chronicles Mag, 10/83. *Mem:* Royal Can Acad Art. *Media:* Acrylic, Oil. *Dealer:* Mr Michel Moreault Dominion Gallery 1438 Sherbrooke St W Montreal PQ Can. *Mailing Add:* 2449 Heather St Duncan BC V9L 2Z6 Canada

HUGHES, PAUL LUCIEN
DEALER, CONSULTANT
b New York, NY, Apr 8, 38. *Study:* NY Univ, BA, 67; Sch Visual Art, 68-69. *Exhib:* State Wyo Fel, 88. *Collections Arranged:* Harry Bertoia Retrospective (guest cur), Colorado Springs Fine Arts Mus, 80; Vance Kirkland retrospective, 28-81; George Rickey, 84, 87 & 90. *Pos:* Dir, Inkfish Gallery, Denver. *Mem:* Alliance for Contemp Art; DADA. *Specialty:* Contemporary abstract art. *Collection:* Bertoia, Anuszkiewicz, Henry Moore, Herbert Bayer, Vance Kirkland, Dave Yust, George Rickey, Philip Tsiaras, Italo Scanga, Werner Drewes and many others. *Mailing Add:* c/o Inkfish Gallery 949 Broadway Denver CO 80203

HUGHES, ROBERT S F
CRITIC, LECTURER
b Sydney, Australia, July 28, 38. *Study:* St Ignatius Col; Sydney Univ, studies in art & archit. *Pos:* Contribr, The Observer, The Spectator, The Sunday Times, The Daily Telegraph & Encounter, in Eng, The Nation & The Sunday Mirror, in Australia, formerly; contribr, The New York Rev of Bks & The New Repub, currently; art critic & sr writer, Time Mag, 70- *Awards:* Frank Jewett Mather Award, Col Art Asn Am, 82 & 85; W H Smith Lit Award, 87; Duff Cooper Prize, 87; Golden Plate Award, Am Acad Achievement, 88. *Publ:* The Shock of the New (8-part TV series on 20th century art), Brit Broadcasting Corp & Pub Broadcasting Corp; The Fatal Shore, 87; Nothing, if not critical, Kropff, 90; Frank Auerback (monogr), 90; Barcelona; and others. *Mailing Add:* c/o Time Mag Rockefeller Ctr New York NY 10020

HUGHEY, KIRK (JOHN KIRK)
PAINTER, PRINTMAKER
b Grand Rapids, Minn, Sept 1, 40. *Study:* Study with Watson Bidwell, Fritz Scholder & Georgia O'Keeffe, St John's Col, Santa Fe, NMex, MA, 79. *Work:* Sheldon Mem Gallery & Christlieb Collection Western Art, Lincoln, Nebr; Mus NMex & Dept Interior, Nat Park Serv Regional Off, Santa Fe; IBM. *Comn:* Western film festival poster, Nat Film Preserve, Telluride, Colo, 81; keynote painting, Nat Guard Heritage Exhib, NMex Nat Guard, Santa Fe, 82; New Mexico Wildflowers (block prints), Mus NMex, Santa Fe, 82; 9 paintings, Klotsche Properties, Santa Fe, 85; 12 paintings, Salinas Nat Monument, Santa Fe, 85-86; Nat Cong Art & Design, 88. *Exhib:* Solo exhibs, Los Llanos Gallery, Santa Fe, 80-83, Fagen-Peterson Fine Art, 82-85, American West, Chicago, 84 & Prairie Lee Gallery, Chicago, 87; Images of the Southwest, Santa Fe Inst Fine Arts, 83; Collector's Choice, Doane Col,

Crete, Nebr, 85; Sharf Gallery, Santa Fe, NMex, 85. *Awards:* NMex Medal of Merit, 82; NMex Cert Appreciation, 82. *Bibliog:* Don Jones (auth), Kirk Hughey/Artist, Santa Fean Mag, 10/81; Sharyn Udall (auth), Images of the neon west, NMex Mag, 7/85; Robert Graybill (auth), The artist and the thing on the hill, Santa Fe Reporter, 10/85. *Media:* Acrylic. *Mailing Add:* c/o Fagan-Peterson Fine Art 7077 Main St Scottsdale AZ 85251

HUGHTO, DARRYL LEO
PAINTER
b Watertown, NY, June 10, 43. *Study:* State Univ NY, Col Buffalo, BS(art educ), 65; Cranbrook Acad Art, MFA(painting), 69. *Work:* Edmonton Art Gallery, Alta; Everson Mus Art; Boston Mus Fine Arts; Mus Fine Arts, Houston; Guggenheim Mus; Abbeyville Press, Westchester, NY; Mus Contemp Art, Houston, Tex. *Comn:* Mural (acrylic on canvas), Charlestown Savings Bank, Boston, 77. *Exhib:* One-man shows, Gallery 99, Bay Harbor Island, Fla, 80, 81, 86 & 87, Salander-O'Reilly Galleries, New York, 81, 82, 83, 84, 86 & 89, Gallery One, Toronto, 91, Stein Bartlow Gallery, Chicago, 92, Galerie Eke London, Montreal, 92; Corcoran Gallery, 77; New Abstract Art, Edmonton Art Gallery, Alta, 77; Theodoran Award Show, Guggenheim Mus, 77; 20th Century Painting & Sculpture, Metrop Mus Art, New York, 79; The New Generation: A Curator's Choice Traveling Exhib, 81; Salander-O'Reilly, New York, 81-; Elca London Gallery, Montreal, Que, 85-; Pre-Post Modern, St Lawrence Univ, Rush Mus, 85; Munson, Williams & Proctor Mus Art Sch, 86; Gallery 99 Miami, Fla, 81-; Gallery One, Toronto, Ont, 81-; Meredith Long, Houston, Tex, 78-; 871 Fine Arts, San Francisco, Calif, 86-; Salander-O'Reilly Galleries, New York, 90. *Teaching:* Teaching asst painting, Cranbrook Acad Art, 68-69; asst prof, Syracuse Univ, 71-79; artist in residence, Va Polytech Inst, Blacksburg, 84; vis artist, Western Mich Univ, Kalamazoo, Mich, 85. *Awards:* Theodoran Award, Guggenheim Found, 77; Humanities Award, Nat Endowment Arts, 83 & 84. *Bibliog:* Ken Carpenter (auth), Third generation abstraction: Darryl Hughto, Arts Mag, 2/75; Kenworth Moffett (auth), The New Generation, Rhineburgh Press, 80; Stephan Pentak (auth), Darryl Hughto, Arts Mag, 5/81; Karen Wilkin (auth), At the Galleries, Partisan Review, 89. *Mem:* Visual Artists & Galleries Asn Inc. *Media:* Acrylic on Canvas. *Dealer:* Salander-O'Reilly Galleries 22 E 80 St New York NY 10021. *Mailing Add:* Rd 2, Box 411 Canastota NY 13032

HUGHTO, MARGIE A
CERAMIST, CURATOR
b Endicott, NY, March 29, 44. *Study:* State Univ NY, Buffalo, BS(art educ), 65; Cranbrook Acad Art, Bloomfield Hills, Mich, MFA(ceramics), 71; with Richard DeVore. *Work:* Boston Mus Fine Arts, Mass; Albright-Knox Art Gallery, Buffalo, NY; Everson Mus Art, Syracuse, NY; Cranbrook Acad Art Mus, Bloomfield Hills, Mich. *Comn:* Ceramic wall pieces, Marina Casino, NJ, 80; ceramic wall pieces, United Energy Resources, Houston, Tex, 81; ceramic wall pieces, Presbyterian Hospital, Philadelphia, Pa, 81. *Exhib:* Language of Clay, Birchfield Ctr, Buffalo, NY, 79-80; Century of Ceramics US, Everson Mus Art, Syracuse, NY, 79-81; Women Artists, Suzanne Brown Gallery, Scottsdale, Ariz, 80; Scripps Invitational, Scripps Col Mus, Claremont, Calif, 81. *Collections Arranged:* New Works in Clay by Contemp Painters & Sculptors (auth, catalog), Am Ceramics, 76, 78 & 81; A Century of Ceramics in the US 1878-1978 (auth, catalog), Am Ceramics, 78. *Pos:* Cur of Ceramics, Everson Mus Art, Syracuse, NY, 73-81; dir, Syracuse Clay Institute, NY, 75-81. *Teaching:* Prof ceramics, Syracuse Univ Sch Art, NY, 71-81. *Bibliog:* Sherry Chayat (auth), The Ceramic Fans of Margie Hughto, Ceramics Monthly, 5/80; Earth, Fire & Water (film), Philip Morris Corporation, 78. *Mem:* Inst Ceramic History. *Media:* Ceramic, Handmade Cotton Paper Pulp. *Res:* Contemporary American ceramics. *Dealer:* Andre Emmerich Gallery 41 East 57th St New York NY 10022. *Mailing Add:* c/o Pondside Press 4 Bollenbecker Rd Rhinebeck NY 12572

HUGO, JOAN (DOWEY)
CRITIC, ADMINISTRATOR
b Weehawken, NJ, Jan 12, 30. *Study:* Simmons Col, Boston, MA BLS, studied performance with Rachel Rosenthal, 80-81 & Rudy Perez, 81-82. *Collections Arranged:* Artwords & Bookworks Traveling Exhib, Los Angeles Inst Contemp Arts, Calif, 78; Letterforms; When Beauty is Enough - A Women's Bldg. *Pos:* Cataloger, Brooklyn Mus Libr, 52-53; librn, Am Libr Paris, Left Bank Br, 53-54; art librn, Otis Art Inst Los Angeles Co, 57-80; Southern Calif ed, Artweek, 79-90; Calif ed, New Art Examiner, 90-; Asst to Provost, Calif Inst Arts (Valencia, Calif), 90- *Teaching:* Instr artist & the book, Otis Art Inst, 77-80, mod art hist, 80-90; instr, Univ Calif, Los Angeles Extension, 82-90 Modernism & Spirituality; History & Theory of Criticism; Guest critic: Claremont Graduate School. *Awards:* Vesta Award, 90 for journalism. *Mem:* Col Art Asn; Art Table; Aso Internationale dos Critiques d'Art; Los Angeles Contemp Exhibs (bd mem) 79-83; Woman's Bldg, 85-88. *Res:* History of artists' books; history of visual communications; contemporary American & European artists, history of performance; public art. *Interests:* Contemporary art, especially the relationships between the arts and social history; the concept of future and the arts; history of performance. *Publ:* Contrib ed, Artweek, Art Issues & Artspace; contribr, spec issue on artists' bks, Dumb Ox, 77; ed, Artwords & Bookworks: A Set of Artists' Postcards, 77. *Mailing Add:* 2601 Waverly Dr Los Angeles CA 90039

HUGUNIN, JAMES RICHARD
CRITIC
b Milwaukee, Wis, June 20, 47. *Study:* Art Ctr Col Design, Los Angeles, 71; Calif State Univ, Northridge, BA, 73; Univ Calif, Los Angeles, MFA, 75. *Work:* Santa Barbara Mus Art; Grunewald Print collection, Univ Calif, Los Angeles; Shaker Seed House, Tyringham, Mass. *Exhib:* Language & Image, Santa Barbara Mus Art, 77; Narrative Art: 1967-1976, Contemp Arts Mus, Houston, 77; Book Exhib, Art Ctr, Sonja Henie--Neils Onstand Found, Hovikodden, Norway, 78; Los Angeles Invitational, Fisher Gallery, Univ Southern Calif, 79; Object, Illusion & Reality, Muckenthaler Gallery, Calif State Univ, Fullerton, 79; Kunstenaarsboeken, Stedelijk Mus, Schiedam, Neth, 81. *Pos:* Founder, ed & publ, Dumb Ox & U-Turn Art Mags, 76-80 & 82-; contrib ed, Obscura Mag, 79-82; Midwest ed, New Art Examiner, 89. *Teaching:* Prof art, Calif Lutheran Col, 77-85; lectr, Chaffey Col, 82, Art Ctr Col Design, 83, Calif Inst Arts, 85 & Sch Art Inst Chicago, 85-86; vis prof, Art Inst Chicago, 85- *Awards:* First Place, Calif Col Photog Exhib, Calif State Univ, Northridge, 74; Purchase Award, Light II, Calif State Univ, Humbolt, 76; David & Reva Logan Grant New Critical Writing, 83. *Bibliog:* Howardina Pindell (auth), article, Print Collectors Newslett, 9-10/77; Marcia Corbino (auth), Contemporary art criticism, Am Art, 10/83. *Mem:* Int Art Critics Asn. *Publ:* Auth, Apocryphal conversations, Afterimage, 6/81; Photography: A bourgeois success story, J Los Angeles Inst Contemp Art, 5-6/82; Joe Deal's Optical Democracy, Reading into Photography, Univ NMex, 82; Meditations on an Uranian Easter egg, Vies, Photog Resource Ctr, 83. *Mailing Add:* 5246 N Bernard Chicago IL 60625

HUI, PAT
PAINTER
b Hong Kong, Aug 25, 43; US citizen. *Study:* Study of Chinese ink painting with Lui Shou-Kwan, 61-64; Univ Hong Kong, BA, 67; Univ Minn, 67-71. *Work:* McDonald Corp, Hong Kong Landmark Ctr. *Exhib:* Shadow of Poetry, Honeywell Corp Gallery, Minneapolis, Minn, 85; Poetic Vision, Alisan Fine Arts, Hong Kong, 87; Lesch Gallery, Minneapolis, 88; Asian Fine Arts, Minneapolis, 89. *Collections Arranged:* Lui Shou-Kwan, 1919-1975, Gallery 80's, Toronto, 80; Nine Chinese Artists, Honeywell Corp Gallery, Minneapolis, Minn, 82; New Visions in Chinese Painting, 84 & Painting, Poetry & Calligraphy, 85, Hui Arts, Minneapolis, Minn; Tradition and Transition, Jewish Community Ctr, Minneapolis, 85. *Pos:* Cur, Gallery 80's, Toronto, 80; dir, Hui Arts, Minneapolis, 82-; steering comt, Asian Art Coun, Minneapolis Inst Arts, 83- *Bibliog:* Laura Weber (auth), Hui Arts, Minnesota Design, 5/83; Mark Stanley (producer), Pat Hui, Video, 5/85; Wilma Wenick (auth), Shadow of poetry, Artnews, Minneapolis, 5/85. *Mem:* Art Dealers Asn Twin Cities (vpres, 83-85, treas, 85); The Minneapolis Inst Arts; Am Art Coun; Walker Art Ctr. *Media:* Watercolor, Ink on Paper and Silk. *Specialty:* Contemporary Chinese artists in all media. *Mailing Add:* Hui Arts 1225 LaSalle Ave Minneapolis MN 55440

HULETT, SIMONNE R
PAINTER, PRINTMAKER
b Blenne, Switzerland. *Study:* Okla State Univ, Stillwater, 46-48; Central State Univ, Edmond, Okla, BA, 71; with Virginia Cobb, Robert E Wood, Fredric Taubes, Charles Reid, Joseph Mugnani, Robert Kaupelis & Douglas Walton. *Work:* Amerax Oil Co, Baptist Hospital & Okla Childrens Hospital, Oklahoma City; Edmond Public Libr & Edmond Hospital, Okla. *Exhib:* Ann Southern Nat Watercolor, La Tech Art Gallery, Rustin, 81; Ann Print & Drawing & Craft Show, Ark Arts Ctr, Little Rock; Southwestern Watercolor, Brookhaven Col, Dallas, Tex, 80-83; Ann Southern Nat Watercolor, Columbia Mus Arts, SC, 80; Fifth Ann Exhib, Burpee Mus, Rockford, Ill, 81; and others. *Awards:* Bronze Award, Tri-state Show, Grumbacher Art, Colo, 79; Ruston Bank Award, Southern Watercolor, 81 & 82; Binney & Smith, Mid-West Watercolor, Binney & Smith Liqutex, 81. *Bibliog:* Martha Stermel (auth), Pen & ink drawings--high light Hulett art, Wichita Falls Times, Tex, 77. *Mem:* Kappi Pi; Individual Artists Okla; Southern Watercolor Soc; Mid-west Watercolor Soc. *Media:* Watercolor, Oil. *Dealer:* Arts Place II 115 Park Place Oklahoma City OK 73103. *Mailing Add:* 2429 NW 59th St Oklahoma City OK 73112

HULICK, DIANA EMERY
HISTORIAN, MUSEUM DIRECTOR
Study: Bryn Mawr, AB, 71; Ohio Univ, MFA, 73; Princeton Univ, with Peter Bunnell, MFA, 78, PhD (McCormick Fel), 84. *Work:* Carleton Col; Stephens Col; Ohio Univ; Photoworks, Boston; Graphic Arts Collection, Princeton Univ. *Exhib:* Smithsonian Inst, Washington, DC, 73; Kansas City Art Inst, 76; New Photographics, 76; Madison Art Ctr, Wis, 77; RI Sch Design, 79. *Collections Arranged:* Waldo Pierce: A New Assessment (auth, catalog), 84; Sabbathday Lake Shakers, Exhib Time & Eternity (with catalog), 85; Through Their Own Eyes, The Personal Portfolios of Edward Weston and Ansee Adams (with catalog). *Pos:* Modernist & gallery dir, Univ Denver, 82-83; dir & cur, Univ Maine, Orono, 83-86; adjudicator, Nat Found Advan Arts, Fla, 83-87; co-ed, Photography as Document: Shaker Spirituality and the Modern Age, Vol 11, NMex Studies Fine Arts, 87; Int Adv Bd, History of Photography (an int quarterly). *Teaching:* Asst prof art hist, Univ Maine, 83-86 & Univ NMex, 88; asst prof photohist, theory & criticism, Ohio State Univ, 86-88; asst prof art, Ariz State Univ, 88- *Awards:* Woodrow Wilson Res Grant Women's Studies, 80; Dayton Hudson Distinguished Vis Artists Carleton Col, 80. *Mem:* Col Art Asn. *Res:* Shaker photography; Diane Forbes, minority and women photographers. *Publ:* Introd, Chronology, Catalog Commentaries, and Bibliography for Waldo Peirce: A New Assessment, pp 9-16, 40-72, Art Collection, Univ Maine, 85; The Transcendental Machine? A Comparison of Digital Photography and Ninettenth Century Theories of Photographic Representation Leonardo, a refereed international quarterly, Vol 23, No 3, pp 419-425, summer 90; Continuity and Revolution: The Work of Ansel Adams and Edward Weston, Through Their Own Eyes: The Personal Portfolios of Edward Weston and Ansel Adams, pp 22-23, Univ Wash, Seattle, 91; From Prohibition to Acceptance: Shakers and Photography in the Nineteenth and Twentieth Centuries, Visual Resources, vol VIII, pp 81-103, fall 91; George Platt Lynes: The Portrait Series of Thomas Mann, History of Photography, an international quarterly, Vol 15, No 2, pp 211-221, fall 91. *Mailing Add:* Sch Art Ariz State Univ Tempe AZ 85287-1505

HULL, CATHY
ILLUSTRATOR, CONCEPTUAL ARTIST
b New York, Nov 4, 46. *Study:* Conn Col, New London, BA, 68; Sch Visual Arts, New York, cert, 70. *Work:* Fourth World Cartoon Gallery, Skopje, Yugoslavia; Collection of Caricatures and Cartoons, Basel, Switz. *Exhib:* Seventeenth Nat Print Exhib, Brooklyn Mus, 70; Soc Illusrs Ann, New York Times Show, 73; one-woman show, 6th World Cartoon Gallery, Skorje, Yugoslavia, 74; Mus De Beaubourg, Paris, France, 77; Women in Design, Pac Design Ctr, Los Angeles, 80; Women in Design Int Az, Scottsdale Ctr for the Arts, Scottsdale, Az, 81; Contemp Graphics, Design & Illus, The Md Inst, Baltimore, 81; Collection of Caricatures & Cartoons Show, Basel, Switz, 80, 82, 90; Contemp Design & Illus Show, Butler Inst Am Art, Youngstown, Ohio, 83; Quebec City Exhib, 85; Bienniale of Humor, Fredikstad, Norway, 87; 6th Int Cartoon Competition, Istanbul, Turkey, 88. *Pos:* Freelance illusr, 71- *Teaching:* Instr, illus & portfolio, Sch Visual Arts, New York, 83- *Awards:* Certificate of Excellence, Am Inst Graphic Arts Inside Show, 71; Silver Award & 2 Certificates of Merit, Soc Publ Designers, 74; Fifty Best Books of the Year Award, 74; Award of Excellence, Soc Newspaper Design, 84 & 85. *Media:* Airbrush, Collage. *Publ:* Contribr & illusr, Graphis #164, 72-73; Print, 5-6/77; Art Direction, 5/77; Nebelspalter, 75-83; V & K, 86. *Mailing Add:* 165 E 66th St New York NY 10021

HULL, GREGORY STEWART
PAINTER
b Okmulgee, Okla, Sept 2, 50. *Study:* Univ Utah, BFA, 73, MFA, 77, studied with Alvin Gittins. *Work:* State Utah Inst Fine Arts, Salt Lake City; Butler Inst Am Art, Youngstown, Ohio. *Exhib:* 7th Intermountain Biennial, Salt Lake Art Ctr, Utah, 75; 52nd Ann, Springville Mus Art, Utah, 76; Utah Mus Fine Arts, Salt Lake City, 76; Munic Art Gallery, Los Angeles, 78; Butler Inst Am Art, Youngstown, Ohio, 81; 64th Ann, Springville Mus Art, Utah, 88; and others. *Awards:* Best Show-Purchase, Utah Painting & Sculpture, 76; 1st Prize, Davis Co Art Ctr, Utah, 76; Am Artists' Golden Anniv Nat Art Competition Winner, 87. *Bibliog:* Stewart Bayle (auth), Art transcending cliches, Utah Holiday Mag, 8/6/76; Suzanne Muchnic (auth), Many called, few chosen for Barnsdall, Los Angeles Times, 5/22/78; Jack Hines (auth), Views of Venice, Southwest Art, 10/88. *Media:* Oil. *Dealer:* Wally Findlay Galleries Int 814 N Mich Ave Chicago IL 60611. *Mailing Add:* 2725 N Oakmont Dr Galleries Flagstaff AZ 86004

HULL, JOHN
PAINTER
b New Haven, Conn. *Study:* Yale Univ, BA, 77, Univ Ill, MFA, 81. *Work:* Metrop Mus Art; Yale Univ Art Gallery; New Mus Contemp Art; Israel Mus, Jerusalem; Greenville Co Art Mus, SC. *Exhib:* Mus Northern Ill Univ, Dekalb, 83; Greenville Co Mus Art, NC, 85 & 86; Rutgers Univ Art Mus, Newark, NJ, 85; Indianapolis Mus Art, 86; Jan Turner Gallery, Los Angeles, Calif, 87; Mus Borough Brooklyn, New York, 87; solo exhibs, Grace Borgenicht Gallery, New York, 89 & 90, Weatherspoon Art Gallery, Greensboro, NC, 89, Yellowstone Art Ctr, Billings, Mont, 89, Nancy Lurie Gallery, Chicago, Ill, 90, J B Speed Art Mus, Louisville, KY, 90 & Irony, Art Gallery of Western Australia, Perth, 90. *Teaching:* Asst prof painting, Yale Univ, currently. *Awards:* Fel, Nat Endowment Arts, 82-86 & 87; Fel Grant, Maryland State Arts Coun, 86-87. *Bibliog:* Suzanne Muchnic (auth), Scapes Exhib: Rooms with too many views, Los Angeles Times, 12/9/85; Paul Richard (auth), Unfamiliar creatures in alien seas, The Wash Post, 2/12/86; Judd Tully (auth), John Hull, Arts, 12/86. *Mailing Add:* c/o Grace Borgenicht Gallery 724 Fifth Ave New York NY 10019

HULTBERG, JOHN
PAINTER
b Berkeley, Calif, Feb 8, 22. *Study:* Fresno State Col, BA, 43; Calif Sch Fine Arts, 47-49; Art Students League, 49-51. *Work:* Metrop Mus Art, Mus Mod Art & Guggenheim Mus Art, New York; Albright-Knox Mus, Buffalo, NY; Stedelijk Mus, Eindhoven; Whitney Mus, New York; Portland Mus, Maine; Corcoran Mus, Wash, DC. *Comn:* Paintings of Newport News Shipyard, Fortune Mag, 57. *Exhib:* One-man shows, Martha Jackson Gallery, New York, 55-72, Corcoran Gallery Art, Washington, DC, 56, ICA Gallery, London, 56, Galerie Dragon, Paris, 56-71 & Oakland Mus, Calif, 60; and many others. *Teaching:* Instr painting, Art Students League, summer 60; instr painting, San Francisco Art Inst, 63-64; artist in residence, Honolulu Art Acad, 66-67. *Awards:* First Prize, Corcoran Biennial, Washington, DC, 55; Benjamin Altman Prize for Landscape, Nat Acad Design, 72 & 85; Nat Endowment Arts Grant, 81; Guggenheim Award, 56; Pollock-Krasner Award, 88. *Bibliog:* Emily Genauer (auth), article in New York Herald Tribune Mag, 55; article in Int Studio, London, 66. *Mem:* Nat Acad Design. *Media:* Acrylic. *Mailing Add:* c/o Anderson Gallery Martha Jackson 101 Buffalo NY 14214

HUMMEL, CHARLES FREDERICK
ADMINISTRATOR
b Brooklyn, NY, Sept 16, 32. *Study:* City Col New York, BA(magna cum laude), 53; Univ Del, MA, 55; Mus Mgmt Inst, Univ Calif, 85. *Pos:* Curatorial asst, H F du Pont Winterthur Mus, Del, 55-58, asst cur, 58-60, assoc cur, 60-67, cur, 67-79, deputy dir for collections, 79-89, deputy dir mus & libr dept, 89-91 (retired). *Teaching:* Adj assoc prof art hist, Univ Del, 64- *Awards:* Winterthur Fel, 53-55; Katherine Coffey Award, Mid-Atlantic Asn Mus, 89; Winterthur Curator Emeritus, 91. *Mem:* Nat Inst Conserv Cult Property; Early Am Indust Asn (dir, 64-); Int Rug Soc (dir, 71); Am Inst Conserv Hist & Artistic Objects; Am Asn Mus (secy, 88-). *Publ:* Auth, With Hammer in Hand, Univ Press Va, 68, 73, 77 & 83; contribr, Furniture to 1790, Britannica Encycl of Am Art, Encycl Brit Inc, 73; auth, A Winterthur Guide to American Chippendale Furniture: Middle Atlantic & Southern Colonies, Crown/Rutledge, 76; auth, Floor coverings in 18th century America, Irene Emery Textile Roundtable, 1975, Textile Mus, 77; coauth, The Pennsylvania Germans: A Celebration of Their Arts, Philadelphia Mus Art, 82. *Mailing Add:* 4403 Kennett Pike Wilmington DE 19807

HUMPFEY, DAVID
PAINTER, CRITIC
b Augsburg, Ger, Aug 30, 55; US citizen. *Study:* NY Studio Sch, 76-77; Md Inst Col Art, BEA, 77; NY Univ, MA, 80. *Work:* Metrop Mus, New York; Carneigie Inst, Pittsburgh; Denver Art Mus; Walker Mus, Minneapolis. *Teaching:* Instr, NY Univ, 90; instr, Univ Calif, Irvine, 92-; Art Ctr, Pasedena, Calif, 92- *Bibliog:* Pamela Wye (auth), Adjusting the Picture, Sufur, 92. *Media:* Acrylic, Oil. *Publ:* Auth, Hairpiece, Art Issues, 90; Stained Sheets, Holy Shroud, Arts, 91. *Dealer:* David McKee Gallery 745 Fifth Ave New York NY 10151. *Mailing Add:* 439 Lafayette St New York NY 10003

HUMPHREY, DAVID AIKEN
PAINTER, PRINTMAKER
b Augsburg, Ger, Aug 30, 55; US citizen. *Study:* New York Studio Sch, 76-77; Md Inst Col Art, BFA, 77; New York Univ, MA, 80. *Work:* Seattle Mus, Wash; Carnegie Inst, Pittsburgh, Pa; Metrop Mus Art, Brooklyn Mus & New York Pub Libr, NY. *Exhib:* Drawings by Young Americans, Nordjylands Kunstmuseum, Aalborg, Denmark, 84; solo exhibs, David McKee Gallery, New York, 84, 85 & 88, Rena Bransten, San Francisco, 87 & Alpha Gallery, Boston, 88; American Art Today, The Figure in the Landscape, Mus Fla Int Univ, Miami, 86; Public and Private: American Prints Today, Brooklyn Mus Art, New York, 86; Inner Images, Colby Col Mus Art, Waterville, Maine, 86. *Teaching:* Instr drawing, Cooper Union, 85. *Awards:* Creative Artist Pub Serv Grant, NY, 79-80; NY State Coun Arts Award, 85; Nat Endowment Arts, 87. *Bibliog:* Ronnie Cohen (auth), David Humphrey, Art News, 12/84; Kenneth Baker (auth), David Humphrey, Art in Am, 1/85; Hollan Cotter (auth), David Humphrey, Flash Art, 12/85; John Yau (auth), David Humphrey, Art Forum, 5/88. *Media:* Oil on Canvas. *Mailing Add:* c/o McKee Gallery 745 Fifth Ave New York NY 10151

HUMPHREY, DONALD GRAY
CURATOR
b Hutchinson, Kans, May 3, 20. *Study:* Univ Kans, BFA; State Univ Iowa, MFA & PhD. *Collections Arranged:* French & American Impressionism, 67; American Sense of Reality, Contemporary Latin American Painting, 69; Texas Collects 20th Century American Art, 71; American Folk Art from the Ozarks to the Rockies, 75. *Pos:* Dir, Philbrook Art Ctr, 59-75, Stark Mus Art, 76-77; chief cur, Mus Fine Arts, Mus NMex, Santa Fe, 79- *Teaching:* Instr art hist, State Univ Iowa, 50-51; asst prof, Okla Univ, 51-57; instr, State Univ Iowa, 57-58; adj prof, Tulsa Univ, 67-72. *Mem:* NMex Asn Mus; Southwestern Art Asn (pres, 72-74); Am Asn Mus; Am Fedn Arts; Asn Art Mus Dirs. *Mailing Add:* 2125 Calle Tecolote PO Box 2087 Santa Fe NM 87505

HUMPHREY, JUDY LUCILLE
GRAPHIC ARTIST, PRINTMAKER
b Columbia, SC, April 6, 49. *Study:* Univ Ga, BFA(art educ), 71, MFA(printmaking), 73. *Work:* Tenn Valley Authority Art-in-Archit, Shiloh, & Knoxville, Tenn; E Tenn State Univ, Johnson City; McDonalds Corp Hqs, Chicago, Ill; Williams House Collection, Winston-Salem, NC. *Exhib:* Boston Printmakers Nat Exhib, Rose Art Mus, Mass, 85; Printmaking Invitational, Tallahassee, Fla, 86; Drawing Invitational, Waterworks Visual Arts Ctr, Salisbury, NC, 86; NC Print & Drawing Invitational, Rowe Gallery, Charlotte, NC, 87; 22nd Ann Nat Print & Drawing Exhib, Peoria, Ill, 88; Oct Show, Asheville Art Mus, NC, 89; 51st Ann Nat Exhib Contemp Am Paintings, Palm Beach, Fla, 89; The Graphic Art of Printmaking, W Gallery, Wichita, Kans, 90; 34th NDak Print & Drawing Ann, Grank Forks, 91; 9th Nat Juried Art Exhib, Wanatachee, Wash, 91; Priva B Gross Int Works on/of Paper Juried Exhib, Bauside, NY, 91; Prints Int, New Canaan, Conn, 91; 21st Int Works on Paper Exhib, San Marcos, Tex, 91. *Teaching:* Prof printmaking & photog, Appalachian State Univ, 73- *Awards:* Purchase Award, 9th Ann Henley Southeastern Spectrum, NC, 90; Merit Award, 72nd Nat Exhib, 91; Purchase Award, 33rd NDak Print & Drawing Ann, 91. *Mem:* Southern Graphics Coun; NC Print & Drawing Soc. *Media:* Pencil, Gouache; Etching. *Mailing Add:* Dept Art Appalachian State Univ Boone NC 28608

HUMPHREY, NENE
SCULPTOR, INSTRUCTOR
b Portage, Wis, Mar 18, 47. *Study:* St Mary's Col, Notre Dame, Ind, BFA, 69; Goddard Col, Boston, MA, 72; York Univ, Toronto, Can, MFA, 78. *Work:* York Univ, Toronto, Ont; Hofstra Univ; Best Products, Va; St Mary's Col, Notre Dame, Ind; High Mus Art, Atlanta, Ga. *Comn:* Enclosed Garden-Landscape (sculpture), Artpark, Lewiston, NY, 80; Meadow Passage-Forest House (sculpture), Morris Mus, Morristown, NJ, 81; Roadrise-Resting Space, Creative Time, New York, 83; Atlanta Road, Atlanta Arts Festival, 84; Passages (sculpture), St Mary's Col, Notre Dame, Ind, 84. *Exhib:* Unending Roads, Hofstra Univ, 83; solo exhibs, Situations, Univ Wis, Oshkosh, 85, Breathing Walls, Alternative Mus, New York, Things in Common, Waterworks Art Ctr, Salisbury, NC, 88 & Sculpture, Sculpture Ctr Gallery, New York, 88; Scale (Small), Rosa Esman Gallery, New York, 88; Sculpture as Companion, Henry Feiwel Gallery, New York, 88; Lines of Vision: Drawings by Contemp Women, Hillwood Gallery & Blum Helman Warehouse, New York, 88; and others. *Pos:* Consult, Art in Public Places, Seattle Arts Commission, 81- *Teaching:* Vis artist, Ill State Univ, Normal, 82, Nova Scotia Col Art & Design, 82. *Awards:* Individual Artist Grant, Conn

Comn Arts, 76; Macdowell Fel, Macdowell Colony, 78; Nat Endowment Arts Grant, 83; Rockefeller Artist Fel, Bellagio, Italy, 87. *Bibliog:* John Caldwell (auth), Modernism in Morristown, New York Times, 8/81; Martin Ries (auth), Ambience/stimuli, in: Re-Dact, An Anthology of Art Criticism, 84; Tom Patterson (auth), Subtle images give Salisbury show its power, Winston-Salem J, NC, 9/11/88. *Mem:* Col Art Asn; fel mem MacDowell Colony. *Publ:* Illusr & contribr, Three stories, Criss-Cross Communications Mag, Colo, 81. *Mailing Add:* 325 W 37th St New York NY 10008

HUMPHREY, S L
PAINTER, ILLUSTRATOR
b Silver City, NMex, Nov 18, 41. *Study:* Western NMex Univ, BA. *Work:* Glendon E Johnson, Am Nat Ins Co, Galveston, Tex; Gerald I Freeman (corp collection), San Jose, Calif; Sen Benny Altamirano, Silver City, NMex; in pvt collection of Dennis Weaver, Calif. *Comn:* Cover for Frontier Days Publ, 73-75; paintings of Rio Grande Valley & settlement of Santa Fe between 1890 & 1900, comn by Clive Edgar, Colo, 75; background painting depicting uses of tools & Western paraphernalia, C O Crum Tool Mus, Henderson, Nev, 75; painting of hist stage line in Southwest Ariz, comn by Juel L Bell, San Diego, Calif, 75. *Exhib:* Women Artists Am West, Saddleback Western Gallery, Santa Ana, Calif, 74-75; George Phippen Mem Show, Prescott, Ariz, 75; Death Valley Exhib, Furnace Creek, Calif, 75; Nat Small Paintings Show, Albuquerque, NMex, 75; NMex State Fair, Albuquerque, 75; and numerous one-woman shows. *Teaching:* Instr painting, Lordsburg Pub Schs, NMex, 63-66. *Awards:* First & Second Place, Southwestern NMex State Fair, 74; First & Second Place, 74 & Second Place, 75, Women Artists Am Western Art Show. *Bibliog:* Mares, mules & mountain bells, Western Horseman Mag, 73; The 32nd El Paso art show, Sundial Sect, El Paso Times, 74; Regina Cooks (auth), article, Southwest Art Mag, 74. *Mem:* NMex Art League; Women Artists Am West; Grant Co Art Guild; Nat League Am Pen Women. *Media:* Oil, Watercolor. *Mailing Add:* PO Box 5001eritage Silver City NM 80062

HUNGERFORD, CONSTANCE CAIN
EDUCATOR, HISTORIAN
b Chicago, Ill, Apr 26, 48. *Study:* Wellesley Col, BA, 70; Univ Calif, Berkeley, MA, 72, PhD, 77. *Teaching:* From instr to prof hist art, Swarthmore Col, Pa, 75-, chmn dept art, 81-87. *Awards:* Am Coun Learned Soc, 78; Am Philos Soc, 80; Am Asn Univ Women, 82-83; NEH, 92-93. *Mem:* Col Art Asn. *Res:* Nineteenth century French painting, specifically Ernest Meissonier (1815-1891). *Publ:* Auth, Meissonier's Souvenir de Guerre Civile, Art Bulletin, 79; Meissonier's first military paintings, Parts I & II, Arts Mag, 80; Meissonier and the founding of the Societe Nationale des Beaux Arts, Art Journal, 89; Meissonier's Siege de Paris & Ruines des Tuileries, Gazette des Beaux-Arts, 90. *Mailing Add:* Dept Art Swarthmore Col Swarthmore PA 19081

HUNG WAH MICHAEL POON
PAINTER, CHOP-ENGRAVER
b Canton, China, Oct 30, 42. *Study:* Sir Robert Black Col, Hong Kong; Hwa Kui Col; Hong Kong Acad Fine Arts. *Work:* Int Young Men's Club, Osaka, Japan; Hong Kong Acad Fine Arts. *Exhib:* Hong Kong Acad Alumnus Club Fine Arts; Hong Kong Art's Festival. *Teaching:* Vpres, Int Studio Chinese Art, 76--88; teacher, Hong Kong Govt Middle Sch. *Mem:* Chinese Art Asn, Hong Kong; Kwong Ngar Calligraphy Soc, Hong Kong. *Media:* All media. *Mailing Add:* 15221 SW 89th Ave Miami FL 33157

HUNISAK, JOHN MICHAEL
HISTORIAN, EDUCATOR
b Troy, NY, June 28, 44. *Study:* Williams Col, BA; NY Univ, MA, PhD. *Teaching:* Instr art hist, Middlebury Col, 70-75, asst prof Baroque & Mod art, 75-78, assoc prof, 79-86, dept chmn, 81-88, prof, 86- & Christian A Johnson prof art, 87-90. *Awards:* Grant-in-aid, Am Philos Soc; travel fel, Am Coun Learned Socs; fel, Nat Endowment Humanities. *Mem:* Col Art Asn. *Res:* Later 19th century French sculpture. *Publ:* Auth, The Sculptor Jules Dalou: Studies in His Style & Imagery, Garland, 77; coauth, Romantics to Rodin (exhib catalog), 80; auth, Dalou's Triumph of the Republic: A study of private and public meanings, Acts 24th Int Cong Hist Art, 82; Rodin, Dalou, and the monument to labor, In: Art the Ape of Nature, Abrams, 81; coauth, The Art of Florence, Abbeville, 88. *Mailing Add:* c/o Dept Art Middlebury Collage Old Chapel Bldg Middlebury VT 05753

HUNKLER, DENNIS
PAINTER, DRAFTSMAN
b Oakland, Calif, Mar 3, 43. *Study:* New Sch Art, Toronto, 65-69; pvt study with Jack Bush, Toronto, 69-70; San Francisco Art Inst, BFA, 72. *Work:* Oakland Mus, Calif; Mus de Arte Contemp Int, Salvador, Bahia, Brazil. *Comn:* Walks of US of A (set design), Jane Brown & Co. *Exhib:* Humboldt Galleries, San Francisco, 74-75; California Printmakers, Printmakers Coun Great Brit, London, 75; Second International Text-Sound-Image Festival, Antwerp, Belg, 78; Phantom Oasis, Mercer Union, Toronto, Can, 81; Papelarte, traveling in Salvador, Brazil, 86. *Pos:* Asst dir, Artists Resource Ctr, Oakland, Calif, 73; mem, adv comt, Jane Brown Found Dance & Related Studies, Oakland, 79- *Teaching:* Instr, figure drawing, Cent Tech Sch, Toronto, 88-89. *Bibliog:* Alexander Fried (auth), The fantasy of three artists, San Francisco Examiner, 12/6/74; Thomas Albright (auth), Unique visions of nature, San Francisco Chronicle, 12/11/74; R F Stepan (auth), Dennis Hunkler's private world, Artweek, Vol 6, No 26. *Media:* Acrylic on Canvas; Pen and Ink. *Dealer:* Art Dialogue Gallery 80 Spadina Ave Toronto Ont Canada M5V 2J3. *Mailing Add:* 117 Coxwell Ave Toronto ON M4L 3B3 Canada

HUNT, BRYAN
SCULPTOR
b Terre Haute, Ind, June 7, 47. *Study:* Otis Art Inst, Los Angeles, BFA; independent study, Whitney Mus Am Art, 72. *Work:* Metrop Mus Art, Guggenheim Mus, Mus Mod Art & Whitney Mus Am Art, New York; Yale Art Gallery, New Haven, Conn; Stedelijk Mus, Amsterdam, Neth; San Francisco Mus Mod Art; Fogg Mus, Cambridge, Mass; Art Inst Chicago; Mus Moderner Kunst, Vienna; and others. *Exhib:* Solo exhibs, Blum-Helman Gallery, New York, 77-79, 81, 83, 85, 90 & 92, Bernier Gallery, Athens, 82, Los Angeles Co Mus Art, 83 & Knoedler Gallery, Zurich, 85, Danielle Templon, Paris, 90 & Tokyo, 90, 91, Orlando Mus Art, Fla, 92; Yale Univ Art Gallery, 82; Inst Contemp Art, Boston, 83; American Sculpture: Three Decades, Seattle Art Mus, 84; Six in Bronze, Brooklyn Mus, 85; A Modern Survey, Cheney Cowles Mem Mus, 86; Four Friends, Aldrich Mus Contemp Art, Ridgefield, Conn, 92; Drawing Redux, San Jose Mus Art, Calif, 92; and many others. *Awards:* Grand Prize, Int Seoul Art Festival, Nat Mus Contemp Art, 90. *Bibliog:* Robin Cembalest (auth), Jacques & Marta Hachivel: Good Vibrations, Artnews, 81-83, 2/91; Margot Hornblower (auth), Something to Stroll About, Time Mag Int Ed, 54-55, 4/29/91; David Bourdon (auth), Forum: Bryan Hunt's Untitled, Rotation Drawing I, Drawing, 32, 7-8/92; and others. *Media:* Construction, Bronze. *Publ:* Auth, Conversations with Nature, Mus Mod Art, New York, 82. *Dealer:* Blum-Helman Gallery 20 West 57th St New York NY 10021. *Mailing Add:* 9 White St New York NY 10013

HUNT, (JULIAN) COURTENAY
PAINTER
b Jacksonville, Fla. *Exhib:* Allied Artists Am; Sarasota Art Asn, Fla; Audubon Artists Am; Soc Four Arts, Palm Beach, Fla; Fla Artist Group Inc, Norton Gallery, Palm Beach; St Augustine Art Asn. *Media:* Oil, Pastel. *Publ:* Artist of Fla, 90. *Dealer:* Gail Stickley Frame Shop Gallery 3545 St John's Ave Jacksonville FL 32205. *Mailing Add:* 2587 Windwood Lane Orange Park FL 32073

HUNT, DAVID CURTIS
MUSEUM DIRECTOR, CURATOR
b Oswego, Kans, Dec 7, 35. *Study:* Univ Tulsa, BA(com design), 58, with Alexandre Hogue, MA(art hist), 68. *Exhib:* Okla Artists Ann, Philbrook Art Ctr, Tulsa, 62-65. *Pos:* Ed, Am Scene Quart, Gilcrease Mus, 65-72, cur art, Gilcrease Inst, Tulsa, Okla, 67-72; cur collections, Stark Mus, Orange, Tex, 72-76; dir, Missoula Mus of the Arts, Mont, 77-80; cur art, Ctr Western Studies, Joslyn Art Mus, Omaha, 80- *Teaching:* Instr mus practices, Univ Tulsa, 70-72. *Awards:* George Wittenborn Mem Award, Art Libr NAm, 85; Silver Medal, Int Bk Exhib, Leipzig, Ger, 89; Okla Bk Award, Okla Libr Asn, 89. *Mem:* Am Asn Mus. *Res:* 19th & 20th century American western artists and works. *Publ:* Coauth, The Art of the Old West, Knopf, 71; contribr, Encyclopedia of the American West, Crowell, 76; coauth, The West as Romantic Horizon, Joslyn Art Mus & Univ Nebr Press, 81; auth, Guide to Oklahoma Mus, Univ Okla Press, 81; Legacy of the West, Joslyn Art Mus and Univ Nebr Press, 82; coauth, Karl Bodmer's America, Univ Nebr Press, 84; auth, The Lithographs of Charles Banks Wilson, Univ Okla Press, 89. *Mailing Add:* c/o Joslyn Art Mus 2200 Dodge St Omaha NE 68102

HUNT, RICHARD HOWARD
SCULPTOR, PRINTMAKER
b Chicago, Ill, Sept 12, 35. *Study:* Art Inst Chicago, BAE, 57. *Work:* Mus Mod Art, Metrop Mus Art & Whitney Mus Am Art, New York; Cleveland Mus Art, Ohio; Art Inst Chicago; Hirshhorn Mus; Mus 20th Century, Vienna, Austria; Nat Mus Art, Washington; Albright Knox Gallery, Buffalo, NY. *Comn:* A Bridge Across and Beyond (welded bronze), Howard Univ, 78; Build-Grow (welded stainless steel), York Col, Queens, NY, 86; Freedman's Column (welded bronze), Howard Univ, Washington, DC; Spatial Interactions (welded bronze), Hunter Mus Art, Chattanooga, Tenn, 91; Build-Grow, Growth Columns, Branching Column and Crane Column (welded bronze), Edward Bennett Williams Bldg, Washington, DC, 92. *Exhib:* Solo exhib, Dorsky Gallery, 68-, Columbia Univ, 81, Westbeth Art Gallery, 81, Fordham Univ, 81 & Brooklyn Artists Cult Asn, 82; retrospective, Mus Mod Art, New York, 71 & Chicago Art Inst, 71; Terry Dintenfass Gallery, New York, 83, 84 & 86; Martin Gallery, Washington, DC, 85; Gwenda Jay Gallery, Chicago, Ill, 91; Louis Newman Gallery, Los Angeles, Calif, 91; Shiduni Gallery, Santa Fe, NMex, 92. *Pos:* Mem, bd gov, Sch Art Inst, Chicago, 85-91. *Teaching:* Asst prof, Sch Art Inst Chicago, 60-62, Univ Ill, 61-63; vis artist, Yale Univ, 64, Northwestern Univ, 68-69 & Washington Univ, 77-78; artist in residence, Eastern Mich Univ, Ypsilanti, 88. *Awards:* Guggenheim Fel, 62-63; Tamarind Artist Fel, Ford Found, 65; Cassandra Found Fel, 70. *Mem:* Am Coun Arts (bd dirs, 74-); Col Art Asn Am (bd dirs, 72-76); Am Acad Rome (bd trustees, 80-82). *Media:* Welded Metal, Cast Metal. *Dealer:* Terry Dintenfass Gallery 50 W 57th St New York NY 10019. *Mailing Add:* 379 W Broadway New York NY 10012

HUNT, ROBERT JAMES
ADMINISTRATOR, EDUCATOR
b Fargo, NDak, Apr 5, 21. *Study:* Univ Iowa, BA, 47, MFA, 50. *Work:* Univ Iowa; Mulvane Art Mus; Des Moines Art Ctr; Friends of Art, Nelson Gallery. *Exhib:* Wichita Art Mus; Mid-America Artists; Kans Free Fair; Am Fedn Arts; Colorado Springs Fine Arts Ctr; plus others. *Pos:* Dir, Mulvane Art Ctr, Washburn Univ, 64-86. *Teaching:* Prof art, Washburn Univ, 50- *Awards:* Purchase Prizes, Wichita Art Mus & Kans State Univ; Mid-Am, Nelson Gallery, 51. *Mem:* Mid-West Col Art Asn; Col Art Asn Am. *Mailing Add:* 1412 Boswell Topeka KS 66604

HUNTER, DEBORA
PHOTOGRAPHER, EDUCATOR
b Chicago, Ill, June 16, 50. *Study:* Northwestern Univ, BA, 72; RI Sch Design, MFA(photog), 76. *Work:* Yale Univ Art Mus; Wesleyan Univ Art Mus; Dallas Mus Art; RI Sch Design, Providence; Amon Carter Mus Art; Houston Mus Fine Art. *Exhib:* Dallas Mus Fine Arts, 79; The New Season, Witkin Gallery, New York; Second Sight, Carpenter Ctr Arts, Harvard, 81; Invisible Light Traveling Exhib, Smithsonian Inst, 80; one-person shows, Delahunty Gallery, Dallas, 80, The Light Factory, Charlotte, NC, 81, Int Mus Photog, 80, Meadows Mus, Southern Methodist Univ, 89 & Emporia State Univ, 89; Directions 1981, Hirshhorn Mus, 81; Mus Contemp Photog, Chicago, 85; Group exhib, Trains & Boats & Planes, Witkin Gallery, New York, 88; Group exhib, Portrayal, Bridge Ctr Contemp Art, El Paso, Tex, 89; two person show, Sitting Pretty, Art Inst Chicago, 92. *Teaching:* Instr, Swain Sch Design, New Bedford, Mass, 75-76; assoc prof photog, Southern Methodist Univ, Dallas, 76-; vis assoc prof Sch Art Inst Chicago, 84-85. *Awards:* Boston Ctr for the Arts Award, Photovisions, 75; First Prize in Photog, Tarrant Co Ann, Ft Worth Art Mus, 76; Mid Am Arts Alliance, NEA, 87. *Bibliog:* Lucy Lippard (auth), From the Center: Feminist Essays on Women's Art, Dutton, 76; David Dillon (auth), From the lighthouse, D Mag, Dallas, 78; article, Artforum, 4/81; article, Chicago Tribune, 12/6/85; article, Dallas Life Mag, Dallas Morning News, 11/5/89; article, Photo J Asahi Camera (Japanese), 8/90. *Media:* Black & White, Color. *Publ:* contribr, Camera, 8-9/75; contribr, Women See Women, Crowell, 76; contribr, A Ten Year Salute, Addison House, 79; contribr, Popular Photog, 8/80. *Dealer:* Witkin Gallery 41 E 57th St New York NY 10022. *Mailing Add:* Dept Art Southern Methodist Univ Dallas TX 75275

HUNTER, JOHN H
PAINTER, PRINTMAKER
b Pa, Sept 26, 34. *Study:* Pomona Col, BA, 56; Claremont Grad Sch, MFA, 58. *Work:* Mus Mod Art, New York; Los Angeles Co Mus; Pasadena Art Mus, Calif; Amon-Carter Mus, Ft Worth, Tex; Nat Gallery Art, Washington, DC; and others. *Comn:* Poster for Tamarind Exhib, Mus Mod Art, Tamarind Lithography Workshop, Los Angeles, 69. *Exhib:* Western Painters Under 35, Univ Calif, Los Angeles, 58; Fulbright Artists Show, US Info Serv, Florence, Italy, 65; Cannes Film Festival, 66; Painters Behind Painters, Calif Palace of Legion of Honor, San Francisco, 67; Drawings, Ft Worth Art Ctr Mus, 69; Decade of Accomplishment, Ill Bell Tel Co, Chicago, 70. *Teaching:* Instr fine art, Ohio State Univ, 60-63; guest artist, Ind Univ, Bloomington, summer 63; prof art, Calif State Univ, San Jose, 65-; guest artist, Tamarind Lithography Workshop, 69 & Lakeside Studios, 79. *Awards:* Fulbright Fel Painting, Florence, 63-64, Renewal Grantee, 64-65. *Bibliog:* Peter Plagens (auth), Possibilities of drawing, Artforum, 10/69; articles, New York Times, Los Angeles Times, Rome Daily Am, Art News & others. *Mem:* Artists Equity Asn. *Media:* Multimedia. *Mailing Add:* Dept of Art Calif State Univ San Jose CA 95192

HUNTER, LEONARD LEGRANDE, III
SCULPTOR, EDUCATOR
b Washington, DC, July 3, 40. *Study:* Univ Miami, BA; Grad Sch Archit, Univ Pa; Univ Calif, Berkeley, MFA. *Work:* Hopkins Ctr, Dartmouth Col. *Comn:* Environmental outdoor hydraulic-kinetic sculpture, Crossroads Plaza, Lexington, Ky, 74. *Exhib:* One-man show, Univ Art Mus, Berkeley, 72; Biennial, New Orleans Mus Art, 73; Annual, Whitney Mus Am Art, 75; Film Festival of the Americas, Virgin Islands, 77; and others. *Pos:* Asst dir, Visual Arts Prog, Nat Endowment Arts, 80-83, acting dir, 81-82. *Teaching:* Assoc prof art, Univ Ky, 72-80, chmn dept art, 78-80; prof art, San Francisco State Univ, 83- *Awards:* Teaching Fel, Univ Ky, 73-74; Golden Venus Medallion, Film Festival of the Americas, 77; and others. *Mem:* Col Art Asn; Nat Asn Artists Orgn. *Mailing Add:* 2105 Cactus Court Walnut Creek CA 94595

HUNTER, MEL
PRINTMAKER, PAINTER
b Oak Park, Ill, July 27, 27. *Study:* Northwestern Univ. *Work:* Japan Trade Bank; Am Heart Asn; Gen Re-Ins Corp; plus others. *Comn:* Several thousand illus comn by publs such as Life, Colliers, Nat Geog, Newsweek & Time-Life Bks, 53-68; 6 major murals, Transp Bldg, New York World's Fair, 64; 12 paintings, Gen Motors Corp, Detroit, 74; 142 eds orig hand-drawn lithographs, 71- *Pos:* Dir, Gallery North Star, Grafton, Vt, 75-83, Atelier N Star, Burlington, Vt, 83-89, & Mel Hunter Graphics, Ferrisburgh, Vt, 75-, Pegasus Fine Art, Ferrisburgh, 82- & Smith-Hunter Gallery, Ferrisburgh, 91-; pres, Aquagraphics Portfolio, Inc (PRWTKIT), Ferrisburgh, 91- *Bibliog:* Susan Ellis (auth), Drawing color separations on surfaced Mylar, Tamarind Tech Papers, 3/74; William G Cotner (auth), Mylar lithography: What it means to you, Decor Mag, 2/81. *Media:* Myla & Grained Plate Glass Lithography, Watercolor. *Specialty:* Contemporary realism. *Publ:* Auth, Making pre-separation effective, Bk Production Indust Mag, 72; Revolution in hand-drawn lithography, Am Artist Mag, 10/77; coauth & publ, The Mylar Method Manifesto, Atelier North Star, 80; auth, The New Lithography: A Complete Guide for Artists and Printers in the Use of Modern Translucent Materials for the Creation of Hand-Drawn Original Fine-Art Lithographic Prints, Van Nostrand Reinhold, 83. *Dealer:* Mel Hunter Graphics (whsl) Smith-Hunter Gallery (retail) Box 1530 Rte 7 Ferrisburgh VT 05456. *Mailing Add:* Rte 7 Ferrisburg VT 05456

HUNTER, PAUL
PAINTER, SCULPTOR
b Paris, France, July 3, 54; Can citizen. *Study:* Laval Univ, Quebec City, BA(vis arts), 77; Concordia Univ, Montreal, MFA, 79. *Work:* Coca-Cola Co, Atlanta, Ga; Quebec Mus; Refco Group Ltd, Chicago, Ill; Lighting Assoc Inc; March & McClennan, Boston, Mass. *Comn:* Mural, St Francis Hosp, Quebec City, 88; murals, Madeleine Islands Hosp, PQ, 92. *Exhib:* CIAC, Montreal, 86; Galerie Graff, Montreal, 87; Les Temps Chauds, Montreal Mus Contemp Art, travelled, France & Belg, 88; Tribute to Tibor de Nagy, Butler Inst Am Art, Youngstown, Ohio, 89; Miniature Environments, Whitney Mus Art at Philip Morris, New York, 89; 79th Ann Exhib, Maier Mus Art, Randolph-Macon Women's Col, Lynchburg, Va, 90; Harmond & Discord: American Landscape Painting Today, Va Mus Fine Arts, Richmond, 90; Paul Hunter in Perspective, Musee du Que, Can; and others. *Awards:* Can Coun Award, 86-87; Pollock-Krasner Found Award, 87; Quebec Govt Award, 88-89. *Bibliog:* John Russell (auth), article, NY Times, 8/11/89; David Waterman (auth), article, Art News, 2/90; Roy Proctor (auth), article, Richmond News Leader, 8/11/90. *Publ:* Auth, Les Temps Chauds (exhib catalog), Montreal Mus Contemp Art, 88; Drawn from Life: Contemporary Interpretive Landscape (exhib catalog), Sewell Art Gallery, Rice Univ, Houston, Tex, 88; Paul Hunter in Perspective (exhib, catalog), Musee du Que, Can, 90. *Mailing Add:* c/o Tibor de Nagy 41 W 57 St New York NY 10019

HUNTER, ROBERT DOUGLAS
PAINTER, INSTRUCTOR
b Boston, Mass, Mar 17, 28. *Study:* Cape Sch Art, Provincetown, Mass, with Henry Hensche; Vesper George Sch Art, Boston; also with R H Ives Gammell, Boston. *Work:* Northeastern Univ, Boston; Tufts Univ; Boston Univ Med Ctr; Mass Inst Technol; Harvard Univ. *Comn:* Epiphany mural, Church St Mary of the Harbor, Provincetown, 56; altar frontal, Emmanuel Church, West Roxbury, Mass, 62. *Exhib:* Acad Artists Show, Springfield, Mass, 61; Am Artist Prof League Show, New York, 66, 67 & 70; New Eng Artists Exhib, Boston, 70 & 74. *Teaching:* Instr fine arts, Vesper George Sch Art, 55-83 & Worchester Art Mus, 70-79. *Awards:* 15 Richard Milton Gold Medals, New Eng Artists Exhib, 54-70; Newington Prize, 66 & 67, Am Artists Prof League; Frederick Thompson Found Award, 76. *Bibliog:* Richard Goetz (auth), Sight sized method, Am Artist, 70. *Mem:* Am Artists Prof League (dir, 60-70); Guild Boston Artists (vpres, 68-73, pres, 73-78); Acad Artists Asn; Copley Soc Boston. *Media:* Oil. *Dealer:* Hammer Galleries 33 W 57th St New York NY. *Mailing Add:* 178 South St Needham MA 02192

HUNTER, ROBERT HOWARD
PAINTER, EDUCATOR
b Auburn, Wash, May 17, 29. *Study:* Ore State Univ, 47-49; Univ Ore, BS & MFA, 49-53; Univ SC, 55-56. *Work:* Ackland Art Ctr, Univ NC, Chapel Hill; Duke Univ, Durham, NC; Greenville Co Mus Art, SC; SC Arts Collection; Pepsico Corp, Purchase, NY. *Exhib:* 159th Ann Painters & Sculptors, Philadelphia, 64; 7th Nat Show Art, Brockton, Mass, 64; Art on Paper, Weatherspoon Art Gallery, NC, 65; 16th Ann Drawing & Small Sculpture Show, Ball State Univ, 70; one-man show, Ackland Art Ctr, Univ NC, Chapel Hill, 68. *Pos:* Gallery dir, Rudolph Lee Gallery, Clemson Univ, 58-68; Ford Found fel, Univ NC, Chapel Hill, 66-67. *Teaching:* Instr figure drawing, Univ Ore, 52-53; prof printmaking, painting & basic design, Clemson Univ, 56-, head dept visual arts 67-71. *Awards:* Guild of SC Artists Awards, 56-63; Springs Art Contest, SC, 61 & 77; 8th Ann Painting of Yr, Atlanta Art Asn, 62. *Mem:* Col Art Asn Am; SC Guild of Artists. *Media:* Acrylic, Wood. *Publ:* Auth, Twenty Lithographs by Robert Hunter, 61; auth, The Shape of R Hunter, 66; illusr, The Binnacle, R Peterson, 67; contribr, Contemporary Artists of South Carolina, 70. *Dealer:* Sound Shore Gallery Stamford Ct. *Mailing Add:* 101 W Park Ave Greenville SC 29601

HUNTER, SAM
HISTORIAN
b Springfield, Mass, Jan 5, 23. *Study:* Williams Col, AB; Univ Florence, cert. *Exhib:* A View from the Sixties: Selections from the Leo Castelli collection and the Michael and Ileana Sonnabend collection (exhib & catalog), Guild Hall Art Mus, East Hampton, NY, 91; The New York School, Arte Americana, 1930-1970, Il Lingotto Mus, Torin, Italy, 92. *Collections Arranged:* Many exhibs at Mus Mod Art, New York, Minneapolis Inst Arts, Rose Art Mus, Jewish Mus, New York & Princeton Art Mus; American Art from the Commodities Collection (catalog), circulating exhib to six Am Mus, 81-82; Aspects of Post-Modernism: Decorative and New Image Art, E R Squibb & Sons Art Galleries, Princeton, NJ, 81; Richard Pousette - Dart, Karel Appel Retrospectives, 86; Mus Art, Ft Lauderdale, Fla, 86-89. *Pos:* Art critic, New York Times, 47-49; ed, Harry N Abrams Inc, New York, 52-53, consult ed, 68-, vpres & ed-in-chief, 71-72; cur, Mus Mod Art, 56-58; dir, Minneapolis Inst Art, 58-60, Rose Art Mus, Brandeis Univ, 60-65 & Jewish Mus, 65-68; fac cur mod art, Princeton Art Mus, 69-; consult, Commodities Corp, Princeton, NJ, 80-; consult & guest cur, Mus Art, Fort Lauderdale, Fla, 85-87; adv, Mus Mod & Contemp Art, Nice, France, 87-89 & M Knoedler & Co, New York, 89-92. *Teaching:* Former instr, Harvard Univ, Univ Calif, Los Angeles, Barnard Col, Columbia Univ & Cornell Univ; asst prof, Univ Calif, Los Angeles, 55-57; assoc prof art hist, Brandeis Univ, 63-65; prof art hist, Princeton Univ, 69-91, emer prof, 91-; Robert Sterling Clark vis prof, Williams Col, 76. *Awards:* Hubbard Hutchinson Fel Critical Studies, Williams Col, 49-52; Guggenheim Fel, 70-71. *Mem:* Col Art Asn Am. *Publ:* Auth, An American Renaissance: Painting & Sculpture Since 1940, 86 & In the Mountains of Japan: The Open Air Museums of Hakone and Utsukushi-Ga-Hara (photogr, David Fin), 88, Abbeville Press; Emerging Art 1990 (exhib catalog), NJ State Mus, Trenton, 90; Larry Rivers, Rizzoli, 90; George Segal, Modern Art: Painting, Sculpture, Architecture, Abrams, 3rd rev ed, 92; Alex Katz & Marino Marini, Arte Americana, 1930-1970, Fabbri, Milan, Italy, 92. *Mailing Add:* 57 Sycamore Lane Skillman NJ 08558-9648

HUNTER-STIEBEL, PENELOPE
ART DEALER, CURATOR
b Washington, DC. *Study:* Barnard Col, BA; Inst Fine Art, NY Univ, MA. *Collections Arranged:* Twentieth Century Decorative Arts Gallery, 71-74 & 78-83, The Grand Gallery Int Exhib (ed, catalog), 74; New Glass Exhib, Metrop Mus Art, 80; The Fine Art of the Furniture Maker (co-auth, catalog), Mem Art Gallery, Rochester, 81; Elements of Style: The Art of the Bronze Mount in the 18th and 19th Century France (auth, catalog), 84, A Bronze Bestiary (auth, catalog), 85 & Menuiserie, the Carved Wood Furniture of 18th Century France, 86, Chez Elle, Chez Lui, At Home in 18th Century France (auth, catalog), 87, Rosenberg & Stiebel Inc; Louis XV & Madame De Pompadour: A Love Affair with Style (auth, catalog), Dixon Gallery, Memphis, Rosenberg & Stiebel; William Beckman: Dossier of a Classical Woman (auth, catalog), Stiebel Mod, Ind Univ Art Mus, 91. *Pos:* Asst cur, Metrop Mus Art, 75-80, assoc cur, 80-83; contrib cur, Philbrook Art Ctr, Tulsa, 82-87; guest cur, Detroit Inst Arts, 83-85; principal, Rosenberg & Steibel Inc, 86- *Res:* Sixteenth through twentieth century decorative arts. *Publ:* Auth, Contemporary art glass, Art News, summer 81; Gustav Serrurier-Bovy, a forgotten master of Art Nouveau, Connoisseur, 11/82; The transcendent materialism of Albert Paley, Mus Fine Arts, Springfield, Mass, 85; Four masters of art deco, Antiques, 8/85; French Furniture of the Eighteenth Century by Pierre Verlet, Univ Press Va, 91; and others. *Mailing Add:* 32 E 57th St New York NY 10022

HUNTINGTON, JIM
SCULPTOR
b Elkhart, Ind, Jan 13, 41. *Study:* Ind Univ, Bloomington, 58-59; El Camino Col, 59-60. *Work:* Addison Gallery Am Art, Andover, Mass; Rose Art Mus, Brandeis Univ; Smith Col Mus, Northampton, Mass; Whitney Mus Am Art, New York; Oakland Mus, Calif; and others. *Comn:* IBM Corp, San Jose, Calif; Insurance Co NAm, Wilmington, Del; Hahn Co, Santa Rosa, Calif. *Exhib:* Corcoran Gallery Art Biennial, Washington, DC & traveling, 65 & 67; Whitney Mus Am Art Painting Ann, 68 & Sculpture Ann, 69; one-man show, Hayden Gallery, Mass Inst Technol, 68, Max Hutchinson Gallery, New York, 71, Parker 470 Gallery, Boston, 72, David McKee Gallery, New York, 75 & 80, Leah Levy Gallery, San Francisco, 80 & 82 & Gallery Paule Anglim, San Francisco, 85; Indiana Influence, Ft Wayne Mus Art, Ind, 84; Princeton Faculty Show, NJ, 85; Boston Arts Festival, 85; Stephen Wirtz Gallery, San Francisco, 88, 89, 91 & 92; Pence Gallery, Los Angeles, 88; and others. *Teaching:* Instr art, Cooper Union, 68 & Hunter Col, 70-72, New York & Princeton Univ, NJ, 78. *Awards:* Grand Prize Award, Sheraton-Boston Competition & Blanche Colman Award, Boston, 65; Nat Endowment Arts Fel, 80-81 & 84-85; Pollock-Krasner Found Grant, 86; Adolph & Esther Gottlieb Found Grant, 86. *Media:* Stone, Cast Iron. *Mailing Add:* 715 Driggs Ave Brooklyn NY 11211

HUNTLEY, DAVID C
PAINTER, ADMINISTRATOR
b Lenoir, NC, Oct 17, 30. *Study:* Univ NC, AB & MACA; Univ Calif, Berkeley; JFK Univ. *Exhib:* City Art Mus St Louis, Mo, 66; Raymond Ducan Gallery, Paris, 66; Ligoa Duncan Gallery, New York, 67; Peoria Art Ctr, 68; Wesleyan Col, Macon, Ga, 69; and many other group & one-man shows. *Pos:* Dir, Univ Mus, Southern Ill Univ, Edwardsville, currently. *Teaching:* Instr hist art, design & art, Limestone Col; prof art, Ala Col, Montevallo; prof & chmn art & design dept, Southern Ill Univ, Edwardsville, formerly. *Awards:* Johnson Award, Birmingham Mus Art, 58; NC Mus Award, Raleigh, 60; Soc Independent Artists St Louis, 66; and others. *Mem:* Mid Am Col Art Asn; Nat Conf Art Admin; Am Asn Univ Prof; St Louis Area Mus Collab (bd dirs); Asn Col & Univ Mus & Galleries (bd dirs); Mid-Am Col Art Asn. *Publ:* Coauth, Louis H Sullivan Architectural Ornament Collection. *Mailing Add:* Univ Mus Southern Ill Univ Box 1150 Edwardsville IL 62026

HUNTOON, ABBY E
SCULPTOR, CRAFTSMAN
b Providence, RI, Sept 8, 51. *Study:* Boston Univ, MFA(ceramics), 83. *Exhib:* Ceramics Now, 27th Ceramic Nat Exhib, Everson Mus, Syracuse, NY, 87-89; Tenth Ann Exhib, Maine Coast Artist, Rockport, 89; 46th Ceramics Ann, Lang Art Scripts Col, Claremont, Calif, 90; one-woman show, Frick Gallery, Belfast, Maine, 90; Frick Gallery, Belfast, Maine, 92. *Awards:* Nat Endowment Arts Visual Artists Grant, 88. *Mem:* Maine Art Comn. *Dealer:* Frick Gallery 139 High St Belfast ME 04915. *Mailing Add:* c/o Sawyer Street Studio 131 Sawyer St South Portland ME 04106

HUOT, ROBERT
PAINTER, FILMMAKER
b Staten Island, NY, Sept 16, 35. *Study:* Wagner Col, Staten Island, 53-57, BSc, 57; Hunter Col, grad art, New York, 61-62. *Work:* Frank Stella, NY; Paula Cooper, New York; William Rubin Collection, New York; Doberman Collection, Munster, Ger; Mus of Mod Art, New York, NY. *Exhib:* Systematic Painting, Guggenheim Mus, New York, 66; The Art of the Real Traveling Exhib, 68 & Recent Acquisitions, 78, Mus Mod Art, New York; Whitney Painting Ann, Whitney Mus, New York, 67 & 69; New Art USA, Mod Mus of Art, Minchem, WGer, 68; Seattle Art Mus, Wash, 69; Modular Painting, Albright-Knox Gallery, Buffalo, NY, 70; one-man shows, Paula Cooper Gallery, New York, 69-74, Millennium, New York, 75 & 79 & State Univ of NY, Albany, 76; Utica Col, 79-80; Hetzler Galerie, WGer, 80-81. *Pos:* Pigment chemist, Sun Chemical Co, Staten Island, 57-58 & 60-62; plant mgr, Neti Art Color, New York, 62-63. *Teaching:* Assoc prof painting, drawing & filmmaking, Hunter Col, New York, 63-81. *Awards:* Nat Coun Arts Grant, New York, 66 & with Twyla Tharp Dance Co, 77. *Bibliog:* S MacDonald (auth), article, 4/79 & An interview with Robert Huot, 2/80, Afterimage. *Media:* Unstretched Canvas; Film. *Dealer:* Filmmakers Coop 175 Lexington Ave New York NY 10016; Max Hetzler Stuttgart WGer. *Mailing Add:* Spurr St RD 1 Box 41 New Berlin NY 13411

HUPP, FREDERICK DUIS
PAINTER, EDUCATOR
b Streator, Ill, Dec 21, 38. *Study:* Univ Ariz, BFA, 62, MFA, 66. *Work:* Tucson Mus Art, Ariz. *Exhib:* Univ Man, Winnipeg, 76; SW Biennial, Mus NMex, Santa Fe, 76; Eight State West Biennial, Grand Junction, Colo, 76; Four Corners Biennial, Phoenix, Ariz, 77; Univ Ariz Art Mus, Tucson, 79; and others. *Pos:* Cur, Univ Ariz Art Mus, 60-61 & Mus Fine Arts, Santa Fe, 62; instr, Fenster Ranch Sch, Tucson, 64-65. *Teaching:* Instr design, Univ Ariz, 68-79; asst prof drawing & painting, Tucson Mus Sch, 68-80, dir educ, 68-70; instr design & drawing, Pima Col, Tucson, 77- *Awards:* Eight West State Biennial Cash Award, Grand Junction, Colo, 74; Four Corners Biennial Cash Award, Phoenix, Ariz, 75; Cash Award, Cedar City Nat, Utah, 76. *Media:* Acrylic, Mixed. *Mailing Add:* 743 N Tenth Ave Tucson AZ 85705

HUPY, ART
CURATOR, PHOTOGRAPHER
b Seattle, Wash, July 8, 24. *Study:* Univ Wash, 46-47; Art Ctr Sch (photog), Los Angeles, Calif, 51-52. *Work:* Whatcom Co Mus, Bellingham, Wash. *Comn:* Logo design, South Seattle Community Col, 70; ten photog murals, Wash Fed Savings, Mt Vernon, 83. *Exhib:* Brussels World's Fair, 58; US Info Agency Exhib, Moscow, USSR, 59; San Francisco Mus Mod Art, 59; Seattle World's Fair, 62; retrospective, Henry Art Gallery, Univ Wash, Seattle, 71; Tacoma Art Mus, Wash, 75; Whatcom Co Mus, Bellingham, 78; Aperature 78, Univ Calif, Berkeley. *Collections Arranged:* Tobey Reflection, Tsutakawa is 75 & Small Treasures of the Northwest Artists, Valley Mus NW Art, La Conner, Wash, 81-86; Skagit Valley Artists (8 shows), Skagit Valley Col Gallery, 81-84. *Pos:* Owner, Arts Gallery, La Conner, Wash, 77-81; founder & dir, La Conner Art Workshops, 78-, Arts Alive, La Conner, 84; founder & cur, Valley Mus NW Art, La Conner, Wash, 81-90, Docent Prog, 81-90, dir & cur, 81-90; dir, Paint La Conner with Jazz, 78-91. *Teaching:* Instr, Burnley Sch Com Art, 60-62, Bush Sch, 68-72, Seattle Community Col, 69 & Quillayute Color Clinic, 74, Wash. *Awards:* 13 advertising art awards Los Angeles & Seattle. *Bibliog:* Paint La Conner with Jazz (film), 78; Various newspaper articles 70-90. *Mem:* Am Soc Mag Photogr; Nat Soc Art Dirs. *Publ:* Publ, Advent Mag, 59; plus numerous photog articles in national mags. *Mailing Add:* Box 557 La Conner WA 98257

HUREWITZ, FLORENCE K
PAINTER, EDUCATOR
b Passaic, NJ. *Study:* Cooper Union Sch Art & Archit, BFA, 76; Art Students League; Am Art Sch. *Work:* Bergen Community Mus, Paramus, NJ. *Exhib:* Biannual Show, NJ State Mus, Trenton, NJ; Invitational for Prize Winners, Jersey City Mus, NJ; American Drawing Biennial, Norfolk Mus Art, Va; Nat Asn Women Artists Travel Oil Show, Pallazzo Vechio, Florence, Italy; Audubon Artists, Nat Acad, New York. *Pos:* Designer stained glass, Rambusch & Co, New York; asst exhib cur, Cooper Union Mus. *Teaching:* Inst fine art painting, Bergen Community Col, Paramus, NJ, 73-85; Art Ctr of N NJ, New Milford, 85- *Awards:* Medal of Honor, Nat Asn Women Artists, 75; Medal of Honor, Nat Asn Women Artists, 86; Jersey City Museum Medal, Painters & Sculptors Soc. *Bibliog:* David Spengler (auth), Woman as an Artist, Bergen Record, 74; Kathy Damecker (auth), Studio Visit--F Hurewitz, Cablevision, NJ, 82; Eileen Watkins (auth), Woman on the Verge, Star Ledger, Newark, 89. *Mem:* Col Art Asn; Nat Asn Women Artists; Womans Caucus for Arts; Artist's Equity of New York. *Media:* Oil. *Dealer:* Kornbluth Gallery Fairlawn Ave Fairlawn NJ 07410. *Mailing Add:* 0-95 Midland Ave Fairlawn NJ 07410

HURLEY, DENZIL H
PAINTER, PRINTMAKER
b Barbados, West Indies, Jan 16, 49. *Study:* Portland Mus Art Sch, BFA, 75; Yale Univ, MFA, 79. *Work:* Brooklyn Mus Art, NY; Metrop Mus Art, New York; San Francisco Mus Mod Art, Calif; Portland Art Mus, Ore. *Comn:* Murals, 76 & 77, prints, 76, City of Portland, Ore. *Exhib:* Oregon Print Annual, Portland Art Mus, 75; 21st Print Biannual, 78-79, 22nd Print Biannual, 81-82, Brooklyn Mus, New York; New Geometry, Del Ctr for Contemp Art, 89. *Teaching:* Lectr printmaking, Yale Sch Art, 79-83; asst prof painting, Scripts Col & Claremont Grad Sch, 84-86; from asst to assoc prof, Hampshire Col, 86- *Awards:* Guggenheim Fel, 80; Pollock-Krasner Found Grant, 89; Nat Endowment Arts Fel, 89. *Bibliog:* Colin Gardner (auth), article, Los Angeles Times, 7/25/86. *Mem:* Col Art Asn. *Media:* Oil; Etching. *Publ:* Contribr, Perspecta 19, MIT Press, 82. *Dealer:* Jack Tilton Gallery 24 W 57th St New York NY 10019; Burnett Miller Gallery 964 N LaBrea Los Angeles CA. *Mailing Add:* 500 West 7 Amherst MA 01002

HURLEY, WILSON
PAINTER
b Tulsa, Okla, Apr 11, 24. *Study:* US Mil Acad, BS, 45; George Washington Univ Law Sch, LLB, 51. *Work:* Fairchild Hall, US Air Force Acad; US Air Force Mus, Wright-Patterson AFB, Ohio; Buffalo Bill Hist Ctr, Cody, Wyo; Nat Cowboy Hall Fame, Okla City; Gilcrease Mus, Tulsa, Okla. *Comn:* Mural (triptych), Metrop Libr, Midwest City, Okla; Albuquerque (diptych), Int Airport. *Exhib:* Nat Acad Western Art, Oklahoma City, 73-88; solo exhibs, Nat Cowboy Hall Fame, 77 & Thomas Gilcrease Mus, Tulsa, 83; solo: retrospective Albuquerque Mus Art & Whitney Mus Western Art, Cody, Wyo, 85; Artists of America, Denver, 81-88. *Teaching:* Scottsdale Artists Sch, 84 & 87. *Awards:* Silver Medal, 73 & 80 & Gold Medal, 77, 78 & 84, Nat Acad Western Art; Prix de West, Nat Acad Western Art, 84. *Bibliog:* Lowell Press, 77; Gilcrease Mag Am Hist & Art, Vol 5, No 2, 83; A retrospective exhib, Lowell Press, 85. *Mem:* Nat Acad Western Art (exec comt, 75-81 & 85-87). *Media:* Oil. *Publ:* Illusr, Without Noise of Arms, Briggs, Northland, 75. *Dealer:* Lloyd M Taggart 64 W Ricks Creek Way Centerville UT 84014; Fenn Gallery Santa Fe NM. *Mailing Add:* 237 Spring Creek Ct NE Albuquerque NM 87122

HURLSTONE, ROBERT WILLIAM
GLASS ARTIST, EDUCATOR
b Chicago, Ill, June 3, 52. *Study:* Ill State Univ, BS, 74; Southern Ill Univ, MFA, 78. *Work:* Corning Mus Glass, NY; Am Crafts Mus, NY; Rahr-West Mus & Civic Ctr, Manitowoc, Wis; Ind Univ Art Mus, Bloomington. *Exhib:* New Glass Traveling Exhib, 78-; Art for Use, Olympics Exhib, Lake Placid & Am Crafts Mus, NY, 80; Small group, Sales Gallery Show, Smithsonian Inst, Washington DC, 80; Ohio Glass Artists, Massillon Mus, Ohio, 80; one-man show, New Works, Habatat Gallery, Mich, 81; American Glass Now, III, touring Japan, 81- *Teaching:* Asst prof glass, 3-D design, Bowling Green State Univ, 78- *Awards:* Mus Dirs Award, Evansville Mus, 77; Third Place Award, Toledo Mus, 81. *Bibliog:* Terri Sharp (auth), Artist profile, Art Craft Mag; Portfolio Section, Am Craft Mag; Photograph of work, Village Voice. *Mem:* Glass Art Soc; Ohio Designer Craftman. *Media:* Glass. *Mailing Add:* Sch of Art Fine Arts Bldg Bowling Green State Univ Bowling Green OH 43403

HURSON, MICHAEL
DRAFTSMAN, PAINTER
b Youngstown, Ohio, 1941. *Study:* Art Inst Chicago, BFA, 63; Oxbow Summer Sch Painting, Saugatuck, Mich, 60 & 61; Yale Univ, Norfolk, Conn, 62. *Work:* Art Inst Chicago; Guggenheim Mus, Whitney Mus Am Art & Metrop Mus Art, New York; Nat Gallery Australia, Canberra. *Exhib:* Chicago & Vicinity, Art Inst Chicago, 61, 63, 64 & 73, Small Scale in Contemp Art, Soc for Contemp Art, 75 & Drawings of the 70's, 77; one-man shows, Mus Contemp Art, Chicago, 72, Mus Mod Art, New York, 74, Daniel Weinberg Gallery, San Francisco, 80, Paula Cooper Gallery, New York, 82, 85-87, 89 & 91, Heath Gallery, Atlanta, Ga, 86, New Prints and Working Proofs, Joe Fawbush Ed, New York, 87; Recent Acquisitions, Metrop Mus Art, New York, 74 & 20th Century Recent Acquisitions, 79; Nine Artists: Theodoron Awards, S R Guggenheim Mus, New York, 77; Am Art Since 1950, Whitney Mus Am Art, New York, 78, Art About Art, 78, New Image Painting, 78, Archit Analogues, 78 & Artists by Artists, 79; Summer Light, Mus Mod Art, New York, 81; New Dimensions in Drawing, Aldrich Mus, 81, Made in New York, City Gallery, New York, 82; Corcoran Gallery Art, Wash, DC, 86; Height x Length x Width: Contemporary Sculpture from the Weatherspoon Collection, Weatherspoon Art Gallery, Univ NC, Greensboro, 91; Art of Our Time-1991, Temple Emanuel, Woodcliff Lake, 91; Act up Benefit Exhib, Matthew Marks, New York, 91; White Columns Benefit Gala and Silent Auction 1992, White Columns, New York, 92; Drawing New Conclusions, Art Inst Chicago, 92; var exhibs at major mus incl Inst Contemp Art, Corcoran Gallery Art, Whitney Mus Am Art; and others. *Awards:* Nat Endowment Arts Grant, 74-75; Theodoron Award, Guggenheim Mus, 77; Vaklova Purchase Award, Mus Contemp Art, Chicago, 80. *Bibliog:* David Salle (auth), New image painting, Flash Art, 3-4/79; Reagen Upshaw (auth), Chicago: Michael Hurson at Dart, Art Am, 9/81; Edward L Saxe (auth), On the margin of society, Am Artists, 9/81; Prudence Carlson (auth), Arch Limner: Michael Hurson, Art in Am, summer 82. *Mailing Add:* c/o Paula Cooper Gallery 155 Wooster St New York NY 10012

HURST, LYNN
PAINTER
b Denver, Colo, 55. *Study:* Eastern Ky Univ, Richmond, BFA, 77; Transylvania Univ, Lexington, Ky; Univ Cincinnati, Ohio; Univ Calif, Santa Barbara, MFA, 82; Pratt Inst, Brooklyn, NY; Univ Ky, Lexington. *Exhib:* Solo shows, Giles Gallery, Eastern Ky Univ, Richmond, 87, Stephen F Austin Univ Gallery, Nacogdoches, Tex, 88, Locus Gallery, St Louis, Mo, 89 & Moody Gallery, Houston, Tex, 89; Galveston Art Ctr, Tex, 91; Sewall Art Gallery, Rice Univ, Houston, Tex, 91; Gallery Dept Art & Art Hist, Univ Nebr, Lincoln, 91; and others. *Teaching:* Lects & workshops, Eastern Ky Univ, Richmond, 87, Stephen F Austin Univ, Nacogdoches, Tex, 88 & Univ Wyo, Laramie, 89. *Awards:* Ford Found Grant, 81; Cult Arts Coun Houston Fel, 89; Nat Endowment Arts Fel, 89. *Bibliog:* Mark Smith (auth), New talent '89, works intrigue and baffle, Austin Am-Statesman, D-3, 5/11/89; Twenty-one Texas artists get fellowships, Houston Chronicle, 8-D, 8/26/89; Shannon Uehling (auth), UNL's art department exhibition colorfully addresses problems, Daily Nebraskan, Lincoln, 9, 2/19/91; and others. *Mailing Add:* c/o Moody Gallery 2815 Colquitt Houston TX 77098

HURST, RALPH N
SCULPTOR, EDUCATOR
b Decatur, Ind, Sept 4, 18. *Study:* Ind Univ, Bloomington, BS & MFA; Ogunquit Sch Painting & Sculpture, Maine, with Robert Laurent. *Work:* Evansville Mus Arts & Sci, Ind; Columbus Mus Arts & Crafts, Ga; Mobile Art Asn Gallery, Ala; Gulf Life Ins Co, Jacksonville, Fla; LeMoyne Art Found Gallery, Tallahassee, Fla. *Comn:* Relief sculpture, Fla State Univ Col Educ, 57; wall relief sculptures, Fla State Univ Union Bldg, Tallahassee, 63; Madonna (sculpture), St Thomas More Cath Church, Tallahassee, 71. *Exhib:* American Sculpture 1951, Metrop Mus Art, New York, 51; Contemporary Sculptors Drawings, Ohio State Univ, 54; Art USA, Madison Sq Garden, New York, 58; Nat Liturgical Art Exhib, San Francisco, 60; Southeastern Art Exhib, High Mus, 67. *Teaching:* Prof art educ & constructive design, Fla State Univ, 53-79, emer prof, 79- *Awards:* Ball Gallery Award, Nat Small Sculpture Exhib, Ball State Univ, 60; Community Purchase Award, Mobile Art Gallery, Ala, 71; Second Award, Maj Fla Artists, Harmon Gallery, Naples, Fla, 79. *Mem:* Artists Equity Asn; Nat Art Educ Asn; Int Sculpture Ctr, Washington, DC. *Media:* Alabaster, Wood. *Dealer:* Foster Harmon Galleries Sarasota FL; Harmon-Meek Gallery Naples FL. *Mailing Add:* c/o Harmon-Meek Gallery II 4262 Gulfshore Blvd Naples FL 33940

HURT, SUSANNE M
PAINTER
b New York, NY. *Study:* Duke Univ; Art Students League, with Frank V Dumond & Kenneth Hayes Miller; Corcoran Sch Art; also with Wayman Adams & A Ginsburg. *Work:* In pvt collections. *Comn:* Portrait, Harold Weill, Weill-Traeger Clinic, New York Hosp, 81; portrait, Col Herbert Nash Dillard, Va Mil Inst Libr, 86; portrait, Claudia Haines Marsh, Pub Welfare Found Inc, Washington, DC, 92. *Exhib:* One-man show, Grist Mill Gallery, Chester, Vt, 76; Cayuga Mus, Auburn, NY, 71; Mus Fine Arts, Springfield, Mass; Hammond Mus, North Salem, NY; Nat Arts Club; and others. *Teaching:* Pvt classes & demonstrations. *Awards:* 1st prize, Anna Hyatt Huntington painting award, 70; Grand Prize, Dept Parks & Recreation, New York, 78; Katherine A Lovell Mem Award, 81; and others. *Mem:* Catharine Lorillard Wolfe Art Club (corresp secy, 71-74); Am Artists Prof League (secy, 87-); Hudson Valley Art Asn; Royal Soc Arts; Nat League Am Pen Women. *Media:* Oil. *Mailing Add:* 299 Riverside Dr New York NY 10025

HURTIG, MARTIN RUSSELL
PAINTER, SCULPTOR
b Chicago, Ill, Aug 11, 29. *Study:* Inst Design Chicago, BS, 52, MS, 57; Atelier 17, Paris, 55. *Work:* Bibliot Nat, Paris; Philadelphia Free Libr; Carroll Reese Mus, Johnson City, Tenn; Honolulu Acad Art; Mus Contemp Art, Chicago. *Comn:* Stained glass windows & mural wall, Union Church, Lake Bluff, Ill, 63; outdoor court sculpture, Waukegan Pub Libr, Ill, 64; lobby relief sculpture, Midwest Iron Works, Chicago, 67. *Exhib:* Nat Print Exhib, Brooklyn Mus, 58 & 68; one-man shows, Flint Inst Arts, 61 & 68, Alonzo Gallery, 66 & 67 & Ecole Spec Archit, Paris, 69; 6th Am Artists Traveling Show, Paris & 12 French cities, 69-70; Jan Cicero Gallery, Chicago, 80, 81 & 83; Mus Mod Art, Paris, 85; Osaka Triennale, Japan, 90. *Teaching:* Asst prof drawing & design, Mich State Univ, 57-62; prof painting, Univ Ill, Chicago, 62-; dir, Sch Art & Design, Univ Ill, Chicago, 82-88, prof painting, currently. *Awards:* Purchase Awards, Carroll Reese Mus, 67 & Honolulu Acad Arts, 71. *Bibliog:* F Schulze (auth), Art news in Chicago, Art News, 11/71; A Goldin (auth), Vitality vs greasy kids stuff, Art Gallery Mag, 4/72; D Guthrie & J Allen (auth), Waging polemical warfare, Chicago Tribune, 4/30/72; Charles Fambro (auth), exhibition review, New Art Examiner, 5/90. *Dealer:* Jan Cicero Gallery 221 W Erie Chicago IL 60610. *Mailing Add:* 1727 Wesley St Evanston IL 60201

HURTUBISE, JACQUES
PAINTER
b Montreal, Que, Feb 28, 39. *Study:* Beaux Art Sch, Montreal, BFA, 60. *Work:* Mass Inst Technol; Peter Stuyvesant Art Found, Amsterdam; Galerie Nat Can, Ont; Art Gallery Ont, Toronto; Vancouver Art Gallery; and others. *Comn:* Murals, Ottawa Univ, 69, Place Radio Can, Montreal, 72 & Ministry of Defense, Ottawa, 72. *Exhib:* 300 Years of Canadian Art, Nat Gallery Can, Ottawa, 67; Art d'Aujourd'Hui, Paris, Rome, Lausanne, Brussels, 68; Seven Montreal Artists, Mass Inst Technol, Cambridge, Gallery Mod Art, Washington & Stratford Festival, Ont, 68; Grand Formats, Musée d'Art Contemporain, Montreal, 70; Birmingham Festival of the Arts, Ala, 79; Mem Univ Art Gallery, St John's, Nfld, 85; Art Gallery, Acadia Univ, Wolfville, NS, 86; Art Gallery NS, Halifax, 86; Beaverbrook Art Gallery, Fredericton, NB, 86; Galerie Restigouche, Campbelton, NB, 87; Confederation Ctr Art Gallery & Mus, Charlottetown, Pei, 87; plus many other one-man & group exhibs. *Pos:* Artist-in-residence, Dartmouth Col, 67. *Awards:* Max Beckmann Scholar, 60; First Prize, Concours Artistique Que, Que Govt, 65; Prize, Expos Hadassah, 68; and others. *Bibliog:* Laurent Lamy (auth), Hurtubise, Lidec, 71. *Mem:* Royal Can Acad Art. *Media:* All. *Mailing Add:* 1226 Chemin Louis Rue St Louis-Terrebonne PQ J0N 1N4 Canada

HURWITZ, MICHAEL H
CRAFTSMAN, MOSAIC ARTIST
b Miami, Fla, Feb 26, 55. *Study:* Boston Univ, BFA, 79. *Work:* Gallery Am Art Renwick Smithsonian, Washington, DC; Mus Fine Arts, Boston, Mass; Mus RI Sch Design, Providence; Art Gallery Yale Univ, New Haven, Conn; Altos De Chavon Found, New York. *Exhib:* New Handmade Furniture, Am Craft Mus, New York, 79; Am Craft Coun Auction, Sothebys, New York, 88; New Am Furniture, Mus Fine Arts, Boston, 89 & Oakland Mus Art, Calif, 90; solo exhibs, Pritam & Eames Gallery, East Hampton, NY, 89 & Peter Joseph Gallery, New York, 92; Masterworks, Peter Joseph Gallery, 91; and others. *Teaching:* Prog head furniture, Univ Arts, Philadelphia, 85-90. *Awards:* Japan Fel 89 & Visual Arts Fel, 90 & 92, Nat Endowment Arts. *Bibliog:* Ed Cooke Jr (auth), New American Furniture, Mus Fine Arts, Boston, 90; Pat Conway (auth), Art For Everyday, Clarkson Potter Pubs, 90; John Updike (auth), Arts & Antiques, 90. *Media:* Furniture Maker, Wood and Other Natural Materials. *Dealer:* Peter Joseph Gallery 745 Fifth Ave New York NY 10151-0407. *Mailing Add:* 234 Market St Philadelphia PA 19106

HURWITZ, SIDNEY J
PAINTER, PRINTMAKER
b Worcester, Mass, Aug 22, 32. *Study:* Sch Worcester Art Mus; Brandeis Univ, BA; Boston Univ, MFA. *Work:* Libr Cong, Washington, DC; Mus Mod Art, New York; DeCordova Mus, Lincoln, Mass; Minneapolis Mus, Minn; Victoria & Albert Mus, London; Nat Mus, Krakow, Poland; and others. *Comn:* Mosaic mural, Skowhegan Sch Art, Maine, 64; ed of woodcuts, Wellesley Col, Mass, 67; six paintings of London, Japan Int Bank, London, 73; ten etchings, Bldg Design & Construction Mag, Chicago. *Exhib:* Am Drawing, Mus Mod Art, New York, 56; Print Biennial, Libr Cong, Washington, DC, 62; Pa Acad, Philadelphia, 64; New Eng Artists, Boston, 71; Martin Sumers Gallery, New York; Mary Ryan Gallery, New York; Franz Bader Gallery, Washington, DC; British Int Print Biennale; and others. *Teaching:* Prof art, Boston Univ, 62- *Awards:* Louis Comfort Tiffany Award,

66; Artist Award, Am Inst Arts & Lett, 69; Mass Found Arts Fel, 76; and others. *Mem:* Col Art Asn Am; Boston Printmakers Soc. *Publ:* Auth, Etchings of Sigmund Abeles, 66 & My woodcut technique, 67, Am Artist; Etchings, Scarecrow Press, 85. *Mailing Add:* Dept Visual Arts Boston Univ Boston MA 02210

HUSEBYE, TERRY L
PHOTOGRAPHER
b El Paso, Tex, Mar 16, 45. *Study:* Univ Wis, Madison, BA, 68, MA, 73, MFA, 79; Univ NM, 73 & 78; studied with Van Deren Coke & Beaumont Newhall. *Work:* Boston Mus Fine Arts; Chicago Art Inst; Int Mus Photog; Mus Mod Art, New York; Corcoran Gallery Art; Dallas Mus Fine Arts; Denver Art Mus. *Exhib:* Solo exhibs, Arco Ctr Visual Art, Los Angeles, 82 & NM Mus Fine Arts, Santa Fe, 82; Summer Light, Light Gallery, New York, 82; Four Color Photographers, Friends Photog, Carmel, Calif, 82; Twentieth Century Photographs from the Museum of Modern Art, Seibu Mus, Tokyo, 82; Color as Form: A History of Color Photography, Corcoran Gallery Art & George Eastman House, Rochester, NY, 82; Contemporary Photography from the Museum Collection, Mus Fine Arts, Houston, 83; Landscapes: Wolf Von Dem Bussche, Terry Husebye, Bernard Plossu, Phoenix Art Mus, 83. *Pos:* Photog coordr, Madison Art Ctr, Wis, 71-72. *Teaching:* Vis lectr, Univ Wis, Madison, 79; vis artist, Kans City Art Inst, 85. *Awards:* Nat Endowment Arts Fel, 81; Guggenheim Fel, 83. *Bibliog:* Contribr, Camera, Lucerne, Switz, 8/74; Dana Asbury (auth), Terry Husebye: Ocotillo Flat, Artspace, fall 82. *Mem:* Soc Photog Educ; Friends Photog. *Dealer:* Etherton Gallery Tucson AZ; Grapestake Gallery San Francisco CA. *Mailing Add:* 2325 Third St Studio 213 San Francisco CA 94107

HUSHLAK, GERALD
COMPUTER ARTIST, PAINTER
b Edmonton, Alta, Feb 15, 45. *Study:* Univ Alta; Univ Calgary, Alta; Univ Calif; Royal Col Art, London, Eng, MARCA. *Work:* Can Coun Art Bank, Ottawa, Ont; San Francisco Mus Mod Art, Calif; Vancouver Art Gallery, BC; Smithsonian Inst, Washington, DC; Alta Art Found. *Exhib:* Glenbow Mus, Calgary; Mendel Mus, Sask; Art Gallery Greater Victoria, BC; York Univ Art Gallery, Toronto; Mus Art Mod, Paris; and others. *Teaching:* Assoc prof painting, Univ Calgary, Alta, 75- *Awards:* Purchase Award, World Print Competition, San Francisco Mus Mod Art, 77. *Bibliog:* Articles, Vanguard Mag, 80, Arts Can, 80, Art Mag & Artweek, 80. *Mem:* Royal Canadian Acad; Royal Can Acad Art. *Media:* Computers; Acrylic. *Mailing Add:* Box 14 Site 24 RR12 Calgary AB T3E 6W3 Canada

HUSTON, PERRY CLARK
CONSERVATOR
b Mo, Jan 4, 33. *Study:* Univ Mo, AB, 55, Medical Sch, 55-57; Nelson Art Gallery, with James Roth, 63-70; special study with Sheldon & Caroline Keck, 68. *Pos:* Assoc conservator, Nelson Art Gallery, 66-70; chief conservator, Kimbell Art Mus, 71- *Teaching:* Supervisor internships, Conserv Grad Progs, Cooperstown & Oberlin Grad Conserv Progs, 72-, teaching consult, 75-77. *Mem:* Fel Am Inst for Conserv Hist & Artistic Works (vpres, 78-79, pres, 80-). *Mailing Add:* 7440 Whitehall Ft Worth TX 76118

HUTCHINGS, LA VERE
PAINTER, INSTRUCTOR
b Idaho Falls, Idaho, Sept 18, 18. *Study:* Brigham Young Univ, 40; Idaho State Col, AA, 41; Chouinard Art Inst, 54-55; Art Students League, 70; John Pike Watercolor Sch, 70; also studied with Sergei Bongart, Jo Rebert & E Hayward Veal. *Work:* Fashion Inst, Los Angeles; Brigham Young Univ Collection; Las Vegas Mus; Laguna Beach Mus. *Comn:* Watercolor, Caldwell Libr Bd, Idaho, 77. *Exhib:* Riverside Mus, Calif, 74 & 76 & 82; Cent Fed Power Plaza Gallery, San Diego, 77; Springville Mus Art, Utah, 77 & 78; Foothills Art Ctr, Golden, Colo, 80; solo exhib, Brigham Young Univ, 83; and others. *Teaching:* Instr, US Armed Forces Inst, Manila, 45-46, Ricks Col, Rexburg, Idaho, 68-69; currently teaching watercolor workshops in various areas of the west. *Awards:* Grumbacher Gold Medal, Ky Watercolor Soc Award & Travel Show, Aqueous, 89; Rex Brandt Award, Watercolor West Mem Show, 88; Art Hardward Award, Rocky Mountain Nat Watermedia Exhib, 92. *Bibliog:* George Hoeper (auth), Gallery features Mother Lode art, Stockton Record, Calif, 8/31/79; Leo Stutzin (auth), A bird to crow about, Modesto Bee, Calif, 11/22/81; Leo Stutzin (auth), Lode watercolorist wins as author too, Modesto Bee, 1/83; La Vere Hutchings paints the Mother Lode, Southwest Art, 1/83; La Vere Hutchings: A love affair, Artwest Mag, 3/4/85; Make your watercolors sing, North Light Pub, 7/86; Beating Foreground Bugaboos, The Artists Mag, 2/91. *Mem:* Nat Watercolor Soc; Watercolor West (vpres, 78-79); Whiskey Painters Am; Soc Western Artists; Midwest Watercolor Soc. *Media:* Watercolor. *Publ:* Basic Watercolor Techniques (included), Northlight Publ Co, 91; Make Your Watercolors Sing, Northlight Publ Co, 86. *Dealer:* Hutchings Gallery Jamestown CA; Haddad's Fine Arts Inc Anaheim CA. *Mailing Add:* PO Box 249 Jamestown CA 95327

HUTCHINS, ROBIN
ART DEALER, GALLERY DIRECTOR
b Newark, NJ, May 26, 38. *Study:* Nat Art Acad, Washington, DC, BFA, 59; Kean Col, Union, NJ, MA, 73. *Teaching:* Lectr, Montclair Hist Soc, NJ, 91; lectr computer art, Fedn, Artists, NJ, 91. *Awards:* ASID Presidential Citation, 90; Daily Point of Lite Presidential Award, AIDS Resource Found, White House, 91. *Mem:* Burgdorf Cult Comn (bd mem, 90-); Maplewood Cult Comn (co-chmn, 88-); Fed Artists NJ; Newark Mus Ballentine House Restoration Comt. *Specialty:* Contemporary American Art. *Mailing Add:* 150 Oakview Ave Maplewood NJ 07040

HUTCHINSON, JANET L
MUSEUM DIRECTOR, COLLECTOR
b Washington, DC, May 2, 17. *Collections Arranged:* Diana Kan, Marc Mellon, Walt Kuhn, Samuel Margolies, Carol Sadowski, Rose W Traines, Carmen Z Simpkins, Nina Buxton, and many others. *Pos:* Owner-dir, Broadlawn Gallery, Camden, Maine, 57-64; cur, Old Merchant's House, New York, 61-62; dir emer, Hist Soc Martin Co, Elliott Mus & House of Refuge, Hutchinson Island, Fla, 65-92. *Mem:* Salmagundi Club, Nat Arts Club, New York. *Publ:* History of Martin County, 75. *Mailing Add:* 1023 NW Spruce Ridge Dr Stuart FL 34994

HUTCHINSON, MAX
ART DEALER, GALLERY DIRECTOR
b Melbourne, Australia, Aug 25, 25. *Study:* Royal Melbourne Inst Technol. *Pos:* Dir, Sculpture Fields, Kenoza Lake, NY, currently. *Specialty:* Contemporary sculpture. *Mailing Add:* c/o Sculpture Fields PO Box 94 Kenoza Lake NY 12750

HUTCHINSON, PETER ARTHUR
CONCEPTUAL ARTIST, ENVIRONMENTAL ARTIST
b London, Eng, Mar 4, 32. *Study:* Univ Ill, BFA, 60. *Work:* Mus Mod Art, New York; Munchengladbach Mus, WGer; Krefeld Mus, Ger; Musée Pompidou, Paris, France; Hoffmann Found, Basel, Switz. *Comn:* Only in America, Sculpture, Philadelphia, 87. *Exhib:* Paricutin Project, John Gibson Gallery, 70; Images: 2 Ocean Projects, 69 & Information, 70, Mus Mod Art; Nature & Art, Krefeld Mus, Haus Lange, Ger, 72; Stedelijk Mus, Amsterdam, 74; Venice Biennale, Am Pavilion, 79; and others; Wilson & Gough Gallery, London, Eng, 89. *Teaching:* Instr, Sch Visual Arts, New York, NY, 77. *Awards:* A & E Gottlieb Found, 87; Nat Endowment Arts Individual Artist Award, 74; Krasner-Pollack Grant, 89. *Bibliog:* Scheldahl (auth), Breadworks as earth works, NY Times, 69; Back to nature, Time, 6/70; James Collins (auth), Story art, New York Mag, 10/74. *Media:* Mixed Media; Organic Materials, Stone. *Publ:* Auth, Earth in upheaval, Arts, 68; Science fiction: an aesthetic for science, Art Int, 68; Is there life on earth, 68 & Foraging: being an account of a hike through the snow-mass wilderness as a work of art, 72, Art Am; Alphabet Cottage Book, OONA Press, Ger, 80; and others. *Mailing Add:* 10 Holway Ave Provincetown MA 02657

HUTCHISON, ELIZABETH S
PAINTER
Study: Otis Art Inst; and with Joseph Mugnaini & Aimee Bourdieu. *Work:* Rice Univ Permanent Collection; Utah State Univ Permanent Collection; Riverside Art Mus Collection, Calif; Am Fedn Social Settlements Permanent Collection, New York; and many others in pvt collections in US & foreign countries. *Exhib:* Nat Watercolor Soc Ann, 66-75; Southern Calif Expo, Del Mar, 69-75; Old Bergen Art Guild, 70-75; Nat Acad Design, New York, 70-72; Nat Watercolor Soc tour of Sweden, 73-74; and many other group & one-man shows. *Awards:* Purchase Award, Watercolor USA, 69, 73 & 74; First Prize in Acrylic, Southern Calif Art for 75, Del Mar; Claire Falkenstein Awards, 73, 78 & 80; and many others. *Mem:* Nat Watercolor Soc (bd mem, 4 yrs, pres, 71-72, juror, 72-73); Women Painters West (juror, 69-72, bd mem, 8 yrs, pres, 73-75). *Media:* Watercolor, Mixed Media. *Dealer:* Albert J Kramer Gallery 3459 Meier St Los Angeles CA 90066. *Mailing Add:* 2200 W Acacia, Apt 404E Hemet CA 92545

HUTCHISON, JANE CAMPBELL
EDUCATOR, HISTORIAN
b Washington, DC, July 20, 32. *Study:* Western Md Col, BA(cum laude), 54; Oberlin Col, MA, 58; Kunsthist Inst, Utrecht, with J G van Gelder, 60-61; Univ Wis, with James S Watrous, PhD, 64. *Work:* Pennell Collection, Libr Cong, Washington, DC. *Exhib:* US Nat Printmakers, Libr Cong, 56. *Collections Arranged:* Dutch & Flemish Paintings from Private Collections, 74 & Graphic Art in the Age of Martin Luther, 83, Elvehjem Mus, Univ Wis, Madison. *Pos:* Libr asst, Toledo Mus Art, Ohio, 58-59; Consult to Rijksprentenkabinet, Amsterdam & Städelsches Kunstinstitut, Frankfurt, 85; consult, Cincinnati Art Mus, 91-92. *Teaching:* Instr art hist, Univ Wis, Madison, 63-64, from asst prof to assoc prof, 64-75, prof, 75- & dept chmn, 77-80 & 92; vis asst prof, Tyler Sch Art, Temple Univ, summer 67. *Awards:* Fulbright Fel, 60-61; Nat Endowment Humanities Grant, 83; Am Coun Learned Soc Grant, 84; Deutscher Akademischer Austauschdienst (DAAD), 89. *Mem:* Col Art Asn; Medieval Acad Am; Midwest Art Hist Soc (secy-treas 81-83, pres 83-); Historians Netherlandish Art; Am Asn Mus. *Res:* Late fifteenth and early sixteenth century Dutch and German engravings. *Publ:* Auth, The Master of the Housebook, Collectors Editions, 72; The housebook master and the Mainz Marienleben, In: A Tribute to Wolfgang Stechow, 76; ed, Early German Artists: The Illustrated Bartsch, plate, Vols 8 & 9, Commentary Vol 9 Part I, Abaris, 80, 81 & 91; auth, Graphic Art in the Age of Martin Luther, Elvehjem Mus, Univ Wis, 83; Ex ungue leonem: The history of the 'Hausbuchmeisterfrage' & The Housebook, Princeton Univ Pres, 85; Albrecht Dürer: A Biography, Princeton Univ Press, 90. *Mailing Add:* Elvehjem Mus Art Univ Wis 800 University Ave Madison WI 53706

HUTSALIUK, LUBO
PAINTER
b Lvov, Ukraine, Apr 2, 23; US citizen. *Study:* Cooper Union Art Sch, 54. *Work:* Palm Springs Desert Mus, Calif; Vt Art Ctr, Manchester; Bibliotheque Nat, Paris, France. *Exhib:* One-man shows, Galerie Norval, Paris, France, 59, Angle du Faubourg, Paris, 63 & Hilde Gerst Gallery, New York, 66; Galerie Royale, Paris, 76; 25 yrs retrospective, USOM Gallery, New York, 80; and others. *Bibliog:* P Imbourg (auth), Art d'Hutsaliuk, J Amateur Art, 64; J Hess Michel (auth), Vibrant paintings of Hutsaliuk, Am Artist, 69. *Mem:* Audubon Artists. *Media:* Oil, Watercolor. *Dealer:* Rolly-Michaux Gallery 943 Madison Ave New York NY 10021. *Mailing Add:* 260 Riverside Dr New York NY 10025

HUTTON, DOROTHY WACKERMAN
DESIGNER, PRINTMAKER
b Cleveland, Ohio, Feb 9, 1899. *Study:* Minneapolis Sch Art, cert; Univ Minn, with Vytlacil, Earl Horter & Hobson Pittman; Acad Andre L'Hote, Paris. *Work:* Smithsonian Inst, Washington, DC; Harvard Univ; and others. *Exhib:* Five Pennell Exhibs, Libr Cong, Washington, DC; Corcoran Gallery Art, Washington, DC; Philadelphia Print Club, Pa; Carnegie Exhib, Pittsburgh; Grand Cent Art Gallery, New York. *Awards:* Silver Medal, Watercolor, Plastic Club, 85. *Mem:* Philadelphia Art Alliance; Am Colorprint Soc (corresp secy, 65-80); Philadelphia Watercolor Club (dir, 65 & 68); Plastic Club. *Media:* All. *Mailing Add:* 203 N Essex Ave Narberth PA 19072

HUTTON, LEONARD
ART DEALER
Pos: Owner & dir, Leonard Hutton Galleries, currently. *Awards:* Presidential Award of Officers Cross (First Class) of Order of Merit, Fed Rep Ger, Bonn, 81. *Mem:* Art Dealers' Asn Am Inc. *Specialty:* German Expressionism and Russian Avant-Garde art. *Mailing Add:* 33 E 74th St New York NY 10021

HUTTON, WILLIAM
MUSEUM CURATOR
b New York, NY, Oct 2, 26. *Study:* Williams Col, BA, 50; Harvard Univ, MA, 52. *Pos:* Asst cur, Toledo Mus Art, 52-65, sr cur, 71-; dir, Currier Gallery Art, 65-68; res staff, Victoria & Albert Mus, London, Eng, 68-71. *Res:* Eighteenth century Meissen porcelain. *Publ:* Ed, Toledo Museum of Art American Paintings, 79. *Mailing Add:* Toledo Mus of Art Box 1013 Toledo OH 43697

HUXTABLE, ADA LOUISE
CRITIC
b New York, NY. *Study:* Hunter Col, AB(magna cum laude); NY Univ; Nine Hon doctorates. *Pos:* Asst cur archit & design, Mus Mod Art, New York, 46-50; contrib ed, Progressive Archit Art in Am, 50-63; archit critic, New York Times, 63-83, mem ed bd, 73-82. *Awards:* Elsie de Wolfe Award, Am Inst Interior Designers, 69; Pulitzer Prize for Distinguished Criticism, 70; Nat Arts Club Lit Award, 71; Macarthur Fel, 82; and others. *Mem:* Am Soc Archit Historians. *Publ:* Auth, Pier Luigi Nervi, Braziller, 60; auth, Classic New York, 64; auth, Will They Ever Finish Bruckner Boulevard?, Macmillan, 70; auth, Kicked A Building Lately?, 76. *Mailing Add:* 33 Neptune Rd Marblehead MA 01945

HYAMS, HARRIET
STAINED GLASS ARTIST, SCULPTOR
b Jersey City, NJ, June 5, 29. *Study:* Rutgers Univ, BA, 50; Columbia Univ, MA, 72; with Zorach, J Hovannes, Marshall Glaser, Lorrie Goulet. *Comn:* mural, Hallmark Bldg, Houston, Tex, 72; stained glass windows, SW Ohio Senior Citizens Inc, Springdale, Ohio, 77; stained glass windows, City of New York, Staten Is, NY, 82; stained glass windows, Saint Vartanantz Church, Ridgefield, NJ, 83; stained glass wall, Harcourt Brace Jovanovich, Orlando, Fla, 84; stained glass skylight for sailing yacht, pvt comn, 91. *Exhib:* Glass America, Lever House, New York, 78; Stained Glass Int, New York, 82; Glass America, New York, 84; one-person show, Harriet Hyams: Stained glass and sculpture, Rockland Ctr Arts, Nyack, NY, 88. *Teaching:* Instr stained glass, Columbia Univ, 72-74. *Awards:* Purchase Award, Columbia Univ, Arthur Wesley Dow, 72; Compendium 1976, Corning Mus, 76. *Bibliog:* Yehuda Yaviv (auth), Film on Stained Glass, Ed Devel Corp, 72; Richard Avidon (auth), Harriet Hyams, Bergdorf Goodman, Glass Arts Mag, 76; Noel Frackman (auth), Review in arts, Arts Mag, 76. *Mem:* Stained Glass Asn Am; NY Experimental Glass workshop; Artist Craftsmen NY. *Media:* Stained Glass. *Publ:* Auth, A sculptor turns to stained glass, Stained Glass, 82; The Chairman's Office, 85-86; From Gallery to Gallery, Stained Glass Quart, summer 89. *Mailing Add:* PO Box 178 Palisades NY 10964

HYDE, ALICE BACH
GRAPHIC ARTIST, PAINTER
b Montgomery, Ala, Jan 7, 39. *Study:* Auburn Univ, Ala, BA, 61; studied with Edgar Whitney, Henry Hensche, Jim Gray, Ed Carlos, Tony Couch, & George Shook. *Work:* Blount Art Collection, First Ala Bank, Weil Brothers Collection, Montgomery, Ala; Walt Disney Art Collection, Orlando; Columbus Mus Art, Ga. *Exhib:* Festival of the Masters, Disney World, Orlando, 88, 90 & 91; Coconut Grove Art Festival, Fla, 88-90 & 92; Ashland Area Gallery, Invitational Only for Award Winners, 90; Beaux Arts Festival of Art, Miami, 90-91; Mainsail Festival of Art, St Petersburg, Fla, 90-91; and others. *Pos:* Illusr State of Ala, 72-86; prof painter, 86- *Awards:* Poster Artist, Winter Park Sidewalk Art Festival, City of Winter Park, 88; Columbus Club Award Excellence, Pastel Soc Am, New York, 89; Award Excellence, Mainsail Festival Art, Festival Comt, 91. *Media:* Pastel. *Dealer:* Art Works Orlando 110 W Colonial Dr Orlando FL 32801. *Mailing Add:* 110 Ichabod Trail Longwood FL 32750

HYDE, SCOTT
PHOTOGRAPHER, PRINTMAKER
b Montevideo, Minn, Oct 10, 26. *Study:* Art Ctr Sch, Los Angeles; Columbia Univ, with Ralph Mayer; Art Students League. *Work:* Mus Mod Art, Metrop Mus Art, Int Ctr Photog, New York; Int Mus Photog, Rochester, NY; Bibliot Nat, Paris. *Exhib:* Synthetic Color, Southern Ill Univ, Carbondale, 74; Mirrors & Windows: Am Photog Since 1960, 78; Master Photogrs Focus Gallery, San Francisco, 81; Off the Press, Col Art Gallery, State Univ New York, New Paltz, 84; City Light, Int Ctr Photog, 86; and others. *Teaching:* Adj prof photog, Cooper Union, 68-70, New York Univ Exten, 71-72 & Manhattanville Col, 72-75. *Awards:* Guggenheim Fel, 65; Creative Artists Pub Serv Prog Grants, 72 & 75. *Bibliog:* Syl Labrot (auth), Scott Hyde photographs, Aperture, 70; Thomas Dugan (auth), Photography between covers, Light Impressions, 75; Naomi Rosenblum (auth), A World History of Photography, 84. *Media:* Offset Lithography. *Publ:* CAPS Book, 75; Auth, Dust Map, 79; auth, The Real Great Society Album, 79. *Mailing Add:* 7411 Dreyfuss Dr Amarillo TX 79121

HYLAND, DOUGLAS K S
MUSEUM DIRECTOR
b Salem, Mass, Oct 7, 49. *Study:* Univ Pa, BA, 70; Univ Del, MA, 76, PhD, 80. *Pos:* Cur painting & sculpture, Spencer Mus Art, Univ Kans, 79-82; dir, Memphis Brooks Mus Art, 82-84; dir, Birmingham Mus Art, 84-91, San Antonio Mus Art, 92- *Teaching:* Asst prof art hist, Univ Kans, 79-82; vis prof, Southwestern Univ, Memphis, 83-84 & Univ Ala, 84- *Awards:* Fels, Kress Found, 78 & Smithsonian Inst, 78-79 & 92; Chevalier Des Arts Et Lettres, 90. *Mem:* Col Art Asn; Asn Art Mus; AAMD; SEMC. *Res:* American and European painting and sculpture of the 19th and 20th centuries. *Publ:* Agnes Ernst Meyer and the avant garde in America, Am Art J, 79; Thomas Hart Benton, 80, Sculpture Catalog, 81 & Marius deZayas: Conjurer of Souls, 81, Spencer Mus Art, Univ Kans; Adelheid Roosevelt: American cubist, J Arch Am Art, 82; Lorenzo Bartolint & American Sculptors, 86; Birmingham Photography Proj, 88. *Mailing Add:* 200 W Jones Ave San Antonio TX 78215

HYMAN, ISABELLE
HISTORIAN, EDUCATOR
b New York, NY, April 19, 30. *Study:* Vassar Col, BA, 51; Columbia Univ, MA, 55; Inst Fine Arts, NY Univ, MA, 66, PhD, 68. *Teaching:* From instr to assoc prof, NY Univ, 63-79, prof hist art, 79- *Awards:* Fel, Villa I Tatti, Florence, 72-73; John Simon Guggenheim Mem Found Fel, 88-89; Fel, Graham Found Advanced Studies Fine Arts, 88-89. *Mem:* Col Art Asn; Soc Archit Historians; Renaissance Soc Am. *Res:* Art and architecture in Renaissance Florence; archit of Marcel Breuer. *Publ:* Ed, Brunelleschi in Perspective, Prentice-Hall, 74; auth, Fifteenth Century Florentine Studies, Garland, 77; articles relating to Italian Renaissance art in scholarly journals; co auth, Architecture: From Pre-History to Post Modernism, Harry N Abrams Inc, 86. *Mailing Add:* Fine Arts Dept 303 Main Bldg NY Univ New York NY 10003

HYMAN, LINDA
ART DEALER, HISTORIAN
b Buffalo, NY, May 11, 40. *Study:* Vassar Col, 58-60; Columbia Univ, with Barbara Novak, BA, 61, MA, 63; City Univ New York Grad Ctr, with Milton Brown, PhD, 78. *Collections Arranged:* New York Crystal Palace, City Univ New York Grad Ctr, 74; Gertrude Greene (auth, catalog), 81, Ernest Fiene (auth, catalog), 81 & Social Art in America 1930-1945 (auth, catalog), 81, ACA Galleries, New York; Arthur Lindberg (auth, catalog), 87 & Oscar Bluemner (auth, catalog), 88, Linda Hyman Fine Arts, New York. *Pos:* Historian, Metrop Mus Mod Art, 67-71; staff, ACA Galleries, 78-82; pvt art dealer & consult, 82- *Teaching:* Asst prof art hist, City Univ New York, Richmond Col, Staten Island, 73-76, Emory Univ, Atlanta, Ga, 76-78. *Specialty:* American and European art, 20th century. *Publ:* Auth, Winslow Homer: America's Old Master, Doubleday, 73; Hiram Powers' Greek slave: High art as popular culture, Art J, 75; American Modernist Landscapes: The Spirit of Cezanne, Linda Hyman Fine Arts, 89. *Mailing Add:* 172 W 79th St New York NY 10024

HYSON, JEAN
PAINTER
b Alvarado, Tex, Mar 4, 33. *Study:* NY Univ with William Baziotes, 52; Art Students League with Yasuo Kuniyoshi, George Grosz & Harry Sternberg, 52-56. *Work:* Walter Barriese Collection, Metromedia, New York; Oakland Art Mus, Calif; Int Banking Ctr, Sutro, Madison & Pillsbury, San Francisco, Calif; City of San Francisco; Levi-Strauss, San Francisco; Container Corp Am, Chicago; Santa Barbara Mus, Calif; Bill Graham, San Francisco. *Exhib:* One-person shows, San Francisco Mus Art, 67, Calif Palace of the Legion of Honor, 69, William Sawyer Gallery, San Francisco, 72, Richmond Art Mus, Calif, 77, Calif Med Asn, 87 & Nat Small Painting Exhib, Boise State Univ, Idaho, 91; Fine Arts Contemp Exhib, Northern Ill Univ, 69; Mus Mod Art Rental & Sales Gallery, New York, 71; California Artists, Western Art Mus Asn, 70 & 92; Collectors Gallery, Oakland Mus, 86. *Teaching:* Instr, Calif Col Arts & Crafts, Oakland. *Awards:* Adolph & Esther Gottlieb Found Grant, 91. *Mem:* Artists Equity Asn, Washington, DC; Mechanics Inst San Francisco. *Media:* Oil, Acrylic. *Mailing Add:* No 5 950 Franklin San Francisco CA 94109

I

IACURTO, FRANCESCO
PAINTER, INSTRUCTOR
b Montreal, Que, Sept 1, 08. *Study:* Fine Arts Sch Montreal; Grande Chaumiere Colarossi, Paris, France, govt scholar; and with Charles Maillard, Ed Dyonnet, John Y Johnstone & others. *Work:* Prov Mus Que; Can House, London, Eng; House of Senate, Ottawa; Rideau Hall, Gov Gen Can; Lt Gov, Que. *Comn:* Fall landscapes, Bank Montreal, London, 71; painting, Janin Construction, Que, 71; pastel, Can Govt, Ottawa, 71; portraits, Louis Albert Vachon, Québec Seminary & Larkin Kerwin, Laval Univ; portraits, ex-Lieutenant Governor Jean Pierre Côté, Mr Richard Guay, Speaker of Parliament, Québec. *Exhib:* Royal Can Acad, Toronto, Ont, 48 & 51 &

Montreal, 60; Spring Exhib, Montreal Mus Art, 52 & 53. *Teaching:* Instr drawing, Cath Sch Comn, 29-33 & Art & Trades Montreal, 29-38; instr painting, Libr Ste Foy, Que, 66- *Awards:* First Medal Art, 28 & Scholar to Europe, 29, Govt Que; Silver Medal, Ministry Exterior, France, 29. *Mem:* Royal Can Acad Arts; Soc Artists Prof Que; Independent Art Asn. *Dealer:* Michel de Kerdour Québec City PQ Can; Arts & Styles 896 Sherbrooke St W Montreal PQ Can. *Mailing Add:* 1232 La Vigerie Quebec PQ G1W 3W7 Canada

IANNETTI, PASQUALE FRANCESCO PAOLO
ART DEALER, COLLECTOR
b Florence, Italy, Apr 10, 40; US citizen. *Study:* Univ Florence; Acad di Belle Arti, Florence; Univ Minn, Minneapolis. *Pos:* Pres, Pasquale Iannetti Inc Galleries, San Francisco. *Teaching:* Lectr fine prints, Col Marin, Kentfield & Univ Calif, Davis. *Mem:* Int Soc Appraisers; Graphic Art Coun, Los Angeles Co Mus & Achenbach Found, San Francisco; Museo Italo Americano, San Francisco (bd dirs). *Specialty:* Fine original prints, drawings and other unique works form the sixteenth century through the twentieth century. *Collection:* Contemporary prints, drawings and paintings; Pre-Columbian and African art; antiquities. *Mailing Add:* 522 Sutter St San Francisco CA 94102

IANNONE, DOROTHY
PAINTER, WRITER
b Boston, Mass, Aug 9, 33. *Study:* Boston Univ BA(phi beta kappa), 57; Brandeis Univ, studied literature & criticism with J V Cunningham, Phillip Rahv & Irving Howe, 58. *Work:* Nat Women's Mus, Washington, DC; Mus Drawings & Prints (Kupferstichkabinet), Berlin, Ger; Ludwig Mus Collection, Aachen, Germany; Bibliotheque Nationale, Paris, France; Kunst Mus, Basel, Switz. *Exhib:* Boxes (Boites), Mus Mod Art, Paris, France, 76; Daily Bul, Fondation Maeght-St Paul De Vence, Mus Mod Art, Paris, France, 76; Dorothy Iannone, Ludwig Mus (Neue Galerie Stadt Aachen), Ger, 80; Listening with the Eyes, Mus Mod Art, Paris, France, 80; Artists' Books, Centre Pompidou (Beaubourg), Paris, France, 85; The Caravan Passes And, Mus Mod & Contemp Art, Nice, France, 91. *Awards:* Berlin Artists' Prog (Deutscher Akademischer Austauschdienst), 76; Senate for Sci & Art Grant, Berlin, 84; Art Found Bonn Grant, 88. *Bibliog:* Barbara Schnierle (auth), Dorothy Iannone, Kunstforum Int, 8/82; Andreas Kaps (auth), Hippy Pattern Handmade, Tageszeitung, Berlin, 3/89; Barbara Wien (auth), John Lennon & Cleopatra, Tip, Berlin, 6/89. *Media:* Acrylic, Gouache. *Publ:* Auth, Story of Bern, Dieter Rot, Dusseldorf, 70; The Berlin Beauties, Mary Dorothy Verlag, Berlin, 78; Dorothy Iannone & Her Mother Sarah Pucci, Ludwig Mus, Aachen, Ger, 80; The Whip, Rainer Verlag, Berlin, 80; Censorship and the Irrepressible Drive Toward Love & Divinity, Ars Viva, Berlin, 82. *Dealer:* Michael Haas Gallery Niebuhrstrasse 5 1000 Berlin 12 Germany. *Mailing Add:* c/o DAAD Jaeger Strasse 23 Berlin 0-1080 Germany

IDA, SHOICHI
PAINTER, PRINTMAKER
b Kyoto, Japan, Sept 13, 41. *Study:* Kyoto Munic Univ Art, BFA(oil painting), 65. *Work:* Nat Mus Mod Art Tokyo, Japan; Mus Mod Art, New York; Mus Cincinnati, Ohio; Mus Mod Art, Chicago; Mus Mod Art, San Francisco. *Exhib:* Ten Selected Artists, Mus Mod Art, Chicago, 80; Japanese Prints of the 20th Century, Portland Mus Art & St Louis Mus, Ore, 83; 25th Anniversary Show for Crown Point Press, Mus Mod Art, New York, 87; Contemp Art Fair, Los Angeles, 88; retrospective exhibs, Mus Portland, Ore, 89 & Art Mus Cincinnati, Ohio, 90. *Media:* Multi Media. *Mailing Add:* 4-5-2 Kagamishhi Okitayama, Kita-ku Kyoto 603 Japan

IDAHERMA (IDAHERMA WILLIAMS)
PRINTMAKER, PAINTER
b Bronx, NY. *Study:* Philadelphia Col Art, BFA(scholar) 59; Pa Acad Fine Art, 60-63; Univ Pa, MFA, 63. *Work:* Rider Col, Lawrenceville, NJ; Sterling Drug Art Collection; Zimmerli Art Mus, Rutgers Univ, NJ, 66; Firestone Libr, Princeton Univ. *Comn:* Symbol (dragonfly design), Churchville Nature Ctr, Pa, 66. *Exhib:* Solo exhibs, NJ State Mus, Trenton, 75, AT&T, Hopewell, NJ, 83, Rider Col, 86 & Image Gallery, 90; Fel Ann Exhib, Pa Acad Fine Arts, 66; Art From NJ, NJ State Mus, Trenton, 69 & 71; Peale House, Pa Acad Fine Arts, 82; FRRIC Int, Montreal, Can, 90; Third Biennial Int Print Exhib, Somerstown Gallery, Somers, NY, 90. *Pos:* Contribr, Del Valley Advance, 66-67; bd mem, Alumni Asn, Pa Acad Fine Arts, 88; vpres, Am Color Print Soc, 88. *Teaching:* Instr painting & drawing, Fleisher Art Mem, Philadelphia, currently; Princeton Adult Sch, currently. *Awards:* Harrison S Morris Mem Fel Watercolor, Pa Acad Fine Arts, 66. *Bibliog:* Linda Holt (auth), Watercolor show a joy, Trentonian, 7/1/75; M Kosich (auth), Artist Uses Different Style of Color in Art, Rider News, Rider Col, 11/21/86; G Suriano (auth), Printmaking - the state of the art, NJ Goodlife Mag, 3/90. *Mem:* Printmaking Coun NJ; Artists Equity; Am Color Print Soc; Philadelphia Watercolor Club; Trenton Artists Workshop Asn; The Print Consortium, St Joseph, Mo. *Media:* Woodblock Prints; Watercolor, Dye on Silk. *Publ:* Auth, Old building transformed, Sch Arts Mag, 11/72; Precautions for elementary and secondary art teachers, Art Hazards News, 9/79; NJ Arts Ann Catalog, NJ State Mus, 86, 88; Princeton Packet, Time Off Mag, Part II, TAWA at Ellarslie, 87. *Mailing Add:* 641 Coppermine Rd Princeton NJ 08540

IDEN, SHELDON
PAINTER, EDUCATOR
b Detroit, Mich, Sept 29, 33. *Study:* Art Inst Chicago; Wayne State Univ, BFA; Cranbrook Acad Art, with Zoltan Sepeshy, MFA. *Work:* Cranbrook Acad Art, Bloomfield Hills, Mich; Ball State Univ, Muncie, Ind; Wayne State Univ, Detroit; Macomb Community Col, Warren, Mich. *Exhib:* Second Biennial, Pa Acad Fine Arts & Detroit Mus Art, 60; Mich Artists Ann, 60-70 & 72 & Other Ideas, 69, Detroit Inst Arts; Drawing & Sculpture Ann, Ball State Univ, 62; All Mich Show, Flint Mus Art, 72. *Pos:* Artist in residence, Mich Coun Arts, 69. *Teaching:* Instr drawing & painting, Wayne State Univ, 63-68; asst prof drawing & painting, Eastern Mich Univ, 68- *Awards:* Fulbright Fel to India, 62; Mus Purchase Award, 70 & Gertrude Kasle Award for Painting, 71, Detroit Inst Arts. *Bibliog:* Hakanson (auth), Made in Detroit, Art Scene, 67 & article, Detroit News, 71; Tall (auth), article, Detroit Free Press, 71. *Media:* Oil, Charcoal. *Mailing Add:* 1440 Gratiot Detroit MI 48207

IGLEHART, ROBERT L
EDUCATOR, WRITER
b Baltimore, Md, Feb 2, 12. *Study:* Md Inst Art, scholar for European study; Johns Hopkins Univ; Columbia Univ, BS(educ); New Sch Social Res. *Pos:* Chmn dept art educ, NY Univ, 46-55; chmn dept, Univ Mich, 55-71; Writer & art critic, 78- *Teaching:* Instr sch art, Univ Wash, 38-41; prof art, Univ Mich, 55-77, emer prof, 77- *Awards:* Nat Gallery Art Medal for Distinguished Serv to Art Educ, 66. *Mem:* Fel Royal Soc Arts; John Dewey Soc; Col Art Asn Am; Nat Art Educ Asn. *Publ:* Auth, numerous articles for prof mag. *Mailing Add:* 117 Dixboro Rd Ann Arbor MI 48105

IGO, PETER ALEXANDER
PRINTMAKER, PAINTER
b Riverhead, NY, Jan 9, 56. *Study:* Univ Calif, Los Angeles, 75; Univ NMex, 76-78; Univ Calif, Berkeley, 79; Belles Artes Nat Inst, Mex, studied lithography, 86. *Work:* Sch Am Res, Mus NMex & First Interstate Bank, Santa Fe; Maxwell Mus Anthrop, Albuquerque, NMex. *Comn:* Paper cast petroglyph, E F Hutton, Santa Fe, NMex, 85; paper cast petroglyph, Hilton Hotel, 85 & Quail Run Develop, Santa Fe, 88. *Exhib:* Solo exhibs, Primitive i Gallery, Chicago, 79, Bank of Santa Fe, 84 & St John's Col, 86; Santa Fe Salon, Santa Fe Festival Arts, 80; Images of the Southwest, Armory Arts, Santa Fe, 81; Museum New Mexico, Santa Fe, 84-85; Paper: In Different Forms, Bank of Santa Fe, 88; Glyphs of New Mexico, Govs Gallery, 89, NMex. *Teaching:* Part time instr, screen printing, Verde Valley Sch, Sedona, Ariz, 80-82 & 84. *Media:* Acrylic on Paper & Canvas, Serigraphy. *Publ:* Auth, Bernique Longley-A Retrospective, Gallery Representation, El Prado Galleries Inc, Sedona, Ariz & Santa Fe, NMex. *Dealer:* Hughes Fisher Art Resources Santa Fe NM. *Mailing Add:* 19 Cerrado Loop Santa Fe NM 87505

IHARA, MICHIO
SCULPTOR
b Paris, France, Nov 17, 28; Japanese citizen. *Study:* Tokyo Univ Fine Arts, BFA, 53; Mass Inst Technol, Fulbright Fel; also with Gyorgy Kepes, 61. *Work:* Wind, Wind, Wind, Kanagawa Mus Mod Art, Kamakura, Japan. *Comn:* Metal screen, Rockefeller Ctr, 78; suspended sculpture, Neiman-Marcus, Beverly Hills, 79, Pavilion Hotel, Singapore, 82, AT&T Long Lines, Atlanta, 82 & Marriott Hotel, New York, 85; plaza sculpture, New World Ctr, Hong Kong, 82; wall sculpture, Harvard Univ, Mass, 86; Tokyo City Hall, 91; and others. *Exhib:* Selection 64, Inst Contemp Art, Boston, 64 & Boston Celebrations, 75; Trends Contemporary Art, Kyoto Mus Mod Art, 68; Ann Exhib, Nat Inst Arts & Lett & Am Acad Arts & Lett, 73; Japanese Artists in America, Tokyo Mus Mod Art & Kyoto Mus Mod Art, 73-74; one-man show, Staempfli Gallery, New York, 77, 80 & 84. *Pos:* Fel, Ctr Advan Visual Studies, Mass Inst Technol, 70-75. *Teaching:* Instr basic design, Musashino Fine Arts Univ, Tokyo, 66-68. *Awards:* Graham Found Fel, 64; Ann Award, Am Acad Arts & Lett & Nat Inst Arts & Lett, 73; First Prize, Fitchburg Libr Art Competition, Mass Coun Arts & Humanities, 74. *Mem:* Japanese Artists Asn. *Media:* Stainless Steel, Brass. *Dealer:* Staempfli Gallery 47 E 77th St New York NY 10021. *Mailing Add:* 63 Wood St Concord MA 01742

IHLE, JOHN LIVINGSTON
PRINTMAKER, EDUCATOR
b Chicago, Ill, Feb 1, 25. *Study:* Univ Iowa, 49, with Maurice Lasansky; Ill Wesleyan Univ, Bloomington, BFA, 50; Bradley Univ, Peoria, Ill, MA, 51, with Ernest Freed; San Francisco State Univ, 54. *Work:* Libr of Cong, Washington, DC; Chicago Art Inst; New York Pub Libr; Achenbach Found for Graphic Arts, Calif Palace of Legion of Honor, San Francisco; Nat Gallery of Art, Washington, DC. *Comn:* Prints (210 each ed), Int Graphic Art Soc, New York, 57, 60 & 61; print, Roten Galleries, Baltimore, Md, 67; print, San Francisco Hosp Comn, San Francisco Art Comn, 73. *Exhib:* One-man shows, San Francisco Mus Art, 60, 66 & 77; Nat Print Exhib, Libr of Cong, Soc Am Graphic Artist, New York & Brooklyn Mus, NY; Nat Print Invitationals, Univ Ky, 61, State Univ NY, Albany, 68, Univ Ill, 70 & Cincinnati Art Mus, Ohio, 73. *Collections Arranged:* Prints of John Ihle (auth, catalogue), Achenbach Found of Graphic Art, 49-62; Ihle: Survey of Work, Univ NDak Art Galleries, 57-76; Traveling Exhibits, Univ NDak, Minot State Col, NDak, Univ Mont, Univ Alta, Calgary & San Francisco Mus Art, 76-77; plus others. *Pos:* Chmn bd, San Francisco Tapestry Workshop, 78- *Teaching:* Prof art & printmaking, San Francisco State Univ, 55-; vis prof printmaking, Univ Alta, Edmonton, 68-69; vis artist printmaking, The Sch Art Inst Chicago, 80. *Mem:* Calif Soc Printmakers (former pres); Color Print Soc. *Media:* All. *Dealer:* Fountain Gallery of Art 117 NW 21st Ave Portland OR 97965. *Mailing Add:* 49 Shell Rd Mill Valley CA 94941

IIMURA, TAKAHIKO
FILMMAKER, VIDEO ARTIST
b Tokyo, Japan, Feb 20, 37. *Study:* Keio Univ, Tokyo, BA(political sci), 59. *Work:* Anthology Film Arch, New York; Centre Beaubourg des Art Plastiques, Paris; Everson Mus, Syracuse, NY; Royal Film Arch, Brussels, Belg; Neuer Berliner Kunstverein, Berlin. *Comn:* Film/video, Metrop Mus Prog for Art on Film, New York, 89. *Exhib:* Japanese Experimental Films, Mus Mod Art, New York, 66; one-man shows, Mus Mod Art, New York, 75,

Centre Beaubourg des Art Plastique, Whitney Mus, New York, 79, Hara Mus, Tokyo, 86, Anthology Film Arch, NY, 89, Mus de Louve, Paris, 90; and many other group and one-man shows. *Teaching:* Vis tutor film, Schiller Col, Berlin, 73, Univ Minn 75-76; vis asst prof film, Kent State Univ, 76; State Univ NY, Binghampton, 78; vis prof, Osaka Univ Arts, Osaka, 85- *Awards:* Spec Prize (for film Onan), 3rd Int Experimental Film Festival, Knokke, Belg, 63; artist-in-residence Grant, Deutscher Akademischer Austamschdienst, Berlin, 73-74; Creative Artist Pub Serv Grant in Film, 75-76. *Bibliog:* Larry Gottheim (auth), 10 Years of Living Cinema, New York, 82; Dominique Noquez (auth), Eloguez Du Cinema Experimental, Centre George Pompidou, Paris, 79; Scott MacDonald (auth), Critical Cinema, Univ Calif, Berkely, 88. *Mem:* Filmmakers Cooperative, New York; Univ Film Asn; Canyon Cinema Cooperative, San Francisco; Art Comt, San Francisco. *Media:* Film, video. *Publ:* Auth, Geijutsu to Higerjutso no Aida (Between Art and Non- Art), Sanichi Shobo, Tokyo, 70; Eizo Jikken No Tameni (For Visual Experimentation), Seido Sha, Tokyo, 86; Film and Video of Takahiko Iimura, Anthology Film Arch, New York, 90. *Mailing Add:* 127 Second Ave No 15 New York NY 10003

IKEDA, YOSHIRO
CERAMIST, EDUCATOR
b Kushikino-City, Kagoshima, Japan, Apr 10, 47; US citizen. *Study:* Portland State Univ, Ore, BS(painting & drawing), 70; Kyoto City Univ Fine Art, Japan, cert, 73; Univ Calif, Santa Barbara, MFA, 77. *Work:* Japanese Govt Ministry Educ, Tokyo; Kyoto City Univ Fine Art, Japan; Utah State Univ, Logan; Calif Polytech State Univ, San Luis Obispo; Topeka Pub Libr, Kans. *Exhib:* El Paso Mus, Tex, 79; Foothills Art Ctr, Denver, 79; Cooperstown Art Asn, NY, 81; Purdue Univ Gallery, West Lafayette, Ind, 81; War Mem Mus, Aukland, NZ, 81; Wichita Mus, Kans, 81; and others. *Teaching:* Instr ceramics, Utah State Univ, 73-74; instr ceramics, Ventura Col, 77-78; asst prof ceramics, Kans State Univ, 78-, area head, 81- *Awards:* First Place Award, Austin Art Asn, 78; Juror's Award, Calif Polytech State Univ, 78; Merit Award, Fletcher Brownbuilt Pottery Guild, 81. *Mem:* Nat Coun Educ Ceramic Arts; Kans Artist Craftsman Asn; Kans Designer Craftsman Asn. *Media:* Clay. *Publ:* Auth, Asymmetrical thrown form, Ceramic Monthly, 6/78. *Dealer:* Marcia Rodell Gallery 11714 San Vicente Blvd Los Angeles CA 90049. *Mailing Add:* 808 Wildcat Ridge Manhattan KS 66502

IKEGAWA, SHIRO
PRINTMAKER
b Tokyo, Japan, July 15, 33; US citizen. *Study:* Tokyo Univ Arts; Otis Art Inst Los Angeles Co, MFA, 61. *Work:* Seattle Art Mus; Brooklyn Mus Art; Metrop Mus Art, New York; Libr Cong & Smithsonian Inst, Washington, DC; and many others. *Comn:* Ed etchings, James B Lancer Corp, 68; three-dimensional print, comn by Mrs Martha Jackson, New York, 69; two ed etchings, Los Angeles Co Mus Art, Graphic Art Coun, 73; prints comn for Int Multiple Exhib, Nomura Display Co, Tokyo, 73; Tale of Genji (color etching), Los Angeles Times, 73; and others. *Exhib:* Int Print Show, Seattle Art Mus, 63-65 & 67-68; Nat Print Exhib, Brooklyn Art Mus, 64 & 66; Pacific Heritage, DeYoung Mem Mus & others, 65; Ann Exhib Watercolors, Prints & Drawings, Pa Acad Fine Arts, 65; CSE Nat Print Exhib, San Francisco Mus Art, 65; Nat Print & Drawing Competition, Dulin Gallery Art, Tenn, 65; Okla Art Ctr, 65 & 67; Ann Exhib Sculpture & Print, Whitney Mus Am Art, 66; 20th Nat Exhib Prints, Libr Cong, 66; Smithsonian Inst Traveling Exhib, 70-73; Printmaking: Process-Innovation, Mus Asn NGrange Co, Fullerton, Calif, 80; Drawing 80, Col St Rose, Albany, NY; Los Angeles Print 1883-1980, Los Angeles Co Mus Art, 80-81; one-person exhib, Los Angeles Inst Contemp Art, 80; and many others. *Teaching:* Asst prof art, Pasadena City Col, 61-67 & Calif State Univ, Los Angeles, 67-76; guest prof, Otis Art Inst Los Angeles Co, 67, prof art & chmn printmaking dept, 76-78; guest prof, Calif Inst Arts, Chouinard Art Sch, 68-71, Calif State Univ, San Francisco, 72, Univ Calif, Berkeley, summer 73, Vancouver Sch Art, BC, summer 74 & Univ Calif, Irvine, 74-75; prof art, Otis Art Inst, Parsons Sch Design, 79- *Awards:* Nat Endowment Arts Fel Printmaking, 74 & Conceptual & Performance Art, 81; Ford Found Fac Enrichment Grants, 77 & 80. *Bibliog:* Leonard Edmondson (auth), Etchings, Van Nostrand Reinhold, 73; article, Southwest Art Gallery Mag, 72; Interview (monograph), Asian Am Studies Ctr, Univ Calif, Los Angeles, 73; and others. *Media:* All. *Dealer:* Martha Jackson Gallery 521 W 57th St New York NY 10019; Comsky Gallery 9777 Wilshire Blvd Suite 815 Beverly Hills CA. *Mailing Add:* 323 E Altadena Drive Altadena CA 91001

IMANA, JORGE GARRON
PAINTER, MURALIST
b Sucre, Bolivia, Sept 20, 30; US citizen. *Study:* Univ San Francisco Xavier, Sucre, MA. *Work:* Nat Mus, La Paz, Bolivia; Univ San Francisco Xavier Mus, Sucre; Nat Mus, Bogota, Colombia; Casa de la Cult, Quito, Ecuador; Bolivian Embassy, Moscow. *Comn:* Hist mural, Bolivian Govt, Junin Col, Sucre, 58; History of Education in Bolivia (mural), comn by Bolivian Govt, Padilla Col, Sucre, 59; Social History in Peru (mural), Constructors Union, Lima, Peru, 61; Ciudad de Dios Sch (mural), comn by students' parents, Lima, 62. *Exhib:* Nat Salon, La Paz, 62; Latin Am Show, Fine Arts Gallery, San Diego, 64; Bolivian Paintings, Mus of Mod Art, Paris, France, 73 & Nat Gallery, Warsaw, Poland, 75; House of Friendship of the Peoples, Moscow, 75; Gallery IDB, Washington, DC, 76; plus 78 one-man shows. *Pos:* Owner, The Artist's Showroom, San Diego. *Teaching:* Prof drawing, Univ San Francisco Xavier, Sucre, 54-60; prof drawing & watercolor, Nat Acad, La Paz, 60-62; dir art dept, Inst Normal Superior, La Paz, 60-62. *Awards:* Nat Award, Nat Show, La Paz, Bolivian Govt, 62; Watercolor Award, Nat Watercolor Show, Lima, Peru, Watercolor Soc, 62; Purchase Awards Oil & Watercolor, Ann Show, San Diego Art Inst, 64. *Mem:* La Jolla Art Asn; San Diego Art Inst; Accademia Italia delle Artie del Lavoro. *Mailing Add:* 3357 Caminito Gandara La Jolla CA 92037

IMBER, JONATHAN
PAINTER, PRINTMAKER
b Baldwin, NY, Oct 1, 50. *Study:* Cornell Univ, BFA, 72; Boston Univ, MFA, 77. *Work:* Boston Mus Fine Arts; Fogg Art Mus, Cambridge, Mass; Rose Art Mus, Waltham, Mass; Currier Gallery of Am Art, Manchester, NH; Broida Trust, Los Angeles, Calif. *Exhib:* Fresh Images, Rose Art Mus, 78; Boston Now, Inst Contemp Art, Boston, 82 & 83; The Figure Again, Currier Gallery of Art, Manchester, NH, 84; Awards in the Visual Arts, Albright Knox Gallery, Buffalo, NY, 85; Expressionism in Boston, 1945-1985, DeCordova Mus, Lincoln, Mass, 86; Jewish Themes-American Contemporary Artists, Jewish Mus, New York, 86; New Eng NOW, DeCordova Mus, Lincoln, Mass, 87-89; solo show, Survey of Paintings, Fitchburg Art Mus, Mass, 90. *Teaching:* Vis artist, Radcliffe Col; Grad Sch, Sch Visual Arts, New York; Boston Mus Sch. *Awards:* Engelhard Award, 85; Mass Artists Fel, 85; Nat Endowment, 87. *Bibliog:* Lois Tarlow (auth), Jon Imber: Painter, Art New Eng, 81; Pam Allara (auth), Issues: new allegory, Art News, 82; William Corbett (auth), Jon Imber, Arts Mag, 5/89; Nancy Stapen (auth), Jon Imber, Artforum, 86; William Leites (auth), Jon Imber, Art in Am, 12/89; John Arthur (auth) Spirit of Place, 89. *Media:* Oil; All. *Dealer:* Victoria Munroe Fine Arts Nine E 84 St New York NY. *Mailing Add:* c/o Nielson Gallery 179 Newbury St Boston MA 02116

IMES, BIRNEY
PHOTOGRAPHER
b Columbus, Miss, Aug 21, 51. *Work:* Bibliotheque Nat, Paris, France; San Francisco Mus Art, Calif; Mus Mod Art & Metrop Mus Art, New York; Art Inst Chicago, Ill. *Exhib:* Friends of Photography, Carmel, Calif, 86; solo exhib, Art Inst Chicago, 87; Real Faces, Whitney Mus Am Art at Phillip Morris, New York, 88; New Southern Photography: Between Myth & Reality, Aperture Found, New York, 89; New Acquisitions--New Work--New Directions, George Eastman House, Rochester, NY, 89. *Awards:* Individual Artist Fels, Nat Endowment Arts, 84 & 88; Photography Award, Miss Inst Arts & Lett, 87 & 90. *Dealer:* Gallery Fine Photography 313 Royal St New Orleans LA 70130; 20th Century Photography Ltd 305 E 63rd New York NY 10021. *Mailing Add:* 802 Third Ave S Columbus MI 39701

IMMONEN, GERALD
PAINTER
b Detroit, Mich, 1936. *Study:* Yale Univ, New Haven, BFA, 60, MFA, 62. *Work:* Memphis Brooks Mus Art; Metropolitan Mus Art, New York. *Exhib:* National Drawing and Print Exhibition, Miami Univ, Oxford, Ohio, 78; Rhode Island Artists, Rhode Island Sch Design, Mus Art, Providence, 81; Prelude to Discoveries and Disclosures, George Ciscle Gallery, Baltimore, Md, 85; Rhode Island Sch Design: Selected Faculty, George Ciscle Gallery, 86; Gerald Immonen: Paintings, Acme Art, San Francico, 87; New Works by Gallery Artists, Charles Cowles Gallery, 87-88; and others. *Teaching:* Prof, RI Sch Design, Providence, currently. *Awards:* Alice Kimball English Fel, Yale Univ, 60; John F Frazier Award for Excellence in Teaching, RI Sch Design, 90. *Mailing Add:* 19 Creighton St Providence RI 02906

IMPIGLIA, GIANCARLO
PAINTER, SCULPTOR
b Rome, Italy, Mar 9, 40; US citizen. *Study:* Tech Sch Photog, Rome; Artistic Lyceum, Rome; Acad Fine Arts, Rome. *Work:* Jane Voorhees Zimmerli Art Mus, New Brunswick, NJ; Snite Mus Art, Notre Dame, Ind; Mus City New York. *Comn:* Five panel mural, Am Insurance Bldg, New York, 75-76; mural, 57th Street Playhouse, New York; two panel mural, Fortunoff Co, New York, 79; five panel mural, Cafe Soc, New York, 87. *Exhib:* Solo exhibs, Rizzoli Gallery, New York & Chicago, 81 & 82, Alex Rosenburg Gallery, New York, 84, Carolyn Hill Gallery, New York, 85, Long Island Focus on Art Show, Old Westbury, NY, 89, RVS Fine Art, Southampton, 89, 9th Annual Philadelphia Art Show, Philadelphia, 89, Gallery Artists Summer Show - RVS Gallery Southampton, 90, Uptown Gallery, New York, 90, Robert Mondavi Winery, Oakville, Calif, 90, Hansen Galleries, New York, 91 & 92, Ministero per i Beni Culturali e Ambientali, Rome, 92 & Deco Gallery, Washington, DC, 92. *Teaching:* Instr, studio seminars. *Awards:* Philadelphia Bowl, 86; Black Tie Award, Am Formal Wear, Inc, 86. *Bibliog:* Kenny Mann (auth), Giancarlo Impiglia - Courage Danger & Leadership - A must for artistic identity, Sun Storm Mag, 5/84; Ronnie Cohen (auth), Giancarlo Impiglia, Art News, 9/84; Laurel Graeber (auth), The Patron Saint of the Formal Wear Industry, Daily News Record, 9/86. *Media:* Acrylic; wood. *Dealer:* Hansen Galleries W Broadway New York NY. *Mailing Add:* 182 Grand St New York NY 10013

INCANDELA, GERALD JEAN-MARIE
PHOTOGRAPHER, MURALIST
b Tunis, Tunisia, Feb 19, 52; French citizen. *Study:* Univ Paris, Nanterre, France, 70-72. *Work:* Getty Mus, Malibu, Calif; Metrop Mus Art & Mus Mod Art, New York; Albright-Knox Mus, Buffalo, NY; Mus Fine Arts, Houston, Tex; Philadelphia Mus Art, Pa. *Comn:* Bronx Zoo Animals, comn by Robert Wooley, New York, 78; View of Central Park, Mus of Mod Art, New York, 79; murals of puppies & penguins, Thermo Electric Co, NJ, 80; paintings, Archer Daniel Midland Co, 83. *Exhib:* Solo exhib, The Kitchen, New York, 81; Corcoran Gallery, Washington, DC, 78; Photo Start, Bronx Mus, New York, 82; Counterpart, Metrop Mus Art, New York & traveling, 82; How to Draw What to Draw, Parrish Art Mus, Southampton, NY, 82; Still Modern After All These Years, Chrysler Mus, Norfolk, Va, 82; Drawing Center, New York & traveling, 82; Museum Modern Art, New York, 83; Museum Modern Art, Oxford, Eng, 86. *Bibliog:* Deborah C Phillips (auth), Gerald Incandela photo images, Print Collector's Newslett, 79; Klaus Kertess (auth), Developing an image, Artforum Mag, 81; Pepe Karmel (auth), Photography: Urban disjunctions, Art in Am, 82. *Publ:* Coauth with Brad Gooch, Pictures-Story, Oakhurst, 81; coauth with Derek Jarman, Caravaggio, Thames & Hudson, 87. *Mailing Add:* 88 Lexington Ave New York NY 10016

INDIANA, ROBERT
PAINTER, SCULPTOR
b New Castle, Ind, Sept 13, 28. *Study:* John Herron Sch Art; Munson-Williams-Proctor Inst; Art Inst Chicago, BFA; Skowhegan Sch Painting & Sculpture; Univ Edinburgh & Edinburgh Col Art, Scotland; Franklin & Marshall Col, Lancaster, Pa, Hon DFA, 70; Ind Univ, Bloomington, Hon DFA, 77; Colby Col, Waterville, Maine, Hon DFA, 81. *Work:* Mus Mod Art, Whitney Mus Am Art, New York; Carnegie Inst Arts, Pittsburgh; Stedelijk Mus, Amsterdam, Neth; Detroit Inst Arts, Mich. *Comn:* Electric mural, New York World's Fair, 64-65. *Exhib:* Mus Mod Art, New York, 61, 63-64; Dunn Int, Tate Gallery, London, 63; Whitney Mus Am Art, New York, 63-67, 69 & 74; Va Mus Fine Arts, Richmond, 74; Hirshhorn Mus, Washington, DC, 74; Corcoran Gallery Art, Washington, DC, 75; 20th Nat Print Exhib, Brooklyn Mus, 77; Art Inst Chicago, 79; Whitney Mus Am Art, 80; Royal Acad, London, 91; Museo Nacional Reina Sofia, Madrid, 92; and others. *Bibliog:* Swenson (auth), Horizons of Robert Indiana, Art News, 66; McCoubrey (auth), Robert Indiana, Univ Pa, 68; Mecklenburg (auth), Wood Works, 84, Weinhardt (auth), Robert Indiana, Harry N Abrams, 90, Smithsonian Inst Press. *Mem:* Royal Soc Arts. *Media:* Oil; Steel. *Publ:* Illusr, Numbers, 68. *Dealer:* Elizabeth McDonald Gallery New York NY; O'Farrell Gallery Brunswick ME. *Mailing Add:* c/o Star of Hope Vinalhaven ME 94863

INDICK, JANET
SCULPTOR
b Bronx, NY, Mar 3, 32. *Study:* Hunter Col, with Robert Motherwell & Dong Kingman, BA(art), 53; The New Sch, with Gregorio Prestopino & Richard Pousette-Dart, 61. *Work:* Bergen Community Mus Art & Sci, Paramus, NJ; Weingroup Equities, NY; Teaneck Jewish Ctr, NJ. *Comn:* Steel sculpture, The Jewish Ctr, Teaneck, NJ, 74; steel menorah, Franklin Lakes Pub Sch, NJ, 80; bronze wall sculpture, 81 & sanctuary & wall, wood menorah, 83, Temple Beth Rison, Wycoff, NJ. *Exhib:* Bergen Mus, Paramus, NJ, 81; Newark Mus, 82; Jersey City Mus, 83; Morris Mus, NJ, 84; Interplay, Summit Art Ctr Invitational, Summit, 86; Edward Williams Gallery, Farleigh Dickinson Univ, NJ, 86; traveling exhibs, 100 Years/100 Works, USA, 89-90, sculpture show, India, 89-90, Nat Asn Women Artists. *Pos:* Mem, Teaneck Adv Bd on the Arts, NJ, 80- *Awards:* Nat Endowment Arts Fel Grant, 81; Sculpture Prize, Nat Asn Painters & Sculptors, 78 & 80; Fel Grant, NJ State Coun Arts, 80-81. *Bibliog:* Articles in The New York Art Rev, 88, Sculpture Fundamentals, 88, Women Artists in America, Appolo Bks, 88. *Mem:* Nat Asn Women Artists (treas); Sculptors League NY (exec bd); New York Soc Women Artists; Artists Equity NY; Sculptors Asn NY. *Media:* Miscellaneous Media. *Publ:* Dictionary of American Painters and Sculptors, Appolo Bks, 88; The Guild, Kraus Sikes Inc, 93. *Dealer:* Lillian Heidenberg Gallery 50 W 57th St New York NY 10019; Kerygma Gallery 38 Oak St Ridgewood NJ. *Mailing Add:* 428 Sagamore Ave Teaneck NJ 07666

INDIVIGLIA, SALVATORE JOSEPH
PAINTER, INSTRUCTOR
b New York, NY, Nov 16, 19. *Study:* Leonardo da Vinci Art Sch; Sch Indust Arts; Pratt Inst, BA; fresco & mural painting with Alfred D Crimi; also with Buck Ulrick, Nicholas Volpe, Earl Winslow & George Harrington, Jr. *Work:* USN Combat Art Collection, Washington, DC; Grumbacher & Sons Collection, New York; Mutual Benefit Life Insurance Co, NJ; Annin Flag Co & Morris Davis Collection, Emily Lowe Found, New York. *Comn:* Assisted Alfred D Crimi with hist mural for Northampton, Mass, 40, Gen Anthony Wayne Mural for Wayne, Pa, 41 & Bowery Mission Mural for Bowery Mission, New York, 42. *Exhib:* Am Watercolor Soc Ann, New York, 53-83; Audubon Artists Ann, New York, 53-88; Joe & Emily Lowe Found Show, 55 & 60; Operations Palette, USN Combat Art, Smithsonian Inst, Washington, DC, 65; Nat Acad Design, New York, 65-75. *Pos:* Art dir, acct exec & vpres, formerly; off comdr, USN combat artist, 61- *Teaching:* Asst & instr, City Col New York, 46-69; private classes, 46-72; instr watercolor, East Williston Libr, New York, 60-72; instr fine & appl arts, Mechanics Inst, New York, 62-66. *Awards:* Pauline Law Award in Oil, Knickerbocker Artists, 74; Gold Medal Watercolor, 75 & Jane Peterson Award in Oil, 76, Allied Artists Am. *Mem:* Artists Fel (pres, 60-63); Am Watercolor Soc (dir, chmn, 53-72); Allied Artists Am (secy, 59-62); Knickerbocker Artists (vpres, 57-59); Audubon Artists. *Media:* Watercolor, Oil. *Publ:* Contribr, Direction, Int Rels Div, Off Info, 66; Watch, USNR, 67; Naval Aviation News, 68; All Hands, Bur Naval Personnel, 69; auth, Watercolor page, Am Artist Mag, 71. *Mailing Add:* 974 Lorraine Dr Franklin Square NY 11010

INGALLS, EVE
INSTRUCTOR, PAINTER
b Cleveland, Ohio, Sept 29, 36. *Study:* Skowhegan Sch Art; Smith Col, BA, 58; Yale Univ Sch Art, BFA, 60, MFA, 62. *Exhib:* Butler Inst Am Art, 66; Vassar Col Art Gallery, 70; Yale-Norfolk, Conn, 72; Art & Archit Gallery, Yale Univ, 77; Contemporary Reflections, Aldrich Mus, 77 & 87; Cleveland Mus, 77, 80 & 86; Connecticut Painting, Sculpture and Drawing Traveling Exhib, 78; SoHo 20 Gallery, New York, 80, 81, 84, 86 & 90; Conn Comn on the Arts, Hartford, 85; Columbus Mus Art, Columbus, Ga, 85; Paula Allen Gallery, New York, 87 & 88; New Brit Mus Am Art, 89; Kulturforum Mönchengladbach, WGer; Conn Biennial, Bruce Mus, Greenwich. *Teaching:* Instr painting & drawing, Silvermine Guild Sch Arts, 72-; vis lectr, Yale Univ, 79; lectr, State Univ NY, Col at Purchase, 85; vis asst prof, Trinity Col, Hartford. *Bibliog:* Virginia Mann (auth), article, 80, Martha Scott (auth), article, 84 & Gregory Galligan (auth), article, 86, Arts Mag; Michael Brenson (auth), rev, New York Times, 86; William Zimmer (auth), rev, New York Times, 89, 91 & 92; and others. *Media:* Mixed. *Dealer:* SoHo 20 Gallery 469 Broome St New York NY 10014. *Mailing Add:* 131 Ansonia Rd Woodbridge CT 06525

INGBER, BARBARA
DEALER, COLLECTOR
b New York, NY, Apr 18, 32. *Study:* NY Univ; Feigan Dramatic Sch. *Pos:* Dir, Ingber Gallery Ltd, 72-89 & Mus Art for Arts Sake, 89- *Mem:* Mus Mod Art; Whitney Mus Am Art; Guggenheim Mus; Metrop Mus; Mus Art for Arts Sake. *Specialty:* 20th century American art. *Collection:* Paintings, drawings, sculpture and photographs by contemporary American artists. *Mailing Add:* 525 E 72nd St New York NY 10021

INGHAM, TOM (EDGAR)
SCULPTOR, PAINTER
b Puyallup, Wash, Feb 23, 42. *Study:* Self Taught. *Work:* Ball State Univ, Muncie, Ind; Univ Puget Sound, Tacoma, Wash. *Comn:* 14 Illus, Playboy Mag, Chicago, Ill, 74-88; poster, British Railways, London, Eng, 85; poster, Seattle Chamber Music Festival. *Exhib:* Puget Sound Area Exhib, Frye Mus Art, Seattle, Wash, 72, 76, 90 & 91; Watergate Exhib, Gallery Borjeson, Malmo, Sweden, 74 & Odanski, Denmark, 75; Ann Exhibs 23, 80 & 25, 83, Soc Illusr, New York; 8th Ann Exhib, Calif Mag, Palo Alto, 83; Physicians for Social Responsibility: Peace Forum & Art Exhib, Calif Polytech, San Luis Obispo, Calif, 86. *Awards:* Gold Medal, 23rd Ann, Soc Illusr, 80; Award of Excellence, 8th Calif Mag Exhib, 83; Third Prize, Puget Sound Area Exhib, Frye Art Mus, 90. *Media:* Pastel Pencil, Pen & Sepia Ink. *Publ:* Contribr, Illusr 23 & 25, Soc Illusr, 82 & 84; Graphics Annual, Graphic Press Corp, Switz, 83; California Art Annual, Calif Mag, 83; Outstanding American Illustrators Today, Graphic-sha, Tokyo, 85. *Mailing Add:* 636 NW 79th Seattle WA 98117

INGLE, JOHN S
PAINTER, EDUCATOR
b Evansville, Ind, Sept 18, 33. *Study:* Univ Ariz, BFA, 64, MFA, 66; Royal Acad Beaux Arts, Brussels, Belgium. *Work:* Metrop Mus Art, New York; Springfield Art Mus, Mo; Evansville Mus Arts & Sci, Ind; Phillip Morris Inc, New York; Chemical Bank, NY; Met Life Insurance Co, NY; Transco Energy Co, Houston; and others. *Exhib:* Contemporary American Realism Since 1960, 81 & Works on Paper From the Collection of Jalene and Richard Davidson, 82, Pa Acad Fine Art; Every Object Rightly Seen, Univ Va Art Mus, Charlottesville, 82; 20th Century American Watercolors Traveling Exhib, Gallery Asn NY State, 83; Contemporary Images Watercolor, Univ Wis, Oshkosh, 83; Realist Watercolor, Univ Conn, Hartford, 83 & Fla Int Univ, 83; solo exhibs, Capricorn Gallery, Bethseda, Md, 79 Tatistcheff & Co, New York, 81, 83, 85 & 88 & Transco Energy Exhib Gallery, Houston, 85; American Realism: Twentieth-Century Drawings and Watercolors, Art, San Francisco, 85; The Recognizable Image, Bruce Mus, Greenwich, Conn, 85; The Eye and the Heart: Watercolors of John Stuart Ingle, 88 & 89; Wadsworth Atheneum, Evansville Mus Arts & Sci, Hunter Mus; Realist Watercolors, Palmer Mus Art, Pa State Univ, University Park, 90. *Teaching:* Prof painting, drawing & design, Univ Minn, Morris, 66- *Bibliog:* Hilton Kramer (auth), Critics choice, New York Times, 1/18/81; James Cooper (auth), article, News World, 1/18/81; John Driscoll (auth), Paradigms of reality, Am Artist, 3/82; Patricia C Johnson (auth), Ingle's watercolors an exhibit not to miss, Houston Chronicle, 2/16/85; Thomas Bolt (auth), John Stuart Ingle, Arts Mag, 11/85. *Media:* Watercolor. *Publ:* Auth, John Camp, the Eye and the Heart, Watercolors of John Stuart Ingle, Rizzoli Publ, 88. *Mailing Add:* c/o Tatistcheff & Co 50 W 57th St 8th Floor New York NY 10019

INGRAM, JUDITH
PAPER ARTIST, SCULPTOR
b Philadelphia, Pa, Oct 12, 26. *Study:* Philadelphia Col Art; printmaking with Carol Summers. *Work:* Del Mus Ann; DuPont Inc; Philadelphia Mus Art; RCA Corp, Eastern US & PR; Emperor Japan; Int Paper Co; Kimberly Clark; Bank Am. *Comn:* Hercules Inc, Wilmington, Del. *Exhib:* Florence Duhl Gallery, New York, 79; Soc of Graphic Artists Ann Exhib; Hooks-Epstein Galleries, Houston, Tex, 79, 81 & 88; Rosenfeld Gallery, Philadelphia, 80, 82, 84, 86 & 89; Sutton Gallery, New York, 81; Philadelphia Print Club; Portland Mus Art, Portland, Maine, 88; and others. *Teaching:* Handmade paper workshops, Univ Del, Univ Pa, Philadelphia Mus Art & Arrowmont Sch Crafts, Gatlinburg, Tenn; Haystack Mountain Sch Crafts, Deer Isle, Maine. *Awards:* 3rd Prize, wall relief, Art Quest '86, Parsons Gallery, New York, 86; Jurors award, Del Ctr Contemp Art, Wilmington, 89. *Bibliog:* Article, in: The Art Fabric Mainstream, by Mildred Constantine & Jack Lenore Larsen. *Mem:* Am Color Print Soc. *Mailing Add:* 142 Smithbridge Rd Glen Mills PA 19342

INJEYAN, SETA L
PAINTER
b Aleppo, Syria, May 3, 46; US citizen. *Study:* Beirut Univ Col, Lebanon, 69; Art Ctr Col Design, Pasadena, Calif, with Richard Diebenkorn, Lorser Feitelson, Llyn Foulkes, Ann McKoy & Peter Alexander, BFA, 75. *Work:* Kaloust Gulbenkian Found, Lisbon, Portugal; Wells Fargo Bank, Los Angeles; Eastern State Hosp, Medical Lake, Wash. *Exhib:* Palos Verdes Art Ctr, Rancho Palos Verdes, Calif, 82; Santa Barbara Mus Art, Calif, 82; Merging One, Santa Monica, Calif, 82; Los Angeles Artcore Gallery, 82; Mona Lisa Gallery, Chiba Ken, Japan, 83; and others. *Awards:* First Place, Armenian Allied Arts Coun, 75; Best Show, Soc Art Ctr Alumni, Art Ctr Col Design, 76; Three Purchases Prizes, Wash State Arts Comn, 83. *Bibliog:* David G Gardner (publ), Contemporary hand-colored photography, Picture Mag, 80; Photography Year, Time-Life, 82; Contemporary photography as phantasy, Am Photogr, 9/83. *Mem:* Artists Equity Asn; Los Angeles Inst Contemp Art; LALMA. *Media:* Miscellaneous media. *Mailing Add:* 5610 Pinecone Rd La Crescenta CA 91214

INOUE, KAZUKO
PAINTER, LECTURER
b Fukuoka City, Japan, Jan 14, 46; US citizen. *Study:* Mich State Univ, BFA & MFA. *Work:* Wichita State Univ Mus Fine Arts, Kans; Mich State Univ; Newark Mus, NJ. *Exhib:* Flint Inst Art, Mich, 73; one-woman shows, Razor Gallery, New York, 74 & O K Harris Gallery, 77; Soho Ctr Visual Artists, 78; Aldrich Mus Contemp Art, Conn, 79; and others. *Teaching:* Vis artist painting & drawing, Mich State Univ, 73; lectr drawing, Eastern Mich Univ, fall 74. *Awards:* Awards, Chautauqua Art Ctr, 70 & Detroit Inst Arts, 72. *Bibliog:* David Shirley (auth), article, 69 & Michael Brenson (auth), article, 84, NY Times; article, Art News, 72; Joseph Dreiss (auth), article, Arts Mag, 74; Michael Brenson (auth), article, NY Times, 5/27/87. *Mem:* Col Art Asn Am. *Media:* Mixed. *Dealer:* Allan Stone Gallery 48 E 86th New York NY. *Mailing Add:* 543 Broadway New York NY 10012

INSLEY, WILL
PAINTER, DRAFTSMAN
b Indianapolis, Ind, Oct 15, 29. *Study:* Amherst Col, BA; Harvard Univ Grad Sch Design, MA(archit). *Comn:* Great Southwest Indust Park, Atlanta, Ga, 68. *Exhib:* One-man shows, Walker Art Ctr, Minneapolis, 68, Albright-Knox Art Gallery, Buffalo, NY, 68, Mus Mod Art, New York, 71, Hause Lange Mus, Krefeld, Ger, 73, Fischbach Gallery, New York, 73, Wurttembergischer Kunstverein, Stuttgart, Ger, 74, Mus Contemp Art, Chicago, 76 & Max Protetch Gallery, New York, 82; The Opague Civilization, Solomon R Guggenheim Mus, New York, 84; Early Wall Fragments, 84, Drawings, 85, & New Wall Fragments, Max Protetch Gallery, New York, 88. *Pos:* Artist in residence, Oberlin Col, 66; art critic, Univ NC, 67-68; art critic, Cornell Univ, 69. *Teaching:* Instr art, Sch Visual Art, 69-88. *Awards:* Nat Found Arts & Humanities Award, 66; Guggenheim Fel, 69. *Bibliog:* The greater context, Tracks, Vol 1 (Nov, 1974); Alison Sky & Michelle Stone (auth), Unbuilt America, McGraw-Hill, 76; Abstract space--the architectural space--the empty building, Tracks, Vol 3, spring, 77; Carter Ratcliff (auth), Fragments for a civilization, Art in Am, Vol 73, 4/75; Maurice Poirier (auth), A realm of logical insanity, Art News, Vol 83, 11/84; Donald Wall (auth), Will Insley: Buildings/ Fragments, Arts Mag, Vol 50, 11/75. *Media:* All. *Dealer:* Max Protetch 560 Broadway New York NY 10012; Annemarie Verna Rontgenstrasse 44 8005 Zurich Switzerland. *Mailing Add:* 231 Bowery New York NY 10002

INUKAI, KYOHEI
PAINTER, SCULPTOR
b Chicago, Ill, July 13, 13. *Study:* Art Inst Chicago; Nat Acad Design; Art Students League. *Work:* Brandeis Univ Mus Fine Art, New York; Portland Mus, Maine; Wichita Univ Mus Art, Kans; Atlantic Richfield Collection, New York; Chase Manhattan Bank Collection, New York; plus many others. *Comn:* Sculptures for shopping malls, Knoxville, Tenn, Monmouth, NJ & North Riverside, Ill. *Exhib:* White House Rotating Exhib; Screenprints 1970, Int Silk Screen Asn, 70; Dixon White Art Ctr, Cornell Univ, 70; ann print exhib, Brooklyn Mus, NY, 71; Am Fedn Arts Traveling Print Show; Wichita Art Asn, Kans, 81; and others. *Awards:* Louis Comfort Tiffany Found Fel. *Media:* Multimedia. *Mailing Add:* 884 West End Ave New York NY 10025

INVERARITY, ROBERT BRUCE
MUSEUM DIRECTOR, PAINTER
b Seattle, Wash, July 5, 09. *Study:* Univ Wash, BA(cum laude), 46; Fremont Univ, MFA, 47, PhD, 48; and with Kazue Yamagishi, Blanding Sloan & Mark Tobey. *Work:* Univ Wash; US Naval Collection, Washington, DC; Arch Am Art, Smithsonian; also in pvt collections. *Comn:* Two mosaics, Univ Wash, 40; cut aluminum decorations, US Naval Airstation, Seattle, 40; six panels, Wash State Mus. *Exhib:* One-man shows & numerous group exhibs, US & Can, 29-39. *Pos:* State dir, Works Progress Admin Fed Art Proj, Seattle, 37-41; official war artist, USN, 43-45; art dir, Boeing Aircraft Co, Seattle, 46-47; dir, Mus Int Folk Art, 49-54; Adirondack Mus, 54-65; Philadelphia Maritime Mus, 69-76. *Teaching:* Cornish Sch, 27-28; dir, Sch Creative Art, Vancouver, Can, 31-33; inst, Univ Wash, 33-37; asst dir, Fred Archer Sch Photog, 47-49; assoc, Sch Am Res, 49-54; res asst, Yale Univ, 51-53. *Awards:* Meritorious Civilian Serv Award, USN, 45; Wenner-Gren Found Grant for Anthrop Res, 51. *Publ:* Auth, Art of the Northwest Coast Indians, Univ Calif Press, 50; ed, Winslow Homer in the Adirondacks, 59; auth & illusr, Visual Files Coding Index, 60; coauth, Early Chinese Art & Its Possible Influence in the Pacific Basin, 72; auth, Catalogue of the Inverarity Collection in the British Museum, 78. *Mailing Add:* 2404 Loring St San Diego CA 92109

IPCAR, DAHLOV
PAINTER, ILLUSTRATOR
b Windsor, Vt, Nov 12, 17. *Study:* Univ Maine, LHD, 78; Colby Col, DFA, 80. *Work:* Brooklyn Mus, Metrop Mus Art & Whitney Mus Am Art, New York; Portland Mus Art, Maine; Colby Col Mus Art, Waterville, Maine. *Comn:* Mural, Patten Free Libr, Bath, Maine, 78; mural, Shriner's Children's Hosp for Crippled Children, Springfield, Mass, 79; mural, Kingfield Elementary Sch, Maine, 80; mural, Narragansett Elementary Sch, Gorham, 81; mural, Poland Springs Community Sch, Maine, 82; and others. *Exhib:* Corcoran Biennial, 37; one-woman shows, Children's Mus, Oakland, Calif, 56, Portland Mus Art, Maine, 59, 63 & 70, Del Art Mus Libr, 76, Frost Gully Gallery, Portland, 77 & 85, Hobe Sound Galleries, Fla, 79, Colby Col Mus Art, 80 & Mus Art, Olin Arts Ctr, Bates Col, Lewiston, Maine, 90; PA & Detroit Ann, 40; Walker Art Mus, Bowdoin Col, Maine,58; Colby Col Mus Art, 74; Maine State Mus, 76; Joan Whitney Payson Art Mus, Westbrook Col, 82-85; and others. *Awards:* Maine State Award, Maine Comn Arts & Humanities, 72; Deborah Morton Award, Westbrook Col, 78; Women Achievement Award, 86. *Bibliog:* Anne Commire (ed), Something About the Author Vol 49, Gale Research; John Clayton (dir), US info Agency, Vision Series #47, 87; Joyce Nakamura (ed), Something About the Author, Vol 8, Gale Research, 89. *Media:* Oil, Watercolor. *Publ:* Auth & illusr, Calico Jungle, Knopf, 65; The Land of Flowers, Viking, 74; Lost & Found, Doubleday, 80; My Wonderful Christmas Tree, Guy Gannett Press, 86; and others. *Dealer:* Thomas R Crotty Frost Gully Gallery 411 Congress St Portland Maine 04101. *Mailing Add:* HCR-33, Box 432 Bath ME 04530

IPOUSTEGUY, (JEAN ROBERT)
SCULPTOR, GRAPHIC ARTIST
b Dun-Sur-Meuse, France, Jan 6, 20. *Study:* Ecole Primaire Superieure, BEPC, 37, Prix Nat Des Arts 7 es Prix hon, 77, Legion D' Honneur, 84. *Work:* Mus Mod Art, New York; Nat Gallery, Londres, Angletree; Nat Gallery of Victoria, Melbourne, Australia; Mus Mod Art, Paris; Mus Beaubourg, Paris; Mus St Pierre, Lyon; and others. *Comn:* Val de Grace, Etat Francais, Paris, 83; A La Lumiere de Chacun, Ambassade de France, Washington, DC, 83; Ministre des Finances, France, Paris, 87; Rimbaud, Paris, 89; Celle, Osnabrück, Allemagne, 92; and others. *Exhib:* Solo Exhib, Sculptures & Dessins, Kunstalle, Darmstadt, 69, Nat Galerie Berlin, Ger, 73, Louisianna Mus, Denmark, 75, Carlbserg Glyptotek, Denmark, 83, Heitland Found, Ger, 89, Dialog, 90 Prague, Czech, 90, Bobigny, Nevers, France, 91 & Oberhausen, Berlin, Allemagne, 92. *Awards:* Prix Bright, XXXII Biennale Venise, M Bright, 64; Dessins, 1er Prix Rijeka, Yogoslavia, 68. *Bibliog:* Gaudibert Pierre (auth), Ipousteguy, Cercle D'Art, Paris, 89. *Mem:* Academie Royal de Belgique. *Media:* All Media. *Publ:* Auth, Leaders et Enfants Nus, Soleil Noir, 70; Ronds Dans L'O et Le Pessimisme, Editions Sigart, 76; Sauve Qui Peut Robin, Crasset, 78; Arcs et Traits, C d'Art-Sarver, 89. *Dealer:* D M Sarber 6 rue du Tresor Paris 75004. *Mailing Add:* 35 Rue Chevreul Choisy-Le-Roi, 94600 France

IPPOLITO, ANGELO
PAINTER, EDUCATOR
b St Arsenio, Italy, Nov 9, 22; US citizen. *Study:* Ozenfant Sch Fine Arts, New York; Brooklyn Mus Art Sch, with Ferren; Meschini Inst, Rome, Italy; also with Afro, Rome. *Work:* Whitney Mus Am Art, Metrop Mus Art; Munson-Williams-Proctor Inst, Utica, NY; Phillips Gallery, Washington, DC; Norfolk Mus Arts & Sci, Va; Milwaukee Mus, Wis; and many others. *Comn:* Mural (oil painting), comn by Singer & Sons, now in collection of Montreal Trust Co, Que, 67. *Exhib:* Young America, Whitney Mus Am Art, 57; Abstract Impressionism, Arts Coun, London, 58; Sao Paulo Bienal, Brazil, 61; American Collages, Mus Mod Art, New York & Beuningen Mus, Rotterdam, 66; Retrospective, State Univ NY, Binghamton, 75; one-man shows, Borgenicht Gallery, New York, 75 & 86; plus others. *Teaching:* Instr painting, Cooper Union, 56-66; artist in residence, Mich State Univ, 66-71; assoc prof art, State Univ NY Binghamton, 71-76, prof art, 76- *Awards:* Fulbright Fel to Florence, Italy, 58; Ford Found Artist in Residence to Arnot Gallery, 65; Tiffany grant, 79; and others. *Bibliog:* Dore Ashton (auth), Arte Americana contemporanea, Commentari, Lionello Venturi Rome, 55; Irving Sandler (auth), Angelo Ippolito Landscapes, Provincetown Advocate, 7/4/57; Alfred Frankenstein (auth), Professors tell a story at Bolles, San Francisco Chronicle, 10/1/61; and others. *Media:* Oil. *Publ:* Contribr, Italy Rediscovered (catalog), Munson-Williams-Proctor Inst, 55; contribr, It Is, spring 58; contribr, Nature in Abstraction, Whitney Mus Am Art, 58; and others. *Mailing Add:* Dept Art State Univ NY Binghamton NY 13901

IPSEN, KENT FORREST
GLASSWORKER, CRAFTSMAN
b Milwaukee, Wis, Jan 4, 33. *Study:* Univ Wis-Milwaukee, BS; Univ Wis-Madison, MS & MFA; also with Harvey K Littleton. *Work:* Milwaukee Art Ctr, Wis; Toledo Mus Art, Ohio; Corning Glass Mus, NY; Chrysler Mus, Norfolk, Va; Chicago Art Inst; and others. *Comn:* First Gov Awards for the Arts, State of Va, 79. *Exhib:* Vidrios, Estudio Actual, Caracas, Venezuela, 74; Wis Directions, Milwaukee Art Ctr, 75; Looking Forward, Fairtree Gallery, New York, 75; Relig & Art, Vatican Mus, 78; New Glass, Int Competition Corning Mus, 79; and others. *Teaching:* Asst prof glassworking, Mankato State Col, Minn, 65-68; assoc prof glassworking, Chicago Art Inst, 68-72; assoc prof glassworking & chmn dept crafts, Va Commonwealth Univ, 73-76, prof, 76- *Awards:* Nat Endowment Arts, US Govt, 72 & 75. *Bibliog:* Lee Nordness (auth), Objects USA, Viking, 71; Ray Grover (auth), Contemporary Art Glass, Crown, 75. *Mem:* Am Craft Coun; Ill Craft Coun (pres, 70-72); Nat Coun Educ in Ceramic Arts; Nat Coun Art Adminr. *Media:* Glass. *Dealer:* Habatat Galleries 28235 Southfield Rd Lathrup Village MI 48076; Heller Gallery 965 Madison Ave New York NY 10021. *Mailing Add:* 715 Bowe St Richmond VA 23220

IPSEN, POUL JANUS
PAINTER, SCULPTOR
b Copenhagen, Denmark, July 20, 36. *Study:* Self-taught. *Work:* State Mus Art, Copenhagen, Denmark; Esbjerg Art Pavillion, Denmark; North Jylland Art Mus, Aalborg, Denmark; Trondheim Art Mus, Norway; The Print Mus, W Coberg, Ger. *Comn:* Painting, auditorium, Lojtegard High Sch, Kastrup, Ger; ceramic relief wall sculpture, Hojsberg-Birkelunds Sch, Albertslund, Denmark, 76; aluminum relief mural, Workers Union Bldg, Copenhagen, 76; aluminum & cement relief mural, Sports Ctr, Hobro, Denmark, 80; mixed media facade mural, Virum High Sch, Virum, Denmark, 85-86. *Exhib:* 2nd Biennale d'Estampe, Mus d'Art Mod, Paris, 70; Wiesbaden Mus, WGer, 71; Engagierte Kunst, State Mus Wien, Vienna, Austria, 72; Art Danois, Musée Grand Palais, Paris, 72; 11th Festival Internationale de la Peinture, Menton Mus, France, 79; Contemporary Danish Painting, traveling USA, 84-85; Gallery Isy Brachof, Paris, France, 88; Sally Hawkins Gallery, New York, 89-90; Intergrafik & Intertriennale, Rostock, WGer, 90; Addok Gallery, New

York, 90. *Awards:* Prize, City of Silkeborg, Denmark, 78; Grant, Danish Banks Confederation, 79. *Bibliog:* Virtus Schade (auth), profile, in: Danish Graphic, 77; Alex Steen & H P Jensen (auths), Danish Art, Palle Fogtdal, Copenhagen, 85, 86 & 87; Palle Smith (auth), 20 Years Poul Janus Ipsen, Gallery Asbaek, Copenhagen, 85-87. *Mem:* Gronningern Art Union, Copenhagen. *Media:* Acrylic. *Dealer:* Segal Gallery 568 Broadway New York NY 10012. *Mailing Add:* 620 Broadway New York NY 10012

IRELAND, PATRICK
CONCEPTUAL ARTIST
b Ireland, 1935. *Work:* Chase Manhattan Bank Collection, Metrop Mus Art, Mus Mod Art, New York; Butler Inst Am Art, Youngstown, Ohio; Mus Art, Univ Ga; Kilkenny Gallery Mod Art, Hugh Lane Gallery Mod Art, Ireland; Nat Gallery Australia. *Exhib:* Solo exhib, Spencer Mus, Univ Kans, Akron Art Inst, Ohio, 80, Fogg Art Mus, Cambridge, Mass, 81, Brooklyn Mus, New York, 82, Butler Inst Am Art, Youngstown, Ohio, 83; Cranbrook Acad, Bloomfield Hills, Mich, 81; Neuberger Mus, Purchase, New York, 82; Brooklyn Mus, New York, 83. *Teaching:* Vis prof, Univ Calif, Berkeley, 67; adj prof, Barnard Col, Columbia Univ, 70. *Awards:* Franklin Murphy lectr, Spencer Mus, Univ Kans, 80. *Mailing Add:* c/o Charles Cowles Gallery 420 W Broadway New York NY 10012

IRENA (IRENE R MIKOL)
PAINTER
b Brooklyn, NY, Oct 20, 12. *Study:* Woodhaven Sch Art, with Bob Barrell, 79; Yuki Tashiro Creative Arts, NY, 80; Arts All Inc, with Marie Pecorella, Richmond Hill, NY, 81-83. *Exhib:* Ann Juried Mem Exhib, Salmagundi Club, New York, 89, 92; NLAPW NY State Exhib, Lever House, New York, 89; Int Art Festival, Dutch Can Soc London, Ont, 90; Audubon Nat Exhib, Nat Arts Club, New York, 90-92; WCA/NLAPW, Sumner Mus, Washington, DC, 91-92; and others. *Awards:* Lee M Loeb Mem Award, 89; Award Excellence, Int Art Festival, Can, 90; Samuel T Shaw Mem Award, 92. *Bibliog:* December Rose Mag (cover), J E Publ, 5-6/88; Bo-Tree Datebook/ Calendar, Int Calendar Group, Asiaprint Ltd, 89. *Mem:* Women's Caucus Arts; Am Artists Prof League; Nat League Am Pen Women (rec secy, 89-); Burr Artists (newsletter ed, 90-); Salmagundi Club (libr comt, 90-91). *Media:* Oil. *Mailing Add:* 89-10 91st St Woodhaven NY 11421

IRVINE, BETTY JO
LIBRARIAN, INSTRUCTOR
b Indianapolis, Ind, July 13, 43. *Study:* Ind Univ, AB, 66, MLS, 69, PhD, 82. *Pos:* Fine arts slide librn, Sch of Fine Arts, Ind Univ, Bloomington, 66-68, asst fine arts libr, 68-69, fine arts librn, 69- *Teaching:* Instr art bibliog, Sch of Fine Arts, Ind Univ, Bloomington, 69- & instr art librarianship, & Info Sci, 86- *Awards:* Officer's Grant, Coun of Libr Resources, Washington, DC, 71. *Mem:* Am Libr Asn (vchmn-chmn-elect art sect, 78-79); Midwest Art Hist Soc (session chmn, 76); Art Libr Soc NAm (chmn, Standards Comt, 83-, vpres, 91 & pres, 91). *Res:* Organization and management of slide libraries; art library planning and design; women in libraries. *Publ:* Auth, Slide Libraries, Colo Libr Unltd, 74, 2nd ed, 79; Organization and management of art slide collections, Libr Trends, 1/75; coauth (with L Korenic), Survey of periodical use in an academic art library, In: Art Documentation, Bulletin Art Libr Soc/ NAm, 10/82; auth, Sex Segregation in Librarianship, Greenwood Press, 86; ed, Facilities Standards for Art Libraries and Visual Resources Collections, Art Libr Soc NA & Colo Libr Unltd, 91. *Mailing Add:* c/o Fine Arts Libr Ind Univ Bloomington IN 47401

IRVING, DONALD J
ADMINISTRATOR, WRITER
b Arlington, Mass, May 3, 33. *Study:* Mass Col Art, BA, 55; Columbia Univ Teachers Col, MA, 56, EdD, 63. *Pos:* Chmn dept art & dir, Peabody Mus Art, George Peabody Col Teachers, Nashville, Tenn, 67-69; dir sch, Sch of the Art Inst Chicago, 69-83; dean, fac fine arts, Univ Ariz, Tucson, 83-90, prof art, 90- *Teaching:* Teacher art, White Plains High Sch, NY, 58-60; instr art, State Univ NY Col Oneonta, 58-60; prof art & dean, Moore Col Art, Philadelphia, 63-67. *Mem:* Nat Asn Schs Art (treas & mem bd dirs, 72-75); Union Independent Cols Art (bd dirs, 72-, chmn bd, 79-); Nat Coun Art Adminr (bd dirs, 73-); Fedn Independent Ill Cols & Univs (bd dirs, 74-). *Res:* Application of industrial materials and techniques to contemporary sculpture. *Publ:* Auth Sculpture: Material and Process, Van Nostrand Reinhold, 70. *Mailing Add:* 10153 E Arizmo St Tucson AZ 85748

IRVING, JOAN
PAINTER, SCULPTOR
b Riverside, Calif, Mar 12, 16. *Study:* Riverside City Col, with Richard Allman, 33-35; Art Ctr Sch, Los Angeles, with Barse Miller & Edward Kaminski, 35-37. *Work:* Metrop Mus Art, New York; Newport Harbor Sch Collection, Calif; Crain Collection, Laguna Beach, Calif; The Buck Collection, Laguna Hills, Calif. *Comn:* Tile mural, Harbor View Sch, Newport Beach, Calif, 49; bronze fountain, comn by E Gene Crain, Laguna Beach, Calif, 72. *Exhib:* Am Watercolor Soc, Nat Acad, New York; Calif Watercolor Soc, Los Angeles Co Mus Art, Calif, 50, 51, 52, 53 & 55; The First 100 Years of the Am Watercolor Soc, Metrop Mus Art, New York, 66; and others. *Pos:* Co-dir, Brandt Painting Workshops, 46-85; chmn, Newport Beach Arts Commission, 50-61; dir, Newport Harbor Art Mus, 60-62. *Awards:* Calif Watercolor Soc Award, 51; James D Phelan Award, 52; Watercolor West Award, 75. *Bibliog:* David W Scott (auth), The Brandts at Blue Sky, Country Beautiful, 7/63; Calif White Paper Painters, Art Gallery, Univ Calif, Fullerton, 76; McClelland E Last (auth), The California Style, Hillcrest Press, 85. *Mem:* Am Watercolor Soc; life fel Royal Soc Arts; hon life mem Laguna Beach Art Asn; hon life mem Watercolor West; hon life mem San Diego Watercolor Soc. *Media:* Watercolor, Oil; Terra-cotta, Wood. *Publ:* Two From California (catalogue retrospective exhib), Riverside Art Mus, Calif, 84. *Mailing Add:* 405 Goldenrod Corona Del Mar CA 92625

IRWIN, GEORGE M
PATRON, COLLECTOR
b Quincy, Ill, May 2, 21. *Study:* Univ Mich, BA, 43; Culver-Stockton Col, Hon DFA, 73; Western Ill Univ, Hon DHL, 90. *Pos:* Chmn bd, Assoc Coun Arts, 62-72 & Ill Arts Coun, 63-71; former mem bd, Ill State Mus & Mus Contemp Art, Chicago; pres, Quincy Soc Fine Arts, 48-78. *Awards:* Distinguished Service Award, Southern Ill Univ, Edwardsville, 81; Nat Honors Award, Nat Trust for Historic Preservation, 83. *Mem:* Life mem Art Inst Chicago; Am Fedn Arts; Nat Trust Hist Preserv; and others. *Collection:* Twentieth century American artists. *Mailing Add:* 1651 Maine St Quincy IL 62301

IRWIN, LANI HELENA
PAINTER
b Annapolis, Md, Oct 27, 47. *Study:* Am Univ, Washington, DC, BFA, 69, MFA, 74. *Work:* Nat Mus Am Art, Washington, DC; Bayly Mus, Charlottesville, Va. *Exhib:* Md Biennial, Baltimore Mus, 74; 19th Area Exhib, Corcoran Gallery Art, Washington, DC, 74; solo exhibs, Washington Proj Arts, 76 & Gallery K, 81, 83 & 86, Washington, DC; Graham Gallery, New York, 77. *Bibliog:* Benjamin Forgey (auth), Irwin: A world of apparent serenity, Washington Star, 5/8/81; Jo Ann Lewis (auth), Views from inside, Washington Post, 5/9/81; Jill Wechsler (auth), Lani Irwin, Am Artist, 6/83. *Media:* Oil. *Dealer:* Gallery K 2010 R St Washington DC 20009. *Mailing Add:* Porziano 68 Assissi 06081 Italy

IRWIN, LISA DRU
PHOTOGRAPHER, PAINTER
b Norfolk, Va, July 27, 53. *Study:* Univ Ga, 71-74; Atlanta Col Art, photography with Ben Davis, 76; San Francisco Art Inst, with Linda Connor, BFA, 77. *Work:* High Mus Art, Atlanta Arts Festival & Nexus Inc, Atlanta, Ga. *Comn:* Photo Mural, Atlanta Hist Soc, 81. *Exhib:* Fogg Art Mus, Harvard Univ, Cambridge, Mass, 80; High Mus Art, Atlanta, 81; solo show, Foto Gallery, New York, 81; Southeastern Ctr Contemp Art, Winston-Salem, NC, 81; Macon Mus Art & Sci, Ga, 81; and others. *Pos:* Com printer, Gamma Photo Lab, San Francisco, 78; photog asst & stylist, Atlanta & San Francisco, 79-81; freelance photogr, Atlanta, 79- *Awards:* 1st Place, North Beach Photog Fair, Columbus Camera, 78; Purchase Award, Arts Festival Atlanta, 80. *Bibliog:* Ben Davis (auth), Watersports, Atlanta Art Papers, 12/80; Judy Henson (auth), Lisa Irwin (review), Art Papers, 11/81. *Media:* Oil; Silkscreen. *Publ:* Contribr, Contemporary Arts Southeast, David Heath, 79; contribr, article, Atlanta Mag, 80; contribr, Brown's Guide to Georgia, 81; contribr, article, Atlanta J, 80-81. *Dealer:* Nexus Galleries Inc 360 Fortune St Atlanta GA 30312. *Mailing Add:* 4742 Thackery Pl NE Seattle WA 98105

IRWIN, ROBERT
ENVIRONMENTAL ARTIST, SCULPTOR
b Long Beach, Calif, Sept 12, 28. *Study:* Otis Art Inst, 48-50; Jepson Art Inst, Los Angeles, 51; Chouinard's Art Inst, Los Angeles, 52-54; San Francisco Inst Art, Hon Dr, 79, Otis-Parson's Art Inst, Hon Dr, 92. *Work:* Art Inst Chicago; Nat Gallery Art, Melbourne, Australia; San Francisco Mus Mod Art, Calif; Mus Mod Art, New York; Whitney Mus, New York; Walker Art Ctr, Minneapolis; Allen Mem Art Mus, Oberlin Col, Ohio; plus others. *Comn:* Mus Contemp Art, Los Angeles. *Exhib:* Matrix, Univ Calif Art Galleries, Berkely, 78; California Perceptions: Light and Space, Calif State Univ, Fullerton, 79; Christo, DiSuvero, Irwin Segal, Neuberger Mus State Univ NY, 79; Painting in Environment, Palazzo Real, Commune di Milano, Italy, 79; Contemporary Art from Southern California, High Mus Art, Georgia, 80; Drawing: The Pluralist Decade, Inst Contemp Art, Univ PA, 80; solo exhibs, Los Angeles Co Art Mus, 81, Fairmont Art Park, Asn, Philadelphia, Pa, 81, Lousiana Mus Art, Humleback, Denmark, 82, Univ Calif, San Diego, 83, Pace Gallery, New York, 85, Wave Hill, New York, 87 & Fisher Gallery, Los Angeles, 89; Seventeen Artists in the Sixties, Los Angelas Co Mus Art, 81; Form and Function: Proposals for Public Art in Philadelphia, Pa Acad Fine Arts, 82. *Teaching:* Instr, Chouinard Art Inst, 57-58; instr, Univ Calif, Los Angeles, 62; instr, Univ Calif, Irvine, 68-69. *Awards:* MacArthur Found Award, 84; Guggenheim fel, 76; MacArthur fel, 84. *Bibliog:* Andrew Yarrow (auth), Whitney Returns to Downtown, The New York Times, 4/16/88; Battling for tenants in a sluggish market, NY Times, 3/4/90; Goings on about town, New Yorker Mag, 3/5/90; David Joselit (auth), Public art & the public purse, Art Am, 7/90. *Media:* All. *Publ:* Auth, Being and Circumstance: Towards a Conditional Art, 85. *Mailing Add:* c/o Pace Gallery 32 E 57th St New York NY 10022

ISAACS, AVROM
ART DEALER, PUBLISHER
b Winnipeg, Man, 26. *Study:* Univ Toronto, BA (polit sci & econ). *Pos:* Dir & owner, Isaacs/Innuit Gallery of Eskimo Art, 70-; assoc fel, Calumet Col, York Univ, 70-; bd dir, Mus Textile, Toronto. *Awards:* LLD York Univ; Order of Can. *Specialty:* The Isaacs/Immuit Gallery, early North American Indian Art and Artifacts; art of the Eskimo of all periods. *Mailing Add:* Isaacs Gallery 179 John St Toronto ON V5T 1X4 Canada

ISAACS, CLAIRE NAOMI
ADMINISTRATOR
b San Francisco, Calif, Feb 12, 33. *Study:* Pomona Col, BA, 54; Ohio State Univ, 54-55; Univ Calif, Berkeley, 62-64; Univ Southern Calif, 71; Claremont Grad Sch, MA(20th century art hist), 75; Harvard Univ, cert art mgt, 77, Coro fel pub affairs for arts mgr, 79. *Collections Arranged:* Children's Book Illustrators (artmobile exhib), 67; Art of the African (traveling exhib), 69; Children's Art From Three Countries: Japan, Iran, USSR, 76; Int Child Art Collection, 1978-83 (auth, catalog), 83. *Pos:* Asst, Art Gallery, Univ Calif,

Berkeley, 61-63; educ supvr, San Francisco Mus Mod Art, 63-66; asst dir & coordr, Visual Art Proj, PACE (Proj to Advance Creativity in Educ), San Bernardino, Inyo & Mono Co Sch, 66-69; dir, Jr Arts Ctr, Munic Arts Dept, Los Angeles, 70-80, Burnsdall Art Ctr, Los Angeles Affairs Dept, 80-83; dir cult affairs, City & Co, San Francisco Arts Comm, 83- *Teaching:* Lectr art for deaf, Univ Calif Exten, Los Angeles, 72. *Awards:* Golden Grate Award, Western Asn Art Mus, 78. *Mem:* Am Asn Mus; Am Asn Youth Mus; Nat Art Educ Asn. *Publ:* Auth, Paul Klee and Galka Scheyer, Artforum, 62; auth, The Art of Borrowing and Distributing Art for the Small Community, Visual Arts Proj, 70; ed, Proceedings of the Conference on Art for the Deaf, Jr League Los Angeles, 75; contribr, The Museum and the Visitor Experience, Western Regional Conf Am Asn Mus, 77. *Mailing Add:* 1737 Pierce St San Francisco CA 94115

ISAACS, RON
PAINTER, INSTRUCTOR
b Cincinnati, Ohio, Oct 14, 41. *Study:* Berea Col, BA, 63; Ind Univ, MFA, 65. *Work:* Am Express, Prudential-Bache, AT&T & Chase Manhattan Bank, New York; Kemper Ins Co Collection, Chicago, Ill. *Exhib:* One-person exhib, Monique Knowlton Gallery, New York, 77-78, 80, 82 & 85, Robert L Kidd Galleries, Birmingham, Mich, 85 & Pittsburgh Ctr for the Arts, 86; More Than Land or Sky: Art from Appalachia, Nat Mus Am Art, Animal Image, Renwick Gallery, Smithsonian Inst, Washington, DC, 81; Realism Invitational, Southeastern Ctr for Contemp Art, Winston-Salem, NC, 82-83; Illusions, Greenville County Mus Art, SC, 84; More Than Meets The Eye: The Art of Trompe L'Oeil, Columbus Mus Art, 85-86; The Medium as Illusion, Calif State Univ, Fullerton, 86; and others. *Teaching:* Instr fine arts, Sue Bennett Col, London, KY, 65-71; prof painting & drawing, Eastern Ky Univ, Richmond, 69- *Awards:* First Purchase Awards, Preview 73, Col of Mount St Joseph, Cincinnati, Ohio, 72, Fifth Berea Drawing Biennial, Berea Col, Ky, 83. *Bibliog:* Harold Olejarz (auth), Ron Isaacs, Arts Mag, 10/78; Madeleine Burnside (auth), Ron Isaacs (rev), Art News, 11/78; Dona Z Meilach (auth), Woodworking: The New Wave, Crown Publ, New York, 81. *Mem:* Am Crafts Coun; Nat Art Educ Asn. *Media:* Acrylic, Birch Plywood. *Dealer:* Monique Knowlton Gallery 153 Mercer St New York NY 10012. *Mailing Add:* 420 Adams Lane Richmond KY 40475

ISAACSON, GENE LESTER
COLLECTOR, HISTORIAN
b Rugby, NDak, June 14, 36. *Study:* Concordia Col, Moorhead, Minn, BA, 58; Univ Northern Colo, MFA, 62; Univ Salzburg Orff Inst, Austria, 63-64. *Pos:* Bd of trustees, Orange Co Ctr Contemp Art & Orange Co Arts Alliance, currently; gallery dir, Rancho Santiago Col, Calif, 85-86, chmn dept art, 92-94. *Teaching:* Chmn dept art, Willamette Univ, 62-63, Santa Ana Col, 64-84; vis assoc prof art hist, Chapman Col, World Campus Afloat, 69-71; ed, Art Forum Newsletter, Calif, 81-91; art hist, Rancho Santiago Col, Santa Ana & Orange Coast Col, Costa Mesa, 85- *Awards:* Profiles in Excellence, Staff Award, R S Col, 92. *Bibliog:* Richard E Ellinger (auth), Design and Color Structure, Int Press, 65. *Res:* Prehistoric and primitive art; African art; oceanic art; art collecting. *Collection:* Extensive survey of West African tribal sculpture; oceanic art, American Indian; United States and European modern painting and graphics. *Publ:* Coauth, Col Exhib Catalogs, Willamette Univ & Santa Ana Col, 62, 68, 72 & 77; auth, Monuments of African Sculpture, Santa Ana Col, 72; articles in Primitive Arts Newsletter, New York, African Arts, Univ Calif, Los Angeles & Western Humanities Rev. *Dealer:* Richard Monsein Gallery 135 Crescent Bay Dr Laguna Beach CA 92651. *Mailing Add:* PO Box 6157 Huntington Beach CA 92646

ISAACSON, LYNN JUDITH
PAINTER, SCULPTOR
b New York, NY, Nov 8, 48. *Study:* Queens Col, with Herb Aach & Louis Finkelstein, MS(art educ), 74; Lehman Col, MFA(painting), 81. *Comn:* Relief construction, Oppenheimer & Co Inc, New York, NY, 81; styrofoam & wood construction, Saratoga Construction Inc, Montreal, Que, 84. *Exhib:* Liberty and the Pursuit of Liberty, Nat Women's Caucus Arts, 86; Lehman College Alumni Show, Lehman Col Art Gallery, Bronx, NY, 86; solo show, Noho Gallery, New York, NY, 86 & 89; Vangarde Gallery, New London, Conn, 88, Noho Gallery, 90; Educ Alliance, New York, 92. *Pos:* Membership secy, Bd Dir, Women's Caucus Arts, 80-86. *Teaching:* Teacher fine arts, Jr High Sch 135, Bronx, NY, 71- *Awards:* Queens Youth Ctr Arts Award, Queens Col, 74. *Bibliog:* Ellen Lee Klein (auth), article, Arts Mag, 9/83. *Media:* Mixed Media on paper based on quilt design. *Publ:* Illusr, Working Big: A Teacher's Guide to Environmental Sculpture (coauths, John Lidstone & Clarence Bunch), Van Nostrand Reinhold Co, 75. *Dealer:* Noho Gallery 168 Mercer St New York NY 10012; Vangarde Gallery 331 Captains Walk New London CT 06320. *Mailing Add:* 229 E 21st St New York NY 10010

ISAACSON, MARCIA JEAN
ARTIST, EDUCATOR
b Atlanta, Ga, Sept 25, 45. *Study:* Univ Ga, Athens, BFA & MFA. *Work:* Minn Mus Art, St Paul; High Mus Art, Atlanta, Ga; Greenville Coun Mus of Art, Greenville, SC; Fla House Rep, Tallahassee; Ala Powers Co; Duke Univ Mus Art, Durham, NC; Eastman Pharmaceuticals, Melvern PA; Arkansas Art Ctr. *Exhib:* Drawings USA, Minn Mus Art, St Paul, 71 & 73; 35 Artists in the SE Traveling Exhib, High Mus Art; Southeastern Graphics Invitational: Drawing, Mint Mus Art, Charlotte, 79; West 79 & 84: Art and the Law, Minn Mus Art, St Paul; Drawing Show, Southeastern Ctr Contemp Arts, Winston-Salem, NC, 82; Kipnis Gallery, Atlanta, 81 & 82; Nat Drawing Invitational, Ark Art Ctr, Little Rock, 86; Ten Years Southeastern Seven, Southeastern Crt Contemp Arts, Winston-Salem, NC, 87; Duke Univ Mus of Art, Durham, NC, Nat Drawing Invitational Emporia State Univ, Emporia, KS. *Pos:* Selection panels, SECCA Grants, Southeastern Ctr Contemp Art, 77, Nat Endowment Arts Fel Grants, 80-81, Ill Art Coun Grants, 85 & Fla Art Coun Grants, 85. *Teaching:* Instr printmaking & drawing, Wesleyan Col, Macon, Ga, 70-73; asst prof drawing, Univ Fla, Gainesville, 73-80, assoc prof, 80- *Awards:* Teacher of the Year, Col Fine Arts, Univ Fla, 77-78; Nat Endowment Arts-Southeastern Ctr Contemp Art Fels, 77; Fla Fine Arts Coun Fel, 79 & 89; Purchase Award, Davidson Col, NC, 73 & State Univ Col, NY, 75. *Media:* Pencil, Charcoal. *Mailing Add:* 617 NE Tenth Pl Gainesville FL 32601

ISAACSON, PHILIP MARSHAL
CRITIC, WRITER
b Lewiston, Maine, June 16, 24. *Study:* Bates Col, BA, 47; Harvard Law Sch, LLB, 50; Bowdoin Col, DFA, 83. *Pos:* Art critic, Maine Sunday Telegram, Portland, 68; mem fed-state adv panel, Nat Endowment for the Arts, 77-; second vpres & mem bd dir, Nat Assembly of State Arts Agencies, 77- *Awards:* Boston Globe-Horn Book Awards, Honor Bk, 89. *Mem:* Maine State Comn Arts & Humanities (chmn, 75-). *Res:* The American eagle as a decorative device; architecture of Maine since 1920; esthetics of architecture. *Publ:* Auth, The American Eagle, NY Graphic Soc, 75; contrib, Marine Forms of American Architecture, Colby Col, 76; auth, Round Buildings, Square Buildings & Buildings that Wiggle Like a Fish, Knopf, 89. *Mailing Add:* 2 Benson St Lewiston ME 04240

ISAACSON, RONALD G
GALLERY DIRECTOR, COLLECTOR
b Chicago, Ill, June 19, 48. *Study:* Northeastern Ill State Univ, BFA, 70. *Exhib:* American Craft Expo, Am Craft Enterprises, St Louis, Mo, 78; Lakefront Festival of Arts, Milwaukee Art Inst, Wis, 79; Monument Sq Art Festival & Wisconsin Designer-Craftsman, Wustum Mus Fine Arts, Racine, 80; Beloit Festival of Art, Wis, 81; Great Lakes Regional Art Expo, Cleveland, Ohio, 82; Marretta Crafts Nat, Ohio, 82; Fountain Sq Arts Festival, Evanston, Ill, 86. *Collections Arranged:* Clay Concepts: Clay as a Vessel, 84, Adornments: Sculptural Jewelry, Gather of Glass: Contemporary Studio Glass & Teapots, 85, Kemenyffy Raku: New Works, 86, Mindscape Galley, Evanston, Ill. *Pos:* Regional mem, Evanston Arts Coun, 74-, adv, grant rev comt, 85-; ed adv, Crafts Report, 79-92; adv, Nat Glass Art Dealers Asn, 83-, arts & bus comt, Evanston Chamber Com, Ill, 84-; co-dir, Mindscape Gallery, Evanston, Ill, currently. *Bibliog:* Sheila Flanagan (auth), A professional approach to fine crafts, 79 & Sharon Shinn (auth), Mindscape collection shows it's stuff to Chicago corporations, 85, Decor Mag; The Gallery as an Art Form, Craft Marketing Yearbk , 84. *Mem:* Nat Crafts Planning Conf (regional mem, 74-); Am Crafts Coun (regional mem, 74-); Ill Arts Coun (regional mem, 74-). *Specialty:* Mixed. *Collection:* Contemporary American crafts 1960-, glass, fiber & ceramics. *Publ:* Coauth, Craft shop design and display marketing techniques, Craft Market News, 78; Publicity: A gallery's point of view, Ceramics Monthly, 80; Reaching new markets tary public relations & stalking the collector, Crafts Report, 85; Glass: The Seductive Media, Am Ceramics Soc, 86. *Mailing Add:* Mindscape Gallery & Studio 1506 Sherman Ave Evanston IL 60201

ISAAK, NICHOLAS, JR
PAINTER, CONSERVATOR
b Manchester, NH, July 5, 44. *Study:* Boston Univ, BFA, 67, MFA, 69; spec study with Walter Murch, Robert Gwathmey & Karl Fortess. *Work:* Va Mus Fine Arts, Richmond; Western Ill Univ, Macomb; Fitchburg Mus Art, Mass; Northern Ill Univ, DeKalb; Bradley Univ, Peoria, Ill; and others. *Exhib:* Pa Acad Fine Arts 164th Ann, 69; one-man shows, Robinson Gallery, Va Mus Fine Arts, 71 & Maxwell Davidson Gallery, New York, 81; Chrysler Mus Art, Norfolk, Va, 72; Print Invitational, Pratt Grahics Ctr, New York, 73; Mod Printmakers, Rochester Inst Technol, NY, 74; 2nd Graphics Biennial, Metrop Mus, Miami, Fla, 75; Fitchburg Mus Art, Mass, 76; Regional Selections, Dartmouth Col Mus, Hanover, NH, 79. *Pos:* Conservator, 79- *Teaching:* Instr printmaking, Norfolk State Col, Va, 69-72; asst prof painting, Boston Univ, Mass, 72-77; assoc prof printmaking & chmn dept, Keene State Col, NH, 77-81. *Awards:* Nat Teaching fel, Dept Health, Educ & Welfare, 69; Cert of Distinction, Va Artists Biennial, Va Mus Art, 71; Rosenthal Found Award, Am Acad & Inst of Arts & Letters, 79. *Media:* Oil; Etching. *Dealer:* Maxwell Davidson Gallery 43 E 78th St New York NY 10021. *Mailing Add:* River Rd No 260 Westmoreland NH 03467

ISENBURGER, ERIC
PAINTER
b Frankfurt am Main, Ger, May 17, 02; US citizen. *Study:* Frankfurt Art Sch. *Work:* Mus Mod Art, New York; Corcoran Gallery Art, Washington, DC; Pa Acad Fine Arts, Philadelphia, Pa; M H De Young Mem Mus, San Francisco, Calif; Wadsworth Atheneum, Hartford, Conn; John Henon Am Inst, Indianapolis, Ind. *Exhib:* Art of Today, 1951, Metrop Mus Art, New York; Pa Acad Fine Arts, Philadelphia; Art Inst Chicago, Ill; Carnegie Inst, Pittsburgh, Pa; eight one-man shows, Knoedler's, New York. *Teaching:* Instr painting, Nat Acad Sch Fine Arts, 59-80. *Awards:* Florence Breevort Eickemeyer Award, Columbia Univ, 80; First Prize & Gold Medal, Corcoran Gallery, Washington, DC; Third Prize, Carnegie Inst, Pittsburg. *Mem:* Academician Nat Acad Design. *Media:* Oil. *Publ:* Auth, article, Am Artist, 48. *Mailing Add:* 140 E 56th St New York NY 10022

ISERMAN, JIM
PAINTER
b Kenosha, Wis, 55. *Study:* Univ Wis, Milwaukee, BFA, 77; Calif Inst Art, MFA, 80. *Comn:* Calendar, Fuji Oil, Osaka, Japan, 90, 91 & 92. *Exhib:* Solo exhib, Flowers, Kuhlenschmidt/Simon, Los Angeles, Calif, 86, Nu-Flowers,

Patty Aande Gallery, San Diego, Calif, 86, Shag Paintings, Feature, New York, 89 & 91, Shag Paintings, Richard Kuhlenschmidt Gallery, Los Angeles, 89; Avant-garde in the '80's, Los Angeles Co Mus Art, 87; Material Conceits, Mint Mus, Charlotte, NC, 90. *Awards:* Fel, Nat Endowment Arts, 84 & 87. *Bibliog:* James Lewis (auth), Home Boys (reproduction), Artforum, p 101-105, 10/91; Peter Schjeldahl (auth), Trend: Sweetness and Light, The Village Voice (reproduction), p 105, 4/14/92; David Pagel (auth), New York Fax (reproduction), Art Issues, p 25-26, 5-6/92; and others. *Mailing Add:* c/o Feature 484 Broome St New York NY 10013

ISHIKAWA, JOSEPH
CONSULTANT, WRITER
b Los Angeles, Calif, July 29, 19. *Study:* Univ Calif, Los Angeles, AB, 42; Univ Nebr. *Collections Arranged:* Jan Saudek: Photographs, 78; Ceremonial Art of West Africa: The Victor DuBois Collection, 78; Irwin Kermen: Collages, 79; Karen Massaro, Clay Paintings & Sculpture, 80; Robert Hanen: Paintings & Constructions, 80; Carl Toth: Photographs, 80; Dominick Labino: Glass, 81; Jiri Anderle, Intaglios & Vladimir Gazovic, Lithographs, 81; 500 Years of German Printmaking, 82; George Bellows Centennial, 82; A Rift in the Curtain: Woodcuts by Tzuu-Hang Chen, 83; Libby Kowalski: Fibers, 84; Works on Paper: Ont & Que, 84; Ivan Picelj: Sculptures, Prints, Paintings, 84; Prints of Peter Takal, 86. *Pos:* From asst cur to cur, Univ Nebr Art Galleries, 43-51; chief cur and asst dir, Des Moines Art Ctr, 51-58; dir, Sioux City Art Ctr, 58-61, Wright Art Ctr, Beloit Col, 61-74 & Kresge Art Ctr, Mich State Univ, 74-86; consult, Sheboygan Arts Found, 66 & Sloan Galleries, Valparaiso Univ, 79. *Teaching:* Emer prof, Alma Col, 79-82, 86, 88. *Awards:* Scandinavian Sem, Am Asn Mus & Fulbright Fels, 65; Beloit Col & Ford Found Humanities Grant, 69; All Univ Res Grant, Mich State Univ, 82. *Mem:* Int Coun Mus; Am Asn Mus; Midwest Mus Conf (vpres, 70, pres, 73-74); Wis Fedn Mus (chmn, 70); Int Coun Fine Arts. *Res:* Influence of Puvis de Chavannes on 20th century painting. *Publ:* Auth, University as tastemaker, Palette, 58; Puvis de Chavannes: Moderne Malgre Lui, Art J, 68; Catalogue Raisonné of the Prints of Peter Takal, Mich State Univ, 86. *Mailing Add:* 8 Vicolo San Silvestro Verona 37100 Italy

ISRAEL, DAVID N
ART DEALER, SCULPTOR
b New Haven, Conn. *Study:* Univ Wis, Madison, BA(art hist), 86; Mass Col Art, 87; Sch Mus Fine Arts, Boston, 87-88. *Exhib:* Grossman, Sch Mus Fine Arts, Boston, Mass, 87 & 88. *Collections Arranged:* The Path to the Beautiful (Brother Thomas porcelains; with catalog), Erie Art Mus, 90; The Past Continues-Two Decades (Sameul Bak; auth, catalog), Koffler Gallery, Toronto, Ont, 90; Vessels from 1980 to 1990 (Brother Thomas; with catalog), Art Gallery Nova Scotia, 91. *Pos:* Assoc dir, Pucker Gallery, Boston, Mass, 88- *Media:* Welded Metal, Mixed Media. *Specialty:* Modern masters, contemporary. *Mailing Add:* c/o Pucker Gallery 171 Newbury St Boston MA 02116

ISROFF, LOLA K
PAINTER
b New York, NY. *Study:* Self taught. *Work:* Wheelabrator-Frye, La Jolla, Calaif; Golden Lamb Inn, Lebanon, Ohio; Akron Art Mus, Ohio; Kaiser Permanente Med Ctr, Cleveland; Metro Health Ctr, Cleveland. *Comn:* Village of Kensington, Wheelabrater-Frye, La Jolla, Calif, 76; Acton Town Hall, Acton Corp, Acton, Mass, 76; Easter Egg Exhib, White House, Washington, DC, 85; Brigham & Women's Hosp, Women's Bd, Boston, 79; Golden Lamb Inn, Lebanon, Ohio, 86. *Exhib:* LKI Collected Work, Canton Art Inst, Canton, Ohio, 72; one-woman show, Akron Art Mus, Akron, Ohio, 75 & Col of Wooster, 90; Firelands Asn Visual Arts, Oberlin, Ohio, 89; Col Wooster Art Mus, Ohio, 90; Akron Art Mus, Ohio, 92; and others. *Awards:* Merit Award, Art News, 50; Girl at Desk, UNICEF, 76; Second Place, Design Contest, Hallmark Cards, 84. *Bibliog:* Jay Johnson & William C Ketchum Jr (coauth), American Folk Art of Twentieth Century, Rizzoli Publ, 83; Anne Graham (auth), House Portraits, Robb Report, 84; Phyllis Tanenbaum (auth), House Portraiture, Coast & Country Hastings, 88. *Mem:* Western Reserve Archit Historian (trustee); Soc Archit Historians. *Media:* Acrylic. *Publ:* Coauth, Old Houses of New York, Defunct, 52; auth, Wonderful World of Ohio, Dept Natural Resources, 66, 67 & 74. *Mailing Add:* 275 N Portage Path Apt 6C Akron OH 44303

ISSERSTEDT, DOROTHEA CARUS
ART DEALER, HISTORIAN
Study: Univ Munich; Univ Freiburg, PhD(art hist); Wheaton Col. *Pos:* Dir, Carus Gallery, currently. *Mem:* Art Dealers Asn Am. *Res:* Medieval art, mainly twelfth and thirteenth century sculpture. *Specialty:* Art of the German Expressionists and art of the twenties; focus on Russian Avant-Garde art 1913-1930. *Mailing Add:* 243 E 82nd St New York NY 10028

ITALIANO, JOÁN
SCULPTOR, LITURGICAL ARTIST
b Worcester, Mass. *Study:* Siena Heights Col, PhB, Studio Angelico, MFA; Barry Univ Miami, Fla; Nino Caruso, Rome, Italy, Beani & Cacia; Pietrasanta, Italy. *Work:* Mount Holyoke Col Mus; Norstar Security Trust, Rochester, NY; Bingham, Dana & Gould, Boston; Int Ctr for Ceramics, Rome, Italy; Brown, Rudnick, Freed & Gesmer, Boston. *Comn:* Our Mother of Joy Fountain, comn by John Cardinal Wright, St Vincent Hosp, Worcester, Mass, 59; Stations of the Cross, comn by architect, Our Lady of Lourdes Church, Milbury, Mass, 62; Tree of Life Fountain, Mary Manning Walsh Carmelite Home, New York, 71; Shrine to the American Saints, Our Lady Good Counsel Church, W Boylston, Mass, 86; memorial panel (ceramic on wood), Mercy Ctr, Worcester, Mass, 90. *Exhib:* Norton Gallery, West Palm Beach, Fla; Salem State Col, 87; Cantor Gallery, Holy Cross Col, Worcester, Mass, 88; Pindar Gallery, New York; and others. *Pos:* Dir, Art Gallery, Barry Col, 56-58; consult liturgical art, Dick Bros Archit Interiors, 62-72; dir, Studio Angelico N, West Boyleston, Mass, 59- & Studio Angelico S, West Palm Beach, Fla, 91- *Teaching:* Instr sculpture, Barry Col, Miami, Fla, 56-58; assoc prof sculpture & ceramics, Col of the Holy Cross, 69-89, chmn fine arts dept, 77-80. *Awards:* First Prize in Sculpture, Palm Beach Art League 37th & 38th Ann; Bachelor Ford Fel, 76; Prize, NE Sculptors Assoc, Boston, 83 & 86; Faculty Fel, 88. *Bibliog:* Vivian Raynor (auth), review, Pindar Show, New York Times, 7/6/84; James Reil (auth), article, Worcester Mag, 5/20/81; George French (auth), Sculptor Joan Italiano's new direction is right on course, Evening Gazette, Worcester, Mass, 10/22/82; and many others. *Mem:* New Eng Sculptors, Asn; Int Sculpture Ctr; Third Order St Dominic. *Media:* All Media. *Dealer:* Art South 4401 Cresson St Philadelphia PA; Pindar Gallery 127 Greene St New York NY. *Mailing Add:* PO Box 175 West Boylston MA 01583

ITATANI, MICHIKO
PAINTER
b Osaka, Japan, May 8, 48. *Study:* Art Inst Chicago, MFA, 76. *Work:* Art Inst Chicago, Mus Contemp Art, Chicago. *Exhib:* Solo exhibs, Alternative Mus, New York, 85, Rockford Mus, Ill, 87; Musee du Que, Can, 88; Asahi Broadcasting Gallery, Japan, 90; Chicago Cult Ctr, 92; Muskegon Mus, 92; Univ Wis, Milwaukee Art Mus, 92; and others. *Teaching:* Prof painting & drawing, Art Inst Chicago, 79- *Awards:* Fel, Nat Endowment Art, 80-81; Ill Arts Coun Artist's Grant, 84 & 85; John Simon Guggenheim Fel, 90-91. *Bibliog:* Haruosanda (auth), article, Mainichi, Japan, 88; Kathryn Hixon (auth), article, Arts Mag, 90; Garret Holg (auth), article, Art News; and others. *Media:* Oil, Silverpoint. *Publ:* NAME Artbook II. *Dealer:* Deson/Saunders Gallery 750 N Orleans Chicago IL 60610. *Mailing Add:* Dept Art Sch Art Inst Chicago Columbus Dr Jackson Chicago IL 60603

ITCHKAWICH, DAVID MICHAEL
PRINTMAKER, ILLUSTRATOR
b Westerly, RI, Aug 18, 37. *Study:* RI Sch Design, BFA. *Work:* John Sloane Study Collection, Univ Del; Charles Dana Mus, Colgate Univ; New York Pub Libr; Munson-Williams-Proctor Inst, Utica, NY; Metrop Mus Art, New York. *Exhib:* Nat Print Exhib, Brooklyn Mus, NY, 70 & 72; Davidson Nat Print Show, Davidson Univ, 73-75; one-man shows, Munson, Proctor, Williams Inst, Utica, NY, 76, Newport Art Asn, RI, 78; Martin Sumers Graphics, 76; Nat Exhib, New York Soc Illusr, 78; and others. *Bibliog:* The visions of David Itchkawich, Intellectual Dig, 2/72; John Mattingly (auth), When Men Were Animals and Animals Were Men: A Study of the Graphic Work of David Itchkawich, Angelica Press, NY, 76; Suzanne Boorsch (auth), The pleasure of creation: The work of David Itchkawich, Print Collector's Newslett, 9-10/78. *Dealer:* Horizon Gallery 45 Christopher St New York NY 10014. *Mailing Add:* 223 E 85th New York NY 10028

ITURRALDE, TERESA
ART DEALER, COLLECTOR
b Mexico City, Mex, Oct 7, 63. *Study:* Univ San Diego, BA, 85. *Pos:* Art dir, Iturralde Gallery, 87-; art consult, Calvin J Goodman, 88- *Teaching:* Teaching asst photog, Univ San Diego, 85 & 86. *Bibliog:* Jeanne Beach (auth), Gallery to feature Latin American art, La Jolla Light, 3/26/87; Daniel Munoz (auth), New Mexico art gallery, La Prensa, San Diego, 4/3/87; Latin Am Art Mag, First Word p 6, & the Latin Am Market p 31, Inaugural Issue, 89; San Diego County, City Mag Local Gallery Owners, Vol 2, p 72, 90; Nancy Kapitanoff (auth), A shared Obsession: Two Sisters Passion for Latin American Art, Los Angeles Times, 5/10/92. *Mem:* World Monuments Found. *Specialty:* Contemporary Mexican and Latin American art. *Collection:* Contemporary art with emphasis on Mexican and Latin American art. *Mailing Add:* 154 N La Brea Ave Los Angeles CA 90036

IVERS, LOUISE H
HISTORIAN, ADMINISTRATOR
Study: Boston Univ, BFA, 64; Univ NMex, MA, 67, PhD, 75. *Teaching:* Prof & chair dept art, Calif State Univ, Dominguez Hills, 71- *Mem:* Soc Archi Historians. *Publ:* Auth, Montezuma Hotel at Las Vegas Hot Springs New Mexico, J Soc Archit Historians, 74; Hotel Castaneda Las Vegas New Mexico, NMex Archit, 76; Indigenous dwellings of Mexico, The Masterkey, 1979; Evolution of modernistic architecture in Long Beach, Southern Calif Quarterly, 86. *Mailing Add:* Calif State Univ Dominguez Hills 1000 E Victoria St Carson CA 90747

IVERSEN, EARL HARVEY
PHOTOGRAPHER, EDUCATOR
b Chicago, Ill, Jan 26, 43. *Study:* Univ Ill, Chicago Circle, BA, 70; RI Sch Design, MFA, 73. *Work:* Mus Mod Art, New York; Univ Colo Art Mus, Boulder; Sheldon Gallery, Univ Nebr, Lincoln; Spencer Art Mus, Univ Kans, Lawrence; Sioux City Art Ctr, Iowa. *Exhib:* The Great West, Denver Art Mus, 77; solo exhib, Mass Col Art, 78, Metropolitan Col, Denver, 78, Kresge Gallery, Mich State Univ, Ann Arbor, 80 & Sioux City Art Ctr, 82; An Open Land, Chicago Art Inst, 83; two-person exhib, Spencer Art Mus, Lawrence, Kans, 83. *Teaching:* Instr photog, Mass Col Art, 73-74; assoc prof design & photog, Univ Kans, Lawrence, 74-, photogr, Univ Theater, 81- *Awards:* Excellence Award Photog, Univ & Col Designers Asn, 76; grant, 76 & fel, 83, Nat Endowment Arts. *Publ:* Illusr, Photo Art Mag, #12 & #14, 81; illusr, Erotic Photography, Demarais Press, 81; illusr, Kansas in Color, Regents Press Kans, 82. *Mailing Add:* Dept Art Univ Kans Lawrence KS 66045

IVES, COLTA FELLER
CURATOR, EDUCATOR
b San Diego, Calif, Apr 5, 43. *Study:* Mills Col, BA, 64; Columbia Univ, MA, 66. *Collections Arranged:* The Great Wave (auth, catalog), 75, Felix Nadar Photographs, 77, The Painterly Print (coauth, catalog), 80, Albrecht Durer and the Holy Family, 82, Eugene Delacroix: Drawings & Prints, 84, Pierre Bonnard: The Graphic Art (coauth, catalog), 89, Metrop Mus Art, New York, NY. *Pos:* Mem staff, Metrop Mus Art, New York, 66-, cur-in-charge, dept prints & illus bks, 75- *Teaching:* Adj prof art hist, Columbia Univ, 70- *Awards:* First Place Award Exhib Catalog, Art Libr Asn New York, 75. *Mem:* Grolier Club, Print Coun Am (exec bd, 76-78, 84-86, vpres, 89-). *Res:* Nineteenth century French prints. *Publ:* Auth, The Flight into Egypt by G D Tiepolo, Metrop Mus Art, New York, 72 Rauschenberg: Photos In and Out City Limits, New York, Universal Ltd Art Ed, 82; French Prints in the Era of Impressionism & Symbolism, Metrop Mus Art, New York, 89; Degas: books in review, Print Collector's Newslett, 85; The Nabis and the French Popular Press, Print Quarterly, 90. *Mailing Add:* Dept of Prints & Photographs Metrop Mus Art New York NY 10028

IVEY, JAMES BURNETT
CARTOONIST, COLLECTOR
b Chattanooga, Tenn, Apr 19, 25. *Study:* Univ Louisville; George Washington Univ; Nat Art Sch. *Work:* Libr Cong, Washington, DC; Syracuse Univ, NY; Albert T Reid Collection, Univ Kans; Mo State Hist Soc; State Hist Soc Wis, Madison. *Collections Arranged:* Cartoons from Gillray to Goldberg, San Francisco Mus Art, 62; Cartoon Museum, Madeira Beach, Fla, 67-68; Cartoon from Hogarth to Herblock, Lock Haven Art Ctr, Orlando, Fla, 71. *Pos:* Political cartoonist, Washington Star, DC, 50-53, St Petersburg Times, 53-59, San Francisco Examiner, 59-66, Rothco Syndicate, 63- & Orlando Sentinel, 67-77; cur & dir, Cartoon Mus, Madeira Beach, Fla, 67-68 & Orlando, Fla, 75-; ed & publ, Cartoon, 71-80. *Teaching:* Adj prof cartooning, Univ Central Fla, 78-82; Rollins Col, 87- *Awards:* Reid Found Fel, 59; Silver T-Square, Nat Cartoonist Soc, 80. *Bibliog:* John Chase (auth), Today's Cartoon, Haiser Press, 63; Maurice Horn (auth), World Encyclopedia of Cartoons, Chelsea House, 80, Contemp Graphic Artists, Gale, 88. *Mem:* Nat Cartoonist Soc (chmn Fla chap, 72-); Am Asn Ed Cartoonists. *Media:* Ink. *Collection:* Original cartoon art, approximately 2000 cartoons representing entire history of the art in twenty countries. *Publ:* Contribr, Freedom & Union: European Cartoonists, 61; Cartoonist Profiles, 70; Cartoon: Pen Mightier than Suit, 71; US History in Cartoon, Int Media, 79; Wash Tubbs, First Adventure Comic Strip, Luna Press, 74. *Mailing Add:* 561 Obispo Ave Orlando FL 32807

IWAMASA, KEN
EDUCATOR, PRINTMAKER
b Manzanar, Calif, Apr 28, 43. *Study:* Calif State Univ, Long Beach, BA, 66, MA, 72. *Work:* El Camino Col; City of Los Angeles; Rio Hondo Col. *Exhib:* One-man shows, Rio Hondo Col, 76 & Old Dominion Univ, 77; World Print Competition, San Francisco Mus Mod Art, Calif, 77; Detroit Nat Print Symposium, Cranbrook Acad Art, 80; Fantastic Art, Castle San Giorgo, Italy, 81; Works on Paper, Cheney-Cowles Mem Mus, Spokane, 81; Artist as Social Critic, Mich State Univ, Ann Arbor, 81; and others. *Teaching:* Asst prof drawing & printmaking, Univ Colo, Boulder, 72- *Awards:* Grants & Purchase Awards from Scott Found, Japan Found & Univ Colo. *Media:* Screen, Lithography. *Dealer:* Miriam Perlman Gallery 505 N Lake Shore Dr Chicago IL 60611; Sebastian Moore Gallery 1411 Market St Denver CO. *Mailing Add:* Dept Fine Arts Univ Colo Boulder Boulder CO 80309

IWAMOTO, RALPH SHIGETO
PAINTER
b Honolulu, Hawaii, Sept 13, 27. *Study:* Art Students League, with John Von Wicht, Vaclav Vytlacil & Byron Browne, 48-49 & 51-53. *Work:* Butler Inst Am Art, Youngstown, Ohio; Sheldon Swope Art Gallery, Terre Haute, Ind; Herbert F Johnson Art Mus, Cornell Univ; State Found on Cult & Arts, Honolulu; Wadsworth Atheneum, Hartford, Conn. *Exhib:* Pa Acad, Philadelphia, 58; Whitney Mus Ann, New York, 58; solo shows, Columbia Mus Art, SC, 59, Elmira Col, NY, 68 & St Mary's Col, Md, 89; Betty Parsons Gallery, New York, 79; Arte Fiera, Bologna, Italy, 78; Bergen Co Mus, NJ, 83; Newark Mus, NJ, 83; Contemp Mus, Honolulu, 90; Open Mind, Wadsworth Atheneum, 91; and others. *Awards:* Purchase Prize, Butler Inst Am Art, 57; Fel, John Hay Whitney Found, 58; Grant, Adolph & Esther Gottlieb Found, 87. *Bibliog:* James Mellow (auth), Art Rev, New York Times, 2/17/73; K Ichida (auth), article, Ichimai Art Mag, Tokyo, 12/80; Helen A Harrison (auth), article, New York Times, 12/29/85. *Media:* Acrylic, Oil. *Publ:* Auth, Octagon Concepts. *Mailing Add:* 463 West St A-1110 New York NY 10014

IZUKA, KUNIO
SCULPTOR, PAINTER
b Tokyo, Japan, Mar 2, 39. *Study:* Otis Art Inst, Los Angeles Co; Art Students League. *Work:* Mus Mod Art Tokyo, Japan. *Comn:* Monumental sculpture, Warner Commun, Los Angeles, 72. *Exhib:* First Int Exhib Mod Sculpture, Hakone Open-Air Mus, Japan, 69; Exhib Contemp Japanese Art, Mus Mod Art, Rio de Janeiro, 71 & Milan, Italy, 72. *Teaching:* Asst instr sculpture, Art Students League, 68-69. *Awards:* Purchase Prize, 50th Anniversary Show, Otis Art Inst Los Angeles Co, 68; Second Prize, Exhib Contemp Japanese Art, New York, 72. *Mem:* Sculptors Guild; Japanese Artist Asn New York. *Media:* Metal; Oil. *Mailing Add:* 2 Allen St New York NY 10002

IZUMI, KIYOSHI
ARCHITECT, EDUCATOR
b Vancouver, BC, Mar 24, 21. *Study:* Univ Man, BArch; Mass Inst Technol, MCP. *Pos:* Mem, Sask Arts Bd, 60; mem bd trustees, Nat Mus Can, Govt Can, 68-74; chmn vis comt, Nat Art Gallery Can, Ottawa, 70-74. *Teaching:* Mem fac environ studies, Univ Waterloo, retired. *Mem:* Academician Royal Can Acad Arts; fel Royal Archit Inst Can. *Publ:* Auth, Some considerations on the art of architecture and art in architecture, Structurist, Univ Sask, Modern Press, No 2. *Mailing Add:* 289 Hiawatha Dr Waterloo ON N2L 2V9 Canada

J

JAAR, ALFREDO
SCULPTOR
b Santiago, Chile, Feb 5, 56. *Study:* Instituto Chileno Norteamericano de Cultura, Chile, 79, Universidad de Chile, Santiago, Chile, 81. *Work:* Found L'Arche de la Fraternite, La Defense, Paris; High Mus Art, Atlanta, GA; La Jolla Mus Contemp Art, CA; Lannan Found, Los Angeles, CA. *Exhib:* Documenta 8, Kassel, WGer, 87; Mus Nat d'Art Mod, Paris, 89; Brooklyn Mus, NY, 89; La Hoya Mus Contemp Art, Los Angeles, 89; San Francisco Mus Modern Art, CA, 90; Betty Rymer Gallery, The Sch Art Institute Chicago, IL, 90; Solo exhibs, Grey Art Gallery, New York, 87, Institute Contemp Art, 88, Galerie Gabrielle, Maubrie, Paris, France, 88, Brooklyn Mus, New York, 89, Galerie Barbara Farber, Amsterdam, Holland, 89, New Mus Contemp Art, New York, 90, Carnegie Mellon Art Gallery, Pittsburgh, PA, 90. *Awards:* John Simon Guggenheim Foun Grant, 85; NY State Coun Arts Grant, 85. *Bibliog:* Anthony Aziz (auth), Fax Art, Artweek, 1/90; David Bonetti (auth), New S F Exhibit is a Fax-finding mission, San Francisco Examiner, 1/15/90, c-7; Joshua Decter (auth), Alfredo Jaar, Diane Brown Gallery, Contemporanea, 9/90, p 97-98; Lisa Gilmer (auth), A Global View of Youth Protest, The Gazette, London, Ontario, 2/9/90; Andy Grundberg (auth), Images of Third-World Dislocation, New York Times, 5/4/90, c-30. *Mailing Add:* 12 Warren St 3rd Fl New York NY 10007

JACHNA, JOSEPH DAVID
PHOTOGRAPHER, EDUCATOR
b Chicago, Ill, Sept 12, 35. *Study:* Univ Mo Photo-Jour Workshop, 57; Ill Inst Technol Inst Design, with Aaron Siskind, Harry Callahan & Frederick Sommer, BS(art educ), 58, MS(photog), 61. *Work:* George Eastman House, Int Mus Photog, Rochester, NY; Art Inst Chicago; Photog Collection, Exchange Nat Bank of Chicago; Mass Inst Technol; Mus Mod Art, New York. *Exhib:* Solo exhibs, Art Inst Chicago, 61, Nikon Salon, Tokyo, 74, Visual Studies Workshop Gallery, Rochester, NY, 79, Chicago Ctr Contemp Photog, 80, Focus Gallery, San Francisco, 81 & Tweed Mus, Duluth, Minn, 86; Photog: Midwest Invitational, Walker Art Ctr, Minneapolis, 73; Photographers and the City, Mus Contemp Art, Chicago, 77; Second Sight, Carpenter Ctr Visual Arts, Harvard Univ, 81; Josephson, Jachna & Siegel: Chicago Experimentalists, San Francisco Mus Mod Art, 88; Vanishing Presence, Walker Art Ctr, Minneapolis, 89. *Teaching:* From instr to asst prof photog, Inst Design, Ill Inst Technol, 61-69; from asst prof to prof photog, Univ Ill, Chicago Campus, 69-; workshops, Peninsula Sch Art, Door Co, Wis, summers 69-71. *Awards:* Fac Grant Color Photog, Univ Ill, Chicago Circle Campus, 72; Ferguson Grant, Friends of Photog, Carmel, Calif, 73; Nat Endowment Arts, 76; John Simon Guggenheim Mem Found Fel, 80. *Bibliog:* Landscape illusions, In: Photography Year 1974, Time-Life Bks, 74; John B Turner (auth), Joseph D Jachna, Photo-Forum, Auckland, NZ, 75; Light Touching Silver (monogr), Chicago Mus Photog, 80. *Publ:* Art in America, New Talent Issue, 62; Camera Mainichi '74-9, 74; Photog & Art-Interactions since 1946, 87; Landscape As Photograph, Yale Univ Press, 85; Vanishing Presence, Walker Art Ctr & Rizzoli, 89. *Dealer:* Stuart Baum 1415 W Wrightwood Chicago IL 60614. *Mailing Add:* Dept Art Univ Ill at Chicago Chicago IL 60680

JACKARD, JERALD WAYNE See Jacquard

JACKSON, BILLY MORROW
PAINTER, EDUCATOR
b Kansas City, Mo, Feb 23, 26. *Study:* Washington Univ, BFA; Univ Ill, Urbana, MFA. *Work:* Metrop Mus Art, New York; Calif Palace Legion of Honor, San Francisco, Calif; Nat Collection, Smithsonian Inst & Nat Gallery Art, Washington, DC; and others. *Comn:* Social Reform & the Progressive Movement, Jane Addams, Ill State Capital, Apringfield, 88-89. *Exhib:* McClung Mus, Univ Tenn, 65-67; Fine Arts Gallery San Diego, Calif, 66; Lehigh Univ, Bethlehem, Pa, 66; Decatur Art Ctr, Ill, 66; 4 Arts Gallery Evanston, Ill, 67; and others. *Teaching:* Prof art, Univ Ill, Urbana, retired, 87. *Awards:* Purchase Prize, Evansville Mus Arts & Sci, 66; Union League Club, Chicago, 67; and others. *Bibliog:* Dr Howard Wooden (auth), Billy Morrow Jackson: Interpretations of Time & Light, Univ Ill Press, Champaign, 90. *Media:* Oil, Watercolor. *Dealer:* Jane Haslem Salon 2025 Hillyer Pl Washington DC 20009. *Mailing Add:* 706 W White Champaign IL 61820

JACKSON, EVERETT GEE
ILLUSTRATOR, PAINTER
b Mexia, Tex, Oct 8, 1900. *Study:* Tex A&M Univ; Art Inst Chicago; San Diego State Col, BA; Univ Southern Calif, MA; also study in Mex. *Work:* Houston Mus Art, Tex; Fine Arts Gallery, San Diego, Calif; Los Angeles Co Mus Art; Pa Acad Fine Arts, Philadelphia. *Exhib:* Am Painting Exhib, Art

Inst Chicago, Ill, 27; Whitney Mus Am Art, New York; Pa Acad Fine Arts, Philadelphia; Los Angeles Co Mus Art; San Francisco Mus Art; retrospective, Inst Nacional de Belas Artes & Inst Nacional de Arqueologia y Historia, Mexico City, 79, San Diego Mus Man, 89; plus others. *Pos:* Bd trustees, Fine Arts Soc, San Diego, 35-80, chmn Latin-Am arts comt, 65-70, acquisitions comt; mem adv bd, Calif State Univ, San Diego, 63-70; col management comm, San Diego Mus Art, 87-88. *Teaching:* Prof art, Calif State Univ, San Diego, 30-63; prof art, Univ Costa Rica, 62. *Awards:* First Anne Bremer Prize, San Francisco Art Asn, 29; First Prize, Leisser Farnham Prize, 30, Fine Arts Gallery, San Diego; Los Angeles Co Mus Art Award, 34. *Mem:* San Diego Art Guild; Am Asn Univ Prof. *Media:* Oil. *Res:* Maya sculpture, Cupan, Honduras, Tikal, Guatemala. *Publ:* Illusr, Wonderful adventure of Paul Bunyon, Ugly Duckling, Popol Vuh, Ramona & American Indian legends, Limited Ed Club & Heritage; auth, Burros and Paintbrushes, 85, Tex A&M Univ Press; Its a Long Road to Comondu, 87; Four Trips to Antiguity, San Diego Univ Press, 91. *Mailing Add:* 1234 Franciscan Way San Diego CA 92116

JACKSON, HARRY ANDREW
PAINTER, SCULPTOR
b Chicago, Ill, Apr 18, 24. *Study:* Art Inst Chicago, 31-38; with Ed Grigware, Cody, Wyo, 38-42; Brooklyn Mus Art Sch, with Hans Hofmann, 46-48; Univ Wyo, Hon Dr, 86. *Work:* Whitney Gallery Western Art, Cody; Vatican Mus, Rome; Minn Inst Arts; Woolarac Mus, Bartlesville, Okla; Am Mus Gt Brit, Bath, Eng. *Comn:* Stampede, 60 & Range Burial, 66 (oil murals), Whitney Gallery Western Art; Sor Capanna (monument), Piazza dei Mercanti, Rome, 62; painted sculpture of John Wayne (for cover), Time Mag, 8/8/69; Sacagawea, Buffalo Bill Historical Ctr, Cody, Wyo; Official Monument to John Wayne (heroic bronze), Beverly Hills, Calif, 84; Sacagewa (patinaed), Santa Barbara, Calif, 85. *Exhib:* Amon Carter Mus, Ft Worth, Tex, 61 & 68; Nat Collection Fine Arts, Washington, DC, 64; Nat Acad Design, New York, 64, 65, 67, 68 & 70; Nat Cowboy Hall of Fame, Oklahoma City, 66 & 70-72; Gilcrease Mus, Tulsa, Okla, 80; retrospective, Buffalo Bill Historical Ctr, Cody, Wyo, 81 & Univ Wyo Art Mus, 87; Palm Springs Desert Mus, Calif, 81; Minneapolis Inst Arts, Minn, 82; J Poole Gallery, London, 82; Trailside Gallery, Scottsdale, Ariz, 83. *Pos:* Off combat artist, USMC, 44-45. *Awards:* Fulbright Grant, 54; Samuel Finley Breese Morse Gold Medal, Nat Acad Design, 68; Silver Medal, Nat Cowboy Hall of Fame, 71. *Bibliog:* M Amaya (auth), article, Connoisseur, 79; L Pointer & D Goddard (auth), Harry Jackson, Abrams Publ, 81; Harry Jackson, Forty Years of his Work 1941-81, Wyo Foundry Studios, 81; Harry Jackson, Thirty Years in Versillia, City Camaiore, Italy, 85; and others. *Mem:* USMC Combat Corresp Asn; Nat Sculpture Soc; Fel Am Artists Prof League; assoc mem Nat Acad Design. *Media:* Oil; Bronze. *Publ:* Contribr monograph catalog, Kennedy Galleries, 69; auth, Lost Wax Bronze Casting, Northland Press, 72 & Van Nostrand Reinhold, 79; Harry Jackson. *Mailing Add:* c/o Buffalo Bill Hist Center 720 Sheridan Ave Cody WY 82414

JACKSON, HERB
PAINTER, PRINTMAKER
b Raleigh, NC, Aug 16, 45. *Study:* Davidson Col, BA, 67; Philips Univ, Marburg, WGer; Univ NC, MFA, 70. *Work:* Brit Mus, London; Libr Cong, Washington, DC; Victoria & Albert Mus, London; Brooklyn Mus Art, NY; Baltimore Mus Art, Md; Whitney Mus Am Art, New York; Minneapolis Inst Arts; Mint Mus, Charlotte, NC. *Comn:* Mural, Vail Commons, Davidson Col, 84; First Union Nat Bank, 88. *Exhib:* One-person exhibs, Mint Mus Art, Charlotte, NC, Springfield Art Mus, Mo, & Fundacao Calouste Gulbenkian, Lisbon, Portugal, Ashville Mus Art, NC; Mint Mus Art, Charlotte, NC, 68, 70-71, 79 & 81; Am Acad & Inst Arts & Letts, New York, 81 & 87; Brooklyn Mus Art, 81; Knoxville World's Fair, Tenn, 82; Contemp Arts Ctr, New Orleans, La, 88; Kunstsammlungen der Veste Coburg, Ger, 88; Lorenzelli Fine Art, Milan, Italy, 89; Exhib Hall of Union Moscow Artists, Moscow, USSR, 89; Samuel P Harn Mus, Gainesville, Fla, 90. *Teaching:* William H Williamson prof fine art, Davidson Col, 69- *Awards:* Southeastern Ctr Contemp Art Grant, 81; Artist Fel, 84. *Bibliog:* Dr Roger Lipsey (auth), Herb Jackson Drawings at the Mint Museum, Arts, 6/83; Dr Donald Kuspit (auth), Herb Jackson: The ArcheologicalSurface, 11/88; Frank Getlein (auth), Herb Jackson: Vitreographs, 8/90. *Mem:* Col Art Asn Am; Southeastern Col Art Conf. *Media:* Acrylic, Graphics. *Dealer:* Jerald Melberg Gallery 119 E 7th St Charlotte NC 28202; Fay Gold Gallery, 247 Buckhead Ave Atlanta GA 30305. *Mailing Add:* Box 2495 Davidson NC 28036

JACKSON, LEE
PAINTER
b New York, NY, Feb 2, 09. *Study:* NY Univ, 1 yr; Art Students League; also with John Sloan & George Luks. *Work:* Metrop Mus Art, New York; Corcoran Gallery Art; Walker Art Ctr, Minneapolis, Minn; Nebr Art Asn, Lincoln; Los Angeles Co Mus Art, Calif; Norfolk Va Mus; Smithsonian Mus, Washington, DC; Butler Art Inst, Youngstown, Ohio. *Exhib:* 56th Ann Paintings, Art Inst Chicago, 46; Whitney Mus Am Art, New York, 49-50; Am Painting Today 1950, Metrop Mus Am, 50; 23rd Biennial, Corcoran Gallery Art, 53; 140th Ann, Nat Acad Design, New York, 65; and many others. *Teaching:* Instr painting & drawing, Sch Art Studies, 47-48; instr painting & drawing, City Col New York, 48-54. *Awards:* Guggenheim Fel, 41; Univ Nebr Art Gallery Purchase Prize, 43; Thomas B Clarke Prize, Nat Acad Design, 51 & 61. *Mem:* Art Students League; Audubon Artists Am; Am Watercolor Soc; Artists Equity Asn; Nat Soc Painters in Casein. *Media:* Oil, Tempera. *Publ:* Contribr, Drawings by American Artists, 47; contribr, Am Artist Mag, 9/53. *Mailing Add:* PO Box 80 Bridgehampton NY 11932

JACKSON, MARION ELIZABETH
HISTORIAN, EDUCATOR
b Saginaw, Mich, July 7, 41. *Study:* Univ Mich, PhD(art hist), 85, with Rudolf Arnheim, Evan Maurer, Marvin Eisenberg & Roy Rappaport. *Collections Arranged:* Inuit Sculpture (auth, catalog), Univ Mich Mus Art, 79; The Vital Vision: Drawings by Ruth Tulurialik (auth, catalog), Art Gallery Windsor, Ont, 86; Contemporary Inuit Drawings, Macdonald Stewart Art Ctr, Univ Guelph, 87; Ruth Weisberg - Paintings, Drawings, Prints 1986-1988, Univ Mich Sch Art, 87; Parr: Drawings, Mt St Vincent Univ, 88. *Pos:* Assoc dean, Univ Mich Sch Art, 86-91. *Teaching:* Lectr, art hist, Eastern Mich Univ, Ypsilanti, 83-84; assoc prof, Univ Mich Sch Art, 86-91, Carleton Univ, Ottawa, Can, 91- *Mem:* Col Art Asn; Native Am Art Studies Asn; Nat Assn for Humanities Educ. *Res:* Native arts, particularly North American Inuit art; folk arts; outsider arts; & art criticism; African American art. *Publ:* Contemp Print Drawings, Macdonald Stewart Art Ctr, 87; Ruth Weisberg: Paintings, Drawings, Prints, 1968-1988, Univ Mich Sch Art, 88; A New Day Dawning: Thirty Years of Cape Dorset Prints, Univ Mich Mus Art, 89; Tyree Guyton: Listen to His Art, Detroit Inst Arts, 90; Auth, Pudlo: Thirty Years of Drawing, Nat Gallery of Can, 90. *Mailing Add:* 190 Globe Ave Apt 3 Ottawa ON 48103 K1S 2C7 Canada

JACKSON, OLIVER LEE
PAINTER, SCULPTOR
b St Louis, Mo, 35. *Study:* Ill Wesleyan Univ, BFA, 58; Univ Iowa, MFA, 63. *Work:* San Francisco Mus Mod Art; Oakland Mus; Seattle Art Mus; New Orleans Mus Art; Crocker Art Mus, Sacramento, Calif. *Comn:* Painting for state off bldg, San Francisco, Calif Arts Coun, 87; marble sculpture for Gen Servs Admin Bldg, Oakland, Calif, 88. *Exhib:* Solo exhib, Seattle Art Mus, 82; Fresh Paint: 15 Calif Artists, San Francisco Mus Mod Art, 82; From the Sunny Side, Oakland Mus, 82; Biennial Exhib, Whitney Mus, 83; An International Survey of Recent Painting and Sculpture, Mus Mod Art, New York, NY, 84; States of War, Seattle Art Mus, Ore, 85; California Figurative Sculpture, Palm Springs Desert Mus, 87; Albright-Knox Gallery, Buffalo, NY, 89. *Pos:* Visiting artist, Art Inst Chicago, 69; artist in residence, Wake Forest Univ, SE Ctr Contemp Art, 80 & NC Sch Arts, Winston-Salem, 80; vis artist, Univ Calif, Santa Barbara, 85, Univ Wa, Seattle, 85, Univ Ill, Champaign, 88, Univ Calif, Berkeley, 89. *Teaching:* Instr, Southern Ill Univ, East St Louis, 67-69, Oberlin Col, 69-70; prof art, Calif State Univ, Sacramento, 71- *Awards:* Award in Painting, Nat Endowment Arts, 80; Nettie Marie Jones Fel, 84. *Bibliog:* Regina Hackett (auth), Oliver Lee Jackson (catalog), SE Ctr Contemp Art, 80; Thomas Albright & Jan Butterfield (co-auth), Oliver Jackson, Seattle Art Mus, 82; Robert Pincus (auth), Oliver Jackson, Iannetti-Lanzone Gallery, San Francisco, 88. *Media:* Oil; Marble. *Dealer:* Eve Mannes Gallery Atlanta GA. *Mailing Add:* 251 Post St No 540 San Francisco CA 94108

JACKSON, RUTH AMELIA
CURATOR
b Paterson, NJ; Can citizen. *Study:* Parsons Sch, Ridgewood, NJ; Holton Arms, Washington, DC; Maret French Sch, Washington, DC; Miss Spauldings, Queensgate, London, Eng. *Collections Arranged:* Auguste Rodin, 63, Mains et Merveilles, 72, Gold for the Gods, 77, The Decorative Scene--Montreal, 1860-1914, 77, Treasures of London, 77 & Spider Woman and the Navajo, 78, Montreal Mus Fine Arts. *Pos:* Pres, Can Guild of Crafts, 72-; cur dec arts, Montreal Mus Fine Arts, 72-79; hon councillor & arch consult, Montreal Mus Fine Arts, 80. *Mem:* Fel Royal Soc Arts. *Publ:* Auth, Galerie Hosmer-Pillow-Vaughan, 69 & Clutch of Curiosities, 70, Can Collector; Mobel, Silber und Keramik aus Quebec, Weltkunst, 74; Canada's Heritage of Silver, Antique Monthly, 76; Traditional Furniture from the Province of Quebec, Apollo, 76. *Mailing Add:* 202-400 Stewart St Ottawa ON K1N 6L2 Canada

JACKSON, SARAH
SCULPTOR, GRAPHIC ARTIST
b Detroit, Mich, Nov 13, 24. *Study:* Wayne State Univ, BA, 46, MA, 48. *Work:* Joseph H Hirshhorn Collection, Washington, DC; Nat Gallery Can, Ottawa; Montreal Mus Fine Arts; Montreal Mus Contemp Arts; Fine Arts Collection, Smithsonian Inst, Washington, DC; Mus Mod Art, New York; Tate Gallery & Victoria & Albert Mus, London; Nat Postal Mus & Mus of Civilization Can. *Comn:* Dancer (bronze), Cloverdale Shopping Ctr, Toronto, 66; Metamorphosis (bronzes) & Mindscape (bronze hanging), Student Union Bldg, Dalhousie Univ; plastic & bronze sculpture, Mt Sinai Hosp, Toronto. *Exhib:* Artist in Residence Ser, Stony Brook Univ, New York, 89; Dreams Come True Exhib, Eye Level Gallery, Halifax, Nova Scotia, 89; Traveling, A Space Exhib, Artware: Artists Books, Toronto, 89; Artitudes, Int Art Competition, Green St Gallery, New York, 89; Copier Art Exhib, London, Olympic, Eng, Copier Art Festival, Tech Univ Nova Scotia, Copier Art Murals and Collectable Prints, Manuge Gallery, Halifax, Copier Art Mural Exhib, Hilton Hotel, Halifax, Nova Scotia, 89; one-woman shows, Micro Hall Art Center, WGer, 89, Westchester Comn Col, Valhalla, NY, 90, Copier Art Bookwords, WCBA, Minneapolis, 90; The Works Art Festival, 90; and many others; Int Soc Copier Artist, New York, 84; Nat Mus Women Arts, Wash, DC, 87; and many others. *Pos:* Artist-in-residence & dir, Arts & Technol Festival, 79- & dir, Summer Arts Celebration, 81-, Tech Univ NS; co-cur, Int Mail/Copier Art Exhib, 85; dir, Int Mail Copier Art Exhib and Art's & Technology Festival, Tech Univ, Nova Scotia, 85, Summer Arts Festival Tech Univ & Copier Arts Festival, Nova Scotia, 86, 87; Initiator & co-cur, Int Mail Copier Art Exhib (with Bookworks), London, Eng, 87. *Teaching:* Lectr, Mexico City Col, 48, London Univ, 54-55, Tate Gallery, London, 54-55, Thomas More Inst, Montreal, 56, Nat Gallery, Ottawa, 57, Toronto Univ, 60-61, YMCA Adult Educ, Toronto, 62, St Mary's Univ, 63, Nova Scotia Col

Art, 70, Dartmouth Adult Educ Div, 72-73 & Univ BC, 79; lectr, Tech Univ, Nova Scotia, 78-89. *Awards:* Award of Excellence, Art Mus Asn Am, 85; Ontario Arts Coun Grant, 74; Grant, Nova Scotia Govt, 90. *Bibliog:* Brian Charent (auth), An interview with Sarah Jackson, Art Mag, winter 74; Guy Robert (auth), Eros et humour chez Sarah Jackson, Vie Des Arts, spring 75; Ramuna Macdonald (dir), Sarah Jackson Halifax (film), Nat Film Bd Can, 80. *Media:* Bronze; Graphics. *Publ:* Auth, Copier Art Bookworks (several titles), poetry & images. *Mailing Add:* 1411 Edward St Halifax NS B3H 3H5 Canada

JACKSON, SUZANNE FITZALLEN
PAINTER, COSTUME DESIGNER
b St Louis, Mo, Jan 30, 44. *Study:* Yale Univ, MFA; San Francisco State Col, BA; Otis Art Inst, Los Angeles, with Charles White; Design Fac, Yale Sch Drama, 87-90. *Work:* NY State Off Bldg, Harlem; Palm Springs Desert Mus, Calif; Mus African-Am Art, Los Angeles; Daniel, Mann, Johnson & Mendenhall, Co, Los Angeles; Indianapolis Mus Art. *Comn:* Peace Bird, Secy State Edmund G Brown, Jr, Sacramento, 72; Stephen Chase, Arthur Elrod & Assoc, Palm Springs, 74; Artful Living, William Chidester Co, Pac Design Ctr, Los Angeles, 75; mural, New Health Ctr, Los Angeles, 79; Design for stained glass window, Dr Vaughn Payne, Los Angeles, 86; and many others. *Exhib:* Joseph H Hirshhorn Mus, Smithsonian Inst, Washington, DC, 77; Barnsdall Munic Art Gallery, Los Angeles, 78; 19-Sixties, Calif Mus African-Am Hist & Cult, Los Angeles, 81-89; Forever Free, Works by African-Am Women Artists (traveling exhib), Ctr Visual Arts, Univ Ill at Normal, origin, 80-82; Joslyn Art Mus, Omaha, Nebr; Montgomery Mus Fine Arts, Ala; Gibbs Art Mus, Charleston, SC; The Art Gallery, Univ Md, Col Park; Indianapolis Mus Art; Mus African-Am Art, Los Angeles, 85; solo exhibs, Calif State Off Bldg, Los Angeles, 81-82; Multi-Cult Art Inst, San Diego, 83; Fashion Moda, New York, 84; Ingber Gallery, NY, 84; Mitzi Landau 20th Century Art, Los Angeles, 84; Sargent Johnson Gallery, San Francisco, 85; Black Like Me Gallery, San Francisco, 86. *Pos:* Vchairperson, Calif Arts Coun, 75-78; Century City Cult Comn, 78-79; artist-coordr, Brockman Gallery Productions CETA Pub Art Prog, 77-78; dir, Int Women's Writing Guild, 79-; proj dir, Cult Exchange Prog, Lagos, Nigeria/Wajumbe Cult Inst, San Francisco, 85-86. *Teaching:* Lectr, Calif Inst Women, 74; Idyllwild Sch Music & Arts, 81-82; chairperson, Fine Arts, painting, drawing & dance, Elliott Pope Prep Sch, 82-85; vis lectr, San Francisco State Univ, 87. *Awards:* Grand Prize, Eyes & Ears Found, Int Yr of the Child Billboards, 79; nominee, First Nat Award in the Visual Arts, 81; fel, Idyllwild Sch Music & Arts, 82-83. *Bibliog:* Contemporary Women Artists, Bo-Tree Publs, 83; The Valley of the Moon, Int Women's Writing Guild, 84; Four Plus One (catalog), Nat Urban League Conf, San Francisco, 86. *Mem:* Int Women's Writing Guild (78-); United Scenic Artists, Local 829; Costume Soc Am; Ctr Study Beadwork. *Media:* Acrylic Wash, Mixed Media. *Publ:* Auth, What I Love (paintings & poetry), Contemp Crafts, 72; Animal (paintings & poetry), continuity transcripts and features, 78. *Mailing Add:* 5733 San Leandro St Oakland CA 94621-4417

JACKSON, VAUGHN L
PAINTER, ILLUSTRATOR
b Raymond, Ohio, Jan 7, 20. *Study:* Am Univ, AA, BA, 69; Corcoran Sch Art, with Richard Lahey, 47-50; Ohio State Univ, 42-43; Columbus Art Sch, 39-40; with Hans Hofmann, Provincetown, summer 55; also with Eliot O'Hara. *Work:* Many in pvt collections. *Comn:* Over 1100 free-lance designs and illustrations in advertising, technical and military publications; displays and visual presentations. *Exhib:* Corcoran Gallery Art, 56; Wash Watercolor Asn, 85, 87, 88, 91 & 92; Salmagundi Club, 89; Penn Watercolor Soc, 89; Ky Watercolor Soc, 89; Midwest Watercolor Soc, 90; and others. *Pos:* Advert artist, Kal, Ehrlich & Merrick Advert Agency, 47-52; artist-illusr, Opers Res Off, Johns Hopkins Univ, 52-55, asst art dir, 55-63; publ art dir, Res Anal Corp, 63-67, visual & graphics mgr, 67-72; visual & graphics mgr, Gen Res Corp, 72, tech publ dir, 72-76; visual dir, System Planning Corp, 76-91; consult designer, caricaturist, illust, 91- *Awards:* Silver Medal, Landscape Club Washington, DC, 55; Award for Outstanding Achievement in Tech Commun, Soc Tech Writers & Publs, 71; First Place, Wash Watercolor Asn Ann, 88. *Mem:* Fairfax Art League; Va Watercolor Soc; Washington Watercolor Asn; Penn Watercolor Soc; Ky Watercolor Soc. *Media:* Watercolor, Acrylic. *Mailing Add:* Ten Penny Studio PO Box 54 Fairfax Station VA 22039

JACKSON, WARD
PAINTER, EDITOR
b Petersburg, Va, Sept 10, 28. *Study:* Richmond Prof Inst, Col William & Mary, BFA & MFA; Hans Hofmann Sch Fine Arts, scholar, 52. *Work:* Nat Mus Am Art, Smithsonian Inst, Washington, DC; Riverside Mus Collection, Rose Art Mus, Brandeis Univ; Elvehjem Art Mus, Univ Wis-Madison; Va Mus Fine Arts, Richmond; NY Univ Art Collection, New York; Solomon R Guggenheim Mus, New York; Wilhelm Lehmbruck Mus, Duisberg, Ger. *Exhib:* One-man show, Va Mus Fine Arts, Richmond, 71 & 73; Inst Contemp Art, Richmond, 80; Schenectady Mus, New York, 81; Geometric Abstraction, 85 & Am Abstract Artists, 50th Ann Celebration, Bronx Mus Arts, 86; Kendall Gallery, New York, 85; J N Herlin Inc, New York, 86; Konkret Sieben, Kunsthaus Nürnberg, WGer, 87; Adlung & Kaiser Galerie, Berlin, Ger, 88; Centro Cultural de la Villa, Madrid, 89; From Mondrian to Minimalism, Marilyn Pearl Gallery, New York, 89-90; Geometric Abstraction & American Minimalism, Solomon R Guggenheim Mus, New York, 90; Mus Morsbroich, Stadtisches Mus, Leverkusen, Ger, 91; Kunsthalle Bremen, Ger, 92; Edwin A Ulrich Mus, Wichita State Univ, Kans, 92. *Pos:* Co-ed, Folio, 49-51, Art Now, New York, 69-72; Adv ed, Art Now Gallery Guide, 69-; archivist & head viewing prog, Solomon R Guggenheim Mus, New York, 55- *Teaching:* Instr art hist, Rollins Col, Winter Park, Fla, 54-55. *Awards:* Fel, Va Mus Fine Arts, 48 & 49; First Prize for painting, New York Ctr Gallery, 56; Nat Endowment Arts Artists Fel, 75-76. *Bibliog:* Ward Jackson Watercolors, Davidson Col, 75; Circular 24/25, Zeitschrift für Kunst und Gestaltung, Bonn, Ger, 78; Christopher Sweet (auth), On Ward Jackson & Helen Koriath (auth), Continuity and Reflexion, Diamonds by Ward Jackson (exhib catalog), Mus Morsbroich, Leverkusen & Kunsthalle Bremen, Ger, 91-92; and others. *Mem:* Am Abstract Artists; Col Art Asn Am. *Publ:* Auth, Art in glass (works of art by Louis Comfort Tiffany), Rollins Col Lit Mag, 55; George L K Morris: Forty years of abstract art, Art J, 72; introd, George L K Morris, The Years 1945-1975, Hirschl & Adler Galleries, New York, 78. *Dealer:* Kendall Gallery 152 Forsyth St 10 New York NY 10002. *Mailing Add:* 152 Forsyth St Apt 3 New York NY 10002-2944

JACOB, MARY JANE
CURATOR, HISTORIAN
b Queens, NY, Jan 5, 52. *Study:* Fla State Univ Study Ctr, Florence, Italy, 72; Univ Fla, Gainesville, BFA, 73; Univ Mich, Ann Arbor, 76. *Collections Arranged:* Magdalena Abakanowicz, 82; Dada and Surrealism in Chicago Collections, 84; Gordon Matta-Clark: A Retrospective, 85; Jannis Kounellis: A Retrospective, 85; British Sculpture since 1965: Tony Cragg, Richard Deacon, Barry Flanagan, Richard Long, David Nash & Bill Woodrow (co-curated with San Francisco Mus Mod Art), 87; all Mus Contemp Art, Chicago & traveling. *Pos:* Curatorial asst, Det Inst Arts, 76-77, from asst cur to assoc cur mod art, 77-80; chief cur, Mus Contemp Art, Chicago, 80-87. *Awards:* Nat Endowment Humanities Fel, 73-74 & 80-81. *Mem:* Nat Women's Caucus Art (adv bd, 79-80); Mich Coun Arts; Art Table Inc, 83- *Res:* 20th century art with emphasis on American art of the 1920's and 1930's and contemporary American and European art. *Publ:* Contribr, The Amazing Decade: Women and Performance Art 1970-1980, Astro Arts Bks, Los Angeles, 83; auth, Anni Albers: A modern weaver as artist, In: The Woven and Graphic Art of Anni Albers, Smithsonian Inst Press, Washington, 85. *Mailing Add:* 710 W Junior Terr No 10 Chicago IL 60613

JACOB, NED
PAINTER, SCULPTOR
b Elizabethton, Tenn, Nov 15, 38. *Study:* Pvt studies with Robert Gilbert, Robert Lougheed & Bettina Steinke. *Work:* Denver Art Mus; Indianapolis Mus Art; Whitney Gallery Western Art, Cody, Wyo; Albrecht Art Mus, St Joseph, Mo; Washburn Univ, Topeka, Kans. *Exhib:* One-man shows, Univ Sask, Saskatoon, Can, 59, Nat Cowboy Hall of Fame & Western Heritage Ctr, Oklahoma City, 72, Birger Sandzen Mem Gallery, Lindsborg, Kans, 76, Whitney Gallery of Western Art, 76, Frye Gallery, Seattle, 79, Coe Kerr Gallery, New York, 82, Wichita Art Mus, 83 & El Paso Mus Art, 83; Twenty-fifth Anniversary Exhib, James Fisher Gallery, Denver, 84. *Teaching:* Guest lectr, painting & figure drawing, Fechin Inst, Taos, NMex, 88-92, Art Students League, Denver, 89-92, Scottsdale Artists Sch, Ariz, 90-92 & Sun Valley Ctr Arts & Humanities, Idaho, 92. *Awards:* John F & Anna Lee Stacy Fel, 74. *Bibliog:* W Bradley (auth), Twenty-five Years--Ned Jacob, Artists of the Rockies, 85; D Medina (auth), Art Talk, Scottsdale, Ariz, 86; O W LaCour (auth), Artists in Quotation, McFarland & Co Inc, Jeffrson, NC, 89. *Mem:* Salmagundi Club, New York; Chelsea Arts Club, London; Nat Arts Club, New York. *Media:* Oil, Charcoal; All. *Mailing Add:* The Old Meeting House PO Box 1047 Skowhegan ME 04976

JACOBOWITZ, ELLEN SUE
CURATOR, DIRECTOR
b Detroit, Mich, Feb 21, 48. *Study:* Univ Mich, BA, 69, MA, 70; Courtauld Inst Art, 70-71; Bryn Mawr Col, PhD. *Collections Arranged:* American Graphics: 1860-1940 (auth, catalog), Rijkmuseum & Philadelphia Mus Art, 82; The Prints of Lucas van Leyden and His Contemporaries (auth, catalog), Nat Gallery Art & Boston Mus Fine Arts, 83; From Mantegna to Goya: Old Master prints from the Berman collection, Philadelphia Mus Art, 85; New Art on Paper, Philadelphia Mus Art, 88. *Pos:* Cur, Philadelphia Mus Art, 72-90; asst dir, Cranbrook Inst Sci, 91- *Awards:* Smithsonian Grants, 77-78; Gold Medal, Netherlands Soc Philadelphia, 83; Fel, Nat Endowment Arts, 87. *Mem:* Print Coun Am (bd mem, 80-83); Print Club Philadelphia (bd mem, 78-84); Illustrated Bartsch (ed & bd mem); Neth-Am Amity Trust (bd mem, 81-). *Res:* Early 16th century Netherlandish printmaking; American printmaking since the late 19th century; contemporary printmaking. *Publ:* Auth, Three Centuries of Chiaroscuro Woodcuts, Pa Acad Fine Arts, 73; contribr, Philadelphia: Three Centuries of American Art, Philadelphia Mus Art, 76; coauth, The Illustrated Bartsch--Lucas van Leyden, Abaris, 81. *Mailing Add:* Philadelphia Mus Art PO Box 7646 Philadelphia PA 19103

JACOBS, DAVID (THEODORE)
SCULPTOR, EDUCATOR
b Niagara Falls, NY, Mar 1, 32. *Study:* Orange Coast Col, AA; Los Angeles State Col, AB & MA. *Work:* Guggenheim Mus & Assyrian Embassy, New York; Mus Art, Richmond, Va; Otterbein Col, Ohio; Valley Mall, Hagerstown, Md; Hofstra Mus, Hempstead, NY. *Comn:* Cloud Fountain (sculptured fountain), Valley Mall Assoc, Hagerstown, Md, 74; bronze relief, Paul Radin Mem, Hofstra Univ Libr, 74; Raingate (sculptured fountain), A Dworkin, Westbury, NY, 75; Ventura High, Deer Park High Sch, NY, 76; Rainframe (sculptured screen), Dawn-Joy Corp, New York, 76. *Exhib:* The Art of Assemblage, Mus Mod Art, New York, 61; 68th Am Exhib, Art Inst Chicago, 66; Sound, Light, Silence, Art That Performs, W R Nelson Gallery, Atkins Mus, Kansas City, 66; Inflatable Sculpture, Jewish Mus, New York, 69; Sound Sculpture, Vancouver Art Gallery, 73; plus many one-man shows, 61-92. *Teaching:* Prof sculpture, Hofstra Univ, 62-, chmn dept fine arts, 82-89; vis critic sculpture, Cornell Univ, New York Prog, 69 & 70, Baruch Col, City Col New York, 77-79. *Awards:* Res grant, Hofstra Univ, 68; Creative Artists

Pub Serv Grant, 73 & 76; Artist-in-Schools Grant, Nat Endowment Arts & NYFA, Central HS, Valley Stream, 79. *Bibliog:* D J Irving (auth), Sculpture: Materials & Processes, Van Nostrand Reinhold, 68; Wayne Craven (auth), Sculpture in America, Crowell, 68; Chichura & Stevens (auths), Super Sculpture: Using Science, Technology and Natural Phenomena in Sculpture, Van Nostrand Reinhold, 74. *Media:* Aluminum, Rubber. *Mailing Add:* Dept of Fine Arts Hofstra Univ Hempstead NY 11550

JACOBS, FERNE K
WEAVER
b Chicago, Ill, 42. *Study:* Claremont Grad Sch, Calif, MFA, 76. *Work:* Royal Scottish Mus, Edinburgh; Am Craft Mus, New York; Mandell Gallery, Los Angeles; The Lannan Found, Palm Beach; RI Sch Design. *Exhib:* One person exhib, Franklin Parrasch Gallery, New York, 91; Four Artist Reflect 1971-1991 (with catalog), The Soc Art in Crafts, Pittsburgh, Pa, 91. *Teaching:* Haystack Mountain Sch Crafts, Deer Isle, Maine, 90; Int Col, Los Angeles, 78- *Awards:* Nat Endowment Arts, 73-74, 77-78, 90-91. *Bibliog:* James Auer (auth), Crafts redefined by new generation, Milwaukee J, 4/26/87; Photogs, Am Craft Mag, 6-7/89; A basket is, Am Craft Mag, 2-3/90. *Mailing Add:* c/o The Sybaris Gallery 301 W Fourth St Royal Oak MI 48067

JACOBS, HAROLD
PAINTER, SCULPTOR
b New York, NY, Oct 29, 32. *Study:* Cooper Union, 53; NY Univ; New Sch Social Res; Sorbonne, Fulbright scholar, 61. *Work:* Whitney Mus Am Art, New York; Portland Art Mus, Ore; Kalamazoo Art Ctr; Philadelphia Mus Art; Pa Acad Fine Arts. *Comn:* Performance sculpture, Group Motion Dance Co; ltd ed, Akiba Acad, Merion, Pa; outdoor mural, Meridian Books, Philadelphia; sculpture, ARA lobby, Philadelphia. *Exhib:* Solo exhibs, Pa Acad Fine Arts, 78 & Portland Ctr Visual Arts, Ore, 81; retrospective, Selected Works 1966-1985, Moore Col Art, 85; VIA Paris, 91; Asphalte, Paris, 92. *Teaching:* Prof painting, Moore Col Art, 66- *Awards:* Nat Endowment Arts Collaboration Grant Visual & Performing Arts, 75; Distinguished Artist Award, Moore Col Art, 83. *Media:* Mixed. *Publ:* Harold Jacobs Selected Works 1966-1985 (exhib catalog & video tape), Moore Col Art, 85. *Mailing Add:* Le Grand Logis Ligre Par Chinon 37500 France

JACOBS, HELEN NICHOLS
PAINTER
b Kent, Conn, Feb 16, 24. *Study:* With Spencer B Nichols & Arthur Maynard. *Exhib:* Audubon Artists, 75 & 87; Kent Art Asn, Conn, 75 & 88; Hudson Valley Art Asn, 78-91; Catharine Lorillard Wolfe Art Club, 80-88; Am Artists Prof League, New York & NJ, 81-88. *Teaching:* Instr oil painting, Ridgewood Adult Sch, NJ, 68-72 & Ridgewood Art Inst, 71-92. *Awards:* Salmagundi Club Award, 81-82; Am Artists Prof League Award, NJ Chap, 87; Hudson Valley Art Asn, 91; and others. *Mem:* Am Artists Prof League; Catharine Lorillard Wolfe Art Club; Kent Art Asn; Hudson Valley Art Asn. *Media:* Oil. *Mailing Add:* 684 Terrace Dr Paramus NJ 07652

JACOBS, JIM
PAINTER, PRINTMAKER
b New York, NY, May 26, 45. *Study:* Boston Univ, BA; Bryn Mawr Col, study with Richmond Lattimore; Harvard Univ; Boston Mus of Fine Arts. *Work:* Rose Art Mus, Brandeis Univ, Waltham, Mass; Chase Manhattan Bank; Arman; Smith Mus. *Exhib:* Expressions of the Seventies, New York, 77; Elizabeth Weiner Gallery, New York, 79 & 80; Danforth Mus, Framingham, Mass, 81; Smith Mus, Springfield, Mass, 81; Gallery Yves Arman, 81 & 82; Oscarsson Siegeltuch & Co, New York, 86; and others. *Pos:* Archivist, Leo Castelli Gallery, 67-68. *Teaching:* Instr vase painting, Boston Univ, 65, Harvard Univ, 66, Bryn Mawr Col, 67; lectr, Boston Mus Fine Arts, Mus Sch, Boston, Harvard Univ; instr vase painting, Bryn Mawr Col, 67. *Awards:* Creative Artists Public Service Program Grant, 81-82. *Bibliog:* Article, Art News, 6/80; article, Arts Mag, 5/81; article, Art Am, 2/83; Michael Komanecky & Virginia Fabbri Butera (coauth), The Folding Image: Screens by Western Artists of the ninteenth & twentieth centuries, (exhib catalog), Yale Univ Art Gallery & Nat Gallery Art, 84. *Media:* Lacquer, Board. *Dealer:* Oscarson Siegeltuch & Co 568 Broadway New York NY 10012. *Mailing Add:* 26 W 20th St New York NY 10011

JACOBS, PETER ALAN
SCULPTOR, EDUCATOR
b New York, NY, Jan 31, 39. *Study:* State Univ NY Col New Paltz, with Ilya Bolotowsky, BS(art educ), 60, MA(art), 62; Vanderbilt Univ-George Peabody Col, EdD(fine arts), 65. *Work:* Bloomsburg State Col, Pa; Col Mainland, Texas City, Tex; Muskingum Col, New Concord, Ohio; George Peabody Mus, Nashville, Tenn; Mus Satire & Humor, Bulgaria. *Exhib:* New Directions in Art, Beloit Mus, Wis; Wis Designer-Craftsman, Milwaukee Art Ctr & Wis Painters & Sculptors, 68 & 69; Southwest Invitational, Yuma, Ariz, 73 & 74; one-man shows, Work on Tour by Ariz Arts & Humanities Comn, Ariz, Tex, Ohio & Wis, 74-75 & Univ Ohio, Univ Colo, Grand Canyon Art Ctr & Univ Wyo Art Mus; Banares Hindu Univ, Varanasa, India, 80; Mostra di Grafica, Soc Delle Belle Arti, Firenze, Italy, 83; 6th International Biennial, Gabrova, Bulgaria, 83; International Salon of Jazz Posters, Bydgoszcz, Poland, 85; 28th Annual Art Zone, Denver, 88. *Collections Arranged:* Ilya Bolotowsky Retrospective, Crossman Gallery, Univ Wis-Whitewater, 68 & Northern Ariz Univ Mus, 73; Andy Warhol, 81, Robert Rauschenberg, 81, Roy Lichtenstein, 82, James Rosenquist, 82, Sam Francis, 83 & Willem de Kooning, 84, Colo State Univ. *Teaching:* Chmn art dept, Univ Wis-Whitewater, 65-70, Northern Ariz Univ, 70-74, Cent Mich Univ, 74-76 & Colo State Univ, 76-86, prof, 88-; head dept art, Univ Wyo, 87-88. *Mem:* Nat Coun Art Adminr (founder & chmn bd dirs, 72-77); Col Art Asn Am; Mich Soc Arts, Lett & Sci (chmn fine arts div, 75); Nat Art Educ Asn; Coun Art Dept Chmn State Wis (pres, 65-70). *Media:* Wood. *Res:* American contemporary Indian arts. *Publ:* Auth, Visual Arts in the Ninth Decade, Nat Coun Art Adminr, 80. *Mailing Add:* 1727 Rangeview Ft Collins CO 80524

JACOBS, RALPH, JR
PAINTER
b El Centro, Calif, May 22, 40. *Study:* With Evelyn Nadeau, Frederic Taubes & Abel G Warshawsky. *Work:* Beirut Art Mus, Lebanon; Continental Telephone Co, Ga. *Comn:* Many pvt collections in Can, Japan, Australia & SAm. *Exhib:* Rosicrucian Mus, San Jose, Calif, 63, 67 & 71; Coun Am Artists Soc Nat Exhib, New York, 64; Nat Exhib, Springville Mus Art, Utah, 65; Soc Western Artists Ann Exhibs, de Young Mus, San Francisco, 65 & 69; Armenian Allied Arts Ann, Los Angeles, 66. *Awards:* State Ann Exhib First Awards, Art League Galleries, Santa Cruz, 63 & 64; Soc Western Artists Ann Second Award for Silhouette in Morning Light, 64; Klumpkey Mem Award for Classic Nude, de Young Mus, San Francisco, 65. *Media:* Oil. *Mailing Add:* PO Box 5906 Carmel CA 93921

JACOBSEN, MICHAEL A
HISTORIAN, EDUCATOR
b Pasadena, Calif, June 4, 42. *Study:* Univ Calif, Santa Barbara, BA, 65, MA, 70; Columbia Univ, PhD, 76. *Pos:* Conservator, Sun Spirit Galleries, Simi Valley, Calif, 90- *Teaching:* Asst prof Renaissance art, Cleveland State Univ, Ohio, 73-77, Univ Ore, 77-79; assoc prof art, Univ Ga, 79-87; vis assoc prof art, Stanford Univ, 87, Univ Calif, Riverside, 88-89; lecturer, Calif Polytechniv Univ, Ponoma, 89-93. *Mem:* Col Art Asn; Southern Calif Art Hist Soc. *Res:* Renaissance art history, Italian 15th century. *Publ:* Auth, A Phimister Proctor, Apelles, 80; Hercules and Antaeus, Source, 81; Mantegna's battle of sea monsters, Art Bull, 12/82; Perspective in Mantegna's early panels, Arte Venenta, 83; Dolphins in Renaissance art, Studies in Iconography, fall 83; Durer's Johannes Kleberger Source, 91. *Dealer:* Sun Spirit Galleries Simi Valley CA. *Mailing Add:* c/o Calif State Polytechnic Univ Art Dept, 3801 W Temple Ave Pomona CA 91768-4071

JACOBSHAGEN, N KEITH, II
PAINTER, PHOTOGRAPHER
b Wichita, Kans, Sept 8, 41. *Study:* Kansas City Art Inst, Mo, BFA; Art Ctr Col Design, Los Angeles; Univ Kans, MFA. *Work:* Sheldon Mem Gallery, Lincoln, Nebr; Univ Kans Mus Art, Lawrence; Mus Art Okla Univ; Oakland Mus, Calif; Pasadena Art Mus, Calif. *Exhib:* A Sense of Place: The Artist & the American Land, Sheldon Mem Art Gallery, Lincoln, Nebr, 74; Southern Ark Univ, Magnolia & Westark Community Col, Ft Smith, Ark, 78; In Respect of Space, Swan River Mus, Paola, Kans, 79; Group, Volga-Consalvo Gallery, Boston, Mass, 79; Corp Exhib, auspices of Minneapolis Art Inst, 79 & NAm Casualty Exhib, 79; and others. *Teaching:* Assoc prof art, Univ Nebr-Lincoln, 68-80. *Awards:* Owen H Kenan Award, 34th Ann Contemp Am Painting, 72; Frank Woods Fel, Univ Nebr, 75. *Bibliog:* Alan Gussow (auth), A Sense of Place: the Artist and the American Land (film), Nebr Educ TV, 74. *Media:* Oil. *Publ:* Contribr, Twelve Photographers: A Contemporary Mid-America Document, Mid-Am Arts Alliance, 78; contribr, Special report: Midwest art, Art in Am, 7-8/79; contribr, Artists work range through human emotions, Kansas City Star, 8/12/79; contribr, Cottonwood Rev, fall 79; contribr, In respect of space, Forum/Kansas City Artists Coalition, 12/79; and others. *Dealer:* Dorry Gates PO Box 7264 Kansas City MO 64113; Charles Campbell Gallery 647 Chestnut St San Francisco CA 94133. *Mailing Add:* 2030 "C" St Lincoln NE 68502

JACOBSON, ARTHUR
PAINTER, PRINTMAKER
b Chicago, Ill, Jan 10, 24. *Study:* Univ Wis, BS, MS(art); Madrid Print Workshop, Spain; London, Eng, 72. *Work:* Pa Acad Fine Art, Philadelphia; Mus NMex, Santa Fe; Ariz State Univ, Tempe; Hastings Col, Nebr; Phoenix Art Mus, Ariz; Dallas Mus, Tex. *Comn:* Exterior mural in marblecrete, Phoenix Jewish Community Ctr, Ariz, 62. *Exhib:* Corcoran Biennial of Painting, Corcoran Gallery Art, Washington, DC, 57; Libr Cong Print Exhib, Washington, DC, 65; Graphics USA, Clarke Col, Iowa, 71; Drawings USA, Minn Mus Art, 75; Watercolor USA, Springfield Mus, Mo, 79; solo exhib, Watercolors, Kerr Ctr, Scottsdale, Ariz. *Teaching:* Prof emer painting & drawing, Ariz State Univ, 56-86; guest prof painting, Univ Wis, 67-68. *Awards:* Purchase awards, Pa Acad Fine Arts & Dallas Mus Art, 65; First Prize for Painting, Phoenix Art Mus, 71. *Mem:* Print Consortium, Kansas City, Mo. *Media:* Oil, Watercolor. *Publ:* Auth, 100 American and European Drawings, Prentice-Hall, 81. *Mailing Add:* 7209 E McDonald Dr No 47 Scottsdale AZ 85250

JACOBSON, FRANK
ADMINISTRATOR
B Philadelphia, Pa, Sept 14, 48. *Study:* Univ Wis, BA, 70; Boston Univ Sch Fine Arts, MFA, 73. *Pos:* Exec dir, Arvada Ctr Arts & Humanities, 79-85; mgr, Theaters & arenas, Denver, 85-87; pres & chief exec off, Scottsdale Cult Coun, 87- *Teaching:* Asst prof theater, Univ Mont, 73-75. *Mem:* Metrop Denver Arts Alliance (pres, 81-83); Asn Performing Arts Presenters (bd, 84-87). *Publ:* Auth, Performing Art Centers - Market the Arts, FEDAPT, 83; Municipal Connections, ACUCAA Bulletin, Vol 29, No 7, 86. *Mailing Add:* Scottsdale Center for the Arts 7383 Scottsdale Mall Scottsdale AZ 85251

JACOBSON, YOLANDE (MRS J CRAIG SHEPPARD)
SCULPTOR
b Norman, Okla, May 28, 21. *Study:* Univ Okla, BFA; also study in Norway, France & Mex. *Work:* Gilcrease Mus Art, Tulsa, Okla; Jacobsen Mus Art,

Norman; State Hist Soc, Reno, Nev; Hist Mus, Carson City, Nev. *Comn:* Sen Patrick McCarran (bronze statue), Statuary Hall, Washington, DC, 61; president's portrait bust, Univ Nev, Reno, 62; bronze portrait sculpture, Makey Sch Mines, Univ Nev, 73; Walter Clark Mem Bronze Portrait, Univ Nev, 81; Bronze Portrait, Wilbur D May Mus, Reno, Nev, 85. *Exhib:* Denver Mus Art, 41; Okla Ann, Tulsa, 42-45; Mid-West Ann, Kansas City, 51; Oakland Mus Art, 56; Silver Centennial, Virginia City, Nev, 61; Mem Exhib, Sheppard Gallery, Univ Nev, 79. *Pos:* Asst ed & bk designer, Univ Nev Press, 63-66. *Awards:* Mid-West Ann, Kansas City, 41; Denver Mus Art, 41; Silver Centennial, Virginia City, 61; Yolande & Craig Sheppard Gallery, Univ Nev, Reno, 79. *Media:* Bronze, Wood. *Mailing Add:* 1000 Primrose St Reno NV 89509

JACOBUS, JOHN M
EDUCATOR, HISTORIAN
b Poughkeepsie, NY, Sept 15, 27. *Study:* Hamilton Col, AB, 52; Yale Univ, MA, 54, PhD, 56. *Teaching:* From instr to asst prof, Princeton Univ, 56-60; from asst prof to assoc prof, Univ Calif, Berkeley, 60-63; assoc prof to prof, Ind Univ, Bloomington, 63-69; prof, Dartmouth Col, 69- *Res:* Nineteenth & twentieth century art, both architecture & painting. *Collection:* Prints & graphic arts from 18th century to present. *Publ:* Auth, Philip Johnson, Braziller, 62; auth, Twentieth Century Architecture: The Middle Years, Praeger, 66; auth, Matisse, Abrams, 73. *Mailing Add:* 5 Hilltop Dr Hanover NH 03755

JACQUARD
SCULPTOR
b Lansing, Mich, Feb 1, 37. *Study:* Mich State Univ, BA & MA. *Work:* Mus Am Art, Andover, Mass; Detroit Inst Arts, Mich; Kresge Mus, Mich State Univ, East Lansing; Kalamazoo Inst Art, Mich; Laumeier Sculpture Park, St Louis; Chicago Inst Art; Ind Univ Art Mus, Bloomington. *Comn:* Sculpture, Chicago Transit Authority, 74. *Exhib:* One-man shows, Detroit Inst Art, 65, Ill Inst Technol, 69, Univ Chicago, 70, Indianapolis Mus, 75, Kalamazoo, 89, S Ben Regional Mus Art, 93 & Grand Rapids Mus Art, 93; Bicentennial Sculpture for a New Era, Chicago, 75. *Teaching:* Assoc prof sculpture, Univ Ill, Chicago Circle Campus, 66-75; prof sculpture, Ind Univ, Bloomington, 75- *Awards:* Guggenheim Fel, 73; Nat Endowment Arts, 80; Lilly Fel, 81. *Media:* Steel, Bronze. *Publ:* Major Color Catalogue of Jacquard & His Art to Accompany Traveling Exhibition. *Mailing Add:* Dept Art Ind Univ Bloomington IN 47405

JACQUEMON, PIERRE
PAINTER
b Lyon, France, Aug 6, 35; US citizen. *Study:* Self-taught. *Work:* Goteborg Mus, Sweden; Magdalene Col, Cambridge, Eng; Mus d'Art Mod, Paris, France; St Paul Sch, NH; Ika-Shika Nat Univ, Tokyo, Japan. *Exhib:* One-man shows, Temple Gallery, London, 62, Bianchini Gallery, New York, 63, Weeden Gallery, Boston, 68, Berkshire Mus, Mass, 69 & Atrium Gallery, Geneva, Switz, 74; Inst Contemp Art, Boston, 70. *Bibliog:* Pierre Jacquemon, Gallerie de Bellecour, Lyon, France. *Media:* Oil. *Dealer:* Phoenix Gallery 30 W 57th St New York NY 10019. *Mailing Add:* 62 E Seventh St New York NY 10003

JACQUES, MICHAEL LOUIS
PRINTMAKER, EDUCATOR
b Barre, Vt, Apr 12, 45. *Study:* Boston Univ, BFA, 67; Univ Hartford Art Sch, MFA, 71; and with David Aronson, Conger Metcalf, Walter Murch & Paul Zimmerman. *Work:* Nat Collection Fine Arts, Smithsonian Mus, Washington, DC; Mus Am Art, Washington, DC; Philadelphia Mus Art; Chrysler Mus, Va; Mus Fine Arts, Boston; and many others. *Exhib:* Silvermine Nat, 80; All on Paper, 80; Acad Artists Asn Exhib, 80 & 81; Audubon Artists Exhib, 80 & 82; Am Artists Prof League Exhib, 82; Boston Printmakers Exhib, 84-85; and many others. *Pos:* Artist-in-residence, ABT Assoc, Cambridge, Mass, 80-81 & Va Mus, 81-82. *Teaching:* Instr art, Emmanuel Col, Boston, 71-73, assoc prof art, 73-88; fine artist, 88- *Awards:* First Prize, Cooperstown Art Asn, 79; Charlotte Printmakers Purchase Award, 79; Am Artist Prof League Prize, 82; Hunterdon Art Ctr Award, 85. *Bibliog:* Paul T Nagand (auth), Michael Jacques-A double career in art, Am Artist Mag, New York, 77; Jeanne B Kissane (auth), Beyond the stereotype, Small Business, Vol IV, No 1, Worcester, Mass, 1/79. *Mem:* Boston Printmakers; Copley Soc. *Publ:* Auth & illusr, Images of Age, ABT Books, 81. *Dealer:* Pucker Safrai Gallery 171 Newbury St Boston MA 02116. *Mailing Add:* 415 Jasmine St Laguna Beach CA 92651

JACQUES, RUSSELL KENNETH
SCULPTOR
b Springfield, Mass, Feb 19, 43. *Study:* Boston Univ, BFA, 66. *Work:* DeCordova Mus, Lincoln, Mass; Abilene Fine Arts Mus, Tex; Mead Mus, Amherst, Mass; Nat Gallery Nova Scotia, Halifax, 89; Boston Univ, 88. *Comn:* Kinetic wood sculpture, Nat Ballet Can, Toronto, 81; stainless steel sculpture, Boston Univ, 82; bronze & stainless steel sculpture, Tex Commerce Bank, Dallas, 82; bronze & stainless steel floor sculpture, First Bank Boston, 83; stainless steel sculpture, Hammerson Can Inc, Toronto, 83; Boston Ballet Co, 79-83. *Exhib:* Stewart Gallery, Dallas, 78, 82 & 83; Counterpoint at the Quadrangle, Springfield Fine Arts, Mass, 82; Boston Mus Fine Arts, 83; Interim I,II & III Chesterwood Outdoor Invitational, Stockbridge, Mass, 83; Abilene Christian Univ, Tex, 83; ISOA Gallery, Greenwich, Conn, 83; and many others. *Teaching:* Instr basic drawing, Holyoke Community Col, 75, instr advan design & compos, 76. *Awards:* Second Place, Best in Show, 71 & Award of Excellence, 78, Springfield Art League, George Walter Vincent Smith Mus. *Bibliog:* Nancy Norcross (dir), The Emerging Artist (film), Mass Arts & Humanities Coun, 80; Outdoor Sculpture in the Berkshires II, Nat Trust Hist Preservation, Libr Congress, 7-9/80; Nancy Goebel (auth), article, Art Voices, 8/81; Claudia Elferdink (dir), Art in Common: Russell Jacques--Sculptor (film), Continental Cablevision Channel 57, Springfield, 83. *Media:* All. *Mailing Add:* 3406 Via Lido Newport Beach CA 92663

JACQUETTE, YVONNE HELENE
PAINTER, PRINTMAKER
b Pittsburgh, Pa, Dec 15, 34. *Study:* RI Sch Design, 52-56, with John Frazier & Robert Hamilton; also with Herman Cherry & Robert Roche. *Work:* Weatherspoon Gallery, NC; Metrop Mus Art, Mus Mod Art, Whitney Mus Am Art, New York; Colby Col Mus; Libr Congress, Washington, DC; Staatliche Mus, Berlin; Mus Art, Carnegie Inst, Pittsburgh, Pa; Am Acad Inst Arts & Letts, New York. *Comn:* Five panel painting in oil, NCent Bronx Hosp, NY, 73; five color lithograph, Horace Mann Sch, Riverdale, NY, 74; mural installation for Fed Bldg & Post Off, Gen Serv Admin, Bangor, Maine, 79-82; Night View Washington DC, Jefferson Mem, 84; Triptych of Minneapolis (mural), First Bank, 85. *Exhib:* Skying, Rutgers Univ Art Gallery, 72; Whitney Painting Ann, Whitney Mus Am Art, 72; Women Choose Women, New York Cult Ctr & US Traveling Show, 72-73; New Image in Painting, Int Biennial, Tokyo, Japan, 74; Small Scale in Contemp Art, Art Inst Chicago, 75; Recent Acquisitions, Drawings, Mus Mod Art, New York, 81; New Work on Paper, Mus Mod Art, New York, 81-82; Brook Alexander Inc, New York, 82, 85, 88 & 89; solo shows, Currents 22, St Louis Art Mus, 83-84, Recent Paintings and Works on Paper, Berggruen Gallery, San Francisco, 84 & 91, Yurakucho Seibu-Takanawa Art, Tokyo, Japan, 85 & Tokyo Nightviews, Brooke Alexnder Inc, New York & Bowdoin Col Mus Art, Maine, 86; Drawings Since 1974, Hirshhorn Mus & Sculpture Garden, Smithsonian Inst, Washington, DC, 84; Survival of the Fittest II, Ingber Gallery, New York, 85-86; 19th Ann Acad-Inst Purchase Exhib, Am Acad & Inst Arts & Letters, New York, 87. *Teaching:* Instr, Moore Col Art, Philadelphia, 72; Vis artist & instr painting, Univ Pa, 72-76 & 79-82; vis artist, Nova Scotia Col Art, 74; instr, Parsons Sch of Design, 75-78; instr, Grad Sch Fine Arts, Univ Pa, Philadelphia, 79-84, Pa Acad Fine Arts Grad Sch Philadelphia, vis critic, 91- *Awards:* Ingram Merrill Grant, 74; Grant Painting, Creative Artists Pub Serv Prog, 79; Am Acad Arts & Letts, 90. *Bibliog:* John Ashbery (auth), The pleasures of paperwork, Newsweek, 3/16/81; Grace Glueck (auth), Painting New York, New York Times, 10/14/83; Leslie Brody (auth), Yvonne Jacquette-aerial art, Tokyo J, 7/85; James R Nelson (auth), Need for Drawings has Never Changed, The Birmingham News, 3/1/87. *Mem:* Artists Equity Asn. *Media:* Oil, Pastel; Miscellaneous. *Publ:* Illusr, Country Rush, Adventures in Poetry, 72; illusr, Aerial, Eyelight Press, 81; Jeff Wright and drawings, Toothpaste Press, 82; Jayne Anne Philips, 84; collabr, (with Rudy Burckhardt, film), Night Fantasies. *Dealer:* Brooke Alexander Gallery 59 Wooster St New York NY 10012. *Mailing Add:* 50 W 29th St New York NY 10001

JAE
SCULPTOR, JEWELRY DESIGNER
b Brooklyn, NY, Jan 9, 47. *Study:* Pace Univ, BA; pvt sculpture study with Bruno Lucchesi, New York & Italy, Jacques Lipschitz, Italy, Evangelous Moustakis, Greece & Manolo, Spain. *Comn:* Garden sculptures, comn by Charles Nissen, London, 82, Lynda McCarthy, S Africa, 83, M Gumpel, US, 84, Valerio Todisco, Italy, 85 & George Farah, US, 86. *Exhib:* Am Hellenic Soc, Athens, Greece, 73; Brooklyn Visits the Met, Metrop Mus Art, New York, 76; Nat Arts Club, New York, 76; Black History Month, US Naval Acad, Annapolis, Md, 77; Brooklyn Mus Art, 77; Salmagundi Club, New York, 77; Int Art Show, Pietrasanta, Italy, 80; and many others. *Teaching:* Instr sculpture, privately, 74-75; lectr art appreciation, 88- *Bibliog:* Article, Chicago Sun Times, 4/77; article, Que Hacemos, Buenos Aires, 4/80; Guerneri (film), The World of Jae, 85, New York. *Mem:* Artists Equity; Salmagundi Club; Int Asn Art; Nat Mus Women in Arts. *Media:* Cast Bronze, Gold; Silver with Gem Stones. *Publ:* Auth, article, Informacion, Alicanti, Spain, 8/88; article, Costa Blanca News, Benedorm, Spain, 8/88; Chicago Sun Times; Novidades, Mex. *Mailing Add:* 48 W 73rd St New York NY 10023

JAEGER, BRENDA KAY
PAINTER, CRAFTSMAN
b Fairbanks, Alaska, July 20, 50. *Study:* Eastern Wash Univ, Spokane, Ill, BA, 72; Whitworth Col, Spokane, Ill, MAT, 75; research with Kohei Fukuda, Japan, 83, 84 & 89; Lower Columbia Col, Longview, Wash, cert Pulp & Paper Technol, 85. *Work:* Alaskan State Coun Contemp Art Bank, Alyeska Pipeline Serv Co & Anchorage Mus Hist & Arts; Dean Witter Reynolds; Ketchikan Pioneers Home, Alaska; Standard Production Co. *Exhib:* The Cheney Cowles Mem Mus, Spokane, Wash; Handmade Paper Works, Anchorage Mus History & Art, Alaska, 79; Int Hand Papermakers Conf, Boston Sch Artisanry, Mass, 80; 8th Nevada Ann: Contemporary Works of Paper, Sierra Nevada Mus Art, Reno, 81; 30th & 32nd Ann Southwest Washington Exhib, 83 & 85, State Capitol Mus, Olympia, Wash; Second Ann Patrons Watercolor Gala, Gallery of the Kresge Fine Art Ctr, Oklahoma City, 84; 45th Ann Exhib Northwest Watercolors, Bellevue Art Mus, Wash, 85; Ann Alaska Juried Watercolor Exhib, 90 & Winter Landscapes, 86, Anchorage Mus History & Art; Stonington Gallery, 86-92. *Pos:* Artist with studio, Brenda Jaeger Art Studio, 78- *Teaching:* Instr art, Whitworth Col, 74-75, Spokane Art Sch, 74-75, Art Arouse Prog, ESD 101, 74-75, Columbia Basin Col, 76-77 & Walla Walla Community Col, 76-77; vis artist, Wash State Cult Enrichment Prog, 75-76, 77-78; instr art, Univ Alaska, Anchorage, 78; pvt instr, 78-; artist-in-educ programs, Alaska, 85-, Utah, 88-92, Iowa, 88-90, Ore, 90-, Aburn, Wash, 90-92; Lower Columbia Col , spring 87 & 88; Lower Kuskokwim Community Col, 88; Univ Alaska Southeast Islands Col, Petersburg, 90. *Awards:* Best of Show, All Alaska Juried Watercolor exhib, 79, 81, 84 & 85; Best of Show,

32nd Ann Southwest Washington Exhib, 85; Allied Arts Juried Painting Show, 87; Eastern Wash Watercolor Soc Juried Competition, 83. *Bibliog:* Schiller (auth), The revolution in paper, Am Artist, 77; Beverly Plummer (auth), How does your garden grow, Fiberarts, 79. *Mem:* Alaska Watercolor Soc; assoc Midwest Watercolor Soc; assoc Am Watercolor Soc; Northwest Watercolor Soc; assoc Nat Watercolor Soc. *Media:* Watercolor, Japanese Handmade Paper. *Publ:* Contribr, Flying Blind: Sunstruck at Merrill Field, & Breakfast, Vol VII, No 3, Calyx, summer 83; Shishaldinskaya, Northward J, Can, 83; illusr, Lake County Diamond, Tim Hunt (auth), Pope in Space, Barbara Blatner (auth) & 17 Toutle River Haiku, James Hanlen (auth), Intertext, 89; auth, Karasuyama Poems, Intertext, Anchorage, Alaska, 94; illusr, Lynx, 89 & 90. *Dealer:* Stonington Gallery Anchorage AK; White Bird Gallery Cannon Beach OR. *Mailing Add:* Box 2152 Longview WA 98632

JAFFE, IRA S
EDUCATOR, CRITIC
b New York, NY, Aug 19, 43. *Study:* Columbia Univ, New York, AB, 64, MFA(cinema), 67; Univ SC, PhD(cinema), 75. *Pos:* Dir, Int Cinema Lect Series & vpres Southwest Film Str, 88, head, Media Arts Prog, Univ NMex, 89. *Teaching:* Lectr cinema, Univ Southern Calif, Los Angeles, 70-72; assoc prof cinema, Univ NMex, Albuquerque, 72-88, prof, 88- *Bibliog:* Leonard J Leff (auth), Reading Kane, Film Quart, Univ Calif Press, fall 85. *Mem:* Soc Cinema Studies. *Res:* Study of Charles Chaplin and Orson Welles; research centering on film theory and on film's relationship to other arts. *Publ:* Auth, Film as the narration of space: Citizen Kane, Literature-Film Quart, 79; Stanley Cavell's pursuit of happiness, Jour Film & Video, 83; Fighting Words: City Lights, Modern Times, The Great Dictator, Univ Press, Ky, 83; Luis Bunuel: The liberty of imagination, Artspace, 85; Fool for love: the shifting frontier, Artspace, 86-87. *Mailing Add:* Col Fine Arts Univ NMex Albuquerque NM 87131

JAFFE, IRMA B
HISTORIAN, EDUCATOR
b New Orleans, La. *Study:* Columbia Univ, BS, MA, PhD. *Pos:* Res cur, Whitney Mus Am Art, New York, 64-65; ed bd, Am Art J, currently; contrib ed, Art News. *Teaching:* Chmn dept art hist, Fordham Univ, 66-77, prof, 66- *Awards:* Nat Endowment Humanities Fel, 73-74; Am Coun Learned Soc, 73 & 82; Award of Merit, Am Asn Mus, 84; Distinguished Serv Award, Fordham Univ, 86. *Mem:* Col Art Asn Am; Am Studies Asn; Northeast Am Soc Eighteenth Century Studies. *Res:* American art. *Publ:* Auth, Joseph Stella, Harvard Univ Press, 70; John Trumbull: Patriot-Artist of the American Revolution, NY Graphic Soc, 75; Trumbull: The Declaration of Independence, Viking-Penguin, 76; Copley's Watson and the Shark, Am Art J, spring 77; The Sculpture of Leonard Baskin, Viking-Penguin, 80; contribr, Am Art J, Art Bulletin, Burlington & Gazette des Beaux-Arts; coauth & ed, Selections from the Permanent Collection of the Arkansas Arts Center, 83; and others. *Mailing Add:* 2514 Fenton Bronx NY 10469

JAFFE, NORA
PAINTER, SCULPTOR
b Urbana, Ohio, Feb 25, 28. *Study:* Dayton Art Inst, Ohio; also with Samuel Adler & David Hare, New York. *Work:* Brooklyn Mus, NY; Pa Acad Fine Arts, Philadelphia; Univ Art Mus, Berkeley, Calif; MacDowell Colony, Peterborough, NH. *Exhib:* Mus Mod Art, New York, 61; Baltimore Mus Art, Md, 63 & 68; Pa Acad Fine Arts, 63-67; Finch Col Mus, New York, 67-71; New Sch Art Ctr, New York, 69-73; Va Mus Fine Arts, Richmond, 70; Gallery Lasson, London, Eng, 70; ArnolFini Art Ctr, Rhinebeck, NY, 78; Vassar Col, Poughkeepsie, NY, 79; Pastoral Gallery, East Hampton, NY, 83; Montclair State Col, NJ, 86 & 90; Virginia Lust Gallery, NY, 90. *Awards:* Second Prize, Gymnasium Show I, New York, 64; MacDowell Colony Residency, 69-70; Grant, Pollock-Krasner Found, 91-92. *Bibliog:* A Note on Nora Jaffe, Caterpillar II, 67; Deborah Curtiss (auth), Introduction to Visual Literacy, Prentice-Hall Inc (in prep). *Mem:* NY Artists Equity. *Media:* Oil; Plaster. *Publ:* Illusr, Caterpillar 13, Caterpillar, 70; Realignment, 74 & The Name Encanyoned River, 78, Treacle Press; Sulfur 4, 82 & Sulfur 5, 83, Calif Inst Technol Press. *Dealer:* Virginia Lust Gallery 61 Sullivan St New York NY 10012. *Mailing Add:* 285 Central Park W New York NY 10024

JAGGER, GILLIAN
PAINTER, SCULPTOR
b London, Eng, Oct 27, 30. *Study:* Carnegie Inst Technol, BFA; Colorado Springs Fine Arts Ctr, with Vytlacil, scholar, 52; Univ Buffalo; Columbia Univ; NY Univ, MA. *Work:* Finch Col Mus, New York; Brompton's, Montreal, Que; Carnegie Inst, Pittsburgh. *Comn:* Portrait comns, 47-51. *Exhib:* Two-man & group shows, Loft Gallery, 55-57; one-man shows, Ruth White Gallery, New York, 61, 63 & 64; Finch Col Mus, 64; Lerner-Heller Gallery, 71, 73, 75 & 77; The Horse: Light & Motion, Lerner-Heller Gallery, New York, 75. *Pos:* Textile designer, Wamsutta Mills, Fruit of the Loom, 55-57. *Teaching:* Lectr art, Radio Free Europe, cols & prof art schs; instr painting, NY Univ, Post Col & New Rochelle Acad, formerly. *Awards:* Guggenheim Fel, 83. *Mailing Add:* Box 188 Kerhonkson NY 12446

JAIDINGER, JUDITH C
PRINTMAKER, PAINTER
b Chicago, Ill, Apr 10, 41. *Study:* Art Inst Chicago, BFA. *Work:* State Found Culture & Arts, Honolulu, Hawaii; Portland Art Mus, Ore; Ill State Mus, Springfield; Okla State Univ, Stillwater; Kemper Group, Long Grove, Ill; Ukrainian Independent Contemp Art, USSR. *Comn:* Wood engraving, Face to Face, Ltd Ed, Penmaen/Busyhaus Publ, 85. *Exhib:* West '79 The Law Exhib, Minn Mus Art; 3rd Int Biennial Print Exhib, Taipei Fine Arts Mus, Taiwan ROC, 87; Interprint '90, Int Print Exhib, LUIV Mus Hist of Religion & Atheism, Ukraine, USSR, 90; 23rd Bradley Univ Print & Drawing Exhib, Ill, 91; Print Club Albany Nat Print Exhib, New York, 92; San Diego Art Inst, Calif, 92; and others. *Teaching:* Instr wood engraving, Office Field & Continuing Educ, Northeastern Ill Univ, 80- *Awards:* Smithsonian Traveling Exhib Award, Contemp Am Drawings V, Norfolk Mus Arts & Sci, 71-74; Purchase Awards, Minot State Col, NDak, 70 & 77; Graphic Award, Int Competition Printmakers, Clary-Miner Gallery, Buffalo, NY. *Mem:* Boston Printmakers; Soc Am Graphic Artists, New York, NY; Soc Wood Engravers, Gt Brit. *Media:* Wood Engraving; Opaque Watercolor, Mixed Media. *Publ:* Engravers Two, Silent Bks, Cambridge, Eng, 92. *Mailing Add:* 6110 N Newburg Ave Chicago IL 60631

JAKSTAS, ALFRED JOHN
MUSEUM CONSERVATOR
b Boston, Mass, Oct 30, 16. *Study:* Harvard Col, AB, 38; Fogg Mus Dept Conservation, with George Stout, Murray Pease & Richard Buck. *Pos:* Conservator, Isabella Stewart Gardner Mus, Boston, Mass, 41-61; Art Inst Chicago, 61-81; consult in conservation, 82- *Mem:* Int & Am Insts Conserv Artistic Objects. *Res:* Study of materials and techniques of painting of various periods. *Publ:* Auth, Problems of Museum Conservation, 63. *Mailing Add:* 10737 Welk Dr Sun City AZ 85373

JALAPEENO, JIMMY (ALBERT J BONAR)
PAINTER, PHOTOGRAPHER
Study: Univ Houston, 64-66; Univ Tex Austin, BFA(painting & photog), 66-69, Russell Lee's asst, 67-68; Univ Calif Davis, MFA(painting & photog), 71-73. *Work:* Towne Club, Dallas; MBank Austin; 3M Corp; Watson & Casey Co; Tex Com Bancshares; and others. *Exhib:* Solo shows, Bois d'Arc Gallery, Austin, 80, Hadler-Rodriguez Gallery, Houston, 83 & 86 & Air Gallery, Austin, 85; Gubernatorial Inauguration group show, 87; Eugene Binder Gallery, Dallas, Tex, 87; Laguna Gloria Art Mus, Austin, 87. *Pos:* Photogr, Tex Hist Comn, Austin, 74- *Teaching:* Lectr basic drawing, Univ Houston Art Dept, 73-74. *Awards:* Nat Endowment Arts Fel, 80. *Bibliog:* Photo portfolio, Riata Mag, 69; drawing portfolio, Calif Quart Mag, spring & fall 72; article, Tex Homes, 1/83. *Mailing Add:* c/o Eugene Binder Gallery 840 Exposition, PO Box 26305 Dallas TX 75226-0305

JAMES, A EVERETTE, JR
COLLECTOR, LECTURER
b Oxford, NC, Aug 22, 38. *Study:* Univ NC, AB, 59; Duke Univ Sch Medicine, MD, 63; Harvard Medical Sch; 66-69; Johns Hopkins Sch Hygiene, 69-71; Harvard Business Sch, 79; Royal Soc Med, London, 74. *Work:* Asheville Art Mus; US Embassies; Greenville Art Mus; Cosmos Club; and others. *Collections Arranged:* The Ahls: An American Art Family (auth, catalog), 81; Collector's Exhib (with catalog), Angus Whyte Gallery, Washington, DC, 81; Spectrum of Portraiture, Centennial Club, Nashville, Tenn, 82; James Collection, 83, Jeannette Cross Collection, 83 & The American Scene, 83, University Club, Nashville; Eugene Healon Thomason Retrospective (catalog), 85; Royster Collection (catalog), 86; Pattie Royster James Collection, 87; Indiana Impressionism (catalog), 89; Collection Antique Waterfowl Decoys, Tenn State Mus, 0; Tonalism and Nocturnes (catalog), 91; James Collection, Cosmos Club, 92. *Pos:* Ed, J Art Med. *Teaching:* Lectr Am Impressionism, Woman's Club, Centennial Club & Dixon Gallery, Memphis, Tenn, 81; instr, Philadelphia Antiques Show & Ark Art Coun, 86. *Bibliog:* James (auth), Uncovering Works of Art, Diagnostic Imaging, 81; Eugene Thompson (auth), How Do You Define a Collector, Collecting News, Vantage Press, 87; Radiography of Painting (monogr), Eugene Healon Thomason: The Ashcan Artist of Appalachia Vantage Press, 89. *Mem:* Nat Trust Historic Preserv; Soc Preservation Tenn Antiquities; Explorer's Club; Cosmos Club. *Res:* Use of imaging techniques to evaluate paintings; visual physiology and art. *Collection:* American impressionism; American landscape. *Publ:* Coauth, Digital Radiography; A Focus on Clinical Unity, 82; coauth, Certain radiographic techniques to evaluate paintings, Am J Roentgenology, 83; coauth, Digital radiography in the analysis of paintings, a new and promising technique, J Am Inst Consev, 83; auth, An introduction to Eugene Healan Thomason: The 'Ashcan Artist' who came to the mountains, Appalachian J, 83; auth, Investing in American Impressionism, MD Mag, 83; Not every canvas is down for the count, Med Econ, 84; A physician's opportunity to contribute to the arts, The Pharos of Alpha Omega Alpha, summer 85. *Dealer:* Vose Gallery Newbury St Boston MA. *Mailing Add:* 519 Belle Meade Blvd Nashville TN 37205

JAMES, BILL (WILLIAM FREDERICK)
ILLUSTRATOR, FINE ARTIST
b Manchester, Conn, Oct 7, 43. *Study:* Syracuse Univ, BFA, 65. *Work:* Dept Commerce, Montgomery, Ala. *Comn:* Mag illus, Tennis Mag, New York, 91; book illus, MacMillan/McGraw Hill, Columbus, Ohio, 91; mag & poster illus, Alfa Romeo, Bloomfield Hills, Mich, 91; brochure illus, Eddie Bauer, Redmond, Wash, 92; mag illus, Golf Illus, Phoenix, Ariz, 92; and many others. *Exhib:* The Flowered Shirt, La Watercolor Soc, 90; Mannequin With Hoop, Watercolor Soc, Ala, 91; Sleeping Sculpture, Southern Watercolor Soc, 92; What, Play Now?, Pastel Soc Am, 92; and many others. *Awards:* Best in Show, La Watercolor Soc, 90; Award in Honor of Juror, Watercolor Soc Ala, 91; Best in Show, Southern Watercolor Soc, 92. *Bibliog:* Bill James (auth), Set your subjects ablaze, Artist's Mag, 88; Bill James (auth), The watercolor page, Am Artist Mag, 89; Carole Katchen (auth), Creative Painting With Pastel, 90 & Greg Albert & Rachel Wolf (coauths), Splash, 90-91, North Light Books. *Mem:* Soc Illusr; Southern Watercolor Soc; Pastel Soc Am; Am Watercolor Soc. *Media:* Pastel, Watercolor; Graphite, Oils. *Publ:* Brochure illus, Weston Hills Country Club, 90; covers, Christmas Gift Catalog, Eddie Bauer, 86, Spring Catalog, Doubleday & Co, 88, Communique Mag, 89; cover illus, Scholastic Mag, 91, Tennis Mag, 91, Golf Mag, 92 & Eddie Bauer, 92. *Mailing Add:* 15840 SW 79th Ct Miami FL 33157

JAMES, CATTI
SCULPTOR, CONSULTANT
b Mount Vernon, NY, Oct 8, 40. *Study:* Boston Univ, BFA; Columbia Univ, MA. *Work:* Harlem Art Collection; Indianapolis Mus Art; NY State Art Collection; Govt Ctr, Plattsburgh, NY; Primary Indust, New York. *Comn:* Mural, Sepia Enterprises, Toledo, 72; costume design, Harry Belafonte Tour, 74 & Walter Nicks Dance Theater & Repertory Co, 74; cover design & book layout, Nat Bd, YWCA, 77; cover design, Girls Clubs Am, 78; cover design & book layout, Nat Bd, YWCA, 79. *Exhib:* Contemporary Black Artists in America, 71 & Whitney Ann, Whitney Mus Am Art, 72; Wild Art Show, PS1, New York, 82; Ritual & Rhythm, Kenkeleba House Gallery, New York, 82; Collage & Assemblage, Gallery Hastings, Hastings-on-Hudson, NY, 83; Exchange of Sources: Expanding Powers, Calif State Stanislaus, Turlock, 83; Artists of the 80s, Los Angeles Co Fair, Pomona, 83. *Teaching:* Art consult, Wiltwyck Sch Boys, 68-70 & Graham Sch, currently; instr anat, Col New Rochelle, 72; lectr African art & workshops on African design. *Awards:* Creative Artists Coun Grant in Painting, NY State Coun Arts, 71. *Bibliog:* Black artists in America (slides), Univ SAla & H Kress Found; Robert Doty (auth), Contemporary Black Artists in America. *Mem:* Am Crafts Coun. *Media:* Wood, Plexiglass. *Publ:* Auth, three articles in Arts & Activities Mag, 67-70; auth, A Black perspective on art, Black Enterprise Mag, 75. *Dealer:* Allan Stone Gallery 48 E 86th St New York NY 10028; Merton D Simpson Gallery 1063 Madison Ave New York NY 10028. *Mailing Add:* 6 Fulton St Hastings-on-Hudson NY 10706

JAMES, CHRISTOPHER P
PHOTOGRAPHER, PAINTER
b Boston, Mass, May 8, 47. *Study:* Cummington Community Arts, 68; Mass Col Art, BFA, 69; RI Sch of Design, MAT, 71. *Work:* Mus Mod Art, New York; Int Mus Photog, George Eastman House, Rochester, NY; Metrop Mus Art, New York; Boston Mus Fine Arts, Mass; Minneapolis Inst Arts Mus; and others. *Comn:* Subway steel enamel panels, Cambridge Arts Coun, 80. *Exhib:* One-man shows, Minneapolis Inst Arts, 77, Int Mus Photog, George Eastman House, 77, Centre d'Art Contemporain, Geneva, 79, Univ Ore Mus Art, 80, Witkin Gallery, NY, 81, 83, 85, 87 & 90; Weston Gallery, Carmel, Calif, 84, 86, 89 & 91, & Lizardi Harp Gallery, Pasadena, Calif, 87, 88 & 90; Mirrors and Windows, Mus Mod Art, New York, 78; Counterparts, Metrop Mus Art, New York, 82; and other one-man shows. *Teaching:* Asst prof photog & design, Greenfield Community Col, 71-78; artist-in-residence, Keene State Col, 77-78; lectr, Mass Inst Technol, Philadelphia Col Art, Univ Ore, Parsons Sch Design & RI Sch Design; instr, Chulalongkorn Univ, Bangkok, Thailand & Rencontres Internationales De La Photographie, Arles; prof, Harvard Univ, 78. *Awards:* Daguerre, Niepce Medal, Phot-Univers USA/USSR, Minister of Foreign Affairs, Paris, 76; Mass Arts Found Fel, 78. *Bibliog:* Hilton Kramer (auth), New York Review, Esman, New York Times, 9/23/77; David Bourdon (auth), New York Review, Esman, Village Voice, 10/10/77; John Russell (auth), New York Review, Witkin, New York Times, 10/21/83. *Mem:* Soc Photog Educ. *Media:* Watercolor, Acrylic Polymer. *Publ:* Contribr, Alternative Photographic Process, Morgan & Morgan, 78; portfolio, Popular Photography, NY, 79; portfolio, American Photographer, NY, 79; cover & portfolio, Camera, Suisse, 4/79. *Mailing Add:* c/o Art Inst of Boston 700 Beacon St Boston MA 02215

JAMESON, DEMETRIOS GEORGE
PAINTER, PRINTMAKER
b St Louis, Mo, Nov 22, 19. *Study:* Corcoran Sch Art, Washington, DC, 46; Washington Univ Sch Fine Arts, BFA, 49; Univ Ill Sch Fine & Appl Arts, Urbana, MFA, 50. *Work:* Portland Art Mus, Ore; Seattle Art Mus, Wash; Denver Art Mus, Colo; Victoria & Albert Mus, London, Eng; Am Embassy, Athens, Greece; and others in pub & pvt collections. *Exhib:* Younger Am Painters, Guggenheim Mus, New York, 54; Northwestern Art Today, Seattle World's Fair, Wash, 62; Corcoran Mus, Washington, DC; San Francisco Mus; Oakland Art Mus, Calif; Tacoma Art Mus, Wash; Butler Inst Am Art, Youngstown, Ohio; Seattle Art Mus; Portland Art Mus, Ore & Denver Art Mus; New Forms Gallery, Athens, Greece; and many others. *Pos:* Tool designer, graphic designer & illusr, US Navy. *Teaching:* Prof art, Ore State Univ, 50-82, prof emer, 82- *Awards:* J T Millican foreign Travel Award, Washington Univ, 50; Awards, Portland Art Mus, Ore & City Art Mus, St Louis, Mo; and many others. *Mem:* Portland Art Asn (pres, 57-58); Artists Equity Asn; Salem Art Asn; Portland Ctr Visual Arts; Corvallis Art Ctr. *Media:* Oil, Watercolor; Lithography. *Publ:* Auth, many articles in Art Digest, Art in Am, Northwest Rev, Painting and Sculpture in the Pacific Northwest & Northwest Art Today. *Mailing Add:* 725 NW 28th St Corvallis OR 97330

JAMESON, PHILIP ALEXANDER
CERAMIST, PAINTER
b Corvallis, Ore, Feb 24, 52. *Study:* Ore State Univ, BFA, 77; Syracuse Univ, MFA, 81. *Comn:* Interior reliefs, State Wash, Battleground, 83 & Cronin & Caplan Realtors, Portland, Ore, 83. *Exhib:* Residency Exhib, Contemp Crafts Gallery, Portland, Ore, 82; 34th Spokane Ann, Cheney Cowles Mus, Wash, 82; Architectural Ceramics, A Documentation, Interart Ctr, New York, 82; Am Nat Ceramics Exhib, Downey Mus Art, Calif, 83; Portland Ctr Visual Arts, 83; Clay for Walls, Renwick Gallery, 83-84. *Teaching:* Instr, Mt Hood Community Col, 83- *Awards:* Purchase Award, Ore State Univ, 77; Ford Found Grants, 79 & 80; Residency Award, Contemp Crafts Asn, 81. *Bibliog:* Cheryl McLean (auth), Installations by Philip Jameson, Ceramics Mo, 83; Raylene Decatur (auth), Clay on the wall, Nat Coun Educ Ceramic Art J, 83. *Mem:* Col Art Asn; Nat Coun Educ Ceramic Art; Contemp Crafts Asn; Northwest Artist Workshop. *Media:* Ceramics. *Mailing Add:* 410 Flynn St Sebastopol CA 95472

JAMISON, PHILIP
PAINTER
b Philadelphia, Pa, July 3, 25. *Study:* Philadelphia Mus Sch Art, grad. *Work:* Pa Acad Fine Arts, Philadelphia; Wilmington Soc Fine Arts, Del; Nat Acad Design, New York; Flint Inst Art, Mich; Frye Art Mus, Seattle, Wash; Nat Air & Space Mus, Washington, DC; Brandywine River Mus, Pa. *Comn:* NASA Artist for Space Shuttle Mission 51-G, 85. *Exhib:* 200 Years of Watercolor Painting in America, Metrop Mus Art, New York, 67; solo exhibs, Hirchl & Adler Galleries, New York, 59-80, Janet Fleisher Gallery, Philadelphia, 77, Newman Galleries, Philadelphia, 82, 84, 86, & 90, Ruthven Gallery, Lancaster, Ohio, 86 & Patricia Carega Gallery, Washingtonn, DC, 85 & 87; and others. *Pos:* Artist, Apollo Soyuz Space Launch, Kennedy Space Ctr, Fla, Nat Aeronautics & Space Admin, 75. *Teaching:* Instr watercolor, Philadelphia Col Art, 61-63. *Awards:* Dana Medal, Pa Acad Fine Arts, 61; Gold Medal of Honor, Allied Artists Am, 64; Nat Acad Design Prize, 67. *Mem:* Am Watercolor Soc; Philadelphia Watercolor Club; Nat Acad Design. *Media:* Watercolor, Oil. *Publ:* Contribr, Am Artist Mag, 62; auth, Capturing Nature in Watercolor, 80; Making Your Paintings Work, Watson-Guptill, 84; A Painting Without Spirit is Like Flat Beer, pvt publ, 88. *Dealer:* Newman Galleries 1625 Walnut St Philadelphia PA 19103. *Mailing Add:* 104 Price St West Chester PA 19382

JAMPOL, GLENN D
PAINTER
b Los Angeles, Calif, July 3, 50. *Study:* Univ Calif, Berkeley, BA, 72, MA, 74, MFA, 75. *Work:* Oakland Mus; San Francisco Mus Mod Art; Mobil Oil Corp, New York; Frederick Weisman Foundation, Los Angeles. *Exhib:* San Francisco Art Inst Ann, 78; solo exhib, San Francisco Art Inst, 79, 80 Langton St, San Francisco, 80 & Baruch Col, City Univ New York, 83; Fresh Paint, San Francisco Mus Mod Art, 82; Klein Gallery, Chicago, 83, 85, 87 & 91; CDS Gallery, New York, 89; Galerie Zindel-Grabner, Berlin, 89. *Teaching:* Art instr, Contra Costa Col, San Pablo, Calif, 75-76. *Awards:* Soc Encouragement Contemp Art Award, San Francisco Mus Mod Art, 77; Nat Endowment Arts Grant, 82. *Bibliog:* J Perrone (auth), MFA candidates--Berkeley, 75 & J Dickson (auth), Glenn Jampol, 80, Art Forum; A Artner (auth), Glenn Jampol, Chicago Tribune, 83; J Tully (auth), Painted fictions (catalog essay), 87. *Media:* Oil, Oil Pastel. *Dealer:* Klein Gallery 356 W Huron Chicago IL 60610; Modernism Gallery 276 Eighth St San Francisco CA 94103. *Mailing Add:* 428 Greenwich St New York NY 10013

JANELSINS, VERONICA
PAINTER, ILLUSTRATOR
b Riga, Latvia, May 20, 10; US citizen. *Study:* State Acad Fine Arts, Riga, grad, 40. *Work:* State Hist Mus Riga; State Art Mus Riga; Baumgarten-Schuler Collection, Stuttgart, Ger; Vitols Collection, Venezuela, Caracas. *Exhib:* Latvian State Art Mus, 40; Expos des Artistes en Exile, Paris, 49; Madonna Festival, Los Angeles, 55; Los Angeles Co Mus, 56; one-man show, Stockholm, 70; plus many others. *Awards:* Madonna Festival Awards, 53 & 55. *Media:* Oil. *Publ:* Many book covers & illus for Gramatu Draugs, Brooklyn. *Mailing Add:* 1298 Monument St Pacific Palisades CA 90272

JANIS, CONRAD
DEALER, COLLECTOR
b New York, NY, Feb 11, 28. *Collections Arranged:* Participated in arranging all exhibitions at Sidney Janis Gallery from New Realism, 62 through Sharp Focus Realism, 72; and others. *Pos:* Co-dir, Sidney Janis Gallery; Gallery owner. *Specialty:* All historic movements in 20th century art to the present. *Collection:* Contemporary American art. *Mailing Add:* Sidney Janis Gallery 110 W 57th St New York NY 10019

JANIS, EUGENIA PARRY
WRITER, HISTORIAN
b July 28, 40, US citizen. *Study:* Univ Mich, with Marvin Eisenberg, BA, 61; Harvard Univ, with Agnes Mongan & Jacob Rosenberg, MA, 63, PhD, 71. *Teaching:* Prof art hist, Wellesley Col, Mass, 68-86 & Univ NMex, Albuquerque, 87- *Awards:* Guggenheim Fel, 74; Am Coun Learned Soc Fel, 80; Decorated Chevalier des Palmes Academiques, Fr Gov, 87. *Res:* Graphic arts of the 19th century; monotypes of Edgar Degas; early artistic photographers in France, the Calotypists; contemporary photographers. *Publ:* Coauth, The Art of French Calotype, Princeton Univ Press, 83; auth, The Art of a Collector: Henri Le Secq Photographer, Musée des Arts & Décoratifs & Flammarion, 86; The Photography of Gustave LeGray, Univ Chicago Press, 88; contribr, Nuclear Enchantment, Photographs of Patrick Nagatani, Univ NMex Press, 91; Joel Peter Witkin, Centre Nat de la Photog, Paris, 91; and others. *Mailing Add:* 815 E Palace Ave No 16 Santa Fe NM 87501

JANJIGIAN, LUCY ELIZABETH
PAINTER, MURALIST
b Jerusalem, Palestine, Dec 14, 32; US citizen. *Study:* Heidelberg Col, Tiffin, Ohio, BA, 55; Emory Univ, Atlanta, Ga, MS, 56; Art Students League, with Robert Hale, 70, Fogerty, 71 & Glasier, 72; study with Victor D'Amico, 72-74; Stacy Wkshp Studio, New York, NY, 74- *Work:* Am Cyanamid Hq, Wayne, NJ; Berliner Handels & Frankfurter Bank, New York, NY; Mekhitarist Mus, Vienna, Austria; Gallery Phillip, Toronto; Arab Bank, New York. *Comn:* Two acrylic murals, St Leon's Church, Fairlawn, NJ, 81; acrylic mural, Armenian Evangelical Union of NAm, Los Angeles, Calif, 85; acrylic mural, Armenian Missionary Asn, Paramus, NJ, 87; Christmas cards & Christmas stamps-American Evangelical Church, New York, 87 & 89. *Exhib:* Mussavi Arts Ctr, New York, 84 & 86; A Remembrance 1915-1985, Washington Plaza Hotel, Washington, DC, 85; Nat Arts Club, Gregg Galleries, New York, 86, 87 & 88; Treasure Room Gallery, New York, 86;

Union Theological Seminary, New York, 88; Armenian Prelacy, New York, 88; Passaic Co Community Col, NJ, 88; Convention Hall Philadelphia PA, 89; Capital Place Gallery, Trenton NJ; Heidelberg Col, Tiffin, OH 90. *Pos:* Mem art comt, Armenian Gen Benevolet Union, Saddle Brook, NJ, 79-; bd trustees, Bergen Mus Arts & Sci, Paramus NJ, 84-90 & Artists for Mental Health, Patterson, NJ, currently. *Awards:* Hon Mention, Bergen County Artists, 70; Hon Mention, Franklin Lakes Art Show, 72; First Place Acrylic Abstract, Gregg Galleries-Nat Arts Club, 81. *Bibliog:* Hope Noah (auth), article, Weekend Times, NJ, 8/88; Sean Siman (auth), The painterly conscience of Lucy Janjigian, Artspeak, 12/1/88; Nancy Kleinhenz (ed), Portraits of Inhumanity - The Advertizer Tribune, Tiffin OH, 10/2/90. *Mem:* Cath Artists of the 80's; Composers, Authors & Artists of Am; Burr Artists; Nat League Pen Women; Westside Arts Coalition & New York Artists Equity Assoc Inc, New York. *Media:* Acrylic. *Mailing Add:* 268 Edgewood Rd Franklin Lakes NJ 07417

JANKO, MAY
PRINTMAKER, PAINTER
b New York, NY, Feb 27, 26. *Study:* Hunter Col, New York, BA, 46, MA, 52; Art Students League, New York, 48-53. *Work:* Metrop Mus Art, New York; Nat Gallery, Washington, DC; United States Info Agency, Bonn, Ger; Cincinnati Art Mus, Ohio. *Exhib:* Nat Prize Print Exhib, Dallas Mus Art, Tex, 54; 14th Nat Exhib of Prints, Libr Cong, Washington, DC, 56; Pa Acad Fine Arts, Philadelphia, 59; American Prints Today, Whitney Mus, New York, Nat Gallery, Washington, DC, Art Inst Chicago, Ill & traveling 15 other major mus, 59; Nat Acad Design, New York, 61 & 84; Int Print Exhib, Taipei City Mus, Taiwan, ROC, 83, 89 & 91. *Pos:* Designer, M Lowenstein, New York, 67-84; asst, Lehman Col Art Libr, 86- *Teaching:* Instr sculpture, DeWitt Clinton Adult Ctr, 53; instr art, New York Jr High Schs, 53-60. *Awards:* Louis Comfort Tiffany Found Fel, 59; Isabel B Markell Award, Audubon Artists-Graphic, 61; Leo Meissner Prize, 159th Ann Exhib, Nat Acad Design, 84; Purchase Award, 61st Nat Exhib, Soc Am Graphic Artists, 85. *Bibliog:* Article, Salon du Brooklyn Museum, La Revue Mod, 8/66. *Mem:* Soc Am Graphic Artists (coun mem, 77); Boston Printmakers Soc; life mem Art Students League, New York; Am Color Print Soc, 88. *Media:* Etching, Lithography; Oils. *Publ:* Ed, League Quart Mag, Art Students League, 51; auth, The land of trolls, Prize Winning Graphics, Vol 4, 66. *Mailing Add:* 2914 Jerome Ave Bronx NY 10468

JANKOWSKI, THEODORE ANDREW
PAINTER, MURALIST
b New Brunswick, NJ, Dec 14, 46. *Study:* Rhode Island Sch Design, 71; Cape Sch Art, 71-73, 80-86. *Work:* State Mus Reserve of Palace of Peter the Great, Leningrad, USSR; Meadows Mus, Southern Methodist, Dallas Tex; Cigna Mus Art Collection, Philadelphia, Pa; Johns Hopkins Evergreen House Perm Collection, Baltimore, Md; Provincetown Art Asn Mus, Mass. *Exhib:* Rollins Col Invitational, Winter Park, Fla, 75; Gasparilla Art Festival, Tampa, Fla, 87; Winter Park Art Festival, Fla, 86 & 87; Hensche & Friends, Michael Ingbar Gallery, New York, 88. *Mem:* Copley Soc, Boston. *Media:* Oil. *Mailing Add:* 1937 Ravenwood Drive Bethlehem PA 18018

JANNETTI, TONY
PRINTMAKER, DESIGNER
b Yonkers, NY, May 27, 47. *Study:* Pratt Inst, BFA, 69. *Work:* Mus Mod Art, New York; Yale Univ Art Gallery, New Haven; Philip Morris Collection, New York; IBM Collection, New York, Dallas, Hartford; Chase Manhattan Bank, New York; Zimmerli Mus, New Brunswick, NJ; and others. *Comn:* Rahini II, Edward Durrell Stone Asn, New York, 80. *Exhib:* Drawing Ctr, New York, 82; Resurrection Show, 55 Mercer St Gallery, New York; Nimbus Gallery, Dallas, Tex, 83-85; Relief Painting in the 80s, Zimmerli Mus, 88; Marcus-Gordon Gallery, 89. *Pos:* Creative consult, Fiji Co, 72-81; founder, Media Wall Design, 88. *Teaching:* Instr, Fordham Univ, 83-84. *Mem:* NY Artist Equity Asn; NY Graphic Artists Guild. *Publ:* Auth, articles in Artforum, 9/81 & 9/86, New York Art Review, 88 & J of the Printworld, 92. *Mailing Add:* Bowery Studios 261 Bowery New York NY 10002

JANNEY, CHRISTOPHER DRAPER
ENVIRONMENTAL ARTIST, SOUND ARTIST
b Washington, DC, Mar 14, 50. *Study:* Princeton Univ, with Michael Graves & James Seawright, BA(archit, visual arts), 73; Mass Inst Techol, with O Piene, MS(environ art), 78. *Work:* Smithsonian Inst. *Comn:* Soundstair on Tour, Three Rivers Art Festival, Pittsburgh, Pa, 79; Soundstair Bonds, Bonds Int, New York, 80; Reach!, Sonic Sports, Fourth Spiel und Klangstrasse Essen, Ger, 82; Heartbeats, 18th St Dance Found, New York, 82; Rainbow Pass, Arquitectonica, Miami, Fla, 88; Double Monocle, Badischer Kunstverein, Karlsruhe, Ger, 88; Miami Airport; East Carolina Univ. *Exhib:* Soundstair, Boston Mus Fine Arts, 79, Walker Art Ctr, 80, Nat Gallery Art, 80, Corcoran Gallery Art, 80, Second Int Electronic Music Conf, Brussels, Belg, 81 & Santa Barbara Mus Art, Calif, 82; Sonic Pass, Miss Mus Art, Jackson, 81; Wall-to-Wall John Cage, Symphony Space, New York, 82; Inside Rhythms, Inst Contemp Art, Boston, 83; Steamshuffle (with catalog), Public Art in America, Philadelphia, Pa, 87; and others. *Pos:* Res fel, Ctr Advan Visual Studies, Mass Inst Technol, 78-; chmn, Inst for Performance Sculpture Inc, 87- *Teaching:* Instr, Mass Coll Art, 84-85 & State Univ NY, Purchase, 87; vis prof, Cooper Union Sch Archit, New York. *Awards:* Nat Endowment Arts Grant, 91; Mass Coun Grant, 91; New England Found Grant, 92. *Bibliog:* Ron Blau (auth), Christopher Janney (film), Sound Sculptor, WCVB-TV, Boston, 4/82; Daria Sommers (auth), The Elephant on the Hill (film), Smithsonian World, PBS, 6/86; Andy Scheleucan (auth), Studio 7 (film), WNEV-TV. *Media:* Sound, Electronics. *Publ:* Articles in The New York Times, 10/84 & 9/86 and People Mag, 10/79. *Mailing Add:* 75 Kendall Rd Lexington MA 02173

JANOWICH, RONALD
PAINTER
b, Baltimore, Md, 48. *Study:* Col Art Md Inst, BFA, 70, MFA, 72. *Work:* Metrop Mus Art, Chase Manhattan Bank & Chemical Bank, New York; Aldrich Mus Contemp Art, Ridgefield, Conn; Bank of Boston; Cleveland Mus Art, Ohio; Tate Gallery, London, Eng; and others. *Exhib:* Small paintings, Nina Freudenheim Gallery, Buffalo, NY, 89; Geometry and Abstraction: An Evolution of Suprematist Thought, Parsons & Lindell Gallery, Helsinki, Finland, 89; Fundamental Abstraction, Cheryl Haines Gallery, San Francisco, 89; Nonrepresentation, Anne Plumb Gallery, New York, 89; Paul Cava Gallery, Philadelphia, 89-90; solo exhibs, Monotypes 1988-90, Pamela Auchincloss Gallery, New York, 90, Galerie Lelong, New York, 90-91, Galerie Malmgran, Goteburg, Sweden, 90, Galerie JMS, Oslo, Norway, 90, Monotypes 1988-90, Gallery Kuranuki, Osaka, Japan, 90 & Compasse Rose Gallery, Chicago, 91; and many other solo & group exhibs. *Bibliog:* Gregory Galligan (review), Art Int, Vol 8, Autumn 89; Kenneth Baker (auth), Forthright, bold abstracts, San Francisco Chronocle, 6/17/89; Kenneth Baker (auth), Abstract Jestures, Artforum, 9/89; H H Arnason (auth), History of Modern Art, 89; Robert Mahoney (auth), Arts, 9/89; and many others. *Media:* Oil. *Publ:* Auth, On Horizontality: A Structural Approach, 82; Brice Marden at Pace, Art Gallery Rev, Fall 82; Contemp Abstract Painting (exhib catalog), Muhlenberg Col, Allentown, Pa, 83; Small Works: New Abstract Painting (exhib catalog), Lafayette & Muhlenberg Cols, 84; Black Oil: Aspects of Dimensionality, J Artists, No 6, spring 86; and others. *Dealer:* Pamela Auchincloss Gallery 558 Broadway New York NY 10012. *Mailing Add:* c/o Garner Tullis Ten White St New York NY 10013

JANOWITZ, JOEL
PAINTER
b Newark, NJ, Nov 29, 45. *Study:* Brandeis Univ, BA, 67; Univ Calif, Santa Barbara, MFA, 69. *Work:* Metrop Mus & Whitney Mus Am Art, New York, NY; Brooklyn Mus, NY; Mass Inst Technol, Cambridge; Mus Fine Arts, Boston. *Comn:* Mural, Alewife Subway Sta, Mass Bay Transportation Authority, Cambridge, 85. *Exhib:* Whitney Biennial, Whitney Mus Am Art, New York, 73; Boston Watercolor Today, 76, A Private Vision: Contemporary Art from the Graham Gund Collection, 83 & Recent Paintings and Sculpture 1944-1984, 85, Mus Fine Arts, Boston, Mass; Hassam Fund Purchase Exhib, Am Acad & Inst Arts & Lett, New York, 80 & 87. *Teaching:* Asst prof, painting & drawing, Brown Univ, Providence, RI, 73-75 & 77; instr painting, Harvard Univ Summer Sch, 80 & 81 & Mus Fine Arts Sch, 85. *Awards:* Artists Fel, Mass State Grants Artists, 75 & 79 & Nat Endowment Arts, 76 & 82; Hassam & Speicher Fund Purchase Award, Am Acad & Inst Arts & Lett, 80 & 87; Artists Fel, New York Found for the Arts, 88. *Bibliog:* Nan Burks Freeman (auth), Boston drawing makes its mark, Drawing, 6/82; Greg Masters (auth), Joel Janowitz, Arts Mag, 12/84; Robert Morgan (auth), New York in Review, Arts Mag, 9/88. *Media:* Oil, Watercolor. *Dealer:* Victoria Munroe Gallery 415 W Broadway New York NY 10012; Barbara Krakow Gallery 10 Newbury St Boston MA 02116. *Mailing Add:* 183 E Broadway New York NY 10002

JANS, CANDACE
PAINTER, PRINTMAKER
b Rockville Center, NY, Oct 22, 52. *Study:* Wheaton Col, Norton, studied with Vaino Kola, BA, 74; Villa Schifanoia Grad Sch Fine Arts, Florence, Italy, MA, 75; RI Sch Design, studied with Wolf Kahn & Irving Petlin, MFA, 79. *Work:* Hunter Mus, Chattanooga, Tenn; Am Express Co, NYNEX, New York; Wheaton Col, Norton, Mass; Cabot Corp, Wellington Mgt Corp, Mass Financial Servs, Boston, Mass; TRW, Inc, Cleveland. *Exhib:* The Mood of New England, Boston Jubilee 350, Copley Soc, Mass, 80; Boston Now, Brockton Mus Triennial, Mass, 80; Contemporary Boston Portraits, Boston Univ Gallery, Mass, 80; Collector's Gallery XVIII, Marion Koogler McNay Art Inst, San Antonio, Tex, 84; Group Show, Bayly Art Mus, Univ Va, Charlottesville, 87; one-man shows, Fischbach Gallery, New York, 84, 86, 89 & Wheaton Col, Mass, 92; and others. *Mem:* Boston Visual Artists Union; Women's Caucus Arts (Boston chap); Boston Athenaeum. *Media:* Acrylic Oil, Lithography. *Mailing Add:* 56 River St Boston MA 02108

JANSCHKA, FRITZ
PAINTER, GRAPHIC ARTIST
b Vienna, Austria, Apr 21, 19. *Study:* Acad Fine Arts, Vienna, with A Paris Guetersloh. *Work:* Albertina, Vienna; Mus XXth Century, Vienna; Philadelphia Mus Art, Pa; Grafische Sammlung, Zurich, Switz; Hist Mus, Vienna. *Comn:* One hundred Etchings to World Literature Editon, Harenberg, Dortmind, WGer; 36 Watercolors to 36 Poems by J Joyce, comn by Clyde Joyce, Vienna, 89. *Exhib:* Pa Acad Fine Arts, Philadelphia, 51-54; Graphische Sammlungen, Zurich, 72; Fantastic Realists, Wiener Schule, Near East & Far East Countries, 72-74; Die Wiener Schule de Phantastischen Realismus, Mus Am Ostwall, Dortmund, Ger, 79; XXth Century, Art Club, Oesterreich Mus, Vienna, 81; one man shows, Orangerie Palais Auersperg, Vienna, 82, Rupertinum Salzburg, Austria, 87 & Illustration's To Sonne & Mond, Gallery at Oper, 89. *Pos:* Vis artist, UNCG, 92. *Teaching:* Prof emer fine arts, Bryn Mawr Col, Pa. *Awards:* M Slaughter Teaching Award, 85; Gold Medal of Merit, City of Vienna, Austria, 89. *Bibliog:* J Norton-Smith (auth), A Tribute to James Joyce's Ulysses, Reading Univ, Eng, 73; Johan Muschik (auth), Janschka Monograph & Vienna school of fantastic realism, Jugend & Volk, Vienna/Munich, 74; Otto Breicha (auth), Der Art Club, Oesterreichs, J & V, Vienna, 81; The Larger Austria, Edition Tusch, Sotrifer, Vienna, 82. *Media:* Oil, Watercolor. *Publ:* Auth, 26 etchings to James Joyce's Ulysses, Rizet, 72; Vom Denken der Dichter, Bibliophile Taschenbuecher, Dortmund, WGer; contribr, After Surrealism, 72, auth, Ulysses Alphabet, 73 & contribr, After Classicism, 73, Propylaen. *Mailing Add:* 707 Simpson St Greensboro NC 27401

JANSEN, ANGELA BING
PRINTMAKER, PAINTER
b New York, NY, Aug 17, 29. *Study:* Brooklyn Col, BA; NY Univ, MA; Atelier 17, New York, with S W Hayter; Brooklyn Mus Art Sch. *Work:* Metrop Mus Art, Mus Mod Art, New York; Philadelphia Mus Art; Art Inst Chicago; Tate Gallery, London, Eng; Worcester Mus, Mass. *Exhib:* Brooklyn Mus Nat Print Exhib, 50, 70 & 76; Nat Exhib of Prints, Libr of Cong, Washington, DC, 69 & 71; Venice Biennial, Italy, 72; Biennial of Graphic Art, Vienna, 72 & 77; Lang of Print, Pratt Ctr, New York, 73; Individual Exhib, Gimpel & Weitzenhoffer, New York, 74; Five Printmakers, Martha Jackson Gallery, New York, 75. *Awards:* Assoc Am Artists Gallery Award, Int Miniature Print Exhib, 71; George Roth Prize, Philadelphia Print Club, 71 & 74; Grant for Printmaking, Nat Endowment Arts, 74-75. *Bibliog:* Article, The Print Collector's Newsletter, 7-8/73; Judith Goldman (auth), The language of print, Review #I, Art Forum, summer 79; Francine Tyler (auth), Angela Jansen, Printmaker. *Media:* Etching. *Dealer:* Witkin Gallery 415 W Broadway New York NY 10012. *Mailing Add:* 1646 First Ave New York NY 10028

JANSEN, CATHERINE SANDRA
PHOTOGRAPHER, EDUCATOR
b New York, NY, Dec 14, 50. *Study:* Cranbrook Acad of Art, Bloomfield Hills, Mich, BFA, 68; Acad di Belle Arti, cert, 69; Temple Univ, MFA, 73. *Work:* Philadelphia Mus of Art; Ctr of Creative Photography; Fine Arts Mus of Honolulu; Frans, Kline & French; Bell of Pa; ARA Co. *Exhib:* Unique Photographs: Multiple Sculpture, Mus of Mod Art, New York, 73; Photo Transfer, Akron Art Inst, Ohio, 73; Three Centuries of American Art, Philadelphia Mus Art, Pa, 76; Soft Sculpture, Living Arts Ctr, Dayton, Ohio, 76; Am Family Portraits, Philadelphia Mus of Art, 76; Breath of Vision, Smithsonian Inst Traveling Exhib, 76-77; and others. *Teaching:* Instr photog, Bucks Co Community Col, Newtown, Pa, 73- *Awards:* Nat Endowment Art Award, Pa State Coun on the Arts. *Mem:* Pa State Coun of the Arts. *Publ:* Illusr, Frontiers in Photography, Time Life, 73; Photography, Upton & Upton, 76; Design Through Discovery, Holt Rinehart & Winston, 77; Photography Catalogue, Harper & Row, 77. *Mailing Add:* c/o Dept Art/Bucks Co Community Col Swamp Rd Newtown PA 18940

JANSON, AGNES
PAINTER, COLLAGE ARTIST
b London, England; US citizen. *Study:* Art Sch, Berlin, Ger; Art Students League, New York; Silvermine Graphic Workshop; Rudolf Baranik Workshop. *Work:* Pepsico, Somers, NY; Canaan Col, NH; Greenburgh Libr, Westchester, NY; Ardsley Methodist Church, NY; Houbigant Co, Ridgefield, Conn & New York; and pvt collections of Malcomb Forbes & Family, Mr & Mrs Edwin Essenfeld, Conn, Mrs Beverly Hughes, NZ, Mr & Mrs Joe Leff, Ariz, Mrs & Mrs Harvey Doliner & Mrs Baruch, NY & Mr & Mrs Walter Hill, NMex. *Exhib:* Solo shows, Mari Gallery, Mamaronek, NY, 69, 82 & 86, Hudson River Mus, 73, 76 & 79, Selected Artists Show, Silvermine Guild of Artists, New Canaan, Conn, 75, Katonah, NY, 76, Pindar Gallery, New York, 79, 81, 83 & 84, Gallery at Chappaqua Libr, 82, Mus Gallery, White Plains Libr, 83; Silvermine Guild of Artists, New Canaan, Conn, 78 & 81; Sarah Lawrence Col, New York; Amos Eno Gallery, New York; Mamaroneck Artist Guild, NY; Stamford Mus, Conn; Dana Point Coastal Arts Coun, Calif; and others. *Teaching:* Adult educ, Ardsley High Sch, 74-77; and pvt classes. *Awards:* Hon Mention, Dana Point Coastal Arts Coun, 91 & 92. *Bibliog:* Article, Arts Mag, 9/83. *Mem:* Dana Point Coastal Arts Coun, Calif. *Media:* Acrylic, Oil; Two-Dimensional Paper, Plywood. *Publ:* Many, auth, newsp articles. *Dealer:* Ann Leonard Gallery Woodstock NY; Alley Gallery San Clemente CA. *Mailing Add:* 3073 Nestall Rd Laguna Beach CA 92651

JANSON, ANTHONY FREDRICK
CURATOR, HISTORIAN
b St Louis, Mo, Mar 30, 43. *Study:* Columbia Univ, BA; Inst Fine Arts, NY Univ, MA; Fogg Mus, Harvard Univ, PhD. *Pos:* Sr cur, Indianapolis Mus Art, 78-83; cur paintings, Ringling Mus Art, Sarasota, 84- *Teaching:* Asst prof, State Univ NY, Buffalo, 73-75; asst prof, Col Charleston, SC, 75-78. *Res:* Dutch 17th century and American 19th century painting. *Publ:* Auth, Instructor's Manual to H W Janson's History of Art, Prentice-Hall, 78; Corot: Tradition and the muse, Art Quart, 78; 100 Masterpieces of Painting in the Indianapolis Museum of Art, Indianapolis Mus Art, 80; The source of David's Anacreon paintings, Sources, 83; Great Paintings from the John and Marble Ringling Museum of Art, Abrams, 86; reviser, H W Janson's History of Art, Abrams, 86. *Mailing Add:* c/o N Carolina Museum Art 2110 Blue Ridge Rd Raleigh NC 27607

JANSS, GLENN COOPER
COLLECTOR
b St Louis, Mo, Feb 29, 32. *Study:* Wellesley Col, BA, 54; grad study, Univ Calif, Los Angeles. *Exhib:* Exhibition of collected works, entitled: American Realism, traveling nationally, 86-87. *Awards:* Woman of the Year Arts Award, Los Angeles Times, 64; Gov's Arts Award of Idaho, 76. *Mem:* Whitney Mus Am Art (nat comt); San Francisco Mus Mod Art (chmn, accessions comt, 84-86); Mus Mod Art, New York (int coun); Nat Gallery (collectors comt); Boise Art Mus (bd trustees). *Collection:* 350 works on paper of 20th century American realism; historical survey, all media. *Publ:* Auth, American Realism, Harry N Abrams Co, New York, 85. *Mailing Add:* PO Box 329 Sun Valley ID 83353

JAQUE, LOUIS
PAINTER
b Montreal, PQ, May 1, 19. *Study:* Inst Appl Arts, Montreal. *Work:* Nat Gallery Can, Ottawa; Montreal Mus Fine Arts; Mus Quebec; Mus d'Art Contemporain, Montreal; Societe Publicite Editoriale Collection, Milan, Italy. *Comn:* Mural, Quebec Pavilion, Expo 70, Osaka, Japan, 70; mural, Maison de Radio-Canada, Montreal, 72; mural, Place de la Bourse, Montreal, 74. *Exhib:* Europa 72, 3rd Int Exhib Painting, Milan, 72; Salon Int d'Art Contemp, Paris, 74 & 75; retrospective, Montreal Mus Fine Arts, 77; solo exhib, Can Cult Ctr, Paris, France, 78; Arte Universal a Traves de los Tempos, Mus Palacio Bellas Artes, Mex. *Teaching:* Instr design & design hist, Inst Applied Arts, Montreal, 59- 83. *Awards:* Jessie Dow Award, Montreal Mus Fine Arts, 60; Can Art Coun Grant to Artist, 64 & 72; Europa 72 Bronze Medal, City of Milan, 72. *Mem:* Founder Soc Prof Artists Que (pres, 64-65); Royal Can Acad. *Media:* Oil, Tempera. *Publ:* Art in New York, Time Mag, 10/31/69; Considerations over a concept, D'ars Mag, Italy, Nos 53 & 54; 16 Quebec painters in their milieu, La Vie Des Arts, 78; Monique Brunet-Weinmann (auth), Louis Jaque: le point de vue d'icare, La Vie Des Arts, spring 85; Monique Brunet-Weinmann (auth), Louis Jaque, 89. *Dealer:* Simon Blais 4521 Clark St Montreal H2T 2T3 PQ; Galerie Frederic Palardy 307 Ste Catherine W Montreal PQ H2X RA3. *Mailing Add:* 6150 Ave de Boise Apt 3G Montreal PQ H3F 2V2 Canada

JARAMILLO, VIRGINIA
PAINTER
b El Paso, Tex, Mar 21, 39. *Study:* Otis Art Inst, 58-61. *Work:* Long Beach Mus Art, Calif; Pasadena Art Mus, Calif; Aldrich Mus Contemp Art, Ridgefield, Conn; Schenectady Mus, NY. *Exhib:* Whitney Mus Am Art Ann, New York, 72; Contemporary Reflections 1971-72, Aldrich Mus Contemp Art, Ridgefield, 72; group exhib, Douglas Drake Gallery, Kansas City, Kans, 75 & one-man show, 76; plus others. *Pos:* Assoc dir & aesthet adv, Hybrid Inc, 72-74. *Awards:* Ford Found Grant, 62; Nat Endowment Arts, 72-73; Creative Artists Pub Serv Prog Grant, 75. *Bibliog:* F Bowling (auth), Outside the galleries: Four artists, Arts Mag, 11/70; Deluxe show, Houston Chronicle, 8/71; C Ratcliff (auth), The Whitney Annual, Part I, Artforum, 4/72. *Mem:* Nat Soc Lit & Arts. *Media:* Acrylic, Oil. *Res:* Religious architecture throughout Europe. *Publ:* Auth, Post-minimal artists, Arts Mag, 9/75. *Mailing Add:* c/o Douglas Drake Gallery 50 W 57th St New York NY 10019

JARDINE, DONALD LEROY
EDITOR, EDUCATOR
b Idaho Falls, Idaho, July 7, 26. *Study:* Weber Col, Ogden, Utah, CA, 48, Assoc Sci, 49; Univ Utah, BS, 50 & MS, 62; Univ Minn, Minneapolis, PhD, 75; studied with Farrell R Collett, Alvin Gittens, Arnold Friberg, Walter Wilwerding, Peter Busa & Reid Hastie. *Work:* Salt Lake Art Barn; Univ Utah; Weber State Col; Univ Minn. *Comn:* General Mills Co. *Exhib:* Utah Artists' Invitational, Ogden, 54-58 & 61; Instructor's Exhib, Salt Lake Art Ctr, 57-60; Asn Prof Artists Ann, Minneapolis, 64-66; People-to-People Exhib, Santiago, Chile, 66; Studio Arts Fac Show, Univ Minn, 68 & 70. *Pos:* Pres, Utah Art Educ Asn, 58-60; ed, The Illustrator, 65- *Teaching:* Art teacher, Bountiful Sr High Sch, Utah, 51-62; assoc dir art educ, Westminster Col, Salt Lake City, 58-60; educ dir art, Art Instr Sch, Minneapolis, 62-; prof career art, Univ Minn, 68-83; dir educ, Palmer Writers Sch, 85- *Awards:* Distinguished Art Award, Weber State Univ. *Mem:* Asn Prof Artists (dir, 65-67); Art Instr Schs (vpres, 77); Art Dir Club; Nat Art Educ Asn (lectr, 74-75). *Publ:* Illusr, The Children's Friend, 55-62; illusr, Tell Me a Story, 60; contribr, Art Instruction School's Textbooks, 62-75; auth, How to Sell Your Artwork, 63; auth, Richard Lack's Atelier, Am Artist, 71; auth, Creating Cartoon Characters, 89, Creating Cartoon Animals, 90, Walter Foster Publ Co. *Mailing Add:* 2390 Wisconsin Ave N Golden Valley MN 55427

JARRARD-DIMOND, TERRY
SCULPTOR, EDUCATOR
b Slater, SC, July 3, 45. *Study:* Winthrop Col, BA, 69; Clemson Univ, MFA, 79. *Work:* SC State Art Collection; Federal Reserve Bank Richmond, Charlotte, NC; Coca Cola Corp Hq, Atlanta, Ga; John Wieland Homes, Inc Collection, Atlanta, Ga. *Comn:* Fiber murals, comn by Harold Cooledge, Clemson, SC, 75 & Richland Mem Hosp, Columbia, SC, 83 & 85; sculpture, Tri-County Tech Col, Pendleton, SC. *Exhib:* Two-artist exhib, Spirit Sq, Charlotte, NC; solo exhib, Ashville Art Mus, NC, 84; Rome Exhib, Palazzo Venezia, Rome, Italy, 84; Woman's Work travelling exhib, Univ Ohio, 87; Surfaces, 300 Galleria, Atlanta, Ga, 88; Fel Recepients, SC State, Mus, Coumbia, SC; This Year's Model, Invitational, Greenville Co Mus Art, SC, 91; Invitational, Columbia Mus Art, SC, 92. *Pos:* Dir, Pickens Co Art Mus, 79-81. *Teaching:* Instr weaving, intro design (two & three dimensional) & sculpture, Greenville Co Mus Art, 81-88; instr drawing, Anderson Col, SC, 81; instr matrix, Lander Col, 83-; vis asst prof sculpture & design, Clemson Univ, SC, 88-89 & 90-91; Anderson design, 87-88; SC Gov's Sch Arts, 80, 82-90. *Awards:* Merit Awards, Shelby Art League Exhib, NC, 82 & NC/SC Fiber Competition, Charlotte, NC, 83; Special Merit Award, First Spartanburg Exhib, SC, 83; Crafts Fel, SCar Arts Comn, 86-87; Hambidge Ctr Creative Studies Fel, Hambidge Ct, Rabun Gap, Ga, 90. *Bibliog:* Sharyn Hyatt & Teresa Mangum (auths), The ceremonial structures of Terry Jarrard-Dimond, Fiber Arts Mag, 7-8/82; Virginia Watson Jones (auth), Contemporary American Women Sculptors: An Illustrated Bio-Bibliography, Oryx Press, 86. *Media:* Mixed. *Dealer:* The Signature Shop and Gallery 3267 Roswell Rd NW Atlanta GA 30305. *Mailing Add:* PO Box 495 Clemson SC 29633

JARVIS, DONALD
PAINTER, INSTRUCTOR
b Vancouver, BC, 1923. *Study:* Vancouver Sch Art, with hon, 48; also with Hans Hofmann, New York, 48 & 49. *Work:* Nat Gallery Can, Ottawa, Ont; Art Gallery Greater Victoria, BC; Vancouver Art Gallery; London Pub Libr & Art Mus; Can Coun Art Bank, Ottawa; and others. *Exhib:* Nat Gallery of Can, 55-65 & 69; Some Painters of the BC Mainland, Art Gallery of Greater Victoria, 65; Int Exhib of Drawings & Prints, Lugano, Switz, 66; one-man show, Vancouver Art Gallery, 49, 55 & 77; Coasts, The Sea and Canadian Art, Stratford, Ont, 79; and others. *Teaching:* Instr painting & drawing, Emily Carr Col of Art, 51-86. *Awards:* Emily Carr Scholar, Vancouver Sch Art, 48; Sr Arts Fel, Can Coun, 61. *Mem:* Royal Can Acad Arts. *Media:* Mixed Media. *Mailing Add:* c/o Bau-Xi Gallery 3045 Granville St Vancouver BC V6H 3J9 Canada

JARVIS, JOHN BRENT
PAINTER
b American Fork, Utah, Nov 28, 46. *Study:* Snow Col, AS, 65; Utah State Univ, BS, 71; Brigham Young Univ. *Work:* Brigham City Mus, Utah; Latter Day Saints Church Mus; Springville Mus Art, Springville, Utah. *Comn:* Painting, Latter Day Saints Church, 84. *Exhib:* Salt Lake Art Ctr Regional Show, 76; Am Watercolor Soc, New York, 76; one-man shows, Brigham Young Univ, Provo, Brigham City Mus, Bertha Eacles Gallery, Ogden, & Trivoli Gallery, Salt Lake City, Utah; Northwest Rendevouse Show, Helena, Mont, 89-90. *Awards:* Merit Award, Utah Painting & Sculpture, Utah Inst Fine Arts, 74; Ann Noye Watercolor, Salt Lake Art Ctr Intermountain, 76; Merit Award, Mormon Art Show, Brigham Young Univ, 77. *Media:* Multimedia, Watercolor. *Dealer:* Lido Gallery Park City Utah. *Mailing Add:* 1355 E 250 North St Pleasant Grove UT 84062

JARVIS, LUCY
CONSULTANT, FILMMAKER
b New York, NY, June 23, 27. *Study:* Cornell Univ; Columbia Univ; New Sch Social Res, New York; Bower Col, LLD. *Pos:* Exec producer, Nat Broadcasting Corp, New York, 60-76; pres, Creative Proj Inc, 76-90; Chmn, Jarvis Theatre & Film Ltd. *Awards:* Chevalier l'Ordre Arts & Lettres, Fr Govt, 69; Int film & TV Festival, New York, 85; Deans Award, Cornell Univ, 90. *Mailing Add:* c/o Creative Proj Inc 555 W 57th St New York NY 10019

JAUDON, VALERIE
PAINTER
b Greenville, Miss, Aug 6, 45. *Study:* Miss State Col Women, Columbus; Univ Am, Mexico City; St Martin's Sch Art, London, Eng; Memphis Acad Art, Tenn. *Work:* Hirshhorn Mus, Washington, DC; Mus Mod Art, New York; Louisiana Mus, Humlebaek, Denmark; Fogg Mus, Cambridge, Mass; Sammlung-Ludwig Mus, Aachen, WGer. *Comn:* Tile work (with Romaldo Giurgola, architect), State Off Complex, Harrisburg, Pa, 76; Three-acre brick & granite paving plan, Munic Bldg, Police Plaza, New York, 88; painting mural, City of Atlanta, City Hall, Ga, 88; Ceramic Mural, Equitable Bldg, New York, 88; and others. *Exhib:* Mus Mod Art, New York; Hirshhorn Mus & Sculpture Garden, Washington, DC, 77; solo exhibs, Pa Acad Fine Arts, 77, Galerie Hans Strelow, Dusseldorf, 80, Corcoran Gallery, Los Angeles, 81, Quadrat Mus, Bottropt Amerika Haus, Berlin, Fed Repub Ger, 83, Dart Gallery, Chicago, 83 & Sidney Janis Gallery, 83, 85, 86 & 88; Nat Gallery, Washington, DC, 80; and others. *Teaching:* Instr, Sch Visual Arts, New York, 83-84 & Hunter Col, New York, 86- *Awards:* Award, Miss Inst Arts & Letters, 81; award & comn, City of New York, 87; vis arts Fel Grant, Nat Endowment for the Arts, 88; Art Award, Excellence in Design, Art Comn, New York, 88. *Bibliog:* Kay Larson (auth), Freezing Expressionism, New York Mag, 4/25/83; Richard Armstrong (auth), article, Artforum, 9/83; John Perreault (auth), Allusive depths: Valerie Jaudon, Art Am, 10/83. *Dealer:* Sidney Janis Gallery 100 W 57th St New York NY 10019. *Mailing Add:* 139 Bowery New York NY 10002

JAVACHEFF, CHRISTO See Christo,

JAWORSKA, TAMARA
FIBER ARTIST, TAPESTRY ARTIST
b Archangelsk, Russia; Can citizen. *Study:* State Acad Fine Arts, Poland, BFA, Fac Art Weaving, MFA; Royal Can Acad Arts, fel academician. *Work:* Nat Mus, Warsaw, Poland; Molsons Brewery, Toronto; York-Hanover Corp, Toronto; JDS Investment Corp, Toronto; Nat Mus A Puschkin, Moscow, USSR; Can Embassy, Ryiadh, Saudi Arabia; Dept External Affairs, Can; Nat Mus, Warsaw, Poland; and many pvt collections. *Comn:* Tapestries-Gobelin, Olympia & York Co, Place Bell Can, Ottawa, 71 & Bank Montreal, Toronto, 75, Metrop Life Ins Co, Ottawa, 77, JDS Finch 1000, Toronto, 76 & var pvt collections in US, Can, Switz, Eng, Sweden & France. *Exhib:* One-person shows, Art Gallery Hamilton, 80 & Nienkamper Art Gallery, Toronto, 80; Can Cult Ctr, Art Gallery, Paris, 81; retrospectives, Ctr Nat de la Tapisserie D'Aubusson, Galerie Inard, Paris, traveling abroad, 81-82, 84, 86, 89 & 91 & Royal Acad Arts, John B Alry Gallery, Toronto, 92; Centennial Exhib RCA, Toronto; and others in Poland, Italy, Switz, WGer, Holland, Mex, Can & Iran. *Pos:* Dir pvt design-weaving art studio, Toronto, currently. *Teaching:* Instr post grad workshop design & weaving, Ont Col Arts, Can. *Awards:* Gold Medal, Int Trienale de Milano, Italy, Int Exhib Interior Design & Archit, 57; Award for Excellence, Wool Gathering, Can Guild Crafts, Montreal, 73; Master Painter Honoris Causa, Academia Italia delle Arti; Gold Medal & First Prize, Int Art Competition, New York, 85. *Bibliog:* Tapestries by Tamara Jaworska (film), CBS Toronto, 70 & Tamara's Tapestry World, CBS Arts & Sci Prog in Film, Toronto, 75; film, Tapestries by Tamara, New Collection, CBC Arts Film, Toronto, 80; film (mini-series), A Modern Country, Tamara's Tapestry World, Textures & Canadian Reflections, Can Broadcasting Co; film, Portrait of the Artist, CHCH TV & CHEX TV; and articles in American & European variety mag, art mag & daily newspapers. *Mem:* Royal Can Acad Arts; Acad Italia del Arti a del Lavoro. *Media:* Handspun Wool, Artificial Yarns. *Dealer:* Centre Nationale de la Tapisserie D'Aubusson Galerie Inard 179 Boulevard St Germain Paris France. *Mailing Add:* 49 Don River Blvd Willowdale ON M2N 2M8 Canada

JAY, BILL
PHOTOGRAPHIC HISTORIAN, CRITIC
b Maidenhead, Berkshire, England, Aug 12, 40. *Study:* Berkshire Col Art, dipl; Univ NMex, MA & MFA; spec study with prof Van Deren Coke & prof Beaumont Newhall. *Work:* Int Mus Photog, Rochester, NY; Bibliotheque Nat, Paris, France; Art Mus, Univ NMex, Albuquerque; plus many pvt collections. *Exhib:* Mod Art, var locations in Brit & Europe, 67; Art Mus, Univ NMex, 76; one-man shows, Micro-Gallery, Phoenix, Ariz & Northlight Gallery, Tempe, Ariz, 77. *Collections Arranged:* Brit Documentary Photog 1850-1970, Brit Coun, 71; The English Scene, Tony Ray-Jones & Sir Benjamin Stone 1864-1914, 71, The Inst for Contemp Arts, London; plus others. *Pos:* Ed/dir, Album Mag, London, Eng, 69-71; dir photog, Inst Contemp Arts, London, Eng, 69-71. *Teaching:* From asst prof to assoc prof art hist, 19th century & 20th century photog, Ariz State Univ, Tempe, Ariz, 74- *Mem:* Soc for Photog Educ (mem bd dirs, 74-78); Royal Photog Soc Gt Brit (mem Royal comn, 72). *Res:* Photography of the 19th and 20th centuries, especially British topographical work of the wet-plate era. *Publ:* Auth, Robert Demachy: Photographs and Essays, 74, Acad Ed; auth, Victorian Cameraman: Francis Frith 1822-1898, 73 & Victorian Candid Camera: Paul Martin 1864-1944, 73, David & Charles; Negative/Positive: A Philosophy of Photography, Kendall-Hunt, 79; Addison House and Photography: Current Perspectives, Light Impressions, 79. *Mailing Add:* Dept Art Ariz State Univ Tempe AZ 85287-1505

JAY, NORMA JOYCE
PAINTER
b Wichita, Kans. *Study:* Wichita State Univ; Art Inst Chicago; Calif State Univ, Long Beach. *Work:* Irvine Found; Edwin Morris Collection; Deloitte, Haskins & Sells. *Exhib:* Am Soc Marine Artists Ann Exhib, 78-90; Grand Central Galleries, New York, 79, 80 & 82; Peabody Mus, Salem, Mass, 81; Mystic Maritime Gallery, Mystic Seaport Mus, Mystic, Conn, 82, 83, 85, 90 & 92; Palm Springs Desert Mus, 84; Newman & Saunders Galleries, Wayne, Pa, 84; Kirsten Gallery, Seattle, Wash, 84; Mariners Mus, Newport News, Va, 85-86; Nat Heritage Gallery Fine Art, Beverly Hills, Calif, 88-90; Maryland Hist Mus, Baltimore, Md, 89. *Awards:* Best Show, Ford Nat Competition, 61; Artists Award, Chriswood Galleries, 73; First Place, Traditional Artists 10th Ann, 76. *Bibliog:* Peter Rogers (auth), review, Sea Hist, winter 80-81; Contemporary Marine Art, Nimrod Press, 81; Rebecca Smith (auth), Norma Jay, West Coast Impressions, Nautical Quart, autumn 84; article, Antiques & Arts Weekly, 12/82; Yacht Portraits, Sheridan House. *Mem:* Fel Am Soc Marine Artists. *Media:* Oil. *Dealer:* Nat Heritage Gallery Fine Art 315 N Rodeo Dr Beverly Hills CA 90210. *Mailing Add:* 13910 SE Hampshire Way Clackamas OR 97015

JEAN, BEVERLY (BEVERLY JEAN STRONG)
PAINTER, ART DEALER
b Eugene, Ore, Oct 1, 27. *Work:* Atlanta Bowe Co, Ga. *Pos:* Owner, Tiqua Gallery, Santa Fe, NMex, currently. *Media:* Oil Painting, Monoprints. *Specialty:* Contemporary paintings; antique folk art; American Indian art; colonial Mexican art. *Mailing Add:* 812 Canyon Rd Santa Fe NM 87501

JEAN-LOUIS, DON (DONALD CHARLES)
SCULPTOR, CONCEPTUAL ARTIST
b Ottawa, Ont, May 17, 37. *Work:* Nat Gallery Can; Montreal Mus Fine Arts; Art Gallery Ont; Can Coun Art Bank; Bakken Mus, Minneapolis. *Comn:* Signage (light sculpture), Coca Cola Can Ltd, Toronto, 77; installation (neon & argon), Fed Govt Can, Toronto, 78; neon sculpture & installation, Can Indust Ltd, Toronto, 80. *Exhib:* Art, Basel, Switz, 74 & Rotterdamse Kunststichting, Holland, 75; From Electrica Fires, Vancouver Art Gallery, 77; Pulse and Process, York Univ, Toronto, 79; Light 4 Play, Harbourfront Art Gallery, Toronto, 79. *Teaching:* Instr photo-electric arts, Ont Col Art, Toronto, summer 78. *Bibliog:* Parkins-Boyle (auth), Art and Architecture, Visual Arts Ont, 82. *Mem:* Royal Can Acad Arts. *Media:* Light. *Mailing Add:* c/o Electric Gallery 226 Steelcase Rd W Markham ON L3R 1B3 Canada

JECK, DOUGLAS A
SCULPTOR
b Jersey City, NJ, 1963. *Study:* Tenn Technol Univ, Cookeville, Tenn, 81-83; Appalachian Ctr Arts & Crafts, Smithville, Tenn, BA, 84-86; Sch Art Inst Chicago, Ill, MFA, 87-89, Fel Award, 89. *Work:* Lamar Dodd Art Ctr, La Grange, Ga. *Exhib:* One-person exhibs, Appalachian Ctr Arts & Crafts, Smithville, Tenn, 85, Connell Gallery/Great Am Gallery, Atlanta, Ga, 91; Death of Innocence, Sarratt Gallery, Vanderbilt Univ, Nashville, Tenn, 87; Doug Jeck & Jacqueline Saccoccio, Sch Art Inst Chicago, Gallery 2, 88, Chicago Fire II, Northwest Arts Coun, 88, New Talent I, 89, Doug Jeck & Lisa Pines, Contemp Art Workshop, 90, Tattoo, Randolph St Gallery, Chicago, Ill, 90; LaGrange National XVI, Lamar Dodd Art Ctr, Ga, 91. *Awards:* Ill Arts Coun Artist Fel, 89; Nat Endowment Arts, Visual Artist Fel Grant, 90. *Bibliog:* Klaus Ottmann (auth), Tattoo, Flash Art, Jan/Feb, 90; Catherine Fox (auth), Clay figures come to life at Connell, Atlanta J & Constitution, Ga, 1/25/91; Jerry Cullum (auth), Douglas Jeck, Art Papers, Vol 15, No 3, 41, May/June, 91. *Mailing Add:* 949 N Hoyne Ave Chicago IL 60622

JEFF
PAINTER, PHOTOGRAPHER
b Oakland, Calif, 1942. *Study:* Univ NMex, BFA, 71; Univ Wis-Madison, MFA, 73. *Work:* Mus Mod Art, Metrop Mus, New York; Art Inst Chicago, Ill; Modema Museet, Stockholm, Sweden; Kunts Mus, Basil, Switz. *Exhib:* Galerie des Glaces/Galerie Sema, Paris, 89; Buda Castle, Budapest, 90; Cultural Ctr Heusden-Zolder, Belg, 91; Guggenheim Gallery, Chapman Col, Orange, Calif, 91; Photo Art Gallery, Burbank, Calif, 91; Vastuskos-Haz, Gyor, Hungary, 91; Denver Art Mus, 93; Musee d'Art Moderne, Bordeaux, France, 93; one-person show, Orange Co Ctr Contemp Art, Santa Ana, Calif, 89. *Teaching:* Adj asst prof, Fashion Inst Technol, 76- *Awards:* Fel, Nat Endowment Arts, 86-87. *Media:* Acrylic, Oil. *Mailing Add:* 114 Fulton St New York NY 10014

JEFFE, HULDAH C
PAINTER
b Dallas, Tex. *Study:* Grand Cent Sch Art; Art Students League; also with Robert Brackman, New York. *Work:* Ga Mus Fine Arts; Columbia Mus Art; Norfolk Mus Art; Sheldon Swope Mus Art; Cornell Univ Med Club. *Exhib:* Salon des Artistes Francaise; Wally Findlay Galleries, New York, Chicago, Beverly Hills & Palm Beach; one-woman exhib, Wally Findlay Galleries, Palm Beach, 89; Wally Findlay Galleries, Int, Chicago, 90. *Pos:* Artist, Hallmark Cards, formerly; ceramist, W Goebel & Co, Bavaria, Ger, formerly; reproductions of original paintings, NY Graphic Soc, formerly. *Awards:* Salon des Artists Francais Awards, Paris, France. *Media:* Oil. *Mailing Add:* 680 S County Rd Palm Beach FL 33480

JEFFERS, WENDY JANE
PAINTER, CURATOR
b Providence, RI, Sept 5, 48. *Study:* Univ Mass, BFA, 71; Pratt Inst, MFA(painting), 74; also attended NY Inst Fine Arts, Art Students League, Tyler Sch Art, Am Univ, New Sch Social Research, Mass Col Art, Columbia Univ, Corcoran Mus Sch, NY Acad Art & Nat Acad Design. *Work:* Port Authority of NY & NJ; Chase Manhattan Bank, New York; Nelson A Rockefeller; Continental Group, Stamford, Conn; Miller, Tabak & Hirsch, New York; pvt collections, Dr & Mrs Jack Aslanian, Mr & Mrs George Demeter, Mr & Mrs William Hayden; and many others. *Exhib:* The Icarus Odyssey, Guadalajara & Mexico City, 79; Wash Square East Galleries, New York Univ, 80; Paperworks 80, Hudson River Mus, Yonkers, New York, 80; AIR Gallery Invitational, New York, 82-85; one-person exhib, Bristol Art Mus, RI, 84; Fairleigh Dickinson Univ, NJ, 84; Sculptures-Drawings, Berkshire Artisans Art Ctr, Pittsfield, Mass, 84. *Collections Arranged:* First Nat City Bank Art Collection, New York, 73-74; Seven Decades at the Colony (auth, catalog), New York, 76; A Curators Choice: A Tribute to Dorothy C Miller, Rosa Esman Gallery, New York, 82; Niles Spencer A Portrait in Words and Images, Archives Am Art, New York, 90; Niles Spencer Exhib, Whitney Mus Am Art, Equitable Ctr, spring 90. *Pos:* Indep Cur, Citibank, New York, 73-74 & 82-; asst to Dorothy C Miller, 74-; artist-in-residence, RI Creative Arts Ctr, 80-83 & Cortona, Italy, 85. *Awards:* Max Beckman Fel, Brooklyn Mus, 71-72; Graduate Fel, Pratt Inst, 73-74; MacDowell Colony Fel, 77. *Bibliog:* John Russell (auth), article, New York Times, 2/5/82; Kay Larson (auth), article, New York Mag, 3/1/82; Michael Kimmelman (auth), Review of Niles Spencer exhib, New York Times, 6/15/90. *Mem:* Col Art Asn. *Media:* Oil, Graphite. *Res:* Working on Catalogue Raisonne of Niles Spencer's painting and sculpture; Working on chronology of Holger Cahill, Dir Fed Art Proj. *Publ:* Auth, Seven Decades of MacDowell Artists (exhib catalog), New York Gallery, 76; Niles Spencer, Whitney Mus Am Art, 90; Dorothy C Miller: A Profile, New Eng Antiques J, 5/90; David Shipley, Visions Mag, 10/91; essay, Holger Cahill & Am Art J Arch Am Art, fall 92. *Mailing Add:* 61-63 Crosby St New York NY 10012

JELLICO, JOHN ANTHONY
DIRECTOR, PAINTER
b Koehler, NMex, June 26, 14. *Study:* Art Inst Pittsburgh, dipl; Univ Pittsburgh, teaching cert; Phoenix Sch Design; Grand Cent Sch Art, New York. *Comn:* Seven relig murals, St Patricks Cath Church, Raton, NMex, 37; 62 chapel murals, Third Air Force, Tampa, Fla, 43-45; 3 paintings, White House, Washington, DC. *Exhib:* Raton Ann Art Show, NMex, 37; Phoenix Art Inst Ann, New York, 38; Art Inst Pittsburgh Exhib, Pa, 40; Taos Art Colony Ann Show, NMex, 41; Gallery Santa Fe, NMex. *Pos:* Asst dir & head illusr, Art Inst Pittsburgh, 46-56; dir, Colo Inst Art, 56-62, pres, 62-72; contrib ed, Am Artist Mag, 68-81; assoc ed, Southwestern Art Mag, 74- *Teaching:* Dir drawing, Colo Inst Art, 56- *Mem:* Hon mem Eugene Fields Soc; Mark Twain Soc. *Publ:* Auth, textbks, Int Correspondence Schs, 59-60; articles in Am Artist Mag, 59-68 & Westerner Mag, 72; contrib & writer, Artists of the Old West & Persimmon Hill, mags; and others. *Mailing Add:* 291 W Belleview Englewood CO 80110

JELLICO, NANCY R
PAINTER, SCULPTOR
b LaGrange, Ga, Sept 22, 39. *Study:* Colo Inst Art, Denver, with John Jellico & Charlie Dye, 60; Univ Denver, with John Witaschek, 81; CA-10 Wkshp, Kerrville, Tex, 86. *Comn:* The Good Things Don't Change (four paintings), 82, sculptures: Bunch Quitter, 83, He Ain't Heavy, 84, Head to Head, 88 & Lendin' a Hand, 90, The Upjohn Co, TUCO Div, Kalmazooo, Mich; Flag design, ProRodeo Hall of Champions & Mus of the Am Cowboy, Colo Springs, 83; archit sculpture (to scale), St Thomas Sem, Denver, Colo, 85, 88 &90. *Exhib:* Mountain Oyster Club's Ann Contemp Western Art Show, Tucson, Ariz, 84-92; Classic-Am Ann Western Art Show & Sale, Beverly Hills, Calif, 87-90; solo exhib, Nat Cowgirl Hall Fame, Hereford, Tex, 90; Women Artists & the West, Tuscon Mus Art, Ariz, 91 & 92; Happy Canyon Western Art Invitational, Pendleton, Ore, 91 & 92; Wyoming Western Images, Murisaki Gallery, Tokyo, Japan, 92. *Pos:* Registrar, Colo Inst Art, Denver, 61-65. *Teaching:* Instr figure drawing & anatomy, Colo Inst Art, 64-65. *Awards:* Warren Richardson Award (first place), 83, C M Charlie Russell Award, 85, Hon Mention, 86, Western Regional Ann Art Show & Sale, Cheyenne, Wyo; Artist of the Year & Best Show/Oil-base Medium, Rushmore Prof Fine Artists Show, Rapid City, SD, 85; Inducted into Colo Inst Art Hall of Fame, Denver, Colo, 91. *Bibliog:* Chan Bergen (auth), article in: Western Horseman Mag, 7/87; Deborah S Borg (auth), article, Equine Images, fall 89; Shirley Behrens (auth), article, Art of the West, 3-4/90. *Mem:* Pastel Soc Am; Pastel Soc SW; Nat Soc Painters Casein & Acrylic; Knickerbocker Artists. *Media:* All Media. *Publ:* Illusr of five art textbooks, Int Correspondence Schs, 60-65; Portrait of Franklin Booth for feature article, Am Artist Mag, 66; Portrait of Pawel Kontny for feature article, Artists Rockies & Golden West Mag, 81; auth & illusr, feature article in: Int Cowboy Mag, Surrey, Eng, 12/87-1/88. *Dealer:* LaPorta Art Gallery Englewood, CO; White Hart Galleries Steamboat Springs CO. *Mailing Add:* Jellico Studio of Western Art 1449 W Littleton Blvd, Suite 204 Littleton CO 80120-7509

JENDRZEJEWSKI, ANDREW JOHN
SCULPTOR, ADMINISTRATOR
b Fremont, Mich, July 1, 46. *Study:* Tyler Sch Art, Rome & Philadelphia, BFA, 68; Wash Univ, St Louis, MFA, 73. *Exhib:* 70th Ind Artists Show, Indianapolis Mus Art, 85; Show Case Show, Water Tower, Louisville, Ky, 85; Omnibus '88 Invitational, Herron Gallery, Indianapolis, Ind, 88; 40th Ann Four State Ilmoian, Quincy Art Ctr, Ill, 90; Midwest Sculpture, South Bend Regional Mus Art, Ind, 90. *Pos:* Mus technician, Univ Mich Mus Art, 73-75. *Teaching:* Prof art & sculpture & art dept chmn, Vincennes Univ Jr Col, 77- *Bibliog:* Steve Mannheimer (auth), The Vincennes group, Indianapolis Star, 10/31/82; Marion Garmel (auth), Strong entries in Omnibus Exhib, Indianapolis News, 7/14/84; Hollis Sigler (auth), Jurer's Statement, 20th Ind Artists Catalog, 85. *Mem:* Nat Asn Sch Art & Design; Mid Am Col Art Asn. *Media:* Miscellaneous. *Mailing Add:* 404 N Fifth St Vincennes IN 47591

JENKENS, GARLAN F
CURATOR, PAINTER
b Stamford, Tex, Aug 26, 49. *Study:* N Tex State Univ, Denton, BFA, 74, MFA, 76; Univ Ore, Eugene, PhD, 82. *Work:* N Tex State Univ Collection, Denton; Koger Corp, Exec Ctr, Little Rock, Ark; Corvallis Art Ctr Collection, Ore; Mountain View Community Col, Dallas, Tex; Worthen Banking Corp, Pine Bluff, Ark. *Exhib:* 8th Ann Achit Drawing & Sculpture Exhib, Delmar Col, Corpus Christi, Tex, 74; Amarillo Competition, Amarillo Art Ctr, Tex, 75; Watermark, Issac Hathaway Fine Art Ctr, Pine Bluff, Ark, 88; Stockton Nat IV, Haggin Mus Art, Calif, 88; Ark Art 91, Henderson State Univ, Arkadelphia, 91; The Arkansas Collection, Univ Ark, Little Rock, 91. *Collections Arranged:* Mark Chagall: Illustrations for the Old Testament (auth, catalog), 88; Frederick Remmington: Illustrator of the Old West (auth, catalog), 89; Drawing: A Survey of the 20th Century (auth, catalog), 90; A Treasury of American Prints (auth, catalog), 91; Dali: The Divine Comedy (50 woodcuts; auth, catalog), 92. *Awards:* Purchase Award, Tex A&I Invitational, 76; Purchase Award, 2nd Ann Juried Exhib, 81; Purchase Award, 5th Nat Biennial, 87. *Mem:* Am Asn Mus; Southeastern Mus Asn; Col Art Asn; Nat Art Educ Asn. *Media:* All. *Mailing Add:* 1600 War Eagle Pine Bluff AR 71603

JENKINS, DONALD JOHN
CURATOR, HISTORIAN
b Longview, Wash, May 3, 31. *Study:* Univ Chicago, BA & MA. *Collections Arranged:* The Woodcut in Japan, 1700-1969, 69 & Japanese Folk Art and Ukiyo-e Prints, 83, Portland Art Mus, Ore; Ukiyo-e Prints & Paintings, The Primitive Period 1680-1745 (auth, catalog), Art Inst Chicago, 71; Louis V Ledoux, Collecting Ukiyo-e Master Prints (auth, catalog), Japan House Gallery, New York, 73; Masterworks in Wood: China and Japan (auth, catalog), Portland Art Mus & Asia House Gallery, New York, 76; Images of a Changing World: Japanese Prints of the Twentieth Century (auth, catalog), St Louis Art Mus, Los Angeles Co Mus Art, Carnegie Inst Mus Art & Portland Art Mus, 83; Perspectives 11, Contemp Japanese Graphics, 88; Portland Art Mus, Ore; Perspectives 13, Shoichi Ida, 89. *Pos:* Asst cur, Portland Art Mus, 66-68, cur, 74-75 & dir, 75-87, cur Asian Art, 87-; assoc cur Oriental art, Art Inst Chicago, 69-74. *Teaching:* Instr art hist, Mus Art Sch, Portland, Ore, 63-65; lectr hist art, Univ Mich, Ann Arbor, 74; vis instr, Dept Art, Univ Chicago, 74. *Mem:* Soc Japanese Arts & Crafts; Int House Japan; Asn Asian Studies, Inc. *Res:* Japanese prints and paintings of the Ukiyo-e School. *Publ:* Coauth, Near Eastern Art in Chicago Collections (catalog), Art Inst Chicago, 74; auth, Handbook of the Asian Collection of the Portland Art Mus, 81; Two Utamaro Prints, Sawers, 82; Ukiyo-e, Kodansha Encycl, Japan, Vol 8, 83; Paintings of the Floating World, The Bulletin of the Cleveland Mus Art, 9/88. *Mailing Add:* Portland Art Mus 1219 SW Park Portland OR 97205

JENKINS, MARY ANNE KEEL
PAINTER, INSTRUCTOR
b Pitt Co, NC, Nov 20, 29. *Study:* Ferree Sch Art, Raleigh, NC; ECarolina Univ, Greenville; NC State Univ Sch Design, Raleigh; San Carlos Art Sch, Mexico City. *Work:* NC Mus Art, Raleigh; Minn Mus Art, St Paul; Glaxo, Inc; Weatherspoon Art Mus; Philip Morris Inc; Equitable Life Assurance; Ray-Chem Corp. *Comn:* Interior mural, Radio Station WPTF, Raleigh, 71; Philip Morris, 82; mural, First Nations Bank, Raleigh Chamber Commerce, 91; portrait collection, NC Mus Hist, 83. *Exhib:* 24th Nat Acad Galleries Ann, New York, 77; Mint Mus Art, Charlotte; Drawings, Minn Mus Art, St Paul; NC Mus Art, Raleigh; Danville Art Mus, Va, 82; Somerhill Gallery,

Chapel Hill, NC, 90; Raleigh Munic Bldg Exhib, 88 & 93. *Teaching:* Instr painting, Dullen Art Ctr, Raleigh; Workshops, NC Mus Art, Raleigh. *Awards:* Third James River Art Exhib First Patron Award, Mariners Mus, Newport News, Va, 69; Drawings USA Purchase Award, Minn Mus Art, St Paul, 71; Purchase Award & Hon Mention, Piedmont Exhib, Mint Mus, Charlotte, NC, 77; Raleigh Art Achievement Award, 87. *Bibliog:* Rubel Romero (auth), Art, Spectator Mag, 6/88; Rubel Romero (auth), Ten Best (All That Was Great in 88) Our Critic's Choices - Deep Perspective, Spectator Mag, 1/89; Blue Greenberg (auth), Jenkins Exhibit: A Whole & It's Parts, The Durham Morning Herald, 4/29/90. *Media:* All painting media. *Dealer:* Peden Gallery II 132 E Hargett St Raleigh NC 27601. *Mailing Add:* 2600 Oxford Rd Raleigh NC 27608-1542

JENKINS, PAUL
PAINTER
b Kansas City, Mo, July 12, 23. *Study:* Kansas City Art Inst & Sch Design, 38-41; Art Students League, 48-52, DH, 73. *Work:* Mus Mod Art, Whitney Mus Am Art & Solomon R Guggenheim Mus, New York; Tate Gallery, London, Eng; Mus Art Mod & Ctr Georges Pompidou, Paris; Stedelijk Mus, Amsterdam, Holland; Mus Western Art, Tokyo, Japan; and others. *Comn:* Medal, Inst French Civilization & Cult, New York Univ, 85; performance of Shaman to the Prism Seen, Paris Opera, 87; painted 2 kilometers of silk for performance at the Great Hall of the People, Peking Prism, 87. *Exhib:* Butler Inst Am Art, Youngstown, Ohio, 86; Musee Picasso Antibes, 87; L'Opera de Paris, 87; Corcoran Gallery Art, Washington, DC & watercolor traveling show: Gimpel Fils Gallery, London; Gallery Art Point, Tokyo; Galarie Patrice Trigano, Paris; Musee de Nice, Galeries de Ponchettes et d'Art; Gimpel Weitzenhoffer Galerie, New York; Houston Mus Fine Arts, Tex; Painted silks, Int Comt for Safeguard of Venice & the Great Wall of China, 88; and others. *Awards:* Golden Eagle Award for Ivory Knife (film), 67; Commandeur Arts & Lettres, France, 83; Art Directors Club Medal, 84; Humanitarian Award, Arts for the Handicapped; Medal, City Menton. *Bibliog:* Albert E Elsen (auth), Paul Jenkins (monogr), Harry N Abrams Inc, New York; Michel Faucher, Claude Fournet, Andre Verdet (auths), Paul Jenkins: Broken Prisms, Shaman to the Prism Seen, Editions Galilee, Paris & Imago Terrae, New York, 89 (illus); Pascal Bonafoux (auth), Paul Jenkins: Conjunctions and Annexes, Editions Galilee, Paris, 91. *Mem:* Century Asn; La Maison Francaise, New York Univ. *Publ:* Co-editor, Observations of Michel Tapie, Wittenborn, 56; auth, Strike the Puma, Gonthier, Paris, 66; coauth, Anatomy of a Cloud, Abrams, 83; auth, dance-drama, Shaman to the Prism Seen, Paris Opera, 5/87; Seven Aspects of Amadeus and the Others, Editions Galilee, Paris, 92. *Mailing Add:* 831 Broadway New York NY 10003

JENNERJAHN, W P
EDUCATOR, PAINTER
b Milwaukee, Wis, June 15, 22. *Study:* Univ Wis, Milwaukee, BS, 46; Univ Wis, Madison, MS, 47; Black Mountain Col, with Josef Albers, 48-50; Acad Grande Chaumiere, Paris, 50; Acad Julian, Paris, 50-51; also with Gerald Wagner, Dornach, Switz, 78 & 81. *Work:* NY Univ; Dulin Gallery Art, Tenn; Univ Mass, Amherst; Adelphi Univ; Nassau Community Col. *Comn:* Stained glass panel, Long Island Jewish Hosp, NY; stained glass mural, comn by Dr Fredrick Lane, Great Neck, NY; stained glass mural(with John Urbain), JFK Airport Int Hotel; murals for eight ships(with Elizabeth Jennerjahn), Mil Sea Transport Serv; painting, Avis World Hq, Garden City, NY. *Exhib:* Exhib Momentum, Chicago; Milwaukee Ann, Univ Wis, Milwaukee; Birmingham Ann, Ala; Dulin Ann, Tenn; Black Mountain Col Invitational, Johnson City, Tenn. *Teaching:* Art teacher, Black Mountain Col, NC, 49-50, Cooper Union, 52-54 & Hunter Col, 53; prof art, Adelphi Univ, 54-; retired, 87. *Awards:* Tiffany Found Grant, 52; Adelphi Univ Humanities Grants, 62, 68 & 84. *Mem:* Nat Drawing Asn. *Media:* Oil, Watercolor. *Publ:* Illusr, Respect for Life, 74; contribr (with Geo K Russell), Laboratory Investigations in Human Physiology, MacMillan, 78. *Dealer:* Rachele Lozzi Fine Art Los Angeles CA. *Mailing Add:* 707 Rainbow Trail Sedona AZ 86336

JENNEY, NEIL
PAINTER
b Torrington, Conn, 1945. *Exhib:* One-man exhibs, Galerie Rudolf Zwirner, Cologne, WGer, 68, Noah Goldowsky Gallery, New York, 70, Blum Helman Gallery, New York, 75 & Matrix Gallery, Wadsworth Atheneum, Hartford, Conn, 75-76; New Image, Whitney Mus Am Art, New York, 78-79; 60-80 Attitudes-Concepts-Images, Stedelijk Mus, Amsterdam, 82; Annina Nosei Gallery, New York, 83. *Bibliog:* Mark Stevens (auth), Neil Jenney: Art is a social science, Portfolio, Vol 4, No 3, 5-6/82; Julia Brown & Bridget Johnson (coauth), Charles and Doris Saatchi: Notes, In: The First Show: Painting and Sculpture from Eight Collections, 1940-1980, Mus Contemp Art, Los Angeles, 83. *Publ:* Auth, Anti-Illusion: Procedures-Materials, Whitney Mus Am Art, 69; When Attitude Becomes Form, Kunsthalle, Bern, 69; article, Allen Mem Art Mus Bulletin, Vol 27, No 3, spring 70. *Mailing Add:* Box 151 Winchester Center CT 06094

JENNINGS, FRANCIS
PAINTER, SCULPTOR
b Wilmington, Del, Feb 27, 10. *Study:* Wilmington Acad Art; Fleischer Mem Sch Art. *Work:* Mural, Del Indust Sch Boys. *Exhib:* Whitney Mus Am Art, New York, 62; Baltimore Mus Art, Md, 63; four shows, Makler Gallery, Philadelphia & Rose Fried Gallery, New York, 60-66; Tenth St Anniversary, Ward Nasse Gallery, New York, 77; Landmark Gallery, New York, 77; and others. *Teaching:* Lectr, Nat Art Teachers Asn Conv, 4/69. *Media:* Acrylic, Oil; All Media. *Publ:* Contribr, The Artist in New York (radio series), 67; You and the Artist (TV series), 69. *Mailing Add:* 55 Greene St New York NY 10013

JENNINGS, JAN
WRITER, MUSEUM ADMINISTRATOR
b Chicago, Ill, Apr 4, 43. *Study:* Northwestern Univ, Evanston, BSJ; Univ Mo-Columbia, grad studies journalism & art. *Pos:* Art writer, San Diego Tribune, Calif, 71-88; mus asst dir, Mingei Int Mus World Folk Art, San Diego, 90. *Mem:* San Diego Mus Art; San Diego Mus Contemp Art. *Publ:* Free-lance writer with contributing features to Southwest Art Mag, Am Artist, Western Art Digest, Art of California, Ranch & Coast. *Mailing Add:* c/o Minei Int-Mus of World Folk Art PO Box 553 La Jolla CA 92038

JENRETTE, PAMELA ANNE
PAINTER, COSTUME DESIGNER
b Ft Bragg, NC, Aug 24, 47. *Study:* Univ Tex, BFA, 69. *Exhib:* Clean, Well-lighted Place (two-artist show), Austin, Tex, 71; Whitney Biennial, New York, 75; Cologne Art Festival, Ger, 75; one-artist show, Artists Space, New York, NY, 75. *Pos:* Studio asst, Lawrence Poons, New York, 71-75. *Awards:* Competition Award, Conde Nast, 69. *Bibliog:* Martha Utterback (auth), Texas, Artforum, 1/71. *Media:* Acrylic, Watercolor. *Mailing Add:* 300 Mercer St No 121 New York NY 10003

JENSEN, BILL
PAINTER
b Minneapolis, Minn, Nov 26, 45. *Study:* Univ Minn, BFA, 68, MFA, 70. *Work:* Whitney Mus Am Art, Metrop Mus Art & Mus Mod Art, New York; Worcester Mus Art, Mass; Fogg Art Mus, Cambridge, Mass; Los Angeles County Mus Art, Calif; Chase Manhattan Bank, New York; J Patrick Lannan Found, Venice, Calif; Saatchi Collection, London; McCrory Corp, Paine Webber Group, New York. *Exhib:* Brooklyn Mus, NY, 71 & 74; Drawing NYC 1978, Inst Contemp Art, Tokyo, 78; The 1970s: New American Painting, traveling in Eastern Europe, New Mus, 79-81 & Whitney Biennial, Whitney Mus, 81, New York; Contemporary Drawings, Univ Calif, Santa Barbara, 81; An Exhibition of Abstract Painting, Art Galaxy, 82; Painting from the Mind's Eye, Hillwood Art Gallery, C W Post Ctr, Greenvale, New York, 83; Drawing with Respect to Painting, New York Studio Sch, 84; Painting as Landscape: Views of American Modernism, 1920-1984, Parrish Art Mus, Southampton, NY, 85; The Spiritual in Art: Abstract Painting 1890-1985, Los Angeles County Mus Contemp Art & Gemeentemuseum, The Hague, 86; solo exhibs, Mus Mod Art, 86, The Phillips Collection, Washington, DC, 87-88, Grob Gallery, London, 91 & Margo Leavin Gallery, Los Angeles, Calif, 91; From Earth to Archetype, Ledisflam Gallery, New York, 90; A Debate on Abstraction: The Persistence of Painting, Bertha & Karl Leubsdorf Art Gallery, Hunter Col, New York, 89; Sightings: Drawing with Color, Pratt Inst, New York, 88-89. *Teaching:* Instr, Univ Minn, 65-70, Brooklyn Mus Art Sch, 71-75 & York Col, Queens, NY, 72-73; instr, Brooklyn Mus Art Sch, 71-75; instr, York Col, Queens, NY, 72-73. *Awards:* Creative Artists Pub Serv Prog, 79; Artist's Fel, Nat Endowment Arts, 85-86. *Bibliog:* Stephen Westfall (auth), Into the Vortex, Art in America, 4/88; Hilton Kramer (auth) Jensen at the Washburn: Timeless Twilight, The New York Observer, 4/4/88; Bill Jensen (auth), Ryder on the storm, Artforum, P 117-121, 12/90. *Media:* Oil, Gouache. *Mailing Add:* Washburn Gallery 41 E 57th St 8th fl New York NY 10022

JENSEN, CLAY EASTON
SCULPTOR, EDUCATOR
b Salt Lake City, Utah, Mar 14, 52. *Study:* Univ Utah, Salt Lake City, BFA, 75; Univ Calif, Berkeley, MA, 78, MFA, 79. *Work:* Oakland Mus, Calif; Crocker Art Mus, Sacramento, Calif. *Comn:* Sculpture, Fed Reserve Bank, San Francisco, Calif, 83; sculpture, Syntex Corp, Palo Alto, Calif, 84; sculpture, AT&T, Pleasanton, Calif, 84; sculpture, William Wilson & Assocs, San Mateo, Calif, 86; sculpture, Dealy, Renton & Assocs, Oakland, Calif, 86. *Exhib:* Solo exhibs, San Francisco Mus Mod Art (with catalog), Calif, 83, Fuller Cross Gallery, San Francisco, 85 & 88, Christopher Grimes Gallery, Santa Monica, Calif, 90, Erickson & Elins Gallery, San Francisco, 92; Utah Mus Fine Arts, Salt Lake City, 75; New Affirmations, Oakland Mus, Calif, 80; MFA Exhib, Univ Art Mus, Univ Calif, Berkeley. *Teaching:* Assoc instr, Univ Utah, Salt Lake City, 75-76; vis fac, Calif Col Arts & Craft, 80-82, asst prof, 87-; guest lectr sculpture, Univ Calif, Berkeley, 84-85; asst prof, San Jose State Univ, 84-85 & 89-90. *Awards:* Fel, Nat Endowment Asn, 78; Soc Encouragement Contemp Art Award, San Francisco Mus Mod Art, 83. *Bibliog:* Alfred Jan (auth), article, in: Images and Issues, 1/84; Suzaan Boettger (auth), rev, in: Art Forum, 4/84; Robert McDonald (auth), Rural Urban Dichotomies, Vol XIIII, No 39, Art Week, 11/19/83; James Scarborough (auth), Galactic Perspective Clay Jensen at Christopher Grimes Gallery, Vol 21, No 35, Artweek, 10/90. *Media:* Painted Steel, Cast Bronze. *Dealer:* Erickson & Elins Gallery San Francisco CA; Morgan Gallery Kansas City MO. *Mailing Add:* 951 62nd St Studio F Oakland CA 94608

JENSEN, DEAN N
DEALER, CRITIC
b Milwaukee, Wis, Oct 9, 38. *Study:* Univ Wis, BA; Roosevelt Univ, Chicago; Univ Chicago. *Collections Arranged:* Center Ring: The Artist (auth, catalog), Milwaukee Art Mus, Columbus Mus Art, NY State Mus, Albany & Corcoran Gallery Art, 81; Material Obsessions: Folk and Outside, Art from Wisconsin Collections (auth, catalog), Milwaukee Inst Art & Design, 89. *Pos:* Art ed & critic, Milwaukee Sentinel, Wis, 67-87; owner, Dean Jensen Gallery, Milwaukee, 87- *Teaching:* Milwaukee Inst Art & Design, 91- *Awards:* Res & Study Fel, Univ Mich, 85-86. *Res:* Contemporary art; Circus as a theme in art. *Publ:* Auth, The Biggest, The Smallest, The Longest, The Shortest, Wis House, 75; Reunion in Hell: The Drawings of Paul Caster, Perimeter Press, 82; contribr, Art News, Arts, Midwest-Art & others. *Mailing Add:* 2824 N Hackett Ave Milwaukee WI 53211

JENSEN, LEO (VERNON)
SCULPTOR, PAINTER
b Montevideo, Minn, July 10, 26. *Study:* Walker Art Ctr, scholar, 46-48. *Work:* Conn Savings Bank; New Britain Mus Am Art, Conn; US Info Agency, Washington, DC; Brown Univ; Walker Art Ctr, Minneapolis, Minn; Mattatuck Mus, Waterbury, Conn; Achenbach Col, San Francisco. *Comn:* Sculpture, Sheraton Hotels, Minneapolis, 63; bronze musicians, United Artists Corp, New York, 67; construction, Macmillan Publ Co, New York, 68; polychrome relief, Gulf & Western Corp, New York, 69; polychrome relief, Med World News, New York, 70. *Exhib:* Solo exhibs, Far Gallery, New York 73, Arras Gallery, New York, 76, A Book Gallery, San Francisco, 78 & Frank Fedele Gallery, New York, 81, Vorpal Gallery, New York, 87, Mattatuck Mus, Waterbury, Conn, 90, Childers Gallery, Ft Lauderdale, Fla, 91; group shows, Butler Inst Am Art, Ohio, 53, Mattatuck Mus, Conn, 90; Mus Mod Art, 64-65, Am Mus Nat Hist, 82, New York; Milwaukee Art Ctr, 65; Nat Portrait Gallery, 81; Chicago Hist Soc, 81; Baseball Hall Fame, 83; Castle Gallery Col, New Rochelle, NY, 87; Mattatuck Mus, Waterbury, Conn, 88; and others. *Pos:* Founder, Wildcat Fine Art Trust, New Haven, Conn, 88. *Bibliog:* M B Scott (auth), The Art & the Sportsman, Renaissance, 68; D Z Meiloch (auth), Contemporary Art With Wood, Crown, 68; H N Abrams (auth), Champions of Am Sport, Smithsonian Inst, 81. *Mem:* Artists Equity Asn. *Media:* Bronze, Wood; Acrylic, Watercolor. *Mailing Add:* PO Box 264 Ivoryton CT 06442

JERGENS, ROBERT JOSEPH
PAINTER, EDUCATOR
b Cleveland, Ohio, Mar 18, 38. *Study:* Cleveland Inst Art; Skowhegan Sch Painting & Sculpture; Yale Univ, BFA & MFA; Am Acad in Rome. *Work:* Cleveland Mus Art; NAm Col, Rome, Italy; Skowhegan Sch Painting & Sculpture; Brooklyn Art Mus; and others. *Comn:* Cleveland Pub Libr, 60 & 89. *Exhib:* Cleveland Mus Art, 57-64; Exhib by US Info Agency; Mus Mod Art, New York; Corcoran Gallery Art, Washington, DC; Mostra Univ, Rome; and others. *Teaching:* Instr design, Cooper Union, formerly; instr drawing, Sch Art & Archit, Yale Univ, formerly; instr design, Cleveland Inst Art, currently. *Awards:* Prix de Rome, 60 & 61; Mary C Page Grant, 61; Prize, Cleveland Mus Art, 61; and others. *Mailing Add:* Cleveland Inst Art 11141 East Blvd Cleveland OH 44106

JERINS, EDGAR
PAINTER
b Lincoln, Neb, June 12, 58. *Study:* Pa Acad Fine Arts, 80. *Exhib:* Los Angeles Fairytales, Calif State Gallery, 81; Wunsch Arts Ctr, Glen Cove, NY, 84; Hecksher Mus, Huntington, NY, 86; 90th Ann Fel Show, Pa Acad Mus, 87; What's in a Face, Pelham Art Ctr, NY, 89. *Awards:* Elizabeth Greenshilds Found Grant, 80; Caroline Gibbons Granger Memorial Award, Pa Acad, 87. *Bibliog:* Helen A Harrison (auth), 76 Artworks review 86 & 87, Islip Mus Show, 89, NY Times. *Mem:* Fel, Pa Acad Fine Arts. *Media:* Oil, Pastel. *Dealer:* Portraits Inc 985 Park Ave New York NY 10028. *Mailing Add:* Rte No 1 234 Palisades New York NY 10964

JERRY, MICHAEL JOHN
EDUCATOR, CRAFTSMAN
b Grand Rapids, Mich, Aug 18, 37. *Study:* Sch Am Craftsman, Rochester Inst Technol, AAS & BFA, 60, MFA, 63; Cranbrook Acad Art, 60-62. *Work:* Wustum Mus Fine Art, Racine, Wis; Mus Contemp Crafts, New York; Metrop Mus of Art, New York. *Exhib:* Objects USA, 69; Int Trade Fair Jewelry Exhib, Munich, Ger, 71; The 6th Goldsmiths Expos, Kersnikova, Yugoslavia, 72; Goldsmiths, Renwick Gallery, Washington, DC, 74; Contemp Metals US, Downey Mus Art, Calif, 85. *Teaching:* Assoc prof metalsmithing, Wis State Univ, Menomonie, 63-70; prof metalsmithing, Syracuse Univ, 70- *Mem:* Am Crafts Coun; Soc NAm Goldsmiths. *Media:* Metal. *Publ:* Contribr, American jewelry, Design Quart, 59; Philip Morton, Contemporary Jewelry, Holt, 69; Objects: USA, Viking, 70; The Craftsman in America, Nat Geog Soc, 75; Metalsmith, Vol 8, fall 88. *Mailing Add:* Dept Art Syracuse Univ Syracuse NY 13244-1010

JERVISS, JOY
PRINTMAKER
b Palmerton, Pa, Feb 14, 41. *Study:* C W Post Col, & Empire State Col; apprentice to Andre Girard. *Work:* Colgate Univ Libr & Syracuse Univ Art Collection, NY; Bibliot Nat, Paris; Miami Mus Mod Art, Fla; Ariz State Univ, Tempe; Princeton Univ Art Mus, NJ; Lehigh Univ Art Galleries, Pa; Art Inst of Zanesville, Ohio. *Pos:* Art exhib dir, N K Winston Corp, New York, 66-73; pres, United Press & Pallet, Northport, NY, 68-; founder, Northport Art League, 71- *Teaching:* Asst instr printmaking, North Shore Community Arts Ctr, Great Neck, NY, 66-68; instr printmaking, Union Free Sch Dist 4, Northport, NY, 70-72; instr, BOCES III, 82-86. *Media:* Etching. *Mailing Add:* 84 Ocean Ave Northport NY 11768

JESS
PAINTER, COLLAGE ARTIST
b Long Beach, Calif, Aug 6, 23. *Study:* Calif Sch Fine Arts, with Clyfford Still, Edward Corbett, David Park, Elmer Bischoff & Hassel Smith. *Work:* Metrop Mus & Mus Mod Art, New York; Art Inst Chicago; Dallas Mus Art, Tex; Philadelphia Mus Art; Los Angeles Co Mus Art. *Exhib:* Assemblage, Mus Mod Art, New York, 61; Pop Art USA, Oakland Art Mus, 63; one-man shows, Mus Mod Art, San Francisco, 68, Mus Contemp Arts, Chicago, 72, Mus Mod Art, New York, 74, Dallas Mus Fine Arts, 77, Arts Club, Chicago, 81 & Ringling Mus, Sarasota, Fla, 83; 70th & 71st Ann, Art Inst Chicago, 72 & 74; Extraordinary Realities, Whitney Mus Am Art, New York, 73; Poets of the Cities, Dallas Mus Fine Arts, 74; Matrix Two, Wadsworth Atheneum, 75; Calif Painting & Sculpture, Mus Mod Art, San Francisco, 76; 8 Artists, Philadelphia Mus Art, 78; Four Seasons, Matrix, Univ Calif, Berkeley, 80; American Accents, Rothman's The Gallery, Stratford, Ont, 83; Comic Art Show, Whitney Mus, 83; and many others. *Awards:* Individual Artist Fed Grant, Nat Endowment Arts, 73. *Publ:* Illusr, Caesar's Gate, (auth, Robert Duncan), Divers Press, Mallorca, 55; Ballads (auth, Helen Adam), Acadia Press, New York, 64; A Book of Resemblances (auth, Robert Duncan), Henry Wenning, New Haven, 66; The Cat and the Blackbird (auth, Robert Duncan), White Rabbit Press, 67; illusr & translr, Gallowsongs, auth, Christian Morgenstern, Black Sparrow Press, 70. *Dealer:* Federico Quadrani c/o Odyssia Gallery New York NY. *Mailing Add:* 3267 20th St San Francisco CA 94110

JESSEN, SHIRLEY AGNES
PAINTER
b Brooklyn, NY, Jan 23, 21. *Study:* New York Sch Applied Design Women, scholar, cert, 39; Fashion Art Inst, Rockefeller Ctr, 40; also with Lou Eisele, Frederick Lehman, Paul Wood & Norman Nodell, 60-79; Huntington Town Art League, 92-93. *Work:* Sotheby Art Auctions; Channels 13: Art & Auctions, 85-87; Channel 21 Art Auctions, 82-85. *Exhib:* Molloy Col, 84; Shelter Rock Libr, 88; Georgia O'Keefe Community Club, 88; Chase Bank, 88; Long Island Art Experience, 5/90. *Pos:* Illusr, Wantagh Parent Teachers Asn, 50-65; illusr, United Cerebral Palsy, 59-75; illusr, Nassau Co Med Soc Auxilary, 59-93. *Teaching:* Expo Films 70-71. *Awards:* Finalist Nat, Am Artist Mag, Grumbacher, 78 & Int Soc Artists, 79; First Prize, South Shore Art League, 81. *Mem:* Freeport Arts Coun; Art Studio Community Club, 89-; Knickerbocker Artists, New York; Int Soc Artists Communicator; Huntington Township Art League, 92-93; Allied Artists Am. *Media:* Oils, Acrylics. *Mailing Add:* 15 St Pauls Crescent Garden City NY 11530

JESSUP, ROBERT
PAINTER
b Moscow, Idaho, July 18, 52. *Study:* Univ Wash, Seattle, BA(art hist), BFA(painting), 75; Univ Iowa, Iowa City, MA(painting), 77, MFA(painting), 78. *Work:* Metrop Mus Art, New York; High Mus Art, Atlanta, Ga; Huntington Art Gallery, Univ Tex, Austin; Roswell Mus & Art Ctr, NMex. *Comn:* Relief painting, comn by Doanld B Anderson, Roswell, NMex, 81; painting, comn by Robert Dornbush, Atlanta, Ga, 85. *Exhib:* Solo exhibs, Roswell Mus, NMex, 81, Nicola Jacobs Gallery, London, Eng, 84, Jan Turner Gallery, Los Angeles, 86, Zola-Lieberman Gallery, Chicago, 86 & Ruth Siegel, Ltd, New York, 86; New Figurative Painting, Asheville Art Mus, NC, 85; Painting & Sculpture Today, Indianapolis Mus Art, Ind, 86; Landscape, Seascape, Cityscape, Contemp Arts Ctr, New Orleans, La, 86. *Teaching:* Lectr & vis artist painting, Ohio State Univ, Columbus, Ohio, 81-82; asst prof painting, Ga State Univ, Atlanta, 82-83 & Cornell Univ, Ithaca, NY, 83-86. *Bibliog:* John Russell (auth), Aspects of the figure, New York Times, 7/2/82; Theodore F Wolff (auth), How artists improve, Christian Sci Monitor, 7/2/86. *Media:* Oil on Canvas & Linen; Charcoal on Paper. *Dealer:* Ruth Siegel Ltd 24 W 57th St New York NY 10019. *Mailing Add:* c/o Zola-Liebermann Gallery 325 W Huron St Chicago IL 60610-3617

JESWALD, JOSEPH
PAINTER
b Leetonia, Ohio, May 17, 27. *Study:* Acad Julian, Paris; with Fernand Leger, Paris; Columbia Univ. *Work:* Hirshhorn Mus; Neuberger Mus; Addison Gallery Am Art; Rockefeller Found. *Pos:* Founder, Montserrat Col Art, Beverly, Mass. *Mailing Add:* 1700 Palmetto Lane Sarasota FL 34236-2422

JEWELL, JOYCE
PAINTER, PRINTMAKER
b Washington, DC, Oct 11, 45. *Study:* Montgomery Col, Md, AA, 65; Am Univ, Washington, DC, BA, 67; George Washington Univ, MFA, 72; Tamarind Inst Lithography, NMex, 74. *Work:* Montgomery County Contemporary Print Collection, Md; Owensboro Federal Savings & Loan Asn, Ky. *Exhib:* 19th Area Exhib, Corcoran Gallery Art, Washington, DC, 74; Irene Leache Mem Art Exhib, Chrysler Mus, Va, 78, 80; Va Printmakers, 1979, Va Mus Fine Arts, 79; 17th Bradley Nat Print & Drawing Exhib, Lakeview Mus, 79; Mid-Am Nat Art Exhib, Owensboro Mus Fine Art, Ky, 80; 22nd Area Exhib: Works on Paper, Corcoran Gallery Art, 80; Collage & Assemblage: A Nat Invitational Traveling Exhib, Miss Mus Art, Jackson, Miss, 81-83; Maryland Biennial: Works on Paper, Baltimore Mus Art, 83-84. *Pos:* Graphic designer, John Hoskins & Assocs, Arlington, Va, 67-71. *Teaching:* Prof design, drawing, etching & lithography, Montgomery Col, Md, 71- *Awards:* Printmaking Award, Montgomery Co Juried Art Show, 78; Mid-Am Volunteers Purchase Award, Owensboro Mus Fine Art, 80; Owensboro Federal Savings & Loan Purchase Award, Mid-Am Nat Art Exhib, 80. *Bibliog:* Article, Gargoyle Mag, No 17/18, 81; Collage & Assemblage, Miss Mus Art, 81. *Media:* Collage. *Mailing Add:* c/o Montgomery Col 7600 Tacoma Ave Takoma Park MD 20912

JEYNES, PAUL
SCULPTOR
b Millburn, NJ, Apr 19, 27. *Study:* Yale Univ, BA, 49; with Frank Eliscu, 74. *Comn:* Tiger-Bronze, US Filter Corp, New York, 76; Cougar & 2 Cubs (lifesize bronze), Rye Country Day Sch, New York, 90. *Exhib:* Society of Animal Artists, 81-91; Wondrous Wildlife, Cincinnati Zoo, Ohio, 83; Audubon Artists, New York, 81; Knickerbocker Artists, New York, 84 & 89; Allied Artists, New York, 84-91; Animals in Art, Humane Soc US, Wash DC, 85; Int Fish and Wildlife Expo, Albany, NY, 86; St Hubert's Giralda, 88-90; Nat Acad Design, 90; Central Park Zoo, NY, 90; Olympia and York, NY, 91. *Pos:* Dir, Art Founders Guild of America Inc, 79-88. *Awards:* First Prize,

Wondrous Wildlife, Cincinnati Zoo, 83; Meiselman Award, Allied Artists, 84, Gold Medal, 85; Eliot Liskin Mem Award, 88; St Hubert's Giralda Award of Distinction, 89; Montana Award, 91. *Mem:* Soc Animal Artists Inc; Allied Artists Am Inc. *Media:* Cast Bronze. *Mailing Add:* 305 E 70th St New York NY 10021

JILG, MICHAEL FLORIAN
PAINTER, PRINTMAKER
b Albert, Kans, June 28, 47. *Study:* Fort Hays State Univ, BA, 69 & MA, 70; Kent State Blossom Festival, with Jack Tworkov, Alex Katz & James Melchert, 70; Wichita State Univ, with John Fincher, MFA, 72. *Work:* Joslyn Art Mus, Omaha, Nebr; Wichita Art Mus, Kans Arts Commission; Purdue Univ Galleries; Alice and Hamilton Fish Libr, Garrison, NY. *Comn:* George Washington Mural Project, Ellis Bicentenial Comt, Kans, 76; St Ann (painting), St Ann Parish, Olmitz,Kans, 81; Sherridan Coliseum, mural proj. *Exhib:* Mid-Am V, Nelson Gallery Art, Kansas City, Mo, 74; Mainstreams 74, Herman Fine Art Ctr, Marietta, Ohio, 74; Selected Kansas Artists, Kans State Capital, Topeka, 77; Allied Artists Am, Nat Acad Galleries, New York, 77-78; 1st Kans Artists Competition, Judicial Bldg, Topeka, 81; Kans Watercolor Soc Five State Exhib, Wichita Art Mus; 11th Ann Paper in Particular Nat Exhib, Columbia Col, Md; The Intaglio Process: Print Consortium Traveling Exhib; Images Women Prints, Embassy of US, Bonn, Germany, 88; Artists: A Kansas Collection, 89. *Teaching:* Prof painting, Ft Hays State Univ, 81- *Awards:* Junior League Omaha Purchase, 70; Purchase Award, Kans Arts Commission, 80; Cash Award, Kans Arts Commission, 81. *Bibliog:* The Best Kansas Arts & Crafts, 88; Erotic Art by Living Artists, 89; A Kansas Collection, 89. *Mem:* Kansas City Artists' Coalition; High Plains Printmakers; Hays Arts Coun (mem bd dirs, currently); Boston Printmakers; Kans Watercolor Soc; Gabinetto Disegni E Stampe Degli Uffizi, Florence, Italy (scholar mem). *Media:* Oil, Acrylic; Intaglio. *Dealer:* Mira Pearlman Gallery Chicago IL; Marial Martyn 829 Arkansas Lawrence KS 66044. *Mailing Add:* Dept Art Ft Hays State Univ 600 Park St Hays KS 67601

JIMENEZ, LUIS ALFONSO, JR
SCULPTOR
b El Paso, Tex, July 30, 40. *Study:* Univ Tex, Austin, BS(art), 64; asst to Seymour Lipton, 66; Ciudad Univ Mexico City, 64. *Work:* Long Beach Mus, Calif; New Orleans Mus, La; Roswell Mus & Art Ctr, NMex; Nat Collection Fine Arts, DC; Metrop Mus Art, New York; Rockefeller Found, New York. *Comn:* Progess I and Progess II, D Anderson & Roswell Mus, 71-75; glass goggles, Sea-Girl, Steuben, New York, 71; Vaquero, Houston, Tex, 81; Sodbuster, Fargo, NDak, 82; Southwest Pieta & Art in Public Places, Albuquerque, NMex; Howl, Wichita State Univ; San Diego Fountain, PY-Vaura Develop Corp, Calif; Cruzando el Rio Bravo, Otis Art Inst, Parsons Sch Design, Los Angeles, Calif. *Exhib:* Human Concern Personal Torment, Whitney Mus, New York, 69; Recent Figure Sculpture, Fogg Art Mus, 71; Whitney Mus Biennial, New York, 71; Richard Brown Baker Collects, Yale Univ Art Mus, Hartford, Conn, 75; Jimenez Retrospective, Contemp Arts Mus, Houston, Tex, 75; Amon Carter Mus Western Art, Ft Worth, Tex, 77; Western States Biennial, Nat Collection Fine Arts, DC, 79; San Diego Mus Art, 83; one-man show, Yares Gallery, Scottsdale, 83; and others; traveling exhib, Hispanic Art in the US, Mus Fine Art, Houston, Tex, Latin America Presence in the US, Bronx Mus Arts & Different Drummers, Hirshhorn Mus, Washington, DC; solo exhibs, Adair Margo Gallery, El Paso, Tex, Betty Mondy Gallery, Houston, Tex, Dallas Mus Art, Phyllis Kind Gallery, New York & Committed to Print, Mus Mod Art, New York. *Teaching:* Prof sculpture, Univ Ariz, currently. *Awards:* Nat Endowment Arts Grant, 77, 81 & 82. *Bibliog:* Quirarte (auth), Mexican American Artists in the US, Univ Tex, 73; Hunter-Jacobus (auth), American Art of 20th Century, Abrams, 73; featured in Newsweek, 8/79, Washington Post, 6/79 & Smithsonian, 4/79; Beardsley, Livingston & Paz (auths), Hispanic Art in the United States; Latin Am Spirit, Abrams. *Media:* Fiberglass Sculpture With a Jazzy Metal-Flake Epoxy Finish & Neon & Lights; Colored Pencil Drawings, Lithographs. *Dealer:* Phyllis Kind Gallery 136 Green St New York NY 10012; Yares Gallery 3625 Bishop Lane Scottsdale AZ. *Mailing Add:* Box 175 Hondo NM 88336

J J (DE LA VERRIÉRE)
GOLDSMITH, SCULPTOR
b Paris, France, Mar 8, 32; US citizen. *Study:* Ecole Nat Art Decoratifs, BA, Paris, France, 49; Escuela de Artes Suntuarias, Barcelona, Spain, 51; London Cent Col, Eng, 57; Pratt Inst, with Prof Albert, MFA, 75; Hunter Col, MA(art hist), 79. *Work:* Cooper Mus, New York; Nat Mus Design; Contemp Crafts Mus; Metrop Mus, New York; Mus Mod Art, New York. *Comn:* Monstrance, Eglise du Gesu, Montreal, 59; Masonic Jewelry, 68, ritual pieces, 70 & commemoration medals, 75, var Masonic Lodges, Ritual Pieces, New York. *Exhib:* Solo exhibs, Pellicone Gallery, Southampton, NY, 82, Goldberg Gallery, NY, 85 & Pompidou Mus, Paris, 85; Caroline Corre Gallery, Paris, 83; Small Works, NY Univ, 83-85; B Fendrick Gallery, Washington, DC, 83; Alan Stone Gallery, New York, 88. *Teaching:* Instr enameling, Haystack Sch Art, 68; asst prof sculpture & electroforming, Pratt Inst, 72-75. *Awards:* First Prize Jewelry, Greenwich Village Outdoor Show, 61-80 & New York Craftsmen, 63, 68-82. *Bibliog:* Ancient Metallurgy in Art, 70; Berber Jewelry in Morocco, 89 & The Hand, 90. *Mem:* New York Craftsmen; Am Crafts Coun; Am Goldsmith Asn. *Media:* Gold, Silver, Precious and Semi-Precious Stones; Rare Woods, Ivory. *Publ:* Auth, Electroforming for Jewelry & Sculpture, 70. *Mailing Add:* 99 MacDougall St No 18 New York NY 10012

JOCDA
PAINTER
b Reynoldsville, Pa, Mar 4, 26. *Study:* Youngstown Univ, AB, with Margaret Evans, David P Skeggs, John Naberezny & Robert Elwell. *Work:* Youngstown Col; Westmar Col; Sioux City Art Ctr; Mo Synod; Des Moines Art Ctr; plus others. *Exhib:* Butler Inst Am Art, 52 & 53; Siouxland Watercolor Exhib, 55-57; Six State Exhib, 55-58; Life of Christ Show, Iowa, 57 & 58; Laas-George Gallery, San Francisco, 61; plus others. *Pos:* Designer, Crest Johnson Studios, Youngstown, Ohio, 53; staff artist, Warren, Ohio, 54; asst dir, Sioux City Art Ctr, 55-61, instr & actg dir, 57-59; arts & crafts coordr, Cent Community Ctr, Columbus, 64-68; free lance, 68- *Awards:* Awards, Trumble Co, 50 & Mahoning Co, 51; Youngstown Col Purchase Award, 52; 11th Iowa Artist Ann Purchase Award, Des Moines Art Ctr, 59. *Mem:* Midwest Mus Conf; fel Inst Arts & Lett; Nat Soc Lit & Arts. *Media:* Oil, Watercolor. *Mailing Add:* 366 Lincoln Ave East Columbus OH 43214

JOELSON, SUZANNE
PAINTER
Study: Bennington Col, BA, 69. *Work:* Eli Broad Collection, Los Angeles. *Exhib:* Solo exhibs, Wolff Gallery, New York, 88, Fernando Alcolea Gallery, Bacelonea, 90 & White Columns, New York, 90; McNeil Gallery, Philadelphia. *Teaching:* Instr painting, Sch Visual Arts, 89- *Awards:* Nat Endowment Arts Fel, 87. *Mailing Add:* 530 Canal St New York NY 10013

JOFFE, BERTHA
DESIGNER
b St Petersburg, Russia; US citizen. *Study:* New York-Phoenix Sch Design, Sch Art League Indust Scholarship, 30-31; City Col New York, BS; Teachers Col, Columbia Univ, MA; NY Univ Inst Fine Arts, Carnegie Tuition Scholarship, 40-42, Art Students League, studied with William Zorach, Winold Reiss & Oronzio Maldarelli. *Comn:* Drapery designs for leading hotels; design on drapery fabric, UN Staff Dining Rm. *Exhib:* Artists for Victory, Metrop Mus Art, New York, 42; Art in Business Exhib, New York, 42; Int Textile Exhib, Weatherspoon Art Gallery, Univ NC, 44; Renaissance Fair, Summit, NJ, 78; Watercolors & Lithographs, On Air Exhib, WNET-TV, New York, 80, 82 & 83; Maplewood Cult Comn Art Exhib, Mem Libr, NJ, 87. *Pos:* Freelance textile designer, 42-; designer women's wear, French Fabrics Co, New York, 62-66; designer home furnishing fabrics, M Lowenstein & Sons, New York, 67-77. *Teaching:* Instr textile & costume design, City Col New York, 40-43; docent art hist, Metrop Mus Art, 41. *Awards:* World Who's Who Commerce & Industry; Int Who's Who Art & Antiques; The World Who's Who Women. *Mem:* Soc Arts, Religion & Contemp Cult, New York. *Media:* Watercolor, Tempera. *Mailing Add:* 77 Parker Ave Maplewood NJ 07040

JOHANNINGMEIER, ROBERT ALAN
PAINTER, WRITER
b St Louis, Mo, Aug 29, 46. *Study:* Kansas City Art Inst, BFA, 68. *Exhib:* Sun Carnival, Mus Fine Art, El Paso, Tex, 67; Allied Artists Am, New York, 80; Audubon Artists Ann Exhib, New York, 80; Grand Nat Exhib, New York, 80 & 81. *Teaching:* Instr, Old Masters Painting Techniques Workshop. *Awards:* First Place, Tri-State Art Exhib, Carlsbad Area Art Asn, NMex, 68. *Bibliog:* Flo Wilks (auth), Radiating harmony, SW Art, 82; Arejas Vitkauskas (auth), American scene, Worldwide News Bur, 83; Trish Garrigus (auth), Art of investing/collecting, Ctr Econ Revitalization, 83. *Media:* Oil. *Res:* Artistic styles and painting techniques from 1400 to the present; topics of special interest to collectors. *Publ:* Auth, The protection of works of art, Art & Commun, 79, Art as investment, 79; auth & illusr, The Art of Investing While Collecting, Art & Commun, 83, Our Culture Crisis, 87 & How to Inspire Our Family and Appreciate Our Heritage, 92. *Dealer:* Cottage Gallery Sixth & Mission Carmel-By-The-Sea CA 93921. *Mailing Add:* 812 N Edwards Carlsbad NM 88220

JOHANSEN, ROBERT
PAINTER
b Kenosha, Wis, Mar 30, 23. *Study:* Layton Sch Art, Milwaukee, Wis. *Work:* Wustum Mus & Johnson's Wax, Racine, Wis; Univ Wis, LaCrosse; Continental Bank of Chicago; NY CTA Chem, Brooklyn. *Comn:* Wausau Insurance Co; Bank One, Milwaukee, Wis. *Exhib:* Am Watercolor Soc Show & Traveling Exhib, New York, 72; Mainstreams '74, Marietta, Ohio; Watercolor USA, Springfield, Mo, 75; Nat Acad Design 150th Ann Exhib, New York, 75; Salmagundi Club, New York; Rocky Mountain Nat Watercolor Show, Colo; Mid-west Watercolor Soc. *Pos:* Aquarellist & advert artist, Snap-on Tools, Kenosha, Wis. *Teaching:* Instr painting, Wustum Mus Fine Arts, 70-73. *Awards:* Top Award, Watercolor Wisconsin, 72; Award of Excellence, Mid-west Watercolor Soc, 84; Marthe T McKinnon Award, Am Watercolor Soc, 87; Ky Watercolor Soc. *Bibliog:* Stephan Bellgraph, Watercolor Wisconsin (film), George Richards, 73; 40 Watercolorists & How They Work, Watson-Guptill. *Mem:* Signature mem Rocky Mountain Nat Watercolor Soc; signature mem Mid-west Watercolor Soc. *Media:* Watercolor. *Publ:* Contribr, Watercolor Page, Am Artist, 3/75; contribr, Palette Talk, Grumbacher, 83; Splash, North Light, 90. *Mailing Add:* 3017 Taylor Ave Racine WI 53405

JOHANSON, GEORGE E
PAINTER, PRINTMAKER
b Seattle, Wash, Nov 1, 28. *Study:* Portland Mus Sch, Ore; Atelier 17, New York. *Work:* Nat Collection, Washington, DC; Chicago Art Inst; New York Pub Libr; Victoria & Albert Mus, London, Eng; Oldham Co Coun, Eng; and many others. *Comn:* Civic Auditorium, Portland, 69; Portland Bldg, 88; City Ctr Parking, Portland, 88; Bremerton High Sch, Wa, 89; Ore State Univ,

Corvallis, 92. *Exhib:* Calif Palace Legion Hon, San Francisco; Am Embassy, London, Eng; Seattle Art Mus; Portland Art Mus, Ore; Univ Ariz, Tucson; Univ Ill; Western NMex Univ; Palm Springs Desert Mus, Calif; Univ Houston, Tex. *Pos:* Pres, Northwest Print Coun, 81-83. *Teaching:* Instr painting & printmaking, Portland Mus Art Sch, 55-80. *Awards:* First Ed Award, Ore Arts Comn, 76; Award, Ore State Fair, Salem, 77; Governors Award for the Arts, 92; and others. *Mem:* Portland Art Asn; Northwest Print Coun (pres, 83). *Media:* Oil, Etching. *Publ:* Creator, Etching and Color Intaglio (film), 73 & Printmaker (film), 76. *Mailing Add:* c/o Elizabeth Leach Gallery 207 SW Pine Portland OR 97204

JOHANSON, PATRICIA
SCULPTOR, ENVIRONMENTAL ARTIST
b New York, NY, Sept 8, 40. *Study:* Brooklyn Mus Art Sch; Art Students League; Bennington Col, BA, 62; Hunter Col, MA, 64; City Col Sch Archit, BS & BArch, 77. *Work:* Mus Mod Art, New York; Storm King Art Ctr, Mountainville, NY; Dallas Art Mus, Tex; Metrop Mus Art, New York; Nat Mus Women Arts, Washington, DC. *Comn:* Ixion's Wheel, State Univ NY Albany, 69; gardens, House & Garden Mag, 69; Cyrus Field (landscape sculpture park), Buskirk, 70-75; Fair Park Lagoon, Dallas, Texas, 81-86; Endangered Garden, Candlestick Cove, San Francisco, 88-93. *Exhib:* Women in Am Archit, Brooklyn Mus, NY, 77; Recent Acquisitions, Mus Mod Art, New York, 79; American Drawings in Black & White, Brooklyn Mus, 80; Recent Acquisitions, Metrop Mus Art, 82; Beyond the Monument, Md Inst Art, Baltimore, 85; Sculpture for Public Spaces, Marisa del Re Gallery, New York, 86; New York Women Artists, NY State Mus, 89; Fragile Ecologies, Queens Mus, New York, 92; Creative Solutions to Ecological Issues, Dallas Mus Natural Hist, 93; and others. *Pos:* Design consult, Consolidated Edison Corp, NY, 72, Yale Univ, 72, Bartholomew Consolidated Sch Corp, Columbus, Ind, 73, Int Year Child Comm, 79, Corning Park, Albany, 82, Fair Park, Dallas, 82, Pelham Bay Park, NY, 84 & Cathedral Sq, Sacramento, 84; San Francisco Clean Water Prog, 88; Pub Art Master Plan, Rockland Co, New York, 90. *Teaching:* Vis prof art, State Univ NY Albany, 69; vis artist, Mass Inst Technol, 74, Oberlin Col, 74 & Alfred Univ, 74; lectr, Colby Col, Maine, 81; West Texas State Univ, Canyon, Tex, 88; Seminar, Yale Univ, 89; Olesen fel, Bennington Col, 91-92. *Awards:* Guggenheim Fel, 70 & 80; Gold Medal, Accademia Italia Delle Arti, 79; Artist's Fel, Nat Endowment Arts, 75. *Bibliog:* Eleanor Munro (auth), Originals: American Women Artists, Simon & Shuster, 79; Laurie Garris (auth), Patricia Johanson, Arts & Archit, Vol III, No 4, 85; Balken, Debra & Lucy R Lippard, Patricia Johanson: Drawings & Models for Environmental Projects, 69-86; Exhib catalogue, Berkshire Mus, Pittsfield, Mass, 87. *Mem:* Global Forum Arts Group, New York. *Publ:* Architecture as Landscape, Princeton J, Vol 2, 85; Civic-minded Landscaping, Heresies, Issue 22, 87; Women Artists tell their own stories, Gallerie, Vancouver, BC, 89; Ann, Public Artists on Public Art, Art J, winter 89; Art and Survival: Creative Solutions to Environmental Problems, Gallerie Monogr, Vancouver, BC, 92. *Mailing Add:* RFD 1 Box 328 Buskirk NY 12028

JOHNS, CHRISTOPHER K(ALMAN)
PAINTER, EDUCATOR
b Racine, Wis, Dec 2, 52. *Study:* Univ Wis, Milwaukee, 71-73; San Francisco Art Inst, BFA, 75; Stanford Univ, MFA, 77. *Work:* Continental Bank, Chicago, Ill; Best Products Co, Richmond, Va; Univ Wis, Platteville; Stanford Univ, Calif; Charles Wustum Mus Fine Art, Racine, Wis. *Exhib:* West-the Law, Minn Mus Art, St Paul, 79 & 80; Hassam Fund Purchase Exhib, Am Acad & Inst Arts, New York, NY, 80; Abstraction in Louisiana, 80 & Festival of New Work, 84, Contemp Art Ctr, New Orleans, La; View from Southeast Wis, Charles Wustum Mus, Racine, Wis, 81; Southern Abstraction, City Gallery, Raleigh, NC, 87; solo exhibs, Union Gallery, La State Univ, Baton Rouge, 83 & Univ Ala, Huntsville, 91. *Teaching:* instr painting, Charles Wustum Mus, 77-78; assoc prof painting & drawing, La State Univ, Baton Rouge, 79- *Awards:* Southern Arts Fedn Artists Fel, 88; Visual Arts Grant, State of Louisiana Arts Div, 86. *Bibliog:* Juliana Harris-Livingston (auth), Abstraction still not convinced, Figaro, New Orleans, La, 8/80. *Media:* Oil. *Dealer:* Jan Cicero Gallery 221 W Erie Chicago IL 60610; Sylvia Schmidt Galleryl, New Orleans, LA. *Mailing Add:* 864 Albert Hart Baton Rouge LA 70808

JOHNS, JASPER
PAINTER
b Augusta, Ga, 1930. *Study:* Univ SC. *Work:* Victoria & Albert Mus, London; Mus Mod Art & Whitney Mus Am Art, New York; Albright-Knox Art Gallery, Buffalo, NY; Wadsworth Atheneum, Hartford, Conn; Mus Mod Art, Paris; San Francisco Mus Mod Art, Calif; Stedelijk Mus, Amsterdam, Neth; Hirshhorn Mus & Sculpture Garden, Washington, DC; Tate Gallery, London; Moderna Museet, Stockholm; Kunst Mus, Basel. *Exhib:* One-man shows, Mud Mod Art, 68, 70 & 92, Cana Art Gallery, Seoul, Korea, 91, Gagosian Gallery, New York, 92, Prints & Drawings from the Castelli Collection, Palaus de Luppe, La Fondation Vincent Van Gogh, Arles, France, 92, Milwaukee Art Mus, Wis, 92, Galeria Weber Alexander Cobo, Madrid, Spain, 92; Mus Contemp Art, Chicago, 71-72; Art Inst Chicago, 74; Walker Art Ctr, Minneapolis, 74; Saidye Bronfman Ctr, Montreal, 80; Pace Gallery, New York, 80; Whitney Mus Am Art, New York, 80; Hirshhorn Mus, Washington, DC, 80; Stedelijk Mus, Netherlands, 80; Margo Leavin Gallery, Los Angeles, 81; Leo Castelli Gallery, New York, 81; Hotel des Arts, Paris, France, 92; Mus Mod & Contemp Art, 92. *Pos:* Dir, Found Contemp Performance Artists, 63- *Bibliog:* C Kelder (auth), Prints: Jasper Johns at Hofstra, Art in Am, 3/73; D Ward (auth), Jasper Johns drawings, Arts Rev, 9/74; J Reichardt (auth), The rendering is the content, Archit Design, 12/74. *Dealer:* Leo Castelli Gallery 420 W Broadway New York NY 10012. *Mailing Add:* c/o Leo Castelli Gallery 420 W Broadway New York NY 10012

JOHNSEN, MAY ANNE
PAINTER
b Port Chester, NY. *Study:* With John Carroll. *Work:* St Mary's Church, Hudson, NY; also in pvt collection of Philip Schyler, Albany, NY. *Comn:* Fire Equipment 1890's (painting), Tsaawassa Fire Dept, Brainard, NY, 53. *Exhib:* Women Artist in Am from 18th Century to Present; Bertrand Russel Int Peace Found Exhib, Nottingham, Eng; A Heritage, Nat Soc Marine Painters Nat Show, Plantations Gallery, Sandwich, Mass; Drawing International, Barcelonia, Spain; Knickerbocker Nat Exhib, New York; Catherine Lollilard-Wolfe Nat Show, New York; Distinguished Marine Painters Gold Medal Show, Franklin Mint Gallery; Int Miniature Art Show, NC, WVa, NMex & Ark; and others. *Awards:* Silvermine Guild Marine Award, 59; First Prize, Columbia Co Fair, 59; Ohio Marine Award, Ohio Miniature Soc, 69; and others. *Bibliog:* Article in La Rev Mod, 68. *Mem:* Assoc mem Miniature Painters, Sculptors & Gravers Soc of Washington, DC; Miniature Art Soc NJ; Am Soc Marine Painters. *Media:* Mixed. *Dealer:* Squillaci Gallery 524 Summit Ave Schenectady NY 12307. *Mailing Add:* Rte 20, PO Box 5 Brainard NY 12024

JOHNSON, ANTOINETTE SPANOS
CURATOR, HISTORIAN
b Birmingham, Ala, June 27, 53. *Study:* Univ Ala, Birmingham, BA, 75; Vanderbilt Univ, MA, 85. *Collections Arranged:* Ed Willis Barnett: Photographs, 86; Vision of the West: The Art of Will Crawford (auth, catalog), Birmingham Mus Art, Ala, 86; Post-Industrial Steel Town (auth, catalog), 88; Birmingham/Hitachi: An Exhib of Contemp Birmingham Artists (auth, catalog), Hitachi, Japan, 89; Michael Ponce de Leon: Prints and Plates (auth, catalog), 90. *Pos:* Ed, Visual Arts Gallery Papers, 80- & contribr, 85-, Univ Ala, Birmingham; instr art hist, 84-; cur, Visual Arts Gallery, 85- *Teaching:* Instr art hist, Univ Ala, Birmingham, 83- *Mem:* Col Art Asn; Southeastern Col Art Asn. *Res:* 19th and 20th Century drawing and illustration. *Publ:* Auth, Vision of the West: The Art of Will Crawford, Birmingham, 86; Birmingham/Hitachi: An Exhibition of Contemporary Birmingham Artists, Birmingham/Hitachi, Japan, 89. *Mailing Add:* 2907 Virginia Rd No 6 Birmingham AL 35223-1253

JOHNSON, AUDEAN
PAINTER, ILLUSTRATOR
b Reading, Pa, June 2, 29. *Study:* Philadelphia Mus Sch Industrial Art, 51. *Bibliog:* Article, Am Artist Mag, 5/87; Victoria Mag, 10/90; posters, Frontline Graphics, San Diego. *Media:* Watercolor. *Publ:* Illustr, Soft as a Kitten, Random House. *Dealer:* Craft Haus Vermont. *Mailing Add:* c/o Eleanor Ettinger 155 Avenue of the Americas New York NY 10013

JOHNSON, BARBARA LOUISE
PAINTER, PRINTMAKER
b Worcester, Mass, Nov 10, 27. *Study:* Univ Miami, Fla, 46-48; Smith Col, Mass, AB, 50; Univ Calif-Berkeley, 51; Univ Mich, BS, 57, MFA, 59. *Exhib:* Nat Print Ann, Hunterdon Mus, Clinton, NJ, 83-87; W Coast Works on Paper, Humboldt State Univ, Arcata, Calif, 87; Ann Competition, El Paso Mus Art, Tex; Biennual Competition, Monterey Penninsula Art Mus, Calif, 89; Japanese Art, Retrete Art City, Finland, 90. *Awards:* Leila Sawyer Mem Award, 87, Shelley Sterling Mem Award, 89 & Medal Honor & Jack Key Cotton Mem Award, 91 Nat Asn Women Artists, New York. *Bibliog:* Jeanne Davidson (auth), Barbara Johnson/artist & printmaker, Print World, spring 87. *Mem:* Calif Soc Printmakers; Los Angeles Printmaking Soc; Nat Asn Women Artist, New York; Carmel Art Asn. *Media:* All. *Mailing Add:* 3548 Greenfield Place Carmel CA 92923

JOHNSON, BARBARA PIASECKA
COLLECTOR
b Staniewicze, Poland, Feb 25, 37. *Study:* Univ Wroclaw, Poland, MA(art hist), 65. *Exhib:* Opus Sacrum, Royal Castle, Warsaw, Poland, 90 & Liechtensteinische Staatliche Kunstsammlung, Vaduz, Liechtenstein, 91; Cultural Heritage in Europe, Jan Vermeer, St Praxedis, Wawel Royal Castle, Krakow, Poland, 91-92; The Badminton Cabinet, Royal Castle, Warsaw, Poland, 92-95. *Pos:* Trustee, dir, chairperson, The Barbara Piasecka Johnson Found, currently; trustee, chairperson, The Paderewski Ctr, currently; pres, Centrum Ignacego Paderewskiego, currently; mem, Chmns Counc Metrop Mus Art, New York, currently; mem, Advisory Comt Nat Gallery Art, Washington, DC, currently; mem, US Dept State Fine Arts Coun, currently; mem, Coun Found Univ Wroclaw, currently; trustee & dir, Atlantic Found & Harbor Branch Found, 72-85; bd mgrs, Wistar Inst Philadelphia, 89-91. *Awards:* St Brother Albert Chmielowski Award, Poland, 90; Award, Foreign Minister of Poland, 91; Gold Medal, Wroclaw Univ, 91. *Bibliog:* David Margolic (auth), Lech's American Angel, NY Times Mag, 10/89; Antoni Dzieduszycki (auth), Love is More Important, Barbara Piasecka Johnson & Eleven Arts Inc (prods, film), 90; Roger M Williams (auth), Wealth in the Service of Poland, Found News, 1-2/91. *Mem:* US Dept State Fine Arts Coun. *Collection:* Paintings 13th-19th Century (emphasis on old masters); Furniture & Decorative Arts 16th-19th Century (emphasis on French Furniture); Sculpture 15th-19th Century. *Publ:* Auth, Opus Sacrum, Religious works from the collection of Barbara P Johnson, Royal Castle Warsaw, Poland, 90 & Liechtensteinische Kustsammlung, Vaduz, 91 & Jan Vermeer, St Praxedis, 91 IRSA, Vienna. *Mailing Add:* 8 Lawrenceville Rd Princeton NJ 08540

JOHNSON, BRENT
PAINTER
b Tyler, Tex, Aug 25, 41. *Study:* Cent State Univ, BFA, 67; Univ Okla; Univ Md. *Exhib:* Watercolor USA, Springfield Art Mus, Mo, 75; Am Watercolor

Soc, Nat Acad Design, New York, 75-81; La Ann, La Mus Art, Shreveport, 76; Delta Art Asn, Ark Art Ctr, Little Rock, 76; San Diego Nat Watercolor Exhib, Cent Fed Tower, 77; Rocky Mountain Nat Watermedia Exhib, Foothills Art Ctr, Golden, Colo, 77; and others. *Pos:* Bd dirs, Oklahoma City Arts Coun, 79-80. *Awards:* Mercantile Bank Award, Watercolor USA, 75; Bus Community Award, Rocky Mountain Nat Watermedia Exhib, 77; John Young Hunter Mem Award, Am Watercolor Soc, 81. *Bibliog:* Lynn Martin (auth), Today's art, Syndicate Mag Inc, 74; Dean G Graham (auth), Outdoor Oklahoma, Okla Dept Wildlife, 1/76; Marcia Lionberger (auth), Oklahoma Art Gallery, Wall & Wall Publ Co Inc, fall 81. *Mem:* Prof Artist Asn Okla (pres, 77-78); Whiskey Painters Am. *Media:* Watercolor, Acrylic. *Dealer:* Temple Art Gallery 1102 S 31st St Temple TX 76501; American Legacy Gallery 5911 Main St Kansas City MO 64113. *Mailing Add:* 513 Sweetgum Oklahoma City OK 73127

JOHNSON, BRUCE (JAMES)
SCULPTOR
b Riverside, Calif, May 6, 44. *Study:* Univ Hawaii, Honolulu, BFA, 66; El Camino Col, Gardena, Calif; Calif Col Arts & Crafts, Oakland, MFA, 70. *Exhib:* James D Phelen Awards Exhib, Calif Palace of Legion of Honor, San Francisco, 69; Western Wash State Nat Drawing & Small Sculpture Exhib, Western Wash State Univ, Bellingham, 70; San Francisco Art Inst Centennial Exhib, 71 & Work on Paper, 73, San Francisco Mus Mod Art; Grids, Inst Contemp Art, Univ Pa, Philadelphia, 72; Eighteen Bay Area Artists, Los Angeles Inst Contemp Art, 76 & Univ Calif, Berkeley Art Mus, 77; Art Hawaii Ann, Honolulu Acad Arts, 78, 79 & 83; Artists Hawaii Cult Exchange Exhib, Ohio & Manila, 80-81. *Teaching:* Instr art, Santa Rosa Jr Col, Calif, 72-76; lectr drawing, Univ Hawaii, Honolulu, 78-79; instr, Honolulu Acad Arts, 81. *Awards:* MacDowell Colony Fel, 71; Young Artist Award, Contemp Art Comt of Oakland Mus Art Guild, 73. *Bibliog:* Judith L Dunham (auth), Johnson and Linhares, Artweek, 3/73; Alfred Frankenstein (auth), She's somebody to watch, San Francisco Chronicle, 4/3/73. *Media:* Wood, Metal. *Dealer:* Nina Owen Ltd 212 W Superior St Ste 202 Chicago IL 60610-3533. *Mailing Add:* c/o Barclay Simpson Fine Arts 3669 Mount Diablo Blvd Lafayette CA 94549

JOHNSON, BUFFIE
PAINTER, LECTURER
b New York, NY, Feb 20, 12. *Study:* Art Students League, 27-28; Univ Calif, Los Angeles, BA, 36; Acad Julien, Paris, 38; S W Hayter Atelier, with Francis Picabia, 38-39. *Work:* Boston Mus Fine Arts; Yale Univ Art Gallery; Nat Collection Fine Arts, Washington, DC; Whitney Mus Am Art & Brooklyn Mus, New York; Guggenheim Mus; San Francisco Art Mus. *Comn:* Murals, Astor Theatre, New York, 59; Knox Murals. *Exhib:* Contemp Am Art Biennial Exhib, Whitney Mus Am Art, 73; one-woman shows, Howard Putzel's 67 Gallery, New Sch Social Res, Betty Parsons Gallery, Max Hutchinson Gallery, New York, 73 & Stamford Mus, Conn, 77; Early Portraits, Bleaker Street Gallery, New York, 89; retrospective, Triton Mus, Santa Clara, Calif, 91. *Teaching:* Instr, Parsons Sch Design, 46-50. *Awards:* First Prize, Salon Int de La Femme, 70; Edward Albee Found Fel; MacDowell Fel; and others. *Bibliog:* David Gascoyne (auth), Gift of Renewal, Resurgence, London, 10/89; Kathryn Allen Rabuzzi (auth), That Old Time Religion, NY Times, 2/5/89; Katy Butler (auth), Sacred Women--Sacred Animals, San Francisco Chronicle, 6/25/89. *Mem:* Group Espace, Paris. *Media:* Oil. *Publ:* Auth, Lady of the Beasts: Ancient Images of the Goddess & Her Sacred Animals, Harper & Row, San Francisco, 88. *Mailing Add:* 102 Greene St New York NY 10012

JOHNSON, CARLA RAE
SCULPTOR, CONCEPTUAL ARTIST
b E Chicago, Ind, Mar 9, 47. *Study:* Ball State Univ, Muncie, Ind, BS, 69; Univ Iowa, Iowa City, MA, 74 & MFA, 75. *Work:* Borough Manhattan Community Col Fine Arts, New York; Heckscher Mus Art, Huntington, NY. *Exhib:* solo exhib, Arts & Life & How I Felt About the Ladder, Meridan Mus Art, Miss, 79 & Studio Equipment Sale, Franklin Marshall Col Art Gallery, Lancaster, Pa, 89; Brooklyn '81, Brooklyn Mus, NY, 80; Lines of Vision, Nat Mus Women Arts, Washington, DC, 90. *Awards:* Second Place Award, Nat Sculpture '79; First Award, Ann Competition, Islip Mus Art, NY, 83; Pollack-Krasner Found Grant, 90. *Bibliog:* Judy Collischan VanWagner (auth), Lines of Vision, Hudson Hill Press, 89. *Mem:* Women's Caucus Art. *Dealer:* Soho 20 Gallery 469 Broome St New York NY 10013. *Mailing Add:* 4211 Ninth St 2nd Fl Long Island City NY 11101

JOHNSON, CECILE RYDEN
PAINTER, PUBLISHER
b Jamestown, NY. *Study:* Augustana Col, AB; Pa Acad Fine Arts; Art Inst Chicago; Am Acad Fine Arts; Univ Colo; Univ Wis. *Work:* Chicago Mus Sci & Indust; Davenport Munic Mus; Macalester Col; General Mills; Minn Mining. *Comn:* Ford Motor Co; Trans World Airlines; Rockefeller Resorts; Jamaican Govt; CBS/World Tennis; and many others. *Exhib:* Am Watercolor Soc; Washington Watercolor Soc; US Info Agency & State Dept Traveling Exhib to Europe, Asia, Africa & South Am; one-man shows, Davenport Munic Mus & Hudson River Mus; US Tennis Open, Nat Stadium, 83; Grand Central Gallery; and others. *Teaching:* Instr workshops, Ghost Ranch, Abiquiu, 82, Bermuda, 83. *Awards:* Catharine Lorillard Wolfe Art Club Gold Medal; Prizes, Am Watercolor Soc, Knickerbocker Artists & others. *Bibliog:* Feature article, Am Artist, 1/83; Kent (auth), 100 Watercolorists, Watson Guptill; Creating in Watercolor (film), Crystal Productions; Feature Article, Am Artist, 5/86. *Mem:* Am Watercolor Soc; Nat Arts Club; Soc Illusr; hon mem Nat League Pen Women; Allied Artists, Audubon Soc. *Media:* Watercolor, Acrylic. *Mailing Add:* Des Artistes One West 67th St New York NY 10023

JOHNSON, CHARLES W, JR
EDUCATOR, HISTORIAN
b New York, NY, Apr 7, 38. *Study:* Westminster Col, BMEd; Union Theol Seminary, MSM; Ohio Univ, PhD, 70. *Teaching:* Asst prof, State Univ NY Col New Paltz, summer 66; From asst prof art hist to assoc prof, 67-81, Univ Richmond, prof, 82-, chmn dept fine arts, 67- *Mem:* Col Art Asn Am; Popular Culture Asn of South. *Mailing Add:* Modlin Fine Arts Ctr Univ of Richmond Richmond VA 23173

JOHNSON, DEAN P
SCULPTOR
Study: SDak State Univ, Brookings, 74-77; Minneapolis Col Art & Design, Minn, 78-79; Univ Wyo, BFA, 80, MA, 81, MFA, 90. *Exhib:* Solo shows, Ctr Contemp Arts, Santa Fe, NMex, 88, Laramie Co Community Col, Cheyenne, Wyo, 89, Casper Col, Wyo, 90 & Nicolaysen Art Mus, Casper, Wyo, 91; Ctr Contemp Arts, Santa Fe, NMex, 90; Wash State Arts Comn, Olympia, 91; Rock Springs Fine Arts Ctr, Wyo, 92; and others. *Awards:* Wash State Arts Coun Comn, 90; Individual Artist Grant, 90 & Fel, 91, Wyo Arts Coun; New Forms: Regional Initiative Grant, Nat Endowment Arts, Rockefeller & Warhol Founds, 92. *Bibliog:* Nancy Melich (auth), Art: range-riding curator hunts best of the west, Wall St J, 28, 8/27/85; Ted Pinkowitz (auth), Installation, constructions, environments, New Art Examiner, 55, 6/88; Thomas Patin (auth), Dean Johnson at the Center for Contemporary Arts, Santa Fe, Artspace, 53, fall 88; and others. *Mailing Add:* 3119 Pioneer Cheyenne WY 82001

JOHNSON, D'ELAINE A HERARD See D'Elaine

JOHNSON, DIANA L
GALLERY DIRECTOR, CURATOR
b New York, NY, July 13, 40. *Study:* Radcliffe Col, Harvard Univ, BA, 62; Brown Univ, MA, 71. *Pos:* Assoc cur prints & drawings, Mus Art, RI Sch Design, 69-76, actg chief cur, 74-76, cur prints, drawings & photogs & chief cur, 76-79, actg dir, 78-79; dir, Brown Univ, David Winton Bell Gallery, 90- *Mem:* Print Coun Am (treas, 82-89); Asn Col & Univ Mus & Galleries (RI rep, 90-); Am Fed Arts (exhib comt). *Publ:* Auth, Spaces (exhib catalog), 78 & Fantastic Illustration and Design in Britain 1860-1930, 79, Mus Art RI Sch Design; Reprise: The Vera G List Collection, 91 & coauth, The Collections of Brown Univeristy, 92, Brown Univ. *Mailing Add:* David Winton Bell Gallery List Art Center Brown Univ 64 College St Providence RI 02912

JOHNSON, (L) DIANE
PAINTER, GRAPHIC ARTIST
b Trenton, NJ. *Study:* Ohio Stae Univ, BA(art educ), 73; Lasalle Exten Univ, cert, 78; studied with Daniel Greene NA, Herman Margllies, NTNL Artist's Sem, 83, 84 & 89. *Work:* R J R Nabisco, Wachovia Bank & Trust, Winston-Salem, NC; Optical Cable Corp, Roanoke Regional Airport, Va; Ethyl Corp, Richmond, Va. *Comn:* Three acrylic paintings, Cent Fidelity Bank, Lynchburg, Va, 88 & 90; pastel painting-interior, Gentry, Locke, Rakes & Moore, Roanoke, Va, 89; acrylic painting-landscape, Coopers & Lybrand, Lynchburg, 92. *Exhib:* solo exhibs, Framery, Lynchburg, Va, 85, Virginia Impressions, Gallery 3, Roanoke, Va, 89; Impressions of Earth & Time, Lynchburg Art Club, Va, 90; Johnson & Schumate, Little Gallery, Moneta, Va, 91; Salmagundi 14th Ann Non-mems Show, New York, 91. *Pos:* Graphic designer/artist, Southwind Studios, Forest, Va, 83-; graphic designer/illus, Wiley & Wilson, Lynchburg, 85-89. *Teaching:* Drawing/painting, Southwind Studios, Forest, Va, 84- *Awards:* Lorna Balian Prize, Winning Children's Book Illusr, Abingdon Press, 87; The Artists Mag Top 100, 1988 Still Life Painting, 89; George Innes Jr Mem Award Pastel, Salmagundi Club, 91. *Bibliog:* Blackburn/Kirsh (auths), article/review, Lynchburg News, 88 & 91; Helen Barranger (auth), Roanoke art as good investment, Roanoker Mag, 90; Whitwell & Winboune (auths), Arts in Review: L Diane Johnson: on show at the Little Gallery at Smith Mountain Lake, Va Southwest Mag, 91. *Mem:* Full mem Pastel Soc Am; Degas Pastel Soc; Midwest Pastel Soc. *Publ:* Illusr, If I Had Long Long Hair, Abingdon Press, 87. *Mailing Add:* 118 White Cypress Dr Forest VA 24551

JOHNSON, DIANE CHALMERS
HISTORIAN, EDUCATOR
b Dubuque, Iowa, Jan 3, 43. *Study:* Harvard Univ, Radcliffe Col, BA(fine arts), 65; Univ Kans, MA(art hist), 67, PhD(art hist), 70. *Teaching:* Asst prof, Col Charleston, 70-75, assoc prof, 75-80, chmn dept art, 70-78, prof fine arts, 80- & chmn dept art hist, 91- *Awards:* Nat Endowment Humanities Res Fel, 81-82; Addlestone Chair Am Art, Col Charleston, 89-91. *Mem:* Col Art Asn Am; Historians Am Art Asn. *Res:* Nineteenth and 20th century European and American art; Art Nouveau and Symbolist art. *Publ:* Coauth, Art as confrontation: the Black man in the art of Gericault, Mass Rev, 69; auth, The studio: a contribution to the nineties, Apollo Mag, 70; Odilon Redon's apocalypse de Saint-Jean, Arts Va, 72; American Art Nouveau, Harry N Abrams Publ, 79; Picasso's Papiers Colles, In: XXVI Int Congress for the History of Art, Univ Pa Press, 89. *Mailing Add:* 59 Smith St Charleston SC 29401

JOHNSON, DONALD RAY
HISTORIAN, PRINTMAKER
b Poteau, Okla, Jan 14, 42. *Study:* Northeast Okla State Col, BA, 63; Univ Okla, MFA, 70 & MA, 71. *Work:* Topeka Publ Lib, Topeka Kans; Baker Art Found; Dickinson State Col, NDak. *Comn:* Lithograph, Kans Cult Arts, 73. *Exhib:* Lithography 1969, Fla State Univ, 69; Images on Paper, Jackson, Miss, 71; Graphics 71, Western NMex Univ, 71; Santa Fe Trail Ctr, Larned, Kans, 81; Ft Hays State Univ, 71; Mulvane Art Ctr, Washburn Univ Topeka, Kans,

88; Baker Art Found, Liberal Kans, 88; and others. *Teaching:* Assoc prof art hist, Emporia Kans State Univ, 70-; chmn, div art, Emporia Kans State Univ, 84. *Awards:* Emporia Kans State Univ Grants, 73, 75, 76, 78, 80-82; Wenner-Gren Found Grant, 83; Kans Comt Humanities Grant, 85. *Mem:* Col Art Asn. *Res:* American West during the 19th century; Santa Fe Trail through Kansas; mound builders in eastern Oklahoma. *Mailing Add:* 1025 E 12th Ave Emporia KS 66801

JOHNSON, DORIS MILLER
PAINTER
b Oakland, Calif, Dec 8, 09. *Study:* Calif Col Arts & Crafts, 32-33; Univ Calif, Berkeley, BA, 34, 34-36. *Work:* Piedmont High Sch Art Gallery, Calif. *Exhib:* Portland Art Mus Invitational, Ore, 40; Carnegie Traveling Show from San Francisco Mus Art, 40-41; Nat Drawing Exhib, San Francisco Mus Art, 70; San Francisco Women Artists Ann Show, One Market Plaza, San Francisco, 79; one-person show, Lucien Labaudt Art Gallery, San Francisco, 73; Crown Zellerbach, San Francisco, 81; Richmond Art Ctr, Calif, 81; San Francisco Women Artists' Opening Gallery, 83; Holloway Howard 20th Century American Art, Artist's of the Berkeley Sch, San Francisco, 92. *Pos:* Founder children's art classes, Art League East Bay, 39; dir, Oakland Art Mus, 39-52, chmn art rental gallery, 56-59; chmn acquisitions comt of activities bd, San Francisco Mus Art, 57-64; mem bd trustees, Calif Col Arts & Crafts, 70-78. *Teaching:* Instr art, Oakland Art Mus, 39-52. *Awards:* 13th Ann San Francisco Women Artists Pres Purchase Prize, San Francisco Mus Art, 38; San Francisco Art Asn Ann Artists Fund Prize, 40; Merit Award, San Francisco Women Artists Painting Show, Zellerbach Plaza Gallery, 82; and others. *Bibliog:* The California Style & California Watercolor Artists, 1925-1955, Hillcrest Press Inc, Beverly Hills, Calif, 10/85; Edan Milton Hughes (publ), Artists in California, 1786-1940, 86. *Mem:* San Francisco Women Artists (pres, 46-48); hon life mem Art League East Bay. *Media:* Mixed; All Media. *Mailing Add:* 329 Hampton Rd Piedmont CA 94611

JOHNSON, DOUGLAS WALTER
PAINTER, PRINTMAKER
b Portland, Ore, July 8, 46. *Study:* Self-taught. *Work:* Permanent Collection, Mus NMex, Santa Fe; Am Nat Collection, Am Nat Ins Co, Galveston, Tex; Univ NMex, Albuquerque; De Vries Insurance Agency, St Joseph, Mich; Hotel Eldorado, Santa Fe, NMex. *Comn:* Rio Grande (mural), El Dorado Hotel, Santa Fe, NMex. *Exhib:* Eight From Santa Fe, 71, Mus NMex, Santa Fe; New Paintings and Prints, Return Gallery, Taos, NMex, 81 & 83; one-man show, Krasl Art Ctr, St Joseph, Mich, 82; Southwest Contemporary Artists, Gumps Gallery, San Francisco, Calif, 85; New Works, Gerald Peters Gallery, Dallas, Tex, 86; Inner Sanctums, Gerald Peters Gallery, Santa Fe, NMex, 88; Contemp miniatures, J N Bartfield Gallery, New York, 89; Birds of Magic, Gerald Peters Gallery, Santa Fe, NMex, 90. *Awards:* Jurors Award, NMex Biennial, Mus NMex, 73; Second Prize Award, Watercolor NMex, NMex Watercolor Soc, 74; Santa Fe Opera Poster, NMex, 81. *Bibliog:* Douglas Johnson, painter, 2/74 & Douglas Johnson, artist, 10/83, Santa Fean Mag; Douglas Johnson, Four Winds Mag, summer 82; Robert Ewing (auth), Douglas Johnson, Gerald Peters Corp; and others. *Media:* Casein on Paper, Clay. *Dealer:* JN Bartfield New York NY; Gerald Peters Gallery Santa Fe NM & Dallas TX. *Mailing Add:* General Delivery Coyote NM 87012

JOHNSON, ERNEST (MELVIN)
PAINTER, INSTRUCTOR
b Hampton, Va, April 18, 24. *Study:* Pratt Inst, cert(illus), 46-49; watercolor workshops with Georg Shook, 76, Edward Betts, 77 & Carl Schmalz, 80. *Work:* Chrysler Mus, Norfolk, Va; Roanoke Mus Fine Arts, Va; Phillip Morris USA, Richmond, Va; Barclays Am, Charlotte, NC. *Exhib:* Irene Leach Mem, Norfolk Mus, Va, 48 & 68; Watercolor USA, Springfield, Mo, 71 & 77; South Watercolor Soc Exhib, 79, 82 & 85; Ky Watercolor Soc Exhib, 80 & 82; Am Watercolor Soc Exhib, 84; Va Watercolor Soc Exhib, 80-84, 86 & 87; Nat Watercolor Invitational, Rockford Col, Ill, 84; Salmagundi Club Ann Non-Members Exhib, 85. *Teaching:* Instr watercolor, WVa Craft Ctr, Ripley, 79, Roanoke Col, 79-81, Longwood Col, Farmville, Va, 82 & James Madison Univ, Harrisonburg, Va, 84. *Awards:* Purchase Awards, Irene Leach Mem, Norfolk Mus, Va, 68 & Watercolor USA, Citizens Bank, Springfield, Mo, 71; Watercolor USA Honor Soc, 86. *Bibliog:* Stevens (auth), Expositions diverses, Rev Mod Arts Vie, 11/67; Shae Avery (auth), Ernest Johnson, portrait of a private person, Roanoker, 5-6/80; Janet Shaffer (auth), Paint-outs, Country Mag, 6/83. *Mem:* Va Watercolor Soc (pres, 80-81); Watercolor Soc, Southern. *Media:* Watercolor, Oil. *Publ:* Illusr, Adventures in Handwriting, Macmillan Co, 71. *Mailing Add:* 7229 Mount Chestnut Rd Roanoke VA 24018

JOHNSON, EUGENE JOSEPH
HISTORIAN
b Memphis, Tenn, May 22, 37. *Study:* Williams Col, BA, 59; NY Univ, MA, 63, PhD, 70. *Teaching:* Prof art, Williams Col, Williamstown, Mass, 65-, chmn art dept, 78-80, 90-91. *Mem:* Soc Archit Hist. *Publ:* Auth, S Andrea in Mantua, the Building History, 75; Charles Moore, Building & Prog, 86; coauth, Memphis: Archit Guide, 90. *Mailing Add:* Dept Art Williams Col Williamstown MA 01267

JOHNSON, GUY
PAINTER
b Fort Wayne, Ind, 1927. *Study:* Fla State Univ, MA, 52. *Exhib:* Solo exhibs, Hundred Acres Gallery, New York, 71 & 72, Gallerie Fabian Carlsson, Gothenberg, Sweden, 74, Stefanatti Gallery, New York, 74, Basel Int Art Exhib, Switz, 78, Galerie d'endt, Amsterdam, Netherlands, 78 & Galerie Arenthon, Paris, 89; Tomasulo Gallery, Union Col, Cranford, NJ, 85; Art in the Armory, New York, 88; Trains and Planes: The Influence of Locomotion in American Painting, traveling exhib, 89-90; 79th Ann Exhib, Maier Mus Art, Randolph-Macon Women's Col, Lynchburg, Va, 90; other one-man exhibs, Louis K Meisel Gallery, 79, 83, 85, 87, 88, 89 & 90. *Teaching:* Murray State Univ, Ky, 53-56, Lee Col, Tex, 56-63, Univ Bridgeport, Conn, 64-68. *Bibliog:* Jose Pierre (auth), Guy Johnson, Editions Pilipacchi, 88; John L Ward (auth), American Realist Paintings 1945-1980, UMI Res Press, 89; Chiong Yiao Chen (auth), A small bite of the Big Apple - Small-scale works of art from New York galleries, Maier Mus Art, Randolph-Macon Women's Col, 90. *Publ:* Les Hyperrealistes Am, Eds Filipacchi, Paris, France, 73; Superrealism, E P Dutton, Co, New York, 75; Superrealist Painting and Sculpture, William Morrow Co, New York, 80; Cover illus, Harper's 5/87; American Realist Painting 1945-1980, UMI Res, Inc, Chicago, 88. *Mailing Add:* c/o Louis K Meisel 141 Prince St New York NY 10012

JOHNSON, HARVEY WILLIAM
PAINTER
b New York, NY, Apr 9, 21. *Study:* Art Students League, 46-49; with Howard Trafton & Robert Johnson; also with Annetta St Gaudens, Cornish, NH. *Work:* Boatmen's Nat Bank, St Louis; Cowboy Artists Am Mus, Kerrville, Tex; Mus Fur Trade, Chadron, Nebr. *Exhib:* Cowboy Artists of America, Oklahoma City, 66-72, Phoenix, Ariz, 73-90; Haley Mem Libr Western Art Show, Midland, Tex, 80-82; Biltmore Celebrity Art Show, Los Angeles, 81-83; Western Heritage Sale, Houston, Tex, 82-83; The Horse in the American West, Ky, 92. *Teaching:* Instr com art, Famous Artists Sch, Inc, 53-72, Cowboy Artists Am Mus, 83, 88. *Awards:* Silver Medal in Oil Painting, 13th & 14th Ann Cowboy Artists of Am, 78 & 79. *Bibliog:* James K Howard (auth), Ten Years With the Cowboy Artists of America, Northland Press, 76; Don Dedera (auth), Visions West, The Story of the Cowboy Artists Museum, 83; Cowboy Artists of America, Desert Hawk, 88. *Mem:* Cowboy Artists of Am (vpres, 75-76 & pres, 76-77). *Media:* Oil. *Publ:* Auth, Western art is fine, SW Art Mag, 80; The sagebrush artist, Horse & Rider, 83; It's that sense of achievement, Art W, 84; Drawer After Drawer of Scrap, SW Art Mag, 86; Canvas Cowboys, Modern Maturity, 92. *Mailing Add:* PO Box 5733 Santa Fe NM 87502

JOHNSON, HOMER
EDUCATOR, PAINTER
b Buffalo, NY, Dec 24, 25. *Study:* Pa Acad Fine Arts with Julius Bloch & Hobson Pittman, 46-52. *Work:* Butler Inst Am Art, Youngstown, Ohio; Smith, Kline & French Labs, Philadelphia; Pa Acad Fine Arts. *Exhib:* Pa Acad Fine Arts Regional, 64; Mus Fine Arts, Springfield, Mass; Pa 71, Harrisburg, 71; one-man show, Philadelphia Art Alliance, 71; Philadelphia Earth Show, Philadelphia Civic Ctr, 73; Am Watercolor Soc Ann Traveling Exhib, 75-76; Univ Del Regional Art Exhib, 77 & 78. *Teaching:* Instr, Pa Acad Fine Arts & Fleisher Art Mem. *Awards:* Cresson Europ Scholar, Pa Acad Fine Arts, 61; Purchase Prize, Am Watercolor Soc, 72; First Prize Aqueous Media, Philadelphia Watercolor Club, 79. *Mem:* Am Watercolor Soc. *Media:* Watercolor, Acrylic. *Mailing Add:* 2120 Spring St Philadelphia PA 19103

JOHNSON, IVAN EARL
EDUCATOR, CRAFTSMAN
b Denton, Tex, Sept 23, 11. *Study:* Univ NTex, BA; Columbia Univ, MA; NY Univ, PhD. *Teaching:* Dir art, Ind Sch Dist, Dallas, Tex, 46-52; prof art educ, Fla State Univ, 52-80; co-dir, Fla State Univ Summer Prog, Oxford Univ, 87-93. *Awards:* Fla State Univ Grant for Study in Denmark, 71; Distinguished Service Awards, Southeastern Arts Asn, 80 & Fla Art Educators Asn, 80; Prof Distinguished Service Award, Miami Univ Oxford, Ohio, 85; Distinguished Fel, NAEA, 80-90. *Mem:* Nat Art Educ Asn; Fla Art Educ Asn (mem bd, 60-61); Fla Coun Arts. *Media:* Fabric, Art History. *Res:* Investigation of evaluation instruments on basic color knowledge. *Publ:* Coauth, Design for Living, Laidlow, 52; auth, Preparation of Art Teachers, Report of Commission on Art in Education, Nat Art Educ Asn, 69; auth, Relevance in art education, J Art Educ, 71; Book ed, Arts & Activities Mag, 70- *Mailing Add:* E 2304 Charles Ct Tallahassee FL 32304

JOHNSON, J SEWARD, JR
SCULPTOR, ADMINISTRATOR
b New York, NY, Apr 16, 30. *Study:* Univ Maine, 51; Harvard Univ, 66. *Work:* Vancouver Mus, Queen Elizabeth Park, BC; Morse Col, Yale Univ; Morris Mus, NJ; Hilton Head Island Inst Arts, SC; Exxon Park, Rockefeller Ctr, New York. *Comn:* The Awakening, Int Sculpture Conf, Washington, DC, 80; The Consultation, Univ Pa Hosp, Philadelphia, 82; four-piece installation, Richard Hughes Justice Complex, Trenton, NJ, 82; Taxi (life-sized bronze), Chemical Bank World Hq, New York, 83. *Exhib:* Mile of Sculpture Exhib, Chicago Arts Fair, 81; Cheltenham Arts Coun, Pa, 82; 12th Int Sculpture Conf, Oakland, Calif, 83; bronze sculpture, Wave Hill Sculpture Park, New York, 83; bronze at Washington Square, Washington, DC, 83-84; World Trade Ctr, New York, 85; Expo 86, Vancouver, BC, 86. *Pos:* Founder & pres, Johnson Atelier Inst, 74-; pres, Int Sculpture Ctr, 78-84. *Awards:* First Place, Design in Steel, US Steel Corp, 69, City Sculpture, Greenwich Art Coun, 82 & Citywide Survey, Washingtonian Mag, 83. *Bibliog:* Steven Brown (auth), article, Life Mag, 80; Steven DiLauro (auth), The foundry that makes sculptors dreams come true, Smithsonian Mag, 82; The Awakening: A narrative in bronze, Pub TV documentary, NJ Network, 82; Celebrating the familiar; the sculpture of J Seward Johnson, Jr, Tenth Avenue Editions. *Mem:* Artists Equity. *Media:* Cast Metal. *Dealer:* Sculpture Placement, Ltd, PO Box 9709, Wash DC 20016. *Mailing Add:* c/o Sculpture Placement PO Box 9709 Washington DC 20016

JOHNSON, J STEWART
CURATOR, CONSULTANT
b Baltimore, Md, Aug 31, 25. *Study:* Swarthmore Col, BA; Univ Del, Winterthur Prog in Early Am Cult, MA; Harvard Univ, Loeb Fel. *Pos:* Cur decorative arts, Newark Mus, 64-68; cur decorative arts, Brooklyn Mus, 68-73, vice dir collections, 70-72; consult contemp glass, Corning Mus Glass, 73-74; cur decorative arts, Cooper-Hewitt Mus Design, 75-76; cur design, Mus Mod Art, New York, 76-86. *Teaching:* Boston Univ, 86-87; FIT, 88-90. *Mem:* Victorian Soc Am (pres, 66-69); Am Friends of Attingham Park (pres, 80-83). *Publ:* Auth, Eileen Gray: Designer, 79; auth, The Modern American Poster, 83. *Mailing Add:* Box 185 Orient NY 11957

JOHNSON, JAMES ALAN
PAINTER, EDUCATOR
b Malden, Mass, Apr 2, 45. *Study:* Mass Col Art, Boston, BFA, 67; Wash State Univ, Pullman, MFA, 70. *Work:* Denver Art Mus, Colo; Franklin Furnace Arch, New York; Nebr Wesleyan Univ, Lincoln; Nat Inst Design, Ahmedabad, India; Tweed Mus, Univ Minn, Duluth. *Exhib:* Artists' Publications, Tweed Mus Art, Univ Minn, Duluth, 81; 1st Int Exhib Visual Poetry, Centro Cult, Sao Paulo, Brazil, 89; A Book in Hand, Arvada Ctr Arts & Humanities, 89; Artist Book Works, Chicago, 90; Multiples, Nexus Gallery, Atlanta, 90; CAGE Gallery, Cincinnati, 91; and others. *Teaching:* Instr graphics, dept archit, Wash State Univ, Pullman, 70; asst prof painting & drawing, Univ Colo, Boulder, 70-78, assoc prof, 78-; asst chmn, 88-91. *Bibliog:* John Fisher (auth), James Johnson at University of Colorado Art Galleries, Artspace, summer 81; Print Collectors Newsletter, 89. *Media:* All media. *Publ:* Auth, Facades, Boulder, 90; Acrostics, Boulder, 90; Dead Air, Boulder, 91; A Thousand Words, Boulder, 91; Words on Works, Leonardo, Vol 25, No 1, 92. *Mailing Add:* Fine Arts Dept Univ Colo Campus Box 318 Boulder CO 80309

JOHNSON, JAMES EDWIN
GRAPHIC DESIGNERS
b Minneapolis, Minn, Feb 18, 42. *Study:* Col St Thomas, Minneapolis; Minn Col Art & Design, with Robroy Kelly & Joe Luca, BFA. *Work:* Minneapolis Col Art & Design; Nat Gallery Fine Arts. *Comn:* Bicentennial pinwheel (outdoor graphic wind piece), Ft Worth Art Mus, Tex, 76; commemorable collage, Dayton-Hudson Found. *Exhib:* Making the City Observable, Int Design Conf, Aspen, Colo, 72; World Crafts Coun, Oaxtepec, Mex, 76; Images of an Era: The Am Poster 1945-1975 Int Traveling Exhib, 76; Exhib of Design Process, Clara M Eagle Gallery, Murray State Univ, 77. *Pos:* Graphic designer, Gen Mills & IBM Corp, 66-70; head graphic design dept, Walker Art Ctr, Minn, 70-78; partner, Johnson plus Johnson Graphic Design, 78- *Teaching:* Instr graphic design, Minneapolis Col Art & Design, 71-79; instr, Hamlin Univ, 74; vis lectr, St Cloud Univ, Univ Minn, Duluth, Bemidje Univ & Moorhead Univ. *Awards:* Cert Distinction, Creativity Eighty, 81; Oliver Award Merit, 81; Champion Papers Award, 82. *Bibliog:* Article, Design Quart 94/95, 75; The show awards exhib, Format Mag, 76; Publication design awards 1977, Soc Publ Designers, 77. *Mem:* Minn Graphic Designers Asn (mem coun, 77); Am Inst Graphic Arts; Soc Publ Designers; Fed Design Registry. *Publ:* Designer, American Indian Art: Form and Tradition, Walker Art Ctr, 72; designers, The Great American Rodeo, Ft Worth Art Mus, 75. *Mailing Add:* 1800 Emerson Ave S Minneapolis MN 55403

JOHNSON, JAMES RALPH
PAINTER, WRITER
b Ft Payne, Ala, May 20, 22. *Study:* Howard Col, BS. *Exhib:* Death Valley Invitational, Calif, 73-81; one-man shows, NMex State Fair Fine Arts Gallery, Albuquerque, 73, 74 & 75; Art Barn Gallery, Ft Worth, Tex, 74; Saddleback Inn Roundup of Cowboy Art, Santa Ana, Calif, 74-82. *Awards:* Award of Merit, Prof Div, NMex State Fair, 73; Gov Purchase Prize, 75 & 77. *Bibliog:* Marian Love (auth), James Ralph Johnson, artist & author, Santa Fean Mag, 4-5/75; Royal Hassrick (auth), Western Painting Today, Watson-Guptill, 75; Peggy and Harold Samuels (auths), Contemporary Western Artists, 82. *Mem:* Artists Equity Asn (vpres, Santa Fe, 73); Am Indian & Cowboy Artists Soc; Grand Cent Art Galleries; Nat Western Artists; Sante Fe Soc Artists. *Media:* Acrylic, Oil. *Publ:* Auth & illusr, The Last Passenger, Macmillan, 56; Utah Lion, Follett, 62; Camels West, McKay, 64; Animal Paradise, 69; The Southern Swamps, 70; plus many others. *Mailing Add:* Box 5295 Santa Fe NM 87501

JOHNSON, JOYCE
SCULPTOR, INSTRUCTOR
b Newton, Mass, July 12, 29. *Study:* Escuela de Artes Oficios y Tecnicos, Madrid, Spain, with Don Ramon Mateu, cert; Sch of Mus Fine Arts, Boston, with Harold Tovish & Oscar Jespers, cert. *Work:* Cushing Acad, Ashburnham, Mass; Cape Cod Conserv, Barnstable, Mass; Provincetown Art Asn & Mus; Habitat, Belmont, Mass. *Comn:* Sculpture, Botanical Gardens, Cornwall, Eng, 85; High Head, Commemorative Plaque, 89. *Exhib:* One-woman exhib, Annhurst Col, South Woodstock, Conn, 74 & Cape Cod Conserv, 83, 85 & 86; 20-Year Retrospective, Wellfleet Art Gallery, Mass, 77; Art in Transition--A Century of the Mus School, Mus Fine Arts, Boston, 77; Schoolhouse Gallery, 87-89; Cape Mus, 88, 91 & 92; Chandler Gallery, 88-91. *Pos:* Asst dir, Beaupre Arts Ctr, Stockbridge, Mass, 59-62; dir-founder, Nauset Sch Sculpture, North Eastham, Mass, 68-71; dir-co-founder, Truro Ctr for the Arts, Mass, 72-82, trustee 72-83, hon trustee, 83-; trustee, Lower Cape Arts Coun, 84-88; writer, Cape Codder Newspaper, currently; found Mem, Peaked Hill Trust to Save Dune Shacks, 85. *Teaching:* Instr sculpture from life, Cape Cod Conserv, Barnstable, Mass, 73-87, Truro Ctr for the Arts, Truro, Mass, 74- & Provincetown Mus Sch, 83-89. *Awards:* First Prize Pictorial Photograph, New Eng Press Assoc, 85; First Prize Sculpture, New Eng Ann, Cape Cod Art Asn, 91. *Bibliog:* Articles, Cape Arts, Vol 1, No 1, Cape Codder, 83 & Cape Cod Times, 83. *Mem:* Provincetown Art Asn (trustee, 76-78). *Media:* Wood Carving, Clay. *Mailing Add:* PO Box 208 Truro MA 02666

JOHNSON, KATE CHAMNESS See O'Meallie, Kitty (Kate Chamness Johnson)

JOHNSON, LEE
PAINTER, EDUCATOR
b Albion, Nebr, Nov 9, 35. *Study:* Minneapolis Col Art & Design, BFA; Skowhegan Sch Painting & Sculpture, with Alex Katz; Univ NMex, MA. *Work:* Denver Art Mus, Colo; Roswell Mus & Art Ctr, Roswell, NMex; Mus of NMex, Fine Arts, Santa Fe; Jonson Gallery, Univ NMex, Albuquerque, NMex; and others. *Exhib:* Watercolor USA, Springfield, Mo, 64; 1st Ann Painting Invitational, Mus of NMex, 68; Masterpieces from the Mus of NMex, McNay Art Inst, San Antonio, Tex, 70; Rocky Mountain Coun on Arts Traveling Exhib, Eight Western States, 72; 8 West Biennial, Grand Junction, Colo, 72-74. *Pos:* Asst dir-cur, Roswell Mus & Art Ctr, NMex, 62-68; dir, Gunnison Coun on Arts & Humanities, Colo, 73-75. *Teaching:* Instr drawing & painting, Eastern NMex Univ, Roswell, 62-67; asst prof drawing & painting, Western State Col, Gunnison, Colo, 68-81, prof art, 84. *Awards:* Five Artists from Colo Traveling Exhib, Rocky Mountain Coun on Arts, 71-72; First Prize Painting, 8 West Biennial, W Co Art Ctr, 74; Artist-in-Residence Grant, Roswell Mus & Art Ctr, 75. *Media:* Acrylic, Watercolor. *Mailing Add:* c/o Dept Art Western State Col Colo Gunnison CO 81230

JOHNSON, LEON BERNARD
PAINTER
b Azania, Africa. *Study:* Michaelis Sch Fine Art. *Work:* The Mural Project, La Plaza Cult Site, #18, Azania, 76; Works on Paper, Brooklyn Mus. *Exhib:* Three Bay Artists, Intersection Gallery, San Francisco; Solo exhibs, Sacred Grounds Gallery, San Francisco, 82, Area X Gallery, New York, 85286, Fervor Gallery, New York, 87, Ombondi Gallery, 89; Art Against Apartheid, Boricua Col, Brooklyn, NY, 85; Voices From Exile, Stuart Levy Gallery, New York, 90. *Awards:* Pollock-Krasner Found Grant, 86; Ruth Chenven Foundation Grant, 89; YADDO Fel, 90. *Bibliog:* Matthew Rose (auth), Leon Johnson, Arts Mag, 4/86. *Publ:* The Languid Body of a Wish, Limited Ed, Nadja Press. *Mailing Add:* 7 E Tenth St New York NY 10003

JOHNSON, LESTER F
PAINTER, EDUCATOR
b Minneapolis, Minn, Jan 27, 19. *Study:* Minneapolis Sch Art; St Paul Art Sch; Chicago Art Inst. *Exhib:* Carnegie Int, Pittsburgh, 64, 68 & 72; Rosc '67, Dublin, Ireland; L'Art Vivant aux Etats-Unis Fondation, Maeght, France, 71; 10 Independents, Guggenheim Mus, New York, 72; Chicago Biennial, 72; 70th Am Exhib, Art Inst Chicago, 72; Minn Mus Art, 73; Whitney Mus Am Art, 73; From the Imagination, Green Mountain Gallery, New York, 78; Homo Sapiens, Alrich Mus Contemp Art, Ridgefield, Conn, 82; Martha Jackson Mem Collection, Nat Mus Am Art, Washington, DC, 85; Gimpel Weitzenhoffer, New York, 90; Donald Morris Gallery, Detroit, Mich, 91; Eva Cohon Gallery, Chicago, 92. *Teaching:* Artist-in-residence, Univ Wis, Milwaukee, 64; adj prof painting, Yale Univ, New Haven, Conn, 64-, dir, studies grad painting, Sch Art & Archit, 69-74. *Awards:* Guggenheim Fel, 72; Guggenheim Fel Painting, 73; Creative Arts Award Painting, Brandeis Univ, 78. *Mem:* Am Acad Design; Coun Am Acad Design. *Mailing Add:* PO Box 7582 Greenwich CT 06836

JOHNSON, LESTER L
PAINTER, EDUCATOR
b Detroit, Mich, Sept 28, 37. *Study:* Univ Mich, BFA, 73, MFA, 74. *Work:* Detroit Inst Arts; Osaka Univ Arts, Japan; Johnson Publ Co & The Masonite Corp, Chicago; Sonnenblick-Goldman Corp, New York; Taubman Co, Inc, Bloomfield Hills, Mich; St Paul Co, Minn. *Comn:* Urban Wall Mural, New Detroit, 74; New Detroit Receiving Hosp, 80; Martin Luther King Community Ctr, Holtzman and Silverman Companies, Farmington Hills, 82; Goodman, Eden, Millender & Bedrosian, 84. *Exhib:* Biennial, Whitney Mus Am Art, New York, 73; Kilimanjaro, Flint Inst Arts, Mich, 73; Henry Ward Ranger Nat Invitational, Nat Acad Design, New York, 77; Passione, Lemberg Gallery, Birmingham, Mich & traveling, 86; Crossroads (with Ed Clark & Al Loving), Buckham Fine Arts Proj, Flint, 88; Amandla, GMI Humanities Art Ctr, Flint, 91. *Teaching:* Prof drawing & painting, Ctr Creative Studies, Col Art & Design, Detroit, 75- *Awards:* John S Newberry Purchase Prize, 54th Exhib Mich Artists, Detroit Inst Arts, 64; The Andrew W Mellon Found Proj Res/Travel Grant, 82 & 84; Mus African-Am Hist, 83; Recognition Award, African-Am Music Festival,90. *Publ:* Contribr, Gil Silverman Selects, Detroit Focus Gallery, 83; Crossroads, Buckham Fine Arts Proj, Flint, Mich, 88. *Mailing Add:* Ctr Creative Studies-Col Art & Design 245 E Kirby St Detroit MI 48202

JOHNSON, LOIS MARLENE
PRINTMAKER, EDUCATOR
b Grand Forks, NDak, Nov 17, 42. *Study:* Univ NDak, BS, 64; Univ Wis-Madison, MFA, 66. *Work:* Philadelphia Mus Art; Elvehjem Art Ctr, Madison; McCray Gallery, Univ NMex, Albuquerque; Univ NDak, Grand Forks; Adolph Behn Mem Collection, New York. *Comn:* Poster, Philadelphia Mus Art, 72. *Exhib:* Soc Am Graphic Artists, New York, 65-67, 70 & 71; Northwest Printmakers Int, Seattle, 68; Am Color Print Soc, 68-72; Silk Screen, Philadelphia Mus Art, 72; 18th Biennial Exhib, Brooklyn Mus, NY, 72; and others. *Teaching:* From asst prof to assoc prof printmaking & chmn

dept, Philadelphia Col Art, 67- *Awards:* Abraham Hankins Award, Am Color Print Soc, 68; Award, Prints in Pa, 69; Eyre Medal, Philadelphia Watercolor Club, 71. *Mem:* Print Club; Am Color Print Soc (coun, 68-72); Philadelphia Watercolor Club (bd dirs, 72); Soc Am Graphic Artists; Philadelphia Art Alliance. *Media:* Intaglio, Silkscreen. *Publ:* Contribr, Artist proof, Pratt Graphic Ctr, 67. *Dealer:* The Print Club 1614 Latimer St Philadelphia PA 19102. *Mailing Add:* Univ Arts 333 S Broad St Philadelphia PA 19102

JOHNSON, MARK M
MUSEUM DIRECTOR
b Rochester, Minn, Dec 10, 50. *Study:* Univ Wis, Whitewater, BA(art hist), 74; Univ Ill, Urbana-Champaign, MA(art hist) & cert arts mus studies, 76. *Collections Arranged:* Idea to Image: Preparatory Studies from the Renaissance to Impressionism (auth, catalog), Cleveland Mus Art, 80; Japanese Woodblock Prints: Themes & Techniques, 80; Cheek and the Arts, 85; The Biting Line: Prints by James Gillray, 86; Woodblock Prints by Un'ichi Hiratsuka (auth, catalog), Muscarelle Mus Art, 86; Classic Bolivian Textiles, 86; Photographs by Yousuf Karsh, 87, American Drawing Biennial, 88, 90 & 92; King William's Praise: Romeyn de Hooghe's Etchings of William III (auth, catalog), 89; Literacy through Art (auth, catalog), 90; Contemporary Abstract Painting: Resnick, Reed, Laufer & Moore, 91. *Pos:* Lectr mus ed, Art Inst Chicago, 76-77; asst cur art hist, Cleveland Mus Art, 77-81; asst dir & cur Europ painting, Krannert Art Mus, Ill, 81-85; dir, Muscarelle Mus Art, Va, 85- *Teaching:* Instr art hist, Cuyahoga Col, Cleveland, 77-81; instr mus studies, Univ Ill, Urbana-Champaign, 81-85; instr art hist & mus studies, Col William & Mary, 85- *Mem:* Am Asn Mus; Col Art Asn; Nat Art Educ Asn; Va Asn Mus. *Publ:* Auth, Abraham van Beyeren's Still Life, Krannert Art Mus Bull, 76; Chardin 1699-1779, Notes on Exhibition, 79 & The Realist Tradition, A Study Guide, 80, Cleveland Mus Art. *Mailing Add:* c/o Muscarelle Mus Art Col of William & Mary Williamsburg VA 23185

JOHNSON, MARTIN BRIAN
ASSEMBLAGE ARTIST, ENVIRONMENTAL ARTIST
b Elmer, NJ, May 2, 51. *Study:* Va Polytechnic Inst; Va State Univ, BArchit, 74; Univ NC, Chapel Hill, MFA, 77. *Work:* Ball State Univ, Muncie, Ind; The Vogel Collection, Nat Gallery Art, Washington, DC; Chrysler Mus, Norfolk, Va. *Exhib:* Four Sharp Artists, Chrysler Mus, Norfolk, Va, 87; Installation, SECCA, Winston-Salem, NC; Newhouse Ctr Contemp Art at Snug Harbor, Staten Island, NY, 88; Enigmatic Constructions-(Retro) Active Art Work(s), Portsmouth Mus, Va, 88; Glimpstone, Peninsula Fine Arts Ctr, Newport News, Va, 90; The Portrait in America, Chrysler Mus, Norfolk, Va, 90; Pleady Entreaty, Va Mus Fine Arts, Richmond, 90; Hesheunisallforone (44 4 x 4S 30 part), Southeastern Ctr Contemp Art, Winston Salem, NC, 92. *Bibliog:* Allan Schwartzman (auth), article, Arts Mag, 1/80; Donald B Kuspit (auth), articles, Art Am, 9/83, Artforum, 5/85; Linda McGreevy (auth), article, Arts Mag, 5/88. *Media:* Mixed. *Mailing Add:* PO Box 29 Virginia Beach VA 23458

JOHNSON, MIANI (MARIANNE) GUTHRIE
DEALER
b New York, NY, July 14, 48. *Study:* Barnard Col, BA. *Pos:* Dir, Willard Gallery, currently. *Media:* All. *Specialty:* Contemporary painting and sculpture. *Mailing Add:* c/o Willard Gallery 12 East 12 St New York NY 10003

JOHNSON, NOTA
PRINTMAKER, PAINTER
b Maryville, Mo, Nov 20, 23. *Study:* Okla State Univ, with Doel Reed, BA, 45; Cincinnati Art Acad, cert(scholar), 46; Univ Tulsa, with Alexandre Hogue, MA, 73. *Work:* Furman Univ, Greenville, SC; Univ Miss, Oxford; Univ Tulsa; Cincinnati Art Acad; Okla State Univ, Stillwater. *Comn:* Carved oak altar gates, 81 & mural, 82, Greek Orthodox Church, Tulsa. *Exhib:* Audubon Artists Ann, 76-84; Nat Acad Design, New York, 77-81; World Art Expos, Hynes Auditorium, Boston, 79; US/USSR Mus, traveling, 79-82; Nat Asn Women Artists Ann, 79-84; First Ann Nat Greek Art Exhib, Springfield, Mass, 83; and others. *Teaching:* Art, Mem High Sch, Tulsa, 68-70; instr art, Tulsa Jr Col, 70- *Awards:* Graphics Award, 18th Ann, Mus Okla, 79; Hortense Ferne Mem Prize, 80 & Alice P Shafer Mem Prize, 82, Nat Asn Women Artists. *Mem:* Life mem Nat Asn Women Artists; life mem Audubon Artists; Visual Arts Comt Tulsa (comt mem, 76-81); Arts & Humanities Coun Tulsa (bd mem, 76-81); Southern Graphics Coun (vpres, 80-82). *Media:* Aquatint, Drypoint; Oil. *Dealer:* Golden Willow Gallery PO Box 3110 Taos NM 87571; Mickelson Gallery 709 G St NW Washington DC 20001. *Mailing Add:* Burgundy Pl 8887 S Lewis Tulsa OK 74137

JOHNSON, RAY
PAINTER
b Detroit, Mich, Oct 16, 27. *Study:* Art Students League; Black Mountain Col, with Josef Albers, Robert Motherwell, Mary Callery & Ossip Zadkine, 45-48. *Work:* Art Inst Chicago; Dulin Gallery; Houston Mus Fine Arts; De Cordova Mus, Lincoln, Mass; Mus Mod Art, New York. *Exhib:* Solo exhibs, Whitney Mus Am Art, New York, 70, Art Inst Chicago, 72, Gertrude Kasle Gallery, 75, Massimo Valsecchi Gallery, Milan, 75, Viewpoints, Minneapolis Walker Art Ctr, 78, Nassau Co Mus Fine Art, 84 & The Ray Johnson New York, Roslyn, 86, More Works by Ray Johnson 1961-1991, Moore Col Art & Design, 91; Mus Fine Arts, Dallas, 74; The Pop Art Show, Royal Acad Arts, London, Eng, 91; Aspects of Collage, Guild Hall Mus, Easthampton, NY, 91; Artists Choice, Mus Mod Art, New York, 91. *Pos:* Founder, New York Corresp Sch Art, 62- *Awards:* Nat Inst Arts & Lett Award, 66; Nat Endowment Arts Grant, 76; Creative Artists Pub Serv Prog Grant, 77; Award Painting, Nat Endowment Arts, 86. *Bibliog:* Becker et al (auth), Happenings, Fluxus, Pop, Nouveau Realism, Rowohlt Verlag GMBH, 65; Al Hansen (auth), A Primer of Happenings and Time/Space Art, Something Else Press, 65; John Russell & Suzi Gablik (auths), Pop Art Redefined, Praeger, 69. *Publ:* Auth, The Paper Snake, 65. *Mailing Add:* 44 W Seventh St Locust Valley NY 11560

JOHNSON, RICHARD A
PAINTER, EDUCATOR
b Minneapolis, Minn, Feb 26, 42. *Study:* Minneapolis Col Art & Design, BFA, 65; Washington Univ, St Louis, Mo, MFA, 67; Am Acad in Rome, fel, painting, Prix de Rome, Italy, 68. *Work:* Longview Mus Art, Tex; R J Reynolds Indus, Winston-Salem, NC; Phillip Morris, New York; Pan Am Life, New Orleans; Katz & Bestoff Inc, New Orleans. *Exhib:* Walker Biennial, Walker Art Ctr, Minneapolis, 66; Tex Painting & Sculpture, Dallas Mus Fine Arts, 71; Photo Realism & Abstract Illusionism, Pittsburgh Arts & Crafts Ctr, 78; Operation Update 1979, Longview Mus, Tex, 79; Reality of Illusion, Denver Mus Art, 79; Illusion, Southeastern Ctr Contemp Art, Winston-Salem, NC, 83. *Teaching:* Chmn, Dept Fine Arts, Univ New Orleans, 79-, instr painting, 80, assoc prof painting, drawing & design, currently. *Awards:* Rockefeller Artist-in-Residence Grant, Southeastern Ctr Contemp Art, Winston-Salem, NC, 80. *Bibliog:* Mary King (auth), Two artists on display, St Louis Post-Dispatch, Mo, 5/74; Ted Calas (auth), Art scene, Figaro Newspaper, New Orleans, 10/79; Harry Schwalb (auth), Trick and treat, Pittsburgher Mag, Vol II, No 8, 79. *Mem:* Artists' Equity Asn La (vpres, 76-78). *Media:* Mixed. *Dealer:* Galerie Simonne Stern 2727 Prytania St New Orleans LA 70130; Watson-DeNagy 1106 Berthea Houston Tex. *Mailing Add:* Fine Arts Dept 2000 Lakeshore Dr Univ New Orleans New Orleans LA 70148

JOHNSON, ROBERT FLYNN
CURATOR, HISTORIAN
b Jersey City, NJ, Mar 20, 48. *Pos:* Cur asst, Worcester Art Mus, Mass, summer 72; asst cur prints & drawings, Baltimore Mus Art, 73-75; cur in chg, Achenbach Found Graphic Arts, Fine Arts Mus San Francisco, 75- *Teaching:* San Francisco Art Inst, 81. *Awards:* Nat Endowment Arts Fel, 75. *Mem:* Print Coun Am; Print & Drawing Soc of Baltimore Mus Art (vpres, 74-75); Bay Area Graphic Arts Coun (adv). *Res:* American prints of the 19th and 20th century; 19th century French drawings. *Publ:* Auth, American Prints, 1870-1950, Univ Chicago Press, 76; Lucian Freud Works on Paper, Thames & Hudson, 89. *Mailing Add:* 126 20th Ave San Francisco CA 94121

JOHNSON, RODELL C
PAINTER, ANIMATOR
b Spring Valley, Minn, July 29, 13. *Study:* Stanford Univ, with Edward Farmer & Daniel Mendelowitz, BA, 37; Walt Disney Prods Sch, with Don Graham, Rico Lebrun, Eugene Fleury & Homer Shoppee, 37-41; also with Joseph Rossi, Zoltan Szabo & Nicholas Reale, 74-75. *Work:* First Nat Bank of NC, Ocean County; NJ Cultural & Heritage Commission, Bay Head; City Hall, First Nat Bank of Toms River, NJ. *Exhib:* NJ Watercolor Soc, 72-73, 76-77 & 80-83; Frye Mus, Seattle, 78; Anchorage Mus, 78; Salmagundi Club Open, New York, 78; Am Watercolor Soc Open; Allied Artists Am; Purdue Univ, 79; and others. *Pos:* Animator, Walt Disney Prods, Burbank, Calif, 37-41 & Famous Studios, New York, 47-49; chief animation branch, US Army Signal Corp Photog Ctr, 41-46; dir & animator, animated commercials, educ & entertainment motion picture studios, New York, 50-78. *Teaching:* Instr watercolor & drawing, Adult Sch, Chatham, NJ, 74-78, Bay Head, NJ, 78-83. *Awards:* John Bermingham Award, NJ Watercolor Soc Ann Open Exhib, 76; NJ Sr Art Exhib Watercolor Award, State Mus NJ, 82 & 83. *Mem:* NJ Watercolor Soc (vpres, 80 & 81); NC Watercolor Soc. *Media:* Watercolor. *Mailing Add:* 1515 Smugglers Cove Lane Vero Beach FL 32963

JOHNSON, RONALD W
HISTORIAN, EDUCATOR
b Rockford, Ill, July, 29, 37. *Study:* Calif State Univ, San Diego, BA, 59 & MA, 63; Univ Calif, Berkeley, MA(hist art), 65 & PhD(hist art), 71. *Teaching:* Asst prof hist art, Univ Iowa, Iowa City, 70-73; prof hist art, Humboldt State Univ, Arcata, Calif, 73; vis instr hist art, Univ Calif, San Diego, 76; vis instr hist art, Univ Calif, Berkeley, 81. *Mem:* Col Art Asn Am. *Res:* Picasso's and late 19th century art; emphasizing conceptual relationships between art and poetry. *Publ:* Auth, Picaasso's old guitarist and the symbolist sensibility, Artforum, 12/74; auth, Dante Rossetti's Beata Beatrix and the new life, Art Bulletin, 12/75; auth, Poetic pathways to Dada: Marcel Duchamp & Jules Laforgue, 5/76, auth, Vincent van Gogh and the vernacular: His southern accent, 6/78 & auth, Picasso's Demoiselles d'Avignon and the theatre of the absurd, 10/80, Arts. *Mailing Add:* Dept Art Humboldt State Univ Arcata CA 95521

JOHNSON, SELINA (TETZLAFF)
MUSEOLOGIST, HISTORIAN
b New York, NY. *Study:* Hunter Col, AB(cum laude); City Col New York, MS(educ); Ctr Human Relations Studies, NY Univ, PhD(museology). *Work:* Bergen Community Mus Art & Sci, Paramus, NJ; Mus Natural Sci, Nantucket Island, Mass. *Comn:* Mem plaque for Hans Christian Andersen Madison, Bergen Mall, 59; Report on Museum Needs & Resources, 68 & Tricentennial History of Bergen County, NJ, 83, Bd Chosen Freeholders. *Exhib:* Fine Arts in Com Art, 3rd Ann Exhib, Freedom House, New York, 59; Painting & Sculpture Ann, Bergen Co Artists' Guild, 60; Photographic Art of Selina Johnson & Louis Davidson, Art Asn, Nantucket Island, Mass, 61; Books Illustrated by NJ Artists, Johnson Libr, Hackensack, NJ, 69; 25th Anniv Exhib, Bergen Community Mus, 81; Measures of Time, Bergen Mus Art & Sci, 86. *Pos:* Founder, dir & first pres, Bergen Community Mus, 56-70; dir,

Mus Natural Sci, Nantucket Island, Mass, 58-65; Bergen Co Cult & Heritage Comnr, NJ, 72-83; cur, Greater Light, Nantucket Island, 73-85, historian & photographer, formerly; biol & med illusr & freelance photographer, City Col New York & Harvard Univ, formerly. *Teaching:* Instr kinesiology & phys educ, Hunter Col, formerly; instr comp anat & biol, NY Univ & City Col New York, formerly; guest lectr landscape archit & natural sci of Nantucket Island, Columbia Univ, formerly. *Awards:* First Prize Art, 51 & First Prize Photog, 65, 67 & 69, NJ State Fedn Women's Clubs. *Bibliog:* Clifford Mische (auth), Museum in Overpeck Park, Bergen Co Park Comn, 56; Georgianne Ensign (auth), The Hunt for the Mastodon, Watts, 71; Barbara Dexter (auth), History of Bergen Community Museum, 83. *Mem:* Life mem Nantucket Hist Asn; Life mem New York Acad Sci; life mem Palisades Nature Asn; life mem Maria Mitchell Asn; life mem Bergen Community Mus. *Publ:* Auth, Creating a Community Museum, 54; Museums for Youth in the United States: Their Origins, Development and Cultural Contributions, Univ Microfilms, 62; ed, Greater Light on Nantucket, Hill House, 73; auth & illusr, Bergen County, NJ--History: The Land and Its First People, Vol I, Bd Chosen Freeholders, 83. *Mailing Add:* Madison House 445 Van Voorhis Rd Morgantown WV 26505-3439

JOHNSON, UNA E
CURATOR, WRITER
b Dayton, Iowa. *Study:* Univ Chicago, PhD, 28; Western Reserve Univ, MA, 37. *Collections Arranged:* All exhibs of prints & drawings, Brooklyn Mus, 41-68. *Pos:* Cur prints & drawings, Brooklyn Mus, 41-68, emer cur. *Awards:* Rockefeller Found Award, 52. *Publ:* Auth, Ambroise Vollard, 44 & rev ed, 77; American Prints, 1660, 50; What is a Modern Print, 56; Twentieth Century Drawings, 1900-, 2 Vols, 64 & American Prints and Printmakers, 1900-, 80; and numerous monogr on mod artists including Bonnard, Rouault, Louise Nevelson & others. *Mailing Add:* 341 W 24th St New York NY 10011

JOHNSON-ROSS, ROBYN
PAINTER
b San Francisco, Calif, Jan 1, 46. *Study:* George Washington Univ, Washington, DC, BA, 68. *Comn:* Corcoran Gallery Art, Washington, DC. *Exhib:* 10+10+10: Washington Artists 1982, Corcoran Gallery, 82; Painting & Sculpture Today, Indianapolis Mus Art, Ind, 84; Peter Miller Gallery, Chicago, 85 & 86; Wanabe Hotel Paintings, Tartt Gallery, Washington, DC & Wash Project Arts, Washington, DC, 86; Dadian Gallery, Wesley Theological Sem, Washington, DC, 90; Rosenberg Gallery, Goucher Col, Baltimore, Md, 92. *Awards:* Fel, Nat Endowment Arts, 87-88. *Media:* Oil. *Mailing Add:* 1706 Lamont St NW Washington DC 20010

JOHNSTON, BARRY WOODS
SCULPTOR
b Florence, Ala. *Study:* Ga Inst Technol, B(arch), 69; Art Students League, with Joseph De Creeft; Pa Acad Fine Arts, with Walker Hancock, Harry Rosen & Tony Greenwood; Nat Acad Fine Arts, with Michael Lantz; also studied in Italy, with Enzo Cardini & Madame Simi. *Work:* The Vatican Mus, Rome; Martin Luther King Libr, Georgetown Univ & Lutheran Church Reformation, Washington, DC; CBN Univ, Va. *Comn:* Medal, Ann Letelier Moffitt Award, Inst Policy Studies, Washington, DC; Journey to Jerusalem, US Citizens Cong, Washington, DC; lobby centerpiece, Fentress Cancer Ctr, Hillside Methodist Hosp, Waco, Tex; Sen Sparkman bust, C of C, Hartsell, Ala; Wedlock (sculpture), Lafayette Ctr, Washington, DC; Mariner, Hampton, Va; Mother & Child, Evanston, Ill. *Exhib:* One-man shows, St John's Church, 75, George Washington Univ Libr, 76, Folger Shakespeare Libr, 79, Washington, DC & City Hall, Hampton, Va, 86; Four Realists, Foundry, Georgetown, 76; Nat Sculpture Soc Ann Group Show, New York, 80-86; Martin Luther King Libr, 83; Allied Artists Am Exhib, New York, 86; Centre Int D'Arte Contemporian, Paris, France, 86; Arts Festival, Castello di Besozzo, Italy, 86; Bucca di Magra, Massa, Italy, 87. *Awards:* Stewardson Award, Pa Acad Fine Arts, 66; Second Prize for Figurative Sculpture, Ga Marble Fest, 83. *Mem:* Nat Sculpture Soc; Founder, Art For Humanity Found (pres, 78-81). *Media:* Clay, Bronze. *Publ:* Auth, articles in Sculpture Rev, winter 85-86 & spring 86, Sculptor's Int, vol 3, 84 & spring 86. *Mailing Add:* 2423 Pickwick Rd Baltimore MD 21207

JOHNSTON, PHILLIP M
CURATOR, MUSEUM DIRECTOR
b Texarkana, Tex, July 24, 44. *Study:* Baylor Univ, BA(cum laude), 66; Southern Methodist Univ, MA, 68; Univ Del, MA, 74. *Collections Arranged:* Victorian Furnishings from Armsmear and the James Goodwin House, 75, American Indian Baskets in the Wadsworth Atheneum, 76, Ancient Art of Peru: the Etherington Collection, 76, Glass from Six Centuries, 76, Art in Seventeenth Century New England (auth, catalog), 77 & Gerrit Thomas Rietveld, Designer (auth, catalog), 80, Wadsworth Atheneum, 80; Courts & Colonies: The William & Mary Style in Holland Eng & Am (co-auth, catalog), Cooper-Hewitt Mus & Carnegie Mus Art, 87- 88; Kansas City Collects Contemp Ceramics (auth, catalog), Nelson-Atkins Gallery, 89. *Pos:* Assoc cur dept decorative arts, Wadsworth Atheneum, Hartford, Conn, 73-75, cur decorative arts, 75-78, chief cur & cur decorative arts, 78-82; cur decorative arts & head antiquities, Oriental & decorative art, Carnegie Mus Art, Pittsburgh, Pa, 82-, dir, 88- *Teaching:* Instr dept English, Hannibal-LaGrange Col, Mo, 67-68 & Southern Methodist Univ, 68-71. *Res:* American silver and furniture, contemporary American ceramics. *Publ:* Auth, A discovery of Thomas Chippendale chairs in America, Connoisseur, 73; ed, English Silver: The Elizabeth B Miles Collection, Wadsworth Atheneum, 76; auth, Eighteenth and nineteenth century American furniture in the Wadsworth Atheneum, Antiques, 79; Dialogues between designer and client: furnishings proposed by Leon Maricotte to Samuel Colt in the 1850s, Winterthur Portfolio, Winter 84; The William and Mary style in New York, Antiques, 88. *Mailing Add:* Carnegie Inst Mus Art 4400 Forbes Ave Pittsburgh PA 15213

JOHNSTON, RANDY J(AMES)
CERAMIST
Study: Univ Minn, Minneapolis, BFA(studio art), 72; studied with Shoji Hamada Mashik, Japan, 75; Southern Ill Univ, Edwardsville, MFA, 90. *Work:* Dustin & Lisa Hoffman, Los Angeles; GTE Telecommunications Corp, Dallas, Tex; Univ Art Mus, Ariz State Univ, Tempe; Univ Art Mus, Univ Minn, Minneapolis; Burke Found, New York; Banff Sch Art, Alberta, Can; and others. *Exhib:* Solo shows, Viterbo Col, LaCrosse, Wis, 83, Wis Acad Sci, Arts & Lett, Madison, 87, Pro Art, St Louis, Mo, 87 & 90; Montgomery Col, Takoma Park, Md, 92; Ore Ceramic Invitational, McMinnville, 92; Manchester Inst Arts & Sci, NH, 92; and others. *Pos:* Studio, River Falls, Wis, 72-; guest cur, Col St Catherine Gallery, St Paul, Minn, 77; consult, Minneapolis Sch Art & Design, Minn, 77, St Cloud State Col, Minn, 78 & adv bd, Northern Clay Ctr, St Paul, Minn, 91. *Teaching:* Guest lectr, var univ & col, 74-92; teacher, Rochester Art Ctr, 73-74 & 76, Univ Minn, Quadna Summer Art Ctr, 76, 78 & 79, Univ Minn Studio Arts, 78-79 & Bergen Sch Art, Norway, 81; vis lectr, Univ Wis-River Falls, 85 & workshop, Univ Wis-Stout, 87; Emily Carr Sch Art, Vancouver, BC, 88; Southern Ill Univ, Edwardsville, 89; spec asst prof, Kansas City Art Inst, Mo, 92. *Awards:* Craftsmen's Apprenticeship, 78-79, Craftsmen's Fel, 78-79 & Visual Arts Fel, 90-91, Nat Endowment Arts; Individual Artist Fel, Proj Grant, Wis Art Bd, 83. *Bibliog:* Am Craft, 12/90-1/91; Fragile Blossoms Enduring Earth, 89; Warren MacKenzie, An Am Potter, 91. *Publ:* Contribr, Early Am Pottery, 77; Wood firing, Vol II, No 1, 83 & article, winter 89, Studio Potter; Between two fires, essay, Am Wood Fired Catalog, Univ Iowa, 91; Portfolio, Ceramics Monthly, 10/91. *Dealer:* Pro Art Gallery St Louis MO; Joan Farrell Collection Washington DC. *Mailing Add:* RR 1 No 234 River Falls WI 54022

JOHNSTON, RICHARD M
SCULPTOR, EDUCATOR
b Kankakee, Ill, Sept 22, 42. *Study:* El Camino Jr Col; Calif State Col, Long Beach, BA; Cranbrook Acad Art, MFA. *Work:* Weber State Col; Salt Lake Co Bar Asn; Cranbrook Acad of Art. *Comn:* Steel wall sculpture, Western Airlines, Los Angeles, 69; bronze wall sculpture, Telemation Inc, Salt Lake City, Utah, 71; gold leaf/steel sculpture, Sun Valley Ski Corp, Idaho, 71; Temple Kol Ami, Salt Lake Int Ctr. *Exhib:* Craftsman USA, Los Angeles Co Mus Art, 66; Nat Crafts Exhib, Univ NMex, 68; Inter-Mountain Biennial, Salt Lake Art Ctr, 70; 73rd Western Ann, Denver Art Mus, 71; Nat Small Sculpture & Drawing Show, San Diego State Col, 72; one-man show, Salt Lake Art Ctr, 80. *Teaching:* Prof, Univ Utah, 68- *Awards:* First Prize, Sterling Silversmiths, 68; Purchase Award, Utah Mus Fine Art, 69; Purchase Award, Salt Lake Art Ctr, 70. *Media:* Metal. *Mailing Add:* 2266 Canyon Dr Colton CA 92324

JOHNSTON, ROBERT HAROLD
ADMINISTRATOR, CRAFTSMAN
b Reading, Pa, July 1, 28. *Study:* Kutztown State Col, BS(art educ), 51; Columbia Univ, MA(fine arts & fine arts educ), 54; Pa State Univ, PhD(ceramic archaeol), 70. *Pos:* Art ed, Biblical Archaeologist, 72-; sr conserv officer, Semetic Mus, Harvard Univ; res consult, Dominican Repub, 83. *Teaching:* Vis lectr art, Grad Sch, Rutgers Univ, 54-58; asst prof art, Lock Haven State Col, Pa, 58-65, chmn & head dept, 58-70, assoc prof, 64-70; prof ceramics, Sch for Am Craftsmen, Rochester Inst Technol, 70-, dean, Col Fine & Applied Arts, 70-, dean, Inst, 82-83. *Awards:* Grant-in-aid res, Am Schs Oriental Res, 73; affil Fulbright scholar, Afghanistan, 73-74; John D Rockefeller Third Found Ceramic & Glass res grant, Afghanistan, 74. *Mem:* World Crafts Coun; Am Crafts Coun; Nat Asn Schs Art; fel Am Anthrop Asn; Am Asn Univ Profs. *Res:* Ceramic archaeology; glass and clay technology. *Publ:* Auth, The aborigines of Cawichnowane, Lock Haven Bulletin, Ser 1(2); auth, The aborigines of Cawichnowane II, Pa Archaeologist, 12/61; auth, A statistical approach to archaeology, New World Antiquity, Vol 11(11-12), Markham House Press Ltd, London, Eng; auth, A statistical analysis of 1113 weapon points from the area related to Cawichnowane, Lock Haven Bulletin, Ser 1(4); auth, The School for American Craftsmen, Handweaver & Craftsman, 3-4/72; and many others. *Mailing Add:* 61 Lime Rock Lane Rochester NY 14610

JOHNSTON, ROY E
PAINTER, HISTORIAN
b Tyrone, N Ireland, June 12, 36. *Study:* Belfast Col Art, BA & NDD, 66; Cardiff Col Art & Univ S Wales, DAE, 69; Trinity Col, Univ Dublin, PhD, 89. *Work:* Ulster Mus, Belfast, N Ireland; Hugh Lane Munic Gallery Mod Art, Dublin, Ireland; Arts Coun Great Britian, London, Eng; Munson-Williams Proctor Inst, Utica, NY; Univ Ulster, Coleraine, N Ireland. *Comn:* Posters for the environment, 70, wall relief, 76 & suite of six drawings, 82, Arts Coun N Ireland, Belfast; tapestry mural, Univ Col Galway, 73. *Exhib:* Irish Imagination, Corcoran Gallery, Washington, DC, 72; Aos Og, Musée d'Art Moderne, Paris, France, 73; Eighth Int Festival of Painting, Cagnes-sur-mer Musée, France, 76; International Connection, Round House Gallery, London, 80; Cleveland Int Drawing Biennial, Middlesbrough Art Gallery, Cleveland, UK, 83; retrospective, Hugh Lane Munic Gallery Mod Art, Dublin, 85; Contrasts, Fung Ping Shan Mus, Hong Kong, 87; Artists of Central New York, Munson-Williams Proctor Inst, Utica, NY, 89. *Teaching:* Lectr, fine art, Univ Ulster, Belfast, 69-87; prof, drawing & painting, Skidmore Col, Saratoga Springs, NY, 87- *Awards:* Carroll Prize Painting, Irish Exhib Living Art, Carroll & Co, 73; Walker Painting Award, An Oireachtas, Dublin Scott, Tallon, Walker, 78; Key Bank Prize, Cooperstown Nat, Key Bank, 88 & 89. *Bibliog:* Dorothy Walker (auth), The Intelligent Eye, Hibernia Review, 72; Dr Brian Kennedy (auth), Roy Johnston 1965-1985, Arts Coun N Ireland, 85; Cyril Barrett (auth), Roy Johnston, Art Monthly, 85. *Mem:* Col Art Asn Am; Nat Asn Sch Art & Design. *Media:* Acrylic, Oil. *Res:* School of Pont-

Aven and the Life and Work of Roderick O'Conor 1860-1940. *Publ:* Auth, Systems and Art, Introspect, 75; Sean Soully, Circa Mag, 82; Roderic O'Conor in Brittany, 84 & Roderic O'Conor: The Elusive Personality, 85, Irish Arts Review; O'Conor Gravures, Arts de L'Ouest, Rennes, 86. *Dealer:* Oliver Dowling Gallery 19 Kildare St Dublin Ireland 2. *Mailing Add:* 62 Greenfield Ave Saratoga Springs NY 12866

JOHNSTON, THOMAS ALIX
PAINTER, PRINTMAKER
b Oklahoma City, Okla, June 4, 41. *Study:* San Diego State Col, BA, 65; Univ Calif, Santa Barbara, MFA, 67; Atelier 17, Paris & Atelier Lacouriere et Frelaut, Paris, 80. *Work:* Henry Art Gallery, Univ Wash & Seattle Art Mus, Seattle; Portland Art Mus; Mod Art Mus, Kobe, Japan; Royal Collection, Riyadh, Saudi Arabia; and others. *Exhib:* One-man show, Whatcom Mus, Bellingham, Wash, 71; 52nd Biennial, Libr Cong, Washington, DC & Blackfish Gallery, Portland, 84;; NW Ann, Seattle Art Mus, 72 & 92, Evergreen State Col, 80, Wash; W Coast Prints, Univ Calgary, Alta, 75; Rochester Inst Technol, 78; Black and White Drawings by 150 Americans 1970-1980, Brooklyn Mus, 80; Davidson Gallery, Seattle, 82 & 91; Francine Seders Gallery, Seattle, 84, 86 & 87; Galerie Jean Claude Riedel, Paris, 89. *Pos:* Dir, Western Gallery, Western Washington Univ, 83-87; auth & ed, Western Gallery News, Western Wash Univ, 83-88. *Teaching:* Prof art, Western Wash Univ. *Awards:* First Place/Graphics, 14th Northern Calif Ann, Calif State Univ, Chico, 70; Purchase Award, 57th NW Ann, Seattle Art Mus, Wash, 72; Artist in Residence, Chateaux Cantenac-Brown Margaux, France, summer 93. *Media:* Intaglio, Acrylic, Oil. *Publ:* Illusr Concerning Poetry, Western Wash Univ, 73-80; The Ventriloquist, R Huff, Univ Press Va, 77; Beyond the veil: The etching of Helen Loggie, Whatcom Mus, 79. *Mailing Add:* c/o Art Dept Western Washington Univ Bellingham WA 98225

JOHNSTON, WILLIAM MEDFORD
PAINTER, EDUCATOR
b Atlanta, Ga, Mar 2, 41. *Study:* Ga State Univ, BA, 65; Fla State Univ, MFA, 67. *Work:* High Mus Art, Atlanta, Ga; Chase Manhattan Bank, New York; Mint Mus Art, Charlotte, NC; Mus Fine Art, Houston, Tex; New Orleans Mus Art, La. *Comn:* Three panel paintings (4 ft x 8ft each) & 350 graphics, Omni Int Hotel, Miami, Fla, 77. *Exhib:* High Mus Art, Atlanta, Ga, 68, 75, 79 & 88; Biennial Piedmont Painting & Sculpture, Mint Mus, Charlotte, NC; 18th Ann Drawing & Small Sculpture Show, Ball State Univ, Muncie, Ind, 72; Tex Fine Arts Asn Ann, Laguna Gloria Art Mus, Austin, 75 & 80; LaGrange Nat Competition, LaGrange Col, Ga, 74, 75, 77 & 90; From Allan to Zucker, Tex Gallery, Houston, 79; Portland Ctr Visual Arts, Ore, 80; 41st Biennial Exhib Contemp Am Painting, Corcoran Gallery, 89; 51st Ann Nat Exhib Contemp Am Painting, Four Arts, Palm Beach, Fla, 89; and others. *Teaching:* Prof painting, Ga State Univ, 67- *Awards:* Purchase Award, 10th Hunter Ann, Chattanooga Art Asn, 69; Soc of Four Arts Award, 32nd Ann Exhib of Contemp Am Painting, 70; First Prize, Greater Midwest Int Exhib IV, Cent Mo State Univ, Warrenburg, 89; Nat Endow for Painting & Works on Paper Fel, Southern Arts Fedn, 90. *Bibliog:* Clyde Burnett (auth), var rev in The Atlanta J, 72-78; John Howett (auth), Medford Johnston, Art Voices S, 1/78; John Howett (auth), The Avant-Garde: 12 in Atlanta, 79; William A Fagaly (auth), The 41st Biennial Exhibition of Contemporary American Painting, Corcoran Gallery, Washington, DC, 89. *Media:* Acrylic. *Mailing Add:* 145 15th St NE Apt 828 Atlanta GA 30361

JOHNSTON, WILLIAM RALPH
HISTORIAN, ADMINISTRATOR
b Toronto, Ont, Feb 15, 36. *Study:* Univ Toronto Trinity Col, Hon BA, 59; NY Univ Inst Fine Arts, MA, 66. *Collections Arranged:* Anatomy of a Chair: Regional Variations in 18th Century Furniture Styles, Metrop Mus, New York, 62; J W Morrice (with catalog), Montreal Mus Fine Arts, Nat Gallery Can, 68. *Pos:* Cur, Robert Lehman Collection, New York, 64-66; gen cur, Montreal Mus Fine Arts, 66-67; asst dir, Walters Art Gallery, 68-85, assoc dir, 85- *Awards:* Fel, Am Wing, Metrop Mus Art, 63-64. *Mem:* Am Ceramic Circle; Victorian Soc Am; Am Fedn Arts. *Res:* 18th & 19th century painting & decorative arts. *Publ:* Coauth, Japonisme, Cleveland Mus; auth, The Nineteenth Century Paintings in The Walters Art Gallery, Baltimore, 82; coauth, Alfred Jacob Miller, Artist on the Oregon Trail, Fort Worth, 82; Masterpieces of Ivory from the Walters Art Gallery, 85; Alfred Sisley, London, 92; and others. *Mailing Add:* Walters Art Gallery 600 N Charles St Baltimore MD 21201

JOHNSTON, YNEZ
PAINTER, SCULPTOR
b Berkeley, Calif, May 12, 20. *Study:* Univ Calif, Berkeley, MFA, 46. *Work:* Mus Mod Art, Whitney Mus Am Art, Metrop Mus Art, New York; Hirshhorn Mus and Sculpture Garden, Washington, DC; Milwaukee Art Ctr, Wis; plus others. *Comn:* Etchings, Int Graphic Arts Soc, New York; drawings, Washington Gallery Mod Art, Washington, DC, 65; etchings, Roten Galleries, Baltimore, Md, 66-67; etching, Los Angeles Co Mus, 81. *Exhib:* One-man retrospective, San Francisco Mus Art, 67; Mitsukoshi Galleries, Tokyo, Japan, 77; Mekler Gallery, Los Angeles, 72, 74, 77, 82, 84 & 88; Worthington Gallery, Chicago, 83, 86 & 88; Retrospective Exhib Paintings, Sculptures, Prints 1950-1992, Fresno Art Mus, Calif, 92; and others. *Teaching:* Instr etching, Colorado Springs Fine Arts Ctr, 54-56 & Univ Judaism, 67; instr painting, Calif State Univ, Los Angeles, 66-67, 69 & 72-73; instr, Otis Art Inst of Parsons Sch of Design, Los Angeles, 78-81; artist-in-residence, Fullerton Col, 82. *Awards:* Guggenheim, 52; Tamarind Fel, 66; Nat Endowment Arts, 82 & 86. *Bibliog:* Jules Langsner (auth), Ynez Johnston, Arts & Archit, 51; Theodore F Wolff (auth), Christian Sci Monitor, 86; John Berry (auth), View from the wind palace, Mankind Mag, 75. *Media:* Oil, Sculpture. *Dealer:* Tom d'Alessandro, Tomlyn Gallery, Tequesta, FL; Eva Maria Worthington 620 N Michigan St Chicago IL 60611. *Mailing Add:* 579 Crane Blvd Los Angeles CA 90065

JOHNSTONE, MARK
PAINTER, CURATOR
b St Louis, Mo, 1953. *Study:* Colo Col, BA, 75; Univ Southern Calif, MFA, 82. *Work:* Calif Mus Photog, Univ Calif, Riverside; Crocker Art Mus, Sacramento, Calif; Centro Documentazioni Arti Visive E Archivo/Rosamilia, San Giorgio, Italy; Biblioteque Nat, Paris, France. *Exhib:* One-man show, Vista: Some Landscape Observations, Calif Mus Photog, Riverside, 81; Ten Year Selection, Martin Schweig Gallery, St Louis, Mo, 87; Recent Work, Min Gallery, Tokyo, Japan, 88; and others. *Collections Arranged:* Eileen Cowin and John Divola, Recent Work, No Fancy Titles, La Jolla Mus Contemp Art, Calif traveling, 85; Frames of Time and Context, 87 & Security Pacific Corp, Los Angeles, Calif, 88-92; Joe Deal: Southern California Photographs, 1976-86, Los Angeles Munic Art Gallery, traveling, 92. *Pos:* Contrib ed, Artweek, 77-; Los Angeles corresp, Afterimage, 81-85; series content adv, The Photographic Vision, KOCE-TV PBS, Huntington Beach, Calif, 83-84; vpres, cur exhibs, Security Pac Corp, Los Angeles, 88-92. *Teaching:* Vis prof photog, Colo Univ, Colorado Springs, summers 79-83; lectr hist photog, Calif State Univ, Fullerton, 81-88. *Bibliog:* Colin Gardner (auth), Calendar-Galleries, Los Angeles Times, 9/6/85; Suzanne Muchnic (auth), A focus on creativity, Los Angeles Times, 3/1/87; Chuck Nicholson (auth), Exploring Culture & Photography, Artneck, 4/29/89. *Media:* Miscellaneous Media. *Res:* Contemporary photography & art. *Publ:* Auth, Landscape: Perceiving the land as image introd, New Landscapes, 81 & The photographs of Larry Burrows, In: Observations: Essays on Documentary Photography, 84, Friends of Photog; Photography, computers, and the man in the stands, Photo-Communique, 9/84; Melting the Material World, Fotokritik, 6/86. *Mailing Add:* 8121 West Blvd Inglewood CA 90305

JOLLEY, DONAL CLARK
PAINTER
b Zion Nat Park, Utah, Oct 20, 33. *Study:* Brigham Young Univ, BS, 59; with Glen Turner, J Roman Andrus. *Work:* First Nat Bank Nev, Reno; San Bernardino County Mus, Redlands, Calif; Aerospace Corp, El Segundo, Calif; Church of Jesus Christ of Latter-Day Saints, Salt Lake City; Brigham Young Univ; Smithsonian Inst. *Exhib:* One-man shows, Brigham Young Univ, 75 & 81 & Univ Nev, Reno, 78; Watercolor West Ann, Riverside Art Ctr Mus, Calif, 75-81; Traditional Artists, San Bernardino Co Mus, Redlands, 76-79 & Fine Arts Inst, 78-79 & 91; Kimball Art Ctr, Park City, Utah, 86; Mid Am Indian Ctr, Wichita, Kans, 90. *Pos:* Jr illusr, Space Technol Lab, Redondo, Calif, 60-61; sr illusr, Aerospace Corp, El Segundo, Calif, 61-71. *Teaching:* Instr painting, San Bernardino Valley Col, 73-81. *Awards:* Brand XII Award, 83; Riverside Centennial Award, 83; Gold medal, 90 & Bronze, 92, Am Indian & Cowboy Artists; and others. *Bibliog:* Fred Kiemel (auth), Making a presentation brochure self-promotion, Camera Life Mag, 5/80; Peggy & Harold Samuels (coauths), Contemporary Western Artists, 82; Patricia Dunsmore (auth), Elan Mag, 11/88. *Mem:* Nat Watercolor Soc; Watercolor West (vpres, 78 & 79); Am Indian & Cowboys Artists. *Media:* Watercolor, Acrylic. *Dealer:* Studio Gallery 26375 Apache Tr Rimforest CA 92378. *Mailing Add:* 26375 Apache Trail Rimforest CA 92378

JONAITIS, ALDONA
HISTORIAN, ADMINISTRATOR
b New York, NY, Nov 27, 48. *Study:* State Univ NY, Stony Brook, BA, 69; Columbia Univ, with Douglas Fraser, MA, 72, PhD, 77. *Exhib:* Chiefly Feasts: The Enduring Kwakiutl Potlatch, Am Mus Nat Hist, 91. *Pos:* Vpres pub progrs, Am Mus Nat Hist, 90- *Teaching:* Prof art, State Univ NY, Stony Brook, 88-90. *Awards:* Chiefly Feasts, Winner, Am Asn Mus Curs Comt Award for Excellence in Exhib, 91. *Mem:* Native Am Art Studies Asn; Appraisers Asn Am; Am Asn Mus. *Res:* Northwest Coast Indian art. *Publ:* Auth, Tlingit Halibut Hooks, Am Mus Natural Hist, 81; Creations of mystics and philosophers, Am Indian Cult & Res J, 81; Art of the Northern Tlingit, Univ Wash Press, 86; From the Land of Totem Poles: The Northwest Coast Indian Art Collection at the American Museum of Natural History, Univ Wash Press, 88; A Wealth of Thought: Fran Boas on Native American Art, Univ Wash Press, 93; Chiefly Feasts: The Enduring Kwakiutl Potlatch, Univ Wash Press, 91. *Mailing Add:* 428 Greenwich St Central Park W 79th St New York NY 10013

JONAS, JOAN
VIDEO ARTIST, CONCEPTUAL ARTIST
b New York, NY, July 13, 36. *Study:* Mount Holyoke Col, Mass; Boston Mus Sch, Mass; Columbia Univ, New York, MFA, 65. *Work:* Mus Mod Art, New York. *Exhib:* The Video Show, Serpentine Gallery, London, 75; Van Abbe Mus, Eindhoven, 75; Mus Mod Art, New York, 75; Assoc Students, Univ Calif, Los Angeles, 75; one-woman shows, Walker Art Ctr, Minneapolis, Minn, 74, Anthology Film Archives, New York, 75 & Inst Contemp Arts, Los Angeles, 75; Mus Fine Arts, Montreal, 80; Volcano Saga, Whitney Mus, Mus Mod Art, Walker Art Ctr & Carnegie Inst, 85-88; Likor Fabric, Kunstwerk, Berlin, 91-92; Artists Mus, Lodz, Poland, 91-92. *Pos:* Guest lectr, Yale Univ, New Haven, Conn, 74, Princeton Univ, 74 & Minneapolis Col Art, Minn; vis artist, Otis Art Inst, Los Angeles, Calif, 75, Minneapolis Col Art & Design, 79, Wright State Univ, Dayton, Ohio, 80 & Long Beach State Col, Calif, 80. *Teaching:* Assoc prof, Hunter Col, 85-88; tutor, Rijksakademie, Amsterdam. *Awards:* Creative Artists Pub Serv Prog, 72, 73 & 75; Nat Endowment Arts Grant, 73 & 75; Maya Dern Award in Video, Am Film Int, 88; Rockefeller Award, 90. *Bibliog:* Wulf Herzgenrath (auth), Video Ein Neue Medium in der Bildenden Kunst, Mag Kunst, Mainz, 7/74; Marcus Guterich (auth), Art Presented According to the Evolution Principle, Kunst Kunst Kunst, Cologne, Ger, 74; Howard Junker (auth), Joan Jonas: The mirror staged, Art Am, 2/81. *Media:* Mirrors; Videotape. *Publ:* Auth, Organic Honey's visual telepathy, Drama Rev, New York, 72; coauth, Show Me Your Dance, Art & Artists, London, 10/73. *Dealer:* Leo Castelli Gallery 420 W Broadway New York NY 10013; Electronic Arts Intermix 536 Broadway New York NY. *Mailing Add:* 112 Mercer St New York NY 10012

JONES, BEN
PAINTER, SCULPTOR
b Paterson, NJ, May 26, 42. *Study:* Sch Visual Arts; NY Univ, MA; Pratt Inst, MFA; Univ Sci & Technol, Kumasi, Ghana, New Sch Social Research. *Work:* Newark Mus, NJ; Howard Univ; Studio Mus, New York, NY; Johnson Publ, Chicago. *Exhib:* Mus Mod Art; Studio Mus in Harlem; Black World Arts Festival, Lagos, Nigeria; Newark Mus, 77; Fisk Univ, 77; Bishop Col, Dallas, Tex, 78; solo shows, Newark Mus & NJ State Mus, 84; group shows, Gallery 62, New York, 83 & Dallas Conv Ctr, 85; and others. *Pos:* Art dir, Urban League Essex Co Exhib, 72. *Teaching:* Prof fine arts, Jersey City State Col, 68- *Awards:* Nat Endowment Arts, 74-75; NJ Arts Coun Grant, 77-78 & 83-84; Delta Sigma Theta-Excellence in the Arts, 85; and others. *Bibliog:* Articles, Art Am, 71; articles, NY Times, 72 & 82-85. *Mem:* World Print Coun; Nat Conf Artists. *Res:* African art and culture in WAfrica and Paris, France. *Mailing Add:* Art Dept Jersey City State Col Jersey City NJ 07305

JONES, CALVIN B(ELL)
PAINTER, MURALIST
b Chicago, Ill, Jan 7, 34. *Study:* Art Inst Chicago; Univ Chicago. *Work:* Inst Positive Educ, Southside Community Art Ctr; Motorola Corp, Scottsdale, Ariz & Chicago, Ill; Beefeater Collection, Detroit. *Comn:* Another Times Voice, Chicago Art Coun, 79; Ceremonies of Heritage Now, Nat Endowment Fine Arts, Chicago, 80; Builders of the Cultural Present, Chicago Coun Fine Arts, 81; Bright Moments-Memories Future, New Regal Theater, 87; Triumphant Celebration, Nat Black Art Festival, 90; and others. *Exhib:* Spokane World Fair, Black Arts Pavilion, Spokane, 75; Int Festac, Western Zone Pavilion, Lagos, Nigeria, 77; Black Esthetics, Mus Sci & Indust, Chicago, 78 & 87; Isobel Neal Gallery Ltd, Chicago, 87 & 88; Chicago Int, Art Expos, 90; Bomani Gallery, San Francisco, Calif, 92. *Awards:* Builders Award, Third World Press, 78 & 87; Arron Douglas Muralist Award, Nat Conf Artists, 79 & 83; Kappa Alpa PSI Achievement Award in Arts, 88. *Mem:* Nat Conf Artists. *Media:* Oil, Mixed Media. *Mailing Add:* 925 W Huron No 103 Chicago IL 60622

JONES, CARTER R(UTHVEN), JR
SCULPTOR
b Mount Kisco, NY, Mar 6, 45. *Study:* Sch Visual Arts, with Edward Giobbi, 64-65; Boston Mus Sch, dipl, 69; pvt study in Paris, 69-71. *Comn:* 25 portraits (sculpted), comn in Boston, New York & Paris. *Exhib:* Equitable Gallery, New York, 80-83. *Teaching:* Instr human & animal anatomy, Sch Visual Arts, New York, 80-82. *Awards:* Art Dirs Award, Art Dirs Am, 79; Youth Award, Nat Sculpture Soc, 80; and others. *Mem:* Nat Sculpture Soc; Soc Artists Anatomists; Am Medallic Sculpture Asn (pres, formerly). *Media:* Clay, Glass. *Mailing Add:* 285 Lafayette St 6th fl New York NY 10012-3324

JONES, CHARLOTT ANN
EDUCATOR, MUSEUM DIRECTOR
b Jonesboro, Ark, May 27, 27. *Study:* Col St Scholastica, BA, 62; NTex State Univ, MS, 70; Pa State Univ, PhD, 78. *Collections Arranged:* Anuskiewicz Silkscreen Prints, 83, Rauschenberg Purina Chow Prints, 83 & Anuskiewicz, Judd, Marisol Prints, 83, Stephens Collection; The Figure and Other Paintings, 83; Paintings and Ceramics, 83. *Pos:* Dir, Mus Ark State Univ 83-; Cur Nat Mus Women Arts, Ark. *Teaching:* Dir children's art, Charlott Jones Sch Art, Jonesboro, Ark, 72-; assoc prof art, Ark State Univ, Jonesboro, 75-90. *Mem:* Nat Art Educ Asn; Ark Art Educ; Am Assoc Mus; Arkansas Women in Higher Education; Ark Mus Asn. *Res:* Free will in art making. *Publ:* Auth, A sister considers chastity, Am, 65; contribr, American Catholics, Am Press, 66; auth, The wellspring of Dylan, English J, 66; Women and art, Delta Kappa Gamma Bulletin, 82; contribr, Gifted and Talented in Art Education (monogr), Nat Art Educ Asn, 83. *Mailing Add:* Arkansas State Univ Mus State University AR 72467

JONES, DAVID LEE
PAINTER, SCULPTOR
b Columbus, Ohio, Feb 26, 48. *Study:* Kansas City Art Inst, BFA, 70; Univ Calif, Berkeley, Marion Davies Fel, 72, MFA, 73; studio asst to Peter Voulkos, 70-72. *Work:* San Francisco Mus Art; Univ Art Mus, Berkeley; DeSaisset Mus & Art Gallery, Univ Santa Clara, Calif; Oakland Mus, Calif. *Exhib:* Recent Acquisitions, Univ Mus, Berkeley, 73; one-man shows, Soc Encouragement Comtemp Art, San Francisco Mus Art, 74 & Michael Walls Gallery, New York, 75; Whitney Biennial Am Painting & Sculpture, Whitney Mus Art, New York, 75; Calif Painting & Sculpture--the Mod Era, San Francisco Mus Art & Nat Collection Fine Arts, Washington, DC, 76-77; New Bay Area Painting & Sculpture (cataloged), Calif State Univ, Northridge, 82; Braunstein Quay Gallery, San Francisco, 84, 87, 91 (catalog) & 92. *Awards:* Soc Encouragement Contemp Art Grant, 74; Individual Artists Grant, Nat Endowment Arts, 74. *Bibliog:* Ellen Lubell (auth), David Jones, Art Mag, 6/74; Al Frankenstein (auth), numerous reviews in San Francisco Chronicle & Examiner. *Media:* Miscellaneous Media. *Mailing Add:* c/o Braunstein Gallery 250 Sutter St San Francisco CA 94102

JONES, DOUG (DOUGLAS MCKEE)
PAINTER, DEALER
b Sewell, Chile, Oct 16, 29; US citizen. *Study:* San Diego Fine Arts & Crafts; San Diego State Col; Los Angeles Art Ctr Col Design, grad; also with Lorser Feitelson, Audubon Tyler, Leon Franks, Sergei Bongart, Harley Brown & Richard Schmid. *Comn:* Portraits, Mayor Charles Dail, San Diego & Mayor Kiyoshi Nakarai, Yokahama, San Diego Chap, Am Inst Architects, 63; 43 portraits, Int Aerospace Hall Fame, San Diego, 64-72; portrait, Gen Claire Chenault, Flying Tigers Asn, 71; portrait, Marie Winzer, Scripps Hosp; and others. *Pos:* Owner & dir, The Jones Gallery, 64- *Awards:* Merit Award, New York Portrait Club, 79. *Mem:* Int Soc Appraisers; Am Soc Appraisers; Am Portrait Soc. *Media:* Oil, Pastel. *Specialty:* Paintings and sculpture by distinguished 19th and 20th century American artists. *Publ:* Auth, article, Southland Artist Mag & illusr cover. *Mailing Add:* The Jones Gallery 1264 Prospect St La Jolla CA 92037

JONES, EDWARD POWIS
PAINTER, PRINTMAKER
b New York, NY, Jan 8, 19. *Study:* Harvard Univ; Art Students League; Acad Ranson, Paris. *Work:* Metrop Mus Art & Mus Mod Art, New York; Corcoran Gallery, Washington, DC; Philadelphia Mus Art; Brooklyn Mus; and others. *Exhib:* Modern Religious Prints, Mus Mod Art Circulating Exhib, 63; Tokyo Print Biennial, Japan, 68; New York World Trade Ctr, 75; Vassar Col, 78; PS 1, 81; Bks & Co, 83; Mead Mus, 83; Marcuse Pfieffer, 85; and others. *Teaching:* Instr art, Loyola Sch, New York, 70-72. *Mem:* Philadelphia Print Club; Munic Art Soc; Artists Equity Asn; Fel Pierpont Morgan Libr (chmn coun, 72). *Media:* Oil, Watercolor; Photo-copier, Etching. *Publ:* Life is Precarious, 88. *Mailing Add:* 925 Park Ave New York NY 10028

JONES, ELIZABETH A B (MRS LUDWIG GLAESER)
SCULPTOR, MEDALIST
b Montclair, NJ, May 31, 35. *Study:* Vassar Col, BA, 57; Art Students League, 58-60; Scuola Arte Medaglia, Rome, Italy, 62-64. *Comn:* Gold medallion, Pope John Paul II, gift of Ital State to Pope, 79; bronze relief, Sabagh Mem, Am Univ Hosp, Beirut, 79; bronze sculpture (multiple), Female Head, Res Lab Inauguration, Revlon Corp, New York, 83; portrait gold medal, Nelson A Rockefeller Ann Pub Serv Award, 88; gold medal, Sloan-Presbyterian Hosp Women, New York, 90; and many others. *Exhib:* Fedn Int Medaille FIDEM, Rome, Madrid, Paris, Athens, Helsinki, Lisbon, Colorado Springs, London, 63-92; solo shows, Tiffany & Co, New York, Houston, Los Angeles, Chicago & San Francisco, 66-68, Univ Md, 81; Smithsonian Inst, Washington & Nat Sculpture Soc, New York, 71, 78 & 88; retrospective, Vassar Col, 82 & Ital Mint, Rome, 89; Tyler Sch Art, Rome, 82. *Pos:* Chief Sculptor-Engraver, US Mint, 81-90. *Awards:* Outstanding Sculptor of the Year, Am Numismatic Asn, 72; Louis Bennet Award, Nat Sculpture Soc, 78; Int Coin of the Year Award, Numismatic News, 83, 84 & 87. *Bibliog:* Velia Johnson (auth), Dieci Anni di Studi Medaglistica, Milan, 79; Giulio Andreotti (preface), Jones-Della Zecca di Roma alla United States Mint (retrospective exhib catalog), Rome, 89; David Bowers (auth), Commemorative Coins of the United States-A Complete Encyclopaedia, Wolfeboro, NH, 91; and many articles in Coin World, Numismatic News, Medaglia & other mags & newspapers in the US & Italy. *Mem:* Fel Am Numismatic Asn; Fedn Int Medaille; Ital Soc Medalists; Am Medallic Sculpture Asn (bd mem). *Media:* Bronze, Precious Metals; Plaster. *Publ:* Contribr, Medals and Coins, Medallic Sculpture, No 5, New York, 89; Reflections on the Gold Coinage of the Twentieth Century, Am Numismatic Soc, COAC Proceedings, No 6, New York, 90. *Mailing Add:* 250 S 17th St Philadelphia PA 19103

JONES, FRANKLIN REED
PAINTER, WRITER
b Needham, Mass, May 18, 21. *Work:* Mus Art, Sci & Indust, Bridgeport, Conn; Conn Audubon Soc, Fairfield; Monarch Capitol Insurance co, Springfield, Mass; Blue Cross Blue Shield Hq, Pittsburgh, Pa. *Exhib:* Invitational Exhib, Univ Utah, 76; Am Watercolor Soc, New York, 77; De Cordova Mus, Lincoln, Mass, 77; Berkshire Mus, Pittsfield, Mass, 77; Ellsworth Nat Exhib, Simsbury, Conn, 77; and others. *Pos:* Asst to dir, Famous Artists Sch, 58-74. *Teaching:* Instr painting, Famous Artists Sch, Westport, Conn, 53-58. *Awards:* Award of Excellence, Ellsworth Gallery, Simsbury Cult Comt, 77; Privet Prize, Adirondack Nat Exhib, 83 & 84; Cert of Merit, 27th Ann Nat Exhib, Soc Illus, 85; and others. *Bibliog:* Fred Whitaker (auth), The Paintings of Franklin Jones, Am Artist Mag, 66. *Mem:* Am Watercolor Soc, Dolphin Fel. *Media:* Acrylic, Watercolor. *Publ:* Contribr, Acrylic Watercolor Painting, 70 & Complete Guide to Acrylic Painting, 71, Watson-Guptill; auth, The Pleasure of Painting, 75 & Painting Nature: Solving Landscape Problems, 78, North Light; illusr, Gray's Sporting J, 77. *Mailing Add:* PO Box 146 Kent CT 06757

JONES, FREDERICK
PRINTMAKER, COMPUTER GRAPHICS ARTIST
b Llanymymech, Wales, Mar 6, 40. *Study:* Cardiff Col Art, Wales; Univ Pittsburgh; Univ Wis-Madison; print workshop, London & Atelier 17, Paris. *Work:* Lakeview Ctr for Arts, Peoria, Ill; Brit Mus, London; Victoria & Albert Mus, London; Krannert Mus, Univ Ill; Southern Ill Univ, Carbondale. *Comn:* Large three part drawing, Ill State Libr, 92. *Exhib:* Int Print Biennial, Seoul, Korea, 71; Mid-Am Exhib, Montreal, Can, 71; Nat Image on Paper Show, Springfield, Ill, 72; Nat Print & Drawing Show, Macomb, 75; Hearland Painters Exhib, Bloomington Art Ctr, Ill, 92. *Teaching:* Lectr design drawing, Chester Col Art, Eng, 66-68; prof printmaking, Western Ill Univ, 68-, gallery dir, 69-71. *Awards:* Painting Award, Container Corp Am, 70; Best of Show, Tri-State Exhib, Muscatine, Iowa, 73; Purchase Award, Ill State Mus, 74. *Bibliog:* Mack Stegmaier (auth), Fred Jones, Am Artist, 2/88. *Media:* Mixed. *Dealer:* J Rosenthal Fine Arts 230 W Superior Chicago IL 60610; Peona Art Guild 1831 N Knoxville Peona IL 61603. *Mailing Add:* c/o Dept Art Western Ill Univ Macomb IL 61455

JONES, GEORGE BOBBY
PAINTER, VIDEO ARTIST
b Louisville, Ky, Oct 30, 46. *Study:* Syracuse Univ with Jim Ridlon, Gary Trento, BFA, 72, with Dr Larry Bakke, MFA, 73; New York Univ, with Howard Conant, Joe Zucker, David Ecker, Shalom Gorewitz & H N Han. *Work:* Herbert F Johnson Mus Art, Cornell Univ; Cayuga Mus Art, Auburn,

NY; Springfield Col Art Gallery; Noyles Art Mus; Antioch Art Gallery, Ohio; and others. *Comn:* Wall mural, Lambros Brothers, Inc, Huntington, WVa, 75; cover design, Options Mag, Fla, 85; Picasso photo montage, Everson Mus, Syracuse, NY, 86. *Exhib:* Invitational, Huntington Art Mus, Hungtington, WVa, 76; Tweed Juried Exhibition, Tweed Art Mus, Duluth, Minn, 77; Hudson River Mus, Yonkers, NY, 79; Schacham Art Gallery, New York, 79; East Hampton Nat Juried Exhib, 81; Toronto Int, 88; Intermedia Thorpe Mus; and many others. *Pos:* Artist & illusr, US Air Force, 64-68. *Teaching:* Asst prof art, Marshall Univ, WVa, 74-76 & Thomas Aquinas Col, New York, 83- *Awards:* First place painting, Rome Int Juried, 63; first place mixed, Westchester Juried Show, 84; video grant, The Kitchen, New York, 75. *Bibliog:* Art in the Eighties, Gallery Guide, 80. *Mem:* Col Art Asn; New York Artists Guild; Am Asn Univ Prof. *Media:* All, Synaesthetic. *Publ:* Auth, Synaesthetic Process Thru Film, Central New Yorker, 72; Characteristics of Multi-Sensory Artists Working in Contemp Visual Arts, UMI Press, 90. *Dealer:* Alan Brown Art Gallery 40 E Hartsdale St Westchester NY. *Mailing Add:* Five N Hudson St Chester NY 10918

JONES, HAROLD HENRY
ADMINISTRATOR, PHOTOGRAPHER
b Morristown, NJ, Sept 29, 40. *Study:* Newark Sch Fine & Indust Arts, dipl, 63; Md Inst Art, BFA, 65; Univ NMex, MFA, 72. *Work:* George Eastman House, Rochester, NY; Univ Art Mus, Univ NMex. *Exhib:* Mus Mod Art, New York, 70; An Exhib: About Self Portraits, Northlight Gallery, Ariz State Univ, 78; The Hand Colored Photog, Philadelphia Col Art, 79; Document Competition, Calif Inst Arts, 79; Attitudes: Photog in the 1970's, Santa Barbara Mus Art, 79; Views of Am, Mus Mod Art, New York, 79; The West Show, Joseph Gross Gallery, Univ Ariz, 79; and many other group & one-man exhibs. *Pos:* Assoc cur, George Eastman House, 70-71; founding dir, Light Gallery, 71-75; founding dir, Ctr Creative Photog, Univ Ariz, 75-77; coordr photog prog, Univ Ariz, Tucson, 77. *Teaching:* Assoc prof art hist, Queens Col, 74-75, Univ Ariz, 77-83. *Awards:* Nat Endowment Arts Photogr Fel, 77. *Mem:* Soc Photog Educ (bd mem, 71-75). *Res:* Aspects of the history of photography. *Collection:* Contemporary photography and related material. *Publ:* Contribr photog, Artweek, 1/78 & 8/78, Contemp Calif Photog, 78, Am Photogr, 8/78 & House & Garden, 1/79. *Mailing Add:* Art Dept Univ Ariz Tucson AZ 85721

JONES, HENRY WANTON
PAINTER, SCULPTOR
b Waterloo, Que, May 11, 25. *Study:* Sir George Williams Sch Art; Montreal Sch Fine Arts, dipl; studied with Dr Arthur Lismer, Gordon Weber & Jacques de Tonnancour. *Work:* McMichael Collection, Kleinburg, Ont; Concordia Col, Montreal; Can Dept External Affairs, Ottawa; Univ New Brunswick, Sackville; Winnipeg Art Gallery, Man. *Comn:* 32-foot high sculpture, reinforced fiberglass & steel, Can Dept Pub Works, for Hull, Que, 72-76. *Exhib:* Solo exhibs, Montreal Mus Fine Art, 58, Winnipeg Mus, Man, 60 & Toronto Mus, 63; retrospective, Concordia Univ, Montreal, 72; Montreal Mus Fine Art, 62 & 63; Musee d'Art Contemporain, Montreal, 70; Musee Rodin, Paris, 70. *Teaching:* Instr painting & drawing, Montreal Mus Fine Arts, 60-67; assoc prof sculpture & drawing, Concordia Univ, 68-88. *Awards:* Jesse Dow Award, Montreal Mus Spring Show, 62; First Prize, Can Group Painters, Montreal Mus, 63; Can Coun Fel, 68 & 72. *Media:* Oil. *Publ:* Le Collectionneur, Spring & Summer 91. *Dealer:* Kastel Gallery 1366 Greene Ave Montreal PQ Canada. *Mailing Add:* 164 Christieville Rd St Sauveur Des Monts Quebec PQ J0R 1R7 Canada

JONES, HERB (LEON HERBERT), JR
PAINTER, PRINTMAKER
b Norfolk, Va, Mar 25, 23. *Study:* William & Mary Col; Univ delle Arti, Dipl Di Merito, 81. *Work:* Univ Va, Charlottesville; NC Nat Bank, Raleigh; Libr Cong, Washington, DC; Chrysler Mus at Norfolk; State Univ NY, Buffalo; and others. *Comn:* 3 Major paintings, Noland Co, Chesapeake, Va, 79; print ward room, USS Dwight D Eisenhower & USS John F Kennedy, 79; print ed, Ducks Unlimited, 81; painting & print ed, Va Mus Marine Sci, 86; Original & Print ed, Luclus J Kellam Jr, Chesapeake Bay, Bridge Tunnel. *Exhib:* Art Buyers Caravan Exhib, Atlanta, Ga, 82; Harborfest, Norfolk, Va, 82-92; one-man shows, Virginia Beach Maritime Hist Mus, 83, Va Mus Marine Sci, 86, 87, Surrey Border Lions Int Club Exhib, Eng, 90 & Norview Lions Int Club Exhib, Norfolk, Va, 91; Mobile Mus, Ala & traveling, 83; Colonial Wildfowl Festival, Williamsburg, Va, 83; Petersburg Area Art League, 90; and other group and one-man shows. *Pos:* One of 100 leaders chosen by US News & World Report to select The Best of America for special issue. *Awards:* First Place Award, 89, Three Awards of Excellence, 89, Painting Industries of the Virginias; First & second Place Awards, Chincoteague Easter Art Festival Watercolor Competition, 89; Great Citizen Hampton Rds, Cox Cable Television, 91; and others. *Bibliog:* Barclay Sheaks (auth), Drawing & Painting the Natural Environment, Davis Publ, 74; conservation & art film, WTVZ-TV, 79; History of international art & profile of contemporary artist, Academie Italia, 81 & World Art Guide, 82-86; articles, Tidewater Virginian, Pace Map, Lifestyle Mag, & Metro Mag; and others. *Mem:* Tidewater Artist Asn; Nat Soc of Arts & Lit; Corresp Academie Europeene des Sci des Arts et Lettres, Paris, France. *Media:* Egg Tempera, Watercolor. *Publ:* Illusr (covers), Va Wildlife Mag, 64-68; and others. *Mailing Add:* 238 Beck St Norfolk VA 23503

JONES, HOWARD WILLIAM
PAINTER, SCULPTOR
b Ilion, NY, June 20, 22. *Study:* Toledo Univ; Columbia Univ; Syracuse Univ, BFA, 48, Cranbrook Acad Art, 53. *Work:* Jewish Mus, New York; Walker Art Ctr; Albright-Knox Mus; Milwaukee Art Inst; St Louis Art Mus. *Comn:* Time Columns: The Sound of Light (wall of light & sound), Whitney Mus Am Art, 68; Retinal Bypass I (sound environment), NJ State Mus, Trenton, 75; Retinal Bypass II (sound environment), Brooks Mem Art Gallery, 77. *Exhib:* Light, Motion, Space, Walker Art Ctr, 67 & Mus Contemp Art, Chicago, 68; solo exhibs, Electric Gallery, Toronto, 71, St Louis Art Mus, 73, Nelson-Atkins Mus, 73, Wadsworth Atheneum, 74 & Forbes Found Mus, 76; Recent Media--Ten Years, Brooks Mem Art Gallery, 77; Art of the Space Era, Huntsville Mus Art, Von Braun Civic Ctr, 78; Soundings, Neuberger Mus, State Univ NY, Purchase, 81-82; Pulse 2, Univ Art Mus, Santa Barbara, Calif, 90; Pulse, Edwin Ulrich Mus Art, Wichita State Univ, Kans, 92; Photons: Phonons: Electrons, Jacksonville Art Mus, Fla, 91. *Teaching:* Instr painting & design, Tulane Univ, 51-54; asst prof, Fla State Univ, 54-57; prof multi-media, Wash Univ, 57-89. *Awards:* Graham Found Fel & Grant, 66-67; New Talent: USA, Art in Am, 66-67; Nat Endowment Arts Fel & Grant, 77. *Bibliog:* Ralph Coe (auth), Post pop possibilities: Howard Jones, Art Int, 1/66 & Breaking the sound barrier, Art News Mag, summer 71; Nat Endowment Arts (producer), Artist in America: Howard Jones (film), Nat Endowment Arts, Corp Pub Broadcasting, 71; Udo Kulterman (auth), Indeterminacy and Light: Unknown Paintings by Howard Jones from the Early 60's, Avant Guarde Mag, No 6, summer 92. *Media:* Sound, Light. *Mailing Add:* PO Box 307 Arcadia MO 63621

JONES, JAMES EDWARD
PAINTER, PRINTMAKER
b Paducah, Ky, Jan 27, 37. *Study:* Philadelphia Col Art, with Henry Pitz, Benton Spruance & Jerome Kaplan, dipl(illus), 60, fel, 56-61, BFA, 61; Univ Pa, with Barnett Newman, Angelo Seveili, David Smith, Richard Stankiewicz & James Van Dyke, MFA, 62. *Work:* Newark Pub Libr, NJ; McDonosh Sch, Md; Dennison Univ; Smith Mason Gallery; and others in England, Monaco, Paris & Logos, Nigeria. *Comn:* Prints, Heritage Mus, Baltimore, Md. *Exhib:* 16th & 18th Area Exhib, Baltimore Mus Art, 63-64; Corcoran Mus Art, 64; Baltimore Co Campus, Univ Md, 79; Smith Mason Gallery, Washington, DC, 79, 80 & 82; Morgan State Univ, 79; Univ Md, Eastern Shore, 83; Morgan State Univ, 83; Last Stop Gallery, Richmond, Va; Burkett Gallery, Md, 88; Senoje Gallery, Baltimore, 90; Morgan State Univ Ann Fac Show, 90, 91 & 92. *Pos:* Dir art gallery, Senoje Consortium, Baltimore, 90-91, exec dir, 91-92. *Teaching:* From assoc prof to prof art educ, painting & printmaking, drawing & visual arts, Morgan State Univ, 62-; instr, Dundalk Community Col, 77-78. *Awards:* Stewart Art Award, NJ State, 56; Univ Pa Fel & Thorton Oakley Creative Achievement Award, 62; Morgan State Univ Grant, 63-68; Huntsville Mus Art, Huntsville Ala Invitational, 80. *Mem:* Jazz Heritage Soc. *Media:* Oil, Encaustic; Engraving, Lithography. *Dealer:* Mirida Rapp Gallery Louisville KY; Print Consortium Kansas City MO. *Mailing Add:* 2930 Silver Hill Ave Baltimore MD 21207

JONES, JOHN PAUL
PAINTER, PRINTMAKER
b Indianola, Iowa, Nov 18, 24. *Study:* State Univ Iowa, with Mauricio Lasansky, BFA, 49, MFA, 51. *Work:* Mus Mod Art, New York; Brooklyn Mus; Nat Gallery Art, Libr Cong, Washington, DC; Los Angeles Co Mus Art. *Exhib:* Art of America in Spain, Madrid, 63; Pittsburgh Int, Carnegie Inst, 64-67; American Painting, Va Mus Arts & Sci, Richmond, 66-70; Tamarind: Homage to Lithography, Mus Mod Art, New York, 69; The New Vein--Europe, Smithsonian Inst, touring in Europe, 69-70; one-man exhibs, Graphics Gallery, 73, Jodi Scully Gallery, 73 & 75, Charles Campbell Gallery, 74 & Univ Calif, Riverside, 75. *Teaching:* Asst prof prints, Univ Calif, Los Angeles, 53-63; prof prints & drawings, Univ Calif, Irvine, 70-82, prof studio art, currently. *Awards:* Graphics Award, Tiffany Found, 51; Creative Printmaking Award, Guggenheim Found, 60. *Bibliog:* Una Johnson (auth), John Paul Jones, Prints & Drawings 1948-1963 (monogr), Brooklyn Mus, 63; Henry Hopkins (auth), John Paul Jones, Painting & Sculpture 1955-1965 (monogr), Los Angeles Co Mus Art, 65; Eugene Anderson (auth), John Paul Jones (monogr), Felix Landau Gallery, Los Angeles, 67. *Dealer:* Mekler Gallery 651 N La Cienega Blvd Los Angeles 90069. *Mailing Add:* c/o The Works Gallery 106 W Third St Long Beach CA 90802

JONES, JUDY VOSS
PRINTMAKER, PAINTER
b Winston-Salem, NC, Dec 26, 49. *Study:* Univ Ga, BFA, 72, MFA, 76. *Exhib:* Birmingham Biennial, Birmingham Mus Art, Ala, 83; Drawing Invitational, Va Mus Art, Richmond, 85; Works on Paper, Nexus Gallery, Atlanta, Ga, 87; Selections From Winstone Press, NC Mus Art, Raleigh, 88; Still-Life/Variations of a Theme, Sarat Gallery, Vanderbilt, Univ, Nashville, Tenn, 89; Visual Arts Fels Retrospective, SC State Mus, Columbia, 90; SC Contemp Artists, Owensboro Mus Fine Art, Ky, 91; and others. *Teaching:* Assoc prof drawing & printmaking, Converse Col, Spartansburg, SC, 76-92. *Awards:* SC Individual Artist Fel, SC Arts Comn, 81 & 87. *Mailing Add:* 230 Milledge Circle Athens GA 30606

JONES, KRISTIN See Jones & Ginzel,

JONES, LOIS MAILOU (MRS V PIERRE-NOEL)
PAINTER, DESIGNER
b Boston, Mass, 1905. *Study:* Boston Mus Sch Fine Arts, scholar, 4 yrs; Boston Normal Art Sch; Designers Art Sch; Harvard Univ; Columbia Univ; Howard Univ, AB; Acad Julien, Paris, with Berges, Montezin, Maury & Adler; Acad Grand Chaumiere, Paris; Colo State Christian Col, Hon PhD, 73; Suffolk Univ, Boston, LHD, 81; Mass Col Art, Boston, Hon PhD, 86, Howard Univ, Wash, DC, Hon PhD, 87. *Work:* Nat Portrait Gallery; Metropo Mus Art; Hirshhorn Mus; Corcoran Gallery Art, Washington, DC; Mus Fine Arts, Boston; Nat Mus Am Art; Nat Womens Mus Art, Wash, DC; and others.

Comn: Designed AKA Commemorative Stained Glass Window, 78 & 366th Regiment Infantry Window, 88, Andrew Rankin Chapel, Howard Univ; mural, The Light, Cook Hall, Howard Univ; portrait of Dr Carter G Woodson, Omega Psi Phi, 84. *Exhib:* Nat Acad Design, New York; Rhodes Nat Gallery, S Rhodesia; Trenton Mus, NJ; San Francisco Mus Art; Salon Artistes Francais, Grand Palais Champs-Elysees, Paris; Phillips Collection, Washington, DC; 60 one-man shows & numerous group shows. *Teaching:* Emer prof design & watercolor painting, Howard Univ, 30-77; head, art dept, Palmer Mem Inst, 28-30; vis prof drawing & painting, Ctr D'Art, Port-au-Prince, Haiti, summer, 55. *Awards:* First Place, Nat Mus Art, Washington, DC, 49, 53, 64; Robert Woods Bliss Landscape Award, Atlanta Univ; First Hon Mention, Salon des Artistes Francaise, 66; Alumni Award, Howard Univ, 78; Women's Caucus Honor Award Outstanding Achievement in Art, 86. *Bibliog:* Karen Peterson & J J Wilson (auths), Women Artists, Harper & Row, 76; Charlotte Rubenstein (auth), American Women Artists, Avon Books & G K Hall, 82; Nancy Heller (auth), Women Artists, Abbeville Press, 87. *Mem:* Fel Royal Soc Arts; Washington Watercolor Asn; Fel Royal Soc Arts, London, Eng; Nat Conf Afro-Am Artists. *Media:* Oil, Acrylic, Watercolor. *Publ:* Auth, Lois Mailou Jones peintures--1937-1951, Georges Frere, Tourcoing, France, 52; Caribbean and Afro-American Women Artists, Budek Films and Slides, Newport, RI, 84. *Mailing Add:* 4706 17th St NW Washington DC 20011

JONES, LOIS SWAN
EDUCATOR, HISTORIAN
b Dallas, Tex, July 3, 27. *Study:* Univ Chicago, PhB, 47, BS, 48, MS, 54; NTex State Univ, PhD, 72; Ctr Univ d'Ete des Pyrenees, Univ Toulouse, summer 75. *Pos:* Conductor, Le Petite Cercle d'Art, Dallas, 60-79; auth, narrator & photogr, Five Nights in Europe, Dallas Country Club, 63-75; co-owner, Swan Jones Prodns, 92- *Teaching:* Lectr art hist, Univ Tex, Arlington, 69-70; from asst prof to prof art hist, NTex State Univ, Denton, 72-92. *Mem:* Art Libr Soc NAm; Col Art Asn; Am Asn Mus; Nat Art Educ Asn; Midwest Art Hist Soc. *Res:* Art bibliography and research methodology; art museums; medieval art. *Publ:* Auth, Art Information: Research Methods & Resources, Kendall/Hunt, 78, rev, 84, 3rd ed, 90; producer multimedia show, Ice Age Art Exhib, Dallas Health & Sci Mus, 80; auth, Self study guides for school age students, Mus Studies J, 83; Art mobiles & suitcase exhibitions, Museologist, 85; Art Libraries & Information Services, Acad Press, 86. *Mailing Add:* 3801 Normandy Dallas TX 75205

JONES, LOU (MARY LOUISE HUMPTON)
PAINTER, SCULPTOR
b West Chester, Pa. *Study:* Pa State Univ, BA(Eng lit), 49; with Gene Davis, 68-72; George Mason Univ, Fairfax, Va, BA(art hist), 77; Corcoran Sch Abroad, Leeds Univ, Eng. *Work:* Phillips Collection, Washington, DC; Northern Va Community Col, Alexandria; Am Embassies, Damascus, Syria, Bern, Switz & Bamako, Mali; Univ DC, Washington. *Exhib:* 19th Area Show, Corcoran Mus, Washington, DC, 74; Va Artists, Va Mus, Richmond, 77 & 79; Enclosures, Foundry Gallery, Washington, DC; Am Drawing Biennial, William & Mary Col, Va, 87; Coastal Exchange Show, Richmond, 88; New Ways to Collage, George Mason Univ, Fairfax, Va; New Work on Paper, Susan Conway Gallery, 90. *Pos:* Panelist, Women Visual Arts, Women's Ctr, Washington, DC, 75, Artists Survival, Univ Md, 78, Am Univ, 79 & Corcoran Sch Art, Washington, DC, Md Inst Art, Baltimore; art consult, Am Corrections, DC, 77-80; dir educ, Athenaeum Mus, Alexandria, Va, 85-; docent, Phillips Collection, Washington, DC, 90. *Teaching:* Instr drawing-mixed media children, Corcoran Gallery, Washington, DC, 75-80; vis prof, Univ Md, 81; lectr, Marymount Univ, Va, 85- & George Mason Univ, 89- *Awards:* Purchase Award, Northern Va Community Col, 75; Fel, Va Ctr Creative Arts, Sweet Briar, 81; Artist Equity Award, Form & Substance. *Bibliog:* Jan Allen (auth), article, Washington Times, 10/83; Pam Kesseler (auth), Yellow and gold, Washington Post, 7/88; Michael Welzenbach (auth), Lou Jones at Conway Carroll, Washington Post, 7/89. *Media:* Paper, Collage. *Dealer:* Susan Conway Carroll Gallery Washington DC 20009; Montana Gallery Alex VA. *Mailing Add:* 329 Maple Ave Falls Church VA 22046

JONES, MARVIN HAROLD
PRINTMAKER, PAINTER
b Flora, Ill, May 19, 40. *Study:* Univ Ill, Urbana; Roosevelt Univ, Chicago; Anderson Col, Ind, BA; Univ Calif, Davis, MA, with Roy DeForest, William Wiley & Peter Saul. *Work:* Libr of Cong, Washington, DC; Confederation Art Gallery, Charlottetown, PEI, Can; Osaka Univ of Arts, Japan; Edmonton Art Gallery, Alta; Univ Dallas, Irving, Tex. *Exhib:* Brit Int Print Biennial, Bradford City Art Gallery, 72, 76, 82 & 86-87; Drawings/USA, Minn Mus of Art, St Paul, 73, 75 & 77; Nat Print Invitational, Brooklyn Mus, NY, 74; Perth Int Drawing Exhib, Western Australian Art Gallery, 75; Miami Int Print Biennial, Miami Art Ctr, Fla, 75; Biennial Int Print Exhib, Print Club of Philadelphia, 77; Int Biennial Graphic Art, Mod Gallery, Ljubljana, Yugoslavia, 79 & 81; Int Triennial of Woodcuts (XYLON), 84-87, 87-89; Mus of Modern Art, Rijeka, Yugoslavia, 88; Moravian Gallery, Brno, Czechoslovakia, 88; Fernsehturm Gallery, Berlin, DDR, 87. *Teaching:* Asst prof printmaking, Univ Alta, Edmonton, 70-72 & Karl Marx Univ, Leipzig, Ger, 81; Prof printmaking, Cleveland State Univ, 76- *Awards:* Ohio Arts Coun Grant, 78 & 80;; Montalvo Ctr for the Arts, 79, 84, & 88. *Bibliog:* Derek M Besant (auth), Satirical graphics by Marvin Jones & John Will, Art Mag, 10/75; Claire Kelly (auth), West coast drawings, Artweek, 3/77; Art in the western reserve, The New Art Examiner, 10/79; Print Voice, Univ Alta. *Mem:* Am Color Print Soc. *Media:* Acrylic. *Mailing Add:* 34580 Sherbrook Park Dr Cleveland OH 44118

JONES, MICHAEL BUTLER
SCULPTOR, FREELANCE CURATOR
b Chicago, Ill, Oct 7, 46. *Study:* Ohio State Univ, BFA, 68, MFA, 78. *Comn:* Ten outdoor murals, Nat Endowment Arts, Dayton, Ohio, 73; 18 outdoor murals in Ohio & Chicago; ten ceramic landscapes, State of Ohio, Columbus, 74; sixteen commerorative bas relief terra cotta panels, Univ Minn, Minneapolis, 85. *Exhib:* Antioch Col, Ohio, 75; Dayton Art Inst, Ohio, 85; Massillon Mus, Ohio, 87; Cleveland Ctr for Contemp Art, Ohio, 88; Cleveland Inst Art, 89; Ohio Univ, 89; Antioch Col, 89. *Collections Arranged:* Film Installations: Works by Paul Sharits, Bill Lundberg, Anthony McCall & Al Wong, 87; Craft As Content: Nat Metals Invitational, 87; Takaaki Matsumoto: Installation Proj & Design Works, 88; Dan Friedman: Installation Proj & Design Works, 91; Printed Matter, 92. *Pos:* Dir, Univ Gallery, Wright State Univ, Dayton, Ohio, 78-82 & Univ Akron, 85-91. *Awards:* Ohio Arts Coun Fel, 80. *Bibliog:* Pam Houk (auth), Gary Bower & Michael Jones, Am Ceramics, 86. *Mem:* Artists' Orgn Cols Ohio; Col Art Asn. *Media:* Clay, Steel. *Publ:* Ed, Athena Tacha: Tape Sculptures, 78 & Regional Fel Recipients Traveling Exhib Cat, Wright State Univ, 79; Ed, Pyramidal Influence in Art, 79, Triad, Sculpture Projects, 81 & Ten Solo Exhibitions, 82, Wright State Univ, Dayton, Ohio; Aspects of Perception, Bard Col & Va Commonwealth Univ, Richmond, 82; coauth, Film Installation Works, Univ Akron, Ohio, 86; Harold Kitner, Univ Akron, 88. *Mailing Add:* 790 Wright St Yellow Springs OH 45387

JONES, NORMA L
PAINTER
b Morrisonville, Ill. *Study:* Univ Houston, Clear Lake City, 75-76; Univ NMex; Univ Mo; Tex Univ; Washington Univ, St Louis; also studied with Rex Brandt, George Post & Edward Betts; Univ NMex. *Work:* Banco de Brazilia, Pondereille Oil Co; Tex Instruments Co, Tenneco; AMACO, Houston; Bank Am, NMex. *Comn:* D Regan, Manhatten, NY; Susan Davis, Las Cruces, NMex. *Exhib:* Am Watercolor Soc, Nat Acad, New York; Watercolor USA, Springfield Mus, Mo; Western Federation, Albuquerque Mus, San Diego & Houston; Watercolor Art Soc Houston; Thompson Gallery, Univ NMex, Kemo Theater Gallery; and others. *Teaching:* Instr, Pickwickian Schs, Houston, Tex & various wkshps in Houston & Albuquerque. *Awards:* Merit Award, Western Fedn, San Diego, 83; Best of Show, Watercolor Show, Thompson Gallery, Univ Mex, 84; First Prize, Collage '86, Pacific Fine Arts Nat Show. *Bibliog:* Article, Le Revue Moderne, Paris, France, 75; articles, Southwest Profile, 84; article, NMex Mag, 5/92. *Mem:* NMex Watercolor Soc Signature Group; Soc Layerists Multi-Media; Southwestern Fedn Watercolorists; North Coast Collage Soc; Am Univ Asn. *Media:* Acrylic, Mixed Media. *Dealer:* Dartmouth St Gallery Albuquerque; Hummingbird Originals Inc Ft Worth TX. *Mailing Add:* 9312 Las Calabazillas NE Albuquerque NM 87111

JONES, PATTY SUE
PAINTER, CURATOR
b New Orleans, La, Aug 18, 49. *Study:* Auburn Univ, 67-69 & 74; Univ Calif, Los Angeles, photog with Robert Heinecken, BA, 72, MA, 74; Univ Wash, with Jack Lenor Larsen, summer 75. *Work:* Yuma Fine Arts Ctr, Ariz. *Comn:* Paintings, Regent Hotels Int, Beverly Hills, Calif, 74; tapestry, Fluor Corp, Irvine, Calif, 78; tapestry, Security Pac Bank, Topanga Canyon, Calif, 79. *Exhib:* Tucson Mus Art, Ariz, 75; Ariz State Univ, Tempe, 79; Security Pac Hq, Los Angeles, 81; Occidental Col, Los Angeles, 81; Los Angeles Inst Contemp Art, 81; and many others. *Collections Arranged:* Robert Delgado, Mural Making: The Process, 80, The Mask: Object and Image, 80, Paper: Cast/Torn/Formed, 80 & California Dada, 80, Old Venice Jail Gallery, Venice, Calif. *Pos:* Dir's coun mem, Yuma Fine Art Ctr, Ariz, 76-77; cur exhibs, Old Venice Jail Gallery, Venice, Calif, 79-81. *Teaching:* Teaching asst, Univ Calif, Los Angeles, 73-74; instr, Ariz Western Col, Yuma, 74-77, Ariz State Univ, Tempe, 75-76 & St Mary's Col, Los Angeles, 82. *Awards:* Purchase Award, 10th Ann Southwestern, 75. *Bibliog:* Laurel Meinig (auth), Artists-in-residence (catalog), Yuma Art Ctr, Ariz, 76; William Wilson (auth), Lint drawings (review), Los Angeles Times, 80. *Media:* Oil. *Publ:* Contribr, Spectrum: New directions in color photography, Univ Hawaii, 79. *Mailing Add:* 5556 Echo St Los Angeles CA 90042

JONES, PIRKLE
PHOTOGRAPHER, EDUCATOR
b Shreveport, La, Jan 2, 14. *Study:* Calif Sch Fine Arts, cert, 49. *Work:* San Francisco Mus Mod Art; Art Inst Chicago; Ctr Creative Photog, Univ Ariz; Yokohama Mus, Japan; Mus Mod Art, New York. *Comn:* Commemorative UN Portfolio, Bank Am, San Francisco, 55; The Story of a Winery, Paul Masson, John Bolles, San Francisco, 59; Courthouses, Bicentennial Proj, Joseph E Seagram Inc, New York, 75. *Exhib:* Photography in the Twentieth Century, Nat Gallery Can, 67; A Photographic Essay on the Black Panthers, De Young Mus Art, 68, Studio Mus Harlem, 70, Hopkins Ctr, Dartsmouth Col, 70 & Univ Calif, Santa Cruz, 70; Octive of Prayer, Mass Inst Technol, 72; The Land, 20th Century Landscapes, Victoria & Albert Mus, 75; Courthouse, Photographs from the Segrams' Collection, Mus Mod Art, New York, 78; Messages From West Coast, Photo Gallery Int, Tokyo, 79; Curator's Choice: By John Humphery, San Francisco Mus Mod Art, 80; Master Photographers: A Sentimental Celebration, Focus Gallery, San Francisco, 81; Awards of Honor, A Documentary Exhibition, San Francisco Arts Commission, Gallery, Bank Am, World Hq, San Francisco, 83; Photography in California: Pushing the Boundaries 1945-1980, San Francisco Mus Mod Art, 84; and others. *Teaching:* Instr photog, Calif Sch Fine Arts, 52-58, Ansel Adams Workshops, Yosemite Nat Park, 66-70 & San Francisco Art Inst, 70- *Awards:* Award Hon Photog, A Documentary Exhib, San Francisco Arts Comn, 83. *Bibliog:* Ansel Adams (auth), article, US Camera

Mag, 10/52; Nancy Newhall (auth), article, Aperture Mag, 56; Robert Holmes (auth), article, Brit J Photog, 10/80. *Publ:* Auth, Portfolio One, Commemoration Signing United Nations Charter, private publ, 55; coauth, Death of a valley, Aperture Mag, 60; The Vanguard, A Photographic Essay on the Black Panthers, Beacon Press, 70. *Mailing Add:* 663 Lovell Ave Mill Valley CA 94941

JONES, RONALD LEE, JR
EDUCATOR, WRITER
b Beckley, WVa, Dec 4, 42. *Study:* Concord Col, BS, 64; Ariz State Univ, MA, 68; Univ Md, PhD, 75. *Pos:* Contrib ed, Art Voices, S Palm Beach, Fla, 78-; chmn, WVa Arts & Humanities Comn, Capitol Complex, Charleston, 78-*Teaching:* Prof art & chmn dept, Shepherd Col, Shepherdstown, WVa, 69-; chmn, Div Creative Arts, Shepherd Col, Shepherdstown, WVa, dean, Sch Arts, currently. *Mem:* Nat Art Educ Asn; Nat Coun Policy Study Art Educ; Col Art Asn, WVa (pres, 71, 72 & 75); Nat Asn Arts Adminr; Nat Asn State Art Agencies; and others. *Res:* Aesthetic response; writing art criticism for art journals. *Publ:* Auth, A re-examination of Mittler's efforts toward modern art attitude, Studies in Art Educ, 75; contribr, Artists in Schools: Analysis and Criticism, Univ Ill Bur Educ Res, 78; auth, Phenomenological analysis effects on aspective perception: a review, Rev Res in Visual Arts, 78; Critical reviews of artists, Art Voices/S 78-80; auth, Phenomenological balance and the aesthetic response, J Aesthetic Educ, 79. *Mailing Add:* PO Box 389 Shepherdstown WV 25443

JONES, RONALD WARREN
ARTIST, CRITIC
b Ft Belvoir, Va, July 8, 52. *Study:* Huntington Col, BA, 74; Univ SC, MFA, 76; Ohio Univ, PhD(art hist), 81. *Work:* Baltimore Mus Art; Moderna Museet, Stockholm, Sweden; Whitney Mus Am Art, Moca, La. *Comn:* Pritzker Park, City of Chicago. *Exhib:* High Mus Art, Atlanta, 86; Metro Pictures, New York, 87-90; Metro Pictures, New York, 87 & 88; Isabella Kacprzak, Koln, 88 & 90; Sebui Mus, Tokyo, 90; Mind Over Matter Whitney Mus Am Art, New York, 90; Linda Cathcart, La; and others. *Teaching:* Yale Univ, 89-; Rhode Island Sch Design, 88-90; Sch Visual Arts, 89-90. *Awards:* Mellon Found Stipend, 83; Fel, Nat endowment Visual Artist, 84. *Bibliog:* Peter Halley (auth), Ronald Jones, Marcel Duchamp, and the New South (catalog essay), San Jose Mus Art; Richard Flood (auth), Ronald Jones (catalog essay), Isabella Kacprzak, Koln; Roberta Smith (auth), The New York Times, 88-90; Eleanor Heartney (auth), Ronald Jones at Metro Pictures, Art in Am, 1/88. *Publ:* Auth, various articles, essays & reviews, in: Artforum, Parkett Arts Mag, C Mag, Art in Am, Artscribe, Flash Art & Real Life Mag. *Dealer:* Metro Pictures 150 Greene St New York NY; Sonnabend Gallery New York NY. *Mailing Add:* 101 Wooster St, 6F New York NY 10012

JONES, RUTHE BLALOCK
PAINTER, EDUCATOR
b Claremore, Okla, June 8, 39. *Study:* Bacone Col, with Dick West, AA; Univ Tulsa, with Carl Coker, BFA; Northeastern State Univ, Tablequah, Okla, MS. *Work:* Mus Am Indian, Heye Found, New York; Indian Arts & Crafts Bd, US Dept Interior, Washington, DC; Heard Mus, Phoenix; Philbrook Art Ctr, Tulsa; Williams Performing Arts Ctr, Tulsa, Okla. *Exhib:* Turtle Show, Niagara, NY, 82; Night of the First Americans, Kennedy Ctr, Washington, DC, 82; Contemporary North American Indian Painting, Mus Natural Hist, Smithsonian Inst, Washington, DC, 82; American Indian Community House, New York, 82; Southeastern Indian Artists, Fine Arts Ctr, Atlanta, Ga, 88; 9th Symposium, Int Soc Polyaesthetic Educ, Schloss Mittersill, Austria, 90. *Teaching:* Instr art, Bacone Col, Muskogee, Okla, 79-85, 87- *Awards:* First for Traditional Indian Painting, Philbrook Mus, 68; Spec Award, US Dept Interior, Okla State Soc; First Painting Award, Red Earth Art Competition, Oklahoma City, 90. *Bibliog:* J Snodgrass (auth), Handbook American Indian Artists, Mus Am Indian, 67; H Meredith (auth), The Bacone School of Art, Chronicles Okla, LVIII, No 1, spring 80; article, Okla Today, Vol 35, No 4, 7-8/85. *Mem:* Southwestern Indian Art Asn, Santa Fe, NMex; Indian Arts & Crafts Asn, Albuquerque, NMex. *Media:* Watercolor, Acrylic, Graphics. *Publ:* Mini Myths and Legends of Oklahoma Indians, Wise, Lu Celia, 78; State of Okalahoma Indian Education Curriculum Guides, 78; Bacone Indian University: A History, Williams & Meredith, 80; The Hill Rag (cover art), 84; Auth, Keepers of Culture, (exhib catalog), Anniston Mus of Natural Hist, Ala, 88. *Dealer:* Native American Art 323 S Main Mall Tulsa OK 74172 74145; Indian Images Box 3621 Evansville IN 47735. *Mailing Add:* 517 S Woodlawn Ave Okmulgee OK 74447

JONES, THEODORE JOSEPH
SCULPTOR, PRINTMAKER
b New Orleans, La, Sept 14, 38. *Study:* Xavier Univ, BA; Mich State Univ, MA; Univ Mont, MFA; Fla A&M Univ, cert; Fisk Univ, cert. *Work:* Johnson Publ Co, Chicago; Mus African Art, Washington, DC; First Am Nat Bank, Nashville. *Exhib:* One-man exhibs, Ala A&M Univ, Normal, 75, Tenn State Mus, 75 & Creatadrama Art Gallery, Bloomington, Ind, 75; 17th Tenn All-State Artists Exhib, Centennial Park Galleries, Nashville, 77; From These Roots Exhib, Tenn State Mus, Nashville, 77; Smith-Mason Galleries, Washington, DC, 77; and many others. *Pos:* Touring artist, Tenn Arts Comn, 70-; art consult, Claiborne Ave Design Team Symp, New Orleans, La, 74-*Teaching:* Instr art, Fla A&M Univ, 65-68; from assoc prof to prof art, Tenn State Univ, 68- *Awards:* Tenn State Univ Grant, 70; Third Place Sculpture, Tenn Art League, 74; Lyzon Galleries Award Graphics, Cent South Exhib, 75. *Bibliog:* Clara Hieronymus (auth), Ted Jones Exhibition, Tennessean Newspaper, 75; Kenneth Weedman (auth), article, Sculpture Quart, 75. *Mem:* Tenn Lit Arts Asn; Southern Independent Artists Asn; Southern Asn Sculptors; Southeastern Graphics Coun; Tennessee Art League. *Publ:* Contribr, Galaxy III Communication Arts Seminar Basic Holography, 74; ed, Faculty exhibition catalogs & brochures, Tenn State Univ, 74-75; auth, Thoughts and Verses (poetry and prints), 75 & Masonite-Printing: A New Approach in Relief Printing, 77, New Dimension Studio, Nashville. *Mailing Add:* c/o Dept Art Tenn State Univ 3500 Centennial Blvd Nashville TN 37209-1561

JONES, THOMAS WILLIAM
PAINTER
b Lakewood, Ohio, Aug 13, 42. *Study:* Cleveland Inst Art, dipl, 64. *Work:* City of Seattle Selects II (For Pub Collection of Seattle City Light, Wash); Rainier Bank Collection, Pac Northwest Bell Collection, Seattle; Pac Car & Foundry & Eddie Bauer, Inc, Seattle. *Comn:* 25 landscape paintings, Gen Tel Co of the Northwest, Everett, Wash, 68; paintings of Old Holland, Western Int Design Serv, St Francis Hotel, San Francisco, 72; paintings for bd dirs, Seattle First Nat Bank, 74; four seasonal landscapes & 60th anniversary catalog cover, Eddie Bauer Inc, Seattle, 75, 80 & 82; Presidential Christmas Card, comn by White House, 85, 86, 87, 88. *Exhib:* One-man show, Frye Art Mus, Seattle, 73; 154th Nat Acad Design, New York, 79; Northwest Art Today, 75, Works on Paper, 75 & Wash Open, 79, Seattle Art Mus; Artists of America, Denver, 81-92; Nat Acad of Western Art, Oklahoma City, 81-92; Celebration of Northwest Art, Gov's Mansion, Olympia, Wash, 84. *Awards:* Ted Kautzky Mem Award, Am Watercolor Soc, 75 & Bronze Medal of Honor, 79; First Place, Water Media, Rocky Mountain Nat, 76; Silver Medal, Nat Acad Western Art, 84 & Gold Medal, 87. *Bibliog:* Barbara Dell (auth), feature article in Artists of the Rockies & Golden West, 12/79; Southwest Art feature article, Southwest Art Inc, 9/85; Patricia Black Bailey (auth), article, US Art, 1/90. *Mem:* Northwest Watercolor Soc (vpres, 74); West Coast Watercolor Soc; Am Acad of Taos, NMex; hon mem Fed Can Artists; Nat Acad Western Art; Santa Fe Watercolor Soc. *Media:* Watercolor. *Publ:* Auth, Watercolor page, Am Artist, 9/79. *Dealer:* Foster/White Gallery 311 Occidental Ave S Seattle WA 98104; Maveety Gallery PO Box 148 Gleneden Beach OR 97388. *Mailing Add:* PO Box 426 Copalis Beach WA 98535-0426

JONES, W LOUIS
PAINTER, SCULPTOR
b Durham, NC, Feb 22, 43. *Study:* Pa Acad Fine Arts; E Carolina Univ, BS; Cranbrook Acad Art, MFA. *Work:* Metrop Life Ins, Boston; RJR/Nabisco Winston-Salem; Exxon; Nations Bank; Citicorp. *Exhib:* Solo exhibs, Arwin Gallery, 66-79, Kornblee Gallery, New York, 77, 78, Greenhill Ctr, Greensboro, NC, 86, Davidson Co Art Guild, 90; American Realism: Realist Invitational, SECCA, Winston-Salem, 83; San Francisco Mus Mod Art, 86; DeCordova & Dana Mus, Lincoln, 86; Univ Tex, Austin, 86; Northwestern Univ, Evanston, 86; Williams Col Mus, Williamstown, Mass, 87; Abron Art Mus, 87; Madison Art Ctr, Wis, 87. *Teaching:* La State Univ, Baton Rouge, 79, Univ SC, Columbia, 80. *Awards:* Purchase Awards, Arnkot Mus, Elmira, 73, Jacksonville Art Mus, 77, Russell Sage Col, Troy, 78, Berkshire Art Mus, Pittsfield, 76, Univ Nebr, Omaha, 78; Grant NY State Coun on the Arts, 73. *Mem:* Nat Soc Painters in Casein; Am Asn Univ Prof. *Media:* Acrylic; Wood. *Publ:* Watercolor 88 by American Artist, Polymer Painting by Russell O Woody, 88. *Dealer:* Marita Gilliam Inc Art Gallery 126 Glenwood Ave Raleigh NC 27603-1704. *Mailing Add:* Rte 4 Box 91-B Asheboro NC 27203

JONES & GINZEL,
SCULPTORS
Jones: b Washington, DC, Aug 1, 56; Ginzel: b Chicago, Ill, July 14, 54. *Study:* Jones: St Martin's, London, 78-79, RI Sch Design, BFA, 79, Yale Univ, MFA, 83; Ginzel: self taught. *Work:* Mus d'Arte Contemporanea, Prato, Italy; Wadsworth Atheneum, Hartford, Conn; Brooklyn Mus, New York; Kunsthalle, Basel, Switz. *Comn:* One Percent for Art Commission, Battery Park City Authority & Metrop Transit Authority, New York, 89-92; Principia, Ore Convention Ctr, Portland, 90; Plethora, Arts Am Prog, New Delhi, India, 91; Diaxiom, Com Sq One, IM Pei & Partners, Philadelphia, Pa, 91; Inner-Arts Grant for Collaborative Work with David Dorfman Dance Co, Nat Endowment Arts, 90-91. *Exhib:* Ad Infinitum, Whitney Mus Am Art at Philip Morris, New York, 85; solo exhibs, Ephemeris, Va Mus Fine Arts, Richmond, Triptych, New Mus Contemp Art, New York, 86, Seraphim, Matrix 99, Wadsworth Atheneum, Hartford, Conn, Charybdis, List Visual Arts Ctr, Mass Inst Technol, Cambridge, 88; Interaction, 88 & Metathesis, Aldrich Mus Contemp Art, Ridgefield, Conn; Charybdis, Waterworks, PS1 Mus, Long Island, NY, 89; Alkahest, Team Spirit, Independent Curators Inc, Neuberger Mus, State Univ, New York, 90. *Teaching:* Ginzel: Instr Sculpture, Sch Visual Arts, New York, 85-; Jones: instr sculpture, Philadelphis Col Art, 86; Both: lectr, Tyler Sch Art, Philadelphia, 87; vis artists, Yale Univ, New Haven, Conn, 88, Cornish Sch Art, Seattle, Wash, 88, RI Sch Design, Providence, 89 & Harvard Univ, Cambridge, Mass, 89. *Awards:* Fulbright Fel, Italy, 83, India 90; Fel, Nat Endowment Arts, sculpture, 86; Fel, Tiffany Found, 91. *Bibliog:* Kristin Jones & Andrew Ginzel (monogr), Kunsthalle, Basel, Switz, 89; Eleanor Heartney (auth), Combined Operations, Art Am, 89; Thomas Kellein (auth), Jones & Ginzel, Kunstforum, 90. *Mem:* Int Sculpture Ctr. *Media:* Mixed Media. *Dealer:* Damon Brandt Gallery 568 Broadway New York NY 10012. *Mailing Add:* 289 Bleecker St New York NY 10014

JONSSON, TED (WILBUR)
SCULPTOR
b Berkeley, Calif, Oct 2, 33. *Study:* Univ Calif Davis, BFA(philos fine art), 52-57; Univ Wash, MFA(sculpture), 62-64. *Work:* City of Seattle, Permanent Works Collection, Wash; Seattle Art Mus, Wash; Manoogian Collection, Detroit, Mich; Fed Reserve Bank San Francisco, Seattle, Wash. *Comn:* Seattle Water Dept (fountain), City of Seattle, Wash, 72; Seattle Int Airport (sculpture), Port of Seattle, Wash, 75; Univ Alaska (sculpture), Alaska Coun

Arts, Anchorage, 76; Olympia Tech Col (sculpture), Wash State Art Comn, 79; Fed reserve, New Plaza (sculpture), Fed Reserve Bank San Francisco, Seattle, Wash, 91. *Exhib:* West Coast Now, Current Art from Western Seaboard, Traveling West Coast Mus Show, 68; Govenor's Invitational Int, Olympia, FWash, 69, 72, 73, 75 & 76; Art in Public Places, Henry Gallery, Univ Wash, 72; Northwest 77, Seattle Art Mus Pavillion, Wash, 77; Northwest Invitational, Artists Today: Part II, Seattle Mod Art Pavillion, 77; Seattle Sculpture 27-87, Bumberbiennial, 87; Northwest Ann, Seattle, 90. *Pos:* Curator, Wash State Capitol Mus, 62-63. *Teaching:* Art instr sculpture, Highline Community Col, Midway, Wash, 68-79; sculpture instr, Calif State Univ, Aumbort, 88-89. *Awards:* First Prize, Pacific Northwest Ann, Spokane Mus Art, 67; Sculpture Award, Ann Exhib Northwest Painting & Sculpture, Seattle Art Mus, 73; Visual Arts Honors Award Outstanding Visual Artist, Wash State Art Comn, 87. *Bibliog:* Charlie B Tomlins (auth), Water Sculpture USA, Univ Tex Press, 86; Louis G Redstone (auth), Art and Architecture & Public Art New Directions, McGraw-Hill, 79. *Mem:* Artist Equity Wash State Chap Nat Affil(vpres 86-92); Int Sculpture Ctr; Artist Trust. *Media:* Stainless Steel. *Dealer:* OK Harris Gallery 383 W Broadway New York NY 10012. *Mailing Add:* 805 NE Northlake Way Seattle WA 98105

JOOST-GAUGIER, CHRISTIANE L
ADMINISTRATOR, HISTORIAN
b Ste Maxime, France; US citizen. *Study:* Radcliffe Col, BA(hon) & MA; Harvard Univ, PhD; Univ Munich. *Teaching:* Asst prof Renaissance art, Tufts Univ, 69-75; prof Renaissance art, NMex State Univ, 75-85, head art dept, 75-81; prof Renaissance art, Univ NMex, 85, chair art dept, 85-87. *Awards:* Fulbright Fel; Delmas Found Grant; Am Asn Univ Women Fel, Italy; Nat Endowment Humanities Grant. *Mem:* Col Art Asn (bd dirs, 81); Nat Coun Arts Administrators (bd dirs); Renaissance Soc Am (coun); Women's Caucus Art (adv bd); Mid Am Col Art Asn; Am Coun Learned Soc; Am Phil Soc. *Res:* Venetian drawings, series of famous men and women; Quattrocento art in Florence and Venice; Lombard architecture. *Publ:* Auth of var articles in Gazette des Beaux-Arts, Art Bull, Zeitschrift für Kunstgeschichte, Commentari, Antichita Viva & Acta Historiae Artium, Artibus et Historiae, Arte Lombarda; The Selected Drawings of Jacopo Bellini. *Mailing Add:* Dept of Art Univ NMex Albuquerque NM 87131

JORDAN, BARBARA SCHWINN
PAINTER
b Glen Ridge, NJ. *Study:* Parsons Sch Design, Paris; Grand Cent Art Sch; Art Students League, with Frank DuMond, Luigi Lucioni & others; Grande Chaumiere & Acad Julian, Paris, France; Columbia Univ; Nat Acad Design. *Work:* Holbrook Collection; Ga Mus Art; Sanford Low Mem Collection; numerous pvt collections. *Comn:* Portraits, incl Queen Sirikit, Princess Margaret & Princess Grace. *Exhib:* Guild Hall, 69, 79 & 81; one-man shows, Bodley Gallery, 71 & 80, Duquesne Univ, 73 & Community Col, West Mifflin, Pa, 73; Summit Art Ctr, NJ, 81; 100 Years of Still Life Painting, Meredith Long Gallery, Houston, 83; Mus Soc Illusr; Marcus Gallery & Gerald Peters Gallery, NMex, 85 & 86; New Brit Mus Am Art, 86; Brandywine Mus, Pa; Mus Am Illustrations, 91; Graphics Gallery, East Hampton, 91-92; Illustration House, New York, 91-92; and others. *Pos:* Founder & chmn art comt, UNICEF, 50-61. *Teaching:* Lectr & instr illus, Parsons Sch Design, 52-54; founder adv coun, Art Instr Sch, 56-70. *Awards:* Prizes, Art Dirs Club, 50 & Guild Hall, 69. *Mem:* Cosmopolitan Club, New York; Soc Illustrators; Philharmonic Soc. *Media:* Oil. *Publ:* Auth, The technique of Barbara Schwinn, 56 & World of fashion art, Art Instr Schs, 68; contribr, Ladies Home J, Good Housekeeping, Colliers, Cosmopolitan, McCalls, Saturday Eve Post & French, Brit, Ger, Belg, Danish & Swed mag, 40-60; and many others. *Dealer:* Gerald Peters Gallery Santa Fe NM. *Mailing Add:* 579 Woodbury Fearrington Village NC 27312

JORDAN, BETH MCANINCH
PAINTER
b Corn, Okla, Nov 23, 18. *Study:* Southwestern State Univ, grad; Tabar Col, Hillsboro, Kans; also with Jack Valle, Millard Sheets & others. *Work:* Okla Art Ctr, Southwest Christian Col, State of Okla Collection of Okla Art & Humanities Coun; Oklahoma City Arts Coun; Kerr Convention Ctr; and over 50 corporate collections. *Exhib:* Okla Nat Printmakers & Watercolor Show, 61; Southwestern Watercolor Soc Regional & Open, Dallas, Tex, 67, 69 & 71; 8 State Exhib Painting & Sculpture Ann, Okla Art Ctr, 71; Watercolor USA, Springfield, Mo, 73 & 79; Okla Artists Ann, Philbrook, Tulsa, 61-72; Butler Inst Am Art, Youngstown, Ohio, 78; one-person show annually for the past 30 yrs; Audubon artists, New York; Nat Womens Show, New York. *Pos:* Art bd, Omiplex, Kirkpatrick Gallery, currently. *Teaching:* Instr painting & drawing, pvt classes, 60-70; instr painting & drawing, Okla Sci & Art Found, 62-66. *Awards:* Southwestern Watercolor Soc Award, 67; First Painting Award, 7th Ann Artists Salon, Okla Mus Art, 68; First Award, 7th Ann Southwestern Watercolor Soc, 71. *Bibliog:* Oklahoma City Key & Oklahoma City Down Towner, 85. *Mem:* Southwestern Watercolor Soc. *Media:* Watercolor, Pencil, Collage. *Dealer:* Norman Wilks Interiors 3839 NW 63rd St Oklahoma City OK 73116; Okla Art Ctr 3113 General Pershing Oklahoma City OK 73107. *Mailing Add:* 1637 Camden Way Oklahoma City OK 73116

JORDAN, GEORGE EDWIN
CRITIC, HISTORIAN
b Ky, Oct 29, 40. *Study:* Univ Ky; Ringling Sch Art, Sarasota, Fla, BFA; ETenn State Univ. *Pos:* Cur, Reece Mus, Johnson City, Tenn, 66-69; cur Am art & registrar, New Orleans Mus Art, La, 69-72; art critic, New Orleans Times-Picayune, La, 74-77, ed World of Art column, 77-79; freelance art writer, lectr, appraiser & consult, 79-; contrib ed, Art & Auction, 81-84; co-ed, New Orleans Art Rev, 82-; auth, Critics Choice monthly column, Go Mag, 83-; guest cur, Seldom Seen Figures, Arts Coun New Orleans, 86. *Teaching:* Guest instr hist contemp painting, Adult Educ, Tulane Univ, 76-79; instr painting & art hist, New Orleans Acad Fine Arts, 84-85. *Res:* Artists who worked in New Orleans and the Southeast, late 18th, 19th and early 20th centuries. *Publ:* Contribr, Louisiana Paintings 19th Century, The William Groves Collection, Groves Press, 71; contribr & coauth, Louisiana portraits, Colonial Dames of Am in La, 76; auth, Louisiana Artists 19th Century, WYES-Educ Television, New Orleans, 72-73; contribr, Encyclopedia of New Orleans Artists, 1718-1918, Historic New Orleans Collection, 87; auth, Josephine Crawford, In: Eight Southern Women Artists (catalog), Greenville County Mus of Art. *Mailing Add:* Jordan Delhaise Gallery 1 Riverside Ave Westport CT 06880

JORDAN, JACK
ADMINISTRATOR, SCULPTOR
b July 29, 27; US citizen. *Study:* Langston Univ, BA; Univ Iowa, MA; Ind Univ, MS; State Univ Iowa, MFA; Okla Univ; Ind Univ, DEd. *Work:* State Univ Iowa Mus, Iowa City; Atlanta Univ Art Mus, Ga; Okla Art Ctr, Oklahoma City; Golden State Ins Co, Calif; Afro-Am Cult Heritage Ctr, Dallas, Tex Anatomy of A Fowl (sculpture), Sutton Estate, Ardmore, Okla. *Comn:* Come Ye Children (sculpture), Bethany United Methodist Church, New Orleans, 71; Mural, Bell Baptist Church, 80; mural, Second Hwy Baptist Church, 81; mural, Guiding Light Baptist Church, 81; mobile mural, 100 yrs struggle for freedom, Nat Afro-Am Mus, Wilberforce, Ohio & wood sculpture, Forgive Them For They Know Not, 92. *Exhib:* New York Archit League & Nat Sculpture Soc; Nat Competitive Art Show, Walker Art Ctr, Minneapolis & El Mira Art Gallery, Pismo Beach, Calif; Nat Art Show, Carnegie Inst Int, Pittsburgh, Pa; Atlanta Art Gallery; Sculpture 81, Counterpoint Guild Nat Exhib of 16 Selected Black Sculptors, New York, 81; New Orleans Mus Art, 89; Downtown Gallery, New Orleans, 90; and others. *Collections Arranged:* Emancipation Centennial Nat Art Exhib, 63; New Orleans Bicentennial Art Exhib, Bicentennial Comn New Orleans, 74; Black Family Bicentennial Art Show, 75. *Teaching:* Head art dept, Claflin Univ, Orangeburg, SC, 49-50, Allen Univ, Columbia, SC, 52-55 & Langston Univ, Okla, 57-61; prof & head art dept, Southern Univ New Orleans, 61-90. *Awards:* Sculpture Awards, Joslyn Art Mus, Omaha, Nebr & Walker Art Ctr, Minneapolis; nine Nat Sculpture Awards, Atlanta Art Gallery, 50-73; and others. *Bibliog:* Cedric Dover (auth), American Negro Art, New York Graphic Soc, 60; Kaye Teall (auth), Black History of Oklahoma, Okla Pub Sch Title III, Elem & Sec Educ Act, 71; Judith W Chase (auth), Afro-American Arts & Crafts, Van Nostrand Reinhold, 71. *Mem:* Okla Art Asn; Nat Conf Artists (vpres, 65, pres, 66-67); Creatadrama Soc; Nat Conf Artists (chmn bd trustees, 83-); New Orleans Ctr Creative Arts (treas, 83-87). *Media:* All. *Mailing Add:* 5545 Congress Dr New Orleans LA 70126

JORDAN, JOHN L (GAUDEAMUS)
SCULPTOR, VIDEO ARTIST
b Houston, Tex, Dec 21, 44. *Study:* Art League of Houston, 66; studied with John Howley, St Kilda, Australia, 83. *Work:* Catskill Alliance for Peace, Woodstock, NY. *Comn:* Billboard mural, US Air Force, Ellington AFB, Tex, 66. *Exhib:* American Natural Pearls, Astrohall Nat Show, Houston, Tex, 82; Homage to Dali with Fried Eggs, Allentown Art Mus, Pa, 88; Hiroshima to Now, Town Hall, Woodstock, NY, 90; Homage to Dali with Fried Eggs, Manhattan Pub, TV-Bruce Greenberg Producer, New York, 91. *Pos:* Artist & designer, Jerusalem Jewels, Hawaii, 77-85; art dir, Gaudeamus Jordan, Woodstock, NY, 88-; art rep, Whitney Morse Art Group, New York, 88-91; producer & host, Ramble On, WATV, Woodstock, NY, 90- *Teaching:* Art teacher, Onteora Sch Dist, Phoenicia, NY, 88-91. *Awards:* Spec Award, Am Fedn Gem & Mineralogical Soc Nat Show, Astrohall, 82; Exhib Award, Allentown Art Mus, Pa, 88. *Bibliog:* Ron Ronck (auth), Arts scene, Honolulu Advertiser, 84; Kevin O'Brian (auth), Woodstock Times, NY, 12/29/88; Sharon Cherve (auth), Woodstocks' Jordan Romances the Stones, Daily Freeman, Kingston, NY, 11/27/89; Artist Creates Dali tribute triptych, Art Bus News, 3/90; Julie Knipe (auth), Judge throws out claim, Globe-Times, Bethlehem, Pa, 5/17/90. *Mem:* Woodstock Artists Assoc, Woodstock Guild of Artists, Woodstock, NY, 89. *Media:* All Media. *Publ:* Encyl Living Artists in Am, 2nd ed, 87; Color Me-No Bikini Atoll (poetry collection), 92; Homage to Dali with Fried Eggs (video), 92. *Mailing Add:* c/o Gaudeamus-Jordan Studios PO Box 1050 Woodstock NY 12498

JORDAN, ROBERT
PAINTER, EDUCATOR
b Floral Park, NY, Sept 22, 25. *Study:* Dartmouth Col, BA; Columbia Univ, MA. *Work:* Addison Gallery of Am Art, Andover, Mass; Nat Air & Space Mus, Washington, DC; St Louis Art Mus; Boston Pub Libr; Washington Univ Art Gallery, St Louis, Mo. *Exhib:* Seven Decades, Addison Gallery, 69; one-man shows, FAR Gallery, New York, 74 & 76-77, Creiger Sesen Gallery, Boston, 80 & Sherry French Gallery, New York, 83, 85, 87, 89 & 91; Am 1976 (traveling exhib), US Dept Interior Bicentennial, 76; Butler Inst Am Art Ann, Youngstown, Ohio, 77; Capricorn Gallery, Bethesda, Md, 80; Night Lights, Taft Mus, Cincinnati, Ohio, 85. *Teaching:* Prof painting & Am art hist, Washington Univ, formerly. *Bibliog:* articles in Arts, 10/83 & 4/85; John Arthur (auth), Spirit of Place: Contemporary Landscape Painting & the American Tradition, Little Brown, 89. *Media:* Oil, Pastel. *Dealer:* Sherry French Gallery 24 W 57th St New York NY 10019. *Mailing Add:* RFD Box 18 Center Conway NH 03813

JORDAN, VANCE
GALLERY DIRECTOR, ART DEALER
b New York, NY, Feb 14, 43. *Study:* Rensselaer Polytech Inst, Troy, NY, BA, 64. *Pos:* Dir, Jordan-Volpe Gallery, New York, currently Curiosities of the

Martin Brothers 1880-1914, 81, Toward the Modern Style: Rookwood Pottery: The Later Years: 1915-1950, 83 & Summers Abroad: The European Watercolors of Francis Hopkinson Smith, 85, Jordan-Volpe Gallery, New York. *Bibliog:* Ulrich W Hiesinger (auth), Impressionism in America: The Ten American Painters, Prestel-Verlag, Munich & Jordan-Volve Gallery, NY, 91. *Mem:* Metrop Mus; Whitney Mus Am Art; Brooklyn Mus. *Specialty:* American paintings 1840-1940; European paintings 1875-1915. *Publ:* Contribr, Abroad: The European Watercolors of Francis Hopkinson Smith, summer 85, 19th and 20th Century Paintings, 89, 50 Recent Acquisitions, 90 & American Selections 1850-1950, 92, Jordan-Volpe Gallery, NY. *Mailing Add:* Jordan-Volpe Gallery 958 Madison Ave New York NY 10021

JORDAN, WILLIAM B
HISTORIAN, CONSULTANT
b Nashville, Tenn, May 8, 40. *Study:* Washington & Lee Univ, BA, 62; NY Univ, MA, 64, PhD, 67. *Pos:* Chmn div fine arts, Meadows Sch of the Arts, Southern Methodist Univ, 67-73, dir, Meadows Mus, 67-81; deputy dir, Kimbell Art Mus, 81-90. *Teaching:* Assoc prof Span art hist, Southern Methodist Univ, 68-75, prof Span art hist, 75-81. *Awards:* Spanish Knight Awards, Order of Isabel la Catolica, 86; Vassari Award, Dallas Mus, 86; Order of Civil Merit, 88. *Mem:* Am Soc of Hispanic Art Hist Studies (gen secy, 76-78); Hispanic Soc of Am. *Publ:* Auth, Juan van der Hamen y Leon, Univ Microfilms, 67; Murillo's Jacob laying the peeled rods before the flocks of Laban, Art News, 68; The Meadows Museum: A Visitor's Guide to the Collection, Meadows Mus, 74; El Greco of Toledo (catalog), Toledo Mus Art, 82; Spanish Still Life in the Golden Age: 1600-1650 (catalog), Kimbell Art Mus, 85; Still Lifes of Juan Sanchez Cotan, Museo del Prado, 92. *Mailing Add:* 3007 Maple No 409 Dallas TX 75201

JORGENSEN, FLEMMING
PAINTER
b Aalborg, Denmark, May 29, 34; Can citizen. *Study:* Art Sch Denmark. *Work:* Can Coun & Nat Gallery Can, Ottawa, Ont; McGill Univ; Univ Victoria; Winnipeg Art Gallery, Man. *Exhib:* 2nd Biennial Int Prints, Paris, France, 70; one-man shows, Marlborough-Godard, Montreal, Que, 72, Gallery Allen, Vancouver, 74, Bau-Xi Gallery, Victoria, 75 & Gallery Mira Godard, Toronto, 76; Kyle's Gallery, 79-83; North Park Studio, Victoria, 85. *Pos:* Vpres, Metholin Int Summer Sch Arts, currently. *Teaching:* Instr, Univ Victoria, BC, Lester B Pearson Col, currently. *Awards:* Can Coun Arts Bursary, 69 & 71. *Dealer:* Gallery Mira Godard 22 Hazelton Ave Toronto ON Can. *Mailing Add:* RR 2 Sydney BC V8L 3S1 Canada

JORGENSEN, ROGER M
SCULPTOR, PAINTER
b St Paul, Minn, June 21, 19. *Study:* Art Inst Chicago, dipl, 46; Art Students League, New York, 50. *Work:* Aldrich Mus, Ridgefield, Conn; Niagara Mus, NY. *Exhib:* Japanese-American Abstract Art, Mus Mod Art, Tokyo, 55; American Abstract Artists, Riverside Mus, New York, 56, NC Mus, Raleigh, 69 & Bronx Mus, NY, 86; Sculpture Now, Heckscher Mus, Huntington, NY, 68; Critic's Choice, Sculpture Ctr, New York, 72; solo exhib, Arnot Art Mus, Elmira, NY, 80. *Awards:* Emily Lowe Purchase Award, 52; Creative Artists Pub Serv Award, 75; Gottlieb Found Grant, 83. *Bibliog:* Corinne Robins (auth), Six artists and the new extended vision, Arts Mag, 9-10/65; John Canady (auth), Art without elevators, NY Times, 4/28/68; Amy Goldin (auth), Look aloft, Art News, 5/68. *Mem:* Am Abstract Artists. *Media:* Acrylic; Aluminum. *Mailing Add:* 15 Butler Pl Brooklyn NY 11238

JORGENSEN, SANDRA
PAINTER, EDUCATOR
b Evanston, Ill, Apr 21, 34. *Study:* Lake Forest Col, BA, 57; Akademie der Bildenden Kunste, Vienna, 58; Art Inst Chicago, MFA, 64. *Comn:* Conrad Sulzer Library Mural, City of Chicago, 85; poster, United Church of Christ, 87. *Exhib:* Richard Gray Gallery, Chicago, 74, 77, 83 & 87; Nancy Lurie Gallery, Chicago, 78; NAME Gallery, Chicago, 78; Art Inst Chicago, 78, 80 & 85; ARC Gallery, Chicago, 79; Hokin Kaufman Gallery,Chicago, 91; and others. *Pos:* Cur, Elmhurst Col Art Collection. *Teaching:* Prof art, Elmhurst Col, 66- *Media:* Oil. *Mailing Add:* 824 Chatham Elmhurst IL 60126

JORGENSON, DALE ALFRED
EDUCATOR, ADMINISTRATOR
b Litchfield, Nebr, Mar 20, 26. *Study:* Harding Col, Ark, philos with J D Bales, BMus, 48; George Peabody Col, Tenn, MA, 50; Ind Univ, aesthetics with John Mueller, PhD, 57; Harvard Univ, cert arts admin, 72. *Pos:* Retired. *Teaching:* Prof aesthetics, Bethany Col WVa, 59-62; dir fine arts, Milligan Col, Tenn, 62-63; head fine arts div & teacher aesthetics, Northeast Mo State Univ, 63-87; retired, 87. *Mem:* Am Soc Aesthetics; Midwest Col Art Asn. *Res:* Aesthetics and elementary aesthetics for contemporary students. *Publ:* Auth, Toward a biblical aesthetic, Christianity Today, 60; The campus and the arts, Proceedings of the Nat Asn Sch Music, 70; Preparing the educator for related arts, Music Educr J, 5/70; The French lieutenant's woman, or to forego manipulation, Christianity Today, 5/11/73; Theological-Aesthetic Roots in the Stone-Campbell Movement, Thomas Jefferson Univ Press, 1/89. *Mailing Add:* 1512 S Cottage Grove Kirksville MO 63501

JOSEPHSON, KENNETH BRADLEY
PHOTOGRAPHER, ASSEMBLAGE ARTIST
b Detroit, Mich, July 1, 32. *Study:* Rochester Inst Technol, BFA, 57; Inst Design, Ill Inst Technol, MS, 60. *Work:* Mus Mod Art, New York; Art Inst Chicago; Ctr Creative Photog, Univ Ariz; Mus Contemp Art, Chicago; Bibliot Nat, Paris. *Comn:* Great Ideas Series (assemblage), Container Corp Am, Chicago, 81; photog mural, SBI, Fla A&M Univ, 86. *Exhib:* The Photographer's Eye, Mus Mod Art, New York 64; solo exhib, Art Inst Chicago, 71, Mus Art, Univ Iowa, Iowa City, 74, Fotoforum, Kassel, Ger, 78 & Mus Contemp Art, Chicago, 83; Painting in the Age of Photography, Kunsthaus, Zurich, 77; Mirrors and Windows, Mus Mod Art, New York, 78. *Teaching:* Prof photog, Art Inst Chicago, 60-; exchange teacher, Konstfackskolan, Stockholm, Sweden, 66-67; assoc prof, Univ Hawaii, Honolulu, 67-68; vis prof, Univ Calif, Los Angeles, 81-82. *Awards:* Fels, Guggenheim Mem Found, 72 & Nat Endowment Arts, 75 & 79; Ruttenberg Arts Found Grant, 83. *Bibliog:* Alex Sweetman (auth), Reading the bread book--a ten page note, Afterimage, 3/74; Floris M Neussüs (auth), Kenneth Josephson: The illusion of the picture, Fotoforum, Kassel, Ger, 78; Lynne Warren & Carl Chiarenza (auths), Kenneth Josephson, Mus Contemp Art, Chicago, 83. *Publ:* Auth, The Bread Book, private publ, 73; contribr, New American imagery, Camera, Switz, Vol 53, No 5, 74; The Photographer's Choice, Addison House, 75; Nude: Theory, Lustrum Press, 79; Kenneth Josephson, Mus Contemp Art, Chicago, 83. *Mailing Add:* c/o Rhona Hoffman Gallery 215 W Superior St Chicago IL 60610

JOVINE, MARCEL
MEDALIST, DESIGNER
b Naples, Italy, July 26, 21; US citizen. *Study:* Univ Naples, Italy, BS; Royal Acad Turin, Italy, BS, 41; also studied with Brunetto Buracchini, Siena, Italy. *Work:* Horse Mus Ky, Lexington; Mus Racing, Saratoga, NY. *Comn:* Five medals celebrating 50th Anniversary of City of Palm Springs, 87; US Capitol Hist Soc celebrating Bicentennial of Constitution, 87, Congress, 88 & Supreme Court, 89; Five dollar Gold coin, US Mint, celebrating Bicentennial of Constitution, 87 & Am athletes at Olympic Games, 88; One dollar Silver coin, US Mint, celebrating 100 Anniversary Eisenhower's birthday, 89; and many more. *Exhib:* Nat Sculpture Soc, Equitable Life Ann, New York, 77-81; Cult Ctr, Sch Art, Demarest, NJ, 80-81. *Pos:* Bd dirs, Cult Ctr, Sch Art, Demarest, NJ. *Awards:* Lindsey-Morris Mem Award, 77 & M H Lamson Prize, 83, Nat Sculpture Soc; Winner, Medal Competition, Am Numismatic Soc, 83 & 87. *Mem:* Nat Sculpture Soc; Fedn Int Medaille. *Media:* Mixed Metals. *Mailing Add:* 270 Harrington Ave Closter NJ 07624

JOW, PAT See Kagemoto, Patricia Jow

JOYAUX, ALAIN GEORGES
MUSEUM DIRECTOR
b Lansing, Mich, Oct 28, 50. *Study:* Mich State Univ, BFA(studio), 75, MFA(studio), 77, MA(art hist), 78. *Collections Arranged:* European Tools From the 17th Century to the 19th Century (auth, catalog), 81; American Naive Painting: The Edgar William and Bernice Chrysler Garbish Collection (auth, catalog), Flint Inst Arts, 82; The Elisabeth Ball Collection of Paintings, Drawings and Watercolors: The George and Frances Ball Foundation (auth, catalog), 83; Childe Hassam in Indian (auth, catalog) 85. *Pos:* Asst dir, Flint Inst Arts, Mich, 78-83; dir, Ball State Univ Art Gallery, 83- *Mem:* Am Asn Museums; Intermuseum Conserv Asn (bd dir). *Res:* Late 19th century European art; Degas. *Mailing Add:* Art Gallery Ball State Univ Muncie IN 47306

JOYCE, J DAVID
PHOTOGRAPHER, SCULPTOR
b Kindersley, Sask, Jan 7, 46. *Study:* Carleton Univ, Ottawa, BA, 69; Univ Ore, Eugene, MA, 72, MFA, 75. *Work:* Seattle Arts Comn Portable Works Collection; City of Seattle; State of Ore; City of Eugene, Ore. *Comn:* Univ Ore Mus Art, Eugene, 82, Hult Ctr Performing Arts, Eugene, 83 & Mid-Valley Arts Coun, Salem, Ore, 83;; photosculpture theatre sets, Eugene Ballet Co, 82; photosculptures, Univ Ore Mus Art, Eugene, 82, Hult Ctr Performing Arts, Eugene, 83 & Mid-Valley Arts Coun, Salem, Ore, 83; City of Eugene, 86 & 88; State of Ore, 86; Seattle Arts Comm, 86; Mahlon Sweet Airport, Eugene, Ore. *Exhib:* Solo exhib, Triton Mus Art, Santa Clara, Calif, 83, Univ Ore Mus Art, Eugene, 85, Northwest Artists Workshop, Portland, Ore, 85, Maryhill Mus, Goldendale, Washington, 86, Ore State Univ, Corvallis, 86, Murcuse Pfeifer Gallery, New York, 87, 89 & Fine Arts Mus, Long Island, NY, 91; Alternative Image II, Kohler Art Ctr, Sheboygan, Wis, 83; Segmentations, Friends Photog, Carmel, Calif, 83; Theatre of Gesture, Los Angeles Ctr Photog Studies, 83; Electrostatics Int, Cleveland State Univ, 84. *Teaching:* Asst prof film, Loyola Univ, Montreal, 75-76; instr mass communication & design, Lane Community Col, Ore, 78- *Awards:* First Place, Washington-Oregon Juried Art Competition, Maryhill Mus, 85; Oregon Artists Fel, 86. *Bibliog:* The Photographic Sculpture of David Joyce, Nat Pub Radio, 7/10/87; articles in Darkroom Photography Mag, 10/85, 1/86 & 2/88. *Media:* Life size photographic and photocopy sculpture. *Dealer:* Marcuse Pfeifer Gallery 568 Broadway Suite 102 New York NY 10012; Susan Spiritus Gallery 3333 Bear St Suite 330 Costa Mesa CA 92626. *Mailing Add:* 990 Madison St Eugene OR 97402

JOYCE, MARSHALL WOODSIDE
PAINTER, INSTRUCTOR
b Medford, Mass, Mar 12, 12. *Study:* Art Inst, Boston. *Work:* Mus Fine Arts South, Mobile, Ala; Cranberry World & Plymouth Plantation, Mass; Peabody Mus, Salem; Mus Fine Arts, Anchorage; and others. *Comn:* Painting & carving, Plymouth Home Nat Bank, 65; painting, Plymouth Pub Libr, 67; calendar series, Davis Standard Co, Pawcatuck, Conn; painting, Kingston Pub Libr, Mass; Sears Tower, Chicago; and other pvt comns. *Exhib:* Marine Painting Nat Competition, Franklin Mint, Philadelphia, 74; Rockport Art Asn, Mass, 74; NShore Art Asn, Gloucester; Cape Cod Art Asn, Barnstable, Mass; Am Soc Marine Artists, New York, 80; Guild Boston Artists, Boston, 80; and others. *Pos:* Demonstrator, workshops, Key West, Fla, Anchorage, Alaska, Mus Fine Arts, Mobile, Ala & Jackson, NH; freelance artist & illusr,

Boston, 36-60; art dir, Gunnar Myrbeck, Quincy, Mass, 61-64. *Teaching:* Instr design illus, Butera Sch Art, Boston, 61-70. *Awards:* Marine Painting Prize, Franklin Mint, 74; Gold Medal of Honor, Rockport Art Asn, 74; 1st Prize, New Eng Watercolor Soc, 80. *Mem:* Rockport Art Asn, Mass; Am Soc Marine Artists; Cape Cod Art Asn; New Eng Watercolor Asn; Guild Boston Artists. *Media:* Oil, Watercolor. *Publ:* Illusr, Skipper Mag, 67; illusr calendars, Davis-Standard Co, Pawcatuck, Conn, 56-57. *Mailing Add:* 5 River St Kingston MA 02364

JOYNER, JOHN BROOKS
HISTORIAN, MUSEUM DIRECTOR
b Baltimore, Md, Nov 24, 44. *Study:* Univ Md, BA, 66, MA, 69. *Collections Arranged:* Asian & African Art, Towson State Univ, 72-73; Permanent Collections, Univ Calgary, 75-76; George Rickey Sculpture, South Bend Art Ctr, 82; Patronage in Southern Art Mus, The Grand Tour, 88; Art of the Eighties: Selections from the Whitney Mus, 90. *Pos:* Dir, Nickle Arts Mus, Univ Calgary, 75-81, South Bend Art Ctr, Ind, 83-87 & Montgonery Mus Fine Arts, 87- *Teaching:* Lectr art hist, Towson State Univ, Baltimore, 72-74, Univ Calgary, Can, 72-80 & Univ Alta, Edmonton, Can, 80-83. *Mem:* Asn Art Mus Dirs; Am Asn Mus; Int Coun Mus. *Res:* 19th-20th century Europe & American painting & sculpture; Arshile Gorky's drawings & Canadian art. *Publ:* Auth, The Drawings of Arshile Gorky (monogr), Univ Md, 69; auth, Stephen Andrews-Banff, Art Mag, 10/77; auth, Printmaking in Alberta, Art Mag, 2/77; ed, the Sculpture of George Rickey (exhib catalog), South Bend Art Ctr, 85; auth, Marion Nicoll RCA, Masters Gallery Ltd, 80. *Mailing Add:* 533 Martha St Montgomery AL 36104

JU, I-HSIUNG
EDUCATOR, PAINTER
b Kiangyin, China, Sept 15, 23. *Study:* Nat Univ Amoy, China, AB(Chinese art), 47; Univ Santo Tomas, Manila, BFA, 55, MA(hist), 68. *Work:* Philippine Cult Ctr, Manila; Nat Mus Hist, Taipei, Taiwan; Int Ctr, Univ Conn; DuPont Art Gallery, Washington & Lee Univ; F&M Ctr, Richmond, Va; and others. *Comn:* 14 paintings, Gulf States Paper Corp Nat Hq, Tuscaloosa, Ala, 70-71; and others. *Exhib:* South-East Asian Art Contest, Manila, 57; Asian Arts Festival, Univ Philippines, Manila, 65; Philippine & Japan Joint Art Exhib, Nat Mus Hist, Taipei, 66; 10th Japan Nan-ga-in Exhib, Tokyo, Kyoto & Osaka Mus, 70; Nat Painting & Calligraph Exhib, Nat Gallery, Taipei, 70 & 74. *Teaching:* Lectr Chinese arts, Univ Maine, Univ NH, Univ Vt, Univ Conn, 68-69 & Va Mus Fine Arts, Richmond, 69-89; prof art, Univ Va & Washington & Lee Univ, 69-89, prof emer, 89- *Awards:* Ring-Tum-Phi Award, Washington & Lee Univ, 71; Art Educator of the Year, Taiwan, 74; Spec Award for Contrib to the Arts, Nat Mus of Hist, Taipai, 78. *Mem:* Col Art Asn Am; Am Asn Univ Prof. *Media:* Ink, Acrylic. *Publ:* Illusr, The Children of Light, 56; auth, About Art, 59; Book of Bamboo, Book of Orchids (2nd & 3rd eds), A Collection of Recent Landscape Paintings by Ju Nat Mus of Hist, Taipai, 76; Book of Chrysanthemum, 84, Book of Plum, 88, Art Farm Gallery, 1st ed; illusr, Beyond the Good Earth, Art Farm Gallery, 91. *Mailing Add:* Art Farm Gallery Rt 5, Box 85 Lexington VA 24450

JUAREZ, ROBERTO
PAINTER
b Chicago, Ill, 1952. *Study:* San Francisco Art Inst, BFA; Univ Calif, Los Angeles, 78-79. *Work:* Newark Mus, NJ; Atlantic Richfield Co, Los Angeles; Gulf & Western, New York; Goldman & Sachs, New York; Rutgers Univ, New Brunswick, NJ; Metrop Mus Art, New York; General Mills Corp, Minneapolis, Minn. *Comn:* 25' X 9 1/2' mural painting, Tri Am, Coral Gables, Fla, 90. *Exhib:* New Wave, New York, Inst Art & Urban Resources, PS1, New York, 81; New Visions, Aldrich Mus, 81; Back to the USA, Kunstmuseum, Luzern, Theinisches Landesmuseum, Bonn & Württembergischer Kunstverein, Stuttgart, 83 & 84; American Artist as Printmaker, Brooklyn Mus, 83-84; An International Survey of Recent Painting and Sculpture (with catalog), Mus Mod Art, New York, 84; New American Painting: A Tribute to James & Mari Michener, Archer M Huntington Art Gallery, Univ Tex, Austin, 84; Blast, 84 & Double Vision, 85, B-Side Gallery, New York; Innovative Still Life, Holly Solomon Gallery, New York, 85; This Way-This Way, Thorpe Intermedia Gallery, Sparkhill, NY, 85; solo exhib, San Francisco Art Inst, Calif, 77, Robert Miller Gallery, New York, 77, 81, 84, 86 & 87, Staller Ctr Arts, State Univ NY, 91; Midtown Payson Galleries, New York, 92; Betsy Rosenfield Gallery, Chicago, Ill, 92; Neuberger Mus, State Univ New York, 92-93. *Pos:* Artist-in-residence, Gulf & Western Co, Altos de Chavon, Dominican Republic, 84; painting workshops, Anderson Ranch, Aspen, 88, 89 & 90. *Teaching:* Vis artist, Pilchuck Glass Ctr, Stanwood, Wash, 91; vis artist, Yale Univ, Norfolk, Conn, 91; vis artist, Anderson Ranch, Snow Mass, Colo, 92. *Bibliog:* Roberta Smith (auth), article, Village Voice, 12/81; Grace Glueck (auth), article, New York Times, 1/28/83; Susan Hapgood (auth), article, Flash Art, 3/83. *Media:* Oil, Acrylic. *Dealer:* Robert Miller Gallery 724 Fifth Ave New York NY 10019. *Mailing Add:* 303 E 8th St New York NY 10009

JUDD, DE FORREST HALE
PAINTER, EDUCATOR
b Hartsgrove, Ohio, Apr 4, 16. *Study:* Cleveland Inst Art, grad, 38, post grad scholar, 39; Colorado Springs Fine Arts Ctr, with Boardman Robinson, 39-42. *Work:* Cleveland Mus Art, Ohio; Dallas Mus Fine Arts, Tex; Beaumont Mus Art, Tex; Univ Tex, Austin; Southern Methodist Univ. *Exhib:* American Painting Today, Metrop Mus Art, 50; Texas Contemporary Artists, Knoedler Gallery, New York, 52; New Accessions, USA, Colorado Springs Fine Arts Ctr, 52; Ten Texas Painters, Frank Perls Gallery, Beverly Hills, Calif, 53; Texas Painting & Sculpture, 20th Century, Southern Methodist Univ, 71. *Teaching:* Prof painting, Southern Methodist Univ, 46-82, prof emer, 82. *Awards:* First Prize, Cleveland Mus Art, 41; E M Dealey Purchase Award, Tex Painters & Sculptors Exhib, 50; First Prize, 2nd Ann Exhib, Beaumont Mus Art, 53. *Media:* Oil, Acrylic. *Mailing Add:* 1620 Piedmont Pl Carrollton TX 75007

JUDD, DONALD CLARENCE
SCULPTOR, ARCHITECT
b Excelsior Springs, Mo, June 3, 28. *Study:* Art Students League, 47-53; Columbia Univ, BS(philos), 53, grad study, 58-61. *Work:* Mus Mod Art, Whitney Mus Art, New York; Walker Art Ctr, Minneapolis, Minn; Los Angeles Co Mus; Albright-Knox Art Gallery, Buffalo; and others. *Comn:* Art Gallery SAustralia, 74, Northern Ky Univ, 77, Linz, Austria, 77 & Muenster, WGer, 77. *Exhib:* One-man shows, Whitney Mus Am Art, (with catalog), 68, Pasadena Art Mus, Calif, 70, Kunsthalle, Bern, 76, Mus STex, Corpus Christi, 77, Watari Gallery, Tokyo, Japan, 78 & Gallery Yamaguchi, Osaka, Japan, traveling, 92-93; New York Painting & Sculpture: 1940-1970, Metrop Mus Art, New York, 69-70; retrospective, Nat Gallery Can, Ottawa, 75; Kunstmuseum Basel, Switzerland; Leo Castelli Gallery, New York, all years; Knight Gallery, Charlotte, NC, 83; Galerie Aronowitsch, Stockholm, 88; Paula Cooper Gallery, New York, 88; Whitney Mus Am Art, New York, 88; Arte Americana 1930-70 (with catalog), Lingotto, Torino, Italy, 92; and others. *Pos:* Contrib ed, Arts Mag, 59-65. *Awards:* Guggenheim Grant, 68; Skowhegan Medal Sculpture, 87; Brandeis Univ Medal Sculpture, 87. *Bibliog:* Ken Johnson (auth), Review Exhibitions, Art in Am, p 104, 6/92; Mark Stevens (auth), Art Oasis, Vanity Fair, p 106-111, 7/92; Franco Fanelli (auth), Basil Transformed, Art Newspaper, No 20, 7-9/92. *Media:* Metal, Plywood. *Publ:* Auth, Nie wieder Krieg, Kunst & Mus J, Vol 2, No 5, p 19-22, 91; Art & Internationalism Prolegomena, Osaka: Gallery Yamaguchi, 92; Specific Objects, Osaka: Gallery Yamaguchi, 92. *Dealer:* Paula Cooper Inc 155 Wooster St New York NY 10012. *Mailing Add:* 101 Spring St New York NY 10013

JUDGE, MARY FRANCES
PAINTER
b Minneapolis, Minn, July 31, 35. *Study:* Col New Rochelle, NY, BA(art), 61; Webster Col, St Louis, Mo; Univ Notre Dame, Ind, MFA(painting), 71. *Work:* Carnegie Mus, Pittsburgh, Pa; Springfield Col Gallery, Ill; Nobles Co Art Ctr, Worthington, Minn; Lee Co Cult Ctr, Ft Myers, Fla; Oak Ridge Mus, Tenn. *Exhib:* Midwest Biennial, Joslyn Mus, Omaha, Nebr, 72; Ann Exhib, Springfield Mus, Mo, 70; Ann Mid-States Exhib, Evansville Mus, Ind, 71; Am Women Artists, Mus Contemp Art, Sao Paulo, Brazil, 80; Brooks Mus Art, Memphis, Tenn, 70 & 71. *Pos:* Mem bd, Dallas Mus Fine Arts, Tex, 76-77. *Awards:* Strathmore Nat Art Award, Scholastic Art Awards, Strathmore Papers, 50; Bixby Portrait Award, St Louis Artists Guild, 71. *Bibliog:* Hedy O'Beil (auth), article, Arts Mag, 10/78; Terry Trucco (auth), article, Art News, 5/79; Marian Courtney (auth), article, NY Times, 6/26/83; Dennis Wepman (auth, article), Manhattan Arts, 89. *Mem:* St Louis Women Artists (bd mem, 72-74); Artist Equity (NY & bd mem Dallas, 74-78). *Media:* All. *Dealer:* Dolly Fiterman Art Gallery 100 University SE Minneapolis MN 55414; Blondie's Contemp Art 72 Thompson St New York NY 10012. *Mailing Add:* PO Box 702 Canal Street Sta New York NY 10013

JUDSON, JEANNETTE ALEXANDER
PAINTER, COLLAGE ARTIST
b New York, NY, Feb 23, 12. *Study:* Nat Acad Design, with Robert Phillip & Leon Kroll; Art Students League, with Vaclav Vytlacil, Charles Alston, Carl Holty & Sidney Gross. *Work:* US State Dept & Hirshhorn Mus, Wash, DC; Brandeis Univ; Mus NMex; Columbia Univ, Brooklyn Mus, Fordham Univ & NY Univ, New York; and many other pub and pvt collections. *Exhib:* One-man shows, Pa State Univ, 69, NY Univ, 69, Syracuse Univ House, New York, 75 & Am Standard Gallery, 80; Key Gallery, New York, 80-83; Bodley Gallery, 67, 69, 71 & 73; and others. *Awards:* Am Soc Contemp Artists Award, 76, 78 & 85, D Feigen Mem Award, 77, Am Soc Contemp Artists; Nat Asn Women Artists Award, 79. *Mem:* Nat Asn Women Artists; Am Soc Contemp Artists; Artists Equity New York. *Media:* Acrylic, Mixed Media. *Mailing Add:* 1130 Park Ave New York NY 10128

JUDSON, WILLIAM D
CURATOR, HISTORIAN
b New London, Conn, Dec 10, 39. *Study:* Williams Col, BA, 60; Oberlin Col, MA, 68; Yale Univ. *Collections Arranged:* 73 var vis artist presentations, 75- *Pos:* Cur film & video, Mus Art, Carnegie Inst, Pittsburgh, 75-; panelist media arts, Nat Endowment Arts, 78-; bd mem, Pittsburgh Filmmakers Inc, 74- *Teaching:* Adj inst film hist, Univ Pittsburgh, 73- *Mem:* Col Art Asn; Ohio Valley Regional Media Arts Coalition (pres, 80-); Am Film Inst; Am Fedn Arts (film adv bd, 78-). *Res:* Early film history; documentary film; experimental film; 20th century art. *Mailing Add:* Carnegie Mus Art 440 Forbes Ave Pittsburgh PA 15213

JUDSON-RHODES, PAMELA
HISTORIAN
b Manchester, Eng, May 1, 27; US citizen. *Study:* Manchester Univ, BA, 50, Univ Pa, PhD(classical archaeol), 68. *Teaching:* Prof classical, medieval & modern art, Women's Studies, West Chester State Col, 70-, chairperson dept art, 79-81. *Awards:* Ital Govt Fel, 65; Fulbright Travel Grant, 65; Am Philos Soc Study Grant, 74; artist-in-residence, British Sch Rome, summer 74; Can Coun Res Grant, 77-80; Westchester State Col Res Grant, 79-80; plus other res grants. *Mem:* Am Inst Archaeol; Inst Studi Romani; Inst Field Archaeol. *Res:* Surface survey in Italy to find new pottery types and land usage in Italy from prehistoric to medieval times. *Publ:* Auth, Survey of the hill country north of Rome, Exped Mag, 70; Notes to slide sets on Roman Forum,

Palestine and Herculaneum, Am Inst Archaeol, 73; Cassia-Claudia Survey, Papers of Brit Sch, Rome, Vol 43, 75; De-forestation and re-forestation in a Central Italian hinterland: Land usage during and after the Roman Occupation, British Archael Reports: Inter Series, 85; coauth, Bridging a seasonal torrent: Geomorphology and archaeology in the Melfa-Liri Valley, Geoarchaelogy, 86. *Mailing Add:* 18 Aiken Ave Princeton NJ 08540

JULES, MERVIN
PAINTER, EDUCATOR
b Baltimore, Md, Mar 21, 12. *Study:* Baltimore City Col; Md Inst Fine & Appl Arts; Art Students League. *Work:* Metrop Mus Art, New York; Art Inst Chicago; Mus Fine Arts, Boston; Portland Art Mus; Libr Cong, Washington, DC; Baltimore Mus Art; Brooklyn Mus; Walker Art Ctr; Fogg Mus; Nat Collection Fine Arts, Washington, DC; Philadelphia Mus; Tel Aviv Mus; Brandeis Univ; plus many other pub & pvt collections. *Exhib:* Carnegie Inst Int, Pittsburgh; San Francisco World's Fair; Artists for Victory, sent to England; Corcoran Gallery Art; Whitney Mus Am Art; one-man exhibs, AFS Gallery, 71, Century Club, New York, 71, Ringwood Manor Asn Arts, NJ, 73, Galerie Macler, Sarasota, Fla, 77 & 80, Cherry Stone Gallery, Wellfleet, Mass, 79, Danco Gallery, Florence, Mass, 79 & Century Asn, New York, 82; two-man exhibs, Provincetown Group, Mass, 73-76; plus many others. *Pos:* Trustee, Cummington Sch Music & Art, Provincetown Art Asn & Fine Arts Work Ctr, Provincetown, Mass, formerly. *Teaching:* Vis artist, Smith Col, 45-46, assoc prof, 46-63, prof, 64-69; prof art & chmn dept, City Col New York, 70-80, prof emer, 80. *Awards:* Res Found Grant, City Univ New York, 76; Fel Grant, City Col New York, 77-78; Fel, MacDowell Colony, 78; and others. *Mem:* Audubon Artists; Soc Am Etchers, Engravers, Lithographers, & Woodcutters; Boston Printmakers; fel Royal Soc Arts; Inst Study Art Educ (governing bd); and others. *Publ:* Auth, many articles in nat art publ. *Mailing Add:* 74-14 Burns St Forest Hills Gardens NY 11375

JULIAN, LAZARO
PAINTER, DESIGNER
b Guadalajara, Mex, Mar 12, 45. *Work:* Mus del Estado de Jalisco. *Exhib:* One-man show, Constructions, Rhoda Sande Gallery, New York, 76 & 77; Iman New York, Mod Art Mus, Ponce de Leon, PR, 76 & Ctr Inter-Am Relations, New York, 76; Primera Muestra de la Plastica Jalisciense, Guadalajara, 77; Artists 77 Int Exhib, Union Carbide Bldg, New York, 77. *Pos:* Dir graphic design dept, Departamento de Bellas Artes del Gobierno del Estado de Jalisco, Mex, 72-73. *Bibliog:* Diana Loercher (auth), Art posing a riddle, Christian Sci Monitor, 3/8/76; Abraham Kein (auth), Conceptual constructions, The Eastsider, New York, 5/26/77; Howard Katzander (auth), Mexican art, Archit Digest, 1/78. *Media:* Acrylic, Cardboard. *Mailing Add:* c/o Rhoda Sande Gallery 220 E 60th St New York NY 10022

JULIO, PAT T
EDUCATOR, CRAFTSMAN
b Youngstown, Ohio, Mar 1, 23. *Study:* Wittenberg Col, BFA, with Ralston Thompson; Univ NMex, MA, with Raymond Jonson & Lex Haas; Univ Colo, with Robert Lister; Ohio State Univ, with Edgar Littlefield; Tex Western Col, with Wiltz Harrison. *Comn:* Stained glass windows, Episcopal Good Samaritan Church, Community Church & pvt collections. *Exhib:* Denver Art Mus, 50 & 63; Pueblo Art Mus, 60; Pueblo Col, 60 & 69; one-man shows, Pueblo Art Mus, 64 & Western State Art Gallery, 69. *Teaching:* Prof art, Western State Col, 71- *Mem:* Col Art Asn Am; Western Art Asn; Am Ceramic Soc; Am Crafts Coun; Inst Indian Studies; and others. *Mailing Add:* 145 Silver Sage Dr Gunnison CO 81230

JUNG, KWAN YEE
PAINTER
b Toysun, China, Nov 25, 32; US citizen. *Study:* Chinese Univ Hong Kong New Asia Col, BA(painting), 61; San Diego State Univ, postgrad studies, 68. *Work:* Springville Mus Art, Utah; Utah State Univ Galleries, Logan; IBM Corp, Austin, Tex; Southern Utah State Col, Cedar; Winsor & Newton, Calif; General Atomic, San Diego. *Exhib:* Calif Nat Watercolor Soc Ann, 72-79; Watercolor USA, 72 & 75; Am Watercolor Soc Ann Exhib, 73-78; Nat Acad Design Ann, 74, 82, 86 & 92; one-man shows, Univ Hong Kong, 75, Edward Dean Mus, Calif, 77 & US Int Univ, San Diego, 83. *Awards:* Nat Watercolor Soc Award, Watercolor West Soc, 75; Am Watercolor Soc Award, 76, 78 & 87; Best of Show, Sumi-E Soc Am, 79; Merit Award, Nat Acad Design, 92. *Bibliog:* Interview, Spectrum-TV 10, San Diego, 82; interview, Artist-TV 51, San Diego, 83; article in SW Art Mag, 1/83; article in Western Arts Digest, 5-6/86. *Mem:* Nat Watercolor Soc; Am Watercolor Soc. *Media:* Watercolor, Oil. *Publ:* Special Focus on California, Art Voices, 2/83; Splash 1 & 2, America's Best Contemporary Watercolor, North Light, 91 & 92; Kwan Y Jung & Yeewah Jung, Art of Calif, 11/92. *Dealer:* 5468 Bloch St San Diego CA 92122. *Mailing Add:* 5468 Bloch St San Diego CA 92122

JUNG, YEE WAH
PAINTER
b Canton, China, Sept 4, 36; US citizen. *Study:* Chung Man Art Sch, WuHun, China, 54-58; Chinese Univ Hong Kong New Asia Col, 58-62. *Comn:* The Tours of Confucius (mosaic painting), Facade of Ambassador Hotel (with Chiu Fung Poon), 59. *Exhib:* Calif Nat Watercolor Soc, 73-74 & 90; Watercolor USA, 73-75 & 88; Nat Acad Design, 74; Butler Inst Am Art, 74; Am Watercolor Soc, 74-75; Redlands Art Asn, 84; San Diego Watercolor Soc, 87. *Awards:* First Place, Southern Calif Expo Art, Del Mar, 71; Calif Nat Watercolor Soc Award, Watercolor USA, 73-78; Watercolor USA Award, Calif Nat Watercolor Soc, 77; First Prize, 25th Art Festival Exhib, 88; Seventh Ann King's Award, Advent Fine Arts Exhib, 89. *Bibliog:* Interview, Spectrum-TV 10, San Diego, 82; article, SW Art Mag, 1/83. *Mem:* Nat Watercolor Soc; Watercolor USA Hon Soc. *Media:* Oil, Watercolor. *Publ:* Auth, Environmental Escape, Southwest Art, 1/83; Splash 1, America's Best Contemporary Watercolor, North Light, 91; Kwan Jung & Yeewah Jung, Art of Calif, 11/92. *Dealer:* 5468 Bloch St San Diego CA 92122. *Mailing Add:* 5468 Bloch St San Diego CA 92122

JURINKO, ANDY (ANDREW FLOYD)
PAINTER
b Phillipsburg, NJ, June 17, 39. *Study:* Kutztown State Col, Pa, 57-58; Philadelphia Mus Col Art, 61-63. *Work:* Sports Mus NEng, Boston, Mass; Nat Baseball Mus & Hall Fame, Cooperstown, NY. *Exhib:* The Grand Game of Baseball, Mus Burough, Brooklyn, NY, 87; Diamonds Are Forever, traveling exhib, 87-90; Diamond Gold, Nat Baseball Mus, 89; Gallery Howoch, New York, 89. *Teaching:* Instr illus, Philadelphia Col Art, 87-88. *Bibliog:* Subject of Sportslook, ESPN, 6/89; Baseball Mag, ESPN, 8/89; New York Mag, 8/92. *Media:* Acrylic, Oil. *Publ:* Diamonds Are Forever, Chronicle Books, 89-90; Summer, Addison Wesley Publ, 90; The Art of Baseball, Harmony Books, 90; Shibe Park, Princeton, 91; Fenway, Putnam, 92. *Dealer:* Gallery Henoch 80 Wooster St New York NY 10012. *Mailing Add:* 125 Cedar St New York NY 10006

JURNEY, DONALD (BENSON)
PAINTER
b Rye, NY, Jan 7, 45. *Study:* Pratt Inst, NY, 71-72; Art Students League, 79. *Work:* Mus City of New York; Hudson River Mus, Yonkers, NY; Bank Am, San Francisco, Calif. *Comn:* Lobby Paintings, Clorox Co, Oakland, Calif. *Exhib:* Berkshire Art Asn, Berkshire Mus, Pittsfield, Mass, 80; Silvermine Guild, New Canaan, Conn, 80; 45th Ann Mid-Year Exhib, Butler Inst, Youngstown, Ohio, 81; Parrish Art Mus, Southampton, NY, 81; 159th Ann Exhib, Nat Acad, NY, 84; 163rd Ann Exhib, Nat Acad, 88. *Awards:* C R Gibson Award, 31st New Eng Exhib, 80; Award of Merit, 62nd Nat Exhib, Springfield Art League, 81; Special Award, 19th Ann Exhib, Putnam Arts Coun, 81. *Bibliog:* Eric Widing (auth), Donald Jurney, 11/82 & M Stephen Doherty (auth), Motifs for landscape painting, 2/84, Am Artist; film, Reflections on the Hudson, CBS-TV, 9/84. *Media:* Oil, Watercolor. *Dealer:* John Pence Gallery 750 Post St San Francisco CA 94109; Five Points Gallery Rt 29 East Chatham NY 12060. *Mailing Add:* Maple Ave Box 813 Sheffield MA 01257

JURSEVSKIS, ZIGFRIDS
SCULPTOR
b Ceresy, Poland, Mar 11, 10; Can citizen. *Study:* Sch Fine Arts & Crafts, Latvia, diploma 30; Art Sch, Liepaja, Latvia, cert, 36. *Work:* Rodman Hall Gallery Collection, St Catharine's, Ontario; Sculptor's Soc of Can Collection, Toronto, Ont. *Comn:* Geese (bronze sculpture), Vitols Tool & Machine Corp, Philadelphia, 78. *Exhib:* Salone Int Del Ceramica, Vicenza, Italy, 60; Art Gallery Hamilton, Ontario, 63 & 66; Winnipeg Art Gallery, BC, 64; McMichael Exhib Gallery, Kleinburg, Ont, 80; Color & Form Soc, 84-88; Sculptor's Soc of Can Shows, 85 & 87-88; Sculptor Soc of Can Traveling Show, London, Paris, Brussels, Budapest, 87. *Pos:* Head ceramics studio, Zigfrid's Art Pottery, Toronto, 57- *Teaching:* Head ceramics dept, Art Sch, Liepaja, Latvia, 36-44. *Awards:* Mem Award, Sculpture 80's, Mary Arthur Huper, 80; World Free Latvians Asn Award, 86; Colour & Form Soc Life Mem Award, 87; and others. *Bibliog:* Suzanne Morrison (auth), Latvian won Canadian handicraft prize at Canadian National Exhibit, Toronto Daily Star, 9/2/65; Velta Toma (auth), Zigfrids Jursevskis, Labietis Mag, No 38, Chicago, 69; Erika Kronbergs (auth), Zigfrids Jursevskis, Latvian Art Mag, 83 & 87. *Mem:* Sculptors Soc Can; Colour & Form Soc; Latvis Soc Artists (treas, 62-75, vpres, 75-); Am Latvian Artists Asn. *Media:* Bronze, Stone. *Mailing Add:* 1425A Bloor St W Toronto ON M6P 3L6 Canada

JUSTIS, GARY (ALLEN)
SCULPTOR
b Wichita, Kans, Apr 4, 53. *Study:* Wichita State Univ, BFA, 77; Sch Art Inst Chicago, MFA, 79. *Work:* Mus Contemp Art, Borg-Warner Corp, Chicago; Ill State Mus, Springfield; Krannert Mus Art, Champaign, Ill; Alexandria Mus Art, La. *Comn:* Wall sculpture, Carson's Int, O'Hare Int Airport, Chicago, 87; sculpture, Carson's Int, O'Hare Int Airport, 90; Garden Park comn, Gary Justis & L J Douglas, Evanston, Ill, 92. *Exhib:* Dimensions Variable, New Mus, New York, 79; solo exhib, Object-Luminosus-Objectus, Mus Sci & Industry, Chicago, 82, Hyperfunctional Icons, Chicago Cult Ctr, 85, Mythos, Beyond Function, Alexandria Mus Art, La, 86, Recent Sculpture, Mus Southeast Tex & The Causal Garden, Compass Rose Gallery, Chicago; Painting & Sculpture Today, Indianapolis Mus, 84; Chicago Art Inst, 84; Ten Years of Collecting, Mus Contemp Art, Chicago, 84; Modern Machines, Whitney Mus Am Art, New York, 85. *Teaching:* Instr sculpture, Sch Art Inst Chicago, 86-; adj asst prof, Univ Ill, Chicago, 88-89; guest lectr, Northwestern Univ, Chicago, 91-93. *Awards:* Edward L Ryerson Fel Award, 79; Nat Endowment Arts Grant, 84; Ill Arts Coun Fel, 84. *Bibliog:* Judith Russi Kirshner (auth), Gary Justis--MSI, Art Forum, 12/82; Dan Cameron (auth), New generation of Chicago artists, Art News, 10/84; Michael Bonesteel (auth), article, Art in Am, 6/85; James Yood (auth), article, Artforum, 12/88; Lauri Dahlberg (auth), article, Dialogue Mag, 90. *Media:* Miscellaneous Media. *Publ:* Auth, Speakeasy, New Art Examiner, Summer 90. *Mailing Add:* 571 W 18th St Chicago IL 60610

JUSZCZYK, JAMES JOSEPH
PAINTER
b Chicago, Ill, Jan 30, 43. *Study:* Univ Ill, Urbana, 60-62; Cleveland Inst Art, BFA(Ford Found Grant), 66; Univ Pa, MFA(fel), 69. *Work:* Chase Manhattan Bank, Merill Lynch Int Zurich, Swiss Bank Corp, Krannert Art

Mus, Univ Ill, Meier & Steinauer AG Zurich. *Comn:* Chromos Electronic AG Zurich, 6/88. *Exhib:* Eight Abstract Painters, Inst Contemp Art, Univ Pa, 78; Geometric Abstraction: A New Generation, Inst Contemp Art, Boston, 81; one-man shows, Gimpel Hanover Galerie, Zurich, Switz, 75-77 & 82, Jan Cicero Gallery, Chicago, 80, 83 & 87, Galerie Knostruktiv Tendens, Stockholm, 82 & 85, ACP Art Coop Palladino, Zurich, Switz, 88, Jan Cicero Gallery, Chicago, Ill, 92; Am Abstract Artists 50th Anniversary Exhib, Bronx Mus Fine Art, NY, 86; Found Constructive and Concrete Art, Zurich, 91. *Pos:* Guest artist-in-residence, Ill State Univ, 79 & Atelierhaus, Zurich, Switz, 86. *Teaching:* Vis artist, Ohio State Univ, 89. *Bibliog:* Klaus Dencker & Garret Holg (auths), Hakin Geometry (exhib catalog), 88; Katrina Vatsella, Pius Sidler & Corey Postiglione (auths), Hakin Geometry II (exhib catalog), 90; Willy Rotzler (auth), Ausstellungskatalog James Juszczyk, Bilder 1990, Rational und Meditativ Zur Malerei von James Juszczyk, 91. *Mem:* Am Abstract Artists; Pro Found. *Media:* Acrylic on Canvas. *Dealer:* Jan Cicero 221 W Erie St Chicago IL 60610; ACP Viviane Ehrhi Galerie Bahnhofquaill CH-8001 Zurich Switz. *Mailing Add:* 74 Grant St New York NY 10013

K

KACERE, JOHN C
PAINTER
b Walker, Iowa, June 23, 20. *Study:* Mizen Acad Art, Chicago, Ill, 38-42; State Univ of Iowa, Ames, 46-51, BFA, 49 & MFA, 50. *Work:* Stedelijk Mus, Amsterdam; Wadsworth Atheneum, Hartford, Conn; Portland Art Mus, Oregon; J B Speed Mus, Louisville, Ky; Daniel Filipacchi, Paris, France; and others. *Exhib:* Walker Art Ctr (traveling), Minneapolis, Minn, 49; Corcoran Gallery, Washington, DC, 63; The Realist Revival, Mus Mod Art, New York, 72; Relativierend Realismus, Stedelijk van Abbemuseum, Eindhoven, Holland, 72; Super-Realist Vision, DeCordova Mus, Lincoln, Mass, 73; Hyperrealistes Americans Fotorealisme, Grafick, Hendendaagse Kunst, Utrecht & Palais van Schone Kunst, Brussels, Belg: Art Inst Chicago; one-man shows, La State Univ, Baton Rouge, 71, 57, Allan Stone Gallery, New York, 63, & O K Harris Gallery, New York, 71, 73, 75, 78, 80, 82, 84, 87 & 89; Brenda Kroos Gallery, Columbus, Ohio, 88; Lavignes-Bastille, Paris, France, 88; Galerie Lavignes Bastille, Paris, France, 91; Amerikansk Kunst efter 1960, Holtegaard, Denmark, 91; Photorealism From Nashville Collections, Cheekwood Fine Arts Ctr, Nashville, Tenn, 92; The Articulated Thumbprint, Boca Raton Mus Art, Fla, 92; and others. *Teaching:* Asst, State Univ Iowa, 49-50; instr, Univ Manitoba, 50-53 & Univ Fla, Gainesville, 53-65; instr, Cooper Union, Parsons Sch Design, 58 & 64, Univ NMex, 64-72, New York Univ, 73-77, Sch Visual Arts, New York, 77. *Bibliog:* Laurent Chalumeau (auth), Portrait: John Kacere, 9/89; Jean-Marie Baron (auth), Paris en Parle: Expositions, 9/89; Art & Antiques, The Dealer as Collector, 96, 3/91. *Publ:* Auth, The End is Art, Oui, Paris, 5/74. *Dealer:* Harris Gallery 383 W Broadway New York NY 10012. *Mailing Add:* 43 Great Jones New York NY 10012

KACHADOORIAN, ZUBEL
PAINTER, EDUCATOR
b Detroit, Mich, Feb 7, 24. *Study:* Meinzinger Art Sch Detroit, 43-44; Saugatuck Summer Art Sch, Mich, 44-45; Skowhegan Sch Painting & Sculpture, Maine, 46; Colorado Springs Fine Arts Ctr, summer 47. *Work:* Detroit Inst Art; Art Inst Chicago; Worcester Mus, Mass; Smithsonian Inst, Washington, DC; William Rockhill Nelson Gallery, Kansas City; and others. *Comn:* Gold leaf & oil altar painting (6 1/2ft X 19ft), St John's Armenian Church Greater Detroit, 67. *Exhib:* Univ Ill, Urbana, 61; Am Ann, Art Inst Chicago, 61; Art USA Now, Johnson Wax Collection, 62; Butler Inst Am Art Ann, Youngstown, Ohio, 64 & 85; Ball State Univ, 73, 74 & 78-81; American Drawing II, Portsmouth, Va, 80. *Pos:* Adv, Common Grounds Detroit, 65-66; art dir, Detroit Repertory Theatre, 70-76; artist-in-the-school, Mich Coun for Arts, 79-82. *Teaching:* Artist-in-residence, Sch Art Inst Chicago, 60-61; instr painting & drawing, Skowhegan Sch Painting & Sculpture, summer 64; instr, Oxbow Sch Painting, Saugatuck, Mich, summer 60, 61, 68 & 69; prof drawing, Wayne State Univ, 67-73. *Awards:* Prix-de-Rome, Am Acad Rome, 56-59; Richard & Linda Rosenthal Award, Nat Inst Arts & Lett, 61; Creative Artist Grant, Mich Coun Arts, 83-84 & 90-91. *Bibliog:* A S Weller (auth), Art USA Now, C J Bucher, 62; Oral History: Archives Am Art, Smithsonian Inst, Washington, DC; Good afternoon Detroit-Kelly & Co, Channel 7, Mich, 84; Full Circle, Educational Channels, Univ Mich, Dearborn, 86. *Mem:* Fel Am Acad Rome. *Media:* Oil, Watercolor. *Dealer:* Old Town Gallery 44 Main St PO Box 2521 Park City UT 84061. *Mailing Add:* 1214 Beaubien Detroit MI 48226

KACHEL, HAROLD STANLEY
MUSEUM DIRECTOR, EDUCATOR
b Elmwood, Okla, Jan 25, 28. *Study:* Panhandle State Univ, Goodwell, Okla, BS; Okla State Univ, Stillwater, MS; Univ Northern Colo, EdD. *Collections Arranged:* Arrangement & cataloging of a minimum of nine exhibs annually. *Pos:* Asst cur, No Man's Land Hist Mus, Goodwell, Okla, 66-68, cur & mus dir, 68- *Teaching:* Instr crafts, Yarbrough Sch, Eva, Okla, 52-57; prof copper tooling & head, Indust Arts Dept, Panhandle State Univ, Goodwell, Okla, 57-90. *Awards:* Distinguished Serv Award, Area Artists Studio, Amarillo, Tex, 76; Teacher of Yr at Panhandle State Univ, Okla Educ Asn, 76; Palette Ward, Artists Studio NW, 82. *Bibliog:* Lee Tucker (auth), A Salute to No Man's Land Hist Mus, Old Timer's News, Keyes, Okla, 6/76. *Mem:* NW Artists Studio. *Mailing Add:* PO Box 307 Goodwell OK 73939

KAERICHER, JOHN CONRAD
PRINTMAKER, EDUCATOR
b Springfield, Ill, June 6, 36. *Study:* Millikin Univ with David Driesbach, BFA, 59; Univ Iowa, with Mauricio Lasansky, Stuart Edie, James Lechay & Robert Knipschild, MFA, 63. *Work:* Univ Iowa; Millikin Univ; Dordt Col; Northwestern Col Iowa; plus pvt collections. *Comn:* Medal, Northwestern Col, 66. *Exhib:* Cent Ill Ann, Decatur Art Ctr, 61-; Gov Off, State Capitol, Des Moines, Iowa, 71; Paper Works, 9th Ann, Waterloo Munic Gallery, 73; Kottler Galleries, New York, 73; Va Polytech Inst Ann, 74; Benjamin Galleries, Chicago, 76; Iowa Printmakers Invitational, Iowa Arts Coun, Des Moines. *Pos:* Gallery dir, Northwestern Col, 63-79, coordr permanent collection, 66- *Teaching:* Assoc prof printmaking & drawing, Northwestern Col Iowa, 63-, chmn art dept, 63-84, 89- *Awards:* Creative Prod Grants, Northwestern Col Iowa, 66, 68, 75, 77, 81 & 84. *Bibliog:* Rev of NY exhib in Park East Periodical, 10/25/73. *Mem:* Mid-Am Col Art Asn; Cols Mid-Am Art Fac Group; Iowa Print Group; Northwestern Printmakers; Found Art Theory & Educ. *Media:* Intaglio, Drawing. *Publ:* Survey of Iowa Printmakers. *Mailing Add:* 202 Arizona NW Orange City IA 51041

KAGAN, ANDREW AARON
HISTORIAN, CRITIC
b St Louis, Mo, Sept 22, 47. *Study:* Washington Univ, AB, 69; Harvard Univ, MA, 71, PhD, 77. *Pos:* Contributing ed, Arts Mag, New York; critic art & architecture, St Louis Globe-Democrat, Mo. *Teaching:* Critic-in-residence, Bennington Col, Vt, 72-73; vis prof art hist, Washington Univ, St Louis, Mo, 80-81. *Awards:* Ford Found Res Grant. *Bibliog:* Art Am, 10/83; Times Lit Suppl (London), 3/84; J Aesthetics & Art Criticism, summer, 84; Contemp Authors, vol 123. *Res:* Paul Klee studies; theory of absolute art; 18th & 20th century art hist, theory, criticism; 19th & 20th century architectural history & criticism. *Publ:* Auth, Paul Klee, Art and Music, Cornell Univ Press, 83, 87; Trova, Abrams, 88; Marc Chagall, Abbeville, 89; Absolute Art, Göttingen, 93; contribr, Dictionary of Art, McMillan; and others. *Mailing Add:* 232 N Kingshighway St Louis MO 63108

KAGEMOTO, HARO
FILMMAKER, PHOTOGRAPHER
b Tokyo, Japan, Jan 9, 52; US citizen. *Study:* Sch Modern Photog, NJ, cert, 72; Univ Hawaii, Manoa, BFA, 77; State Univ NY, New Paltz, MFA, 79. *Work:* Everson Mus Fine Art, Syracuse, NY; Erie Art Mus, Mich; Libr of Cong, Washington, DC; Calif Mus Photog, Santa Barbara; Guggenheim Mus, New York. *Exhib:* Prints & Drawing Invitational, Mariam Graves-Mugar Gallery, New London, NH, 81; Leisure Am, Tampa Mus Art, Fla, 83; Classical Photographs, Boston Mus Art, 83; Dada Duchamp Exhib, Colby-Sawyer Col, New London, NH, 83; Alaskan Mail Art Exhib, Ketchikan Arts Coun, 83 & 84; Games 92, St Cloud, Minn, 92; and others. *Pos:* Production mgr & asst dir, Wonderland Productions, San Francisco, 83-88, dir, 89- *Teaching:* Instr etching-intaglio, Communications Village, Kingston, NY, 77-79; vis artist photo-silkscreen, Univ Calif, Berkeley, 80-83; vis lectr printmaking, San Francisco State Univ, 83. *Mem:* Am Film Inst. *Mailing Add:* 2806 Truman Ave Oakland CA 94605

KAGEMOTO, PATRICIA JOW
PRINTMAKER, PHOTOGRAPHER
b New York, NY, Feb 20, 52. *Study:* State Univ NY, New Paltz, BFA, 75; Printmaking Workshop, New York, studied with Robert Blackburn, 84. *Work:* Collection of Bellevue Hosp, New York; Printmaking Workshop, New York. *Comn:* Intaglio print eds, Communications Village Ltd, Kingston, NY, 75. *Exhib:* Mohawk-Hudson Regional, Univ Art Gallery, State Univ NY, Albany, 76, Schenectady Mus, 77, Albany Inst Hist & Art, New York, 78; Invitational Art Exhib, Ctr Galleries, Albany, NY, 83; Affirmations of Life, Kenkeleba House, New York, 84; In a Stream of Ink, Col Art Gallery, State Univ NY, & Alumni Printmakers' Invitational, New Paltz, NY, 84; All Media I, Woodstock Artists' Asn, NY, 85 & 91. *Pos:* Consult printer, Printmaking Workshop, New York, 84; exhibition auditor, NY State Coun Arts, New York, 84-87; gallery asst, Watermark/Cargo Gallery, Kingston, NY, 88-91. *Teaching:* Instr etching & color viscosity, Commun Village Ltd, Kingston, NY, 75-80; vis artist color viscosity printing, State Univ Col, Fredonia, NY 78; dir children's print workshop linocuts, Woodstock Libr, NY, 89. *Awards:* Am the Beautiful Award, Printmaking, Am the Beautiful Fund, 76; First & second place, graphics, Sullivan Cultural Ctr, Catskill Art Soc, 83; Ulster Co Decentralization Grant, Intaglio Prints, NY State Coun Arts, 89. *Bibliog:* Graphic Arts, Educ Audio Visual Inc, 77; Liam Nelson (auth), Harris and Jow Merit High Watermarks, The Daily Freeman, 89; Steven Kolpan (auth), Intaglio Dragons, Woodstock Times, 89. *Media:* Color Viscosity Intaglio Prints. *Mailing Add:* 2806 Truman Ave Oakland CA 94605-4847

KAGLE, JOSEPH L, JR
PAINTER, MUSEUM DIRECTOR
b Pittsburgh, Pa, May 2, 32. *Study:* Carnegie Mus Sch Art, 38-51; Dartmouth Col, AB, 55; Univ Colo, MFA, 58. *Work:* Southeast Ark Arts & Sci Ctr, Pine Bluff; Alcoa Collection, Pittsburgh; Nat Mus Taiwan, Taipei; Kimon Friar Collection, Athens, Greece; Sanford Besser Collection, Little Rock, Ark. *Comn:* Concrete mural, Hafa Adai Theatre, Agana, Guam, 72-73; mosaic mural, State Arts Coun, Univ Guam, 74; concrete mural, Nat Endowment for Arts, Agana, Guam, 75; acrylic painting, Bank of Guam, Agana, 75; sculptures, comn by lawyer in Guam, 75. *Exhib:* One-man show, US Info Serv Lincoln Ctr, Taipei, Taiwan, 75; Image of the South Pacific, Nat Mus Taiwan, Taipei, 76; NY State Ann, Arnot Mus, 77; Lakeview Series, Southeast Ark Arts & Sci Ctr, Pine Bluff, 79; retrospective, Hopkins Ctr, Dartmouth Col, Hanover, NH, 80. *Collections Arranged:* Buddhist Hell Scrolls (auth, catalog), travel exhib throughout South, 80; John Howard and Friends, group

show of minority art, 80; Southeast Ark Arts & Sci Ctr Permanent Collection, 80; Wildlife Collection Ann Exhib, 80; Arkansas Annual, 80. *Pos:* Exec dir, Southeast Ark Arts & Sci Ctr, 78- *Teaching:* Assoc prof art & chmn dept, Keuka Col, Keuka Park, NY, 64-68; assoc prof & artist-in-residence, Wash State Univ, 65-66; assoc prof art, World Campus Afloat, 68-69; prof art & chmn dept, Univ Guam, 70-76. *Awards:* First Award in Painting, Cheney Cowles Mus, 66; Pac Artist of Yr, Am Inst Architects, Pac Chap, 77; Grant, Found Proj Scholar, 83 & 84. *Bibliog:* State Council on the Arts Artists of Guam, Nat Endowment for Arts, 74; Getting better all the time, PB Com (Paul Greenberg), 78; Work by J Kagle, Dartmouth Col, 80. *Mem:* Col Art Asn; Am Mus Asn; Southeast Mus Asn; Mid-Southern Watercolorists. *Media:* Acrylic, Watercolor. *Collection:* Oriental and modern American art. *Publ:* Auth, The Twenty-Four Hour Day, China Press, 75; Osiik is Dead, Glimpses, Guam, 76; contribr, The Future is Now, Com Press, 80; auth, Long walks at twilight and dawn, Islands Mag, 80; The good old boy of art, Art Consortium, 80. *Dealer:* Art Center 1300 Cellege Dr Waco TX 76708. *Mailing Add:* 3400 O'Brien Circle Waco TX 76708

KAHAN, ALEXANDER
DEALER, CONSULTANT
Study: State Univ NY. *Pos:* Owner, Alexander Kahan Fine Arts Ltd, New York, currently. *Mem:* Appraisers Asn Am. *Specialty:* Paintings and graphics of 19th and 20th century. *Collection:* Appel, Matta, Dubuffet, De Chirico, Riopelle, Calder, Dufy, Jenkins, Miro, Francis, Chagall, Picasso, Renoir, Lautrec, Marini & Stella. *Mailing Add:* 565 West End Ave New York NY 10024

KAHAN, LEONARD
DEALER, PAINTER
b Bronx, NY, Jan 21, 35. *Study:* Pratt Inst, BFA, 57; Brooklyn Col, MFA, 64. *Pos:* Owner, L Kahan Gallery, Inc, currently. *Mem:* Appraisers Asn Am. *Media:* Acrylic, Collage. *Specialty:* African art. *Mailing Add:* L Kahan Gallery Inc 560 Broadway Suite 508 New York NY 10012

KAHAN, MITCHELL DOUGLAS
MUSEUM DIRECTOR, HISTORIAN
b Richmond, Va, May 1, 51. *Study:* Univ Va, BA, 73; Columbia Univ, univ fel, 73, MA, 75; City Univ New York Grad Sch, univ fel, 75-76, MPhil, 79, PhD, 83. *Collections Arranged:* Art Inc: American Paintings from Corporate Collections (coauth & ed, catalog), Montgomery Mus & Brandywine Press, 79; American Paintings of the Sixties and Seventies: Selections from the Whitney Museum of American Art (auth, catalog), Montgomery Mus, 80 & Roger Brown (coauth, catalog), 80; Nicholas Africano (auth, catalog), 83 & Heavenly Visions: Art of Minnie Evans (auth, catalog), 86, NC Mus. *Pos:* Cur painting & sculpture, Montgomery Mus Fine Arts, Ala, 78-82; cur Am & contemp art, NC Mus Art, 82-86; dir, Akron Art Mus, 86-; vpres, Intermuseum Conservation Asn, 88-90, pres 90-92. *Awards:* Helena Rubinstein fel, Whitney Mus Art, 76; Smithsonian fel, Nat Collection Fine Arts & Hirshhorn Mus, 76-78; Nat Endowment fel, 87. *Res:* American art, contemporary art. *Publ:* Robert Colescott: Pride & Prejudice in A Retrospective, San Jose Mus, 87. *Mailing Add:* Akron Art Mus 70 E Market St Akron OH 44308

KAHN, A MICHAEL
PAINTER, DESIGNER
b Russia, July 4, 17; US citizen. *Study:* Pratt Inst, Brooklyn, MFA; Art Students League, cert; Univ Mex, dipl; Univ Lima Bellas Artes, dipl; also with Robert Brackman, Ogden Pleisner & Chaves Morado; fresco in Mexico. *Work:* Judah L Magnes Mus, Berkeley, Calif; Los Angeles Mus; Matson Navig Co Collection, San Francisco; Peruvian Cult Ctr, Lima; Pomeroy Collection; also in pvt collections around the world. *Comn:* Graphics for Europe & Far East, Off of Surgeon Gen, Washington, DC. *Exhib:* One-man shows, US Info Serv Cult Ctr, US Info Serv, Lima, Peru, 51 & On Israel, Pomeroy Gallery, San Francisco, 68 & Barry Univ, Miami, Fla, 86; Exhib, Judah L Magnes Mus, Berkeley, 57 & Art of Israel, 70; US Info Serv Hellenic Am Exhib, Athens, Greece. *Bibliog:* E M Polley (auth), Sacred Cows, Art & Artist Mag, San Francisco, 69; Alexander Fried (auth), A Michael Kahn, Lively Arts-San Francisco Examr, 70; Allen Gadol (auth), A Michael Kahn, Directions in Art, Miami, 72. *Mem:* Am Artists Group, New York; Artists Club of San Francisco; Art Dirs Club San Francisco; Nat Writers Club; Am Asn Travel Ed. *Media:* Oil, Acrylic. *Mailing Add:* 5 Island Ave Miami Beach FL 33139-1302

KAHN, ANNELIES RUTH
CERAMIST, CRAFTSMAN
b Dresden, Ger, Aug 17, 27; US citizen. *Study:* RI Sch Design, BFA; Tex Woman's Univ, MA. *Exhib:* Seventh Int Exhib Ceramic Art, Smithsonian Inst, Washington, DC, 58; Ann Area Competition, Corcoran Gallery, Washington, DC, 59; 22nd Ceramic Nat Traveling Show, Everson Mus, Syracuse, 62 & 68; Am Craftsmen's Coun Exhib, Oakland, Calif, 63; Form and Quality, Int Exhib, Munich, Ger, 64-69. *Pos:* Designer & glaze analyst, Calif Art Tile Co, Richmond, 51-52; asst to dir, Gump's Gallery, San Francisco, 52-53 & Fine Art Gallery, Dallas, 64-66. *Teaching:* Instr ceramics, Md Art Inst, Baltimore, 57-59 & Southern Methodist Univ, 64-69; instr ceramics & sculpture, Mountain View Col, Tex, 70-74. *Awards:* Craft Horizons Award, Smithsonian Inst, 58; First Prize, Corcoran Gallery, 59; 16th Tex Crafts Exhib Top Award, Dallas Mus Fine Arts, 74; and others. *Bibliog:* Creation in Clay (film), KERA TV, 68. *Mem:* Tex Designer Craftsmen (secy, 71, vpres, 74-75); Dallas Craft Guild; World Crafts Coun; Am Craftsmen Coun. *Dealer:* Contemporary Gallery 2800 Routh St Dallas TX 75201. *Mailing Add:* 7831 La Sobrina Dallas TX 75248

KAHN, NED M
ENVIRONMENTAL ARTIST, SCULTPTOR
b New York, NY, Feb 16, 60. *Study:* Univ Conn, Storrs, BA, 82. *Work:* NC Mus Life & Sci, Durham; Exploratorium Mus, San Francisco; Parc De La Villette, Paris, France; Saibu Mus Art, Fukouka, Japan; NY Hall Sci, Queens. *Comn:* Regenerating landscape, Wash State Arts Coun, Puyallup, 90; greenhouse proj, San Francisco Arts Comn, 91; Vortex Tower, Liberty Sci Ctr, Liberty Park, NJ, 92; wavespout (breathing sea), City of Ventura, Calif, 93; primordial garden, Chevron Corp, San Francisco, 94. *Exhib:* Multimediale 2, Ctr Art, Karlsruhe, Ger, 91; Rotunda Gallery, Canary Wharf, London, Eng, 92; NC Mus, Durham, 92; Momentum Gallery, Ventura, Calif, 92; Mole Antonelliana, Torino, Italy, 92; and others. *Pos:* Artist-in-residence, Exploratorium Mus, San Francisco, 82-, Headlands Ctr Arts, Calif, 87-88, NY Hall Sci, Queens, 88-89. *Awards:* Artist-in-Residence Grant, Headlands Ctr Arts, 87-88; Sculpture Fel, Nat Endowment Arts, 91; Bernard Osher Cult Award, Jewish Community Endowment, 92. *Bibliog:* Adam Gopnick (auth), Talk of the town: twister, New Yorker Mag, 11/88; Bruce Weber (auth), Works in progress, NY Times Mag, 3/89; Jeff Greenwald (auth), Local color, SF Mag, 3/90. *Media:* Environmental. *Mailing Add:* 264 Downey St San Francisco CA 94117

KAHN, PETER
PAINTER, GRAPHIC DESIGNER
b Leipzig, Ger, July 5, 21; US citizen. *Study:* With Hans Hofmann, 47-49; NY Univ, BS & MA. *Work:* Utica Mus; Va Mus; White Mus; Cornell Univ; Univ Notre Dame Gallery. *Exhib:* Art USA 1954, Va Mus, 54; New Graphic Art Traveling Show, Holland, 65; Natural Vision, Columbia Univ, 68; retrospective, Hobart Col. *Teaching:* Asst prof, La State Univ, Baton Rouge, 51-53; assoc prof & chmn dept, Hampton Inst, Va, 53-57; prof graphics & paintings, Cornell Univ, 57-68, prof art hist, 72-84, emer prof, 84-; Mellon prof, Calif Inst Technol, 78; Hamburg, 85-86. *Awards:* Gov Award, Va Mus, 56; First Prize for Graphics, Binghamton Mus, 58; First Prize, Utica Mus, 59 & 60. *Media:* Graphics. *Publ:* Auth, The golden section fallacy, Leonardo, Paris, fall 80; Letters Lines & Pages, 82. *Mailing Add:* Dept Art Hist Cornell Univ Ithaca NY 14853

KAHN, ROBIN
PAINTER
b New York, NY, Jan 17, 61. *Study:* Barnard Col, Columbia Univ, BA (art hist), 82; Pratt Inst, MFA, 85. *Exhib:* Bienniale, Everson Mus Art, Syracuse, NY, 88; Marta Cervera Gallery, New York, 89; All Quiet on the Western Front, Galerie Antoine Candua, Paris, 90; Galerie Sophia Ungers, Köln, Ger, 90; Project Room, White Columns, New York, 90. *Awards:* Support Grant, Art Matters Inc, 88; Fel Grant, Nat Endowment Arts, 89. *Bibliog:* Roberta Smith (auth), The Group Show as Crystal Ball, NY Times, 7/6/90; Kim Levin (auth), Best Picks, Village Voice, 7/24/90. *Media:* Miscellanous Media. *Mailing Add:* 114 Mercer New York NY 10012

KAHN, SUSAN B
PAINTER
b New York, NY, Aug 26, 24. *Study:* Parsons Sch Design; also with Moses Soyer. *Work:* Albrecht Gallery Mus, St Joseph, Mo; Montclair Mus, NJ; Butler Inst Am Art, Youngstown, Ohio; Reading Mus, Pa; Joslyn Art Mus, Omaha, Nebr. *Comn:* Two Paintings, M Riklis, chmn Rapid Am Corp, 86-87. *Exhib:* One-person shows, ACA Galleries, New York, 64, 68, 71, 76, & 80, Albrecht Art Mus, St Joseph, Mo, 74 & New York Cult Ctr, 74; Nat Acad Design, 70; Butler Inst Am Art, 73; St Peter's Col Art Gallery, Jersey City, NJ, 78; Heidi Neuhoff Gallery, 89; and others. *Awards:* Nat Arts Club Award, 67; Famous Artists Sch Award, 67 & Anne Barnett Mem Prize, 81, Nat Asn Women Artists; Solveig S Palmer Award, 87; Dorothy Schweitzer Award, 90. *Bibliog:* Marshall Matusow (auth), Art Collectors Almanac, Jerome E Treisman, 65; Lincoln Rothschild (auth), Susan Kahn, Asn Univ Presses Inc, 80. *Mem:* Artists Equity Asn; Nat Asn Women Artists. *Media:* Oil. *Publ:* Contribr, How to Paint a Prize Winner, 65. *Dealer:* Heidi Neuhoff Gallery 999 Madison Ave New York NY 10021. *Mailing Add:* 870 United Nations Plaza New York NY 10017

KAHN, TOBI AARON
PAINTER, SCULPTOR
b New York, NY, May 8, 52. *Study:* Hunter Col, New York, BA(summa cum laude), 76; Pratt Inst, New York, MFA, 78. *Work:* Solomon R Guggenheim Mus, Jewish Mus & Swiss Bank Corp, New York; Rose Art Mus, Boston, Mass; Ft Wayne Mus, Ind; Nat Gallery Art, Washington, DC. *Comn:* Paintings, Mitchell & Co, Boston, 85; painting, First City Corp, New York, 86; sculptures for set designs, Solomons Dance Co, 88, Muna Iseng Dance Proj, Elizabeth Swados, 90. *Exhib:* New Horizons in American Art, Guggenheim Mus, New York, 85; A View of Nature, Aldrich Mus, Ridgefield, Conn, 86; The New Romantic Landscape, Whitney Mus Am Art, Stamford, Conn, 87; Chosen Space, Cleveland Ctr Contemp Art, 88; Art on Paper, Weatherspoon Art Gallery, Greensboro, NC, 88; Golem! Danger, Deliverance & Art, Jewish Mus, New York, 88; Contemp Landscapes: Five views, Waterworks Visual Arts Ctr, Salisbury, Va; Eco-92, Mus Mod Art, Rio de Janeiro, Brazil, 92; and others. *Teaching:* Lectr, Sch Visual Arts, New York, 86- *Bibliog:* Douglas Dreishpoon (auth), Tobi Kahn, the essence of vision, Arts Mag, 1/85; Michael Brenson (auth), article, NY Times, 11/6/87; Susan Kandel & Elizabeth Hayt-Adkins (coauths), article, Art News, 1/88. *Mem:* Col Art Asn. *Media:* Acrylic; Wood, Bronze. *Publ:* Illusr, Tikkun Mag, Vol 1, No 2, Nan Fink Publ, 86; Jerusalem, Broadway Play Publ Inc, 88. *Dealer:* Mary Ryan Gallery 24 W 57th St New York NY 10019. *Mailing Add:* 12-23 Jackson Ave Long Island City New York NY 11101

KAHN, WOLF
PAINTER
b Stuttgart, Ger, Oct 4, 27. *Study:* New Sch Social Res, with Stuart Davis; Hans Hofmann Sch; Univ Chicago, BA, 51. *Work:* Whitney Mus Am Art, Mus Mod Art & Metrop Mus Art, New York; Houston Mus Fine Arts; Los Angeles Co Mus Art, Calif; Brooklyn Mus, NY. *Comn:* 2000 K Street, Washington, DC, 87; The Four Seasons, AT&T Hq, New York, 85. *Exhib:* Ann, Whitney Mus Am Art, 58 & 59; Univ Ill Biennial, 58-60; Bloedel Bequest, Whitney Mus Am Art, 77; one-man shows, RI Sch Design, Providence, 79 & Landscapes, San Diego Mus, Calif, 84; Chicago Arts Club, 81; Am Pastels, Met Mus, NY, 89; Recent Paintings, Ft Lauderdale Mus Art, 90; Recent Acquisitions from the Metropolitan Museum, Queens Mus, New York; One-man show, Ft Lauderdale Mus Art, Fla (traveling), 90-91; NJ Ctr Visual Arts, Summit, 91. *Teaching:* Vis assoc prof painting, Univ Calif, Berkeley, 60-61; artist-in-residence, Dartmouth Col, 84. *Awards:* Fulbright scholar to Italy, 63-65; Guggenheim fel, 66; Art Award, Am Acad Arts & Lett, 79. *Bibliog:* Wolf Kahn (auth), Hans Hoffmann's Good Example, spring 92, Milton Avery's Good Example, spring 83, Art J; Lawrence Campbell (auth), Wolf Kahn at Grace Borgenicht, Art Am, 11/89. *Mem:* Nat Acad Design; Amer Acad & Inst Arts & Lett. *Media:* Oil, Pastel. *Publ:* Hans Hofmann's good example, Art J, 82; Pastel Light, Station Hill Press, 83; Milton Avery's good example, Art J, 83; Autocratic & Democratic Stillife Paintings, Am Artist, 2/86; Hans Hofmann-Teacher for the NY School, Art Am, 10/90; Hofmann's Mixed Messages, Art Am, 11/90. *Dealer:* Grace Borgenicht 724 5th Ave New York NY 10019; Asn Am Artists 20 W 57th St New York NY 10019. *Mailing Add:* 813 Broadway New York NY 10003

KAIDA, TAMARRA
PHOTOGRAPHER
b Lienz, Austria, 1946. *Study:* Goddard Col, Plainfield, Vt, BA, 74; State Univ NY, Buffalo, MFA, 79. *Work:* Ctr Creative Photog, Tucson, Ariz; Int Mus Photog, George Eastman House, Rochester, NY; Santa Fe Mus Fine Arts, NMex; Mus Mod Art, NY; Polaroid Corp, Cambridge, Mass; and others. *Exhib:* Curator's Choice, Lieberman and Saul Gallery, New York, 89; Current Works, Gallery Kansas City Artists Coalition, Mo, 89; group show, Anderson Ranch Arts Ctr, Aspen, Colo, 89; solo exhib, Fine Arts Gallery, Rhode Island Sch Design, 89 & OPSIS Found Gallery, NY, 90; Arizona Photographs: The Snell and Wilmer Collection, Ctr Creative Photography, 90; Photographic Book US, 91. *Collections Arranged:* Contemporary European Portraiture, Northlight Gallery, Ariz State Univ, Tempe, 83; Mixed Signals: Photographs with Text (co-cur Rod Slemmons), Northlight Gallery, Ariz State Univ, Tempe, 88. *Pos:* Asst dir educ dept, Int Mus Photog at George Eastman House, Rochester, NY, 76-79. *Teaching:* Vis lectr, Ariz State Univ, 79-80, asst prof, 80-85, assoc prof, 85- *Awards:* Fel, Nat Endowment Arts, 86; Photography Fel, Ariz Comn Arts. *Publ:* Coauth (with Rita Dove), The Other Side of the House, Pyracantha Press, Ariz State Univ Sch Art, 88; auth, Tremors from the Faultline, Visual Studies Workshop Press, 89. *Dealer:* Etherton Gallery Tucson AZ; Califia Books San Francisco CA. *Mailing Add:* 534 N Orange St Mesa AZ 85201

KAIMAN, CHARLES
PAINTER
b New York, NY, July 12, 47. *Study:* Art Students League of New York, with Edwin Dickinson, Jean Liberté & Sol Wilson, 60-66; New York Univ, BS, 69; study with Joseph De Martini & Gerritt Hondius. *Exhib:* Solo exhibs, AAA Gallery, Detroit, Mich, 72 & Roko Gallery, New York, NY, 75; Allied Artists Ann, New York, 75 & 77; Jersey City Mus, NJ, 78; Audubon Artists Ann, New York, 81; Recent Paintings, Prince Street Gallery, 82 & Blue Mountain Gallery, 84, 87 & 88, New York. *Pos:* Treas, Prince St Gallery, 81-83 & Blue Mountain Gallery, 88- *Media:* Oil, Watercolor. *Dealer:* Blue Mountain Gallery 121 Wooster St New York NY 10012. *Mailing Add:* c/o Blue Mountain Gallery 121 Wooster St New York NY 10012

KAINEN, JACOB
PAINTER, PRINTMAKER
b Waterbury, Conn, Dec 7, 09. *Study:* Art Students League, with Nicolaides, 26; NY Univ Eve Sch Archit, 36-38; Pratt Inst, grad, 30; Corcoran Sch Art, hon DFA, 92. *Work:* Whitney Mus Am Art, Metrop Mus Art & Mus Mod Art, New York; Art Inst Chicago; Phillips Collection, Nat Mus Am Art, Washington, DC; and many others. *Exhib:* Corcoran Gallery Art Painting Biennial, 57; one-man shows, Roko Gallery, New York, 64-66, Pratt Manhattan Ctr, New York, 72, Lunn Gallery, Washington, DC, 76-79 & 81-82; Print Retrospective 1938-1978, Assoc Am Artists, New York, 78; Jacob Kainen, Five Decades as Painter, Nat Collection Fine Arts, 79; Recent Paintings, Middendorf Gallery, Washington, DC, 86, 88 & 89. *Bibliog:* Jacob Kainen (film), Nat Mus Art, Smithsonian Inst, 82; Harry Rand (auth), Jacob Kainen, Arts Mag, 83. *Media:* Oil. *Mailing Add:* 27 W Irving St Chevy Chase MD 20815

KAISER, BENJAMIN
SCULPTOR, DESIGNER
b Tel Aviv, Israel, July 2, 43; US citizen. *Study:* San Jose State Univ, BA, 77, MFA, 79. *Work:* Mus Contemp Art in Glass, Valencia, Spain; City Palo Alto, City San Jose, Calif. *Comn:* Fountain, Villa Monterey Country Club, Phoenix, 82; glass panels, Rolm Corp, San Jose, Calif, 83. *Exhib:* New Glass Int Exhib, Corning Mus Art, 79; Contemporary Glass--Australia, Canada, USA and Japan, Nat Mus Mod Art, Kyoto & Tokyo, Japan, 81; International Directions in Glass Art, Art Gallery Western Austalia, Perth, 82; Sculptural Glass, Tucson Mus Art, 83; Vicointer 83, Mus Contemp Art in Glass, Valencia, Spain, 83. *Teaching:* Instr glass-blowing, Bezalel Acad Art & Design, Jerusalem, 72-74. *Media:* Glass, Stainless Steel. *Mailing Add:* 9209 Wallaceton Elk Grove CA 95624

KAISER, CHARLES JAMES
PAINTER, GRAPHIC ARTIST
b Milwaukee, Wis, Mar 10, 39. *Study:* Layton Sch Art, Milwaukee; Univ Wis-Milwaukee, BFA, MS & MFA; painting with John Colt, Robert Burkert & Laurence Rathsack. *Work:* Wustum Mus, Racine, Wis; Union Art Gallery, Univ Wis-Milwaukee; Civic Art Collection, Munic Bldg, Springfield, Ill; Marquette Univ & Miller Brewing Co Corp, Milwaukee. *Comn:* Portrait, Pres of Mount Mary Col, Milwaukee, Wis, 82. *Exhib:* Five shows, Watercolor USA, Springfield, Mo, 62-72; Northwest Miss Valley Artists Invitational, Ill State Mus, Springfield, 66; Calif Nat Watercolor Soc, Laguna Beach, 70 & 72-73; Exhib Contemp Am Painting, Palm Beach, Fla, 70; Chicago & Vicinity, Chicago Art Inst, 71; Wis Directions, 75 & 78, Wis Artists Make Toys, 79 & Drawing: The Fundamental Art, 81, Milwaukee Art Mus. *Teaching:* Assoc prof art, Mount Mary Col, 73- *Awards:* Calif Nat Watercolor Soc Purchase Award, Butrijamp Found, 70; Madison Salon Graphic Art Drawings & Prints Award, Wis State J; Wis Watercolor Soc Award for Excellence, 71. *Mem:* Calif Nat Watercolor Soc; Wis Watercolor Soc; Wis Painters & Sculptors. *Media:* Watercolor; Prismacolor Pencil. *Dealer:* Bradley Galleries 2639 N Downer Ave Milwaukee WI 53211; Cudahy Gallery Wis Art Milwaukee Art Mus. *Mailing Add:* 5028 N Diversey Blvd Milwaukee WI 53211

KAISER, DIANE
SCULPTOR, EDUCATOR
b Brooklyn, NY, May 27, 46. *Study:* Brandeis Univ, BA(Hon Scholar); Columbia Univ, MFA; additional study with Peter Grippe & Sahl Swarz. *Work:* Columbia Univ. *Comn:* Amherst Arts Lottery, 90 & 92. *Exhib:* Contemporary Reflections, Aldrich Mus Contemp Art, Ridgefield, Conn, 75; Mus Fine Arts, Springfield, Mass, 81; 14 Sculptors Gallery, New York, 85; Outdoor Sculpture of Chesterwood, Mass, 86-87; Outdoor Sculpture of Stamford Mus & Nature Ctr, Conn, 88; solo exhib, Mus Fine Arts, Springfield, Mass, 89; Outdoor Sculpture at Bradley Palmer State Park, Mass, 92; and others. *Collections Arranged:* Drawings & prints, independent exhib prog, Comt Visual Arts Inc, New York, 77; The Living Room: sculpture and furniture, 14 Sculptors Gallery, New York, 86. *Teaching:* Chmn & instr art dept, Chapin Sch, New York, 70-79, St Hilda's & St Hugh's Sch, New York, 90-; vis artist, Dwight-Englewood Sch, NJ, 76; instr, Northfield-Mount Hermon Sch, Northfield, Mass, 79-80; lectr art dept, Smith Col, Northampton, Mass, 80-83; asst prof art, Elms Col, Chicopee, Mass. *Awards:* MacDowell Colony Fel, 73. *Mem:* Col Art Asn. *Media:* Clay, Wood. *Publ:* Contribr, Children, Clay & Sculpture. *Mailing Add:* 345 Elm St Northampton MA 01060

KAISER, KAREN
PAINTER, DESIGNER
b Leadville, Colo, Oct 6, 45. *Study:* Univ Colo, Denver, 66; Colo Inst Art, 72; private study with Jon Zahourek, 73-75; Judy Chicago, 76; Len Chmiel, Buffalo Kaplinski & Robert Harvey, malaga, Spain, 87-88. *Work:* Tatiana PoPova Private Collections, USSR; Bacardi & Co Ltd, Malaga, Spain. *Comn:* Coyote Tales (murals), USPHS Indian Hosp, Crown Point, NMex; children's poster & book, Eye of Moon Publ, Denver, Colo, 84; off advert poster, Washington, DC, 85 & Sepia in Flaming June (poster), Boston, Mass, 86, comn by Nat Ctr Homeopathy; Symbolic mural, Archetypos, Art & Dream Study Center, Denver, Colo, 86. *Exhib:* Biennial Exhib, Denver Art Mus, Colo, 75; Art on the Grasslands, Wright Ingraham Inst, Parker, Colo, 77; solo exhibs, Kenneth Bunn Studio, Denver, 77, Ft Lewis Col, Durango, 81 & Petroleum Club Denver, 84, Colo; Introductions 78, Charles Campbell Gallery, Oakland Mus, Calif, 78; 5 Women from Colorado, Aspen Inst, 78; Bacardi Cortijo, Malaga, Spain, 88; Arri BaBa Gallery, inaugural show, 89, Malaga, Spain. *Pos:* Vpres, Artists Equity, 74-75; designer, William Thach Studios, Inc, 74-84 & 87-88; exec secy, Am Inst of Homeopathy. *Teaching:* Private instruction drawing, 80- *Awards:* First Place Watercolor, 65 & First Place Oil Painting, 66, Fine Arts League, La Junta, Colo. *Bibliog:* James Mills (auth), Nossaman uses Amaryllis to record drama of life-death, Denver Post, 77; Peter Patton (auth), Of emotion and identity, Artweek, 78; Barbara Whipple (auth), Patterns in the life cycle: The art of Karen Nossaman, Am Artist Mag, 79; Sur, Malaga, 88. *Media:* Mixed. *Publ:* Illusr, cover design, Bravo Mag, 79 & Houston Symphony Mag, 84; contribr, Promoting and Selling Your Art, 83; coauth & illusr, A Magical Journey, Un Viaje Májico, Eye of Moon Publ, 85. *Dealer:* Mussavi Art Ctr 623 Broadway New York NY 10012; Studio III Gallery Ruidoso NM 88345. *Mailing Add:* 1585 Glencoe Denver CO 80220

KAISER, VITUS J
PAINTER
b Erie, Pa, May 3, 29. *Study:* NC State Col; Veterans Sch, Erie, with Joseph Plavcan; Univ Pittsburgh. *Work:* Erie Pub Libr. *Exhib:* Am Drawing Biennial, Norfolk Mus, Va, 71; Albright-Knox Art Gallery, Mem Gallery, Buffalo, 72; Butler Inst Am Art, 73; American Drawings III, Portsmouth, Va, 80; American Drawings, Smithsonian Inst traveling exhib, 81; and others. *Mem:* Erie Art Mus; Soc Watercolor Painters Pa; and others. *Media:* Multimedia. *Mailing Add:* 551 W 26th St Erie PA 16508

KAISH, LUISE
SCULPTOR, PAINTER
b Atlanta, Ga. *Study:* Syracuse Univ, with Ivan Mestrovic, BFA & MFA; Escuela Pintura y Escultura, Mexico City, Mex; Taller Grafico. *Work:* Whitney Mus Am Art, New York; Jewish Mus, New York; Rochester Mem Art Gallery, NY; Smithsonian Inst; Metrop Mus Art, New York; Nat Mus Am Art, Washington, DC. *Comn:* Ark of Revelations (bronze), Temple B'rith Kodesh, Rochester; Great Ideas of Western Man & Walter Paepke Award Sculpture, Container Corp Am; Christ in Glory (bronze), Holy Trinity

Mission Sem, Silver Spring, Md; ark doors, menorahs, eternal light (bronze), Temple Beth Shalom, Wilmington, Del; Continental Grain Co, New York. *Exhib:* Sculpture USA, Metrop Mus Art, New York; Recent Sculpture USA, Mus Mod Art, New York; Albright-Knox Mus, Buffalo; Hopkins Ctr, Dartmouth Col, Hanover, NH; Whitney Biennials, Whitney Mus Am Art, New York; one-man shows, Minn Mus Art, Staempfli Gallery, New York, Rochester Mem Art Gallery & Jewish Mus, New York; plus others. *Pos:* Artist-in-residence, Hopkins Ctr, Dartmouth Col; vis artist, Univ Wash, Seattle & Univ Haifa, Israel. *Teaching:* Prof sculpture & chmn div painting & sculpture, Columbia Univ, New York, 80- *Awards:* Guggenheim Fel Creative Sculpture; Louis Comfort Tiffany Grant Creative Sculpture; Rome Prize Fel in Sculpture, Am Acad, Rome. *Mem:* Sculptors Guild. *Media:* All. *Dealer:* Staempfli Gallery 47 E 77th St New York NY 10021. *Mailing Add:* c/o Staenfli Gallery 415 W Broadway New York NY 10012

KAISH, MORTON
PAINTER, EDUCATOR
b Newark, NJ, Jan 8, 27. *Study:* Syracuse Univ, BFA; Acad de la Grande Chaumiere, Paris; Ist d'Arte, Florence; Accad delle Belle Arti, Rome. *Work:* Brooklyn Mus, NY; Indianapolis Mus; Whitney Mus Am Art; Atlantic Richfield Corp, New York; Nat Mus Arts, Smithsonian Inst, Washington, DC. *Exhib:* Young American Printmakers, Mus Mod Art, New York, 53; one-man shows, Staempfli Gallery, New York, 64-89 & New Sch Social Res, 74; Art Inst Chicago, 64; Whitney Mus Ann Am Painting, 66; Am Inst Arts & Lett, 66, 73 & 74; US Info Serv, Italy, 72; Minn Mus Art, 75; Springfield Mus Art, 75; Taft Mus, 82; USIA Jerusalem, Israel, 85. *Teaching:* Prof painting & drawing, Fashion Inst Technol, State Univ NY, 73-; instr, New Sch, 74-77 & Art Students League, 74-; artist-in-residence, Dartmouth Col, 74 & Univ Haifa, Israel, 85; vis prof, Queens Col, 79, Univ Wash, Seattle, 79 & Boston Univ, 87; vis artist, Columbia Univ, 86; FIT, Univ Florence, 90 & 92. *Awards:* Appointed: New York State Univ Fac Exchange Scholar, 87; Benjamin Altman Landscape Prize, Nat Acad Design, 89; Nat Acad Design, 92. *Bibliog:* J Gruen (auth); article, Arts Mag, 11/83; R Bass (auth), article, Art News 11/83; R Martin (auth), article, Arts Mag, 11/86. *Mem:* Academican Nat Acad Design; Artists Fel; Century Asn. *Media:* Oil, Acrylic. *Dealer:* Staempfli Gallery 415 W Broadway St New York NY 10012. *Mailing Add:* 610 West End Ave New York NY 10024

KAKAS, CHRISTOPHER A
PRINTMAKER, PAINTER
b Dayton, Ohio, Dec 11, 41. *Study:* Miami Univ, Ohio, BFA, 66; Univ Iowa, MA, 68, MFA, 69. *Work:* Minneapolis Inst Art; Sheldon Mem Art Gallery, Univ Nebr, Lincoln; Mus Art & Archit, Univ Mo, Columbia; Cleveland Mus Art, Ohio; Rockford Col, Ill; and others. *Exhib:* Metrop Mus, Coral Gables, Fla, 80; Univ SDak, Vermillion, 80; one-man shows, Hiestand Art Gallery, Miami Univ, Oxford, Ohio, 80, Mongomery Mus Fine Arts, Ala, 82 & Sarratt Gallery, Vanderbilt Univ, Nashville, Tenn, 86; Rockford Int, Rockford Col, 83; 40th NAm Print Exhib, Brockton, Mass, 88; Biennial Exhib Contemp Southern Art, Huntsville, Ala, 88; Artists Proof, 89; Greenville Mus Art, NC, 89. *Teaching:* Asst prof, Syracuse Univ, NY, 75-76; asst prof art, Western Ky Univ, Bowling Green, 76-78; assoc prof, printmaking, Univ Ala, Tuscaloosa, 78- *Awards:* Purchase Awards, 1st Ann Nat Print Exhib, San Diego State Univ, 68, 2nd Ann Nat Print Exhib, Ga Comn Arts, 71 & 4th Annual Nat Print Exhib, Moravian Col, 85; Award, Rockford Int, 83; Award, 6th Alabama Works on Paper, 85. *Mem:* Col Art Asn; Los Angeles Printmaking Soc; Southern Graphics Coun. *Media:* Intaglio, Lithograph; Gouache, Acrylic. *Dealer:* Miriam Perlman Inc Lake Point Tower Suite 1902 505 N Lake Shore Dr Chicago IL 60611; Maralyn Wilson Gallery 2010 Cahaba Rd Birmingham AL 35223. *Mailing Add:* Dept of Art PO Box 870270 Univ Ala Tuscaloosa AL 35487-0270

KALB, MARTY JOEL
PAINTER, EDUCATOR
b Brooklyn, NY, Apr 13, 41. *Study:* Mich State Univ, BA, 63; Yale Univ, BFA, 64; Univ Calif, Berkeley, MA, 66. *Work:* J B Speed Mus, Louisville, Ky; Univ Mass; Ohio Wesleyan Univ; Dayton Art Inst. *Exhib:* One-man show, Akron Art Inst, 75 & Canton Art Inst, 81; Wright State Univ, Ohio, 82; Denison Univ, Ohio, 82; Columbus Mus Art, Ohio, 82 & 86; Ohio Univ, Lancaster, 88; and others. *Teaching:* Instr, Univ Ky, 66-67; assoc prof painting, Ohio Wesleyan Univ, 67-81, prof, 81- *Awards:* Ohio Arts Coun grant, 79-80; Columbus Art League Exhib Painting Award, 86. *Bibliog:* Articles, New York Times, 10/12/80, Dialogue, 6 & 7/81, 4/82, 12/82, 12/87, 11/88 & Columbus Dispatch, 10/85, 4/89, 12/89, 3/90. *Mem:* Col Art Asn Am. *Media:* Acrylic, Pastel. *Publ:* Auth, Collaborative Acoustic Installation, Wexner Ctr, Ohio State Univ, 87; feature story, Art of Our Time, Dayton Art Inst, 87; review, The Photographs of Joseph Albers, Allen Mem Art Mus, 1/3/88; rev, Art in Europe and America, Wefner Ctr, Ohio State Univ, 5/90. *Dealer:* Roberta Kuhn Gallery 641 N Hish St Columbus OH 43215; Deson Saunders 750 N Orleans Chicago IL 60610. *Mailing Add:* 165 Griswold St Delaware OH 43015

KALI (HANNA WEYNEROWSKI)
PAINTER
b Warsaw, Poland; US citizen. *Study:* Warsaw Acad Fine Arts, grad, 35-39; Acad Royale des Beaux Arts, Brussels, Belgium, grad, 45-47. *Exhib:* One-man shows, Palais Des Beaux Arts, Brussels, Belgium, 47, Calif Palace Legion Honor, 55 & DeYoung Mem Mus, San Francisco, 62. *Awards:* First Prize, Western Ont Exhib, London. *Mem:* Hon mem Artists Equity Asn. *Mailing Add:* 191 Robinhood Drive San Francisco CA 94127

KALINA, RICHARD
PAINTER, PRINTMAKER
b New York, NY, May 21, 46. *Study:* Univ Pa, BA, 66. *Work:* Indianapolis Mus Art; Norton Gallery Art, Palm Beach, Fla; Lehman Brothers Kuhn Loeb, Inc & New York Univ, New York; Amstar Corp; Pa Acad Fine Arts; and others. *Exhib:* Solo exhibs, O K Harris Gallery, New York & Jack Glenn Gallery, Los Angeles, 70, Tibor de Nagy Gallery, New York, 79, 80, 82 & 84, Piezo Electric (with catalog), New York, 86 & 87, Elizabeth McDonald Gallery, New York, 88-89 & Diane Brown Gallery & Ledis Flam Gallery, 92; Sidney Janis Gallery, New York, 90; Lennon Weinberg Gallery, New York, 92; Pamela Auchincloss Gallery, New York, 92; Diane Brown Gallery, New York, 92; and others. *Teaching:* Lectr, Art New York City Prog, State Univ NY, 77, Montclair State Col, 91 & Yale Univ, Norfolk, Conn, 91; painting panel discussion, NY, 79 & Morton G Neumann Family Found, NY, 80; panel discussion, Sch Visual Arts, New York, 81, New Sch, 88, Hunter Col, 89 & Inst Contemp Art, PS1, 90; sem, Aspen Inst Humanistic Studies, Baca, Colo, 82; studio lectr, Bates Col, 89 & Drew Univ, 90; art hist fac, Bennington Col, Vt, 89-90, panel discussion, 91; artist-in-residence, Fordham Univ, Col Lincoln Ctr, New York, 90; vis artist, Glassel Sch Art, Houston Mus Art, Tex, 91 & New York Univ, Grad Sch Art, 91. *Awards:* Visual Arts Fel, Nat Endowment Arts, 92. *Bibliog:* Robert C Morgan (auth), The new end game, 1-3/92 & Alain Kirili (auth), Interview with Richard Kalina, 4-5/92; Steven Henry Madoff (auth), A new lost generation, Art News, 4/92; Richard Kalina, Bomb, winter 92. *Media:* Oil on Canvas. *Mailing Add:* 44 King St New York NY 10014

KALISHER, SIMPSON
PHOTOGRAPHER
b New York, NY, July 27, 26. *Study:* Ind Univ, BA, 48. *Work:* Mus Mod Art, New York; Art Inst Chicago; George Eastman House, Rochester, NY. *Exhib:* Photography at Mid-Century, George Eastman House, Rochester, NY, 58 & travelling; Four Directions in Photography, Albright-Knox Art Gallery, 64; History of the Picture Story, Mus Mod Art, New York, 67; 12 Photographers of the Social Landscape, Poses Inst, Waltham, Mass, 68; Harlem on My Mind, Metrop Mus Art, New York, 68; Photography in America, Whitney Mus, 75; Photography as Social Literture, Farmingham Valley Arts Ctr, Avon, Conn, 78; Mirrors and Windows, Mus Mod Art, New York, 78 & travelling, 78-80; Discovering America, Art Inst Chicago, 78; solo exhib, Voltaire Gallery, New Milford, Conn, 80. *Teaching:* Instr photog, Sch Visual Arts, New York, 80-83. *Bibliog:* Hugh Edwards (auth), Railroad Men, Infinity, 3/62; Thomas H Garver (auth), 12 Photographers of the American Social Landscape, 67; Robert Doty (ed), article, Photogr in America, 74. *Mem:* Am Soc Mag Photogr. *Publ:* Auth, Railroad Men: Photographs and Collected Stories, Clarke & Wag, 61; Propaganda and Other Photographs, Addison House, 76; illusr, Clinical Sociology, 79. *Dealer:* Witkin Gallery 41 E 57th St New York NY 10022; Keith de Lellis New York NY 10128. *Mailing Add:* Roxbury CT 06783

KALLIR, JANE KATHERINE
ART DEALER, WRITER
b New York, NY, July 30, 54. *Study:* Brown Univ, Providence, RI, AB, 76. *Pos:* Dir, Galerie St Etienne, New York, 79- *Mem:* Art Dealers Asn Am; Art Table. *Res:* Austrian & German expressionism; international naive art, especially in its relationship to modernism. *Specialty:* Klimt, Schiele, Kokoschka, Kubin, Kollwitz, Grandma Moses, Modersohn-Becker, Corinth, Sue Coe. *Publ:* Auth, Arnold Schoenberg's Vienna, Rizzoli, 84; Viennese Design and the Wiener Werkstaete, Braziller, 86; Gustav Klimt: 25 Masterworks, 89; Egon Schiele: The Complete Works, 90; Richard Gerstl/Oskar Kokoschka, 92. *Mailing Add:* c/o Galerie St Etienne 24 W 57th St New York NY 10019

KAM, MEI K
PAINTER, INSTRUCTOR
b Chungshan, Guangdong, China, Aug 7, 38; US citizen. *Study:* New York Univ, Cert Interior Decor, 67; Art Students League, New York, 77-78; Edgar Whitney Workshop, New York, 79-82. *Work:* Pastel Soc Am, Nat Art Club, New York. *Comn:* Watercolor paintings, US Coast Guard, Washington, DC, 84-85. *Exhib:* Three Contemporary Artists, New York Univ Prog Bd, 86; 121st Exhib, Am Watercolor Soc, New York, 88; Hudson Vally Art Asn Ann, Westchester Co Ctr, 82-88; Audubon Artists Ann, Nat Art Club, New York, 80 & 88; Nat Acad Design, 92. *Teaching:* Instr watercolor, Salmagundi Club, New York, 82-85 & Jackson Heights Art Club, Queens, NY, 85-86; instr pastel, Pastel Soc Am, New York, 87. *Awards:* Award of Excellence, Charles Davis Mem Fund, 85; Artist Fel Award, Elizabeth K Ellis, 86 & 87; Morilla Canson Talens Award, Pastel Soc Am, 87. *Bibliog:* Dorothy Hall (auth), Art and Artists, Park East, 1/82; Palmer Poroner (auth), The Problem of Conservative Art, ArtSpeak, 4/16/84. *Mem:* Salmagundi Club; Pastel Soc Am; Hudson Valley Art Asn; Knickerbocker Artists; US Coast Guard Artists; Audubon Artists Inc. *Media:* Watercolor, Pastel. *Publ:* Contribr, Readers' pictures exhibited, The Artist (Eng), 8/81; Drawing with Pastels by Ron Lister, Prentice-Hall, 82. *Dealer:* Greene Art Gallery 29 Whitfield St Guilford CT 06437. *Mailing Add:* 45-23 Union St Flushing NY 11355

KAMEN, REBECCA
SCULPTOR, EDUCATOR
b Philadelphia, Pa, July 8, 50. *Study:* Pa State Univ, BS, 72; Univ Ill, MA, 73; RI Sch Design, MFA, 78. *Work:* Uniweave Co Showroom, Chicago; IBM, Baltimore, Md & Raleigh, NC; Tower Construction, Bethesda, Md; Gannett Corp, Roselyn, Va; Advisors Financial, Vienna, Va. *Comn:* Welded steel sculpture, Lynhaven Career & Vocational Ctr, Columbia, SC, 75; welded steel sculpture, Lancaster High Sch, Lancaster, SC, 75; laminated wood wall relief,

Pa State Univ, 76. *Exhib:* Works on Paper, 80, Collage on Paper, 81, Corcoran Gallery Art; Collage and Assemblage, Miss Mus Art, Jackson, 81; Artscape, Baltimore, 83; Alexandria Sculpture Festival, Va, 83; Fresh Paint, Pleiades Gallery, New York, 83; Summer Sculpture, Gallery K, Washington, DC, 83; Sculpture Installation, Washington & Lee Univ, 84; Recent Sculpture, J Walter Thompson Gallery, New York & Brody's Gallery, Washington, DC, 86; Sculpture '86, Art Trust, Washington, DC, 86; Joe Guy/Rebecca Kamen, Leslie Cecil Gallery, New York, 87; Primitivism, Artscape 1987, Baltimore, MD, 87; Rebecca Kamen: Recent Painting & Sculpture, Winston Gallery, Washington, DC, 88. *Pos:* Artist-in-residence, SC Arts Comn, 74. *Teaching:* Assoc prof sculpture, Northern Va Community Col, Alexandria, 78- *Awards:* Artscape, Award, 83, Citicorp Financial Inc, 83; award, Alexandria Sculpture Fest, Alexandria, Va, 83; Sculpture Award '84, Washington, DC, 84. *Bibliog:* Clarissa K Wittenberg (auth), Washington, DC, Art Voices, 80; Jack Perlmutter (auth), Collage on paper at Corcoran Gallery of Art, Art Voices, 81; Nancy G Heller, Washington, DC, Arts Mag, 83. *Mem:* Int Sculpture Ctr; Washington Sculptors Group. *Media:* Wood, Steel. *Dealer:* Brody's Gallery 1706 21st St Washington DC 20009. *Mailing Add:* 5000 17th St N Arlington VA 22207

KAMIHIRA, BEN
PAINTER
b Yakima, Wash, Mar 16, 25. *Study:* Art Inst Pittsburgh; Pa Acad Fine Arts, 48-52, J Henry Schiedt traveling scholar, 52. *Work:* Whitney Mus Am Art, New York; Pa Acad Fine Arts, Philadelphia; Ringling Mus, Sarasota, Fla; Colorado Springs Fine Arts Ctr, Colo; Dallas Mus Fine Arts; Brooklyn Mus, NY; Okla Art Mus. *Exhib:* One-man exhibs, Forum Gallery, New York, 66, 73 & 76, Galleria La Medusa, Rome, Italy & touring throughout Italy, 78, Pa Acad Fine Arts, Woodmere Art Mus, Philadelphia, Pa, Gallery Urban, New York, Peale House Gallery, Philadelphia, Pa; Nat Acad Design; Pa Acad Fine Arts; Corcoran Gallery Art, Washington, DC; Butler Inst Am Art, Youngstown, Ohio; Mus Mod Art, New York; Pa Acad Fine Arts; Carnegie Inst, Pa; Whitney Mus, New York; Greensville Mus; Philadelphia Mus Art; and others. *Teaching:* Instr drawing & painting, Pa Acad Fine Arts & Pa State Univ, formerly; artist in residence, Rice Univ, Houston, Tex, formerly. *Awards:* Saltus Gold Medal, Range & Fund Purchase Award; Nat Acad Design Purchase Prize, New York; Lippincott Prize, Nat Acad Design; Award Merit, Butler Inst Am Art. *Mem:* Fel Pa Acad Fine Arts; academician Nat Acad Design. *Media:* Oil on Canvas. *Publ:* Auth, American Artist, Art in America, New York Times, Realities, San Diego Mag & Time, currently. *Mailing Add:* c/o Gerold Wunderfish & Co 50 W 57th St 12th Fl New York NY 10019

KAMINSKY, JACK ALLAN
PHOTOGRAPHER, PRINTMAKER
b New Brunswick, NJ, Sept 8, 49. *Study:* Brooklyn Col, BS, 72, MFA(fel), 75. *Work:* LaGrange Col, Ga; Arch Am Art, Smithsonian Inst, Washington, DC. *Comn:* Graphic designs, Off of Neighborhood Govt & New York Mass Transit Authority for Eastern Pkway Subway Sta, 74. *Exhib:* Brooklyn Scenes by Brooklyn Artists, Brooklyn Mus Community Gallery, 79; Summer Exhib, Salmagundi Club, New York, 79; Doors & Chairs & Windows, Snug Harbor Cult Ctr, Staten Island, NY, 79; Never Fail Imagery Show, Sch Mus Fine Arts, Boston, 80; Invitational, Henry Hicks Gallery Ltd, Brooklyn, NY, 81; Rotunda Gallery, Brooklyn Borough Hall, Brooklyn, 82; Queens Mus Commercial Gallery, Queens, NY, 83; Brooklyn Mus, Brooklyn, NY, 84; Gallery 72, Omaha, Nebr, 85; Wiesner Gallery, Brooklyn, NY, 87; Soho Photo Gallery, NY, 88; Lever House, NY, 88; Stuhr Mus, Grand Island, Nebr, 90; Gov's Mansion, Lincoln, Nebr, 90. *Pos:* Photogr, Aunt Len's Doll & Toy Mus, 74-; gallery asst, Ann Kendall Richards Inc, New York, 81-88; photogr, PEN, NY, 84-; asst dir photo dept, Baby Togs, NY, 88- *Teaching:* Head graphics & photog dept, Brooklyn Mus Art Sch, 73-85; instr photog, Pratt Inst Continuing Educ, Brooklyn Botanic Gardens, 85; Long Island Univ, Continuing Educ, Brooklyn, NY & The Educ Alliance, New York, 85- *Mem:* US Coast Guard Artists; Salmagundi Club. *Publ:* NY Woman Mag, 88. *Mailing Add:* 1760 Marine Pkwy Brooklyn NY 11234

KAMM, DOROTHY LILA
PAINTER, WRITER
b Chicago, Ill, Apr 6, 57. *Study:* Northern Ill Univ, BFA, 79; Sch Art Inst Chicago, MFA, 84. *Comn:* 21-piece dessert set, comn by Mrs Beverly Rushin, Port St Lucie, Fla, 88; napkin rings, comn by Mrs Fara Gold, Vero Beach, Fla, 88; tiles, comn by Dr Burton Bussard, Laingsburg, Mich, 89; 9-piece dresser set, comn by Dr & Mrs Michael Dennis, Ft Pierce, Fla, 89; set of 33 name stands, comn by Mr & Mrs Tommy Bruhn, Ft Pierce, Fla, 90. *Exhib:* Art-i-ture: Furniture by Artists, Ctr Arts, Stuart, Fla, 90 & 91; The Lighthouse Gallery, 90. *Teaching:* Instr basic design & advance interior design, MacCormac Jr Col, Chicago, Ill, 81-84; instr color light & sound, Dayton Art Inst, Dayton, Ohio, 85; instr china painting, Art Gallery, Smithfield Col, Stuart, Fla, 88- *Awards:* Purchase Award, 26th Ann Lighthouse Gallery Art & Craft Festival, 89. *Bibliog:* Florence Pion (auth), Porcelain artist has turned dream into a reality, Ft Lauderdale Sun-Sentinel, 6/8/90; Jolinda Porfidio (auth), Local Artist Gaining Fame for Porcelain Work, The New Tribune, 4/15/91; For Mother, with Love, Traditional Home Mag, 4/91. *Mem:* Int Porcelain Artists & Teachers Inc; Art Assocs of Martin Co, Inc; Inter-Soc Color Coun; Nat League Am Pen Women, (vpres membership, 90-92); Am Asn Univ Women. *Media:* Porcelain. *Publ:* Auth, Being creative, 88 & Forget-me-not plate, 90, China Decorator; Marketing your finished product: Part I, II, III, 89 & Pricing your artwork, 89, Porcelain Artist; The art of china painting, The Pen Women, 90; Sunday Afternoon, Forget-me-not Tea Service, 7-8/90, Designing Porcelain Sets from Interior Finishes, 5-6/91, Iridescent Dreams, Brit Porcelain Artist Mag, 7-8/92; ed, Dorothy Kamm's Porcelain Collector's Companion, 92. *Mailing Add:* PO Box 8212 Port St Lucie FL 34985

KAMPF, AVRAM S
EDUCATOR, CURATOR
b Jan 1, 20. *Study:* New York Univ, BA, 51; New Sch Social Res, MA, 53; PhD, 62; Columbia Univ, with Meyer Schapiro, Rudolph Wittkover & Julius Held. *Collections Arranged:* Avraham Ofek, Paintings (auth, catalog), Catherine Noren, The Camera of My Family (auth, catalog), Luise Kaish, Sculpture (auth, catalog), 73 & Jewish Experience in the Art of the 20th Century, 75-76 (auth, catalog), Jewish Mus, New York. *Pos:* Chief cur, Jewish Mus, New York, 71-76; dir & founder, Haifa Univ Art Gallery, Israel , 78-85. *Teaching:* Prof art hist, Montclair State Col, 57-; assoc mem art hist, Columbia Univ, 61-65; vis prof art hist, Hebrew Univ, Haifa Univ, Jerusalem, 76- *Awards:* Fulbright lectr, Hebrew Univ, 66; Kenneth B Smilen Literary Award, Jewish Mus, 84; Mus Award Original Res, Israel Mus, 85. *Mem:* Col Art Asn; Interfaith Forum on Religion & Archit; Hebrew Union Congregation-Comn Art & Archit. *Res:* Jewish motifs in Twentieth Century art. *Publ:* Auth, Contemporary Synagogue Art, Jewish Publ Soc, 65; The Jewish Mus, An institution adrift, Judaism, 68; Aspects of the relationship to architecture, painting and sculpture, Scripta Hierosolymitana, 72; Jewish Experience in the Art of the Twentieth Century, Bergin & Garvey, 84; Ardon, the Bauhaus and the search for transcendence, Tel Aviv Mus, 85. *Mailing Add:* 372 Central Park S New York NY 10025

KAMROWSKI, GEROME
PAINTER, SCULPTOR
b Warren, Minn, Jan 29, 14. *Study:* St Paul Sch Art; Art Students League; New Bauhaus; Hans Hofmann Sch, New York. *Work:* Mus Mod Art, Whitney Mus Am Art & Metrop Mus, New York; Detroit Inst Art; Phillips Mem Gallery; plus others. *Comn:* Aerial sculpture, Univ Hosp, Ann Arbor; Gateway Crown (aerial sculpture), Ann Arbor; Constellations (mosaic), Detroit People Movers, Joe Louis Sta. *Exhib:* Surrealism Reviewed, Heywood Gallery, London; one-man shows, Betty Parsons, New York, 42, Galerie Creuze, Paris, 51 & Monique Knowlton Gallery, New York, 78, Joan Washburn Gallery, New York, 87, Convulsive Beauty, Whitney Mus, 88; Surrealism, Rutgers Univ Mus of Art, 77; Am Abstract Artists, Univ NMex Mus of Art, 77; plus many others. *Awards:* Founders Prize, Detroit Inst Art; Guggenheim Fel, 37; Racknam Fel, 72; Mich Coun Arts, 88. *Bibliog:* Andre Breton (auth), Surrealisme et la Peinture, Brentano's; Evan M Maurer & Jennifer L Bayles (coauth), Gerome Kamrowski--A Retrospective Exhibition, Univ Mich Mus. *Mailing Add:* 1501 Beechwood Dr Ann Arbor MI 48103

KAMYS, WALTER
PAINTER, EDUCATOR
b Chicago, Ill, June 8, 17. *Study:* Art Inst Chicago, 43, with Hubert Ropp & Boris Anisfeld; also with Gordon Onslow-Ford, Mex, 44. *Work:* Yale Univ; Mt Holyoke Col; Smith Col; Fogg Art Mus; Regional Contemp Art Collection, Fargo, ND; plus others. *Exhib:* One-man shows, Bertha Schaefer Gallery, New York, 55, 57 & 60, New Vision Ctr Gallery, London, Eng, 60 & East Hampton Gallery, NY, 70; Recent Drawings, USA, Mus Mod Art, 56; 22nd Int Watercolor Biennial, Brooklyn Mus, 63; Inst Contemp Art, Boston, 66; Smithsonian Inst, 68; retrospective, Herter Art Gallery, Univ Mass, 86; Works on Paper, Nada-Mason Gallery, Mount Herman Sch, Northfield, Mass, 90. *Teaching:* Instr art, Putney Sch, Vt, 45; G W V Smith Art Mus, Springfield, Mass, 47-60; prof painting & drawing, Univ Mass, 60-, dir, Art Acquisition Prog, 62-74. *Awards:* Boston Art Festival Award, 55; Award, Drawing & Small Sculpture Shows, Ball State Teachers' Col, Art Gallery, Muncie, Ind, 61-62; Westfield State Col Purchase Prize, 68. *Bibliog:* Harriet Janis & Rudi Blesh (auth), Collage: Personalities, Concepts, Techniques, Chilton, 62; Morris Risenhoover & Robert T Blackburn (auths), Artists as Professors, Conversations with Musicians, Painters, Sculptors, Univ Ill Press, 76; The Societe Anonyme & The Preir Bequest, Yale Univ. *Media:* Watercolor. *Mailing Add:* N Main St Sunderland MA 01375

KAN, DIANA
PAINTER, LECTURER
b Hong Kong, Mar 3, 26; US citizen. *Study:* With Chang Dai Chien, China, 46; Art Students League, with Robert Johnson & Robert B Hale, 49-51; Ecole Beaux Arts, Paris, with Paul Lavelle, 52-54. *Work:* Nat Acad Design, Metrop Mus Art, New York; Philadelphia Mus Art; Nelson Gallery, Atkins Mus, Kansas City, Mo; Nat Hist Mus, Taiwan. *Comn:* Lotus painting, Nat Hist Mus, Taiwan, 71. *Exhib:* Royal Acad Arts, London, Eng, 64; Royal Soc Painters, London, 64; Nat Acad Design, New York, 67-86; one-man shows, Elliott Mus, 67, 74 & 86, Nat Hist Mus, Taiwan, 71 & New York Cult Ctr, 72; Hobe Sound Galleries, Fla, 76 & 86; Nat Arts Club, 79; and others. *Teaching:* Instr watercolor, Art Students League, New York, 85. *Awards:* Henry Gasser Mem Award, Allied Artists Am; John Pike Mem Award, Nat Acad Design, 87; Silver Medal of Honor, 88, Gold Medal of Honor, Distinguished Achievement, 90, Knickerbocker, NY. *Bibliog:* Sheila Elliot (auth), The art of Chinese painting--Diana Kan, Artists Mag, 8/86; Shu-I (auth), Profile of Diana Kan, Cosmopolitan Mag, 2/87; Daria Sommers (dir), Eastern Spirit, Western World: A Profile of Diana Kan (film), Elliot Mus Production, Stuart, Fla, World Premiere, Mus Fine Art, Boston, 88. *Mem:* Assoc mem Nat Acad Design; Fel Royal Soc Arts, London, Eng. *Media:* Watercolor. *Publ:* Auth, How and Why of Chinese Painting, 74; auth, articles, Am Artists Mag, 74 & 86. *Dealer:* Grand Central Art Galleries 24 W 57th St New York NY 10019; Hobe Sound Galleries 11900 SE Dixie Hwy Hobe Sound FL 33455. *Mailing Add:* The Nat Arts Club 15 Grammercy Park S New York NY 10003

KAN, KIT-KEUNG
PAINTER
b Kuangtung Province, China, Dec 7, 43. *Study:* Studied Chinese painting with Leung Pak-Yu, Chou Yat-Fung and Kan Maytin, 58-62; Univ Md, PhD, 75. *Work:* Hong Kong Mus Art; Int Monetary Fund, Washington, DC. *Exhib:* Contemporary Hong Kong Art, Hong Kong Mus Art, 69-70; one-man shows, Robert Brown Contemp Art, Washington, DC, 86, 87, 89 & 91, Hsiung Shih Gallery, Taipei, 88 & 91, Roberts Gallery, Tawson State Univ, Baltimore, 89 & 92 & Alisan Fine Art, Hong Kong, 90; Len Bellinger, Kathryn Markel Gallery, New York, 85,; Tai-kueng Kan, Hong Kong Art Ctr, 86; Hsiung Shih Biennial Invitational, Hsuing Shih Gallery, Taipei, 87. *Awards:* First Prize, Watercolor, Open Art Competition, Chatham Gallery, Hong Kong, 64; First Prize, Ann Fine Art Exhib, Greater Reston Art Ctr, Va, 82. *Mem:* Artist Equity; Coalition Washington Artists. *Media:* Chinese Ink, Watercolor on Rice Paper. *Dealer:* Robert Brown Contemporary Art 1005 New Hampshire Ave NW Washington DC 20037; Hsiung Shih Gallery 385 Tunhwa S Rd Suite 1008 Taipei Taiwan. *Mailing Add:* 6809 Tammy Ct Bethesda MD 20817

KAN, MICHAEL
HISTORIAN, ADMINISTRATOR
b Shanghai, China, July 17, 33; US citizen. *Study:* Columbia Col, BA(art hist & archeol), 53; State Univ NY Agr & Tech Col Alfred, MFA(ceramics & sculpture), 57; Columbia Univ, MA(art hist), 69, MPhil, 74. *Collections Arranged:* African Art & Simpson Collection, Brooklyn Mus, 70; guest cur, Ancient Art of West Mexico, Los Angeles Co Mus Art, 70; curatorial consult, African Art Tribal Art from West Africa, Portland Mus, 71; curatorial consult, Pre-Columbian Art in the Collection of Jay C Leff, Allentown Mus, 72; Detroit Collects African Art, 77; Treasures of Ancient Nigeria: Legacy of 2000 Years, 79. *Pos:* Assoc cur primitive art, Brooklyn Mus, 68-70, cur, 70-73, chief cur, 73-76; cur African, Oceanic & New World cult, Detroit Inst of the Arts, 77- *Teaching:* Lectr art hist, Univ Calif, Berkeley, 64-66; lectr art Eastern Asia, Finch Col, 66-67; lectr African art, NY Univ, 70- *Mem:* Mus Collaborative Inc (trustee, 75); Am Asn Mus. *Res:* The art of early cultures of pre-Columbian Peru and pre-Columbian Mexico; African art education. *Publ:* Contribr, Early Chinese Art and the Pacific Basin, 68; auth, African Sculpture, 70; coauth, Ancient Art of West Mexico, 70. *Mailing Add:* Detroit Inst Arts 5200 Woodward Ave Detroit MI 48202

KANE, BILL
ASSEMBLAGE ARTIST, PHOTOGRAPHER
b Holden, Mass, Feb 18, 51. *Study:* Univ Mass, BA, 73; San Francisco State Univ, MA, 78. *Work:* Museum fur Moderne Kunst, Frankfort, Germany; San Francisco Mus Mod Art; Carnegie Mellon Institute, Pittsburgh, Pa; The Oakland Mus, Calif; Stanford Univ, Calif. *Comn:* Neon installation, Washington Project Arts, Washington, DC, 81; photo/neon mixed media, Southland Corp, Dallas, Tex, 82; mixed media, sculpture, Heathman Hotel, Portland, Ore, 84; photo/neon mixed media, Cognata & Assocs, San Francisco, 84; photo/neon mixed media, N W Ayer Advert, New York, 89. *Exhib:* Contemporary Glass, Nat Mus Tokyo & Kyoto, 81; International Directions in Glass Art, Nat Gallery Victoria, Melbourne, Australia, 83; Examining the Perimeters of 20th Century Photog, San Francisco Mus Mod Art, 85; dalla Pop Art Americana, alla Nuoua Figurazuove, Padiglione d'Art Cont, Milano, Italy, 87; Explorations, extending the boundaries of cont photography, Mus Contemp Photog, Chicago, 87; Am Art Today, Fla Int Univ Art Mus, Miami, 92. *Awards:* Photog fel, 80 & painting fel, 91, Nat Endowment Arts; Photog Award, Eyes & Ears Found, 79 & 84. *Bibliog:* Bill Kane-Photo/Neon Works, Boca Raton Ctr Arts, 82 & Foster Goldstrom Inc, 83; Carl Little (auth), Bill Kane at Foster Goldstrom, Art Am, 12/89. *Media:* Neon, Paint, Wood. *Dealer:* Foster Goldstrom 560 Broadway New York NY 10012. *Mailing Add:* 314 Waverly Ave Brooklyn NY 11205-3615

KANE, BOB PAUL
PAINTER
b Cleveland, Ohio, July 11, 37. *Study:* Cornell Univ; Art Students League, with Will Barnet; Pratt Inst. *Work:* Cincinnati Art Mus; Mus Munic St Paul de Vence, France; Joseph H Hirshhorn Collection; Palm Springs Desert Mus; Pa Acad Fine Arts. *Exhib:* Collector's Choice, Okla Art Ctr, 68; Biennial of the Painters of the Mediterranean, Nice, France, 73; Biennial of Menton, France, 73; Bertha Schaefer Gallery, New York, 68, 70, 72 & 74; Galerie Marcel Bernheim, Paris, 70, Albright-Knox Mus, 73; Ankrum Gallery, Los Angeles, 69, 74, 79 & 81; plus many others. *Teaching:* Instr painting & art hist, Mt Clair Col, 69-70; instr painting & art hist, NY Univ, 69-70. *Bibliog:* Richard Boyle (auth), Bob Kane, Mus Munic St Paul de Vence, 72. *Media:* Oil. *Dealer:* Bertha Schaefer Gallery 41 E 57th St New York NY 10022; Ankrum Gallery 657 N La Cienega Blvd Los Angeles CA 90069. *Mailing Add:* 125 Riverside Dr No 2F New York NY 10019

KANE, MARGARET BRASSLER
SCULPTOR
b East Orange, NJ, May 25, 09. *Study:* Syracuse Univ; Art Students League; also with John Hovannes; Colo State Christian Col, Hon PhD, 73. *Work:* US Maritime Comn; Limited Ed Lamp Co; and numerous pvt collections. *Comn:* Plaque for Burro Monument, Fairplay, Colo. *Exhib:* Lever House, New York, 59-79, 87-90; Chicago Art Inst; New York Metrop Mus; Whitney Mus Am Art, New York; Philadelphia Mus Int Sculpture Exhibs; Pa Acad Fine Arts; plus others. *Pos:* Juror, Am Mach & Foundry Co, 57. *Teaching:* Lectr, Creative Approach to Sculpture. *Awards:* First Anna Hyatt Huntington Prize, 42 & Medal of Hon for Sculpture, 51, Nat Asn Women Artists; Henry O Avery Prize, NY Archit League, 44; Owl Award Arts, Nat League Am Pen Wowen Inc, 91; plus others. *Bibliog:* Greenwich Mag, Dec, 91. *Mem:* Nat Asn Women Artists; Greenwich Arts Coun; Silvermine Guild Artists; fel Int Inst Arts & Lett; Pen & Brush, Inc, Mem Emer, 92. *Media:* Wood, Marble. *Publ:* Contribr ann reproductions, Greenwich Time Publ, 50-77; auth, article, Am Artists, 1/70; reproductions, In: Contemporary Stone Sculpture, Crown, 71; reproductions of wood carvings used by McGraw-Hill, 73; Am References (artists), 89. *Mailing Add:* 30 Strickland Rd Cos Cob CT 06807

KANEGIS, SIDNEY S
DEALER
b Winthrop, Mass, Sept 6, 22. *Study:* Boston Mus Fine Art Sch. *Pos:* Owner & dir, Kanegis Gallery, Boston, 50- *Specialty:* Modern master graphics. *Mailing Add:* 244 Newbury St Boston MA 02116

KANGAS, GENE
SCULPTOR, AUTHOR
b Concord, Ohio, May 22, 44. *Study:* Miami Univ, BFA; Bowling Green Univ, MFA; Univ Ky. *Work:* Butler Inst Am Art, Ohio; City Miami, Fla; City Upper Arlington, Ohio; Case Western Reserve Univ & Cleveland Pub Libr, Cleveland. *Comn:* Sculptures, Cuyahoga Co Justice Ctr, Cleveland, Ohio, 77, Frank J Lausche State Off Bldg, Cleveland, 80, Case Western Reserve Univ, Cleveland, 81, Dade Co, Miami, Fla, 83, Coral Springs, Fla, 84, Boynton Beach, Fla, 85. *Exhib:* Sculpture Invitational, Art Acad Cincinnati, 80; City of Upper Arlington Sculpture Invitational, Columbus, Ohio, 82; Art Assemblage, Columbus, Ohio, 82; Invitational Sculptor Exhi; and numerous group and one-man exhibs. *Teaching:* Instr sculpture, Univ NC, 68-71; asst prof sculpture, Cleveland State Univ, 71-75, assoc prof, 75-84, prof, 84- *Awards:* Univ Res Grant, Univ NC, 68-70; First Prize in Sculpture, Cleveland Mus Art, 75; RCAC Res Grant, Cleveland State Univ, 91-93; and others. *Bibliog:* Hollander (auth), Plastics for Artists and Craftsmen; Campen (auth), Outdoor sculpture in Ohio; McCelland (dir), Public Sculpture of Cleveland (film), 82. *Media:* Metal, Wood. *Publ:* Coauth, Decoys; A North American Survey, Hillcrest Publ, 83; Decoys, Collector Bks, 91; Collectors Guide to Decoys, Wallace-Homestead Publ, 92; New World Folk Art, Cleveland State Univ Publ, 92. *Mailing Add:* Cleveland State Univ Euclid Ave at East 24th Cleveland OH 44115

KANIDINC, SALAHATTIN
CALLIGRAPHER, DESIGNER
b Istanbul, Turkey, Aug 12, 27. *Study:* Defenbaugh Sch Lettering, under Roger I Defenbaugh; Zanerian Col Penmanship, text lettering under John P Turner; State Univ Iowa, cert lettering, under Prof Meyer; Univ Minn, cert lettering; Univ Calif, cert advert. *Work:* The White House, Washington, DC; Independence Hall, Philadelphia; Franklin Mint Mus Medallic Art, Franklin Center, Pa; Peabody Inst Libr, Baltimore, Md. *Comn:* Presidential designs, Tiffany & Co, New York, 70; Genius of Michelangelo Medals, Franklin Mint, 71; medal design, Fedr Turkish-Am Socs, New York, 73; Christmas Card Design, UNICEF, New York, 73 & 91; postage stamp designs, United Nations, 78, 82 & 86; and others. *Exhib:* 1000 Yrs of Calligraphy & Illumination, Baltimore, 59; Bertrand Russell Centenary Int Art Exhib, London, 72-73. *Pos:* Chief calligrapher, Deniz Basimevi MD, Istanbul, Turkey, 50-61; lettering artist, Buzza-Cardozo, Anaheim, Calif, 62-64; asst art dir, Rust Craft Publ, Dedham, Mass, 64; lettering specialist-designer, Tiffany & Co, New York, 64-72; owner-creative dir, Kanidinc Int, New York, 72- *Awards:* First Prize, Ann McKay Christmas Card Contest, 74. *Mem:* Int Asn Master Penmen & Teachers Handwriting; Int Ctr Typographic Arts; Queens Coun Arts; Soc Scribes & Illuminators; Int Graphological Soc; Handwriting Analysts Int. *Media:* Ink, Gouache. *Publ:* Contribr, Alphabet Thesaurus, Vol II, III, 65-71; contribr, Turkish-Am Encycl Dig. *Mailing Add:* 33-44 93th St Jackson Heights NY 11372

KANOVITZ, HOWARD
PAINTER
b Fall River, Mass, Feb 9, 29. *Study:* Providence Col, BS, 49; RI Sch Design, 49-51; with Franz Kline, 51-52; Inst Fine Arts, NY Univ, 59-61. *Work:* Whitney Mus Am Art, New York; Ludwig Mus, Cologne, Ger; Hirshhorn Mus & Sculpture Garden; Mus Boymans-Van Beuningen, Rotterdam, Holland; Metrop Mus Art, New York; and others. *Comn:* The Opening, 180 Beacon Corp, Boston, 67; A Death in Treme, Florists Transworld Delivery Collection, Detroit, 71; Collector's Wall, F K Johnssen, Essen, Ger, 71. *Exhib:* Whitney Mus Am Art Ann, New York, 72; Dokumenta 6, Kassel, Ger, 77; Guild Hall, Easthampton, 78; Hamburg Kunstverein, Hamburg, Ger, 79; Akad der Kunste, Berlin, Ger, 79; Kestner-Gesellschaft, Hannover, 79; Parrish Art Mus, Southampton, 88; Art Mus, Fla Int Univ, Miami, 89. *Teaching:* Instr painting & design, Brooklyn Col, 61-64; instr 2-D design, Pratt Inst, 64-66; prof painting, Southampton Col, 77-78; Sch Visual Arts, New York, 80-85. *Awards:* Berlin Deutscher Akademischer Austauschdienst Fel, 79-80. *Bibliog:* Peter Sager (auth), Neve Formen des Realismus, Mag Kunst, 71; Sam Hunter (auth), Howard Kanovitz's new paintings, 4/75 & Michael Florescu (auth), Kanovitz, the new work, 2/79, Arts Mag. *Media:* Acrylic. *Dealer:* Marlborough Gallery 40 W 57th St New York NY 10019. *Mailing Add:* 463 Broome St New York NY 10013

KANTER, LORNA J
PAINTER, PRINTMAKER
b Passaic, NJ, Apr 10, 31. *Study:* Am Art Sch, AAS (4 yr merit cert completion), 62; Pratt Graphics Art Ctr (scholar), 63; Art Students League (scholar), 77-80. *Work:* White House, Washington, DC; Ronald W Reagan Libr, Simi Valley, Calif; Intrepid Sea/Air/Space Mus, New York; Douglas MacArthur USO, New York; Colonial Williamsburg Found, Va,. *Comn:* Portrait of Gen Douglas MacArthur & George Washington, comn by Military Order of Purple Heart, Intrepid Mus, New York, 85; Two Portraits of Pres

Ronald Reagan, comn by Military Order of Purple Heart, White House Washington, DC & Intrepid Mus, New York, 86. *Exhib:* 17th Ann Knickerbocker Artists, Nat Arts Club, New York, 64; Travelling Exhib, Fairleigh Dickinson Univ, Teaneck, NJ, 64; 30th Ann Painters & Sculptors Soc NJ, Jersey City Mus, 71; Libby Girl Among the Flowers, Cartier Inc, New York, 86; Realism Today, Am Artist Mag Nat Competition, Carol Siple Gallery, Denver, Colo, 88-89. *Teaching:* Portraiture & Drawing, Am Art Sch, New York, 65-66. *Awards:* Green Ribbon, Nat Arts Club, Knickerbocker Artists, 64; Artist Yr Award, Salmagundi Club, Beaux Arts, Inc, 84; National Competition, Award, Am Artist Mag, 88-89. *Bibliog:* Mermelstein (auth), Dreams of gold & ancient queens, Herald-News, 85; A portrait of courage, NY Post, 85; Daryln Brewer (auth), Er-satz masterpieces for your home, NY Times, 90. *Mem:* New York Artists Equity; Beaux Arts Inc; life mem, Art Students League. *Media:* Drawing Mediums, Oil. *Publ:* Auth, Pain & TMJ: The Experience & Survival of a Patient, Mod Nutrition News, 87; Col Craig House Garden, (lithographs world-wide), ART Inc, 89. *Mailing Add:* 24 Janice Terr Clifton NJ 07013

KAPLAN, FREDERIC CLARK
PAINTER, ILLUSTRATOR
b Philadelphia, Pa, Jan 2, 48. *Study:* Pa Acad Fine Art, 67-68 & 78-79; Philadelphia Col of Art, 81. *Work:* Nat Park Service, Valley Forge, Pa; Am Red Cross, Philadelphia, Pa. *Comn:* Mural, SCS Indust, Ocala, Fla, 78; film & illustrs, Animation Arts Assoc, Philadelphia, Pa, 79. *Exhib:* Solo exhibs, Flight Through Surrealism, Temple Univ, 71, Beethoven Nine, Gallery at the Philadelphia, 90, Goforth Rittenhouse Galleries, 91; Am Artist Nat Competition, Am Artist Mag, New York, 78; Art at the Armory, Philadelphia Armory, 90. *Pos:* Art dir, Lawrence Factor Inc, Miami, Fla, 83-84; Herder's Cutlery Inc, Malvern, Pa, 84-87; ed/artist, Kane Communications, Upper Darby, Pa, 88-89. *Awards:* Joseph Milner Honor Award, 66, Joseph L Milner Merit Award, 67, Philadelphia Civic Ctr, Pa; Semi-finalist, Am Artists Nat, 78. *Bibliog:* Helen Schaeffer (auth), Surrealist trancends reality, News of Delaware County, 90; Folcroft Artist Interprets Beethoven Classics, Interboro News, 90; Lisa Marum (auth), Beethoven's Fifth on Oil, Classical Mag, 91. *Media:* Oil, Ink. *Publ:* Illustr, The End of the Dream, DAW Bks, 72; auth, Ballpoint as an art medium, Podium II, 74; Volitional Romanticism, Arts Objectively, 76; illustr, Children of a Fanad Chieftan, Nuttall Press, 88; contribr, Art Matters Inc, 90. *Dealer:* Nat Broadcast Music Co's Gallery at Philadelphia 2401 Pennsylvania Ave Philadelphia PA 19103. *Mailing Add:* PO Box 0083 Folcroft PA 19032-0083

KAPLAN, ILEE
PRINTMAKER, ADMINISTRATOR
b Los Angeles, Calif. *Study:* Univ Calif, Berkeley, BA; Calif State Univ, Long Beach, MA. *Exhib:* Solo exhibs, Folk dance, 81, New Woodcuts, 87 & Night Life Series, 89, Studio 1617, Los Angeles; Four Views of the Figure, Fine Arts Gallery, Cerritos Col, Norwalk, Calif, 86; group show, Carson-Sapiro Gallery, Denver, Colo, 87; Summer Visions, Gallery 209, Redondo Beach, Calif, 88; Praise Her by Her Works: Jewish Women Artists, Univ Southern Calif Hillel Gallery, Los Angeles, 88; At the Edge: Nat Print & Drawing Echib, Tex Fine Arts Asn, Austin, 89; Recent Woodcuts, Nazareth Col, Mich, 89; Procession, Dance, St Lukes Acad Music & Art, 90; Recent Works, Chamberlain Gallery, San Juan Capistrano, Calif, 91. *Pos:* Adminr, Brockman Gallery Productions, Los Angeles, 82-84; mem adv bd, Mus Studies prog, Rancho Santiago Community Col, Canta Ana, Calif, 88; assoc dir, Univ Art Mus, Calif State Univ, Long Beach, 84-; steering comt, Pub Corp Art, Long Beach, Calif, 86, 87 & 88; grant rev panelist, Inst Mus Serv, 92; selection panel, Long Beach Adv Comt Pub Art, 92. *Teaching:* Instr art, Calif State Univ, Dominguez Hills, Carson, 83; lectr, Calif State Univ, Long Beach, 85 & 88. *Awards:* Fel, Nat Endowment Arts, 87; Fel, Calif Arts Coun, 90. *Bibliog:* A brand-new arts council celebrates Jewish artists with its first show, Los Angeles Times, 11/18/88; Kaplan's work is strong, Kalamazoo Gazette, 11/89; People fire Kaplan's palette, Press Telegram, 9/91. *Mem:* Pub Corp Arts; Angel's Gate Cult Ctr; Am Asn Mus. *Publ:* Auth, The arts in Long Beach, Long Beach Citizen News. *Dealer:* Studio 1617 1617 Silverlake Blvd Los Angeles CA 90026. *Mailing Add:* 1865 Ashbrook Ave Long Beach CA 90815

KAPLAN, JACQUES
COLLECTOR, DEALER
b Paris, France, Oct 22, 24. *Study:* Sorbonne Univ, France, PhD. *Awards:* Croix de Guerre. *Bibliog:* Articles in New York Times, 66, Life Mag, 68, Time & Newsweek. *Collection:* Contemporary American art, 19th century European art and the Old Masters. *Mailing Add:* 170 E 78th St New York NY 10021

KAPLAN, JEROME EUGENE
PRINTMAKER
b Philadelphia, Pa, 1920. *Study:* Philadelphia Col Art, dipl; also with Paul Froelich & Benton Spruance. *Work:* Libr Cong, Washington, DC; Philadelphia Mus Art; Nat Gallery Art, Washington, DC; New York Pub Libr. *Comn:* Portfolio, White House Etchings, for President Jimmy Carter, 80. *Exhib:* 4th Int Prints, Ljubjana, Yugoslavia, 61; Am Prints Today, Print Coun Am, 62; First Biennial Int l'Estampe, Epinal, France, 71; 25th Nat Exhib, Washington, DC, 77; 57th Nat, Soc Am Graphic Artists, New York, 79; and 19 one-man exhibs. *Teaching:* Prof printmaking, Philadelphia Col Art, 48-91, chmn dept, 70-80, retired, 91. *Awards:* Guggenheim Fel, 61; Fel, Tamarind Lithography Workshop, 62. *Mem:* Print Club Philadelphia; Artists Equity Asn; Soc Am Graphic Artists. *Media:* Intaglio, Lithography. *Publ:* Illusr, The Bucket Rider, 72; illusr, From a Housewife's Diary, 78; illusr, Charlie in the House of Rue, 80. *Dealer:* Print Club 1614 Latimer St Philadelphia PA 19103. *Mailing Add:* Univ of the Arts Broad & Pine Sts Philadelphia PA 19102

KAPLAN, JULIUS DAVID
ADMINISTRATOR, HISTORIAN
b Nashville, Tenn, July 22, 41. *Study:* Wesleyan Univ, Middletown, Conn, BA; Columbia Univ, MA & PhD. *Collections Arranged:* Symbolism, Europe and America at the End of the 19th Century, 80, Gaston Lachaise, Sculpture and Drawings, 80, Kate Steinitz, Art and Collection, Avant-Garde Art in Germany in the 1920's and 1930's, 82 & Selections from The Edward-Dean Museum of Decorative Arts, 84, Art Gallery, Calif State Univ, San Bernardino; The Evans Collection of Oriental Ceramics, 88; The Dechter Collection of Greek Vases, 89. *Teaching:* Lectr, Colby Col, Waterville, Maine, 66; asst prof, Univ Calif, Los Angeles, 69-77; assoc prof art hist, Calif State Col, San Bernardino, 77-, chmn dept, 78-82, prof, 82-, assoc dean, graduate prog 86-, dean, graduate studies, 89- *Awards:* Grant-in-aid, Am Coun Learned Socs, 77; Nat Endowment Arts Grant, 81; Calif Art Coun Grant, 81, 82 & 83; Fine Arts Comt, City of San Bernardino, Calif, 88. *Mem:* Col Art Asn; Art Historians Southern Calif. *Res:* Academic and official art in France, 1850-1900. *Publ:* Auth, The religious subjects of James Ensor 1877-1900, Revue Belge d'Archaeol d'Hist l'Art, 66; auth, Gustave Moreau, Los Angeles Co Mus Art, 74; auth, Gustave Moreau, UMI Res Press, 82. *Mailing Add:* Dept Art Calif State Univ 5500 University Pkwy San Bernardino CA 92407

KAPLAN, KATHERINE
ART DEALER
b New York, NY. *Study:* Haverford Col, Pa, BA, 86. *Pos:* Assoc dir, Kraushaar Galleries, New York, 91- *Specialty:* Twentieth century American art. *Publ:* Coauth, Kraushaar Galleries catalogs. *Mailing Add:* c/o Kraushaar Galleries 724 Fifth Ave New York NY 10019

KAPLAN, LEO
ASSEMBLAGE ARTIST, COLLAGE ARTIST
b Binghamton, NY, Jan 21, 12. *Study:* Rochester Inst Technol, 32. *Work:* Chase Manhattan Bank, New York; Everson Gallery, Syracuse; Memorial Art Gallery, Rochester, NY; Skidmore Col, Saratoga Springs, NY; Eastman Kodak Co; Welch's, Westfield, NY; Xerox Corp, Stamford, Conn; Bausch & Lomb, Rochester, NY. *Comn:* The Humanities, Monroe Community Col, Rochester, NY, 66; AMF Inc, White Plains, NY, 78; Kodak Centennial, Lincoln First, Rochester, 79; Regents Publ, New York, 83; Rochester Tel Co, 85. *Exhib:* One-man shows, Two Rivers Gallery, Binghamton, NY, 68 & Univ Miami Calder Gallery, 90; Miss Mus Art, Jackson, 81; Hunter Mus, Chattanooga, 82; Roanoke Mus Fine Art, 82; Mus Art, Ft Lauderdale, 82, 83 & 88; Tampa Mus, 83; and others. *Awards:* Best of show, Brockport State Univ, 66; Ida Abrams Award, Mem Art Gallery, Finger Lakes, 71; Merit Award, 82, Hortt Jurors Award, 90, Ft Lauderdale Mus, Fla, 90. *Dealer:* Alan Brown Gallery Hartsdale NY 10530; Oxford Gallery Rochester NY 14607. *Mailing Add:* 5310 Buttonwood Ct Tamarac FL 33319

KAPLAN, MARILYN FLASHENBERG
PAINTER
b Brooklyn, NY. *Study:* Syracuse Univ, BFA; Columbia Univ Teachers Col, MA, 54. *Work:* New York Port Authority, Japan Air Lines & Lanvin-Charles of the Ritz Collection, New York; Nat Collection of Fine Arts, Smithsonian Inst, Washington, DC; Johnson & Johnson Collection, New Brunswick, NJ. *Comn:* Poster, No More War by Personality Posters, New York for Nat Peace Movement, 69; painting, Mass Blue Cross & Blue Shield Hq, 84. *Exhib:* Nat Acad Design, New York, 70, 72 & 75; New Eng Ann, Silvermine, Conn, 72 & 73; Images of an Era: The American Poster 1945-1975, Corcoran Gallery Art, Washington, DC, 76; Smithsonian Inst Traveling Bicentennial Art Exhib, Inst Contemp Art, London, Eng, Musee des Arts Decoratifs, Paris, France, Palazzo Delle Esposizione, Rome, Italy & Stedelijk Mus, Amsterdam, Neth; solo exhib, Isis Gallery, Manhasset, NY, 88, Jericho Pub Libr, NY, 89. *Teaching:* Art coordr elem & jr high sch art, Croton-Harmon Schs, NY, 54-56. *Awards:* Invitational Show Award, Hofstra Univ, NY, 66; Second Prize Oils, Heckscher Mus, NY, 72; Benjamin Altman Landscape Prize Painting, Nat Acad Design, 75; and many others. *Bibliog:* Gary Yanker (auth), Prop Art; Images of an Era: The American Poster 1945-1975 (catalogue), Nat Collection of Fine Arts, Smithsonian Inst; Robert Carlsen (auth), Encounters: Themes in Literature, McGraw-Hill. *Media:* Acrylic, Oil. *Dealer:* Isis Gallery 609 Plandome Rd Manhasset NY 11030. *Mailing Add:* 26 Birchwood Park Dr Jericho NY 11753

KAPLAN, MURIEL
SCULPTOR, COLLECTOR
b Philadelphia, Pa, Aug 15, 24. *Study:* Cornell Univ, BA, 46; Sarah Lawrence Col, Grad Work, 58-60; Oxford Univ, Eng, cert, 71; Art Student's League, NY, 75-88. *Work:* Columbia Univ Law Libr, New York, NY; Brandeis Univ, Waltham, Mass; Lyndon Johnson Libr, Univ Tex, Austin; John F Kennedy Sch, Jerusalem, Israel. *Comn:* Two rotating steel sculptures, Trans Lux Corp, Norwalk, Conn, 66 & 68; portrait busts, Judge Simon Rifkind, 67 & Vera List, 75 & Charles E Smith, 90; two steel sculptures, Empire State Construct Co, Tarrytown, NY, 72. *Exhib:* Allied Artists Am Annual, Nat Acad Art, New York, 58-73; Nat Asn Women Artists Annual, Fed Bldg, New York, 66-85; Artists and Engineers in Technology, Brooklyn Mus, NY, 68; Sculptor's Guild, Lever House, New York, 72; Nat Asn Women Artists Exhib, Bergen County Mus, NJ, 74; Artist's Guild, Norton Mus Art, Palm Beach, Fla, 81-90; Folk Art Exhib, Barrington Mus, Delray Beach, Fla, 84; Art in Public Places, Govt Ctr, West Palm Beach, Fla, 85-86 & 88. *Pos:* Secy, Comt to Estab Art Mus, Westchester, NY, 56-58; co-chair, First Televised Art Auction, WNET, New York, 64; mem, Comt Art in Pub Places, Palm Beach, Fla, 83-84; art adv bd, Boca Raton Mus Art, Fla, 88-; bd dir, Palm Beach County, Coun Arts, 92. *Teaching:* Instr portrait sculpture, pvt studio, 66-70 & Arts Coun, Palm Beach, Fla, 86; instr, Armory Sch, 87- *Awards:* Sculpture Prize, Nat Asn Women

Artists Ann, 66; Robert Kennedy Humanitarian Award, University Settlement House, New York, 68; Portrait Award, Allied Artists Am Ann, 69; First Prize Sculpture, Barrington Mus Art, 84; Sculpture Prize, Norton Art Mus, 88. *Bibliog:* Eve Sharbutt (auth), Sculptor creates from structural steel, Assoc Press, 8/12/73; Dorothy Ann Flor, Casted characters, Ft Lauderdale Sun Sentinel, 5/17/84; Muriel Kaplan Keeps Ahead in the Sculpture Business, Arts Mag, 7/92. *Mem:* Art Students League; Nat Asn Women Artists; Artist's Guild, Palm Beach; Palm Beach County Count Arts; Norton Gallery & Sch Arts, Lect Sponsor. *Media:* Steel, Clay. *Dealer:* Portraits Inc 985 Park Ave New York NY 10028. *Mailing Add:* 339 Garden Rd Palm Beach FL 33480

KAPLAN, PENNY
SCULPTOR, PRINTMAKER
b New York, NY. *Study:* Hunter Col; Columbia Univ, studied with Prof Brilliant & Miriam Shapero; New York Univ studied with Krishna Reddy. *Work:* Everson Mus, Syracuse, NY; Nassau County Arts Mus, NY; Hofstra Univ, Hempstead, NY; Pace Col White Plains, NY; Westchester County Courthouse, White Plains, NY. *Comn:* Sculpture, Westchester County, NY, 76; sculpture, St Peters Church, New York, 82; sculpture, State of Conn, 85, 89. *Exhib:* Int Sculpture Conference, Washington, DC, 80 & 82. *Mem:* Artists Representing Environmental Art (secy 85-90); Soho 20 Gallery (bd dir); Sculptors Guild. *Media:* Steel. *Mailing Add:* c/o Soho 20 469 Broome St New York NY 10013

KAPLAN, SANDRA
PAINTER, PRINTMAKER
b Cincinnati, Ohio, May 23, 43. *Study:* Art Acad Cincinnati, with Julian Stanczak, 60-61; Pratt Inst, with Richard Lindner & Lennart Anderson, BFA(with hons), 65; City Univ New York, 68-70. *Work:* ALCOA Pittsburgh, Pa; Am Express Co, Inverness Park, Colo; Hyatt Regency Hotel, Dubai, United Arab Emirates; Blue Cross, Blue Shield, Denver; Neiman Marcus Corp Hqs, Los Angeles. *Comn:* Vail Athletic Club, 79; Prince Khalid, 5-panel watercolor, Standard Textile Corp, Cincinnati; monotypes, Fairmont Hotels, San Jose & Chicago, 87; watercolors, Marriot Hotel, Hong Kong; Art in Public Places, watercolor, Colo Coun Arts, 89. *Exhib:* Fifteenth Street Gallery, Denver, 80; Inkfish Gallery, Denver, 79, 80 & 82; Janus Gallery, Santa Fe, 81 & 83; Ventana Gallery, Santa Fe, 85-90; Dubins Gallery, Los Angeles, 88 & 90; Eva Cohon Galleries Ltd, Chicago & Highland Park, 89; Olson Larsen Gallery, Des Moines, Iowa, 90; Arvada Ctr Arts, 91; Nicolaysen Art Mus, Casper, Wyo, 92. *Teaching:* Instr painting & design, Arapahoe Community Col, 74-75; art instr, Metro State Col, 77-78; guest art instr, Denver Univ, 78-79. *Awards:* First Place, Rocky Mountain Regional Print Show, 82; Ludwig Vogelstein Found Grant, Phillip Morris Fel, Yaddo Artists Colony, 86; Best of Show, Colo Art Expo. *Bibliog:* Roberta McIntyre (auth), A summer's garden, Focus, Santa Fe, 10/87; Carole Katchen (auth), Watercolor, the very large picture, Artists Mag, 9/88; Lynn Kari Petrich (auth), Painting floral subjects, Am Artist/Watercolor, 89. *Media:* Watercolor; Oil. *Publ:* Illusr, Rationale, 65; contrib, Art Work, No Commercial Value, Grossman, 71; Landscapes, (catalog) Arvada Ctr Show, 91; Human and/or Nature, (brochure) Nicolaysen Mus, 92. *Dealer:* Sharks Inc 2020 9th St Boulder Colo 80302; Dubins Gallery 11948 San Vicente Blvd Los Angeles Calif 90049. *Mailing Add:* Dubins Gallery 11948 San Vincente Blvd Los Angeles CA 90049

KAPLAN, STANLEY
PRINTMAKER, MURALIST
b Brooklyn, NY, Sept 4, 25. *Study:* Cooper Union Sch of Art, cert fine arts, 49; NY Univ, BS, 52; Pratt Inst, New York, MS, 68. *Work:* Metrop Mus of Art, New York; Brooklyn Mus, New York Pub Libr; Columbia Univ; Philadelphia Mus Art; Newark Mus Art. *Comn:* Murals, Int Tel & Tel Community Develop Corp, New York & Fla, 73, 74 & 75; mural, Manuche's Restaurant, New York, 62. *Exhib:* One-man show, Shelter Rock Libr, Albertson, NY, 80; Libr of Cong, Washington, DC, 51, Audubon Artists, 66, Nat Acad of Design, New York, 71, Kennedy Gallery, 71 & Assoc Am Artists Gallery, 72; and others. *Pos:* Mgr, Tortoise Press, 78- *Teaching:* Art teacher, Levittown Pub Schs, NY, 54-59; prof art, Nassau Community Col, Garden City, 66- *Awards:* Sixth Ann Competition Award, Port Washington Pub Libr, 71; Purchase Award, Soc Am Graphic Artists 55th Nat Print Exhib, 77. *Mem:* Soc Am Graphic Artists (vpres, 72-74, pres, 76-78). *Mailing Add:* c/o Dept Art 1 Education Dr Nassau Comm Col Garden City NY 11530

KAPLINSKI, BUFFALO
PAINTER
b Chicago, Ill, May 25, 43. *Study:* Art Inst Chicago; Am Acad Art. *Work:* Denver Pub Libr, Johns-Manville, United Bank & Petro-Lewis, Denver. *Comn:* Fredrick Ross Co, Denver; Prudential Bache Securities, Denver. *Exhib:* 98th Ann, Am Watercolor Soc, New York; 162nd Ann, Pa Acad Fine Arts, Philadelphia; 27th Exhib, Audubon Artists, New York; 15th-18th Ann, Nat Soc Painters in Casein; High Country in Art, Boulder Pub Libr, 79; Wilderness and Wildlife--Nature Conservancy, Aspen, Colorado Springs & Denver, 79; East Meets West, Jewish Community Ctr, Denver, 84; Rotary Artists of America, Denver, 88, 89 & 90. *Teaching:* Instr, Colo Inst Art, Univ Denver; instr watercolor, Art Students' League, Denver, currently. *Awards:* 15th Ann Exhib Hon Mention, Nat Soc Painters in Casein; Southwestern Watercolor Soc Purchase Award, Southern Methodist Univ Fine Arts Ctr; Southwestern Biennial Hon Mention, NMex Arts Mus, Santa Fe. *Bibliog:* Article in Am Artist Mag, 8/72; article, Artists Rockies, 9/77 & 10/83; Harold & Peggy Samuels, Contemp Western Artists, 11/82; articles in Am Artist, 6/84 & Art West Mag, 9-10/84. *Media:* Acrylic, Watercolor. *Mailing Add:* PO Box 44 Elizabeth CO 80107

KAPROV, SUSAN
PAINTER, MURALIST
b New York, NY, Aug 11, 46. *Study:* City Col New York, BA, 67; Dartmouth Col, Hanover, NH, MA, 68. *Work:* Mus Mod Art & Metrop Mus Art, New York; Corcoran Gallery Art, Washington, DC; Nat Mus Am Art, Washington, DC; Brooklyn Mus; Rose Art Mus; Gernsheim Col, Waltham, Mass. *Comn:* Austin Co, Atlanta, Ga; Reeves Communication Corp, NY, 81; NASA, Washington, DC, 81 & 92; Prudential Insurance Co, 82; Hexcel Corp, 83; City of New York; Port Authority, NJ, 90; Liberty Sci Ctr, 92. *Exhib:* Prints: Acquisitions 1973-76, Mus Mod Art, New York, 77; one-man show, Hayden Planetarium, New York, 78 & Brooklyn Mus, 81; Recent Acquisitions, Nat Mus Am Art, Washington, DC, 78; Art-Technol, Philadelphia Print Club, 79 & 92; Alternative Imaging Systems, Everson Mus, Syracuse, NY, 79; installation, Granite Gallery, Nat Mus Am Art, 83-84; Fay Gold Gallery, Atlanta, 90; Neikrug Gallery, NY, 92; Midtown Y Gallery, 92. *Teaching:* Sch Visual Arts, New York, 92. *Awards:* MacDowell Colony Fel, 71 & 73; Ossabaw Island Proj Fel, 73; Creative Artists Pub Serv fel, NY State Coun on Arts, 79-80. *Bibliog:* Donald Saff (auth), History of American Printmaking, Holt, Rinehart, Winston, 77; Ellen Lubell (auth), article, Art in Am, 81; V Butera (auth), article, Arts Mag, 81. *Mem:* Am Inst Architects. *Media:* Oil; Encaustic, Acrylic Photomontage on Aluminum. *Mailing Add:* 149 Willow St Brooklyn NY 11201

KAPSALIS, THOMAS HARRY
PAINTER, SCULPTOR
b Chicago, Ill, May 31, 25. *Study:* Sch Art Inst Chicago, BAE, 49, MAE, 57; Fulbright Grant, Ger, 53-54. *Work:* Main Bank, Chicago, Ill; Elmhurst Col, Ill; Art Inst Chicago, Ill; Ill State Mus, Springfield. *Exhib:* Chicago & Vicinity Exhib, 12 times, 50-81 & Contemp Drawings from 12 Countries, 52, Art Inst Chicago; 27th Biennial Exhib Contemp Painting, Corcoran Gallery Art, Washington, DC, 61; Visions-Painting & Sculpture: Distinguished Alumni 1945 to Present, Art Inst Chicago, 76; two-person exhib, Art Inst Chicago, 79; Chicago: Some Other Traditions, Madison Art Ctr, Wis, 83; Artists Choose Artists, 83, Hyde Park Art Ctr, Chicago; one-man shows, NAME Gallery, 85 & Roy Boyd Gallery, Chicago, 86 & 88; faculty sabbatical exhib, Art Inst Chicago, 87; int art expn, Navy Pier, Chicago, 86; American Prints 1900-1960, Art Inst Chicago, 92. *Teaching:* Prof drawing & painting, Art Inst Chicago, 52-; lectr painting, Northwestern Univ, Chicago & Evanston, 58-71. *Awards:* Huntington Hartford Found Grant, 56 & 59; Pualine Palmer Prize, 60 & Jule F Brower Prize, 69, Art Inst Chicago. *Bibliog:* Meilach & Seiden (auth), Direct Metal Sculpture, Crown, 66; Meilach & Hinz (auth), How to Create Your Own Designs, Doubleday, 75. *Media:* Oil, Watercolor; Bronze. *Mailing Add:* 5204 N Virginia Ave Chicago IL 60625

KARAFEL, LORRAINE
WRITER, CRITIC
b Orange, NJ, Nov 29, 56. *Study:* Univ of Paris IV, Sorbonne, France 76; Ecole du Louvre, Paris, France, 76 & 77; Univ Florence, Italy, 77; Rutgers Col, New Brunswick, NJ, BA, 78; New York Univ Inst Fine Arts, MA, 84; Columbia Univ, Sch of Arts, MFA, 87. *Pos:* Assoc cur spec exhib progs, Nat Gallery of Art, Washington, DC, 90- *Teaching:* Instr, Parsons Sch Design, New York, 86-90; vis lectr, Rutgers Col, New Brunswick, NJ, 89- 90; lectr, George Mason Univ, Fairfax, Va, 92- *Mem:* Int Art Critics Asn, Am Branch. *Publ:* Contribr, Sculptors Drawings Over Six Centuries, The Drawing Ctr, 81; auth, Bernard Maisner, Arts Mag, 86; auth, Master of the Moulin Rouge, Art News, 86; auth, Memphis-Milano at the Cooper-Hewitt Mus, Art News, 86; contribr, paintings in the Louvre, Stewart, Tabori & Chang, 87. *Mailing Add:* 12 E 95th St New York NY 10128

KARAWINA, ERICA (MRS SIDNEY C HSIAO)
PAINTER, STAINED GLASS ARTIST
b Ger; US citizen. *Study:* Studied in Europe; also with Frederick W Allen & Charles J Connick, Boston. *Work:* Contemp Mus, Honolulu; Mus Mod Art, New York; Boston Mus Fine Arts; Libr Cong, Washington, DC; Honolulu Acad Arts; State Found Cult Arts. *Comn:* Crux Gemmata (faceted glass in concrete), Manoa Valley Church, Honolulu, 67; six windows of faceted glass, St Anthony's Church, Kailua, Oahu, Hawaii, 68; This Earth is Ours (faceted glass), News Bldg Foyer, Honolulu Advertiser, 72; translucent glass mosaic murals, Hawaii State Off Bldg, Honolulu, 75; ceiling (faceted glass), Circuit Ct, Honolulu, 84; Hawaii, Hawaii (faceted glass mural), Campus Ctr, Diamond Head, Kapiolani Col, Honolulu, 88. *Exhib:* Dance Int, Rockefeller Ctr, New York, 37; Competition of State of Mass, New York's Fair, 39; Protestant Orthodox Ctr, New York World's Fair, 64; one-man shows, China Int Inst, Taipei, Taiwan, 56 & Contemp Arts Ctr, Honolulu, 77; Ryan Gallery, Kailua, 81; plus others. *Pos:* Draftsman stained glass, Connick Studios, Boston, 30-33; designer stained glass, Burnham Studios, Boston, 35-38. *Teaching:* Butera Sch of Art, Boston, 47-48. *Awards:* John Poole Mem Prize, Honolulu Acad Arts, 52; James C Castle Award, Narcissus Art Festival, Honolulu, 61. *Bibliog:* Jean Charlot (auth), Exhibition of stained glass, 5/53; Joanne Shaw (auth), Echoes of universality, Vol 72, No 9, Paradise of Pac; Francis Haar & Murray Turnbull (ed), Artists of Hawaii, Vol II, 77; Hawaii Doe (vcr cassette), Karawina, 85. *Mem:* Honolulu Print Makers; Honolulu Acad of Arts; Hawaii Artists League; fel Int Inst Arts. *Media:* Stained Glass. *Publ:* Contribr, From Maui to Mainz, 56-57 & From Hawaii to Holland, 63, Stained Glass. *Mailing Add:* 1434 Punahoi St No 437 Honolulu HI 96822-4721

KARDON, CAROL
PAINTER, INSTRUCTOR
b Mt Vernon, NY. *Study:* Art Students League, New York, 55-56; Bennington Col, Vt, BA, 56; Univ Pa, Grad Sch Fine Arts, spec student, 70; also studied

with Wolf Kahn, Dan Greene & Albert Handell, Barnes Found, Merion, Pa. *Work:* Bryn Mawr Col, Pa; AT&T Co; Pepsico Co; Kidder Peabody Co; Shell Oil Co; and others. *Exhib:* Cheltenham Award Show, Mus Philadelphia Civic Ctr, Pa, 80 & Cheltenham Art Ctr, Pa; one-woman shows, Gross McCleaf Gallery, Philadelphia, Pa, 80-82 & 84 & Gallery Ave Kobe, Nishinomiya Hyogo, Japan, 87; Great Swamp XXV Exhib, Nabisco Brands Corp, East Hanover, NJ, 85; Ann Exhib, Pastel Soc Am, New York, 86, 87, 89 & 92; group show, Neville-Sargent Gallery, Chicago, Ill, 89-92. *Teaching:* Pastel & color, Main Line Ctr Arts; landscape workshop in Santa Fe, NMex, Pa Acad Fine Arts, Philadelphia, 91. *Awards:* Painter in Residence, Millay Colony, Austerlitz, NY, 79; Rosenfeld Award, Cheltenham Award Show, 83; Pew Found Grant, Art Alliance, Philadelphia, Pa, 93. *Mem:* Pastel Soc Am. *Media:* Pastel, Oil. *Mailing Add:* 248 Beech Hill Rd Wynnewood PA 19096

KARDON, JANET
MUSEUM DIRECTOR, CURATOR
b Philadelphia, Pa. *Study:* Temple Univ, BS(educ); Univ Pa, MA(art hist), Moore Col Art, Doctor Humanities, 84. *Collections Arranged:* Line (cataloged), Sch of Visual Arts, New York, 76; Seventies Painting (cataloged), Philadelphia Col Art, 78, Siah Armajani (cataloged), 78, Alice Avcock (cataloged), 78 & Point (cataloged), 78; Masks Tents Vessels Talismans (cataloged), Inst Contemp Art & Urban Encounters: Art Architecture Audience (cataloged), 80; Drawings: The Pluralist Decade (cataloged), Venice Biennial, 80; Machineworks: Acconci, Aycock, Oppenheim (cataloged), 80-81; Robert Zakanitch (cataloged), 81; David Salle (cataloged), 86; Robert Kushner, 87; Robert Mapplethorpe: The Perfect Moment, Inst Contemp Art, 88; Building a Permanent Collection: A Perspective on the 1980's, Explorations: The Aesthetic of Excess (auth, catalog) Costumes by Pat Oleszko, Am Craft Mus, 90. *Pos:* Dir exhib, Philadelphia Col of Art, 76-78; dir, Inst Contemp Art, Univ Pa, 79-89; dir, Am Craft Mus, NY, 89. *Teaching:* Lectr Am art & 20th century art, Philadelphia Col of Art, 68- *Awards:* Nat Endowment Arts Res Grant, 78. *Bibliog:* Lisa Hammel (auth), Crafty Lady, Avenue, 2/90; Helen L Kohen (auth), Director defends the fine art of American craft, Miami Herald, 4/1/90; Edward J Sozanski (auth), Janet Kardon's new venue, Philadelphia Inquirer, 8/19/90; and others. *Mem:* Col Art Asn; Pa Coun Arts; Am Asn Mus; Asn Art Mus Dirs. *Res:* Twentieth century; post-World War II; earthworks performance sculpture. *Publ:* Auth, Janet Kardon interviews some modern maze makers, Arts Int, 4-5/76. *Mailing Add:* American Craft Museum 40 W 53rd St New York NY 10019

KARIYA, HIROSHI
CONCEPTUAL ARTIST
b Kamaishi, Iwate Pref, Japan, Apr 14, 48. *Work:* Inst Contemp Art Univ Pa, Philadelphia; McCarthy Arts Ctr, St Michaels Col, Winooski, Vt; Kubu Mus, Mooka, Japan. *Exhib:* 11th Japan Art Festival, Henry Gallery, Univ Wash, Seattle, 76; 13th Contemp Art Exhib, Tokyo Metrop Mus, Japan, 77; World Print Competition, San Francisco Mus Art, 77; 12th Ljubljana Int Biennial, Mus Mod Art, Ljubljana, Yugoslavia, 77; Fifth Int Exhib Graphic Art, Kunstverein zu Frechen, WGer, 78; Fourth Int Drawing Bienneale, Camden Arts Ctr, London, 79; Sound Show, Project Studios One, New York, 79; Sutra: One thing in everything; Everything in one thing, Univ Pa, Philadelphia, 90. *Bibliog:* Kay Larson (auth), Sound Show, Village Voice, 10/29/79; Kunie Sugiura (auth), News from New York, Bijutsu Techo, 7/89; Edward J Sozanski (auth), Contemplating creation, rebirth, Philadelphia Inquirer, 3/18/90. *Media:* Multi Media. *Mailing Add:* 143 S Eighth St No 3B Brooklyn NY 11211

KARLEN, PETER H
EDUCATOR, WRITER
US citizen. *Study:* Univ Calif, Berkeley, BA(hist), 71; Univ Calif, Hastings Col Law, JD, 74; Univ Denver Col Law, MS(law & society), 76. *Pos:* Art attorney, self-employed, 78-86, pub coun, 86-; writer, syndicated Artlaw column, 79-; contrib ed & columnist, Artweek, 79-, Art Calendar, 89-; Art Cellar Exchange, 89-; Equine Images, 92- *Teaching:* Lectr law & the arts, Univ Warwick Sch Law, 76-78; adj prof, Univ San Diego Sch Law, 79-84; adj prof, Western State Univ Col Law, 76, 79, 80, 88 & 92. *Mem:* Artists Equity; Am Soc Aesthetics; Brit Soc Aesthetics; Volunteer Lawyers Arts, NY. *Res:* Property rights in aesthetic creations; expert opinions, fakes & forgeries; artist's moral rights. *Publ:* Auth, What is art? A sketch for a legal definition, Law Quart Rev, 78; Legal aesthetics, Brit J Aesthetics, 79; Moral rights in California, Univ San Diego Law Rev, 82; Aesthetic quality & art preservation, J Aesthetics & Art Criticism, 83; Fakes, forgeries, & expert opinions, Jour Arts Mngmt & Law, 86; Appraiser's Responsibility for Determining Fair Market Value, Cloumbia - VLA, J Law & Acts, 89. *Mailing Add:* 1205 Prospect Suite 400 La Jolla CA 92037

KARLSTROM, PAUL JOHNSON
HISTORIAN, ADMINISTRATOR
b Seattle, Wash, Jan 22, 41. *Study:* Stanford Univ, BA(Eng lit), 64; Univ Calif, Los Angeles, MA(art), PhD, 73. *Collections Arranged:* Venice Panorama (auth, catalog), Grunwald Ctr for Graphic Arts, Univ Calif, Los Angeles, 69; Archives of American Art, California Collecting, (auth, catalog), Oakland Mus, Calif, 77; Louis M Eilshemius in the Hirshhorn Museum Traveling Exhib (auth, catalog), 78; Claude Buck (auth, catalog), Glastonbury Gallery, San Francisco, 83. *Pos:* Asst cur, Grunwald Ctr for the Graphic Arts, Univ Calif, Los Angeles, 67-70; guest cur, Smithsonian Inst Traveling Exhib Serv, Washington, DC, 77; dir, West Coast Regional Ctr, Arch Am Art, Smithsonian Inst, San Francisco, 73-91, San Marino, 91-; mem adv bd, Humanities West; bd dirs, Bay Area Video Coalition. *Teaching:* Instr Renaissance to mod art, Calif State Univ, Northridge, 72-73; vis instr mus practices, Calif Col Arts & Crafts, Oakland, 76. *Awards:* Samuel H Kress Fel, Nat Gallery Art, Washington, DC, 70-71; Acad Distinction, Col Fine Arts, Univ Calif, Los Angeles, 74. *Mem:* Col Art Asn Am; Humanities West; Calif Hist Soc (edit bd); Bay Area Video Coalition (bd). *Res:* American art and culture, 19th and 20th century. *Publ:* Auth, Louis Michel Eilshemius, Harry N Abrams, 78 Vol 20, No 2, 80; Los Angeles in the 1940s: Post-modernism and the visual arts, Southern Calif Hist Soc Quart, winter 87; The Spirit in the Stone: Visionary Art of James W Washington, Jr, Univ Washington Press, 89; Turning the Tide: Early Los Angeles Modernists 1920-1956, Santa Barbara Mus Art, 90; Fletcher Benton, Harry N Abrams, 90. *Mailing Add:* c/o Arch of Am Art de Young Mus Huntington Libr, 1151 Oxford Rd San Marino CA 91108

KARN, GLORIA STOLL
PAINTER, INSTRUCTOR
b New York, NY, Nov 13, 23. *Study:* Art Students League; also with Eliot O'Hara & Samuel Rosenberg. *Work:* Yale Univ; Brooklyn Mus; Pittsburgh Pub Schs; Carnegie Inst Mus Art. *Exhib:* Assoc Artists Pittsburgh Ann, 49-; Butler Inst Am Art Ann, 61; one-man shows, Pittsburgh Plan for Art, 65, Carnegie Inst Mus, 66 & North Hills Art Ctr, 78, 83 & 91; Sacred Arts Show, St Stephens, Pittsburgh, 66. *Teaching:* Instr painting & collage, North Hills Art Ctr, 65-; instr, Community Col Allegheny Co, 73-79. *Awards:* Carnegie Inst Purchase Prize, 60; Westinghouse Purchase Prize, 66; North Hills Art Ctr Achievement Award, 83. *Mem:* Assoc Artists Pittsburgh; Group A, Pittsburgh (pres, 66-70); Pittsburgh Ctr Arts (bd mem, 69-72); North Hills Art Ctr (bd mem, 70-72 & 78-80, pres, 80-81). *Media:* Oil, Watercolor. *Mailing Add:* 151 Louise Rd Pittsburgh PA 15237

KARNES, KAREN
CERAMIST, CRAFTSMAN
b New York, NY, Nov 17, 25. *Study:* Brooklyn Col, BA, 46; NY State Col Ceramics, Alfred Univ, 51; Sesto Fiorentino, Italy, 50-51. *Work:* Am Crafts Mus, New York; Everson Mus, Syracuse, NY; Metrop Mus Art, New York; Del Mus Art, Wilmington; Philadelphia Mus Art, Pa; and others. *Comn:* Fireplace, sink & garden seats, comn by Jack Lenor Larsen, Easthampton, NY, 62. *Exhib:* High Styles: Am Design Since 1900, Whitney Mus Am Art, New York (traveling), 85; Kamper Gallery, Kansas City Art Inst, Mo, 86; N Eng Ceramic Vessels, Westminster Gallery, Boston, Mass, 86; Art in Craft Today: Poetry of the Physical, Am Craft Mus, New York, 86; The Arts at Black Mt Col, Grey Art Gallery, New York (traveling), 87; Fired with Enthusiam, Campbell Mus, Camden, NJ (traveling), 87; one-person exhib, Hadler/Rodriguez Gallery, La, 81, New York, 81, 82 & 85, The Hand and the Spirit, Scotsdale, Ariz, 86, Stratton Arts Festival, Stratton, Vt, 86 & Garth Clark Gallery, New York, 87, 90; and many others. *Collections Arranged:* Salt Glazed Ceramics, Hadler Rodriguez Gallery, 77. *Teaching:* Instr, clay seminar/workshop, Bloomsburg State Univ, Pa, Penland Sch Crafts, 71; art craft workshop, Soc Ed, Eng, 70 & 73, kiln workshop, Bowling Green State Univ, Ohio, 73; craftsman-in-residence, Hunter Col, CUNY, 75-76, Del Art Mus, 76; instr, Royal Col Art, London, 77, Southampton Col LI Univ, summer prog 78-80; Frog Hollow Craft Ctr, Middlebury, Vt, 80-82, 85 & 89; Camberwell Sch Art, London, 86. *Awards:* Am Crafts Coun Fel, 76; Nat Endowment Arts Fel, 76, 88; Nat Coun Ceramic Fel, 80; Artists Fel, Vermont Coun on the Arts, 88; and others. *Bibliog:* Reggie Hynes (auth), Karen Karnes Workshop, Ceramic Review, 82; Mary E Harris (auth), The Arts at Black Mountain Col, MIT Press, Cambridge, Mass, 87; Zelanski & Fisher (coauths), Appreciating the Visual Arts, John Calmann & King, 88. *Dealer:* Garth Clark Gallery. *Mailing Add:* c/o Garth Clark Gallery 24 W 57th St New York NY 10019

KARNIOL, HILDA
PAINTER
b Vienna, Austria, Apr 28, 10; US citizen. *Study:* With Olga Konetzny-Maly & A F Seligman, Vienna, 25-28; Acad for Women, 26-30. *Work:* Delaware Art Ctr, Wilmington; Lincoln Sch, Honesdale, Pa; US Dept Health, Educ & Welfare; Lewisburg Art Coun, Pa; Lycoming Col, Williamsport, Pa; State Univ, Bloomsburg, Pa; Susquehanna Univ, Selinsgrove, Pa. *Comn:* Portraits of presidents of Susquehanna Univ, Dr Benjamin Kurz, Dr Henry Ziegler, Dr & Mrs Gustave W Weber, & Dr John I Woodruff. *Exhib:* Pa State Mus, Harrisburg, 54; Adha Artzt Gallery, New York, 60; Drexel Inst Technol, 60; La Salle Col, 64; La State Univ, New Orleans, 71; over 100 solo exhibs. *Teaching:* Instr painting, Susquehanna Univ, 58-75. *Awards:* First Prize in Portraiture, Berwick Art Ctr, Pa, 65; Artist-in-residence, Fed Govt Cult Enrichment Prog, 67; First Merit & Purchase Prize, Lewisburg Art Asn, 75 & 78; Distinguished Citzenship Award, Susquehanna Univ, 88. *Bibliog:* L E L (auth), Art & artists, gallery guide, New York-J Am, 11/60; Sigmund Stoler (auth), Upstate artist's 14th show, Harrisburg Patriot, 67; Michael Lenson (auth), The realm of art, culture mirror, Newark Sun News, 11 /67. *Mem:* Susquehanna Art Soc; Pi Delta Phi; Soc d'Honneur Francaise. *Media:* Oil, Watercolor, Acrylics. *Publ:* Illusr, Melusine & illusr, The Nose, 29, Adolf Synek; auth, From the Sketchbook of Hilda Karniol, Standard, 70. *Mailing Add:* Veranda Club 6061 Palmetto Circle N Boca Raton FL 33433

KARP, AARON S
PAINTER
b Altoona, Pa, Dec 7, 47. *Study:* State Univ NY Col Buffalo, BA, 69; Ind Univ, MFA, 73. *Work:* Guggenheim Mus, New York; Southeastern Ctr Contemp Art, Winston-Salem, NC; Albuquerque Mus & Univ NMex Art Mus, Albuquerque; Ackland Art Ctr, Chapel Hill, NC; Roswell Mus, NMex. *Exhib:* Recent Acquisitions, Solomon R Guggenheim Mus, New York, 82; one-man exhibs, Janus Gallery, Santa Fe, NM, 88 & 90, Watson Gallery, Houston, Tex, 89, Katherina Rich Perlow Gallery, New York, 89 & 91, State Univ NY, Albany, NY, 90, Barclay Simpson Gallery, Lafayette, Calif, 90; Emerging

Artists 1978 to 1986: Selections from the Exxon Series, Guggenheim Mus, New York, 87; Hothouse, Kohler Art Ctr, Sheboygan, Wis, 88; East Side-West Side; Artists from Two Coasts, Helander Gallery, Palm Beach, Fla, 88; Major Works, Robischon Gallery, Denver, Colo, 89; Abstraction, Eve Mannes Gallery, Atlanta, Ga, 90. *Pos:* Oper supervisor, Guggenheim Mus, 74-75; dir, E Carolina Univ Gallery, Greenville, NC, 77-79. *Teaching:* Asst prof, Univ NMex, Albuquerque, 79-84. *Awards:* Artist-in-Residence Grant, Roswell Mus & Art Ctr, NMex, 81; Research Allocation Grants, Univ NMex, Albuquerque, 82; Exxon Corp Purchase Award, Guggenheim Mus, New York, 83. *Bibliog:* Diane Waldman (auth), Emerging Artists 1978 to 1986: Selections from the Exxon Series (catalog), Solomon R Guggenheim Mus, 87; Louise Krasniewicz (auth), review, The Times Union, Albany, NY, 3/17/90; Sandy Ballatore (auth), Aaron Karp, Artspace, 9-10/90. *Media:* Acrylic. *Dealer:* Helander Gallery 415 W Broadway NY 10012; 350 S County Rd Palm Beach FL 33480. *Mailing Add:* 7811 Guadalupe Trail NW Albuquerque NM 87107

KARP, RICHARD GORDON
PAINTER, LECTURER
b Brooklyn, NY, May 17, 33. *Study:* City Col New York, BBA(advert) & MA(fine art); Brooklyn Mus Art Sch, with John Bageris. *Work:* Aankoop Gemete, Stedlijk Mus, Amsterdam, Neth; Northern Ill Univ, DeKalb. *Exhib:* Stedlijk Mus, Amsterdam, 70; RAI Exhib, Amsterdam, 70; Heckscher Mus, Huntington, NY, 74; Viridian Gallery, New York, 77; Parrish Mus, South Hampton, NY, 78. *Bibliog:* Julie Attkiss (auth), Karp, riding his intuition, Holland Herald, 3/69. *Mem:* Visual Artist & Gallery Asn; Artists Equity. *Media:* Oil & Mixed Media. *Dealer:* Ronald Hunnings Inc 139 Spring St New York NY 10012; Kunsthandel K 276 Keizersgracht 276 Amsterdam Netherlands. *Mailing Add:* 1201 Queen Anne Rd Teaneck NJ 07666

KARPEL, ELI
SCULPTOR
b New York, NY, Oct 25, 16. *Study:* City Col New York, BA; Univ Calif, Los Angeles, MA; Univ Southern Calif; Ohio State Univ; with Chaim Gross. *Work:* Palm Springs Desert Mus; Hirshhorn Mus, Washington, DC; Storm King Mountain Mus, Mountainville, NY; Skirball Mus, Los Angeles; over 300 pvt collections including Rona Barrett, Vidal Sassoon, Dinah Shore, Frank Sinatra and Barbra Streisand; Jewish Mus, New York. *Exhib:* One-man shows, Ankrum Gallery, 72, 78, 80 & 85, Pierce Col, 73 & 82 & Gumps Gallery, San Francisco, 79 & 82. *Teaching:* Lectr art, Univ Calif, Los Angeles, 50-53; prof art, Pierce Col, Los Angeles, 58-82. *Media:* Bronze & other materials. *Dealer:* Ankrum Gallery 657 N La Cienega Los Angeles CA 90069. *Mailing Add:* 689 Brooktree Rd Santa Monica CA 90402

KARPOWICZ, TERRENCE EDWARD
SCULPTOR, KINETIC ARTIST
b East St Louis, Ill, May 11, 48. *Study:* Albion Col, BA, 70; Univ Ill, Champaign, MFA(Fulbright Hays Fel), 75. *Work:* Northern Ill Univ; Gov State Univ, Ill; Kemper Collection, Chicago. *Comn:* Per Cent for Arts, State Ill, Northeastern Ill Univ, 82; Univ Ill Med Ctr, 90. *Exhib:* Chicago & Vicinity, Art Inst Chicago, 74; Sixth Dollhouse Invitational, Corcoran Gallery Art, 80; 33rd Ill Invitational, Ill State Mus, Springfield, 81; Int Mile of Sculpture, Navy Pier, Chicago, 82-83. *Teaching:* Instr sculpture, Art Inst Chicago, 79-81 & Univ Ill, Chicago Circle, 83-. *Awards:* Nat Endowment Arts Fel, 80 & 82; Illinois Fel, 85; Int Art Symposium, Soviet, Ga, 91. *Bibliog:* Alan Artner (auth), Mystery dogs freewheeling show, Chicago Tribune, 80; Ann Morgon (auth), article, Art Int, 82; Paul Richards (auth), It's a dream--sculptors on paper, Washington Post, 83. *Mem:* Chicago Artists Coalition. *Media:* Wood, Stone. *Mailing Add:* 1802 N Damen Ave Chicago IL 60647

KARSH, YOUSUF
PHOTOGRAPHER
b Armenia, Dec 23, 08; Can citizen. *Study:* With John H Garo, Boston; hon degrees from 21 univs among others. *Work:* Metrop Mus Art, New York; Mus Mod Art, New York; Nat Portrait Gallery, London, Eng; St Louis Art Mus, Mo; Nat Gallery Can, Ottawa, Ont; Biblioreque Nat, Paris; Chicago Art Inst; Boston Mus Fine Arts; Huntington Mus, Calif. *Exhib:* One-man shows, Boston Mus Fine Arts, 68, Corcoran Gallery Art, 69, Seattle Art Mus, 70, Mus Mod Art, Tokyo, 71-81, Mus Sci & Industry, Chicago, 77-79, Mus Photogr & Film, Bradford, Eng, Int Ctr Photogr NY, 83 & Nat Portrait Gallery, London, 83; plus many others, including Nat Gallery of Australia & Canada & Alberta, Can. *Pos:* Photog adv, Expo 70, Osaka, Japan, 69-70; trustee, Photog Arts & Sci Found, 65-72. *Teaching:* Vis prof photog & fine arts, Ohio Univ, 68-70; vis prof photog & fine arts, Emerson Col, 72-73. *Awards:* Can Coun Medal, 65; Centennial Medal, 67; Order of Can, Can Govt, 68; Rochester Sci Mus Fel, 72; Silver Shinola Award, Boston Univ, 83; Companion of Can, Can Govt, 90. *Bibliog:* Forsee (auth), Yousuf Karsh, In: Five Famous Photographers, 70; featured article, Reader's Digest, 2/77; featured on Sixty Minutes, Columbia Broadcasting System, 5/77; Harry Rasky (dir), Karsh: The Searching Eye (film), 85. *Mem:* Hon fel Royal Photog Soc; Dutch Treat Club, New York; Rideau Club, Ottawa; Royal Can Acad Arts; Prof Photog Asn Can; Century Club; hon fel Prof Photog Am. *Publ:* Auth, Karsh Portraits, 76; Karsh Canadians, 78; Karsh: a Fifty Year Retrospective, 83; American Legends, 92. *Mailing Add:* Karsh Photog Studio 6th Floor Chateau Laurier Ottawa ON K1N 8S7 Canada

KARWELIS, DONALD CHARLES
PAINTER, INSTRUCTOR
b Rockford, Ill, Sept 19, 34. *Study:* Univ Calif, Irvine, with Robert Irwin, BA, 69, with Robert Morris, MFA, 71. *Work:* Long Beach Mus Art, Calif; Paul Schorr III, Lincoln, Nebr; Laguna Art Mus & County Mus Art, Los Angeles; Coopers & Lybrand, Houston, Tex; Newport Harbor Art Mus, Calif. *Comn:* Sculpture, T Ayres, Newport Baech, Calif, 83. *Exhib:* Orange Co Ctr Contemp Art, 81; Los Angeles Co Mus Art, 84; Kirk de Gooyer Gallery, Los Angeles, 84; Irvine Fine Arts Ct, 86 & 90; Newport Harbor Art Mus, 79 & 86; Lithuanian Art Mus, Lemont, Ill, 90; LJ Gallery, Newport Beach, Calif, 89; and many others. *Teaching:* Lectr sculpture, Univ Calif, Irvine, 69-71 & 86-87; lectr drawing & painting, Riverside City Col, 71-72. *Awards:* Nat Defense Educ Act Res Grant, 70; Nat Endowment Arts Grant, 76. *Bibliog:* Melinda Wortz (auth), article, Artnews, 4/83; Christine Fryman Schwable (auth), article, Images & Issues, 9-10/83; Cathy Curtis (auth), article, Los Angeles Times, 10/28/89. *Media:* Acrylic, Multimedia, Oil. *Publ:* Contribr, Los Angeles Artists' Publ, 73; auth, Color, 75; Speaking to the enemy, Artweek, 9/5/87. *Mailing Add:* 202-K E Stevens Santa Ana CA 92707

KARWOSKI, RICHARD CHARLES
PAINTER, EDUCATOR
b Brooklyn, NY, Oct 3, 38. *Study:* Pratt Inst, with Richard Lindner & Jacob Landau, BFA, 61; Columbia Univ, MA, 63. *Work:* Okla Art Ctr, Oklahoma City; Everson Mus, Syracuse, NY; Wichita Mus, Kans; Detroit Art Inst, Mich; Butler Inst Am Art, Youngstown, Ohio. *Exhib:* Watercolor USA, Springfield, Mo, 80; Winterscape, Guild Hall Mus, East Hampton, NY, 81-82; Pittsburgh Watercolor Soc Ann, 81-83; Pelham Arts Ctr, NY, 83; Guild Hall Mus, 50 Artists View the South Fork, East Hampton, 85-86; Retrospective: 1970-86, Saatchi & Saatchi Compton Advert Inc, New York, 86; Michigan Watercolor Soc, Drasl Art Ctr, 86; Wagner Col, Kade Gallery, Staten Island, NY, 87; Retrospective: 1963-1988, Aritawagh Hall, Springs, East Hampton, 88; Watercolor Bright & Beautiful, Guild Hall Mus, 88; and others. *Pos:* Dir, Grace Gallery, New York City Tech Col, Brooklyn, 70-80, assoc dir, 81; adv comn mem, Art & Design High Sch, New York, 77-, pres, Alumni Asn, 80-. *Teaching:* Prof painting & design, New York City Tech Col, 69-. *Awards:* Okla Watercolor Soc President's Award, 84; Nat Arts Club Salzman Award, 85; Northlight Book Award, Wamaroneck Artist Gold, 85; and others. *Bibliog:* Chauncey Howell (reporter), NBC News, 74; John Perrault (ed, critic), article, SoHo Weekly News, 11/27/75; Helen A Harrison (auth), article, New York Times, 2/3/80. *Mem:* Salmagundi Club; Pa Soc Watercolor Painters; Audubon Soc of Artists; Nat Arts Club; NY Artists Equity (bd dirs, 82-84). *Media:* Watercolor, Oil. *Publ:* Auth, The contour color method, The Artists Mag, 4/86; Contribr, Art in Society, The Arts Academe, Univ Wis, 76; auth, Am Artist Mag Watercolor page, Bill Publs, 3/79; contribr, Footwear, Van Nostrand, 79; illusr, The Intimate Hour (bk jacket), Avery, 79; auth, The Watercolor Page, Am Artist Mag, Mar 79; contribr, Pratt Reports, Pratt Inst, spring, 81; auth, Watercolor Bright and Beautiful, Watson Guptill, 10/88. *Dealer:* Nancy Stein Art Consult New York NY; Gallery East East Hampton NY. *Mailing Add:* c/o Thornapple Corp Art Assocs 1409 Silverside Rd Wilmington DE 19810

KASAK, NIKOLAI
PAINTER, SCULPTOR
b Russ; US citizen. *Study:* City Col Arts, Warsaw, BFA; Acad Fine Art, Vienna, MFA; Acad Fine Art Sch Advan Study, Rome, dipl. *Work:* Mus Fine Art, Baranowicze & Minsk; McCrory Collection & Mus Mod Art, New York; Smithsonian Inst Arch Am Art, Washington, DC; NJ State Mus; Tel Aviv Mus. *Exhib:* Guggenheim Mus, New York; Mus Mod Art, Buenos Aires & Denis Rene Gallery, Paris, 61; Constructivism and Geometric Tradition: Albright-Knox Art Gallery, Buffalo, NY, 79; Dallas Mus Fine Arts, 80; La Jolla Mus, Calif, 80; San Francisco Mus Mod Art, Calif, 80; Mus Art, Carnegie Inst, Pittsburgh, 81; Milwaukee Art Ctr, 81; Beyond the Plane: American Constructions 1930-1965, NJ State Mus, Trenton & Univ Md, 83-84; 50th Anniversary of American Abstract Art 1936-1986, Bronx Mus, NY, 86; Galeria Nazionale d'Arte Moderna, Rome; Trends in Geometric Abstract Art, Tel Aviv Mus, 86; A Living Tradition: 23 Am Abstract Artists Traveling Show, Eastern-Western Europe, Bronx Mus, NY, Cultural Presentation of the USA, 88-92; Detroit Art Ctr, Mich, 81. *Awards:* First Prize for Warsaw Emblem, City Hall Warsaw; First Prize for Mural, City Hall Baranowicze; Prize for Painting-Construct, Art Club Rome. *Bibliog:* Robert Kramer (ed), The Art of Kasak (monogr), New York, 68; Artisti Contemporanei, Rome, 82; John E Bowlt (auth), From Action to Dymamic Silence: The Art of Nikolai Kasak (monogr), Los Angeles, 91. *Mem:* Am Abstr Artists. *Media:* Space & Matter. *Publ:* Auth, Physical art--Action of positive & negative space, (manifesto), 46; Storia de Pitture Contemporanee, Domani, Rome, 48; Arte fisico-constructivo, Arte Madi, Buenos Aires, 52. *Mailing Add:* 5648 Delafield Ave Bronx NY 10471

KASH, MARIE (MARIE KASH WELTZHEIMER)
PAINTER, GRAPHIC ARTIST
b Akron, Ohio, May 5, 60. *Study:* Cent State Univ, Edmond, Okla, BA(com art), 82; studies with Alan Flattman & Sally Strand. *Work:* Goddard Art Ctr, Ardmore, Okla; Corp: Laureate Psychiatric Clinic & Hosp, Tulsa, Okla; Gable & Gotwals, Attorneys at Law, Tulsa, Okla; Am Bank & Trust, Edmond, Okla; Lawyers Title Oklahoma City Inc. *Comn:* Pvt portrait, comn by Jim Schuelein, Oklahoma City, 88; pvt portrait, comn by Mr & Mrs Sherwood Taylor, Norman, Okla, 89-90; pvt protrait, comn by Dr & Mrs Blair Cunnyngham, Edmond, Okla, 89; pvt portrait, comn by Ms Susan Ivester, Norman, Okla, 89; pvt portrait, comn by Mr & Mrs Bill Hodges, Edmond, Okla, 91. *Exhib:* 8th, 9th, 11th Ann Juried Exhibs, Pastel Soc Southwest, Dallas, 88, 89 & 91; solo exhibs, Plain Indians & Pioneers Mus, Woodward, Okla, 89 & Goddard Art Ctr, Ardmore, Okla, 93; Diverse Works on Paper, ArtPlace, Oklahoma City, 90; two-person exhib, M A Doran Gallery, Tulsa, 91; Pastels '92, 7th Ann Nat Juried Exhib, Midwest Pastel Soc, Chicago, 92. *Pos:* Graphic media artist, Okla Water Resources Bd, Oklahoma City, 84-88. *Awards:* Stephen Leitner, Esq Award, 19th Ann Open Exhib, Pastel Soc Am,

91; First Award Excellence, 11th Ann Exhib, Pastel Soc Southwest, 91; First Place, Pastel, Okla Art Guild, 92. *Bibliog:* Bill Hommel (auth), Rev, Okla Gazette, 11/29/89; John Brandenburg (auth), Exhibit features simpler things, 11/30/89 & John Brandenburg (auth), Exhib a mixed-media bag, 8/5/90, Daily Oklahoman. *Mem:* Pastel Soc Am; assoc mem Knickerbocker Artists; Pastel Soc Southwest; Okla Art Guild. *Media:* Pastel, Watercolor. *Dealer:* M A Doran Gallery 3509 S Peoria Tulsa OK 74105; L A Thompson Gallery 2611 Worthington St Dallas TX 75204. *Mailing Add:* 2724 NW 45th Oklahoma City OK 73112

KASHDIN, GLADYS SHAFRAN
PAINTER, EDUCATOR
b Pittsburgh, Pa, Dec 15, 21. *Study:* Art Students League, with Stefan Hirsch; Univ Miami, BA(magna cum laude), 60; Fla State Univ, with Karl Zerbe, MA, 62, PhD(humanities), 65. *Work:* Tex Tech Mus, Lubbock; Tampa Pub Libr; Columbus Mus Arts, Ga; Tampa Int Airport; Futan Univ, Shanghai, China; Kresge Mus Art, East Lansing, Mich; Tampa Mus Art. *Comn:* Silkscreen eds, LeMoyne Art Found, Tallahassee, Fla, 70, 71 & 73. *Exhib:* 28th Ann Brooklyn Mus, 44; one-woman shows, 2nd & 3rd Southeastern Ann, High Mus, Atlanta, 47, Palm Beach Art League, Norton Gallery, West Palm, 48-63 LeMoyne Art Found, Tallahassee, 66-74, Columbus Mus Arts, Ga, 73, 76 & 83, Univ SFla, 75 & 81, Tex Tech Mus, 78; Fla Dept of State, Tallahassee 85 & 86; Kresge Mus Art, E Lansing, Mich, 87; Ferris State Univ, Mich, 89. *Pos:* Photogr, Shafran Co, NY & Fla, 38-60. *Teaching:* Instr & dir oil painting, Adult Educ, Palm Beach Co, Fla, 56-60; instr watercolor, Thomasville Art Guild, Ga, 61-62; prof humanities, Univ SFla, Tampa, 65-87, Humanities Visual Arts Workshops, 66-71, prof emeritus humanities, 87- *Awards:* Merit Award, Palm Beach Art League, 58, 60 & 63; Gold Medal, Univ Miami, 60; Citizens Award, Mus Advisory Bd, Hillsborough County, 84. *Bibliog:* Dr Hans Juergensen (auth), Kashdin's Everglades series, 73 & Herb Allen (auth), Local rivers series theme, 75, Tampa Tribune; Pam Renner (auth), Gladys Kashdin: An artist in her sun-lit years, Bay Life, 79. *Mem:* Tampa Mus Art; Metrop Mus Art. *Media:* Watercolor, Acrylic. *Publ:* Auth, A new approach to a humanities-visual arts workshop, Humanities J, fall 70; Life long education for women--general & liberal studies from their point of view, Perspectives, winter 74; Women artists and the institution of feminism in America, SEASA, 79. *Mailing Add:* 441 Biltmore Ave Temple Terrace FL 33617

KASKEY, RAYMOND JOHN
SCULPTOR, ARCHITECT
b Pittsburgh, Pa, Feb 22, 43. *Study:* Carnegie Mellon Univ, BA(archit), 67; Yale Univ, Sch Art & Archit, also sculpture with Erwin Haver, 69. *Work:* Mus Mod Art, New York; First Interstate Bank, Ore; Kaiser Permanente, Portland, Ore. *Comn:* sculpture, Portland Bldg, Ore, 85; sculpture, Harold Washington Library Ctr, Chicago, 90; sculpture, Nat Law Enforcement Officers Memorial, Washington, DC. *Exhib:* Nat Sculpture Soc Ann, Equitable Gallery, New York, 80 & 81; Barbara Fendrick Gallery, Washington, DC; John Nichols Gallery, New York, 86; Barbara Fendrick Space, New York, 88. *Teaching:* Asst prof arch & design, Univ Md, College Park, 69-76; vis critic, Yale Univ, New Haven, Conn, spring 77 & Kans State Univ, Manhattan, spring 78. *Awards:* Mrs Louis Bennett Prize, 82 & Henry Hering Mem Medal, 86, Nat Sculpture Soc; Creative & Performing Arts Award, Univ Md, 70 & 72. *Bibliog:* video, Portlandia, Rogers Cable Network, Ore; Hail, Portlandia, Art News, 12/85; article, Archit Mag, 12/85; article, Newsweek, 7/86; article, Mus & Arts, 10/88. *Mem:* Nat Sculpture Soc; Am Inst Archit. *Media:* Bronze, Stone. *Dealer:* Barbara Fendrick Gallery 3059 M St NW Washington DC 20007. *Mailing Add:* 2221 Hall Pl NW Washington DC 20007

KASLE, GERTRUDE
CONSULTANT, COLLECTOR
b New York, NY, Dec 2, 17. *Study:* Art Students League, with John Barber; NY Univ; Univ Mich; Ctr Creative Studies, Detroit; Wayne State Univ, BS(art educ). *Pos:* Assoc dir & partner, Franklin Siden Gallery, 64-65; pres, Gertrude Kasle Gallery, 65-77; mem comt visual arts & mus, Mich Coun Arts, 71; adj cur art, Marie Selby Mus of Botany & Art, 79-80; trustee, Arts Found Mich. *Awards:* Distinguished Alumni Award, Wayne State Univ, 68; President's Cabinet Award, Univ Detroit, 77. *Mem:* Patron Detroit Inst Arts (Founders' Soc); Nat Soc Lit & Arts; Artists Equity Asn; hon bd mem Friends Mod Art, Detroit Inst Art. *Mailing Add:* 26705 Irving Franklin MI 48025

KASNOWSKI, CHESTER N
COLLAGE ARTIST, CONCEPTUAL ARTIST
b Perth Amboy, NJ, Jan 23, 44. *Study:* Dayton Art Inst, Ohio, BFA, 71; Tulane Univ, New Orleans, La, MFA, 73. *Work:* Brooklyn Mus, NY; Guggenheim Mus & Whitney Mus Am Art, New York; Stedelijk Mus, Amsterdam. *Exhib:* One-person exhibs, Ball State Univ, Muncie, Ind, 74 & McKissick Mus, Columbia, SC, 78; Contemp Arts Ctr, New Orleans, La, 78; Dartmouth Col Galleries, Hanover, NH, 79; Class Portrait, Robert Hull Fleming Mus, Burlington, Vt, 81; Invitational, Franklin Furnace, New York, 82. *Awards:* Nat Endowment Arts Grant, 74; Drawing Grant, 78 & Spec Mention, Illuminated Thoughts Exhib, 79, Vt Coun Arts. *Mem:* Col Art Asn. *Media:* Mixed. *Dealer:* Bertha Urdang Gallery 23 E 74th St New York NY 10021. *Mailing Add:* Box 14 Weston VT 05161

KASS, DEBORAH
PAINTER
b San Antonio, Tex, 52. *Study:* Art Student's League, 68-70; Whitney Mus Independent Study Prog, 72; Carnegie-Mellon Univ, BFA (painting). *Work:* Guggenheim Mus; Cincinnati Mus; La Jolla Mus, Calif; Prudential Col; Progressive Corp; First Bank Minneapolis; Commodities Corp. *Exhib:* Baskerville & Watson, 86; Scott Hanson Gallery, 88; Simon Watson, 90; Fiction/Non Fiction, 92. *Teaching:* Distinguished vis artist, RI Sch Design, 90, 91; vis artists, Art Inst, Chicago, 93. *Awards:* Fel, Nat Endowment Arts, Painting, 87; Fel, Painting New York State Coun on the Arts, 91; Art Matters, 92. *Bibliog:* Michael Brenson (auth), New York Times, 1/24/84; Dan Cameron (auth), Second nature new paintings by Deborah Kass, ARTS, 4/86; Co-eds (Jerry Saltz & Alfred Vandermark), New York's new artist, Beyond Boundaries, 87 and others. *Publ:* Auth, In Her Own Voice, Bomb mag, fall, 87 & Roundtable Projs, part 1 & 2, spring & summer, 88; Roberta Smith (auth), Women Artists Engage Me Enemy, New York Times, 8/16/92. *Dealer:* Echo Press 1805 E Tenth St Bloomington IN 47407. *Mailing Add:* 137 W Broadway New York NY 10013

KASS, JACOB JAMES
PAINTER
b Brooklyn, NY, Jan 24, 10. *Study:* Self-taught. *Work:* Lowe Mus Art, Univ Miami, Coral Gables; Va Polytech Inst & State Univ. *Exhib:* Solo exhib, Lowe Mus Art, Univ Miami, Coral Gables, 82, Brevard Art Ctr & Mus, Melbourne, Fla, 83 & Va Polytech Inst & State Univ, 83; Mus Art & Hist, San Juan, PR, 88; Utah Mus Fine Arts, Salt Lake City, 88; Tampa Mus, Fla, 89; Fed Reserve Bd Bldg, Washington, DC, 90; Tiffany's & Co, New York; and others. *Awards:* Nat Endowment Arts Fel, 81. *Bibliog:* John Yau (auth), Jacob Kass at Allan Stone, Art in Am, summer 81; Theodore Wolff (auth), The many masks of modern art, Christian Sci Monitor, 6/9/83; Objects en Derive, Georges Pompidou, France, 84; Diamonds Are Forever, Albany, NY, 88. *Mem:* Southeastern Ctr Contemp Art, N Salem; Fla Gulf Coast Art Ctr; Folk Art Soc New York. *Media:* Oil and Magna on Steel Saw Blades. *Publ:* Three contemporary masters, Folk Art Traditions, 1-3/90; Folk Art Messenger, Vol 5, 92. *Dealer:* Allan Stone Gallery 48 E 86th St New York NY; Nancy Hoffman Gallery 429 W Broadway New York NY 10012. *Mailing Add:* 1005 Imperial Palm Dr Largo FL 34641

KASS, RAY
PAINTER
b Rockville Centre, NY, Jan 25, 44. *Study:* Univ NC, BA, 67, MFA(painting), 69; also painting with Keith Crown. *Work:* Addison Gallery Am Art, Andover, Mass; Smith Col Mus, Northampton; Boston Pub Libr; Griffith Art Ctr, St Lawrence Univ, Canton, NY; Tufts Univ Med Ctr, Boston. *Exhib:* One-man shows, Calif State Univ, Humboldt, 70, Allan Stone Gallery, New York, 72, 75, 77 & 81, Addison Gallery Am Art, 74, Osuna Gallery, Washington, DC, 79 & Southeastern Ctr Contemp Art, NC, 80; 4 Artists Sponsored by Inst Contemp Art, Boston City Hall, 72. *Pos:* Guest cur, Phillips Collection, Washington, DC, 80-83. *Teaching:* Asst prof painting, Calif State Univ, Humboldt, 69-71; guest lectr, Landscape Workshop, Univ NH, Durham, summer 73; asst prof painting, Va Polytechnic Inst, Blacksburg, Va, 76-81, assoc prof, 81- *Awards:* Norfolk Biennial Painting Prize, Norfolk Mus, Va, 68; Blanche E Colman Found Award, 73-74; Individual Artists Grant, Nat Endowment Arts, 81; and others. *Bibliog:* John Canaday (auth), Ray Kass at Allan Stone Gallery, New York Times, 6/3/72; John Yau (auth), Ray Kass, article, Art Am, summer 81. *Mem:* Col Art Asn Am. *Media:* Watercolor, Oil. *Dealer:* Allan Stone Gallery 48 E 86th St New York NY 10028. *Mailing Add:* RR 2 No 725 Christianburg VA 24073

KASSMAN, SHIRLEY
PAINTER, EDUCATOR
b Hamburg, NY, July 29, 29. *Study:* Albright Art Sch, Buffalo, NY, with Seymour Drumlevitch in painting, cert, 50; State Univ Col Buffalo, NY, BS(art educ), 51, MS(art educ), 58. *Work:* Penny Collection, Rochester Mem Art Gallery, NY; Ithaca Col, NY; Springfield Col, Mass; Burchfield Art Ctr, Buffalo, NY. *Comn:* Hyatt Regency Hotel, Buffalo, NY, 83. *Exhib:* Women Are Many Faces, Everson Mus, Syracuse, NY, 74; Albright-Knox Art Gallery, 75, 78, 79, 84 & 86; 55th & 56th Erie Art Ctr Ann, Pa, 78 & 79; one-person shows, Chautaugua Art Asn, 79, Members Gallery, Albright-Knox, 82, Calif State Univ, Bakersfield, 84 & Artists Gallery, Buffalo, NY 86 & 88; Upton Gallery, State Univ NY, Col Buffalo, NY, 81; retrospective, Burchfield Art Ctr, 87. *Collections Arranged:* Patteran Artists Traveling Exhib, Burchfield Ctr, Buffalo, 75-77. *Teaching:* Prof design & women in art, State Univ NY, Buffalo, 58- *Awards:* State Univ NY Grants, 74 & 75; Gold Medal Patron Award, Buffalo Soc Artists, 83; Creative Artists Pub Serv Prog Grant, NY State Coun Arts, 84. *Bibliog:* Dr Judith Herman (auth), Shirley Kassman: Feminist artist, Spree Mag, 79. *Mem:* Buffalo Soc Artists (vpres, 77-78, pres, 78-79); Patteran Artists; Western NY Women's Art Registry; Women's Caucus for Art; Coalition of Womens Art Orgn. *Media:* Oil Pastel, Oil. *Dealer:* Barbara Schuler Assoc Buffalo NY; Ruth Bachofner Gallery Los Angeles CA. *Mailing Add:* 231 Anderson Pl Buffalo NY 14222

KASSOY, BERNARD
PAINTER, PRINTMAKER
b New York, NY, Oct 23, 14. *Study:* City Col New York, BSS(cum laude), MSE(fine arts); Cooper Union Art Sch, grad, 37; also with John Ferren, Isaac Soyer & Arthur Osver. *Work:* Workmans Circle Community House, Bronx, NY; Butler Inst Am Art, Youngstown, Ohio; Slater Mem Mus, Norwich, Conn; Arch Am Art; Univ Ga Mus; pvt collections, Sri Lanka, England, Italy, US & Sicily; Bocour Artists Colours; Lehman Col Arch, Hist Bronx, photos and interview tapes. *Comn:* Birdiness (film photog & editing), Bd Educ, High Sch Music & Art, New York, 57; Stage set design for Fiddler on the Roof, Apricot Theatre, NY, 88. *Exhib:* Showcase, Bronx Coun Arts, New York, 68-69; Nat Acad Design, New York, 68 & 75; 28 Contemporaries, Bronx Mus Arts, New York, 71; Int Sculpture Exhib, Pietrasanta, Italy, 76 & Forte dei Marmi, Italy, 76; one-man shows, Ward-Nasse Gallery, New York, 79, Mid-

Hudson Art & Sci Ctr, Poughkeepsie, NY, 79, Vladeck Hall Gal, Bronx, NY Retrospective, 89 & Woodcuts, Pioneer-Smithy Gallery, Cooperstown, NY, 91; Ward Nasse Gallery, NY, 86; Bronx Mus Arts, NY, 85-86; Pioneer Gallery, Cooperstown, NY, 88. *Pos:* Painter, Fed Art Proj, NY, 36. *Teaching:* Instr fine arts, High Sch Music & Art, 39-72; instr lithography, City Col New York, 66-67; instr lithography, Nat Acad Design, 68; instr painting & mem fac, Harriet FeBland Advan Painters Workshop, New Rochelle, NY, 74- *Awards:* Merit Award, 58th Ann, Art Dirs Club, 79; Award Merit, Pastel Soc Am, 81; Award in Painting, Am Soc Contemp Artists Ann, 84; Florian Kramer Mem Award in Painting, City Col Art Alumni Exhib, 85; Artist Fel, Va Ctr Creative Arts, 86 & 88. *Bibliog:* Contemporary Graphic Artists, 87. *Mem:* Artists Equity Asn New York (bd dirs, 62-, secy, 75-78); Contemp Artists Guild; Am Soc Contemp Artists (vpres, 83-85); Pastel Soc Am; Int Asn Artists, UNESCO (delegate, US comt). *Media:* Oil, Watercolor; Woodcut, Lithography. *Publ:* Illusr, ed drawings, NY Teacher News, 50-60; Therapeutic Dance/Movement, Human Sci Press, 79. *Dealer:* Pioneer Gallery Cooperstown NY. *Mailing Add:* 130 Gale Pl Bronx NY 10463

KASSOY, HORTENSE
SCULPTOR, PAINTER
b Brooklyn, NY, Feb 14, 17. *Study:* Pratt Inst, grad; Columbia Univ Teachers Col, with Oronzo Maldarelli, BS & MA; Am Artists Sch, with Chaim Gross. *Work:* Slater Mem Mus, Norwich, Conn; Bocour Artists Colors, Inc; Amalgamated Houses; Arch Am Art. *Comn:* Maternal Force (marble sculpture), Amalgamated Housing Coop Towers, Bronx, NY, 71. *Exhib:* Nat Acad Design, New York, 71; 28 Contemporaries, Bronx Mus Art, 71, Ann, 72, Year of the Woman, 75; Brooklyn Mus, Contemp Artists Guild, 74; 150th Ann, Nat Acad Design, 75; solo exhibs, Caravan House Gallery, New York, 75, Women in the Arts Gallery, 78, Vladeck Gallery, 81 & 85, Ward-Nasse Gallery, 86 & Pioneer Gallery, Cooperstown, NY, 87; Int Sculpture Exhib, Forte dei Marmi, 76, Pietrasante, 76, Italy; Am Soc Contemp Artists Ann, 79-91; Between the Wars, Bronx Mus, NY, 85-86; Palisades Gallery Inaugural Exhib, Hudson River Mus, 82. *Pos:* Chmn visual arts, Bronx Coun Arts, 73-76; corresp secy, US Comt, Int Asn Art (UNESCO), 79-89. *Teaching:* Instr sculpture, painting & 3D design, Evander Childs High Sch, Bronx, 61-72; instr sculpture, Harriet FeBland Advan Workshop, 75-80. *Awards:* Grumbachers First Prize in Watercolor, Painters Day at World's Fair, 40; Erlanger Award in Sculpture, 80 & Rizzoli Award in Sculpture, 83, Am Soc Contemp Artists, 90; Fel, Va Ctr Creative Arts, 86, 88 & 89. *Mem:* Artists Equity Asn, New York (bd dirs, 71-75 & 79-83, vpres, 75-79 & adv bd, 89-91; Contemp Artists Guild; Am Soc Contemp Artists (assoc pres, 87-89 & vpres, 90-92). *Mailing Add:* 130 Gale Pl Apt 6B Bronx NY 10463

KASTEN, KARL ALBERT
PAINTER, PRINTMAKER
b San Francisco, Calif, Mar 5, 16. *Study:* Marin Col; Univ Calif, AB & MA; Univ Iowa, with Lasansky; Hans Hofmann Sch Art. *Work:* Victoria & Albert Mus, London, Eng; Mus Mod Art, New York; Auckland City Mus, New Zealand; Mus Beaux-Arts, Rennes, France; Los Angeles Co Art Mus; and others. *Comn:* Painting, Reno, comn by Carter R King, 90. *Exhib:* Fifth Contemporary Printmakers, Univ Ill, Champaign, 56; Art Inst Chicago Am Painting Ann, 60; Contemporary American Painting & Sculpture, Univ Ill, 69; Achenbach Found Graphic Arts, San Francisco, 75; World Print III Traveling Exhib, 80-81; National Printmaking Invitational, Fla State Univ; and others. *Teaching:* Instr painting & drawing, Univ Mich, 46-47; asst prof painting & drawing, San Francisco State Col, 47-50; prof painting & graphics, Univ Calif, Berkeley, 50-82, emer prof art, 83- *Awards:* Oakland Art Mus Women's Bd Purchase Prize, Western Painters Exhib, 54; Creative Arts Inst Fel, 64 & 71; Tamarind Lithography Fel, 68; plus others. *Bibliog:* Meilach & Ten Hoor (auth), Assemblage & Collage, Crown, 73; A Kurasaki (auth), Modern Woodcut Techniques, Kyoto, Japan, 78; McClelland and Last (auths), The California Style, Hilcrest, 85; and others. *Mem:* Calif Soc Printmakers (coun mem, 72-76); Berkeley Art Ctr (bd mem). *Dealer:* Wenniger Graphics 174 Newburg St Boston MA 02116; Jan Holloway Gallery San Francisco CA. *Mailing Add:* 1884 San Lorenzo Ave Berkeley CA 94707

KASTNER, BARBARA H
PAINTER
b Perryton, Tex, Dec 2, 36. *Study:* San Antonio Art Inst, 75-78; Tex Tech Univ, BS, 59, MS 64. *Work:* Nebr Wesleyan Univ, Lincoln; Omaha Airport Authority, Nebr; Pillsbury Int Hq, Minneapolis; AT&T, Northwestern Bell Tel Co, Omaha, Nebr; CONAGRA, Omaha, Nebr; Northwestern Bell Tel Co, Omaha, Nebr; Norwest Corp, Omaha, Neb. *Exhib:* Rocky Mountain Nat Watermedia Exhib, Foothills Art Ctr, Golden, Colo, 79, 82, 83, 92; Nat Watercolor Soc Exhib, Brea Civic & Cult Ctr, Los Angeles, 81, 82, 89; Watercolor USA, Springfield Art Mus, Mo, 83; Ann Exhibs, Nat Acad Design, New York, 84, 90 & 92; Allied Artists Am Exhib, Nat Arts Club, New York, 86; Am Watercolor Soc Exhib, New York, 77, 82, 83, 85, 90 & 91. *Pos:* Bd dirs, Tex Watercolor Soc, San Antonio Watercolor Soc, 77-79; chairperson, Juror Search Comt, Rocky Mountain Nat Watermedia Exhib, Golden, Colo, 92; Juror of Awards, Am Watercolor Soc, 91; Appointed Mem of Evergreen Area Coun for the Arts, Evergreen, Colo, 92-95. *Awards:* Jane Peterson Award, Allied Artists Exhib, 87; Ogden M Pleissner Mem Award, Nat Acad Design Nat Exhib, 90; Walser Greathouse Medal, Am Watercolor Soc Exhib, 90. *Bibliog:* Roger Catlin (auth), Flatness of summer landscape transformed into art, Omaha World Herald, 7/25/82; Stephen Doherty (auth), Five ways to strengthen your landscapes, Watercolor '91, Am Artist's Mag, spring; Carole Katchen (auth), Dramatize Your Paintings With Tonal Value, Northlight Publ, 93. *Mem:* Am Watercolor Soc (juror awards, 91); Nat Watercolor Soc; Evergreen Coun Arts; Alliance for Contemp Art, Denver, Colo. *Media:* Casein, Acrylic. *Publ:* Contribr, Impact, The Art of Nebraska Women, Impact Inc/Nebr Arts Coun, 88; auth, Making night scenes sparkle, Artists Mag, 4/91; contribr, Five ways to strengthen your landscape, Watercolor '91, Am Artists Mag, 4/91; Contributed to Dramatize Your Paintings with Tonal Value, by Carole Katchen Northlight Publ, 93. *Mailing Add:* 30012 Troutdale Ridge Rd Evergreen CO 80439

KASUBA, ALEKSANDRA
ENVIRONMENTAL ARTIST
b Lithuania, Jan 10, 23; US citizen. *Study:* Art Inst Kaunas, Lithuania, 41-42; Acad Fine Rrts, Vilnius, Lithuania, 42. *Work:* Atlanta Univ Collection; Delgado Mus Art, New Orleans; Mus Contemp Crafts, New York; Johnson's Wax Collection; Bank Calif; and others. *Comn:* White marble wall, Container Corp Am, Chicago, 69; 20th Century Environment, Carborundum Mus Ceramic, Niagara Falls, 73; Int Furnit Exhib, Paris, 80; Brick Relief, New York, 81; Old Post Office Plaza Pavement, Washington, DC, 81; World Trade Ctr, New York, 86. *Exhib:* One-man show, Waddell Gallery, New York, 66 & Univ City Science Ctr, Philadelphia, 89; Experiments in Art & Technology, Brooklyn Mus Art, 68; Contemplative Environments, Mus Contemp Crafts, New York, 70; Space Shelters for Senses, New York, 71-72; Spectral Passage, De Young Mem Mus, San Francisco, 75; Women in Am Archit, Brooklyn Mus, 77; Art in Science, Philadelphia Art Alliance, 78; Transformations in Modern Architecture, Mus Mod Art, 79; Am Women Artists: The 20th Century, Knoxville Mus Art, Ky, 89. *Pos:* Consult, Nat Endowment Arts, 80. *Teaching:* Instr creative processes & elements art in archit scale, Sch Visual Arts, 71-72; instr stretched fiber structures, Cranbrook Acad Art, 76. *Awards:* Am Inst Archit Citation, Artist-Archit Collab, 71; Citation for Innovative Space Treatment, Women's Archit Auxiliary & New York Chap Am Inst Archit, 72; Nat Endowment Arts Fel, 83. *Bibliog:* Rita Reif (auth), article, New York Times, 5/11/71; James D Morgan (auth), article, Archit Rec, 8/71; Ronald Najman (auth), Saturday Revue, 8/12/72; and others. *Publ:* Contribr, Report on Art & Technology Program of the Los Angeles County Museum of Art, 71; Underground Interiors, Quadrangle, 72; Women in American Architecture & Design, Whitney Publ, 77. *Mailing Add:* 335 Greenwich New York NY 10013

KATANO, MARC
PAINTER
b July 17, 52. *Study:* Calif Col Arts & Crafts, Oakland, BFA(with distinction), 75. *Exhib:* Calif Palace Legion Honor, San Francisco, 74; Sun Gallery, Hayward, Calif, 77; Calif Col Arts & Crafts, Oakland, 78; Berkeley Arts Ctr, 80; solo exhibs, Stephen Wirtz Gallery, San Francisco, 80, 83, 86 & 87, Calif State Univ, Hayward, 82, Studio Marconi, Milan, Italy, 83, Plaza Gallery, Bank Am, San Francisco, 84, San Jose Inst Contemp Art, 85, Richard Green Gallery, New York, 86 & 88 & Mary Wright Gallery, Dallas, 87; E B Crocker Art Mus, Sacramento, 81; Mus Mod Art, San Francisco, 81; Calif State Univ, Hayward, 82; Traditions Transformed, Oakland Mus, 84; American Woodcuts: Revival and Innovation, traveling exhib in Europe, World Print Coun, 84; Cultural Frontiers Across the Pacific, Dominican Col, San Raphael, Calif, 85; California Directions in Painting, Visual Arts Ctr, Alaska, Anchorage, 85. *Awards:* KQED Award, Crown Zellerbach Inc, 80; award, Soc Encouragement Contemp Art, 81. *Bibliog:* Knute Stiles (auth), Marc Katano at Stephen Wirtz, Art Am, 11/83; Knute Stiles (auth), Marc Katano, Art Am, 11/83; Mark Katano Recent Paintings, Arts & Antique Collector, 6/85; Stephen Westfall (auth), review, Arts Mag, 5/87. *Media:* Oil. *Mailing Add:* c/o Stephen Wirtz Gallery 49 Geary St San Francisco CA 94108

KATAYAMA, TOSHIHIRO
PAINTER, DESIGNER
b Osaka, Japan, July 17, 28. *Study:* Self-taught. *Work:* Fogg Art Mus, Harvard Univ, Cambridge, Mass; Seibu Mus Mod Art, Tokyo; Rose Art Mus, Brandeis Univ, Waltham, Mass; Tokyo Munic Mus; De Cordova Mus, Lincoln, Mass; Ohara Mus Art, Kurashiki, Japan; Toyama Mus Mod Art, Japan. *Comn:* mural, Metrop Boston Transit Authority, State St Sta, 76; marble floor design (135' x 200'), NS Bldg, Tokyo, 82; relief mural with stainless steel pipes (23' x 60'), Akasaka Prince Hotel, Tokyo, 83; Theatre curtain-tapestry design (33' x 66'), Sonic City Hall, Ohmiya, 88; granite wall sculpture (26' x 100'), Ohara Mus Art, Kurashiki, Japan, 91; grand floor landscape design, including steel scculpture (33' x 15' x 35') & water fall, Panasonic Hdq Off, Tokyo, 92. *Exhib:* Graphic Image, Cent Mus Mod Art, Tokyo & Kyoto Nat Mus, Japan, 73 & 74; one-man shows, American Institute of Graphic Arts, NY, 68, Rose Art Mus, Brandeis Univ, 71, Kunstler Haus, Wine, Austria, 77 & Nantenshi Gallery, Tokyo, 78, 80, 83, 86 & 89; and others. *Pos:* Art dir, Nippon Design Ctr, Tokyo, 60-63; graphic designer, Geigy, Basel, Switz, 63-66; dir, Carpenter Ctr Visual Arts, Harvard Univ, 90- *Teaching:* Sr lectr graphic design, Carpenter Ctr for Visual Arts, Harvard Univ, Cambridge, 66- *Bibliog:* George Kepes & Ivan Chermaeff (auth), Work by Toshi, Graphic Design, Number 50, 73; The Work of Toshi Katayama, Kajima Inst Publ Co, 81; and many others. *Mem:* Alliance Graphique Int (head official, Zurich, 75). *Media:* Mixed. *Publ:* Coauth, Twelve Persons in Graphic Design Today, Bijutsu Shuppan-Sha, 69; coauth, Three Notations, Rotations with Mr Octavio Paz, Harvard Univ, 74. *Dealer:* Nantenshi Gallery 3-6-5 Kyobashi Chuo-Ku Tokyo Japan. *Mailing Add:* c/o Carpenter Ctr Harvard Univ 24 Quincy St Cambridge MA 02138

KATCHEN, CAROLE LEE
PAINTER
b Denver, Colo, Jan 30, 44. *Study:* Ripon Col, Wisc; Univ Colo, Boulder, BA(cum laude), 65. *Work:* Northwest Community Hosp, Arlington Heights, Ill; AGIP, Houston, Tex; Cherry Creek Nat Bank, Denver Symphony Orchestra, Denver, Colo; John Madden Corp, Englewood, Colo. *Exhib:* Solo exhibs, Centro Colombo-Americano, Bogota, Colombia, 74 & Mus

Southwest, Midland, Tex 82; 8 State Exhib Painting & Sculpture, Okla Art Ctr, Oklahoma City, 78; Midwestern Printmaking & Drawing, Tulsa Libr, Okla, 78; Rocky Mountain Nat Watermedia, Foothills Art Ctr, Golden, Colo, 80; Alliance Contemp Art, Denver Art Mus, 82; Pastel Soc Am Ann, Nat Arts Club, New York, 90. *Pos:* Contrib ed, Today's Art & Graphics, New York, 80-81 & The Artist's Mag, Cincinnati, 86- *Awards:* Outstanding Achievement in Art, West Valley Col, 70; Outstanding Working Woman, US Dept Labor, 82; Kans Pastel Soc Award, Pastel Soc Am, 90. *Bibliog:* John Jellico (auth), Drawing from life, Am Artist Mag, 9/75; Betty Harvey (auth), Carole Katchen, Artists of the Rockies, 76; Barbara Moss (auth), Profile, Design Notes, 92. *Media:* Pastel. *Publ:* Auth & illusr, I Was a Lonely Teenager, Scholastic, 65; auth, Figure Drawing Workshop, 85, Painting Faces & Figures, 86; Creative Painting With Pastel, North Light Books, 90. *Dealer:* Saks Gallery 3019 E Second Ave Denver CO 80206. *Mailing Add:* 1426 S Armacost No 4 Los Angeles CA 90025-2222

KATO, KAY
CARTOONIST
Study: Pa Acad Fine Arts; Am Acad Dramatic Arts. *Work:* NJ Gov Brendan Byrne; Newark Pub Libr Spec Collections, 57 cartoon originals from weekly column, depicting library programs & events, 92. *Comn:* Cover, Am Tel & Tel Mag, 54; book jacket for The Television-Radio Audience and Religion, 55; cover, Today's Living, New York Herald-Tribune, 57; also covers for Christian Sci Monitor, Sat Eve Post & others. *Exhib:* One-woman shows, R C Vose Galleries, Boston, Boston Pub Libr, Newark Pub Libr, Newark Mus & Montclair State Col, Belleville Pub Libr, 89; At Man and His World, Int Salon of Cartoons, Montreal, Que, 75-88; two-woman show, NJ Blood Ctr, East Orange, 81; Montclair Art Mus; travelling shows, West Caldwell Pub Libr, Livingston Pub Libr & Passaic Pub Libr, 92; and others. *Teaching:* Instr, Cambridge Ctr Adult Educ, Mass, 44-47; instr, South Orange & Maplewood Adult Sch, 63. *Awards:* First Prize Award for Cartoons, NJ State Fedn Women's Clubs, 77 & 78; Plaque Award, Newark Mus Paleontology Prog, 79 & Livingston Hist Soc, 90. *Bibliog:* Essex Co Libr Prog, Channel 3, Cablevision TV, 79. *Mem:* Graphic Artists Guild. *Publ:* Contribr, This Week, Nation's Bus, NY Times Mag, Parade, Am Weekly & others; Staten Island Advance, 77; auth, weekly cartoon column, Star Ledger, Newark; Kay Kato at Montclair State Col, Montclair State Col, 88; contribr, Marriage and Family Reality, Harper & Row, 89; and others. *Mailing Add:* 60 Chapman Pl PO Box 134 Glen Ridge NJ 07028

KATSIFF, BRUCE
PHOTOGRAPHER, MUSEUM DIRECTOR
b Philadelphia, Pa, Dec 10, 45. *Study:* Philadelphia Col Art, 64-65; Rochester Inst Technol, BFA, 68; Pratt Inst, MFA, 73; Oxford Univ, 85-87. *Work:* George Eastman House, Rochester, NY; Am Arts Doc Ctr, Exeter, England; Allentown Art Mus, Pa; Erie Art Mus, Pa. *Exhib:* Photog as Printmaking, Mus Mod Art, New York, 68; Vision & Expression, Int Mus Photog, 69; Philadelphia Mus Art, 70; Underground Gallery, New York, 70; Pa Acad of Fine Arts, 73; Pa Photogrs, Allentown Art Mus, 87; Am Photogrs; Taingin, China, 87; Pa Acad Fine Arts, 90. *Pos:* Eastman Kodak, 67-69; dir, James A Michener Art Mus, 90- *Teaching:* Prof art, Bucks Co Community Col, 69-, chmn art & music, 75-89 & Thomas Edison Col, 76-78. *Bibliog:* Gene Thorton (auth), Photography Review, New York Times, 70; A D Coleman (auth), article, Village Voice, 71. *Mem:* Col Art Asn; Soc Photographic Educators. *Mailing Add:* River Rd Lumberville PA 18933

KATSOULIDIS, PANAGIOTIS
GRAPHIC ARTIST
b Greece, 33. *Work:* Hellenic Can Trust; Atlantic Bank, New York; Nat Bank Greece, Chicago Br; Nat Gallery Greece, Athens; Mus Nat Hist, New York. *Exhib:* Biennale, Sao Paolo, Brazil, 65 & 67; 10th Int Salon, Paris, 69; Greek Art Now, CNA Gallery, Chicago, 74; Biblioteque Nat, Paris, 78; China - Greece, Hellenic Found, Rodi Karkazis Gallery, Chicago, 84; and others. *Pos:* Prof graphic art, Technol Inst. *Mailing Add:* c/o Rodi Karkazis Gallery 168 N Michigan Ave No 300 Chicago IL 60601

KATZ, ALEX
PAINTER
b New York, NY, July 24, 27. *Study:* Cooper Union; Skowhegan Sch; Colby Col, Maine, Hon Phd, 85. *Work:* Mus Mod Art, Metrop Mus Art, Whitney Mus Art, New York; Art Inst Chicago; Los Angeles Co Mus Art, Calif; Brooklyn Mus, NY; Philadelphia Mus Art, Pa; and others. *Comn:* Mural, Harlem Sta, Chicago. *Exhib:* Retrospective exhibs, Wadsworth Atheneum, 71, Whitney Mus & Va Mus, 74-75 & 86; 32nd Biennial Exhib Contemp Am Painting, Corcoran Gallery Art, Washington, DC, 71; Queens Mus, Flushing, New York, 80; Recent Drawings, Mus Mod Art, New York, 81; print retrospective, Brooklyn Mus, NY, 88; Seibu Mus Art, travelling, Tokyo, Japan, 88; NC Mus Art, travelling, Raleigh, 90; drawing retrospective, Mus Art, Munson-Williams-Proctor Inst, travelling, Utica, NY, 91; and others. *Teaching:* Adj prof, Yale Univ, 62-63, New York Univ, 83-84. *Awards:* St Gaudens Medal, 80; Skowhegan Award, 80; Award for Art in Pub Places, Chicago Bar Asn, 85; and others. *Bibliog:* Robert Rosenblum & Richard Marshall (coauth), Alex Katz, Rizzoli/Whitney, 86; Donald Kuspit (auth), Alex Katz: Night Paintings, Abrams, 91; Sam Hunter (auth), Alex Katz, Rizzoli, 92; and others. *Mem:* Am Acad and Inst Arts & Letters, 88. *Media:* All. *Mailing Add:* c/o Marlborough Gallery 40 W 57th St New York NY 10019

KATZ, EUNICE
PAINTER, SCULPTOR
US citizen. *Study:* Art Students League, with Harry Sternberg; Sculpture Ctr, with Dorothea Denslow; also with Angelo di Benedetto, Frederick Taubes, Donald Pierce & Edgar Britton. *Work:* US State Dept Art Embassies Prog, Washington, DC; Temple Emanuel Collection, Denver, Colo; Denver US Nat Bank; Hillel House, Boulder; Children's Hosp, Pittsburgh, Pa; Petro-Lewis, Denver, Colo. *Comn:* Stained glass window, BMH Congregation, Denver, 67 & 13' walnut & bronze tablet, 75; stained glass window, East Denver Orthodox Congregation, 68; four figure sculpture (bronze), Beth Israel Hosp, 70; two stained glass windows, Hebrew Congregation, Wichita, Kans, 72. *Exhib:* Allied Artists Am, Nat Acad, 49-66; Nat Soc Painters & Sculptors, NJ, 64; NAm Sculpture Exhib, Golden, Colo, 79; one-man shows, Pietrantonio Gallery, New York, 65 & La Salle Univ, Philadelphia, 65; Denver Art Mus; Art Mus of NMex; Wadsworth Atheneum, Conn; Laguna Gloria Mus, Tex. *Teaching:* Instr drawing & painting, Studio Classes, 57-65. *Awards:* Merit Award, Rocky Mountain Liturgical Arts, 58; Patron's Award, Art Mus NMex Biennial, 66; First Place Award, Am Asn Univ Women, 66. *Bibliog:* KRMA TV Fine Artist Series, Educ TV, 66; Woman artists of the Southwest, Artist Mag, 73. *Mem:* Allied Sculptors Colo; Artists Equity (secy, Denver Chap, 63-64); Rocky Mountain Liturgical Arts; Greater Denver Coun Arts & Humanities; Am Fedn Arts. *Media:* Oil; Bronze. *Dealer:* Saks Galleries 3019 E Second Ave Denver CO 80206. *Mailing Add:* 3131 E Alameda Ave Denver CO 80209

KATZ, HILDA (HULDA WEBER)
PAINTER, WRITER
b June 2, 09; US citizen. *Study:* Nat Acad Design; New Sch Social Res, scholar, 40 & 41; Accad Sci, Lett & Arts, Milan, Italy, Hon Dr, 74. *Work:* NY State Mus Albany; US Nat Mus; Met Mus Art, Jewish Mus, Brooklyn Mus Art, New York Pub Libr, New York Mus City, New York; Libr Congress; Nat Col Fine Arts; New Britian Mus Am Art; Israel Mus, Jerusalem; Ft Lewis Col Art Mus, Colo; Nat Mus Am Art, Lib Cong, Air & Space Mus, Smithsonian Inst, Washington, DC; Boston Pub Libr; Nat Gallery Art. *Exhib:* Venice Biennial, US Pavilion, Italy, 40; Corcoran Gallery Art Biennial, Washington, DC; Boston Pub Libr Invitations to Turin, Venice, Florence & Naples, Italy & France & Israel; US Info Agency Exhib to Europe, Asia, Mid East & Africa; Soc Am Graphic Artists-Japan & Ecuador Invitational Exchanges; Brooklyn Mus, NY; Children's Mus, Hartford, Conn; Bezalel Nat Mus, Israel; and many others. *Teaching:* Lectr & demonstrations in painting & graphics for art associations until 1951. *Awards:* Six Purchase Awards, Libr Cong; Prize, Soc Am Graphic Artists; Honor Award Plaque, Exec & Prof Hall of Fame, 66; Purchase Awards, Univ Minn, Metrop Mus Art, Univ Maine Col & NY Pub Libr; Metrop Mus Art Fel; Nobel Designate 74, 75 & 78; and others. *Bibliog:* Report & studies in history of art, Nat Gallery Art, 67-69; article, Nat Air & Space Catalog, 71; America in the War (catalog), Libr Cong, 83. *Mem:* Soc Am Graphic Artists; Nat Asn Women Artists; Artist Equity Asn; fel Metrop Mus Art; hon mem Acad Sci, Lett & Arts, Milano, Italy; plus others. *Media:* Oil, Watercolor, Prints. *Mailing Add:* 915 West End Ave Apt 5D New York NY 10025

KATZ, LEANDRO
ASSEMBLAGE ARTIST, FILMMAKER
b Buenos Aires, Arg, June 6, 38; US citizen. *Study:* Univ Nac Buenos Aires, BA, 61; Pratt Graphic Arts Ctr, 65-67. *Work:* Rare Book Collection, Houghton Libr, Harvard Univ; Ruth & Marvin Sackner Arch, Fla; Mus Mod Art Rare Book Libr, New York; Ira Wool Collection. *Comn:* Banco de la Provincia de Buenos Aires, New York. *Exhib:* Structure, John Gibson Gallery, New York, 78; Cineprobe, Mus Mod Art, New York, 79; The Lunar Alphabet, Clocktower, New York, 80; Metropotamia, PS1, Long Island City, 81; The Judas Window, Whitney Mus Am Art, 82; Orpheus Beheaded, RI Sch Design Mus, 83; 1987 Whitney Biennial Exhib, Whitney Mus Am Art; The Decade Show, New Mus Cont Art, 90. *Pos:* Guest cur, PS1, 79-; mem advisory bd, Mus Contemp Hispanic Art, currently. *Teaching:* Fac mem pre-Columbian art, Sch Visual Arts, New York, 71-; fac mem semiotics & cinema, Brown Univ, 81-; fac mem, film dept, New Sch Social Res, New York, 86-; fac mem, Dept Commun, William Paterson Col, currently. *Awards:* Fels, Nat Endowment Arts, 79 & Guggenheim Found, 80, Jerome Found, 82, Art Matters, 87, New York Found Arts, 89 & Council Arts, 90. *Bibliog:* Ted Castle (auth), Verbal art speaks up, Flash Art, 11/80; Lucy Lippard (auth), Overlay, Pantheon Books, 83; Dore Ashton (auth), American Art Since 1945, Oxford Univ Press. *Mem:* Asn Independent Film & Video. *Media:* Photography, Language Assemblages. *Publ:* Auth, Es Una Ola, Ed Sudamericana, 68; Self Hypnosis, TVRT Press, 75; The Milk of Amnesia, CEPA & The Visual Studies Workshop Press, 85; 27 Windmills, Viper's Tongue Books. *Mailing Add:* 25 E Fourth St New York NY 10003

KATZ, MORRIS
PAINTER
Study: Ulm, Ger & Gunsburg; with Hans Facler; Art Students League. *Work:* Evansville Mus Arts & Sci, Ind; Jr Col Albany, NY; Butler Inst Am Art, Youngstown, Ohio; St Lawrence Univ Giffiths Art Ctr, Canton, NY; Univ Art Gallery, State Univ NY Binghamton. *Exhib:* Instant Art Shows, more than 10,000 throughout the world. *Teaching:* Instr, Learning Annex, New York. *Mem:* Am Guild of Variety Artists; Int Platform Asn; Artists Equity Asn; Int Arts Guild Monaco; Am Fedn Television & Radio Artists. *Media:* Oil, Pencil. *Publ:* Auth, Paint Good and Fast, Sterling. *Mailing Add:* 247 W 29th St New York NY 10001-5202

KATZ, TED
PAINTER, EDUCATOR
b Philadelphia, Pa, July 29, 37. *Study:* Franklin & Marshall Col, AB, 59; Art Students League, 61-65; Acad Grande Chaumiere, Paris, 64-65; Harvard Univ, Grad Sch Educ, 68-72, EdM, 69, EdD, 72. *Exhib:* John F Kennedy Ctr; Demuth Found; Philadelphia Col Art; Moore Col Art; Millersville Univ. *Pos:* Fel, Grad Sch Educ, Harvard Univ, 68-72; dir Aesthetic Education Proj, Northwest Regional Educ Lab, Portland, Ore, 71-72; dir, Ford Found Proj, Inst Am Indian Arts, Santa Fe, NMex, 72-75; dir, Appalachia Regional Arts Prog, NC Arts Coun, Raleigh, NC; chief educ div, Philadelphia Mus Art, Pa, 77-84; dep dir, Ore Art Inst, Portland, 84-86. *Teaching:* lectr, Philadelphia Col Art, 78-84. *Awards:* Grant, Carnegie Corp; Grant, Ford Fund; Grant, Nat Endowment Arts. *Bibliog:* Howard Taubman (auth), Awakening the defeated, New York Times, 11/12/66; Museums as Schools, Newsweek, 10/15/79; Museums for a New Century, a Report of the Commission on Museums for a New Century, Am Asn Mus, Washington, DC, 84. *Media:* Aquamedia. *Publ:* Auth, Art as a Reflection of Human Concerns and Other Common Denominators, In: Museums, Adults & the Humanities: A Guide for Educational Programming, Am Asn Mus, Washington, DC, 81; Museums & Schools: Partners in Teaching, Pa Dept Educ, Harrisburg, 84; The Philadelphia Museum of Art Institute as research and development, Arts & Learning Spec Interest Group Proceedings J, Am Educ Res Asn, 84; coauth, Understanding & Creating Art (with Golstein, Kowalchuk & Saunders), West Pub Co, St Paul, Minn, 2nd ed, 91. *Dealer:* Butters Gallery Ltd 223 NW 9th Ave Portland OR 97209; Foster/White Gallery 311 1/2 Occidental Ave S Seattle WA 98104. *Mailing Add:* 411 Rydal East Jenkintown PA 19046

KATZEN, HAL ZACHERY
DEALER
b Baltimore, Md, July 16, 54. *Study:* San Francisco Col Art; Johns Hopkins Univ; Md Inst Col Art, BFA, 76. *Pos:* Asst dir, B R Kornblatt Gallery, Baltimore, Md, 76-78; assoc dir, Transworld Art, Alex Rosenberg Gallery, formerly. *Specialty:* Contemporary art, American painting and sculpture. *Mailing Add:* 305 E 40th St New York NY 10016

KATZEN, LILA (PELL)
SCULPTOR, EDUCATOR
b New York, NY, Dec 30, 32. *Study:* Art Students League; Cooper Union; also with Hans Hofmann, New York & Provincetown, Mass. *Work:* Nat Mus Am Art, Nat Gallery Art, Smithsonian Inst, Washington, DC; Town of Greenwich, Conn; Norton Art Gallery, Palm Beach, Fla; Fordham Univ, Lincoln Ctr, New York; Birmingham Mus Art, Alta; Wadsworth Atheneum, Hartford, Conn; and numerous pvt collections. *Comn:* Bilevel Symphony (sculpture), comn by Dept Housing & Urban Develop, Miami, Fla, 79; Floten Escort (sculpture), comn by Gen Serv Agency, Rodino Bldg, Newark, NJ, 82; Royal Naval Airport, Jidda & Jubail, Saudi Arabia; Royal Guest House, Al-Batan, Saudi Arabia; Wand of Inquiry (sculpture), Brandeis Univ, Waltham, Mass, 83; and others. *Exhib:* Biennial of Contemporary Painting and Sculpture, Whitney Mus Am Art, New York, 73; Mus Fine Arts, St Petersburg, Fla, 80; Metrop Mus Art Ctr, Coral Gables, Fla, 80; Phillips Collection, Washington, DC, 81; Women Artists Invitational, Philadelphia Col Art, Pa, 83; solo exhibs, Double Rainbow, World Expo, Brisbane, Australia, 88, Palm Beach Gardens City Hall, Fla, 89, Prince of Fire & Dancing Mask, Fordham Univ, Lincoln Ctr, New York, 89, Maya Queen Empowered, Dante Park, New York, 89, Favorite Graces, Queens Mus, Flushing Meadows, NY, 89 & Dawn Double Rainbow, Chicago Int Art Expos, Navy Pier, Ill, 90; City of Stamford Sculpture Gardens, Conn, 91; David Anderson Gallery, Buffalo, NY, 91; Axis Gallery, Philadelphia, 92; Muscarelle Mus Art, Williamsburg, Va, 92; Univ NC, Chapel Hill, 92. *Teaching:* Instr, 2-D design-media, sculpture, art & perception, Md Inst Col Art, 62-80. *Awards:* Nat Endowment Grant, 73; Goodyear Fel, 74; Creative Arts Award, Am Asn Univ Women, 74; Greenwich Environ Award, Greenwich Arts Coun, 79; First Prize-Institutional Setting, Nat Garden Show, Washington, DC, 83. *Bibliog:* Eleanor Munro (auth), Originals: American Women Artists, Simon & Schuster, 79. *Mem:* Archit League, New York; Col Art Asn; Municipal Art Soc, New York. *Media:* Various Metals, Concrete. *Mailing Add:* 459 Washington St New York NY 10013

KATZENBERG, DENA S
CONSULTANT, CURATOR
b Baltimore, Md. *Study:* McCoy Col of Johns Hopkins Univ; New York Sch of Interior Design. *Collections Arranged:* Great Am Cover-Up: Counterpanes of the 18th & 19th Century (auth, catalog), 71, Contemp Egyptian Folk Tapestries, 73, Blue Traditions: Indigo Dyed Textiles & Related Cobalt Glazed Ceramics from the 17th Century through the 19th Century (auth, catalog), 73-74, And Eagles Sweep Across the Sky: Indian Textiles of the North American West (auth, catalog), 77, Baltimore Album Quilts (auth catalog), 81-82, Imperial Costume from the Manchu Dynasty, 82, Baltimore Mus of Art. *Pos:* Consult Cur, Baltimore Mus Art, currently. *Mem:* Centre Int d'Etude des Textiles Anciens, Lyon, France; Needle & Bobbin Club, New York. *Res:* History of Indigo dye, Irish textile printing and manufacturing; North American Indian weaving; Baltimore album quilting. *Collection:* Textiles. *Publ:* Auth, Copper plate-printed Irish textile, Antiques, 4/77. *Mailing Add:* 22 Blythewood Rd Baltimore MD 21210

KATZIVE, DAVID H
ADMINISTRATOR
b San Francisco, Calif, Mar 23, 42. *Study:* Brown Univ, BA; Univ Chicago, MA. *Pos:* Chief educ div, Philadelphia Mus of Art, 70-76; consult, Art Park, Lewiston, NY, 74-; asst dir, Brooklyn Mus, 76-81; dir, DeCordova Mus, 81-*Teaching:* Instr art hist, Univ Chicago Exten, 66-68 & Ill Inst Technol, Chicago, 68-70. *Mem:* Am Asn Mus; Col Art Asn; Art Mus Asn; Asn Art Mus Dirs. *Mailing Add:* 57 Hicks St Brooklyn NY 11201

KATZMAN, HERBERT
PAINTER, INSTRUCTOR
b Chicago, Ill, Jan 8, 23. *Study:* Art Inst Chicago, cert. *Work:* Mus Mod Art & Whitney Mus Am Art, New York; Art Inst Chicago; Hirshhorn Mus, Washington, DC; Crocker Art Mus, Sacramento, Calif. *Exhib:* Fifteen Americans, Mus Mod Art, New York, 52; New Decade, Whitney Mus, 54; Venice Biennial, Italy, 57; Carnegie Biennial, Pa Acad Fine Arts. *Teaching:* Instr painting & drawing, Sch Visual Arts, New York, 69-87. *Awards:* Grants, Nat Coun Arts & Humanities, 66, Guggenheim, 68 & New York Coun Arts, 76. *Bibliog:* Articles in Art, USA & Viking, 63; Eric Protter (auth), Painters on Painting, Dunlap, 63. *Media:* Oil. *Dealer:* Dintenfass Gallery 50 W 57th St New York NY 10021. *Mailing Add:* c/o Terri Dintenfass 50 W 57th New York NY 10019

KAUFFMAN, (CAMILLE) ANDRENE
PAINTER, MURALIST
b Chicago, Ill, Apr 19, 05. *Study:* Art Inst Chicago, BFA, 39, MFA, 41; Univ Chicago; Ill Inst Technol, 41; Univ Ill, Chicago, 52; also with Andre L'Hote, Paris. *Work:* Art Inst Chicago; Rockford Col; Elmhurst Art Mus; State Mus, Springfield, Ill; Sears Tower, Chicago; and others. *Comn:* Murals (oil on canvas), Works Progress Admin & US Treas Dept, Burbank & Hirsch High Sch, Cook Co Hosp, Ida Grove & Iowa Post Off Bldgs, 34-42; bas reliefs (wood or stone), Works Progress Admin, schs & field houses, Oak Park & Evanston, Ill, 34-42; murals (ceramic tile), Rockford Col, Rockford, Ill, 51-52; murals (ceramic) & stained glass window, Third Unitarian Church Chicago, 55-69; drawing & sculpture, Jane Adams Medal of Rockford Col, Chicago. *Exhib:* One-woman shows, Vanderpoel Gallery, Chicago, 70, Univ Club, Chicago, 74, Elmhurst Col, 77, Loyola Univ, Chicago, 85, Truman Col, 86, Monmouth Col, Ill, 87 & Elmhurst Art Mus, 90; Loyola Univ Chicago, 85; Feds Exhib, Truman Col, 86; Whitney Mus; Mus Modern Art; Brooklyn Mus; Carnegie Inst, Pittsburgh; Nat Soc Mural Painters Design Ctr, New York & Moscow, Russia; 1933 a Century of Progress to the Focus V exhib, Art Inst, Chicago, 87; and many others. *Teaching:* Prof, Art Inst Chicago, 27-67, chmn div fine arts, 63-66, emer prof, 67-; prof painting, sculpture, ceramics & hist art, head art dept & chmn arts div, Rockford Col, Ill, 42-58. *Awards:* John Quincy Adams Fel Europe, Art Inst Chicago, 27; Achievement Award, Women's Caucus Art, 83; $500 Award, Senior Citizens Art Network Exhib, State of Ill Bldg, Chicago, 90. *Bibliog:* Prof John Hayward (narrator), Third Church Trilogy (TV prog), Channel 11, Chicago, 8/59; Donald Key (auth), Kauffman show rich in color, Milwaukee J, 9/17/61; subject of TV doc, Don't Miss, NBC, 3/16/86. *Mem:* Arts Club Chicago; Nat Soc Mural Painters; Chicago Soc Artists; Am Asn Univ Profs; Col Art Asn. *Media:* Acrylics, Ceramic Glaze; Oil, Watercolor. *Mailing Add:* 411 N West Ave Elmhurst IL 60126

KAUFFMAN, ROBERT CRAIG
PAINTER, SCULPTOR
b Los Angeles, Calif, Mar 31, 32. *Study:* Univ Southern Calif Sch Archit, 50-52; Univ Calif, Los Angeles, MA, 56. *Work:* Whitney Mus Am Art, New York; Tate Gallery Art, London, Eng; Art Inst Chicago; Los Angeles Co Mus Art; Pasadena Art Mus, Calif; and others. *Exhib:* The 1960's, Mus Mod Art, New York, 67; California Prints, Mus Mod Art, New York, 72; Corcoran Biennial, 73; 71st Am Exhib, Art Inst Chicago, 74; Whitney Downtown, 74; Univ Ill, 74; Inst Contemp Arts, Los Angeles, Calif, 75; Fullerton Art Gallery, Calif State Univ, 79; Whitney Mus Am Art, 80; Va Commonwealth Univ, Richmond, 81; Asher/Faure, Los Angeles, Calif, 81; La Jolla Mus, Calif, 81; and others. *Teaching:* Assoc prof painting & sculpture, Univ Calif, Irvine, 67-72; instr painting & sculpture, Univ Calif, Berkeley, 69 & Sch Visual Arts, New York, 70-71. *Awards:* US Govt Fel for the Arts, 67; 69th Am Exhib First Prize, Art Inst Chicago, 70. *Bibliog:* Jane Livingston (auth), Recent works by Craig Kauffman, 69 & Review of Kauffman show, 70, Artforum. *Media:* Acrylic, Plastic. *Publ:* Coauth, Transparency, Reflection, Light, Space, 71. *Dealer:* Pace Gallery 32 E 57th St New York NY 10022. *Mailing Add:* Dept Art Univ Calif Irvine CA 92717

KAUFMAN, GLEN
PRINTMAKER
b Ft Atkinson, Wis, 32. *Study:* Univ Wis, BS, 54; Cranbrook Acad Art, MFA, 59; State Sch Arts & Crafts, Copenhagen, Denmark, 60. *Work:* Am Craft Mus; Art Inst Chicago; Helen Allen Collection, Univ Wis, Madison; Itami City Craft Ctr, Hyogo, Japan; Juraku Mus, Kyoto, Japan. *Exhib:* Solo exhibs, Fiberworks, Berkeley, Calif, 87, Madison-Morgan Cult Ctr, Madison, Ga, 88, Allrich Gallery, San Francisco, Calif, 88 & 90 & Gallery Gallery, Kyoto, Japan, 89; Tour of Africa, Smithsonian Inst Traveling Exhib Serv, 88-91; Tour of Europe, USIA Arts Am Prog, 89-91; Itami Craft Ctr, Osaka, Japan, 89 & 90. *Pos:* Head, Dept Fabric Design, Cranbrook Acad Art, Bloomfield Hills, Mich, 61-67. *Teaching:* Assoc prof art, Univ Ga, Athens, 67-72, prof art, 72-; vis lectr, Sch Textiles, Royal Col Art, London, Eng, 76. *Awards:* Univ Ga Creative Res Medal, 88; Silver Prize, Itami Craft Ctr, Osaka, Japan, 89; Nat Endowment Arts Visual Artists Fel Grant, 90. *Bibliog:* Carolyn Price Dyer (auth), Glen Kaufman: a synthesis of two worlds, Fiberarts, summer 89; Tomio Sugaya (auth), Columbus and the egg, Sansai, 10/89; Jeon Myung-OK (augh), A fiber artist introduces his work, 10/89 & Experience seen through a grid: Glen Kaufman, 12/89, Monthly Crafts. *Mailing Add:* c/o Moriyo Shimabukuro 190 Harben Pl Athens GA 30606

KAUFMAN, IRVING
PAINTER, EDUCATOR
b New York, NY, Oct 4, 20. *Study:* Art Students League; NY Univ, BA & MA. *Work:* Univ Mich Mus Art; Saginaw Mus Art; Ohio State Univ; Parke-Davis Co; Columbia Univ Law Libr. *Exhib:* Various group shows and one-man

exhibs. *Teaching:* Assoc prof art, Univ Mich, Ann Arbor, 56-64; prof art, City Col New York, 64-86, emer prof, 86-; vis prof art educ, Teachers Col, Columbia Univ, New York, 86. *Awards:* Manual Barkan Award, Nat Art Educ Asn, 81; Lowenfeld Mem Lectr, Nat Art Educ Asn, 88. *Mem:* Inst Study Art in Educ (pres, 72); Col Art Asn Am; Univ Coun Art Educ. *Media:* Oil. *Publ:* Auth, Art & Education in Contemporary Culture, 66; contribr, Concepts in Art Education, 70; New Ideas in Art Education, 72; ed, Arts Issue, Curriculum Theory, Network, 74; contribr, Arts in Society, 75; auth, Studies In Art Educ, 88; and others. *Dealer:* Rehn Gallery 655 Madison Ave New York NY 10021. *Mailing Add:* 3 Perigee Path East Hampton NY 11937

KAUFMAN, JANE
PAINTER, LECTURER
b New York, NY, May 26, 38. *Study:* Cornell Univ, 56-58; NY Univ, BA, 60; Hunter Col, MA, 65. *Work:* Whitney Mus Am Art, New York; Wooster Mus Fine Arts, Mass; Mus Mod Art S Australia, Canberra; Brooklyn Mus, NY; Aldrich Mus Contemp Art, Ridgefield, Conn; and others. *Exhib:* One Man's Choice, Dallas Mus Fine Arts, Tex, 69; Highlights of 1970 Season, Aldrich Mus Contemp Art, Ridgefield, Conn, 70; one-person show, Whitney Mus Am Art, New York, 71; Lyrical Abstraction, 71, The Struct of Color, 71 & Ann, 73, Whitney Mus Am Art; Corcoran Gallery Art, 72 & 73; Critic's Choice, Lowe Art Gallery, Syracuse Univ, NY & Munson-Williams-Proctor Inst Mus Art, Utica, 77; Decorative Art: Recent Works, Douglas Col Gallery, New Brunswick, NJ, 78; Intricate Struct-Repeated Images, Tyler Sch Art, Philadelphia; and many others. *Teaching:* Instr fine arts, New York Pub High Schs, 60-69; Lehman Col, Bronx, NY, 69-70, Bard Col, Annandale-on-Hudson, NY, 71-73 & Brooklyn Mus Art Sch, 72-73; lectr, Queens Col, 73-74; vis artist, workshops & lect, var cols & univs, US & Can, 74-; instr fine arts, Cooper Union Sch Art, New York, 81- *Awards:* Guggenheim Fel, 74; Nat Endowment for Arts Fels, 79; Creative Artists Pub Serv Prog Grant for sculpture, 81. *Mailing Add:* c/o Bellas Artes 584 Broadway New York NY 10012

KAUFMAN, JOE
ILLUSTRATOR, WRITER
b Bridgeport, Conn, May 21, 11. *Study:* Lab Sch Indust Design; also with Herbert Bayer. *Exhib:* Art Dirs Club, 43-60; Soc Illustrators, 45; one-man shows, Fleisher Art Mem, Philadelphia, 50 & Parsons Sch of Design, New York, 78. *Mem:* Soc Illustrators. *Publ:* Illusr, I Spy With My Little Eye, McGraw-Hill, 70; auth & illusr, Busy People, 73; How We Born, How We Grow, Work, Learn, 75; About the Big Sky, High Hills, Rich Earth, Deep Sea, 78; Wings, Paws, Hoofs and Flippers, 81; Slimy, Creepy, Crawly Creatures, 85; and others. *Mailing Add:* 18 W 70th St New York NY 10023

KAUFMAN, LORETTA ANA
SCULPTOR, INSTRUCTOR
b New York, NY, Feb 17, 46. *Study:* Palm Beach Jr Col; Univ Tampa. *Work:* San Angelo Mus Art, Tex; Westpoint Pepperell Inc, New York; Spartanburg Regional Med Ctr, SC; NationsBank, London, Eng; Environ Res Found, Washington, DC. *Exhib:* Solo exhibs, Exhibit A Gallery, Savannah Col Art & Design, Ga, 87, New Work, Piedmont Craftsmen Ctr, Winston-Salem, NC, 90; Wyoming Clay Show, Nicolaysen Art Mus, Casper, Wyo, 89; Handmade for the 90's, Berkshire Mus, Mass, 90; Perspectives Gallery, Va Tech, Blacksburg, 91; NCECA Clay Nat, Ariz State Univ Art Mus, Tempe, Touring, 91-92. *Pos:* Cur, Tri State Sculptors Exhib, Spartanburg Co Arts Ctr, SC, 91. *Teaching:* Instr, sculpture, Greenville Co Mus Art, SC, 88-; vis artists ceramics, Greenville Co Sch Dist, 89-90; artists in residence sculpture, Shriner's Hosp Crippled Children, Greenville, SC, 90-91. *Awards:* First Place, 3rd Ann Monarch Tile Nat Ceramics Competition, 88; Purchase Award, 2nd Ann NCNB Exhib, 89. *Bibliog:* Ann Spencer (auth), Exhibit to feature noted sculpture, Charlotte Observer, NC, 12/29/89; Olivia Fowler (auth), Interview with a Sculptor, Montgomery, AL Lakeside Living Mag, 90; Dr Kathryn Bennett (auth), Tri State Sculptors, Atlanta Art Papers, 5-6/91; and others. *Mem:* Tri State Sculptors Educ Asn; Artists Equity Asn; Women's Caucus Art. *Media:* Clay. *Publ:* Contribr, Monarch tile national, Ceramics Monthly, 11/1/88. *Dealer:* Novus Gallery 116B Bennett St NW Atlanta GA 30309. *Mailing Add:* 426 Lake Eljema Dr Piedmont SC 29673

KAUFMAN, LORI HOKIN
ART DEALER, COLLECTOR
b Chicago, Ill, Apr 29, 51. *Study:* Purdue Univ, BA(art hist), 73. *Pos:* Asst dir, Hokin Gallery, Chicago, 73-81; pres & owner, Hokin/Kaufman Gallery, 82- *Mem:* Art Dealers Asn Am; Chicago Art Dealer Asn. *Specialty:* 20th century painting and sculpture; Unique, artist designed furniture. *Collection:* Contemporary paintings; Primitive art. *Mailing Add:* 210 W Superior Chicago IL 60610

KAUFMAN, MICO
SCULPTOR
b Romania, Jan 3, 24; US citizen. *Study:* Acad Fine Arts, Rome & Florence, Italy, 47-51. *Work:* Bronze sculpture, Rouses Mem, Lowell, Mass, 80; Homage to Women (bronze sculpture), Hist Nat Park, Lowell, Mass, 84; Claude Debussy (bronze sculpture), Univ Mass, Lowell Campus, Mass, 87; Ann Sullivan (bronze sculpture), Tewksbury, Mass, 85; bronze sculpture, Muster Park Fountain, Tewksbury, Mass, 92; Helen Keller (bronze sculpture), Agawam, Mass, 92. *Comn:* Official Ford VPres Commemorative Medal, 73; Official Ford Pres Commemorative Medal, 74; 200 Bicentennial Medals, Danbury Mint; Official Pres Reagan/VPres Bush Medal, 85; Official Pres Bush Commemorative Medal, 89. *Exhib:* Int Fedn Medal Producers, Lisbon & Port, 79, Florence, Italy, 83, Stockholm, Swed, 85, Commemorative Medal, Colo, 87, Freedom British Mus, London, Eng, 92; Prudential Art Festival, New Eng Sculpture Soc, 69; retrospective, Am Numismatic Soc, 92. *Teaching:* Instr sculpture, Boston Ctr Adult Educ, 59-62, New Eng Sch Art, Boston, 69-70 & Nashua Arts & Sci, 70-71; instr sculpture, New Eng Sch Art, Boston, 69-70 & Nashua Arts & Sci, 70-71. *Awards:* Alma & Ulysses Ricci Award for Best Conservative Painting or Sculpture, Rockport Art Asn, 67; Sculptor of Year, Houston, Tex, 78 & J Sanford Saltus Award for Signal Achievement in Art of the Medal, Am Numismatic Soc, 92. *Bibliog:* Ann Schecter (auth), Vivid sculptural works, 11/19/67 & Perlinax (auth), Maggie Walker Medal, 11/11/71, Lowell Sun, Mass; Brenda Badolato (auth), The sculpture of Mico Kaufman, Lawrence Eagle Tribune, Mass, 6/18/68. *Mem:* Nat Sculpture Soc; New Eng Sculpture Asn; Cambridge Art Asn; Rockport Artists Asn. *Media:* Bronze, Stainless Steel. *Publ:* Auth, The Making of Mold Block and Case, 60; Your most penetrating portrait ever, Nat Sculpture Rev, 72. *Mailing Add:* 23 Marion Dr Tewksbury MA 01876

KAUFMAN, NANCY
ART ADVISOR, WRITER
b Woonsocket, RI. *Study:* Boston Univ, AB(art hist), 60; Univ Calif, Berkeley, art & archit hist. *Comn:* Matt Mullican (mural, 70's), Zeckendorf Co, 89; Hanny Roseman, bronze wall relief, 45, J P Morgan & Co, 90. *Collections Arranged:* NY City Transit Authority, Livingston Plaza Facility, 92; Haight Gardner Poor & Havens, 87. *Pos:* Dir visual arts referral serv, Creative Artists Pub Serv prog, 74-79; bd dirs, Ctr for Arts Info, 78; partner, Kaufman Randolph Tate, Fine Art Services, 79-83; pres, Nancy Kaufman Fine Art Servs, 83- *Teaching:* Mem fac, New Sch Social Res, 84-86. *Bibliog:* At home with art, House Beautiful, 83-86. *Mem:* Art Table (bd dir, 90-); Asn Prof Art Adv (bd dir 83-88). *Mailing Add:* 305 W 86th St New York NY 10024

KAUFMAN, STUART MARTIN
PAINTER, ILLUSTRATOR
b Brooklyn, NY, Dec 1, 26. *Study:* Pratt Inst, New York, 45-46; Art Students League, New York, 46-48; study with Howard Trafton, Frank V DuMond & Frank Reilly. *Work:* Newark Mus Art, NJ; Minneapolis Inst Fine Art, Minn; Metrop Mus Art, Lehman Collection. *Exhib:* Annual Invitational, Montclair Mus, NJ, 57-64; Selected New Jersey Artists, Newark Mus, 58, 59, 64 & 65; Invitational Exhib, Chicago Art Inst, 61; Realistic American Art, Butler Inst Am Art, Youngstown, Ohio, 62; Fine Arts Festival, San Diego Mus, Calif, 64; 20th Century Realists, Hirschl & Adler Gallery, New York, 65; Annual Exhib, Nat Acad Design, New York, 66; Invitational Annual Exhib, Soc Illusrs, New York, 66; Davis Gallery, NY. *Pos:* Illusr (book cover paintings), Simon & Schuster, 61-83, CBS Publ-Fawcett, 70-82, Dell Publ, 83-86, Warner Publ, 84-86 & St Martins Press, 86. *Awards:* George R Beach Prize, 58 & Traditional Oils, 64, Montclair Mus Art; Guri Seaver Mem Award, Art Inst Chicago, 61. *Bibliog:* Esther Forman Singer (auth), Figure paintings of Stuart Kaufman, Am Artist, 72. *Media:* Oils. *Mailing Add:* 6050 S Verde Trail, Apt 403 Boca Raton FL 33433-4466

KAUFMANN, RICK
DIRECTOR, CURATOR
b Apr 28, 47. *Study:* Self-taught. *Collections Arranged:* Sixty solo exhibs from 1987-1992, Art et Industrie, New York; group shows, 10th Anniversary Exhib, 90 & 1980/1990, 90, Art et Industrie, New York; American Art Furniture, Osaka, Japan, 90; Art Furniture New York, Fukoka, Japan, 90; Spider Web/The Tattoo, Calabana, New York, 92; Fine Art/Functional Art (auth, catalog), Turbulance Gallery, New York, 93. *Pos:* Owner, Richard Kaufmann Antiques, Ann Arbor, Mich, 67-70; dir & co-owner, Kaufmann Rust Decorative Arts, New York, 70-76; founder & dir, Art et Industrie, New York, 76- *Teaching:* Pt-time lectr, Parsons Sch Design, New York, 81 & 84. *Awards:* Industrial Design Soc Awards, 82, 84, 85 & 86. *Mem:* Nat Arts Club; Am Antiq Soc; Am Hist Preserv Soc; Functional Art Soc (founder); Mus Seating & Art Progs Int (pres). *Res:* Synthesizing art and design into radical new forms. *Specialty:* Functional, decorative and fine art. *Publ:* Auth, Forrest Myers Retrospective (exhib catalog), 89; Michelle Oka Doner (exhib catalog), 90; Furniture Design for the Ninties, PCB Int, 90; Gloria Kisch (exhib catalog), 91; Elenora Triggboff (exhib catalog), 91. *Mailing Add:* c/o Turbulance Gallery 812 Broadway New York NY 10003

KAUFMANN, ROBERT CARL
ART LIBRARIAN
b Birmingham, Ala, Apr 27, 37. *Study:* Birmingham Southern Col, Ala, BS(Fr & hist), 61; Sch Libr Serv, Columbia Univ, New York, MSLS, 65, MA candidate in art hist, 65-69. *Pos:* Asst librn, Fine Arts Libr, Columbia Univ, New York, 64-68, fine arts librn, 68-69; librn, Cooper-Hewitt Mus, Smithsonian Inst, New York, 65-; art libr, Div Art, Donnell Br, New York Pub Libr, 69; art & archit librn, Yale Univ, New Haven, Conn, 71-74. *Awards:* Joe Delmore Langston Award, Ala Libr Asn, 63; Comt to Rescue Italian Art Res Fel, Bibliot Naz Centrale, Florence, Italy, 69-71. *Mem:* Victorian Soc Am; Art Libr Soc NAm. *Res:* Nineteenth century furniture and decorative arts; subject headings for twentieth century decorative arts. *Mailing Add:* 220 W 93rd St New York NY 10025

KAULITZ, GARRY CHARLES
PAINTER, PRINTMAKER
b Rapid City, SDak, Oct 6, 42. *Study:* Rochester Inst Technol, BFA & MFA. *Work:* Hyatt Regency Collection; Gallery Today Collection, Indianapolis, Ind; State of Ky; City of Louisville, Ky; Art Inst Chicago; Humana Inc; Am Life Insurance. *Comn:* Steeltect Industs, Louisville; Norton Hosp, Louisville. *Exhib:* One-man shows, J B Speed Art Mus, Louisville, 71, Bellarmine Col, Ky, 76 & 90 & Brookhaven Col, Tex, 79; Int Miniature Print Exhib, New York, NY, 78; Print Club of Philadelphia, 79-80; Freichen International Print Exhib, 80; Crackow Biannual, 80; and others. *Teaching:* Prof printmaking,

Louisville Sch Art, 68-82; vis artist, Brookhaven Col, Tex, 79, 83 & 88 & Southern Ill Univ, 79; guest speaker, Detroit Print Symposium, 80; instr, Univ Louisville, 87- *Awards:* Evansville Mus Ann Exhib Award, 68; Arthur D Allen Mem Award, Regional Fine Arts Biennial, 71; Alsmith Fel, 92. *Bibliog:* Sarah Lansdell (auth), Review of work, 2/71 & Linda Bousch (auth), A printmaker's excursion into fact & fantasy, 2/75, Courier-J & Times. *Media:* Oil, Serigraphy. *Publ:* Auth, A Portfolio of Prints & Poems, pvt publ, 73. *Mailing Add:* 1244 S Brook St Louisville KY 40203

KAUPELIS, ROBERT JOHN
PAINTER, EDUCATOR
b Amsterdam, NY, Feb 23, 28. *Study:* State Univ NY Col Buffalo, BS; Albright Art Sch, cert; Teachers Col, Columbia Univ, MA & DEd. *Work:* Duke Univ Mus; Univ Mass; Atlanta Art Inst; NY Univ Art Collection; Mich State Univ; and others. *Exhib:* Katonah Gallery, Katonah, NY, 70, 75, 78 & 79; over 50 one-man shows incl Image South Gallery, Atlanta, Ga, 77-79 & 82, Schenectady Mus, 80, Andre Zarre Gallery & Hudson River Mus, New York, 83; Emporia State Univ, Emporia, Kans, 85; Univ Alaska, Fairbanks, 86; Kingsboro Community Col, Brooklyn, 87; Jack Gallery, New York, 87, 88, 90; Gallery Camino Real, Boca Raton, Fla, 90; Alan Brown Gallery, Hartsdale, NY, 90; Circle Gallery, Chicago & Denver, 90. *Pos:* Bd trustees, Silvermine Guild Arts Ctr & mem col bd, Studio Arts Comt Advan Placement Prog. *Teaching:* Prof art, NY Univ, 56-85; retired. *Awards:* Prize for Sculpture, New Eng Ann, 69; Painting Prize, Silvermine New Eng Ann, 73, First Prize, 79 & 80; and others. *Bibliog:* Herbert Livesey (auth), The Professors, Charterhouse, 75; Gerald M Monroe (auth), Teaching drawing: The personal approaches of Robert Kaupelis, Drawing, 5-6/79 & American Artist, 8/81; Ruth Bass (auth), article, Arts, 9/83. *Mem:* Silvermine Guild Artists; Univ Coun on the Arts. *Media:* Acrylic, Oil. *Publ:* Auth, Learning to Draw, 66 & Experimental Drawing, 80, Watson-Guptill. *Dealer:* Reece Gallery 24 West 57th St New York NY 10019; Circle Gallery Soho 468 W Broadway New York NY 10012. *Mailing Add:* 988 Barberry Rd Yorktown Heights NY 10598

KAWA, FLORENCE KATHRYN
PAINTER
b Weyerhaeuser, Wis, Feb 24, 12. *Study:* Minneapolis Sch Art, 30-34; Univ Wis, Milwaukee, BS, 40; La State Univ, Baton Rouge, MA, 44; summers, Black Mountain Col, 44, Columbia Univ, 46-48, Cranbrook Acad Art, 51, Mass Inst Technol, 56 & Leeds Col Art, England, 70. *Work:* Univ Wis, Madison; La Art Comn, Baton Rouge; US Info Agency for Am Embassies; Pub Bldgs Admin for Marine Hosps; Hoover State Office Bldg, Des Moines, Iowa. *Exhib:* Int Watercolor Biennial, Brooklyn Mus, 51, 55, 57, 59 & 61; Ann Exhib Contemp Am Sculpture, Watercolor & Drawings, Whitney Mus Art, New York, 53; Nat Competition Watercolors, Drawings & Prints, Metrop Mus Art, New York, 53; Contemp Watercolor in the US, sponsored by US Embassy Cult Div, France, 53; 20th Century American Graphic Arts, US Info Agency Touring Foreign Mus, 56-57; one-man show, Des Moines Art Ctr, 76. *Teaching:* Asst prof painting & design, Fla State Univ, 46-62; prof painting & design, Drake Univ, 64-78, emer prof, 78- *Awards:* Edmundson Award for Best Work in Any Medium, Des Moines Art Ctr, 70, Esther & Edith Younker Award, 77; 13th Midwest Biennial Purchase Award & Best in Show, Joslyn Mus, Omaha, 74; plus others. *Media:* Oil, Watercolor. *Dealer:* Olson-Larsen Gallery 203 Fifth St West Des Moines IA 50265. *Mailing Add:* 41 W Byrne Roswell NM 88201

KAWABATA, MINORU
PAINTER, INSTRUCTOR
b Tokyo, Japan, May 22, 11. *Study:* Tokyo Acad Fine Art, grad, 34; also study in Paris & Italy, 37-39. *Work:* Albright-Knox Art Gallery, Buffalo, NY; Everson Mus Art, Syracuse, NY; Guggenheim Mus; Mus Mod Art, Sao Paulo, Brazil; Mus Mod Art, Tokyo. *Exhib:* Guggenheim Int, New York, 59 & 64; Everson Mus Art, 74; Mus Mod Art, Kamakura, Kamakurashi, Japan, 75; Juda Rowan Gallery, London, 80; retrospectives, Nat Mus Mod Art, Kyoto, 92 & Ohara Mus Kurashiki, 92. *Teaching:* Prof painting, Tama Univ Art, Japan, 50-58; prof painting, drawing & compos, New Sch Social Res, 60- *Awards:* Rhythm of Brown, Guggenheim Mus, 59; Work, Mus Mod Art, Sao Paulo, 60; Work B, Mus Mod Art, Kamakura, 61. *Bibliog:* Kramer (auth), article, 11/23/74, Raynor (auth), article, 3/7/80 & John Russell (auth), article, 10/16/81, New York Times. *Dealer:* Jack Tilton Gallery 24 W 57th St New York NY 10019. *Mailing Add:* 463 West St New York NY 10014

KAWASHIMA, TAKESHI
PAINTER, SCULPTOR
b Takamatsu City, Japan, Jan 13, 30. *Study:* Musashino Univ Art, 51-56; Art Students League New York, 66. *Work:* Mus Mod Art, New York; Ohara Mus Art, Kurashiki; Tokyo Metrop Mus Art; Japanese Sch New York, 85; Toyama Prefectural Mus Art, Toyama City, 89; Tokushima Prefectural Mus Mod Art, Tokushima City, 88; and others. *Comn:* Miki-cho Town Hall, Kagawa, Japan, 83; Kagawa Prefectural Hall, 86; The Long-Term Credit Bank Japan, Ltd, Chicago, 88; Tokyo Life Insurance Co, Ltd, Tokyo, 89; Takamatsu City Libr, Takamatsu City, 92; and others. *Exhib:* Aldrich Mus Contemp Art, Ridgefield, Conn, 67; Nat Mus Art, Osaka, Japan, 77; Tradition & Today, Bargen Mus Art Sci, NJ, 83; Japan: Dynasty '83, Sante Webster Gallery, Philadelphia, 83; Japanese Contemporary Painting, 1960-1980, Mus Mod Art, Gunma, 84; retrospective show (solo), Takamatsu City Mus Art, Takamatsu City, 89; and others. *Collections Arranged:* Hosetsu Ohtsuka Calligraphy (auth, catalog), 82. *Awards:* Silvermine Prize, 18th Ann New Eng Exhib, New Canaan, Conn, 67. *Bibliog:* Udo Kulterman (auth), The new painting, Frederick A Praeger, 69; Joseph Love (auth), Art Int, 71; John Canaday, New York Times, 72. *Media:* Acrylic, Oil, Watercolor; Stone. *Publ:* Contribr, Decoration art, 72 & The base of sculpture, 78, Shincho-Sha; New York for twelve years, Shikoku Shinbun, 76; auth, I Love New York, essay, US Japan Publ New York, Inc, 104, 92; contribr, Exclusive, Soho, Seikatsu-no-tome-sha, 54, 89; Chronicle of Art, Vol 6 1976-1989, Mainichi News Paper, 74-75, 91. *Dealer:* Nantenshi Gallery 3-6-5 Kyobashi Chuo-ku Tokyo Japan. *Mailing Add:* 11 Mercer St, 2F New York NY 10013

KAWECKI, JEAN MARY
SCULPTOR, GALLERY DIRECTOR
b Liverpool, Eng, June 24, 26; US citizen. *Study:* Liverpool Col Art, Eng; Art Career Sch, New York; also with Douglas Prizer. *Work:* Hoffman LaRoche Pharmaceutical Co. *Comn:* Wall sculpture, First Montclair Housing Corp, 83; Site-Specific Works for Temple Anshemeth, New Brunswick, 87. *Exhib:* Nat Miniature Soc, Nutley, NJ, 75; Audubon Artists, Nat Acad Design, New York, 78; Newark Mus, 78; Nabisco World Hq, 79; solo show, NJ Inst Technol, 80-; Bergen Mus, 81; Montclair State Col, 90; and others. *Pos:* Free lance illusr mag, London, Eng, 46-51, Sol Vogel & Am-Mitchell Publ, New York, 51-53, Tobias Meyer & Nebenzahl, New York, 58-66; co-founder & dir, Doubletree Coop Art Gallery, Upper Montclair, 74-88. *Awards:* Patrons Award, Hudson Artists at the Bergen Mus, 76; Sculpture Award, Audubon Artists at Nat Acad Galleries, New York, 78; First Prize, St John's Ann Juried Show, Newark, 79, 86. *Bibliog:* Anne Betty Weinshenker (auth), M & A on Art, NJ Music & Arts, 12/76. *Mem:* Artists Equity Asn NJ & NY; Doubletree Coop Gallery (dir & chmn hanging comt & spec shows, 74-88). *Media:* Found Stone, Metal & Epoxy. *Dealer:* Sheila Nussbaum Gallery Millburn NJ. *Mailing Add:* 28 Mountainside Park Terr Upper Montclair NJ 07043

KAY, REED
PAINTER, EDUCATOR
b Boston, Mass, Mar 29, 25. *Study:* Sch Mus Fine Arts, Boston, dipl, 49, with Karl Zerbe; also with Oskar Kokoschka. *Exhib:* New Eng Regional Drawing, Smith Col Mus Art, 65; Am Fedn Arts Nat Exhib, 66; Urban Aesthetics, Queens Mus, NY, 76; A Selection of Am Art, Inst Contemp Art, Boston, 76; Art in Transition, Mus Fine Arts, Boston, 77; one-man exhib, Alpha Gallery, Boston, 78, 83 & 90; Circle Gallery, Washington, DC, 86. *Teaching:* Instr painting, Sch Mus Fine Arts, Boston, 51-56; instr painting techniques, Skowhegan Sch Painting, Maine, 52-60; instr painting, Boston Univ, 56, prof painting, 68- *Awards:* James William Paige Traveling Fel, 50-51; Artist Fel Grant for painting, Nat Endowment Arts, 81-82. *Media:* Oil, Gouache. *Res:* Effects of painter's materials & media on aesthetic qualities of pictures & on the way they change with age. *Publ:* Auth, The Painter's Companion, Webb Bks, 61; contribr, World Bk Encycl, 71-88; The Painter's Guide to Studio Methods & Materials, Doubleday, 72 & rev ed, Prentice-Hall, 83. *Dealer:* Alpha Gallery 14 Newbury St Boston MA 02116. *Mailing Add:* 109 Rawson Rd Brookline MA 02146

KAYE, DAVID HAIGH
TEXTILE ARTIST, DESIGNER
b Kingston, Ont, 1947. *Study:* Ont Col Art, Toronto, AOCA; Univ Guelph, BA; Cranbrook Acad Art, Bloomfield Hills, Mich, MFA. *Work:* Jean A Chalmers Collection of Contemp Can Crafts, Ont Crafts Coun, Toronto; Can Coun Art Bank, Ottawa; Nat Mus Mod Art, Kyoto, Japan; Massey Found Collection, Ottawa; Prudential Insurance Co Am, Toronto. *Comn:* Linen & Jute (tapestry), comn by P Farlinger, Glouchester News, Toronto, 74; Relief Illusion (tapestry), comn by L Gladstone, Videogenic Corp, Toronto, 81; Relief Illusion Number Two (tapestry), comn by Helena Hernmarck & Niels Diffrient, Ridgefield, Conn, 82. *Exhib:* 100 Yrs: Evolution of the Ontario College of Art, Art Gallery Ont, Toronto, 76; Fiberworks, Cleveland Mus Art, Ohio, 77; Fiber Works: Americas & Japan, Nat Mus Mod Art, Kyoto & Tokyo, Japan, 77 & 78; Engaged Reliefs, Macdonald Stewart Art Ctr, Guelph and traveling, 82-83; Canada Mikrokosma, Barbican Ctr, London, Eng, 82 & Textilmuseum, Krefeld, WGer, 83; Tapices Canadienses Contemporaneos, Palacio de Cristal, Madrid, Spain, 83; Here and Now-Canadian Fibre Art, Cambridge Arts Ctr, Cambridge, Ont, 86; and others. *Awards:* Lt-Gov's Medal, Grad Medal, Ont Col of Art, 72; Can Coun Short-Term Grant, Ottawa, 75 & 78; F Javier Sauza Arts Award, 80; Craftsmen Grant, Ont Arts Coun, Toronto. *Bibliog:* M E Bevlin (auth), Design Through Discovery, Holt, Rinehart & Winston, 77; S W Keene (auth), Toronto artist seeks integrity of idea, materials, technique, Weaving & Fiber News, Homer, NY, 80; J Parkin (auth), Art in Architecture, Visual Arts, Ont, 82. *Mem:* Visual Arts Ont; Ont Crafts Coun. *Media:* Natural Fibers, Mixed Media. *Mailing Add:* 128 Dovercourt Rd Toronto ON M6J 3C4 Canada

KAYE, GEORGE
PAINTER, EDUCATOR
b Malden, Mass, Nov 21, 11. *Study:* Swain Sch Design; Brooklyn Mus Art Sch; Brooklyn Col, BA; City Col New York Grad Sch; NY Univ, MA. *Work:* Philathea Col Mus, London, Ont; Dept Educ Film Libr, Mus Mod Art, New York. *Exhib:* One-man show, Wave Hill, New York, 79; Images Art Gallery, Briarcliff Manor, NY, 81; Trisdonn Contemp Gallery, Nyack, NY; Riverdale Gallery, New York, 85, 86 & 92. *Pos:* Asst dir art, 59-68, dir, 68-73, Bd Educ, New York; consult art, Mayor's Off, New York, 65-66, Dept Pub Events, 66-73; cult dir, Coun Supv & Adminr Bd Educ, New York, 75- *Teaching:* Instr art, New York City Pub Schs, 34-53; chmn dept art, High Sch Music & Art, New York, 53-59; lectr art educ, NY Univ, 60-62; lectr hist art, Pratt Inst, 65-66 & Bronx Community Col, 67-68. *Awards:* Cert Appreciation, New York City Soc Osteopathic Physicians & Surgeons, 70; Citations, NY State Educ Dept, 72; New York Pub Schs, 82. *Bibliog:* J M McCormick (auth), Gallery reviews in New York, Pictures on Exhib, 3/66; J Gollin (auth), Reviews & previews, Art News, 3/66. *Mem:* Nat Art Educ Asn (local chmn, 72); NY

State Art Teachers Asn (New York City liaison, 59-72); New York Sch Art League, NY (trustee, 60-); NY State Coun Adminr Art Educ (vpres, 63-72); NY Soc Exp Study Educ (chmn art sect, 63-72). *Media:* Mixed. *Publ:* Contribr, Color in education, Color Eng, 64; ed, Art & the Young Child, 68; ed, Creative Crafts for Today, 70; coauth & ed, A Child's Story of Vincent Van Gogh, 70; auth, Pastels, Pitman Pub, 74. *Dealer:* Reece Galleries 24 W 57th St New York NY 10019. *Mailing Add:* 3333-F Henry Hudson Pkwy Apt PHC Bronx NY 10463

KAYE, MILDRED ELAINE
PRINTMAKER, INSTRUCTOR
b New York, NY, Sept 24, 29. *Study:* Ind Univ, Ind, 51; Montclair State Col, MA, 77. *Work:* John Herron Inst, Indianapolis; Leonard Bocour Co Collection, Garnerville, NY; Ind Univ Permanent Collection, Bloomington; Montclair State Col Permanent Collection, Upper Montclair, NJ; Am Cult Ctr, Taipei, China. *Exhib:* Nat Asn Jewish Women, Fairleigh Dickinson Univ, Teaneck, NJ, 81; Passaic Community Col, 87; Jacob Javits Ctr, 89; Mari Ann, 92; Weiss Art Ctr, 92; and others. *Pos:* Art ed, Am Book Co, 52-56; graphic designer, Guy-Mar Printing, 65-72. *Teaching:* Instr graphic arts, Art Ctr NJ. *Awards:* First Prize, Mari Ann; Second Prize, Salute Small Works; Second Prize, Pavillion Gallery; and others. *Bibliog:* Segment on exhibit (film), NJ Nightly News, 11/81; Henry Doren (auth), The face of the coin, NJ Artform, 12/81; Art in Orange County, 83; The New York Art Review. *Mem:* Salute to Women in the Arts; Art Ctr Northern NJ; Nat Asn Women Artists; Nat Print Consortium. *Media:* Serigraph, Collograph. *Publ:* Auth, The want ad, 10/80, The other side of the coin, 12/80, The layout and paste-up, self taught, 8/81, Introduction to typography, 10/81 & Introduction to copyfitting, 2/82, NJ Artforms; dir, The Carousel, an Idyl (animated film), 86; Life Cycles: 2 Flatworms (scientific animated film), 86. *Dealer:* Mari Gallery 133 E Prospect Ave Mamaroneck NY 10543. *Mailing Add:* 87 Kern Pl Saddle Brook NJ 07662

KAYSER, THOMAS ARTHUR
CONSULTANT, DESIGNER
b Milwaukee, Wis, Oct 4, 35. *Study:* Layton Sch Art, 58; Cranbrook Acad Art, 59; Mus Mgt Inst, Berkeley, 80. *Collections Arranged:* The American Indian/The American Flag, 76; The Art of Haute Couture, 78; German Expressionism from Western Michigan, 79; Kalamazoo Collects Photography, 80; Super Realism from the Morton G Neumann Collection, 81; New Image/Pattern & Decoration from the Morton G Neumann Collection, 83; A Century of Caring, 86; Light Dreams, Kalamazoo Inst Arts, Mich, 87; The Cutting Edge, 88; John Himmelfarb: Meetings in the Garden, 89. *Pos:* Asst dir, Flint Inst Arts, Mich, 65-78; exec dir, Kalamazoo Inst Arts, Mich 78-89; pres, Tom Kayser & Assoc, 89- *Mem:* Am Asn Mus; Art Mus Asn; Mich Mus Asn; Mich Coun Arts (chmn adv bd); hon mem & founder, Dirs Art Mus Mich; Midwest Mus Asn. *Mailing Add:* 2132 Rambling Rd Kalamazoo MI 49008

KAZ (LAWRENCE KATZMAN)
DESIGNER, CARTOONIST
b Ogdensburg, NY, June 14, 22. *Study:* Univ Pa, BS; Art Students League, with Reginald Marsh. *Pos:* Pres & chmn bd, Kaz Inc, 47-; bus mgr, Cartoonist; chmn, Int Cong Comics; dir, World Bus Coun & Metrop Pres Orgn & Princeton Rev, Nat Cartoonists Soc, currently. *Awards:* Silver Cup of City of Bordighera, Italy, 59; Palma d'Oro, 66; Silver T-Square, Nat Cartoonists Soc. *Mem:* Art Students League; Nat Cartoonists Soc; Cartoonists Guild. *Publ:* Auth & illusr, Nellie the Nurse, 58, Calling Nurse Nellie, 61 & Nellie's Laff-In, 68; auth & illusr, For Doctors Only, Eng, 60; Prima y Dopo i Pasti, Italy, 60; and other bks & cartoons in mags & newspapers throughout the world; illusr, greeting cards & bks, Gibson-Buzza. *Mailing Add:* 101 Central Park W New York NY 10023

KAZ, NATHANIEL
SCULPTOR, INSTRUCTOR
b New York, NY, Mar 9, 17. *Study:* Art Students League, with George Bridgman, Samuel Cashwan & William Zorach. *Work:* Metrop Mus, Whitney Mus & Brooklyn Mus, NY; NY Univ, New York; Larry Aldrich Mus, Conn. *Comn:* Wood relief, US Treas Dept, US Post Off, Hamburg, PA; cast aluminum relief, Binghamton Col, NY; limestone relief carving, Vine St Temple, Nashville, Tenn; Gordian Knot (bronze relief), Northern Valley Englewood Savings Bank, Leona, NJ; four cast bronzes & large wood carving, Temple Beth Emeth, Albany, NY; and others. *Exhib:* Whitney Mus Am Art, New York; Metrop Mus Art, New York; Mus Mod Art, New York; Art Inst Chicago; Pa Acad; Philadelphia Mus Fine Arts, Pa; World's Fairs, Chicago, New York & San Francisco, 39; Univ Nebr; Nat Acad Design, NY, 74, 76, 79, 81, 86, 88. *Teaching:* Instr sculpture, Art Students League of NY, currently. *Awards:* Grant, Nat Inst Arts & Lett; First Prize, Nat Monument Competition, UN Gen Assembly; Sculpture Prize, Brooklyn Mus, NY, 48 & 52; Alfred G B Steel Mem Prize, 148th Ann Exhib, Pa Acad Fine Arts, 53; Medals of Honor, Audubon Artists, 60, 81, 83, 84 & 87; Agop Agopoff Award, Nat Acad Design, 88. *Bibliog:* Ray Wisniewski (dir), A Small Bronze Mask: A Portrait of the Sculptor Nathaniel Kazas Revealed in His Work (film), George C Arcaro, 56. *Mem:* Sculptor's Guild; life mem, Art Students League; Audubon Artists; Nat Sculpture Soc Fel; Assoc Nat Acad Design. *Media:* Bronze, Marble. *Mailing Add:* Art Students League 215 W 57th St New York NY 10019

KAZOR, VIRGINIA ERNST
CURATOR
b Detroit, Mich, Sept 28, 40. *Study:* Univ Southern Calif, BA, MA. *Collections Arranged:* Separate Realities (catalog), 73; 24 From Los Angeles (with catalog), 74; Dreams for Sale: The Great Work of Hollywood Still Photographers 1927-1949, 76; Greene and Greene: Architecture and Related Design of Charles Sumner Greene and Henry Mather Greene, 1894-1934 (with catalog), 77; The Barnsdall Projects: Drawings by Frank Lloyd Wright, 80; Frank Lloyd Wright: Designs for Hollyhock House, 86; Frank Lloyd Wright in Los Angeles 1919-1926: An Architecture for the Southwest (with catalog), 88. *Pos:* Curatorial asst mod art, Los Angeles Co Mus Art, 65-68; cur, Los Angeles Munic Art Gallery, 70-78 & Frank Lloyd Wright's Hollyhock House, 78- *Mem:* Los Angeles Bicentennial Orgn (chmn mus comt, 74-); Soc Archit Hist, Southern Calif Chap (pres, 81-83, exec bd, 83-86). *Mailing Add:* Hollyhock House Los Angeles Munic Art Gallery 4804 Hollywood Blvd Los Angeles CA 90027

KEANE, BIL
CARTOONIST
b Philadelphia, Pa, Oct 5, 22. *Work:* Bil Keane Original Cartoon Collection, Syracuse Univ; Mus Cartoon Art, Greenwich, Conn. *Pos:* Staff artist, Philadelphia Eve Bull, 45-59; creator & nat syndicated cartoonist, The Family Circus & Channel Chuckles. *Awards:* Best Syndicated Panel Cartoonist, Nat Cartoonists Soc, 69, 71 & 74. *Mem:* Nat Cartoonists Soc; Newspaper Comics Coun; Cartoonists Guild. *Media:* Pen and Ink. *Publ:* Auth, Pasghetti & Meat Bulbs, 81, Can I Have a Cookie, 82, Jeffy's Lookin at Me, 82 & Go To Your Room, 82, Fawcett; auth, That Family Circus Feeling, Andrews & McMeel, 82; and many others. *Mailing Add:* 5815 E Joshua Tree Lane Paradise Valley AZ 85253

KEARL, STANLEY BRANDON
SCULPTOR
b Waterbury, Conn, Dec 22, 13. *Study:* Yale Univ, BFA, 41, MFA, 42; Univ Iowa, PhD, 48; study in Rome, Italy, 9 yrs. *Work:* Iowa State Univ; Univ Minn, Duluth; Naz Galeria, Rome, Italy; Nat Mus, Stockholm, Sweden; Mus Goteborg, Sweden; plus others. *Exhib:* One-man shows, Beaux Art Gallery, London, 56, Hudson River Mus, Yonkers, 64, Guild Hall Mus, East Hampton, NY, 82, Ingber Gallery, New York, 84, Benton Gallery, Southampton, NY, 86 & 91, Benson Gallery, Bridgehampton, NY, 88 & Benton Gallery, New York, 91; Penthouse Exhib, 60 & Art Lending Libr Exhib, 65, Mus Mod Art, New York; Whitney Mus Am Art Ann, New York, 62; US Info Agency, Bangkok, Thailand; Grand Cent Mod, New York, 65 & 68; Art in Am Embassies Abroad, selected by Mus Mod Art, New York, 68; Art in Embassies Program, US State Dept, 79; Nat Acad Design, 84. *Pos:* Fulbright exchange prof to Univ Rome, Italy, 49-50. *Teaching:* Lectr, Univ Minn, Duluth, 47-48; lectr, Pratt Inst, 67. *Awards:* Hudson River Mus Sculpture Award, 63; Silvermine Guild Asn Ann Award, 67; Sculpture Award, Ludwig Vogelstein Found Inc, 82-83; First Prize in Sculpture, Guild Hall Mus, East Hampton, NY, 85; Gulf & Western Corp Found Award, 85. *Bibliog:* Michel Seuphor (auth), The Sculpture of This Century, Dictionary of Modern Sculpture, A Swemmer, Ltd, London, 59; New York Art Review, Third Ed, Les Krantz, 88; Dictionary of American Sculptors, Apollo, 84. *Mem:* Col Art Asn Am; Sculptors Guild; Artists Equity Asn. *Media:* Cast Bronze. *Dealer:* Ingber Gallery 415 W Broadway New York NY 10012. *Mailing Add:* 344 Sprain Rd Scarsdale NY 10583

KEARNEY, JOHN (W)
SCULPTOR
b Omaha, Nebr, Aug 31, 24. *Study:* Cranbrook Acad Art, Bloomfield Hills, Mich, 45-48; Univ Stranieri, Perugia, Fulbright Grant Italy & Ital Govt Grant Sculpture, 63-64. *Work:* Norfolk Art Mus, Va; Detroit Children's Mus; Minn Mus, St Paul; Edwin A Ulrich Mus of Art, Wichita, Kans; New Sch Social Res, New York; Standard Oil Bldg & Mus Sci & Indust, Chicago. *Comn:* Large outdoor sculptures, Wichita State Univ, Chicago, Chicago Park Dist, Wichita Coliseum & Lincoln Park Zoo, Chicago, 82; King Ranch, Tex; Interfirst Plaza, Houston; Crown Manufacturing Corp, West Chicago, Ill. *Exhib:* Corcoran Biennial, Washington, DC, 55; Am Fulbright Artists, Palazzo Venezia, Rome, 64; Painting & Sculpture Today, John Herron Mus, Indianapolis, 65; one-man shows, ACA Galleries, New York, 65,69,72,74,76 & 79, Ill Inst of Technol, 76, Ulrich Mus of Art, Wichita, 76 & Contemp Art Workshop, Chicago, 81 & 84; Soc Contemp Am Art Exhib, Art Inst Chicago, 66; two-man show, Art Inst Chicago, 77; Cherrystone Gallery, Wellfleet, Mass, 80 & 92; Goldman-Kraft Gallery, Chicago, 85; Group Gallery, 87, Berta Walker Gallery, Provincetown, Mass, 92. *Pos:* Dir, Contemp Art Workshop, Chicago, 51-90, pres, 92; mem adv bd, Art Inst Art Rental & Sales Gallery, Art Inst of Chicago. *Teaching:* Instr sculpture, Contemp Art Workshop, Chicago, 50-70 & Mundelein Col, 70-71; vis artists, Am Acad in Rome, 85 & 92. *Awards:* Man of Year, Adult Educ Coun Chicago, 62; Fulbright Award, Italy, 63 & 64; Ital Govt Grant, 63 & 64. *Bibliog:* TV docs, ABC-TV, Eyewitness Chicago, 6/5/76, Off the Record (with Rob Weller), 81, CBS-TV, Two on Two, 12/11/83 & WGN-TV, Chicago's Very Own (with Mike Curtis), 1/8/92; articles, People Mag, 10/16/89, Chicago Mag, 6/89, Chicago Sunday Tribune, 5/10/92. *Mem:* Provincetown Art Asn & Mus (vpres, 62-70); Fine Arts Work Ctr, Provincetown (adv bd). *Media:* Bronze, Steel. *Dealer:* ACA Gallery 21 E 67th St New York NY 10021; Contemporary Art Workshop 542 W Grant Pl Chicago IL 60614. *Mailing Add:* 830 Castlewood Terr Chicago IL 60640

KEARNEY, LYNN HAIGH
ADMINISTRATOR, GALLERY DIRECTOR
b Chicago, Ill, Nov 16, 27. *Study:* Northwestern Univ, BA, 49; Harvard Univ/Harvard Bus Sch, 78. *Pos:* Admin dir, Contemp Art Workshop, Chicago, 51-80, co-dir, 80- 91, dir, 92-; trustee, Francis Parker Sch, Chicago, 81-84, Provincetown Art Asn & Mus, 80-84, Dedalus Found (Robert Motherwell Found), 91-92; panelist, Chicago Off Fine Arts. *Bibliog:* Beverly Price (auth),

Off the Record with Rob Weller, ABC/TV documentary, 5/81; Barbara Varro (auth), Man who turns bumpers into beasts, Chicago Sun Times, 3/22/81. *Mem:* Provincetown Arts Asn & Mus (trustee 80-84); Chicago Artists Coalition; Nat Asn Artists. *Specialty:* Young emerging artists, all media. *Publ:* Auth, Bumper Art, Body Engineering J, 10/76. *Mailing Add:* 830 Castlewood Terrace Chicago IL 60640

KEARNS, JAMES JOSEPH
SCULPTOR, PAINTER
b Scranton, Pa, Aug 7, 24. *Study:* Art Inst Chicago, BFA, 51. *Work:* Mus Mod Art & Whitney Mus Am Art, New York; Newark Mus Art; NJ State Mus, Trenton; Nat Collection Fine Arts, Smithsonian Inst & Hirshhorn Mus, Washington, DC; Hirshhorn Mus, Washington, DC. *Exhib:* Nat Inst Arts & Lett, 59; Whitney Mus Am Art Ann, 59-61; Johnson Wax Collection, World Tour, 62-67; Pa Acad Fine Arts, Philadelphia, 64-65; The Figurative Tradition, Whitney Mus Am Art, 80; one-man shows, Rider Col, NJ, 87, Dir Choice, Hunterdon Art Ctr, 87 & Trenton State Mus, 88. *Pos:* Mem bd gov, Skowhegan Sch Painting & Sculpture, 64-70. *Teaching:* Instr drawing, painting & sculpture, Sch Visual Arts, 60-; instr sculpture, Fairleigh-Dickinson Univ, 62-63; instr painting & sculpture, Skowhegan Sch Painting & Sculpture, summers 62-65. *Awards:* Nat Inst Arts & Lett Grant, 59. *Bibliog:* Selden Rodman (auth), Conversations With Artists, Devin Adair, 57 & The Insiders, La State Univ, 60; Lee Nordness (auth), Art USA Now, Viking, 63. *Media:* Bronze, Fiberglass. *Publ:* Illusr, Can these bones live, New Directions, 60; illusr, The Heart of Beethoven, Shorewood Press, 62. *Dealer:* Grippi Gallery 315 E 62nd St New York NY 10021. *Mailing Add:* 452 Rockaway Rd Dover NJ 07801

KEAVENEY, SYDNEY STARR
LIBRARIAN, EDUCATOR
b Grand Rapids, Mich, Nov 12, 39. *Study:* Wellesley Col, BA(art hist), 61; Simmons Col, MS(libr sci), 64; Rutgers Univ, PhD(libr & info sci), S L A Plenum Scholar, 83. *Pos:* Fine arts librn, Boston Pub Libr, Mass, 62-66. *Teaching:* Prof art & archit dept, Pratt Inst Libr, Brooklyn, NY, 66-91, lectr art info & picture resources, 68-80, asst dean libr, 91- *Mem:* Special Libr Asn (pres, NY chap, 73-74); Art Librn Soc NAm; Art Librn Soc NY (chmn, 77). *Res:* Methods in art and architecture research. *Interests:* Modern art, architecture and American art. *Publ:* Auth, American Painting: An Information Guide, 74 & ed, Art and Architecture Information Guide Series, 74-80, Detroit, 14 vols; Contemporary Art Documentation, Scarecrow Press, 86. *Mailing Add:* Pratt Inst Libr Brooklyn NY 11205

KECK, HARDU
PAINTER, ADMINISTRATOR
b Tallinn, Estonia, Apr 6, 40. *Study:* Yale Univ Sch Music & Art, 61; Wesleyan Univ, Middletown, Conn BA, 62; RI Sch Design, Providence, RI, MFA, 64. *Work:* Galleria Nazionale d'Arte Mod, Rome; RI Sch Design Mus Art, Providence; Yale Univ, Conn; pvt collection, Lessing J Rosenwald, Philadelphia; Olivetti Corp, Ivrea, Italy. *Comn:* Fireman's Fountain, Providence, RI, 75; City mural, Old Stone Bank, Providence, RI, 84. *Exhib:* Galleria Nazionale d'Arte Moderna, Rome, 68; Konkretistu, Galerie Umeni, Prague, Czech, 69; Qui Arte Contemporaine, Rome, 69; Sarnano International Graphic Exhib, Italy, 69; Six Artists, Hayden Gallery, Mass Inst Technol, Cambridge, Mass, 73; Choice, Yale Univ, Conn, 77; Estnik Varld festival, Stockholm City Gallery, Swed, 80. *Pos:* VPres, Acad Affairs, RI Sch Design, Providence, 90. *Teaching:* Prof design, RI Sch Design, Providence, 84-90. *Awards:* Second Prize, Acireale Int Invitational, Italy, 68; Purchase Prize, Sarnano Int, Italy, 69 & Am Artists in Italy, US Info Serv, Rome, 75. *Bibliog:* Gordon Brown (auth), article, Arts Mag, 11/73; Jeremy Gilbert-Rolfe (auth), article, Artforum, 12/73; Edith Schloss (auth), article, Int Herald-Tribune, Paris, 79. *Mem:* Provincetown Art Asn; Newport Art Asn. *Media:* Acrylic, Oil. *Publ:* Collabr, Hardu Keck catalog, Galleria II Bilico, 68; auth, Reflections on common and uncommon ground, In: Discipline in Art Education, Brown Univ-RI Sch Design, 86. *Dealer:* Crista Pelin Galerie Lepinrinne 2 Helsinki 93 Finland 00930. *Mailing Add:* 26 Main St Noank CT 06340

KECK, JEANNE GENTRY
PAINTER
b Goochland County, Va, Nov 29, 38. *Study:* William & Mary Col, 58-59; Dayton Art Inst, 74-75; Berkshire Sch Contemp Art, 91; Vt Studio Ctr, 92; special study with Don Dennis, Fred Leach, Nita Engle, Glen Bradshaw, Al Brouillette, Robert Lassig, Ed Betts, Frank Webb, Maxine Masterfield & Marilyn Phillis. *Work:* Green Brokers, Englewood, Colo; Ford Aerospace & Communication Corp, Hanover, Md; Fed Reserve Bank, Baltimore, Md; Anne Arundel Hosp, Annapolis, Md; Nation's Bank, Charlotte, NC; and others. *Exhib:* One-person show, Springfield Art Mus, Ohio, 78-79, Twentieth Century Gallery, Williamsburg, Va, 86, Md Fed Arts, Annapolis, 84 & 87, C Grimaldis Gallery, Baltimore, Md, 89 & Md Hall Creative Arts, Annapolis, 89; Am Watercolor Soc, Salmagundi Club, New York, 84; San Diego Watercolor Soc Int Exhib, Grossmont Col Art Gallery, El Cajon, Calif, 85; Ga Watercolor Soc 6th Int Exhib, 85; La Watercolor Soc, 15th & 16th Int Exhibs, Int Trademart, New Orleans, 85-86; Southern Watercolor Soc, Oklahoma City, 86; Ruby Blakeney Gallery, Savage Md, 91; Virginia Lynch Gallery, Tiverton, RI, 92. *Teaching:* Instr painting, Fairborn Art Asn, Ohio, 77-81; instr watercolor, brush & palette, Wright-Patterson AFB, Ohio, 80. *Awards:* Bronze Medal, Ohio Watercolor Soc, 84; Silver Award, Mid Atlantic Regional, 84; Second Award, Southern Watercolor Soc, 86. *Bibliog:* Critics Corner (tv Show), PBS, Baltimore, 85; Mark St John Erickson (auth), Economy & expression, Williamsburg Gazette, Va, 86; Marilyn Phillis (auth), Watercolor Techniques for Releasing the Creative Spirit, 92. *Mem:* Md Fedn Art (mem bd dirs, 82-86); Ohio Watercolor Soc; Baltimore Watercolor Soc (juror, 84); Ga Watercolor Soc; Pa Soc Watercolor Painters; Annapolis Watercolor Club (pres, 83-84, vpres, 84-86). *Media:* Acrylic, Oil. *Publ:* Auth, Making Color Sing, Watson-Guptill, 86. *Dealer:* C Grimaldis Gallery Baltimore MD; Virginia Lynch Gallery Tiverton RI. *Mailing Add:* 1117 Kalmia Ct Crownsville MD 21032

KECK, SHELDON WAUGH
EDUCATOR, CONSERVATOR
b Utica, NY, May 30, 10. *Study:* Harvard Univ, BA, 32; Fogg Art Mus, apprentice in restoration, 32-33; Hamilton Col, DFA, 76. *Pos:* Conservator, Brooklyn Mus, 34-61; private consult & lectr painting conservation. *Teaching:* Dir art conserv, NY Univ Conserv Ctr, 61-65, prof fine arts, 64-66; prof art conserv, Cooperstown Grad Progs, State Univ NY Col Oneonta, 69-81; retired, 81. *Awards:* Fulbright Fel, 59; Guggenheim Fel, 59-60. *Mem:* Cooperstown Art Asn; Int Inst Conserv Hist & Artistic Works (mem coun, pres, 74-80); Int Coun Mus; Am Inst Conserv Hist & Artistic Works (pres, 72-74). *Publ:* Auth, numerous articles in professional journals & art periodicals on exam & conservation of paintings. *Mailing Add:* 31 River St Cooperstown NY 13326

KEECH, JOHN H
PAINTER
b Winston-Salem, NC, May 28, 43. *Study:* Washington Univ, BFA, 65; Univ Iowa, MFA, 68. *Work:* Masur Mus Art, Monroe, La; The Stephens Collection & Ark Art Ctr, Little Rock; Muhlenberg Col, Allentown, Pa. *Exhib:* Hassam Purchase Fund Exhib, Am Acad & Inst Arts & Lett, New York, 78; Glass Backwards, Kohler Mus Art, Sheboygan, Wis, 79; Third ann Fla Nat, Fla State Univ, Tallahassee, 88; In Search of Am Experience, Fed Plaza, New York, 89; New Am Talent, Laguna Gloria Art Mus, Austin, Tex, 89; Vehicles for New Forms/New Functions, Arrowmont Gallery, Gatlinburg, Tenn, 90. *Teaching:* Asst prof painting & drawing, Ark State Univ, 68-78, assoc prof, 78-89, prof, 89- *Awards:* Best of Show, 10th Monroe Nat Ann Exhib, Masur Mus Art, La, 73; Merit Awards, Multiple Media Exhib, Erie Art Ctr, 74 & Spar Nat Art Exhib, 83; Third Ann Fla Nat, Fla State Univ, Tallahassee; New Am Talent, Austin, Tex, 89; 22nd Bradley Nat Print & Drawing Exhib, Peoria, Ill; Nat Endowment for Arts Fel Award, Mid-Am Art Alliance, 92. *Media:* Oil, Plexiglass. *Publ:* Auth, Jazz-Eye, private publ; contrib, Two Untitled Works, River City Review, 85. *Mailing Add:* PO Box 43 State University AR 72467

KEELER, DAVID BOUGHTON
PAINTER
b Cleveland, Ohio, Feb 11, 31. *Study:* Cleveland Inst Art, dipl; Case Western Reserve Univ, Cleveland. *Work:* Cleveland Inst Art, Ohio; Cleveland Art Asn; Nat Mus Am Art, Washington, DC. *Exhib:* Cleveland Mus Art Regional, 60-63, 65, 67, 74 & 76; Butler Inst Am Art Nat, Youngstown, Ohio, 60 & 62; Corcoran Gallery of Art, Washington, DC, 65 & 69; one-man shows, 323 Gallery, Alexandria, Va, 65; Studio Gallery, Alexandria, Va, 66; Barbara Fielder Gallery, Washington, DC, 76; Wolfe St Gallery, Alexandria, 77; Studio Gallery, Washington, DC, 83; Curzon Gallery, Boca Raton, Fla, 89 & 91; Soc Four Arts Nat, Palm Beach, Fla, 91. *Pos:* Preparor & exhib designer, Cleveland Mus Art, 61-64; tech asst to cur, Nat Collection Fine Arts, Washington, DC, 66-71 & chief exhib & design, 72-85. *Bibliog:* Andrew Hudson (auth), article, Washington Post, 10/65 & 10/66; Ben Forgey (auth), article, Washington Evening Star, 4/76. *Media:* All Media. *Mailing Add:* 399 NE 20th St Boca Raton FL 33431

KEELING, HENRY CORNELIOUS
PAINTER, EDUCATOR
b St Albans, WVa, Sept 4, 23. *Study:* Pratt Inst, BFA(interior design); NY Univ; Hans Hofmann Sch Fine Art, New York; Art Students League; Marshall Univ, MA(fine art); also with Bernard Klonis, Reuben Tam, Leo Manso & Victor Kandell. *Work:* Parkersburg Art Ctr, Parkersburg, WVa; Charleston Art Gallery of Sunrise, WVa; WVa Arts & Humanities Coun, Charleston; Herbert M Rothchild Collection, New York; WVa State Col. *Comn:* Three paintings & mural, Consolidated Gas Corp, Clarksburg, WVa, 67; two paintings, Roanoke Indust Savings & Loan Corp, Va, 68; mural, New River Bank & Trust Co, Oak Hill, WVa, 80. *Exhib:* Brooklyn Mus Art Sch Ann, 54 & 55; Invitational, Parkersburg Art Ctr, 76-77; Invitational Relig Show, WVa State Col, 77; one-man shows, Gallery 4, Charleston, WVa, 78, 80 & 81, Morris Harvey Col, 78 & Ghent Gallery, Norfolk, Va, 80. *Teaching:* Assoc prof & head dept, Univ Charleston, formerly. *Awards:* Purchase Awards for Graphics, Charleston Art Gallery, 71 & WVa Arts & Humanities, 71; Merit Award, Parkersburg Art Ctr, 77. *Mem:* Provincetown Art Asn; WVa Allied Artists. *Media:* Watercolor, Collage. *Mailing Add:* 4410 Washington Ave SE Charleston WV 25304

KEENA, JANET LAYBOURN
PAINTER
b St Joseph, Mo, Sept 11, 28. *Study:* Univ Kans; Univ Calif, Los Angeles; Am Acad Art, Chicago. *Work:* Albrecht Mus, St Joseph, Mo; Park Col, Parkville, Mo; Dart Drug Hq, Los Angeles. *Exhib:* Albrecht Art Mus, 72; Ark Art Ctr, Little Rock, 72; Int Traveling Show Americana, Am Art by Mid-West Artists, 72; Richmond Mus, Va, 79; Nat Arts Club, New York. *Teaching:* Artist-in-residence, William Jewell Col, 73. *Awards:* First Publ Award, Fine Arts Discovery Mag, 70; First Prize, Renwick Mus Award, Nat Arts Club Ann, Mo State Fair, 71 & 72 & Northern Va Community Col. *Bibliog:* Donald Hoffmann (auth), Art in Mid-America, Kansas City Star, 5/69 & 5/74; Jean Trusty (auth), Art, Kansas City Squire Mag, 4/71; R C Seine (ed), Contemporary American Artists, La Rev Mod, Paris, 11/71. *Mem:* Nat Arts Club, New York; Washington Women's Art Asn. *Media:* Oil, Watercolor. *Mailing Add:* 7501 Range Rd Alexandria VA 22306

KEENE, PAUL
PAINTER
b Philadelphia, Pa, Aug 24, 20. *Study:* Philadelphia Mus Sch & Univ Pa, 39-41; Tyler Sch Art, Temple Univ, 45-48; Acad Julien, Paris, 49-51; Whitney Fel, 52-54. *Work:* Pa Acad Fine Arts, Philadelphia; Philadelphia Mus; Howard Univ; Morgan State Col; Bowdoin Col. *Comn:* History of University (mural), Johnson C Smith Univ; medal for Am Negro Commemorative Soc, Philadelphia. *Exhib:* Pa Acad Fine Arts, 52-53 & 68-69, Lagos Mus, Nigeria, 61; Master Series, Carnegie Libr, Pittsburgh, 70; one-man show, Festac-Lagos, Nigeria, 79; Painting Show, Morgan State Univ, Baltimore, Md, 80; Alfred Deshong Mus, Widener Univ, 81. *Teaching:* Prof painting, Centre D'Art, Port-au-Prince, Haiti, 52-53; assoc prof drawing & painting, Philadelphia Col Art, 54-68, chmn basic art prog, 63-66; prof drawing & design, Bucks Co Community Col, Newton, 68- *Bibliog:* Briskin (auth), New talent art in America, Art in Am, 54; Lewis-Waddy (auth), Black artists on art, Contemp Crafts, 71. *Media:* Mixed. *Mailing Add:* 2843 Bristol Rd Warrington PA 18976

KEENER, POLLY LEONARD
ILLUSTRATOR, WRITER
b Akron, Ohio, July 14, 46. *Study:* Conn Col, New London, BA, 68; Kent State Univ, 67; Princeton Univ, NJ with Kurt Weitzman, 68. *Work:* Stan Hywet Hall Found & West Point Market, Akron, Ohio. *Exhib:* Lyman Allan Mus, New London, Conn, 68; 13th Ann Baycrafters Show, Baycrafters Gallery, Bay Village, Ohio, 75; Group Christmas Show, Mus Nat Hist, Cleveland, Ohio, 79; Our Own Show, Soc Illus Mus Am Illus, New York, 91. *Pos:* Pres, Keener Corp, Akron, Ohio, 77-; mem, bd trustees, Stan Hywet Hall Found, Akron, 79-; part-time graphic designer, freelance, 79- *Teaching:* Instr, soft sculpture, Univ Akron, 79-84, cartooning, 79-; cartooning, Northeastern Ohio Univs Col Med, 92. *Awards:* Woman of the year, in Creative Arts, Women's Hist Week, 89. *Bibliog:* Maggi Anderson (auth), Food for thought, West Side Leader, 2/16/88; Sally Carter (auth), No age limit for cartooning says Akron's Polly Keener, Sr Focus Newspaper, 7/92; Christopher Noxon (auth), Professor Cartoon, The Cape Codder, 8/4/92. *Mem:* Soc Illusrs, New York; Col Art Asn, New York; Nat Cartoonists Soc, New York. *Media:* Pen and Ink, Watercolor. *Res:* History, techniques & psychology of cartooning. *Publ:* illusr, Eat Dessert First, Fairlawn Press, 87; auth, Interview with Mischa Richter, Cartoonists Profiles Mag, 88; illusr, It's Our Serve, Jr League, Long Island, 89; auth, Cartooning, Prentice Hall, 92; illus, 80 & Great Ideas for Making Money At Home, Walker & Co, New York, 92; and others. *Mailing Add:* 37 Elmdale Ave Akron OH 44313

KEENEY, ALLEN LLOYD
EDUCATOR, MUSEUM DIRECTOR
b Salt Lake City, Utah, July 19, 33. *Study:* Colo Inst Art; Univ Wyo, BA; studied design with Robert Russin. *Comn:* Three hist landscapes, Sweetwater Co Mus, Green River, Wyo, 70; Western design, Antler Hotel, Newcastle, Wyo, 60. *Exhib:* One-man shows, Wyo Artists's Asn, 60 & Community Fine Arts Ctr, 67. *Collections Arranged:* 353 original art works owned by Sch Dist Number One, Sweetwater Co, Wyo. *Pos:* Asst dir, Community Fine Arts Ctr, 66-69, dir, 70-91; retired. *Teaching:* Instr art, Weston Co Pub Schs, 57-60; chmn dept art, Sch Dist Number One, Sweetwater Co, Wyo, 60-91; retired. *Awards:* Merit Award, Sweetwater Co Libr Asn. *Mem:* Wyo Art Educ Asn (vpres, 68-69, pres, 69-70); Nat Art Educ Asn; Colo & Wyo Mus Asn; Wyo Artist's Asn; Sweetwater Co Art Guild. *Media:* Oil, Sculpture. *Collection:* North American art 1900-1986. *Mailing Add:* 1509 Sublet St Rock Springs WY 82901

KEERL, BAYAT
PAINTER, PHOTOGRAPHER
b Basel, Switz, March 21, 48, US citizen. *Study:* Layton Sch Art, Milwaukee, Wis, BFA, 70; Rutgers Univ, MFA, 72. *Work:* Am Express Co, World Hq, New York; Union Bank of Switz, New York; Zimmerli Art Mus, New Brunswick, NJ. *Awards:* Nat Endowment Arts, 81 & 87. *Bibliog:* Ann Wooster (auth), Photo/Alchemy (exhib catalog), Freidus Gallery, 82; Jill Kyle (auth), Painted Photography, Spot Mag, 86; Jo Ann Lewis (auth), Galleries, Washington Post, 88. *Media:* Oil on Photograph. *Mailing Add:* 71 Mercer St New York NY 10012

KEEVER, KIM
PAINTER, PRINTMAKER
b New York, NY, May 13, 50. *Study:* Old Dominion Univ, Norfolk, Va, BS, 71. *Work:* Mus Mod Art, New York; Chrysler Mus, Norfolk, Va. *Exhib:* Davidson Nat Print Exhib, Davidson, NC, 75; New York, Centro Arte & Communication, Buenos Aires, Arg, 84; Irene Leach Exhib, Chrysler Mus, Norfolk, Va, 86; Recent Acquisitions, Mus Mod Art, New York, 86; M-13 Gallery, New York, 86; Brody's Gallery, Washington, DC, 88. *Bibliog:* Everett Potter (auth), Kim Keever & Promises, Promises, Arts Mag, 86; Klaus Ottman (auth), Supermannerism, Flash Art, 86. *Media:* Acrylic, Oil; Block Printing. *Publ:* Auth-illusr, Yes & No, Prints & Poetry, Kaldewey Press, 82. *Dealer:* M-13 Gallery 72 Greene St New York NY 10012. *Mailing Add:* 204 E Seventh St New York NY 10009

KEHLMANN, ROBERT
CRITIC
b Brooklyn, NY, March 9, 42. *Study:* Antioch Col, Ohio, BA, 63; Univ Calif, Berkeley, MA, 66. *Work:* Corning Mus Glass, NY; Leigh Yawkey Woodson Art Mus, Wausau, Wis; Hessisches Landes Mus, WGer; Am Craft Mus, NY; Mus Art Decoratifs, Lausanne, Switz; Hokkaido Mus Mod Art, Japan; Mus Für Zeitgenössische Glasmalerei, Langen, WGer; Toledo Mus Art, Ohio. *Exhib:* Americans in Glass, Leigh Yawkey Woodson Art Mus, Wausau, Wis, 78 & 81; New Stained Glass, Mus Contemp Crafts, New York, 78; New Glass, Corning Mus Glass, NY, 79; International Directions in Glass Art, Art Gallery Western Australia, Perth, 82; Sculptural Glass, Tucson Mus Art, Ariz, 83; Oakland Mus, Calif, 86; Craft Today USA, Am Craft Mus, New York, 89-90; Hist Am Glass, Corning Mus, Glass, New York, 89. *Collections Arranged:* Current Trends in Glass (auth, catalog), Walnut Creek Civic Art Gallery, Calif, 80; Emerging Artists in Glass (auth, catalog), Calif Crafts Mus, Palo Alto, 81; Glass Art Nat, Downie Mus Art, Calif, 86. *Pos:* Contributing ed, Glass Art Mag, Oakland, Calif, 75-76; ed, Glass Art Soc J, Seattle, Wash, 81-84; contrib ed, New Glass Work Mag, 87-88. *Teaching:* Instr Glass Design, Calif Col Arts & Crafts, Oakland, Calif, 78-80, 90 & Pilchuck Glass Ctr, Stanwood, Wash, 78-80; instr design, Miasa Bunka Ctr, Miasa, Japan, 85. *Awards:* Craftsman's Fel Grant, Nat Endowment Arts, 77; Art Critic's Fel Grant, Nat Endowment Arts, 78. *Bibliog:* Grace Glueck (auth), Art People, The New York Times, 2/10/78; Lindsay Stamm Shapiro (auth), American Stained Glass now, Craft Horizons, 2/78; Johannes Schreiter (auth), Die Glasbilder von Robert Kehlmann, Neues Glas, 3/81; Interview: Robert Kehlmann, Stained Glass Art, Japan, fall 85; Paul Smith (auth), Poetry of the Physical, Craft Today, 86; Susanne K Frantz (auth), Contemp Glass, H N Abrams, 89. *Mem:* Glass Art Soc (bd dir, 80-84 & 89-92). *Media:* Glass. *Res:* Twentieth century stained glass. *Publ:* Auth, Schaffrath: Stained glass and mosaic, Craft Horizons, 2/78; Stained glass in the USA today, Canada Crafts, 10-11/78; Glasfenster der siebziger jahre, Kunst Und Kirche, Linz, Austria, 4/79; The legacy of Johan Thorn Prikker, 4/15/85 & Glass of the 80s, 8/87, Am Craft; 20th Century Stained Glass: A New Definition, Kyoto Shoin Co Ltd, Kyoto, Japan, 92. *Dealer:* Dorothy Weiss Gallery 256 Sutter St San Francisco CA 94108. *Mailing Add:* 2207 Rose St Berkeley CA 94709

KEHOE, PATRICE
PAINTER
b Atlanta, Ga, Feb 13, 52. *Study:* Duke Univ, 70-72; Univ of NC, Chapel Hill, BFA, 73; Wash Univ, St Louis, Mo, MFA, 77. *Exhib:* 22nd Area Exhib: Works on Paper, Corcoran Gallery of Art, Washington, DC, 80 & The Washington Show, 85; Maryland Biennial, Baltimore Mus Art, Md, 80; Twenty from Washington, Univ of Houston, Tex, 82; one-person shows, Osuna Gallery, Washington, DC, 83, 86 & 88; Ten Washington, DC Painters, Southeastern Ctr Contemp Art, Winston-Salem, NC, 86; two-person show with W C Richardson, Va Mus Fine Arts, Richmond, 86; Recollections: Washington Artists at WPA, 1975-88, DC, 88; Works of Distinction: Selected Donations and Lends, Nat Mus Women Arts, Washington, DC, 91. *Teaching:* Assoc prof painting & drawing, Univ of Md, College Park, 77- *Awards:* First Prize, Md Biennial, Baltimore Mus of Art, 80; Louis Comfort Tiffany Award, 82; Visual Arts Fel Grant, Nat Endowment Arts, 88. *Bibliog:* Lee Fleming (auth), The Washington show, Art News, 85; Jane Addams Allen, Am impressive showcase for DC duo, The Washington Times, 86; Alice Thornson (auth), Kehoe's biological motifs continue their evolution, The Washington Times, 88; Howard Risati (auth), Patrice Kehoe, Artforum, 91; Mary McCoy (auth), A shift of energy, an earthly glow, Washington Post, 90. *Mem:* Washington Project for the Arts, DC. *Dealer:* Jones Troyer Fitzpatrick Gallery Washington DC 20009. *Mailing Add:* 4309 Sheridan St University Park MD 20782

KEISTER, STEVE (STEPHEN LEE)
SCULPTOR
b Lancaster, Pa, Aug 22, 49. *Study:* Tyler Sch Art, Philadelphia & Rome, BFA, 70, MFA, 72. *Work:* Whitney Mus Am Art; Mus Contemp Art, Chicago; Dallas Mus Fine Arts; Lannan Found, West Palm Beach, Fla; Mus Contemp Art, Los Angeles; High Mus Art, Atlanta; Milwaukee Art Mus. *Exhib:* New Work-New York, New Mus, 78; Eight Sculptors, Albright-Knox Gallery, Buffalo, 79; solo exhib, Options, Mus Contemp Art, Chicago, 80; Biennial, 81, Selected Painting & Sculpture Acquired Since 1978, 82 & Minimalism to Expressionism, 83, Whitney Mus Am Art; Beelden-Sculpture 1983, Rotterdam Arts Coun, Neth, 83; Language, Drama, Source & Vision, New Mus, New York, 83. *Teaching:* Instr, Sch Visual Arts & New York Univ. *Awards:* Pollock Krasner Found Scholar, 87; Nat Endowment Arts Fellowship, 88. *Bibliog:* Peggy Kutzen (auth), article in Arts Mag, 5/81; Prudence Carlson (auth), Otherworldly geometrics, Art in Am, 10/81; Jeanne Silverthorne (auth), article in Artforum, 1/83. *Media:* Plywood, Miscellaneous Media. *Publ:* Steve Keister: Recent Work (exhib catalog), 88; Steve Keister: Sculpture (exhib catalog), Nina Freudenheim Gallery, Buffalo, 90. *Mailing Add:* 46 Laight St New York NY 10013

KELDER, DIANE M
HISTORIAN, CRITIC
b New York, NY, May 23, 34. *Study:* Queens Col, AB, 55; Univ Chicago, MA, 57; Bryn Mawr Col, PhD, 66. *Collections Arranged:* Drawings by the Bibiena Family, Philadelphia Mus Art, 68 & Finch Col Mus, 68; Five Centuries of Stage Design, Finch Col Mus, 71. *Pos:* Asst cur prints & drawings, Philadelphia Mus Art, 66-67; ed, Art J, 73-80. *Teaching:* Instr art hist, Queens Col, 60- & Finch Col, 67-71; prof art hist, Col Staten Island, 71-; Grad Ctr, CUNY, 79- *Awards:* Fanny Workman Fel, Am Asn Univ Women, 62-63; Jr Humanist Fel, Nat Endowment Humanities, 71; Ingram Merrill Found Award, 72; Gladys Krieble Delmas Found, 78, 82. *Mem:* Int Art Critics Asn; Col Art Asn. *Interests:* Baroque stage design; late 18th century painting; graphic art from the 16th through the 20th centuries; French Impressionism. *Publ:* Auth, Rembrandt, McGraw-Hill, 70; The French Impressionists and Their Century, 70 & ed, Stuart Davis, 71, Praeger; contribr, Ferdinando Galli Bibiena's Architettura Civile, Blom, 71; The Great Book of French Impressionism, Abbeville, 80; The Great Book of Post-Impressionism, Abbeville, 86. *Mailing Add:* c/o Col of Staten Island 130 Stuyvesant Pl Staten Island NY 10301

KELEMEN, PAL
HISTORIAN
b Budapest, Hungary, Apr 24, 1894; US citizen. *Study:* Univ Ariz, DHL; Univ Budapest; Univ Munich; Univ Paris; mus res in Budapest, Vienna, Florence, London, Madrid & Seville. *Pos:* Survey trips, US Dept State, Mex, Cent Am & Europe, 33-; mem comn for protection & salvage of artistic & hist monuments in war areas, World War II. *Teaching:* Lectr, Nat Gallery Art, Metrop Mus Art & other mus & univs; spec lect tour, US Dept State, Europe & the Near East. *Awards:* Comdr, Order of Merit, Ecuador. *Bibliog:* Pal Kelemen (auth), SMRC, Ariz State Mus, 81. *Mem:* Fel Royal Anthrop Inst; mem var sci socs in US, Latin Am & Europe. *Res:* Early Christian art; pre-Columbian and colonial art in Latin America. *Publ:* Auth, Ancient, Colonial Art of the Americas, Dutch, 62, Ger, 64, Fr, 65, Span, 67, Port, 69; auth, Art of the Americas, 69 & 70, Hungarian, 80; auth, Peruvian Colonial Painting, 71; contribr, Folk Baroque in Mexico, 74, Vanishing Art of the Americas, 77 & Stepchild of the Humanities, 79, Encycl Britannica, Stauffacher's World Art History & others. *Mailing Add:* 1241 Silverado St La Jolla CA 92037

KELLAR, JEFF
SCULPTOR
b Washington, DC, Sept 25, 49. *Study:* Univ Pa, BA, 71, film with Rudy Burkhardt. *Work:* Univ S Maine, Gorham, Maine; Portland Mus Art, Maine. *Comn:* Arc Temple Bet Ha-Am, Portland, Maine, 87; exterior sculpture for the Percent for Art Prog, Kennebunk Sch System, Kennebunk, Maine, 90; interior sculpture, Sanford Sch System, Sanford, Maine, 90; interior sculpture, Freeport Sch System, Maine, 92; interior sculpture, Belfast Sch System, Maine, 92. *Exhib:* Artist Designed Furniture, Norton Gallery Art, W Palm Beach, Fla, 86; Ten, Portland Mus Art, Portland, Maine, 88; Interstices, Farnsworth Mus, Rockland, Maine, invitational, 89; Art That Works, travelling exhib, 14 mus across the country, 90-93; solo exhib, Gallery Camino Real, Boca Raton, Fla, 91; and others. *Pos:* Adv panel, Maine Arts Comn, 88-91; Gov's Adv Bd, Maine Aspirations Compact, 88. *Teaching:* Artist-in-Residence, Sculpture, Univ S Maine, Gorham, 87; Instr, Haystack Mountain Sch Crafts, 87. *Awards:* Daphne Award, Indust Design Award, Hardwood Inst, 81; Design Award, Maine Times Design, Maine Times, 87. *Bibliog:* Sherry Miller (auth), Ten, Portland Mus Art, Art New Eng, 6/88; Shirley Jacks (auth), rev, Art New Eng, 7-8/90; Martha Severins (auth) essay, Portland Mus Art Bull, 11/90; and others. *Mem:* Int Sculpture Ctr. *Media:* Miscellaneous Media. *Publ:* Contrib, Designing Furniture, Taunton Press, 89; Maine Art Now, Dog Ear Press, 90. *Dealer:* Barridoff Gallery 26 Free St Portland ME 04101-3926. *Mailing Add:* PO Box 4770 Portland ME 04112

KELLAR, MARTHA ROBBINS
PAINTER, INSTRUCTOR
b Alamogordo, NMex, Nov 23, 49. *Study:* Murray State Univ, Ky, 67-69; NMex State Univ, Alamogordo, spec study with Ramon Froman, Albert Handell, David Leffel, Sherrie McGraw, 79-81. *Comn:* Oil portraits of Dean Fred Downs, Dean Bryce Brisbane & Dean Gus Guthrie, Col Bus Admin & Econ, NMex State Univ, Las Cruces, 92. *Exhib:* Pastel Soc Am Nat Open, Nat Arts Club, New York, 85-86 & 87; Salmagundi Club Non-Member Exhib, New York, 86 & 87; Catherine Lorillard Wolfe Art Club Ann Exhib, Nat Arts Club, New York, 87. *Teaching:* Instr pastel, oil painting, Kellar Art Studio, La Luz, NMex, 86-; instr figure drawing, Eastern NMex Univ/Ruidoso, NMex, 91- *Awards:* Andrews/Nelson/Whitehead, Pastel Soc Am Nat Open, 85; J B McReynolds Mem, Salmagundi Club Non-Members Exhib, 87; Degas Award, Pastel Soc West Coast Nat Open, 89. *Bibliog:* Steve Wall (auth), Unity, harmony & clarity: the life and work of Martha Kellar, Mountain Passages Mag, winter/spring 92. *Mem:* Pastel Soc Am; Pastel Soc West Coast. *Media:* Oils, Pastels. *Dealer:* Canyon Gallery Carrizo Canyon Rd PO Box 1897 Ruidoso NM 88345; Edie's 2001 Triplett St Owensboro KY 42303. *Mailing Add:* Three Robin Lane La Luz NM 88337

KELLER, FRANK S
PAINTER
b Minneapolis, Minn, Aug 31, 51. *Study:* Creighton Univ, Nebr, 69-70; Univ Minn, Minneapolis, BA, BFA, 74; Pratt Inst, MFA, 77. *Work:* Phillips Collection; Mus Art, Carnegie Inst, Pittsburgh; Mus Fine Arts, Houston; Edwin A Ulrich Mus Art, Wichita, Kans. *Exhib:* Minnesota Artists, Rochester Art Ctr, 72 & 74; Baltimore Mus Art, 75; solo exhibs, 57th St Galleries, New York; Ariz Nat Painting Exhib, Scottsdale Ctr Arts, 78; Art in Embassies, Dept State, Am Embassy, Bonn, WGer, 79-; American Works on Paper: 100 Years of American Art History Traveling Exhib, 83-85. *Awards:* Purchase Award, Baltimore Mus Art, 75. *Bibliog:* Ann Sargent Wooster (auth), article, Art News, 5/77; Peter Frank (auth), article, Village Voice, 1/2/78; Christa Lancaster (auth), Frank Keller: Tending the formal tradition, Arts Mag, 11/81. *Mem:* Visual Artists & Galleries Asn. *Media:* Drawing. *Publ:* Auth, Frank Keller-Paintings 1975-1981 (exhib catalog), 81. *Mailing Add:* 57 Thompson St 6A New York NY 10012

KELLER, MARTHA
PAINTER
Study: Boston Univ, 66-68; Tyler Sch Art, 67; Maryland Inst Col Art, BFA, 70. *Exhib:* One-man shows, Lepofsky Gallery, Baltimore, Md, 74, Johns Hopkins Univ, Baltimore, 76, Albuquerque Arts Ctr, Univ NMex, 78, Whitaker Found Mus, Palermo, Italy, 82 & Stephen Rosenberg Gallery, New York, 86, 87 & 89; Biennial, Baltimore Mus Art, 77; PS 1, Inst Art & Urban Resources, Arte Fiera Internationale, Bologna, Italy, 80; Small Works, 80 Washington Sq East Gallery, New York, 81; Abstract Presence, Defacto Gallery, New York, 85; The Gold Show, Genovese Gallery, Boston, 88. *Awards:* Ludwig Vogelstein Found, 87; MacDowell Colony Fel, 89; NY Found Arts Fel, 89; Nat Endowment Arts, 89. *Bibliog:* Eleanor Heartney (auth), ArtNews, 2/88; Stephen Westfall (auth), Art in America, 3/88. *Mem:* Abstr Am Artists Asn. *Mailing Add:* c/o Stephen Rosenberg Gallery 115 Wooster St New York NY 10012

KELLEY, DEBORAH MAVERICK
PAINTER
b Detroit, Mich, Jan 15, 53. *Study:* L'Accademia di Belli Arti, Perugia, Italy, 74; Sch Art, Univ Mich, BFA, 75; Tyler Sch Art, Temple Univ, MFA, 79. *Work:* Prudential Life, New York, NY. *Exhib:* Nature as Image, Orgn Independent Artists, New York, 84; 17 Artists View the City, Park Atrium, Olympia York, New York, 84; Artist's Toys, Vanderwoude Tananbaum Gallery, New York, 85 & 86; Fifth Annual Exhib, Mus Hudson Highlands, Cornwall-on-Hudson, 86; Sragow Gallery, New York, 86. *Awards:* Ellen Battel Stoekel Fel, Yale Univ, 75; Artist-in-Residence, Millay Colony Arts, 86. *Mem:* New York Artists Equity; Orgn Independent Artists. *Media:* Oil; Charcoal. *Dealer:* Sragow Gallery 436 E 11th St New York NY 10009. *Mailing Add:* 121 Cedar St San Antonio TX 78210

KELLEY, DONALD CASTELL
GALLERY DIRECTOR
b Boston, Mass. *Study:* Sch of Mus Fine Arts, Boston, dipl; Yale Univ, BFA & MFA. *Pos:* Gallery dir, Boston Atheneum, 68- *Interests:* Work of 20th century American contemporary artists and photographers. *Mailing Add:* Boston Atheneum 10 1/2 Beacon St Boston MA 02108

KELLEY, DONALD WILLIAM
PRINTMAKER, SCULPTOR
b Tulsa, Okla, July 20, 39. *Study:* Univ Tulsa, with Alexandre Hogue & Duayne Hatchett, BA, 62; Claremont Grad Sch, MFA, 66; Univ NMex with Garo Antreasian, 66; Tamarind Lithography Workshop, Los Angeles, 66-69. *Work:* Cincinnati Art Mus; Los Angeles Co Mus Art, Los Angeles; Mus Mod Art, New York; Norton Simon Mus Art, Pasadena, Calif; Nat Gallery Art, Washington, DC; Univ NMex Art Mus, Albuquerque, NMex. *Exhib:* One-man shows, Not in New York Gallery, Cincinnati, 75, Antioch Col, 75 & Cincinnati Invitational Awards Exhib, Cincinnati Art Mus, 75; Alternative Landscape, Contemp Art Ctr, Cincinnati, 72; Environ Sculpture--Proposals for Sawyer Point Park, Contemp Arts Ctr, Cincinnati, Ohio, 77; Persistent Vision, Claremont Grad Sch, 85. *Teaching:* Assoc prof art, Univ Cincinnati, 69-75, currently; vis artist lithography, Antioch Col, 75. *Bibliog:* Jules Engel & Ivan Dryer (auth), Look of a lithographer (film), Tamarind Lithography Workshop, 69; Kristin L Spangenberg (auth), Cincinnati Invitational Awards Exhibition: Drawings and Prints, Midwest Art, 3/75. *Media:* Lithography. *Mailing Add:* c/o Fine Arts Dept Univ Cincinnati 839 Rm C Dept Art & Archit Cincinnati OH 45221

KELLEY, MIKE
PAINTER
b Detroit, Mich, 1954. *Study:* Univ Mich, Ann Arbor, BFA, 76; Calif Inst Art, Valencia, MFA, 78. *Exhib:* Word Works, Minneapolis Col Art & Design and Walker Art Ctr, Minneapolis, 83; Biennial, 85, Recent Drawing, 88 & Whitney Biennial, 89, Whitney Mus Am Art, New York; Currents 7: Work in Action, Milwaukee Art Mus, Concord Gallery, NY, 85; Spectrum: Natural Settings, Corcoran Gallery Art, Washington, DC, 86; Contemp Diptychs: Divided Visions, Whitney Mus Am Art, Conn, 87; Avant-Garde in the Eighties, Los Angeles Co Mus Art, 87; Awards in the Visual Arts 7, Los Angeles Co Mus Art & traveling, 88; solo exhibs, Galeria Juana de Aizpuru, Madrid, 91, Jablonka Galerie, Cologne, 91, Galerie Peter Pakesch, Vienna, 91, Basel Kunsthalle, Switz, 92, Inst Contemp Art, London, 92, capMusee, Bordeaux, France, 92 & Portikus, Frankfurt, 92; Aldrich Mus Contemp Art, Ridgefield, Conn, 91; Songs of Innocence/Songs of Experience, Whitney Mus Am Art, Equitable Ctr, New York, 92; Recent Narrative Sculpture, Milwaukee Art Mus, Wis, 92; Post Human, Musée d'Art Contemporain, Pully/Lausanne, Switz, 92; Ars Pro Domo, Mus Ludwig, Cologne, 92; Schurmann Sammlung, Ludwig Forum fur Int Kunst, Aachen, Ger, 92; Re: Framing Cartoons, Wexner Art Ctr, Ohio State Univ, Columbus. *Bibliog:* William S Bartman & Miyoshi Barosh (eds), Mike Kelley, Art Press, 92; Diedrich Diederichsen (auth), Yet another discovery: Mike Kelly in video, no 31, p 77-79, 92, Rane Relyea (auth), Wild Kingdom, no 31, p 82-85, 92, Bernard Marcadé (auth), The world's bad breath, no 31, p 97-99, 92 & Julie Sylvester (auth), interview, Talking failure, no 31, p 100-103, Parkett; Catherine Liu (auth), Just pathetic, p 95-96, 4/92 & Colin Gardner (auth), Helter skelter at the temporary contemporary, p 103-104, 4/92, Artforum; and others. *Mailing Add:* c/o Metro Pictures 150 Greene St New York NY 10012

KELLEY, RAMON
PAINTER
b Cheyenne, Wyo, Feb 12, 39. *Study:* Colo Inst Art. *Work:* Santa Fe Art Mus, NMex; Marietta Col, Ohio; Mus Native Am Cult, Spokane, Wash; Tex Tech Univ Mus, Lubbock; Charles & Emma Frye Mus Fine Art. *Exhib:* Ann Exhib, Am Watercolor Soc, 71-77; Mainstreams, Marietta, Ohio, 72, 75 & 76; Allied Artists Am, 72, 73 & 74; Nat Arts Club Pastel Exhib, 74; Pastel Soc Am, 75-79; and others. *Awards:* Artists & Dealers Award, Mus Native Am Cult, 79; Mem Award Portrait, Pastel Soc Am, 79; Best of Show Medal, Kalispell Art Show & Auction, 79; and others. *Mem:* Pastel Soc Am (juror, 78). Nat Arts Club; Am Watercolor Soc (nat juror); Allied Artists Am; Pastel Soc Am. *Media:* Oil, Watercolor. *Publ:* Contribr, Am Artist Mag, 3/69 & 12/72 & Southwest Art Mag, 11/73; contribr, Joe Singer's How to Paint Figures in Pastel, Watson-Guptill, 76; coauth, Ramon Kelley Paints Portraits & Figures, Watson-Guptill, 77. *Dealer:* Canyon Rd Art Gallery 710 Canyon Rd Santa Fe NM 87501. *Mailing Add:* c/o Ventana Art Inn at Loreto 211 Old Santa Fe Trail Santa Fe NM 87501

KELLY, ARLEEN P See Schloss, Arleen P

KELLY, CYNTHIA FERENCE
GALLERY DIRECTOR, PAINTER
b Harrisburg, Pa. *Study:* Art Inst Pittsburgh; Carnegie-Mellon Univ, Pittsburgh, BFA(Edgar Roth Scholar, Women's Alumni Scholar), 78. *Pos:* Dir, Forbes St Gallery, Pittsburgh, 76-77 & Hewlett Gallery, Carnegie-Mellon Univ, Pittsburgh, 77-79; exec dir, Green Hill Ctr NC Art, Greensboro, 79-89, Darte, 91- *Mem:* Am Crafts Coun; Piedmont Craftsmen; NC Mus Coun; Am Asn of Mus; Southeastern Mus Coun. *Specialty:* Contemporary visual arts. *Publ:* Auth, Arts is a 4 letter word, 3/80 & The Penland School of Crafts, 9/80, Arts J; auth catalog essay, A Survey of NC Fiber Arts & Textile Design, 82. *Mailing Add:* 2507 Kingwood St Pittsburgh PA 15234

KELLY, ELLSWORTH
PAINTER, SCULPTOR
b Newburgh, NY, May 31, 23. *Study:* Pratt Inst, 41-42; Boston Mus Sch, 46-48; Ecole Des Beaux-Arts, Paris, 48-49. *Work:* Metrop Mus Art, Whitney Mus Am Art, Guggenheim Mus & Mus Mod Art, New York; Art Inst of Chicago, Ill; Mus Contemp Art, Los Angeles; Stedelijk Mus, Amsterdam, Holland; Nat Gallery of Art, Washington, DC; Tate Gallery, London; Philadelphia Mus Art; St Louis Art Mus, Mo; and others. *Comn:* Mural, UNESCO, Paris, 69; sculpture, Friends of the Park, Chicago, Ill, 81; 2 sculptures, General Moragues Plaza & single sculpture, El Parc de la Creuta del Coll, comn by City of Barcelona, Spain, 85- 87; sculpture, Mus Fine Arts, Houston, 86; Walker Art Ctr, Minneapolis, Minn, 88; painting, Morton H Meyerson Symphony Ctr, Dallas, Tex, 89. *Exhib:* Documenta III, 64, Documenta IV, 68, Documenta IX, Kassel, WGer, 92; XXXIII Biennale, Venice, Italy, 66; Albright-Knox Art Gallery, Buffalo, NY, 72; Mus Mod Art, New York, 73, 78 & 90; Whitney Mus Am Art, New York, 82; St Louis Mus Art, 83; Musee Nat d'Art Moderne, 80, Galerie du Jeu de Paume, Paris, France, 92; Works on Paper, Mod Art Mus, Ft Worth, Tex, 87; A Print Retrospective, Detroit Inst Art, 87; Overholland Mus, Amsterdam, Holland, 89; Art Inst Chicago, 89; Gallery Kasahara, Osaka, Japan, 90; Portikus, Frankfurt, WGer, 90; Westfalisches Landesmuseum, Munster, Ger, 92; Nat Gallery Art, Wash, 93. *Awards:* Tokyo Int Educ Ministry Award, 63; Chevalier de L'Ordre des Arts et des Lettres, French Repub, 87; Officier de l'Ordre des Arts et des Lettres, Fr Repub, 92. *Bibliog:* John Coplans (auth), Ellsworth Kelly, Abrams, 72; Diane Upright (auth), Ellsworth Kelly: Works on Paper, Ft Worth Mod Art Mus, Tex, 87; Yves-Alain Bois, Jack Cowart, Alfred Pacquement (auths), Ellsworth Kelly: les annees francaises, 1948-1954 (exhib catalog), Galerie Nationale du Jeu de Paume. *Mem:* Nat Inst Arts & Lett. *Publ:* Auth, Fragmentation and the single form, Artists Choice, Mus Mod Art, NY, 90. *Dealer:* Blum Helman Gellery Inc 20 W 57th St New York NY 10019. *Mailing Add:* c/o Leo Castelli Gallery 420 W Broadway New York NY 10012

KELLY, FRANKLIN WOOD
CURATOR, HISTORIAN
b Richmond, Va, June 1, 53. *Study:* Univ NC, Chapel Hill, BA(art hist), 74; Williams Col, Mass, Kress Fel, MA(art hist), 79, Univ Del, Newark, PhD(art hist-outstanding dissertation), 85. *Collections Arranged:* Problems in Connoisseurship and Conservation, Minneapolis Inst Arts, 85; The Early Landscapes of Frederic Edwin Church (with catalog), Amon Carter Mus, 84; Frederic Edwin Church (with catalog), Nat Gallery Art, 89-90. *Pos:* Cur asst, Va Mus, Richmond, 75-77; assoc cur paintings, Minneapolis Inst Arts, 83-85; asst cur Am art, Nat Gallery Art, Washington, DC, 85-87, cur Am art, 87-88; cur collections, Corcoran Gallery of Art, Washington, DC, 88-90; cur Am & Brit painting, Nat Gallery Art, Washington, DC, 90. *Teaching:* Univ Md, 90 & Princeton Univ, 91; adj assoc prof, Univ Md, 91. *Awards:* Kress Fel, Ctr Advan Study, Nat Gallery Art, Washington, DC, 81-83. *Mem:* Col Art Asn. *Res:* American art, specializing on 19th century landscape painting, especially that of Frederic Edwin Church. *Publ:* auth, Portraits of John Durand, Antiques Mag, 82; Thomas Cole's paintings of Mount Etna, Arts in Va, 83; The Early Landscapes of Frederic Edwin Church, 87; Frederic Edwin Church & The National Landscape, 88; Frederic Edwin Church, 89. *Mailing Add:* Dept Am Art Nat Gallery Art Washington DC 20565

KELLY, ISAAC PERRY
EDUCATOR, PHOTOGRAPHER
b Orlando, Fla, June 2, 25. *Study:* Univ Hawaii; Univ Fla, BD, 53, MEd, 55; Peabody Col, EdD, 65. *Comn:* Tapestry (woven), comn by Mrs Ed Buerk, Delray Beach, Fla, 75; tapestry (woven), comn by Dr William Chovan, Cullowhee, NC, 75; tapestry (woven), Pryory Sch, Jamaica, West Indies. *Exhib:* Photography and fiber exhibitions in the Southeast USA, three photographic exhibitions in Denmark, and one in China. *Pos:* State supvr art, Dept Pub Instr, Raleigh, NC, 63-68; bd dirs, Campbell Folk Sch; head, Dept Art, Western Carolina Univ, 68-76. *Teaching:* Assoc prof art educ & weaving, Western Carolina Univ, 68-90. *Awards:* Outstanding NC Art Educator, 85. *Mem:* Assoc Artists NC (pres, 73-75); NC Art Educ Asn (pres, 77-79); Handweavers Guild Am; Int Soc Educ Arts; NC Crafts Asn; Nat Art Educ Asn; life mem, NC Art Soc. *Media:* Weaving, Photography. *Publ:* Auth, Art Education in North Carolina, 65. *Mailing Add:* Box 755 Cullowhee NC 28723

KELLY, JAMES
PAINTER
b Philadelphia, Pa, Dec 19, 13. *Study:* Pa Acad Fine Arts, Philadelphia; Barnes Found, Merion, Pa; Calif Sch Fine Arts, San Francisco. *Work:* San Francisco Mus Art; Mus Mod Art, New York; Los Angeles Mus Art; Univ Mass, Boston; Westinghouse Corp, Salem, NC & Pittsburgh, Pa. *Exhib:* San Francisco Mus Art Painting Ann, 55-58; Minneapolis Inst Art, Minn, 57; Los Angeles Co Mus Art, 68; Huntsville Mus of Art, Ala, 77; one-man shows, Albright Col, Reading, Pa, 66, Long Island Univ, Brooklyn, NY, 68, East Hampton Gallery, New York, NY, 69 & Westbeth Galleries, New York, 71-72, Col Notre Dame, Belmont, Calif, 90; Art in the San Francisco Bay Area (with catalog), 45-80, Oakland Art Mus, Oakland, Calif, 85. *Teaching:* Lectr painting, Univ Calif, Berkeley, summer 56. *Awards:* Ford Found grant lithography, 63; Nat Endowment Arts grant painting, 77-78; Grant, The Peter & Madeleine Martin Found for Creative Arts, San Francisco, 90. *Bibliog:* Mary Fuller McChesney (auth), A Period of Exploration, San Francisco, 45-50, Oakland Art Mus, 73; Thomas Albright (auth), Art in the San Francisco Bay Area 1945-1950: An Illustrated History, Univ Calif Press, 85; Tony Novelozo/John Natsoulas (auth), Lyrical Vision: The 6 Gallery, 1954-1957, Natsoulas/Novelozo Gallery, Davis Calif, 90. *Media:* Acrylic, Oil. *Mailing Add:* 463 West St New York NY 10014

KELLY, MARY
CONCEPTUAL ARTIST
b Ft Dodge, Oowa, June 7, 41. *Study:* Col St Teresa, Minn, BA, 63; Pius XII Inst, Florence, Italy, MA, 65; St Martins Sch Art, London, 68-70. *Work:* Zurich Mus, Switz; Australian Nat Gallery, Canberra; Arts Coun Gr Brit; Tate Gallery, London, Eng; Art Gallery of Ont, Can, Vancouver Art Gallery, New Museum, New York. *Comn:* New Hall, Cambridge Univ, New Museum, New York. *Exhib:* Solo exhibs, Postmasters Gallery, New York, 89 & 93, New Mus Contemp Art, New York, 90, Vancouver Art Gallery, Can, 90, Knoll Gallery, Vienna & Budapest, 91, Mackenzie Art Gallery, Can, 92, Herbert Johnson Mus Art, Cornell Univ, 92, C Zilkha Gallery, Wesleyan Univ, 92; Barbara Toll Fine Art, NY, 90, The Decade Show, New Mus, 90; Shocks to the System, South Bank Ctr, London, Eng, 91; Whitney Mus Am Art, 91; Carnegie Mus Art, 92; So Oder So Nicht Sein, Forum Stadpark, Graz, Austria, 92; Univ Mus, Santa Barbara, 92; Post Masters Gallery, New York, 93. *Pos:* Dir studio, independent study program, Whitney Mus Am Art. *Awards:* Visual Arts Award, Arts Coun Gr Brit, 77; Nat Endowment Art; Visual Arts Award, Greater London Arts Asn, 80. *Bibliog:* Parveen Adams (auth), The Art of Analysis, Fall, No 58, 10/91; Emily Apter (auth), Fetishism and Visual Seduction in Mary Kelly's Interim, Fall, No 58, 10/91; Laura Mulvey (auth), Impending Time: Mary Kelly's Corpus, Lapis, 92. *Media:* Miscellaneous Media. *Publ:* Auth, Pecunia Olet, Top Top Stories, City Lights Books, San Francisco, 91; Magiciens de la Mer(d), Art Forum, New York, 91; Gloria Patri, Wesleyan Univ, Pvt Publisher; On Display, Not Enough Gees and Gollies to Describe It, No 35, Parkett, 92. *Mailing Add:* 24 W 76th St Apt 3-R New York NY 10023

KELLY, MOIRA
CURATOR, WRITER
b Newcastle on Tyne, Eng, Jan 29, 51. *Study:* Univ Newcastle on Tyne, Eng, with prof Kenneth Rountree ARA, also spec study of Inigo Jones and the English Mask, BFA(hons), 74. *Work:* Northern Arts Collection, Newcastle on Tyne, Eng. *Collections Arranged:* William J Carey Collection, Univ Tex, Dallas, 79; Traveling Exhib, The Subjective Eye (auth, catalog), 80-81; Eight in the Eighties (auth, catalog), Britain Salutes New York, 83; New Wood, Sir John Makepiece Trust, 83; Collision, Lawndale Art & Performance Ctr, Houston, Tex, 84. *Pos:* Res, Spencer A Samuels Inc, New York, 74-76; dir, AIR Gallery, 76-79 & Moira Kelly Fine Art, 79-83, London, Eng, Lawndale Art & Performance Ctr, Univ Houston, Tex, 83-86; auth, various revs & catalogs, Art Monthly, The Guardian & Artscribe, 78- *Teaching:* Visiting lecturer of art law & management, colleges, and universities throughout Britain & the US including Chelsea, St Martins, Syracuse, Univ Tex, Dallas & Univ Houston, Tex, also studio teaching. *Awards:* Virgin Mary Travelling Scholar, 70-74; Northern Artist's Award, Regional Arts Asn, 74; Res Award (New York), British Coun, 77. *Bibliog:* William Packer (auth), Opening up, Financial Times, London, 80; Hetty Eingzig (auth), Women Gallery Directors, Harpers, London, 81; Edward Lucie Smith (auth), Moira Kelly, Illustrated London News, 81. *Publ:* Coauth, The Rothko wrangle, Art Monthly, London, 78; auth, Hugh O'Donnel: New Paintings, Artscribe, 79; The Chicago Art Fair, Economist, 85. *Mailing Add:* 119 Calhoun St Washington Depot CT 06794

KELLY, ROBERT JAMES
PAINTER, GRAPHIC ARTIST
b Billings, Mont, June 26, 58. *Study:* Moorhead State Univ, BA, 80; Sch Commun Arts, 91. *Work:* Southern Plains Indian Art Mus, Anadarko, Okla; Northern Wolf Mus, Sci Mus Minn & Smithsonian Inst, Ely. *Comn:* Wolf dance costume (with Wolf Feather Artist Cooperative), Sci Mus Minn, Ely, 83; mixed media sculpture, (with Wolf Feather Artist Cooperative), First Bank, Duluth, 84; GBW O/C painting, pvt collector, Minneapolis, 89; mapping servies O/C, pvt collector, Minneapolis, 90; three paintings, Arusa Inc, Minneapolis, 91. *Exhib:* 7th Annual Art From the Earth, Galleria, Norman, Okla, 83; Heart of the North, Raven Gallery, Edina, Minn, 84; Invitational Exhibit, Southern Plains Indian Art Mus, Anadarko, Okla, 85; Artist Soc Int Exhib, Juried, San Francisco, 87; Transmutations, Red Gallery, Minneapolis, 90. *Mem:* Minn Artists Asn. *Media:* Oil on Canvas, Pastel on Paper. *Mailing Add:* 18097 Liv Lane Eden Prairie MN 55346-4108

KELLY, WILLIAM JOSEPH
DRAFTSMAN, PAINTER
b Buffalo, NY, May 4, 43. *Study:* Philadelphia Col Art, BFA; Prahran Col Adv Educ; Nat Gallery Sch, Australia, MA. *Work:* Victorian Trades Hall Council, Melbourne, Australia; Lehigh Univ; Accademia de Belle Art, Perugia, Italy; Australian Nat Gallery, Canberra; Victorian Arts Ctr; and many others. *Exhib:* Ann Exhib, Albright-Knox Art Gallery, Buffalo, 63; one-man shows, Prince St Gallery, New York, 74, Accad de Belle Arti, Perugia, Italy, 75 & William Kelly: Realism in Transition, Butler Inst Am Art, 82; Tapestry & the Australian Painter, Nat Gallery, Melbourne, 79; Australian Printmaking,

Brown Univ, 80; Invitational, New York Studio Sch Galleries, 80; Gerstman-Abdallah Fine Arts, Cologne, WGer, 86; William Kelly: Survey, Victorian Arts Centre, 90; and others in Can, Sweden, Japan, Denmark, Korea, Hungary & Gr Brit. *Pos:* Dean sch art, Victorian Col Arts, Melbourne, 75-81. *Teaching:* Instr, Victorian Col Arts & Nat Gallery Sch, Melbourne, Australia, Philadelphia Col Art & others. *Awards:* Fulbright Grant, 68-69; Fulbright Fel, 69-70; Fel Visual Arts & Soc Sci, Phillip Inst Tech; Australian Film Comn Grant, 83. *Bibliog:* Robert Godfrey (auth), Towards Human Intent, Westminster Col, 80; Walter Brayman & Myron Brody (auths), Conversation with William Kelly, Forum Mag, 3/80; and others; Dr Louis Zona (auth), William Kelly: Realism in Transition, Butler Inst Am Art; and others; Janet McKenzie (auth), William Kelly, Art and Australia, Sydney, autumn/winter, 86; Wayne Tindall (dir), William Kelly/Painter & Projects, Video Documentary 30 min, 87. *Media:* Acrylic; Charcoal. *Publ:* Auth, Two Who Responded, Art & Artists, London, 4/76; Drawing Now, Artist's Choice Mus Newslett, New York, 4/80; Photomontage of a painting, Leonardo, winter 80; Imaged art: The subjectified aspect in the age of new figuration, Artists Choice Mus J, New York, fall 82; Intro to Contemporary Australian Drawing, Macmillan Co, 86. *Dealer:* c/o Artsco PO Box 368 Prahran Melbourne Australia 3181. *Mailing Add:* PO Box 368 Prahran 3181 Australia

KELM, BONNIE G
MUSEUM DIRECTOR, ADMINISTRATOR
b Brooklyn, NY, Mar 29, 47. *Study:* Buffalo State Univ Col, BS(art educ), 68; Bowling Green State Univ, MA(art hist), 75; Ohio State Univ, PhD(arts admin), 87. *Collections Arranged:* Art in Columbus-50 Years, Columbus Mus Art, 80; Three Views from Columbus (with catalog), Arts Consortium, Cincinnati, 81; Artworks: A Tribute to Women Artists (with catalog), Columbus Cult Arts Ctr, 83; Connections: An International Exhibition of Visual Arts & Cultural Artifacts), (with catalog), Ohio State Univ Galleries, 85; Into the Mainstream: Contemporary American Folk, Naive and Outsider Art), (with catalog), Miami Univ Art Mus, 90; Traditions, Transitions & Transformations, Yearlong Exhib Prog, 92. *Pos:* Pres, bd trustees, Columbus Inst Contemp Arts, Columbus, Ohio, 77-82; dir, The Bunte Gallery, Franklin Univ, Columbus, Ohio, 78-88; Miami Univ Art Mus, Oxford, Ohio, 88-; bd trustees, Ohio Mus Asn, 92- *Teaching:* Prof art hist, Franklin Univ, Columbus, Ohio, 78-88; vis prof art ed/admin, Ohio State Univ, Columbus, 80-83; assoc prof arts admin, Miami Univ, Oxford, Ohio, 88- *Awards:* Fulbright Award, USIA & Netherlands Am Comn for Educ Exch, 88; Eleanor A Gelpi Award, YWCA Women of Achievement, 87; NEH Summer Sem Fel, 92. *Bibliog:* Becky Stiles Belt (auth), With a little help from my friends, Columbus Homes & Lifestyles, 5-6/84; Kathleen Mullen (auth), There's more to art & life than meets the eye, Business First Mag, 10/84; Cynthia Crane (auth), Bonnie's Gallery, Columbus Monthly, 11/85. *Mem:* Am Asn Mus; Int Comt Mus; Col Arts Asn; Ohio Mus Asn; Midwest Art Hist Soc. *Publ:* Contribr, Good art, bad art & the elusive question of quality, Artspace, Ohio Arts Coun, 86; Art Openings as Cultural Rituals, Public policy & arts administration, Vol 3, Nat Art Educ Asn, 89; Into the Mainstream: Contemporary American Folk, Naive & Outsider, Miami Univ Art Mus, 90; Aminah Robinson, Kunstforum Int, 91; Traditions, Transitions & Transitions, Visual Arts Res, 92. *Mailing Add:* Miami Univ Art Mus Patterson Ave Oxford OH 45056

KELMAN, MAUREEN (S)
SCULPTOR, EDUCATOR
b Cleveland, Ohio, July 14, 52. *Study:* Monmouth Col, BA, 74; Univ Mass, Dartmouth, MFA, 81; Haystack Mountain Sch Crafts, with Walter Nottingham, 83, Margaret Prentice, 84 & Kai Chan & Betty Oliver, 88; research & study in Japan, with Shioko Fukumoto, Sieki Kikuchi & Sadako Sakurai, 87. *Work:* Cannabis Press Collection, Kasama, Japan. *Comn:* 30 fabric banners, Community Col RI, Warwick, 86; 7 woven sculptures, comn by Elizabeth Webbing, Pawtucket, RI, 86. *Exhib:* Fiber Crosscurrents, John Michael Kohler Arts Ctr, Wis, 84; New England Fiber Arts, Newport Art Mus, RI, 85; Int Textile Fair Exhib, Kyoto, Japan, 87; Influences-Innovations, Torpedo Factory Art Ctr, Alexandria, Va, 92; Contemporary Shibori, Int Shibori Symp, Nagoya, Japan, 92; and others. *Teaching:* Assoc prof art dept, Community Col RI, Warwick, 81-92; instr surface design, RI Sch Design, Providence, 90; instr weaving & basketry, Frissell Mus, Oaxaca, Mex, 91-92. *Awards:* Spec Mention Award, May Show, Cleveland Mus Art, 80; Visual Artist's Fel, Nat Endowment Arts, 90. *Mem:* Col Art Asn; Am Craft Coun. *Media:* Fiber. *Mailing Add:* 216 Eighth St Providence RI 02906

KELMENSON, LITA
SCULPTOR, EDUCATOR
b Buffalo, NY, June 30, 32. *Study:* Albright Art Sch, Cert, 53; State Univ NY, Buffalo, BS, 54; Queens Col, NY, MS, 64. *Work:* Mari Galleries of Westchester Ltd, Mamaroneck, NY. *Exhib:* Nat Asn Women Artists Exhib, Bergen Community Mus, NJ, 83 & Monmouth Mus Fine Arts, NJ, 87; Int Competition, Mussavi Art Ctr, New York, 85; Invitational Exhib, Nat Educ Asn, Washington, DC, 87; Nassau Co Mus Fine Arts, Roslyn, NY, 88; Invitational, In the Best Tradition, Heckscher Mus. *Pos:* Adv bd, Islip Art Mus, 76-79. *Teaching:* Vis lectr plastic sculpture, Adelphi Univ, Garden City, NY, 74; asst prof, Hofstra Univ, Hempstead, NY, 75-76; adj prof, Nassau Community Col, Garden City, NY. *Awards:* Special Award, Nassau County Mus Fine Art, 88; Chase Manhattan Award for Works on Paper, 89; Medal Honor & Amelia Peabody Mem, Nat Asn Women Art, Amelia Peabody Estate, 90. *Bibliog:* Helen Harrison (auth), New approaches to social art, NY Times, 1/10/82; Malcolm Preston (auth), Social commentaries, Newsday, 1/12/82; Phyllis Braff (auth), Inner concepts, outer forms, NY Times, 1/15/89. *Mem:* Nat Asn Women Artists; Artist-Craftsmen New York; Orgn Independent Artists. *Media:* Wood, Polyester Resin. *Publ:* Auth, A wholesome commitment, The Graphic, 82; A sense of Mexico, Spanish Today, 85, Nat Art Educ Asn J, 85; An historical perspective, NY State Art Teachers Asn J, 88. *Dealer:* Corp Art Assoc Ltd 270 Lafayette St New York NY 10012. *Mailing Add:* 199 N Marginal Rd Jericho NY 11753

KELSO, DAVID WILLIAM
PRINTMAKER, ART DEALER
b Van Nuys, Calif, Jan 29, 48. *Study:* Univ Calif, Riverside, BA, 69; Univ Calif, Berkeley Extension with Kathan Brown, 71. *Work:* Rutgers Archives, Zimmerli Mus, New Brunswick, NJ; US Dept of State, Washington, DC. *Exhib:* Folio 73, San Francisco Mus Mod Art, Calif, 73; Prints California, Oakland Mus, Calif, 75; Third and Sixth Hawaii Nat Print Exhib, Honolulu Acad Arts, 75 & 83; Art in Public Places, Cheney Cowles Mem Mus, Spokane, WA, 77; Bay Area Fine Art Presses, Walnut Creek Civic Arts Gallery, Walnut Creek, Calif, 78; Six Printmakers, San Francisco Mus Mod Art, Calif, 78; Selections from the Rutgers Archives, Grolier Club, New York, 85; Process Prints, Richmond Art Ctr, Calif, 86. *Pos:* Founder, dir, Made in California Intaglio Press, Oakland, 80- *Awards:* Purchase award, Northwest Int Small Format Print Exhib, Artist Services, 78. *Media:* Intaglio Printmaking. *Specialty:* Contemporary intaglio prints (primarily Calif Artists). *Publ:* Auth, Frank Lobdell: Proofing for Prints, Print Collector's Newsletter, 88. *Dealer:* Betsy Senior Fine Art 55 Crosby St New York NY 10012; Olga Dollar Gallery 210 Post St San Francisco CA 94108. *Mailing Add:* 3246 Ettie St No 16 Oakland CA 94608

KEMBLE, RICHARD
PRINTMAKER, SCULPTOR
b Erie, Pa, Nov 7, 32. *Study:* Trenton State Col, NJ, BA; Pratt Graphics Art Ctr, study with Carol Summers. *Work:* Art in the Embassies; Firestone Libr, Princeton Univ; Allentown Art Mus, Pa; Mus Mod art, Thessaloniki, Greece; IBM; Newark Mus, NJ; NJ State Mus, Trenton; US Info Agency. *Comn:* Sculpture, Mercer Hosp, Trenton, NJ; altarpiece & vestments, St Andrews Church, Yardley, Pa, 72; cake, Mus Contemp Crafts, New York, 73; Circle F Industry, Trenton, 73; sculpture, Gloucester Co Col, NJ, 75. *Exhib:* Albright Knox Art Gallery, Buffalo; Mus Mod Art, Sao Paulo, Brazil; Kameoka Art Exhib, Kyoto, Japan; Gallery Daberkow, Frankfurt, Ger; Philadelphia Mus Art, Pa. *Teaching:* Instr printmaking, Pratt Inst, 67-78, Long Beach Island Found Arts & Sci, Loveladies, NJ, 73; artist-in-residence, North Country Sch, 73-80 & NJ State Coun Arts, 74-75. *Awards:* Purchase Award, NJ State Mus, 70; Printmaker's Fel, Nat Endowment Arts, 74-75; NJ State Coun Arts Grant, 78. *Bibliog:* Mary Midura (auth), Renaissance man leads the good life, Trentonian, 12/71; Burton Wasserman (auth), Kemble's woodcuts, Camden Courier Post, 10/73; Experimente mit dem Druckstock, Frankfurt Allgemeine Zeitung, Ger, 76; Richard Kemble Woodcuts (catalog), Int Print Soc, New Hope, Pa, 84; Franz Geierhaus (auth), The Creative Act, Int Print Soc, New Hope, pa, 85; film doc, Richard Kemble, Media Ctr Trenton State Col, NJ, 85. *Mem:* Pratt Graphic Arts Ctr; Soc Am Graphic Artists; Am Color Print Soc. *Publ:* Auth, The Quiet Forest (portfolio), Forager House Studio, Washington Crossing, Pa, 77. *Dealer:* Assoc Am Artists 20 W 57th St New York NY 10019; Int Print Soc New Hope PA 18938. *Mailing Add:* c/o Forager House Studio Box 82 Washington Crossing PA 18977

KEMENYFFY, STEVEN
CERAMIST, EDUCATOR
b Budapest, Hungary, Aug 18, 43; US citizen. *Study:* Augustana Col, Rock Island, Ill, BA, 65; Univ Iowa, Iowa City, MA, 66, MFA, 67. *Work:* Everson Mus, Syracuse, NY; State Univ NY, Geneseo; Butler Inst Am Art, Youngstown, Ohio; Smithsonian Inst, Washington, DC; Cincinnati Art Mus, Ohio; Erie Art Mus, Pa. *Comn:* Ceramic wall murals (with Susan Kemenyffy), Rohm & Haas Pharmaceutical, Philadelphia, Pa; Kaiser Permanente Med Ctr, Irvine, Calif; Int Fur Co, Montgomery, Ala; Scott Enterprises, Erie, Pa; Penn Bank, McBrier Properties Group, Erie, Pa; and numerous private commissions. *Exhib:* Ceramics '70 Plus Wovenforms, Everson Mus, Syracuse; Ceramic Sculpture Invitational, Univ of NC, Chapel Hill, 77; Soup Soup, Beautiful Soup, Campbell Mus, Camden, NJ, 83; 75 Yrs of Pittsburgh Art, Its Influences, Carnegie-Mellon Univ, Pa, 85; Pattern & Decoration Contemporary Approaches, Craftsman Potters Asn, London, Eng, 88; A Festival of Ceramics, Rufford Craft Ctr, Nottinghamshire, Eng, 88; Nat Ceramics 88, New Zealand Soc Potters Inc, Wellington, NZ, 88; Raku-Arts, Kansas City Contemporary Art Ctr, Kansas City, Mo, 89; Exhib 280: Works OffWalls, Huntington Mus Art, WVa, 89; J M Kohler Art Ctr, Sheboygan, Wis, 90; Celebrating Clay, Miller Gallery, Cincinnati, Ohio, 90; Cent Pa Festival of the Arts Crafts Nat 24, Zoller Gallery, State Col, Pa, 90; Traveling Craft Exhib, Pittsburgh, Pa, 90; Miller Gallery, Cincinnati, Ohio, 92; Ceramics Invitational Exhib, Kipp Gallery, Ind Univ Pa, 92; Am Crafts, Cleveland, Ohio, 92; Figurative Clay, Claytrade, Portland, Ore, 92. *Teaching:* Prof Ceramics, Edinboro State Col, Pa, 69-, Edinburgh Art Col, Edinburgh, Scotland, 85, Miami Univ, Oxford Ohio, 86, San Diego Potters Guild, Calif, 87, Nat Ceramics 88, Wellington, NZ, 88, Ringling Sch Art & Design, Sarasota, Fla, 88; Int Experimental Ceramic Studio, Kecskemet, Hungary, 87, Congresso Nacional De Technicas Para Arte Ceramica, San Paulo, Brazil, 89, Phoenix Col, Ariz, 90, Bussum, Holland, 90, Fla Community Col Jacksonville S Campus, Fla, 90; Kingston, RI, 91, Walnut Creek, Calif, 91, Toronto, Ont, Can, 91, Renwick Gallery Nat Mus Am Art, Smithsonian Inst, Washington, DC, 91, Eastern Ky Univ, Lexington, 92. *Awards:* Cash Ceramic Award, Cleveland May Show, Cleveland Mus Art, 72; Nat Endowment Arts Grant, 77; Assoc Artists of Pittsburgh Ann Award, Carnegie Mus, 83. *Bibliog:* John Gibson (auth), Contemporary Pottery Decoration, Chilton Bk Co, Radnor, Pa, 87; Steve Branfman (auth), Raku, A Practical Approach, Chilton Bk, Randnor, Pa, 91; Susan Peterson (auth), The Craft & Art of Clay, Prentice Hall, Englewood Cliffs, NJ, 92. *Mem:* Nat Coun Educ Ceramic Arts; Pittsburgh Craftsman Guild; Pa Guild Craftsmen; Assoc Artists Pittsburgh. *Media:* Clay. *Dealer:* Sybil Robins Craftsman Gallery Scarsdale NY; Fenton Moore Buffalo NY. *Mailing Add:* 4570 Old State Rd McKean PA 16426

KEMENYFFY, SUSAN B HALE
CERAMIST
b Springfield, Mass, Oct 4, 41. *Study:* Syracuse Univ, New York, BFA, 63, study with Robert Marks; Univ Iowa, Iowa City, MA, 66, study with Mauricio Lasansky, MFA(with hons), 67. *Work:* Everson Mus, Syracuse, NY; Cincinnati Art Mus; Canton Art Inst, Ohio; Erie Art Mus, Pa. *Comn:* Ceramic wall murals (with Steven Kemenyffy), Rohm & Haas Pharmaceutical, Philadelphia, Pa, 88; Int Fur Co, Montgomery, Ala, 88; McBrier Properties Group, Erie, Pa; private commissions. *Exhib:* Contemporary Raku Ceramics: Tradition Transformed, Nat Council on Educ For the Ceramics Arts Invitational, San Antonio, Tex, 86; Pattern & Decoration Contemporary Approaches, Craftsmen Potters Asn, London, Eng, 87; San Diego Potters Guild, Calif, 87; A Festival of Ceramics, Rufford Craft, Nottinghamshire, Eng, 88; Nat Ceramics 88, NZ Soc Potters, Inc, Wellington, NZ, 88; Susan & Steven Kemenyffy, Ceramic Images, Brodigan Gallery, Groton Sch, Mass, 88; Raku-Transforming the Tradition, Nat Coun on Education for the Ceramic Arts, Kansas City Contemp Arts Ctr, Kansas City, Mo, 89; Multi, Media Show, Am Crafts, Cleveland, Ohio, 90; Celebrating Clay, Miller Gallery, Cincinnati, Ohio, 90; J M Kohler Art Ctr, Sheboygan, Wis, 90. *Teaching:* Escuela Madrilena de Ceramica de la Moncloa; Edinburgh Col Arts Edinburgh, Scotland, 85; Miami Univ, Oxford, Ohio, 86; Ringling Sch Art & Des, Sarasota, Fla, 88; lectr at numerous univs and art asns, 78- *Awards:* Nat Endowment Arts Grant, 73; Assoc Artist's Pittsburgh Award, Carnegie-Mellon Mus, 81, 83 & 87; Ann Ceramic & Small Sculpture Show Award, Butler Mus Art, Youngstown, Ohio, 82. *Bibliog:* Regis Brody (auth), Energy Efficient Ceramics, Watson-Guptill Publ, 82; Harriet Gamble (auth), Arts and Activities, 2/86; John Gibson (auth), Contemporary Pottery Decoration, Chilton Book Co, 87. *Media:* Clay, Graphics. *Dealer:* Sybil Robins Craftsman Gallery Scarsdale NY; Fenton Moore Buffalo NY. *Mailing Add:* 4570 Old State Rd McKean PA 16426

KEMP, FLO
PRINTMAKING
b Oct 21, 41. *Study:* Montclair State Col, NJ, BA, 63; Hofstra Univ, NY, MA, 73. *Work:* Securities Exchange Comn, Manhattan Savings Bank, New York; United Jersey Bank, NJ. *Comn:* Seiskeya Ballet Prog Cover, Seiskeya Ballet Studios, St James, NY; Gurneys Resorts Etching, Gurney's Inc, Montauk, NY. *Exhib:* 100 Years-100 Artists, Nat Asn Women Artists Travel Exhib, Fine Arts Mus South, Mobile, Ala, Chattanooga Regional Hist Mus, Tenn & Longview Mus Art, Tex, 89-90; Nat Travel Printmaking Exhib, Mus SW, Midland, Tex & Jesse Besser Mus; Marbella Art Gallery Exhib, New York, 91; The Environment, Elaine Benson Gallery, Bridgehampton, NY, 92. *Pos:* Vpres, Northport Galleries, NY, 88-90; chmn, Nat Travel Print Exhib, Nat Asn Women Artists, 90-92. *Awards:* Purchase Award, Nat Works on Paper, Terrance Gallery, 87; Landscape Award, Washington Square, New York, 91. *Mem:* Nat Asn Women Artists; Huntington Art League; Smithtown Arts Coun; East End Arts Coun. *Media:* Etching. *Mailing Add:* Box 2202 Setauket NY 11733

KEMP, PAUL ZANE
EDUCATOR, SCULPTOR
b Apache Creek, NMex, Nov 6, 28. *Study:* NMex Highlands Univ, BA, 50, MA, 54; Cranbrook Acad Art, MFA, 60. *Exhib:* Third Ann Prints, Drawings & Crafts, Ark Arts Ctr, Little Rock, 69; Am Graphics 69, Col of the Pac, 69; Nat Graphic Arts & Drawing Show, Wichita Art Asn, Kans, 69; Northwest Printmaker's Int, Seattle, 69; Tex Fine Arts Asn Ann Citation Show, Austin, 69 & 70; 8th Baytown Annual, Tex, 74; Metals Invitational Show, 81 & Blue Bonnets and Other Flora, 86, Cult Activities Ctr, Temple, Tex; The Art Ctr Cent Tex Biennial, Waco, Tex, 89. *Teaching:* Asst prof art, Baylor Univ, 61-64, assoc prof, 64-69, prof, 69- *Awards:* Jurors Choice, Tex Fine Arts Asn Citation Show, 69 & 70; Purchase Entry, Ark Art Ctr, 69; Cash Award, 8th Baytown Ann, 74. *Media:* Sheet Metal, Miscellaneous Media. *Publ:* Contribr & illusr, Tex Trends Art Educ, spring 69. *Mailing Add:* Dept of Art Baylor Univ Waco TX 76706

KEMPE, RICHARD JOSEPH
COLLECTOR, CURATOR
b New York, NY, Oct 28, 22. *Study:* New York Univ, BS, 47; PhD, 53; Univ Oslo, cert, 48. *Collections Arranged:* Metrop Young Artists Show, Nat Arts Club, 58 & 59; Sch Paris Exhib, Nat Arts Club, 63; Books and Graphics of the Cobra Artists, City Gallery, New York City Dept Cult Affairs, 86. *Pos:* UN Delegate to World Conf on Intellectual Property (WIPO), Stockholm, 67. *Mem:* Franklin Furnace Arch Inc (int adv comt, 85-). *Interests:* Modern and contemporary art, collection also contains extensive group of artists' books, currently emphasizing artwork of young Mexican artists. *Publ:* Ed, Cobra Prints Cobra Books, Franklin Furnace Arch Inc, 86; contribr, Hendrik Glintenkamp: un debujante norteamericano en Mexico, 1917-1920, Inst Nac de Bellas Artes, Mexico, 87. *Mailing Add:* Rio Lerma 156-502 Mexico 06500 Mexico

KEMPNER, HELEN HILL
COLLECTOR, PATRON
b Houston, Tex, Jan 30, 38. *Pos:* Bd trustees, Contemp Arts Mus, Houston, 77-, vpres, 77-78, secy, 78-79, pres, 79- *Collection:* Contemporary paintings and sculpture; primitive, mostly African art. *Mailing Add:* Contemp Art Mus 5216 Montrose Blvd Houston TX 77006

KENDA, JUANITA ECHEVERRIA
PAINTER, WRITER
b Tarentum, Pa, Nov 12, 23. *Study:* Stephens Col; Art Students League; Temple Univ, BFA; Univ Hawaii; also with Jon Corbino, Sam Hershey, Boris Blai, Raphael Sabatini, Jean Charlot, George Bridgman & others. *Work:* Hawaiian State Found Cult Art. *Comn:* Murals, Straub Clinic & Children's Hosp, Honolulu. *Exhib:* Honolulu Painters & Sculptors, 60 & 61; Moorestown Friends Sch, 61; Univ Hawaii, 65; Galeria Santiago, San Juan, PR, 67; Downtown Gallery, 79; and many others. *Collections Arranged:* Art of Hawaii Children, circulated by Smithsonian Inst, 60-64. *Pos:* chmn sch art exhib, Honolulu Acad Arts, 50-, head creative art sect, 49-63; state prog spec, State Dept Educ, Honolulu, 63-64; community relations officer, East-West Ctr, 68-70; pres, Downtown Gallery Ltd, 69-82. *Teaching:* Instr workshop, Hawaii Summer Sch, 51; instr, Univ Hawaii Sch Educ, 65-66, watercolor, Honolulu Acad Arts. *Awards:* Hon Consul of Mex in Hawaii. *Mem:* Hawaii Painters & Sculptors League; Asn Art Mus; Pac Art Asn; Nat Art Educ Asn; Int Comt Mus; Hawaii Watercolor Soc; and others. *Media:* Watercolor, Etching. *Publ:* Auth & illusr, Art and art education in Hawaii & Art guide for Hawaii, Sch Arts Mag; auth & illustr, Curriculum outline--elementary art and curriculum outline--secondary art, Dept Educ, State of Hawaii; contribr to Paradise of the Pacific; auth, Art guide for preschool and kindergarten, San Diego Schs, Calif, 71; and others. *Mailing Add:* 3708 Lurline Dr Honolulu HI 96816

KENDALL, (MS) MICHAEL
ADMINISTRATOR, EDUCATOR
Study: Drexel Univ, BA, 74; NY Univ, MA, PhD; Scuola Int di Grafica, Venezia, Italy. *Work:* US Mission to the United Nations, New York; African Mus, Smithsonian Inst; Howard Univ & Nat Aeronautic and Space Admin Collection, Washington, DC; Studio Mus in Harlem, New York; Schomburg Ctr for Res in Black Am Cult, NY Pub Libr. *Pos:* Asst cur, Drexel Univ Hist Costume Collection, Philadelphia, Pa, 70-74; dir recreation & fine arts prog, Presbyterian Senior Servs, New York, 79-80; Getty Ctr Educ in Arts, 89-90, prog officer, 90- *Teaching:* Art teacher, United Nations Int Sch, New York, 84-86; asst prof, Montclair State Col, NJ, 86-90. *Awards:* Faculty Merit Award, Montclair State Col, 89; Student Chap Sponsor Award of Excellence, Nat Art Educ Asn, 89; Painting Fel, Yaddo Artist Colony, 82. *Bibliog:* Leo Krasner (auth), The eye is the first circle, Brooklyn Affairs, Vol 2, No 2, 3/85. *Mem:* Col Art Asn; Am Asn Mus; Nat Art Educ Asn. *Publ:* Auth, The resurrection of Edmonia Lewis, Afro-Am, 3/81; Exploring the temple of love: Robert Longo at the Brooklyn Museum, Brooklyn Affairs, Vol 2, No 4, 5/85. *Mailing Add:* 300 S Gramercy Pl No 103 Los Angeles CA 90020

KENDALL, THOMAS LYLE
CERAMIST, EDUCATOR
b St Louis, Mo, Apr 30, 49. *Study:* Ill State Univ, BS, 71, MS, 73. *Work:* Ill State Univ, Normal; Kalamazoo Inst Arts, Mich; Mich Arts Coun, Lansing; Cooper Hewitt, NY. *Comn:* Large scale out door sculptures, Battle Creek, Mich, 89. *Exhib:* Columbus Mus Art, Ohio, 75 & 79; Marietta Col, Ohio, 78; Raku V-Nat, Peters Valley, NJ, 79; solo exhib, Craft Alliance Gallery, St Louis, Mo, 81; Mich Ceramics, 83; Functional Ceramics Invitational, St Louis, 85; Wooster Col, 86. *Collections Arranged:* Contemporary Ceramics: The Artist's Viewpoint (auth, catalog), 77. *Pos:* Dir, Sch Kalamazoo Inst Arts, 83-92, fac, 73-92. *Teaching:* Chmn, Dept Ceramics, Kalamazoo Inst Arts, Mich, 73-90. *Awards:* First Place, Battle Creek Craft Biennial, 79; Purchase Award, Kalamazoo Art Competition, 83; Cash Award, Mich Ceramics, 83. *Mem:* Nat Conf Educ Ceramic Arts; Am Crafts Coun; Kalamazoo Area Ceramists Asn; Nat Asn Sch Art & Design. *Media:* Clay. *Publ:* Auth, Computerized glass calculation, Ceramics Monthly, 12/83. *Mailing Add:* 10936 Three Mile Rd Plainwell MI 49080

KENDRICK, MEL
SCULPTOR
b Boston, Mass, 1949. *Study:* Trinity Col, Hartford, BA, 71; Hunter Col, New York, 73. *Work:* Metrop Mus Art, Whitney Mus Am Art, Brooklyn Mus, New York; Addison Gallery Am Art, Andover, Mass; Storm King Ctr, Mountainville, NY; Centro Cult Art Contemporaneo, Mexico City, Mex; Walker Art Center, Minneapolis, Minn; High Mus Art, Atlanta, GA. *Exhib:* Solo exhibs, John Weber Gallery, New York, 83, 85, 87, 89 & 92, Margo Leavin Gallery, Los Angeles 84, 88 & 90, Barbara Krakow Gallery, Boston, Mass, Univ Mass Gallery, 86, Contemp Arts Mus, Houston, 86, St Louis Art Mus, Mo, 87, Galeria 57, Madrid, Spain, 87, C Grimaldii Gallery, Baltimore, MD, 90 and others; Biennial Exhib, Whitney Mus Am Art, 85; Art of the 80s, Metrop Mus Art, New York, 88; Four American: Aspects of Current Sculpture, Brooklyn Mus, New York, 89; Baltimore Mus Art and Grimaldis Gallery, MD, 90; John Weber Gallery, New York, 92; Guild Hall Mus, New York, 92; and others. *Awards:* Grants, Creative Artists Pub Serv Prog, 74 & 78; Nat Endowment Arts, 78 & 81. *Bibliog:* Michael Boodro (auth), Mel Kendrick's Calculated Risks, Art News, p 104-109, 5/91; Michael Kimmelman (auth), In Westchester, Sculpture Meets Nature, NY Times, 7/19/91; Kay Larson (auth), Summer Stock, New York, p 60, 9/2/91; Miles Beller (auth), Interlocking Parts, Art News, No 13, p 24, 4/9/92; Jed Perl, Through a Blighted Landscape, New Criterion, 9/92. *Dealer:* John Weber Gallery 142 Greene St New York NY 10012. *Mailing Add:* 134 Duane St New York NY 10007

KENNA, MICHAEL
PHOTOGRAPHER
b Widnes, Cheshire, Eng, Nov, 20, 53. *Study:* Upholland Col, Lancashire, Eng, 65-72; Banbury Sch Art, Oxfordshire, 72-73; Col Printing, London, HND Distinction, 73-76. *Work:* Australian Nat Gallery, Canberra; Bibliotheque Nationale, Paris, France; San Francisco Mus Mod Art; Fox Talbot Mus, Lacock, Eng; Milwaukee Art Mus; Victoria & Albert Mus, London. *Exhib:* Arbres, Georges Pompidou Ctr, Paris, France, 82; solo exhibs, Fox Talbot Mus, Lacock, Wiltshire, Eng, 83 & Bampton Arts Ctr,

Oxfordshire, 84; 20th Century Photographs, Hololulu Acad Arts, Hawaii, 84; Madison Art Ctr, Wis, 85; Chateau d'Eau Mus, Toulouse, France, 86; Nicephore Niepce Mus, Chalon-Sur-Saone, France, 86; Gallery Min, Tokyo, Japan; Photographers Gallery, London, 87; Mus Ludwig, Cologne & Kunstverein Gottingen, Fed Repub Ger, 87. *Teaching:* Friends of Photography, San Francisco, Calif. *Awards:* Friends of Imogene Cunningham Award, San Francisco, Calif, 81; KQED/Zellerbach Award, San Francisco, Calif, 81. *Bibliog:* Jean Francois Chevrier (auth), Michael Kenna: Photographs, Stephen Wirtz Gallery & Weston Gallery, 84. *Publ:* Michael Kenna 1975-1987 (exhib catalog), Gallery Min, Tokyo, Japan; Michael Kenna - Night Walk, San Francisco Friends of Photography. *Mailing Add:* PO Box 590202 San Francisco CA 94159

KENNEDY, GENE (EUGENE MURRAY)
PHOTOGRAPHER, EDUCATOR
b San Diego, Calif, Mar 13, 46. *Study:* San Diego State Univ, BA, 69, MA, 76. *Work:* Mus Mod Art, New York; Cent Wash Univ; San Diego Natural Hist Mus & San Diego State Univ, San Diego; Hallmark Contemp Collection, Kansas City; Calif State Libr. *Exhib:* One-man shows, Moore Col Art, 83 & 89, San Diego Nat Hist Mus, 83, Lightwork Gallery, Sacramento, 86, 87 & 89, Northern Ill Univ, 87, Univ Calif Exten, 88, Univ the Paciic, 88; group exhibs, San Francisco Camerawork, 83, Purdue Univ, W Lafayette, 85, Mus Contemp Photog, 85; and others. *Collections Arranged:* Robert Bechtle: Reference and Realism in Four Modes, 78, Fletcher Benton Sculpture, 79 & Helen Levitt: Color Photographs, 80, Tom Holland: Works from 1969-1979, 80, Manuel Neri: Twenty Years, 81 & Helen Shirk: Metalwork, 81, Grossmont Col Gallery, El Cajon, Calif. *Pos:* Dir, Art Gallery Grossmont Col, 73-81; The Darkroom, Sacramento, 86- *Teaching:* Instr photog, San Diego State Univ, 70-73, Grossmont Col, El Cajon, Calif, 72-81, Univ Calif, San Diego, 82-83, Maine Photographic Workshops, 82; Univ The Pacific, 87-88; Univ Calif, Davis, 89; Sierra Col, Rocklin, Calif, 89-91; Cosumnes River Col, Scramento, 90-91. *Awards:* Spec Award of Excellence, Moore Col Art, 83; Nat Endowment Arts Grant, 84. *Bibliog:* Portfolio: Photographs by Gene Kennedy, J Am Photog, 3/85; Jan Haag (auth), Gene Kennedy: Ravaged Landscapes, View Camera Mag, 3/89; Gary F Kurutz (auth), Violations of the Landscape: The California Photography of Gene Kennedy, Calif State Libr Found Bull, 7/90. *Mem:* Soc Photographic Educ; Friends of Photog. *Media:* Photography. *Publ:* Ed, Garry Winogrand, 76, ed & illusr, Carol Shaw-Sutton: Crossing Over, 78, Viewpoint: Ceramics 1978 & 1979, 78 & 79 & ed, Helen Levitt: Color Photographs, 80, Grossmont Col Publ. *Dealer:* The Darkroom 708 57th St Sacramento CA 95819. *Mailing Add:* 708 57th St Sacramento CA 95819

KENNEDY, HARRIET FORTE
PAINTER, SCULPTOR
b Cambridge, Mass. *Study:* Northeastern Univ, BA, 77; Harvard Univ, Cert, 74. *Work:* Walter Reed Army Med Ctr, Washington, DC; Mass Col Pharmacy; Smith-Mason Gallery, Washington, DC. *Exhib:* Mus Sch, Boston, Mass, 63 & 64; Mus Fine Arts, Boston, Mass; Afro-Am Artists, Mus Nat Ctr, Boston; NJ State Art Mus, Trenton, NJ; Mus Sci & Indus, Chicago, Ill; The Alchemi Gallery, Boston; Smith Mason Gallery, Washington, DC. *Pos:* Asst registr, Mus Fine Arts, Boston, 68-73; asst dir/registr & cur, Boston Gallery, Mus Nat Ctr Afro-Am Artists, 73- *Teaching:* Prof, art history, Northeastern Univ, 79-80; lectr art history, Mass Col Art, 80-83, Simmons Col, 89-90. *Mem:* Am Asn Mus; African Am Mus Asn; Nat Conf Artists; Medford Arts Coun. *Publ:* Auth, Van Ein Stam Our Common Origins, 72; An Independent Woman: Met A Warnick Fuller Cat, 86. *Mailing Add:* Nat Ctr Afro-American Artists Inc 300 Walnut Ave Boston MA 02119

KENNEDY, J WILLIAM
PAINTER
b Cincinnati, Ohio, Aug 17, 03. *Study:* Art Acad Cincinnati; Carnegie Inst Technol, AB; Univ Ill, MFA. *Work:* Portraits, Ind Univ, Bloomington & Univ Ill, Champaign; A E Staley Co, Decatur, Ill; Withrow High Sch, Cincinnati. *Comn:* Portraits: Pres Herman B Wells, 62, VPres Joseph Franklin, 63 & Dean Edmundson, 64, Ind Univ, Bloomington & Dean Carl Brandley, 67 & Col Leslie A Bryan, 69, Univ Ill, Champaign. *Exhib:* 1st, 2nd & 3rd Nat Exhibs, Rockefeller Ctr, New York; San Francisco World's Fair; Corcoran Biennial; two Pa Acad Fine Arts Ann; Richmond Biennial, Va. *Teaching:* Prof art, Univ Ill, Champaign, 26-70. *Awards:* Merit Award, Fla Gulf Coast Art Ctr, 72; Hon Mention, Milwaukee Art Gallery; First Prize in painting, Decatur Art Ctr. *Mem:* Provincetown Art Asn; Fla Gulf Coast Art Ctr. *Media:* Vinyl. *Mailing Add:* 1414 Monte Carlo Dr Clearwater FL 33546

KENNEDY, JAMES EDWARD
PAINTER, SCULPTOR
b Jackson, Miss, Sept 30, 33. *Study:* Ala State Univ, BS; Ind Univ, MAT(painting); Spring Hill Col. *Work:* Johnson Publ Co Collection, Chicago. *Exhib:* Atlanta Univ Nat Exhib, 60-64; Eastern Shore Art Gallery, 67; Birmingham, Ala Festival Arts Centennial Exhib, 72; Ala State Univ, 72; Univ WFla, 73. *Teaching:* Prof art hist & painting, Univ S Ala, Mobile, 68-, chmn dept art, currently; guest instr Afro-Am art, Morehead State Univ, Minn, summer 72. *Awards:* Afro-Am Art Slide Grant, 69 & Ethnic-Am Minority Art Slide Libr Grant, 71, Samuel H Kress Found. *Bibliog:* Afro-American Artists, Boston Pub Libr, 73. *Mem:* Nat Conf Artists; Col Art Asn Am. *Publ:* Coauth, An Afro-American Slide Project, Art J, 70-71 & An Afro-American Art and Artist's Finders Index, Am Revolution Bicentennial Comn, Washington, DC, 73. *Mailing Add:* Dept Art Univ South Ala 307 University Dr Mobile AL 36688

KENNEY, DOUGLAS
CERAMIST, CLAY SCULPTOR
b San Diego, Calif, 1962. *Study:* San Diego Mesa Col, AA, 83; San Diego State Univ, BA, 85; Rochester Inst Technol, Scholar, 87, MFA(ceramics), 89. *Comn:* Three custom relief tile disks on plywood, comn by Carole Kraus, 92. *Exhib:* Dimensions 88, 90 & 92, Lenexa, Kans; Wichita National, Kans, 88; Octagon 20th Anniversary Exhib, Ames, Iowa, 89; New York Int Gift Fair, 89 & 90; Definitions in Clay, San Antonio, Tex, 90; solo exhibs, Perspectives of Clay, RIT Libr, 88, Perspectives Previews, Minneapolis, Minn, 90, Douglas Kenney Ceramics, Gallery Authentique, Roslyn, NY, 91, Recent Ceramic Work, Turquoise Coyote, San Antonio, Tex, 91, Turquoise Coyote, San Antonio, Tex, 92, Creative Arts Gallery, San Antonio, Tex, 91 & 92, Gallery Authentique, Roslyn, NY, 92; Am Crafts Enterprises Show, Baltimore, Md, 89; Just Fired/Nat Coun Educ Ceramics AAS, Tempe Arts Ctr, Ariz, 91; Tokyo Crafts Expo '92, Japan. *Teaching:* Instr ceramics, San Antonio Col, 89-92; guest lectr, Univ Calif-Davis, 90; guest lectr/workshop, Univ Tex, San Antonio, 91. *Awards:* Patron Purchase Award, Wichita Nat, 88; Wallace Mem Libr Purchase Award, 89. *Mem:* Col Art Asn; Am Craft Coun; Nat Coun Educ Ceramic Arts. *Media:* Clay; Enamel on Metal. *Publ:* Am Craft, Gallery Sect, B/W photo, 12/89, 1/90 & 8-9/92; Art Calender Mag, B/W cover photo & statement, 12/90; Raku: A Practical Approach, B/W photo & statement, Chilton Bk Co, 91; Raku Integrations, Ceramics Mo, 6-8/91; color photog, Deco Deco, Japanese Interior Design Mag, 2/92. *Mailing Add:* 2503 Jackson Keller No 121 San Antonio TX 78230

KENNEY, ESTELLE KOVAL
ART THERAPIST, PAINTER
b Chicago, Ill, Feb 15, 28. *Study:* Sch Art Inst Chicago, with Joshua Kind, BFA, 76, MFA, 78; registered art therapist, ATR; Chicago Inst Psychoanalysis, TEP grad, 78; Loyola Univ Chicago, 82- *Work:* Ill State Mus, Springfield; Union League Club Chicago. *Exhib:* The Chicago Connection, traveling, 76-77; Contemp Issues--Works on Paper by Women, Woman's Bldg, Los Angeles, plus others, 77-78; solo show, Renaissance Soc, Bergman Gallery, Univ Chicago, 80; Navy Pier, Chicago, 80; Artists Urban Gateways, 81; and others. *Pos:* Art therapist, Grove Sch Handicapped, Lake Forest, Ill, 72-77, New Triar E & C, Spec Educ, Winnetka, Ill, 77-78, Cove Sch Learning Disabled, Evanston, Ill, 79-81 & North Shore Inst Therapy through Arts, Winnetka, Ill, 79-81; contrib ed, Format Mag, 78- *Teaching:* Art therapy lectr, Univ Ill Circle Campus, Chicago, 77 & Nat Col Educ, Evanston, Ill, 77; dir art therapy prog, Loyola Univ Chicago, 81- *Awards:* First Purchase Prize, Union League Club of Chicago, 74 & Ill State Mus, Springfield, 75. *Mem:* Ill Art Educ Asn; Nat Art Educ Asn; Am Art Therapy Asn; Ill Art Therapy Asn (pres). *Media:* Enamel, Watercolor. *Publ:* Auth, Joshua Kind: Naive painting in Illinois, Format Mag. *Dealer:* Sonia Zaks Gallery 620 North Michigan Ave Chicago IL 60611. *Mailing Add:* Loyola Univ Lake Shore Campus 6525 N Sheridan Rd Chicago IL 60626

KENNON, ARTHUR BRUCE
EDUCATOR, EDITOR
b Mine la Motte, Mo, Feb 18, 33. *Study:* Southeast Mo State Univ, BS, 58, Southern Ill Univ, MFA, 67, Univ Mo, Specialist Art Educ, 74. *Pos:* Coord first ABC Art Program, St Louis Art Mus, Ferguson-Florissant Sch Dist, 91-92; Evaluator Fine Arts Survey, State La Dept Educ, Arts/Humanities Div, 91. *Teaching:* Dir Art Educ, Desloge Mo Pub Schs, 59-64; coordr art, Ferguson & Florissant Mo Schs, 64-; adj fac art & educ, Webster Univ, Webster Groves, Mo, 70. *Awards:* Art Educator of the Year, Mo Art Educ Asn, 78; Outstanding Contributions to Art Educ, Nat Arts Educ Asn, 79; Host Comt, NAEA Conv, Kansas City, 90. *Bibliog:* Jean Dean (auth), Art Leaders, Northwest Journal, 10-10-88; Clarissa Start (auth), Creative Way, St Louis Post Dispatch, 7-15-88; Garnet Leader (auth), Our New President, The Sketch Book, Spring 88; John Archibald (auth), Art Kennon, St Louis Post-Dispatch, 11/89. *Mem:* Royal Soc Encouragement Arts (Fellow); life mem Kappa Pi Int Hon Art Fraternity (pres-current); Mo Art Educ Asn (pres, 76-78); St Louis Art Supervisors Asn (pres, 65-67); Berkeley Community Teachers Asn (pres 66-67 & 72-73). *Publ:* Auth, Art is Basic, Kappa Pi, 87; Andy Warhol, Kappa Pi Sketch Book, Spring 87; ed, The Sketch Book of Kappa Pi (mag) Kappa Pi, 76-; auth, Arts Integration in the Elementary Curriculum, La Dept Educ, 92. *Mailing Add:* 9231 Paul Adrian Dr Crestwood MO 63126

KENOJUAK (ASHEVAK)
PRINTMAKER, SCULPTOR
b Ikerasak, Baffin Island, NT, Dec 25, 33. *Work:* Nat Gallery Can, Ottawa, Ont; Mus Man, Ottawa; Toronto Dominion Bank, Ont; Amon Carter, Ft Worth, Tex; McMichael Collection, Ont. *Comn:* Metal plaque, Alcan Can, 64; murals, Expo 67, Montreal & Expo 70, Osaka, Japan. *Exhib:* Winnipeg Art Gallery, 75; Musee d'ethnographie, Neuchatel, Switz, 76; and others. *Awards:* Order of Can, Govt Can. *Mem:* Royal Can Acad of Arts. *Media:* Lithography, Engraving; Stonecut. *Publ:* Auth, Kenojuak, Nat Film Bd, 61; Kenojuak, Blodgett, Mintmark Press. *Dealer:* West Baffin Eskimo Coop Ltd Cape Dorset NT X0A 0C0 Can. *Mailing Add:* General Delivery Cape Dorset NT X0A 0C0 Canada

KENT, H LATHAM
PAINTER
b Mass, June 20, 30. *Study:* Vesper George Sch Art, 51, Boston, Mass; apprentice with Artie McKenzie, Fla. *Exhib:* Coral Gables Art Gallery, Coral Gables, Fla; Int Boat Show Art Exhibs, Miami Beach, Fla; Gingerbread Sq Gallery, Key West, Fla; Acacia Gallery, W Bridge Water, Mass; Aries East Gallery, Brewster, Mass; and others. *Pos:* Artist, Steve Hannagan, New York 51-54 & Bronzini of New York, 54-57; pres & off, Southern Chapter, Am

Arist Prof League, formerly; Com artist, Coco-Cola, Union Pacific Railroad, Libbey Glassware & Admiral, formerly. *Mem:* Copley Soc, Boston, Mass; Int Soc Marine Painters, Fla; Am Artists Prof League, SFla (pres, 78-83). *Media:* Oil. *Mailing Add:* 7 Windsong Landing Chatham MA 02633

KENTON, MARY JEAN
PAINTER
b Fayette County, Pa, 1946. *Study:* Pomona Col, Claremont, Calif, BA, 68; San Francisco Art Inst, MFA, 74. *Work:* Mattress Factory, Pittsburgh, Pa. *Comn:* Painting, The Floating Rectangles, comn by John Cage, 90. *Exhib:* Geometry of Color, Laughlin House Property, Fayette County, Pa, 89; Mary Jean Kenton: A Survey, 1973-1990, Allegheny Col Art Galleries, Meadville, Pa, 90; Carnegie Int 1991, Carnegie Mus Art & Mattress Factory, 91-92, Mary Jean Kenton & David Nyzio, Mattress Factory, Pittsburg, Pa, 92-93. *Pos:* Ed (for Pittsburgh), New Art Examiner, 86- *Awards:* Fel in Art Criticism, Pa Coun Arts, 88 & 91. *Bibliog:* Robert Raczka (auth), Mary Jean Kenton's Freedom (with limits), Penn State J Contemp Criticism, University Park, Pa, 34-38; Michael Odom (auth), A cage without Bars, In Pittsburgh, Pittsburgh, Pa, 10/16-10/22/91; Sheena Wagstaff (auth), Earth Colors, Pittsburgh Mag, Pittsburgh, Pa, 22-23, 8/92. *Media:* Oil & Acrylic, Watercolor. *Publ:* Auth, Mary Jean Kenton: The Geometry of Color, pvt publ, 89; Points of View IV: Artist's Choice (catalog, essay), Westminster Col Art Gallery, New Wilmington, Pa, 92. *Mailing Add:* Box 42 Merrittstown PA 15463

KENYON, COLLEEN FRANCES
PHOTOGRAPHER, ADMINISTRATOR
b Dunkirk, NY, Aug 6, 51. *Study:* Skidmore Col, Saratoga Springs, NY, BS, 73; Ind Univ, Bloomington, with Henry Holmes Smith in photog, MFA, 76. *Work:* Mus Mod Art, New York; Int Mus Photog, George Eastman House, Rochester, NY; Ind Univ, Bloomington; Metrop Mus Art, New York. *Exhib:* Mirrors & Windows: Am Photog Since 1960, Mus Mod Art, New York, 78; one-person show, Foto Gallery, New York, 80, Camerawork Gallery, San Francisco, 80, Sacred Childern, ARCO Ctr Visual Art, Los Angeles, Calif, 80, Color & Hand-Colored Photographs, Silver Image Gallery, 81 & Catskill Ctr Photog, Spring 82; 15 years retrospective, Kleinert Gallery, Woodstock, NY, 86; Pleasures & Terrors of Domestic Comfort, Mus Mod Art, New York. *Collections Arranged:* Correspondents, Catskill Ctr for Photog, Woodstock, NY, 78 & Color in Question, 79; Six X Six, Kingston Artist Group, 84; The Still Life, The Moving Hand, Greene Co Coun Arts, 85. *Pos:* Dir educ, Ctr for Photog, Woodstock, NY, 78-80, exec dir, 81- *Teaching:* Instr photog, Slippery Rock State Col, Pa, Jan-May, 77; instr photog, Bard Col, Annandale, NY, winter 79. *Awards:* Creative Artists Pub Serv Prog Fel; NYFA Fel; Polaroid Studio Grant. *Bibliog:* Lawrence Audette (auth), Ulster Arts, Ulster Co Coun on Arts, 79; Portfolio, (interview & photogs), Darkroom Mag, 5-6/80. *Mem:* Soc for Photog Educ; Women's Caucus for Art. *Media:* Photography; Painting. *Publ:* Contribr (work featured), Alternative Photographic Processes, Morgan & Morgan, 78, Self-Portrayal, Friends of Photog, 79, Popular Photography Annual 1979, Popular Photog, 79 & Ulster Arts, Ulster Co Coun on Arts, 79; auth, Portfolio (interview & photographs), Darkroom Mag, 80. *Dealer:* Photofind Woodstock NY. *Mailing Add:* Box 77 Rte 212 Shady NY 12479

KEOUGH, JEFFREY
DIRECTOR
b Concord, Mass, Oct 30, 53. *Study:* Sch of the Mus Fine Arts, Boston, Mass. *Pos:* Dir of Exhibs, Mass Col Art, currently. *Mailing Add:* Mass Col of Art North Hall Gallery 621 Huntington Ave Boston MA 02115

KEPALAS (ELENA KEPALAITE)
SCULPTOR, PAINTER
b Vilnius, Lithuania; US citizen. *Study:* Ont Col Art, Toronto; Brooklyn Mus Sch Art. *Work:* Pa Acad Fine Arts, Philadelphia; Univ Mass Art Gallery, Amherst; Libr & Mus Performing Arts, Lincoln Ctr, NY; Lithuanian Mus, Adelaide, Australia; Mus Mod Art Lending Serv, New York. *Comn:* Bronze bust, Mr Louis Horst, New York, 62; bronze bust, Mrs Gunilla Kessler, New York, 71; bronze bust, Mr Robert Spring, 87; bronze reliefs of 4 American Saints: Frances Cabrini, John Newmann, Elizabeth Ann Seton & Isaac Jogues, 92. *Exhib:* Pa Acad Fine Arts, Philadelphia, 68; Silvermine Guild Artists Ann, New Canaan, Conn, 69; Jersey City Mus, NJ, 69-71; Phoenix Gallery, New York, 70, 72, 74, 76, 78-81 & 84. *Awards:* First Prize, Coun Advan Lithuanian Cult, Chicago, Ill, 78; Accademico d'Italia con Medaglia d'Oro, Salsomaggiore, Italia, 80; Doris Kreindler Mem Award, Am Soc Contemp Artists, 83. *Bibliog:* Edgar Buonagurio (auth), Elena Kepalas, Art Mag, 6/79; Elena Kepalas Bronze Sculptor, New York Arts J, 79; Palmer Poroner (auth), Discoveries in Arts, Art Speak, 11/81. *Mem:* Am Soc Contemp Artists; Metropolitan Painters & Sculptors. *Media:* Bronze; Acrylic, oil. *Mailing Add:* 99-05 59th Ave Apt No 1F Rego Park NY 11368

KEPES, GYORGY
PAINTER, EDUCATOR
b Selyp, Hungary, Oct 4, 06. *Study:* Royal Acad Fine Arts, Budapest, MFA, 28; RI Sch Design, Hon PhD, 81. *Work:* Univ Ill; Dallas Mus Fine Arts; Albright-Knox Art Gallery, Buffalo, NY; Mus Mod Art & Whitney Mus Am Art, New York; Gyorgy Kepes Mus, Egar, Hungary, 91; and many others. *Comn:* Murals, Grad Ctr, Harvard Univ, Travelers Ins Co, Los Angeles, Sheraton Hotel, Dallas & Chicago, Children's Libr, Fitchburg, Mass & Church of Redeemer, Baltimore; and many others. *Exhib:* Art Inst Chicago; San Francisco Mus Art; Mus Fine Arts, Houston; Nat Collection Fine Arts, Washington, DC; Whitney Mus Am Art, New York; one-man shows, Dartmouth Col, 77, Prakapas Gallery, New York, 77, Hayden Gallery, Mass Inst Technol, 78 & Alpha Gallery, Boston, 80, 81 & 83; and many others. *Collections Arranged:* Designed exhib, Arts of the United Nations, Art Inst Chicago, 64; designer sect of Triennale de Milano, 68. *Pos:* Head light dept, Chicago Inst Design, 37. *Teaching:* Head light & color dept, New Bauhaus, 37-38; instr, Chicago Inst Design, 38-43; prof visual design, Mass Inst Technol, 46-80, dir, Ctr Advan Visual Studies, 67-74, Inst prof emer, 71-; vis prof, Harvard Univ, 64-66 & 79; artist in residence, Am Acad Rome, 74-75. *Awards:* Guggenheim Fel, 60-61; Medaglia d'Oro, Convengo Int Artisti Critici e Studiosi d'Arte, 66; Fine Arts Award, Am Inst Architects, 68; IAFA Award, Ill Acad Fine Art, 92. *Mem:* Nat Inst Arts & Lett; fel Am Acad Arts & Sci. *Media:* Acrylic, Oil. *Publ:* Auth, Language of Vision, 44 & The New Landscape, 56, Paul Theobald & Co; ed, Visual Arts Today, 60; Vols I-VII, In: Vision & Value Series, Braziller, 65, 66 & 72. *Mailing Add:* 90 Larchwood Dr Cambridge MA 02138

KEPETS, HUGH MICHAEL
PAINTER, PRINTMAKER
b Cleveland, Ohio, Feb 6, 46. *Study:* Carnegie-Mellon Univ, BFA, 68; Ohio Univ, MFA, 72. *Work:* Metrop Mus Art, New York; Philadelphia Mus Fine Arts; Cleveland Mus Art; Libr Cong, Washington, DC; Yale Univ Art Gallery. *Comn:* Cover, Paris Rev 65, spring 76; City Walls Inc, New York, 76; Outdoor three dimensional wall painting, Three Rivers Arts Festival, Pittsburgh, 82. *Exhib:* Cleveland Mus Art, 68-81; Brooklyn Mus, NY, 72 & 76; 35th Midyear Show, Butler Inst Am Art, 72; Works on Paper, Va Mus Fine Arts, Richmond, 74; Boston Printmakers 27th Annual, Boston Mus Fine Arts, 75; West '79/The Law, Minn Mus Art, St Paul, 79; Am Acad Arts & Lett, New York, 78 & 80; One-man shows, Fischbac Gallery, New York, NY, 74, 76, 78, Marcus/Gordon Assoc, Pittsburgh, 81, Roger Ramsay Gallery, Chicago, 84, 88, David Adamson Gallery, Washington, DC, 86, Randall Beck Gallery, Boston, 86; plus many others group and solo exhibitions. *Awards:* Nat Endowment Arts Grant, 76; Cleveland Arts Prize, 79; Creative Artists Pub Serv Grant, 80. *Dealer:* Orion Ed 270 Lafayette St New York NY 10012. *Mailing Add:* 134 E 16 St New York NY 10003

KEPNER, RITA
SCULPTOR, ADMINISTRATOR
b Binghamton, NY, Nov 15, 44. *Study:* Elmira Col, NY, 62-63, Harpur Col, State Univ NY, BA, 66, Okla Univ, 88; Accademia Bedriacehse Calvatore, Italy, hon MFA, 84; Seattle Pac Univ, 90; Western Wash Univ, 91-92. *Work:* Warsaw Mus, Poland; Seattle City Collection, Wash; Kenmore Libr; Washington Mutual, Seattle; Children's Hosp, Seattle. *Comn:* Wood Sculpture, City of Znin, Poland, 77; wood sculpture, City of Zalaegerszeg, Hungary, 77; bronze sculpture, Develop Authority, Seattle, 78; granite sculpture, Seattle Publ Libr, 78. *Exhib:* Artist in the City, Seattle Art Mus, Wash, 77; Int Sculptors, Znin, Poland, 76 & Zalaegerszeg, Hungary, 77; Am Artist in Poland, Zoliborg Mus, Warsaw, 81; Am Artist in Wiesbaden, Die Roemer, Ger, 88. *Pos:* Artist-in-residence, Seattle, 75, 77-78. *Teaching:* Instr Sculpture Experimental Col, Univ Wash, 72-74; instr sculpture, Evergreen Col, Olympia, Wash, 74-78. *Awards:* Appointed Visual Arts Ambassador-informal-between USA & Poland, 76-81; Kosciuszko Found Travel Grant Award Winner, 75, 76, 79, 81. *Bibliog:* Something Happened in Seattle, NEA Newsletter, 76; David Miller (dir), Rita Kepner Sculptor, 81; Who's Who in the World, 92-94. *Mem:* Bainbridge Island Arts Coun (founder, 86); Int Artists Asn UNESCO, Paris; Artists Equity Asn; Int Artists Coop, Edelvecht, Ger. *Media:* Wood, Stone. *Publ:* Contribr, Northwest Art, The Arts, Leonardo Mag, Poland Mag, Polska Panorama, Seattle Post Intelligencer. *Mailing Add:* 6681 Flagler Rd Nordland WA 98358

KERMES, CONSTANTINE JOHN
PAINTER, PRINTMAKER
b Pittsburgh, Pa, Dec 6, 23. *Study:* Carnegie-Mellon Univ, BFA; also with Victor Candell, Leo Manso & Frank Lloyd Wright. *Work:* Storm King Art Ctr; Notre Dame Art Mus, South Bend, Ind; Stockmanshove Mus, Damme, Belgium; Pa State Univ, University Park; Sabbathday Lake Shaker Community, Maine. *Comn:* Murals, Pa Hist & Mus Comn, Cornwall Mus, 68; Fontrier Found, Paris; assemblage murals, Ford New Holland, Pa & Brussels, Belg; Farm & Indust Equip Inst, Wrigley Bldg, Chicago. *Exhib:* Solo exhibs, Grimaldis Gallery, Baltimore, 79, Reading Mus, 80, ten solo shows at Seligmann Gallery, New York & Demuth Found Gallery, Lancaster, Pa, 87; Design Rev, Smithsonian Inst, Washington, DC, 69; Pa Watercolor Soc, 79, 80, 84 & 85; Hancock Shaker Mus, Pittsfield, Mass, 89; and many others. *Awards:* Design Awards, Am Iron & Steel Inst, 65, 69, 73 & 75; Traveling Exhib Painting Prize, Petrol Industs, 71; Award Oxford, Md Ann Exhib, 91 & 92. *Bibliog:* Morse (auth), Shakers & Worlds People, Dodd Mead, 80; Horgan (auth), Shaker Holy Land, Harvard Press, 82; S Stein (auth), Shaker Experience in America, Yale Univ Press, 92. *Media:* Oil, Watercolor; Woodcut, Lithography. *Publ:* Auth, Shaker Architecture, 70; auth & illusr, American Icons, 75; Folk images of rural Pennsylvania, Pa Folklife, 6/75 & 6/81; Symbols of Love in Folk Art, 87. *Dealer:* Jacques Seligmann Gallery 5 E 57th St New York NY 10022. *Mailing Add:* 981 Landis Valley Rd Lancaster PA 17601

KERN, ARTHUR (EDWARD)
EDUCATOR, SCULPTOR
b New Orleans, La, Oct 27, 31. *Study:* Tulane Univ La, BA, 53, MFA, 55. *Exhib:* One-man shows, Ariz State Univ, 74 & Int Sculpture Conf, Tulane Univ, 76; South Houston Gallery, New York, 75. *Teaching:* Asst prof drawing, Univ Southwestern La, 67-69; assoc prof painting & sculpture, Tulane Univ La, 69-, assoc chmn dept art, 72- *Mailing Add:* 1730 Pine St New Orleans LA 70118

KERNE, BARBARA DAVIS
PAINTER, PRINTMAKER
b New York, NY, Jan 1, 38. *Study:* Brooklyn Col, BA, 58; Univ Md, MA, 69. *Work:* Corcoran Gallery Art, Libr Cong & US Dept State Art Bank, Washington, DC; Norton Gallery Art, West Palm Beach, Fla; Franz Masereel Ctr Graphic Arts, Kasterlee, Belg; Portland Mus Art, Ore; Univ Tenn, Knoxville. *Comn:* painting, Art Pub Archit Montgomery Co, Rockville, Md, 87; painting, Grand Hyatt Hotel, Washington, DC, 87; painting, Signet Bank, Corp Hqs, Washington, DC. *Exhib:* Solo exhibs, Prints and collages, 79 & Paintings, 88-90, Franz Bader Gallery, Washington, DC, Paintings, 82, Etchings, 85, Jane Haslem Gallery, Washington, DC, Paintings, Montgomery Col, Rockville, Md, Paintings, Addison-Ripley Gallery, Washington, DC, 93; California 88, Calif Soc Printmakers, Mill Col Art Gallery, Oakland, 88, Somar Gallery, San Francisco, 90 & Berkeley Art Ctr, Calif, 91; 63rd SAGA Nat Print Exhib, Galleries Fed Plaza, New York, 89; Contemporary American Printmaking, Selby Gallery, Ringling Sch Art, Sarasota, Fla, 92; Lynne Ward Mem Travelling Exhib, Portland Mus Art, Ore, 92; Irene Leach Mem Exhib, Chrysler Mus Art, Norfolk, Va, 92; and many others. *Teaching:* Prof art, Montgomery Col, Rockville, Md, 72- *Awards:* Best in Show, Purchase, Art on Paper, Md Fedn Arts, 84; Best in Show, Purchase, Mid-Am Biennial, Owensboro Mus Art, 86; Fel, Franz Masereel Ctr Graphic Arts, Kasterlee, Belg, 87; Fel, Virginia Ctr Creative Arts, Sweet Briar, Va, 91-93. *Bibliog:* Gail Forman (auth), Coloring the garden serene, Washington Post, 10/3/86; Cintia Cabib (dir), Barbara Davis Kerne (video), public television, 87; Cintia Cabib (auth), Barbara Davis Kerne, printmaker, Montgomery Cable, 87; A A Every (dir), Barbara Kerne, Educator/Artist (video), public television, 92. *Mem:* Soc Am Graphic Artists; Calif Printmakers Soc; Col Art Asn; S Graphics Coun Bd 90-91 (secy, 89-90); Coalition Washington Artists (secy, 88, 89, 90 & 91). *Media:* Oil; Intaglio. *Dealer:* Addison-Ripley Gallery Ltd 9 Hillyer Ct NW Washington DC 20008. *Mailing Add:* 10409 Lloyd Rd Potomac MD 20854

KERNS, ED (JOHNSON), JR
PAINTER
b Richmond, Va, Feb 22, 45. *Study:* Va Commonwealth Univ, BFA; Md Inst Col Art, Baltimore, with Grace Hartigan, MFA. *Work:* Aldrich Mus Art, Ridgefield, Conn; Chase Manhattan Bank, New York; Edward Albee Found, New York; Citicorp, New York; Corcoran Gallery, Washington, DC. *Exhib:* Albright-Knox Art Gallery, Buffalo, NY, 71 & 72; one-man shows, A M Sachs Gallery, 72 & 74 & Rosa Esman Gallery, 76-87; Brooklyn Mus, NY, 74; Grey Art Gallery, New York Univ, NY, 77; Dayton Art Inst, Ohio, 77; Ctr Arts, Muhlenberg Col, Allentown, Pa, 77 & 81; San Francisco Mus Mod Art, 78; Pa Acad Fine Arts, 82; and others. *Pos:* Eugene H Clapp Prof Humanities, Dept Art, Lafayette Col, Easton Pa. *Teaching:* Prof art, Lafayette Col, Easton, Pa, 80- *Awards:* Art Achievement Key, Va Commonwealth Univ, 67; Artist of the Year, Larry Aldrich Assoc, New York, 71. *Bibliog:* Articles, Art News, 12/84, Arts Mag, 1/79 & Artforum, 1/80. *Mem:* Col Art Asn. *Media:* Acrylic, Collage. *Publ:* Coauth (with Loder), Guerillas of Grace, Luriamedia Press, 84; Tracks in the Straw, Luriamedia Press, 85; Eavesdropping on the Echoes, Luriamedia Press, 87. *Dealer:* Rosa Esman Gallery 70 Green St New York NY 10012. *Mailing Add:* Dept Art Lafayette Col Easton PA 18042

KERNS, GINGER
PAINTER, EDUCATOR
b Brooklyn, NY, July 3, 1948. *Study:* New York Univ, BA, 70; Northwestern Univ, MA, 74. *Work:* Metrop Mus Art, New York. *Comn:* Portraits, Gantt Found, Chicago, Ill. *Exhib:* Theory & Practice, Mus Mod Art, 78; Everson Mus Art, Syracuse, NY, 83; Laguna Art Mus, Laguna Beach, Calif, 88. *Teaching:* Prof, Univ Calif, Berkeley, 87- *Mem:* Cowboy Hall of Fame. *Mailing Add:* Univ Calif at Berkeley Berkeley CA 94720

KERR, JAMES WILFRID
PAINTER, CONCEPTUAL ARTIST
b New York, NY, Aug 7, 1897. *Study:* Poppenhusen Inst, College Point, NY, 14; New York Sch Fine & Appl Art, 20-2 Social Res, 33-34; study with Howard Giles & Camilio Egas, Ecuador, Jacques Maroger, Louvre, Paris. *Work:* Mus City New York; Joslyn Art Mus, Omaha; Newark Mus, NJ; NMex State Fair Permanent Art Collection, Albuquerque; Albuquerque Mus; and others. *Exhib:* Painting in the United States, Carnegie Inst, Pittsburgh, 49; Art USA, Madison Sq Garden, New York, 58; Allied Artists Am Ann, New York, 61, 62 & 63; Albuquerque Exhib, Mus NMex, Santa Fe, 61; 47th Ann Nat Art Exhib, Mus Art, Springville, Utah, 71. *Pos:* Founder & owner, Fairbairn Publ, New York, 25-40; art dir, Harry Doehla Co, Fitchburg, Mass, 45-50. *Teaching:* Asst instr art, NY Sch Fine & Appl Art, summer 21; dir art educ, Kerr Summer Sch Art, Detroit, summers 23-24; spec lectr art educ, Syracuse Univ, summer 32. *Awards:* First Altman Prize, Nat Acad Design, New York, 45; Purchase Prize, NMex State Fair, Albuquerque, 63; Silver Medal, Am Vet Soc Artists, New York, 63. *Mem:* Salmagundi Club; Allied Artists Am; Am Vet Soc Artists; Artists Equity Asn; Presidents Club, Western Mich Univ, Kalamazoo; Archives Am Art, Detroit. *Media:* Oil. *Publ:* Contribr, Art recovery, Sch Arts Mag, 33; coauth, Historic design for modern use, 38; auth, Modern lettering, 39. *Dealer:* Grand Central Art Galleries 24 W 57th St New York NY 10017. *Mailing Add:* 7017 Bellrose Ave NE Albuquerque NM 87110

KERRIGAN, MAURIE
SCULPTOR, PAINTER
b Jersey City, NJ, Apr 28, 51. *Study:* Moore Col Art, Philadelphia, Pa, BFA, 73; Art Inst Chicago, MFA, 77; Whitney Mus Am Art, 77. *Work:* Philadelphia Mus Art & Please Touch Mus, Philadelphia, Pa; Lanon Found, Palm Beach, Fla; Phillips Collection, Smithsonian Inst, Washington, DC; Nat Women's Mus, Washington, DC; Best Corp Collection, NC. *Comn:* Mural, Candy Corns Visit Chicago, Pippers Alley, Chicago, Ill, 76; exterior sculpture, Three Boats, Reading Mus, Reading, Pa; sculpture, The Muse 34th Vessel, Am Express Col, New York. *Exhib:* Chicago & Vicinity, Art Inst Chicago, Ill, 77; Contemp Drawings, Philadelphia Mus Art, Pa, 79; Projects IV, Inst Contemp Art, Philadelphia, Pa, 80; Awards in the Visual Arts I, Nat Mus Am Art, Washington, DC, 82-83; De Moines Art Ctr, 82-83; Denver Art Mus, 82-83; one women show, Rockin, Philadelphia Mus Art, 87, Walkin, Pennsylvania Acad Fine Art, 89. *Pos:* Pres, Kerrigan Painting Co. *Awards:* Artist Fel, Pa Coun Art, 82; MacDowell Colony Fel, 86 & 87; Penny McCall Found Award, 87. *Bibliog:* Jean Silverthorne (auth), Maurie Kerrigan, Arts, 12/79; Ann-Sargent Wooster (auth), Maurie Kerrigan at Touchstone, Art in Am, 12/81; Wendy Slatkin (auth), Maurie Kerrigan, Arts, 5/83. *Mem:* Women's Caucus Art; Int Sculpture Ctr. *Media:* Handmade Paper, Oil Pastels. *Dealer:* Max Hutchinson Gallery 131 Green St New York NY 10012. *Mailing Add:* 2426 Lombard St Philadelphia PA 19146

KERSLAKE, KENNETH ALVIN
PRINTMAKER, EDUCATOR
b Mt Vernon, NY, Mar 8, 30. *Study:* Pratt Inst, 50-53, with Calvin Alberts & Philip Guston; Univ Ill, Urbana, with Lee Chesney, BFA, 55 & MFA, 57; Tamarind Lithography Workshop with Garo Antreasian, 64. *Work:* Libr Cong, Washington, DC; Brooklyn Mus, NY; Nat Gallery Art, Washington, DC; Samuel P Harn Mus Art, Gainesville, Fla; Boston Mus Fine Arts; plus others. *Exhib:* 30 Years of Am Printmaking, 20th Ann Exhib of Prints, Brooklyn Mus, NY; one-man show, Oxford Gallery, Eng; Am Prints & Printmaking, Pratt Graphic Ctr, New York; Graphics Invitational, Mint Mus, Charlotte, NC, 81; 30 American Printmakers, Ohio State Univ, Columbus; solo exhibs, Univ SC at Spartenburg; and others. *Teaching:* Distinguished serv Prof & Head Printmaking, Prog, Univ Fla, Gainesville, 58-; artist-in-residence, Univ Mo, Columbia, summer, 81; prof art, Univ Ga Studies Abroad Prog, Cortona, Italy, summer, 82; artist-in-residence, Univ Tex, Austin. *Awards:* Distinguished Fac Award, Univ Fla, 79; Grant, Frans Masereel Graphic Centrum, Kasterlee, Belgium; Teacher of Yr, Col Fine Art, Univ Fla, 87. *Bibliog:* H Williams (auth), Notes for a Young Painter, Prentice-Hall, 63; R Fichter (auth), Three Florida artists using photography, Fla Arts, 5/78; portfolio, Art Visions, Winter Park, Fla. *Mem:* Boston Printmakers; Print Club, Philadelphia; Soc Am Graphic Artists; Southern Graphic Coun, Pres, 90-92; Fla Printmaking Soc (bd dirs). *Media:* Intaglio and Painting. *Dealer:* Barbara Gillman Gallery Miami FL; Gallery Contemporania Jacksonville FL. *Mailing Add:* 1114 NW 36th Dr Gainesville FL 32605

KERSWILL, J W ROY
PAINTER
b Bigbury, Eng, Jan 17, 25; US citizen. *Study:* Plymouth Col Art, Eng; Bristol Col Art, scholar. *Work:* Wyo State Art Gallery; Mus Mountain Man; Grand Teton Natural Hist Asn Nat Park, Wyo; Jefferson Nat Expansion Mem, St Louis, Mo; Dept Interior Nat Collection, Washington, DC. *Comn:* Hist murals, Alpenhof Teton Village, Wyo, First Nat Bank, Englewood, Colo & Key Bank, Cheyenne, Wyo. *Exhib:* Am Artists Prof League Ann, New York, 50- *Mem:* Am Artists Prof League; Artist Equity Asn. *Media:* Watercolor, Oil. *Dealer:* Buffalo Trail Gallery PO Box 2014 Jackson WY 83001. *Mailing Add:* Box 2440 Jackson WY 83001

KERTZER, ANITA ELIZABETH
PAINTER, SCULPTOR
b Ottawa, Ont, Can. *Study:* Ottawa Sch Art; Banff Sch Fine Arts; Ringling Sch Art, Fla. *Work:* Parliamentary Portrait Gallery, Ottawa, Can. *Exhib:* Salon de Paris, Louvre (Grand Palais), Paris, France, 86; Fed Brit Artists, Pall Mall, London, Eng, 86-92; Pastel Int, Casa Loma, Toronto, Ont, 87; Nouveaux Maitres de L'image, Vieux-Ports, Montreal, Que, 89; North America's Most Innovative Pastel Painters; Ill Mus Art, Quincy, 90; retrospective, Univ SFla, Sarasota, 92. *Pos:* Pres, Pastel Soc Can, 84- *Teaching:* Instr portrait, Manatee Art League, Fla, 86-92. *Awards:* Mention Honorable, Salon de Paris, Institut de France, 86; Giffuni Plaque, Nat Arts Club, Pastel Soc Am, 87; First Prix Pastel, Nouveaux Maitres Image, APAQ, Que, 89. *Mem:* Pastel Soc Can (pres, 87-); Pastel Soc Am; Can Conf Arts; Soc Pastellistes France; Sarasota Art Asn, Fla. *Media:* Oil, Pastel. *Mailing Add:* Winding Way RR 2 Box 64 Ottawa ON K2C 3H1 Canada

KERZIE, TED L
PAINTER
b Tacoma, Wash, May 10, 43. *Study:* Wash State Univ, Pullman, BA, 65; Claremont Grad Sch, Calif, MFA, 72; Calif State Univ, Bakersfield, MAH. *Work:* Power Mus, Sydney, Australia; Wayne Anderson Collection, Boston; Luigiani Rossi Collection, Milan, Italy; Arco Collection Visual Arts, Los Angeles; Reader's Digest Collection, New York; Stouffers, Capital Group, Los Angeles; Merv Griffin, Palm Desert. *Comn:* Stouffers, Dion-Ross. *Exhib:* Solo show, Cirrus Gallery, Los Angeles, 80, Sherry Franklin Gallery, Santa Monica, Calif, 91; Arco Collection Visual Arts, Los Angeles, 81; M M Shinno Gallery, Los Angeles, 81; Nagasaki Prefecture Mus, Japan, 81; Tengin Salon Gallery, Fukuoka, Japan, 81; Ten Calif Colorist Traveling Exhib; Valerie Miller Gallery, Palm Desert, Directors Guild, Hollywood, Calif. *Collections Arranged:* Los Angeles Abstract Painting (catalog), Univ Calif, Riverside, 80. *Teaching:* Asst prof fine arts, Scripps Col & Claremont Grad Sch, Calif, 73-76; prof fine arts, Calif State Col, Bakersfield, 76-, summer arts, 86- *Bibliog:* William Wilson (auth), article, 80 & Suzanne Munchnic (auth), article, 8/81, Los Angeles Times; Melinda Wortz (auth), article, Art News, 80 & 83; Pick of the week, LA Weekly, 11/91. *Mem:* Aircraft Owners & Pilot Asn; Angel Flight Pilots. *Media:* Acrylic. *Mailing Add:* c/o Dept Art California State Collage 9001 Stockdale Hwy Bakersfield CA 93309

KESSLER, ALAN
PAINTER, SCULPTOR
b Philadelphia, Pa, Oct 15, 45. *Study:* Philadelphia Col Art, BFA; Yale Univ Summer Sch, Norfolk, Conn, Yale fel, 66; Md Inst Col Art, Baltimore, Hoffberger fel painting, MFA, 69. *Work:* Am Fedn Arts, New York; NY Univ Collection; Brockton Art Mus, Mass; Rose Art Mus, Brandeis Univ; State Univ NY Col Cortland. *Exhib:* One-man shows, Brown Univ, 77, O K Harris Gallery, New York, 77, 79 & 80, Everson Mus Arts, Syracuse, NY, 78 & Morgan Gallery, Kansas City, Mo, 78; Directions, Hirshhorn Mus, Washington, DC, 79; Real, Really Real, Super Real, Directions in Contemporary American Realism, 81 & 82; and others. *Teaching:* Instr painting & drawing, Md Inst Col Art, 68-69; instr, Hudson River Mus, 74; asst prof art, Brown Univ, 77-82. *Awards:* First Prize in Painting, Acad Arts, Easton, Md, 68; Elizabeth T Greenshields Mem Found Grant in Painting, Montreal, 74; Artist in Residence Grant, Nat Endowment Arts, Del State Arts Coun, 75-76. *Bibliog:* Gregory Battcock (auth), Super Realism a Critical Anthology, Dutton, 75; Vivian Radnor (auth), Art: While waiting for tomorrow, New York Times, 10/23/77; Kim Levin (auth), Preview exhibition wood sculpture, O K Harris Gallery, Arts Mag, 10/77. *Media:* Polychrome, Wood. *Mailing Add:* 305 Cerito Santa Fe NM 87501

KESSLER, HERBERT LEON
EDUCATOR
b Chicago, Ill, July 20, 41. *Study:* Univ Chicago, BA, 61; Princeton Univ, MFA, 63, PhD, 65. *Teaching:* From asst prof to prof hist art, Univ Chicago, 65-76; Charlotte Bloomberg prof & chmn dept, Johns Hopkins Univ, 76- *Awards:* Fel, Medieval Acad Am, 91- *Mem:* Medieval Acad Am; Col Art Asn; sr fel Dumbarton Oaks. *Res:* Medieval art. *Publ:* Ed, Studies in Classical and Byzantine Manuscript Illumination, Univ Chicago Press, 71; auth, Illustrated Bibles from Tours, 77 & The Cotton Genesis, 86, Princeton Univ Press; Frescoes of the Dura Synagogue & Christian Art, Dumbarton Oaks, 90. *Mailing Add:* Dept Hist Art Johns Hopkins Univ Baltimore MD 21218

KESSLER, JANE Q
CURATOR, WRITER
b Charlotte, NC, June 14, 46. *Study:* ECarolina Univ, BS, 69; Yale Univ Printroom, 82; Boston Pub Libr Printroom, 83. *Collections Arranged:* Harvey Littleton: Glass, 78; Southeastern Graphics Invitational (auth, catalog), 79-82; Southeastern Contemporary Metalsmiths (auth, catalog), 80 & 81; Contemporary American Prints from the Permanent Collection of the Mint Museum (auth, catalog), 83; Ida Kohlmeyer: Thirty Years (auth, catalog), 83; Southern Comfort/Discomfort, 87, Made in America, 88, Va Beach Arts Ctr; Counterbalance: LeWitt, Tinguely, Peart, Bechtler Gallery, 91; RSV: 6 Artists Respond, Bechtler Gallery, 92. *Pos:* Cur exhibs, 78-84, cur contemp art, Mint Mus, 84-88; principal partner, Curs' Forum, 88-; bd dir, Penland Schs. *Awards:* Prof Fel Grant, Nat Endowment Art Mus. *Bibliog:* Interview, New Arts Examiner, 86. *Mem:* NC Print & Drawing Soc (pres bd, 83); Southeastern Col Arts Conf (bd dirs, 82-85); Southern Graphics Coun; World Print Coun; Am Crafts Coun Southeastern Assembly; Southeastern Mus Coun. *Res:* Regional exhibitions of prints, drawings and crafts; history of American prints; southern art; American crafts; crafts of the Southern Highlands. *Publ:* Ed, Ida Kohlmeyer: Thirty years, Mint Mus, 84; auth, Unmaking it, Art Papers, 85; Arturo Sandoval, Am Craft, 88; Rude Osonik, Am Craft, 90; Randy Schull, NC State Univ. *Mailing Add:* 10300 Mt Olive Rd Mt Pleasant NC 28124

KESSLER, JON A
SCULPTOR
b Yonkers, NY, Jan, 57. *Study:* State Univ NY, Purchase, BFA, 80; Whitney Mus Independent Study, Studio Prog, NY, 81. *Exhib:* Solo exhibs, Luhring Augustine Gallery, New York, 90 & 92, Galerie Max Hetzler, Koln, 92, Nanba City Hall, Osaka, 92, Spiral Garden, Tokyo, 92, Kunstverein, Hamburg, 93; Mus Mod Art, Whitney Mus Am Art, New York, 92; Hayward Gallery, London, Eng, 92; Prospect, 93, Kunstverein, Frankfurt, 93. *Bibliog:* Patrick Furse (auth), Doubletake at the Hayward, Spotlight, Vol 1, No 2, 92; William Feaver (auth), One More with Feeling, Observer, 2/23/92; Elizabeth French Bigham (auth), John Kessler, Tema Celeste, summer, 92. *Dealer:* Luhring Augustine 130 Prince St New York NY 10012. *Mailing Add:* 412 11th St Brooklyn NY 11215

KESSLER, LEONARD H
ILLUSTRATOR
b Akron, Ohio, Oct 28, 21. *Study:* Carnegie Inst of Tech, BFA(painting & design), 49. *Awards:* New York Times 10 Best Illus Children's Books, 54, 55 & 57. *Mem:* Soc of Illusr; Graphic Artists Guild; Author's League; Authors Guild; Soc Children's Books Writers. *Media:* Pen and Ink, Watercolor, Gouache. *Publ:* Auth & illusr, Superbowl, 80, Old Turtle's Baseball Stories, 82, The Big Mile Race, 83, Old Turtle's Winter Games, 83 & Old Turtle's Book of Jokes & Riddles, 86, Greenwillow Bks; Here Comes the Strikeout, Harper & Row, 65; Old Turtle's Soccer Team, Greenwillow; Old Turtles, 90 Knock-Knock, 91 Greenwillow; Here Comes Strikeout rev ed, 92, Harper & Row. *Mailing Add:* 6 Stoneham Ln New City NY 10956

KESSLER, MARGARET JENNINGS
PAINTER
b Auburn, Ind, Aug 15, 44. *Exhib:* Top 100, Nat Arts for the Parks Show, travelling, 89. *Teaching:* Instr, painting workshops in NMex, Wis, Tex, nationwide & Bermuda. *Awards:* Best of Show, Artists & Craftsmen Assoc, Dallas, 81, 84, 85, 87 & 92; Best traditional painting, Hoosier Salon, Indianapolis, 83; Silver, 82, Bronze, 83, Gold Medal, 89, Grumbacher Art Awards; Hon Mention, Am Artist's Prof League, Salmagundi Club, New York, NY, 84. *Bibliog:* Article, Southwest Art Mag, 12/84. *Mem:* Artists & Craftsmen Assoc (pres, 85-86). *Media:* Oil. *Publ:* North Light Mag, 4/85 & The Artists' Mag, 1/85, 2/85 & 1/88; contribr, cover, The Artist's Mag, 2/85; Painting Better Landscapes, Watson-Guptill Publ, New York, 87. *Dealer:* Southwest Art Gallery 706 Preston Forest Shopping Ctr Dallas TX 75230. *Mailing Add:* 330 Ridgehaven Place Richardson TX 75080

KESSLER, SHIRLEY
PAINTER
b New York, NY. *Study:* Art Students League. *Work:* Iowa State Mus, Iowa City; Nashville Mus Art, Tenn; Asheville Mus Art, NC; Norfolk Mus Art, Va; Bulter Inst Am Art; Mus Art Vallobra, Brussels, Belgium; Mus Art, Forternes, Norway. *Exhib:* Museo Nacional Bellas Artes, Buenos Aires, 63; Am Watercolor Soc Ann, 64 & Audubon Artists, 65, Nat Acad Design, New York; 1st Int Exhib Women Painters, Cult Ctr, Cannes, France, 66; Int Peinture de Saint Germain-des-Pres, Paris, 70; Festival Int d'Art, Italy, 85. *Awards:* Palmes d'Or Promotion Queen Fabiola, Belg, 75; Grand Prix Humanitaire de France & Medaille d'Argent with Laureate Dipl, Int Arts Festival, De Saint Germain-des-Pres, France, 75; Medal of Merit, Nat Soc Painters Casein & Acrylic, 83; USA Ann Award, Nat Asn Women Artists, 85. *Bibliog:* Archives of American art, Smithsonian Inst, 70. *Mem:* Nat Asn Women Artists (pres, 67-70, permanent adv bd, 71-); Nat Soc Painters Casein & Acrylic (bd dirs, 70-); Soc D'Encouragement au Progress (USA permanent officer, 70-); Audubon Artists (bd dirs, 80-). *Media:* Acrylic, Watercolor. *Publ:* Auth, Paris Critique, Arts Int, 86. *Mailing Add:* 6290 Water Lilly Lane No FH Boynton Beach FL 33437-4928

KESTER, LENARD
PAINTER
b New York, NY, May 10, 17. *Work:* Brooklyn Mus, NY; Toledo Mus, Ohio; Denver Mus, Colo; Boston Mus Fine Arts, Mass; Everson Mus Art, Syracuse, NY; and others. *Comn:* First Nowell (painting), Life, 47; Pictorial Record of Pacific Northwest, Louis Comfort Tiffany Found, 49; Man's Musical Heritage (mural), Mayo Clin, Rochester, Minn, 53; stained glass windows, Billy Rose Mausoleum, NY, 67; First Nowell, Life Mag, 12/22/47. *Exhib:* Five exhibs, Los Angeles Mus, 43-55; Art Inst Chicago, 47; Carnegie Inst, Pittsburgh, 47-49; six exhibs, Nat Acad Design, New York, 51-66; Corcoran Gallery Art, Washington, DC, 57; and many others. *Teaching:* Pvt instr & pub lect. *Awards:* First Prize, Storm in the Canyon, Los Angeles Mus, 43; Saltus Gold Medal for Merit, November 7th, Nat Acad Design, 58; First Prize, Venice Reflections, Calif State Expos, 71; plus many others. *Bibliog:* Janice Lovoos (auth), The art of Lenard Kester, Am Artist, 2/59. *Mem:* Assoc Nat Acad Design; Am Watercolor Soc. *Media:* Oil, Watercolor, Gouache. *Mailing Add:* 1117 N Genesee Ave Los Angeles CA 90046

KETCHAM, HENRY KING (HANK)
CARTOONIST
b Seattle, Wash, Mar 14, 20. *Study:* Univ Wash, 38. *Work:* Albert T Reid Collection; William Allen White Found, Univ Kans; Achenbach Found for Graphic Arts, Calif Palace Legion Hon; Boston Univ Libr. *Pos:* Animator, Walter Lantz Prod, 38-39, Walt Disney Prod, 39-42; co-designer, Dennis the Menace Playground, Monterey, Calif, founder, Playart Found, 69. *Awards:* Billy De Beck Award as outstanding cartoonist, 52; Cert for Best Comic Mag, Boys' Club Am, 56; Silver T-Sy Award, Nat Cartoonist Soc, 78. *Mem:* Nat Cartoonists' Soc. *Interests:* Donor, Hank Ketcham Collection to Boston University Libraries. *Publ:* Auth & illusr, Dennis the Menace ann bk collection, 54-; auth & illusr, daily syndicated cartoon, Dennis the Menace, US & foreign newspapers, 51-; contribr, cartoons to nat newspapers; auth, I Wanna Go Home, McGraw-Hill, 65; The Merchant of Dennis, Abbeville, 90. *Mailing Add:* c/o Field Newspaper Syndicate PO Box 800 Pebble Beach CA 93953

KETCHAM, RAY WINFRED, JR
DEALER, DESIGNER
b Hartford, Ala, Dec 4, 22. *Study:* Ringling Sch Art, Fla, 46-48. *Comn:* Home Calendar, Coca-Cola Company, 55-67; mural, Delta Airlines, 66. *Pos:* Owner, Ray Ketcham Gallery, 66- *Awards:* Freelance Artist of the Year, Professional Artists Asn Atlanta Inc, 65. *Specialty:* Nineteenth & early twentieth century American & European paintings. *Mailing Add:* 540 Forestdale Drive NE Atlanta GA 30342

KETCHUM, ROBERT GLENN
PHOTOGRAPHER, CURATOR
b Los Angeles, Calif, Dec 1, 47. *Study:* Univ Calif, Los Angeles, with Heinecken & Teske in photog, BA(design, cum laude), 70; Brooks Inst, 71; Calif Inst Arts, MFA(photog), 74. *Work:* Mus Mod Art & Metrop Mus Art, New York; Los Angeles Co Mus Art, Los Angeles; Nat Mus Am Art & Corcoran Gallery, Washington, DC. *Comn:* Seafarm (book), comn by Harry N Abrams, Int Ocean Inst, New York, 77; portfolio, traveling exhibit, Lila Acheson Wallace Fund, New York, 82-84; color portfolio of Alaska, The Wallace Ford Fund, New York, 82-84; Chattahoochee Suite, Cousins Properties, Atlanta, Ga, 85-87; color portfolio, Cleveland Found, Gund Found, Akron Art Mus, Ohio, 86- *Exhib:* White House, Washington, DC, 79; Smithsonian Traveling Exhib Service, 80-84; Am Photogr and Nat Parks Traveling Exhib, 81-83; one-man exhib, Sheldon Mem Art Gallery, Lincoln, Nebr, 84; Lyndon Johnson Library, Austin, Tex, 84; Nat Mus Am Art, 85; and others. *Pos:* Cur, Nat Park Found, DC, 78-; bd trustees, Los Angeles Ctr Photog Studies, 75-81, pres & exec dir, 79. *Teaching:* Founder & teacher photog workshop, Sun Valley Ctr Arts & Humanities, 71-73; instr photog, Calif Inst Arts, 75; instr & adv bd, Appalachian Arts Ctr, Highlands, NC, 82- *Awards:* Nat Park Found Award, 78 & 79; Mat Res Award, Ciba-Geigy, 79;

NY State Coun on the Arts Grant, 85. *Bibliog:* Suzanne Muchnic (auth), Ketchum, Evert at Municipal, Los Angeles Times, 6/14/83; Gene Thorton (auth), Critics choice/photography, New York Times, 12/29/85; Margaret Moorman (auth), New York Reviews/Robert Glenn Ketchum, Art News, 3/86. *Mem:* Friends Photog. *Media:* Cibachrome Color Prints, Books. *Publ:* Coauth, Outerbridge, Los Angeles Ctr Photog Studies, 76; auth, Photographic Directions: Los Angeles 1979, Security Pac Bank, 79; Landscape Photographers and America's National Parks, Nat Park Found, 79; The Hudson River and the Highlands, Aperture, 85. *Mailing Add:* 696 Stone Canyon Rd Los Angeles CA 90077

KETNER, JOSEPH DALE
MUSEUM DIRECTOR, CURATOR
b Anderson, Ind, Oct 30, 55. *Study:* Ind Univ, BA, 77, MA, 80. *Collections Arranged:* Grace Hartigan, 81 (with catalog), 81; Beautiful, Sublime & Picturesque (with catalog), 84; Architectural Ceramics (with catalog), 85; Carl F Wimar (with catalog), 91; Columbus of the Woods (with catalog), 92. *Pos:* Cur-registr, Ft Wayne Mus Art, Ind, 79-82; cur, 82 & dir, 89-, Washington Univ Gallery Art. *Mem:* Midwest Art Hist Soc, Univ Mus Comt (co-chair, 92); incorporating mem, St Louis Area Mus Collaborative. *Publ:* Auth, Continuing Search of Grace Hartigan, Artnews, 81; Robert S Duncanson: Late Literary Landscapes, Am Art J, 83; coauth, Beautiful, Sublime, & Picturesque, Washington Univ, 84; Carl F Wimar: Chronicler of the Missouri, R Amon Carter/Abrams, 91; auth, Emergence of the African-American Artist, Univ Mo, 93. *Mailing Add:* Washington University Gallery of Art One Brookings Dr, Campus Box 1214 St Louis MO 63130

KETTNER, DAVID ALLEN
ARTIST, EDUCATOR
b Sunman, Ind, Oct 19, 43. *Study:* Skowhegan Sch Painting and Sculpture, 64; Cleveland Inst Art, BFA, 66; Ind Univ, MFA, 68. *Work:* Pa Acad Fine Arts; Philadelphia Mus Art, Pa; Rutgers Univ, Col Arts & Sci, Camden, NJ. *Exhib:* Six Self-Portraits 1975 Series, Whitney Mus Am Art, New York, 76; 41st Int Eucharistic Congress Liturgical Arts Exhib, Civic Ctr, Philadelphia, 76; Philadelphia Houston Exchange, Inst Contemp Art, Philadelphia, 76; Recent Acquisitions, Philadelphia Mus Art, 77; Am Drawing Show, Fine Arts Gallery, San Diego, Calif, 77; Contemp Drawing, 78 & A Bach Transcription, 81, Pa Acad Fine Arts. *Teaching:* Assoc prof painting & drawing, Philadelphia Col Art, 68- *Bibliog:* Victoria Donohue (auth), article, Philadelphia Inquirer, 10/9/81. *Mailing Add:* Dept Painting Broad & Pine Sts Univ of the Arts Philadelphia PA 19102

KEVESON, FLORENCE
PAINTER, ILLUSTRATOR
b New York, NY. *Study:* Cooper Union Art Sch, art degree; Art Students League, Ford Found Scholar; also with Sidney Gross & Leo Manso. *Exhib:* Albany Inst Hist Art Ann, 68-72; solo exhib, Silvermine Guild Artists, 69 & Marist Col, 72; Wadsworth Atheneum Mus Ann, 69-77; Berkshire Mus Ann, Pittsfield, Mass, 70-80; Painters & Sculptors NJ, Bergen Mus, Paramus, NJ, 70-83; Butler Inst Ann, 72; Nat Arts Club, 82-89. *Pos:* Illusr, Conde Nast Publ, 49-52; free-lance illusr, 53- *Awards:* Shandoff Award, Berkshire Ann, 70; G Paley Award, Nat Asn Women Artists Ann; Michael M Engel Award, Am Soc Contemp Artists. *Mem:* Audobon Artists; Am Soc Contemp Artists. *Media:* Oil. *Publ:* Illus in Vogue, McCalls, Good Housekeeping & Glamour. *Dealer:* Rudolph Galleries 24 Mill Hill Rd Woodstock NY 12498. *Mailing Add:* 314 E 201 St Bronx NY 10458

KEVORKIAN, RICHARD
PAINTER
b Dearborn, Mich, Aug 24, 37. *Study:* Pa Acad of Fine Arts, Philadelphia, 58; Richmond Prof Inst, BFA(painting), 61; Calif Col of Arts & Crafts, Oakland, MFA(painting), 62. *Work:* Philip Morris, USA, Richmond, Va; Walter Rawls Mus, Courtland, Va; Southeastern Ctr for Contemp Art, Winston-Salem, NC; First & Merchants Nat Bank, Richmond; Bank & Trust of Wachovia, NC. *Exhib:* Painting in the South, 1564-1980, traveling exhib, Va Mus, Richmond, Birmingham Mus Art, Birmkngham, Ala, Nat Acad Design, New York, JB Speed Art Mus, Louisville, Ken & New Orleans Mus Art, La; Southern Abstraction: Five Painters, Traveling Exhib, Univ Tenn, Clemson Univ, NC State Univ & Cheekwood Fine Arts Ctr, Nashville, Tenn; Contempany Art Acquisitions, Equitable Gallery, New York; 35 Southeastern Artists, High Mus, Atlanta, Ga, 76; Southeast 7, Southeastern Ctr Contemp Art, Winston-Salem, 77. *Pos:* vis artist, Nat Col Art & Design, Dublin Ireland; Central School Art and Design, London, London, Eng; Loughborough Col Art, Leister, Eng; Winchester, Col Art, Eng; Ulster Col, Belfast, Northern Ireland. *Teaching:* Instr painting, Richard Bland Col, Petersburg, Va, 61-64; prof & chmn dept of painting & printmaking, Va Commonwealth Univ, Richmond, 64- *Awards:* Individual Sr Artists Grant (painting), Nat Endowment Arts, 72; Southeastern Ctr Contemp Arts Grant (painting), 76; Guggenheim Fel Painting, 78. *Mem:* Nat Coun of Art Adminr. *Media:* Oil, acrylic. *Dealer:* Aaron Gallery 1717 Connecticut Ave NW Washington DC 20009. *Mailing Add:* 325 N Harrison St Richmond VA 23220

KEY, TED
CARTOONIST
b Fresno, Calif. *Study:* Univ Calif, Berkeley. *Work:* Brandywine Mus; George Arents Research Libr; Syracuse Univ; Int Mus Cartoon Art. *Pos:* Creator, Hazel, daily panel syndicated by King Features; creator, Peabody's Improbable History; creator, Bullwinkle & Rocky show; ideas for many Saturday Evening Post covers. *Awards:* Best Syndicated Panel, Nat Cartoonists Soc, 77. *Publ:* Auth & illusr, 18 Hazel bks, The Biggest Dog in the World, Phyllis, Many Happy Returns & Squirrels in the Feeding Station; auth, Cat From Outer Space, Walt Disney Prod; Million Dollar Duck, Walt Disney Prod; Gus & So'M I, Walt Disney Prod; D12 & L12, two-page feature for 10 years, Jack & Jill Mag, books, biweekly posters, Econ Press, over 25 years. *Mailing Add:* 1694 Glenhardie Rd Wayne PA 19087

KEYSER, ROBERT G
PAINTER
b Philadelphia, Pa, July 27, 24. *Study:* With Fernand Leger, Paris, 49-51. *Work:* Philadelphia Mus Art; Philips Gallery, Washington, DC; Munson-Williams-Proctor Inst, Utica, NY; Pa Acad Fine Arts; Col William & Mary. *Exhib:* Solo exhibs, Yale Univ Art Gallery, 62, Galleria Temple Univ, Rome, 77 & Col William & Mary, 78; Robert Keyser: Ten Years (1977-1987), traveling exhib, 87-88; Univ Pa, 91. *Teaching:* Prof painting & drawing, Univ of the Arts, Philadelphia, 58-91. *Awards:* Ballinglen Arts Found Fel, Bally Castle, County Mayo, Ireland, 92-93. *Bibliog:* Charles LeClair (auth), The Art of Watercolor, Prentice-Hall, 85; Charles LeClair (auth), Color in Contemporary Painting, Watson-Guptill, 91. *Media:* Oil, Watercolor. *Dealer:* Dolan/Maxwell 154 Wooster St New York NY; Dolan/Maxwell 2046 Rittenhouse Sq Philadelphia PA 19103. *Mailing Add:* 1291 E Sawmill Rd, RD 4 Quakertown PA 18951

KEYSER, WILLIAM ALPHONSE, JR
CRAFTSMAN, EDUCATOR
b Pittsburgh, Pa, July 30, 36. *Study:* Carnegie-Mellon Univ, Pittsburgh, BS, 58; Sch for Am Craftsman, Rochester Inst of Tech, MFA(furniture design), 61. *Work:* Univ Collection, Univ of Nebr, Lincoln; Am Crafts Mus, New York; Artpark, Lewiston, NY; Eastman Kodak Co, Rochester, NY; Memorial Art Gallery, Rochester NY. *Comn:* Subway Benches, Sculptures, Mass Bay Transportation Auth, 84; complete sanctuary furnishings, St Mary's Church, Rochester, NY, 87; Rochester Top 100, annual award sculpture, Peat Marwick & Rochester Chamber of Commerce, 87-92; baptistry, St Joseph's of Penfield, NY, 87; reception desk, Bausch & Lomb Bldg, RIT, Rochester NY. *Exhib:* Am Craft Mus, NY, 62, 66, 69, 79 & 84; New Furniture - Ten Artists, Carnegie Mus, Pittsburg, Pa, 83; Bentwood Today, RI Sch Design Mus Art, 84; Am Contemporary Works in Wood, The Dairy Barn, Athens OH, 87 & 89; Nat Invitational Furniture Show, Mendeocino CA, 87 & 90. *Teaching:* Prof furniture design, Sch for Am craftsman, Rochester Inst of Technol, 62-, chmn crafts, 81-89. *Awards:* Young Americans Award, Am Crafts Coun, 62; Gertrude H Moore, Rochester Finger Lakes, 72; Craftsmen's Fel, Nat Endowment for the Arts, 75. *Bibliog:* Lee Nordness (auth), Objects USA, 70; Jonathan Fairbanks (auth), American Furniture 1620 to the Present, 81; Dona Z Meilach (auth), Woodworking: The New Wave, Crown Publ, 81; and others. *Mem:* Am Crafts Coun; Empire State Crafts Alliance. *Media:* Wood. *Publ:* Auth, Steam Bending--Heat and Moisture Plasticize Wood, 77 & auth, Portfolio: W A Keyser, The Challenge of Churches, 79, Fine Woodworking Taunton Press. *Dealer:* Pritam & Eames East Hampton NY; Snyderman Gallery Philadelphia Pa. *Mailing Add:* Rochester Inst Tech Rochester NY 14623

KHACHIAN, ELISA A
PAINTER
b Worcester, Mass, May 6, 35. *Study:* RI Sch Design, BS, 57; Fairfield Univ, graphic art, 82; Silvermine Col Art. *Work:* Pvt collection for Town of Fairfield, Conn. *Exhib:* 100 Women, 100 Works, 100 Years (travelling show), Nat Asn Women Artists, 88; Juried Exhib, Javitts Ctr, Nat Asn Women Artists, NY, 88; Conn Watercolor Soc, New Britain Mus Am Art, 90; First Show Mus, Katonah Mus, NY, 92; Conn Women Artists, New Britain Mus Am Art, 92; and others. *Pos:* Art asst, RI Sch Design, Spec Talents, 56-57; art educ, W Concord Sch System, 57-58. *Teaching:* Problem solving, Darien Art Soc, 87-91. *Awards:* Charles H Fischer Prize, Brush & Pallette Ann, 88; Conn Women Artists Award, Merchants Bank & Trust, 89; Seven Awards, 50th Ann Conn Watercolor Soc, 90. *Mem:* Nat Asn Women Artists; Silvermine Guild Ctr for the Arts; Conn Women Artists; Conn Watercolor Soc; New Haven Paint & Clay. *Media:* Watercolor, Acrylic. *Mailing Add:* 213 Hollydale Rd Fairfield CT 06430

KHALIL, CLAIRE ANNE
PAINTER
b Boston, Mass, Feb 20, 44. *Study:* Emmanuel Col, BA, 65; Acad di Belle Arte, Florence, Italy, 65-66. *Work:* Am Stock Exch, New York; Janss Found, Sun Valley, Idaho; Venus--the Bittkers-New Haven, Conn, 75. *Comn:* Red Brick House, comn by Gloria Garfinkel, New York, 81; Sweet Briar, comn by Stephanie Axinn, New York, 82; The House of the Three Gables, comn by Carol Butz, New York, 82; Sun Valley and the Janss Collection with Dove, comn by Glenn Janss, Idaho, 84. *Exhib:* Focus on Realism: Selections from the Collection of Glenn C Janss, traveling exhib throughout US, 85; Fireworks: American Artists Celebrate the Eighth Art, Butler Inst Am Art, Youngstown, Ohio, 85. *Bibliog:* Alvin Martin (auth), American Realism--Twentieth Century Drawings and Watercolors, San Francisco Mus Mod Art & Harry N Abrams, 86. *Dealer:* Nancy Hoffman 429 W Broadway New York NY 10012. *Mailing Add:* c/o Nancy Hoffman Gallery 429 W Broadway New York NY 10012

KHEEL, CONSTANCE
PAINTER
b New York, NY, 45. *Study:* Bennington Col, Bennington, Vt, BA(painting & sculpture), 67. *Work:* Nat Gallery Mod Art, Santa Domingo, Dominican Repub; The Newark Mus, NJ; Herbert F Johnson Mus Art, Ithaca, NY; Aldrich Mus Contemp Art, Ridgefield, Conn; Mint Mus Art, Charlotte, NC. *Exhib:* Harcus-Krakow Gallery, Boston, Mass, 80; Andre Zarre Gallery, New York, 82, 84 & 86; Nina Freudenheim Gallery, Buffalo, NY; Ana Sklar

Gallery, Miami, Fla; solo exhibs, Williams Col Mus Art, Mass, 89, Tobia Kraa Gallery, Upper Monclair, NJ, 89, R V S Fine Art, S Hampton, NY, 89, Boinayel Galleria de Arte Santa Domingo & Distal Gallery Troy, NY; Inst de Cultura Puertorquena, San Juan, 90; Nat Asn Women Artists, New York, 90; R V S Fine Art, S Hampton, NY, 90. *Awards:* Fel, Nat Endowment Arts, 87. *Mem:* Nat Asn Women Artists. *Dealer:* Reece Gallaries 24 W 57th St New York NY 10019. *Mailing Add:* RD 1, BOX 262 Buskirk NY 12028

KHOURI, GRETA MATSON See Matson, Greta

KIAH, VIRGINIA JACKSON
PAINTER, MUSEUM DIRECTOR
b East St Louis, Ill, June 3, 11. *Study:* Philadelphia Mus & Sch Art, 27-31, dipl; Art Students League, 29-32, study with Louis Bouche, Robert Brackman & Vincent Dumonde; Columbia Univ, AB, 49 & MA, 50; Dr Humanities, Savannah Col Art & Design, 86. *Comn:* portrait of Finley Wilson, Elks, Washington, DC, 40; portrait of Judge Thomas L Griffith, comn by self, Los Angeles, Calif, 41; two portraits of Mrs Thomas Dyett, comn by Thomas Dyett, New York, 52; portrait of Rev Harry Hoosier, Washington Delaware Conf, Methodist Church Retreat, Gulfside, Miss, 54; portrait of Vpres, Ga State Univ, Urban Life Bldg, 79. *Exhib:* Philadelphia Mus & Sch Art Ann Exhib, 30; Baltimore Mus Art Ann Md Artists Show, 35; Nat Columbia Motion Pictures Portrait Painting Contest Prizewinners Exhib, Eggleston Galleries, New York, 37; Art Students League Ann Show, 37; Southern Regional Art Show, Williamsburg, Va, 69; one-person show, US House of Representatives, 86. *Collections Arranged:* Marie Dressler Exhib, Kiah Mus, Savannah, Ga; African Art & William H Johnson Pastel & Print Collection, Found, New York. *Pos:* Founder & dir, Kiah Mus, Savannah, Ga, 59-; chmn, Comt for the Ga United Nations Arts, 74-75; founder & dir, Lillie Carroll Jackson Mus, Baltimore, Md, 74-79. *Teaching:* Instr art & chmn dept, Cuyler, Beach & Scott Jr High Schs, 51-62. *Awards:* Nat Conf of Artists Distinctive Merit, 60-62, 68 & 70-72. *Bibliog:* Dr K B Raut (auth), Mrs Virginia Kiah--artist, Kiah Mus, Savannah Mag, Joseph Chauhan Publ, 1/71; Burchart, Denilov, Naeve & Taylor (auths), Treasures of America, Reader's Digest Asn, 74; Helen C Smith (auth), She couldn't go to museums so she started one, Atlanta Constitution Newspaper, 11/9/74. *Mem:* Nat Conf Artists; Savannah Ga 36th St Improv Asn; Ga Coastal Mus Asn; and others. *Media:* Oil. *Publ:* Auth, Gone fishing, Afro-Am Newspaper Mag, 55; auth, Black artists, Savannah Mag, 72; auth, Ulysses Davis: Folk Sculptor, Southern Folklore Quart, Univ Fla, 78. *Mailing Add:* 505 W 36th St Savannah GA 31401

KIDD, REBECCA MONTGOMERY
PAINTER
b Muncie, Ind, Nov 29, 42. *Comn:* Double portrait, comn by Delegate & Mrs Robert Bloxom, Mapsville, Va, 73; film illus, Effective Educ Systems, Essexville, Mich, 75; children's portrait, comn by Mr & Mrs Stephen B Tankard, Exmore, Va, 84; Civil War era portrait, comn by Mr & Mrs Louis Floyd, Exmore, Va, 86; double portrait, comn by Mrs Joanne Vankesteren Smith, Onancock, Va, 88. *Exhib:* The Pentagon, Arlington, Va, 74; Int Cong on Arts & Commun Exhib, Queen's Col, Univ Cambridge, Eng, 82; Int Platform Asn Conv Art Exhib, Hyatt Regency, Washington, DC, 84; solo exhib, Eastern Shore Chap Va Mus, Eastern Shore Community Col, Melfa, Va, 87. *Awards:* Popular Choice Award, & Merit Award, IPA Conv Exhib, 84. *Bibliog:* Art by Rebecca Kidd shown, Daily Times, Salisbury, Md, 1/17/82; Artist Rebecca Kidd recieves IPA Awards, Eastern Shore News, Va, 8/23/84. *Mem:* Visual Artists & Galleries Asn. *Media:* Oils, Pastels. *Dealer:* Roadside Gallery Main St Melfa VA. *Mailing Add:* 9 Lake St Onancock VA 23417

KIDRICK, VALERIE ANNE
MUSEUM DIRECTOR, GALLERY DIRECTOR
b Craig, Colo, Dec 07, 61. *Study:* Univ Utah, BA, 85, MA, 90. *Collections Arranged:* Southern Utah Invitational, summer 89-90; Set, stage & costumes, Shakespearean Festival, summer 89-90. *Pos:* Dir, Braithwaite Gallery, Cedar City, Utah, 88-; bd mem, Cedar City Arts Coun, Utah, 88; state rep, Western Mus Conference. *Teaching:* instr Art History, Southern Utah Univ. *Mem:* Utah Mus Asn; Am Federation of the Arts; Am Asn Mus. *Mailing Add:* Braithwaite Fine Arts Gallery Southern Utah Univ 351 W Center St Cedar City UT 84720

KIEFERNDORF, FREDERICK GEORGE
PAINTER, EDUCATOR
b Milwaukee, Wis, May 12, 21. *Study:* Univ Wis, BA & MS. *Work:* Springfield Art Mus, Mo; Mo State Hist Soc Permanent Collection (painting requested 75); Wis Salon Art, Madison; Sch Ozarks, Point Lookout, Mo; Pittsburgh State Col, Kans. *Exhib:* Watercolor USA, Springfield, Mo, 67, 68, 71 & 79; Ann Delta Show, Little Rock, 67 & 74; Ten Painters of Missouri, Traveling Exhib, Mo State Coun Arts, 68; Springfield Art Mus Midwest Exhib, 72; retrospective exhib, Park Central Gallery, 81; two-man show, Jordan Creek Gallery, 85; show of drawings & paintings, Springfield Art Mus, 88. *Teaching:* Prof art, Southwest Mo State Univ, 53-81. *Awards:* Purchase Award, Springfield Art Mus, 56 & 65 & Award of Merit, 67; Purchase Award, Sch Ozarks, 70 & Award of Merit, 81. *Bibliog:* Edgar A Albin (auth), article in Art Voices/South, 7-8/78; Edgar A Albin (auth), article in Springfield Mag, 1/87; Gregory Thielen (auth), Journeys Near & Far, Springfield Art Mus, 88. *Media:* Polymer, Vinyl Cement. *Mailing Add:* 1748 Madaline Springfield MO 65804

KIEFFER, MARY JANE
PAINTER
b Chicago, Ill. *Study:* Am Acad Art, 37-38; Maholy-Nagi Sch Design; Art Inst Chicago. *Comn:* Numerous pvt comns. *Exhib:* Pasadena Soc Artists Ann, Riverside Art Mus, 68; Invitational, Nat Acad Design, New York, 68; Utah State Univ, Logan, 74-80; Brand XII, Brand Libr, Glendale, Calif; Nat Watercolor Soc Ann, Palm Springs Mus, Calif; Rocky Mountain Nat, Colo Art Mus; Downey Mus, 90; Los Angeles Co Century Gallery. *Awards:* First Award & Purchase Award, Laguna Art Mus, 74, Bruggen Ann Award, 76 & Del Mar Col Ann Award, 79, Nat Watercolor Soc, 55-85; Purchase Award, Utah State Univ Gallery, Logan. *Mem:* Nat Watercolor Soc (pres, 77-78); Pasadena Soc Artists (pres, 81-82). *Media:* Watercolor. *Publ:* Contribr, Expressive Watercolor Techniques, Davis, 82. *Mailing Add:* 1252 Inverness Pasadena CA 91103

KIELKOPF, JAMES ROBERT
PAINTER
b St Paul, Minn, July 13, 39. *Study:* Minneapolis Sch Art, BFA, 65; Grand Marias Art Colony, summer 63; Skowhegan Sch Painting, summer 64. *Work:* Walker Art Ctr, Minneapolis Inst Art. *Comn:* First Bank Minneapolis, Minn, 82; Republic Bank, Houston, Tex, 83; 3M Corp, St Paul, Minn, 90. *Exhib:* Walker Art Ctr Biennial, 64 & 66; Minneapolis Inst Art Biennial, 67; Interchange, Dallas Mus Fine Arts, Tex, 72; Landmark Ctr, St Paul, 79; Minneapolis Inst of Art, Minn, 86;; SDak Art Mus, Brookings, 90. *Media:* Acrylic, Oil. *Dealer:* Thomas Barry Fine Arts 400 First Ave N Suite 304 Minneapolis MN 55401. *Mailing Add:* 1963 Ashland St Paul MN 55104

KIENHOLZ, LYN
PATRON, ADMINISTRATOR
b Chicago, Ill. *Study:* Sullins Col; Md Col Women. *Collections Arranged:* Echange Entre Artistes (catalog), Mus Art Mod, Paris & Europ tour, 82-83; California Sculpture Show (catalog), Olympic Arts Festival, Los Angeles & Europ tour, 84-85; Cowin-Divola (catalog), La Jolla Mus Contemp Art & nat & Europ tour, 85-87; Off the Beaten Track (brochure), Wight Gallery, Univ Calif, Los Angeles, 88; Chinese Influence on West Coast Artists (catalog), Taiwan Mus Art, 88; Lee Miller Photographer (book), Corcoran Gallery Art, nat & int mus tour, 89-93; Individual Realities (catalog), Sezon Mus Art, Tokyo & Japan tour, 91. *Pos:* Asst to artist Edward Kienholz, 66-74; exec dir, Beaubourg Found, Ctr Pompidou, Paris, 77-81; founder & chmn, Calif-Int Arts Found, Los Angeles, 81- *Bibliog:* Hunter Drohojowska (auth), Carrying a torch for Olympic artists, Los Angeles Herald Examiner, 7/31/83; Suzanne Muchnic (auth), Lyn Kienholz puts sculpture on a pedestal, Los Angeles Times, 6/2/84; Carolyn Mitchell (auth), It Takes ability and connections to establish an arts Foundation, Chattanooga Times, 12/24/85; Jody Leader (auth), C/IAF on a roll, Los Angeles Reader, 7/11/86; Suzanne Muchnic (auth), Museum leaders to get eyeful of Los Angeles, Los Angeles Times, 9/18/90. *Mem:* Artists Equity; Comite Int Musées d'Art Moderne. *Interests:* All forms of contemporary art. *Mailing Add:* 2737 Outpost Dr Los Angeles CA 90068

KIKER, EVELYN COALSON
PAINTER, INSTRUCTOR
b Belzoni, Miss, May 17, 32. *Study:* Delta State Col, BS(educ), 69; Univ Miss, MA, 71, PhD, 81. *Work:* Miss State Univ, Starkville; Miss Univ Women, Columbus. *Exhib:* Mid-South Exhib, Brooks Mem Art Gallery, Memphis, Tenn, 64 & 65; Arts & Crafts Show, Miss Art Festival, Jackson, 65 & 66; Belzoni Group, Ahda Artzt Gallery, New York, 67 & Meridian Mus Art, Miss, 72; Jr Col Art Teachers, Jackson Municipal Art Gallery, Miss, 70. *Teaching:* Miss Delta Jr Col, Moorhead, 69- *Awards:* Best in Show, Miss Collegiate Exhib, 67; Purchase Award, Miss Art Colony, Commercial Nat Bank, Laurel, Miss, 78; Second Prize, Laurel Art in the Park Comt, 79. *Bibliog:* R Stephens (auth), L'Art a L'Etranger: Expositions diverses, La Revue Moderne, 11/65; C N White (auth), Reviews & previews, Art News, 2/67; O C McDavid (auth), O C McDavids gallery talk, Clarion-Ledger/Jackson Daily News, 10/29/72. *Mem:* Miss Art Colony; Delta Br Nat League Am Pen Women. *Media:* Oil, Acrylic. *Mailing Add:* Miss Delta Community Col Moorhead MS 38761

KIKUCHI-YNGOJO, ALAN
PHOTOGRAPHER, COLLAGE ARTIST
b San Francisco, Calif, Feb 6, 49. *Study:* Diablo Valley Col, 67-69; Univ Calif, Davis, BA, 71, MFA, 75. *Work:* Metrop Mus Art, Alternative Mus, New York; Clarence Kennedy Gallery, Polaroid Corp, Cambridge, Mass; Cleveland Mus Art; Erie Art Ctr, Pa. *Exhib:* Contemporary Icons, San Francisco Mus Mod Art, 75; Beyond Photography, Alternative Mus, New York, 80; US Art Now, Gotesborgs Konstforening, Sweden, 81; Painting and Sculpture Today, Indianapolis Mus Art, 82; Counterparts, Metrop Mus Art, New York, 82; solo exhib, Triton Mus Art, Santa Clara, Calif, 82; Recent Acquisitions, Clarence Kennedy Gallery, Polaroid Corp, Cambridge, Mass, 83; Seven American Artists, Cleveland Mus Art, 83. *Awards:* Nat Endowment Arts Fel, 81. *Bibliog:* Grace Glueck (auth), article in New York Times, 1/15/82; Lynn Zelevansky (auth), article in Art News, 4/82; Christopher French (auth), Redefining figures, Art Week, 7/3/82. *Dealer:* Hal Bromm Gallery 90 W Broadway New York NY 10013. *Mailing Add:* 290 Lafayette St New York NY 10012

KILAND, LANCE EDWARD
PAINTER, PRINTMAKER
b Fargo, NDak, Nov 27, 47. *Study:* Moorhead State Univ, BA, 69; Southern Ill Univ, MFA, 71. *Work:* Walker Art Ctr, Minneapolis; Art Inst Chicago. *Exhib:* Mid-States Art Exhib, Evansville Mus Art, Ind, 70; Manisphere,

Winnipeg Art Gallery, Manitoba, 74; Red River Ann Exhib, Plains Art Mus, Moorhead, Minn, 81; Bewildered Image, Minneapolis Inst Arts, 82; Biennial Exhib, Whitney Mus Am Art, New York, 83; Rooted in NDak, NDak Mus Art, Grand Forks, 84; 39th Biennial Am Painting, Corcoran Gallery Art, Washington, DC, 85; Viewpoints, Walker Art Ctr, Minneapolis, 85; Recent Acquisitions: Emerging Artists, Walker Art Ctr, Minneapolis, 86; Print & Drawing Exhib, Minneapolis Inst Arts, 88; Landmark Editions, NDak Mus Art, Grand Forks, 91; New Acquisitions, Art Inst Chicago, 91. *Teaching:* North Hennepin Community Col, Minneapolis. *Bibliog:* Eleanor Heartney (auth), Lance Kiland, 1/84 & Mason Riddle (auth), Lance Kiland, 10/85, Arts Mag; Chris Waddington (auth), Lance Kiland at Thomson, Art in Am, 6/89. *Media:* Oil; Lithograph & Woodcut. *Dealer:* Thimmesh Gallery 25 N Fourth St Suite 201 Minneapolis MN 55401. *Mailing Add:* 3153 Bloomington Ave S Minneapolis MN 55407

KILIAN, AUSTIN FARLAND
PAINTER, EDUCATOR
b Lyons, SDak, Sept 19, 20. *Study:* Augustana Col, SDak, BA, 42; Univ Iowa, MFA, 49; Acad Montmartre, Paris, with Fernand Leger, 51; Mexico City Col, 52; Ohio State Univ, 55; Univ Calif, Los Angeles, 66. *Work:* D D Feldman Collection, Dallas; Univ Iowa Galleries, Iowa City. *Exhib:* Laguna Gloria Mus Citation Regional, Austin, Tex, 58; Art Asn New Orleans, Delgado Mus, 59; Made in Tex by Texans, Dallas Mus Contemp Arts, 59; San Diego Art Instr Show, Art Ctr La Jolla, Calif, 61; Inland Empire Country Club Fac Exhib, San Bernardino, 81; Living Desert, Palm Desert, Calif, 85; and others. *Collections Arranged:* Waco Art Forum Mus Regional Shows, 59; San Diego Art Guild Shows, Fine Arts Gallery, 61; Art In All Media, Southern Calif Expos, Del Mar, 63-70; Col of the Desert Shows, 70- *Pos:* CEO, Kilian Studios, 88- *Teaching:* Instr photog, Univ Idaho, 49-50; head dept art, Dillard Univ, 50-53; asst prof, Baylor Univ, 53-59; chmn dept art, Calif Western Univ, 59-64; assoc prof, Col Desert, Calif, 70-86, head dept art, 86-87 & prof emer, 87- *Awards:* Art Asn New Orleans Third Award, Delgado Mus, 52; Sons of Herman Award, San Antonio, Tex, 55; Purchase Award, D D Feldman Exhib, 68. *Bibliog:* Henry Burnett & Orville Voigt, Today Painting (Video Series), Col Desert, 80-85; William Hemmerdinger (auth), Collectors, Palm Springs Life Mag, 12/81. *Mem:* Art Hist Southern Calif; Palm Springs Desert Mus; Col Art Asn Am; Am Fedn of Arts. *Media:* Collage, Oil. *Publ:* Auth, Catalog loan exhibition of notable works from the Metropolitan, 52, Culture makes a face, KABC-TV, Hollywood, 62, The Two Californias (catalog), 63, Southern California Exposition, Art in All Media (catalogs), 63-70 & article, San Diego Eve Tribune, 6/14/64. *Mailing Add:* 73286 Juniper Street Palm Desert CA 92260-4702

KILLEEN, MELISSA HELEN
DEALER, GALLERY DIRECTOR
b Binghamton, NY, Oct 28, 55. *Study:* Syracuse Univ, NY, BFA(cum laude), 76; Johnson Atelier Tech Sch Sculpture, NJ, cert, 78. *Collections Arranged:* Wood Biennial (twelve wood designer-craftsmen; auth, catalog), 78, 80 & 82; Monumental Sculpture Traveling Exhib, 79 & 82; Monumental Weaving, 83; Com Bank, Hq & Br, NJ; Traveler's Mortgage Serv Hq, Cherry Hill, NJ; Jefferson Bank, Philadelphia, Pa. *Pos:* Craft coordr, By Hand Crafts Gallery, NJ, 76-77; mgr, Richard Kagan Gallery, Pa, 78-79; dir & owner, The Gallery at 401, Magnolia, NJ, 79-; owner & dir, Landsman Gallery, 82-; vpres, ArtMarkit Inc, 82-; appraiser, Am Soc Appraisals, 88. *Teaching:* Asst dept chairperson ceramic shell & plastics, Johnson Atelier, NJ, 76-79. *Mem:* Sr mem Am Soc Appraisers; Am Craft Coun. *Specialty:* Contemp fine art, monumental sculpture and graphic art, corporate art consultation, appraisals. *Mailing Add:* c/o Landsman Gallery 401 S White Horse Pike Magnolia NJ 08049

KILLMASTER, JOHN H
PAINTER, ENAMELIST
b Allegan, Mich, Dec 2, 34. *Study:* Soc Arts & Crafts, Detroit, Mich; Hope Col, BA; Univ Guanajuato, Mex, Cranbrook Acad Art, MFA. *Work:* Boise Gallery Art & Boise Cascade World Hq Collection, Boise, Idaho; FMC Corp; Idaho First Nat Bank; Sunshine Mining; and others. *Comn:* Sculpture, Portland Arts Comn, 78-79; murals, Wash State Art Comn, 79. *Exhib:* San Francisco Mus Mod Art, Calif, 79-80; Nat Mus Am Art, Smithsonian Inst, 79-80; Newport Harbor Mus, Calif, 80; Denver Art Mus, 80; Art from Idaho (with catalog), Nat Mus Am Art, 83; Enamels Int, Long Beach Mus Art, Calif, 85; Int Juried Art Competition, Mussavi Art Gallery, New York, 85; Massana-Soldevila First Int Enamel Exhib, Barcelona, Spain, 88; Creativkreis Int Email Exhib, Jerusalem & WGer, 88-89; Int Enamel Exhib, Australia, 90. *Pos:* Illusr & designer, Ladriere Art Studio, Detroit, 58-61. *Teaching:* Asst prof painting, Ferris State Col, 69-70; prof art, Boise State Univ, 70-; instr art, Grand Marais Art Colony, Minn, 85. *Awards:* Purchase Awards, Idaho Artists Ann, Boise Art Mus, 70, 74, 76 & 77; Western States Art Found fel & grant, 74; Governors Award for Excellence in the Arts, 78. *Bibliog:* Crafts in Architecture, West States Art Found, 81-82. *Mem:* NW Designer Craftsman Asn; Nat Enamelist Guild, Washington, DC; Enamelists Guild West, San Diego; Enamalist Soc (mem, bd trustees). *Media:* Acrylic, Enamel. *Dealer:* Ochi Gallery Boise ID; American Art Resources Stamford CT. *Mailing Add:* 1910 University Dr Boise ID 83725

KILROY, MARY A
ADMINISTRATOR, CURATOR
Study: Manor Junior Col, AS, St Joseph Univ, BA, Temple Univ, Sem Prog for Mgt Develop Sch Business. *Pos:* Dir, Fine Arts Prog & Adv Bd Design, Redevelopment Authority, City of Philadephia, 70-; consult for numerous cities in developing guidelines & formulating legislation for "Percent for Public Art" programs, including Pittsburgh, Pa, Phoenix, Ariz & Atlantic City, NJ, 82-; adv & cur, Fed Reserve Bank of Philadelphia Collection, 85-; mem, Mayors Adv Comt on Sculpture, 85-; Gov's Adv Comt Chmn on Sculpture, 89. *Bibliog:* Auth, 498 Hardworking Women, Philadelphia, 89. *Mem:* Art Table; Pa Arts Coalition (mem bd dirs, 86-); Citizens for Arts in Pa (mem bd dirs, 83-); Nexus Found for Art (mem bd dirs, 83-); COLLAB, Del Valley Design Orgn (mem, bd dir, 90-). *Mailing Add:* Fine Arts Prog Adv Bd Design 1234 Market St 8th floor Philadelphia PA 19107

KIM, PO (HYUN)
PAINTER
b Korea; US citizen. *Study:* Univ Ill, MFA, 57. *Work:* Chicago Art Inst, Ill; Solomon R Guggenheim Mus, New York; Okla Art Ctr; Tenn Fine Art Ctr; NJ Power & Lighting Co. *Exhib:* Painting & Sculpture Today, Indianapolis Mus Art, Ind, 78; one-man shows, Kornblee Gallery, New York, 61, Squibb Gallery, Princeton, NJ, 79, Gallery Mod Art Int, Munich, West Germany, 80 & Art Alliance, Philadelphia, Pa, 80; Korean Drawing Now, Brooklyn Mus, NY, 81; A Feast for the Eyes, Heckscher Mus. Huntington, NY, 81. *Teaching:* Instr, New York Univ, 61-62. *Media:* Oil, Acrylic. *Mailing Add:* 417 Lafayette St New York NY 10003

KIMBALL, WILFORD WAYNE, JR
LITHOGRAPHER, DRAFTSMAN
b Salt Lake City, Utah, July 15, 43. *Study:* Southern Utah State Col, BA, 68; Univ Ariz, MFA, 70; Tamarind Inst, Albuquerque, NMex, fel printing, 70-71, Master Printer, 71. *Work:* Tamarind Collection, Albuquerque, NMex; Brooklyn Mus; Libr Cong, Washington, DC; Lessing J Rosenwald Collection, The Philadelphia Mus of Art & Nat Gallery Fine Arts, Washington, DC. *Exhib:* Brooklyn Mus Biennial Print Exhib, New York, 78; 56th Ann Philadelphia Competition, The Print Club, 80; Colorprint USA, Texas Tech Univ, Lubbock, Tex, 80; Tenth Anniversary Exhib, Tyler Mus Art, Tex, 81; one-man shows, Phoenix Art Mus, Ariz, 81, Art Mus STex, 81 & Thirty Am Printmakers Invitational, Univ Gallery Fine Art, Ohio State Univ, 82; Seventh British Int Print Biennale, Cartwright Hall, Bradford, W Yorkshire, Eng, 82; and others. *Pos:* Artist-in-residence, Roswell Mus & Art Ctr, NMex, 72. *Teaching:* Lectr lithography, Univ NMex, 71; vis lectr lithography, Univ Wis, Madison, 72-73 & summers 73 & 74; asst prof lithography & drawing, San Diego State Univ, 73-74; asst prof lithography, Calif State Univ, Long Beach, 74-75; asst prof lithography & drawing, Univ Tex San Antonio, 75-77; lectr lithography, San Diego State Univ, 77-78; prof lithography, Ariz State Univ, Tempe, 78-84 & Brigham Young Univ, Provo, Utah, 84-; prof lithography, Brigham Young Univ, 84- *Awards:* William H Walker Purchase Award, 55th Philadelphia Ann, 79; Purchase Awards, 17th Bradley Nat Print & Drawing Exhib, 79 & Vermillion '79 Nat Print & Drawing Competition, 79. *Media:* Lithography. *Mailing Add:* 185 South 1300 East Pleasant Grove UT 84062

KIMBRELL, LEONARD BUELL
HISTORIAN
b Archibald, La, Aug 3, 22. *Study:* Northwestern State Univ, La, BA, 42; Univ Ore, MS, 50, MFA, 54; Univ Iowa, PhD, 65. *Work:* Univ Ore, Eugene; Portland Art Mus, Ore. *Pos:* Contrib ed, Artweek, 71-81; art critic, NW Mag, 81-; Art appraiser. *Teaching:* Prof art, Eastern Ore Col, 54-61; prof art, Portland State Univ, 61-, head dept art & archit, 76-84; Prof Emer, 93. *Awards:* Purchase Award, Portland Art Mus, 53. *Mem:* Col Art Asn; Soc Archit Historians. *Res:* Cranach's nudes in the light of Luther's ethics; Alexander Pope as failed painter; guide to art in the Pacific Northwest; Rodins at Maryhill. *Publ:* Auth, Some new light on Astoria Column, Festshrift: Marion Ross, Soc Archit Historians, 76. *Mailing Add:* Dept Art Portland State Univ PO Box 751 Portland OR 97207

KIMES, DON
PAINTER, EDUCATOR
b Oil City, Pa, Nov 18, 50. *Study:* Westminster Col, BA, 75; Univ Pittsburgh, grad studies, 75-77; Brooklyn Col City Univ New York, MFA, 80; NY Studio Sch, cert, 78; studied with Agostini, Bell, Campbell, McNeil, Vicente, Heliker, Matter & Carone. *Work:* Chautauqua Inst, NY; Westminster Col Gallery, Pa; NY Studio Sch, NY; IBM Corp, NY; Conn State Univ; Watkins Gallery, Am Univ, Washington, DC. *Exhib:* Solo exhibs, Prince Street Gallery, New York, 79, 80, 82, 84 & 86, 88 & 90, Michael Rockefeller Gallery, State Univ NY, Fredonia, 88, Chautauqua Inst, 88, 89 & 90 Watkins Gallery, Washington, DC, 89; Paperworks, Brooklyn Mus, NY, 82; Critic's Choice, Arsenal Gallery, New York, 84; 20th Anniversary Retrospective, NY Studio Sch Galleries, New York, 85; Nat Acad Design, New York, 86; Baltimore Mus, Md, 86. *Teaching:* Instr painting, State Univ NY, Stonybrook, 79; instr painting, NY Studio Sch, New York, 80- & chmn bd govs, 83-85; artistic dir, Chautauqua Inst Sch Arts, 85-; Artist-in-Residence, Conn State Univ, 87-88; assoc prof art, dept chmn, Am Univ, Washington, DC, 88- *Awards:* Visual Fel, Edna St Vincent Millay Found, 85; Visual Deleg, Jurmala Conf-Cult Exchange, Soviet Union, 86. *Bibliog:* Lawrence Alloway (auth), Critic's Choice, Arsenal Gallery, NY, 83; John Arthur Shanks (auth), Popolopen Metaphor, Sunstorm Press, 86; Cynthia Kraman (auth), Don Kimes , The Artist as Philosopher, Sunstorm Mag, 88. *Media:* Oil, Acrylic. *Publ:* Auth, In Praise of Space: 19th Century American Landscape, Westminster Press, 76; From Landscape to Collage, Ecker Press, 86; coauth, Chadakion Review, An Interview with Agostini & Portfolio Reproduction. *Dealer:* Gaumann-Cicchino Gallery Box 475 Orleans MA 02853. *Mailing Add:* c/o Prince Street Gallery 121 Wooster St New York NY 10012

KIMMEL-COHN, ROBERTA
DEALER, WRITER
b Milwaukee, Wis, Feb 1, 37. *Study:* Sophie Newcomb Col, with George Rickey; Univ Wis; Boston Univ Sch Fine & Appl Arts, BFA. *Pos:* Art dir, McGraw-Hill Publ Co, New York, 61-62, Macmillan & Co, 64-65 & Walker & Co, 65-67; pres, Roberta Kimmel Advert, New York, 67-; partner, Kimmel/Cohn Photog Arts, New York, 74- *Bibliog:* Surrealism in advertising, Art Dir Mag, 70; article in Art Dir Ann, 72; People in the news, New York Times, 74. *Specialty:* Photography; Man Ray; nineteenth and twentieth century art. *Publ:* Auth, Erste Landung, portfolio of photographs by George Grosz, 77; Man Ray: Vintage Photographs, Rayographs and Solarizations, 77; In Artist's Homes, Clarkson Potter Inc. *Mailing Add:* 41 Central Park W New York NY 10023

KIMMELMAN, HAROLD
SCULPTOR
b Philadelphia, Pa, Feb 20, 23. *Study:* Cape Sch Art, Provincetown, Mass; Pa Acad Fine Art, Philadelphia. *Comn:* Helios Flame, Sun Oil Corp Hq, Radnor, Pa, 76; Burst of Joy, The Gallery, Philadelphia, 77; Marino Monument, Casa Enrico Fermi Corp, Philadelphia, Pa, 77; Man Helping Man, Am Col Cardiology, Bethesda, Md, 79; Hol; Hand in Hand, Merck Sharp & Doehme, West Point, Pa, 88. *Exhib:* Pa Acad Fine Arts, 68; Philadelphia Civic Ctr Show, 71. *Awards:* Braverman Karp Prize for sculpting, 68; May Audubon Prize for sculpting, 69. *Bibliog:* Sculpture of a City, Walker Publ Co, 74. *Mem:* Artists Equity Asn (pres, Philadelphia Chap, 72); fel Pa Acad Fine Arts. *Media:* Stainless Steel, Bronze. *Publ:* Drexel Univ, Vol I, Philadelphia, Pa, 86. *Mailing Add:* 538 W Carpenter Lane Philadelphia PA 19119

KIMURA, JOAN ALEXANDRA
PAINTER, DRAFTSMAN
b Los Angeles, Calif, July 10, 34. *Study:* Art Ctr Col Design, cert, 55; Univ Alaska, BFA; Syracuse Univ, MFA, 84. *Work:* Anchorage Mus Art, Atlantic Richfield Co & Sohio Alaska Petroleum Co, Anchorage; Alaska State Mus, Fairbanks & Juneau. *Comn:* Univ Alaska, Anchorage, comn by State of Alaska, 81; Nunaka Sch, 84 & Bear Valley Sch, 86, comn by Municipality of Anchorage. *Exhib:* Conn Acad Fine Arts Show, Hartford, 68, 71, 72, 74, 77 & 82; Nat Acad Design Show, New York, NY, 69; one-person exhibs, Charles Z Mann Gallery, New York, 69, Alaska Methodist Univ, 72, Anchorage Mus Hist Art, 75, 83 & 88 & West Broadway Gallery-Alternate Space, New York, 81 & 83. *Pos:* Mem bd dirs, Anchorage Mus Hist & Art, 81-88, mem acquisition comt, 88- *Teaching:* Instr art, Anchorage Community Col, 78-87; prof art, Univ Alaska, Anchorage, 87- *Awards:* Sage Allen Award, Conn Acad Fine Art, 71; Best of Show, All Alaska Show, Anchorage Mus, 76; First Prize, Pac Northwest Figure Drawing Competition, Visual Arts Ctr Alaska, 86. *Bibliog:* Revs, Arts Mag, 9-10/69; Will Grant (auth), art rev, Artspeak, 12/1/83. *Mem:* Conn Acad Fine Art. *Media:* Oil; Drawing. *Mailing Add:* Anchorage Community Col/Dept Art 2533 Providence Ave Anchorage AK 99508

KIMURA, RIISABURO
PAINTER, PRINTMAKER
b Yokosuka, Japan, Oct 13, 24. *Study:* Yokohama Univ, 47; Hosei Univ, Tokyo, 54. *Work:* Mus Mod Art, New York; Nat Mus Mod Art, Kyoto, Japan; US Info Agency; City of Hamburg, WGer. *Comn:* Print ed, Brooklyn Mus, 75. *Exhib:* USA Pavillion Expo 70, Osaka, Japan; Japanese Artists in the Americas, Nat Mus Mod Art, Kyoto, Japan, 74; one-man shows, Gallery Mod Art, Munich, Ger, 77, Int Mod Art, Gallery, Munich, 82, Kyoto, Osaka, Kobe, Japan, 87, Chino Gallery, New York, 89, JICC, Washington, DC, 91, Gallery Aunkan, Osaka, Japan, 91 & Artra Gallery, New York, 92; Frank Fedele Fine Arts, New York. *Awards:* Int Biennal Print Award, Tokyo, 70. *Bibliog:* Art News, 10/79; Interior Design, 1/79; Art Am, 3/80. *Mailing Add:* 463 West St New York NY 10014

KIMURA, SUEKO M
PAINTER
b Hawaii. *Study:* Univ Hawaii, BA & MFA; Chouinard Art Inst; Columbia Univ; Brooklyn Mus Sch Art; Art Students League. *Work:* State Found Cult & Arts; Contemp Arts Ctr; State Dept Educ Artmobile; Kaiser Hawaii-Kai Develop Co; Honolulu Acad Art; and others. *Exhib:* One-man shows, George Hall Gallery, Contemp Arts Ctr & Crossroads Gallery; Brooklyn Mus; San Diego Art Mus; Bibliot Am, Bucharest; Kyoto Mus Mod Art. *Teaching:* Emer prof art, Univ Hawaii, 52-77. *Awards:* Honolulu Printmakers, 62; Easter Art Show, 62, 65 & 68; Purchase Prizes, State Found Cult & Arts, 68, 69 & 72; plus others. *Bibliog:* Artists of Hawaii, Vol 1, Haar & Neogy, 74; Am Women Artists, 84. *Mem:* Hawaii Painters & Sculptors League; Honolulu Printmakers. *Media:* Oil, Acrylic. *Publ:* Illusr, cover design & drawings, Philosophy & Cult, East & West, 62. *Mailing Add:* 2567B Henry St Honolulu HI 96817

KIMURA, WILLIAM YUSABURO
PAINTER, PRINTMAKER
b Seattle, Wash, June 28, 20. *Study:* Hollywood Art Ctr, 39; Cornish Sch Art, Seattle, 40; also with Adolph Kronengold, Danny Pierce, Junichiro Sekino, Bill Richie & Evan Phoutrides. *Work:* Fine Art Mus, Alaska Methodist Univ, Color Ctr Gallery, Anchorage. *Comn:* Homage to Salmon (aluminum welded sculpture), Anchorage CofC, 79; Stainless Steel Welded Sculptural Fountain, Balanced Arcs, Anchorage, 81. *Exhib:* Smithsonian Traveling Exhib, USA & Europe, Washington, DC, 62; one-man shows, Anchorage Fine Art Mus, 71, prints, The Gallery, Anchorage, 77 & Painting & Prints, Anchorage Fine Arts Mus, 78; Ann All Alaska Exhib Artists & Craftsmen, 65-72; Wenatchee Apple Blossom Festival, Wash, 71. *Teaching:* Instr painting, Anchorage Community Ctr, 59-60 & Anchorage Community Col, 61-63; artist in residence, Alaska Methodist Univ, 66, assoc prof art, 73; artist in residence, Visual Arts Ctr of Alaska, 77. *Awards:* Mel Kohler Award in Painting, Ann All Alaska Exhib, 66; Prints Alaska Award, Alaska Coun Arts, 76; First Award in Prints, All-Alaska Juried Art Exhib, 76 & 77. *Bibliog:* Paintings & Prints, Alaska Methodist Univ, 63; Woodcuts & Prints, Mel Kohler Gallery, 64; Paintings & Prints, Anchorage Fine Art Mus, 71. *Mem:* Life mem Alaska Artist Guild (pres, 63-65). *Dealer:* Artique Ltd 314 G St Anchorage AK 99501. *Mailing Add:* 1025 W 11th Ave Anchorage AK 99501

KIND, JOSHUA B
EDUCATOR, CRITIC
b Philadelphia, Pa, Nov 5, 33. *Study:* Univ Pa, Philadelphia, BA, 55; Columbia Univ, PhD, 67. *Pos:* Chicago ed, Art News, New York, 64-70; dir, Oxbow Summer Sch Art, Saugatuck, Mich, 67-68; contrib ed, New Art Examiner, Chicago, 75- *Teaching:* Instr art hist, Northwestern Univ, Evanston, Ill, 59-62; instr humanities, Univ Chicago, 62-65; vis prof art hist, Sch of Art Inst Chicago, 64-76; asst prof art hist & humanities, Ill Inst Technol, Chicago, 65-69; prof art hist, Northern Ill Univ, DeKalb, 69- *Awards:* Nat Endowment for the Arts Critics Fel, 77. *Mem:* Col Art Asn; Soc Architectural Historians. *Res:* Modernism; creativity and the avant-garde; Renaissance inconography; modern architecture. *Publ:* Auth, Rouault, 69; Art and the corps of women, 3/78 & The corruption of Norman Rockwell, 1/79, New Art Examiner; contribr, World Bk Year Book & Encyclopedia Britannica Yr Bk, 70-; contrib, Contemp Artists, 1st, 2nd & 3rd ed; contrib, Int Dict of Art and Artists, vol 2, 90. *Mailing Add:* 5619 Dunham Rd Downers Grove IL 60515

KIND, PHYLLIS
ART DEALER
b New York, NY. *Study:* Univ Pa, AB; Univ Chicago, MA. *Pos:* Dir, Phyllis Kind Galleries, Chicago, 67-, New York, 75- *Mem:* Am Art Dealers Asn. *Specialty:* Representing major Chicago artists introducing exhibitions and selected works by other major contemporary American & Russian artists, also specializing in Outsider and Art Brut. *Dealer:* Phyllis Kind Gallery 136 Greene St New York NY 10012. *Mailing Add:* c/o Phyllis Kind Gallery 136 Greene St New York NY 10012

KINDAHL, CONNIE
WEAVER, CRAFTSMAN
b Decatur, Ill. *Study:* Univ Ill. *Comn:* Prudential Insurance Co, Wash, DC, 84; Med W Community Health Plan, Chicopee, Mass, 84; Alpha Chi Omega Sorority, Amherst, Mass, 84; Harvard Community Health Fac, W Roxbury, Mass, 86; Dow Chemical Co, Chicago, Ill, 86. *Exhib:* 2-man show, Western New Engl Col, Springfield, Mass, 83; Wichita Nat Decorative Arts Exhib, Wichita, Kan, 85; 8th Ann Vahki Exhib, Mesa, Ariz, 86; Fiber/Fiber, Convergence 86, Toronto, 86; Rugs: Contemporary Handwoven Floorcoverings, Mus Am Textile Hist, North Andover, Mass, 86. *Teaching:* Instr rug weaving, Weavers Guild Boston, 84-86 & Auagusta Heritage Ctr, Davis & Elkins Col, 88. *Awards:* Chairmans Choice in Fiber, Wesleyan Potters, 82, Special Recognition Award, Nassau Co NY Fiber Arts Forum & Exhib, 85 & First Prize in Rugs, New Eng Weavers Seminar, 85. *Bibliog:* Elizabeth French (auth), Connie Kindahl, Shuttle Spindle & Dyepot Handweavers Guild Am, 86. *Mem:* Am Craft Coun; Handweavers Guild Am; Worcester Craft Ctr; Leverett Craftsmen & Artists. *Media:* Fiber. *Publ:* All White Overshot Rug, spring, 82, Rugs on a Three-End Block Draft, Weavers J, spring 84; Boundweave Rug on an Overshot Threading, Shuttle Spindle & Dyepot, 86. *Mailing Add:* 364 Daniel Shays Hwy Pelham MA 01002

KINDERMANN, HELMMO
PHOTOGRAPHER, PAINTER
b Lancaster, Pa, Oct 11, 47. *Study:* Tyler Sch Fine Art, Temple Univ, BFA, 69; study of photog, Visual Studies Workshop, Rochester, NY, 71-73; State Univ NY Buffalo, MFA, 73. *Work:* Miss Art Asn, Jackson; Visual Studies Workshop, Rochester, NY; St Lawrence Univ, Canton, New York; Alternative Mus, New York. *Exhib:* Images, Dimensional, Movable, Transferable, Akron Art Inst, Ohio, 73; New Approaches, Ctr for Exploratory and Perceptual Arts, Buffalo, NY, 75; New Photographics/76, Cent Wash State Col, Ellensburgh, 76; Photo/Synthesis, Herbert F Johnson Mus of Art, Ithaca, NY, 76; Auto as Icon, Int Mus Photog, George Eastman House, Rochester, NY, 79; and others. *Pos:* Cur, US Eye Photo Exhib, Nat Fine Arts Comt, XIII Olympic Winter Games, Lake Placid, NY, 78- *Teaching:* Asst prof photog, Lake Placid Sch Art, Ctr for Music, Drama & Art, NY, 73-81. *Awards:* Purchase Prize, Images on Paper, Miss Art Asn, 71. *Mem:* Soc for Photog Educ; Col Art Asn Am; Photog Instr Asn; Friends of Photog. *Publ:* New Photographics/76, Cent Wash Col, 76; contribr, Works and Process, CMDA Publ Co, 76; contribr, Photo/Synthesis, Herbert F Johnson Mus Art, 76; contribr, The Photograph Collectors Guide, Lee Witkin & Barbara London, NY Graphic Soc; contribr, Uniquely Photographic, Quiver No 5, Honolulu Acad Arts; and others. *Mailing Add:* 1830 Rose Tree Lane Havertown PA 19130

KING, ELAINE A
CURATOR, HISTORIAN
b Oak Park, Ill, Apr 12, 47. *Study:* Northern Ill Univ, BA, MA; Columbia Col, Chicago, photog hist with Arthur Siegel; intern, George Eastman House, summer 77; Northwestern Univ, PhD, 86, with Howard Becker, Leland Roloff, Charles Kleinhaus & Donald Kuspit & Jim Brekenridge. *Collections Arranged:* Barry Le Va, 66-88; Mich Gerhard, Drawings & Sculpture, Michael Gatlin, 82-89; Notley Maddox (auth, catalog), 81; Jo Mielziner-Sketches, from the collection of Jules Fisher (auth, catalog), 83; Ed Paschke: New Paintings (auth, catalog), 83; Mel Bochner: 1973-1985, 85; Mel Bochner,

Abstraction-Abstraction, 86; From Los Angeles--David Amico & Mark Lere, 86; Robert Wilson: Drawings from the Civil Wars, 86; Hilla and Bernd Becher: Industrial Monuments, 86; Martin Puryear (catalogue), Elizabeth Murray, Drawing Tishan Hsu, 8 year summary, 86-88; New Generations, Chicago, 90 & New York, 91; five Artists at the Airport, 92. *Pos:* Cur, Dittmar Mem Gallery, Northwestern Univ, 77-81; dir, Hewlett Art Gallery, Carnegie-Mellon Univ, 81-89; corresp ed, Dialogue Mag, 84-89; dir, Carnegie-Mellon Univ Art Gallery, 85-91; independent cur, freelance, 91-; art critic in residence, Del Ctr Contemp Art, Wilmington, 92. *Teaching:* Lectr art dept, Northwestern Univ, 77-81; assoc prof art hist, Carnegie-Mellon Univ, 81- *Awards:* Pa Coun Arts; Nominator Award, Visual Arts, 88 & 89; Mid-Atlantic Arts Found, Fel Panel, 91. *Mem:* Col Art Asn; Art Table & Am Asn Mus, Mountain Lake Criticism Symp (bd dirs, 81-91); Int Asn Art Critics; Am Asn Historians Am Art. *Publ:* Hermitage, Quiescence & Enigma, Magdalena Jetolova (exhib booklet), Carnegie Mellon, 91; A Precarious Balance of Being (exhib catalog), New Generations: New York, Carnegie Mellon, 91; Sowers of Myth: Time Change, Perception (catalog), Chicago Cult Ctr, 91; The NEA: A Misunderstood Patron, Prentice Hall Anthology Contemp Issues: Multicultural Issues, winter 92; King, Elaine--, The Homeless: Reality, Spectacle, PC?, Pittsburgh, 4/92. *Mailing Add:* 5604 Fair Oaks St Pittsburgh PA 15217

KING, ELEANOR (ELEANOR KING HOOKHAM)
PAINTER, PRINTMAKER
b Marlow, Okla, April 5, 09. *Study:* Okla City Col, with Martha Avey, 23; Acad Cult France, Dr Hon Causa, 80; Elmhurst Col, Hon Dr Art, 87. *Work:* Mus Nat Mod Art & Mus Mod Art de la Ville, Paris; Univ Ind Art Mus, Bloominton; Ill Wesleyan Univ Mus Art; St Lawrence Seaway, John Vanderpoel Mus, Chicago; Elmhurst Col, Ill; Art Mus, Pensacola, Fla. *Comn:* 40 ft mural, comn by Oak Brook Polo Club, Chicago, 88. *Exhib:* Int Feminine, Mus Art Ville Paris, 68; Int Art Feminine, Mus Athens, Greece, 68; Int Expo, City Hall, Nice, France, 71; Woman Artists, Palais Goblein, Paris, 72; Int Exposition Art, Bruxelles, Belg, 73-75; Int Artists, Sony Art Mus, Osaka, Japan, 79-83; Beverly Art Ctr Mus, Chicago, 90. *Teaching:* Privately, 26-80. *Awards:* Medaille D'Or, Arts, Sciences & Lettres, Accad Ital, Parma, 79 & 88; Medaille Gold, Grand Prix Humanitaire France, 83; Gold Medal, Istituto D'Arte Contemp Di Milano, Italy, 88. *Bibliog:* Elmhurst (producer), film, Continental Cable Vision, 82; John Knudson (producer), film, Cable Vision, Harper Col, 82. *Mem:* Elmhurst Artists Guild (pres, 51-52 & 71-73); Elmhurst Fine Arts & Civic Ctr Found (pres, 75-); Acad Arts, Sci & Lett, France; Nat Soc Arts & Lett. *Media:* Watercolor, Oil; Etching, Lithography. *Publ:* Auth, Color-La Couleur, Paris, 76 & rev ed, USA, 85. *Dealer:* Galerie Bernheim-Jeune 83 Faubourg St Honore Paris France. *Mailing Add:* 289 Adelia St Elmhurst IL 60126

KING, LYNDEL IRENE SAUNDERS
DIRECTOR, ADMINISTRATOR
b Enid, Okla, June 10, 43. *Study:* Univ Kans, BA, 65; Univ Minn, MA, 71, PhD, 82. *Pos:* Asst dir, Art Mus, Univ Minn, 76-78, dir, 78-; dir, Exhibs & Mus Relations, Control Data Corp, 79-81; exhib coordr, Nat Gallery Art, 80; dir, Art Mus, Univ Minn, 81- *Teaching:* Art hist, Mus Studies, Univ Minn. *Mem:* Art Mus Asn (bd secy, 83); Asn Art Mus Dirs; Am Asn Mus; Asn Col & Univ Mus & Galleries; Am Fed Arts, (bd). *Res:* Nineteenth century England, especially interaction of arts and society. *Publ:* Auth, Exhibition diplomacy, Mus News, 79; Museums and special exhibitions, Art J, 80; The industrialization of taste: The Artunian of London, UMI Research Press, 85. *Mailing Add:* 110 Northrop Auditorium Univ Minn Minneapolis MN 55455

KING, MARY ETTA See Houston, Mary Etta (King)

KING, MYRON LYZON
DEALER
b Hampton Bays, NY, Oct 22, 21. *Study:* David Lipscomb Col, Peabody Col, BA. *Pos:* Lyzon Pictures & Frames, Inc, Nashville. *Specialty:* Contemporary American art; Sterling Strauser, Paul Lancaster, Malva and David Burlink. *Mailing Add:* 932 Evans Rd Nashville TN 37204

KING, PATRICK J
ART DEALER, CURATOR
b St Joseph, Mo, Nov 8, 51. *Study:* Kansas City Art Inst & Sch Design, BFA, 74; Mo Western State Col; Parsons Sch Design. *Collections Arranged:* Fiber Structures & Fabric Surfaces (coauth, catalog), Herron Sch Art, Indianapolis, 79; American Artists/Indianapolis (ed, catalog), Ball State Univ, Muncie, Ind, 83. *Pos:* Asst dir, Herron Sch Art Gallery, Indianapolis, 79-81; dir exhibs, Editions Limited Gallery, Indianapolis, 81-82; dir & owner, Patrick King Contemporary Art, Indianapolis, 82. *Awards:* Traci Award (to recognize the advancement of culture in Indianapolis), Metropolitan Arts Coun. *Mem:* Founding mem Indianapolis Art Galleries & Dealers Asn, 89-90. *Res:* Painting, sculpture and textile work completed within the last decade. *Publ:* Ed, To Dance: Recent Paintings and Drawings by Mary Beth Edelson with Performance in Mind (exhib catalog), Patrick King Contemp Art, Indianapolis, 84. *Mailing Add:* Patrick King Contemp Art 427 Massachusetts Ave Indianapolis IN 46204

KING, RAY
SCULPTOR, STAINED GLASS ARTIST
b Philadelphia, Pa, July 4, 50. *Study:* Burleighfield House, Loudwater, Bucks, Eng, 75-76. *Work:* Nat Mus Am Art, Washington, DC; Victoria & Albert Mus, London, Eng; Corning Mus Glass, Corning, NY; Best Products, Richmond, Va; Chasco Co, Jericho, NY; DuPont de Nemours E I & Co, Wilmington, Del. *Comn:* Solar Wing (prism projection piece), GSA, US Courthouse & Fed Bldg, San Jose, Calif, 83; Light Sails (light activated wall sculpture), Orlando Airport, Fla, 84; stained glass windows, Univ Alaska, Fairbanks, 85; carved glass murals, Pew Charitable Trust, Philadelphia, Pa, 87; Saturn Lamps (bronze & glass lights), Rainbow Room, New York, 87; Aurora Window, canopy & sconces, The Cosmopolitan, Philadelphia, 89; Cosmos, wall mounted, illuminated frieze in bronze & glass, Graduate Hosp, Philadelphia, 89. *Exhib:* World Glass 1982, Hokkaido Mus Mod Art, Sapporo, Japan, 82; Ornamentalism, Hudson River Mus, Yonkers, NY, 83; solo exhibs, New Works, Heller Gallery, New York, 84, Works in Glass, Metal & Light, Royal Inst Brit Architects, London, Eng, 86 & Illuminated Sculpture, Sanske Gallerie, Zurich, Switz, 88; Kulturhuset, Stockholm, Sweden, 85; Poetry of the Physical, Richmond Mus Art, Va, 88; Architectural Art, Am Craft Mus, New York, 88; Contemp Philadelphia Artists, Philadelphia Mus Art, 90. *Pos:* Panelist, fel grants, Nat Endowment Arts, 81; mem bd dirs, New York Experimental Glass Workshop, 81-88. *Awards:* Nat Endowment Arts Fel, 84; Pa Coun Arts Fel, 86; Edwin Guth Mem Award, Illuminating Engineering Soc, 88. *Bibliog:* Patrick Reyntiens (auth), The Technique of Stained Glass, B T Batsford, 77; Robert Jensen & Patricia Conway (auths), Ornamentalism, Clarkson N Potter, 82; Patricia Conway (auth), Art for Everyday, Clarkson N Potter, 90. *Mem:* Int Sculpture Soc; Am Craft Coun. *Media:* Glass, Metal. *Mailing Add:* 603 S 10th St Philadelphia PA 19147-1917

KING, WILLIAM DICKEY
SCULPTOR
b Jacksonville, Fla, Feb 25, 25. *Study:* Univ Fla, 42-44; Cooper Union Art Sch, 45-48; Brooklyn Mus Art Sch, 49; Academia dei Belle Arti, Rome, 49-50; Cent Sch, London, 52. *Work:* Univ Calif; Cornell Univ, Ithaca, NY; Hunter Mus, TN; Syracuse Univ, NY; Los Angeles Co Mus, Calif; Brandeis Univ, Waltham, Mass; Metrop Mus Art, Whitney Mus & Solomon R Guggenheim Mus, New York; and many pvt collections. *Comn:* Murals, SS United States, 52 & Banker's Trust, New York, 60; sculptures, Miami-Dade Jr Col, Fla, 72, State Univ NY, Potsdam, 73-74, Detroit Med Ctr, 79, Madison Art & Civic Ctr, Wis, 79 & Lincoln Libr, Ft Wayne, Ind, 80, Palo Alto, Calif, 86 & Fla State Coun Arts, Lakeland, Fla, 87. *Exhib:* Whitney Mus Am Art, Mus Mod Art & Guggenheim Mus, New York; Philadelphia Mus Art; Los Angeles Co Mus Art; retrospective, San Francisco Mus Art, Calif, 70 & 74; solo exhibs, San Francisco Mus Art, 70, Wadsworth Atheneum, Hartford, 72, Hunter Mus, Chatanooga, Tenn, 87, Peconic Gallery, New York, Brunnier Gallery & Mus, Iowa, 90, Extension Gallery Inc, NJ & Hokin Gallery Inc, Fla, 91; Cranbrook Acad Art, Bloomfield Hills, Mich, 74 & 76; Nat Acad Design, New York, 89; Brenan Col Galleries, Gainsville, Ga, 91; Coming of Age of Am Sculpture, Lehigh, Pa, 91-92; Mus Art, Ft Lauderdale, Fla, 92. *Teaching:* Instr sculpture, Brooklyn Mus Sch Art, 52-55; lectr sculpture, Univ Calif, Berkeley, 65-66; instr sculpture, Art Students League, 68-69, Univ Pa, 72-73 & State Univ NY, 74-75. *Awards:* Fulbright Fel, 49-50; St Gaudens Medal, Cooper Union, 64; Creative Artists Pub Serv Proj Grant, 74; Gold Medal, Nat Acad Design, New York, 86. *Bibliog:* S Schwartz (auth), New York letter: William King, Art Int, 11/72; John Sanders (auth), Photography Year Book 1973, London, 72; Hilton Kramer (auth), The Age of the Avant-Garde, London, 74. *Dealer:* Terry Dintenfass Inc 18 E 67th St New York NY 10021. *Mailing Add:* 17 E 96th St New York NY 10028

KINGMAN, DONG
PAINTER, ILLUSTRATOR
b Oakland, Calif, Mar 31, 11. *Study:* Lingnan Sch, Hong Kong, with Sze Tu-Wai, 26; Fox & Morgan Art Sch, Oakland; Acad Art Col, San Francisco, Hon LHD, 87. *Work:* Metrop Mus Art, Mus Mod Art & Whitney Mus Am Art, New York; Boston Mus Fine Arts, Mass; M H De Young Mus, San Francisco; Art Inst Chicago; Addison Gallery Am Art; Butler Art Inst; Cranbrook Acad Art; Brooklyn Mus Art, NY; Honolulu Acad Art, Hawaii; Pa Acad Fine Arts, Philadelphia; Tweed Gallery, Univ Minn, Duluth; Wadsworth Atheneum, Hartford, Conn; and others. *Comn:* Murals, Hilton Hotel, New York, 63, mosaic, Pres Hotel, Hong Kong, 64, Bank Calif, San Francisco, 68 & Boca Raton Hotel, Fla, 70; 55 Days in Peking, 63, Flower Drum Song, 61 & title paintings for major motion pictures; tapestry designed for Ambassador Hotel, Hong Kong, 74; Lincoln Savings Bank, New York; and others. *Exhib:* Am Watercolor Soc; San Francisco Art Asn; Metrop Mus Art Watercolor Exhib; Whitney Mus Am Art Ann; Columbus Mus Arts & Crafts, Ga. *Teaching:* Instr art, Columbia Univ, 46-54; instr watercolor & hist Chinese art, Hunter Col, 48-53; fac mem, Famous Artists Sch, Westport, Conn, 54-; Hewitt Travelling Painting Workshop, 57- *Awards:* Dolphin Medal Award, Am Watercolor Soc, 87; Paul Remmey Award, Am Watercolor Soc, 90; Mary Pleissner Award, Am Watercolor Soc, 91; and others. *Bibliog:* James Wong Howe (dir), Dong Kingman (film), 54; Alan D Gruskin (auth), The Watercolors of Dong Kingman, Crowell Co, 58; Helena Kingman (auth), Dong Kingman;s Watercolors, Watson-Guptill, 90. *Mem:* Am Watercolor Soc; West Coast Watercolor Soc; Dutch Treat Club. *Media:* Watercolor, Acrylic. *Publ:* Illusr, Johnny Hong in Chinatown, 52; City on the Golden Hill, 67; The Effect of Gamma Rays on Man-in-the-moon Marigolds, 71; dir, Hongkong Dong (film), 75; auth, Paint the Yellow Tiger, Sterling Publ, 91; and others. *Dealer:* Conacher Galleries 134 Maiden Lane San Francisco CA 94108. *Mailing Add:* 21 W 58th St New York NY 10019

KINGSLEY, APRIL
CRITIC, LECTURER
b New York, NY, Feb 16, 41. *Study:* Inst Fine Arts, NY Univ, BA(art hist) & MA; City Univ NY Grad Ctr, 86, M Phil, ABD. *Pos:* Asst cur, Mus Mod Art, New York, 70-71; assoc cur, Pasadena Art Mus, Calif, 71-72; critic, Soho Weekly News, NY, 75-77, Village Voice, 77-79 & Newsweek, 79; cur, Sculpture Ctr, New York, 80-; assoc ed, Art Express Mag, 81-82. *Teaching:*

Instr ideas in art, Sch Visual Arts, 73-, RI Sch Design, 83, Queens Col, 85-86 & City Col, 85-86. *Bibliog:* Judy K Collischan van Wagner (auth), Women Shaping Art, 84- *Mem:* Int Art Critics Asn. *Res:* Conceptual art; Abstract Expressionism; Ashcan realism. *Publ:* Afro-American Abstraction, 82; Robert Beauchamp, 84; Adolph Gottlieb Works on Paper Retrospective, 86; 300 Years of American Paintings: The Montclair Art Museum Collection, 89; The Turning Point: The Abstract Expressionists and the Transformation of American Art, 92. *Mailing Add:* 246 W 16th St New York NY 10011

KINGTON, L(OUIS) BRENT
SCULPTOR, EDUCATOR
b Topeka, Kans, July 26, 34. *Study:* Univ Kans, BFA, 57; Cranbrook Acad Art, MFA, 61. *Work:* Mus Contemp Crafts, New York; Krannert Art Mus, Univ Ill, Urbana; Univ Wis-Milwaukee; Renwick Gallery, Smithsonian Inst, Washington, DC; Ill State Mus, Springfield; and others. *Comn:* Memphis Botanical Garden, Tenn; Friendship Hall, Nakajo, Japan; Rend Lake Col, Ina, Ill. *Exhib:* North American Goldsmiths, Renwick Gallery, Smithsonian, Washington, DC, 74; American Crafts for the Vatican Museum, Rome, 78; Towards a New Iron Age, Victoria & Albert Mus, London, 82; Craft Today, Poetry of the Physical, Am Craft Mus, New York, 86; The Eloquent Object, Philbrook Art Ctr, Tulsa, Okla, 87; City on a Hill: 20 Years of Artists at Cortona, Italy, 89; Artists from Illinois, Kunstlerhas Palas, Bregenz, Austria, 91; and others. *Pos:* Dir, Sch Art & Design, Southern Ill Univ, Carbondale. *Teaching:* Prof metal smithing, Southern Ill Univ, Carbondale, 61- *Awards:* Craftsman Fel, Nat Endowment Arts, 75 & 82; Award Excellence, 36th Ann Wabash Valley Exhib, Swope Art Gallery, 80; Artist Fel, Ill Arts Coun, 85; and others. *Mem:* Soc NAm Goldsmiths (pres, 70-74); Am Crafts Coun (trustee, 76-80); Artists-Blacksmiths Asn NAm (dir, 75-79). *Media:* Metals. *Dealer:* Kay Garvey Gallery 230 W Superior Chicago IL 60610; Bellas Artes 301 Garcia at Canyon Rd Santa Fe NM 87501. *Mailing Add:* Sch Art Southern Ill Univ Carbondale IL 62901

KINIGSTEIN, JONAH
PAINTER, DESIGNER
b New York, NY, June 26, 23. *Study:* Cooper Union Art Sch, 41-43; Grande Chaumiere, Paris, 47-51; Belle Arte, Rome, Fulbright Fel, 53-54. *Work:* Mus Mod Art, New York; Albright-Knox Art Gallery, Buffalo, NY; Nelson Gallery Art; Washington Mus; Ain Herod Mus, Tel-Aviv, Israel; also in pvt collections. *Exhib:* Butler Inst Am Art, Youngstown, Ohio, 56; Young Americans, Whitney Mus Am Art, New York, 57; Nat Acad Arts & Lett, 68; one-man shows, ACA Gallery, 68 & Rittenhouse Gallery, Philadelphia, 75; Washington Irving Gallery, New York, 82; Art & the Law, Landmark Ctr, St Paul, Minn, 82; Rittenhouse Gallery, Philadelphia, 82; Pindar Gallery, New York, 88 & 92; Student Univ Art Gallery, Univ Mass, 90; and others. *Teaching:* Brooklyn Mus Art Sch, 70. *Awards:* First Prize, Silvermine Guild, 59; Louis Comfort Tiffany Found Award, 62; Perkins-Elmer Prize, 62; and others. *Mailing Add:* 105 E Ninth St New York NY 10003

KINNAIRD, RICHARD WILLIAM
PAINTER, EDUCATOR
b Buenos Aires, Arg, Nov 19, 31; US citizen. *Study:* Univ Mich, Ann Arbor, 49-51; Carleton Col, Northfield, Minn, BA, 53; Art Inst Chicago, 52; Univ Ill, with Lee Chesney, MFA, 58. *Work:* Seattle Mus of Art; NC Mus of Art, Raleigh; Hanes Knitting Corp & R J Reynolds Corp, Winston-Salem, NC. *Comn:* Thomas Wolfe Mem Sculpture, class gift to Univ NC-Chapel Hill, 66; pediment sculpture, Mint Mus of Art, Charlotte, NC, 72. *Exhib:* Award Winners Exhib of Chicago No-Jury Show, Art Inst of Chicago, 57; Southeastern Ann Painting & Sculpture, High Mus, Atlanta, Ga, 66; Experimental Media, Corcoran Gallery of Contemp Art, Washington, DC, 70; Painting & Sculpture Exhib, Mint Mus of Art, 71; Third Ann Contemp Reflections, Aldrich Mus of Contemp Art, 73; solo exhibs, Sandhurst Art Coun, Aberdeen, NC, 78 & Rowan Art Ctr, Salisbury, NC, 79; Selections from the Collection, Aldrich Mus Contemp Art, Ridgefield, Conn, 78; Patron Art Patron, Southeastern Ctr Contemp Art, 79; Exhib of Works by Tenn Valley States Artists, Tenn Valley Auth Washington Visitors Ctr, DC, 79. *Collections Arranged:* Univ Evansville Fine Arts Exhib, Ind, 73. *Teaching:* Instr printmaking & etching, Auburn Univ, Ala, 60-64; from instr to assoc prof painting, Univ NC, 64-76, prof painting, 76- *Awards:* Purchase Award, Third Ann Contemp Reflections, Aldrich Mus of Contemp Art, 74; First Painting Award, Spring Mill Ann Art Exhib, Spring Mills Corp, Lancaster, SC, 76; First Award, 40th Ann NC Artists, NC Mus of Fine Art, Raleigh, 77. *Media:* Acrylic, Oil. *Mailing Add:* c/o Dept Art Univ NC Chapel Hill NC 27514

KINNEE, SANDY
PAINTER, PRINTMAKER
b Port Huron, Mich, Mar 30, 47. *Study:* Univ Mich, Ann Arbor, BFA(printmaking), 69, grad study, 70; Wayne State Univ, Detroit, MFA(printmaking), 76; Atelier 17, Paris, France, 79. *Work:* Metrop Mus Art, New York; Mus NMex, Santa Fe; Evergreen State Col; Portland Art Mus; Allen Art Mus, Oberlin, Ohio; Madison Art Ctr, Wis; State Off Bldg, Columbus, Ohio. *Exhib:* Works on Handmade Paper, Mus Mod Art, New York, 76; Paper as Medium, Smithsonian, traveling, 78-80; Fans, Philadelphia Mus Art, Pa, 79; one-man shows, Mather Gallery, Case Western Reserve Univ, Cleveland, Ohio, 82, Lambert/Miller, Phoenix, Ariz, 82, Tracy Felix Artspace, Colorado Springs, Colo, 85 & 86, Marcus/Gordon, Pittsburgh, Pa, 87, Gallery Two Nine One, Atlanta, Ga, 87, Coburn Gallery, Colo Col, Colorado Springs, Colo, 89 & Peter M David Gallery, Minneapolis, Minn, 90; The Men Among Us, Peter M David Gallery, Minneapolis, Minn, 86; Four Graphic Artists, Joslyn Art Mus, Omaha, Nebr, 87; William Campbell Contemp Art, Fort Worth, Tex, 89; Virginia Miller Galleries, Coral Gables, Fla, 89. *Teaching:* Printmaking, Colo Springs Fine Arts Ctr, Colo, 77-78; Basic Studio, Colorado Fine Arts Ctr, Colo, 79 & Colo Col, Colorado Springs, 86; Painting, Papermaking, Printmaking, Concepts of Drawing and Basic Studio, Univ Colo, Colorado Springs, 78-80. *Awards:* Purchase Award, Southwest Biennial, Mus NMex, Santa Fe, 78; Printmakers Fel, Western States Art Found, 79; Pollack Krasner Found Grant, 87. *Bibliog:* Jules Heller (auth), Papermaking, Watson-Guptill, 78; Virginia Butera (auth), Sandy Kinnee, Arts Mag, 6/81; Suzanne M Singletary (auth), Sandy Kinnee, fans and kimonos, Artspace, 1/82. *Media:* Handcolored Intaglio on Handmade Paper; Watercolor. *Publ:* Papermaking (film), Crystal Productions, Aspen, Colo, 80; An Introduction to Printmaking (slide ser) & Printmaking with Basic Equipment (slide ser) Crystal Production, Aspen, Colo, 83; auth, Fans, bridges, kimonos and the role paper plays in my work, Print Club, Philadelphia, 81; Printmaking (film), Crystal Prod, Aspen, Colo, 83. *Dealer:* Orion Editions 270 Lafayette St New York NY 10012; Peter M David Gallery Minneapolis MN. *Mailing Add:* 1202 N Institute Colorado Springs CO 80903

KINNEY, GILBERT HART
COLLECTOR, ADMINISTRATOR
b New York, NY, May 11, 31. *Study:* Yale Univ, BA, 53 & MA, 54; John F Kennedy Sch, MPA, 73. *Pos:* Trustee, 74-77, 78- & chief exec officer, 77-78, Corcoran Gallery of Art, Washington, DC; trustee, Archs Am Art, 74-88, 89-91, pres, 78-82; trustee, Am Fed Arts, 78; dir, Am Arts Alliance, 85-91; trustee, Yale Art Gallery, 91- *Collection:* Major emphasis post-war American painting and sculpture, also European 20th century painting and sculpture, East Asian ceramics, South and Southeast Asian sculpture especially bronzes. *Mailing Add:* 1231 31st St NW Washington DC 20007

KINOSHITA, GENE
ARCHITECT
b Vancouver, BC, Jan 18, 35. *Study:* Univ BC, BArch (honors), 59; Yale Univ, MArch, 62. *Comn:* Detention Ctr, Ont Govt, 74; Royal Ont Mus Expansion, 75-83; Ont Col Art expansion & renovations, 77-85; Law Libr, Univ Toronto, 86-91; McMaster Univ Art Gallery & Libr, Hamilton, Ont, 89-91; Scis Complex, Univ Western Ont, London, 89-91. *Exhib:* Travelling Exhib Can Art Mus, Royal Can Acad Arts, 67; Can Unit Masonry Awards Prog Travelling Exhib Can, 72; Ont Masons Rels Coun, Travelling Prov Exhib, 73; Am Inst Arch & Am Correctional Asn Traveling Show, 80; Royal Can Acad Gallery, 87. *Pos:* Pres, Moffat Kinoshita Assocs Inc, Architects, 65-; Royal Can Acad Arts (pres, 84-88). *Awards:* Ont Asn Archit Award of Excellence for Royal Ont Mus & N York Aquatic Ctr, 87 & 89; Merit Award for Alumni Ctr, Univ Guelph, Ont, 89; Award of Excellence, Ont Asn Architects, 89; and many others. *Mem:* Ont Asn Archit; academician Royal Can Acad Arts; Ont Col Art (hon trustee); Greater Toronto Arts Award Found, (pres, 92-94); Visual Arts Ont; and others. *Publ:* Auth, The ROM: A new lease on life, Canadian Collector, 7-8/82; auth, Museums are for people, the evolution of a design concept, Rotunda Mag, Vol 15, No 2, 82. *Mailing Add:* 278 Sheldrake Blvd Toronto ON M4P 2B6 Canada

KINSEL, MICHAEL LESLIE
MUSEUM DIRECTOR
b Council Bluffs, Iowa, May 5, 47. *Study:* Augustana Col, Rock Island, Ill, BA, 69; Univ Chicago, MBA, 73; Lutheran Sch Theology, Master Divinity, 73, DD, 75. *Pos:* Asst dir, Lutheran Sch Theology, Chicago, 70-73; vpres, Knophurst Co, Chicago, 73-74; proj dir, Western Heritage Soc, Omaha, 74-78; dir, Western Heritage Mus, Omaha, 78-88; assoc develop dir, Univ Cinn Found, 92- *Teaching:* Instr, Creighton Univ, 82. *Mem:* Am Asn Mus Dirs; Mountain Plains Mus Conf. *Mailing Add:* 621 Mehring Way Cincinnati OH 45202

KINSMAN, ROBERT DONALD
MUSEUM DIRECTOR, HISTORIAN
b Bridgeport, Conn, Sept 13, 29. *Study:* Columbia Univ, BS, 58, MA(art hist), 66. *Collections Arranged:* Jimmy Ernst Retrospective (auth, catalog), 63 & Lyonel Feininger: The Formative Years (auth, catalog), 64, Detroit Inst Arts; The Sculpture of Primitive Peoples (auth, catalog), Mary Washington Col, Univ Va, 66; Leroy Lamis Retrospective (auth, catalog), 79 & Julius Schmidt Retrospective (auth, catalog), 80, Sheldon Swope Art Gallery, Terre Haute, Ind. *Pos:* Asst cur, Nat Gallery Art, Washington, DC, 61-62; cur contemp art, Detroit Inst Arts, 63-65; mus dir, Mary Washington Col, Univ Va, Fredericksburg, 66-68; dir, Sheldon Swope Art Gallery, Terre Haute, Ind, 78-85; bd dirs, Arts Illiana Inc, 81-85; dir, Metrop Mus & Art Ctr, Coral Gables, Fla, 85-86; dir, Mus Cartoon Art, Rye Brook, NY, 87-88. *Teaching:* Instr art hist, Mary Washington Col, Univ Va, Fredericksburg, 62-63, asst prof, 66-68; asst prof, State Univ NY, Albany, 68-77. *Awards:* Faculty Research Fel, State Univ NY Research Found, 71. *Mem:* Am Asn Mus; Col Art Asn Am; Am Asn Univ Prof. *Res:* American and European painting and sculpture since 1850. *Publ:* Auth, Recent lithographs by James McGarrell, 80; John Rogers Cox retrospective, 82; Contemporary art from the collection of International Minerals & Chemical Corp, 83; An American in Paris: Drawings, prints and watercolors by Herman Armour Webster, 83; Recent sculpture by Julius Schmidt, Sheldon Swope Gallery, Terre Haute, Ind, 85. *Mailing Add:* 32 Bouton St E, Apt 3 Stamford CT 06907

KINSTLER, EVERETT RAYMOND
PAINTER, INSTRUCTOR
b New York, NY, Aug 5, 26. *Study:* Nat Acad Design, New York; Art Students League, with DuMond; also, John Johansen & Jas Montgomery Flagg; Rollins Col, Hon DFA, 83. *Work:* Metrop Mus Art, New York; Carnegie Inst, Pittsburgh; Brooklyn Mus; Smithsonian Inst, Washington, DC; Mus City New York; Blount Collection, Ala; Cowboy Hall Fame, Okla; and

others. *Comn:* Portraits of Pres George Bush; Secy State James Baker; official White House Portrait of Pres Gerald R Ford & Pres Ronald Reagan; portraits of John Wayne & Katherine Hepburn; and others. *Exhib:* One-man shows, Grand Cent Art Galleries, 58 & 83, Lotos Club, New York, 72, Lluisa Gallery, Mich, 81, Artists of Am, Denver, 81-90 & Rollins Col, Fla, 83; exhib Ann, Nat Acad Arts, etc; and ann exhibs of Am Watercolor Soc, Nat Acad Arts, etc. *Teaching:* Instr painting & drawing, Art Students League, 70-75. *Awards:* Artists Fel, 86; Nat Arts Club, 59-67; Silver Medal, Audubon Artists, 88; and others. *Bibliog:* Articles in Am Artist, 1/72 & 7/84, People, 7/14/76, Saturday Evening Post, 82, Southwest Art, 3/82, Artists oif the Rockies, summer 83 & Art Times, 4/88, NY Times 12/89. *Mem:* Audubon Artists; Allied Artists; Century Asn; Life mem, Players Club; Life mem, Lotos Club; and others. *Publ:* Illusr, Opera Companion, Dodd, 61 & Verdi, 63; auth, Painting Portraits, Watson-Guptill, 87; Painting Faces, Figures & Landscapes, Watson-Guptill, 81. *Dealer:* Susan Conway Gallery 1214 30th St NW Washington DC 20007. *Mailing Add:* 15 Gramercy Park New York NY 10003

KIOUSIS, LINDA WEBER
PAINTER, ILLUSTRATOR
b Cleveland, Ohio. *Study:* Cleveland Inst Art, dipl; Case Western Reserve Univ, BS, MA. *Work:* Univ Mo Hosp & Clinic, Columbia; Ohio Watercolor Soc; Salem Pub Libr, Ohio; Arches Paper Co; Binney & Smith Inc, Pa. *Exhib:* Mainstream America: Collection of Phil Desind, Butler Inst Am Art, Youngstown, Ohio, 87; Am Realism, Parkersburg, WVa, 89; Choices and Decisions, Chelsea Galleries, Beachwood, Ohio, 90; Watercolor Now, Springfield Art Mus, Mo, 91; Watercolor USA, Mo, 91; 34th Ann Chautauqua Nat Exhib Am Art; Woman's Touch, Glass Growers Gallery, Erie, Pa, 91; Art Inspired by Architecture, Great Northern Corp Ctr, Ohio, 92; Graphic Watercolors, Sandusky Cult Ctr, Ohio, 92. *Awards:* Silver Medal, Pa Watercolor Soc, 88; Award for Excellence, Watercolor, Ohio, 88; Springfield Art Mus Award, Watercolor USA, Mo, 91. *Bibliog:* Marilyn Phillips (auth), Watermedia Techniques for Releasing the Creative Spirit. *Mem:* Ohio Watercolor Soc; Pa Watercolor Soc; Watercolor USA Hon Soc; Nat Asn Women Artists. *Media:* Transparent Watercolor. *Mailing Add:* 8968 Snow Rd Parma OH 44130-2117

KIPNISS, ROBERT
PAINTER, PRINTMAKER
b New York, NY, Feb 1, 31. *Study:* Art Students League; Wittenberg Col; Univ Iowa, BA & MFA; Wittenberg Univ, hon PhD, 79; Illinois Col, hon PhD, 89. *Work:* Whitney Mus Am Art, New York; Chicago Art Inst; Yale Univ Art Gallery; Libr Cong, Washington, DC; Albright-Knox Mus, Buffalo, NY; Nat Collection Fine Arts, Smithsonian Inst, Washington, DC; Cleveland Mus, Ohio. *Exhib:* One-man shows, Allen R Hite Inst, Univ Louisville, 65, Museo de Arte Moderno La Tertulia, Colombia, 75 & Hirschl & Adler Galleries, New York, 77; Recent Acquisitions, Whitney Mus Am Art, 72; Int Exhib of Original Drawings, Mus Mod Art, Rijeka-Dolac, Yugoslavia, 76; III Bienal Americana de Artes Graficas, Museo La Tertulia, Cali, Colombia, 76; Retrospective, Asn Am Artists, New York, 77. *Awards:* Medal Honor, Audubon Artists, 82; Prize, Nat Acad Design, 76, 80 & 81. *Bibliog:* Robert Kipniss: The Graphic Works, Abaris Books, 80. *Mem:* Nat Acad Design; Soc Am Graphic Artists. *Media:* Oil; Mezzotint, Etching. *Publ:* Illusr, Poems of Emily Dickinson, Thomas Y Crowell, 64; Collected Poems of Robert Graves, Anchor Doubleday, 66; Poems of Rilke, Limited Ed Club, 81. *Dealer:* Merrill Chase Galleries 620 N Michigan Ave Chicago IL 60611; Gerhard Wurzer Gallery 5701 Memorial Dr Houston TX 77007. *Mailing Add:* Hudson House Box 7099 Ardsley-on-Hudson NY 10503

KIPP, LYMAN
SCULPTOR
b Dobbs Ferry, NY, Dec 24, 29. *Study:* Pratt Inst, 50-52; Cranbrook Acad Art, 52-54. *Work:* Whitney Mus Am Art, New York; Albright-Knox Art Gallery, Buffalo; High Mus of Art, Atlanta, Ga; Univ Ala, Huntsville; State NY Albany Mall. *Comn:* Sculpture for Post Off & Fed Off Bldg, Van Nuys, Calif; sculpture, Village Lake Placid, NY; Grosse Pointe Libr, Mich. *Exhib:* Four Whitney Mus Am Art Sculpture Ann, 64-70; Sculpture in Environment, New York, 67; Cool Art, 68 & Highlights of the Season, 68, Larry Aldrich Mus, Conn; Art of the Real, Mus Mod Art, New York & London, 68, & Paris & Berlin, 69; Change of View, Larry Aldrich Mus, 75; Sculpture in the Constructivist Tradition, Hamilton Gallery, NY, 77; Urban Structures-Monumental Sculpture, Nat Endowment Arts Traveling Exhib originated in Akron, Ohio, 77-79; Art in Public Places, Ferris State Col, Mich, 79. *Teaching:* Instr sculpture, Bennington Col, 60-63; asst prof sculpture, Hunter Col, 63-66, prof & chmn dept, 75-; prof sculpture & chmn dept, Lehman Col, 66-75. *Awards:* Guggenheim Fel, 66; Fulbright Grant, 66; City Univ Fac Res Awards, 70 & 75. *Mailing Add:* c/o Ianuzzi Gallery 34505 N Scottsdale Rd Scottsdale AZ 85282

KIPP, ORVAL
PAINTER, EDUCATOR
b Hyndman, Pa, May 21, 04. *Study:* Carnegie-Mellon Univ, AB(with hon), 32, Teachers Col, Columbia Univ, AM, 35, Univ Pittsburgh, PhD, 49. *Work:* Ind Univ Pa Mus; Pa high schs. *Comn:* Painting, Sutton Hall; painting of Mary Lesch, registrar of Ind Univ Pa alumni; portraits of three past pres for Ind Univ, Pa. *Exhib:* Am Fedn Arts Traveling Exhib; Am Artists Prof League Grand Nat, 72; Three Rivers Arts Festival, Pittsburgh; Carnegie Mus; Greensburg Art Club, Westmoreland Colo Mus, 86; and others. *Pos:* Bd dirs, Indiana Univ Mus, Pa. *Teaching:* Instr art, Indiana Univ Pa, 36-41, dir art dept, 41-60, chmn, 60-64, prof, 60-69, prof emer, 69-; artist-in-residence, Kiski Sch, 64-69; instr, Ivy Sch of Prof Art, 64-69; lectr, Trick or Treat in Art Education, Ind State Art Teachers, Indianapolis. *Awards:* Prizes, Indiana Art Asn, 47-57; Spec Jury Award, Pittsburgh Soc Art, 68. *Mem:* Eastern Art Asn; Assoc Artists Pittsburgh; Indiana Art Asn, hon mem; Pa Art Educ Asn; Pittsburgh Watercolor Soc; and others. *Media:* Watercolor, Oil. *Mailing Add:* 3285 Dawson St Pittsburgh PA 15213

KIPPENBERGER, MARTIN
PAINTER
b Dortmunt, Ger, 53. *Exhib:* Berlinart 1961-1987, Mus Mod Art, New York, 87; Refigured Painting: The German Image 1960-88, Toledo Mus Art, travelled to Guggenheim, New York, Kunstmuseum Dusseldorf & Schirn Kunsthalle, Frankfurt, 88; New Prints from Germany, St Louis Art Mus, 88; solo shows, Wiener Festwochen, Vienna, David Nolan Gallery, New York, Karsten Schubert Gallery, London, Koelnischer Kunstverein, Cologne, Kunstraum Daxer, Muenchen & Galerie Wewerka & Weiss, Berlin, 91 & Metro Pictures, New York, 92; Gulliver's Travels, Galerie Sophia Ungers, Cologne, 91; Buchstaeblich, Von der Heydt Mus, Wuppertal, 91; Models of Reality, Harris Mus, Lancashire, 91; Allegories of Modernism, Mus Mod Art, New York, 92; and others. *Bibliog:* Martin Kippenberger-Ten Years After, Taschen Verlag, Cologne, 91; Heavy Burschi (exhib catalog), Koelnischer Kunstverein, Cologne, 91; Tiefes Kehlchen (exhib catalog), Wiener Festwochen, Vienna, 91; and others. *Publ:* Auth, Untouched and Unprinted Paper, Printed Matter Inc, New York, 90; Eine Handvoll vergessener Tauben, Galerie Graesslin-Erhardt, Frankfurt Pharmakon, Makuhari Messe/Kikuko Amagasaki, Tokyo, 90; Fred the Frog Rings the Bell Once a Penny Two a Penny Hot Cross Buns, Galerie Max Hetzler, Cologne, 91; Kippenberger: The Canary Searching for a Port in the Storm, David Nolan Gallery, New York, 91; Hotel Hotel, Verlag der Buchhandlung Walter Koenig, Cologne, 92; and others. *Mailing Add:* c/o Metro Pictures 150 Greene St New York NY 10012

KIRBY, KENT BRUCE
PRINTMAKER, PHOTOGRAPHER
b Fargo, NDak, Dec 31, 34. *Study:* Carleton Col, with Albert Elsen, BA, 56; Univ NDak, with Robert Nelson, MA, 59; Univ Mich, with Emil Weddige, MFA, 70. *Work:* Detroit Inst Arts; Guggenheim Mus, New York; Philadelphia Mus Art; Grand Rapids Art Mus, Mich; Cranbrook Art Mus, Bradley Univ. *Comn:* Prints, comn by Joseph Kinnebrew, Carl Toth, Irwin Hollander, Phil Davis, Brian Blount & Thomas Cooper. *Exhib:* Bradley National, Bradley Univ, 85; Print Invitational, Univ Dallas, 85 & Univ Ala, 88; Nat Mus Am Hist, 88-89; Stockton Nat Print & Drawing Exhib, Haggin Mus Art, Stockton, Calif, 90; Illuminance '92, Nat Competitive Exhib Photog Art, Fine Arts Ctr, Lubbock, Tex, 92; and others. *Teaching:* Instr drawing & painting, Muskingum Col, 59-61; instr, Wilkes Col, 61-62; prof printmaking & photos & chmn dept art, Alma Col, 62-90, chmn fine arts div, 73-74, Charles A Dana prof art, 76-90. *Awards:* Newberry Libr Res Fel, 74; Mich Coun Arts Grants, 75, 79 & 81; Nat Endowment Arts Grant, 76. *Bibliog:* Joyce Macrorie (auth), Collotype, Print Rev 6, winter 77. *Mem:* Col Art Asn Am; Artists Equity. *Media:* Collotype. *Res:* Light print press to revive collotype technique; publishing works by American Artists. *Publ:* Auth, Art, technology & the liberal arts college, Art J, spring 70; The collotype printing process: A proposal for its revival, In: Leonardo, Vol, 9, Pergamon Press, 76; Studio Colotype: Continuous Tone Printing for the Artist, Printmaker & Photographer, Heliochrome Press, Dalton, Mass, 88. *Dealer:* Chicago Center for the Print, IL. *Mailing Add:* Light-print Press 9667 W Van Buren Rd Riverdale MI 48877

KIRK, JEROME
SCULPTOR, KINETIC ARTIST
b Detroit, Mich, Apr 3, 23. *Study:* Mass Inst Technol, BS. *Work:* San Francisco Mus Mod Art; Sheldon Art Gallery, Univ Nebr; Phoenix Art Mus, Ariz; Storm King Art Ctr, Mountainville, NY; and others. *Comn:* Twenty-Three maj sculpture comn in pub places; Phoenix Bird Ascending & Tiered Orbits, Civic Plaza, Phoenix, 71; Silver Orbit, Storm King Art Ctr, 73; Waves, Monterey Conf Ctr, Calif, 77; Solar Semaphore, Lincoln, Nebr, 79; Standing Waves, Univ Calif, Berkeley, 80; Avion, Koll Ctr, Irvine, Calif; Torsive Undulations in Space, TRW Hq. *Exhib:* De Young Mus Collectors Show, 65; Contemp Am Painting & Sculpture, Krannert Art Mus, Champaign, Ill, 67; Santa Barbara Mus, 69; Storm King Art Ctr, 73; Painting & Sculpture Today, Ind Mus Art, 76; Sculpture Potsdam, NY, 77; Sheldon Art Gallery, Univ Nebr; 26 solo and 57 group exhibs. *Bibliog:* Selleck (auth), Principles of Design, 75; Robinette (auth), Outdoor Sculpture, 76; Brommer & Horn (auths), Art in Your World, 77. *Media:* Aluminum, Stainless Steel. *Publ:* Aurora Variant, Leonardo, Vol 24 No 1, 91. *Dealer:* Louis K Meisel Gallery 141 Prince St New York NY; Erickson & Elins Fine Art 345 Sutter San Francisco CA. *Mailing Add:* 874 41st St Oakland CA 94608

KIRK, MICHAEL
PRINTMAKER, INSTRUCTOR
b New York, NY, Oct 31, 47. *Study:* Rutgers Univ, NJ, BA(art hist), 69; Pratt Inst, MFA(printmaking), 73. *Work:* Philadelphia Mus of Art; Boston Mus of Fine Arts; Nat Collection of Fine Arts, Washington, DC; Brooklyn Mus; Libr of Cong, Washington, DC. *Exhib:* The 18th & 19th Nat Print Exhib, Brooklyn Mus, 72 & 73; A New York Album, Brooklyn Mus, 79; Prints in Sequence, State Mus of NJ, Trenton, 77; Primera Bienal del Grabado de America, Maracaibo, Venezuela, 78; One-man exhibs, Ctr Music, Drama & Art, Lake Placid, 82, Murisori Williams Proctor Mus, Utica, 82 & Kiva Gallery, New York, 83; and others. *Pos:* Bd dir, KIVA Found Art, New York, 87- *Teaching:* Instr printmaking, Parsons Sch of Design, Manhattan, 73-, Rutgers Univ, 83- *Awards:* New York Found Art Artists fel, 86. *Mem:* Soc Am Graphic Artists. *Mailing Add:* c/o Park Gallery 174 N Hurstbone Louisville KY 40207

KIRKPATRICK, DIANE
HISTORIAN
b Grand Rapids, Mich, June 28, 33. *Study:* Vassar Col, BA, 55; Cranbrook Acad Art, MFA, 57; Univ Mich, Ann Arbor, MA, 65, PhD, 69. *Collections Arranged:* Chicago: The City and Its Artists, Univ Mich Art Mus, Ann Arbor, 78. *Pos:* Manuscript & layout ed, Fideler Publ Co, Grand Rapids, Mich, 57-58; dir children's educ, Grand Rapids Art Mus, Mich, 60-62; dir film & video studies, Univ Mich, 77-78. *Teaching:* asst prof to assoc prof, Univ Mich, 72-82, prof, 82- *Mem:* Col Art Asn Am; ACM SIGGRAPH; Soc Photog Ed. *Res:* Contemporary art, including photography, film, video and computers. *Publ:* Auth, Generative systems in contemporary visual art, Generative Lit & Generative Art, 82; On the trail of time with Sonia Landy Sheridan, Lightworks, 82; Religous photography in the Victorian age, 83 & Science, Art, and the human image, 85, Mich Quart Rev; Holography and the art-technology scene, Holography Redefined, 84. *Mailing Add:* Hist of Art Dept Univ Mich 110 Tappan Hall Ann Arbor MI 48109-1357

KIRKWOOD, MARY BURNETTE
PAINTER
b Hillsboro, Ore, Dec 21, 04. *Study:* Univ Mont, BA; Univ Ore, MFA; Harvard Univ Sch Fine Arts, art hist with Prof Paul J Sachs; Royal Art Sch, Stockholm, Sweden, with Prof Otte Skold; Art Students League, with Reginald Marsh; also with Joseph Stefanelli & Robert Goldwater, Paris. *Work:* Cheney Cowles Mus, Spokane, Wash; Boise Art Gallery, Idaho; IBM Corp; Bank of Idaho; Boise Cascade Corp. *Comn:* Murals for agr sci bldg, 48 & libr, 52, Univ Idaho. *Exhib:* West Coast Juried, Seattle Art Mus, 62; West of the Mississippi Exhib, Colorado Springs, 63; Intermountain Exhib, Salt Lake City Art Ctr, 63 & 65; Fifty States Exhib, Burpee Art Mus, Rockford, Ill, 66; Western States Exhib, Denver Art Mus, 71; plus others. *Teaching:* Prof art, Univ Idaho, 30-70. *Awards:* Third Prize for Miercoles Santo, Pac Coast Ann, Wenatchee, Wash, 63; Best of Show for El Cristo de la Columna, 63 & Second Prize for Trampoline, 66, Cheney Cowles Mus, Spokane, Wash. *Mem:* Portland Art Asn; Idaho Art Asn. *Media:* Oil. *Mailing Add:* 812 Apple Lane Moscow ID 83843

KIRSCHENBAUM, BERNARD EDWIN
SCULPTOR
b New York, NY, Sept 3, 24. *Study:* Cornell Univ; Inst Design, Chicago, BA. *Work:* Storm King Art Ctr, Mountainville, NY. *Comn:* Sculptures, Spectrum II, Mass Inst Technol, Cambridge, 68 & Walkthrough, J Patrick Lannan Found, Palm Beach, Fla, 69. *Exhib:* Sculpture in Environment, Cent Park, New York, 67; Cool Art: Abstraction Today, Newark Mus, NJ, 68; Painting & Sculpture Today, Indianapolis Mus Art, 70; Three New York Artists, Corcoran Gallery Art, Washington, DC, 73; Sculpture in the Fields, Storm King Art Ctr, 74. *Awards:* Guggenheim Fel Sculpture, 72. *Dealer:* Sculpture Now Inc Max Hutchinson 142 Greene St New York NY 10012. *Mailing Add:* 180 Park Row New York NY 10038

KIRSCHENBAUM, JULES
PAINTER, EDUCATOR
b New York, NY, Mar 25, 30. *Study:* Brooklyn Mus Art Sch. *Work:* Butler Inst Am Art, Youngstown, Ohio; Whitney Mus Am Art, New York; Weatherspoon Art Gallery; Des Moines Art Ctr, Iowa; Everhardt Mus, Scranton, Pa; Met Mus Art, New York; Hirshhorn Mus, Washington, DC. *Comn:* Hist of Iowa, Cent Nat Bank, Des Moines, 64. *Exhib:* Drawings USA, Mus Mod Art, New York, 34; Whitney Mus Am Art Ann, 55; Painting USA: The Figure, Mus Mod Art, New York, 63; Artists Abroad, Paintings from Whitney Collection, 69; Gov Exhib Nine Iowa Artists, 71. *Teaching:* Artist in residence, Des Moines Art Ctr, 63-67; prof painting, Drake Univ, 67-; vis prof art, Temple Univ, 72-73. *Awards:* Fulbright Fel, 56; First Prize for Figure Painting, Nat Acad Design, 57; First Prize for Oils, Butler Inst Am Art, 60. *Bibliog:* The figure, Time, 62. *Media:* Acrylic, Egg Tempera. *Dealer:* Forum Gallery 1018 Madison Ave New York NY 10021. *Mailing Add:* Art Drake Univ 25th St & University Ave Des Moines IA 50311

KIRSHNER, JUDITH RUSSI
CURATOR, CRITIC
b St Louis, Mo, Nov 24, 42. *Study:* Barnard Col, BA, 64; Bryn Mawr, MA, 69. *Collections Arranged:* Claes Oldenburg, The Mouse Mus, 77; June Leaf-Retrospective, 78; Gordon Matta-Clark, Circus-Caribbean Orange, 78; Vito Acconci-Retrospective: 1969-80, 80; Contemporary Chicago Painters-Two Decades, 86. *Pos:* Chief cur, Mus Contemp Art, Chicago, 76-81; cur, Terra Mus Am Art, 85-86. *Teaching:* Asst prof art criticism & contemp art, Sch of the Art Inst Chicago, 81- *Mem:* Col Art Asn; Int Art Critics. *Publ:* Auth, Tom Otterness' frieze, 83 & Non-u-ment: Gordon Matta-Clark, 85, Artforum; The possibility of an avant-garde, Formations, 85; numerous reviews in Artforum and numerous mus catalog essays. *Mailing Add:* 5658 S Blackstone Ave Chicago IL 60637

KIRSTEN, NICHOLAS
VIDEO ARTIST
b Seattle, Wash, 1947. *Study:* Univ Was, 65-66. *Work:* King County; Pacific Northwest Bell; Peoples Nat Bank; Rainier Bank; Safeco Ins Co. *Exhib:* Stillwater Gallery, Seattle, 83; Return Gallery, Taos NMex, 84; Mysterium Gallery, Boulder, Colo, 88; solo shows, Kirsten Gallery, Seattle, 79-81, 83, 85 & 88. *Pos:* Dir, Kirsten Gallery, Invisible Frame Shop & Kirsten Gallery Publ, 77- *Mailing Add:* 5022 Roosevelt Way NE Seattle WA 98105

KIRSTEN-DAIENSAI, RICHARD CHARLES
PAINTER, PRINTMAKER
b Chicago, Ill, Apr 16, 20. *Study:* Art Inst Chicago; Univ Wash; also study in Japan, 58-89. *Work:* Seattle Art Mus; Bell Tel Co; Libr of Cong, Washington, DC; Metrop Mus Art, New York; Tokyo Mus Mod Art, Japan. *Exhib:* Seattle Art Mus, numerous shows, 45-69; Frye Mus, Seattle, 60-65 & 69; Gov Invitational, 67; Collector's Gallery, Bellevue, Wash, 67; Richard White Gallery, Seattle, 68; Kirsten Gallery, Seattle, 75-89; plus many others. *Awards:* Purchase Prize, Univ Ore, 68; Purchase Prize, Seattle First Nat Bank, 69; plus others. *Bibliog:* Article, Arts Asia Mag, 1-2/79. *Mem:* Northwest Watercolor Soc (pres, 68 & 69); Artists Equity (pres, Seattle Chap, 52-56), Seattle Chap mem, 89. *Media:* Watercolor, Acrylic; Mixed Media. *Mailing Add:* c/o Kirsten Gallery 5320 Roosevelt Way NE Seattle WA 98105

KISCH, GLORIA
SCULPTOR
b New York, NY, Nov 14, 41. *Study:* Sarah Lawrence Col, BA, 63; Boston Mus Sch, 64-65; Otis Art Inst, Los Angeles, BFA & MFA, 69. *Work:* Mildura Art, Victoria, Australia; Milwaukee Art Mus; Newport Harbor Art Mus, Calif; Denver Art Mus; Los Angeles Co Art Mus; Equitable Corp; Neuberger Mus, Purchase, NY; Va Mus Fine Arts, Richmond. *Comn:* Sidney & Francis Lewis; Harty Mountain Products Corp; Community Bank, Holyoke, Mass. *Exhib:* Solo exhibs, Newport Harbor Art Mus, Newport Beach, Calif, 74, Art et Industre, New York, 89 & 90; Inst Contemp Art, Los Angeles, 78; Inst Art & Urban Resources, PS1, Long Island City, NY, 80; Milwaukee Art Mus, Wis, 81; Queens Mus, New York; Robert Moses Plaza at Lincoln Ctr, New York, 87. *Publ:* The Rocker, Bernice Steinbaum (auth), Rizzoli Publs; International Furniture Design for the 90's, Libr Applied Design; Product Design 4, Libr Applied Design. *Mailing Add:* 620 Broadway New York NY 10012

KISKADDEN, ROBERT MORGAN
PAINTER, EDUCATOR
b Tulsa, Okla, Dec 6, 18. *Study:* Univ Kans, BFA, 47; Ohio Wesleyan Univ, MA, 49. *Work:* Wichita Art Mus, Kans; Birger Sandzen Mem Gallery, Lindsborg, Kans; Bloomfield Collection, Wichita State Univ; Kansas 4-H Found, Rock Springs; Kans State Univ, Manhattan; also in other pub & pvt collections. *Exhib:* Art USA, Madison Square Garden, 58; Ann Juried Exhib, Kans Watercolor Soc; National Invitational Drawing Exhib; Small Oil Painting Juried Exhib, Wichita Art Asn; One man show, Carmel Fine Art Gallery, 88. *Teaching:* From asst prof to prof painting, Wichita State Univ, 49-84, asst dean, Col Fine Arts, 71-84, emer prof, 84-; pvt lessons. *Awards:* Ted Hawkins Award, 73, Purchase Award, 74, Cash Award, 77 & Honorary Mention, 79, Ann Kans Watercolor Soc Exhib; Award of Excellence, 80 & Second Place, 84, Wichita Art Asn; Fourth Place, Small Oil Painting Exhib, 85. *Mem:* Wichita Artists Guild (past pres & mem bd); Kans Watercolor Soc; Kans Acad Oil Painters; Wichita Art Asn; Wichita Art Mus. *Media:* Oil, Watercolor. *Mailing Add:* 4000 Rio Rd No 67 Carmel CA 93923-8634

KISSEL, WILLIAM THORN, JR
SCULPTOR
b New York, NY, Feb 6, 20. *Study:* Harvard Univ, BA, 44; Pa Acad Fine Arts, 51-53; Barnes Found, Merion, Pa, grad, 53; Rinehart Grad Sch Sculpture, with Sidney Waugh, Cecil Howard & Bruce Moore, grad, 58. *Comn:* Granite Mem, Montclair, NJ, 56; many bronze animal sculptures, Eastern US, 65-70. *Exhib:* Mass Sculptor's Exhib, Beverly, Mass, 58; Am Artists Prof League Grand Nat, Lever House, New York, 64 & 66; Nat Acad Design Exhibs, New York, 65-68 & 71; Nat Sculpture Soc Exhibs, Lever House, 67 & 70; Md Arts Coun Exhib & State Tour, 71 & 72. *Awards:* Speyer Awards, Nat Acad Design, 66 & 68; Am Artists Prof League Award, 66. *Bibliog:* Articles, Am Art Stone, 59 & La Rev Mod, Paris, 66. *Mem:* Nat Sculpture Soc; fel Am Artists Prof League. *Media:* Bronze, Marble. *Mailing Add:* 223 Valley Rd Owings Mills MD 21117

KITAJ, R B
PAINTER, PRINTMAKER
Chagrin Falls, Ohio, 32. *Study:* Ruskin Sch, Univ Oxford, dipl, 60; Royal Col Art, grad, 62; Univ London, Hon Dr, 82. *Work:* Mus in the US & Europe. *Exhib:* One-man shows, Marlborough Fine Art, London, 63, 70, 74, 80 & 85-86, Marlborough Gallery, New York, 65, 79 & 85-86, Ikon Gallery, Birmingham, 77, Marlborough Galerie, Zurich, 77, Beaumont-May Gallery, Hopkins Ctr, Hanover, 78, Hirshhorn Mus Sculpture Garden & Smithsonian Inst, Washington, DC, 81; Retrospective (with catalog), Hirshhorn Mus, Washington, DC, 81; Kunsthalle, Dusseldorf, 82; and others. *Teaching:* Vis lectr, Slade Sch, Univ London; vis prof, Univ Calif, Berkeley & Univ Calif, Los Angeles. *Awards:* Cooper Union Citation, New York, 82; Skowhegan Medal for Drawing, New York, 85. *Bibliog:* James Faure Walker (auth), R B Kitaj, interview, Artscribe, No 5, 77; M Livingstone (auth), R B Kitaj, Phaidon-Rizzoli, London & New York, 85. *Mem:* Inst Arts & Letters, New York; Royal Acad London; Nat Acad Design. *Publ:* Co-narrator (with Christopher Finch), R B Kitaj (film), Arts Coun Gt Brit, London, 67; auth, Mainly about using photos re: the prints, Art Artists, 11/69; Wings (recent sculpture and buildings), Los Angeles Co Mus Art, 71. *Mailing Add:* c/o Marlborough Fine Arts Ltd 6 Albermarle St London W1X 4BY England United Kingdom

KITAO, T KAORI
HISTORIAN, EDUCATOR
b Jan 30, 33; US citizen. *Study:* Univ Calif, Berkeley, AB(archit), 58, MA(art hist), 61; Harvard Univ, PhD(art hist), 66. *Pos:* Chmn, Swarthmore Col. *Teaching:* Asst prof hist archit, RI Sch Design, 63-66; asst prof art hist, Swarthmore Col, 66-68, assoc prof, 68-75, prof, 75- *Mem:* Col Art Asn; Soc Archit Historians; Soc Cinema Studies; Semiotic Soc Am; Int Soc

Comparative Study Civilizations (vpres, 80-83). *Res:* Philadelphia architecture; comparative semiotics, east and west; Bernini and Baroque Rome. *Publ:* Auth, Circle and Oval in the Square of St Peter's, NY Univ Press, 74; contribr, La prospettiva rinascimentale, Centro Di, Florence, 80. *Mailing Add:* Dept Art Swarthmore Col Swarthmore PA 19081

KITNER, HAROLD
EDUCATOR, PAINTER
b May 18, 21; US citizen. *Work:* Akron Art Mus; Kent State Univ; Canton Art Inst; Akron Univ; Cleveland Mus; S Fla Art Ctr. *Exhib:* Simultaneous one-man shows & retrospective, Kent State Univ; recent works, Canton Art Inst, 79, Kuban Galleries, 83 & 84; Don Drumm Art Gallery, 86; Retrospective, Akron Univ & Ohio Univ, 88-89, Father & Son, Miami, 90. *Pos:* Art critic, Akron Beacon J, 48-61; dir, Blossom-Kent Art Prog, 67-; chmn, Vis Artist Prog, Miami Beach, 89. *Teaching:* Prof painting & drawing, Kent State Univ, 47-79, chmn painting & sculpture dept, 50-67, chmn sch art, 64-65, prof emer, 79-; vis prof, South Fla Art Inst, 86, Kent State Univ, 88 & Boca Raton Mus, 89; dir, Inst S Fla Art Ctr, 89-91; emer prof, New World Sch, 92. *Media:* Oil, Casein. *Publ:* Catalog, Libr Cong, 88. *Dealer:* Gallery Camino Real 399 Camino Gardens Blvd Boca Raton FL; The Art Place 9900 S W 140 St Miami Fl 33176. *Mailing Add:* 800 SFAC Lincoln Rd Miami Beach FL 33139

KITTREDGE, NANCY (ELIZABETH)
PAINTER
b Ellsworth, Maine, Nov 12, 38. *Study:* Vesper George Sch Art, Boston, 56-57; Univ NH, Durham, 57-59; Univ Maine, Orono, BA, 61; Univ Miami, Coral Gables, Fla, MA, 63. *Work:* Household Corp, Chicago; R L Kotrozo Inc, Scottsdale, Ariz; Indust Metals South Inc, New Orleans; Dow Theory Lett Inc, La Jolla, Calif; Luce, Forward, Hamilton & Scripps, San Diego; Univ Maine, Orono. *Comn:* Portrait, Univ Maine Theatre Dept, Orono, 76. *Exhib:* Yokohama-San Diego, Women's Jr Col Arts, Yokohama, Japan, 79; solo exhibs, San Diego Mus Art, 81 & 90; Women's Invitational Exhib, John Douglas Cline Gallery, Phoenix, 81; Ankrum Gallery Invitational, Los Angeles, 82; Women in Art Exhibition, Nairobi, Kenya, 85; San Francisco Art Exchange, 86; JJ Brookings Gallery, San Jose, 87; Schwartz Cierlak Gallery, Santa Monica, 88; New Port Harbor Mus, 88; New Connections: An Exhibition of Painting and Sculpture, Mt San Antonio Col, Walnut, Calif, 91; Contemporary Artists' Artists, Sylvia White Contemporary Art, Los Angeles, 91; Dogs/Doghouses and Other Fine Containers, Joy Horwich Gallery, Chicago, 91; Local Productions: Painters of San Diego County, Mathes Cult Ctr for the Arts, Escondido, Calif, 92; Points of View: Five San Diego Artists, Lyceum Gallery, San Diego, 92. *Teaching:* Instr Tulane Univ, New Orleans, 68-69. *Mem:* San Diego Art Guild (mem bd, 76-77 & 82-83); Artists Equity. *Media:* Oil, Mixed Media. *Publ:* American Artists: An Illustrated Survey of Leading Contemporary Americans, Krantz Publ Co, Chicago, 85; San Diego Artists, Artra Pub Inc, Encinitas, Calif, 88; The California Art Review, 2nd ed, Am References Publ Corp, Chicago, 89. *Dealer:* Joy Horwich Gallery 226 E Ontario Chicago IL 60611; David Zapf Gallery 2400 Kettner Blvd San Diego CA 92101. *Mailing Add:* 13646 Mira Montana Dr Del Mar CA 92014

KITZINGER, ERNST
HISTORIAN
b Munich, Ger, Dec 27, 12; US citizen. *Study:* Univ Rome, 31-32; Univ Munich, PhD, 34; Swarthmore Col, DHL, 69; Univ Warwick, 89; Univ Rome, 92. *Pos:* Asst, Brit Mus, London, Eng, 35-40; Dumbarton Oaks Ctr for Byzantine Studies, Washington, DC, 41-67. *Teaching:* A Kingsley Porter univ prof, Harvard Univ, 67-79. *Mem:* Medieval Acad Am; Col Art Asn Am; Archeol Inst Am; Ger Archaeol Inst; Am Philos Soc; and others. *Res:* Early Christian, Byzantine & medieval art. *Publ:* Auth, The Mosaics of Monreale, 60; auth, The Art of Byzantium and the Medieval West, Selected Studies, 76; auth, Byzantine Art in the Making, 77; auth, Early Medieval Art in the British Museum, third ed, 83; auth, The Mosaics of St Mary's of the Admiral, Palermo, 90. *Mailing Add:* 14 Richmond Rd Oxford 0X1 2JJ England United Kingdom

KLABUNDE, CHARLES SPENCER
PRINTMAKER, PAINTER
b Omaha, Nebr, Oct 1, 35. *Study:* Univ Nebr, Omaha, BFA, 58; Univ Iowa, Iowa City, MFA, 62; studied with Mauricio Lasansky. *Work:* Metrop Mus Art, Mus Mod Art & Pierpont Morgan Libr, New York; Philadelphia Mus Art; Art Inst Chicago; and many others. *Comn:* Prints, Assocs Am Artist, New York, 71, 72 & 74. *Exhib:* Minneapolis Mus Art, 68; Brooklyn Mus Art, 69; Whitney Mus Am Art, 70; Sheldon Mem Art Gallery, Lincoln, Nebr, 72; The Print Club, Philadelphia, 80; Galerie Lucie Weill, Paris, 84; New Orleans Acad Fine Arts, 86; and many others. *Teaching:* Asst prof printmaking, The Cooper Union, New York, 68-75. *Awards:* Guggenheim Fel, 71-72; Purchase Awards, Davidson Nat Print and Drawing Competition, 73 & The Print Club, Philadelphia, 75; Nat Acad Design, 79. *Media:* Etching, Engraving; Oil. *Publ:* Illusr, The Lost Ones, Samuel Beckett (auth), 84. *Dealer:* French Country Pottery 52 Bridge St Frenchtown, NJ 08825. *Mailing Add:* 25 Fifth St Frenchtown NJ 08825

KLARIN, WINIFRED ERLICK
PAINTER, JEWELER
b Portland, Maine, Dec 8. *Study:* Portland Mus Fine Art, Hayloft scholar, 30; Vesper George Sch Art, Boston, grad, 33; Soc Arts & Crafts, Detroit, 58-60; Wayne State Univ, 58-62; Cranbrook Grad Sch Art, 63. *Work:* US Libr Cong, State Dept, Washington, DC; Owens-Corning Fiberglass Corp, Toledo, Ohio; Steel Case Corp, Grand Rapids, Mich; First Fed Savings & Loan, Detroit; Masco Corp, Ypsilanti, Mich. *Exhib:* One-woman shows, J B Speed Art Mus, Louisville, Ky, 69, Long Boat Key Art Ctr, Fla, 78 & Eliot Gallery, Fla, 85; Eckerd Col, 82; Art Ctr Show, 83-90; Temple Beth El Art Show, Fla, 83-90; ARS Univesalis Gallery, Ybor City, Fla, 85; Mind's Eye Gallery, St Petersburg, Fla, 92; Sable Palms Gallery, Gulfport, Fla, 92; and others. *Pos:* Vis artist, Eckerd Col, St Petersburg, 74-75. *Awards:* Awards, Art Ctr, St Petersburg, 78 & 81; Award winner, Beaux Arts Gallery, Seminole, 90. *Bibliog:* We Scroll, St Petersburg, 92; Aspec rev, Eckerd Col, 92; Betty Jean Miller (auth), St Petersburg Times, 3/5/92; Betty Jean Miller (auth), Gulfport Gabber, 2-3/92; Steve Baal (auth), Senior News, 6/92; and others. *Media:* Multimedia. *Mailing Add:* 5950 Pelican Bay Plaza No 203 Gulfport FL 33707

KLAUBER, RICK
PAINTER
b July 7, 50. *Study:* Bard Col, with Murray Reich, BA, 72. *Exhib:* One man show: Artists Space, New York, 75 & Long Point Gallery, Provinctown, Mass, 77, 79 & 81; Albright-Knox, Buffalo, NY, 81; The Drawing Room, AFR Fine Arts, Washington, DC, 88; Crosscurrents, Fine Arts Work Ctr, Provincetown, Mass, 90; White Columns, New York, 90; Behind Bars, Threadwaxing Space, New York, 92; Universal Fine Objects, Provincetown, Mass, 92; and others. *Teaching:* Guest teacher drawing & painting, Bard Col, 84-85; School Visual Arts, 85-87; teacher drawing, Parsons Sch Design, 89-90. *Bibliog:* B H Friedman (auth), article, New York Review, 77; John Yau (auth), article, Art in Am, 81; B H Friedman & Chris Busa (auth), Crosscurrents: the New Generation, East Hampton Ctr for Contemporary Art, 90. *Media:* Oil. *Publ:* Contribr, A bird is more (catalog on Robert Motherwell), Im Irker Gallery, St Gal, Switz, 71; auth, article on Fritz Bultman, Provincetown Arts, 86; contribr, Rosebud, Mudfish, 88. *Mailing Add:* 57 Prince St New York NY 10012

KLAUSNER, BETTY
DIRECTOR, CURATOR
b New York, NY, Aug 18, 28. *Study:* Wells Col, BA, 50. *Collections Arranged:* Masami Teraoka Erotica, 1968-1984, 84; Llyn Foulkes: Portraits, 86; Terry Allen, Big Witness (Living in Wishes), 87; Michael Singer, 87; Joan Snyder Collects Joan Snyder, 88; Home Show, 88. *Pos:* Dir, Contemp Graphics Ctr, Santa Barbara Mus Art, 78-81, Santa Barbara Contemp Arts Forum, 84-92. *Mailing Add:* 7 W La Guerra St Santa Barbara CA 93101

KLAVANS, MINNIE
PAINTER, SCULPTOR
b Garrett Park, Md, May 10, 15. *Study:* Wilson Teachers Col, BSEd, 35; with pvt instr in silversmithing, 51-55; painting with Laura Douglas, 58-60; Am Univ, 60-64; with Luciano Penay, 65-70; Corcoran Gallery Art, plastics with Ed McGowin, 70-71. *Work:* Nat Collection Fine Arts, Corcoran Gallery Art, Nat Endowment Arts, Nat Mus Am Art, Nat Mus Women in Arts, White House Exhib Rotating Prog, Smithsonian Inst, Washington, DC; Baltimore Mus Art, Md; Mus Contemp Art, Madrid, Spain; and private collections. *Exhib:* One-person shows, Cisneros Gallery, New York, 67, Inst Hispanic Cult, 68, Mus Mod Art, Bilbao, Spain, 69; Chrysler Mus Art, Norfolk, Va, 72; Int Art Exhib, Asn Int des Defense des Artistes, Amsterdam, 81; Woman's Nat Democratic Club, 82; Art as Book as Art, Md State Arts Coun, Baltimore, Md, 84; Tally Richards Gallery, Palm Desert, Calif, 84; Cosmos Club, Washington, DC, 85; Kathleen Ewing Gallery, Washington, DC, 85. *Awards:* First Prize for silversmithing, Smithsonian Inst, 53 & 55; Spec Award, Baltimore Mus Art, 67. *Mem:* Artists Equity Asn. *Dealer:* Mickelson Gallery 707 G St NW Washington DC 20001; 0010453x0ery Kensington MD 20795. *Mailing Add:* 2134 Bancroft Pl NW Washington DC 20008

KLAVEN, MARVIN L
PAINTER, EDUCATOR
b Alton, Ill, Apr 8, 31. *Study:* State Univ Iowa, BA & MFA. *Work:* Univ Iowa; Millikin Univ; Mayer Collection, Gilman Collection & Ill Bell, Chicago. *Exhib:* 24 Illinois Artists, 67; Chicago Sun Times Exhib, 68; 21st NMiss Valley Art Exhib, 68; Artists Who Teach, 69; Contemp Am Painting & Sculpture, 69. *Pos:* Dir, Decatur Art Ctr, Ill, 61-69 & Kirkland Art Gallery, 69- *Teaching:* Asst prof drawing, Northern Ill Univ, 59-61; prof art dept, Millikin Univ, 61- *Awards:* Tiffany Found Grant, 64. *Media:* Acrylic, Silk Screen. *Mailing Add:* Art Dept Millikin Univ 1184 W Main St Decatur IL 62522

KLECKNER, SUSAN
PHOTOGRAPHER, FILMMAKER
b New York, NY, July 5, 41. *Study:* Art Students League, with Landes Lewitin; City Univ New York; Pratt Inst. *Comn:* Birth Film, Women's Interart Ctr & NY State Coun Arts, New York, 72; Another Look, Teleprompter & Women's Video Service, NY, 72; Desert Piece, Women Artist Filmakers, 82; media, Feast or Famine, Interart Theatre, 83. *Exhib:* Brooklyn Mus, NY, 72; film Festival, Whitney Mus Am Art, New York, 73 & Mod Mus, Paris, France, 74; Wild Art Show, Project Studio One, New York, 82; AIR Gallery, 82; Moonmade Space, 83; West 22nd St Show, 83. *Pos:* Dir photog workshop, Community Resource Ctr, NY, 68-70; co-dir, Women's Liberation Cinema, 70-71; founding coordr, Women's Interart Ctr, New York, 70-71; video ed, Women's Video News Service, 72-73; artist-in-residence, Cummington Sch Arts, 74 & Women's Interart Ctr, 82; co-dir, Workshops for Women, 80-83. *Teaching:* Asst chmn photog, Pratt Inst, New York, 70-74; consult writing, City Univ New York, 72-73; dir, Fresh Film Ctr Photog, NY Univ Undergrad Film Sch, New York, 73-74; instr, NY Inst Photog, 78-80, Int Ctr Photog, 82-, New York Univ/Int Ctr Photog grad prog, 83 & New York Univ performance studies, 83. *Awards:* Grant, Whitney Mus, NY State Coun Arts, 72. *Bibliog:* Gazzette, Ms Mag, 73; Rochelle Ratner (auth), Beyond the limits, Soho Weekly News, 80; Carrie Rickey (auth), Third

wave, Village Voice, 81. *Mem:* Women Artists in Revolution; Feminists in the Arts; Womens Caucus Art; Peacock Brigade; Professional Women Photogr. *Media:* Video, Xerography; Pastel, Watercolor. *Publ:* Auth, A personal decade, Heresies, No 16, 83. *Dealer:* New Yorker Films 43 West 61st St New York NY 10011. *Mailing Add:* 329 E 94th St New York NY 10128

KLEEMANN, RON
PAINTER
b Bay City, Mich, July 1937. *Study:* Univ Mich, BS(design), 61. *Work:* Guggenheim Mus, Mus Mod Art, New York; Hirshhorn Mus, Washington, DC; Indianapolis Mus Art; Univ Va Art Mus; Air & Space Mus, Washington, DC; and others. *Comn:* Painting for reproduction, Corvette catalog, 86. *Exhib:* Mus Contemp Art, Chicago, 71; Wichita Mus, Wichita State Univ, Kans, 75; New Acquisitions, Mus Mod Art, New York, 77; Flint Inst Fine Arts, 78; Louis K Meisel Gallery, New York, 79, 83 & 92; Rich Perlow Gallery, New York, 87; R H Love Galleries, Chicago, 87; Cheekwood Fine Arts Ctr, Nashville, Tenn, 92. *Pos:* Official Artist, Indianapolis 500, 77-79. *Bibliog:* Andrea Mikotajok (auth), American Realists at Louis K Meisel, Arts Mag, 1/75; articles, Indianapolis News, 4/77 & Chicago Tribune, 10/77. *Mailing Add:* c/o Louis K Meisel Gallery 141 Prince St New York NY 10012

KLEIDON, DENNIS ARTHUR
EDUCATOR, DESIGNER
b Chicago, Ill, Sept 20, 42. *Study:* Bradley Univ, Peoria, Ill, 60-61; Univ Ill, Champaign, 61-64; Ill Wesleyan Univ, Bloomington, BFA(com art), 66; Ill State Univ, Normal, MS(sculpture), 67. *Work:* Massillon Mus, Ohio; Northern Ill Univ, DeKalb; Ill State Univ; Numa Ltd, Akron. *Comn:* Commemorative sculpture wall piece (wood, assemblage), Akron Nat Bank & Trust, Tuchman, Canute, Ryan & Wyatt, Architects, Rolling Acres Shopping Ctr, 76; promotional design, Scheeser & Buckley, Inc, Akron, 76; illustration, Hesselbart & Mitten Advert, Akron, 75 & Alsides, Inc, Akron, 75. *Exhib:* All-Ohio Exhib, Canton Art Inst, 71 & 72; Images, Nat Drawing Competition, Baldwin Wallace Col, Berea, Ohio, 72; Cleveland Invitational Exhib, Cooper Sch of Art, 72 & Lake Erie Col, 73; one-man show, Akron Art Inst, 76; and others. *Pos:* Designer/deliniator, Wight & Assoc, Downers Grove, Ill, 65-66 & Richard R Cramer, Architects, Hinsdale, Ill, 67; pres, Kleidon & Assoc, 75- *Teaching:* Instr drawing, Univ Ill, Champaign, 67-69; From assoc prof to prof graphic design, Univ Akron, 69- *Awards:* Res grants, Univ Akron, 70 & 77; First Place/Painting, All-Ohio Exhib, Canton Art Inst, 71; Merit Award/Design, Nat Univ & Col Designers Asn Design Competition, 75. *Bibliog:* Tex Tech Univ, Color Print USA (filmstrip), 71; Packaging education: The case for cooperation, Boxboard Container Mag, 11/79. *Media:* Acrylic, Vinyl. *Dealer:* Gallery 200 200 W Mound Columbus OH 43223. *Mailing Add:* 4670 Granger Rd Akron OH 44333

KLEIMAN, ALAN
PAINTER, SCULPTOR
b Brooklyn, NY, Feb 20, 38. *Study:* Richmond Prof Inst, BFA; Cranbrook Acad Art, MFA; study with Oscar Kokoschka, Salzburg, Austria. *Work:* Mus Mod Art, Whitney Mus Am Art, Metrop Mus Art, New York; Carnegie Mus, Pittsburgh, Pa; Boston Mus Fine Art, Mass. *Comn:* Abstract fresco, Richmond City Fathers, Va, 57; rubber paint pool mural, comn by Mr & Mrs Pechenik, York, Pa, 60; abstract painted wall, Detroit Archit League, Mich, 65; abstract painted wall, City Walls, New York, 72. *Exhib:* Biennale, Sao Paulo, Brazil, 68; Silvermine, Conn, 70; Carnegie Inst Int, Pittsburgh, 71; In The Realm of the Monocramatic, Chicago & New York, 79; Painting About Painting, Paterson Col, NJ, 81; and others. *Pos:* Asst publicity dir, Artist Tenents Asn, 60-67; vpres, Grand St Artist Group, 70-75; chmn, Soho Artifacts, 71-75. *Awards:* First Prize for Print, Boston Arts Festival, 59; Creative Artists Pub Serv fel & CETA grant, 78. *Bibliog:* Hans Van Deljen (auth), Alan Kleiman paints Europe, Frie Folkes, Amsterdam, 56. *Media:* Watercolor, Oil. *Publ:* Auth, Painting Provincetown water, The Beacon, 61; Investigations into the light of red color, Arts, 76; Light dazzle and glow, The Soho Artist. *Dealer:* Area Code Gallery 31 Wooster St New York NY 10013. *Mailing Add:* 70 Grand St New York NY 10013

KLEIN, CECELIA F
HISTORIAN, EDUCATOR
b Pittsburgh, Pa, June 5, 38. *Study:* Oberlin Col, BA, 60, MA, 67; Columbia Univ, PhD with Douglas Fraser, 72. *Collections Arranged:* Art of Pre-Columbian Am, Meadow Brook Art Gallery, Oakland Univ, Rochester, Mich, 76; Mother, Worker, Ruler, Witch: Cross-Cultural Images of Women, Mus Cult Hist, Univ Calif, Los Angeles, 80. *Teaching:* Asst prof art hist, Oakland Univ, Rochester, 72-76; assoc prof art hist, Univ Calif, Los Angeles, 76-88, prof, 88- *Mem:* Col Art Asn; Asn Latin Am Art. *Res:* Pre-Columbian art history, with emphasis on Aztec art/iconography. *Publ:* Auth, To Bleed Forever: The Function of Stone-Carved Images of Aztec Royal Blood-letting Rites (article), World Art: Themes of Unity in Diversity, Pa State Univ Press, Vol III, 575-584, 89; Gaining Respect: Native American Art Studies and the Humanities, Native Am Art Studies Asn Newsletter, 6/89; Feathered Serpents and Flowering Trees: Reconstructing the Murals of Testihuacan (rev), Fine Arts Mus San Francisco, African Arts, XXIII, 90; Depictions of the Dispossessed: Image and Self-image of Euroamerica's Colonized Natives, Art J, 90; Snares and Entrails: Mesoamerican Symbols of Sin and Instruments of Social Control, Res: Anthropology and Aesthetics, Vol 19-20, 90/92. *Mailing Add:* c/o Dept Art Hist 3209 Dickson Univ Calif 405 Hilgard Ave Los Angeles CA 90024-1417

KLEIN, DORIS
PRINTMAKER, SCULPTOR
b New York, NY, Nov 10, 18. *Study:* Art Students League, with Sidney Gross; Works Progress Admin Sch, with James Leschay & Anton Refregier; also sculpture with Maurice Glickman. *Work:* Univ Maine Permanent Collection; New Sch Permanent Collection, New York, NY. *Exhib:* Mus Belles Artes, Arg, 63; Maxwell Gallery, San Francisco, 67; Audubon Artists, 68; Roko Gallery, New York, 68-72; and many others. *Awards:* Best of Show, Jersey City Mus, 63-66; Marion K Haldenstein Mem Prize, Nat Asn Women Artists, 68; Grumbacher Award, Mamaroneck Artists Guild, 69. *Bibliog:* Hilton Kramer (auth), Rev of Roko show, New York Times, 68; Betty Chamberlain (auth), Philharmonic Hall program, 72. *Mem:* Nat Asn Women Artists. *Media:* All. *Mailing Add:* 235 W 76th St New York NY 10023

KLEIN, ELLEN LEE
PAINTER, WRITER
b New York, NY. *Study:* City Col New York, BA; Pratt Inst, MFA. *Work:* Thirteen Collection, New York; Hofstra Mus, Long Island, NY. *Exhib:* solo exhibs, Green Mountain Gallery, New York, 73 & Maples Gallery, Fairleigh Dickinson Univ, 74; Hudson River Mus Ann, Yonkers, NY, 77; Terrance Gallery Nat All On Paper Show, Palenville, NY, 83; Sotheby's Thirteen Collection, Channel 13 Auction, New York, 83; 15th Ann Art Show, Fairleigh Dickinson Univ, 83; Cornell Med Ctr, New York, 92. *Pos:* Adminr, Sch Fine Arts, Nat Acad Design, New York, 80-; critic & writer, Arts Mag, New York. *Teaching:* Instr drawing & art hist, High Sch Music & Art, New York, 72-73; adj prof contemp art, Jersey City State Col, 74; instr painting, Usdan Ctr Creative & Performing Arts, Wyandanch, NY, 80; dir, Art Alumni Asn of City Col, New York; adv, Robeson Ctr Gallery, Rutgers Univ, Newark, NJ. *Bibliog:* Lawrence Campbell (auth), article, Art News, 9/73; Klein at Phoenix, Park East, 3/76; Nina Ffrench-Frazier (auth), Gallery guide, Westsider, 4/27/78. *Mem:* Col Art Asn Am; Artists Equity; Am Asn Mus; Art Alumni Asn; Int Council Mus. *Media:* Oil, Paper Collage. *Publ:* Auth, Toby Buonagario: More optical bounce to the ounce, 86, Beneath the surface of Terence La Noue, 86, All kinds of rational questions: An interview with Michael Goldberg, 86 & Debra Weier - in all Dimensions, 88, ARTs Mag; Manhattan Spotlight on Furman J Finck, Manhattan Spotlight, 4/88. *Mailing Add:* 139-12 84th Dr Briarwood NY 11435

KLEIN, ESTHER M
PATRON, COLLECTOR
b Philadelphia, Pa, Nov 3, 07. *Study:* Temple Univ, BS, LHD, 80; Univ London. *Pos:* Ed, Philadelphia Art Alliance Bull; art critic, WPEN(daily radio prog); founding dir, Long Beach Island Found Arts & Sci, NJ. *Awards:* Gimbel Award, 75; Art Alliance Award of Merit, given jointly to Esther & Philip Klein, 75; Distinguished Daughters of Pa. *Mem:* Life mem Pa Acad Fine Arts; life mem Philadelphia Print Club; Philadelphia Art Alliance (comt mem). *Interests:* Donor of annual prizes to Print Club and Clothesline Exhibit to encourage young Philadelphia artists. *Collection:* Philadelphia artists. *Mailing Add:* 135 S 18th Street Philadelphia PA 19103

KLEIN, GWENDA J
DEALER, WRITER
b San Francisco, Calif, Nov 10, 49. *Study:* Colo Col, BA, 71, MAT, 72. *Collections Arranged:* Contemporary Mexican Prints Travelling Exhib, Art Mus Asn Am, 80-83. *Pos:* Arts columnist, Peninsula Mag, 78-80; Kaleidoscope, KTEH-TV, San Jose, Calif, 78-81; dir & co-owner, Klein Gallery, Chicago, 81-86; private art dealer, 86-88; owner & dir, Gwenda Jay Gallery, Chicago, 88- *Mem:* Chicago Art Dealers Asn. *Specialty:* Contemporary American painting and sculpture. *Publ:* Auth, Francisco Zuniga, Oakland Mus, 77; auth, article, New Art Examiner, 80. *Mailing Add:* Gwenda Jay Gallery 301 W Superior Chicago IL 60610

KLEIN, LYNN (ELLEN)
PAINTER, PHOTOGRAPHER
b San Francisco, Calif, April 14, 50. *Study:* Univ Minn, BA, 74, MA, 76, Cite Internationale des Arts, Paris, 84-86. *Work:* Minneapolis Inst Arts; Philadelphia Mus Art; Atlantic Richfield Co, Los Angeles, Oakland Mus Calif; Am Tel & Tel, New York; Bibliotheque Nat, Dept des Estampes et de Photographie, Paris; Morgan Guaranty Trust, New York; Dayton Hudson, Minneapolis; plus others. *Comn:* Mural, Mayo Clinic, Rochester, Minn, 77, Saks Fifth Avenue, Denver, Colo, 90, Bank of the Orient, San Francisco, Calif, 89; Bank of the Orient, San Francisco, 89; Saks Fifth Ave, Denver, Colo, 90. *Exhib:* West 81, Art & Law, 81, Lighter Shade of Pale, 90, Minn Mus Art, St Paul; solo exhibs, Cameraless Prints, Coffman Gallery, Univ, Minn, Minneapolis, 82, The Print Club, Philadelphia, Pa, 85, & Foster White Gallery, Seattle, 89; Phelan Award Exhib Printmaking, World Print Coun, San Francisco, 83; Photograms & Photographs, Los Angeles Ctr Photog Studies, 83; Photog Invitational, Tweed Mus Art, 83; Lensless Photography, Franklin Inst, Philadelphia, 83; Printed by Women, Port Hist Mus, Philadelphia, 83; 38th Salon de la Jeune Peinture, Grand Palais Paris, France, 87; Contemporary Textiles: Traditional Roots, Minneapolis Inst Arts, 88; Textile Arts International: Rauschenberg, Samarst & Klein, 90; and others. *Teaching:* Instr design, Univ Minn, 74-84. *Awards:* Minn State Arts Bd Grant, 78; Photog Fel, Film in the Cities Gallery, 83; James P Phelan Art Award, World Print Coun, 83; Rockefeller Found Fel, 84-86. *Bibliog:* Frank Cebulski (auth), The Phelan Awards, 8/27/83; Charles Talley (auth), A cautious progress, 9/18/88, Artweek; World Print Coun Awards, J Print World, 6/83; Capturing Light by David Skarjune, Vinyl Arts, 1/88; Contemporary textiles: traditional roots, Minneapolis Soc Fine Arts Mag, 5/88. *Media:* Miscellaneous Media. *Publ:* Double/Absent, No 15, Vermillion Editions, Diptych, 83. *Dealer:* Allrich Gallery 251 Post St San Francisco CA 94108; Steven Anderson Vermillion Editions Ltd 2919 Como SE Minneapolis MN 55414. *Mailing Add:* 240 Beach Dr Marrowstone Island Nordland WA 98358

KLEIN, MICHAEL EUGENE
HISTORIAN, WRITER
b Philadelphia, Pa, July 30, 40. *Study:* Rutgers Col, New Brunswick, NJ, BA, 62; Columbia Univ, New York, MA, 65, PhD, 71. *Collections Arranged:* John Covert, 1882-1960 (auth, bk), Smithsonian Inst Press, 76. *Pos:* Vis cur, Hirshhorn Mus, 76. *Teaching:* Asst prof art hist, State Univ NY, Brockport, 71-73; asst prof, Univ SC, 73-77; asst prof, Western Ky Univ, 77-80, assoc prof, 81- *Mem:* Col Art Asn Am; Southeastern Col Art Conf; Midwestern Art Hist Soc. *Res:* American art of early 20th century, especially John Covert; Arnold Friedman. *Publ:* Auth, John Covert's time: Cubism, Duchamp, Einstein, a quasi scientific fantasy, summer 74 & John Covert's studios in 1916 and 1923, fall 79, Art J; Scotese collection at the Columbia Museum of Art, Southeastern Col Art Conf J, fall 74; auth, John Covert and the Arensberg circle, Arts Mag, 5/77. *Mailing Add:* Dept of Art Western Ky Univ Bowling Green KY 42101

KLEIN, SANDOR C
PAINTER, SCULPTOR
b New York, NY, Oct 27, 12. *Study:* Nat Acad Design; Acad Julien, Paris; Beaux-Arts, Paris; Acad Fine Arts, Vienna; Royal Acad Art, Budapest; Am Acad Rome, fel, 31. *Work:* Smithsonian Inst Mus Am Art & The Pentagon, Washington, DC; Albany State Mus, NY; Luxembourg Mus; Fine Arts Mus of South, Mobile, Ala. *Comn:* Portraits of Hon Schuyler Otis Bland, Chmn Maritime & Fisheries Comn, 46, Gen Nathan F Twining, Chmn Joint Chiefs of Staff, 61 & Gen Curtis E LeMay, USAF Chief of Staff, 62, comn by US Govt; Eleanor Roosevelt, comn by Am Cancer Soc, 63; Armand Hammer, Occidental Co, 67. *Exhib:* Paris Salon; Carnegie Inst Int; plus others in the US & abroad. *Teaching:* Instr painting, Nat Acad, New York, Beaux Arts & Acad Julien, Paris. *Awards:* Pulitzer Prize for Painting, 31; Silver Medal, Paris Salon; Medal, Int Biennale, Venice, 32; Oscar D'Italia, 85. *Media:* Oil. *Mailing Add:* c/o Belanthl Gallery 142 Court St Bronxville NY 11201

KLEINBAUER, W EUGENE
HISTORIAN
b Los Angeles, Calif, June 15, 37. *Study:* Univ Calif, Berkeley, with Walter Horn, BA & MA, 59; Princeton Univ, with Richard Krautheimer & Kurt Weitzmann, PhD, 67. *Pos:* Chmn visual arts adv panel, Ind State Art Comn, 75-76; bd dir, Midwest Art History Soc, 80-82; pres, Internat Ctr Medieval Art, 87-90. *Teaching:* Asst prof hist art, Univ Calif, Los Angeles, 65-72; chmn dept fine arts, Ind Univ, 73-76, chmn arts admin prog, 73-75 & fall 78, prof hist art, 77- & prof Near Eastern languages & cultures, 85-; Sam & Ayala Zacks vis prof hist of art, Hebrew Univ, Jerusalem, 78; assoc dir, Henry Hope Sch Fine Arts, Ind Univ, 88-92; Chmn dept hist art, Ind Univ, 92-95. *Awards:* Nat Endowment Humanities Fel, 76-77. *Mem:* Col Art Asn Am; Int Ctr Medieval Art (mem bd dir, 70-73, 74-77 & 81-83, ed, GESTA, 80-83, pres, 87-90); Medieval Acad Am; US Nat Comt Byzantine Studies; Nat Soc Arts & Letters; Cent Ind Soc, Archeol Inst Am (pres, 77-80); Speculum (ed bd, 90-). *Res:* Specialist in medieval art and architecture; historiography of Western art. *Publ:* Ed, Modern Perspectives in Western Art History, Holt Rinehart, 71; ed, E Kitzinger, Art of Byzantium & Medieval West, Ind Univ, 76; auth, Research Guide to the History of Western Art, Am Libr Asn, 82; Early Christian and Byzantine Architecture, GK Hall, 92; numerous scholarly articles & reviews. *Mailing Add:* Sch of Fine Arts Ind Univ Bloomington IN 47405

KLEINBERG, SUSAN
PAINTER, SCULPTOR
b Phoenix, Ariz. *Study:* Hunter Col with Bob Morris & Tony Smith, MA, 72. *Work:* Los Angeles Co Mus, Calif; Cincinnati Mus, Ohio; La Jolla Mus, Calif; Am Ctr Paris, France; IBM, New York & Paris, France. *Comn:* Park-slides, Pomona, Calif, 75; Triptich paintings, Liebman, Adolph, Cherne, New York, 87, Rainen Corp, San Francisco, 88 & Media Ctr for Human Rights, New York, 90; 2 paintings, comn by Mrs L Levin, Los Angeles, Calif, 87; painting, Colo Open Lands, Land Trust, 89; painting, Univ Calif, San Diego, 91. *Exhib:* Los Angeles Co Mus, Calif, 79; Mass Inst Technol, Boston, 82; Mus Mod Art, New York, 82; La Jolla Mus, Calif, 83; Castelli Gallery, New York, 85; Sarah Lawrence Col Mus, New York, 87; Light/Walls, Am Ctr Paris/Beauborg, France, 87; Orton Collection, Cincinnati Mus, Ohio, 88; Sarabhai Collection, Ahmedabad, India. *Awards:* Nat Endowment Arts, 77; Max Beckman Award, Brooklyn Mus, 80; City des Arts, Paris, 86. *Media:* Mixed media. *Mailing Add:* 250 85th St 14-H New York NY 10024

KLEINMAN, SUE
PAINTER, LECTURER
b New York, NY. *Study:* Pratt Inst, Brooklyn, BFA; Caton-Rose Inst Fine Arts; New Sch Social Res, New York; Mus Mod Art, New York, with Zoltan Hecht & Donald Stacey; also with Raphael Soyer & Anthony Toney. *Work:* Brown Univ, RI; Fairleigh Dickinson Univ, Rutherford, NJ; Maimonides Hosp, Brooklyn; Mus Art, Ft Lauderdale, Fla. *Exhib:* Knickerbocker Art, 59 & Audubon Art, 60, Weiner Gallery, New York; one-woman shows, Lord & Taylor Gallery, New York, 76, Pompano Recreation Ctr, Pompano Beach, Fla, 80 & Pompano Beach Pub Libr, 83, 85, 86, 89 & 91. *Pos:* Lectr & docent, Ft Lauderdale Mus Art, 73-88; instr art appreciation, Century Village, 84-85; vpres, Mus Art; vpres & prog chmn, Bnoi Bneth; bd dirs, On-Pompano Chap. *Awards:* Bronze Medal, Village Art Ctr, 58; Silver Medal, Trade Bank New York. *Bibliog:* Jane Jaffe (auth), article, Manhattan E, 65; Dorothy Hall (auth), article, Park E, 69; Saint-Evermond (auth), article, France-Amerique, 69; Pompano Monday Paper, 87. *Mem:* Artists Equity Asn; Nat Women's Art Asn; Broward Art Guild; Boca Raton Art Ctr; ORT. *Media:* Oil and Palette Knife. *Dealer:* Contextual Gallery 813 E Los Olas Blvd Ft Lauderdale FL 33301. *Mailing Add:* 405 N Ocean Blvd Pompano Beach FL 33062

KLEINSMITH, BRUCE JOHN See Nutzle, Futzie (Bruce John Kleinsmith)

KLEINSMITH, GENE (EUGENE DENNIS)
PAINTER, WRITER
b Madison, Wis, Feb 22, 42. *Study:* Augustana Col, SDak, with Palmer Eide & Ogden Dalyrymple, BA(art), 63; Northern Ariz Univ, Flagstaff, with Dr Donald Bendel & Dr Peter Jacobs, MA(art), 69; Univ Nev, Las Vegas, 70-; Univ Calif, 71. *Work:* Ariz Western Col & Yuma Art Ctr, Yuma, Ariz; Los Angeles Co Mus, Los Angeles; Mus Int delle Ceramiche, Faenza, Italy; Calif Designer-Craftsman; Victoria & Albert Mus, London, Eng; and others. *Comn:* Facade for church, Ascension Lutheran Church, Ft Collins, Colo, 63; ceramic sculptures, Univ Wis-Madison, 66, Marcia Rodell Gallery, Los Angeles, Calif, 84. *Exhib:* Nat Endowment Traveling Exhib, Southern Calif, 70 & 80; Am Bicentennial Exhib, Paris, France, 76; Clay as Art, Ariz Comn Arts & Humanities, Flagstaff, 80, 81 & 83; Art USA, Charlottesville, Va, 83; one-man show, Los Angeles Art of the Olympiad, Marcia Rodell Gallery, Calif, 84 & Art in the Sun, Victor Valley Art Gallery, 90. *Collections Arranged:* Am Bicentennial Exhib, Paris, France, 76, Art in the Sun, Victor Valley Art Gallery, 90; Artist-in-Residence programs, Victor Valley Col, 72-88. *Teaching:* Instr acrylics & drawing, San Bernardino Valley Col, Calif, 67-71; chmn & instr acrylics & drawing & art hist, Victor Valley Col, Victorville, Calif, 71- *Awards:* European Honorariums, 88, 89 & 90; Victor Valley Col Educator of the Year, 92; San Bernardino Co Gold Medal, 92. *Bibliog:* Richard Notkin (auth), The Artist as Social Critic, 82; Gene Kleinsmith, Victor Valley Mag, 85; Du Cote de la Vie, Le Ceramic Moderne Mag, Paris, France, 7/85; Art Deserves Its Place in the Sun, San Bernadino Sun Newspaper, 2/24/90. *Mem:* Nat Coun on Educ Ceramic Arts; Am Crafts Coun; Nat Coun Art Adminr; Inst for Ceramic Hist; Southern Calif Designer-Craftsmen; Los Angeles County Art Mus. *Media:* Acrylics, Mixed Media. *Res:* Aesthetic and technical information to sustain a meaningful interchange of dialogue and consequence. *Publ:* Auth, Earth, Fire and Water, 76 & Clay's the Way, 78, rev ed, 81 & 86, Victor Valley Col Press; Rudy Autio, 80 & Artist as Innovator, 9/83, Ceramics Monthly; William C Alexander, Nat Coun Educ Ceramic Arts J, 10/83; Americans in Clay, 86; An Artists Dialogue, 90; and others. *Dealer:* Gallery II 218 W Main St Charlottesville VA 22901. *Mailing Add:* 13624 Quapaubw Apple Valley CA 92308

KLEMENT, VERA
PAINTER, EDUCATOR
b Danzig, Poland, Dec 14, 29; US citizen. *Study:* Cooper Union Sch Art & Archit, grad, 50. *Work:* Mus Mod Art, Jewish Mus, New York; Philadelphia Mus Art; Ill State Mus, Springfield; Univ Tex; Continental Bank, Chicago; Ill State Bldg, Chicago; Nothern Trust Bank, First Nat Bank, Chicago; Art Inst, Chicago; Jewish Mus, New York. *Comn:* Ed of etchings, NY Hilton/Rockefeller Ctr, 61; 27 1/2 ft & 2 ft painting, Kemper Ins Co, Long Grove, Ill, 75. *Exhib:* Modern Art in US, Mus Mod Art Travelling Exhib, New York, 56; Art Inst Chicago, 67; Ill State Mus, 74; Walker Art Ctr Invitational, Minneapolis, Minn, 77; Jewish Mus, New York, 82; Terra Mus Am Art & Renaissance Soc, Chicago, 87; one-woman show, Spertus Mus, 87; group show, Ill State Mus, Springfield, 90; and others. *Teaching:* Instr painting, Univ Ill, 68-69; asst prof art, Univ Chicago, 69-78, assoc prof, 78-86, prof, 87- *Awards:* Louis Comfort Tiffany Found Grant, 54; Ill Arts Coun Grant, 81, 84, 87; Guggenheim fel, 81-82; Nat Endowment for the Arts, 87. *Bibliog:* William S Lieberman (auth), Printmaking & the American woodcut today, Perspectives USA, 53; Amy Goldin (auth), Vitality vs greasy kid stuff, Art Gallery Mag 4/72; article in Artists' Writings, publ by NAME, 77; Dore Ashton (auth), Two Part Connection: Vera klement's Painting, Arts Mag, 3/84, retrospective catalog, A Question of Drawing, 89; James Yood (auth), Vera Klement, Artforum, 89. *Media:* Oil. *Dealer:* Roy Boyd Gallery Chicago IL; Walter Bischoff Stuttgart Ger. *Mailing Add:* 727 S Dearborn Chicago IL 60605

KLETT, MARK
PAINTER
b Albany, NY, Sept 9, 52. *Study:* St Laurance Univ, BS, 74; State Univ NY, MFA, 77. *Work:* Mus Mod Art, New York; Los Angeles Co Mus Mod Art, Calif; Art Inst Chicago, Ill. *Exhib:* On the Art of Fixing a Shadow, Nat Gallery Art, Washington, DC, 89; Between Home & Heaven, Nat Mus Am Art, Smithsonian Inst, 92; Revealing Territory, Amon Carter Mus, Ft Worth, Tex, 92. *Teaching:* Acad prof, Ariz State Univ, 82- *Awards:* Art Fel, Nat Endowment Arts, 79, 82 & 84; Visual Arts Fel, AVA, 85; Creative Arts Award, Brandeiss Univ, 90. *Mem:* Soc Photog Educ; Phoenix Art Comn. *Dealer:* Pace Macgill 32 E 57th St New York NY 10022. *Mailing Add:* 1136 S Ash Tempe AZ 85281

KLINDT, STEVEN
ADMINISTRATOR
b Davenport, Iowa, Dec 18, 47. *Study:* Sch of Art, Univ Iowa, BA(studio art), 70, MA(photog), 74. *Collections Arranged:* Photograph Invitational, Galesburg Civic Art Ctr, Ill, 76; Proposals for Lake Sculpture, Evanston Art Ctr, Ill, 77; New American Photography (auth, catalog), Columbia Col, 82. *Pos:* Dir, Galesburg Civic Art Ctr, 74-76, Evanston Art Ctr, 76-79, Chicago Ctr Contemp Photog, Columbia Col Galleries, 79-83, Mus Contemp Photog, Columbia Col, 83-84, Tweed Mus Art, Duluth, Minn, 84-89, Exec Dir, Queens Mus Art, New York, 89- *Teaching:* Mus studies MA program, Columbia Col, Chicago, 79-84; Visual Arts Admin, New York Univ, 92- *Mem:* Col Art Asn; Am Asn Mus; Asn Art Mus Dirs. *Publ:* Ed, Jerry N Uelsmann, Photographs from 1975-1979, Columbia Col, Chicago, 80; Light Touching Silver-Photographs, Columbia Col, Chicago, 80; and others. *Mailing Add:* The Queens Museum New York City Bldg Flushing Meadows, Corona Park NY 11368

KLINE, HARRIET
PAINTER, PRINTMAKER
b New York, NY, Sept 25, 16. *Study:* Hunter Col, BA; also with Isaac Soyer; Art Students League, with Robert Philipp & Morris Kantor; China Inst, NY, with Prof Y C Wang, 45-59. *Work:* Grey Art Ctr, NY Univ; State Art Collection, Dresden, Ger; State Univ NY Col Oswego; Western New Eng Col, Springfield, Mass; Scarsdale Nat Bank; and others. *Exhib:* Silvermine Nat Exhib, Silvermine Guild, New Canaan, Conn, 59, 74, 86 & 89; Nat Asn Women Artists, Nat Acad, New York, 59-; solo exhibs, Selected Artists Gallery, New York, 60-75, Paper Work, 38th Ann, Butler Inst Am Art, 74 & Katonah Gallery, NY, 80; First Exhib American Graphics, Albertinum Mus, Dresden, 80; First Nat Asn Women Artists, traveling show, Israel & Egypt, 82; Solo Moneyworks, Automation House, NY, 84, Schiller-Wapner galleries, New York, 88, Katonah Gallery, NY, 89 & Lobby Gallery, New York, 92; Five Moneyworks Canvases, windows, Tiffany & Co, 89 &92. *Teaching:* Instr, pvt classes, 59-68. *Awards:* Nat Asn Women Artists Works on Paper, 70, 72, 78, 80, 84 & 90; Am Soc Contemp Artists Watercolors & Graphics Award, 79, 83 & 84, Works on Paper, 89; and others. *Mem:* Nat Asn Women Artists; Am Soc Contemp Artists; life mem Art Students League. *Media:* Watercolor; Moneyworks. *Publ:* Article, Artspeak, 5/16/88; articles, NY Times, 5/22/88, 2/12/89 & 8/15/92; article, The Numismatist, 5/88; article, Coinage Mag, 6/88; article, Intercorp, 10/13/89; and others. *Dealer:* Note: Moneyworks is a registered trademark; all rights reserved by artist. *Mailing Add:* 390 Heathcote Rd Scarsdale NY 10583

KLINE, RICHARD R
SCULPTOR, HOLOGRAPHY
b Three Rivers, Mich. *Study:* Mich State Univ, MFA, 64; Ox Bow Sch Art; Art Inst Chicago, with Abraham Rattner. *Work:* Everson Mus Art, Syracuse, NY; Richard DeMarco Gallery, Edinburgh, Scotland. *Exhib:* Everson Mus Art, Syracuse, NY, 74; Henri Gallery, Washington, DC, 74; Colgate Univ, Hamilton, NY, 76; Edinburgh Art Festival, Scotland, 80; Graham Gallery, Houston, Tex. *Teaching:* Prof, Cent Mich Univ, Mt Pleasant, 64-, chmn, Dept Art, 79-87. *Bibliog:* Film event (review), Village Voice, 72; 55 Mercer Street (review), Art News, 72. *Mem:* Col Art Asn; Nat Coun Art Adminrs. *Media:* Mixed Media. *Mailing Add:* Art Dept Cent Mich Univ Mt Pleasant MI 48859

KLINE, RONALD WAYNE
PRINTMAKER, PUBLISHER
b New Market, Va, Apr 2, 49. *Study:* Atlanta Col Art, BFA, 78; Fla State Univ, with William Walmsley, MFA, 81; Tamarind Inst, Albuquerque, NMex, with John Sommers, master printer cert, 83. *Work:* Washington Post Collection; Chattahoochee Valley Art Mus, Lagrange, Ga; Coca-Cola Co. *Comn:* Collab with folk artist to create original 5-color lithograph, Nat Bus Comt Arts, New York, 84; Collab with contemp artist to create original 4-color lithograph, High Mus Art, Atlanta, Ga, 85. *Exhib:* Reflex and Reflection, Washington Proj Arts, Washington, DC, 83; Political Art Show, Nexus Gallery, Atlanta, Ga, 84; Lagrange Nat XV, Chattahoochee Valley Art Asn, 90; Multiples Show, Nexus Contemp Art Ctr, Atlanta, 90; The Red Clay Survey, The Huntsville Mus Art, Ala. *Pos:* Dir and master printer, Rolling Stone Press, Atlanta, 84- *Teaching:* prof lithography, Atlanta Col Art, 85-92. *Awards:* Individual Artists Grant, Fulton Co Arts Coun, 90 & 92; Purchase Award, Lagrange Nat XV, 90. *Bibliog:* Catherine Fox (auth), Atlanta's Rolling Stone Press gathers ink, Atlanta J, 12/27/87 & Atlanta Constitution, 12/27/87; Paul Evens (auth), Original lithographs: Published by Rolling Stone Press, Art Paper, Atlanta, 1/89; Laura Lieberman (auth), the alchemy of lighography, Southern Accents Mag, 9/89. *Mem:* Southern Graphic Coun. *Media:* Lithography. *Mailing Add:* Rolling Stone Press 432 Calhoun St NW Atlanta GA 30318

KLING, JEAN LOUISE
CURATOR, ADMINISTRATOR
b Niles, Mich, Sept 7, 39. *Study:* Pomona Col, BA(with honors), 61; Claremont Univ Col, 63; Catholic Univ, 65-69; Trinity Col, 70. *Collections Arranged:* Alice Barney, Cosmos Club & Alice Pike Barney & Her Friends, Nat Mus Am Art, 79, Alice Pike Barney: Bringing Culture to a Provincial Capital, Studio House, 82, Pastels from Studio House, Studio House, 84 & Alice Pike Barney: The Paris Years, 86, Washington, DC; Edwin Scott, Cosmos Club, Washington, DC, 79; 14 Washington Women Artists, Market V Gallery, Washington, DC, 79; Covers from Washington Review, Landsburg Art Ctr, Washington, DC, 81; 200 Years of Worship & Witness: Christ Church Washington Parish, Summer Sch & Christ Church, Washington, DC, 90. *Pos:* Registr, Alice Pike Barney Collection & Barney Studio House, Washington, DC, 64-80, cur Barney Studio House, 81-; assoc ed, DC Gazette, 70-75; admin dir, Capital Hill Arts Workshop, 71-78; producer & moderator, Washington Review of the Arts on the Air, 75-78; man ed, Washington Review of the Arts, 75-81. *Teaching:* Theater, Captial Hill Arts Workshop, Washington, DC, 73-78 & 88. *Awards:* Special Achievement Award, Nat Mus Am Art, Smithsonian Inst, Washington, DC, 84 & 85; Community Arts Achievement Award, Capital Hill Arts Workshop, Washington, DC, 84; Walter Graham Award, Capital Hill Arts Workshop, Washington, DC, 92. *Bibliog:* Sarah-Booth Conroy (auth), Barney studio house, Washington Post, 1/90. *Mem:* Treas, Capital Hill Arts Workshop (bd dirs, 73-75); pres & treas, Friends Wash Review Arts (bd dirs, 84-88); bd dirs, Eddie Davis Mem Scholar, Duke Ellington Sch Performing Arts, 92. *Res:* Alice Pike Barney (biog), Visual Theater Arts from 1880-1930; architectural & social history, Christ Church, Washington Parrish. *Publ:* Barney Studio House, Smithsonian Inst, 81, 83, 85; Pastel Portraits from Studio House, Smithsonian Inst, 84; auth, artist, Alice Pike Barney: Bringing Culture to the Capital, Washington History, Vol II, no 1, Hist Soc Washington, DC, spring, 90. *Mailing Add:* 404 10th St SE Washington DC 20003

KLIPPER, STUART DAVID
PHOTOGRAPHER
b Bronx, NY, Aug 27, 41. *Study:* Univ Mich, Col Lit, Sci & Arts, BA, 62, Col Archit & Design, 62-63. *Work:* Minneapolis Inst Art; Walker Art Ctr, Minneapolis; Art Inst Chicago; Mus Fine Arts, Boston; Mus Mod Art, New York; and others. *Comn:* Anasazi Plates, Univ Mich; Cray I Computer, Cray Res Inc; The World in a Few States, First Bank Systems, Minneapolis. *Exhib:* One-man shows, Color & Black & White Photographs, 1971-74, O K Harris Works of Art, New York, 75, Multiple Strip Images, Walker Art Ctr, Minneapolis, 78, Recent Work, Minn Mus Art, Minneapolis, 80, Art Inst Chicago, 80 & Douglas Kenyon Gallery, 80 & Three Photog Groups, 1978-79, Minn Mus Art, 80; 20th Century Am Photogr, Atkins Mus Fine Art, Kansas City, 74; Am Photog in the 70's, Art Inst Chicago, 79; Duluth Photogrs, Tweed Mus; George Eastman House, Rochester, 82; Minn Mus Art, 82; and others. *Collections Arranged:* Seven Photogr (guest-cur), Art Gallery, Macalester Col, St Paul, Minn, 78. *Teaching:* Instr photog, Minneapolis Col Art & Design, 70-71, vis prof, 74-75 & 78; vis prof photog, Colo Col, Colorado Springs, 78, 79, 80, 89. *Awards:* Nat Endowment Arts Photogr Fel, 79; J S Guggenheim Mem Found Photogr Fel, 79-80, 89-90; Bush Found Visual Arts Fel, 80-81; and others. *Mem:* Minn Artists' Exhib Prog. *Publ:* Contribr, Midwest Invitational Catalogue, Walker Art Ctr, 74; auth, The History of Photography in Limericks, privately publ, 77; contribr, Minnesota Survey: Six Photographers Catalogue, Minneapolis Inst Art, 78; auth, The Art of the Twin Cities, Portfolio Mag, summer 80. *Mailing Add:* 5044 Xerxes Ave S Minneapolis MN 55410-2226

KLITZKE, THEODORE ELMER
EDUCATOR, HISTORIAN
b Chicago, Ill, Nov 4, 15. *Study:* Art Inst Chicago, BFA, 40; Univ Chicago, BA, 41, PhD, 53; Kansas City Art Inst, Hon DFA, 80. *Teaching:* Instr art hist, Univ Chicago, 46-47; asst prof art hist, State Univ NY Col Ceramics, Alfred Univ, 53-59; prof art hist & chmn dept art, Univ Ala, Tuscaloosa, 59-68. *Mem:* Am Studies Asn; Col Art Asn Am; Soc Archit Historians; fel Nat Asn Sch Art. *Res:* Social history of American art; 19th century French art; German expressionism; history of prints and drawings. *Publ:* Contribr, reviews in Col Art J & Art Bull, 59-; contribr, Alexis de Tocqueville and the Arts in America, Festschrift Ulrich Middeldorf, 68; auth, Melville Price Retrospective: 1920-1970, Frame House Gallery, 70; contribr, Hermann Wilhelm (catalog), 72. *Mailing Add:* 7918 Sherwood Ave Baltimore MD 21204

KLOBE, TOM
GALLERY DIRECTOR, EDUCATOR
b Minneapolis, Minn, Nov 26, 40. *Study:* Univ Hawaii, BFA, 64, MFA, 68; Univ Calif, Los Angeles, 72-73. *Work:* State Found Culture & Arts, Contemp Mus & Honolulu Acad Arts, Honolulu, Hawaii; City of La Mirada, Calif; Nat Orange Show Collection, San Bernadino, Calif; Downey Mus Art, Calif. *Comn:* Onizuka Ctr Int Astronomy, Hawaii. *Exhib:* Artists of Hawaii, Honolulu Acad Art, 67 & 68; 9th Ann Southern California Exhib, Long Beach Mus Art, 71; Calif-Hawaii Regional, Fine Arts Gallery, San Diego, 71, 72 & 76; Ann Purchase Prize Competition, Riverside Art Mus, Calif, 72-74 & 76; solo exhib, Downey Mus Art, Calif, 74. *Collections Arranged:* Woven Menagerie (auth, catalog), Orange Coast Col, 76; Pranas Domsaitis, 78, Akari by Noguchi, 78, Koa Furniture of Hawaii, 81, Egyptian Antiquities, 82, Greek and Russian Icons (with video), 85, Woven Passage: The Silk Route, 87, The Art of Polish Posters, 87, Univ Hawaii Art Gallery; Crossings, 89, Hawaii & France; The Art of Asian Costume, 88; The Image and the Word, 90. *Pos:* Actg dir, Downey Mus Art, Calif, 76; dir, Univ Hawaii Art Gallery, Honolulu, 77- *Teaching:* Assoc prof design & Islamic & Medieval art hist, Univ Hawaii, Honolulu, 77- *Awards:* Best in Exhib Design, Koa Furniture of Hawaii, 81, Greek and Russian Icons, 84, 2nd Int Shoebox Sculpture Exhib, 85, Print Casebooks 6-8, The Art of Micronesia, 86 & The Art of Polish Posters, 87. *Mem:* Hawaii Mus Asn; Nat Asn Mus Exhib. *Publ:* Ed International Shoebox Sculpture Exhibitions, 82, 85 & 88, Univ Hawaii Art Gallery. *Mailing Add:* Univ Hawaii Art Gallery Honolulu HI 96822

KLONARIDES, CAROLE ANN
VIDEO ARTIST, CURATOR
b Washington, DC, Apr 2, 51. *Study:* Va Commonwealth Univ, Richmond, BFA(painting & printmaking), 73; Whitney Mus Independent Study Prog, New York, 72-73; New Sch Social Res, New York, MA(media studies), 83. *Work:* Mus Mod Art, New York; Ctr Georges Pompidou, Paris, France; Donnell Media Ctr, NY Pub Libr, New York; Mus Art, RI Sch Design, Providence; Contemp Arts Mus, Houston, Tex. *Comn:* 60 second video psa, Nat Asn Artists' Orgn, New York, Art Against AIDS, AmFAR; 6 1/2 minute video art tape, Channel Four, NYSCA, NYFA, United Kingdom, 88; 11 two-three minute videos, Olympia & York, New York, 88; 11 41 minute video, Wexner Ctr Visual Arts & BBC2 (United Kingdom). *Exhib:* Video: Heroes/Anti-Heroes, Contemp Arts Mus, Houston, Tex, 84; San Sabastion Film/Video Festival, San Sebastion, Spain, 84; Video Recent Acquisitions, Mus Mod Art, New York, 86; Films on Art, A Festival at the Mus Boymans-Van-Beuningen, Rotterdam, 86; Documenta 8, Kassel, Ger, 87; Digital Visions: Computers & Art, Everson Mus Art & IBM, Syracuse, NY, 87; Ghosts in the Machine, Channel Four, London, Eng, 88; Meet the Makers, Donnell Media Ctr, New York, 88; Reflections, Films by Artis, 7 Festival International Du Film Sur l'Art, Montreal Can, 89; Electronic Landscapes, Nat Gallery Can Ottawa Ontario, 89; Reconstructed Realms, Long Beach Mus Art, CA, 89; Video and the Computer, MOMA, NYC, 89; Into The Nineties: New Works/New Spaces, Wexner Ctr Visual Arts, Columbus, OH, 90; ImageWorld, Art and Media, Whitney Mus Am Art, 90. *Pos:* Programming dir, MCTV, 80-82; dir, Baskerville & Watson Gallery, New York, 83-87. *Awards:* Nat Endowment Arts Fel, New Genres, 87; NY Found Arts Fel, Collaboration

(MICA-TV), 87. *Bibliog:* Marvin Heiferman & Lisa Phillips (auth), Imageworld, Whitney Mus Am Art 89-90; Regina Cornwell (auth), TV or Not TV, Contemporanea, 10/89 p 58-63; Robert H Pelfrey (auth), Art & Mass Media, Harper & Row, 85. *Mem:* Pub Art Fund (panelist, 88); Nat Endowment Arts (panelist, 88, site visitor, 89); Community Access Advisory Commt Brooklyn Community Access Television; New York Found Arts (bd gov). *Publ:* "Television for Real", Center Quarterly No 38, Volume 10, Number 2, Center for Photography at Woodstock, 89, 23-25; "It's Evening in America", Luso-Americanos de Arte Contemporanea, 7/4/89. *Dealer:* Electronic Arts Intermix 536 Broadway 9th Fl New York NY 10012. *Mailing Add:* c/o Long Beach Mus Art Media Art Ctr 2300 E Ocean Blvd Long Beach CA 90803

KLOPFENSTEIN, PHILIP ARTHUR
MUSEUM DIRECTOR, PAINTER
b Lake Odessa, Mich, Apr 28, 37. *Study:* Mich State Univ, with Abraham Ratner & Linsey Decker, BFA; Western Mich Univ, with Harry Hefner, MFA; Harvard Univ, Arts Admin Cert. *Exhib:* State Ark Educ Dept Traveling Exhib, 76-; Mid Southern Watercolor Soc Ann, 72-74. *Collections Arranged:* John Henry Byrd (1840-1880), Southeast Ark Arts & Sci Ctr, Pine Bluff, 70; Ernest Trova One-Man Exhib, 71; Art Inc II (Am paintings from Am corp collections), 80. *Pos:* TV writer & teacher, Ark Educ TV, Conway, 68-69; dir, Southeast Ark Arts & Sci Ctr, 70-76; exec dir, Augusta Richmond Co Mus, Ga, 77-79; dir, Montgomery Mus Fine Arts, Ala, 79-82; vice pres, Res and Reclamation, 83-88. *Teaching:* Instr, Paw Paw Pub Sch, Mich, 63-65; instr painting, watercolor & art educ, Little Rock Univ, 65-68; instr art hist, Auburn Univ, Montgomery, 84-85, Glenwood Pub Sch, 89- *Mem:* Am Asn Mus; Southeastern Mus Conf (regional rep, 74-75); Am Asn Mus. *Media:* Watercolor, Acrylic. *Res:* John Henry Byrd. *Publ:* Auth, John Henry Byrd (1840-1880), 71. *Mailing Add:* PO Box 1388 Glenwood AZ 71943

KLOSS, GENE (ALICE GENEVA GLASIER)
ETCHER, PAINTER
b Oakland, Calif, July 27, 03. *Study:* Univ Calif, Berkeley, AB(hon in art), 24; Calif Sch Fine Arts, 24-25; Calif Sch Arts & Crafts. *Work:* San Francisco Art Mus, Calif; Metrop Mus Art, New York; Smithsonian Inst, Washington, DC; Mus Tokyo, Japan. *Comn:* Prints, Soc Print Connoisseurs, New York, 49; prints, Print Club Albany, NY, 52; prints, Soc Am Graphic Artists, New York, 53; prints, Print Makers Calif, Los Angeles, 56. *Exhib:* Three Centuries of Art in United States (in collab with Mus Mod Art, New York), Paris, 38; Nat Acad Design Ann, New York, 50-; Three Am Regionalist Printmakers, Pratt Graphic Ctr, NY, 76; one-man shows, Muckenthaler Cult Ctr, Fullerton, Calif, 80, Roswell Mus, 82, WTex Mus, 84 & Corcoran Gallery Art, Washington, DC, 88. *Awards:* Purchase Award, Libr Cong, 53; Fower Prize, 60 & Purchase Prize, 61, Print Club Albany; Anonymous prize, Nat Acad Design, 61. *Bibliog:* Mary Carrol Nelson (auth), Intaglios by Gene Kloss, Am Artist, 2/78. *Mem:* Academician Nat Acad Design; Soc Am Graphic Artists; Philadelphia Watercolor Club; Albany Print Club. *Media:* Oil, Watercolor. *Publ:* Illusr, The Great Kiva, 80 & Gene Kloss Etchings (catalog), 81, Sunstone Press, 81. *Mailing Add:* Box 33 Taos NM 87571

KLOSS, WILLIAM
HISTORIAN, WRITER
b Cleveland, Ohio, Dec 23, 37. *Study:* Oberlin Col, BA, 62, MA, 68; Univ Mich, 72. *Collections Arranged:* More than Meets the Eye: the Art of Trompe l'Oeil (with catalog), Columbus Mus Art, Ohio, 85. *Pos:* Exhib coordr, Smithsonian Inst Traveling Exhib Ser, 74-78; founder & dir of tours, Washington Art Assoc Inc, 78- *Teaching:* Asst prof art hist, Univ Va, Charlottesville, 69-72; lectr art hist, Smithsonian Inst Assoc Prog, 78- *Awards:* Fulbright Scholar for Study of Art Hist in Rome, US Govt, 67-69; Presidential Appt, Comt for Preservation of White House, 90. *Mem:* Col Art Asn of Am. *Publ:* Auth, Treasures from the National Museum of American Art, 85, Smithsonian; auth, Figural Images of Theodore Robinson, Paine Art Ctr, 87; auth, Samuel F B Morse, Harry N Abrams, 88; principal contribr, Treasures of State, 91 & auth, Art in the White House: A Nation's Pride, Harry N Abrams, 92. *Mailing Add:* 1824 Wyoming Ave NW Washington DC 20009

KLOTZ, SUZANNE
PAINTER, SCULPTOR
b Shawno, Wis, Oct 15, 44. *Study:* Washington Univ, St Louis, 62-64; Kansas City Art Inst, 64-66, BFA, 66; Univ Mo, Kansas City, 66-67; Tex Tech Univ, 70-72, MFA, 72. *Work:* Nat Mus, Smithsonian Inst; Spencer Art Mus, Lawrence, Kans; Scripps Col, Claremont, Calif; Baha'i Nat Ctr, Wilmette, Ill; Am Craft Mus, NY; San Francisco Mus Mod Art. *Comn:* Sculpture, Roosevelt Park, Phoenix, Ariz. *Exhib:* one-person exhibs, Scottsdale Ctr Arts, 78, Phoenix Art Mus, 81 Spencer Art Mus, Lawrence, Kans, 82 & Mus STex, Corpus Christi, 83; Boise Gallery Art, Boise, Idaho; Cheney Cowles Mem Mus, Spokane, Wash; Ohio State Univ, Columbus; Purdue Univ, Lafayette, Ind; Ben Gurion Univ Negeu Beer, Sheva, Israel; Elaine Horwitch Gallery, Scottsdale, Ariz, 93. *Teaching:* Instr painting, drawing & design, Angelo State Univ, San Angelo, Tex, 72-75, assoc prof, 85-86; asst prof drawing & design, Scripps Col, Claremont, Calif, 76-78; vis prof, Univ Tex, San Antonio, spring 85; vis sculptor, Ariz State Univ, Tempe, 85-86 & Univ Utah, 91-92. *Awards:* Craftsman Fels, 76 & 78 & Performance Grant, 83, Nat Endowment Arts; and others. *Bibliog:* Hubert Crehan (auth), Dream houses & fanciful creatures of Suzanne Klotz, St Louis Post Dispatch, Mo, 74; Berman & Pinto (auths), Creative Exploration Series, Merrick, 75; and many articles in various magazines. *Media:* Mixed. *Publ:* Coauth, Everything's the Same, Country Western Press, 77; coauth, Everything's Different, 78. *Dealer:* Elaine Horwitch Gallery 4211 N Marshall Way Scottsdale AZ 85251. *Mailing Add:* 300 Birch Blvd Sedona AZ 86336

KLUVER, BILLY (JOHAN WILHEM)
ADMINISTRATOR
b Monaco, Nov 13, 27; Swedish citizen. *Study:* Royal Inst Technol, Stockholm, EE; Univ Calif, Berkeley, PhD. *Work:* Mus Mod Art, New York; Kunsthaus, Zurich, Switz; Centre George Pompidou, Paris, France; Mus Ludwig, Cologne, WGer; and others. *Collections Arranged:* Four Americans, Mod Museet, Stockholm, 62; Art 1963--A New Vocabulary (cur), Arts Coun YMHA, Philadelphia, 62; American Pop Art, Mod Museet, Stockholm, 64; Some More Beginnings (cur), Brooklyn Mus, NY, 68; The New York Collection for Stockholm, Mod Museet Stockholm, 73; What Are You Working On Now? 1960-1970, PS 1, New York, 83. *Pos:* Mem tech staff, Bell Tel Lab, Murray Hill, NJ, 58-68; co-founder & pres, Experiments in Art and Technol, 66- *Awards:* Royal Order of Vasa, New York Collection for Stockholm, Govt Sweden, 74. *Bibliog:* Jill Johnston (auth), Marmelade Me, E P Dutton, 71; Douglas Davis (auth), Art and The Future, Praeger, 73; Calvin Tomkins (auth), The Scene, Viking Press, 76. *Publ:* Contribr & ed, Pavilion, Dutton, 72; Circle of Montparnasse, Universe, 85; auth, A Day with Picasso, Art in Am, 86; contribr, Perpetual Motif, Art of Man Ray, Abbeville, 88; coauth, Kikis Paris, Harry N Abrams, 89. *Mailing Add:* 69 Apple Tree Rd Berkeley Heights NJ 07922

KNAPP, SADIE MAGNET
PAINTER, SCULPTOR
b New York, NY, July 18, 09. *Study:* NY Training Sch Teachers, lic; City Col New York; Brooklyn Mus Art Sch; Atelier 17; Sculpture Ctr. *Work:* Ga Mus Art, Athens; Norfolk Mus Art, Va; Riverside Mus, New York. *Comn:* Mural, fired enamel painting on steel, Kew Gardens Civic Ctr, NY, 77. *Exhib:* Corcoran Gallery Art, Washington, DC; Baltimore Mus; Pa Acad Fine Arts, Philadelphia; Butler Inst Art, Youngstown, Ohio; solo exhib, Hollywood Mus, Fla, 74; Nat Competition, Mus of Four Arts, Palm Beach, Fla, 85; and others in Can, Eng, France, Switz, Arg, Mex, Japan, India, Scotland & Italy. *Collections Arranged:* Exchange exhibits arranged for women artists of Japan, 60 & artists of Argentina & Mexico, 65 & Nat Asn Women Artists--both exhibs shown in var foreign & domestic mus. *Teaching:* Instr enamels, Worcester Crafts Ctr, 63. *Awards:* Baltimore Mus Award, 56, 58 & 61; Grumbacher Award for Painting, Nat Acad Design, 68; Awards (two), Am Heritage Art Exhib, 77; Cramer Prize, 80; and others. *Mem:* Nat Asn Women Artists (vpres, 61-65, pres, 65-67); Nat Soc Painters in Casein & Acrylics; Artists Equity Asn; and others. *Media:* Acrylic, Oil; Metal, Cast. *Mailing Add:* 162 Somerset H West Palm Beach FL 33417

KNAPP, TOM
SCULPTOR, PAINTER
b Gillette, Wyo, Sept 28, 25. *Study:* Santa Rosa Jr Col, Calif; Calif Col Arts & Crafts, Oakland; Art Ctr Sch, Los Angeles. *Work:* Whitney Gallery Western Art, Cody, Wyo; Indianapolis Mus Art; Heritage Libr, Bank of Alaska, Anchorage; Mescelero Tribe, Mescalero Indian Reservation, NMex; Midland Nat Bank Collection, Tex. *Comn:* Paul Stock Mem, Stock Found, Cody, Wyo, 72; Gladys Porter Zoo, Brownsville, Tex; El Paso Mus Art; Capt Bill McMurrey (state), Tex Ranger Mus, San Antonio, 5/86; Cherokee Nat Hist Soc; Midland Mus Art, Midland, Tex; Benson Park, Loveland, Colo; lifesize bronze football figure, Rose Bowl Hall Fame, Tournament Roses, Pasadena, Calif; Cahuilla Indian Reed Gatherer (lifesize bronze), Palm Desert, Calif; and others. *Pos:* Animator, Walt Disney Studios, 54-56; com artist, Mountain States Telephone, 67-68 & 69-70. *Bibliog:* Barbara Funkhouser (auth), A sculptor casts his bronzes, El Paso Sun Dial Mag, 74; Marilyn Watson (auth), Pouring in the Hondo Valley, NMex Mag, 2/78; Kay Mayer (auth), Dancers of Ruidoso, Art West Mag, 3/82. *Mem:* Am MENSA; Audubon Soc; World Wildlife Fund; NY Zoological Soc. *Media:* Bronze; Drawing. *Mailing Add:* Box 510 Ruidoso Downs NM 88346

KNAUB, RAYMOND L
PAINTER, INSTRUCTOR
b Gering, Nebr, July 6, 40. *Study:* Baylor Univ, 58-60; Univ Nebr, Lincoln, BFA, 63; Univ Colo, Boulder; also with Frederick Mizen, David Seyler & Frank Sampson. *Work:* United Bank of Colo; Dixon Paper Co; Colo Pub Employees Retirement Asn; W Tex Mus Asn Collection; Monaghan Farms Inc; US Embassy, Moscow. *Comn:* Georgetown Loop Railway (poster), Georgetown Soc, Colo. *Exhib:* Denver Art Mus, 72 & 73; 20th Nat Soc Painters Acrylic & Casein, New York, 73; 61st Allied Artists Am, New York, 74; Rocky Mountain Nat Watermedia Exhib, Golden, Colo, 75; Mountain Oyster Club Art Show; Western Heritage Art Fair, Littleton. *Teaching:* Instr art, Jefferson Co Schs, Lakewood, Colo, 68- & Red Rocks Community Col, Denver, 71-73. *Bibliog:* Feature article in Southwest Art Mag, 9/78 & 9/89; Western Art Dig, 11-12/86; Art-Talk, 8-9/89. *Media:* Oil. *Publ:* Illusr, Colorado Homes & Lifestyles, winter 87. *Dealer:* Saks Gallery Denver CO; Zaplin-Lampert Gallery Santa Fe NM. *Mailing Add:* 14332 N Wesley Cr Lakewood CO 80228

KNECHT, JOHN
FILMMAKER, VIDEO ARTIST
b Iron Ridge, Wis, Mar 5, 47. *Study:* Univ Wis, Oshkosh, BS, 72; Idaho State Univ, MFA, 74. *Work:* Queens Mus, New York. *Exhib:* Solo shows, Millennium, 79, Collective for Living Cinema, 80, Mus Mod Art, New York, 85, Alternative Mus, New York, 92; Frames, Hunter Gallery, New York, 80; Film as Installation, Clocktower Gallery, New York, 80; Int Forum des Jungen Films, Berlin, WGer, 81; Edinburgh Film Fest, Edinburgh, Scotland, 81 & 84; 2nd Video Biennial, Mus Mod Art, 88; and others. *Pos:* Chair, art & art hist, Colgate Univ, 91- *Teaching:* Asst prof, Univ Okla Sch Art, 74-79; assoc prof, Colgate Univ Dept of Art & Art Hist, 81-; vis lectr, Brown Univ, spring 81. *Awards:* Lightworks Grant, 83; New York Found for the Arts

Video Fel, 89; New Forms Fel Rockefeller & Nat Endowment Arts, 90. *Bibliog:* Mick Eaton (auth), Continuing the adventures of Adrian Block, Film Bulletin, London, 2/83; Lucy R Lippard (auth), A Different War, Real Comet Press; Robert Doyle (auth), Artists of Conscience, John Knecht: Iron. *Media:* Film, Video. *Publ:* Friction/non-friction cinematograph, winter 91; Muses & fuses: Trama in the Technosphere, artists space catalogue on the w ork of Les LeVeque. *Mailing Add:* Box 83 Hamilton NY 13346

KNIEF, HELEN (JANET) JEANETTE
PAINTER
b Brooklyn, NY, July 16, 07. *Study:* Art Students League, with Bridgeman, l'Olinsky & S Dickinson; Brooklyn Mus Art Sch, with Victor Candell, David Stone Martin; Nat Acad Sch, with Robert Phillip; Phoenix Sch Design; Pratt Inst. *Work:* Work in over 200 pvt collections. *Comn:* Portrait, pres Flushing Savings Bank, NY, 54; portrait, police comnr, Nassau Co Police Dept, 55; portrait, seven grandchildren, comn by Mrs John Ryan, Baldwin, NY, 64-74; portrait, Phillip Chasin, shown in his honor at Waldorf Astoria Dinner, 74; portrait, Mr B C Cobb, comn by Mrs Carl Miller, New York, 74; and many others. *Exhib:* Brooklyn Mus, NY, 57; Long Beach Arts Asn, NY, 69-70; Country Art Gallery, 70-91; Nat Acad Gallery, New York, 70-71; Lever House, Union Carbide, NY, 71-72; Garden City Galleries, Kans, 75; one-man show, Fitzgerald Gallery, Westhampton Beach, 92; and others. *Teaching:* Pvt adult classes, 68-72. *Awards:* Numerous, including First Prize, Kathy, Malverne Artists Long Island, 68; First Prize, Walled Garden & Second Prize, The Garden, Long Beach Art Asn, 70; and numerous others. *Bibliog:* Catharine L Wolfe (auth), Jeanne Paris, Long Island Press, 71. *Mem:* Catharine Lorillard Wolfe Art Club; Malverne Artist Long Island; Art League Nassau Co; Long Beach Art Asn (bd dirs). *Media:* Oil, Pastel. *Publ:* Article, Long Island Press, 58; article, Long Island New Owl, 58-75; article, Malverne Herald, 68; article, Long Island Entertainer; Nassau Star & Independent, 71. *Mailing Add:* 20 Skyview Place Melville NY 11474

KNIFFIN, RALPH GUS
GRAPHIC ARTIST
b San Carlos Reservation, Ariz, Nov 21, 46. *Study:* Inst Am Indian Art, Santa Fe, NMex, dipl; study with Allan Houser, Charles Loloma, Otellie Loloma & Fritz Scholder. *Work:* Gila Co Court House, Globe, Ariz; Sentry Ctr, Scottsdale, Ariz; San Carlos Indian Hosp, Ariz; Gallo Winery, Modesto, Calif; United Bank, Tempe & Phoenix, Ariz. *Exhib:* All Indian Art Show, Gallery La Luz, Alamagordo, NMex, 74; Scottsdale Nat Indian Art Exhib, Scottsdale, Ariz, 75 & 76; Nat Indian Art Show, Heard Mus, Phoenix, Ariz, 76; Invitational in Drawing, Heard Mus, Phoenix, Ariz, 77. *Awards:* Best of Show, Gallery La Luz, Alamagordo, NMex, 74; First Place, Scottsdale Nat Art Exhib, Ariz, 76; First Place Spec in Graphics, Heard Mus, Phoenix, Ariz, 76. *Bibliog:* Articles in Carefree Enterprise, 74 & Phoenix Cent News, 75; Maggie Wilson (auth), New Artist Stunned by Limelight Status, Ariz Repub, 76. *Media:* Pen & Ink. *Mailing Add:* c/o Gallery 3 3819 N Third St Phoenix AZ 85012

KNIGHT, CHRISTOPHER ALLEN
CRITIC, ADMINISTRATOR
b Westfield, Mass, Nov 23, 50. *Study:* Hartwick Col, NY, with Prof Bruce Kurtz, BA, 72; State Univ NY, Binghamton, with Dr Albert Boime, MA, 76. *Collections Arranged:* The Modern Chair (cataloged), Origins & Evolution, 1840-1940, 77; The Angel of Mercy (cataloged), Eleanor Antin Installation, 77. *Pos:* Cur, La Jolla Mus Contemp Art, Calif, 76-79; asst pub info dir, Los Angeles Co Mus Art, Calif, 79-80; art critic, Los Angeles Herald Examiner, 80-89 & Los Angeles Times, 89- *Teaching:* Vis lectr renaissance & mod art, State Univ NY at Binghamton, 76; vis instr mod art, Hartwick Col, Oneonta, NY, 76; vis instr, Claremont Grad Sch, Claremont, Calif, 82. *Awards:* Nat Endowment Arts Fel, 73-74 & 84; Art World Award, Manufacturers Hanover Trust, 82, 84, 86, 87 & 91. *Mem:* Col Art Asn; Int Asn Art Critics. *Res:* Early 20th century concepts of American modernism; post-1960 American art and media. *Publ:* auth, The Elusive Image: Eight Artists, Michael C McMillen, Walker Art Ctr, 79; The Word Made Flesh: L A Pop Revisited, In: Art in Los Angeles: 17 Artists in the Sixties, Los Angeles Co Mus Art, 81; On native ground: US modern, Art in Am, 10/83; The Persistant Observer, In: 25 Years of Space Photography, W W Norton & Co, 85; Panofsky's Hat, In: The Barry Lowen Collection, Los Angeles Mus Contemporary Art, 86. *Mailing Add:* 6851 Iris Circle Los Angeles CA 90068

KNIGHT, JACOB JASKOVIAK
PAINTER, ILLUSTRATOR
b Worcester, Mass, Feb 26, 38. *Study:* Self-taught. *Work:* West Point Pepperell, New York; General Electric Co; Rockefeller Collection, New York; Hugh Heffner Collection; Exxon, New York. *Comn:* Historical paintings (murals), Salem Cross Inn, West Brookfield Mass, 83, Town of Spencer, Mass 87 & Town of Palmer, Mass, 90; James Beard Regional American Calendar, Workman, 83; hist mural, Quaboag Plantation, 91. *Exhib:* One-man shows, Art Dir Club, New York, 74, Main St Gallery, Nantucket, Mass, 75, Hubris Galley, New York, 78, Adam L Gimbel Gallery, New York, 83 & Saks 5th Ave, New York, 83-84. *Bibliog:* Fred Karden (auth), The artist as his own man, Worcester Telegram & Gazette, Mass, 69; Leslie Powell (auth), Art: Primative, Villager, Greenwich Village, 70; Valerie Brooks (auth), Love & magic: The naive style in illustrations, Print Mag, 74. *Media:* Oil and Acrylic. *Publ:* Illusr, What's gone right with the United Nations, Vista, UN Mag, 73; illusr, All things bright and beautiful, McCalls, 74; illusr, We must decide which species will go on forever, Smithsonian, 76; illusr, A very quiet horror, Playboy, 77. *Mailing Add:* c/o Brookfield Gallery of Fine Arts 39 Upper River St Brookfield MA 01506-0417

KNIGHT, JOHN
CONCEPTUAL ARTIST
b Los Angeles, Calif, Mar 26, 45. *Study:* Univ Calif, Los Angeles, BA, 70; Univ Calif, Irvine, MFA, 73. *Work:* Stedelijk Stadtisches Van Afbemuseum, Eindhoven, NL; Art Inst Chicago. *Exhib:* Documenta 5, 72 & Documenta 7, 82, Fredericiuvm Kunsthalle, Kassel, WGer; Attitudes 72-Southern Calif, Pasadena Mus Art, 72; Southland Video Anthology, Long Beach Mus Art, Calif, 75; 74th American Exhib, Art Inst Chicago, Ill, 82. *Teaching:* Instr studio, Nova Scotia Col Art & Design, formerly, Otis Art Inst, Los Angeles, 76-77; instr studio, Southern Calif Inst Archit, 76- *Mailing Add:* c/o Marian Goodman Gallery 24 Fifth Ave New York NY 10011

KNIGHT, TOM (THOMAS LINCOLN), JR
EDUCATOR, PHOTOGRAPHER
b Oakland, Calif, June 17, 25. *Study:* Humboldt State Univ, BA, 50, MA(art educ), 56. *Exhib:* Faculty Shows, Humboldt State Univ, 56-88; US Arts Comn Photog Exhibs, Washington, DC, 68 & 70; one man shows, Univ Nev, Reno, 68, 69 & 70, Col of the Redwoods Gallery, Eureka, Calif, 79 & Micheocan State Mus, Morelia, Mex, 79, Univ Glasgow Art Mus, Scotland, 82, Reese Bullen Gallery, Humboldt State Univ, 88; Refocus 70, Univ Southern Calif, 70; two-man show, Teatro Juarez, Guanajuato, Mex, 81; Third Annual Invitational Exhib, Humboldt Cult Ctr, Eureka, Calif, 83; Rufino Tamayo Gallery, Nat Mus Art, Mex, 84; Micheocan State Mus, Morelia, Mex, 90; group exhib, Humboldt State Univ Faculty, Glasgow Sch Art, 90. *Teaching:* Prof photog & art, Humboldt State Univ, Calif, 56-; vis prof photog, Univ Nev, Reno, summers 68 & 69, Grand Valley State Col, summer 71; photog workshop, Glasgow Sch Art, Scotland, 86 & 89. *Awards:* Meritorious Teaching Award (art), Humboldt State Univ, 87. *Publ:* Photog, Anza's bones in Arizona, J West, Vol VII, No 3; photog (back cover), Imogene Cunningham & Margery Mann's Imogene Cunningham-Photographs, Univ Wash, 70; photogr, British Photogr J, 76; photogr, Photo Metro, 83; Retrospective catalog, Portrait of Elmer Bichoff, Painter, San Francisco, 90. *Mailing Add:* 76 California Ave Arcata CA 95521

KNIGIN, MICHAEL JAY
PAINTER, PRINTMAKER
b Brooklyn, NY, Dec 9, 42. *Study:* Tyler Sch Art, BFA. *Work:* Whitney Mus Art, New York; Nat Collection Fine Arts, Washington, DC; Copper Hewitt Mus, NY; Albright-Knox Art Gallery, Buffalo; Portland Mus Fine Arts, Ore; US Dept State, Washington, DC; Mus Modern Art, Mexico City; Taiwan Mus; Citibank, Chicago & New York; NASA Art Collection. *Exhib:* Smithsonian Inst, Washington, DC, 69; Albright-Knox Art Gallery, 70; Mus Mod Art Lending Serv, New York, 71; Recent Acquisitions, Whitney Mus Am Art, New York, 71; Sch Worcester Art Mus, Mass, 72; Israel Mus, Jerusalem, 76; Taiwan Mus, 77; Mus Mod Art, New York, 78; Nat Soc Illusr Show, 78-79; US Dept of State, Washington, DC, 79; Foreign Corresp Club, Tokyo, 79; Brooklyn Mus, 83; Guild Hall Mus, East Hampton, NY, 90; NASA Gallery, Cape Kennedy, Fla; and many exhibs both US & abroad. *Teaching:* Prof, Pratt Inst, currently. *Awards:* Ford Found Grant, Tamarind Lithography Workshop, 64; NASA Art Team, 89-90. *Bibliog:* Benjamin Forgey (auth), article, Washington Star, 12/10/78; Elizabeth Stevens (auth), article, Baltimore Sun, 1/21/79; Jane Rees (auth), article, Asahi Evening News, Japan, 10/17/79. *Mem:* Soc Am Graphic Artists; Jimmy Ernst Artists Alliance. *Media:* All; Lithography. *Publ:* Coauth, The Technique of Fine Art Lithography, 70; auth, Local Choice, Pratt Graphics Ctr, 72; The Contemporary Lithographic Workshop Around the World, Van Nostrand, Mexico City News, 85. *Mailing Add:* PO Box 95 Wainscott NY 11975

KNIPPERS, EDWARD
PAINTER, PRINTMAKER
b Oklahoma City, Okla, Sept 7, 46. *Study:* Pa Acad Fine Arts, 67; Sorbonne, Paris, 68; Asbury Col, Wilmore, Ky, BA, 69; Int Summer Acad Fine Arts, Salzburg, Austria, with Zao Wou-ki, 70, with Otto Elgau & Wolfgang Zeiszner, 76; Univ Tenn, Knoxville, MFA, 73; S W Hayter's Atelier 17, Paris, fel, 80. *Work:* Int Summer Acad Fine Arts, Salzburg, Austria; Tenn Fine Arts Ctr, Cheekwood, Nashville; Vanderbilt Univ, Nashville; Billy Graham Mus, Wheaton, Ill; Univ Okla Mus Art, Norman. *Exhib:* Solo exhibs, Tenn Fine Arts Ctr, Cheekwood, Nashville, 74, Patmos Gallery, Toronto, 75, Univ Ky, Lexington, 82, Foxhall Gallery, Washington, DC, 82 & 86, & Wheaton Col, Ill, 83 & 86, Va Mus Fine Arts, 86-87; J B Speed Mus, Louisville, Ky, 77; Fresh Paint Traveling Exhib, 77-79; Los Angeles Co Mus, 85-86; New Expressionism, SE Ctr Contemp Art, Winston-Salem, NC, 87; Univ Okla, Norman, Okla, 90; Roanoke Mus Fine Arts, Va, 90; Greenbelt Invitational, Castle Ashby, Northhampton, Eng, 92. *Pos:* Co-ed, Christians in Visual Arts Newslett, 80- *Awards:* Salzburg Prize, Int Summer Acad Fine Arts, Austria, 76; Fel Award, Va Mus Fine Arts, Richmond, 87-88; Va Prize for painting, Va Comn Arts, hon mention, 89 & 90. *Bibliog:* Howard N Fox (auth), Setting the stage, Los Angeles Co Mus Art catalog, 85; Timothy Verdon (auth), Violence & Faith in Art of Edward Knippers, Univ Okla Mus Art; Frederick R Brandt (auth), Spiritual Impact-The Paintings of Edward Knippers, Va Mus Fine Arts. *Mem:* Christians Visual Arts (bd dirs, 80-). *Media:* Oil; Intaglio, block prints. *Mailing Add:* 2408 Washington Blvd Arlington VA 22201

KNIPSCHER, GERARD ALLEN
PAINTER, GRAPHIC ARTIST
b New York, NY, July 9, 35. *Study:* Calif Col Arts & Crafts, BFA (with hon); Acad Art, San Francisco; Sch Fine Art, San Francisco; Sch Visual Arts, New York; also with Richard Diebenkorn. *Work:* Calif Col Arts & Crafts, Oakland, Calif; NACAL Operation Palette, US Navy Combat Art Collection, DC; M H De Young Mem Mus, San Francisco. *Comn:* Launch US second moon shot, Apollo XII, Cape Kennedy, Fla, comn by US Naval Combat Art, 69; US Navy

Amphibious Exercise Operation Exotic Dancer, Onslow Beach, NC, 74; portrait & drawings of Lt Al Cisnernos, first pilot of Mex-Am heritage to fly with US Navy Blue Angels flight demonstration team, Pensacola, Fla, 75; portraits Mario, Gala & Ronnie Broeders, comn by Mr Mario Broeders, Buenos Aires, Arg, 75. *Exhib:* Nat Acad Design Ann Exhib, New York, 67 & 71; 60th Ann Exhib Allied Artists Am, Inc, New York, 73; Nat Arts Club Open Oil Exhib, New York, 75; Am Artists Prof League, Lever House, NY, 75; Am Fortnight Exhib, Hong Kong, 75. *Pos:* Chmn art comt, Salmagundi Club, currently. *Teaching:* Instr figure painting, Salmagundi Club, currently. *Awards:* Allied Artists Am Award, 73; Macown Tuttle Mem Prize, Salmagundi Club, 74; Sara Boal Mem Award, Am Artists Prof League, Grand Nat Exhib, 79. *Mem:* Salmagundi Club; Artists Fellowship (vpres, 73-75); Navy League US; Hudson Valley Art Asn; Am Artists Prof League. *Media:* Oil, Graphite Pencil. *Mailing Add:* P O Box 418 Highland Mills NY 10930

KNIPSCHILD, ROBERT
PAINTER
b Freeport, Ill, Aug 17, 27. *Study:* Univ Wis, BA, 49; Cranbrook Acad Art, MFA, 51. *Work:* Pa Acad Fine Arts, Philadelphia; Baltimore Mus Art, Md; Phillips Gallery & Hirshhorn Mus, Washington, DC; Cranbrook Mus, Bloomfield Hills, Mich. *Exhib:* American Painting Today, Metrop Mus Art, New York, 51; Pa Acad Fine Arts Ann, 51; Carnegie Inst Int, Pittsburgh, 52; Container Corp Am, 63; 50 Artists from 50 States, Am Fedn Arts, 65. *Teaching:* Vis artist, Am Univ, 52; instr painting, Univ Conn, 54-56; asst prof, Univ Wis-Madison, 56-60; assoc prof, Univ Iowa, 60-66; prof painting, Univ Cincinnati, 66-90, prof emer, 90- *Awards:* Purchase Awards, Libr Cong, 51, Pa Acad Fine Arts, 51 & Am Fedn Arts, 63. *Bibliog:* Patricia Boyd (auth), Exhibition of Robert Knipschild, Christian Sci Monitor, 11/3/69. *Mem:* Mid Am Col Art Asn; Nat Asn Schs Art. *Media:* Oil. *Dealer:* Piedmont Gallery W Riverside Dr Augusta KY 41002; Birckhead Gallery 342 W Fourth St Cincinnati OH 45202. *Mailing Add:* 1159 Hillcrest Rd Cincinnati OH 45224

KNOBLER, LOIS JEAN
SCULPTOR, PAINTER
b New York, NY, Feb 2, 29. *Study:* Syracuse Univ Col Fine Arts, BFA; Fla State Univ, MA. *Work:* Worcester Mus, Mass; Fla State Univ Mus; St Lawrence Univ, NY. *Exhib:* Art for US Embassies, Inst Contemp Art, Boston, 66; St Lawrence Univ Acquisition Exhib, NY, 74; William Benton Mus, Univ Conn, Storrs, 75; two-person show, Hillyer Gallery, Smith Col, Northampton, Mass, 76; solo exhib, Atrium Gallery, Univ Conn, Storrs, 83; American Traditions in Watercolor, Worcester Art Mus, Worcester, Mass, 87; Topographies, Moore Col Art, Philadelphia, Pa, 89. *Awards:* Greater Hartford Civic Arts Festival Award, 72. *Bibliog:* Joyce Brodsky (auth), catalog essay, Univ Conn, 83; Zelanski & Fisher (coauth), Shaping Space, Holt, Rinehart & Winston, 86; American Traditions in Watercolor: The Worcester Art Mus Collection, Abbeville Press, 87. *Media:* Miscellaneous Media. *Mailing Add:* 2041 Wallace St Philadelphia PA 19130

KNOBLER, NATHAN
SCULPTOR, EDUCATOR
b Brooklyn, NY, Mar 13, 26. *Study:* Newark Sch Fine & Indust Art; Ohio State Univ; Syracuse Univ, BFA, 50; Fla State Univ, MA, 51. *Work:* US Info Agency; Smith Col Mus, Northampton, Mass; Munson-Williams-Proctor Mus, Utica, NY; Fla State Univ; Slater Mus, Norwich, Conn. *Comn:* Silver Award Sculpture, Int Silver Co, Meriden, Conn; Silver Award Sculpture, G Fox & Co, Hartford, Conn. *Exhib:* Pa Acad Fine Arts Nat Print Show, Philadelphia; Brooklyn Mus Nat Print Show, NY; Drawing Soc Traveling Nat; Selection 1964, Inst Contemp Art, Boston; Surreal Images, De Cordova Mus, Lincoln, Mass, Smith Col & Allentown Mus, Pa. *Teaching:* Prof art, Univ Arts, Philadelphia, Pa, currently. *Mem:* Col Art Asn Am. *Media:* Stone, Bronze; Wood. *Res:* Art appreciation and criticism; drawing perception. *Publ:* Auth, The Visual Dialogue, rev ed 81; El Dialogo Visual, 70, rev ed, 80. *Mailing Add:* 2041 Wallace St Philadelphia PA 19130

KNODE, MARILU
CURATOR, ADMINISTRATOR
b Calgary, Alberta, Can, Aug 4, 59; US citizen. *Study:* Univ Grenoble, France, 81-82; Univ Kans, Lawrence, BA(art hist), 81; City Col New York, MA(mus studies), 84. *Collections Arranged:* Tony Craig Sculpture (mid-career retrospective; with Paul Schimmel), 90; Different Stories (selections from permanent collection), 91; Mapping Histories (group show with Anne Ayres, auth, catalog), 91-92; Personal Inventory, Ellen Birrell & Nick Vaughn (auth, catalog). *Pos:* Sr cataloger, Mus Mod Art, New York, 84-88; asst cur, Newport Harbor Art Mus, Calif, 89-91, assoc cur, 91-92. *Mem:* Am Asn Mus; Western Mus Conf. *Publ:* Contrib, Tony Cragg Sculpture: 1975-1990, 90, auth, Third Newport Biennial: Mapping Histories, 91, Sarah Seager, 93, Newport; auth, Interview with Nayland Blake, J Contemp Art, Newport, 92; and others. *Mailing Add:* 2511 E 17th St Long Beach CA 90804

KNOEBEL, DAVID JON
SCULPTOR
b Elysburg, Pa, July 19, 49. *Study:* Yale Univ, with William Bailey, BA, 72; Skowhegan Sch, with William Stankiewicz, 72; also with George Sugarman, 79-82. *Work:* Indianapolis Mus Art. *Exhib:* Nat Sculpture Competition, Univ SC, Columbia, 78; Nat Small Works Competition, NY Univ, 79; Nat Sculpture Show, Md Inst Art, Baltimore, 80; Pool Proj, Artist's Space, New York, 80; Painting & Sculpture Today, Indianapolis Mus Art, 80; one-man show, Baruch Col, State Univ NY, 82; Gold Show, Mus Mod Art, New York, 82; Smart Art, Harvard Univ, 85; Primo Piano, Rome, Italy, 86. *Teaching:* Vis artist, Marymount Int Sch, Rome, Italy, 85. *Bibliog:* Kay Larson (auth), Voice choices, Village Voice, 1/28/80; Tiffany Bell (auth), article, Arts Mag, 3/80; Helen Harrison (auth), Four forms of light, New York Times, 6/13/82. *Media:* Misc Media, Wood. *Publ:* Auth, Coal tipples: Photographs by the Bechers, Shamokin News Item, Pa, 12/20/75; contribr catalog statement, Painting & Sculpture Today, Indianapolis Mus, 80; auth catalog statement, Light, Islip Art Mus, 82. *Mailing Add:* RD 1 Box 317 Elysburg PA 17824

KNOLL, ISABEL A GIAMPIETRO See Giampietro, Isabel (Isabel A Giampietro Knoll)

KNOPF, DONNA BRAVERMAN See Braverman, Donna (Donna Braverman Knopf)

KNOPP, HANS-GEORG
DIRECTOR
b Jan 13, 45; Ger citizen. *Study:* Tubingen, Baccalaureat, 65; Univ Vienna & Univ Marburg, Hon Dr Philos, 73. *Pos:* Prog dir, Bombay 75-80, dir, Colombo, 80-81, head language dept, Jakarta, 82-85, dir, Singapore, 85-86, language dept, Munich, 87-91, dir, Chicago, 91- , Goethe Institut. *Mem:* Ger Studies Asn; Chicago Coun For Relations (bd mem, 92). *Mailing Add:* Goethe Institute Chicago 401 N Michigan Ave Chicago IL 60611

KNORR, JEANNE BOARDMAN
PAINTER, EDUCATOR
b Chambersburg, Pa. *Study:* Indiana Univ Pa, BS; Columbia Univ Teachers Col, MA; Art Students League, scholar; Ohio State Univ, PhD(painting). *Work:* Dallas Theol Sem, Tex; Lakeview Ctr Arts, Peoria, Ill; Ohio State Univ Mus Collections, Columbus; First & Merchants Bank Collection, Richmond, Va; Norfolk State Univ, Va. *Comn:* Fabric wall hanging, St Paul's Episcopal Cathedral, Peoria, 69; fabric wall, Computer Ctr, Norfolk & Western Railroad, Roanoke, Va, 78; and many fabric wall hangings in pvt collections in Ill, NY & Va. *Exhib:* one-man exhibs, Robinson House, Va Mus, Richmond, 72, Peninsula Art Asn, 80; Crafts Invitational, Bank of Va, Norfolk, 77; Artists Invitational, Hermitage Found, Norfolk, Va, 77; Fiber Invitational, Portsmouth Art Ctr, Va, 81; and others, 82-88; Tidewater Artists Mems exhib, Norfolk, Va, 90-92. *Teaching:* Assoc prof art, Norfolk State Col, 69-86. *Awards:* Artist of Distinction in crafts, 70 & in sculpture, 71, Va Mus; Third & Fourth Ann Crafts Fabric Award, Norfolk, Va, 73 & 74. *Bibliog:* Dona Meilach (auth), Creative stitchery, 8/71 & Soft sculpture, 74, Craft Horizon Mag; Cornelia Justice (auth), rev of exhibs at Studio Gallery, 4/66; Elyse & Mike Sommer (auth), A new look at crochet, 75; and others. *Mem:* Am Craftsmen Coun; Tidewater Artists Asn. *Media:* All media. *Publ:* Contribr, Directions, Ill Art Educ Asn, 70. *Mailing Add:* 730 Maury Ave Norfolk VA 23517

KNOTT, DEE D
PAINTER, ILLUSTRATOR
b Flint, Mich, May 6, 43. *Study:* Mich State Univ, 61-62; Kendall Sch Design, 62-63. *Work:* Nat Watercolor Soc First Half Century Collection, Palos Verdes, Calif; Utah State Univ Arts Ctr, Provo; Marriott Corp, Mich, 90; Ferris State Univ, Big Rapids, Mich; Mich Artists Collection, Battle Creek Art Mus; Isuzu Corp Hq, Mich, 90. *Comn:* Paintings, Gen Motors, Detroit, 80, Nat 4-H Bldg, Washington, DC, 86, Mich Spec Olympics, Detroit, 86 & Cleo Laine Album Cover, Milton Keynes, Eng, 88; 5 paintings for the Premier of China, comn by Lee Iacocca, Detroit, 88. *Exhib:* 37th Nat Exhib, Butler Inst Am Art, Youngstown, Ohio, 78; Ga Watercolor Soc, Mus Arts Sci, Macon, Ga, 83; Retrospective/Knott, Detroit Inst Arts, 84; RI-Japan Exhib, Kawakami, Tokyo, Japan, 85; Watercolor USA, Springfield Art Mus, Mich, 85; Adirondacks Nat Exhib Am Watercolors, Old Forge, NY, 90. *Awards:* Art League of Chicago Award, Midwest Watercolor Soc, 85; Huntington Bronze Medal, Catherine Lorillard Wolfe Nat Exhib, 86; Todah Moshe Award, Adirondack Nat Exhib Am Watercolors, 88. *Bibliog:* Gregory J Galligan (auth), Lilies, Rochester Times, 88; Sylvia Krissoff (auth), The Knott touch, Grand Rapids Press, 88; Corinne Abatt (auth), Dee Knott sees a beautiful gentle world, Birmingham Essentric, 88. *Mem:* Am Watercolor Soc; Nat Watercolor Soc; Rocky Mountain Nat Watermedia Soc; Catherine Wolfe Art Club Soc; Am Soc Marine Artists. *Media:* Transparent watercolor. *Publ:* auth, Capturing the moment, Artist Mag, 85; illus, Christmas Journey, Am Libr Soc Asn, Mich, 90; Cleo Laines Word Tour Publ, 90. *Dealer:* Hobe Sound Galleries PO Box 1840 Hobe Sound FL 33455. *Mailing Add:* 11004 Hartland Rd Fenton MI 48430-2576

KNOWLES, ALISON
PERFORMANCE ARTIST, PRINTMAKER
b New York, NY, Apr 29, 33. *Study:* Middlebury Col, Vt, 52-54; Pratt Inst, 54-57, Hon BFA; Manhattan Sch of Printing, 62. *Work:* Mus of Mod Art Bk Collection, New York; Oakland Mus, Calif; Jean Brown Archives, Tyringham, Mass. *Comn:* The Identical Lunch (two self-portraits), comn by Alberto Zopellari, 77; Leone D'oro (silkscreen ed), comn by Francesco Conz, 78. *Exhib:* The Big Book, Mus of Contemp Art, Chicago, 67; The Identical Lunch, Galerie Inge Baecker, Bochum, Ger, 73; Collections from the Full Moon, Galerie Rene Block, Berlin, De Appel, Amsterdam, 74; SumTime, Everson Mus, Syracuse, NY, 74; 03 23 03, Mus of Fine Art, Montreal, Can, 77; Walker Art Ctr performance, exhib, Univ Minn, 80; one-man shows, The Book of Bean, Franklin Furnace, NY, 82, A Finger Book, Lighthouse Blind, NY, 85-86, Ruth & Marvin Sackner Archive, Miami Beach, Fla, 86, Unique Cloth & Paper Works, Nordyllands Kunstmuseum, Aalborg, Denmark, Finger Book 2 & Palimpsest Prints, 87-88, Seven Indian Moons, 90, Emily Harvey Gallery, NY; and others. *Teaching:* Dir graphics lab, Calif Inst of the Arts, Valencia, 70-72. *Awards:* Guggenheim Fel, 68; Nat Endowment Arts, 81 & 85; Travel Grant, Deutscher Acad, Ger, 83; Teaching Residency, Sommerakademie für Bildende Kunst, Salzburg. *Bibliog:* William Wilson

(auth), The Big Book, Art in Am, 7-8/68; Charlie Morrow (auth), Living music, Soho Weekly News, 74; Tom Johnson (auth), Shoes, shoestrings & Gertrude Stein, Village Voice, 78. *Mem:* Printed Ed; The Performance Workshop. *Media:* Serigraphy, Silkscreen. *Publ:* Auth, More By Alison Knowles, unpublished ed, 76; Gem Duck, Pari & Dispari, 78; Natural Assemblages and the True Crow, Visual Studies Workshop Press, Rochester, NY, 80; A Bean Concordance, Printed Eds, 83; coauth (with George Brecht), The Red, The Green, The Yellow, The Black and The White, Brussels Ed, Lebeer-Hossman, 83. *Mailing Add:* 122 Spring St New York NY 10012

KNOWLES, ELIZABETH
SCULPTOR
b St Louis, Mo, 58. *Study:* Pomona Col, Claremont, Calif, BA, 81; Sch Art Inst Chicago, MFA, 83. *Exhib:* Charting the Inner Terrain, Pratt Inst, Brooklyn, NY, 91; December Selections, Orgn Independent Artists, New York, 91; Medium Matters, Citicorp, New York, 91; One person show, C&A Gallery, New York, 91; Sculpture 91, Highland Park, Rochester, NY, 91; and many others. *Awards:* Artist's Space Grant, 90; Lancaster Group Award, NY, 91; Va Ctr Creative Arts Fel, Sweet Briar, Va, 92; and others. *Bibliog:* Mike Krippendorf, rev, The New Art Examiner, 2/84; Margaret Moorman (auth), Multitude of styles at Queens Mus show, New York Newsday, 1/8/88; Phyllis Braff (auth), Lines Redefining Space, NY Times, 4/19/89; Tom Patterson (auth), 3 Sculptors Take Risks, Winston-Salem J, 3/18/90; Sherrye Lohn (auth), Form Overtakes Function, St Louis Post- Dispatch, 5/13/90. *Media:* Mixed Media. *Publ:* Tim Patterson (auth), Three sculptors take risks and produce a curious and challenging exhibitin, Winston-Salem J, 3/18/90; Chris Redd (auth), Upstairs, downstairs, Triad Style, 3/21/90; Sherrye Cohn (auth), Craft as art: form overtakes function, St Louis Post Dispatch, 5/13/90; Margo Shermeta (auth), Meeting ground (catalogue essay), Forum, St Louis, 90; Helen Harrison (auth), A widely varied response to the Notion of Motion, NY Times, 10/28/90. *Mailing Add:* 259 W 85th St No 4 New York NY 10024

KNOWLES, RICHARD H
PAINTER, EDUCATOR
b Evanston, Ill, June 29, 34. *Study:* Grinnell Col; Northwestern Univ, Evanston, BA, 56; Ind Univ, MA, 61, studied with James McGarrell, Leon Golub. *Work:* Ind Univ, Bloomington; Ark State Univ; State of Tenn Collection, Reece Mus, Nashville; Brooks Mem Mus Art, Memphis, Tenn. *Exhib:* Solo show, Loyola U, New Orleans, 87; Six Americans, Ark Art Ctr, Little Rock, 64; 50 States Exhib & Tour, Rockford Art Asn & Am Fedn Arts, 65-67; 40 Tenn Artists Exhib & Tour, 68-69; Am Painters & Sculptors, Colgate Univ, 75; Edinburgh Arts Festival, Scotland, 80; Two-person show, Memphis Ctr Contemp Art, 88. *Pos:* Pres, Mid-Am Col Art Assoc, 86, 88; Publ, Untitled (art jour), currently. *Teaching:* Asst prof art, Univ Ark, 61-65; prof art, Memphis State Univ, 66- *Awards:* Best Entry for Ark Artist, Delta Ann, 61 & 62; Painting Prize, Mid-South Exhib, 72. *Media:* Acrylic, Oil. *Mailing Add:* Dept Art Memphis State Univ Memphis TN 38152

KNOWLES, SUSAN WILLIAMS
CURATOR, CRITIC
b Washington, DC, Sept 1, 52. *Study:* Vanderbilt Univ, BA, 74, MA, 86; Peabody Col, MLS, 75. *Collections Arranged:* The American Scene: 1900-1950 Traveling Print Show (auth, catalog), 83; A Decade of British & American Screenprints Traveling Show (auth, catalog), 85; A C Webb: The Skyscraper Drawings Architectural Perspectives (auth, catalog), 86; Spirit & Form: William Edmondson & Puryear Mims, 88; The Best Folk of Nashville, 88; Small Sculpture & Works on Paper from Nashville Collections, 89; Hatch Show Print Originals, 89; Nashville Collects Red, 90. *Pos:* Registrar & art librn, Fine Arts Ctr, Cheekwood, Tenn, 81-85, cur collections, 85-87; visual arts coordr, Metro Nashville Arts Comn, Tenn, 87-92; cur, Tenn Exhib, Nat Mus Women Arts, 92-94. *Teaching:* 20th century art hist, O'More Col Design, 92. *Mem:* Col Art Asn; Am Asn Mus. *Publ:* Revs, New Art Examiner, 85-92; auth, Signatures Section: Center Stage Mag, 87-88; Living Artists: Four Installations, Knoxville Mus Art, 90; Pinkney Herbert (exhib catalog), Univ Little Rock, Ark; monthly art column, Nashville Scene, 91-92. *Mailing Add:* 758 Roycroft Pl Nashville TN 37203

KNOWLTON, DANIEL GIBSON
RESTORER, CONSERVATOR
b Washington, DC, Nov 14, 22. *Study:* With Marian U M Lane, Washington, DC; Boston Arts & Crafts, grad. *Work:* Univ Chicago Libr; Brown Univ Libr, Providence, RI; Dumbarton Oaks Libr, Washington, DC; Harvard Univ Libr; Cornell Univ Libr; Ann Mary Brown Mem Libr, Providence, RI. *Comn:* Epistle (gold & leather binding), Grace Church, Providence, 56; The Anguish of the Jews (gold & leather binding), comn by Ciro Scotti, Vatican Libr, 68. *Exhib:* Hand bookbinding exhibs, Corcoran Gallery Art, 58; one-man shows, Bristol Hist Soc RI, 69, RI Sch Design, 71 & 75 & Ctr Bk Arts, New York, 75; Rockefeller Libr, Brown Univ, 81 & 91; Providence Hist Soc, 81 & 91; and others. *Pos:* Bookbinder, Brown Univ, 56-; owner & bookbinder, Daniel G Knowlton Co, Longfield Studio, Bristol, RI, 74-92. *Teaching:* Instr bookbinding, Daniel G Knowlton Co Longfield Studio Home Bindery, 74-92. *Bibliog:* Yankee Damon (auth), article in Yankee Mag, 62; Ann Banks (auth), article in Brown Alumni Monthly, 71; Interview, Educational TV 36, Providence, RI, 74 & TV News WJAR-TV, 90. *Mem:* Miniature Painters, Sculptors & Gravers Soc, Washington, DC; Guild Book Workers, New York; Ctr Book Arts, New York. *Media:* Bookbinding. *Mailing Add:* 1202 Hope St Bristol RI 02809

KNOWLTON, GRACE FARRAR
SCULPTOR, PHOTOGRAPHER
b Buffalo, NY, Mar 15, 32. *Study:* Smith Col, BA(art), 54; Columbia Univ Teachers Col, MA(art educ), 81. *Work:* Metrop Mus Art, New York; Newark Mus, NJ; Corcoran Gallery Art; Houston Mus Fine Arts; Victoria & Albert Mus, London, Eng. *Comn:* Pottery prototypes for Appalachian Workshops, Am Fedn Arts, New York, 71. *Exhib:* One-man shows, Henri Gallery, Washington, DC, 73, Razor Gallery, New York, 74, Parsons-Dreyfuss Gallery, New York, 79, Aaron Berman Gallery, 81, Susan Harder Gallery, 83, Twining Gallery, 85-86 & 87, Witkin Gallery, 86 & 87, Bill Bace Gallery, 89, Smith Col Mus Art, Mass, 92 & M-13, New York, 92; Metrop Mus Art, New York, 82; Aldrich Art Mus, Ridgefield, Conn, 86; Independent Curators Inc, New York, 90; M-13, New York, 91. *Pos:* Asst to cur graphic arts dept, Nat Gallery Art, Washington, DC, 54-57. *Teaching:* Instr art, Arlington Co Pub Schs, 57-60. *Awards:* Pub Art Fund Inc, 87; Outdoor Installation Proj Grant, EHampton Ctr Contemp Art, 89. *Bibliog:* Ken Johnson (auth), Grace Knowlton at Bill Bace, Art Am, 1/90; Christine Liotta (auth), Sculpture: A Natural Order, The Hudson River Mus, Yonkers, 9-10/91; Roberta Smith (auth), The New York Times, 4/24/92. *Media:* Clay, Metal. *Publ:* Auth, Grace Knowlton, Layers and Traces (exhib catalog), Smith Col Mus Art, 4-8/92. *Dealer:* Twining Gallery 568 Broadway New York NY 10012; Witkin Gallery 415 W Broadway New York NY 10012. *Mailing Add:* RD 1 Box 215 Palisades NY 10964

KNOWLTON, JONATHAN
PAINTER, EDUCATOR
b New York, NY, Feb 22, 37. *Study:* Yale Univ, BA; Univ Calif, Berkeley, MA. *Work:* Mus Mod Art, New York; Victoria & Albert Mus, London; Univ Calif Art Mus, Berkeley; La Jolla Mus Fine Art, Calif; Oakland Mus, Calif; Montreal Mus Fine Arts, Ont. *Exhib:* Survey '68, Montreal Mus Fine Arts, 68; 17th Nat Print Exhib, Brooklyn Mus, 70; Edmonton Art Gallery, 72; John Bolles Gallery, San Francisco, 73; Latitude 53, Edmonton, 75; Front Gallery, Edmonton, Alta. *Teaching:* Assoc prof drawing & painting, Univ Alta, 66-90. *Awards:* Purchase Award, Los Angeles Co Mus Art, 61; Fulbright Grant, 64-65; Can Coun Grant, 68-69. *Bibliog:* Phylis Matousek (auth), Knowlton travels many roads, Edmonton J, 11/14/84; The Nuclear Glare Has Its Own Beauty in A-Bomb, Soc, 89; Elizabeth Beauchamp (auth), Knowlton retrospective sheds light on local talent, Edmonton J, 6/1/90. *Media:* Acrylic, Oil, Watercolor. *Publ:* Auth, Riding the mainstream of modern imperatives, Interface, Vol 2, No 9, 11/79. *Dealer:* Vik Gallery Edmonton. *Mailing Add:* c/o Dept Art & Design Univ Alberta Edmonton AB T6G 2C9 Canada

KNOX, ELIZABETH
PAINTER
b June 13, 44. *Study:* Parsons Sch Design; New Sch Social Res; Art Students League, with Robert Beverly Hale. *Exhib:* Biennial Contmp Am Painting & Sculpture, Whitney Mus Am Art, New York, 75; Fourth Ann Long Island City Open Studios Exhib, NY, 89; RedFining Visionary Art, Doma Gallery, Soho, NY, 89; group exhib, John Davis Gallery, SoHo, NY, 88; Art on Paper, Weatherspoon Art Gallery, Univ NC, Greensboro, 88; Long Island City Artists Invitational, Studio K Gallery, NY, 87. *Bibliog:* Ann Weber (auth), Elizabeth Knox: Beyond the world of things, Vision Mag, 80; Eileen Watkins (auth), Hoboken inspires exhibits, Newark Star-Ledger, 83. *Mailing Add:* c/o Round Top Ctr for the Arts-Round Top Gallery Business Rte 1 Box 1316 Damariscotta ME 04543

KNOX, GEORGE
HISTORIAN, WRITER
b London, Eng, Jan 1, 22. *Study:* Courtauld Inst Art, Univ London, BA, MA & PhD. *Collections Arranged:* Tiepolo Bicentenary Exhib, Fogg Art Mus, Cambridge, Mass, 70; Tiepolo Drawings, Staatsgalerie, Stuttgart, 70; Tiepolo: Tecnica e Immaginazione, Palazzo Ducale, Venice, 79; Piazzetta: Disegni, Incisioni, Libri, Manoscritti, Fondazione Giorgio Cini, Venice, 83; Piazzetta, A Tercentenary Exhibition, Nat Gallery Art, Washington, DC, 83; 18th Century Venetian Art in Canadian Collections, Vancouver Art Gallery, 89. *Teaching:* Instr, Slade Sch Art, Univ London, 50-52; instr, King's Col, Newcastle, Univ Durham, 52-58; instr, Queen's Univ, Ont, 69-70; prof fine arts & head dept, Univ BC, 70-87, prof emer. *Mem:* Can Comm for the Hist of Art; Comite Int d'Histoire de l'Art; Ateneo Veneto. *Interests:* Venetian 18th century art, particularly the drawings of the Tiepolo family, Piazzetta & Pellegrini. *Publ:* Auth, Catalogue of the Tiepolo Drawings in the Victoria & Albert Museum, 60; Domenico Tiepolo: Raccolta di Teste, Udine, 70; Giambattista & Domenico Tiepolo , The Chalk Drawings, Oxford, 80; Robert Lehman Collection VI: Italian 18th Century Drawings, New York, 87. *Mailing Add:* 3495 W 11th Ave Univ Brit Columbia Vancouver BC V6R 2K1 Canada

KNUDSEN, CHRISTIAN
PAINTER, PRINTMAKER
b June 3, 45; Danish citizen. *Study:* Sir George Williams Univ, BFA, 69. *Work:* Mus Fine Arts & Musee D'Art Contemporain, Montreal; Art Gallery Ont, Toronto; Vancouver Art Gallery, BC; Can Coun Art Bank, Ottawa. *Comn:* Painting, Govt Can Post Off, Quebec, 78. *Exhib:* Concordia Univ, Montreal, 74; Vancouver Art Gallery, 78; Montreal Mus, Que, 79; Glenbow Mus, Calgary, 80; Agnes Etherington Art Ctr, Kingston, Ont, 81. *Bibliog:* David Burnett (auth), Knudsen at Godard, Art Am, 1/78; David Burnett (auth), Christian Knudsen, Parachute No 11, summer 78; Robert Swain (auth), Christian Knudsen, Agnes Etherington Art Ctr, Kingston, Ont, 81. *Media:* Mixed Media; Silkscreen. *Dealer:* Mira Godard Gallery 22 Hazelton Toronto ON M5R 2E2 Can. *Mailing Add:* 3827 Drolet Rd Montreal PQ H2W 2L3 Canada

KNUTSSON, ANDERS
PAINTER
b Malmö, Sweden, May 8, 37; US citizen. *Study:* Malmö Tech Col, Sweden, BSME, 67; Cincinnati Art Acad, 69. *Work:* Albright-Knox Art Gallery; Arkivmuseet, Lund, Sweden; Fleming Mus, Univ Vt, Burlington; Moderna Museet, Stockholm, Sweden; Univ Maine Mus Art, Orono; Williams Col Mus Art, Williamstown, Mass; and many other pub & pvt collections. *Exhib:* One-man shows, Helen Day Art Ctr, Stowe, Vt, 87, Keith Green Gallery, New York, 87, Gates of Light, Williams Col Mus Art, Williamstown, Mass, 88, Bennett Siegel Gallery, New York, 90, edition Hylteberga, Skurup, Sweden, 90, Lightscapes, Univ Maine Mus Art, Orono, 90 & Stephen Solovy Gallery, Chicago, and many others; Bjõn Olsson Gallery, Stockholm, Sweden, 89; Frank Bernaducci Gallery, New York, 89; Lillian Heidenberg Gallery, New York, 91; Art Now Gallery, Gothenburg, Sweden, 92; Lõwenadler Gallery, Stockholm Art Fair, Sweden, 92; and many others. *Bibliog:* Lisa Yokana (auth), Gates of Light, Williams Col Mus Art, 89; Carlo McCormick (auth), Anders Knutsson and the Promise of Light, Anders Knutsson Lightscapes/Ljusskap, Univ Maine Mus Art, 90; Barnaby Ruhe (auth), Another Conceptual Category, Anders Knutsson: Lightscapes/Ljusskap, Univ Maine Mus Art, 90; and many others. *Media:* Oil, Wax. *Mailing Add:* 93 Lexington Ave Brooklyn NY 11238

KOBAYASHI, HISAKO
PAINTER
b Tokyo, Japan, Jan 23, 46. *Study:* Univ Hawaii, BFA, 78; Pratt Inst, MFA, 80. *Exhib:* Brooklyn Artists, Brooklyn Mus, New York, 80; Tradition and Today, Bergen County Mus, NJ, 82; New Directions, Newark Mus, NJ, 83. *Awards:* Semi finalist, CAPS Grants Awards, New York State, 81, 82. *Bibliog:* Review, OCS News, 88, Downtown, NY Free Press, 89 & NY Yomuri Press, 90. *Mem:* Nat Asn Women Artists; Japanese Artist Asn of New York (vpres, 90-). *Media:* Oil, All Media. *Mailing Add:* 55 Great Jones St New York NY 10012

KOBER, ALFRED JOHN
EDUCATOR, SCULPTOR
b Great Bend, Kans, June 3, 37. *Study:* Dodge City Col, AA, 58; Ft Hays State Col, BS(art), 60 & MS(art), 66. *Work:* Boise Gallery Art, Idaho; Ft Hays State Col. *Comn:* Two outdoor sculptures, Boise State Univ, 71 & 72; stainless steel sculpture, Bank of Idaho, Boise, 72; welded steel sculpture, Boise Cascade World Hq, Boise, 74; sculpture for Veterans Park, Boise, comn by Idaho Veterans, 76; stainless steel sculpture, Atlantic Richfield, Denver, 78. *Exhib:* Ann Exhib Northwest Artists, Seattle, Wash, 69-74; Mainstreams, 72 & 77; LaGrange Nat Competition II, Ga, 75; 21st Ann Drawing & Small Sculpture Show, Ball State Univ, 75. *Teaching:* Instr art, Hutchinson Community Jr Col, Kans, 66-68; assoc prof sculpture, Boise State Univ, 68-78, assoc prof, 78, prof, 79. *Awards:* Purchase Award, Grover M Hermann Fine Arts Ctr, Marietta, 72; Award of Excellence, Marietta Col, 72; Award, Ball State Univ, 75. *Mem:* Boise Art Asn. *Media:* Mixed. *Mailing Add:* c/o Dept Art Boise St Univ 1910 Univ Dr Boise ID 83725

KOCAR, GEORGE FREDERICK
PAINTER, ILLUSTRATOR
b Cleveland, Ohio, Sept 28, 48. *Study:* Cuyahoga Community Col, Cleveland, Ohio, AA, 75; Cleveland State Univ, Cleveland, Ohio; BA, 77; Syracuse Univ, NY, MFA, 83. *Work:* Cleveland State Univ; Cent Mo State Univ, Warrensburg; Metro Gen Hosp, Cleveland, Ohio; Butler Inst Am Art, Youngstown, Ohio. *Exhib:* May Show, Cleveland Mus Art, Ohio, 79, 81-83 & 87; Butler Mid-Year Exhib, Butler Inst Art, Youngstown, Ohio, 81-85, 87; Watercolor USA, Springfield Mus Art, Mo, 90; one-person show, Kent State Univ, Ohio, 86, Erie Art Mus, Pa, 86, Central Mo State Univ, Warrensburg, 87, Trumball Art Guild, Warren, Ohio, 90 & Lake Erie Col, Painsville, Ohio, 92; Without Words, Ariel Gallery, New York, 88; No Neo (exhib, catalog), Pa State Univ, Zoller Gallery, Univ Park, 89; Living Color, Earth Art Gallery, Tokyo, Japan, 90; Satire & Commentary: the art of Yolanda Daliz, George Kocar & Mary Lou Greene, Bruce Gallery, Edinboro Univ, Pa, 91; Personalities, two-person show, Ariel Gallery, New York, 91. *Pos:* Pres, Kocar Art, Bay Village, Ohio; master designer, Am Greeting Corp, 84- *Teaching:* Part-time fac, Akron Univ, Ohio & Cleveland Inst Art. *Awards:* Gold Medal Painting, Int Art Competition, 112 Greene St, New York. *Bibliog:* John Byrum (auth), Kocar and Soppeland at Fine Arts Asn, Dialogue, 9-10/89; Daniel S Hodgson (auth), Post-Revolutionary Visions: The Spectacle of Subversion, NO NEO catalog essay, 8/89; Sidney Gilbert (auth), Personalities, Artspeak, 8/89. *Mem:* New Orgn Visual Arts, Cleveland, Ohio; Saving & Preserving Arts & Cultural Environ, Cleveland, Ohio; FAVA, Oberlin, Ohio; Cleveland Ctr Contemp Art, Ohio. *Media:* Acrylic, Watercolor. *Publ:* Illusr, Us against them, NY Times, 83; Is That You Laughing Comrade?, Citadel Press, 86; auth-illusr, Vacationing with a bunch of Maine-iacs, Cleveland Plain Dealer, 86; auth, Painting the world at large & Fine Art & Illustration-Bridging the Gap, 86, Artist's Mag; illusr, Cooking with Humor. *Dealer:* Powerhouse Gallery 2000 Sycamore Cleveland OH 44113; Agora Gallery 560 Broadway New York NY. *Mailing Add:* 24213 Lake Rd Bay Village OH 44140

KOCH, ARTHUR ROBERT
PAINTER, EDUCATOR
b Meriden, Conn, Feb 26, 34. *Study:* Wesleyan Univ; RI Sch Design, with John Frazier, BFA, 57; Univ Wash, MFA, 61. *Exhib:* Art: USA: 59, New York; US Info Agency Painting Show, Europe, 62-66; Tex Painting & Sculpture of the 20th Century, 70-71. *Teaching:* Instr studio, Univ NH, 57-59; instr studio, El Centro Col, Dallas, 66-70; head dept studio art, Meadows Sch Arts, Southern Methodist Univ, 70-, assoc prof design & painting, 78- *Awards:* Ft Worth Art Ctr Award, 70. *Mem:* Dallas Area Artists Equity Asn (pres, 70-71); Artists Equity Asn (vpres, 71); Blue Bonnets Anonymous (chmn, 71-72); Tex Asn Schs Art. *Dealer:* Contemp Fine Arts Gallery 2425 Cedar Springs Dallas TX 75201. *Mailing Add:* c/o Div Art Owens Art Ctr Southern Methodist Univ Dallas TX 75275

KOCH, EDWIN E
SCULPTOR, PAINTER
b New York, NY, Feb 21, 15. *Study:* Mus Mod Art Sch; also with E Kramer. *Work:* Butler Inst of Am Art, Youngstown, Ohio. *Exhib:* Am Watercolors, Drawings & Prints, Metrop Mus Art, 52; Int Exhib Watercolors, Prints, Drawing, Pa Acad Design, 52; Int Watercolor Exhib, Brooklyn Mus, 53; Nat Acad Design, 58-75; var one-man shows. *Awards:* Framemakers Award, Silvermine Guild Artists, 62; Medals of Honor for Watercolor, 70 & Oils, 72, Painters & Sculpture Soc NJ; Grumbacher Award, Audubon Artists, 79. *Bibliog:* Brian O'Doherty (auth), One-man show, 62 & John Canady (auth), One-man show, 66, New York Times. *Mem:* Audubon Artists; Nat Soc Painters in Casein & Acrylic (bd dirs, 75-); Knickerbocker Artists (vpres, 77-78); Painters & Sculptors Soc NJ (vpres, 74-); Am Vet Soc Artists (treas, 70-75). *Media:* Oil, Casein. *Mailing Add:* RD-1 Box 76 Hoagberg Hill Rd Wallkill NY 12589

KOCH, GERD (HERMAN)
PAINTER, EDUCATOR
b Detroit, Mich, Jan 30, 29. *Study:* Wayne State Univ, BFA; Univ Calif, Los Angeles; Univ Calif, Santa Barbara, MFA. *Work:* Santa Barbara Art Mus; Los Angeles Co Mus Art; Univ Mont; Va State Mus Fine Art; Calif State Univ Long Beach. *Comn:* Design of Ash Grove (folk music cabaret), 58. *Exhib:* Los Angeles Co Mus Art Ann, 59; solo exhibs, Esther Robles Art Gallery, Los Angeles, 59, 61, 63 & 65, Esther Bear Art Gallery, 65 & 67, Carnegie Art Mus, 88 & Momentum City Art Gallery, 91; Art or Anti Art, Occidental Col, 65; Univ NC, 66; Butler Inst Am Art, Youngstown, Ohio, 66; Calif Palace of Legion of Honor, San Francisco, 67; Calif Arts Festival, 68; and others. *Teaching:* Prof painting & drawing, Ventura Col, 60-61 & 67-; instr, Univ Calif Exten, 66- *Awards:* Purchase & First Award, Los Angeles Co Mus Art, 59; Calif State Fair First Award, 63; M Grumbacher Inc Purchaser Award, Nat Watercolor Soc, 56 & Purchase Award, 76. *Mem:* Nat Watercolor Soc; Ventura Art Asn. *Media:* Oil, Acrylic. *Mailing Add:* c/o Dept Art Ventura Col 4667 Telegraph Rd Ventura CA 93003

KOCH, PHILIP
PAINTER, INSTRUCTOR
b Rochester, NY, Mar 30, 48. *Study:* Oberlin Col, BA, 70; Ind Univ, MFA, 72. *Work:* Minn Mus Art, St Paul; Ind Univ Fine Arts Mus, Bloomington. *Exhib:* Solo exhibs: C Grimaldis Gallery, Baltimore, 80 & 83, Gross McCleaf Gallery, Philadelphia, 81-82, Meredith, Long & Co, Houston, 84, 84, 88 & 92, Steven Scott Gallery, Baltimore, 89, Jane Haslem Gallery, DC, 89 & 91, Payne Gallery, Bethlehem, Pa, 90, Sazama Gallery, Chicago, 90; The figure in the Landscape, Artists Choice Mus, New York, 85; Chicago Realists, Sheldon Swope Art Mus, Terra Haute, Ind, 92; C Grimaldis Gallery, Baltimore, 81 & 83; Meredith Long & Co, Houston, 84, 86 & 88; The Figure & the Landscape, Artists' Choice Mus, New York, 85; Paintings by Bernard Chaet, Philip Koch & Gaber Peterdi, Jane Haslem Gallery, Washington, DC, 88;; Solo exhibs, Jane Haslem Gallery, Wash, Dc, 89 & Payne Gallery, Moravian Col, Bethlehem, Pa, 90. *Teaching:* Instr painting, Cent Wash State Col, 72-73 & Md Inst Col Art, 73- *Awards:* Purchase Prize, Minn Mus Art, 75; Union Independent Cols Art Nat Teaching Fel, 76; Ford Found Fac Enrichment Grant, Md Inst, 79; Mellon Grant, 84. *Media:* Oil, Watercolor. *Publ:* Auth, Direct painting outdoors, Am Artist, 4/82. *Dealer:* Meredith Long & Co 2323 San Felipe Houston TX 77019; Jane Haslem Gallery Washington DC. *Mailing Add:* 4823 Hawksbury Rd Baltimore MD 21208

KOCH, ROBERT
HISTORIAN, WRITER
b New York, NY, Apr 7, 18. *Study:* Harvard Univ, AB, 39; NY Univ, MA, 53; Yale Univ, PhD, 57. *Teaching:* Prof art hist, Southern Conn State Univ, 56-79, prof emer, 79- *Awards:* Fac Scholar Award, Southern Conn State Univ, 74. *Res:* Art nouveau in France, Spain, Latin America and the US. *Publ:* Auth, articles in Art in Am, 62, 64 & 65 & Antiques, 74; Louis C Tiffany, Rebel in Glass, 64; contrib, Artistic America, Tiffany Glass and Art Nouveau, 70; auth, Louis C Tiffany's Glass-Bronzes-Lamps, 71; Louis C Tiffany's Art Glass, 77. *Mailing Add:* 143 Hoyt St Stamford CT 06905

KOCH, VIRGINIA See Greenleaf, Virginia

KOCHER, ROBERT LEE
PAINTER, EDUCATOR
b Jefferson City, Mo, Dec 19, 29. *Study:* Univ Mo-Columbia, AB & MA; also with Fred Shane & Paul Brach, Post Grad; Univ Iowa, Iowa City with Jean DeMarko & Robert Knipschild. *Comn:* Religious Feasts, Culver-Stockton Col Dining Hall, 57; outdoor sculpture, Duane Arnold Residence, Cedar Rapids, Iowa. *Exhib:* Mid-Am Ann, Kansas City, Mo, 60; All Iowa Artists, Des Moines Art Ctr Ann, 63-75; Miss Corridor Competition, Renwick Gallery, Washington, DC, 80; 32 one-person exhibs, Nat Surface Design Competition. *Pos:* Dir, New York Term Coe Col, 78-80. *Teaching:* Prof art, Coe Col, 59-, Marvin D Cone Prof, 87- *Awards:* First Prize Painting, All Iowa Artists, Des Moines Art Ctr, 69; Younkers Award. *Bibliog:* Andrew Dolkart (auth), The Old Executive Building: A Victorian Masterpiece, Govt Publ Review, 85. *Mem:* Cedar Rapids Art Ctr (bd dirs, 61-81); Cedar Rapids Marion Coun Arts; Friends Adv Bd, Univ Iowa Mus Art, 86-90. *Media:* Acrylic, Watercolor. *Mailing Add:* 1955 Park Ave SE Cedar Rapids IA 52403

KOCHERTHALER, MINA
PAINTER
b Munich, Ger; US citizen. *Study:* Columbia Univ; Art Students League, with Mario Cooper; Nat Acad Design Sch Fine Art, with Ralph Fabri. *Work:* Norfolk Mus Arts & Sci; also in many pvt collections. *Exhib:* Royal Soc Painters Watercolours, London, 62; 200 Yrs Watercolor Painting Am, Metrop Mus Art, New York, 66-67; Mus Acuarela, Mexico City, 68; Butler Inst Am Art, 70; Can Soc Painters Watercolour, 71-72. *Pos:* Deleg, US Comt Int Asn Arts, New York, 60-62; volunteer, Landauer Collection, NY Hist Soc, 87. *Awards:* John J Karpick Mem Medal, Audubon Artists, 62; seven prizes, Nat Soc Painters Casein & Acrylic, 58-77; Grumbacher Polymer Award, Catharine Lorillard Wolfe Art Club, 71; and many others. *Mem:* Hon mem Am Watercolor Soc (rec secy & coordr chmn, 62-82); Audubon Artists; Nat Soc Painters Casein & Acrylic (vpres, 62-84, dir, 84-); Allied Artists Am (rec secy, 74-78, mem coordr, 78-86); Catharine Lorillard Wolfe Art Club. *Media:* Acrylic. *Mailing Add:* 124 W 79th St New York NY 10024

KOCHHEISER, THOMAS H
CURATOR, EDUCATOR
b Galion, Ohio, June 10, 56. *Study:* Ohio State Univ, BA (distinction in art hist), 79; Oberlin Col, MA(art hist), 87. *Collections Arranged:* Joan Semmel, from Emblematic Woman Exhib Ser, 11-12/86; Mark Jackson: Paintings, 10/87; Rachel Rosenthal: The Objects Show, 1-2/88; Hannah Wilke: A Retrospective (catalog), 3/89; Komar & Melamid, 3/90. *Pos:* Dir, Gallery 210, Univ Mo, St Louis, 86- *Teaching:* Lectr art hist & gallery mgt, Univ Missouri, St Louis, 85- *Mem:* Col Art Asn. *Res:* Contemporary art with emphasis on feminism, sexuality and political art. *Publ:* Ed, Hannah Wilke - A Retrospective (exhib catalog), Univ Missouri Press, 89. *Mailing Add:* Art Dept Univ of Mo St Louis MO 63121

KOCHKA, AL
MUSEUM DIRECTOR, ADMINISTRATOR
b Paterson, NJ, June 28, 28. *Study:* Newark State Teachers Col, NJ, BS, 49; William Paterson Col NJ, MA, 68. *Pos:* Dir, NJ Coun Arts, Trenton, 76-78, Sangre de Cristo Arts & Conf Ctr, Pueblo, Colo, 79-84, Amarillo, Tex, 84-87 & Muskegon Mus Art, Muskegon, Mich, 88- *Teaching:* Art teacher, Kinnelon High Sch, NJ, 63-68; art educ consult, NJ State Dept Educ, Trenton, 68-74, dir arts & humanities, 74-76. *Awards:* Art Educator of Yr, Art Educators NJ, 73; Mitchell A Wilder Award, Tex Asn Mus, 87. *Bibliog:* Frances Traher (auth), Sangre de Cristo Art Center hits its stride, Art West, Vol 6, 83. *Mem:* Am Asn Mus; Mich Asn Mus; Midwest Mus Conf; Tex Asn Mus (bd trustees, 83-84); Mich Mus Asn (bd trustees, 91-92). *Publ:* Contribr, Dan Coen: The Lamar Series, Colorado Springs Fine Arts Ctr, 84; ed & contribr, Georgia O'Keeffe and Her Contemporaries, 85, Eight Modern Masters, 85 & Holy Family through the Ages, 86, Amarillo Art Ctr. *Mailing Add:* 297 W Clay Apt 203 Muskegon MI 49440

KOCHMAN, ALEXANDRA D
CERAMIST, SCULPTOR
b Poltava, Ukraine, USSR, 36. *Study:* Fashion Inst Technol, New York, AAS, 62; Northeastern Ill State Univ, Chicago, BA, 72; Univ Ill, Chicago, MFA, 78. *Work:* Ill State Mus, Springfield, Ill; State Ill Ctr Governor's Off, Chicago, Ill; Burroughs Corp, Dallas, Tex; Milwaukee Pub Mus, Wis; Amoco Corp, Chicago, Ill. *Comn:* Sculptural vessels, Swiss Bank, Chicago, Ill, 84; mural, Lincoln Properties Corp, Oakbrook, Ill, 86; ceramic wall sculpture, Barack, Forrazzano & Kirschbaum, Chicago, Ill, 87; Siemens Medical Systems (mural), Schaumburg, Ill, 87; wall sculpture, St Volod & Olha Church, Chicago, Ill, 88. *Exhib:* Illinois Crafts, Ill State Mus, Springfield, Ill, 81; A Survey of Illinois Clay, Lakeview Mus, Peoria, Ill, 82; Ceramic Nat, Downey Mus Art, Los Angeles, Ca, 84; Ceramics by A D Kochman, Evanston Art Ctr, Ill, 85; Artemisia Gallery, Archit Ceramics, Chicago, Ill, 86; Chicago Fire 2, Navy Pier N, Chicago, Ill, 88; New Art Forms, Navy Pier, Chicago Ill, 88; Women in Visual Arts, 89, Outstanding American Craftsmen, 90, Judith Racht Gallery, Harbert, Mich; New Horizons in Art, North Shore Art League, Skokie, Ill, 90;; Chicago Street Gallery, Lincoln, Ill. *Pos:* Consult, Milwaukee Pub Mus, Wis, 80. *Teaching:* Adj asst prof art & sculpture, Rosary Col, River Forest, Ill, 83- *Awards:* First Award, Oakbrook Invitational, Oakbrook C of C, 82; Governor's Purchase Award, Ill State Prof Exhib, State Ill, 86; First Award, Ill State Exhib, Springfield, 89. *Bibliog:* Randi Sherman (auth), Alexandra D Kochman exhibition, Chicago Artist Coalition News, 81; Garret Holg (auth), Alexandra D Kochman ceramics, New Art Examiner, 85; Yuri Myskiv (auth), Alexandra D Kochman and the world in balance, Ukrainian Weekly Rev. *Mem:* Chicago Artists' Coalition (bd mem, 82-82); Ukrainian Inst Mod Art (art juror, 79-). *Mailing Add:* 5453 N Virginia Ave Chicago IL 60625

KOCHTA, RUTH MARTHA
ART DEALER, PAINTER
b Ridgewood, NY, Jan 5, 24. *Study:* Queens Col, New York, 65-68; Art Students League with Julian Levi, Rudolph Baranik, Bruce Dorfman & Leo Manso, 69-75. *Work:* First & Merchants Bank, Richmond, Va; Nat Bank NAm, New York; Fairleigh Dickinson Univ, Teaneck, NJ; Philathea Mus, Can; General Electric, Pittsfield, Mass. *Exhib:* Nat Acad, New York, 69; Audubon Artists Ann Exhib, New York, 70; Philathea Mus, Can, 72; Elizabet Ney Mus, Austin, Tex, 72; Heckscher Mus, Huntington, NY, 74; Wadsworth Atheneum, Hartford, Conn, 75; New Britain Mus, Conn, 75. *Pos:* Dir, Imperial Gallery, New York, 80-82; owner/dir, Clark Whitney Gallery, Lenox, Mass, 83- *Media:* Oil. *Specialty:* Contemp paintings and sculpture. *Mailing Add:* 25 Church St Lenox MA 01240

KOCSIS, JAMES PAUL
PAINTER, PUBLISHER
b Buffalo, NY, April 27, 36. *Study:* Philadelphia Col of Art, Univ of the Arts, dipl, 58. *Work:* Lessing J Rosenwald Collection, Nat Gallery Art, Libr of Cong, Washington, DC; Albright-Knox Art Gallery, Buffalo, NY; Victoria & Albert Mus, London; pvt collections of HM Elizabeth, Queen of Eng, His Royal Highness Charles, Prince of Wales, The Right Hon Lord Kenneth Clark & Nancy & Ronald Reagan, Presidential Collection, The White House; Kendal Mus, Eng; and others. *Exhib:* One-man shows, Igneous Man Exhib I, Columbia Mus Art, SC, 74 United World Col Adriatic, Trieste, Italy & Southern Africa, Mbabane, 85, US Int Univ-Europe, London, 85, Univ Glasgow, Scotland, 85, James Joyce Mus, Dublin, Ireland, 85, Kendal Mus, Eng, 86; US Mission to the UN, New York, 90; Sopot, Poland, 91; Gdansk, Poland, 91-92; Ger Am Inst: Sparkasse Saarbrucken; Goethe Inst Am House, Frankfurt, Ger, 92; and others. *Pos:* Illusr, children's books, 61-68; illusr & designer for Random House Publ & 20th Century Fox, 67; publ of catalogues, books, color prints & posters for nat & int distribution. *Teaching:* Instr drawing & pictoral composition, Philadelphia Col of Art Univ of the Arts, 65-67; lectr, Philadelphia Col of Art Univ of the Arts, Kutztown State Teachers Col, civic & social groups. *Awards:* Am Inst Graphic Arts Biannual Award, 68. *Bibliog:* Jim Smith (auth), Portrait of an artist who set out to make it on his own-James Paul Kocsis, Buffalo News Mag, 10/22/78; Kocsis, The Art of James Paul Kocsis (monogr), Paragon Press, 81; Albert Hofammann (auth), James Paul Kocsis, Sunday Call-Chronicle, 11/1/81. *Media:* Oil on Linen. *Mailing Add:* PO Box 20782 Lehigh Valley PA 18002-0782

KODNER, MARTIN
ART DEALER, CONSULTANT
b St Louis, Mo, Nov 25, 34. *Study:* St Louis Col Pharmacy, BS, 56. *Pos:* Dir, Gallery of the Masters, St Louis, Mo, currently. *Mem:* Am Appraisers Asn, New York. *Specialty:* American and European art of the 19th and 20th centuries; masters of the old west; impressionists. *Publ:* Auth, Oscar E Berninghaus, Gateway Heritage Publ, winter 83-84; Carl (Charles) Wimar, Gateway Heritage Publ. *Mailing Add:* Gallery of The Masters Inc 9918 Clayton Rd St Louis MO 63124

KOEHLER, HENRY
PAINTER
b Louisville, Ky, Feb 2, 27. *Study:* Yale Univ, BA, 50. *Work:* Calif Palace Legion Honor, San Francisco; Speed Mus Art, Louisville, Ky; Parrish Art Mus, Southampton, NY; Thomasville Cult Ctr, Ga. *Comn:* Baseball murals, NY Mets, Shea Stadium, 64. *Exhib:* One-man shows, Calif Palace Legion Honor, 66 & Speed Art Mus, 67; Wildenstein, London, 71, 73, 76 & 78; The Horse in Art, Santa Barbara Mus Art, Calif, 74; Alken Racing Hall Fame, 78; Galerie La Cymaise, Paris, 82, 84, 87 & 91; Spink & Son, London, 90 & 92. *Pos:* Trustee, Parrish Mus of Art, Southampton, NY. *Mem:* The Brook, NY; Whites, The Beefsteak, London; Century Asn, New York. *Media:* Oil. *Dealer:* Authur Ackermann & Son 50 E 57 St New York NY 10022; Galerie La Cymaise 174 Rue De Faubourg St Honore 75008 Paris. *Mailing Add:* 80 N Main St Southampton NY 11968

KOEHLER, RONALD GENE
SCULPTOR
b Jackson, Mo, Sept 30, 50. *Study:* Southeast Mo State Univ, Cape Girardeau, BS(art educ), 72, MAT, 75; Memphis State Univ, Tenn, with Harris Sorrelle, MFA(sculpture), 80. *Work:* Ark Arts Ctr, Little Rock; Del Mar Col, Corpus Christi, Tex; Tenn All-State Artist Collection, Nashville; W Palm Beach Int Airport, Fla; Dublin Laurens Mus, Ga. *Comn:* Platter of Greed (welded steel), First Nat Bank, Cleveland, Miss, 82; cemetery sculpture (welded steel), comn by Mary Salley, Dublin, Ga, 86; sculpture installation, Our Lady of Victories Catholic Church, Cleveland, Miss, 91. *Exhib:* Am Contemp Works in Wood, Dairy Barn Southeastern Cult Art Ctr, Athens, Ohio, 89; 22nd Ann, Del Mar Col, Corpus Christi, Tex, 88; Visual Articulation '88, Tex A&M Univ, Col Sta, 88; Contemp Am Wood, Banaker Gallery, Walnut Creek, Calif, 89; The 9th Ann Wood Show, Durham, Ont, Can, 92; Regional Selections - Defining Ideas, Arrowmont Sch Arts Crafts, Gatlinburg, Tenn, 91; one-man shows, Fragmented Surfaces, Memphis Brooks Mus Art, Tenn, 92 & Sculpture, Bellarmine Col, Louisville, Ky, 92; Just Plane Screwy: Metaphysical & Metaphorical Tools by Artists, Wustum Mus Fine Art, Racine, Wis, 92. *Teaching:* Instr design, Memphis State Univ, Tenn, 78-80; instr sculpture, Delta State Univ, Cleveland, Miss, 80-82, assoc prof sculpture & printmaking, 84-; staff asst, Arrowmont Sch Arts & Crafts, Gatlinburg, Tenn, 82-84. *Awards:* Purchase Awards, E Tenn State Univ, 86, Del Mar Col, Corpus Christie, Tex, 88 & Cottonlandia Mus, Greenwood, Miss, 91; Visual Artist Fel-Miss Arts Comn, 91-92. *Bibliog:* featured artist, Fine Wood Working Mag, No 62, 1/87 & Gallery section, Am Craft Mag, Vol 47, No 4, 8/87; Arthur Williams (auth), Sculpture: Technique-Form-Content, Davis Publ, 89; Richard Morris (auth), Regional Selections: Defining Ideas, Art Papers, vol 15, no 3, 5-6/91. *Mem:* Int Sculpture Award; Am Crafts Coun; Craftsman Guild Miss. *Media:* Wood, Metal. *Publ:* Auth, Natural Dyes on Handmade Paper, Delta State Univ, 82. *Mailing Add:* 400 S Bolivar Cleveland MS 38732-3745

KOENIG, CATHERINE CATANZARO
PAINTER
b Buffalo, NY, Aug 25, 21. *Study:* Buffalo Fine Arts Acad; Albright Art Sch, with Philip Elliot, Isaac Soyer, Ralston Crawford & Charles Burchfield, dipl, 42. *Work:* Albright-Knox Art Gallery; Burchfield Art Ctr, Buffalo, NY; Libr Cong; Okla Art Ctr, Oklahoma City; Ball State Univ Gallery, Muncie, Ind; Butler Inst Am Art, Youngstown, Ohio. *Exhib:* Brooklyn Mus Print Ann, 48, Int Watercolor Show, Brooklyn Mus, 53; Nat Watercolor Show, Pa Acad Fine

Arts, 51, 53 & 57; Butler Int Am Art Midyear Painting Show, 54, 72 & 75, Invited Artist, 90; Nat Drawing Show, Okla Art Ctr, 73, 76, 77 & 80; Nat Print & Drawing Exhib, Dulin Gallery Art, 77 & 80; solo exhib, Albright-Knox Art Gallery, 80, Ball State Univ Art Gallery, 81 & Butler Inst Am Art, 91; 150 Years of Western NY Painting, Albright-Knox Art Gallery, 87; two-person show, Mem Art Gallery Rochester, 87; 52nd Butler Inst Ann, 88 & 89. *Teaching:* Instr watercolor, Art Inst Buffalo, 46-56; lectr figure drawing, Millard Fillmore Col, State Univ NY, Buffalo, 61-79; instr, Niagara Co Community Col, 78-81. *Awards:* Nat Drawing Show Award, Delmar Col, Tenn, 80; Purchase Award, Ball State Univ 26th Nat Drawing Show, 80; Award winner, Butler Inst Am Art Midyear Show, 88. *Media:* Egg Tempera, Pastel. *Dealer:* Nina Freudenheim Gallery Buffalo NY. *Mailing Add:* 18 E Girard Blvd Kenmore NY 14217

KOENIG, ELIZABETH
SCULPTOR
b New York, NY, Apr 20, 37. *Study:* Sorbonne, Paris, 57; Wellesley Col, BA, 58; Yale Univ, MD, 62; Art Students League, New York, with John Hovannes, 63-64; Corcoran Mus Sch Art, with Heinz Warnecke & John Rood, 64-67. *Work:* Curator's Collection, Eugene O'Neill Mem Theater Found, Waterford, Conn; Art Students League, New York. *Comn:* Tenn marble carving, Washington Hebrew Cong, Washington, DC, 78; monumental bronze sculpture for front of Admin Bldg, George Meany Ctr Labor Studies, Silver Spring, Md, 82. *Exhib:* Ten Sculptors, Washington Womens Arts Ctr, Washington, DC, 77; retrospective 1963-1978, Lyman Allyn Mus, New London, Conn, 78 & Rotunda, Pan-Am Health Orgn, Washington, DC, 78; Finalist Exhib, Outdoor Sculpture Competition, Rockville Munic Gallery, Md, 78; 11th Ann Sculpture Conf, Meridian House Int, Washington, DC, 80; Sculpture & Prints, Cath Univ Am, 80. *Collections Arranged:* The Mystique of Metal, Art Barn, Nat Park Serv, Washington, DC, 85. *Awards:* First Prize for Sculpture, 70 & Second & Third Prizes for Sculpture, 71, Tri-State Regional Sculpture Exhib, Montgomery Co Art Asn. *Bibliog:* Patricia Raymer (auth), From iron to gold, Washington's metal artists, Washingtonian Mag, 75; Robert Spring (auth), New projects: Sculpture for the George Meany Center, In: The Artists Foundry for Practicing Sculptors, Vol 5, No 1, 82. *Mem:* Artists Equity Asn, Washington, DC (vpres, 77-83); life mem Art Students League, New York; Int Sculpture Ctr. *Publ:* Auth, Sculpture--Elizabeth Koenig, Retrospective Exhibition 1963-1978, Lee Douglas Assoc, 78; auth, Monumental torso, Washington Artists News, 81. *Dealer:* Foxhall Gallery 3301 New Mexico Ave NW Washington DC 20016; Miller Gallery 2715 Erie Ave Cincinnati OH 45208. *Mailing Add:* 9014 Charred Oak Dr Bethesda MD 20817

KOENIG, JOHN FRANKLIN
PAINTER
b Seattle, Wash, Oct 24, 24. *Study:* US Army Univ, France, 45; Univ Wash, 48. *Work:* Mus Art Mod, Paris, France; Ctr Nat Art Contemp, Paris; Mus Western Art, Tokyo; Seattle Art Mus; Mus Art Contemp, Montreal; Musee National d'Art Moderne, Ctr National d'Art et de Culture Georges Pompidou; Nat Mus Art, Osaka, Japan; Musee del'Etat, Luxembourg. *Comn:* Mural & glass windows (with Wogenscky), CHU Hosp, St Antoine, Paris, 65. *Exhib:* Galerie Arnaud, 52-74; Carnegie Inst Int, Pittsburgh, 64; retrospective, Seattle Art Mus, Wash, 70; one person exhibs, Fuji Television Gallery, Tokyo, 77, Tacoma Art Mus, 80, Paris Art Ctr, 82, Galerie Treize, Montreal, 83, Galerie Kutter, Luxembourg, Greg Kucera Gallery, Seattle, 83, Nat Gallery Iceland, Rekajavik, 85 & Carolyn Staley Gallery, Seattle, 86; and others. *Pos:* Cur, Seattle Parks Dept Centennial, 84 & John Pence Gallery, San Francisco, 84. *Teaching:* Artist-in-residence, Sch Appl Arts, Istanbul, 76. *Awards:* Student Show Prize, Univ Wash, 48; Third Prix Artistes Etrangers, Mus Art Mod, Paris, 59; Prix Critiques Art de Presse Parisienne, 1st Biennale Paris, 59; Names Officer de l'Ordre des Arts et es Lettres, France, 86. *Bibliog:* Pierre Restany (auth), John Franklin Koenig, Galerie Arnaud, Paris, 60; Michel Ryon (auth), John Franklin Koenig, Galerie Arnand, Paris, 69; Liliane Thorn-Petit (auth), John Franklin Koenig, Radio-Television Luxem, Bourgeoise, 75; film, Fuji Televison, Tokyo, Japan, 77. *Media:* Acrylic, Oil. *Publ:* Coauth, John Franklin Koenig, 65 & 70; ed, La Danse Contemporaine, Fayard, Paris, 80. *Mailing Add:* 400 18th Ave E No A Seattle WA 98112

KOENIG, PETER L
PAINTER, CURATOR
b Hungary, Sept 10, 33. *Study:* Mass Col Art, BFA, 59; Cranbrook Acad Art, MFA, 61; Harvard Univ, EdM, 71; further study-Warsaw Acad Fine Arts; Boston Univ; Mass Inst Technol. *Work:* RI Col, Providence; Univ NDak, Grand Forks; Weber State Col, Ogden, Utah; Prahran Col, Melbourne, Australia; Ctr Contemp Art, Great Falls, Mont. *Exhib:* Butler Inst Am Art, Youngstown, Ohio, 63; Boston Arts Festival, 64; Pa Acad Fine Arts, Philadelphia, 66; solo exhib, Harvard Univ, Cambridge, Mass, 71, Ctr Contemp Art, Great Falls, Mont, 85, Univ Hawaii, 91, Fitchburg Mus, Mass, 92, Heritage Plantation of Sandwich, Mass, 92, Mass Col Art, 93; Salt Lake Art Ctr, Utah, 75. *Collections Arranged:* Utah Artist Today, Brigham Young Univ, Utah, 77; Rodger P Kingston: Photographs, Univ Ark, 80; Rituals of the Land, Art Complex Mus, Duxbury, Mass, 86; New Horizons: 19th Century American Marine Painting (auth, catalog), Art Complex Mus, Duxbury, 88; Falmouth: A Visual Legacy, Cape Mus Fine Arts, Mass, 88. *Pos:* Dean, Art Dept, Prahran Col, Melbourne, Australia, 76-79; cur, Art Complex Mus, Duxbury, Mass, 85-89. *Teaching:* Prof painting & drawing, RI Col, Providence, 63-67; chmn art dept, Wheelock Col, Boston, 67-71 & Weber Col, Utah, 71-76; prof, Univ Ark, 79-82; lectr, Univ Hawaii, 90. *Awards:* Provincetown Workshop Fel, Mass, 61; McDowell Fel, 64; Fulbright Grant, 64-65; US Bicentennial Grant, 76. *Mem:* Am Asn Mus; New Eng Mus Asn; Col Art Asn Am; Falmouth Artists Guild; Honolulu Acad Fine Arts. *Media:* Acrylic, Photography. *Publ:* Auth, Rituals of the Land: Native American Art of the Colorado Plateau, Art Complex Mus, 86; Falmouth: A Visual Legacy, Teaticket Press, 87. *Dealer:* Picchi Gallery Piazza di Brancoli Lucca Italy 55050; Gallery 333 North Falmouth MA. *Mailing Add:* Box 456 Falmouth MA 02541

KOENIG, ROBERT J
MUSEUM DIRECTOR
b Jersey City, NJ, June 6, 35. *Study:* Pratt Inst, BS(art educ), 57; Yale Univ, BFA, 59, MFA, 61; New Sch Soc Res; Columbia Univ Sch Gen Studies; Gen Elec Mgt Prog Mus Adminrs. *Pos:* Exhib designer, Newark Mus, NJ, 61-63; asst dir, Morris Mus Arts & Sci, 69-76; from asst dir to assoc dir, Montclair Art Mus, NJ, 76-80, dir, 80-; juror/evaluator, AAM Accreditation Comm, NJ State Coun on Arts & Inst Awards, 85-88; Md State Coun Arts, 87; Vietnam Mem Comp, 88; dir, Noyes Mus, Oceanville, NJ, 91- *Teaching:* Instr art, Pub Schs, Union City, NJ, 63-69, Bloomfield Col, NJ, 89-90, Montclair State Col, NJ, 88-89, Univ Pa, 90, Berkshire Sch Contemp Art, North Adams, Mass, 92; adj prof, Stockton State Col, Pomona, NJ, 92- *Awards:* First Prize, Grad Painting, Yale Univ, 60; Excellence Award, NJ Art Dir's Club, 90; Silver Medal, The Song of the Loom, Leipzig Int Bk Exhib, 90. *Mem:* MAAM, Gov NJ; Am Asn Mus; Nat Trust His Preservation; NJ Mus Coun (bd of dir), 85-87; Long-range Planning Comm, 87-88; AAMD (chmn, Accreditation comn); Nat Arts Club; Yale Club, New York; Nat Arts Club, New York. *Mailing Add:* c/o Noyes Mus Lily Lake Rd Oceanville NJ 08231

KOEPNICK, ROBERT CHARLES
SCULPTOR, EDUCATOR
b Dayton, Ohio, July 8, 07. *Study:* Dayton Art Inst, dipl; Cranbrook Acad Art; also with Carl Milles. *Work:* Dayton Art Inst; Dayton & Montgomery Pub Libr; Portrait of Max Rudolph, Cincinnati Music Hall. *Comn:* Pillar of Faith (bronze sculpture), Bethany Lutheran Village, Centerville, Ohio, 85-86; 2 bronzes, Simon Kenton & Chief Little Turtle, Covington, Kentucky, Greater Cincinnati Bicentennial Celebration; Right Staff Memorial, Air Force Mus, Dayton, Ohio, 90; Kussnerius Memorial, David Church Cemetery, Kettering, Ohio, 92; portrait of Rudy Dudon, Mutual Tool & Die, Pres, Dayton, Ohio 92. *Exhib:* Pa Acad Fine Arts, Philadelphia; Art Inst Chicago; Metrop Mus Art, New York; Nat Acad Design, New York; Syracuse Mus Fine Arts, NY; two-man show, Shillito-Rikes Art Gallery, 83; and others. *Pos:* Tech adv, Ohio Art Coun, 68- *Teaching:* From instr to prof sculpture, Dayton Art Inst, 36-41 & 46-74, emer prof, 74-; vis sculptor, Mt St Joseph Col, 51-55 & Antioch Col, 53-54. *Bibliog:* Richard Camden (auth), Outdoors Sculptures in Ohio, 80. *Mem:* Dayton Soc Painters & Sculptors; Cincinnati Liturgical Art Group. *Media:* All Media. *Mailing Add:* 1134 E Lower Springboro Rd Lebanon OH 45036

KOESTNER, DON
PAINTER
b St Paul, Minn, Nov 28, 23. *Study:* Minneapolis Sch Art, four yrs. *Work:* Brown County, Minn Courthouse; Dakota Co Minn Libr; Minn State Historical Soc Permanent Collection. *Comn:* Mural, St Olaf's Church, Minneapolis, 50; diorama-mural, Goodhue Co Hist Soc, Red Wing, Minn, 69. *Exhib:* Am Artists Prof League, 68; Classical Realism Show, Springville Mus Art, Utah, 82; Amarillo Art Ctr, Tex, 83; Maryhill Mus Art, Goldendale, Wash, 83; The Painters of Light, Dallas, Tex, 83; Classical Realism Conf Show, Heritage Art Gallery, Alexandria, Va, 86; one-man show, Heritage Art Gallery, Alexandria, Va, 87; Lancaster Art Festival, Lancaster, Ohio, 88. *Teaching:* Instr oil painting & drawing, Minn Mus Art Sch, 70-75 & Atelier Lack, Minneapolis, 75-85. *Awards:* Grumbacher Award, Ogunquit Art Ctr Nat Exhib, 64; First Prize for oil painting, Minn State Fair, 66; Award, Am Artists Prof League, 68. *Mem:* Am Soc Classical Realism. *Media:* Oil. *Publ:* Essay, Landscape Painting, Realism in Revolution, Taylor Publ, Dallas, Tex, 85. *Dealer:* Beard Art Galleries 1112 Nicollet Ave Minneapolis MN 55403; Heritage Gallery 228 S Washington St Alexandria VA 22314. *Mailing Add:* 138 B Hwy 61E Silver Bay MN 55614

KOGA, MARY
PHOTOGRAPHER
b Sacramento, Calif, Aug 10, 20. *Study:* Art Inst Chicago, MFA; Univ Chicago, MA; Univ Calif, Berkeley, BA. *Work:* Art Inst of Chicago; San Francisco Mus of Mod Art; Exchange Nat Bank, Chicago; J P Seagram Collection, New York; Kimberley Clark, Wis; Mus Contemp Photog, Chicago; Balch Inst, Philadelphia; Knox Col, Ill; Sioux City Art Ctr; Art Mus STex, Corpus Christi. *Exhib:* One-man shows, Knox Col, Galesburg, Ill, 86, Ill Wesleyan Univ, Bloomington, 88, Univ NJ, Rutgers, 88, Shado Gallery Ore, 77, Utah State Univ, 79, Pittsburgh Film-Makers Gallery, 83, J B Speed Art Mus, Louisville, Ky, 85, Truman Col, Chicago, 85, Santa Fe Ctr for Photography, 90, Adams Gallery, Dunkirk, NY, 90, Camera Club of New York, 91, Art Mus STex, Corpus Christi, 92; San Francisco Mus Mod Art, 73 & 78; Art Inst Chicago, 73 & 84-85; Women of Photography, San Francisco Mus Art, Wellesley Col Mus, Univ Wis, 75, Univ Michigan, 78; Los Angeles Co Mus Nat Hist, 80; Sch Mus Fine Art, Boston, 80; Field Mus Nat Hist, Chicago, 83; Carnegie Mus Nat Hist, Pittsburgh, 83; Houston Ctr, Photography, 88; Sioux City Art Ctr, 87; Univ Wis, Green Bay, 88-90; Rockford Col Art Dept, 91; Soc for Contemp Photo, 91; Cleveland Photog Workshop Gallery, 92. *Teaching:* Asst prof, Univ Chicago, 59-69; mem fac, Columbia Col, 73-80. *Awards:* Ill Art Coun Award, 75, 79 & 84; Nat Endowment Arts, 82; Chicago Off, Fine Art, 88-90. *Bibliog:* Chicago: The City and its Artists, 1945-78, Univ Mich, 78; The Human Condition, Temple Univ, 80; Women of Photography, San Francisco Mus Mod Art, 75. *Mem:* Soc Photog Educ; Friends Photog; Photographic Soc, Art Inst Chicago. *Media:* Color Photographs; Black & White. *Dealer:* Ill Artisans Shop State Ill Bldg Chicago IL; Stuart Baum Chicago FT Wayne Museum SR Gallery; Artworks SR Gallery Rock Island; Artsouth Phila; Consultart Vero Beach FL. *Mailing Add:* 1254 Elmdale Ave Chicago IL 60660

KOGAN, DEBORAH
PAINTER, ILLUSTRATOR
b Philadelphia, Pa, Aug 31, 40. *Study:* Philadelphia Col Art; Pa Acad Fine Arts, 58-62; Univ Pa, Albert C Barnes Found, 62-64. *Work:* Drexel Univ, Philadelphia, Pa; Libr Cong, Washington, DC; Univ Minn, Minneapolis; Free Libr Philadelphia; Montgomery Co Col, Center Square, Pa. *Comn:* Graphic murals, Chase Manhattan Bank, 69. *Exhib:* Pa Acad Fine Arts Bienniel, 67 & 69; Philadelphia Artists, Philadelphia Mus Art, 73, 74 & 79; 110th Exhib Am Watercolor Soc, Nat Acad of Design, New York, 77; American Women in Fine Arts, Moore Col Art, Philadelphia, 77; Mus Philadelphia Civic Ctr, 78; US-Israeli Exchange Exhib, Tel Aviv, 78; Albright Col, 80; Rosenfeld Gallery, Philadelphia, 80, 81 & 85; also many one-woman shows. *Teaching:* Univ the Arts, Philadelphia, currently. *Awards:* Tiffany Grant, 68; Am Inst of Graphic Arts Award for Illustration, 76; Drecel Citation, 87; Purchase Award, Millersville State Col; Carolyn W Field Award for Children's Lit, 88. *Bibliog:* Paul West (auth), Children's books, New York Times, 77; Books Books Books, Philadelphia Col Art, 78; 21 Women Artists, Muse, 79; and others. *Mem:* Artists Equity Asn (mem bd dir, 77-79); Women's Caucus for Art; Muse: Woman's Collab (mem bd dirs, 77-80); Authors Guild. *Media:* Acrylic; Mixed. *Publ:* Illusr, I Have a Sister, My Sister is Deaf, 77, illusr, That is That, 79 & illusr, Through Grandpa's Eyes, 80, Harper & Row; auth & illusr, Sunday Morning We Went to the Zoo, Harper & Row, 81; illusr, Little Tree, Crown Publ, 87; auth & illusr, My Dog Trip, 87; My Daddy was a Soldier, 90; Star Gazing Sky, 91. *Mailing Add:* 810 Southampton Ave Wyndmoor PA 19118

KOGER, IRA MCKISSICK
COLLECTOR, PATRON
b Charleston, SC, Dec 5, 12. *Study:* Col Charleston, BS, 33; Univ SC Law Sch; Rollins Col, hon DFA; Univ SC, LLD, Univ NFla, DLitt. *Exhib:* Genteel Tradition, Painting Exhibition, Rollins Col, Winter Pk, Fla (cataloged); Chinese Ceramic (travelling exhib), Ringling Mus, Sarasota, Fla (cataloged) Exhibited in Museums in Columbia, Savannah, Nashville, Memphis, Little Rock, Norfolk, Richmond, College Park (Md), Charlotte, Tampa, Jacksonville, Orlando. *Collections Arranged:* Celebration of the Art of the Oriental Potter (cataloged), Jacksonville Art Mus, 73. *Pos:* Hon trustee, Jacksonville Art Mus, Fla; trustee, Ringling Mus & Rollins Col. *Interests:* Oriental porcelain. *Collection:* American paintings; French 19th century paintings; Oriental and English ceramics, English and American furniture. *Mailing Add:* 3986 Boulevard Ctr Dr Jacksonville FL 32207

KOHL, BARBARA
PRINTMAKER, PAINTER
b Milwaukee, Wis, Feb 10, 40. *Study:* Univ Wis Madison, BS(art hist); Univ Wis Milwaukee. *Work:* Milwaukee Art Ctr. *Comn:* Painting, comn by Golda Meier, 77. *Exhib:* Wis Painters & Sculptors, Milwaukee Art Ctr, 65; Washington Art, Washington Armory, DC, 77 & 78; New York Show, Allen Park Gallery, 77; Janus Gallery, Washington, DC, 78; Alex Rosenberg Gallery, 78-79; Voices of Past, Women in Jewish Art, Jewish Community Ctr, Washington, DC, 79. *Teaching:* Asst trainer of docents in art hist, Milwaukee Art Ctr, 78- *Awards:* Pub Television Auction Award for Best in Show, 77. *Media:* Color and Fabric on Paper; Oil on Canvas. *Collection:* Milton Avery oils, Morris Lewis, Dubuffet, Hockney, Ralph Fasanella, Wayne Thiebold, Hepworth, Suttman, Saul Steinberg. *Mailing Add:* 777 N Prospect Milwaukee WI 53202

KOHLER, RUTH DEYOUNG
MUSEUM DIRECTOR, CURATOR
b Chicago, Ill, 41. *Study:* Smith Col, Northhampton, Mass, BA; Univ Hamburg, Ger; Kunsthochschule, Hamburg, Ger; Banff Sch of Fine Arts; Univ Wis, Madison; Lakeland Col, LHD, 84. *Pos:* Dir & mem, Kohler Found, Inc, Wis, 60-, pres 85-; asst dir, John Michael Kohler Arts Ctr, Sheboygan, Wis, 68-72, dir, 72-; mem, Wis Arts Bd, Madison, 73-81 & chmn, 74-77; mem, Wis Am Revolution Bicentennial Comn, Madison, 74-77; mem visual arts panel, Nat Endowment Arts, Washington, DC, 75-, mem visual arts mus panel, 76-78, mem, Selection Panel for Percent Art Prog Madison, Wis, 86. *Teaching:* Instr printmaking, Univ Alta, Calgary, Can, 64-66. *Awards:* Fel, Wis Acad Sci, Art & Letts, Madison. *Mem:* Nat Coun on Ed for Ceramic Arts, 90; hon bd Jamaes Renlick Alliance, Smithsonian Inst, 90; hon mem Col Fel Am Crafts Coun, 92. *Mailing Add:* 608 New York Ave Sheboygan WI 53081

KOHLMEYER, IDA (R)
PAINTER, SCULPTOR
b New Orleans, La, Nov 3, 12. *Study:* Newcomb Col, New Orleans, BA, 33, MFA, 56; also with Hans Hofmann, 56. *Work:* Mus Fine Arts, Houston, Tex; High Mus Art, Atlanta, Ga; Corcoran Gallery Art & Nat Collection, Smithsonian Inst, Washington, DC; Brooklyn Mus Art, Metrop Mus Art & Jewish Mus, New York; San Francisco Mus Art; plus many others. *Comn:* Krewe of Poydras, New Orleans, 83. *Exhib:* Painting in the South: 1564-1980, Va Mus; American Women: 20th Century, Lakeview Ctr Arts & Sci, Peoria, Ill, 72; North, East, West, South & Middle, Moore Col Art, Philadelphia, 75; Thirty Years-Traveling Retrospective (with catalog), Mint Mus, Charlotte, NC; one-women shows, Allene Lapides Gallery, Santa Fe, NMex, Tucson Mus Art, Ariz, Gimpel Fils, London, Eng; and many others. *Teaching:* Instr drawing & painting, Newcomb Col, 56-64; assoc prof painting, Univ New Orleans, 73-75. *Awards:* Ford Found Purchase Award, 28th Corcoran Biennial Am Art, 63; Mus Purchase Award, High Mus, Atlanta, 63 & 66; Artists of SE & Tex Biennial Award, New Orleans Mus Art, 75; Outstanding Achievement in Visual Arts Award, Nat Women's Caucus for the Arts, 81; plus many others. *Bibliog:* Ida Kohlmeyer: New dimensions, Arts Mag, 4/82; Ida Kohlmeyer, Times Picayune, 4/83; Theodore F Wolff (auth), The Art of Ida Kohlmeyer-A Message of Friskiness and Joy, Christian Sci Monitor, 9/10/84; Ida Kohlmeyer Sculpture 1968-1985, Newcomb Col, Tulane Univ & New Orleans Mus Art, 85; Roger Green (auth), Ida Kohlmeyer Month, Art News, summer 85; Ida Kuhlmeyer Thirty Years, Mint Mus, 83. *Media:* Oil, Mixed Media; Wood, Welded Metal. *Dealer:* Gimpel & Weitzenhoffer 1040 Madison Ave New York NY 10021; Gimpel Fils 30 Davies St London England WIYILG. *Mailing Add:* 11 Pelham Ave Metairie LA 70005

KOHN, MICHAEL BUNDY
ART DEALER, CRITIC
b Los Angeles, Calif, Sept 20, 58. *Study:* Univ Calif, Los Angeles, BFA(art hist), 80; Inst Fine Arts, New York Univ, MA(art hist), 84. *Pos:* US ed, Flash Art Mag, 83-85; co-owner & dir, Garet/Kohn Gallery, New York, 83-84; owner, Michael Kohn Gallery, Los Angeles, 85- *Teaching:* Teaching asst, art hist, New York Univ, 83; vis teacher, Art Ctr, Pasadena, 86. *Awards:* Hill Rebay Fel, Guggenheim Mus, 83. *Res:* Recurring themes and motifs of historical styles in contemporary art and current social context. *Specialty:* Contemporary art from Europe, New York and Los Angeles. *Publ:* Auth, Carlo Maria Mariani and Neoclassicism, 1/82 & Mannerism and contemporary art, 3/84 Arts Mag; Styles and their social context in the East Village, Univ Calif, Santa Barbara Mus (exhib catalog), 10/84; Romantic visions, 1/85 & Hypermannerism, 6/86, Flash Art Mag. *Mailing Add:* 920 Colorado Ave Santa Monica CA 90401

KOHN, MISCH
PAINTER, PRINTMAKER
b Kokomo, Ind, Mar 26, 16. *Study:* John Herron Art Inst, BFA, 39; also with Jose Clemente Oroszco & Leopoldo Mendez, Mexico City, 43. *Work:* Bibliot Nat, Paris; Victoria Mus, Melbourne, Australia; Whitney Mus Am Art, Mus Mod Art, Metrop Mus Art, New York; and others. *Exhib:* Art Inst Chicago, 51, 60 & 70; Los Angeles Co Mus Art, 61; Mus Nat Art Mod & Bibliot Nat, Paris, 59; retrospective, Ford Found & Am Fedn Arts, 61; one-man exhibs, David Stuart Gallery, 63-66 & Zabriskie Gallery, New York, 72-77; and many others. *Teaching:* Assoc prof art, Ill Inst Technol, 53-65, prof art, 65-70; prof, Calif State Univ, Hayward, 72-80. *Awards:* Guggenheim Fel, 67; Philadelphia Print Club, 69; Mark Rothko Found Grant, 71; and others. *Bibliog:* Gabor Peterdi (auth), Printmaking: Methods Old and New, Macmillan, 59; S W Hayter (auth), About Prints, Oxford Univ Press, 62. *Mem:* Print Coun Am; Nat Acad Design; and others. *Mailing Add:* 1860 Grove Way Castro Valley CA 94546

KOHN, WILLIAM ROTH
PAINTER, EDUCATOR
b St Louis, Mo, Aug 23, 31. *Study:* Wash Univ, BFA, 49; Atelier 17, Paris, with S W Hayter, 54; Mills Col, MA, 60. *Work:* Springfield Art Mus, Mo; St Louis Art Mus; Carlton Col, Minn; Dalhousie Art Gallery, Halifax; Chase Manhattan Bank. *Comn:* Mural, Am Automobile Asn, Mo, 78; Mayor's Award for the Arts (print), Arts & Humanities Comn, St Louis, 81. *Exhib:* Seventy-Ninth & Eighty-First Ann Painting & Sculpture Show, San Francisco Mus, 60 & 62; Mid Am Show, Nelson Gallery, Kansas City & St Louis Art Mus, 65-67; one-man shows, Loretto Hilton Gallery, Webster Col, 70, Mobile Art Gallery, Ala, 73, Terry Moore Gallery, St Louis, 76 & Ex Convento Del Carmen, Guadalajara, Mex, 79, Currents, St Louis Art Mus, 80, Alcazar Palace, Seville, Spain, 86, Jan Cicero Gallery, Chicago, 88 & Elliot Smith Gallery, St Louis, 88; Int Exhib Graphic Art, Mus Art, Ljubljana, Yugoslavia, 71; Midwest Invitational, Krannert Mus, Univ Ill, 76; Salon de Octubre, Casa de la Cultura, Guadalajara, Mex, 79 & 82; Randall Gallery, St Louis, Mo, 90. *Teaching:* Prof painting & design, Wash Univ, 63- *Awards:* Fulbright Hays Grant to India, 65; Mo State Coun Arts Grant, 77; 1st Prize, St Louis Posters, First St Forum, 82. *Bibliog:* Robert W Duff (auth), Art Museum debut for William Kohn, St Louis Post Dispatch, 4/25/80; Francisco Correal (auth), Bill Kohn: El Ultimo viajero romantico, Guia 16, Spain, 6/25/86; Patricia Rice (auth), William Kohn puts Seville on campus, St Louis Post Dispatch, 11/21/86. *Mem:* Art Coord Coun (chmn St Louis Area, 75-76); St Louis Artists Coalition. *Media:* Acrylics, Watercolor. *Publ:* Auth, Pilgrimage to Rocio, St Louis Post Dispatch, 11/30/87; Poloma Blanca, Washington Univ Mag, summer 88. *Dealer:* Elliot Smith 360 N Skinker St Louis Mo 63112; Jan Cicero 221 W Erie Chicago IL 61610. *Mailing Add:* 6100 Kingsbury St Louis MO 63112

KOHUT, LORENE
PAINTER
b La Port, Tex, Nov 16, 29. *Study:* With Coulton Waugh & John Gould. *Work:* Court Gen Sessions, Washington, DC; Pa State Univ; Fred Clark Mus, Carversville, Pa; Del State Col; Wesley Col. *Exhib:* Ogunquit Arts Ctr 49th Nat, Maine, 69; Hudson Valley Art Asn, 42nd & 43rd Nat, White Plains, NY, 69-70; Nat Acad Design, NY, 70; Catharine Lorillard Wolfe Nat, New York, 80; Am Artist Prof League Grand Nat Exhib, 81. *Awards:* Gold Medal Oils, Hudson Valley Art Asn, 69; Gold Medal, watercolor, Catharine Lorillard Wolfe Nat, 80; Gold Medal, oil, Am Artist Prof League Grand Nat Exhib, 81. *Mem:* Artists Equity Asn; Am Artist Prof League. *Media:* Mixed Media, Alkaloid. *Dealer:* Extra Touch of Class Alexandria VA 22312. *Mailing Add:* 706 Garwood St Smithville TX 78957

KOLBA, STAHANOUCH TAMARA See St Tamara

KOLBOWSKI, SILVIA
CONCEPTUAL ARTIST, PHOTOGRAPHER
b Buenos Aires, Arg, 1953. *Study:* Hunter Col, BA. *Exhib:* Artist's Space, New York, 80; Nature Morte Gallery, New York, 85 & 86; Whitney Mus Am Art, 87, 88, 89 & 90; Postmasters Gallery, New York, 88, 89 & 92; Material

Ethics, Milford Gallery, New York, 88; Interim Art, London, 88; New Directions, S Bitter-Larkin Gallery, New York, 90; Marginal Practices, Gracie Mansion Gallery, New York, 90; Galerie Roger Pailhas, Paris, 92. *Awards:* New York Found Arts Grant, 86; Nat Endowment Arts, 89. *Bibliog:* Roberta Smith (auth), Subtle ways to eat your cake and have it too, NY Times Gallery Rev, 10/8/89; Barbara Moore (auth), Folio Artist's Publications, 89; Joshua Decter (auth), Decoding the Museum, Flash Art, 11-12/91; Josefina Ayerza (auth), Silvia Kolbarski, Lacanian Ink, New York, No 3, 91; Silvia Kolbowski: Projects, Border Ed, New York, 92. *Mailing Add:* c/o Postmasters 80 Greene St New York NY 10012

KOLDORF, IRENE JANET
SCULPTOR
b Newark, NJ, Aug 8, 25. *Study:* Pratt Inst, Brooklyn, NY, 43-44; Kean Col, Union, NJ, BA(art educ), 70; Rutgers-Newark Mus Training Prog, cert, 80. *Work:* Am Soc Parenteral & Enteral Nutrition, Washington, DC; Breaux Mart, New Orleans, La; Pvt Collections, Lorraine Gerson, New York, NY. *Comn:* Metal figures, Temple Sha'Arey Shalom, comn by the Lippy family, Springfield, NJ, 82. *Exhib:* Double Images, Port Washington Pub Libr, Port Washington, NY, 85 & Monmouth Mus, Monmouth, NJ, 85; Art by Design, Princeton, NJ, 88; Monmouth Mus, Lincroft, NJ, 89; Trenton City Mus, NJ, 89; Zimmerli Mus, East Brunswick, NJ, 89; and others. *Pos:* Founder & corresp secy, Springfield Asn Creative Arts, Springfield, NJ, 63-68. *Teaching:* Teacher sculpture, Westfield Summer Wkshp, NJ, 75-84; docent humanities, Newark Mus, NJ, 80-; artist-in-residence, Artists League Cent NJ, 85 & 86, 90 & 92; demonstr sculpture, East Brunswick-TV Channel 8, 85, 86 & 90. *Awards:* Best in Show, Springfield Asn Creative Arts, NJ, 65; Hon mention, Middlesex County Mus, NJ, 85; Second Place, Wahington Sq Outdoor Art Exhib, New York, NY, 85; Awards, Catherine Lorillard Wolfe Art Club & Nat Arts Club, New York, 90 & 92. *Bibliog:* Ann Betty Weinshenker (auth), article, NJ Music & Arts, 78. *Mem:* Sculptors Asn NJ (docent, 81-82, secy, 83-, pres, 88-89); Artists League Cent NJ; Int Sculpture Ctr, Washington, DC; Women's Caucus Arts; Summit Art Ctr, NJ; Sculptor Asn (pres, NJ, 88-). *Media:* Wood, Stone, Metal. *Mailing Add:* 21 Garden Oval Springfield NJ 07081

KOLISNYK, PETER
PAINTER, SCULPTOR
b Toronto, Ont, Nov 30, 34. *Study:* Western Tech Sch Toronto, Ont, with Fred Fraser, Julius Griffith, Margaret Aitken & George Griffin, 51-54. *Work:* Art Gallery Ont, Toronto; Art Bank, Can Coun, Ottawa; Winnipeg Art Gallery, Man; Queen's Silver Jubilee Art Collection, Govt Ont, Toronto; Ukrainian Inst Mod Art, Chicago. *Comn:* Agnes Etherington Gallery, Queens Univ, Kingston, Ont; Peterboro Art Gallery. *Exhib:* One-man exhibs, Art Gallery Ont, 77-78, Mercer Union, Toronto, 83 & Art Gallery Lindsay, 83; Montreal Mus Fine Arts, 60, 62, 67 & 69; Fourth Biennial Exhib Can Art, Nat Gallery Can, Ottawa, 61; Art Gallery Ont, Toronto, 67, 69, 70, 72 & 77; Albright-Knox Art Gallery, 68; A Plastic Presence, San Francisco Mus Art, and others, 69-70; 49th Parallels--New Canadian Art, Mus Contemp Art, Chicago, and others, 71; Contemporary Outdoor Sculpture, Guildwood Hall, Toronto, 82; Rational Alternatives, Harbourfront Art Gallery, Toronto, 83; Works on Paper, Ukrainian Inst Mod Art, Chicago, 83; and many others. *Pos:* Cur, Cobourg Art Gallery, 64-69; trustee, Art Gallery Ont, 82- *Teaching:* Dir & lectr art, Glendon Col, York Univ, Toronto, 75-; instr, Prison Arts Found, Kingston, Ont, 78 & Emily Carr Col Art, Vancouver, 82- *Awards:* Sculpture Award, Ont Soc Artists, 72; Can Coun Sr Arts Grant, 75-76; Ont Arts Coun Grants, 75, 77-79 & 81-83. *Bibliog:* Clara Hargittay (auth), article, Art Mag, 5-7/82; David Nasby & Fern Bayer (coauth), Art for Architecture, Govt Ont, 82. *Mem:* Can Artists Representation Ont; Can Soc Painters Watercolour; Ont Soc Artists; Royal Can Acad Arts. *Media:* Watercolor; Miscellaneous. *Mailing Add:* c/o Ukranian Inst Mod Art 2320 W Chicago Ave Chicago IL 60622

KOLLER-DAVIES, EVA
ASSEMBLAGE ARTIST, PAINTER
b St Peternov, Rumania, Jan 29, 25; Can citizen. *Study:* Central Tech Sch, 43; Ontario Col Art, Toronto, 68-70; Univ Toronto, 72-73. *Work:* Permanet collection, Ctr Arts, Vero Beach, Fla, 92. *Exhib:* Traveling exhib, Ont Soc Artists, 76; Five Abstract Artists, Gallery of Riverside Theatre, Vero Beach, Fla, 86; solo exhib, Indian River Community Col Gallery, Fla, 86, Gallery of Brevard Community Col, Melbourne, Fla, 88 & McAlpine Ctr Arts, Ft Pierce, Fla, 89; Florida Artists, Ctr for Arts, Vero Beach, 88; Ont Soc Artist, McDonald Gallery, Toronto, 88. *Media:* Acrylic, Mixed Media. *Mailing Add:* 788 Acacia Rd Vero Beach FL 32963

KOLLIKER, WILLIAM AUGUSTIN
PAINTER, PRINTMAKER
b Bern, Switz, Oct 12, 05; US citizen. *Study:* Berner Secundar Schule, Bern; Nat Acad Design, Md Inst; Boston Sch Art, Grand Cent Art Sch; Art Students League; Univ Tex, El Paso. *Work:* Univ Tex El Paso; Grumbacher Collection, New York; El Paso Nat Bank; El Paso Fed Savings & Loan; El Paso Chamber of Commerce; Kemp Fork, El Paso Mus Art, El Paso, Tex. *Comn:* Mosaic mural, El Fed Savings & Loan, El Paso, 64; design of bronze eagles, Amistad Dam, Del Rio, Tex, 68; gold medal, 69 & bronze plaques, 70, Chamizal Settlement. *Exhib:* Santa Fe Mus Art, 58; NMex State Univ; Las Cruces Art Ctr, 74; one-man shows, El Paso Mus Art, Inst Nat de Bellas Artes Museo de Arte E Historica, 74, Abilene Fine Arts Mus, 75, Museo De Arte E Distoria-Intl Friendship exhib, The Tissot Galleries, Florisant, US Dept Interior, Washington, DC (bicentennial celebration), 76, Gallery 1, Midland, Tex, Roswell State Bank, NMex, 77, Ojo del Sol, El Paso, Tex, 82, Univ Tex El Paso, & Coronado State Bank, 82; Barry Stevens Gallery, New York; 5 artists group show, El Paso Mus Art; Sun Carnival Art Exhib, El Paso; Grumbacher Travelon Exhib, New York; Bus Man's Art Show, El Paso, Tex; 25th Ann Tex Painting & Sculpture Exhib, Dallas Mus Art. *Pos:* Dir art, Cunningham & Walsh Advert Agency, New York, 52-54, White & Shuford, El Paso, 54-65; art dir & art ed, Am Weekly, New York, 34-52. *Teaching:* Instr com art, Univ Tex, El Paso, 60-63; mem fac staff, El Paso Mus Art, 73-88. *Awards:* Twice awarded the city of El Paso Conquistador Award; First place Rio Bravo Watercolor Exhib UT El Paso Centennial Mus. *Mem:* Watercolor Soc El Paso. *Media:* Watercolor. *Collection:* Pre-Columbia artifacts and graphic collection. *Publ:* Illusr, Aesop's Fables, 40; Adventures in Puddle Muddle, 41. *Mailing Add:* 3812 Hillcrest Dr El Paso TX 79902

KOLTUN, FRANCES LANG
COLLECTOR, LECTURER
b New York, NY. *Study:* Brooklyn Col, BA; Columbia Univ, MA. *Pos:* Ed, writer & broadcaster, NBC & Syndicated Radio on Collecting, 70- *Mem:* Drawing Soc. *Collection:* Nineteenth and twentieth century drawings and etchings. *Publ:* Numerous articles on art. *Mailing Add:* 45 E 66th St No 4N New York NY 10021

KOMAR, VITALY See Komar and Melamid

KOMAR AND MELAMID
CONCEPTUAL ARTIST, LECTURER
b Moscow, USSR, Komar Sept 11, 43, Melamid July 14, 45. *Study:* Stroganov Inst Art & Design, Moscow, USSR, 67. *Work:* Tel Aviv Mus, Israel; Stedeliyk Mus Amsterdam; Guggenheim Mus, Mus Mod Art & Metrop Mus Art, New York. *Exhib:* Solo exhibs, Wadsworth Atheneum, Hartford, Conn, 78, Mus Mod Art, Oxford, Eng, Mus Decorative Art, Paris, France, 85, Neuen Gesellschaft für Gildende Kunst, Berlin, 88, Brooklyn Mus, 90; Counterparts and Affinitees, Metrop Mus Art, New York, 82; Reallegory, Chrysler Mus, Norfolk, Va, 83; An International Survey, Mus Mod Art, New York, 84; The Biennale of Sydney, Australia, 86; Documenta 8, Kassel, 87; Fifty Years of Collecting: An Anniversary Selection, Sculpture of the Modern Era, Solomon R Guggenheim Found, 87; F I A C Paris, 89; Brooklyn Mus, 90. *Teaching:* Instr visual art, Moskov Regional Art Schole, 68-76. *Awards:* Grant, Nat Endowment Arts, 82. *Bibliog:* Umberto Eco (auth), Bevente Breznev Cola, L'Espresso, 76; Robert Hughes (auth), Through the ironic curtain, Time Mag, 10/25/85; Gary Indiana (auth) Komar and Melamid confidential (cover story), Art in Am, 6/85; Jan Frazier (auth), Profile, The New Yorker, 12/86; Jean-Hubert Martin (auth), L'art da da da de Komar et Melamid, Art Press, N103, 5/86; Carter Ratcliff (auth), Komar and Melamid, Abbeville Press, 89. *Publ:* Coauths, The barren flowers of evil, 3/80 & In search of religion, 5/80, Artforum; Death Poems, NGBK-Nichen, Ger, 88. *Dealer:* Ronald Feldman Gallery 33 Mercer St New York NY 10013. *Mailing Add:* 718 Broadway, No 5D New York NY 10003

KOMARIN, GARY
PAINTER
b New York, NY, Sept 14, 51. *Study:* Albany State Univ, studied with Richard Stankiewicz, BA, 73; New Sch Social Res, 74; New York Studio Sch, studied with Paul George, 74; Art Students League, studied with Gabriel Laderman, 75; Brooklyn Mus Sch, 75; Boston Univ Sch Fine Arts, studied with Philip Guston, MFA(painting), 77. *Work:* AT&T, New York; Boston Univ; Stevens Corp, Ark; United Bank Houston; Prudential Ins Co; and others. *Comn:* Painting for Clarendon House Project, Liebman & Liebman, New York, 80; painting on paper, comn by chmn bd trustees, Kimball Art Mus, Ft Worth, Tex, 85; Chris Thompson album (cover painting), Atlantic Records. *Exhib:* Solo exhibs, Mus Art, Univ Ore, Eugene, 81, Maxwell Davidson Gallery, New York, 85, Helander Gallery, Palm Beach, 88, Brian Reddy, Little Silver, NJ, Sandler/Hudson Gallery, Atlanta, Ga, 91, Klarfeld/Perry Gallery, New York, 92 & others; East Village and New York-New Work (with catalog), Moos Art, Fla, 85; Best of Season, Helander Gallery, Fla, 86; Dog Days of Summer, Littlejohn Smith Gallery, New York, 86; Morris Mus Biennial, NJ, 88; and others. *Teaching:* Asst prof painting & drawing, Hobart & William Smith Cols, Geneva, NY, 77-78, Univ Ore, 80-81 & Southern Methodist Univ, Dallas, 81-84. *Awards:* Finalist, Int Art Competition, Los Angeles, 83; 1st Prize, 19th Ann Painting Competition, Houston, 83; Philip Hulitan Award, Soc of Four Arts, Palm Beach, 86. *Bibliog:* Carol Everingham (auth), A comical view of American dream lost, Houston Post, 11/85; Pam Perry (auth), Stories in paint, Atlanta Constitution, 11/85; W Zimmer (auth), The mentor shines through at show in Little Silver, 87, Summer splendors outside the city, 87, New York Times; Eileen Watkins, Surrealist loads canvas with images so viewer can find something new, New York Times, 87; and others. *Mem:* Col Art Asn. *Media:* Oil on Canvas, Oil on Paper. *Dealer:* Klarfeld/Perry 472 Broone St New York NY 10012. *Mailing Add:* 6 Kevin Dr Flanders NJ 07836

KOMODORE, BILL
PAINTER
b Athens, Greece, Oct 23, 32; US citizen. *Study:* Tulane Univ La, BA, 55 & MFA, 57; Hans Hofmann Sch, Provincetown; also with Mark Rothko. *Work:* Whitney Mus Am Art; Des Moines Art Ctr, Iowa; Nat Gallery Art; Walker Art Ctr; Milwaukee Mus Art; Hamilton Gallery Art, Ont, Canada; Dallas Mus Art, Tex. *Exhib:* The Responsive Eye, Mus Mod Art, 64; Albright-Knox Art Gallery, Buffalo, NY, 65 & 68; Whitney Mus Am Art, New York, 65 & 68; Marcia Tucker's The Art of the Invisible, Visual Arts Gallery, New York, 70; one man shows, Haydon Calhoun Gallery, Dallas, 61, Howard Wise Gallery, NY, 65 & 67, Automation House, New York, 73, D W Gallery, Dallas, 81, 83 & 84 & Eugene Binder Gallery, Dallas, 87; retrospective show, Mary Washington Col, 75; Made in Texas, Univ Tex, Austin, 79; 12 Artists

from North Texas, Dallas Mus Fine Arts, 79; Texas Time Machine, Cullen Cutz, Houston, 86; First Texas Triennial (with catalog), Contemp Arts Mus, Houston, 88; Texas II, San Francisco Mus Modern Art, 88; three-man show (McManaway, Komodore, Gummelt), Baylor Univ Gallery, Waco, Tex, 90; The Vessel, Dallas, Tex, 90. *Teaching:* Vis artist, Mary Washington Col, 73-76, Richland Col, Arts Magnet High Sch, Dallas, 77-78, Brookhaven Col, Dallas, 81-90, Dallas Theatre Ctr, 81-84 & Univ Tex, Dallas, 82-88; painter, prof, Southern Methodist Univ, 90- *Awards:* Bausch & Lomb Sci Award, 50; Houston Mus Award, Dallas Mus of Fine Arts, 60; Tex Comn on Arts Grant, 79-80. *Bibliog:* Robert Trout (interviewer), Op art, CBS News, 64; Cyril Barrett (auth), An introduction to optical art, Studio Vista, 71; R P Warren (auth), Ballad of a Sweet Dream of Peace: A Charade for Eastern, Press Works, Dallas, 81; Janet Kuther (auth), article Dallas Morning News, 1/30/86; Melissa Morrison (auth), article Dallas Morning News, 8/90. *Media:* Oil, Watercolor. *Publ:* Illusr, Fishes of Lake Pontchartrain, Tulane Univ Press, 54; contribr, Contemporary American Painting and Sculpture, Univ Ill Press, 65; Young America, 1965, Whitney Mus Am Art, 65. *Mailing Add:* c/o Southern Methodist Univ Div Art Rm 1640 0AC Dallas TX 75275

KONI, NICOLAUS
SCULPTOR, LECTURER
b Hungary, May 6, 11; US citizen. *Study:* Acad Fine Art, Vienna, Austria, dipl anat fine art; Masters Sch, Paris; Masters Sch, Florence, Italy. *Work:* Bronze sculptures, Fountain of the Night, Okla Art Ctr; bust, J V Forrestal, Forrestal Bldg & Annapolis Naval Mus; Marian Anderson, Metrop Opera Lincoln Ctr, New York & Kennedy Ctr Performing Art, Washington, DC; The Freedom of Man, Sen Margaret Chase Smith Libr, Washington, DC; and others. *Comn:* Bronze sculpture of C Walter Nichols, NY Univ Bus Admin Sch; marble portraits, R Reynolds, Wake Forest Col, Winston-Salem, NC & M W Green, West Tex Mus, Lubbock, Tex; monumental bronze, American Indian, comn by Seminole Slub, Palm Beach, Fla; bronze sculpture, Dr Walter Nausboune, Palm Beach Good Samaritan Hosp; bronze monument, American Indian, Seminole Club, W Pal Beach; stone carving Marshal R Pilsindski (Pres of Free Democratic Poland). *Exhib:* Whitney Mus Am Art, New York; Birmingham Mus Fine Art, Ala; Parrish Art Mus, Southampton, NY; Milch, Weintraub Gallery, New York; Int Expos of Sculpture (sponsored by Smithsonian Inst), Paris. *Teaching:* Instr sculpture, Graham-Eckes Sch, Palm Beach, formerly; lectr, Univ Bridgeport, formerly; instr fine art, Univ Mo, Columbia, formerly. *Awards:* First Prize in Art, Eighth Ann Art Festival, Parrish Art Mus; Knighthood of the Order of St George by Prince Henry, Imperial House of Byzantine, 92. *Bibliog:* Pierre Bourdell (forward), Nicolaus Koni, A Sculptor Bringing Out the Spirit Asleep in Matter (film), New York Fine Arts Coun; Nicholas Koni--Classical Sculptor in the Modern World (film). *Mem:* Nat Sculpture Soc; Quilleis Art Soc. *Media:* Miscellaneous Media. *Dealer:* Studio & Sculpture Garden East Gate Montauk Highway Westhampton NY 11977; Weitraub Gallery Madison Ave New York NY. *Mailing Add:* 146 Australian Ave Palm Beach FL 33480

KONOPKA, JOSEPH
PAINTER
b Philadelphia, Pa, Oct 6, 32. *Study:* Cooper Union, grad, 54; Columbia Univ, 55. *Work:* Butler Inst Am Art, Youngstown, Ohio; Mus City of New York; Nat Mus, Warsaw, Poland; Nat Mus, Cracow, Poland; NJ State Mus; Peabody Mus, Salem, Mass; and others. *Exhib:* Butler Inst Am Art, 74, 77, 79, 82, 84 & 87; Brooklyn Mus, 76, 78 & 81; Hunterdon Art Ctr, Clinton, NJ, 78-83, 85 & 90; Recent Acquisitions, 81, Drawing from Permanent Collections, 82 & On the 20th Century, 83, Monclair Art Mus, NJ; Capricorn Galleries, Bethesda, Md, 81 & 91; Newark Pub Libr, 87-88; Atlantic City Art Ctr, 89 & 90; Bergen Mus, Paramus, NJ 91; and others. *Pos:* Scenic artist, NBC TV, Late night with David Letterman. *Awards:* Purchase Awards, Newark Mus, 68 & NJ State Mus, 70; Medal Honor, NJ Painters & Sculptors Soc, 71; Purchase Awards, Ocean City Art Ctr, NJ, 70 & Atlantic City, NJ, 71. *Bibliog:* articles, Arts Mag, 2/73 & 12/75; Sunday New York Times, 76 & Newark Star-Ledger, 10/79 & 1/82; article, NJ Art Form Mag, 3-4/81. *Mem:* Assoc Artists NJ (vpres, 77-85); United Scenic Artists, NY. *Media:* Acrylic. *Dealer:* Capricorn Gallery 4849 Rugby Ave Bethesda MD 20814. *Mailing Add:* 26 Snowden Pl Glen Ridge NJ 07028

KONRAD, ADOLF FERDINAND
PAINTER
b Bremen, Ger; US citizen. *Study:* Newark Sch Fine & Indust Art, NJ; Cummington Sch, Mass; Newark State Col, Hon DFA. *Work:* Newark Mus; Springfield Mus Fine Art, Mass; Montclair Art Mus, NJ; Nat Acad Design, New York; NJ State Mus, Trenton. *Comn:* Mural, Veterans Nursing Facility, NJ State Coun Arts, Paramus, NJ, 86. *Exhib:* Am Painting Today, Metrop Mus Art, 50 & Whitney Mus Am Art Ann, 52, New York; Butler Inst Am Art, Youngstown, Ohio, 56; Pa Acad Fine Arts Painting Exhib, 64; Mainstream 70, Marietta Col, Ohio, 70; Mus Fine Arts, Springfield, Mass, 73; retrospective exhibs, Montclair Art Mus, NJ & State Mus, Trenton, 80. *Teaching:* Adj instr painting, Newark State Col, 72; artist in residence, Somerset Co Col, NJ, 76-80. *Awards:* Tiffany Found Fel Creative Painting, 61; Andrew Carnegie Prize, Nat Acad Design, 67; NJ Symphony Ann Arts Award, 69. *Bibliog:* An artist looks at Newark, Newark Mus, 66; Henry Gasser (auth), Adolf Konrad, painter of the American scene, Am Artist, 11/68; Visions on Canvas (film), Gibson Gallery, Caldwell, NJ, 89. *Mem:* Nat Acad Design; Artists Equity Asn; Assoc Artists NJ. *Media:* Oil. *Mailing Add:* c/o The Magenta Gallery 131 Washington St PO Box 55 Rocky Hill NJ 08553

KONZAL, JOSEPH
SCULPTOR
b Milwaukee, Wis, Nov 5, 05. *Study:* Beaux-Arts Inst Design, New York; Art Students League, with Max Weber & Robert Laurent, 26-31. *Work:* Tate Gallery Art, London; Whitney Mus Am Art, New Sch Social Res, New York, Smithsonian Inst, Washington, DC, New Jersey State Mus, Trenton, New Jersey; Canton Art Inst, Ohio; Storm King Art Ctr, Mountainville, NY; Gen Serv Admin Bldg, Washington, DC; Norton Gallery Art, W Palm beach, Fla. *Comn:* Sculpture, Blossom Music Ctr, Cuyahoga Falls, Ohio, 72; Outdoor Sculpture, Gen Servs Admin, Art & Archit Prog, Fed Off Bldg, Dayton, Ohio, 77. *Exhib:* Six Ann Shows, 48-68 & Geometric Abstraction in America, 62, Whitney Mus Am Art; Recent Sculpture, Mus Mod Art, New York, 58; one man exhibs, Bertha Schaefer Gallery, NY, 60, 63, 65, 67 & 71, Canton Art Inst, Ohio, 74, Andre Zarre Gallery, New York, 78 & 80 & Berman/Daferner Gallery, New York, 92; NJ State Mus Ann, 65-71; May Show for Ohio Artists, Cleveland Mus Art, 72 & 75; Boston Mus Fine Arts; Larry Aldrich Mus, Conn; Am Acad & Inst Arts & Lett, 81, 82 & 83. *Teaching:* Instr, Newark Sch for Fine & Indust Arts, Queens Col, New York, Adelphi Univ, Malloy Col, Brooklyn Mus Art Sch & Kent State Univ, formerly. *Awards:* Guggenheim Fel for Creative Work in Sculpture, 65-66; Sculpture Competition Prize for Nassau Co Ct House, John F Kennedy Mem Cult Ctr, 68; Adolph & Ester Gottlieb Found Grant, 82. *Mem:* Sculptor's Guild. *Media:* Metal, Wood. *Mailing Add:* 160 E Third St New York NY 10009

KOONS, DARELL J
EDUCATOR, PAINTER
b Albion, Mich, Dec 18, 24. *Study:* Bob Jones Univ, BS, 51; Western Mich Univ, MA, 55; Eastern Mich Univ. *Work:* Butler Inst Am Art, Youngstown, Ohio; Mint Mus Art, Charlotte, Gov Mansion, Columbia, SC State Art Collection Mus Art, SC; Gibbes Gallery, Charleston, SC. *Exhib:* Acquavella Galleries, New York, 64 & 66; Springfield Mus Art Nat, Mass, 65; Soc Four Arts Nat, Palm Beach, Fla, 67; one-man shows, Mint Mus, Charlotte, NC, Wash Co Mus Art, Hagerstown, Md, Columbus Mus, Columbus, Ga, Jesse Besser Mus, Alpena, Mich; Art Embassies Prog, US State Dept, 90. *Teaching:* Instr art, Homer Community Schs, 52-54; Bob Jones Univ, 55- *Awards:* Purchase Awards, Guild SC Artists, 63, Davis Assocs, Chattanooga, Tenn, 65 & Wake Forest Univ Gallery Contemp Art, 65. *Bibliog:* Steve Yates (auth), Greenville's noted barn painter, Sandlapper, 3/68. *Mem:* Greenville Art Asn & Guild; Guild SC Artists. *Media:* Watercolor, Acrylic. *Mailing Add:* 6 Yancy Dr Greenville SC 29615

KOOPALETHES, OLIVIA (OLIVIA KOOPALETHES ALBERTS)
PAINTER, PRINTMAKER
b New York. *Study:* Cooper Union for the advancement of Sci & Art, New York, 43, 44, 45; study with Wallace Harrison, New York, 46-49; Atelier Gernand Leger, Paris, 49; Atelier Andre Lhote, Paris, 50; Roberto DeLamonica, 76-79, Krishna Reddy, New York Blackburn Workshop, 80 & Shou Ping Liao, 81, Tenafly, NJ. *Exhib:* solo-shows, Maurice Pin Libr, Fair Lawn, NJ, 84, On Paper, New City Libr, New York, 89; 100 Years/100 Works, Nat Asn Women Artist, Islip Art Mus, New York, 89; Foreign exhib, Nat Asn Women Artists, Sanskir Kendra Mus, Ahemdebad, India, 89; Montclair State Art Gallery, NJ, 92; League of Transient Beauty, Aspects of Flowers, Invitational, Lever House, New York, 92; Critical Eye, Am Soc Contemp Artists, Broome St Gallery, 92; Ridgewood Art Inst, NJ, 92; Nat Asn Women Artists traveling print show, 92-93. *Teaching:* Monitor printmaking, Robert DeLamonica Art Ctr, 79-81, Shou Ping Lian Art Ctr, Tenafly, NJ, 81-82. *Awards:* Elizabeth Morse Genius Award, Nat Asn Women Artists, 81; Cecil Shapiro Mem Award, Nat Asn Women Artists, 85; Dr Wu & Elsie Ject-Key Mem Award, Nat Asn Women Artists, 92; Honorable Mention, Montclair State Art Gallery. *Bibliog:* David Spengler (auth), An eye pleasing exhibit, The Record, 2/16/81; John Zeaman (auth), Creativity with crayons, Bergen Record, 1/3/88; Martin Parsons (auth), American Society of Contemporary Artists lights up Westbeth, Artspeak, 4/16/90; League of Transient Beauty Aspects of Flowers, video, Lever House, New York, 92. *Mem:* Nat Asn Women Artists (hist, 6/87-5/91); Am Soc Contemp Artists; Printmaking Coun of NJ; Art Ctr Watercolor Affiliates. *Media:* Wax Crayon, Colored Pencil; Encaustics. *Publ:* Contribr, Pages of Revelation, Artbuilders Inc, 86; 100 Years: A Centennial Celebration of National Association of Women Artists, Nassau County Mus Fine Arts, Roslyn Harbor, NY, 88. *Mailing Add:* Cambridge Way Alpine NJ 07620

KOOYMAN, RICHARD E
CRAFTSMAN
b Grand Rapids, Mich, Oct 1, 56. *Study:* Grand Valley State Univ, BFA, 79; Ohio State Univ, MFA, 82. *Exhib:* Nerron Mus Art, Indianapolis, Ind, 87; Objects Gallery, Chicago, 87, 88 & 90; Clark Gallery, Boston, 89; Detroit Gallery Contemp Craft, Detroit, 89; Urban Inst Contemp Art, Grand Rapids, Mich, 90; Chicago Int Art Forms, Navy Pier, Chicago, 90; The Bridge (ser), Soc Contemp Craft, Pittsburgh, Pa, 91; Washington Craft Show, Smithsonian Inst, Washington, DC, 91. *Awards:* Mich Coun Arts, 88; Nat Endowments Arts, 89. *Mem:* Am Craft Coun; Col Art Asn; Nat Coun Educ Ceramic Arts. *Mailing Add:* PO Box 2284 Frankfort MI 49635

KOPF, SILAS
CRAFTSMAN
b Warren, Pa, 1949. *Study:* Princeton Univ, AB(archit), 72; with Wendall Castle, 74-76; Ecole Boulle, France. *Work:* Gannett Corp; Scovill Corp; pvt Collections of Anne & Ronald Abramson, Washington, DC, Walda & Sydney Bestoff, New Orleans, La, Janice & Robert Diamond, New York, NY, Sylvia & Donald Gerson, Ft Myers, Fla and many others. *Comn:* Craft work, Steinway & Sons, New York. *Exhib:* Wisteriahurst Mus, Holyoke, Mass, 86;

Workbench Gallery, New York, 86; A C E Crafts at the Armory, New York, 87; Artful Objects: Recent American Craft, Ft Wayne, Ind, 89. *Awards:* Craftsman's Fel, Nat Endowment of Arts, 88. *Bibliog:* Articles in fine woodworking, Am Craft, NY Times, Boston Globe, Art in New Eng, La, Marqueterie (France) & Art and Practices of Marquetry (Britian). *Mailing Add:* c/o Gallery Henoch 80 Wooster St New York NY 10012

KOPPELMAN, CHAIM
PRINTMAKER, EDUCATOR
b New York, NY, Nov 17, 20. *Study:* Am Artists Sch; Art Col Western Eng, Bristol; Ozenfant Sch Fine Arts; Aesthetic Realism with Eli Siegel & Ellen Reiss. *Work:* Victoria & Albert Mus, London; Mus Fine Arts, Caracas, Venezuela; Mus Mod Art, Metrop Mus Art & Whitney Mus Am Art, New York; and many others. *Exhib:* Merida Rapp Graphics, Louisville, Ky, 85; 161st Ann, Nat Acad, 86; 10th Int Small Works Ann, NY, 86; Print Club, Philadelphia, 88; Alternative Mus, NY, 88; Brooklyn Mus, 89; and others. *Pos:* Consult, Aesthetic Realism Consultations, 71- *Teaching:* NY Univ, 47-55, Brooklyn Col, 50-60, State Univ NY, New Paltz, 52-58 & Sch Visual Arts, 59- *Awards:* 3rd Int Miniature Print Exhib Prize, 68; Creative Artists Pub Serv Grant, 76; Cannon Prize, Nat Acad, 86 & 89; 10th Ann Int Small Works Exhib Award, 86; Philadelphia Mus Purchase Award, Print Club, 87; Prize, Nat Acad, 89. *Bibliog:* Barry Schwartz (auth), The New Humanism, Praeger, 74; Una Johnson (auth), American Prints and Printmakers, Doubleday; Fritz Eichenberg (auth), The Art of the Print, Abrams, 76; Joan Lukach (auth), Hilla Rebay: In Search of the Spirit in Art, 83. *Mem:* Nat Acad Design; Soc Am Graphic Artists (former pres). *Media:* Etching, Miscellaneous Media. *Publ:* Co-auth, Aesthetic Realism: We Have Been There, 69; auth, This Is the Way I See Aesthetic Realism, 69; illusr, Damned Welcome, Definition, 72; contribr, Sunstorm Mag, 85; auth, J of the Print World, 87, 88, 89 & 92. *Dealer:* Susan Teller Gallery 568 Broadway New York NY 10012. *Mailing Add:* 498 Broome St New York NY 10013

KOPPELMAN, DOROTHY
PAINTER, CONSULTANT
b New York, NY, June 13, 20. *Study:* Brooklyn Col; Am Artists Sch; Art Students League; studied Philosophy of Aesthetic Realism with Eli Siegel, founder, now with Ellen Reiss. *Work:* Yale Univ, New Haven, Conn; Hampton Inst, Va. *Exhib:* Mus Mod Art, New York, 62; one-woman show, Terrain Gallery, 61; three-person show, The Kindest Art, 70; San Francisco Mus Mod Art, Calif; 161st Ann Juried Exhib, 86, 165th Juried Exhib, 90, Nat Acad Design, New York; Hudson Guild, 88 & 90; Allied Am Artists; plus many others. *Pos:* Dir, Terrain Gallery, 55-73 & Visual Arts Gallery, 62-64; pres, Aesthetic Realism Found Inc, 73-87. *Teaching:* Instr art, Adult Educ, Brooklyn Col, 52-75; consult Aesthetic Realism, 71-; instr, Nat Acad, Sch Fine Arts, 88 & 89. *Awards:* First Prize for Painting, City Ctr Gallery, 57; Prize Painting, Brooklyn Soc Artists, 60; Tiffany Found Grant, 65-66. *Bibliog:* Emily Genauer (auth), article, NY Herald Tribune, 62; revs, Art News, 59, 61 & 62, NY Times, 62. *Mem:* Women's Caucus Art; Artist's Equity; Allied Am Artists. *Media:* Oil. *Publ:* Coauth, Aesthetic Realism: We Have Been There, 69; illusr, Children's Guide to Parents & Other Matters, 71; Van Gogh, Sunstorm, 84. *Mailing Add:* 498 Broome St New York NY 10013

KOPRIVA, SHARON
PAINTER, SCULPTOR
b Houston, Tex, Feb 11, 48. *Study:* Univ Houston, with J Alexander & J Surls, BS, 70. *Work:* Mus Fine Arts, Sante Fe, NMex; Mus Fine Arts, Houston, Tex. *Comn:* Grant, City of Houston, Tex, 80; sculpture, ZZ Top, Billy Gibbons, Houston, 90. *Exhib:* Mus Fine Arts, Sante Fe, NMex, 86; Ctr Contemp Art, Mexico City, 87; Art Mus S Tex, Corpus Christi, 87; Laguna Gloria Art Mus, Austin, 89; Mus SE Tex, Beaumont, 91; and others. *Pos:* Bd mem, Orange Show Found, Houston, 89- *Teaching:* Teach Fel, Univ Houston, 81;; Vis Artist, Tex Tech & NDak State Univ, 90. *Awards:* First Place, Blaffer Gallery, Univ Houston, 88;; Sculpture Grant, Diverse Works, Houston, 90. *Bibliog:* D Tennant (auth), article in: Artspace, 86; S Bell (auth) & Gambrell (auth), articles in: Art Am, 87 & 89; Ed Hill (auth), article, Art Forum, 90. *Media:* Oil, Pencil; Bone, Paper-Mache. *Dealer:* Allan Stone Gallery New York NY 10016. *Mailing Add:* 1317 Arlington Houston TX 77008

KORAS, GEORGE
SCULPTOR
b Florina, Greece; US citizen. *Study:* Sch Fine Arts, Athens, Greece, dipl, 55; study in Paris & Rome, 55; Art Students League, 57; with Jacques Lipchitz, 55-59. *Work:* W P Chrysler Collection; Provincetown Mus, Mass; Norfolk Mus, Va; Nat Mus Athens, Greece, 78. *Comn:* Cast bronze sculptures, Bd Educ, Queens, NY, 71 & Bd Educ, Bronx, 72 & 74. *Exhib:* Panhellenios Zapeion, Athens, Greece, 49; Brooklyn Mus, NY, 60; Pa Acad Fine Arts, Philadelphia, 64; Silvermine Guild Artists, New Canaan, Conn, 67; Consulate General of Greece, 79. *Teaching:* Prof art, State Univ NY, Stony Brook, 66- *Awards:* Brooklyn Mus, 60, Pa Acad Fine Arts, 64 & Hofstra Univ, 65. *Bibliog:* Radio interview, produced on Voice of Am, New York, 72; G Koras Sculptor (TV film), produced by NY State Coun Arts, 72; Nat Radio-Television of Greece, 79. *Mem:* Audubon Artists. *Media:* Bronze. *Mailing Add:* Staller Ctr Art Gallery SUNY-Stony Brook Main Stony Brook NY 11794

KORD, VICTOR GEORGE
ADMINISTRATOR, PAINTER
b Satu Mare, Romania, Sept 16, 35; US citizen. *Study:* Cleveland Inst Art; Yale Univ, BFA, 58, MFA, 60. *Work:* Whitney Mus Am Art, New York; Cleveland Mus Art, Cleveland; Aldrich Mus, Ridgefield, Conn; Madison Art Ctr & Univ Wis, Madison, Wis; Elvehjem Art Ctr, Univ Wis. *Exhib:* Chicago Art Inst, 62; solo exhibs, Richard Gray Gallery, Chicago, 67, Univ SFla, Tampa, 68, Galerie Ricke, Cologne, Ger, 70 & Univ Ill, Champaign, 70; Cleveland Mus Art, Ohio, 68; Lyrical Abstraction, Whitney Mus Am Art, New York, 71; New American Abstract Painting, Vassar Col, Poughkeepsie, NY, 72; Invitation 77 - Ten Painters, Walker Art Ctr, Minneapolis, 77; Made in Virginia, Reynolds-Minor Gallery, Richmond, 84; group exhib, Kathryn Sermas Gallery, New York, 90; two-man show, Kathryn Sermas Gallery, New York, 90; and others. *Pos:* Co-ed, New Arts Examiner, Richmond Off, 83-87. *Teaching:* Univ Ill, Champaign, 60-65; Univ Wis, Madison, 65-81, chair, 79-81; chair & prof, Va Commonwealth Univ, Richmond, 81-87; chair & prof art, Cornell Univ, Ithaca, NY, 87- *Awards:* Guggenheim Fel, 62. *Mem:* Fed Arts Coun Richmond, Va (bd dirs, 83-87). *Mailing Add:* 710 Triphammer Rd Ithaca NY 14850

KOREN, EDWARD B
CARTOONIST, ILLUSTRATOR
b New York, NY, Dec 13, 35. *Study:* Columbia Univ, BA, 57; Atelier 17, Paris, with S W Hayter; Pratt Inst, MFA, 64; Union Col, LHD, 84. *Work:* Fogg Mus, Cambridge, Mass; Princeton Univ Mus; RI Sch Design Mus; US Info Agency; Libr Congress; and others. *Exhib:* Exposition Dessins d'Humeur, Soc Protectrice d'Humeur, Avignon, France, 73; Art from the New York Times, Soc Illusr, New York, 73; Art from the New Yorker, Grolier Club, 75; Terry Dintinfass Gallery, New York, 75-77, 79 & 91; Koren: Prints and Drawings 1954-1981 Traveling Exhib, State Univ Albany, 82-83; and others. *Teaching:* Adj prof art, Brown Univ, 64- *Awards:* Third Prize, Biennale Illusr, Bratislava, Czech, 73; Ten Best Childrens Books of the Year, New York Times, 73; Prix d'Humour, Soc Protectrice d'Humour, Avignon, France, 76; John Simon Guggenheim Fel, 70-71. *Mem:* Authors Guild; Soc Am Graphic Artists. *Media:* Pen & Ink. *Publ:* Illusr, Noodles Galore, Basic Bks, 77; Dragons Hate to Be Discrete, Knopf, 78; How to Eat Like a Child, 78 & Teenage Romance, 81, Viking; auth, Well, There's Your Problem, 80 & Small Ensembles, 83, What About Me? 90, Pantheon; Do I Have to Say Hello?, Viking, 90; and others. *Mailing Add:* c/o The New Yorker 25 W 43rd St New York NY 10036

KORENIC, LYNETTE MARIE
LIBRARIAN
b Berwyn, Ill, Mar 29, 50. *Study:* Univ Wis, Madison, MFA, 79 MA, Libr Sci, 81, MA, Art History, 84. *Pos:* Asst Art Librn, Fine Arts Libr, Ind Univ, 82-84, Arts Libr, Univ Calif, 84-88; head arts libr, Univ Calif, Santa Barbara, 88- *Mem:* Art Libr Soc N Am (secy 83-84, vpres 89, pres 90, past pres, 91; Col Art Asn; Am Libr Asn. *Publ:* Coauth, Survey of Periodical Use in an Academic Art Library, 82, Grant Development Strategies for Large and Small Libraries, 90, ARLIS/NA Publ. *Mailing Add:* Univ Calif Arts Libr Santa Barbara CA 93106

KORMAN, BARBARA
SCULPTOR, ASSEMBLAGE ARTIST
b New York, NY, Apr 8, 38. *Study:* Art Students League; NY State Col Ceramics; Alfred Univ, BFA(cum laude), 59, MFA(Grad Fel), 60. *Work:* In many pvt collections throughout the world. *Exhib:* Albright-Knox Art Gallery, Buffalo, NY, 60; Nat Acad Design, New York, 73-77; Metrop Mus Art, New York , 76; Bronx Mus, NY, 77 & 79; Queens Mus, NY, 81; Overseas Press Club, NY, 88; Tiffany & Co Windows, NY, 92; and others. *Teaching:* Fel painting & basic 2-D design, NY State Col Ceramics, 59-60; teacher & dir ceramics, Ceramic Workshop, Berkshires, summer 59; teacher sculpture & stage design, NY Bd Educ, 61-91. *Awards:* Int Women's Yr Award, 75-76; House Heydenryk Prize Sculpture, 74; Outstanding Art Educator Award, 77; Jeffrey Childs Willis Mem Prize Sculpture, 84. *Mem:* Nat Asn Women Artists; New York Artists Equity; Int Sculpture Ctr; Westchester Coun Arts. *Media:* All. *Mailing Add:* 357 E 201st St Bronx NY 10458

KORMAN, HARRIET R
PAINTER
b Bridgeport, Conn, Dec 10, 47. *Study:* Skowhegan Sch Painting & Sculpture, summer 68; Queens Col (NY), BA, 69. *Work:* Weatherspoon Art Gallery, Univ NC, Greensboro; Solomon R Guggenheim Mus, New York. *Exhib:* Solomon R Guggenheim Mus, 71; Whitney Ann Exhib Painting, Whitney Mus Am Art, New York, 72 & 73; one-person shows, Copley Gallery, Los Angeles, 74, 112 Greene St Gallery, New York, 75 & Daniel Weinberg Gallery, San Francisco, 76 & 78; Willard Gallery, New York, 76 & 80. *Teaching:* Adj faculty, Fashion Inst Technol, New York, 88-; prof, Art Dept Queen's Col, City Univ New York, 89- *Awards:* Theodoron Found Award, 71; Nat Endowment for the Arts Fel Grant, 74. *Bibliog:* Jeanne Siegel (auth), article in Art News, 72; Roberta Smith (auth), article in Artforum, 75; Hilton Kramer (auth), rev, New York Times, 1/18/80. *Mailing Add:* c/o Lennon Weinberg Inc 580 Broadway New York NY 10012

KORNBLATT, BARBARA RODBELL
DEALER
b Baltimore, Md, Jan 25, 31. *Study:* Community Col Baltimore, AA; Goucher Col, with Hilton Brown, BA. *Pos:* Dir, B R Kornblatt Gallery, Washington, DC. *Bibliog:* Articles in Sun, 5/26/76, News Am, 9/23/79 & Baltimore News Am, 11/2/80. *Specialty:* Contemporary American sculpture, prints and painting. *Mailing Add:* 3512 Old Court Rd Baltimore MD 21208-3123

KORNBLAU, GERALD
ART DEALER, CONSULTANT
b New York, NY, Aug 12, 28. *Specialty:* American 19th century folk art; paintings, sculpture, pottery and decorated furniture; weathervanes, quilts. *Mailing Add:* 305 E 61st St New York NY 10021

KORNBLUM, MYRTLE
PAINTER, PRINTMAKER
b Chicago, Ill, Aug 18, 09. *Study:* Washington Univ, St Louis; Univ Miami, Coral Gables, studied with Hans Hoffman. *Exhib:* City Art Mus, St Louis, Mo, 60-62; Print Club New York, 60; Art USA, Madison Sq Garden, New York, 60; Libr Cong, Washington, DC, 63; Silvermine Printmakers, New Canaan, Conn, 65; Atkins Mus Fine Art, Kansas City, Mo; Joslyn Mus, Omaha, Nebr; one-woman shows, St Louis Artists Guild, 70-81 & Norton Gallery, St Louis, Chicago, Kansas City, Madrid & Haifa; and others. *Awards:* First Prize, New Testament Show, Temple Israel, St Louis Co, Mo, 70; Second Prize, 70 & First Energy Prize, 75, St Louis Artists Guild. *Mem:* St Louis Artists Guild; Acad Prof Artists; Community Women Artists. *Media:* Collagraph, Woodcut. *Mailing Add:* 550 Coeur De Royal Dr St Louis MO 63141

KORNBLUTH, FRANCES
PAINTER, COLLAGE ARTIST
b New York, NY, July 26, 20. *Study:* Brooklyn Col, BA, 40; Brooklyn Mus Art Sch, 55-59; Pratt Inst, MAE, 62. *Work:* Chrysler Mus, Norfolk, Va; Aetna & Cigna Collections, Hartford, Conn; Quinebaug Valley Community Col, Danielson, Conn; Doctor;s Coun, New York; Gestalt Inst, Cleveland, Ohio. *Exhib:* 158th Ann Exhib Pa Acad Fine Arts, Philadelphia, 63; 32nd & 42nd Conn Artists Ann, Slater Memorial Mus, Norwich, Conn, 75 & 85; Joan Whitney Payson Gallery Art, Portland, Maine, 83; 78th Ann Exhib, Conn Acad Fine Arts, William Benton Mus, Storrs, 88; Connecticut Vision, Mattatuck Mus, Waterbury, 89. *Teaching:* Lectr art, Univ Conn, 70 & 71 & Annhurst Col, Woodstock, Conn, 79-80; instr & dir gifted educ, Thompson Publ Sch, Conn, 72-76. *Awards:* Grumbacher Award, 59; Medal of Honor, Catherine & Henry J Gaisman, 61 & Elizabeth Ringus Fulda Memorial, 68; Knox Found Finalist for Commission, Hartford, 90. *Bibliog:* Philip Gould (auth), Monhegan: Summer Light Islands Mag, 10/89; Jude Schwendenwein (auth), Color & Light Permeate Kornbluth Show, Hartford Courant, Conn, 6/15/91; Susan Wadsworth (auth), Frances Kornbluth: Paintings & Constructions, Art New England, Boston, Mass, 8-9/91. *Mem:* Nat Asn Women Artists; Conn Acad Fine Arts; Women Artists Monhegan Island; Northeast Conn Art Guild. *Media:* Acrylic, Oil. *Publ:* Auth, Monhegan: Summer Light, Islands Mag, 10/89. *Dealer:* Artworks Gallery 30 Arbor St Hartford CT; Leader Associates 7 Nottingham Rd Wayne NJ 07470. *Mailing Add:* 134 Buckley Hill Rd North Grosvenor Dale CT 06255

KORNETCHUK, ELENA
DEALER, HISTORIAN
b Ger, June 10, 48; US citizen. *Study:* Univ Md, College Park, BA, 70; Univ Iowa, MA, 72; Georgetown Univ, PhD, 82. *Collections Arranged:* The Graphics of Estonia, Latvia and Lithuania, Russian Images Ltd, 78, Contemporary Russian Painting, 78 & Kaplan's Lithographs, 79; Retrospective of Anatolii Kaplan, Russian Images Ltd, Pittsburgh, 79. *Pos:* Partner, Masterworks Int, Chicago, 76-78; pres, International Images, Ltd (aka Russian Images, Ltd), Sewickley, Pa, 78-; lectr, contemp art in the USSR, Univ Pittsburgh, 85-; mem, bd dirs, Carnegie-Mellon Univ Art Gallery, Pittsburgh, 85-; cur Eastern Europ Art, New Eng Ctr Contemp Art, Brooklyn, Conn, 86- *Teaching:* Instr Russian lang, lit & cult, Univ Iowa, 70-72 & Univ Md, College Park, 73-75. *Mem:* Asn Advan Slavic Studies, Stanford, Calif, 71-; World Affairs Coun, Pittsburgh, 78-; Sweetwater Art Ctr, Sewickley, Pa (bd dirs, 80-84); Asn Advan Baltic Studies, Mahwah, NJ, 82-; Am Coun Study Islamic Soc, Villanova, Pa, 85-; Am Latvian Artists Asn, New York, 85- *Specialty:* Contemporary art from Russia, Latvia, Estonia, Bulgaria and other countries of Eastern Europe. *Collection:* Contemporary art from the USSR, Japanese wood engravings. *Publ:* Auth, Contemporary Russian printmaking: An overview, Graphics Mag, 10-11/79; Contemporary Soviet prints: A national diversity, Print News, 10/80; Inars Helmust and the Latvian graphic tradition, spring 82, Nature printing: Robert Little and Renata Sawyer, spring 83, Prints today: Holland summer, 83 & The watercolors of Dzemma Skulme, spring 86, J Print World. *Mailing Add:* International Images Ltd 514 Beaver St Sewickley PA 15143-1779

KORNMAYER, J GARY (JOHN)
PAINTER, PHOTOGRAPHER
b Omaha, Nebr, July 10, 34. *Study:* San Diego State Univ, 59-61; Nat Univ, San Diego, BA, 70, MA(audio-visual commun), 74. *Work:* Riverside Art Mus, Calif. *Comn:* Tex Hist, Nat Univ, San Diego, 73 & Am Hist of Slavery, 74. *Exhib:* One-man shows, Noho Gallery, New York, 75-78, Inst Mex NAm Relaciones Cult, Mexico City, Inst Allende, San Miguel Allende, Mex, 80 & San Diego Art Inst, 89 & 92; Calif-Hawaii Biennial, Fine Arts Gallery, San Diego, 76; San Diego Art Inst; and others. *Pos:* Photogr, Gen Dynamics Corp, San Diego, 58-60, sr audio-visual commun, 60-69, mgr graphics commun, 80-92. *Awards:* Distinctive Merit, San Diego Art Director's Soc, 65; Second Place, Fine Arts Gallery San Diego, 68; First Place Purchase Award, Riverside Art Mus, 70. *Bibliog:* Hedy O'Beil (auth), J Gary Kornmayer, artist, Arts Mag, 10/77; Hal Gray (auth), Horizons, Channel 39, 12/77; In the Public Interest, City of San Diego, Channel 2, 1/78. *Mem:* San Diego Fine Arts Soc-Art Guild (mem bd dirs, 68-70); Span Village Art Asn (mem bd dir, 72-74, pres, 74-78); San Diego Art Inst (mem bd dirs, 90-92). *Media:* Mixed Media. *Dealer:* Knowles Gallery 7420 Girard Ave La Jolla CA 92037. *Mailing Add:* 3436 Park W Lane San Diego CA 92117

KOROT, BERYL
PAINTER, VIDEO ARTIST
b New York, NY, Sept 17, 45. *Study:* Univ Wis, 63-65; Queens Col, BA, 67. *Work:* Chase Manhattan. *Comn:* Videoskulptor, Kolnischer Kunstuerein, Zurichkunsthaus, Berliner Kunstverein, 89; Carnegie Inst Art, Points of Departure: Origins in Video, Pittsburgh, 90. *Exhib:* Solo exhibs, Everson Mus, Syracuse, 75 & 79, Castelli Gallery, New York, 77 & Whitney Mus, 80; Documenta 6, Kassel, Ger, 77; Yesterday and After, Musee des Beaux Arts, Montreal, 80; Burden, Kos, Korot, San Francisco Art Inst, 81; John Weber Gallery, New York, 86; Planes of Memory, Long Beach Mus Art, Calif, 88; Time and Memory: Video Art and Identity, Jewish Mus, 88; and others. *Teaching:* Sch Visual Arts, 76-78. *Awards:* Creative Artists Pub Serv Grant, 72 & 75; Nat Endowment for the Arts Grant, 75, 77 & 79; NYSCA grant, 78. *Bibliog:* Jeff Perrone (auth), Text and Commentary (rev), Art Forum, 5/77; Grace Glueck (auth), articles, The NY Times, 6/75, 3/18/77, 12/5/80; Christopher Knight (auth), Moving pictures and 'Planes of Memory' (rev), Los Angeles Herald Examiner, 2/14/88; John Russel, review, NY Times, 7/29/88. *Publ:* Ed, Radical software, Vol I & Vol II, Gordon & Breach Sci Publ, 72-74; Video Art, Harcourt, Brace, Jovanovich (in press). *Mailing Add:* 258 Broadway Apt 7E New York NY 10007

KOROW, ELINORE M See Bieber, Elinore Maria Korow

KORSHAK, YVONNE
HISTORIAN, EDUCATOR
b Chicago, Ill. *Study:* Radcliffe Col, BA, 58; Univ Calif, Berkeley, with D A Amyx, H Chipp, J K Anderson & J Bony, MA(classical archeol), 66, PhD(art hist), 73. *Collections Arranged:* Selections from the Adelphi Univ Art Collection (co-ed, catalog), 79. *Teaching:* Prof, Adelphi Univ, 75-, chairperson dept art & art hist, 79-82, dir mus studies prog, 79- *Awards:* Award Merit, 88, President's Award, 90, Adelphi Univ; Award Merit, Am Ash Mus. *Mem:* Charter mem Long Island Art Historians Asn; Col Art Asn Am; Archeol Inst Am; Asn Ancient Historians; Am Soc 18th Cent Studies. *Res:* Eighteenth-nineteenth century French painting; classical Greek art; iconography and hidden imagery. *Publ:* coauth, Selections from the Permanent Collections of the Arkansas Arts Center, 83; auth, Realism and Transcendent Imagery: Van Gogh's Crows over the Wheatfield, Pantheon 43, 85; Frontal Faces in Attic Vase Painting of the Archaic Period, Chica, 87; The Liberty Cap as a revolutionary symbol in America and France, Smithsonian Studies in Am Art, 10/87; "Paris and Helen" by Jacques Louis David: Choice and judgement on the eve of the French Revolution, Art Bull, 3/87. *Mailing Add:* 1025 Fifth Ave New York NY 10028

KORTENHAUS, LYNNE M
CONSULTANT, CURATOR
b Long Branch, NJ, Jan 11, 51. *Study:* RI Sch Design, Providence, BFA, 73, MFA, 75; Florence, Italy, independent study, 74-75, hons. *Pos:* Asst dir, Arvest Galleries, Boston, Mass, 75-78; art consult, pvt-corp insts in Boston, 78-79; New Eng rep, Phillips Fine Art Auctioneers & Appraisers, 79-82; dir marketing & corp sales, Haley & Steele Gallery, 83-84, fine arts consult & cur, 84- *Teaching:* Instr lithography, RI Sch Design Printmaking Workshop, 73-75. *Bibliog:* Article in Corporate Artnews, 6/85; article in Designers West, 8/85. *Mem:* Appraisers Asn Am (bd dirs); Appraisers Registry; Newbury St League (vpres & auction chairperson). *Media:* Appraisal. *Mailing Add:* 6 Mt Vernon Ave Charlestown MA 02129

KORTHEUER, DAYRELL
PAINTER, CONSERVATOR
b New York, NY, July 25, 06. *Study:* Art Students League, with Frank DuMond, George Bridgman & John Carroll; Nat Acad Design, with Charles Hawthorne. *Work:* Portraits, Landscapes Merchant's Asn, New York; Mint Mus Art; Emory Univ; Univ NC; Hickory Mus Art, NC, 81; and others. *Exhib:* Carson-McKenna Gallery, Charlotte, NC, 69; Mint Mus Art, 74; Betty Graham Gallery, Charlotte, NC, 80; Waterworks Visual Arts Ctr, Salisbury, NC, 89; Moring Art Ctr, Asheboro, NC, 91; Appalachian Cult Ctr Mus, Boone, NC, 92. *Awards:* Nat Arts Club Prizes, 28; Mint Mus Art Awards, 41 & 42; Gold Medal, Blowing Rock Art Asn, 54 & Award, 55. *Mem:* fel Am Inst Conserv Hist & Artistic Works; NC State Art Soc; Mint Mus Art. *Media:* Oil, Watercolor. *Mailing Add:* c/o Southminster 8919 Park Rd Charlotte NC 28210

KORTLANDER, WILLIAM
PAINTER
b Grand Rapids, Mich, Feb 9, 25. *Study:* Mich State Univ, BA; Univ Iowa, MA & PhD. *Work:* Columbus Mus Art, Ohio; Schumacher Gallery, Capital Univ, Columbus, Ohio; Zanesville Art Inst, Ohio; Huntington Mus, WVa; Chemical Bank & AT&T, New York. *Comn:* Painting, Bernice & Harold Steinbaum, Old Westbury, New York, 80. *Exhib:* Dallas Mus Fine Arts, Tex, 58, 59 & 61; Pa Acad Fine Arts, Philadelphia, 65; Wadsworth Atheneum, Hartford, Conn, 65; Corcoran Gallery, Washington, DC, 68; Baltimore Mus, Md, 68; A M Sachs Gallery, New York, 79; one-man show, Haber/Theodore Gallery, New York, 80, 82 & 84 & Foster Harmon Gallery, Sarasota, Fla, 86 & 87; Nat Mus Am Art, Smithsonian Inst, Washington, DC, 81; The Shanghai Exchange, Shanghai Teachers Univ, Peoples Repub China, 88; The Contemporary Landscape, Cumberland Gallery, Nashville, Tenn, 88. *Teaching:* Instr art hist, Lawrence Univ, 54-56; asst prof art hist, Univ Tex, Austin, 56-61; vis asst prof art hist, Mich State Univ, summer 61; prof painting, Ohio Univ, 61- *Awards:* Painting of Year, Mead Corp, 65; Baker Award, Ohio Univ, 67. *Bibliog:* Doc, Kortlander & Kortlander, WOUB TV, Athens, Ohio, 84; Nicholas Roukes (auth), Acrylics Bold & New, Watson Guptil, 86. *Media:* Multimedia. *Publ:* Auth, Painting with Acrylics, Van Nostrand Reinhold, 73. *Mailing Add:* 7414 Angel Ridge Rd Athens OH 45701

KORZENIK, DIANA
WRITER, EDUCATOR
b New York, NY, Mar 15, 41. *Study:* Vassar Col, Oberlin Col, with Linda Nochlin, Rosemarie Beck, Wolfgang Lotz & Wolfgang Stechow, BA; Yale Art Sch, Norfolk, Conn; Columbia Univ; Harvard Univ, with Rudolph Arnheim, EdD. *Comn:* J P Getty Trust; Art-Making & Education. *Collections Arranged:* Exhibitions on Nineteenth Century America, 86 & Drawn to Art: Fruitlands, 88, Univ NH. *Pos:* Prof, adv, Am Art Educ, Am Antiquarian Soc. *Teaching:* Prof, Dept Art Educ, Mass Col Art, Boston, 72- *Awards:* Fel, Woodrow Wilson-Ford Found, 62; L L Winship Lit Award, Boston Globe, 86; City of Boston Pro Arts Serv in the Arts Award, 92. *Bibliog:* David Perkins (auth), Project Zero, J Aesthetic Educ; Howard Gardner (auth), Art, Mind & Brain & Artful Scribbles, Basic Books Inc. *Mem:* Nat Art Educ; Caucus Social Theory & Art Educ; Mus Fine Arts; Ephemera Soc Am; Col Art Asn; Women's Caucus Art. *Media:* Painter. *Publ:* Auth, Drawing & socialization, 79 & Child art: Historical perspective, 81, Art Educ; Drawn to Art-A 19th Century American Dream, Univ Press New Eng, 86; Framing the Past, Nat Art Educ Asn, 92; Art Making & Education, Ill Univ Press, 93. *Mailing Add:* c/o Art Educ Dept Mass Col Art, 621 Huntington Ave Boston MA 02115

KOS, PAUL JOSEPH
SCULPTOR, EDUCATOR
b Rock Springs, Wyo, Dec 23, 42. *Study:* San Francisco Art Inst, BFA, 65, MFA, 67. *Work:* Ft Worth Art Mus, Tex; Mus Mod Art, Mus Conceptual Art, San Francisco; Inst Contemp Art, Univ Pa; Austrian Govt, Ganz, Austria. *Comn:* Floating (sculpture), Winery Lake, Napa, Calif, 68, Wind (sculpture), 69 & Performance (sculpture), 70. *Exhib:* One-man show, M H De Young Mem Mus, San Francisco; Bienal Sao Paulo, Brazil, 73 & 75; Trigon 74, Neue Galerie am Landesmuseum Joanneum, Ganz, Austria, 74; Art Now '74, John F Kennedy Ctr Performing Arts, Washington, DC, 74; Whitney Biennial, Whitney Mus Am Art, New York, 75; Paris Biennial, 77; Univ Mus, Berkeley, Calif, 80. *Teaching:* San Francisco Art Inst, 78- *Awards:* Nat Endowment Fel, 74 & 76. *Mailing Add:* c/o San Diego State Univ Dept of Art Univ Art Gallery San Diego CA 92182-0214

KOSCIANSKI, LEONARD J
PAINTER, EDUCATOR
b Cleveland, Ohio, April 20, 52. *Study:* Cleveland Inst Art, BFA, 77; Univ Calif, Davis, MFA, 79. *Work:* Metrop Mus Art, New York; Philadelphia Mus Art; Cleveland Mus Art; Chase Manhattan Bank; Newport Harbor Mus, Calif; Milwaukee Mus Art; Chicago Art Inst. *Exhib:* Beast: Animal Imagery in Recent Painting, PS 1, New York, 82; one-man shows, Karl Bornstein Gallery, Santa Monica, 81, 83, 85 & 87, Phyllis Kind Gallery, 83, 84, 86, 87, 88, 89, 90 & 91 Newport Harbor Mus, Calif, 84, Greenville Co Mus Art, SC, 88, Brady Galler, Washington, DC, 89, Arthur Roger Gallery, New Orleans, 90 & 92, Fendrick Gallery, Washington, DC, 91 & Robert Berman Gallery, Santa Monica, 92; New Narrative Paintings, Metrop Mus Art, New York, 83; Narrative Paintings, Mex City, 84; Innocence & Experience, Greenville County Mus Art, SC, 85; The 1980's: A New Generation, Metrop Mus Art, New York, 88; American Art Today: Contemporary Landscape, Art Mus, Fla Int Univ, Miami, 89; Since 1980: New Narrative Painting, Phoenix Mus Art, Ariz; Harmony and Discord: American Landscape Today, Va Mus Fine Arts, Richmond, Va; Twenty Years of Landfall Press, Landfall Gallery, New York; The Landscape in Twentieth-Century American Art, traveling, Tampa Mus Art, Fla, Greenville Co Mus Art, SC, Madison Art Ctr, Wis, Grand Rapids Art Mus, Mich, 92. *Teaching:* Asst prof art, Univ Tenn, Knoxville, 80-84 & Univ Md, College Park, 84-87; lectures & workshops at numerous institutions. *Awards:* Fels, Awards Visual Arts, 83 & Nat Endowment Arts--Southeastern Ctr Contemp Arts, 83; Individual Artist Fel, Nat Endowment Arts, 85 & 89; Rockefeller Found Scholar, Bellagio, Italy. *Bibliog:* Helen L Kohen (auth), Landscape Show Rich in Tradition, The Miami Herald, 1/15/89; Alan G Artner (auth), Cinematic Canvas: Koscianski's predator art employs many idioms of film, Chicago Tribune, 2/16/89; Pat Van Gelder (auth), Animals as subjects in Contemporary Art, Am Artist, 5/89. *Media:* Oil on Canvas, Pastel on Paper. *Dealer:* Phyllis Kind Gallery Greene St New York NY. *Mailing Add:* 1712 S Harbor Ln Annapolis MD 21401

KOSCIELNY, MARGARET
SCULPTOR, PAINTER
b Tallahassee, Fla, Aug 13, 40. *Study:* Tex Woman's Univ, with Toni Lasalle; Univ Ga, BA(art hist) & MFA, with Irving Marantz, Joseph Schwarz & Charles Morgan. *Work:* Jacksonville Art Mus. *Comn:* Omni, Norfolk, Va, 75; Hyatt Hotel, Washville, 76; Fla Senate, 78; Atlanta Airport, 80; AT&T, Jacksonville, 83; Stage Set Designs, The Magic Flute, Univ NMex, 87; and others. *Exhib:* Two-man exhib, Contemp Gallery, St Petersburg, 75; Four Jacksonville Artists, Cummer Gallery, Fla, 76; one-person shows, Vanderbuilt Univ, Nashville, Tenn, 77, Univ Conn, 81 & Univ NMex, 87; Flight Patterns, Third Florr Gallery, Atlanta, Ga, 80; and many others. *Pos:* Asst to dir, Cummer Gallery Art, 69-74; cur, Kamal Col, Jacksonville, Fla, 78- *Teaching:* Instr printmaking, Jacksonville Univ, 67 & Jacksonville Art Mus, 68. *Awards:* Nat Endowment Arts Grant Fla Arts Coun, 76; Nat Competition, Atlanta Airport Comn, 79. *Bibliog:* Photos & Essays, Kalliope, 79. *Media:* Plexiglass, Assemblage; Pastel. *Mailing Add:* 14 E Fourth St No 1123 New York NY 10012

KOSHALEK, RICHARD
MUSEUM DIRECTOR
b Wausau, Wis, Sept 20, 41. *Study:* Univ Wis, Madison; Univ Minn, Minneapolis, BA(archit), MA(art hist). *Collections Arranged:* 9 Artists-9 Spaces (auth, catalog), 70; Stephen Antonakos: Outdoor Neons, 75; Dan Flavin: Drawings, Diagrams & Spaces, 75; Larry Bell: The Iceberg & It's Shadow, 75; Robert Irwin: Continuing Responses, 75-76; The Great American Rodeo (auth, catalog), 76 & 77; Ronald Bladen: Outdoor Sculpture Proposals, 78; Warburton Ave: The Architecture of a Neighborhood, 78; John Mason: Installations From the Hudson River Series, 78; Richard Serra: Elevator 80; and many others. *Pos:* Cur, Walker Art Ctr, Minneapolis, 67-72; asst dir, Nat Endowment Arts, 72-73; dir, Ft Worth Art Mus, 74-76; dir, The Hudson River Mus, 76-80; deputy dir, Mus Contemp Art, Los Angeles, 80- *Awards:* IBM Int Fel; Nat Endowment Arts Fel. *Mem:* Art Prog, Chase Manhattan Bank; Yale Univ Coun Comt on Art Gallery & Brit Art Ctr. *Publ:* Auth, Midwest Photographers, Walker Art Ctr, 72. *Mailing Add:* c/o Mus Contemp Art 250 S Grand Ave Calif Plaza Los Angeles CA 90012

KOSS, GENE H
SCULPTOR, EDUCATOR
b La Crosse, Wis, Nov 17, 47. *Study:* Univ Wis, River Falls, BS; Tyler Sch Art, Temple Univ, Philadelphia, MFA. *Work:* The Lannan Found, Palm Beach, Fla; Univ Wis, La Crosse; Tyler Sch Art, Temple Univ, Philadelphia; One Canal Place, New Orleans; New Orleans Mus Art. *Comn:* Ceramic sculpture, Schie Eye Inst, Philadelphia, 76. *Exhib:* Third Biennial Lake Superior Int Craft Exhibit, Tweed Mus Art, Minn, 75-77; Marietta Col Crafts Nat, Ohio, 76; 55th Ann Exhib, Meadows Mus Art, Shreveport, La, 77; one-man shows, Univ Southwestern La, Lafayette, 76, Newcomb Art Sch, Tulane Univ, New Orleans, La, 77, Arthur Roger Gallery, 84 & Perception Gallery, Houston, 86; two-man show, Glass & Ceramic Sculpture, Circle Gallery, New Orleans, La, 78; and others. *Collections Arranged:* Louisiana Craftsmen Show, 77-78 & Glass & Ceramics Student Show, 77-78, Newcomb Art Sch, Tulane Univ, New Orleans. *Pos:* Cur, Nat Glace Sculpture Exhib, Perception Gallery, 84; exhib coordnr, Glass Invitational Contemp Art Ctr, 85. *Teaching:* Instr glass, Tyler Sch Art, Temple Univ, Philadelphia, summer 76; assoc prof ceramics & glass, Newcomb Art Sch, Tulane Univ, New Orleans, 76- *Awards:* Best of Show, Five State Ceramic Exhib, Minn Clay Co, 74; Sculpture Award, Marietta Col Crafts Nat, 77; Award of Excellence, La Craftsmen Show, La Craft Coun, 77. *Bibliog:* Joel Myers (auth), New American glass, Craft Horizons, 8/76; Fred Adams (auth), Glass, Glass Mag, 6/77; Michael Flaherty (auth), Ceramic activities, Ceramics Mo, 9/77. *Mem:* Glass Art Soc; Am Crafts Coun; Nat Coun on Educ in Ceramic Arts; Contemp Art Ctr; La Crafts Coun (mem standards comt bd, 77-78). *Media:* Glass, Ceramics. *Publ:* Auth, The techniques of manufacture, In: Vasilike Ware: An Early Bronze Age Pottery Style in Crete, Paul Astroms Forlag, Sweden, 77. *Dealer:* Perception Galleries Glass Art Houston TX; Arthur Roger Galleries New Orleans LA. *Mailing Add:* Tulane Univ La New Orleans LA 70118

KOSTA, ANGELA
ASSEMBLAGE ARTIST, WRITER
US citizen. *Study:* Art Inst Chicago, 76-78; primarily self-taught. *Exhib:* Art Inst Chicago, 62 & 77; solo exhib, Main St Art Gallery, Chicago, 65, Spectrum Gallery, 83 & San Diego Mus Art, 85-88, San Diego; Chicago Cult Ctr, 78; Gallery 8, La Jolla, 81; Circle Gallery, San Diego, 87; Tijuana Cultural Ctr, Mex, 87; Yokohama Citizens' Gallery, Japan, 92. *Awards:* Purchase Award, New Horizons Art, North Shore Art League, 77; Best of Show Awards, Artists Guild Ann, San Diego Mus Art, 87 & 88; San Diego Art Inst, 89. *Bibliog:* Miller (auth), article, Los Angeles Times, 6/2/82; Lewinson (auth), article, San Diego Union, 4/7/83; Ollman (auth), article, Los Angeles Times, 11/20/87. *Mem:* Artists Equity Asn; San Diego Artists Guild; San Diego Mus Contemp Art. *Media:* Mixed Media; Collage, Drawing. *Publ:* Paper art, Fiberarts Mag, 84; Abakanowicz retropective, 11/6/84 & Judy Chicago's project, 7/7/85, San Diego Union; Banham by design, Reader, 4/24/86; Teacher/student interface: two views of education, Fiberarts Mag, 87. *Mailing Add:* 3151 Mooney St San Diego CA 92117

KOSTABI, MARK
PAINTER, SCULPTOR
b Los Angeles, Calif, Nov 27, 60. *Study:* Fullerton Community Col, 78; Calif State Univ, Fullerton, 79-81. *Work:* Mus Mod Art, New York, NY; Seibu Mus, Tokyo, Japan; Memphis Brooks Mus Art, Tenn; Metrop Mus, NY. *Comn:* Mural, Limelight, Chicago, Ill, 85; shopping bag design, Bloomingdales, New York, 86; Twist Soda Label, 86. *Exhib:* Solo exhibs, Newport Beach, Calif, 81 & Ronald Feldman Gallery, New York, 86; The East Village Scene (with catalog), Inst Contemp Art, Philadelphia, Pa, 84; Painting and Sculpture Today, Indianapolis Mus Art, Ind, 84; American Art Now: Painting in the 1980's, Columbus Mus Arts & Sci, Ga, 84; 10th Street and Avenue B: East Village Art Today, Newport Beach, Calif, 84; Public and Private: American Prints Today, Brooklyn Mus, 86; Say Less and Say Yes (solo exhib, with catalog), Seibu, Tokyo, Japan, 86. *Awards:* Proliferation Prize, East Village Eye, 84. *Bibliog:* Walter Robinson (auth), Mark Kostabi at Hal Bromm, Art in Am, 84. *Media:* Oil on Canvas. *Publ:* Auth, Kostabi, self publ, 81; illusr, East Village 85, 85 & auth, Upheaval, 85, Pelham Press; Soho New York, Egret Press, 86. *Dealer:* Ronald Feldman 31 Mercer St New York NY 10013. *Mailing Add:* Kostabi World 544 W 38th St New York NY 10018

KOSTECKA, GLORIA
PAINTER
b Bloomfield, NJ, Dec 7. *Study:* Am Art Sch, New York; Traphagen Sch Fashion, New York. *Exhib:* Federated Art Asn Exhib, NJ State Mus Cultural Ctr, Trenton, 77; Nat Soc Painters Casein & Acrylic 24th Exhib & Nat Audubon Soc Exhib, Nat Acad Galleries, New York, 77 & 78; Am Artists Professional League, Bergen Co Mus, NJ, 80; Nat Soc Painters Casein & Acrylic 28th Ann Exhib, Nat Arts Club, New York, 81 & 85. *Awards:* Travel Awards, Nat Soc Painters Casein & Acrylic, 81-85 & Wash Square Outdoor Art Exhib, 81-83. *Mem:* Nat Soc Painters Casein & Acrylic; Am Portrait Soc. *Media:* Acrylic, Pencil. *Mailing Add:* 23 Elmwood Dr Clifton NJ 07013

KOSTELANETZ, RICHARD
MEDIA ARTIST, WRITER
b New York, NY, May 14, 40. *Study:* Brown Univ, AB(with honors), 62; Kings Col, London, Fulbright Scholar, 64-65; Columbia Univ, MA, 66. *Work:* Book-Art Books: Mus Mod Art; Humanities Res Ctr, Univ Tex, Austin; Videotapes: Anthology Film Archives, New York; Franklin Furnace, New York. *Comn:* Videotapes Synapse, Syracuse Univ, 75; holograms, Cabin Creek Ctr, Work & Environ Studies, 78; audiotapes, Westdeutscher Rundfunk, 82, 83 & 89; audiotapes, Am Pub Radio, St Paul, Minn, 84; holograms, Dennis Gabor Lab, Mus Holography, 85. *Exhib:* Imaged Words & Worded Images, New York Univ, 70; one-man shows, Video Writing, Anthology Film Archives, New York, 75 & 76, Visual poems, Nonsyntactic Prose, Minimal Fiction, Numerical Art, Chistopher Stephens, New York, Univ Toledo, 75-77; Audio Art, The Kitchen, New York, 78; Book Art, PS 1, Long Island City, New York & Tulsa Public Libr, 78; Wordsand (retrospective work in several media), Simon Fraser Univ, Univ Alta, Cornell Col, Calif State Univ, Miami Dade Community Col, Vassar Col, 78-81; and many others. *Collections Arranged:* Language & Structure in North Am, traveling exhib throughout Can & US, 75-77. *Pos:* Co-founder & publ, Assembling & Assembling Press, 70-82; stipendiat, DAAD Berliner Kunstperprogramm, Ger, 81-83. *Teaching:* Vis prof, Am studies & eng, Univ Tex, Austin, 77. *Awards:* Guggenheim Fel, 67; Visual Arts Grant, 76, 78, 79 & 85 & Media Arts Grant, 81, 82, 85, 86, 89 & 90, Nat Endowment Arts; DAAD Berliner Kunstlerprogramm, 81-83; and others. *Bibliog:* Tom Johnson (auth), Intermedia Lives, Village Voice, 10/4/76; George Myers Jr (auth), Scavenger Art & Richard Kostelanetz, An Introduction to Modern Times, Lunchroom, 82. *Mem:* Nat Artworkers; Found Independent Video & Film; Int Asn Art Critics; PEN. *Media:* Video, Film; Books, Holography. *Res:* Polyartistry; literary intermedia (sound & visual poetry). *Publ:* Auth, Wordsand, Simon Fraser Gallery (with R K Eds) 78; Conversing with Cage, 89; Writings About John Cage, 93; John Cage: Writer, 93; Wordworks: Poems New & Selected, 93; and many others. *Mailing Add:* PO Box 444 Prince St Sta New York NY 10012

KOSTER, MARJORY JEAN
PRINTMAKER
b Grand Rapids, Mich, Feb 9, 26. *Study:* Univ Mich Exten Night Sch, 47-64; Pratt Graphic Workshop, New York, summer 64. *Work:* Metrop Mus Art, New York; Brooklyn Mus Art, NY; Art Inst Chicago; Detroit Art Inst, Mich; Grand Rapids Art Mus, Mich; and others. *Exhib:* Ann Exhib Prints & Drawings, Oklahoma Art Ctr, 67; 7th Ann Mercyhurst Col Nat Graphics Exhib, Erie, Pa, 67; 3rd Nat Print & Drawing Exhib, Western Mich Univ, Kalamazoo, 68; 16th Nat Print Exhib, Brooklyn Mus, 68; 1st Nat Print Exhib, Honolulu, 71. *Mem:* Nat Inst Arts & Lett. *Media:* Woodcut. *Mailing Add:* 940 Maynard Ave NW Grand Rapids MI 49504

KOSTIUK, MICHAEL MARION, JR
PHOTOGRAPHER
b Paris, Tex, Dec 9, 44. *Study:* Univ Tex, Austin, 63-66; Md Inst Art, Baltimore, 69; Visual Studies Workshop, Rochester, NY, 73. *Work:* Mus Fine Arts, Boston; Dallas Mus Fine Arts; New Orleans Mus Art; Whitte Mus, San Antonio Mus Asn, Tex; Humanities Res Ctr, Univ Tex, Austin. *Comn:* Photographic documentary, Finch Col Mus Art, New York, NY & Amon Carter Mus, Ft Worth, Tex, 72; limited ed, photographic portfolio, Polaroid Corp, Cambridge, Mass, 75; photographic 3-D art work, Art Mus S Tex, Corpus Christi, Tex, 76; public transit art work, Inst Contemp Art, Philadelphia, Pa, 80. *Exhib:* Attitudes: Photography in the 1970's, Santa Barbara Mus Art, 79; Libros de Artistas, Nat Libr, Madrid, Spain, 82; Philadelphia Art Alliance, Pa, 82; Les E'tats Du Livre, Caroline Corre Gallery, Paris, France, 83; Cleveland Inst Art, Ohio, 84; Univ Chicago Libr, 86. *Pos:* Proj dir, Bookworks: 1982 Conf, Philadelphia, 81-83; artist-in-residence, Ctr Performing Arts, Pa State Univ, Univ Park, Pa, 87. *Awards:* Fel Special Proj, Pa Coun Arts, 86; Artist Performance Residency Award, Yellow Springs Inst, Chester Springs, Pa, 86. *Bibliog:* Dave Simpson (auth), Four Texans: About Photography, San Antonio Mus Asn, 77; Jon Holmes (auth), Deep in the heart of Texas, Camera, 8/77; Tom Livesay (auth), Young Texas Artist Ser, Artspace, fall 77. *Media:* Miscellaneous. *Publ:* Contribr, Darkroom Dynamics: a Guide to Creative Darkroom Techniques, Van Nostrand, Reinhold, Curtin & London, 79; co-auth, Two by two, Houston City Mag, Tex, 79. *Dealer:* Tony Zwicker Books & Bookart 15 Gramercy Park New York NY 10003. *Mailing Add:* 4207 Avenue G Austin TX 78751

KOSTYNIUK, RONALD P
SCULPTOR, EDUCATOR
b Sask, July 8, 41. *Study:* Univ Sask, BSc & BEd; Univ Alta, BFA; Univ Wis, MS & MFA. *Work:* Edmonton Art Gallery, Alta; Saskatoon Art Gallery, Sask; Kresge Art Found, Detroit, Mich; Can Coun Art Bank, Ottawa, Ont; Dalhousie Univ, Halifax, NS. *Comn:* relief mural, exec off Paul Albertsen Ltd, Winnipeg; sculptors, Assoc Bldg, Calgary; sculptors, City of Edmonton Recreational Complex, Edmonton. *Exhib:* One-man shows, Mem Univ, St John's, Nfld, 73, Sarnia Art Gallery, Ont, 74, Univ Moncton, NB, 74, Mt St Vincent Univ, Halifax, NS, 75 & Univ Calgary, Alta, 78. *Teaching:* Prof design & sculpture, Univ Calgary, Alta, 71-, head grad studies, dept art. *Awards:* Can Council Arts Bursary, 69; Foreign Exchange Scholar, External Affairs Govt Can, 78; Killam Resident Fel, Univ Calgary, 79. *Bibliog:* Jan Van der Marck (auth), Relief sculpture, 69; John Stocking (auth), Relief sculptures, Arts Mag, 75; John Graham (auth), Kostyniuk's reliefs, Vie des Arts, 75; Marion Andres (auth), Kostyniuk's constructed reliefs, Art Post, 86. *Mem:* Royal Can Acad Art; Univ Art Asn; Can Conf of the Arts. *Media:* Plastics, Metals. *Publ:* Auth, The Evolution of the Constructed Relief 1913-1979 & Art and Sources, Univ Calgary. *Mailing Add:* 4907 Viceroy Dr Calgary AB T3A 0V2 Canada

KOSUTH, JOSEPH
CONCEPTUAL ARTIST
b Toledo, Ohio, Jan 31, 45. *Study:* Toledo Mus Sch of Design, 55-62; Cleveland Art Inst, 63-64; Sch of Visual Arts, New York, 65-67. *Work:* Mus of Mod Art, New York; Nat Gallery of Can, Ottawa, Ont; Tate Gallery, London, Eng; Solomon Guggenheim Mus, New York; Whitney Mus of Am Art, New York. *Comn:* The Brooklyn Museum Collection: The Play of the Unmentionable, Grand Lobby, Brooklyn Mus, NY, 90; Ex Libris Frankfurt, 90; Ex Libris J F Champollion, 91; Ex Libris Robert Musil, City of Esslingen, 92. *Exhib:* One-man shows, Leo Castelli Gallery, NY, 88, Knoll Galleria, Budapest, 88, Galerie Le Gall Peyroulet, Paris, 89, Galeria Juana de Aizpuru, Madrid, 90, Galeria Comicos, Lisbon, 90, Margo Leavin Gallery, Los Angeles, 90, The Brooklyn Mus, NY, 90, Prague: Office of the President, Czechloslovakia, Prague Castle, 92, Smithsonian Inst, Hirshhorn Mus & Sculpture Garden, Wash, DC, 92. *Pos:* Rev critic, Arts Mag, New York, 67; Am ed, Art-Lang J, New York, 69-73; bd mem, Franklin Furnace, New York, currently. *Teaching:* Fac mem, Sch Visual Arts, New York, 68-; prof, Hocschule für Bilden Künst, Hamburg, Ger, 88-, Kunstakademie, Stuttgart, 90- *Bibliog:* Catherine Millet (auth), Joseph Kosuth, Flash Art, 2-3/71; Elizabeth Baker (auth), JK: Information Please, Art News, 2/73; Bruce Boice (auth), Kosuth: two shows, Artforum, Vol II. *Publ:* Auth, The Play of the Unmentionable: An Installation by Joseph Kosuth at the Brooklyn Museum, New Press in asn with the Brooklyn Mus, NY 92; Podobenstvi (Ex Libris, Kafka)/Parable (Ex Libris, Kafka) Joseph Kosuth (exhib catalog), Off of the Pres, Czechloslovakia, Prague Castle, 92; A Room with 23 Qualities, Ed Cantz, Stuttgart, 92; Ex Libris, J F Champollion (Figeac), Artpress and Centre des Arts Plastiques, Paris, France, 91; Art after Philosophy and After: Collected Writings, 1966-1990, MIT Press, Mass, 91. *Dealer:* Leo Castelli Gallery 420 West Broadway New York NY 10012. *Mailing Add:* 591 Broadway New York NY 10012

KOTALA, STANISLAW WACLAW
PAINTER, LIBRARIAN
b Boleslawiec, Poland, Sept 27, 09; US citizen. *Study:* Inst Design, Poland, dipl, 37; Acad Fine Arts, Cracow, Poland, with K Sichulski & P Dadlez, 38-39; Acad Fine Arts, Dusseldorf, Ger, with T Champion & W Heuser, BA, 49; Rutgers Univ, New Brunswick, MLS, 65. *Work:* Dom Wojska Polskiego, Warszawa, Poland; Mus Slaskie, Katowice, Poland. *Exhib:* Int Festival, Polish Arts Exhib, Edinburgh, Gt Brit, 47; Polish-Am Artist Exib, Kosciuszko Found, New York, 50; Nat Exhib Paintings by Am Artists of Polish Descent, Alliance Col, Cambridge Springs, Pa, 51; Plastyka za Drutami, Warszawa, 63; one-man show, Samuel Fleisher Art Mem, Philadelphia, 60. *Pos:* Artist-painter, Cordey China Art Studio, Philadelphia, 52-59; art ref librn, Free Libr Philadelphia, 59-79; retired. *Teaching:* Dir art hist, Inst Art Teachers, Dossel, Ger, 43-44; instr com art, Com High Sch, Lippstadt, Ger, 46-47. *Awards:* First Award, Off Club, 45; First Prize, Acad Fine Arts, Dusseldorf, 48. *Bibliog:* W Borzecki (auth), W zwierciadle sztuki, Nowy Swiat, 10/15/50; W Denkowski (auth), S W Kotala lecture, Gwiazda, 2/6/69. *Mem:* Am Libr Asn. *Media:* Watercolor, Oil. *Publ:* Illusr, Nasz Plomyczek, 46; Wiadomosci, 46. *Mailing Add:* 8147 Revere St Philadelphia PA 19152

KOTIK, CHARLOTTA
CURATOR, HISTORIAN
b Prague, Czech, Dec 13, 40; US citizen. *Study:* Kunsthistorisches Inst, Univ Wien, 65; Charles Univ, Prague, BA(art hist), 66, MA(art hist), 68. *Collections Arranged:* Jiri Kolar: Transformations (auth, catalog), 78; On Paper, About Paper (auth, catalog), 80; Jennifer Bartlett (auth, catalog), 80; Figures: Forms and Expressions (auth, catalog), 81; Fernand Leger: Retrospective (auth, catalog), 82; John Cage: Scores and Prints (coauth, catalog), 82; Charles Clough, Recent Work (auth, catalog), 83; Second Western States Exhib (auth, catalog), 84; Expendable Ikon: Works by John McHale (auth, catalog), 84; Francois Morellet: Systems (auth, catalog), 84; Working in Brooklyn: Sculpture (auth, catalog), 85; Monumental Drawing: Works by 22 Contemporary Americans (auth, catalog), 86; Third Western States Biennal (auth, catalog), 86; Working in Brooklyn: Painting (auth, catalog), 87; 4 Americans: Aspects of Current Sculpture (auth, catalog), 89; Working in Brooklyn: Installations (auth, catalog), 91; Grand Lobby Installation Series (auth, brochures), 84- *Pos:* Cur asst, Jewish Mus, 58-61 & Nat Gallery, 61-64, Prague, Czech; assoc & asst cur, Nat Trust, Prague, Czech, 67-70; cur, Albright-Knox Art Gallery, Buffalo, 70-83; cur, Brooklyn Mus, NY, 82-, chair dept painting & sculpture, 92- *Teaching:* Tutor fine arts, Empire State Col, Buffalo, NY, 77-79; adj asst prof, State Univ NY Buffalo, 79-83; instr art hist, Sch Visual Arts, New York, 90- *Awards:* Frederick R Weisman Art Found Award for outstanding achievement in contemp art, 91; Munic Art Soc Cert of Merit for the Grand Lobby Ser, 91; Nat Endowment Arts & US Info Agency, selected to curate Louise Bourgeois, the exhib to represent US in the 1993 Venice Biennale. *Mem:* Am Asn Mus, Round Table; Art Table Inc; Nat Endowment Arts (panelist & field rep); Arts Action Coalition, New York (bd dir); City Arts Workshop Inc, New York (bd dir). *Res:* Contemporary American art and architectural history. *Publ:* Co-auth, Contemporary Art 1942-72, Collection Albright-Knox, 72; Albright-Knox Art Gallery, Paintings and Sculpture from Antiquity to 1942, 78; Fernand Leger, Abbeville Press, 81; contrib auth, The Play of the Unmentionable: An Installation by Joseph Kosuth at The Brooklyn Museum, New Press, with Brooklyn Mus, 92. *Mailing Add:* Dept Painting & Sculpture Brooklyn Mus Brooklyn NY 11238

KOTOSKE, ROGER ALLEN
PAINTER, SCULPTOR
b South Bend, Ind, Jan 4, 33. *Study:* Univ Notre Dame, Ind, 50-52; Univ Denver, Colo, BFA, 54, MA, 56. *Work:* Rockhill Nelson Gallery, Kansas

City, Mo; State Univ NY Col Oswego; Denver Art Mus; Franklin Mint, Philadelphia. *Comn:* Large outdoor sculpture, City of Denver, 68. *Exhib:* Artist Teacher Today USA, State Univ Oswego, NY; one-man shows, Pollock Gallery, Southern Methodist Univ, Dallas, 69 & James Yu Gallery, New York, 76; Report from Soho, Grey Gallery, New York, 76; Contemp Am Painting & Sculpture, Indianapolis Mus Art, 78; Ill Painters Traveling Exhib, 81-; 22nd Biennial Works on Paper Exhib, Univ Del, Newark, Del, 86; Int Exhib, Chinese Nat FA, Beijing, 87; Greater Midwest Int III, Mo, 88. *Teaching:* Prof art, Univ Denver, 58-68 & Univ Ill, Urbana, 68- *Awards:* Purchase Awards, Nelson-Atkins Mus, 59 & State Univ Oswego, NY, 68. *Bibliog:* Meilach & Kowal (co-auth), Sculpture Casting, Crown Publ, 72; Meilach (auth), The Artist Eye, Regnery Press, 72; Verhelst (auth), Sculpture: Tools, Materials and Techniques, Prentice-Hall, 73 & 88. *Mem:* FATE; CAA. *Media:* Acrylic; Wood. *Mailing Add:* 1611 W White St Champaign IL 61820

KOTTEMANN, GEORGE & NORMA
COLLECTORS
Dr Kottemann, b St Louis, Mo, Aug 17, 31; Mrs Kottemann, b Springfield, Ill, Jan 1, 32. *Collection:* Contemporary paintings, prints and sculpture. *Mailing Add:* 3300 N Bigelow Peoria IL 61604

KOTUN, HENRY PAUL
ART THERAPIST
b Uniontown, Pa, July 31, 31. *Study:* Mus Art Sch, Hagerstown; Syracuse Univ; Corcoran Sch Art, Washington, DC; George Washington Univ, MA, 66. *Comn:* Stage sets for hist pageant, Rogers Co, Ohio, 62-63. *Exhib:* Cumberland Valley Exhib, Co Mus, Hagerstown, Md, 56-68; Md Craft Coun Traveling Exhib, 65; Land of Pleasant Living, WCBM Gallery, Baltimore, Md, 69; Easton Acad Fine Arts, Md, 69. *Collections Arranged:* 200 yrs Am Interiors, 76; Art in Bloom, 78; Antique Laces, 79; Three Views thru Six Eyes, 80; Contemp English Landscapes, 81; Paintings by James Voshell, 81; and others. *Pos:* Color designer & consult, Jurica Bros Biol & Zool Charts, Chicago, 50-52; dir, The Gallery, Hagerstown, 66-70; dir, Washington Co Mus Fine Arts, 70-84; art therapist, PHP Corp, Va, 84-88; Cedar Ridge Childrens Home, RICA, Baltimore. *Teaching:* Instr, Washington Co Bd Educ, Md, 55-70; instr ceramics & sculpture, Mus Art Sch, Hagerstown, 66-68; instr art appreciation, ceramics & sculpture, Hagerstown Jr Col, 66-69; instr crafts, Shepherd Col, 67-68. *Awards:* Mus, Award Sculpture, Washington Co Mus Fine Arts, 68. *Mem:* Am Asn Mus; Washington Co Arts Coun (pres, 67-70); Nat Art Educ Asn. *Mailing Add:* 428 N Potomac Hagerstown MD 21740

KOTZKY, ALEX SYLVESTER
CARTOONIST
b New York, NY, Sept 11, 23. *Study:* Art Students League, 41. *Pos:* Free-lance commercial artist, 46-57; cartoonist syndicate strip Duke Hand, 58-59, syndicate strip Apt 3-G, Field Enterprises, 61- *Mem:* Nat Cartoonists Soc. *Mailing Add:* 203-17 56th Ave Bayside NY 11364

KOVATCH, JAK
PRINTMAKER, EDUCATOR
b Los Angeles, Calif, Jan 17, 29. *Study:* Univ Calif, Los Angeles, 46; Chouinard Art Inst, Los Angeles, 47-49; Calif Sch of Art, Los Angeles, 49-50; Univ Southern Calif, Los Angeles, 51; Los Angeles City Col, 55-56; Art Students League, spec study with Michael Ponce de Leon, 72 & 75. *Work:* Fogg Mus Art, Harvard Univ; Libr Congress; Joseph Hirshhorn Collection; Fairfield Art Collection, Town Hall, Conn; John Slade Ely House Collection, New Haven; Art Mus, Joinville, Brazil; Univ Miss. *Exhib:* Los Angeles Co Mus Art, 49, 54 & 55; Boston Mus Fine Arts, 54; Libr Congress, 54; Butler Inst Am Art, 54; M H de Young Mem Mus, San Francisco, Calif, 54; Mus Mod Art, New York, 56; Wadsworth Antheneum, Hartford, Conn, 58 & 72-76 & 79; Audubon Artists Inc, Nat Acad Galleries, New York, 73 & 78; Nat Acad Design Exhib, 77 & 80; Boston Ctr Arts, 76; Honolulu Acad Arts, Hawaii, 77 & 85; Print Club, Philadelphia, Pa, 78; Metrop Mus Art, Tokyo, Japan, 87 & 88; Taiwan, Rep of China, 88 & 91; Barbican Art Ctr, London, Eng, 89; and 500 others. *Pos:* Student asst, Lynton Kistler Lithography Studio, Los Angeles, 52-53; animation dept, Walt Disney Prod Inc, Burbank, Calif, 53-54. *Teaching:* Instr, Famous Artists Schs Inc, Westport, Conn, 57-59, New York City Col Exten Div, 59-60; Prof Design, Univ Bridgeport, Conn, 62-; ethyl prof, Indust Design, 88- *Awards:* Mellon Found Fel, Yale Univ, 79, 81 & 82; Zinn Ltd Award, Audubon Artists, Nat Arts Club, New York, 81, Audubon Artists Medal Honor, 88; Conn Comn Arts Grant, 84-85; and 125 others. *Mem:* Audubon Artists; Artists Equity; Westport Arts Ctr Conn; Los Angeles Printmaking Soc; Silvermine Ctr Arts; and others. *Media:* Multimedia, Painting. *Dealer:* Silvermine Ctr for Arts Inc 1037 Silvermine Rd New Canaan CT 06880. *Mailing Add:* 34 Sasco Creek Rd Westport CT 06880

KOVATCH, RONALD R
CERAMIST
Study: Kansas City Art Inst, BA, 76; Southern Ill Univ-Edwardsville, MFA, 87. *Work:* Kansas City Art Inst, Mo; St Mary's Col, South Bend, Ind; Evansville Mus Art & Sci, Ind; Marian Col, Indianapolis; Valparaiso Univ, Ind; Univ Wis, Whitewater. *Exhib:* Solo exhibs, Lill St Gallery, Chicago, 90, Univ Notre Dame, ISIS Gallery, Ind, 91, Gallery Nine, Univ Ill, Urbana-Champaign, 91, and others; group shows, Seventh Ann San Angelo Nat Ceramics Competition, San Angelo Mus Fine Arts, Tex, 92; Fresh Ideas from Familiar Faces, Ill Ceramic Invitational, Parkland Col Art Gallery, Champaign, 92; Containers Revisited, Nat Coun Educ for the Ceramic Arts, Tyler Art Gallery, Tyler Sch Art, Temple Univ, Philadelphia, 92; and many others. *Pos:* Owner/operator, pottery studio, Vernon, Ind, 78-85; many workshops & lectrs, 88-91. *Teaching:* Vis artist/instr ceramics, Sch Art Inst, Chicago, 88; vis asst prof ceramics, Sch Fine Arts, Ind Univ, Bloomington, 88-89; asst prof ceramics, Univ Ill, Urbana-Champaign, Sch Art Design, 89- *Awards:* Visual Artist Fel Grant, Nat Endowment Arts, 90; Visual Artist Fel, Ill Arts Coun, 91. *Mailing Add:* 303 N Orchard St Urbana IL 61801

KOVINICK, PHILIP PETER
WRITER, HISTORIAN
b Detroit, Mich, July 4, 24. *Study:* Calif State Univ, Chico, BA & MA. *Collections Arranged:* Canyons, Arroyos & Oases: Desert Landscape in Southern California, 1900-1985, 85; Reaching the Summit: Mountain Landscapes in Calif, 1900-1986, 86. *Mem:* Collegium Western Art (pres); Laguna Art Mus Hist Collections Coun (charter mem); Archives Am Art. *Res:* Art and artists of the American West, 1819 to present. *Publ:* Auth, South Dakota's other Borglum, SDak Hist, 71; The Woman Artist in the American West, 1860-1970 (catalog), 76; coauth, Women artists: The American frontier, Art News, 12/76; The Women Artist & the American West, 1850's-1970's, Univ Tex Press (in prep). *Mailing Add:* 4735 Don Ricardo Dr Los Angeles CA 90008

KOWAL, CAL (LEE)
CURATOR, PHOTOGRAPHER
b Chicago, Ill, Sept 4, 44. *Study:* Univ Ill, Chicago (art & art hist), 67; Ill Inst Technol, Inst Design, MS (photog), 71. *Work:* Art Inst Chicago, Ill; Cincinnati Art Mus, Ohio; De Cordova Art Mus, Lincoln, Mass; Miami Art Mus, Oxford, Ohio; Chase Manhattan-Ohio Banks, Cincinnati. *Comn:* Silkscreen, SHV NAm, Cincinnati, Ohio, 81; Collaborative Effort (with Peter Bodnar III), Louisville Water Tower Art Asn, 85. *Exhib:* National Photographic Invitational, Anderson Gallery, Richmond, Va, 75; OK Art, Contemp Art Ctr, Cincinnati, Ohio, 76; solo exhibs, True-False, Carl Solway Gallery, Cincinnati, 83 & Univ Dayton, Ohio, 85; Representation Strategies in Contemporary Photography, Southern Ill Univ, Carbondale, 85; 5 in Color: The Constructed Photograph, Warren Lee Ctr, Vermillion, SDak, 86. *Collections Arranged:* Daniel Brown Collection, Middlebury Col, Vt, 81; All Ohio Photography File, Art Acad Cincinnati, 83; Extended Vision (auth, catalog), Ponderosa, Inc, Dayton, Ohio, 84. *Pos:* Cur photog, Carl Solway Gallery, 82-86. *Teaching:* Sr fac photog & drawing, Art Acad Cincinnati, Ohio, 71-; guest prof, Miami Univ, Oxford, Ohio, 76-78; vis artist, Sch Art Inst, Chicago, 84-85. *Awards:* Artist-in-Residence, Syracuse Univ, 77; Ohio Arts Coun Fel, 82; Soc Contemp Photog Award, Current Works, Kans, 85. *Mem:* Contemp Art Ctr (bd trustees); Soc Photog Educ (Midwest bd). *Media:* Mixed Media & Drawing; Photographic Assemblages. *Publ:* Auth, Book Full of Spoons, Rose-Pose Publ, 75; T-Shirts Are Tacky, 76; This Space Reserved, 79; Soft Color, portfolio, Self-Publ, Cincinnati, Ohio, 84; Unfamiliar House Series, 86. *Dealer:* Carl Solway Gallery 314 W 4th St Cincinnati OH 45202. *Mailing Add:* 2543 Cleinview Ave Cincinnati OH 45206

KOWAL, DENNIS J
WRITER
b Chicago, Ill, Sept 9, 37. *Study:* Art Inst Chicago; Univ Ill, Chicago Circle; Southern Ill Univ, BS, 61, MFA, 62. *Work:* Gillette Corp, Boston; Lakeforest Col, Ill; Inst Contemp Art, Boston; Babson Col, Wellesley, Mass; Bank New Eng Corp hq, Boston; and many others. *Comn:* Monuments, Milton Acad, Mass, 78, Newsweb Corp, Chicago, 78, Ravina Festival Pavilion 80, Nat Fire Protection Asn, Batterymarch Park, Mass, 80-81, Federal Reserve Bank, Boston, 82. *Exhib:* Dorsky Gallery Ltd, New York, 74; One-man exhib, Mead Art Mus, Amherst Col, Mass, 78, NC Mus Art, Raleigh, 78, Gilbert Gallery Ltd, Chicago, Ill, 79, Boston Fine Arts Gallery, Mass, 84 & Beaulieu Art Gallery, Cambridge, Mass, 88; Robert Freidus Gallery, New York, 77; Worthington Gallery, Chicago, 77-78; Mead Art Mus, Amherst Col, Mass, 78; NC Mus Art, 78; Gilbert Gallery Ltd, Chicago, 79; and many others. *Pos:* Artist-in-Resident, Dartmouth Col, 70-71, Univ Ga, 73, Amherst Col, 77-78, Milton Acad, 77, Maudslay State Park, Newburyport, Mass, 88- *Teaching:* Prof sculpture, Columbus Col Art, Ohio, 63-64, Univ Ill, Champaign, 66-70 & Mass Col Art, Boston, 71-72; vis lectr, Univ Ga, 73. *Awards:* Numerous awards, 70-; Artist-in-Resident & Fel, Yaddo, Saratoga Springs, NY, 70, Macdowwell Colony, Peterborough, NH, 65, 72, Vietnam Veterans Mem Commonwealth, Mass, 86-; Nat Endowment Arts Matching Grant, Babson Col, Wellesley, Mass, 76. *Bibliog:* Eva Jacob (auth), The Real Paper, Boston, 3/77; article, Portrait of the artist-The Boston art market and sculptor Dennis Kowal, 77; Rituals of celebrations, Dennis Kowal, Decade Mag, 79; and numerous others. *Mem:* Inst Contemp Art, Boston, Chicago; Boston Visual Artists Union; and others. *Media:* Multi. *Publ:* Contribr, Contemporary Wood Sculpture, 68, contribr, Contemporary Stone Sculpture, 69 & auth, Casting Sculpture, 72, Crown; auth, Artists speak, NY Graphic Soc, 76; The Link, An Artist of Modern Time, Boston Univ Press, 88; Public Art in Greater Boston, Harvard Common Press,. *Mailing Add:* 508 S Osprey Ave Sarasota FL 34236

KOWALKE, RONALD LEROY
PAINTER, PRINTMAKER
b Chicago, Ill, Nov 8, 36. *Study:* Univ Chicago, 54-56; Art Inst Chicago, 54-56; Rockford Col, BA, 59; Cranbrook Acad Art, MFA, 60. *Work:* Mus Mod Art & Metrop Mus Art, New York; Libr Cong & Nat Gallery, Washington, Dc; Rockford Col, Ill. *Exhib:* Nat Print Exhib, Calif Soc Etchers, San Francisco Mus Art, 65; 15th Ann Print Exhib, Brooklyn Mus, 66; New Directions 1982, Hawaii Artist League, Amfac Plaza Gallery, 82; Hawaii '82-Works on Paper, Univ Hawaii, Hilo, 82; Hawaii Craftsman '82, Amfac Plaza Gallery, 82; two-man exhib, Structures, Art Loft Gallery, Hawaii, 83; Easter Arts Festival, Ala Moana Art Ctr, Hawaii, 83. *Teaching:* Instr design, Northern Ill Univ, 60-61; instr drawing, design & printmaking, Swain Sch Design, New Bedford, Mass, 61-64; assoc prof art, Univ Hawaii, 69-72, prof, 72- *Awards:* Purchase Awards, Honolulu Acad Arts, 69 & 71; Faculty Res Grant, Univ Hawaii, 69 & 70; Faculty Travel Grants, Univ Hawaii, 79 & 82. *Bibliog:* Dantes Inferno: A Portfolio of Ten Etchings, Impressions Workshop, Boston, 70; Gentle Words and Gentle People: A Portfolio of Ten Etchings, Univ Hawaii, Honolulu, 71; Artists of Hawaii, Vol 11, Univ Hawaii Press, 77. *Mem:* Honolulu Printmakers. *Dealer:* Associated American Artists Inc 663 Fifth Ave New York NY 10022; Ferdinand Roten Inc 123 W Mulberry Baltimore MD 21201. *Mailing Add:* 1590 Ulupil St Kailua HI 96734

KOWALSKI, DENNIS ALLEN
CONCEPTUAL ARTIST
b Chicago, Ill, May 14, 38. *Study:* Univ of Ill, Chicago (archit), 55-57; Sch Art Inst Chicago, BFA(sculpture), 62; Sch Art Inst Chicago, MFA(sculpture), 66. *Work:* Gov State Univ; Ill State Univ; Art Inst Chicago; Mus Contemp Art, Sidley & Austin, Chicago; Prudential, Newark, NJ. *Comn:* Outdoor sculpture, Univ of Chicago, 75. *Exhib:* Art Inst Chicago, 65-66, 75 & 80; one-man shows, NAME Gallery, 76 & 80, Marianne Deson Gallery, Chicago, 78, 81, 83, 86 & 89, Deson/Saunders Gallery, Chicago, Art Acad Cincinnati, 91 & Robert Morrison Gallery, New York, 92; Semaphore Gallery, New York, 83; Experimental Art Exhib, Young Artists Club, Budapest, 86; Redefining the Object, Cleveland Ctr Contemp Art & Wright State Univ, Dayton, Ohio; Generations I Chicago, Carnegie Mellon Univ Gallery, Pittsburg, Pa; West Art and the Law, traveling, 91; and many others. *Teaching:* Assoc prof sculpture, Univ of Ill, Chicago, 70- *Awards:* Nat Endowment Arts Fel Grant, 75; Grant, Ill Arts Coun, 80, Fel, 80 & 84. *Bibliog:* Alan Artner (auth), articles in Chicago Tribune, 10/7/83 & 4/25/86 & 6/2/89; Garret Holg (auth), rev, Art News,9/89; Tim Porges (auth), Contemporanea, Chicago Reviews, 5/90; James Yood (auth), rev, New Art Examiner, 12/91; Kathryn Hixson (auth), rev, 11-12/91. *Dealer:* Dart Gallery 700 N Carpenter Chicago IL 60610; Robert Morrison Gallery 59 Thompson New York NY 10012. *Mailing Add:* 4134 N Damen Ave Chicago IL 60618

KOWALSKI, LIBBY R
FIBER ARTIST, EDUCATOR
Chicago, Ill, Jun 29, 40. *Study:* Millikin Univ, BA, 62; Colorado State Univ, BFA, 79; Cranbrook Acad Art, MFA, 81. *Work:* Kresgie Art Mus, E Lansing, Mich; Dowd Fine Arts Gallery, Cortland, NY; IBM, Southfield, Mich; Unisys, Washington, DC; General Motors, Detroit, Mich. *Exhib:* Fiber Structure Nat, Downey Art Mus, Downey, Calif, 88; Black & White, Gayle Willson Gallery, Southhampton, New York, 89; Small Works Invitational, Ctr for Tapestry Arts, New York, 89; Fiber Explorations, State Univ New York, Stony Brook, 89; solo exhib: Space/Place/Fragment, Ctr Tapestry Arts, New York, 91; and others. *Teaching:* Assoc prof weaving & surface design, State Univ New York, Cortland, NY, 82-; fibers, Chautauqua Sch Art, summers 87-91; designer/owner, CTD Studio, Hand Weaving & Design Studio, New York, 89-; adj fibers, Grad Prog, Syracuse Univ, 91. *Awards:* Visual Artists Prog Grant, New York State Coun on Arts, 85; Computer Graphics, Stipend, Research Found State Univ New York, 86. *Bibliog:* Else Regensteiner (auth), Geometric Design in Weaving, Schiffer Publ, 86; Tom Milligan (auth), Libby Kowalski: her work (film), WSKG, 4/90. *Mem:* Am Craft Coun; Col Art Asn. *Media:* Fibers. *Publ:* Contribr, Fiberarts Design Book, 80; contribr, Ithaca Women's Anthology, 89. *Dealer:* Yaw Gallery, Birmingham, Mich; Interart Ctr New York NY. *Mailing Add:* c/o CTD Studio 41 Union Sq W Suite 502 New York NY 10003

KOWALSKI, RAYMOND ALOIS
PAINTER
b Erie, Pa, June 21, 33. *Study:* Pa State Teachers Col, Edinboro; Cleveland Inst Art, BFA, 77. *Work:* State of Pa Educ Syst. *Exhib:* May Show, Cleveland Mus Art, 69-71 & 83; Preview 71, Mt St Joseph's Col, Cincinnati, 71; Butler Mus Show, Youngstown, Ohio; one-man show, Green Mansion Gallery, Cleveland, 79, Bluffton Col, Ohio, 79, Ohio Mus Beachwood, 87; Ohio State Fair, 79; Willoughby Fine Arts Ctr, Ohio, 79; Shaker Hist Mus, 90. *Pos:* Designer, Am Greetings Corp, Cleveland, 59-65, art dir, 65-, managing art dir, 73-, dir, Creative Planning, 81, dir design, 83; Exec dir design, 85. *Teaching:* Instr design, Cooper Sch Art, Cleveland, 69-70; instr painting for local art groups, 70-; guest critic, RI Sch Design, Sr Proj, 90; guest instr, Columbus Col Art & Design, Parsons Sch Design, 92. *Awards:* Award, Jewish Community Ctr Ann, Cleveland Heights, 79; Award, Erie Art Ctr Ann, Penn, 79; Ohio State Fair, 81; and others; Fine Arts Show Awards, B P Am Gallery, Cleveland Ohio, 87 & 88; Am Greetings Corp Fine Arts Show, Cleveland Playhouse Gallery. *Bibliog:* Helen Borsick (auth), article in Cleveland Plain Dealer Suppl, 68; Ray Kowalski--painter of houses, Wonderful World Ohio, 10/69; Ray Kowalski-House Painter, WKYC-TV, Cleveland. *Mem:* Soc Illusrs. *Media:* Acrylic, Collage, Watercolor. *Dealer:* Alan Gallery Cleveland OH. *Mailing Add:* 2780 Berkshire Rd Cleveland Heights OH 44106

KOZLOFF, JOYCE
PAINTER, MOSAIC ARTIST
b Somerville, NJ, Dec 14, 42. *Study:* Carnegie Inst Technol, BFA, 64; Columbia Univ, MFA, 67. *Work:* Brooklyn Mus, Metrop Mus Art, Mus Mod Art, New York; Nat Gallery Art, Washington, DC; Neue Galerie Sammlung Ludwig, Aachen, Ger; Ball State Univ Art Gallery, Muncie, Ind; and many others. *Comn:* Home Savings Am, Los Angeles & Community Redevelopment Agency of the City of Los Angeles, 89; Pasadena, The City of Roses, Maguire Thomas Partners, Plaza las Fuentas, Pasadena; I S 218, NY Percent for Art Program, Art Comn City of New York, 91; History of Visual Style in Hollywood Movies, 7th and Flower Station, Southern Calif Rapid Transit District's Metro Rail Proj, 91-93; and others. *Exhib:* one-woman exhibs, Everson Mus, 79, Mint Mus, 80, Renwick, Smithsonian Inst, 80-81, Joslyn Mus, 82, Inst Contemp Art, Philadelphia, 83 & Del Mus, Wilmington, 84, Lorence-Monk Gallery, NY, 90 & Nina Freudenheim Gallery, Buffalo, 90; Arts on the Line, Hayden Gallery, Mass Inst Technol, 80; Printed Art: A View of Two Decades, Mus Mod Art, New York, 80; A Private Vision: Contemporary Art from the Graham Gund Collection, Mus Fine Arts, Boston, 82; Soft as Silk, Wadsworth Atheneum, 82; Back to the USA, Lucerne Mus, Switz, 83; On 42nd St, Whitney Mus Am Art at Philip Morris, New York, 84; Not Just Black & White, City Gallery, New York, 85; Jewish Community Mus, San Francisco, 86; Making their Mark: Women Artists Today, A Documentary Survey 1970-1985, traveling, 88-90. *Teaching:* Instr ACE prog, Queens Col, Flushing, NY, 71-72; instr, Sch Visual Arts, 73-74, Art Inst Chicago, 75, Syracuse Univ, 77 & Univ NMex, 78; instr, Washington Univ, St Louis, Mo, 86; instr, Cooper Union, New York, 90; instr, Rutgers Univ, New Brunswich, NJ, 92. *Awards:* Nat Endowment Arts Grant Painting, 77 & Grant Drawing, 85; Yaddo Fel, Saratoga Springs, NY, 84; Rockefeller Found Grant, Bellagio, Italy, 92. *Bibliog:* Eleanor Heartneg (auth), A necessary transgression, The New Art Examiner, 11/88; Allan Schwartzman (auth), Monumental trouble, Elle, 9/89; Peggy Phelan (auth), Grimes of Passion, Artforum, 5/90; and many others. *Mem:* Heresies Collective; Public Art Fund, NY (advisory bd, 84-86); Col Art Asn (bd dirs, 85-89). *Media:* Ceramic Tiles, Glass Mosaic. *Publ:* Auth, Thoughts on my art, In: Name Book I, Name Gallery, Chicago, 77; coauth (with Valerie Jaudon), Art hysterical notions of progress and culture, Heresies IV, winter 78; auth, Frida Kahlo at the Neuberger Museum, Art in Am, 5-6/79. *Dealer:* Barbara Gladstone Gallery 152 Wooster St New York NY 10012. *Mailing Add:* 152 Wooster St New York NY 10012

KOZLOFF, MAX
PHOTOGRAPHER, WRITER
b Chicago, Ill, June 21, 33. *Study:* Univ Chicago, BA, 53, MA, 58; Inst Fine Arts, NY Univ; Fulbright scholar, France, 62-63. *Exhib:* One-man shows, Holly Solomon Gallery, New York, 77, 79 & 80, Marlborough Gallery, New York, 82, PPOW Gallery, 93. *Pos:* Art critic, The Nation, 61-69; NY corresp, Art Int, 62-64; contrib ed, Artforum, 63-74, exec ed, 74-76. *Teaching:* Instr, Calif Inst Arts, 70-71 & Yale Univ, 74; prof photog, Sch Visual Arts, New York, 89-; and many others. *Awards:* Pulitzer Fel Critical Writing, 62-63; Frank Jewett Mather Award Art Criticism, 66; Guggenheim Fel, 68-69; Nat Endowment Arts Criticism Fel, 84; Int Ctr Photog Writing Award, 90. *Publ:* Auth, Renderings: Essays on a Century of Modern Art, 68; Jasper Johns, 69 & rev ed, 72; Cubism Futurism, 74; Photography and Fascination, 79; The Privileged Eye, 87; contribr art & photog criticism to major jour; Duane Michals Now Becoming Then, Twelve Trees Press, 90. *Mailing Add:* 152 Wooster St New York NY 10012

KOZLOW, RICHARD
PAINTER
b Detroit, Mich, May 5, 26. *Study:* Cass Tech, Detroit; Detroit Soc Arts & Crafts. *Work:* Ohio Univ Mus Art, Athens; Butler Art Mus; Smithsonian Nat Mus Am Art, Washington, DC; Spanish Nat Libr Collection, Madrid; State Mich Libr, Archives Mus, Lansing, 88; and others. *Comn:* Sky Series (three paintings), Ford Motor Co, NAAO Bldg, Dearborn, Mich, 80; The Opera's Not Over (painting), Yaffe Assocs, Southfield, Mich, 81; Great Ideas of Western Man Series, Container Corp Am; Wine labels (five paintings), Muer Corp Restaurants, 89-90; painting, Mona Lizautuers-Les Auteur Restaurant, Royal Oak, Mich, 90. *Exhib:* Solo exhibs, Retrospective, Detroit Inst Arts, 64, Retrospective, Art Gallery Windsor, Ont, 77, Ohio Univ, Athens, 82 & Am Embassy, Madrid, Spain, 84; Mich Artists Exhib, Detroit Inst Arts, 50, 53, 58, 63 & 64; Regional Ann, Butler Inst Am Art, Ohio, 52; 20th Century Am Art, San Diego Mus, Calif, 68; Lithographs from Mourlot Graphics, Hudson River Mus, NY, 70; travelling exhib, Nat Inst (Mex) Bellas Artes - San Miguel Allende, Aguas Calientes & Guanajuato, 91; and others. *Teaching:* Instr & dept head, Detroit Soc Arts & Crafts, 50-60; instr special workshops, Birmingham-Bloomfield Art Asn, Mich, 70-79, & 90; artist in residence, Inst Allende, San Miguel Allende, Gto, Mexico, formerly; instr special travel workshops, Costa Rica, 81, Smokey Mountains, 81 & Mexico, 82. *Awards:* Founders Award, Mich Artist Exhib, Detroit Inst Arts, 63; Mich Found Arts Award, 82. *Bibliog:* Louise Brunner (auth), Landscape painting of Richard Kozlow, Am Artist Mag, 56; Wendon Blake (auth), Complete Guide to Acrylic Painting, Watson-Guptill; L J Feinberg (auth), cover painting & biog, J Am Med Asn, 1-26/90. *Media:* Acrylic, All. *Publ:* Auth & illusr, Of Man's Inhumanity to Man, Lark Press, 65. *Dealer:* Rubiner Gallery West Bloomfield MI. *Mailing Add:* 176 Suffield Ave Birmingham MI 48009

KOZLOWSKI, EDWARD C
PAINTER, DESIGNER
b Bridgeport, Conn, Mar 11, 27. *Study:* Butera Sch Fine Art, 47; Whitney Sch Art, portrait with Simka Simkovitch, dipl, 51; Yale Sch Design, color with Josef Albers, BFA, 54. *Work:* Yale Univ, New Haven, Conn. *Exhib:* Connecticut Yale Artists, Yale AA Gallery, New Haven, 76; 2nd Ann Int Soc Arts, Foothills Art Ctr, Golden, Colo, 79; 27th Ann Nat Soc Painters Casein & Acrylic, Nat Arts Club, New York, 80; 3rd Ann, Salmagundi Club, New York, 80; 156th Ann, Nat Acad Design, New York, 81. *Pos:* Staff artist, Bridgeport Post, Conn, 47-54; advert designer, Int Silver Co, Meriden, Conn, 54-56; dir packaging develop, Warner Packaging, Bridgeport, Conn, 56-64; owner, Edward C Kozlowski Design Inc, New York, 64-83. *Teaching:* Instr design, Pratt Inst, Brooklyn, 65-69 & Parson Sch Design, 83-86. *Awards:* Best Show, 20th Ann, Barnum Festival Soc, 80; Best Acrylics, 20th Ann, Barnum Festival Soc, 80; Frederick Lowey Award, Salmagundi Club, 81. *Mem:* Salmagundi Club; Conn Classical Arts; Am Inst Graphic Arts; Advertising Club Fairfield Co (pres, 64-65). *Media:* Acrylic, Watercolor; Conte Pencil, Lithograph. *Publ:* Coauth, The package designer looks at packaging materials, Packaging Design, 64; contribr, Changing times, Indust Design, 75; auth, Job sheet: A better link between packager and marketer, Product Mgt, 76. *Dealer:* Art/Place 400 Center St Southport CT; Moviehouse Gallery Main St Millerton NY. *Mailing Add:* 74 Columbine Dr Trumbull CT 06611

KOZMON, GEORGE
PAINTER, PRINTMAKER
b Cleveland, Ohio, Apr 22, 60. *Study:* Cleveland Inst Art, Ohio, BFA, 82. *Work:* Cleveland Mus Art, Ohio; Erie Art Mus, Pa; DuPont, Detroit, Mich; IBM, Armonk, NY; Butler Inst Am Art, Youngstown, Ohio. *Comn:* Painting

(paper, 3ft x 4ft), BP Am, Cleveland, 84; canvas (4ft x 6ft), Goodyear Tech Ctr, Akron, 85; Dyptich on Masonite (3ft x 5ft), Haliburton Corp, Dallas, Tex, 86; painting on masonite (3ft x 5ft), Turner Construction, Columbus, 86; 5 (5ft x 8ft) canvases, Univ Hosp, Cleveland, Ohio, 89. *Exhib:* Cleveland Mus Art, 82-86; one-person shows, Cleveland Ctr Contemp Art, 83 & Robert L Kidd Gallery, Birmingham, Mich, 84-85, 88 & 91, Mary Bell Gallery, Chicago, 87, 89 & 92 & Scottsdale, Ariz, 89; Sande Webster Gallery, Philadelphia, 89 & 91; Gov Residence Invitational, Columbus, 85; The Artist Obsessed: Architecture Perceived, Fendrick Gallery, Washington, DC, 86; One-man show, Quan/Schieder Gallery, Toronto. *Teaching:* Vis lectr, Mid Am Col, Art Asn, 84; instr, drawing & archit, Cleveland Inst Art, 85-86. *Awards:* Ohio Coun Individual Fel, 84-85; Ohio Arts Coun Visual Artists Fel, 84, 87 & 91; Nat Endowment Arts Individual Artists Fel, 87-88; and others. *Bibliog:* Gerorge Kozmon (video), Goodyear, 84; Showing a new perspective, Birmingham Eccentric, Mich, 5/85; Jo Ann Lewis (auth), A brush with buildings, Washington Post, 4/12/86. *Mem:* New Orgn Visual Arts; World Fedn Hungarian Artists. *Media:* Acrylic on Paper & Aluminum. *Publ:* Auth, Art in the Midwest, Am Artist, 84; City whites, Cleveland Mag, 84; Drawing a line of departure, Cleveland Mus Art, 84; and numerous catalogues. *Mailing Add:* 4567 Ammon Rd South Euclid OH 44143

KRACZKOWSKI, PHIL
SCULPTOR
b Chelsea, Mass, Nov 28, 16. *Study:* RI Sch Design, 38. *Work:* Smithsonian Inst, Washington, DC; Mus Medallic Art, Wroclaw, Poland. *Comn:* Statue, comn by William O Sweet, Ottawa, Can, 63; plaque, comn by Lady Bird Johnson, Austin, Tex, 63; bust, J Edgar Hoover Soc, Washington DC, 64; Curtis E Lemay Soc, Omaha, Nebr, 66; The Explorers Club, New York, 69. *Exhib:* 34th Ann Exhib Nat Sculpture Soc, New York, 67; Worcester Nat Mus, Mass, 67. *Awards:* New England Mfg, Jewelers & Silversmith Asn, 36; Sculpture, Providence Art Club, 72; First Prize, Dedham Art Guild, 78. *Mem:* Assoc Mem Nat Sculpture Soc. *Publ:* Sculptor Kraczkowski, Western Horseman, 7/67; The Sculptors of Philip Kraczkowski, Am Artists, 8/69; A Sculptor's Hobby, Yankee, 10/72; Sculpture with a smile, Christian Sci Monitor, 1/72. *Mailing Add:* C Robin Blanchard P O Box 223 Attleboro MA 02703

KRAKOW, BARBARA L
DEALER
b Boston, Mass, June 9, 36. *Study:* Boston Univ, BA, 58. *Pos:* Owner & dir, Barbara Krakow Gallery, Boston, currently; art adv panel, Internal Revenue Service, 80-84; membership comt, Art Dealers Asn Am, 85-; bd mem, Art Auction AIDS Action Comt, 85, co-chairperson, 86. *Teaching:* Lectr, Harvard Arts Mus, 11/86. *Awards:* Honored by Boston YWCA, Tribute to Women Entrepreneurs, 86. *Mem:* Art Table Inc; Art Dealer Asn Am. *Specialty:* American art 1945 to present, paintings, sculpture, drawings and prints. *Mailing Add:* Barbara Krakow Gallery 10 Newbury St Boston MA 02116

KRAMER, BURTON
DESIGNER, EDUCATOR
b New York, NY, June 25, 32. *Study:* Inst Design, Ill Inst Technol, BSc(visual design), 54; Yale Univ Sch Fine Arts, MFA(design), 57; also with Josef Albers & Paul Rand. *Work:* Smithsonian Inst, North Am Life Assurance. *Comn:* Identity program design, Can Broadcasting Corp, Copps Coliseum, Reed Paper, Can Craft Coun, Teknion Furniture, Science North, Nat Res Coun Can, Onex Packaging, Gemini Group & St Lawrence Centre Arts. *Exhib:* Biennial Graphic Design, Brno, Czech, 70, 74 & 78; Can Graphic Design, Tokyo, Japan, 75; Spectrum Can, Montreal, 76; VI Poster Biennale, Warsaw, Poland, 76; RCA Designers 78, Toronto, 78; Graphic Designer Can Best of '80's, Art Dirs Show, Toronto, 85. *Pos:* Chief designer, Halpern Advert, Zurich, Switz, 62-65; dir corp graphics, Clairtone Sound Corp, 66-67; pres, Kramer Design Assocs Ltd, Marketing Commun & Design, currently. *Teaching:* Mem design fac, Ont Col Art, 78- *Awards:* Gold Medal Award, Int Typographic Composition Asn, 71; Gold Medal Award, Art Dir Club, 73 & 75; Graphic Designers Can, 85. *Bibliog:* Article, Studio Mag, Toronto, 85; First Choice, Tokyo, 89; Idea Mag, Tokyo, 92. *Mem:* Royal Can Acad Art; fel Graphic Designers Can (pres, 75-77); Alliance Graphique Int; Am Inst Graphic Arts. *Publ:* Auth, Typographic eye, New York, 74; auth & contribr, Top trademarks and symbols of the world, Milan, 74; auth & ed, Idea Mag, Tokyo, 75 & 85; auth, Canadian Interiors, Toronto, 75; Appl Arts Quart, 90. *Mailing Add:* Burton Kramer Design Asn Ltd 103 Dupont St Toronto ON M5R 1O4 Canada

KRAMER, GERTRUDE M
DEALER
b Ger; US citizen. *Pos:* Vpres & asst dir, Arras Gallery, Ltd, New York, 71- *Specialty:* Contemporary art. *Mailing Add:* c/o Arras Gallery Ltd 24 W 57th St New York NY 10019

KRAMER, HILTON
CRITIC
b Gloucester, Mass, Mar 25, 28. *Study:* Syracuse Univ, BA; Columbia Univ; New Sch Social Res; Harvard Univ; Ind Univ. *Pos:* Assoc ed & feature ed, Arts Digest, 54-55; managing ed, Arts Mag, 55-58, ed, 58-61; chief art critic & art news ed, New York Times, formerly. *Teaching:* Lectr art today. *Publ:* Auth, The Age of the Avant-Garde, Farrar, Straus & Giroux, 74; contribr, Arts Mag, Partisan Rev, Commentary, New Repub, New York Rev Bks, Encounter, Art in Am, Artforum, The Hudson Rev, Artscanada & others. *Mailing Add:* 850 Seventh Ave Suite 503 New York NY 10019

KRAMER, JAMES
PAINTER
b Columbus, Ohio, Oct 24, 27. *Study:* Cleveland Sch Art; Western Reserve Univ; Ohio State Univ. *Work:* Monterey Peninsula Mus Art, Calif; Georgetown Hist Soc, Colo; United Bank Denver; Univ Nevada, Reno; Colo Heritage Ctr Mus, Denver; Mus Western Art, Denver; Bank Belen, NMex. *Comn:* Illustration, Trail Guide, Ventana Chapter, Sierra Club, 69; program cover, Orchestra Santa Fe, 84-85; Sixth Street (watercolor), Georgetown Soc, 85. *Exhib:* Mus Western Art, Denver, Colo, 84; Southwestern Realism, NMex Mus Fine Art, Santa Fe, 90 & Taiwan Mus, 91; American Art in Miniature, Gilcrease Mus, Tulsa, Okla, 90; Millicent Rogers Mus, Taos, NMex, 92; Royal Watercolour Soc, London, Eng, 92; and others. *Teaching:* Watercolor workshop, Mont Art Educ Asn, Great Falls, 74; watercolor workshop, Soc Western Artists, Fresno, Calif, 75 & Ghost Ranch, Abiquiu, NMex, 80; instr, Valdes Art Workshp, Santa Fe, NMex, 85- & Scottsdale Artists' Sch, Ariz, 86-88. *Awards:* Gold Medal, Calif Art Club, 73; Silver Medal, Nat Acad Western Art, 89; Frederic Remington Award, Nat Acad Western Art, 91; and others. *Bibliog:* Stephen M Parks (auth), James Kramer, skill can destroy soul, Art Lines, 9/84; Suzanne Deats (auth), James Kramer, Focus/Santa Fe, 6-7/87; John Villani (auth), Watercolorist displays stroke of genius, NMex Mag, 5/92. *Mem:* Nat Acad Western Art; Santa Fe Watercolor Soc. *Media:* Watercolor. *Publ:* Contribr, The Watercolor Page, Am Artist Mag, 73; contribr, 40 Watercolorists & How They Work, 76 & Executive Diary, 76, Watson-Guptill; Painting Small & Watercolor and Gouache (films), Okla Co Libr, 77. *Dealer:* Nedra Matteucci-Fenn Galleries Santa Fe NMex. *Mailing Add:* 631 Calle de Valdes Santa Fe NM 87501

KRAMER, LINDA LEWIS
SCULPTOR, COLLECTOR
b New York, NY, Mar 25, 37. *Study:* Scripps Col, Claremont Calif, with Paul Soldner, BA, 59; Sch Art Inst, Chicago, MFA, 81. *Work:* Mus Contemp Art, Chicago; Purdue Univ, W Lafayette; Univ Ill, Carbondale. *Exhib:* Chicago Sculpture Int, Art Expo, 83 & 84; one-woman show, Three Cultures, Red, Yellow & Blue, Univ Ariz, Tuscon, 84; Alternative Spaces, Mus Contemp Art, Chicago, 84; 80th Exhib, Art Inst, Chicago, 84; Material & Metaphor, Chicago Pub Libr Cultural Ctr, 86; Still Light, Evanston Art Ctr. *Pos:* Mem bd dirs, Lill Street Gallery, Chicago, 82-86 & prog chmn, 83-84; comt mem, Evanston Art Ctr Exhibs, 91- *Awards:* Arts & Riverwoods Award, 78th Chicago Vicinity, 80; Ill Arts Coun Grant, 84; Levy Found Prize, 80th Chicago & Vicinity Exhib, 84. *Bibliog:* Janet Koplos (auth), Linda Kramer-Profile, Am Ceramics, 84; Diane Douglas (auth), Material & Metaphor, Chicago Pub Libr Cultural Ctr, 86; Patty Carroll (auth), Spirited Visions, Univ Ill Press, 91. *Mem:* Mid-west Clay Guild (vpres, 86, treas, 90). *Media:* Misc media, Installations. *Collection:* Chicago imagists first and second generation hairy who school. *Publ:* Auth, Natural & Cultural Energy, Leonardo Mag, 87. *Dealer:* Printworks Gallery 311 West Superior Chicago IL 60610. *Mailing Add:* 370 Glendale Ave Winnetka IL 60093

KRAMER, LOUISE
MURALIST, SCULPTOR
b New York, NY. *Study:* Cooper Union, cert, 44; Hofstra Univ, BA, 68; Hunter Col, MA, 70. *Work:* Nassau Community Col, Hempstead, NY; Mus Fine Art, Univ Iowa, Iowa City; Brentwood High Sch, NY. *Comn:* Mural, Int Ladies Garment Workerts' Union, Local 23-25, NY, 85. *Exhib:* Two Women Sculptors, RI Univ Gallery, Kingston; Emerging Real, Storm King Art Ctr, Mountainville; one-woman show, Nassau Co Mus Fine Arts, Roslyn; Women Choose Women, NY Cultural Ctr; Calif Col Arts & Crafts Print Show, San Francisco Mus Art; Printmaking, New Forms, Whitney Mus, New York; AIR Gallery, New York, 75, 78, 81, 83 & 85; Working Women, Am Fedn State Co & Munic Employees; 18th Nat Print Exhib, Brooklyn Mus, 86. *Teaching:* Artist-in-residence, sculpture, Univ Iowa, Iowa City, 78; lectr sculpture, Arrandale Sch, Great Neck, NY. *Awards:* North Shore Community Arts Award, Great Neck, 75; Fel Printmaking, NY State Coun Arts, 76; Nat Endowment Arts Fel Printmaking, 76. *Bibliog:* Lizzie Borden (auth), Louise Kramer, Artforum, 72; Kate Linker (auth), Louise Kramer, Arts Mag, 5/77. *Mem:* Women in the Arts; Women's Caucus Arts. *Media:* Steel, Brass. *Dealer:* AIR Gallery 63 Crosby St New York NY 10012. *Mailing Add:* 26 Beaver St New York NY 10004

KRAMER, MARGIA
CONCEPTUAL ARTIST, VIDEO ARTIST
b Brooklyn, New York. *Study:* Art Students League; Brooklyn Col, BA; Inst of Fine Arts, New York Univ, MA(art hist); performanc/dance study with Yvonne Rainer & Simone Forti,. *Work:* Mus Mod Art, New York; Allen Mem Art Mus, Oberlin, Ohio; New York Pub Libr; Univ Calif, San Diego; Temple Univ; Carnegie/Mellon. *Comn:* Secret (video), Ill Arts Coun, Chicago, 81; Progress (Memory) I (video), Visual Studies Workshop, Rochester, NY, 83; New Wozzeck (video) Jerome Found, 85; Obelisk for Raymond Williams (pub sculpture), Pub Art Fund Inc, New York, 88; I a Wo/Man (multi-media), San Francisco Artspace, 89. *Exhib:* Jean Seberg-The FBI-The Media, Mus Mod Art, New York, 81; Progress (Memory) II, Whitney Mus Art, 84; Surveillance, Los Angeles Contemp Exhibs (LACE), 87; Social Engagement: Women's Video in the 80's, Whitney Mus Art, 87; Democracy and Politics, Dia Art Found, 88; Committed to Print, Mus Mod Art, 88; A Different War: Vietnam in Art, Akron Art Mus, traveling exhib, 89-92; Making Their Mark: Women Artists move into the Mainstream 1970 to 1985, Cincinnati Art Mus, traveling exhib, 89-90. *Pos:* Television studio technician, Morgan Guaranty Trust Co & WNYC-TV Channel 31, 82-83; ed, Upfront Mag, 84-85; panelist, New York Found for the Arts, 86. *Teaching:* Vis asst prof, painting & drawing, Duke Univ, 79-80; asst prof painting & drawing, Univ of Ill, Chicago, 80-81; asst prof film & video, Univ of Hartford, 83-84; artist in residence, Mass Inst

Technol, 89. *Awards:* Artists Fel, Nat Endowment Arts, 76, 82 & 90; Fel, NY Found Arts, 88; Fel Mass Coun Arts Humanities, 89. *Bibliog:* Lucy Lippard (auth), Get the Message? A Decade of Art for Social Change, 84 & A Different War: Vietnam in Art, 90; Branda Miller & Deborah Irmas et al (auths), Surveillance, 87; Deborah Wye (auth), Committed to Print, Social and Political Themes in Recent American Printed Art, 88. *Mem:* Asn of Ind Video & Filmmakers, Inc; Col Art Asn. *Media:* Multi-media, Video; Graphics, Books. *Publ:* Coauth (with Vanalyn Green), Against Inner Exile, Upfront Mag, No 2, winter 81/82; auth, Disinformation Warfare, A Breaking of Codes in Painting and Video, Red Bass Mag, No 10, Fla, winter/spring 86; Cracking the Concrete: Interventionist Posters, Upfront Mag, winter 86/87; Andy Warhol et al, The FBI File on Andy Warhol, 88; The Warhol File, Andy Warhol: Film Factory, London, 89. *Dealer:* Video Data Bank Art Inst Chicago Jackson Blvd & Columbus Dr Chicago Ill; Printed Matter Inc 7-9 Lispenard St New York NY. *Mailing Add:* 17 White St New York NY 10013

KRAMER, REUBEN
SCULPTOR
b Baltimore, Md, Oct 9, 09. *Study:* Rinehart Sch Sculpture, Europ traveling scholar, 31 & 33; Am Acad Rome; Acad Grand Chaumiere. *Work:* Baltimore Mus Art, Md; Corcoran Gallery Art, Washington, DC; Peale Mus, Baltimore; Harvard Univ Law Libr; Univ WVa Dental Hall. *Comn:* Statue of Supreme Court Justice Thurgood Marshall, 80. *Exhib:* Prix Rome Exhib, 36; Nat Art Week, IBM Corp, Md, 41; Int Sculpture Show, Philadelphia, 49; Nat Inst Arts & Lett, 64; 35 Years of Sculpture & Drawings, Retrospective Exhib, Jewish Community Ctr, Baltimore, Md, 74; 50-Yr Retrospective of Reuben Kramer's Art, Baltimore Mus Art, 78. *Teaching:* Pvt instr sculpture, 39-; instr sculpture, Adult Educ, Baltimore City Col & Polytech Inst; head dept sculpture, Am Univ, 51-52. *Awards:* Prix de Rome, Am Acad Rome, 34; Nat Inst Arts & Lett Grant, 64; Statue Award, nat competition, 77; Alumni of Year & Hon Exhib, Md Inst Col Art, 85. *Bibliog:* Alton Balder (auth), Six Maryland Artists, Balboa Publ, 55; Man the Maker (film), WMAR-TV, Baltimore, 61; Theodore L Low (auth), The Art of Reuben Kramer, Walters Art Gallery, 63. *Mem:* Artists Equity Asn (vpres, 68). *Media:* Bronze. *Mailing Add:* 121 Mosher St Baltimore MD 21217

KRAMRISCH, STELLA
CURATOR, EDUCATOR
b Mikulov, Czech; US citizen. *Study:* Univ Vienna, PhD; Univ Chicago, PhD(hon), 84; Columbia Univ, PhD(hon), 85; Univ Pa, LLD (hon). *Collections Arranged:* Art of Nepal (auth, catalog), Asia House, New York, 64; Unknown India: Tribal & Ritual Art (auth, catalog), Philadelphia Mus Art, 68; Manifestations of Shiva (auth, catalog), Philadelphia Mus Art, 81; Painted Delight (auth, catalog), Philadelphia Mus Art, 86. *Pos:* Ed, J Indian Soc Oriental Art, 32-50; emer cur, Indian & Himalayan art, Philadelphia Mus Art, 54-; ed, Artibus Asiae, 60- *Teaching:* Prof Indian art, Univ Calcutta, 23-50; lectr Indian art, Courtauld Inst, Univ London, 37-40; prof SAsian art, Univ Pa, 50-69; adj prof Indian art, Inst Fine Arts, NY Univ, 64- *Awards:* Padma Bhushan Award, India, 82; Charles Lang Freer Medal, 85. *Bibliog:* Joseph Dye (auth), Marsyas, Vol 17, 75; B S Miller (auth), Exploring India's Sacred Art, Univ Pa Press, 83. *Publ:* Auth, Indian Sculpture, 32 & 81; The Hindu Temple, 46 & 76. *Mailing Add:* Philadelphia Mus of Art PO Box 7646 Philadelphia PA 19101

KRANE, SUSAN
CURATOR, HISTORIAN
b Gary, Ind, June 8, 54. *Study:* Carleton Col, BA(magna cum laude), 76; Columbia Univ, MA, 78. *Collections Arranged:* Judy Pfaff (auth, catalog), 82; Surfacing Images: The Paintings of Joe Zucker (auth, catalog), 82; Mario Merz (auth, catalog), 84; Jan Kotik: The Painterly Object (auth, catalog), 84; Structure to Resemblance: Works by Eight American Sculptors (coauth, catalog); Hollis Frampton: Recollections/Recreations (coauth, catalog), 84; The Wayward Muse (auth, catalog), 87; Art at the Edge: Creighton Michael (auth, catalog), 87; Art at the Edge: Sherrie Levine (coauth, catalog), 88; Southern Expressions: A Sense of Self (auth, catalog), 88; Art at the Edge: Houston Conwill (auth, catalog), 89; Southern Expressions: Points of View (coauth, catalog), 89; Art at the Edge: Ida Applebroog (auth, catalog), 89; Lynda Benglis: Dual Natures (auth, catalog), 91; Art at the Edge: Joel Otterson (auth, catalog), 91; Southern Expressions: Tales Untold (coauth, catalog), 91; Max Weber: The Cubist Decade, 1910-1920 (coauth, catalog), 91; Art at the Edge: Barbara Ess (auth, catalog), 92. *Pos:* Rockefeller Found Intern, Walker Art Ctr, Minneapolis, 78-79; asst cur, Albright-Knox Art Gallery, Buffalo, NY, 79-82, assoc cur 83, cur 83-87; cur, 20th Century Art, High Mus Art, 87. *Teaching:* Adj prof art hist, State Univ NY, Buffalo, 80-86; adj prof, Emory Univ, Atlanta, 88. *Mem:* Art Table. *Publ:* Auth, Albright-Knox Art Gallery--The Painting and Sculpture Collection, Acquisitions Since 1972, Hudson Hills Press, New York, 87; Saving Graces, David Schirm, Buscaglia-Castellani Art Gallery, Niagara Falls, NY, 89; Striking Out: Another American Road Show , Scoring in Heaven, Aperture, New York, 91; Graven Images in Barbara Rowe, Castellani Art Mus, Niagara Falls, NY, 91; Matrix: Nene Humphrey, Winthrop Univ, Rock Hill, SC, 92. *Mailing Add:* c/o High Mus Art 1280 Peachtree Atlanta GA 30309

KRANKING, MARGARET GRAHAM
PAINTER, INSTRUCTOR
b Florence, SC, Dec 21, 30. *Study:* Am Univ, Washington, DC, BA(summa cum laude, Clendenin Fellow in Art Hist), 52. *Work:* Fed Nat Mortgage Asn, AT&T & Wall St J, Washington, DC; Triton Investment Co Inc; Philip Morris USA; Nat Coun Educ, Washington, DC; and others. *Comn:* Portrait, Rear Admiral Harold C Train & Admiral Harry D Train II, comn by Mrs Harold C Train, Washington, DC, 71; portrait, Dr Cecile Bolton Finley, Univ Va, Mrs Joseph V Marcoux, Alexandria, Va, 79; Charles H Jones, 83 & Harry A Tow, 85, Water Pollution Control Fed, Washington, DC; Children's Nat Med Ctr, Washington, DC. *Exhib:* 7th Ann Area Show, Corcoran Gallery Art, Washington, DC, 52; Maryland Biennial, Baltimore Mus Art, 74 & 76; one-man shows, Dunbarton Col Art Gallery, Washington, DC, 72, Spectrum Gallery Inc, 74, 76, 78, 79, 81, 83, 85, 87, 90 & 92; Philip Morris USA, Richmond, Va, 82, 83 & 86; Watercolor USA, Springfield Art Mus, Mo, 85, 87 90 & 92; Rocky Mountain Nat Watermedia Exhib, Foothills Art Ctr, Golden, Colo, 85, 86 & 88; Lombardi Cancer Res Ctr, Washington, DC, 92; Rocky Mountain Nat, 92; and others. *Pos:* Asst to head of publications, The Nat Gallery of Art, 52-53; official US Coast Guard artist, 86- *Teaching:* Guest instr, Amherst Col, Mass, 85. *Awards:* First Place, Area 87 Exhib Paintings & Graphics, Fairfax Co Coun Arts, Va, 87; Ross Family Award, Adirondacks Nat Exhib Am Watercolor, Old Forge, NY, 88; George Gray Award, US Coast Guard Art Prog, 91; and others. *Bibliog:* Carl Schmalz (auth), Finding and Improving Your Painting Style, Watson-Guptill, New York, 86;; Kim Wells (auth), Member of the issue, N Light Mag, 7/90; Ginny Baier (auth), The color gray, Watercolor 92, spring; Charles Sullivan (auth), Numbers at Play, Rizzoli, New York, 92. *Mem:* Artists Equity; Potomac Valley Watercolorists (pres, 81-83); Southwestern Watercolor Soc; Southern Watercolor Soc; Nat Watercolor Soc. *Media:* Watercolor, Pastel. *Publ:* Auth, The watercolor page, Am Artist Mag, 5/88. *Dealer:* Spectrum Gallery Inc 1132 29th St Washington DC 20007; McBride Gallery 215 Main St Annapolis MD 21401. *Mailing Add:* 3504 Taylor St Chevy Chase MD 20815

KRANTZ, LES (LESLIE J)
EDITOR, PUBLISHER
b St Louis, Mo, Dec 20, 45. *Study:* San Francisco State Univ, 63; Univ Mo, BA, 68. *Pos:* Publ, The Krantz Co, Chicago, currently; ed, The Chicago Art Review, 77-79 & 82-89, The New York Art Review, 78-82 & 88, The Washington DC Art Review, 80-, The California Art Review, 81-84, The Texas Art Review, 82- & The Southwest Art Review, 83-, Krantz Co; ed/publ, Portrait of Chicago, 81, Am Artists, 85 & 89, Am Art Galleries, 85, Am Photogr, 85, & Am Architects, 86; pres, Am References, Inc, currently. *Bibliog:* John Greenwater (dir), Literary Critic (film), PBS, 80; Jo Ann Lewis (auth), article, Washington Post, 81; Allen Artner (auth), article, Chicago Tribune, 81; Bill Maruel (auth), article, Dallas Times Herald, 83; Gale Research (auth), Contemporary Authors, 86; LA Times, 5/19/88; Wall St Journal, 5/20/88; NY Times, 6/2/88; Time Mag, 5/88. *Mem:* Chicago Artists Coalition; Art Inst Chicago; Mus Contemp Art, Chicago. *Publ:* Jobs Rated Almanac, 88. *Mailing Add:* 2210 N Burling St Chicago IL 60614

KRASHES, BARBARA
PAINTER, DIRECTOR
b New York, NY. *Study:* Art Students League, with Reginald Marsh, Julian Levi & Vaclav Vytlacil; NY Univ, BS; Hunter Col, NY; Educ Alliance, with Chaim Gross; New Sch Social Res, New York. *Work:* Ulrich Mus Art, Wichita, Kans; St Lawrence Univ Mus, Canton, NY; Am Can Co, New Jersey; Walter Kiddie Constructors, Inc, New York; Hood Mus Art, Dartmouth Col, Hanover, NH. *Exhib:* Art: 1965, Am Express Pavilion, New York World's Fair; Am Abstract Artists, Riverside Mus, NY, 68; Fordham Univ at Lincoln Ctr, New York, 80; NY Univ, 80; Hyde Collection, Glens Falls, NY, 78. *Pos:* Art dir, Adult Educ Ctr, New York. *Awards:* George B Bridgman Mem Scholar, Art Students League. *Bibliog:* Art World Problems (tape), Today's World, Fordham Univ, 73. *Mem:* Fedn Mod Painters & Sculptors, Inc (pres, 70-74); life mem Art Students League; NY Artists Equity Asn, Inc. *Media:* Mixed-Media, Acrylic. *Publ:* Contribr, Art '65 Lesser Known & Unknown Painters, Young Am Sculpture-East to West, 65; contribr, The New York Arts Calendar (spec issue) for New York World's Fair Am Express Show, 65; contribr, Feigin Memorial Collection (catalog), St Lawrence Univ, 71; Female Artists in the United States: A Research and Resource Guide to Women Painters 1900-1985, Rutgers Univ,86. *Mailing Add:* 77 W 85th St New York NY 10024

KRASNYANSKY, ANATOLE LVOVICH
PAINTER, ARCHITECT
b Kiev, Ukraine, USSR, Feb 26, 30; US citizen. *Study:* Kiev State Inst Fine Art & Archit, MA, 53. *Work:* Kiev State Artist's Union Collection, Ukraine, USSR; Dalzell Hatfield Gallery Collection (Int Watercolor Masters), Los Angeles; Stanford Univ, Palo Alto, Calif; Los Gatos Mus, Calif; Dyansen Galleries; and others. *Comn:* Restovration of Potemkin and Marble Palases, State, St Peterburg, Russia, 52-53; Central Art Pavilion, Exhibs Artists Union, State, Kiev, Ukraine, 55-58; Restovration of Historical Alexandria Park, State, Uman, Ukraine, 61-68; Metro Station Politechnical Inst, State, Kiev, Ukraine, 69; Ampitheatre & Corp Bldg, Renaissanse Guild Inc, Long Beach, Calif, 84-85. *Exhib:* Russian Artist's in USA, Stanford Univ, Palo Alto, 81 & comtemp Russian Artists, UCLA; solo exhibs, Stanford Univ, Palo Alto, 82 & Dyansen Galleries, Beverly Hills & Coho, NY, 88-90; Contemporary Russian Artists in Exile, Univ Calif, Los Angeles, 82; Russian Art in USA, Los Gatos Mus, Calif, 82; group & solo exhibs, Dyansen Galleries, Boston, San Diego & Washington, DC, 88-91; and others. *Pos:* Principal archit designer, Inst Tech Aesthetics, Dept Interior Design, Kiev, Ukraine, 68-74; principal designer & art dir, Central Ukraine Pavilion Republican Exhibs, Kiev, 74; set designer, Universal Studios, Hollywood, 78-84; independent consult archit design & presentation, Univ Calif, Los Angeles, 83; dir design & art, Renaissance Guild Inc, Long Beach, Calif, 84. *Teaching:* Lectr aesthetic design & art, Kiev Inst Technical Aesthetic, Ukraine, 69-73. *Awards:* First Prize, Interiors and Art for Metro, Politechnical Inst, State, 60; Second Prize, Monument of Potemkin Uprising in Odessa, State, Ukraine, 65; ABC Certif Appreciation Prof Contribution Acad Award Shows, Hollywood, 76-77. *Media:* Watercolor, Acrylic. *Dealer:* Dyansen Galleries of USA 131 Varick St New York NY 10012. *Mailing Add:* 871 S Bundy Dr Los Angeles CA 90049

KRATINA, K GEORGE
SCULPTOR
b New York, NY, Feb 12, 10. *Study:* Syracuse Univ, BS, 32, MS, 33; Yale Univ, BFA, 37. *Comn:* Ceramic relief, St Bonaventure Univ, NY; wood statues, St Paul Cathedral, Los Angeles; sanctuary mosaic sculptures, Fac Chapel, Fr Judge Sem, Va; steel sculpture, Adath Israel Temple, Merion, Pa; Uncle Sam heroic monument, Troy, NY, 80; and many others. *Teaching:* Prof design, Sch Archit, Rensselaer Polytech Inst, 63-77, emer prof archit & art, 77-; prof, Div Art & Archit, Cooper Union, formerly; prof, 3D & Sculptures, Yale Univ, formerly, prof emer, currently. *Awards:* Prix de Rome, 38; Nat Prize for Sculpture Competition for Cath Welfare Bldg, Washington, DC, 40; 3 Awards for Collaboration Excellence, Am Inst Architects, 41, 58 & 60; and many more. *Mem:* Fel Nat Sculpture Soc; Nat Sci Soc; Nat Forestry Soc. *Mailing Add:* RD Box 110 Pitts Rd RR 1 Old Chatham NY 12136

KRATZ, MILDRED SANDS
PAINTER
b Pottstown, Pa. *Study:* With Whitney & Burns, Portugal & Greece. *Work:* Franklin Mint Mus; General Mills; Goodyear Inc; Fitchburg Mus; Motorola; and others. *Comn:* Franklin Mint. *Exhib:* Nat Acad Design, New York, 73-90; 105 one-woman shows incl, Fitchburg Art Mus, Mass, 75; Wistariahurst Mus, Holyoke, Mass, 79; Dyer-York Mus, Saco, Maine, 80; Canton Art Inst, Ohio, 80; William Penn Mus, Pa; Watercolor USA, Ger, 93. *Teaching:* Artist-instr, Queen Elizabeth II, New York to Eng, 75. *Awards:* Six gold medals, misc exhibs, 75-88; Pa Senatorial Citation, 77; Grumbacher Award, Watercolor USA, 82; Awards, Water Soc Ohio, 83-85. *Bibliog:* Mildred Sands Kratz - Contemporary Artist, PBS Show. *Mem:* Hon Soc Watercolor USA; Am Watercolor Soc; Am Artist Prof League; Pottstown Area Artists Guild (co-founder & pres, 66); Ohio Watercolor Soc; Allied Artists Am. *Media:* Watercolor. *Publ:* Illusr, Nat Antiques Rev, 71; Stories of French Creek, 73; auth, Watercolor page, Am Artist Mag, 73; illusr, Prints, 83; Palette Mag, 83; Stitchery, 86-92. *Dealer:* Gallery II Exton PA 19341; Gallery Madison 90 New York 10028. *Mailing Add:* 5 Mourar Dr Spring City PA 19475-3430

KRAUS, (ERSILIA) ZILI
SCULPTOR, JEWELER
b Sat Chinez, Timisoara, Romania; US citizen. *Study:* Graphic Sketch Club, Philadelphia, Pa, 28-30; Nat Acad Design with Leon Kroll, 30-32; Barnes Found, Pa, 33-35; Samuel S Fleisher Art Mem with Frank Gasparro, 62-74; Inst Allende, San Miguel de Allende with Enrique Lopez, 72-81. *Work:* Cinnaminson Town Hall, NJ; Burlington Co Libr, Westhampton, NJ. *Comn:* Resurrection (mural), Calvin Presbyterian Church, Pa, 35; Yearbook (cover illustration), Columbia Univ Sch Health & Admin, New York, 67. *Exhib:* Earth Edge, Painting, Montreal Mus Fine Art, Quebec, 56; Sculpture, Fleisher Art Mem, Philadelphia, Pa, 67-72; sculpture, Woodmere Art Mus, Philadelphia, Pa, 68-86, jewelry, 80-85; sculpture, Cheltenham Art Ctr, Pa, 70-84; sculpture, Da Vinci Art Alliance, Philadelphia, Pa, 72-84; sculpture, Burlington City Cult & Heritage Comn, Mt Holly, NY, 84-87. *Collections Arranged:* Membership Show, Cinnaminson Art Centre, 66-67; Triboro Artists, Burlington Co Libr, 69; jewelry, Cheltenham Art Ctr, Pa, 85; jewelry, Woodmere Art Mus, Philadelphia, 83-92. *Pos:* Textile designer, Shapiro & Co, New York, 45-48. *Teaching:* Instr painting, Art League Long Island, Queens, NY, 50-51; instr painting, Northern Burlington City Region High Sch, Columbus, NJ, 64-65; instr beginning & advanced painting, Cinnaminson High Sch, NJ, 65-76. *Awards:* First Prize, jewelry (man's neckpiece), Woodmere Art Mus, Phildelphia, 83 & 91; Oscar d'Italia, sculpture, Accademia Italia, Italy, 85; Purchase, ring, Cheltenham Twp Art Ctr, Pa, 85. *Mem:* Woodmere Art Mus, Philadelphia, Pa; Da Vinci Art Alliance, Philadelphia; Cheltenham Township Art Ctr, Cheltamham, Pa; Nat Mus Women Arts, Washington, DC. *Media:* Wood, Pastel; Metal, Gem Stones. *Interests:* Designing creative jewelry (men's and women's). *Publ:* Burlington Co Times, 91. *Mailing Add:* 503 Wayne Drive Cinnaminson NJ 08077

KRAUSE, BONNIE JEAN
MUSEUM DIRECTOR, CURATOR
b La Crosse, Wis, Sept 20, 42. *Study:* Viterbo Col, BA, 64; Southern Ill Univ, MS, 68. *Collections Arranged:* US Grant: Man of Peace, Man of War, traveling exhib, 83; From Mother to Daughter: Ethnic Patterns in Handwork, 84; Bits and Pieces: Southern Illinois Tradition in Rag Rugs, traveling exhib, 90; Olynthus 348 B C: The Destruction and Resurrection of a Greek City, traveling exhib, 92. *Pos:* Dir, Ill Ozarks Graft Guild, Southern Ill Univ, 80-81, cur hist, Univ Mus, 81-85, sr develop specialist, 85-90; dir univ mus, Univ Miss, 90- *Teaching:* Instr art marketing, Southern Ill Univ, 74-76. *Mem:* Ozark States Folklore Soc; Miss Hist Soc; Miss Folklore Soc; Miss Mus Asn; Am Mus Asn. *Publ:* Auth, The Legend of Dug Hill, Mid-Am Folklore, 82; Trouble is a One-Eyed Mule: Tales Between the Rivers, produced/toured play, 82; Family of the Hills: The Bridgemans of the Pine Hills, US Forest Serv, 85; coauth, German Americans in the St Louis Region 1840-60, Mo Hist Soc, 89. *Mailing Add:* University of Mississippi University Museums University MS 38677

KRAUSE, GEORGE
PHOTOGRAPHER
b Philadelphia, Pa, Jan 24, 37. *Study:* Philadelphia Col Art. *Work:* Mus Mod Art, New York; Bibliot Nat, Paris; Libr Cong, Washington, DC; Philadelphia Mus Art; Houston Mus Fine Art. *Exhib:* Five Unrelated Photographers, Mus Mod Art, New York, 63; one-man shows, George Eastman House, Rochester, NY, 75, Mus Bellas Artes, Caracas, Venezuela, 76, Witkin Gallery, New York, 78, Houston Mus Fine Art, 78, Am Acad Rome, 79 & Pa Acad Fine Art, Philadelphia, 82; one-man Retrospective, Houston Mus Fine Art, 92. *Teaching:* Assoc prof photog, Bucks Co Community Col, Newtown, Pa, 73-75; prof photog, Univ Houston, 75-; dir photog workshops, Venice Photog Biennale, Italy, summer 79; artist in residence, Am Acad Rome, 79-80. *Awards:* Grants Guggenheim Found, 76 & 77; Prix de Rome, 76; Nat Endowment Arts, 73 & 79. *Bibliog:* Mark Power (auth), George Krause I, Monog Toll & Armstrong, 72; Nancy Hellebrand (auth), I Nudi-George Krause, Photo Rev, 80; Arno Minkkinen (auth), article, Contemp Photogr, 81; Anne Tucker (auth), George Krause: A Retrospective, Rice Univ Press. *Mem:* Am Acad Rome. *Publ:* Illusr, The photographer's eye, 66 & Looking at pictures, 73, Mus Mod Art; auth, I Nudi (catalog), Mancini, 80. *Dealer:* Harris Gallery 1100 Bissonnet Houston TX 77005. *Mailing Add:* Univ Houston Univ Park 4800 Calhoun Houston TX 77004

KRAUSE, LAVERNE ERICKSON
PAINTER, PRINTMAKER
b Portland, Ore, July 21, 24. *Study:* Univ Ore, BS, 46; Mus Art Sch, Portland, 52-58; Pratt Graphic Ctr, New York, summer 66. *Work:* Seattle Art Mus; Portland Art Mus; Salt Lake Art Ctr, Utah; La State Univ Union, Baton Rouge; Deichmanske Bibliotek, Oslo, Norway; plus others. *Exhib:* One-person shows, Deichmanske Bibliotek, Oslo, 74, Rockford Col, Ill, 74 & Delta State Univ, 78; Artists of Oregon, Portland Art Mus Ann, 49-; six shows, Int Printmakers, Seattle Art Mus, 60-71; West Coast Graphics, Univ Ky, circulated by Smithsonian Inst, 71-72; Atelier Nord Exhib, Oslo, 75 & 82; Ore Pavillion, Expo '86, Vancouver, BC. *Teaching:* Vis artist, Mt Angel Col, Ore, summer 65; from asst prof to prof painting & printmaking, Univ Ore, 66-; vis assoc prof, La State Univ, Baton Rouge, summer 70. *Awards:* Ford Found Purchase Prize for Painting, 64; Governor's Arts Award, 80; Wurlitzer Found Grant, 81; Eugene Arts Foun Arts & Letts Award, 85. *Mem:* Artists Equity Asn (nat pres, 69-70); Col Art Asn Am; Portland Art Asn; NW Print Coun. *Media:* Oil, Acrylic; Etching, Monoprint. *Publ:* Illusr, Clouded Sea (etchings), 71, Deady & Villard (etchings), 74 & Portraits, Friends, Artists (etchings & woodcuts), 79, Press 22. *Dealer:* Fountain Gallery Art 117 NW 21st Ave Portland OR 97210. *Mailing Add:* 3295 W 16th Ave Eugene OR 97402

KRAUSHAAR, ANTOINETTE M
DEALER
b New York, NY. *Pos:* Dir emer, Kraushaar Galleries, currently. *Specialty:* Twentieth century American art. *Mailing Add:* 724 Fifth Ave New York NY 10019

KRAUSS, ROSALIND E
CRITIC, HISTORIAN
b Washington, DC, Nov 30, 40. *Study:* Wellesley Col, BA, 62; Harvard Univ, PhD, 69. *Collections Arranged:* Joan Miro: Magnetic Fields, Guggenheim Mus, 71; 200 Years of American Sculpture, Whitney Mus Am Art, 76; Richard Serra, Mus Mod Art, New York, 85. *Pos:* Assoc ed, Artforum, 71-76; ed, October Mag, 76- *Teaching:* Assoc prof art hist, Mass Inst Technol, 65-71; lectr, Princeton Univ, 72-74; prof, Hunter Col, 75-90, Columbia Univ, 92- *Awards:* Guggenheim Found Fel, 71; Mather Award Criticism, Col Art Asn, 72. *Res:* Theory and criticism of modernist art; history of photography. *Publ:* Auth, Terminal Iron Works: Sculpture of David Smith, MIT Press, 71; Passages in Modern Sculpture, Viking Press, 77; Sculpture of David Smith: Catalog Raisonne, Garland Press, 78; The Originality of the Avant-Garde and Other Modernist Myths, MIT Press, 84. *Mailing Add:* 12 Greene St New York NY 10013

KRAUTH, HARALD
PAINTER
b Eberbach, Ger, June 29, 23; US citizen. *Study:* Paedagogium, Bad-Godesberg, Ger, Abitur, 42; studied with Keh Haber, 46-52; Dartmouth Col, with Hannes Beckmann, 70-74; Goddard Col, MA, 73; Union Grad Sch, PhD, 78. *Exhib:* Painters of Bonn, Mus City Bonn, Ger, 51; Vt Invitational, Norwich Univ, 69, 70 & 72-; solo exhibs, Goddard Col, 73 & Dartmouth Col, 74; Vt Artists, Fleming Mus, 76. *Teaching:* Assoc prof & chmn dept philos, religion & fine arts, Norwich Univ, 68-90. *Bibliog:* Richard Wolkomir (auth), A Vermont artist & designer, Christian Sci Monitor, 75. *Mem:* Col Art Asn Am; Copley Soc Boston. *Media:* Tempera, Oil. *Publ:* Auth, The Weston Priory, Liturgical Arts, 70; Artistic Photography, Methods & Techniques, Amphoto, 76. *Dealer:* Charles Fenton Gallery Woodstock VT 05091. *Mailing Add:* Turkey Hill Northfield VT 05663

KRAVIS, JANIS
DESIGNER, ARCHITECT
b Riga, Latvia, Oct 20, 35; Can citizen. *Study:* Sch Archit, Univ Toronto. *Exhib:* Royal Can Acad Arts, Nat Gallery Can, Ottawa, 70. *Awards:* Ont Tourist Accommodation Award, 67; Ont Eedee Design Award, 67; 25 Year Merit Award in Archit Excellence, Ont Asn Archit, 91. *Mem:* Ont Asn Architects; Asn Can Indust Designers; Royal Can Acad Art; Royal Archit Inst Can. *Mailing Add:* 38 Cedarbank Crescent Toronto ON M3B 3A4 Canada

KRAVITZ, WALTER
SCULPTOR, PAINTER
b Chicago, Ill, Oct 25, 38. *Study:* Art Inst Chicago, BFA(fel), 64; Syracuse Univ, MFA, 67. *Comn:* Suspended sculptures, Washington DC Conv Ctr, 86 & Niagara Falls, NY wintergarden; pyramid with lights & sound, Artpark, New York, 83; stairwell installation, Washington Proj Arts, 83; Muddy Branch Sch, Montgomery County, Md. *Exhib:* Installations, Washington Proj Arts, 81; Ten From DC, Lawndale Ctr, Univ Houston, 82; PS1, New York, 82; Franz Bader Gallery, Washington, DC, 86-88; SE Ctr for Contemp Art, 87. *Teaching:* Prof design & painting, Philadelphia Col Art, 69-74; prof painting & drawing, George Mason Univ, 76- *Mailing Add:* 614 A St SE Washington DC 20003

KRAVJANSKY, MIKULAS
PAINTER, PRINTMAKER
b Rudnay, Czech, May 3, 28; Can citizen. *Study:* Acad Muzas Art, Bratislava, Czech, PSV, 57. *Work:* Nat Mus Slovakia, Bratislava; Inst Scenography, Int Mus, Prague; Royal Ont Mus, Toronto. *Comn:* Stucco mural, Nitra City Hall, Czech, 55; mobile sculpture, Dept Rec & Parks, Bratislava, 59; mural, Toronto City Hall, 69. *Exhib:* Binale of Fine Arts, Sao Paolo, Brazil, 57 & 61; Scenography, Int Culture Ctr, Cairo, Egypt, 66; ETC Opera Designs, Nat Opera, Budapest, Hungary, 67; Nat Canadian Exhib, Toronto, 72; Group of Contemporarists, tour of SAm cities, 72; Art Expo, Javitz Comr Ctr, New York, 80-88; one man shows, Dyansen Galleries, New York, Los Angeles, San Francisco, San Diego, New Orleans & Boston. *Pos:* Head scenographer, State Theatre, Presov, Czech, 59-64; head art & design dept, Czechoslovak TV, Bratislava, 64-68; artistic dir, Black Box Theatre of Can, 69-78. *Teaching:* Lectr scenography, Acad Arts, Bratislava, 57-58; asst prof design, Acad Muzas Art, Bratislava, 65; asst master art-design, Humber Col, Toronto, 69-75. *Bibliog:* Stage Design Throughout the World Since 1950; Harap, London, 60; Genesis (film), Gregor Film, Toronto. *Media:* All Media; Intaglio. *Dealer:* Dyansen Corp 3 E 54th St New York NY 10022; Metrop Art Assoc 346 New Yor Ave Huntington NY 11743. *Mailing Add:* c/o P C Hart Gallery 337 E Indiantown Rd Suite 16 Jupiter FL 33477

KREBS, PATSY
PAINTER
b Oakland, Calif. *Study:* Claremont Grad Sch, MFA, 76. *Work:* Santa Barbara Mus Art, Calif. *Exhib:* Four Californians, La Jolla Mus Contemp Art, Calif, 77; Dealers' Choice, McNay Art Mus, San Antonio, Tex, 86; 20th Century Watercolors, Long Beach Mus, Calif, 88; In Celebration: 50th Anniversary Gifts, Santa Barbara Mus Art, 92; Black & White, Riverside Art Mus, Calif, 92. *Teaching:* San Francisco Art Inst. *Awards:* Support Grant, Adolph & Esther Gottlieb, 86; Support Grant, Nat Endowment Arts, 91; Support Grant, Marin Arts Coun, 92. *Bibliog:* Pamela Hammond (auth), Patsy Krebs: the fullness of abstraction, Art Space Mag, 92. *Media:* Acrylic and Watercolor on Paper and Canvas. *Dealer:* The Haines Gallery 49 Geary St San Francisco CA 94108. *Mailing Add:* PO Box 446 Inverness CA 94937

KREBS, ROCKNE
SCULPTOR
b Kansas City, Mo, Dec 24, 38. *Study:* Kans Univ, Lawrence, BFA, 61. *Work:* Phillips Collection, Smithsonian Inst, Corcoran Gallery Art, Hirshhorn Mus & Sculpture Garden, Washington, DC; Philadelphia Mus Art, Pa; Ft Worth Art Mus, Tex; Contemp Art Ctr, Cincinnati, Ohio. *Comn:* The Laser, City St Petersburg, Fla, 75; The White Tornado (solar environmental sculpture), GSA New Federal Bldg, Topeka, Kans, 79; Still Green (laser environment), Disneyland Hotel, Anaheim, Calif, 79; Urban scale neon, The Miami Line (one-quart mile long neon), Miami, Fla, 87; Crystal Willow (24 ft x 19 ft glass, steel & searchlight sculpture), 88. *Exhib:* Sculpture Am Directions, Nat Mus Am Art, Washington, DC, 75; The Source: An Urban Scale Laser Enviroment, Nat Mall, Washington, 80; Solar Environment, US Botanical Gardens, Washington, DC, 81; Urban scale lasers: Columbus, Oh, 82, Mt Wilson to CALTECH, Pasadena, 83, Fountain Sq, Cincinnati, Oh, 84, Madison, Wis, 86, Memorial Art Gallery & Univ Rochester, NY, 87, Byrd Pk, Richmond, Va, 89 & others through 92; Laser Dance, Lisner Auditorium, Wash, DC, 85; Laser exhibs: Cleveland Ctr Contemp Art, Ohio, 87 & Okla Art Ctr, Okla City, 88. *Pos:* Bd dir, Washington Project Arts, 80-84, & Coalition of Washington Artists, Washington, DC, 82- *Awards:* Individual Artist Fel Grant, Nat Endowment Arts, 70; J S Guggenheim Fel, 72; Night Beautiful Award, Fla Power & Light Co, 87; Illumination Engineering Soc Award, 87; Distinguished Merit Award, Md Col Art & Design, outstanding leadership Behalf Artists Rights, Md, 89. *Bibliog:* Paul Richard (auth), The city at night is light, Washington Post & News Serv, 73; Nina Felshin (auth), article, Art Int, 5/74. *Media:* Light. *Publ:* Coauth, Rockne Krebs, Artist on Their Art, 68 & Walter Hopps, and Nina Felshin, Three Washington Artists, 70, Art Int; Jane Livingston, Art & Technol Catalog, Los Angeles Co Mus, 71; Nina Felshin, Projected Images (catalog), Walker Art Ctr, 74; Sam Hunter, American Art, Abrams, 79. *Mailing Add:* 1428 V St NW Washington DC 20009

KREILICK, MARJORIE E
MOSAIC ARTIST, EDUCATOR
b Oak Harbor, Ohio, Nov 8, 25. *Study:* Ohio State Univ, BA, 46, MA, 47; Cranbrook Acad Art, MFA, 52; apprentice to Gulio Giovanette, Rome, 56; Am Acad in Rome, FAAR, 63. *Work:* Joslyn Mus, Omaha, Nebr; Columbia Mus Art, SC. *Comn:* Marble pebble mural, Wonderland Shopping Ctr, Livonia, Mich, 59; ten marble murals, State Off Bldg, Milwaukee, 63; mosaic foucault pendulum, Augustana Univ, Sioux Falls, SDak, 67; marble mosaic mural, Mayo Clinic, Rochester, Minn, 69; marble mosaic pool, Telfair Acad Arts & Sci, Savannah, Ga, 73. *Exhib:* Palace of Expos, Rome; Minn Mus Art, St Paul; solo show, Archit League, New York; Fairweather Hardin Gallery, Chicago. *Teaching:* Instr-docent design, Toledo Mus Art, 48-51; from instr to prof design-sculpture, Univ Wis-Madison, 53-92, prof emer, 92- *Awards:* Univ Wis Grant, 60; Prix de Rome, Am Acad in Rome, 61. *Mem:* Nat Soc Mural Painters; Int Asn Contemp Mosaicists, Ravenna, Italy. *Media:* Marble Mosaic. *Publ:* Contribr, Art in Architecture, 69. *Dealer:* Fairweather Hardin 101 E Ontario Chicago IL 60611. *Mailing Add:* 2713 Chamberlain Ave Madison WI 53705

KREITZER, DAVID MARTIN
PAINTER
b Ord, Nebr, Oct 23, 42. *Study:* Concordia Col, BS, 65; San Jose State Univ, MA, 67. *Work:* Santa Barbara Mus, Calif; San Diego Mus, Calif; Joseph Hirshhorn Found, Washington, DC; Sheldon Gallery, Univ Nebr. *Comn:* Woman's Place & US Army Corps of Engrs, covers for Atlantic Mag, 70; California & the War, cover for Motorland Mag, 70; Tristan und Isolde (opera posters), Seattle, 81. *Exhib:* One-man shows, American Art Since 1850, 68, Maxwell Gallery, San Francisco, Ankrum Gallery, Los Angeles, 71, 75, 77 & 79-81, Gumps Gallery, San Francisco, 81; Benedictine Art Awards, New York, 69; 6th Mobile Ann, Ala, 71; Adelle Mus Fine Arts, Dallas, 83. *Teaching:* Instr painting, San Jose State Col, 68; instr life drawing, Poly State Univ, San Luis Obispo, Calif, 83. *Awards:* Ciba-Geigy Award, 71. *Bibliog:* Currant Mag, 6/75; Am Artist, 4/82. *Media:* Watercolor, Oil. *Dealer:* Summa Gallery 527 Amsterdam Ave NY 10024. *Mailing Add:* 1442 12th St Los Osos CA 93402

KREMPEL, RALF
PAINTER, ASSEMBLAGE ARTIST
b Groitzsch, Saxony, Ger, June 5, 35. *Exhib:* Le Salon des Nations, Ctr Int d'Art Contemp, Paris, 85; Art Contemporain Cabinet des Dessins, Espace Delpha, Paris, 86; Galerie Salammbo-Atlante, Paris, 87, 88, 89, 90; Galerie ouverte tous les jours, y compris le dimanche de 10 h a 13 h et de 14 h a 19 h, Paris. *Pos:* Inventor & designer of Visual Commun Syst, world-wide message relay & depicting method employing colors rather than letters in transmission & presentation. *Awards:* Invité d'Honneur, Le Salon des Nations, SOCAP, Geneva, Switz, 85. *Mem:* The Mus Soc. *Media:* Acrylic, Polymer Point Pens; Acrylic Sheet, Vinyls. *Publ:* Auth, numerous patent bulletins & statements; auth, 2 USA & European Patents and 3 Registered Trademarks: Visual Communication System, Krempel Code & Art with a Message. *Dealer:* San Francisco Painter Magnate Rincon Ctr San Francisco CA 94119-3368; Galerie Salammbo-Atlante 18 rue des Coutures Saint-Gervais 75003 Paris France. *Mailing Add:* 2400 Pacific Ave San Francisco CA 94115-1275

KREN, MARGO
PAINTER, EDUCATOR
b Houston, Tex, Dec 1, 39. *Study:* Univ Wis, Madison, BS, 66; Univ Iowa, MFA, 79. *Work:* Nelson Gallery/Atkins Mus, Kansas City, Mo; El Paso Mus Art, Tex; Minot State Univ, NDak; Nation Mus Women Arts, Washington, DC; Western Univ Mich, Kalamazoo; Yellow Freight Systems Inc, Kansas City, Kans. *Exhib:* Narrative/Personal Visions, Downey Mus Art, Los Angeles, 85; Kansas Collection, Nat Mus Women Arts, Washington, DC; Deutsch-Amerikanisches Inst, Regensburg, Ger, 88; South Bend Art Ctr, Ind, 89; Univ Cent Fla, Orlando , Fla, 91; and others. *Pos:* Panelist, Arts Midwest/NEA Regional Visual Arts Fel Selection, 88; Mid-Am Art Alliance panelist, Nat Endowment Arts Regional fels, 92. *Teaching:* Assoc prof painting, drawing & design, Kans State Univ, Manhattan, 71-; artists residences, Ragdale Found, Lake Forest, Ill, 86, Va Ctr Creative Arts, Sweet Briar, 87 & Yaddo, 89. *Awards:* Nat Endowment Arts Grant, 82; Gov Art Award, 89; Kans State Univ Distinguished Grad Fac Mem Award,89-90. *Bibliog:* Novelene Ross (auth), Margo Kren/dreams and memories, Women Artist News, winter 86-87; Andrew Svedlow (auth), Within the mask: contemplation of works by Georgia O'keeffe and Margo Kren, Kans Quart, Vol 19, No 4, 87. *Mem:* Kansas City Artist Coalition (pres, 82-83); Nat Women's Caucus for Art; Col Art Asn. *Media:* Acrylic, Oil. *Publ:* Auth, Philomene Bennett, a Kansas City artist, 82 & Michael Meyers, a Chicago performance artist, 85, Kans Quart. *Dealer:* Ben Pickard Gallery Oklahoma City OK; Anderson-O'Brien Gallery Omaha NE. *Mailing Add:* 823 Bertrand Manhattan KS 66502

KRENECK, LYNWOOD
PRINTMAKER, EDUCATOR
b Kenedy, Tex, June 11, 36. *Study:* Univ Tex, BFA, 58, MFA, 65. *Work:* Fine Arts Gallery San Diego, Calif; Wichita Art Asn Galleries, Kans; Print Collection, Philadelphia Mus Art; Springfield Art Mus, Mo; Art in Embassies Prog, US State Dept; Okla Art Ctr; High Mus, Atlanta. *Exhib:* Libr of Cong Nat Print Show, 75; 30 American Printmakers, Ohio State Univ, 81-82; British Biennial, 82; New American Graphics III, 83; Printmaking, The Tallahassee Invitational, Fla, 85; one-man show, Univ Del, 85; Small Print Exhib, Purdue Univ, 86; Soc Am Graphic Artists Nat Exhib, New York, 86; and many others. *Teaching:* Prof printmaking, Tex Tech Univ, 65- *Awards:* Boston Printmaker's Ann Exhib, 78, 79; Okla Print & Drawing Exhib, 79; Purchase Awards, Ann Prints, Drawings & Crafts Exhib, Ark Art Ctr, 81; Works on Paper Int Exhib, Auburn Univ, 86 & North Dakota Print & Drawing Show, Univ NDak, 86. *Mem:* Southern Graphics Coun; Boston Printmakers; Philadelphia Print Club; Los Angeles Print Soc; Soc Am Graphic Artists. *Media:* Serigraphy, Silkscreen. *Res:* Research and development of techniques for new water base screen print inks; Visiting Artist in Residence, Ohio State University, 1986 to enhance R & D; Various articles and manual published in 1988. *Mailing Add:* 5224 14th St Lubbock TX 24916

KRENS, THOMAS
MUSEUM DIRECTOR, EDUCATOR
b New York, NY. *Study:* Williams Col, BA, 69; State Univ NY, Albany, MA, 71; Yale Univ, MPPM, 84. *Collections Arranged:* Jim Dine Prints: 1970-1977 (coauth, catalog), 77; The Prints of Helen Frankenthaler (ed, catalog), 80; Drawings of Robert Morris 1960-1980 (auth, catalog), 82; Radical Painting-American & European Contemp Paintings (auth, catalog), 83; The Restoration of Thomas Hart Benton, 85. *Pos:* Trustee, Williamstown Regional Art Conserv Lab, 83-85; stategic planning consult, Brooklyn Mus, 84-86; consult, Art & Architecture Thesaurus, Getty Art Hist Info Proj, 85-86. *Teaching:* Asst prof contemp art, Williams Col, 72-80, lectr, 80- *Mem:* Asn Art Mus Dirs. *Mailing Add:* c/o Solomon R Guggenheim Mus 1071 Fifth Ave New York NY 10128

KRENTZIN, EARL
SCULPTOR, SILVERSMITH
b Detroit, Mich, Dec 28, 29. *Study:* Wayne State Univ, BFA, 52; Cranbrook Acad Art, MFA, 54; Royal Col Art, London, Fulbright Fel, 57-58. *Work:* Detroit Inst Art, Mich; Cranbrook Galleries, Bloomfield Hills, Mich; St Paul Art Ctr, Minn; Jewish Mus, New York; Mus Contemp Crafts, New York. *Comn:* Enamel plaque, Gloria Dei Lutheran Church, Detroit, 54; Menorah, Temple Israel, Detroit, 63; metal sculpture, Westland Shopping Ctr, Detroit, 65; plus many pvt comn of silver sculptures. *Exhib:* One-man shows, Kennedy Galleries, New York, 68-75, Detroit Inst Art, 78 & Oshkosh Mus, 82; NJ State Mus, Trenton, 70; Jewelry USA Traveling Exhib, Am Crafts Mus, 84-; Masters Am Metalsmithing Mus Ornamental Metalwork, Memphis, 88; Toys Designed by Artists, Ark Arts Ctr, Little Rock, 89, 90, 91 & 92; and others. *Teaching:* Instr art, Univ Wis-Madison, 56-60; vis prof silversmithing, Univ Kans, 65-66; vis prof metalwork, Fla State Univ, 69. *Awards:* Tiffany Grant, 66; Nat Decorative Arts Exhib, Wichita Art Ctr, Kans, 66; Fulbright Fel, 57-58. *Bibliog:* Article, Am Mag, 11-12/82. *Media:* Miscellaneous Media. *Publ:* Auth, Centrifugal casting, Craft Horizons Mag, 11/54. *Dealer:* Donna Jacobs Gallery Birmingham MI 48011. *Mailing Add:* 412 Hillcrest Grosse Pointe MI 48236

KRESTENSEN, ANN M
CERAMIST, PAINTER
b Baltimore, Md, April 4, 39. *Study:* Md Inst Art, 60. *Comn:* Ceramic vesseles & triptych (silk painting), ALB Fed Bank, Las Cruses & Corrales, NMex, 85. *Exhib:* Baltimore Regional Show, Baltimore Mus Art, Md, 60; Everson Mus Gift Gallery Show, Everson Mus, Syracuse, NY, 82. *Pos:* Craft rep, MNex Arts & Crafts Fair, 79-81; Southwest Arts & Crafts Festival, 88-90. *Awards:* New Concept Award, Baltimore Regional Show, 60; Merit Award, NMex Clay, 83. *Mem:* Am Crafts Coun. *Media:* Clay, Painting. *Mailing Add:* PO Box 686 Placitas NM 87043

KRETSINGER, MARY AMELIA
GOLDSMITH, PRINTMAKER
b Emporia, Kans, Sept 29, 15. *Study:* Univ Kans, Lawrence, AB, 37; State Univ Iowa, Iowa City, MA, 41; grad study, Columbia Univ, New York & Ind Univ, Bloomington. *Work:* Johnson Wax Co Collection Contemp Am Art, Racine, Wis; Goldsmith's Hall, London; Mus Contemp Crafts, New York; Wichita Art Asn Galleries; Rochester Mem Gallery, NY. *Comn:* Gold & enamel box for pres award, Beech Air Corp, Wichita, 66; tabernacle and wall cross, St Peter's Church, Southwest Harbor, Maine, 70; crucifix & candleholders, Brandeis Univ Catholic Chapel, Waltham, Mass, 70; processional cross & font, Our Lady of Perpetual Help, North Windham, Maine, 71; baptismal font cover, St Andrew's Church, Emporia, Kans, 79. *Exhib:* Philadelphia Art Alliance, 57-60; State Dept Europe, 60; Int Exhib Mod Jewelry, Goldsmiths Hall, London, 61; Int Handicrafts Exhib, Stuttgardt, WGer, 67; Objects USA, Lee Nordness Gallery, New York, 70; Art Gallery Ont, 71; Art of Cloisonne, Lowe Mus, Univ Miami, Fla, 72; Art of Enamels, Gallery State Col New York & Metrop Mus, New Paltz, 73; Exhib Liturgical Arts, 41st Int Eucharistic Cong, Philadelphia Civic Ctr, 76. *Teaching:* Assoc prof metalsmithing design, Emporia State Univ, Kans, 49-63; instr enameling, Brookfield Craft Ctr, Conn, 59 & 66; instr enameling, Worcester Craft Ctr, Mass, 63 & 65; instr cloisonne enameling, Young Women's Christian Asn, Dallas, 65; instr silversmithing & enameling, Wichita Art Asn, 69-71. *Awards:* Best in Show, Mid West Designer Craftsman, 59; Purchase Awards, Mus Contemp Crafts, 68, Wichita Art Asn, 69, Goldsmith's Hall, London, 69, Johnson Wax Co, 71 & Univ Neb, 76. *Bibliog:* Phillip Morton (auth), Contemporary jewelry, Holt, Rinehart & Winston, 2nd ed, 76; Thelma Newman & J H Newman (auths), The Container Book, Crown Publ, New York, 77; Lee Nordness (auth), Objects USA, Viking Publ, New York, 77. *Media:* Gold, Enamel. *Mailing Add:* 911 Market St Emporia KS 66801

KREZNAR, RICHARD J
SCULPTOR, PAINTER
b Milwaukee, Wis, May 1, 40. *Study:* Univ Wis, BFA; Brooklyn Col, MFA; Inst Allende, Mex. *Work:* Walker Art Ctr, Minneapolis; Milwaukee Art Mus, Wis; Univ Wis-Madison; Colgate Univ, Hamilton, NY; Sidney Lewis Best Co; and others. *Exhib:* Pa Acad Fine Arts, 63; Butler Inst Am Art, Youngstown, Ohio, 65; Milwaukee Art Mus, 66; Wis Directions, Milwaukee Art Mus, 75; Brooklyn Col Art Dept Past & Present, Robert Schoelkopf Gallery, New York, 77; The Mat Dominant--Some Current Artists & Their Media, Pa State Univ, University Park, 77; Small is Beautiful (traveling show), Freedman Gallery, Albright Col; one-man shows, Paley & Lowe Inc, 72 & O K Harris Gallery, New York, 74, 76 & 83; Transparent Structures, Thorpe Intmedia Gallery, Sparkill, NY, 83; Mattingly-Baker Gallery, Dallas, Tex; and others. *Teaching:* Instr studio art courses, Brooklyn Col, 64-73, asst prof, 74-79; instr, Parsons Sch of Design, 78; instr sculpture, Skowhegan Sch Painting & Sculpture, 78; instr sculpture, Philadelphia Col Art, 80-82 & Cooper Union, NY; vis artist, Univ Wis-Milwaukee, 84. *Awards:* Ford Found Purchase Award, 62 & 64; Prizes, Milwaukee Art Ctr, 62, Wis Salon of Art, 63 & Walker Art Ctr, 64. *Dealer:* O K Harris Gallery 383 West Broadway New York NY 10012. *Mailing Add:* PO Box 218 Maver Rd Callicoon Center NY 12714

KRIEGER, FLORENCE
SCULPTOR, PAINTER
b New York, NY. *Study:* Cooper Union Art Sch, BA, 35; Nat Acad Fine Arts, 40; Art Students League, 45; study with Jose DeCreeft & Robert Brackman. *Comn:* Medals, Bd Educ, New York, 35; Art Students League, 63; steel & bronze scorpion & lion, Crewe Group of Companies, New York, 70; bronze wall hangings, Elisofon Gallery, New York, 75; bronze menorah & eternal light, Westminster Chapels, New York, 80. *Exhib:* The Dream, Riverside Mus, New York, 52; Peace, Allied Artists, New York, 55; solo exhib, Long Island Univ Gallery, Brooklyn, NY, 63; The American, Nat Acad Design, New York, 75; Wind Song, Pacem in Terris Gallery, UN, New York, 79; Mother Love, Salmagundi Club, New York, 83; Pray for Peace, Knickerbocker Artists, New York, 84; Women, Audubon Artists, New York. *Pos:* Dir, Fine Arts Sculpture Co, New York; pvt lessons in painting, 86-90. *Teaching:* Instr sculpture, NY Sch Indust Art, 38-42 & Gallery 7, Brooklyn, 80-86. *Awards:* Merit Award, Riverside Mus, Civil Serv Comn, 52; Salmagundi Club Award, Second Ann Exhib, 79; Knickerbocker Mem Award, 34th Ann Exhib, 84; Merit Award, Brooklyn Mus. *Bibliog:* Close Up article, New York Post, 80; John Korez (auth), profile, Villager, 81. *Mem:* Catherine Lorillard Wolfe Art Club Inc; Knickerbocker Artists; Nat Asn Women Painters & Sculptors; Audubon Artists; Am Artists Prof League. *Media:* All. *Publ:* Auth, article, 90th Anniversary Catherine Lorillard Art Club, NY Times. *Dealer:* Ed Elisofon Galleries 115 E 9th St New York NY. *Mailing Add:* Gallery 7 & Art Studios 8759 19th Ave Brooklyn NY 11214

KRIEGER, RUTH M
PAINTER, PRINTMAKER
b Newark, NJ, May 17, 22. *Study:* With Stuart Davis, 41; Moses Soyer, 42; Newark State Col, BA, 43. *Work:* State Mus, Trenton, NJ; Miss Art Asn, Jackson; Rosenberg Libr, Galveston, Tex; Burndy Engineering Co, Norwalk, Conn; Montclair State Col, NJ. *Exhib:* Conn Acad, Hartford Atheneum, Conn, 71; Audubon Artists, Nat Acad Gallery, New York, 71; Boston Printmakers, Boston Mus Fine Arts, Mass, 72; Ann Small Sculpture & Prints, Butler Inst, Youngstown, Ohio, 72; Assoc Artists of NJ, Montclair Art Mus, NJ, 74; Drawing Invitational, Hunterdon Co Art Ctr, Clinton, NJ, 81; Assoc Artists of NJ, Nabisco Galleries, Parsippany, NJ, 81. *Awards:* Clyde L Carnahan Award, 70 & 72; Second in Oils, Nat Acad New York, 70 & Conn Acad Ann, 71. *Mem:* Assoc Artists of NJ (pres 78-80, bd mem 74-); Artists Equity Asn of NJ. *Media:* Oils, Acrylic; Seriagraph, Cliche Verre. *Dealer:* Little Gallery Raleigh NC. *Mailing Add:* 454 Prospect Ave No 142 West Orange NJ 07052

KRIEGER, SUZANNE BARUC
PAINTER, LECTURER
b Jan 31, 24. *Study:* Studied oil painting with Esphere Slobotkina; self-taught batik. *Work:* Nassau Community Col, NY; Schoenfeld Med Art Asn, New York, NY. *Comn:* Mural, Radium Treatment Room, Franklin Gen Hosp, Valley Stream, NY, 66; murals & decorations, Saddle Rock School Disco, Great Neck, NY 75; vignette for brochure, Designers Showcase, 84 & 85. *Exhib:* Parrish Art Mus, Southhampton, NY, 68; Arts Festival, Nat Arts Pavilion, New York, NY, 70; Festival of Arts, Brooklyn Mus; Art Exhib, Heckscher Mus, Huntington, NY; Versions of Our World Today, Donnell Libr, New York, 80; Salmagundi Club, New York; New York State Pre-Biennial Art Exhib, Lever House, New York, 83; Art Exhibition of the 80's, Union Carbide Bldg, New York; Nassau Co Fine Arts Mus. *Teaching:* Instr arts & crafts, Creative Develop Prog, 7-11 Club, Great Neck, NY, 66-71 & Summer Wkshp, Saddle Rock Elem Sch, 66-72; instr seniors art, Continuing Educ Res Ctr, Queens, NY. *Awards:* First Prize Batik, Salmagundi Club, 75; Second Prize Watercolor, 44th Nat Art League Spring Exhib, 80. *Bibliog:* Jeanne Paris (auth), review, Long Island Press, 70; A Smith (auth), Wall with a view, New York Daily News; Malcom Preston (auth), Unusual work, Newsday, Long Island. *Mem:* Nat Asn Am Pen Women; Long Island Craftsman Guild; Nat Art League; Artists Net-Work Long Island. *Media:* Batik; Pen and Ink. *Publ:* Contribr, Little Neck Then and Now, Banner Publ, 84. *Dealer:* Glass Gallery 315 Central Park W New York NY 10025. *Mailing Add:* 40 Schenck Ave Great Neck NY 11021

KRIENKE, DOUGLAS ELLIOT
ART DEALER, CONSULTANT
b Summit, NJ, Mar 31, 47. *Study:* Wilkes Col, BA, 73. *Pos:* Dealer-dir-owner, Whistler Gallery Inc, Basking Ridge, NJ, 74- *Bibliog:* Marion Filler (auth), Ridge Gallery explores contemporary realism, Morristown Daily Record, 4/80; David Shirey (auth), The art sampler, New York Times, 6/80; Eye on the arts (film), 11/81 & State of the Arts, 5/84, NJ Pub Television. *Specialty:* Eighteenth, nineteenth and twentieth century fine American paintings, including J F Murphy, A T Britcher, A H Wyant, J M Culverhouse, A Jacobsen, W T Richards, William Hart, William Matthew Prior, George H Bought on, Hudson River, Folk Art and Modernist paintings. *Collection:* 19th and 20th century American and European painting. *Publ:* Ten catalogs for gallery exhibitions including American Paintings & Fifty Years of American Paintings. *Mailing Add:* Whistler Gallery Inc 88 S Finley Ave Basking Ridge NJ 07920

KRIENKE, KENDRA-JEAN CLIVER See Cliver, Kendra-Jean (Kendra-Jean Cliver Krienke)

KRIENSKY
PAINTER, WRITER
b Glasgow, Scotland, July 27, 17; US citizen. *Study:* Boston Mus Fine Arts, 36-40, with Alma O LeBrecht; Art Students League, 48-49; Escuela Tech Mex, 50-51. *Work:* Pushkin Mus, Moscow; Alfred Khouri Mem Collection, Norfolk Mus, Va; Lincoln Ellsworth Collection; also in many pvt collections, US, China, USSR & Mex. *Comn:* Peace cards consisting of paintings or drawings with poetry. *Exhib:* Am Watercolor Soc; Nat Acad Design; Inst Mex-Norte Am Relac Cult; one-man shows, Knoedler Gallery, White House, Washington, DC & Art Inst Chicago; 15 Year retrospective, Frick Art Libr, Univ Conn; and many others. *Awards:* First Prize, Inst Mex-Norte Am Relac

Cult, 50; and others. *Mem:* Visual Artists & Galleries Asn; Artist's Equity. *Media:* Oil, Pen & Ink. *Publ:* Auth, The Way is Peace, The Road is Love (drawings, paintings & poems), Gibson, 73; auth, The art of Art (painting & prose--formerly titles Visions of Hope & Faith), 76. *Mailing Add:* 463 West St New York NY 10014

KRIENSKY, MORRIS E See Kriensky

KRIESBERG, IRVING
PAINTER
b Chicago, Ill, Mar 13, 19. *Study:* Art Inst Chicago, BFA, 41; Escuela de Artes Plasticas, Esmeralda, Mexico City; NY Univ, MA, 72. *Work:* Mus Mod Art, Whitney Mus Am Art, Jewish Mus, New York; Detroit Inst Art; Chase Manhattan Bank, New York; Cincinnati Mus Art; Rose Mus Boston; Nat Mus Am Art, Washington, DC. *Comn:* Mural, Beth Emet, Evanston, Ill, 72; Peace Dove Banner, New York Cult Ctr, 82. *Exhib:* One-man shows, St Louis Mus Art, Mo, 53, Everson Mus, 80, Rose Mus, Boston, 81 & Washington Univ Art Gallery, St Louis, 82; 16 Americans, Mus Mod Art, New York, 54; 10 Independents, Guggenheim Mus, New York, 71; Am Mus Asn, 86-87. *Teaching:* Prof painting, Yale Grad Sch, 62-70 & State Univ NY, 71-76. *Awards:* Fulbright Grant, 65-66; Guggenheim Mem, 76; Nat Endowment Arts, 81; NY Found, 91. *Bibliog:* Allan Kaprow (auth), Kriesberg & Nature, Art Int, 6/64; Dore Ashton (auth), Kriesberg Dinterfass Gallery, 78; Geo Preston (auth), Kriesberg, Arts Mag, 12/87. *Mem:* Nat Acad Design. *Media:* Oil. *Publ:* Auth, Looking at Pictures, Ford Found, 56; Art, The Visual Experience, Pitman, 65; Working with Color, Van Nostrand Reinhold, 86. *Dealer:* Katharine Rich-Perlow Gallery 560 Broadway New York NY 10012. *Mailing Add:* 160 Sixth Ave New York NY 10013

KRIGSTEIN, BERNARD
PAINTER, ILLUSTRATOR
b New York, NY, Mar 22, 19. *Study:* Brooklyn Col, BA, 40. *Exhib:* One-man shows, Harry Salpeter Gallery, New York, 64 & 67, Harbor Gallery, Cold Spring Harbor, 66, 73 & 78, Fashion Inst Technol, New York, 70, Adirondack Ctr Mus, Elizabethtown, NY, 79 & Grace Gallery, NY Tech Col, 82; Brooklyn Mus, New York; Allied Artists; Am Watercolor Soc, 65, 68 & 72; Nat Acad Design, 74 & 80; Pratt Graphic Ctr Travelling Exhib, 82-84; Mus Mod Art; and many others. *Teaching:* Instr painting & drawing, High Sch Art & Design, New York, 62-70 & 71-81; asst prof fine art, Fashion Inst Technol, State Univ NY, 70-71. *Awards:* Grumbacher Gold Medal, 81 & Lee Loeb Mem Awards, 85, Allied Artist of Am; Ralph Mayer & Bocour Awards, 81 & Robert Simmons Award, 85, Am Soc Contemp Artists; President's Award, Painters & Sculptors Soc, NJ, 81; David Humphries Mem Award, Allied Artists Am, 87. *Bibliog:* Jerry West, publ & John Benson, ed, Squa Tront-Special Issue: Bernard Krigstein, Cambridge, Mass, 75; and others. *Mem:* Allied Artists; Pastel Soc Am (bd dirs); WPA Artists; Artists Equity Asn NY (mem bd dirs, 77, 78 & 79); Audubon Artists. *Media:* Miscellaneous. *Publ:* Illusr, Manchurian Candidate, McGraw; Various Fables from Various Places, Capricorn-Putnam; Buccaneers & Pirates of Our Coasts, Random; Boy's Life Mag, New York Times Mag, Am Heritage, Saturday Evening Post & Columbia Records; Comic Art Show (exhib catalog), Whitney Mus, 83; De Overlevende, Zetel Publ, Nijmegen, Neth; contribr, Contemporary Graphic Artists, Gale Res, 87. *Mailing Add:* 140-21 Burden Crescent Jamaica NY 11435

KRIMS, LES
PHOTOGRAPHER, EDUCATOR
b Brooklyn, NY, Aug 16, 42. *Study:* Cooper Union, New York, BFA; Pratt Inst, Brooklyn, MFA. *Work:* Mus Mod Art, New York; Nat Gallery Can, Ottawa; Musee Nat d'Art Moderne, Centre Georges Pompidou, Paris; George Eastman House, Rochester, NY; Bibliot Nat, Paris. *Exhib:* One-man shows, George Eastman House, 69 & 71, Galerie Delpire, Paris, 74 & Fictcryptokrimsographs, Light Gallery, New York, 75; two-man show, Witkin Gallery, New York, 69 & 72; Color As Form, A History of Color Photography, George Eastman House, Rochester, NY, 82; American Images, Barbican Art Gallery, London, Eng, 85; Staging the Self-Portrait, Photography 1840-1985, Nat Portrait Gallery, London, Eng, 86; Photography, a Facet of Modernism (with catalog), Mus Mod Art, San Francisco, 86; Photographs from the Nat Mus Mod Art, Kyoto Japan, 87. *Teaching:* Assoc prof art, Buffalo State Col, 69-81, prof, 81- *Awards:* State Univ NY Res Found Grant & Grant-in-Aid, 70 & 71; Nat Endowment Arts Fel, 71, 72 & 76; NY State Coun Arts Grant, 71, 73 & 75. *Bibliog:* Article, Photo Image, Japan, 70; 7 Corriere Della Sera, Italy, 90; Det iscenesaha Fotografi, Denmark, 92. *Media:* Dye Coupler, Silver Prints. *Publ:* Auth & illusr, The Incredible Case of the Stack O'Wheats Murders, 72; The Little People of America 1971, 72; Making Chicken Soup, 72; Fictcryptokrimsographs, 75; Idiosyncratic Pictures, 80. *Mailing Add:* 187 Linwood Ave Buffalo NY 14213

KRINSKY, CAROL HERSELLE
HISTORIAN, EDUCATOR
b Brooklyn, NY, June 2, 37. *Study:* Smith Col, BA, 57; NY Univ, MA, 60, PhD, 65. *Teaching:* Prof fine arts, NY Univ, 65- *Awards:* Am Coun Learned Soc Travel Grant, 81; Nat Jewish Book Award, 85; Millard Meiss Publ Award, 88. *Mem:* Soc Archit Historians (NY chap pres, 79-81, nat pres, 84-86); Col Art Asn; Planning Hist Group; Int Ctr Medieval Art; Columbia Sem on the City. *Res:* Recent native American architecture; architecture in New York and Chicago; European synagogue architecture. *Publ:* Auth, Seventy-Eight Vitruvius manuscripts, J Warburg & Courtauld Inst, Univ London, 67; Vitruvius De Architectura, Wilhelm Fink Verlag, 69; Rockefeller Center, Oxford Univ Press, 78; Synagogues of Europe: Architecture, History & Meaning, Archit Hist Found, MIT Press, 84; Gordon Bunshaft of Skidmore, Owings & Merrill, Archit Hist Found, MIT Press, 88. *Mailing Add:* 370 First Ave New York NY 10010

KRISTENSEN, GAIL MARIE
CERAMIST, ENAMELIST
b Miltown, Wis, Mar 3, 24. *Study:* Univ Minn, Minneapolis, 42-43 & 51-54; Iowa State Univ, Ames, 43-45; Drake Univ, Des Moines, 45-47. *Work:* Walker Art Ctr, Minneapolis; Minn Mus Art, St Paul; Denver Fine Arts Ctr; Greenville Fine Arts Mus, SC. *Comn:* Wall relief, Univac Corp, St Paul, Minn, 72; ct yard fountain, Unity Church, St Paul, 73; ceramic wall relief, Pacemaker Inc, St Paul, 77; ceramic wall relief, Production Credit Asn, River Falls, Wis, 78; ceramic wall relief, Pentair Corp, St Paul, 79; ceramic wall reliefs, Sentinal Savings & Loan, 84 & Maricopa Cnty Hwy & Transportation Bldg, 90, Phoenix, Ariz, Scottsdale Ins Co, 85; fountain sculptures, private homes, Phoenix, 86, Scottsdale, 87 & Tempe, 88. *Exhib:* Nat Ceramic Competition, Mus Mod Art, New York, 68; Kristensen Ceramics, Minn Mus Art, St Paul, 68 & 73; Nat Ceramic Expo, Milwaukee Art Ctr, Wis, 69; Exhib '70, Columbus Gallery Fine Arts, Ohio, 70 & Exhib '79, 79; Kristensen Ceramics, Minneapolis Inst Art, Minn, 74; Am Crafts, Gallery of Art Asn, Springfield, Ill, 80; Int Acad Ceramics Expo, Kyoto Mus, Japan, 80; Int Ceramic Art Symposium, Oslo, Norway, 90; and others. *Pos:* Com artist, Meredity Publ Co, Des Moines, Iowa, 56-57; guest Am artist-in-residence, Wurkunst Sch, Weisbaden, Ger, 62-64. *Teaching:* Resource instr, Univ Minn & numerous local cols & univs, 65-67; adj asst prof art, Macalester Col, 68-82. *Awards:* Nat Merit Awards, Am Craft Coun, 66 & 70; Purchase Award, Brooks Mem Gallery, 71; Ariz Governors Award for Clay Work, 90. *Bibliog:* P Roghenberg (auth), Enamels on Metal, 69 & Complete Book of Ceramic Art, 72, Crown Publ Co; B Young (auth), Ceramics by Kristensen, Ceramic Mo, 72. *Mem:* Artists' Equity Asn (local vpres, 76-79); Am Craft Coun; hon mem Int Acad Ceramics, Switz; Minn Sculptors Soc; Int Sculpture Assoc. *Media:* Clay, Glass. *Publ:* Auth, articles, Ceramic Mo Mag, 4/67, 1/68 & 11/68; auth, Am Craft, 8/92. *Dealer:* Elain Horwitch Galleries Hwy 179 Sedona AZ 86336; Elenor Jecks Gallery 6344 E Broadway Tucson AZ 85710. *Mailing Add:* 360 Cathedral Rock Trail Sedona AZ 86336

KROLL, DAVID
PAINTER
b Phoenix, Ariz, Feb 27, 56. *Study:* San Francisco Art Inst, BFA, 80; Art Inst Chicago, MFA, 86. *Work:* First Nat Bank Chicago; Gund Collection, Cambridge, Mass; Microsoft Corp, Redmond, Wash; Philip Morris Mgt Corp, New York; Prudential Ins Co, Newark, NJ. *Exhib:* One-man exhibs, Sch Art Inst Chicago, 85, NAME Gallery, Chicago, 88, Betsy Rosenfield Gallery, Chicago, 89, 91 & 93, Betsy Rosenfield Gallery, Chicago Int Art Expo, 90 & Jamison/Thomas Gallery, New York, 92; Revelations: Artists Look at Religion, Gallery 2, Sch Art Inst Chicago, 91; Still Alive: Contemporary Still Life, Rockford Col Art Gallery, Ill, 91; Light, Milwaukee Inst Art & Design, 92; Artfair/Seattle, Betsy Rosenfield Gallery, Seattle, 92; From America's Studio: Drawing New Conclusions, Betty Rymer Gallery, Sch Art Inst Chicago, 92; May 1992, Betsy Rosenfield Gallery, Chicago Int Art Expo, 92; Nature Fabrilis, Steibel Modern, New York, 92; and others. *Teaching:* Vis artist painting, Art Inst Chicago, 86-91. *Bibliog:* Wade Wilson (auth), David Kroll, New Art Examiner, 12/91; Susan Snodgrass (auth), David Kroll at Betsy Rosenfield Gallery, Art Am, 1/92; Holland Cotter (auth), Nature Fabrilis, NY Times, 7/3/92. *Media:* Oil on Linen. *Mailing Add:* c/o Betsy Rosenfield Gallery 212 W Superior St Chicago IL 60610

KRONENGOLD, ERIC A
PHOTOGRAPHER, EDUCATOR
b Long Island, NY, June 29, 35. *Study:* San Francisco State Univ, BA, 66, MA, 70. *Work:* Bibliot Nat, Paris, France; Ctr Creative Photog, Univ Ariz; Chicago Art Inst; Ariz Comn Arts; Hayden Gallery, Mass Inst Technol. *Exhib:* Octave Prayer, Hayden Gallery, 72; Attitudes: Photog in the 70's, Santa Barbara Mus Art, Calif, 79; Am Vision, Washington Square E Gallery, New York, 79 & NY Univ, 80; Arboretum, Boulder Ctr Visual Arts; Shwayder Gallery, Univ Denver; Auraria Higher Educ Complex, Denver; and others. *Teaching:* Prof art photog, Ariz State Univ, Tempe, 70- *Bibliog:* Article, New Orleans Time, 4/79; and others. *Mem:* Soc Photog Educ. *Media:* Black & White Print, Color Print. *Publ:* Contribr, Young Photographers, Univ NMex Press, 68; Modern Photography, Vol 34, No 9, 70; Octave of Prayer, Aperture One, MIT Press, 72; Object and Image, Prentice-Hall, 2nd ed; auth, New America, a review, Vol 3, No 1, Univ NMex Press. *Mailing Add:* Sch Art Ariz State Univ Tempe AZ 85287

KRONSNOBLE, JEFFREY MICHAEL
PAINTER, EDUCATOR
b Milwaukee, Wis, Feb 9, 39. *Study:* Univ Wis-Milwaukee, BS, 61; Univ Mich, Ann Arbor, MFA, 63. *Work:* Mus Fine Arts, St Petersburg, Fla; Addison Gallery Am Art, Andover, Mass; Nat Gallery Art, Washington, DC; Fla Capitol Bldg; New Orleans Mus Art; and others. *Comn:* Portrait, Univ S Fla Med Sch. *Exhib:* Chicago & Vicinity Exhib, Art Inst Chicago, 61-63; one-man shows, New Orleans Mus Art, 67, Univ Fla, Gainesville, 75 & ACA Galleries, New York, 79 , 81, 84 & 86; 25 Yr Retrospective Exhib, Polk Mus Art, Lakeland, Fla, 90. *Teaching:* Prof art, Univ SFla, 63- *Awards:* Thomas B Clarke Prize, Nat Acad Design, New York, 80; William A Paton Prize, Nat Acad Design, New York, 81. *Bibliog:* Barbara Gallati (auth), Jefferey Kronsnoble, Arts, 12/81; Katherine Duncan (auth), Jeffrey Kronsnoble, A Retrospective, Catalogue Essay, Polk Mus Art. *Media:* Mixed, Charcoal. *Dealer:* Barbara Gillman Miami FL; Clayton Galleries Tampa FL. *Mailing Add:* 908 S Dakota Ave Tampa FL 33606

KROPF, JOAN R
CURATOR, LECTURER
b Cleveland, Ohio, Aug 4, 49. *Study:* Cleveland Art Inst; Cooper Sch Art; Cuyahoga Community Col; St Petersburg Jr Col; Eckerd Col. *Collections*

Arranged: Worked with others to assemble and arrange, Important Writings of Dali, 74, Cancelled Graphic Plates, 75, Hiram College Graphics Show, 76, Erotic Art by Dali, 76, Dali's Anamorphoses, 77, Dali/Hasman Photography Exhib, 78, Important Dali Statements & Surrealist Documents, 79, Women: Dali's View, 79, Homage to Gala, 82, Secret Life Drawings, 82 & Flor Dali, 83; Lucas Collection 85, Dali's Divine Comedy, 85, Dali Sculpture, 86, Surrealist Drawings, 88, Many Faces of Dali- Lacroix Photographs, 89; The Alchemy of the Philosophers, 90. *Pos:* Asst dir, Salvador Dali Mus, Cleveland, 71-75, dir, 76-82, cur, 83-89, co-exec dir, 90 & cur, 92. *Mem:* Am Asn Mus. *Publ:* Auth, Secret Life Drawings, 82 & Flor Dali (photographs), 83, Salvador Dali Mus; auth, Dali's Divine Comedy, Surrealist Drawings, Docent Training Manual. *Mailing Add:* c/o Salvador Dali Mus 1000 Third St S St Petersburg FL 23701

KRUEGER, LOTHAR DAVID
PAINTER, EDUCATOR
b Two Rivers, Wis, Sept 19, 19. *Study:* Milwaukee State Teachers Col, Wis, BS, 42; Univ Wis-Madison, MS, 47; Univ Iowa, with Mauricio Lassansky in printmaking, grad, 50; Ohio State Univ, Columbus, grad art hist, 53. *Work:* Wis Mem Union, Madison; Am Inst Architects, Ark Arts Ctr, First Nat Bank Little Rock & Pulaski Savings & Loan, Little Rock, Ark. *Exhib:* 6 Ann Exhibs Art, Springfield Art Mus, Mo, 48-67; 9 Midwestern Delta Exhibs, Ark Art Ctr, Little Rock, 60-75; St Paul Art Ctr, 63 & 64-65; 10th Midsouth Exhib, Brooks Mem Gallery, Memphis, Tenn, 65; Ann, Ark Arts Ctr, Little Rock, 80; 22nd Ann, Oklahoma Arts Ctr, 80; and others. *Collections Arranged:* Am Inst Architects Art Collection, Ark Artist Exhib, traveling since 66; Arts, Crafts & Design Fair, Ark Distinguished Artists Collectors Exhib, 74. *Pos:* Vpres, Ark Educ Asn, 65-66, pres, 66-68. *Teaching:* Instr painting & drawing & ed, Northern Iowa Univ, Cedar Falls, 47-51; prof painting & drawing, Univ Ark, Fayetteville, 53-81, prof emer, 81- *Awards:* First Place, Ark Artist Exhib, Am Inst Architects, 60-61 & 77; Honorable Mention, 12th Ann Delta Regional, Ark Arts Ctr, 69; Purchase Prize, Ark Arts Ctr, 80. *Bibliog:* Edgar A Albin (auth), An expert in abstract expressionism, Ark Democrat, 61 & The Arts, Sunday News & Leader, Springfield, Mo, 72. *Media:* Acrylic, Watercolor. *Mailing Add:* 720 E Skyline Dr Fayetteville AR 72701

KRUG, HARRY ELNO
PRINTMAKER, EDUCATOR
b Oshkosh, Wis, Aug 20, 30. *Study:* Univ Wis-Milwaukee, BFA; Univ Wis-Madison, MS. *Work:* Libr of Cong, Washington, DC; Nelson-Atkins Art Gallery, Kansas City, Mo; US Info Agency; Springfield Art Mus, Mo; Ohio Univ Galleries. *Exhib:* 22nd Am Color Print Exhib, Am Color Print Soc, 63; 6th Nat Print Exhib, Silvermine Guild Artists, New Canaan, Conn, 67; 19th Ann Exhib, Boston Mus Fine Arts, Mass, 68; Teacher-Artist Today, State Univ NY Col Oswego, 69; Hopman, Krug, Ecker, Galerie Feursee, Stuttgart, 70. *Pos:* Crafts dir, Spec Serv, Ger. *Teaching:* Prof & chmn printmaking, Pittsburgh State Univ, currently. *Awards:* Mid-Am Ann Purchase Award, Nelson-Atkins Art Mus, Kansas City, 60; Sonia Watter Award, Am Color Print Soc, Pa, 62; Prize for Graphics, Jersey City Mus, NJ, 68. *Mem:* Boston Printmakers; Philadelphia Print Club. *Media:* Serigraphy, Lithography. *Mailing Add:* c/o Dept Art Pittsburgh State Univ Pittsburg KS 66762

KRUGER, BARBARA
CONCEPTUAL ARTIST, FILM CRITIC
b Newark, NJ, Jan 26, 45. *Study:* Syracuse Univ; Parsons Sch Design; Sch Visual Arts. *Exhib:* Whitney Mus Am Art, New York, 73, 82, 83, 85, 87 & 89; Castello di Rivoli, Turin, Italy, 89; Pennsylvania Acad Fine ARts, Philadelphia, 89; Denver Art Mus, Colo, 89; Mus 20th Century, Vienna, Austria, 89; Ctr Georges Pompidou, Paris, France, 89; Mus Contemp Art, Los Angeles, Calif, 89; Rheinhalle, Koln, WGer, 89; Frankfurt Kunstverein and Schirn Kunsthalle, Frankfurt, WGer, 89; solo exhibs, Crousel/Hussenot Gallery, Paris, 87, Monika Spruth Gallery, Koln, WGer, 87 & 90, Nat Art Gallery, Wellington, New Zealand, 88, Mary Boone Gallery, New York, 89, Galerie Bebert, Rotterdam, Netherlands, 89, Fred Hoffman Gallery, Santa Monica, Calif, 89, Duke Univ Mus Art, Durham, NC, 90; and many other group & solo exhibs. *Collections Arranged:* Pictures and Promises, The Kitchen, New York, 81; Artists' Use of Language, Franklin Furnace, New York, 83; Creative Perspectives in American Photography, Hallwall's Gallery, Buffalo, NY, 83. *Teaching:* Vis artist, Calif Inst Art, Art Inst Chicago & Univ Calif, Berkeley. *Awards:* Creative Artists Serv Progr Grant, 76-77; Nat Endowments Arts Grant, 83-84. *Bibliog:* Robert C Morgan (auth), Barbara Kruger, Arts Mag, 4/89; Carol Squires (auth), Diversionary (Syn) tactics/Barbara Kruger has a way with words, Bijutsu Techo, 4/89; Therese Lichtenstein (auth), Barbara Kruger's After-Effects: The Politics of Mourning, Art and Text, 7/89; Frederick Garber (auth), Re Positioning: The Syntaxes of Barbara Kruger, Univ Hartford Studies in Lit, 9/89; and many others. *Media:* Mixed. *Publ:* Auth, Picture/Readings, 79; No Progress in Pleasure, 82; contribr, film criticism, Artforum. *Mailing Add:* c/o Mary Boone Gallery 417 W Broadway New York NY 10012

KRUKOWSKI, LUCIAN
PAINTER, EDUCATOR
b Brooklyn, NY, Nov 22, 29. *Study:* Brooklyn Col, BA, 52; Yale Univ, BFA, 55; Pratt Inst, MS, 58, PhD, 77. *Work:* St Louis Art Mus, Mo; Fogg Mus, Mass; San Francisco Art Mus, Calif. *Comn:* Outdoor wall painting, Nat Endowment Arts, St Louis, 72; outdoor wall painting, H B E Corp Bldg, St Louis, 83. *Exhib:* Staempfli Gallery, 58 & 62 & Cee-je Gallery, New York, 67; Loretto Hilton Gallery, 70, Moore Gallery, St Louis, 75 & 78 & Burns Gallery, St Louis, 81; Long Island Univ, New York, 85; Messing Gallery, St Louis, Mo, 92. *Teaching:* Prof art, Pratt Inst, 55-69, chmn dept fine arts, 67-69; prof art & dean, Sch Fine Arts, Washington Univ, 69-77, prof philos, 77- *Mem:* Am Soc Aesthetics; Am Philos Asn. *Publ:* A basis for attributions of art, J Aesthetics Art Criticism, fall 80 & Artworks that end and objects that endure, winter 81; commentary on Beardsley's fiction as representation, Synthese 46, 81; Adorno & atonal music (rev), Bucknell, 84; Art and Concept, Univ Mass Press, 87; Aesthetic Legacies, 92. *Mailing Add:* 24 Washington Terr St Louis MO 63112

KRULIK, BARBARA S
DIRECTOR
b June 13, 55. *Study:* Pa State Univ, Univ Park, BA. *Collections Arranged:* Oil Sketches from the Ecole des Beaux Arts, 87; Painters by Painters, Portraits from the Uffizi Gallery, 88; 19th Century Polish Painting, 88; Women in Mex, 90; Helene Schjerfbeck: Finland's Modernist Rediscovered, 92; Hallowed Haunts: The Drawings & Watercolors of Charles Addams, 91-92. *Pos:* asst dir, 83-89, Nat Acad Design, interim dir, 89-90, deputy dir, 90-92; guest cur, New York City AIA Archit Design Awards exhib, 86, 87 & 90; assoc dir, Forum Gallery, 92- *Teaching:* Guest lectr, Fashion Inst Technol & Mus Studies Prog, 87 & 88; Univ Pa, continuing educ, 92. *Mem:* Am Assoc Mus; Int Coun Mus. *Mailing Add:* 200 E 28th St New York NY 10016

KRUMHOLT, ANN
PAINTER, SCULPTOR
b Troy, NY, Jan 9, 33. *Study:* La Art Inst, with Norma Routt. *Work:* Ronald Reagan, White House, Wash, DC. *Comn:* Oil Rig, Bradex Oil Co, Baton Rouge, La, 82; Racoon, Julianne Ziefle for Billy Vera, Los Angeles, Calif, 87; Cocker Spaniel, comn by Mr & Mrs Thomas Bartlett, Baker, La, 87; Seascape, Gary I, comn by Mr & Mrs Ken Dunham, Greenwell Springs, La, 88; Seacastle, H A Lloyd, Plaquemine, La, 90. *Exhib:* Am Bank, Fly the Coup, 82; City Lights, Visual Art Alliance, Houston, Tex, 90 & 91. *Teaching:* Children's basic art, LSU Union. *Awards:* Freddie Trophy, Dobe Dabbers, 87, Best of Show, 87 & First Place, 87; First Place Oils, Acad Arts Festival, Plaquemine, La, 89; Visual Art Alliance, Houston, Tex, 90. *Bibliog:* Anne Price (auth), LSU Vet Sch Exhib, State Times Morning Adv, 10/87; Linda Crum Ebert (auth), Local Artist, 87. *Mem:* Visual Arts Alliance, Houston, Tex; River City Festivals Asn, Baton Rouge, La. *Media:* Acrylic, Oil; Clay, Porcelain. *Mailing Add:* 20525 Wagner Dr Zachary Baton Rouge LA 70791

KRUSHENICK, JOHN
PAINTER, PRINTMAKER
b New York, NY, Mar 18, 27. *Study:* City Col New York; Art Students League, with Johnson, Hale, Browne & Vytlacil; Hans Hofmann Sch Fine Arts, New York; Univ Wis, BFA. *Work:* Mus Mod Art & Bank St Col Educ, New York; Weatherspoon Gallery, NC; Ft Wayne Mus Art, Ind. *Comn:* Playground Equipment, Crescent Ave Pre-School, Ft Wayne, Ind, 78. *Exhib:* Mus Mod Art, Tokyo, Hiroshima & Kyoto, 59; Martha Jackson Gallery, 71; New York Civil Liberties Show, Leo Castelli-Downtown, 72; 10th Street New York City, 77; Ft Wayne Mus Art, 78; Channel 13 Benefit Auctions, 83-84; 10 Park Gallery Montclair, NJ, 90. *Pos:* Owner & dir, House of Brata Frames & Brata Gallery Coop, 57-64; dir & cur, Dorsky Gallery, 70-71; mem mus adv panel, Ind Arts Comn, 75-76; dir, Mus Art, Fort Wayne, Ind, 75-78; art critic, News-Sentinel, Ft Wayne, 78-79; assoc, CS Schulte, Resource-Corp Art Collections, MJ, 81; Dupont Graphic Arts, NJ, 90. *Teaching:* Adj instr studio crafts & procedures, Cooper Union, 68-69; assoc prof mus & gallery procedures & dir, Fine Arts Gallery, Univ Wis-Milwaukee, 72-75; instr adult educ art conserv, Pequannock, NJ, 82, Montclair NJ. *Awards:* Golden Brush Award, Wis Art Guild, 74. *Bibliog:* John Canaday (auth), Embattled Critic; Irving Sandler (auth), Triumph of American Painting & New York Painters and Sculptors of the 50's; Fred Mcdarral (auth), Artists World. *Mem:* Eight St Art Club, New York, 58-60; College Art Asn, 73-78; Am Asn Mus, 74-80. *Media:* All Media. *Publ:* Contribr, Mus News, 6/73; Mid-West Art, 12/74; contribr catalogue, First International Mail Exhibition, Bway Galleries, Milwaukee, Wis, 3/77; auth, transcript lecture, Collections Users View, Asn Ind Mus, 9/77; auth & designer catalogs, Ilya Bolotowsky & Western Artists of Taos, New Mexico, Ft Wayne Mus Art, 78; auth, various articles in local NJ papers, Fin & Feather Club Pequannock between 84 and 86. *Mailing Add:* 7 Windsor Pl Upper Montclair NJ 07043

KRUSHENICK, NICHOLAS
PAINTER
b New York, NY, May 31, 29. *Study:* Art Students League, 48-50; Hans Hofmann Sch, New York, 50-51. *Work:* Metrop Mus Art, Whitney Mus Am Art & Mus Mod Art, New York; Los Angeles Co Mus Art; Albright-Knox Art Gallery, Buffalo, NY; Aldrich Mus Contemp Art, Ridgefield, Conn; Walker Art Ctr, Minneapolis, Minn; San Francisco Mus Art, Calif; Libr Cong, Washington, DC; Va Mus Fine Arts, Richmond; Art Gallery Ont, Can; and others. *Comn:* Large painting, State Univ NY Albany, 69. *Exhib:* One-man shows, Fishbach Gallery, New York, 65, Pace Gallery, 67, 69, 71, Walker Art Ctr, Minneapolis, Minn, Portland Ctr Visual Arts, Ore, 74, Aldrich Mus, Ridgefield, Conn, 81 & Daniel Newberg Gallery, New York, 90; The 1960's, Mus Mod Art, NY, 66; Systemic Painting, Guggenheim Mus, NY, 66; Tamarind Print Show, Mus Mod Art, NY, 69; Aldrich Mus, Ridgefield, Conn, 71, 75 & 79; Biennial Contemporary American Painting, Whitney Mus, NY, 73; San Francisco Mus Art, Calif, 74; Contemporary Collectors, Aldrich Mus, Ridgefield, Conn, 77; Homage to Hans Hofmann, Metrop Mus Art, NY, 78; Print Show, Brooklyn Mus, NY, 78; Cartoon Show, Whitney Mus Downtown, NY, 79; New Acquisitions, Whitney Mus, NY, 79; Penthouse Exhib, Mus Mod Art, NY, 79; Baskerville & Watson Gallery, NY, 86; Richard Green Gallery, NY, 87; Group Show, Daniel Newburg Gallery, New York, 90; Geometric Abstraction, Marc Richards Gallery, Santa Monica, Calif, 90; Rope, Fernando Alcolea Gallery, Barcelona, 91; and others. *Pos:*

Art critic, Yale Univ, 69-70. *Teaching:* Vis artist, Univ Wis, 69; artist-in-residence, Dartmouth Col, 69; artist, Cornell Univ, 70. *Awards:* Tamarind Lithography Award, 65; Guggenheim Found Fel, 67. *Media:* Acrylic, Oil. *Mailing Add:* 140 Grand St New York NY 10013

KRUSKAMP, JANET
PAINTER, INSTRUCTOR
b Grants Pass, Ore, Dec 10, 34. *Study:* Chouinard Art Inst, Los Angeles and pvt study. *Work:* Rosicrucian Egyptian Mus, San Jose & Triton Mus Art, Santa Clara, Calif; Springville Mus Art, Utah; Alexandria Mus Art, La; La Grange Col, Ga; and others. *Comn:* Seven paintings, Cowden Ranch, 74; painting, Burger King, 75; Challenge-Cook Brothers, 76; two paintings, Jet Air, Inc, 76; painting, Anning-Johnson & Co, 89; Bicentennial Event, comn by San Jose Bicentennial, 76. *Exhib:* Soc Western Artists Ann, M H De Young Mus, San Francisco, 71; Soc Western Artists, Rosicrucian Egyptian Mus, 72; Mainstreams, Marietta Col, Ohio, 75; solo exhibs, Springville Mus Art, Utah, 78, San Jose Mus Art, 80 & Charles & Emma Frye Mus Art, Washington, 74; San Jose Mus Art, Calif, 80; Redding Mus Art, Calif, 80; and others. *Pos:* Art juror. *Teaching:* Pvt painting instr, currently. *Awards:* Soc Western Artists Ann First Place Oils, 70; Trustees' Award & Andy Trophy, Grand Galleria Nat Art Competition, Seattle, 72 & First Prize & Purchase Prize, 73; and others. *Bibliog:* Janice Lovoos (auth), Janet Kruskamp's America, Southwest Art, 6/75; Ted Bredt (auth), A romantic display, Calif Today, 76; Susan Thomas (auth), Women that make a special difference, San Jose Mag, 79; and others. *Mem:* Nat Mus Women Arts, Washington, DC; Los Gatos Art Asn (pres, 69). *Media:* Oil, Egg Tempera. *Publ:* Auth, Painting from your own photos, another view, North Light Mag. *Dealer:* Center Art Galleries-Hawaii Inc PO Box 15577 Honolulu HI 96830-5577; Marjorie Cahn Gallery PO Box 2065 Los Gatos CA. *Mailing Add:* 1627 Hyde Dr Los Gatos CA 95030

KUBLER, GEORGE ALEXANDER
HISTORIAN, CURATOR
b Los Angeles, Calif, July 26, 12. *Study:* Yale Univ, BA, 34, MA, 36, PhD, 40. *Teaching:* Prof hist art, Yale Univ, 38- *Awards:* Latin Am Studies Asn Award, 92. *Bibliog:* Thomas Reese (ed, intro), Collective Essays, 85. *Res:* Pre-Columbian and colonial Latin American art; art of Spain and Portugal. *Publ:* Auth, Religious Architecture of New Mexico, 40; Mexican Architecture of the Sixteenth Century, 48; coauth, Art & Architecture of Spain & Portugal, 59; auth, Art & Architecture of Ancient America, 62; The Shape of Time, 62; Building the Escorial, 83. *Mailing Add:* 56 High St New Haven CT 06520

KUBOTA, SHIGEKO
VIDEO CURATOR, VIDEO ARTIST
b Niigata, Japan, Aug 2, 37. *Study:* Univ Tokyo, BA(sculpture), 60. *Exhib:* Video Sculpture: Duchamp's Grave, The Kitchen, New York, 75, Seattle, Wash, 75, Everson Mus, Syracuse, NY, 76, Acad Kunste, Berlin, WGer, 76 & Am Mus Moving Image, Long Island, NY, 91; Nude Descending a Staircase, Seattle, 76 & Dokumenta 6, Kassel, Ger, 77; Video Sculptures, Rene Block Gallery, New York, 77; Fur Augen und Ohren, Akademie der Kunste, Berlin, 80; Video Classics, Bronx Mus, NY, 81; Takanawa Mus, Karuizawa, Japan, 81; Nat Video Fest, Kennedy Ctr Performing Arts, Washington, DC, 82; Biennial Exhib, Whitney Am Art, New York, 83; Louisiana Mus, Copenhagen, Denmark, 84; Tamayo Mus, Mexico City, 85; Museum Villa, Stuck, Munich, WGer, 86; solo exhib, Piezo Electric, Venice, Calif, 86, Am Mus Moving Image, Astoria, NY, 91, Hara Mus Contemp Art, Tokyo, Japan, 92 & Stedelijk Mus, Amsterdam, Holland, 92; Sydney Biennale, Australia, 90; Artec 91, Nagoya, Japan, 91; Nat Mus Art, Osaka, Japan, 92. *Pos:* Video cur, Anthology Film Archives, 74- *Teaching:* Mem video art fac, Sch of Visual Arts, New York, 78-; artist-in-residence video, Sch Art Inst Chicago, 81, 82 & 84. *Awards:* Fel, Nat Endowment Arts, 78 & 80; Fel, NY State Coun Arts, 80, 82 & 84; Guggenheim Fel, 87. *Bibliog:* James Addams Allen (auth), Japanese tradition woven into video installation, Washington Times, 12/83; Brooke Adams (auth), Profile, Art in Am, 2/84; Michael Shapiro (auth), The Japanese in New York (Manhattan catalog), Vol 1, p 42, spring/summer 90. *Publ:* Auth, Marcel Duchamp & John Cage, Takeyoshi Miyazawa, 70. *Dealer:* Rene Block Gallery 1000 Berlin 5 Schaperstrabe 11 Berlin Ger. *Mailing Add:* 110 Mercer St New York NY 10012

KUCHAR, KATHLEEN ANN
PAINTER, EDUCATOR
b Meadow Grove, Nebr, Feb 4, 42. *Study:* Kearney State Col, BA, 63; Ft Hays Kans State Col, MS, 66; Brooklyn Mus Art Sch, Max Beckmann Mem scholar, 66-67, with Reuben Tam, 67; Wichita State Univ, MFA, 74. *Work:* Wichita State Univ Art Gallery; Ft Hays State Univ Art Gallery; Nebr Arts Collection; Crescent Cardboard Co Collection; Biblical Arts Ctr, Dallas, Tex. *Exhib:* Watercolor USA, Springfield Art Mus, Mo, 68, 79, 80, 84 & 85; one-person show, Nat Design Ctr, New York, 68; Am Watercolor Soc Exhib, New York, 79; one-person show, Biblical Arts Ctr, Dallas, Tex, 88; Group show, Ariel Gallery, New York, 88. *Teaching:* Instr art, Minden Pub Schs, Nebr, 63-65; assoc prof painting-design, Ft Hays State Univ, 67-78, prof, 78- *Awards:* Best in Show, Tri State Watercolor Exhib, Wichita Art Mus, 79 & 81; Fel painting, Mid-Am Alliance, 86; Purchase Award, Nat Watercolor Soc, 83 & 85; Fel Nat Emdowment Arts, 86. *Bibliog:* Rev in Art News, 68 & Art Rev, 69; Female Artists, Past & Present, Women's Hist Res Ctr, Inc, 74; Rev in Manhattan Arts, 88; New York Art Rev, 88. *Mem:* Rocky Mountain Nat Watermedia Soc; Kans Watercolor Soc; Nat Watercolor Soc; Watercolor-USA-Honor Soc. *Media:* Acrylic; Lithography. *Dealer:* Anderson-O'Brien Gallery Omaha NE; Leedy Voulkos Gallery Kansas City MO. *Mailing Add:* 2202 Fort St Hays KS 67601

KUCHEL, KONRAD G
ADMINISTRATOR
b Salem, Mass, Aug 25, 37. *Study:* Bowdoin Col, AB, 60; Inst Fine Arts, New York Univ, MA, 63. *Pos:* Asst to dir & ed, Mus Bulletin, Mus Art, RI Sch Design, 63-64; coordr loans, Exhib Dept, Am Fedn Arts, 65-69 & 76-86, dir exhibs, 69-75. *Mem:* Am Asn Mus. *Mailing Add:* 43 W 74th St Apt 5B New York NY 10023

KUCHTA, RONALD A
MUSEUM DIRECTOR, LECTURER
b Lackawanna, NY, June 23, 35. *Study:* Cape Cod Sch Art, Provincetown, Mass, 53-57; Kenyon Col, Gambier, Ohio, BA, 57; Western Reserve Univ, Cleveland, Ohio, MA(art hist), 62; Mgt Inst, Cornell Univ, 79. *Collections Arranged:* Modern Mexican Painting, 70; Tantra (with catalog), 70; Interior Vision, European Abstract Expressionism, 1945-1960 (with catalog), 70; Animals in African Art (with catalog), 73; 15 Abstract Artists--Los Angeles, 73; New Works in Clay, 76; Provincetown Painters, 77; Diversions of Keramos: American Clay Sculpture 1925-1950, 83; Robert Beauchamp: American Expressionist, 84; Syracuse China Ctr Study Am Ceramics, 87; Continuity and Transformation, Contemporary Japanese Ceramics, 92. *Pos:* Cur, Chrysler Art Mus, 61-68, Santa Barbara Mus Art, 68-74; dir, Everson Mus Art, 74- *Teaching:* Adj prof museology, Syracuse Univ, 74- *Awards:* Outstanding Serv Educ, Northeastern Baptist Asn, 83; Service to the Arts Award, Cult Resources Coun, Syracuse, 92. *Mem:* Am Asn Mus Dir; Int Coun Mus; Nat Arts Club, New York; Nat Conf Educ Ceramic Art; Int Acad Ceramics, 92. *Publ:* Auth, introd to The Diversions of Keramos: American Clay Sculpture 1925-1950, 83, Robert Beauchamp, American Expressionist, 84 & American Ceramics Now, 87, Everson Mus Art; American Ceramics: The Collection of Everson Mus Art, Rizzoli, 89;; Fragile Blossoms, Enduring Earth, Japanese Influences on American Ceramics, 1880's-1980's, 89; Ceramics, Art and Perception, Sydney, 91; Tradition and Invention in Contemporary Ceramics, Ceramic Review, London, 92; and others. *Mailing Add:* Everson Mus Art Syracuse NY 13202

KUCZUN, ANN-MARIE
PAINTER, ILLUSTRATOR
b Springfield, Mass. *Study:* Bay Path Jr Col, ABS; Univ Colo, Boulder. *Work:* Pratt Community Col, Kans; E F Hutton & Co, Colo; US West, Colo & Wyo; Ellsworth Hist Soc, Kans. *Comn:* Bookcover, Roberts-Rinehart Inc, Boulder, Colo; bookcover, Natural Resources Ctr, Boulder, Colo; illus & bookcover, Island Press, Covelo, Calif. *Exhib:* San Diego Watercolor Soc Nat, 80; Buell Gallery, 83; Kansas Pastel Soc, 84; one-person show, Univ Northern Colo, 84; Sangre De Cristo Arts & Conf Ctr, Colo, 88-89; Univ Colo-Boulder, 89. *Pos:* Freelance illusr, Univ Colo, John H Breck, Inc, Buxton Corp, WWLP/TV, Roberts Rinehart Inc Publ; pub, Roberts-Rhinehart Inc. *Bibliog:* Illus feature in Colorado Mag, 9-10/77; feature with color photos in Boulder Daily Camera, 9/16/77 & 6/17/79; Southwest Art, 5/88; Business Plus, 4/11/89. *Media:* Watermedia, Pastel; All. *Publ:* Contribr, Collaging with Paper, 78 & Printworld Inc, 81. *Dealer:* William Havu Fine Arts 2565 Blake St Denver CO; J-Michael Galleries 3916 W 50th St Edina MN. *Mailing Add:* 930 Miami Way Boulder CO 80303

KUEHN, EDMUND KARL
PAINTER, LECTURER
b Columbus, Ohio, Aug 18, 16. *Study:* Columbus Art Sch, cert, 38; Art Students League, cert, 39. *Work:* Columbus Gallery Fine Arts; Capital Univ, Battelle Mem Inst. *Exhib:* Keny & Johnson Gallery, 82-90. *Collections Arranged:* Paintings from Columbus Homes, 63; Jean Crotti in Retrospect, 65; The Gordian Knot, 67; Works by David Blythe, 68. *Pos:* Cur, Columbus Gallery Fine Arts, 39-43, asst dir, 62-67, cur collections, 67-76. *Teaching:* Asst prof drawing & painting, Ohio State Univ, 46-47; assoc prof drawing & painting, Columbus Col Art & Design, 52-62. *Mem:* Columbus Art League; Am Asn Mus. *Media:* Miscellaneous media. *Mailing Add:* 828 City Park Ave Columbus OH 43206

KUEHN, FRANCES
PAINTER
b New York, NY, Feb 16, 43. *Study:* Douglass Col, Rutgers Univ, BA, Rutgers Univ, New Brunswick, MFA. *Work:* J B Speed Art Mus, Louisville, Ky; Weatherspoon Art Gallery, Univ NC; Power Inst, Univ Sydney, Australia; Allen Mem Art Mus, Oberlin, Ohio; New Jersey State Mus, Trenton; and others. *Comn:* Portrait for private collection, 72. *Exhib:* Whitney Mus Ann, 72 & Biennial, 73; one-woman shows, Douglass Col Libr, 73, Max Hutchinson Gallery, 73 & 74 & A M Sachs Gallery, New York, 78; Contemporary Portraits by Well-Known American Artists, Lowe Art Mus, Coral Gables, Fla, 74; Selections in Contemporary Realism, Akron Art Inst, Ohio, 74. *Teaching:* Artist-in-residence, Rice Univ, 80. *Awards:* NJ State Coun Arts Artist's Fel, 78-79; Nat Endowment Arts Artist's Fel, 82-83. *Bibliog:* Phyllis Derfner (auth), Frances Kuehn, Art Spectrum, 2/75; Lynn Miller & Sally Swenson (auths), Lives and Work, Talks with Women Artists, Scarecrow Press, 81. *Media:* Acrylic. *Mailing Add:* 789 West End Ave, Apt 4D New York NY 10025-5417

KUEHN, GARY
SCULPTOR, GRAPHIC ARTIST
b Plainfield, NJ, 1939. *Study:* Drew Univ, NJ, BA(art hist), 62; Rutgers Univ, NJ, MFA, 64. *Work:* NJ State Mus, Trenton; also in pvt collections of Richard P Kaplan, New York, Roy Lichtenstein, New York & Robert Scull, New York. *Exhib:* One person exhibs, Douglas Drake Gallery, Kansis City, 74, 76, 80, 82, 87, 89 & 91, Art Galaxy, New York, 85, Margarete Roeder Gallery, New York, 86 & 90, Galerie Julie Kewenig, Frechen, Ger, 86 & 88,

Rudolf Zwirner Gallery, New York & Koln, Ger, 86 & Galerie Sylvia Menzel, Berlin, Ger, 87; Elements of Style, New York, Deson-Saunders Gallery, Chicago, Ill, 89; Aus Meiner Sicht, Galerie Rolfe Ricke, Kolnisher, Kunstuerien, Ger, 89; Made in New York, Williams Ctr Arts, Easton, Pa, 89; New Aquisitions, Lehmbruch Mus, Duisberg, Ger, 91; Galerie Rudolf Zwirner, Koln, Ger, 91; Gallery Artists, Douglas Drake Gallery, New York, 92; Kuehn Marioni Smith, Margarete Roeder Gallery, New York, 92; and many others. *Teaching:* Instr, Fairleigh Dickinson Univ, NJ, 65, Drew Univ, NJ, 65-68, Sch of Visual Arts, New York, 68, Hochshule fur Bildende Kunst, Braunschweig, Ger, 70, & Douglass Col, 73; prof, Rutgers Univ, 73. *Awards:* Nat Endowment Arts Grant, 77; DAAD Fel, Berlin, 79; Greenburger Award, 90. *Dealer:* Margaret Roeder Gallery 545 Broadway New York NY 10012. *Mailing Add:* 133 W 24th St New York NY 10011

KUEHNL, CLAUDIA ANN
GOLDSMITH
b Kenosha, Wis, Aug 11, 48. *Study:* Philadelphia Col Art, Pa, BFA, 70; State Univ NY Col, New Paltz, MFA, 74. *Exhib:* Contemp Am Gold-Silversmiths, Corcoran Gallery Art, Washington, DC, 72; Southern Tier Arts & Crafts Exhib, Corning Mus, NY, 74; Contemp Crafts of the Americas Int Exhib, Ft Collins, Colo, 75; Mex Exhib, Univ Mex, Mexico City, 75; Silver & Goldsmithing in Am Exhib, Lowe Art Mus, Univ Miami, Coral Gables, Fla, 76; NAm Goldsmiths Exhib, Phoenix Art Mus, Ariz, 77; Jewelry & Metal Objects from the Society of North American Goldsmiths (Europ traveling show); Quadrum Gallery, Chestnut Hill, Mass, 83-88; Gene Barth Gallery, Oklahoma City, 85; Cross Creek Gallery, Malibu, Calif, 86; Fergus-Jean Gallery, Columbus, Ohio, 89. *Teaching:* Instr art appreciation & asst prof in two dimensional design & drawing, Suffolk Co Community Col, Selden, NY, 75-; asst prof metalsmithing & jewelry, Southampton Col, NY, 76-79 & Art Dept Drawing; tech mgr, Gesswein, Thailand, 89-90. *Awards:* Nat Endowment Arts Fel, Crafts, 75-76. *Mem:* Soc NAm Goldsmiths; Am Crafts Coun; NY State Craftsmen Inc. *Media:* Gold, Stone. *Publ:* Jewelry concepts, Technology, Oppi Untrach; auth, Murray Bouid, Jewelry Making; Metal Smith, spring 87. *Dealer:* Works Gallery Jobs Lane Southampton NY 11968; Works Gallery 1250 Madison Ave New York NY 10128. *Mailing Add:* Quogue St Box 622 Quogue NY 11959

KUEMMERLEIN, JANET
FIBER ARTIST
b Dearborn, Mich, Jan 10, 32. *Study:* Detroit Soc Arts & Crafts, 50-51; Cranbrook Acad Art, with Harry Osaki, 51-52. *Work:* Chicago Art Inst; Rochester Inst Technol; Ga Inst Technol; Smithsonian Nat Gallery Art; 3M Corp. *Comn:* Fiber relief sculpture, Gen Serv Admin, Richmond, Calif, 76; fiber mural, Williams Ctr, Tulsa, 80 & State Bar Calif, Sacramento, 80; fiber & sculpture, State Fed Savings, Tulsa, 82; fiber relief sculpture, Richardson-Vicks, Shelton, Calif, 83; fiber relief, Z J Loussac Libr, Anchorage, Alaska; fiber mural, DuPont, Wilmington, Del. *Exhib:* Five Fiber Artists, Sheldon Mem Gallery, Lincoln, Nebr, 63; Objects USA Travelling Exhib, US & Europe, 69; Forms in Fibre, Chicago Art Inst, 71; American Craft Exhib, Dallas Mus, 72; Craft Invitational, San Diego Mus Fine Art, 74; Art in Worship, Mus Contemp Crafts, New York, 74; Women, Fiber, Clay & Metal, Bronx Mus, 77; Fiberworks, Cleveland Mus, 78. *Collections Arranged:* Contemporary Crafts (auth, catalog), Rockhurst Col, 64. *Awards:* Awards, Univ Kans, 65-69 & Am Inst Archit, 69-71, 75-79 & 88. *Bibliog:* Louise Schulteis (auth), Artist in fiber, Kansas City Star, 71; Irene Reynolds (auth), Fiber artist, Kansan Mag, 76. *Mem:* Mo Coun Arts; Am Craft Coun. *Media:* Fiber. *Publ:* Contribr, Textile Art in the Church, Abingdon Press, 71; contribr, Quilting, Patchwork, Applique, Trapunto, 74 & Soft Sculpture, 74, Crown; contribr, The Place of Art in the World of Architecture, Chelsea House, 80; contribr, Sewing Machine Craft Book, Van Nostrand Reinhold, 80. *Mailing Add:* 7701 Canterbury Prairie Village KS 66208

KUH, HOWARD
PAINTER
b New York, NY, 1899. *Study:* Art Students League; Marine painting with Jay Conaway, Maine; painting with S M Adler, New York. *Work:* Butler Inst Am Art, Youngstown, Ohio; Slater Mem Mus, Conn; Tweed Mus & Minneapolis Mus, Minn; Stratford Col, Va; Evansville Mus Arts & Sci. *Exhib:* Audubon Artists, Nat Acad of Design, New York; Riverside Mus; New Eng Ann, Silver Mine, Conn; Avery Mem Mus, Hartford, Conn; one-man shows, Roko Gallery & Bodley Gallery. *Mem:* Am Soc Contemp Artists; Artists Equity NY. *Mailing Add:* 45 Christopher St No 16B New York NY 10014

KUH, KATHARINE
CRITIC, CONSULTANT
b St Louis, Mo, July 15, 04. *Study:* Vassar Col, BA; Univ Chicago, MA(art hist); NY Univ; also five hon PhDs. *Pos:* Owner & dir, Katharine Kuh Gallery, Chicago, 36-42; cur mod art, Art Inst Chicago, 42-59; art ed, Sat Rev, 59-77; art consult, First Nat Bank Chicago, 68-79. *Publ:* Auth, Art Has Many Faces, 51, auth, The Artist's Voice, 61 & auth, The Open Eye, 70, Harper & Row; Leger, Univ Ill, 58; Break-Up: The Core of Modern Art, NY Graphic, 65. *Mailing Add:* 140 E 83rd St New York NY 10028

KUHLENSCHMIDT, RICHARD EDWARD
DEALER
b Cleveland, Ohio, Feb 27, 51. *Study:* Calif State Univ, Fullerton, BA, 75. *Pos:* Cur exhibs, Bowers Mus, Santa Ana, Calif, 77-79; owner & dir, Richard Kuhlenschmidt Gallery, Los Angeles, 80- *Bibliog:* Karen Back (auth), Best of Los Angeles, Los Angeles Weekly, 9/83. *Specialty:* Contemporary Los Angeles and New York artists. *Mailing Add:* 1630 17th St Santa Monica CA 90404

KUHLMAN, WALTER EGEL
PAINTER, EDUCATOR
b St Paul, Minn, Nov 16, 18. *Study:* St Paul Sch Art, with Cameron Booth; Univ Minn, BA; Tulane Univ; Calif Sch Fine Arts; Acad Grande Chaumiere. *Work:* San Francisco Mus Mod Art; Oakland Mus, Calif; NY Metrop Mus Art; Nat Mus Art, Wash, DC; Mus Mod Art, Rio de Janiero; De Saisset Mus, Santa Clara, Calif; Minnesota Mus Art; The Art Inst Calif; and many others. *Exhib:* One-man shows, The Carlson Gallery Historic Survey of Bay Area Abstr Expressionist Art, San Francisco, 45-60, Calif Palace of the Legion of Hon, 56-64, Walker Art Center, Minneapolis, Stanford Univ Gallery, Santa Barbara Mus Art, Charles Campbell Gallery, San Francisco, 81, 83, 85; 20-yr Retrospective, De Saisset Mus, 69, 40-yr Retrospective, Sonoma State Univ Gallery; San Francisco Mus Mod Art, 3-man show; Painting & Sculpture of the Modern Era, Smithsonian Inst; NY World's Fair; San Francisco Mus Mod Art; Period of Exploration, Oakland Mus, Calif, 73; Bolles Gallery, San Francisco; UC Davis, Directions in Bay Area Painting, A Survey of Three Decades; and others. *Teaching:* Stanford Univ; Calif Sch Fine Arts; Univ NMex, 60-65; Univ Santa Clara, 66-69; prof painting & chmn dept art, Sonoma State Univ, Calif, 69- *Awards:* Fel, Cummington Found, Mass, 42, Graham Found, Chicago, 57, Calif Arts Coun, 83, Maestro Award; Calif Arts Coun Award, Outstanding Calif Working Artist & Teacher; Tiffany Found, NY; Graham Found, Chicago. *Media:* Oil, Monoprints. *Mailing Add:* 27 Glen Ct Sausalito CA 94965

KUHN, AUDREY GRENDAHL
PRINTMAKER, GRAPHIC ARTIST
b Chicago, Ill, May 3, 29. *Study:* Univ Mich, Ann Arbor, BA(design), 52; Skidmore Col, 72; Russel Sage Col, Troy, NY, grad study art educ & printmaking, 73-75. *Work:* Mus Mod Art, Haifa, Israel; Mayo Clinic, Rochester, Minn; Norton Simon Co, New York; Corp Sci & Technol, Indianapolis; Hudson Valley Community Col, Troy, NY. *Exhib:* Graphic Artists NY, State Univ NY, Albany, 78; Mohawk Hudson Regional, Albany Inst Hist & Art, 78; Artexpo NY, Jacob Javits Ctr, New York, 79-89; solo exhib, Ctr Gallery, Albany, 85; group exhib, Ctr Gallery, Albany, 92; Print Club Albany Ann, Schenectady Mus, 92. *Awards:* First Prize, Albany Artists Show, 76; Second Prize, Stockade Art Show, Stockade Asn, 91; Second Prize, Art in the Park, Saratoga Co Arts Coun, 92. *Bibliog:* Sharon Shinn (auth), Mixed media prints, 3/89 & Monotypes: the unique prints, 3/91, Decor Mag. *Mem:* Print Club Albany (treas & chmn presentation print comt, 89-91); Designer Crafts Coun Schenectady Mus; Graphic Artists New York (treas, 76); Southern Vt Art Cr; Ctr Galleries, Albany. *Media:* Serigraph with Intaglio. *Dealer:* Towne Gallery Main St Lenox MA 01240. *Mailing Add:* Ten Valdepenas Lane Clifton Park NY 12065

KUHN, BOB
DRAFTSMAN, PAINTER
b Buffalo, NY, Jan 28, 20. *Study:* Pratt Inst, 3 yrs; Art Students League. *Work:* Nat Cowboy Hall Fame, Oklahoma City; Genesee Country Mus, Rochester, NY; Wildlife World Mus, Monument, Colo. *Exhib:* One-man show, Abercrombie & Fitch, New York, 65 & two-man show, 67; one-man show, Tryon Gallery, Nairobi, Kenya, 73; Animals in Art, Royal Ont Mus, Toronto, 75. *Awards:* Gold Medal, Silver Medal, Nat Acad Western Art; Gold Medal, Nat Cowboy Hall Fame; Three Medals of Honor, Soc Animal Artists. *Mem:* Soc Animal Artists. *Media:* Acrylic on Masonite. *Publ:* Auth, Animal Art of Bob Kuhn, Watson-Guptill, 73; contribr, Classic African Animals, Winchester, 73. *Mailing Add:* c/o Wildlife of the Am W Art Mus 110 N Center St PO Box 2984 Jackson Hole WY 83001

KUHN, MARYLOU
EDUCATOR, PAINTER
b South Bend, Ind, Oct 18, 23. *Study:* Layton Sch Art; Univ Wis; Art Inst Chicago; Ohio State Univ, univ fel, 53, BSc & PhD; Teachers Col, Columbia Univ, MA. *Exhib:* LeMoyne Art Found, 65-; Ind Univ, 74; Gulf Coast Jr Col, 75; Fla A&M Univ, 76. *Pos:* Ed, Fla Art News, 60-62; ed, Southeastern Arts Bulletin, 62-64; Regional ed, Art Educ J, 64-66, co-ed, Studies in Art Educ, 70-73, sr ed, 73-75; treas, Sem Res in Art Educ, 76-78. *Teaching:* Prof art educ, Fla State Univ, 51-, chmn dept art, currently; guest lectr art educ, Inst Educ, Univ London, 66-67; distinguished vis prof, Southern Ill Univ, Carbondale, 78; retired. *Mem:* Int Soc Educ Through Art; Nat Art Educ Asn; Women's Caucus Art (pres, 78-79); Adult Educ Asn USA; Am Coun Arts; Am Fedn Arts. *Media:* Encaustic, Watercolor. *Res:* Community and adult art education, curriculum and teacher education in art, philosophy and theory. *Publ:* Auth, Standards and criteria, Adult & Exten Art Educ, 66; auth chap, In: Behavioral Emphasis in Art Education, 75; auth, Priorities for arts in everyday living and education, Registry Vol 16; auth, Philosophical base for lifelong learning, In: Life-Long Learning in Visual Arts, 80; auth, Women, work and cultural equality, In: Ninth Decade in Visual Arts, 80. *Dealer:* LeMoyne Art Found 125 N Gadsden St Tallahassee FL 32303. *Mailing Add:* 1403 Betton Rd Tallahassee FL 32312

KUJUNDZIC, ZELJKO D
CERAMIST, SCULPTOR
b Subotica, Yugoslavia, Oct 23, 20; Can citizen. *Study:* Royal Col Art, Budapest, Hungary, BA, 44; Inst Fine Arts, Budapest, MFA, 46, with Jeno Barchai. *Work:* Nat Mus, Geneva, Switzerland; Bellevue Art Mus, Wash; Pa State Univ, University Park & Fayette Campus; Univ BC, Vancouver; Kyoto City Mus, Japan; and others. *Comn:* Thunderbirds, monument, Univ Brit Columbia, Can, 67; Reverence (mural), Prov Hosp BC, Nelson, 68; Ceramic mural, First Fed Bank, Pittsburgh, Pa, 73; libr mural, Pa State Univ, Uniontown, 74; Holocaust Mem, B'nai B'rith, Uniontown, Pa, 81. *Exhib:* One-man exhibs, Art Inst Pittsburgh Gallery, 81, Nehan Gallery, New York,

87-88, New Orleans, 88, Confluence Gallery, Twisp, Wash, 89, Goastal Arts League Gallery, Half Moon Bay, Calif, 89, Osoyoos Art Gallery, Can, 90, Gallery Kootenays, Nelson, Can, 90, Toussowasket Gallery, Kelowna, BC, Can, 90, Netherbow Gallery, Edinburgh, Scotland, 90 & Gulacsy Gallery, Budapest, Hungary, 90; Am Numizmatic Soc New York, 89; Gardens Art Gallery, Bellingham, Wash, 89; John Blackaird Gallery, Toronto, Can, 90; Juried exhib, Fedn Int Medaille, British Mus, London, Eng, 92; and others. *Pos:* Pres, Okanagan Contemp Artists, 66-68; exec dir, Pioneer Crafts Coun, Mill Run, Pa, 70-71. *Teaching:* Assoc prof, Pa State Univ, Uniontown, 68,79, prof emer, 82; sculpture workshop partic, Nat Univ Mex, 79; Raku Workshop, Wenatchee Valley Col, Wash, 81; lectr, Escuela Nac de Ceramica, Madrid & Barcelona, Spain. *Awards:* Merit Awards, Expo 67 Can, Nat Crafts Coun Can, 67 & Int Ceramics, Nat Mus Art, Poland, 73; Purchase Award, Int Medalist Exhib, Nat Gallery Art, Poland, 76; Bronze Medal, Int Medalist Juried Exhib, Stockholm, Sweden, 85. *Bibliog:* Anne Payne (auth), Kujundzic, Arts West, 66; Ray Turner (auth), Art with Zeljko, CHBC-TV, 67-68; Philip R Shepherd (auth, feature), Z Kujundzic, Onion, Toronto, 77; M Krstic (auth), article, La Ceramique Moderne, 85; Elaine Purchase (auth), Documentary: The Life and Works of Z Kujundzic, KOMO-TV, Seattle, Wash, 85 & 86; Judit Acsay (auth), Z Kujundzie, Uj Tükör, Budapest, Hungary, 87. *Mem:* Int Acad of Ceramics, Switz; Sculptors Soc of Can; Sculptors Soc of BC (regional rep); Mesa Int Prof Artists Asn; NW Designer Craftsmen, 84- *Media:* All. *Publ:* Auth (autobiog), Torn Canvas, Richard Patterson, 57, paperback ed, 64; Paolo Soleri, Art & You, 73; Experimental solar kilns, Ceramic Mo, 75; Cuire au soleil, l'Atelier des Metiers d'Art, Paris, 76; Les ceramistes americains, La Ceramique Moderne, Paris, France, 82; Antonio Vivas Zamorano (auth), Z Kujundzic: Ceramica, Madrid, Spain, 84. *Mailing Add:* 605 Juniper St Oroville WA 98844

KULICKE, ROBERT M
CRAFTSMAN, PAINTER
b Philadelphia, Pa, Mar 9, 24. *Study:* Philadelphia Col Art; Tyler Sch Arts, Temple Univ; Academie Leger, Paris, 49-51. *Work:* Philadelphia Mus Art; Hirshhorn Mus & Sculpture Garden; Mus Art, Pa State Univ. *Exhib:* Silvermine Guild, 64; Art Inst Chicago; Dayton Art Inst, Ohio; 100 Years of American Realism, Am Fedn Arts, 65; Whitney Mus Am Art, New York, 69; one-man exhibs, Kornblee Gallery, New York, 70-73, Davis & Long Co, New York, 74-80, Mus Art, Penn State Univ, 78, Davis & Langdale Co, New York, 81-90, Columbia Mus Art & Sci, SC, 83, John C Stoller & Co, Minneapolis, Minn, 85 & John F Warren, Philadelphia, 88. *Teaching:* Instr, Univ Calif, 64 & 70; instr, Jewelry Arts Inst, New York, 64-, dir, 74- & assoc, 87- *Awards:* Int Design Award, Am Inst Interior Designers, 68; assoc mem Nat Acad Design, 88. *Media:* Oil, Pastel. *Mailing Add:* c/o Davis & Langdale 231 E 60th St New York NY 10022

KULTERMANN, UDO
ART HISTORIAN, ARCHITECT
b Stettin, Ger, Oct 14, 27. *Study:* Univ Greifswald, Ger, 47-50; Univ Munster, 50-53. *Exhib:* Monochrome Painting, 60, Ad Reinhardt, Francesco Lo Savio & Jef Verheyen, 61, Glass Chain, 62, City Art Mus, Leverkusen, Ger. *Pos:* Dir, City Art Mus, Leverkusen, Ger, 59-64; consult to art collectors, galleries and govt agencies. *Teaching:* Prof hist & theory archit, Washington Univ, 67-, Ruth & Norman Moore Prof Archit, 86- *Awards:* Distinguished Fac Award, Wash Univ, 85. *Res:* Art and Reality From Fiedler to Dernida; History of art history; African culture; Third World architecture; Eastern European Architecture. *Publ:* Auth, Art Events & Happenings, Matthew, Miller & Dunbar, 71, I Contemporanei, Mondadori, 79, Architecture in the Seventies, Archit Press, 80; Architects of the Third World, 80, Contemp Architecture in Eastern Europe, Dumont, 85; History of Art Theories, Wissenschftliche Buchferellschoft, 86; Visible Cities-Invisible Cities, Wash Univ, 88; History of Art History, Agaris, 93. *Mailing Add:* Washington Univ Campus Box 1079 St Louis MO 63130

KUMLER, KIPTON (CORNELIUS)
PHOTOGRAPHER, LECTURER
b Cleveland, Ohio, June 20, 40. *Study:* Cornell Univ, BEE, 63, MEE, 67; Mass Inst Technol, with Minor White, 68-69; Harvard Univ, MBA, 69; spec study with Paul Caponigro, 70. *Work:* Mus Mod Art, Metrop Mus Art, New York; Mus Fine Arts, Boston; Victoria & Albert Mus, London; Int Mus Photog, George Eastman House, Rochester, NY. *Comn:* Essay on Danish Archit in Frederiksted, St Croix, Landmark Soc, 75-76; Photog Surv, Del Water Gap, Nat Endowment Arts, 76-77. *Exhib:* Recent Acquisitions, Boston Mus Fine Arts, 74; Addison Gallery Am Art, 74; solo exhibs, NJ Mus, Trenton, 78, Photog Place, Philadelphia, 79, Cronin Gallery, Houston, 80, Harcus Krakow Gallery, Boston, 80 & Worcester Art Mus, Mass, 80; and others. *Collections Arranged:* Traveling Exhib, Nat Endowment Arts Survey Work, NJ, 77-78. *Teaching:* Instr photog, Project Inc, Cambridge, Mass, 69-72; instr advan photog, Maine Photog Workshops, Rockport, 77-80. *Awards:* Nat Endowment Arts Photog Survey Grants, Peters Valley, NJ, 76-77 & Boston Hist Survey, 80-81; Mass Coun Arts Photog Fel, 77. *Publ:* Contribr, Camera, Lausanne, Switz, 70; contribr, Popular Photography, 75; auth, Kipton Kumler: Photographs, 75 & Plant Leaves, 78, David Godine; contribr, Print Letter, Zurich, 77. *Dealer:* Marcuse Pfeifer Gallery 825 Madison Ave New York NY 10016; Harcus Gallery 7 Newbury Boston MA 02116. *Mailing Add:* 28 Beaver Pond Rd PO Box 639 Lincoln MA 01773

KUN, NEILA
PHOTOGRAPHER
b Philadelphia, Pa, Feb 8, 51. *Study:* Tyler Sch Art, Temple Univ, BFA, 72. *Work:* Bibliotheque Nat, Paris, France; New York Pub Libr; Del Co Community Col; Lehigh Univ; Villanova Univ, Pa. *Comn:* Sculpted obverse coin of the realm, Guyana one penny piece, Franklin Mint, Pa, 77; sculpted coin for Queen Elizabeth's silver anniversary for Brit Virgin Island, Franklin Mint, Pa, 79. *Exhib:* two-person show, Del Co Community Col, Media, Pa, 82; Philadelphia Art Alliance, Pa, 84; Artists Equity Triennial, Port of Hist Mus, Philadelphia, 84, 88; Univ City Arts League, Philadelphia, 85; Alexandria Mus, La, 85; 63rd Annual Competition, Print Club, Philadelphia, 87-88; Works on Paper, Beaver Col, 89; Mems Show, Philadelphis Art Alliance, Pa, 90; Art at the Armory, Philadelphia, Pa, 90. *Awards:* Abbington Photo Show, 87; Award of Merit, Artists Equity Show, 88; Award of Merit, Artists Equity Show, 88. *Mem:* Soc Photog Educ; Friends Photog; Artists Equity; Print Club, Philadelphia. *Publ:* article, Popular Photog, 2/90. *Mailing Add:* 223 S Springmill Rd Villanova PA 19085

KUNC, KAREN
PRINTMAKER, EDUCATOR
b Omaha, Nebr, Dec 15, 52. *Study:* Univ Nebr-Lincoln, BFA, 75; Ohio State Univ, MFA, 77. *Work:* Nat Mus Am Art, Smithsonian Inst, Washington, DC; Libr Congress, Washington, DC; Worcester Art Mus, Mass; Sheldon Memorial Art Gallery, Univ Nebr, Lincoln; Nat Art Libr, Victoria & Albert Mus, London, Eng. *Exhib:* World Print III, San Francisco Mus Mod Art, Calif, 80; One-woman shows, Columbus Mus Art, Ohio, 83, Sheldon Mem Art Gallery, Lincoln, Nebr, 84; 7th Hawaii Nat Print Exhib, Honolulu Acad Arts, 85; 17th Int Biennial Graphic Art, Mednorodini Graficni Likovni Ctr, Ljubljana, Yugoslavia, 87; Relief Printing in the 1980's, Zimmerli Art Mus, Rutgers Univ, New Brunswick, NJ, 88; Imprimatur, Greenville Co Mus Art, SC, 88; Tradition & Innovation 1500-1989, Calif Palace Legion of Honor, San Francisco, 89. *Pos:* Gallery dir, Univ Nebr, 88- *Teaching:* Assoc prof printmaking, Univ Nebr, Lincoln, 83-; vis asst prof, Univ Calif, Berkeley, 87; vis artist/teacher, Carleton Col, Northfield, Minn, 89. *Awards:* Fel Nat Endowment Arts, 84; First Prize, Graphica Atlantica, Reykjavik, Iceland, 87; Purchase Award, Univ Del, 88. *Bibliog:* Kyle MacMillan (auth), Lincoln Printmaker, Omaha World Herald, 4/3/88; Michael Welzenbach (auth), article, Washington Post, 6/3/89; Nancy N Rice (auth), Karen Kunc; William Yonker, New Art Examiner, 6/90. *Mem:* Col Art Asn; Ctr Book Arts; Print Club; Calif Soc Printmakers; Boston Printmakers. *Media:* Woodcut. *Publ:* Coauth, ed, Polish Prints: A Contemporary Graphic Tradition, Univ Nebr-Lincoln Dept Art & Art History, 89. *Dealer:* Mary Ryan Gallery 452 Columbus Ave New York NY 10024. *Mailing Add:* RR No 1 Box No 71 Avola NE 68307

KUNSCH, LOUIS
PAINTER, COLLAGE ARTIST
b Bronx, NY, Dec, 37. *Study:* Art Students League New York, 61-65, Sch Visual Arts, NY, 70-72. *Exhib:* Audubon Artists, NY; Staten Island Mus; Ball State Univ, Ind; Jamaica Arts Ctr; Berkshire Mus, Mass; Purdue Univ, Ind; solo shows, Main Street Gallery, Brewster, NY, 75, Long Beach Libr, 77, The Exhibitionists, Jamaica, 77, PS 1, Long Island City, 79. *Mem:* Artists Equity New York; Hunters Point Community Artists. *Mailing Add:* Ten/Twenty Art Space 10-20 45th Rd Long Island City NY 11101

KUNSTLER, MORTON
PAINTER, ILLUSTRATOR
b New York, NY, Aug 28, 31. *Study:* Brooklyn Col; Univ Calif, Los Angeles; Pratt Inst, cert, 50. *Work:* USAF Mus, Boulder, Colo; San Mateo Co Historical Mus, Calif; US House Reps, US Senate & The White House, Washington, DC; Lowie Mus Anthrop, Berkeley, Calif; Nassau Co Mus Fine Arts, Roslyn, NY; Mus Am Hist, Smithsonian Inst, Washington, DC. *Comn:* Paintings, National Geographic, Washington, DC, 66-69; six paintings, American Cyanamid, NJ, 71-76; four paintings, NY Bank for Savings, New York, 76; seven paintings, Rockwell Int, Pa, 80; Cram & Foster, 80. *Exhib:* One-man shows, Hammer Galleries, New York, 77, 79, 81-82, 85-86 & 89, USN Mem Mus, Washington, DC, 79 & 82 & Pittsburgh Ctr Arts, Pa, 81; Mus Westward Expansion, St Louis, 89; Dunnegan Gallery, Bolivar, Mo, 91; Hammer Galleries, 92; Nat Military Park, Gettysburg, 92; Hall Valor Mus, New Market Battlefield, Va, 92; and others. *Bibliog:* Painting America, LI Goodliving, 9/88; Mort Kunstler, Braniff Mag, 1/89; Mort Kunstler's American Heritage, The Virginian, 7/89; Images of the Civil War, the Paintings of Mort Kunstler, Gramercy, 92; Video-Images of the Civil War, the Paintings of Mort Kunstler, Reda Productions, 92; and others. *Media:* Oil, Watercolor. *Dealer:* Hammer Galleries 33 W 57th St New York NY 10019. *Mailing Add:* Cove Neck Oyster Bay NY 11771

KUOPUS, CLINTON
PAINTER, EDUCATOR
b Detroit, Mich, Dec 8, 42. *Study:* US Navy Photog Intelligence Sch, 63; Eastern Mich Univ, Mich State Univ, Wayne State Univ. *Work:* Mich Educ Asn; Hiram Col, Ohio; J Walter Thompson Advert Agency; Lake Erie Col Permanent Collection; Pub Collection, Cedar City, Utah. *Exhib:* Source Detroit Exhib, Cranbrook Mus Art, Bloomfield Hills, Mich, 76; May Show Exhibs, Cleveland Mus Art, Ohio; Butler Inst Am Art, Youngstown, Ohio, 79; 38th Cedar City Nat, Utah, 79; Print Collaboration-Stewart and Stewart, Detroit Inst Art 91 & Kansas City Art Mus, 91-92. *Pos:* Photog interpreter, US Navy, 62-66; fac/admin, Parsons Sch Design, 83- *Teaching:* Photog intelligence training petty off, US Navy, 64-66; instr visual art, Bloomfield Hills Schs, Mich, 70-75; asst prof art, Lake Erie Col, Painesville, Ohio, 75-80, 82-83; adj fac, Youngstown State Univ, 80-82 & Univ Akron, 81-82; foundations fac, Parsons Sch Design, 83-, dir of exhib, 88- *Bibliog:* Art Editor (auth), article, Detroit Free Press, 73; Weekly art criticism, Detroit News, 73-74; Helen Cullinen (auth), article, Cleveland Plain Dealer, 76-78. *Mem:* Mich Watercolor Soc (bd dirs & dir exhibs, 72-74); Mich Art Educ Asn; Phi Kappa Phi Hon Soc; Am Asn Univ Profs. *Media:* Multimedia. *Mailing Add:* PO Box 6475 Yorkville Sta New York NY 10128

KUPER, YURI (YURI KUPERMAN)
PAINTER
b Moscow, USSR, July 5, 40; British citizen. *Study:* Academy of Art, Moscow. *Work:* Pushkin Mus, Tretiakov Gallery, Moscow; Nat Found Contemp Art, Ministry of Cult, Paris; Nat Gallery, Oslo; Bank of Am; Univ Chicago; Nat Libr of Congress, Wash, DC; Thew Sainsburg Collection, Univ Norwich; Veno Royal Mus, Kiyoharu Shirakaba Mus, Tokyo. *Exhib:* Centre Culturel, Jerusalem, 72, Haaken Galerie, Oslo, 81, Claude Bernard Galerie Paris, 83-88, New York, 86-89, Krugier Galerie, Geneve, Switz, 83, Galerie Rambert, Paris, 89; solo-show, Yoshii Gallery, Tokyo, 91 & 92, Yoshii Found-Kiyoharu Mus, 91, Valois Gallery, Paris, 91, Hesdin Gallery, Paris, 92, Yoshii Gallery, New York, 92, Sala Alternativa Gallery, Caracas, 92. *Bibliog:* David Newman (auth), Arts, 3/81; John Russel (auth), Maugunal exhib, NY Times, 10/83; John Berger (auth), Vuri Kuper Paintings, Claude Bernard, 10/83. *Publ:* Illust, L'Angoisse du Roi Solomon, Emile Ajar (auth), 79; Notre Dame de Paris performed at the Nat Theatre, L'Opera de Paris, 88; Tristane and Isolde, Imprimerie Nationale, Paris in the series Le Livre de Art, 89; My Sister, Life, Boris Paternak (auth), Ltd-Eds Club, New York, 90; Nouvelles de la Russie Rouge, Imprimerie National, Paris, 91-92. *Mailing Add:* 6 Place Furstemberg 75006 Paris France

KUPFERMAN, MURRAY
PAINTER, SCULPTOR
b Brooklyn, NY. *Study:* Pratt Inst; Nat Acad Design. *Work:* St Vincent Col, Latrobe, Pa; Brooklyn Mus; New Rochelle Col, NY; Smithsonian Inst, Washington, DC; La Monte Dougherty Geol Observ. *Comn:* Undersea murals, Caravelle Hotel, St Croix, VI & Hotel Bonaire, Dutch W Indies. *Exhib:* The White House, Washington DC; Wash Co Mus Fine Arts; Children's Mus, Brooklyn, NY; Maritime Col; Yonkers Mus, NY; Brooklyn Col. *Teaching:* Instr art appreciation & painting, Brooklyn Tech; instr painting, Educ Alliance. *Awards:* Allied Artists; Audubon Artists. *Mem:* Am Watercolor Soc; Allied Artists Am; League of Present Day Artists; Audubon Artists; Nat Soc Painters in Casein; plus others. *Media:* Casein, Acrylic; Brass, Plastics. *Mailing Add:* 1270 E 19th St No 5L Brooklyn NY 11230

KURAHARA, TED N
PAINTER, EDUCATOR
b Seattle, Wash, July 16, 25. *Study:* St Louis Sch Fine Arts, Washington Univ, with Paul Burlin, BFA, 51; Bradley Univ, Peoria, Ill, with Leon Engers, MA, 52. *Work:* NY Univ, New York; Des Moines Art Ctr, Iowa; Springfield Art Ctr, Ill; Univ Sidney, Australia; Brooklyn Mus; Huntington Gallery, WVa; and others. *Exhib:* Occidental Col, Los Angeles, 80; Woodside-Braseth Gallery, Seattle, 80; Anders Tornberg, Lund, Sweden, 81, 84 & 91; Leif Stahle Gallery, Paris, France, 87; Anita Shapolsky Gallery, NY, 87, 90 & 92; and others. *Teaching:* Prof art, Grad Fine Art, Pratt Inst, Brooklyn, NY; assoc prof art, Pratt Inst, Brooklyn, 70-, chairperson painting & drawing dept, 80-83. *Awards:* Yaddo Fel, 78; Guggenheim Found Grant, 85; Nat Endowment Arts Grant, 86. *Bibliog:* Donald B Kuspit (auth), Kuraharas Paintings, 84; J Sans (auth), A propos du travail de Kurahara, L'oeilk, Paris. *Media:* Acrylic, Mixed Media. *Dealer:* Anita Shapolsky Gallery New York NY; Anders Tornberg Gallery Lund Sweden. *Mailing Add:* 78 Greene St New York NY 10012

KURHAJEC, JOSEPH A
SCULPTOR
b Racine, Wis, Oct 13, 38. *Study:* Univ Wis, BS, 60, MFA, 62. *Work:* New Sch Social Res, New York; Espanol Mus Contemp Art, Madrid, Spain; Mus Mod Art, New York; Chicago Art Inst; Walker Art Ctr, Minneapolis, Minn. *Comn:* Bronze cone, Allan Stone, Purchase, NY, 71; bronze sculpture, Norman Shaifer, Brooklyn Heights, NY, 71. *Exhib:* Am Fedn Art Traveling Exhib, 64; Sculpture Ann, Whitney Mus Am Art, New York, 64, Young America, 65; Espanol Mus Contemp Art, 69; Ten Independents, Guggenheim Mus, New York, 72; Basel Art, 76. *Teaching:* Asst prof, Cornell Univ, 65-66; asst prof, Newark Sch Indust & Fine Art, 67-69; asst prof, Univ Wis-Stout, 71-73, State Univ NY, New Paltz, 73-74, Lo Studiolo, Rome, 74-83. *Awards:* Int Fur Designers Award, 83. *Mem:* Sculptors Guild, New York. *Mailing Add:* 178 Rue Raymond Losserand Apt 3104 Paris 75014 France

KURKA, DONALD FRANK
PAINTER, ADMINISTRATOR
b Chicago, Ill, July 29, 30. *Study:* Syracuse Univ, BFA, 52; Art Inst Chicago, MFA, 56; NY Univ, PhD, 68. *Comn:* IBM; Hosp Corp Am; Hilton Hotels; Stouffers, Tenn Valley Authority. *Exhib:* Contemporary Prints, Libr Cong, 55; solo exhib, McClung Mus, Univ Tenn, Knoxville, 78; Hunter Mus, Chattanooga, Tenn, 81 & Here & Now,Greenville Cty Mus Art, SC, 89; Southern Realism, Miss Mus Art, Jackson, 80 & Montgomery Mus Art, 80; Cheekwoon Fine Arts Ctr, Nashville, Tenn, 87; Mus Art, Evansville, Ind, 88; Biennial V, Birmingham Mus Art, Ala, 89; Phobias, print show, Reece Mus, Tenn, 89. *Teaching:* Prof painting, Southampton Ctr, Long Island Univ, 69-77, dir, Div Fine Arts, 73-77; prof & head dept art, Univ Tenn, Knoxville, 77- *Awards:* Vandergrift Award, Art Inst Chicago, 55; Founders Day Award, NY Univ, 68; Best in Show, Long Island Painters, Hecksher Mus, 73; Art-in-residence, Univ of Ga, Study abroad prog, Cortuna, Italy, fall, 90. *Mem:* Nat Coun Art Adminr; Nat Asn Schs Art & Design; Col Art Asn. *Media:* Acrylic, Oil. *Publ:* Auth, Fact, Fiction, Fantasy-Exhib Catalog essay, Ewing Gallery, Univ Tenn, 87. *Dealer:* A R T S Inc Nashville Tenn; E C May & Co Washington DC. *Mailing Add:* 622 Buttonwood Dr Longboat Key FL 34228-2904

KURLANDER, HONEY W
PAINTER, INSTRUCTOR
b Brooklyn, NY. *Study:* Parsons Sch Design; NY Univ; Pratt Inst, Brooklyn, BA. *Work:* De Seversky Conf Ctr, Greenvale, NY; Dietz Mus, Wasserberg, Ger; C W Post Col Art Ctr, Brookville, NY; Gregory Mus Traveling Collection, Hicksville, NY; Reddon Collection, Paris, France. *Comn:* Western scenes of horses & oil drilling, Rotan-Mosle, Tulsa, Okla, 81; Waldorf Astoria, NY & Stanford Ct, Calif, Hospitality Valuation Serv Inc, Mineola, NY, 83-87; Roslyn, Turn of the Century (2 murals), Jolly Fisherman, Roslyn, NY, 84; Fulton Street Ferry Landing (mural), Thomas M Quinn & Sons Inc, Astoria, NY, 85; Centennial Celebration of the Statue of Liberty, Dietz Art Ltd, New York, 86. *Exhib:* Long Island Artists, The Heckscher Mus, Huntington, NY, 66-68; Exposition Intercontinental, The Palace, Monaco, 65; Traveling Art Exhib, Gregory Mus, Hicksville, NY, 70-; solo exhib, Adelphi Univ, Alumni House Gallery, Garden City, NY, 77; First International Art Competition, Am Artist Mag, Marion, Ohio, 78; NLAPW Nat Exhib, Goethe Hall, Sacramento, Calif, 78; Exhib of Oil Paintings, Salmagundi Club, New York, 78; Celebration of the Arts, Nassau Mus Fine Art, Roslyn, NY, 83. *Pos:* Freelance textile designer, 49-58; Freelance children's bk illustr, 50-60. *Teaching:* Instr, painting, E Meadow High Sch, New York, 58-60 & Kurlander Studio, Old Westbury, NY, 59- *Awards:* Best of Show, Malverne Artists 28th Ann, Greenwich Savings Bank, 72; Best of show, NY State Juried Art Exhib, Lever House, 87; Best of show, C W Post, 90. *Bibliog:* Tom Cullen (auth), Looking back-the art of success, Long Island Com Rev, 9/72; Jeanne Paris (auth), Many faces of nature, Newsday, 9/79; Malcolm Preston (auth), Two definitely modern realists, Newsday, 4/84. *Mem:* Nat League Am Penwomen; Salmagundi Club; Art League Nassau Co. *Media:* Acrylic, Oil. *Dealer:* Robley Gallery Old Northern Blvd Roslyn NY 11576; Garden City Galleries Ltd 923 Franklin Ave Garden City NY 11530. *Mailing Add:* 6 Kings Dr Old Westbury NY 11568

KURTZ, BRUCE D
HISTORIAN, CURATOR
b Bozeman, Mont, May 18, 43. *Study:* San Francisco Art Inst, BFA, 64; Univ Iowa, MA, 66, MFA, 67. *Collections Arranged:* El Arte Narrativo (with catalog), 85; Altered Egos : Samaras, Sherman, Wegmanm (auth, catalog); American Art of the 1980's: Eli & Edythe Broad Collection (auth, catalog); New Narrative Painting: Metropolitan Museum of Art Collection, Four Contemporary Mexican Painters (auth, catalog), 86; Postmodern Visions in American Architecture, 86; Keith Haring, Andy Warhol & Walt Disney, 91; Phoenix Art Mus, Ariz. *Pos:* Cur 20th Century art, Phoenix Art Mus, Ariz, 85- *Teaching:* Instr art hist, Southern Ill Univ, 67-69; assoc prof art hist, Hartwick Col, Oneonta, NY, 69-85. *Awards:* Art Critic's Fel Grant, Nat Endowment Arts, 75 & 76. *Mem:* Nat Arts Club; Asn Int Critiques Art (Am sect). *Res:* International contemporary art. *Publ:* Contribr, Video Art, Harcourt-Brace Jovonovich, 76; auth, Spots: The Popular Art of American Television Commercials, Arts Commun, 77; contribr, The writings of Robert Smithson, NY Univ Press, 79; auth, Paikvision, Artforum, 10/82; Visual Imagination: An Introduction to Art, 87 & Contemporary Art, Prentice-Hall, 65-90, 92; and numerous essays in art periodicals. *Mailing Add:* 1625 N Central Ave Phoenix AZ 85004

KURTZ, ELAINE
PAINTER
b Philadelphia, Pa, June 10, 28. *Study:* Philadelphia Col Art, BA, 50; Barnes Found, Merion, Pa, 64-65. *Work:* Philadelphia Mus Art, Pa; Hirshhorn Mus & Sculpture Garden, Washington, DC; Portland Mus Art, Portland, Maine; Nat Mus Am Art, Washington, DC; Herbert Johnson Mus Art, Cornell Univ. *Exhib:* solo exhibs, Osuna Gallery, Washington, DC, 80, 82, 84 & 88, Rosenthal Fine Arts Ltd, Chicago, 85 & Gross McCleaf Gallery, Philadelphia, 86, 88 & 91; 10 Year Anniversary, Herbert F Johnson Mus, Ithaca, NY, 83; Pertaining to Philadelphia, Philadelphia Mus Art, 84; Selections from the Martha Jackson Memorial Collection (with catalog), Nat Mus Am Art, 85; Anita Shapolsky Gallery, New York, 87 & 90; Inaugural Exhib, Part I & Part II, Anderson Gallery, Buffalo, NY, 91; and others. *Awards:* Silver Star Alumni Award for Painting, Philadelphia Col Art, 77. *Bibliog:* Judith Stein (auth), Elaine Kurtz, Arts Mag, 78; Jo Ann Lewis (auth), Abstracts by Elaine Kurtz, Wash Post, 82; Maximum Impact Minimalism, Wash Post, 88. *Media:* Acrylic on Canvas, Mixed Media on Canvas. *Dealer:* Gross McCleaf Gallery Philadelphia PA; Osuna Gallery Washington DC. *Mailing Add:* 17 E 16th St 8th Floor New York NY 10003

KURYLUK, EWA
PAINTER, SCULPTOR
b Cracow, Poland, May 5, 46. *Study:* Acad Fine Arts, Warsaw, MFA & MA, 70. *Work:* Bibliotheque Nationale, Paris; Graphische Sammlung Albertina, Vienna, Austria; Nat Mus, Warsaw, Poland; Kettle's Yard Mus, Cambridge, Eng; Bass Mus Art, Miami Beach, Fla. *Comn:* Wall piece, Fels Nat Humanities Ctr, Res Triangle Park, NC, 89. *Exhib:* Textile Sculpture, Mus des Beaux Arts, Lausanne, Switz, 85; 40th Int Festival, Richard Demarco Gallery Edinburgh, 86; Membranes of Memory, Centro de Arte y Comunicacion, Buenos Aires, 86; Fourth Int Triennale Drawing, Mus Archit, Wroclaw, Poland, 88; Polish Women Artists and the Avant-garde, Nat Mus Women in Arts, Washington, DC, 91; and others. *Pos:* Ed, Cashiers Littéraíres, Paris, 82- & Formations, 83- *Teaching:* Prof acad film, Lodz, 79-80, Inst Applied Theater Sci, Giesseh, WGer, 86, New Sch, New York, 88- & Univ Calif San Diego, 92. *Awards:* Rockefeller Fel, Nat Humanities Ctr, 88; Bronze Medal, 4th Int Triennale Drawing, 88; Asian Cult Coun Fel for Japan, 91. *Bibliog:* Grace Glueck (auth), Ewa Kuryluk, NY Times, 4/13/84; Jan Kott, E White & E Grabeka (coauths), The fabric of memory, Ewa Kuryluk: Cloth works 1978-1987, Formations, 87. *Mem:* Int Art Critics Asn; PEN. *Media:* All Media, Cloth. *Mailing Add:* 504 W 110 St Apt 3A New York NY 10025

KURZ, DIANA
PAINTER, EDUCATOR
b Vienna, Austria; US citizen. *Study:* Brandeis Univ, BA(fine arts, cum laude); Columbia Univ, MFA(painting). *Work:* Corcoran Gallery Art, Washington, DC; Rose Art Mus, Brandeis Univ, Mass; Brooklyn Botanic Garden, Brooklyn, NY. *Comn:* Mural, comn by Howard Finkelstin, New York, 85. *Exhib:* Brooklyn Mus, 75; solo exhibs, Snug Harbor Cult Ctr, 82, Rider Col, 84, Alex Rosenberg Gallery, New York, 84, Palais de Justice, Aix-En-Provence, France, 86, Mercer Co Community Col, 90 & Thomas Ctr Gallery, Gainesville, Fla, 91; A M Sachs Gallery, New York, 83; Ingber Gallery, New York, 85; Transco Gallery, Houston, 88; Koslow/Rayl Gallery, Los Angeles, 88; group exhib, Grand Central Gallery, New York, 89, USSR Artists Union Gallery, Moscow, 90; and others. *Teaching:* Lectr drawing, Philadelphia Col Art, 68-73; adj lectr art, Queens Col, NY, 71-76; vis prof art, Pratt Inst, 73; vis asst prof, Univ Colo, 78; vis asst prof art, State Univ NY Stony Brook, 79; vis artist painting, Va Commonwealth Univ, 80; vis artist painting, Cleveland Inst Art, 80-81, Sch Art Inst Chicago, 87, Oxbow Sch Art, Mich 88 & Vermont Studio Ctr, 90. *Awards:* Fulbright Grant to France, 65-66; Creative Artists Pub Serv Grant, 77; MacDowell Fel, 77; Am Ctr Residency, Paris, 85-86. *Bibliog:* Lawrence Alloway (auth), catalog, Queens Col, 72; Sandra Langer (auth), Arts Mag, 2/84; Lawrence Campbell, Art in Am, 5/84. *Mem:* Women's Caucus Art; Col Art Asn. *Media:* Oil, Watercolor. *Publ:* Mother Massage, Dell Publ, 92. *Mailing Add:* 152 Wooster St New York NY 10012

KUSAMA, YAYOI
SCULPTOR, PAINTER
b Matsumoto City, Japan, 29; US citizen. *Study:* Art Students League, New York, 57; Kyoto Arts & Crafts Sch, Japan, 59. *Work:* Chrysler Mus, Provincetown, Mass; Stedelijk Mus, Amsterdam. *Exhib:* Solo exhibs, Fuji Television Gallery, Tokyo, 84, Missoni Boutique, Yura Kucho-Marion Seibu, Tokyo, 85, Tamagawa-Takashimaya, Tokyo, 86, Musee Municipal Dole, 87, Soul Burning Flashes, Fuju Gallery, 88, Ctr Int Contemp Art, New York, 90 & Oxford Mus, Eng, 90; Le Japon des Avantgarde, Centre Georges Pompidou, Paris, 86; Japanese Art Today, San Diego Mus, 86; Opening Show, Meguro Mus Art, Tokyo, 87; Objet, Tsukashin Hall, Osaka, 87; Second Int Contemp Art Fair, Los Angeles, 88; Chicago Int Art Expos, 88; Art-Kites Traveling Show, 88-92; and many others. *Pos:* Pres & founder, Japan Ed Co, 77- *Publ:* Publ, Between Heaven and Earth, 88; Woodstock Phallus Cutter, 88. *Mailing Add:* c/o Ctr Contemp Arts 724 Fifth Ave New York NY 10019

KUSHNER, DOROTHY BROWDY
PAINTER, PRINTMAKER
b Kansas City, Mo. *Study:* Kansas City Teachers Col, BS, 37; Columbia Univ, MA, 38; Art Students League; Art Inst Chicago; Kansas City Art Inst. *Work:* Pasadena Art Mus; Univ Ill; Va Mus Fine Arts; Los Angeles Cedars-Sinai Collection; Palmcrest House, Long Beach. *Exhib:* Libr of Cong, 60; Boston Mus Fine Arts, 65; Calif State Fair, 69; Nat Acad Design, 71; Nat Watercolor Soc, 72-83; Santa Monica Libr Gallery, 85. *Teaching:* Instr art, Kansas City Pub Schs, Grover Cleveland High Sch, New York, 40-46 & Pasadena City Col, 69- *Awards:* Laguna Beach Art Asn; Nat Watercolor Soc, 70 & 79; Pasadena Soc Artists Award, 70. *Mem:* Am Color Print Soc; Nat Watercolor Soc; Los Angeles Art Asn; Laguna Beach Art Asn; Pasadena Soc Artists. *Media:* Acrylic, Watercolor. *Mailing Add:* 1447 17th St No 1 Santa Monica CA 90404

KUSHNER, ROBERT ELLIS
PAINTER
b Pasadena, Calif, Aug 19, 49. *Study:* Univ Calif, San Diego, BA. *Work:* Brooklyn Mus, NY; Denver Art Mus, Colo; Mus Moderner Kunst, Palais Leichtenstein, Vienna; Tate Gallery, London, Eng; Whitney Mus Art, Mus Mod Art, Metrop Mus Art, New York; Philadelphia Mus Art; Milwaukee Art Mus; Los Angeles Co Mus Art; Kitakyushu Mus, Japan. *Exhib:* Whitney Ann, Whitney Mus Am Art, 75, 81 & 85; Sentimental Fables, Mus Mod Art, New York, 81; raveling, Inst Contemp Art, Boston, 83; Made In America: 200 Years of Drawing, Minneapolis Inst Arts, Minn, 83; Contemp Figuration, Art Adv Serv Exhib, Mus Mod Art, New York, 84; A New Beginning, Hudson River Mus, New York, 85; Galleria Capricorni, Venice, Italy, 85, Galerie Rudolf Zwirner, Koln, Ger, 86 & 88, Retrospective: ICA, Philadelphia, Pa, Speed Mus, Louisville, Aspen Art Mus, 87-88; Homage to Mozart, Galerie Ropac, Salizburg, Austria, 85, Connecticut Collects: American Art Since 1960, Whitney Mus, Conn, 86; Americana, Groniger Mus, The Netherlands, 87; Early Concepts of the Last Decade, Holly Solomon Gallery, New York, 87; Wichita Art Mus, 88; and others. *Bibliog:* Vicky Alliata (auth), Da New York la moda erotica e assurda di Bob Kushner, Luomo, 4/74; Amy Goldin (auth), The new Whitney Biennial: pattern emerging?, Art in Am, 5/75; Douglas Blau (auth), Robert Kushner, Flashart, 1-2/80; Georg Jappe (auth), Just for survive, Kunstforum Int, 5/83; Dan Cameron (auth), A Whitney wonderland, Arts Mag, summer 85; Roberta Smith (auth), Early Concepts of the Last Decade at Holly Solomon Gallery, The NY Times, 9/25/87 plus many others. *Media:* Oil, Bronze. *Publ:* Contribr, Dimensions of Black, 70; Unnatural Acts 5, Unnatural Acts Press, 74; The Wonnerful World of Food, Sweet 16 Press, 78; The New York Hat Line, Bozeaux of London Press, 79 & Persian Poems, 81; and others. *Dealer:* Holly Solomon Gallery 724 Fifth Ave New York NY 10019. *Mailing Add:* 17 E 16th St New York NY 10003

KUSNERZ, PEGGY ANN F
LIBRARIAN, EDUCATOR
b Detroit, Mich, Jan 12, 47. *Study:* Univ Mich, BA(art hist), 71, MLS, 71, MA(Am cult), 82, PhD(am cult), 92. *Collections Arranged:* Images of Old Age 1790 to Present (coauth, catalog), SITES Exhib, 79. *Pos:* Head libr exten serv & mus libr, Univ Mich, 72-80, head art, archit libr & computer lab, 80- *Teaching:* American Culture: Research Methods, Univ of Mich. *Mem:* Art Libr Soc NAm; Asn Archit Sch Librns; Am Studies Asn; Soc Photog Educators. *Res:* History of photography; art & architecture libraries; art bibliography. *Interests:* History of photography & panoramic photography. *Publ:* Auth, Selection and acquisition of slides in special libraries, Picturescope, 72; Elsa Fuller: Perceptions of another era, Chronicle, Mich, 74; Oral history, 79 & Collection evaluation techniques in academic art library, 83, Drexel Libr Quart; ed, Architecture Library of the Future, Ann Arbor Univ of Mich Press, 89. *Mailing Add:* 804 Sycamore Ann Arbor MI 48104

KUSPIT, DONALD BURTON
HISTORIAN, CRITIC
b New York, NY, Mar 26, 35. *Study:* Columbia Univ, BA; Yale Univ, MA(philos); Univ Frankfurt, PhD; Pa State Univ, MA(art); Univ Mich, PhD(art hist). *Pos:* Contrib ed, Artforum; ed, Art Criticism, currently; contrib ed, Contemporanea, Wolkenkratzer; ed bd, Centennial Review & Sculpture Now. *Teaching:* Prof art, State Univ NY Stony Brook, 78- *Awards:* Can Coun Leave Fel, 68-69; Nat Endowment Humanities Younger Humanist Fel, 73-74; Guggenheim Mem fel, 77-78. *Mem:* Col Art Asn Am; Am Soc Aesthet. *Res:* Modern art and contemporary criticism. *Publ:* Auth, The new subjectivism art in the 1980s (UMI Res Press), 88; Louise Bourgeois, Random House, 88; Alex Katz at Night, Abrams, 90; The Cult of the Avant-garde Artist, Cambridge Univ Press, 93; Primordial Presences: The Sculpture of Karel Appel, Abrams, 93; & others. *Mailing Add:* Dept Art State Univ NY Stony Brook NY 11794

KUTNER, JANET
CRITIC, WRITER
b Sept 20, 37; US citizen. *Study:* Stanford Univ, 55-57; Southern Meth Univ, BA, 59. *Pos:* art critic, Dallas Morning News, 70- *Awards:* Art Critics Award, Nat Endowment Arts, 76-77; Art Critics Fel, Nat Gallery Art, 91. *Mem:* Am Asn Mus; Int Coun Mus; Art Table. *Publ:* Coauth, David McManaway, Contemp Art Mus, Houston, 73; auth, James Surls, Tyler Mus Art, 74; various reviews of Texas exhibits for Artnews Mag, 75- *Mailing Add:* Dallas Morning News Communs Ctr Dallas TX 75265

KUVSHINOFF, BERTHA HORNE
PAINTER, SCULPTOR
b Dunganess, Wash, Aug 29, 15. *Work:* Tacoma Art Mus, Wash; Phoenix Art Mus, Ariz; Evansville Art Mus, Ind; Eureka Col Mus, Ill; Miami Art Mus, Fla. *Exhib:* Seattle Russian Ctr, 66; Cath Ctr Gallery, Baltimore, Md, 67; Edmonds Art Gallery, Wash, 70; Eureka Col Gallery, Ill, 71; Int Depeinture, Paris. *Awards:* Silver Medal, 70 & Gold Medal, 71, Acad Int Tommasso Companelia, Rome, Italy. *Bibliog:* Visual Arts, Seattle Times, 7/30/70; article, Roanoke Rev, 9/23/71; Hartland of Nebraska Living, Grand Island Independent, 4/1/72; plus others. *Media:* Oil. *Mailing Add:* 121 1/2 Yale Ave N Seattle WA 98109

KUVSHINOFF, NICOLAI
PAINTER, SCULPTOR
b Siberia, Russia, Dec 19, 10; US citizen. *Work:* Seattle Art Mus, Wash; Atlanta Art Mus, Ga; Omaha Art Mus, Nebr; Santa Fe Art Mus, NMex; Tacoma Art Mus, Wash. *Exhib:* Novikoff Found Fine Arts, Seattle, 61-72; Hutzler's Westview Exhib Hall, Baltimore, Md, 65 & 67; Tacoma Allied Arts, Wash, 66; Seattle Russian Ctr, 66; Stuhr Mus, Grand Island, Nebr, 72; Tacoma Art Mus, Wash; Lima Mus Mod Art, Peru. *Awards:* Silver Medal, 70 & Gold Medal, 72, Acad Int Tommasso Campanella, Rome, Italy. *Bibliog:* Articles in Int Herald Tribune & Le Monde, Paris, 57 & Art News, New York, 60, plus others. *Media:* All. *Publ:* Auth, Art Book, Libr Cong, Washington, DC, 59; Drawings, 66. *Mailing Add:* 121 1/2 Yale Ave N Seattle WA 98109

KUWAYAMA, GEORGE
CURATOR, HISTORIAN
b New York, NY, Feb 25, 25. *Study:* Williams Col, BA; Inst Fine Arts, NY Univ; Univ Mich, MA. *Collections Arranged:* Arts Treasures from Japan (auth, catalog), 65; Contemporary Japanese Prints (auth, catalog), 72; Ceramics of Southeast Asia (auth, catalog), 72; Ancient Ritual Bronzes of China (auth, catalog), 76; Chinese Jade from Southern California Collections (auth, catalog), 77; Chinese Ceramics: The Heeramaneck Collection (auth, catalog), 73; The Joy of Collecting: Far Eastern Art from the Lidow Collection (auth, catalog), 80; The Bizarre Imagery of Yoshitoshi (auth, catalog), 80; Far Eastern Lacquer (auth, catalog), 82; Japanese Ink Painting (auth, catalog), 85; Shippo: The Art of Enameling in Japan (auth, catalog), 87; The Quest for Eternity: The Sculptural Development of Ceramic Funerary Figures in China (ed & contribr), 87; Imperial Taste: Chinese Ceramics from the Percival David Foundation, The significance of Chinese Ceramics in the East and West (ed & contribr), 89; Ancient Mortuary Traditions of China (ed), 91; New Perspectives on the Art of Ceramics in China (ed), 92. *Pos:* Cur Oriental art, Los Angeles Co Mus Art, 59-63, sr cur Far Eastern art, 63- *Teaching:* Instr Chinese painting, Univ Calif, Los Angeles, 62; instr Far Eastern painting, Univ Southern Calif, 63. *Awards:* Freer Fel, Univ Mich, 55; Hackney Fel, Am Oriental Soc, 56; Inter-Univ Fel, Ford Found, 57. *Mem:* Asn Asian Studies; Chinese Art Soc; Japan Soc; Int House Japan; Col Art Asn. *Res:* Far Eastern art and archaeology. *Publ:* The Korean celadon, Vol III, No 3 & Korean art in Western collections: The collection of Robert Moore, Vol IV, No 1, Korean Culture; Object of the month: Chinese carved lacquer tray in the Los Angeles County Museum of Art, Orientations, Vol XIV, No 7; The Great Bronze Age of China: A Symposium, Los Angeles Co Mus Art, 83; Archaeological Objects, Ceramics and Lacquer Works, Arts of Asia, 3-4/89; Beauty and Utility: the Lacquered Baskets of China, Orientations, 11-12/89. *Mailing Add:* Los Angeles Co Mus Art 5905 Wilshire Blvd Los Angeles CA 90036

KUWAYAMA, TADAAKI
PAINTER
b Nagoya, Japan, Mar 4, 32. *Study:* Tokyo Univ Art, BFA, 56. *Work:* Albright-Knox Art Gallery, Buffalo, NY; Worcester Art Mus, Mass; Wadsworth Atheneum, Hartford, Conn; Larry Aldrich Mus, Ridgefield, Conn; Herron Art Mus, Indianapolis. *Exhib:* Carnegie Int, Pittsburgh, 61-67; Formalist Show, Washington Gallery Mod Art, Washington, DC, 63; Systemic Show, Guggenheim Mus, New York, 66; New Forms & Shapes of Color, Stedelijk Mus, Amsterdam, 67; Plus by Minus, Today's Half-Century, Albright-Knox Art Gallery, 68. *Awards:* Nat Coun Arts Grant, 69; Adolph & Esther Gottlieb Found Grant, 86. *Media:* Acrylic, Oil. *Mailing Add:* 136 W 24th St New York NY 10011

KWAK, HOON
PAINTER
b Seoul, Korea, July 9, 41; US citizen. *Study:* Fine Art Col, Seoul Nat Univ, BFA, 63; Calif State Univ, Los Angeles, MA, 80, Long Beach, MFA, 82. *Work:* Security Pac Nat Bank, Los Angeles; Exec Life Insurance, Los Angeles; Mod Art Mus, Seoul, Korea; Manatt, Phelps, Rothenberg & Tunney Co, Los Angeles; Bear Stearns & Co, Los Angeles. *Comn:* Paintings, Conrad Hilton, Chicago, 85 & Compri Hotel, Aurora, Colo, 85. *Exhib:* Spokane Nat exhib, Cheney Cowles Mem Mus, Spokane, 81; 6 Artists, Nagasaki Prefecture Mus, Nagasaki, Japan, 81; 61st Nat Watercolor Soc exhib, Palm Springs, Calif, 81; New Comers, 81 & Only Los Angeles, 86, Los Angeles Municipal Art Gallery; Show-1 Winter, 81, Additional Space Expose V, 82 & 1 To 1, 85, Rental Gallery, Los Angeles County Mus Art. *Awards:* Purchase Award, Minot State Col, NDak, 81; Past Pres Award, Nat Watercolor Soc, 81; Invitational Exhib Award, Pensacola Col, 82. *Media:* Acrylic, Oil. *Mailing Add:* 1 Coveview Dr Ranch Palos Verdes CA 90247

KWIECINSKI, CHESTER MARTIN
EDUCATOR, PAINTER
b Youngstown, Ohio, July 7, 24. *Study:* Kansas City Art Inst, BFA & MFA; Kansas City Univ; Youngstown Univ. *Work:* Butler Inst Am Art, Youngstown, Ohio; El Paso Mus of Art, Tex. *Comn:* Historical murals, McSorley Colonial, Pittsburgh, Pa, 54; murals (with Bill Rakocy), Colonial House and Congo Rm, Youngstown, Ohio, 60 & Alberini Restaurant, Niles, Ohio, 65. *Exhib:* Mo State Fair, 49 & 50; Albright-Knox Gallery Art, Buffalo, NY, 52; El Paso Regional show, 76; one-man show, Butler Inst Art, Youngstown Ohio, 62. *Pos:* Mus dir, Abilene Fine Arts Mus, Tex, 73-80. *Teaching:* Instr, Warren City Schs, Ohio, 54-66; assoc prof painting, Col of Artesia, NMex, 67-71. *Awards:* Best Local Art, New Year Show, Butler Inst Am Art, 42; Purchase Award, Carlsbad Art Asn, NMex, 68; Purchase Award, Hobbs-LLano Estacado, Hobbs Art Asn, NMex, 69. *Mem:* Am Asn Mus; Tex Asn Mus; Permian Basin Mus Asn, 78. *Media:* Watercolor, Oil. *Publ:* Guest art ed, Abilene Reporter News, 74; auth, articles, Pigment & Form, 64. *Mailing Add:* 4010 Potomac Abilene TX 79605

KWONG, EVA
SCULPTOR, CERAMIST
b Hong Kong, Feb 9, 54. *Study:* Oxbow Summer Sch Painting, Saugatuck, Mich, 74; RI Sch Design, Providence, BFA, 75; Tyler Sch Art, Temple Univ, MFA, 77. *Work:* Cranbrook Art Mus, Bloomfield Hills, Mich; Finnish Craft Mus, Helsinki, Finland; Butler Inst Am Art, Youngstown, Ohio; Slippery Rock State Univ, Pa. *Exhib:* One-woman shows, The Clay Place, Pittsburgh, 77 & 81, Gallery II, Wash State Univ, Pullman, 79, Pittsburgh Ctr for the Arts, 85, Univ Akron, Ohio, 86, Eells Art Gallery, Blossom Music Ctr, Cuyahoga Falls, Ohio, 87 & Ill Wesleyan Univ, Bloomington, Ill, 90; Anagama Exhib, Hunterdon Art Ctr, Clinton, NJ, 81; Teabowl Invitational, The Craft Alliance, St Louis, 84; Gummeson Gallery, Stockholm, Sweden, 86; Eccentric Visions, Xavier Univ, Cincinnati, 90; All Ohio Show, Canton Art Inst, Canton, Ohio, 90; Couples, Soc Contemp Crafts, 91, The Clay Place, Pittsburgh, Pa, 92; Evasive Vase, 91, 100 Cups Invitational, 92, Teapots: Contemp View, PRO Art, St Louis, Mo, 92; All Ohio Award Winners, Lakeside Gallery, Mich, 91; Dramatic Expressions, Cain Park Art Gallery, 91, Robert Mihaly, Eva Kwong, Don Harvey, Busta Gallery, Cleveland, Ohio, 91; Am Wood Fire '91, Univ Iowa Mus Art (catalog), Iowa City, 91; Kirk Mangus, Eva Kwong, Sybaris Gallery, Royal Oak, Mich, 91; For the House & Garden, Pewabic Pottery, Detroit, Mich, 92; Ceramics Invitational, Ind Univ Pa, 92; Tyler Sch Art Ceramics Alumni Exhib, 92, Archie Bray Found Benefit, Owen/Patrick Gallery, Philadelphia, Pa, 92; Made in Ohio, Bowling Green State Univ, Ohio, 92; Lill St Gallery, Navy Pier, Chicago, Ill, 91 & 92. *Teaching:* Grad teaching assistanship, Tyler Sch Art, Philadelphia, 75-77; instr, Spokane Falls Community Col, Spokane, Wash, 80 & Pittsburgh Arts Ctr Arts, 80; instr for numerous drawing & ceramic workshops throughout US & abroad. *Awards:* Arts Midwest, Nat Endowment Arts Regional Fel, 87; Ohio Arts Coun Fel, 88; Nat Endowment Arts, 88. *Bibliog:* Bruce Metcalf (auth), Eva Kwong (rev), Am Ceramics, Vol 5, No 3, 54; Michael Jones (auth), Eva Kwong (article), Dialogue, Jan/Feb, 86; article, Monthly Craft Mag, Seoul, Korea, Vol 1, No 9, 54-55, 11/88. *Media:* Clay, Paper. *Dealer:* William Busta Gallery 2021 Murray Hill Rd Cleveland OH 44106; Sybaris Gallery 301 W Fourth St Royal Oak MI 48067. *Mailing Add:* 320 Rellim Dr Kent OH 44240

KYRA
ENVIRONMENTAL ARTIST, PAINTER
b China, Apr 22, 47; US citizen. *Study:* Ariz State Univ, BFA, 73; Fla State Univ, MFA, 75. *Work:* Southern Regional Courthouse, Hollywood, Fla; Art & Cult Ctr Hollywood, Fla; Bass Mus Art, Miami Beach. *Comn:* Drawing (color pencil), Broward Co Art in PP, Ft Lauderdale, 81; drawing, site specific sculpture, Metro-Dade Art in Pub Places, Fla, 86. *Exhib:* Prof Women Artists Fla, Lowe Art Mus, Coral Gables, 76; Women's Mus, Lincoln Ctr, New York, 77; 23rd Ann M Allen Hortt Mem Competition & Exhib, Mus Art, Ft Lauderdale, Fla, 82; one-person exhibs, The Magic Circle Series 1978-1985, Nova Univ, 85, Great American Goddess Coatlicue, 85, In Quest of the American Goddess Coatlicue, 86 & Sun Goddess: Emergence of Myth, 86, Broward Community Col, Great Goddess Chicomecoatl, Art & Cult Ctr, Hollywood, Fla, 87, Cosmic Goddess Chiocomecoatl/Demeter, Dupont Gallery, Washington & Lee Univ, Va, 88, Great Goddess Rhea, Malia, Crete, Greece, 88, Great Goddess Chicomecoatl/Shakti, Rim Inst, Payson, Ala, 88; and many others. *Pos:* Pres, Coalition Women's Art Orgn, 85-89, vpres 89-; pres, Southeastern Women's Caucus Art, 85-90. *Teaching:* Prof art, Broward Community Col, 76- *Awards:* Outstanding Artist SE, Am Art-SE Mag, 78; Fla Arts Coun Fel Grant, Tallahassee, 82; Barbara Deming Mem Fund Grant, 86; and others. *Bibliog:* Alessandra Comini (auth), The Hierarchy in Art and Art History, WAN, 83; Eleanor Tufts (auth), American Women Artists, Garland Publ, 84; Patrice Wynn (auth), The Womanspirit Sourcebook, Harper & Row, 88; Gloria Orenstein (auth), The Reflowering of the Goddess, Pergamon Press, 90. *Mem:* Col Art Asn Am; Women's Caucus Art (nat, regional vpres, 84-86 & Miami chap, presently); Fla Asn Community Col. *Media:* Performance Art, Site-specific Sculpture. *Publ:* The Magic Circle Goddess series, Women of Power, spring 87; article, New Renaissance, 88; article, Cathartic, spring 88; auth, Censored: The male nude, Women Artists News, 83; Estella Lauter (auth), Women as Mythmakers Revisited, Quandrant Vol XXIII, No 1, 90; and others. *Mailing Add:* PO Box 6735 Hollywood FL 33021

L

LABAT, TONY
CONCEPTUAL ARTIST, SCULPTOR
b Nov 14, 51. *Study:* San Francisco Art Inst, BFA, 78, MFA, 80. *Work:* Mus Mod Art, New York; George Pompidou, Paris, France; Long Beach Mus Art, Calif; Newport Harbor Art Mus, Newport Beach, Calif; Open Heim Collection, Bonn, Ger. *Comn:* Installations, Works Progress Admin, Washington, 85, Capp St Proj, San Francisco, 87 & Mus Contemp Art, Los Angeles, 88. *Exhib:* American Art of the late 80's traveling exhib, Boston & Europe, 88; Fuller-Gross Gallery, San Francisco, Calif, 88; Bay Area Media, San Francisco Mus Mod Art, 90; Idealist, Ingrid Raab Gallery, Berlin, 90. *Teaching:* Prof performance/video, San Francisco Art Inst, 85-; prof media, Univ Calif, San Diego, 86-87. *Awards:* Grant, Nat Endowment Arts, 87; Fleishhacker Found Grant, 87; Engelhard Award, Boston, 88; Asn Visual Artists. *Bibliog:* Jan Butterfield (auth), Object Poem, Henry Art Gallery, 86; Alfred Jan (auth), A Critique of Culture, High Performance, 87; Carlo McCormick (auth), Tony Labat, Artspace, 87. *Media:* Performance, Video. *Mailing Add:* 880 Jamestown San Francisco CA 94124

LABLE, ELIOT
SCULPTOR
b Apr 24, 37. *Study:* New Sch, 70-73; Brooklyn Mus Art Sch, 72-73. *Exhib:* Reflections Ann, Aldrich Mus Contemp Art, 76; solo exhib, Frank Marino Gallery, New York, 79-81; 55 Mercer St Gallery, 84 & 86-92; Gallerie Pelen, Helsinki, Finland, 87, 88; Gallerie Ostermahl, Stockholm, Sweden, 88; Contemp Mus Costa Rica (auth, catalog), 92; Impremo Atelier Print Show (auth, catalog), Helsinki, Finland, 92; and others. *Teaching:* Mem fac, Brooklyn Mus Art Sch, 78-85, LaGuardia Col, 85- *Awards:* Comt Visual Arts Grant, 78; New York Found Arts Grant, 82; Nat Endowment Arts Artist in Residence Grant, 83. *Bibliog:* Barnaby Ruhe (auth), Falling show, Art World, 3/83; Michael Brenson (auth), article, NY Times, 6/88; William Zimmer (auth), article, NY Times, 7/88; Enrique Tovar (auth), La Nacion, review, 2/92; Kivirinta (auth), Helsing in Sanomat, review, 1/92; and others. *Media:* Miscellaneous. *Publ:* Auth, Galerie (catalog), Pelin, 88. *Mailing Add:* 152 W 25th St New York NY 10001

LA BOBGÄH, ROBERT GORDON
PRINTMAKER, SCULPTOR
b Montreal, Que, Nov 22, 36. *Study:* Concordia Univ, Montreal, BA, 62; Western Mich Univ, Kalamazoo, MA, 67. *Work:* Nat Gallery Alvethorpe, Libr Congress, Washington, DC; Nat Gallery Can, Ottawa; Philadelphia Mus Art; Erie Art Mus, Pa. *Comn:* Ceramic murals, Hamburg Bros, Pittsburgh, Pa 77; stages of the cross in ceramic, Immaculate Conception Church, Clarion, Pa, 78. *Exhib:* Los Angeles Printmaking Soc, Grunwald Ctr, Univ Calif, Los Angeles, 86; Works on Paper, 3rd Floor Gallery, Oakland, Calif, 86; Masks, Kipp Gallery, Indiana, Pa, 86; Blatent Image Silver Eye, Pittsburgh, Pa, 87; Carnegie Inst Art, Pittsburgh, Pa, 87 & 92; and others. *Teaching:* Instr, Pittsburgh Ctr Arts, Pa, 88-91. *Awards:* Purchase Award, Erie Art Mus, 87; Jurors Award, Auburn Works on Paper, Ala, 86 & Westmoreland Mus Art, 86; Gloria Fitzgibbons Award, Pittsburgh, 92. *Mem:* Soc Sculptors, Pittsburgh; Pittsburgh Soc Artists; Assoc Artists, Pittsburgh; Philadelphia Print Club. *Media:* All Media; Metal, Cast. *Publ:* Coauth, The Paper Bird Handmade Book, Pvt publ, 72. *Dealer:* Carson St Gallery Inc Pittsburgh PA 15203. *Mailing Add:* 319 S Atlantic Ave Pittsburgh PA 15224-2310

LABRIE, CHRISTY
STAINED GLASS ARTIST
b Portsmouth, NH, June 24, 43. *Study:* Boston Ctr Adult Ed, Sacred Heart Hosp Sch Nursing, Manchester. *Work:* Eucharistic Chapel, Mary E Sheehan Ctr, Watertown, Mass; Carmelite Monastery, Concord, NH; LaSalette Shrine, Attleboro, Mass. *Comn:* Numerous pvt comns. *Exhib:* Southhampton

Glassworks & Galerie, Palm Beach, Fla; Sheafs Warehouse Mus, Portsmouth, NH. *Teaching:* Classes, lectures & assembly, Archdiocesan Choir Boy Sch, Cambridge, Mass. *Mem:* Our Lady's Rosary Makers. *Publ:* Illustr, cover artist, Yankee Mag, 1/76 & Our Lady's Missionary, 10/76, Soul Mag, 9-10/86; Christmas card, Healing & Restoration Ministry, 90 & 91; contribr, Randy the Rooster (children's book); coauth of several abstracts & papers publ in sci/med j. *Mailing Add:* 45 Washington Rd Rye NH 03870

LACHAPELLE, JOSEPH ROBERT
SCULPTOR, EDUCATOR
b Little Fall, Minn, July 12, 43. *Study:* Wayne State Univ, Detroit, Mich, BS, 67; Ohio State Univ, Columbus, MFA, 70, PhD, 77. *Exhib:* Va Artists, Richmond Mus, 72; Nat Invitational, Madison Art Ctr, 72; Artists in Wood, Ohio State Univ & Univ Ky, 74; Columbus Mus Art, Ohio, 74, 75 & 76; one-man show, Centro de Arte y Comunicacion, Buenos Aires, 82; Hudson River Mus, 82. *Pos:* Asst gallery dir, Ohio State Univ, 75-76. *Teaching:* Instr sculpture, Western Ill Univ, 70-71; instr sculpture, Hampton Inst, Va, 71-74; asst prof sculpture, New York Univ, 77- *Awards:* Purchase Award, Western Ill Univ, 71. *Mem:* Col Art Asn. *Media:* Wood, Light. *Publ:* Auth, Conflict between research and practice, 82 & auth, Creativity research: Its sociological and educational limitations, 83, Studies Art Educ. *Mailing Add:* 63 Inwood Dr Nanuet NY 10954

LACK, RICHARD FREDERICK
PAINTER, INSTRUCTOR
b Minneapolis, Minn, Mar 26, 28. *Study:* Minneapolis Sch Art; R H Ives Gammell Studios, Boston. *Work:* Maryhill Mus Fine Arts, Washington; Elizabeth T Greenshields Mem Found Collection, Montreal, Que; Springville Mus Art, Utah; Newark Mus Art, NJ. *Comn:* Six portraits of Joseph P Kennedy, Jr, comn by Ambassador Kennedy & Kennedy Found, New York; portraits of Gov Wendell Anderson and Gov Albert Quie. *Exhib:* Allied Artists Am, 53; Boston Arts Festival, 53 & 54; Nat Acad Design Ann, 55; Twin City Biennial, Minneapolis Inst Arts, 62; Am Artists Prof League Nat, 67-73. *Teaching:* Dir & instr painting & drawing, Atelier Lack, Minneapolis, 69- *Awards:* First Prize, Copley Soc, Boston, 62; Gold Medal, Am Artists Prof League, 67 & 73 & Margaret Fernald Dole Prize for Best Portrait, 72; and others. *Bibliog:* D Jardine (auth), Richard Lack's atelier system of training painters, Am Artist Mag, 6/71. *Media:* Oil, Pastel. *Publ:* Auth, On the Training of Painters and Notes on the Atelier Program, 79 & Classical Realism, The Other Twentieth Century, 82, Atelier Lack Inc; Realism in Revolution, Taylor, 85; ed adv & contribr, Classical Realism Quart. *Mailing Add:* 5827 Louis Ave Minnetonka MN 55343

LACK, STEPHEN
PAINTER, FILMMAKER
b Aug 27, 46. *Study:* Columbia Univ, New York, with Tony Padovano, 66; McGill Univ, BA, 67; Inst Allende, San Miguel, Mexico, MFA, 68. *Work:* Australian Art Gallery, Canberra; Chase Manhattan Bank, Chemical Bank, New York; Dept External Affairs, Ottawa, Can; Progressive Corp, Cleveland, Ohio; Print div, New York Pub Libr; Quadracci Col, Imperial Oil, Pewaukee, Wis. *Comn:* Mural, Societe Int Transporte Aeronautique, Switzerland, 88; Artes Magnus, Ancienne Manufacture Royale, De Limoges, France; Rutgers Archives Print-making, Voorhees Zimmerleig Mus, New Brunswick, NJ; Grey Art Gallery, New York. *Exhib:* Mostra Internazionale di Arti Visive Promossa dai Bologna, Italy, 85; A Brave New World: 40 NY Artists, Udstilungsbygningen, Copenhagen & Lund, Sweden, 85; Drawings, Bemis Found, Omaha, 87; Forum, Zurich Art Fair, Switzerland, 87; Seibu, Japan, 89; Simon Dresdrere Gallery, Toronto, Ont, 89; Selections: Chemical Bank, and Porcelaine Pastforms, Present Tense, F I T, New York, 89; Motion as Metaphor, Virginia Beach Ctr Arts, Va, 91; Stephen Rosenberg Gallery, New York, 92; Recent Acquisitions, Rutgers Archives, Voorhees Mus, New Brunswick, NJ, 92. *Teaching:* Artist-in-residence, Banff Inst, Alta, Can, 87; studio workshop, Long Island Univ, 88; artist-in-residence, Ford Motor Co, Dearborn, Mich. *Awards:* Nat Endowment for the Arts, 87; Canada Council Award, 91. *Bibliog:* Allan Moyle (dir), The Rubber Gun, St Lawrence Films, 77; Jonathan Seliger (auth), Stephen Lack's credible polarities, Arts Mag, 4/86; Timothy Cohrs (auth), Stephen Lack print portfolio, Arts Mag, 4/88; Eileen Myles (auth), Steven Lack: one man show, Art Am, 12/89. *Media:* Paint on Canvas. *Publ:* Auth, Just Get Me Out of Here, Eldindean Press, 87. *Dealer:* Stephen Rosenberg Gallery 115 Wooster St New York NY; Simon Dresdnere Gallery 12 Hazelton Ave Toronto Ont CN M5R 2E2. *Mailing Add:* 9 Willow Ave Rockleigh NJ 07647

LACKEY, JANE W
FIBER ARTIST
b 1948. *Study:* Calif Col Arts & Crafts, BFA, 74; Cranbrook Acad Art, MFA, 79. *Work:* Chubb Insurance Group, NJ; Sigal Corp, Washington, DC; Corpus Christi Nat Bank, Tex. *Exhib:* Solo exhibs, Pacific Basin Sch Textile Arts, Berkeley, Calif, 76, Elements Gallery, New York, 83 & Hokin/Kaufman Gallery, Chicago, Ill, 88; Interlochen Acad Art, Interlochen, Mich, 79; Nimbus Gallery, Dallas, Tex, 83; Sch Art Gallery, Kent State Univ, Kent, Ohio, 85; Am Craft Mus, Inaugural Exhib, New York, nat tour, 87-88; Musee des Arts Decoratifs, Paris, France, 89, intl tour, 89-90; Musee Cantonal des Beaux-arts, Lausanne, Switz, 89; Chairman Exhibition, Charlotte Crosby Kemper Gallery, Kans City Art Inst, Kansas City, Mo, 90; Perspectives from the Pacific Rim, Bellevue Art Mus, Wash, 91; Domestic Ontogeny: New Textile Forms, Oliver Art Ctr, Oakland, Calif, 92; Nine Women, Dart Gallery, Chicago, Ill, 92. *Pos:* Guest cur, Muskegon Mus Art, 79; juror, Wichita Art Mus, 81; juror, Lawrence Arts Ctr, 82; co-cur, Charlotte Crosby Kemper Gallery, Kansas City Art Inst, 92; juror, Art Ctr, 91; juror, Adams Mem Gallery, 88. *Teaching:* Prof & dept chair, Fiber Dept, Kansas City Art Inst, 80-; lect, Sch Art Inst, Chicago, Ill, 91. *Awards:* Nat Endowment Arts, 84 & 88; US/France Exchange, Nat Endowment Arts, 89. *Bibliog:* Charles Talley (auth), Textural Limits, Artweek, 15-16, 9/13/90; Mary Merkel-Hess (auth), Review, Fiberarts, Vol 18, 91; W Logan Fry (auth), Review, Fiberarts, Vol 18, No 5, 64-65, 92. *Mailing Add:* 625 W 63rd St Kansas City MO 64113

LACKTMAN, MICHAEL
CRAFTSMAN, JEWELER
b Philadelphia, Pa, Mar 1, 38. *Study:* Pa State Col, 57-61; Cranbrook Acad of Art, Bloomfield Hills, Mich, 61-63; Kunsthaandverskolen, Copenhagen, Denmark, 65-66. *Work:* Pa State Col, Millersville, Pa; Cranbrook Acad Art, Bloomfield Hills, Mich. *Comn:* Liturgical metalry, Redeemer Lutheran Church, Livermore, Calif, 71; Kiddusch cup, Brandeis Univ, Waltham, Mass, 63. *Exhib:* California Design VI, Crocker Art Mus, Sacramento, 69; California Design XI, Pasadena Art Mus, 71; Metal Experience, Oakland Art Mus, Calif, 71; 4th Int Jewelry Exhib, Schmuckmuseum, Pzorheim, Ger, 72; Diamond Today: Int Jewelry Exhib, New York, 75. *Teaching:* Asst prof design, Univ Calif, Berkeley, 66-73, Univ Chile, Santiago, 72-73; prof jewelry & metalsmithing, Univ Wis-Milwaukee, 73- *Awards:* Louis Comfort Tiffany Grant, 63; Ford Found Grant, 72-73; Nat Endowment Humanities Grant, 75. *Bibliog:* Articles & photographs of work, Art & Archit, 71 & Playboy Mag, 75. *Mem:* Am Craftsman Coun; San Francisco Bay Asn; Sterling-Silversmiths Guild Am; Scand-Am Found; Col Art Asn. *Media:* Jewelry, Metals. *Mailing Add:* Dept of Art Univ of Wis Milwaukee WI 53201

LACOM, WAYNE CARL
PAINTER, GRAPHIC ARTIST
b Glendale, Calif, Oct 11, 22. *Study:* Art Ctr Sch, 42; Chuoinard Art Inst, 43-44; Jepson Art Inst, 45-46. *Work:* Brand Libr Gallery, Glendale, Calif, Los Angeles Unified Sch Dist. *Comn:* Bronze sculpture, Flamingo Hotel, Las Vegas, 70; painting, Hawaiian Airlines, Honolulu, 71; stained glass window, comn by Mr & Mrs Taub, Encino, Calif, 72; painting, Security Pacific Bank, Glendale, Calif, 75. *Exhib:* Artists of Los Angeles & Vicinity, Los Angeles Co Mus Art, Calif, 50; Watercolor Exhib, Santa Barbara Art Mus, Calif, 52; Pasadena Mus Art, Pasadena, Calif, 53; Denver Mus Art, Colo, 54; Cuernavaca Art Mus, Mex, 55; Lahaina Restoration Found Mus, Lahaina, Hawaii, 88. *Pos:* Pres, Int Art Serv, 78- *Teaching:* Instr watercolor, Los Angeles Unified Sch Dist, Adult Educ, 47-78. *Awards:* First Place, Glendale Art Asn, 48; Best of show, Catalina Art Fest, 89. *Bibliog:* The Creative Hand (video), Los Angeles Unified Sch Dist, 73. *Mem:* Nat Watercolor Soc (pres, 65-66); Artists for Educ Action (treas, 67-73). *Media:* Watercolor, Acrylic. *Publ:* Transparent Watercolor, 73 & Landscapes, 77, Davis Publ; Palette Talk, Grumbacher, 75; The California Style, Hillcrest Press, 85; The California Romantics, Artra, 86. *Dealer:* Village Gallery 120 Dickenson St Lahaina HI 96761. *Mailing Add:* 16703 Alginet Place Encino CA 91436

LACY, SUZANNE
CONCEPTUAL ARTIST, EDUCATOR
b Wasco, Calif, Oct 21, 45. *Study:* Univ Calif, Santa Barbara, BA; Fresno State Col; Calif Inst Arts, MFA; study with Judy Chicago, Sheila de Bretteville & Allan Kaprow. *Exhib:* Solo exhib, Montgomery Gallery, Pamona Col, 83; Video Art: A History, Mus Mod Art, New York, 83; Social Art Exhib, Banff Art Atr, Alta, Can, 85; La Jolla Mus Contemp Art, 87; Monument and Memorial, New Langton Arts, San Francisco, 88; Making Space, Presentation House, Vancouver, Can, 88; Committed to Print, Mus Mod Art, New York, 88; Art and the Law, The W Collection, St Paul, Minn, 90; Ageless, The Women's Bldg, Los Angeles. *Teaching:* Minneapolis Col Art & Design, 85-86; Sch Art Inst Chicago, 86; vis artist, Carleton Col, 87; dean, Sch Fine Arts, Calif Col Arts & Crafts. *Awards:* Nat Endowment Arts Grants, 79, 81 & 85; Fel, Calif Arts Coun, 89. *Bibliog:* Moira Roth (auth), The Crystal Quilt, Art Am, 88; Paige Bruhn & Douglas Hoppe (auth), Interview with Suzanne Lacy, P-Form, 2-5/90; Diana Rico (auth), The Edges of the World, Mother Jones, 6/90. *Mem:* Los Angeles Inst Contemp Art; The Woman's Bldg (mem bd, 74-79); Women's Caucus Arts (nat bd, 80-82). *Media:* Theatrical and non-theatrical performance; conceptual photography, books and video. *Publ:* Coauth, Political Performance Art, Heresies No 17, 85; auth, Fractured Space, In Art in the Public Interest, MIT Press, 89; Skeptical of the Spectacle, The Act, Vol 2 No 1, 90. *Mailing Add:* Calif Col Arts & Crafts 5212 Broadway Oakland CA 94618

LADER, MELVIN PAUL
HISTORIAN, EDUCATOR
b Auburn, NY, Jan 30, 47. *Study:* State Univ NY, Albany, BA, 69, MA, 72; Univ Del, PhD, 81. *Teaching:* Prof art hist, George Washington Univ, 78- *Awards:* Mus Fel, Smithsonian Inst, 77-78; Fel, Rockefeller Found, 78. *Mem:* Col Art Asn; Arch Am Art. *Res:* Abstract expressionism; twentieth century American art; modern art patronage. *Publ:* Auth, Graham, Gorky, DeKooning and the Ingres revival in America, 78, Howard Putzel: Proponent of surrealism and abstract expressionism in America, 82 & Arshile Gorky's The artist and his mother, 1/84, Arts Mag; Arshile Gorky, Abbeville, NY, 85; Peggy Guggenheim's Art of This century in Peggy Guggenheim's Other Legacy (exhib catalog), Solomon R Guggenheim Mus, 87. *Mailing Add:* Dept Art George Washington Univ 801 22nd St NW Washington DC 20052

LADERMAN, GABRIEL
PAINTER, EDUCATOR
b Brooklyn, NY, Dec 26, 29. *Study:* Atelier 17, with S W Hayter 49 & 52; Hans Hofmann Sch Fine Arts, 49; with DeKooning at studio, 49-50; Brooklyn Col, BA, 52; Cornell Univ, MFA, 57. *Work:* Meade Mus, Amherst, Mass; Glen C Janss Collection, Boise Art Mus; Nat Gallery Art, Washington, DC; FMC Corp, Chicago; Cleveland Mus Art; Mus Fine Arts, Boston; and pvt

collections of Edward Pillsbury, Robert Natkin, Malcolm Holtzman, William Bailey & Davidson Collection; plus others. *Exhib:* Brooklyn Mus, 58 & 59; American Sense of Reality, Milwaukee Art Ctr, 69; Trends in Contemporary Realist Painting, Boston Mus Fine Art, 74; one-person exhibs, Inst of Int Educ, UN, New York, 78, Nat Mus Malaysia, Kuala Lumpur, 82, Cornell Univ, 82, Meade Mus, Amhurst Col, Mass, 83, Joel Berger Gallery, Provincetown, Mass, Contemp Realist Gallery, San Francisco, 87 & 90 & Jessica Darraby Gallery, Los Angeles, 87; Contemporary American Realism Since 1960, Pa Acad Fine Arts, traveling to Va Mus Fine Arts, Oakland Mus, Gulbenkian, Lisbon & Germanische Nationalmuseum, Nuremberg, 81; Narrative Painting, Fla Int Univ Mus, Miami, 88; Joel Berger Gallery, Provincetown, Mass, 88; 100th Anniversary Exhib, Pratt Inst, New York City Gallery, traveling to Brooklyn Campus, 88; The Nude, One Penn Plaza, New York, 88; Storytelling: Narrative Painting, NJ Ctr for Visual Arts, 88; Objects Observed: Contemporary Still-life, Gallery Henoch, New York, 90. *Pos:* Provost's tenure comt, Yale Univ, 82; juror, Nat Endowment Arts, 83, NY State Coun on Arts, 85-86; invited commentator, MacArthur Found, 86, 87 & 88; invited judge, Univ Va, 88. *Teaching:* Asst prof, State Univ NY, 57-59, Pratt Inst, 59-68; artist in residence, La State Univ, 66-67; prof, Queens Col, 66- , chmn, 79-82; visiting prof, grad sch, Yale Univ, 68-69, 81, 83 & 89; faculty, Skowhegan Sch Painting & Sculpture, 70 & 71; instr painting, Tanglewood Inst, 73 & Yale-Norfolk Sch, 74; founding dir summer landscape prog, Queens Col, 80-81; visiting critic & guest lectr at many colleges, univs and institutions throughout US, Australia & Asia. *Awards:* Fulbright Fel to Italy, 62-63; Nat Endowment Arts Sr Fel, 81-82, 82-83 & 86-87; Ingram Merrill Found, 75-77 & 84; J S Guggenheim Fel, 88. *Bibliog:* Don Gray (auth), Laderman at Schoelkopf, Artworld, 86; Jed Perl (auth), review article, New Criterion, 87; John L Ward (auth), American Realist Painting 1945-1980 (2 reproductions), UMI Res Press, Ann Arbor, 89. *Media:* Oil, Pastel. *Publ:* Auth, Outer Light, Ann XXXV, Artnews, 11/69; Unconventional Realists, Part II, Sculpture, Artforum, 70; Notes from the Underground, Artforum, 70; Use and Misuse of the Past and Too Recent Past, Artforum, 71; Morandi, Col Art J, summer 82. *Dealer:* Schoelkopf Gallery 825 Madison Ave New York NY 10021. *Mailing Add:* c/o Tatistcheff & Co 50 W 57th St 8th Fl New York NY 10019

LADOUCEUR, PHILIP ALAN
ADMINISTRATOR, DIRECTOR
b Syracuse, NY, Nov 6, 50. *Study:* State Univ NY, MA, 80; studied with Kenneth Lindsay & Albert Boime. *Collections Arranged:* Six Women Artists, 92; 92 Visions of Color, 92; Dan Leary: Works on Paper, (auth, catalog), 92; Modern Prints (auth, catalog), 92. *Pos:* Dir, BlandenMem Art Mus, 91- *Mem:* Am Asn Mus; Col Art Asn. *Mailing Add:* Blanden Memorial Art Museum 920 Third Ave S Fort Dodge IA 50501

LAEMMLE, CHERYL
PAINTER
b Minneapolis, Minn, Aug 11, 47. *Study:* Humboldt State Univ, BA, 74; Washington State Univ, MFA, 78. *Work:* Eli Broad Family Found; Metrop Mus Art & Chase Manhattan Bank, New York; Tamayo Mus, Mexico City, Mex; Frederick R Weismann Found; Corcoran Mus Art, Washington, DC; Walker Art Ctr, Minneapolis; Gen Mills, Minneapolis, Minn; High Art Mus. *Exhib:* Solo exhibs, Nat Mus Women Arts, Washington, DC, 89, Rena Bransten Gallery, San Francisco, 89,Fay Gold Gallery, Atlanta, Ga, 89 & 92, Mus Art, Washington State Univ, Pullman, 90, Terry Ditenfass Gallery, New York, 91, Greg Kucera Gallery, Seattle, 90 & 92, Peril, Allene LaPides Gallery, Santa Fe, NMex, 92; Self Image, Sharpe Gallery, New York, 83; New-New York Phoenix Art Mus, Ariz, 83; An Int Survey of Recent Painting & Sculpture, Mus Mod Art, New York, 84; Inst Contemp Art, Univ Pa, Philadelphia & Lowe Art Mus, Coral Gables Fla, 84; From New York, Ace Contemp Exhib, Los Angeles, Calif, 88; Making Their Mark; Women a Move in the Mainstream 70-85, Cincinnati Art Mus, 89; Real Illusion, Whitney Mus Art at Equitable Ctr New York, 90; In the Looking Glass, Mint Mus Art, Charlotte, NC, 91; La Femme Surreal & the Frozen Narrative, Visual Arts Ctr, Calif State Univ, Fullerton, 91; I, Myself & Me, Twentieth Century & Contemp Self Portraits, Midtown Payson Galleries, New York, 92; and many other one-man & group exhibs. *Awards:* Fel, Creative Artists Pub Serv Prog, 80; Vera G List Award, 84; Painting Fel, Nat Endowment Arts, 85-86 & 86-87. *Bibliog:* Lisa Peters (auth), article, Arts Mag, 5/83; Richard Armstrong (auth), article, Art Forum, summer 83; Ronny Cohen (auth), article, Art News, summer 83; William Zimmer (auth), Art walk, Village Voice, 4/1/86. *Dealer:* Fay Gold Gallery 247 Buckhead Ave Atlanta GA 30305. *Mailing Add:* 735 E 9th St New York NY 10009

LAESSIG, ROBERT
PAINTER, ILLUSTRATOR
b NJ, 1920. *Study:* Art Students League; also study in Ger. *Work:* Cleveland Mus Fine Arts, Ohio; Butler Inst Am Art, Ohio; Norfolk Mus, Va; Springfield Inst Fine Arts, Ohio; Akron Art Inst, Ohio. *Comn:* Official White House Christmas card, comn by President & Mrs Johnson, 64-68; Official Christmas card, Gov Celeste Ohio, 82-86. *Exhib:* Philadelphia Watercolor Soc, 64-70; Allied Artists, New York, 70-72; Pittsburgh Watercolor Show, 78; Ohio Watercolor Show, 78-79; Am Watercolor Show, 79. *Pos:* Pres, Robert Laessig Fine Arts Co, West Richfield, Ohio, 69-71 & Quail Ravine Studios, Inc, Peninsula, Ohio, 85-89. *Awards:* Prizes, Am Watercolor Soc, 70 & 71, Wichita Centennial, 70 & Pittsburgh Watercolor, 80; Gold medal, Ohio Watercolor Soc, 87 & 88; and numerous others. *Mem:* Nat Acad Design; Am Watercolor Soc; Ohio Watercolor Soc. *Mailing Add:* 5026 Hawkins Rd Richfield OH 44286

LAFON, DEE J
PAINTER, SCULPTOR
b Ogden, Utah, Apr 23, 29. *Study:* Weber State Col; Univ Utah, BFA, 60, MFA, 62; also with Francis de Erdley, Phil Paradise & Marquerite Wildenhain. *Work:* Utah State Fine Art Collection, Salt Lake City; Okla Art Ctr, Oklahoma City; Philbrook Art Mus, Tulsa, Okla; Univ Okla, Norman; Dillard Collection, Univ NC, Greensboro. *Comn:* Wood sculpture, Univ Okla, 72. *Exhib:* Am Drawing Bienniale, Norfolk, Va, 69; Int Miniature Prints Show, Pratt Graphic Ctr, New York, 70; Midwest Bienniale, Omaha, Nebr, 72; one-man shows, Springfield Art Mus, Mo, 78 & Goddard Art Ctr, Ardmore, Ore, 78. *Teaching:* Instr ceramics & drawing, Weber State Col, 62-64; assoc prof painting & drawing, ECent State Col, 64-, chmn dept art, 79- *Awards:* Eight State Exhib Purchase Award, 70; Hon Mention, Midwest Bienniale, 72; Tulsa Regional Painting & Drawing Award, 72. *Mem:* Okla Designer Craftsman. *Media:* Oil, Multi-media. *Dealer:* Oklahoma Art Ctr 3113 General Pershing Blvd Oklahoma City OK 73118; Ben Pickard Gallery 541 NW 39th St Oklahoma City OK 73118. *Mailing Add:* 904 Tarkington Circle Norman OK 73071

LAGER, FANNIE
SCULPTOR, COLLECTOR
b New York, NY, Nov 14, 11. *Study:* Brooklyn Col, painting with Nancy Ranson, 39-41; Brooklyn Mus Art Sch, painting with Isaac Soyer, 42-70 & sculpture with Toshio Odate, Barney Hodes & Lee Ackerman, 74-81; Sculpture Ctr, sculpture with Shulamith Brumer, 71-73. *Exhib:* Second Ann Open Juried--Non Members, Salmagundi Club, New York, 79; one-women shows, Atlantic Gallery, Brooklyn Mus Art Sch, 78, Brooklyn & Soho, NY, 79 & 81; Knickerbocker Artists 29th Ann, Nat Arts Club, New York, 79; Brooklyn 1980, Community Gallery, Brooklyn Mus, NY, 80; First open show for sculpture, Salmagundi Club, 82. *Awards:* Excellence Award, Sculpture Ed Alliance, 86. *Bibliog:* Sheila H Jacobs (ed), Retirees---Aetna Life & Casualty, 3-4/81 & Kevin Flood (auth), Second career fills her retirement years, 9-10/82, Aetna Circle; Denise Bibro (auth), 3 Dimensions by 3, Artspeak, 6/81. *Mem:* Assoc mem Audubon Artists; New York Artists Equity Asn Inc; Salmagundi Club (82-88, resigned, 88); Inst Retired Prof New Sch Social Res; Charter mem Nat Mus Women Arts. *Media:* Wood, Stone. *Collection:* American contemporary impressionism. *Dealer:* Dorsey's Art Gallery 533 Rogers Ave Brooklyn NY 11225; Spiral Gallery 637 Vanderbilt Ave Brooklyn NY 11238. *Mailing Add:* 2215 Newkirk Ave Apt B5 Brooklyn NY 11226

LAGORIA, GEORGIANNA MARIE
MUSEUM DIRECTOR, CURATOR
b Oakland, Calif, Nov 3, 53. *Study:* Gonzaga Univ, Florence, Italy, 74; Santa Clara Univ, Calif, BA, 75; Univ San Francisco. *Collections Arranged:* The Candy Store Gallery (with catalog), 80, Contemporary Hand Colored Photographs (with catalog), 81, Northern California Art of the Sixties (with catalog), 82 & Artist and the Machine 1910-1940 (with catalog), 86, de Saisset Mus, Santa Clara, Calif; Judy Dater: Twenty Years, traveled through US & Spain, 86. *Pos:* Asst dir, de Saisset Mus, Santa Clara Univ, Calif, 78-83, dir, 83-86; dir, Palo Alto Cult Ctr, Calif, 86-91; adv bd, Wiegand Gallery, Col of Notre Dame, Belmont, Calif; consult, 91- *Awards:* Publication Support Grant, Ahmanson Found, 81; Nat Endowment Arts, 85-86. *Mem:* ArtTable; California Asn Mus (bd 87-89); Western Mus Conf of Am Asn Mus. *Res:* Modern and contemporary art, craft, and design with an emphasis on the West Coast. *Publ:* Contribr, Judy Dater: Twenty Years, Univ Arizona, 86. *Mailing Add:* 47-665 Mapelle Rd Kaneohe HI 96744

LAGORIO, IRENE R
PRINTMAKER, PAINTER
b Oakland, Calif, May 2, 21. *Study:* Calif Col Arts & Crafts, Oakland, 38-39; Univ Calif, Berkeley, AB & MA, 42; Columbia Univ, 45. *Work:* Monterey Art Comn Conf Ctr Collection, Calif; Monterey Peninsula Mus of Art Collection; Northern Calif Savings & Loan Collection; Germanischen Mus & Libr Collection, Nuremberg, Ger; Sunset Cult Ctr Collection, Carmel, Calif. *Comn:* jewel painted mural, Lloyd Ctr, Portland, Ore, 60; mosaic murals, SS President Roosevelt, Am Pres Lines, 61; metal sculpture mural, Seaside, Ore, US Bancarp, 64; mosaic mural, Soc Nat Bank, Cleveland, Ohio, 69; mosaic mural design, Episcopal Condominium, Los Gatos, Calif, 70. *Exhib:* Metrop Mus Art Watercolor Exhib, 53; Am Color Print Soc Ann, Philadelphia, 72; US Info Serv Traveling Color Print Exhib, throughout Europe, 72; one-man shows, Onstage and Backstage at Sunset Ctr, Marjorie Evans Gallery, Sunset Ctr, Carmel, Calif, 79 & Fluoro Paint & Printers Ink, Monterey Peninsula Mus Art, Calif, 80; and others. *Pos:* Cur educ dept, Calif Palace of Legion of Honor, 50; dir, Achenbach Found Graphic Arts, 51-55; art critic & artist, Monterey Peninsula Herald, Weekend Mag, 75-89. *Teaching:* Spec lectr, Univ Calif Exten Courses, 60- *Awards:* Chapelbrook Found Grand for Graphic Proj, Boston, 69; Best in Show, Monterey Peninsula Mus Art 7th Competitive, 71. *Bibliog:* E Loran (auth), The San Francisco scene, Art News, 53; G Dorfles (auth), Modern painters in USA, Domus Mag, 54; Exposition de San Francisco, La Rev Mod, 60. *Mem:* Carmel Art Asn (pres, 72-); Arts Assoc Found (dir, 61-). *Media:* Serigraphy, Silkscreen. *Publ:* Illusr, This Open Zoo-A Bestiary, Salamander, 71; Moving to Monterey, Kaskaskia Press, 88; illustr & poems, Art History's Innovators, Arina Press, 92. *Mailing Add:* First & Mission Sts Box 153 Carmel CA 93921

LAGUNA, MARIELLA
PAINTER, PRINTMAKER
b New York, NY. *Study:* NY Univ (archit); New Sch; Brooklyn Mus Art Sch; Adelphi Univ; Pratt Graphic Ctr. *Work:* Rockefeller Family; Brooklyn Col; also in many pvt & indust collections. *Comn:* Portraits & wall paintings, pvt & indust. *Exhib:* Pa Acad Fine Arts, Philadelphia, 64; Allied Artists Am Ann,

64; Nat Acad Design Ann, 64; Salvatora Rosa, Naples, Italy, 72; Pallazzo Vechio, Florence, Italy, 72; and many others. *Pos:* Colorist, Lawrence Laguna Architect, 60-; interior designer (free lance). *Teaching:* Instr art, Baldwin, Oceanside, Rockville Centre Pub Schs continuing educ workshops, 57- *Awards:* Gold Medal (First Prize), Hofstra Univ, 61; 16 Resident Fels including Yaddo & The Edward MacDowell Colony, 65, 69, 73, 75 & 77, 5 Resident Fels including Helen Wurlitzer Found, Taos, NMex & Montalva Ctr, Saratogo, Calif; Medal of Honor, Nat Asn Women Artists, 67; Annual Award, Am Soc Contemp Artists, 83 & 89, and many others. *Bibliog:* Newspaper interviews, Taos, Long Island Press, News Day, San Jose Mercury News, Calif & others. *Mem:* Artist Equity of New York, Inc; Nat Asn Women Artists, Inc; New York Soc Women Artists; Contemp Artists. *Media:* Oil, Acrylic; Etching. *Mailing Add:* 324 Christopher St Oceanside NY 11572

LA HOTAN, ROBERT L
PAINTER
b Cleveland, Ohio, 1927. *Study:* Columbia Univ, Brevoort-Eickmeyer fel, 50-53. *Work:* Lehigh Univ, Bethlehem, Pa; Northern Trust Co, Kansas City, Mo; Univ NC; Hirshhorn Collection; Hamilton Col. *Exhib:* Corcoran Biennial, 56; Dallas Mus Contemp Art, 58; Rochester Mem Art Gallery, 66; one-man show, Lehigh Univ, 69; Kraushaar Galleries, 69, 72, 75, 78, 81, 84, 87, 90 & 93; Hull Gallery, Washington, DC, 79 & 82. *Teaching:* Instr, Dalton Sch, New York, 56-92. *Awards:* Fulbright Fel to Ger, 53-55; Purchase Awards, Am Acad Inst Arts & Letters, 73-77; Benjamin Altman Prize (landscape), Nat Acad Design, 88. *Media:* Oil, Watercolor. *Dealer:* Kraushaar Galleries 724 Fifth Ave New York NY 10028. *Mailing Add:* 865 West End Ave New York NY 10025

LAHR, J(OHN) STEPHEN
PAINTER, EDUCATOR
b Lincoln, Nebr, Aug 5, 43. *Study:* Univ Nebr, Lincoln, BFA, 68, with James Eisentrager, MEd, 72, EdD, 79. *Work:* Univ Nebr, Omaha; Joslyn Art Mus, Omaha; Pensacola Jr Col, Fla, 86. *Exhib:* Paper in Particular, Columbia Col Gallery, Mo, 81, 82 & 83; Mid-Four Regional Competition, Nelson Gallery Art, Atkins Mus, Kansas City, Mo, 81 & 82; Watercolor Missouri, William Woods Col, Fulton, 83 & 84; two-person exhib, Joslyn Art Mus, Omaha, 83; Kans Watercolor Soc Ann Competition, Wichita Art Mus, 85; Pensacola Nat Landscape Exhib, 86; Ga Watercolor Soc Ann Nat Exhib, Macon Mus Arts & Sci, 89 & 92. *Collections Arranged:* Missouri Folk: Their Creative Images, Folk Arts Exhib, 82; Sichaun Fine Arts Acad Exhib, Fine Arts Gallery, Valdosta State Col, Ga, 86 & 89; Valdosta Work on Paper I and II, Fine Arts Gallery, 88-89; Artoberfest (juried exhib), Cult Arts Ctr, 91. *Pos:* State art dir, Nebr Dept Educ, Lincoln, 74-79. *Teaching:* Instr art, Lincoln Pub Sch, Nebr, 69-72 & Univ Nebr, Lincoln, 72-73; asst prof art educ & studio, Univ Nebr, Omaha, 78-80; asst prof art educ & painting, Univ Mo, Columbia, 80-85; assoc prof, head dept art & gallery dir, Valdosta State Col, Ga, 85-89, prof art dept, 91. *Awards:* Purchase Awards, Joslyn Art Mus, 80 & Univ Nebr, Omaha, 82; Pensacola Nat Pruchase Award, 86. *Mem:* Nat Art Educ Asn; Am Watercolor Soc; Ga Art Educ Asn (bd mem); Ga Watercolor Soc; Ga Citizens for the Arts (exec bd mem); Lowndes/Valdosta Arts Comn (bd mem). *Media:* Watercolor, Acrylics. *Res:* Methods of art instruction; Art Teaching practices; Art educator profiles. *Publ:* Auth, Handbook for Art Education, Nebr Dept Educ, 78; Who teaches art: Report of recent surveys, In: Studies in Art Educ, Nat Art Educ Asn, 83-84; Health Hazards in the Artroom, EAEA J, 91. *Mailing Add:* Dept Art Valdosta State Col Valdosta GA 31698

LAI, WAIHANG
PAINTER, INSTRUCTOR
b Hong Kong, Jan 7, 39. *Study:* Chinese Univ Hong Kong, BA, 64; Claremont Grad Sch & Univ Ctr, MA, 67. *Comn:* Painting of McBryde Mill, A&B Inc, 75 & 77. *Exhib:* Watercolor USA, Springfield Art Mus, Mo, 69; The Best in the West, Edward-Dean Mus, Calif, 70; Philadelphia Watercolor Club Exhib, Philadelphia Civic Ctr Mus, 72; one-man shows, Phoenix Art Mus, Ariz, 67, Kauai Mus, Hawaii, 71, 72 & 92, Kahana Kii Fine Art Gallery, 82 & Princeville Galleries, Hawaii, 85, Kilohana Galleries, Hawaii, 89; Am Watercolor Soc Ann Exhib, 85. *Teaching:* Vis prof art, Ariz State Univ, Tempe, summer 67; asst prof art, Maunaolu Col, Maui, Hawaii, 68-70; assoc prof, Kauai Community Col, 70- *Awards:* Hon Mention, Hong Kong Art Exhib, Univ Hong Kong, 59-61; First Award for Watercolor, 1st Ann Spring Festival Fine Arts, Rowland Heights, Calif, 68; First Place for Watercolor, Maui Co Creative Arts Exhib, Hawaii, 68. *Mem:* Am Watercolor Soc; Philadelphia Watercolor Club; Kauai Watercolor Soc (pres); Kauai Oriental Art Soc (pres, currently). *Media:* Watercolor, Acrylic. *Publ:* Auth, The Chinese Landscape paintings of Waihang Lai, 66; The Watercolors of Waihang Lai, 67 & Waihang Lai, Watercolor Calendar, 78. *Mailing Add:* PO Box 363 Lihue HI 96766

LAICO, COLETTE
COLLAGE ARTIST, PAINTER
b New York, NY. *Study:* Art Students League; Marymount Col, Haystack Mtn Sch Art & Crafts. *Comn:* Paintings, Am Int Life Assurance Co, New York, 89. *Exhib:* Monmouth Mus Fine Arts, Monmouth, NJ, 87; Ann Exhib Silvermine Guild Gallery, New Canaan, Conn, 86, 87, 88, 89, 90, 91 & 92; Ann Nat Asn Women Artists, New York, 87, 88, 89, 90, 91 & 92; Connecticut Gallery, Marlborough, 88, 89 & 90; Hudson River Mus, Yonker, NY, 89. *Teaching:* Instr art/craft, Westchester Art Workshop, 71-86; instr colonial art/crafts, Westchester Comm Col, 76-80; instr quilting, Scarsdale Adult Sch, 79-88. *Awards:* Gerald Kandler Mem Award, Womans Club Whiteplains, 89 & Mamaroneck Artists Guild, 86; Elizabeth Morse Genius Award, 88 & Sara Winston Mem Award, 92, Nat Asn Women Artists; Randolf Ghitwood Award, Greenwich Art Soc, 92. *Bibliog:* Dorethy Friedman (auth), Artist Explores "Arts", Greenwich Time, 1/19/90; Janet Koplos (auth), article, Advocate & Greenwich Time, 2/18/90. *Mem:* Silvermine Guild Ctr Arts; Stamford Art Asn; Artists Equity Asn; Nat Asn Women Artists; Am Craft Coun. *Media:* Mixed Media. *Mailing Add:* 21 Saxonwood Park Dr White Plains NY 10605

LAING, RICHARD HARLOW
ADMINISTRATOR, ARTIST
b Ypsilanti, Mich, Apr 19, 32. *Study:* Eastern Mich Univ, BS(art); Wayne State Univ, MA(printmaking, sculpture); Pa State Univ, DEd(art educ). *Comn:* Fountain (bronze & stainless), comn by Paul Vortman, Denton, Tex, 62; wall sculpture, comn by Blazier Comn for Civic Ctr, Denton, Tex, 66; three stainless steel sculptures, Pa State Univ, University Park, 67-68; bronze sculpture fountain, Ewing-Miller Assoc, Terre Haute, Ind, 68; 10 piece stained glass design & construction, Elizabeth's Restaurant, Meadville, Pa, 77. *Exhib:* Am Inst of Architects Exhib, Rice Univ, Houston, 67; 16th Ann Nat Drawing & Small Sculpture, Muncie, Ind, 70; Wabash Valley Regional Exhib, Terre Haute, Ind, 71; Allegheny Col Galleries, Pa, 78; Theil Col Galleries, Grove City, Pa, 78; Butler Mus Art, Youngstown, Ohio, 79. *Pos:* Develop specialist cult affairs, ECarolina Univ, Greenville, 83- *Teaching:* Instr design shop, Col Art & Design, Univ Mich, 54-55; instr studio art & humanities, Edsel Ford High Sch, 55-60; asst prof studio art & art educ, NTex State Univ, 60-68; art head dept & assoc prof, Ball State Univ, Muncie, Ind, 68-71; prof & chair, Edinboro State Col, Pa, 71-79; dean & prof, ECarolina Univ, Greenville, NC, 79- *Awards:* First Cash Prize/Painting, Eastern Ind Artist Exhib, Muncie Art Asn, 69 & 71; Community Arts Award, Greenville, NC, 80. *Mem:* Col Art Asn. *Media:* Mixed. *Mailing Add:* 204 Pineview Dr Greenville NC 27834

LAIOU, ANGELIKI E
EDUCATOR
b Athens, Greece, Apr 6, 41. *Study:* Univ Athens, 58-59; Brandeis Univ, BA(summa cum laude), 59-61; Harvard Univ, MA, 62, travel grants, 64-65, PhD, 66. *Pos:* Dir, Dumbarton Oaks, Washington, DC, 89- *Teaching:* Instr, Univ La, New Orleans, 62; instr, Harvard, 66-69, asst prof, 69-72, prof Byzantine hist, 81-; assoc prof, Brandeis, 72-75; prof, Rutgers, 75-81; vis prof, Princeton, 81. *Awards:* Guggenheim Fel, 71-72 & 78-79; Rutgers Univ Res Coun grants; Am Coun Learned Soc Fel, 88-89. *Mem:* Phi Beta Kappa; Medieval Acad Am; Am Comt Byzantine Studies; Greek Comt Study South-Eastern Europe; Am Sch Classical Studies Athens. *Mailing Add:* Dumbarton Oaks Research Collection and Library 1703 32nd St NW Washington DC 20007

LAIRD, E RUTH
SCULPTOR
b Houston, Tex, Mar 21, 21. *Study:* Cranbrook Acad Art, Bloomfield Hills, Mich, with Maija Grotell, summer 51 & 53-55. *Work:* Mus Contemp Crafts, New York; Everson Mus & Iroquois China Collection, Syracuse, NY; Children's Mus, Detroit; Cranbrook Mus, Mich. *Comn:* Altar Sculpture, Meditation Chapel, Rice Univ, Houston, 63 & Mem Sculpture, 75; Fountain, New Harmony, Ind, 65; Baptismal Fountain, St Basil Church, Angelton , Tex, 65. *Exhib:* One-woman shows, Univ Houston, 57, NMex Highlands Univ, 59, Laguna Gloria Mus, Austin, Tex, 65 & Mus Fine Arts, Houston, 67; Syracuse Int Traveling Exhib, New York, 57. *Teaching:* Instr ceramic sculpture, St Thomas, Houston, 55-57 & Univ Houston, 55-58; asst dean & instr ceramic sculpture, Mus Fine Arts Sch, Houston, 58-68. *Awards:* Tex Swed Cult Found Summer Study-Travel Grant, Int Designers' Conf, 55; Iroquois China Award, Int Exhib, Everson Mus, 57; Woman of Year Outstanding Contrib Fine Arts, Theta Sigma Phi, Houston, 68. *Bibliog:* Dr William Pryor (dir), The Arts in Houston (TV show), 60; Campbell Geeslin (auth), Emerging reputations, Am Artist, 62; The American Ceramist, Craft Horizon, 62. *Media:* Clay, Stone. *Dealer:* Handmakers The Galleria 5015 Westheimer Rd Houston TX 77027. *Mailing Add:* 205 South Orange St Fredericksburg TX 78624

LAKE, JERRY LEE
PHOTOGRAPHER, EDUCATOR
b Manhattan, Kans, Apr 1, 41. *Study:* Va Commonwealth Univ, Richmond Professional Inst, BFA, 66; Ohio Univ, Athens, MFA, 68. *Work:* Corcoran Gallery Art, 69; Kodak Corp, 85; Bibliotheque Nat, Paris, 84-85; Nat Inst Health, 86. *Exhib:* One-man shows, Sign of Jonah Gallery, Washington, DC, 69 & Northern Va Community Col, 69; Fac Exhib, Corcoran Gallery Art, 68-70; Corcoran Gallery Art, 69; Unpeopled Spaces Traveling Exhib; Biennial Exhib, Va Mus, 81; In Celebration: Art at George Washington University, The Art Barn, Washington, DC, 82; Fac Show, Dimock Gallery, Washington, DC, 83-90; The Ritz, Washington DC Proj Arts, 83; 1734 Gallery, 83; Best of Kathleen Ewings Gallery, 83 & 86; Nat Juried Exhib, NY, 84. *Teaching:* Dir photog prog, Corcoran Sch Art, 68-71; head photog section, George Washington Univ, 71-; prof photo, George Washington Univ. *Bibliog:* Benjamin Forgey (auth), Designed for design, Washington Post, 83; Jo Ann Lewis (auth), Professorial pictures, Washington Post, 83. *Mem:* Soc Photog Educ; Int Photog Soc; Am Asn Col Prof. *Publ:* Contribr photog, Horizon Mag, 75-76 & America Mag, 76; contribr cover photog, Environmental Action, 12/77. *Dealer:* Kathleen Ewing Gallery 1609 Connecticut Ave Washington DC 20009. *Mailing Add:* George Wash Univ Washington DC 20052

LAKE, RANDALL
PAINTER, PRINTMAKER
b Long Beach, Calif, Aug 2, 47. *Study:* Acad Julian, Paris, 67; Univ Colo, BA, 69; Ecole Superieure Beaux Arts, Paris, 72; Atelier 17, Paris, 72-73; Univ Utah, MFA, 77. *Work:* Springville Mus Art, Utah; Am Embassy, Am Libr, Paris; Utah State Arts Collection. *Comn:* Oil paintings of Jerusalem, Mormon

Church, Salt Lake City, 79; portrait Willard Eccles, Weber State Col, 81; portrait Nellie Tayloe Ross, Wyo State Capitol, Cheyenne, 82; portrait Dr Leonard W Jarcho, Univ Utah Med Sch, 83; Val A Browning, St Benedict's Hosp, Ogden, Utah, 85; Mayor Ted Wilson, City & Co Bldg, Salt Lake City, 86. *Exhib:* Salon D'Automne, Grand Palais, Paris, 70 & 72; Salon De Mai, Musee D'Art Mod, Paris, 72; Utah Painting & Sculpture, Mus Fine Arts, Univ Utah, Salt Lake City, 75-76; Intermountain Biennial, Salt Lake Art Ctr, 76; Assoc Utah Artists Bicentennial Exhib, Salt Palace, Salt Lake City, 76. *Pos:* Assoc dir, Guthrie Inst Fine Arts, 73-78, painter in residence, 80- *Teaching:* Assoc instr, Univ Utah, 76-78; Scottsdale Artists' Sch, 92-93. *Awards:* First Place, Assoc Utah Artists Bicentennial Exhib, 76; Purchase Award, Deseret News Show, 78, Utah Arts Co, 84; Gold Medal, April Salon, Springville Mus Art, 81; Purchase Award, Utah Arts Coun, 84. *Bibliog:* Genevieve Breerette (auth), A travers les galeries, Le Monde, 71; Lois Collins (auth), Painters of the Guthrie, Expression Mag, 81; Diane Casella Hines (auth), Randall Lake-traditional realist, Am Artist Mag, 2/3/84; article, Randall Lake-Revivalist, Southwest Art Mag, 9/85. *Media:* Oil, Pastel; Gouache. *Dealer:* John Pence Gallery 750 Post St San Francisco CA 94109. *Mailing Add:* 158 E 200 South No314 Salt Lake City UT 84111

LALLY, JAMES JOSEPH
DEALER, CONSULTANT
b Mt Vernon, NY, Apr 18, 45. *Study:* Harvard Univ, BA, 67; Columbia Univ, MBA, 68, MIA, 70. *Pos:* Dir, Chinese Works of Art Dept, Sotheby Parke Bernet NY, Inc, formerly, dir, Sotheby Parke Bernet Hong Kong, Ltd, formerly; pres, Sotheby's NAm, formerly, J J Lally Co, currently. *Specialty:* Chinese works of art (ceramics, archaic bronzes, jades, sculpture, paintings and the minor arts). *Mailing Add:* JJ Lally & Co 41 E 57th St New York NY 10022

LA LUMIA, FRANK
PAINTER
b Chicago, Ill, Aug 9, 48. *Study:* Am Acad Art, 72-73. *Work:* Mus NMex, Santa Fe; Americana Mus, El Paso, Tex; Southern Utah State Coll, Cedar City. *Exhib:* Nat Watercolor Soc Annual, Laguna Beach Mus Art, Calif, 78; one-man show, Charles & Emma Frye Mus, Seattle, 79; two-man show, Americana Mus, El Paso, Tex, 87. *Bibliog:* Jay Murphy (auth), feature article, SW Art, 89. *Mem:* Nat Watercolor Soc. *Media:* Oil, Watercolor. *Dealer:* Michael Wigley Gallery 1111 Paseo de Peralta Santa Fe NM 87501; Taos Art Gallery PO Box 1007 Taos NM 87571. *Mailing Add:* PO Box 3237 Pojoaque Sta Santa Fe NM 87501

LAMA, ALBERTO DE
PAINTER, PRINTMAKER
b Havana, Cuba. *Study:* De La Salle Sch, Havana; Univ Havana; Am Acad Art, Chicago, with William Mosby & Joseph Vanden Broucke, AA; Northeastern Ill Univ, Chicago, BA. *Work:* Pullman Bank Art Collection, Chicago; Home Fed Savings Art Collection, Chicago; Stop Publicidad, Caracas, Venezuela; Jim Walter Corp, Tampa, Fla; Delta Airlines, Atlanta, Ga. *Comn:* Corp Portraits, Celotex Corp. *Exhib:* Ill State Fair Prof Art Exhib, 67 & 70; Munic Art League Chicago, 66 & 70; Galeria Sans Souci, Caracas, 73 & 76; Wildlife Gallery, Minocqua, Wis, 73-79; Talisman Gallery, 76; and others. *Pos:* Pres, Graphic Direction Inc, Tampa Fla. *Teaching:* Instr painting & drawing, Am Acad Art, 69-74. *Awards:* Diamond Awards 70 & 71 & Gold Medal, 70 & 75, Palette & Chisel Acad Fine Arts; Harriet Bitterly Mem Award, Chicago, Ill, 76. *Mem:* Palette & Chisel Acad Fine Arts (bd dirs, 70-); Regent Art League, Chicago, Ill; Municipal Art League, Chicago, Ill. *Media:* Oil; Etchings. *Dealer:* Graphic Direction Inc 3005 Horatio Tampa Fl 33609. *Mailing Add:* 3005 Horatio St Tampa FL 33609

LA MALFA, JAMES THOMAS
SCULPTOR, EDUCATOR
b Milwaukee, Wis, Nov 30, 37. *Study:* Univ Wis, Madison, BS, 60, MS, 61 & MFA, 62; studied sculpture with Leo Steppat & printmaking with Alfred Sessler. *Work:* Memphis Acad Art; Univ Wis, La Crosse; Neville Art Mus, Green Bay, Wis. *Comn:* Relief sculpture, Phillips Hall, Univ Wis, Eau Claire, 66; sacred sculpture, Wittenberg Univ, Ohio, 68. *Exhib:* The States First Ann, Neville Pub Mus, Green Bay, Wis, 65; Springfield Art Ctr, Ohio, 67; Print & Drawing Nat, Minot State Teachers Col, NDak, 70; 29th Northeastern Wis Art Ann, Green Bay, 70; 23rd Ohio Ceramic & Sculpture Ann, Butler Inst Art, 71. *Teaching:* Instr visual arts, Univ Wis-Eau Claire, 63-66 & Wittenberg Univ, 66-69; asst prof, Univ Wis, Green Bay, 69-72; assoc prof, Univ Wis Ctr, Marinette, 72- *Awards:* A System of Sculpture Invitational, Univ Wis, Milwaukee Art Dept, fall 91. *Bibliog:* J J (auth), article, Art News, 4/64; Pierre Mornand (auth), Expositions diverses review, Rev Mod, 11/71. *Mem:* Coalition of Active Sculpture Teachers. *Media:* Multi. *Mailing Add:* Univ Wis Ctr-Marinette 750 W Bay Shore St Marinette WI 54143

LAMANTIA, JAMES
EDUCATOR, COLLECTOR
b New Orleans, La, Sept 22, 23. *Study:* Tulane Univ La, BSArch, 43; Harvard Univ Grad Sch Design, BArch, 47; Skowhegan Sch, 47. *Pos:* Prof archit, Tulane Univ, currently. *Awards:* Prix de Rome, 48-49; Fulbright fel, Italy, 49-50; Fulbright prof archit, Univ Jordan, Amman, 78-79. *Bibliog:* Equal arts of James Lamantia, Archit Forum, 52. *Media:* Oil. *Collection:* English drawings and paintings of the 19th century; architectural drawings; Piranesi prints. *Mailing Add:* 539 Bienville St New Orleans LA 70130

LAMANTIA, PAUL (CHRISTOPHER) ZOMBEK
PAINTER
b Chicago, Ill, Jan 20, 38. *Study:* Art Inst Chicago, BFA, 66, MFA, 68. *Work:* Koffler Found Collection, Nat Collection Fine Arts, Smithsonian Inst; Jean Duboffet Collection, Paris; Dennis Arian Collection, Mus Contemp Art, Chicago; Art Inst of Chicago, Ill; David & Alfred Smart Gallery. *Exhib:* Violence in Recent American Art, Mus Contemp Art, Chicago, 68; What They're Up To In Chicago Traveling Exhib, Nat Gallery Can, Ottawa, 72-73; North, East, South & Middle: An Exhibition on Contemporary American Drawing, Corcoran Gallery Art & Ft Worth Art Mus, 75-76; The Chicago Connection Traveling Exhib, E B Crocker Art Gallery, Sacramento, 76-77; Works on Paper, Art Inst Chicago, 77; Chicago Currents, Koffler Found Collection, Nat Collection Fine Arts, Smithsonian Inst, 79-80; Selections from the Dennis Adrian Collection, Mus Contemp Art, Chicago, 82; retrospective, Hyde Park Art Ctr, Chicago, 82; Chicago--Some Other Traditions Traveling Exhib, Madison Art Ctr, Wis, 83-85. *Awards:* Logan Prize, Art Inst Vicinity Show, Chicago, 84. *Bibliog:* Peter Frank (auth), Hunting the emergent American: On the trail of the Exxon National, Nat Art Guide, 1/81; David Elliott (auth), Cunning painter of the smart set, Chicago Sun-Times, 3/29/81; Dennis Adrian (auth), Sight Out of Mind, Essays & Criticism on Art, UMI Research Press, 10/85. *Media:* Oil, Mixed Media. *Dealer:* Sonia Zaks Gallery 620 N Michigan Chicago IL. *Mailing Add:* 315 W Concord Pl Chicago IL 60614

LAMARCA, HOWARD J
DESIGNER, EDUCATOR
b Teaneck, NJ, July 11, 34. *Study:* Cooper Union Art Sch, scholar, 52-56, cert graphic arts, 56; Columbia Univ, BFA, 60; Syracuse Univ, grad asst, 60-62, MFA, 62. *Collections Arranged:* James Gordon Irving-Painter, 71; Grant Reynard-Painter, 71; Charles Shedden, Sculptor-Ralph Didriksen, Painter, 71; George Fish, Painting-Shirley Yudkin, Paintings, 72; Marion Lane, Painting Retrospective, 72; Arnoldo Miccoli-Painter, 73; Sam Weinik-Painter, 74; Erna Will-Sculptor; Eleanor Smoler-Painter, 74; Batiks--Giovanna Bellia La Marca, Co Col Morris, 76; Batik & Calligraphy Exhibit, Dwight-Englewood Sch, 85. *Pos:* Advert art dir, Givaudan Advert, New York, 57-; dir, Bergen Community Mus, 71-74; sem dir Europ advert, Paris, France, Dusseldorf & Frankfurt, Ger, Zurich, Switz & Milan, Italy, 78-84; European Art Tour, Milano, Venice, Florence, Rome, 90. *Teaching:* Asst prof art, Trenton State Col, 74-80; assoc prof art, Co Col of Morris, 74; adj asst prof, Parsons Sch Design, 79-81; chmn art dept & prof art, C W Post Ctr, Long Island Univ, 80-; lectr, Musashino Art Univ Tokyo, Meiji Gakuin Univ, Yokohama & Tokyo. *Awards:* Graphics Design Award, New York, 79 & 81. *Mem:* Soc Scribes; Art Dir Club NY; Col Art Asn Am; Am Inst Graphic Arts; Univ & Col Design Asn. *Media:* Graphics, Calligraphy. *Publ:* Auth, An analysis of Gauguin's-What are We? Where Do We Come From? Where Are We Going?, Artist Mag, London, 3/62; An analysis of the facade of San Marco, Eleven Mag, spring 72; Some Thoughts on Design, City Univ New York, 74; Ethics & aesthetics, Focus, 76; Another Hillwood, Ventures in Res, 2/86. *Mailing Add:* Three Crescent Ave Cliffside Park NJ 07010

LAMARRE, PAUL
CONCEPTUAL ARTIST, SCULPTOR
b Detroit, Mich. *Study:* Univ Mich, BFA, 78. *Work:* ICA, London, Eng; New Mus Contemp Art, New York; Montecarotto Mail Art Mus, Italy. *Comn:* Bldg installation, comn by Andrew Klink, Los Angeles, 89-90; bldg installation, comn by Helen Jacobs, New York, 90. *Exhib:* one-person shows, Hallwalls, Buffalo, NY, 83 & Dooley Le, Cappellaine Gallery, New York, 92; Starving Artists Cook Book, Anthology Film Archives, New York, 89; EIDIA Show, Barbara Braathen, New York, 89; New Fabricants, Richard Green Gallery, Los Angeles, 90; Store Show, Richard/Bennett Gallery, Los Angeles, 91; Value, New York, 91; and others. *Awards:* CAPS Fel, New York, 82; Video Fel, New York Found, 87. *Bibliog:* Luca Neri (auth), Il Ricettario Dell Artista, Lei Mag, 89; Robert Mahoney (auth), Quiet desperation, Arts Mag, 89; Judd Tulley (auth), Art speak, Taxi Mag, 89; Hal Rubenstein (auth), Mirabella Mag, 91. *Mem:* Asn Independent Video & Filmakers; NY Artists Equity Asn; Media Alliance. *Media:* Installations, Video. *Publ:* Coauth, Starving Artists' Cook Book, EIDIA Publ, 91; Starving Artists' Banquet, NY Times, 92. *Mailing Add:* PO Box 11 Prince St Sta New York NY 10012

LAMB, ALBERTA CARMELLA See Cifolelli, Alberta (Alberta Carmella Lamb)

LAMB, DARLIS CAROL
SCULPTOR, PAINTER
b Wausa, Nebr. *Study:* Univ Nebr, Omaha; Creighton Univ, Omaha; Red Rocks Community Col; studied sculpture with Stanley Bleifield, Lloyd Glasson & Francisco Zuniga; Columbia Pacific Univ, BA, MA. *Work:* Gannett Found, Denver; Nebr Hist Soc, Lincoln; First Fed Savings & Loan Asn of Lincoln, Omaha; Benson Park Sculpture Garden, Loveland, Colo; Am Lung Asn. *Comn:* Bas reliefs, Eisenhower Tunnel, Colo Hwy Dept, Denver, 78; Spirit of Health (sculptures, bas reliefs & medallions), Am Lung Asn, Colorado Springs & Denver, Colo, 84-86; sculpture, Loveland High Plains Arts Coun, Colo, 88. *Exhib:* Northern Am Sculpture Exhib, Foothills Art Ctr, Golden, Colo, 83, 84, 86, 87, 90 & 91; Nat Sculpture Soc, Park Ave Atrium, New York, 85 & 91; 161st Exhib, Nat Acad Design Gallery, New York, 86; Lincoln Ctr Sculpture Garden, Ft Collins, Colo, 88; 49th Exhib, Audubon Artists, New York, 91. *Teaching:* Terracotta sculpture, Carrizo Art Sch-Ruidoso, NMex, 90 & 92 & Loveland Fine Arts Acad, Loveland, 92. *Awards:* First Place (sculpture), Jewish Community Ctr, 86; Sculpture Award, North Am Sculpture Exhib, 90; C Percival Dietsch Award, Nat Sculpture Soc, 91. *Bibliog:* Jim Mills (auth), Dimensions, Denver Post, 81; Beth Fennell (auth),

Interviews with the artists, Foothills Art Ctr Communique, 12/82; Jo Cole (auth), In the arts-Darlis Lamb, The Villager, 1/6/83; Carole Maree Hoffman (auth), Darlis Lamb, Craft Range Mag, 5-6/83; Gary Michael (auth), article, Southwest Art Mag, 1/89; Betty Lane (auth), Footprints in the sand, Elan Mag, 5/90. *Mem:* Am Artists Prof League; Catharine Lorillard Wolfe Art Club; North Am Sculpture Soc. *Media:* Clay, Cast Metal; Watercolor, Oil. *Dealer:* Gallery East PO Box 641 Loveland CO 80537. *Mailing Add:* 5515 S Kenton Way Englewood CO 80111

LAMBERT, ED
PRINTMAKER, PAINTER
b Atlanta, Tex, Jan 27, 49. *Study:* Tex Tech Univ, BFA & MFA. *Exhib:* Pratt Graphic Ctr Int Minature Print Exhib, 75; Mach I Int Print Exhib, Metrop Mus Art, Miami, Fla, 75; one-man shows, M E's Gallery, Houston, 83 & Charlton Art Gallery, San Antonio, 86; Animal Magnetism, Nueva Street Gallery, San Antonio, 90. *Teaching:* Prof printmaking, Del Mar Col, Corpus Christi, Tex, 74-, chmn art dept, 80- *Bibliog:* Joseph A Cain (auth), Profile, Art Voices South, 7-8/80; Dan Goddard (auth, rev), San Antonio Express News, 7/19/90. *Media:* Etching, Airbrush. *Dealer:* Nueva Street Gallery 507 E Nueva St San Antonio TX 78205. *Mailing Add:* 607 Del Mar Corpus Christi TX 78404

LAMBRECHTS, MARC
PAINTER, PRINTMAKER
b Lier, Antwerp, Belg, Sept 14, 55. *Study:* Higher St Lucas Inst, Brussels, Belg; Art Sch, Bratislava, Czech (govt scholarships); Pratt Inst, New York. *Work:* Aldrich Mus Contemp Art, Conn; Flemish Community, Belgium. *Comn:* Portfolio of Etchings, Rotary Club, Antwerp, Belg, 81 & Univ Brussels, 89. *Exhib:* Solo exhibs, Gallery Fontainas, Brussels, Belg, 88, Arts Club Washington, DC, 89, Tibor de Nagy Gallery, New York, 91, A Taste of Belgium, Bryamdt Galleries, Atlanta, Ga, 91, Hugieia Art Gallery, Belg, 92; Recent Acquisitions, Aldrich Mus Contemp Art, Conn, 88; Hudson River Open '89, Hudson River Mus, New York, 89; Art of Northeast USA, Silvermine Galleries, Conn, 91; A Taste of Belgium, Bryant Galleries, Atlanta, Ga, 91; 100 Years Belgian Art, L'Arc de Defence, Paris, France, 90; VUB, Free Univ Brussels, Belg, 91. *Awards:* Medal & Cert Excellence, USA Major Art Competition, Los Angeles, 87; Cert Excellence, printmaking, Int Art Competition, New York, 87; First Prize, Young Belgian Graphic Artists, Rotary Club. *Bibliog:* Patrick Conrad (dir), Sanciveria, VTM, 92; Hugo Brutin (auth), Marc Lambrechts, Art Cult & Catalog, 92. *Media:* All Media; Etching. *Dealer:* Tibor de Nagy Gallery 41 W 57th St New York NY 10019. *Mailing Add:* 30 St Felix St Apt 1C Brooklyn NY 11217

LAMELL, ROBERT (C)
PAINTER, ARCHITECT
b Oradea, Romania, Nov 21, 13; US citizen. *Study:* Hindenburg Polytech, Oldenburg, Ger, 35; Royal Hungarian Polytech Univ, Budapest, dipl, 41. *Comn:* Murals, restaurants, Carynthia, Austria, 46-47; murals, St Anthony Hosp, Denver, 57; mural, Okla Tile Co, Oklahoma City, 60; mural, Utica Bank & Trust Co, Tulsa, 75. *Exhib:* One-man shows, Kleinmayr Galleries, Klagenfurt, Austria, 48 & Ashville Mus Art, NC, 53; Okla Art Ctr, Oklahoma City, 60; Arts Place II, Okla Art Ctr, Oklahoma City, 82; Mabel-Gerrer Art Mus, Shawnee, Okla, 83; Norick Art Ctr, Olkahoma City, Okla, 87. *Pos:* Deliniator & designer, C L Monnot Jr & Assoc, archit, Oklahoma City, 55- *Teaching:* Instr watercolor, Gaetches Studio, Okla City. *Awards:* Best Show, Fidelity Bank, 81; Strathmore Award, Watercolor Oklahoma, 82; Dick Blick Award, Tri-State Exhib Kans Watercolor Soc, 83. *Mem:* Okla Art Guild; Okla Watercolor Asn; Am Inst Archit; Pastel Soc Okla. *Media:* Acrylic, Oil; Watercolor. *Dealer:* The House Gallery 5536 N Western Oklahoma City OK 73116. *Mailing Add:* 2640 Wilshire Blvd Oklahoma City OK 73116

LAMIS, LEROY
SCULPTOR, EDUCATOR
b Eddyville, Iowa, Sept 27, 25. *Study:* NMex Highlands Univ, BA, 53; Columbia Univ Teachers Col, MA, 56. *Work:* Albright-Knox Mus; Des Moines Art Ctr; Whitney Mus Am Art; Joseph H Hirshhorn Collection, Washington, DC; Larry Aldrich Mus. *Comn:* NY State Coun Arts Award, 70. *Exhib:* Whitney Mus Am Art Sculpture Ann, New York, 64, 66 & 68; Responsive Eye, Mus Mod Art, New York, 65; Art Today, Albright-Knox Art Gallery, Buffalo, 65; one-man shows, Staempfli Gallery, New York, 66, 69 & 73 & Traveling Show, 69, J B Speed Mus, Louisville, John Herron Mus, Indianapolis, La Jolla Mus Art, Calif; Neuberger Collection, Smithsonian Inst & RI Sch of Design, 68; Am Sculpture, Univ Nebr, Lincoln, 70; Artists at Dartmouth, New City Hall, Boston, Mass, 71. *Pos:* Found & pres, PC Art Inc. *Teaching:* Asst prof, Cornell Col, 56-60; prof sculpture, Ind State Univ, Terre Haute, 61-; artist in residence, Dartmouth Col, 70. *Mem:* Am Abstract Artists. *Media:* Plastics; computer art. *Mailing Add:* 3101 Oak Terre Haute IN 47803

LAMONTAGNE, ARMAND M
SCULPTOR, PAINTER
b Pawtucket, RI, Feb 3, 38. *Study:* Studied in Florence, Italy. *Comn:* Bronze bust, Gerald R Ford Mus, Dearborn, Mich; 7-foot wood sculptures of Babe Ruth, 84 & Ted Williams, 85, Baseball Hall of Fame, Cooperstown, NY,; portrait of gov, Providence, RI, 87; life size wood sculptures of Larry Bird, Bobby Orr, Carl Yastrzemski, New Eng Sports Mus. *Awards:* Russell Grinell Found Grant, 64. *Media:* Wood. *Mailing Add:* 405 Burgy Rd N North Scituate RI 02857

LA MONTE, ANGELA MAE
PAINTER
b New Britain, Conn, 1944. *Study:* Catan-Rose Inst Fine Arts,Cert, 67; Nat Acad Fine Arts, Study with Hugh Gumpel, 69; City Col, New York, MFA, 77; Bank St Col, MS, 82. *Exhib:* The $100 Gallery-Third Show, 78; Malcolm King Faculty Exhib, Harlem State Off Bldg Gallery, 81; Art '84 Tobago, Int Art Convention, Trinidad-Tobago, WI, 84; Boniface Gallery, Cathedral of St John the Divine, New York, 86; Castillo Gallery, New York, 87; Gallery M, New York, 87; Gallery Art 54, New York, 88. *Teaching:* Prof art, painting & drawing, Malcolm King Col, New York, 79-89, chairperson art dept, 84-89. *Awards:* Louis Comfort Tiffany Found Scholar Award, 69; Louis La Beaume Award, Nat Acad Fine Arts, 70; Art Alumni Pres Award, City Col New York, 83. *Mem:* Orgn Independent Artists. *Media:* Oil; Miscellaneous. *Publ:* Art exhibit to benefit Malcolm-King, New York Voice, 9/81; article, New Britain Herald, 9/86; article, Hartford Courant, 9/87; article, Amsterdam News, 1/88. *Mailing Add:* 149 W Fourth St Apt 2B New York NY 10012

LAMPITOC, ROL PONCE
PAINTER, PRINTMAKER
b Laoag City, Philippines; Can citizen. *Study:* Univ Philippines Sch Fine Arts, 52; Univ Windsor, 74; Nat Art Seminars, with John Howard Sanden, cert, 80. *Work:* Malacanang Palace & US Embassy, Manila, Philippines; St Claire Col Art Collections, Windsor, Ont; Univ Toronto, Chemical Eng, Ont; Centenary Hosp, Scarborough, Ont; Univ Toronto's Emmanuel Theological Col, Ont. *Comn:* Vpres Diosdado Macapagal, comn by Paldo Bustamante, Quezon City, Philippines; Mayor Richard Daley (portrait), comn by Philippine Consul Gen Sulit, Ill; Pres Harry Truman (portrait), US Embassy, Manila, Philippines; Bishop Georgiji (life-size portrait), Serbian Orthodox Diocese, Can; Prof Silcox Woodsworth, Woodsworth Col, Toronto, Ont. *Exhib:* SEast Asian Art Conference, Art Asn Philippines, Manila, 57; Art Gallery, Windsor, Ont, 74; Pastel Soc Am, Nat Arts Club, New York, 74, 76, 77 & 79; 6th Int Art Friendship, Int Friendship Asn Japan, Tokyo, 81; Philipino Artist North Am, Nat Archives, Ottawa, Ont, 81; Pastel Soc Can Nat Arch, Ottawa, Ont, 88. *Pos:* Serigraphist, Quezon City, Philippines; asst art dir, Piercell Merchandising, Windsor, Ont, 73-80; painter & master printer, Atelier Lampitoc, Agincourt, Ont, 80- *Teaching:* Instr painting, St Clair Col Continuing Educ, 73-74; instr painting, Windsor Art Gallery, 74. *Awards:* First Prize, Art Asn Philippines, 72; First Prize & most popular piece, Blue Mountain Found Arts, Collingwood, Ont, 87; First Prize, Maison Dela Culture, Pastel Soc Can, 89. *Bibliog:* Dorothy Hall (auth), Art & artists, Park East, 1/10/77; Liane Faulder (auth), Famed in the Philippines, Toronto Star, Ont, 7/31/84; Carlota Rubio (auth), Art to Live with, Vision Hispano Americana, 1/15/88; and others. *Mem:* Visual Arts Ontario; Pastel Soc Canada; Portrait Club New York; Philipino Artists Group. *Media:* All; Serigraphy, Silkscreen. *Dealer:* Five Signatures 111 Queen St E Suite 340 Toronto ON M5C 1S2; Harbour Gallery. *Mailing Add:* 25 Tunmead Sq Scarborough ON M1B 1X1 Canada

LANCASTER, MARK
PAINTER
b Yorkshire, Eng, May 14, 38. *Study:* Dept of Fine Art, Newcastle Univ, Eng, 61-65. *Work:* Victoria & Albert Mus & Tate Gallery, London; Arts Coun of Northern Ireland, Belfast; Allen Art Mus, Oberlin, Ohio; Art Gallery of S Australia, Adelaide; Mus of Mod Art, New York. *Exhib:* British Drawings: The New Generation, Mus Mod Art, New York, 67; Six Artists (toured Britain), Victoria & Albert Mus, London, 67; Young British Artist (traveling), Mus Mod Art, New York, 68; British Painting, Hayward Gallery, London, 75; one-man shows, Rowan Gallery, London, Eng, 65, 67, 71, 73, 75 & 80, Walker Art Gallery, Liverpool, Eng, 73 & Multiples, New York, 75; Tate 79, Tate Gallery, London,; Am Painting: the 80's, Grey Art Gallery, New York, 79. *Pos:* Artist-in-Residence, King's Col, Cambridge, Eng, 68-70; designer, Merce Cunningham Dance Co, New York, 74-80, artistic adv, 80-84, artist & designer, 85- *Teaching:* Instr, Dept of Fine Art, Newcastle Univ, Eng, 65-66; Bath Acad of Art, Corsham, Wiltshire, Eng, 66. *Awards:* Purchase Prize, British Int Print Biennale, Bradford, 70; NY Dance & Performance Award, 89. *Bibliog:* Mark Lancaster, Betty Parsons Gallery, article in New York Times, 10/74; John Russell (auth), Lancaster sets the stage for Cunningham, Art Am, 7-8/79; Richard Shone (auth), Mark Lancaster, Burlington Mag, 7/80; and others. *Mailing Add:* c/o Cunnungham Dance Found 55 Bethune New York NY 10014

LANCEL MCELHINNEY, JAMES
PAINTER
b Abington, Pa, Feb 3, 52. *Study:* Skowhegan Sch of Painting & Sculpture, 73; Tyler Sch of Art of Temple Univ, BFA, 74; Yale Sch of Art, MFA, 76. *Exhib:* Candidates for Art Awards, Am Acad & Inst of Arts & Letters, New York, 79; Challenge Exhib, Fleisher Art Mem, Philadelphia Mus Art, 83; 20th Juried Exhib, Allentown Art Mus, Pa, 86; Printmaking: East-West, Sichuan Fine Arts Inst, China, 86; 163rd Ann Exhib, Nat Acad Design, New York, 88; one-person shows, Gross McCleaf Gallery, Philadelphia, 86-87, Almquist Gallery, New Preston, Conn, 87, Jessica Darraby Gallery, Los Angeles, 87, Addison Ripley Gallery, Washington, DC, 87, Washington Studio Sch, DC, 87, J Rosenthal Fine Arts, Ltd, Chicago, 88, Perkins Ctr Arts, Moorestown, NJ, 88, Hahn Gallery, Philadelphia, 90 & Goforth Rittenhouse Galleries, Philadelphia, 91; Contemp Philadelphia Artists, Philadelphia Mus Art, 90; The Figure, R H Love Gallery, Chicago, 89; Re-Figure, Levy Gallery, Moore Col Art, Philadelphia, 90; Contemp Philadelphia Artists, Philadelphia Mus Art, 90; Linda Hayman Gallery, Boca Raton, Fla, 91. *Awards:* Purchase Award, Camden County Cult Asn, Haddon Heights, NJ; Ben and Lorraine Alexander Award, Cheltenham Ann Juried Exhib, Pa, 86; Visual Arts Fel, Nat Endowment Arts, 87. *Bibliog:* Edward J Sozanski (auth), Using the

Human Figure to Examine Issues, Philadelphia Inquirer, 3/15/90; A Philadelphia Exhib Worth the Effort? Philadelphia Inquire, 4/29/90; David James (auth), Society, Philadelphia Inquirer, 1/29/91. *Media:* Oil. *Publ:* Contribr, newsletter, Japanese Sword Soc US, 81; Token to Rekishi, Nihon Token Hozon Kai, 84; auth, exhib review, Spectacular Helmets of Japan, Metalsmith, Soc NAm Goldsmiths, spring 86; coed, Art and Sword, Japanese Sword Soc US, 88. *Dealer:* J Rosenthal Fine Arts 212 W Superior St Chicago IL 60610. *Mailing Add:* 313 Fulton St PO Box 40174 Philadelphia PA 19106

LAND, ERNEST ALBERT
PAINTER, DESIGNER
b Hamilton, Ont, Sept 21, 18; US citizen. *Work:* NASA Space Mus, Washington, DC; Grumbacher Collection Fine Art; IBM Collection Fine Art, New York; Marietta Col, Ohio; Butler Inst Am Art, Youngstown, Ohio. *Comn:* Mural, USA Corps Engrs, Seattle World's Fair, 60; nine murals on hist solid propellants, USN Mus, Indian Head, Md, 62-63; exhib, Work of Dr Leakey, Olduvai Gorge, Africa (with Robert Widder & Ken Hopkins), Nat Geog Explorers Hall, 63-64. *Exhib:* Butler Inst Am Art Ann, Youngstown, Ohio, 70; Mainstreams Int, Marietta Col, Ohio, 70 & 72; Allied Artists Am 58th Ann, Nat Acad Design Galleries, 71; Am Artists Prof League Grand Nat, 71. *Pos:* Dir art & designer scenics, US Info Agency TV & Film Serv, Washington, DC. *Teaching:* Lectr, Chase Manhattan Bank, New York, 54-55; lectr, Am Tel & Tel, New York, 55-62. *Awards:* John J McDonough Award, Butler Inst Am Art, 72; Best in Show & First Prize, Mainstreams, Marietta Col, 77; Lester Cook Mem Prize, 77. *Bibliog:* Joseph Grumbacher (auth), Twenty-one paint in polymer, M Grumbacher, 65; Gutierrez & Roukes (auth), Painting with Acrylics, Watson-Guptill, 65; Joseph Giacalone (auth), Leonardo would have us use polymer, Syndicate Mag, 66. *Mem:* Life fel Royal Soc Art, London; fel Am Artists Prof League; Art League Northern Va. *Media:* Oil. *Publ:* Illusr, US Senate Comt Aeronaut & Space Sci, US Govt Printing Off, 63. *Dealer:* Capricorn Galleries 4849 Rugby Ave Bethesda MD 20814. *Mailing Add:* c/o Capricorn Galleries 4849 Rugby Ave Bethesda MD 20814

LAND, SARAH AGNES RILEY See Riley-Land, Sarah (Sarah Agnes Riley Land)

LANDAU, JACOB
PAINTER, PRINTMAKER
b Philadelphia, Pa, Dec 17, 17. *Study:* Philadelphia Col Art, with Earl Horter & Franklin Watkins, cert, 38; New Sch Social Res, with Erich Fromm, Rudolf Arnheim & Eugene O'Neill, Jr, 48-49 & 52-53. *Work:* Mus Mod Art, New York; Whitney Mus Am Art; Metrop Mus Art; Libr of Cong; Philadelphia Mus Art; and others. *Comn:* Ten stained glass windows, Keneseth Israel Synagogue, Philadelphia, 71; Meditation on Love & Death (lithograph), NJ State Arts Coun, 75; and others. *Exhib:* The Figure, Recent Paintings USA, 62 & Tamarind--Homage to Lithography, 69, Mus Mod Art, New York; Human Concern-Personal Torment, Whitney Mus Am Art, 69; one-man shows, Jorgenson Auditorium, Univ Conn, 71, Hopkins Hall, Ohio State Univ, 73 & ACA Gallery, New York, 76; Am Acad Arts & Lett, 73 & 74; Graphic Retrospective, NJ State Mus, 81; Drawing Retrospective, Ryder Col, Laurenceville, NJ, 88; and others. *Teaching:* From instr to assoc prof, Pratt Inst, 57-68, prof graphic art, 68-86, founder, Univ-Without-Walls Proj, prof emer, 86- *Awards:* Nat Arts Endowment Sabbatical Grant, 66; Guggenheim Found Fel, 68; Ford Found Travel-Study Grant, 75; NJ State Coun Arts Fel, 87. *Bibliog:* H C Pitz (auth), Jacob Landau, Am Artist, 10/56; Jacob Landau, Current Biog, 12/64; Barry Schwartz (auth), Tiger of wrath--Jacob Landau, Arts Soc, spring-summer 71; and others. *Mem:* Soc Am Graphic Artists; Visual Artists & Galleries Asn; Nat Acad Design; adv bd, Brandywine Workshop; trustee, Roosevelt Arts Proj. *Media:* Watercolor; Woodcut, Lithography. *Publ:* Auth, Charades, Tamarind Lithography Workshop, 65; Yes-no, art-technology, Wilson Libr Bull, 9/66, The Necessity of Art in Education, World Futures, Vol XXI, Nos 1, 2, 85; Holocaust, Assoc Am Artists, 68; illusr, Out of the whirlwind, Union Am Hebrew Congregations, 68; illusr, Selected Writings of Hoffmann, Univ Chicago, 69; and others. *Dealer:* Martin Sumers Graphics 50 W 57th St New York NY 10019. *Mailing Add:* 2 Pine Dr Roosevelt NJ 08555

LANDAU, MITZI
DEALER, CURATOR
b New York, NY, Sept 18, 25. *Study:* NY Univ, BA, 45. *Collections Arranged:* Gaston Lachaise sculptures & drawings; Edward Muybridge, Picasso Vollard Suite, Margaret Bourke- White, Joseph Albers, Louis Sullivan, Billboard Art. *Pos:* Cur, Gaston Lachaise Found, Art Dealers Asn, 67-; founder, Travelling Exhib Serv; mem bd dir, Los Angeles Munic Art Gallery; lectr Gaston Lachaise & mod sculpture, var mus, pub groups & docents. *Mem:* Col Art Asn; Asn Am Mus. *Specialty:* Art of the 19th & 20th century, American and European sculpture, paintings, drawings and master photography. *Mailing Add:* 1625 Thayer Ave Los Angeles CA 90024

LANDAU, MYRA
PAINTER, MURALIST
b Bucarest, Rumania; Mex citizen. *Study:* Studied with Oswaldo Goeldi, Authodactic engraving on metal in painting. *Work:* Mus Mod Art, Mexico; Pinqcoteca del Estado, Sao Paulo, Brazil; Casa de Las Americas, Habana, Cuba; Univ Veracruzana, Xalapa, Mexico; Casas de Cultura, Mexico; and others. *Exhib:* Mus Mod Art, Mexico City, 75 & 87; Centro de Estudios del er Mundo, Mexico City, 77; Casa de La Cultura, Recife-Pe, Brazil, 78; Gallery Arte Global, Sao Paulo, Brazil, 78; Mus Mod Art, Salvador, Brazil, 78; Mus Carrillogil, Mexico City, 79; Univ Metrop Mexico City, 80; Ctr Cult Mexique, Paris, 83; Instituto Italo, Latino Americano, Roma, Italia. *Pos:* Docente-Facultad de Artes Plasticas, 74-75; investigadora, Inst de Investigaciones; esteticas, Univ Veracruzana, 75- *Bibliog:* Teresa del Conde (auth), 12 Expresiones plasticas de hoy, Bancreser, 11/88; Raul Renan & Berta Taracena (auth), 67; Diez años de la Galeria Metropolitana, Univ Autonoma Metropolitana, 89. *Mem:* Foro de Arte Contemporaneo, Mexico City. *Media:* Linen, Pastels. *Publ:* Si Sabes Ver, Univ Veracruzana, 76; Textos Legirles Ritmos Ile Gibles, Univ Veracruzana, 85; Ritmos, Univ Autonoma Nacional de Mexico, 86. *Mailing Add:* Alfaro 6 Xalapa Veracruz Mexico

LANDERS, BERTHA
PAINTER, PRINTMAKER
b Winnsboro, Tex. *Study:* Sul Ross Col, BS(art); Colorado Springs Fine Arts Ctr, Colo, grad study with Arnold Blanch, Adolf Dehn, Boardman Robinson & Henry Varnum Poor; Art Students League, grad study with Reginal Marsh. *Work:* Dallas Mus Art; Denver Mus Art; Libr Cong, Washington, DC; Witte Mem Mus, San Antonio, Tex; Ft Worth Art Ctr, Tex; Corpus Christi Mus, Tex; Los Angeles Co Mus Art; Valley House Gallery, Dallas, Tex; Am Scene Gallery, Austin, Tex; Brighton Press & Gallery, San Diego, Calif; and others. *Exhib:* Dallas Allied Arts Show Ann, 36-45; Nat Print Ann, New York, 42-57; Nat Acad Design, New York, 43-44; Corpus Christi Nat Exhib, Tex, 45; Nat Gallery, Washington, DC, 46; Brooklyn Art Mus Exhib, 53; and others. *Pos:* Cur & cataloguer, Mrs A A Zonnie Print Collection, 42-49; pres, Tex Women Printmakers, 44-46; art librn, Dallas Pub Libr, 46-49; art librn, Kansas City Pub Libr, Mo, 50-58. *Awards:* Painting Purchase, Corpus Christi Nat Exhib, 45; Print Purchase, Libr Cong, 45; Painting Purchase, Denver Art Mus, 47. *Bibliog:* Albert Reese (auth), American Prize Winning Prints of the 20th Century, 49. *Mem:* Charter mem Nat Mus Women Arts, Washington, DC; San Diego Print Club. *Media:* Printing, Etching, Aquatinting & Lithography; Oil, Watercolor. *Dealer:* Kennedy Galleries 20 E 56th St New York NY 10022. *Mailing Add:* 12567 Caminto de la Gallarda San Diego CA 92128

LANDFIELD, RONNIE (RONALD T)
PAINTER
b Bronx, NY, Jan 9, 47. *Study:* Art Students League, 62-63; Kansas City Art Inst, Mo, 63; San Francisco Art Inst, 64-65. *Work:* Mus Mod Art, Whitney Mus Art, Metrop Mus Art, New York; Hirshhorn Mus of Art, Washington, DC; RI Sch of Design Mus, Providence; Walker Art Ctr, Minneapolis, Minn. *Comn:* Mural (painting 11 ft x 20 ft), Westinghouse Corp & I Chermayoff, Pittsburgh, Pa, 70. *Exhib:* Whitney Ann & Biennial Exhib of Am Painting, New York, 67, 69 & 73; Lyrical Abstraction, Whitney Mus of Am Art, 71 & Aldrich Mus of Contemp Art, Ridgefield, Conn, 71; Art for Your Collection, RI Sch of Design, Providence, 71; Recent Acquisitions, Mus of Mod Art, New York, 72; one-man shows, Andre Emmerich Gallery, New York, 73-75 & 75, Linda Farris, Seattle, Wash, 78, 79, 81, 84, 87 & 89, Sarah Rentschler Gallery, New York, 78 & 79 & Medici-Berensen, Miami, Fla, 79; Charles Cowles Gallery, New York, 80, 82-84; Hokin Gallery, Miami, Fla, 85 & 87; Hokin-Kaufman Gallery, Chicago, 85 & 87; Stephen Haller Fine Arts, New York, 87, 88, 89 & 90. *Teaching:* Instr fine arts, Sch of Visual Arts, New York, 75-89. *Awards:* Gold Medal, San Francisco Art Inst, Calif, 65; Cassandra; Nat Endowment Arts, 83. *Bibliog:* Whee Kim (auth), A personal definition of pictorial space, Arts Mag, 11/74; Noel Frackman (auth), article, Arts, Vol 50, No 1, 9/75; Phyllis Tuchman (auth), article, Art News, Vol 77, No 3, 3/78. *Media:* Acrylic, Watercolor. *Dealer:* Stephen Haller Fine Arts 415 W Broadway New York NY 10012. *Mailing Add:* 31 Desbrosses St New York NY 10013

LANDIS, ELLEN JAMIE
CURATOR, HISTORIAN
b Chicago, Ill, May 6, 41. *Study:* Univ Calif, Berkeley, BA; Univ Vienna, 60-61; NY Univ, Inst Fine Arts, MA. *Exhib:* Reflections, 88; Common Ground: Suites, 88-89; Museum Menagerie, 91; E I Couse, 91; Unbroken Threads, 92; and others. *Collections Arranged:* Homage to Rodin (coauth, catalog), Los Angeles Co Mus Art, Los Angeles, 67; Rodin Bronzes from the Collection of B Gerald Cantor (auth, catalog), Am Fedn Art, 70; Vincent Van Gogh, Baltimore Mus Art, 70; Four Americans in Paris: The Collections of Gertrude Stein and Her Family, Baltimore Mus Art, 71; Early 20th Century European Masterpainters, 77, Indian Art Today (auth, catalog), 77, Metro Youth Art (auth, catalog), 77 & Albuquerque Artists I (auth, catalog), 77, Mus Albuquerque; Reflections of Realism (auth, catalog), 79 & Katachi: Form and Spirit in Japanese Art, 80, Albuquerque Mus; Here and Now, 35 Artist in New Mexico (auth, catalog), 81, West-Southwest (auth, catalog), 82, In Place, 82, Eve Laramee, 83 & Hiroshige, 83 Albuquerque Mus, Wilson Hurley, 85; Adventures West, 89; Printers Impressions, 90. *Pos:* Adv bd, Artspace Mag, 78-; actg cur, Robert Gore Rifkind Collection, Beverly Hills, Calif, 70 & 71-72; bd dirs, Actors Theater, Albuquerque, NMex, 79-81; bd trustees, Comprehensive Art Publ, Ohio, 80- *Teaching:* Lectr introd to art, Yuba Col, Marysville, Calif, 76-77. *Awards:* The Chris Award, Homage to Rodin, Film Coun Greater Columbus, 69. *Bibliog:* Contemporary Personalities, Accademia' Italia' Delle Arti e Del Lavoro, 82; International Who's Who of Professional & Business Women, 1st ed, autumn 88. *Mem:* Col Art Asn; Am Asn Mus. *Res:* Centralized research in areas of 19th Century and 20th Century art. *Publ:* Co-auth, The David E Bright Collection, Los Angeles Co Mus Art, Los Angeles, 67; Matisse in Baltimore, Television Spec, 71; Carl Redin (exhib catalog) 84 & Wilson Hurley: A Retrospective Exhibition (exhib catalog), 85, Albuquerque Mus. *Mailing Add:* 7112 Osuna NE Albuquerque NM 87109

LANDREAU, ANTHONY NORMAN
ADMINISTRATOR
b Washington, DC, Apr 2, 30. *Study:* Cath Univ Am, with Kenneth Noland; Black Mountain Col, NC, with Kline, Fiore & Rice, BA, 54. *Collections*

Arranged: Smithsonian Travelling Exhib Serv, 69-71; Carnegie Inst, 78-79; Textile Mus, 83-85. *Pos:* Exec dir, Textile Mus, Washington, DC, 67-75; cur educ, Carnegie Inst Mus Art, Pittsburgh, 75-81; pres, Int Collection Inc, 81-88; grad studies prog Antropology, Temple Univ, Philadelphia, 88. *Teaching:* Instr weaving-design, Black Mountain Col, 54-56; lectr hist of textiles, Univ Md, 75. *Awards:* Near E Res Ctr Grant, rug studies in Turkey, 73; Nat Endowment Arts prof fels, study in Turkey, 73 & study in USSR, 75; Turkish res proj, Nat Endowment Humanities, 80. *Mem:* Am Asn Mus; Archaeol Inst Am; Col Art Asn; Am-Turkish Asn (bd mem, 74-); Iran-Am Soc (bd mem, 74-). *Res:* Folk weaving, particularly in the Middle East. *Publ:* auth, Yoruk, The Nomadic Weaving Tradition in the Middle East, Carnegie Inst, 78; auth, Carpets and rugs, Encycl Americana, 80; Flowers of the Yayla, Textile Mus, 83. *Mailing Add:* 2019 Spring Garden St Philadelphia PA 19130

LANDRY, ALBERT
DEALER
b New York, NY, Oct 9, 19. *Study:* Columbia Univ, MA(art hist); Atelier Leger, Paris, France. *Pos:* Dir, Galerie Villand-Galanis, Paris, 50-54; dir, Assoc Am Artists, 54-58, Albert Landry Galleries, New York, 58-64 & J L Hudson Co Art Gallery, Detroit, 64; vpres, Marlborough-Gerson Gallery, 69; former dir, Landry-Bonino Gallery; dir, New York Art '73; pvt dealer for 20th century corporate art collections, currently; Fine Arts Consult. *Specialty:* Contemporary American and European art. *Mailing Add:* 22 E 36th St No 5C New York NY 10016

LANDRY, RICHARD MILES
PHOTOGRAPHER, VIDEO ARTIST
b Cecilia, La, Nov 16, 38. *Study:* Univ Southwestern La, with Calvin Harlan, BME. *Exhib:* Whitney Mus Biennial, 72; Brazil Biennial, 73; Xerox Art in Evolution, 73; Los Angeles Co Mus, 74; ICA Gallery, Philadelphia, 75. *Awards:* Creative Artists Award, 74; Creative Artists Pub Serv Award for Mixed Media, 74; Nat Endowment Arts Grant for Video, 75. *Dealer:* Leo Castelli Gallery 420 W Broadway New York NY 10021. *Mailing Add:* 125 Cedar St Apt 8S New York NY 10006

LAND-WEBER, ELLEN E
PHOTOGRAPHER, EDUCATOR
b Rochester, NY, Mar 16, 43. *Study:* Univ Iowa, Iowa City, BA(art hist), MA & MFA(creative photog). *Work:* Int Mus of Photog, George Eastman House, Rochester, NY; San Francisco Mus Mod Art, Calif; New Orleans Mus Art; Libr Cong, Washington, DC. *Comn:* Bicentennial Doc Proj on Archit of Courthouses in US (in collab with 23 other photogrs with assigned geog areas), Seagram's Inc, New York, 75-76. *Exhib:* One-person shows, San Francisco Mus Mod Art, 78, Bard Col, Annandale on Hudson, NY, 79, Focus Gallery, San Francisco, 80 & Shadai Gallery, Tokyo, 83; Women of Photog, San Francisco Mus Mod Art, Calif, 75-76; Photog Synthesis Nat, Herbert Johnson Mus, Cornell Univ, Ithaca, NY, 76; Electroworks, George Eastman House, Rochester, NY, 79. *Teaching:* Instr photog, Univ Calif Extension, Los Angeles, 70-74; asst prof photog, Humboldt State Univ, Arcata, Calif, 74-79, assoc prof, 79-83, prof, 83-. *Awards:* Nat Endowment Arts Photographer's Fel, 74, 79 & 82. *Mem:* Soc for Photog Educ (nat treas, 79-81, nat secy, 81-83). *Publ:* Illusr, Vision & Expression, Horizon Press, 69; Women of photography: an historical survey, San Francisco Mus of Mod Art, 75; Translations, Herbert F Johnson Mus, Ithaca, NY, 79; Courthouse, a Photographic Document, Horizon Press, 79; The Passionate Collector, photographs by Ellen Land-Weber, Simon & Schuster, 80. *Mailing Add:* 790 Park Place Arcata CA 95521

LANDWEHR, WILLIAM CHARLES
MUSEUM DIRECTOR
b Milwaukee, Wis, Sept 19, 41. *Study:* Univ Wis-Stevens Point, BS, 63; Univ NDak, MA, 68. *Collections Arranged:* Barry Le Va: Six Blown Lines (Accumulation Drift), Art Ctr Gallery, Univ Wisconsin-Stout, Menomonie, 69; Richard Hunt: Small Sculpture-Drawings-Lithographs (auth, catalog) Quincy, Ill, Art Ctr, 72; Realism in NC, Mint Mus, Charlotte, 74; The Lithographs & Etchings of Phillip Pearlstein (auth, catalog raisonne), Springfield Art Mus, Mo, 86; Robert Cottingham: A Print Retrospective 1972-1986 (auth, catalog raisonne), Springfield Art Mus, Mo, 86; Watercolor USA 1986-The Monumental Image (auth, catalog), Springfield Art Mus, Mo, 86. *Pos:* Cur, Art Ctr Gallery, Univ Wisconsin-Stout, Menomonie, 68-69; dir, SDak Art Mus, Brookings, 69-71, Quincy Art Ctr, 71-73, Springfield Art Mus, Mo, 76-87 & Paine Art Ctr & Arboretum, Oshkosh, Wis 89-; cur exhibs, Mint Mus, Charlotte, NC, 73-76; exec dir, Lakeview Mus Arts & Sci, Peoria, Ill, 87-89. *Teaching:* Instr art, SDak State Univ-Brookings, 69-71; lectr art, Western Ill Univ-Macomb, 72-73; Cent Piedmont Community Col, Charlotte, 73-75. *Mem:* Am Asn Mus; Am Federation Arts (trustee, 78-80); Midwest Mus Conf; Wis Fed Mus. *Publ:* Auth, The Villain as Hero, Southwest Art, 6/75; ed, Selections from the Permanent Collection of the Springfield Mus, Mo, 80; auth, American Watercolors from the Collection of the Springfield Mus, Mo, 87; Ellen Murray: The Collection Series, Mid-America Arts Alliance, Kansas City, Mo, 88; Exercising Tight Control: The Watercolors of Peggy Flora Zalucha, Am Artist, 10/90. *Mailing Add:* 2055 Carlton Rd Oshkosh WI 54904-9335

LANE, ALVIN S
COLLECTOR
b Englewood, NJ, June 17, 18. *Study:* Univ Wis, PhB; Harvard Univ Law Sch, LLB; New Sch Social Res, with Seymour Lipton. *Pos:* Chmn comt on art, New York Bar Asn, 63-65; mem bd overseers fine arts, Brandeis Univ, 66-70; mem adv bd to NY Atty Gen on Art Legis, 66-71; secy & trustee, Aldrich Mus Contemp Art, 69-76, dir & vpres, 79; Soho Ctr for Visual Artists Inc, 74-83; bd dirs, Artists Equity Asn, New York, Creative Artists Public Service Program, Inc, 82-84; Drawing Committee, Whitney Mus Am Art, 91. *Collection:* Mod & contemp sculpture and sculptors' drawings. *Publ:* Auth, How the bar can assist the art community, New York Bar Asn, 65; The case of the careless collector, Art in Am, 65; Disclosure on disclosure, Print Collector Newslett, 74. *Mailing Add:* 35 E 38th St New York NY 10016

LANE, JOHN RODGER
MUSEUM DIRECTOR, HISTORIAN
b Chicago, Ill, Feb 28, 44. *Study:* Williams Col, BA, 66; Univ Chicago, MBA, 71; Harvard Univ, AM, 73, PhD, 76. *Collections Arranged:* Stuart Davis: Art and Art Theory, Brooklyn Mus & Fogg Art Mus, 78; Modernist Art from the Edith and Milton Lowenthal Collection, Brooklyn Mus, 81; Robert Bourdon: Auto Rex, Carnegie Inst, 82; The Groups: Paintings by Archie Rand, Carnegie Inst, 83; Abstract Painting and Sculpture in America, Carnegie Inst, San Francisco Mus Mod Art, Minneapolis Inst Art & Whitney Mus, 83-84; Carnegie International, Carnegie Inst, 85; Ross Bleckner, 88 & Don Van Vliet, San Francisco Mus Mod Art, 88. *Pos:* Asst dir, Fogg Art Mus, 74; exec asst to dir, Brooklyn Mus, 75-78, adminr curatorial affairs, 79, asst dir curatorial affairs, 80; dir, Mus Art, Carnegie Inst, 80-87, San Francisco Mus Mod Art, 87-. *Teaching:* Teaching fel art hist, Harvard Univ, 73-75. *Mem:* Col Art Asn; Am Asn Mus; Int Coun Mus; Asn Art Mus Dirs. *Res:* 20th century American Art. *Publ:* Auth, New York: The Brooklyn Mus, Stuart Davis: Art and Art Theory, 78; co-ed (with Susan C Larsen), Abstract Painting and Sculpture in America 1927-1944, Carnegie Inst & Harry N Abrams, Inc, 83; co-ed (with Saskia Bos & John Caldwell), 1985 Carnegie International, Carnegie Inst, 85; contribr, The Barney A Ebsworth Collection Catalog, SLouis Art Mus, 87; Stuart Davis, American Painter, The Metrop Mus Art, 91. *Mailing Add:* c/o San Francisco Museum of Modern Art Van Ness at McAllister St San Francisco CA 94102

LANE, LOIS
PAINTER, PRINTMAKER
b Philadelphia, Pa, Jan 6, 48. *Study:* Yale Summer Sch Music & Art, 68; Philadelphia Col Art, BFA, 69; Yale Univ Sch Art & Archit, MFA, 71. *Work:* Whitney Mus Am Art, & Mus Mod Art, New York; Albright-Knox Gallery, Buffalo, NY; Des Moines Art Ctr, Iowa; Mus Fine Art, Houston; Nat Gallery of Art, Washington, DC. *Exhib:* One-person exhibs, Willard Gallery, New York, 77, 79, 80, 83, 87 & 89, Akron Mus Art, Ohio, 80 & Nigel Greenwood Gallery, London, John Berggruen Gallery, San Francisco, 87 & Barbara Mathes Gallery, New York, 88 & 89; New Image Painting, 78-79 & Biennial, 79, Whitney Mus Am Art, 84; Ten Artists/Artists Space, Neuberger Mus, Purchase, NY, 79; Painting & Sculpture Today, Indianapolis Mus Art, 80; A New Bestiary: Animal Imagery in Contemp Art, Va Mus, 81; Back to the USA, traveling to var Ger mus, 83; Recent Acquisitions, Mus Mod Art, New York, 83; Philadelphia Mus Art, Pa, 88; NY St Mus, Albany, 89; Rhode Island Sch Design, Providence, 90. *Awards:* NY State Coun Arts Creative Artists Pub Serv Prog Grant, 77; Nat Endowment Arts fel painting, 78. *Bibliog:* Jeanne Siegal (auth), Arts, 11/80; Brian Wallis (auth), Arts, 1/81; Carolyn Kinder Carr (auth), introd to The Image in American Photography & Sculpture 1950-1980, Akron Art Mus; Lois Nesbitt (auth), Artnews, 9/88. *Media:* Oil; Etching; Monotypes. *Publ:* Contribr, New Image Painting, Whitney Mus, 78; American Painting: the Eighties, Barbara Rose/Vista Press, 79. *Mailing Add:* c/o Barbara Mathes Gallery 851 Madison Ave New York NY 10021

LANE, MARION JEAN ARRONS
PAINTER, INSTRUCTOR
b Brooklyn, NY. *Study:* Brooklyn Mus Art Sch, with Manifred Schwartz & Reuben Tam; Pratt Inst, NY; Art Students League, with Morris Kantor; William Paterson Col, NJ, BA; Rutgers Univ, MFA. *Exhib:* Brooklyn Mus Alumni Exhib, 58; Work by New Jersey Artists, Newark Mus Triennial, 61 & 85; Art from New Jersey, NJ State Mus, Trenton, 68 & 70; Lincoln Ctr, Philharmonic Hall, New York, 68; New Talent, Kraushaar Gallery, New York, 75; Pleiades Gallery, New York, 76 & 77; Women's Caucus for Art, Fed Plaza, New York, 82; New York Univ, 84; City Without Walls Gallery, Newark, NJ, 84; Maurice Pine Libr, Fairlawn, NJ, 86; Kerygma Gallery, NJ, 89; Williams Ctr, Rutherford, NJ, 90. *Teaching:* Instr, art appreciation & drawing, Bergen Community Col, 80-86; art therapist, 86-90. *Awards:* Essex Award, Painters & Sculptors Soc, Jersey City Mus, 65; NJ State Coun Arts Fel Grant, 83 & 88; Edward Albee Found Fel, 83. *Bibliog:* Hedy Obeil Pazz (auth), article, Arts Mag, 10/77; Deborah Jerome (auth), article, Record, 82; Eileen Watkins (auth), article, in: Newark Star Ledger, 4/86 & 9/90. *Mem:* Life mem Art Students League. *Media:* Acrylic, Sheetmetal. *Mailing Add:* 441 Hawthorne Pl Ridgewood NJ 07450

LANE, ROSEMARY LOUISE
PRINTMAKER, SCULPTOR
b San Francisco, Calif, Dec 6, 44. *Study:* Calif Col Arts & Crafts, Oakland, with Ralph Borge, Robert Bechtle & Roy DeForrest, BFA, 66; Calif State Univ, Hayward, 70; Univ Ore, with Laverne Krause & Ken Paul, MFA, 73. *Work:* Univ Ore Art Gallery, Eugene. *Comn:* Artwork, comn by Martha Dupont, The Sanctuary, Wilmington, Del, 89-90. *Exhib:* 59th, 60th & 61st Soc Am Graphic Artists National, Cooper Union, New York, 82, Hutchings Gallery, Greenvale, NY, 83, Firehouse Gallery, Garden City, NY, 85; Int Juried Art Exhib, Mussavi Gallery, New York, 85; 5th, 10th, 12th, 13th, 15th & 17th Nat Print & Drawing Exhib, Minot State Univ, NDak; 7th Nat Open Juried Exhib Contemp Spiritual Art, Marywood Col, Visual Arts Ctr, Scranton, Pa, 87; 3rd Int Biennial Print Exhib, Taipei Fine Arts Mus, Taiwan, China, 88; Nat Print Exhib '88, Trenton State Col, NJ; Colorprint USA, Nat Curated Invitational Exhib, Univ Tex, Lubbock, 83, 86, 88 & 91; Ten Years

of Excellence Individual Artists Fel Recipients, Del Div ARts, Carvel Bldg & Rehobeth Art League, 91. *Teaching:* Vis instr printmaking, Univ Ore, Eugene, 73-74; from instr printmaking, drawing & papermaking to asoc prof, Univ Del, Newark, 74-87, area coordr, 74-93, prof, 88- *Awards:* Merit Award, Int Juried Art Exhib, Mussavi Gallery, New York, 85; Award, 5th, 15th & 17th Nat Print & Drawing Exhib, Minot State Col, NDak; Individual Artist's Fel Grant, Del State Arts Coun, 85 & 86. *Bibliog:* Lisa Lyons (auth), Rosemary Lane, Artvoices, 1-2/80; Patricia Wright (auth), Rosemary Lane/ Muse Gallery, Art Express, 12/81; Penelope Bass Cope (auth), Artist goes with her feminine instincts, Wilmington J, 11/83. *Mem:* Soc Am Graphic Artists; Los Angeles Printmaking Soc; Philadelphia Print Club; Int Graphic Arts Found. *Media:* Bichromate Prints; Handmade Paper Casts. *Mailing Add:* 50 Cummings Ct Bear DE 19701

LANE, WILLIAM
PAINTER
b Kalamazoo, Mich, Jan 12, 36. *Study:* Univ Calif Los Angeles, BA, 58, MA, 61. *Work:* Home Savings & Loan Collection, Los Angeles, Calif; Security Pac Bank, Los Angeles, Calif; Toronto Dominion Bank, Los Angeles, Calif; Price, Waterhouse & Co, Los Angeles, Calif. *Exhib:* One-man shows, Palos Verdes Art Mus, 69, La Jolla Mus Art, 67, Studio Cafe, Corona Del Mar, 88, St Luke's Episcopal Church, Long Beach, Calif, 89; InterAmerican Culture, Honduras, 81; 20th Century European & Am Watercolors, Long Beach Mus Art, Calif, 88; Five Southern California Painters, Am Cult Ctr, Taipei, Taiwain, 90; 6 + 35, FHP Hippodrome Gallery, Long Beach, Calif, 91; Seductive Geometry, Los Angeles Abstr Art, Olga Dollar Gallery, San Francisco, Calif, 91; Aspects of Figural Painting in Southern California, Tatistcheff Gallery, Santa Monica, Calif, 91. *Teaching:* Prof art, Rio Hondo Col, Whittier, Calif, 69-; vis asst prof painting, Univ Calif Los Angeles, 76-77; prof painting, Riottende Col, Whittier, Calif, currently. *Awards:* Purchase Awards, City Art Festival, Los Angeles, 60, 66; Nat Endowment Arts Fel, 87. *Media:* Acrylic, Watercolor. *Mailing Add:* 2203 E 10th St Long Beach CA 90804

LANG, AVIS
EDITOR, CURATOR
b Chicago, Ill, Jan 18, 44. *Study:* Univ Mich, Ann Arbor, BA, 65, MA(art hist), 68. *Collections Arranged:* Pork Roasts: 250 Feminist Cartoons Traveling Exhib, US, Can & Europe, 81-; Mirrorings: Women Artists of the Atlantic Provinces Traveling Exhib, Can, 82-83. *Pos:* Managing ed, Heresies: A Feminist Publication on Art and Politics, 89- *Teaching:* Lectr, Univ BC, Vancouver, 68-78, Banff Ctr, Alta, 80 & NSCAD, Halifax, formerly; asst prof, Simon Fraser Univ, Burnaby, BC, 83; adj lectr, City Univ New York, 92-93. *Res:* Women artists of the past; feminist concerns; cartoons; contemporary Canadian art. *Mailing Add:* 202 W 78th St 3E New York NY 10024

LANG, CAY
PHOTOGRAPHER
b Long Beach, Calif, Feb 5, 48. *Study:* Calif State Univ, Fresno, BA, 76; San Francisco Art Inst, MFA, 79. *Work:* Mediateque, Henin Veaumont, France; De Saisset Mus, Santa Clara, Calif; Los Angeles Co Mus Art; Bibliotheque Nat, Paris, France. *Exhib:* Laguna Beach Mus Art, Calif, 85; Camden Art Ctr, London, Eng, 85; Mus Mod Art, Ft Mason, San Francisco, 86; De Saisset Mus, Santa Clara, Calif, 88; Palais de Tokyo, Paris, 88. *Teaching:* Univ Calif Berkeley Exten, 90; Calif State Univ, San Francisco Exten, 90; Univ Calif, Davis, spring 91 & 92. *Awards:* Fel, MacDowell Colony, 87; Proj Grant, Polaroid Corp, 87; Visual Arts Fel, Am Pen Women, 88-89. *Bibliog:* Hans Eberhard Hess (auth), Blumenwunder aus Kalifornien, Phototecnik Mag, 4/86; Portfolio, Photo Design, 7/88; Evelyn Roth (auth), Body language, Am Photogr, 7/88. *Dealer:* Galerie Michele Chomette 24 Rue Beauborg 75003 Paris France; Benteler-Morgan Gallery, Houston, Tex. *Mailing Add:* 1506 62nd St Emeryville CA 94608

LANG, DANIEL S
PAINTER
b Tulsa, Okla, Mar 17, 35. *Study:* Northwestern Univ, Evanston; Univ Tulsa, BFA, with Alexandre Hogue; Univ Iowa, MFA, 59, with Mauricio Lasansky. *Work:* Mus Mod Art, New York; Art Inst Chicago; Libr Cong, Washington, DC; Nelson-Atkins Mus Fine Art, Kansas City; Victoria & Albert Mus, London; and others. *Comn:* Beneficial Management Group, NJ, 82. *Exhib:* Boston Mus Fine Arts, 61; Gimpel & Weitzenhoffer, New York, 75; Fischbach Gallery, New York, 77, 79 & 80; Graphik Int, Stutgart, WGer, 79; David Findlay Gallery, New York, 81; Sherry French Gallery, New York, 84; Hokin Gallery, Palm Beach, Fla, 91; William Hardie Gallery, Glasgow, Scotland, 92. *Teaching:* Asst prof painting, Art Inst Chicago, 62-64, Wash Univ, 64-65; vis artist, Ohio State Univ, 68-69, Univ SFla, fall 72; adj prof, Univ Utah, 84- *Media:* Multimedia. *Publ:* Auth, Daniel Lang: Trees/Water/ Silence, A selection of paintings from 1975 through 1986, 86. *Mailing Add:* 38 W 56th St No 5 New York NY 10019

LANG, J T
PRINTMAKER, EDUCATOR
b Maple Shade, NJ, Dec 24, 31. *Study:* Philadelphia Col Art, Cert; Tyler Sch Art, BFA, BS(educ) & MFA; Barnes Found, with Violette De Mazia; also with Toshi Yoshida, Hirooyuki Tajima & Yuji Abe, Tokyo. *Work:* Philadelphia Mus Art; Cincinnati Mus Art; Birmingham Mus Art; State Dept, Washington, DC; Philadelphia Libr Collection. *Comn:* Large ed/woodcut, Print Club Philadelphia, 65; Exodus (litho ser), Pearl Fox Gallery of Elkins Park, 71; color litho ed, La Salle Col, Philadelphia, 74; John Baptist de La Salle, La Salle Col, Philadelphia, 81. *Exhib:* Japan Print Soc Ann, Tokyo, 62, 63, 65 & 66; one-man print shows, Yoseido Gallery, Tokyo, 65 & Birmingham Mus, Ala, 74; USA Print Workshop Exhib, Cincinnati, 67; Am Color Print Soc Ann, Philadelphia, 68-81. *Teaching:* Asst prof Western cult, Aoyama G Univ, Tokyo, 63-67; vis lectr printmaking, Tyler Sch Art, Philadelphia, 68-70; asst prof printmaking & Asian art hist, LaSalle Col, Phildelphia, currently. *Awards:* Purchase Award, Pa Acad Fine Arts, 69; Outstanding Printmaker Award, Philadelphia Bd Educ, 73; Tyler Art School Award of Honor, 84. *Bibliog:* Dorothy Grafly (auth), Summer print show, Sun Bull, Philadelphia, 7/30/67; Richard L Bell (auth), Prints of J T Lang (video tape), Springfield High Sch, 4/71; Sally Ann Harper (auth), Lang/printmakers, La Salle Collegian, 3/27/73. *Mem:* Am Color Print Soc (coun mem, 72-); Philadelphia Print Club; Col Art Teacher's Asn; Philadelphia Watercolor Club, 87- *Media:* All. *Dealer:* Pearl Fox Gallery 104 Windsor Ave Melrose Park Philadelphia PA 19126. *Mailing Add:* LaSalle Univ Philadelphia PA 19141

LANG, MARGO TERZIAN
PAINTER
b Fresno, Calif. *Study:* Stanford Univ; Fresno State Univ; Ariz State Univ; Prado Mus, Madrid, Spain; also spec study with Edgar Whitney, Dong Kingman, Rex Brandt, George Post, Millard Sheets & others. *Work:* Over 50 paintings in US Embassies worldwide; and many others. *Comn:* Sunrise Tomorrow (cross superimposed on desert sunrise) comn by J Parker Nicholson, Glass & Garden Church, Scottsdale, Ariz, 71; Arizona Scenes, Pepsi Cola Bldg. *Exhib:* Int Platform Asn, Washington, DC, 70-75; Phoenix Art Mus, 70 & 71; one-person shows, Guadalajara, Mex, 68, Grand Cent Galleries, New York, 68 & 69, Corcoran Mus, 74, Brussels, Belg, 74 & Hammer Galleries, New York, 77; and others. *Awards:* Ann Competition Award, Grand Cent Galleries, 68 & 69; Best of Show Award, 70 & Silver Medal of Excellence, 71, Int Platform Asn; Honored by US Dept State for 25 Yrs of Exhibiting Paintings in Embassies Worldwide, 89. *Mem:* Nat Soc Arts & Lett; Nat Soc Lit & Arts; Am Artists Prof League; Ariz Watercolor Asn. *Media:* Oil, Watercolor. *Publ:* Twenty-Five Years at the US Department of State, 64-89, Art in Embassies Catalog, Paris, France. *Dealer:* Hammer Galleries 525 Park Ave New York NY 10021. *Mailing Add:* 6127 Calle del Paisano Scottsdale AZ 85251

LANG, RODGER ALAN
SCULPTOR, EDUCATOR
b Chicago, Ill, Feb 9, 42. *Study:* Cornell Col, BA(art); Univ Wis-Madison, with Don Reitz & Harvey Littleton, MA(art) & MFA. *Work:* Brooks Mem Art Gallery, Memphis, Tenn; Mesa Col, Grand Junction, Colo; American Craft Mus, New York City. *Comn:* Ceramic tile wall mural, US West Corp, 78; ceramic tile wall mural, State of Colorado, 80. *Exhib:* Objects: USA The Johnson Collection of Contemporary Crafts, Traveling Exhib, 69; Clayworks: 20 Americans, Mus Contemp Crafts, New York, 71; Contemporary Crafts of the Americas, Colo State Univ & Orgn Am States, 75; Civilizations, Kohler Arts Ctr, Sheboygan, Wis, 77; 20 Colo Artists, Denver Art Mus, 77; Clay Az Art Int: II, international traveling exhib, 86-87; Figure & Landscape: Western Am Ceramicists, Denver Art Mus, 86. *Teaching:* Instr, Cleveland Inst Art, 66-70; assoc prof, Metrop State Col, 70-77, prof, 77- *Bibliog:* Rose Slivka (auth), Laugh-in in clay, Craft Horizons, 10/71; Civilizations in clay, Craft Horizons, 12/77; The Old Pecos Mus, Ceramics Mo, 4/90. *Mem:* Nat Coun Educ Ceramic Arts. *Media:* Ceramics, Wood, Mixed Media. *Dealer:* Inkfish Gallery Paul Hughes 949 Broadway Denver CO 80203. *Mailing Add:* 1655 Hoyt St Lakewood CO 80215

LANG, WENDY F
ADMINISTRATOR, PHOTOGRAPHER
b Cleveland, Ohio, Feb 15, 38. *Study:* Antioch Col, BA(design), 61; Stanford Grad Sch, MA, 63. *Work:* Nara Mus, Japan. *Exhib:* Butler Inst Am Art, Youngstown, Ohio, 78; Canton Inst Art, Ohio, 78; Friends Photog, 78; Downey Mus Art, Los Angeles Ctr Photog Studies, 78; Tenth Ann Int Photog Meet, Arles, France, 79; and many others. *Pos:* Bd dirs, Cameravision, Los Angeles, 76-80; mem bd trustees, Los Angeles Ctr Photog Studies, 78-; coordr, Photog Mus, Los Angeles, 79-80. *Teaching:* Inst community serv, Los Angeles City Col, 79-84. *Bibliog:* Photographic Artists & Innovators, 83. *Mem:* Soc Photog Educators; and others. *Publ:* Contribr, Communication Arts, London Records, 74; Rufus, 78 & Shards, 79, Small Press; co-illusr, Ballet Box, RCA Records, 79; contribr & coauth, Sequences: Baptism of Eros II, Peterson's Photog, 6/79. *Mailing Add:* 1231 Kipling Ave Los Angeles CA 90041

LANGAGER, CRAIG T
PAINTER, SCULPTOR
b Seattle, Wash, July 5, 46. *Study:* Minn State Univ, Bemidji, BS(art), 71; Univ Ore, Eugene, MFA(art), 74. *Work:* Brooklyn Mus Art, NY; Denver Art Mus, Colo; Metrop Mus Art, New York; Winnipeg Art Gallery, Manitoba, Can; Univ Colo Galleries, Boulder. *Comn:* One Percent for Art Purchase, Seattle Arts Comn, Wash, 78; wall relief, comn by Ann Gerber, Seattle, Wash, 79; sculpture, comn by Gordon Hanes, Winston-Salem, NC, 82; sculpture, Niagara Frontier Transporation Authority, Buffalo, NY, 82-83. *Exhib:* Wave Hill '81: Tableaux, Wave Hill Outdoor Sculpture Exhib, Bronx, NY; Painting & Sculpture Today, Indianapolis Mus Art, Ind, 82 & 86; New York, E Fla State Univ, Metrop Mus & Art Ctr, Coral Gables, & Phoenix Art Mus, 82-83; solo exhib, Critical Distance: Cloning for a New Society, Inst Contemp Art, Boston, 82 & Security Pac Gallery, Seattle, 91-92; 3-person show, Dialogues, Winnipeg Art Gallery, 84; Body and Soul: Aspects of Recent Figurative Sculpture, Contemp Art Ctr, Cincinnati, Ohio, 85 & traveled 85- 87, Art Mus Asn Am, San Francisco, Calif; Solo installation, Security Pacific Gallery, Seattle, 91-92. *Pos:* Coord, Earthworks: Land Reclamation as Sculpture Symp, King Co Arts Comn, Seattle, Wash, 78-79. *Teaching:* Chmn, fine arts dept, Cornish Inst, Seattle, Wash, 76-78; vis artist, sculpture, Syracuse Univ,

NY, winter 82; Univ Colo, Boulder, spring 85; vis prof, sculpture & painting, Western Wash Univ, Bellingham, 89-90. *Awards:* Minn State Arts Grant, Minn Coun Arts, Minneapolis, 75; Whitney Found Grant, New York for Dartington Col Arts, Eng, 77. *Bibliog:* Kim Levin (auth), Craig Langager, Critical Distance-Cloning for a New Society, (catalog essay) Issues, New Allegory II, Inst Contemp Art, Boston, 82; Shirley Madill (auth), Dialogues, Winnipeg Perspective 84, Grauer, Langager, McEwen, (catalog essay), Winnipeg Art Gallery, Man, 84; Sarah Rogers-Lafferty (auth, catalog essay), Body and Soul, Aspects of Recent Figurative Sculpture, Contemp Arts, Cincinnati, 85. *Dealer:* Ruth Siegel Inc 24 W 57th St New York NY 10019. *Mailing Add:* 2970 N Shore Dr Bellingham WA 98226

LANGER, SANDRA LOIS (CASSANDRA)
HISTORIAN, CRITIC
b Woodridge, NY, Dec 18, 41. *Study:* Univ Miami, BA, 67, MA, 69; NY Univ, PhD, 74. *Collections Arranged:* Beyond Survival: Old Frontiers, New Horizons; Robert R Presto Collection, New York Empire State Mus, NY. *Pos:* Contrib critic, Art Papers, 74-79; independent art hist & critic, New York, 86; co-dir, Psych-Arts Soc, currently; art adv & appraiser, free-lance writer, critic, grants & publ adv, currently. *Teaching:* Asst prof mod-contemp art, Fla Int Univ, 73-78; asst prof to assoc prof, Univ SC, Columbia, 78-86; vis, assoc prof, Hunter & Queens. *Awards:* Smithsonian Post-Doctorial Fel, Nat Mus Art, 84. *Mem:* Col Art Asn; Women's Caucus for Art (adv bd, 75-77, 79-); Nat Women's Studies Asn; Int Asn Art Critics; Am Soc Journalists & Authors. *Res:* John F Kensett a critical biography; Deconstructing Romaine Brooks; critical overview; contemporary art and criticism, feminism and post modernism. *Publ:* co-ed & contribr, Feminist Art Criticism: An Anthology, UMI Res Press, 88; Turning points & striking places: Feminist art criticism, Col Art Journal, 91; The Many Masques of Eve, Hillwood Art Gallery, 91; Mother and Child in Art, Cresent/Random House Bks, 91. *Mailing Add:* 32-22 89th St Apt 605 Flushing NY 11369-2179

LANGFORD, SHERRY K
ENVIRONMENTAL ARTIST, PAINTER
North Platte, Nebr, Oct 29, 44. *Study:* Private study with G Leslie Smith, 67-70, Kansas City Art Inst, 69-72. *Work:* Searcy Co Bank, Marshall, Ark; Tenneco, Houston, Tex. *Comn:* Great Blue Heron, NW Ark Audubon Soc, Fayville, Ark, 84; Red Wolf, Wolf Sanctuary, Eureka, Mo, 87; River Otters, Little Rock Zoo, 87; Mountain Lion, Little Rock Zoo, 92; Mexican Wolf, Wolf Sanctuary, Eureka, Mo, 92; and others. *Exhib:* Okla Wildlife Art Festival, Camelot Hotel, Tulsa, Okla, 82-91; Arts Crafts & Design Fair, Robinson Conv Ctr, Little Rock, Ark, 82-92; Art Happening, St Louis, Mo, 84-92; Cheyenne Audubon Wildlife Exhib, Conv Ctr, Cheyenne, Wyo, 85; Wildlife Art Walk, St Louis Zoo, Mo, 85-88; Nat Wildlife Art Fest, Doubletree Inn, Overland Park, Kans, 88-92; and others. *Collections Arranged:* One-woman Exhibition, Fort Smith Art Ctr, 86 & 89. *Pos:* Litho-artist, Hallmark Cards, 62-64. *Awards:* Best of Show, Okla Wildlife Art Fest, 88 & 91; Best of Show, Nat Wildlife Art Exhib, 88; Artist of Year, Ark Wildlife Fed, 88, 91 & 92; Best of Show, Red River Revel, Shreveport, La, 89; Best of Show, Best Bald Eagle, Best Pencil, Okla Wildlife Art Festival, 90. *Bibliog:* Doris Freyder (auth), Wildlife Artist, Ozarks Mountaineer, 10/82; Terry Horton (auth), article, Arkansas Out of Doors, 10/88. *Mem:* Eureka Springs Guild of Artists & Craftspeople. *Media:* Pencil, Watercolor. *Publ:* Illusr, Trees, Shrubs & Vines of Arkansas, Ozark Soc; A Shadow in the Forest, J B George, Vantage Press. *Dealer:* White Oak Studio HC 79 Box 152 Marshall AR 72650; The Spinning Wheel 32 N Main Eureka Springs AR 72632. *Mailing Add:* c/o White Oak Studio Rt 1 Box 152 Marshall AR 72650

LANGLAND, TUCK
SCULPTOR, EDUCATOR
b Minneapolis, Minn, Oct 6, 39. *Study:* Univ Minn, BA(art), 61, MFA(sculpture), 64. *Work:* Ind Univ, Univ Notre Dame, South Bend; Midwest Mus Am Art, Elkhart, Ind; St Paul Acad & Summit Sch, Minn; Minn Mus, St Paul. *Comn:* William J Karnes (bronze), Beatrice Foods, Chicago, 69; Autumn (bronze), Portland, Ind, 74; Violin Woman (bronze), South Bend, Ind, 82; Polymnia (bronze), Ft Wayne, Ind, 84; Madeline Bertrand (bronze), Niles, Mich, 87. *Exhib:* One-man shows, Kalamazoo Inst Art, Mich, 77, St Catherine's Col Gallery, St Paul, Minn, 77, Small Bronzes, traveling, Eng, 77-78, Tweed Mus, Duluth, Minn, 78, Reflections, South Bend Art Ctr, Ind, 80 & Mid-West Mus Am Art, Elkhart, Ind, 84; Concurrent Themes, South Bend Art Ctr, 87; and others in US & Eng. *Teaching:* Asst lectr sculpture, Carlisle & Sheffield Cols of Art, Eng, 64-67; asst prof sculpture, Murray State Univ, 67-71; assoc prof & chmn dept fine arts, Ind Univ, South Bend, 71-82, prof, 82-; vis lectr, Stoke-on-Trent, Eng, 77-78. *Awards:* First Prize, Midwest Mus Am Art, 79; Outstanding Sculpture, Hoosier Salon, 80, 82 & 84-87; Best of Show, Northern Ind Arts Asn, 83; Liskin Prize, Nat Sculpture Soc, 85. *Mem:* Artists Equity; Fel, Nat Sculpture Soc. *Media:* Bronze. *Publ:* Auth, Practical Sculpture, Prentice Hall, Englewood Cliffs, NJ, 88. *Mailing Add:* 12632 Anderson Rd Granger IN 46530

LANGMAN, RICHARD THEODORE
GALLERY DIRECTOR
b Philadelphia, Pa, June 9, 37. *Study:* Cornell Univ, 54-55; Univ Calif, Berkeley, BA(urban design), 60. *Collections Arranged:* Alice Neel, Paintings, 74; Clayton Pond, Paintings & Graphics, 74; Graphics of the 70's (Int Graphics Show), 75 & Craft Art (Nat), 77, Langman Gallery; Bruce Evans, Paintings, SICA, 78 & 80, Constructions, 80; Andy Warhol, Paintings & Graphics, 83. *Pos:* Dir, Langman Gallery, Jenkintown, Pa. *Specialty:* Contemporary painting and sculpture. *Mailing Add:* 218 Old York Rd Jenkintown PA 19046

LANGSDORF, MARTYL SCHWEIG See Martyl (Martyl Schweig Langsdorf)

LANIGAN-SCHMIDT, THOMAS
ASSEMBLAGE ARTIST, INSTRUCTOR
b Elizabeth, NJ, Jan 16, 48. *Study:* Pratt Inst, Brooklyn, NY, 65-66; Sch Visual Arts, New York, 67; studied pvt with Jack Smith & Charles Ludlam, 70-74. *Work:* Metrop Mus Art, New York; Albright Knox Mus, Buffalo, NY; Mus d'Art Contemporain, Lausanne, Switz; Ludwig Mus, Aachen, Ger; Nelson Atkins Gallery, Kansas City. *Exhib:* Venice Biennale, The Pluralist Decade, USA Pavillion, Venice, Italy, 80; 20th Century Art from the Metrop Mus New York, Queens Mus, Flushing, NY, 83; Arte, Ambiente, Scena, Venice Bienale Italy, 84; Content: A Contemporary Focus, Hirshorn Mus & Sculture Garden, Washington, DC, 84; Sacred Images in Secular Art, Whitney Mus, New York, 86; Contemporary Diptychs, Whitney Mus (Equitable), New York, 87; Americana Installation, Groninger Mus, Neth, 87; 1991 Biennial Exhib, Whitney Mus Am Art, New York, 91. *Pos:* Bd govs, Skowhegan Sch Painting & Sculpture, 91- *Teaching:* Instr MFA prog, Sch Visual Arts, 89-; resident artists studio, Skowhegan Sch Painting & Sculpture, 91- *Bibliog:* Robert Atkins (auth), The center show, Village Voice, 5/26/89; Roberta Smith (auth), The return of Tzarina Tatlina, NY Times, 4/24/92; Tzarina Tatlina, New Yorker, 4/92. *Media:* Scotch Tape, Plastic Wrap. *Publ:* Contribr, Ornamentalism, Robert Jensen & Patricia Conway (auths), Oitter/Crown, 82; Once a Catholic, Peter Occhigrasso (auth), Houghton/Mifflin, 88. *Dealer:* Holly Solomon Gallery 724 Fifth Ave New York NY 10019. *Mailing Add:* 309 W 47th St New York NY 10036

LANMON, DWIGHT P
MUSEUM DIRECTOR, CURATOR
b Pueblo, Colo, July 28, 38. *Study:* Knox Col, Galesburg, Ill, 56-58; Univ Colo, Boulder, BA, 58-60; Univ Calif, Los Angeles, 61-66; Univ Del, Winterthur, MA, 66-68. *Pos:* Asst cur ceramics and glass & in charge of conservation, H F duPont Winterthur Mus, Del, 68-73, dir & trustee, 92-; deputy dir-collections, Corning Mus Glass, NY, 73-81, dir, 81-92; bd mem, Census of Stained Glass, 80-92; trustee, Rockwell Mus, 83-92, pres, 88-92. *Mem:* Int Coun Mus (glass comt, 77-); Int Asn Hist Glass (secy gen, 81-85); Asn Art Mus Dirs; fel, Soc Antiquaries (London). *Media:* Glass. *Specialty:* American decorative arts, 1640-1860. *Publ:* Coauth, John Frederick Amelung, 76 & 92; Paperweights: Flowers Which Clothe the Meadows, 78. *Mailing Add:* Winterthur Mus Winterthur DE 19735

LA NOUE, TERENCE
PAINTER, EDUCATOR
b Hammond, Ind, Dec 4, 41. *Study:* Ohio Wesleyan Univ, BFA, 64; Hochschule für Bildende Künste, West Berlin, Fulbright Scholar, 65; Cornell Univ, MFA. *Work:* Roy Neuberger Mus, Purchase, NY; Corcoran Gallery Art, Washington, DC; Indianapolis Mus Art; Carnegie Inst; Whitney Mus Am Art, Guggenheim Mus, Brooklyn Mus & Mus Mod Art, New York; Albright-Knox Gallery. *Exhib:* Philadelphia Mus Art; Carnegie Int, Pittsburgh; Albright-Knox Gallery, 71; Indianapolis Mus Art, 72; one-man shows, Nancy Hoffman Gallery, 74-78 & 80, Galerie Farideh Cadot, Paris, 77, 78 & 80, Arts Club Chicago, 83, Siegel Contemp Art, New York, 83, 85-88 & 90, Andre Emmerich, 88-89 & 92, Heland-Wetterling Gallery, Stockholm, Sweden; 9th Paris Biennial Am Art, 75; Philadelphia Mus Art, 77; 34th Corcoran Biennial of Am Painting; Iran-Am Soc, 78; Ochi Gallery, Sun Valley, Calif, 92; and others. *Teaching:* Asst prof art, Trinity Col, 67-72; assoc prof art & head dept, La Guardia Col, 72-84. *Awards:* Nat Endowment Art Grant, 72 & 83; Guggenheim Fel, 82. *Bibliog:* Numerous articles in Art in Am, Arts Mag, NY Times & Art News, 76- *Media:* Acrylic on Canvas. *Mailing Add:* c/o Andre Emmerich Gallery 41 E 57th St New York NY 10022

LANSDON, GAY BRANDT
PRINTMAKER, JEWELER, METALSMITH
b San Antonio, Tex, Dec 6, 31. *Study:* Univ Houston, Tex, BFA, 65; Mus of Fine Arts Sch, Houston, 66-68; Sam Houston State Univ, MFA, 75. *Work:* Univ Houston, Univ Ctr; Sam Houston State Univ; Shell Oil Co; Xerox Corp; Price Waterhouse; and others. *Comn:* 16 paintings, comn by Dr Robert Stewart, Houston, 67; serigraph, comn by Jean Geeslin, Huntsville, Tex, 69; three printed fiber panels, Bellville State Bank, Tex, 72. *Exhib:* SW Crafts Biennial, Mus Santa Fe, NMex, 71; 15th Ann Tex Craftsman, Dallas Mus Fine Arts, 71; Colorprint USA, Lubbock, Tex, 75; Third Nat Print Exhib, Univ Southern Calif, Los Angeles, 75; 14th Midwest Biennial, Joslyn Art Mus, Omaha, Nebr, 75; Purdue Univ Small Print Exhib, 76; Five Texas Jewelers, Austin, 92. *Teaching:* Instr art, Houston Mus of Fine Arts, Tex, 69-71; art dept fac, Univ Houston, Cent Campus, 71-82, coordr printmaking, 76-82; mem fac continuing educ, Univ Tex, Austin, currently. *Awards:* Jurors' Merit Awards, SW Graphics Invitational, 72 & Dimension X, 76, Houston Art League; First Prize, Baytown Ann, 78. *Bibliog:* Kit Van Cleave (auth), Gay Lansdon: Mixed-media printmaking, Today's Art, 2/77. *Media:* Mixed. *Dealer:* Artisans Gallery at the Arboritum 1000 Research Blvd Suite 258 Austin TX 78759. *Mailing Add:* 11631 River Oaks Trail Austin TX 78753

LANSDOWNE, JAMES FENWICK
PAINTER
b Hong Kong, Aug 8, 37. *Study:* LLD-hon, Univ Victoria. *Work:* Ulster Mus, Belfast; Montreal Mus Fine Arts; Art Gallery of Greater Victoria; Beaverbrook Found; Audubon House, New York. *Exhib:* Lab Ornithol, Cornell Univ, 68; Nat Mus Natural Hist, Smithsonian Inst, Washington, DC, 69; Animals in Art, Royal Ont Mus, Toronto, 75; retrospective, Vancouver Art Gallery, 81; Scripps Inst Oceanography, La Jolla, Calif, 81; and others. *Awards:* Order of Canada. *Mem:* Royal Can Acad Arts. *Media:* Gouache. *Publ:* Coauth, Birds of Northern Forest, 66; Birds of Eastern Forest, Part I, 68 & Part II, 70; auth, Birds of the West Coast, Part I, 76 & Part II, 80; illusr, Rails of the World, 76. *Mailing Add:* 941 Victoria Ave Victoria BC V8S 4N6 Canada

LANSNER, FAY
PAINTER, TAPESTRY ARTIST
b Philadelphia, Pa. *Study:* Tyler Sch Fine Art, 45-47; Art Students League, 47-48; Hans Hofmann Sch, 48-50; also with Leger & L'Hote, Paris, 50-51. *Work:* Weatherspoon Art Mus, Greensboro, NC; NY Univ Art Collection; Corcoran Gallery Art, Washington, DC; Newsweek, Metrop Mus, New York; Neuberger Mus, State Univ NY Col, Purchase; and others. *Exhib:* Corcoran Gallery, Washington, DC, 67; Albright-Knox Art Gallery, Buffalo, NY, 67; Mus Mod Art, New York, 68, 69 & 71; 17th Brooklyn Mus Print Ann, NY, 70; Women in the Arts, Stamford Mus, Conn, 72; Women Choose Women, New York, 72; Hofmann Students, Metrop Mus Art, New York, 78; Poets & Painters, 79; one-person exhib, Denver Mus, Ingber Gallery, New York, 80. *Bibliog:* Harold Rosenberg (auth), Hofmann students, Art News Ann, 63; Doris Reno (auth), Lansner paintings show, Times Herald Post, 66; Fay Lansner (monogr), Essay 13, Guest Conversation, I Sandler, 77. *Publ:* Auth, Barbara Riboud, Craft Horizons Mag, 4/72. *Dealer:* Marlborough Graphics 40 W 57th St New York NY 10022; Arras Gallery 29 W 57th St New York NY 10019. *Mailing Add:* 317 W 80th St New York NY 10024

LANTZY, DONALD MICHAEL
ADMINISTRATOR, PRINTMAKER
b Wilmington, Del, May 8, 42. *Study:* Philadelphia Col Art, Pa, BFA, 65; Temple Univ, Tyler Sch Art, MFA, 69. *Work:* Temple Univ, Philadelphia, Pa; West Chester State Col, Pa. *Exhib:* Solo exhib, Pa Acad Fine Arts, 77 & Gross/McCleaf Gallery, 79, Philadelphia, Pa; US Int Studies, Naples, Italy, 81; Temple Abroad, Rome, Italy, 81; Lowe Art Gallery, Syracuse, NY, 83. *Pos:* Assoc Dean, Tyler Sch Art, Philadelphia, Pa, 74-75 & dir, Temple Abroad, 79-82; Dean, Col Visual & Performing Arts, Syracuse Univ, Ny, 82- *Media:* Drawing, Painting. *Mailing Add:* Syracuse University 200 Crouse College Syracuse NY 13244-1010

LANYON, ELLEN
PAINTER, PRINTMAKER
b Chicago, Ill, Dec 21, 26. *Study:* Art Inst Chicago, with Joseph Hirsch, BFA, 48; State Univ Iowa, with M Lasansky, MFA, 50; Courtauld Inst, Univ London, with Helmut Reuhman. *Work:* Art Inst of Chicago & Mus Contemp Art, Chicago; Walker Art Ctr, Minneapolis; Nat Collection, Smithsonian Inst; Metrop Mus Art & Brooklyn Mus, New York; McNay Art Inst, San Antonio, Tex; Des Moines Art Ctr; Madison Art Ctr; Krannert Mus. *Comn:* Container Corp Am: Great Ideas, US Dept Interior Bicentennial Exhib; Workingmans Coop Bank, Boston, 81; State Ill Bldg, Chicago, 83; Perregrin (bronze), Southern Ill Univ Foundry, Carbondale, 86; State Capitol, Springfield, Ill, 89. *Exhib:* Art Inst Chicago, 46-81; Recent Painting USA: The Figure, Mus Mod Art, New York, 62; solo exhibs, Richard Gray Gallery, 68-85, Susan Caldwell Inc, New York, 82-83, Name Gallery, Chicago, 83 & 25-year retrospective (traveling exhib), Krannert Mus, Univ Ill, 87-88; Landscape, Whitney Mus; American Realism, San Francisco Mus Art, 85; Realism & Realities, Voorhees Mus, Rutgers Univ, 89; Pretto-Berland Hall, NY Struve Gallery, Chicago, 90; Locks Gallery Philadelphia, Berland-Hall, NY, 92; and others. *Pos:* Mem, Col Art Asn Bd Dirs, 78-82; CAA Art Journal Ed Bd, 81- *Teaching:* Instr painting & dir, Ox Bow Summer Sch of Painting, Saugatuck, Mich, 60-; vis artist-lectr, Stanford Univ, 73 & Univ Calif, Davis, 73 & 80; vis artist & fel, Inst Arts & Humanistic Studies, Pa State Univ, 74; vis artist, State Univ Iowa; instr painting, State Univ NY Purchase, 78-, Parsons Sch Design, 79-80 & Sch Visual Arts, 80-83; instr painting, Cooper Union, 79-82, assoc prof, 83- *Awards:* Nat Endowment Arts Grant, 74 & 87; Yaddo Fel, 74-75 & 76; Hereward Lester Cooke Found, 81. *Bibliog:* Donald Kuspit (auth), Strange Games (catalog essay), 87; Christopher Lyon (auth), Recent Drawings, 90; Eleanor Heartney (auth), Monograph Essay, 92; and others. *Mem:* Col Art Asn (bd dirs, 77-81). *Media:* Acrylic, Prismacolor; Lithography. *Publ:* The Weasel by Annie Dillard, 82; White Walls, autumn 82; Mirabai Versions by Robert Bly, 84; Niagara Solo Press, NY, 90; Elements, Pondside Press, Rhinebeck, NY, 91. *Dealer:* Printworks Ltd 311 W Superior Chicago 60610. *Mailing Add:* 138 Prince St New York NY 10012

LA PELLE, RODGER
PAINTER, DEALER
b Philadelphia, Pa, July 31, 36. *Study:* Univ Pa; Pa Acad Fine Arts. *Work:* Free Libr Philadelphia, Pa; Munson-Williams-Proctor Mus, Utica, NY; Mus Mod Art, New York. *Exhib:* Nat Exhib, Pa Acad Fine Art, Philadelphia, 58, Calif Palace of Legion Honor, San Francisco, 62 & San Francisco Art Mus, Calif, 63; La Pelle Galleries, 85-88. *Pos:* Owner, Roger La Pelle Galleries. *Awards:* Silver Medal, Cologne, Ger, 56; Cresson Traveling Scholar, Pa Acad Fine Art, 61; Moss-Graff Prize, Cheltenham Ann Exhib, 88. *Mem:* Fel Pa Acad Fine Arts (pres, currently). *Media:* Oil. *Specialty:* Contemporary painting, sculpture and graphics. *Mailing Add:* c/o La Pelle Galleries 122 N Third St Philadelphia PA 19106-1802

LAPENA, FRANK RAYMOND
PAINTER, EDUCATOR
b San Francisco, Calif, Oct 5, 37. *Study:* Chico State Univ, AB(art); San Francisco State Univ, life credential educ(art); also with tribal elders and medicine men-traditionalists; Sacramento State Univ, MA. *Work:* Indian Arts & Crafts Bd, Washington, DC; Southern Plains Indian Mus, Anadarko, Okla; Crocker Mus, Sacramento, Calif; Mus Mod Art, New York; Univ Utah, Salt Lake City. *Comn:* There is Remembering (chap heading-painting, In: The Human Condition), Scott, Foresman & Co, 73; Bear Dancer (cover painting, In: Tracks), Henry Holt & Co, 88. *Exhib:* One-man show, Calif Indian Days, Calif Expos, Sacramento, 77; Fetishes, San Francisco Mus Art, 75; Am Indian Art Heritage, Art Inst of Chicago, 77; Indian Images travelling exhib, Univ NDak, Grand Forks, 77; Am Indian Art Now, Wheelwright Mus, Santa Fe, NMex, 78; The Real People, Am Indian, group show, Havana, Cuba, 79; Philbrook Art Ctr, Tulsa, Okla; 20-yr retrospective, Wheelwright Mus, Santa Fe, 88. *Pos:* Alternate mem art, Calif Comn Teacher Preparation & Licensing, State Calif, 72; bd mem, Ctr Arts of Indian Am, Washington, DC, 74-; comnr, Calif Hist Capitol Comn, 85- *Teaching:* Instr art & photog, Shasta Community Col, Redding, Calif, 69-71; assoc prof art hist, Calif State Univ, Sacramento, 71-; vis prof Indian art hist, Lethbridge Univ, Alta, Can, summer 74. *Awards:* Best Painting Award, October Art Festival, Davis, 80; Purchase Award, 57th Ann Crocker-Kingsley Exhib, 82; First Place & Purchase Award, St John's Ann Religious Art Festival, Sacramento, 82; and others. *Bibliog:* Jamake Highwater (auth), The Sweet Grass Lives On, Lippincott & Crowell, 80; Wade & Strickland (auths), Magic Images: Contemporary Native American Art, Univ Okla Press, 81 & Four Winds, spring 82; The Extension of Tradition, Crocker Mus, 85. *Mem:* Native Am Indian Artists; Native NAm Indian Artists; Int Soc Preserv Black & White Photog; Int Native Coun Arts, New York. *Media:* Mixed, Acrylic. *Res:* Culture and arts of the traditional and evolving arts and crafts of California tribal people. *Publ:* Contribr, Wintu Indian, In: Handbook of North American Indian, 20 vols, Smithsonian, 76; ed, Legends of the Yosemite Miwok, Yosemite Natural Hist Asn, 82; A native American's view of rock art, Ancient Images on Stone: Rock Art of the Californias, UCLA Press, 82; Introduction & The World Is a Gift of My Elder, Extension of Tradition, Crocker Mus, 85; The World Is a Gift, Handmade Book, Limestone Press, San Francisco, 87. *Mailing Add:* 1531 42nd St Sacramento CA 95819

LA PIERRE, THOMAS
PAINTER, PRINTMAKER
b Toronto, Ont, Dec 28, 30. *Study:* Ont Col Art, AA; Ecole Beaux Arts; Atelier 17. *Work:* Montreal Mus Fine Art, PQ; Sir George Williams Univ; Art Gallery Hamilton, St Catherines & Art Gallery Ont, Ont. *Exhib:* Sao Paulo Biennial, 63; Focus on Drawing, Art Gallery Ont, 65; Price Fine Art Awards Exhib, 70; Atlantic Provinces, 74; W Coast traveling exhib, Burnaby Art Gallery; Dimensions of Realism, Milan, Italy, 78; Sichuan Fine Art Inst, Chong Quing, China, 88; Rodman Hall, St Catherines, Ont, 88. *Teaching:* Instr drawing & painting, Ont Col Art, 58- *Awards:* Ont Soc Artists Award, 68; Price Fine Art Award, 70; Can Soc Painters in Watercolour Honour Award, 78, 79 & 80. *Bibliog:* William McElcheran (auth), Dialogue with demons, Arts Can, 70; Robert Percival (auth), 20th Century mystic, Art Mag, 75; Paul Duval (auth), article in Art Mag, 76 & 77. *Mem:* Can Soc Painters in Watercolour; Royal Can Acad Arts. *Media:* Oil, Watercolor. *Publ:* Limited edition bk, lithographs, drawings & paintings, 1975-1980. *Mailing Add:* Ont Col Art 110 McCaul St Toronto ON M5T 1W1 Canada

LAPINSKI, TADEUSZ (A)
PRINTMAKER, EDUCATOR
b Rawa Mazowiecka, Poland, June 20, 28; US citizen. *Study:* Acad Fine Arts, Warsaw, Poland, MFA, 55. *Work:* Mus Mod Art, New York; Nat Collection Fine Arts & Nat Gallery, Washington, DC; Mus Mod Art, Tokyo; Albertina Mus, Vienna; plus others. *Comn:* Washington Portfolio, Washington DC Print Club & Soc of Graphic Arts, 74. *Exhib:* Am Print in Venice, 77; one-man exhibs, Baak Gallery, Cambridge, Mass, 79, Bacardi Art Gallery, 79, Forum Gallery, Zagreb, Yugoslavia & Klevit Gallery, Washington, DC; Central Inst Art, Beijing, Peoples Repub China, 88; Mus City Torun, Poland, 92. *Teaching:* Assoc prof lithography, Univ Md, 72-82, prof, 83- *Awards:* First Prize, Int Print Festival Vienna, 78; Second Prize, World Print, Paris, 80; Outstanding Achievement Award, 81 & Honor Awards, 86, Univ Md; Statua Victory, World Prize Calvatone, Italy, 85. *Bibliog:* Fritz Eichenberg (auth), The Art of the Prints, Abrams, 77; Jane Haslem (ed), American Paintings and Graphics, Washington, DC; Lillian Dobbs (auth), Lapinski prints are unique, hard to find, Miami News, 11/16/79. *Mem:* Soc Am Graphic Artists; Painters Sculptors Soc of NJ (vpres, 72-76); Washington Printmakers Soc; Soc Graphic Arts, New York. *Dealer:* F Bader Gallery 2124 Pennsylvania Ave NW Washington DC 20037. *Mailing Add:* 10413 Eastwood Ave Silver Spring MD 20901

LA PLANT, MIMI
PAINTER, PRINTMAKER
b San Francisco, Calif, Jan 7, 43. *Study:* Col of Marin, 68; Santa Rosa Jr Col, AA, 72; Univ Calif, Berkeley, BA, 74; Humboldt State Univ, MA, 82; Univ Calif Santa Barbara, MFA, 91. *Work:* Humbolt Cult Ctr, Eureka, Calif; Humboldt State, Santa Barbara Mus Art. *Comn:* Monotypes, Bank of Del Mar, Calif, 83 & Prudential Life Insurance Co, & Bank of Colo, 84; six monoprints, Dow Chemical, San Diego, Calif; large monotype, ANA Hotel, Japan 85. *Exhib:* West Coast Works On/Of Paper 87 & 88; Crocker-Kingsley Ann, Crocker Mus, Sacramento, Calif, 86; Locus, San Luis Obispo Art Ctr, 92; 3 Abstract Painters, Foxhall Gallery, Washington, DC, 92; Introductions 92, Weintraub, Sacto, Calif; and others. *Pos:* Dir educ, The Ink People, Eureka, Calif, currently. *Teaching:* Instr, Col Redwoods, Eureka & Mendocino Art Ctr, Mendo, Calif; Humboldt State Univ. *Bibliog:* Belle McDonnell (auth), Mimi La Plant: An artist for all seasons, Times Standard Newspaper, 7/88. *Mem:* Redwood Art Asn (bd dirs, 87-88); The Ink People; Mendocino Art Ctr; Calif Art Asn; Calif Art Found, Santa Barbara. *Media:* Oil, Acrylic; Monotype. *Publ:* Auth, Monoprint: Painting or printing, Mendocino Art Ctr Mag, 7/87. *Dealer:* San Francisco Mus Mod Art Rental Gallery San Francisco CA; Judith Weinbraub 1723 J St Sacramento CA 95814. *Mailing Add:* PO Box 14383 Santa Barbara CA 93107

LAPLANTZ, DAVID
JEWELER, SCULPTOR
b Toledo, Ohio, June 12, 44. *Study:* Bowling Green State Univ, with Hal Hasselschwert, BS(art), 66; Cranbrook Acad Art, with Richard Thomas,

MFA, 69; Southern Ill Univ, with Alex Bealer, 70. *Work:* St Paul Art Ctr, Minn; Nat Mus Mod Art, Kyoto, Japan; Nat Mus Am Art, Smithsonian Inst, Washington, DC; Am Craft Mus; Schmuck Mus, Pforzheim, Ger. *Comn:* Commemorative (scale model of house), Civil Rights Group, Detroit, 67. *Exhib:* Copper, Bronze & Brass Competition, Univ Ariz Mus Art, Tucson, 77; 3rd Profile of US Jewelry, Tex Tech Univ, Lubbock, 77; For the Table Top, 80-83 & Contemporary American Jewelry: US Info Agency Arts America, 85-87, traveling shows, Am Craft Mus; Gold as Gold-Alternative Materials in American Jewelry, Renwick Gallery, Smithsonian Inst, Washington, DC, 81-84; Contemporary Jewelry-the Americas, Australia, Europe, Japan, Nat Mus Mod Art, Tokyo & Kyoto, Japan, 84; Jewelry USA, Nat Competitive Exhib, Am Crafts Mus & NAm Goldsmiths Soc, 84-86; Sixth Int Jewelry Ornament for the Head and Hair Competition, Pforzheim, Ger, 85-86; and others. *Teaching:* Instr, Inst Am Indian Arts, Santa Fe, NMex, 67-68, Kent State Univ, 77-78 , Colo State Univ, 69-70, San Diego State Col, 70-71 & Humboldt State Univ, 71- *Awards:* Fulbright Scholar, New Zealand, 85; Merit Award, North Am Goldsmith Biennial Exhib, Phoenix Art Mus, Ariz. *Bibliog:* Articles in Crafts Horizons, 69-70 & 75, Goldsmith J, 80 & Art Craft Mag, 80; article, Ornament Mag, Vol V, No 4, 82; Chuck Evans (auth), Jewelry: Contemporary Design & Techniques, Davis Publ, 83; Peter Dormer & Ralph Turner (coauth), The New Jewelry-Trends and Traditions, Thames & Hudson, London, 85. *Mem:* Am Craftsman's Coun; Friends of Calif Design; Soc NAm Goldsmiths. *Media:* All. *Publ:* Contribr, Body Jewelry-International Perspective, 73; Contemporary Jewelry, rev ed, 76; Jewelry Concepts & Technology, 83; auth, Artists Anodizing Aluminum, Press de LaPlantz, 88; ed, Jewelry Metalwork Survey, 1991, Press de LaPlantz, 91. *Mailing Add:* 899 Bayside Cutoff Bayside CA 95524

LAPLANTZ, SHEREEN
WEAVER, INSTRUCTOR
b Glendale, Calif, Feb 9, 47. *Study:* Los Angeles State Univ, BA, 68; Cranbrook Acad Art, 69. *Work:* Mendocino Art Ctr, Calif; Murray St Univ. *Exhib:* Virginia Beach Arts Ctr, Va, 82; Eve Mannes Gallery, Atlanta, 82; Seattle Ctr, 83; one-person show, Murray St Univ, Ky, 83; Gallery 8, La Jolla, 83; and others. *Pos:* Publ, Press de LaPlantz, Bayside, Calif, 81- *Teaching:* Instr fiberarts, Col Redwoods, Eureka, Calif, 74-77. *Awards:* Textiles Awards, Spring Show, Redwood Art Asn, 73 & 75; Cash Award, Calif Crafts IX, Crocker Art Gallery, 75. *Bibliog:* Dona Meilach (auth), Basketry Today, Crown, 79; Fiberarts Design Book, Hastings House, 80; Fiberarts Design Book II, Hastings House, 83. *Mem:* Handweavers Guild Am; Am Crafts Coun. *Media:* Fiber, Reed. *Publ:* Auth, Baskets and curls, Shuttle, Spindle & Dyepot, 81; auth & ed, Plaited Basketry-The Woven Form, Press de LaPlantz, 82; contrib ed, ARC, 82; auth, Handwoven, Basketry Materials Guide, 83; auth, The artist in business, Humboldt Bay Sheep & Wool Newsletter, 83; and others. *Mailing Add:* 899 Bayside Cutoff Bayside CA 95524

LAPOINTE, FRANK
PAINTER, PRINTMAKER
b Port Rexton, Nfld, May 11, 42. *Study:* Ont Col of Art, AOCA, 66. *Work:* Can Coun Art Bank, Pub Works, Canada; Univ Ore, Corvallis; Nat Gallery Can, Ottawa; Art Gallery Ont, Toronto. *Comn:* Nfld postcard ser: What do you think of Jack?, Mem Univ Art Gallery Jubilee Portfolio, St John's, Nfld, 75; stainless steel & aluminum mirror sculpture, Fed Bldg, Grand Falls, Nfld, 79; lithograph portfolio, Can Saltfish Corp, 81; lithograph ed, For Sale, Mem Univ, St Johns, Nfld, 85; lithograph ed, Contrasts, Nfld Teachers' Asn, 90. *Exhib:* Nfld Artists, Can Cult Ctr, Paris, 85; 5 Salon Des Vendanges De Cognac, Cognac, France, 85; 25 Years of Art, Nat Touring Show, Mem Univ Art Gallery, 86; Door as a Circular Passage, Mem Univ Gallery, St John's, Nfld, 86; Out of the Studio, Mem Univ Gallery, St John's, Nfld, 90; Nfld Art, Salle de la Renaissance, Bordeaux, France, 92. *Pos:* Asst cur & art specialist, Art Gallery, Mem Univ, St John's, Nfld, 70-72, cur, 72-73; resident printmaker, St Michael's Printshop, Nfld, 81-82; guest cur, Art Gallery, NS Halifax, 83; visual arts coordr, Sound Symp, St John's, Nfld, 83, 88 & 90; colour/design consult, Enterprise Nfld, 91-92. *Teaching:* Instr painting & printmaking, Dundas Valley Sch of Art, Dundas, Ont, 69-70; lectr, aesthet design, Mem Univ, St John's, Nfld, 88, 90 & 91. *Awards:* Silver Medal, 67 & Bronze Medal, 68, Nfld Arts & Lett, Govt Nfld; Can Coun Grant, 77; Can Coun Grant, 86. *Bibliog:* Joe Bodolai (auth), Visit to Newfoundland, 75-76 & Peter Bell (auth), Frank Lapointe/Gerald Squires, 76-77, Artscanada; Peter Bell (auth), Oberheide, Wright, Lapointe, Vie des Arts, Montreal, winter 76; Visions Artists and the Creative Process, TV Ont, 82. *Mem:* Can Soc of Painters in Watercolor; St Michael's Printshop; Artists' Coalition Nfld; Nfld Sound Symp. *Media:* Watercolor, Acrylic; Lithography, Etching. *Mailing Add:* Tors Cove Southern Shore NF A0A 4A0 Canada

LA PORTA, ELAYNE B
PAINTER, PRINTMAKER
b Wilton, Conn. *Study:* Lesnick Sch Art with Steve Lesnick, 68-79; pvt study with Arnold Hitchcock, 68 & Cliff Segerclum, 68; Acad Fine Arts, Florence, Italy, 69. *Work:* Biblical Arts Ctr, Dallas, Tex; Villonova Univ, Pa, 91. *Exhib:* Villanova Univ Pa, 91; Univ New Orleans, La, 91; Paul VI Inst Arts, Washington, DC, 91; Marion Libr, Dayton, Ohio, 91; West Bend Gallery Fine Arts, Wis, 92. *Bibliog:* Beije Howell (auth), Historical biblical art by Elayne La Porta, Santa Monica Outlook, 10/80; Judee Quillum (auth), Elayne La Porta Artist, Art Voices South, 1/80; A D Hopkins (auth), Elayne La Porta Biblical Artist Las Vegas Review J, 11/83. *Mem:* Catholic Fine Arts Soc, New York; Catholic Artists of the 90's, New York; Midwest Asn Relig Talent Inc, Milwaukee, Wis; Int Registry Relig Women Artists, Fresno, Calif. *Dealer:* Vernon Fine Arts 1738 Treble Humble TX 77338. *Mailing Add:* 443 Blackridge Dr Henderson NV 89015

LAPOSKY, BEN FRANCIS
DESIGNER, VIDEO ARTIST
b Cherokee, Iowa, Sept 30, 14. *Work:* Sanford Mus, Cherokee, Iowa; Univ Okla, Norman; Mus Sci & Technol, Tel Aviv, Israel. *Exhib:* Light as a Creative Medium, Carpenter Ctr, Harvard Univ, 66; Cybernetic Serendipity, Inst Contemp Art, London, 68; On the Eve of Tomorrow, Computer Art, Hannover, Ger, 69; Computer Graphics Art Exhib, Rhinelander Gallery, New York, 76; Computer Art Exhib, Univ Waterloo Galleries, Can, 77; Cybernetic Symbiosis, computer art exhib, Univ Calif, Berkeley, 79; plus others. *Awards:* Art Dirs Club Medal, New York, 57. *Bibliog:* Electronic Gayety, Fortune Mag, 12/56; H Franke (auth), Computer Graphics-Computer Art, Phaidon, London, 71; Andrew Kagan (auth), Ben F Laposky: Midwestern pioneer of absolute light form, Arts Mag, 6/80. *Media:* Kinetic Light Assemblages, Photography. *Publ:* Auth, Electronic abstracts: Art for space age, Proc Iowa Acad Sci, 58; Oscillographic design, Perspective Mag, London, 60; Oscillons: Electronic abstractions, Leonardo Mag, Oxford, 69 & Kinetic Art, 74; contribr, Ruth Leavitt, ed, Electronic Abstractions in Artist & Computer, Harmony Bks, 76; Magic squares: A design source, Leonardo Mag, Eng, 78. *Mailing Add:* 301 S Sixth St Cherokee IA 51012

LARAMÉE, EVE ANDRÉE
SCULPTOR, CONCEPTUAL ARTIST
b Los Angeles, Calif, Jan 6, 56. *Study:* San Diego State Univ, BA, 78; San Francisco Art Inst, MFA, 80. *Work:* Guggenheim Mus, New York; Albuquerque Mus Art, NMex; Islip Art Mus, East Islip, NY; Fine Arts Mus Long Island; MacArthur Found, Chicago, Ill. *Comn:* Site-Specific Installation, Zilkha Gallery, Wesleyan Univ, Middletown, Conn, 90; Site-Specific Installation, Mus Contemp Art, Chicago, Ill, 92. *Exhib:* Eve Laramée, Albuquerque Mus Art, NMex, 83; Personal Environments, Mus NMex, Santa Fe, 86; Strange Attractors: Signs of Chaos, New Mus Contemp Art, New York, 89; Revered Earth, Contemp Arts Mus, Houston, Tex, 90; A Natural Order, Hudson River Mus, Yonkers, NY, 90; Eve Andrée Laramée: New Sculpture, John Gibson Gallery, New York, 91; Red Cross, Artists Mus, Berlin, Ger, 92; Art at the Armory: Occupied Territory, Mus Contemp Art, Chicago, Ill, 92. *Teaching:* Adj prof sculpture, New York Univ, 89-92; part-time prof art grad studies, RI Sch Design, 92-93; vis prof sculpture, Mass Inst Technol, Cambridge, 92. *Awards:* Fel, New York Found Arts, 89; Fel, Art Matters Inc, 90; Sculptor-in-Residence at Chesterwood, Guggenheim Mus, 92. *Bibliog:* Barbara Bloemink (auth), A Natural Order, Hudson River Mus, 90; Suzi Gablik (auth), Revered Earth, Ctr Contemp Art, Santa Fe, 90; Beryl Wright (auth), Occupied Territory, Mus Contemp Art, 92. *Mem:* Nat Asn Artists Orgn, Washington, DC; Blast/The X Art Found, New York (artist adv bd). *Media:* All; Installation. *Publ:* Auth, Notes on Sculpture, Albuquerque Mus, 83; The Eroded Terrain of Memory, Zilkha Gallery, Wesleyan Univ, 90; Inventing Wilderness: The National Parks, New Observations Mag, 91; Artists Project, J Contemp Art, 92. *Dealer:* John Gibson Gallery 568 Broadway New York NY 10012. *Mailing Add:* 118 Java St Brooklyn NY 11222

L'ARCHEVEQUE, ANDRE ROBERT
PAINTER, ILLUSTRATOR
b Montreal, Que, Apr 12, 23. *Study:* Ecole des Beaux Art, Montreal, MA, 42, Sir George Williams Sch Art, 43, Famous Artists Sch, New York, 49. *Work:* City of Montreal Pub Collection, Que; Chateau de Ramezay Mus, Montreal; Govt of Can Pub Collection, Ottawa; Texaco Can, Toronto; Bankers Asn Can, Montreal. *Comn:* Great Moments, large painting, Prudential Insurance Co, Toronto, Ont, 72; painting, Arab Repub Egypt, Cairo, 85; design for Quebec Pavillion, World Exhib, Govt of Que, 68. *Exhib:* Traveling exhib across US & Can, 75; solo exhibs, retrospective, Montreal, Toronto & Ottawa, 82 & Chateau de Ramezay Mus, Montreal, 85. *Pos:* Ed illusr, Pocket Books, 48-58; Advert illusr, 52-72. *Awards:* First Prize, Watercolor & Drawing Exhib, Vancouver Air Command. *Bibliog:* Guy Boulizon (auth), Poetry of Nature, catalog, 82; videocassette, Prudential Insurance Co, 82; Nathalie Legris (auth), Andre L'Archeveque, Editions Marcel Broquet. *Media:* Oil, Acrylic; All Media. *Publ:* Illusr, World Book Encyl, 76; auth & illusr, Meditation, Bernard Desroches, 87. *Dealer:* Galerie Bernard Desroches 1144 Sherbrooke St Montreal PQ H7R 1K4 Canada. *Mailing Add:* 56 Les Erables Laval sur le Lac PQ H7R 1A4 Canada

LARICO, BENJE
PAINTER
Study: Albuquerque, NMex, 73; Whitney Mus Independent Study Prog, 74; Wash Univ, St Louis, Mo, BFA, 72; Bennington Col, Vt, MA, 76. *Exhib:* Salon de Montrouge, France, 84; Daniel Weinberg Gallery, Los Angeles, Calif, 84; Am Acad Rome, Italy, 85; Abstractions in Process, Artists Space, New York, 87; Nordster Collection, Grey Gallery, New York, 88; Trisha Brown Benefit Auction, Paula Cooper Gallery, New York, 90; Molica Gallery, New York & Rome, Italy, 92. *Awards:* Prix de Rome, Am Acad Rome, 84-85; Grant, NY Found Arts, 88; Grant Painting, Nat Endowment Arts, 89. *Mailing Add:* 358 Broadway New York NY 10013

LARK, RAYMOND
DRAFTSMAN, PAINTER
b Philadelphia, Pa, June 16, 39. *Study:* Philadelphia Mus Sch Art; Dobbins Voc, Philadelphia; Temple Univ, BS; Los Angeles Tech Col; Univ Colo, LHD, 85. *Work:* Libr Cong; Mus African & African-Am Art & Antiquities, Buffalo, NY; and many others. *Comn:* Universal City Studios, Calif, 64-65; Movie Land Wax Mus & Palace of Living Arts, Buena Park, Calif, 64-65; Blue Cross Insurance Co, 67 & CBS-TV Studios, Los Angeles, 73; and others. *Exhib:* Smithsonian Inst, 71; NJ State Mus, Trenton, 71; Libr Cong, 73; Guggenheim Mus, 75; Honolulu Acad Arts, Hawaii, 75; Metrop Mus Art, New York, 76;

Univ Calif Ctr Afro-Am Studies, Los Angeles, 83; Salon Nations Centre Int D'Art Contemporain, Paris, 83; Univ Colo, 84; Utah Mus Fine Arts, Salt Lake, 89; Dickinson Univ, NDak, 89; Triton Mus Art, Santa Clara, Calif, 90. *Collections Arranged:* Black Sculpturing Exhibition, Charles W Bowers Mem Mus (auth, catalog), Santa Ana, Calif, 69; Five Black Artists Exhibit, Florenz's Art Gallery, Hollywood, 69; Nine American Artists Exhibit (auth, catalog), Emerald Gallery, Hollywood Beach, Fla, 70; and others. *Pos:* Pres, Art West Assoc Inc, Calif, 68-70. *Teaching:* Univ Calif, Los Angeles, 83; Calif Mus Afro-Am Hist & Cult, 83; Albany State Col, Ga, 88; and others. *Awards:* Proclamations, President Nixon, 72, President Ford, 75 & President Carter, 77; Nat Endowment Arts Grant, 76; Arco Atlantic Richfield Found Grant, 84; Colo Humanities Prog Grant, 84; plus others. *Bibliog:* Robert J Rhodes (auth), Raymond Lark: A study in determination, Southwest Art, 3/82; Fred Anderson (dir), Raymond Lark: From rags to riches (film), ABC-TV Calif, 2/2/83; Melody Jackson (dir), Raymond Lark: Good Day Los Angeles (film), KTTV-TV Calif, 2/19/83; Tom Thompson (dir), Raymond lark & Betye Saar: Two-part doc on Afro-Am Art (film), KCET-TV News Calif, 2/23/88 & 2/24/88; Ray Gonzales (dir), Dr Raymond Lark and Al Hornsby: Pacesetters (film), KTLA-TV Calif, 3/20/88; Lisa George (dir), Raymond Lark at Albany State Col (film), WALB-TV News (NBC) GEorgia, 4/15/88; Wilfred D Samuels (auth), Raymond Lark: American Artist of Tradition and Diversity, Univ Utah Press, 89. *Media:* Oil, Pencil. *Res:* Graphic art masters, Afro-Am Art. *Publ:* Contribr, Drawings and paintings by an Afro-American artist, Leonardo, 82; auth, The Selected Writings of Raymond Lark, 89-90; and many others. *Mailing Add:* PO Box 76169 Los Angeles CA 90076-0169

LARKIN, EUGENE
DESIGNER, EDUCATOR
b Minneapolis, Minn, June 27, 21. *Study:* Univ Minn, BA & MA. *Work:* Mus Mod Art, New York; Nat Gallery Art & Libr Cong, Washington, DC; Art Inst Chicago; Addison Gallery Am Art, Andover, Mass; Nat Collection of Fine Arts, Smithsonian Inst, Washington, DC; and others. *Comn:* Int Graphic Arts Soc; Gen Mills Corp; Bus Wk; Minneapolis Soc Fine Arts; US Info Agency. *Exhib:* US Info Agency Traveling Exhib to Iran, Italy, France, Spain & Ger; one-man shows, Minneapolis Inst Art & Hamline Univ, 68; State Univ NY Albany, 69; Univ Calif, Long Beach, 69; Univ Minn, 74, 78, 81, 87, 91 & 92; Anderson & Anderson Gallery, 91 & 92. *Teaching:* Instr, Kans State Col, Pittsburg, 48-54; head printmaking dept & chmn fine arts div, Minneapolis Sch Art, 54-69; prof, Design Dept, Univ Minn, Minneapolis, 69-91. *Awards:* Walker Art Ctr, 60 & Washington Watercolor & Print Exhib, 63; Rockford Biennial, 83; plus many others. *Mem:* Am Asn Univ Prof; Col Art Asn Am. *Media:* Woodcuts, Lithographs, Oil. *Publ:* Auth, Design: The Search for Unity, William C Brown, 88. *Mailing Add:* 64 Groveland Terr Minneapolis MN 55403

LARKIN, (DR) JOHN E, JR
COLLECTOR, PATRON
b St Paul, Minn, Nov 8, 30. *Study:* Univ Minn, BS & MD; Harvard Univ. *Pos:* Former trustee, Minn Mus Art, Minn Soc Fine Arts & Minn Inst Art; benefactor, Minn Inst Art, Minn Mus Art & Univ Minn Mus; accessions comt, Minn Inst Art. *Collection:* American art. *Mailing Add:* 7 Yellow Birch Rd Dellwood White Bear Lake MN 55110

LARMER, OSCAR VANCE
PAINTER, EDUCATOR
b Wichita, Kans, July 11, 24. *Study:* Minneapolis Sch of Fine Arts, cert painting; Univ Kans, BFA; Wichita State Univ, MFA. *Work:* Nelson Gallery of Art, Kansas City, Mo; Kans State Univ, Manhattan; Wichita State Univ, Kans; Wichita Art Asn Gallery; Kans Univ, Lawrence; and others. *Comn:* Medallion, Kans State Col Centennial, Manhattan, 61; President's Medallion, Kans State Univ, 74; painting, Kans 4-H Found, Kans State Univ, 77. *Exhib:* Mid-Am Exhib, Nelson Gallery Art, Kansas City, Mo, 52-70; Watercolor USA, Springfield Art Mus, Mo, 57 & 68; Rocky Mountain Exhib, Denver Art Mus, Colo, 65; 45th Ann 17-State Exhib, Springfield, Mo, 75; Nat Watercolor Exhib, La Watercolor Soc, 76; Works of Art on Paper, Nat-Western Ann, Western Ill Univ, Galesburg, 76; Summer Invitational, Nelson Gallery of Art, Kansas City, Mo, 77, 79, 81, 84 & 86; Kansas Landscapes-Touring Invitational, 85-86; Burke Armstrong Gallery, Taos, NMex, 91-92. *Pos:* Asst dir, Wichita Art Mus, Kans, 53-55. *Teaching:* Prof drawing & painting, Kans State Univ, Manhattan, 56-89, head art dept, 67-71, emeritus prof, 90- *Awards:* Purchase Awards, Smoky Hills Art, Hadley Med Ctr, 77, Kans Watercolor Soc, United Bank & Trust, 77, Prairie Exhib, 83 & Showcase Manhattan, 90; Winner, Kansas Postcard Series No 13, 90. *Bibliog:* V W Bell (auth), The Kansas Art Reader, Univ Kans Press, 76. *Mem:* Nat Col Art Asn; Mid-Am Col Art Asn; Kans Watercolor Soc; Kans Fedn of Art. *Media:* Watercolor, Oil. *Publ:* Coauth, A Foundation for Expressive Drawing, Burgess Publ, 83. *Mailing Add:* 2441 Hobbs Dr Manhattan KS 66502

LAROCHE, LYNDA L
CRAFTSMAN, DESIGNER
b Urbana, Ill, May 23, 47. *Study:* Montgomery Col, AA, 69; Univ NMex, BFA, 71; Indiana Univ, MFA, 76. *Work:* Indiana Univ Art Mus; Indianapolis Mus Art. *Exhib:* Fine Art Jewelry in America, Cross Creek Gallery, Malibu, 86; Twice Gifted, Workbench Gallery, New York, 86; US Metal, San Francisco State Univ, 89; Art: Jewelry and Metalsmithing, Col Design, Iowa State Univ, Ames, 89; Fortunoff Silver Competition, New York, 90; Nat Metals Exhib, Mesa Arts Ctr, Ariz, 90; Expressions: Jewelry in the 1990's, Contemp Arts Ctr, Cincinnati, 91; The Collector's Eye, Am Craft Mus, New York, 91. *Pos:* Adv Panel for the Crafts, Indiana Arts Comn, 83-86; bd mem, Soc N Am Goldsmiths, 88-92. *Teaching:* Vis asst prof, Indiana Univ, 78-79, 86 & 90, Montgomery Col, 79 & 88, Miami Univ, Oxford, Ohio, 88-89, SDak State Univ, 92. *Awards:* First Prize, Sterling Design Competition, Sterling Silversmiths Guild Am, New York, 76; Nat Endowment Arts, 88. *Media:* Sterling Silver, Gold. *Publ:* Auth, Master Metalsmith: Alma Eikerman, Metalsmith, winter 83; Randy Long: Recent Metalwork, Metalsmith Exhib Review, fall 84. *Mailing Add:* 915 Eighth Ave Brookings SD 57006-1317

LARRAZ, JULIO F
PAINTER
b Havana, Cuba, Mar 12, 44. *Work:* Westmoreland Co Mus Art, Greensburg, Pa; Archer M Huntington Art Gallery, Univ Tex, Austin; Pa State Univ, Philadelphia; Mus Arte Mod, Bogota, Colombia; Mus Monterrey, Mexico, 87. *Exhib:* One-man shows, FAR Gallery, 74 & 77, Hirschl & Adler Galleries, 79 & 80, Nohra Haime Gallery, New York, 83, 84, 85, 88, 90 & 92; Childe Hassam Fund Purchase, Am Acad Arts & Lett, New York, 74; Museo de Arte Moderno, Bogota, Colombia, 86; Frances Wolfson Art Gallery, Miami-Dade Community Col, Fla, 89; Krannert Art Mus, Univ Ill, Champaign, 92. *Awards:* Cintas Found Fel, Inst Int Educ, 75; Am Acad Arts & Lett Award, 76. *Bibliog:* Barbara Duncan (auth), Lines of Vision, Washington, DC, 69; David Bourdon (auth), New York reviews Julio Larraz, Art Am, 3/87; Ruth Bass (auth), New York reviews Julio Larraz, Art News, 10/88; Edward Sullivan (auth), Julio Larraz, Hudson Hills Press, NY, 89. *Media:* Oil, Watercolor. *Publ:* Contrib, The Eye Witness to Space, Abrams, 70; illusr, The Perfect Wagnerite, Time-Life Bks, 72; The Whitehouse Enemies, New Am Libr, 73; contribr, Still the flypaper of politics, New York Times Mag, 74; New York Mag. *Dealer:* Nohra Haime Gallery 41 E 57th St New York NY 10022. *Mailing Add:* c/o Nohra Haime Gallery 41 E 57th St 6th floor New York NY 10022

LARSEN, CARL ERIK
CONSULTANT, EDUCATOR
b Vienna, Austria, Oct 10, 11; US citizen. *Study:* Inst Superieur Hist Art & Archeol, Brussels, Belg, BA; Cath Univ Louvain, MA & PhD; restoration with Jef Lammens, Ghent & Jules Defort, Brussels. *Pos:* Dir & ed-in-chief, Pictura; Belg Govt Cult Mission in Brazil, 46-47. *Teaching:* Res prof art, Manhattanville Col Sacred Heart, 47-55; instr, Sch Gen Studies Exten Div, City Col New York, 48-55; from lectr to vis prof, Georgetown Univ, 55-58, assoc prof fine arts, 58-63, prof fine arts, 63-67, head dept fine arts, 60-67; prof hist art, Univ Kans, 67-80, dir, Ctr Flemish Art & Cult, 70-80, prof emer art hist, 80-; guest prof, Univ Salzburg, Austria, 88. *Awards:* Knight's Cross, Order of Leopold & Order of the Crown, Belg; Laureate, Inst France, Prix Thorlet, 62; mem, Jury Taras Shevshenko Mem, Washington, DC. *Mem:* Appraisers Asn Am; Asn Dipl Hist Art & Archeol, Cath Univ Louvain. *Res:* History of northern baroque and northern renaissance art. *Publ:* Auth, Frans Post, Interprete du Bresil, Colibris Editoria, Amsterdam-Rio de Janeiro, 62; coauth with Jane P Davidson, Calvinistic Economy and 17th Cent Dutch Art, Univ Kans Publ, 79; auth, Rembrandt, Peintre de Paysages: Une Vision Nouvelle, Publ d'Histoire l'Art & l'Archeologie Univ Louvain, 83; 17th Cent Flemish Painting, Luca Verlag, Feren, WGer, 85; The Paintings of Anthony Van Dyck, two vols, Luca Verlag, WGer, 88; and others. *Mailing Add:* Kajetaner Platz 5/5/11 Salzburg A-5020 Austria

LARSEN, D DANE
CERAMIST, SCULPTOR
b Oct 21, 50. *Study:* Harvard Univ, BA, study with William Reimann, Rudolf Arnheim & Buckminster Fuller; Univ Calif, Study with Ron Nagle; San Francisco State Univ, MA, study with Charles McKee, Hayward King, Dale Roush, Daniel Rhodes & Paul Soldner. *Work:* San Francisco State Univ Ceramics Collection; Carpenter Ctr for the Visual Arts, Harvard Univ, Cambridge, Mass; Oakland Mus, Calif; Prieto Gallery, Mills Col, Oakland. *Exhib:* Calif Ceramics & Glass, Oakland Mus; The Calif Craftsman, Monterey Peninsula Mus Art, Monterey, Calif; Marietta Col Crafts Nat, Grover M Hermann Fine Arts Ctr, Marietta, Ohio; Designer-Craftsman Nat, Richmond Art Ctr, Calif; Calif Crafts X, E B Crocker Gallery & Mus, Sacramento; Nat Cone Box Show, Kans Univ Union Gallery, Lawrence. *Pos:* Consult & dir of ceramics prog, San Rafael City Recreation Dept, 77- *Teaching:* Instr ceramics, Col of Marin, Kentfield, Calif, 76- & Columbia Jr Col, Calif, summer 77; Art Acad, San Francisco, Calif, 80-84. *Awards:* Cash Awards, Calif Craftsman, 76, San Jose Mus Art, 76 & 76 & Civic Arts Gallery, 77. *Mem:* San Francisco Potters Asn; Am Crafts Coun; Col Art Asn. *Media:* Clay, Wood. *Dealer:* Meyer, Fort Mason Ctr San Francisco CA 94123. *Mailing Add:* PO Box 150973 San Rafael CA 94915-0973

LARSEN, JACK LENOR
DESIGNER, WRITER
b Seattle, Wash, Aug 5, 27. *Study:* Univ Wash, BFA, 50; Cranbrook Acad Art, MFA, 51. *Work:* Mus Mod Art, New York, NY; Victoria & Albert Mus, London, Eng; Stedelijk Mus, Amsterdam, Holland; Cooper-Hewitt Mus Decorative Arts & Design, New York; and others. *Comn:* Theatre curtain, comn by Charles Luchman Assoc for Phoenix Civic Plaza, Concert Hall, Ariz, 72. *Exhib:* One-man show, Mus Decorative Art, Copenhagen, Denmark, 76; retrospectives, Stedelijk Mus, Amsterdam, 68, Mus Fine Arts, Boston, Mass, 71, Renwick Gallery, Washington, DC, 72 & Fashion Inst Technol, New York, 78; 30 Yrs of Creative Textiles, Mus des Arts Decoratifs, Pavillon de Marsan, Louvre, Paris, 81. *Collections Arranged:* Co-dir, Wall Hangings, Mus Mod Art, New York, 70. *Pos:* Chmn, Haystack Sch, 76-81; pres, Am Crafts Coun, 81. *Teaching:* Dir fabric design dept, Philadelphia Col Art, 61-63; artist in residence, Royal Col Art, London, 75; affiliate prof, Univ Wash. *Awards:* Neiman-Marcus Award, Distinguished Serv in the Field of Fashion; Trailblazer Award, DIFFA; Collab Award for Excellence in Design. *Mem:* Am Crafts Coun (bd trustees, 54-, pres, 81-90, pres emer, 90-); Royal Soc Art, London; hon fel Am Inst Interior Designers; Mem Art Club Chicago; Life

Mem Metrop Mus Art; Color Asn of US (adv bd). *Publ:* Fabrics for Interiors, 75; auth, The Dyer's Art, 76; coauth, The Art Fabric: Mainstream, 81; Interlacing: The Elemental Fabric, Kodahsha; Material Wealth: Living with Luxurious Fabrics, 89. *Mailing Add:* 41 E 11th St New York NY 10003

LARSEN, JOHN CHRISTIAN
EDUCATOR, LIBRARIAN
b Menominee, Mich. *Study:* Univ Mich, BDes, 50, MA(art hist), 51, MALS, 55, PhD, 67. *Pos:* Reference librn, Fine Arts Dept, Detroit Pub Libr, Mich, 54-57; head art div, Mich State Libr, Lansing, 57-61; art reference, Am Libr Asn. *Teaching:* Instr bibliog fine arts, Sch Libr Sci, Univ Mich, Ann Arbor, 65-68; asst prof bibliog visual arts, Col Libr Sci, Univ Ky, Lexington, 68-71; asst prof lit fine arts, Sch Libr Serv, Columbia Univ, New York, 71-77; assoc prof bibliog visual arts, Sch Libr Sci, Northern Ill Univ, De Kalb, 77-88. *Mem:* Art Libr Soc NAm; Am Libr Asn; Asn Col & Res Libr; Victorian Soc Am (bd mem, 75-76). *Res:* Use of information resources in visual arts. *Interests:* Evaluation of reference materials treating visual arts; education of art librarians. *Publ:* Auth, A seminar in fine arts bibliography, J Educ Librarianship, 70; The use of art reference sources in museum libraries, Spec Libr, 71; The education of fine arts/music librarians, Libr Trends, 75; Museum Librarianship, Shoe String Press, 85; Researcher's Guide to Archives, Shoe String Press, 88. *Mailing Add:* 4000 N Charles St Baltimore MD 21218

LARSEN, MERNET RUTH
PAINTER, EDUCATOR
b Houghton, Mich, June 2, 40. *Study:* San Francisco Art Inst, with Nathan Olivera, 60; Univ Fla, with Hiram Williams, BFA, 62; Univ Ill, 62-63; Ind Univ, with James McGarrell & William Bailey, MFA, 65. *Work:* Univ Okla; Okla Art Ctr; Fla House of Rep; General Telephone Co; Ind Univ. *Exhib:* Thirteen Young Artists You Should Collect, Okla Art Ctr, 65; Mid-Am Ann, Nelson Gallery, Kansas City, Mo, 66; Realism & Figuration, Fla State Univ Mus, Tallahassee, 71; All Fla Painters, St Petersburg Mus, 76; one-person show, Mont State Art Gallery, Bozeman, 77; Realism & Metaphor, Jacksonville Mus and others, 80; Artists Choice, Swain Sch Design, 82; Southern Absraction, New Orleans & Raleigh, NC, 87. *Teaching:* Vis instr, Univ Okla, Norman, 65-67; prof painting & drawing, Univ SFla, 67-; instr, Cath Univ Milan, Rome, Italy, summer 70; vis artist painting, Ridgewood Sch Art, NJ, 73-74 & Mont State Univ, Bozeman, winter, 77; vis asst prof drawing, Yale Univ, fall 76; instr, Yale, Norfolk, 79. *Awards:* Fel Nat Endowment, 88, 89. *Media:* Oils, Acrtlic. *Mailing Add:* Art Dept FAH 110 Univ S Fla Tampa FL 33620

LARSEN, PATRICK HEFFNER
PAINTER, SCULPTOR
b Port Arthur, Tex, July 11, 45. *Study:* Lamar Univ, BBA, 68; Sam Houston State Univ, teacher cert, 69; Stephen F Austin State Univ, MA, 70, MFA, 73. *Work:* Stephen F Austin State Univ, Nacogdoches, Tex; First Nat Bank of Ark, Little Rock; Univ Cent Ark, Conway. *Exhib:* Okla Art Ctr, Oklahoma City, 70 & 72; 16th & 17th Ann Delta Exhib, Ark Art Ctr, Little Rock, 73 & 74; one-man shows, Ft Smith Art Ctr, Ark, 75 & SArk Art Ctr, El Dorado, 76; 54th Ann Exhib, Meadows Mus of Art, Shreveport, La, 76; Rocky Mountain Ann Watercolor Exhib, Foothills Art Ctr, Golden, Colo, 77; Ariz Nat Painting Exhib, Scottsdale Art Ctr, Ariz, 77. *Teaching:* Asst prof painting, drawing, sculpture, watercolor & design, Univ Cent Ark, Conway, 70-80, assoc prof, 80- *Awards:* First Place & Purchase Award, Fifth Ann Ark Artist Exhib, Southeastern Ark Art Ctr, 72; First Place in 19th Invitational Exhib of Ann Ark State Festival, 76; Top Award, 18th Ann Ark Oil Painting Exhib, 77. *Mem:* Nat Art Educ Asn; Ark Art Educ Asn. *Media:* Acrylic, Watercolor; Wood. *Mailing Add:* Univ Cent Ark 6 Salem Rd Conway AR 72032

LARSEN, ROBERT WESLEY
PAINTER
b Aurora, Ill, Nov 22, 23. *Study:* Kansas City Inst Art, 46-47; Detroit Sch Arts & Crafts, 47-50; Ringling Sch Art, 50-51. *Work:* High Mus; Polk Mus Art, Lakeland, Fla. *Exhib:* Tenth Southeast Exhib, High Mus, 55; Gulf Caribbean Exhib, Houston Mus Fine Arts, 56; Art in Embassies Prog, US Dept State, 66; solo exhibs, Columbia Mus Art, SC, 67, Columbus Mus Art, Ga, 68 & Hodgell Hartman Gallery, 80; Polk Mus Exhib, Lakeland, Fla, 79. *Teaching:* Instr painting, Ringling Sch Art & Design, Fla, 66- *Awards:* First Prize, Tenth Southeast Exhib, High Mus, 55 & Fla Festival Art, Lehigh Acres Asn, 64; Spec Award, Soc Four Arts, Ft Lauderdale, Fla, 67. *Bibliog:* Jeanette Crane (auth), Robert Larsen at Hodgell Hartman, 78; Robert Larsen artist, Sarasota Town & Country Mag, 11-12/78; featured article, Am Artist Mag, 12/84. *Media:* Oil. *Dealer:* Hodgell Hartman Gallery 46 S Palm Ave Sarasota FL 33577. *Mailing Add:* 1395 40th St Sarasota FL 34234

LARSEN, SUSAN C
CURATOR, HISTORIAN
b Chicago, Ill, Oct 3, 46. *Study:* Knox Col, Galesburg, Ill, 64-66; Northwestern Univ, BA, 68, MA, 72, PhD, 75; Graves Found Fel, 80. *Collections Arranged:* Wallworks, Univ Southern Calif Gallery, 81; Abstract Painting and Sculpture in America 1927-44 (auth, catalog), Mus Art, Carnegie Inst, Pittsburgh, Pa, 83; Edward Hopper, Whitney Mus, 89; Art in Place: 15 Years of Collecting, Whitney Mus, 89. *Pos:* guest lectr, series of lectures on Richard Diebenkorn, Los Angeles Co Mus Art, Los Angeles, 77; mem adv bd, Archives Am Art. *Teaching:* Asst prof hist of art, Carleton Col, Northfield, Minn, 74-75; from assoc prof to prof hist of art, Univ Southern Calif, Los Angeles, 75-; cur permanent collection, Whitney Mus Am Art, New York, 88-90; adjunct cur permanent collection, Whitney Mus Am Art, 90-91. *Mem:* Col Art Asn Am; Am Studies Asn; Southern Calif Art Historians Asn. *Res:* Abstract art of the 1930's; WPA in New York City; contemporary art in California; American folk art. *Publ:* Coauth, A Conversation with Richard Diebenkorn, J Los Angeles Inst Contemp Art, summer 77; auth, exhib catalogue, Vija Celmins, Newport Art Mus, 12/79; Richard Tuttle, Baxter Art Gallery, 79; C Y Twombly, Newport Art Mus, 10/81; Selections from 8 Collections (catalog), Mus Contemp Art, Los Angeles, 83; coauth, Art in Place, Whitney Mus Am Art, 89; regular contribr, Art News Mag, Artweek & Artforum. *Mailing Add:* 360 Laurinda Long Beach CA 90803

LARSON, BLAINE (GLEDHILL)
PAINTER, INSTRUCTOR
b Salt Lake City, Utah, July 13, 37. *Work:* Corcoran Gallery Art, Washington, DC; Rochester Art Mus, NY; Nat Collection Fine Arts, DC. *Exhib:* Seven one-man shows, Jefferson Place Gallery, Washington, DC & Diane Brown Gallery, 77 & 78; Ten Washington Artists, Edmonton Art Mus, 70; Int Art Wash Exhib, 77 & 78; Gesture on Paper, Corcoran Mus, 80; Jack Rasmussen Gallery, 81; On Going Dialogue, Andrew Hudson & Blaine Larson, Corcoran Gallery Art, 81; and others. *Teaching:* Chmn painting, Corcoran Sch Art, 70- *Bibliog:* Ben Forgey (auth), articles in Washington Star & Art News; Jack Perlmutter (auth), article, Art Voices South, 5-6/80. *Media:* Acrylic. *Mailing Add:* Dept Drawing & Art 500 17th St NW Corcoran Sch Washington DC 20006

LARSON, JANE (WARREN)
CERAMIST, WRITER
b San Francisco, Calif, June 2, 22. *Study:* Swarthmore Col; Univ Rochester, BA(Eng, cum laude); Univ Calif, Los Angeles, sculpture with Anna Mahler; Antioch Univ, Visual Arts Ctr, MFA(ceramics). *Work:* Wash Co Mus of Art, Hagerstown, Md; Oak Ridge Community Art Ctr, Tenn; Collection of Works by Maryland Artists, Univ of Maryland. *Comn:* three outdoor murals with waterfalls (8' x 20', 8' x 13', 4' x 19'), Guest Quarters Hotel, Bethesda, Md, 86; murals, Pierson, Ball & Dowd Law Off, Washington, DC, 86; ceramic mural (4' x 10'), Fed City Shelter, Washington, DC, 88; columnar ceramic mural (8' x 1 1/2' x 1 1/2'), Nat Acad Engin & Sci, Beckman Ctr, Irvine, Calif; columnar mural (5' x 1' x 1'), Johns Hopkins Sch Int Studies, Washington, DC; outdoor wall mural (3' x 30') Energy & Life, Art Ctr, Oak Ridge Tenn, 92. *Exhib:* Int Sculpture Conf, Washington, DC, 90; one-person shows, Ceramics, Science & Art, Am Asn Advan Sci, Washington, DC, 90; Maryland's Best 1986, Rockland Arts Ctr, Ellicot City, 86; Making the square ceramic form, Full Circle Gallery, Alexander, Va, 88; Seven Artists, Studio Gallery, Washington, DC, 91; Sculpture on the Grounds, Rockville Civic Ctr Mansion, Rockville, Md, 92; Water Features, Franklin Sq Exhib Space, Washington, DC, 92; one-person show, Clay Tales from the Living Earth, Studio Gallery, Washington, Dc, 92. *Teaching:* Instr ceramics, Oak Ridge Community Art Ctr, Tenn, 63-66; workshops, slab construction, Kiln Club of Washington, DC, 81; Potter's Guild, Annapolis, Md, 81; instr slab ceramics, Inst Learning Retirement, Am Univ, Washington, DC, 83-84 & 86. *Awards:* Purchase Award, Objects 73, Western Colo Ctr for the Arts, 73; First Prize, Ceramic Guild Juried Show, 87. *Bibliog:* Bethesda artist's flowers will bloom forever here, The Chronicle, Bethesda, Md, 5/8/85; C Stapleton (auth), Tomorrow's antiques, The Washingtonian, 5/79; L Ellicott (auth), Jane Larson, Clay Tales, EyeWash, 2/92. *Mem:* Artists Equity; Kiln Club Washington, DC; Bethesda Ceramic Guild, Md; Int Sculpture Ctr. *Media:* Stoneware Clay, Ancient Glazes. *Res:* Art objects of the past that take the squared vessel form. *Collection:* Origins of modern ceramics, particularly Japanese Iga, Hanada, Leach & Picasso. *Publ:* Auth, A Tennessee mural, 6/68, Ceramics at Expo 70, 6/70, Hamada legacy, 10/70 & Collecting ceramics, 5/72, Ceramics Mo; Can we consider beauty?, Crafts Horizons, 6/73; Waterfall Murals, Tile World, fall 87; Bethesda: An artist's perspective, New Art Examiner, 4/87; Ceramics & the Homeless, Ceramics Mo, 4/89. *Mailing Add:* 6514 Bradley Blvd Bethesda MD 20034

LARSON, JUDY L
CURATOR
b Glendale, Calif, Mar 9, 52. *Study:* Univ Calif, Los Angeles, BA, 74, MA, 78. *Collections Arranged:* American Engravings before 1820 (with catalog), Am Antiquarian Soc, 79-84; Enchanted Images (auth, catalog), Santa Barbara Mus, 80; American Illustration (auth, catalog), Glenbow Mus, 85-86; Georgia Printmakers, (auth, catalog), High Mus, Atlanta, Ga, 86. *Pos:* Sr cataloger, Am Antiquarian Soc, Worcester, Mass, 79-84; cur Am Art, High Mus, Atlanta, Ga, 85- *Teaching:* Lectr hist prints, Assumption Col, fall 84 & Emory Univ, spring 86. *Res:* 18th and 19th century American Painting, federal period printmaking & illustration 1880-1925. *Publ:* Contribr, William M Harnett Metrop Mus Art, New York, 265-275, 92. *Mailing Add:* c/o High Mus Art 1280 Peachtree St Atlanta GA 30309

LARSON, KAY L
CRITIC, WRITER
b Cedar Rapids, Iowa, Sept 18, 46. *Study:* Pomona Col, Claremont, Calif, with Mowry Baden, BA(philos, art practice), 69. *Pos:* Art critic/writer, Real Paper, Cambridge, Mass, 72-75; assoc ed, 75-78; art critic/writer, Village Voice, 79-80; art critic, New York Mag, 80- *Teaching:* Instr, NY Univ, 90- *Awards:* Nat Endowment Arts Critic Grants, 78 & 80. *Mem:* Int Art Critics Asn. *Mailing Add:* c/o New York Magazine 755 Second Ave New York NY 10017

LARSON, PHILIP SEELY
SCULPTOR, EDUCATOR
b Ventura, Calif, July 21, 44. *Study:* Univ Minn, Minneapolis, BA, 66; Columbia Univ, PhD, 71. *Comn:* Interior design & installation, Collection of Keyboard Instruments, Schubert Club, Landmark Ctr, St Paul, 79. *Exhib:* Hanson-Cowles Gallery, Minneapolis, 77; Glen Hanson Gallery,

Minneapolis, 79 & 81; Emergent Americans, Guggenheim Mus, New York, 81; Mus Art, RI Sch Design, 83; Thomson Gallery, Minneapolis, 83; and others. *Collections Arranged:* Burgoyne Diller, 71; DeKooning: Drawings & Sculptures (auth, catalog), 74; Naives/Visionaries (auth, catalog), 74; World Architecture in Minnesota, 78; Prairie School Architecture in Minnesota, Iowa and Wisconsin (auth, catalog), 82. *Pos:* Cur, Walker Art Ctr, Minneapolis, 70-75; frequent contribr, Print Collector's Newsletter. *Teaching:* Prof, Minneapolis Col Art & Design, 75- *Awards:* Artist's Fel, Nat Endowment Arts, 79 & 81. *Media:* Cast Bronze, Cast Iron. *Mailing Add:* c/o Thomson Gallery 321 Second Ave N Minneapolis MN 55401

LARSON, SIDNEY
PAINTER, CONSERVATOR
b Sterling, Colo, June 16, 23. *Study:* Univ Mo, AB & MA; Univ Okla; also with Thomas Hart Benton. *Work:* State Hist Soc, Mo; Munic Bldg, Jefferson City, Mo; Columbia Col; Columbia Pub Libr. *Comn:* Social History of Phelps Co, Rolla Daily News, Mo, 52; Social History of Insurance, Shelter Ins Co, Columbia, Mo, 59; Social History of Ceramics & Metal, Riback Industs, Columbia, 67; mural, Munic Bldg, Jefferson City, Mo, 85; mural, Guitar Bldg, Columbia, Mo. *Pos:* Mus cur, State Hist Soc, Mo, 61- *Teaching:* Instr, Oklahoma City Univ, 50-51; Univ Mo-Columbia, summers; prof art, Columbia Col, 51- *Awards:* Huntington Hartford Found, 62; Distinguished Serv Award, State Hist Soc, Mo, 89; Mo State Arts Coun Award, 91. *Mem:* Nat Soc Mural Painters; Am Inst Conserv Hist Artistic Works. *Res:* Private, federal, state and municipal painting restorations. *Publ:* Auth, Introduction to Fred Shane Drawings, 64; articles on Thomas Hart Benton, 69, 74 & 75 & auth, Conservation of a Bingham, 72, Mo Hist Rev; Chap in: Thomas Hart Benton Artist-Writer-Intellectual, 89. *Mailing Add:* 2025 Crestridge Dr Columbia MO 65203

LARSON, WILLIAM G
PHOTOGRAPHER, EDUCATOR
b North Tonawanda, NY, Oct 14, 42. *Study:* State Univ NY, Buffalo, BS(art), 64; Inst Design, Ill Inst Technol, Chicago, MS(photog), with Aaron Siskind & Wynn Bullock, 67. *Work:* Mus Mod Art, New York; Philadelphia Mus Art; New Orleans Mus Art; Smithsonian Inst, Washington, DC; Nat Gallery Art, Sidney, Australia. *Exhib:* Portraits in Photog, Mus of Mod Art, New York, 69; The Expanded Photograph, Philadelphia Mus of Art, 72; Sewn, Stitched & Stuffed, 73, Mus of Contemp Crafts, New York; Unique Photographs, Sculpture Multiples, Mus of Mod Art, New York, 73; Light & Lens, Hudson River Mus, Yonkers, NY, 73; Three Centuries of Am Art, Philadelphia Mus of Art, 76; Locations in Time, Int Mus of Photog, Rochester, 77; Electroworks, Int Mus Photography, Rochester, 79; American Color Photography, Gallerie Rudolf Kicken, Koln, Ger, 80; Whitney Biennial, Whitney Mus Am Art, New York, 81; The Still Life, Mus Mod Art, New York, 81; and others. *Collections Arranged:* Moholy-Nagy Photographs (75 photographs with monogr picture ed), Claremont Col, 75. *Teaching:* Prof & dept chmn photog, Tyler Sch of Art, Temple Univ, Philadelphia, 67- *Awards:* Nat Endowment Arts, 71 & 79; Guggenheim Fel, 82. *Bibliog:* Rourke & Davis (auths), New Frontiers in Color, Newsweek, 4/76; Skip Atwater (auth), William Larson--Time & Structure, Afterimage, Rochester, 12/76; David Featherstone (auth), Tension through color, Artweek, San Francisco. *Publ:* Contribr, Three Centuries American Art, Philadelphia Mus Art, 76; auth, Fire Flies, Gravity Press, 76; ed, Quiver, Temple Univ, 77; contribr, One of a kind, Polaroid Corp, 79; auth, Big Pictures, Little Pictures, Gravity Press, 80; and others. *Dealer:* Light Gallery 724 Fifth Ave New York NY 10019. *Mailing Add:* 120 Hopwood Rd Collegeville PA 19426-2844

LARZELERE, JUDITH ANN
TAPESTRY ARTIST
b Ann Arbor, Mich, Mar 17, 44. *Study:* Radcliff Col, 62-64; Univ Mich, BA, 67; Rutgers Univ, MFA, 74. *Work:* Iowa State Univ Libr, Ames; Am Craft Mus, New York; Radcliffe Col Harvard Univ, Cambridge, Mass. *Comn:* Banners, Phillips Andover Acad, Andover, Mass, 81; silk wallhanging, Teradyne, Nashua, NH, 82; silk walllhanging, Biogen, Cambridge, Mass, 83; wallhanging, Putnam Investors, Boston, Mass, 88; wallhanging, Harper Indust, Inc, New York, 88. *Exhib:* Quilt National, Dairy Barn Art Ctr, Athens, Ohio, 81, 83, 85, 87 & 89; Contemp Am Quilts in Japan, Nitsu Osaka Art Ctr, Osaka, Japan, 85; Contemp Am Quilts, Hopkins Ctr Art Mus, Dartmouth Col, Hanover, NH, 86; Space: New Form New Function, Arrowmont Sch Art, Gatlinburg, Tenn, 86; Quilt Nat '87, Am Craft Mus, New York, 87; Contemp Quilts, Boston Univ Art Gallery, Mass, 87; Quilts Not To Sleep With, Wilson Art Ctr, Rochester, NY, 88. *Pos:* Studio artist, 78- *Teaching:* Penland Sch, NC, 90; Arrowmont Sch, Gatlinburg, Tenn, 90; Haystack Sch, Deer Isle, Maine, 91. *Awards:* Purchase Prize, A Banner Year, Iowa State Univ, 83; Best in show, 85, third prize, 86, Newburyport Arts Lottery Arts Show, Mass. *Bibliog:* Nancy North Strickland (auth), New England Quilters, Quilting Today #5, 88; Judith Nasatir, Contemp Quilts, Interior Design Mag, 2/89. *Mem:* Am Craft Coun. *Media:* Contemporary quilts, Strong Color. *Publ:* Auth, Beyond log cabin, Threads, Tauton Press, 2/86; contribr, Fiber Expressions: The Contemporary Quilt, Schiffer Pub, 87; America's Glorious Quilts, Hugh Lauter Levin, 87; Fiberarts Design Book III, Lark Press, 88; auth, Quilting strip by strip, Threads, Tauton Press, 8/88. *Dealer:* The Works Gallery 319 South St Philadelphia Pa 19147; Maveety Gallery PO Box 148 Gleneden OR 97388. *Mailing Add:* c/o Kendall Ctr 226 Beech St Belmont MA 02178

LASANSKY, LEONARDO
DRAFTSMAN, PRINTMAKER
b Iowa City, Iowa, Mar 29, 46. *Study:* Univ Iowa, BGS, 71, MA, 72 & MFA, 72; also with Byron Burford & 15 Stuart Edie. *Work:* Brooklyn Mus, New York; Princeton Univ Mus; Philadelphia Mus Art; Achenback Collection, San Francisco; Nat Mus, Krakow, Poland; Libr of Cong, Washington, DC; Mus of Art, Grenchen, Switz; Minneapolis Inst Art; Nat Gallery of Art, Washington, DC; Hood Mus, Dartmouth Col. *Comn:* Portrait, Christopher Columbus, James Ford Bell Libr. *Exhib:* Minneapolis Inst Art, Minn, 77; Am Drawing 1927-1977, Minn Mus Art, St Paul, 77; Hassam Fund Purchase Exhib, Am Acad Inst Arts & Lett, New York, 79; 21st Nat Print Exhib, Brooklyn Mus, New York, 79; Int Print Biennale, Krakow, Poland, 80; Am Drawing in Black & White, Brooklyn Mus, New York, 80-81; Int Book Design Exhib, Mus Kunsthandwerks, Leipzig, Ger, 82; 7th Nat Print Exhib, Univ Calif, Los Angeles, 82; one-man show, Dartmouth Col, Hood Mus, 82; Univ Mich, Ann Arbor, 85; Forum Gallery, New York, 86; Premio Int, eiella, Italy, 87; Bienal de San Juan, Grabado Lationamericano, Puerto Rico, 88-; Am Embassy, Belgrade, Yugoslavia, 89-90; Prefectural Mus Art, Fukuoka, Japan, 90. *Pos:* Adv panel, Minn State Arts, 88-90. *Teaching:* Prof art, Hamline Univ, 72-, chmn fine arts div, 80-85, acting chmn art dept, 90-91; artist-in-residence, Dartmouth Col, 82. *Awards:* Purchase Award, 5th Nat Hawaii Print Exhib, Honolulu, 80; Purchase Award, 4th Miami Int Print Exhib, Fla, 80; Distinguished Alumni Award, Univ Iowa, 81; Drawing Award, Berkshire Mus, Pittsfield, Mass, 82; and others. *Bibliog:* Lane Stiles (auth), article, Projekt Mag, Warsaw, Poland, 3/81. *Media:* Intaglio. *Mailing Add:* Print Dept Hamline Univ 1536 Hewitt St Paul MN 55104

LASANSKY, MAURICIO L
PRINTMAKER, DRAFTSMAN
b Buenos Aires, Arg, 14; US citizen. *Study:* Superior Sch Fine Arts, Arg; Iowa Wesleyan Col, Hon DA, 59; Pac Lutheran Univ, Hon DFA, 69; Carleton Col, Northfield, Minn, Hon DA, 79; Coe Col, Iowa, Hon DFA, 85. *Work:* Art Inst Chicago; Mus Mod Art, NY; Libr Cong, Washington, DC; Uffizi Gallery, Florence, Italy; Mus Arte Contemp, Madrid, Spain; and over 100 univs & galleries, US & abroad. *Exhib:* One-man shows, Mauricio Lasansky: Selections from 30 Years of Printmaking, The Nazi Drawings, Palace Fine Arts, Mexico City, 69, Dickinson Col, Carlisle, Pa, 72 & 74, Third Int Biennial Mexico, 80, and over 160 others; Whitney Mus Am Art, New York, 71; and others. *Pos:* Virgil M Hancher chair (emer), Univ Iowa, 67. *Teaching:* Dir, Free Fine Arts Sch, Villa Maria, Cordoba, Arg, 36 & Taller Manualidades, Cordoba, 39; vis lectr, Univ Iowa, 45, asst prof art, 46, assoc prof, 47, prof, 48-, res prof, 65-67, Virgil M Hancher Distinguished Prof, 67-71, res prof, 71-72; Lucas lectr, Carleton Col, 65. *Awards:* Guggenheim Fel, 43, 44, 45, 53 & 63; Distinguished Teaching of Art Award, Col Art Asn, 80; Nominated for Wolf Found Award in the Arts, Jerusalem, Israel,82; Hon Award Arts & Humanities Comn for the Aging, 83; Acadamician, Nat Acad Arts & Design, New York, 90. *Bibliog:* Kevin Kelly (producer & dir), Lasansky Printmaker, Univ Iowa Video Ctr. *Mem:* Col Art Asn Am (bd dirs, 70-); life mem Nat Acad Design; Nat Acad Fine Arts, Buenos Aires, Argentina; Fel, Inst Advan Study, Indiana Univ, Bloomington. *Media:* Etching. *Mailing Add:* 216 E Washington St Iowa City IA 52240

LASCH, PAT
SCULPTOR
b New York, NY, Nov 20, 44. *Study:* Queen Col, NY, BA, 70; Ga State, MFA, 90. *Work:* Queens Col, City Univ New York; Mus Mod Art, Metrop Mus Art, New York; Oberlin Mus, Ohio; Prudential Insurance Co, NJ; Rutgers Univ, New Brunswick, NJ. *Comn:* Hommage: 1929-1979 (sculpture), Mus Mod Art, New York, 79. *Exhib:* Solo exhibs, AIR Gallery, New York, 73, 77, 79 & 80, Kathryn Markel Gallery, New York, 81, 84 & 85; Lerner Heller Gallery, New York, 81; Albright-Knox Gallery, Members' Gallery, Buffalo, NY, 84; McIntosh Drepdale Gallery, Washington, DC, 85; Marilyn Pearl Gallery, New York, 88, 90 & Paridiso, Il Ponte Gallery, Rome, Italy; Contemporary Women: Consciousness & Content, Brooklyn Mus Art Sch, NY 77; Out of the House, Whitney Mus Am Art Downtown, New York, 78; 10th Anniversary Exhibition, Marilyn Pearl Gallery, New York, 86; Saints and Sinners: Contemporary Responses to Religion, DeCordova Mus, Lincoln, Mass, 86-87; Sculpture of the Eighties, Queens Mus, NY, 87; Ironies: Figure & Still Life in Sculpture, Marilyn Pearl Gallery, New York, 90; The Cooked & the Raw, Thomas Segal Gallery, Boston, Mass; and other solo exhibs. *Pos:* Guest panelist, Soho Ctr Visual Arts, New York, 77. *Teaching:* Parson's Sch Design, 78-88, RI Sch Design, 89-90 & Univ Mass, Amherst, 91- *Awards:* Prize, Am Acad Rome, 82-83; Special Proj, NY St Coun Arts, 84-85; Pollock-Krasner, 87; and others. *Bibliog:* Ellen Lubell (auth), When a good gallery folds, Village Voice, 4/11/85; Vivien Raynor (auth) article, NY Times, 10/4/85; Jeff Weinstein (auth), It's heaven when you, Village Voice, 10/22/85. *Media:* Mixed. *Publ:* Auth, AIR, Artforum, 11/80, 70; If You Make A Mistake Put A Rose On It, 85. *Dealer:* Kathryn Markel Gallery 50 W 57th St New York NY; Marilyn Pearl Gallery 420 W Broadway New York NY 10012. *Mailing Add:* 463 West St #228G New York NY 10014

LASKA, DAVID
DESIGNER, PAINTER
b Richmond, Va, Apr 10, 20. *Study:* Art Students League (Hale); Newark Sch Fine & Indust Arts. *Comn:* Portrait of Nathan S Kline, Nathan S Kline Inst, Orangeburg, NY, 80. *Exhib:* Hudson River Contemp Artists, Hudson River Mus, Yonkers, NY, 83; 35th Art of NE USA, Silvermine Guild, New Canaan, Conn, 84; Somers Gallery, Somers, NY, 85; Mari Gallery Memaroneck, NY, 86; Lotus Club, New York, 87; Municipal Hall, Larchmont, NY, 88; 35th Nat Soc Painters in Casein & Acrylic, Nat Arts Club, New York, 88. *Awards:* Henry Hoppin, 28th New Eng Ann; Perkin Elmer Corp, 35th Art NE USA, 84; Marion de Solamendez, 35th Nat Soc Painter in Casein & Acrylic, 88. *Bibliog:* Robert Cohen (auth), Resident makes splash with waterfront scenes, Gannett Westchester Newspapers, 8/13/88. *Mem:* Nat Soc Painters Casein & Acrylic (vpres, 80-88); New York Artists Equity Asn (bd dirs, 82). *Media:* Acrylic. *Mailing Add:* 127 Cooper Dr New Rochelle NY 10805

LASKE, LYLE F
SCULPTOR, EDUCATOR
b Green Bay, Wis, May 10, 37. *Study:* Univ Wis, Platteville, BS, 59; Univ Wis, Madison, MS, 61 & MFA, 65; Univ Minn, 68. *Work:* Plains Art Mus, Moorhead, Minn. *Exhib:* Solo exhib, Walker Art Ctr, Minneapolis, Minn, 66; Artists of Central NY, Everson Mus Art, Syracuse, 71; Draw and Small Sculpture Show, Ball State Univ, Ind, 74; Miss River Crafts Show, Memphis, Tenn, 77; Am Woodcarvers, Craft Ctr, Worchester, Mass, 78; New Handmade Furniture, Am Craft Mus, New York, 79; Beyond Folk, Minneapolis Inst Art, Minn, 84. *Teaching:* Instr, Wis State Univ, Platteville, 62-64; prof sculpture, Moorhead State Univ, Minn, 65-; assoc prof, New York State Univ Col Oneonta, 70-71. *Media:* Wood. *Publ:* American woodcarvers, Craft Horizons, 4/78; Air-powered tools, Fine Woodworking, 1-2/79; Some abrasive facts, Fine Woodworking, 3-4/80; Woodworking: The New Wave, Crown Publ, 81; Fine Woodworking Techniques 3, The Taunton Press, 81. *Mailing Add:* Art Dept Moorhead State Univ Moorhead MN 56560

LASKER, JOE (JOSEPH L)
PAINTER, ILLUSTRATOR
b Brooklyn, NY, June 26, 19. *Study:* Cooper Union Art Sch, cert, 39. *Work:* Whitney Mus Am Art, New York; Philadelphia Mus Art; Springfield Mus, Mass; Joseph H Hirshhorn Collection, Washington, DC; Calif Palace of Legion of Honor, San Francisco; and others. *Comn:* Murals, US Pub Works Admin, Post Off, Calumet, Mich, 41, Milbury, Mass, 42 & Henry St Settlement Playhouse, New York, 48. *Exhib:* Pa Acad Fine Arts Ann, 47-53; Whitney Mus Am Art Ann, 47-58; Nat Acad Design Ann, New York, 47-82; Krawshaar Galleries, New York, 51-; and others. *Teaching:* Assoc prof painting, Univ Ill, 52-53. *Awards:* Prix de Rome Fel, Am Acad Rome, 50 & 51; Guggenheim Fel, 54; Nat Inst Arts & Lett Grant, 68; Nat Acad Design, 80. *Bibliog:* 19 Young Americans, Life, 3/20/50; Goodrich & Baver (auth), American art of our century, Praeger, NY, 61; Figurative Tradition, Whitney Mus Am Art, New York, 61. *Mem:* Nat Acad Design. *Media:* Oil, Watercolor. *Mailing Add:* c/o Kraushaar Gallery 724 Fifth Ave New York NY 10019

LASKER, JONATHAN
PAINTER
b Jersey City, NJ, 1948. *Study:* Sch Visual Arts, NY, 75-77; Calif Inst Arts, Valencia, Calif, 77. *Work:* Mus Ludwig, Cologne; The Corcoran Gallery of Art, Washington, DC; The Hirshhorn Mus & Sculpture Garden, Smithsonian Inst, Washington, DC; Wacoal Art Ctr, Tokyo. *Exhib:* one-man shows, Landmark Gallery, New York, 81, Annette Gmeiner, Kirchzarten, Ger, 84, Michael Werner, Cologne, Ger, 86, Anders Tornberg, Lund, Sweden, 87, Gian Enzo Sperone Gallery, Rome, 88 & Massimo Audiello Gallery, New York, 89; Art at the End of the Social, Rooseum, Malmö, Sweden; Daniel Newburg Gallery, New York, 89; Scott Hanson Gallery, 90; Sperone-Westwater Gallery, New York, 91; Thaddaeus Ropac Gallery, Paris, 92. *Awards:* Nat Endowment Arts, 87 & 89; New York Found Arts, 89. *Bibliog:* Barbara MacAdam (auth), Artnews, 2/90. *Mailing Add:* c/o Massimo Audiello Gallery 436 E 11th St No 5 New York NY 10007-4519

LASKIN, MYRON, JR
CURATOR, HISTORIAN
b Milwaukee, Wis, Apr 7, 30. *Study:* Harvard Univ, AB, 52, AM, 54; Inst Fine Arts, NY Univ, PhD, 64. *Collections Arranged:* Fountainebleau, Nat Gallery Can, 73. *Pos:* Cur Europ art, Nat Gallery Can, 68; cur paintings, J Paul Getty Mus, Malibu, Calif, 84-89. *Teaching:* Asst prof art hist, Washington Univ, 61-66. *Awards:* Italian Govt Grant, NY Univ, 59-60; Villa I Tatti Fel, 65-67, Kress Fel, 66-67, Harvard Univ. *Res:* Italian 16th and 17th century painting. *Publ:* Contribr, Burlington Mag, Art Bulletin, Arte Illustrata & others. *Mailing Add:* J Paul Getty Mus Art PO Box 2112 Santa Monica CA 90406

LASSAW, IBRAM
SCULPTOR, PAINTER
b Alexandria, Egypt, May 4, 13; US citizen. *Study:* Sculpture Ctr, 26-30; Beaux Arts Inst Design, 30-31; City Col New York; Long Island Univ, Hon Dr Arts, 89. *Work:* Albright-Knox Art Gallery, Buffalo; Baltimore Mus Art; Whitney Mus Am Art & Mus Mod Art, New York; Mus Mod Art, Rio de Janeiro, Brazil; Carnegie Mellon Univ, Pittsburg, Pa; Nat Collection Fine Arts, Smithsonian, Washington, DC; Wichita Art Mus, Kans. *Comn:* Sculpture, comn by Percival Goodman for Beth El Temple, Springfield, Mass; Baldachin & altar screen, House of Theology of Franciscan Fathers, Centerville, Ohio; hanging sculpture for lobby, Hilton Hotel, New York; sculpture for Beth El Temple, Providence, RI, Temple of Aaron, St Paul, Minn & Temple Anshe Chesed, Cleveland, Ohio, plus others. *Exhib:* Recent Acquisitions, Whitney Mus Am Art, New York; Two Hundred Years of American Sculpture, Whitney Mus Am Art, New York, 76; Five Distinguised Alumni, Hirschhorn Mus, 82; solo exhibs, Lafayette Col, Pa, 83, Benton, South Hampton, NY, 86 & Harmon Meek gallery, Fla, 92; Abstract Painting and Sculpture in American, Mus Art, Carnegie Inst, 83, San Francisco Mus Mod Art, 84 & Whitney Mus Am Art, 84; The Third Dimension, Sculpture of the New York School, Whitney Mus Am Art, 84; Space Explorations, retrospective 1929-1988, Guild Hall Mus, East Hampton, NY, 88; II Biennale Internazionale Di Scultura Contemporanea Di Matera Italia, 90; Manny Silverman Gallery, Los Angeles, 92; Edwin A Ulrich Mus Art, Wichita, Kans, 92; and many others. *Pos:* Fed Arts Proj, Pub Works Admin, 33-42. *Teaching:* Instr sculpture, YMHA, 92nd St, New York, 35-36 & Am Univ, 50; artist in residence, Duke Univ, 62-63; vis artist, Univ Calif, Berkeley, 65-66; adj fac, Southampton Col, 66-; vis prof, Brandeis Univ, Waltham, NY, 72 & Mt Holyoke Col, 78; also pvt classes in studio. *Bibliog:* Peter Selz (auth) Art in Our Time, Abrams, 82; 25 Artists, Univ Publ Am, Frederick, Md, 82; and many others. *Mem:* Founder Am Abstract Artists (pres, 46-49); Artists Club; Am Acad & Inst Arts & Lett, 84. *Dealer:* Harmon-Meek Gallery 386 Broad South Naples FL 33940. *Mailing Add:* 678 Fireplace Rd East Hampton NY 11937

LASTER, PAUL
COLLAGE ARTIST, PAINTER
b Flint, Mich, Oct 14, 51. *Work:* The Brooklyn Mus; Chase Manhattan Bank, New York; Gota-Gruppen, Stockholm; Magasin 3, Stockholm; Reader's Digest Asn, Pleasantville, NY. *Exhib:* One-man shows, Robbin Lockett Gallery, Chicago, 86, Galerie Arch, Amsterdam, 88, Pence Gallery, Santa Monica, 89 & 90, Hirschl & Adler Modern, 90; Four Artists, Soho Ctr for Visual Artists, New York, 82; The More Store, Jack Tilton Gallery, New York, 84; The Art of Appropriation, The Alternative Mus, New York, 85; Beyond the Image, First Street Forum, St Louis, 87; Northwestern Collects, Mary & Leigh Block Gallery, Evanston, Ill, 90. *Bibliog:* Paul Laster, treads a painterly path to reality, NY Times, 3/23/90; Lisa Liebermann (auth), Goings on About Town, The New Yorker, 3/26/90. *Mailing Add:* c/o Hirschl & Adler Modern 420 W Broadway New York NY 10021

LASUCHIN, MICHAEL
PRINTMAKER, PAINTER
b Kramatorsk, USSR, July 24, 23; US citizen. *Study:* Rostow Col Art, USSR, 40-41; Philadelphia Col Art, BFA; Tyler Sch Art, Temple Univ, MFA. *Work:* Libr Cong, Washington, DC; Philadelphia Mus Art; Nat Libr Print Collection, Paris; Mus Mod Art, Barcelona; Brooklyn Mus Art; and others. *Comn:* Print, Print Club Philadelphia, 74; print, Pratt Graphics Ctr, New York, 80. *Exhib:* 11th Int Exhib Graphic Arts, Mus Mod Art, Ljubljana, Yugoslavia, 75; 3rd Int Drawing Biennale, Cleveland, Eng, 77; 12th Int Print Biennale, Crakow, Poland, 88; Ninth Norwegian Int Print Triennale, Fredrikstad, Norway, 89; Interprint Lviv '90, Lviv, USSR, 90. *Teaching:* Prof printmaking, Univ Arts, 72- *Awards:* Grumbacher Gold Medal Award, Nat Watercolor Soc, 81; Purchase Award, Honolulu Acad Fine Art, 85; Venture Fund Award, Melon Found, 87. *Bibliog:* Cynthia B Frost (auth), Paintings suggest, Daily Pennsylvanian 11/20/74; Bill Southwell (auth), Exhibiting new talent, Drummer, 4/22/75; Dorothy Grafly (auth), Art contrasts, Art in Focus, 4/75. *Mem:* Boston Printmakers; Nat Watercolor Soc; Soc Am Graphic Artists; Am Color Print Soc; and others. *Media:* Watercolor, Printmaking. *Publ:* Contribr, Folio '76. *Dealer:* The Plum Gallery 1800 E Lancaster Ave Paoli PA 19301. *Mailing Add:* 120 E Cliveden St Philadelphia PA 19119

LATOS-VALIER, PAULA
MUSEUM DIRECTOR, ADMINISTRATOR
b Philadelphia, Pa, Feb 6, 46. *Study:* Univ Dijon, France, Propedeutique Equivalent, 66; Univ New Hampshire, BA(magna cum laude), 67; Yale Univ, MPhil, 71. *Comn:* Banner Ser, Humphrey Browning & McDougall, Boston, Mass, 75; Indoor Banners, Ocean Spray Cranberry, Mass, 75-76; Boston Plaza Banners, Ctr Plaza Assoc, Mass, 75-76; Theatre District Banners, City of Boston, Mass, 77; Haymarket Square Banners, Boston City Hall, Mass, 77. *Exhib:* Food Show, Inst Contemp Art, Boston, 72; New Talent/New England, DeCordova Mus, Lincoln, Mass, 73; Libr Cong Nat Print Exhib & Tour, Smithsonian Inst, Washington, DC, 73-74; New England Artists, Mass Inst Tech, Cambridge, 73; Flags, Banners & Kites Int, Allied Arts Seattle, Wash, 77; View From Down Under, Ministry Arts Regional Gallery Tour, Melbourne, Australia, 79-80. *Pos:* Asst dir, Boston Visual Artists Union Gallery, 74-76; mgr int art exhibs, Australian Gallery Dirs Coun, Sydney, 79-81; asst dir to exec officer, Biennale Sydney, 81-89; mgr int visual arts, Australia Coun, Sydney, 89-90; dir, Art Gallery Western Australia, Perth, 90- *Teaching:* Inst, drawing & design, DeCordova Mus Sch, Lincoln, Mass, 74-77; lectr, Exhibition & Gallery Mgt, City Art Inst, Sydney, 85-87. *Bibliog:* Mike van Niekerk (auth), New gallery dir has a clear vision, West Australian, 7/6/90. *Mem:* Col Art Asn; Art Mus Asn Australia (pres, 90-); Coun Australian Mus Asn (vpres, 90-). *Publ:* Auth, Crafty Animals, Ellsyd Press, Sydney, 87; Alphabet Animals, Sterling Publ, NY, 89. *Mailing Add:* Art Gallery of Western Australia Perth Cultural Center Perth WA 6000 Australia

LATTANZIO, FRANCES
PHOTOGRAPHER, EDUCATOR
b Detroit, Mich, Oct 2, 49. *Study:* Univ Mich, BFA, 71, MFA, 73. *Work:* Bank of Ind & Vincennes Univ, Ind; Madison Plaza Corp & Hyatt Int Corp, Chicago; Ind State Univ, Terre Haute. *Exhib:* One-person exhib, Quincy Col, Ill, 86; Midwest Photograph Invitational VI, Univ Wis, Green Bay, 90; Creative Images, Indianapolis Art League, 88; The Known/The Unknown, Briscoe Gallery, Miss State Univ, 88; Hand-Manipulated Photography, Buckham Fine Arts Proj, Flint, Mich, 89. *Teaching:* Assoc prof photog, Ind State Univ, Terre Haute, 75-; adj asst prof photog, St Mary of the Woods Col, Ind, 80. *Awards:* Engraph Award, Engraph Inc, 81. *Bibliog:* Cheryl Bopp (auth), article, Arts Insight, 3/80. *Mem:* Col Art Asn; Soc Photog Educ; Friends of Photog; Arts Illiana. *Media:* Silver Prints; Hand-colored. *Publ:* Illusr, Figurative Contexts, Turman Gallery, 83. *Mailing Add:* 1500 S Sixth St Terre Haute IN 47802

LAUB, STEPHEN
SCULPTURE
b Oakland, Calif, July, 10, 45. *Study:* Univ Calif, Berkely, BA, 69, Ma, 70. *Work:* Mus Mod Art & Donnelle Media Ctr, New York Pub Libr, New York; GOT A Gruppen AB (consortium), Stockholm, Sweden; Kunsthaus, Zurich, Switz. *Exhib:* The Sense of Self Traveling Exhib, 78-80; Extended Photog, Fifth Biennale, Vienna Mus, Austria, 81; Venice Biennale 1984, Venice Exhib Hall, Italy, 84; Spatial Relationships, Mus Mod Art, New York, 85; Alles und noch viel mehr, Kunstmuseum, Bern, Switz, 85; Art on the Beach, Creative

Time, Hunters Point, NY, 87; Images of Am Pop Culture, Laforet Mus, Tokyo, 89; On the Edge: Photography & Sculpture, Cleveland Ctr Contemp Art, Ohio, 90. *Teaching:* Asst prof sculpture, Rutgers Univ, NJ, 87- *Awards:* Fulbright Fel, Italy, 71-72; Artist's Fel, Nat Endowment Arts, 78-79; Artist's Fel, New York Found Arts, 89-90. *Bibliog:* J Hoberman (auth), Recent exhibitions, Village Voice, 7/30/85; Roberta Smith (auth), Stephen Laub, NY Times, 3/25/88; Charles Hagen (auth), Stephen Laub at Koury Wingate, Artforum, summer 88. *Media:* Wood. *Dealer:* Koury Wingate Gallery 578 Broadway New York NY 10012. *Mailing Add:* 176 W Houston St No 20 New York NY 10014

LAUB-NOVAK, KAREN
SCULPTOR, PAINTER
b Minneapolis, Minn, Aug 25, 37. *Study:* Carleton Col, Northfield, Minn, BA; State Univ Iowa, with Mauricio Lasansky, MFA; Sch Vision, Salzburg, Austria, with Oskar Kokoschka. *Work:* Carleton Col; Yale Univ; St Vincent's Archabbey; Continental Bank, Chicago; Pac Sch Relig; and others. *Comn:* 12-ft bronze statue of Norman Borlaug, 1971 Nobel Peace Prize Winner, Cresco, Iowa; portrait of David Stockman, OMB, US Govt, 84; bronze statuettes for Ann Awards, Iowa Bio-Technol Asn, 89; Bronze Crucifix, Paulist church, Grand Rapids, Mich, 89. *Exhib:* One-woman shows, Rochester Art Ctr, Minn, 70, Rockefeller Found, 74, Univ Tenn, 74, Pac Sch Relig, 74 & Yale Univ, 75, Des Moines Art Ctr; William Sawyer Gallery, San Francisco; Los Robles Gallery, Palo Alto, Calif; and many others. *Pos:* Freelance illusr, Books, Mag & Newspapers; ed adv, Momentum Mag; freelance writer, various publ. *Teaching:* Instr drawing, Carleton Col, 61-62; lectr, Georgetown Univ, Stanford Univ, Syracuse Univ, Mt Vernon & Univ Calif, Riverside. *Awards:* Kokoschka Award, Salzburg, Austria. *Bibliog:* L P Ruotolo (auth), A new apocalypse, Motive Mag, 66. *Mem:* Artists Equity. *Publ:* Illusr, Skunk named Zorrie (children's bk), 72; Art Creativity & The Sacred (Book) Essay; The Art of Deception (article); various other articles. *Mailing Add:* 3211 Northampton St NW Washington DC 20015

LAUCK, ANTHONY JOSEPH
SCULPTOR, EDUCATOR
b Indianapolis, Ind, Dec 30, 08. *Study:* John Herron Art Sch, Indianapolis, dipl prof grade in sculpture; Corcoran Sch Art, Washington, DC, cert advan study in sculpture & painting; Art Students' League, NY, also with Oronzio Maldarelli, Ivan Mestrovic, Carl Milles, Hugo Robus & Heinz Warneke. *Work:* Pa Acad Fine Arts, Philadelphia; Corcoran Gallery Art, Washington, DC; Butler Inst Am Arts, Youngstown, Ohio; Indianapolis Mus Art; Gary Art Ctr, Ind; Grand Rapids Mus, Mich. *Comn:* Set of facet windows, Congregation of Holy Cross, Ind Prov, Moreau Sem Chapel, Univ Notre Dame, 53; limestone image of Our Lady of the Univ, Univ Notre Dame, 63; 12 stained glass windows, Ursuline Motherhouse, Chatham, Ont, Can, 64; Basswood Sculpture Triptych, St Joseph Hosp, Mishawaka, Ind. *Exhib:* Fairmount Park Art Asn Int Exhib, Philadelphia, 48; Nat Exhib Art, Pa Acad Fine Arts, 49 & 53; Ind Artists' Exhib, Indianapolis Mus Art, 50, 51, 54 & 56; Audubon Artists, Nat Acad Arts, NY, 52-75; Mus Midwestern Am Art, Elkhart, Ind. *Collections Arranged:* The Work of John B Flannagan, Art Gallery, Univ Notre Dame, 61, The German Expressionists, 70 & The Graphic Work of Georges Rouault (with introd), 72. *Pos:* Conf planning comt, Mid-Am Col Art Asn, 67-72; comt acquisitions, Snite Mus Art, Notre Dame Univ. *Teaching:* Chmn art dept, Univ Notre Dame, 50-73; dir, Art Gallery, Univ Notre Dame, 54-74. *Awards:* Monk at Prayer (limestone), Pa Acad Art, 53; The Wife of Lot (terra cotta), Indianapolis Mus Art, 54; Whirlpool Nat Sculpture Competition, Krasl Art Ctr, St Joseph, Mich, 86- *Bibliog:* Dean A Porter (auth), Anthony Lauck: Sculptor, 70 & Edward Fischer (auth), The many facets of Anthony Lauck, 73, Univ Notre Dame Art Gallery Publ. *Media:* Wood, Stone. *Dealer:* David Mann 249 E 48th St New York NY 10017. *Mailing Add:* Moreau Seminary Notre Dame Univ Notre Dame IN 46556

LAUF, CORNELIA
CURATOR, ART HISTORIAN
b May 26, 61. *Study:* Oberlin Col, BA, 83; Columbia Univ, MA, 85; PhD, 92. *Collections Arranged:* Natura Naturata (An Arument for Still Life), Josh Baer Gallery, New York, 89; Flux Attitudes (auth, catalog), New Mus Contemp Art & Hallwalls, 92; The Wealth of Nations (auth, catalog), Warsaw, 92. *Pos:* Independent cur, 87- *Awards:* Wolfgang Stechow Mem Prize, Oberlin Col, 81-82, Oberlin Col Alumni Fel, 85-86; University Fel, 83-84, President's Fel, 84-86, Columbia Univ Travel Grant, 86, Samuel H Kress Fel, 89-90, Columbia Univ. *Publ:* Auth, Joseph Berrys, Seven Days (rev), 11/88; Franz Erhard Walther, Arts, 2/89; Talents and Gewgaws, Artscribe, 9-10/89; On reading some drawings of Reuys, Arts, 3/90; Collection Handbook, Guggenheim Mus, 92; Andre Cadere, Mus Mod Art, Paris & PSI, New York, 92. *Mailing Add:* 591 Broadway New York NY 10012

LAUFER, SUSAN
PAINTER
b Tuckahoe, New York, 50. *Study:* Art Students League, New York, 68; Boston Univ, Mass, BFA, 72; New York Univ, MA, 75. *Work:* Albright Knox Art Gallery; Brooklyn Mus; Denver Mus Art; Detroit Inst Art; Metrop Mus Art, New York; Screen Actors Guild, Los Angeles; Harris Bank, Chicago; Southeast Bank, Miami, Fla; and others. *Exhib:* Solo shows, Univ Conn, 90, Germans van Eck Gallery, New York, 90 & 91, Ctr Contemp Art, Chicago, 91 & 92, Betsy Senior Fine Arts, New York, 92; Chicago Mus Contemp Art, Ill, 91; Denver Art Mus, Colo, 92; Cleveland Ctr Contemp Art, Ohio, 92; and others. *Teaching:* Vis lectr, var univ, mus & col. *Awards:* Ferkauf Found, New York, 85; Ariana Found, Endowment, New York, 85; Nat Endowment Arts, 92. *Bibliog:* Gregory Galligan (auth), Susan Laufer (exhib catalog), Germans van Eck Gallery, New York, 90; Marilyn Fox (auth), Link to post modernism, Reading Eagle, Pa, 19, 6/9/90; John Davies Delmar (auth), A cast of artists who shape in plaster, Newsday, 6/19/90; and others. *Publ:* Illustr, The Ruin Revived, Branden Press, Boston, Mass, 86; contribr, The Richard Maslow Collection (exhib catalog), 87; auth, Lines of Vision (exhib catalog), 89; illusr, Stone Heart (cover), No 26, fall 89 & auth, Literature and the Visual Arts, No 27, fall 89, Pequod, Nat Poetry Found, New York; Lifeline Series (cover), Storyline Press, 92. *Mailing Add:* 53 Crosby St New York NY 10012

LAUGHLIN, MORTIMER
PAINTER
b San Francisco, Calif, July 24, 18. *Study:* Hollywood Art Ctr, Calif, 41; Abbott Art Sch, Washington, DC, 45; Art Students League, New York, 46. *Exhib:* Mus Mod Art, New York; Stamford Mus, Conn; San Francisco Mus Art, Calif; Newport Art Asn, RI; Silvermine Art Asn, Conn; Albany Inst Hist Art, NY; Art USA, New York; one-man shows, Bartholet Gallery, 80-84, 85, 88 & 90 & Gelabert Gallery, 91. *Media:* Mixed Media. *Dealer:* Gelabert Gallery 255 West 86th St New York NY 10024. *Mailing Add:* Rd 1 Box 8 Susquehanna PA 18847

LAURENT, JOHN LOUIS
PAINTER, EDUCATOR
b Brooklyn, NY, Nov 27, 21. *Study:* With Walt Kuhn, 46-48; Syracuse Univ, BFA, 48; Acad Grande Chaumiere, Paris, 48-49; Ind Univ, MAT, 54. *Work:* Univ Ill; First Nat Bank, Boston; De Cordova & Dana Mus, Lincoln, Mass; Addison Gallery Am Art, Andover, Mass. *Comn:* Great Bay Area Mural, Univ NH; Dove & Fish (two panels), St George's Church, York, Maine, 68; cover paintings, L L Bean, Freeport, Maine, 89. *Exhib:* One-man show, Addison Gallery Am Art, Andover, Mass, 72; St Paul's Sch, Concord, NH, 78; Art in Embassies Prog, Dept of State, Washington, DC, 79-82; Barridoff Galleries, Portland, Maine, 82 & 87; Payson-Weisberg Gallery, New York, 83; Midtown Gallery, New York, 85 & 86; and others. *Teaching:* Asst dir drawing & painting, Ogunquit Sch Painting & Sculpture, summers 46-60; asst prof drawing & painting, Va Polytech Inst, 50-53; prof drawing & painting, Univ NH, 54- *Awards:* Louis Comfort Tiffany Found Grant, 62; Nat Coun Arts Award, 66-67; City of Manchester Prize, Currier Gallery, NH, 70. *Bibliog:* Peter Cox (auth), A talk with John Laurent, 69 & The best of Maine at Frost Gallery, 69, Maine Times; Edward Betts (auth), Creative Seascape Photog & Creative Landscape Photog, Watson-Guptill Publ. *Mem:* Barn Gallery (bd dirs, 68-88); York & NH Art Asns. *Media:* Acrylic, Oil. *Dealer:* Frost Gully Gallery 411 Congress St Portland Maine 04101. *Mailing Add:* PO Box 1628 Ogunquit ME 03907

LAURIDSEN, HANNE H7L
PAINTER, SCULPTOR
b Esbjerg, Denmark; US citizen. *Study:* Univ Calif, San Diego with Eleanor Antin, Italo Scanga, Alan Kaprow, Newton & Helen Harrison, MFA, 82, Univ Calif-Berkeley, BA, 80. *Work:* NECCA Mus, Conn, Paterson Mus, NJ. *Exhib:* The Onion Universe, LaJolla, Calif, 82; Who is the Monster?, travelling exhib to New York & Europe, 84-85; People & Animals in Movement, Ismael Gallery, New York, 88; Art for Amnesti, Germans van Eck Gallery, 90; Paintings of New York & Other Fantasies, Rockefeller Townhouse Gallery, 92. *Teaching:* Teacher, drawing, sculpture, painting, Guild Hall Mus, E Hampton, NY, 83-86. *Awards:* Grants, Ford Found & Louis B Mayer Found, 82. *Bibliog:* Grace Gluck (auth), 3 offbeat shows with a conceptual bend, New York Times, 11/21/82; Kay Larson (auth), The Healing Power of Art (catalog), Pratt Gallery, New York, 82; Harriet Shapiro (auth), article, People Mag, 4/4/88. *Media:* Miscellaneous Media. *Publ:* Auth, Shadows, High Performance, Los Angeles, spring-summer, 82. *Dealer:* Ismael Gallery 221 A Center St York NY 10012. *Mailing Add:* 517 E 11th St New York NY 10009

LAVADOUR, JAMES
PAINTER
b Adams, Ore, 1949. *Work:* Seattle Art Mus, Wash; Portland Art Mus, Ore; The Heard Mus, Phoenix, Ariz; Wash State Arts Comn, Olympia; Seattle Arts Comn, Wash. *Comn:* Art in Public Places, Wash State Arts Comn, Olympia, 83, 85 & 87; NW Major Works Project, 89, Seattle Arts Comn, Wash. *Exhib:* Northwest Now, Tacoma Art Mus, Wash, 86; Crossed Cultures: 5 Contemporary Native Northwest Artists, Seattle Art Mus, Wash, 89; Northwest Viewpoints: James Lavadour, Portland Art Mus, Ore, 90; Shared Visions: Native American Sculptors and painters in the 20th Century, The Heard Mus, Phoenix, Ariz, 91; Land, Spirit, Power: First Nations at the National Gallery of Canada, Nat Gallery Can, Ottawa, Ont, 92. *Awards:* Ore Arts Fel, Ore Arts Comn, 86; Nat Printmaking Fel, Rutgers Univ, 90; Betty Bowen Mem Recognition Award, Seattle Art Mus, 91. *Bibliog:* Linda E Evans (auth), The Undiminished Landscape, Security Pacific Gallery, San Francisco, Calif, 90; Iona Chelette (auth), Northwest Southwest: Prainted Fictions, Palm Springs Desert Mus, 90; Margaret Archuleta (auth), Shared Visions, The Heard Mus, 91. *Media:* Oil on Linen. *Mailing Add:* c/o Elizabeth Leach Gallery 207 SW Pine St Portland OR 97204

LAVATELLI, CARLA
SCULPTOR, WEAVER
b Rome, Italy, Aug 21, 28; US citizen. *Study:* Santa Maria degli Angeli teaching degree, Rome, Italy, 46. *Work:* Nat Gallery, Rome; Phillips Collection, Washington, DC; Stanford Univ Law Bldg; H E Leone, Pres Repub Italy; Freiburgh Univ, Botanical Gardens, Ger. *Comn:* Marble & bronze sculptures, Shah of Iran, Park & Mus Mod Art, 68-76; bronze sculptures, Upjohn Pharmaceuticals, Kalamazoo, Mich, 70; portraits in bronze, SAS Ranier of Manaco & Princess Grace & 3 children, 71; bronze &

stainless steel sculpture, Brown Univ, Plaza Sci Bldg, 83-85; Paper, Cord, Reeds Installation Centennial Cathedral, St John the Divine, New York, 86; and others. *Exhib:* Spoleto, Palazzo Collicola, Italy, 66; solo shows, Hakone Mus, Japan, 72-73; Alexander Iolas, New York, 72; Phillips Collection, Washington, DC, 74; San Francisco Mus Art, 75-76; Gimpel & Weitzenhoffer, New York, 76; permanent exhib, 140 Thompson, New York & Working Place, Sculpture Garden, Camaiore, Italy, 88-; and others. *Bibliog:* Lorenza Trucchi (auth), Lavatelli at Carpine, Momento Sera, 65; Ruggero Orlando (auth), Contemporary Art From NY (film), Rai Italian TV, 70; Gene Baro (auth), Carla Lavatelli Ritmi Spaziali, Washington Post, 74; Carlo Lavatelli Herrmann, Festa (film), 86; Happening for Peace in XVI Century Monument in Pistola, Italy (film), Dami Assocs, 91- *Publ:* Auth, The Work of Carla Lavatelli, 1970-84, 85; A Cotton Bag Full of Stardust, handmade ltd ed by artist, 82. *Mailing Add:* 140 Thompson St New York NY 10012

LAVENTHOL, HANK
PAINTER, PRINTMAKER
b Philadelphia, Pa, Dec 22, 27. *Study:* Yale Univ, with Robert Georges Eberhard, BA(sculpture); Acad Belli Arti, Florence, Italy. *Work:* Yale Univ Art Mus, New Haven, Conn; Rosenwald Collection, Nat Gallery Fine Arts, Washington, DC; Print Collection, New York Pub Libr; Lowe Mus Art, Univ Miami, Coral Gables, Fla; Duke Univ Mus; Citicorp, Forbes Mag & Cigna Corp, Warburg Pincus, New York; and others. *Comn:* Image du Rose (etching), 72, Assoc Am Artists, New York; Ruth (four-color etching), Commentary Bk Soc, New York, 71; seven color etchings, George Visat, Paris, 72; 9 ed (color etching), New York Graphic Soc, Greenwich, Conn, 72-78; 12 ed (color etching), Original Print Collectors Group, New York, 75-80. *Exhib:* Philadelphia Mus Art, 68; Atheneum of Philadelphia, 73; Mickelson Gallery, Washington, DC, 73; Nat Arts Club, New York, 75; Best Prints, 73-78, Bibliot Nat, Paris; Frank Fedele Fine Arts, New York, 79, 80 & 81; and many other group & one-man shows in US & Europe; Werner Gallery, New York, 89. *Bibliog:* E Benezit (auth), Dictionanaire Des Peintres, Gravuers, 76. *Mem:* Artists Equity Asn New York; Circulo Bellas Artes, Palma de Mallorca; Visual Artists & Galleries Asn. *Media:* All; Etching, Mazzotint. *Publ:* Le Miroir aux alouettes', Ed Georges Visat, Paris, 72; Les Crises, Reves D'Enfant, Eyedeas, portfolios etchings, Hanover Atelier, 80. *Dealer:* Hanover Atelier RD 1 Box 44 Hanover St Yorktown Hts NY; Werner Gallery 201 E 87th New York NY. *Mailing Add:* RFD 1 Hanover St Yorktown Heights NY 10598

LAVERDIERE, BRUNO E
SCULPTOR
b Waterville, Maine, May 13, 37. *Work:* Patrick Lannan Found; Everson Mus, Syracuse, NY; Columbus Mus, Ohio; Am Craft Mus, New York. *Exhib:* Mus Contemp Crafts, 77; Everson Mus, Syracuse, NY, 77; Fine Arts Gallery, State Univ NY-Cortland, 91; Franklin Parrasch Gallery, New York 91. *Teaching:* Adj Instr, Adirondack Community Col, 77- *Awards:* Nat Endowment Arts, Grants, 76; NY Found Fel, 87. *Mailing Add:* 497 A Stony Creek Rd Hadley NY 12835

LAVIER, BERTRAND
CONCEPTUAL ARTIST, PRINTMAKER
b Chatillon-sur-Seine, France, 49. *Work:* Huntington Mus Art, WVa. *Exhib:* One-man shows, Ctr Nat d'Art Contemp, Paris, France, 75, Kunsthalle, Berne, Switz, 84, Musee d'Art Mod de la Ville de Paris, France, 85; Dokumenta VII, Kassel, Ger, 82; Space Invaders, Musee des Beaux Arts Montreal, Can, 86. *Awards:* Gudrun Indoden (auth), Kunstforum, 12/79; Germano Celant (auth), A brush with the real, 10/85 & Daniel Soutiff (auth), Grenoble/Bertrand Lavier, summer 88, Artforum. *Media:* Mixed. *Mailing Add:* c/o Crown Point Press 568 Broadway New York NY 10012

LAVIN, IRVING
HISTORIAN
b St Louis, Mo, Dec 14, 27. *Study:* Cambridge Univ, Eng, 48-49; Washington Univ, BA, 49; NY Univ, MA, 52; Harvard Univ, MA, 52, PhD(Sheldon Fel), 55. *Teaching:* Lectr hist art, Vassar Col, 59-62; from assoc prof to prof, NY Univ, 63-73; prof, Sch Hist Studies, Inst for Adv Study, 73- *Awards:* Fulbright Fel, 61-63; Am Coun Learned Soc Fel, 65-66; Guggenheim Found Grant, 68-69. *Mem:* Fel Am Acad Arts & Sci; Corpus Ancient Mosaics Tunisia (mem steering comt, 69-); Nat Comt for the Hist of Art; Comite int d'histoire de l'art. *Res:* Art of late antiquity; Renaissance and Baroque sculpture. *Publ:* Auth, Bernini and the Crossing of Saint Peter's, Arts, Archaeol Inst Am & Col Art Asn Am, 68; Five new youthful sculptures by Gianlorenzo Bernini and a revised chronology of his early works, 68, Bernini's death, 72 & Divine inspiration in Caravaggio's two St Matthews, 74, Art Bull; Bernini and the Unity of the Visual Arts, Oxford Univ Press, 80; Drawings by Gianlorenzo Bernini from the Museum der Bildenden Künste, Princeton Univ Press, 81. *Mailing Add:* Inst for Advanced Study Princeton NJ 08540

LAVIN, MARILYN ARONBERG
EDUCATOR, HISTORIAN
b St Louis, Mo, Oct 27, 25. *Study:* Washington Univ, BA, 47, MA, 49; Univ Rome, cert, 52; Inst Fine Arts, NY Univ, PhD, 73. *Teaching:* Prof hist art, Princeton Univ, 75-; vis prof, Yale Univ, 78 & Univ Md, 79-80. *Awards:* Charles Rufus Morey Book Award, Col Art Asn, 77. *Mem:* Col Art Asn Am (mem bd dirs, 79-83); Renaissance Soc. *Res:* Italian Renaissance painting with special interest in work of Piero della Francesco and history of fresco painting. *Publ:* Auth, The Corpus Domini Altarpiece of Urbino, Art Bull, 67; Piero Della Francesca: The Flagellation, Penguin, Viking, 72; 17th Century Barberini Documents & Inventories of Art, NY Univ Press, 75; Piero della Francesca's Baptism of Christ, Yale Univ Press, 81; The Eye of the Tiger: Department of Art & Architecture, Princeton Univ Press, 83. *Mailing Add:* Dept Art & Archeol McCormick Hall Princeton Univ Princeton NJ 08544

LAW, C ANTHONY
PAINTER
b London, Eng, Oct 15, 16; Can citizen. *Study:* With Franklin Brownell, Ottawa, Frederick Varley, Percyval Tudor-Hart, Quebec & expeditions with Frank Hennessey, Ottawa; St Mary's Univ, Halifax, NS, Hon DLitt, 81. *Work:* Nat War Mus, Ottawa; Can House, London, Eng; Dalhousie Univ Art Gallery, Halifax, NS; Univ NB Art Gallery, Fredricton; Heritage Mus, Dartmouth, NS; Maritime Mus Atlantic, Halifax; Canada House, London, Eng; Nova Scotia Centennial Collection; and others. *Comn:* Two paintings, New Court House, NS, 75. *Exhib:* Royal Can Acad, 39-71; Nat Art Gallery, London, Eng, 44; Nat Gallery Can, 46; Biennal 1970, Atlantic Provinces Art Circuit; Can Soc Watercolours Traveling Show, Art Gallery Nova Scotia, 80; Retrospective, Centennial Art Gallery, NS Mus Fine Art, 68; one-man show, Mall Galleries, London, 79, Artic Watercolours; and others. *Pos:* Artist-in-residence, St Marys Univ, Halifax, NS, 68-80; vchmn bd dir, Art Gallery, NS, 75-78, chmn bd dir, 78-; dir bd, Talent Trust NS, 75-; mem bd governors, NS Col Art & Design, 88-90. *Awards:* Jessier Dow Award, Montreal Mus of Fine Arts, 39-50. *Mem:* NS Soc Artists; Visual Art NS; Can Artist Representation. *Media:* Oil, Watercolor. *Dealer:* Yaneff Gallery 119 Lsabella St Toronto ON M4Y 1P2 Can; Kensington Paperworks Galleries 817-17th Ave SW Calgary AB T2T 0A1 Can. *Mailing Add:* 8 Halls Rd Halifax NS B3P 1P3 Canada

LAWALL, DAVID BARNARD
HISTORIAN, MUSEUM DIRECTOR
b Detroit, Mich, Aug 27, 35. *Study:* Oberlin Col, BA, 56; Princeton Univ, MFA, 59 & PhD, 66. *Collections Arranged:* A B Durand 1796-1886 (auth, catalog), Montclair Art Mus, 71; Small Paintings Toward a Renewal of Classicism, 74-79, Anton Refregier (auth, catalog), 77, Image of Post-Modern Man, 79 & Ernest Fiene/Leon Kroll (auth, catalog), New Still Life & Landscape Painting (auth, catalog), 87, New York Gallery Show, 88, Univ Va Art Mus. *Pos:* Cur, Univ Va Art Mus, 71-85, dir, 85-90. *Teaching:* Instr, Univ Mo, Columbia, 60-61; instr, Ohio State Univ, Columbus, 61-64, asst prof, 64-68; assoc prof, Univ Va, Charlottesville, 69- *Awards:* Fel, Nat Endowment Humanities, 69. *Mem:* NY Acad Art (exec bd, 81-). *Publ:* Auth, Asher Durand: Art and Art Theory, 77 & Asher Durand: Catalog of Paintings, Garland, 78; coauth, Leon Kroll, A Spoken Memoir, Univ Va Press, 83. *Mailing Add:* 108 Bollingwood Rd Charlottesville VA 22903

LAWRENCE, HOWARD RAY
DESIGNER, EDUCATOR
b San Francisco, Calif, Mar 21, 36. *Study:* Univ Calif, Berkeley, BA(Arch), 62, MA(sculpture), 64. *Pos:* Archit apprenticeship, US, 65-69. *Teaching:* Asst prof archit, San Francisco City Col, 69-70, Hampton Inst, Va, 70-71, Univ Kans, 71-72, Pa State Univ, 72-, Birmingham Polytech, Eng, 78 & St Martin's Sch of Art, London, 81. *Awards:* Harry Lord Ford Sculpture Prize, Univ Calif, 64. *Mem:* Asn Col Sch Archit; Environ Design Asn. *Media:* All. *Mailing Add:* Architecture University Park PA 16802

LAWRENCE, JACOB
PAINTER, MOSAIC ARTIST
b Atlantic City, NJ, Sept 7, 17. *Study:* Harlem Art Workshop, 34-39; Am Artists Sch, 38; Denison Univ, Hon DFA, 70; Pratt Inst, Hon DFA, 72. *Work:* Mus Mod Art, Am Acad Arts & Lett, Whitney Mus Am Art, Metrop Mus Art, New York; Phillips Mem Gallery, Washington, DC. *Comn:* Three paintings, Fortune Mag, 8/48; painting, Container Corp Am, 53; lithograph, Benrus Watch Co, 67; portrait of Jesse Jackson for cover, Time Mag, 4/70; Olympic poster, Ed Olympia 1972, Munich, Ger, 72; Community, mosiac mural, GSA, 89; Incident in Life of Harold Washington, mosiac mural, Harold Washington Libr, 90; plus others. *Exhib:* Migration Series, Mus Mod Art, New York, 44; John Brown Series, Am Fedn Art Traveling Exhib, 47; retrospective, Brooklyn Mus, 61 & Whitney Mus Am Art, 74; one-man shows, Brandeis Univ, 65, Seattle Art Mus, 74, Birmingham Mus Art, 74, St Louis Art Mus, 74 & New Orleans Mus Art, 75; Toussaint L'Overture Series, Fisk Univ, 68; retrospective traveling exhib, Seattle, Wash, Washington, DC, Oakland, Calif, Dallas, Tex, Atlanta, Ga & Brooklyn, NY, 87-88; Africa & S Am traveling exhib, 89-90. *Pos:* Mem, Wash State Arts Comn, 74 & 77; mem app by pres, Nat Endowment for the Arts Coun, 77- *Teaching:* Instr painting, Black Mountain Col, summer 47 & Pratt Inst, 56-71; prof painting, Univ Wash, 71-83, prof emer, 83- *Awards:* Guggenheim Fel, 46; Nat Inst Arts & Lett Grant, 53; Brooklyn Art Bks Children Citation for Harriet and the Promised Land, 73; Presidents for Art Award, President Bush, 90; Divine Award, mural for Jamacian Social Security Bldg. *Bibliog:* Alain Locke (auth), And the migrants kept coming, Fortune Mag, 41; Aline B Saarinen (auth), Jacob Lawrence, Am Fedn Arts, 60; Bearden & Henderson (auth), 6 Black Masters of American Art, Zenith, 72; Ellen Hawkins Wheat (auth), Jacob Lawrence American Painter. *Mem:* Artists Equity Asn New York (past pres); Nat Inst Arts & Lett; Black Acad Arts & Lett; Hampton Inst. *Media:* Acrylic, Egg Tempera. *Publ:* Illusr, One Way Ticket, 49; Harriet and the Promised Land, 68; Aesops Fables, 70. *Dealer:* Francine Seders Gallery 6701 Greenwood Ave N Seattle WA 98103. *Mailing Add:* 4316 37th Ave NE Seattle WA 98105

LAWRENCE, JAMES A
PAINTER, PHOTOGRAPHER
b San Mateo, Calif, May 23, 10. *Study:* Univ Calif, Davis, grad, 33; Art Ctr, Los Angeles, art & photog, with Barse Miller, Will Connell & Charles Kerlee, 35-37; Chouinard Art Inst, Los Angeles, with Phil Paradise & Ricco Lebrun, 38; Art Students League, 40; New York Sch Mod Photog; also with illusr Louis J Rogers, San Francisco, 34. *Work:* Ford Collection, Dearborn, Mich; Calif Hist Soc. *Comn:* Ford Times Publications 1948-1960, Inc, 60. *Exhib:*

One-man shows, Reed Galleries, New York, 41, Gump Galleries, San Francisco, 43 & Univ Nev, 53; Golden Gate Int Exhib, San Francisco; Art Inst Chicago; Metrop Mus Art, New York; Los Angeles Co Mus Art; and others. *Pos:* Tech photogr, Pagano Inc, New York, 40-41; mem, Nev State Coun Arts, 67-71. *Teaching:* Guest instr watercolor, Stanford Univ, spring 48; also pvt students in watercolor at var periods. *Awards:* Cert Merit & Gold & Silver Medals, Golden Gate Int Exhib, 40-41; Am Artists Prof League, 42; Terry Art Inst Award; and others. *Mem:* Nat Watercolor Soc. *Media:* Watercolor. *Publ:* Contribr, Ford Times, Sunset Mag, US Camera & Carson Valley-Historical Sketches; photogr, Sunset Mag, Calif, 40-49; Calif Art Rev, 1st ed, 90. *Mailing Add:* Rock Creek Ranch 1198 Centerville Lane Gardnerville NV 89410

LAWRENCE, JAYE A
SCULPTOR, CRAFTSMAN
b Chicago, Ill, Jan 8, 39. *Study:* Univ Ariz, BFA, 60; Ariz State Univ, MFA, 75. *Work:* Ariz State Univ Collection, Tempe; Pac Lutheran Univ Collection, Tacoma, Washington, DC; Yuma Fine Arts Asn Collection, Ariz. *Exhib:* Americana, 76 & Gifts That Artists Give, 76, Mus Mod Art, San Francisco, Calif; Leather Forms: Functional to Fantastic, Grosmont Col, El Cajon, Calif, 81; 32nd Allied Craftsman Exhib, San Diego Mus Art, Calif, 81; Forms of Leather, Arrowmont Sch Art & Crafts Gatlinburg, Tenn, 82; group show, Tex Sch Fine Arts Asn, Lubbock, Tex, 83; Leather Works, Sawtooth Ctr for Visual Design, Winston-Salem, NC; Spectrum Gallery, San Diego, Calif, 81; Invitational Exhib, Munic Art Ctr, Lubbock, Tex, 87; Innerskins/Outerskins: Gut & Fishskins, San Francisco Craft & Folkart Mus, Calif, 87, traveling, 87 & 88; The Container Untamed, 87, Chairs Acoss the Media, 88, Gardner Gallery, San Diego, Calif; Teapot Image, Faith Nightingale Gallery, San Diego, Calif, 89; and many others. *Teaching:* Instr leather art, Grossmont Col, El Cajon, Calif, 81. *Awards:* Best of Show, 3rd Ann Phoenix Jewish Community Ctr Show, 69; Purchase Award, 4th Ann SWestern, 69; 12th Ariz Ann Award, 69; First Award Region XX, Tex Fine Arts Asn, Lubbock, Tex, 82. *Bibliog:* Marilyn Hagberg (auth), Jaye & Les Lawrence, 10/73 & Erik Gronborg (auth), Jaye Lawrence, 8/74, Craft Horizons; Carolyn Russell (auth), Rope forms sculpture, Daily Times Advocate, 4/28/74. *Mem:* Am Crafts Coun; Allied Craftsmen San Diego (corresp secy). *Media:* Rawhide, Hog Casing; Wood. *Dealer:* Virginia Breier Gallery 3091 Sacramento St San Francisco CA 94115; Signature Gallery 3693 Fifth Ave San Diego CA 92103. *Mailing Add:* 2097 Valley View Blvd El Cajon CA 92019

LAWRENCE, LES
CERAMIST, SCULPTOR
b Corpus Christi, Tex, Dec 17, 40. *Study:* Southwestern State Col, Okla, BA, 62; Tex Tech Univ; Ariz State Univ, MFA(ceramics), 70. *Work:* Whitty Mus, San Antonio; Phoenix Art Mus, Ariz; E B Crocker Art Gallery, Sacramento, Calif; Pac Lutheran Univ, Tacoma, Wash; Ariz State Univ Collection, Tempe; Sheraton Hotel, Los Angeles, Calif; Southern Conn State Univ. *Exhib:* Viewpoint 80, Mus Tex Tech Univ, Tex, 79; Les Lawrence, Southplains Col, Tex, 82; Am Crafts Traditions, San Francisco Airport, Calif, 84; Ceramic Festival II, Univ Art Collections, Ariz State Univ, 85; The Cup Exhib, Salem Art Asn, Ore, 86; 200 Tea Pots, Springfield Art Asn, Ill, 87; Birthday Party, Kohler Art Ctr, Sheboygan, Wis, 88; Ceramic Ivitational, Sikes Gallery, Millersville Univ, Pa, 89; Visiting Artist, Monarch Tile Nat Exhib, San Angelo Tex Mus Art, Tex, 90; Ceramic Conjunction, Long Beach Mus Art, Calif, 77; Great Am Foot, Mus Contemp Crafts, New York, 78; and others. *Teaching:* Instr ceramics-sculpture, Hardin-Simmons Univ, Abilene, Tex, 66-68; prof ceramics, Grossmont Col, El Cajon, Calif, 70-; vis artist, Northern Iowa Univ, Cedar Falls, 88. *Awards:* Tex Watercolor Soc 16th Ann First Purchase Award, San Antonio Art League, 67; First Purchase Award, Region 20 Tex Fine Arts Asn, 68; Calif Crafts IX Purchase for E B Crocker Art Gallery, 75; Distinguished Alumni, South Plains Col, Tex, 87. *Bibliog:* Marilyn Hagberg (auth), Jaye & Les Lawrence, 10/73 & Erik Gronborg (auth), Les Lawrence, 6/75, Craft Horizons; Les Lawrence, Ceramics Monthly, 4/74. *Mem:* Am Crafts Coun; Allied Craftsmen San Diego (secy, 74); Nat Coun Educ for Ceramic Arts. *Media:* Clay. *Dealer:* Lawrence Arts 2097 Valley View Blvd El Cajon CA 92019. *Mailing Add:* 2097 Valley View Blvd El Cajon CA 92021

LAWRENCE, MICHAEL
PAINTER, SCULPTOR
b Los Angeles, Calif. *Study:* Bard Col, NY, 61-62; with Jacques Lipchitz; Univ Calif, Los Angeles, BFA, 65. *Work:* Cuenca Mus, Spain; Atelier Dalmas, Paris, France; Bard Col, Annandale, NY; Los Angeles Co Mus Art, Los Angeles. *Comn:* Hyatt, New Brunswich; Lou Ann Baurer, San Francisco, Calif; Garden for Lewis Carroll (sculpture), J Spielman, New York, 72; bronze of James Douglas Morrison, Los Angeles, 80; La Vie (mural), F Warthman, Palo Alto, 86. *Exhib:* James Joyce, Sequier Gallery, Madrid, 68; Kidnapping, Mus Mod Art, New York, 72; Fantasy & Jam, Greer Gallery, 72; Ruth Schaffner, Los Angeles, Calif; Wenger Gallery; one-man show, Circus, Wenger Gallery, Los Angeles, 88. *Teaching:* Chmn art dept, Concord High Sch, Los Angeles, Calif, 85. *Awards:* Nat Soc Arts & Letters, 61; Huntington Hartford Fel, 64. *Bibliog:* Ray Bradbury (auth), Fourth of Julies, Ruth S Schaffner Gallery, 74. *Media:* Oil; Bronze, Clay. *Publ:* Coauth, interview in Frank Mag, 86. *Dealer:* Susy Locke 201 Estates Dr Piedmont CA 94611. *Mailing Add:* 918 N San Vicente Blvd Los Angeles CA 90069

LAWRENCE, RODNEY STEVEN
PAINTER, ILLUSTRATOR
b Flint, Mich, Feb 20, 51. *Study:* Flint Community Jr Col; Univ Mich, BFA(magna cum laude), 73. *Comn:* Painting, First Nat Park Bank, Livingston, Mont, 74; illus, Dept Interior, Washington, DC, 82; Hamilton Collector Plates, 88. *Exhib:* C M Russell Mus, Great Falls, Mont, 76-79; Nat Wildlife Art Show, Kansas City, 80; Birds in Art National Tour, Leigh Yawkey Woodson Mus, Wausau, Wis, 83; Wildlife: The Artist's View, 90. *Teaching:* Ann Wildlife Artists Workshop, Kellogg Bird Sanctuary, Augusta, Mich; Beartooth Wildlife Workshop, Big Timber, Mont, 92. *Awards:* Mich Wildlife Artist of Year, Mich United Conserv Clubs Art Contest, 81; Trout Stamp Design Winner, Trout-Salmon Stamp Contest, 81, 87 & 92 & Duck Stamp Winner, Waterfowl Stamp Contest, 83 & 90, Mich Dept Nat Resources. *Bibliog:* Subject of many TV interviews on work and awards won, 81-86; Am interview with wildlife artist Rod Lawrence, Small-Towner, 83; Go mid-west young man, Midwest Art, 84; Who's Who mag, 11/88; Traverse Mag, 11/89. *Mem:* Outdoor Writers Asn Am; Ducks Unlimited. *Media:* Acrylic on Panel, Oil. *Publ:* Illusr, Fred Bear's Field Notes, The Adventures of Fred Bear, Doubleday, 76; Complete Guide to Walleye Fishing, Willow Creek Press, 80; The Pigeon River Country, Asn Pigeon River Country, 85; Bear Paw Tackle (catalog cover), 91. *Dealer:* Mill Pond Press Inc 310 Center Court Venice FL 34292. *Mailing Add:* Rte 1 Box 373 M-72 E Kalkaska MI 49646

LAWRENCE, SIDNEY S
PAINTER, WRITER
b San Francisco, Calif, 1948. *Study:* Univ Calif-Berkeley, BA(art history), 72; Univ Calif-Davis, 72-74, MA, 80. *Work:* Sallie Mae (Student Loan Marketing Asn); Lerner Development Cos; Federal Reserve Bank, Richmond, Va; Sally de Sousa, Rostrevor, Ireland; Pamela Watson, Sydney, Australia. *Exhib:* Solo exhib, Gallery K, Washington, DC, 83, 85, 88 & 92; Options '83, Washington Project for Arts; Edges of Humor, Sawhill Gallery, James Madison Univ, Va; From the Potomac to the Anacostia: Art and Ideology in the Washington Area, Washington Project for Arts, 89; Art Against AIDS--Washington, DC, 90. *Pos:* Researcher & consult, Fine Arts Mus, San Francisco & Oakland Mus, 71-72; co-dir, Memorial Union Art Gallery, Univ Calif-Davis, 72-74; actg pub affairs officer, Nat Mus Am Art, Washington, DC, 74; pub affairs officer, Hirshhorn Mus & Sculpture Garden, Smithsonian Inst, Washington, DC, 75- *Bibliog:* Alice Thorson (auth), Galleries, Washington Times, 9/29/88; Florence Rubenfeld (auth), Sidney Lawrence, Mus & Arts Washington, 9-10/88; Pat Kolmer (auth), Sidney Lawrence: Wall Reliefs and Drawings, Wash Rev, 6-7/92. *Publ:* Co-auth, Music in Stone: Great Sculpture Gardens of the World, Scala Bks, 84; auth, Art after modern art, 10/84, What a relief! New forms in art, 2/86, Artists collect, 9/87, Marching to a different drummer in art, 6/88, Photographs--the artists secret weapon, 5/89, The 80's--world of paradox echoed in art, 3/90, & Latin Legacy--how four pioneers fueled modern art, 6/92, Smithsonian News Service; Houston Conwill--Markings on the Sand, Hirshhorn Works 1989, Washington, DC, 90. *Mailing Add:* Hirshhorn Mus & Sculpture Garden Independence Ave at Eighth St SW Washington DC 20560

LAWRENCE, SPENCER
DRAFTSMAN, PRINTMAKER
b Bronx, NY, Feb 26, 49. *Study:* Sch Visual Arts, New York, cert, 71; RI Sch Design, Providence, BFA, 73. *Work:* Univ Art Mus, Berkeley, Calif; Printmaking Workshop, New York. *Comn:* Heroes of Black History, John Hope Settlement House, Providence, RI, 73. *Exhib:* Atlanta Life Insurance Competition, Ga, 82; Society American Graphic Arts, Cooper Union, New York, 82; Taipei Fine Arts Mus (with catalog), Taiwan, 83; Dillard Univ, New Orleans, 84; Afro-American Mus Life & Cult, Dallas, 84; Through a Master Printer (with catalog), Columbia Mus, SC, 85 & Miss Mus, Jackson, 86; Louise Nevelson & Young Artist, Soc Arts & Lett, Nat Art Club, New York, 86. *Awards:* Harlem Cult Coun Award, New York, 76. *Bibliog:* Article, in: Metrop Mus Art Bull, New York, 12/68; article, in: Art Dirs J, 73. *Mem:* Soc Arts & Lett, New York; Printmaking Workshop, New York. *Media:* Mixed; Watercolor, Colored Pencil. *Dealer:* Delawrence Maine Gallery 85 Beaver Street New York NY. *Mailing Add:* Sherry Washington Gallery 1274 Library St Detroit MI 48226

LAWRENCE, SUSAN
ART DEALER, CONSULTANT
b New York, NY, Dec 10, 39. *Study:* Univ Kans, BA, 61. *Pos:* Dir, Lawrence Gallery, Kansas City, Mo, 76-84; co-dir, Batz-Lawrence Gallery, Kansas City, Mo, 84-88; Lawrence Fine Art, Kansas City, Mo, 88-; bd dir, UM-KC Gallery Art, Kansas City, Mo, 88- & Film Soc Greater Kansas City, 91- *Mem:* Kansas City Art Gallery Asn (pres, 83-84, treas, 86); Westport Gallery Asn, Kansas City, Mo (founder & pres, 78-83); Contemp Art Soc, Kansas City (secy, 86). *Specialty:* Contemporary fine art, paintings, sculpture and original prints by American and European artists, including regional artists. *Mailing Add:* 804 W 48th Ste 305 Kansas City MO 64112

LAWSON, EDWARD PITT
ADMINISTRATOR
b Newton, Mass, Sept 12, 27. *Study:* Bowdoin Col, BA; Inst Fine Arts, NY Univ, AM. *Pos:* Curatorial asst, Toledo Mus Art, 56-57, supvr art educ, 57-59; asst cur, The Cloisters, 59-62; asst dir, Montreal Mus Fine Arts, 62-67; dir, Tucson Art Ctr, 67-69; admin asst, Int Exhibs Found, 69-70; asst dir, Am Asn Mus, 70-72; chief, dept educ, Hirshhorn Mus & Sculpture Garden, 73- *Teaching:* Instr, Toledo Mus Art Sch of Design, 54-56; vis lectr, Sir George Williams Univ, 63-67; lectr, Univ Ariz, 68-69; lectr, Northern Va Community Col, 73 & Smithsonian Assocs, 74-; spec vis lectr, George Washington Univ, 74- *Awards:* Belg-Am Summer Fel, 56; Metrop Mus Art Travel Grant, 61; Montreal Mus Travel Grant, 65. *Mem:* West Mus League (vpres, 68-69); Am Asn Mus; Can Mus Asn (coun mem, 63-67); PQ Mus Asn (vpres, 63-65, pres, 65-67). *Mailing Add:* Smith Hall of Art Acad Ctr 801 22nd St NW George Washington Univ Washington DC 20052

LAWSON, THOMAS
PAINTER, WRITER
b Glasgow, Scotland, 1951. *Study:* Univ St Andrews, MA, 73; Univ Edinburgh, MA, 75; Grad Sch City Univ New York, Phil, 79. *Work:* Chase Manhattan Bank, New York; Brooklyn Mus, NY; Emory Univ, Atlanta; Univ Colo, Boulder; Arts Coun Gt Brit, London. *Comn:* Temporary mural, Manhattan Munic Bldg, Dept Gen Serv, New York; temporary mural, Dunstan Soap Works, Type & Wear Mus Servs, Gateshead, Eng, 90; sculpture, Circulo de Bellas Artes, Madrid, 91. *Exhib:* The Image Scavengers, Inst Contemp Art, Univ Pa, Philadelphia, 82; La Forme e L'Informe, Galleria d'Arte Mod, Bologna, Italy, 83; The Heroic Figure, Contemp Art Mus, Houston, 84; Correspondences, Laforet Mus, Tokyo, Japan, 86; Sydney Biennale, Art Gallery New South Wales, Sydney, Australia, 86; Painting, Brooklyn Mus, Brooklyn, 87; Mus Contemp Art, La Jolla, Calif, 87; A Forest of Signs, Mus Contemp Art, Los Angeles, 89. *Pos:* Cur Consult, The Drawing Ctr, NY, 78-81; ed, Real Life Mag, NY, 79- *Teaching:* Instr, Sch Visual Arts, NY, 81-89; vis artist, Calif Inst Arts, spring 87-89, dean, 90-; grad instr, Rhode Island Sch Art Design, 87-88. *Awards:* Nat Endowment Arts Fel, 82-83, 85-86 & 88-89; Proj Grant, Art Matters Inc, 86-87; Proj Grant, NYSCA, 89. *Bibliog:* Richard Martin (auth), article, 11/84 & Ronald Jones (auth), article, summer 85, Arts Mag; Jeanne Silverthorne (auth), Third Eye Centre (monogr & exhib catalog), Glasgow & Anthony Reynolds, London, 90. *Mem:* Col Art Asn; Artists Equity; Nat Asn Artist Run Orgn. *Media:* All. *Publ:* Auth, Making some distinctions, Flash Art, 79; auth, Going places, Real Life Mag, 80; auth, Last exit: Painting, 81 & The dark side of the bright light, 82, Artforum; The Snake Pit, 86 & Bandits/Space Vampires, 88, Artforum, 3/86; Guilt by Association, IMMA, Dublin, 92. *Dealer:* Anthony Reynolds Gallery 5 Dering St London W1. *Mailing Add:* 1200 S Highland Ave Los Angeles CA 90019

LAWTON, FLORIAN KENNETH
PAINTER, CONSULTANT
b Cleveland, Ohio, June 20, 21. *Study:* Cleveland Sch Art, 42 & 48-50; John Huntington Polytech Inst, 48-49; Cleveland Col, 48-49. *Work:* Cleveland Mus Art; Massilon Must Art, Ohio; Miami Univ, Oxford, Ohio; pvt collection of King Kahlid, Saudi Arabia; Arthur Andersen Co; Cleveland Mus Art; Massilon Mus Art, Ohio; and others. *Comn:* Cleveland Citiscape, Ohio Bell Tel Co, 79; Rotek Co, Hamburg, Ger, 88; Nat Engineering Co, Cleveland, Ohio; TAW Inc, Cleveland; Carpet & Co, New York; and others. *Exhib:* Cleveland Mus Art, 78-84; Butler Mus Am Art Nat, Youngstown, Ohio, 77-88; Nat Watercolor Soc, All-West Traveling Exhib, Los Angeles, 77-80; Salmagundi Club, New York, 78-80; Ky Watercolor Soc, Owensboro Mus, 79; retrospective, Butler Mus Am Art, Youngstown, Ohio, 89; Am Watercolor Soc, NY; Watercolor USA, Springfield, Mo; and others. *Pos:* Art consult, Cleveland, Ohio, 72-; adv, Orange Arts Coun, Ohio, 77-; critic, 82- *Teaching:* Instr painting & watercolor, Cleveland Inst Art, 81-; instr watercolor, Orange Arts Coun, Ohio, 77- *Awards:* Grand Buckeye Leaf Award, Nat Watercolor Soc, 81; Peoples Choice Award, Great Lakes Regional, 82; First Prize & Larry Quackenbush Award, Hudson Ann, 82; Ohio Watercolor Soc, 80-84, 86, 88; Boston Mills Ann First, 86-87, 88, 89. *Bibliog:* Modern art review, Revue Mod Desarts, Paris, France, 6/70; Amish Romance (doc film), Scripps-Howard TV, Hiram Col, 75. *Mem:* Ohio Watercolor Soc; Am Watercolor Soc; Ky Watercolor Soc; Midwest Watercolor Soc; Nat Watercolor Soc. *Media:* Mixed. *Publ:* Auth, Watercolor page, In: American Artist, Watson-Guptill, 70; featured artist, fine arts prints, Mill Pond Press, Venice, Fala. *Dealer:* Gallery One Mentor OH; Mill Pond Press Venice FL. *Mailing Add:* 410-29 Willow Cirle Aurora OH 44202

LAWTON, JAMES L
SCULPTOR, EDUCATOR
b Louisville, Ky, July 28, 44. *Study:* Louisville Sch Art, Ky; Murray State Univ, Ky, BSc; Kent State Univ, Ohio, MFA. *Work:* Western Mich Univ, Kalamazoo; City Hartland, Mich. *Comn:* Three Trusses Plus (painted steel sculpture), Cass Park, City Detroit, 77-78. *Exhib:* A Road Show, juried, Contemp Art Inst Detroit, 85-86, Traveling; Artist Who Teach, juried, Centennial Art Exhib Nat Asn State, Univ & Land Grant Cols, Fed Reserve Bd Art Gallery, Washington, DC, 87; First Alumni Invitational Exhib, Murray State Univ, 88; solo exhib, Left Bank Gallery, Flint, Mich, 89; Saginaw Art Mus, Mich, 91; Invitational, Structure, Object Event, The Art Ctr Battle, Creek, Mich, 92. *Teaching:* Prof Sculpture, Mich State Univ & Kresge Art Ctr. *Awards:* Mich State Univ Grants, 68 & 79; Best in Show, 22nd Ann Paint & Sculpting Competition, Lansing, Mich; '89 Col Res Leave & Grant Awards. *Bibliog:* Brian McGillinary (article) Towne Courier, Lansing, Mich, 12/89; Corinne Abatt (article), Eccentric News Paper, Rochester, Mich, 12/89; Darlene B Damp (article), The Saginaw News, Mich, 9/91. *Dealer:* Bay St Galley Northport MI. *Mailing Add:* Dept Art Mich State Univ East Lansing MI 48824

LAWTON, NANCY
PAINTER, GRAPHIC ARTIST
b Calif, Feb 28, 50. *Study:* Calif State Univ, San Jose, BA, 72; Mass Col Art, MFA, 80. *Work:* Ark Art Ctr Mus; The Brooklyn Mus; Chicago Art Inst; H J Heinz Corp; Ill Bell Tel Corp. *Comn:* Portrait of H J Heinz, Heinz Corp, Pittsburgh, 84. *Exhib:* solo exhib, Brooklyn Mus, 83; American Drawings in Black and White: 1970-1980, 80 & Gene Baro Collects, 83, Brooklyn Mus; Drawing, Ark Art Ctr Mus, Little Rock, 84; The Art of Drawing III, Staempfli Gallery, New York, 84; gallery artists, Victoria Munroe Gallery, New York, 85 & 87; Realism Today, Nat Acad Design & Butler Inst Am Art, 88. *Teaching:* Instr printmaking, Mass Col Art, Boston, 79-80, instr drawing, 80-81; artist in reidence, Noble & Greenough Sch, Boston, 90. *Awards:* Mellon Found Scholar, 82; Creative Artist Pub Serv Award, 83; Grant, New York Arts Develop Fund, 85. *Bibliog:* Jack Bresnahan (auth), From the light to the dark, Boston Herald Sunday Mag, 79; Timmi Pierce (auth), Nancy Lawton: A representational artist, Staten Island Coun Arts, 85; Elizabeth Carpenter (auth), Realism Today: American Drawings from the Rita Rich Collection (catalog), Nat Acad Design, 8/14/90. *Media:* Pencil on Paper. *Dealer:* Victoria Munroe Fine Art Ltd 9 E 84th St New York NY 10028. *Mailing Add:* 9501 York Rd Monterey CA 93940

LAWTON, THOMAS
HISTORIAN, EDITOR
b Somerset, Mass, Feb 5, 31. *Study:* RI Sch Design, 49-50; Durfree Tech Inst, BS(design), 53; State Univ Iowa, MFA, 59; Harvard Univ, 59-63, PhD, 70; Stanford Chinese Language Training Ctr, 63-64. *Pos:* Assoc cur Chinese art, Freer Gallery Art, 67, cur Chinese art, 70, asst dir, 71-77, dir, 77-87, dir Freer Gallery Art and Arthur M Sackler Gallery, 82-87, senior res scholar, 87-; vice exec secy, Nat Palace Mus, Taipei, Taiwan, 70. *Teaching:* Instr Chinese art, Smithsonian Assoc, 70 & George Washington Univ, 70-71 & 74-75, Franklin P Murphy Lecturer, 89; lectr, Harvard Univ, Cambridge, Mass, Princeton, NJ, Yale Univ, New Haven, Conn, Univ Va, Charlottesville, Oxford Univ, Eng, Shanghai Mus, Shanghai, Mus Rietberg, Zurich, Switzerland. *Awards:* Fulbright, 63-66; John D Rockefeller 3rd Fund, 66-67; Charlottesville/Albemarle Found for the Encouragement of the Arts, 87. *Publ:* Auth, Chinese Figure Painting, Freer Gallery Art, Washington, DC, 73; Chinese Art of the Warring States Period, Freer Gallery Art, Washington, DC, 82; co-auth, Asian Art in the Arthur M Sackler Gallery: The Inaugural Gift, Arthur Sackler Gallery, Washington, DC, 87; New Perspectives on Chu Culture in the Eastern Zhou Period; ed, Arthur M Sackler Gallery, Washington, DC, 91; co-auth, Freer: A Legacy of Art, Freer Gallery Art, Washington, DC, 93. *Mailing Add:* Freer Art Gallery Jefferson Dr at 12th St SW Washington DC 20560

LAXSON, RUTH
CONCEPTUAL ARTIST
b Roanoke, Ala. *Study:* Auburn Univ; Atlanta Col Art. *Work:* Mus Mod Art, NY; New York Pub Libr; Yale Univ; Getty Ctr, Malibu, Calif; Sackner Collection, Miami; Victoria & Albert Mus, London; Univ Alta, Edmonton. *Exhib:* Aging-Its Process-Its Perception, Jamestown Gallery, NY, 90; Paperworks 91/SE Quinlan Arts Ctr, Gainesville, Ga, 91; Boundless Vision, San Antonio Art Inst, 91; Old Wives Tales, Tula Found, Atlanta, 91; solo exhib, Some Things Are Sacred, Atlanta Col Art Libr, 91. *Awards:* Nat Endowment Arts Exhib Grant, 80; DeKalb Coun for the Arts Grant, 86. *Bibliog:* Betty Bright (auth), Arts least fragile vehicle, Art Papers, 5-6/90; Glen Harper (auth), Some things are sacred, Atlanta Col Art, Afterimage, 10/91; Virginia Warren Smith (auth), interview, Atlanta Constitution, 9/91 & Art Papers, 3-4/92; Judith Hoffberg (auth), Some things are sacred, little tyrannies, Umbrella Mag, 12/91; and others. *Mem:* Atlanta Col Art Alum; Nexus Contemp Arts Ctr. *Media:* Printmaking, Multimedia. *Publ:* Little Tyrannies, 90; Where is Everybody?, 90; Imaging, 91; Some Things are Sacred, 91; Wheeling, 92; and others. *Mailing Add:* PO Box 190731 Atlanta GA 31119-0731

LAY, PATRICIA ANNE
SCULPTOR
b New Haven, Conn, Aug 14, 41. *Study:* Rochester Inst Technol, MFA; Pratt Inst, BS. *Work:* NJ State Mus, Trenton; Rochester Inst Technol; IBM; Rutger Univ. *Comn:* Montclair State Col, 85 & 92. *Exhib:* Solo Shows, Douglass Col Women Artists Series, 73, NJ State Mus, 74, Jersey City Mus, 87 & Condeso/Lawler Gallery, New York, 92; Contemporary Reflections, Aldrich Mus, Ridgefield, Conn, 75; Whitney Mus Am Art Biennial, 75; AIR Gallery, New York, 81; NJ Arts Inclusion Prog 1978-84, Jane Voorhees Zimmerli Art Mus, NJ, 84; Structures: 13 New Jersey Artists, Montclair Art Mus, 84; Noyes Mus, NJ, 89; and others. *Teaching:* Asst prof sculpture, State Univ NY Buffalo, 68-69; instr ceramics, Wagner Col, 69-71; lectr ceramics, Hunter Col, 71-72; assoc prof ceramics, Montclair State Col, 72- *Awards:* NJ State Coun Fel in Sculpture, 84 & 88. *Bibliog:* Leon Nigrosh (auth), Claywork, 75 & Low Fire: Other Ways to Work in Clay, 80, Davis Publ; Susan Peterson (auth), The Craft & Art of Clay, Prentice Hall, NJ, 92. *Media:* Clay, Metal. *Mailing Add:* Fine Arts Dept Montclair State Col Valley Rd Upper Montclair NJ 07043

LAYMON, CYNTHIA J
ASSEMBLAGE ARTIST, INSTRUCTOR
b Gary, Ind, Feb 17, 48. *Study:* Ind Univ, Bloomington, BA, 70; Southern Ill Univ, MFA, 77. *Work:* US Embassy, Madrid; Ala Power & Light, Birmingham; Cincinnati Bell Info Syst; IBM, Raleigh, NC; Deloitte, Haskins & Sells, Baltimore; Eastman Pharmaceutical Collection, Malvern, Pa; Orlando Int Airport, Fla; Seabury & Smith, Washington, DC; Landmark Clubs, Dallas, Tex; and others. *Comn:* McCann Erickson Inc, New York; IBM, Rockville, Md; Deloitte, Haskins & Sells, Baltimore, Md; USA Today, Washington, DC. *Exhib:* A Common Ground, Alexandria Mus, La, 81; New American Graphics, Al Batha Mus, Am Cult Ctr, Am Embassy & Legation Mus, Morocco, 82-83; Paper/Fiber VI, VII & XIII Nat Exhib, The Arts Ctr, Iowa City, 83-89; Craft Invitational, Southeast Ctr Contemp Art, Winston-Salem, NC, 83; Contemp American Fibers, Redding Mus, Calif, 83; touring exhib, Spotlight, 85-86; Tampa Triennial, Tampa Mus, Fla, 85; Cynthia Laymon: Transitions, Contemp Craft Gallery, Louisville, Ky, 89; Off the Wall, Mus York Co, Rock Hill, SC, 90. *Teaching:* Asst prof studio art, Lake Erie Col, 77-79; assoc prof, Univ NC, Greensboro, 79- *Awards:* Dirs Prize, Audubon Artists, NY; Award & Merit Award, Survey Illinois Fibers, Handweavers Guild Am & Lakeview Mus, 78; Award of Excellence, NC/SC Fibers Competition, Charlotte Handweavers Guild, 80. *Bibliog:* Gilda Morina Syverson (auth), Cynthia Laymon: Fiber/paper constructions, Fiberarts Mag,

7-8/82; Joan Michaels-Paque (auth), Cynthia Laymon: Pleated interplay, Fiberarts Mag, 9-10/85. *Mem:* Col Art Asn; Am Craft Coun; NC Fiber Arts Asn (treas, 79-81, educ dir, 81-82); Tri-State Sculptors Guild; NC Print & Drawing Soc; and others. *Media:* Mixed. *Mailing Add:* Univ NC at Greensboro 1000 Spring Garden Greensboro NC 27412

LAYNE, BARBARA J
SCULPTOR, INSTRUCTOR
b Seattle, Wash, Jan 12, 52. *Study:* Univ Colo, BFA, 79; Univ Kans, MFA, 82. *Work:* SC State Art Collection, Columbia; Cent d'Art Graphique, Romainmotier, Switz; Fed Reserve Bank Richmond, Charlotte, NC. *Exhib:* Solo exhibs, Southeastern Ctr Contemp Art, Winston-Salem, NC, 84, Second St Gallery, Charlottesville, Va, 87 & 1078 Gallery, Chico, Calif, 88; Portrait of the South, Palazzo Venezia, Rome, 84; Musée Cantonal des Beaux Arts, Lausanne, Switz, 85; Galerie Maya Behn, Zurich, Switz, 85; Fibers East-Fibers West, Fiberworks Ctr, Berkeley, Calif, 85; Postscriptum-Librifibra, Studio E Gallery, Rome, 86; New Directions in Paper, Mendocino Arts Ctr, Calif, 86; Leopold-Hoesch Mus, Duren, WGer, 86; Artists Who Teach, Fed Reserve Bd, Washington, DC, 87; Contemporary Directions in Fiber, Southern Arts Fedn, traveling exhib, 87-88; Paper: New Directions, Gallery Contemp Art, Colorado Springs, Colo, 88. *Teaching:* Asst prof fiberart, Univ SC, Columbia, 82-89; asst prof fibres, Concordia Univ, Montreal, 89- *Awards:* Purchase Award, South Carolina, State of the Art, 86. *Mem:* Surface Design Asn; Am Crafts Coun. *Media:* Mixed. *Publ:* Auth, Paper Art in America, Leopold Hoesch Mus, Duren, WGer, 86. *Mailing Add:* Dept of Sculpture, Concordia Univ, VA262 1395 Rene Levesque Montreal PQ H3G 2M5 Canada

LAYTON, RICHARD
PAINTER, DEALER
b Wilmington, Del, Apr 15, 29. *Study:* With Frank E Schoonover & Carolyn Wyeth; Philadelphia Mus Col Art. *Work:* In many bus and pvt collections in US and abroad. *Comn:* Ten murals, incl Univ Del & E I du Pont de Nemours & Co; designer of 1973 Am Revolution Bicentennial Comn Medal. *Exhib:* Corcoran Gallery Art, Washington, DC; Am Watercolor Soc; Audubon Artists; Pa Acad Fine Arts, Philadelphia; Del Art Mus; plus many others. *Collections Arranged:* Sixteen regional & nat exhibs incl N C Wyeth Exhib, Pa State Mus, Harrisburg, 65, Brandywine Heritage, 71 & N C Wyeth Exhib, 72, Brandywine River Mus. *Pos:* Former cur, Brandywine River Mus, Chadds Ford, Pa; pres, Del Arts Soc, currently; pres, Brandywine Editions, Ltd; bd dirs, Christian Sanderson Mus, Chadds Ford, Pa. *Bibliog:* Del Today Mag, 5/71. *Mem:* Nat Soc Mural Painters. *Specialty:* Brandywine & Wyeth art; illustrators of the Howard Pyle school. *Publ:* Auth, Introduction to North Carolina Wyeth, Crown, 72. *Mailing Add:* Christian C Sanderson Museum Rte 100 N Chadds Ford PA 19317

LAZAROF, ELEANORE B See Berman, Eleanore (Eleanore B Lazarof)

LAZARUS, FRED, IV
ADMINISTRATOR
b New York, NY, Jan 1, 42. *Study:* Claremont Men's Col, BA, 64; Harvard Univ, MBA, 66. *Pos:* Exec asst to chmn, Nat Endowment for Arts, 75-78; pres, Md Inst Col Art, 78- *Awards:* Mayor's Award, 88. *Mem:* Md Independent Cols & Univs Asn; Am Coun for the Arts (sec); Afro-Am (bd mem); Nat Coalition for Educ in the Arts (chmn, 87-89); Partners for Livable Places (trustee emer); and others. *Mailing Add:* Md Inst Col of Art 1300 W Mt Royal Ave Baltimore MD 21217

LAZENBY, DEXTER
CONCEPTUAL ARTIST
b Overbrook, Pa, 55. *Study:* Conn Col, 73; Univ Md, College Park, 75; Tufts Univ & Sch Mus Fine Arts, BFA, 79; Sch Mus Fine Arts, Boston, Mass, 81 & 83. *Work:* Mus Fine Arts & First Church of Christ Scientist, Boston, Mass; Tufts Univ, Medford, Mass; Whitehead Inst Biomedical Res, Cambridge, Mass; Prudential Insurance Co Am. *Exhib:* Solo exhibs, Nielsen Gallery, 83, 86 & 90, Foster Gallery, Mus Fine Arts, 85, Boston, Mass; Travelling Scholars, Mus Fine Arts, Boston, Mass, 83 & 87; Currents, Inst Contemp Art, Boston, Mass, 89; Exploring the Figure through Sculptured Forms, Newport Art Mus, RI, 90; Common Ground II: Sculpture, Hurst Gallery & Nielsen Gallery, 90; Summertime Exhib, Nielsen Gallery, Boston, Mass, 92; Nielsen Gallery, Boston, Mass, 92; Frick Gallery, Belfast, Maine, 92; and many others. *Awards:* Visual Artists Fel for Sculpture, Nat Endowment Arts, 86; Pollack-Krasner Found Grant, 87; Engelhard Award, 88. *Bibliog:* Robert Taylor (auth), Sculpture at De Cordova Explores Edge of 90's, Sunday Boston Globe, 1/7/90; Nancy Stapen (auth), Ancient Art Meets Today in Exhibit, Boston Herald, 3/16/90; David Raymond (auth), De Cordova Museum and Sculpture Park, Lincoln Sculpture on the Edge, Art New England, 3/90; and many other reviews. *Mailing Add:* c/o Nielsen Gallery 179 Newbury St Boston MA 02116

LEA, LAURIE JANE
SCULPTOR, GRAPHIC ARTIST
b Atlanta, Ga, May 7, 48. *Study:* Newcomb Col, with Frank Boles, 66-67; Univ Colo, Boulder, with Gene Matthews & Frank Sampson, BFA, 70; Univ Ga, Athens, apprenticed with William Thompson, 78-79. *Work:* Ga Arts Coun, State Art Collection, Ga; Macon Mus Arts & Sci, Ga; Danville Mus Fine Art & Hist, Va. *Exhib:* Art on Paper, Weatherspoon Gallery, Univ NC, 73; Invitational Show, Mem Arts Ctr, Atlanta, Ga, 74; American Drawings, Smithsonian Inst Exhib, Portsmouth, Va, 76; Georgia Sculpture Exhib, Athens, Ga, 78; Nat Asn Art Sch Invitational, Univ Ga, 80; The Great Garden Sculpture Show, Sculptural Arts Mus, Atlanta, 82; USA: Portrait of the South, Palazzo Venezia, Rome, Italy, 84; Birmingham Biennial, Birmingham Mus Art, Ala, 85; National Women Artists Invitational, Clemson Univ, 86; Ut Och In, Malmo Kuntshall, Malmo, Sweden, 86; At the Edge, Laguna Gloria Art Mus, Austin, Tex, 89. *Pos:* Art dir, Common Cup Alternative Art Space, Atlanta, 72-77; bd dirs, Ga Artists Int Exhib Fund, 84-87, Fulton Arts Coun, Atlanta, Ga, 84-87. *Teaching:* Vis artist, Atlanta Pub Schs & Trinity Schs, 74-81. *Awards:* Purchase Award, Atlanta Arts Festival, 72; First Place Heritage Award, Ga Comn Nat Bicentennial Celebration, 76; Best in Show, Southern Watercolor Soc Sixth Ann Exhib, Pensacola Mus Art, 82. *Bibliog:* Creating an Artwork (videotape), WETV 30, PBS, 83. *Media:* Man-made Materials; Mixed. *Dealer:* Fay Gold Gallery 3221 Cains Hill Place NW Atlanta GA 30305. *Mailing Add:* 135 Plymouth St No 6A Brooklyn New York NY 11201

LEA, STANLEY E
PRINTMAKER, PAINTER
b Joplin, Mo, Apr 5, 30. *Study:* Pittsburg State Univ, BFA; Univ Ark, MFA. *Work:* Smithsonian Inst & Libr Cong, Washington, DC; Brit Mus, London; Inst Mex Norteamericano, Mexico City; Mus Fine Arts, Houston. *Comn:* Collagraphs, Hyatt Regency Hotel, Houston, 72; paintings, Ft Worth Nat Bank, 73, Citizens Bank, Richards, Tex, 74, Am Nat Bank, Austin, 74 & USAA Bldg, San Antonio, 74; City of Hunstville (mural), Bradford Hotel, Dallas, Tex. *Exhib:* 48th Ann Soc Am Graphic Artists, New York, 67; Mainstreams Int, Marietta, Ohio, 68; Watercolor USA, Springfield, Mo, 69; 148th Ann Nat Acad Design, New York, 73; Nat Color Print USA, Lubbock, Tex, 74. *Teaching:* Prof printmaking & painting, Sam Houston State Univ, Huntsville, Tex, 61-; vis prof, Mus Fine Arts, Houston, 68-71. *Awards:* Arts Nat, Tyler, Tex, 62; 4th Ann Print & Drawing, Ark Art Ctr, 70; Award, 68th Nat Texas Fine Arts, 79. *Bibliog:* Gerald F Brommer (auth), Art of Collage, Davis, Publ, Inc, 78. *Mem:* Col Art Asn; Southern Graphics Coun. *Media:* Collagraphs, Mixed Media Collage; Mixed Media. *Dealer:* Sol Del Rio 1020 Townsend San Antonio TX 78209; Valley House Gallery 6616 Spring Valley Rd Dallas TX 75240. *Mailing Add:* 3324 Winter Way Huntsville TX 77340

LEA, TOM
PAINTER, WRITER
b El Paso, Tex, July 11, 07. *Study:* Art Inst Chicago, 24-26; study in Italy, 30 & NMex, 33-35; Baylor Univ, hon LittD, 67; Southern Methodist Univ, hon LHD, 70. *Work:* Dallas Mus Fine Art, Tex; El Paso Mus Art, Tex; State Capitol, Austin, Tex; Pentagon War Art Collection; Humanities Res Ctr, Univ Tex, Austin; also in pvt collections. *Comn:* Murals, US Court House & Pub Libr, El Paso, US Post Off Bldgs, Pleasant Hill, Mo, Odessa, Tex & Washington, DC. *Exhib:* One-man shows, Ft Worth Art Ctr, Tex, 61 & El Paso Mus Art, 63 & 71; Inst Texan Cult, San Antonio, 69. *Pos:* Artist & war corresp, Life Mag, 41-46. *Media:* All. *Publ:* Auth & illusr, The Brave Bulls, 49, The Wonderful Country, 52, The King Ranch, Vols I & II, 57, The Primal Yoke, 60, The Hands of Cantu, 64, A Picture Gallery, 68 & In the Crucible of the Sun, 74, Little; and others. *Mailing Add:* 2401 Savannah St El Paso TX 79930

LEACH, ELIZABETH ANNE
ART DEALER, WRITER
b Salinas, Calif, Mar 2, 57. *Study:* Scripps Col, Claremont, Calif, BA, 79; study with Arthur Stevens, Roland Reiss & Carl Hertel. *Collections Arranged:* Architecture of Monterey Peninsula (coauth, catalog), Monterey Mus, 76; Permanent Collection, Heathman Hotel, 84; co-cur, Curator's Choice, Ore Art Inst, 86; cur, Corporate Collections, Ore Business Committee Arts, Heathman Hotel, 86 & 89; cur, Photography Collection, Tonkin Torp Galen Marmaduke & Booth, 90. *Pos:* Asst dir, Galerie de Tours, Pebble Beach, Calif, 76; consult for archit survey, Hollywood Revitalization Comt, 78; dir, Elizabeth Leach Gallery, Portland, Ore, 81-, chair, Visual Arts Comt, Artquake, 87-89; adv bd, Artfair Seattle, 90- *Bibliog:* Megan McMorran (auth), Leach Will Agree, Bus J Mag, 8/13/84; Dorothy Smith (auth), article, in: Daily J Commerce, 11/8/84; Stephanie Martin (auth), article, in: Pac Northwest Mag, 4/85; Randy Gragg (auth), A Gallery for Our Time, Oregonian, 5/91. *Mem:* Portland Ctr Visual Arts (bd mem, 84-); Ore Art Inst; Chair of Visual Art Comt Artquake, 87. *Specialty:* Contemporary fine art. *Publ:* Auth, Art as an investment, Inst Managers & Prof Women, 81. *Mailing Add:* c/o Elizabeth Leach Gallery 207 SW Pine St Portland OR 97204

LEACH, MADA (MADELINE KLEIMAN)
PAINTER
b Chicago, Ill, Dec 3, 39. *Study:* Duke Univ, 59; Meredith Col, BFA, 71; Art Inst Chicago, BFA & BAE, 64. *Work:* Cincinnati Bell Collection, Ohio; Louisville Arts Collection, Ky; Universal Bank, Orange, Calif; Strohmeier Collection, Frankfurt, Ky. *Comn:* Mural, Allergan Pharmaceutical, Irvine, Calif, 88. *Exhib:* Aqueous '81, Ky Watercolor Soc, Frankfurt Libr, Ky, 81; Cincinnati Bicentennial, Cincinnati Art Mus, Ohio, 81; Laguna Art Festival, Laguna Beach, Calif, 83-89; Traditionalist Show, Brea Ctr Arts, Brea, Calif, 84; Newport Festival of the Arts, Newport Beach, Calif, 86. *Teaching:* Art instr, Art Inst Chicago, 64-65, Oakpark Schs, Ill, 65-68 & North York Bd Educ, Ont, Can, 75-80. *Awards:* Best of Show, Nature Interpreted, Josephine Rollman Mus, Cincinnati, 80; Strathmore Paper Award, Ohio Watercolor Soc, 81; Art Club Trust Award, Ky Bluegrass Competition, 82. *Media:* Watercolor, Acrylic. *Dealer:* Art Angles 3411 E Chapman Ave Orange Ca 92669. *Mailing Add:* c/o Art Angles 3411 E Chapman Ave Orange CA 92669

LEADER, GARNET ROSAMONDE
ADMINISTRATOR
b Bessemer, Ala. *Study:* Maryville Col, Tenn, AB; Columbia Univ, MA(fine arts); Peabody Col, Tenn; Univ Tenn; Art Students League, New York, with

Reginald Marsh; Univ Ala, AA. *Exhib:* Birmingham Asn Art, Ala; Ala State Fair Art Exhib, Birmingham; Miss Univ for Women, Columbus. *Pos:* Pres, Bessemer Art Club; pres emer, retired, Kappa Pi Int Hon, 38-68, pres, retired. *Teaching:* Instr arts & crafts, Birmingham Pub Schs, 28-71. *Mem:* Birmingham Art Asn; Watercolor Soc Ala; Nat Art Educ Asn; fel Royal Soc Arts, London. *Publ:* Contribr, Design Mag & Sketch Book. *Dealer:* Lassetter & Co Birmingham AL 35203. *Mailing Add:* 5117 Main St Bessemer AL 35020

LEAF, JUNE
PAINTER, SCULPTOR
b Chicago, Ill, 1929. *Study:* Roosevelt Univ, Chicago, BA, 54; Inst Design, Chicago, MA, 54; DePaul Univ, LHD, 84. *Work:* Mus Mod Art, New York; Art Inst Chicago & Mus Contemp Art, Chicago, Ill; Smithsonian Inst, Washington, DC; Madison Art Ctr, Wis; Col Cape Breton, Sydney, NS, Can. *Exhib:* Torment, Whitney Mus Am Art, New York, 70; Alternative Realities in Contemp Am Art, Univ Minn, Katherine Nash Gallery, Minneapolis, 81; solo exhibs, Col Cape Breton Art Gallery, Sydney, NS, 82, Dalhousie Art Gallery, Halifax, NS, 82, NDak Mus Art, 83, Optica Gallery, Montreal, Can, 85, Edward Thorp Gallery, New York, 85 & 88, A Survey of Painting, Sculpture and Works on Paper, 1948-1991, travelling, Wash Proj Arts, DC, 91 & Works on Paper, 1969-1970, Va Lust Gallery, New York, 91; Edward Thorp Gallery, New York, 86-92; Pratt Inst, Brooklyn, NY, 88; Phyllis Kind Gallery, Chicago, Ill, 89. *Pos:* Instr painting & drawing, Art Inst Chicago, 54-58, Parson Sch Art & Design, New York, 66-68. *Awards:* Can Coun Arts Award, 78 & 84; Engelhard Award, 86; Nat Endowment Arts, 89. *Bibliog:* Paul Richard (auth), June Leaf's epiphanies & other delights, Wash Post, 4/14/91; John Yau (auth), Original desire, ARTS Mag, 11/91; Nancy Stapen (auth), June Leaf's emphatically female figure Imagery, Boston Globe, 12/91. *Media:* All Media. *Mailing Add:* c/o Edward Thorp Gallery 103 Prince St New York NY 10012

LEAF, RUTH
PRINTMAKER, INSTRUCTOR
b New York, NY. *Study:* New Sch Social Res, New York, with Anthony Toney; Atelier 17 with William Stanley Hayter. *Work:* NY Univ; US Info Agency; Bowdoin Col Mus Art; Colgate Univ. *Exhib:* Sala Exposiciones, Escuela Nac Artes Plasticas, 67; Boston Mus, 70; De Cordova Mus, Mass, 71; Soc Am Graphic Artists, New York, 71; Galerie Art & Gravure, Paris, 72. *Pos:* Consult, Colby Col, Maine. *Teaching:* Instr intaglio, NShore Community Art Ctr, 69- *Awards:* Purchase Awards, Libr Cong, 46, Hofstra Univ, 63 & Olivet Col, 67. *Bibliog:* Ron Perkins (auth), Artists at Work--Filmstrip 4, Jam Handy Sch Serv, 70; Interview with artist, Art in the World radio prog, Nassau Community Col. *Mem:* Soc Am Graphic Artists; Boston Printmakers; Silvermine Artists Guild; Print Club, Philadelphia; Am Color Print Soc. *Media:* Graphics, Paper Works. *Publ:* Auth, Intaglio Printing Techniques, Watson-Guptill; Etching, Engraving & Other Intaglio Techniques, Dover. *Mailing Add:* 40-30 235th St Douglaston NY 11363

LEAKE, EUGENE W
PAINTER
b Jersey City, NJ, Aug 31, 11. *Study:* Yale Univ Sch Art & Archit; Art Students League. *Work:* Baltimore Mus Art; J B Speed Art Mus, Louisville, Ky; Wash Co Mus, Hagerstown, Md; Corcoran Gallery Art, Washington, DC; Owensboro Mus fine Arts, Ky. *Bibliog:* Craig Hankin (auth), The Maryland Landscapes of Eugene Leake, Johns Hopkins Univ Press, 86. *Media:* Oil. *Dealer:* C Grimaldis Gallery 928 Charles St Baltimore MD 21239. *Mailing Add:* Turner Rd Monkton MD 21111

LEARY, DANIEL
DRAFTSMAN, PRINTMAKER
b Glens Falls, NY, July 20, 55. *Study:* Antioch Col, Yellow Springs, Ohio, BFA, 79; Syracuse Univ, MFA, 87. *Work:* Libr Cong, Washington, DC; Metro Mus Art, New York; Minneapolis Inst Arts, Minn; Munson-Williams Proctor Inst Mus Art, Utica, NY; Walker Arts Ctr, Minneapolis, Minn. *Exhib:* One-man shows, Breedlove Gallery, Ft Smith, Ark, 84 & 85, Comart Gallery, Syracuse Univ, 85 & 87, Hyde Collection, Glens Falls, NY, 90, Printworks Gallery, Chicago, 88 & 91 & Blanden Mem Art Mus, Ft Dodge, Iowa, 92; Munson-Williams-Proctor Inst Mus Art, Utica, NY, 89; Vero Beach Ctr Arts, Fla, 89; Jane Voorhees Zimmerli Art Mus, Rutgers Univ, 90; Bradford Art Mus & Galleries, West Yorkshire, Eng, 90; Contemp Art Ctr, Cincinnati, Ohio, 91. *Awards:* New York Found Arts, 88; Nat Endowment Arts, 89; Glens Falls Found, 89. *Bibliog:* Alan G Artner (auth), Leary portraits etched with discernment, Chicago Tribune, 1/6/89; Gordon Ligocki (auth), Young artist drawing powerful figures, The (Hammond, Indiana) Times, 8/24/90; Alan G Artner (auth), Leary drawings reflect rare craft, insight, Chicago Tribune, 10/4/91. *Media:* Etching, Miscellaneous Media. *Mailing Add:* PO Box 136 Hudson Falls NY 12839

LEATHERDALE, MARCUS ANDREW
PHOTOGRAPHER
b Montreal, Que, Sept 18, 52. *Study:* Ecole Des Beaux Arts, Montreal, 70-73; Art Ctr, Los Angeles, BFA, 74; San Francisco Art Inst, BFA(hon student), 75-77. *Work:* Madison Art Ctr, Wis; Australian Art Gallery, Canberra; New Orleans Mus Art, La; Vienna Mus Mod Art, Austria. *Exhib:* Solo exhibs, London Regional Art Gallery, Ont, 83, Rheinisches Landes Mus, Bonn, Ger, 84, Greathouse Gallery, New York, 84, 85, 86 & 87, Claus Runkel Fine Arts, London, Eng, 88, Wessel O'Connor Gallery, New York, 89 & Fay Gold Gallery, Atlanta, Ga, 90; Brent Sikkema, New York, 90; Artur Rogers Gallery, New Orleans, 91. *Awards:* Nat Endowment Arts Award for Photog, 84. *Bibliog:* John Sturman (auth), Marcus Leatherdale ritual, Artnews, 86; Brook Adams (auth), Marcus Leatherdale 1984-1987, Greathouse Gallery, New York, 88; Peggy Cypher (auth), Marcus Leatherdale, Arts, 89. *Dealer:* Fahey-Klein Gallery Los Angeles CA; Brent Sikkemma Fine Arts 155 Spring St New York NY 10012. *Mailing Add:* 281 Grand St No 3 New York NY 10002

LEATHERS, WINSTON LYLE
PAINTER, PRINTMAKER
b Miami, Man, Dec 29, 32. *Study:* Univ Man, BFA, 56, Univ Mex, 57-58; Man Teachers Col, 60; Univ BC, 61. *Work:* Can Coun Collection; Winnipeg Art Gallery; Univ of Fife, Scotland; Edmonton Art Gallery. *Comn:* Environmental wall mural, Roghmans Ltd, Winnipeg, 73; low relief concrete wall mural, Porv of Man, Portage La Prarie, 77; mural, IKOY Archit Partnership, Winnipeg, Man, 77; low relief wall mural, BACM Co Ltd, Winnipeg, 78. *Exhib:* Paris Int Print Exhib, France, 72; Bermuda Biennial, 72; Brit Fedn Int, 73; Int Print Exhib, Zurich, Switz, 74; Manisphere Int, Moorehead, Minn, 75. *Collections Arranged:* Univ of Mex, Contemp Gallery of Art, Mexico City, 57; University of BC, 61; Western Canadian Art Circuit Traveling Exhib, Winnipeg Art Gallery, 66-67; British Fedn of Artist Gallery, London, Eng, 68; Winnipeg Art Gallery, 74. *Pos:* Man art curric revision comt, Prov of Man, 61-66; art adv, Libr Comn, City of Winnipeg, 76- *Teaching:* Prof design & drawing, Univ of Man, 69- *Awards:* Sr Can Coun Grant for Printmaking, 67-68 & Proj Grant for Printmaking, 73, Can Coun; Purchase Award, Man Soc Artists, Winnipeg, 76. *Bibliog:* Prof Vann (auth), Perspective--Winston Leathers, Univ Man, 69; Philip Fry (auth), Manitoba Artists, Winnipeg Art Gallery, 72; Ann Davis (auth), Cosmic Variations--Winston Leathers, Winnipeg Art Gallery, Bulletin Mag, 6/75. *Mem:* Can Artists Representation (pres, 72); Royal Can Acad Arts; Brit Fedn of Artists, Eng; Can Soc of Printmakers; Can Soc of Graphic Artists. *Dealer:* Thomas Gallery Osborne St Winnipeg MB Can. *Mailing Add:* 55 Roslyn Crescent Winnipeg MB R3L 0H6 Canada

LEAVITT, THOMAS WHITTLESEY
MUSEUM DIRECTOR
b Boston, Mass, Jan 8, 30. *Study:* Middlebury Col, AB, 51; Boston Univ, MA, 52; Harvard Univ, PhD, 58. *Collections Arranged:* New Renaissance in Italy (with catalog), Pasadena, Calif, 58; Piet Mondrian (with catalog), Santa Barbara, Calif, 65; American Portraits in California Collections (with catalog), Santa Barbara, 66; Brücke (with catalog), Cornell Univ, 70, Georg Kolbe, 72; Seymour Lipton, 73; Directions in Afro-American Art, 74; Painting Up Front, 81; Masters of Contemporary Art in Poland, 86. *Pos:* Asst to dir, Fogg Art Mus, 54-56; exec dir, Fine Arts Comn, People to People Prog, 57; dir, Pasadena Art Mus, 57-63; dir, Santa Barbara Mus Art, 63-68; dir, Andrew Dickson White Mus Art, Cornell Univ, 68-72, dir mus prog, Nat Endowment for Arts, 71-72, mem mus adv panel, 72-75; trustee, Am Fedn Arts, 72-; dir, Herbert F Johnson Mus Art, Cornell Univ, 73-91; mem mus panel, NY State Coun Arts, 75-78 & 80-81. *Teaching:* Lectr Am art, Univ Calif, Santa Barbara, 64-65; prof hist art, Cornell Univ, 68- *Mem:* Col Art Asn Am; Am Asn Mus (coun mem, 76-79, vpres, 80-82, pres, 82-85); Asn Art Mus Dirs; Independent Sector (bd mem, 80-84); Am Fedn Arts; Williamstown Regional Art Conserv Lab (pres, 85-87, bd dirs, 88-). *Res:* American 19th & 20th century painting. *Publ:* Auth, The Crisis in Museums, 71; George Loring Brown (catalog), 73; Let the dogs bark, George Loring Brown and the critics, Am Art Rev, 1-2/74; and others. *Mailing Add:* H F Johnson Mus of Art Cornell Univ Ithaca NY 14853

LEAVITT, WILLIAM
PAINTER
b Washington, DC, Nov 27, 41. *Study:* Univ Colo, BA, 63; Clairmont Grad Sch, MFA, 67. *Work:* San Diego Mus Contemp Art, La Jolla, Calif; Boysmans Mus, Rotterdam, Holland. *Teaching:* Instr post studio art, Col Inst Art, 75-76. *Awards:* Art Fel New Genre, Nat Endowment Arts, 91. *Dealer:* Richard Kuhlenschmidt Gallery 1630 17th St Santa Monica CA 90405. *Mailing Add:* 4320 W Second St Los Angeles CA 90004

LEBECK, CAROL E
CERAMIST
b Spokane, Wash, Sept 8, 31. *Study:* Univ Calif, Los Angeles, MA(ceramics); Swed State Sch Design, Stockholm, Sweden, HKS(ceramics). *Work:* Los Angeles Co Cult Art Asn, Brand Libr, Los Angeles; Marietta Col, Ohio; Univ Ariz. *Exhib:* California Women in Crafts, Craft & Folk Art Mus, Los Angeles, 77; California Crafts X, Crocker Art Gallery, Sacramento, 77; Viewpoint: Ceramics, 1978, Grossmont Col Gallery, El Cajon, Calif; Celebrations Gallery Invitational: Dinner for Eight, San Diego, 79; West Coast Clay Spectrum, Security Pac Bank, Los Angeles, 79; and many others. *Teaching:* Instr ceramics, Grossmont Col, El Cajon, Calif, 62-85. *Awards:* Fel, Swed Am Found Grant, 58; Purchase Award, Marietta Crafts Nat, 75; Award of Merit, California Crafts X, 77. *Mem:* Am Crafts Coun; Allied Craftsmen of San Diego (corresp secy, 75). *Media:* Clay, Mixed. *Mailing Add:* 7108 Stanford Ave La Mesa CA 92041

LEBEY, BARBARA
PAINTER, PRINTMAKER
b Newark, NJ, Feb 28, 39. *Study:* Sarah Lawrence Col, BA, 59, Emory Univ Sch Law, JD, 70. *Work:* Princeton Univ Art Mus, NJ; Carter Presidential Ctr, Atlanta; Robert B Coggins Collection of Woman Artists, Marietta, Ga; Vanderbilt Collection; Newark Mus Art; Hunter Mus; Albany Mus, Ga, 90. *Comn:* Floral Still Life, comn by President & Mrs Jimmy Carter, 86; Seacoast Garden (painting), comn by Pat Conroy, 87; Springtime in Buckhead (commemorative print), Greater Atlanta C of C, Buckhead Sesquicentennary, 88; Walter B Ford Collection, 90. *Exhib:* Rablen West, Vero Beach, Fla, 90;

Little Acorn Gallery, Dunwoody, Ga, 90; Leon Loard Gallery Fine Arts, Montgomery, Ala, 90; Foster Harmon Galleries, Sarasota, Fla, 92; Omell Galleries, London, St James, Eng, 92; and others. *Awards:* Purchase Award, Sussex Co Art Competition, 61; Gold Medal, Artists in New Eng, Vt Co Arts, 85; Award of Merit, Robert B Coggins Collection, Trammel Crow Co, 88. *Bibliog:* Diana Brown (auth), Gardens of painted delights, Southern Homes, 87; Robert Nesbitt (auth), Artist realizes her dream, Inside Buckhead, 87. *Mem:* Atlanta Artists Club; Collectors Club, High Mus Art, Atlanta. *Media:* Oil, Watercolor; All Media. *Mailing Add:* 3065 E Pine Valley Rd NW Atlanta GA 30305

LEBOFF, GAIL F
PHOTOGRAPHER
b Brooklyn, NY, June 6, 50. *Study:* State Univ Ala, 71-73; New York Univ, BS, 80, MA(studio art-photo), 82. *Work:* Coca-Cola Collection, Atlanta, Ga. *Comn:* Work in Genre of Art Work, comn by Poumans, Queens, NY, 85-86. *Exhib:* New Works, Bergen Mus Art & Sci, NJ, 83; Print Collection Color, Brooklyn Mus, NY, 84; Seeing is Believing, Alternative Mus, New York, 85; Images of Icon (traveling exhib), Johnson & Johnson, NJ, 86-87; Taking Liberty, NY State Mus, Albany, 86; Chairs, Witkin Gallery, New York, 87. *Teaching:* Instr, Sch Visual Arts, New York, currently. *Mem:* Women's Caucus Art; Soc Photogr Educ. *Mailing Add:* 451 Broome St No 12W New York NY 10013

LEBRON, MICHAEL A
CONCEPTUAL ARTIST, GRAPHIC ARTIST
b St Louis, Mo, July 19, 54. *Study:* Cooper Union, BFA, 76. *Work:* Mus Mod Art, New York, NY. *Awards:* New York Fine Arts Award, 86; David Dinkins Excellence in Arts Award, 87; Nat Endowment Arts Fel, 90. *Bibliog:* Richard Goldstein (auth), A spectre is Haunting the MTA, Village Voice, 82. *Mailing Add:* 36 Cooper Sq No 7F New York NY 10003

LE BRUN, CAROL
CRITIC, DEALER
b Rochester, NY, May 2, 42. *Study:* Marymount Manhattan Col, BA, 64. *Pos:* Art ed & critic, Boston Herald Traveler, Mass, 66-72 & Boston Herald Am, 72-73; art critic, Christian Sci Monitor, 73-; pub relations dir, Boston Arts Festival, 85; vpres, Aruest Galleries, Inc, Boston, 73-81. *Res:* Turn of the century American impressionists, New England artists & 19th & 20th century European artists. *Publ:* Contribr, Sunday Herald Traveler Mag, Boston Arts Mag, Europe Mag, Sunday Herald Am Mag, Christian Sci Monitor, Quincy Patriot Ledger & Boston Herald. *Mailing Add:* 770 Boylston St Boston MA 02199

LECHAY, JAMES
PAINTER
b New York, NY, July 5, 07. *Study:* Study with Brother Myron Lechay. *Work:* Art Inst Chicago; Nat Collection Fine Arts, Smithsonian Inst; Des Moines Art Ctr; Pa Acad Fine Arts, Philadelphia; Mus Art, Univ Iowa; plus others. *Exhib:* Metrop Mus Art, New York; Art Inst Chicago; Pa Acad Fine Arts; Carnegie Inst, Pittsburgh; Toledo Mus Art; Denver Art Mus; Palace of the Legion of Honor, San Francisco; Walker Art Ctr, Minneapolis. *Teaching:* Prof art, Univ Iowa, 45-75; instr, Stanford Univ, summer 51 & Skowhegan Sch Painting & Sculpture, summer 63; vis prof, Chinese Univ of Hong Kong, 76; Studio Art Sch, Samos, Greece, 86-88. *Awards:* Childe Hassam Fund Purchase Award, Am Acad Arts & Lett, 74; Ranger Fund Purchase Prize, Nat Acad Design, 79; Palmer Mem Award, Nat Acad Design, 81; plus others. *Bibliog:* Vie des Arts, 6/89; Provincetown Arts, 90. *Mem:* Nat Acad Design. *Media:* Oil, Watercolor. *Dealer:* Kraushaar Galleries 724 Fifth Ave New York NY 10019. *Mailing Add:* Box 195 Wellfleet MA 02667

LECHTZIN, STANLEY
GOLDSMITH, EDUCATOR
b Detroit, Mich, June 9, 36. *Study:* Wayne State Univ, BFA; Cranbrook Acad Art, Bloomfield Hills, Mich, MFA. *Work:* Mus Am Crafts, New York; Detroit Inst Arts; Schmuckmuseum Pforzheim, Ger; Philadelphia Mus Art; Goldsmiths Hall, London; Yale Univ. *Comn:* Silver mace, Temple Univ, 66; Longwood Col, 74; paten, 41st Int Eucharistic Cong, Philadelphia, 76. *Exhib:* One-man shows, Mus Contemp Crafts, New York, 65, Lee Nordness Galleries, NY, 69, Int Jewelry Exhib, Tokyo, Japan, 73 & Goldsmiths Hall, London, 75; Philadelphia: Three Centuries of Am Art, Philadelphia Mus Art, Pa, 76; 20th Century Jewelry, Electrum Gallery, London, Eng, 85; Hong-ik Ann Exhib, Walker Hill Art Ctr Mus, Seoul, Korea. *Teaching:* Prof metalsmithing, Tyler Sch Art, Temple Univ, 62-, chmn metals/jewelry 62-, chmn dept crafts, 65-79 & 85-88. *Awards:* Luis Comfort Tiffany Found Award in Crafts, 67; Nat Endowment Arts Craftsmen's Grant, 76 & 85; Pa Governor's Award in Crafts, 84. *Bibliog:* Karl Schollmayer (auth), Neuer Schmuck, Ernst Wasmuth-Verlag, Ger, 74; C E Licka (auth), Stanley Lechtzin: Technic and the organic paradigm, Metalsmith, summer 82; Michael Dunas (auth), Conversations on Technology, Philosophy of the Physical, Metalsmith, summer 88. *Mem:* Soc NAm Goldsmiths (mem bd dirs, 70-75); Am Crafts Coun; Col Fels Am Crafts Coun. *Media:* Metal, Plastic. *Res:* Electroforming of gold jewelry; computer aided design & manufacture for crafts. *Publ:* Auth, Electrofabrication of metal, Craft Horizons, 64; contribr, Metal Techniques for Craftsmen, 68; auth, Museum of Contemporary Crafts (brochure), 69; contribr, Contemporary Jewelry, 70. *Dealer:* Galerie Jocelyne Gobeil Montreal Que Can. *Mailing Add:* Temple Univ Tyler Sch Art Beech & Penrose Ave Elkins Park PA 19126

LECKY, SUSAN
PAINTER
b Los Angeles, Calif, July 19, 40. *Study:* Univ Southern Calif, BFA; also European travel. *Work:* Los Angeles Co Mus; Bloomington Fed Savings & Loan, Bloomington, Pontiac & Streator Br. *Exhib:* Joslyn Mus, Omaha, 72; solo exhibs, Univ Ill, Champaign, Ill, 77, Millikin Univ, Decatur, Ill, 83, Eastfield Col, Mesquite, Tex, 85, Conduit Gallery, Dallas, Tex, 86 & E Tex State Univ, Commerce, Tex, 86, Brazos Gallery, Richland Col, Callas, Tex, 91, The Art Center, Waco, TX, 92; Winter Invitational, Norris Cult Arts Ctr, St Charles, Ill, 83; Looking at the Earth, Nat Air & Space Mus, Smithsonian Inst, Washington, DC, 86-87; 21st Bradley Nat Print & Drawing Exhib, Bradley Univ, Peoria, Ill, 87; 21st Nat Drawing & Small Sculpture, Delmar Col, Corpus Christi, Tex, 87 & 92; two-person exhibs, Clifford Gallery, Dallas, Tex & Univ Tulsa, Okla, 88; Tex Woman's Univ, Denton, 89; 32nd Ann Delta Art, Ark Arts Ctr, Little Rock, 89; Halpert Biennial, 90; Appalachian State Univ, Boone, NC, 90; 7th Ann State Competition, Lubbock Fine Arts Ctr, Tex, 91; Arlington Mus Art, Tex, 91; Painting Invitational-3-person, Martin Mus Art, Baylor Univ, Waco, Tex, 91; 18th Ann Competition, Masur Mus Art, Monroe La, 91. *Pos:* Restorer, Univ Ill Libr, 73-; art critic, New Art Examr, 76-78; pub lect, Millikin, Decatur, Ill, 83, Eastfield Col, Mesquite, Tex, 85; East Tex Univ, Commerce, 86; Univ Tulsa, 86; Richland Col, Dallas, 89; Tex Woman's Univ, Denton, 89, Webster Univ St Louis, 91, Art Ctr, Waco, Tex, 92. *Teaching:* Vis artist, Univ Tulsa, Okla, 88. *Bibliog:* Joe Kagle (dir), The Studios (video), Art Ctr, Waco, Tex, 92. *Media:* Acrylic, Colored Pencil. *Mailing Add:* PO Box 95 Ladonia TX 75449

LE CLAIR, CHARLES
PAINTER, EDUCATOR
b Columbia, Mo, May 23, 14. *Study:* Univ Wis, BS & MS, 35; Acad Ranson, Paris, 36; Columbia Univ, 40-41. *Work:* Butler Art Inst; Carnegie Inst Mus; Albright-Knox Art Gallery; Provincetown Art Asn & Mus; McNay Art Inst, San Antonio. *Exhib:* Butler Inst Am Art, Youngstown, Ohio, 51, 56 & 71; Whitney Mus Am Art, New York, 51-56; Int Watercolor Exhib, Brooklyn Mus, 59; Nat Acad Design Ann, 60; Pa Acad Fine Arts, Philadelphia, 63 & 65; Am Acad & Inst Arts & Lett, 78. *Teaching:* Assoc prof painting, Chatham Col, 46-52, chmn dept art, 46-60, prof painting, 52-60; dean, Tyler Sch Art, Temple Univ, 60-74, prof painting, 60-81, chmn dept painting & sculpture, 79-81, prof emer, 81- *Awards:* Ten Awards, Assoc Artists Pittsburgh, 46-; Ford Found Fel Advan Educ, 52-53; Pennell Mem Award, Pa Acad Fine Arts, 65. *Media:* Oil, Watercolor. *Publ:* Auth, A Salute to William Pitt (catalog), Chatham Col, 58; A Salute to William Pitt (catalog), Chatham Col, 58; Education of the Artist, Alumni Rev, Temple Univ, 1/62; The Art of Watercolor: Techniques and New Directions, Prentice-Hall, 85; Color in Contemp Painting, Watson-Guptill, 91. *Mailing Add:* 2052 Lombard St Philadelphia PA 19146

LEDERMAN, SHEYA NEWMAN See Sheya

LEDERMAN, STEPHANIE BRODY
PAINTER, DRAWINGS
b New York, NY. *Study:* Univ Mich Sch Archit & Design; Finch Col, BS(design); C W Post Ctr, Long Island Univ, MA(studio art), 75. *Work:* Newark Mus, NJ, Chase Manhattan Bank, Mus Mod Art, New York, NY; Prudential Insurance Co, NJ, Health & Hosps Corp, NY; Insurance of NAm, New York. *Comn:* edition of 100 small artworks, Franklin Furnace, New York, NY, 83; poster, funded by Nat Endowment Arts Alternative Mus, New York. *Exhib:* American Narrative Story Art 67-77, Contemp Arts Mus, Houston, 77-79; Great Am Foot, Mus Contemp Crafts, New York, 78-80; Artists Postcards II, Cooper-Hewitt Mus, New York, 78-80; Words & Images, Philadelphia Col Art, 79; Penthouse Aviary, Mus Mod Art, New York, 80; A New Bestiary, Inst Contemp Art, Va Mus, Richmond, 81; New Acquisitions, Newark Mus, NJ, 83; Domestic Tales, Univ Mass, 84; Rape, Ohio St Univ, 85; Butler Libr, Metrop Mus Art, New York, 85; The Clocktower, New York, 86, Queens Mus, 87; Am Acad Arts & Letts Purchase Exhib, New York, 88; On the Cutting Edge, Fine Arts Mus, Long Island, New York, 89; 4 Gallery Artists, Katzen Brown Gallery, New York, 90; The 80's, A Post Pop Generation, Southern Alleghenies Mus Art, Loretto, Pa, 90; Landscape in Question, Hartwick Col, Oneonta, New York, 90; New York Artists Bookworks, Mus Modern Art Libr, New York, 90; solo exhib, Kathryn Markel, 79, 81 & 83, Real Art Ways, Hartford, Conn, 84, San Francisco Airport, Calif, 86, Queensboro Community Col, New York, 88, Alfred Univ, New York, 90. *Pos:* Docent, Queens Mus, 82- *Teaching:* vis artist, Hunter Sch Visual Arts, Long Island Univ, 77- *Awards:* Line Grant, Nat Endowment Arts & NYSCA Funds, 84; Ariana Found, 85; Percent For Art, 88; Purchase Award, Hassam & Speicher, Am Acad & Inst Arts & Lett, 88. *Bibliog:* Janis Edwards (auth), Extensions of the Book, Art Week, 8/10/85; Peter Stack (auth), Airport Shoe: One Show Fits All, San Francisco Chronicle, 12/87; Karin Lipson (auth), article, Newsday, 7/22/88. *Media:* Oil. *Publ:* Auth & illusr, Chocolate Cake, 79 & He Doesn't Walk Funny-He Wore Corrective Shoes, 79, pvt publ; Romantic couplet (the hustle) (portfolio), Paris Rev, 79; Spring Chicken, Artifacts at End of Decade, 81; The adventuress tries fantasy, Whitewalls, 83; Domestic Screams, 85. *Mailing Add:* 822 Madison Ave No 4 New York NY 10021

LEE, AMY FREEMAN
PAINTER, LECTURER
b San Antonio, Tex, Oct 3, 14. *Study:* St Mary's Hall, San Antonio, grad, 31; Univ Tex, Austin, 31-34; Incarnate Word Col, 34-42, Hon LittD, 65. *Work:* D D Feldman Collection, Univ Tex Mus, Austin; Smith Col Mus Fine Arts, Mass; Ft Worth Art Ctr, Tex; Norfolk Mus Arts & Sci, Va; McNay Art Mus, San Antonio, Tex; and others. *Comn:* Camelia Award Painting, Joskes of

Texas, San Antonio, 71. *Exhib:* Tex Watercolor Soc, McNay Art Mus, San Antonio, 83 & 85; Nat Soc Painters in Casein & Acrylic, Nat Art Club, New York, 85; Int-30th Anniversary Exhib-Arte, AC, Monterrey, Mex, 85; solo exhibs, Incarnate Word Col, 81 & 85, Sol del Rio Gallery, San Antonio, Tex, 87 & 89; Hors de Concourt, 40th Anniversary Exhib, Tex Watercolor Soc, McNay Art Mus, San Antonio, 89; McNay Art Mus, San Antonio, Tex, 91; Invitational Exhib, Arte AC, Monterrey, Mex, 92; and others. *Pos:* Art critic, San Antonio Express-News, 39-41; art critic, KONO Radio Sta, San Antonio, 47-52; ed critic, KTSA Radio Sta, San Antonio, 79-80. *Teaching:* Lectr, Trinity Univ, 54-57, San Antonio Art Inst, 55-57 & Our Lady of Lake Col, 69-; lectr English & aesthetics, Humane Ethics-Incarnate Word Col, San Antonio, 66-; vis scholar, St Mark's Sch, Dallas, Tex, 89. *Awards:* Elected to Tex Women's Hall of Fame-Arts & Humanities by the Gov of Tex, Austin, 84; First Living Treasure San Antonio Award, Ctr Peace Through Cult, 88; 20th Anniversary Medal, Univ Tex Health Sci Ctr, San Antonio, 89; Gov's Appointment, Tex Comt Humanities, 92; and others. *Bibliog:* To See a World (documentary), 84 & Reality is Becoming, 85, CBS. *Mem:* Int Soc Educ Through Art; SW Watercolor Soc; Int Soc Aesthetics; Children's Fine Arts Ser, San Antonio, Tex (adv bd, 90); Mex Cult Inst, San Antonio, Tex (adv bd, 90); and others. *Media:* Watercolor, Drawing. *Publ:* Auth, Creativity and the Human Spirit, Univ Tex Press, Austin, 73; On the Fifth Day: Animal Rights and Human Ethics--A Game for all Seasons, Acropolis Books, Washington, DC, 77; Winging with the Wild, White Bird (exhib catalog), McNay Art Mus, San Antonio, 1/86; Modern Alchemists, Newsletter, Am Inst Architects, Washington, DC, 92; What's New? (foreword), Tex Watercolor Soc Exhib Catalog, 92. *Dealer:* L & L Gallery 1107 N Fourth St Longview TX 75601; Sol Del Rio Art Gallery 1020 Townsend Ave San Antonio TX 78209. *Mailing Add:* 127 Canterbury Hill San Antonio TX 78209

LEE, BALDWIN S
PHOTOGRAPHY
b New York, NY, Feb 17, 51. *Study:* Mass Inst Technol, BS, 72, with Minor White; Yale Univ Sch Art, MFA, 75; with Walker Evans. *Work:* Mus Mod Art, New York; Univ Mich Mus Art, Ann Arbor; Univ Ky Art Mus, Lexington; Yale Univ Art Gallery, New Haven, Conn; Nat Trust for Historic Preservation. *Exhib:* America's Uncommon Places, Washington, DC, 87; New Southern Photography: Beyond Myth and Reality, Burden Gallery, New York, 89; Personae: Contemporary Portraiture and Self-Portraiture, Islip Art Mus, NY, 89; Baldwin Lee: Photographs of Black Southerners, 1983-1988, Univ Mich Art Mus, Ann Arbor, 91 & Univ Kan Mus Art, Lawrence, 92; The Sporting Life, High Mus Art, Atlanta, Ga, 92. *Teaching:* Asst prof photog, Yale Univ, New Haven Conn, 75-79; hd photog dept, asst prof photog, Mass Col Art, Boston, 79-82; prof photog, Univ Tenn, Knoxville, Tenn, 82-; visiting prof, Mass Inst Technol, 91-92. *Awards:* Nat Endowment Arts Fel, 84 & 90; John Simon Guggenheim Mem Fel, 84. *Mailing Add:* 105 Balboa Circle Oak Ridge TN 37830

LEE, BRIANT HAMOR
HISTORIAN, EDUCATOR
b New Haven, Conn, May 6, 38. *Study:* Carnegie-Mellon Univ; Adelphi Univ, BA; Acad de Belle Arti, Rome, Cert de Frequenza; Univ Italiana per Stranieri-Perugia; Ind Univ, MA; NY Univ; Mich State Univ, PhD. *Comn:* Over 100 theatrical productions, Scenographer, (in collaboration with staging dir); 25 theatrical productions, staging dir & scenographer, 64- *Pos:* Design engineer, Kliegl Lighting, New York, 63-64; Ed, Jour of Empirical Research in Theatre, 80-85. *Teaching:* Instr scenography, US Int Univ, San Diego, Calif, 62-63; asst prof scenography, Bradley Univ, Peoria, Ill, 67-68; assoc prof theatre, Bowling Green State Univ, Ohio, 68- *Mem:* Am Theatre Asn; Speech Commun Asn; Am Soc for Theatre Res; Ohio Theatre Alliance; Ohio Community Theatre Asn. *Media:* Watercolor, Ink. *Res:* Late 18th century European theatre architecture and theatrical staging. *Publ:* Auth, Pierre Patte, Late 18th century lighting innovator, Theater Survey, 76; The origins of the box set in the late 18th century, Theatre Survey, 78; Corrugated Scenery, Oracle Press, 82; Understanding Microcomputers & Microcomputer Wordprocessing, 85, Bowling Green State Univ. *Mailing Add:* 336 S Church St Bowling Green OH 43402

LEE, CAROLINE D
CURATOR, CONSULTANT
b Dallas, Tex, Nov 27, 34. *Study:* Stephens Col, Columbia, Mo, 52-53; Univ Ariz, Tucson, 53-55; Tex Christian Univ, Fort Worth, 55; Univ Tex, Austin, 55; San Antonio Art Inst, Tex, Painting Dept, 68-69 & Ceramics Dept, 70; Trinity Univ, San Antonio, Painting Dept Tex, 70-71, Univ Tex, Art Hist/ Grad Painting, San Antonio, 78-79; Univ Mex, Exten, San Antonio, Tex, 79. *Collections Arranged:* Elizabeth Maddox Theatre, 84; San Antonio Survey, Transco Energy Co Houston, Tex, 86; Caroline Lee Gallery, Houston, Tex, 86-88; Haitian Ritual Art, Economos Fine Art, Santa Fe, NMex, 88; Chrysallis Art & Design, Sante Fa, NMex, 89; Prison Art, Taos, NMex, 92. *Pos:* Dir, Southwest Craft Ctr Gallery, San Antonio, 71-75; owner & dir, Objects Gallery, San Antonio, 80-84, Caroline Lee Gallery, San Antonio, Tex, 84-88, Exvoto Gallery, San Antonio & Houston, Tex, 85-86; mgr, Chrysallis Art & Design, Santa Fe, NMex, 89; private consult to collectors, architects, designers, 88-90; artist consult, Clay & Fiber Gallery, Taos, NMex, 90; cur, Taos Inn, NMex, currently. *Teaching:* Integration of Abilities, 70-71; hon inst, Trinity Univ, San Antonio, Tex, 70-71. *Awards:* Award Excellence, Houston Designer-Craftsmen Exhib, 79; Second Prize Mixed Media, Tex Women Artists, Nat Orgn Women, 80; Archives of Am Art, Smithsonian Inst, Washington, DC, 83- *Bibliog:* Don Wilcox (auth), El Dia de los Muertos, Am Craft Mag, 10-11/84; Susan Freudenheim (auth), Altar egos, Tex Homes Mag, 10/85; John Howell (auth), The explicit image, Art Forum, 4/86. *Mem:* Bd, Santa Rosa Children's Hosp Volunteer Orgn, McNay Mus Art, San Antonio Art League, Witte Mus Art & Tex Sculpture Symposiums. *Publ:* Auth, Texas: The future climate for crafts, Tex Crafts, 79; The new decade: The emergent shape, Tex Designer Craftsmen, spring 80. *Mailing Add:* Caroline Lee Gallery PO Box 1449 Taos NM 87571

LEE, CATHERINE
SCULPTOR, PAINTER
b Pampa, Tex, Apr 11, 50. *Study:* San Jose State Univ, BA, 75. *Work:* Stadtische Galerie im Lenbachhaus, Munich; Mus Mod Art, NY; Tate Gallery, London; Mus Art, Carnegie Inst, Pittsburgh; US Dept State, Washington, DC. *Exhib:* Selected Works, Albright-Knox Mus, Buffalo, NY, 87; Artists in the Abstract, Weatherspoon Gallery, Univ NC, Greensboro, 90; Biennale de Sculpture, Monte Carlo, Monaco, 91; Geteilte Bilder, Das Diptychon in der neuen Kunst, Mus Folkwang, Essen, Ger, 92; Stadtische Galerie im Lenbachhaus, Munich, 92; Neue Galerie der Stadt Linz, Austria, 92; and many others. *Teaching:* Artist-in-residence, Minneapolis Col Art & Design, Minn Inst Art, 82; vis asst prof painting, Univ Tex, San Antonio, 83; adj asst prof, Columbia Univ, New York, 86-87. *Awards:* Creative Artists Pub Serv Prog Fel Painting, 78; Nat Endowment Arts, Painting Grant, 89. *Bibliog:* John Russell (auth), Bright young artists, New York Times, 5/18/86; Demetrio Paparoni (auth), A Conversation with Catherine Lee, Tema Celeste, 2/92; David Carrier & Helmut Friedel (auths), Catherinne Lee, Outcasts, Stadtische Galerie im Lenbachhaus, Munich, 92. *Media:* Bronze; Oil. *Dealer:* Galerie Karsten Greve Wallrafplatz 3 5000 Koln Ger; Galerie Karsten Greve 5 Rue Debelleyme 75003 Paris France. *Mailing Add:* 106 Spring St New York NY 10012

LEE, DORA FUGH
PAINTER, SCULPTRESS
b Peking, China, Aug 16, 30; US citizen. *Study:* With Prince Pu Ju, Chao Meng-chu & Yen Shao-Hsiang, Peking, China; additional study with sculptor, Pietro Lazzari, Washington, DC. *Work:* China Inst, New York; Pearl Buck Found, Philadelphia; Smithsonian Inst & Nat Cathedral, Washington, DC; The Willard Hotel, Washington, DC; Johns Hopkins Medical Ctr, Baltimore, Md; Nat Portrait Gallery, Smithsonian Inst; and others. *Comn:* Sears House, Washington, DC. *Exhib:* Watercolor USA, Springfield, Mo, 75; Mainstreams, Marietta Col, Ohio, 76; Am Watercolor Soc Traveling Exhib, 76-92; Franz Bader Gallery, Washington, DC, 76-92; Md Acad of Arts, Easton, 77. *Teaching:* Pvt lessons in Chinese traditional painting & calligraphy, Capitol Hill & Smithsonian Inst, Washington, DC, 70-; Chinese calligraphy, George Washington Univ. *Awards:* Best of Show, 68, First Prize/Watercolor, 71 & 72, Montgomery Co Art Asn Traveling Exhib, Am Watercolor Asn, 76; North Light Award, Nat Sumei Soc, 85. *Mem:* Washington Watercolor Asn; Nat League Am Pen Women; Am Watercolor Soc. *Media:* Oil, Watercolor; Clay. *Dealer:* Franz Bader Gallery 1701 Pennsylvania Ave NW Washington DC 20037; Gallery 90 1248 Madison Ave New York NY 10128. *Mailing Add:* 6305 Orchid Dr Bethesda MD 20817

LEE, ELEANOR GAY
PAINTER
b Atlanta, Ga. *Study:* Nat Acad Design Sch Fine Art. *Work:* Mus City New York; Mus Fine Art, Hickory, NC; Mus Fine Art, Greenville, SC; River Edge Mus, Can; John St Methodist Church, New York; and others. *Exhib:* Guild Hall, East Hampton, NY, 63; Burr Galleries, New York, 71; Nat Biennial Composers, Authors & Artists Am, 71; Catharine Lorillard Wolfe Art Club Open, 71; Governor's Mansion, Jackson, Miss, 81; and others. *Pos:* Dir one-man shows, Burr Galleries, 57-64; attendant, Thompson Gallery, New York, 66-69. *Awards:* First Prize, 71 & Second Prize, 79, Composers, Authors & Artists Am; 4th Prize, 7th Regiment Armory, Company K, 80; and others. *Mem:* Burr Artists (founding pres, 71); Catharine Lorillard Wolfe Art Club (pres, 50-53); Composers, Authors & Artists Am (nat pres, 79-81); hon mem Gotham Painters; and others. *Media:* Oil, Pastel. *Mailing Add:* Nat Arts Club 15 Gramercy Park S New York NY 10003

LEE, ELLEN WARDWELL
CURATOR
b Indianapolis, Ind, Feb 5, 49. *Study:* Smith Col, Northampton, Mass, BA, 71. *Collections Arranged:* William McGregor Paxton, 79; The Aura of Neo-Impressionism: WJ Holliday Collection, 83; More than Red, White and Blue: Am Paintings from the Permanent Collection of Indianapolis Mus Art, 89; Seurat at Gravelines: The Last Landscapes, 90. *Pos:* Assoc cur painting & sculpture, Indianapolis Mus Art, 75-84, cur, 84-89 & sr cur, 89-91, chief cur, 91- *Mem:* Am Asn Mus; Int Coun Mus. *Res:* Late 19th early 20th century American & European painting and sculpture. *Publ:* Coauth, Alfred Thompson Bricher, 1837-1908, Indianapolis Mus Art, 73; William McGregor Paxton, NA, Indianapolis Mus Art, 79; auth, The Aura of Neo-Impressionism: The WJ Holliday Collection, Indianapolis Mus Art & Ind Univ Press, 83; Seurat at Gravelines: The Last Landscapes, Indianapolis Mus Art, 90; Seurat Centenary (bk revs), Art J, Vol 51, No 2, 104-107, Summer 92. *Mailing Add:* Indianapolis Museum of Art 1200 W 38th St Indianapolis IN 46208

LEE, GERALDINE See Hooks, Geri

LEE, JANIE C
DEALER
b Shreveport, La, Apr 22, 37. *Study:* Sarah Lawrence Col, BA, 59. *Mem:* Art Dealers Asn Am (vpres, 84-86, bd dirs, 84-88). *Specialty:* Twentieth Century modern American and European Art, specializing in drawings. *Publ:* Auth, Master Drawings 1918-1985, spring 86; Ink Drawings 1890-1986, spring 87; Master Drawings, 1877-1987, spring 88; Abstract Expressionist Drawings 1941-1955, fall 88; Master Drawings 1859-1989, fall 89. *Mailing Add:* 1209 Berthea St Houston TX 77006

LEE, LI LIN
PAINTER
b Jakarta, Indonesia, Oct 11, 55; US citizen. *Study:* Univ Pittsburgh, BS, 78. *Work:* Ameritech Servs, Chicago; Arthur Anderson & Co, Chicago; Art Inst Chicago; Philip Morris Co Inc, New York; Prudential Ins Co Am, Newark, NJ. *Exhib:* Solo Exhibs, LaSorda-Iri Gallery, Los Angeles, 88, Reicher Gallery, Barat Col, Lake Forest, Ill, 89, Tilden-Foley Gallery, New Orleans, 89, E M Donahue Gallery, New York, 89, 90, 91 & 92, Li-Lin Lee, New Works, Richard Iri Gallery, Los Angeles, 90, Betsy Rosenfield Gallery, Chicago, 90 & 92; Artfair/Seattle, Betsy Rosenfield Gallery, 92; Wall Project, Sculpture Center, Benefit Exhib, New York, 92; The Rectangled Bank, E M Donahue Gallery, New York, 92; May 1992, Betsy Rosenfield Gallery, Chicago Int Art Expo, Chicago, 92; and others. *Bibliog:* S G (auth), Li Lin Lee at Blum Helman Gallery, LA Times, 5/89; John Yau (auth), Li Lin Lee at E M Donahue Gallery, Artforum, summer 89; John Brunetti (auth), Li Lin Lee at Betsy Rosenfield Gallery, New Art Examiner, 5/92. *Media:* Oil on burlap, Enamel on wood. *Dealer:* E M Donahue Gallery 560 Broadway No 304 New York NY 10012. *Mailing Add:* c/o Betsy Rosenfield Gallery 212 W Superior St Chicago IL 60610

LEE, MARGARET F
PAINTER
b South St Paul, Minn, May 19, 22. *Study:* Rochester Art Ctr, with Adolph Dehn, Arnold Blanch & Robert Birmelin, 60-74; John Pike Watercolor Sch, Woodstock, NY, 72; watercolor with Zoltan Szabo, 74; Japanese woodblock with Toshi Yoshida, 74; Univ Minn, BA(art), 75. *Work:* YMCA-YWCA Permanent Collection, Rochester, Minn. *Exhib:* One-man show, Augsburg Col, Minneapolis, 73; 17th & 18th Int, Galerie Int, New York, 73-74; Mainstreams USA, Marietta Col, Ohio, 74; American Painters in Paris, French Ministry & Paris City Coun, 75; Arts of Asia Gallery, Rochester, Minn, 75-77; and others. *Teaching:* Lectr Japanese Sumi-e, Winona Art Ctr, Minn, 74; instr Japanese painting, Rochester Art Ctr, 74. *Awards:* First Place, Northern Lights 75, St Paul, 75; Award of Excellence, Arts Omnibus, 76, St Paul; Award, Midwest Watercolor Soc Exhib, Minn Mus of Art, St Paul, 77. *Mem:* Minn Artists Asn; Sumi-e Soc Am, New York; Twin City Watercolor Soc, Minneapolis, MN. *Media:* Acrylic, Sumi Ink. *Dealer:* Callaway Galleries Inc Center St & SW First St Rochester MN 55901. *Mailing Add:* 145 E Eighth St Zumbrota MN 55992

LEE, NELDA S
DEALER
b Gorman, Tex, July 3, 41. *Study:* Tarleton State Col, AA, 61; N Tex State Univ, BFA, 63; Tex Tech Univ, Lubbock, grad study, 65 & San Miguel de Allende Art Inst, Mex, 65. *Work:* Delgado Mus of Art, New Orleans, La; El Paso Mus of Art, Tex. *Comn:* Portrait of late Sam Jones, Supt Rising Star Pub Sch, comn by Student Coun, 66; designed terrazo marble floors, Sweetwater High Sch, comn by Balfour Co, Tex, 67; student ctr, Tarleton State Univ, comn by Student Coun, Stephenville, Tex, 68. *Exhib:* Artist of SE in Tex, Delgado Mus Art, New Orleans, La, 64; Tex Fine Arts Asn Traveling Exhib, 64-67; Int Designer-Craftsmen Exhib, El Paso Mus, Tex, 65; Tex Watercolor Soc Exhib, Elizabeth Ney Mus, San Antonio, Tex, 67. *Collections Arranged:* President Carter's Inaugural Reception Exhib, The Capitol, Washington, DC, 77. *Pos:* Owner-operator, Nelda Lee Inc, 69- *Teaching:* Chairperson art dept, Ector High Sch, Odessa, Tex, 63-68. *Awards:* First Place Sculpture, Artist of the SE in Tex, Delgado Mus of Art, 64; First Place Design, Int Designer-Craftsmen Exhib, 65; First Place Mixed-Media, Tex Fine Arts Exhib, 65. *Bibliog:* Scheryl Vannoy (auth), Texas art dealer stages exhibition at Capitol, San Angelo Standard Times, 77; article, SW Art Mag, 80; Carrie Steenson (auth), A rare work of art, Business Mag, 81. *Mem:* Am Soc of Appraisers; Tex Asn Art Dealers (pres, 79-81); Int Soc Appraisers. *Specialty:* Eighteenth--twentieth century English and American masters. *Publ:* Auth, History of Art in Odessa, Texas, Permian Basin Hist Ann, 69; coauth, Painter of a vanishing America, SW Art, 74. *Mailing Add:* PO Box 4268 Odessa TX 79760-4268

LEE, ROBERT J
PAINTER, EDUCATOR
b Oakland, Calif, Dec 26, 21. *Study:* Acad Art, San Francisco, with Richard Stephens, Hamilton Wolf. *Work:* US Air Force Hist Soc; Mt Holyoke Mus, Mass; Springfield Mus Fine Arts, Mass; Evanston Mus, Ill; Columbia Mus Art, SC; USAF. *Exhib:* Calif Palace Legion of Honor, San Francisco, 46; Art Inst Chicago, 47-49; Butler Inst Am Arts, Youngstown, Ohio; Conn Acad Fine Arts, Hartford; Smithsonian Inst, Washington, DC, 71; 200 Yrs Am Illus, New York Hist Soc, 77; 25 one-man shows in galleries. *Teaching:* Instr illus, Pratt Inst, 55-57; assoc prof painting & design, Marymount Col, NY, 62- *Awards:* First Prize Gold Medal of Honor, Allied Artists, 60; Award of Excellence, Soc Illusr, 67; First Prize Painting, Putnam Arts Coun, 81. *Mem:* Soc of Illus. *Publ:* Illusr ltd ed, Our Town, 76; illusr, A Fable, Franklin Press, 76; Poets on Pain and Sensation, A Colish Press, 80; The Braggin' Dragon, DLM Teaching Resources, 89; The Magic Pumpkin, H Hold Publ, 89. *Dealer:* Charles A Pace 10202 Piping Rock Houston TX 77042. *Mailing Add:* c/o Marymount Col Dept Art Tarrytown NY 10591

LEE, ROBERT M
PAINTER, SCULPTOR
b Alamogordo, NMex, Aug 13, 33. *Study:* Studied drawing with Randall Davey. *Work:* Koshare Indian Mus, La Junta, Colo; Boatman's Nat Bank, St Louis, Mo; Albuquerque Mus, NMex; Albuquerque Int Airport Collec. *Comn:* John Henry (Horse of the Year), Nat Asn State Racing Comnr, 82; Winner Golden Slipper Stakes, Sydney Turf Club, Australia, 85. *Exhib:* Mountain Oyster Club Art Exhib, Tucson, Ariz, 73-84; The West in Paint & Bronze, Mo Athletic Club, St Louis, 74-75; The Enduring West, 78 & West-Southwest, 82, Albuquerque Mus, Tex; Margaret Jamieson Presents, St Vincent Hosp Benefit, Santa Fe, NMex, 79-81; NMex State Fair Cowboy Classic, Albuquerque, 81-85; Preview 82, Tex Art Gallery, Dallas, 82. *Awards:* Second Place, Nat Artists Contest, Saturday Evening Post, 79. *Bibliog:* Ed Ainsworth (auth), The cowboy in art, World Publ Co, 68; Flo Wilks (auth), Bob Lee-at home on the ranch, SW Art, 7/79. *Media:* Oil; Cast Metal. *Mailing Add:* 19716 N Hwy 85 Belen NM 87002

LEE, ROGER
EDUCATOR, CURATOR
b Vancouver, BC, Dec 1, 42. *Study:* Univ BC, BA, 64 & MA(fel), 66. *Collections Arranged:* Line in Chinese and Japanese Art, Norman Mackenzie Art Gallery, Univ Regina; Sculpture in Movement, Evelyn Roth; Contemp Traditional Chinese Painting, 88; Farmer Paintings from Jilin, 90. *Teaching:* Assoc prof art hist, Univ Regina, 66- *Mem:* Univ Art Asn Can; CAA. *Res:* Contemporary & Asian (Chinese). *Publ:* A Brief History of Western Art, Jinan, China, 81; Contemporary Traditional Chinese Paintings, Mackenzie Nat Gallery, 90; Inside the Outer Gate, Farmer Painting from Jilin Province, Dunlop Art Gallery, 92. *Mailing Add:* Dept Visual Arts Univ Regina Regina SK S4S 0A2 Canada

LEE, SHERMAN EMERY
MUSEUM DIRECTOR
b Seattle, Wash, Apr 19, 18. *Study:* Am Univ, BA & MA; Western Reserve Univ, PhD. *Pos:* Cur Far Eastern art, Detroit Inst Art, 41-46; with dept arts & monuments div, Civil Info & Educ Sect, Gen Hq, Supreme Comdr, Allied Powers, Tokyo, 46-68; asst dir to assoc dir, Seattle Mus Art, 48-52; cur Oriental art, Cleveland Mus Art, 52-, dir, 58-83. *Teaching:* Lectr art hist, Univ Wash, 48-52; Case Western Reserve Univ, 58, prof art, 62-; adj prof, Univ NC, Chapel Hill, currently. *Awards:* Legion of Honor; Order of the North Star; Order of the Sacred Treasure, Third Class. *Mem:* Asn Art Mus Dirs (past pres); Am Acad Arts & Sci; Asia Soc (trustee). *Publ:* Auth, Japanese Decorative Style, 61; History of Far Eastern Art, 64; coauth, Chinese Art Under the Mongols, 68; auth, Reflections of Reality in Japanese Art, 83; Past and Present: East and West, 83; and others. *Mailing Add:* 102 Dixie Dr Chapel Hill NC 27514

LEEBER, SHARON CORGAN
ART DEALER, CONSULTANT
b St Johns, Mich, Oct 1, 40. *Study:* Univ Wyo; Cent Mich Univ; Nat Open Univ, Washington, DC; Trinity Univ. *Work:* Las Cumbres, Acapulco, Mex; Univ Tex, Dallas & Arlington; Dallas Mus Fine Arts; Arlington City Libr, Tex. *Comn:* Univ Tex, Arlington, 76; Arlington City Hall, Tex, 76; large welded male, Incarnate Word Col, San Antonio, Tex, 77. *Exhib:* Tex Fine Arts Nat, Austin, 69; one-man retrospective show, Elizabet Ney Mus, Austin, 71; Tex Sculpture & Painting, Dallas, 71; Dallas Art, City Hall, Dallas, Tex, 78; Big Name Artists Show, Dallas, 78 & 79. *Pos:* Pres, Archit Arts Co, 81-; trustee, Florentine Found Art, 85- *Teaching:* Instr photog, El Centro Col, Tex, 72-82. *Awards:* Purchase Awards, Shreveport Mus, 69 & Dallas Mus Fine Arts, 78; Purchase Award, Dallas Mus Fine Arts, 78. *Bibliog:* Thelma Neuman (auth), The Mirror Book, 78; L Haacke (auth), Art is more comfortable, Dallas Times Herald, 3/30/78; High Profile - Dallas Morning News, 92. *Mem:* Nat Sculptor's Asn; Artists Equity Asn (secy, Dallas Chap, 71-72); Engrs, Artists & Technologists; Tex Fine Arts Asn; Tex Soc Sculptors; and others. *Media:* Welded Steel, Glass. *Publ:* Nat Asn Indust & Off Parks Publ Series: How to Acquire for Your Development, #5, 87. *Dealer:* Contemporary Gallery 2800 Routh St The Quadrangle Dallas TX 75201. *Mailing Add:* 6410 Dykes Way Dallas TX 75230

LEEDS, ANNETTE
PAINTER
b Boston, Mass. *Study:* Mass Col Art, grad; Art Students League; Brooklyn Mus, with Moses Soyer; also with Paul Puzinas, Howard Boesendahl & Wang Dawen. *Exhib:* Chinoh Gallery, 88; Bonwit Teller, 88; Tweed Gallery, 88; St John's Univ, 91; AGA Gallery, 92; and others. *Teaching:* Pvt instr, 68- *Awards:* First Prize, Am Pen Women; First Prize, Artists Inc, 79; Second Prize, Nat Arts Club, 83; Best in landscape, Catharine Lorillard Wolfe Art Club, 89. *Mem:* Catharine Lorillard Wolfe Art Club; Burr Artists; Nichibei Fukinkai; Alliance Queens Artists. *Media:* Oil, Watercolor. *Mailing Add:* 116-17 Union Turnpike Forest Hills NY 11375

LEEDY, JIM (JAMES A LEEDY)
CERAMIST, PAINTER
b Letcher County, Ky, Nov 6, 29. *Study:* William & Mary (now Va Commonwealth), BFA, 57; Southern Ill Univ, MFA, MS, 58; Mich State Univ, MA(art hist), 59. *Work:* Am Craft Mus, New York; Nelson-Atkins Mus Art, Kansas City; Everson Mus Art, Syracuse; Ariz State Univ Mus, Tempe; John Michael Kohler Arts Ctr, Sheboygan, Wis. *Comn:* Sky Art, Mo Arts Coun/Am Inst Architects, Kansas City, 79; As the Phoenix Rose From Its Own Ashes So Can Man, Pori Int Jazz Festival, Finland, 87; ceramic mural, Himeji Int Cult Ctr, Japan, 88. *Exhib:* Solo shows, Am Craft Mus, New York, 68, John Michael Kohler Art Ctr, Sheboygan, Wis, 71, Contemp Art Ctr, Kansas City, Mo, 90 & Rochester Arts Ctr, Minn, 91; Surrealism, Retretti Arts Ctr, Suomi, Finland, 87; Raku-Transforming the Tradition, Kansas City, Contemp Art Ctr, Mo, 89; Contemporary American Ceramics, Nelson-Atkins Mus, Kansas City, Mo, 90. *Teaching:* Prof art hist, Univ Mont, Missoula, 59-64; prof art hist, Ohio Univ, Athens, 64-68; prof sculpture, Kansas City Art Inst, 68- *Awards:* Nat Endowment Arts, Major Fel, 90. *Bibliog:* Matthew Kangas (auth), Prehistoric modern, Am Craft, 6-7/90; Laura Caruso (auth), Material, Process and Paradox: The Art of Jim Leedy, Leedy Voulkos Gallery, 91. *Mem:* Hon mem, Nat Coun Educ Ceramic Arts. *Media:* Paint. *Dealer:* Leedy Voulkos Gallery 1919 Wyandotte Kansas City MO 64108. *Mailing Add:* C-12 Rt 4 Lake Lotawana MO 64063

LEEPA, ALLEN
PAINTER, EDUCATOR
b New York, NY, Jan 9, 19. *Study:* Am Art Sch New York, scholar; Art Students League; New Bauhaus, Chicago, scholar; Columbia Univ, BS, MA & EdD(scholar, dean's fel); Sorbonne & Grande Chaumiere, Paris. *Work:* South Bend Mus Art, Ind; Royal Acad, Scotland; Grand Rapids Mus, Mich. *Comn:* Mural, Ingham Co Arts Comn, State Wide Mich Competition, 84. *Exhib:* Mus Mod Art, New York, 53; Sao Paulo Biennale, Brazil, 63; one-man show, Galerie La Cour d'Ingres, Paris, 63; Mus Art Mod, Paris, 64 & 65; Retrospective, Hofstra Univ, 65; and many others. *Teaching:* Instr art, Hull Sch, Chicago, 37-38; Brooklyn Art Ctr, 39-41; Brooklyn Mus & Metrop Mus Art, 40-41; prof art, Mich State Univ, 45- *Awards:* Painting, Fulbright Award, Paris; Childe Hassam Painting Award, Am Acad Arts & Lett, 69; Ford Found Grant, 70; Statewide Mural Competition, Mich, 80; Painting, Ford Found, SAm; and others. *Bibliog:* Michael Seuphor (auth), Abstract Painting, 62 & Dictionary of Abstract Art, 63, Abrams. *Mem:* Am Asn Univ Prof; Mich Acad Arts, Sci & Lett. *Media:* Acrylic on Canvas. *Publ:* Auth, The Challenge of Modern Art, Barnes, 49 & 61; contribr, articles in Humanities in Contemp Life, 60, New Art, 66, Minimal Art, 68 & New Ideas in Art Educ, 73; auth, Abraham Rattner, Abrams, 74; and others. *Dealer:* Leepa Gallery of Fine Arts 210 S Pinellas Ave Tarpon Springs Fla. *Mailing Add:* 1873 Wacassassa St Tarpon Springs FL 34689

LEEPER, DORIS MARIE
SCULPTOR, PAINTER
b Charlotte, NC, Apr 4, 29. *Study:* Duke Univ, BA, 51. *Work:* Nat Mus Am Art, Washington, DC; Miss Mus Art, Jackson, Miss; Columbus Mus Art, Ohio; 180 Beacon Collection, Boston, Mass; Wadsworth Atheneum, Hartford, Conn. *Comn:* Fiberglass sculpture, Alpert Investment for Forum 303, Arlington, Tex, 71; 160 modular unit wall sculpture, Hunter Mus Art, Chattanooga, Tenn, 73-75; enamel painting, Int Bus Machines, Atlanta, Ga, 76; concrete sculpture, Regional Serv Ctr, Jacksonville, Fla, 78; stainless steel wall sculpture, Orlando Int Airport, Fla, 83. *Exhib:* One-person shows, Hunter Mus Art, Chattanooga, 75 & 79, Ringling Mus Art, Sarasota, 76, Southeastern Ctr Contemp Art, Winston-Salem, NCar, 77, Norton Gallery Art, West Palm Beach, Fla, 79, Anniston Mus Natural Hist, Ala, 80, Atlantic Ctr Arts, New Smyrna Beach, Fla, 84; Six Florida Sculptors, Thomas Ctr, Gainesville, Fla, 89; Five Sculptors, Stetson Univ, Deland, Fla, 91; 2nd Int Ephemeral Sculpture Exhib, Fortaleza, Brazil, 91-92; and many others. *Awards:* Nat Endowment Arts Grant, 72; Artist-in-Residence Fel, Rockefeller Found, 77; Fine Arts Coun Fla Grant, 77. *Bibliog:* An interview with Doris Leeper, Enjoy, 73; Virginia Watson Jones (auth), Contemporary American Women Sculptors, Oryx Press, 86; Charlotte S Rubinstein (auth), Am Women Sculptors. *Mem:* Atlantic Ctr Arts, New Smyrna Beach, Fla (mem adv coun & founder); LaNapoule Art Found, France (int adv coun); Volusia Co Cult Arts Adv Bd, Fla. *Media:* All; Miscellaneous. *Dealer:* Albertson-Peterson Gallery 329 Park Ave S Winter Park FL 32789; Art Sources Inc 927 Lincoln Rd Miami Beach FL 33139. *Mailing Add:* 806 N Peninsula New Smyrna Beach FL 32169

LEEPER, JOHN PALMER
MUSEUM DIRECTOR
b Denison, Tex, Feb 4, 21. *Study:* Southern Methodist Univ, BS, 42; Harvard Univ, MA, 47. *Pos:* Keeper, W A Clark Collection, Corcoran Gallery Art, 48, asst dir, 48-49; dir, Pasadena Art Mus, 50-53, Marion Koogler McNay Art Mus, San Antonio, Tex, retired. *Teaching:* Instr art hist, Dexter Sch, Boston, 46, Univ Southern Calif, 51, Pasadena Sch Fine Arts, 52 & Trinity Univ, 56-57; adj prof, Div Art & Design, Univ Tex, San Antonio. *Mem:* Am Asn Mus; Asn Art Mus Dirs; Tex Soc Arts & Lett; Am Inst Designers. *Publ:* Auth, Everett Spruce, 59; Otis Dozier, 60; ed, The autobiography of Jose Clemente Orozco, 62; auth, A Caribbean sketchbook by Jules Pascin, 64. *Mailing Add:* 6000 N New Braunfels San Antonio TX 78209

LEE-SISSOM, E
PAINTER
b Oakland, Calif, Feb 11, 34. *Study:* Art Instruction, Inc; Watkins Inst; Univ Tenn. *Work:* Parthenon Galleries & Mus, Tenn State Mus & Opryland Hotel's Collection Tenn Art, Nashville; Sunkist Corp Off, Atlanta, Ga; Tenn Valley Authority Corp Offices & Visitors Ctr, Knoxville, Tenn. *Comn:* Painting, Cookeville General Hospital, Tenn, 81. *Exhib:* 26th Nat Soc Painters Casein & Acrylic, Am Acad & Inst Arts & Letters, NY, 79; 22nd Traveling, Nat Soc Painters Casein & Acrylic, 79-80; 2nd Ann Open, Salmagundi Club, New York, 79; Grand Nat, Am Artists Prof League, New York, 79 & 80; one-woman show, Parthenon Galleries, Nashville, Tenn, 79 & 81. *Awards:* Third Award, 17th Tenn All-State, 77; Grand Award, 13th Central S, 78; Lyzon Art Gallery, 16th Central South, 81. *Mem:* Assoc mem Nat Soc Painters Casein & Acrylic; Am Artists Prof League; Tenn Art League; Cumberland Arts Soc Cookeville Tenn (bd dirs, 75-80). *Media:* Acrylics. *Publ:* Contribr, Tennessee Conservationist, Tenn Dept Conserv, 78; contribr, Int Soc Artists Communicator, Billboard Publ, 79; illusr cover, Key: Nashville, Silversmith, 82; contribr, Nashville!, Advantage Publ, 83. *Mailing Add:* 1151 Shipley Church Rd Cookeville TN 38501

LEE-SMITH, HUGHIE
PAINTER, INSTRUCTOR
b Eustis, Fla, Sept 20, 15. *Study:* Art Sch Detroit Soc Arts & Crafts, Scholastic Mag Scholar; Cleveland Inst Art, cert, 38; Wayne State Univ, BS(art educ), 53; John Huntington Polytechnic Inst. *Work:* Detroit Inst Arts, Mich; Wadsworth Athenaeum, Hartford, Conn; Lagos Mus, Nigeria; Mus of Int Art, Sophia Bulgaria; NJ State Mus; and many others. *Comn:* mural, NJ State Commerce Bldg, New Jersey State Council on the Arts, 88; Mosiac Tile Mural, McPherson Bldg, The Prudential and Deansbank Investment Corp, Washington, DC, 89. *Exhib:* Detroit Inst Arts Regional, 48-57; Butler Inst Am Art; Greenville Mus Art & Am Inst Arts & Letts; Boston Mus Nat, 70; An American Dream World: Romantic Realism 1930-1955, Whitney Mus, 75; Princeton Univ Mus, 75; Art the Law, West Collection (traveling exhib). *Teaching:* Instr painting, Grosse Pointe War Mem, Mich, 56-66 & Vt Acad, summer 68; instr drawing & painting, Princeton Country Day Sch, NJ, 63-65; artist in residence, Howard Univ, 69-71; instr, Art Students League, 72-, Karamu House, Cleveland, Ohio & Vermont Acad, Saxtons River. *Awards:* Allied Artists Am Prize, 58; Clarke Prize, Nat Acad Design, 58; Len Everette Mem Award, Audubon Artists, 86; Binney & Smith Award, Audubon Artists, 83. *Bibliog:* The metaphysical world of Hughie Lee-Smith, Am Artist, 10/78; article, Link, Cleveland Inst Art, 81; Art of Hughie Lee-Smith and Jacob Lawrence, Pub TV, 82. *Mem:* Artist Equity Asn (bd mem dir, 82-84); Audubon Artists (pres, 80-82); Artist Fel (vpres, 84-88); Nat Acad Design (coun mem, 86-); Fedn Mod Painters & Sculptors. *Media:* Multimedia. *Mailing Add:* 152-A Chatham Dr Cranbury NJ 08512

LEESON, TOM
PAINTER, SCULPTOR
b Chicago, Ill, Mar 16, 45. *Study:* Ball State Univ, BS, 68, Univ Calif, Los Angeles, MA, 71. *Work:* Los Angeles Co Mus Art, Calif; Santa Monica City Col Art Gallery, Calif. *Comn:* Painting comn by Lynda Resnick, Los Angeles, 86. *Exhib:* Current Concerns, Part 2, Los Angeles Inst Contemp Art, 75; The Object Observed, Los Angeles Munic Art Gallery, 78; Deja Vu: Masterpieces Updated, travelling exhib, Western Asn Art Mus, 83; Setting the Stage, Los Angeles Co Mus, 85-86; one person exhib, Ovsey Gallery, Los Angeles, Calif, 86 & 89. *Teaching:* Vis lectr drawing, Univ Calif, Los Angeles, 77-79, lectr, 83-90, vis asst prof, 91-92; vis lectr drawing & sculpture, Univ Calif, Santa Barbara, 82. *Bibliog:* Howard Fox (auth), Setting the Stage, Los Angeles Co Art Mus Art, 85; David Helfrey (auth), Suspending disbelief, Visions Mag, Spring 88. *Media:* Oil, Acrylic; All Media. *Dealer:* Ovsey Gallery 170 S La Brea Los Angeles Calif 90036. *Mailing Add:* 4748 W Washington Blvd Los Angeles CA 90016

LEET, RICHARD See Leet, Richard Eugene

LEET, RICHARD EUGENE
MUSEUM DIRECTOR, PAINTER
b Waterloo, Iowa, Sept 11, 36. *Study:* Univ Northern Iowa, BA, 58, MA, 65, with Ansei Uchima, Ted Egri, Paul R Smith & John Page; Univ Iowa, 61-64, with Stuart Edie & Robert Knipschild. *Work:* Mus Art, El Paso, Tex; Charles H MacNider Mus, Mason City, Iowa; Waterloo Munic Galleries, Iowa; Des Moines Art Ctr; Sioux City Art Ctr, Iowa. *Exhib:* Ann Iowa Artists Exhib, Des Moines Art Ctr, 58-80; Ann Midyear Show, Butler Inst Am Art, Youngstown, Ohio, 69, 75 & 77; Midwest Biennial, Joslyn Art Mus, Omaha, 72, 74 & 76; Spiva Art Ctr, Joplin, Mo, 77; Tweed Mus Art, Minn, 80; John Nelson Bergstrom Art Ctr, Neenah, Wis, 81; Pillsbury Corp, American Art: Challenge of the Land, Minn, 81; 20 Year Retrospective of Watercolors (touring), Sioux City Art Ctr, Iowa, 85; Mabee-Gerrer Mus Art, Shawnee, Okla, 87; Watercolor USA, Springfield Mus of Art, Mo, 88. *Pos:* Mus dir & founding dir, C H MacNider Mus, 65- *Teaching:* Instr art, Oelwein Community Schs, Iowa, 58-65; instr painting & drawing, C H MacNider Mus, Mason City, Iowa, 65- *Awards:* Purchase Award, Mus Art, El Paso, 71; Esther & Edith C Younker Painting Award, Iowa Artist's Show, Des Moines Art Ctr, 78; First Place, 88, 2nd Place, 89 Ann Iowa Watecolor Soc Exhib. *Bibliog:* Bruce Bienemann (auth), Spiritscapes: Recent Paintings by Richard Leet (exhib catalog), Mabee-Gerrer Mus Art, Shawnee, Okla, 87; Mark Stegmaier (auth), An Artful Balance, Lowan Mag, Vol 36, No 3, 50-54, 3/88; Kristin Buehner (auth), MacNider Plus Leet equals 26 Years of excellence in the arts, Mason City Globe Gazette, Iowa, 4/92. *Mem:* Am Asn Mus (coun, 83-84); Midwest Mus Conf (pres, 72-73); Iowa Arts Coun (mem coun, 70-76); Iowa Mus Asn (pres 78-80); Iowa Watercolor Soc (signature mem). *Media:* Watercolor. *Publ:* Auth & ed, Monthly column, Mason City Globe Gazette, 68-86; portfolio, Selections from the Yucatan sketch books of Lawrence Mills, 81; auth, Selections from the McMichael Canadian Collection (catalog), 82; He Pulled Lots of Strings, Monograph accomp Bil Baird Memorial Exhib, 88; auth & designer, 25 Selections American Art, Charles H MacNider Mus (collection catalog), 91. *Dealer:* Percival Galleries Inc Walnut at Sixth Valley Nat Bank Bldg Des Moines IA 50309. *Mailing Add:* 1149 Manor Dr Mason City IA 50401

LEETARU, ILSE
PRINTMAKER
b Tallinn, Estonia, Oct 27, 15; US citizen. *Study:* Deutshe Meistershule, Munich, Ger, 48-49; Sch Visual Arts New York, 63-66; Grande Chaumiere, Paris, 67-70; Neo Sch, New York, 90. *Work:* Hosp Corp Am, Nashville; Scott Publ Co & Skaolden Law Co, New York; Tartu Art Mus, Estonia; Kanagawa Prefectural Gallery, Yokohama, Japan; Tallinn Art Mus, Estonia. *Exhib:* Artistes USA, Galeries R Duncan, Paris, 76, 78, 81; Nat Asn Women Artists USA, Am Cult Ctr, Tel Aviv, Israel, 81 & Cairo, Egypt, 82; Nat Asn Women Artists, Dept Cult Affair, New York Gallery Exhib, 81; Estonian Art, Civic Ctr, Toronto, Can, 85; Galeria Cultura, Campinas, Brazil, 88; Hanga Ann, Metrop Mus, Tokyo, 85, 87; solo print exhib, Art Mus, Tartu, Estonia, 90 & Art Mus, Tallinn, Estonia, 91. *Awards:* Prix de Paris, R Duncan, 76, 78; First Prize, Nat Asn Women Artists, 78; Medaille de Bronze, Akademia r Duncan, Paris, 81. *Bibliog:* Endel Koks (auth), Estonian graphic artist, Stcokholm, Sweden, 79; P Reets (auth), Estonian art in exile, Stockholm, Sweden, 80. *Mem:* Nat Asn Women Artists. *Media:* All Media. *Dealer:* Artfull Eye M F Glintock 12 N Union St Lambertville NJ 08530. *Mailing Add:* 3240 Riverdale Ave Bronx NY 10463

LEETE, WILLIAM WHITE
PAINTER
b Portsmouth, Ohio, June 12, 29. *Study:* Yale Univ, BA, 51, BFA, 55 & MFA, 57. *Work:* De Cordova Mus, Lincoln, Mass; Cleveland Mus, Ohio; Worcester Mus, Mass; Univ Mass. *Exhib:* New Eng Contemp Artists, Boston, 63 & 65; Silvermine Guild, Conn, 66; Art in Embassies, Inst Contemp Arts, Boston, 66; Structured Art, De Cordova Mus, 69; Young New England Painters, John & Mabel Ringling North Mus, Fla; Portland Mus & Currier Gallery, Manchester, 69. *Teaching:* Assoc prof art, Univ RI, 57-74, prof, 74- *Media:* Acrylic. *Dealer:* Lenore Grey 15 Meeting St Providence RI 02903; Ward-Nasse Gallery 178 Prince St New York NY 10013. *Mailing Add:* Dept Art F207 Univ RI Kingston RI 02881

LEFCOURT, IRWIN
DEALER
b New York, NY, Jan 15, 10. *Study:* Nat Acad of Design, New York; Art Students League. *Pos:* Asst cur graphic art div, Smithsonian Inst, Washington, DC, 39-41; owner & dir, Art Fair Gallery, Larchmont, 57- *Mem:* Appraisers Asn of Am. *Specialty:* Modern and old master graphics; Japanese prints; Fin de Siecle posters. *Mailing Add:* 3 Washington Sq Larchmont NY 10538

LEFEBVRE D'ARGENCE, RENÉ-YVON
MUSEUM DIRECTOR, WRITER
b Plouescat, France, Aug 21, 28. *Study:* Col St Aspais, Fountainebleau; Lycée Albert Sarraut, Hanoi; Ecole Libre des Sci Polit; Sorbonne; Pembroke Col, Cambridge; Breveté de Ecol Nat Langues Orientales Vivantes, Licencié-es-Lettres. *Collections Arranged:* Avery Brundage Collection, 63-; Chang Dai-Chien (with catalog), 72; Hans Popper Collection (with catalog), 73; Exhib Archaeol Finds People's Repub China, 75; 5000 Years of Korean Art (ed & coauth, catalog), 79; Treasures from the Shanghai Museum, 6,000 Years of Chinese Art (ed, catalog), 83. *Pos:* Cur, Musee Cernuschi, Paris, 53; mem, Ecole Francaise d'Extrême-Orient, 54; cur, Blanchard de la Brosse Mus, Saigon & Louis Finot Mus, Hanoi, 54-58; Quai d'Orsay grant, Taiwan, 59; Asiatic Collections, M H De Young Mem Mus, San Francisco, 64; dir, Avery Brundage Collection, 65-68; dir & chief cur, Asian Art Mus San Francisco, 69-85; bd mem, Asian Art Found, 85; bd mem, Inst Sino-Am Studies; pres, Fr-Am Bilingual Sch; vpres, Chinese-Am Bilingual Sch, 81- *Teaching:* Prof art hist, Univ Calif, Berkeley, 62-65. *Awards:* Chevalier de l'ordre National de Merite, France, 70; Order Cult Merit, Korea, 80; Chevalier de la Legion d'Honneur, France, 83. *Publ:* Auth, Avery Brundage Collection, Chinese, Korean & Japanese Sculpture, 74; Bronze Vessels of Ancient China in the Avery Brundage Collection, 77; ed & coauth, Museum & University Collections of Asian Art in the San Francisco Bay Area, 77; 5000 Years of Korean Arts, 79; Treasures from the Shangha Museum, 6000 Years of Chinese Art, 83; and others. *Mailing Add:* Kerfelice Herbignac 44410 France

LE FEVRE, RICHARD JOHN
PAINTER, DESIGNER
b Rochester, NY, Feb 11, 31. *Study:* Rochester Inst Technol, BS, 55, MFA, 67. *Work:* State of Tenn, Nashville; Fall Creek Falls State Park, Tenn; E Tenn State Univ; Univ Tenn, Knoxville; Nat Bank NC, Charlotte. *Comn:* Oil, St Stephen's Church, Rochester, 60; acrylic on Plexiglas, Church of Epiphany, Rochester, 65; polymer, Marine Midland Bank, Rochester, 65; acrylic on Plexiglas, Capital Cadillac Corp, Atlanta, Ga, 70; acrylic on Plexiglas altarpiece, Tyson Episcopal Ctr, Knoxville, Tenn, 71. *Exhib:* Appalachian Corridors Exhib 1, Va, 68; Experiments in Art and Technology, High Mus, Atlanta, 69; Midsouth Competition, Parthenon Mus, Nashville, 70; Art USA 2, Univ Northern Ill, 71; Tenn Arts Comn, Dulin Gallery, Knoxville, 72. *Pos:* Designer, Todd Co, Rochester, 54-55 & S M Crossett, Rochester, 55-58; pres, Le Fevre Studios, Rochester, 58-65. *Teaching:* Dir arts & graphic arts, Rochester Inst Technol, 65-67; assoc prof design & area coord, Univ Tenn, Knoxville, 67- *Awards:* Purchase Award, Carroll Reece Mus, 71; Purchase Award, Mint Mus, 71; First, Second & Third Prizes, Graphic Art Show, Knoxville, 79; and over 50 awards in design. *Media:* Acrylic, Watercolor. *Mailing Add:* Rte 1 Lefevre/Heard Lane Seymour TN 37865

LEFRANC, MARGARET (MARGARET LEFRANC SCHOONOVER)
PAINTER, ILLUSTRATOR
b New York, NY. *Study:* Art Students League, NY; Kunstschule des Westerns, Berlin, Ger; Acad Grande Chaumiere, Paris, France; Acad Russe Paris; study with Andre l'Hote, Charles Bissiere, Antoine Bourdelle & Richard Merrick. *Work:* Hall of Fame, Oklahoma City; Univ Okla Press, Norman; Lowe Gallery, Univ Miami, Fla. *Exhib:* Pa Acad Fine Arts, Philadelphia, 36; New York World's Fair Fine Arts Exhib, 39; solo shows, Okla Art Ctr, 50 & Meridith Hunter Gallery, 81; Southwestern Ann, Tulsa, 52; Ann Exhib NMex Artists, Mus NMex, 56; Lowe Gallery Ann, Univ Miami, Fla, 62; Governor's Gallery, Santa Fe, NMex, 92; and others. *Pos:* Founder & dir, Guild Art Gallery, New York, 35-37; designer, colorist & stylist, Gilman Fabrics, Inc, New York, 38-42; liaison secy to cur, Cooper Union Mus, New York, 43-45. *Teaching:* Metrop Mus & Art Ctr, Miami, 83. *Awards:* Illustration Award, 50 Best Bks of Yr, Libr Cong, Washington, DC, 48; Hon Mention, Rodeo of Sante Fe, Mus of NMex, 55; Hon Mention, Temple Betham Invitational, Miami, Fla, 72. *Mem:* Artists Equity Asn (mem bd dirs, 60-76, pres, 61-63 & 65-67); Fla Artists Group. *Media:* Oil, Watercolor; Line, Graphics. *Res:* Pueblo pottery design for synoptic series of San Ildefonso pottery. *Publ:* Illusr, Maria, the Potter of San Ildefonso, Univ Okla Press, 48; Indians on Horseback, T Y Crowell, 48; Indians of the Four Corners, T Y Crowell, 52; ed, Songs of the Tewa, Sunstone Press, 76; illusr, Dance Around the Sun, T Y Crowell, 77. *Mailing Add:* 627 Camino de la Luz Santa Fe NM 87501

LEHMAN, ARNOLD L
MUSEUM DIRECTOR, ART HISTORIAN
b New York, NY, July 18, 44. *Study:* Johns Hopkins Univ, BA, 65, MA, 66; Yale Univ, MA, 68, PhD, 73. *Collections Arranged:* Archit of World Fairs (auth, catalog), Dallas Mus Fine Arts, Tex, 72; Boom or Bust, Am Painting from World War I through 1939, 74; Art Deco, 74; Judaica from Am Collections, 75; The Vanderbilts: Collectors, 75; Am Magic Realists (auth, catalog), 76; World of Haitian Printing, (auth, catalog), 77; 50 Years of Cuban Painting, 77; Oskar Schlemmer (ed, catalog). *Pos:* Chester Dale Fel, Metrop Mus Art, New York, 69-70; dir, Urban Improvements Prog, New York, 70-73; Parks Coun, New York, 73-74; Metrop Mus & Art Ctr, Miami, Fla, 74-79; Baltimore Mus Art, Md, 79- *Teaching:* Lectr art hist, Cooper Union Sch Art & Archit, New York, 69-71; Hunter Col, City Univ New York, 71-72. *Mem:* Am Asn Mus Dirs (pres, trustee). *Res:* American architecture and urban planning; American painting, 20th century; late 19th century French painting. *Mailing Add:* Baltimore Mus Art Art Museum Dr Baltimore MD 21218

LEHMAN, MARK AMMON
EDUCATOR, SCULPTOR
b Philadelphia, Pa, Apr 12, 30. *Study:* Philadelphia Col Art, BFA, 60; Tyler Sch Art, MFA, 62; Columbia Univ, 64- *Comn:* Head of J F Kennedy, Students of Trenton State Col, 65. *Exhib:* NJ State Mus Ann, 66 & 67; Columbia Univ, 66 & 77; Pa Guild Craftsmen Traveling Exhib, 67; NJ Designer Craftsmen, NJ State Mus, 68; Centenary Col, 76. *Teaching:* Asst prof art hist, ceramics & sculpture, Trenton State Col, 63- *Awards:* NJ Tercentenary Exhib Award, 64. *Mem:* NJ Designer Craftsmen. *Media:* Clay. *Publ:* Auth, Article pertaining to ceramic kiln burners, Studio Potter, 75. *Mailing Add:* Dept of Art Trenton State Col Hillwood Lakes Trenton NJ 08625

LEHR, JANET
DEALER
b New York, NY, June 7, 37. *Study:* New York Univ, BA, 55; Brooklyn Law Sch, LLB/JD, 58. *Pos:* Co-partner, Gallery 6M, 62-72; owner, Janet Lehr Inc, 72-; co-owner, Vered Gallery, East Hampton, NY, 88- *Mem:* Founding mem Asn Int Photog Art Dealers; Antiquarian Booksellers Am. *Res:* Photographically illustrated books of the 19th century. *Specialty:* Fine vintage photographs of both the 19th and 20th century; exceptional contemporary. *Publ:* Auth, Talbot's Role in the History of Photography, Antiquarian Bookman, J Chernofsky, 78; John Thomson, History of Photography, 1/80; and 32 catalogs. *Mailing Add:* 891 Park Ave New York NY 10021

LEHR, MIRA T(AGER)
PAINTER
b New York, NY, Sept 22, 38. *Study:* Vassar Col, BA, 56; Boston Mus Sch, 57; pvt study with Robert Motherwell & James Brooks, 68 & 69. *Work:* Bass Mus, Miami Beach, Fla; Univ Tex, Tyler; Vassar Col Mus, Poughkeepsie, NY; Bacardi Collection, Miami, Fla. *Comn:* Large scale wall piece, Art Enterprises Inc, Chicago, 86; monoprints, Interterra Corp, Miami, 88. *Exhib:* Women Caucus Art Travels, Philadelphia Art Alliance, Pa, 82; A Century of Women's Achievements, La Worlds Fair, New Orleans, 85; Ann Hortt Mem, Ft Lauderdale Mus, Fla, 86 & 89; Ann Exhib Contemp Am Paintings, Soc of 4 Arts, Palm Beach, Fla, 87-90; The Way of the Women Artist, Hollywood Art & Cult Ctr, Miami, Fla, 89; Cuban Mus, Miami, Fla, 89. *Pos:* Chmn, Continuum Inc, 80-89 & Art in Public Places, Miami Beach, Fla, 85-91; trustee, Art in Public Places, Dade Co, 86-90. *Awards:* Best in Show, Visions Aquarius, Prof Artists Guild, 80; Purchase Award, First Ann Works on Paper, Univ Tex, 86; Purchase Award, Belmont Towbin Found, 90. *Bibliog:* Giulio V Blanc (auth), Bombs & Oranges, Discovering Miami's Explosive Art Scene, Arts Mag, 11/90; Linda Nochlin (auth), article, Best Mag, 10/5/90; Elisa Turner (auth), Luria group poses lively dialogue, Miami Herald, 6/6/90. *Mem:* Womens Caucus Art (bd dirs, 83-86); Nat Asn Women Artists. *Media:* Acrylic, Mixed Media. *Dealer:* Gloria Luria Gallery 1033 Kane Concourse Bay Harbor FL 33154; Jaffe Baker Gallery 608 Banyan Trail Boca Raton FL 33431. *Mailing Add:* 5215 Pine Tree Dr Miami Beach FL 33140

LEHRER, LEONARD
PAINTER, LITHOGRAPHY
b Philadelphia, Pa, Mar 23, 35. *Study:* Philadelphia Col Art, BFA, 56; Univ Pa, MFA, 60. *Work:* Mus Mod Art & Metrop Mus Art, New York; Nat Gallery of Art & Libr Cong, Washington, DC; Philadelphia Mus Art; Cleveland Mus Art; Sprengel Mus, Hannover, WGer. *Comn:* Paintings, Kreissparkasse, Hildesheim, WGer, 90. *Exhib:* Brooklyn Mus Print Show, 72; one-man shows, Utah Mus Fine Arts, 73 & 82 & Marian Locks Gallery, Philadelphia, 74, 77 & 84; Galerie Kuhl, Hannover, Ger, 79, 82 & 91; 4th Miami Int Print Biennial, 80; 7th Int Print Biennial, Bradford, Eng, 82; and others. *Teaching:* Prof art & chmn dept, Univ NMex, 70-74; prof art, Univ Tex, San Antonio, 74-77; prof art & dir, Sch Art, Ariz State Univ, Tempe, 77-90, dir, Visual Arts Res Studios, 84-90; chair, Dept Art & Art Prof, New York Univ, 91. *Awards:* First Prize, Fourth Miami Int Print Biennial, 80; Heitland Found Prize, Celle, WGer, 80; Gold Medal Award, Nat Soc Arts & Letters, 81; and others. *Bibliog:* V D Coke (auth), The Painter and the Photograph, Univ NMex Press, 72; Fritz Eichenberg (auth), The Art of the Print, Abrams, 76; E A Quensen (publ), The Art of Leonard Lehrer, WGer, 86. *Mem:* Col Art Asn Am. *Media:* Oil, Lithography. *Dealer:* Galerie Kuhl Hannover Ger; Orion Editions NY. *Mailing Add:* Chair, Dept Art & Art Professions, New York Univ Barney Bldg #300, 34 Stuyvesant St New York NY 10003

LEIBER, GERSON AUGUST
PRINTMAKER
b Brooklyn, NY, Nov 12, 21. *Study:* Art Students League; Brooklyn Mus Art Sch. *Work:* Metrop Mus Art, New York; Whitney Mus Am Art, New York; Nat Gallery Art, Washington, DC; Libr Cong, Washington, DC; Boston Mus Fine Arts. *Comn:* Print eds, Assoc Am Artists & Int Graphic Arts Soc. *Exhib:* Am Prints Today, USA, New York, 59; Cincinnati Int Biennial, 60; American Prints, in Russia, Rome, Italy, Mexico City, Mex & Salzburg, Ger; Libr Cong Exhibs; and many others. *Teaching:* Instr graphics & illus, Newark Sch Fine & Indust Art, 61-68. *Awards:* Tiffany Fels, 57 & 60; Audubon Medals of Honor for Graphics, 63-65; Am Nat Print Exhib Prize, Assoc Am Artists Gallery. *Bibliog:* Frank Getlein (auth), Bite of the Print, Potter, 63; Hooten & Kaiden (auth), Mother and Child in Modern Art, Meredith Corp. *Mem:* Assoc Nat Acad; Soc Am Graphic Artists (pres, 78-80); Audubon Artists. *Media:* Intaglio. *Publ:* Illusr, Crisis (poem), Oxhead Press, 69. *Mailing Add:* 7 Park Ave New York NY 10016

LEIBERT, PETER R
CERAMIST, SCULPTOR
b New York, NY, Mar 13, 41. *Study:* Buffalo State Univ, BS(art educ), 63; Indiana Univ, MS(art educ), 67, MFA(ceramics, with distinction), 67. *Exhib:* one-man shows, Portogallo Gallery, New York, 69, Cooper Union, New York, 71 & Kogei Gallery, Dobbs Ferry, NY, 74; American Crafts Nat, Currier Gallery Art, Manchester, NH, 81; Gallery at Workbench, New York, 87; New Port Art Mus, RI, 88; Pritman & Eams Gallery, East Hampton, Long Island, 88. *Teaching:* Artist in residence, Haystack Mountain Sch Crafts, Deer Isle, Maine, 78; prof ceramics, Conn Col, 67-, chmn dept art, 78- *Awards:* Purchase Prize, Rose Arts Festival, Norwich, Conn, 70-78 & 83; Best in Clay, 22nd Ann Exhib, 78 & First Prize for Sculpture, New Eng Regional Exhib, 83, Mystic Art Asn. *Mem:* Am Crafts Coun; Nat Coun Educ Ceramic Arts; Soc Conn Craftsmen. *Media:* Ceramics; Mixed. *Publ:* Illusr, Back to gum prints, Camera 35, 70 & A portfolio of photography, Pukka, 70; contribr, The artist as photographer, Conn Col Alumni News, 71. *Mailing Add:* Dept Art Conn Col Box 5473 270 Mohegan Ave New London CT 06320-4196

LEIBOVITZ, ANNIE
PHOTOGRAPHER
b 1950. *Exhib:* Nat POrtrait Gallery, Washington, DC, 91; Int Ctr Photog, New York, 91; Phoenix Art Mus, Ariz, 92; Mus Art, Ft Lauderdale, Fla, 92; Inst Contemp Art, Boston, Mass, 92; Southeastern Ctr Contemp Art, Winston-Salem, NC, 92; Joslyn Art Mus, Omaha, Nebr, 93; Friends of Photography, Ansel Adams Ctr, San Francisco, Calif, 93; Jacksonville Mus Art, Fla, 93; Utah Mus Fine Arts, Salt Lake City, 93. *Pos:* Photographer, Rolling Stone Mag, ten yrs, chief photographer, 73- *Publ:* Auth (introduction by Tom Wolfe), untitled, forthcoming. *Dealer:* Sidney Janis, 110 West 57th Street, New York, NY 10019. *Mailing Add:* 55 Van Dam New York NY 10013

LEIBOWITZ, BERNICE
PAINTER, EDUCATOR
b Brooklyn, NY, Nov 2, 29. *Study:* Hunter Col, BA, 50, MA, 53; Art Students League, 55. *Work:* Schering-Plough Collection, Madison, NJ, 81 & 82. *Exhib:* Affiliate Group Show, Newark Mus, NJ, 78; Art of the North East, Silvermine Art Guild, New Canaan, Conn, 90; The New Romanticism, Pleiades Gallery, New York, 90; Art From New York City, Hispano 20 Gallery, Barcelona, Spain, 90; Art Educators as Artists, Glassboro State Col, NJ, 90. *Pos:* Bd dir, Arts Ctr, 80-, chmn, 89- *Teaching:* Instr fine art, Bergen Community Col, 74- *Bibliog:* Meredith Hall (auth), Bernice Leibowitz' Haunting Images, Art Speak, 3/90; Eileen Watkins (auth), Celebration of Spring, Sun, Star Ledger, 2/87; Carnival of Color, Manhattan Arts, 11/87. *Mem:* Nat Asn Women Artists; Artists Equity. *Media:* Acrylic. *Mailing Add:* 144 N Terrace Place New Milford NJ 07646

LEICESTER, ANDREW JOHN
ENVIRONMENTAL ARTIST
b Birmingham, Eng, Mar 5, 48. *Study:* Portsmouth Polytechnic, England, BA, 69; Manchester Polytechnic, England, MA, 70; Univ Minn, Minneapolis, MFA, 72. *Work:* Walker Art Ctr; Sheldon Mem Art Gallery. *Comn:* Paradise (watergarden), Colo Territorial Correctional Facility, Canon City, 86; Cincinnati Gateway (park entrance), Bicentennial Commons, Cincinnati, 88; Riverwalk at Piers 3 & 5 (promenade and overlook), Philadelphia, Pa, 90; Genetic Eng Bldg (roof, facade and atrium), Iowa State Univ, Ames, 90; Zanja Madre (watergarden), Los Angeles, 92. *Exhib:* Invitation, 75 & The River--Images of the Mississippi, 76, Walker Art Ctr; Proposals for Sawyer Point, Contemp Art Ctr, Cincinnati, 77; Artpark, Lewiston, NY, 78; Art on the Beach, Creative Time, Battery Park, New York, 80; Artists Gardens & Parks, Hayden Gallery, 81; Nature-Sculpture, Wurttembergischer, Kunstverein, Stuttgart, WGer, 81; The Artist As Social Designer, Los Angeles County Mus Art, 85; The Texas Landscape 1900-1986, Mus Fine Arts, Houston, 86. *Pos:* Bd dirs, Pub Art St Paul, Minn. *Teaching:* Instr sculpture & drawing, Carleton Col, Minn, 73-74; instr sculpture, Minneapolis Col Art & Design, 75-80; instr, Sch Landscape Archit, Univ Minn, St Paul, 85; vis fel, Royal Melbourne Inst Technol, Australia, 86. *Awards:* Fel, Minn Arts Bd, 80-81, Nat Endowment Arts, 81-82, Bush Found, 77, 83, 90 & McKnight Found, 85. *Bibliog:* John Beardsley (auth), The New Urban Landscape, Earthworks and Beyond, Abbeville Press, 89; Garth Rockcastle (auth), Ethics in Paradise, VIA Mag, Vol 10, 90; Donlyn Lyndon (auth), Conceiving a Courtyard, PLACES Mag, Vol 6, No 3, 90. *Media:* Mixed. *Publ:* Double Crossing, a George Washington Memorial for Dade County Courthouse, Flagler St, Miami, 87; Cincinnati Gateway, Main Entrance to Bicentennial Commons Part, Cincinnati, 88; Riverwalk at Piers 3 & 5, Delaware Avenue, Philadelphia, 90. *Mailing Add:* 1500 Jackson St NE Minneapolis MN 55413

LEIGH, HARRY E
SCULPTOR, PAINTER
b Buffalo, NY, Nov 7, 31. *Study:* Albright Art Sch, dipl, 52; State Univ New York, Buffalo, BA, 53; painting with Richard Pousette-Dart, 56-60; Columbia Univ, MA, 59. *Work:* Va Mus Fine Art, Richmond; Birchfield Collection, Buffalo. *Exhib:* Albright-Knox Art Gallery, Buffalo, NY, 52, 53 & 57; Everson Mus, Syracuse, 61; one-man shows, Brata Gallery, New York, 67 & 69, Berkshire Mus, Mass, 71, OK Harris Gallery, New York, 74 & 78 & Ramapo Col, Mahwak, NJ, 87; Projected Artist at Work, Finch Col Mus, New York, 71; Rockland Ctr Arts, Nyack, NY, 82; Mt Aramah Exhib, Arden, NY, 86; Anita Shaposky Gallery, Jim Thorp, Pa, 88. *Teaching:* Painting teacher, Rockland Community Col, Suffern, NY, currently. *Awards:* MacDowell Fel, artist-in-residence, 68-70, 72, 74-75, 83, 85 & 86; Yaddo Fel, artist-in-residence, 72, 79, 80 & 87; Creative Arts Prog Serv Fel, 78-79; Hand Hollow Found Fel, 80; Artist-in-residence, Thorpe Intermedia Gallery, 88. *Bibliog:* Martin Last (auth), rev, Art News, 1/69; Elizabeth Frank Perlmutter (auth), article, Art News, 9/74; Grace Glueck (auth), Harry Leigh & Keith Long, New York Times, 5/12/78. *Mem:* MacDowell Fel Comt (treas). *Media:* Wood, Bricks; House Paint, Oil. *Dealer:* OK Harris Gallery 383 W Broadway New York NY 10012. *Mailing Add:* 66 Haverstraw Rd Suffern NY 10901

LEIGH, JACK DAVID
PHOTOGRAPHER
b Savannah, Ga, Nov 8, 48. *Study:* Univ Ga, BA, 72. *Work:* NY Univ; Gibbes Art Gallery; Telfair Acad Arts & Sci, Savannah, Ga; Coca-Cola USA; Fed Reserve Bank. *Exhib:* one-man shows, NY Univ Sch Arts, 82, Gibbes Art Gallery, 83 & Telfair Acad Arts & Sci, 86; The Face of the South, Mus Palazzo Venezia, Rome, Italy, 85; Fay Gold Gallery, 88. *Teaching:* Instr, Southern Images Photo Workshops. *Awards:* Distinction Award, Am Asn Mus; Award of Excellence, Am Inst Graphics Arts; Southern Arts Fedn, Nat Endowment for the Arts Photograph Fel. *Bibliog:* Vivien Raynor (auth), article, NY Times, 2/82; Kathryn Livingston (auth), Review, Am Photog, 6/84; Katie McGrail (auth), Boston Herald (review), 86. *Mem:* Soc Photog Educ. *Publ:* Auth, Oystering: A Way of Life, Carolina Art Asn, 83; The Ogeechee: A River and Its People, Univ Ga Press, 86; Nets & Doors: Shrimping in Southern Waters, Southern Images, 89. *Mailing Add:* 132 E Oglethorpe Ave Savannah GA 31401

LEIGHTON, DAVID S R
ADMINISTRATOR
b Regina, Sask, Feb 20, 28. *Pos:* Dir, Sch Fine Arts, Banff Ctr, 70-82; Dir, Nat Ctr for Mgt Res Develop, Univ Western Ont, 86- *Mailing Add:* c/o Nat Ctr for Mgt Res Develop Univ Western Ont London ON N6A 3K7 Canada

LEIGHTON, PATRICIA MACINNES
ENVIRONMENTAL ARTIST, SCULPTOR
b Greenock, Scotland, July 8, 50; Brit citizen. *Study:* Edinburgh Col Art, Scotland, BA(drawing & painting), 70-74; Sch Fine Art, Poznan, Poland, with Prof Magdalena Abakanowicz, MA, 74-76. *Work:* Univ Glasgow, Scotland; St Albans Abbey, Eng; Kyoto Mus, collab with Neagu, Japan; Djerassi Found, Woodside, Calif; Grizedale Gallery in the Forest, Hawkshead, Eng. *Comn:* Wake, comn by Carl Djerassi, Woodside, Calif, 84; Silurian Cant & Vigil, Grizedale Forest & Northern Arts, Cumbria, Eng, 86; Meall A Chairn, Glasgow Garden Festival, Scotland, 88; Seven Runes, Broward Co Cult Affairs Coun, Ft Lauderdale, 90-92; Motorola-M8, Motorola, Easter Inch, Scotland, 92-93. *Exhib:* Edinburgh Arts 76, Fruitmarket Gallery, Scotland, 77; Five Artist Exhib, Arsenali Gallery, Amalfi, Italy, 79; solo exhibs, AIR Gallery, London, Eng, 80, Third Eye Ctr, Glasgow, Scotland, 82, Newcastle Polytechnic Gallery, Eng, 83 & Kala Inst, Berkeley, Calif, 83; Wall to Wall, Smith Art Gallery & Mus, Stirling, Scotland, 88; 2nd Int Ephemeral Sculpture Exhib, Democrito Rocha Found, Fortaleza-Ceara, Brazil, 91. *Awards:* Artist-in-Residence Fel, Scottish Arts Coun, 77-79; Artist-in-Residence, Djerassi Found, 83-84; Sculptor in Residence, Grizedale Forest, Eng, Northern Arts & Forestry Comn, 86. *Bibliog:* Franco Zagari (auth), L'Architetettura del Giardino Contemporaneo, De Luca Edizioni d'Arte, 88; Graeme Murray (auth), Art in the Garden, Edinburgh, 89; Bill Grant & Paul Harris (auths), The Grizedale Experience, Canongate Press, 91. *Media:* All. *Mailing Add:* 40 Renwick St New York NY 10013

LEIN, MALCOLM EMIL
ADMINISTRATOR, DESIGNER
b Havre, Mont, July 19, 13. *Study:* Univ Minn, BArch. *Collections Arranged:* Fiber, Clay and Metal Biennial, 52-; Drawings USA, Biennial, 61-; Goldsmith, 70; The Introspective Italian, 71; Fifty Years of American Drawing, 77. *Pos:* Dir & pres, Minn Mus Art, 47-79. *Teaching:* Lectr, Macalester Col, St Paul, Minn, 47-50. *Mem:* Am Asn Mus. *Mailing Add:* 6200 E Hummingbird Lane Scottsdale AZ 85253

LEIPZIG, ARTHUR
PHOTOGRAPHER
b Brooklyn, NY, Oct 25, 18. *Study:* Photo League, 42; Paul Strand Workshop, 46. *Work:* Mus Mod Art, New York; Brooklyn Mus; Nat Gallery Art, Ottawa; Art Inst Chicago; Eastman House, Rochester, NY; Int Ctr Photog; Long Island Univ; Nat Mus Am Art, Washington, DC; Bank Am Art Prog, San Francisco; Bibliotheque Nationale, Paris; Consolidated Freightways Collection, San Francisco. *Exhib:* New Faces, 46, Xmas Sale of Photographs, 53, Family of Man, 55 & From the Mus Collection, 58, Mus Mod Art, New York; Photography as a Fine Art, Metropolitan Mus Art, New York, 61 & 62; Eastman House, Rochester, NY, 73; retrospective, Nassau Mus Fine Art, Roslyn, NY, 75; Photo League, Int Ctr Photog, 78, Mus City New York Plays, 88, Frumkin Adams Gallery, New York, 90; Photographs of Jewish Life

Around the World, Nassau & Queens Mus, NY, 82; Int Photog Art Exhibs, Beijing, China, 83; Daniel Wolf Gallery, Street Photograph, 86; Brooklyn Mus, Classic Photograph Mus Collection, 87; Hist Photog from Calif Collection, San Francisco, 89; one-man show, Photofind Gallery, New York, 90; Musee de la Civilisation, Quebec City, 90. *Pos:* Staff photogr, PM Newspaper, 42-46 & Int News Photo, 46-47. *Teaching:* Dir photog & prof art, Long Island Univ, 68- *Awards:* Nat Urban League Award, 67; res grant, 80-81 & Trustees Award Scholarly Achievement, 82 & 89, Long Island Univ; Excellence in teaching, David Newton, 89. *Bibliog:* Jacob Deschin (auth), Six great teachers, 35 M Photog, 74; Documentary Photography, Time Life Books, 83. *Mem:* Am Soc Mag Photogr. *Publ:* Contribr, US Camera Ann, 53, 54, 56 & 60; The Family of Man, Mus Mod Art, 55; Photography Yearbook, Fountain Press Ltd, 57, 59, 62 & 72; The Family of Children, Ridge Press, 77; auth, Photography & social change, Ventures in Res, 78; Sarah's Daughters, 88. *Mailing Add:* 378 Glen Ave Sea Cliff NY 11579

LEIS, MARIETTA PATRICIA
PAINTER
b Newark, NJ. *Study:* Univ Calif, Santa Monica Community Col, Parson, 78-82; Univ NMex, Albuquerque, MA, 85 & MFA, 88. *Work:* Mount Sinai Hosp, New York; Sunrise Develop Corp, Palm Springs, Calif; First Outerstate Bank, Albuquerque, NMex; Daytona Hilton, Fla; Compus Computer Serv, Dallas, Tex. *Exhib:* CHABOT Col, Hayward, Calif, 88; Collection 89-90, Ft Wayne Mus Art, Tenn, 89; Marietta Patricia Leis, Columns, St John's Col, Santa Fe, NMex, 90; Art of Albuquerque, Albuquerque Fine Arts Mus, NMex, 90; Arlingtons Winterfest, Arlington Mus Art, Tex, 90; St Johns Col, NMex, 90; Eastern NMex Univ, 92; and others. *Teaching:* Instr art & drawing, Univ NMex, Albuquerque, 85-88, art & contemp art, 88- *Awards:* Artist Grant, Artist Space, New York, 89; At The Edge, Touring Citation, Laguna Gloria Art Mus, Tex, 89; Hon Distinction, Int Art Biennial-Mus, Hisico, Capranica, Italy. *Bibliog:* W Clark (auth), Whats New?, Arts & Albuquerque J, 11/2/90; K Bennett (auth), Live Long & Make Art, Arts Plus, Albuquerque Voice, 11/7/90; L Allison (auth), Leis Uncovers the Illusion, New Mexican, Pasatiempo, 11/9/90. *Mem:* Albuquerque United Artists; Col Art Asn; Nat Asn Women Artists. *Media:* Oil, All Media. *Dealer:* John Cacciatore Dir Dartmouth St Gallery 3011 Monte Vista NE Albuquerque Neex 87106. *Mailing Add:* PO Drawer D Corrales NM 87048

LEITHAUSER, MARK ALAN
PAINTER, PRINTMAKER
b Detroit, Mich, June 22, 50. *Study:* Wayne State Univ, BA, 72, MA, 73, MFA, 74. *Work:* Nat Gallery Art; Brooklyn Mus; Libr Cong. *Exhib:* Michigan Focus, Detroit Inst Arts, 74; Boston Printmakers Nat Show, DeCordova Mus, Lincoln, Mass, 76; 30 Years of American Printmaking, Brooklyn Mus, 76; Nat Printmakers Show, Libr Cong, 77; In Celebration of Prints, Philadelphia Art Alliance, 80; Nat Print & Drawing Competition, Dulin Gallery Art, Knoxville, Tenn, 81; American Perspective, 81 & Close Focus, 87, Nat Mus Am Art; Recent Acquisitions on Paper, Corcoran Gallery Art, 81; solo exhibs, Coe Kerr Gallery, 89 & 92, Chrysler Mus, 93 & Corcoran Gallery, 93; Refiguring Nature, Mus Contemp Art, Ft Worth, 91. *Pos:* Deputy Chief Design, Nat Gallery Art, 74- *Awards:* Purchase Award, Nat Print Show, Libr Cong, 75, Nat Printmakers Show, Nat Mus Am Art, 77 & Nat Print & Drawing Exhib, Dulin Gallery Art, 81; Leslie Cheek Design Award, 88; Presidential Design Award, 84 & 88. *Media:* Painting, Etching. *Dealer:* Hom Gallery 2103 O St NW Washington DC 20037; Coe Kerr Gallery 49 E 82nd St New York NY 10028. *Mailing Add:* 3614 Idaho Ave NW Washington DC 20016

LEKBERG, BARBARA HULT
SCULPTOR
b Portland, Ore, Mar 19, 25. *Study:* Univ Iowa, BFA & MA, with Humbert Albrizio; Simpson Col, hon DFA, 64. *Work:* Montclair Mus Art, NJ; Des Moines Art Ctr, Iowa; Knoxville Art Ctr, Tenn; Whitney Mus Am Art; General Electric Collection, Fairfield, Conn. *Comn:* Three interior sculptures, Beldon-Stratford Hotel, Chicago, 53; three interior sculptures, Socony-Mobil Co, New York, 55; lobby relief, Riedl & Freede Advert, Clifton, NJ, 64; life-size figures, Bayfield Clark, Bermuda, 71 & 74; Orpheus (10 ft work), Simpson Col, Iowa, 84; life size figure, Trafalgar House Realty, New York, 86; and others. *Exhib:* Five Pa Acad Fine Arts Ann, Philadelphia, 50-62; New Talent, Am Fedn Arts Traveling Show, 59-60; Recent Sculpture USA, Mus Mod Art, New York, 59; one-man shows, Sculpture Ctr, New York, 59, 65, 71, 75, 77 & 83; traveling solo show, Birmingham Mus Art, Ala & Columbia Mus Art, SC, 73; retrospective, Mt Holyoke Col Mus, Mass, 78; Contemporary Sculpture at Chesterwood, Stockbridge, Mass, 88. *Teaching:* Fac, Col New Rochelle, 80-84;; Philadelphia Col Art, 81- *Awards:* Am Inst Arts & Lett Grant, 56; Guggenheim Found Fels, 57 & 59; Margaret Hexter Prize, Nat Sculpture Soc, 88. *Bibliog:* Interview, Hudson Valley Cable TV, 81; The Figure (film), Nat Sculpture Soc, 83; Virginia Watson-Jones (auth), Contemporary American Women Sculptors, Oryx Press, 86. *Mem:* Sculptors Guild; Nat Sculpture Soc; Nat Acad Design. *Media:* Bronze, Steel. *Dealer:* Sculpture Ctr 167 E 69th St New York NY 10021. *Mailing Add:* 911 Stuart Ave Mamaroneck NY 10543

LELAND, WHITNEY EDWARD
PAINTER, EDUCATOR
b Washington, DC, Apr 12, 45. *Study:* Memphis Acad Arts, BFA; Univ Tenn, Knoxville, MFA. *Work:* Springfield Art Mus, Mo; Hunter Mus Art, Chattanooga, Tenn; Nat Mus Am Art, Smithsonian Inst, Washington, DC; Ark Art Ctr, Little Rock; Chase Manhattan Bank, New York. *Exhib:* Western Asn Art Mus, traveling exhib, 79-81; Southern Abstraction: Five Painters, traveling exhib, 83-84; Watercolor USA 1986: The Monumental Image, Springfield Art Mus, Mo, 86; 10 Years of Southeast Seven, SE Conf Contemp Art, Winston-Salem, NC, 87; solo exhib, Cumberland Gallery, Nashville, 90. *Teaching:* Asst prof, Univ Tenn, Knoxville, 70-78, assoc prof, 78-86, prof painting, 86- *Awards:* Fel Grant, nat Endowment Art, SE Conf Contemp Art, 77; Nominated, Eighth Ann Awards Visual Arts, SE Conf Contemp Art, Winston-Salem, NC, 88; Arches & Rives Paper Award, Arjo Wiggins USA, Springfield Art Mus, 92. *Bibliog:* Bennett Schiff (auth), In a Tobacco City the Arts are Put in Place-Out Front, Smithsonian, Vol 9, No 10, 1/79; Don Kurka (auth), Southern Abstraction, Art Papers, Vol 8, No 2, 3-4/84; Faith Heller (auth), Ten Years of 'Southeast Seven': An Abundance of Individual Visions, Arts J, 1/88. *Media:* Acrylic, Watercolor. *Dealer:* Cumberland Gallery Nashville Tenn. *Mailing Add:* Art Dept Univ Tenn-Knoxville Knoxville TN 37996

LEM, RICHARD DOUGLAS
PAINTER
b Los Angeles, Calif, Nov 24, 33. *Study:* Univ Calif, Los Angeles, BA; Calif State Univ, Los Angeles, MA; Otis Art Inst; Calif Inst Arts; also with Rico LeBrun & Herbert Jepson. *Work:* San Diego Fine Arts Gallery. *Exhib:* California: South, San Diego Fine Arts Gallery, 65; two-man show, Palos Verdes Art Gallery, 68; Lynn Kottler Galleries, New York, 73; Galerie Mouffe, Paris, France, 76; Le Salon des Nations, Paris, France, 84; plus others. *Awards:* Los Angeles Fine Arts Soc & Art Guild Award for Painting, 65. *Media:* Oil, Watercolor. *Publ:* Auth, illusr, Miles Journey, 83. *Mailing Add:* 1861 Webster Ave Los Angeles CA 90026

LEMER, ELLEN TERRY
DEALER, COLLECTOR
b Brooklyn, NY, Dec 27, 43. *Study:* Ithaca Col, 61-64; Hofstra Univ, BA, 65; NY Sch Interior Design, cert, 71. *Work:* Brooklyn Mus. *Collections Arranged:* Ideas '79, Resources Coun Show, 79. *Pos:* Art consult, Bass & Lemer, New York, 79- & MMT Sales Inc, New York, 80- *Bibliog:* O Gueft (ed), article, Interiors, 12/79. *Specialty:* Contemporary paintings, constructions, fiber objects and sculpture plus some ethnic art. *Collection:* Works by younger contemporary artists: Neda al Hilali, Leslie Goldberg, David Kraisler, Lee Milmon, Beth Ames Swartz and Jim Waid. *Mailing Add:* 120 E 81st St No 93 New York NY 10028

LEMIEUX, ANNETTE ROSE
CONCEPTUAL ARTIST, PAINTER
b Norfolk, Va, Oct 11, 57. *Study:* Northwestern Conn Community Col, AA, 77, Hartford Art Sch, Univ Hartford, Conn, BFA, 80. *Work:* Mus Mod Art, Chase Manhattan Bank, Dannheisser, New York; Rooseum, Malmö, Sweden; Okla Art Mus, Okla City; Elaine Dannheisser Found, New York; Israel Mus, Jerusalem, Israel. *Exhib:* Whitney Biennial, Whitney Mus Am Art, New York, 87 & 89; Colleccion Sonnabend, Centro d'Arte Reina Sofia, Madrid, Spain, 87; solo exhibits, Wadsworth Mus, Hartford, Conn, 88 & The Appearance of Sound, Ringling Mus, Sarasota, Fla, 89, New Mus, New York, 89, Galerie Monika Sprü, Köln, WGer, 90, Rhona Hoffman Gallery, Chicago, 90, Josh Baer Gallery, New York, 91, Stichting De Appel, Amsterdam, Holland, 92; Art at the End of the Social, Rooseum, Malmö, Sweden, 80; Curents, Inst Contemp Art, Boston, Mass, 87; Extreme Order, Lia Ruma Galerie, Naples, Italy, 87; Coleccion Sonnabend, Centro d'Arte Reina Sofia, Ministerio Cult, Madrid, Spain; Reprised De Vues, Halle Sud/Geneve, Geneva, Switz, 88; Art and the End of the Social, Rooseum, Malmo, Sweden, 88; Nat Mus Am Art, Smithsonian Inst, Washington, DC, 89; San Francisco Mus Mod Art, Calif, 90; Albright Knox Mus, Buffalo, NY, 89; Corcoran Gallery, Washington, DC, 90; Newport Harbor Art Mus, Newport Beach, Calif, 90; Oklahoma City Art Mus, Okla, 91; Josh Baer Gallery, New York, 92; More Than One Photography, Mus Mod Art, New York, 92. *Teaching:* Visiting artist & lecturer at mus, schools & organizations for the past 7 years. *Awards:* New York Fel for Painting, 87; Nat Endowments Arts Painting Grant, 87 & 91; Mies van der Rohe Stipendium, Kaiser-Wilhelm Mus, Krefeld, Ger, 92. *Bibliog:* Renee Steenbergen (auth), Annette Lemieux at De Appel, NRC Handelsblad (Dutch), 2/92; Holland Cotter (auth), Annette Lemieux and Annette Messager, New York Times, 4/24/92; Kim Levin (auth), Annette Lemieux/Annette Messager, The Village Voice, Voice Choices, 5/5/92. *Publ:* Beyond Boundaries (Jerry Saltz, auth), Rizzolli, 86; Contribr, Unexpressionism (Germant Celant, auth), Rizzolli, 88; Memoirs of a Survivor, ZG Publ, Brooke Alexander Inc, 89. *Dealer:* Josh Baer Gallery 270 Lafayette St New York NY 10012. *Mailing Add:* 153 W 27th St No 1005 New York NY 10001-6203

LEMIEUX, BONNE A
PAINTER
b Elmwood Park, Ill, Aug 3, 21. *Study:* Los Angeles Art League, 82-83; Studied with Jake Lee, 82-83; Los Angeles Valley Col, 82-84. *Work:* City of Los Angeles Permanent Art Collection; Norwalk City Hall, Calif; Ernie Pyle Sch, Bellflower, Calif; Salvation Army Tabernacle, Hollywood. *Comn:* Portrait of Mayor, City of Norwalk, 90; Hist Bldg, walleck, Shave, Stanard & Blender, Woodland Hills Calif, 90. *Exhib:* 119th Ann Am Watercolor Exhib, Salmagundi Club, New York, 86; Women Painters W, Univ Del, Newark, 87; Am Contemp Masters Invitational, Dr Sun Yat-Sen Mem Hall, Taipei, Taiwan, 87; Old Bergen, Ky Highlands Mus, Ashland, 87; Artists Soc Int, E Co Performing Arts Ctr, El Cajon, Calif, 89. *Teaching:* Art instr watercolor, Creative Art Ctr, Burbank, 91- *Awards:* Best of Show, Valley Artists Guild, 80; Art Store & More Award, 86; Bronze Medal, Artists of the Southwest, 88. *Bibliog:* David Kozinski (auth), Bonnie LeMieux, versatile artist, Artists Market, 76; Ernest Kay (ed), Bonnie LeMieux, The World Who's Who of Women, 86; Judy Shay (auth), Arts Glendale News Press, 89. *Mem:* Valley Watercolor Soc; Women Painters W; San Fernando Valley Art

Club (vpres, 77 & pres, 78); Women Artists W; assoc mem Am Watercolor Soc. *Media:* Watercolor, Oil. *Dealer:* Los Angeles Art Asn Galleries 825 N La Cienega Blvd Los Angeles CA 90046. *Mailing Add:* 2370 Laurel Canyon Blvd Hollywood CA 90046

LEMIEUX, IRENEE
PAINTER
b Quebec, Can, Aug 3, 31. *Study:* Laval Univ; Conserv de Musique de Quebec, Montreal; Fontainebleau, France. *Work:* La Minerve, Quebec. *Exhib:* Third Salon Int de la Riviera, Grasse, France; 3rd Salon Int de la Cote d'Azur, Chateau des Requiers; 2nd Salon Int du Carnaval de Nice; 2nd Salon Int de Baden-Baden, Allemagne, 73; 7th Grand Prix Int Painting & Sculpture, Antibes, 74; among others. *Awards:* First Prize with Gold Medal, 3rd Salon Int de la Cote d'Azur, 73; Spec First Prize with Gold Medal, Acad de Lutece, Paris, 73; Second Prize with Silver Medal, 7th Grand Prix Int Painting & Sculpture, 74; and others. *Bibliog:* Roland Laznikas (auth), article, 3/73 & Raymond Clermont (auth), article, 6/74, La Rev Mod, Paris; and others. *Mem:* Asn Beaux-Arts Cannes. *Media:* Acrylic. *Mailing Add:* 5 Ave du Pont Scott Quebec PQ G1N 3S3 Canada

LEMON, ROBERT S, JR
EDUCATOR, HISTORIAN
b Pittsburg, Kans, Oct 1, 38. *Study:* Univ Mo, Kansas City, BA, 62; Ohio Univ, MA, 69 & PhD, 75. *Pos:* Mem, Orlando Airport Art Selection Comt, Orlando Aviation Authority, Fla, 83-89; mem, bd visitors, Cornell Fine Arts Mus, Rollins Col, 82- *Teaching:* Prof art hist, Rollins Col, Winter Park, Fla, 73-, chmn, art dept, 80- *Mem:* Southeastern Col Art Conf (bd dirs, 86-); Col Art Asn. *Res:* Twentieth century American painting and sculpture. *Publ:* Auth, An interview with Lowell Nesbitt, Art Voices South, 78; The Figurative Pretext: A Comparative Explication of the Fiction of Alain Robbe-Grillet and the Painting of the Photo Realists, University Microfilms, 80; American Printmakers of the 30's (exhib catalog), Cornell Fine Arts Mus, 81; Photo Realism: Logical evolution from post-painterly abstraction, Southeastern Col Art Conf Rev, 87; Reliefs and Menhirs: The Sculpture of J G Naylor (exhib catalog), Univ Gallery of Gainesville, Fla, 88. *Mailing Add:* Rollins Col 2684 Winter Park FL 32789

LENGYEL, ALFONZ
HISTORIAN, WRITER
b Godollo, Hungary, Oct 21, 21; US citizen. *Study:* Univ Budapest, JD, 48, 48-50; San Jose State Col, BA(art hist), 58, MA(art hist), 59; Inst Art & Archeol, Univ Paris, PhD(summa cum laude),64; London Inst Applied Res, Hon JD, 75. *Pos:* Adj cur, Detroit Inst Arts, 68-72. *Teaching:* Mem fac, Univ Md Europ Div, Paris & Heidelberg, 63-68; prof art hist & classical archeol, Wayne State Univ, 68-72; prof & dir archeol prog, Northern Ky Univ, 72-77; dean & prof, Inst Mediterranean Art & Archeol, 77-82; coordr art hist & museology prog, Rosemont Col, 82-; prof art hist & cur, Goebel's Print Collection, Eastern Col, 85-87; adv prof, Fudan Univ, Shanghai, China, 87-; consult prof, Xian Jiaotong Univ, Xian, China, 88; Pres, Fudan Mus Found, 89-; US dir, Sino-Am Field Sch Archeol, Xian, China. *Awards:* Rockefeller Grant, Vienna, 57; S H Kress Grant, 67; Smithsonian Grant, 68; Gold Medal, Brazil Acad Humanities, 75. *Mem:* Int Coun Mus, Paris; Renaissance Soc Am; Am Asn Mus; Col Art Asn Am; Archeol Inst Am. *Publ:* Auth, Quattrocento, Kendall-Hunt, 72; coauth, L'Art et le Monde Moderne, Larousse, 72; Lexicon der Kristlichen Ikonographie, Herder Verlag, 73; ed & coauth, The Archaeology of Roman Pannonia, Ky Univ Press, 80; Selected prints from the Goebel's Collection, Eastern Col, 89; and others. *Mailing Add:* 1522 Schoolhouse Lane Ambler PA 19002-1989

LENHARDT, SHIRLEY M
PAINTER
b St Louis, Mo, Oct, 6, 34. *Study:* Univ Mo, BS(art ed), 74, MA (painting), 79, MFA (painting), 81. *Work:* Univ Mo Women's Ctr, Columbia, Mo; Univ Mo Chancellors Collection, Columbia, Mo. *Exhib:* Am Art Ann Middletown Fine Arts Ctr, Middletown, Ohio, 81-85; Ann Juried Nat Exhib, Ga Tech, Atlanta, 81 & 86; Vineyard Theatre Gallery, New York, 84; New Orleans Art Asn Nat, 84 & 88; Nepenthe Mundi Soc, Wichita, Kans, 86, 87, 88; Important Mo Women Artists, travelling exhib, 86; Missouri Women Artists, St Louis Univ, 91. *Collections Arranged:* Water: Moods & Reflections, 84, Shiao-Cai-Li-Chinese Artist, 86 & Salubi Onakufe-Nigerian Artist (auth catalog), 86 Hawthorn Gallery. *Pos:* Columbia Comm on the Arts, Columbia, Mo, 82-86 & Dir, Hawthorn Gallery Art, 84-87. *Teaching:* Columbia Adult Educ Painting, 70-, Drawing 75-81, Univ Mo, Columbia. *Awards:* Best of Show-Gold Medal, Black Forest Sch Creative Art, Int Exhib, 81; First Prize, Sno-Bird Gallery Nat Exhib, 86; First Prize, Emerald City Classic VI-VII, Nepenthe Mundi Soc, 87, 88. *Bibliog:* Tim Stokesberry (auth), A Matter of Style, Travel Host Mag, 5/85; Shawna Stallcup (auth), Images of Women, Columbia Missourian, 9/6/85. *Mem:* Columbia Art League Exec Bd, 91-92. *Media:* Acrylic, Oil; Watercolor. *Mailing Add:* 1118 St Christopher Columbia MO 65203

LENKER, MARLENE N
PAINTER, COLLAGE ARTIST
b Passaic, NJ, Mar 07, 32. *Study:* Fairleigh/Dickenson Univ, AA, 51; Montclair State Col, MA, 76. *Work:* Bergen Mus, Paramus, NJ; Montclair State Col, Upper Montclair, NJ; St Barnabas Medical Ctr, Livingston, NJ; Pepsico - Headquarters, Purchase, NY; Hewlitt Packard Headquarters, Fort Worth, Tex. *Comn:* Okla State Bank, Okla; ASEA, Brown Boveri Inc, NJ. *Exhib:* One-woman shows, David Gary Ltd, NJ, 83, Snug Harbor Cult Ctr, NY, 85, Adelle Taylor Gallery, Dallas, Tex, 86, Reece Galleries, New York, 87, Nathans Gallery, NJ, 89, Bloomfield Cult Ctr, NJ, 91 & David-Gary Gallery, NJ, 92; Miniature International, DeBello Gallery, Toronto, Can, 89; Miniature Invitational, Old Church Cult Ctr, Demarast, NJ, 90; Hummerick Mus, Cincinnati, Ohio, 90; Northcoast Collage Soc, Cincinnati Mus, Ohio, 90. *Pos:* Pres, West Essex Art Asn, 70-73. *Teaching:* Instr, Caldwell Col, Caldwell, NJ, 77-79. *Bibliog:* Skye Griffith (auth), Lyrical Landscapes, Staten Island Advance, 85; J Taylor Basker (auth), Art Review, NY Art Forms, 87; Eileen Watkins (auth), A Sense of Special, Star Ledger, 89. *Mem:* Nat Asn Women Artists (selection jury, 82-83); Artists Equity - New York Chapter; Soc of Layerists in Multimedia; North Coast Collage Soc; New Jersey Watercolor Soc. *Media:* Acrylic, Oil. *Publ:* Illusr, New Jersey Goodlife, Rene B Timpone, 88; contribr, New York Art Review, Krantz, 89; Layering - An Art of Time and Space, 91. *Dealer:* Adelle M Gallery 3317 McKinney Ave Dallas TX 75204. *Mailing Add:* 28 Northview Terr Cedar Grove NJ 07009

LENNON, TIMOTHY
PAINTING CONSERVATOR
b Chicago, Ill, Sept 18, 38. *Study:* Loras Col, BA; Univ Notre Dame, MA; Art Inst Chicago. *Pos:* Conservator, Art Inst Chicago, 80- *Mem:* Fel Am Inst Conserv Artistic & Hist Works; Int Inst Conserv Artistic & Hist Works. *Mailing Add:* Art Inst Chicago Michigan Ave at Adams St Chicago IL 60603

LENSSEN, HEIDI (MRS FRIDOLF JOHNSON)
PAINTER, LECTURER
b Frankfurt, Ger; US citizen. *Study:* Uffizi, Florence, Italy, copy degree, 25; Berlin State Acad Fine Arts, cert, 29; pvt study in Paris, France; also with Count Merveldt, Rome, 32-33; Acad Rossi, Florence; Ecole Arts et Metiers, Paris. *Work:* Berlin Mus; Kunsthalle, Mannheim; Springfield Mus Art, Utah. *Comn:* More than 100 comns, US & Europe. *Exhib:* Audubon Artists, 44 & 45; one-man show, Lynn Kottler Gallery, 54 & 70 & Walt Kuhn Gallery, 83; Show of Pastels, Kingston, NY, 80; Ann Leonard Gallery, Woodstock, NY, 86; Joshua Gallery, Kingston, NY; Paradox-Gallery, Woodstock, 86; and others. *Teaching:* Instr art & co-dir, Am Sch Design, New York, 37-42; lectr art, City Col New York Adult Educ, 45-58 & Franklin Sch Prof Arts, 52-57; instr art & lectr, Hunter Col, 49-51. *Awards:* Arthur Brown Gold Medal Oil Painting, 54. *Bibliog:* Marthe Davidson (auth), article, Art News, 37; Emily Genauer (auth), article, World Telegram New York, 40. *Mem:* Woodstock Artists Asn; life mem Mark Twain Soc. *Media:* Oil, Pastel. *Publ:* Auth & illusr, Art and Anatomy, J J Augustin, Inc & Barnes & Noble, 44; auth, Hands in Nature and Art, Studio Publ. *Mailing Add:* 34 Whitney Dr Woodstock NY 12498

LENT, BLAIR
ILLUSTRATOR, WRITER
b Boston, Mass, Jan 22, 30. *Study:* Boston Mus Sch, Cummings Mem travel fel to Switz & Italy, 1 yr, Bartlett travel fel to USSR, grad(hons). *Work:* Boston Pub Libr; Kerlan Collection, Univ Minn. *Comn:* Why the Sun and the Moon Live in the Sky (animated film), ACI Films, New York, 71; Christmas card design, UNICEF. *Exhib:* Solo Show, Wiggin Gallery, Boston, 70; Work by Five Major American Illustrators, Univ Art Gallery, Albany, NY, 72; Contemp Am Illusr Children's Bks, Rutgers Univ, 74-75; Brattleboro Mus, Vt, 80; Univ Conn, Storrs, 82. *Awards:* Silver Medal, Bienal Int Arte Grafice, Sao Paulo, Brazil, 65; Bronze Medal, Bienale Illustrators, Bratislava, Czech, 69; Caldecott Medal, Am Libr Asn, 73. *Bibliog:* Lee Hopkins (auth), Books Are By People, Citation, 69; Anne Commire (auth), Something About the Author, Gale, 72; and others. *Publ:* Auth & illusr, From King Boggen's Hall to Nothing-at-all, Little, 67; auth (pseud Ernest Small) & illusr, Baba Yaga, Houghton Mifflin, 66; illusr, The Funny Little Woman, Dutton, 72; auth & illusr, Bayberry Bluff, Houghton Mifflin, 84. *Mailing Add:* 10 Dana St No 208N Cambridge MA 02138

LEON, DENNIS
SCULPTOR, EDUCATOR
b London, Eng, July 27, 33; US citizen. *Study:* Temple Univ, BSc(educ), 56; Tyler Sch Art, MFA, 57. *Work:* Philadelphia Mus Art; Oakland Mus Art; San Francisco Mus Mod Art. *Comn:* Chevron Corp, 86. *Exhib:* Pa Acad Fine Arts, 56, 64 & 68; Philadelphia Mus Art; James Willis Gallery, 73; Univ Calif, Davis, 74; JPL Fine Arts, London, Eng, 75; Am 76, San Francisco Mus Mod Art, 77; Hanson-Fuller Golden Gallery, San Francisco, 77, 79, 81-82 & 84-85; San Jose Mus Art, 81; and others. *Teaching:* Prof sculpture, Philadelphia Col Art, 60-72 & Calif Col Arts & Crafts, 72-; vis artist, Sheffield Polytech, Eng, 75 & 76. *Awards:* Guggenheim Fel, 67; Nat Inst Arts & Lett Award, 67; MacDowell Fel, 81; Djerassi Found Fel, 83 & 84; and others. *Media:* Mixed Media. *Publ:* Auth, Paul Harris, 73. *Dealer:* Fuller Goldeen Gallery 228 Grant Ave San Francisco CA 94108. *Mailing Add:* 1254 E 12 St Oakland CA 94606

LEON, RALPH BERNARD
PAINTER, ILLUSTRATOR
b Atlantic City, NJ, Mar 10, 32. *Study:* Pratt Inst, BFA, 57; Ecole de Musique et Beaux Arts de Fontainebleau, Walter Damrosch Scholar, 58; La Grande Chaumiere, Paris, France, with Henri Goetz. *Work:* Found, State Univ NY Binghamton; Pentagon Art Collection, Washington, DC. *Exhib:* Butler Inst Am Art Ann, Youngstown, Ohio, 56, 73 & 74; one-man shows, Somerset Art Asn, Bernardsville, NJ, 76, Mayans Gallery, 84, 86, 89 & 92, Santa Fe; Santa Fe Six, Fenn Gallery, NMex, 77; Armory Show, Santa Fe, 77; Santa Fe Festival of Arts, 79 & 80; 30 Year Retrospective, Ernesto Mayans Gallery, Santa Fe, 82; Southwest '85, NMex Mus Fine Art, Santa Fe, 85. *Pos:* Illusr & art dir, Airscoop (flight safety mag), USAFE, Wiesbaden, 59-69; graphic artist, US Bureau Land Mgt, 76- *Awards:* Benjamin Altman Prize & Ranger Fund Purchase Prize, Nat Acad, New York, 74; Leon Lehrer Mem Award, Allied Artists Am Ann Exhib, New York, 75. *Bibliog:* Maiariv, Tel Aviv Daily, 71; Suzanne Deats (auth), Art, Santa Fe Reporter, 84; David Bell (auth), Art Market, Albuquerque, 86. *Media:* Oil. *Dealer:* Ernesto Mayans Gallery 601 Canyon Rd Santa Fe NM 87501. *Mailing Add:* 1707 Callejon Zenaida Santa Fe NM 87501

LEONARD, JOANNE
PHOTOGRAPHER, EDUCATOR
b Los Angeles, Calif, 1940. *Study:* Univ Calif, Berkeley, BA, 62; San Francisco State Col, 63-64. *Work:* US State Dept; Am Arts Doc Ctr, Exeter, England; San Francisco Mus Art; Int Mus Photog, Rochester, NY; Stanford Univ Mus, Palo Alto; Crocker Art Mus, Sacramento, Calif; Oakland Mus; and numerous pvt collections. *Exhib:* One-person shows, M H De Young Mem Mus, 68, San Francisco Art Inst, 74, Calif, Laguna Gloria Art Mus, Austin, Tex, 80 & Orange Coast Col Photo Gallery, Costa Mesa, 84; Photo Trans Form, San Francisco Mus Mod Art, 81; Vision & Expression, George Eastman House, Rochester, NY, 69-70; San Francisco Mus Art, 71, 75, 82 & 85; Summer Light, Light Gallery, New York, 72; Seattle Art Mus, Wash, 76; Whitney Mus Am Art, New York, 78; Franklin Inst, Philadelphia, 83; Santa Barbara Mus Art, Calif, 82, 83 & 86; Detroit Inst Arts, 92; Univ Mich Mus Art, 92. *Teaching:* Lectr, San Francisco Art Inst, 73-75 & Mills Col, Oakland, Calif, 82-83 & 86; prof art, Univ Mich Sch Art, Ann Arbor, 78- *Awards:* Phelan Award, 71; Nat Endowment, Photog Surveys Grant, 77; Josephine Nevins Keal Award, Univ Mich, 81. *Bibliog:* N W Janson (auth), History of Art, Abrams, New York, 86; de la Croix, Tansey & Kirkpatrick (auth), Gardner's Art through the Ages, Harcourt, Brace & Javonovich, San Diego, 91; Lucy Lippard (auth), Lost & Found (catalog essay), 92; and others. *Mem:* Soc Photog Educators; Col Art Asn. *Publ:* Sexual Discourses: From Aristotle to AIDS 1989, Univ Mich Press, 92. *Mailing Add:* Sch Art Univ Mich Ann Arbor MI 48109

LEONARDI, HECTOR
PAINTER, EDUCATOR
b Waterbury, Conn, Jan 18, 30. *Study:* RI Sch Design, BFA; Yale Univ, MFA. *Work:* Univ Notre Dame; Univ Bridgeport; Santa Fe Mus; Mattatuck Mus; Mus Boca Raton. *Exhib:* Albright-Knox Art Gallery, Buffalo, 66; Spectrum Gallery, New York, 72 & 73; Razor Gallery, New York, 74 & 75; Benson Gallery, Bridgehampton, NY, 76; Roy G Biv Gallery, New York, 78; Art Latitude Gallery, New York, 79; and others. *Teaching:* Instr color, design, drawing & painting, Univ Bridgeport, formerly; instr color, Parsons Sch Design, formerly. *Media:* Oil, Acrylic. *Mailing Add:* 334 W 20th St New York NY 10011

LEOPOLD, SUSAN
SCULPTOR, ASSEMBLAGE ARTIST
b Chicago, Ill, July 13, 60. *Study:* Sch Visual Arts, BFA, 82. *Work:* Brooklyn Mus, New York; Chase Manhattan Bank; First National Bank Chicago, Ill. *Exhib:* New Sculpture: Icon & Environment, traveling exhib, Independent Curators Inc, 83-84; one-woman show, Carnegie Mellon Univ Art Gallery, Pittsburgh, Pa, 87; The World is Round: The Artist & The Expansive Vision, traveling exhib, 87-89; Boxes, Containers & Vessels, Atlanta Col Art, Ga, 88; Homage to Edward Hopper, Baruch Col Art Gallery, New York, 88; Miniature Environments, Whitney Mus Am Art, New York, 89. *Awards:* Rhodes Family Award, Sch Visual Arts, 82; Indo-American Fel, 89. *Bibliog:* Michael Brenson (auth), A bountiful season in outdoor sculpture reveals a new sensibility, NY Times, 7/18/86; David Rimanelli (auth), Susan Leopold at John Weber, Art Forum, 12/88; John Russell (auth), Some masterly work of microscopic stature, NY Times, 8/11/89. *Media:* Mixed Media. *Mailing Add:* c/o John Weber Gallery 142 Greene St New York NY 10012

LERE, MARK ALLEN
SCULPTOR
b La Moure, NDak, May 13, 50. *Study:* Metrop State Col, Denver, Colo, BFA, 73; Univ Calif, Irvine, MFA, 76. *Work:* Mus Mod Art & Chase Manhattan Bank, New York; Mus Contemp Art, Los Angeles Co Mus Art & Fed Reserve Bank, Los Angeles, Calif. *Comn:* Untitled installation, Calif Arts Coun, Sacramento, 80; doorway installation, Community Redevelopment Agency, Los Angeles, Calif, 86; outdoor sculpture, City of Irvine, Calif, 88; Seattle Scatter, outdoor sculpture, City of Seattle, Wash, 90; garden sculpture, Kaohsiung Mus Art, Taiwan; Seattle Scatter Proj, City Seattle, Wash (5 locations), 92; and many others. *Exhib:* Aperto, 84, Venice Biennale, Italy; Solo Exibs, Mus Contemp Art, Los Angeles, Calif, 84-85, Carnegie-Mellon Univ, Pittsburgh, Pa, 86, NDak Mus Art, Grand Forks, 89-90, John Berggruen Gallery, San Francisco, Greg Kucera Gallery, Seattle, Wash, 91, Margo Leavin Gallery, Los Angeles, 92; Anniottanta, Mus Mod Art, Bologna, Italy, 85; Prospect 86, Frankfurter Kunstverein, Frankfurt, WGer; Avant Garde in the 80's, Los Angeles Co Mus Art, Calif, 87; Figurative Impulses, Santa Barbara Mus Art, Calif, 88; Gli anni Ottanta e Novanta dalla collezione Panza di Biumo, Museo Cantonale d'Arte, Lugano, Switz, 92. *Awards:* Visual Artists Fel in Sculpture, Nat Endowment Arts, 84 & 88. *Mem:* Col Arts Asn. *Dealer:* Margo Leavin Gallery 812 N Robertson Blvd Los Angeles CA 90069. *Mailing Add:* 2447 N Claremont Ave Los Angeles CA 90027

LERMAN, DORIS (HARRIET)
PAINTER, SCULPTOR
b Newark, NJ. *Study:* Inst Mod Art; Napeague Inst Art; also with Victor D'Amico & William Baziotes. *Work:* Guild Hall, East Hampton, NY. *Comn:* Poster, Guild Hall, Exhib, Mus Mod Art, 55. *Exhib:* One-man show, Gallery 84, New York, 71, 73, 75 , 78, 81 & 86; Artists of the Spring, East Hampton, 73-88; Circulating Exhib, Suffolk Co Schs, 75; Invitationals, Guild Hall, East Hampton, 77-81; Benson Gallery, Bridgehampton, 77-80; and others. *Pos:* Mem bd dirs & pres, Victor D'Amico Inst Art, 73-85; Chmn, several Guild Hall Mus projs. *Awards:* Hon Mention, Guild Hall, 65 & 74; Best in Mixed Media, Guild Hall, 78. *Mem:* Parrish Mus; Guild Hall. *Media:* Miscellaneous. *Mailing Add:* 6212 Crathie Lane Bethesda MD 20816

LERMAN, LEO
WRITER, HISTORIAN
b New York, NY, May 23, 14. *Pos:* Feature ed, Vogue, 72-83; ed-in-chief, Vanity Fair, 83; ed adv, Condé Nast Publ, Inc, 84- *Teaching:* Lectr, TV & radio; lectr art of biog & writing of children's bks, NY Univ. *Awards:* Lotus Club Award for the Museum--100 Years of the Metropolitan Museum of Art, 69. *Res:* Italian Renaissance; international 19th century social history art, especially 1830-1914. *Publ:* Auth, Leonardo da Vinci: Artist & Scientist, Bobbs-Merrill, 40; Michelangelo: A Renaissance Profile, Knopf, 41; The Museum-100 Years of the Metropolitan Museum of Art, Viking, 69; contribr, Vogue, New York Times, Atlantic Monthly, Sat Rev, Gourmet & others. *Mailing Add:* 350 Madison Ave New York NY 10017

LERMAN, ORA
PAINTER, SCULPTOR
b Campbellsville, Ky, Mar 14, 38. *Study:* Antioch Col, BA; Pratt Inst, with Calvin Albert, MFA; Art Students League, with Theodoros Stamos; Brooklyn Mus, with Reuben Tam. *Work:* Jewish Mus, New York, Reader's Digest Corp, Pleasantville, NY, Ponlain Mus, Vernon, France. *Exhib:* One-woman shows, Prince Street Gallery, 71, 72, 74 & 76 & Bernice Steinbaum Gallery, 82, New York; 20 Fulbright Artists, Inst Int Educ, NY, 75; Works on Paper, Brooklyn Mus, 75; Sons & Others, Women See Men, Queens Mus, 75; Jewish Themes: Contemporary American Artists, Jewish Mus, New York, 86; The Nature of the Beast, Hudson River Mus; Fantastic Journeys, Staller Ctr Arts, Stonybrook, NY. *Pos:* Pres, Women's Caucus Art, 78-80. *Teaching:* Mem fac, sculpture, New Sch Social Res, 67-69; prof art, Suffolk Co Community Col, 71-91. *Awards:* MacDowell Colony Fel; State Univ NY res grants; Ossabaw Found Fel; Andrew Mellon Fel; Fulbright Fel, Japan; Indo-Am Fel; Readers Digest Artist-in-Residence at Giverny Grant. *Bibliog:* Lawrence Campbell (auth), articles, Art News, 4/71 & 10/73; John Gruen (auth), article, Soho Weekly News, 10/75; Joan Marter (auth), article, Arts Mag, 5/82; L Campbell (auth), article, Art in Am, 11/82; Karen Lipson (auth), article, Newsday, 5/11/88; Diane Ketcham (auth), article, NY Times, 1/15/89. *Mem:* Col Art Asn Am; Women in the Arts. *Media:* Oil, Watercolor; Wax, Clay. *Publ:* Auth, the Elusive Subject: Joan Mitchell & Reflections on Van Gogh, Arts Mag, 9/90. *Mailing Add:* 463 West St No 1013 New York NY 10014

LERNER, ABE
BOOK DESIGNER
b New York, NY, Sept 14, 08. *Exhib:* Cooper Union (bk designs), 48; YMCA (photographs), Newburyport, Mass, 74-75; New York Community Col, 75; Grolier Club (bk designs), 89. *Pos:* Asst prod mgr, Viking Press, 37-42; art dir & prod mgr, World Publ Co, Cleveland & New York, 42-50 & 54-64; chmn, Trade Bk Clin, Am Inst Graphic Arts, 53-54; chmn, 50 Bks of Yr Comt, 55; dir design & prod, The Macmillan Co, 64-71, ed art bks, 71-74; free lance designer & production consult, currently; ed & East Coast corresp, Fine Print. *Teaching:* Lect series on design problems and their solution for young bk designers, Am Inst Graphic Arts; instr bk design & prod, Am Inst Graphic Arts, 41-42; instr bk design & prod, Columbia Univ, 53-54. *Awards:* Bks included in Fifty Books of the Year, eight yrs, 38-54; Trade Bk Clin monthly selections, 38- *Mem:* The Grolier Club; The Typophiles (pres). *Publ:* Auth, Fine Print, Passim, 77; Assault on the Book, Bird & Bull Press, 79; Form and Content, Angelica Press, 79; Grolier Gazette, 87; California Printing, Part III, Book Club Calif, 87. *Mailing Add:* 101 W 12th St New York NY 10011

LERNER, ABRAM
MUSEUM DIRECTOR
b New York, NY, Apr 11, 13. *Study:* NY Univ, BA; also var art schs, New York & Florence. *Exhib:* One-man exhib, Davis Gallery, New York; Brooklyn Mus; Pa Acad Fine Arts; ACA Gallery, New York; Peridot Gallery, New York. *Pos:* Asst dir, ACA Gallery, 45-55; asst dir, Artists Gallery, 55-56; cur, Hirshhorn Collection, 56-67, dir, Hirshhorn Mus & Sculpture Garden, Smithsonian Inst, 67-84; retired, 84- *Awards:* Founding Dir Emer, Hirshhorn Mus; Commander, Order Orange-Nassau; Chevalier L'Ordre Arts & Lettres. *Mem:* Arch Am Art (adv bd). *Publ:* Contribr mag & mus catalogs; auth, Gregory Gillespie, 77; ed, The Hirshhorn Mus & Sculpture Garden (inaugural catalog), Abrams, 74. *Mailing Add:* 98 Lewis St Southampton NY 11968

LERNER, ALEXANDRIA SANDRA
PAINTER
b Philadelphia, Pa. *Study:* Pa Acad Fine Arts, cert, 75; Philadelphia Col Art, BFA, 76. *Work:* Philadelphia Mus Art, Pa; Rutgers Univ, NJ; Art Inst Chicago, Ill; Houghton Libr, Harvard Univ; Franklin Furnace Archive, New York; Southern Alleghenies Mus. *Exhib:* 25 Pa Women Artists, Southern Alleghenies Mus, 79; Artists Books, Tweed Mus, Minn, 80; Speaking Volumes, AIR Gallery, New York, 80; Small Works, Washington Square East Gallery, New York, 81; Three American Artists, ABF Gallery, Germany, 81; A Contemporary Survey Art Books, Southern Alleghenies Mus, Loretto, Pa, 81; solo exhibs, Beyond the Garden Wall, Marian Locks Gallery, Philadelphia, 82 & Philadelphia Art Alliance, 89; Rutger's Nat, 85 & 86, Philadelphia Art Now, Philadelphia Mus Art, 90, Port Hist Mus, Philadelphia, 90; Philadelphia Art Now, Philadelphia Mus Art, 90; Port of Hist Mus, Philadelphia, Pa, 90. *Collections Arranged:* Erotic Art, Nexus Gallery, Philadelphia, 80; Bookworks (auth, catalog), Nexus Gallery, Philadelphia, 80; A Contemporary Survey Art Books (auth, catalog), Philadelphia Art Alliance, 81; Women in Art, William Penn Mus, Pa, 81. *Pos:* Co-dir, Artist Book Project, Nat Endowment Arts & Pa Council Grants, 80-; co-dir, SYNAPSE: A Visual Art Press, Pa, 80-; mem bd, New Art Examiner, 84-88; dir, McNeil Gallery, Philadelphia, 85-88. *Awards:* Stedman Fund Purchase Prize, Rutgers Univ, 76; Philadelphia Mus Purchase Prize,

Cheltenham Art Ctr, 80; Purchase Award, Art Inst Chicago, 81. *Bibliog:* Ann Jarmusch (auth), The real realisme/Philadelphia's new image, Art News, 3/81; Martha Giever (auth), Artists books, alternative space or precious object?, Afterimage, 5/82; Edward Sozanski (auth), Works of Intensity by Sandra Lerner, Philadelphia Inquirer, 5/89; Miriam Siedel (auth), Sandra Lerner, New Art Examiner, 9/82. *Mem:* Found for Today's Art/Nexus (trustee 76-); Philadelphia Art Alliance (chmn 80-85); Fel Pa Acad Fine Arts; Citizens Arts in Pa; Artists Equity. *Media:* Fresco. *Publ:* Auth, Ruffled Passions, Visual Art Press, 80. *Dealer:* Caroline Lee Box 1449 Taos NM 87571. *Mailing Add:* Box 5304 Taos NM 87571

LERNER, LOREN RUTH
LIBRARIAN
b Montreal, Que, Nov 4, 48. *Study:* McGill Univ, BA, 69, MLS, 75; Univ Mich, MA(art hist), 72. *Pos:* Fine arts librn, Concordia Univ, Montreal, Que, 75-, head, libr media ctr & visual arts bibliographer, 81-, spec servs, 92- *Teaching:* Lectr, Dept Art Hist, Concordia Univ, 82-; co-lectr, Grad Sch Art & Info Studies, McGill Univ, winter 88. *Mem:* Art Libr Soc NAm (Can Regional Rep, 82-85). *Res:* Art and architecture in Canada; Can film lit. *Publ:* Auth, On Rudolf Arnheim & Ernst Gombrich (annotated bibliographies), Can Rev Art Educ, 81; Canadian Art Publications: History and Recent Developments, Art Libr J, spring 83; coauth with Elizabeth Sacca, Visual Arts Reference and Research Guide, Perspecto Press, Montreal, 83; auth, Collection evaluation in fine arts libraries, in: Current Issues in Fine Arts Collection Development, Art Libr Soc NAm, Tucson, 84; Other disciplines and art: an overview based on oral evidence, Art Libr J, Vol XII, No 4, 87; Memoires et theses en histore de l'art canadien & Annales d'histoire de l'art canadien, J Can Art Hist, vol X, No 1, 87; co-ed, Art and Architecture in Canada: A Bibliography (Univ Toronto Press, 91). *Mailing Add:* Concordia Univ Norris Libr 1455 de Maisonneuve Blvd W Montreal PQ H3G 1M8 Canada

LERNER, MARILYN
PAINTER
b Milwaukee, Wis, Sept 19, 42. *Study:* Univ Wis, Milwaukee, BA, 64; Pratt Inst, New York, MFA, 66. *Work:* Merrill Lynch; McCrory Corp; Chase Manhattan Bank; Prudential Life Insurance; Progressive Corp. *Exhib:* Solo exhibs, John Good Gallery, New York, 87 & 89, Robert Morrison Gallery, 92; John Good Gallery, 87; Pratt Manhattan Gallery, New York, 88-; Traveling Univ Galleries, Spain, 88-; Inst N Am Studies, Barcelona, 88-; Fiction/Nonfiction, New York, 90; Painting Between the Sacred and the Profane, Rhamel Gallery, Koln, Ger, 90; Marilyn Lerner/Jill Levine, Fiction/Nonfiction, New York, 90. *Teaching:* Assoc prof sculpture, Baruch Col, New York, 80-; instr painting, Sch Visual Arts, New York, 89- *Awards:* Nat Endowment for the Arts, 87; NY Found for the Arts, 90; Fullbright, Indo-Am Fel, 90-91. *Bibliog:* Terry R Meyers (auth), Controlled substance, Marilyn Lerner's recent paintings, Arts Mag, 9/89; John Yau (auth), rev, Art Forum, 5/89; Mary Jones (auth), Arts Mag, rev & illus, 2/91. *Media:* Oil Paint, Oil Pastel. *Mailing Add:* 133 W 21st St New York NY 10011

LERNER, MARTIN
CURATOR, HISTORIAN
b Brooklyn, NY, Nov 14, 36. *Study:* Brooklyn Col, BA, 59; Inst Fine Arts, New York, 62-65. *Collections Arranged:* Indian Miniatures from the Jeffrey Paley Collection (auth, catalog), 74; Bronze Sculptures from Asia (auth, catalog), 75; Blue and White: Early Japanese Export Ware (auth, catalog), 76-77; Along the Ancient Silk Routes, Central Asian Art from Berlin, 82; Notable Acquisitions of Indian & Southeast Asian Art, Metrop Mus Art, 82; Indian and Southeast Asian Art from the Kronos Collections (auth, catalog), Metrop Mus Art, New York, 84; The Lotus Transcendent (auth, catalog), Metrop Mus Art, 91. *Pos:* Asst cur Oriental art, Cleveland Mus Art, 66-72; vchmn in charge of Far Eastern art, Metrop Mus Art, New York, 72-76 & cur, Indian & Southeast Asian art, 76- *Teaching:* Asst prof Oriental art, Univ Calif, Santa Barbara, 65-66 & Case-Western Univ, Cleveland, 68-71. *Res:* Indian and Southeast Asian art. *Publ:* Auth, Bronze Sculptures from Asia (exhib catalog), Metrop Mus Art, 75; Blue and White: Early Japanese Export Ware (exhib catalog), Metrop Mus Art, 78; Early Chola Bronze at the Norton Simon Mus Art at Pasadena, Chhavi, Vol II, 81; The Flame and the Lotus, Abrams, 84; coauth (with W Felton), Thai and Cambodian Sculpture: From the 6th to 14th Centuries, Philip Wilson, 89. *Mailing Add:* Metrop Mus Art Fifth Ave at 82nd St New York NY 10028

LERNER, NATHAN BERNARD
PHOTOGRAPHER, PAINTER
b Chicago, Ill, Mar 30, 13. *Study:* Nat Acad Art, Chicago; Art Inst Chicago; New Bauhaus, Chicago; Sch Design Chicago, BA; also with Archipenko, Moholy-Nagy and G Kepes. *Work:* George Pompidou Ctr, Paris, France; Bauhaus-Archiv, Berlin, Ger; Nihon Univ, Tokyo, Japan; Metrop Mus Art & Mus Mod Art, New York, Art Institute of Chicago,; and others. *Exhib:* One-man shows, Mus Sci & Indust, Chicago, 74, Pentax Mus, Tokyo, Japan, 75, Bauhaus Archiv, Berlin, Ger, 76, Inst Contemp Art, Boston, 79 & Chicago Cult Ctr, 84; Photogr & the City, Mus Contemp Art, Chicago, 76 & 79; Lazlo Moholy-Nagy Exhib, Georges Pompidou Centre, Paris, 77; Recent Acquisitions, Int Mus Photog, George Eastman House, Rochester, NY, 77, Amon Carter, Ft Worth, Tex, Mus Contemp Art, San Francisco, Ctr Photog Art, New York, Photog Gallery Int, Tokyo, Japan, San Francisco Mus Art & Milwaukee Mus Art; Whitney Mus Art, NY, 88; and others. *Teaching:* Instr photogr, Sch Design, Chicago, 39-43; instr product design, Inst Design, Chicago, 45-49, dean fac & students, 45-49. *Bibliog:* Gerald Fromberg (auth), Nathan Lerner--The Bauhaus Years (film), Bradley Univ, Peoria, Ill, 74; Elaine A King (auth), Nathan Lerner--Photographer, Midwest Art, 76. *Mem:* Artists Guild of Chicago. *Media:* All. *Publ:* Auth, Space in Your Pictures, Minican Photog, 42; coauth (with Gyorgy Kepes), Light as a medium of expression, Encyclopedia of Arts, 45. *Dealer:* Edwin Hoak Gallery 200 W Superior St Chicago IL; Ehlens Caudill Gallery Inc 750 N Orleans St Chicago IL. *Mailing Add:* 849 W Webster Ave Chicago IL 60614

LERNER, SANDRA
PAINTER, COLLAGE ARTIST
b New York, NY. *Study:* Pratt Graphic Ctr, New York, 66-68; Hofstra Univ, BA, 78; Kampo Kaikan, with Soshi Kampo, Kyoto and Sumera, Japan, 81; studied painting with Leo Manso, Jerry Okomoto and Harry Sternberg, studied calligraphy & philos with Soshi Kampo Harada, Kampo Kaikan, Kyoto & Sumera, Japan, 81. *Work:* AT & T; Aldrich Mus, Ridgefield, Conn; Jonathan Ingersol Mus, Laurel, Miss; World Study Mus, Fukuoka, Japan; Kampo Kaikan Mus, Kyoto, Japan; Art Group Int; and others. *Comn:* LAND (environ stage set for Eiko & Koma; with Eiko & Koma & Robert Mirabel), Rockefeller Found Multi-Arts Production Fund, 92. *Exhib:* Works on Paper, Brooklyn Mus, NY, 75, Dubins Gallery, Los Angeles, 87; Contemporary Reflections, Aldrich Mus Contemp Art, Ridgefield, Conn, 76; Acquisitions Plus, Aldrich Mus Contemp Art, Ridgefield, Conn, 78 & 81; Carlsberg Glyptothek Mus, Copenhagen, Denmark, 80; Betty Parsons Gallery, 81; Mus Fine Arts, Houston, Tex, 82; one-woman shows, Betty Parsons Gallery, 82, Gallery Don, Fukuoka, Japan, 84, Kamp Kaikan Mus, Kyoto, Japan, 84, Dubins Gallery, Los Angeles, 86 87 & 89, Kaufman Gallery, Houston, Tex, 86 & 91, Pace Univ, Peter Fingesten Gallery Fine Arts, New York, 87 & June Kelly Gallery, New York, 90 & 92; Folding Screens, John Szoke Gallery, New York, 88 & Silvermine Gallery, Stanford, Conn, 88; Dubins Gallery, Los Angeles, 91; Mus Contemp Art, Hiroshima, Japan, 91; and others. *Pos:* 0rtist in residence, Nassau Co Bd Coop Educ, 75; art coordr, Friends Sch, Old Westbury, NY, 75- *Teaching:* Lectr, Nassau Co Mus Fine Arts. *Awards:* Purchase Grant, Aldrich Mus Acquisition, Nat Endowment Arts, 78; Consult on the Arts, NY State Senate Spec Comt Arts, 78-86; Stipend to lectr in Japan, Int Commun Agency Grant, 81. *Bibliog:* Barnaby Ruhe (auth), Art World, 11/15/87; Dennis Wepman (auth), Sandra Lesner's Abstractions, Manhattan Arts, 11/87; Donald Kuspit (auth), Sensibility of Transcendence (exhib catalog), 90 & Mist Series (exhib catalog), 92, June Kelly Gallery; and others. *Media:* Oil, Acrylic; Mixed Media. *Dealer:* June Kelly Gallery 591 Broadway New York NY 10012; Dubins Gallery 11948 San Vicente Blvd Los Angeles CA 90049. *Mailing Add:* Ten E 18th St New York NY 10003

LERNER, SANDY R
PAINTER, LITHOGRAPHER
b Pa, May 13, 18. *Study:* Lafayette Col, BA; Pratt Inst, MFA; Art Students League; Nat Univ Mex; Washington Univ; also with Diego Rivera, Orozco, Fred Conway, Frank Reilly, Hans Hofmann & Zorach. *Work:* Smithsonian Inst & Navy Mus, Washington, DC; Brooklyn Navy Yard, NY; Tel Aviv Mus, Israel; Pratt Inst, Brooklyn; and others. *Comn:* Portrait, Massons of New York; portrait, 9th Regement of New York. *Exhib:* Nat Arts Club; Burr Artists; Audubon Artists; Salmagundi Artists; NJ Prof Artists; and others. *Pos:* Exec dir, Art Restoration Tech Inst; ed, Shrine Mag, currently. *Teaching:* Instr, Pratt Inst, Parsons Sch Design, New Sch Soc Res, currently. *Mem:* Salmagundi Club; Burr Artists; Col Art Asn Am (vpres, 69-70); Am Inst Art & Conserv; Int Inst Conserv Hist Works & Fine Arts; and others. *Media:* Oil, Mixed. *Mailing Add:* 220 E 65th St No 6H New York NY 10021

LEROY, HUGH ALEXANDER
SCULPTOR
b Montreal, Quebec, Can, Oct 9, 39. *Study:* Sir George Williams Univ, Montreal, dipl, 60; Montreal Mus Fine Arts, Sch Art & Design, studied with Arthur Lismer; McGill Univ, Montreal, studied with Louis Dudek, 76-77. *Work:* Nat Gallery & Can Coun Art Bank, Ottawa; Montreal Mus Fine Arts & Mus d'Art Contemporaine, Montreal; Ont Arts Coun, Toronto; Dept of Defense, Ottawa; Concordia Univ, Montreal. *Comn:* Sculpture, McGill Univ, Montreal, 73; sculpture, York Univ, Toronto, 74; sculpture, Fed Govt Can, Ottawa, 74; sculpture, Banff Ctr, Alta, 78; Ministry Govt Serv Public Works, New Justice Bldg, Ottawa. *Exhib:* Solo exhibs, Galerie Godard-Lefort, 69, & Waddington Galleries, 72, Montreal, Que, Eye Level Gallery, Halifax, NS, 82, Wynick Tuck Gallery, Toronto, 84 & Toronto Sculpture Garden, 87,; Canadian Pavilion, Expo 67, Montreal, 67; Art from 80 Spadina, Artspace, Petersborough, Ont, 85; Installation Piece, Wynick/Tuck Gallery, Toronto, 86; Chinese Exchange Exhib, Zhejiang Acad, China, 86; 49th Parallel, New York, 89. *Pos:* Dean, fine arts dept, Montreal Mus Sch Art & Design, 66-69; chmn, sculpture dept, Ont Col Art, Toronto, Can, 69-70; dir, MFA program, visual arts dept, York Univ, North York, Ont, 83-86. *Teaching:* Assoc prof, visual arts, York Univ, Toronto, 74-75, 77-78 & 81-89; sculpture instr, Banff Centre, Alberta, 79; Nova Scotia Col Art Design, Halifax, 81; vis lectr, Importance of Intuition, Sheridan Col, Toronto, 85; A Search for Personal Imagery, Dundas Valley Sch Art, 85. *Awards:* First Purchase Prize, Can Pavilion, Expo '67, Can Coun, 67; UNESCO Fel, 68; Royal Can Acad Fel, 75. *Bibliog:* John Bentley Mays (auth), A Muscular Surge in Daring Hues, Globe & Mail, Toronto, 5/7/87; Christopher Hume (auth), The Toronto Star (rev), 1/19/89; Donna Lypchuk (auth), Hugh LeRoy, Olga Korper Gallery, C Mag #21, spring 89. *Media:* Mixed. *Publ:* Contribr, What the Dickens--, Archit Canada, Toronto, 67. *Mailing Add:* c/o Olga Korper Gallery 17 Morrow Ave Toronto ON M6R 2H9 Canada

LEROY, LOUIS
PAINTER
b Yuma, Ariz, Aug 18, 41. *Study:* Univ Ariz, with Andrew Ruch, BFA, 70. *Exhib:* Chicano Affirmation & Resistance, White Gallery, Unic Calif, Los Angeles, 90. *Pos:* Owner, Salsa Graphics Studio, San Antonio, 80- *Awards:* Chrystal Stairs Award, Asn Am Cult, 88. *Mem:* Asn Am Cult (Found bd mem, 85-). *Dealer:* Dagen Della Gallery Old Market Square San Antonio TX. *Mailing Add:* 3111 N Zarzamora St San Antonio TX 78201

LESCH, ALMA WALLACE
TAPESTRY ARTIST, EDUCATOR
b McCracken Co, Ky, 1917. *Study:* Murray State Univ, BS, 41; Louisville Sch Art, 59-61; Univ Louisville, MEd, 62. *Work:* Objects: USA, Johnson Collection; J B Speed Art Mus, Louisville, Ky; Evansville Mus of Art, Ind; Mint Mus, Charlotte, NC; Flint Inst Art, Mich. *Comn:* Draperies, Bernheim Forest Nature Mus, Clermont, Ky, 62; wall hangings, First Presby Church, Columbus, Ind, 70 & Citizens Fidelity Bank, Louisville, 72; tapestry, Meldinger Tower, Louisville, 83; Druthers' Restaurant, Louisville, Ky, 84. *Exhib:* Fabric Collage, Mus Contemp Crafts, New York, 65; Fine Art of Collage, Kunstegewerbemus, Zurich, Switz, 68; Objects: USA, Smithsonian Inst, 70; 1st World Crafts Exhib, Toronto, Ont, 74; Alma Lesch: Retrospective, Liberty Nat Bank, Louisville, Ky, 84; New Works in Fiber, Contemp Crafts Gallery, Louisville, Ky, 89; 200 Years of Kentucky Crafts, Owensboro Mus Fine Art, Ky, 92; plus others. *Teaching:* Assoc prof textiles, Louisville Sch Art, 61-78; instr vegetable dyeing, Haystack Mountain Sch Crafts, Deer Isle, Maine, summers 66 & 70, Philadelphia Col Textiles, Memphis Acad Art, summer 67 & Indian Sch, Santa Fe, 72; instr, Arrowmont Sch Crafts, Gatlinburg, Tenn, 70-77; adj prof, Univ Louisville, 75-82. *Awards:* Distinguished Work Award, World Crafts Coun, 74; Best of Show, Evansville Mus Art, 78; Ky Governor's Art Award, 87. *Bibliog:* Lee Nordness (auth), Objects: USA, Viking, 70; Portraits without Faces (film), Ky Arts Comn, 77-78; Phyllis George (auth), Kentucky Crafts, 89. *Mem:* World Crafts Coun; Am Crafts Coun; fel Ky Guild Artists & Craftsmen; Louisville Craftsmen Guild. *Media:* Textiles. *Publ:* Auth, Vegetable Dyeing, Watson-Guptill, 70. *Dealer:* Liberty Gallery 416 W Jefferson St Louisville KY 40202; Ky Art & Craft Found 609 W Main St Louisville KY 40202. *Mailing Add:* PO Box 67 Shepherdsville KY 40165

LESH, RICHARD D
PAINTER, INSTRUCTOR
b Grand Island, Nebr, May 3, 27. *Study:* Univ Nebr; Univ Denver, BA & MA; Mexico City Col. *Work:* Omaha Nat Bank. *Exhib:* Midwest Biennial, 58; Nebraska Centennial, Joslyn Mus, Omaha, 67 & Sheldon Gallery, Lincoln, 68; Nebr Wesleyan Univ Painting Ann, Lincoln, 78. *Pos:* Pres, Nebr Art Coun, 68-69. *Teaching:* Instr painting & head dept art, Wayne State Col, 51-79, Colo State Univ, 82-88. *Awards:* Second Prize Painting, Midwest Biennial, Joslyn Mus, 55; First Prize Painting, May Show, Sioux City Art Mus, 58; First Prize Painting, Heritage Mus, Omaha, 79. *Mem:* Col Art Asn Am; Nebr Art Teachers Asn. *Media:* Acrylic, Lacquer. *Mailing Add:* 1205 Lory St Ft Collins CO 80524

LESHER, MARIE PALMISANO
SCULPTOR
b Reading, Pa, Sept 20, 19. *Study:* Art Students League; Berte Fashion Studio, Philadelphia, Pa; Mus of Fine Arts Sch & Univ, Houston, Tex. *Work:* Beaumont Art Mus, Tex; Laguna Gloria Art Mus, Austin, Tex; Carver Mus, Tuskegee, Ala; Reading Pub Mus, Pa; San Jacinto Col North, Houston, Tex. *Exhib:* Seventh Ann Eight State Exhib, Okla Art Ctr, Oklahoma City, 65; 28th Ann Nat Exhib, Jersey City Mus, NJ, 69; 22nd Ann, Butler Inst of Am Art, Youngstown, Ohio, 70; Catharine Lorillard Wolfe Art Club Ann, New York, 73, 79 & 81; Nat Sculpture Soc 40th & 41st Ann, New York, 73 & 74; Int Women's Arts Festival, New York, 76; 14th Biennial, Joslyn Mus of Art, Omaha, Nebr, 76; and many others. *Pos:* Advert mgr & art dir, Lowensteins, Memphis, Tenn, 45-46, Levy's, Houston, Tex, 46-50, Sakowitz, Houston, 50-52, Battelstein's, 59-60. *Teaching:* Instr sculpture, Sculptors Workshop, Houston, 72-73. *Awards:* First Award, Tex Fine Arts Asn, 73; First Purchase Award, Tri-State Exhib, Beaumont, Tex, Mobil Found, 75; Prix de Paris, 78; and others. *Bibliog:* Reva Remy (auth), L'Art a l'estranger, La Revue Mod, Paris, 6/68; Helen Anderson (auth), The sculptress, Houston Post, 3/68; Marie David (auth), Please do touch!, Houston Chronicle, 6/69. *Mem:* Artists Equity, New York & Philadelphia; Tex Soc Sculptors Int (dir, 73-); Fashion Group (secy-treas, 47-48); Knickerbocker Artists New York; and others. *Media:* Multi. *Dealer:* Sol Del Rio 1020 Townsend Ave San Antonio TX 78209. *Mailing Add:* 10130 Shady River Rd Houston TX 77042

LESHYK, TONIE
SCULPTOR, DRAFTSMAN
b Toronto, Ont, July 5, 50. *Study:* Sheridan Col Sch Design, Mississauga, Ont, dipl, high hons, 73; Ont Col Art, dipl, high hons, 75, study with Colette Whitten & Ann Whitlock. *Work:* Art Bank, Can Coun Arts, Ottawa; Art Gallery Brant, Brantford, Ont. *Exhib:* Vancouver Art Gallery, BC, 74; Toronto-Los Angeles Exchange, Los Angeles Inst Contemp Art, 79; Small Sculpture (with catalog), 82 & The Shelter Drawings: Out of the Studio, 85, Harbourfront Gallery, Toronto; A Portrait Southern Alberta Art Gallery (with catalog), Lethbridge, Alta, 83; Shelter, Burlington Cult Ctr, 86; Scale, Alta Col Art Gallery, Calgary, 86; Bollinger-Leshyk, Oakville Galleries, 87. *Collections Arranged:* Guest cur, ACT Powerhouse, Montreal-Toronto Exchange, 79; Artist's Choice, Glendon Gallery, Toronto, 80. *Teaching:* Artist-in-residence, Activity Ctr, Art Gallery Ont, Toronto, 79-82; instr, mixed media & visual arts, North York, Ont, summers, 83-88, head prog, 83 & 86; instr, Found Drawing I & III, Univ Guelph, 86-87. *Awards:* Design Can Award, 74; Ont Arts Coun Proj Award, 79 & 88; Can Coun Arts Grants, 83 & 86. *Bibliog:* Otto Rapp (auth), Tonie Leshyk at the Southern Alberta Art Gallery, Artmag, No 63/64, 83; Marshall Webb (auth), Ghost house: In memoriam to a worthy opponent, Vanguard, 4/84; Val Greenfield (auth), No peace, no shelter, C Mag, No 8, winter 86. *Media:* Plaster, Mixed Media. *Publ:* Auth, Your Skilled Weapon, self-publ, 85. *Mailing Add:* 924 Ossington Ave Toronto ON M6G 3V1 Canada

LESKO, DIANE
CURATOR, HISTORIAN
US citizen. *Study:* State Univ NY, Binghamton, AB, 71, MA, 75, PhD, 81. *Pos:* Cur collections, Mus Fine Arts, St Petersburg, Fla, 85-89; sr cur collections & exhibs, 89- *Teaching:* Asst prof art Hist, Lycoming Col, Williamsport, Pa, 78-85. *Awards:* Phi Beta Kappa. *Mem:* Col Art Asn; Womens Caucus Art; Am Asn Mus. *Res:* Nineteenth and twentieth century European and American art. *Publ:* Auth, Il Faut Etre de Son Temps: Charles Negre as painter-photographer in mid-19th century France, Arts, 81; James Ensor, the Creative Years, Princeton Univ Press, 85; James Ensor and Symbolist Literature, Art J, 85; Jon Corbino: An Heroic Vision, 87; Gari Melchers: A Retrospective Exhib, 90. *Mailing Add:* 7600 Bayshore Dr NO 206 St Petersburg FL 33706

LESLIE, JOHN
PAINTER, PHOTOGRAPHER
b July 11, 23. *Study:* Murrell Dobbins Tech, with Harry Brodsky, 38-41; Philadelphia Graphic Sketch Club, Fleisher Art Mem, 39-42, Philadelphia Mus Sch Indust Art, Philadelphia Col Art, 44; Penn State Univ, 82. *Work:* Philadelphia Mus Art, Philadelphia Maritime Mus; US Dept State, Art Embassies Prog, Washington, DC; Westmoreland Mus Art, Greensburg, Pa; Reading Pub Mus & Art Gallery, Pa. *Comn:* Collaborative Designer, Gimbel Brothers Thanksgiving Day Parade, Philadelphia, Pa, 45; window dioramas, Bonwit Teller, 45-50, Philadelphia Eagles Football Team, Pa, 46; theatrical stage sets, Bessie V Hicks Sch Dramatic Arts, Philadelphia, 46; mural, Philadelphia Savings Fund Soc, 48. *Exhib:* 41st, 45th & 50th Ann Exhib, Woodmere Art Mus, Philadelphia, Pa, 80, 85 & 90; 27th Ann Exhib, Ursinus Col, Collegeville, Pa, 83; 3rd Ann Exhib Pastel Paintings, Philadelphia Sketch Club, Philadelphia, Pa, 87; 1st Ann Galeria Exhib, NY Passenger Ship Terminal, NY, 88; 10th Ann NY Art Expo, Jacob Javits Convention Ctr, NY, 88. *Pos:* Art dir, Duplex Display & Manufacturing Co, Philadelphia, Pa, 47-54; designer, Leslie Creations, Lafayette Hill, Pa, 54-67; creative dir, Kopy Kat Inc, Ft Washington, Pa, 68-77; art dir, Jesse Jones Indust Inc, Philadelphia, Pa, 78-79. *Teaching:* Lectr, Galerie Marjole', Sanatoga, Pa, 87. *Awards:* Artistic Merit Award, Playboy Mag, 58; King Prussia Award, Cult Ctr Upper Merion, Pa, 66; Distinguished Serv Art Award, Citizens Comt Pub Educ, Philadelphia, 81. *Bibliog:* Paulette Lind Torres (auth), John Leslie is an artist who doesn't feel a need to exhibit, Reading Eagle, 2/17/85; Thomas Becnel (auth), Captured on canvas: John Leslie's talents have many outlets, Sarasota Herald Tribune-New York Times, 1/29/89; Alan Bennett (auth), Crystal mall concept: Leslie's plan for sculptured, functional downtown malls, Charlotte Sun Herald, 2/19/90. *Mem:* Oil Pastel Asn, NY; Philadelphia Print Club; Woodmere Art Mus, Philadelphia; Englewood Camera Club, Fla; Boca Grande Art Alliance, Fla. *Media:* Oil Pastel, Soft Pastel; Photography. *Publ:* Illusr, Artist Honored: shows at world's largest art exhibition, Venice Gondolier, 3/19/88; Englewood artist tapped for prestigious Oil Pastel Asn, Boca Beacon, 3/25/88; Artist enters Hall of Fame, Gulfshore Life Mag, 5/89; Mus acquires works of area painter, Evening Phoenix, 9/28/89; Bonwit's closing recalls artist's window displays during 1940's and 50's, Rotonda Rev, 7/90. *Dealer:* Blueberry Hill 6318 Zeno Circle Port Charlotte FL 33981. *Mailing Add:* 6318 Zeno Circle Port Charlotte FL 33981-5399

LESLIE, SEAVER
PAINTER, INSTRUCTOR
b Boston, Mass, Aug 22, 46. *Study:* RI Sch Design, BFA, 69 & MA, 70; with Peter Blake, London, Eng, 73-74. *Work:* Fogg Art Mus, Cambridge, Mass; The Continental Corp, Simpson, Thatcher & Bartlett, New York; Chase Manhattan Bank, New York; Chemical Bank, New York. *Comn:* Art Park, Lewiston, NY, 75. *Exhib:* Nat Arts Club Invitational Drawing, New York, 80; Manhattan, Whitney Mus, New York, 82; New Talent New York, Sioux City Art Mus, 85-; Glen Ganss Collection, Mus Mod Art, 86 & American Realism, Watercolors & Drawings, 86, Mus Mod Art, San Francisco; De Cordova Mus, Lincoln, Mass. *Teaching:* Instr painting, RI Sch Design, 71-81, Parsons Sch Design, 80-82, Wellesley Col, 83-84; artist-in-residence, Univ Calif, San Diego, 84-85, 87-88 & Univ Tenn, Knoxville. *Awards:* Second Prize Painting, Providence Art Club, Hilton Kramer, 70. *Bibliog:* Addison Parks, (auth), Seaver Leslie, Arts Mag, 80; Edward Sozanski (auth), Seaver Leslie, Providence J, 82; Daniel Schulman (auth), Seaver Lesie, Arts Mag, 83. *Media:* Oil, Watercolor. *Publ:* West by East, RI Sch Design, 70; 12 Points--Putting the Case for Customary Weight and Measure, Am Customary Weight & Measure, 79. *Mailing Add:* Old State Farm Wiscasset ME 04578

LESNICK, STEPHEN WILLIAM
PAINTER, INSTRUCTOR
b Bridgeport, Conn, Mar 22, 31. *Study:* Silvermine Col Art, BA, Art Career Sch, BA; also with Revington Arthur, Jon McClelland, Jack Wheat & Gail Symon; studied watercolor with Herb Olsen. *Work:* Elk's Western Helldorado Art Collection, Nev; Burndy Libr Arts & Sci, Norwalk, Conn. *Comn:* Indust paintings, Burndy Libr Art & Sci, 59; portrait of Gov mansion, Gov Paul Laxalt, Carson City, 68; commemorative coin (Boulder Dam), Elks Lodge, Las Vegas, 71-78; medallion series, Nev State Mus, 77- *Exhib:* All New Eng Art Exhib, Conn, 55; Layout & Design Int Art Competition, Japan, 63; Ann Conn Relig Art Exhib, 63 & 64; Ann Am Watercolor Soc Show, 68; Helldorado Western Art Exhib, Nev, 68; and thirty-three one man shows. *Pos:* Layout designer, Vacart Art Studio, Stamford, Conn, 60-65; art dir, Kelley & Reber Advert, Las Vegas, 65-66; illusr, E G & G, Inc, Las Vegas, 66-73; art ed, Las Vegas Sun, 70-; syndicated newspaper columnist, Art for Everyone; illusr, Marine Corps Gazette; one of founders, Las Vegas Art Mus; owner, Lesnick Art Products. *Teaching:* Instr art, Desert Art League, Boulder City, 65-66; instr art, Las Vegas Art League & Artists & Craftsmans Guild, Nev, 65-68 & Clark Co Community Col; owner & instr, Lesnick Art Studio,

Las Vegas, 65- *Awards:* Int Design Show, Japan, 63; Conn Relig Show, Hallmark Greeting Cards, 63 & 64; First Prize, Nev Bicentennial Commemorative Medallion, Franklin Mint, 72; Purchase Prize, Barum Fest; First Prize & Purchase Award, Helldorado Western Art Show; Region I Winner ($3000), Nat Arts in the Parks, 87. *Bibliog:* Articles in Desert Scope, 69-71. *Mem:* Nev State Watercolor Soc; Soc NAm Artists. *Media:* All Media. *Mailing Add:* 1127 Westminster Ave Las Vegas NV 89119

LESSEPS, TAUNI DE
PAINTER, SCULPTOR
b Paris, France, Mar 10, 20; US citizen. *Work:* Three bronzes, The White House; Lausanne Mus, Switz; Hirshhorn Mus, Washington, DC; also works in pvt collections of Princesa Jose de Baviera y Borbon, Madrid, Spain, Mr & Mrs Nicholas du Pont & Capt J Y Cousteau; and others. *Comn:* Headless Horseman (metal), Sleepy Hollow Country Club, Scarborough, NY; Scenic View of London (mural), Cumberland Court, London, Eng; entire collection in solid 18-karat gold & silver, F J Cooper, Philadelphia, Pa; sculptures, Baccarat Crystal of France; three fountains, Spastic Children's Hosp, Kuwait. *Exhib:* Osawa Gallery, Tokyo, Japan, 75; one-man shows, Bruce Mus & Bell Gallery, Greenwich, Conn, 77; Kottle Gallery, French Embassy & Vernay-Jussel Galleries, New York, 78; Centre for the Arts, Vero Beach, Fla, 88. *Awards:* Nominated Academician of Italy with Gold Medal, Belli Arte, Beaux Arts, 79. *Mem:* Soc Illusr; Nat Art Mus of Sport. *Media:* Acrylic, Oil. *Mailing Add:* 452 Worth Ave Palm Beach FL 33480

LESTER, MICHELLE
TAPESTRY, PAINTING
b Cleveland, Ohio, June 28, 42. *Study:* Cleveland Inst Art, BFA, 65; Syracuse Univ, NY, MFA(design), 67. *Work:* Rockefeller Collection, New York; Ky Mus, Bowling Green. *Comn:* 3M Co, Washington , DC, 83; Texaco, Inc, New York, 85; Neiman Marcus, Dallas, Tex, 85; Metrop Life, Philadelphia, Pa, 88; EI Dupont Nemours & Co; and others. *Exhib:* Solo exhibs, Kaufmann Graphics, Los Angeles, 76, Modern Masters Tapestries, New York, 83 & Gallery 10, Scottsdale, Ariz, 85-87; Contemporary Fiber Art, Newark Mus, NJ, 78; Landscape: New Views, Herbert Johnson Mus, Cornell Univ, Ithaca, NY, 78; National Miniature Fibers, Santa Fe & traveling, 79; French Culinary Inst, NY, 87; Educ Testing Serv, Princeton, NJ, 92; and others. *Pos:* Designer/display artist, Larson Design Studio, New York, 71-73; asst to Ruth Kaufmann, Ruth Kaufmann Gallery, New York, 71-76. *Teaching:* Instr textiles, weaving & design, Rochester Inst Technol, NY, 68-71; instr weaving & dyeing, Brooklyn Mus Art Sch, NY, 71-77; instr fibers, Parsons Sch Design, New York, 79-83 & New York Univ, 83. *Awards:* Merit Award, National Mini Tapestry Show, The Gathering, Kansas City, Mo, 78. *Bibliog:* P K Preston (auth), articles, Fiber Arts Mag, 3-4/78 & 1/79; Betty Freudenheim (auth), New York Times, 3/3/88. *Mem:* Am Crafts Coun; New York Guild Graphic Artists. *Publ:* Contribr, Family Creative Workshop, 72-76 & McCall's How to Weave It, 74, Plenary Publ; Book of Crafts and Hobbies, 81, How to Do Just About Everything, 85 & Back to Basics, 85, Reader's Digest. *Mailing Add:* 15 W 17th St New York NY 10011

LETENDRE, RITA
PAINTER
b Drummondville, Que, Nov 1, 28. *Study:* Ecole Beaux Arts, Montreal; P E Borduas, Montreal. *Work:* Mus Art Contemporain, Montreal; Mus Beaux-Arts, Montreal; Long Beach Mus Fine Arts, Calif; Rose Art Mus, Brandeis Univ, Waltham, Mass; Mus Que. *Comn:* Wall painting, Calif State Col, Long Beach, 65; mural, Greenwin of Toronto, 71; wall painting, Benson & Hedges, Neil-Wyick Col, Toronto, 71; mural, J D S Investment, Sheridan Mall, Pickering, Ont, 72. *Exhib:* Internationalism des Arts, Mus Beaux-Arts, 60; 5 Festival di due Mondi, Spoleto, Italy, 62; IV Biennale Can Painting, Tate Gallery, London, Eng, 63; Can Pavilion Expo 67, Montreal, 67; Que Pavilion, World's Fair, Osaka, Japan, 70; and others. *Awards:* Le Prix de Peinture, Concours Artistique Que, 61; Que Bourse de Recherche, 67; Can Arts Coun Sr Grant Award, 71. *Bibliog:* C Delloye (auth), Rita Letendre, Art Aujourdhui, 62; D Travers (auth), Rita Letendre wall painting, Arts & Archit, 66; Jules Heller (auth), Printmaking Today, Holt, Rinehart & Winston, 71. *Mem:* Royal Can Acad Art. *Media:* Acrylic. *Mailing Add:* 288 Sherbourne St Toronto ON M5A 2S1 Canada

LETTENSTROM, DEAN ROGER
PAINTER, EDUCATOR
b Superior, Wis, Sept 12, 41. *Study:* Univ Wis, Superior, BFA, 67; Univ Dallas, Irving, Tex, MA, 68; Skowhegan Maine, 68; Ohio State Univ, Columbus, Ohio, MFA, 69; MacDowell Colony, 73. *Work:* Chicago Art Inst Libr, Ill; Huntington Mus & Galleries, WVa; Tweed Mus Art, Duluth, Minn; Lutheran Brotherhood Co, Minneapolis; Ohio State Univ Galleries, Columbus. *Exhib:* Texas Painting & Sculpture, Dallas Mus Fine Arts, Dallas, Tex, 68; Iowa Arts Ann, Des Moines Art Ctr, Iowa, 70; American Artists in Europe, Prato, Italy, 73; Small Works Nat, NY Univ Galleries, NY, 80; 16th Ann All Media, Brea Mus, Fullerton, Calif, 82; Eight State Biennial, Sioux City Art Ctr, Iowa, 83; Texas Fine Arts National, Laguna Gloria Mus, Austin, Tex, 84; La Grange National XI, La Grange, Ga, 86. *Teaching:* Assoc prof painting, Drake Univ, Des Moines, Iowa, 70-73; instr painting, Minneapolis Col Art Design, 77-78; assoc prof painting, Univ Minn, Duluth, 79- *Awards:* Arts Coun Award, Dayton Art Inst, 69; Purchase Award, Lutheran Insurance, 70; Best Painting, Iowa Ann, Des Moines Art Ctr, 71. *Mem:* Col Art Asn Am. *Mailing Add:* Art Dept Univ Minn Duluth MN 55812

LE VA, BARRY
SCULPTOR
b Long Beach, Calif, 1941. *Study:* Calif State Univ, Long Beach, 60-63; Los Angeles Col Art & Design, 63; Otis Art Inst, Los Angeles County, BFA, 64, MFA, 67. *Work:* Whitney Mus, Mus Mod Art, New York; Rijksmuseum Kröller-Müller, Otterloo, Neth; Philadelphia Mus Art; Chicago Art Inst. *Exhib:* Solo exhibs, Tex Gallery, Houston, 85 & 89, Daniel Weinberg Gallery, Los Angeles, 86 & 89, Galerie Fred Jahn, Munich, WGer, 88, David Nolan Gallery, New York, 89 & 90, Rijkmuseum Kröller-Müller, 88, Carnegie-Mellon Art Gallery, Pittsburgh, 88 & High Mus Atlanta, 89; Drawings from the 80's, Carnegie Mellon Univ Art Gallery, Pittsburgh, 87; Barbara Gladstone Gallery, New York, 87; 1967: At the Crossroads, Inst Contemp Art, Univ Pa, Philadelphia, 87; Points of Contact, Laurie Rubin Gallery, New York, 87; Early Conceps of the Last Decade, Holly Soloman Gallery, New York, 87; Tex Variations, David Nolan Gallery, New York, 90; American Drawings from 1980, Leverksen Mus, Ger, 90; Sonnabend Gallery, New York, 91; and others. *Teaching:* Instr, Minneapolis Col Art & Design, 68-70; instr adv sculpture, Princeton Univ, 73-74; instr grad sculpture, Yale Univ, 76. *Awards:* Young Talent Grant, Los Angeles County Mus, 68; Fel Sculpture, Guggenheim Found, 74; Nat Endowment Arts Fel, 76. *Bibliog:* Vivien Raynor (auth), Art: Twisted chains from Barry Le Va, New York Times, 3/13/81; Klaus Kertess (auth), Barry Le Va's sculpture: Ellipsis and ellipse, Artforum, 1/83; Therese Lictenstein (auth), Works on paper, Arts, 1/84; David Lurie (auth), American eccentric abstraction, 1968-1972, Arts Mag, 3/86; Stephen Ellis (auth), At order's edge, Art Am, 7/86; Ronny Cohen (auth), A new look at big drawing, Drawing, 9-10/86. *Publ:* Auth, Notes on a piece by Barry Le Va, Studio Int, 11/71. *Dealer:* David Nolan Gallery New York NY 10012. *Mailing Add:* 160 W 24th St, No 5C New York NY 10011

LEVEE, JOHN H
PAINTER, SCULPTOR
b Los Angeles, Calif, Apr 10, 24. *Study:* Art Ctr Sch & Chenard Sch, Los Angeles; Univ Calif, Los Angeles, BA, 48; New Sch Social Res, with Stuart Davis, Abe Rattner & Kunyoshi, 48-49; Acad Julian, Paris, grand prix, 51. *Work:* Mus Mod Art, Whitney Mus Am Art & Guggenheim Mus, New York; Corcoran Gallery Art, Washington, DC; Mus Mod Art, Paris; plus many others in pub & pvt collections. *Comn:* Wall, Architects, Chateau Vaudreuil, Paris, 71-72; walls, Bank Credit Com, Paris, 72-73; floor design, Sch Marne-le-Vallee, Paris, 75; walls & banners, Prudential Life Insurance Co, Los Angeles, 77; wall, (1700 sq ft), Col Chateauchinon, France, 86. *Exhib:* Corcoran Gallery Art, 56-58; New Acquisitions, 57 & Young Am Painters, 57-58, Mus Mod Art, New York; Whitney Mus Am Art, 57, 58 & 66; Haifa Mus Art, Israel, 63; Phoenix Art Mus, Ariz, 64; Krannert Art Mus, Univ Ill, 65; Walker Art Ctr, Minneapolis, 65; Tel Aviv Mus, Israel, 69; Palm Springs Mus, Calif, 77; Mus Mod Art, Toufouse, France, 93; plus many others. *Teaching:* Vis prof art, Univ Ill, 64-65, Washington Univ, 67, NY Univ, 67-68 & Univ Southern Calif, 70. *Awards:* purchase award, Commonwealth Va Biannual, 66; Ford Fel, Tamarind Workshop, 69; Four Prizes, Woolmark Found, 74-75. *Media:* Acrylic; Plexiglas. *Collection:* African, pre-Columbian and contemporary painting and sculpture. *Dealer:* Gallerie Callu-Merile 17 Rue des Beaux Arts Paris 6; Gallerie Le gall Peyroulet 18 Rue Keller Paris 11. *Mailing Add:* 119 rue Notre Dame des Champs Paris France

LEVEN, ANN R
ADMINISTRATOR
b Canton, Ohio, Nov 1, 40. *Study:* Brown Univ, AB, 62; studio work at RI Sch of Design; Harvard Bus Sch, MBA, 64; Fogg Mus. *Work:* Brown Univ. *Pos:* Asst treas, 70-72 & treas, 72-79, Metrop Mus Art, New York; Mus Aid Panel (mem), New York State Coun on the Arts, 77-79; adv comt, Art Dept, Brown Univ; trustee, Artist's Choice Mus, 79-87; vpres, Chase Manhattan Bank, 79-83; staff liaison, Nat Endowment Art; dir, Twyla Tharp Dance Found, 82-87 & Am Art's Alliance, 90-92; treas, Smithsonian Inst, 84-90; overseer, Hood Mus-Hopkins Ctr, Dartmouth Col, 84-91, chmn bd, 88-91; deputy treas, Nat Gallery Art, 90- *Teaching:* Fac, Columbia Business Sch, 75- *Awards:* Minnie Nelen Hicks Prize, Brown Univ; NY State Outstanding Young Woman, 76. *Mem:* Womens Forum; Art Table; Am Asn Mus. *Mailing Add:* Nat Gallery Art Washington DC 20565

LEVENSON, RUSTIN S
CONSERVATOR
b Toledo, Ohio, July 19, 47. *Study:* Wellesley Col, BA, 69; Fogg Art Mus, Harvard Univ, cert conserv, 72. *Pos:* Conservator, Can Conserv Inst, 73-74 & Nat Gallery Can, 74-77, Ottawa, Ont; asst conservator, Metrop Mus Art, New York, 77-80; pres & head conservator, New York Conserv Assoc, 80-; Fla Conserv Assoc, 86- *Mem:* Fel Int Inst Conserv; fel Am Inst Conserv (chmn Paintings group, 83-84); Nat Inst Conserv. *Publ:* Auth, Emergency conservation, Ont Mus Bull, 74; Conservation of a portrait by A Cuyp, Harvard Univ, 76; coauth, Adhesives for strip lining 20th century paintings, Nat Gallery Can, 76; A new method for strip lining, UNESCO, 78; Materials and techniques of early Quebec painters, J Can Art Hist, 83; A New Method for Loose Lining Contemporary Paintings, AIC, 87. *Mailing Add:* 13291 Old Cutler Rd Miami FL 33156

LEVERING, ROBERT K
PAINTER, COLLAGE ARTIST
b Ypsilanti, Mich, May 22, 19. *Study:* Univ Ariz, AB, 42; Art Inst Chicago, 43; Art Students League, 55-56; Brooklyn Mus Sch Art with Reuben Iam, 59-61. *Work:* USAF Collection, Pentagon, Washington, DC; also in pvt collections. *Comn:* Portraits of Kennedy, Eisenhower, U Thant, Martin Luther King & Dag Hamerskjold; portraits, pres Am Express; portraits, pres Wells & Fargo; and other public & pvt comns. *Exhib:* Seven exhibs, New York

City Ctr Gallery; Soc Illustrators Gallery, New York; Brooklyn Mus, 61; Mikelson Gallery, Washington, DC, 68; NY Art Dirs Club Exhib, 69. *Teaching:* Guest critic & lectr, Parsons Sch Design, 65-70, instr painting & drawing, 76-93. *Awards:* Gold Medal, 69 & Merit Awards, Soc Illusr; Citation, NJ Art Dirs Club, 69; Soc Publ Designers Award, 69. *Media:* Oil; Graphics, Miscellaneous Media. *Publ:* Illusr, leading nat mag, bks, newspapers, advert & ed. *Mailing Add:* 330 E 79th St No 10-D New York NY 10021

LEVI, JOSEF
PAINTER
b New York, NY, Feb 17, 38. *Study:* Univ Conn, BA, 59; Columbia Univ, 60. *Work:* Mus Mod Art, New York; Albright-Knox Gallery, Buffalo, NY; Aldrich Mus Contemp Art, Ridgefield, Conn; Krannert Art Mus, Univ Ill, Urbana; Des Moines Art Ctr; Corcoran Gallery, Washington, DC; Brooklyn Mus, NY; Newark Mus, NJ; and many others. *Exhib:* One man shows, Stable Gallery, NY, 66 & 68-70, Art Club, Chicago, Ill, 67, Gertrude Kasle Gallery, Detroit, Mich, 71, AM Sachs Gallery, 75, 76 & 78 & O K Harris Gallery, New York, 83, 85, 87, 90 & 92; Images Gallery, Toledo, Ohio; Summer Exhib, Studio Mus, NY, 68; Warren Benedek Gallery, New York, 73; Art Fair, Basel, Switz, 73; Mus Art, RI Sch Design, Providence, 76; Deja Vu: Masterpieces Updated, Western Asn Art Mus, 81-82; Westheimer Collection, Okla Art Ctr, Oklahoma City, 88; and others. *Teaching:* Artist-in-res, Appalachian State Univ, Boone, NC, 69 & Pa State Univ, University Park, 76. *Awards:* Purchase Award, Univ Ill, Urbana, 66; Selected for New Talent USA, Art Am, 66. *Bibliog:* William Wilson (auth), In the eye of the beholder, Art News, 2/70; J Patrice Marandel (auth), Preface for Silkscreen Portfolio, Domberger, 71; Allen Ellenzweig (auth), Still life with art history: The collage paintings of Josef Levi, Arts Mag, 12/76; Martha Scott (auth), Josef Levi, Arts Mag, 3/85. *Mem:* New York Artists Equity Asn. *Media:* Acrylics, Graphite on Paper. *Dealer:* O K Harris 383 W Broadway New York NY 10021; Adams Middleton Gallery Dallas TX. *Mailing Add:* 171 W 71st St New York NY 10023

LEVICK, (MR & MRS) IRVING
COLLECTORS
Collection: Contemporary American and European artists, including Gatch, Weber, Dove, Hartley, Rivers, Levine, Marin, Weinberg, King, Knaths, Shahn, Roth, Tam, Greene, Guerero, Avery, Dubuffet, Levee, Nikos, Nicolson, Sutherland, Marini, Fraser, Francis, Wiley, Buggiani, Kinley, Lawrence, Appel, Corneille, Severini, Kinigstein, Katzman, Rouault, Graves, Brice, Heerup, Wols, Bauermeister, Jimmy Ernst, James Wines, Lynn Chadwick, Saul Steinberg, Davies, Seymour Drumlevitch, Harriet Grief and others. *Mailing Add:* 78 New Amsterdam Ave Buffalo NY 14216

LEVIN, GAIL
HISTORIAN, PHOTOGRAPHER
b Atlanta, Ga, Feb 19, 48. *Study:* Sorbonne, Paris, 68; Simmons Col, BA(art hist), 69; Tufts Univ, MA, 70; Rutgers Univ, PhD(art hist), 76. *Work:* High Mus Art, Atlanta; Ctr for Photog, Woodstock, NY. *Exhib:* Solo exhibs, Mem Art Gallery, Univ Rochester, NY, 85, Cedar Rapids Art Mus, Cedar Rapids, Iowa, 86, Univ Iowa Mus Art, Iowa City, 87, Peale House Gallery, Pa Acad Fine Arts, Philadelphia, 87-88 & Univ Art Collections, Ariz State Univ, Tempe, Ariz, 88. *Collections Arranged:* Morgan Russell: Synchromist Studies, 1910-1922, Mus Mod Art, New York, 76; Synchromism and Am Color Abstraction, 1910-1925, Whitney Mus Am Art, 78; Abstract Expressionism: The Formative Years, traveling exhib, 78; Edward Hopper: Prints and Illustrations, 79 & Edward Hopper: the Art and the Artist, traveling exhib, 80; Visions of Tomorrow: New York and American Industrialization in the 1920s-1930s, Isetan Mus Art, Tokyo & traveling, 88; Marsden Hartley in Bavaria, Emerson Gallery, Hamilton Col, Clinton, NY, traveling, 89-90. *Pos:* Cur, Edward Hopper Collection, Whitney Mus Am Art, 76-84. *Teaching:* Instr, New Sch for Social Res, 73-75; asst prof art hist, Conn Col, New London, 75-76; vis asst prof, Graduate Sch, City Univ New York, 79-80; Will & Ariel Durant Prof Humanities, St Peter's Col, Jersey City, NJ, 87-88; assoc prof, Baruch Col, New York, 86-88; prof, Baruch Col & grad sch of City Univ, New York, 89- *Awards:* Nat Endowment Humanities Grant, 84, 89 & 92; John Sloan Mem Found, 91; Yale Univ Grant, 92-93. *Bibliog:* Ron Peck (dir), Edward Hopper (film, based on conversations with Gail Levin), Arts Council of Great Britain, 81; Atlanta J, 12/1/85. *Mem:* Int Asn Art Critics; PEN Freedom to Write; Col Art Asn Am. *Res:* Edward Hopper: a biography and catalogue raisonne; Marsden Hartley: a catalogue raisonne. *Interests:* Modern American and European art. *Publ:* Auth, Edward Hopper: The Complete Prints, 79, Edward Hopper as Illustrator, 79 & Edward Hopper: The Art and the Artist, 80, Norton; auth & photogr, Hopper's Places, Knopf, 85; Twentieth Century American Painting, The Thyssen-Bornemisza Collection, Sotheby, 87 & Harper & Row, 88; Marsden Hartley in Bavaris, Univ Pres New England, 89; Theme and Improvisation: Kandinsky and The American Avant-garde, 1912-1950, Bulfinch Press, 92. *Mailing Add:* 125 E 84th St No 2D New York NY 10028

LEVIN, HUGH LAUTER
PUBLISHER, DEALER
b Rye, NY, July 2, 51. *Study:* Univ Pa, BA, 73, Wharton Sch, MBA, 84. *Pos:* Pres, Hugh Lauter Levin Assoc Inc, 74-; dir, Abrams Original Editions, 76-83, vpres, Harry Abrams, Inc, 81-83. *Mem:* Fine Art Publs Asn (treas, 82-85); Orgn Ind Artists. *Specialty:* Publication of contemporary prints and illustrated books. *Mailing Add:* 2507 Post Rd Southpost CT 06490

LEVIN, KIM
CRITIC
US citizen. *Study:* Vassar Col, AB; Yale-Norfolk Summer Sch Art; Columbia Univ, MA. *Pos:* Ed assoc, Art News, New York, 65-73; contrib ed, Arts Mag, 73-; NY corresp, Opus Int, 73-77; NY corresp, Flash Art, 80-84; contribr, Village Voice, 80- *Teaching:* Lectr drawing, Philadelphia Col Art, 67-70; lectr drawing & painting, Parsons Sch Design, New York, 69-72. *Awards:* Art/World Award for Distinguished Newspaper Criticism, 86. *Mem:* Int Asn Art Critics (vpres, 84-90, pres, 90-92, secy, 91-). *Publ:* Contribr, Light in Art, Collier, 69; Super Realism, 75 & New Artists Video, 78, Dutton; auth, Lucas Samaras, Abrams, 75; contribr, Theories of Contemporary Art, Prentice-Hall, 85; auth, Beyond Modernism, Harper & Row, 88; contribr, Beyond Walls & Wars: Art, Politics & Multi-Culturalism (essays), Midmarch Press, 92. *Mailing Add:* 52 W 71st St New York NY 10023

LEVIN, MORTON D
PRINTMAKER, PAINTER
b New York, NY, Oct 7, 23. *Study:* City Univ New York, BS(art educ); studies in Paris, France; painting with Andre Lhote, sculpture with Ossip Zadkine, etching & engraving with Stanley W Hayter & etching with Federico Castellon; studied lithography, Pratt Graphic Arts Ctr, New York. *Work:* New York Pub Libr; Libr of Cong, Washington, DC; Hist of Med Div, Nat Libr Med, Md. *Comn:* Mural, Stained Glass, L Natali Inc, 79. *Exhib:* Northwest Printmakers 18th & 21st Ann, Seattle Art Mus, 46-49; 4th-7th Ann Nat Exhib of Prints, Libr of Cong, 46-49; Nat Acad Design & Soc Am Etchers, Gravers, Lithographers and Woodcutters, Inc, 46-48; 46th Ann Watercolor & Print Exhib, Pa Acad Fine Arts, 48; Salon de Mai, Musee D'Art Mod, Paris, France, 51; Biennale Int d'Arte Marinara, Pallazzo del Academia, Genoa, Italy, 51; one-man shows, Galerie Breteau, Paris, France, 52, Winston Gallery, San Francisco, 77, 79-85 & 86-90 & Winston Gallery, 91-92; and others. *Teaching:* Founder, dir & instr printmaking & painting, Morton Levin Graphics Workshop, San Francisco, Calif, 72- *Awards:* Hon Mention, 21st Ann Northwest Printmakers, Seattle Art Mus, 49; Bryan Mem Prize, The Villager Travel Exhib, New York, 64; Third Prize, Washington Sq Art Exhib, Inc, 64. *Media:* Etching, Woodcut; Watercolor, Oil. *Publ:* Contribr, Yellow Silk, No 34, summer 90. *Dealer:* Winston Gallery 780 Sutter St San Francisco CA 94109. *Mailing Add:* 1416 Broadway Apt 6 San Francisco CA 94109

LEVINE, DAVID
CARTOONIST, PAINTER
b Brooklyn, NY, Dec 20, 26. *Study:* Tyler Sch Fine Arts; Hans Hoffman Sch. *Work:* Hirshhorn Mus & Sculpture Garden, Washington, DC; Cleveland Mus, Ohio; Brooklyn Mus, NY; Fogg Art Mus, Cambridge, Mass; Nat Portrait Gallery, Washington, DC; Metrop Mus Art, New York. *Exhib:* Whitney Mus Am Art Sculpture & Drawing Ann, 60 & 63; David Levine & Aaron Shikler, Brooklyn Mus, 71; Butler Inst Am Art, 58, 60, 72; Caricature Show, Am Cult Ctr, Paris, 79; Philips Gallery, DC, 80; Caricatures Eng 19th century authors, Morgan Libr, 81; Caricatures & Watercolors, Ashmolean Mus, Oxford, Eng, 87; with Aaron Shikler, Claude Bernard Gallery, 88; and others. *Awards:* Thomas B Clarke Prize, Nat Acad Design, 62; Guggenheim Fel; Gold Medal for Graphics, Am Acad & Inst Arts & Letters, 92. *Bibliog:* P A Dreyfus (auth), The double image of David Levine, Am Artist, 71. *Mem:* Century Asn. *Media:* All Media. *Publ:* Illusr, The Man from MALICE, 66; Pins and Needles, 69; No Known Survivors, David Levine's Political Plank, 70; New York Rev Books; NY Mag; The Arts of David Levine, Knopf, 78. *Mailing Add:* 161 Henry St Brooklyn NY 11201

LEVINE, EDWARD
PAINTER
b Detroit, Mich, Jan 10, 28. *Study:* Wayne State Univ, Southlands Sch Design. *Work:* Ameritech, Detroit, Mich; Mich Bell Tel, An Ameritech Co, Detroit, Mich; Miller, Canfield, Paddock & Stone, Bloomfield Hills, Mich. *Exhib:* Solo exhibs, Xochipilli Gallery, Birmingham, Mich, 86, 88 & 90; Macomb Community Col, Mt Clemens, Mich, 87; Animal Life in Contemporary Art, House of Reps, Washington, DC, 88; Urban Scenes of the 80's, De Waters, Flint, Mich, 88; Urbanology, Nat Exhib on Art & The City, Detroit, Mich, 89; and others. *Awards:* Nat Endowment Arts; Silver Scarab, Scarab Club, 85. *Media:* Acrylic, Oil. *Dealer:* Xochipilli Art Gallery 568 N Woodward Ave Birmingham MI 48009. *Mailing Add:* 700 Lockwood Rd Royal Oak MI 48067

LEVINE, ERIK
SCULPTOR
b Los Angeles, Calif, Oct 31, 60. *Study:* Univ Calif, Los Angeles, 82; Calif State Univ, Northridge, 80-81. *Work:* Walker Art Ctr, Minneapolis, Minn; LA Mus Mod Art, Humlebaek, Denmark; High Mus Art, Atlanta, Ga; Albright-Knox Art Gallery, Buffalo, NY; Chase Manhattan Bank, New York. *Comn:* Round House (sculpture garden), Walker Art Ctr, Minneapolis, Minn, 90. *Exhib:* Enclosing the Void: 8 Contemp Sculptors, Whitney at Equitable Ctr, New York, 88; one-man shows, Louisiana Mus Mod Art, Humlebaek, Denmark, 89 & Fundacio Joan Miro, Barcelona, Spain, 89; 1989 Biennial Exhib, Whitney Mus Am Art, New York, 89; Awards in the Visual Arts 8, traveling, High Mus Art, Atlanta, Ga & La Jolla Mus Contemp Art, Calif, 89. *Awards:* Nat Endowment Arts, 88; NY Fdn Arts, 88. *Bibliog:* Renate Cornu (auth), Erik Levine, Halle Sud, Barcelona, 89; Richard Armstrong, Richard Marshall, Lisa Phillips (auth), 1989 Whitney Biennial, Whitney Mus Am Art, 89; Michael Kimmelman (auth), Erik Levine at Diane Brown Gallery, New York Times, 89. *Dealer:* Diane Brown Gallery 560 Broadway New York NY 10012. *Mailing Add:* PO Box 1187 Long Island City NY 11101

LEVINE, JACK
PAINTER
b Boston, Mass, Jan, 3, 15. *Study:* Study with Dr Denman W Ross, 29-31; also with Harold Zimmerman; Colby Col, Hon DFA, 46. *Work:* Metrop Mus Art, New York; Mus Mod Art, New York; Walker Art Ctr, Minneapolis; Art Inst Chicago; Whitney Mus Am Art, New York; Vatican Mus, Rome, Italy; Barnanisiza-Physsens, Spain. *Exhib:* Retrospectives, Inst Contemp Art, Boston, 53, Whitney Mus Am Art, New York, 55 & Palacio Bellas Artes, Mexico City, Mex, 60; annually, Carnegie Inst, Pittsburgh & Art Inst Chicago; Corcoran Gallery Art, Washington, DC; Mus Mod Art, New York; Mus Fine Arts, Boston; Pa Acad Fine Arts; one-man show, DeCordova Mus, Lincoln, Mass, 68; Jewish Mus, New York, 90; Mid Town Gallery, New York, 90. *Teaching:* Lectr, Art Inst Chicago, Skowhegan Sch Painting & Sculpture, Univ Ill, Pa Acad Fine Arts, Am Art Sch, New York & Cleveland Mus Art Sch; Home Video & TV Show, Feast of Pure Reason, Ch 13, PBS, New York. *Awards:* Guggenheim Fel, 45 & 46; Corcoran Gallery Art Award, 59; Altman Prize, Nat Acad Design, 75; plus others. *Mem:* Nat Inst Arts & Lett; Artists Equity Asn; Am Acad Arts & Sci; Nat Acad Arts & Lett; and others. *Mailing Add:* 68 Morton St New York NY 10014

LEVINE, LES
VIDEO ARTIST, MEDIA SCULPTOR
b Dublin, Ireland, Oct 6, 35; US citizen. *Work:* Nat Gallery Can, Ottawa, Ont; Metrop Mus Art, Whitney Mus Am Art, Mus Mod Art, New York; Philadelphia Mus Art; Indianapolis Mus Art; Nat Gallery Australia, Canberra. *Comn:* Contact (sculpture), Gulf & Western Indust, 69. *Exhib:* One-man exhibs, Slipcover, Walker Art Ctr, 67, Star Garden, Mus Mod Art, New York, 67, I Am Not Blind, Wadsworth Atheneum, 76, Prayer Rug, Philadelphia Mus Art, 79, We Are Not Afraid, Lower Manhattan Cult Coun, NY Subways, 81, Blame God Inst Contemp Art, London, Eng, 85, Media Proj & Pub Advert, Mai 36 Gallery, Luzern, Switz, 88; Documenta, Kassel, Ger, 77 & 87; Everson Video Revue, Everson Mus, Syracuse, 80; San Francisco Int Video Festival, 83; Committed to Print, Mus Mod Art, NY, 88; Consume or Perish & Pray for More, New York Found Arts, New York Subways, 89; Public Mind: Les Levine's Media Sculpture and Mass Ad Campaigns, Everson Mus, Syracuse, 90; Ease Pain, NY Found Arts, New York, 92. *Collections Arranged:* Open To New Ideas (organizer), Jimmy Carter Collection, Ga Mus Art, Athens, 77. *Pos:* Pres, Mus Mott Art, Inc, 71- *Awards:* First Prize for The Star Machine, Sculpture Biennale, Art Gallery Ont, 68; Nat Endowment Arts Fel, 74 & 80; Video Award, New York State Coun Arts, 80; and others. *Bibliog:* David Bourdon (auth), Plastic art's biggest bubble, Life Mag, 8/69; Barbara Cavaliere (auth), Les Levine's ads---and more ads, Arts Mag, 3/81; Vivien Raynor (auth), Not Afraid in the Subway, New York Times, 5/21/82; and others. *Media:* Videotape; Gold, Multimedia. *Publ:* The poets' encyclopedia, Unmuzzled Ox, Vol 4, No 4, New York, 79; publ, Media: The Bio Tech Rehearsal for Leaving the Body, Alberta Col Art, 79; Biennale van de la Critique, Palais des Beaux Arts, Antwerpen Charleroi, 79; auth, Handmade Etchings by Les Levine, Artist Profusions, 81; Blame God, Inst Contemp Art, London, Eng, 85; and others. *Mailing Add:* 20 E 20th St New York NY 10003

LEVINE, MARILYN ANNE
SCULPTOR
b Medicine Hat, Alta, Can, Dec 22, 35. *Study:* Univ Calif, Berkeley, MA, 70, MFA, 71. *Work:* Montreal Mus Fine Arts; Nat Mus Mod Art, Kyoto & Tokyo; San Francisco Mus Mod Art; Israel Mus, Jerusalem; Australian Nat Gallery, Canberra. *Comn:* Sculpture/mural, Pac Enterprises, Los Angeles, 90. *Exhib:* Fuller Goldeen Gallery, San Francisco, 71, 75, 80 & 83; one-man shows, O K Harris Gallery, New York, 74, 76, 79, 81, 84 & 85; GalerieD; Canada Trajectories, Mus Art Mod, Paris, 73; retrospectives, Norman McKenzie Art Gallery, Regina, 74 & Inst Contemp Art, Boston, 81; Illusion & Reality, Australian Nat Gallery; Galerie Alain Blondel, Paris, 81; and others. *Teaching:* Asst prof sculpture & ceramics, Univ Utah, 73-76; vis lectr, Univ Calif, Berkeley, 75-80. *Awards:* Gold Medal, XXVII Concorso Int della Ceramica Arte, 69; Ceramics Int Medal, 73; Nat Endowment Arts Fel, 76 & 80; and others. *Bibliog:* Nancy Foote (ed), The photo realist--12 interviews, Art in Am, 11-12/72; Susan Peterson (auth), The ceramics of Marilyn Levine, Crafts Horizons, Vol 37, 2/77; Hiroshi Matsubara (auth), American west coast artist, Marilyn Levine, Contemp Sculpture, Tokyo, 6/78. *Media:* Clay. *Dealer:* O K Harris Gallery 383 W Broadway New York NY 10012. *Mailing Add:* c/o John Natsoulas Gallery 140 F St Davis CA 95616

LEVINE, MARION LERNER
PAINTER
b London, Eng, Oct 31, 31; US citizen. *Study:* Art Inst of Chicago, BFA, 54, study with Paul Wieghardt, Max Kahn, Vera Berdich. *Work:* Citibank; Bank Am; Bellevue Hosp; Brooklyn Mus; US State Dept; Bryn Maur Col. *Comn:* Printed Editions (6 etching) for Orion Editions, New York, 85, 86, 88, 90, 91, 92. *Exhib:* one-woman shows, Watercolors, Foundry Gallery, Washington, DC, 80 & Paul Klapper Libr, Queens Col, NY, 81; Albright-Knox Mus, Buffalo, NY, 81; Springfield Art Mus, 83; Perlow Gallery, New York, NY, 86; Butler Inst Am Art, Youngstown, Ohio, 87; Carey Arboretum, 90; Prince St Gallery, New York, 92; and others. *Teaching:* Lectr watercolor, Sch Gen Studies, Brooklyn Col, 76-80; instr drawing, Univ Calif, Los Angeles, 77; vis artist, Art Inst Chicago, 81; instr painting, Col Staten Island, City Univ New York, 81-82. *Awards:* Adolf & Esther Gottlieb Grant in Painting, 81; Creative Artists Pub Serv Program Fel, 83; Nat Endowment Arts Fel, 86; and others. *Bibliog:* Ruth Bass (auth), Art rev, Art News, 79; Anselm Hollo (auth), The Shelves of Paradise, Marion Lerner Levine's Watercolors, 79; June Cutler (auth), Marion Lerner Levine, Am Artist, 84; and others. *Mem:* Col Art Asn; Womens Caucus Art. *Media:* Oil, Watercolor. *Dealer:* Orion Editions Gallery 270 Lafayette St New York NY 10012. *Mailing Add:* 359 Sixth Ave Brooklyn NY 11215

LEVINE, MARTIN
PRINTMAKER, EDUCATOR
b New York, NY, May 14, 45. *Study:* Calif Col Arts & Crafts, MFA; State Univ NY, Buffalo, BS. *Work:* Smithsonian Inst, Washington, DC; Brooklyn Mus; Mus Fine Arts, Boston; Art Inst Chicago, Ill; Victoria & Albert Mus, London, England; and many others. *Comn:* Two etchings of hist landmark (with ADI Gallery, San Francisco), Clorox Co, Oakland, Calif, 76; edition of etchings, Union League Club, Chicago, 83 & Pratt Graphics Ctr, NY, 81 & 84. *Exhib:* Nat Acad Design Ann Exhib, 74, 76-79 & 86; 30 Years of American Printmaking, Brooklyn Mus, NY, 76; Int Print Biennale, Cracow, Poland, 78 & 86; Int Grafik Biennale, Frechen, WGer, 78, 80, 82 & 86; XV Int Bienal, Sao Paulo, Brazil, 79; Chicago & Vicinity, Art Inst Chicago, 81 & 85; Int Print Exhib, Taiwan, Republic of China, 83 & 85; Soc Am Graphic Artists Nat Print Exhib, 81, 85 & 86; and many others. *Teaching:* Asst prof, Northwestern Univ, Evanston, 79-85 & State Univ NY, Stony Brook, 86- *Awards:* Purchase Award, 24th Nat Exhib of Prints, Libr Cong, 75; Nat Endowment Arts Printmaking Fel Grant, 77. *Bibliog:* Article, Bldg Design, London, 83; article & cover, Arts Rev, London, 83. *Mem:* Boston Printmakers; Calif Soc Printmakers; Audubon Artists; Soc Am Graphic Artists. *Media:* Intaglio, Lithography. *Publ:* Auth, (catalog), Am Cult Ctr, Embassy of the USA, Tel Aviv, Israel, 85. *Mailing Add:* 25 Cornwallis Rd East Setauket NY 11733

LEVINE, MELINDA (ESTHER)
CRITIC, EDITOR
b Buffalo, NY, Apr 18, 47. *Study:* State Univ NY, Buffalo, BA, 70; State Univ NY, Stony Brook, 70-71. *Pos:* Asst ed, Artweek, 80-81, managing ed, 81-82; cur, Art Gallery Notre Dame, Belmont, Calif, 82; art critic, San Francisco Mag, 82-83, Berkeley Gazette, 82-83 & San Francisco Focus, 83-84. *Mem:* Int Asn Art Critics; Media Alliance; Northern Calif Art Writers Guild. *Res:* West Coast contemporary art, particularly that of Northern California and the California clay movement. *Publ:* Articles in San Francisco Focus, San Francisco, Images & Issues, Am Craft & Artweek. *Mailing Add:* 456 61st St Oakland CA 94609

LEVINE, SHEPARD
PAINTER, EDUCATOR
b New York, NY, June 21, 22. *Study:* Univ NMex, BA & MA; Univ Toulouse, France. *Work:* Parnassus Hall, Athens, Greece; Ore State Univ; Arkia Airlines, Israel. *Exhib:* Am Graphic Arts Asn; Brooklyn Mus; Henry Gallery, Univ Wash; San Francisco Mus Art; Portland Art Mus, Ore; Spokane Art Mus; and others. *Teaching:* Lectr to mus & pvt groups; prof art, Ore State Univ, formerly, emer prof, currently. *Awards:* Purchase Award, Univ Ore. *Mailing Add:* 3750 NW Hayes Ave Corvallis OR 97330

LEVINE, TOM
PAINTER, PRINTMAKER
b Cincinnati, Ohio, Nov 16, 45. *Study:* Miami Univ, Oxford, Ohio, BA, 67; Univ Denver, MBA, 68; Univ Cincinnati, MFA, 74. *Work:* Mus Mod Art, New York; Cincinnati Art Mus; New York Pub Libr; Andover Col, Mass; Mass Inst Technol, Cambridge. *Comn:* Stage set (three paintings), Chase Manhattan Bank, New York, 81; painting, Heidelberg Inc, Cincinnati, 92. *Exhib:* Recent Acquisitions, Cincinnati Art Mus, 83; solo exhibs, Galerie Weunsche, Bonn, 86, Galerie Ursus-Presse, Dusseldorf, 88, 90, & 92, Segacho Exhib Space, Tokyo, 90 & Munic Gallery, Esch Luxembourg, 90; In Defense of Sacred Lands, Harcus Gallery, Boston, 87; Drawings, Lorence-Monk Gallery, New York 91; Print & Drawing Coun Exhib, Minneapolis Inst Art, 91; and others. *Media:* Oil. *Mailing Add:* PO Box 698 Canal St New York NY 10013

LEVINE, TOMAR
PAINTER
b New York, NY, Mar 24, 45. *Study:* City Col New York, BA, 66; Brooklyn Col NY, MFA, 74. *Work:* New York Acad Med; Chemical Bank, New York; AT&T, New York; Guy Carpenter & Co Inc, New York; INA Corp, New York. *Exhib:* New American Still Life, Westmoreland Co Mus Art, Greensburg, Pa, 79; Painted Light, Reading Mus, Reading, Conn, 83; Artists' Choice: The First Eight Years, Artists' Choice Mus, New York, 84; Am Realism-20th Century Drawings & Watercolors, San Francisco Mus Mod Art, San Francisco, Calif, 85; 161st Ann Exhib, Nat Acad Design, New York, 86; Deutsch-Amerikanisches Inst, Munic Gallery, Regensburg, WGer, 88-89. *Awards:* Yaddo Fel, 84; Fel, Va Ctr Creative Arts, 85; Cummington Community Arts, 91. *Bibliog:* Bill Sullivan (auth), Tomar Levine, Arts Mag, 83. *Mem:* NY Artists' Equity. *Media:* Egg Tempera, Acrylic Oil. *Mailing Add:* 191 Claremont Ave No 43 New York NY 10027

LEVINSON, JOEL D
PHOTOGRAPHER, CONCEPTUAL ARTIST
b Conn, April 24, 53. *Study:* Univ Calif, Berkeley, BA(communications), 75, MA(visual arts), 77. *Work:* Yale Art Mus; Winnipeg Art Gallery; Mus fur Kunst und Gewerbe; Minneapolis Inst Arts; Boston Mus Fine Arts; Bibliotheque National. *Exhib:* Addison Gallery Am Art, 80; Minneapolis Inst Arts, 82; Denver Art Mus, 83; Palm Springs Art Mus, 84; Solo exhibs, Amerika Haus, Berlin, 87, Crocker Art Mus, 88, Marsha Mateyka Gallery, 89, J B Speed Art Mus, Louisville, 82, O K Harris, New York, 82, Art Mus STex, Corpus Christi, 83, Sprengel Kunstmus, Hanover, WGer, 85 & Milwaukee Art Mus, Wis, 86. *Awards:* Eisner Award, Univ Calif, 78. *Bibliog:* Content/Context, Artforum, 12/88; Media Art/Constructive Photography, Art, 1/89; Robert C Morgan (auth), Joel Levinson and the loss of representation, New Art Int, 2-3/90. *Media:* Photography, Collage-Montage. *Publ:* Auth, Joel D Levinson (photogr), PM Publ, 82; The Making of a Collection, Minneapolis Inst Arts, Aperture, 84; Fleamarkets, Braus Ed, 87; People and Places, Milwaukee Art Mus, 87. *Dealer:* Eric Frank Gallerie Geneva Switzerland. *Mailing Add:* 2442 N Gower St Los Angeles CA 90068

LEVINSON, MIMI
PAINTER, LECTURER
b Kenosha, Wis, June 6, 40. *Study:* Carnegie-Mellon Univ, with Roger Anliker, BFA, 62; San Jose State Col, Frick Scholarship, 64. *Work:* Ga Railroad Bank Collection, Augusta; Mesa Vista Hospital, San Diego, Calif; New Delhi Handi Crafts Mus, India. *Comn:* Stained glass wall mosaic, Casselhoff's, Pitsburgh, Pa, 62; painted fabric mural, Kaiser-Permanente, San Diego, Calif, 78; batiks, Hillcrest Psychotherapy Ctr, San Diego, Calif, 80. *Exhib:* Craftman's Guild Shows, Arts & Crafts Ctr, Pittsburgh, Pa, 66-67; Art Guild All Media, San Diego Mus Art, Calif, 75 & 81; Calif Crafts XI, E B Crocker Art Mus, Sacramento, 79; Exchange Exhib, Yokohama Art Ctr, Japan, 79; Textile Kunst, Krefeld, Ger, 88; Fibers Exhib, Brand Mus, Glendale, Calif, 91; duo solo shows, Jewish Community Ctr, San Diego, Calif, 91-92; Fibre Meets Fiber, Mansfield Mus, Eng, 92. *Teaching:* Instr art, Sunnyside Sch, Pittsburgh, Pa, 62-67; workshop leader batik-weaving, Convergence 76, Pittsburgh, Pa, 76; instr cult arts, Jewish Community Ctr, San Diego, Calif, 79-91; San Diego State Univ extended studies, 89-92. *Awards:* First Prize, Augusta Art Asn, 71; Purchase Prize, Ga Railroad Bank, 72; Third Prize, Weaver's Guild, 75. *Bibliog:* Dan Coyro (auth), Batik: How to turn wax and dye into art, The Sentinel, 75; Jan Jennings (auth), Natural history museum, San Diego Evening Tribune, 78; Elise Miller (auth), Womanism to surrealism, San Diego Mag, 79. *Mem:* Allied Craftsmen; Am Crafts Council; Artists Equity; Calif Fibers (chmn, 77); San Diego Mus Art Guild. *Media:* Batik, Mixed. *Publ:* Contribr, Crafts 1976, Southern Calif Designer Inc, 76; Exotic Needlework, Crown, 78. *Mailing Add:* 1730 Alta Vista Way San Diego CA 92109

LEVINSON, MON
SCULPTOR, PAINTER
b New York, NY, Jan 6, 26. *Work:* Whitney Mus Am Art, New York; Joseph H Hirshhorn Collection, Washington, DC; NY Univ Art Collection; Rose Art Gallery, Brandeis Univ; Brooklyn Mus, NY; Albright-Knox Art Gallery, Buffalo, NY. *Comn:* Objects & 69; sculpture, Pub Sch 166, New York, 67; mural-sculpture, Housing & Redevelop Bd, Demountable Vest Pocket Parks, New York, 69; and others. *Exhib:* Plus by Minus, 68 & Paper about Paper, 80, Albright-Knox Gallery, Buffalo, NY; A Plastic Presence, Milwaukee Art Ctr, Wis, New York & San Francisco, 69-70; Whitney Mus Am Art Sculpture Ann, 70 & 73; Storm King Arts Ctr, Mountainville, NY, 72 & 75; Hirshhorn Collection, 74; Rosa Esman Gallery, New York, 76 & 77; Getler Pall Gallery, New York, 81; Fine Arts Mus, Long Island, 81; Amdre Zarre Gallery, New York, 89. *Teaching:* Vis artist, C W Post Col, 70-72 & 76-77. *Awards:* Cassandra Found Award, 72; Creative Artists Pub Serv Prog Award, NY State Coun Arts, 74; Nat Endowment Arts Fel, 76. *Mailing Add:* 309 W Broadway New York NY 10013

LEVINTHAL, DAVID LAWRENCE
PHOTOGRAPHER
b San Francisco, Calif, March 8, 49. *Study:* Stanford Univ, AB, 70; Yale Univ, MFA, 73; Mass Inst Tech, SM, 81. *Work:* Mus Mod Art, New York; Corcoran Gallery Art, Washington, DC; Los Angeles Co Mus Art, Calif; Amon Carter Mus, Fort Worth, Tex; Nat Gallery New Zealand, Wellington. *Exhib:* Photography and Art, Los Angeles Co Mus Art, 87; Avant-Garde in the 80's, Los Angeles Co Mus Art, 87; Surrogate Selves, Corcoran Gallery, Washington, DC, 89; Photography of Invention, Nat Mus, Washington, DC, 89; Constructed Realities, Kunstverein, Munich, Germany, 89; Devil on the Stairs, Inst Contemp Art, Philadelphia, Pa, 91; More Than One Photography, Mus Mod Art, New York, 92; Instant Imaging Stories, Mus Mod Art, Vienna, Austria, 92. *Teaching:* Instr, photog, Univ Neada, Las Vegas, 75-76. *Awards:* Artists Grant, Nat Endowment Arts, 90-91. *Bibliog:* Andy Gundberg & Kathy Gauss (coauths), Photo & Art & Anne Hoy (auth), Fabrications, Abbeville Press, 87; Terrie Sultan (auth), Surrogate Selves, Corcoran Gallery, 89. *Mem:* Col Art Asn. *Publ:* Coauth (with Garry Trudeau), Hitler Moves East, Sheed Andrews & McMeel, 77; illustr, Modern Romance, Univ San Diego, 85; Centric 35: David Levinthal, Calif State Long Beach, 89; American Beauties, Laurence Miller, 90. *Dealer:* Lawrence Miller Gallery 138 Spring St New York NY 10012. *Mailing Add:* 251 W 19th St, No 6-C New York NY 10011

LEVITT, ALFRED
PAINTER, PREHISTORIAN
b New York, NY, Aug 15, 94. *Study:* Columbia Univ; Art Students League; Acad Grand Chaumiere, France; also with Hans Hofmann, New York. *Work:* Neveh-Sha'anan Mus, Haifa, Israel; plus many other pvt collections in Europe & US. *Exhib:* Butler Inst Am Art, Youngstown, Ohio, 46; Pa Acad Fine Arts, Philadelphia, 48; Brooklyn Mus Exhibs, 47, 51, 53 & 59; Whitney Mus Am Art, New York, 49, 53 & 55; one-man shows, Babcock Galleries, New York, 45 & 46, Art Alliance Philadelphia, 47 & Terry Dintenfass Galleries, 83; Permanent Collection, Metrop Mus Art, New York, 92; and many others. *Pos:* Coord chmn, Mod Artists Cape Ann, Mass, 47; founder, dir & instr, Ecole Mod de Provence, St Remy de Provence, France, 49-50 & 59-62. *Teaching:* Lectr cave art, NY Univ, Cooper Union, Archaeol Inst Am at Wagner Col, North Shore Soc Archaeol Inst Am, New York Pub Libr, Philadelphia Art Alliance & also in France; lectr mod art. *Awards:* Chevalier de L'ordre des Arts et Lettres for Outstanding Studies of Stone Age Cave Art, Fr Govt, 75. *Mem:* Archaeol Inst Am; Soc Prehistorique L'Ariege, France; Fel MacDowell Colony; life mem Archaeol Soc Staten Island. *Res:* Various researches of cave art and prehistory; extended visits and studies of the drawing, engraving, painting and sculpture of Stone Age artists in France, Spain and Italy; made extensive studies of prehistoric engravings on boulders in Valcamonica, Brescia, Italy, 80. *Mailing Add:* 505 La Guardia Pl New York NY 10012

LEVITT, HELEN
PHOTOGRAPHER, FILMMAKER
b New York, NY, 1918. *Work:* Mus Modern Art, New York; Metro Mus Art, New York; Boston Mus Fine Arts; Corcoran Gallery Art; Mus Fine Arts, Houston. *Exhib:* Solo exhibs, Mus Modern Art, 43 & 74, Nexus Gallery, Atlanta, 76, Sidney Janis Gallery, 80, Corcoran Gallery Art, 80 & Boston Mus Fine Arts, 83. *Awards:* Guggenheim Fel, 59, 60 & 80; Ford Found Fel, 64; Nat Endowment Arts Fel, 76. *Bibliog:* Walker Evans (auth), Quality: Its image in the arts, Atheneum, 69; John Szarkowski (auth), Looking at Photographs, Mus Mod Art, New York, 73; Roberta Hellman & Marvin Hosking (auths), Color Photographs by Helen Levitt, Grossmont Col, 80. *Publ:* Coauth (with James Agee), A Way of Seeing, Horizon, 81. *Dealer:* Daniel Wolf Gallery 30 W 57th St New York NY; Jeff Fraenkel Gallery 55 Grant Ave San Francisco CA. *Mailing Add:* c/o Laurence Miller Gallery 138 Spring St New York NY 10012

LEVY, BERNARD
DEALER
b New York, NY, Feb 10, 17. *Study:* NY Univ, BA, 37. *Pos:* Pres, Bernard & S Dean Levy Inc, 73- *Bibliog:* On Madison Avenue, Fortune Mag, 12/47; Rita Reif (auth), Antiques, NY Times, 10/76; Douglas Villiers (auth), Next Year in Jerusalem, Viking Press, 76. *Mem:* Art & Antique Dealers League Am (pres, five yrs). *Specialty:* American paintings; American antique furniture; silver; English and American ceramics. *Mailing Add:* Bernard & Dean Levy Inc 24 E 84th St New York NY 10028

LEVY, DAVID CORCOS
ART HISTORIAN, EDUCATOR
b New York, NY, Apr 10, 38. *Study:* Columbia Col, BA, 60; New York Univ, MA, 67, PhD, 79. *Work:* Guggenheim Mus, New York. *Pos:* Exec dean, Parsons Sch Design, New York, 70-89; chancellor, New Sch Social Res, New York, 89-90; pres & dir, Corcoran Gallery Art, Washington, DC, 91- *Mailing Add:* 16 E 23rd St New York NY 10010

LEVY, HILDA
PAINTER, SCULPTOR
b Pinsk, Russia. *Study:* Univ Calif, Berkeley, AB; Pasadena City Col; Jepson Art Inst; Univ Calif, Los Angeles; also with Adolph Gottlieb. *Exhib:* Nat Gallery Can, Ottawa, Ont; Libr of Cong, Washington, DC; Butler Inst Am Art, Youngstown, Ohio; San Francisco Mus Art & M H de Young Mem Mus, San Francisco; one-woman show, Calif Palace Legion Hon, Pasadena Mus & McNay Inst, Calif; and others. *Awards:* 40 local & nat awards. *Bibliog:* Edward Reep (auth), Content of Watercolor, Reinhold; Lawrence C Goldsmith (auth), Watercolor Bold & Free, Watson Guptill; Les Krantz (ed), Calif Art Rev, Am References. *Mem:* Nat Watercolor Soc; Bay Printmakers. *Media:* Wood, Jewelry. *Mailing Add:* 2411 Brigden Rd Pasadena CA 91104

LEVY, MARGARET WASSERMAN
SCULPTOR
b Dec 13, 1899; US citizen. *Study:* Wellesley Col, BA, 22; Bryn Mawr Col, 23; Philadelphia Sch Occupational Therapy, 23-24; Stella Elkins Tyler Sch Art; Pa Acad Art. *Work:* Pa Acad Fine Arts, Philadelphia; Philadelphia Mus Fine Arts, Pa; Drexel Univ, Pa; Woodmere Art Gallery, Philadelphia; Valley Agr Col; also many pvt collections incl: Ambassador & Mrs Shelby Davis, Princess de Nescemi and Mrs Haakov Styrie; and others. *Comn:* Bronze sculpture, Julius Rosenwald II for Alverthorpe Park, Pa, 70; polyester & resin sculpture, Leon Berkowitz for Delaware Valley Col Agriculture, Pa, 76; bronze, Mossand Leatherbee Architects for Blackwell Mansions Park, Pa; whale for playground, Re-development Authority City Philadelphia, Pa; Little Persian Goat Plicare, St Peters Sch, Pa, 77; elephant, Germantown Friends Sch, Young adult Germantown Friends Sch. *Exhib:* Ann Exhibs, Pa Acad Fine Arts, 50, 52, 60, 61, & 72; Third Philadelphia Arts Festival, Philadelphia Mus Art & Pa Acad Fine Arts, 62; Nat Acad Design, New York, 63 & 81; Artists Equity Exhib, Mus Civic Ctr, Philadelphia, 71 & 81; Bodley Gallery, New York, 83; one-woman shows, Lehigh Univ Mus, Bethelem, 62, Provident Trust Co, 67 & Marion Lock Gallery, 83 Philadelphia, Pa; Wellesly Col Art Gallery, Wellesly, Mass. *Pos:* Bd mem, Woodmere Art Gallery, currently. *Teaching:* Instr Woodmere Art Gallery. *Awards:* Lloyd Van Sciver Mem Prize for best work, Ann Juried Exhib, 61; Honorable Mention, Woodmere Art Gallery, 62 & 63; Second Prize, Exhib by Soc Am Pen Women, Smithsonian Inst. *Mem:* Artists Equity, Philadelphia (bd mem); Philadelphia Art Alliance (sculpture comt). *Publ:* Article, Sculpture 73 Drexel Inst Mag, 64; contribr, Changing Sculpture Concepts, Wellesley Alumnae, 72. *Mailing Add:* 1016 Westview St Philadelphia PA 19119

LEVY, MARK
WRITER, HISTORIAN
b New York, NY, June 24, 47. *Study:* Clark Univ, BA, 68; Ind Univ, MA, 70, PhD, 77. *Pos:* Comnr, Alameda Co Art Comn, 85-86. *Teaching:* Asst prof, Kenyon Col, 74-79 & Univ Nevada, 80-81; prof, Calif State Univ, Hayward, 81-; vis prof advan art theory, Grad Prog, San Francisco Art Inst, 84-89. *Awards:* Samuel Kress Dissertation Fel, 73; Nat Endowment Humanities Fel, 77; Fullbright-Hays Grant, summer 91. *Mem:* Col Art Asn; Northern Calif Art Critics Guild (steering comt, 83); Int Asn Art Critics. *Res:* Contemporary California art. *Publ:* Auth, Joan Brown the Golden Age, San Diego State Univ, 86; The Shaman is a Gifted Artist, High Performance, fall 88; Rilke, Letters on Cezanne, San Francisco Rev of Books, fall 88; Squeak Carnwath, Artspace, 1/2/89; Wayang Kulit as a model for performance art, High Performance, summer 89; and others. *Mailing Add:* 3555 Monterey Blvd Oakland CA 94619

LEVY, PHYLLIS H
PAINTER
b Brooklyn, NY, June 20, 27. *Study:* Cooper Union Art Sch, cert; San Francisco State, AB(art), MA(art educ); Colo Springs Fine Arts Ctr (scholar); Calif Sch Fine Arts (scholar). *Work:* Israel Mus, Jerusalem. *Exhib:* 15th Ann Watercolor, San Francisco Mus Art, Calif, 51; 26th Ann Women, San Francisco Mus Art, Calif, 51; Am Watercolor Drawings & Prints, Metrop Mus, New York, 52; 2nd Ann Exhib, Richmond Art Ctr, Va, 53; NJ Artists, Newark Mus, 55; 71st Ann Exhib, Nat Collection Fine Arts, Washington, DC, 64. *Teaching:* Teacher art, Montgomery Co Public Sch, 69-78. *Awards:* San Francisco Art Asn Prize, 51. *Mem:* Artists Equity Asn. *Media:* Acrylic, Mixed Media. *Mailing Add:* 9202 Friars Road Bethesda MD 20817

LEVY, S(TEPHEN) DEAN
DEALER, GALLERY DIRECTOR
b New York, NY, Nov 17, 42. *Study:* Yale Univ, BA, 64. *Pos:* Vpres, Bernard & S Dean Levy, Inc, 73- *Bibliog:* On Madison Avenue, Fortune Mag, 12/47; Rita Reif (auth), Antiques, New York Times, 10/76; Douglas Villiers (auth), Next Year in Jerusalem, Viking Press, 76. *Mem:* Art & Antique Dealers League. *Specialty:* American paintings, antique furniture, silver; English and American ceramics. *Mailing Add:* Bernard & Dean Levy Inc 24 E 84th St New York NY 10028

LEVY, TIBBIE
PAINTER
b New York, NY, Oct 29, 08. *Study:* Cornell Univ, with Arshile Gorky, AB; Art Students League; Acad Grand Chaumiere & Acad Andre Lhote, Paris, France; NY Univ, JD. *Work:* Contemp Art Soc Gt Brit; Mus Mod Art, Madrid, Barcelona & Bilbao, Spain; Princeton Univ Mus; Cornell Univ Mus; plus 40 other mus. *Exhib:* Bodley Gallery, New York, 60-70; Galerie Ror Volmar, Paris, 61; Sala Nebli, Madrid, 62; Galeria Forum, Madrid, 63; Portal Gallery, London, Eng, 63 & 65; plus others. *Teaching:* Lectr art. *Media:* Oil. *Dealer:* Bodley Gallery 787 Madison Ave New York NY 10021. *Mailing Add:* 2 Sutton Pl S New York NY 10022

LEW, FRAN
PAINTER
Study: Brooklyn Col, with Philip Pearlstein, BA(art), 66; Boston Univ Sch Fine & Applied Art, MFA, 68; Int Ctr Paintings & Costume Design, Palazzo Grassi, with Gregory Battcock, Master (glassblower) Seguso, Venice, Italy, 78; Art Student's League, with Daniel Greene, Robert Beverly Hale & John Howard Sanden, 78-79; Reilly League of Artists, NY, with Cesare Borgia, 79-84. *Work:* Governor's Mansion, Albany, NY; Consulate Israel, New York; United Jewish Asn-Fedn Jewish Philanthropics, Westchester, NY. *Comn:* Portrait Trilogy--Golda Meir, David Ben Gurion, Moshe Dayan, IAD Peace Comt, New York, 82; portrait, Interpublic Group of Companies, New York, 84; portrait, comn by du Vigneaud family, Scarsdale, NY, 88; portrait, NY, Am Cancer Soc, New York, 86; portrait, Coalition of Italo-Am Asn, New York, 90. *Exhib:* Palazzo Grassi Int Ctr Painting & Design Exhib, Venice, Italy, 78; Am Artists Mag Golden Anniversary Exhib, John Pence Gallery, 87; solo exhibs, Manhattan Borough President's Art Gallery & Pen & Brush Club, New York, 89. *Teaching:* Instr art, Am Int Sch, Israel, 71-72; instr portrait drawing, Adult Educ, Katonah, White Plains, NY, 80-82. *Awards:* Gold Medal, Knickerbocker Artists, 84; Corporate Prize, Am Artist Mag Golden Anniversary Nat Competition, 87; Solo Award-Best in Show, Pen & Brush Oil Exhib, 87. *Bibliog:* Fritz Henning (ed), Member of the Issue, Northlight Mag, 6/83; eds, Drawings in the Golden Anniversary National Art Competition, Am Artist Mag, 6/87; Edward Rubin (auth), article, Manhattan Arts, 10/89. *Mem:* Knickerbocker Artists; Hudson Valley Art Asn; Catherine Lorillard Wolfe Art Club; Pen & Brush Club; life mem, Art Students League. *Media:* Oil. *Dealer:* Grand Central Art Galleries 24 W 57th St New York NY 10019. *Mailing Add:* 150 Lake St 6C White Plains NY 10604

LEW, WEYMAN
PAINTER, PRINTMAKER
b San Francisco, Calif, Feb 17, 35. *Study:* Univ Calif, Berkeley, BS, 57; San Francisco Art Inst, with Jay deFeo, 65-66. *Work:* M H de Young Mem Mus, San Francisco; Univ Calif Mus, Berkeley; Inst Arte Contemporaneo, Lima, Peru; Santa Barbara Mus Art, Calif; Oakland Art Mus, Calif; Brooklyn Mus. *Comn:* Univ Calif Mus, Berkeley, 74. *Exhib:* One-man shows, M H De Young Mem Mus, 70, Inst Contemp Art, Lima, Peru, 70, Santa Barbara Mus Art, 71, Art Gallery Greater Victoria, BC, Can, 72, Bonython Art Gallery, Sydney, Australia, 72-75, Sande Webster Gallery, Philadelphia, 72, 74, 77, 80 & 84 & Int Art Exhib Hall, Beijing, China, 91; and many others. *Pos:* Dir, Kelley Galleries, San Francisco, 68. *Teaching:* Guest instr painting, drawing & serigraphy, M H de Young Mem Mus Art Sch, 70-71. *Awards:* Merit Award, San Francisco Art Festival, 80; Distinguished Award for Cult, Chinese Cult Found San Francisco, 91. *Bibliog:* Thomas Albright (auth), reviews in San Francisco Chronicle, 68-70, 73 & 77; Ken Wang (auth), An artist who can take a line and have it do anything he wants, San Francisco Examiner, 8/10/83. *Mem:* Calif Soc Printmakers. *Media:* Ink, Watercolor; Etching. *Publ:* Auth, Weyman Lew Sketches Away, Triton Assocs, 81; Weyman Lew, of Peoples and Places, Chinese Cult Found San Francisco, 91; Echoes of Oxford, illustrations by W Lew, Phillip Carlson, 91. *Mailing Add:* 2810 Pacific Ave San Francisco CA 94115

LEWANDOWSKI, EDMUND D
PAINTER, ADMINISTRATOR
b Milwaukee, Wis, July 3, 14. *Study:* Layton Sch Art, 31-35. *Work:* Addison Gallery Am Art, Andover, Mass; Brooklyn Mus, NY; Boston Mus Fine Arts; Mus Mod Art, New York; Corcoran Gallery Art, Washington, DC; plus many others. *Comn:* Polanki Fountain, Milwaukee Civic Ctr, Wis, 70; mural, First Wis Ctr, Milwaukee, Wis, 73; Polish-American Bicentennial Graphics, Polish Nat Alliance, Chicago, Ill, 75; 4 mosaic murals, Vet Mem, Milwaukee War Mem, 76; mural, St Lukes Hosp, Milwaukee, Wis, 79. *Exhib:* Art Inst Chicago; Carnegie Inst, Pittsburgh; Corcoran Gallery Art, Washington, DC; Pa Acad Fine Arts, Philadelphia; Phillips Collection, Washington, DC; plus others. *Pos:* Fac, Layton Sch Art, 47-49; from prof painting to head, Dept Art, Fla State Univ, 49-54; pres, Layton Sch Art, 54-72; chmn, Dept Art, Winthrop Col, 73-84, artist in residence, 84- *Teaching:* Prof, Layton Sch Art, 45-49; prof painting, Fla State Univ, 49-54, head dept, 52-54; dir, Layton Sch Art; chmn dept art, Winthrop Col, Rock Hill, SC, 79- *Awards:* Merit Award, SC Bicentennial Comn, 76; Purchase Award, SC Art Comn, 76; Distinguished Achievement in the Field of Art Award, Am Coun Polish Cult Clubs, 79; plus many others. *Bibliog:* Andrew C Ritchie (auth), Abstract painting and sculpture in America, Mus Mod Art, 51; Nathaniel Pousette-Dart (ed), American Painting Today, Hastings House, 56; John I Baur (auth), Revolution and Tradition in Modern American Art, Harvard Univ, 59. *Mem:* Wis Painters & Sculptors; Polish-Am Artists. *Publ:* Contribr, annual report cover, Falk Corp, 58; 10 Distinguished Am Artists, New York Times, 6/58; Ford Times, 10/61; cover, The Diplomat, 12/61; cover, Wis Architect, 11/63; Images of America, Univ Wash Press; 50 yrs of painting, H V Allison Galleries, New York, 90. *Dealer:* H V Allison Galleries New York NY. *Mailing Add:* 537 Meadowbrook Lane Rock Hill SC 29730

LEWCZUK, MARGRIT
PAINTER
Study: Queens Col, New York, NY, 52. *Exhib:* Solo exhibs, Brooklyn Mus, NY, 75, John Davis Gallery, Akron, Ohio, 82, Thorden Wetterling Gallery, Stockholm, Sweden, 87, Pamela Auchincloss Gallery, New York, 87, 89 & 92, Dolan Maxwell Gallery, Philadelphia, Pa, 88 & Bjorn Wetterling Gallery, Gottenburg, Sweden, 91; Munson-Williams Proctor Mus, New York, 81; Faculty Invitational, Bennington Col, Vt, 83; Works on Paper, Allport Gallery, San Francisco, Calif, 89. *Awards:* Nat Endowment Arts, 89. *Media:* Oil on Linen, Charcoal Pastel on Paper. *Publ:* Exhib Catalogues for Pamela Auchincloss Gallery, 87 & Thorden Wetterling Gallery, 87. *Mailing Add:* c/o Pamela Auchincloss Gallery 558 Broadway New York NY 10012

LEWENZ, LISA
ENVIRONMENTAL ARTIST, PHOTOGRAPHER
b Baltimore, Md, Apr 1, 55. *Study:* Philadelphia Col Art, 73-74; Kans City Art Inst, 76-77; Art Inst Chicago, BFA, 78; Calif Inst Arts, MFA, 82. *Work:* City of Salem Collection, Mass; New Eng Holocaust Found Collection, Boston; Mus Contemp Arts, Baltimore, Md; Hallmark Collections, Kans City; Tisch Photo Collections, New York Univ. *Comn:* John A Logan Col, Ill Arts Coun, Carbondale, 85. *Exhib:* New Chicago Photographers, Mus Contemp Photog, Chicago, 84; Appearances, Minneapolis Int Art, Minn, 84; Empty Chairs & Hallways, Ledel Gallery, New York, 87; solo exhib, A View from Three Mile Island, San Francisco Camerawork, Calif, 87, A Letter without Words, 92 St Gallery, New York, 89, Towards a More Perfect Union, Baltimore Mus Art, Md, 92; Other Rooms, The Kunstraum, Washington, DC, 90; Visual AIDS, Mus Contemp Arts, Baltimore, Md, 90. *Collections Arranged:* Site Works, St Mary's Gallery, 87; Constructions, 90, Contemporary Puerto Rican Painting, 90, Fifth Annual National Print & Drawing Exhibit, Gormley Gallery, 91. *Pos:* Dir, Unit One photog prog, Univ Ill, Champaign, 85-87, Gormley Gallery, Col Notre Dame Md, Baltimore, 90-91; dir/coordr, site specific sem, St Mary's Col, Md, 87-88. *Teaching:* Vis lectr photog, Minneapolis Col Art & Design, 84; vis asst prof photog, Univ Ill, Champaign-Urbana, 85-87, New York Univ, 92. *Awards:* Ferguson Award, Towards a More Perfect Union, Friends Photog, 90; Nat Endowments Arts, Mid Career Fel & US/France Award, LaNapoule, France, 90; Fulbright Hays Scholar, Sr Res Award Ger, Ger & Coun Int Exchange Scholars, 93. *Bibliog:* Jim Hugunin (auth), A problem of nuclear Phahl-out, Houston Ctr for Photog J, 86; Deborah Bright (auth), The Contest of Meaning: Critical Histories of Photography, Richard Bolton (ed), MIT Press, 89; John Pfahl & Sandra Olson (auths), Tainted Prospects: Photographers & the Compromised Environment, Castellani Art Mus, 91. *Mem:* Soc Photog Educ; Md Art Place, Baltimore (exec bd dir, 88-92); Col Art Asn; Baltimore Artists Housing Coop (co-pres, bd dir, 90-); Friends Photog. *Media:* Interdisciplinary Arts, Photography; Film, Video. *Publ:* Auth, 1984 A View from Three Mile Island, No Net Productions, 83; contribr, Nuclear Power, A Weapon for the Enemy, UCLA Press, 84; Visions Issue: Environmental Action, 85; Friends of the Earth Journal, 86. *Mailing Add:* 244 E 23rd St No 3A New York NY 70010

LEWIN, BERNARD
DEALER, COLLECTOR
b Ger; US citizen. *Study:* With Kurt Wagner, Berlin. *Exhib:* Ann shows, Castaneda, Cora, Coronel, Tamayo and others. *Pos:* Art dir, B Lewin Galleries, Palm Springs, Calif, 60- *Awards:* Twenty-fifth Anniversary of Mexican Masters, City of Los Angeles; Lifetime Achievement Award, First Int Gallery Invitational, Chicago. *Mem:* Art Dealers Asn. *Specialty:* Mexican masters, Tamayo, Siqueiros, Merida, R Martinez, R Coronel, Diego Rivera, Felipe Castenada, Gustavo Montoya and others. *Collection:* Mexican masters, American and European. *Mailing Add:* Lewin Galleries 210 S Palm Canyon Dr Palm Springs CA 92262-6312

LEWIS, CAROLE
SCULPTOR
b London, Eng, Dec 28, 34, US citizen. *Study:* Hana Geber Workshop, apprentice to Hana Geber, 79-82,. *Work:* Am Collection, Mus Int Art, Sophia,

Bulgaria; Gen Electric Corp, Fairfield, Conn; Mus Hudson Highlands, Cornwall, NY; Starrett City Assoc, Brooklyn, NY; Seicomart Corp, Sapporo, Japan; and others. *Exhib:* Group shows, Cleveland Mus Nat Hist, Cleveland, Ohio, 84; Dimensional Whimsey, Pelham Art Ctr, Pelham, NY, 86; American Image-A Hundred Years of Figurative Sculpture, Port Hist Mus, Philadelphia, Pa, 87; Creature & Creatures Great & Small, Elaine Benson Gallery, Bridgehampton, NY, 85 & 87-90; Nat Acad Design 163rd Ann Exhib, New York, 88;; Images Gallery, Briacliff Manor, NY, 89; Shidoni Bronze Gallery, Tesugne, NMex, 89. *Awards:* Medal Honor for Sculpture, Nat Asn Women Artists Ann Exhib, 87; Alma Kline Award, Audubon Artists Ann Exhib, 89; Pietro & Alfred Montana Award, Nat Sculpture Soc Ann Exhib, 91. *Mem:* Sculptors Guild; Nat Asn Women Artists; Nat Sculptors Soc, Fel; Audubon Artists. *Media:* Terra Cotta, Clay; Metal, Bronze. *Mailing Add:* 368 W 246th St Bronx NY 10471

LEWIS, DON S, SR
ART DEALER, PAINTER
b July 21, 19; US citizen. *Study:* Carnegie Mus, Pittsburgh; painting with Virginia Cuthbert. *Exhib:* One-man show, Gallerie Int, New York, 67. *Pos:* Chmn & lectr on investment art & conserv, Aushew Gallery, Virginia Beach, 54- *Mem:* Nat Soc Lit & Arts; Am Asn Mus; Am Fedn Arts; Int Inst Conserv Hist & Artistic Works. *Media:* Metal, Acrylic. *Specialty:* Nineteenth and twentieth century American paintings. *Mailing Add:* 5548 Sajo Farm Rd Virginia Beach VA 23455

LEWIS, DONALD SYKES, JR
ART DEALER, PAINTER
b Norfolk, Va, Dec 13, 47. *Study:* Randolph-Macon Col, Ashland, Va, BA(fine arts); Univ Va, MA(hist of art). *Work:* Central Fidelity Bank, Norfolk, Va; Randolph-Macon Col, Richmond; Sears, Roebuck & Co, Chicago, Ill. *Exhib:* Second Ann Invitational Juried Show, Gallery II, Norfolk, 77; 57th Ann Nat Apr Salon, Springville Mus Art, Utah, 81; Randolph-Macon Col, Ashland, Va 85. *Pos:* Vpres, Auslew Gallery, Inc, Norfolk, 73-76, dir, 76-83, pres, 83-; adv comt, Chrysler Mus, currently. *Teaching:* Instr Am art, Hermitage Mus, Norfolk, 75, 78 & 79 & Old Dom Univ, 75-76. *Bibliog:* Hampton Roads Virginia Guide to Visual Artists, Grunwald & Radcliff, 84. *Mem:* Archives Am Art; Assoc Am Inst Conserv Hist & Artistic Works. *Media:* Oil. *Res:* Cataloging works of Herman Ottomar Herzog and his son, Lewis E Herzog. *Specialty:* 19th & 20th century American art & European Art. *Publ:* Auth, Emily Nichols Hatch (catalog), 74 & foreword, In: Carolyn Wyeth (catalog), 12/74, Auslew Gallery, Inc; Herman Herzog, Southwest Art Rev, 75; contribr, Carolyn Wyeth Exhibition Catalogue, R W Norton Art Gallery, Shreveport, La, 1/76; auth, Herman Herzog (1831-1932), German landscapist in America, Am Art Rev, 7-8/76; American Paintings of Herman Herzog (exhib catalog), Brandywine River Mus, 9/12-11/22. *Mailing Add:* 5309 Argall Ave Norfolk VA 23508

LEWIS, DOUGLAS
HISTORIAN, CURATOR
b Centreville, Miss, Apr 30, 38. *Study:* Lawrenceville Sch, NJ, dipl, 56; Yale Col, BA, 59 & 60; Clare Col, Cambridge Univ, BA, 62, MA, 66; Yale Univ, MA, 63, PhD, 67; Am Acad Rome, Chester Dale fel, 64, dipl, 65. *Collections Arranged:* African Sculpture, 70, The Far North (Am Eskimo & Indian Art), 73, The Drawings of Andrea Pallido Traveling Exhib, 81, Renaissance Small Bronze Sculpture and Associated Decorative Arts (with catalog), 83 & Italian Sculpture of the Fourteenth through the Seventeeth Centuries, 84, Renaissance Master Bronzes (with preface to catalog), 86, Nat Gallery Art. *Pos:* David E Finley fel Venetian art, Nat Gallery Art, Washington, DC, 65-68; cur sculpture, Nat Gallery Art, 68-; vchmn, Citizens Stamp Adv Comt, US Postal Serv, 85- *Teaching:* Asst prof baroque & romantic art, Bryn Mawr Col, 67-68; asst prof renaissance & baroque art, Univ Calif, Berkeley, spring 70; sem leader renaissance archit, Folger Inst, Renaissance Sem, Washington, DC, spring 72; adj prof, Renaissance & baroque art, Johns Hopkins Univ, 73-77; prof Renaissance art & archit, Univ Calif, Berkeley, fall 79; lectr, Iowa State Univ, Ames, 80; vis lectr, Georgetown Univ, 80-; Univ of Md, 89-91. *Awards:* Copley Medal, Smithsonian Inst, 81. *Mem:* Fel Am Acad in Rome; Soc Archit Historians; Col Art Asn Am; Belg-Am Educ Found; Centro Palladiano, Vicenza; and others. *Res:* Art and architecture in Renaissance Venice; monographic studies on Michele Sanmicheli, Jacopo Sansovino, Andrea Palladio, Baldassare Longhena, Francesco Muttoni & Galeazzo Mondella (Moderno). *Publ:* Auth, The Late Baroque Churches of Venice, 67 & Garland, 79; The Drawings of Andrea Palladio, Nat Gallery Art, 81; coauth, Renaissance Master Bronzes, SITES, 86. *Mailing Add:* Nat Gallery of Art Washington DC 20565

LEWIS, ELIZABETH See Sprang, Elizabeth

LEWIS, ELIZABETH MATTHEW
STAINED GLASS ARTIST, WRITER
b Charleston, SC. *Study:* Richmond Prof Inst, Va; Purdue Univ, Lafayette, Ind, BA; sculpture course at Barry I, Wales, Glamorgan Educational Comt; Univ London; Pratt Inst, MLS; Teachers Col, Columbia Univ, EdD; Inst Arts Admin, Harvard Univ, cert; Ctr Medieval & Renaissance Studies, Oxford, cert(stained glass). *Work:* Ball State Univ Art Gallery, Muncie, Ind; Miami Mus Mod Art. *Comn:* Bronze reliefs, George's Restaurant, Indianapolis, Ind, 51; mural, Loeb Playhouse, Mem Union, Purdue Univ, 52; mural, First Fed Savings & Loan, Lafayette, Ind, 58; ceramic relief, United Methodist Church, Lafayette, Ind, 61; mem stained glass window, Second Presby Church, Ft Lauderdale, 82. *Exhib:* One-man shows, Lafayette Art Ctr, Ind, Ft Wayne Union Bank, Ind, Miami Mus Mod Art, Ft Lauderdale Art Ctr, 64 & Hollywood Art Mus, 83, Fla. *Collections Arranged:* Four Generations of Waughs: An American Family of Artists 1827-1970, 70, Illustrators of the American West, loan from the collection of George Goodstadt, 75, Drawings by Al Hirschfeld, 76 & Military Medicine and the Wound Man (with Gordon E Mestler), 76, US Military Acad. *Pos:* Co-partner, Lewis Workshop Studios, Kokomo, W Lafayette, Ind, 50-62; fine arts librn, US Military Acad, West Point, NY, 67-78; cur slides, Dept Art, City Col New York, 71; dir, Lyon Productions Ltd, Ft Lauderdale, Fla, 77-; educ asst, Mus of Art, Ft Lauderdale, Fla, 87-88. *Teaching:* Instr painting, Ind Univ Extension, Kokomo, 50-52; sr lectr art, US Military Acad, 67-78. *Awards:* Patent, Graphics Retrieval Systems, 78; Sculpture Prize, Broward Art Guild, 80; Flori Award, Fla Independent Filmmakers, 80. *Mem:* Col Art Asn; Am Asn Mus; Am Asn Univ Prof; Fla Artists Equity (bd dir, 82-86); Fla Prof Artists, 86- *Res:* Color in visual perception; design for transparent media; filming the making of antique glass. *Interests:* Research in slumped glass and experimental models of contemporary cathedral glass set in aluminum. *Publ:* Auth, A Summer School in Wales, Art Educ, 66; A Cost Study of Library Color in Microimage Storage and Retrieval, DC Col, 74; filmmaker, Sun Song: The mosaic art of John de Groot, 75; ed, Military Medicine and the Wound Man: A Graphic Display of the Wound Man Through History, US Military Acad, 76, J of Micrographics, 76; auth, Stained Glass (bk review), The Cadet Chapel, winter 87. *Mailing Add:* 1500 NE 18th Ave Ft Lauderdale FL 33304

LEWIS, ELMA INA
ADMINISTRATOR
b Boston, Mass, Sept 16, 21. *Study:* Emerson Col, BLI, 43; Boston Univ, MEd, 44; Emerson Col, Hon LHD, 68; Anna Maria Col, Hon LHD, 71; Boston Col, Hon LHD, 71; Colby Col, Hon DFA, 72; Harvard Univ, Hon ArtD, 72. *Pos:* Founder & dir, Elma Lewis Sch Fine Arts, Boston, 50- & Nat Ctr Afro-Am Artists, Boston, 68- *Awards:* Outstanding Woman's Award, Campfire Girls Am, 70; Mayor's Citation, City of Boston, 70; Henry O Tanner Award, Black Arts Coun Calif, 71; plus others. *Bibliog:* Margo Miller (auth), Black Boston's Miss Lewis: Art czarina with a needle, Boston Globe, 4/18/68; Caryl Rivers (auth), Black America's Barnum, Hurok & Guthrie, New York Times, 11/17/68; A century of New England news photos, Boston Globe Mag, 1/77. *Mem:* Fel Black Acad Arts & Lett; Gov Task Force on Arts & Humanities; Metrop Cult Alliance, Boston; Mass State Dept Educ Adv Bd. *Publ:* Contribr, Who Took the Weight, Little, 72; auth, At the crossroads: Doom or bloom, Forum Mag, 72; Celebrating us little people, Boston Rev of Arts, 9/72. *Mailing Add:* 15 Homestead St Roxbury MA 02121

LEWIS, GLENN A
SCULPTOR, CONCEPTUAL ARTIST
b Chemainus, BC, Oct 26, 35. *Study:* Vancouver Sch Art, dipl, 58. *Work:* Vancouver Art Gallery; Nat Gallery of Can, Ottawa; Air Can, Montreal; Can Coun Art Bank, Ottawa. *Comn:* Bronze Dog, City of Vancouver, 72; plastic boxes (mural), Govt Can, Nat Sci Libr, Ottawa, 73. *Exhib:* 8 Closets, 70, Bewilderness-Origins of Paradise (with catalog), 78 & Art in Vancouver 1931-1983, 83, Vancouver Art Gallery, BC; Canada Trajectoiries 73, Musee Moderne de la Ville de Paris, France, 73; Hier et Apres, Montreal Mus Fine Arts, Que, 80; Paradise, Nat Film Bd Can, Ottawa, 80; Museums by Artists, Art Gallery Ont, 83; Le Paradis, La Chartreuse-CIRCA, Villeneuve-Les Avignon, France, 83. *Pos:* Arts adminr, Western Front Soc, Vancouver, 73-87; mem media arts adv comt, Can Coun, Ottawa, 86-87; mem bd trustees, Vancouver Art Gallrey, 86-87; head, media arts section, Canada Coun, Ottawa, 87-90. *Teaching:* Instr ceramics art methods, Univ BC, 64-67, instr ceramics & sculpture, Fine Arts Dept, Univ BC, 71-74; vis prof ceramics, Alfred Univ, 70-71. *Awards:* Grants, Art Gallery of Ont, 67 & Vancouver Art Gallery, 68; Winnipeg Ann Prize, Winnipeg Art Gallery, 68; Senior Canada Council, 76, 81. *Bibliog:* Alex Mogelon (auth), Art in Boxes, Van Nostrand Reinholt, 74; Philip Monk (auth), Rev of Hier et Apres, McLeans Mag, 6/2/80; John Bentley Mays (auth), Visions: Contemporary Art in Canada, Douglas & McIntyre, 83. *Mem:* Vancouver Artists League. *Media:* Miscellaneous. *Publ:* Auth, Journey Through an Earthly Paradise, 78 & Japanese Gardens, 82, Impressions Mag; Performance by Artists, Art Metropole, 79; The Mythological Design of the Garden Path, Sect A Mag, 85. *Dealer:* Coburg Gallery 314 Water St No 2 Vancouver BC. *Mailing Add:* R R2 Site 21 C-12 Gibsons BC V0N 1V0 Canada

LEWIS, GOLDA
ASSEMBLAGE ARTIST, PAPERMAKER
b New York, NY. *Study:* With Vaclav Vytacil, Hans Hofmann & Jack Tworkov; Papermaking with Douglas Howell. *Work:* Ciba-Geigy Chem Co, Ardsley, NY; Madden Corp, New York; Hercules Powder Co, Wilmington, Del; Foundations of Paper Hist, Haarlem, Holland; Cheney Pulp & Paper Co, Franklin, Ohio; and others. *Exhib:* Handmade Paper, Points & Unique Works, Mus Mod Art, New York, 76; New Ways with Paper, Nat Collection Fine Arts, Smithsonian Inst, Washington, DC, 77-78; solo exhibs, Int Biennale of Paper, Duren, WGer, Galerie Faust, Geneva, Switz, 86, Discerning Images Gallery, Montclair, NJ, 87 & Gallery Inter-Am Develop Bank, Washington, DC, 88; Form and Substance, NJ Ctr Visual Arts, Summit, 88; Nat Sch Art, Brussels, 89; Koninklijke Bibliotheek, Royal Libr, Holland, 89; Aaron Gallery, Washington, DC, 89; Petit Format De Papier, Cul-Des-Sarts, Couvin, Belg, 89; Paper in Art, Nysted Kunstforening, Int Paper Art Biannual, Denmark, 89; and others. *Pos:* Built, equipped & consult, Papermaking Dept, Wildcliff Mus, New Rochelle, NY, 77. *Teaching:* Instr, Ballard Sch, New York, 61-71; lectr, Marymount Manhattan Col, 71; Am Fedn Arts rent an artist workshop on paper and artists working in paper, 74; lectr & workshops handpapermaking, Univ Mass, Amherst, 78; lectr, Univ Costa Rica, San Jose, 83 & 84, Leopold Hoesch Mus, Duren, WGer, 86, NJ Ctr Visual Arts, Summit, 88. *Awards:* NY State Coun Arts Grant, 71; Award, Clayworks, 80;

Florsheim Fund Grant, 92. *Bibliog:* Thelma Newman (auth), Innovative Printmaking, Crown Publs, 77; Bernard Toale (auth), The Art of Papermaking, Davis Publs, 83; International Paper Art Biannual (catalog), Nysted, Denmark, 89; and others. *Media:* Handmade Paper. *Publ:* Auth, 77 Hand Papermaker's Conf, Women Artists Newsletter, 1/78. *Mailing Add:* 31 Union Sq W Studio 9C New York NY 10003

LEWIS, JOHN CHAPMAN
PAINTER, INSTRUCTOR
b Washington, DC, Sept 26, 20. *Study:* Corcoran Sch Art, 38-40. *Work:* Corcoran Gallery Art, Phillips Collection & Nat Collection Fine Arts; High Mus Art, Atlanta, Ga; NC Mus Art, Raleigh. *Exhib:* Corcoran Biennial, Corcoran Gallery Art, 49, 51, 55, 61 & 63 & one-man show, 64; Young Am Painters, 50 & Am Painting Today, 50, Metrop Mus Art, New York; one-man shows, NC Mus Art, Raleigh, 50, Baltimore Mus Art, 53 & Phillips Collection, 73; Trends in Watercolor Today, Italy & the US, Brooklyn Mus, 57; Am Paintings from the Phillips Collection, The White House, Washington, DC, 77-78. *Teaching:* Instr painting & drawing, Corcoran Sch Art, 49-50, 53-58; artist-in-residence studio art, Marymount Col Va, Arlington, 66-84; retired, 84. *Awards:* First Award Painting, Golden Anniversary Exhib, Isaac Delgado Mus, New Orleans, 51 & 16th Area Exhib, Corcoran Gallery Art, 63. *Bibliog:* Harriet Griffiths (auth), Painting with feeling, 1/24/60 & Benjamin Forgey (auth), Lewis' harmonious reveries, rev of Phillips Exhib, 5/30/73, Washington Star; Leslie Judd Ahlander (auth), Review of one-man show, Corcoran Gallery, Wash Post, 3/1/64. *Mailing Add:* 304 E Congress St Charles Town WV 25414-1320

LEWIS, JOHN CONARD
SCULPTOR, GLASSBLOWER
b Berkeley, Calif, Mar 13, 42. *Study:* Univ Calif, Berkeley, BA, 68, MA, 72, studied with Peter Voulkos, Marvin Lipofsky & Ron Nagle. *Work:* Ariz State Univ Art Mus, Tempe; Tacoma Art Mus, Wash; Univ Wis-Madison Mus Art. *Exhib:* Am Glass Now, Toledo Mus Art, Ohio, 73; Statements, Oakland Mus Art, Calif, 73; Collectors Exhib, Mus Contemp Crafts, New York, 74; Contemp Crafts of the Americas, Colo State Univ, Boulder, 76; Nat Glass Invitational III, Univ Wis-Madison, 76; and others. *Collections Arranged:* New American Glass Focus WVa, Huntington Art Gallery, WVa, 76. *Awards:* Purchase Awards, Corning Mus Glass, NY, 70, Designer-Craftsman Ann, Richmond Art Ctr, 70 & Blown Glass Invitational, Tacoma Art Mus, Wash, 71. *Mem:* Am Crafts Coun; Glass Art Soc. *Media:* Blown Glass, Cast Glass. *Mailing Add:* c/o Brendan Walter Gallery 1001 Colorado Ave Santa Monica CA 90401

LEWIS, LOUISE MILLER
GALLERY DIRECTOR, EDUCATOR
b St Louis, Mo, Dec 4, 40. *Study:* Univ Calif, Berkeley, BA, 63; Univ NMex, Albuquerque, MA(french), 66, MA(art history), 72. *Collections Arranged:* Perimeters: Prints & Poetry from the Arts in Corrections programs, Public Conscience/Private Mind, Anna Bialobroda, Chinese Garden of Chang ta Ch'ien, Odyssey: an installation in neon by Jan Sanchez, Calif State Univ, Northridge, 90. *Pos:* Cur, asst dir, Univ NMex Fine Arts Mus, 66-72; assoc dir, Calif State Univ Northridge Art Gallery, 72-80, dir, 80- *Teaching:* Asst prof, Calif State Univ, Northridge, 72-79, assoc prof, 79-83, prof art hist, 83- *Res:* Art and the media. *Publ:* Auth, California Video in Xle Biennale de Paris, Muse̍e d'Art Moderne, 80; Video in Southern California, No 26, 80 & Future Video: Max Olney, No 38, 83, Los Angeles Inst Contemp Arts J; Future Video: Max Olney, LAICA Journal, 83; Where Art the Daumiers of Video Art, Media Arts, 85; June Wayne: Recent Work, World Print News, 85. *Mailing Add:* California State University/Northridge Art Gallery 18111 Nordhoff St Northridge CA 91330

LEWIS, MARCIA
JEWELER-METALSMITH, INSTRUCTOR
b Washington, DC, Oct 7, 46. *Study:* Corcoran Sch, Washington, DC; San Diego Univ, Calif; Calif State Univ, Long Beach. *Work:* Mus Contemp Crafts, New York; Oakland Mus Art; Renwick Gallery Mus Am Art, Smithsonian Inst. *Exhib:* Int Handwerks Messe, Munich, Ger 71; Am Metalsmiths, DeCordova Mus, Lincoln, Mass, 73; Kunstindustri Mus, Copenhagen, Denmark, 73; Goldsmiths 74, Smithsonian Inst, Washington, DC, 74; Crafts of the NAmericas, Colo State Univ & Smithsonian Inst, 75; Calif Design 12, Los Angeles, 76. *Pos:* Apprentice goldsmith, Ingrid Hansen, Zurich, Switz, 71-72; asst silversmith, Tony Laws Studio Ltd, Londin, Eng, 72-73. *Teaching:* Instr metalsmithing & gen crafts, Univ Wis, Whitewater, 73-75 & San Jose State Univ, Calif, 75-76; assoc prof art, Long Beach City Col, Calif, 78- *Awards:* Sterling Silversmiths Award, Design Competition, Silversmiths Guild, 69; George C Marshall Mem Fel, Denmark-Amerika Fondet, 72; Nat Endowment Arts Award, Washington, DC, 76. *Bibliog:* Beverly Edna Johnson (auth), Biographical, Los Angeles Times Home Mag, 72; Thelma Newman (auth), Containers, Crown Publ, 77; Oppi Untracht (auth), Jewelry Techniques for Craftsmen, Doubleday, 78. *Mem:* Soc NAm Goldsmiths. *Media:* Metal. *Publ:* Auth, Wearable aluminum ornaments, Calif State Univ, Long Beach, 77. *Mailing Add:* Dept Art Long Beach City Col 4901 E Carson St Long Beach CA 90808

LEWIS, MARY
SCULPTOR
b Portland, Ore, June 18, 26. *Study:* Univ Ore, 45-50, BS(sculpture), 49; Ore Div Am Asn Univ Women Mabel Merwin fel, 50, Syracuse Univ, with Ivan Mestrovic, tech asst to Mestrovic, 51-53, MFA, 53. *Comn:* Bird (mahogany & copper) & Skunk Cabbage (marble), Waterbury Club, Conn, 64; Madonna & Child (maple relief), St Joseph's Church Chapel, Roseburg, Ore, 78; The Holy Family (maple relief), St Frederic's Church, St Helens, Ore, 85; Mysteries of the Rosary (15 bronze reliefs), Peace Garden, The Grotto, Portland, Ore, 89. *Exhib:* 12th & 14th Ann New Eng Exhibs, Silvermine Guild Artists, New Canaan, Conn, 61 & 63; 62nd & 63rd Ann Exhib, New Haven Paint & Clay Club, John Slade Ely Ctr, New Haven, 63 & 64; Retrospective, Fine Arts Gallery, Lower Columbia Col, Longview, Wash, 81; Liturgical Arts, Invitational Exhib, Marylhurst Col, Ore, 84; Gallery Genesis, Chicago, Ill, 88. *Pos:* Staff artist, GAF Corp Photo Div, Portland, Ore, 70-76. *Teaching:* Asst prof sculpture, Nat Col Arts, Pakistan, 58-60. *Awards:* Tiffany Traveling Scholar, 53; Fulbright Lectr, 58 & 59. *Bibliog:* Virginia Watson-Jones (auth), Contemporary American Women Sculptors, Oryx Press, 86,. *Mem:* Liturgical Arts Resource Ctr. *Media:* Wood, Stone. *Publ:* Coauth & illusr, The Little Yellow Dinosaur, 71, illusr, In the Beginning--the Bible Story of Creation, Adam & Eve, Cain & Abel, 72, Jesus Christ, His Youth, Disciples, Miracles, 75, GAF View-Master. *Mailing Add:* 74394 Wortman Rd Rainier OR 97048

LEWIS, MICHAEL H
PAINTER, EDUCATOR
b Brooklyn, NY, Aug 10, 41. *Study:* State Univ NY Col, New Paltz, painting with Ben Bishop, George Wexler & Ilya Bolotowsky, BS, 63, MFA, 75; Mich State Univ, MA, 64. *Work:* Fogg Mus Art, Harvard Univ; Albertina Mus, Vienna, Austria; Portland Mus Art, Maine; Univ Maine Mus Art, Orono, Maine. *Comn:* Oil portrait, comn by Edmund S Muskie, 83; cover paintings for The Magus of Strovolos, Homage to the Sun & Fire in the Heart (all by Kyriacos Markides), 86, 87 & 90. *Exhib:* Solo shows: Uptown Gallery, New York, 80 & 88, 91, 93 & Congress Square Gallery, Portland, Maine, 86, 87-90 & 92; Fogg Art Mus, Harvard Univ, 87-89; three-Person show, Am Ctr, Sapporo, Japan 91; Levinson/Kane Gallery, Boston, Mass, 91, 92; Steven Scott Gallery, Baltimore, Md, 92; and others. *Pos:* Mem, Maine Comn Arts & Humanities, 72-78, visual arts adv panel, 79-81. *Teaching:* Instr art, Kingston City Pub Schs, NY, 64-66; prof painting & drawing, Univ Maine, Orono, 66-, chmn, Dept Art, 75-81, acting assoc dean col arts & sci, 81-83, chmn, Dept Art, 87- *Awards:* Video Work of Art Grant, Maine State Arts Comn & Maine Pub Broadcasting Network, 83; New Eng Found Arts/Nat Endowment Arts-Regional Fel, Visual Artists (drawing), 90-91. *Bibliog:* Carl Little (auth), Metamorphosis: 4 Artists Reflect Maine's New Aesthetic, Art New Eng, 7-8/90; Carl Little (auth), Michael H Lewis at the Univ Maine Mus Art, Art in Am, 9/1/90; Philip Isaacson (auth), A Painter Colors His World, and Ours, and Makes it Soft; Maine Sunday Telegram, 5/10/92; and others. *Media:* Oil, Video. *Mailing Add:* 104 Bennoch Rd Orono ME 04473

LEWIS, NAT BRUSH
PAINTER, INSTRUCTOR
b Boston, Mass, Dec 17, 25. *Study:* Pembroke Col, Brown Univ & RI Sch Design, AB; Art Students League; watercolor with Mario Cooper; also with Henry Gasser Art. *Work:* Am Asn Univ Women, Somerset Hills, NJ; Bloomfield Art League, NJ; Bergen Mus Arts & Sci. *Exhib:* NJ Watercolor Soc; Am Watercolor Soc, New York; Am Artists Prof League Grand Nat; Salmagundi Club Exhib; Hudson Valley Art Asn; and others. *Teaching:* Adj prof Art, Seton Hall Univ, 84- *Awards:* Solo Exhib Award, Salmagundi Club, 79; NJ Watercolor Soc, 68, 74, 79, 80, 82, 88, Silve Medal Hon, 91; Hudson Valley Art Asn, 91. *Mem:* NJ Watercolor Soc (pres, 73-75); Am Artists Prof League; Hudson Valley Art Asn; Nat Asn Women Artists; NJ Miniature Soc and others. *Media:* Watercolor, Oil. *Mailing Add:* 51 Overlook Rd Caldwell NJ 07006

LEWIS, PHILLIP HAROLD
CURATOR
b Chicago, Ill, July 31, 22. *Study:* Art Inst Chicago, BFA, 47, Univ Chicago, MA, 53, PhD, 66; Australian Nat Univ, Fulbright Fel, 53-54. *Collections Arranged:* Anthrop, geol & hist exhibs, Grout Hist Mus, Waterloo, Iowa, 55; What is Primitive Art, Field Mus Natural Hist, 58, estab Hall of Primitive Art, 61, with exhibs Primitive Artists Look at Civilization, The Human Image in Primitive Art & Australian Aboriginal Art: Arnhem Land, from collection of Louis A Allen, Palo Alto, Calif. *Pos:* Field res proj primitive art, New Ireland, 53-54, 70 & 81; asst cur primitive art, Field Mus Natural Hist, 57-59, assoc cur, 60, cur, 61-67, cur primitive art & Melanesian ethnol, 68- *Teaching:* Lectr anthrop, Univ Chicago, 67-71; lectr, Eve Div, Northwestern Univ, Chicago, 73. *Awards:* Chicago Natural Hist Mus Fel, 50-51, 54-55; Wenner-Gren Mus Res Fel, 68; Nat Sci Found Res Grant, 69-71; Nat Endowment Art Res Fel Mus Profs, 81. *Mem:* Fel Am Anthrop Asn; fel Royal Anthrop Inst Gt Brit & Ireland. *Publ:* Auth, A Definition of Primitive Art, Vol 36, 61 & The Social Context of Art in Northern New Ireland, Vol 58, 69, In: Fieldiana, Field Mus Nat Hist; Changing memorial ceremonial in Northern New Ireland, J Polynesian Soc, Vol 182, No 2; Art in Changing New Ireland: Exploring the Visual Art of Oceania, Univ Press Hawaii, Honolulu, 378-391, 79; A Malanggan Figure in the Permanent Collection (in) Tryptych, The Mus Soc, M H DeYoung Mem Mus, Fine Arts Mus San Francisco, 11/88, 12/88 & 11-13, 6/89; Chap 12, In: Art, and Identity in Oceania, Univ Hawaii Press, Honolulu, 149-163, 90. *Mailing Add:* Field Mus Natural Hist Roosevelt Rd & Lake Shore Dr Chicago IL 60605

LEWIS, RONALD WALTER
PAINTER, INSTRUCTOR
b Atlanta, Ga, Jan 27, 45. *Study:* Ala Col, BS(art & bus), 67. *Work:* Birmingham Mus Art, Ala; Fayette Art Mus, Ala; Jefferson State Col, Birmingham; Sylacauga Mus, Ala; Columbus Mus, Calif. *Exhib:* Ala Watercolor Soc, Birmingham Mus Art, 71-77; Dixieland Watercolor & Drawing Show, Montgomery Mus Art, Ala, 73; Watercolor USA, Springfield Art Mus, Mo, 73-74; Rocky Mountain Nat Watercolor, Golden, Colo, 76;

Mainstreams, Marietta Col, Ohio, 76-77; Southern Watercolor Soc, Nashville, Tenn, 77; and others. *Teaching:* instr watercolor & oil, Mountain Brook Community Sch, Ala, 76- *Awards:* Seventy-five awards including Ala Watercolor Soc & Southern Watercolor Soc. *Bibliog:* Stevens (auth), Ronald Lewis Paintings, La Revue Mod, Paris, 9/73. *Mem:* Ala Watercolor Soc (vpres, 73-74); Birmingham Art Asn (mem bd, 76-); Southern Watercolor Soc; Am Watercolor Soc. *Media:* Miscellaneous Media. *Publ:* Illusr, My Country Roads & Pappa's Old Trunk, 11/81, Buck Publ Co; Birmingham Mag, 7/83; Southern Accents Mag, winter 83; Artist's Mag, 4/90. *Dealer:* Dumonde Fine Art New York; Horizon Galleries Houston TX. *Mailing Add:* 2728 Ossa Wintha Dr Birmingham AL 35243

LEWIS, SAMELLA SANDERS
PAINTER, HISTORIAN
b New Orleans, La, Feb 27, 24. *Study:* Hampton Inst, BS; Ohio State Univ, MA & PhD; Tunghai Univ, Taiwan; Fulbright fel, 62; Univ Southern Calif, 64-66; NY Univ Inst Fine Arts, 65; Hampton Univ, Va, LHD, 90. *Work:* Oakland Mus, Calif; Baltimore Mus Fine Arts; Va Mus Fine Arts, Richmond; High Mus, Atlanta, Ga; Atlanta Univ Mus Contemp Art. *Exhib:* Joseph Hirshhorn Collection, Palm Springs Mus, 69; Dimensions of Black, La Jolla Mus Art, 70; Two Generations of Black Artists, Calif State Univ, Los Angeles, 70; Smithsonian Inst Traveling Print Exhibs, 80-83; Print Club Invitational, Philadelphia, Pa, 83. *Collections Arranged:* Media, Style & Tradition - The California Artists, 81 & Wildlife Sculpture, A Bayou Heritage, 82, Calif Mus Afro-Am Hist & Cult; Artist-teachers, Univ Southern Calif, Santa Monica Place, 83; African Images in the New World, Los Angeles Calif, 83; Richard Hunt: Sculptures & Drawings, 86 & Jacob Lawrence: Paintings & Drawings, 89-91, Arts Am. *Pos:* Coordr educ, Los Angeles Co Mus Art, 69-70; ed-in-chief, Int Rev African-Am Art, 85; pres, Oxum Int, 87; art ed, Black Art Mag, 78. *Teaching:* Prof fine arts & head dept, Fla A&M Univ, 53-58; prof humanities & art hist, State Univ NY, 58-68; prof art hist, Scripps Col, 69, emer prof, 84- *Awards:* NY State-Ford Found Grant, 65; Ford Found Research Grant, 81-82; Prof of Yr Award, Scripps Col, 84; Honor Award, Women's Caucus Art, 89. *Bibliog:* The Black Artists (film), Afrographics, 68; Focus, KNBC-TV, 68; article, Los Angeles Times, 70. *Mem:* Col Art Asn Am; Nat Conf Artists (co-chairperson, 70-73). *Res:* African, Asian and Afro-American art. *Collection:* Rare African works, including Bakuba in the 1890's; Caribbean and African-American Works. *Publ:* Co-ed, Black Artists on Art, Vols I & II, 69 & 71; auth, Art: African American (textbk), Harcourt, 76; The Art of Elizabeth Catlett, Mus African Am Art, 84. *Dealer:* Alan S Lewis & Associates Fine Arts. *Mailing Add:* c/o Nat Conf Artists, Mich Chap Fisher Bldg No 216 3011 W Grand Blvd Detroit MI 48202

LEWIS, STANLEY
SCULPTOR, PRINTMAKER
b Montreal, Que, Mar 28, 30. *Study:* Montreal Mus Fine Arts, 48-51; Inst Allende, San Miguel, Mex, scholars, 52-55; Elizabeth T Greenshields Mem Found grant, Florence, Italy, 56-59. *Work:* Nat Gallery Can, Ottawa; Montreal Mus Fine Arts; Jerusalem Mus, Israel; Samuel Zacks Collection; Primal Portraits (5 stone cut prints), Los Angeles Mus Natural Hist; and others. *Comn:* Sleeping Spirit (lava boulder), 53, standing nude (white marble), 53 & The Corngrinder (gray marble), 54, Inst Allende; late Samuel Bronfman, Can Jewish Cong, 66. *Exhib:* One-man shows, Montreal Mus Fine Arts, 52 & 59, Israel Art Auction Gallery, Tel Aviv, 65 & Nat Gallery Can, 71; Atelier J Lukacs, Montreal, 75, 76 & 78. *Teaching:* Instr sculpture, McGill Univ Sch Archit, 52, Montreal Mus Fine Arts, 61-63 & Saidye Bronfman Art Ctr, Montreal, 61-; lectr, The Eskimo Artist, Nat Film Bd, Montreal, 75. *Awards:* Prize, Concours Artistiques, Que, 59. *Bibliog:* Peter Olwyer (auth), article, Can Art, fall 55; Earle Birney (auth), article, Sat Night, 55; Folch (auth), article, Vie Arts, summer 59. *Mem:* Founding mem Que Sculptors' Asn; hon rep Int Acad Leonardo da Vinci. *Media:* Stone. *Res:* Contributed original research on Michelangelo's childhood and marble carving techniques to writing of Irving Stone's The Agony and the Ecstasy. *Publ:* Auth, The Stone Speaks, 53; Hands to Create Wonders, 61; Space, Man and Stone, 69. *Mailing Add:* Apt 4 4131 Cote des Neiges Rd Montreal PQ H3H 1X1 Canada

LEWIS, VIRGINIA ELNORA
MUSEUM DIRECTOR, HISTORIAN
b Sault Ste Marie, Ont, Apr 7, 07; US citizen. *Study:* Wellesley Col, 26-28; Univ Pittsburgh, AB, 31, AM, 35; Carnegie Inst Technol, cert, 33; Harvard Univ; Brit Mus Dept Prints, with Arthur M Hind, summer 38. *Pos:* Actg head, Frick Fine Arts Dept, Univ Pittsburgh, 40-63, cur exhibs, 46-47, head librn, Frick Fine Arts Libr, 63-65, asst dir, Frick Fine Art Bldg, 65-67; dir, Dennis Art Gallery, Raymond Moore Found, Mass, summer, 53 & dir, Frick Art Mus, 70-85; consult dir, Westmoreland Co Mus Art & Woods Marchand Found, Greensburg, Pa, 54-56; retired, 85. *Teaching:* Prof fine arts, Univ Pittsburgh, 57-67, emer prof, 77- *Awards:* Distinguished Daughters Pa, 77; Kaufmarus Salute Women of the Year, Pittsburgh, Port Gozelb. *Mem:* Soc Archit Hist; Women's Press Club, Pittsburgh; chmn Selection Comt Walter Read Hovey Award; Pittsburgh Found (exec bd mem); Fricks Art Pittsburgh Publ Libr. *Publ:* Auth, Russell Smith: Romantic Realist, Univ Pittsburgh Press, 57; ed, Walter Read Hovey, auth, The Arts in Changing Societies: Reflections Inspired by Works of Art in the Frick Art Museum, 72 & Treasures of the Frick Art Museum, 75, Frick Art Mus, Pittsburgh; auth, Firenze, In: The Pittsburgh Bibliophiles Pilgrimage to Italy, Pittsburgh Bibliophiles, 76. *Mailing Add:* 401 S Dallas Ave Pittsburgh PA 15208

LEWIS, WILLIAM ARTHUR
PAINTER, EDUCATOR
b Detroit, Mich, Mar 20, 18. *Study:* Col Archit & Design, Univ Mich, BDesign, 48. *Work:* Butler Inst Am Art, Youngstown; Grand Rapids Mus Art; Univ Mich Grad Sch; Grinnell Col; and others. *Comn:* Watercolor series, McNary Sr Serv Ctr, Detroit, 87; oil painting, Grand Rapids City Hall, 71; acrylic paintings, Soc Mfg Engrs, Dearborn, Mich, 71 & Grand Rapids Jr Col, 86; three portraits, 1st Unitarian Church, Ann Arbor, Mich, 90. *Exhib:* Five Ann Exhibs, Butler Inst Am Art, 54-65; Drawing USA, Mus Mod Art, 56; Corcoran Gallery Biennial, Washington, DC & Am Fedn Art Tour, 57; one-man show, The Last Year of the Civil War, Detroit Hist Soc, Mint Mus, Madison Col, Va, Eastern Mich Univ, Dearborn Hist Mus & others, 62-65; Drawing USA, St Paul Art Ctr, 63 & 66. *Pos:* Assoc dean, Sch Art, Univ Mich, Ann Arbor, 66-75 & 84-85; dir, Comn Accreditation, Nat Asn Schs Art, 72-75; chief reader, Advanced Placement Studio Art, Col Bd-ETS, 78-81. *Teaching:* Prof art, Sch Art, Univ Mich, Ann Arbor, 64-86, prof emer. *Awards:* Rackham Sch Grad Studies Fac Res Grants for Last Year of the Civil War, 60-62; J M W Turner, 64. *Bibliog:* Hazen Schumacher (auth), The Painting Professor, Univ Mich TV Studios, 62; Louise Bruner (auth), Feelings of an artist, Toledo Blade, 64. *Mem:* Fel Nat Asn Schs Art & Design; Mich Watercolor Soc. *Media:* Watercolor, Acrylics. *Publ:* Auth & illusr, The Civil War--A contemporary approach, Dimension, spring 62; illusr, cover & article, Limnos, summer 69. *Dealer:* De Graaf Fine Art Inc 300 W Superior Chicago IL 60610; Preston Burke Galleries Inc 240 E Grand River Detroit MI 48226. *Mailing Add:* 2550 Traver Blvd Ann Arbor MI 48105

LEWIS, WILLIAM R
INSTRUCTOR, PAINTER
b Osceola, Iowa, Sept 23, 20. *Study:* Drake Univ, BFA, 49; Univ Wash; Ariz State Univ, MA, 52. *Work:* Ariz Western Col, Yuma; Glendale Community Col, Ariz; Scottsdale Civic Ctr, Ariz. *Exhib:* Ariz Ann, Phoenix Art Mus, 61-68; Butler Art Mus Ann Midyear Show, 62; Am Watercolor Soc Ann, 63-65; Southwestern Invitational, Yuma, 67-72; Watercolor USA Traveling Show, 68. *Teaching:* Chmn dept art, S Mountain High Sch, Phoenix, 64-81. *Awards:* Ariz Ann First in Watercolor, Phoenix Art Mus, 62. *Mem:* Ariz Watercolor Asn (pres, 63-64). *Media:* Watercolor. *Mailing Add:* 313 E 15th St Tempe AZ 85281

LE WITT, SOL
PAINTER
b Hartford, Conn, 1928. *Study:* Syracuse Univ, BFA, 49. *Work:* Stedelijk Mus, Amsterdam, Holland; Albright-Knox Art Gallery, Buffalo, NY; Art Gallery Ont, Toronto; Los Angeles Co Mus Art, Los Angeles, Calif; Mus Mod Art, New York; also many international museums. *Comn:* Indoor structure, Port Authority Allegheny Co, Pittsburgh, Pa, 84; outdoor structure, Art in Public Places, Chicago, Ill, 85; wall drawings, Equitable Hq, New York, 85 & Bankers Trust, London, Eng, 88; lobby floor, Theatre Royal de la Monngie, Brussels, Belgium, 86; Disney Develop Women Co, Orlando, 91. *Exhib:* Sculpture Ann, Whitney Mus Am Art, New York, 67; Guggenheim Mus & Mus Mod Art, 71, Walker Art Ctr, 72 & 88, New York; San Francisco Mus Art, 75; retrospective travelling exhib, Mus Mod Art (exhib catalog), New York, Mus Contemp Art, Montreal, Krannert Mus, Champaign, Mus Contemp Art, Chicago & La Jolla Mus, Calif, 78-79; Wall Drawings 1968-1981, Wadsworth Atheneum, Hartford & Paula Cooper Gallery, New York, 81; Wall Drawings & Structures, Stedelijk Mus, (exhibit catalog), Amsterdam, 84; Drawings 1958-1992, Haags Gemeentemuseum, 92; and many other one-man & group shows. *Teaching:* Instr, Mus Mod Art Sch, 64-67 & Cooper Union, 67. *Bibliog:* E C Goosen (auth), The Art of the Real USA 1948-1968, Mus Mod Art, 68; Lucy R Lippard (auth), Minimal Art, Haags Gemeentemuseum, 68; Susanna Singer (auth), Sol LeWitt Wall Drawing, Kunsthalle, Bern, 92; and others. *Publ:* Auth, I am still alive: On Kawara, Studio Int, 70; Sentences on conceptual art, 7/71 & Sol Le Witt, 6/73, Flash Art, Milan; All wall drawings, Arts Mag, 2/72; Sentences on conceptual art, Uber Kunst, Cologne, WGer, 74; Lines in Two Directions & in Five Colors with All Their Combinations, Walker Art Ctr, 88. *Dealer:* John Weber Gallery 142 Greene St New York NY 10012. *Mailing Add:* c/o Susanna Singer 50 Riverside Dr New York NY 10024

LEWTON, VAL EDWIN
DESIGNER, PAINTER
b Santa Monica, Calif, May 23, 37. *Study:* Claremont Univ Col, Calif, MFA, 62. *Work:* Nat Mus Am Art, Washington, DC; Corcoran Gallery, Washington, DC; and others. *Comn:* Air shaft mural, DC Art Works, 88. *Exhib:* Ten Plus Ten, Corcoran Gallery Art, 82; The Washington Show, Corcoran Gallery Art, 85; From the Anacostia to the Potomac, WPA, Washington, 89; one-man shows, Plum Gallery, Kensington, Md, 83-85, Addison Ripley, Washington, 90, and others. *Collections Arranged:* Exhibition Designer for Robert Rauschenburg Retrospective, Nat Mus Am Art, 76; Decorative Designs of Frank Lloyd Wright, 77, Renwick Gallery, 77, The Masterpieces of Louis Comfort Tiffany, Renwick Gallery, 89, Albert Pinkham Ryder, Nat Mus Am Art, 90; and others. *Pos:* Chief design & production, Nat Mus Am Art-Smithsonian Inst, 73- *Teaching:* Lectr art, Univ Calif, Riverside, 62-63 & Georgetown Univ, Washington, DC, 81- *Bibliog:* Harry Rand (auth), The watercolors of Val Lewton, Arts Mag, 5/80; and others. *Media:* Acrylic, Watercolor. *Publ:* Auth, Washington Review (column), 75- *Dealer:* Addison Ripley Gallery Nine Hillyer Ct Washington DC 20008. *Mailing Add:* 627 K St NW Washington DC 20001

LEYS, DALE DANIEL
EDUCATOR, DRAFTSMAN
b Sheboygan, Wis, Dec 10, 52. *Study:* Yale Univ, 73; Layton Sch Art, Milwaukee, BFA, 74; Univ Wis, Madison, MA, 75, MFA, 77. *Work:* Evansville Mus Arts & Sci, Ind; Kentucky Fried Chicken, Louisville, Ky; A B Chandler Med Ctr, Lexington, Ky; Hyatt Regency Hotel, Frankfort, Ky; Hospital Corp Am, Nashville, Tenn; Budd Co, Shellbyville, Ky; Univ Ky, Mus

Art; Nationsbank, Charlotte, NC. *Exhib:* Evansville Mus Arts & Sci, Ind, 77, 78 & 80; Ball State Univ Art Gallery, Muncie, Ind, 78 & 83; Rutgers Univ, NJ, 80; Greenville Mus, SC, 81; Davenport Mus, Iowa, 81; J B Speed Art Mus, Louisville, Ky, 82; Cheekwood Fine Arts Ctr, Nashville, Tenn, 84; Nat Drawing Invitational, Univ Tenn, Knoxville, 84 & Wake Forest Univ, Winston-Salem, NC, 88; Canton Art Inst, Ohio, 86; Univ SC, Columbia, 87; Univ Ark, Little Rock, 88; Marshall Univ, Huntington, WVa, 89; Dale Leys Recent Drawing, Heike Pickett Gallery, Lexington, Ky, 90; Univ Mo, Columbia, 92; Springfield Art Mus, Mo, 92. *Teaching:* Prof drawing, Murray State Univ, 77- *Awards:* Drawing Award, State Univ NY, Potsdam, 77; Graphics Award, Mid States Exhib, Evansville Mus, 80; Purchase Award, Appalachian State Univ, Boone, NC, 83; 1986 Regional Competitive Exhib Award, Paducah, Ky, 86; Drawing Excellence Award, All Ky Art Exhibit, Lexington. *Bibliog:* Jerry Spieght (auth), Dale Leys: Ideas and his work, Sch Arts, 78 & Dale Leys, Art Voices S, 78; Dialogue Mag, 90; Art Papers, 91. *Media:* Mixed Media. *Mailing Add:* Dept Art Murray State Univ University Station Murray KY 42071

LHOTKA, BONNY PIERCE
PAINTER
b La Grange, Ill, July 14, 42. *Study:* Bradley Univ, BFA, 64. *Work:* United Banks, Rocky Mountain Energy, Midland Savings & Loan, Denver; First Nat Bank, Boise; Nat Conf State Legislations, Charles Swabb, IBM, US West United Air Lines, Johnson Space Ctr, Mariott Hotels. *Exhib:* Allied Artists Am, Nat Acad Design, New York, 74, 76 & 77; Nat Watercolor Soc, Palm Springs Desert Mus, Calif, 74-81; Am Watercolor Soc, Nat Acad Design, 77; Nat Acad Design Exhib, 77, 79 & 81; one-man show, Wyo State Art Gallery, Cheyenne, 79. *Teaching:* Instr abstract watermedia & acrylic, Colo Watercolor Soc, summer 77 & Colo Artist Workshops, summer 78. *Awards:* First Nat Top Ten, Am Artist Mag, 78; Strathmore Awards, Strathmore Paper Co, 79; Century Award of Merit, Rocky Mountain Watermedia Exhib, 81. *Mem:* Nat Watercolor Soc; Audubon Artists; Nat Soc Painters in Casein & Acrylics; Rocky Mountain Nat Watermedia Soc. *Media:* Watermedia; Acrylic. *Publ:* Contribr, Watercolor page, Am Artist Mag, 77; Watercolor, The Creative Experience by Nochis, North Light, 79; article, Southwest Art Mag,3/81; Creative Seascape Painting, Watson Guptill; The Guild 5, 6 & 7, Kraus Sikes Inc, Madison, Wis, 90-92. *Dealer:* Ruth Bachofnen Gallery 1926 Colorado Ave Santa Monica CA 90401. *Mailing Add:* 5658 Cascade Pl Boulder CO 80303

LI, CHU-TSING
HISTORIAN
b Canton, China, May 26, 20; US citizen. *Study:* Univ Nanking, China, BA (Eng lit), 43; Univ Iowa, MA(Eng), 49, PhD(art hist), 55; post-doctoral res, Harvard Univ, 59 & Princeton Univ, 60. *Pos:* Res cur, Nelson Gallery Art, Kansas City, 68-; fac cur, Spencer Mus Art, Lawrence, Kans, 66- *Teaching:* From instr to prof art hist, Univ Iowa, Iowa City, 54-66; prof Oriental art, Univ Kans, Lawrence, 66-, chmn, Dept Hist Art, 72-78, Judith Harris Murphy Distinguished prof art hist, 78-90; Judith Harris Murphy Distinguished Prof Art His Emeritus, 90- *Awards:* Phi Tau Phi (Chinese Scholastic Hon Soc), Phi Beta Kappa (hon), Phi Beta Delta (Hon Soc Int Scholars). *Mem:* Col Art Asn; Midwest Art Hist Soc; Asia Soc; Asn Asian Studies. *Res:* Chinese painting of the Sung, Yuan, Ming, Ch'ing, and Modern Period. *Publ:* Auth, The Autumn Colors on the Ch'iao and Hua Mountains, 65 & A Thousand Peaks and Myriad Ravines: Drenwatz Collection, 74, Artibus Asiae; Liu Kuo-sung, Development of a Modern Chinese Artist, 69 & contribr, Five Chinese Painters: Fifth Moon Exhibition, 70, Nat Gallery Art, Taipei, Taiwan; auth, Trends in modern Chinese painting, Artibus Asiae, 79; ed, Chinese Scholar's Studio: Artistic Life in the Late Ming Period, London: Thames and Hudson, 87; ed, Artists and Patrons: Some Social and Economic Aspects of Chinese Painting, Seattle: Univ Wash Press, 89. *Mailing Add:* Univ Kans Lawrence KS 66045

LIAO (SHIOU-PING LIAO)
PAINTER, PRINTMAKER
b Taipei, Taiwan, Sept 2, 36. *Study:* Nat Taiwan Normal Univ, Taipei, BA, 59; Tokyo Univ Educ, Japan, MA, 64; Ecole Nat Superienredes Beaux Arts, Paris, 65-68. *Work:* Nat Mus Mod Art, Tokyo, Japan; Victoria & Albert Mus, London, Eng; Musee Municipal d'Art Mod, Paris, France; Cincinnati Art Mus, Ohio; New York Pub Libr; Metrop Mus Art, New York. *Comn:* Mural, Cathy Hospital, Taipei, 76; mural, Howard Plaza Hotel, Taipei, 83. *Exhib:* Salon de Mai & Salon d'Antonne, Musee Municipal d'Art Mod, Paris, France, 68; Nat Print, Brooklyn Mus, New York, 70; one-man shows, Taft Mus, Cinncinnati, 70, Calif Palace Legion Honor, San Fransisco, 73, Mus Mod Art, Liege, Belgium, 92 & Taiwan Mus Art, 92; Int Print Biennial, Nat Mus Mod Art, Tokyo, Japan, 70; Oversize Print, Whitney Mus Am Art, New York, 71; Int Print Exchange Exhib, Mus Art, Soeul, Korea, 79; Five from the Orient, Bergen Co Mus, Paramus, NJ, 81. *Collections Arranged:* Paintings by Leading Overseas Artist (auth, catalog), Hong Kong Mus Art, 82; Contemporary Printmaking Asn (auth, catalog), Singapore, 82; The Art of Shiou-ping Liao, Taiwan Mus Art, 92. *Teaching:* Vis prof printmaking, Tsukuba Univ, Japan, 77-79; Daemen Col, Amherst, NY, 78; adj prof painting & printmaking, Seton Hall Univ, NJ, 79-; vis prof, Nanjing Inst Art, Spring 91. *Awards:* Silver Medal, Salon des Artistes Francais, Paris, 65; De Cordova Mus Purchase Prize, Boston Printmaker Show, 71. *Bibliog:* The Art of Shiou-ping Liao, Taiwan Mus Art, 92. *Mem:* Soc Am Graphic Artists; Chinese Graphic Soc Taipei (bd dir, 74). *Media:* Mixed Media; Watercolor, Oil. *Publ:* Auth, The Art of Printmaking, 74 & ppreciation of Modern Prints, 76, Taipei Lion Art Book Co. *Mailing Add:* Seton Hall Univ/Dept Art & Music 400 S Orange Ave South Orange NJ 07079

LIBBY, GARY RUSSELL
MUSEUM DIRECTOR, EDUCATOR
b Boston, Mass, June 7, 44. *Study:* Univ Fla, studied with Jerry Uelsmann, AA, BA, studied with Philip Hultman, MA; Tulane Univ, studied with Leo Steinberg, MA. *Collections Arranged:* Audubon: Birds & Animals, 75, The Third Empire Porcelains and Silver, 77 & Artistic Taste in Pre-Castro Cuba, (auth, catalog), 77, Mus Arts & Sci, Daytona Beach, Fla; 400 Years of Prints, Eight Cuban Masters, Sampson Hall Gallery, Stetson Univ, Deland, Fla, 77; Salon & Picturesque Photography in Cuba, 89. *Pos:* Dir, Mus Arts & Sci, Daytona Beach, Fla, 77- *Teaching:* Instr, Tulane Univ, New Orleans, La, 68-71; asst prof humanities-art hist, Stetson Univ, 72-73, asst prof art hist surv, 72-77, vis prof, 77-85. *Mem:* Southeast Col Art Conf; Col Art Conf; Col Art Asn; Am Asn Mus. *Res:* Latin American: Cuban and Caribbean, 19th century English and American painting; Pre-Columbian ceramics. *Collection:* Pre-Columbian, etchings, engravings, 19th century painting. *Publ:* Auth, Pat Bannister: Mysterious world of women, 1/78, Mort Kunstler: Careful research-----, 5/78, Cuban art, 6/78, Bruce Elliott Roberts, 1/79, Perry Cosentino: An interview, 2/80, Southwest Art Mag, Berlin Porcelain, 12/90 & Cuban Painting, Int Fine Art Collector Mag, 1/91; Ed, Alexander Archipenko: Themes and Variations, Mus Arts & Sci, Daytona Beach, Fla, 90. *Mailing Add:* c/o Mus Arts & Sci 1040 Museum Blvd Daytona Beach FL 32014

LIBERI, DANTE
PAINTER, SCULPTOR
b New York, NY, Oct 15, 19. *Study:* Acad Fine Arts, Montecatini, Italy. *Comn:* Grand Ballroom, Willard Hotel, Washington, DC; murals, Doral Spa, Miami Beach, Fla; La Reserve Restaurant, New York. *Exhib:* Knickerbocker Artists, New York, 52; one-man shows, Galleria Vannucci, Pistoia, Italy, 70, Galleria Ghelfi, Montecatini, Italy, 72, Bottega D'Arte, Quarrata & Galleria San Luca, Verona, Italy, 79; Art Expo (sculpture), New York & Los Angeles, 89 & 90; plus others. *Awards:* First Prize for Sculpture, Oper Democracy. *Media:* Oil. *Publ:* Illusr, New Yorker Mag, 43; auth, Sculpture, Meisner Gallery, Farmingdale, NY. *Dealer:* Meisner Gallery, Farmingdale, NY; Riggs Gallery La Jolla CA. *Mailing Add:* 2591 Laguna Cyn Rd Laguna Beach CA 92656-1223

LIBERMAN, ALEXANDER
PAINTER, SCULPTOR
b Kiev, Russia, 1912; nat US. *Study:* Painting with Andre L'Hote, Paris, France, 29-31; Ecole Special d'Archit with August Perret, 32; Ecole Beaux-Arts, Paris, 32-33; RI Sch Design, DFA(hon), 80. *Work:* Mus Mod Art, New York; Albright-Knox Art Gallery, Buffalo; Art Inst Chicago; Tate Gallery, London, Eng; Nat Collection Fine Arts, Washington, DC; and many others. *Comn:* Windward, Miami, Fla, 84; Olympic Iliad, Seattle, Wash, 84; Stargazer, San Diego, Calif, 84; Galaxy, Oklahoma City, 85; Aura, Palm Beach, 86; Faith Jerusalem, Israel, 87; Ulysses, Los Angeles, Calif, 88. *Exhib:* One-man shows, Mus Mod Art, New York, 60, Vernissage, Rome, 78, Greenberg Gallery, St Louis, 79, Landau Alexander Gallery, Los Angeles, 79 & Arts Gallery Limited, Baltimore, 79; Mus Mod Art, New York, 62, 64, 65, 67, 68 & 69; Contemp Am Sculpture Ann, Whitney Mus Am Art, 69; Pure and Clear, Philadelphia Mus Art, 69; Retrospectives: Painting and Sculpture, Corcoran Gallery Art, Washington, DC & Mus Fine Arts, Houston, 70; Color As Language, Mus Mod Art, New York, 75; Black and White are Colors, Pomona Col, Calif, 79; and others; Miro in Am, Mus Fine Arts, Houston, TX, 82; Selected Recent Aqcquisitions, Metrop Mus Art, New York, 83; Aldrich Mus, Ridgefield, CT, 85; Tel Aviv Mus, Israel, 86; Lanzone Gallery, San Francisco, CA, 87. *Pos:* Ed dir, Conde Nast Publ, 62- *Awards:* Chevalier, Legion Honor, France. *Bibliog:* Barbara Rose (auth), Alexander Liberman (monogr), Abbeville Press, 81. *Publ:* Auth, The Artist in His Studio, 60 & Greece, Gods and Art, 68, Viking. *Dealer:* Andre Emmerich Gallery 41 E 57th St New York NY 10022. *Mailing Add:* 173 E 70th St New York NY 10021

LICCIONE, ALEXANDER
PAINTER, GRAPHIC ARTIST
b Rochester, NY, Jan 28, 48. *Study:* Acad di Belle Art di Brera Milan, Italy Fine Art Int, 69-72; Fla Atlantic Univ, Boca Raton, BFA, 78. *Work:* Pvt Collection, Brescia & Melfi (Potenza), Italy; murals, CitiBank, New York; ceramic statues, Dime Bank, New York; New Sch for Soc Res, New York; New York Pub Libr; ABC TV; Avalanche Pictures, New York. *Comn:* Sports outdoor mural, 76 & several cover illus, 78, Indian River Community Col, Ft Pierce, Fla; cover painting, Rochester Boxing Asn, 80 & Rochester Sesquicentennial Inc, 84, NY; Hilton Hotel, New York; Foreign Channel 31/HBO, ABC TV; TV announcer's box, Yankee Stadium. *Exhib:* Detailing the Subject Matter, Theatrical Prop House, New York, 83; Ariel Art Gallery, New York, 88-90; ABC TV, CBS TV, Universal Pictures, Guiding Light Soap Opera; Children Television Workshop - Square One, 92; American 500 Contemp Exhib, Centro Cultura Recoleta, Buenos Aires, Argentina, 92; and others. *Awards:* Int Platform Asn Bd Gov Award, 92. *Bibliog:* Giancarlo Politi: International Art Diary, 90; Alex Liccione Paints in 3D, video, Art Seen Art Video, 90. *Mem:* Nat Stereoscopic Asn; Orgn Independent Artists, New York; Art Initiatives at Tribeca, New York. *Media:* Oil, Watercolor. *Publ:* Auth, Stereo (3-D) realism in oil, Nat Stereo World Mag. *Mailing Add:* 48-35 43rd St Apt 5B Woodside NY 11377

LICHACZ, SHEILA ENIT
PAINTER
b Monagrillo, Panama, Oct 9, 42; US & Panamanian citizen. *Study:* Our Lady of the Lake Univ, San Antonio, Tex, BS, 65; Inter-Am Univ, PR, MA(educ), 68. *Work:* El Escorial, Madrid, Spain; Presidential Palace, Panama; Nat Bank

Panama; Mus Man, Panama City; Univ Tex, Austin; Nat Gallery Contemp Art Int Collection, Mus Art, San Jose, Costa Rica; Chase Manhattan Bank, Panama; and many others. *Comn:* Painting, Archdiocese Panama for John Paul II, 83; mural, Riverbend Baptist Church, Austin, Tex, 85. *Exhib:* US Embassy, Panama, 79; Nat Inst Cult, Panama, 80 & 81; Latin Am Art Exhib Gallery, Univ Tex, Austin, 81; Mus Mod Art Latin Am, Washington, DC, 81; Our Lady of the Lake Univ, San Antonio, 82; State Capitol, Austin, Tex, 82 & 83; Santa Fe East Gallery, NMex, 84. *Pos:* Dir & cur, Lichacz Living Mus, currently. *Bibliog:* C Alzola (auth), Sheila Lichacz, Vanidades Mag, 10/81; Catherine Wilner (auth), Sheila Lichacz: our lady of the pots, Houston Art Scene, spring 83; David Bell (auth), Santa Fe Letter, Art Space, Southwestern Contemp Arts Quart, winter 84-85. *Mem:* Tex Asn Mus. *Media:* Pastel. *Mailing Add:* c/o Ventanna Fine Arts 211 Old Santa Fe Trail Santa Fe NM 87501

LICHAW, PESSIA
PRINTMAKER
Study: Technion Tel-Aviv, Israel, BA, 64; Betzalel Acad, Jerusalem, 69-70; Art Students League, 76-80. *Work:* Jerusalem Mus. *Comn:* Images reproduced, Marriott Hotel, Tex, 84, Hyatt Hotel, New York, 86 & Sheraton Hotel, Philadelphia, Pa, 88; Originals, Gurneys Inn, Montauk, NY, 87 & City Bank, New York, 88-90. *Exhib:* Duke Univ, NC, 80; Nassau Community Col, Long Island, NY, 80; Queens Mus, New York, 82; traveling show State Univ NY, Buffalo, NY, 82 & Weschester, NY, 82; Bergen Community Mus, NJ, 83. *Awards:* Purchase Prize & Merit Scholarship, 77; Honorable mention, Nassan Community Col, 81; Mem prize, Nat Asn Women Artists, 84. *Bibliog:* Malcolm Preston (auth), Five approaches to graphics, Newsday, 2/7/80; Jeanne Paris (auth), Glen Cove's a gallery, Newsday, 4/18/80; Helen A Harrison (auth), Many shades of white, New York Times, 1/11/81. *Mem:* Nat Asn Women Artists; Artist Network Great Neck; Printmaking Workshop, New York; Art Students League, New York. *Media:* Monoprints. *Mailing Add:* Nine Hampton Ct Lake Success NY 11020

LICHT, EVELYN M
PAINTER, SCULPTOR
b New York, NY, Mar 4, 05. *Study:* Art Students League, 24; Hunter Col, 20-24; Rutgers Univ, 27-32; Academia de Belle Arte, Perugia, Italy, 62-69; New Sch Social Research, 68-72; Art Workshop with Randall Morgan, Sant' Agata, Italy. *Work:* Everson Mus & John Mayfield Libr, Syracuse, NY; Hinkhouse Collection, Eureka Col, Ill; Philadelphia Mus Art, Pa; Mus Cathedral of St John, New York; Mus of City of New York; Mus Contemp Art, Cathedral of St John, New York. *Comn:* Homage Dal Vesuvio, Serrento Palace Hotel, Italy, 81. *Exhib:* Women Sculptors, Grammercy Arts Club, New York, 63; Contemp Religious Art, Community Church, New York, 64; Women Watercolorists, Lever Bldg, New York, 64; Casein Artists, Union Carbide Bldg, New York, 65; Contemp Landscapes, Katonah, New York, 65; Butler Inst, Cleveland; Chas Mann Gallery, New York. *Pos:* Chmn, Kihbutz Scholarship Art, 64-70; dir art gallery, United Fedn New York, 66-70. *Teaching:* Instr art, Teaneck, NJ, 24-29; supervisor art, District 18, Bronx, NY, 48-50; chmn art, Kieran Jr High, 50-60. *Bibliog:* Shea Tenenbaum (auth), Art of Evelyn Licht, Montreal Chronicle, 73; articles, in, Mexico City Tribune, Israel Art News & Art News, NY. *Mem:* Artists Equity; Arts Int; Arts Interaction; Nat Art Club; charter mem Nat Mus Women Arts; charter mem Libr of Manuscripts, Col, Syracuse Univ. *Media:* Oil, Watercolor; Bronze. *Dealer:* Glass Gallery 315 Central Park West New York NY 10025. *Mailing Add:* 90 La Salle St New York NY 10027

LICHTENBERG, MANES
PAINTER
b New York, NY. *Study:* Art Students League; with Fernand Leger, Paris; Acad Grande Chaumiere, Paris. *Exhib:* Philadelphia Acad Fine Arts; Nat Acad Design, New York; Mus Mod Art, Paris; Allied Artists Am, New York; Mus l'Ile de France, Paris. *Awards:* Prix Othon Friesz, Paris, 61; Gold Medal of Honor, Allied Artists Am, 64; Prix Maurice Utrillo, Utrillo Found Int, Paris, 64. *Mem:* Allied Artists Am; Am Watercolor Soc. *Media:* Watercolor, Oil. *Mailing Add:* 47 Golfivew Ct Homosassa FL 34446-8815

LICHTENSTEIN, GARY
PAINTER, PRINTMAKER
b Oct 23, 53; US citizen. *Study:* Syracuse Univ, BA, 73; San Francisco Art Inst, with Robert Fried, BFA, 75; Antioch col West, MFA, 78. *Work:* De Sassait Art Mus, Univ Santa Clara, Calif; Light of Sweden Found, Gotegorg; San Francisco Mus Mod Art; Univ Conn Art Gallery; Wadsworth Athenium, Hartford, Conn. *Exhib:* New York Art Expo, 79; Boston World Art Exhib, 79; Washington Int Art Fair, 80; New York Int Exhib Contemp Art, 81; San Francisco Int Art Expo, 81. *Pos:* Pres & owner, Soma Fine Art Press. *Teaching:* Guest lectr art of Robert Fried, San Francisco Art Inst, 79; printmaking workshop, San Francisco Mus Mod Art, 80; instr printmaking, Univ Calif, Berkeley, 81-86. *Bibliog:* Documentary video: California Art Scene, San Francisco Ctr for Visual Studies, 85. *Media:* Oil base; Serigraphy. *Mailing Add:* c/o Soma Fine Art Press 665 Third St, Suite 225 San Francisco CA 94107

LICHTENSTEIN, ROY
PAINTER, SCULPTOR
b New York, NY, Oct 27, 23. *Study:* Ohio State Univ, BFA, 46, MFA, 49; Hon DFA, Calif Inst Arts, Valencia, 77, Ohio State Univ, 88 & Bard Col, 89. *Work:* Solomon R Guggenheim Mus, New York; Whitney Mus Am Art, New York; Mus Mod Art, New York; Stedelijk Mus, Amsterdam, Holland; Metrop Mus, New York; and many others. *Comn:* Brushstroke murals, Dusseldorf Univ Med Ctr, 70; Mermaid (sculpture), Theatre Performing Arts, Miami Beach, Fla, 79; Brushstrokes in Flight, Equitable Life Assurance Bldg, Whitney Mus Art, New York, 85; Coups de Pinceau, Caisse des Depots & Consignations, Paris, 88; mural, Tel Aviv Mus Art, Israel, 89. *Exhib:* Whitney Mus Am Art, New York, 65, 67, 68, 70, 72, 73, 74, 75, 77, 78, 80, 82, 83, 84, 85 & 87; Solomon R Guggenheim, New York, 65, 76; Mus Mod Art, New York, 66, 67, 68, 74, 76, 80, 85, 88; Venice Bienale, 66; one-man shows, Centre Nationale d'Arte Contemporain (traveling), Paris, 75-76, Inst Contemp Art, Boston, 79, Portland Ctr Visual Arts, 80, St Louis Art Mus, 81, Fundacion Juan March, Madrid, 82, Walker Art Ctr, Minneapolis, Minn, 86, The Drawings of Roy Lichtenstein, Mus Mod Art (traveling), New York, 87-88 & Interiors, Leo Castelli Gallery, New York, 92; Corcoran Gallery Art 36th Biennial, Washington, DC, 79; Hirschorn Mus, Washington, DC, 80; Brooklyn Mus Art, New York, 81; Nat Mus Am Art, Smithsonian Inst, Washington, DC, 84; Frank Stella, Roy Lichtenstein, Palacio Velazquez, Madrid, Spain, 91; Roy Lichtenstein: Haystacks, Tom Wesselman: Drawings and Steel Drawings, Galerie Martine Queval & Galerie Joachim Becker, Paris, France, 92. *Teaching:* Instr, Ohio State Univ, 46-51; asst prof, State Univ Oswego, 57-60 & Douglass Col, Rutgers Univ, 60-63. *Bibliog:* John Coplans (ed) Roy Lichtenstein, 72; Jack Cowart (auth), Roy Lichtenstein 1970-1; Laurence Alloway (auth), Lichtenstein, 83; plus many others. *Mem:* Am Inst Arts & Letts. *Dealer:* Leo Castelli Gallery 420 W Broadway New York NY 10012. *Mailing Add:* c/o Leo Castelli Gallery 420 W Broadway New York NY 10012

LICHTNER, SCHOMER FRANK
PAINTER, PRINTMAKER
b Peoria, Ill, Mar 18, 05. *Study:* Milwaukee State Teachers Col, with Gustave Moeller, 24; Art Inst Chicago, 26; Art Students League, with Boardman Robinson, 27; Univ Wis, Madison, art history with Oscar Hagen, 29-30. *Work:* Milwaukee Art Mus, Wis; Univ Wis Union Gallery, Madison; Wustum Mus, Racine, Wis; Milwaukee Journal, Wis; White House (selected by Pres Roosevelt), Washington, DC. *Comn:* Murals, Walker Jr High, Milwaukee, Wis, 34; murals, Sheboygan Post Off, WPA Treas Dept, Wis, 38; mural, Stokely Canning Co, Wis, 52; mural, Northern & Marine Bank, Milwaukee, Wis, 55; Gov's Award (serigraph), Madison, Wis, 85. *Exhib:* Milwaukee Art Mus, Wis, 62, 84 & 90; Artists of Chicago & Vicinity, Art Inst Chicago, 63; Art Inst Chicago; Davidson Nat Print & Drawing, Stowe Gallery, NC, 72; Wisconsin Directions, Milwaukee Art Mus, 75; Wisconsin Painters & Sculptors, Univ Wis Fine Arts Gallery, 80; Am Show, Art Inst Chicago; Carnegie Int, Carnegie Inst, 30, Pittsburgh, Pa; Ballet Art, Performing Art Ctr, 83 & Bradley Galleries, 83, Milwaukee; Taliesim, Spring Green, Wis, 87; 100 Years Wisconsin Art, 88; Ballerina & Cow, sculpture, Chicago Int Expo, Posner Gallery, 90. *Teaching:* Instr drawing & design, Univ Wis, 60-69. *Awards:* Serigraph, Wis Salon, Madison, 50; Award for Painting, Mr & Mrs Jule E Brower, Chicago Artists & Vicinity, Art Inst Chicago, 64; Award for Painting, Wis Painters & Sculptors, 65. *Bibliog:* Richard Olney (auth), Schomer Lichtner Drawings, 64; Dennis Stone (auth), The light touch of Schomer Lichtner, Art Scene, 68; James Auer (auth), Fifty Years in Art, The Lichtner- Grotenrath Story, Wis Trails, 84. *Media:* Acrylic, Casein; Serigraph, Etching. *Publ:* Auth, Schomer Lichtner Drawings, Gallery Press, 64; Schomer Lichtner Spotted Cow Drawings, 69 & Schomer Lichtner Drawings from the Nude, 74, Spotted Cow; Schomer Lichtner Alphabet Drawings, 73 & Ballerinas' Holiday, 79, self publ. *Dealer:* Bradley Galleries 2639 N Downer Ave Milwaukee WI 53211; Seuferer Chosy Gallery 218 N Henry St Madison WI 53703. *Mailing Add:* 2626A N Maryland Ave Milwaukee WI 53211

LIDDLE, NANCY HYATT
MUSEUM DIRECTOR, CONSULTANT
b Martinsville, Ind, Aug 27, 31. *Study:* Ind Univ, AB. *Collections Arranged:* The Sculpture of Richard Stankiewicz 1953-1979; Edward Koren: Prints and Drawings, 82; Thom O'Connor: Prints and Drawings, 83; The Faces of the City: Albany Portraits from Three Centuries, 86; Our Land/Ourselves: Am Indian Contemp Artists, 91; Swiss Poster Art from the Ciba-Geigy Collection, 92. *Pos:* Vpres, 327 Gallery, Albany, NY, 59-63; art critic, Knickerbocker News, Albany, NY, 64-65; asst dir, Univ Art Gallery, State Univ NY, Albany, 66-77, dir, 77-93. *Teaching:* Lectr, State Univ NY, Albany, currently. *Awards:* Chancellors Award, State Univ NY, 80; Preservation Award, Hist Albany Found, 81. *Mem:* Albany Inst Hist & Art; Hist Albany Found; Am Asn Mus; Gallery Dirs Coun, State Univ NY; The Cosmopolitan Club, New York. *Mailing Add:* Univ Art Mus State Univ NY Albany NY 12222

LIEBER, THOMAS ALAN
PAINTER
b St Louis, Mo, Nov 5, 49. *Study:* Univ Ill, BFA, 71, MFA, 74. *Work:* Guggenheim Mus, Mus Mod Art, New York; San Francisco Mus Mod Art; Los Angeles Mus Mod Art; Tate Gallery, London; Cleveland Art Mus. *Exhib:* The Aesthetics of Grafitti, San Francisco Mus Mod Art, Calif, 78; Fresh Paint, San Francisco Mus Mod Art, 82; New Perspectives in American Painting, Guggenheim Mus, 78-88; San Francisco Bay Area Paintings, Univ Nebr, Lincoln, 84; Contemp American Monotypes, Chrysler Mus, Norfolk, Va, 85; Maine Collects, Farnsworth Mus, Rockland, Maine, 89. *Teaching:* Vis prof, Stanford Univ, 89; Vt Studio Sch, Johnson, Vt. *Awards:* Nat Endowment Arts, 75. *Bibliog:* Robert McDonald (auth), Physically finds its place, 76 & Tom Liebers environmental paintings, 77, Art Week; John Russell (auth), Younger Americans, New York Times, 83. *Media:* Oil, Watercolor. *Dealer:* John Berggruen 228 Grant San Francisco CA. *Mailing Add:* c/o John Berggruen 228 Grant St San Francisco CA 94108

LIEBERMAN, LAURA CROWELL
WRITER, ADMINISTRATOR
b Oak Ridge, Tenn, Apr 7, 52. *Study:* Pomona Col,72; Swarthmore Col, BA, 74. *Collections Arranged:* Atlanta Women Artists: A Personal Survey, Atlanta Art Workers' Gallery, 78; 36 Women Artists (coed, catalog), Peachtree Ctr Gallery, Atlanta, 78; Nine Diverse Directions: Atlanta, Ga Southern Col, 83. *Pos:* Artist-in-residence, Ga Coun for Arts & Humanities, Atlanta, spring, 77; artist-in-residence, Atlanta Women's Art Collective, 77-78; ed-in-chief, Atlanta Art Workers' Coalition Newspaper, 78-80; ed-in-chief, Atlanta Art Papers, Inc, 80-83 & Words Art Inc, 82-84; arts ed, Southern Accents, 84-88; publicist, Great Am Gallery, 88-92; dir, The Atlanta Arts Clearinghouse, 92- *Bibliog:* Karen Wantuck (auth), Subjective (catalog), 78; Sherry Baker (auth), 36 women artists, Atlanta Gazette, 4/78; Clyde Burnett (auth), A personal survey, Atlanta J-Constitution, 7/78. *Mem:* Atlanta Women's Art Collective; Southeastern Women's Caucus for Art (panelist, 79); Whittier Mill Village Asn. *Res:* Contemporary art in Atlanta, Georgia and the Southeast. *Publ:* Co-ed, Other Harmonies, Atlanta Women's Poetry Workshop, 77; auth, Five Atlanta women artists, Southern Quart, Univ Southern Miss, 79; ed, Contracts for Artists, 83; and others; auth, William Christenberry: A Retrospective (catalog essay), 90; London to Atlanta: International Exchange (catalog), 91; ed, City Arts update (newsletter), 92. *Mailing Add:* 3 Spring Circle NW Atlanta GA 30318

LIEBERMAN, LOUIS (KARL)
SCULPTOR, DRAFTSMAN
b Brooklyn, NY, May 7, 44. *Study:* Brooklyn Mus Art Sch, cert, 64; Brooklyn Col, BA, 62; RI Sch Design, BFA, 69. *Work:* Metrop Mus Art, New York; Staten Island Mus, Richmond, NY; Philadelphia Mus Art, Pa; Aldrich Mus, Ridgefield, Conn; Brooklyn Mus, NY; and others. *Comn:* Wall relief, Aldrich Mus Contemp Art, Ridgefield, Conn, 73; Wall relief, Kenan Ctr, NY State Coun on Arts, Lockport, NY, 73; and others. *Exhib:* Solo exhibs, Root Art Ctr, Hamilton Col, Clinton, NY, 80, Harm Bouckaert Gallery, New York, 81; List Art Ctr, Hamilton Col, Clinton, NY, 82; Ellen Price, New York, 82, John Davis Gallery, Akron, Ohio, 83 & 85, Columbus Mus Art Collectors Gallery, Ohio, 84, John Davis Gallery, New York, 86; One Cubic Foot, Thomas J Watson Libr, Metrop Art Mus, New York, 83; A Sigh of Relief, Wilson Art Ctr, Rochester, NY, 87; Stephen Rosenberg Gallery, New York, 87-88; New Art on Paper, Hunt Paper Collection, Philadelphia Mus Art, Pa, 88; Paper Thick, Erie Art Mus, Pa, Art Mus, Santa Cruz, Calif, Hunter Mus, Chattanooga, Tenn, 88-89; Black, Gray and White, Henry Feiwel Gallery, New York, 89. *Pos:* Contribr art critic, New York Arts J, 78-79. *Teaching:* Adj lectr drawing, Brooklyn Col, NY, 71-78; adj lectr sculpture/design, Lehman Col, Bronx, 72-75; vis artist sculpture, Ill State Univ, Normal, 79; vis artist, Hamilton Col, Clinton, New York, 82. *Awards:* New York Found Arts, 84-85; Pollock-Krasner Found, 87; Adolph and Esther Gottlieb Found, 89-90; and many others. *Bibliog:* Brian Riverman (auth), article, Dialogue, 7/84 & 8/84; Holland Cotter (auth) articles, Arts Mag, 11/85, Art Am, 1/87; Stephan Westfall (auth) article, Arts Mag, 2/87. *Media:* Multimedia. *Mailing Add:* 16 Greene St New York NY 10013

LIEBERMAN, MEYER FRANK
PAINTER, PRINTMAKER
b New York, NY, Aug 28, 23. *Study:* Art Students League, with Reginald Marsh; Pratt Graphics Ctr, with Andrew Stasik. *Work:* Jewish Mus, New York; Presidential Residence, Jerusalem; Columbia Univ, New York; Brooklyn Col, New York; Woodstock Hist Soc, Woodstock, NY. *Exhib:* Coney Island, Mus City New York, 55; Drawing USA, Mus Mod Art, New York, 56; one-man shows, Bodley Gallery, 78, Night Gallery, 81, Terrance Gallery, 81; Work Art Gallery, Saugerties, NY, 86. *Teaching:* Instr drawing, painting & composition, Art Life Craft Studios, New York, 64-68; instr drawing, collage painting & composition, Temple Emanu-El, Yonkers, NY, 66-74; instr drawing, painting & composition, Flatbush Jewish Ctr, Brooklyn, 67-78; instr, Temple Emanuel, Kingston, NY, 78-80; Gifted & Talented Prog, Onteora School Dist, New York, 85- *Mem:* Woodstock Artists Asn; Barrett House, Poughkeepsie, NY. *Media:* Oil, Watercolor. *Mailing Add:* 648 Zena Rd Woodstock NY 12498

LIEBERMAN, WILLIAM S
CURATOR
b Paris, France, Feb 14, 24. *Study:* Swarthmore Col, BA(hons), 43; Harvard Univ, with Paul J Sachs, 44-45. *Collections Arranged:* Mus Mod Art exhibs, Four Americans in Paris: The Collection of Gertrude Stein and Her Family, 70; Modern Masters: Manet to Matisse, 75; Art of the 20's, 79; Modern Masters, Euopean Paintings from the Museum of Modern Art (auth, catalog), 80; Metrop Mus Art exhibs, Henry Moore; 60 Years of His Art (auth, catalog), 83; Aspects of the City, 84; Balthus, 84; Paul Klee, 88 & Boccioni, 88-90; Twentieth Century Modern Masters: The Jacques and Natasha Gelman Collection, 89-90; The Arts of Mexico: Splendors of Thirty Centuries, 90-91; The Fauve Landscape, 91; Magritte, 92. *Pos:* Mem staff, Dept Exhibs & Publ, Mus Mod Art, New York, 43, asst to dir mus collections, 45-49, assoc cur prints & illus bks, 49-53, cur prints, 53-66, cur painting & sculpture, 67-69, dir painting & sculpture 69-71, dir drawings, 71-79; chmn, Dept 20th Century Art, Metropolitan Mus Art, New York, 79- *Awards:* Chevalier de l'Ordre des Arts et des Lett, Repub France. *Mem:* Grolier Club; Am Fedn Arts; Cassandra Found; Drawing Soc; Int Graphic Arts Soc; and others. *Collection:* Eighteenth century silver boxes, Japanese prints of the Meiji era. *Publ:* Auth, Picasso: Blue & Rose Periods, Abrams, 54; Matisse: 50 Years of His Graphic Art, Braziller, 56; Edvard Munch, Los Angeles Co Mus Art, 69; Redon: Prints & Drawings & Jacques Villon, Mus Mod Art; introd, Pollock: The Last Sketchbook, Johnson Reprint Corp, 82. *Mailing Add:* Metropolitan Mus Art Fifth Ave at 82nd St New York NY 10028

LIEBERMANN, PHILIP
PHOTOGRAPHER, EDUCATOR
b Brooklyn, NY, Oct 25, 34. *Study:* Mass Inst Technel, BS & MS, 58, PhD(linguistics), 66. *Work:* Brooklyn Mus, NY; Mus RI Sch Design, Providence; Albright Knox Gallery, Buffalo, NY; Silver Bullet Gallery, Providence; Providence Athenaeum, RI. *Comn:* Photographs for book, Soc Creative Altruism, Boston, 59; photographs, Theater on the Green, Wellesley, 62; Book-Walking in Switzerland, The Mountaineers, Seattle, 85-87; US of the Alpine Tourist Comn. *Exhib:* Boston Arts Festival, Mass, 65, 66 & 67; Carl Siembab Gallery, Boston, 66; B Urdang Invitational Travelling Exhib, 84; Animal in Photography 1845-1985, Invitational Photographers' Gallery, London, 86; B Urdang Gallery 82, 84, 86, 89 & 92. *Teaching:* Prof linguistics & cognitive sci, Brown Univ, 74-, adv photog, 82-84, George Hazard Crooker prof, 92- *Awards:* Young Photog Award, Time-Life, 65; Sullivan Award, J Banigan Sullivan, 84 & 86; Guggenheim Fel, 87. *Media:* Black & White Photography. *Publ:* Co-Auth, Walking in Switzerland, Mountaineers, 87. *Dealer:* Bertha Urdang 23 E 74th St New York NY 10021. *Mailing Add:* 141 Elton St Providence RI 02906

LIEBLING, JEROME
PHOTOGRAPHER, FILMMAKER
b New York, NY, April 16, 24. *Study:* Brooklyn Col, with Walter Rosenblum, Milton Brown & Art Reinhardt; New Sch Social Res, with Lew Jacobs & Paul Falkander. *Work:* Mus Mod Art, New York; Corcoran Gallery Art; Boston Mus Fine Art; Libr Cong; Minneapolis Inst Art. *Exhib:* The Photo League, Int Ctr Photog, New York, 78; Mirrors and Windows, Mus Mod Art, New York, 78; 14 Northeast Photographers, Boston Mus Fine Arts, 78; solo exhibs, Corcoran Gallery Art, 80, Fogg Art Mus, 82 & Portland Art Mus, Maine, 83; American Children, Mus Mod Art, New York, 81; Northeast Perambulations, Addison Gallery, 82. *Teaching:* Prof photog & film, Univ Minn, Minneapolis, 49-69 & Hampshire Col, 70-83; prof photog, Yale Univ, 76-77. *Awards:* Fels, Guggenheim Found, 77 & 81 & Nat Endowment Arts, 79. *Bibliog:* Estelle Jussim (auth), No 15, Friends Photog, 77; Alan Trachtenberg (auth), Jerome Liebling--Photographs, Univ Mass Press, 82. *Mem:* Soc Photog Educ (trustee, 73-78); Univ Film Study Ctr (vpres, 75-77). *Publ:* Coauth, Face of Minneapolis, Dillon Press, 66; illusr, Photography Current Perspectives, Mass Rev, 77. *Dealer:* Photofind 138 Spring St New York NY 10012. *Mailing Add:* 39 Dana St Amherst MA 01002

LIEBMAN, DR SARAH
EDUCATOR, PAINTER
b Brooklyn, NY. *Study:* Brooklyn Col, BA, 76, with Sam Gelber & Jerome Viola, MFA, 78, with Philip Pearlstein & Lee Bonticou; Pratt Inst, Grad Fel Fine Art, 77, with Richard Bove & Dr Ralph Wickiser; Teachers Col, Columbia Univ, EdM, 86, EdD, 90, with Justin Schorr & Maxine Green. *Exhib:* Mid East Traveling Exhib, Cult Affairs Ctr, US Embassy, Israel & Egypt, 81; Nat Asn Women Artists, 81-82; Ann Exhib, Catherine Lorillard Wolfe Art Club, New York, 82; Nat Coun Art Jewish Life, Lever House, New York, 83; Nat Asn Women Artists, Bergen Mus Art & Sci, Paramus, NJ, 83 & New York, 83-84; solo exhib, Macy Gallery, Columbia Univ, New York, 85. *Teaching:* Instr drawing & painting, Sephardic Community Ctr, 81-84; instr art hist appreciation, Brooklyn Col, NY, 83-87; instr art hist, appreciation & drawing, Univ Conn, 91-92. *Awards:* Marilyn Freeman Award, Brooklyn Col, 75; Elizabeth Elanger Award, Nat Asn Women Artists, 81; Binney & Smith Award, Catherine Lorillard Wolfe Art Club, 82. *Mem:* Nat Asn Women Artists; Nat Art Educ Asn; Audubon Artists; Artists Equity. *Media:* Oil, Pastel. *Mailing Add:* 1717 Avenue N Brooklyn NY 11230

LIEBMAN, NORMAN
PAINTER
b Newark, NJ, Oct 9, 33. *Study:* Rutgers Univ, AB, 55; Chautauqua Art Inst, 81-86. *Work:* Mus Art, Ft Lauderdale, Fla; Boca Mus Art, Fla; Mayo Clinic Found, Rochester, Minn. *Exhib:* Hortt, 31, 32 & 34, Mus Art, Ft Lauderdale, Fla, 89, 90 & 92; Boca Mus Art 39th Ann Show, Boca Mus, Fla, 90; Society of Four Artists, Soc 4 Arts Mus, Palm Beach, Fla, 90. *Awards:* All Fla Prize, Boca Mus Art, 90. *Mem:* SFla Art Ctr. *Media:* Acrylic, Oil. *Mailing Add:* 16 Island Ave 7C Miami Beach FL 33139

LIEBOWITZ, JANET
PAINTER, SCULPTOR
b New York, NY. *Study:* Art Students League; Am Art Sch; studied with Robert Reed, New Haven. *Work:* Elmira Col, NY; Bocour Artist Color Collection, New York; Butler Art Inst, Youngstown, Ohio; Albrecht Gallery, St Joseph, Miss; Griffith Art Inst, St Lawrence Univ, Canton, NY. *Exhib:* Artists Choice, Women for the Arts Found, New York, 77; Silvermine Gold of Art Ctr, Phoenix Gallery, New York; Elmira Col, NY; Wadsworth Atheneum, Hartford, Conn. *Collections Arranged:* Papyrus Abstracts, Wesport Weston Arts Coun, 82; Selections in Contemp Art, Wesport Weston Arts Coun, 83. *Awards:* Painters prize, Painters & Sculptors Soc NJ, 68; Nat Asn Women Artists, NY; Reginald March Scholar Art Students League. *Bibliog:* Michael Benedict (auth), Art Int, 66; John Caldwell (auth), Art Forms of Paperwork, NY Times, 8/82. *Mem:* Nat Asn Women Artists; Penwomen, Boca Raton Chapter; Lighthouse Gallery, Tequesta, Fla; Artists Equity; Prof Artist Guild of Boca Raton Mus, Fla. *Media:* All. *Dealer:* Silvermine Guild of Artists New Canaan Conn. *Mailing Add:* Six Northwoods Lane Boynton Beach FL 33436

LIFSON, HUGH ANTHONY
PAINTER, EDUCATOR
b New York, NY, Nov 7, 37. *Study:* Studio 10, with Irving Marantz, 53-59; Univ Wis, with Warrington Colescott & S Zingale, 55-56; Wesleyan Univ,

with R Limbach, AB, 59; Ind Univ, 60; Pratt Inst, with Robert Richenberg & James McGarrell, 61. *Work:* Cedar Rapids Mus Art, Iowa; State Univ NY, Postdam; Wesleyan Univ, Middletown, Conn; St Leo Col, Fla; Davenport Munic Art Gallery, Iowa. *Comn:* Environment, Cedar Rapids Art Ctr, Iowa, 69. *Exhib:* One-person shows, Ohio State Univ, Columbus, 72, Ward Nasse Gallery, New York, NY, 78; Mid American Annual, St Louis Munic Mus, Mo, 68 & Nelson Atkins Mus, Kansas City, 84; USA The Figure, Mus Mod Art, New York; South Bend 20th Century Ctr, Ind, 81. *Teaching:* Prof, Cornell Col, Mt Vernon, Iowa, 84 & 86- *Bibliog:* Richard Kostelanetz (auth), Metamorphosis, Assembling Press, 81. *Media:* Acrylics, Polyofinics; Computer Graphics. *Dealer:* Computer Studio 30 E 10th St New York NY 10003. *Mailing Add:* 219 Sixth Ave N Mt Vernon IA 52314

LIGHT, KEN
PHOTOGRAPHER, EDUCATOR
b Bronx, NY, Mar 16, 51. *Study:* Ohio Univ, Athens, Ohio, BGS, 73. *Work:* Int Ctr Photography, New York; San Francisco Mus Mod Art, Calif; Calif Hist Soc, San Francisco; Int Polaroid Collection, Boston; Fed Reserve Bank, San Francisco. *Comn:* Libr Congress, Am Folklife Ctr, 89 & 90. *Exhib:* Work, Oakland Mus, Calif, 77; Faces Photographed, San Francisco Mus Mod Art, 84; New Documentary Photog, USA Images Gallery, Cincinnati, Ohio, 89; San Joaquin Co Hist Soc & Mus Arts Station, Tifton, Ga, 90; Mus Contemp Art, Morelia, Mex, 90; Nev Mus Art-Wiegand Gallery, 93; Italian Americans in the West, Libr Cong, 94; one-man exhibs, The Eye Gallery, San Francisco, 91, Chovnick Gallery, New York, 91 & Pac Tel Corp Plaza Gallery, Walnut Creek, Calif, 92. *Teaching:* Fac photog, San Francisco Acad Art 76-; lectr photog, Univ Calif, Berkeley 82- *Awards:* Nat Endowment Arts Photogrs Fel, 82 & 86; Dorothea Lange Fel, 87; Thomas M Stoke Int Journalism Award, 90; Cannon Photo Esaysity Award, Univ Mo, 92. *Bibliog:* Roger Minick (auth), Images of Work, (catalog), San Jose Mus Art, 78; Paul Raedeke, To the Promised Land, Arrival Mag, 87; Mark Lapin (auth), Light on the Border, Photo District News, 88. *Mem:* Soc Photog Ed; Am Fed Teachers. *Publ:* Contribr, The Circle of Life, Harper Collins Publ, 91; Mexico Through Foreign Eyes, W W Norton, 92; Time for a Witness, East Bay Guardian, 1/92; Granta, No 40, fall 92; Image Mag, San Francisco Examiner, 7/12/92. *Mailing Add:* 3107 Deakin St Berkeley CA 94705

LIGHTON, LINDA
SCULPTOR, INSTRUCTOR
b Kansas City, Mo, Mar 10, 48. *Study:* Monterrey Inst Technol, Mex, 65-66; Fontainbleau Sch Fine Arts, France, 67; Factory Visual Arts, Seattle, Wash, with Margaret Ford & David Furman, 71-74; Western Wash State Col, Bellingham, 75; Univ Idaho, Moscow, 75-77; Kansas City Art Inst, with Clary Illian & Akio Takamori, 77 & 86; Kansas City Art Inst, BFA, 87-89. *Work:* Kahn Steel, Kansas City, Mo; also pvt collection of the Crown Prince of Brunei. *Exhib:* Dimensions 87, Lenexa Nat, Kansas, 87; Cross Roads Ceramics, Kansas City, Mo, 89; Chicago Int Art Expo, 90; New Art Forms, Chicago, Ill, 90; Fed Reserve Bank, Kansas City, Mo, 90; and others. *Pos:* journalist, Nat Coun Educ Ceramic Arts J, 85-89. *Teaching:* Guest lectr ceramic art, Univ Idaho, Moscow, 78-79 & Shawnee Mission East, Shawnee Mission, Kans, 84; Arts Partners (artist-in-residence prog), Kansas City, Kans & Mo secondary schs, 86-91; Artist in Educ, State Mo; Childrens Workshop Lenexa Nat Art Show, Kans, 92. *Awards:* Jurors Award, Galeria Mesa, Ariz, 86; First Prize, Hidden Glen Art Show, Olathe, Kans, 89; First Prize, Kaw Valley Arts Show, Kansas City, Kans, 90. *Bibliog:* Donald Hoffman (auth), Ceramics, Kans Star, 3/19/89; Rick Hellman (auth), Ceramist's work takes on new look; new meaning, Kans City Jewish Chronicle, 3/23/90; Laura Caruso (auth), Seeking Innerconnections, Kans City Star, 9/2/90. *Mem:* Nat Coun Educ Ceramic Arts; founding mem, Kansas City Contemp Art Ctr, Kans; Kansas City Artist Coalition; Arts Partners of Kansas City (dir, bd mem & secy); Kansas City Clay Guild. *Media:* Clay, Metal. *Publ:* Auth, numerous articles in, Nat Coun for Educ of Ceramic Arts J. *Dealer:* Morgan Gallery 819 Walnut Kansas City MO 64106. *Mailing Add:* 4620 Charlotte Kansas City MO 64110-1565

LIJN, LILIANE
SCULPTOR, WRITER
b New York, NY, Dec 22, 39. *Study:* Ecole de Louvre, Paris, Sorbonne, Paris. *Work:* Tate Gallery, London, Eng; Mus de la Ville de Paris, France; Centre Nat d'Art Contemporain, Paris; Arts Coun Great Brit, London; Victoria & Albert Mus, London. *Comn:* Kinetic sculpture, Peter Stuyvescent Corp & Arts Coun Great Brit, Warwick Univ, Coventry, Eng, 72; Circle of Light, Milton Keynes Shopping Arcades, Eng, 79; Split Spiral Spin, Birchwood Sci Park, Warrington New Town, Eng, 79; Extrapolation, Norfolk & Norwich Triennial Festival, Norwich, 82; Carbon Black, Nat Chemical Labs, London Argo, N H Schroder, Poole Dorset, 88. *Exhib:* Mus d'Art Mod, Paris, 67; Electra, Mus d'Art Mod, Paris, 83; 20th Century Drawings & Watercolors, Victoria & Albert Mus, London, 85; Livres d'Artistes, Centre George Pompidou, Paris, 85; Technologia e Informatica, Venice Biennale, Venice, 86; Imagine the Goddess, Fisher Fine Arts, London, 87; Licht und Transparenz Mus, Bellerive, Zurich, Switz, 88; Nagoya Biennale Artec, Japan, 89; and others. *Teaching:* Mem coun mgt, Byam Shaw Art Sch, 83-90. *Awards:* Alecto Print Award, Bradford Print Biennale, 76; Publishing Award, Art Coun GB, 81; Award, Arts Coun Bursary Holography, 82. *Bibliog:* Cyril Barrett (auth), Art as research: the experiments of L Lijn, Studio Int, Vol 173 (June, 1967); Vera Lindsay (auth), Liliane Lijn in discussion with Vera Lindsay, Studio Int, Vol 177 (May, 1969); Joan Murray (auth), Beyond the image: Liliane Lijn, Fireweed 5 & 6, Woman & Language, Toronto, 80; Jasia Reichardt (auth), Liliane Lijn (catalog essay), Fisher Fine Art, 86; Phillipa Scott (auth), New Sculpture (catalog), Gillian Jason Gallery, London, 90. *Media:* All Industrially Used Materials. *Publ:* Auth, Inside & out: notes on anti-gravity koans, Flash Art, Milan, Italy, 2/71; Reflections: Three Poems, Time Zone, Grosseteste Rev, 71; What is art?, Ostrich No 9, Northumberland, 9/73; Six Throws of The Oracular Keys, Ed de la Nepe, Paris, 82; Crossing Map, Thames & Hudson, 83; Imagine the Goddess, A Rebirth of the Female Archetype in Sculpture, Leonardo, Vol XX, No 2. *Dealer:* Fisher Fine Art Ltd 30 King St Saint James's London SW1. *Mailing Add:* 28 Camden Sq London NW1 9XA England United Kingdom

LIKAN, GUSTAV
PAINTER, INSTRUCTOR
b Srb, Yugoslavia, May 1, 12; US citizen. *Study:* Akad der Bildenden Kunste, Munich, Ger; Franz Hals Mus, Haarlem; Louvre, Paris. *Work:* Moderna Galerija & Strossmayer Mus, Zagreb, Yugoslavia; Mestrovic Mus, Split, Yugoslavia; Kunstlerhaus Mus, Salzburg, Austria; Kunstmuseet, Copenhagen, Denmark. *Comn:* Murals of schs, comn by Eva Peron, Buenos Aires, 50, Cordoba, 51 & Mendoza, Arg, 51, mural of a hosp, comn by Eva Peron, 50 & mural of a church, Buenos Aires, 51. *Exhib:* Nat Mus Vienna, 41; one-man shows, Merrill Chase Galleries, Chicago, 64, Laguna Gloria Art Mus, Austin, Tex, 76, Abilene Fine Arts Mus, Tex, 76 & Am House, Heidelberg, WGer, 83; Concord Gallery, Austin, Tex, 84; Dougherty Art Ctr, Austin, Tex, 86; Katolik Univ, Hamburg, WGer, 84, 85; Gallery Las Brisas, Acapulco, Mex, 87; Merrill Chase Gallery, Chicago, 88-90. *Teaching:* Prof fine art, Chicago Acad Fine Art, 60-67, Laguna Gloria Mus Fine Art, Austin, Tex, 69-78, Austin Community Col, 82- *Bibliog:* Article, Third Coast, 9/10/83. *Media:* Graphic & Acrylic Painting. *Publ:* Auth, Art Classes 2,5: Meaning, Method & Media, 72; Likan Drawings, 73; also auth, articles in bks & newspapers in Austria & Yugoslavia. *Dealer:* Merrill Chase Galleries Ltd 620 N Michigan Ave Chicago IL 60611. *Mailing Add:* 1407 Ridgecrest Dr Austin TX 78746

LI LAN
PAINTER
b New York, NY, Jan 28, 43. *Work:* Seibu Art Mus, Tokyo, Japan; Ohara Mus Art, Kurashiki, Japan; Parrish Art Mus, Southampton, NY; William Benton Mus Art, Storrs, Conn; Heckscher Mus, Huntington, NY; and others. *Exhib:* Solo shows, Natenshi Gallery, Tokyo, Japan, 71, 74, 77, 80 & 85, Robert Miller Gallery, New York, 78, Asher/Faure Gallery, Los Angeles, 80 & 82, O K Harris Gallery, New York, 83, 85 & 87, Franz Bader Gallery, Washington, DC, 89 & William Benton Mus Art, Storrs, Conn, 90; Late Twentieth Century Art Traveling Exhib, Sydney & Frances Lewis Found, 78-85; Am Acad & Inst Arts & Lett, New York, 83 & 87; Yun Gee and Li-Lan: Paintings by a Father & Daughter, Southampton Campus Fine Arts Gallery, Long Island Univ, NY, 88; Drawing on the East End, 1940-1988, Parrish Art Mus, Southampton, NY, 88; William Benton Mus Art, Storrs, Conn, 90. *Awards:* Artists Grant, Artists Space, NY, 88 & 90. *Bibliog:* Gerrit Henry (auth), article, Art in Am Mag, 4/86; Barbara Delatiner (auth), article, NY Times, 6/26/88; Helen Harrison (auth), aticle, NY Times, 3/8/92. *Media:* Oil, Drawings. *Publ:* Auth, Canvas with an Unpainted Part, An Autobiography, Asahi Newspaper Publishing, Tokyo, 76. *Dealer:* OK Harris Gallery 383 W Broadway New York NY 10012. *Mailing Add:* PO Box 1194 East Hampton NY 11937

LILES, CATHARINE (BURNS)
PAINTER, PATRON
b Macon, Ga, 44. *Study:* Wesleyan Col BFA(magna cum laude), 79; Mercer Univ, MLS, 89; with Constantine Chatov, Rhett English & Ann Adams. *Work:* Univ Tex Medical Sch, Houston; Art by Am Women, Louise and Alan Sellars Collection, Marietta, Ga; King & Spalding Attys, Wasington, DC; Arnall Golden Gregory Atty, Macon, Ga. *Comn:* Macon Symphony, Southern Bel Co. *Exhib:* Solo Exhibs, People & Places, Middle Ga Col, 81, Faces & Figures, Mercer Univ, 82 & Pittura dal Muro, JH Webb Gallery, Macon, Ga, 84; Who Am I?, Mus Arts & Scis, Macon, Ga, 83; Paintings by American Women, Mus Arts & Scis, 83, Brenau Col, Gainesville, Ga, 91, Etowah Art Coun, Cartersville, Moultrie Art Ctr & Kennesaw Col, Marietta, Ga, 92; Art by American Women, Brenau Col, Gainesville, Ga, 91, Knoxville Mus Art, Tenn, 92 & St Petersburg Mus Art, Fla, 93. *Pos:* Owner & Pres, Markwell Inc, Healthcare Marketing Liles & Assoc, 82-; pres, Macon Arts Alliance; bd dirs, Macon Mus Arts & Scis. *Teaching:* Instr, figure drawing & portrait painting, Mercer Univ, 1/83-9/83. *Awards:* Hon Mention, Winter Arts Festival, Middle Ga Art Asn, 73, 90 & 92; Best in Show Print, Addy Award, Ad Club Central Ga, 87 & 88; Outstanding Alumni Award, Wesleyan Col, 91. *Bibliog:* Paul E Sternberg (auth), Paintings by American Women: Selections from the Collection of Louise & Alan Sellars, 89 & Art by American Women, 91. *Mem:* Macon Arts Alliance; assoc mem Am Watercolor Soc; Middle Ga Art Asn; assoc mem Nat Watercolor Soc; Ga Watercolor Soc. *Media:* Watercolor, Oil. *Dealer:* Art By American Women 2120 Cornerstone Lane Marietta GA 30064; JH Webb Gallery Vineville Ave Macon GA 31204. *Mailing Add:* 2653 Stanislaus Circle Macon GA 31204

LILES, RAEFORD BAILEY
PAINTER, SCULPTOR
b Birmingham, Ala, July 20, 23. *Study:* Birmingham-Southern Col; Auburn Univ, BSEE, 49; Atelier Fernand Leger, Paris, France, 49-51. *Work:* Musee d'Art Mod, Eliat, Israel; Andrew Dickson White Mus Art, Cornell Univ; Corcoran Gallery Art, Washington, DC; Amos Andersons Konstmuseum, Helsingor, Finland; Alfred Khouri Collection, Norfolk Mus, Va; and others. *Comn:* Silk screen series, East Hampton Gallery, NY, 67; also pvt collections. *Exhib:* Salon d'Art Independent & Art Libre, Paris, 51; Salon Nouvelle Reality, Mus Mod Art, Paris, 55; Mirco Salon d'Avril, Iris Clert, Paris, 56; Mus Art; Birmingham Mus, 72; and others. *Awards:* Prize, Students of Leger, 51; First Prize, Alpine Gallery, 58. *Bibliog:* Turpin (auth), L'Orleanais Dans Les Art, 52; Orinese (auth), Tour D'Expositions Combat, 55; Brown (auth), Review of expositions, Art Mag, 68. *Mem:* Birmingham Art Asn; Ala Watercolor Soc. *Media:* All Media. *Mailing Add:* 484 W 43rd St Apt 121C New York NY 10036

LILJEGREN, FRANK
PAINTER, INSTRUCTOR
b New York, NY, Feb 23, 30. *Study:* Art Students League, with John Groth, Dean Cornwell & Frank J Reilly. *Work:* Manhattan Savings Bank, New York; Am Educ Publ Inst, New York; New Britain Mus Am Art, Conn; Art Students League, New York. *Comn:* Pastel Portrait, First Presby Church, Van Wert, Ohio. *Exhib:* Coun Am Artists Soc, Lever House, New York, 64 & 67; Salmagundi Club, New York, 64-68; Acad Artists Asn, Springfield Fine Arts Mus, Mass, 66-70; O S Ranch Exhib, Tex, 77-80; Fort Wayne Mus Art, Ind, 79; and others. *Teaching:* Instr painting, Westchester Co Art Workshop, White Plains, 66-77, Art Students League, 73-74, Wassenberg Art Ctr, Van Wert, Ohio, 77-80, Wright State Univ, 81- *Awards:* Allied Artists Am Awards; Frank V Dumond Award, Salmagundi Club, 65 & 67; Medal of Merit for Oil Painting, Today's Art Mag, 71. *Bibliog:* Jo Mary McCormick-De Guyton (auth), Frank Liljegren and his old friends, Am Artist Mag, 2/72; Ralph Fabri (auth), Medal of merit winner in 58th A A A annual, Today's Art Mag, 3/72. *Mem:* Allied Artists Am (corresp secy, 67, exhib chmn, 68-76, pres, 70-72, dir, 72-76); Artists Fel; Salmagundi Club; life mem Art Students League. *Media:* Oil, Pastels. *Dealer:* Mongerson Wunderlich Galleries 704 N Wells St Chicago Ill 60610. *Mailing Add:* 203 S Cherry St Van Wert OH 45891

LILYQUIST, CHRISTINE
EGYPTOLOGIST, CURATOR
b Glendale, Calif, Aug 15, 40. *Study:* Pomona Col, BA, 62; NY Univ, MA, 65, PhD, 71. *Collections Arranged:* Dir, Dendur Temple Installation, Metrop Mus Art, New York, 72-78, dir, Egyptian Reinstallation, 72-83, consult, Renovation of the Cairo Mus, 75-77 & cur, Mus Consortium for the Exhib Treasures of Tutankhamun, 75-79. *Pos:* Asst cur Egyptian dept, Metrop Mus Art, New York, 70-72, assoc cur in charge, 72-74 & cur, 74-; consult, New York City Dept Park & Rec (Cleopatra's Needle), 78-80. *Mem:* Col Art Asn. *Res:* Egyptian gold, Middle Kingdom arts. *Publ:* Ed, Tutankhamun Exhib Publ, Metrop Mus Art, New York, 76; auth, Ancient Egyptian Mirrors: From the Earliest Times Through the Middle Kingdom, Munchner Aegyptologische Studien 27, 79. *Mailing Add:* Dept Egyptian Art Metrop Mus Art Fifth Ave at 82nd St New York NY 10028

LIMA, JACQUELINE (DUTTON)
PAINTER, DRAFTSMAN
b Niagara Falls, NY, Oct 28, 49. *Study:* Swain Sch Design, New Bedford, MA, BFA, 78; Brooklyn Col, City Univ New York, MFA, 80. *Comn:* Hand painted wearable buttons, Rotunda Gallery: Jackie Battenfield, Brooklyn, NY, 85. *Exhib:* Brooklyn 85, Brooklyn Mus, NY, 85; Hobart & William Smith Col, Geneva, NY; The World is Round, Houston Gallery; Panoramas, Hudson River Mus, Col Art Gallery, State Univ NY, New Paltz, NY, Albany Inst Hist & Art, Albany, NY, Arts & Sci Ctr, Nashua, NH, Parrish Art Mus, Southhampton, NY & Del Art Mus, Wilmington, 87-88; Interior Spaces, Newport Art Mus, Newport, RI, 88. *Collections Arranged:* AMMO, The Brooklyn Landscape, 84 & Masters of War, 85, Artist Exhibit Space; House & Home, 1 Main Street for Brooklyn Waterfront Artists Coalition, 90. *Pos:* Cur & co-dir, AMMO Artist Exhib Space, 84-86; dir, Blue Mountain Gallery, NY, 85-90; cur, Brooklyn Water Front Artists Coalition, 88-90. *Teaching:* Instr drawing, Pratt Inst, 83; instr painting, Kingsborough Community Col, 84-89; drawing, New Jersey Ctr Visual Arts, 90. *Awards:* Charles W Shaw Award, Brooklyn Col, 79 & 80; Dr Maury Leibovitz Art Award, Lotos Club, Artists Welfare Fund, 86. *Bibliog:* Review of the World is Round, Contemporary Panoramas, Vivian Raynor, The New York Times, Jan 89; Review, Jed Perl (auth), The New Criterion, May 90; Tracy Garrity (auth), On the waterfront, Phoenix, Brooklyn, NY, 86. *Mem:* Col Art Asn; Women's Caucus for Art; Brooklyn Waterfront Artists Coalition (bd dir, 85 & 86, rec secy, 87, vpres, 88, pres, 89, consult, 90). *Media:* Oil. *Publ:* The World is Round, (catalog), Contemporary Panoramas, HR Mus, ll/87. *Dealer:* Lee Pope Somerstown Gallery Somers NY. *Mailing Add:* 79 Hudson Ave Brooklyn NY 11201

LI MARZI, JOSEPH
PAINTER, GRAPHIC ARTIST
b Chicago, Ill. *Study:* Art Inst Chicago. *Work:* Mus Fine Arts, Springfield, Mass. *Comn:* Historical, Fed Govt, Fed Bldg, Wapokeneta, Ohio, 37; mil hist of army co, Fed Govt, Staten Island, NY, 42; story of food, Royal Scarlet Foods, New York, 51; indust uses of Gen Cables, Inc, New York, 52. *Exhib:* Art Inst Chicago Nat; Brooklyn Mus Nat; Pa Acad Fine Arts Nat; one-man shows, Contemporary Arts, New York, Simon's Rock, Mass & Lehman Gallery, Red Rock, NY, 75; Cleveland Inst Art; Mus Mod Art, New York; Libr Arts Ctr, Newport, NH; Berkshire Mus, Pittsfield, Mass; Spencertown Acad, NY. *Teaching:* Instr painting, High Sch Art & Design, New York, 52-73. *Awards:* Hon Award, Mural Competition, Fed Govt, 37. *Mem:* Painters & Sculptors Soc NJ; Audubon Artists, New York; Am Soc Contemp Artists Inc, New York. *Media:* Oil, Graphics. *Dealer:* Ella Lerner Gallery 17 Franklin St Lenox MA 02140. *Mailing Add:* Box 144 East Chatham NY 12060

LIMONE, FRANK
CONCEPTUAL ARTIST
b Brooklyn, NY, Aug 14, 38. *Study:* St Louis Univ, BA, 69; Tyler Sch Art, Philadelphia, MFA, 72. *Work:* Walker Art Ctr, Minneapolis; Des Moines Art Ctr; High Mus Art, Atlanta, Ga; Collection of Dial Finance & Collection of Am Rep Insurance Co, Des Moines, Iowa & Scottsdale, Ariz; Meredith Corp, Des Moines, Iowa & Kansas City, Mo. *Exhib:* One-man exhib, Hudson River Mus, NY, 85. *Pos:* Lectr. *Awards:* Mid-Career Sculpture Grant, Nat Endow for Arts, 81. *Bibliog:* Graham W J Beal (auth), Walker Art Ctr Arch, 79; Holliday T Day (auth), Frank Limone at Roy Boyd, Art in Am, 10/79; Victoria Melcher (auth), Frank Limone at Douglas Drake, Kansas City Star, 2/79, 10/81; Fade to Black (film), KCMO-TV, CBS, 11/81. *Media:* All media. *Mailing Add:* 774 Mamaroneck Ave White Plains NY 10605

LIMONT, NAOMI CHARLES
PRINTMAKER, INSTRUCTOR
b Pottstown, Pa. *Study:* Pa Acad Fine Arts, BFA; Pratt Graphic Ctr, with Michael Ponce de Leon; Barnes Found; Univ Pa, BFA; Tyler Sch Art, with Romas Viesulas, MFA; also with Jerome Kaplan. *Work:* Philadelphia Mus Art & Pa Acad Fine Arts; Yale Univ; Eastern Mennonite Col, Va; Univ Southern Calif; Rutgers Univ, NJ. *Comn:* Mural, St Christopher's Children's Hosp, Philadelphia, 65; Creation (folio of prints), Philadelphia Print Club, 67; Folio '76 (bicentennial folio), Graphics Guild, Cheltenham, Pa, 75; Polio of Prints, The Centennial of Sun Printing Co, 80. *Exhib:* The Earth Art Show, Philadelphia, 75; Int Biannual Print Show, Print Club, 77; Eye on the Seventies, Philadelphia Mus Art, 79; Int Miniature Print Exhib, New York, 79; Nat Print Exhib, Cedar City, Utah, 78; and others. *Teaching:* Artist-in-res, Lock Haven State Col, 81; instr graphics, Abington Art Ctr, 84-89. *Awards:* Sun Oil Award, Earth Art Exhib, 75; Stella Drabkin Award & Bronze Medal, Am Color Print Soc, 76; Grumbacher Award, 81. *Bibliog:* Bagnell & Sosin (coordrs), The Tyler Show working women artists from Tyler School of Art, Samuel Paley Libr, Temple Univ, 73; review, Art News, 9/80; review, Art Voices, 3-4/81. *Mem:* Philadelphia Print Club; Philadelphia Art Alliance; Artists Equity Asn; Am Color Print Soc (pres); Philadelphia Watercolor Club. *Dealer:* Richard Rosenfeld Gallery 113 Arch St Philadelphia PA 19106. *Mailing Add:* RD 2 PO Box 249 Barto PA 19504

LIN, MAYA Y
SCULPTOR
Study: Yale, BA, 81, MA(archit), 86, Hon Dr Fine Arts, 87. *Work:* Los Angeles Co Mus Art; Vietnam Veterans Mem, Washington, DC. *Exhib:* Am Women Artists - Par II, The Younger Generation, Sidney Janis Gallery, New York, 84; Jane Voorhees Zimmerli Art Mus, Rutgers State Univ, NJ, 85; Avant-Garde in the Eighties, Los Angeles Co Mus Art, 87; 60's-80's Sculpture Parallels, Sidney Janis Gallery, 88; Group Exhib, Rosa Esman Gallery, New York, 90. *Pos:* Design consult, Cooper-Lecky Partnership, Washington, DC, 81-82; archit designer, Peter Forbes & Assocs, Boston, 83, Batey & Mack, San Francisco, 84; archit apprentice, Fumihiko Maki & Assocs, Tokyo, 85; design assoc, Peter Forbes & Assocs, New York, 86-87; Maya Lin Studio, New York, 87- *Teaching:* Archit studio instr, Phillips Exeter Acad, summer 82; head teaching asst, Yale Art Hist Dept, 84-85; vis prof, Yale Col Seminar, 86; vis lectr, Harvard Univ, Sch Landscape Design, Cambridge, Mass, 88. *Awards:* Henry Bacon Mem Award, AIA, 84; Nat Endowment Arts, 88; Design 100 - Elements of Style, Metrop Home, 90. *Bibliog:* Alice Hall (ed), Vietnam Mem, Nat Geographic, 5/85; Jonathan Coleman (auth), Time Mag, 11/6/89. *Mailing Add:* c/o Sidney Janis Gallery 110 W 57th St New York NY 10019

LINCOLN, RICHARD MATHER
CERAMIST, EDUCATOR
b Ann Arbor, Mich, Mar 1, 29. *Study:* Potters Guild, Ann Arbor, with Rhoda Le Blanc Lopez & J T Abernathy. *Work:* Dallas Mus Fine Arts; Witte Mus, San Antonio, Tex; Detroit Inst Arts; Davenport Art Ctr, Iowa. *Comn:* Mural, Apparel Mart, Dallas; mural, Ft Worth Children's Hosp, Tex; light fixtures, The Quadrangle, Dallas. *Exhib:* Eight Ceramic Nat & Int Exhibs, Everson Mus, Syracuse, NY, 54-68; Young Americans, New York, 56; Fiber, Clay & Metal, St Paul, Minn, 60; Miami Ceramic Nat, 60; five S Cent Regional Exhibs, Santa Fe, NMex, 62-71. *Teaching:* Assoc prof ceramics, Tex Christian Univ, 63- *Awards:* Third Pottery Prize, Young Americans, 56; Purchase Award, Univ Mich Mus, 56; First Pottery Award, SCent Regional Exhib, 62. *Bibliog:* Texas potter--Richard Lincoln, Designers W, 11/70. *Mem:* Am Craftsmen Coun. *Mailing Add:* 4759 Westcreek Dr Ft Worth TX 76133

LINDEMANN, EDNA M
MUSEUM DIRECTOR EMERITUS, EDUCATOR EMERITUS
b Buffalo, NY. *Study:* Univ Buffalo, BS(art); Albright Art Sch; Northwestern Univ, MA, 40; Cranbrook Acad Art; Columbia Univ, EdD, 56. *Collections Arranged:* Burchfield Int Exhib, 68; Charles Clough: Selections 1972-81, 83; 150 Years of Portraitive in Western NY, 81; Charles Cary Rumsey, Sculptor: 1879-1922, 83; Niagara Falls, New Impressions, 85; Burchfield and His Colleagues, 89. *Pos:* Dir cult affairs, State Univ NY Col Buffalo, 65-68; dir, Charles Burchfield Ctr, 68-85; chmn, Gallery, Asn NY State, 70-72, mem bd dirs, 72-77; Burchfield Ctr Coun, 68- *Teaching:* Instr art educ, NY Univ, 49-56; prof design, State Univ NY Col Buffalo, 56-85. *Awards:* Focus Award for Outstanding Contribution to Cult Affairs, Western New York-Buffalo Courier Express, 76; Citizen of the Year Award, Buffalo News, 85. *Mem:* Gallery Asn of New York State (found mem & chmn, 72-75); Burchfeild Art Ctr, Buffalo, NY (found dir, dir emer current); Art Appraisers Asn. *Publ:* Auth, Our Legacy of Art in Western New York, 72; ed, Edwin Dickinson, 77; Roycroft: Spirit for Today, 77; The American Landscape: Paintings by Allen D'Arrangelo, 79; Burchfield and his Colleagues: Artist/Dealer/Collector, 89. *Mailing Add:* 52 Behm Rd West Falls NY 14170

LINDENBERG, MARY K
PAINTER, INSTRUCTOR
b New York, NY, Feb 2, 21. *Study:* Hunter Col, BA, 42. *Comn:* Christmas Cards, 92, Courage Cards. *Exhib:* Brockton Art Mus, Mass, 80; Newport Art Mus, RI, 81; Three-person Show, Providence Art Club, RI, 85; RI Watercolor Soc, Pawtucket, 88; Bierstadt Art Soc, New Bedford, Mass, 88. *Pos:* Co-founder, Mass Art Week, 57- *Teaching:* Instr watercolor, New Bedford

YWCA, 78-, Southeastern Mass Univ, 85. *Awards:* First Prize, Brockton Art Mus, 80; Prize for watercolor, Greater Fall River Art Asn, 90; First Prize for drawing, Bierstadt Art Soc, 88. *Bibliog:* Eleanor Roth (auth), Do artists have special perceptions?, AIM Mag, 74; article, Surprising ingredient of creativity, Living Mag, Singapore, 79. *Mem:* Bierstadt Art Soc; Marion Art Ctr; Westport Art Group; Greater Fall River Art Asn. *Media:* Watercolor, acrylic. *Publ:* Auth, mem issue, North Light Mag, 80, 83 & 91; Variations on a theme of nature, Palette Talk Mag, 84; Getting started in teaching, Draw Mag, 86. *Dealer:* Lopoukhine Gallery Inc 125 Newbury St Suite 4 Boston MA 02116. *Mailing Add:* 20 Emerald Dr North Darmouth MA 02747

LINDERMAN, EARL WILLIAM
PAINTER
b Endicott, NY, Jan 1, 31. *Study:* Albright Art Sch & NY State Univ Col, BS, 53; Pa State Univ, MEd, 56, EdD, 60. *Work:* Valley Nat Bank Art Collection, Phoenix; William C Brown Publ Co, Dubuque, Iowa; Portland Art Mus, Ore; Lowe Art Gallery, Univ Miami; Eckerd Col, St Petersburg, Fla; and others. *Exhib:* One-man shows, Tally Richard's Gallery Contemp Art, Taos, NMex, 78-83; Marilyn Butler Fine Art, Scottsdale, Ariz, 80-84; Aberbach Fine Art, New York, 82; Salon D'Automne, Grand Palais,Paris, France, 82; Elaine Horwitch Galleries, Scottsdale, Ariz, 84-86; C G Rein Galleries, Scottsdale, Ariz, 88-92, Houston, 90-92, St Paul, Minn, 90 & Santa Fe, NMex, 90-91; and others. *Teaching:* Prof painting & drawing, Ariz State Univ, Tempe, 66- *Awards:* Bronze Vessel Second Award, Plains Art Mus, Moorhead, Minn, 79. *Bibliog:* Jim O'Rourke (auth), Earl Linderman, 1972-1982 Retrospective, Plains Art Mus, 82. *Media:* Oil, Pastel. *Publ:* Auth, Invitation to Vision, 67, coauth, Developing Artistic and Perceptual Awareness, 4th ed, 79 & auth, Teaching secondary School Art, 2nd ed, 80, William C Brown; coauth, Crafts in the Classroom, Macmillan Publ Co, 77, 84; auth, Linderman: The True and Incredible Adventures of Doctor Thrill, Paradise House, 84. *Mailing Add:* 5301 N 69th Pl Paradise Valley AZ 85253

LINDGREN, CHARLOTTE
SCULPTOR
b Toronto, Ont, Feb 1, 31. *Study:* Univ Mich, BS; Can Coun studies in Finland, Sweden & Eng. *Work:* Can Dept External Affairs, Ottawa; York Univ, Toronto; Winnipeg Art Gallery; Confederation Ctr Art Gallery, Charlottetown, PEI; McLaughlin Gallery, Oshawa. *Comn:* Ten Light Nets, Queen's Col, Nfld, 68; IBM Headquarters Conference Room, Toronto, 68; woven sculpture, Expo '70, Can Dept External Affairs, Osaka, Japan, 70; sculpture, CBC Bldg, Montreal, 74; wall sculpture, Fed Fisheries Bldg, 77. *Exhib:* Montreal Mus Fine Arts, 66; Nat Art Gallery, Ottawa, 67; Expo '67, Montreal, 67; Int Tapestry Biennials, Lausanne, Switz, 67 & 69; Art Gallery of Ont, 74; Can House, London, 76; Can Colt Centre, Paris, France, 76; Harbourfront, Toronto, 80; IV Triennale, Poland, 81; Barbican Centre, London, Eng, 82; and others. *Pos:* Mem adv arts panel, Can Coun; consult, Nat Capitol Commission, 78, Pangnirtung Tapestries, 78-81; Vice-pres, Royal Academy, 78-81. *Teaching:* Mem fac, NS Col Art & Design, 78-79 & 81-82 & Banff Ctr Fine Arts, 79; vis prof, Royal Col Art, London, 83. *Awards:* Haystack Sch Scholar Award, 64; Can Coun Arts Award, 65; First Prize Award, Perspective Competition Centennial Comn, Govt Can, 67; Ont Arts Coun Award, 87. *Bibliog:* C Fraser (auth), article, 6/66 & J Graham (auth), article, 7/71, Arts Can; L Rombout (auth), article, Vie Art, winter 67; J Murray (auth), article, Arts Atlantic, winter 80. *Mem:* Royal Can Acad Artists; Can Artists' Representation (NS rep). *Media:* Miscellaneous. *Mailing Add:* 1557 Vernon St Halifax NS B3H 3M8 Canada

LINDMARK, ARNE
PAINTER, INSTRUCTOR
b Poughkeepsie, NY, Oct 26, 29. *Study:* Pratt Inst; also watercolor with Edgar Whitney. *Work:* Huntington Gallery, WVa. *Exhib:* Am Watercolor Soc Traveling Exhibs, 66-79; Nat Arts Club Ann, 69-71; Allied Artists Am, 71-72; Mainstreams 72, Marietta, Ohio, 72; Am Watercolor Soc Exchange Show, Sydney, Australia, 79. *Teaching:* Instr painting & watercolor, Huntington Gallery, summer 71; instr, South West Watercolor Soc, Dallas, 78-79, Mid-West Watercolor Soc, Wis, 79, Houston Art Group, 80, Pocono Pines Workshos, Pa, 82 & 83 & Seven S St Workshops, Rockport, Mass, 83. *Awards:* Samuel J Bloomingdale Mem Award, 73 & Edgar A Whitney Award, 74, Am Watercolor Soc; Ranger Fund Purchase Award, Nat Acad Design, 79. *Bibliog:* Wendon Blake (auth), Acrylic Watercolor Painting, Watson-Guptill, 70; Margit Malstrom (auth), Arne Lindmark, master of the watercolor scene, Am Artist Mag, 1/71; Frank Webb (auth), Watercolor Energies, 83. *Mem:* Am Watercolor Soc; Allied Artists Am; Hudson River Art Asn; Duchess Co Art Asn; Nat Acad Design. *Media:* Watercolor. *Mailing Add:* 101 Forbus St Poughkeepsie NY 12603

LINDQUIST, EVAN
PRINTMAKER, EDUCATOR
b Salina, Kans, May 23, 36. *Study:* Emporia Kans State Univ, BSE, 58; Univ Iowa, MFA, 63. *Work:* Whitney Mus Am Art, New York; Uffizzi, Florence, Italy; Albertina Mus, Vienna, Austria; Nelson-Atkins Art Mus, Kansas City; Art Inst Chicago. *Exhib:* Prints by Seven, Whitney Mus Am Art, New York, 71; Boston Printmakers Ann Exhib, 71-75; two-men circulating exhib, Ark Arts Coun, 79-81; Opera Bevilacqua La Masa, Venice, Italy, 77; Gallerie V Kunstverlag Wolfbrum, Vienna, Austria, 79; Ark Arts Ctr, Little Rock, 83, 86 & 87; and others. *Teaching:* Prof art, Ark State Univ, Jonesboro, 63- *Awards:* More than 60 awards including Boston Printmakers, 71-74 & Potsdam Prints, NY State Univ Potsdam, 72. *Mem:* Visual Artists & Galleries Asn; Boston Printmakers; The Print Club, Philadelphia; Soc Am Graphic Artists; Southern Graphics Coun. *Media:* Engraving, Woodcut. *Dealer:* Gallery V Kansas City. *Mailing Add:* 4300 Hickory Lane Jamesboro AR 72401

LINDQUIST, MARK
SCULPTOR
b Oakland, Calif, May 16, 49. *Study:* New England Col, BA, 71; Pratt Inst; Fla State Univ, MFA, 90. *Work:* Metrop Mus Art, New York; High Mus Art, Atlanta, Ga; Dallas Mus Art, Tex; Nat Mus Am Art, Washington, DC; Philadelphia Mus Art; and others. *Comn:* Sculpture, Brockton Art Mus, Mass, 85. *Exhib:* The Art of the Turned Bowl, Renwick Gallery, Smithsonian Inst, 78; solo shows, Brevard Art Mus, Melbourne, Fla, 86, Franklin Parrasch Gallery, New York, 89, Mendelson Gallery, Washington Depot, Conn, 91, Gail Severn Galley, Ketchum, Idaho, 92 & Snyderman Gallery, Philadelphia, 92; Ob'Art, Les Ateliers d'Art, Paris, 86; The Poetry of the Physical, Am Craft Mus, New York & travelling, 86-88; Mus Fine Arts, Boston, 91; and others. *Teaching:* Instr welding & three-dimensional design, New Eng Col, 70-71; head of woodworking, Craft Ctr, Worcester, Mass, 77-78; assoc prof, Sch Archit, Fla A&M Univ, 88-89. *Awards:* MacDowell Colony Fel, NH, 79. *Bibliog:* Nancy Means Wright (auth), Mark Lindquist: The Bowl Is a Performance, Am Craft Mag, 10/11/80; Siegfried Ehrmann (auth), Portrat: Melvin und Mark Lindquist, Holz und Elfenbein, Ger, 84; Janet Koplos (auth), Mark Lindquist at Franklin Parrasch, Art in America, 4/90. *Mem:* Phi Kappa Phi. *Media:* Wood. *Publ:* Auth, Spalted Wood, 77, Turning the Spalted Bowl, 78 & Harvesting Burls, 84, Fine Woodworking Mag; Sculpting Wood, Davis Press, 86. *Mailing Add:* Rte 2, Box 247 Quincy FL 32351

LINDROTH, LINDA
PHOTOGRAPHIC ARTIST, CURATOR
b Miami, Fla, Sept 4, 46. *Study:* Douglass Col, BA(art), 68; Rutgers Univ, MFA(art), 79; also with Gordon Matta Clark & Garry Winogrand. *Work:* Mus Mod Art, Metrop Mus Art & Mus City of New York, New York; Bibliot Nat, Paris; NJ State Mus, Trenton; Polaroid Corp; Price Waterhouse Co, New York; Ctr Creative Photog, Tucson, Ariz. *Exhib:* solo exhibs, Newark Mus, NJ, 85-86, City Spirit Artists/The New Haven Found, 86 & Photo Structures 1982-1986, Aetna Inst Gallery, Hartford, Conn, 87; 1992 Exhib Photog, Berkshire Art Mus, Pittsfield, Mass, 92; Homeless, A Visual Dialogue, Artspace, New Haven, Conn, 92; New York/New Haven, Artspace, 92; The New Eng Holocaust Mem Competition Gund Gallery, Harvard Grad Sch Design, Cambridge, Mass, 92; Notes from the Material World: Contemporary Photomontage, John Michael Koehler Art Ctr, Sheboygan, Wis, 92. *Pos:* Founder & dir, Gallery Jazz Inc Art Gallery, New Haven, Conn, 84-87; guest cur, Aetna Inst Gallery, Hartford, 87; co-curator, The Pump House Gallery, Hartford, 90-93. *Teaching:* Instr photog, Douglass Col, New Brunswick, NJ, 77-79. *Awards:* Grant, Found Contemp Performance Arts In, 90; Ann Design Rev Award, ID Mag, 90 & 91; Proj Grant for Archaeology/Body/City, New Forms Regional Initiative, New Eng Found Arts, 92. *Bibliog:* Ann R Langdon (auth), New and Improved: New York/New Haven Rattles Viewers Cages for a Change, New Haven Advocate, 6/25/90; 1991 Ann Design Review, ID/Int Design Mag, 7-8/91; Catalina Island: Twenty Six Miles and Thirty Four Years Away, Photog Insight, J II, no 4, 92. *Publ:* Contribr, New Jersey Photography, 74 & Photographic Process as Medium, 76, Rutgers Univ; Artists Books USA, Independent Cur Inc, 78. *Mailing Add:* 219 Livingston St New Haven CT 06511

LINDSAY, ARTURO
SCULPTOR, PAINTER
b Colon, Panama, Sept 29, 46; US citizen. *Study:* Cent Conn State Univ, BA, 70; Univ Mass, MFA, 75; New York Univ, doctoral studies ongoing. *Work:* Nat Union Cuban Writers & Artists, Havana; Slater Mem Mus, Norwich, Conn; Barnett-Aden Collection, Washington, DC; Royal-Athena Galleries, New York; Univ Mass, Amherst. *Comn:* Homage to our Musicians (mural), Craftery Gallery, Hartford, 78; Cinque (mural), Amistad Cultural Resource Ctr, Hartford, 78. *Exhib:* Through Young Black Eyes, Wadsworth Atheneum, Hartford, 72-73; Caribbean Festival Arts, Nat Union Cuban Writers & Artists Mus, Havana, Cuba, 79; Black & Hispanic Art in Conn, Slater Mem Mus, Norwich, 80; Art in the Southwest, African Am Mus, Dallas, 81; Artists of the 80's, Los Angeles County Mus, 83; Houston Artists, Midtown Art Ctr, 84; African Am Art in Pub & Pvt Collections in Atlanta, The High Mus, 84; Caribbean Art: African Currents, Mus Contemp Hispanic Art, Soho, NY, 86; Encuentro de Escultura, Museo de Arte Contemporaneo, Panama City, Panama; Plexus, Santuary of Saitria, Sardinia, Italy. *Pos:* Dir & owner, Galeria Arturo, Hartford, Conn, 79-83; exec dir, Midtown Art Ctr, Houston, 83-84; asst dir, Royal-Athena Galleries, New York & Beverly Hills, 84- *Teaching:* Instr, Univ Hartford, Univ Conn & NH Col. *Awards:* First Prize, Atlanta Life Ann Exhib & Competition, Atlanta Life Insurance Co, 81. *Bibliog:* Jay Whitsett (dir), Looking Better, Conn Pub Television Show, 78; James Miller (auth), Ancestry & the Art of Arturo Lindsay, Int Rev of African Am Art, 85. *Mem:* Int Sculpture Ctr; Col Art Asn Am; Nat Conf Artists; Art Against Apartheid; Plexus. *Media:* Cast Metal; Multi-Media. *Mailing Add:* 4026 Birchwood Cove Decatur GA 30034

LINDSAY, KENNETH C
HISTORIAN, WRITER
b Milwaukee, Wis, Dec 23, 19. *Study:* Univ Wis, PhB, 41, scholar, 47, MA, 48, PhD, 51; Ecole du Louvre, Fulbright fel, 49. *Collections Arranged:* Marshall Glasier, An Exhibition of Paintings & Drawings, 59; Jean Leppien, Paintings, Watercolors, Graphic Works, 64; Architectural Process, Works of James Mowry, 67; The Works of John Vandelyn, 70; Angello Ippolito, Retrospective, 75. *Pos:* Mem, NY State Comn Arts, 66-67; coun archit & urban design, Binghamton, 67-68. *Teaching:* Asst surv, Univ Wis, 47-49; instr, Williams Col, 50-51; prof, State Univ NY Binghamton, 51- *Awards:* NY State Res Found Grants, 67, 69 & 72. *Res:* Modern American painting. *Publ:* Co-auth, Method in Breughel's paintings, J Aesthet & Art Criticism, 15: 376-386; auth, Kandinsky in 1914 New York, Art News, 55:; Kandinsky in Russia (catalog), Guggenheim Mus, 63; Les themes l'inconscient, XXe Siecle, 27: 46-52; Millet's Winnower rediscovered, Burlington Mag, 74; plus others. *Mailing Add:* Dept Art State Univ NY Binghamton NY 13901

LINDSTROM, GAELL
PAINTER, EDUCATOR
b Salt Lake City, Utah, July 4, 19. *Study:* Univ Utah, BS; Calif Col Arts & Crafts, MFA; also with Roy Wilhelm, Gloucester, Mass. *Work:* Utah State Univ; Southern Utah State Col. *Comn:* Murals, Southern Utah State Col & Cedar City Pub Libr; mosaic mural, Utah State Univ Forestry Bldg, 61. *Exhib:* Am Watercolor Soc, 53 & 57; Calif Watercolor Soc, 57. *Collections Arranged:* Maynard Dixon Exhib, Southern Utah State Col, 55; Nat Ceramic Exhib, 57 & 58 & Nat Painting Exhib, 58, Utah State Univ. *Teaching:* Prof art, Southern Utah State Col, 53-56, Utah State Inst Fine Arts, 57-61 & Utah State Univ, 57-85. *Awards:* Prizes & Purchase Awards, Utah State Fair, 52-54; Utah State Art Inst, 54; Am Watercolor Soc, 57. *Mem:* Am Watercolor Soc; Nat Watercolor Soc. *Media:* All. *Mailing Add:* 3800 Juniper Circle Hurricane UT 84737-2824

LINHARES, JUDITH
PAINTER
b Pasadena, Calif, Nov 21, 40. *Study:* Calif Col Arts & Crafts, BFA, 63, MFA, 70. *Work:* Calif Palace Legion of Honor; Mills Col Art Gallery; Frederick Wiseman Found, Los Angeles; San Francisco Mus Mod Art. *Comn:* Airport, City of San Francisco. *Exhib:* Paintings on Paper, San Francisco Mus Mod Art, 72; Bad Painting, New Mus, New York, 78; Paradise Lost, Paradise Regained, Venice Biennale, Italy, 84; Fatimah and or Fred, Greenville Co Mus Art, SC, 85; Calif A-Z, Butler Inst Am Art, Youngstown, Ohio, 90. *Teaching:* Sch Visual Arts. *Awards:* Adaline Kent Award, San Francisco Art Inst, 76; Nat Endowment Arts Grant, 79 & 87. *Bibliog:* Dan Cameron (auth), Judith Linhares weaves a spell, Arts Mag, 12/85; Thomas Albright (auth), Art in the San Francisco Bay Area, Univ Calif Press, 85; Wendy Beckett (auth), Contemp Women Artists, 88. *Media:* Oil on Canvas, Gouache on Paper. *Mailing Add:* c/o John Davis Contemp Art 59 Walker St New York NY 10013

LINHARES, PHILIP E
CURATOR
b Visalia, Calif, Aug 8, 39. *Study:* Calif Col of Arts & Crafts, BFA, MFA, 66; post-grad study in Florence, Italy, 72. *Exhib:* San Francisco Mus of Art, Calif, 65; Nev Art Gallery, Reno, 77; La Mus, Copenhagen, Denmark, 77; one-man shows, Berkeley Gallery, San Francisco, 70, Lone Mountain Col, San Francisco, 77 & Oakland Mus, 79; and others. *Pos:* Curatorial asst, Oakland Mus of Art, Calif, 67; dir exhib, San Francisco Art Inst, Calif, 67-77; artist-in-residence, South of Market Cult Ctr, San Francisco, 77-; dir, Mills Col Art Gallery, 78- *Publ:* Auth, articles in Currant Mag, 75-76; California Communication, Sydney Biennale Exhib catalogue, Australia, 76. *Mailing Add:* c/o The Oakland Mus 1000 Oak St Oakland CA 94607

LINK, HOWARD ANTHONY
CURATOR
b Rochester, NY, Dec 18, 34. *Study:* Pa State Univ, BAppArts, MA(art hist); Univ Pittsburgh, PhD(art hist). *Collections Arranged:* Utamaro & Hiroshige (auth, catalog), 76-77 & The Theatrical Prints of the Torii Masters (auth, catalog), Japan, 77. *Pos:* Assoc cur of Oriental art, Honolulu Acad of Arts, 71-74, keeper of Ukiyo-e Print Ctr, 71-, cur Asian art, 74-82, sr cur, 83-87, sr cur emer, 87- *Teaching:* Instr art hist, Sophia Univ, Tokyo, Japan, 66-67, asst prof art hist, 67-70; assoc prof art hist, Univ Hawaii, Hilo, 70-71. *Awards:* Nat Best Lect Series Award, Cherry Blossom Festival, Univ Hawaii, 71; Senate, State Hawaii, Pub Serv as Cur, 87 (retirement). *Mem:* Oriental Art Soc of Hawaii; Ukiyo-e Soc Japan; Ukiyo-e Soc Am. *Res:* Torii Sch of Ukiyo-e; Rimpa paintings and Nikuhitsu; Utagawa Hirosnige. *Publ:* Auth, The Art of Shibata Zeshin: The Mr and Mrs James E O'Brien Collection at the Honolulu Academy of Arts, Robert G Sawers Publ, 79; Exquisite Visions: Rimpa Painting from Japan, Honolulu Acad Arts, 82; Waves and Plagues: The Art of Masami Teraoka, Chronicle Books, 88; Utagawa Hirioshige: The James A Michener Collection, Kokusai Art, 92; Selected Japanese Geure Paintings in Western Collections, Kodansha, 92. *Mailing Add:* 414 Florian Way Spring Hill FL 34609

LINK, LAWRENCE JOHN
PAINTER, WRITER
b Oklahoma City, Okla, Sept 2, 42. *Study:* Univ Okla, BA, 65, MFA, 68. *Work:* San Francisco Mus Art; Smithsonian Inst; Osaka Univ Arts, Japan; Chase Manhattan Bank, New York; Ore State Univ Mus. *Comn:* Lithographs, World Print Orgn, 74. *Exhib:* 12 Ann Exhib Prints & Drawings, Okla Art Ctr, 70; 2nd Ann Hawaii Nat Prints Exhib, Honolulu Acad Arts, 73; World Print Competition 73, San Francisco Mus Art, 73; Nev State Mus, 75; Corcoran Gallery, Washington, DC, 75; one-man show, Fred Jones Mem Mus, Okla, 78; Bold Statements: Painting, Southeastern Ctr Contemp Art, NC, 80; Pontiac Art Ctr, Mich, 83; Robert L Kidd Gallery, Birmingham, Mich, 87. *Pos:* Mich ed, New Art Examiner, 83- *Teaching:* Prof, Western Mich Univ, 77- *Awards:* Purchase Award, World Print Competition, 73. *Bibliog:* Article, Image and meaning, New Art Examiner, 6/84; Article, Information Technolopgy, The Chronicle of Higher Education, 7/8/92; Article, Higher Ed Still a NeXT Priority, NeXTWORLD, summer 92. *Media:* Oil, Acrylic. *Publ:* Auth, Comment, Am Craft, 8/86; Walter Darby Bannard, Arts Mag, 10/86; The problem of imitation, New Work, 10/87; Font styles, ClarisWorks J, 10/92; Start thinking about fonts, ClarisWorks J, 2/92. *Mailing Add:* 3382 Sandra Dr Kalamazoo MI 49004

LINK, PHYLLIDA K
GRAPHIC ARTIST, PAINTER
b New York, NY, May 2, 40. *Study:* Sorbonne, Paris, France, art certificate, 60, City Univ NY, BA, 62, MA, 66 & 87. *Work:* Pen & Brush Club, Nat Arts Club, World Trade Center, Avanti Gallery, New York; Glyptothek Mus, Copenhagen, Denmark. *Exhib:* Staten Island Mus, Juried Ann, 82; Pastellists-Women, Pen & Brush Club, New York, 84-89; Lever House Gallery, Pastel Soc Am Mems, New York, 87; Nabisco Gallery, Pastel Soc of Am Mems, East Hanover, NJ, 88; Milburn Playhouse Gallery, Pastel Soc Am Mems, Milburn, NJ, 90; and others. *Teaching:* Prof, St Peter's Col, Jersey City, 86- & Hudson Co Comn Col, 88- *Awards:* NY Public Libr Award for Best Libr Exhib Ann, 79; Pastel Soc of Am Salmagundi Club, New York, 81; Cert, Lever House, New York, 82. *Mem:* Pastel Soc Am, New York; Nat Mus Women Arts, Washington, DC. *Media:* Pastel, Watercolor. *Mailing Add:* c/o Ketchel 208 E Broadway Apt J 203 New York NY 10002

LINK, VAL JAMES
JEWELER, EDUCATOR
b Shreveport, La, Apr 28, 40. *Study:* Cranbrook Acad Art, Bloomfield Hills, Mich, MFA; Univ Tex, Austin, BFA; Del Mar Jr Col, Corpus Christi, Tex, AA. *Work:* Ark Art Ctr Mus, Little Rock; Sarah Campbell Blaffer Gallery, Univ Houston; Mus Contemp Crafts Touring Exhib, NY; Denver Art Mus & Am Crafts Coun Touring Exhib. *Comn:* Sic Holloware & jewelry works, comn by Mr C A Harlan, Birmingham, Mich, 67-68; commemorative cup, comn by Univ Houston for Mrs Sarah Blaffer, 73; sculptural awards, Am Petrol Inst, Washington, DC, 73 & 74; seven major jewelry pieces, comn by Kenneth Helfand, Mill Run, Pa, 74-75; and others. *Exhib:* The Goldsmith 70 Exhibition, Minn Mus Art, St Paul; Inter-D III, Crafts 74 Int, McAllen Int Mus, Tex, 74; Reprise, Int Exhib Metalsmithing Work, Cranbrook Acad Art, 75; Contemp Metalcrafts, Clifford Gallery, Pittsburgh Arts & Crafts Ctr, Pa, 77; Soc NAm Goldsmiths Nat Metalsmith 77, Phoenix Art Mus, Ariz & Henry Gallery Fine Arts, Univ Wash, Seattle, 77; American Goldsmiths--Now, Soc NAm Goldsmiths, Steinberg Gallery, Washington Univ, 78; and others. *Teaching:* Instr jewelry & metal, Interlochen Arts Acad, Mich, 67-70; assoc prof & head jewelry & metal area, Univ Houston, 70- *Awards:* First Place, 15th Tex Crafts Exhib, Dallas Mus Fine Arts, 71; Ark Art Ctr Mus Purchase Award, 71-72. *Bibliog:* Lisa Hammel (auth), Thank technology, New York Times, 6/20/70; Murray Bovin (auth), Photographic representation of work, In: Silversmithing, Bovin Publ, 4th ed, 73. *Mem:* Soc NAm Goldsmiths; Sterling Silversmiths Guild Am; Am Contemp Arts & Crafts Slide Libr; Am Crafts Coun; Tex & Houston Designer Craftsmen. *Media:* Gold, Silver. *Mailing Add:* c/o Dept Art Univ Houston 4800 Calhoun Rd Houston TX 77004-4893

LINN, JOHN WILLIAM
ADMINISTRATOR, WRITER
b Shanghai, China, May 25, 36; US citizen. *Study:* Art Inst Chicago; San Diego State Univ, BA & MA; Univ Ga, PhD; worked with Edmund B Feldman and Albert Christ-Janer. *Work:* San Diego State Univ Gallery, Calif; Paul Sargent Gallery, Eastern Ill Univ, Charleston; First Nat Bank, Springfield, Ill. *Exhib:* Ill State Fair Exhib, Springfield, 77; Provincetown Nat Print & Drawing Exhib, Mass, 77; Hot Springs Art Ctr Exhib, 91; Delta Exhib, Ark Arts Ctr, 91; Texarkana Exhib, 92; & others. *Collections Arranged:* Seven State Bicentennial Exhibition, Paul Sargent Gallery, Eastern Ill Univ, 9/77. *Pos:* Dir & owner, Art Cellar Gallery, San Diego, Calif, 65-67. *Teaching:* Assoc prof art hist, Eastern Ill Univ, 67-77, chmn dept art, 75-77; prof art hist & dean fine arts, Henderson State Univ, 77-90; dir, Joint Educ Consortium, 90- *Awards:* Best in Show, All San Diego Co Collegiate Exhib, San Diego State Univ, 63 & Del Mar Southern Calif Exhib, Del Mar Co Fair, 67; First Place, San Diego Co Exhib, San Diego Art Guild, John Paul Jones, 66; and others. *Bibliog:* Naomi Baker (auth), John Linn, San Diego Union, 64; Charlotte Steen (auth), Art rev, Art Forum, 65; Donovan Mailey (auth), Art Cellar Gallery, San Diego Mag, 65. *Mem:* Nat Coun Art Adminrs; Am Coun Arts. *Res:* Using the phenomenological method of art criticism in the analysis of art, particularly Chinese landscape painting. *Publ:* Auth, In praise of brevity, Acad Forum, 83; Arts of Asia, Christian Sci Monitor (several publ); numerous articles in Acad Forum & Art Papers. *Mailing Add:* c/o Henderson State Univ Dept Art Arkadelphia AR 71923

LINN, JUDY
PHOTOGRAPHER
b Detroit, Mich, June 28, 47. *Study:* Pratt Inst, NY, BFA, 69. *Work:* Getty Collection, Los Angeles, Calif; Detroit Art Inst; Dallas Mus Fine Art. *Exhib:* Dallas Mus Fine Arts, Tex, 76; 4 Photographers, Padigione d'Arte Contemporanea, Milan, Italy, 80; New York, New Wave, PS 1, Queens, 81; Recent Work, Susane Hilberry Gallery, Birmingham, 82; Flowers, Detroit Art Inst, Mich, 85; Chain Reaction, Gallery 55, New York, 85; India Observed, Sandra Berler Gallery, Chevy Chase, Md, 86. *Teaching:* Adj asst prof photogr, Pratt Inst, Brooklyn, NY, 74-85. *Bibliog:* Oriole Farb (auth), article, Mass Rev, summer 74; Patti Smith (auth), Babel, Putnam, NY, 78; Sam Wagstaff (auth), A Book of Photographs, Grey Press, 78. *Dealer:* Sandra Berler 7002 Connecticut Ave Chevy Chase MD 20815. *Mailing Add:* 252 Elizabeth St New York NY 10012

LINN, STEVEN ALLEN
SCULPTOR
b Chicago, Ill, May 3, 43. *Study:* Univ Ill, BS(floricult & ornamental hort). *Work:* Indianapolis Mus Art; Milwaukee Art Mus; Univ Va; Bayley Art Mus; Albany Art Mus, Ga; Mus des Arts Decorative Lausanne, Switz; Nat Baseball Hall of Fame; Mus of Craft & FolK Art, Los Angeles, Calif. *Comn:* One Colorado Plaza, Pasadena, Calif, 91; Louis & Susan Meisel Outdoor Sculpture Collection, Sagaponic, NY, 92; Fair Dept Stores, Worcester, Mass. *Exhib:* Indianapolis Mus Art, 78; Whitney Mus Am Art, 79 & 80; Rochester Mem, 79; Newport Art Mus, 79 & 86; Shidoni Outdoor, 81; Milwaukee Art Mus, 81; Corcoran Gallery Art, 82; Nat Baseball Hall Fame, 85; and others.

Teaching: Lectr theatre design, Smith Col, Northampton, Mass, 68-69; tech instr sculpture, Univ Calif, Santa Cruz, 71-74; asst prof, Pratt Inst, Brooklyn, NY, 86- *Awards:* Ward Sculpture Prize, Berkshire Mus, 68; Rome Prize, Am Acad in Rome, 75; MacDowell Colony Fel, 80; Pollock-Krasner Found Award, 85. *Bibliog:* Betty Freudenheim (auth), Trend in art glass; other materials, NY Times, 1/9/86; Ferdinand Hampson (auth), Glass: State of the Art II, 88; Cover, Art Today Mag, Summer 89; Nancy Kapitanoff (auth), Works pay tribute to special leaders, Los Angeles Times, 5/24/92. *Mem:* Int Sculpture Ctr. *Media:* Bronze, Glass. *Dealer:* Louis K Meisel Gallery 141 Prince St New York NY 10012; Kurland/Summers Gallery 8742 Melrose Los Angeles CA 90069. *Mailing Add:* 101 Crosby St New York NY 10012

LINTAULT, ROGER PAUL
EDUCATOR, SCULPTOR
b New York, NY, June 13, 38. *Study:* State Univ NY New Paltz, BS(art) with distinction, 60; Southern Ill Univ, MFA(sculpture & ceramics), 62. *Work:* Honolulu Acad Arts, Hawaii; Mus Contemp Crafts, New York; Warner Brothers Records, Los Angeles, Calif; Calif State Univ, San Bernardino. *Exhib:* Craftsmen USA, Los Angeles Co Mus Art, Calif, 66; Looking West 1970, Joslyn Art Mus, Omaha, Nebr, 70; one man show, Esther-Robles Gallery, Los Angeles, 75; Calif State Univ, San Bernardino, 79 & Fullerton, 81; Janus Gallery, Los Angeles, 79. *Teaching:* Asst prof art, Univ Hawaii, Honolulu, 65-68; lectr art, Calif State Univ, Long Beach, 68-69; prof art, Calif State Univ, San Bernardino, 69-, chmn dept, 72-77. *Awards:* First & Purchase Prizes, All Calif Art Exhib, Nat Orange Show, 74. *Bibliog:* Don Woodford (auth), Truth, illusion and Roger Lintault, 4/26/75, Artweek; Louis William Fox (auth), article, Artweek, 1/13/79; Suzanne Muchnic (auth), article, Ten tales of architecture, Los Angeles Times, 2/9/79. *Media:* Metal, Cast. *Mailing Add:* c/o Dept Art 5500 University Pkwy Calif State Univ San Bernardino CA 92407

LIONNI, LEO
SCULPTOR, PAINTER
b Amsterdam, Holland, May 5, 10; US citizen. *Study:* Univ Genoa, Italy, PhD; Hon Degree, Cooper Union, 91. *Work:* Philadelphia Mus Art; Mus Mod Art, Metrop Mus Art, New York. *Exhib:* Four American Graphic Artists, Mus Mod Art, New York, 53; Venice Biennale, 72; Klingspor Mus, Ger, 73; Baukunst Gallery, Cologne, Ger, 74; Staempfli Gallery, New York, 77 & 78; Verona Mus, 79; Galleria d'Arte Moderna, Bologna, 90; and others. *Pos:* Art dir, NW Ayer & Son, Philadelphia, 39-48 & Fortune, 48-60. *Awards:* Art Dir of the Year, Nat Soc Art Dirs, 55. *Media:* Bronze; Oil. *Publ:* Auth & illusr, Little Blue & Little Yellow, 59, Swimmy, 63, Frederick, 66, Alexander & with Wind-Up Mouse, 69, Taccuino di Lionni, 72 & Parallel Botany, 77. *Mailing Add:* 35 E 85th St New York NY 10028

LIPMAN-WULF, PETER
SCULPTOR, PRINTMAKER
b Berlin, Ger, Apr 27, 05; US citizen. *Study:* State Acad Fine Arts, Berlin, with Ludwig Gies. *Work:* Metrop Mus Art & Whitney Mus Am Art, New York; Nat Gallery Art, Washington, DC; Brit Mus, London; Berlinische Gallerie, Berlin; Albertina, Vienna. *Comn:* Bronze busts of Bruno Walter & Karl Bohm, Metrop Opera, New York, 58 & 72 & ceramic wall relief, New York City Tech Col; St Andrew (ceramic), St Andrew Lutheran Church, Chicago, 67; Joy of Life (ceramic relief), Mill Lane High Sch, Farmingdale, NY, 68; bronze bust of Pablo Casals, Corcoran Gallery Art, Washington, DC, 74; St Michael Chapel, Rutgers Univ, NJ. *Exhib:* Pa Acad Fine Arts Ann, 50-64; Whitney Mus Am Art Ann, 50-68; Goethe House, New York, 69 & 74; Guild Hall, East Hampton, NY, 74; Widener Univ, Chester, Pa, 79 & 80; Rutgers Univ, New Brunswick, NJ, 80; Elaine Benson Gallery, Bridgehampton, NY, 84 & 88. *Teaching:* Prof sculpture, Adelphi Univ, 61-77, emer prof, 77- *Awards:* Guggenheim Fel, 49-50; Olivetti Award, Silvermine Guild Artists, 62; Widener Medal, Widener Univ. *Mem:* Silvermine Guild Artists; Jimmy Ernst Artist Assoc. *Media:* Bronze, Engraving. *Publ:* Auth, Wall and space, 71, Artist as teacher in America, 72, On teaching a fundamental course of sculpture, 73, On my illustrations of Goethe's Faust, 75 & Artist-in-residence in a secondary sch, 77, Leonardo Mag. *Dealer:* Elaine Benson Bridgehampton NY 11932; Vered Gallery East Hampton NY 11937. *Mailing Add:* Whitney Rd Sag Harbor NY 11963

LIPOFSKY, MARVIN B
SCULPTOR, GLASS ARTIST
b Barrington, Ill, Sept 1, 38. *Study:* Univ Ill, Urbana, BFA; Univ Wis-Madison, MS & MFA. *Work:* Kunstgewerbe Mus, Berlin; Mus Bellerive, Zurich, Switz; Nat Mus Mod Art, Kyoto, Japan; Corning Mus Glass, NY; Oakland Art Mus, Calif; Hokkaido Mus Mod Art, Japan; Los Angeles Co Mus; and many others. *Comn:* Glass, plastic, metal twin panels, Metro Media Bldg, Los Angeles, 69; Frank Lloyd Wright, Calif Col Arts & Crafts Founders Award, 72; reception sculpture, Pacific Enterprises, Los Angeles, 90. *Exhib:* One-man shows, Gallery Marionie, Kyoto, Japan, 78 & 87, Florence Duhl Gallery, New York, 79, S M Galerie, Frankfurt, 81, Galerie L, Hamburg, 81, Betsy Rosenfield Gallery, Chicago, 82 & Holsten Galleries, Palm Beach, 85 & 87; Reiley/Hawk Gallery, Cleveland, Ohio, 88; Leo Kaplan Ltd, New York, 89; Union of Bulgaria Artists, Sofia, 91. *Pos:* Ed, Glass Art Soc J, 76-80. *Teaching:* Asst prof design, Univ Calif, Berkeley, 64-72; prof & head glass dept, Calif Col Arts & Crafts, Oakland, 67-87; vis prof, Rietveld Acad, Amsterdam, Holland, 70, Bazalel Acad Art, Jerusalem, Israel, 71, Univ Calif Los Angeles, 73, Pilchuck Sch Glass, Stanwood, Wash, 74, 77, 81 & 88, Colo Mountain Col, Summervail, 81 & 83 & Miasa Bunka Ctr, Miasa, Japan, 87; vis artist, Konstfack Skolen, Stockholm, Sweden, 89 & Univ Ceramic & Glass, Helsinki, Finland, 89. *Awards:* Purchase Awards, Toledo Mus Art, 68 & Northern Ill Univ, 69; Nat Endowment Arts Fels, 74 & 76; Col Fels, Am Craft Coun, 91; plus others. *Bibliog:* Marvin Lipofsky, Pilchuck Series, 1984-85 (exhib catalog), Holsten Galleries, 85; Czechoslovakian Series (exhib catalog), Maurine Littleton Gallery, 85; Series Otaru (exhib catalog), D Erlien Gallery, 88; Maria Porges (auth), Artist and educator Marvin Lipofsky, Neves Glass, 4/91; Cheryl White (auth), Marvin Lipofsky: Roving ambassador of glass, Am Craft Mag, 10-11/91; and others. *Mem:* Int Comt Artists in Glass; hon life mem Glass Art Soc (pres, 78-80). *Mailing Add:* 1012 Pardee Berkeley CA 94710

LIPPARD, LUCY ROWLAND
WRITER
b New York, NY, Apr 14, 37. *Study:* Smith Col, BA, 58; NY Univ Inst Fine Arts, MA, 62; Moore Col Art, Hon DFA, 72, San Francisco Art Inst, Hon DFA, 85. *Pos:* contrib ed, Art Am. *Teaching:* Adj prof, Univ Colo, Boulder, 87- *Awards:* Guggenheim Fel, 68; Nat Endowment Arts Grant, 72-73 & 76-77; Penny McCall Found award, 89; Medal, Smith Col, 92. *Mem:* Heresies Publ Collective; Printed Matter Inc; Alliance for Cult Democracy; Nat Writers Union. *Publ:* Auth, Fro8 The Center, 76; Overlay, 83; Get the Message? 85; Mixed Blessings: New Art in a Multicultural America, 90; A Different War: Vietnam in Art, 90; Partial Recall, 92. *Mailing Add:* 138 Prince St New York NY 10012

LIPPINCOTT, JANET
PAINTER, PRINTMAKER
b New York, NY, May 16, 18. *Study:* Colorado Springs Fine Art Ctr; Art Students League; San Francisco Art Inst; also with Emil Bisttram, Taos, NMex, 49. *Work:* Utah Fine Arts Mus, Salt Lake City; Columbia Fine Arts Mus, SC; Denver Art Mus, Colo; Roswell Mus & Art Ctr, NMex; Albuquerque Mus, NMex; Fine Arts Mus, Santa Fe, NMex. *Exhib:* Colo State Col, Greeley, 61; Denver US Nat Ctr, Colo, 63; St John's Col, Santa Fe, 68, 80 & 88; Britton Gallery, Denver, Colo, 80; Col Santa Fe, NMex, 81; Enthios Gallery, Santa Fe, NMex, 86; Fagen-Peterson Gallery, Scottsdale, Ariz, 87, 88, & 89; Fletcher Gallery, Santa Fe, NMex, 90. *Teaching:* Instr, Santa Fe Community Col, NMex, 85- *Awards:* Atwater Kent Award, Palm Beach, Fla, 63; Southwestern Biennial Award, Santa Fe, 66; Arts in Residence, Durango, Colo, 68. *Bibliog:* Artist of the month, Southwest Art Gallery Mag, 5/72. *Mailing Add:* c/o Fletcher Gallery 668 Canyon Rd Santa Fe NM 87501

LIPPMAN, JUDITH
GALLERY DIRECTOR, EDUCATOR
b New York, NY, June 11, 29. *Study:* Syracuse Univ, BA, 49. *Collections Arranged:* Maryland Art in Legislative Spaces (auth, catalog), 80 & Maryland Art & Artists (auth, catalog), 81, Gen Assembly Md. *Pos:* Guest lectr, Col Notre Dame, Md, 74-76; dir & cur, 20th Century Am Art, Meredith Gallery Contemp Art, Baltimore, 77-; mem, Artistic Properties Comn, State of Md, 77-80; Capitol arts coordr, Gen Assembly Md, 80-; lectr, New Sch Social Res, New York, 80-81, Johns Hopkins Univ, 83-, Md Inst Col Art, 85. *Mem:* Am Inst Architects; Artists Equity Asn. *Specialty:* Contemporary American art and fine crafts. *Publ:* Coauth, Gene Davis, Ed Baynard, Dorothy Gillespie, 80, Arts Gallery. *Mailing Add:* Meredith Gallery Contemp Art 805 N Charles St Baltimore MD 21201

LIPPMANN, JANET GURIAN
GALLERY DIRECTOR, PAINTER
b New York, NY, May 10, 36. *Study:* Brooklyn Col, with Ilya Bolotowsky, Ad Reinhardt, Kurt Seligman, John Russell, Mark Rothko & Burgoyne Diller, BA(art educ), 56, MA(art educ), 60; NY Univ, with Knox Martin. *Work:* Reader's Digest Asn, Inc. *Exhib:* One-person exhib, Janet at Giverny, 86, Tuscana, 88, The River Gallery, Irvington on Hudson, New York & Enchantment, Nat Art Club, New York, 91; Nat Arts Club, 89-91; Conoissuer Gallery, Rhinebeck, NY, 92; Goodman Gallery, Southampton, NY, 91-92. *Pos:* Founder, pres & dir, The River Gallery, Irvington-on-Hudson, NY, 74-89; founder, pres & dir, Janet Lippmann Fine Arts, 89- *Teaching:* Instr art, Bayridge High Sch, 56, Traphagen Elem Sch, Mt Vernon, NY, 62-63; instr, Children's Art Series, Mt Vernon, 64-71; pvt instr, Adult Art Classes, Tarrytown, NY, 71-73. *Awards:* Honorable Mention, Nat Arts Club, 89. *Mem:* Nat Arts Club, New York; Hudson River Contemp Artists. *Media:* Oils, Pastels. *Specialty:* Paintings by American and international artists. *Publ:* Auth, Painting in Giverny, Am Artist, 3/88. *Mailing Add:* c/o Janet Lippmann Fine Arts 8 N Dutcher St Irvington-on-Hudson NY 10533

LIPPOLD, RICHARD
SCULPTOR
b Milwaukee, Wis, May 3, 15. *Study:* Art Inst Chicago, BFA, 37; Univ Chicago; Univ Mich. *Work:* Metrop Mus Art, Mus Mod Art, New York; Detroit Art Inst; Wadsworth Atheneum; Whitney Mus. *Comn:* Retiring room, King of Saudi Arabia, Riyadh, 76; Ad Astra, Nat Air & Space Mus, Washington, DC, 76; seven sculptures, Iran, 77-78; sculpture, Four Seasons Restaurant, Seagram Bldg, New York, 82; Shinto Temple, Kyoto, Japan, 82-83; 250 ft high work, Park Avenue Atrium Bldg, New York; 16-stories high outdoor work, Seoul, SKorea, 86; Construction, comn by Montrone family, La Jolla, Calif, 91; outdoor sculpture (32' high), comn by collector Dr Martanni, Bologna, Italy. *Exhib:* Fifteen Americans, Mus Mod Art, New York, 52; Salute to France, Mus d'Art Mod, Paris, 55; The New Decade, Whitney Mus Am Art, New York, 55; Portraits of Speakers, Arts Club Chicago, 75; Post-War Am Sculptors, Nat Collection Fine Arts, Washington, DC, 75; Am Directions, Smithsonian Inst, Washington, DC, 75; 200 Yrs Am Sculpture, Whitney Mus Am Art, New York, 76; Art in Archit, Meadow Brook Art Gallery, Rochester, Mich; Pvt Images: Photographs by Sculptors, Los Angeles Co Mus Art, Los Angeles, Calif, 78; 100 Artists 100 Years Centennial Exhibition, Art Inst Chicago, 79; A Tribute to Dorothy Miller's

A Curator's Choice, New York, 82; Venice Biennale, 88; Retrospective, Haggerty Mus Art, Milwaukee, Wis, 90, Untitled Construction, Emerald Shapery Ctr, San Diego, Calif, 90. *Teaching:* Head art dept, Trenton Jr Col, 47-52; prof art, Hunter Col, 52-65. *Awards:* Creative Arts Award, Brandeis Univ, 58; Silver Medal, Architects League New York, 60; Fine Arts Medal, Am Inst Architects, 70; and others. *Bibliog:* Brian O'Dougherty (producer), Richard Lippold (TV film), Boston Educ TV, 60; The sun and Richard Lippold (TV film), New York TV, 69. *Media:* Wire, Metal. *Mailing Add:* PO Box 248 Locust Valley NY 11560

LIPSCHULTZ, MAURICE A
COLLECTOR
b Chicago, Ill, Aug 5, 12. *Pos:* Mem bd gov, Mus of Contemp Art, Chicago & Mus Art, Ft Lauderdale; mem art vis comt, Smart Gallery, Univ Chicago; mem art bd, Spertus' Mus & D'Arcy Gallery, Loyola Univ. *Mem:* Mus Art, Ft Lauderdale, Fla; Fla Atlantic Univ; Mus Contemp Art, Chicago. *Collection:* Primarily contemporary; specializing in structurist art and large scale sculpture. *Mailing Add:* 2001 N Ocean Blvd Boca Raton FL 33431

LIPSCOMB, GUY FLEMING, JR
PAINTER, INSTRUCTOR
b Clemson, SC, Apr 11, 17. *Study:* Univ SC, BS, 38; 40 watercolor workshops, 67-92; Art Students League, 75. *Work:* Univ SC; Mus Washington, Ga; LaGrange City Mus, Ga; Columbia Col, SC; Rice Mus, Georgetown, SC. *Exhib:* Southern Watercolor Soc Regional, 78-83; Am Watercolor Soc, New York, 79; Watercolor USA Nat, Springfield, Mo, 79; Rocky Mountain Nat, Golden, Colo, 80; Butler Inst Am Art, 80; Nat Arts Club, New York, 80; Allied Artists Nat, New York, 81; and many others. *Teaching:* Instr watercolor & painting, Columbia Mus Art workshops and throughout USA & Can. *Awards:* Best of Show, Ky Nat Watercolor Soc, 82; Am Artists Prof League Award, New York, 82; Second Award, Guild SC Artists, 83; Gold Medal Knickerbocker Artist, 86; and many others. *Mem:* Southern Watercolor Soc (secy, 81-83); Salmagundi Club; signature mem, Midwest Watercolor Soc; Allied Artists New York; signature mem, Ga Watercolor Soc; signature mem, SC Watercolor Soc. *Media:* Watercolor, Oil. *Publ:* Contribr, Art Voices, 82; North Light Mag. *Mailing Add:* 1717 W Buchanan Columbia SC 29206

LIPSKI, DONALD G
SCULPTOR
b Chicago, Ill, May 21, 47. *Study:* Univ Wis, Madison, BA,(hist)Cranbrook Acad Art, MFA, 73. *Work:* Metrop Mus Art, New York; Walker Art Ctr, Minneapolis; Boston Mus Fine Art, Mass; San Antonio Art Mus, Tex; Menil Collection, Houston, Tex. *Exhib:* Solo exhibs, Projects, Mus Mod Art, New York, 79 & Focus, Ft Worth Art Mus, Tex, 80; Seven Artists, Neuberger Mus, Purchase, NY, 81; Awards Exhib, Am Acad & Inst Arts & Lett, New York, 83; Awards in Visual Arts, travelling exhib, Tex, Mich & Fla, 84; The End of the World, New Mus Contemp Art, New York, 84; Working in Brooklyn, Brooklyn Mus, NY, 85; Sculpture Inside & Outside, Walker Art Ctr, Minneapolis, Minn, 88. *Teaching:* Asst prof, Univ Okla, Norman, 73-77. *Awards:* Fel, Nat Endowment Arts, 78 & 84; Awards in Visual Arts, 84; NY Found Arts, 86; Guggenheim Fel, 88. *Bibliog:* Donald Kuspit (auth), Donald Lipski, German Vaneck Gallery, 85; H H Arnason (auth), History of Modern Art, 3rd ed, Abrams, 86; John Russel (auth), Turning the plain into fantasy, New York Times, 3/15/87. *Media:* All Media. *Dealer:* Rhona Hoffman Gallery Chicago IL. *Mailing Add:* 1061 Manhattan Ave Brooklyn NY 11222

LIPSON, GOLDIE
SCULPTOR, PAINTER
b New York, NY, Nov 18, 05. *Study:* With Carl Nelson; fresco painting, Mex, 51. *Work:* Randolph-Macon Womens Col. *Comn:* Fresco murals, San Miguel Inst, Mex, 51; mural in oil, comn by Mr & Mrs Samuel Carson, Purchase, NY, 60; murals in tile, cement & oil, Orchid Spring, Winter Haven and Lake of the Hills, Fla, 68-82; outdoor sculptures, Winter Haven & Orchid Springs, Fla. *Exhib:* Metrop Mus Art, New York, 40; one-person shows, Uptown Gallery, 42-45, Charles Barzansky Gallery, New York, 46-67, Ridge Art Asn, 75-; retrospectives, County Ctr, White Plains, NY, 53, Barzansky Gallery, 67, Ridge Art Cult Art Ctr, Winter Haven, Fla, 70 & Melvin Gallery, Fla Southern Univ, 80; Nat Asn Women Artists Traveling Show, US & Europe, 67; and others. *Pos:* Presently engaged in writing and lecturing. *Teaching:* Dir art classes, YMCA, Lake Wales, Fla, 86-87, Studio Workshop, Fla, 66-88. *Awards:* First Prize, New Rochelle Art Asn, 48-50; Top Prize in Oil, 48 & Prize for Colored Print, 57, Westchester Co Ctr. *Bibliog:* Mae McKinley (ed), Many Faces of Goldie, pvt publ, 78. *Mem:* Artists Equity; Fla Artists Equity; Nat Mus of Women in the Arts. *Media:* All. *Publ:* Auth & illusr, Rejuvenation, 63, We, 65 & Beyond Yoga, rev ed 77; illusr, Yoga, Youth and Reincarnations, 65; auth, Rejuvenation through Yoga, rev ed 78. *Mailing Add:* 724 Master Piece Rd Lake Wales FL 33853

LIPTON, BARBARA B
MUSEUM DIRECTOR, CURATOR
b Newark, NJ. *Study:* Univ Iowa, BA(art hist); Univ Mich, studied Oriental art with James Plummer, MA; Rutgers Univ, MLS. *Exhib:* One-woman photog exhib, Newark Mus, NJ, 78; Am Mus Nat Hist, New York, 81; Anchorage Mus, 81. *Collections Arranged:* Whaling Days in New Jersey (auth, catalog), 75 & Survival: Life and Art of the Alaskan Eskimo (auth, catalog), 77-78, Newark Mus, NJ; Images of the Alaskan Eskimo, New England Found Arts, 80-82; Arctic Vision: Art of the Canadian Inuit (traveling exhib, auth, catalog), Govt Canada, 84-86; Treasures of the Tibetan Mus, 88. *Pos:* Art libr dir, Newark Mus, NJ, 70-75, spec proj consult 76-82; asst dir, Castle Gallery, Col New Rochelle, 83-84; guest cur, Govt Canada, 84-86; dir, Jacques Marchais Ctr Tibetan Art, 85- *Teaching:* Instr, sch continuing ed, Pratt Univ, Brooklyn, NY, 79; instr eskimo art, New Sch, New York, NY & Univ Vt, 86. *Mem:* Am Asn Mus; Mid-Atlantic Asn Mus. *Res:* Whaling history; life and art of the Alaskan and Canadian Eskimo; New Jersey history; archival Eskimo films; Tibetan art and history. *Collection:* Eskimo art and artifacts. *Publ:* Coauth, Westerners in Tibet, Newark Mus, 73; auth, John Cotton Dana and the Newark Museum, 79; exec producer, Village of No River (film), 81; Tibetan Visual Art in White Lotus, 91. *Mailing Add:* 282 Scotland Rd South Orange NJ 07079

LIPTON, LEAH
HISTORIAN, EDUCATOR
b Kearny, NJ. *Study:* Douglass Col, Rutgers Univ, BA, 49; Harvard Univ, MA, 50. *Collections Arranged:* Around the Station: The Town and the Train (with catalog), 78 & Family Connections: Portraits by Chester Harding (auth, catalog), 81, Danforth Mus Art, Framingham, Mass; A Truthful Likeness: Chester Harding and his Portraits (auth, catalog), Nat Portrait Gallery, 85; Charles Hopkinson: Pictures from a New England Past (auth, catalog), Danforth Mus Art, 88-89; Three New England Painters: Hosmer, Pooke, Woodward (auth, catalog), Danforth Mus Art, 91. *Pos:* bd dirs & adj cur Am Art, Danforth Mus Art, 80- *Teaching:* Prof art hist, Framingham State Col, Mass, 70- *Awards:* Distinguished Serv Award, Framingham State Col. *Mem:* Col Art Asn; Soc Archit Historians. *Res:* 19th and 20th century American art & architecture; portrait painting in America especially New England; life and career of Chester Harding (1792-1866); American women artists, 1900-1940. *Publ:* Auth, William Dunlap, Samuel F B Morse, John Wesley Jarvis & Chester Harding: Their careers as itinerant portrait painters, 81, The brief life of the Boston Artists' Association, 1841-1851, 83 & Chester Harding and The Life Portrait of Daniel Boone, 84, Am Art J; Chester Harding in Great Britain, Antiques, 84; Yankee Painters in the South, Southern Quart, 88. *Mailing Add:* Dept Art Framingham State Col 100 State St Framingham MA 01701

LIPTON, SONDRA SAHLMAN
PAINTER, SCULPTOR
b New York, NY. *Study:* NY Univ, sculpture with Vincent Glinsky. *Work:* Pres Lyndon B Johnson Libr & in private collections of Mrs Pierre du Pont II, Paul Mellon, Mrs Seward Mellon, Jacqueline Kennedy Onassis, Mrs Sybil Harrington. *Media:* Oil. *Mailing Add:* 501 E 87th St New York NY 10128

LIPZIN, JANIS CRYSTAL
FILMMAKER, PHOTOGRAPHER
b Colorado Springs, Colo, Nov 19, 45. *Study:* Ohio Univ, BFA; NY Univ; Univ Pittsburgh, MLS; San Francisco Art Inst, MFA; Pittsburgh Filmmakers Workshop. *Exhib:* Solo exhibs, Anthology Film Archives, 81 & 83 & Mus Mod Art, New York, 85; PS 1, New York, 88; Art Gallery Ontario, Can, 90; Pacific Film Arch, Berkeley, Calif, 90; Mus Mod Art, New York, 91; Stadkino, Vienna, Austria, 92. *Pos:* Media cur, Anne Bremer Mem Libr, San Francisco Art Inst, 74-76, chair dept filmmaking, 85-91; bd dirs, Canyon Cinema Coop, 81-83; contribr ed, Artweek, 81-84; bd dir, Found Art in Cinema, San Francisco, 83-90; consult, Univ Wisc, Milwaukee, 91. *Teaching:* Asst prof art in film & photog, Antioch Col, 76-80; prof filmmaking, San Francisco Art Inst, 78-; vis artist, San Francisco State Univ, 81. *Awards:* Ohio Arts Coun Individual Artist Grant, 78; Nat Endowment Arts Individual Artist Grant, 83; NEA Inter/Arts, New Genres with Sonoma County Found, 90-91. *Bibliog:* Jeff Fraenkel (auth), Janis Crystal Lipzin: A filmmaker's retrospective, San Francisco Chronicle, 78; Manohla Dargis (auth), The eight & narrow, Village Voice, 89. *Mem:* Canyon Cinema Coop; NY Filmmakers Coop; Col Art Asn; Experimental Film Coalition. *Media:* Photography & Film. *Publ:* Auth, Talking with Joyce Wieland, Cinemanews, 78; Performing performance, Artweek, 11/14/81; Looking for gems, Artweek, 81; Tribute to James Broughton, San Francisco Int Film Festival catalog; auth, Addressing urban issues, Artweek, 83. *Dealer:* Canyon Cinema Coop 2325 Third St Suite 338 San Francisco CA 94107; NY Filmmakers Coop 175 Lexington Ave New York NY 10016. *Mailing Add:* San Francisco Art Inst 800 Chestnut St San Francisco CA 94133

LIS, JANET
PAINTER
b Cleveland, Ohio, Jan 9, 43. *Study:* Cleveland Inst Art, scholar, 57-61; Ohio Univ Sch Fine Arts, BFA, 65. *Work:* Hollywood Mus Art, Fla; Southeastern Ctr Contemp Art; Lauren Rogers Mus, Miss; Brevard Co, Fla Art Pub Places Prog, Savanna's Clubhouse, Merritt Island; State of Fla Art Pub Bldg Prog, Fla Regional Off Bldg, Miami. *Comn:* First United Methodist Church & First Church of Nazarene, Pompano Beach, Fla. *Exhib:* Scottsdale Watercolor Biennial, 80; Watercolor USA, 80 & 81; Piedmont Biennial, Mint Mus, Charlotte, NC; Ga Watercolor Soc Exhib, Columbus Mus Art, 81; Aqueous, Ky Watercolor Soc, 81; Realist Invitational, Southeastern Ctr Contemp Art, 83; Mainstream America, 87 & 88 & Ann Mid-year Show, Butler Inst Am Art; San Diego Watercolor Soc Ann, 89. *Teaching:* Boca Mus, Boca Raton, Fla. *Awards:* Purchase Awards, Southeastern Ctr Contemp Art, 79, Eastman Mem Found, Lauren Rogers Mus, 79; Cash Awards, Watercolor USA, 80 & Arts Assembly of Jacksonville, 81; Cash award, Ann Mid-year Show, Butler Inst Am Art, 88. *Bibliog:* Lorraine Huber (auth), The colorful world of Janet Lis, Fiesta Mag, 9/75; Mary Crowe Dorst (auth), article, Art Voices, 11-12/81. *Mem:* Southern Arts Fedn; Fla Watercolor Soc. *Media:* Acrylic on Paper. *Dealer:* Capricorn Galleries 4849 Rugby Ave Bethesda MD 20014. *Mailing Add:* 12 Sunset Lane Pompano Beach FL 33062

LISK, PENELOPE E TSALTAS
PAINTER, PRINTMAKER
b New York, NY, June 16, 59. *Study:* Bryn Mawr Col, Pa, AB(fine art printmaking), 81, with Fritz Janschka; Cranbrook Acad Art, Bloomfield Hills, Mich, MFA(printmaking), 85, with Steve Murakishi. *Work:* Detroit Inst Art, Mich; Nelson Atkins Mus, Kansas City, Kans; Newport Harbour Art Mus, Calif; Cranbrook Acad Art Mus, Bloomfield Hills, Mich; Muskegon Mus Art, Mich. *Exhib:* Three Philadelphia Painters, Am Col, Bryn Mawr, Pa, 87; one-person shows, Limited Impressions, Cabrini Col, 88 & Chilton Co, 90, Radnor, Pa; Drawing '89, Trenton State Col, NJ, 89; 4 artists show, Villanova Univ, Pa, 90; Pavillion Gallery, Mem Hosp, Pennsauken, NJ, 92. *Collections Arranged:* Centennial Exhib, Baldwin Sch, 89. *Pos:* Gallery Asst, Noël Butcher Gallery, Philadelphia, Pa, 85-87. *Awards:* Purchase Prize, Nat Drawing, Mercer Co Cult & Heritage Comn, 87; 2nd Prize-Painting, Impressions VIII, Main Line Chamber Com & Sun Oil Co, 88. *Mem:* Print Club, Philadelphia; Pa Counc Arts. *Mailing Add:* 2421 N Feathering Rd Media PA 19063

LISKER, SARA
DESIGNER, CRAFTSMAN
b Odessa, Russia, July 31, 18; US citizen. *Study:* Pa Acad Fine Arts, 35-39; Univ Pa, 35-36; Philadelphia Col Art, with Jack Lenor Larsen, 61-64. *Work:* Del Art Mus, Wilmington. *Exhib:* Crafts 1970, Boston Mus Fine Arts, 70; Craftsmanship, Franklin Inst, Philadelphia, 70-71; Craftsman 73, Civic Ctr Mus, Philadelphia, 73; Clothing to Be Seen, Mus Contemp Crafts, New York, 74; Marianne Deson Gallery, Chicago, 80; Philadelphia Art Alliance, 81. *Teaching:* Vis lectr, Batik-Moore Col Art, 65, 66 & 67. *Awards:* Purchase Prize, Kentmere Mus, Wilmington Fine Arts Soc, 67; Cash Award, Harrisburg State Festival, 73. *Mem:* Charter mem Philadelphia Crafts Group (bd dirs & exhib chmn, 75-78). *Media:* Fabric, Wax. *Publ:* Contribr, Clothing Decoration, Lane Publ, 77. *Mailing Add:* 127 Fitzwater Philadelphia PA 19147

LIST, CLAIR ZAMOISKI
CURATOR, ARTS ADMINISTRATOR
b Baltimore, Md, Dec 2, 53. *Study:* Univ Pa, BA & MA, 75. *Collections Arranged:* Images of the 70's: 9 Washington Artists (auth, catalog), Corcoran Gallery Art, 80 & John Dickson-Ed Mayo (auth, catalog), 80; 22nd Area Exhib: Works on Paper, 80; Personal Narratives: Will Brunner-John Ryan, 80; Collage on Paper, 81; Corcoran After Hours, 81; Narrative Wood, 81; On-going Dialogue: Andrew Hudson-Blaine Larson, 81; Video, 82, 38th Corcoran Biennial Exhibition of American Painting, (with catalog), 83 & Watercolors Washington (with catalog), 84, Corcoran Gallery Art. *Pos:* Curatorial asst, Solomon R Guggenheim Mus, New York, 76-78, curatorial coordr, 78; assoc cur contemp art, Washington Region, Corcoran Gallery Art, DC, 79-84; dir, Mayors Adv Comm Art Culture, Baltimore, Md, 87- *Mem:* Col Art Asn. *Mailing Add:* 21 S Eutaw St Baltimore MD 21201

LIST, VERA G
PATRON, COLLECTOR
b Boston, Mass, Jan 6, 08. *Study:* Simmons Col. *Pos:* Trustee & vpres, New Mus Contemp Art; life trustee, New Sch Social Res, currently; Coun Arts, Mass Inst Technol; hon bd mem, Jewish Mus; dir, Albert A List Found. *Awards:* Louise Waterman Wise Award, 64; NY State Coun on Arts Award to Albert A List Found for List Art Poster Prog, 69; Hadassah's Woman of Valor Award; Mayor, New York Award, Arts & Culture, 86. *Media:* Sculpture, Painting. *Interests:* Established List Art Poster Program; many gifts of art to New York museums and others. *Collection:* Contemporary sculpture and painting. *Mailing Add:* Byram Shore Rd Greenwich CT 06830

LISTER, ARDELE DIANE
VIDEO ARTIST
b Calgary, Alta, Jan 21, 50. *Study:* Univ BC, BA, 70, MAABD, 73. *Work:* Stedelijk Mus, Amsterdam; Donnell Libr, & Mus Mod Art, New York; Art Bank, Ottawa; Acad Kunst, Berlin; Washington Proj Arts, Washington, DC; Nat Gallery, Can; La Jolla Mus Contemp Art. *Comn:* Artists Television Workship, Banff Ctr, Can. *Exhib:* New Narrative, Mus Mod Art, New York, 83; Pompidou Ctr, Paris, 87; Infermental traveling exhib, worldwide, 87 & 88; Univ Calif, Santa Cruz, 88; Internat Fest de Film et Video des Femmes, Montreal, 89; Nat Gallery Can Ottawa, 89 & 90; Brooklyn Mus, 90 & 91; Long Beach Mus Art, 92; Vancouver Art Gallery, 92; and others. *Pos:* Ed, Criteria, 74-78. *Teaching:* Instr, Monclair State Univ, NJ, 84, Sch Visual Arts, NY, 90; instr TV arts, Ctr Media Arts, New York, 84-86; prof video, Rutgers Univ, 91- *Awards:* Selected Work, Tokyo Video Festival, 81 & 82; Prize, 3 Rivers Arts Festival, 86 & 89; First Prize, Daniel Wadsworth Mem Festival, 87; Biannual Int Video Festival, Medellin, Columbia, 88. *Bibliog:* Ann Sargent Wooster (auth), Video art?, Afterimage, 82 & Views by Women Artists, New York City, 82; Victor Ancona (auth), Video art, Videography, 3/83; Brian Johnson (auth), Hot art in a cool medium, Maclean's Mag, 3/3/86. *Mem:* Women in Film, NY; Media Alliance. *Publ:* Auth, article, Heresies, 77; coauth, Performance by Artists, Art Metropole, 79; auth, article, Independent, 79; rev, FELIX, 91. *Dealer:* Video Data Bank Columbus Dr & Jackson Blvd Chicago IL 60603; The Kitchen 512 W 19th St New York NY 10011. *Mailing Add:* 202 15th St Brooklyn NY 11215

LITTLE, JAMES
PAINTER, PRINTMAKER
b Memphis, Tenn, July 21, 52. *Study:* Memphis Acad Arts, BFA, 74; Syracuse Univ, MFA(fels), 76. *Work:* Ark Arts Ctr, Little Rock; Everson Mus Art; Brooks Mus Art; Twentieth Century Fund, New York; Mrs RaFaella de Ussia Collection, Mex; and others. *Comn:* Oil painting, Stephen Mallory Assoc, New York, 77. *Exhib:* Solo exhib, Everson Mus, 76; Works on Paper, Albright-Knox Art Gallery, 83; Liz Harris Gallery; Chrysler Mus; Alice Bingham Gallery, Memphis; RI Mus Art, Directions in the 1990's, 90; and many others. *Teaching:* Asst drawing, Syrcuse Univ, 74-76; instr drawing & painting, Memphis Acad Arts, 77-78. *Awards:* Creative Artists Pub Serv Grant, 81. *Media:* Oil on Linen or Canvas. *Dealer:* June Kelly Gallery 591 Broadway New York NY; Sid Deutsch Gallery 29 W 57th St New York NY. *Mailing Add:* 315 Seventh Ave New York NY 10001

LITTLE, KEN DAWSON
SCULPTOR, EDUCATOR
b Canyon, Tex, April 8, 47. *Study:* Tex Tech Univ, BFA, 70; Univ Utah, MFA, 72. *Work:* Everson Mus; Phoenix Art Mus; Contemp Arts Found, Honolulu; Lannan Found, Palm Beach; Mus Contemp Craft; Ariz State Univ; Utah Mus Fine Art; plus many others. *Comn:* Woodland Park Zoo (outdoor work), Seattle Art Comn, Wash, 91. *Exhib:* solo traveling exhib (with catalog), Selected sculptures, 82-85 & 86; one-man shows, Memorial Art Ctr, Iowa, Cheney Cowles Art Mus, Spokane, Wash, Portland Ctr Visual Arts, Ore, 86, Fabric Workshop, Philadelphia, Pa, 88 & 89, Jennifer Pauls Gallery, Sacramento, Calif, 90 & Diverseworks, Houston, Tex, 91; An installation, The Elements of Progress: Dream Escape, Blue Star Art Space, San Antonio, Tex, 89; Telltale Heart (with catalog), Washington Project for the Arts, DC, 90; Roswell Mus & Art Ctr, NMex, 91; Yellowstone Art Ctr, Billings, Mont, 91; Art Gallery, North Tex State Univ, Denton, 91. *Teaching:* Grad teaching asst, Univ Utah, 71-73; instr art, Univ South Fla, 72-74; asst prof Univ Mont 74-78; vis prof, Alfred Univ, NY, 78; vis prof, Univ Calif, Davis, 79; assoc prof, Univ Mont, Chmn, 78-80; asst prof, Univ Okla, Norman, 80-85; asst prof, Univ Tex San Antonio, 88- *Awards:* Western States Arts Found Fel, 77; Nat Endowment Arts Fel, 82-83 & 88-89. *Bibliog:* Elizabeth Skidmor Sasser (auth), Ken Little at the San Antonio Art Inst, Artspace Mag, Vol 8, No 3, 84; Dave Hickey (auth), Ken Dawson Little: A Beastiary of damaged goods, Art Space Mag, summer 85; Mike Welzenbach (auth), What Makes Us Tick: The Tell Tale Heart at the WPA, rev, Washington Post, 3/15/90. *Mem:* Contemp Arts San Antonio (mem bd, 90-). *Media:* Mixed. *Dealer:* Jennifer Pauls Gallery Sacramento Calif; Barry Whistler Fine Arts Dallas Tx. *Mailing Add:* 257 W Hermine San Antonio TX 78212

LITTLE, POLLY A
PAINTER
b St Joseph, Mo, Nov 13, 54. *Study:* Mo Western State Col, BA, 76; Univ NMex, BFA, 78, MA, 80. *Work:* Preston North Financial Ctr, Dallas, Tex; Zale's Corp Am, Huntington, Calif; Atlantic Richfield Corp, Los Angeles; Continental Ill Bank & Trust, Houston, Tex; Int Bus Machines, Irving, Tex. *Comn:* Oil on Canvas, Preston North Financial Ctr, 83. *Exhib:* one-woman shows, Tex Christian Univ, 83, Mattingly Baker Gallery & Dallas Mus Art, 84; Paintings & Works on Paper, 500X, Dallas, 86; Madonna Project, San Antonio Art Inst, 86; Figurative Messages, Art Ctr, Waco, Tex, 87; Daily Dramas, Ruth Wiseman, Dallas, 89; Dialogues II, Artist's Gallery, Buffalo, NY, 89; Expose Yourself, Hallwalls, Buffalo, NY, 92. *Pos:* Asst dir, Mattingly Baker Gallery, 80-82. *Teaching:* Teaching artist, Tex Women's Univ, Denton, 83-84; asst prof, Northlake Col, Irving, Tex, 85-88; arts in educ, Inst West NY, 90-92. *Awards:* Cash awards, SW Printing & Drawing Exhib, 78, Art Mus S Tex, 82, Art Mus of SW, 83; Lift Grant, Buffalo & Erie Co Arts Coun, 90. *Bibliog:* Expressions: Artist takes a somber view of human condition, Dallas Times Herald, 2/29/84; Message from Madonna, Dallas Morning News, 10/19/85; Expatriots Return Home, Dallas Morning News, 4/24/89; Little & Lavatelliat the Artists Gallery, Buffalo News, 9/8/89. *Media:* Oil on Canvas; Woodcuts. *Dealer:* Gallery 44 1916 13th St Boulder CO 80302. *Mailing Add:* 85 Catherine St Williamsville NY 14221

LITTLE CHIEF, BARTHELL
PAINTER, SCULPTOR
b Lawton, Okla, Oct 14, 41. *Work:* Southwestern Mus Los Angeles, Calif; Southern Plains Mus, Anadarko, Okla; Morris Mus, Morristown, NJ; Mus Art, Univ Okla, Norman; Okla Hist Soc, Oklahoma City. *Comn:* Terra-cotta sculpture, US Dept Interior, Washington, DC, 69; tempera painting, US Dept Interior, Washington, DC, 81; fiberglass sculpture, US Dept Interior, Washington, DC, 85. *Exhib:* Am Indian Artist, Philbrook Art Mus, Tulsa, Okla, 78; Vestiges and Resurgence, Morris Mus, Morristown, NJ, 79; Am Contemp Paintings Traveling Exhib, SAm, 79; one-man show, Mus Art, Univ Okla, Norman, 79; Am Indian Art 1980's, Native Am Ctr Living Arts, Niagara Falls, NY, 81. *Media:* Tempera, Gouache; Terra-Cotta, Bronze. *Publ:* Auth, Kiowa Voices, Tex Christian Univ Press, 83. *Dealer:* Barbara Gallery 135 Palace Ave Sante Fe NM 87501. *Mailing Add:* Rt 3 Box 109A Anadarko OK 73005

LITTLER, CHARLES ARMSTRONG See Rubylee, (Charles Armstrong Littler)

LITTLETON, HARVEY K
EDUCATOR, SCULPTOR
b Corning, NY, June 14, 22. *Study:* Univ Mich, BDesign; Brighton Sch Art, Eng; Cranbrook Acad Art, MFA; Philadelphia Col Arts, Hon DFA. *Work:* Toledo Mus Art, Ohio; Victoria & Albert Mus, London; Mus Mod Art & Metrop Mus Art, New York; Kunstmuseum, Dusseldorf, WGer; Philadelphia Mus Art, Pa. *Exhib:* Objects USA, Johnson Wax Collection, 69-72; 15th Triennale Exhib Archit & Decorative Art, 74; New Glass, Corning Mus Glass, 79-81; retrospectives, Mint Mus Art, 79 & Renwick Gallery, Smithsonian Inst, 84; and others. *Pos:* Bd trustees, Pilchuck Sch, Wash, Penland Sch, NC, currently. *Teaching:* Instr ceramic art, Toledo Mus Art Sch Design, 49-51; prof art, Univ Wis-Madison, 51-77, emer prof, 77-, chmn dept

art, 64-67 & 69-71, univ res grants, 54, 57, 62, 72 & 75. *Awards:* Louis Comfort Tiffany Found Grant, 70-71; Nat Endowment Art Fel, 78-79; Gold Medal, Am Crafts Coun, 83; NC Governor's Award for Fine Arts, 87. *Bibliog:* Colescott (auth), Harvey Littleton, 59 & Dido Smith (auth), Off hand glassblowing, 64, Craft Horizons; Joan Falconer Byrd (auth), Pioneer in American studio glass, Am Craft, 2-3/80; Harvey K Littleton, A Retrospective Exhib, High Mus Art, 84. *Mem:* Fel Am Crafts Coun (trustee, 57 & 59-64); hon mem Nat Coun Educ in Ceramic Arts; hon mem Glass Art Soc; Corning Mus Glass; hon life mem Am Ceramic Soc. *Media:* Glass. *Publ:* Auth, Erwin Eisch, 63 & Glass in the Ozarks, 73, Craft Horizons; Glassblowing--a Search for Form, Van Nostrand Reinhold, 72. *Mailing Add:* Rte 1 PO Box 843 Spruce Pine NC 28777

LITTRELL, DORIS MARIE
DEALER
b Apache, Okla, April 30, 28. *Pos:* Owner, Okla Indian Art Gallery, currently. *Specialty:* Native American arts, with emphasis on Oklahoma Indian artists and craftsman. *Mailing Add:* 3927 S Barnes Pl Oklahoma City OK 73119

LITWIN, RUTH FORBES
SCULPTOR, PAINTER
b Omaha, Nebr, Apr 14, 33. *Study:* San Antonio Col, Tex, 50; Richland Col, Dallas, 78; Southern Methodist Univ, Dallas, with Wilbert Verhelst, 79, Brookhaven Col, Dallas, Tex, with Don Taylor, 91-92; Western Ky Univ, with Ivan Schieferdecker & Laurin Northesen, 91. *Work:* Jewish Home for the Aged, Dallas; Artists Postcards & Albums from the International Festivals in Copenhagen & Nairobi, Nat Mus Women Arts, Washington, DC, 90. *Comn:* Memorial (cast bronze) & Eternal Light (cast bronze), Mem Ctr Holocaust Studies, Dallas, 83. *Exhib:* Arts Place, Okla Art Ctr, Oklahoma City, 88; 32nd Invitational, Longview Mus Arts Ctr, Tex, 91; Kirkpatrick Ctr, Oklahoma City, 91; Expanding Visions, Sumner Sch Mus Archives, Washington, DC, 92; 19th Ann Competition, Masur Mus, Monroe, La, 4 state, 92; Nat Competition, South Bend Art Ctr, Ind, 92; and others. *Awards:* Honorable Mention, Seventh Ann Tex Fine Arts Asn Exhib, 80; Second Place, Richardson Civic Art Soc, 82; Juror's Choice Award, Tex Fine Arts Asn State Citation & Travelling Exhib, 83. *Bibliog:* Bob Cox, NCTV Newscope, 88; Dallas Times Herlad, Art Rev, Tex, 88; Marcie Inman (photogr), ARTimes, Irving, Tex, 8/92. *Mem:* Tex Fine Arts Asn (dir, 78-79, pres, 80-82, state bd, 82-86); D'Art Visual Art Ctr, Dallas (charter mem, 81); Tex Sculpture Asn (bd mem, 83, mem bd dirs, 84-85); Nat Artists Equity Asn Inc; Women's Caucus Art (bd mem, 84-86, vpres programming, 86). *Media:* All. *Publ:* Auth, Tough Issues in Women's Art, The Washington Post, Washington, DC, 2/22/91. *Mailing Add:* 11174 Russwood Circle Dallas TX 75229

LITZ, JAMES C
PAINTER
b Buffalo, NY, Sept 17, 48. *Study:* Self-taught. *Work:* Mus D'Art Naif, Paris, France; Fenmore House, NY State Hist Soc, Cooperstown, NY; Mengei Int World Folk Art Mus, La Jolla, Calif; Vietnam Vets Art Group; New York State Hist Soc, Buffalo; and others. *Exhib:* Nat Int exhibs, Clary Miner Gallery, Buffalo, NY, 87-90; Vietnam Vets Arts Group Nat Touring Exhib, 87-98; The Magic of Naive Art Touring Exhib, 87-88; Mid-west Mus Am Art Touring Exhib, 87-88; 42nd Western NY Albright Knox Exhib, Buffalo, NY, 88 & 90; Burchfield Art Ctr Folk Art Exhib, Buffalo, 88; La Cite Naifs Hotel de Ville salon Richelieu Exhib, Paris, 89; Nat Baseball Exhib, Gallery 53, Cooperstown, NY, 90. *Awards:* Partner's Press Award, Albright Knox Western NY Exhib, 88; First Prize, Cooperstown Art Asn 55th Nat Art Exhib, 90. *Mem:* Cooperstown Art Asn; Mus Am Folk Art, NY. *Media:* Acrylic, Watercolor. *Dealer:* Benjamans Art Gallery 419 Elmwood Ave Buffalo NY 14222; Vern Stein Fine Arts 5735 Main St Williamsville NY 14221. *Mailing Add:* 1724 Como Park Blvd Depew NY 14043

LIU, HO
COLLECTOR, PAINTER
b Canton, China, Mar 20, 17; US citizen. *Study:* Lingnan Univ, Canton, BA; George Washington Univ, MA. *Collection:* Chinese calligraphy, painting and porcelain. *Mailing Add:* 1946 Hopewood Dr Falls Church VA 22043

LIU, HUNG
PAINTER
b Changchun, China, Feb 7, 48. *Study:* Beijing Teachers Col, China, BFA, 75; Cent Acad Fine Art, Beijing, MFA equivalent, 81; Univ Calif, San Diego, MFA, 86. *Work:* Dallas Mus Art; San Jose Mus Art; San Francisco Arts Comn. *Comn:* Moscone Conv Ctr, San Francisco. *Exhib:* Solo exhibs, Sittings, Bernice Stienbaum Gallery, Goddesses of Love & Liberty, Nahan Contemp, New York, Bad Women, Rena Bransten Gallery, Resident Alien, Capp St Proj, San Francisco. *Pos:* Asst prof art, Mills Col, Oakland, Calif. *Teaching:* Lessons in drawing and painting. *Awards:* Nat Endowment Arts, 89 & 91; Capp Street Project Stipend, 88; Artists Award, Contemp Art by Women of Color, 90. *Mem:* Col Art Asn. *Publ:* Numerous articles in Art forum & Artweek between 88 & 92. *Dealer:* Bernice Steinbarn 132 Green St New York NY 10012; Rena Bransten 77 Geary St San Francisco CA 94108. *Mailing Add:* Dept Art Mills College 5000 McArthur Blvd Oakland CA 94613-1399

LIU, KATHERINE CHANG
PAINTER, PRINTMAKER
b Kiang-si, China; US citizen. *Study:* Univ Calif, Berkeley, MS, 66. *Work:* Va Mus Fine Arts; Roanoke Mus Art, Va; State Collection Baja, Calif, Mex; Utah State Univ. *Exhib:* Solo shows, Louis Newman Galleries, Los Angeles, Los Angeles Artcore, State Univ NY, Pa State Univ, Harrison Mus, Utah, Roanoke Mus Art & others; Nat Watercolor Soc Ann, Laguna Beach Mus & Palm Springs Mus 79-87; Allied Artists Am, Nat Acad Arts & Letts, New York, 86 & 87; Nat Soc Painters Casein & Acrylic, Nat Art Club, New York, 85 & 86; Los Angeles Artcore Invitational, 88; State of the Art, Parkland Col, Ill, 89; Artist by Artists, Merging One Gallery, Santa Monica, Calif, 89; plus many others. *Pos:* Invited juror & lectr for over 50 nat & regional exhibs & orgns. *Teaching:* Instr watercolor, Roanoke Mus Art, Va, 75-79, Conejo Valley Art Mus, 80-82 & watercolor groups, US. *Awards:* Second Award, Nat Watercolor Soc, 79; Best-in-show, Nat Watercolor Soc mem Show, 84; Gold Medal, Allied Artists Am, New York, 86. *Bibliog:* Sylvia Moore (auth), Yesterday & Tomorrow: California Women Artists, Midmarch Arts, 89; MJ Van De venter (auth), Katherine Liu, Art Gallery Int, 1- 2/90; Nita Leland (auth), The Creative Artist, Watson-Guptill Publ, 90. *Mem:* Watercolor USA Hon Soc; Nat Watercolor Soc. *Media:* Watercolor, Monotype; Mixed. *Publ:* Auth, The California Romantics, Robert Perine, Antra Publ, 87; Exploring Painting, Davis Publ; Painting the Spirit of Nature, Watson-Guptill; Watercolor and Collage Workshop, Watson-Guptill. *Dealer:* Louis Newman Galleries Los Angeles CA. *Mailing Add:* 1338 Heritage Pl Westlake Village CA 91362

LIVESAY, THOMAS ANDREW
MUSEUM DIRECTOR, ADMINISTRATOR
b Dallas, Tex, Feb 1, 45. *Study:* San Francisco Art Inst, 63-65; Univ Tex, Austin, BFA, 68, MFA, 72; Harvard Univ, 78. *Collections Arranged:* Five Austin Artists (with catalog), 74; The Amarillo Competition, 75 & 77; Charles Burchfield Selected Works (with catalog), 75; Henri Matisse Etchings, 75; American Masters, 75; Warren Davis Retrospective (with catalog), 75; American Images, 76, with Nat Endowment for the Humanities; Young Texas Artists Series, 76-78. *Pos:* Tech staff, Univ Tex Art Mus, Austin, 66-70; cur, Elisabeth Ney Art Ctr, Austin, 70-73; dir, Longview Mus & Art Ctr, Tex, 73-75; cur, Amarillo Art Ctr, 75-77, dir, 77-80; asst dir admin, Dallas Mus Fine Arts, 80-85; dir, Mus NMex, 85- *Teaching:* Univ Okla, MLS/me prog, 87- *Awards:* Roy Crane Award Fine Arts, Univ Tex, Austin, 68. *Mem:* Am Asn Mus; Tex Asn Mus (pres, 83-85). *Res:* Twentieth century American art with particular emphasis on sculpture. *Publ:* Coauth, Larson-Walsh-Sculpture, 74; auth, Young Texas Artists Series, 78; American Images, 78; coauth, Made in Texas, 79; auth, Russell Lee, 79; Ruth Abrams, New York Univ, 86. *Mailing Add:* Box 2087 Santa Fe NM 87501

LIVET, ANNE HODGE
ADMINISTRATOR, CRITIC
b Ft Worth, Tex, Jan 23, 41. *Study:* Wellesley Col, Mass, 59-61; Univ Tex, Austin, 61-62; Tex Christian Univ, Ft Worth, BA, 72, MA, 74. *Collections Arranged:* Brazos River: a Television Exhibition with Robert Rauschenberg, Viola Farber and David Tudor, Ft Worth Art Mus, 77, The Record as Artwork: from Futurism to Conceptual Art (ed & contribr, catalog), 77 & Stella Since 1970 (ed, catalog), 78; David McManaway: Works-Twenty Years (auth, catalog), Univ Gallery, Meadows Sch Arts, Southern Methodist Univ, Dallas, 79; The Works of Edward Ruscha (auth, catalog), San Francisco Mus Mod Art, Calif, 81; Infotainment, 18 Artists from New York (auth, catalog); Art Against AIDS (ed, catalog); The New Urban Landscape (co-cur & auth, catalog), World Financial Ctr. *Pos:* Dir performing arts, Ft Worth Art Mus, 74-78 & cur, 75-78; co-founder with Stephen Reichard, Livet Reichard Co Inc, 79- *Awards:* Nat Endowment Arts Fel Mus Prof, 76; Inst for Art & Urban Resources Fel, New York, 78-79. *Publ:* Ed & contribr, Contemporary Dance, Abbeville Press, 78; Contemporary Art Southeast, Vol II, No 2, 79. *Mailing Add:* c/o Livet Reichard Co Inc 11 Harrison St New York NY 10013

LÍVÍCK, STEPHEN
PHOTOGRAPHER
b Castleford, Eng, Feb 11, 45; Can citizen. *Study:* Self-taught. *Work:* Can Mus Contemp Photog, Ottawa; Mus Mod Art, New York; George Eastman House, Rochester, NY; Carnegie Mus Art, Pittsburgh, Pa; Corcoran Gallery Art, Washington, DC. *Exhib:* Solo exhibs, George Eastman House, Rochester, NY, 75 & 77, Nat Film Bd Can, Ottawa, 76, 77, 82 & 83, Baltimore Mus Art, 78, McIntosh Gallery, Univ Western Ont, London, 81, MacDonald Stewart Art Ctr, 83 & Can Mus Contemp Photog, Ottawa, 92; Persona (with catalog), Nickle Arts Mus, Calgary, 82; Seeing People, Photogrs Gallery, London, Eng, 84; Contemporary Canadian Photography, Nat Gallery Can, Ottawa, 85; Corcoran Gallery Art, Washington, DC, 89. *Awards:* Several grants, Can Coun & Ont Arts Coun. *Bibliog:* David Livingstone (auth), Photography, MacLean's, 11/80 & 9/81; David Scopic (auth), Gum Bichromate Book, 91; Calcutta, Can Mus Contemp Photog, 92; and others. *Media:* Gum Bichromate Printing. *Mailing Add:* 22A Maitland St Third Floor London ON N6B 3L2 Canada

LIVINGSTON, JANE S
CRITIC, CURATOR
b Upland, Calif, Feb 12, 44. *Study:* Pomona Col, BA(art hist), 65; Harvard Univ, MA(fine arts), 66. *Pos:* Cur mod art, Los Angeles Co Mus Art, 67-75; corresp ed, Art in Am, 70-; chief cur, Corcoran Gallery Art, 75-, assoc dir, 78-; mem mus adv panel, Nat Endowment for the Arts, 77- *Mem:* Asn Am Mus; Col Art Asn; Int Coun Mus; Friends of Photog (bd, 79-). *Publ:* Coauth, Art & Technology, Viking Press & Los Angeles Co Mus Art, 70; auth, Manuel Alvarez Bravo, Godine, 78; coauth, Black Folk Art in America, Corcoran Gallery Art, Washington, DC, 82; L'Amour Fou: Photography and Surrealism, Abbeville Press & The Corcoran Gallery Art, 85; The Indelible Image: Photographs of War-1846 to the Present, Harry N Abrams & The Corcoran Gallery Art, 85. *Mailing Add:* 2700 Q St NW Washington DC 20007

LIVINGSTON, MARGARET GRESHAM
ADMINISTRATOR, PATRON
b Birmingham, Ala, Aug 16, 24. *Study:* Vassar Col, AB, 45; Univ Ala, MA, 46. *Pos:* chmn bd,78-86 & chmn comp on collections, 86-Birmingham Mus Art. *Awards:* Silver Bowl Award for Contrib Arts, Birmingham Festival Arts, 67; Woman of Year, Birmingham, Ala, 86. *Mem:* Am Asn Mus (ed comt & pub relations, 81); Birmingham Festival Arts (vpres, 78-79). *Interests:* Art history, education, board administration & organization and publication of museums. *Collection:* American graphics and drawings. *Publ:* Co-ed, Bull Mem Birmingham Mus, 71-74 & Birmingham Festival Arts Bull, 71-77, Birmingham Mus. *Mailing Add:* 12 Country Club Rd Birmingham AL 35213

LIVINGSTON, SIDNEE
PAINTER
b New York, NY. *Study:* Nat Acad Design. *Work:* Princeton Univ; Everhart Mus, Pa; Univ Miami, Fla; Univ Miss; Columbus Mus, Ga; and others. *Exhib:* Art Inst Chicago; Butler Art Inst; Philadelphia Acad Fine Arts; St Louis Mus, Mo; Libr of Cong, Washington, DC; three solo traveling shows (monotypes); and many others. *Awards:* Mildred Tommy Atkins Prize, 71 & Award-Oil, 77, Asn Women Artists; MacDowell Colony Fel; First Prize Watercolor, NJ Painters & Sculptors. *Mem:* Artists Equity Asn, New York; Nat Asn Women Artists. *Media:* Oil, Watercolor. *Mailing Add:* 50 E 89th St No 23B New York NY 10128

LIVINGSTONE, BIGANESS
PAINTER
b Cambridge, Mass. *Study:* Mass Col Art, BFA(painting), 50; Univ Wis-Madison, MFA(painting), 80. *Work:* Chase Manhattan Bank Collection, New York; Merrimack Co Courthouse, NH; Neville Mus, Wis; Radcliffe Col, Cambridge, Mass; Sheraton Hotel Corp, Boston; Shiff Hardin & Waite, Chicago, Ill; Engineering Bldg, Univ Wis-Madison Art Prog, Wis Arts Bd. *Comn:* Mural, Pierce Chapel, Lenox, Mass, 66. *Exhib:* Bronx Mus Art, 74; Fitchburg Art Mus, Mass, 76; Bergstrom-Mahler Mus, Wis, 78; Duluth Art Inst, Minn, 79; One Ill Ctr, 81; Zollal/Lieberman Gallery, Ill, 81; Elvehjem Mus, Wis, 84; Milwaukee Art Mus, 86; Minneapolis Art Mus, 86; Del Ctr Contemp Art, 89; one-man shows, DeCordova Mus, Mass, 58, Groton Sch, Mass, 60, Harvard Univ Divinity Sch, 66, Fitchburg Art Mus, 76, Bergstrom-Mahler Mus, Wis, 78, Priebe Gallery, Univ Wis-Oshkosh, 90, David Barnett Gallery, Milwaukee, Wis, 92. *Pos:* Regional dir, City Spirit Grant, NH Comn Arts, 75; mem, adv bd, Cudahy Gallery, Milwaukee Art Mus, 84-85; mem, Wis Arts Bd, 85. *Teaching:* Lectr art, Colby-Sawyer Col, NH, 63-65; asst prof art, Newton Col, Mass, 65-75; prof art, Univ Wis, Fox Valley, 76- *Awards:* Grant, Radcliffe Inst Independent Study, Radcliffe Col, Mass, 65; Univ Wis Res Grant, 84, 85, 89 & 90; Wis Arts Bd Grant, 82 & 91. *Bibliog:* Ted Farah (auth), Art collecting for fun and profit; Bartlett Hayes (auth), Tradition becomes innovation; Who's Who in American Education, Nat Reference Inst, 92-93. *Mem:* NH Art Asn (pres, 75). *Media:* Acrylic, Oil. *Mailing Add:* Art Dept Univ of Wisconsin-Fox Valley Menasha WI 54952

LIVINGSTONE, JOAN
SCULPTOR, EDUCATOR
b Portland, Ore, May 29, 48. *Study:* Beloit Col, Wis, 66-67, Portland State Univ, BA, 72, Cranbrook, Acad Art, Bloomfield Hills, Mich, MFA, 74. *Work:* Cranbrook Acad Art Mus, Peat Marwick Exec Ed Ctr, Chicago, The Robert Efannebecker Collection, Lancaster, Pa, Burke Hoffman Law Offices, Kansas City, Mo. *Comn:* Buchner's Woyzeck, 71 & Shakespeare's King Lear, 72, set designs, Portland Shakespeare Co, Ore; Ionesco's Exit the King, set design, Androgyna Theatre Co, Portland, 76. *Exhib:* Solo exhibs, Installation: Harlequin, Fiberworks Gallery, Berkley, Calif, 84, Figures and Curtains: 1980-84, 341 W Superior St, Chicago, Ill, 84, Joan Livingstone: Sculpture from 1980-85, Contemp Craft Assoc, Portland, Ore, 85, Joan Livingstone: Recent Sculpture and Collage, Tyler Gallery, Tyler Sch Art Temple Univ, Elkins Pk, Pa, 86, Joan Livingston: Recent Sculpture, 88, and Joan Livingstone: New Sculpture, 90, Artemisia Gallery, Chicago; Mesh: Five Chicago Sculptors, Foster Gallery, Fine Arts Center, Univ Wisconsin-Eau Claire, Wis, 89; Armor: Seven Chicago Sculptors, Randolph St Gallery, Chicago, 89; Crossroads: Contemp Fiber, The Gallery of Contemp Art, Univ Colo, Colo Springs (catalog), 90; USA/Columbia: Fibers, Fla State Univ Gallery and Mus, Tallahassssee, traveling to Bogota, Medellin, Calle, Columbia through 91 (catalog); and many others; Sculpture Textile, 12th Biennial, Mus Cantonal des Beaux Arts, Lausanne, Switz, 85; Imagining Form: Six Sculptors, State of Ill Art Gallery, Chicago, 88. *Pos:* Artist-in-residence, Banff Ctr Art, Alta, Can, 82-87; panelist, Imagining Form: Six Sculptors, State of Ill Auditorium, Chicago, 88; lectr, Progr for Artisanry, New Bedford, Mass, 88. *Teaching:* Asst prof fiber, Kansas City Art Inst, Mo, 76-80; head fiber dept, Cranbrook Acad Art, Bloomfield Hills, Mich, 80-82; assoc prof fiber debt, Art Inst Chicago, 83- *Awards:* Artists Fel, Ill Arts Coun, 89; Fel, The Louis Comfort Tiffany Found, 89; Fel, The Howard Found, Brown Univ, RI, 90. *Bibliog:* Jeff Abell (auth), Imagining Form, New Art Examiner, Vol XV, No 7, 4/88; David McCracken (auth), Gallery Scene: Exhibit shows diversity of artists' approach, Chicago Tribune Friday Section, 2/26/88; Suzanne Richerson (auth), Paper/Fiber XI, New Art Examiner, Vol XV, No 11, summer 88. *Media:* Mixed Media. *Publ:* New synthesized images, Impulse: New Images in Fabric, Detroit Artists Market, 84; Katarina Weslien: Transformations & other everyday events, Payson Gallery, 87; Keynote at Convergence, Chicago Artists Coalition News, Vol XVI, No 10, Chicago, 88. *Dealer:* Artemisia Gallery Chicago IL. *Mailing Add:* Sch of the Art Inst of Chicago 37 S Wabash Chicago IL 60603

LLORENTE, LUIS
PAINTER, DESIGNER
b Santander, Spain; US citizen. *Study:* Sch Indust Arts & Sch Visual Arts, Columbia Univ; also with Anthony Thieme & Umberto Romano. *Work:* USN Combat Art Collection, Washington, DC; Neighborhood Med Ctr, Bronx, NY; also in many pvt collections. *Comn:* Bathyscaph Trieste, San Diego Naval Base, USN, 61; atomic submarine, Rota Naval Base, Spain, 64; Gemini V Recovery, Aboard USS Lake Champlain, 65; USS New Jersey, Philadelphia Navy Yard, 68; US Marines Distributing candy to children, 69. *Exhib:* Audubon Artists, Nat Acad Design, 60-61 & Am Watercolor Soc, twelve times & seven travel awards, 60-79; Mus de la Marine, Paris, 63; Smithsonian Inst & Dept of State Exhib Hall, Washington, DC, 65; and others. *Awards:* Ford Times Award, Am Watercolor Soc, 75; Louis E Seley Award, Salmagundi Club, 78; Alicia Sutherland Award, Knickerbocker Artists, 79. *Bibliog:* John Smee (auth), Portrait of an artist, Chronicle, New York, 61; Mann Sierra (auth), American-Spaniard paints in Rota Naval Base, Alerta, Santander, Spain, 64. *Mem:* Artists Fellowship; Am Watercolor Soc (asst corresp secy, 71-); Knickerbocker Artists (1st vpres, 77-); Salmagundi Club; Am Vet Soc Artists. *Media:* Watercolor, Oil. *Mailing Add:* 245 Ft Washington Ave New York NY 10032

LOAR, PEGGY A
MUSEUM DIRECTOR, ADMINISTRATOR
b Cincinnati, Ohio, May 14, 48. *Study:* Univ Cincinnati, BA(art hist), 70, MA, 71. *Collections Arranged:* Indiana Stoneware (auth, catalog), Indianapolis Mus Art, 72; Bulgarian Medieval Jewelry, Dunbarton Oaks, 81; American Impressionism, Petit Palais, Paris, 82; Master Drawings from the National Gallery of Ireland, 83; The Precious Legacy: Judaic Treasures from the Czechoslovak State Collections, 83; Jamaican Art: 1922-1982, 83. *Pos:* Cur educ, Indianapolis Mus Art, 72-, asst dir, 77-; proj dir, Learning Mus, Nat Endowment Humanities, Washington, DC, 75-, mem nat bd consult, 77-; prog dir, Inst Mus Serv, Washington, DC, 77-78, asst dir, 78-87; dir, Smithsonian Inst Traveling Exhib Service, 81-; dir, Wolfsonian Found, 87- *Teaching:* Lectr art hist, Univ Cincinnati, 70-71; lectr art appreciation & art criticism, Ind Univ & Purdue Univ, Indianapolis, 75-77; guest lectr, Herron Sch Art, Indianapolis & Depauw Univ, Greencastle, Ind, 75-78. *Awards:* Nat Endowment Arts Grants, Ind Pottery, 75 & Role of Humanities in Art Mus Educ, 76; Nat Endowment Humanities, Learning Mus Program, 81; Grants, fel, Japan Found, Swedish Inst, Aspen Inst for Humanistic Studies & John Hopkins Sch Int Studies, Bologna. *Bibliog:* Adele Silver (auth), Issues related to museum education: Curators/directors and educators interface, Midwest Mus Conf, Vol 36, No 4; Priscilla Brouillette (auth), Loar adds new enthusiasm, Vision, Ind Comt Humanities, 77. *Mem:* Ind Comt Humanities; Am Asn Mus; Indianapolis Art League Found; Int Coun Mus; Soc Women Geographers. *Res:* Museum education; Indianapolis Museum of Art accessions and collections; humanities curriculum. *Publ:* Auth, Arts and the three Rs/43, Mus News, 9-10/76; Issues, Midwest Mus Conf, Vol 36, No 4; Sculpture Eleven, Vol 5, No 3 & A Maze of Opportunities, Vol 6, No 1, Ocular Mag; Success through sharing: The team approach to cultural understanding, In: Education 10, Int Coun Mus, 82-83; coauth, General operating support for women: Problems in paradise, J Col & Univ Law, Vol 7, No 3-4e; auth, Interview with John David Mooney, Sculpture Int, 1/85. *Mailing Add:* Wolfsonian Foundation 1001 Washington Ave Miami Beach FL 33139

LOBDELL, FRANK
PAINTER
b Kansas City, Mo, 21. *Study:* St Paul Sch Fine Art, Minn, 38-39; Calif Sch Fine Art, 47-50; Acad Grande Chaumiere, Paris, 50-51. *Work:* Los Angeles Co Mus, Stanford Mus, San Francisco Mus Art & Oakland Mus Art, Calif; Nat Gallery, Washington, DC. *Exhib:* 3rd Biennial of Sao Paulo, Brazil, 55; International Art of a New Era, Osaka, Japan, 58; Kompas 4, West Coast USA, Van Abbemuseum, Eindhoven, 70; 32nd Biennial Am Painting, Corcoran Gallery Art, Washington, DC, 71; San Francisco Mus Art, 83. *Teaching:* Prof art, Stanford Univ, 66- *Awards:* Nealie Sullivan Award, San Francisco Mus Art, 60; Tamarind Fel, 66; Award Merit, Am Acad Arts & Letters, 88. *Bibliog:* Michel Tapie (auth), Frank Lobdell, David Anderson, Paris, 66; Walter Hoppe (auth), Frank Lobdell 1948-1965, Pasadena Art Mus, 66; Gerald Nordland (auth), Frank Lobdell, San Francisco Mus Art, 69. *Media:* All. *Dealer:* Campbell-Thiebaudt Gallery 645 Chestnut St San Francisco CA 94133. *Mailing Add:* 2754 Octavia San Francisco CA 94123

LOBELLO, PETER
SCULPTOR, GRAPHIC ARTIST
b New Orleans, La, Nov 18, 35. *Study:* Sch Archit, Tulane Univ, 53-55, Newcomb Sch Art, 54-55. *Work:* Aldrich Mus Contemp Art; Geneva Mus Art, Switz; Phoenix Art Mus; Plains Art Mus, Moorhead, Minn; New Orleans Mus Art. *Comn:* Sculptures, Chateau Bellereve, Geneva, 74, Villa Savoia, Geneva, 76 & Hyatt Hotels Corp, New York, 80; bronze sculpture for Privy Coun Chamber, New Istana Palace, Bandar Seri Begawan, 84; Atrium sculpture, Madison Equities and Gery Advertising, New York, 85; Anodized aluminum lobby sculpture, One Paydras Plaza, New Orleans, 86. *Exhib:* Contemporary Reflections 73, Aldrich Mus Contemp Art, 73; Selections from the Art Lending Service, Mus Mod Art Penthouse Gallery, New York, 78; Prospectus: 1970s, Aldrich Mus Contemp Art, 79; Robert Kidd Gallery, Detroit, 80; 21st Midwestern Invitational, Plains Art Mus, Moorhead, Minn, 80; Alexander Rosenberg Gallery, New York, 80; Inaugral Show, Alexander Carlson Gallery, New York, 80; Rutgers Univ, 83; and others. *Bibliog:* Paul Goldberger (auth), 42nd St: The Grand Hyatt, New York Times, 9/22/80; Isabel Forgang (auth), At home with sculptor Peter Lobello, New York Daily News Tonight, 10/15/80; Ada Louise Huxtable (auth), Architecture view: Two new triumphant hotels, New York Times, 10/19/80. *Mailing Add:* 71 Grand St New York NY 10013

LOBERG, ROBERT WARREN
PAINTER, INSTRUCTOR
b Chicago, Ill, Dec 1, 27. *Study:* City Col San Francisco, AA, 50; Univ Calif, Berkeley, BA, 52, MA, 54; San Francisco State Univ, 52; Hans Hofmann Sch Art, Provincetown, Mass, 56; studied painting with Carl Kasten, Ward Lockwood, John Haley, Erle Loran, James McCray, Glen Wessels, Worth Ryder, Felix Ruvolo, William Calfee, Carl Holty & Kyle Morris. *Work:* Art Inst Chicago; San Francisco Art Comn; Henry Gallery, Univ Wash, Seattle; Oakland Art Mus, Calif; Gallery Mod Art, Washington, DC; Portland Art Mus, Ore; and many pvt collections. *Exhib:* San Francisco Mus Art Ann, 55-; Fifty California Artists, Whitney Mus Am Art, New York, 62, Walker Art Ctr, Minneapolis, Albright-Knox Art Gallery, Buffalo & Des Moines Art Ctr, Iowa, 63, organized by San Francisco Mus Art & Los Angeles Co Mus; one-man shows, Staempfli Gallery, New York & Primus-Stuart Galleries, Los Angeles, 62, Henry Gallery, Univ Wash, Seattle, 64, Berkeley Gallery, San Francisco, 67-68, Both-Up Gallery, 73, 75-76, Berkeley Art Ctr, 77, San Jose Mus Art, 78, Sun Gallery, Hayward, 83 & Victor Fischer Galleries, Oakland, Calif, 86; US Info Agency Exhib, Paris, France, 64; Watercolors from the California Collection: 130 Years of Watercolor, Oakland Mus, 77; Egyptian Show, Rental Gallery, San Francisco Mus Art, 79; Gallery Paule Anglim, San Francisco, 79-81; Victor Fischer Gallery, San Francisco & Oakland, 89-90; and many other one-man & group exhibs. *Pos:* Exhib designer, Am Mus Natural Hist, 56-57, San Francisco Mus Mod Art Rental Gallery, 70- *Teaching:* Lectr art, Univ Calif, Berkeley, 55, 56, 59 & 65, Contra Costa Col, San Pablo, 71, Univ Calif, Davis, 71-72, Calif Col Arts & Crafts, Oakland, 81-82 & Santa Rosa Jr Col, 83-84; instr painting & drawing, Calif Col Arts & Crafts, Oakland, 61-63 & San Francisco Art Inst, 63-66; instr art, Univ Calif, Berkeley, 65 & Acad Art Col, San Francisco, 70; vis fac, Dept Art, Univ Wash, Seattle, 67-68; pvt instr, 72-79. *Awards:* Yaddo Found Scholar, 57; MacDowell Colony Scholar, 59 & 60; Fine Arts Merit Award, San Francisco Art Festival, 76; Nat Endowment Arts Fel, 82; and many others. *Bibliog:* Numerous reviews in various magazines including, Artforum, Artweek, NY Times, Washington Times, Art News, 63-; Dorothy Burkhart (auth), rev, Artweek, 86. *Publ:* Contribr, Prize-Winning Oil Paintings, Book II, Allied Publ Inc, Tenn, 60; plus many catalogs, 62- *Mailing Add:* 2020 Vine St Berkeley CA 94709

LOCHNAN, KATHARINE A
CURATOR, WRITER
Ottawa, Can, Aug 18, 46. *Study:* Univ Toronto, BA, 68, MA, 71; Courtauld Inst, Univ London, Eng, PhD, 82; Univ Calif, Berkeley, cert mus mgt, 87, Ryerson Polytechnical Inst, cert bus admin, 91. *Pos:* Cur asst, Royal Ont Mus, 68-69; asst cur, Art Gallery Ont, 69-75, cur prints & drawings, 76-; volunteer asst, Brit Mus, 75-76. *Teaching:* 19th & 20th century prints, art hist dept, Univ Toronto, spring 93. *Awards:* J Paul Getty Trust Scholar, 87; Award of Merit, Ryerson Polytechnical Inst, 91. *Mem:* Print Coun Am (bd mem, 80-82); London House Asn Can (chmn bd, 81-84); William Morris Soc Can (vpres, 84-85); Toronto Hist Bd, 90- *Res:* Whistler's etchings and lithographs; 19th century French and English prints, drawings and watercolors, William Morris and Arts and Crafts Movement, Symbolism. *Publ:* Auth, The Etchings of James McNeill Whistler, Yale Univ Press, 84; The Thames from its source to the sea: an unpublished portfolio by Whistler and Haden, Studies Hist Art, 86; Les Lithographes de Delacroix pour Faust et le theatre anglais de annees 1820, Nouvelles de l'Estampe, 86; Whistler's Etchings and the Sources of His Etching Style, 1855-80, Garland Publ, 88. *Mailing Add:* 21 Mackenzie Crescent Toronto ON M6J 1S9 Canada

LOCKE, MICHELLE WILSON
CURATOR, HISTORIAN
b Dallas, Tex, June 10, 47. *Study:* Trinity Univ, San Antonio, Tex; Univ Tex, Austin, BFA. *Pos:* Lectr-librn, Art Mus of STex, Corpus Christi, 72-76, cur, 76-79. *Mem:* Am Asn of Mus; Col Art Asn. *Res:* Fifteenth Century French illuminated manuscripts. *Mailing Add:* 207 Leming Ave Corpus Christi TX 78404

LOCKHART, ANNE IVEY
MUSEUM DIRECTOR, CURATOR
b Ashland, Ohio, Feb 26, 43. *Study:* Flora Stone Mather Col, Western Reserve Univ, BA, 64; Case Western Reserve Univ, MA, 67. *Collections Arranged:* Contemporary Prints (auth, catalog), 74, Modern Drawings (auth, catalog), 75, Seven Artists: Contemporary Drawings (auth, catalog), 78 & Sculpture Outside in Cleveland (auth, catalog), 81, Cleveland Mus Art; The Nude, Univ Mich Mus Art, 82. *Pos:* Asst cur, Cleveland Mus Art, 74-81; cur western art, Univ Mich Mus Art, Ann Arbor, 81-84; dir, Univ Gallery, Memphis State Univ, Tenn, 84-87; mus consult, 87-92; Bakersfield Mus Art, Calif, 92- *Teaching:* Lectr, Univ Mich, 82-84; asst prof art hist & museology, Memphis State Univ, Tenn, 84-87. *Mem:* Print Coun Am. *Res:* Compiling a catalogue of prints after Guercino drawings. *Publ:* Auth, Four engravings by the master with the banderoles, 73 & Three monotypes by Edgar Degas, 77, Cleveland Mus Bull; Moe Brooker, exhib catalog, New Gallery Contemp Art, Cleveland, 80; coauth, Sculpture Outside in Cleveland, NOVA, 81; auth, The Passion of Rodin: Sculpture from the B Gerald Cantor Collection, 88. *Mailing Add:* 1667 Central Ave Memphis TN 38104

LOCKS, MARIAN
ART DEALER, COLLECTOR
b Philadelphia, Pa. *Study:* Univi Pa; New York Univ; New Sch Soc Research; Moore Col, hon DFA, 90. *Pos:* Coordr, Ann New Talent Exhibs, Marian Locks Gallery, Philadelphia, Pa, 69-88, founding dir & dir emer, 68-; corp art adv & curator, Philadelphia, Pa, 69- *Awards:* Hunt Award & Outstanding Women in the Arts, 85; Art Matters Award & Excellence in the Arts, 88. *Mem:* Pa Acad Fine Arts; Inst Contemp Art, Univ Pa; assoc Philadelphia Mus Art; Art Table; Philadelphia Art Dealers Asn. *Specialty:* Gallery is internationally recognized as a showcase for contemporary area artists and 20th century masters. *Collection:* 20th century contemporary. *Mailing Add:* 600 Washington Square S Philadelphia PA 19106

LOEFFLER, CARL EUGENE
EDITOR, VIDEO ARTIST
b Cleveland, Ohio, Nov 14, 46. *Work:* San Francisco Mus Mod Art; Mus Mod Art, New York; Tex Tech Univ, Lubbock. *Exhib:* La Mamelle Inc 1975-80, San Francisco Mus Mod Art, 80; Performance Art, Mus Contemp Art, Chicago, 80; Video Art: A History, Mus Mod Art, New York, 83. *Collections Arranged:* Performance Art, 80; Watching Television, 83. *Pos:* Founding dir, La Mamelle Inc, 75- & Contemp Art Press, 75-; ed, Art Com Mag, 81- *Teaching:* Instr performance studio, Acad Art Col, 76- *Awards:* Artist Space Grant, 77-83 & Critics Fel, 80, Nat Endowment Arts. *Media:* Telecommunications, Print. *Res:* Performance art; television art; telecommunications in the arts. *Publ:* Auth, Performance Anthology, Contemp Arts Press, 80. *Mailing Add:* Rincon Annex PO Box 3123 San Francisco CA 94119

LOEHLE, BETTY BARNES
PAINTER
b Montgomery, Ala, Mar 21, 23. *Study:* Auburn Univ, Ala, 40-42; Harris Sch Art, Nashville, Tenn, 42-46; Evanston Art Ctr, Ill, 63-67. *Work:* Ga Council Arts & Humanities, Atlanta; DeKalb Community Col, Clarkston, Ga; R J Reynolds Tobacco Co, Winston-Salem, NC; Coca-Cola Int, Atlanta. *Exhib:* Hunter Ann, Hunter Mus Art, Chattanooga, Tenn, 77; Piedmont Show, Mint Mus, Charlotte, NC, 77; Artists in Ga, High Mus, Atlanta, 78; Southern Watercolor Soc, 76-79, 81-85 & 89; Ala Watercolor Soc, 79-81, 83, 85 & 89; Ga Watercolor Soc, 79 & 81-87; Ky Watercolor Soc, 81, 83 & 85; Art in Ga, Albany Mus, Ga, 81. *Awards:* Purchase Award, Olin Mills Corp, Hunter Mus, 77; Hans Hofman Award, Southern Watercolor Soc, 79; Award, Southern Watercolor Soc, 80, Ga Watercolor Soc, 80, 82, 83, 85, 87 & 88. *Bibliog:* Pat Hetzler (auth), Betty Barnes Loehle, Art Voices Mag, 5-6/81. *Mem:* Artists Assocs Inc (pres 78 & 79); Atlanta Artists Club; Southern Watercolor Soc; Ala & Ky Watercolor Socs; Ga Watercolor Soc (bd dir, 80-87). *Media:* Mixed. *Dealer:* Abstein Gallery 558 14th St NW Atlanta GA 30318. *Mailing Add:* 2608 River Oak Dr Decatur GA 30033

LOEHLE, RICHARD E
PAINTER, ILLUSTRATOR
b Atlanta, Ga, Mar 9, 23. *Study:* Atlanta Col Art, 40; Harris Sch Art, grad cert, 48; Evanston Art Ctr, Ill, 67. *Work:* High Mus Art; Montgomery Mus Art, Ala; Ala Watercolor Soc, Birmingham; Ga Coun Arts & Humanities; Chicago Artists Guild. *Exhib:* Ga Artists Show, High Mus, 74 & 76; Southern Watercolor Soc, Columbus Mus, 78 & 82; Ga Watercolor Soc, Macon Mus, 82; Ky Watercolor Soc, Owensboro Mus, 83; Southern Watercolor Soc, Asheville Mus, NC, 83; and others. *Awards:* Purchase Prize, Dixie Ann, Montgomery Mus Art, 72; Best in Show, Atlanta Arts Festival, 73 & Southern Watercolor Soc, 80 & 83. *Bibliog:* Edith Coogler (auth), Prize-winning artist, Atlanta Constitution, 6/28/70; S Coleman & C Anderson (auths), article, Southern Watercolor Soc Newslett, 83; Richard and Betty Loehle, Parallel Careers, Nat Television, Mod Maturity, No 252. *Media:* Oil, Acrylic; Watercolor. *Publ:* Coauth, Great American Depression Book of Fun, Harper & Row, 81. *Dealer:* Portrait Brokers of Am Inc 36 Church St Birmingham AL 35213. *Mailing Add:* 2608 River Oak Dr Decatur GA 30033

LOESER, THOMAS
SCULPTOR
b Boston, Mass, May 27, 56. *Study:* Haverford Col, BA, 79; Boston Univ, BFA, 82; Univ Mass, N Dartmouth, Mass, MFA, 92. *Work:* Mus Art, RI Sch Design, Providence; Cooper Hewitt Mus, Brooklyn Mus, New York; Mus Fine Arts, Boston; Yale Univ Art Gallery, New Haven. *Exhib:* Furniture by British American & French Designers, Victoria & Albert Mus, London, Eng, 84; Material Evidence, Smithsonian Inst, Washington, DC, 85; Furniture for Postmodern Age, Queens Mus, New York, 85; Poetry of Physical, Am Craft Mus, New York, 86; Grand Prix des Metiers d'Art, Hall d'Exposition des Archives Nat, Montreal, Can, 87; Craft Today--USA, Musee des Arts Decomfits, Paris, France, 89; New Furniture in America, Mus Fine Arts, Boston, Mass, 89 & 91; Art That Works, Mint Mus Art, Charlotte, NC, 90; one-person show, Peter Joseph Gallery, New York, 92; Gallery NAGA, Boston, Mass, 92; Gallery Design Madison, Univ Wis, 92; Univ Mass, Dartmouth Art Gallery, Mass, 92. *Pos:* Bd trustees, Haystack Mountain Sch, Maine, 88-; juror, Festival at the Lake Crafts Show, Oakland, Calif, 90, Ill Arts Coun, 91; panelist, Nat Endowment Arts, 92. *Teaching:* Instr Fine Arts, RI Sch Design, 87-88, Univ Wis, Madison, 91-92; asst prof, Univ Wis, Madison, 92-; numerous lectures & workshops at various universities & institutions. *Awards:* Visual Artists Fel Grant, Nat Endowment Arts, 84, 88 & 90; Japan-US Creative Artist Exchange Fel, 92. *Bibliog:* Arts and Crafts, Korea, 3/92; NAGA Spotlighting Studio Furniture, Boston Globe, 5/20/92; Style, House Beautiful, 7/2. *Media:* Wood, All Media. *Publ:* Auth, Speakeasy, New Art Examiner, 9/92. *Mailing Add:* 1068 Curtis St Albany CA 94706

LOEWER, HENRY PETER
WRITER, ILLUSTRATOR
b Buffalo, NY, Feb 13, 34. *Study:* Albright Art Sch, Univ Buffalo, with Lawrence Calcagno & Anne Coffin Hanson, BFA, 58. *Work:* Hunt Inst for Botanical Doc, Carnegie-Mellon Univ, Pittsburgh, Pa; Catskill Art Soc, Hurleyville, NY. *Exhib:* Int Exhib of Botanical Drawings, Hunterdon Art Ctr, Clinton, NJ, 77; 4th Int Exhib of Botanical Art, Carnegie-Mellon Univ,

Pittsburgh, Pa, 77-78; one-man show, Horticultural Soc of New York, 77. *Awards:* First Place, Garden Writers Am, 81, 84 & 92. *Media:* Pen and Ink, Watercolor. *Publ:* Illusr, Wildflower Perennials for Your Garden, Hawthorn, 76; auth & illusr, Gardens by Design, Rodale, 86; A Year of Flowers, Rodale, 89; A World of Plants, Abrams, 89; The Wild Gardener, 91. *Mailing Add:* PO Box 15610 Asheville NC 28813

LOFTUS, PETER M
PAINTER
b Washington, DC, Oct 27, 48. *Study:* Md Inst Col Art, BFA, 71; Univ Pa, 74. *Work:* Glen C Janss Collection; San Jose Mus Art, Calif; Hunter Mus, Chatanooga, Tenn. *Exhib:* American Realism: 20th Century Drawings & Watercolors, San Francisco Mus Mod Art, traveling exhib, 85; Contemporary Americian Realism, Columbus Mus Arts & Sci, Ga, 85; The Realist Landscape, Robeson Art Ctr Gallery, Rutgers Univ, 85; The Subject is Water, Newport Art Mus, 88; The Face of the Land, Southern Allegheny Mus Art, 88; New Horizons in American Realism, Flint Inst Arts (traveling exhib with catalog), 91. *Teaching:* Vis lectr painting, Univ Calif, Santa Cruz, 76-88. *Bibliog:* Fredy Kaplan (auth), Portfolio of regional landscapes, Am Artist, 2/84; Alvin Martin (auth), American Realism: 20th Century Drawings & Watercolors, Abrams, 86; West Art & the Law, West Publ Co, 87. *Mem:* Col Art Asn Am. *Media:* Watercolor, Oil. *Dealer:* Fischbach Gallery 24 W 57 St New York NY; Contemporary Realist Gallery 23 Grant 6th Floor San Francisco CA 94108. *Mailing Add:* 729 Western Dr Santa Cruz CA 95060

LOGAN, DAVID GEORGE
METALSMITH, EDUCATOR
b Milwaukee, Wis, June 14, 37. *Study:* Univ Wis-Madison, BS, 63, with Arthur Vierthaler, MFA, 68; Univ Ill-Urbana, with Robert von Neumann, Jr, MA, 67. *Comn:* Art in Worship (slide series), Am Crafts Coun. *Exhib:* Michiana Crafts Competition, Lafayette, Ind, 72; 37th Ann Nat Crafts Competition, Cedar City, Utah, 78; Nat Invitational Exhib, Northern Mich Univ, 79; Nat Print & Small Sculpture Exhib, Copus Christi, 81 & 83; Marietta Crafts Nat, Ohio, 82; and others. *Teaching:* Art, Oregon Pub Schs, Wis, 63-66; asst prof art, Mich State Univ, 68-79; vis artist metalsmithing, Northern Mich Univ, summer 71 & 74; assoc prof art, ETenn State Univ, 79- *Awards:* Jewelry Award, Westchester Art Soc, NY, 70; Ascension Lutheran Church Award for Liturgical Jewelry, East Lansing, 73; Haas Found Award, Nat Print & Small Sculpture Exhib, 83. *Mem:* Mich Art Educ Asn (pres, 71-72, ed newslett, 73-74); Nat Art Educ Asn; Am Crafts Coun; Soc NAm Goldsmiths; Tenn Art Educ Asn (bd mem, 81-). *Media:* Non-ferrous Metals, Glass. *Mailing Add:* RR4 Box 1705 Elizabethton TN 37643

LOGAN, GENE ADAMS
SCULPTOR, PAINTER
b Kickapoo, Kans, June 14, 22. *Study:* Southwest Mo State Univ, BS, 49; Univ Southern Calif, PhD, 60; Univ Ore, 65; Univ Kans, MFA, 67; also with Elden Tefft & Jan Zach. *Work:* El Camino Col Sculpture Garden, Torrance, Calif; included in over 300 pvt collections. *Comn:* Sculpture, Chase Nat Ins Co, Springfield, Mo, 66; sculpture, Westmont Industs, Santa Fe Springs, Calif, 75; sculpture, City of La Mirana, Calif, 77; office bldg, Am Alliance for Health, Physical Educ, Recreation & Dance, Reston, Va, 85. *Exhib:* One-man shows, Ankrum Gallery, Los Angeles, 70-72, 75, 78 & 82; Pioneer Mus & Haggin Galleries, Stockton, Calif, 78; Zantman Art Galleries, Carmel, Calif, 79, Palm Desert, Calif, 89; Townhouse Gallery, New Orleans, 80, 88; Crowther of Syon Lodge, London, Eng, 80. *Teaching:* Prof art anat, Southwest Mo State Univ, Springfield, 67-69; prof life drawing, Pasadena Sch Fine Arts, Calif, 70. *Awards:* First Award Sculpture, All-Calif Exhib, Laguna Beach, 60 & 61; Sculpture Gold Medal Award, Calif State Fair & Expos, Sacramento, 62. *Bibliog:* Michael Leopold (auth), Beverly Hills Mag, 4-5/78; Irene Lagorio (auth), Art & artists, Monterey Peninsula Herald, 2/9/79; Sharon Apfelbaum (auth), Art, Palm Springs Life Mag, 2/80; and others. *Media:* Brazed Sheet Copper, Bronze; Acrylic. *Dealer:* Zantman Art Galleries Sixth & Mission Carmel CA 93921; 73-925 El Paseo Palm Desert CA 92260. *Mailing Add:* 1551 W 13th St Suite 215 Upland CA 91786

LOGEMANN, JANE MARIE
PAINTER, PRINTMAKER
b Milwaukee, Wis, Nov 12, 42. *Study:* Layton Sch of Art, Milwaukee, Wis, 61; Univ Wis, Milwaukee, BA, 63. *Work:* Milwaukee Art Mus, Wis; James Michener Collection, Univ Tex, Austin; Stanford Univ Art Mus, Calif; Zimmerli Art Mus, Rutgers Univ, New Brunswick, NJ; Mus Mod Art & Jewish Mus Art, New York. *Exhib:* Solo video show, Everson Mus, Syracuse, NY, 75; Southland Video Anthology, Long Beach Mus, Calif, 75; In the Shadow of Duchamp, Grolier Club, New York, 79; Mapped Art, Independent Cur Inc, New York, 81; Merronom, Contemp Art Mus, Barcelona, Spain, 81; Rutgers Archives for the Printmaking Studios, Zimmerli Art Mus, New Brunswick, NJ, 83; Lenore Gray Gallery, Providence, RI, 88; 100 Drawings by Women, CW Post Col, Long Island Univ, NY, 89; Anthony Ralph Gallery, New York, 91; AAA, Ulrich Mus, Wichita, Kans, 92. *Collections Arranged:* Diversity-NY Artists (auth, catalog), Univ RI, fall 85; American Abstract Artists: New Work: New Mem, 87. *Bibliog:* Peter Frank (auth), revs, Artnews, 11/79; Jacqueline Brody (auth), revs, Print Collector's Newslett, 11/82. *Mem:* Am Abstract Artists (mem bd dirs, 86-). *Media:* Acrylic, Oil. *Publ:* Auth & illusr, Abstracts-Book III, 78; ed, Ecology and feminism issue, Vol 4, Art Heresies, 81; Art in New York Today: Idea Mag, Toyko, Japan, 8/88. *Mailing Add:* 35 Bond St New York NY 10012

LOISELLE, BERNARD ROGER
PAINTER, MUSEUM DIRECTOR
b Haverhill, Mass, May 16, 19. *Study:* Corcoran Sch Art, Washington, DC, with Eugene Weisz, Richard Lahey & Kenneth Stubbs, 37-40. *Work:* Portrait, Civic Ctr Mansion, Rockville, MD. *Comn:* Mural, Villa Rosa Restaurant, comn by Richard Pellicano, Wheaton, Md, 60; Idyll of Autumn (landscape), 81 & The Fisherman (painting), 84, Rockville Civic Ctr, Md; plus numerous portraits commissioned by various individuals. *Exhib:* Washington Soc Oil Painters, 62-68 & Mercury, 70, Smithsonian Inst, Washington, DC; Rockville Gallery, Md, 84; Foxhall Sq, Washington, DC, 85. *Collections Arranged:* Paintings by John Clendening (auth, catalog), Artist Air & Space Mus, 83; Paintings by Denny Arant (auth, catalog), 85 & Zehra Rehmutulla Post (auth, catalog), 86, Rockville Art League (auth, catalog), 85, Rockville Civic Ctr, Md; plus numerous monthly shows. *Pos:* Dir, Rockville Munic Art Gallery & Civic Ctr, Md, 56- *Teaching:* Instr art, Dept Justice, Washington, DC, 54-65, Rockville Civic Ctr, 68-76 & Jewish Community Ctr, Md, 76-86. *Awards:* First Place Awards, Dept Justice, Washington, DC, 56 & Rockville Art League, 71; Bader Award, Smithsonian Show, DC Soc Oil Painters, 62. *Bibliog:* Article, Loiselle family art, Rockville Newspaper, 64; Unveiling Mansion Portrait of former Mrs Maryland, Virginia Moore & artist Gardell Christensen, Civic Ctr, 9/11/88; Unveiled portraits of Mrs John Eggener, 5/90, Joseph Monto, 7/90, Mrs Glory Lawe Compton, 7/90. *Mem:* Life mem Washington Landscape Painters Club; Am Portrait Soc; Mont Co Art Asn. *Media:* Oil. *Mailing Add:* 17060 King James Way Apt 801 Gaithersburg MD 20877

LOMAHAFTEWA, LINDA JOYCE
PAINTER, INSTRUCTOR
b Phoenix, Ariz, July 3, 47. *Study:* Inst Am Indian Arts, Santa Fe, NMex; San Francisco Art Inst, BFA & MFA. *Work:* Ctr Arts Indian Am, Washington, DC. *Exhib:* Riverside Mus, New York, 65; Mus NMex, Santa Fe, 65-66; Ctr Arts Indian Am, 67-68; San Francisco Art Inst Spring Show, 70-71; Scottsdale Nat Indian Art Exhib, Ariz, 70-71. *Teaching:* Asst drawing, San Francisco Art Inst, 70; painting instr, Assoc Am Indian Arts, San Francisco, summer 72; asst prof Native Am studies, Calif State Col, Sonoma, 72-; lectr, Native Am Studies, Univ Calif, Berkeley, 74-76; instr painting, Inst Am Indian Arts, Santa Fe, NMex, 76- *Awards:* Hon Mention for Oil Painting, Mus NMex, 65; First Place in Graphic Arts Purchase Award, Ctr Arts Indian Am, 67; Third Place in Drawing, Scottsdale Nat Indian Art Exhib, 70. *Bibliog:* Lloyd E Oxendine (auth), 23 contemporary Indian artists, Art in Am, 7-8/72. *Media:* Acrylic, Oil. *Publ:* Illusr, Indian Mag, 71; Weewish Tree, Am Indian Historian Press, 71; contribr, Art in Am, 72. *Mailing Add:* Inst Am Indian Arts St Michael's Dr Santa Fe NM 87501

LOMBARD, ANNETTE
PAINTER, INSTRUCTOR
b New York, NY, Jan 25, 29. *Study:* Art Students League, with Louis Bouche, 65-66, Daniel Green, 76-78 & David Leffel, 80-82. *Work:* Mt Calvary Fire Baptized Holiness Church, Brooklyn, NY; Pa State Univ, Hazelton; Calvary Hosp; US Navy, Pentagon, Washington, DC; and pvt collection of Willis R Casey, dir athletics, NC State Univ, Raleigh. *Exhib:* Vet Soc Am, Customs House Mus, World Trade Ctr, New York, 79 & 81; Chung-Cheng Cult Ctr, St John's Univ, Long Island, NY, 80; solo pastel exhib, Salmagundi Club, New York, 80; Pastel Exhib, Pen & Brush, New York, 81 & 82; Pastel Soc Am, Lever House, New York, 82; and others. *Collections Arranged:* Fifth & Sixth Ann Non-Member Exhibs (with catalog), Salmagundi Club, 82 & 83. *Teaching:* Free-lance instr still life, anat & portraits, 71- *Awards:* Gold Medal, Grand Nat Exhib, Am Artists Prof League, 77; Salmagundi Club Award, 82; Pen & Brush Award, Knickerbocker Artists, 83. *Mem:* Salmagundi Club; Am Artists Prof League; Pastel Soc Am; Artists Fel; US Navy Art Coop & Liaison Comn. *Media:* Mixed. *Mailing Add:* c/o Salmagundi Club 47 Fifth Ave New York NY 10003

LONDIN, BARBARA
PAINTER
b New York, NY. *Study:* Art Students League, with George Grosz & Reginal Marsch, 50; New Sch Soc Res, with Julian Levi, 64-67. *Work:* Bass Mus, Miami Beach, Fla; Chrysler Mus, Norfolk, Va; Mint Mus, Charlotte, NC; NY Cult Ctr; Rose Mus, Brandeis Univ, Waltham, Mass. *Comn:* Mural, comn by Robert Londin, New York, 70. *Exhib:* One-women show, Mint Mus, Charlotte, NC, 73 & Dreitzer Mus, Brandeis Univ, Waltham, Mass, 75; The 80's - A Post Pop Generation, Southern Alleghanies Mus Art, 90. *Pos:* Pres, Phoenix Gallery, 88-90; rep, bd asn, Artist Run Galleries, 92. *Awards:* Cert Excellence, I A C, 88. *Mem:* Artist Equity. *Media:* Acrylic. *Publ:* Wilson Libr Bull. *Mailing Add:* c/o Phoenix 568 Broadway Suite 607 New York NY 10012

LONDON, ALEXANDER
COLLECTOR, ILLUSTRATOR
b Paris, France; US citizen. *Study:* Lycee Mantaigne, Paris; Univ Pa, MS; Columbia Univ. *Pos:* Pres, Marstin Printing Corp, 69-; publ, Electronic & Appliance Co, 70-; exec dir, Imprimerie Centrale Commerciale, Paris, 70- *Awards:* Ten typographical & printing design awards, 56-79; spec awards for illus in Kalevala, 54 & design of Holocaust catalog, 79. *Collection:* French Impressionists; French Montparnasse; American contemporary. *Publ:* Illusr, Kalevala, 54; contribr & illusr var catalogs & art mag. *Mailing Add:* 350 Central Park W No 10C New York NY 10025

LONDON, ANNA
GRAPHIC ARTIST, SCULPTOR
b Poland, July 2, 13; US citizen. *Study:* Brooklyn Col, BA, 33; Columbia Univ, MA, 35; Ruth Leaf Workshop, 70-75. *Work:* Firehouse Gallery, Nassau Community Col, Garden City, NY; Berkshire Mus, Pittsfield, Mass. *Exhib:* Heckscher Mus, Huntington, NY, 75; C W Post Col, Greenvale, NY, 73 & 78; Parrish Mus, Southampton, NY, 79; Hudson River Mus, NY, 85; Cork Gallery, Lincoln Ctr, NY, 80-90; and others. *Awards:* Purchase Awards, Firehouse Gallery & Berkshire Mus; Prize, Nat Asn Women Artists. *Bibliog:* Ruth Leaf (auth), Intaglio Printmaking Techniques, Watson-Guptill, 76. *Mem:* Nat Asn Women Artists; Hempstead Harbor Artist Asn; Nat Mus Women Arts, Washington, DC. *Media:* Monprints; Clay. *Dealer:* Graphic Eye Gallery 301 Main St Port Washington NY 11050. *Mailing Add:* 33 Larch Dr Manhasset Hills NY 11040

LONDON, BARBARA
CURATOR
b Glen Cove, NY, July 3, 46. *Study:* Hiram Col, Ohio, BA, 68; Inst of Fine Arts, New York Univ, MA, 72. *Collections Arranged:* Projects: Video I-XXXII, 74-81, Loren Madsen, 75, Peter Campus, 76, Nam June Paik, 77, Bookworks, 77 (Sachs Gallery), Projects: Shigeko Kubota, 78, Video Viewpoints, 78-90, Laurie Anderson, 78, Donald Lipski, 79, Video from Tokyo to Fukui and Kyoto (auth, catalog), 79 & Sound Art, 79, Mus Mod Art, New York, Music Video 85, Bill Viola, 87, Barbara Steinman, 89, Gary Hill, 90; Tony Cokes, 91, Thierry Kuntzel, 91, Jana Sterbak, Mus Mod Art, 92. *Pos:* Asst int prog, Mus Mod Art, New York, 71-73, curatorial asst dept of prints & illus bks, 73-77, cur video prog, 77- *Teaching:* Film Dept, NY Univ, 79-82. *Awards:* Fel, Nat Endowment Arts, 88. *Publ:* Auth, Video Letter of Shuntaro Tanileawa and Shuji Terayama, Camera Obscura, Los Angeles, 90 & Fall, 91; A Few Reflections on High Definition Video and Art, HDTV, Union Square Press, New York, 90; Gary Hill, Image Forum, Tokyo, 91; Electronic Explorations, Art in America, 5/92; Techno-Visions: Tradition and the Avant-Garde, Art 20/21 & Earthly Paradise: The Paintings of Po Kim, Seoul, Korea, 92. *Mailing Add:* 106 W 87th St No 5B New York NY 10024

LONDON, PETER
PAINTER, EDUCATOR
b New York, NY, June 27, 39. *Study:* Queens Col, BA, 61; Columbia Univ, MFA, 62, EdD, 68. *Work:* Columbia Univ; Concordia Univ; Queens Col. *Comn:* Stainless steel sculpture, John Bowne High Sch, New York, 69. *Exhib:* Collection of Final Portraits, Nat Holocaust Mus, Washington, DC, Concordia Univ, Univ Maui, Columbia Univ & Turo Synogogue. *Pos:* Pres, Pub Arts Coun, Mass, 75-79; post doctoral fel, Lesley Col, Cambridge, Mass; art critic, New Bedford Mag; ed bd, Sch Arts Eastern Regional Dir, NAEA. *Teaching:* Asst prof art & art educ, Concordia Univ, 67-71; prof art & art educ, Mass Univ, Dartmouth, 71- *Awards:* Traveling Fel to Israel, 83-84. *Mem:* Nat Art Educ Asn; Int Soc for Educ through Art; Int Art Educ Asn; NEng Art Therapy Asn. *Media:* Charcoal, Pastel. *Publ:* Auth, Taming of the American Imagination, Nat Art Educ Asn J, 74; Towards a New Philosophy of Art Education, Art for the Primary Level, 74; Trust and Education, Southeastern Mass Union J, 75; Alternative Careers in Art, Careers in Art, 79; No More Secondhand Art, Showbhalia, 89; Art as Transformation, NAEA J, 5/92. *Dealer:* Galerie Don Steward Sherbrook St W Montreal PQ Can. *Mailing Add:* Southeastern MA Univ North Dartmouth MA 02747

LONG, BERT L, JR
SCULPTOR
b Houston, Tex, Sept 27, 40. *Study:* Univ Calif-Los Angeles, 72. *Work:* Huntington Gallery Mus Univ Tex, Austin; Mus Fine Arts, Houston, Tex; Dallas Mus Art, Tex; Bell Telephone, Houston, Tex; Metrop Mus Art, New York; and many others. *Comn:* Neighbor (ice, 21000 lbs), Laguna Gloria Mus, Texarkana, Tex; Security (ice, 50000 lbs), City of Austin, Nat Arts Week, 11/16/87; Creativity (ice, 22000 lbs), Abilene, Tex, 88; Texas Artist of the Year (ice, 32000 lbs), Houston Art League, 90; Roma Contemporanea (ice, 60000 lbs), Contemp Arts Mus, Houston, Tex, 91. *Exhib:* Solo exhibs, Dallas Mus Art, Tex, 88, Tex A&M Mem Student Ctr, Col Sta, Tex & Barry Whistler Gallery, Dallas, 89, Allan Stone Gallery, New York, 90, Lew Allen Gallery, Santa Fe, NMex & Contemp Arts Mus, Houston, 91 & Bert in the New World, Lyons Matrix Gallery, 92; Now, Then, Again, Dallas Mus Art, Tex, 90; Duke Univ Mus Art, Durham, NC, 90; Studio Mus Harlem, New York, 90; Northwest x Southwest: Painted Fictions, Palm Springs Desert Mus, 90; Artists of Conscience: 16 years of social and political commentary, Alternative Mus, New York, 91. *Awards:* Rome Prize Fel, 90-91. *Bibliog:* Jenny Read (auth), Bert Louis Long: a profile, Wanted in Rome, 7/10/91; Jane Aker (auth), Painting the Social Landscape, Santa Fe Reporter, Vol 17, 10/23-29/91; Don Fabricant (auth), Finding their own Voices, The Santa Fe Sun, 11/91. *Media:* Ice. *Publ:* Auth, Forerunners and Newcomers: Houston's Leading African American Artists, Southern Univ, Tex, 11/89; Mixed Blessings: Contemporary Art and the Cross Cultural Process by Noted Art Critic & Writer Lucy Lippard, New York, fall 90; Guest Information, Dallas Mus, fall, 90; American Academy in Rome, Ann Exhib, 91; Mental Asylum, Contemp Arts Mus, Bayou Book Series, 1/92. *Mailing Add:* c/o Hiram Butler Gallery 2318-2320 Portsmouth Houston TX 77098

LONG, ELECTRA
PAINTER, DRAFTSMAN
b Mount Sterling, Ky, Oct 21, 43. *Study:* Acad Art Col, San Francisco State Univ, BA, 70, MA, 76; Art Students League; Nat Acad Design. *Work:* Portrait of William Scranton III, State Senate Bldg, Harrisburg, Pa; portrait of Katharine D McCormick, Stanford Univ Med Sch, Calif. *Comn:* Dr Gurnam SS Brard, Piedmont, Calif, 87; Portraits, comn by Gerald Winer, 88, James Lindsay, 88 & Ronald Knecht, 89; Larry Abrams, New York, 90. *Exhib:* Solo exhibs, Stage II Theatre, Walnut Creek, Calif, 83 & Art Students League, New York, 88; Menlo Park Eleventh Ann Exhib, 83 & Soc Wester Artists Ann Exhib, Hall of Flowers, 84, Rosicrucian Mus, Calif; David Hardy & Friends Exhib, Piedmont, Calif, 8; About Faces, Civic Arts Ctr Exhib, Walnut Creek, Calif, 87; Salmagundi Club Show, New York, 89. *Teaching:* Instr writing & communications, San Francisco Community Col, 74-88. *Awards:* Best of Show, Newark Days Art Show, 82 & 84; Anna Elizabeth Klumpke Mem Award, Soc Western Artists Ann Show, San Francisco, 87; Signature Award, Soc Western Artists. *Mem:* Art Students League; Soc Western Artists (signature mem); Mensa Int; Int Soc Philos Inquiry. *Mailing Add:* 1000 North Point San Francisco CA 94109

LONG, FRANK WEATHERS
PAINTER
b Knoxville, Tenn, May 7, 06. *Study:* Art Inst Chicago, 25-27; Pa Acad Fine Art, 27-28; Acad Julien, Paris, 28-29. *Work:* Nat Collection, Smithsonian Inst, Washington, DC; Int Bus Machines Corp, New York; Berea Col, Ky; Univ NMex; Univ Ky. *Comn:* Two-Panels, Univ Ky Libr, 31; ten-panels, Fed Bldg, Louisville, Ky, 33, one-panel, US Post Offices, Drumwright, Okla, 36, Morehead, 39, Berea, 40, Ky, Crawfordsville, Ind, 42 & three-panels, Hagerstown, Md, 38, Treas Dept, Fed Govt; one-panel, Davidson Col Libr, 35. *Exhib:* Media 1966, Walnut Creek Mus, Calif, 66; Hemisfair Preview Exhib, San Antonio, Tex, 67; Nat Crafts Exhib, NMex Western Univ, 72; Crafts VII Exhib, 77 & One Space, Three Visions, 79, Mus of Albuquerque; One-man retrospective, Univ Ky; and others. *Pos:* Dir, Alaska Off of Indian Arts & Crafts Bd, Juneau, 51-57; field rep, SW Off of Indian Arts & Crafts Bd, Gallup, NMex, 57-59, Albuquerque, 62-69. *Teaching:* Instr lapidary, Univ NMex. *Awards:* First Prizes, Southwest Biennial, 63, NMex State Fair, 63, 65 & 67 & NMex Crafts Biennial, 64 & 66. *Mem:* NMex Designer-Craftsmen (Albuquerque chap pres, 69). *Media:* Gem Material; Metal. *Publ:* Auth & illusr, Herakles, The 12 Labors, Black Archer Press, 31; The Creative Lapidary, 77 & Lapidary Carving, 82, Van Nostrand Reinhold. *Mailing Add:* 1836 Florida NE Albuquerque NM 87110

LONG, JENNY
ART DEALER
b Ft Worth, Tex, June 26, 55. *Study:* Finch Col, AA, 75; Sarah Lawrence Col, Bronxville, BA, 77. *Pos:* Asst dir, Meredith Long Contemp, New York, 77-79, dir, 79-80; mgr, Adam L Gimbel Gallery, New York, 81-83; adminr, Christie, Manson & Woods Int, Am Paintings Dept, 84-86; adminr, Meredith Long & Co, Houston, Tex, 86- *Specialty:* 19th and 20th century American Art. *Mailing Add:* 6363 San Felipe St No 258 Houston TX 77057

LONG, MEREDITH J
DEALER
b Joplin, Mo, Sept 14, 28. *Study:* Univ Tex, BA, 50, Law Sch, 50-51, 53-54. *Pos:* Munic arts comnr, Houston; pres, Meredith Long & Co, Houston, 57- *Mem:* Alley Theatre, Houston (pres, bd); Houston Ballet Found (bd mem); Archives Am Art (bd mem). *Specialty:* 19th and 20th century American art. *Publ:* Ed, Americans at Home and Abroad Catalogue, 71; Tradition and Innovation--American Paintings 1860-1870, 74; Americans at work and play, 80. *Mailing Add:* 2323 San Felipe Houston TX 77019

LONG, ROSE-CAROL WASHTON
HISTORIAN, ADMINISTRATOR
b New London, Conn, Mar 1, 38. *Study:* Wellesley Col, BA, 59; Yale Univ, MA(hist art), 62, PhD(hist art), 68. *Collections Arranged:* Twentieth Century Prints, Godwin-Ternbach Mus, 83. *Teaching:* Lectr, Queens Col & Grad Ctr, City Univ New York, 67-69, asst prof, 69-78, assoc prof, 79-83, prof art hist, 84- *Awards:* Nat Endowment Humanities Fel, 72-73; Am Coun Learned Soc Grant, 72-73 & 82-83; Guggenheim Fel, 83-84. *Mem:* Col Art Asn; Am Fedn Arts. *Res:* Pioneers of 20th century abstract painting; Kandinsky; German Expressionism. *Publ:* Auth, Kandinsky: The Development of an Abstract Style, Clarendon Press, Oxford, 80; Occultism, Anarchism & Abstractions: Kandinsky's Art of the Future, Art J, spring 87; Scholarship: Past, Present & Future Directions, German Expressionist Prints and Drawings, The Robert Gore Rifkind Ctr for German Expressionist Studies, 2 Vols, Los Angeles Co Mus Art, 89; auth & ed annotation, German Expressionism: Documents from the End of the Wilhelmine Empire to the Rise of National Socialism, G K Hall, Macmillan, 92. *Mailing Add:* 161 W 15th St No 6J New York NY 10011

LONGAKER, JON DASU
EDUCATOR, WRITER
b Davos, Switz, Jan 5, 20; US citizen. *Study:* Univ Pa, BA(fine arts), 41; Barnes Found, Merion, Pa, 46-47; Cinquantenaire Mus, Brussels, Belg Am Educ Found, summer 51; Columbia Univ, 47-52. *Pos:* Art critic, Richmond Times-Dispatch, Va, 56-64 & 72-74, drama critic, 65-; columnist on arts, Commonwealth Mag, Richmond, 67-80; mem, State Art Comn, Richmond, 70-74. *Teaching:* Instr art appreciation, Barnes Found, Merion, Pa, 50-51; prof art hist, Randolph-Macon Col, Ashland, Va, 53-; Am Univs, Aix-en-Provence, France, 64-65. *Res:* Islamic art, architecture and crafts. *Publ:* Auth, Painting in the South--a Double Portrait, Inst Southern Cult, Longwood Col, 61; Strive and succeed, Arts in Va, 70; Art, Style and History: A Selective History of Art, Scott, Foresman, 70. *Mailing Add:* 133 Beverly Rd Ashland VA 23005

LONGHURST, ROBERT E
SCULPTOR
b Latham, NY, Feb 23, 49. *Study:* Adirondack Community Col, AS, 69; Kent State Univ, BA(archit), 75. *Comn:* Sticks & Stones (environ construct, wood & granite) pvt residence, Lake Placid, NY, 89; Blast (14' high granite & stainless steel), ensign-Bickford Ind, Simsbury, Conn, 92. *Exhib:* One man shows, Randall Galleries, New York, 82 & Lollis Newman Galleries, Beverly Hills, Calif, 86. *Awards:* Friends Am Art, Butler Inst Am Art, 79; Helen Eisler Mem Award, Audubon Ann, 80. *Bibliog:* Alice Gilborn (auth), Reaching for Perfection, Adirondack Life, 9/83; Dick burrows (ed), A New Twist, Fine Woodworking, 8/91. *Mem:* Int Sculpture Ctr, Washington, DC. *Media:* Wood, Stone. *Mailing Add:* Potterbrook Rd RFD Box 351 Chestertown NY 12817

LONGLEY, BERNIQUE
PAINTER, SCULPTOR
b Moline, Ill. *Study:* Art Inst Chicago, grad(Byron Lathrop traveling fel), 45; Inst de Allende, San Miguel de Allende, Mex, 71; Santa Fe Sch Arts & Crafts, 75. *Work:* Mus NMex, Santa Fe; Dallas Mus; Fine Arts Ctr, Colorado Springs, Colo. *Comn:* Murals, comn by Alexander Girard, Santa Fe, 59; murals, La Fonda Del Sol, NY, 60. *Exhib:* Int Watercolor Show, Art Inst Chicago, 48; NMex Mus Fine Arts Invitational Show, 68; Kermezaar Festival, El Paso, Tex, 75; Santa Fe Festival Arts, 77-81; Margaret Jamison Presents, 79-80; solo exhibs, Gov Gallery, NMex State Capital; retrospective, Santa Fe East Gallery, NMex, 82; Quiet Realities - I & II, 85-86; Contemporary Realism, Leslie Levy Gallery, Scottsdale, 85; one-woman show, Santa Fe East Gallery, Santa Fe, NMex, 88; Hickory Mus, Hickory, NC, 89. *Awards:* Honorable Mention, Art Inst Chicago, 48; Honorable Mention, Denver Mus Art Regional Show Sculpture, 48; Purchase Prize, 53 & Honorable Mention, 65, Mus NMex. *Bibliog:* Bernique Longley-A-Retrospective, Gallery Representation, El Prado Galleries Inc, Sedona, Ariz & SAnta Fe, NMex. *Mem:* Alumni Asn - Asn Inst of Chicago. *Media:* Oil, Acrylic. *Publ:* Auth, Suite of Lithographs, Tamarind Inst, 72. *Mailing Add:* 427 Camino del Monte Sol Santa Fe NM 87501

LONGO, ROBERT
PAINTER
b Brooklyn, NY, 53. *Study:* State Univ Col NY, Buffalo, BFA, 75. *Work:* Mus Mod Art, New York; Walker Art Ctr, Minneapolis, Minn; Tate Gallery, London; Art Inst Chicago; Guggenheim Mus, New York; Menil Collection, Houston; and many others. *Exhib:* Empire: A Performance Trilogy, Corcoran Gallery Art, Washington, DC, 81; Eight Artists: The Anxious Edge, Walker Art Ctr, Minneapolis, 82; Focus on the Figure: Twenty Years, Whitney Mus, New York, 82; New Figuration in America, Milwaukee Art Ctr, 82; 1983 Biennial, Whitney Mus, New York, 83; The New Art, Fate Gallery, London, 83; An International Survey of Recent Painting and Sculpture, Mus Mod Art, NY, 83; The Human Condition: Biennial III, San Francisco Mus Mod Art, 84; Currents, Inst Contemp Art, Boston, 84; Performance Works 1977-1981, Brooklyn Mus, NY, 85; The American Exhibtion, Art Inst Chicago, 86; Monumental Drawing: Works by 22 Contemporary Americans, Brooklyn Mus, NY, 86; Avante-Garde in the Eighties, Los Angeles County Mus Art, 87; one-person exhibs, Metro Pictures, NY, 88 & 90; Mus Boymans van Beuningen, Rotterdam, 88; Seibu Contemp Art Gallery, Tokyo, 89; Los Angeles County Mus Art (catalog), traveled to Mus Contemp Art, Chicago & Wadsworth Atheneum, Hartford, Conn, 89; Linda Cathcart Gallery, Los Angeles, 89 & 91; Gallerie Daniel Templon, Paris, 90; Tex Gallery, Houston, 91 & Hamburg Kunstverein, Hamburg, 91; Affinities and Intuitions: The Gerald S Elliot Collection of Contemporary Art, Art Inst Chicago, 90; Compassion and Protest: Recent Social and Political Art from the Eli Broad Family Foundation Collection, San Jose Mus Art, 91; Power, Indianapolis Mus Art, 91; Allegories of Modernism: Contemporary Drawing, Mus Mod Art, New York, 92. *Bibliog:* Owen McNally (auth) Monsters in the Gallery, The Hartford Courant, Hartford, Conn, 6/9/90, sect B, B1 & B5; Susan White (auth), Robert Longo: A Baby of the NEA, The Hartford Advocate, Conn, 6/4/90, 3; Timothy W Luke (auth), Shows of Force: Power, Politics, and Idology in Art Exhibitions, Duke Univ Press, Durham, NC & London, 92. *Mailing Add:* 85 South St New York NY 10038

LONGO, VINCENT
PAINTER, PRINTMAKER
b New York, NY, Feb 15, 23. *Study:* Cooper Union, Cert 46; Brooklyn Mus Art Sch, 49-50. *Work:* Libr Congress, Washington, DC; Mus Mod Art, Brooklyn Mus Art, Whitney Mus Am Art, New York; Nat Gallery Art, Washington, DC. *Exhib:* Two Decades of Am Prints, Brooklyn Mus, NY, 69; One-man retrospectives, 15 Year Print Retrospective, Corcoran Gallery & Detroit Inst Art, 70; Whitney Mus Painting Ann, New York, 71; Am Drawings, Whitney Mus, New York, 73; Color in the Graphic Arts, Libr Congress, Washington, DC, 74; Thirty Years of Am Prints, Brooklyn Mus, NY, 76; Am Prints Process & Proofs, Whitney Mus, New York, 81; The Perstistence of Painting, Ulrich Mus, Wichita, Kan, 92. *Teaching:* Prof art, Bennington Col, Bennington, Vt, 57-67, Hunter Col, New York,67- *Awards:* Fullbright Fel, 51; Fel Guggenheim, 71; Grant Nat Endowment Arts, 73. *Bibliog:* Gene Baro (auth), Print Retrospective (catalog essay), Corcoran Gallery, 70; Judith Goldman (auth), American Prints: Process & Proofs; Louis Lomonaco (auth), Artes et Metier Graphique, Flammarion, 92. *Mem:* Am Abstract Artists. *Publ:* Auth, A Debate on Abstraction (exhib catalog), Hunter Col, 88. *Dealer:* Condeso-Lawler 76 Greene St New York NY 10012. *Mailing Add:* 50 Greene St New York NY 10013

LONGOBARDI, PAM
PAINTER, PRINTMAKER
b New Jersey, 1958. *Study:* Exch student, Univ Utah, 78; Univ Ga, BFA (studio art), 81; Mont State Univ, Bozeman, MFA, 85. *Work:* Burroughs-Wellcome Pharmaceuticals, Raleigh, NC; Miami Metrop Mus & Art Ctr, Coral Gables, Fla; Pratt Inst, New York; Deloitte-Touche and Agnes Scott Col Permanent Collection, Atlanta, Ga; Instituto de Estudios Norte Americans, Barcelona, Spain. *Exhib:* Solo exhibs, Brunswick Gallery, Missoula, Mont, 87, Inst de Estudios Norte Americanos, Barcelona, Spain, 87, Ewing Art Gallery, Univ Tenn, Knoxville, 88, Gray Art Gallery, ECarolina Univ, Greenville, 89, Merwin Gallery Art, Ill Wesleyan Univ, Bloomington, 89, San Francisco Mus Mod Art Rental Gallery, Calif, 90, Artemisia Gallery, Chicago, 90, Kathryn Sermas Gallery, New York, NY, 91 & 92, Lowe Gallery, Atlanta, 91 & Santa Monica, Calif, 92; Miniatures: Small Works, Mus Gallery, San Francisco Mus Mod Art, 87; Contemp Am Drawing, Fine Arts Gallery, Wake Forest Univ, Winston-Salem, NC, 88; Power of Interpretation, Agnes Scott Col, Atlanta, Ga, 89; Living Artists: Installations, Knoxville Mus Art, Tenn, 90. *Teaching:* Guest artist & inst, Mont State Univ, Bozeman, 86; vis artist, Chicago Art Inst, 86, Dartmouth Col, Hanover, NH, 88, Univ Chapel Hill, NC, 88, Univ Northern Iowa, Cedar Falls, 89, Mason Art Ctr, San Francisco, 89 & La State Univ, Baton Rouge, 90; artist-in-schools, Mont & Nev Arts Couns, 86-87; guest artist, Knoxville Mus Art, 87, Southeastern Col Art Conf & Southern Graphics Coun, Univ Tenn, Knoxville, 87, Western Carolina Univ, Cullowhee, NC, 87; asst prof art, Univ Tenn, Knoxville, 87- *Awards:* Purchase Awards, NMiami Mus Art, Coral Gables, 84 & Pratt Graphics Ctr, New York, 85; First Place Award Printmaking, Calif State Univ Art Mus, Long Beach, 85; Res Fel Abroad/ Spain, Univ Tenn, Knoxville, 89. *Bibliog:* Paul Govern (auth), Drawing Conclusions, Winston-Salem Spectator, 3/16/88; David Ribar (auth), Installations, Artpapers, 90; Peggy Cyphers (auth), Pam Longobard: NY in Review, ARTS, summer, 91. *Publ:* Contribr, Scientific American, Vol 250, No 4, 84; Infinity Mag, Vols 2, 3, 4 & 5, 84-86; auth & contribr, Images of nature and power: Named and nameless, Vol 2, Peabody Review, 90; contribr, Divided World, La State Univ Printmaking Dept, 90; The Persistance of Myth, Wycross Press, Auburn, Ala, 90. *Dealer:* Kathryn Sermas Gallery New York NY; Lowe Gallery Santa Monica CA. *Mailing Add:* 2524 Jefferson Ave Knoxville TN 37914

LONGO-MUTH, LINDA L
PAINTER, INSTRUCTOR
b Nyack, NY, Mar 25, 48. *Study:* Univ Roma, Italy, 69; Southern Conn Univ, New Haven, BS, 70; independent study, Paris, France, 71; Montclair State Col, NJ, MA, 75. *Work:* Cathedral St John the Divine, New York; Assoc Neurologists, Plainfield, NJ; Global Petroleum Corp, Waltham, Mass. *Exhib:* Extended Visions, Fashion Inst Tech, New York, 88; Shared Visions, IBM Gallery Sci & Art, New York, 89; Artists with Disabilities, Cork Gallery, Avery Fisher Hall, Lincoln Ctr, New York, 90-91; Against The Odds, MetLife Corp Gallery, New York, 91; Triumph of Spirit, Stock Exchange Bldg, Citibank, Wall St, New York, 91. *Pos:* Bd advs, Resources for Artists with Disabilities, New York, 90-92 & bd dirs, 92- *Teaching:* Instr studio art, Ramapo Central Sch Dist, Suffern, NY, 70-87; instr art therapy, Multiple Sclerosis Southern NY, 88. *Awards:* Zvita & Joseph Akston Found Award, 91 & Dorothy Seligson Mem Award, 92, Nat Asn Women Artists; Guy Forde Mony Penney Award, Helen Hayes Hosp, 92. *Bibliog:* Robert Samuels (auth), Showing the true colors, in a new career, Gannett Newspapers, 7/2/89; Susan Leavitt (producer), video, CBS Affiliate WJW Life choices television prog, 91; Leslie Boyd (auth), Rockland artist profile in courage, Gannett Newspapers, 12/26/91. *Mem:* New York Artists Equity; Artists Space, NY; Nat Asn Women Artists; Arts Coun Rockland, Spring Valley, NY; NY Soc Women Artists. *Media:* Acrylic-on-Canvas. *Publ:* Contribr, NJ Rehab mag cover, 12/89; Mental and Physical Disbility Law Reporter, Am Bar Asn, Washington, DC, vol 16 no 3, 5-6/92. *Mailing Add:* 4 Reina Lane Valley Cottage NY 10989

LONGSTAFFE, JOHN RONALD
COLLECTOR
b Toronto, Ont, Apr 6, 34. *Exhib:* Selected View: Longstaffe Collection 1958-1984, Vancouver Art Gallery, 85. *Pos:* Pres, Vancouver Art Gallery, 66-68; vchmn, Nat Mus Can, 68-69, dir, 75-79. *Awards:* Award of Merit, Canadian Mus Asn, 78. *Interests:* Aid to Vancouver Art Gallery's and National Gallery of Canada's permanent collections. *Collection:* Contemporary Canadian art; contemporary international graphics. *Mailing Add:* 21-4771 Cordova Bay Rd Victoria BC V8Y 2J7 Canada

LONGSTREET, STEPHEN
PAINTER, HISTORIAN
b New York, NY, Apr 18, 07. *Study:* New York Sch Fine & Appl Art, 27; also with Matisse & Bonnard & sketching with Pascin, Grosz, Arp & Feitelson, Paris, 27-29 & 33-38. *Work:* San Francisco Mus; Yale Univ; Jazz Mus New Orleans; Los Angeles Art Asn; Mus Mod Art; and others. *Comn:* Stage sets, RexRoth Poetry Jazz, 52; stage sets, Areut Gabby Ballet, 53. *Exhib:* Nu-World Shows, Balbac Gallery, Paris, 40-60; San Francisco Mus Show, 65; Santa Barbara Mus Show, 67; Southern Calif Ann, 70; Paideia Galleries, Los Angeles, 71; one-man shows, Brooks Mem Mus, Memphis, Tenn, 78, Wolf Galleries, Munich, Ger, 80, Gallery 170, Los Angeles, Calif & Rutgers Univ, New Brunswick, NJ, 86, The Jazz Scene, Regenstein Mus, Univ Chicago, 90, Look at My Walls, Senior Eye Gallery, Long Beach, Calif, 90; plus others. *Pos:* Ed-in-chief, The Great Draftsmen (30 vols), 65-75; bd dir, Viewpoints Inst. *Teaching:* Lectr, Los Angeles Art Asn, 50-; prof art, Viewpoints Inst, 65-; prof mod arts, Univ Southern Calif, Los Angeles, 69, 73-78; lectr, Los Angeles Co Mus; co-published Jazz A to Z (art & text). *Awards:* Winader Foundation

First Prize Watercolors, 30; First Prize Oils, Am Art Festival, 46; Second Prize Drawings, Midwest Antiwar Soc, 69. *Mem:* Los Angeles Art Asn (pres, 72-75); Writers Guild Film Soc; co-founder Los Angeles Co Mus Art Graphic Soc; co-founder Functionists West with Fielelson & Lundberg. *Media:* Oil, Collage. *Collection:* Daumier prints; Rowlandson; Goya; Japanese prints. *Publ:* auth, Geisha, Pocket Bks, rev ed, 77; lib of congress, Jazz Collection, 80; illusr & text, From Storyville to Harlem, Rutgers Univ Press; auth & illusr, Magic Trumpeter, Zephyr Press, 88; auth & illusr, Jazz Dictionary, Catbird Press, 89. *Mailing Add:* 1133 Miradero Rd Beverly Hills CA 90210

LONGVAL, GLORIA
PAINTER
b Tampa, Fla, Feb 7, 31. *Study:* Am Art Sch, New York, NY, with Raphael Soyer, 51-52; Art Students League, with Robert Brackman, 52-53; Nat Acad Design, with Robert Philip, 55-58. *Work:* Los Angeles Free Clinic; Wifredo Lam Centro, Havana, Cuba. *Comn:* Drawing for Int Decade of Women, Woman Tours, Los Angeles, Calif, 75; portraits (oil), Boris & Polia Pillin, Los Angeles, 76; portrait, Sharon Davis, Los Angeles, 77; portrait (oil), Dr Gerald Newmark, Los Angeles, 80. *Exhib:* Personae, Calif State Univ, Los Angeles, 85; Contemporary Latino Artists, Polytech Sch, Pasadena, 86; Women's Hist Month, Rotunda of City Hall, Los Angeles, 86; Nat Exhib Contemp Women Artists, Warm Gallery, Minneapolis, Minn, 86; one-person show, April Sgro-Riddle Gallery, Los Angeles, 88, Los Angeles Artcore Gallery, 89; William Grant Still Art Ctr, Los Angeles, 89; Self Help Graphics, Galeria Otra Vez, Los Angeles, 89; Lancaster Mus, Calif, 90; Galeria Nueva, Los Angeles, 91; Cuarta Bienal De La Habana, Museo Nacional, Cuba, 91; Univ Judaism, Los Angeles, 92; La Raza Cósmica, Los Angeles, 92. *Pos:* Contrib ed, Los Angeles Artcore News, 86; adv bd, Los Angeles Poetry Festival, 90-92; cur, Latin Diaspora, Art N Barbee Gallery, Los Angeles, 92. *Teaching:* Instr painting, Sch Fine Arts, Univ Judaism, 68-71; guest instr, Los Angeles Children's Mus, 87-88. *Awards:* First Hon Mention, 50 Best Drawings, Bodley Gallery, New York, 59; First Hon Mention, Nat Acad Allied Artists Am, 59; First Prize, Multi Media Mini, San Bernardino County Mus, 83. *Bibliog:* Gloria Williams (auth), Surveying the Figure, Art Week, 85; Shifra M Goldman (auth), Yesterday and Tomorrow, Calif Women Artists, 89; Margaret Lazzari (auth), Curriculum viva, Visions Art Quart, 92. *Mem:* Artists Equity; Los Angeles Artcore (vpres, 86-87); Women's Caucus for Art. *Media:* Acrylic, Oil. *Dealer:* Galería Las Americas 912 E Third St Suite 402 Los Angeles CA 90013. *Mailing Add:* 1328 N Ogden Dr Los Angeles CA 90046

LONIDIER, FRED SPENCER
PHOTOGRAPHER, EDUCATOR
b Lakeview, Ore, Feb 19, 42. *Study:* Yuba Col, Marysville, Calif, AA, 62; San Francisco State Col, BA, 66; Univ Calif, San Diego, MFA(photog & mixed media), 72; also with David Antin. *Work:* Long Beach Mus Art, Calif; Faith Flam, Studio City, Calif; Oakland Mus, Calif; Los Angeles Video Libr, Calif; Southern Calif Libr Social Studies & Research. *Exhib:* One person shows, I Like Everything Nothing But Union, South Bay Regional Ctr, 84, Houston Ctr Photog, Tex, 84, US Fed Bldg, City Pub Libr, 85, Rutgers Univ Labor Educ Ctr, New Brunswick, NJ 85-86, Ironworkers Union, Local 657, 86, Univ & Col Labor Educ Asn, 86 & Calif Fedn Teachers, 89; The Other America, Festival Hall, London, UK, 86; Four Days in the 60's, San Francisco State Strike 20th Reunion, 87; San Diego Fac Exhib, Mandeville Gallery, 88; Pressing Engagements: Socially Oriental Photography (catalog), Tuttle Gallery, McDonough Sch, Md, 89; Visual Sociology, Mendenhall Gallery, Whittier Col, Calif, 90; Work Prints: The Eye of the Photojournalist, Rough Gallery, 90; and many others. *Pos:* Vis artist, Rhode Island Sch Design, Providence, 83; consultant Eye Gallery, San Francisco, Calif, 85. *Teaching:* Lectr photog, Univ Calif, San Diego, 72-75, assoc prof & asst, 82- *Awards:* San Diego Acad Senate Res Grant, Univ Calif, 75-76, 78-80, 81, 82, 83-84, 86-87, 88-89, 89-90; Nat Endowment Arts Fel, 80-83; Labor Coun Award, San Diego - Imperial Counties Labor Coun, 89. *Bibliog:* Abigail Solomon-Godeau (auth), Photography at the Dock: Essays on Photographic History, Institutions and Practices, Univ Minn Press, Minneapolis, 89; Blaise Tobia (auth), Undermining documentary, Afterimage, 9/90; Martin Spence (auth), Images of Labor, Uppnet News, Vol 3 No 3, 91. *Mem:* Los Angeles Inst Contemp Art; Col Art Asn Am. *Media:* Photo Text Installation, Slides & Video. *Publ:* Auth, Pointing to some problems, pointing to the future, Obscura, Vol 2, No 5, 83; contribr, Art & Idealogy (catalog), New Mus, New York, 84; coauth, Union Made: Artists Working with Unions, Upfront, NYPADD, New York, 83-84; Working with Unions in Culture in Contention, Real Comet Press, 85; contribr, Working with Unions II, in Democratic Communications in the Information Age, Garamound Press, Can, 1/90. *Mailing Add:* Univ Calif Visual Arts Dept (B-027) La Jolla CA 92093

LOOK, DONA
SCULPTOR
b Mequon, Wis, 1948. *Study:* Univ Wisconsin, Oshkosh, BA, 70. *Work:* Philadelphia Mus Art; Arkansas Arts Ctr, Little Rock; Erie Art Mus, Pa; Am Craft Mus, New York. *Exhib:* group show, Perimeter Gallery, Chicago, Ill, 83; Philadelphia Craft Show, Philadelphia Mus Art, 86; Craft Today, traveling exhib, 86-89; Tactile Vessel, Am Craft Mus, New York, 89; Artful Objects, Fort Wayne Mus Art, Ind, 89; Meeting Ground, The Forum, St Louis, Mo, 90. *Awards:* Fel Nat Endowment Arts, 88. *Bibliog:* Craft Today: Poetry of the Physical, Am Craft Mus, 86; Dona Look, Am Craft Mag, 85; Jack Lenor Larson (auth), The Tactile Vessel, Erie Art Mus, 89. *Media:* Fiber. *Mailing Add:* c/o Perimeter Gallery 750 N Orleans Chicago IL 60610

LOONEY, NORMAN
SCULPTOR
b Seattle, Wash, Oct 31, 42. *Study:* Calif State Univ, Long Beach, MFA(drawing & painting). *Work:* World Expo, 88. *Comn:* Security Pacific Nat Bank, Calif; Calif State Univ, Long Beach; Environetics Int, Los Angeles; Innovax Methods Group, Los Angeles; Naples Prof Ctr, Long Beach. *Exhib:* Los Angeles Co Mus Art; NC Mus Art, Raleigh; Birmingham Mus Fine Art, Ala; Montgomery Mus Art, Ala; Hunter Mus Art, Tenn; Miti Gallery, Stockholm, Swed, 77; Soc Prom Contemp Art, Athens, Greece, 77; Okla Art Ctr, Oklahoma City, 77; The Texas Thirty, Nave Mus, Victoria, Tex, 77; and others. *Pos:* Artist-in-resident, City Long Beach, Calif, 79-80. *Teaching:* Lectr, univs & cols in southern Calif & Southwest Tex State Univ. *Awards:* Trask Found Fel, Yaddo, NY, 77; Project Grant, Robinson Gallery, Houston, 78; Ossabow Island Project, Ga, 79; and others. *Media:* Mixed. *Mailing Add:* 1105 E Third St Long Beach CA 90802

LOONEY, ROBERT FAIN
CURATOR, LIBRARIAN
b Rocky Mount, NC, July 20, 25. *Study:* Univ NC, BA, 53, MA, 55, MS, 60. *Pos:* Librn, Art Dept, Free Libr Philadelphia, 61-64, cur, Print Collection, 64-85; retired. *Mem:* Mus Arts & Humanities Div & Picture Div, Spec Libr Asn (chmn, 72-73); Philadelphia Print Club (bd dirs, 76-85). *Res:* Early American prints; modern prints. *Publ:* Auth, Old Philadelphia in Early Photographs, Dover, 76; ed, Philadelphia Printmaking: Prints Before 1860, Free Libr Philadelphia, 76; coauth, The Prints of Benton Murdoch Spruance, Univ Pa Press, 86. *Mailing Add:* 427 N 20th St Philadelphia PA 19130

LOPEZ, MICHAEL JOHN
CERAMIST
b Los Angeles, Calif, Oct 19, 37. *Study:* Los Angeles City Col, 56-60; Calif Col Arts & Crafts, BFA & MFA, 63. *Work:* Oakland Mus, Calif; E B Crocker Art Gallery, Sacramento, Calif. *Comn:* Leslie Ceramics Supply Co, Berkeley, Calif. *Exhib:* 18th Nat Decorative Arts & Ceramics Exhib, Wichita Art Asn, Kans, 64; 23rd & 24th Ceramic Nat, Everson Mus Art, Syracuse, NY, 64 & 65 & traveling show, 65; Media 72, Western State Craft Competition, Civic Arts Gallery, Walnut Creek, Calif, 72; Calif Design 76, Pac Design Ctr, Los Angeles, 76. *Teaching:* Instr ceramics, Calif Col Arts & Crafts, 65-70 & Diablo Valley Col, 70- *Awards:* Am Craftsmen Coun Award of Merit, 2nd Biennial Calif Craftsman Exhib, Oakland Mus, 63; First Place Ceramics, Chicago Festival Art, 63; Asn San Francisco Potters Award, 71. *Bibliog:* Jacinto Quirarte (auth), Mexican American Artists, Univ Tex, 73. *Mem:* Asn San Francisco Potters. *Media:* Clay. *Mailing Add:* c/o Dept Art, Diablo Valley Col 321 Gulf Club Rd Pleasant Hill CA 94523

LOPEZ, RHODA LE BLANC
SCULPTOR, EDUCATOR
b Detroit, Mich, Mar 16, 12. *Study:* Detroit Art Acad, Wayne State Univ; Cranbrook Acad Art, with Maija Crotell; Scripps Col. *Work:* Detroit Inst Arts; Univ Wis-Madison; Scripps Col, Claremont, Calif; Juvenile Ct, City San Diego. *Comn:* Many banks & pvt & pub collections; fountain, All Souls Episcopal Church, San Diego; hist murals, San Diego, Calif; Home Fed Savings & Loan, San Juan Capistrano; Ramada Inn, Old Town, SDak. *Exhib:* Syracuse Nat, 49-55; Mich Craftsmen Ann, Detroit, 49-58; five shows, Scripps Invitational, 53-66; Allied Craftsmen Ann, San Diego, 60-76; Design 8-11, Pasadena, 65, 68 & 71; and many maj shows, US and abroad. *Pos:* Med artist, Univ Mich Med Sch, 53-59; founder & dir, Clay Dimensions, San Diego, 69-84. *Teaching:* Instr ceramics, Ann Arbor Potters Guild, Mich, 50-59, La Jolla Mus Art Ctr, Calif, 60-65 & Univ Calif Exten, San Diego, 65-78, Mira Costa Jr Col & Clay Dimensions, San Diego, Calif; lectr, Pac Arts Conf, 67; lectr series, San Diego Co Pub Schs, 72. *Bibliog:* Rhoda Le Blanc Lopez, Designers West, 71; Valerie Hatch (auth), article in Art West, 71; Marie Stanton (auth), A visit into Rhoda Lopez world of clay, San Diego Union, 1/72; and many others. *Mem:* African Arts Soc; Contemp Arts Soc, Retired OWL (Olders Women's League); SDak Mus Fine Arts & Retired Allied Craftsmen Teachers. *Media:* Clay. *Mailing Add:* 1020 Pacific Beach Dr San Diego CA 92109

LOPINA, LOUISE CAROL
PAINTER
b Chicago, Ill, Nov 24, 36. *Study:* Chicago Art Inst; Purdue Univ, BS; study with Lawrence Harris & Don Dennis. *Work:* Cincinnati Nat Hist Mus & Cincinnati Club, Cincinnati; Hartwood Club; Nissequoque Golf Club, St James, Long Island, New York; G & R Tackle Co. *Comn:* Dioram A Blackgroups: Asistencia Mission, San Bernardino Co Mus, 92. *Exhib:* Private exhibs, The Cincinnati Club, 81, Nissequoque Golf Club, NY, 86; Soc Animal Artists Exhibs, anns 72-90; Nature Interpreted, Cincinnati Mus Natural Hist, 80, 82 & 84; Wondrous Wildlife, Cincinnati Zoo, 83; Outdoor Expo, Albany, NY, 85; Nature of the Beast, Southern Alleghenies Mus Art, 86; Prestige Gallery: 1st & 2nd Ann Original Art Showcase, Can; Artist's Registry Exhib, The Dog Mus, 92; Whaletail, East African Wildlife Soc, 92; Wildlife West Art Festival, San Bernardino Co Mus Found. *Teaching:* Instr drawing & painting, USAF Acad-Officer's Wives Club, 72-75. *Awards:* Best in Show, Nat Nature Art Exhib, 78, 79 & 82; Selection for commemorative print, Snow Leopard Symposium, India, 86. *Bibliog:* Al Rosen & Faith Every (dirs), Louise Lopina's Art on the Wild Side, television feature program, 2/78; article, A sampling of assorted artists, Dayton Mag, 5-6/81. *Mem:* Nat Audubon Soc; Nature Conservancy; Soc Animal Artists (exhib co-chmn); Old English Sheepdog Club Am. *Media:* Oil, Watercolor. *Publ:* Illusr, A Cook's Tour of the Air Force Academy Vol II, AFA Officer's Wives Club, 72; The Complete Old English Sheepdog, Howell Book House, 76; Reptiles and Amphibians of Aullwood & Wild Flowers of Aullwood, Nat Audubon, 78; View from the top: Snow leopards, Color Print, 82; Old English Sheepdogs, 85; Shetland Sheepdogs, 88; Bulldog, 90. *Mailing Add:* 7 Calle Agua San Clemente CA 92673

LORAN, ERLE
PAINTER, WRITER
b Minneapolis, Minn, Oct 3, 05. *Study:* Univ Minn, 22-23; Minneapolis Sch Art, grad, 26; Chaloner Found Scholar Study Europe, 26-30; also with Hans Hofmann, New York, 54; Minneapolis Sch Art & Design, Hon MFA. *Work:* Univ Art Mus, Univ Calif, Berkeley; Smithsonian Inst, Washington, DC; San Francisco Mus Art; Denver Art Mus; and others. *Exhib:* Sixteen American Cities, Mus Mod Art, New York, 33; Five shows, Contemporary American Painting, Whitney Mus Am Art, New York, 37-52; American Painting & Sculpture, 38 & Int Exhibs Watercolors, 39-46, Art Inst Chicago; six shows, Krannert Art Mus, Univ Ill, 49-69; Recent Watercolors, Oakland Mus, 81; Paule Anglim Gallery, 88; John Berggruen Gallery, 89; Univ Art Mus, Berkeley,Calif, 91; and others. *Teaching:* Prof art, Univ Calif, Berkeley, 36-81, chmn dept art, 52-56, emer prof art, 81- *Awards:* Bronze Medal, Pepsi-Cola Nat, New York, 48; Artists' Coun Prize, San Francisco Mus Art, 56; Purchase Prize, Krannert Art Mus, 65; and others. *Bibliog:* Forbes Watson (auth), American Painting Today, Am Fedn Arts, 39; Allen S Weller (auth), Contemporary American Painting, Univ Ill, 49-69; Nathaniel Pousette-Dart (auth), American Painting Today, Hastings House, 56. *Mem:* Arts Club, Univ Berkeley, Calif. *Media:* Acrylic, Watercolor. *Publ:* Auth, Cézanne's Composition, Univ Calif Press, 43; Cézanne, Les Peintres Celebres, Ed Art Lucien Mazenod, Geneva & Paris, 48 & rev ed, 85; Trial by juries, Art News, 12/52; Cézanne in 1952, Art Inst Chicago Quart, 2/52; Cézanne and Lichtenstein: Problems of transformation, Artforum, 9/63. *Mailing Add:* 10 Kenilworth Ct Berkeley CA 94707

LORBER, D MARTIN H B
CONSULTANT
b Macon, Ga, July 22, 43. *Study:* Univ NC, BA, 65; CCNY, BS, 92. *Mem:* Nippon Bijutsu Token Hozon Kyokai; Oriental Ceramic Soc; Asia Soc, New York; Pres Coun; Token Soc, Great Britain. *Interests:* Japanese Swords & Fittings; Korean, Sung ceramics; Impressionist & Post-Impressionist paintings. *Publ:* Auth, The Eugene W Kettering Collection of Japanese Metalwork, Dayton Art Inst, 75; Japanese sword fittings, 5/77 & Japanese Buddhist paintings, 7/78, Arts of Asia; coauth, 100 Masterpieces from the Collection of Dr Walter Ames Compton, Christie's, 2/92; coauth, Parts I, II & III, In: Japanese Swords & Swords Fittings, Christie's, 92. *Mailing Add:* 304 E 20th St New York NY 10003

LORBER, RICHARD
CRITIC, EDUCATOR
b New York, NY, Dec 9, 46. *Study:* Columbia Col, with Meyer Schapiro & Lionel Trilling, BA(lit & art hist), 67; Columbia Univ, with Meyer Schapiro & Linda Nochlin, MA(art hist), 70, EdD(art), 77. *Pos:* Ed, Dance Scope Mag, 74-; contrib ed, Arts Mag, 75-; community liaison, Mus of Mod Art, 76-77; critic & contribr, Artforum, Arts Mag, 77-; adv panelist, NY State Coun on Arts, 78-; proj dir, Nat Video Clearinghouse, 79-; consult, Electronic Arts Intermix, 81; pres, Fox-Lorber Assoc Inc, 81- *Teaching:* Instr art hist, Parsons Sch of Design, 74-77; asst prof art & art educ, Grad Sch of Educ, New York Univ, 77-79. *Publ:* Coauth, The Gap, McGraw-Hill, 68; auth, articles in Arts in Soc & Filmmakers Newsletter, 77; contribr, Video Art, Dutton, 78; article, Videodance, Millenium Film J, 12/81. *Mailing Add:* 419 Park Ave S New York NY 10016

LORBER, STEPHEN NEIL
PAINTER, PRINTMAKER
b New York, NY, Aug 30, 43. *Study:* Pratt Inst, BFA; Brooklyn Col, MFA; Yale Univ, Stoekel fel, 64. *Work:* Chicago Art Inst; Okla Art Ctr, Oklahoma City; Western NMex Univ, Silver City; Roswell Mus & Art Ctr, NMex; Am Tel & Tel Co; Chase Manhattan Bank, New York; and others. *Exhib:* Weatherspoon Art Gallery, Univ NC, Greensboro; one-man shows, Milliken Gallery, New York, 81, 83 & 85; William Proctor Mus, Utica, NY, 82; Contemporary Arts Ctr, New York, 82; Fendrick Gallery, Washington, DC, 83; David Settler Gallery, Houston, Tex, 84; Robert L Kidd Assocs, Birmingham, Miss, 85; John Szoke Gallery New York, 87; Goddard Ctr Arts, Ardmore OK, 89; Chicago Intl Art Expos 89,90. *Awards:* Artist in Residence Grant, Roswell Mus & Art Ctr, NMex; Yaddo Fel, 71 & 75; Nat Endowment Arts Fel, 76-77. *Bibliog:* Garrit Henry (auth), Art News, summer 76; Allen Ellenweog (auth), Arts Mag, 9/77; Stephen Yoskowitz (auth), Arts Mag, Vol 55, No 9, 5/81. *Media:* All. *Mailing Add:* RD 3 Box 198 Greenwich NY 12834

LORCA DI CORCIA, PHILIP
PHOTOGRAPHER
Study: Boston Mus Fine Arts, dipl, 75, post grad certif, 76; Yale Univ, MFA, 79. *Work:* Fogg Art Mus; Boston Mus Fine Arts; Yale Univ Art Gallery; Biblioteque Nationale, Paris; Mus Mod Art, Metrop Mus Art, New York; Los Angeles Co Mus Art; San Francisco Mus Mod Art; Addison Gallery Am Art, Andover, Mass. *Exhib:* Solo shows, Zeus Arte, Milan, Italy, 85 & Photogrs Gallery, London, 91; Univ Toronto Art Gallery, 91; Metrop Mus Art, 91; Pleasures and Terrors of Domestic Comfort, MOMA, 91-92; More Than One Photography, MOMA, 92. *Awards:* Photogr Fel, Nat Endowment Arts, 80, 87 & 89; Guggenheim Fel, 87-88. *Mailing Add:* 55 Hudson St No 8D New York NY 10013

LORCINI, GINO
SCULPTOR, MURALIST
b Plymouth, Eng, July 7, 23; Can citizen. *Study:* Montreal Mus Sch Art. *Work:* Nat Gallery Can, Ottawa; Mus Art Contemporain, Montreal; Chase Manhattan Bank, New York; Art Gallery Ont, Toronto; Matsushita Corp, Tokyo; and others. *Comn:* Mural, Nat Arts Ctr, Ottawa, 68; mural, Montreal Forum, Que, 69; fountain sculpture, Ste Anne's Hosp, PQ, 70; sculpture, Nat Defence Bldg, Ottawa, 72; Ontario Prov Court House, London, 73; Bell Canada, Trinity Square, Toronto, 84; Congress Ctr, Ottawa, 85; CFPL Broadcasting Sta, London, Ont, 87. *Exhib:* Op from Montreal, Fleming-Hull Mus, 66; Sculpture 67, Toronto, 67; Surv 68, Montreal, 68; one-man traveling exhib, Atlantic Provinces Mus, Can, 69; 3-D Into the 70's, Art Gallery Ont, Toronto, 70; Constructivist Heritage, Harbourfront Gallery, Toronto, 81; and other group & one-man shows. *Teaching:* Asst prof painting & sculpture, McGill Univ, 60-68; resident artist, Univ Western Ont, 69-72. *Awards:* Jessie Dow Award, Montreal Mus Fine Arts, 65; Arts Award, Can Coun, 68. *Bibliog:* M Gaulin (auth), Sculptor Lorcini, Time, 68; D Sanders (auth), Gino Lorcini, Bus Quart, 71. *Mem:* Royal Can Acad Arts Coun. *Media:* Aluminum, Bronze. *Publ:* Coauth, Creative response, McGill J Educ, 67. *Mailing Add:* 326 Old Brock Rd Greensville ON L9H 5H6 Canada

LORD, CAROLYN MARIE
PAINTER
b Los Angeles, Calif, Oct 6, 56. *Study:* Painting Workshops, with Millard Sheets, George Post, Rex Brandt, Robert E Wood, 76-83; Principia Col, Elsah, Ill, BA(fine arts), 78; San Francisco Tapestry Workshop, with Jean-Pierre Larochette, 81. *Work:* Principia Col, Elsah, Ill; Scripps Col, Claremont, Calif; Kaiser Permanente, Pleasanton, Calif; Bank A Levy, Ventura, Calif. *Comn:* Painting for label, and auction, Beringer Brothers Vineyards, St Helena, Calif, 85. *Exhib:* One-woman shows, Northeastern Nev Mus, Elko, 85 & 90; Watercolor USA Watercolor Now, Springfield Art Mus, Mo, 91; Watercolor Biennial, Triton Mus, Santa Clara, Calif, 92; Midwest Watercolor Soc, Neville Pub Mus, Green Bay, Wis, 92; Gardens Real and Imagined, Sun Gallery, Hayward, Calif, 92; and others. *Awards:* Adirondack Award Second Place, Adironack Nat Exhib, Rouse Co, Baltimore, 87; Juror's Award Second Place, San Diego Watercolor Soc, 88; Springfield Mus Cash Award, Watercolor USA, 88. *Bibliog:* Sandy Preston (auth), Carolyn Lord, US Art Mag, 1-2/89; Lynn Kari Petrich (auth), Painting floral subjects, Watercolor '89, Am Artist, winter, 89; Robin Worthington (auth), The lightness of being artistic, San Jose Mercury News, 3/21/90. *Mem:* Watercolor USA Hon Soc; Nat Watercolor Soc; WatercolorWest; Westcoast Watercolor Soc; Eastbay Watercolor Soc. *Media:* Watercolor on Paper. *Publ:* Illusr, Musings of a fence painter, 2/3/86, View at the end of the walk, 9/1/87 South seas Romeo and Juliet, 9/27/88, The Home Forum, Christian Sci Monitor; contribr, Exploring Painting, Davis Publ, 88. *Dealer:* Stary-Sheets Fine Art Galleries 14988 San Canyon Ave Suite 1-5 Irvine CA 92718. *Mailing Add:* 1993 DeVaca Way Livermore CA 94550

LORD, MICHAEL HARRY
DEALER, CURATOR
b Milwaukee, Wis, Nov 19, 54. *Study:* Univ Wis-Milwaukee. *Pos:* Asst to dir, Irving Galleries, 68-77; owner & dir, Michael H Lord Gallery, 78- *Mem:* Milwaukee Art Dealers Asn (pres, 81-); Wis Coalition Arts & Human Needs (bd dirs, 83-). *Specialty:* Contemporary American art; masters in photography and sculpture. *Mailing Add:* 420 E Wisconsin Milwaukee WI 53202

LORELLI (SVOBODA), ELVIRA MAE
SCULPTOR, PAINTER
b Upland, Calif, May 31, 27. *Study:* Pomona Col, BA, 50; Claremont Grad Sch, Scripps Col, MA(art educ), 61; Claremont Grad Sch & Univ Ctr, MA(art), 69. *Work:* Trona High Sch, Calif; Barstow Centennial Park, Calif. *Comn:* Murals, USO Club House, 76, Baptist Church, 80, Methodist Church, 84, Barstow, Calif; stained glass window, St Joseph Church, Barstow, 86; bronze reliefs, Rotary Club, Barstow, 90. *Exhib:* Around the World, Nat Art Appreciation Soc, New Orleans, 84; Chaffee Community Art Show, Ont Mus & Gallery, Calif, 86; Fine Arts Inst Ann Art Show, Mus Art, San Bernardino Co, Calif, 87; Sixth Ann Fine Arts Show, SW Sculptors Asn, Victoriville, Calif, 88; Calico Fine Arts Show, Calico Ghost Town, Calif, 84-92; and others. *Teaching:* Dept head art & art instr, Barstow Community Col, 62-82; art instr, Univ Calif, Riverside, 78-87 & Chapman Col, 79-84. *Awards:* Nat Art Appreciation Soc, 84. *Bibliog:* Barbara Phillips (auth), Artists of Cool Water Ranch, Daggett, Calif, 87-; Around the World, Nat Art Appreciation Soc, 84. *Mem:* Southwest Sculptors; Gem Carvers Guild Int; Fine Arts Inst; Chaffee Community Art Asn. *Media:* Bronze; Watercolor, Oil. *Publ:* Auth, Artists USA Inc, 1977-78, 77; Directory of Portrait Artists, Am Portrait Soc, 85. *Mailing Add:* 29205 Exeter St Barstow CA 92311

LORENTZ, PAULINE
PAINTER, INSTRUCTOR
b Newark, NJ. *Study:* Newark Sch Fine & Indust Arts, NJ, grad; Art Students League; also with John R Grabach. *Exhib:* Am Artists Prof League Grand Nat, New York, 65, 67-69 & 86-92; Expos Intercontinentale, Monaco & Dieppe, France, 67-68; 24th Am Drawing Biennial, Norfolk Mus Arts & Sci, Va, 71; Nat Exhib, Mus Fine Arts, Springfield, Mass, 71-73; Smithsonian Traveling Exhib, US, 71-73. *Teaching:* Instr, Summit Art Ctr, NJ, 62-87, Art Ctr NJ, Orange, 73-80 & NJ Ctr Visual Arts, 87- *Awards:* Gold Medals for Drawing, 67, 69 & 70, Catherine Lorillard Worlfe Art Club; Am Artists Prof League Gold Medal Graphics Award, 67 & 90, Gold Medal Oil Painting; Arts Atlantic Award, Gloucester, Mass, 72; and many others. *Bibliog:* Philbrook Smith (auth), article, NJ Mus & Arts Mag, 2/64; article, Palette Talk, Vol 32, 77; article, Am Artist Mag, 4/84. *Mem:* Am Artists Prof League (pres, NJ chap, 85-88, dir, 86-); Catharine Lorillard Wolfe Art Club; Hudson Valley Art Asn, NY; Acad Artists Asn, Mass; Rockport Art Asn, Mass. *Media:* Oil, Charcoal. *Mailing Add:* 20 Southview Dr Berkeley Heights NJ 07922

LORING, JOHN
PAINTER, PRINTMAKER
b Chicago, Ill, Nov 23, 39. *Study:* Yale Univ, BA, 60; Ecole des Beaux Arts, Paris, 61-64; printmaking with Johnny Friedlaender, Paris, 62-64. *Work:* Metrop Mus Art, Whitney Mus Am Art, Mus Mod Art, New York; Art Inst Chicago; Boston Mus Fine Arts. *Comn:* Mural, US Customs Serv, Main Hall, US Customhouse, World Trade Ctr, New York, 74; three posters, New York Cult Ctr, 74; murals, Prudential Life Insurance Co, Eastern Home Off, Woodbridge, NJ, 76; outdoor mural proj, Nat Endowment Arts, Scranton, Pa, 77; murals, Nat Hq, Western Savings, Philadelphia, 79. *Exhib:* Silkscreen: History of a Medium, Philadelphia Mus Art, 71; Realism Now, New York Cult Ctr, 72; one-man shows, Baltimore Mus Art, 72 & Long Beach Mus Art, Calif, 75; Biennale of Graphic Art, Ljubljana, Yugoslavia, 73 & 77; Intergrafia 74 & 76, Krakow, Poland; Painting & Sculpture Today, Indianapolis Mus Art, 74; Silkscreen Prints, Chicago Art Inst, 75; Pace Editions, New York, 77. *Pos:* Art ed, Deleg World Bulletin, UN, 72; contribr, Print Collector's Newsletter, 73-75 & Art in Am, 77-; assoc ed & contribr, Arts Mag, 73-; contrib ed, Archit Digest, 76-; design dir & sr vpres, Tiffany & Co, 79- *Teaching:* Distinguished vis prof art, Univ Calif, Davis, 77. *Awards:* Fourth Prize, Intergrafia 74, Krakow; Edith Wharton Award, Design & Art Soc, New York, 88. *Bibliog:* Ellen Lubell (auth), John Loring, 2/74 & Mario Amaya (auth), John Loring, 2/78, Arts Mag; Robert Hughes (auth), Murals without walls, 6/79. *Media:* Oil; Photo Silkscreens. *Publ:* Auth, Marisol Prints (catalog), New York Cult Ctr, 73; David Hockney: Drawings (catalog), Dayton's Gallery 12, 74; coauth, Multiples, Neuen Berliner Kunstvereins, 74; Tiffany Taste, 86, Tiffany's 150 Years, 87, The Tiffany Wedding, 88 & Tiffany Parties, 89, Doubleday. *Mailing Add:* 860 Fifth Ave New York NY 10021

LOSAVIO, SAMUEL
SCULPTOR, PAINTER
b Baton Rouge, La, Mar 15, 52. *Study:* La State Univ, BFA, 73, MFA, 79. *Work:* Valencia Community Col, Orlando, Fla. *Exhib:* Surrealism Continued & Southeast 7-11, Southeastern Ctr Contemp Art, Winston-Salem, NC, 88; Louisiana Abstractions, Contemp Art Ctr, New Orleans, 88; Birmingham Biennial V, Birmington Mus Art, 89; 22nd Bradley Nat Print & Drawing Exhib, Bradley Univ, 89; Working on Paper, Contemp Am Drawing, High Mus Art, Atlanta, 90. *Teaching:* Asst prof, found coordr, Univ Fla, 90. *Awards:* Purchase Award, Col Mainland, 85; Fel, Nat Endowment Arts, 87; Southeastern Ctr Comtemp Art Fel, RJ Reynolds, 87; Nat Endowment Arts Fel, 89; Juror's Award, Orlando Mus Art, Ann Juried Exhib, 90. *Mailing Add:* 2621 NW 69th Terr Gainesville FL 32606

LOTHROP, KRISTIN CURTIS
SCULPTOR
b Tucson, Ariz, Feb 8, 30. *Study:* Bennington Col, BA; also sculpture with George Demetrois, 4 yrs. *Exhib:* Nat Sculpture Soc, 67-71; Hudson Valley Art Asn, 68; Nat Acad Design, 68-71; Allied Artists Am, 69. *Awards:* Mrs Louis Bennett Award, Nat Sculpture Soc, 67; Thomas R Proctor Award, Nat Acad Design, 68, Daniel Chester French Award, 70; Dessie Greer Prize, Nat Acad Design, 69; Liskin Purchase, Nat Sculpture Soc, 86. *Mem:* Nat Sculpture Soc; New England Sculptors' Asn. *Media:* Bronze, Wood, Stone. *Mailing Add:* 17 Bridge St Manchester MA 01944

LOTRINGER, SYLVERE
WRITER
b Paris, France, Oct 15, 38; US citizen. *Study:* Ecole Pratique des Hautes Etudes, Paris, BA & MA, 65, PhD 67. *Pos:* Sr mellon critic, CAL Arts, Calif, 90-91; vis critic, Art Ctr, Pasadena, 91-92. *Teaching:* Prof French Lit & Philo, Columbia Univ, 72- *Publ:* Auth, Foreign Agent Art & Theory, Merve Verlag, Berlin, 91; Photography & Death, Interrupted Life, New Mus Contemp Art, 91; Art & The Commodification of Theory, Flash Art, Milan, 91; Hyperreal, Jean Raudrillard, Disappearance of Art, St Martin's Press, 92; Immaculate Conception, Artscribe, London, 92. *Mailing Add:* 522 Philosophy Hall Columbia University New York NY 10027

LOTTERMAN, HAL
PAINTER, EDUCATOR
b Chicago, Ill, Sept 29, 20. *Study:* Univ Ill, BFA, 45; Univ Iowa, MFA, 46. *Work:* Butler Inst Am Art, Youngstown, Ohio; Akron Art Inst; Ohio Univ; Ball State Univ; Mulvane Art Ctr, Topeka, Kans. *Exhib:* Metrop Mus Art, New York, 50; Carnegie Inst Int, Pittsburgh, 52; Pa Acad Fine Arts Am, Philadelphia, 53; Nat Acad Design Ann, New York, 54; Art USA 58, New York, 58. *Teaching:* Instr art, Univ Iowa, 47-50; instr art, Toledo Mus Art, 50-56; prof art, Univ Wis-Madison, 65-86, prof emer, 86- *Awards:* Tiffany Fund Painting Scholar, 51; Univ Iowa Purchase Award, 57. *Media:* Oil. *Mailing Add:* 2337 Atwood Ave Madison WI 53704

LOTTES, JOHN WILLIAM
EDUCATOR, ADMINISTRATOR
b Minneapolis, Minn, Apr 8, 34. *Study:* Concordia Jr Col, St Paul, Minn, AA, 53; Minneapolis Sch Art, BFA, 60; Hochschule Gestaltung, Ulm, Ger, 58-59; Univ Iowa, 67; Minneapolis Col Art & Design, Hon MFA, 73; William Jewel Col, Hon LL, 82. *Pos:* Dean col & registr, Kansas City Art Inst, 66-68, pres, 70-83; dir planning & develop, Corcoran Gallery & Sch Art, Washington, DC, 68-69; asst to pres acad affairs, Calif Col Arts & Crafts, Oakland, 69-70; comnr, Munic Arts Comn, Kansas City, 79-83; bd dirs, Kansas City Arts Coun, 79-83, treas, 79-80, pres, 80-83; pres, Minneapolis Soc Fine Arts, 83-86; consult, School of Visual Arts, New York, 86-87; pres, Ore Sch Arts & Crafts, Portland, 87- *Teaching:* Chmn indust design, Minneapolis Sch Art, 62-63; asst prof indust design, Kansas City Art Inst, 64-66. *Awards:* Citation, Mid Am Col Art Asn, 83. *Mem:* Life mem, Fel Nat Asn Sch Art (bd dirs, 72-83, pres, 79-81); Portland Arts Alliance (pres, 90); Col Art Asn, 72- *Mailing Add:* c/o Art Inst Southern Calif 2222 Laguna Canyon Rd Laguna Beach CA 92651

LOTZ, STEVEN DARRYL
PAINTER, EDUCATOR
b Los Angeles, Calif, Dec 28, 38. *Study:* Univ Calif, Los Angeles, BFA, 61; Univ Fla, Gainesville, with Hiram Williams, MFA, 63; Acad Fine Arts, Vienna, Austria, 65-66. *Work:* Jacksonville Art Mus, Fla; Orlando International Airport; His Royal Highness, Prince Phillip, London; Palace Hotel, Lake Buena Vista; Universal Studios, Orlando. *Comn:* Fla Solar Energy Ctr; Walt Disney World, Fla. *Exhib:* Solo exhibs, Jacksonville Art Mus, Fla, 70, Galerie Zeitgendssische Kunst, Hamburg, WGer, 73 Orlando Mus Art, Orlando Fla, 73 & traveling exhib, Ringling Mus Art 74-76; Allalachian State Univ, NC, 90; Stetson Univ, Deland, Fla, 88; Univ of Tampa, Fla, 89. *Teaching:* Asst prof drawing & painting, Jacksonville Univ, Fla, 66-68; chmn, Univ Cent Fla, Orlando, 68-78, prof drawing & painting 68-; vis exchange instr, Edinburgh Col Art, 78-79 & 80-81. *Awards:* First Prize, Jacksonville Arts Festival, 65; First Prize, Ocala Arts Festival, Ocala Nat Bank, 69; State Fla Grant. *Bibliog:* Roger Ortmayer (dir), Space Cathedral (film), CBS TV, New York, 72; Frank Martin (auth), article, Art Voices South, 11-12/79; Egberdien Van Rossum (auth), article, Bres 99 Mag, 4/83. *Media:* Oil, Acrylic. *Mailing Add:* Dept Art Univ Cent Fla, Box 25000 Orlando FL 32816

LOUGHLIN, JOHN LEO
PAINTER
b Worcester, Mass, Apr 11, 31. *Study:* Worcester Art Mus Sch; Clark Univ, AB, 57; Bridgewater State Col, EdM, 64; also with Eliot O'Hara, Edgar Whitney & Barse Miller. *Work:* M & M Karolik Collection, Boston Mus Fine Art; Cumberland RI Housing for Elderly; Old Colony Savings Bank, Providence, RI; US Naval War Col, Newport, RI; Gen Elec Corp, Schenectady, NY. *Exhib:* Boston Arts Festival, 55; Acad Artists Show, Springfield, Mass, 59; Bristol Art Mus Show, RI, 70; Am Watercolor Soc, Nat Acad Design Galleries, New York, 71 & 83; Providence Art Club Open Watercolor Show, 72. *Pos:* Illusr cartogr, Nat Geog Mag, 58-59; head dept art, US Naval War Col, 61-68; art dir, WSBE-TV, Providence, 68-88. *Teaching:* Pvt instr, 69-; vis lectr watercolor, Providence Col, 70-72. *Awards:* Gold Medal, Providence Watercolor Club, 83; Chas P Fonda Award, Rockport Art Asn, 83; Medal of Honor, Oil Painting, Acad Artists, 86. *Bibliog:* Articles, Am Artist Mag, 6/88. *Mem:* Assoc Am Watercolor Soc; Providence Art Club; RI Watercolor Soc (vpres, 70-72, pres, 72); artist mem Rockport Art Asn; Allied Artists, New York. *Media:* Oil, Watercolor. *Publ:* Illusr, Nat Geog Mag, 58; Mass Wildlife Mag, 59; contribr & illusr, Salt Water Sportsman Mag, 59; illusr, Naval Rev, 67; New Eng Sch Develop Coun Publ. *Dealer:* Limerock Studio & Gallery Lincoln RI 02865. *Mailing Add:* 124 Angell Rd Lincoln RI 02865

LOVE, FRANCES TAYLOR
WRITER, PUBLISHER
b Salina, Kans, Apr 25, 26. *Study:* Univ Tex, BA(journalism & speech); studied television writing, Univ Houston; sem in Gt Brit & other Europ study, Smithsonian Inst. *Collections Arranged:* Steamboats Along the Louisiana Bayous (auth, catalog), 69, 19th Century Painters in Louisiana (auth, catalog), 72, Louisiana French Furnishings: 1750-1830 (ed, catalog), 74, Haitian Voodoo Art (auth, catalog), 76 & Victorian Decorative Arts in Louisiana (auth, catalog), 77, Art Ctr Southwestern La. *Pos:* Pub relations dir, Lafayette Art Asn, 60-63; dir, Art Ctr Southwestern La, Lafayette, 65-83. *Res:* Louisiana colonial decorative arts; Texas and Louisiana decorative art and architecture; Victorian decorative art. *Publ:* Auth & ed, My Home is Austin, Texas, 58 & Here is South Louisiana, 65, Tribune Press. *Mailing Add:* PO Box 51998 Lafayette LA 70505

LOVE, JIM
SCULPTOR
b Amarillo, Tex, 1927. *Work:* Menil Collection, Houston; Mus Mod Art, New York; Whitney Mus Am Art, New York; Univ Houston, University Park; Hobby Airport, Houston; Mus Fine Arts, Houston. *Exhib:* Dallas Mus Contemp Art; Mus Mod Art, New York; Mus Fine Arts, Houston; Whitney Mus Am Art, New York; Contemp Arts Mus, Houston; Rice Univ Mus, Houston; and others. *Media:* Steel. *Dealer:* Janie C Lee Gallery 1209 Berthea Houston TX 77006. *Mailing Add:* 5009 Blossom St Houston TX 77007

LOVE, RICHARD HENRY
DEALER, HISTORIAN
b Schneider, Ind, Dec 27, 39. *Study:* Univ of Md, Europe; Bloom Col, Chicago Heights, Ill; Univ of Ill, Chicago; Northwestern Univ, Evanston, Ill; Villa Schifanoia, Florence, Italy; independent study in Europe. *Comn:* Murals, Flak Kaserne Bldg, US Army, Augsburg, Ger, 62 & Dorchester Club, Ramada Inn, Dolton, Ill, 65. *Exhib:* Springfield Art League 67th Nat Exhib, George Walter Vincent Smith Art Mus, Mass, 86; Art for Peace, Univ Union Art Gallery, Calif Polytech State Univ, San Luis Obispo, Calif, 87; Fourth Ann Artspace Nat, Artspace, Sacramento, Calif, 87; Inalienable Rights, Alienable Rights, Contemp Art Workshop, Chicago Artists Coalition, Chicago, Ill, 89; Lake Worth, Fla Art League, 49th Anniversary Nat Juried Art Competition, 90; solo-exhib, Midwest Mus Am Art, Elkhart, Ind, 91. *Pos:* Art critic, Star-Tribune Newspaper, Chicago Heights, Ill, formerly; art commentator, WNIB, WBBM & WEFM radio, Chicago, formerly, WCIU TV, Chicago, 78-; pres & owner, R H Love Galleries, Inc, Chicago, 67-; chmn bd, Haase-Mumm Publ Co, Chicago, 81- & Amart Book and Catalog Distributing Co, 81-; television producer & host, Am Art Forum, Cent Educ Network & World Net, US Info Agency. *Teaching:* Instr art, Park Forest, Ill; prof art hist, Prairie State Col, Chicago Heights, Ill; commentator art hist & RH Love on American Art, WCTU-TV, Chicago, 77-87. *Bibliog:* Victoria Lautman (auth), An American Cache at Chicago's RH Galleries, Archit Dig, Los Angeles, Calif, 11/87; Bob Herguth (auth), Chicago Profile: Richard H Love, Chicago Sun-Times,

9/4/87; Sherri Gilman (auth), Gallery Owner Strives to Promote American Artists, Inside Lincoln Park, Chicago, 11/29/89. *Mem:* Trustee, Lincoln Acad Ill; Ill Arts Coun, Exhib Develop Comt (chmn, 90); Ill Acad Fine Art (pres). *Media:* Oil, Acrylic. *Res:* 18th, 19th & 20th century American art, most particularly American Impressionism; American impressionists, masters of American impressionism, Theodore Earl Butler, Louis Ritman, Lawton Parker; John Barber, Robert Goodnough, Kenneth Noland. *Specialty:* 18th, 19th & 20th century American paintings; contemporary American paintings. *Publ:* Auth, Harriet Randall Lumis: 1870-1953 (exhib catalog), 77, William Chadwick (1879-1962) (exhib catalog), 78, Cassatt: The Independent, 80, R H Love Galleries; John Barber: The Artist, The Man, 81 & Theodore Earl Butler: Emergence from Monet's Shadow, 83, Haase-Mumm Publ; Louis Ritman, From Chicago to Giverny: How Louis Ritman was Influenced by Lawton Parker and other Midwestern Impressionists, Haase-Mumm Publ, 90. *Mailing Add:* c/o R H Love Galleries 100 E Ohio Chicago IL 60611

LOVEJOY, MARGOT R
MULTI-MEDIA, EDUCATOR
b Campbellton, NB, Can, Oct 21, 30. *Study:* Mt Allison Univ, with Alex Colville & Lauren Harris, 47-49; St Martins Sch Art, London, cert(design & illus), 50; Pratt Graphics Ctr, with Ponce de Leon, Stasik & Zimilies, 66-71. *Work:* Bibliotheque Nat, Paris; Dresden Mus, Ger; Hunterian Mus, Glasgow; Mus Mod Art Libr Collection & Neuberger Mus, New York. *Comn:* Prints, John Barton Fine Arts, New York, 65-72; membership print, Pratt Graphics Ctr, 69; etchings, Nabis Fine Arts, New York, 73-74. *Exhib:* Solo exhibs, Atlantic Prov Art Gallery Asn, traveling exhib, NB Mus, Can 75-76, Soho 20, 84, PS1 Mus, Inst Contemp Art, 87, Labyrinth, East End Arts, 88 &R Alternative Mus, Islip Art Mus, New York, 92; Digital Visions, IBM Galleries, New York, 88; Committed to Print, Mus Mod Art, New York, 88; On the Cutting Edge, Fine Arts Mus Long Island, Hempstead, NY, 89; Philadelphia Print Club Invitational, Pa, 89; Burning in Hell, Franklin Furnace, 91, Artists of Conscience, Alternative Mus, 91, At the Intersection of Cinemat the Book, Granary Books, New York, 92; Mostra da Gravura Mostra America, Curitiba, Brazil, 92. *Teaching:* Instr, Pratt Graphics Ctr, New York, 72-79 & Parsons Sch Design, New York, 75-78; prof fine art, State Univ NY, Purchase, 78- *Awards:* Special Project Grant, Art Matters Inc, 89; NY State Coun Arts Media Grant, 92. *Bibliog:* Helen Harris (auth), Back to the future, as seen by a black box, New York Times, 4/12/92; Artists of conscience, Art News, 4/92; Nancy Princenthal (auth), Cinematic books, bookish cinema, Print Collector's Newsletter, Vol XXIII, No 1, Mar-Apr. *Mem:* Soc Am Graphic Artists (vpres, 83); Col Art Asn; Women's Caucus Art. *Media:* Projection Installation; Mixed Media. *Publ:* Auth, Labyrinth, Ctr Ed, State Univ NY, Purchase, 90; The Politics of Presence (exhib catalog), Alternative Mus, New York, 90; Black Box (exhib catalog), Islip Art Mus, 92; Thoughts on Technology, the Book Arts & Postmodernism (essay for exhib); Off the Shelf and Online, MCBA, Minneapolis, 92. *Mailing Add:* 166-04 81st Ave Jamaica NY 11432

LOVELESS, JIM
PAINTER, EDUCATOR
b Saginaw, Mich, Apr 24, 35. *Study:* DePauw Univ, AB, 57; Ind Univ, MFA, 60. *Work:* Munson-Williams-Proctor Inst, Utica, NY; Ithaca Col Mus of Art, NY; Oneida Valley Nat Bank, Hamilton, NY; Chase Manhattan Bank, New York; Colgate Univ, Hamilton, NY. *Exhib:* Munson-Williams-Proctor Inst Ann, Utica; one-man shows, Kalamazoo Col, Mich & Everson Mus, Syracuse, NY, 77 & Gettysburg Col, Pa, 90; New Visions Gallery, Ithaca, NY, 89; and others. *Teaching:* Asst prof studio & art hist, Hope Col, Holland, Mich, 60-64 & Univ Ky, Lexington, 64-66; prof studio & art hist, Colgate Univ, Hamilton, 66- *Awards:* Heffner Award, Grand Rapids Mus of Art Ann, 62; Yaddo Fel; Millay Colony Fel, 86. *Mem:* Col Art Asn. *Media:* Watercolor, Acrylic. *Mailing Add:* Dept Fine Arts Colgate Univ Hamilton NY 13346

LOVELL, MARGARETTA MARKLE
CURATOR, HISTORIAN
b Pittsburgh, Pa, Oct 30, 44. *Study:* Smith Col, BA, 66; Univ Del, MA, 75; Yale Univ, PhD, 80. *Collections Arranged:* American Painting, 1730-1960: A Selection from the Collection of Mr & Mrs John D Rockefeller, 3rd, Nat Mus Western Art, Tokyo, 82; William Morris: The Sanford and Helen Berger Collection, Univ Mus, Univ Calif, Berkeley, 84; Venice: The American View, 1860-1920, Fine Arts Mus San Francisco & Cleveland Mus, 84-85. *Pos:* Cur Am painting, San Francisco Mus, 81-85. *Teaching:* Actg instr, Am art, Yale Univ, 77-80, asst prof, 80-81; asst prof Am art, Univ Calif, Berkeley, 81-90; Dittman prof Am studies, Col William & Mary, 90-92; assoc prof hist art, Univ Calif, Berkeley, 92- *Awards:* Ralph Henry Gabriel Prize, Am Studies Asn, 81; Am Coun Learned Socs Grant, 89; Nat Endowment Humanities Res Fel, 89-90. *Publ:* Auth, Reading Portraits: Social Images and Self-Images in Eighteenth-Century American Family Portraits, Winterthur Portfolio, winter 87; A Visitable Past: Views of Venice by American Artists 1860-1915, Univ Chicago Press, 89; Such Furniture as Will be Most Profitable: The Business of Cabinetmaking in Eighteenth-Century Newport, Winterthur Portfolio, spring 91. *Mailing Add:* Dept Hist Art-405 Doe Libr Univ Calif Berkeley CA 94720

LOVELL, TOM
PAINTER, ILLUSTRATOR
b New York, NY, Feb 5, 09. *Study:* Syracuse Univ, BFA. *Work:* Explorers Club, New York; US Merchant Marine Acad, King's Point, NY; Nat Cowboy Hall Fame, Oklahoma City. *Comn:* Hist paintings, US Marine Corps, 45, Life Mag, 61, Nat Geog Soc, Washington, 65-68 & Abell-Hanger Found, Midland, Tex, 69-73. *Exhib:* Soc Illustrators, New York, 63; solo exhib, Syracuse Univ Centennial, Lubin House, 70; Nat Cowboy Hall Fame, 73-83, Retrospective Show, 92. *Awards:* Prix West, Cowboy Hall Fame, 74 & 86; Gold Medals, Cowboy Artists Am, 75-77 & 80 & Nat Acad Western Art Show, 76-78 & 82-83. *Bibliog:* Norman Kent (auth), Tom Lovell & his work, Am Artists. *Mem:* Soc Illustrators; Cowboy Artists Am; Nat Acad Western Art. *Media:* Oil. *Publ:* Auth, Persimmon Hill, Nat Cowboy Hall Fame. *Mailing Add:* 3 Tano Rd RR 4 Santa Fe NM 87501

LOVING, AL
PAINTER, COLLAGE ARTIST
b Detroit, Mich, Sept 19, 35. *Study:* Univ Ill, BFA, 63; Univ Mich, MFA, 65. *Work:* Metrop Mus Art & Whitney Mus Am Art, New York; Detroit Inst Art, Mich; Toledo Mus Art, Ohio; Albright Knox Art Gallery, Buffalo, NY. *Comn:* Painting, JFK Int Airport, New York, 70; painting, comn by Nelson Rockefeller, Albany, NY, 73; mural, Renaissance Comt, Detroit, Mich, 73; painting, VA Hospital, Bronx, NY, 80; ceramic wall, City of Detroit, Mich, 85. *Exhib:* One-person show, Whitney Mus Am Art, New York, 69; Living Am Artistss, Gallery Maight, traveling, Paris, France, 71; Art from the 50's to the 60's, Metrop Mus Art, New York, 79; Afro-Am Abstractions, travelling, PS1, Long Island City, NY, 81; London - New York, Polytech, traveling, Manchester, Eng, 83; The Appropriate Object, Albright Know Gallery & traveling, Buffalo, NY, 88. *Teaching:* Artist-in-residence painting, Skowhegan Sch Painting, 81 & Va Commonwealth Univ, 85-86; asst prof painting, City Univ NY, 88- *Awards:* NY State Coun Arts Award, 86; Guggenheim Fel, 86; Nat Endowment for the Arts, painting, 70, 75 & 85. *Media:* Acrylic, Handmade Paper. *Dealer:* June Kelly Gallery 591 Broadway New York NY 10012. *Mailing Add:* c/o GR N'Namdi 161 Townsend Birmingham MI 48009

LOVING, RICHARD MARIS
PAINTER, EDUCATOR
b Vienna, Austria, Jan 27, 24. *Study:* Fieldston Sch, Riverdale, NY, 39-42; Bard Col, Annandale, NY, 43-44; New Sch Soc Res, 46. *Work:* Art Inst Chicago; Joslyn Art Mus, Omaha, Nebr; First Nat Bank Chicago; Kemper Art Collection, Chicago; Borg-Warner Corp, Chicago; Mus Contemp Art, Chicago; and others. *Comn:* Enamel triptych, Concordia Col, River Forest, Ill, 67; enamel & stainless wire, Graver Water Conditioning, Union, NJ, 68; vitreous enamel mural, Union Tank Car Corp, Chicago, 70. *Exhib:* Abstract, Symbol, Image, Ill Arts Coun Traveling Exhib; Chicago & Vicinity Drawings & Prints, Art Inst Chicago, 68 & 69; Collector's Choice Exhib, Joslyn Art Mus, Omaha, Nebr, 68; Contemporary Art in Midwest, Univ Notre Dame, 69; Karlsruhe-Chicago, Karlsruhe, WGer, 79; Chicago; Some Other Traditions, 83-85; Traveling Exhib, Abstract-Symbol-Image, Ill Arts Coun. *Pos:* Founding ed, Chicago-Art-Write. *Teaching:* Prof painting & drawing, Sch Art Inst Chicago, 63- *Awards:* Nat Endowment Arts Fel. *Media:* Oil on Canvas or Wood Paneling. *Dealer:* Roy Boyd Gallery 215 W Superior St Chicago IL 60610. *Mailing Add:* 1857 W Armitage Ave Chicago IL 60622

LOWE, HARRY
ADMINISTRATOR, DESIGNER
b Opelika, Ala, Apr 9, 22. *Study:* Auburn Univ, BA, 43, MFA, 49; Cranbrook Acad Art, 51 & 53. *Collections Arranged:* Stuart Davis Memorial, Nat Collection Fine Arts, Washington, DC, Art Inst Chicago, Univ Calif Art Galleries, Los Angeles & Whitney Mus Am Art, New York, 65; Deputy Commissioner, US Exhib, Venice Biennale, 66; The Charles Sheeler Exhibition, Philadelphia Mus Art & Whitney Mus Am Art, 69. *Pos:* Dir, Tenn Fine Arts Ctr, Nashville, 59-64; cur, Dept Exhib & Design, Nat Mus Am Art, 64-72, asst dir opers, 72-74, asst dir, 74-81, acting dir, 81-82, deputy dir, 82-84, deputy dir emer, 84. *Teaching:* Prof art, Auburn Univ, 49-59; fac, Sem for Hist Adminrs, Williamsburg, Va, 65, 67-71. *Mem:* Nat Trust Hist Preserv; Skowhegan Sch Painting & Sculpture (mem adv comt). *Mailing Add:* 802 A St SE Washington DC 20003

LOWE, J MICHAEL
SCULPTOR, EDUCATOR
b Cincinnati, Ohio, Aug 18, 42. *Study:* Ohio Univ, BFA; Cornell Univ, MFA. *Work:* Butler Inst Am Art, Ohio; State Univ NY Col Potsdam; Cornell Univ; St Lawrence Univ (NY); Tyler Mus, Tex. *Comn:* St Lawrence Univ, 85. *Exhib:* Sculpture Now, Inc, New York, 78; solo exhib, Ohio Northern Univ, 83; San Diego Art Inst, Calif, 87 & 90; NAm Sculpture Exhib, Colo, 88 & 92; San Bernardino County Mus, Calif, 89; two person show, R F Brush Gallery, St Lawrence Univ, 89; and others. *Teaching:* Instr fine arts, St Lawrence Univ, 66-67, asst prof, 67-72, chmn dept, 71-87, assoc prof, 72-78, prof, 78- *Awards:* Purchase Awards, Tyler Mus Art, 70, Butler Inst Am Art, 72 & Clinton Co Govt Bldg, 76; Second Award Sculpture, Cooperstown Art Asn, 91. *Bibliog:* Dictionary of American Sculptors: 18th Century to the Present, Apollo Press. *Mem:* Col Art Asn Am. *Media:* Welded Metal. *Mailing Add:* Dept of Fine Arts St Lawrence Univ Canton NY 13617

LOWE, MARVIN
PRINTMAKER, PAINTER
b Brooklyn, NY, May 19, 27. *Study:* Juilliard Sch; Brooklyn Col, BA, 54; Univ Iowa, MFA, 60. *Work:* Philadelphia Mus Art; Brooklyn Mus; Indianapolis Mus Art; Libr Cong; Nat Collection Fine Arts, Smithsonian Inst; New York Pub Libr; and 88 others. *Comn:* Paintings, Purdu Univ, West Lafayette, Ind, 90. *Exhib:* Libr Cong, 60, 62 & 65; Mus Mod Art, New York, 65; Brooklyn Mus, 67; Philadelphia Mus Art, Nat Print Exhib, 68 & 72; two-person show, Am Embassy, Ankara, Turkey, 74; solo exhibs, Weyhe Gallery, New York, 76, Zriny Gallery, Chicago, 77-83, Sheldon Swope Art Mus, Terre Haute, Ind, 79 & 85, Printworks Ltd, Chicago, 87 & Purdue Univ, 88; Indianapolis Mus Art, 82-83; Kunstzentrum, Glende/Reinbek, Fed Repub Ger, 88; Privatgalerie Plewisast, Hamburg, Fed Repub Ger, 88; and many others.

Teaching: Prof fine arts, Ind Univ, Bloomington, 68- *Awards:* Fel, Nat Endowment Arts Artists Award, 75; Ford Found Grant, 79; Ind Arts Comn Artists' Fel, 87; and others. *Bibliog:* Thelma Newman (auth), Innovative printmaking, Crown Publ, 75; article in Print Collector's Newsletter, 7-8/83; articles in Printwork, 84-86; American Artists, New York Art Review & Chicago Art Review, Am References Publ, 89. *Mem:* Soc Am Graphic Artists. *Media:* Printmaking, Painting. *Dealer:* Printworks Ltd W Superior St Chicago IL 60610. *Mailing Add:* 2750 S Spicewood Lane Ind Univ Bloomington IN 47401

LOWENTHAL, CONSTANCE
HISTORIAN, ADMINISTRATOR
b New York, NY, Aug 29, 45. *Study:* Brandeis Univ, BA, 67; Inst Fine Arts, NY Univ, AM, 69, PhD, 76. *Pos:* Asst mus educator, Metrop Mus Art, New York, 78-85; Exec dir, Int Found Art Res, New York, 53-; bd dirs, Int Art & Antiques Loss Register, Ltd, Ctr Educ Studies. *Teaching:* Fac mem art hist, Sarah Lawrence Col, Bronxville, 75-78. *Mem:* Col Art Asn. *Publ:* Auth, Lorenzo Ghiberti, Encycl Britannica 3, 74; Conrat Meit's Judith and a Putto at Brou, Marsyas, 74; Conrat Meit's Busts of Philbert le Beau, Festschrift Yvonne Hackenbroch, 83; Rev of Limewood Sculptors of Renaissance Germany, M Baxandall (auth), Renaissance Quart, 83; contribr, Art Crime Update, The Wall Street Journal, 12/88. *Mailing Add:* Int Found Art Res 46 E 70th St New York NY 10021

LOWNEY, BRUCE STARK
PAINTER, PRINTMAKER
b Los Angeles, Calif, Oct 16, 37. *Study:* NTex State Univ, BA; San Francisco State Univ, MA; Univ NMex, asst to Garo Antreasian; Tamarind Lithography Workshop. *Work:* Minneapolis Inst Art; Art Inst Chicago; Art Mus Univ NMex, Albuquerque; Oklahoma City Art Ctr; Libr Cong Collection, Washington, DC; and others. *Exhib:* Whitney Mus Am Art Print Exhib, New York, 70; one-man shows, Martha Jackson Gallery, New York, 71, Hills Gallery, Santa Fe, 73 & Univ NDak, Grand Forks, 74; 23rd Nat Exhib Prints, Libr Cong, 73; and others. *Teaching:* Instr, Minneapolis Col Art & Design, Fort Lewis Col, Univ NMex & Univ Tex, Austin, formerly. *Awards:* Louis Comfort Tiffany Found Graphics Art Award, 69; Nat Endowment Arts Grant, 74; Western States Arts Found fel, 79; and others. *Media:* Oil, Lithography. *Mailing Add:* 800 Oso Ridge Route Grants NM 87020

LOWRY, BATES
HISTORIAN, MUSEUM DIRECTOR
b Cincinnati, Ohio, June 21, 23. *Study:* Univ Chicago, PhB, 44, MA, 53, PhD, 56. *Pos:* Ed, Monogr Series, Col Art Asn, 57-59 & 65-68 & Art Bulletin, 65-68; dir, Mus Mod Art, New York, 68-69; mem bd dirs, Comt for Nat Mus Building Arts, 78-80; dir, Nat Bldg Mus, Washington, 80-87. *Teaching:* Asst prof art, Univ Calif, Riverside, 54-57, Inst Fine Arts, New York Univ, 57-59; prof art & chmn dept, Pomona Col, 59-63, Brown Univ, 63-68 & Univ Mass, Boston, 71-80; mem, Inst Advan Study, 71; distinguished vis prof, Univ Del, Newark, 88-89. *Awards:* RI Gov's Award for Contribution to Arts, 67; Grand Off, Star of Solidarity, Italy, 68; Guggenheim Fel, 72. *Mem:* Soc Archit Historians (bd dirs, 59-61, 63-65); Art Historians Southern Calif (pres, 61-63); Comt to Rescue Italian Art (co-founder); Am Fedn Arts (trustee, 69-71); Dunlap Soc (pres, 74-); Col Art Asn (bd dirs, 62-65). *Publ:* Auth, The Visual Experience, 61; Renaissance Architecture, 62; Muse or Ego, 63; Architecture of Washington, DC, 77-79; Building a National Image, 85. *Mailing Add:* 255 Massachusetts Ave Boston MA 02115

LOY, JOHN SHERIDAN
PAINTER
b St Louis, Mo, Nov 4, 30. *Study:* Colorado Springs Fine Art Ctr, Colo; Wash Univ Sch Fine Arts, BFA, 54; Cranbrook Acad Art, Bloomfield Hills, Mich, MFA, 58. *Work:* Munson-Williams-Proctor Inst, Utica, NY; Utica Col, NY; Lincoln-Rochester Bank Collection, Rochester, NY; Hayes Nat Bank, Clinton, NY; Savings Bank Utica. *Exhib:* Artists Cent NY, Munson-Williams-Proctor Inst, 60-70; Albany Inst Hist & Art Regional, NY, 69; Everson Mus Regional, Syracuse, NY, 70; Cooperstown Art Asn Ann, NY, 71; 2 person exhib, Munson-Williams-Proctor Inst, 85. *Pos:* Prog dir, Peoples Art Ctr, St Louis, 59; gallery dir, Munson-Williams-Proctor Inst Sch Art, Utica, NY, 78-86. *Teaching:* Instr drawing, Wash Univ, 59; instr drawing & painting, Munson-Williams-Proctor Inst, 60-91. *Awards:* First Painting Prize, Cooperstown Art Asn, 71, 74, 76 & 77; Grand Prize, Cooperstown Art Asn, 83; Residency, Cité Internationale des Arts, Paris, 91. *Media:* Oil. *Mailing Add:* 13 Fountain St Clinton NY 13323

LOYD, JAN BROOKS
SCULPTOR, GOLDSMITH
b Quanah, Tex, Jan 28, 50. *Study:* Columbia Col, Mo, AA, 70; Southern Ill Univ, Carbondale, BA, 72, MFA, 74. *Work:* Ark Art Ctr, Little Rock; Mint Mus Art, Charlotte; Nat Ornamental Metal Mus, Memphis; Southern Ill Univ Mus, Carbondale. *Comn:* Bronze & steel cross, St Barnabus Episcopal Church, Denton, Tex, 75; eight bronze panels, NC Dept Com-NC Arts Coun, Charlotte, 82; mixed metal interior reliefs, Aeronca Corp, Charlotte, 85. *Exhib:* The Goldsmith, Renwick Gallery, Smithsonian Inst, Washington, DC, 74; Feria Mundial de la Plata, Univ Mex Mus, Mexico City, 74; The Metalsmith, Phoenix Art Mus, 77; solo exhib, Southeastern Ctr Contemp Art, Winston-Salem, 80; Young Americans: Metal, Mus Contemp Crafts New York, 80; Toward a New Iron Age, Victoria & Albert Mus, London, Eng, 82; American Metal Work, Kyoto Mus Traditional Indust, Japan, 83; USA-Portrait of the South, Palazzo Venezia, Rome, Italy, 84. *Teaching:* Instr metal, Southern Ill Univ, Carbondale, 74-77; asst prof, Univ NC, Charlotte, 77-83. *Awards:* Designer-Craftsmen Award, NC Artists Exhib, NC Mus Art, 79; Merit Awards, 12th Competitive Exhib, Fayetteville Mus, 84 & Metal Sculpture Exhib, Millersville Univ, 84. *Bibliog:* Julie Hall (auth), Tradition and Change: The New American Craftsmen, E P Dutton, 76; Thelma R Newman (auth), The Container, Crown Publ, 76; Jane Kessler (auth), Jan Brooks Loyd, Art Papers, 80. *Mem:* Am Craft Coun (vpres, bd trustees, 86); Soc NAm Goldsmiths; Artists-Blacksmiths Asn NAm; NC Art Advocates. *Media:* Metal. *Mailing Add:* PO Box 264 Newell NC 28126

LUBBERS, LELAND EUGENE
SCULPTOR, EDUCATOR
b Stoughton, Wis, June 6, 28. *Study:* St Louis Univ, AB, MA, PhL & STL; Univ Paris, Dde l'U Paris; Acad Grande Chaumiere, Paris. *Work:* Duchesne Col, Omaha, Nebr; Sheldon Gallery, Univ Nebr, Lincoln; Seattle Opera Asn, Wash; Art in Embassies Prog, US State Dept; Jacksonville Art Mus, Fla. *Comn:* Outdoor fountain, City Omaha, 69; sculptured constructions, Canisius Col, NY, 70; crucifix group (wrought iron), St John's Church, Omaha. *Exhib:* One-man shows, Automated Junk Sculpture Exhib, Sheldon Mem Art Gallery, 65, Jacksonville Art Mus, 67 & Frye Art Mus, Seattle, 68; Ward-Nasse Gallery, New York, 74 & 77; Sheldon Gallery, Lincoln, 74-77; SW State Univ, Marshall, Minn, 77; Art About Information, University Gallery, Omaha, 85. *Pos:* Pres, Satelite Communications for Learning, currently. *Teaching:* Prof fine arts, founder & head dept, Creighton Univ, 65-72, dir, telecomunications art, 82-89. *Awards:* Three time Award Winner, Best Sculptures, Midwest Biennial, Joslyn Mus, Omaha; Chevalier Dans L'Ordre de Palmes Academiques, France. *Bibliog:* Robert Reilly (auth), Jesuit junkman, Critic Mag, 2-3/68; John Wain (auth), To Lee Lubbers in Omaha, In: Letters to Five Artists, Viking, 70; Larry Austin (auth), Caritas: Symphony of the gigantic hammered welded aluminum imitation earth volumes, Source, 11/70. *Mem:* Asn Int Dde l'U Paris; Nebr Art Educ Asn; Assoc Artists Omaha; Nebr Arts Coun (dir, 66-72). *Media:* Metals. *Publ:* Auth, L'image publicitaire actuelle et ses origines, Univ Paris, 63. *Mailing Add:* Telecommunications Dept 2400 California St Omaha NE 68178

LUBELL, ELLEN
CRITIC, WRITER
b Brooklyn, NY, Apr 7, 50. *Study:* State Univ NY at Stony Brook, with Lawrence Alloway, BA, 71. *Pos:* Contrib ed, Arts Mag, 72-79; dir, Landmark Gallery, New York, 73-75; ed/publ, Womanart Mag, Brooklyn, 76-78; art critic, Soho Weekly News, New York, 77-79; free lance contribr, Art Am, 81-84; art critic, Village Voice, New York, 84-; free lance contribr, Newsday, 88-91; dir commun, Inform, New York, 91- *Teaching:* Instr art criticism & art journalism, Sch Visual Arts, New York, 79-80. *Awards:* Art Critics Fel, Nat Endowment Arts, 78. *Bibliog:* Corinne Robins (auth), The women's art magazines, Art Criticism, Vol 1, No 2, 79; Cynthia Nadelman (auth), Women artists: Self-images, Art News, 82; Grace Glueck (auth), Private gone public, NY Times, 6/28/85. *Mem:* Int Asn Art Critics; Art Table. *Res:* To explore the relationship between fine arts and popular culture and the meaning of this differentiation in contemporary society. *Publ:* Auth, Whatever happened to the women's artist movement, Womanart Mag, 77; Can museums collect contemporary sculpture? Soho Weekly News, 79; Park Slope: An Overview (catalog), Brooklyn Mus, 80; The corporate collector, 84 & Dia Foundation shaken, 85, Village Voice; Politics before culture in the Bronx, 87, Painting by numbers, 88 & Sudden Impasto, 89, Village Voice; Corporations and art: they mean business, 90, Variety. *Mailing Add:* 161 Prospect Park W Brooklyn NY 11215

LUBOWSKY, SUSAN
DIRECTOR
b Brooklyn, NY, Jan 16, 49. *Study:* Pratt Inst, BFA, 70, MFA, 75. *Collections Arranged:* Constructivism and the Geometric Tradition, McCrory Corp, traveling exhib, 77-80. *Pos:* Asst cur, McCrory Corp, NY, 77-80; asst dir, Queens Mus, 80-82; branch dir, Whitney Mus at Philip Morris, 82-88 & Whitney Mus at Equitable Ctr, 87-88; dir, Visual Arts, Nat Endowment Arts, 89-92, Southeastern Ctr Contemp Art, Winston-Salem, NC, 92- *Teaching:* Instr art hist & gallery dir, State Univ NY, Brockport, 75-77; adj prof art, New York Univ, 86-88. *Mem:* Art Table Inc. *Res:* 20th century American art, specialization in the 1920s, 1930s and contemporary art. *Publ:* Auth, Figures of Mystery (exhib catalog), Queens Mus, 82; auth, Three American Families: A Tradition of Artistic Pursuit, 83, Alexander Calder: Selections from the Permanent Collection, 84, The Surreal City, 1930s-1950, 85, coauth, Yasuo Kuniyoshi, 86 (all exhib catalogs), Whitney Mus & auth, George Ault Voids and Enclosures, Sculpture Since the 60's, 88; Spaces '88, Mus d'Arte Contemporanea, Prato, Italy, 88. *Mailing Add:* c/o Southeastern Ctr Contemp Art 750 Marguerite Dr Winston-Salem NC 27106

LUCA, MARK
PRINTMAKER
b San Francisco, Calif, Oct 14, 18. *Study:* San Francisco State Univ, with John Gutmann, AB(hon), 40; Columbia Univ, MA(fine arts), 48; Univ Calif, Berkeley, PhD(mus educ), 58. *Work:* Achenbach Found, Calif Palace Legion Hon; Art Mus & Morrison Libr, Univ Calif, Berkeley; Oakland Mus & Mills Col Art Gallery, Oakland, Calif. *Exhib:* Calif Palace Legion Hon Invitational, 61; Print, Painting & Sculpture Exhib, Richmond Art Ctr, Calif, 62, 63, 68 & 71; Oakland Mus Art Ann, 63 & 68; one-person exhib, Panoras Gallery, New York, 66 & US Cult Inst, Lima, Peru, 80. *Pos:* Cur, Mus Italo Am, San Francisco, 81-82. *Teaching:* Instr art, State Univ NY, Potsdam, 48-50 & Sacramento State Univ, 55-56; lectr art educ, Univ Calif, Berkeley, 58-78. *Bibliog:* Articles, Art Week, 8/21/71, Westart, 2/22/74 & Lima Times, Peru, 11/14/80. *Mem:* Calif Soc Printmakers; Calif Writers Club (pres, Berkeley chap, 84-85). *Media:* Collagraph, Lithography. *Publ:* Illusr, Back to the Cave, 56 & auth & illusr, San Francisco: Seven Stages, 58, Peregrine Press; coauth,

Understanding Children's Art, Charles Merrill, 67; Art Education: Strategies, Prentice-Hall, 68; auth, chap, in: The Museum as Educator, Museums, UNESCO, 73; San Francisco: Autobiography, Star Rover House, 84. *Dealer:* Piedmont Gallery 4121 Piedmont Ave Oakland CA 94611. *Mailing Add:* Seven N Knoll, No 8 Mill Valley CA 94941

LUCAS, BONNIE LYNN
PAINTER, INSTRUCTOR
b Syracuse, NY, Sept 20, 50. *Study:* Wellesley Col, BA, 72; Rutgers Univ, MFA, 79. *Work:* Zimmerli Art Mus, Rutgers Univ. *Comn:* Temple Soc Concord (synagogue), Syracuse, NY, 88; Commissioned Assemblage (To Life). *Exhib:* Solo exhibs, Leverett House, Harvard Univ, 76, Kathryn Markel Gallery, New York, 79 & Avenue B Gallery, New York, 85, 86 & 87; Art on Paper, Weatherspoon Gallery, Univ NC, Greensboro, 78; People 81, Hudson River Mus, Yonkers, NY, 81; Basic Needs, Islip Mus, East Islip, NY, 85; The Doll Show: Artist's Dolls & Figurines, Hillwood Art Gallery, C W Post, Long Island Univ, 85; Tangents: Art in Fiber, Col Art, Baltimore, MD, 87; Frontiers in Fiber: The Americans, NDak Mus Art, 88; Alice and Look who else, Through the looking Glass, Bernice Steinbaum Gallery, New York, 88; Lone and Charity: The Tradition of Caritas in Contemporary Painting, Sherry French Gallery, New York, 89; Assemblages from the Permanent Collection, Jane VoorkeesZimmerli Art Mus, Rutgers Univ, New Brunswick, NJ, 89. *Teaching:* Lectr, Montclair State Col, NJ, 83 & Jane Voorhees Zimmerli Art Mus, Rutgers Univ, 84; vis artist, Appalachian Univ, Boone, NC, 87, Univ Ariz Tempe, 88; Workshop artist, Artpark, Summer, 88; instr, Parsons Sch Design Continuing educ, New York, 88-; vis artist, Am Acad Rome, 89. *Awards:* Stevens Traveling Fel, Wellesley Col, 89; Grant, Art Matters Inc, 90. *Bibliog:* and many articles and reviews in Artworld, Arts Mag, New York Times, Artnews, Artspeak, Womanews, Village Voice & Newsday from 1979 to 1988; Joan Marter (auth) Review, Art Mag, Summer, 87; Michael Brenson (auth), Cosmopolitan Artworks along suburban byways, NY Times, 8/4/89. *Media:* Oil, Watercolor. *Mailing Add:* 37 Spring St New York NY 10012

LUCAS, CHRISTOPHER
CONCEPTUAL ARTIST
b Durham, NC, 58. *Study:* Yale Summer Sch Music & Art, 79; Kans Univ, BA, 80. *Work:* High Mus Art, Atlanta, Ga; Carnegie Mus Art, Pittsburgh, Pa; Chemical Bank, New York; Chase Manhattan, New York; Prudential Insurance Company of America. *Exhib:* Solo exhib, John Good Gallery, New York, 86, 87, 89, 91 & 92; John Good Gallery, New York, 85, 86, 87 & 88; Jan Turner Gallery, Los Angeles, 86 & 87; Provocative Abstraction: New Painting New York, Karl Bornstein Gallery, Santa Monica, Calif, 90; Int Biennal of Paper Art, traveling Denmark, Japan & Canada, 90; group exhib, Mario Diancono Gallery, Boston, 91. *Awards:* Fel, Nat Endowment Arts, 87-88; Pollock-Krasner Found, 88; Fulbright Fel, Repub of Korea, 90-91. *Bibliog:* Patricia Lowry (auth), Carnegie Exhibition Revives Art of Abstraction, Pittsburgh Press, 88; Robert Mahoney (auth), Christopher Lucas, Arts Mag, 9/89; Claudia Roth Pierpont (auth), Now Voyager: Discovering new physical and spiritual dimensions, 10/89. *Mailing Add:* c/o John Good Gallery 532 Broadway New York NY 10012

LUCAS, GEORGETTA SNELL
PAINTER
b Harmony, Ind, July 25, 20. *Study:* Ind State Univ, BS, 42; Butler Univ, MS, 64; Ind Univ & John Herron Sch Art, 60-65. *Work:* Ind Univ/Purdue Univ Med Ctr & Indianapolis Public Sch Collection; Ind State Univ Permanent Collection, Terre Haute; Alpha Delta Kappa Int Headquarters, Kansas City, Mo; Theta Xi Fraternity House, General Motors Inst, Flint, Mich. *Comn:* Noah Loading Ark, mural, comn by William Plummer, Frankfurt, Germany, 74; Reflections, memorial oil painting, M S D Perry Admin, Indianapolis, 78; Masonic Lodge No 1-1809, comn by Bridgeport Lodge No 163, Ind, 90. *Exhib:* New York World's Fair, Bourbon St Gallery, La Pavilion, 64; Nat Asn Women Artist traveling show, Fine Arts Acad, Calcutta, India, 65; Nat Asn Women Artist show, Casino Municipale Gallery, Cannes, France, 66; Mid State Exhib, Evansville Mus, Ind, 70; 100th Yr Celebration Show, Nat Asn Women Artists, Jacob Javits Bldg, New York, 89. *Pos:* Lectr, Int Platform Asn, Washington, DC, 75, 77-78, 82 & 84; lectr, Art Educators Asn Ind, 76; lectr, Prof Educators Ind Conv, 78; lectr, Ind Fedn Art Clubs, 88; lectr, Ind Sch Women's Asn, 88. *Teaching:* Inst art, Plainfield City Schs, Ind, 46-49 & 50-52; Metro Sch Dist of Wayne, Indianapolis, 52-68; Metro Sch Dist of Perry Twp, Indianapolis, 68-81. *Awards:* Indiana Artist/Craftsmen, 74; Silver Award, Int Platform Art, 78; Best of Show, Nat League Am Pen Women, 83. *Bibliog:* Leonidas Smith (auth), Hoosier artist, Indianapolis Star Mag, 8/65; Donald Frick (auth), Batik-Filmstrip-TV Cube, Indianapolis Mus Art, 74; Mary Slayton (auth), Shares love of art, music, The Plainfild Messenger, 5/17/90. *Mem:* Nat Asn Woman Artist; Nat League Am Pen Women (Ind art chmn, 84-); honorary life mem, Ind Artist/Craftsmen Inc (pres, 79-84 & 87-89); Int Platform Asn (chmn art comt, 86-); honorary life mem Ind Fedn Art Clubs (pres, 85-87). *Media:* Batik, Oil. *Publ:* Illustr, Why So Sad, Little Rag Doll?, E C Seale, 63; contribr, Former harmony resident receives VIP treatment, Brazil Daily Times, 8/3/67; Georgetta Snell Lucas art work presented to ISU, The Tribune, 73; Art teachers to see demonstration, Daily Herald, 3/22/76. *Mailing Add:* 9702 W Washington Indianapolis IN 46231

LUCCHESI, BRUNO
SCULPTOR
b Lucca, Italy, July 31, 26; US citizen. *Study:* Inst Arte, Lucca, MFA, 53. *Work:* Pa Acad Fine Arts, Philadelphia; Dallas Mus Fine Arts; Ringling Mus, Sarasota, Fla; Hirshhorn Mus, Washington, DC; Whitney Mus Am Art, New York. *Comn:* Sculpture, Trade Bank, New York; sculpture, Cornell Univ. *Exhib:* Whitney Mus Am Art, New York; Pa Acad Fine Arts; Corcoran Gallery Art, Washington, DC; Nat Inst Arts & Lett; Brooklyn Mus, NY; plus others. *Teaching:* Instr, Acad Fine Arts, Univ Florence, Italy, 52-57; instr, New Sch Social Res, 62- *Awards:* Watrous Gold Medal, Nat Acad Design, 61; Gold Medal, Nat Arts Club, 63; S F B Morse Medal, Nat Acad Design, 65; and others. *Mem:* Sculptors Guild; Artists Equity Asn; Nat Acad Design; Am Asn Univ Prof. *Dealer:* Forum Gallery 1018 Madison Ave New York NY 10021. *Mailing Add:* 30 Fifth Ave No 4J New York NY 10011

LUCE, C(HARLES BEARDSLEY)
CONCEPTUAL ARTIST
b Phoenix, Ariz, June 15, 47. *Study:* Amherst Col, BA, 69, Univ Wash, MAT, 71. *Work:* The City of Seattle, Seattle Art Mus, Wash; Libr Cong, Washington, DC; Prudential Insurance Co, Newark, NJ; Bell Tel Co & Gen Elec Co, Chicago, Ill; NYNEX, New York; Sackner Archive of Concrete & Visual Poetry, Miami, Fla. *Exhib:* The Cyclonic Collapse of the Teahouse, 78 & Aether House, 79, Seattle Art Mus; Luise Ross, New York, 84; Fuji Art Salon, Tokyo, Japan, 85; Stokker-Stikker Gallery, New York, 86; Gracie Mansion, New York, 90-91; Dessont Saunders, Chicago, 91; and others. *Pos:* Dean etymology, Inst Study of Etymological Lessons, New York, 79 & St Ann's Sch, Brooklyn. *Awards:* Art Matters, 89; John Simon Guggenheim Fel, 91. *Bibliog:* John Paoletti (auth), Charles Luce: Light truths, Arts Mag, 4/82. *Media:* Mixed. *Dealer:* Gracie Mansion Gallery 442 E Ninth St Suite 4 New York NY 10009; MIA Gallery 536 First Ave S Seattle WA 98104. *Mailing Add:* 142 Henry St No 8W New York NY 10002

LUCERO, MICHAEL (LEWIS)
SCULPTOR
b Tracy, Calif, Apr 1, 53. *Study:* Humboldt State Univ, Arcata, Calif, BA, 75; Univ Wash, Seattle, MFA, 78. *Work:* Metrop Mus Art, New York; Seattle Art Mus; Museo Tamayo, Mexico City; San Francisco Mus Mod Art; New Mus Contemp Art, New York; Everson Mus, Syracuse, NY. *Exhib:* Solo exhibs, Charles Cowles Gallery Inc, New York, 81, 83, 84 & 86, Linda Farris Gallery, Seattle, Wash, 82 & 87, Hokin Kaufman Gallery, Chicago, 83 & 86, Fuller Goldeen Gallery, San Francisco, 85, ACA Contemp, New York, 88 & Contemp Arts Ctr, Cincinnati, Ohio, 90; Contemporary Cutouts, Whitney Mus Am Art, New York, 88; Ceramic Tradition: Figuration, Palo Alto Cult Arts Ctr, Calif, 89; two-man show, Reese Bullen Gallery, Hombolt State Univ, Arcata, Calif, 89; Explorations - The Aesthetics of Excess, Am Craft Mus, New York, 90; Figures in Ceramics, La State Univ Art Gallery, Baton Rouge, 90; Natural Image, Stanford Mus & Nature Ctr, Conn, 90; Seattle Art Mus, Wash; Nat Mus Contemp Art, Seoul, Korea; Corcoran Gallery Art, Washington, DC; Mus Fine Arts, Boston, Mass. *Teaching:* Instr, New York Univ, 79-80 & Parsons Sch Design, 81-82; guest lectr, RI Sch Design, Providence, 79, Wake Forest Univ, Winston-Salem, NC, 80. *Awards:* Nat Endowment Arts, 79, 81 & 84; Creative Artists Public Service Program Fel, 81; Nettie Marie Jones Fel, Ctr Music, Drama & Art, Lake Placid, NY, 83. *Bibliog:* William Zimmer (auth), A new figure on the horizon, Am Ceramics, winter issue; The figure; a celebration, Grand Forks Herald, 11/13/81; John Perreault (auth), Good for the figure, Soho News, 12/1/81. *Mailing Add:* c/o Fay Gold Gallery 247 Buckhead Ave NE Atlanta GA 30305

LUCEY, JACK
PAINTER, EDUCATOR
b San Francisco, Calif, Feb 11, 29. *Study:* Acad Art Col, San Francisco, 55; San Francisco Art Inst, 59; San Francisco State Univ, BA, 76. *Work:* USAF Mus, Nellis, Nev; Naval Aviation Mus, Pensacola, Fla; Hall of Justice Bldg, San Francisco; Trans World Airlines, New York; Calif Hwy Patrol Collection, Sacramento, Calif. *Comn:* Murals of Alaska, Pac Orient Lines, San Francisco, 72; London Illus, Trans World Airlines, New York, 74; Irish Countryside Paintings; Irish Tourist Bd, Dublin, 75; US Coast Guard Aircraft Scene, US Coast Guard Air Sta, San Francisco, 77. *Exhib:* 29th Ann Soc Western Artists, M H De Young Mus, San Francisco; San Francisco Art Festival, Civic Ctr, 76; Zellerbach Invitational, Zellerbach Plaza, San Francisco, 76; Industrial Graphics Int, San Jose, 77; Watercolor Technique, Marin Co Watercolor Soc, Mill Valley, Calif, 77; Third Falkirk Ann, Falkirk Cult Ctr, San Rafael, Calif, 78; one-man show, Agura Art, Collection of 36 paintings and Drawings Representing California Agriculture Today, Calif Mus Design & Industry, Los Angeles, 86. *Collections Arranged:* Veterans Mem Mus, 79; one-man shows, Sport's Art, Zellerbach Art Mus, 80 & Aviation Art, Bohemian Club, San Francisco, Calif, 81. *Pos:* Graphics artist, Shell Oil Co, San Francisco, 52-56; art dir, Independent J, San Rafael, Calif, 56- *Teaching:* Instr art, Acad Art Col, San Francisco, 76-77; instr illus, Col Marin, 75-; instr graphics, Indian Valley Col, Novato, Calif, 78- *Awards:* First Place Illus, San Jose State Univ, Calif, 77. *Mem:* Col Art Asn; Soc Western Artists; San Francisco Soc Commun Arts; Artists in Print; North Bay Advert Commun. *Media:* Oil, Watercolor. *Publ:* Illusr, The Alamo, Reader's Digest, 73; San Francisco Giants, San Francisco Mag, 78; Chemical facts of life, Standard Oiler Mag, Standard Oil of Calif, 78. *Dealer:* Allport Assoc Gallery 1000 Magnolia Ave Larkspur CA 94939. *Mailing Add:* 84 Crestwood Dr San Rafael CA 94901

LUCHS, ALISON
CURATOR, HISTORIAN
b Washington, DC, Oct 5, 48. *Study:* Vassar Col, Poughkeepsie, NY, BA, 70; Johns Hopkins Univ, Baltimore, PhD, 76. *Pos:* Res asst, Ctr Advan Study Visual Arts, Washington, DC, 80-83, asst cur sculpture, 82-89, assoc cur early European sculpture, 89- *Teaching:* Asst prof Swarthmore Col, Pa, 76-77; asst prof, Syracuse Univ, NY, 77-80. *Awards:* Robert H Smith Res Leave Grant, 88; Ailsa Mellon Bruce Nat Gallery Art Curatorial Sabbatical Fel, Ctr Advan Study Visual Arts, 92-93. *Res:* Italian Renaissance, all media; local Washington, DC, architecture; medieval decorative arts. *Publ:* Auth, Cestello:

A Cistercian Church of the Florentine Renaissance, Garland, New York, 77; translr, Martin Wackernagel's The World of the Florentine Renaissance Artist, Princeton, 81; auth, Stained Glass Above Renaissance Altars, Zeitschrift für Kunstgeschichte, 85; Tullio Lombardo's Ca' d'Oro relief: a self-portrait with the artist's wife?, Art Bull, 89; The Convent of Sta Maria Maddalena de'Pazzi and its Works of Art, Florence, 90-91. *Mailing Add:* c/o Sculpture Dept Nat Gallery Art Washington DC 20565

LUCIER, MARY
VIDEO ARTIST, PHOTOGRAPHER
b Bucyrus, Ohio, Jan 25, 44. *Study:* Brandeis Univ, BA, 65. *Work:* Whitney Mus Am Art; Stedelijk Mus, Amsterdam; Nat Gallery, Can; Am Film Inst; San Francisco Mus Mod Art. *Comn:* Equinox (video installation), Grad Ctr, City Univ New York, 79; Planet (video installation), Hudson River Mus, 80; Winter Garden (video installation), Lower Manhattan Cult Coun, New York, 82; Noah's Raven (video installation), Toledo Mus Art, 93. *Exhib:* Solo exhibits, Whitney Mus Am Art, 81, 85 & 86, Carnegie Inst, Pittsburgh, 83, Wadsworth Atheneum, Hartford, 86, Dallas Mus Art, 87, Mus Contemp Art, Los Angeles, 88, Greenberg Wilson, New York, 89 & 91 & City Gallery Contemp Art, Raleigh, NC, 91; Biennial Exhib, Whitney Mus Am Art, 83; Mus Mod Art, New York, 83; Walker Art Ctr, Minneapolis, Minn, 87; San Francisco Mus Mod Art, Calif, 88; Kolnischer Kunstverein, Berlin, 89; Hudson River Mus, Yonkers, NY, 90, 2nd Biennale of Nagoya, Japan, 91; Univ Galleries, Ill State Univ, 90; Whitney Mus Am Art, Greenberg Wilson, New York, 91; 2nd Biennale Nagoya, Japan, 91; Ronald Feldman Fine Arts, New York, 92; and others. *Pos:* Artist in residence, WNET Channel 13, New York, 82. *Teaching:* Instr video art, Sch Visual Arts, 79-83, New York Univ, 88-; vis artist, Minneapolis Col Art & Design, 80, Cleveland Inst Art, 82, San Francisco Art Inst, 84, New York Univ, 88-90 & State Univ NY, Purchase, 92. *Awards:* Jerome Found Grant, 82; Media Arts Grant, Nat Endowment Arts, 83; Media Grant, NY State Coun Arts, 83; Guggenheim Mem Found Grant, 90; and others. *Bibliog:* John Miller (auth), Mary Lucier, 2/90 & Kirby Gookin (auth), Mary Lucier, 4/91, Artforum; Arlene Raven (auth), Refuse refuge, Village Voice 1/15/91; Ann-Sargent Wooster (auth), The garden in the machine, Arts Mag, 4/92; and others. *Mem:* Media Alliance, NY (bd mem, 81-82); Parabola Arts Found Inc (bd mem & secy, currently). *Publ:* Contribr, Women's Work, Allison Knowles, 75; ed & contribr, Video Art, Harcourt Brace Jovanovich, 76; contribr, Scenarios, Assembling, 80; Illuminating Video, Aperture, 91. *Dealer:* Greenberg Wilson New York NY. *Mailing Add:* 223 W 20th St No 4A New York NY 10011

LUCK, ROBERT
CURATOR, INSTRUCTOR
b Tonawanda, NY, Oct 31, 21. *Study:* Univ Buffalo, BFA, 47; Harvard Univ, MA, 49; Inst Meschini, Rome, Italy, cert painting, 50; Attingham Summer Sch, England, 62. *Pos:* Cur, Cincinnati Art Mus, 54-55; dir, Akron Art Inst, 55-56; Telfair Acad Arts & Sci, Savannah, Ga, 56-57; asst dir, Am Fedn Arts, 58-72; cur, Contemp Wing, Finch Col Mus Art, 73-75; vis cur, Neuberger Mus, State Univ NY, Purchase, 78-79 & Cooper-Hewitt Mus, 80-84; asst, dept print & photog, Metrop Mus Art, 84-87. *Teaching:* Instr, Toledo Mus Art, 52-54; instr art hist, Parsons Sch Design, 73-78; instr, Pratt Inst Sch Continuing Educ, New York, 78-80. *Mailing Add:* 150 E 27th St Apt 1-G New York NY 10016

LUCKNER, KURT T
CURATOR
b Stafford Springs, Conn, Dec 29, 45. *Study:* Georgetown Univ, AB(art hist); Stanford Univ, MA(art hist). *Collections Arranged:* Silver for the Gods: 800 Years of Greek and Roman Silver (int loaned exhib), Toledo Mus Art, Ohio, Nelson Gallery, Kansas City, Mo & Kimball Mus Art, Ft Worth, Tex, 77-78. *Pos:* Asst cur ancient art, Stanford Univ Mus, summer 69; curatorial asst, Toledo Mus Art, Ohio, 69-70, asst cur, 70-73, cur ancient art, 73- *Mem:* Col Art Asn; Archaeol Inst Am (pres, Toledo Chap, 71-75). *Publ:* Auth, Art of Egypt-part I, Vol 14, No 1 & part II, Vol 15, No 3, Greek vases: Shapes & uses, Vol 15, No 3, African art, Vol 16, No 2 & Greek gold jewlery, Vol 17, No 1, Toledo Mus News. *Mailing Add:* PO Box 1013 Toledo OH 43697

LUDMAN, JOAN HURWITZ
WRITER, RESEARCHER
b Brooklyn, NY, Feb 1, 32. *Study:* Barnard Col, BA, 53; C W Post Col, Long Island Univ, MA, 71. *Pos:* Assoc, Mason Fine Prints, Glen Head, NY, 72-86. *Res:* American and European original prints; compiling catalog, Raisonne Paintings of Fairfield Porter. *Publ:* Coauth (with Lauris Mason), Print Reference Sources: A Select Bibliography 18th-20th Centuries, 75, 2nd ed, 79 & The Lithographs of George Bellows: A Catalogue Raisonne, 77, Kraus-Thomson Orgn Ltd; contribr, Cecile Shapiro, auth, Fine Prints: Collecting, Buying and Selling, Harper & Row, 76; co-ed (with Lauris Mason), Print Collector's Quart: An Anthology of Essays on Eminent Printmakers of the World, 77, Kraus-Thomson Orgn Ltd; auth, Fairfield Porter: A Catalogue Raisonne of his Prints, Highland House Publ, Inc, 81. *Mailing Add:* 74 Hunters Lane Westbury NY 11590

LUDMER, JOYCE PELLERANO
LIBRARIAN, HISTORIAN
b New York, NY. *Study:* Hunter Col, BA; Univ Calif, Los Angeles, with Carlo Pedretti, MLS & MA(art hist). *Pos:* Humanities bibliographer, Calif State Univ, Northridge, 70-72; librn, Elmer Belt Libr Vinciana, Univ Calif, Los Angeles, 73-; head librn, Art Libr, Univ Calif, Los Angeles, 75- *Mem:* Art Libr Soc NAm (vchmn & chmn elect, 78-79); Col Art Asn; Am Libr Asn; Asn Col & Res Libr. *Res:* Leonardo da Vinci studies; art bibliography. *Interests:* Renaissance, classical & baroque art history; art bibliography. *Mailing Add:* 10626 Holman Ave Los Angeles CA 90024

LUDTKE, LAWRENCE MONROE
SCULPTOR
b Houston, Tex, Oct 18, 29. *Study:* Univ Houston, BS; Coppini Acad Fine Art, San Antonio, with Waldine Tauch. *Work:* USAF Acad; Central Intellegence Agency Hq; White House; Pentagon; Lifesize Bronzes, Lyndon B Johnson Libr. *Comn:* Charging Bronze Rams, Johnson & Johnson Inc, San Angelo, Tex, 66; Dr Denton Cooley (bronze bust), St Lukes Hosp, Houston, 69; Eddie Wokecki (bronze bas relief), Rice Univ, Houston, 69; Pieta (bronze group), St Marys Sem, Houston, 74; Fiona O'Donnell (bronze bust), comn by Dr Manus O'Donnell, Houston, 74; works comn by President Ronald Reagan, John Wayne, General Robinson Risner, Maury Maucrick, Robert Kennedy and Martha Mitchell. *Exhib:* Nat Cowboy Hall of Fame. *Teaching:* Scottsdale Artist Sch, 89. *Mem:* Fel Nat Sculpture Soc; Coppini Acad Fine Arts; Royal Acad Brit Sculptors (corresp mem). *Media:* Bronze, Marble. *Mailing Add:* 10127 Whiteside Houston TX 77043

LUDWIG, ALLAN I
PHOTOGRAPHER, HISTORIAN
b New York, NY, June 9, 33. *Study:* Yale Univ, with Josef Albers, Charles Seymour, Jr & Erwin R Goodenough, BFA, 56, MA, 60, Bollingen Found fel, 60-63, PhD, 64. *Work:* Agfa Corp Collection; Mus Fine Arts, Houston, Tex; Los Angeles Co Mus Art, San Francisco Mus Mod Art; Espace Photographique de Paris; Tokyo Inst Technol; Mus Mod Art, Metrop Mus, New York; Mus Photog Arts, San Diego. *Exhib:* Solo exhibs, Twining Gallery, New York, 87, White Columns, New York, 87 & 88, O'Kane Gallery, Houston, Tex, 88, XYZ Gallery, Ghent, Belg, 89, Farideh Cadot Gallery, New York, 88 & 90, Northern Light Gallery, Ariz State Univ, Tempe, 90, Galerie Farideh Cadot, Paris, France, 91, Pamela Auchincloss Gallery, New York, 92; group exhibs, Insect Politics, Hallwalls, Buffalo, NY, 90, Animals, Houston Ctr for Photog, Tex, 90, Photography: 1980's Discovery & Invention, Art, 21-90, Basel Switz, 90, Natural History & Formaldehyde Photog, Musee Zoologique de l'Universite Louis Pasteur, Strasbourg, France, 90 & Natur Mus Senchenberg Forschungs Institut, Frankfort, WGer, 91; Motion & Document, Sequence & Time, Addison Gallery Am Art, Andover, Mass, 91; The Interrupted Life, The New Mus, New York, 92. *Collections Arranged:* Repulsion: The Aesthetics of the Grotesque, Alternative Mus, 86. *Pos:* Chmn bd, Alternative Mus, New York, 78-83, mem exec bd, 83-88; dir, Ludwig Portfolios, 81-88. *Awards:* Photog Fel, NJ State Coun Arts, 89-90; Grant, Agfa Corp, 90; Nat Endowment Arts Fel, 91. *Bibliog:* Photography 150 Years: Its Light and Shadow, Col of Art, Nihon Univ, Tokyo Inst Technol, 178, 89; Kunstforum, pp 142-145, 3-4/90; Kath McQuaid (auth), Photo Surrealism, South End News, 2/15/90. *Media:* Platinum Printing, Silver Gelatin Printing. *Publ:* Auth, Graven Images, Wesleyan Univ Press, 66 & 75; Holy Land USA, The Clarion, summer 79; Beyond Photography I, II, 81 & 82 & Seeing Is Believing, 12/85-1/86, Alternative Mus; Sermons in Stone, Franco Maria Ricci, 11/84; Repulsion: The Aesthetics of the Grotesque, Alternative Mus, 86. *Dealer:* Pamela Auchincloss Gallery 558 Broadway New York NY 10012; Galerie Farideh Cadot 77 Rue Des Archives 75003 Paris France. *Mailing Add:* 55 Prince St New York NY 10012

LUDWIG, EVA
SCULPTOR
b Berlin, Ger, May 25, 23; US citizen. *Study:* Greenwich House Pottery, with Lu Duble, 58-62; Sculptor's Workshop, with Harold Castor, 64; Craft Students League, wood sculpture with Domenico Facci, 68; Queens Col, sculpture with Richard Miller, 80-81. *Exhib:* Nonmem Exhib, Nat Sculpture Soc, New York, 72; Ann, 81 & Artist of the Month, 82, Woodstock Guild Craftsmen; Catherine Lorillard Wolfe Art Club Exhib, 83, 84, 88, 89, 90, 91 & 92; Pen & Brush Sculpture Exhib, 86, 87 & 88; Alliance Queens Artists, 88, 89, 90 & 91; solo exhib, Queens Col Art Ctr, 92; and others. *Awards:* Best in Wood, 69 & Bert Wangler Mem Award, 72, Woodstock Guild Craftsmen; First Prize in Sculpture, Cooperstown Art Asn, 71. *Bibliog:* Holding Ideas Into Art, Q C Quad, 5/18/92; B Gogel (auth), Ludwig's Sculptures on Exhibition at Q C Art Center. *Mem:* Alliance Queens Artists; Catherine Lorillard Wolfe Art Club. *Media:* Wood, Clay. *Mailing Add:* 57-44 164th St Flushing NY 11365

LUEBBERS, LESLIE LAIRD
MUSEUM DIRECTOR, HISTORIAN
Study: Wellesley Col, AB, 67; Johns Hopkins Univ, MA, 69; New York Univ, Inst Fine Arts, MA, 87. *Collections Arranged:* World Print Three, 80 & World Print Four, 83, San Fancisco Mus Mod Art; Am Woodcuts, USIA European Tour, 84-87; Mind & Matter, USIA Asian Tour, 89-92; Carroll Cloar & Art History: Komar & Melamid, Memphis State Univ, 91. *Pos:* Dir, World Print Coun, San Francisco, Calif, 79-84; dir, Int Art Projects, San Francisco & New York, 85-90; dir, Univ Gallery, Memphis State Univ, Tenn, 90- *Res:* Prints: 19th & 20th centuries, contemporary art & architecture. *Publ:* Auth, American Woodcuts: Revival and Innovation, USIA/World Print, 83; Mind and Matter: New American Abstraction, USIA/World Print Coun, 90; Jean Fautrier: Prints of the Forties, Print Collector's News Letter, 91; American Abstraction in the 90's & Into the Abstract World (article), Taipei Fine Arts Mus, 92; Jean-Paul Riopelle: Prints and the Legend, Print Collector's News Letter, 92. *Mailing Add:* Memphis State University University Gallery Memphis TN 38152

LUECKING, STEPHEN JOSEPH
SCULPTOR, EDUCATOR
b Belleville, Ill, Aug 11, 48. *Study:* Quincy Col, Ill, BFA, 70; Bradley Univ, Peoria, Ill, grad study, 71; Miami Univ, Oxford, Ohio, MFA, 73. *Work:* Ill State Mus, Springfield. *Comn:* Miami Sun Reservoir (with Margaret

Lanterman), Miami Univ & Nat Endowment Arts, Oxford, Ohio, 80; Upwells, Univ Ill, 90. *Exhib:* Ill Arts Coun, traveling, 78; Fed Ctr Mus, Chicago, 78; Ill State Mus, Springfield, 78; Art Inst Chicago, 79; Contemp Arts Ctr, Cincinnati, 80; Chicago Cult Ctr, 81; Rockford Art Mus, 89; Roy Boyd Gallery, Chicago, 90. *Collections Arranged:* Seven Sculptors, 78 & Stuart Court Installations (auth, catalog), 81-82, DePaul Univ; Paul Caponigro & Charles Ross, Archaeoastronomy Am Conf, St John's Col, 79. *Pos:* Reviewer & essayist, New Art Examiner, 86-; Visual Arts Panelist, Ill Arts Coun 87, & 88. *Teaching:* Asst prof, Purdue Univ, West Lafayette, Ind, 74-76; assoc prof, DePaul Univ, Chicago, 76-; vis artist, Sch Art Inst Chicago, 79 & 86. *Awards:* Clussman Prize, Art Inst Chicago, 78; project grants, Ill Arts Coun, 78, 80 & 81; Pougialis Award, Columbia Col, 81. *Bibliog:* Alan Artner (auth), The Nation: Chicago, Art News, summer, 77; Holliday T Day (auth), Chicago Invitational, Art Am, 11/78; Wendy Hoffman-Yuni, article, New Art Examiner, 3/79. *Media:* Steel, Iron. *Publ:* Contrib, Sculpture Mag, 89-90; Am Crafts, 90; Am Ceramics, 91-92. *Dealer:* Roy Boyd 215 West Superior Chicago IL 60610. *Mailing Add:* Dept Art DePaul Univ 25 E Jackson Blvd Chicago IL 60604

LUEDERS, JIMMY C
PAINTER, INSTRUCTOR
b Jacksonville, Fla, July 4, 27. *Study:* Pa Acad Fine Arts, William Emlen Cresson Mem traveling scholar, 50, Henry Schiedt Mem scholar, 51. *Work:* Pa Acad Fine Arts; Philadelphia Mus Art; Sch Pharmacy & Tyler Sch Art, Temple Univ; Moore Col Art, Philadelphia. *Exhib:* Butler Art Inst, Youngstown, Ohio; Am Fedn Art Traveling Exhib Art Schs, 56; Metrop Young Artist Show, Nat Arts Club, New York, 60; Nat Acad Design, New York, 60; Nat Inst Arts & Lett, New York, 69. *Teaching:* Instr painting, Pa Acad Fine Arts, 57- *Awards:* Third Hallgarten Prize, Nat Acad Design, New York, 60; Percy M Owens Mem Award for Distinguished Pa Artist, 80. *Media:* Acrylic. *Dealer:* Ben Mangel Gallery 1714 Rihenhouse Sq Philadelphia PA 19103. *Mailing Add:* c/o Pa Acad Fine Arts Broad & Cherry Sts Philadelphia PA 19102

LUINO, BERNARDINO
PAINTER
b Latina, Italy, Mar 27, 51. *Study:* Accademia di Belle Arti, Rome & Florence, Italy, MA. *Comn:* Mural, Presso II Centro Incontri Marentino Fiat, Torino, Italy. *Exhib:* Solo exhibs, Galleria Lo Zibetto, 80, Galleria II Fante di Spade, 82, Milan, Italy; Biennale di La Spezia, La Spezia, 80; VII Nat Biennal of Figurative Art, Piacenza; I Int Biennal of Graphic Art, Museo Civico Riva del Garda, Centro Int, della Grafica Venezia, Trento, 82; Grafica Italiana Contemporanea, Quadriennale Nazionale d'Arte di Roma, traveled USA and Canada, 82; XXIV Biennale Nazionale d'Art, Palazzo della Permanente, Milan, Italy, 89. *Media:* Oil on Panel. *Publ:* Illustr, Luino, Fotolito Savaresi, 85. *Mailing Add:* c/o Gallery Henoch 80 Wooster St New York NY 10012

LUISI, JERRY
SCULPTOR, INSTRUCTOR
b Minneapolis, Minn, Oct 7, 39. *Study:* Nat Acad Design, cert, 68-72; Art Students League. *Work:* NY State Gov Mansion, Albany; Agriculture Hall Fame, Kansas City, Mo; nat Acad Design, New York. *Comn:* BASF Corp, Parsippany, NJ, 81-83; Armento Archit Arts, Buffalo, NY, 87; Franklin Mint, 88; Medallic Art, 89; Reseal, New York, 89. *Exhib:* Nat Acad Design 70, 74 & 81; Allied Artists Am, 71, 72 & 75; Nat Sculpture Soc, 74-; Mus Fine Arts, Springfield, Mass, 77; Salmagundi Club, 80 & 81; Artists Prof League, New York, 89; and others. *Pos:* Deleg, Fine Arts Fedn, New York, 78-80; ed sculpture, Aristos Mag, 83. *Teaching:* assoc prof, Fine Arts Prog, Fashion Inst Technol, 72- & Nat Acad Design, 79-82. *Awards:* Greenshields Found Grant, 72 & 75; Anna Hyatt Huntington Award, Hudson Valley Art Asn, 80; John Gregory Award, Nat Sculpture Soc, 80; and others. *Bibliog:* Articles, Nat Sculpture Rev, fall 80. *Mem:* Nat Sculpture Soc; Acad Artists Asn; life mem Art Students League; Artists Prof League, New York. *Media:* Clay, Bronze. *Mailing Add:* Dept Fine Arts Fashion Inst Technol 227 W 27th St New York NY 10001

LUITJENS, HELEN ANITA
INSTRUCTOR, PAINTER
b Bakersfield, Calif. *Study:* Univ Redlands, BA; Univ Southern Calif, MA; Univ Hawaii, scholar, 63; Univ Calif, Los Angeles; Inst Art San Miguel de Allenda. *Work:* Munic Art Dept, Los Angeles; Inst Mex Norteamericano de Relaciones Cult, Mexico City; Anderson Konstmuseum, Helsinki, Finland; Konst Salongen Kavaletten, Uppsala, Sweden; Union Bank, Los Angeles. *Exhib:* Inst Mexicano Norteamericano de Relaciones Cult, 69; Konst Salongen Kavaletten, 73; Nat Watercolor Soc, Laguna Beach, Calif, 74; Pac Cult Mus Pasadena, 74; Palos Verdes Art Mus, 75. *Teaching:* Chmn dept art, Paul Revere Jr High, Los Angeles, 55-72; teacher pvt classes, 72-79; lectr painting & drawing, Chapman Col World Campus Afloat; lectr art hist, E Mediterr, Black Sea, Panama Canal & Alaska Cruises, 75. *Awards:* 30 awards in art shows in Southern California, 65-75. *Mem:* Nat Watercolor Soc (mem bd, corresp secy, 75); Women Painters West; Arizona Artists Guild; Los Angeles Art Asn Watercolor West; Ariz Watercolor Asn. *Media:* Watercolor. *Publ:* Contribr, Mosaics, Drawing, Elegant Era, Los Angeles Times & Better Homes & Gardens. *Dealer:* Challis Gallery Laguna Beach CA. *Mailing Add:* 9818 Lindgren Ave Sun City AZ 85373

LUKAS, DENNIS BRIAN
PAINTER, EDUCATOR
b Hamilton, Ont, Can, June 21, 47. *Study:* St Michael's Sch Cantorum, Toronto, Dipl(ancient music); Doon Sch Fine Art, Ont, with Henri Masson, Carl Schaefer & Tony Onley; McMaster Univ, with Tony Urquhart; Montreal Mus Sch Fine Art, with Arthur Lismer, grad dipl; Atelier 17, Paris, France, with Stanley Hayter. *Work:* Munson-Williams-Proctor Inst, Utica, NY; Art Gallery Hamilton, Ont; Bibliot Nat, Paris; Montreal Mus Fine Arts; Art Gallery Greater Victoria, BC; and many others. *Exhib:* One-man show, Stable Gallery, Montreal Mus Fine Arts, Can, 70; Retrospective Eleven Yrs, McKenzie Gallery, Trent Univ, Peterborough, Ont, 74; Peripheries, Mus d'Art Contemporain, Montreal, 74; Young Contemporaries, Art Gallery of London, Ont, 75; Forum 76, Montreal Mus Fine Arts, 76; On View Visual Arts Ont (touring 14 mus), 76-77; traveling exhib, Ctr Cult, Drummondville, Que, 80; Gallery 76, Ont Col Art, Toronto, 80; and others. *Teaching:* Instr drawing & painting, Montreal Mus Sch, Que, 71-74; lectr drawing & painting, Univ Toronto, Ont, 75-76; vis asst prof drawing & painting, Hamilton Col, Clinton, NY, 76-78. *Awards:* Can Coun Awards, 67, 68 & 72; Ont Arts Coun Awards, 74-76, 78, 80, 82-84; A J Casson Award, Seneca Col, Willowdale, Ont, 78. *Bibliog:* Catharine Bates (auth), article, Montreal Star, 73; David Lehman (auth), Dennis Lukas Recent Work to 1977, Hamilton Col Ed; Andre Dupont & Henri Barras (coauth), Lukas, Ctr Cult, Drummondville, Que, 80. *Mem:* Niagara Artists Co; Montreal Mus Fine Arts (gov & benefactor); Governor Art Gallery of Greater Victoria, BC. *Media:* All. *Mailing Add:* 51 Main St W Grimsby ON L3M 1R3 Canada

LUKASIEWICZ, RONALD JOSEPH
PRINTMAKER, SCULPTOR
b Pittsburgh, Pa, Apr 20, 43. *Study:* Carnegie-Mellon Univ, BFA; Univ Ga, MFA. *Work:* Pittsburgh Pub Schs, Pa; Dow Chemical Co, Midland, Mich; City of Athens, Ga; Bankers Trust Co, NC; and others. *Comn:* Suite of serigraphs, 73 & bound book of serigraphs, 73, Dow Chemical Co, Midland, Mich; modular sculpture, Scorpio Rising Workshop, Farmington, Ga, 73; modular sculpture, City of Athens, Ga, 77; suite of serigraphs, Thornet Furniture, Dallas, 81. *Exhib:* 10th Ann Piedmont Graphics Exhib, Mint Mus of Art, Charlotte, NC, 73; Assoc Artists Ann Show, Carnegie Mus, Pittsburgh, Pa, 73; Medals, Banners, Ribbons, Pittsburgh Arts & Crafts Ctr, Pa, 74; Ga Nat, Lyndon House Galleries, Athens, 76; Moving Parts & Captured Light, The Third Floor, Atlanta; Spectrum I, Lyndon House Art Ctr, Athens, Ga, 80; Western Carolina Univ, Cullowhee, NC, 81; Corvoll Reese Mus, 86; Color as Theory, Goethe Inst, Atlanta, Ga, 88; and others. *Pos:* Dir cult activities, Athens, Ga, 74-76; preparator, Ga Mus of Art, Univ Ga, 76-87; dir, Climax Press, 83- *Awards:* Purchase Award, Assoc Artists of Pittsburgh, Pittsburgh Pub Schs, 72; Award, Lyndon House Art Ctr, 81. *Bibliog:* D Miller (auth), Exhibit review, Pittsburgh Post Gazette, 74; J Chappell (producer), Scorpio Rising (16mm film doc), 74; Screen Printing Today, WGTV Television, 74. *Mem:* Col Arts Asn; Assoc Artist of Pittsburgh; Athens Art Asn. *Mailing Add:* 350 Belmont Rd Athens GA 30605

LUKIN, SVEN
PAINTER
b Riga, Latvia, Feb 14, 34. *Study:* Univ Pa. *Work:* Albright-Knox Art Gallery, Buffalo, NY; Los Angeles Co Mus Art; Larry Aldrich Mus, Ridgefield, Conn; Univ Tex, Austin; Whitney Mus Am Art, New York; and others. *Exhib:* Univ Ill, Urbana, 65; Torcuato di Tella, Buenos Aires, Arg, 65; New shapes of Color, Stedelijk Mus, Amsterdam, Holland, 66; Univ Colo, Denver, 67; Painting: Out From the Wall, Des Moines Art Ctr, Iowa, 68; New Work, Los Angeles Co Mus Art, 78; Gallery Face, Tokyo, 87; Mus Foreign Art, Riga, Latvia, 87; and others. *Awards:* Guggenheim Fel, 66; Pollock-Krasner Found Grant, 90. *Bibliog:* Sam Hunter (ed), New Art Around the World, Abrams, 66; Allen S Weller (auth), The Joys & Sorrows of Recent American Art, Univ Ill, 68; Gregory Battcock (ed), Minimal Art: a Critical Anthology, Dutton, 68. *Mailing Add:* 807 Ave of the Americas New York NY 10001

LUKOSIUS, RICHARD BENEDICT
PAINTER, CRAFTSMAN
b Waterbury, Conn, Oct 26, 18. *Study:* Yale Univ, with Josef Albers, BFA & MFA. *Work:* Slater Mus, Norwich, Conn; Univ Conn Health Ctr, Farmington. *Exhib:* New Eng Artists, Slater Mus, Norwich, Conn, 68; Contemp Drawings, Univ Conn, Storrs, 71; Frascati Gallery, Stonington, Conn, 77; Sculpture & Drawings by Conn Artists, Slater Mus, Norwich, 79; Invitational Print Exhib, Mystic Art Gallery, Conn, 79; and many other group & one-man shows. *Teaching:* Prof painting, drawing & graphic design, Conn Col, 54-84, emer prof, 84- *Awards:* First Prize Logo Design for Peabody Mus, Yale Univ, New Haven, Conn, 84. *Media:* Acrylic. *Mailing Add:* 65 Rainbow Dr Uncasville CT 06382

LUMBARD, JEAN ASHMORE
DEALER
b Clinton, SC. *Study:* Columbia Univ, New York. *Specialty:* Contemporary art; watercolors, pastels, drawings, original prints, paintings on canvas, tapestries and sculpture by international artists with emphasis on American artists. *Mailing Add:* 17 E 96th St New York NY 10128

LUMBERS, JAMES RICHARD
PAINTER
b Toronto, Ont, Can, Oct 8, 29. *Study:* Ont Col of Art, OCA, 50; study with William Maltman, Toronto. *Work:* Ont Govt; Tenn-Ness Antiques; Sun Oil Co; and numerous other corporate & pvt collections in USA and Canada. *Comn:* Portraits, John Diefenbaker, 72, Chief Dan George, 73, 83 & 85, The Toronto Symphony Orchestra, 85, Hockey Greats: Gordie House & Wayne Gretzky, 91, Sir Edmund Hillary, 92. *Exhib:* One man shows, Royal Ont Mus, Toronto, Can; Ont Sci Ctr, Toronto; Kennedy Galleries Inc, New York, 72; Nature Can, Nat Mus Can, 73, 76-78; Sportsman's Edge Gallery, New York, 78; McMichael Can Collection, Toronto Dominion Ctr; Le Moyne Art Found, Tallahassee, Fla, 78. *Pos:* Graphic designer, James Lumbers Graphics

Ltd, Toronto, 62-; dir, Can Chap Explorer's Club, currently. *Awards:* Statue, Juvenile Diabetes Found, 90; Winner of the Can Collectible of the Year, 91. *Bibliog:* Global Network News Hour, 89; Can Press, 89; Documentaries on PBS (Fla). *Mem:* Fel Explorers Club, New York. *Media:* Acrylic. *Publ:* over 50 works in ltd eds; Decor Mag & Art Bus News, 87-92; Feature Art Impressions, spring, 87. *Dealer:* Newport Editions Willowdale Can. *Mailing Add:* c/o Blink Bonnie Gallery Cherry Hill Rd Grafton ON K0K 2G0 Canada

LUMMUS, CAROL TRAVERS
PRINTMAKER
b Hyannis, Mass, Nov 2, 37. *Study:* Colby Sawyer Col, New London, NH, AA, 57; Mass Col Art, Boston; Univ of Geneva, Switz; study color with Hannes Beckmann, Dartmouth Col, Hanover, NH. *Work:* Univ Wis, Madison, Wis; Lund-Wassmer Springfield Mus Collection, Salt Lake City, Utah; Arts Bank, Concord, NH; Art Unexpected Places, Coun Arts, Concord, NH. *Exhib:* Living With Crafts Ann, League NH Craftsmen, Concord, NH, 73-90; solo exhib, Manchester Inst Arts, NH, 75-77; Nat Cape Coral Ann, Fla, 75; NH Art Ann, Currier Mus Art, Manchester, 75; three-women show, Colby Sawyer Col, New London, NH, 76; St Gaudens Nat Site, Cornish, NH, 83; Nat Asn Women Artists, New York, 85; Instituto-Brasil-Estados Unidos Exchange, N Ceara, Brazil, 85. *Pos:* Illusr, Cincinnati Mag, Ohio, 64-67. *Awards:* Oil award, Fitchburg Mus Art, Mass, 73; Rosmond DeKalb Award, Currier Mus Art, 75. *Mem:* League NH Craftsmen; Cape Cod Performing Arts Asn, (bd dirs); NH Comn Arts (advisory panel); Silvermine Guild Arts, Conn; Nat Asn Women Artists, NY. *Media:* Intaglio print. *Publ:* Illusr, Editiones del Norte (cover/book), Hanover, NH, 68. *Dealer:* Southern Editions 927 Gallery 906 Royal St New Orleans LA 70116. *Mailing Add:* c/o 927 Gallery 906 Royal St New Orleans LA 70116

LUMSDEN, IAN GORDON
DIRECTOR
b Montreal, Que, June 8, 45. *Study:* McGill Univ, Montreal, BA, 68; Mus Mgt Inst Univ Calif, Berkeley, 91. *Collections Arranged:* The First Decade (with catalog), Confedn Ctr Art Gallery & Mus, Charlottetown, PEI, 75; Wallace S Bird Mem Collection (with catalog), Beaverbrook Art Gallery, Fredericton, NB, 75; Bloomsbury Painters & Their Circle (US & Can traveling exhib), 76-78; The Queen Comes to New Brunswick: Paintings & Drawings by Molly Lamb Bobak (Can traveling exhib), 77-78; Drawings by Jack Weldon Humphrey (Can traveling exhib), 77-79; The Murray and Marguerite Vaughan Inuit Print Collection (Can traveling exhib), 81-82; 20th Century British Drawing, Beaverbrook Art Gallery, 86; Drawings by Carol Fraser 1948-1986 (Can traveling exhib), 87-88; Gainsborough in Canada (with catalog), 91. *Pos:* Cur art dept, New Brunswick Mus, St John, NB, 69; cur & dir, Beaverbrook Art Gallery, 69-; dir, Arts Atlantic, 77-; dir, Can Cult Property Export Rev Bd, 82-85, 49th Parallel Ctr for Contemp Can Art, New York, 89-92. *Mem:* Can Art Mus Dirs Orgn (pres, 83-85); Can Mus Asn (secy-treas, 73-75); Atlantic Prov Art Gallery Asn (chmn, 70-72); Secondary Art Sub-Comt for NB Schs; Am Asn Mus; 49th Parallel Ctr Comtemp Can Art Prog Comt. *Res:* 19th & 20th century Canadian art; 20th century British painting. *Publ:* Auth, Warkov, No 66 & Forrestall: de l'expressionnisme a l'hyperrealisme, No 67, Vie des Arts; Artist in New Brunswick: George Neilson Smith, Can Antiques Collector, 5-6/75; L'agrandissemene du Beaverbrook, Vie des Arts, Vol XXIX, No 116, 84. *Mailing Add:* 725 George St Fredericton NB E3B 1K6 Canada

LUND, DAVID
PAINTER, EDUCATOR
b New York, NY, Oct 16, 25. *Study:* Queens Col (NY), BA; New York Univ. *Work:* Toronto Art Gallery; Whitney Mus Am Art; Chase Manhattan Bank, NY; Baltimore Mus, Md; Corcoran Gallery Art, Washington, DC; Montclair Mus, NJ; Johnson Mus, Cornell Univ, Ithaca, NY. *Exhib:* Whitney Mus Am Art, New York, 58, 60-62 & 77; twenty-one one-man shows, Grace Borgenicht Gallery, NY, 60-83; Baltimore Mus, Md, 60; Albright-Knox Art Gallery, Buffalo, NY, 63; Pa Acad Fine Arts, Philadelphia, 65, 66 & 69; Nat Collection Fine Arts, White House, 66-69; Am Acad Arts & Lett, 69-70, 76 & 77; Kent State Univ, Ohio, 69 & 71; Denver Art Mus, Colo, 70; Smithsonian Inst, Washington, DC, 70, 72 & 73; and many others. *Pos:* Consult, Creative Artists Pub Serv Program, 79-81. *Teaching:* Instr painting, Cooper Union Art Sch, 55-74; Parsons Sch Design, 63-69; asst prof painting, Columbia Univ, 69-; vis prof, Boston Univ, 75-76. *Awards:* Fulbright Grant Italy, 57-59; Ford Found Purchase Prize, Whitney Mus Am Art, 61; Childe Hassam Purchase Award, Am Acad Arts & Lett, 69 & 78. *Bibliog:* M D Keyishian (auth), David Lund Arts, 82; Barbara Rosecrance (auth), Landscape as metaphor: The recent work of David Lund, Arts, 84; Gregory Galligan (auth), New Landscape: Paintings by Daniel Lund, Arts, 87; and others. *Mem:* Nat Acad; Artists Equity NY. *Media:* Oil, Pastel. *Publ:* Contribr, Nuove Tendenze Della Pittura Astratta American, Mondo Occidentale, Rome, 59; Nuove Tendenze--, I Quatro Soli, Turin, 59; Artists on Architecture, Architecture, Am Inst Architects, 5/85. *Dealer:* Olga Dollar Gallery 210 Post St San Francisco CA; Lederman Fine Arts 309 Court St Hoboken NJ. *Mailing Add:* 470 West End Ave New York NY 10024

LUND, JANE
PAINTER, PRINTMAKER
Study: Pratt Inst, 56. *Work:* Nelson Gallery Found, Kansas City, Mo; de Saisset Mus, Santa Clara, Calif; De Cordova Mus, Lincoln, Mass; Boston Mus Fine Art, Mass. *Exhib:* Perspectives on Contemporary American Realism, Pa Acad Fine Arts, Philadelphia & Art Inst Chicago, 83; Artists Choosing Artists, Artists Choice Mus, New York, 85; Collected Visions, Fed Reserve Bank, Boston, 86; one-woman show, Forum Gallery, New York, NY, 88; Jane Lund Art Scene Series, Springfield Mus Fine Arts, Mass, 89; Monocular Vision: New England Realist Artists, Inaugural Exhib, Fitchburg Art Mus, Mass, 89; Jane Lund: Watercolor Constructions, Hart Gallery, Northampton, Mass, 90; The Object: Found, Observed, Imagined, Fitchburg Art Mus, Mass, 91. *Teaching:* Instr drawing, Berkshire Community Col, Pittsfield, Mass, 72-81. *Awards:* Fel, Mass Coun Arts & Humanities, 79; Bunting Inst Radcliffe Col, 85-86; Artist's Fel, Nat Endowment for the Arts. *Bibliog:* Pastel paintings of Jane Lund, Mass Rev, spring 77; Eight women portrait artists, Mass Rev, summer 83; A realist portfolio, New Eng Monthly, 10/85. *Media:* Highly Finished Pastels, Lithographs; Watercolor Constructions. *Dealer:* Forum Gallery Inc 1018 Madison Ave New York NY 10021. *Mailing Add:* Norton Hill Rd Ashfield MA 01330

LUNDBERG, WILLIAM
PAINTER
b Albany, Calif, 1942. *Study:* San Jose State Univ, Calif, BA(art), 64; Univ Calif, Berkeley, MA(art), 66. *Work:* Mus Art, RI Sch Design; also numerous pvt collections. *Exhib:* One-man shows, Whitney Mus Am Art, New York, 82, Artpark, Film Sculpture Comn, Lewiston, NY, 84, Carnegie Inst Mus Art, Pittsburgh, Pa, 84, Emily Davis Gallery, Univ Akron, Ohio, 87, Espace Lyonnais d'Art Contemporain, Lyon, France, 87; group shows, Blue Star Gallery, San Antonio, 87, Ringling Mus Art, Sarasota, Fla, 87, Contemp Arts Mus, Houston, 88; and others. *Teaching:* Teacher, New Eng Col, Arundel, Eng, 71-74; Md Inst Col Art, Baltimore, 83; Parsons Sch Design, New York, 84-85; Univ Tex-Austin, 85- *Awards:* John Simon Guggenheim Mem Found Fel, 81; Artists Grant, NJ Coun Arts, 85; Summer Res Award, Univ Tex, 88; Teaching Excellence Award, Col Fine Arts, 88. *Mailing Add:* 602 E 49th St Austin TX 78751

LUNDE, KARL ROY
HISTORIAN, WRITER
b New York, NY, Nov 1, 31. *Study:* Columbia Univ, BA, MA & PhD. *Pos:* Dir, The Contemporaries, New York, 56-65. *Teaching:* Instr art hist, Sch Gen Studies, Columbia Univ, 57-70; prof art hist, William Paterson Col NJ, 70- *Res:* Italian Renaissance bronzes; 19th century romantic art in Scandinavia; 20th century American painting. *Publ:* Contribr, Arts Mag, 75-85; contribr, Drawing Mag, 79-; auth, Isabel Bishop, 75 & Richard Anuszkiewicz, 77, Abrams; contribr, Drawing Mag, 79-; auth, The Graphic Works of Robert Kipniss, Abaris Bks Inc, 80; John Day, Tenth Ave Ed Inc, 84 & Nat Neujean, Atelier Vokaer, Brussels, 86. *Mailing Add:* Dept Art William Patterson Col 300 Pompton Rd Wayne NJ 07470

LUNDEBERG, HELEN
PAINTER
b Chicago, Ill, June 24, 08. *Study:* With Lorser Feitelson. *Work:* Los Angeles Co Mus Art, Calif; San Francisco Mus Art; Joseph H Hirshhorn Collection; Sheldon Mem Art Gallery, Lincoln, Nebr; Nat Mus Am Art, Washington, DC. *Exhib:* Fantastic Art, Dada, Surrealism, Mus Mod Art, New York, 36-37; Whitney Mus Am Art, New York, 62, 65 & 67; Painting & Sculpture in Calif: The Mod Era, San Francisco Mus Mod Art & Nat Collection Fine Arts, Washington, DC, 76-77; First Western States Biennial Travelling Show, 79 & 80; Lorser Feitelson and Helen Lundeberg Retrospective Exhib, San Francisco Mus Mod Art, 80; Helen Lundeberg Since 1970, Palm Springs Desert Mus, 83; California Contemporary, Monterey Peninsula Mus, 83; Aspects of California Modernism 1920-1950, Fed Reserve Bd Gallery, Washington, DC, 86; solo exhibs, California Contemporary, Laguna Art Mus, 87, A Birthday Celebration, Los Angeles Co Mus Art, 88 & A Retrospective, Sesnon Art Gallery, Univ Calif Santa Cruz, 88; Elders of the Tribe, travelling exhib, 87-89; Turning the Tide, travelling exhib, 90-92. *Awards:* Award for Outstanding Achivements in the Visual Arts, Women's Caucus Art, 81. *Bibliog:* Eleanor Munro (aut), Originals: American Women Artists, Simon & Schuster, 79; Diane Moran (auth), Helen Lundeberg: the sixties and seventies, Art Int, 5/79; Charlotte S Rubinstein (auth), American Women Artists, Hall & Co, 82; Ilene Susan Fort (auth), Helen Lundeberg: A Birth Celebration (exhib catalog), Los Angeles Co Mus Art, 88; and others. *Media:* Acrylic & Oil. *Dealer:* Tobey C Moss 7321 Beverly Blvd Los Angeles CA 90036. *Mailing Add:* 8307 W Third St Los Angeles CA 90048

LUNDEEN, GEORGE WAYNE
SCULPTOR
b Holdrege, Nebr, Aug 26, 48. *Study:* Hastings Col, Nebr, BA, 71; Univ Ill, MFA(sculpture), 73; Accademia de Belle Arte, Italy, 74. *Work:* Nebr State Collection, Kearney; People's Republic China, Nat Gallery, Peking; Holdrege, Nebr. *Comn:* Life-size Sculpture, Ben Franklin, Univ Pa, 87; Life Size Sculpture, Gene Sarazen, Atlanta Nat Golf Course, 88; two life size sculptures, Nike Inc, Beaverton, Ore, 90. *Exhib:* North Am Sculpture Exhib, Foot Hills Art Ctr, 79-86; Allied Artists Am Ann, New York, 80-87; Nat Sculpture Soc Ann, New York, 80-88; Nat Acad Design Ann, New York, 80-86; Am Western Art Exhib, Peking Arts Gallery, China, 81. *Pos:* Fulbright-Hays Scholar, Florence, Italy, 73-74; artist-in-residence, Tex A & M Univ, 78-79. *Awards:* Silver Medal, Nat Sculpture Soc, 82; Gold Medal, Nat Acad Design, 82; Art Castings of Colorado Award, NAm Sculpture Exhib, 83; North American Sculpture Exhib, John Cavenaugh Memorial Award, 86; Allied Artists Members & Associates Award, 87. *Bibliog:* John Jellico (auth), G W Lundeen, Artist of the Rockies & Golden West, spring 81; M Lantz & T Morgan (auths), The western art of 12 western sculptors, Nat Sculpture Review, fall, 80; Libby James (auth), George Lundeen, Southwest Art, 5/83. *Mem:* Nat Sculpture Soc; Allied Artists Am. *Media:* Bronze, Terra-cotta. *Dealer:* Loveland Sculpture Gallery 338 E 4th St Loveland CO 80537. *Mailing Add:* 338 E Fourth St Loveland CO 80537

LUNDIN, NORMAN K
PAINTER
b Los Angeles, Calif, 1938. *Study:* Sch Art Inst Chicago, BA, 61; Univ Chicago, 61; Univ Cincinnati, MFA, 63; Univ Oslo, Norway, 63. *Work:* Mus Mod Art, New York; Detroit Inst Arts; Brooklyn Mus Art; Seattle Art Mus; Achenbach Found; Fine Arts Mus, San Francisco. *Exhib:* Solo exhibs, Allan Stone Gallery, New York, Space Gallery, Los Angeles, Stephen Haller Fine Art, NY, Long Beach Mus Art, Calif, (catalog), Adams-Middleton Gallery, Dallas, American Realism, San Francisco Art Mus, (catalog), Sources of Light, Henry Art Gallery, Seattle; Whitney Mus Am Art, New York; Barnsdale Gallery, Los Angeles Munic Mus; Seattle Art Mus. *Pos:* Vis artist, Hornsey Col Art, London, Eng, 69-70, Wash State Univ, Pullman, 73, Ohio State Univ, Columbus, 75, San Diego State Univ, 78 & Brighton Col Art, Eng, 79. *Teaching:* Prof art, Univ Wash, Seattle, 64- *Awards:* Grants, Fulbright Found, 63-64, Ford Found, 78-79 & Nat Endowment Arts, 83; Wash State Visual Artists Fel, Tiffany Found. *Bibliog:* Bruce Guenther (auth), Fifty Northwestern Artists, San Francisco Chronicle Books, 83; Lynn Gamwell (auth), West Coast Realism, Laguna Beach Mus Art, 83; Robert Flynn Johnson (auth), Norman Lundin: A Decade of Drawing & Painting, Univ Wash Press, Long Beach Mus Art, 90. *Media:* Oil, Acrylic. *Dealer:* Stephen Haller Fine Art 415 W Broadway New York NY 10012; Francine Seders Gallery Seattle. *Mailing Add:* 3419 E Denny Way Seattle WA 98122

LUNEAU, CLAUDE
SCULPTOR
b Paris, France, 1935; Can citizen. *Work:* Can Coun Art Bank; Laurentian Univ, Sudbury; Windsor Art Gallery; Holdbrooks Holdings, Toronto; Mus of Civilization, Ottawa. *Exhib:* Solo exhibs, Mira Godard Gallery, Toronto, Ont, 82 & 84, Moosart Gallery, Miami, Fla, 86; Mendal Gallery, Saskatoon, Sask, 83; Glenbow Mus, Calgary, Alta, 83; Equinox Gallery, Vancouver, BC, 88; Robertson Galleries, Ottawa, Ont, 88; 49th Parallel, New York, 89; Structure: Claude Luneau & Greg Murdock, Gallery/Stratford, Ont, 90. *Awards:* Can Coun Project Cost Grant, 83, 84 & 85; Ont Arts Coun Material Assistance Grant, 83 & Traveling Cost Grant, 86. *Bibliog:* Christopher Hume (auth), Essays in whimsy, 8/14/82, Heavy Metal, 8/31/84, Toronto Star; From the Heart: Folk Art in Canada, McLelland & Stewart, Toronto, 83; Peter Day (auth), Claude Luneau, Can Art, spring 86. *Mailing Add:* c/o Olga Korper Gallery 17 Morrow Ave Toronto ON M6R 2H9 Canada

LUNSFORD, JOHN (CRAWFORD)
HISTORIAN, CURATOR
b Dallas, Tex, Apr 15, 33. *Study:* Harvard Univ, AB(Eng lit), 54; Columbia Univ, MA(pre-Columbian art hist & archaeol), 67. *Collections Arranged:* The Clark and Frances Stillman Collection of Congo Sculpture (with catalog), 69; Arts of Oceania (with catalog), 70; The Romantic Vision in America (with catalog), 71; African Art from Dallas Collections (with catalog), 72; The Gustave and Franyo Schindler Collection of African Sculpture (with catalog), 75; Nora and John Wise Collection of Pre-Columbian Art, 76. *Pos:* Curator, Dallas Mus Art, 68-80, sr cur, 80-86. *Teaching:* Adj prof art hist, Southern Methodist Univ, Dallas, 67- *Res:* The arts of pre-Columbian Meso-America and West and Central Africa; pre-Columbian Central and South America; native American art. *Mailing Add:* Dept Art Hist, Meadows Sch Arts Southern Methodist Univ Dallas TX 75275

LUNTZ, IRVING
DEALER
b Milwaukee, Wis, Jan 9, 29. *Study:* Northwestern Univ. *Pos:* Pres & dir, Irving Galleries, Inc, Palm Beach, Fla, 59- *Mem:* Art Dealers Asn Am; Appraisers Asn Am. *Res:* Nineteenth and twentieth century American and European painting; sculpture and graphics. *Mailing Add:* 332 Worth Ave Palm Beach FL 33480

LUPORI, PETER JOHN
EDUCATOR, SCULPTOR
b Pittsburgh, Pa, Dec 12, 18. *Study:* Carnegie-Mellon Univ, BFA, 42; Univ of Minn, MS(educ), 47; studied with Joseph Bailey Ellis & John Rood. *Work:* The Walker Art Ctr, Minneapolis, Minn; Ball State Teachers Col Art Gallery, Muncie, Ind; North Hennepin Community Col Art Gallery, Fridley, Minn; Albert Lea Pub Libr, Minn; Minn Alumni Asn Art Gallery, IDS Ctr, Minneapolis. *Comn:* Crucifix & Madonna (aluminum), Stations (ceramic), Holy Childhood Church, St Paul, Minn, 56-58; ten stained glass windows, First Methodist Church, Monmouth, Ill, 61; Medicine Int (ceramic bas-relief), Fairview-Southdale Hosp, Edina, Minn, 65-67; 24 stained glass windows, Minnehaha United Methodist Church, Minneapolis, Minn, 66; Creation (ceramic bas-relief), Westminster Presbyterian Church, Minneapolis, 82; St Joseph tryptich (ceramic bas-relief), St Joseph Hosp, Dickinson, NDak, 84; Bishop Wipple (bronze), St Cornelia Church, Morton, Minn. *Exhib:* Ann Assoc Artist of Pittsburgh, Carnegie Inst of Art, Pa, 40-62; Biennial Exhib of Paintings & Prints, Walker Art Ctr, Minneapolis, 47-49; 1st Biennial Exhib Prints & Drawing, Minneapolis Inst of Arts, 50, 52-54; Six-State Sculpture Exhib, Walker Art Ctr, 47, 51; Ann Local Artists Exhibs, Minneapolis Inst of Arts, 47-48, 50-52; 16th Ceramic Ann Nat Exhib, Syracuse, NY, 51; Fine Arts Exhib, Minn State Fair Art Gallery, St Paul, 46-; one-man show, St Paul Mus of Art, 52. *Teaching:* Instr sculpture, Univ of Minn, Minneapolis, 46-49; asst prof, sculpture, Col of St Thomas, St Paul, Minn, 49-51; prof sculpture, The Col of St Catherine, St Paul, 47- *Awards:* 2nd award in sculpture, Prix de Rome, NY, 41; Carnegie Inst Prize for Sculpture, Assoc Artists of Pittsburgh, 49; Emily Arsenberg Award, Asn Artists Pittsburgh, 62. *Mem:* Artists Equity Asn; Soc Minn Sculptors; Minn Artists Asn; Pittsburgh Artists Asn. *Media:* Ceramic, Wood. *Mailing Add:* 5118 12 Ave S Minneapolis MN 55417

LUPPER, EDWARD
PAINTER
b NJ, Jan 4, 36. *Study:* With Wesley Lea, Frenchtown, NJ; Trenton Jr Col; Parsons Sch Design, New York; Calif Col Arts & Crafts, Oakland; San Francisco Art Inst; San Francisco State Col; M H de Young Mem Mus Sch, 78. *Work:* Bear Paintings, Teddy Bear Mus, Naples, Fla. *Comn:* Two paintings, Scott Newhall Collection, 80 & 82; Annedeen Hosiery Mills, 88. *Exhib:* Baltimore Mus Art, 55; Tucson Art Ctr, Ariz, 59; Fort Worth Art Ctr, 60; San Francisco Mus Art, 60; Am Embassy, Belg, 77-78; solo exhibs, Naples Art Gallery, Naples, Fla, 86, 87, 88, 89, 90, & 91, 92 & 93. *Pos:* Artist, card line, Posters, Sunrise Publ, 88-89 & 90-93. *Awards:* Huntington Hartford Found Fel, 64. *Bibliog:* Article, San Francisco Chronicle, 60, San Francisco Examr, 62 & 65 & Seattle Times, 71; articles in Naples Daily News, 86 & Naples Times, Fla, 86, 87, 88, 89 & 90-92. *Media:* Casein, Oil. *Publ:* Auth, articles in Playgirl, 74, Apartment Life, 9/74, Popular Gardening Indoors, 77, Eaton Paper Corp, 77-78, Sunrise Publ, 79-80, Gulfshore Life & Naples Guide, 86 & 91-92, Am Artist, 88, Artist Mag, 89,; brochure, Delta Shiva Corp, 87-88. *Dealer:* Phillips Flynt Galleries 2121 Westheimer Houston TX 77098; The Naples Art Gallery 275 Broad Ave S Naples FL 33940. *Mailing Add:* 1255 Pacific San Francisco CA 94109

LURAY, J
COLLAGE ARTIST, PAINTING
b Columbus, Ohio, Apr 14, 39. *Study:* Ohio State Univ; Columbus Col Art & Design, BFA(advert), 62. *Work:* Nat Educ Asn, KPMG Peat Marwick, Cleveland, Ohio; Marketing Mix Inc, St Louis, Mo; Commun Satellite Corp, Washington, DC; Magna Group, Inc, Belleville, Ill. *Comn:* Field Res & Engineering, Inc, Springfield, Va; Monsanto Co, St Louis, Mo; Hilco Technols, St Louis, Mo; Barnes Hosp, St Louis, Mo; May Dept Store Inc, St Louis, Mo. *Exhib:* 19th Area Exhib, Corcoran Gallery Art, Washington, DC, 74; 51st Nat Exhib, Watercolor Soc Ala; 52nd Ann Int Traveling Exhib, NW Watercolor Soc; 15th Ann Salamagundi Art Exhib, New York; 71st Ann Exhib, Nat Watercolor Soc, Brea, Calif; Grand Exhib, Soc Artists, Akron, Ohio; and others. *Pos:* Advert designer, W P Simpson, Columbus, 60-62, Paul L Devaney Studio, Columbus, 62-69 & Designers Two, 69-92. *Awards:* St Louis Artists Guild Mems Award, 92; Howard Manville Award, NW Watercolor Soc, Kirkland, Wash, 92; Strathmore Award, 89, Thomas Award, 90 & Five State Award, 92 Kans Watercolor Soc Five State Exhib. *Bibliog:* Martin Sharter (auth), Art & singular images, Atlanta Mag, 73. *Mem:* Women's Caucus Art, Washington, DC & St Louis, Mo; St Louis Artists Coalition; St Louis Artists Guild; Art League Inc, Alexandria, Va; sig mem, Nat Watercolor Soc. *Media:* Miscellaneous. *Dealer:* Boody Fine Arts Inc 10706 Trenton Ave St Louis MO 63132. *Mailing Add:* 14727 Chermoore Dr Chesterfield MO 63017-7901

LURIA, GLORIA
DEALER, CONSULTANT
b New York, NY. *Study:* Pratt Inst; Art Students League; Skidmore Col, BS. *Pos:* Owner-dir, Gloria Luria Gallery, Miami, Fla, 66- *Mem:* Art Dealers Asn SFla. *Specialty:* Contemporary paintings; sculpture; graphics; tapestries. *Mailing Add:* 5770 Miami Lakes Dr Miami Lakes FL 33014

LURIE, BORIS
PAINTER, SCULPTOR
b Leningrad, Russia, July 18, 24; US citizen. *Exhib:* Drawings USA, Mus Mod Art, New York, 59; Tenth Street New York Cooperative Movement, Houston Art Mus, Tex, 60; New York Library, Mus Mod Art, 62; Recycling Exhib, Israel Mus, Jerusalem, 78; Arts & Politics, Karlsruehe Mus, Ger, 78; Counterculture Art, Am Info Serv, Paris,78; Graffiti-art, Nassauischer Kunstverein, Weisbaden, Ger, 89. *Bibliog:* Ray Wishniewski (dir) Doom Show (film), New York, 62. *Media:* All. *Publ:* Auth, Leonardo, London, 78; coauth, No! art, Ed Hundertmark, Cologne/Berlin, Ger, 88. *Dealer:* Galerie & Ed Hundertmark Cologne WGer Bruesselerstrasse 29. *Mailing Add:* 48 E 66th St New York NY 10021

LURIE, SHELDON M
DRAFTSMAN, GALLERY DIRECTOR
b Kingston, NY, Dec 10, 42. *Study:* RI Sch Design, BFA, 63; Md Inst Col Art, MFA, 66. *Work:* Am Soc Hq, Teheran, Iran; Consulate US, Casablanca, Morocco; Miami-Dade Community Col, Fla. *Comn:* Sackner Archieves of Concrete & Visual Poetry. *Exhib:* Dibujos: S M Lurie, Centro Colombo Americano, traveling, 83; Miami Three: Lurie, Levy, Ward, Rowe Art Ctr, Charlotte; solo exhib, Drawings, Pub Libr, Coral Gables, Fla, 86; Visual Arts Gallery, Pensacola, Fla, 88. *Collections Arranged:* New Figure Drawing, Twelve Latin American Artists (auth, catalog), 84; Elena Presser: Bach's Goldberg Variations, traveling (auth, catalog), 85-; Perceptions: Black & White, Work by Three Artists (auth, catalog), 86; plus curated fifty other exhibs. *Pos:* Dir galleries, Miami-Dade Community Col, Fla, 80-; art writer, Nouveau Mag, 88- *Teaching:* Instr drawing, Md Inst, Baltimore, 63-64; instr drawing & design, Vernon Co Jr Col, Newport, RI, 65-68 & Miami-Dade Community Col, Fla, 81- *Awards:* People's Prize, Ann Exhib, Newport Art Asn, 66, 67 & 69; Fla Endowment Humanities, 82 & NMex Art Coun, 83, America Is A Negro Child. *Bibliog:* Bea Moss (auth), Artist brushes with adventure, Miami Herald, 2/12/82; Joseph Traugott (auth), Arts, Albuqueraue J, 8/28/83; Paula Harper (auth), Art review, Miami News, 10/12/84. *Mem:* Cultural Exec Coun; Fla Art Mus Dir Asn. *Media:* Graphite on Paper. *Specialty:* Contemporary art with specialization on younger unknown artists; contemporary art from Latin America. *Publ:* Illusr, America Is A Negro Child: Race Poems & Drawings, Mesa Verde Press, 81; auth, The Invitation of the Self Portrait, Miami-Dade Community Col, 82; Jean Ward and the Observers As Steel Works, Gillman Gallery, 84. *Mailing Add:* 771 NE 116th St Biscayne Park FL 33161

LUSK, PATRICIA A
PAINTER, ADMINISTRATOR
b Carleston, SC, Sept 16, 45. *Study:* Univ SC, BFA, 76; studied with, Ed Betts, Al Brouillette, Jeanne Dobie, Babara Nechis, Charles Reid, Christopher Schink, Ralph Smith, Doris White & Robert Wood. *Work:* Cryovac (W R Grace) Inc, Greenville, SC; Greenville Mem Hosp; Stratford Col of Fine Arts, Hilton Head; Coca Cola, New York; Albritton, Tampa, Fla; Truffles, Hilton Head Island, SC; Nine pieces, St Francis Hosp, Greenville; painting of Osprey, Pub Ed-Art Comm, Hilton Head, 85 & 86. *Exhib:* Gibbs Mus, Charleston, SC, 80 & 83; York County Mus, Fort Mill, 82; Florence Mus, SC, 84; Spartanburg Art Mus, 86; Headley Whitley Mus, Lexington, Ky; Nevelle Mus, Wis; and others. *Pos:* Organizer, Jackson Art Workshops for Children, Greenville, 75-77; dir & designer studio space, Stratford Col of Fine Arts, 85- *Teaching:* Instr painting, Tempo Gallery, Greenville, 83-84 & Hilton Head Art League, 84-86; Recreation Ctr, Beaufort, SC; Hilton Head Island Art Workshops. *Awards:* Merit Award, SC Watercolor Soc, 83; Grumbache Silver Medal for Excellence, Beaufort Ann Exhib, 85. *Bibliog:* Elisa Krautter (auth), Musings, Island Packet, 5/27/85; Jeffery Hall (auth), The Artists series, Hilton Head Report, 5/9/86. *Mem:* Am Watercolor Soc; SC Watercolor Soc (pres, 86-87). *Media:* Watercolor. *Publ:* Contribr, Island Packet, 87-90, Islander Mag, 88, Island Scene Mag, 90 & US Art, 90. *Dealer:* Alicia Roman Baynard Cover Rd Hilton Head Island SC 29928. *Mailing Add:* 22 Plantation Dr Hilton Head Island SC 29928

LUSKER, RON
PAINTER, DESIGNER
b Chicago, Ill, Jan 28, 37. *Study:* Sch Art Inst Chicago, 54-60; Univ Ill, Chicago Circle, Ill State Gen Assembly scholar, 57-62; Univ Chicago, 62-63; Southern Ill Univ, Carbondale, BA, 65, MFA, 66. *Work:* Univ NC; Price Waterhouse, Chicago; Chase Manhattan; Southern Ill Univ; Aldrich Mus Contemp Art. *Exhib:* 14th Ann Painting & Sculpture Exhib, Peoria Art Ctr, Ill, 66; 70th Ann Midwest Painting Exhib, Art Inst Chicago, 67; Convocation Arts, Sculpture, State Univ NY Albany, 68; 4th Ann Art Exhib Sculpture, Staten Island, 69; Eastern Seaboard Regional 3rd Ann Sculpture Exhib, 70; plus others. *Teaching:* Instr art, Southern Ill Univ, Carbondale, 65-67; asst prof art, State Univ NY Stony Brook, 68-72; assoc prof art, Kingsborough Community Col, 72-74. *Awards:* Grad Sch for Sculpture Fel & Grant in Aid, State Univ NY Stony Brook, 69 & 70. *Bibliog:* Malcolm Preston (auth), Assemblages display intellectual fantasy, Newsday, 5/21/69; Claire White (auth), Exhibition review, Craft Horizons, 6/70; Albert Boime (auth), Cosmic artifacts: The work in lucite of Ron Lusker, Art J, winter 72. *Mem:* Am Craftsmen Coun; Col Art Asn Am; Ctr Study Democratic Insts. *Media:* Acrylic, Oils. *Publ:* Auth, New York: The season in sculpture, 8/70, The green meadow school, 8/70, The jewelry of Marci Zelmanoff, 12/70 & Attitudes, Brooklyn Museum, 70, Craft Horizons Mag. *Mailing Add:* 85 Mercer St New York NY 10012

LUTES, JIM (JAMES)
PAINTER
b Ft Louis, Wash, Dec 5, 55. *Study:* Wash State Univ, BA, 78; Art Inst Chicago, BFA 82. *Work:* Mus Contemp Art, Chicago; Ruth Nath, tom Biscotto, Lynne Warren, Jin Soo Kim, Regan Hiserman, James & Edie Cloonan, Chicago; Mus Contemp Art, Ghent, Belg. *Exhib:* Solo exhibs, Dart Gallery, Chicago, 86, 87, 88, 91 & 92, Michael Kohn Gallery, Los Angeles, 89 & Univ Mo, St Louis, 90, S Bitter-Larkin Gallery, New York, 92; Los Angeles County Mus, Los Angeles, 88; Mus Contemp Art, Chicago, 89; Human, Suburban Fine Arts Ctr, Highland Park, Ill, 91; Documenta IX (catalog), Ger, 92. *Teaching:* Vis artist, Art Inst Chicago, 83- *Awards:* Anna Louis Raymond Travelling Fel, 82; Awards in Visual Arts, 88. *Bibliog:* Articles in Art Paper 12/85, 1/86; Two decades of painting in Chicago, New Art Examiner, 12/87; Kathryn Hixson (auth), Jim Lutes, Arts Mag, 12/88; Carla McCormick (auth), Jim Lutes: Fat Chances, Artforum, 12/88; Alan G Artner (auth), Is Painting Dead, Chicago Tribune, 4/92. *Media:* Oil, Watercolor. *Dealer:* Dart Gallery 750 N Orleans No 303 Chicago IL 606010. *Mailing Add:* 2253 S Troy St Chicago IL 60623-3455

LUTZ, MARJORIE BRUNHOFF
SCULPTOR
b Cincinnati, Ohio, Jan 25, 33. *Study:* Art Students League, with Sidney Simon; Duke Univ. *Work:* Southern Vt Art Ctr, Manchester. *Comn:* Early Bird, Todd Hunter Develop Corp, welded steel abstract, Taft Steel Corp, New York, 81. *Exhib:* Ann Fall Show, Southern Vt Art Ctr, Manchester, 77-90; Energy Art, Foothills Art Ctr, Golden, Colo, 82; Lehman Libr, Fordham Univ, 82; Am Soc Contemp Artists Traveling Show, 84; solo show, Southern Vt Art Ctr, 84; Javits Fed Ctr, 83; Northstar Gallery, Stratton, Vt, 87-88; Chesterwood, Stockbridge, Mass, 89-90. *Teaching:* Instr sculpture, Southern Vt Art Ctr, Manchester, Vt. *Awards:* Doris Kriendler Mem Award, Am Soc Contemp Artists, 83. *Mem:* Am Soc Contemp Artists; Southern Vt Art Ctr, (dir, 88-93, vpres, 88, pres, 89-92); Screen Dir Guild. *Media:* Wood, Stone. *Dealer:* Bartholet Gallery 55 E 76th St New York NY 10021. *Mailing Add:* PO Box 14 Shushan NY 12873-0014

LUTZ, WINIFRED ANN
SCULPTOR, ENVIRONMENTAL ARTIST
b Brooklyn, NY, May 6, 42. *Study:* Cleveland Inst Art, BFA, 65; Atelier 17, with Stanley William Hayter, 65; Cranbrook Acad Art, MFA, 68. *Work:* Cleveland Mus Art; Albright-Knox Art Gallery; Chicago Art Inst; Desert Mus, Palm Springs, Calif; Crocker Gallery, Sacramento; Newark Mus, NJ; Int Paper Corp, New York; Jan van Eyck Akademie, Maastricht, Metherlands; Mount Holyoke Col Art Mus, Mass; Nat Bank of Chicago. *Exhib:* One-man show, Paper Reliefs, Am Craft Mus, New York, 75, Marilyn Pearl Gallery, 77-79, 84-85, 86, 88 & 90 New Am Paperworks, Int Traveling Invitational Exhib, 82-86, Paper as Image, Arts Coun of Great Britain, 83 & Dolan-Maxwell Gallery, Philadelphia, 90; Handmade Paper Objects, Santa Barbara Mus Art, Calif, 76; Handmade Paper, Prints & Unique Works, Mus Mod Art, New York, 76; Wood, Nassau Co Mus, Long Island, NY, 77; New Ways with Paper, Nat Collection Fine Art, DC, 78; Paper about Paper, Albright-Knox Art Gallery, Buffalo, New York, 80; Int Biennale Paper Art, Leopold-Hoesch Mus, Duren, Ger, 86 & 88; Light Cycle, Visual Arts Ctr of Alaska, Anchorage, 86; A Point of View--A Vista, Hewlett Gallery, Carnegie-Mellon Univ, Pittsburgh, 86; Paper Art, Mus Provencial, Hasselt, Belg, 88; Paper Makes Space, Nordyllandi Kunst, Denmark, 89 +251 Grand Lobby Installation, Brooklyn Mus, 90; A Natural Order, Hudson River Mus, Yonkers, NY, 90. *Teaching:* Asst prof sculpture, Yale Sch Art, 75-81, assoc prof, 81-82; assoc prof sculpture, Tyler Sch Art, 82- *Awards:* Nat Endowment Arts Fel, 84; Creative Time Inc Project Grant, 89; Pa Coun Arts, 89; Francis J Greenburger Found, 90. *Bibliog:* Jean Feinberg (auth), Findings of Winifred Lutz, Craft Horizons, 4/79; Jules Heller (auth), Papermaking, Watson-Guptill, 78; Maureen Bloomfield (auth), Nuances of number, Dialogue, an Art J, 11-12/85; Kotik (auth), The cutting edge, Kalamazoo Ctr for Arts, 88; Peter Gruen (auth), Viewpoint, Vol 9, No 6, Dialogue, 11-12/86; Bloemink (auth), A Natural Order, Hudson River Mus, 90. *Mem:* Col Art Asn. *Media:* All. *Publ:* Auth, Felting, Am Crafts Mag, 8-9/80; Casting to Acknowledge the Nature of Paper, Int Conf Hand Papermakers, Carriage House Press, 81; appendix of Non-Japanese Fibers for Japanese Papermaking, Weatherhill, 83; Surface Is A Function Of Distance, catalog essay, the Detroit Inst Arts Founders Soc, 88; Shrinking To Expand, Carriage House Press, 88. *Dealer:* Marilyn Pearl Gallery 420 W Broadway New York NY 10012. *Mailing Add:* c/o The Printclub & Gallery Store 1614 Latimer St Philadelphia PA 19103

LUX, GLADYS M
PAINTER, EDUCATOR
b Chapman, Nebr, 1899. *Study:* Kearney State Col, SS, 18; Univ Nebr, BFA, 25, AB, 33, MA, 35; Art Inst Chicago, SS, 29. *Work:* Peru State Col; Doane Col; Pub Schs, Kearney, Nebr; Artists Guild Collection, Lincoln, Nebr; Wesleyan Univ, Nebr. *Exhib:* Regional shows, Omaha, Minneapolis, Kansas City, Wichita & Topeka, 27-67; Art Inst Chicago, 36; Rockefeller Ctr, 36-38; New York World's Fair, 39; Joseph Pennell Mem Print Exhib; Art & Artists in Nebraska, 82, Great Plains 1930-1939 (traveling exhib), 85-86, Inflation-Sheldon Mem Art Gallery, Univ Nebr. *Teaching:* Instr art methods, Summer Schs, Univ Nebr, Lincoln, 23-25, Sioux City High Sch, 25-27; chmn dept art, Nebr Wesleyan Univ, 27-33 & 36-66, asst prof art, 36-50, assoc prof, 50-66, artist in residence, 66-67. *Awards:* Nebr Art Teachers Asn Serv Award, 69; Gov Arts Award, Nebr Arts Coun, 79; Distinguished Serv Award, Nebr Retired Teachers Asn, 80; Lincoln Mayor's Special Arts Award, Lincoln Arts Coun, 86. *Bibliog:* Article, Art Digest, 36-38; World's Fair exhibit, New Yorker, 39. *Mem:* Lincoln Artist Guild (past pres, secy); Nebr Art Teachers Asn (past pres, vpres). *Media:* Watercolor, Oil. *Res:* Purchased and renovating 1914 City Hall, University Place, Nebraska; historical conservation and building to become University Place Galleries. *Publ:* Auth, Symbols of Good Neighbors, Christ of the Andes, Candle Beam, 43; European arts seen internationally, Western Arts Asn Bull, 55; Students Exhibits, 59; illusr, In a Tall Land, 63; The baby doll, an evolution, 72 & Our hobby with TLC, 74, In: United Federation Doll Clubs Book 5. *Mailing Add:* c/o Milder Manor 1750 S 20th St Lincoln NE 68502

LUZ, VIRGINIA
PAINTER
b Toronto, Ont, Can, Oct 15, 11. *Study:* Cent Tech Sch. *Work:* Robert McLaughlin Gallery, Oshawa, Ont; Can Dept External Affairs; Can Embassies; J S McLean Collection; London Art Mus; also in many pvt collections. *Exhib:* Ont Soc Artists, 45-83; Can Women Artists Show (travelling exhib to New York & Can), 47-49; Can Soc Painters in Watercolour, 47-75; Can Tours; Can Group Painters; Tribute to Ten Women, Sisler Gallery, Toronto, Ont, 75; and others. *Teaching:* Instr illus, Cent Tech Sch, Toronto, 40-74, dir art, 69-74. *Mem:* Ont Soc Artists; Royal Can Acad; Can Soc Painters in Watercolour. *Media:* Watercolor. *Mailing Add:* 113 Delaware Ave Toronto ON M6H 2S9 Canada

LYFORD, CABOT
SCULPTOR, PAINTER
b Sayre, Pa, May 22, 25. *Study:* Skowhegan Sch Art, summer 47; Cornell Univ, BFA, 50; Sculpture Ctr, New York, 50-51. *Work:* Lamont Gallery, Exeter, NH; Addison Gallery Am Art, Andover, Mass; Wichita Mus, Kans; Colby Col, Waterville, Maine; New England Ctr Continuing Educ, Durham, NH; Ogunquit Art Mus; Portland Mus Art, Maine; Hunter Mus, Chattanooga, Tenn; over 150 pvt collections. *Comn:* Sculpture, Mt Sunapee Summit, NH, 64; Harbor Sculpture (black granite), Portsmouth, NH, 75; black granite whale, Prescott Park, Portsmouth, NH, 79; sculpture, Voc Tech, Stratham, NH, 83; Albacore Park Submariner Mem, Portsmouth, NH; and others. *Exhib:* Payson Mus, Portland, Maine; RI Festival, Providence; NH Art Asn, Manchester; Addison Gallery, Andover, Mass; Fitchburg Art Mus; Univ NH; and others. *Teaching:* Instr sculpture, Phillips Exeter Acad, NH, 63-86. *Awards:* Prizes, City Manchester, 70 & NH Architects Asn, 71 & 74-77; Sculpture Prize, Nat Acad Design, 90. *Media:* Stone, Wood; Watercolor. *Publ:* Contribr, Contemporary Stone Sculpture, 71. *Dealer:* Midtown Payson Galleries 745 Fifth Ave New York NY 10151; Hobe Sound Galeries Hobe Sound FL 33455. *Mailing Add:* Box 104, Rte 2 New Harbor ME 04554

LYLE, CHARLES THOMAS
ADMINISTRATOR
b Duluth, Minn, July 16, 46. *Study:* Univ Minn, James Wright Hunt scholar, 67-68, BA(cum laude), 68; Univ Del, Hagley fel, 68-70, MA(Am hist), 71. *Collections Arranged:* New Jersey Arts & Crafts: The Colonial Expression (with catalog), 72; American Crafts: The New Jersey Contribution, 75; American Folk Art, 75. *Pos:* Dir, Monmouth Co Hist Asn, Freehold, NJ, 71-78 & Hist Soc Del, 80-; dir mus, Nat Trust for Historic Preservation, 78-80; dir, Md Hist Soc, Baltimore, 90- *Teaching:* Vis inst, Mus Studies Dept, Univ Del; instr Am decor arts prior to 1900, Lincroft, NJ, 75-76. *Awards:* Scholar Am Friends, Attingham Summer Sch, 77; Hugley Fel, Univ Del, 68-70. *Bibliog:* Buildings and furniture of the Monmouth Co Hist Asn, Antiques, 1/80. *Mem:* Am Asn Mus; Middle Atlantic Asn Mus; Am Asn State & Local Hist; Nat Trust Hist Preserv; Nat Soc Fund Raising Exec. *Mailing Add:* Md Hist Soc 201 W Monument St Baltimore MD 21201

LYMAN, THOMAS WILLIAM
EDUCATOR, HISTORIAN
b Chicago, Ill, Apr 28, 26. *Study:* Univ Ill, BS, 49; Univ Chicago, PhD, 64. *Teaching:* Instr art hist, Art Inst Chicago, 60-65, dir admissions, 60-64; assoc prof, Southern Ill Univ, 65-67; from assoc prof to prof, Emory Univ, 62-, chmn, Art Hist Dept, 77-79, 81-82 & 88-89. *Awards:* Nat Endowment Humanities Fel, 80, Res Grant, 81-82. *Mem:* Col Art Asn; Medieval Acad Am. *Publ:* Auth, Architectural portraiture and Jan Van Eyck's Washington Annunciation, Gesta, 81; Saint-Sernin, Viollet-le-Duc et la theorie de l'harmonie des proportions, Gazette Beaux-Arts, 81; La table d'autel de Bernard Gilduin et son ambience orginelle, 82; French Romanesque Sculpture: An Annotated Bibliography, G K Hall, 87; Opus ad quadratum vs opus ad triangulum in 5-aisled romanesque churches, Artistes, Artisans et Production Artistique au Moyen Age, II, 88. *Mailing Add:* 1767 E Clinton Rd NE Atlanta GA 30307

LYNCH, BETTY
PAINTER, INSTRUCTOR
b McAlester, Okla. *Study:* Univ Tex, BA, 38; workshops with Robert E Wood, 72-88; also with Leonard Brooks, Rex Brandt & Charles Reid, Eliot O'Hara, Millard Sheets. *Work:* Mus Southwest, Midland, Tex; Art Asn Richmond, Ind. *Exhib:* Tex Watercolor Soc, Witte Mem Mus, San Antonio, 67, 68, 75, 82 & 83; Sun Carnival Art Exhib, El Paso, Tex, 67; Southwestern Print & Drawing Exhib, Dallas Mus Fine Arts, 69; Western Fedn Watercolor Soc, San Antonio, Tex, 79 & Phoenix, Ariz, 82 & Lubbock, Tex, 90; Am Watercolor Soc, 83, 85, 87 & 88. *Teaching:* Workshop instr watercolor, Okla, Calif, Kans, Fla, NMex, Wis, Mich, Colo, Nev, England & Spain, 77-83 & Artists Coop Workshops, France, 85; instr watercolor, La Romita Sch, Terni, Italy, 83, 84, 85, 87, 88, 89, 90, 92 & 93. *Awards:* Purchase Prize, Tex Watercolor Soc, 83; Ed Whitney Award, Am Watercolor Soc, 87; Best-In-Show, Watercolor Art Soc, Houston, 90. *Bibliog:* Florence Hutchinson Lonsford (auth), Spotlight on Kappa artists, The Key, 82. *Mem:* Tex Watercolor Soc; Midland Arts Asn; San Antonio Watercolor Group; Am Watercolor Soc. *Media:* Watercolor, Graphic Artist. *Publ:* Auth, Watercolor page, Am Artist Mag, 80; Travel Tips From the Pros, Am Artist Mag, 85; Featured in Western Art Digest's Watercolor Edition, 5/86. *Dealer:* Baker Gallery Fine Art 13th & Ave L Box 1920 Lubbock TX 79408. *Mailing Add:* 1500 Harvard Midland TX 79701

LYNCH, GERALD
SCULPTOR
b Philadelphia, Pa, Jan 26, 44. *Study:* Maryknoll Seminary Col, BA, 61-65; Philadelphia Col Art, 66 & 69; Nat Cathedral, 74 (stone carving apprentice). *Work:* Noyes Mus Fine Art, Oceanville, NJ; Cape May Co, NJ; Semeco Collection Contemp Art, Warsaw, Poland. *Comn:* Life size marble carving, Cathedral St Peter & Paul, Philadelphia, PA, 79; sculpture & stone carving, Nat Cathedral, Washington, DC, 81 & 82; 56 ft bas-relief, Tropicana Transportation Ctr, Atlantic City, NJ, 86; life-sized marble carving, Archit Prog, Cape May Co, NJ, 88. *Exhib:* Nat Shows at Nat Acad Design, New York, Am Inst Arts & Lett, Nat Arts & Salmagundi Club, 75-87; one-man show, House Rep, Cannon House Rotunda, Washington, DC, 82, Noyes Mus Fine Art, NJ, 85 & 88 & Eisenwerk Gallery, Philadelphia, Pa, 90; Trenton City Mus, NJ, 88; Ruth Zafrir Gallery, Philadelphia, Pa, 92. *Teaching:* Adj prof art, Atlantic Comm Col, NJ, 89-90; sculptor-in-residence, The Carving Studio, West Rutland, Vt, 90; instr, Marble Carving Symposium, Marble, Colo, 91 & 92. *Awards:* Gold Medal (sculpture), Allied Artists Am 62nd Ann Show, 75; Gold Medal, Ocean City Art Ctr Seventh Ann Show, 78; Art Symposium, Polish Sculpture Ctr, Oflonsko, Poland, 91. *Bibliog:* Burton Wasserman (reviewer), Art Matters, State of the Arts Prog, NJ Network TV; contribr, Academy Award Winning Doc, The Stone Carvers. *Media:* Marble, Bronze. *Mailing Add:* 206 E New York Ave Villas NJ 08251

LYNCH, MARY BRITTEN
PAINTER
b Pruden, Ky, Sept 30, 32. *Study:* Univ Tenn, Chattanooga, BA; Provincetown Workshop, Mass, studied with Leo Manso & Victor Candell; Univ Tenn, Knoxville, 65; Long Island Univ, Southampton, NY. *Work:* First Am Nat Bank, Nashville; Coca Cola Corp, Atlanta; South Central Bell, Atlanta; Tenn Valley Authority; Univ Tenn, Chattanooga. *Exhib:* Okla Arts Ctr, Oklahoma City, 74; solo traveling show, Southeast & West, 79-80; Nat Watercolor Soc, Calif; Miss State Col for Women; State Univ New York; Purdue Univ; and others. *Pos:* Founder, Lenoir City Arts Festival, Tenn, 63; Visual Arts Adv Panel Tenn Arts Comn. *Teaching:* Instr watercolor & acrylics, Hunter Mus Art, Chattanooga, 69-77, Watercolor Workshop, Univ Tenn, Chattanooga, 75, 85 & 86 & Chattanooga Christian High Sch, 80-86, Girl's Preparatory Sch & Baylor Sch, Chattanooga. *Awards:* Top Award, Tenn Watercolor Soc, 90; Cash Award 91 & Purchase Award, 92, Tenn Watercolor Soc; Exhib South, Gainesville, Fla, 92; and others. *Bibliog:* Southern Artisans (film for TV), 73. *Mem:* New York Artists Equity Asn; founding mem Tenn Watercolor Soc (founder, 69, treas, 70, vpres, 71, pres, 72-); Nat Watercolor Soc, Calif. *Media:* Watercolor, Acrylic. *Publ:* New York Art Rev 88; Biog Dir of Am Artists; Women in Art; Am Artist Mag Watercolor, 90. *Dealer:* Art South Montgomery AL; MaryAnna Thomison Asn Atlanta Ga. *Mailing Add:* 1505 Woodnymph Trail Lookout Mountain TN 37350

LYNCH, TOM (THOMAS MICHAEL)
PAINTER, INSTRUCTOR
b Chicago Ill, Feb 22, 50. *Work:* Neville Pub Mus, Wis; Burpee Art Mus, Rockford, Ill; Sagamon State Univ, Springfield, Ill; Standard Oil Corp, Chicago; and others. *Comn:* A Man and His City (paintings), Chicago Coun Fine Arts, 78; Portrait of a City (paintings), IBM Corp, Green Bay, Wis, 79 & Calumet City, Ill, 80; Chicago at Night & Chicago Harbors (paintings), Chicago Coun Fine Arts, 80; Spectrolith Corp Calendar; Five menu covers for Wag Restaurant; and others. *Pos:* Consulting dir, Am Int Art Ctr, Des Plaines, Ill, 81-; dir art, Ill Watercolor Soc, currently; consult, Hunt Speedball Products, Crescent Cardboard Co, & Raphael Brushes, currently; consult, Savoir-Faire Co, Calif & Lanaquadrelle Paper, France. *Teaching:* Instr watercolor, Dillman's Sand Lake Lodge, Wis, 79-81, 82-86, Northwestern Ohio Watercolor Soc & Southwest Watercolor Soc, Dallas, 81-86 & Southern Ariz Watercolor Soc, Tucson & Phoenix, 81-86, tools of the trade instr, currently. *Awards:* Graphic Art Award, Chicago Artist Guild, 79; First Place, Int Soc Artists, 80; Ochs Award Co Orange Co Watercolor Soc. *Bibliog:* Steve Fosdick (auth), Chicago at night, Herald, 5/81; Leona Toppel (auth), Profile, Downtown News, 12/81; Steve Doherty (auth), article, Am Artists, 5/81; Linda Rhodes (auth), profile, Ozark Mag, 2/85; Sue McGarry (auth), Group profile, Southwest Art, 5/85; Fred Klein (auth), Profile, Wall St J. *Mem:* Soc Am Impressionists (exec comt). *Media:* Watercolor. *Publ:* Auth & illusr, Watercolor lesson with Tom Lynch, Crafts & Things Mag, 81; auth, Watercolor page, Am Artist Mag, 81; illusr, Winter in Sleepy Hollow, Ford Times Mag, 81; contribr, Ford Times, 1/82, 4/82 & 12/82 & Readers Digest, 82; auth, The Magic of Watercolor, 82; Saluagh techniques, Am Artist, 4/86. *Dealer:* Richard Jamiolkowski 151 Laurel Ct Wheeling IL 60090. *Mailing Add:* 605 N Chestnut Arlington Heights IL 60004

LYNCH-NAKACHE, MARGARET
PAINTER
b Hartford, Conn, Dec 17, 32. *Study:* RI Sch Design, BFA, 54; Beaux-Arts, Paris, cert, 56; Atelier Chapelain-Midy. *Work:* L'Ambassade du Liban, Paris; Our Lady Victory Church, Centerville, Mass; Les Embrunts, Les Essembres, France; Georgetown Univ Hosp, Washington, DC;; Inst Keguruan Dan Ilum Pendidikan, Yogyakarta, Indonesia. *Comn:* Blown Tulips, Sargi, Dakar, Senegal, 78; Paris Cityscape, Cameron, Royal Oak, Mich, 78; Roses, Dagommer Cie, Paris, 78; Madonna, Ostronic, Potomac, Md, 79; Green Dunes, McDonald, Wellesley, Mass, 83. *Exhib:* One-person show, La Galerie du Meridien, Paris, 79, Hunter House, Vienna, Va, 82 & Georgetown Univ Hosp, Washington, DC, 85 & 87; All New England, 79; Coun of Arts Invitational, Colvin Mill Run, Va, 80; Long Branch Nature Ctr, 81; Cape Cod Art Asn, 83; Sandscape Gallery at Munson Meeting, Chatham, Mass, 88; and others. *Pos:* Artist, Universal Films, New York, 56-57 & Girl Scouts USA, Hq New York, 59-61; artist-in-residence, Art Barn, DC, 79; pres, Network For Artists, Kindred Art Collection & Host Exhib Ltd, McLean, Va, 79-85. *Awards:* Second Place, Cape Cod Art Asn, 56; Second Place, McLean Art Club, 79; Second Place, Dennis Art Festival, 81; Purchase Prize, Herdon Fine Art Exhib, 89. *Bibliog:* L Chauvin (auth), Margaret Nakache, Galerie Jardin des Arts, 2/75; E Holgren (auth), Whisperings and sharings, Alexandrian Mag, spring 78; J de Recqueville (auth), Carnet des arts, Paris-Tel, 1/79. *Mem:* bd mem McLean Project for the Arts. *Media:* Watercolor, Oil. *Publ:* Contribr, Cadette Girl Scout Handbook, Girls Scouts USA, 63; auth, Art royalties, Int Herald Tribune, 5/16/77; Art game letters, Washington Post Mag, 11/5/78. *Mailing Add:* PO Box 68 West Hyannisport MA 02672

LYNDE, STAN
CARTOONIST, ILLUSTRATOR
b Billings, Mont, Sept 23, 31. *Study:* Univ Mont; Sch Visual Arts, New York, 56-57. *Exhib:* The Evolution of Rick O'Shay, Yellowstone Co Fine Arts Ctr, Billings, Mont, 63; The Paintings of Stan Lynde, Midland Nat Bank, Billings, 75. *Pos:* Creator, auth & artist comic strip, Rick O'Shay, Chicago Tribune-New York News Syndicate Inc, 58-77 & Latigo, Field Newspaper Syndicate, 79-83. *Awards:* Inkpot Award Achievement in Comic Arts, 77; Mont Gov Award Arts, 83. *Bibliog:* A History of the Comic Strip, 68; Comics of the American West, 77; articles, Cartoonist Profiles Mag, 69, 70, 79, & 81. *Mem:* Nat Cartoonist's Soc; Comic Arts Prof Soc. *Media:* Pen & Ink; Oil. *Publ:* Auth, Rick O'Shay and Hipshot--The Great Sunday Pages, Tempo Bks, 76; Rick O'Shay, Hipshot, and Me, Cottonwood Graphics, 90. *Mailing Add:* 2340 Trumble Creek Rd Kalispell MT 59901

LYNDS, CLYDE
SCULPTOR, PAINTER
b Jersey City, NJ, June 22, 36. *Study:* Art Students League, 58-63; Frank J Reilly Sch, New York, 63-68. *Work:* Nat Mus Am Art, Washington, DC; Wadsworth Atheneum, Hartfield, Conn; Jacksonville Mus, Fla; New York Univ; Marion Koogler McNay Art Inst, San Antonio, Tex. *Comn:* Sculpture, Schneider Children's Hosp, New Hyde Park, NY, 88; sculpture, World Expo, Brisbane, Australia, 88; sculpture, State of New Jersey, NJ Mem Veterans Home, 90; sculpture, AT&T Guardian Ctr, New York, 91; sculpture, Nogales Border Sta, Nogales, Ariz, 92; and others. *Exhib:* Solo exhibs, Babcock Galleries, NY, 69, 71, 73 & 75, Corcoran Gallery Art, Washington, DC, 73,

Wallace Wentworth Gallery, Washington, DC, 85 & 87, OK Harris Works of Art, New York, 86, 88 & 91 & Yoh Art Gallery, Osaka, Japan, 92; Aldrich Mus, Conn, 88; La Musee de la Civilization, Que, Can, 89; Stadtmuseum, Dusseldorf, Ger, 90; Univ Calif, 90; group exhib, Nicaf, Yokohama, Japan, 92. *Pos:* Bd dir, Bermant Found. *Awards:* First prize, Monmouth Col, 68; First prize & Medal of Honor, Painters & Sculptors Soc, NJ, 68; NJ State Coun Arts Fel, 84; Fels, NJ State Coun on Arts, 84 & 88. *Bibliog:* Sculpture Mag, 4/89 & 7/90. *Media:* Miscellaneous Media; Acrylic, Oil. *Publ:* Frederick Morgan, auth, Drawings, Poems of the Two Worlds, Verona, Italy. *Dealer:* O K Harris Gallery 383 W Broadway New York NY 10012; Yoh Art Gallery Osaka Japan. *Mailing Add:* 20 Franklin Ave Wallington NJ 07057

LYON, ROBERT F
SCULPTURE, ADMINISTRATOR
b Queens, NY, Sept 3, 52. *Study:* Mercer County Community Col, AA, 72; Trenton State Col, BA, 74, Tyler Sch Art, MFA, 77. *Work:* New Orleans Mus Art, La; Mercer Co Heritage Commission, Trenton, NJ; Kohler Co, Wis; Lamar Dodd Art Ctr, La Grange, Ga; Pan Am Insurance Co, New Orleans, La. *Comn:* Bronze, clay reliefs, Rouse Co, Portland, Ore, 89. *Exhib:* One man exhibs, Arthur Roger Gallery, New Orleans, 89, McIntosh Gallery, Atlanta, Ga, 90 & Artists Alliance Lafayette, La, 92; Triennial, New Orleans Mus Art, La, 80; Southern Exposure, Alternative Mus, New York, 85; Southeastern Exhib, Fine Arts Mus South, Mobile, Ala, 90; Lamar Dodd Art Ctr, LaGrange, Ga, 90; Art Works About Art, John Michael Kohler Arts Ctr, Sheboygan, Wis, 90; Out Door Sculpture Tour, Univ Tenn, Knoxville, Tenn, 90; Invitational Sculpture Exhib, Southeastern Col Art Conf, Memphis, Tenn, 91. *Pos:* Bd dir, Baton Rouge Gallery, 88- *Teaching:* Prof sculpture, La State Univ, Baton Rouge, 78- *Awards:* Project/Exhib Grant, Southeastern Col Art Conf, 89; artist-in-residence, Banff Ctr, 89; artist-in-residence, Sculpture Space, Utica, NY, 93. *Bibliog:* Charlotte Speight (auth), Images in Clay Sculpture, Harper & Row, 83; Susan Wechsler (auth), A house is not always a home, Am Ceramics, 86; Robert Speer (auth), Two makes more, CN & R, 89. *Mem:* Int Sculpture Ctr; Col Art Asn; Southeastern Col Art Conf; Baton Rouge Gallery (bd dirs, 88-); Nat Coun Art Admin. *Media:* All Media. *Publ:* Coauth, Vaselike Ware: An early Bronze Age pottery style in Crete, Paul Astroms Forlag, 79. *Dealer:* Arthur Roger Gallery 432 Julia St New Orleans, LA 70130. *Mailing Add:* 1506 S Eugene St Baton Rouge LA 70808

LYONS, BEAUVAIS
PRINTMAKER, EDUCATOR
b Hanover, NH, Feb 24, 58. *Study:* Alfred Univ, 77; Univ Wis-Madison, BFA, 80; Ariz State Univ, MFA, 83. *Work:* Grunwald Ctr Graphic Arts, Los Angeles, Calif; Herbert F Johnson Mus Art, Cornell Univ, Ithaca, NY; Madison Art Ctr, Wis; Kohler Art Libr, Madison, Wis; Univ SDak-Vermillion. *Exhib:* Fla State Univ, Tallahasee, 89; Rare Discoveries from the Hokes Archives, Cheekwood Fine Arts Ctr, Nashville, Tenn, 90; James Madison Univ, Harrisonburg, Va, 91; Salem Col, Winston-Salem, NC, 91; Selections from the Hokes Archives, Print Club, Philadelphia, Pa, 92; and others. *Pos:* Dir, Hokes Archives, 83- *Teaching:* Vis asst prof art, Weber State Col, Ogden, Utah, 84-85; asst prof, Univ Tenn, Knoxville, 85-89, assoc prof, 89. *Awards:* Purchase Award, Los Angeles Printmaking Soc, 84; Southern Arts Fedn/Nat Endowment Arts Regional Fel, 88. *Bibliog:* Roy H Behrens (auth), Design in the Visual Arts, 84 & Illustration as an Art, 85, Prentice-Hall; Jacqueline Brody (auth), article, Print Collectors Newslett, 5-6/90. *Mem:* Southern Graphics Coun; Col Art Asn. *Media:* All Media. *Publ:* Auth, The excavation of the apasht: Artifacts from an imaginary past, Leonardo J, Vol 18, No 2, 85; Speakeasy, New Art Examiner, Vol 17, No 5, 1/90; Artistic Freedom and the University, Art J, Vol 50, No 4, winter 91. *Mailing Add:* Dept Art-Univ Tenn 1715 Volunteer Blvd Knoxville TN 37996-2410

LYONS, FRANCIS E, JR
ART DEALER, LECTURER
b Detroit, Mich, Feb 14, 43. *Study:* Oakland Univ, BA, 68; City Col San Francisco, studied archit, 73; Montgomery Col, Md, 74. *Pos:* Co-founder & owner, Xochipilli Gallery, Rochester, Mich, 70-72; gallery rep & nat mgr, Marson Galleries, Baltimore, Md, 74-81; pres & owner, Frank Lyons Collection, Baltimore, Md, 81-; consult & interim dir, Venable-Neslage Gallerie, Washington, DC, 92- *Teaching:* Lectr, prints & printmaking, numerous cols, univs & art ctrs, 76- *Specialty:* 19th and 20th century prints and photographs; Japanese ukiyo-e and sosaka-hanga; early photography. *Mailing Add:* 6 Hyot Ave Glens Falls NY 12801

LYONS, JOAN
PHOTOGRAPHER
b New York, NY, Mar 6, 37. *Study:* Alfred Univ, BFA, 57; State Univ NY, Buffalo, MFA, 73. *Work:* Visual Studies Workshop, Rochester, NY; Ctr Creative Photog, Tucson, Ariz; Mus Mod Art, New York; San Francisco Mus Mod Art; Minneapolis Art Inst. *Exhib:* In Sequence, Mus Fine Arts, Houston, 82; Facets of the Collection, Mus Mod Art, San Francisco, 83; one-woman show, Ctr Creative Photog, Tucson, 84; Beyond Words, Art of the Book, Mem Art Gallery, Rochester, 86; Evocative Presence, Mus Fine Arts, Houston, 88; La Camera Ciega, Mus Art Contemp, Seville, Spain, 88; New photomontage, Cranbook Acad Art, Bloomfield Hill, Minn, 88. *Pos:* Dir, Visual Studies Workshop Press, 72- *Teaching:* Adj instr visual studies, Visual Studies Workshop, 75-, State Univ NY, Brockport, 86- *Awards:* CAPS Fel, NY, 75 & 81. *Bibliog:* Tom Dugan (auth), Photography Between Covers, Light Impressions, 80; Ann Tucker (auth), Target Collection, Mus Fine Arts, Houston, 84; Joan Foncuberta (auth), Phot Visions No 15, Barcelona, Spain. *Mem:* Soc Photog Educ. *Publ:* Auth Ten self-pub artist's bks, 72-; ed, Artist's Books, a Critical Anthology & Source Book, Visual Studies Workshop Press, 86. *Dealer:* Visual Studies Workshop 31 Prince St Rochester NY 14607. *Mailing Add:* 176 Rutgers St Rochester NY 14607

LYONS, LISA
CURATOR, HISTORIAN
b Minneapolis, Minn, Dec 13, 50. *Study:* Northwestern Univ, Evanston, Ill, BA(art hist), 72; Columbia Univ, New York, MA(art hist), 73. *Collections Arranged:* Scale & Environment: 10 Sculptors (contribr, catalog), 77, Nicholas Africano, 78, Eight Artists: The Elusive Image (auth, catalog), 79, Close Portraits (auth, catalog), 80, The Anxious Edge (auth, catalog), 82, Wegman's World (auth, catalog), 82, Walker Art Ctr, Minneapolis; 39th Biennial Cont Painting (auth, catalog), 85, Corcoran Gallery Art, Washington, DC; Nicholas Africano: Innocence & Experience (auth, catalog), 91, Siah Armajani: The Poetry Garden & Recent Works, 92 & Chris Burden and Lynn David, 92, Lannan Found, Los Angeles, Calif. *Pos:* Fel, Toledo Mus Art, Ohio, 73-74; Rockefeller Found Fel, Walker Art Ctr, Minneapolis, 75-77, asst cur, 77-78, cur, 79-82; dir acquisitions, Mus Fund, Minneapolis, 83-89; dir art progs, Lannan Found, Los Angeles, Calif, 89- *Publ:* Auth, Henri Matisse: 1914-1917, Arts Mag, 5/75; An interview with James Byrne, Studio Int, 5-6/76; contribr, The river: Images of the Mississippi, Walker Art Ctr, 76; Auth, Chuck Close, Rizzoli Int Publ, 87. *Mailing Add:* c/o Lannan Found 5401 McConnell Ave Los Angeles CA 90066

LYSUN, GREGORY
PAINTER, RESTORER
b Yonkers, NY, Oct 24, 24. *Study:* Art Students League, with Louis Bouche, Edwin Dickinson, John Groth, Robert Beverly Hale & Reginald Marsh, 47-53. *Work:* Art Students League; Berkshire Mus, Pittsfield, Mass; New Britain Mus Am Art, Conn; De Cordova Mus, Lincoln, Mass; Butler Inst Am Art, Youngstown, Ohio. *Comn:* Portrait of Ruth Taylor, Westchester Community Serv Coun, Inc, White Plains, NY, 75; restoration work of 6 paintings by Edward Gay, comn by Mrs S Gay Linville, Scarsdale, NY, 81; restoration work of painting by John Steuart Curry, comn by Eugene Curry, Armonk, NY, 81; restoration of John Stewart Curry's Portrait of a Gypsy, Jefferson Co Hist Soc, Oskaloosa, Kans, 82; restoration work of the Pieta, statue, comn by St Joseph's Church, Bronxville, NY, 91. *Exhib:* 35 Years in Retrospect, 1936-1970, Butler Inst Am Art Midyear Show, 71; 67th Ann Exhib Conn Acad Fine Arts, Wadsworth Atheneum Mus, Hartford, Conn, 77; Art Teachers Juries Exhib, Neuberger Mus, State Univ NY, Col at Purchase, 77; From the 1920's to the present, works from the League's permanent collection, Art Students League, New York, 77; Directors Choice Exhib, selections from DeCordova Mus, Lincoln, Mass, 78; Ann Allied Arts Am, 85; 75th Nat Exhib, Conn Acad Fine Arts, William Benton Mus, Storrs, Conn, 88; and others. *Teaching:* Instr painting & drawing, Westchester Art Workshop, Co Ctr, White Plains, NY, 69-, Pelham Art Ctr, 78- & State Univ NY Col, Purchase, 82-; instr painting & drawing & chmn, Dept Art, Fairview-Greenburgh Community Ctr, Greenburgh, NY, 72- *Awards:* Alice Collins Dunham Award, Best Portrait, 73rd Nat Exhib, Conn Acad Fine Arts, 83; Purchase Prize, 31st Ann Nat, Butler Inst Am Art, 83; Conn Acad Prize, 76th Ann Exhib, Conn Acad Fine Arts, 86; and others. *Bibliog:* Winifred B Bell (auth), Paintings by Gregory Lysun, Berkshire Eagle, 71; Helen Ganz Spiro (auth), Art students follow teacher's example, 82 & Painter takes students to a different world, 83, Gannett Westchester Newspapers. *Mem:* Life mem Art Students League; Allied Artists Am; life fel Am Artists Prof League; Conn Acad Fine Arts; Hudson Valley Art Asn. *Media:* Oil. *Publ:* Auth, The construction of a painting, Palette Talk, 79. *Mailing Add:* 481 Winding Rd N Ardsley NY 10502

LYTLE, RICHARD
PAINTER, EDUCATOR
b Albany, NY, Feb 14, 35. *Study:* Cooper Union; Yale Univ, BFA & MFA; also with Josef Albers. *Work:* Mus Mod Art, New York; Yale Art Gallery; Nat Collection Art, Washington, DC; Minneapolis Mus Fine Arts; Cincinnati Art Mus. *Comn:* Concrete relief mural, Fairfield Univ, 65. *Exhib:* 16 Americans, Mus Mod Art, New York, 59; Seattle World's Fair, 62; Whitney Mus Am Art Ann, New York, 63; Art: USA: Now, SC Johnson Collection, World Tour, 63-; one-man show, De Cordova Mus, Lincoln, Mass, 74; Hopkins Ctr, Dartmouth Col, 86; plus others. *Teaching:* Instr art, Yale Univ, 60-63, assoc prof, 66-81, prof 81-, actg dean, Yale Sch Art, 80-81 & 90; dean, Silvermine Col Art, 63-66. *Awards:* Fulbright Grant to Italy, 58; Prof Achievement Citation & Augustus St Gaudens Award, 85, Cooper Union. *Bibliog:* Art: USA: NOW, Viking Press, 63; 16 Americans, Mus Mod Art, 59. *Media:* Oil, Watercolor. *Dealer:* Munson Gallery 35 Whitney Ave New Haven CT 06510. *Mailing Add:* Dept Art Yale Univ New Haven CT 06520

LYTTON, CONSTANCE B
PRINTMAKER, PAINTER
b New York, NY. *Study:* Col William & Mary; Art Students League with Rudolph Baranik; Ruth Leaf Studio Atelier 778. *Work:* Wesleyan Univ, Middletown, Conn; Univ Chicago. *Exhib:* Solo exhib, Davison Art Ctr, Wesleyan Univ, Middletown, Conn, 66; Butler Institute of American Art Traveling Exhib, Youngstown, Ohio, 88; The Larger Print, Midge Karr Gallery, NY Inst Technol, Westbury, 90; Mus Southwest, Midland, Tex, 90; Port Washington, NY Libr 91; ARC Gallery, Chicago, 92; and others. *Pos:* Co-Dir, Prints Etc, Whitestone, NY. *Awards:* Juror's Award, Conn Women Artist Ann, 74. *Mem:* Artist Equity; Nat Asn Women Artist; Hempstead Harbor Art Asn. *Media:* Etching, Monoprint; Mixed Media. *Dealer:* Skidmore Asn 645 Snowden Lane Princeton NJ. *Mailing Add:* 21 Schenck Ave Great Neck NY 11021

M

MAAS, MARION ELIZABETH
PAINTER
b Brooklyn, NY, Feb 27, 30. *Study:* Pratt Inst, BS, 51; New York Univ; Frank Reully Sch Art. *Exhib:* The Garden, Mill Pond House, St James, LI, NY, 89; 100 Years 100 Works Nat Asn Women Artists traveling exhib, Islip Art Mus, East Islip, NY, 89, Fine Arts Mus, Mobile, Ala, 89, Chattanooga Regional Mus, Tenn, 89, Longview Mus Art, Tex, 89, Kirkpatrik Art Ctr, Oklahoma City, 90; Centennial Celebration, Jehangir Art Gallery, Bombay & Baroda, India, 89-90. *Awards:* Best in show, Nat Art League, 86; First Prize, Nat Asn Women Artists, 87. *Mem:* Nat Asn Women Artists; Catherine Lorillard Wolfe Art Club. *Media:* Acrylic, oil. *Dealer:* Discovery Art Gallery 3 Brewster St Glen Cove NY 11542. *Mailing Add:* 85-57 67th Rd Rego Park NY 11374

MAASS, RICHARD ANDREW
MUSEUM DIRECTOR
b New York, NY, Apr 11, 46. *Study:* Univ Wis, Madison, BA(Am hist), 68; New Sch for Social Res, New York, MA, 72; Cooperstown Grad Prog, MA(mus admin), 73. *Pos:* Ecol supvr, Mus City New York, 70-71; asst prog dir, S St Seaport Mus, New York, 71-72; dir, Fresno Arts Ctr, 73-80; exec dir, Tucson Mus of Art, 80-85; dir, Tampa Mus Art, 85- *Awards:* Fel, Sem for Hist Adminr, Colonial Williamsburg, 71; Fel, Harvard Bus Sch Arts Admin Sem, 73. *Mem:* Am Asn Mus; Fla Art Mus Dir Asn; Southeastern Mus Conference (bd mem); Asn Art Mus Dir. *Mailing Add:* Tampa Mus Art 601 Doyle Carlton Dr Tampa FL 33602

MCADOO, CAROL WESTBROOK
CERAMIST, PAINTER
b Colonial Heights, Va, Dec 28, 37. *Study:* Self taught. *Work:* Lauren Rogers Mus, Laurel, Miss; NCNB Art Collection, Charlotte, NC; P Hanes Collection, Winston-Salem, NC; AT&T Corp; Coca-Cola Corp. *Comn:* Mag cover, Brown's Guide to Georgia, Atlanta, 73. *Exhib:* Piedmont Painting & Sculpture, Mint Mus Art, Charlotte, NC, 71; 4th Realist Exhib, Southeastern Ctr Contemp Art, Winston-Salem, NC, 72; Rogers Mus Exhib, Lauren Rogers Mus, Laurel, Miss, 72; one-woman exhibs, Mint Mus Art, Charlotte, NC, 73 & Wilson Arts Coun, NC, 75; Soc Four Arts, Palm Beach, Fla, 73; Catherine Lorillard Wolfe, Nat Arts Club, New York, 80. *Teaching:* Private lessons. *Awards:* 3rd Place, Cape Coral Nat Exhib, 71; Purchase Award, Lauren Rogers Mus, 72; 1st Place Painting, 23rd Ann Poplar Lawn Art Festival, 81. *Mem:* Nat Soc Painters Casein & Acrylic; South Cobb Arts Alliance; SEastern Ctr Contemp Art. *Media:* Clay; Acrylic. *Publ:* Auth, Reflections of the Outer Banks, Island Publ House, 76. *Dealer:* Edward L Greene Box 265 Manteo NC 27954. *Mailing Add:* 5070 Sunset Trail NE Marietta GA 30067

MCALLISTER, GERALDINE E
GALLERY DIRECTOR
b Asher, Okla, Sept 22, 25. *Study:* Univ Calif, San Diego, BA, 72, MFA, 74. *Pos:* Dir, Mandeville Gallery, Univ Calif, San Diego, 75- *Mem:* Nat Soc Arts & Lett; Univ Calif & San Diego Alumni Asn (pres). *Mailing Add:* Mandeville Gallery B-027 Univ Calif San Diego La Jolla CA 92093

MACARAY, LAWRENCE RICHARD
PAINTER, EDUCATOR
b Elsinore, Calif, May 8, 21. *Study:* Whittier Col, BA, 51; Calif State Univ, Long Beach, MA, 55. *Work:* Bowers Mus, Santa Ana, Calif; San Bernardino Co Mus Art; Bertrand Russell Peace Found, Nottingham, Eng; Spectrum Press, Orange, Calif; pvt collection of art critic, William Wilson, Los Angeles Times. *Comn:* Location oil paintings of Eng & Ireland, 75. *Exhib:* New Talent, New York, Los Angeles Co Mus Art, 71-72; Bertrand Russell Centenary Art Exhib, Nottingham, 73; Southern Calif Regional Print & Drawing Exhib, 73, 74 & 76; Long Beach Mus Art, 80; Joslyn Ctr Arts, Torrance, Calif, 82; Grants Pass Mus Art, Ore, 83; Prize Winner, La Mirada Festival of the Arts, 84; one man show, Joslin Fine Arts Gallery, Torrance, Calif, 85; El Camino Col Exhib, 87. *Pos:* Art & travel ed, Torrance Press-Herald, Calif, 63-70. *Teaching:* Prof drawing & painting, El Camino Col, 62-88. *Awards:* Prize for Art Unlimited, Downey Mus Art, Calif, 74; Southern Calif Exposition Prize, Del Mar, 74; All Calif Art Exhib Prize, 76. *Media:* Oil. *Mailing Add:* 1431 E La Palma Ave Anaheim CA 92805

MACAULAY, DAVID ALEXANDER
DESIGNER, ILLUSTRATOR
b Burton on Trent, Eng, Dec 2, 46. *Study:* RI Sch Design, BArchit, 69. *Work:* Cooper Hewitt Mus, New York; Toledo Mus Art; Mus Art, RI Sch Design. *Exhib:* Ann Int Exhib Children's Bk Illus, Bologna, Italy, 76-77; 200 Years Am Illus, Mus of Hist, New York, 77; Buildingbooks, 77 & Drawing the Line, 78, Montclair Art Mus, NJ; Children's Book Art, Monterey Peninsula Mus Art, Calif & Triton Mus Art, Santa Clara, Calif, 78-79. *Pos:* Free lance graphic designer & illusr, 72- *Teaching:* Instr 2-dimensional design, RI Sch Design, 74-76, adj prof illus, 76-85, chmn dept, 77-79; vis lectr, Yale Univ, 78-79; vis instr drawing, Brown Univ, 82-; vis prof art, Wellesley Col, 85- *Awards:* Caldecott Hon Medal, Am Libr Asn, 74 & 78; Deutscher Jungenbuchpreis (Best non-fiction picture book), Ger, 75; Medal, Am Inst of Archit, 78. *Bibliog:* Paul Goldberger (auth), Schede/Libri, Abitare, Edtrice Segesta, Milan, 5/76 & How to build a castle, New York Times, 11/77; Stefan Kanfer (auth), Books, Time Mag, 11/77. *Mem:* Providence Preserv Soc (trustee). *Media:* Pen & Ink. *Publ:* Auth & illusr, Cathedral, The Story of Its Construction, 73, City, A Story of Roman Planning and Construction, 74, Underground, 76, Great Moments in Architecture, 78, Motel of the Mysteries, 79, Help! Let Me Out, 82, Mill, 83, The Amazing Brain, 84 & Baaa, 85, Houghton Mifflin; and many publications internationally. *Mailing Add:* c/o Space Gallery of Archit 39 W 67th St New York NY 10023

MACAULAY, THOMAS S
ENVIRONMENTAL ARTIST, SCULPTOR
b Marshfield, Wis, Jul 2, 46. *Study:* St Olaf Col, BA, 68; Univ Iowa, MA, 70, MFA, 71. *Exhib:* Solo exhibs, Twining Gallery, New York, 87,Harvard Univ, Cambridge, Mass, 88, Ind Univ, Bloomington, 89, Contemp Mus, Honolulu, 90, Univ Colo, Boulder, 90, La Pietra, Honolulu, 91 & USE Western Reserve Univ, 92. *Teaching:* Prof sculpture, Wright State Univ, Dayton, Ohio, 73- *Awards:* Fel, Guggenheim Mem Found, 84; Fel, Asian Cult Coun, 87; Fel, Fulbright Scholar Research, Japan-US Educ Comn, 91. *Bibliog:* Donald Kuspit & Betty Collings (coauth), Macaulay's Sculptural Views of Perceptual Ambiguity, Dayton Art Inst, 86; Donald Kuspit (auth), Thomas Macaulay: The Circle Squared, Univ Del, 90; Ann Bremner (auth), Thomas Macaulay A Year, Southern Ohio Mus. *Mem:* Artist's Organization (pres, 87-92). *Media:* Environmental Installation, Miscellaneous Media. *Publ:* Auth, Hawall Architect: Art in Architecture, Hawaii Coun-Am Inst Architects, 3/90. *Dealer:* Twining Gallery 568 Broadway New York NY 10012. *Mailing Add:* 5510 S Scarff Rd New Carlisle OH 45344

MCAULEY, SKEET
PHOTOGRAPHER, EDUCATOR
Monahans, Tex, Mar 7, 51. *Study:* Sam Houston State Univ, BA, 76; Ohio State Univ, MFA, 78. *Work:* Int Ctr Photog, New York; New York Pub Libr, NY; Mus Fine Arts, Houston, Tex; Rose Art Mus, Brandeis Univ, Waltham, Mass; Tyler Mus Art, Tex; Nat Mus Am Art, Washington, DC; Dallas Mus Art, Tex; Amon Carter Mus, Ft Worth, Tex; Ctr Creative Photog, Tucson, Ariz. *Exhib:* Solo exhibs, Simon Lowinsky Gallery, New York, 89, Amon Carter Mus, Ft Worth, Tex, 89, Burden Gallery, New York, 89, Barry Whistler Gallery, Dallas, Tex, 89, Calif Mus Photog, Riverside, 91, Heard Mus, Amherst, Mass, 91, Moody Gallery, Houston, Tex, 92, Dallas Mus Art, Tex, 92; Janet Borden Gallery, New York, 89; The State I'm In, Dallas Mus Art, Tex, 91; Fotografia Am del SXX, Sala de Exposiciones de la Fundacion 'La Caixa', Madrid & Centre Cultural de la Fundacion 'La Caixa', Barcelona, Spain, 91; Who Discovered Whom, Islip Art Mus, NY, 92; Between Home and Heaven, Nat Mus Am Art, Washington, DC & Carnegie Mus Art, Pittsburg, Pa, 92; This Sporting Life, High Mus Art, Atlanta, Ga & Sarah Campbell Blaffer Gallery, Houston, Tex, 92. *Teaching:* Instr photog, Spring Hill Col, Mobile, Ala, 78-79, Tyler Jr Col, Tyler, Tex, 79-81; assoc prof photog, Univ NTex, Denton, 81- *Awards:* Nat Endowment Arts Individual Artist Fels, 84 & 86; Polaroid Artist Support Grant, Polaroid Corp, 88. *Bibliog:* Charles Hagen (auth), Tricky Attempts to Juggle Esthetics & Politics, NY Times, 6/14/92; High Mus Art, This Sporting Life, 1878-1991, Atlanta, Ga, 92; Merry Foresta (auth), Between Home & Heaven, Contemporary American Landscape Photography, Nat Mus Am Art, Washington, DC, 92. *Publ:* Sign Language: Contemporary Southwestern Native America, Aperture Press, 89. *Dealer:* Barry Whistler Gallery 2909-A Canton St Dallas TX 75226. *Mailing Add:* 303 N Winnetka Dallas TX 75208

MACBIRD, ROSEMARY (SIMPSON)
PAINTER
b St Joseph, Mo, Nov 19, 21. *Study:* Art Inst Chicago, 41-43; also with Robert Wood, 82, Zoltan Szabo, 82 & Charles Reid, 83. *Comn:* Watercolors, Santa Barbara Bank, Calif, 81, Lawrence Stewart, Phoenix, Ariz, 82, Norman G Oliver, Hollywood, Calif, 83, Bonnie & Alan Kay, Los Angeles, 90 & Barbara Alter, Newport Beach, Calif, 92. *Exhib:* Knickerbocker Artists Ann Exhib, Salmagundi Club, New York, 83-84; Catherine Lorillard Wolfe Women Artists of America, 84-85; Allied Artists Am Ann Exhib, Nat Arts Club New York, 84-85; Orange Co Fair Ann Art Exhib, Juror & exhibitor, Santa Ana, Calif, 89; US Dept Immigration & Naturalization Serv Centennial Art Exhib, Images of American Immigration, a three year traveling exhib, Georgetown Univ Art Gallery, Washington, DC, Ellis Island New York, Atlanta Fulton Co Libr, Atlanta, Ga, John F Kennedy Mus & Libr, Boston, Mass, Transamerica Tower, San Francisco, Calif, Natural Hist Mus, Los Angeles, Calif, 91-93; and others. *Awards:* Santa Fe Fed Bank Purchase Award, Watercolor West Ann Exhib, 80; Grumbacher Gold Medal & Cash Award, Knickerbocker Artists Ann Exhib, 83; Best Watercolor Artist in Show Award, Art-a-Fair Festival, 89; and others. *Mem:* Nat Watercolor Soc; Knickerbocker Artists; Am Soc Marine Artists; San Diego Watercolor Soc; Costa Mesa Art League. *Media:* Watercolor, Oil. *Dealer:* Watercolor Gallery 1415 S Coast Hwy Laguna Beach CA 92651; Lu Martin Galleries 372 N Coast Hwy Laguna Beach CA 92651. *Mailing Add:* 913 Q Ronda Sevilla Laguna Hills CA 92653

MCBRYDE, SARAH ELVA
PAINTER, PRINTMAKER
b Columbus, Ohio, July 2, 42. *Study:* Syracuse Univ; Washington Univ, St Louis, Mo, BFA, study with Fred Becker & Arthur Osver; Washington Univ scholar, Skowhegan Sch Painting & Sculpture; Am Univ, Washington, DC, MFA. *Comn:* Mural on Hotel, San Blas Islands, Panama, Cent Am; paintings, Mrs & Mrs Harry B Willis, Panama City, Cent Am & Mrs Hestlene Martin, Washington, DC; mural, Transemantics, Inc, Washington, DC; and others; portraits of Giambattista Vico and others, Centro di Studi Vichiani, Naples, Italy; portrait on silk of G B Vico, NY Inst for Vico Studies, 89. *Exhib:* Batik Exhib, Martin Luther King Libr; Washington, New Archit, Washington, DC, 83; Potomac Craftsmen Gallery, Torpedo Factory Art Ctr, 83; Nat Zoo: Gallery & Bookstore, 83; Greenspring Gallery, Alexandria, Va, 86; Artists Equity Awards Exhib, 88; Concepts Gallery, Bethesda, Md, 90. *Pos:* Gallery asst, Stuttman Art Gallery, Washington, DC, formerly; art division, Martin Luther King Mem Libr, currently. *Awards:* Design Award, Am Libr Asn, 82. *Bibliog:* Paul Richard, Art Review, Washington Post, 10/77. *Mem:* Artists Equity; Am Soc Picture Prof. *Media:* Egg Tempera, Acrylic; Batik. *Publ:* Illusr (covers), Nat Educ Asn Publ, Sci & Children Mag; covers, Weekender Mag, Washington Star Newspaper, 76-78. *Mailing Add:* 10130 Falls Rd Potomac MD 20854

MCCABE, MAUREEN M
COLLAGE ARTIST
Study: RI Sch Design, Providence, BFA, 69; Cranbrook Acad Art, Bloomfield Hills, Mich, MFA, 71. *Work:* RI Sch Design; Wadsworth Atheneum, Hartford, Conn; Samuel Greenbaum & Kogod Collection, Washington, DC. *Exhib:* One-person shows, Gallery K, Washington, DC, 72, 75, 79, 82, 84, 87 & 89, Allan Stone Gallery, New York, 77 & Marianne Deson Gallery, Chicago, 84; Renwick Gallery, Smithsonian Inst, 81; Neuberger Mus, 82; Washington Project for the Arts, 83; Art Expo Chicago, 83; Museo Tamayo, Mexico City; New England Now, traveling exhib to six New England states, 88-89. *Teaching:* Prof studio art, Conn Col, New London, 71- *Awards:* Yaddo Fel, 75; Residence Grant, Cite des Arts, Paris, 77-78; Individual Artist Grant, Conn Comn Arts, 80; MacDowell Fel, 88; Rockefeller Fel, Bellagio, Italy, 88. *Dealer:* Gallery K 2010 R St NW Washington DC 20009. *Mailing Add:* 50 Old Norwich Rd Quaker Hill CT 06375

MCCAFFERTY, JAY DAVID
VIDEO ARTIST, PAINTER
b San Pedro, Calif, Feb 21, 48. *Study:* Los Angeles State Col, BA; Univ Calif, Irvine, MFA. *Work:* Los Angeles Co Mus Art; Long Beach Mus Art. *Exhib:* Southland Video Anthology Traveling Show, Long Beach Mus Art, 75; one-man shows, Grapestake Gallery, San Francisco, 78 & Cirrus Gallery, Los Angeles, 79; Baudoin Lebon, Paris, France, 80; Los Angeles Co Mus Art, 81; Cirrus Gallery, Los Angeles, 85 & 90; Works Gallery, Long Beach, Calif, 89. *Teaching:* Vis lectr art, World Campus Afloat, Chapman Col, 74; instr to prof, Los Angeles Harbor Col, Wilmington, Calif, 76-; instr, Claremont Col Grad Sch Art, 78; vis lectr, Univ Calif, Irvine, 80. *Awards:* New Talent Award, Los Angeles Co Mus Art, 74; Nat Endowment for the Arts Fel, 76. *Bibliog:* Joseph Youth (auth), Los Angeles, Art Int, 1/75; article, Art News, 9/83. *Media:* Sun, Paper. *Dealer:* Cirrus 542 S Alameda Los Angeles CA 90013; Galerie Krebs Bern Munstergasse 43 Bern Switzerland. *Mailing Add:* 1017 Beacon St San Pedro CA 90731

MCCALL, ANN
PAINTER, PRINTMAKER
b Toronto, Ont, Can, Dec 12, 41. *Study:* McGill Univ, Montreal, BA, 64; Univ Pittsburgh, 71-74; Concordia Univ, Montreal, BFA, 78. *Work:* DeCordova Mus, Lincoln, Mass; Vancouver Art Gallery, BC; Winnipeg Art Gallery, Man; Can Coun Art Bank, Ottawa; Mus Lodz, Poland. *Exhib:* Rockford Int, Ill, 79, 81 & 83; World Print III, San Francisco, 80; Norwegian Int Print Biennial, Frederikstad, Norway, 80, 82 & 84; Biennale Graphic Art, Ljubljana, Yugoslavia, 81 & 83; 7th & 8th British Int Print Biennial, Bradford, Eng, 82 & 86; Listowel Int Print Biennale, Listowel, Ireland, 86; Cracow Print Biennale: Cracow, Poland, 78, 80, 88; Premio de Grabado Maximo Rames, Ferrol, Spain, 87 & 90; Int Print Bienale, LVIV, Russia, 90. *Awards:* Purchase Award, Burnaby Biennale, BC, 77; Merit Awards, Boston Printmakers Exhib, 77 & 83. *Bibliog:* Diana Nemiroff (auth), article, Vie des Arts, 78; Giles Daigneault & Ginette Deslauriers (coauth), Ann McCall, In: La Gravure au Quebec 1940-1980, 80; Virginia Nixon (auth), article, The Montrealer, 82. *Mem:* Boston Printmakers; Print & Drawing Coun Can; Visual Arts Ont; Royal Can Acad Arts; Conseil Québecois de L'Estampe. *Media:* Acrylic; Silkscreen. *Dealer:* Galerie Waddington & Gorce Inc 2155 Mackay Montreal PQ; Gallery Sheila Roth 276 Avenue Rd Toronto ON. *Mailing Add:* c/o Galerie Waddington & Gorce 2155 Mackay Montreal PQ H3G 2J2 Canada

MCCALL, ANTHONY
FILMMAKER
b London, Eng, Apr 14, 46. *Study:* Whitgift Sch, Croydon, Eng, 56-64; Ravensbourne Col Art & Design, Bromley, Kent, Eng, 64-68, BA(first class hons), 68. *Work:* Royal Belgium Film Arch, Brussels; Arts Coun of Gt Brit, London; Mus of Mod Art, New York. *Exhib:* Documenta, Kassel, Ger, 77; Film as Film, 1910 to the Present, Kunstverein, Cologne, 78; Int Film Theory Conf 5, Univ Wis-Milwaukee, 79; Edinburgh Int Film Festival, 80; Berlin Film Festival, 81; and others. *Teaching:* Instr, London Col Printing, 70-71; vis lectr avant-garde film theory, New York Univ Dept of Cinema Studies, 77. *Awards:* Marie-Josi Prize 5th Int Experimental Competition, Knokke, Belg, 75; Creative Artists Prog Serv Grant, 76; Film Production Grant, New York State Coun Arts, 81; and others. *Bibliog:* Annette Michelson & P Adams Sitney (coauth), A on Knokke and the independent filmmaker, Artforum, 5/75; Jane Weinstock (auth), The subject of argument, Downtown Rev, Vol 1, No 1; E Ann Kaplan (auth), Feminist approaches to history, psychoanalysis and cinema in Sigmund Freud's Dora, Millennium Film J, fall/winter 81; and others. *Mailing Add:* 11 Jay St New York NY 10013

MCCALL, ROBERT THEODORE
ILLUSTRATOR, PAINTER
b Columbus, Ohio, Dec 23, 19. *Study:* Scholar, Columbus Fine Art Sch, Ohio, two yrs. *Work:* Phoenix Art Mus, Ariz; Art Mus Univ NMex, Albuquerque; Collection of US Air Force, Col Smithsonian Inst Washington, DC; Arizona Indust Comn Bldg, Phoenix; Glendale Pub Libr, Ariz. *Comn:* Four Paintings for the film 2001 A Space Odyssey, MGM Film Corp, now in Nat Air & Space Mus, Washington, 68; Twenty-three commemorative stamps, US Postal Serv, 72-88; The Space Mural, A Cosmic View (2100 sq ft, in the Lobby), Smithsonian Inst for the Nat Air & Space Mus, Washington, DC, 76; Three Decades of Achievement (10 ft x 20 ft mural in visitors ctr), Nat Air & Space Admin, Hugh L Dryden Flight Res Ctr, Edwards, Calif, 77; Opening the Space Frontier--the Next Giant Step, mural, mus at Johnson Space Ctr, Houston, Tex, 78-79; The Prologue and the Promise (mural), Disney's EPCOT Ctr, Fla; Expanding the Frontiers of Flight (mural), VA Air & Space Str, Hampton, Va, 92. *Exhib:* Am Watercolor Soc, 65; Space Art, Nat Gallery Art, Washington, DC, 70; Air & Space, Grand Cent Art Galleries, New York, 78; one-man show, Space Artist Robert McCall, Phoenix Art Mus, Ariz, 71; retrospective, Scottsdale Ctr Arts, Ariz, 81; Exhib, Nat Air & Space Mus, Smithsonian Inst, 84; and many other one-man shows. *Pos:* Art dir, The Black Hole (motion picture), Walt Disney, 79; conceptual designer, Star Trek, the Motion Picture, Paramount Pictures, 79. *Teaching:* Many speaking engagements. *Awards:* Soc Illusrs Hall of Fame, New York, 88; Honoree Award, Scottsdale Mem Hosp, 89; Stellar Award for Space Achievement, Rotary Club, Houston, Tex, 90. *Bibliog:* Pat Dreyfus (auth), Space Artist Robert McCall, Am Artist, 70; Joe Stacy (auth), Worlds Premier Aerospace Artist, Ariz Highways Mag, 73; Air & Space, Smithsonian, 90. *Mem:* Soc Illusr, New York (Air Force art prog chmn, 63-64, secy, 66). *Media:* Watercolor, Ink; Oil, Acrylic. *Publ:* Illusr many articles & covers for Life, Saturday Evening Post, Nat Geographic Mag, Popular Sci, Newsweek, Readers Digest, Colliers & others, 56-90; co-auth (with Isaac Asimov), Our World in Space, NY Graphic Soc, 74; A Vision of the Future, The Art of Robert McCall, Harry Abrams, 83; illusr, Pioneering the Space Frontier, Bantam Books, 86; The Art of Robert McCall, Bantam-Doublday, 92. *Mailing Add:* 4816 Moonlight Way Paradise Valley AZ 85253

MCCALLUM, CORRIE (MRS WILLIAM HALSEY)
PAINTER, PRINTMAKER
b Sumter, SC, Mar 14, 14. *Study:* Univ SC, cert fine arts, 36; Boston Mus Sch, with Karl Zerbe. *Work:* La State Univ, Baton Rouge; SC Arts Comn, State Collection; Columbia Mus Arts, SC; Ford Motor Co; SC State Mus. *Comn:* Mural, Home Federal Bank, 62. *Exhib:* Contemporary Artists of South Carolina (with catalog), Greenville Mus; one-man show, Concourse Gallery, State St Bank, Boston, Mass, 71; Art in Transition, Boston Mus Fine Arts, 77; Southeastern Contemp Art, Winston Salem, NC, 88; Gibbes Mus Art, Charleston SC, 89; Spoleto Festival USA, 91 & 92. *Pos:* Emer printmaker, Southern Graphics Coun, 84. *Teaching:* Cur art educ for Charleston Co, Gibbes Art Gallery, 60-69; instr painting & drawing, Newberry Col, SC, 69-71; instr painting, drawing & printmaking, Col Charleston, 71-79. *Awards:* Purchase Prize for Drawing, Mint Mus Graphics Ann, 64; Painting Award, Guild SC Artists Ann, 65; Scientific Educ Found Grant for Travel & Study Around the World, 68. *Bibliog:* Jack Morris (auth), Contemp Artists of South Carolina, 70; Art in Transition, Boston Mus, 77. *Publ:* Illusr, Dutch Fork Farm Boy, & 50 Years Along the Way, 68, Univ SC; coauth, A Travel Sketchbook, R L Bryan Co, 71. *Dealer:* Kunstsalon Wolfsberg Bederstrasse 109 Zurich Switz; Halsey-McCallum Studio 20 Fulton St Charleston SC 29401. *Mailing Add:* 26 Archdale St Charleston SC 29401

MCCALLUM, STEVEN DOUGLAS
PAINTER, PRINTMAKER
b Alliance, Ohio, July 8, 51. *Study:* Kent State Univ, with Adja Yunkers, Julian Starczak & Dore Ashton, BFA, 73, MFA, 75. *Work:* Butler Inst Am Art, Youngstown, Ohio; Sydney & Frances Lewis Found, Richmond, Va; Michener Collection, Kent, Ohio; DIOP Collection, Dakar, Senegal, Africa; Inköpta Konstverk, Goteborg, Sweden. *Comn:* Tropicana Corp, Brandonton, Fla. *Exhib:* One-man shows, Canton Art Inst, Ohio, 78, Hansen Gallery, New York, 79 & 80, Helander Gallery, Palm Beach, Fla, 87, Cooper Gallery, Tampa, Fla, 88, Butler Inst Am Art, Youngstown, Ohio, 88, Allan Stone Gallery, New York, 85, 88 & 90 & Tampa City Ctr, 92; Duke Univ, Durham, NC, 88; Cooper Galery, Tampa, Fla, 88-90; Stylt Gallery, Goteburg, Sweden; Painters & Sculptors on View, ABC/Capital Cities, New York, 90; and others. *Pos:* Studio asst, Al Held, 80-81, Helen Frankenthaler, 81-82, James Rosenquist, 82-84; exhib installation, Leo Castelli Gallery, 83-84. *Teaching:* Adj prof, Kent State Univ, Youngstown State Univ, Univ Akron, 76-80; vis artist painting workshop, Ohio Arts Coun, 78. *Bibliog:* Louis Zona (auth), Steven McCallum (exhib catalog), 10/88; Stephen Westfall (auth), Steven McCallum at Allan Stone, Art Am, 12/88. *Media:* Acrylic, Oil; Serigraphy. *Dealer:* Allan Stone Gallery 48 E 86th St New York NY. *Mailing Add:* PO Box 484 Aripeka FL 34679

MCCANN, CECILE NELKEN
CRITIC
b New Orleans, La. *Study:* Vassar Col; Tulane Univ; San Jose State Univ, Calif, BA & MA; Univ Calif, Berkeley; also with Herbert Sanders, Robert Fritz, Shoji Hamada & Peter Voulkos; hon dr San Francisco Art Inst, 89. *Work:* City of San Francisco; San Jose City Col; San Jose State Univ; Mills Col, Oakland; State of Calif, Sacramento. *Exhib:* Everson Mus Art, Syracuse, 62 & 64; one-woman shows, Crocker Art Mus, Sacramento, 65 & Calif Col Arts & Crafts, Oakland, 66; Calif Design, Pasadena Mus Art, 65 & 68; Wichita Design Craftsmen, Kans, 66; and others. *Pos:* Ed & publ, Artweek, Oakland, 69-89. *Teaching:* San Jose State Univ & Calif State Univ, Haywood, 64-65, Chabot Col, 65-68, Laney Col, 60-69. *Awards:* Critic's Grant, Nat Endowment Arts, 75; Media Award, Bay Area Coalition for Visual Arts, 88; Vesta Award, Woman's Bldg, Los Angeles, 88. *Mem:* Col Art Asn; Int Asn Art Critics; Art Table. *Publ:* Contribr, Craft Horizons, 71 & 73; contribr, William Wiley, Opus, France, 73; auth, Ken Friedman (catalog essay), Yugoslavia, 74; contribr, Art in America, Artweek, currently. *Mailing Add:* 244 Colgate Ave Kensington CA 94708

MCCANNEL, (MRS) MALCOLM A
COLLECTOR
b Minneapolis, Minn, Nov 20, 15. *Study:* Smith Col, BA; Minneapolis Sch Art. *Pos:* Bd mem, Walker Art Ctr, Minneapolis, currently. *Collection:* Contemporary American sculpture and painting. *Mailing Add:* 1520 Waverly Pl Minneapolis MN 55403

MCCARRON, PAUL
ART DEALER
b Mason City, Iowa, June 15, 33. *Study:* Art Inst Chicago, BA, 58, MFA, 59. *Res:* 16th to 20th century fine prints and drawings; Rembrandt; 16th century Italian prints; 17th century mezzotints; Martin Lewis. *Publ:* Auth, Martin Lewis: The Graphic Work (catalog) & Martin Lewis: Catalogue of the Retrospective Exhibit, Kennedy Galleries, 73; Lithographs by Honore Daumier (catalog), Paul McCarron, 81. *Mailing Add:* 1014 Madison Ave New York NY 10021

MCCARTHY, DENIS
PAINTER
b New York, NY, Feb 21, 35. *Study:* Cooper Union, 59-64; Yale Univ, BFA & MFA, 64-66. *Work:* Work in pvt collections only. *Exhib:* Painting Ann, 70 & Biennial Exhib, 73, Whitney Mus Am Art; Exhib, O K Harris, New York, 72; Spring Exhib, Aldrich Mus, Ridgefield, Conn, 73; Automation House, New York, 76; Hundred Acres Gallery, New York, 77; New York Acad Sci, 78; one-man show, 55 Mercer Gallery, New York, 78 & NY State Col, Old Westbury, NY, 80. *Teaching:* Instr drawing, Sch Visual Arts, New York, 67-72 & New York Univ, 76-77; instr painting & printmaking, Hunter Col, 71- *Mailing Add:* 147 Spring St No 5 New York NY 10012

MCCARTHY, DENNIS
SCULPTOR, EDUCATOR
b Chicago, Ill, Oct 27, 21. *Study:* Kansas City Art Inst, BFA, 49, MFA, 50; St Benedict's Col, Atchison, Kans, AB, 51; with Frederic Taubes, 66-70; with Elden Tefft, Kans Univ, 82-90. *Work:* St Theresa Convent, Decatur, Ill; St Benedict's Abbey, Muchnic Gallery & Maur Hill Prep Sch, Atchison, Kans; Allen Fieldhouse, Univ Kans, 87. *Comn:* Kansas Monk (bronze), 57 & mosaic murals, 58, St Benedict's Col, Atchison, Kans; mosaic mural, St Elizabeth Parrish, Kansas City, Mo, 60; corpus & cross, Maur Hill Chapel, 63 & entrance cross, Maur Hill Prep Sch, 83, Atchison, Kans; Portrait of a Nurse, VA Hosp, Leavenworth, Kans. *Exhib:* Bronze Exhib, Kans Univ, Lawrence, 82; Kans Sculptor's Exhib, Johnson Co Community Col, Overland Park, 84; Sculpture Exhib, Wichita Art Mus, Kans, 85 & 86; Outdoor Sculpture Exhib, Lawrence, Kans, 87;; Wyandotte Co Libr, Sculpture Show, 88, 89 & 90. *Pos:* Trustee, Kans State Art Exhib Serv, Manhattan, 58-60; treas, Kans Sculptors Asn, 84-85, pres, 85-86. *Teaching:* Instr wood sculpture, Kans City Univ, 53-54; instr art, St Benedict's Col, Atchison, 56-71; prof art, Benedictine Col, Atchison, 71-88. *Awards:* Purchase Award, River Bend Art Fair, Atchison, 86; Atchison Art Asn (charter mem, 64-). *Media:* All. *Mailing Add:* Rte 2 Box 14 Atchison KS 66002

MCCARTHY, DORIS JEAN
PAINTER, INSTRUCTOR
b Calgary, Alta, Can, July 7, 10. *Study:* Ont Col Art, 30; Cent Sch Arts & Crafts, London, Eng, 35. *Work:* Art Gallery Ont, Toronto; London Art Gallery, Ont; Royal Art Collection, Windsor Castle, Eng; Ont Centennial Collection; and others. *Comn:* Mural, Toronto Pub Libr, 33; mem bk, Malvern Col, Toronto, 48; creche figures, Church of St Aldan, Toronto, 48; fabric banner Trinity, St James Cathedral, Toronto, 75; wall hangings, St Aidan's Church, Cana Place, Toronto. *Exhib:* Ont Soc Artists Ann, 33-; Royal Can Acad Ann, 34-; Can Soc Painters Watercolor, 38-; various solo shows, 32 & Wynick/Tuck Gallery, 82, Toronto; and others. *Teaching:* Instr drawing, painting & hist art, Central Tech Sch Toronto, 33-, asst head, 68-72. *Awards:* Order of Canada, Women Artist of the Year, Ont Soc Artists, 83; Fel Ont Col Art, 90-; Order of Ont, 92. *Bibliog:* Gary Michael Dault (auth), Vivacious artist pins down Artic air, Toronto Star, 3/77; John Bentley Mays (auth), Portraits of the edge of the world, Globe & Mail, Toronto, 10/31/80; Doris McCarthy: Heart of a Painter (doc film), W Wacko Productions, Gasper, Alta. *Mem:* Royal Can Acad; Ont Soc Artists (pres, 65-68); Can Soc Painters in Watercolor (pres, 56-57); Fedn Can Artists; Prof Artists Can (chmn, 67-69). *Media:* Oil, Watercolor. *Publ:* Auth, A Fool in Paradise, an Artists Early Life & The Good Wine, An Artist Comes of Age, Macfarlane, Walter E Ross, 91. *Dealer:* Wynick/Tuck Gallery 80 Spadina Ave Fourth Floor Toronto ON M5V 2J3 Canada. *Mailing Add:* One Meadowcliff Dr Scarborough ON M1M 2X8 Canada

MCCARTHY, KATHLEEN
SCULPTOR
b Pittsburg, Pa. *Study:* Cornell Univ, BFA, 74; Ind Univ, Bloomington, MFA, 77. *Comn:* Permanent site specific installations in five elevated subway stations, Metrop Transportation Authority New York, Queens, 89-92. *Exhib:* Solo exhibs, Lead Head, Window installation, Pub Image Gallary, New York, 83, Falling Dream, White Columns Gallery, New York, 85, In the President's Board Room, CW Post, Long Island Univ, Pub Art Prog, Greenvale, NY, 87, Gracie Mansion Gallery, New York, 90 & San Francisco Airports Comn, 91; Art What Thou Eat: Images of Food in American Art, Edith C Blum Art Inst, Bard Col, Annandale-on-Hudson, New York & New York Hist Soc, New York, 90; Critical Mass, Md Inst, Baltimore, 91; Troubled Sleep: Houses of Spirit/Memories of Ancestors, Woodlawn Cemetery, Bronx, NY, 92; Between the Sheets, PPOW, New York, 92; Object Choice, Hallwalls, Buffalo, NY, 92. *Awards:* Individual Artists Grant, Nat Endowment Art, 88 & 90; Funded Residency Grant, Sculpture Space, Utica, NY, 89; Weber Found Grant, 92. *Mailing Add:* 325 W 37th St New York NY 10018

MCCARTIN, WILLIAM FRANCIS
PAINTER
b New York, NY, Dec 9, 05. *Study:* Art Students League, with Richard Lahey, five yrs; New Sch Social Res, one yr. *Work:* Allentown Mus, Pa; Portland Art Mus, Maine. *Exhib:* Gallery Contemp Arts, Pittsburgh; Maine Coast Artists, Rockport, 70; 7 from Monhegan, Phillips Exeter Acad, NH, 70; Joseph De Meers Ltd, Hilton Head, SC, 71; solo exhibs, Beaumont Art Mus, Tex, 71, Alonzo Gallery, 71, 75 & 79; and others. *Awards:* Tiffany Found Grant, 25; John Newman Medal, Casein Soc, 60; Nat Endowment Arts Fel, 77. *Media:* Acrylic. *Publ:* Auth, article, Arts Mag. *Mailing Add:* 41 Union Sq W New York NY 10003

MCCARTY, LORRAINE CHAMBERS
PAINTER, INSTUCTOR
b Detroit, Mich. *Study:* Detroit Art Acad, Wayne State Univ, with G Alden Smith; Meinzinger Art Acad; Stephens Col, with Albert Christ-Janer, also with Glen Michaels, Emil Weddidge, Robert Wilbert & Adolph Dehn. *Work:* Butler Mus Am Art, Youngstown, Ohio; Smithsonian Nat Air & Space Mus; Muskegon Mus Art, Mich; Northwood Inst, Midland, Mich; Stephens Col; Int Women's Air & Space Mus, Ohio; and others. *Comn:* Painting, Bohn Copper & Brass, Detroit; painting, R L Polk Co Int Hq, Detroit, 73; painting, Wyandotte Paint Products, Troy, Mich, 74; murals, Int Women's Air & Space Mus, Ohio, 77 & Lear Siegler, 88. *Exhib:* Butler Mus Am Art Ann, 67 & 70-74; Womanart, Saginaw Mus Arts, Mich, 74; Fed Aviation Admin, DC, 77; Dayton Art Inst, Ohio, 78; Battle Creek Art Ctr, Mich, 78; Smithsonian Air & Space Mus, DC, 80-82; Flint Inst Traveling Exhib, 83; and 43 solo exhibs. *Pos:* Mem, Arts Cult Coun, Oakland Co, Mich, 75-; designer & adv, Int Women's Air & Space Mus, Ohio. *Teaching:* Instr painting, Flint Inst Arts, 70-; instr, Grosse Pointe War Mem, Mich, 70-79; instr oil painting, Art Ctr, Pontiac, Mich, 75- *Awards:* Purchase Prize, Butler Mus, 67; Cooke Found Fel, 83; Mich Coun Arts Grant, 83. *Bibliog:* Joy Hakenson (auth), Abstract artists focus on a real world, Detroit News, 79; Corinne Abatt (auth), Flight's romance captured, Birmingham Eccentric, Mich, 79; Cheryl Beller (auth), Take off just beginning, Royal Oak Daily Tribune, 79. *Mem:* Mich Acad Arts, Sci & Lett; Mich Watercolor Soc; Detroit Soc Women Painters & Sculptors; Scarab Club, Detroit; Artists Equity; and others. *Media:* Acrylic, Oil. *Mailing Add:* 1112 Pinehurst Ave Royal Oak MI 48073

MCCAUGHEY, ARNOLD PATRICK
DIRECTOR, ADMINISTRATOR
b Belfast, Ireland, Feb 10, 43. *Study:* Scotch Col, Melbourne, Australia, 54-60; Ormond Col, Univ Melbourne, BA, 65; Monash Univ, hon Dr Letts, 88. *Pos:* Art critic, The Age, Melbourne, 54-60; dir, Nat Gallery Victoria, Melbourne, 81-87, Wadsworth Atheneum, Hartford, Conn, 88-; coun trustees, Australian Nat Gallery, currently. *Teaching:* Fel, Monash Univ, Melbourne, 67-69 & fel fine arts, 72-73; vis prof Australian studies, Harvard Univ, 86-87. *Awards:* Harkness Fel, 69-71. *Mem:* Am Asn Museums; Asn Art Mus Dirs; Australian Coun Arts (visual arts bd); Int Cult Corp Australia. *Publ:* Auth, Australian Abstract Art, Nat Gallery, 68; The Australian Impressionist Painters of the Heidelberg School - The Jack Manton Collection, Oxford Univ Press, 79; Fred Williams, Bay Bks, 80. *Mailing Add:* Wadsworth Atheneum 600 Main St Hartford CT 06103

MCCAULEY, GARDINER RAE
ADMINISTRATOR, PAINTER
b Oakland, Calif, Aug 8, 33. *Study:* Calif Col Arts & Crafts, studied with Hamilton Wolf, 48-51; Univ Calif, Berkeley, BA, 55, MA, 57, studied with Milton Resnick, David Park, Esteban Vicente, Erle Loran & Corrado Marca-Relli. *Exhib:* Ann Exhib of San Francisco Art Asn, San Francisco Mus Art, 55-57; Bay Area Invitational, Calif Palace of the Legion of Honor, San Francisco, 58; one-man shows, Berkeley Gallery, San Francisco, 64 & Columbia Art League Galleries, 81; Artists of Ore, 67, 70, 72; Spectrum, Portland Art Mus, Ore, 70; Stephens Faculty, Merril Chase Gallery, Chicago, 74; Marymount Manhattan Col, NY, 78; Area Painters, Art Gallery, Univ Mo-Columbia, 78; and others. *Pos:* Crafts dir, US Spec Serv, France & Ger, 59-62; exec dir, Montalvo Ctr Arts, Saratoga, 82-89. *Teaching:* Lectr drawing, Univ Calif, Berkeley, 62-65; instr art, Univ Santa Clara, Calif, 64; asst prof painting & drawing, Lewis & Clark Col, Portland, Ore, 66-72; head dept art, painting & drawing, Stephens Col, Columbia, Mo, 72-82; vis artist, Barnfield Col, Eng, 80. *Awards:* Juror's Prize, San Francisco Art Asn Ann, San Francisco Mus Art, 63; James D Phelan Found Award, Calif Palace of Legion of Honor, San Francisco, 65; Firestone-Baars Found Grant, 80. *Bibliog:* Joanna Magloff (auth), From the Berkeley Gallery, 12/63, Elizabeth Polley (auth), San Francisco: Gardiner McCauley & Howard Margolis, 3/64, Artforum; Anita Ventura (auth), Pop, Photo & Paint, Arts Mag, 4/64. *Mem:* Nat Coun Art Adminrs; Col Art Asn Am; Mid-Am Col Art Asn; Am Asn Univ Profs. *Media:* Acrylic, Oil. *Publ:* Auth, Introduction to Masayuki Imai: Ceramic Art, Saratoga Villa Montalvo, 85. *Mailing Add:* 948 The Alameda Berkeley CA 94707

MCCHESNEY, CLIFTON
PAINTER, EDUCATOR
b Gary, Ind, Feb 8, 29. *Study:* Am Acad Art, dipl; Ind Univ, with Jack Tworko, BS; Cranbrook Acad Art, with Zolton Sepeshy, MFA. *Work:* Detroit Inst Art; Cranbrook Acad Art, Bloomfield Hills, Mich; Univ Ryuukus, Okinawa, Japan; Biwako Mus, Otsu, Japan; Ginza Nova Gallery, Tokyo, Japan; and others. *Exhib:* 24 Ann, Soc Contemp Arts, Chicago Art Inst, 64; one-man shows, Benni Gallery, Kyoto, 67 & Ginza Nova Gallery, Tokyo, Japan, 75; Arwin Galleries, Detroit, 80; Freeman Gallery, East Lansing, Mich, 81 & 82; Western Mich Univ, 84; Central Mich Univ, 85; and others. *Pos:* guest artist, Kalamazoo Art Ctr, Mich, summer 64; Vis artist, State Univ NY Albany, fall 65; instr, Leland summer workshop, 65, 66, 80-89. *Teaching:* Prof painting & drawing, Mich State Univ, East Lansing, 60-91. *Awards:* Purchase Awards, Detroit Inst Arts, 61 & Purdue Univ, 70; Travel Grant to Japan, Ford Found, 74; Distinguished Faculty Award, Col Arts & Letts, Mich State Univ, 85. *Bibliog:* Man and Humanity (film), Mich State Univ, 71; Spec

American Issue, Arts Mag, Vol 39, No 7; article in, Geijutsu Seikatsu, No 4, 75. *Media:* Acrylic, Pencil. *Dealer:* Lansing Art Gallery Lansing MI; Stephen Rosenberg Gallery New York. *Mailing Add:* 5301 Horstman Rd Williamston MI 48895

MCCHESNEY, MARY FULLER See Fuller, Mary (Mary Fuller McChesney)

MCCHESNEY, ROBERT PEARSON
PAINTER, MURALIST
b Marshall, Mo, Jan 16, 13. *Study:* Washington Univ Art Sch, with Fred Conway; Otis Art Inst, Los Angeles. *Work:* Whitney Mus; Chicago Art Inst; Oakland Art Mus; Muskegon Mus Art, Mich; San Francisco Mus Mod Art; Harrison Mus Art, Utah State, Logan; and others. *Comn:* Wall decoration, USS Monterey; mural, Social Serv Admin Bldg, San Francisco, Calif, 77. *Exhib:* Art Inst Chicago Ann, 47-61; Sao Paulo Third Biennial, 55; Corcoran Gallery Art, 57; Calif Palace Legion Hon, 62; Expo 70, Osaka, Japan, 70; Retrospective, San Francisco Art Comn Gallery, 74; 19 Yrs, Calif State Univ, Hayward, 77; Calif Art Mus, Santa Rosa, Calif, 88; and others. *Teaching:* Instr, San Francisco Art Inst, formerly. *Awards:* Purchase Prizes, San Francisco Art Comn, 50 & 69; Purchase Prize, Whitney Mus Am Art, 55; Prize, San Francisco Mus Art, 60. *Media:* Acrylic. *Dealer:* Madison St Gallery Petaluma CA; Annex Galleries Santa Rosa CA. *Mailing Add:* 2955 Sonoma Mountain Rd Petaluma CA 94952

MCCHRISTY, QUENTIN L
PAINTER, DESIGNER
b Cushing, Okla, Jan 24, 21. *Study:* Okla State Univ, with Doel Reed, BA; Cincinnati Acad Art, with Helwhig & Crawford. *Work:* Philbrook Art Ctr, Tulsa, Okla; Joslyn Mus Art, Omaha, Nebr; Butler Inst Am Art, Youngstown, Ohio; Pa State Univ, State College; Watercolor, Mr & Mrs Weller Collection, Guilford Col, Greensboro, NC, 90-91. *Comn:* Murals, Ft Worth Children's Mus & Wesley Found, Methodist Church, Stillwater, Okla; designed decorations glassware, Bartlett Collins, mfrs domestic & export glassware; plus others. *Exhib:* 26th Biennial, Corcoran Gallery, Washington, DC, 59; Contemporary American Art, Oklahoma City, 60; All City Arts Festival, Los Angeles, Calif, 60-; Audubon Artist Nat Galleries, New York, 62; Pa Acad Fine Arts, Philadelphia, 63; La Salon Des Nations A Paris France, 85; plus others. *Pos:* Art dir, Ft Worth Children's Mus, 50; Nat Artist Show judge, 65. *Teaching:* Instr drawing, Okla State Univ; instr art, Ft Worth Children's Mus. *Awards:* Purchase Award, 47, Prize, 48 & Ruskin Award, 62, Philbrook Art Ctr; Butler Mus Art Friends of Art Award, 60; Painting Exhib Awards, Wind River Valley Nat Show, Dubois, Wyo, 61 & 65; Art Horizons Certificate of Excellence, New York, 88; Artitudes Certificate of Excellence, New York, 89. *Mem:* Int Platform Asn. *Media:* Transparent Watercolor, Oil; Ink. *Publ:* Artist article, La Revue Moderne Publ, Paris, France, 60; four pen drawings, Am Artist Mag, New York, 6/8/64; article & illus, Enciclopedia Internazional Degli Artisti, Carlo Bugatti, Ancona, Italy, 70-71; Art Diary, Giancarlo Politi, Milan, Italy, 90. *Mailing Add:* 183 Ocean Pky-1A Brooklyn NY 11218

MCCLAIN, MATTHEW
CURATOR, WRITER
b Des Moines, Iowa, Mar 26, 56. *Study:* Univ Mont Inst Intensive Humanitarian Study, cert, 75; Univ Cincinnati Col Design, Archit & Art, BA(art hist), 78; Whitney Mus Am Art, 78-79, Rubinstein fel, 78-79. *Exhib:* Symbolist Mood Around 1900 (auth, catalog), Whitney Mus Am Art, New York, 78, Indust Sights, 79 & Enclosure & Concealment (auth, catalog), 79; Urban Encounters (auth, catalog), Inst Contemp Art, Philadelphia, 80 & Made in Philadelphia III (auth, catalog), 80. *Collections Arranged:* Symbolist Mood Around 1900, Whitney Mus Am Art, New York, 78, Indust Sights, 79 & Enclosure & Concealment, 79; Urban Encounters, Inst Contemp Art, Philadelphia, 80 & Made in Philadelphia III, 80; John C Gregory: Recent Works, Grey Gallery, Philadelphia, Pa, 81; Maureen Garvin: Ruffles and Roses, Wallingford Art Ctr, Pa, 82; Susan Chyrsler White and Sam Karen Norgard, Kling Gallery, Philadelphia, 82. *Pos:* Pub Info Mgr, Contemp Arts Ctr, Cincinnati, 76-78; curatorial intern, Whitney Mus Am Art, 78-79; cur/adminr, Inst Contemp Art, Philadelphia, 79-80; columnist, Philadelphia City Paper. *Mem:* Col Art Asn Am. *Mailing Add:* 1218 Locust St Philadelphia PA 19107

MCCLAIN, ROBERT LEE
ART DEALER, GALLERY DIRECTOR
b Tokyo, Japan, Oct 24, 53; US citizen. *Study:* Kans State Univ, BA(journalism), 76. *Pos:* secy/bd dirs, Houston Art Dealers Asn, 90; spec adv, Mayors Arts Task Force, Houston, 91-92. *Teaching:* Lectr, Glassell Sch Art, Mus Fine Arts, Houston. *Awards:* Nominee, Rhodes Scholar, 75. *Specialty:* Contemporary American & European paintings & sculpture. *Mailing Add:* 2627 Colquitt Houston TX 77098

MCCLANAHAN, JOHN D
PAINTER, EDUCATOR
b Salina, Kans. *Study:* Bethany Col, Lindsborg, Kans, BFA; Univ Iowa, Iowa City, MFA. *Work:* Art Mus, Univ Iowa, Iowa City; Weatherspoon Art Gallery, Univ NC, Greensboro; Mint Mus Art, Charlotte, NC; Baylor Univ, Waco, Tex; Seguin Art Ctr, Tex. *Exhib:* Watercolor USA, Springfield Art Mus, Mo, 66-69, 72-75, 79 & 81; one-man exhib, Mint Mus Art, 71; Mid-Am Art Exhib, Owensboro, Ky, 79, 82 & 86; Baylor Univ, 81 & 83; Art Ann Two, Okla Art Ctr, Oklahoma City, 81; Biennial Nat Small Painting Exhib, Mullaly-Matisse Galleries, Birmingham, Mich; Kans Nat Small Painting Exhib, Ft Hays State Univ, Kans, 84 & 87; 2nd Ann Int Exhib Miniature Art, Del Bello Gall, Toronto, Can, 87; 30th Ann Delta Art Exhib, Ark Art Ctr, Little Rock, Ark, 87. *Teaching:* Instr painting, Stephen F Austin State Univ, Nacogdoches, Tex, 64-67; from asst prof to assoc prof painting, Queens Col, Charlotte, NC, 67-76, chmn dept art, 75-76; prof painting, Baylor Univ, Waco, Tex, 76-, acting dir visual arts, 85-89, chmn dept art, 89- *Awards:* Purchase Prizes, Tex Painting & Sculpture Exhib, 77 & 82 & Fifth Biennial Five State Exhib, 79. *Mem:* Col Art Asn Am; Tex Fine Arts Asn. *Media:* Water Media, Collage. *Mailing Add:* Sch of Art Baylor Univ Waco TX 76798-7263

MCCLEARY, MARY FIELDING
COLLAGE ARTIST, EDUCATOR
b Houston, Tex, Feb 27, 51. *Study:* Tex Christian Univ, Ft Worth, BFA, 72; Univ Okla, Norman, MFA, 75. *Work:* Miami Univ Mus, Oxford, Ohio; Gihon Found, Dallas, Tex; IBM Corp, Houston, Dallas & Corpus Christi, Tex; First Int Bank, Houston, Tex; State of Okla Art Collection, Oklahoma City. *Exhib:* Boston Printmakers 27th Ann Nat Exhib, Boston Mus Fine Arts, 75; Houston Women, Contemp Arts Mus, Houston, Tes, 75; Works on Paper: Southwest 1978, Dallas Mus Fine Arts, 78; Paperworks, Witte Mus, San Antonio, Tex, 79; Made in Tex, Huntington Art Gallery, Univ Tex, Austin, 79; one-man shows, Watson/de Nagy & Co Gallery, Houston, Tex, 79, 80, 83, 85 & 86; Tyler Mus Art, Tyler, Tex, 82; Mattingley Baker Gallery, Dallas, Tex, 82 & 85; Dimensional Paper, 85 & Transpositions/Collaborations, 86, San Antonio Art Inst; The Narrative Figure, Addison-Ripley Gallery, Washington, DC, 87; From the Object: Still Life Themes & Variations, Glassell Sch Fine Arts, Houston, Tex, 87; Bernice Steinbaum Gallery, New York, 88; The Texas Exhibit, Nat Mus Women Arts, Washington, DC, 88, Laguna Gloria Art Mus, Austin, Tex, 89; Mid-America Biennial, Nelson-Atkins Mus, Kansas City, Mo, 88; Texas Realism, Art Mus Southeast Tex, Beaumont, 89. *Pos:* Gallery dir, Stephen F Austin State Univ, 79-82. *Teaching:* prof art, Stephen F Austin State Univ, Nacogdoches, Tex, 75- *Awards:* First Place Award, Blaffer Gallery, Univ Houston, Tex, 77; Purchase Prize, Miami Univ, Oxford, Ohio, 78; Second Place Award, Assistance League of Houston, Tex, 78; Mid-America Alliance/Nat Endowment Arts Fel, 88-89. *Bibliog:* Alexis Krasilorsky (dir), From the heart (film), Gihon Found, Dallas, 81-82; Susan Freudenheim (auth), Mary McCleary, Tex Homes, 2/86; Fran Kalmykor (ed), Mary McCleary, Inquirer: Houston's Chronicle of the Arts, 11-12/86. *Media:* Mixed Media on Paper, Painting. *Dealer:* The Watson Gallery 3510 Lake Houston TX 77098. *Mailing Add:* c/o Lynn Goode Gallery 2719 Colquitt Houston TX 77098

MCCLELLAN, DOUGLAS EUGENE
PAINTER
b Pasadena, Calif, Oct 10, 21. *Study:* Art Ctr Sch, Los Angeles, Calif; Colorado Springs Fine Arts Ctr, with Boardman Robinson & Jean Charlot; Claremont Grad Sch, MFA. *Work:* Los Angeles Co Mus Art; Los Angeles Co Fair Asn; Pasadena Art Mus. *Exhib:* Libr Cong, 48; San Francisco Mus Art, Calif, 49-52; Los Angeles Co Mus Art, 49-55; Metrop Mus Art, New York, 50; Pa Acad Fine Arts, Pa, 53; Corcoran Gallery Art, Washington, DC, 53; Pacific Coast Biennial, 55; Carnegie Inst of Technol, Pittsburgh, Pa, 55 & 57; Whitney Mus Am Art, New York, 57; one-man shows, Felix Landau Gallery, 53-59, Pasadena Art Mus, 54 & Univ Calif, Riverside, 55. *Teaching:* Instr, Chaffey Col, 50-59, Otis Art Inst, Los Angeles, Calif, 59-61, Scripps Col & Univ of Calif, Santa Cruz; prof art, Univ Calif, Santa Cruz, 70- *Awards:* Painting Prize, Los Angeles Co Mus Art, 50 & 53; Nat Orange Show, 54. *Mailing Add:* 4150 Glen Haven Rd Soquel CA 95073

MCCLELLAND, JEANNE C
PRINTMAKER, PAINTER
b Edmeston, NY. *Study:* Albright-Knox Sch Fine Arts, Buffalo, dipl; State Univ NY Col Buffalo, BS(art educ); Munson-Williams-Proctor Inst, Utica, NY; Hartwick Col, Oneonta, NY; State Univ Col NY, Oneonta. *Work:* Mus Fine Arts, Springfield, Mass; St John Fisher Col (NY); Holyoke Mus, Mass; Munson-Williams-Proctor Inst, Utica, NY. *Exhib:* One-person show, State Univ NY Col, Oneonta; Boston Printmakers, Mass; Studio Sch & Gallery, Int Mini Print Exhib, 86-88; Int Graphi Arts Found, Mini Print Exhib, New York; Nat Small Print Exhib; and others. *Mem:* Munson-Williams-Proctor Inst; Cooperstown Art Asn; Roberson Ctr-Arts & Sci; Int Graphic Arts Found, Darien, Conn. *Mailing Add:* 17 Sharon St Sidney NY 13838

MCCLENDON, MAXINE (MAXINE MCCLENDON NICHOLS)
PAINTER, CRAFTSMAN
b Leesville, La, Oct 21, 31. *Study:* Univ Tex, Austin; Tex Women's Univ; Pan Am Univ. *Work:* Mus Int Folk Art, Santa Fe, NMex; IBM Collection; Lauren Rogers Mus Art, Laurel, Miss; Ark Arts Ctr, Little Rock; McAllen Int Mus, McAllen, Tex. *Comn:* Tex Instruments, Houston, 79; Union Bank of Switz, 80; Hyatt Regency Hotel, Ft Worth, Tex, 81; Continental Plaza, Ft Worth, Tex, 82; panels, Four Corners, Dallas, Tex, 86. *Exhib:* 16th Tex Crafts Exhib, Dallas Mus Fine Arts, 74; 8th & 9th Ann Southwestern Area Exhibs, Mus Southwest, Midland, Tex, 74 & 75; Fourth Nat Crafts Exhib, Marietta Col, 75; Invitational Biennial, Beaumont Art Mus, Tex, 76; 19th nat, El Paso Mus Art, Tex, 76; McAllen Int Mus, 76; Southwest Craft Ctr, Tex Designer/Crafts Ctr, San Antonio, 78; and others. *Pos:* Cur Mex Folk Art, McAllen Int Mus, 74-80. *Awards:* Best in Exhib, 6th Ann Prints, Drawings & Crafts, Ark Art Ctr, 74; Award of Excellence, Houston Designer/Craftsman, 76; Judges Award, Fourth Marietta Nat, 75. *Mem:* Am Crafts Coun (state rep, 76-80); Tex Designer/Craftsmen (pres, 73-74). *Media:* Acrylic, Oil. *Dealer:* Adelle M Fine Art 3317 McKinney Ave Dallas TX 75204. *Mailing Add:* 2018 Sharyland Rd Mission TX 78572

MCCLENNEY, CHERYL ILENE
ADMINISTRATOR
b Chicago, Ill, July 18, 48. *Study:* Art Inst Chicago, BFA, 69. *Work:* Solomon R Guggenheim Mus, New York. *Pos:* Cur coordr, Solomon R Guggenheim Mus, 70-74; asst prog dir, Mus Collab Inc, 74-76; asst comnr, New York City Dept Cult Affairs, 76-78; dir mus prog, Nat Endowment Humanities, 78-83; asst dir prog, Philadelphia Mus Art, currently. *Teaching:* Instr, Art Inst Chicago, 68-69. *Mem:* Am Asn Mus; Am Asn State & Local Hist; African-Am Mus Asn. *Mailing Add:* Philadelphia Mus Art PO Box 7646 Philadelphia PA 19101

MACCLINTOCK, DORCAS
SCULPTOR
b New York, NY, July 16, 32. *Study:* Smith Col, AB; Univ Wyo, AM. *Comn:* Trophy, Collie Club Am Found, 88. *Exhib:* Cleveland Mus Natural Hist, 84; Calif Acad Sci, 86; Animal Imagery, St Hubert's Giralda, 87-89; Wildlife Images, Central Park Zoo Gallery, New York, 90; Art and The Animal, Cleveland Mus Natural Hist, 91; and others. *Pos:* Res assoc, Calif Acad Sci, San Francisco; cur affil, Peabody Mus, Yale Univ, New Haven, Conn. *Awards:* Smith Col Medal, 87. *Mem:* Soc of Animal Artists Inc (mem exec bd, 76-85, jury, 76-). *Media:* Plastilene, Clay. *Publ:* Auth, Squirrels of North America, Van Nostrand, 70; A Natural History of Giraffes, 73, A Natural History of Zebras, 76, Horses as I See Them, 80, A Natural History of Raccoons, 81, A Raccoon's First Year, 82, African Images, 84, Phoebe the Kinkajou, 85 & Red Pandas, 88, Scribners. *Mailing Add:* 33 Rogers Rd Hamden CT 06517

MCCLURE, CONSTANCE
PAINTER, PROFESSOR
b Huntington, WVa, Feb 12, 34. *Study:* Ringling Sch of Art, Sarasota, Fla; Skowhegan Sch of Painting & Sculpture, ME; Col of Mt St Joseph, BA; Univ Cincinnati, MFA. *Work:* Cincinnati Zoological Soc; Bell Telephone Co, Cincinnati; Cincinnati Art Mus; Federated Dept Stores, Cincinnati; Gennadeion Libr, Am Sch Classical Studies, Athens, Greece; Litton Industries, Hebron, Ky. *Comn:* Portrait of conductor, Cincinnati Symphony Orchestra, 70; 18 ft canvas mural, Ohio Nat Bank, Columbus, 76; portrait of pres, Mt St Joseph Col, Ohio, 77. *Exhib:* Ohio Women Artists: Past & Present, Butler Inst of Am Art, Youngstown, Ohio, 76; 14 Cincinnati Artists, Tampa Bay Arts Ctr, Fla, Peachtree Ctr, Atlanta, Ga & Contemp Arts Ctr, Cincinnati, 76; Cincinnati Art Mus, 81; Daniel Brown's Collection, Middlebury Col, Vt, 81; Graphic Collection of Daniel Brown, Hunter Mus Art, Chattanooga, Tenn. *Collections Arranged:* Drawing & Print Awards Exhib, Cincinnati Art Mus, 75; Regional Proj, Contemp Arts Ctr, Cincinnati, 73; Frescoes: Working People, Arts Consortium, Cincinnati, 91. *Teaching:* Prof painting, Art Acad of Cincinnati, 74- *Awards:* Best in Show, Cincinnati Zoo Arts Festival, 65-68 & 73; First Prize-Drawing, Exhib 180, Huntington Mus Art, 66; Purchase Prize, Jewish Community Ctr Invitational, 68. *Bibliog:* Sally Webster (auth), Regional project, Cincinnati Post, 10/73; Monica Geran (auth), Balancing the scales, Interior Design, 12/80; Jane T Stanton & Colleen M Wood (auths), Constance McClure, Frescoes-Working People (catalog), 91. *Media:* Oil, Buon Fresco. *Mailing Add:* 2356 Park Ave Cincinnati OH 45206

MCCLURE, THOMAS F
SCULPTOR, EDUCATOR
b Pawnee City, Nebr, Apr 17, 20. *Study:* Univ Nebr, BFA, 41; Wash State Col, 41; Cranbrook Acad Art, MFA, 47. *Work:* Seattle Art Mus; Syracuse Mus Fine Arts, NY; Detroit Inst Arts; Wright Mem Ctr, Beloit Col, Wis; DeWaters Art Mus, Flint, Mich. *Comn:* Welded bronze relief, Victor Gruen Assocs, Eastland Shopping Ctr, Detroit, 56; cast bronze relief, DeWaters Art Ctr, 58; welded bronze free standing scultpure, Albert Kahn Assocs, Univ Mich Undergrad Libr, Ann Arbor, 59; ten cast bronze relief sculptures, Congregation Shaarey Zedek, Detroit, 69; large cast bronze sculpture, Mich Blue Cross Bldg, Detroit, 74; and others. *Exhib:* Pa Acad Fine Arts Ann, Philadelphia & Detroit, 58; Contemporary Sculpture 1961, Cincinnati Art Mus & John Herron Art Inst , 61; Drawings USA, St Paul, Minn, 61; one-man exhibs, Gilman Galleries, Chicago, 68, 70 & 75, Arwin Gallery, Detroit, 76, Flint Inst Art, 78, Elaine Horwitch Gallery, Sedona, 87; Neon & Kinetic Art, Mus Kinetic Art, Los Angeles, 87. *Teaching:* Instr design, Sch for Am Craftsmen, Alfred, NY, 47-48; asst prof drawing & design, Univ Okla, 48-49; prof sculpture, Univ Mich, 49-79. *Awards:* First Prize for Painting, Northwest Artists Ann, Seattle, 43; Prize in Sculpture, 12th Nat Ceramics Ann, Syracuse, 47; Founders Prize in Sculpture, 45th Mich Artists Ann, Detroit, 54. *Media:* Metal. *Dealer:* Elaine Horwitch Galleries 4211 N Marshall Way Scottsdale AZ 85251. *Mailing Add:* 2406 Pine Cove Rd Prescott AZ 86301

MCCOLLEY, SUTHERLAND
CONSULTANT, DESIGNER
b Philadelphia, Pa, Oct 17, 37. *Study:* Westminster Choir Col, BMus, 60, MMus, 62; NY State Coun Arts Mus Training Prog, 70; Intermus Conserv Lab, 73; Harvard Univ Inst Arts Admin, 73; Int Mus Studies Prog, 74, Mus Exchange Prog, 76. *Pos:* Researcher, M Knoedler & Co, 67-69; cur art, Hudson River Mus, Yonkers, NY, 69-76; dir, Dulin Gallery Art, Knoxville, 78-80; arts adv, Tenn Valley Authority, Knoxville, 80-81; consult, Sutherland Co, East Hampton, NY, 82- *Awards:* City Knoxville Mayor's Award, 81. *Mem:* Univ Club, New York. *Publ:* Auth, The Works of James Renwick Brevoort, 72. *Mailing Add:* PO Box 155 Wainscott NY 11975

MCCOLLUM, ALLAN
SCULPTOR, PAINTER
b Los Angeles, Calif, 1944. *Work:* Mus Mod Art; Metrop Mus Art; Chicago Art Inst; Los Angeles Mus Contemp Art; Detroit Inst Art. *Exhib:* Julian Preto Gallery, New York, 87-90; Galerie Yvon Lambert, Paris, 80, 88 & 90; John Weber Gallery, New York, 88-92; Studio Trisorio, Naples, 89; Galerie Fahnemann, Berlin, 90; Image World: Art & Media Culture, Whitney Mus Art, New York, 89; 1991 Carnegie International, Carnegie Mus Art, Pittsburgh, 91-92; Allegories of Modernism: Contemporary Drawing, Mus Mod Art, New York, 92; many more solo & group exhibs, 69-90. *Awards:* Nat Endowment Arts, 87, 88, 89 & 90. *Bibliog:* Mathilde Roskam (auth), Allan McCollum at the Van Abbemuseum, Eindover, Flash Art, 1/2/90; Dorothy Spears (auth), Allan McCollum, Artform, summer 90; Kim Levin (auth), Allan McCollum, Village Voice, 3/20/90. *Media:* Miscellaneous Media. *Mailing Add:* c/o John Weber Gallery 142 Greene St New York NY 10012

MCCOLLUM, MIKE L
PAINTER, PRINTMAKER
b Hoquiam, Wash, June 22, 39. *Study:* Humboldt State Col, Arcata, Calif, BA, 67; Univ Calif, Berkeley, MA, 69, MFA, 73. *Work:* Bank of America, San Francisco Mus, DeYoung Mus & Security Pacific Bank, San Francisco; Brooklyn Mus, NY. *Comn:* Five paintings, Valley Bank, Nev, 80. *Exhib:* Solo exhib, De Young Mus, San Francisco, Calif, 73; Area X Gallery, New York, 84; World Print Coun, San Francisco, 85; Wenniger Gallery, Boston, Mass, 88; Allied Arts Gallery, Las Vegas, Nev, 90. *Teaching:* Dean col fine & performing arts, 89- *Awards:* Visual Arts Award, Nat Endowment Arts, 80. *Mem:* Int Coun Fine Arts; Deans Nat Coun Art Adminr. *Dealer:* Magnolia Editions Gallery 2527 Magnolia Oakland CA 94607. *Mailing Add:* Univ Nev-Las Vegas 4505 Maryland Pkwy Las Vegas NV 89154

MCCONNELL, MICHAEL PATRICK
SCULPTOR
b Troy, Ohio, Dec 4, 48. *Study:* Ohio Univ, Athens, BFA(sculpture), 70, MFA(sculpture), 74. *Work:* Butler Inst Am Art, Youngstown, Ohio; Laguna Gloria Art Mus, Austin, Tex; Currier Gallery Art, Manchester, NH; Meadows Mus Art, Shreveport, La; Zanesville Art Ctr, Ohio. *Comn:* Sculpture, NH Comn Arts, 83. *Exhib:* Mainstreams, Marietta Col, Ohio, 75 & 76; Int Craft, Tweed Mus Art, Duluth, Minn,77; Drawing and Small Sculpture, Ball State Univ Art Gallery, Muncie, Ind, 77, 78, 79 & 81; Grand Prix Int d'Art Contemp de Monte-Carlo, Nat Mus Monaco, 80 & 82. *Teaching:* Assoc prof sculpture, Univ NH, 76- *Awards:* Sculpture Award, Marietta Col, 76; Finalist, Int Competition, Johnson Atelier Inst, 79; Award of Merit, Saenger Nat, Univ Southern Miss, 78. *Media:* Welded Steel, Cast Bronze. *Mailing Add:* 9 Faculty Rd Durham NH 03824-2706

MCCORISON, MARCUS ALLEN
LIBRARIAN
b Lancaster, Wis, July 17, 26. *Study:* Ripon Col, BA, 50; Univ Vt, MA, 51; Columbia Univ, MS, 54; Col Holy Cross, LHD, 92; Univ Vt, LHD, 92; Clark Univ, Hon Dr Litt, 92. *Collections Arranged:* A Society's Chief Joys (auth, catalog), Grolier Club, Newberry Libr, Univ Calif, Los Angeles, 68-70. *Pos:* Librn, Kellogg-Hubbard Libr, Montpelier, Vt, 54-55; chief rare bk, Dartmouth Col, Hanover, NH, 55-59; head spec collections, Univ Iowa, Iowa City, 59-60; librn, Am Antiq Soc, Worcester, Mass, 60-91, dir, 67-89, pres, 89-, pres emer, 92; trustee, Fruitlands Mus, 80-89, Old Sturbridge Village, 81- & Historic Deerfield, 91. *Teaching:* Adj, Clark Univ. *Awards:* Pepys Medal, Ephemera Soc, London, 80; Ripon Col, Distinguished Alumni Award, 89; Columbia Univ, Sch Lit Serv, Distinguished Alumni Award, 92. *Mem:* Century Asn; Rare Bk Sect, Asn Col & Res Libr (chmn, 65); Independent Res Libr Asn (chmn, 72-73 & 78-80); Grolier Club (councillor, 79-84); Bibliog Soc Am (pres, 80-84). *Res:* History of American printing, publishing, book trades, including American prints. *Interests:* American prints in all media prior to year 1877. *Collection:* American prints of the 18th and 19th century. *Publ:* Auth, Vermont Imprints, 1777-1820, Am Antiq Soc, 63; auth, 1764 Catalogue of the Redwood Library, Yale Univ Press, 65; ed, The history of printing in America, Imprint Soc, 70. *Mailing Add:* Am Antiq Soc 185 Salisbury St Worcester MA 01609

MCCORMICK, PAM(ELA ANN)
SCULPTOR
b Grand Rapids, Mich, Jan 7, 46. *Study:* San Jose State Univ, BA, 72, study with Sam Richardson, MA, 72; Stanford Univ, post-grad study in art hist, 76. *Comn:* Floating water sculpture, Artists Representing Environmental Art, New York, 84; Drawing Water from a Rock, Central Park, New York, 84; World Win, water sculpture, Harbor Festival, New York, 85; Apollo Muses, sculpture, comn by Lila Tyng, New York, 86; Sculpture in the Mall, Corcoran Art Gallery & Washington Sculptors' Group, Washington, DC, 86. *Exhib:* Environmental Arts Projects, Morris Mus, Morristown, NJ, 80; Captured by Gypsy Moths, Central Park, New York, 81; New Sculpture: Icon & Environment (with catalog), Guild Hall, EHampton, NY & traveling, 84; Aldrich Mus (with catalog), Ridgefield, Conn, 85; Video Contemporary New York, Athens, Greece, 85; A Salute to Halley's Comet, Light Gallery, New York, 86; Four Sculptors (with catalog), Pub Art Trust, Washington, DC, 86; Vista, Lambert's Cove, Martha's Vineyard, Mass, 86; Balance of Power (stage set), Unconventional Constitutional Convention, Cooper Union, New York, 86; Sculpture Symposium on the Mall, Corcoran Gallery & Washington Sculptors Group, 86. *Awards:* Nat Endowment Arts Fel, 74; Award of Distinction, Audubon Naturalist Soc, 86. *Bibliog:* Grace Glueck (auth), article, New York Times, 9/80; article, Women's Art J, New York, 6/82; article, Artspeak, New York, 5/84; Karl Lunde (auth), Art and the environment, Arts Mag, New York, 3/85; Paul Richards (auth), article in

Washington Post, 9/18/86. *Mem:* Int Sculpture Soc; Artists Representing Environmental Arts; Artists Equity. *Media:* Water, Stone,. *Publ:* Illusr, Palace Peeper, Gilbert & Sullivan Soc, New York, 12/85. *Mailing Add:* 97 Wooster St New York NY 10012

MCCORMICK, ROD
SCULPTOR
Study: Tyler Sch Art, Philadelphia, Pa, BFA, 74; RI Sch Design, Providence, MFA, 78. *Exhib:* Solo show, Owen Patrick Gallery, Philadelphia, Pa, 90; Univ Arts, Philadelphia, Pa, 91; Meredith Gallery, Baltimore, Md, 91; Leo Kaplan Mod, New York, 92. *Pos:* Owner, Mail & McCormick-Designers & Makers of Fine Jewelry, Philadelphia, 82-88. *Teaching:* Univ Arts, Philadelphia Col Art & Design, Pa, 81-, assoc prof, currently. *Awards:* Venture Fund Grant, Philadelphia Col Arts, 87, Univ Arts, 90, Pa; Nat Endowment Arts Fel, 90; Fel, Pa Coun Arts, 91. *Bibliog:* Michael Dunas (auth), Rod McCormick-lamps, sculpture, lighted sculpture, Metalsmith, 41, fall 90; Tom Csaszar (auth), Review-Rod McCormick, New Art Examiner, 37, 2/91. *Mailing Add:* P O Box 29578 Philadelphia PA 19144

MCCOSH, ANNE KUTKA (MRS DAVID MCCOSH)
PAINTER, PRINTMAKER
b Danbury, Conn. *Study:* Art Students League, with Kenneth Hays Miller, Kimon Nicolaides & Eugene Fitsch. *Work:* Portland Art Mus, Ore; Am Red Cross, Washington, DC; Univ Ore Art Mus, Eugene, Ore. *Exhib:* Seattle Art Mus, 45; Exhib Watercolors, Drawings & Prints, Metrop Mus Art, New York, 52; Portland Art Mus, 70, 72 & 73; Pac Northwest Art Ann, Eugene, Ore, 72; Earthworks-Artworks, Kerns Art Ctr, Eugene, 77; Mus Art, Univ Ore, 77; Tacoma Mus Art, 91; and others. *Teaching:* Instr painting & drawing, M I Kerns Art Ctr, Eugene, 60-81. *Awards:* Tiffany Fel, 30; G R D Traveling Scholar, 34. *Mem:* Art Students League. *Media:* Oil; Lithography. *Publ:* Ed, David McCosh Retrospective Exhibition, 85. *Mailing Add:* 1870 Fairmount Blvd Eugene OR 97403

MCCOUBREY, SARAH
PAINTER
b New Haven, Conn, Sept 5, 56. *Study:* Univ Pa, BA, BFA, MFA, 81. *Exhib:* One-man shows, More Gallery, Philadelphis, Pa, 85, Leslie Cecil Gallery, New York, 89, Comfort Gallery, Haverford Col, Pa, 90 & Robert Brown Contemp Art, Washington, DC, 90; BAUhouse Gallery, Baltimore, Md, 90; Cheekwood Nat Contemp Painting Competition, Tenn, 91; Botanical Gardens & Fine Arts Ctr, Cheekwood, Nashville, Tenn, 91. *Teaching:* Inst painting, Corcoran Sch Art, Washington, DC, currently. *Awards:* Nat Endowment Arts Grant, 89; Md Covernant for Arts, 90. *Media:* Acrylic, Oil. *Dealer:* Robert Brown Contemp Art 1005 New Hampshire Ave Washington DC. *Mailing Add:* 104 Elm Ave Takoma Park MD 20912

MCCOY, ANN
MURALIST, DRAFTSMAN
b Boulder, Colo, July 8, 46. *Study:* Univ Colo, BFA, 69; Univ Calif, Los Angeles, MA, 72. *Work:* Metrop Mus Art, Whitney Mus Am Art, New York; Hirshhorn Mus, Washington, DC; Los Angeles Co Art Mus; Art Inst Chicago; Nat Gallery Australia; Lannan Found, Fla. *Comn:* Mural in pencil, Harris Bank. *Exhib:* 10 Years of Contemporary Art Acquisitions, Los Angeles Co Art Mus, 73; Whitney Mus Am Art, New York, 73; Painting & Sculpture Today, Contemp Art Ctr, Cincinnati, 74; 71st Am Exhib, Art Inst Chicago, 74; one-person exhibs, Inst Contemp Art, Boston, 75, Arts Club Chicago, 79, Roy Boyd Gallery, Chicago, 79 & Margo Leavin Gallery, Los Angeles, 79; America 1976, Corcoran Gallery Art, Washington, DC, Wadsworth Atheneum, Hartford, Conn & Fogg Art Mus, Cambridge, Mass, 76; 31st Ann Exhib, Brooklyn Mus, 78; Still Modern After All These Years, Chrysler Mus, Norfolk, Va, 82; Memento Mori, Moore Col Art Gallery, Philadelphia, Pa, 85; Myths & Symbols, Bruno Facchetti Gallery, New York, 86; Second Sights, San Francisco Mus Mod Art, 86. *Teaching:* Instr, Sch Visual Arts, 77-, Barnard Col, 80- & Columbia Univ, 85-, New York. *Awards:* Nat Endowment Arts, 78; Prix de Rome, 89-90; AVA Award, 89-90. *Bibliog:* William Wilson (auth), Integrity fails to make shift from LA to NY, Los Angeles Times, 10/17/82; Mark Schipper (auth), Ann McCoy, Art Scene, 12/84; Michael Brenson (auth), They seek spiritual meaning in an age of skepticism, New York Times, 5/11/86. *Media:* Pencil. *Publ:* Auth, Alice Baber: Light as subject, 9-10/80 & The daemon and the night sea, 11-12/80, Art Int; Maura Sheehan's urban artifacts, Arts Mag, 11/85. *Dealer:* Eugene Bindy Gallery PO Box 26305 Dallas Tex 75226; Herstand and Co New York. *Mailing Add:* PO Box 1491 Stuyvesant Sta New York NY 10009

MCCOY, KATHERINE BRADEN
DESIGNER, EDUCATOR
b Decatur, Ill, Oct 12, 45. *Study:* Mich State Univ, BA, 67. *Comn:* Poster & catalog, Detroit Inst Arts, 73-76; archit signage & graphic design, Pontiac Silver Dome, Mich, 75-79; package design & signage, Tivoli Ltd, Birmingham, Mich, 77; environ design, Univ Mich, 78-79. *Exhib:* Commun Graphics Shows, Am Inst Graphic Arts Gallery, New York, 72, 76 & 79, Five Years of Posters, 79 & Covers Show, 79; Artists in Residence, Cranbrook Acad Art, Bloomfield Hills, Mich, 78; Station 100, Chicago, 78-81. *Collections Arranged:* Knoll and Herman Miller: The Development of Contemporary Furniture (auth, catalog), Cranbrook Acad Art, 75 & Design in Michigan (auth, catalog), 77; International Graphic Design Education, Icograda Chicago, 78. *Pos:* Designer, Unimark Int, Detroit, 67-68; sr designer, Chrysler Corp Identity Off, Detroit, 68-69; sr designer, Omnigraphics, Boston, 69-70; sr designer, Designers & Partners, Detroit, 70-71; partner, McCoy & McCoy, Detroit, 71-; bd ed, Indust Design Mag, 76- *Teaching:* Co-chmn, Dept Design, Cranbrook Acad Art, 71- *Awards:* Industrial Design Excellence Award, 80; I Award, Interiors Mag, 80; Showroom of the Year Award, Inst Business Designers, 80. *Bibliog:* Articles, Graphic Design Educ, 81, Interiors Mag, 82 & Novum Grebrauschgraphik, 82. *Mem:* Indust Designers Soc Am (pres, 83-84); Am Inst Graphic Arts; Soc Typographic Arts. *Publ:* Auth & ed, Projects and Processes, Cranbrook Acad Art, 76; Design in Michigan, Wayne State Univ Press, 78. *Mailing Add:* Dept Design Cranbrook Acad Art 500 Lone Pine Rd Box 801 Bloomfield Hills MI 48013

MCCOY, MICHAEL DALE
DESIGNER, EDUCATOR
b Eaton Rapids, Mich, Sept 16, 44. *Study:* Mich State Univ, BA, 66; Wayne State Univ, MA, 68. *Work:* Am Inst of Graphic Art, New York; Cranbrook Acad Art Mus, Bloomfield Hills, Mich; Cooper Hewitt Mus, New York; Philips Design Ctr, Neth; JIDA, Tokyo. *Comn:* Archit graphics, Pontiac Silverdome, Mich, 76; furniture, Knoll Int, New York, 78; Experimental dealership design, Chrysler Corp, Detroit, 78; interior design, Univ Mich, 79; furniture, Interior Ctr, Tokyo. *Exhib:* Commun Graphics, Am Inst Graphic Arts, New York, 74, 76 & 79; Cranbrook Art Mus, 77, 78 & 83; Cooper-Hewitt Mus Design, New York, 81; Progressive Archit Furniture Exhib, 81. *Pos:* Partner, McCoy & McCoy Design Consult, Bloomfield Hills, Mich, 71- *Teaching:* Co-chmn design dept, Cranbrook Acad Art, Bloomfield Hills, Mich, 71- *Awards:* Ann Design Rev Awards, Indust Design Mag, 71-80; Print Casebooks Award, Print Mag, 76-78; Design Excellence Award, Industrial Designers Soc Am, 80. *Bibliog:* Cranbrook comes back, 9/82 & Office of the year, 5/83, Interiors Mag. *Mem:* Indust Design Soc Am. *Publ:* Coauth, Problem Solving in the Man-Made Environment, Cranbrook Acad Art, 74. *Mailing Add:* Cranbrook Acad Art Box 801 Bloomfield Hills MI 48303-0801

MCCOY, PAT A
WRITER, CRITIC
b Seattle, Wash. *Study:* Ctr Mod Psychoanalytic Studies, cert; NY Univ with Ross Bleckner, Achille Bonito Oliva & Gillo Dorfles, 83. *Pos:* Art lectr to mus, univs & galleries, New Arts Prog, Pa & Atlantic area, 91- *Teaching:* Lectr Eng, City Univ, New York, 85-88 & John Jay Col Criminal Justice, 88-91. *Awards:* NY State Found Arts, 87; Mid-Atlantic Grant, 92; Nat Endowment Art Grant, 92. *Mem:* Soc Mod Psychoanalysts. *Res:* Cultural study & analysis pertaining to art, aesthetics, "interior of individual" in post modern & modern eras. *Publ:* Auth, East Village: dead or alive, Artscribe Mag, 87; Disrupted narrative, 88 & Modern lexicon, 89, Arts Mag; Art Criticism Today (Round Table ed), M/E/A/N/I/N/G, 92; Innovations in Child Mental Health-rev, J Mod Psychoanalysis, 92. *Mailing Add:* 630 E 14th St Apt 3 New York NY 10009

MCCOY, WIRTH VAUGHAN
PAINTER, EDUCATOR
b Duluth, Minn, Dec 16, 13. *Study:* Univ Minn, BA, 37; Univ Iowa, MFA, 48; Acad Grande Chaumiere, cert painting & design, 51; Calif Sch Fine Art, 49; Acad Montmartre, 50; also with James Lechay, Maurice Lasansky, Mark Rothko, Yasuo Kunioshi & others. *Work:* Portland Art Mus; Seattle Art Mus; Mineral Industs Mus, Pa State Univ; Univ Iowa; Wash State Univ. *Exhib:* Artists Ore, Portland, 54; Centennial Exhib, Kansas City Art Inst, 62; Spokane Int Art Exhib, 64; one man show, Mus Art, Pa State Univ, 79; retrospective, Zoller Gallery, Pa State Univ, 80. *Pos:* Bd dir, Palmer Mus Art, Pa State Univ, 88- *Teaching:* Asst prof painting & drawing, Ore State Univ, 48-53; prof painting & drawing, resident artist & dir, Wash State Univ Ctr, 53-64; head dept art, Pa State Univ, 64-71, prof art, 71-79, emer prof, 79- *Mem:* Col Art Asn Am; Cent Pa Festival Arts (bd dirs); Peale Club Philadelphia; Pa Acad Fine Arts; Art Alliances Cent Pa. *Media:* Acrylic, Oil. *Mailing Add:* 932 E McCormick State College PA 16801

MCCRACKEN, JOHN HARVEY
SCULPTOR, PAINTER
b Berkeley, Calif, Dec 9, 34. *Study:* Calif Col Arts & Crafts, BFA, 62, grad work, 57-65. *Work:* Mus Mod Art, Whitney Mus Am Art & Guggenheim Mus, New York; Los Angeles Co Mus; Art Inst Chicago; Art Gallery Ont, Toronto; Honolulu Acad Art, HI; Milwaukee Art Ctr, Wis; Musee d'Art Contemp de Montreal, Can; San Francisco Mus Art, Calif. *Exhib:* Primary Structures, Jewish Mus, New York, 66; American Sculpture of the Sixties, Los Angeles Co Mus Art, 67; 5th Guggenheim Int Exhib, Guggenheim Mus, 67; Art of the Real, Mus Mod Art, New York, 69; 69th Am Exhib, Art Inst Chicago, 70; Mus Contemp Arts, Chicago, 70; Documenta, Kassel, WGer, 72; one-man shows, Hoffman Borman Gallery, Santa Monica, Calif, 87, Newport Harbor Art Mus, Newport Beach, 87, Fine Art Gallery, Irvine, Calif, 87, The Sculpture of John McCraken, 1965-1986, PS 1, 89; Carnegie Int, 91; Carnegie Mus Art, Pittsburg, 91-92; Sonnabend Gallery, New York, 92; and others. *Teaching:* Asst prof sculpture & painting, Univ Calif, Irvine & Los Angeles, 65-68; asst prof sculpture, Sch Visual Arts, New York, 68-69; asst prof sculpture & painting, Hunter Col, 71-82. *Awards:* Nat Endowment for the Arts Award, 68. *Bibliog:* Edward Leffingwell (ed), The Sculpture of John McCraken 1965-1986 (catalog), PS 1 Gallery; Mollet Vieville (auth), Ghislain (catalog, solo exhib), Galerie Froment & Putman, Paris, 5/92; Carnegie International 1991, The Carnegie Mus Art, Pittsburgh, 91. *Media:* Fiberglass, Wood. *Dealer:* Fred Hoffman Gallery 912 Colorado Ave Santa Monica CA 90401. *Mailing Add:* 10001 E First St Los Angeles CA 90012

MCCRACKEN, PHILIP
SCULPTOR
b Bellingham, Wash, Nov 14, 28. *Study:* Univ Wash, BA; sculpture with Henry Moore, Eng, 54. *Work:* Detroit Inst Art; Whitney Mus Am Art, New York; United Nations Asn, New York; St Louis Art Mus, Mo; Anchorage Mus Art, Alaska. *Comn:* Norton Bldg, Seattle, Wash, 79; Kankakee State

Hosp, Ill, 61; Swinomish Indian Tribal Ctr, LaConner, Wash, 64; Fed Bldg, Gen Serv Admin, Seattle, Wash, 76; King County King Dome, Seattle, Wash, 78. *Exhib:* One-man shows, Seattle Art Mus, 61, Victoria Mus, BC, 64, La Jolla Mus Art, Calif, 70 & Anchorage Mus Art, 70; group shows, Corcoran Gallery Art, 66; Rutgers Univ, 68; Grand Rapids Art Mus, 69; Acad & Inst Arts & Letters, New York, 86; and many others. *Awards:* Norman Davis Award, 57; Artists of the Year, Wash State, 64; Irene Wright Mem Award, Seattle Art Mus, 65. *Bibliog:* Dore Ashton (auth), Modern American Sculpture, Abrams, 67; James J Kelly (auth), The Sculptural Idea, Burgess Press, 70; Colin Graham (auth), Philip McCracken, Univ Wash Press, 80. *Media:* All Media. *Dealer:* Kennedy Galleries 40 W 57th St New York NY 10019. *Mailing Add:* Guemes Island Anacortes WA 98221

MCCREADY, ERIC SCOTT
ADMINISTRATOR, EDUCATOR
b Vancouver, Wash, Mar 14, 41. *Study:* Univ Ore, BS, 63, BA, 65, MA, 68; Univ Pavia, Italy, BA, 65; Univ Del, PhD(art hist), 72; Wintherthur Summer Inst. *Teaching:* Asst prof art hist, Bowling Green State Univ, 72-75; Asst prof art hist, Univ Wis-Madison, 75-79; assoc prof art hist, Univ Tex, Austin, 79-89; assoc prof, Univ Ore, presently. *Mem:* Assoc Art Mus Dir; Soc Archit Historians (mem decorative arts chap); Mid-West Art Hist Soc; Victorian Soc Am. *Res:* American art. *Publ:* Auth, The Nebraska State Capitol: Its Design, Background and Influence, Nebr State Hist Soc, 74; Tanner and Gilliam: Two American black painters, Negro Lit Forum, 74; Richard Taliaferro: 18th Century Virginia Architect, Univ Ore Press, 77; Bertram Goodhue: Master of many arts (rev), J Soc Archit Historians, 78. *Mailing Add:* 16 Westbrook Way Eugene OR 97405

MCCREADY, KAREN (KAREN MCCREADY NOBLET)
DEALER, WRITER
b Beaver Falls, Pa, May 2, 46. *Study:* Austin Col, Sherman Tex, BA, 68; Aspen Inst Humanistic Studies, with Alan Kaprow, 69; Parsons Sch Design, 71. *Collections Arranged:* Lehman Brothers, Kuhn Loeb corp art collection, 78-82; Contemp American Ceramics: Twenty Artists (auth catalog), Newport Harbor Art, Newport, Calif, 86. *Pos:* Dir, Pace Editions, Inc, New York, 72-82; dir, Crown Point Press, Calif & New York, 82- *Teaching:* Lectr, Collectors' Inst New Sch Soc Res, NY, fall 78; instr printmaking, Sch Vis Arts, New York, spring 83. *Mem:* Art Table, Inc (vpres, 90). *Res:* Survey of contemporary porcelain and its use in the studio setting today. *Specialty:* Contemporary American prints. *Collection:* Contemporary English & American ceramics; antique English & Japanese ceramics; art deco ceramics. *Publ:* Auth, 8 for the 80's, Quay Gallery, 80; coauth with Jan Axel, Porcelain: Tradition and New Visions, Watson-Guptill Publ, 81. *Mailing Add:* 39 Bond St New York NY 10012

MCCUE, HARRY
PRINTMAKER, CRAFTSMAN
b New York, NY, Sept 27, 44. *Study:* Pratt Inst, with Romano, Blaustien & McNeil, BFA, 67; Univ Colo, Boulder, with Roland Ries & William T Wiley, MFA, 69. *Work:* Univ Colo, Boulder; Univ Pa, Edinboro. *Comn:* Set design (collabr, D Smyth), Cornell Dance Group, Ithaca, NY, 84; cart design & construction, Mystic Seaport Mus, Conn, 84; design carriage, NY State Hist Soc, Cooperstown, 85; design pastel drawings & prints, New Statler Hotel Complex, Cornell, Ithaca, NY. *Exhib:* Arnot Mus, Elmira, NY, 77; Bevier Gallery-Rochester Inst Technol, 78; solo exhibs, Art Gallery, Adelphi Univ, 80, Schweinfurth Mus, Auburn, NY, 86 & Herbert F Johnson Mus, Cornell Univ, NY, 87; Munson-Williams-Proctor Gallery, Utica, NY, 82; Everson Mus, Syracuse, NY, 85; New Visions Gallery, Ithaca, NY, 86-90; Edinboro Univ, Pa, 87. *Pos:* Asst slide librn, Univ Colo, Boulder, 68. *Teaching:* Instr painting, drawing & printmaking, State Univ NY, Geneseo, 69-72; instr drawing & printmaking, Ithaca Col, 73-77, chmn art dept, 78- *Awards:* F&M Schaeffer Art Award, Schaeffer Brewing Co, 66; Lodestar Grant, Ithaca Col, 84; Grant, Horizon Bank, 85. *Bibliog:* Malcolm Preston (rev), Newsday, 10/7/80; Wellikof (auth), American Historical Supply Catalog, Schocken Press, 84. *Mem:* World Print Coun; Col Art Asn; Nat Arts Coun; Carriage Asn Am; Pastel Artists NY. *Media:* Intaglio Prints, Oil. *Publ:* Marquis Who's Who East, 22nd ed. *Mailing Add:* 2422 Skinner Rd Lodi NY 14860

MCCULLOCH, FRANK E
PAINTER, PRINTMAKER
b Gallup, NMex, Aug 24, 30. *Study:* Univ NMex, BA, 53; Princeton Univ, 53-54; NMex Highlands Univ, 55; Inst Allende, Mex, MFA, 65. *Work:* Amarillo Art Ctr, Tex; Mus Albuquerque; Roswell Mus & Art Ctr, NMex; Mus Fine Arts, Univ NMex, Albuquerque; Inst Allende, San Miguel, Mex. *Comn:* Don Quixote Proj, One Percent For Arts Prog, Albuquerque, 82; acrylic, Cent Bank Cooperatives, Denver, 83. *Exhib:* Southwest Biennial, Mus NMex, Santa Fe, 63, 67, 74 & 76; one-man exhibs, Roswell Mus & Art Ctr, NMex, 79, Governors Gallery, State Capitol, Santa Fe, 81, Munson Gallery, Santa Fe 84, 88, RSV Gallery, Southampton, NY, 83, Dartmouth St Gallery, 88, 89 & 91, Conrad Gallery, Galveston, Tex, 91 & La Galleria del Carraresi (Civic Mus), Treviso (Venice) Italy, 91; Here & Now, Mus Albuquerque, 80; 46th Ann Midyear Exhib, Butler Inst Am Art, 82; Artists of Albuquerque, Mus Albuquerque, NMex, 90; and others. *Teaching:* Mem fac art, pub schs, Albuquerque, 56-, Inst Allende, Mex, 63-65, Univ NMex, 70-73 & Southern Methodist Univ, 77. *Awards:* Second Award, Fiesta Biennial, Mus NMex, 59; First Award, Inst Allende Exhib, Mex, 64; Grumbacher Award & Fifth Award, Nat Sun Carnival Exhib, El Paso Mus, 68. *Bibliog:* Larry Smith (dir), Four Plates, Ten Colors, (film), 83; Sandy Ballatore (auth), article, NMex Mag; Mary Carrol Nelson (auth), article, Southwest Art. *Mem:* Albuquerque Arts Bd, 88. *Media:* Oils on Canvas; Lithography, Handmade Paper. *Publ:* Auth, Raymond Jonson, Artspace, 81. *Dealer:* Munson Gallery 653 Canyon Rd Santa Fe NM 87501; Mill St Gallery Aspen. *Mailing Add:* 203 14th SW Albuquerque NM 87102

MCCULLOUGH, DAVID WILLIAM
PAINTER, SCULPTOR
b Springfield, Mass, Dec 28, 45. *Study:* Boston Inst of the Arts, Mass, 63-64; Aspen Sch of Contemp Art, Colo, summer 68, with Wilbur Neiwald & Doris Cross; Kansas City Art Inst, Mo, BFA(printmaking, painting), 70; Univ Mich, 69, with printmaker, Emil Weddige; Calif Inst of the Arts, 70, with Allan Kaprow & Dick Higgins. *Work:* Continental Insurance Co, New York; Sony Corp, Parkridge, NJ; Joslyn Art Mus, Omaha; Indianapolis Mus Art; Kemper Insurance Co, Chicago. *Comn:* Sculptural fountain, Am Petrofina Oil Co, Dallas, 74; three monumental sculptures, Tex Comn Arts & Humanities, 74. *Exhib:* Dallas Mus of Fine Arts Bicentennial, 71; Okla Art Mus, Oklahoma City, 71; South by SW Exhib, Ft Worth Art Mus, 72; Tyler Mus of Art, 74; Beaumont Art Mus, Tex, 75; Joslyn Art Mus, Omaha, Nebr, 76; Amarillo Art Ctr, 77; and others. *Teaching:* Artist in residence video-audio, Western Wash State Col, Bellingham, 76; artist in residence painting & sculpture, Santa Fe Contemp Art Sch, NMex, 76; lectr, Kansas City Art Inst, 82, Minneapolis Sch Art & Design. *Awards:* First Prize, Painting/Sculpture Biennial, Dallas Mus of Fine Arts, 71; First Prize, Univ Tex, Arlington, 76; Best of Show, Meadows Art Mus, Shreveport Art Guild, La, 77. *Bibliog:* Museum People, KERA-TV film, 74; Victoria Melcher (auth), David McCullough, Arts Mag, 1/76; Sarah Burns (auth), David McCullough, Arts Mag, 1/82. *Media:* Acrylic; Sand, Mixed. *Dealer:* Virginia Miller Galleries 169 Madiera Ave Coral Gables Fla 33134; Patrick King Contemporary Art 427 Massachusetts Ave Fort Wayne Ind 46204. *Mailing Add:* c/o Virginia Miller Galleries 169 Madiera Ave Coral Gables FL 33134

MCCULLOUGH, JOSEPH
ADMINISTRATOR, PAINTER
b Pittsburgh, Pa, July 6, 22. *Study:* Cleveland Inst Art, dipl, 48; Yale Univ, with Lewis York, 49-50, BFA, 50, with Josef Albers, 50-51, MFA, 51; Univ Evansville, Ill, hon DFA, 80. *Work:* Cleveland Mus Art; Ohio Univ; Syracuse Univ; Youngstown Pub Schs, Ohio. *Comn:* Stained glass windows, St Edmund Roman Cath Church, Warren, Mich, 69. *Exhib:* Corcoran Biennial Exhib, Washington, DC, 55; Audubon Artists Ann Exhib, New York, 56; Contemp Am Painting & Sculpture, Univ Ill, 57; All Ohio Painting & Sculpture Show, Dayton Art Inst, 67; Cleveland Arts Prize Exhib, 71. *Pos:* Pres, Cleveland Inst Art, 55-89, pres, emer, 90; trustee, Minneapolis Col Art & Design, currently; trust adv, Sculpture Ctr, Cleveland; sec, Access to the Arts, Cleveland. *Awards:* Spec Award for Painting, Cleveland Mus Art, 58; Purchase Award for Painting, Dayton Art Inst, 67; Cleveland Arts Prize for Visual Arts, Women's City Club Cleveland, 71. *Mem:* Cleveland Art Asn (secy, 55-88); Nat Asn Schs Art (pres, 62-65); Col Art Asn (bd dirs, 63-68); Osaka Univ Arts, Japan (hon trustee, currently). *Media:* Acrylic, Watercolor. *Publ:* Contribr, Art in Cleveland Architecture, AIA Handbook to Cleveland Architecture, Reinhold, 58; The Enamelist, Kenneth Bates, World, 66. *Mailing Add:* 2637 Wellington Rd Cleveland Heights OH 44118

MCCURDY, MICHAEL CHARLES
ILLUSTRATOR, DESIGNER
b New York, NY, Feb 17, 42. *Study:* Sch Mus Fine Arts, Boston; Tufts Univ, Medford, Mass, BFA, 64, MFA, 71. *Work:* New York Pub Libr; Boston Pub Libr & Mus Fine Arts, Boston; Univ Tex, Austin. *Comn:* Print, Lincoln Conserv Comn, Mass, 81; print, Art Soc, Cleveland Mus Natural Hist, 81; Albnay Print Club, NY, 86; Rochester Print Club, 92. *Exhib:* Solo exhib, Michael McCurdy & Penmaen Press, Boston Athenaeum, Mass, 76; The Artist & the Book, Wenneger Graphics, Boston, 82; International Exhibition of Wood Engraving, Hereford City Art Gallery, Eng, 84; Univ of Mo Libr, 88; Elizabeth Stone Gallery, Birmingham, MI, 92; and others. *Teaching:* Instr drawing, Boston Sch Mus Fine Arts, 66-67; instr drawing & graphics, Concord Acad, Mass, 72-75; instr fine printing, Wellesley Col, Mass, 76. *Awards:* Bronze Medal, Book Award, Die Schonste Bucher Aus Aller Welz, Leipzig, 83; Ten Best Illustrated Children's Books, New York Times, 86. *Bibliog:* Fritz Eichenberg (auth), article, Illus 63 Mag, Ger, 76; Mary Peterson (auth), Penmaen Press, NAm Rev, 81; Eunice Agar (auth), Michael McCurdy and Penmaen Press, Am Artist, 86. *Mem:* Soc of Printers, Boston. *Media:* Book Arts, Wood Engraving. *Publ:* Illusr, The Man Who Planted Trees, Chelsea Green, 85; auth & illusr, Toward the Light, Porcupine's Quill, 82; illusr, The Winged Life, Sierra Club Books, 86; The Owl-Scatterer, Atlantic Monthly, 86; auth & illusr, The Illustrated Harvard, Globe Pequot Press, 86. *Mailing Add:* 66 Lake Buel Rd Great Barrington MA 01230

MCDANIEL, CRAIG MILTON
ADMINISTRATOR, PAINTER
b Norfolk, Va, Sept 14, 48. *Study:* Univ Pa, BS, 70; Univ Mont, MFA, 75; Ohio State Univ, MFA(painting), 86. *Work:* Sheldon Swope Art Mus, Terre Haute, Ind. *Exhib:* Focus: Craig McDaniel, Gov Ohio's State Residence, Columbus, 87; In Indiana, Indianapolis Art Mus, 91; Craig McDaniel & Anita Bracalante, Ind Arts Comn, 91; Town & Country, Mansfield Art Ctr, Ohio, 92; two-person shows, South Bend Regional Art Mus, Ind, 93 & New Harmony Gallery Contemp Art, Ind, 93. *Collections Arranged:* Hurry Sundown: The 1930's (catalog with Jean Robertson), 79; Six Guns and Tomahawks (catalog with Jean Robertson), 81; The Last Laugh, 83; Object As Subject (exhib catalog), 89; Exploring Maps (catalog with Jean Robertson), 92. *Pos:* Founding dir (with Jean Robertson), Southern Ohio Mus & Cult Ctr, Portsmouth, 78-84; dir progs dept, Columbus Mus Art, Ohio, 85-88; dir, Turman Art Gallery, Ind Stat Univ, 88- *Teaching:* Asst prof drawing/painting & mem fac, Sch Grad Studies, Ind State Univ, Terre Haute, 88- *Awards:* Merit Award, Water Tower Ann, Louisville Visual Arts Asn, 91; Visual Artist Fel, Ind Arts Comn, 91 & 92; Award of Excellence, 48th Ann Wabash Valley Exhibit, Swope Art Mus, 92. *Bibliog:* Sarah Rogers Lafferty (auth), Selections: Six in Ohio, Contemp Arts Ctr, 82; Robert Flott (auth),

Arts Spotlight, Terre Haute Tribune-Star, 10/91; Portfolio: Craig McDaniel, Arts Ind, 10/91. *Media:* All. *Publ:* Auth, Under Intense Scrutiny (exhib catalog), Turman Gallery, 90. *Mailing Add:* Indiana State University, Turman Gallery Fine Arts Bldg Terre Haute IN 47809

MCDARRAH, FRED WILLIAM
PHOTOGRAPHER, EDITOR
b Brooklyn, NY, Nov 5, 26. *Study:* New York Univ, BA(journalism), 54. *Work:* Albright Knox Collection. *Exhib:* Solo exhibs, International Jack Kerouac Gathering, 58-60, Musie de Quebec, Can, 87, Photographs of the Artists' World, 58-62, Anita Shapolsky Gallery, New York, 88, The Power of Documentary Photography, Hartnett Gallery, Univ Rochester, 89, New York Sch Action Painters, Antioch Col, 89 & Rock 'n Roll Art & Artifacts, Mus Art, Sci & Indust, Bridgeport, 89; Greenwich Village: The Fifties & Sixties, New York City Gallery, Queens Mus, 89; The Formative Decade: 1964-1974, G Ray Hawkins Gallery, Los Angeles, 89; Andy Warhol System-Pub-Pop-Rock, Found Cartier, Jouy-en-Josas, Paris, France, 90; Intellectual History of Greenwich Village, Pollock-Krasner Mus, East Hampton, 90; Jack Kerouac Traveling Writers, Saint-Malo Int Festival, France, 91; and others. *Pos:* Freelance writer, photogr & picture ed, Village Voice, 59; bk reviewer, ASMP Infinity Mag, 72-73, Photo District News, 85-88, picture prof, 90- *Awards:* Fel in Photogr, John Simon Guggenheim Mem Found Award, 72; Page One Award Best Spot News Photo, New York Newspaper Guild, 71 & 80. *Bibliog:* Profile Currents, Univ Rochester, 11/7/88; Village eye-fast track, New York Mag, 6/26/89; Jerry Tallmer (auth), Visions from the east village, New York Post, 7/23/89; The Still Photograph, Images Inc, Vol 4, Nos 2 & 3, 89; Carol Wheeler (auth), A Chronicler of the beats, East Hampton Star, 10/4/90; Assoc Press, 8/4/92. *Mem:* New York Press Photogr Asn; Am Soc Picture Prof; Nat Press Photogr Asn; Authors Guild, Inc; New York Press Club. *Publ:* Auth, The Artists World in Pictures, Shapolsky Books, 61 & 88; Stock Photo & Assignment Sourcebook, Second Ed, 84; Kerouac & Friends: A Beat Generation Album, William Morrow, 84, new ed translated Japanese, Schichosha Ltd, Tokyo, 90; Museums in New York, 5th ed, St Martin's Press, rev ed, 90; Grennwich Village Guide, Acapella Ltd, 92. *Mailing Add:* 505 LaGuardia Pl New York NY 10012

MACDONALD, BETTY ANN
PRINTMAKER, ENVIRONMENTAL ARTIST
b Brooklyn, NY, Aug 2, 36. *Study:* Adelphi Univ, BA, 58; Columbia Univ, MA, 60; Chinese Inst, 76-78. *Work:* Libr Cong; Corcoran Gallery; Nat Mus Am Hist (Smithsonian Inst); Mus Mod Art, Buenos Aires, Arg; Am Cult Ctr, New Delhi, India. *Comn:* Mural, comn by Washington Women's Investment Club, Washington, DC. *Exhib:* New England Artists Exhib, J F Kennedy Bldg Govt Ctr, Boston, 80; 63rd Nat Art Exhib, Mus Fine Arts, Springfield, Mass, 82; 34th Nat Exhib Boston Printmakers, DeCordova Mus, 82; 40th Anniversary Exhib, Nat Arts Club, New York, 82; Graphic New Hampshire, Plymouth State Col, 84; Los Angeles Printmaking Soc Exhib, Univ HI, Hilo, HI, 85; Prizewinners Exhib, Judicial Ctr, Fairfax, Va, 85; one-person shows, Dept Interior, Geological Survey, Reston, Va, 89, Washington Printmakers Gallery, Washington, DC, 89, Bird-In-Hand Gallery, Washington, DC, 92 & Pushkin Mus, Moscow, Russia, 92. *Teaching:* Instr art, Montshire Mus, 76-83, Lebanon Col, 83-84 & Smithsonian Inst, 85-92. *Awards:* Past President's Award 63rd Nat Exhib, Springfield Art League, 82; First Prize Printmakers VII, Wash Women's Art Ctr, 85; State Prize Copley Soc Exhib, Nat League of Am Pen Women, 86. *Bibliog:* Nancy G Heller (auth), Heat at Women's Art Ctr, Wash Post, 3/28/85; Pamela Kessler (auth), Plum Gallery, Wash Post, 3/18/88; Mary McCoy (auth), Washington Printmaker Gallery, Washington Post, 8/22/91. *Mem:* Life mem Art Student League; Nat Asn Women Artists; Los Angeles Printmaking Soc; Washington Area Printmakers. *Media:* Miscellaneous Media. *Publ:* Contribr, Tilt: An Anthology of New England Women's Writing and Art, New Victoria Publ, 75; Orig Print Calender, Wash Area Printmakers, 87, 88, 89 & 90; William & Mary Rev, 92; book cover, Adagio for Trumpet and Strings, Arsis Press. *Dealer:* Bird in Hand 323 Seventh St SE Washington DC 20003; Washington Printmakers Gallery 2106 R St Washington DC 20008. *Mailing Add:* 7222 Vistas Ln McLean VA 22101

MACDONALD, BRUCE K
EDUCATOR, HISTORIAN
Study: Trinity Col, BA, 61; Harvard Univ, MA, 67 & PhD, 73. *Collections Arranged:* Photographs Before Surrealism, Mus Mod Art, New York, 68; Nineteenth Century Painting from the Museo de Arte de Ponce, Mass Inst Technol, 74. *Pos:* Dir, Exhibs, Mass Inst Technol, Cambridge, Mass, 74-75; dean, Sch of the Mus Fine Arts. *Mem:* Photogr Resource Ctr, Inc (bd trustees); For Spacious Skies, Inc (bd trustees). *Publ:* Contributing Auth, Brassai, Mus Mod Art, 68; The Quarry by Gustave Courbet, Boston Mus Fine Arts Bull, 69; Nineteenth Century Painting from the Museo de Art de Ponce, Mass Inst Technol, 74; contribr, Visual Dharma: The Buddhist Art of Tibet, Shambala, 75. *Mailing Add:* Sch of the Mus Fine Arts 230 The Fenway Boston MA 02115

MACDONALD, COLIN SOMERLED
WRITER, PUBLISHER
b Ottawa, Ont, Mar 5, 25. *Study:* Self taught artist; also study with Mabel May. *Exhib:* One-man show, Little Gallery, Photog Stores, Ottawa, Ont, 62; Ottawa Born Artists, Univ Ottawa, 67. *Pos:* Ed & publ, Dictionary Can Artists, 67-; pres-dir, Can Paperbacks Publ Ltd, 74- *Awards:* Exploration Program Research Award, Can Coun, 85; Publisher Award, Can Coun, 82; Wintario/Heritage Ont grant, 87; plus others. *Bibliog:* W Q Ketchum (auth), Faces of Ottawa, Ottawa J, 3/70; Nancy Baele (auth), One-man dictionary of artists, The Ottawa Citizen, 6/90. *Res:* Biographical information on living and dead Canadian visual artists with bibliography and critical comments. *Publ:* Auth, Dictionary of Canadian Artists, Vols I-VII, 67-89. *Mailing Add:* 17 Gwynne Ave Ottawa ON K1Y 1X1 Canada

MACDONALD, KEVIN JOHN
PAINTER, PRINTMAKER
b Washington, DC, July 2, 46. *Study:* Montgomery Jr Col, Takoma Park, Md, 64-66; George Washington Univ, BFA, 69; Corcoran Sch of Art, Washington, DC, 69. *Work:* Metrop Mus Art, New York; Corcoran Gallery Art, Washington, DC; Phillips Collection, Washington, DC; Hirshhorn Mus Art; Nat Mus Am Art, Washington DC; and others. *Exhib:* Am Drawings, 76 & Images of the 70's (with catalog), 80, Corcoran Gallery Art, Washington, DC; Fifth Davidson Nat, Davidson Col, NC, 76; Md Biennial, Baltimore Mus Art, 76, 78 & 80; Drawing Show, Phillips Collection, Washington, DC, 77. *Pos:* Chmn, Wash Proj for the Arts, DC. *Bibliog:* Martha Wright (auth), article, Art Int, 1/78; David Tannous (auth), article, Art in Am, 5/78; Charlotte Moser (auth), article, Art News, 10/81; and others. *Media:* Oil, Colored Pencil. *Dealer:* Adamson Editions 406 7th St NW Washington DC 20004. *Mailing Add:* 8207 Georgia Ave 5th Silver Spring MD 20910

MCDONALD, ROBERT HERWICK
CURATOR, MUSEUM DIRECTOR
b Philadelphia, Pa. *Study:* Univ Calif, Berkeley, BA & MA, Mus Mgt Inst. *Pos:* Contribr ed, Artweek, 73-88; dir, Daniel Weinberg Gallery, San Francisco, 74-76; admin asst dir, Univ Calif Art Mus, Berkeley, 77-79; chief cur, La Jolla Mus Contemp Art, 79-82 & Laguna Art Mus, 84-85, Calif; dir, Art Mus Santa Cruz, Calif, 82-84; critic, LA Times (San Diego ed), 85-87; dir, de Saisset Mus, Santa Clara, Calif, currently. *Teaching:* Instr Europ cult hist, Univ Calif, Riverside, 67-71 & Calif State Univ, Hayward, 71, 72 & 74; Intro Art Hist & Appreciation, Univ San Diego, 86-87. *Awards:* San Diego Press Club Award, 82, Phi Beta Kappa. *Mem:* Col Art Asn; Am Art Fedn; Am Assn Mus; Int Asn Art Critics (US); Calif Confederation Arts. *Res:* Contemporary American art, California artists. *Publ:* Auth, Craig Kauffman-A Comprehensive Survey 1957-1980, Fels Contemp Art, Los Angeles, 81; Christo: Collection on Loan from the Rothschild Bank AG, Zurich, Introduction, 82 & Rooms and Stories: Recent work by Terry Allen, 83; D J Hall Selected Works 1974-1985, Los Angeles Munic Art Gallery, 86; Sense of Place: D J Hall, F Scott Hess, John Valadez, Fisher Gallery, Univ Southern Calif, Los Angeles, 87; Morris Graves: Works of Fifty Years, de Saisset Mus Santa Clara Univ, Calif, 90. *Mailing Add:* c/o Santa Clara Univ De Saisset Museum 500 El Camino Real Santa Clara CA 95053

MACDONALD, ROBERT R
DIRECTOR, HISTORIAN
b Pittsburgh, Pa, May 11, 42. *Study:* Univ Notre Dame, BA, 64, MA, 65; Univ Pa, MA, 70. *Collections Arranged:* New Haven Colony Furniture (ed, catalog), New Haven Hist Soc, 72; La Portrait Gallery (ed, catalog), 81 & Sun King: Louis XIV and the New World (ed catalog), 84, La State Mus. *Pos:* Dir, New Haven Hist Soc, 71-74, La State Mus, 74-85 & Mus City New York, 85- *Teaching:* Assoc fel Am civilization, Yale Univ, 73-74; instr mus studies, Tulane Univ, 81; lectr mus studies, NY Univ, 86- *Awards:* Order of Arts & Lett, French Repub, 85; Order of Isabella Catolica, Govt Spain, 85. *Mem:* Am Asn Mus (pres, 85-87); Am Asn State & Local Hist (mem coun, 78-80). *Res:* American folk art, social and cultural history. *Mailing Add:* c/o Museum of the City of New York Fifth Ave at 103rd St New York NY 10029

MACDONALD, SCOTT
CRITIC, EDUCATOR
b Easton, Pa, Oct 10, 42. *Study:* DePauw Univ, BA, 64; Univ Fla, MA, 66, PhD, 70. *Teaching:* Asst prof humanities, Univ Fla, 69-70; from asst prof to prof film & Am lit, Utica Col, 71-, dir, Art Gallery, presently. *Res:* Research regarding avant-garde filmmakers. *Specialty:* Upstate New York artists whose work poses a challenge to the local Utica-Rome community. *Publ:* Auth, The expanding vision of Larry Gottheim's films, 78; Surprise, The films of Robert Huot, Quart Rev Film Studies, 80; Interview with Taka Iimura, Part 1, Art & Cinema, 80; Interview with Robert Huot, Afterimage, 80; and others. *Mailing Add:* 5 Sherman St New Hartford NY 13413

MCDONALD, SUSAN STRONG
PAINTER, PRINTMAKER
b Rochester, NY, Aug 18, 43. *Study:* Sweet Briar Col, BA, 65; studied with Kathan Brown, 68-71; Yoshida Hanga Acad, 71-74. *Work:* Walker Art Ctr, Minneapolis Inst Art & Univ Minn Gallery, Minneapolis; Michael C Rockefeller Gallery, Fredonia, NY; Western Regional Post Off, San Francisco. *Comn:* YWCA Award Prints, St Paul, 89. *Exhib:* Photoetchings from Crown Point Press, Ames Gallery, Berkeley, 71; Oakland Mus Art, 74; Japan Printmakers Asn Ann Exhib, Tokyo, 75; Portrait of an Artist, Minneapolis Inst Art, 81; Five Minneapolis Artists, Tweed Mus Art, 82; WARM: A Landmark Exhib, Minn Mus Art, St Paul, 84; Women's Art Registry, 86; solo exhib, Soho 20, Invitational, 87, 4th Ann Minn Artists' Exhib, 87, Kew Studios, London, Eng, 88 & Hogarth Club London, 88, Out of Control: Artists Bks, ARC Gallery, Chicago, 90. *Pos:* Scientific illusr, Univ Calif, Berkeley, 69-71; muralist, Wall Painting Artists Inc, 78-81. *Teaching:* Instr, Int Sch Sacred Heart, Tokyo, Japan, 71-74, Metro State Univ, Minneapolis, Minn, 79-90, North Hennepin Community Col, 83-90, Split Rock Arts Prog, Univ Minn, 84-89. *Awards:* CUE Award, City Minneapolis, 82; WARM Mentor Scholarships, 83, 86 & 89; One month residency fel for printmaking, Ucross Found, 87. *Bibliog:* Diane Hellekson (auth), Using the figure, 1/85 & Margot Kreil Galt (auth), Delving into the self and finding the bones of us all, 1/86, Artpaper; Sharon Zweigbaum (auth), Susan McDonald tackles Lay issues, Vol 3, No 5, FAN, 5/86. *Mem:* Founding mem Womens Art Registry Minn. *Media:* Acrylic, Oil; All Media. *Publ:* Auth, State: State of the art/art: Art of the state, Craft Connection, 75; Harmony Hammond: A ten year retrospective, 81, In the studio, 83 & Fitting into the fifties, 83, WARM J; Making art: Political and personal change, 84 & Mystery in art , 12/85, Exhibition or Carnival, 4/86 & Ritual & Tradition, Vol 6, No 8, 4/87, Art paper. *Dealer:* Asato Art Tokyo Japan. *Mailing Add:* 1056 Thirteenth Ave SE Minneapolis MN 55414

MACDONALD, WILLIAM L
ARCHITECTURAL HISTORIAN
b Putnam, Conn, July 12, 21. *Study:* Harvard Col, AB, Harvard Univ, AM & PhD(Emerton Fel, Shaw Fel & Morse Fel); Am Acad Rome, ACLS. *Pos:* Exec secy, Byzantine Inst, 50-54. *Teaching:* Prof art & archit, Yale Univ, 56-65 & Smith Col, Northampton, Mass, 65-81. *Awards:* Bryant Found Grant; Fel, Am Acad in Rome; A D Hitcock Prize, 86; Kevin Lynch/MIT Award, 89. *Mem:* Soc Prom Roman Studies, London; Soc Archit Historians (dir, 58-64); Soc Libyan Studies, London; Am Asn Archit Bibliogr; Am Inst Archaeol; fel Am Acad Rome. *Res:* History of architecture; ancient, early Christian, Baroque & American architecture. *Publ:* Auth, Early Christian Architecture, 62; Northampton Massachusetts Architecture & Buildings, 75; The Pantheon: Meaning and Progeny, 76; assoc ed, Princeton Encyclopedia of Classical Sites, 77; auth, Piranesi's Carceri: Sources of Invention, 79; The Architecture of the Roman Empire, Vol 1, rev ed 82, Vol 2, 86. *Mailing Add:* 3811 39th St NW Washington DC 20016

MACDONELL, CAMERON
PAINTER, MURALIST
b Elmira, NY, May 29, 38. *Study:* State Univ NY Col Educ Buffalo, BS(art educ), studied with John Davidson, Mort Grossman, Larry Calcognio & Trevor Thomas; independent study, Santa Barbara, Calif. *Work:* IBM Collection, Owego, NY; City of Santa Barbara, Calif; Chemung Canal Collection. *Comn:* Life of Mark Twain (collages), Bill Manos, Elmira, NY, 88; The Vinyard (mural), Granny's Restuarant, 88; The Homesteand (mural), Granny's Restuarant, 89; Music is Life (mural), Chuck Clarks, 91; Work Flow (mural), Artistic Greetings, 91. *Exhib:* Regional, Albright Knox Art Gallery, NY, 60; Regional, Santa Barbara Mus Art, Calif; Our Town Gallery, Santa Barbara, 74; Goleta Galleria, Calif, 75; one-man show, 76, regional group show, 76-79, Arnot Art Mus, Elmira, NY; Artists Gallery, Elmira, NY, 79-81; Clemens Ctr, Elmira, NY, 83; Chemung Canal Gallery, 88; NUS Traveling Exhib, 90 Group show. *Pos:* Art dir marketing develop, Art Frame Publ, Santa Barbara, Calif, 70-76; mgr Econoline advert, Asn Retarded Children, Elmira, NY, 77-81; Graph artist, Robinson Bldg Materials, 81-90. *Teaching:* Instr, Studio 605, 84-90. *Awards:* Silver Medallions, Bicentennials, City of Santa Barbara & Co of Santa Barbara, 76; Artistic Serv Award, OMRDD, NY, 79; Citation, State of New York, Arts In the Park, 80. *Bibliog:* Larry Griffis, Jr (auth), World of art, Buffalo Courier Express, 61; Lee Batten (auth), California Artists, Art Fame Publ, 75; Tom Page (auth), Brush with Greatness, Elmira Star Gazette, 1/91. *Mem:* Southern Tier Arts Asn (co-chmn, 79-80); Founder of the Arts in the Park, An Ann Event, Elmira, NY. *Media:* Woodcuts, Oil. *Publ:* Illusr & contribr, Sethmaterial, Prentice Hall, 70; contribr, Reflections, 72 & illusr, Salvang, 75, Art Fame Publ. *Dealer:* The Sturdivant Gallery 912 Southport St Elmira NY 14904; Art & Frame Gallery Water St Elmira NY 14901. *Mailing Add:* Studio 605 605 Yale St Elmira NY 14904

MCDONNELL, JOSEPH ANTHONY
SCULPTOR, PAINTER
b Detroit, Mich, Oct 20, 36. *Study:* Univ Notre Dame, with Ivan Mestrovic, BFA & MFA; Acad Belli Arte, Florence, Italy. *Work:* Milwaukee Pub Mus; Snite Mus, Univ Notre Dame. *Comn:* Sculpture, Station Plaza, Trenton, NJ, 90; mural, Chicago Bank Commerce, Standard Oil Bldg, 75; Deptford Mall, NJ, 75; relief sculpture, Tallyrand Bldg, Tarrytown, NY, 82; sculpture, Waterway Tower, Irving, Tex, 82; suspended kites, One Countryside Place, San Antonio, Tex, 83; IBM, Gaithersburg, Md, 87; Stele IX, Dulles Off Park, Va, 88; sculpture fountain, Silver Spring, Md, 88; and others. *Exhib:* One man shows, McNay Art Inst, San Antonio, 64, Flint Art Inst, Mich, 64, John Wanamaker Fine Arts Gallery, Philadelphia, 70 & Katonah Gallery, NY, 79; Hastings on Hudson, Snite Mus, Univ Notre Dame, 80; Paige Gallery, Dallas, 82; Century Assoc, New York, 84. *Pos:* Critic & asst ed, Artworld, 84- *Teaching:* Instr, Col New Rochelle, NY, 82-83. *Awards:* Dept of Housing & Urban Development Award, Nat Community Art Competition, 73; Award, New Eng Silvermine Exhib, 76 & 77. *Bibliog:* Article, Philadelphia Inquirer, 11/1/70; Harriet Schiff (auth), article, Detroit News, 9/17/71; Louis G Redstone (auth), New Directions in Shopping Centers and Stores, McGraw-Hill, 73; and others. *Media:* Multi. *Mailing Add:* 34 Garden St Cold Spring NY 10516

MCDOUGAL, IVAN ELLIS
PAINTER, INSTRUCTOR
b Lometa, Tex, June 29, 27. *Study:* Schreiner Inst, Kerrville, 47; Trinity Univ, San Antonio, 48; Am Acad Art, Chicago, 49. *Work:* McNay Art Mus, San Antonio. *Exhib:* Western Fedn Watercolor Soc Ann, Albuquerque Art Mus, 76; San Antonio Art League, Koehler Cult Ctr, 78; Rocky Mountain Nat Watermedia Exhib, Foothills Art Ctr, Golden, Colo, 80; Southern Watercolor Soc, La Tech Univ Gallery, Ruston, 81; San Diego Watercolor Soc; and others. *Teaching:* Instr watercolor, Jewish Community Ctr, 78-92. *Awards:* Juror's Award, San Diego Watercolor Soc; Patron Purchase, Watercolor USA, 87; Top 100 in Arts for the Parks Competition, 90 & 92; and others. *Mem:* San Antonio Art League; Tex Watercolor Soc; San Antonio Watercolor Group; Contemporary Artists Group. *Media:* Watercolor, Acrylic. *Publ:* Contribr, The Texas hill country, interpretations of 13 artists, North Light Mag, Tex A&M Univ Press, 81; contribr, Pecos to Rio Grande, Tex A&M Univ Press, 83. *Dealer:* Sol Del Rio Art Gallery 1020 Townsend San Antonio TX 78209. *Mailing Add:* 6850 Oxford Trace San Antonio TX 78240

MACDOUGALL, ANNE
ART DEALER, PAINTER
b Winchester, Mass, Apr 27, 44. *Study:* Abbot Acad; Randolph-Macon Woman's Col, AB(art); Syracuse Univ, grad study in art. *Work:* Boston Univ, Mus Fine Arts, Boston; Va Mus Fine Arts; DeCordova Mus, Lincoln, Mass; Indianapolis Mus. *Exhib:* Boston Printmaker's Nat, 74, 76 & 77; Nat Print, Trenton State, 79; Drawings, DeCordova Mus, 80; Nat Print & Drawing, NDak State, 81; Addison Gallery Am Art, 81. *Pos:* Dir, G W Einstein Gallery, New York. *Awards:* Va Ctr Fel, 78; MacDowell Fel, 80; Purchase Award, Berkshire Mus, 81. *Bibliog:* Robert Taylor (auth), article, Boston Globe, 9/21/72; Meryle Secrest (auth), article, Washington Post, 4/5/75; Paul Ciano (auth), article, Jewish Advocate, 2/8/78 & 6/81. *Mem:* Nat Asn Women Artists; Boston Printmakers; Boston Visual Artists Union; Cambridge Art Asn (vpres, 72-73). *Media:* Watercolor. *Mailing Add:* 98 Riverside Dr New York NY 10024

MACDOUGALL, PETER STEVEN
CERAMIC ARTIST, SCULPTOR
b Willimantic, Conn, Oct 23, 51. *Study:* Northwestern Conn Community Col, 70-72; Alfred Univ, New York, BFA, 75; Wichita State Univ, Kans, MFA, 77. *Work:* Downey Mus Art, Downey, Calif; Elrich Mus, Wichita State Univ; Nelson Gallery, Alfred Univ, New York; and others. *Exhib:* Copperstown Ann, Copperstown Art Asn, New York, 79-80; Fingerlakes Show, Mem Art Gallery, Rochester, 80; Everson Mus, Syracuse, NY, 80; Artworks Gallery, Hartford, Conn, 81; Univ Dallas, Irving, Tex, 81; and others. *Teaching:* Instr ceramics, Wichita Art Asn, 76-78; asst prof, State Univ NY, Oswego, 78-82; asst prof, Middle Tenn State Univ, 82-87. *Awards:* Craft Award, Northwestern Community Col, 72; Jury Award, Hartford Civic Art Show, 75; Third Place, Adironack Invitational, 81. *Mem:* Col Arts Asn; Nat Coun Educ Ceramic Arts; Am Craft Coun. *Media:* Clay. *Dealer:* Hanover Gallery New York NY. *Mailing Add:* Backshore Rd Round Pond ME 04564

MCELROY, JACQUELYN ANN (MCELROY-EDWARDS)
PRINTMAKER, EDUCATOR
b Rice Lake, Wis, June 28, 42. *Study:* Univ Minn; Univ Mont, BA, 65, MA, 66, MFA, 67. *Work:* Dulin Gallery Art, Knoxville, Tenn; Pillsbury Co, Minneapolis; Winnipeg Art Gallery, Man, Can; Plains Art Mus, Moorhead, Minn; Okla Art Ctr, Oklahoma City; and others. *Exhib:* Midwest Biennial Exhib, Joslyn Mus, Omaha, Nebr, 74; 2nd Miami Graphics Int, Coral Gables, Fla, 75; Artist as Social Critic, Miriam Perlman Inc, Chicago, Ill, 81; Art & the Law, Minn Mus & Western Publ Co, 81; Printed by Women, Women's Caucus Art, Philadelphia, 83; The Americans Are Coming, Art Warehouse, Winnipeg, Can, 85; 62nd Ann Spring Salon, Springville Art Mus, Utah, 87; NJ Art Ctr Nat Show, 88; Critical Choices, Univ Art Galleries, Univ SDak, 90. *Teaching:* Prof art hist & printmaking, Univ NDak, Grand Forks, 68-, asst dean, 79-84 & 91-92, chmn visual arts, 86- *Awards:* Purchase Awards, Art & the Law, Minn Mus & Western Publ Co, 80, Challenge of the Land, Pillsbury Co, 81 & Tempo Gallery, Appleton, Wis, 83. *Bibliog:* Just Plain Art, Plains Art Mus Publ, Minn, 90. *Mem:* Nat Conf Art Admin; Grand Forks Arts & Humanities Coun; Am Asn Univ Prof; Col Art Asn. *Media:* Serigraphy. *Dealer:* Rourke Art Gallery 523 S Fourth Moorhead MN 56560; Browning Arts 22 N 4th Grand Forks ND 58201. *Mailing Add:* RR 1 Box 63C Thompson ND 58278-9741

MCEVILLEY, THOMAS
WRITER, CRITIC
b Cincinnati, Ohio, July 13, 39. *Study:* Univ Cincinnati, BA, 63, PhD, 68; Univ Washington, MA, 65. *Exhib:* 84 Seasons, Oil and Steel Gallery, New York, 84; Cracked Transparency, Middelburg, Holland, 10/84; Cracked Transparency II, Kunstmuseum, Bern, Switz. *Pos:* Contrib ed, Artforum, 82- *Teaching:* Assoc prof art hist , Rice Univ, 70- *Awards:* Nat Endowment, Arts Critic's Grant, 84-85. *Bibliog:* Jo Goldberg (auth), Leonard Pearlson, Artforum, 9/87; Nancy Spero (auth), Everson Mus, Artforum, 5/88; Hermann Nitsch (auth), David Nolan, summer 88. *Res:* Contemporary art; art and philosophy; iconography; art theory. *Publ:* Auth, The Yale Lectures, Yale Univ Sch Art, 92; Diogenes of Sinope, Peter Koch Printer, 92; The Arimaspea, McPherson & Co, 93; Thornton Dial, The Tiger Paintings, Abrams, 93; Yves Klein, Conquistador of the Void, Schirmer-Mosel Verlag, 93. *Dealer:* c/o Artforum 65 Bleecker St New York, NY 10012. *Mailing Add:* Box 20752 Tompkins Sq Sta New York NY 10009

MCEWEN, JEAN
PAINTER
b Montreal, Que, Dec 14, 23. *Work:* Mus Mod Art, New York; Walker Art Ctr, Minneapolis; Albright-Knox Art Gallery; Ottawa Mus; Toronto Mus; and others. *Comn:* Stained glass window, Sir George Williams Univ, 66; murals, Toronto Airport & Plase Arts, Montreal, 67; mural, Bank Scotia (head office), Montreal, 91. *Exhib:* One-man shows, Gallery Godart-Lefort, Montreal, four times, 62-69, Gallery, Montreal, 63, Gallery Moos, Toronto, four times, 63-69 & Mayer Gallery, Paris, 64; Dunn Int Exhib, Tate Gallery, London, 63; Retrospective, Mus Fine Arts, Montreal, 87. *Pos:* Univ Concordia. *Teaching:* Lectr painting, Concordia Univ. *Awards:* Quebec Art Competition, 62; Jessie Dow Award, Montreal Spring Show, 64. *Bibliog:* Color in Depth (catalog), Mus Fine Arts, Montreal. *Media:* Oil, Watercolor. *Publ:* Illusr, La Pain Quotidien, 64; illusr, Les Iles Reunies, 73. *Dealer:* Mira-Godard Ltd 22 Hazelton Toronto ON Can; Waddington & Garce 1504 Sherbrooke W Montreal. *Mailing Add:* 3908 Parc Lafontaine Rue Montreal PQ H2L 3M6 Canada

MCFADDEN, DAVID REVERE
CURATOR
Study: Univ Minn, BA(magna cum laude), 72, MA, 78. *Collections Arranged:* The Education of Craftsmen: Silver, 75; Exotic Entrepreneurs:Trade with the Orient, 76; Cooper-Hewitt Collections of Decorative Arts (auth, catalog), 78-84, Scandinavian Modern: 1880-1980

(auth, catalog), 82, English Majolica, 82, Tiffany Studios Medalwork, 83, Design in the Service of Tea, 84 & Wine: Celebration and Ceremony, 85; L'Art De Vivre, 89; Flora Danica, 90. *Pos:* Cur, Minneapolis Inst Arts, 74-78 & Cooper-Hewitt Mus, 78- *Teaching:* Cooper-Hewitt/Parsons MA program, 82- *Awards:* Knight First Class, Order of Lion of Finland, 84; Knight Commander, Order of Northern Star, Sweden, 88; Chevalier, Ordre des Arts et des Lettres, France, 89. *Mem:* Worshipful Co Goldsmiths; Decorative Arts Soc; Soc Silver Collectors; founder Decorative Arts Asn. *Res:* Nineteenth century decorative arts and ceramics; twentieth century design. *Collection:* Porcelain, 79, The Cooper-Hewitt Collection: Glass, 79 & The Cooper-Hewitt Collection: Furniture, 79. *Publ:* Auth, Recent Acquisitions in Silver: A Petrie and D Willaume, 75, An Aldobrandini Tazza: A Preliminary Study , 77 & Scandinavian Modern Design 1880-1980, 84, Minneapolis Inst Bull; L'Art De Vivre: Decorative Arts and Designs in France 1789- 1989, 89. *Mailing Add:* 120 E 89th St New York NY 10028

MCFADDEN, MARY
COLLECTOR, DESIGNER
b New York, NY, Oct 1, 38. *Study:* Columbia Univ: Traphagen Sch of Design. *Work:* Lannan Found, Palm Beach, Fla; Metrop Mus Art Costume Inst, New York. *Collections Arranged:* Biet Giorgis Trust, Lannan Found. *Pos:* Ed, Vogue Mag, S Africa, 65-68, US, 71-74; contribr, Rand Daily Mail, 69-70; pres, Mary McFadden Inc, 74- & Mary McFadden Jewels, 78-; pres & cur, Lannan Found, Palm Beach, Fla, 74-82; chmn, Mary McFadden Collection. *Teaching:* Instr fashion, Fashion Inst of Technol, New York, 76; instr chic, Hunter Col, 77 & instr style, Cooper-Hewitt Mus of Decorative Arts & Design, New York, 77. *Awards:* Legendary Women Award, Birmingham, Ala, 77; Coty Hall of Fame, 78; Gov Award, RI Sch Design, 78. *Media:* Silk. *Collection:* Ancient artifacts from Egypt, Greece and Madagascar; sculpture from Africa; Oriental artifacts and furniture; contemporary American art, including painting by Tom Wudl, Robert Mangold, sculpture by Mark di Suvero, Kenneth Shores & Isamu Noguchi; Indian 16th century miniatures, ancient textiles. *Publ:* Auth, var articles on Iran, Haiti, Madagascal, Ethiopia Burma, India, Kashmir, Usbzcistan-Tashkent & Easter Island, Vogue USA, 71; Mirabella, 89. *Mailing Add:* 264 W 35th St New York NY 10001

MCFARLAND, LAWRENCE D
PHOTOGRAPHER
b Wichita, Kans, Sept 1, 42. *Study:* Kansas City Art Inst, MO, BFA, 73; Univ Nebr, Lincoln, MFA, 76. *Work:* Ctr Creative Photog, Tucson; Int Mus Photog George Eastman House, Rochester, NY; Mus Mod Art, New York; Amon Carter Mus, Ft Worth, Tex; Carpenter Ctr Arts, Harvard, Cambridge, Mass. *Exhib:* Solo show, Int Mus Photog, Rochester, NY, 80; Road & Roadside, Chicago Art Inst, Ill, 87; The Evidence of Man, Amon Ctr Mus, Ft Worth, Tex, 89; Arizona Photographers, Ctr Creative Photog, Tucson, 90; Past/Present, Mus Fine Art, Houston, Tex, 92; 1992 New Orleans Triennial, New Orleans Mus Art, La, 92; and others. *Teaching:* Assoc prof photog, Univ Tex, 85- *Awards:* Nat Endowment Arts Fel, 79, 85 & 91. *Mem:* Soc Photog Educ. *Publ:* Contribr, Young American Photographers, Lustrum Press, Vol 1, 74; Kansas Album, Kans Banker Asn, 77; An Openland: Photographs of the Midwest, 83 & The Making of a Collection: Photographs from the Collection of Minneapolis Institute of Art, 84, Aperture; In Spite of Everything, Yes, Univ NMex Press, 86. *Dealer:* Ethenton/Stern Gallery 135 S Sixth Ave Tucson AZ. *Mailing Add:* 2913 Clearview Austin TX 78703

MCFARREN, GRACE
PAINTER
b Philadelphia, Pa, Feb 6, 14. *Study:* Sch Design for Women; Graphic Sketch Club; Pierce Jr Col, Philadelphia; study with Clayton Bachtel, Peter Dubaniewicz, Joseph McCullough, Marion Bryson & Doris Peters, Clevelnad, Ohio; Del Art Ctr, Wilmington, with Robert McKinney, 60; study with Edgar Whitney, New York, 69. *Work:* Univ Del; Hagley Mus; DuPont de Nemours & Co; Nelson Rockefeller Collection; three Wilmington Banks; Mrs David Craven Collection; and others. *Exhib:* Ann May Show, Cleveland Art Mus; Dayton Art Mus Lending Libr of Paintings; Smithsonian Inst, Washington, DC; Am Watercolor Soc, Univ Del; Philadelphia Mus Art; Del Mus Art; Juror's Choice Exhib, Univ Del, 86; and others. *Pos:* Founder, Wilmington Circulating Gallery of Paintings, dir, formerly. *Teaching:* Lectr, Univ Del Days for Women Exten, four yrs; lectrs & demonstrations, studio group in Wilmington & univ women's group. *Awards:* Three Purchase Prizes, Univ Del Ann Regional Shows; First, Second & Hon Mention, Chester Co Art Asn; Best in Show, Nat League Am Pen Women Nat Show & Rehoboth Art League; and others. *Mem:* Am Watercolor Soc. *Media:* Watercolor, Acrylic. *Mailing Add:* 3 Winterbury Circle Wilmington DE 19808

MCFARREN, MARIA NAZARETH See Naza (Maria Nazareth McFarren)

MCFEE, JUNE KING
EDUCATOR
b Seattle, Wash, June 3, 17. *Study:* Whitman Col, 35-37; Univ Wash, BA, 39; Cent Wash Col, MEd, 54; Stanford Univ, EdD, 57; Archipenko Sch Art; Cornish Sch Art; also with Amede Ozenfant; Eastern Mich Univ, Hon Dr, 82. *Exhib:* Seattle Art Mus; Seattle Artists Summer Shows; Wash State Invitational; Stanford Art Gallery Fac Exhibs. *Pos:* Ed, Studies in Art Educ. *Teaching:* From instr to asst prof art educ, Stanford Univ, 55-63; vis assoc prof, Ariz State Univ, 64-65; from assoc prof to prof art educ & dir, Inst Community Art Studies, Univ Ore, 65-77, head, Dept Art Educ, 77-83. *Awards:* Art Educr Yr, Miami Univ, 81; Nat Art Educ Asn Distinguished Serv Award, 83 & Fel, 84. *Mem:* Nat Art Educ Asn (pres, Pac Region, 67-69); Soc Res in Art Educ; Coun Policy Studies Art Educ. *Publ:* Auth, Preparation for Art, Wadsworth, 70; Art, Culture & Environment, Kendall-Hunt, 80; Cultural Influences on Aesthetic Experiences in Arts and Cultural Diversity, Holt Rinehart Winston, 80; Art abilities, In: Int Encycl Educ, Eng, 85; Cultural dimensions in the teaching of art, in: The Foundations of Aesthetics, Art and Art Education, Praeger, 88. *Mailing Add:* 750 Chorro No 9 San Luis Obispo CA 93401

MCGAHEE, DOROTHY BRAUDY See Braudy, Dorothy

MCGARRELL, JAMES
PAINTER, EDUCATOR
b Indianapolis, Ind, Feb 22, 30. *Study:* Ind Univ, AB, 53; Skowhegan Sch Painting & Sculpture, 53; Univ Calif, Los Angeles, MA, 55; Stuttgard Acad Fine Arts, Ger, Fulbright fel, 56. *Work:* Whitney Mus Am Art, New York; Mus Mod Art, New York; Centre Georges Pompidou; Mus Hamburg, Ger; Joseph Hirshhorn Mus, Washington, DC; Metrop Mus Art, New York; Pa Acad, Philadelphia; and others. *Exhib:* Carnegie Inst Int, 58 & 82; New Images of Man, Mus Mod Art, New York, 59; Dokumenta III, Kassel, Ger; Americans, Art Inst, Chicago; Venice Biennale, 68; Art About Art, Whitney Mus, 78; The Human Figure in Contemporary Art, Contemp Arts Ctr, New Orleans, 82; Five Whitney Mus annuals & biennials; and others. *Pos:* Bd gov, Skowhegan Sch, 81- *Teaching:* Vis artist, Reed Col, 56-59; prof fine arts, Ind Univ, 59-80, Skowhegan Sch Painting & Sculpture, 64-68 & Washington Univ Sch Fine Arts, 81-; artist-in-residence, Dartmouth Col, spring 93. *Awards:* Guggenheim Found Fel, 64; Nat Endowment Arts Award, 66, Fel 85; Nat Acad Design, 92; and others. *Bibliog:* Giovanni Testori (auth), McGarrell, Claude Bernard (Paris), 67; Norman Geske (auth), Venice 34, the Figurative Tradition in Recent American Art, Smithsonian, 68; James McGarrell talks with Paul Cummings, Drawing, 7-8/85; Thomas Bolt (auth), James McGarrell's universe, Arts Mag, 4/86. *Mem:* Col Art Asn Am (bd dirs, 70-74). *Media:* All. *Publ:* Auth, Towards an art of eloquence, Artists Choice Mus Newletter, spring 82. *Dealer:* Frumkin Adams Gallery 50 W 57th St New York NY 10022; Galerie Simonne Stern New Orleans and Atlanta. *Mailing Add:* Sch Fine Arts, Box 1031 Washington Univ St Louis MO 63130

MCGARRY, PATRICIA JOSEPHINE
INSTRUCTOR, SCULPTOR
b Chicago, Ill, May 23, 47. *Study:* Univ Ill, Urbana, BFA, 70; Sch Art Inst Chicago, MFA, 72. *Comn:* Mural, Echo Special Educ Cooperative, South Holland, Ill, 74. *Exhib:* Art Inst Chicago, 72; Milwaukee Lakefront Art Festival, Wis, 72, 75 & 76; Beaux-Arts Designer Craftsman, Columbus, Ohio, 73; Six on Six, NAME Gallery, Chicago, 80; two-person show, ARC Gallery, 82; Potters Exhib, Springfield Art Asn, Ill, 82; and others. *Teaching:* Prof art, Thornton Community Col, South Holland, Ill, 77-82. *Awards:* Midwest Crafts Award, Nat Home Fashions League, 71; Second Place, Greater Fall River Art Asn, 72. *Mem:* Chicago Artists Coalition; Am Craftsman Asn. *Media:* Clay. *Mailing Add:* 621 Escanaba Ave Calumet City IL 60409

MCGARRY, SUSAN HALLSTEN
EDITOR, WRITER
b Minneapolis, Minn, June 27, 48. *Study:* Univ Minn, BA, 74, MA(art hist), 78. *Pos:* Freelance arts writer & critic, 78-; ed, Southwest Art Mag, 79- *Res:* Artists living and working in the Western U S. *Publ:* Coauth, Taking Stock: Painting & Sculpture by G Harvey, Somerset House, 86; contrib, The Cowboy Artists of America, Desert Hawk, 88. *Mailing Add:* 3718 Grennoch Lane Houston TX 77025

MACGAW, WENDY
SCULPTOR
b Detroit, Mich, Nov 16, 55. *Study:* Univ Mich Sch Art, BFA, 77; Cranbrook Art Acad, MFA, 79. *Work:* Detroit Inst Arts, Albert Kahn & Asn, Architects. *Exhib:* Young Americans: Award Winner, Am Craft Mus, New York, 82; Steel-Glass Sculpture: Wendy MacGaw, Detroit Int Art, Mich, 85; Invitational Metal Show, 3 Rivers Art Fest, Pittsburgh, Pa, 85; Glass America, Heller Gallery, New York, 85; Mich Nat Endowment Art Fest, 1965-85, Detroit Focus Gallery, 86; Detroit Artists: Update, Cranbrook Art Mus, Bloomfield Hills, 86; Detroit Artists Artemesia, 88; Glass, 88. *Pos:* Co-owner, Artpack Serv, Detroit, Mich, 84-; mem, Speech, Detroit, 84. *Teaching:* Asst prof design, Ctr Creative Studies, Detroit, 79-; instr fine arts, 3-D Design, Wayne State Univ, Detroit, 83-84; instr art & writing, Detroit Inst Art, Mich, 83-84; self-employed, currently. *Awards:* Award winner, Young Americans: Metal, 80; Nat Endowment Arts Fel, 82-83 & 86-87; Creative Artist Grant, Mich Coun Arts, 84-85; Mich Coun Arts, 88- *Mem:* Detroit Focus; Founders Soc Detroit Inst Arts. *Media:* Metal, Glass. *Dealer:* Lemberg Gallery N Woodward Ave Birmington MI 48009. *Mailing Add:* 28201 Wellington Farmington Hills MI 48334

MCGEE, WINSTON EUGENE
PAINTER, EDUCATOR
b Salem, Ill, Sept 4, 24. *Study:* Univ Mo, BJ, 48 & MA, 49; Univ Wis; Ecole Superieure Beaux-Arts, 50-51; Atelier-M Jean Souverbie, French Nat Acad, 51; Fulbright Scholar to Paris, 51. *Work:* Whitney Mus Am Art, New York; Calif Palace of Legion of Honor, San Francisco; Philadelphia Mus Art; Smithsonian Inst, Washington, DC; Indianapolis Mus Art, Ind. *Comn:* Relief painting, Mo State Hist Soc, Columbia; mural, Trinity Cathedral, Cleveland, Ohio; mural, David Leach estate, Madison, Ohio; Sara Beck Mem, Lake Erie Col, 78; Calif Wall, ceramic mural, Turlock Centennial Found, Calif. *Exhib:* one-man show, Mitchell Mus, Mt Vernon, Ill, 74; 50th Yr Anniversary Traveling Show, Cleveland Mus, 68; Lincoln Fine Arts Ctr Dedication Exhib, 70; Atelier II, La Defense, Paris, France, 78; Calif State Univ-Stanislaus, Turlock, 78; Abante Fine Arts Gallery, Portland, Ore, 88. *Pos:* Head, Dept

Art, Lake Erie Col, 52-69; actg chmn art, Cleveland State Univ, 69-72, fac in painting, 72-76; prof & chmn art dept, Calif State Univ, Stanislaus, 77-93. *Awards:* Cleveland Mus May Show Jury Award, 68; Annie McEntree Norton Award Painting & Graphic, Univ Mo; Gold Medal, Academie Italia delle Arti, 84; Res & Creative Grant, CSUS, 86. *Bibliog:* Articles, Graphic Artists, 72 & 75; article in Mo State Hist Soc Bulletin, 9/75; Materials & Techniques of 20th Century Artists, Cleveland Mus Art, 77. *Mem:* Cleveland Coun Arts; Cleveland Art Community; New Orgn for Visual Arts; fel Int Inst Arts & Lett (Switz). *Media:* Oil, Acrylic. *Publ:* Urban Crafts, PBS-TV, 76; Winston McGees Abstract Images, Art Seen, David Howard Production, San Francisco Ctr Visual Studies, 92; California Wall (film), Winsu Prod, 88. *Dealer:* Abante Fine Arts Gallery 204 SW Yamhill Portland OR. *Mailing Add:* Dept Art Calif State Univ Stanislaus 801 Westmonte Vista Ave Turlock CA 95380

MCGEEHAN, BETTY
SCULPTOR
b Passaic, NJ, Jan 27, 34. *Study:* Art Students League, with Jose deCreeft, 78; NY Sch Social Res, 84; Pratt Inst, New York, 86. *Work:* James Michener Art Mus, Doylestown, Pa; Noyes Mus, Oceanville, NJ; Nabisco Food Group Inc, Parsippany, NJ; Fla Palm Air Resorts, Pompano Beach; Overlook Hosp, Summit, NJ. *Comn:* Marble sculpture (5') & bronze sculpture (8'), United Telecommuns Inc, Kansas City, Mo, 84; bronze bas relidt (5' x 3'), Deloitte/Touch, Parsippany, NJ, 88; aluminum wall sculpture (6'), Toyota Motor Corp Hq, New York, 90; 2 wall sculptures (38" each), AT&T Capitol Corp, Morristown, NJ, 92. *Exhib:* 100 Years/100 Works, traveling show, Islip Art Mus, NY, Longview Mus Art, Tex, Chattanooga Mus, Tenn & Fine Art Mus S, Mobile, Ala, 89; one-woman show, Fairleigh Dickinson Univ, Rutherford, NJ, 91; NJ Ctr Visual Arts Int, Summit, 91; Divrsity & Vision, Snug Harbor Cult Ctr, Staten Island, NY, 92; Transformation of Matter into Art, NY Nat Acad Scis, 92. *Awards:* First Prize Ann Exhib, NJ Ctr Visual Arts, 86; Honorable Mention, Sculpture Exhib, Pen & Brush, New York, 88; Fel, Vt Studio Colony, Johnson, 88. *Bibliog:* Eileen Watkins (auth), Chatham sculptor, 84 & Explore interior scapes, 90, Star Ledger, NJ. *Mem:* Sculptors Asn NJ (pres, 83-84 & 90); Sculptors League (bd mem, 89-92); Nat Asn Women Artists; Allied Artists Am; Womens Caucus Arts. *Media:* Welded & Cast Metal, Found Objects. *Dealer:* Gross McCleaf Gallery 127 S 16th St Philadelphia PA 19102. *Mailing Add:* 147 Huron Dr Chatham NJ 07928

MCGILL, FORREST
HISTORIAN, MUSEUM ADMINISTRATOR
b East Orange, NJ, Oct 25, 47. *Study:* Cornell Univ, BA, 69; Univ Mich, MA, 73, PhD(Fulbright-Hays res award), 77. *Pos:* Coordr pub prog, Univ Mich Mus Art, Ann Arbor, 77-78; asst dir, Archer M Huntington Art Gallery, Univ Tex, Austin, 80-; dir, Mus Art & Archaeol, Univ Mo, currently. *Teaching:* Vis instr Asian art, Oakland Univ, Mich, 78; vis asst prof, Univ Colo, Boulder, 79; adj asst prof, Univ Tex, Austin, 79- *Mem:* Col Art Asn; Am Asn Mus; Am Comt South Asian Art. *Res:* Buddhist art in Southeast Asia. *Publ:* Coauth, A Catalog of the Mr and Mrs Henry Jewett Greene Memorial Collection of Far Eastern Ceramics, Univ Mich Mus Art, 74. *Mailing Add:* Mary Washington Col Galleries Fredericksburg VA 22401-5358

MACGILLIS, ROBERT DONALD
PAINTER, PRINTMAKER
b Bayonne, NJ, June 30, 36. *Study:* Mech Inst, New York; Newark Sch Fine Arts, NJ. *Work:* Grover M Hermann Fine Arts Ctr, Marietta Col; Bayonne Pub Libr; Caldwell Art Ctr, Caldwell Col; Univ Conn; Nabisco Co Pub Art Collection, East Hanover, NJ. *Comn:* US Navy Art & Combat Liaison, Washington, DC, 80. *Exhib:* Allied Artists Am, New York; Acad Artists, Springfield, Mass; Conn Watercolor Soc, Hartford; Am Watercolor Soc, New York; and others. *Pos:* Indust artist, Gen Dynamics Elec Boat Div, Groton, Conn, 60-75. *Awards:* Over 70 awards for nat & regional juried exhibs; Gold Medal for graphics, Acad Artists, 78; Louis E Sealey Award, Salmagundi Club, 80; and others. *Mem:* Salmagundi Club; Am Artists Prof League; Artists Fel; Conn Watercolor Soc; Hudson Valley Artists. *Media:* Watercolor, Oils; Miscellaneous Media. *Publ:* Auth articles,Art Times,75. *Dealer:* Wright Gallery Cape Porpoise ME. *Mailing Add:* 96 School St Groton CT 06340

MCGILVERY, LAURENCE
BOOK DEALER, PUBLISHER
b Los Angeles, Calif, May 21, 32. *Study:* Pomona Col, BA, 54. *Pos:* Mem adv bd, Artbibliographs Mod, Santa Barbara, 73 & Who's Who in Am Art & Am Art Dir, 78. *Mem:* Art Libr Soc of NAm; Antiquarian Booksellers Asn Am; San Diego Booksellers Asn. *Res:* Art periodical indexes and art bibliographies. *Publ:* Auth, Artforum, 1962-1968: A Cumulative Index to the First Six Volumes, McGilvery, 70; coauth, several other bibliographies. *Mailing Add:* PO Box 852 La Jolla CA 92038

MCGINNIS, CHRISTINE
PAINTER, PRINTMAKER
b Philadelphia, Pa. *Study:* Pa Acad Fine Arts; Fleisher Art Mem. *Work:* Mus Nat Sci, Philadelphia; Civic Ctr Mus, Philadelphia; Free Libr Philadelphia; Am Embassy, Dublin, Ireland; Pa Acad Fine Arts. *Exhib:* Philadelphia Art Mus Regional Exhib, 64; Brooklyn Art Mus 14th Nat Exhib, New York, 65; Am Express Pavillion, New York World's Fair, 66; Libr Cong 20th Nat, Washington, DC, 67; Washington Art Mus, 77-81; Art Expo Traveling Show, 80-83; one-person show, Roger LaPelle Galleries, 82, 84, 86, 89 & 90; Touchstone Gallery, Washington, DC, 88; Phoenix Gallery, New York, 88. *Teaching:* Fleisher Art Memorial, Philadelphia; Sch Art League, Philadelphia; Wynne Art Ctr, Philadelphia. *Awards:* Award, Albany Print Club, 68; First Prize, Pa Acad, 74; Secoond Prize, Allentown Mayfair Festival, 92. *Bibliog:* Margaret Holbern Ellis (auth), The Care of Prints and Drawings, 78; The Woodmere Art Museum: Index to the Permanent Collection, 86. *Mem:* Fel, Pan Am Festival Asn & Pa Acad Fine Arts. *Media:* Acrylic, Graphics. *Publ:* Illusr, Ctr City Mag, 63; Promenade Mag, 68; Audubon Mag, 70; Decor Mag, 78; Imfad Cat, 77-80. *Mailing Add:* 5929 Devon Pl Philadelphia PA 19138

MCGLAUCHLIN, TOM
SCULPTOR
b Beloit, Wis, Sept 14, 34. *Study:* Univ Wis, BS, 59, MS(art), 60; pottery with James McKinnell, Univ Iowa, 62; Oriental art hist, Univ Washington, 66-67. *Work:* Corning Mus Glass, NY; Toledo Mus Art, Ohio; Musee des Arts Decoratifs de la Ville de Lausanne, Switz; Nat Mus Mod Art, Kyoto, Japan; Kunst Mus, Dusseldorf, WGer; and others. *Comn:* Clouds of Joy (23' glass sculpture), Webstrand Ldt, Toledo, Ohio, 84; glass sculpture, Glass Capitol Columns, Crosby Gardens, Toledo, 86; glass & stainless steel sculpture, A Mountain for Toledo, Rotary Club Toledo, 88. *Exhib:* Glass Aus USA, Glasmuseum Frauenau, WGer, 79; American Glass Now II, touring Japan, 80; Glass: Artist and Influence, Detroit Art Inst, 81; Nat Mus Mod Art, Kyoto, Japan, 81; Thirty Years of New Glass, 1957-1987, Corning Mus Glass, NY, 87; Int Exhib Glass 88, Kanazwa, Japan; and others. *Pos:* Chmn art dept, Cornell Col, Mt Vernon, 68-71. *Teaching:* Prof art, Cornell Col, Mt Vernon, Iowa, 61-71; prof & dir glass prog, Toledo Mus Art, 71-84. *Awards:* Ohio Arts Coun Grant, 79. *Bibliog:* Glass at Wagman, St Louis Globe Democrat, 4/23-24/82; Losken M Feuerzauber (auth), Glas aus USA, Kunst und Handwerk, WGer, 11-12/79. *Mem:* Glass Art Soc; Am Crafts Coun; Int Sculpture Ctr. *Media:* Glass; Steel. *Mailing Add:* 2527 Cheltenham Toledo OH 43606

MCGOUGH, CHARLES E
PRINTMAKER, EDUCATOR
b Elmhurst, Ill, Aug 2, 27. *Study:* Southwestern Univ; Ray Vogue Commercial Art Sch, dipl; Univ Tulsa, BA & MA; NTex State Univ; also with Hardin Simmons. *Work:* Boston Mus; Philbrook Mus; Dallas Mus Fine Arts; Little Rock Mus Fine Arts. *Comn:* Genre mural, Southern Hills Country Club, Tulsa, Okla, 56; mural, ETex State Univ, Commerce, 63; mural, Goodfellow AFB, San Angelo, Tex, 64; several graphic works, First Nat Bank, Dallas, Tex, 65; several graphic works, Southwestern Life Ins Co, Dallas, 67. *Exhib:* Nat Serigraph Ann, Brooklyn Mus Art, 63; Drawing USA, Walker Art Ctr, 66; Nat Print Ann, Boston Mus Fine Arts, 67; Southwest Print & Drawing Ann, Dallas Mus Fine Arts, 67, 68 & 70; Nat Print & Drawing Ann, Okla Art Ctr, 69-72. *Pos:* Owner, McGough Advert Co, 45-50; art dir, Crane Advert, Tulsa, 50-52. *Teaching:* Instr art, N R Crogier Tech High Sch, Dallas, 52-56; prof & head art dept, ETex State Univ, 56- *Awards:* Graphic Purchase Award, Boston Univ Mus Show, 65; Southwest Print & Drawing Ann Award, Dallas Mus Fine Arts, 67; Graphic Purchase Award, Nat Print Ann, Okla Art Ctr, 71. *Mem:* Southwest Print & Drawing Soc; Tex Asn Schs Art. *Media:* Graphics. *Publ:* Auth, Print painting, Dallas Morning News, 67; Serigraphy, Dallas Times Herald, 68; Serigraph & the total image, Tex Trends Art Educ, 68. *Dealer:* Cushing Galleries 2723 Fairmount St Dallas TX 75201. *Mailing Add:* 1603 Walnut St Commerce TX 75428

MCGOUGH, STEPHEN C
MUSEUM DIRECTOR, HISTORIAN
b San Angelo, Tex, Dec 12, 49. *Study:* E Tex State Univ, 70; Stanford Univ, with Albert E Elsen on Rodin, Ensor, AB, 72, AM, 75, PhD(art hist), 81. *Collections Arranged:* Rodin's Monument to Balzac (with catalog), 72-73; The Stamp of Whistler (with catalog), 79; Hiroshige: 100 Views of Edo (with catalog), 82; The Graphic Image: German Expressionist Prints (with catalog), 82-83. *Pos:* Cur mod art, Allen Mem Art Mus, Oberlin Col, 76-79; assoc dir, Elvehjem Mus Art, Univ Wis, 81-88; dir, Univ Ore Mus Art, 88- *Teaching:* Mus training & connoisseurship, Univ Wis, Madison, 81-83. *Mem:* Am Asn Mus; Col Art Asn Am; Ore Mus Asn. *Res:* 19th and 20th century Northern European and American art; extensive research in Belgian art, 1860-1910; history of prints. *Publ:* Coauth, Rodin and Balzac, Cantor/Fitzgerald, 73; coauth & ed, Hiroshige: 100 Views of Edo, Univ Wis, 82; The Graphic Image: German Expressionist Prints, Univ Wis, 83; auth, James Ensor's The Entry of Christ into Brussels in 1889, Garland, NY, 85; coauth, James Ensor, Musee du Petit Palais, Paris, 90. *Mailing Add:* Univ Ore Mus Art Eugene OR 97403-1223

MCGOVERN, ROBERT F
PAINTER, SCULPTOR
b Philadelphia, Pa, Apr 1, 33. *Study:* Philadelphia Col Art, Pa, with Benton Spruance. *Work:* Mus Art, Free Libr, Philadelphia; Rare Bk Collection, Cornell Univ, Ithaca, NY. *Comn:* Portraits of Bishop Lorenz Grassel & Mathew Carey, Am Cath Hist Soc, Philadelphia, 76; carving of Bishop Neumann, Bishop Neumann High Sch, Philadelphia, 77; banner of St John Neumann, comn by Sister of St Francis for use at Canonization, Rome, Italy, 77; wood relief of St John Neumann for Daylesford Abbey, Paoli, Pa, 78. *Exhib:* Prints & Drawings, Philadelphia Art Alliance, 62; Print Club, Philadelphia, 63; Am Color Print Soc, Philadelphia, 73-77; Liturgical Arts, 41st Int Eucharistic Cong, 77. *Pos:* Co-chmn found prog, Philadelphia Col Art, 76- *Teaching:* Prof drawing design & anatomy, Philadelphia Col Art, 56-82, prof painting, currently. *Mem:* Philadelphia Print Club; Artists Equity (pres, Philadelphia Chap, 64-65); Am Color Print Soc. *Media:* Wood Carving, Woodcuts; Oil. *Publ:* Auth, rev, Religious Art in 20th Century--An Understanding, Pax Romano, Fribourg, Switz, 65; coauth, Saturday Waiting, 60 Pen & Ink Drawings, Fortress Press, Philadelphia, 70; auth, A Re-emergence of religious art in the seventies, Dimension Mag, Philadelphia, 74; illusr, Uncommon Book of Prayer, Seabury Press, 78. *Mailing Add:* 120 Woodside Ave Narberth PA 19072

MCGOWIN, ED (WILLIAM EDWARD)
PAINTER, SCULPTOR
b Hattiesburg, Miss, June 2, 38. *Study:* Univ Southern Miss, BS, 61; Univ Ala, MA, 64. *Work:* Whitney Mus Am Art & Guggenheim Mus, New York; Hirshhorn Mus, Nat Collection Fine Arts & Corcoran Gallery, Washington, DC. *Comn:* permanent outdoor sculpture, Gen Serv Admin, Jackson, Miss, 78; outdoor sculpture, Artpark, Lewiston, NY, 84; permanent outdoor sculpture, Veterans Admin, Indianapolis, 85; Percent for Art, New York, 92. *Exhib:* Solo exhibs, Corcoran Gallery Art, 62 & 75 (with catalog), Baltimore Mus Art (with catalog), 72, Mus Mod Art, Paris, 78, Cranbrook Acad Art Mus, Bloomfield Hills, Mich, 83, Ctr Fine Arts, Miami, 87, Gracie Mansion Gallery, New York, (catalog), 89 & Boca Raton Mus Art, Fla, (catalog), 91; Whitney Mus Am Art, New York, 66 & 76; Projects & Proposals of the 70's, PS 1, New York, 77; Cagnes-sur-Mer Mus, Cagnes, France, 78; Guggenheim Mus, New York, 83; Space Framed II, Harvard Univ, Cambridge, Mass, 84; Nat Acad Sci Wash, DC, Wichita Art Mus, Kans, 88; Miss Mus Art, (catalog), 89. *Teaching:* Prof art, State Univ NY, Old Westbury, 76-89. *Awards:* Grants, Nat Endowment Arts, 67 & 80, Cassandra Found, 72; Miss Arts & Lett Award, Miss Arts & Lett Comt, 80. *Bibliog:* Susan Freudenhime (auth), The Southern Voice, Ft Worth Art Mus, Tex, 81; Timothy Eaton (auth), Ed McGowin Painting, Boca Raton Mus Art, Fla, 91. *Media:* Mixed Media. *Dealer:* Gracie Mansion Gallery 167 Avenue A New York NY 10009. *Mailing Add:* 96 Grand St New York NY 10012

MCGRAIL, JEANE KATHRYN
PAINTER, PRINTMAKER
b Minneapolis, Minn, May 1, 47. *Study:* Univ Wisc, River Falls, BS, 70; Cranbrook Acad Arts, MFA, 72; Sch of Art Inst, Chicago. *Exhib:* Cicchinelli Gallery, New York, 80-82; Evanston Art Ctr, Ill, 81; solo exhibs, Gallery at the Commons, Chicago, Ill, 82, Truman Col, 91 & Carl Jung Inst 92; Printmaking & Drawing Exhib, Harper Col, Palatine, Ill, 84; Country Side Art Ctr, Arlington Heights, Ill, 84, 85 & 86; Perceptions of the Other, S Shore Cult Ctr, Chicago, 90; Artemesia Gallery, Chicago, 91; Prince Street Gallery, New York, 92; Ceres Gallery, New York, 92; Art at 12 White, New York, 92. *Pos:* Ed, CAG Newsletter, Miami, Fla, 78-80. *Awards:* Award, Art Auction Exhib, N Miami, Fla, 80; Chicago Cultural Arts Grant, 92. *Mem:* Chicago Artists Coalition; Women's Caucus for Arts; Ill Art Educ; Col Art Asn. *Dealer:* McGrail Studios 1339 W Rosedale Chicago IL 60660. *Mailing Add:* PO Box 6211 Evanston IL 60204

MACGREGOR, GREGORY ALLEN
PHOTOGRAPHER
b La Crosse, Wis, Feb 13, 41. *Study:* Univ Calif, San Francisco, MA(photog), 71; with Jack Welpott & Don Worth. *Work:* San Francisco Mus Mod Art, Calif; Oakland Mus, Calif; Chicago Art Inst, Ill; Mus Mod Art & Whitney Mus, New York. *Exhib:* Deus Ex Machina, Friends of Photog, Carmel, Calif, 75; On the Go, Fine Arts Mus, San Francisco, Calif, 78; Attitudes in the 70's, Santa Barbara Mus Art, Calif, 79; Recent Work, O K Harris Works of Art, New York, 79 & 82; American Tractor, Foster Goldstrum Fine Arts, San Francisco, 82; San Francisco Mus Mod Art, 82, 83, 87 & 88. *Teaching:* Asst prof & chmn photog, Lone Mountain Col, San Francisco, Calif, 70-78; asst prof photog, Calif State Univ, Hayward, 80-84. *Bibliog:* Ted Hedypath (auth), The real as surreal, Artweek, 2/25/80; Jim Hughes (auth), Proofsheet, Popular Photog, 6/80; Mark Levy (auth), article, Images & Issues, 10/82. *Mem:* Soc Photog Educ. *Publ:* Illusr, Points of view, New West, 11/79; contribr, Darkroom Dynamics, Curtin-London, 79; auth, Explosions, Headlands Press, 80; article, Art Comn, 6/83; illusr, Darkroom Mag, Vol 4, No 8, 82; and others. *Dealer:* O K Harris 383 W Broadway New York NY 10012; Equivalents Gallery 1822 Broadway Seattle WA. *Mailing Add:* 12100 Montecito No 145 Los Alamidos CA 90720

MCGREW, BRUCE ELWIN
PAINTER
b Wichita, Kans, Oct 20, 37. *Study:* Wichita State Univ, Kans, BFA; Univ Ariz, MFA, 64. *Work:* Nat Park Serv, Three Rivers, Calif & Haleakala Nat Park, Maui, Hawaii; Univ Minn, Morris; Univ Kansai, Osaka, Japan; Univ Ariz, Law Sch. *Comn:* oil landscape, Georgetown Leather, Washington, DC, 77; watercolor, Pennie Edmonds Law Firm, New York, 77. *Exhib:* Kiosko del Arte, Hermosillo, Mex, 78; Maggie Kress Gallery, Taos, NMex, 79; Marion Locks, Philadelphia, 81; Colorado Springs Fine Arts Ctr, Colo, 81; Univ Ark, Fayetteville, 81; and others. *Teaching:* Instr painting & drawing, Univ Minn, Morris, 64-66; prof art, Univ Ariz, Tucson, 66-; artist-in-residence, Nat Park Serv, Sequoia & Kings Canyon Nat Park, Three Rivers, Calif, summer 75 & Haleakala Nat Park, Maui, Hawaii, summer 76; mem staff watercolor workshop, Summervail Art Workshop, Vail, Colo, summer 77; mem staff drawing & watercolor workshop, Univ Tex, El Paso, 4/78 & Guadalajara Summer Sch, Univ Ariz, 79. *Awards:* Fac Res Support in Humanities & Sociology, Univ Ariz, Tucson, 72-73; Purchase Awards, 13th Ann Cedar City Exhib, Utah, 74 & Ninth South Western Invitational Yuma Fine Arts Asn, Ariz, 75. *Media:* Watercolor, Oil. *Publ:* Contribr, Oracle: A Voluntary of Poems and Prints, Oracle Press, 74. *Dealer:* Marion Locks Gallery 1524 Walnut Philadelphia PA 19102. *Mailing Add:* Box 160 Oracle AZ 85623

MCGREW, R BROWNELL
PAINTER
b Columbus, Ohio, Sept 6, 16. *Study:* Otis Art Inst, 36-40; Concordia Col, St Paul, Minn, DLitt, 81; Valparaiso Univ, Ind, MFA, 92. *Work:* Mus Northern Ariz, Flagstaff; Cowboy Hall of Fame, Oklahoma City, Okla; Palm Springs Desert Mus, Calif; Cowboy Artists Mus, Kerrville, Tex; Eiteljorg Mus, Indianapolis, Ind; Gilcrease Mus, Tulsa, Okla; Russell Mus, Great Falls, Mont; Gene Autry Western Heritage Mus, Los Angeles, Calif. *Exhib:* Solo exhib, Laguna Beach Art Mus, 78; Mus Native Am Cult, Spokane, 81; Anschutz Collection, Tuscon Art Mus, 85; retrospective, Gilcrease Mus, Tulsa, Oka; and many others. *Bibliog:* R Brownell McGrew, The Lowell Press, 78. *Mem:* Fel Am Inst Fine Arts; life mem Soc Western Artists; emer mem Cowboy Artists of Am. *Media:* Oil, Charcoal, Pencil. *Dealer:* O'Brien's Art Emporium 7122 Stetson Scottsdale AZ 85251. *Mailing Add:* PO Box 448 Sonoita AZ 85637

MCGUIRE, MAUREEN
DESIGNER, STAINED GLASS ARTIST
b Flushing, NY, July 13, 41. *Study:* NY State Col Ceramics, Alfred Univ, BFA, 63; Pope Pius XII Inst, Florence, Italy (affil Rosary Col, Ill), Cardinal Spellman scholar & MA, 64; workshop, with Ludwig Schaffrath, Berkeley, Calif, 75. *Comn:* Design for large tapestry, La Casa De Cristo Lutheran Church, Paradise Valley, Ariz; leaded stained glass windows & laminated glass screen wall, St Matthew's United Methodist Church, Bowie, Md; faceted glass window, skylights, mosaic walls, exterior concrete bas relief sculptures, interior design, furniture design incorporating flower display system, St Francis Cemetery Resurrection Mausoleum; commercial installation: 15 faceted glass windows, Paradise Valley Mall, Paradise Valley, Ariz; residential installation: leaded glass window & light fixtures, Logan Van Sittert residence, Phoenix; and many others. *Pos:* Apprentice designer-craftsman, Glassart Studio, Scottsdale, Ariz, 64-69; independent artist-designer, Phoenix, 69- *Awards:* Honor Awards, Nat Conf Relig Archit, 68 & Interfaith Forum Relig, Art & Archit, 79. *Bibliog:* Ann Patterson (auth), Stained glass: The art, Ariz Repub, 9/30/79. *Mem:* Stained Glass Asn Am; Interfaith Forum Relig, Archit & Arts; Am Craft Coun; Ariz Stained Glass Asn. *Media:* Leaded and Faceted Stained Glass; Mosaics in Glass. *Publ:* Auth-illusr, The case for the independent designer, Stained Glass Quart, 4/80. *Mailing Add:* 924 E Bethany Home Rd Phoenix AZ 85014

MCHAM, SARAH BLAKE WILK
HISTORIAN, EDUCATOR
b Boston, Mass. *Study:* Institut d'Art et Archéologie, Paris, France, 65-66; Smith Col, BA, 66; Inst Fine Arts, New York Univ, PhD, 77. *Teaching:* Asst prof art hist, Rutgers Univ, 78-84, assoc prof, 84-86, chmn, 86-90, prof, 92- *Awards:* Am Philoso Soc Grant, 81 & 86; Am Coun Learnd Soc, 84. *Mem:* Col Art Asn; Renaissance Soc Am. *Res:* Italian Renaissance sculpture and painting. *Publ:* Ed, Central Italian Sculpture, 1400-1500: An Annotated Bibliography, GK Hall, 86; auth, The political meaning of Dontello's "Dovizia," Artibus et historiae, Vol 14, 86; Donatello's tomb of Pope John XXIII, In: Life and Death in 15th Century Florence, Duke Univ Press, 89; Donatello and the High Altar in the Santo, IL60, Essays honoring Irving Lavin, M A Lavin, ed, Italica Press, 90; The Chapel of St Anthony in Padua and the Development of Venetian Renaissance Sculpture, Cambridge Univ Press, 93. *Mailing Add:* Dept Art Hist Voorhees Hall Rutgers Univ New Brunswick NJ 08903

MACHETANZ, FRED
PAINTER, LITHOGRAPHER
b Kenton, Ohio, Feb 20, 08. *Study:* Ohio State Univ, AB, 30, MA, 35; Chicago Art Inst, 30-32; Am Acad, Chicago, 30-32; Art Students League, 45; Univ Alaska, Hon DFA, 73; Alaska Pac Univ, LHD, 83, Ohio State Univ, LHD, 84. *Work:* Rasmuson Libr, Univ Alaska; Glenbow Found, Alta Mus, Calgary; Anchorage Hist & Fine Arts Mus; Northwest Indian Ctr, Gonzaga Univ; Frye Art Mus, Seattle. *Comn:* Scripps Inst Res Ship, Alpha Helix, 63; Dept Interior, Washington, DC, 69; Inst Arctic Biol, Univ Alaska, 71; Mat Su Col, Univ Alaska; Eben Hobson (portrait), N Slope Borough, Fairbanks, 81. *Exhib:* One-man shows, Univ Alaska, Fairbanks & Anchorage, Frye Mus, Seattle, Anchorage Hist & Fine Arts Mus, St Louis Mus Sci & Nat Hist, Artists Am Show Col Hist Mus Denver, Soc Animal Artists Travel Tours, 90-92. *Pos:* Distinguished assoc art, Univ Alaska. *Teaching:* Univ Alaska, 63-74. *Awards:* Silver Medal, NAm Wild Animal Art Exhib, 79; Artist of Yr, Am Artist Mag, 81. *Bibliog:* Stephen Doherty (auth), '81 artist of the year, Am Artist, 81; Sara Machetanz (auth), The Fifty Stone Lithographs of Fred Machetanz, Mill Pond Press, 83; Tom Davis (auth), Muktuk & Margueritas, Wild Life Art News, 91. *Mem:* Soc Animal Artists. *Media:* Transparent oil on board; Lithograph on stone. *Publ:* Auth & illusr, Panuck, Eskimo Sled Dog, 39 & auth & illusr, On Arctic Ice, 41, Scribners; illusr, Rick of High Ridge, 52; Where Else but Alaska, 54; A Puppy Named Gih, 57; Robbie and the Sled Dog Race, 64. *Dealer:* Tennys Owens Artique Ltd 314 G St Anchorage AK 99501. *Mailing Add:* PO Box 2589 Palmer AK 99645

MACHIN, ROGER
SCULPTOR
b Leicester, Eng, Jan 29, 55. *Study:* Brighton Polytechnic, MA, 78, Sch Inst Arts Chicago, MFA, 80. *Work:* De Paul Univ, Chicago; Niagara Univ, Niagara Falls, NY; Long Island Univ, CW Post Campus, NY; Taylor Univ, Upland, NY. *Exhib:* One & two person exhibs, NAME Gallery, Chicago, Ill, 79, De Paul Univ, Chicago, Ill, 81, Foster Gallery, Univ Wis, Eau Claire, 82, Marianne Deson Gallery, Chicago, Ill, 85, Ill Wesleyan Univ, Bloomington, 89 & Turman Gallery, Ind State Univ, Terra Haute, 92; Aggregate, State Ill Gallery, Chicago, 86; Exterior/Interior, Rockford Art Mus, Ill, 86; Eccentric Machines, Kohler Art Ctr, Sheboygan, Wis, 87; Down to the Sea, New House Gallery, Staten Island, NY, 87; Sculpture Chicago Alumni Exhib, Ill, 87; Movers & Shakers, DePree Art Ctr, Holland, Mich, 88; Summer Hydra, Compass Rose Gallery, Chicago, 89; Sculpture: Part II, Betsy Rosenfield Gallery, Chicago, Ill, 90; Sculpture Invitational, Greater Lafayette Mus Art, Ind, 91; Sculpture, Ricky Renier Gallery, Chicago, Ill, 91; Exploring Maps, Turman Gallery, Ind State Univ, Terra Haute, 92; and other group & solo exhibs. *Pos:* Asst to Loren Madsen, 78-84; Proj mgr contemp installations,

Westin Maui & Westin Kauai, 87 & Hyatt Regency Waikoloa, Hawaii, 88. *Teaching:* Instr, Univ Wis, Eau Claire, 82, Chelsea Sch Art, London, Eng, 83, W Surrey Col Art, Eng, 87, Brighton Poly Tech, Sussex, 87, Reading Univ, Eng, 87 & Ill State Univ, Normal, 88; head sculptor, Evanston Art Ctr, Ill, 88. *Awards:* Individual Artist Grant, Ill Arts Coun, 84, 85 & 86; Visual Arts Fel, sculpture, Nat Educ Asn, 86 & 88; Uncross Found Fel, Wyo, 89. *Bibliog:* Steve Lueckina (auth), Chicago sculpture: A nuts and bolts eloquence, New Art Examiner, 10/88; Corey Postigilione (auth), summer hydra at compass Rose Gallery (rev), Dialogue, 12/89; many other mag & newspaper articles & revs. *Mailing Add:* 2556 W Thomas Chicago IL 60607

MACHIORLETE, PATRICIA ANNE
PAINTER
b Jersey City, NJ. *Study:* Fairleigh Dickinson Univ, BS, 67; Art Ctr NJ, 81; also workshops with Barbara Nechis & Arthur Barbour. *Work:* Allied Signal Corp, Morris Township, NJ; Pub Serv Elect & Gas Co, Newark, NJ; NJ Am Water Co, Short Hills, NJ; Drakes Cakes, Wayne, NJ; The Lanid Corp, Parsippany, NJ. *Comn:* 3 Water Colors, comn by Mr Neil Vanderdusen, Pres, Sony Corp Am, Mendham, NJ, 86. *Exhib:* 15th Ann Sasmagundi Club, 84 & 89 & Knickerbocker Artists, 84 & 89, New York; one woman show, Beneficial Mgt Corp Gallery, Peapack, NJ 87; NJ Watercolor Soc, Monmouth Mus, Lincroft, NJ, 88-91; NAWA Travel Exhib, Mus Southwest, Sewanee, TN, 91-92; 71st Ann Nat Watercolor Soc, Brea Civic Ctr, Calif, 91; 49th Ann Audubon Artists, Nat Arts Club, New York, 91. *Pos:* Bd Dirs, NJ Watercolor Soc & Newsletter Ed, 91- *Awards:* Monmouth Mus Award, 46th Annual NJ W C Soc Exhib, 88; Grumbacher Medallion, Leonardo Da Vinci, 83. *Mem:* Nat Asn Women Artists (bd dir), Chairperson, 91-93; Garden State Watercolor Soc; Miniature Soc NJ; Essex Watercolor Soc; NJ Watercolor Soc. *Media:* Watercolor. *Mailing Add:* 133 Autumn Ridge Rd Bedminster NJ 07921

MCHUGH, ADELIZA SORENSON
DEALER, COLLECTOR
b St George, Utah, Apr 29, 12. *Study:* Spec study with Robert Arneson, Roy De Forest, David Gilhooly, Gladys Nilsson, Jim Nutt & Maija Peeples. *Collections Arranged:* Roy De Forest Drawings, San Francisco Mus & Whitney Mus, New York. *Pos:* Dir, Candy Store Gallery, Folsom, Calif, 62- *Specialty:* Contemporary American art. *Collection:* Californian ceramic sculpture, American primitive drawings of today; California paintings. *Publ:* Contribr, Adeliza and the candy store bunch, Connoissur, 11/87; The candy store-Folsom, House Garden, 3/88; German Tour Guide Marco Polo Kalifornien, 91. *Mailing Add:* 2249 Columbia St Palo Alto CA 94306

MCILROY, CAROL J
PAINTER, DEALER
b Sandpoint, Idaho, Feb 21, 24. *Study:* Univ Colo, with John Pellew; Univ NMex, with Joe Morello, Daniel Green, Arthur Sussman & Sam Smith. *Work:* Am Bank Com, Albuquerque NMex; NMex Jr Col. *Exhib:* Mainstreams, 69; Regional Art Exhib, Phoenix, 71; McAddo II Gallery, Prescott, Ariz, 73; Stamford Art Exhib, Tex; Concetta D Gallery, Albuquerque, NMex. *Pos:* Chmn standards comt, NMex Arts & Crafts Fair, 72-73; mem, Bicentennial Art Comt, 75; co-owner, Galeria del Sol. *Awards:* First Prize Landscape, 4th Regional Art Exhib, Phoenix, 71; Magnifico, Albuquerque, 92; Gov's Exhib, Albuquerque, 92. *Mem:* Am Artists Prof League; Artists Equity (vpres, 71-72); NMex Art League. *Media:* Oil. *Mailing Add:* 8907 Los Arboles Ave NE Albuquerque NM 87112

MCILVAIN, DOUGLAS LEE
EDUCATOR, SCULPTOR
b Mt Holly, NJ, July 26, 23. *Study:* Tyler Sch Fine Arts, Temple Univ, BFA & BS, Tyler Sch Fine Arts Rome; New York Univ, MA(art educ); also with Raphael Sabatini, Jose De Creeft& Bruno Lucchesi. *Work:* Monmouth Col; Merrill Lynch, Princeton, NJ; Tyler Sch Fine Arts Rome; Stanford, Conn Forum; Georvgin Ct Col. *Comn:* Four portraits, Health Hall of Fame, 80; Bell Tel Labs, 82; Jack Leiner Archit Design, 83; Portrait, Roosevelt Hosp, 89; Statue for ARC, NJ, 91; and others. *Exhib:* Pa Acad Art, 60; Morris Mus, NJ, 82; Art Expo, New York, 83; Monmouth Mus, NJ, 85-88 & 92; Phoenix Gallery, New York, 92; Guild Creative Arts, 92; and others. *Pos:* Art designer, Monmouth Mus, 78-79. *Teaching:* Assoc prof art, Georgian Ct Col, 68-86. *Awards:* First Prize, Jersey City Mus, 61; First Prize, Red Bank Festival Arts, 61-62, 64-65, 67, 69-71 & 73; First Prize, Guild of Creative Arts, 89. *Mem:* Sculpture Asn NJ; Guild Creative Arts; Art Alliance; Am Asn Univ Prof; Int Sculpture Ctr. *Media:* Bronze, Wood. *Mailing Add:* 40 Whitman Dr Red Bank NJ 07701

MCILVAIN, FRANCES H
PAINTER, GALLERY DIRECTOR
b Newark, NJ, May 11, 25. *Study:* Tyler Sch Art, Temple Univ, BFA & BS, 47, Temple Univ Rome, with Charles LaClair, 65; Phildalephia Mus Sch Art, with W Emerton Heitland, 48; with Marid Cooper, 75, Nicholas Reale, 80, Marilyn H Philis, 89 & Frank Webb, 90. *Work:* Temple Univ, Philadelphia, Pa; Bell Laboratories, Holmdel, NJ; Continental Group Computer Hq, Conn; Firmenich Corp, Princeton, NJ; Nabisco Brands, E Hanover, NJ. *Comn:* Mural of Noah's Ark, First Presbyterian Church, Red Bank, NJ, 60; paintings, Atchison Sch, Tinton Falls, NJ, 70 & 81; mural, Monmouth Mus, Lincroft, NJ, 80. *Exhib:* Monmouth Co Arts Coun Ann, Monmouth Mus, Lincroft, NJ, 80, 85 & 90; Garden State Watercolor Soc, Princeton, NJ, 81-90; Nabisco Brands USA Gallery, 82 & 87; Art Expo, New York, 83; 43rd Ann Open Show, NJ Watercolor Soc, 85 & 88-90. *Pos:* Halsted & Van Vechten/Advert, 52-58. *Teaching:* Instr art, Rancocas Valley Regional High Sch, Mt Holly, NJ, 47-53; instr art, Tinton Falls Sch, NJ, 63-83. *Awards:* Best in Show, Henry Luhrs Award, 80; Monmouth Arts First Prize, 83, Second Prize, 85; Best in Show, 88. *Mem:* Guild Creative Arts, (bd mem, 75-92); Monmouth Arts Found; Am Watercolor Soc; NJ Watercolor Soc (1st vpres, 79-86, pres, 92-94); Trenton Artists Workshop Asn, Garden State Watercolor Soc. *Media:* Watercolor, Collage. *Mailing Add:* 40 Whitman Dr Red Bank NJ 07701

MCILVANE, EDWARD JAMES
STAINED GLASS ARTIST, GLASS BLOWER
b New York, NY, July 5, 47. *Study:* St John's Univ, New York, BS(Art Educ), 75, RI Sch Design with Dale Chihuly & James Carpenter, MFA(Glass), 78. *Work:* Pilchuck Sch, Stanwood, Wash; Patrick Lannon Found, Palm Beach, Fla. *Comn:* Lobby windows, Temple Beth-El, Providence, RI, 82; chapel windows, Good Shepherd of Hills, Cave Creek, Ariz, 84; exec off windows, Bank of Boston, Mass, 85; two leaded glass skylight windows, Ctr Law & Soc, Stonehill Col, N Easton, Mass, 90; Lobby windows, Presby World Hq, Louisville, Ky, 92. *Exhib:* Young Americans in Clay & Glass, Mus Contemp Crafts, New York, 78; Das Bild in Glas (with catalog), Hessiches Landsmuseum, Darmstadt, WGer, 79; Art in Craft Media: The Haystack Tradition, travelling exhib, 81; 3-Dimensions, Univ Tex, El Paso, 85; A History of Excellence, Newport Art Mus, RI, 87. *Teaching:* Instr stained glass, Haystack Mountain Sch Crafts, 77 & RI Sch Design, 78-; prog coordr, stained glass, Pilchuck Sch, 78. *Awards:* Crafts Fel, 80 & Design Fel, 86, RI State Coun Arts; Visual Artists Fel, Nat Endowment Arts, 83. *Bibliog:* K & F Breydert (auths), Ars Pro Deo, SMI, Paris, 86; Kemp & Perron (auths), Architectural Ornamentalism, Whitney Libr Design, 87. *Mem:* Am Crafts Coun. *Publ:* Contribr, artist's statement, In: Art in Craft Media, Bowdoin Col Press, 81; auth, New perspectives on glass in architecture, Glass Art Soc J, 87. *Dealer:* Heller Gallery Greene St New York NY 10012. *Mailing Add:* Table Rock Rd No PL-13 Lincoln RI 02865-3921

MCINERNEY, GENE JOSEPH
PAINTER
b Easton, Pa, Jan 6, 30. *Work:* Miniature Art Soc of NJ, Nutley; Fred Clark Mus, Carversville, Pa; Meadowbrook Sch, Philadelphia, Pa. *Comn:* Bicentennial Calendar, Northampton Co, Pa, Bicentennial Comn, 75. *Exhib:* Painters & Sculptore Soc NJ, Jersey City Mus, 71, 72 & 74; Miniature Painters, Sculptors & Gravers Soc, Washington DC Arts Club, 72 & 73; Nat Soc Painters in Casein & Acrylic, Nat Acad, New York, 72-75; Mainstreams Int, Marietta, Ohio, 72 & 73; Butler Inst Am Art, 84, 85 & 86. *Awards:* First Prize, Atlantic City Nat Boardwalk Show, 70; Mainstreams Award of Excellence, Marietta Col, 72; Presidents Prize, Painters & Sculptors Soc NJ, 74. *Bibliog:* Art, Gene McInerney, La Rev Mod, 11/72. *Media:* Acrylic, Watercolor. *Publ:* Taking Advantage of Acrylics, Watercolor, An Artist Publ, fall 91. *Dealer:* Capricorn Gallery 4849 Rugby Ave Bethesda MD 20814; Bernard Picture Co New York NY. *Mailing Add:* Northlight Studio 315 Brodt Rd Bangor PA 18013

MCINTOSH, GREGORY STEPHEN
PAINTER
b Ojai, Calif, May 7, 46. *Study:* Santa Clara Univ, BA, 68 & MA, 71. *Work:* Libr Congress, Washington, DC; Muskegon Mus Art, Mich; Calif Palace Legion of Hon, San Francisco; San Francisco Mus Mod Art; Los Angeles Co Mus Art; Oakland Mus, Calif. *Comn:* Jazz at Ojai, Commemorative Fine Art Posters, 81 & 82; mural, US Post Office, 83; US Olympic Comt fine art commem poster, 84. *Exhib:* Solo exhibs, Expressions, Fred Segal's, Santa Monica, 87, Gregory Stephen McIntosh: Paintings, Ojai Art Ctr Gallery, Calif, 88 & Jewish Community Ctr, Cleveland Heights, Ohio, 89, Atmospheres, Park Gallery, Ft Lauderdale, Fla, 88, Atmospheric Expressions, Waterstreet Gallery, Mystic, Conn, Gregory Stephen McIntosh: Works on Paper, Springfield Art Asn, Ill & Gouache & Pastel, Bernard's Township Libr, Basking Ridge, NJ, 89; Somerset Art Asn Exhib, Far Hills, NJ, 88 & 90; Affaire in the Gardens, Beverly Hills, Calif, 88-91; Boca Raton Mus Art, Fla, 88, 91 & 92; Festival of the Masters, Walt Disney Corp, Fla, 89; Artist Show, Novometro Gallery, Cleveland, Ohio, 90; Elements, Kneeland Gallery, Sun Valley, Idaho, 91; Miami Beach Festival Art, Fla, 91-92; Calif Gold Coast Watercolor Soc Ann Competition, Ojai Ctr Arts, Calif, 92; Art & Healing, Lipsett Gallery, Nat Ins Health, Bethesda, Md, 92. *Awards:* Painting Grant with Walter Ruhlman, funded by California Arts Coun, 83; Purchase Award, Coconut Grove Art Asn, 88; best show, Kalamazoo Inst Arts, 90; artist in residence, Paris, France, 91. *Bibliog:* McIntosh sky scapes will be displayed at Maturango Museum during March, Daily Independent, 3/87; Beate Bermann-Enn (auth), In Search of Landscape Lost, Art Scene vol 8 no 4, 12/88. *Mem:* Pastel Soc Am (full mem, 90). *Media:* Gouache & Pastel on Paper, Oil on canvas. *Dealer:* Anca Colbert. *Mailing Add:* PO Box 961 Ojai CA 93023

MACIVER, LOREN
PAINTER
b New York, NY, Feb 2, 09. *Study:* Art Students League, 19. *Work:* Whitney Mus Am Art, Metrop Mus Art, Mus Mod Art, New York; Corcoran Gallery Art, Washington, DC; Addison Gallery Am Art, Andover, Mass; and others. *Comn:* S S Argentina, 49. *Exhib:* Venice Biennale, 67; Tolouse Mus Fine Arts, 67; Mus Beaux Arts, Lyons, France, 68; Mus Art Mod Ville de Paris, 68; Mus Ponchettes, Nice, France, 68; Corcoran Gallery Art; Whitney Mus Am Art, New York; Mus Mod Art, New York; and others. *Awards:* First Prize, Art Inst Chicago, 61; Purchase Prize, Krannert Art Mus, Univ Ill, 63; Lee Krasner Award, 91; and others. *Mem:* Nat Inst Arts & Lett. *Media:* Oil. *Dealer:* Pierre Matisse Gallery 41 E 57th St New York NY 10022. *Mailing Add:* 61 Perry St New York NY 10014

MCIVOR, JOHN WILFRED
PRINTMAKER, PAINTER
b Henderson, Ky, July 17, 31. *Study:* Murray State Univ, 49-50; Univ Ill, BFA(summa cum laude), 57, fel, 57-59, MFA, 59. *Work:* Albright-Knox Art Gallery, Buffalo, NY; Am Fedn Arts, New York; Libr Cong, Washington, DC; State Univ NY Albany; Jacksonville Mus, Fla. *Comn:* Exterior (with David Hatchett), Buffalo Rehab Comn, 71. *Exhib:* 100th Anniversary Show of Land Grant Colleges, Kansas City Art Inst, 68; Master Drawings & Watercolors Since the 15th Century, Albright-Knox Art Gallery, 69; North of the Penn Line, traveling show to mus of Northeast, 69-71; Am Fedn Arts Traveling Exhib, 70-71; Watercolors Since 1900, Birmingham Mus Art, Ala, 72. *Pos:* Founder, Team Workshop, Buffalo. *Teaching:* Asst prof art, Auburn Univ, 59-63; prof art, State Univ NY Buffalo, 63-; vis prof, Southern Ill Univ, spring 70. *Awards:* Fac Fel, State Univ NY Res Found, 70 & 72. *Bibliog:* Edward Reep (auth), The Content of Watercolor, Reinhold, 69. *Mailing Add:* 159 11th St Atlantic Beach FL 33233

MACK, CHARLES RANDALL
EDUCATOR, HISTORIAN
b Baltimore, Md, May 23, 40. *Study:* Univ NC, Chapel Hill, AB, PhD (hist art). *Work:* Ed, Art Hist Series, Camden House, Inc, 89- *Collections Arranged:* Classical Art from Carolina Collections (auth catalog), Columbia Mus Art, SC & NC Mus Art, Raleigh, 74; A Campus Collects (auth catalog), Univ SC Mus, Columbia, 80; H Robert Bonsack: Figure Studies, Goethe Inst, Atlanta traveling exhib, 81-82; Turned to Tradition: Southeastern Folk Pottery Today (auth catalog), Columbia Mus Art, SC, 88; Paper Pleasures: Five Centuries of Drawings and Watercolors (auth catalog), Univ SC Mus, Columbia, 92. *Pos:* gen consult ed, Dictionary of Artist's Biography, 90; co-ed, Southeastern Col Art Conf Review, 73-75. *Teaching:* Prof ancient & Renaissance art, Univ SC, Columbia, 70-, William J Todd, Prof Italian Renaissance, 92- *Awards:* Comt to Rescue Ital Art Internship, Florence, 68-69; Kress Found Res Fel, Rome, Italy, 69-70, Grant, 84; Am Coun Learned Soc Trav Grant, 82, 89; Nat Endowment Humanities Grant, 84, 89. *Mem:* Col Art Asn; Southeastern Col Art Conf (pres 75-76, bd mem 84-87); Southeastern Chap Soc Archit Historians (bd mem 84-87, pres 91-92); Southeastern Renaissance Conf; Renaissance Soc Am. *Res:* Fifteenth century Italian architecture; Renaissance art; Etruscan and Roman art; Southeastern folk pottery. *Publ:* Auth, The Rucellai Palace: Some new proposals, Art Bull, 74; Brunelleschi's Spedale degli Innocenti rearticulated, Architectura, 81; Pienza: The Creation of a Renaissance City, Cornell Univ, 87; Nicholas V and the Rebuilding of Rome: Reality & Legacy, Papers in Art Hist from Pa State Univ, 87; The Bath Palace of Nicholas V at Viterbo, Papers in Art Hist from Pa State Univ, 92. *Mailing Add:* Dept of Art Univ SC Columbia SC 29208

MACK, DANIEL R
CRAFTSMAN, DESIGNER
b Rochester, NY, Dec 23, 47. *Study:* Univ Toronto, BA, 70; The New Sch, New York, MA, 75; self-taught woodworker. *Work:* Cooper Hewitt Mus; Am Craft Mus; Mus Fine Arts, Houston. *Exhib:* Am Craft Mus, 87, 91 & 92; Cooper Hewitt Mus, 92. *Teaching:* Teacher rustic woodworking, Anderson Ranch Arts Ctr, Snowmass, Colo, 87- *Awards:* Fel, NY Found Arts, 86 & 90; Fel, Mid-Atlantic Arts Found, 88. *Bibliog:* Rustic revival, Washington Post, 5/85; William Bryant Logan (auth), Rococo rustic, House & Garden, 11/86; many other articles in national magazines. *Media:* Natural Form Wood. *Publ:* Making Rustic Furniture, Sterling/Lark 92. *Mailing Add:* 3280 Broadway New York NY 10027

MACK, RODGER ALLEN
SCULPTOR, EDUCATOR
b Barberton, Ohio, Nov 8, 38. *Study:* Cleveland Inst Art, BFA, 61; Cranbrook Acad Art, Bloomfield Hills, Mich, MFA, 63; Acad Belle Arti, Florence, Italy, Fulbright Grant, 63-64. *Work:* Munson-Williams-Proctor Inst, Utica, Everson Mus Art, Syracuse, NY; St Lawrence Univ; State Univ NY Col Fredonia; Hamline Univ; Museu d'Art Contemporani, Barcelona, Spain. *Comn:* Plaza sculpture, Mkt Plaza, North Little Rock, 68; Syra cast bronze, Dellplain Hall, Syracuse Univ, 69. *Exhib:* One-man shows, Galleria Arte, Florence, 64, Krasner Gallery, New York, 70-81, Sid Deutsch Gallery, New York, 84, Everson Mus, 84 & Museu Dioces'a de Barcelona, 92; Sculpture Invitational, Rochester Inst Technol, 75; and others. *Teaching:* Instr sculpture, Arks Sch Art/Drama, Little Rock, 64-68; assoc prof sculpture, Syracuse Univ, 68-77, prof, 77-, dir, Sch Art, 82-91; dean, Triangle Trust Workshop, Pine Plains, NY, 83- *Awards:* Nat Endowment Arts Award, Nat Coun Arts, 67; CAPS Grant, NY State Coun Arts, 77-78; Ford Found Grant, 80-81. *Bibliog:* John Canaday (auth), article, New York Times, 1/70, 1/71 & 1/72; Michael Brenson (auth), rev, NY Times, 2/84. *Media:* Bronze, Steel. *Mailing Add:* 408 S Franklin St Syracuse NY 13202

MCKAY, ARTHUR FORTESCUE
PAINTER, EDUCATOR
b Nipawin, Sask, Sept 11, 26. *Study:* Alta Col Art; Acad Grande Chaumiere, Paris; Columbia Univ; Barnes Found, Pa. *Work:* Nat Gallery, Ottawa, Ont; Art Gallery Ont, Toronto; Montreal Mus Fine Arts, Que; Vancouver Art Gallery, BC; Nat Gallery Can. *Exhib:* Five Printers from Regina, Nat Gallery Ottawa, 61; Post Painter Abstraction, Los Angeles Co Mus, 64; Religious Art Today, Regis Col, 65; Images of a Canadian Heritage, Vancouver Art Gallery, 67; retrospective exhib, Norman MacKinzie Art Gallery, 68; Nat Gallery of Can, 81. *Teaching:* Assoc prof art, Univ Regina, 51- *Awards:* Humanities Res Coun Grant, 57 & 58; Can Coun Sr Fel, 63. *Bibliog:* C Greenberg (auth), Art on the prairie, Arts Can Mag, 9/63; T Fenton (auth), Canada's Art McKay, Artforum, 12/68. *Media:* Watercolor, Oil. *Publ:* Auth, Emma Lake Artists Workshop, Arts Can, 64 & 82. *Mailing Add:* 2865 Angus St Regina SK S4S 1N7 Canada

MCKAY, JOHN SANGSTER
EDUCATOR, ADMINISTRATOR DESIGN, COLLAGE
b Farmers City, Ill, May 30, 21. *Study:* Univ Ill, Urbana-Champaign, BFA, 47; Inst Design, Chicago, Ill, cert, 48; Univ Buffalo, 50. *Teaching:* Instr design, Albright Art Sch, Buffalo, 47-54; asst dean design, Sch Fine Arts, Wash Univ, 54-68; prof visual arts, Univ Kans, 68-86, assoc dean Sch Fine Arts, 68-75, dir grad studies, Dept Design, 77-80, acting chmn, 80-82, assoc chmn, 83-86; retired. *Mem:* Fel Nat Asn Schs Art (pres, 69-72); Am Coun Arts Educ (bd dirs, 69-72); Int Coun Fine Arts Deans; Lawrence Kans Community Arts Coun (chmn, 73-74). *Media:* Paper, Watercolor. *Publ:* Co-auth, Nat Asn Schs Art Bull, 72. *Mailing Add:* 4745 S Atlantic Ave Ponce Inlet FL 32127

MCKAY, RENEE
PAINTER
b Montreal, Que; US citizen. *Study:* Inst Pedagogique, Montreal; McGill Univ, Montreal, BA, 41; studied with Ben Shahn, Morris Davidson & Joe Jones. *Work:* Slater Mem Mus, Norwich, Conn; Norfolk Mus, Va; Butler Inst Am Art, Youngstown, Ohio; Lydia Drake Libr, Pembroke, Mass. *Exhib:* Open Ann, Newark & Montclair, NJ; Nat Asn Women Artists Traveling Show, Butler Inst Am Art, Youngstown, Ohio; Nat Asn Women Artists Ann & Audubon Ann, Nat Acad Galleries, New York; Nat Asn Women Artists, Lever House & Union Carbide, New York; Weyhe Gallery, New York, 79. *Teaching:* Instr art, Peck Sch, Morristown, NJ, 55-57. *Awards:* Watercolor Award, 75 & Oil Award, 80, Audubon Artists; Acrylic Award, Nat Soc Painters Casein & Acrylic, 83; and others. *Mem:* Audubon Artists (pres, 79-80); Artists Equity Asn (vpres, 79-81); Nat Asn Women Artists (adv bd, 74-76); Nat Soc Painters Casein & Acrylic; Nat Arts Club; and others. *Media:* Acrylic, Watercolor. *Mailing Add:* 200 E 66th St New York NY 10021

MCKEAN, HUGH FERGUSON
PAINTER, EDUCATOR
b Beaver Falls, Pa, July 28, 08. *Study:* Pa Acad Fine Arts; Art Students League; Ecole Beaux-Arts, Fontainebleau, France; Rollins Col, BA & DFA; Williams Col, MA; Stetson Univ, LHD; Brevard Col, D Ed; Univ Tampa, LLD. *Work:* Toledo Mus Art; Univ Va. *Exhib:* Soc Four Arts, Palm Beach, Fla, 48; Allied Artists Am, 49; Exhib, Atlanta, Ga, 49; Second Nat Exhib Am Painting, New York; numerous ann exhibs; Fla Fedn Art. *Pos:* Dir, Morse Mus Am Art, Rollins Col, 42-, actg pres, 51-52, pres, 52-69, chmn bd, 69-75; dir, Winter Park Land Co, 52-; trustee, Ringling Mus, Fla; trustee, Edyth Bush Charitable Found, 75-88; pres, Charles Hosmer Morse Found (reorganization of the Morse Mus Am Art, removed from Rollins Col to Winter Park, Fla), 76- *Teaching:* From asst to prof art, Rollins Col, Winter Park, Fla, 35-45. *Awards:* Prizes, Fla Fedn Art, 31 & 49; Cervantes Medal, Span Inst; Decoration of Honor, Rollins Col, 42; Best Fla Landscape, 49; John Young Award, Orlando Area Chamber of Commerce, 67. *Mem:* Fla Fedn Art (pres, 51-52); Louis Comfort Tiffany Found (trustee); NH Art Asn; Orlando Art Asn; Am Fedn Arts; Fla Arts Coun; and others. *Publ:* Auth, The Lost Treasures of Louis Comfort Tiffany, Doubleday & Co, 80. *Mailing Add:* 930 Genius Dr Winter Park FL 32789

MCKEE, DAVID MALCOLM
ART DEALER
b Cumbria, Eng, Oct, 8, 37. *Pos:* Dir, David McKee Gallery, currently. *Mem:* Art Dealers Asn Am. *Specialty:* Postwar and contemporary painting and sculpture, mainly American, including Philip Guston, Jake Berthot, Harvey Quaytman, Sean Scully & William Tucker. *Mailing Add:* David McKee Gallery 745 Fifth Ave New York NY 10151

MCKENNA, GEORGE LAVERNE
CURATOR
b Detroit, Mich, Dec 7, 24. *Study:* Univ Ore, 43-44; Univ Calif, 48-49; Univ Chicago, 50; Wayne State Univ, Mich, AB, 48, MA, 51. *Collections Arranged:* Repeated Exposure: Photographic Imagery in the Print Media (auth, catalog), 82; Posters and Modern Color Prints, 85; Expressionism in the Graphic Arts, 85; Art by Chance: Fortuitous Impressions (auth, catalog), 89. *Pos:* Registrar, Nelson-Atkins Mus Art, 52-82, cur prints & photogs, 60-, cur drawings, 85- *Mem:* Print Coun Am; Am Asn Mus. *Publ:* Auth, 22 spec exhib brochures, 82-92, ed, Calendar of Events, 53-82 & co-ed, Handbook of Collections, 5th ed, 73, Nelson-Atkins Mus. *Mailing Add:* Nelson-Atkins Mus Art 4525 Oak St Kansas City MO 64111-1873

MCKENZIE, ALLAN DEAN
EDUCATOR, HISTORIAN
b Pendleton, Ore, Aug 17, 30. *Study:* San Jose State Univ, BA(com art), 52; Univ Calif, Berkeley, MA(art hist), 55; Inst Fine Arts, NY Univ, PhD(art hist; Fulbright Scholar), 65. *Teaching:* Instr medieval art, NY Univ, 57-64; asst prof medieval & classical art, Univ Wis, Milwaukee, 64-66; assoc prof medieval art, Univ Ore, 66-74, prof, 74-; emer, 88. *Awards:* Founders' Day Award, NY Univ, 66; Travel Grants, Univ Ore, 66, 67 & 71; Grant for Poland, Int Res Exchange Bd, New York, 73; Samuel H Kress Found Grant for Egypt, 86. *Mem:* Col Art Asn, 57-86; Archeol Inst Am (Eugene Chap pres & secy, formerly); Int Ctr Medieval Art; Medieval Acad Am, 75-82; Am Asn Advan Slavic Studies. *Res:* Russian and Byzantine painting; Medieval art. *Publ:* Auth, Greek & Russian Icons, Northwest, 65; Russian Art: Old and New, Univ Ore, 68; Provincial Byzantine painting in Attica, Cahiers Arch, 82; Russian Icons in the Santa Barbara Museum of Art, 82; Icons of Russia, Maryhill Mus Art, 86; Sacred Images & The Millennium; Christianity & Russia (AD 988-1988), 88. *Mailing Add:* Dept Art Hist Univ Ore Eugene OR 97403

MACKENZIE, DAVID, IV
PAINTER
b Los Angeles, Calif, Nov 8, 42. *Study:* Orange Coast Col, Costa Mesa, Calif, AA; San Francisco Art Inst, BFA & MFA; also with Ron Nagle & Tom Holland. *Work:* Oakland Mus Art, Calif. *Exhib:* One-man shows, San Francisco Art Inst, 73, Grapestake Gallery, San Francisco, 75, 76 & 80 & A Ten Year Survey, Bluxome Gallery, San Francisco, 83; 18 Bay Area Artists, Art Mus, Univ Calif, Berkeley, 75; Whitney Biennial, Whitney Mus Am Art, 75; Tough Stuff, San Francisco Mus Mod Art, 83; Bay Area Painting, San Francisco, 84; Sheldon Mem Art Gallery, Univ Nebr, Lincoln, Nebr; David Mackenzie, Angles Gallery, Santa Monica, Calif, 89; Natural Order, Art in General, New York, 91. *Pos:* Guest cur, Los Angeles Inst Contemp Art, Los Angeles, 76 & San Francisco Art Inst, 78; guest organizer, San Francisco Art Inst, 83. *Awards:* Nat Endowment Arts Grant, 75. *Bibliog:* Peter Frank (auth), On the Trail of the Exxon National, Nat Arts Guide, Vol 3, No 1, 81. *Mailing Add:* 315 Columbia St Brooklyn NY 11231

MACKENZIE, HUGH SEAFORTH
PAINTER
b Toronto, Ont, June 19, 28. *Study:* Ont Col Art; Mt Allison Univ, BFA. *Work:* Montreal Mus Fine Arts, PQ; Art Gallery Ont & Univ Toronto, Toronto; Univ Waterloo; London Art Gallery, Ont; House of Commons, Ottawa. *Comn:* Portrait of L B Pearson, Dept State, Ottawa, 68. *Exhib:* One-man shows, Morris Gallery, Toronto, 63-77 & Univ Waterloo, 75; Art Gallery Ont, 58-59, 61, 68 & 70; Montreal Mus Fine Arts, Que, 64 & 70; Ann Exhib Contemp Can Artists, Art Gallery of Hamilton, 70-72; Lithographs in collabr with NS Col Art, Nat Gallery Can, 71; Bau-Xi Gallery, Toronto, 81, 82, 83, 85 & 86. *Teaching:* Instr art, Ont Col Art, 68- *Awards:* J W G Forster Award, Ont Soc Artists, 61; Can Coun Award, 70. *Bibliog:* Dauct (auth), article, Arts Can, spring 72; Hale (auth), article, Arts Mag, 2/70; Duval (auth), High Realism in Canada, Irwin Clarke & Co, Ltd, 74. *Mem:* Assoc Royal Can Acad. *Media:* Tempera, Etching. *Mailing Add:* 84 MacPherson Ave Toronto ON M5R 1W8 Canada

MCKENZIE, MARY BETH
PAINTER
b Cleveland, Ohio, July 30, 46. *Study:* Mus Fine Arts, Boston, 64-65; Cooper Sch Art, 65-67; Nat Acad Design, 69-74. *Work:* RJ Reynolds Corp Collection; Hesse Collection; Danish Bank, Mus of the City of New York, Metrop Mus, New York; Nat Mus Am Art, Washington, DC; Butler Inst Am Art, Youngstown, Ohio. *Exhib:* Solo exhibs, Nat Arts Club, 76 & FAR Gallery, 80, New York; Frank Caro Gallery, New York, 88; Joseph Keiffer Gallery, 91. *Teaching:* Instr painting, Nat Acad Design, 81- *Awards:* Greenshields Found Grant & Stacey Found Grant, 78; Thomas B Clarke Prize, Nat Acad Design Ann, 81. *Bibliog:* Harvey Stein (auth), Artists Observed, Harry Abrams, 86. *Mem:* Allied Artists; Audubon Artists; Pastel Soc Am. *Media:* Oil. *Publ:* Auth, A Painterly Approach, Watson-Guptil, NY, 87. *Dealer:* Frank Caro Gallery 41 E 57th St New York NY 10022. *Mailing Add:* 525 W 45th St New York NY 10036

MCKESSON, MALCOLM FORBES
PAINTER, SCULPTOR
b Monmouth Beach, NJ, July 24, 09. *Study:* Harvard Col, AB(art), 33; Art Career Sch, 51-53; Art Students League, 55; New York Univ, MA(art educ), 56; NY State Teachers Col, New Paltz. *Work:* ABN Bank. *Exhib:* Bodley Gallery, 61; Nat Arts Club, 65-69; Lynchburg Art Ctr, 69; Burke Rehabilitation Ctr, White Plains, NY, 80; Town of Greenburgh, NY, 81; Twilight Artist, Twilight Park, Haines Falls, NY; Nat Arts Club, New York; and others. *Teaching:* Instr art, New York Pub Schs, 56-60. *Awards:* Art Comt Award in Oil Painting, Nat Arts Club, 76. *Mem:* Composers, Authors & Artists New York (past pres); Burr Artists; Eleanor Gay Lee Gallery Found, New York (past pres). *Media:* Watercolor, Oil; Wood, Acrylic. *Interests:* Architectural and landscape subjects; construction of 1 1/2 ton sailing model of English historic galleon of 1610. *Mailing Add:* 22 E 29th St New York NY 10016

MCKIE, TODD STODDARD
PAINTER
b Boston, Mass, Apr 25, 44. *Study:* RI Sch Design, BFA(painting), 66. *Work:* Philip Morris, USA; Mass Inst Technol; Fogg Mus, Cambridge, Mass; Lincoln Ctr for the Performing Arts & Chase Manhattan Bank, New York; Mus Fine Arts & Wellington Mgt Co, Boston, Mass. *Comn:* Mural (90ft x 40ft), City of Boston, 72. *Exhib:* Eat Art, Contemp Art Ctr, Cincinnati, Ohio, 72; Boston Collects Boston, Mus Fine Arts, 73; Works on Paper, Fogg Art Mus, Harvard Univ, Cambridge, Mass, 74; Biennial Exhib, Whitney Mus Am Art, New York, 75; Painted in Boston, Inst of Contemp Art, 75; Boston Watercolor Today, Mus Fine Arts, Boston, 76; Collectors Collect Contemporary, Inst Contemp Art, Boston, 77; Rose Art Mus, Brandeis Univ, 90. *Awards:* Colman Award, Blanche E Colman Found, 72; Creative Artists Fel, Mass Arts & Humanities Found, 74 & 89. *Bibliog:* Carl Belz (auth), The grid and the buffet, Art Am, 3/72; David Greenberg (auth), Big art, Running Press, Philadelphia, 77. *Media:* Oil, Ceramics. *Dealer:* Helander Gallery W Broadway New York NY; Barbara Singer Fine Art 18 Sparks St Cambridge MA 02138. *Mailing Add:* 117R Magazine St Cambridge MA 02139

MCKIM, WILLIAM WIND
PRINTMAKER, PAINTER
b Independence, Mo, May 13, 16. *Study:* Kansas City Art Inst, with Thomas Hart Benton & John S DeMartelly. *Work:* William Rockhill Nelson Gallery; Kansas City Art Inst. *Comn:* Wildlife panorama, Kansas City Mus, 62; lithograph, Mid-America Art Asn; lithograph, Print Soc, Nelson Gallery, 84. *Exhib:* Art of Two Cities, Kansas City & Minneapolis, 66; one-man show, Kansas City Art Inst & Albrecht Gallery, St Joseph, Mo, 67-68; 10 Missouri Painters Traveling Exhib, 68-69; Mid Am Artists Exhib, St Louis & Kansas City, 68 & 70; Printmakers Traveling Exhib, 69. *Teaching:* Instr drawing, Kansas City Art Inst, 45-48, instr lithography, 48-58, prof lithography, 58-86; retired. *Awards:* D M Lighton Award, Midwestern Ann, Kansas City, 40; New York State Fair Award. *Media:* Lithography; Tempera. *Mailing Add:* 8704 E 32nd St Kansas City MO 64129

MCKINLEY-HAAS, MARY
PAINTER, DESIGNER
b St Louis, Mo. *Study:* Smith Col, AB; studied at Art Students League with Norman Lewis; studied at Nat Acad Design with Robert Phillip. *Work:* Fontbonne Col, St Louis; Piermont Mills, New York; Northern Trust, Naples, Fla. *Exhib:* Solo exhibs, Tarlowe Gallery, Westhampton Beach, NY, 74, Fontbonne Col Gallery, St Louis, 77, Gallery Yssa (Ludlow-Hyland), New York, 79 & 81, Vered Int Gallery, E Hampton, NY, 81 & Netherlands Bank, New York, Univ Tex, Austin, 88 & 92, RVS Fine Art, Southampton, NY, 90, TSS Gallery, New York, 92; Parrish Art Mus, Southampton, NY, 75 & 78; Water Mill Mus, NY, 83; Vered Gallery, E Hampton, NY, 85; Nabisco Brands Gallery, E Hanover, NJ, 89; Queens Col Art Ctr, Flushing, NY, 91. *Pos:* Head, Costume Design Dept, ABC-TV, New York, 68-73; costume designer, CBS-TV, New York, 75-77. *Bibliog:* Carol Huneke (auth), Union exhib captures beauty of Southeast, Daily Texan, 9/21/88; Robert Long (auth), Perspectives, Southampton Press, 6/7/90; Christine Lyons (auth), Honoring the artists of the Hamptons: Mary McKinley-Hass, Davis Papers, 6/1/90. *Mem:* Women in the Arts; United Scenic Artists. *Media:* Oil, Mixed Media; Monotype. *Publ:* Auth, articles, in: Women in the Arts Newslett, 84-86. *Dealer:* RVS Fine Art 24 Job's Lane Southampton NY 11968. *Mailing Add:* 280 Lafayette St New York NY 10012

MCKINNEY, DONALD
DEALER
b New York, NY, May 2, 31. *Study:* Columbia Univ, 54-57; London Univ, 60-62. *Pos:* Pres, Marlborough Gallery, New York, 74-78; dir, Hirschl & Adler Mod Galleries, 81- *Specialty:* American and European contemporary art. *Publ:* Contribr, Jackson Pollack Catalogue Raisonne, Yale Univ Press, 78; coauth, Mark Rothko, Kunsthaus Zurich, 71. *Mailing Add:* c/o Hirschl & Adler Mod Galleries 851 Madison Ave New York NY 10021

MCKINNEY, TATIANA LADYGINA
PAINTER, INSTRUCTOR
b Smolensk, Russia; US citizen. *Study:* Acad Vinogradov, Riga, Latvia, cert, 30; Escola Nacional de Belas Artes, Brazil, 45-48; New Col Fine Arts Inst, Sarasota, Fla, with Balcomb Greene, James Brook & Marca Relli, cert, 67. *Work:* Dartmouth Col, Hanover, NH; The Apostolic Delegation, Washington, DC; The Vatican Collection; New Col Art Gallery & Fine Arts Soc, Van Wezel Hall, Sarasota, Fla. *Comn:* Painted mural hanging, Chapel, St Francis Seminary, Milwaukee, Wis; painted mural hanging, comn by Archdiocese of Washington, DC and presented to Pope John Paul II; painted mural hanging, comn by Bishop Nevins, Venice, Fla; painted mural hanging, St Martha's Church, Sarasota, Fla. *Exhib:* Salao Nacional de Belas Artes, Mus Nacional, Rio de Janeiro, Brazil, 55; Florida Arts Invitational, Cummer Gallery Art, Jacksonville, 66; Four Arts National Exhibit, Four Arts Soc, West Palm Beach, Fla, 66; Florida Arts Invitational, Lowe Art Mus, Univ Miami, Coral Gables, Fla, 68; XIII Salon International, Mus d'Art Contemp, Clermont-Ferrand, France, 81; Invitee d'Honneur, Salon International, Palais des Beaux Arts, Charleroi, Belg, 86; Kobi Mus, Japan, 89; Cyipros & Totaumtue, 92. *Pos:* Prog dir, Venice Area Art League, Fla, 68-71. *Teaching:* Instr art & painting, Venice Area Art League, Fla, 68-, Paul VI Inst, Washington, DC, 81-83, artist in residence, 50-91. *Awards:* Bronze Medal, Salao Nacional de Belas Artes, Mus Nacional, Rio de Janeiro, Brazil, 55; Best of Show, Arts Coun Southwest Fla, Edison Col, 70. *Bibliog:* Article, Tatiana McKinney at Interchurch, About Town Column, New Yorker Mag, 7/24/79; Father Thomas F Fait, Painting to be exhibited, Catholic Standard, 11/11/82; Monseignor Michael Farina, Tatiana McKinney, 11/82 & Tatiana McKinney does it again, 85, Paul VI Inst Lett. *Mem:* Artists Equity; Fla Artists Group; Venice Area Art League (vpres, bd mem, 65-70); Sarasota Fine Arts Coun (bd mem, 66-72); Nat Asn Am Pen Women. *Media:* Oil, Acrylics with Metal Leaf. *Dealer:* Paul VI Inst Arts Washington DC 20036. *Mailing Add:* 409 Darling Drive Venice FL 33595

MCKINNICKINNICK, MARGARET I
PAINTER, PRINTMAKER
b Marlboro, Mass, Feb 2, 24. *Study:* Silvermine Guild Sch Art; lithography with Hiroshima Morimoto, Westbeth Workshop, New York. *Work:* Town Hall, Westport, Conn; City Hall & Norwalk Community Col, Norwalk, Conn; Gen Elec Co, Fairfield, Conn; Silvermine Ctr Arts; Dorems & Co, New York. *Comn:* Etching, Friends Silvermine Ctr Arts, 80. *Exhib:* One-man shows, Vassos Gallery, Silvermine Guild Calleries, New Canaan, Conn, 82 & 86, Art Place Gallery, Southport, 83 & 85, Fairfield Pub Libr, 84, Conn Gallery, Marlbouough, 90 & Cast Iron Gallery, New York, 91-92; Hampshire Col Gallery, Amherst, Mass, 81; Works on Paper, Adelphi Univ, Garden City, Long Island, 81; New England Watercolor Soc Exhib, Mus of Art, Sci & Indus, Bridgeport, 82 & 89; Trustee's Choice, Aldrich Mus, 83; In the Family, Lyman Allyn Mus, New London, 84; Adelphi Univ Manhattan Ctr, New York, 90. *Teaching:* Instr art, Mus Mod Art, New York, 65-69, Calhoun Sch, New York, 70-75 & Sacred Heart Univ, 81-84. *Awards:* Print Award, Berkshire Mus, Pittsfield, Mass, 81. *Bibliog:* Russell Jinishian (auth), Artist lays it on the line, Bridgeport Sunday Post, 9/25/83. *Mem:* Silvermine Guild Ctr Arts (mem bd trustees, 78-81); Westport-Weston Coun Arts; Art Place, Southport, Conn. *Media:* Acrylic, Oil; Etching. *Mailing Add:* 42 Maple Lane Greens Farms CT 06436

MACKINTOSH, SANDRA
SCULPTURE, COLLAGE ARTIST
b Detroit, Mich, July 2, 44. *Work:* Guggenheim Mus; Brooklyn Mus, NY; Newark Mus, NJ; Hood Mus, Dartmouth Col, NH; Goldman Sachs, New York. *Exhib:* Constructed Sculpture in Wood, Brooklyn Mus, 92. *Media:* Wood. *Dealer:* Cordier & Ekstrom 417 E 75th St New York NY 10021. *Mailing Add:* 396 Joy Rd Woodstock NY 12498

MCKNIGHT, THOMAS FREDERICK
PAINTER, PRINTMAKER
b Lawrence, Kans, Jan 13, 41. *Study:* Wesleyan Univ, Middletown, Conn, BA(art); Columbia Univ. *Work:* Davison Art Ctr, Wesleyan Univ; New York State Mus, Albany; Smithsonian Inst, Washington, DC; Metrop Mus Art, New York. *Comn:* Paster & print, US Constitution Bicentennial, 89; prints, America's Cup, 92; paintings & prints, Urban Fair, Kobe, Japan, 93. *Exhib:* One-man shows, Basel Art Fair, 75-77, Tomic Galerie, Dusseldorf, Ger, 76, Hartmann Gallery, Munich, Ger, 77 & Newport Art Asn, RI, 81; Graphic Biennial, Llubljana, Yugoslavia, 81; Seibu, Tokyo, Japan, 89; Davison Art Ctr, Weslyan Univ, 88; and many others. *Bibliog:* Thomas McKnight's World, A Vision of Earthly Happiness, Abbeville Press, NY, 87; Thomas McKnight: Windows on Paradise, (introd by Annie Gottleib), Abbeville Press, NY, 90; Thomas McKnight, Treville Press, Tokyo, 90. *Media:* Casein; Serigraphy. *Mailing Add:* c/o Chalk & Vermilion Fine Arts Ltd 200 Greenwich Ave Greenwich CT 06830

MCKOY, VICTOR GRAINGER
SCULPTOR
b Fayetteville, NC, Apr 21, 47. *Study:* Clemson Univ, BS(biology), 70, Sch of Archit, two years. *Work:* Charleston Mus, SC; Ward Found Mus, Salisbury State Col, Md; Gibbes Art Gallery, Charleston, SC. *Exhib:* Birds of the Wood, Am Mus Nat Hist, 74; Expressions of Nature in Art, Greenville Mus Art, SC, 75 & Columbia Mus Art, SC, 75; Bird Sculpture Birmingham Mus Art, Ala, 76; The Artist and the Animal, High Mus Art, Atlanta, Ga, 77; Wild America, Kodak Gallery, New York, 78; one-man show, Hammer Galleries, New York, 76, Gibbes Art Gallery, SC, 84 & Coe Kerr Gallery, NY, 84; Birds in Art, Leigh Yawkey Woodson Art Mus, 85. *Bibliog:* Rodger Schroder (auth), Grainger McKoys carved birds, Fine Wood Working Mag; Pat Robertson (auth), Oyster House connection, Sporting Classics Mag, 9/83; Thomas Hoving (auth), My Eye, Connoisseur Mag, 2/85. *Media:* Wood and oil paint. *Mailing Add:* Rt 3 Box 278 Sumter SC 29154

MCLAUGHLIN, JEAN WALLACE
ADMINISTRATOR, CONSULTANT
b Charlotte, NC, Dec 19, 50. *Study:* Univ NC, Chapel Hill with George Kageris, BA, 72, Calif Col Arts & Crafts, with Lia Cook, 83-85, Penland Sch with Diane Itter, 86, NC State Univ, Sch Design, 87-88, Grad Sch, 90- *Exhib:* Subtext, NC Mus Art, Raleigh, 89. *Pos:* Prog dir, Arts & the Handicapped Prog, NC Dept of Admin, 78- 79; visual arts dir, NC Arts Coun, 79-82 & 85-; contrib ed, Sculptor's Int, 82-85. *Mem:* Am Crafts Coun; Am Mus Coun; New Langton Arts (bd mem, 83-85); Nat Asn Artists Orgn; NC World Ctr (coun mem, 88-). *Publ:* Auth, Art in the Churches & Synagogues of NC, NC Dept Cult Resources, 76; interview with Magdalena Abakanowicz & Understanding in contemporary craft movement, interview with Carl Djerassi, Sculpture Mag, 85; ed, New Works: A Public Art Project Planning Guide (Patricia Fuller, auth), Durham Arts Coun, 88. *Mailing Add:* 600 N Boundary St Raleigh NC 27604

MCLEAN, JAMES ALBERT
EDUCATOR, PRINTMAKER
b Gibsland, La, Nov 25, 28. *Study:* Southwestern La Inst, AB, 50; Southern Methodist Univ, BD, 53; Tulane Univ, MFA with J L Steg, 61. *Work:* Seattle Mus Art, Wash; The High Mus, Atlanta, Ga; Brooklyn Mus, NY; Olivet Col, Mich; Minot State Col, ND. *Exhib:* 33rd, 35th, 36th & 38th Northwest Printmakers Int, Seattle Mus, Wash, 62, 64, 65 & 67; 14th, 15th, 19th & 20th Nat Print Exhibs, Brooklyn Mus, 64, 66, 74 & 76; Nat Print & Drawing Exhibs, Minot State Col, 73-76; Colorprint, USA, Tex Tech Univ, Lubbock, 74-76; Spec Interest Group on Computer Graphics, 88; Postive/Negative Exhib, E TennState Univ, 88; Small Print Exhib, Purdue Univ, 88; SIGGRAPH, 88, 89; Artware, Cebit, Hanover, WGer, 89. *Teaching:* Assoc prof gen art, LaGrange Col, Ga, 63-66; prof printmaking, Ga State Univ, Atlanta, 66- *Awards:* Purchase Award, Northwest Printmakers Int, 64, Western NMex Univ Nat Print Exhib, 73 & Minot State Col Nat Print & Drawing Exhib, 76; First prize, Glassboro State Col, 90. *Bibliog:* Illus in: Fritz Eichenberg (auth), The Art of the Print, Abrams, 76, Gene Baro (auth), 30 Years of American Printmaking, Brooklyn Mus. *Media:* Silkscreening. *Dealer:* Heath Gallery 416 E Paces Ferry Atlanta GA 30305. *Mailing Add:* 1256 Dunwoody Knoll Dr Dunwoody GA 30338

MCLEAN, RICHARD THORPE
PAINTER, EDUCATOR
b Hoquiam, Wash, Apr 12, 34. *Study:* Calif Col Arts & Crafts, BFA, 58; Mills Col, MFA, 62. *Work:* Guggenheim Mus, New York; Mus Boymans-Van Beuningen, Rotterdam; Whitney Mus Am Art, New York; Va Mus Fine Arts, Richmond; Utrecht Mus, Holland. *Exhib:* 22 Realists, Whitney Mus Am Art, 70; Sharp Focus Realism, Sidney Janis Gallery, New York, 72; Documenta 5, Kassel, Ger, 72; Working in Calif, Albright-Knox Art Gallery, Buffalo, NY, 72; Tokyo Biennale, 74; New-Photo Realism, Wadsworth Atheneum, Hartford, Conn, 74; Contemp Images in Watercolor, Akron Art Inst, Ohio, 76; Painting & Sculpture in Calif: The Mod Era, San Francisco Mus Mod Art & Smithsonian Inst, 76; Thirty Yrs of Am Art, 1945-1975, Whitney Mus Am Art, New York, 77; and many others. *Teaching:* Prof painting & drawing, San Francisco State Univ, 63- *Awards:* Nat Endowment Arts, 86. *Bibliog:* Alwynne Mackie (illusr), New realism and the photographic look, Am Art Rev, 11/78; Christine Lindey (illusr), Superrealist Painting & Sculpture, William Morrow & Co, 80; Louis K Meisel (auth), Photorealism, Harry N Abrams, 80. *Media:* Oil, Watercolor. *Dealer:* O K Harris Works of Art 383 W Broadway New York NY 10012. *Mailing Add:* 5840 Heron Dr Oakland CA 94618

MCLEOD, STEPHEN
EDUCATOR, CRITIC
b Dallas, Tex, Dec 17, 57. *Collections Arranged:* Morris Louis Mem Exhib, 63, Francis Bacon, 63 & Int Award Exhib, Guggenheim Mus; Barnett Newman: The Stations of the Cross, 66; Jean Dubuffet, 66. *Pos:* Art ed, Sheep Meadow Press, 83-84; The Nation, 68-80; asst ed, Art R Bowker, New York, 88-89. *Teaching:* Instr, Methodist Univ; prof art, Columbia Univ, New York; prof iconography, St Joseph's Sem, Dunwoodie, 91- *Awards:* Foreign Leader Grant, US State Dept, 68. *Res:* 20th century American art and art criticism. *Publ:* Auth, The Venice Biennale 1895-1978, 78. *Mailing Add:* St Joseph's Sem Seminary Ave Yonkers NY 10704

MCMAHON, JAMES EDWARD
DEALER
b New York, NY, Jan 1, 37. *Study:* Hofstra Col, BA. *Pos:* Owner, Gallery Madison 90, currently. *Specialty:* American art of the 19th and 20th centuries; American illustrators. *Mailing Add:* 514 E 88th New York NY 10128

MCMANUS, JAMES WILLIAM
SCULPTOR, GALLERY DIRECTOR
b Glenwood Springs, Colo, Jan 1, 42. *Study:* Colo State Univ, BFA, 65; Univ Washington, MFA, 67. *Work:* Oakland Art Mus; San Diego Art Mus, Calif; Reading Art Ctr, Eng; Henry Art Mus, Univ Washington; 3M Corp, Chicago. *Comn:* Expo '74, Spokane, Wash; Admin Bldg, Wash State Hwy Comn, Olympia; Electro-Develop Corp, Seattle. *Exhib:* Six-man traveling exhib, Brit Art Coun, 73-75; Allrich Gallery, San Francisco, 77; Selected Works 1967-1977, de Saisset Mus, Univ Santa Clara, Calif, 77; Calif State Univ, Fresno, 77; Allrich Gallery, San Francisco, 79; Oakland Art Mus, 81. *Collections Arranged:* California Realism, 19th & 20th Century Comparison, 78; Mel Ramos, 79; Stanton Macdonald Wright, 80; Adja Yunkers, 80; Rodin's Burghers of Calais, 81; Alice Hutchins Survey, 82. *Teaching:* Teaching asst, Univ Wash, 67, instr art, 67-68; prof art & gallery dir, Calif State Univ, Chico, 68-; vis prof art, High Wycombe Col Art, Eng, 71-72. *Awards:* Fac Res Grant, Calif State Univ, Chico, 69; Fulbright-Hays Grant, Eng, 72. *Bibliog:* John Marlowe (auth), article, Current Art Mag, 6/75; James W McManus (30 min video tape), Calif State Univ, Chico, 77; Kevin Star (auth), article, San Francisco Examiner, 11/18/79; and others. *Media:* Bronze, Steel, Aluminum. *Dealer:* Allrich Gallery 251 Post St San Francisco CA 94133. *Mailing Add:* Dept Art Calif State Univ Chico CA 95929-0820

MCMILLAN, CONSTANCE
PAINTER, ILLUSTRATOR
Study: Bennington Col, painting with Karl Knaths & sculpture with Simon Moselsio, BA, 46; Mills Col, painting with William Gaw & ceramic sculpture with Antonio Prieto, fel, 53-55, MA, 55. *Exhib:* Slusser Gallery, Univ Mich, Ann Arbor, 80; Pindar Gallery, New York, 85; Il Mercate Galleria, Milan, Italy, 86; Galleria 9, Cologne & Spe-resta Del Carline, Bologna, Italy, 86; solo exhibs, Cornerstone Gallery, Conn, 86-89, Atlantic Gallery, New York, 87 & Phoenix Gallery, New York, 89. *Teaching:* instr painting, design & art hist, Emma Willard Sch, Troy, NY, 52-53; instr painting & design, Angell Sch, Ann Arbor, 62-63. *Awards:* First Prize, Morris Gallery, New York, 56; Grad Fel, Mills Col, Calif. *Mem:* Ann Arbor Art Asn. *Media:* Oil, Gouache; Charcoal, Pastel. *Publ:* Illusr, Chikka, 62, Ponies for a King, 63, Reilly & Lee; illusr, Memory of a Large Christmas, Norton, 62; drawing reproduced record cover, Gateway Summer Sounds, Folkways Records, 82. *Dealer:* Phoenix Gallery 568 Broadway New York NY. *Mailing Add:* 2760 Heather Way Ann Arbor MI 48104

MCMILLAN, STEPHEN WALKER
PRINTMAKER, PHOTOGRAPHER
b Berkeley, Calif, Dec 21, 49. *Study:* Hornsey Col Art, London, Eng, 70-71; Univ Calif, Santa Cruz, AB, 72, BFA, 75. *Work:* Brooklyn Mus, NY; Achenbach Collection, San Francisco; Oakland Mus, Calif; Mem Mus, Petah-Tiqua, Israel; US Embassy, Tokyo, Japan; Portland Art Mus; Stanford Univ Libr, Palo Alto, Calif; and others. *Exhib:* US Info Agency Two Yr Traveling Exhib in 8 Japanese Cities, US Embassy, Tokyo, 77-78; 21st Nat Print Exhib, Brooklyn Mus, 78; 17th Bradley Nat Print & Drawing Exhib, Lakeview Mus, Peoria, Ill, 79; 31st Ann Boston Printmakers Exhib, De Cordova Mus, Lincoln, Mass, 79; New Aquisitions, Achenbach Collection, San Francisco, 80; Fourth Miami Int Print Biennial, Metrop Mus, Miami, Fla, 80. *Awards:* Purchase Awards, San Francisco Art Comn, 78, Davidson Gallery, Seattle, Wash, 78 & Los Angeles Printmaking Soc, 78. *Mem:* Calif Soc Printmakers. *Media:* Etching, Lithograph. *Mailing Add:* 1525 Arlington Blvd El Cerrito CA 94530

MCMILLEN, MICHAEL C(HALMERS)
ENVIRONMENTAL ARTIST, SCULPTOR
b Los Angeles, Calif, Apr 6, 46. *Study:* Calif State Univ, Northridge, BA; Univ Calif, Los Angeles, MA & MFA. *Work:* Australian Nat Gallery, Canberra; Art Gallery New South Wales, Australia; Los Angeles Co Mus Art; Oakland Mus, Calif; Guggenheim Mus, New York. *Exhib:* Eight Artists from Los Angeles, San Francisco Art Inst, Calif, 75; Sounds: Environments by Four

Artists, Newport Harbor Art Mus, Newport Beach, Calif, 75; Biennial of Sydney, Art Gallery New South Wales, Australia, 76; Los Angeles in the 70s, Ft Worth Art Mus, Tex, 77; one-man shows, Inner City, Los Angeles Co Mus, Los Angeles, 77 & Whitney Mus Am Art, New York, 78; Eight Artists: The Elusive Image, Walker Art Ctr, Minneapolis, 79; Art in Los Angeles-The Museum as Site, Los Angeles Co Mus, 81; New Perspectives in American Art: Exxon Nat Exhib, Guggenheim Mus, 83; 38th Corcoran Biennial: Exhibition of American Painting, Corcoran Gallery Art, 83. *Teaching:* Lectr at var inst, 74- *Awards:* travel grant, Biennale of Sydney, Australia Coun, 76; Nat Endowment Arts Fel, 78; Young Talent Award, Los Angeles Co Mus Art, 78. *Bibliog:* Melinda Wortz (auth), Inner City of the Mind, Art News, 2/78; Christopher Knight (auth), Some recent art and archit analogue, Los Angeles Inst Contemp Art J, 2/78; Christopher Knight (auth), Michael C McMillen, Arts & Archit, Fall 81. *Publ:* Auth, True confessions, Los Angeles Inst Contemp Art J, 75; contribr, Choke, Choke Publ, 76; auth, Special effects breakdown, Los Angeles Inst Contemp Art J, 77. *Mailing Add:* c/o Barry Whistier 2909 A Canton Gallery Dallas TX 75226

MCMULLAN, JAMES BURROUGHS
ILLUSTRATOR, GRAPHIC ARTIST
b Tsingtao, China, June, 14, 34; US citizen. *Study:* Cornish Art Sch, Seattle, Wash; Pratt Inst, New York, BFA, 58. *Work:* Libr Cong, Washington, DC. *Exhib:* Push Pin Retrospective, The Louvre, Paris, France, 70; Century of American Illustration, Brooklyn Mus, NY, 72; Maps Show, Mus Natural Hist, New York, NY, 77; International Poster Biennale, Polish Mus, Warsaw, 84; World's Most Memorable Posters, UNESCO, Grand Palais, Paris, 86; Five Masters of the Contemporary Poster, Lowell Gallery, New York, 87; solo exhibs, Giraffics Gallery, East Hampton, New York, 88 & Margo Feiden Gallery, New York, NY, 88; Art of Illustration Show, Headley-Whitney Mus, Lexington, Ky, 88; Twenty Best American Illustrators, Seoul, Repub Korea, 88. *Pos:* Illusr, Push Pin Studios, New York, NY, 65-68. *Teaching:* Instr illus, Sch Visual Arts, New York, NY, 71-84, instr drawing, 82-, master degree prof, 84-85. *Awards:* Gold Medal, 81, Hamilton King Award, 87 & Silver Medal, 88, Soc Illusrs; ANDY Award, Advert Club New York, 88. *Bibliog:* Richard Coyne (auth), James McMullan, Communication Arts Mag, 5-6/74; Michael Patrick Hearn (auth), The Art of the Broadway Poster, Ballantine Bks, 80; Ko Noda (dir), The Art of James McMullan, Van Gough Video, 83; S Chwast & S Heller (ed), The Art of New York, 84; S Heller (auth), Innovators of American Illustration, Van Nostrand Reinhold, 86; My life in the theater, Print Mag, 5/6/88. *Mem:* Am Inst Graphic Arts (dir, 74-76, vpres, 76-77); Soc Illusrs; Am Illus (adv bd, 85-). *Media:* Watercolor. *Publ:* Ed, Realism in illustration, 2/78 & auth, New York neighborhoods: A student project, 78, Print Mag; auth, Revealing Illustrations, Watson-Guptill, 81; The Gant ad, How Mag, 1/85; Realism and design, Am Inst Graphic Arts J, 85. *Mailing Add:* 222 Park Ave S Apt 10B New York NY 10003

MCNALLY, SHEILA JOHN
EDUCATOR, HISTORIAN
b New York, NY, Dec 10, 32. *Study:* Vassar Col, BA; Univ London; Univ Kiel; Univ Munich; Harvard Univ, PhD, 65. *Pos:* Prin investr, Excavations Diocletian's Palace, Split, Yugoslavia, 68-; dir, Excavations, Akhmim, Egypt, 78- *Teaching:* Prof art hist, Univ Minn, Minneapolis, currently. *Awards:* Fulbright Res Grants, Ger, 53-54 & Yugoslavia, 67-68. *Mem:* Col Art Asn (bd dirs, 75-79); Midwest Art Hist Soc; Archaeol Inst Am; Libyan Soc; Women's Archaeol Caucus. *Res:* Late Roman art. *Mailing Add:* 124 SE Bedford St SE Minneapolis MN 55414

MCNAMARA, JOHN
PAINTER
b Cambridge, Mass, Feb 16, 50. *Study:* Mass Col Art, BFA(painting), 71, MFA(painting), 77. *Work:* Mus Fine Arts, Boston; Rose Art Mus, Brandeis Univ; Metrop Mus Art, New York; Honolulu Acad Fine Art; Visual Art Ctr MIT, Cambridge, Mass. *Exhib:* Rose Art Mus, Waltham, Mass, 78; Boston Now, Inst Contemp Art, Boston, 81-83; one-man show, Exhib Space, New York, 82, Stavaridis Gallery, Boston, 83-85, 87 & 89, & Bess Cutler Gallery, New York, 84-86; Tucson Mus Contemp Art, Ariz, 92. *Teaching:* Instr, Mass Col Art & San Francisco Art Inst. *Awards:* Mass Arts & Humanities Grant, 80-83, 86, & 89; Nat Endowment Arts Fel, 81; Awards in Visual Arts II Fel, 82. *Bibliog:* Theodore Wolff (auth), The home forum, Christian Sci Monitor, 4/7/83; Nancy Stapen (auth), John McNamara, Art Forum, 1/88; David Bonetti (auth), John McNamara, Art News, 2/88. *Media:* Oil on Canvas. *Dealer:* Nina Nielsen Gallery Boston MA. *Mailing Add:* 1150 Sanchez St San Francisco CA 94114

MCNAMARA, MARY JO
HISTORIAN, EDUCATOR
b Troy, NY, Jan 23, 50. *Study:* Vassar Col, AB, 72; Stanford Univ, MA, 75, PhD, 83. *Pos:* Cur, Vassar Col Art Gallery, 76-78. *Teaching:* Instr art hist, Vassar Col, Poughkeepsie, NY, 76-78; lectr, Univ Wis-Milwaukee, 78-79; instr, Oberlin Col, Ohio, 79-80; acting asst prof, Univ Calif, Irvine, 80-83; vis asst prof, Univ Calif, Riverside, 84; asst prof, Wayne State Univ, 84- *Awards:* Cantor-Fitzgerald res grant, 75-76. *Mem:* Col Art Asn. *Res:* Modern Art. *Publ:* Coauth, Rodin's Burghers of Calais, The Cantor-Fitzgerald Group, Los Angeles, 77. *Mailing Add:* 1451 Bennaville Birmingham MI 48009

MCNAMARA, WILLIAM PATRICK, JR
PAINTER, PRINTMAKER
b Shreveport, La, Sept 3, 46. *Study:* Centenary Col La, BA, 69; NMex Highlands Univ, MA, 72. *Work:* Centenary Col La; First Nat Bank, Shreveport, La; Ark Art Ctr, Little Rock; Springfield Art Mus; Phillips Petroleum Co, Tulsa, Okla. *Exhib:* Delta Art Exhib, Ark Arts Ctr, Little Rock, 80 & 84-88; Watercolor USA, 80 & 82-87 & A View from the Mountain, 89, Springfield Art Mus, Mo; Butler Inst Am Art, 82 & 83; Rocky Mountain Nat Watermedia Exhib, Foothills Art Ctr, Golden, Colo, 85; Watercolor West Nat, Riverside Nat Mus, Redlands, Calif, 85; Nat Watercolor Soc, Brea, Calif, 87 & 91; Watercolor Retrospective, Ark Arts Ctr, Little Rock, 89. *Teaching:* Instr drawing & composition, Centenary Col La, 73-76. *Awards:* Award Merit, Watercolor USA, Springfield Art Mus, Mo, 80; SMMA Purchase Award, The Monumental Image, Springfield Art Mus, Mo, 86; Binney-Smith Award, Nat Watercolor Soc, Brea, Calif, 87. *Bibliog:* M Stephen Doherty (auth), Watercolor today: Ten contemporary artists, Am Artist, 2/83; Elizabeth B Leonard (auth), Painting the Landscape, 84 & Mary Suffudy (ed), Sketches Techniques, 85, Wastson-Guptill; Dan Morris (auth), McNamara Ventures into Monumentalism, Ark Gazette, 6/86; Donald Harrington (auth), Songs of sunlight & water, Ark Times, 7/89. *Mem:* Watercolor USA Honor Soc; Nat Watercolor Soc. *Media:* Watercolor. *Publ:* Auth, Watercolor page, Am Artist, 5/83. *Dealer:* Capricorn Galleries 4849 Rugby Ave Bethesda MD 20814; M A Doran Gallery 3509 S Peoria Tulsa OK. *Mailing Add:* HC-33 Box 52 Pettigrew AR 72752

MCNARY, OSCAR L
PAINTER, COLLECTOR
b San Antonio, Tex, Mar 23, 44. *Study:* San Antonio Jr Col, Tex; Tex Southern Univ; Southern Methodist Univ; Warren Hunter's Sch Art. *Exhib:* Ninth Biennial, Five State Art Exhib, Port Arthur, Tex, 87; Galerie Gorpal Invitational, Dallas, Tex, 88; 45th Ann Painting Competition, Abilene Fine Arts Mus, 89; Beverly Gordon Gallery Invitational exhib, 89 & 90; Tex Watercolor Soc Exhib, San Antonio, Tex, 86; and many others. *Awards:* Mixed Media First Place Award, Waco Art Ctr, 84; Purchase Award, Dallas City Hall, Tex, 85; Best of Show Award, Art Community Ctr, Corpus Christi, 78; and many others. *Bibliog:* Article, Art Voices South, 9-10/80. *Media:* Acrylic, Oil. *Mailing Add:* PO Box 832627 Richardson TX 75083

MCNEALY, ROBERT
PAINTER, SCULPTOR
Study: Cornish Sch Appl Arts, Seattle, 61-62; Idaho State Univ, 68; York Univ, Toronto, MFA, 85. *Work:* Art Gallery Ont & York Univ, Toronto; Jan Van Eyck Acad, Maastricht, Netherlands; Munic Van Reekum Gallery Mod Art, Apeldoorn, Netherlands. *Comn:* Church Facade and Stations of The Cross, St Matthews Church, Pocatello, Idaho, 66. *Exhib:* Four Painters, Art Gallery Ont, Toronto, 79; Vestiges of Empire (with catalog), Camden Arts Ctr, London, 84; Drawing Installation, Saidye Bronfman Ctr, Montreal, 85; Fire and Ice, Binz 39, Zurich, 85; Active Surplus: The Economy of the Object (catalog), Power Plant, Toronto, New York, 87-88; Architettura: Astrazione, Robert McNealy, Bernie Miller & Elspeth Pratt (catalog), Sala Uno, Rome, Italy, 88; A Meeting, An exhib by Canadian & Dutch artists (catalog), Stichting Artichoc, Found Artichoc, Oss, Netherlands, 89. *Pos:* Founding mem Mercer Union Parallel Gallery (pres, 82-83). *Teaching:* Instr, Banff Ctr, Alta, 79; instr sculpture, York Univ, Toronto, 83-84; instr, Emely Carr Sch Art, Vancouver, BC, Canada, 88- *Awards:* Samuel C Sarrick Purchase Award, York Univ, 85. *Bibliog:* John Bentley Mays (auth), Installation reaffirms McNealy's strength, The Globe & Mail, 3/20/85. *Media:* Multi-Media Environmental. *Dealer:* S L Simpson Gallery 515 Queen St W Toronto ON M5V 2B4 Can. *Mailing Add:* c/o S L Simpson Gallery 515 Queen St W Toronto ON M5V 2B4 Canada

MCNEIL, DEAN S
SCULPTOR
b Geneva, Ill, 1957. *Study:* Antioch Col, Yellow Springs, Ohio, 75-79. *Exhib:* Physics, Piezo Electric Gallery, New York, 86; one-man shows, Utopia/Dystopia, Scott Hanson Gallery, 88, Call & Talk, Paula Allen Gallery, 89, Sculpture for the Dead, Scott Hanson Gallery, 90 & Pioneers of Safety, Univ Art Mus, Univ Calif, Santa Barbara, 91; group show, John Davis Gallery, New York, 88; Linda Cathcart Gallery, Santa Monica, 89 & 90; All Quiet on the Western Front?, Antoine Candau Gallery, Paris, 90; Outside America, Fay Gold Gallery, Atlanta, 91. *Awards:* Nat Endowment Arts, 88. *Bibliog:* Kim Levin (auth), The Village Voice, 5/16/86, 9/21/88. *Mailing Add:* 140 Sullivan St New York NY 10012

MCNEIL, GEORGE J
PAINTER, PRINTMAKER
b New York, NY, Feb 22, 08. *Study:* Pratt Inst, Brooklyn, 27-29; Art Students League, 30-31 & 32-33; Hans Hofmann Sch Fine Art, 33-36; Teachers Col, Columbia Univ, MA, 43, EdD, 52, Pratt Inst, DFA (hon), 85; Maryland Inst Col Art, DFA (hon), 88; Univ Hartford, DFA (hon), 90. *Work:* Mus Mod Art; Nat Mus, Havana, Cuba; Newark Mus Art; Walker Art Ctr, Minneapolis; Whitney Mus Am Art; Metrop Mus Art; Nat Mus Am Art; plus others. *Exhib:* Mus Mod Art, New York, 36, 51, 63-64 & 69; Whitney Mus Am Art Ann, 53, 57, 61 & 65, The 1930s, 68; US Info Agency Pan-Am Exhib, circulated Latin Am, 61-62; Pa Acad Fine Arts, 62; Wadsworth Atheneum, Hartford, Conn, 62; Art Inst Chicago, 63; plus many other group & one-man shows. *Awards:* Nat Coun Arts Award, 66; Guggenheim Fel, 69; Am Acad Arts & Lett Award, 82. *Mem:* Am Inst Acad Arts & Letter, 89. *Media:* Oil, Acrylic. *Mailing Add:* 195 Waverly Ave Brooklyn NY 11205

MACNEILL, FREDERICK DOUGLAS
PAINTER
b Boston, Mass, Sept 28, 29. *Study:* Vesper George Sch Art, 52-54, with Alphonse J Shelton, 69 & Arthur Safford, 70. *Work:* First Nat Bank, John Hancock Life Insurance Co & First Church Christ Scientist, Boston; Otis Elevator Co, New York; Raytheon Corp, Lexington, Mass. *Exhib:* Southern Vermont Art Ctr, Manchester, 82; solo exhibs, Guild Boston Artists, Mass,

82-84; Hudson Valley Art Asn, Westchester County Ctr, White Plains, NY, 85; Arts for the Parks, Jackson, Wyo, 91 & 92; Mystic Int Exhib, Conn, 92; and others. *Pos:* Instr, Needham Art Ctr, Mass, 83-83. *Awards:* Martin Hannon Mem Award, Salmagundi Club, 82; Elliot Liskin Award, 84, George O Davies Silver Medal, 85, Rockport Art Asn; Sigmond Koslow Memorial Award, 90; Peg Leg Award, 90. *Bibliog:* Article in Yankee Mag, 78; Print Catalogue, NY Graphic Soc Ltd, 84. *Mem:* Guild Boston Artists; Allied Artists Am; Am Artists Prof League; Rockport Art Asn; Hudson Valley Art Asn. *Media:* Oil, Watercolor. *Mailing Add:* 23 Dana Rd Concord MA 01742

MACNELLY, JEFFREY KENNETH
CARTOONIST, SCULPTOR
b New York, NY, Sept 17, 47. *Study:* Univ NC. *Pos:* Mem staff, Richmond News Leader, 70-81; creator, comic strip Shoe, currently; ed cartoonist, Chicago Tribune, 81- *Awards:* Pulitzer Prize as Editorial Cartoonist, 72, 78, & 85; Reuben Award, Nat Cartoonist Soc, 79 & 80. *Mem:* Am Asn Ed Cartoonists; Nat Cartoonists Soc. *Media:* India Ink, Watercolor; Bronze. *Publ:* Auth, MacNelly, The Pulitzer Prize Winning Cartoonist: a Specially Selected Collection, Westover, 72; Directions, Andrews McNeel, 83; eleven published collections of Shoe. *Mailing Add:* Tribune Media ServInc 64 E Concord St Orlando FL 32801

MCNICKLE, THOMAS GLEN
PAINTER
b New Castle, Pa, Oct 17, 44. *Study:* Edinboro State Col, BS(art), 66, MEd(studio), 72. *Work:* Butler Inst Am Art; Hoyt Inst Fine Art, New Castle, Pa. *Exhib:* Am Artists Prof League Grande Nat, New York, 82 & 83; Views of Youngstown, Butler Inst Am Art, 82; Audubon Artists Ann, Nat Arts Club, New York, 83, 84 & 85; Am Watercolor Soc Ann Exhib, 84; Watercolor USA, Springfield, Mo, 84 & 85. *Collections Arranged:* Forty Watercolors (auth, catalog), from collection Butler Inst Am Art, 82; Hoyt Nat Painting Show (auth, catalog), 84 & 85. *Teaching:* Instr art, Weshannock Twp Schs, New Castle, Pa, 66-; instr painting, Hoyt Inst Fine Art, New Castle, Pa, 66-; private workshops watercolors, 79- *Awards:* Award Excellence, Black Forest Inst, Exhib, 82; Second Prize Watercolor, Terrance Gallery Nat Exhib, 82; Ford Motor Co Fund Award, Mich Watercolor Soc Ann, 85. *Mem:* Nat Watercolor Soc; Pa Soc Watercolor Painters; Pittsburgh Watercolor Soc (bd dirs, 83); Knickerbocker Artists, New York. *Media:* Watercolor. *Mailing Add:* RD No 3 Volant PA 16156

MCOWEN, C LYNN
ART DEALER, COLLECTOR
b Long Beach, Calif, July 12, 53. *Study:* Calif State Univ, BA, 77; studied with Master Painter, People Republic China, 85-86; pvt study with Calvin J Goodman in Art Marketing. *Pos:* Dir graphics & printing, East End Arts & Humanities Coun, Childrens Inst Res & Design Ctr, 77-79; graphic illusr, State Univ NY, Stony Brook, 79-84. *Mem:* UCLA Art Coun. *Specialty:* Contemporary paintings, prints & drawings from the People's Republic of China. *Collection:* Variety of paintings, prints, drawings & sculpture done by contemporary artists from the People's Republic of China. *Dealer:* Mayoon Fine Asian Art 6409 W 6th St Los Angeles CA 90048. *Mailing Add:* 934 N Holliston Ave Pasadena CA 91104

MCOWEN, CAROL M
ART DEALER, COLLECTOR
b Denver, Colo, Dec 23, 27. *Study:* Private study with Calvin Goodman (art marketing), 88; Calif State Univ, Long Beach, MA(Chinese art hist). *Pos:* Owner, MAYOON, Fine Asian Art, South Pasadena, Calif. *Mem:* Long Beach Art Mus (mem Friends Coun, 80-88); Los Angeles Co Art Mus (docent, 82-84); Univ Calif Art Coun, Los Angeles; Metrop Mus Art. *Res:* Contemporary landscape painting in the Peoples' Republic of China: 1976-1986. *Specialty:* Fine Asian art, specializing in contemporary Chinese prints & paintings. *Collection:* Variety of contemporary paintings, drawings & prints from China. *Mailing Add:* 7326 S Marina Pacifica Long Beach CA 90803

MCPHERSON, BRUCE RICE
EDITOR, PUBLISHER
b Atlanta, Ga, Oct 12, 51. *Study:* Brown Univ, AB, 73; Annenberg Sch Commun, Univ Pa, 75. *Pos:* Ed & publ, McPherson & Co (Documentext, Treacle Press), 74- *Res:* Avant-Garde, 1958-present, principally United States, especially concerned with happenings, fluxus, performance art, cinematography and related areas. *Publ:* Ed, More than Meat Joy: Complete Performance Works and Selected Writings, by Carolee Schneemann, 79 & Something Else Press: An Annotated Bibliography, by Peter Frank, 82, Documentext. *Mailing Add:* PO Box 1126 Kingston NY 12401-0126

MACPHERSON, KEVIN
PAINTER
b New Jersey, Apr 9, 56. *Study:* N Ariz Univ, BFA, 78; Scottsdale Artists Sch, 86- *Exhib:* Plein Air Painters Am, 87, 88, 89, 90 & 91; Mesa Southwest Mus, 88; two-man show, Venture Fine Arts, Tucson, Ariz, 89 & 91; solo exhibs, Taos Art Gallery, NMex, 89, O'Brien's Art Emporium, Scottsdale, Ariz, 89 & 92; Taos, Impressionist Show, 89, 90, 91 & 92; Ctr Arts Southwest, Santa Fe, NMex, 90. *Teaching:* Taos Art Inst, 7/89; oil painting workshops, Scottsdale Artists' Sch, 90, 91, 92 & 93; Macpherson & Vinella workshop, 91 & 92. *Awards:* Best of Show, Amarillo Nat Landscape Competition, 87; Stacey Scholar, 90; Best Landscape, Oil Painters Am, 92. *Bibliog:* Artists' worth watching (article), Art Talk, 2/88; article, Art of the West, 11-12/88 & 11-12/89; Southwest Art, 11/89. *Mem:* Plein Air Painters Am; Spectrum; Oil Painters Am. *Media:* Oil. *Mailing Add:* Valle Escondido Box 55 Rt 1 Taos NM 87571

MCPHERSON, LARRY E
PHOTOGRAPHER, EDUCATOR
b Newark, Ohio, May 1, 43. *Work:* Mus Mod Art, New York; Art Inst Chicago & Exchange Nat Bank, Chicago, Ill; Int Mus Photog at George Eastman House, Rochester, NY; New Orleans Mus Art, La; Mus Fine Arts, Houston. *Exhib:* One-man shows, Art Inst Chicago, Ill, 69, 78 & 81; Vision and Expression, George Eastman House, Rochester, NY, 69; Mirrors & Windows, Mus Mod Art, New York, 78; Farbwerke, Kunsthaus Gallery, Zurich, Switz, 80; Contemp Am Color, Galerie Rudolf Kicken, Koln, Ger, 80; Color as Form: A History of Color Photography, Corcoran Gallery & George Eastman House, 82; The Nature of the Beast, Hudson River Mus, Yonkers, NY, 89; 1992 Trienial, New Orleans Mus Art, 92. *Teaching:* Assoc prof photog, Memphis State Univ, Tenn, 78. *Awards:* Nat Endowment Arts Fel Photog, 75 & 79; Guggenheim Fel Photog, 80. *Bibliog:* Nathan Lyons (auth), Vision and Expression, Horizon Press, 69; Candida Finkel (auth), review, Afterimage, 10/78; Elaine King (auth), article, Camera Mag, 80. *Mem:* Soc Photog Educ. *Dealer:* Kurts Bingham Gallery 766 S White Station Rd memphis TN 38117; A Gallery of Fine Photography 322 Royal St New Orlenas LA 70130. *Mailing Add:* Dept Art Memphis State Univ Memphis TN 38152

MCQUEEN, JOHN
CRAFTSMAN
b Champagne, Ill, 43. *Study:* Univ SFla, BA, 71; Tyler Sch Art, Temple Univ, Philadelphia, MFA, 75. *Work:* Cooper-Hewitt Mus, New York, NY; Minneapolis Inst Art; Philadelphia Mus Art; Renwick Gallery, Smithsonian Inst, Washington, DC; Wadsworth Atheneum, Hartford, Conn. *Exhib:* Recent Acquisitions, Philadelphia Art Mus, 79; The Art Fabric Mainstream, San Francisco Mus Mod Art, Calif, 81; The Art Fabric Mainstream, San Francisco Mus Mod Art, Calif, 81; solo exhibs, Kans City Art Inst, Mo, 83, Bellas Artes Gallery, Santa Fe, NMex, 87, Garth Clark Gallery, New York, 89 & Los Angeles, 90; Fiber R/Evolution Exhib, Milwaukee Art Mus, Wis, 85; Craft Today USA (with catalog), Mus de Arts Decoratifs, Paris, France, 89; Artful Objects: Recent American Crafts, Ft Wayne Art Mus, Ind, 89; The Vessel: Studies in Form and Media, Craft & Folk Art Mus, Los Angeles, Calif, 89; and others. *Awards:* Fels, Nat Endowment Arts, 77, 79 & 86; NY Found Arts, 88. *Bibliog:* Bill Hynes (ed), Crafts Symposium and Robert L Pfannebecker: Contemporary American Craft Exhibition, Shippensburg Univ, Pa, 89; Victoria Geibel (auth), The Evolving Basket, Metropolis, pp 68-73, 6/89; and others. *Publ:* Auth, Craft Today: Poetry of the Physical, Am Crafts Mus, 88; Poetry in the Round, Surface Design, pp 22-23, spring 89. *Mailing Add:* c/o Garth Clark Gallery 170 S La Brea Ave Los Angeles CA 90036

MCQUILLAN, FRANCES
PAINTER, INSTRUCTOR
b Chicago, Ill. *Study:* New York Sch Fine & Appl Art, dipl; Caldwell Col, BA; Art Students League; Fairleigh Dickinson Univ; Montclair Art Mus Adult Sch. *Exhib:* Conn Acad Fine Arts; Allied Artists Am; Expos Intercontinental Exhib, Dieppe, France & Monaco; Am Artists Prof League; Montclair Art Mus Exhib. *Pos:* Illusr, Peerless Fashions, New York, 32-37; freelance window display, New York, 38-39. *Teaching:* Instr drawing, watercolors, oils & acrylics, Montclair Art Mus, NJ, 50-; instr drawing, Montclair Adult Sch, 67-70; instr oil painting, Yard Sch Art, Montclair, 67-70 & 83. *Awards:* Silver Medal Oil Painting, Knickerbocker Artists, 53; First Prize Watercolors, Am Artists Prof League, 70; First Prize Oils, Art Ctr of NJ. *Mem:* NJ Watercolor Soc; Am Artists Prof League; Art Ctr of NJ. *Media:* All Media. *Mailing Add:* 3 Godfrey Rd Montclair NJ 07043

MCREYNOLDS, (JOE) CLIFF
PAINTER, INSTRUCTOR
b Amarillo, Tex, Jan 26, 33. *Study:* San Diego State Univ, BA, 59, MA, 60. *Work:* Chicago Art Inst. *Comn:* Portrait of pres, Mesa Col, San Diego, Calif, 75. *Exhib:* Drawings USA Traveling Exhib, Minn Mus Art, St Paul, 75; Alternative Realities, Mus Contemp Art, Chicago, Ill, 76; Calif Painting & Sculpture--the Modern Era, San Francisco Mus Mod Art, 76; Juried Drawing Exhib, Chicago Art Inst, 77; Fourth Triennial--India Traveling Exhib, New Delhi, 78 & Tokyo, Japan, 79; For God's Sake--Cliff McReynolds, San Jose Mus Art, Calif, 83; Downey Mus Art CA, 87; Venice Arts Festival Venice CA, 88; Biola Univ La Mirada CA, 88; SDTYAE and traveling, Yukohama, Japan, 92; others. *Pos:* Illusr, Psychol Today, 70-73, Esquire Mag, 73, Visions, 77 & Omni Mag, 78-79. *Teaching:* Instr drawing, Mesa Col, San Diego, 69- *Awards:* Best in Show, Del Mar Exhib, 63; Best in Show, All Calif Exhib, 63 & First Prize, Calif-Hawaii Regional, 72, Fine Arts Gallery, San Diego. *Bibliog:* Marilyn Hagberg (auth), McReynolds--sharp satirist, San Diego Mag, 2/67; Jan Jennings (auth), One man show on view, San Diego Union, 12/71; State of the Arts, Dr Gene Edward Veith Jr, 91. *Media:* Oil, Pencil. *Publ:* Auth, All Things New, Revelation Art, 80; Auth, Wonders of the Visible World, Critique of America 3/88. *Mailing Add:* 6311 Dowling Dr La Jolla CA 92037

MCREYNOLDS, KIRK See St Maur, Kirk (Kirk Seymour McReynolds)

MCSHEEHY, CORNELIA MARIE
PRINTMAKER, PAINTER
b Floral Park, New York, Aug 10, 47. *Study:* Mass Col Art, Boston, BFA, 69; State Univ NY, Albany, MA, 72. *Work:* Libr Cong, Washington, DC; Univ NDak, Grand Forks; State Univ NY, Potsdam; Minot State Col, NDak; Tex Tech Univ, Lubbock; Univ Okla, and others. *Exhib:* Print & Drawing Ann, Univ NDak, 72, 74, 77 & 83; Boston Printmakers, De Cordova Mus, Lincoln, Mass, 73; 18th Print Exhib, Brooklyn Mus, 73; Calif Palace Legion Honor,

San Francisco, 73; Print Exhib, Libr Cong, 75; Mus Fine Arts, Boston, 76; New American Graphics 2 & 3, Madison Art Ctr, 82-84; Printed by Women, Port Hist Mus, Philadelphia, 83; Solo exhibs, Cleveland State Univ, Ohio, 83, Providence Col, RI, 84, Gould Acad, Maine, 85 & Tokio Studios, Los Angeles, 86; Brit Int Print Biennial, WYorkshire, 86; Contemporary Am Prints, US Consulate, Leningrad, Russia, 86; Wild, Wild Wit, Boston, 87; Univ Conn, Storrs, 87; Cameron Univ, 88; SUNY-Albany, NY, 88. *Teaching:* Instr printmaking, Mass Col Art, Boston, 72-75; asst prof, Brown Univ, 76-77; prof, RI Sch Design, 77-, head printmaking prog, 79- *Awards:* Nat Endowment Arts Grant Printmaking, 75-76; Visual Artist Residency, MacDowell Colony, 83; Mellon Fac Res Grant, Polaroid Corp Grant, 85, 86, finalist, Mass Coun Arts, 87; numerous purchase awards in current nat and international exhib. *Bibliog:* Ross Romano (auth), The Collograph, 80. *Mem:* Boston Printmakers; Col Art Asn; Women's Caucus Art; MacDowell Colony Fel. *Media:* Printmaking, Multi Media. *Publ:* Contribr, Art Now, Inc, 76- *Mailing Add:* 48 Mt Vernon St Boston MA 02108

MCSHINE, KYNASTON LEIGH
CURATOR, CRITIC
b Port of Spain, Trinidad, Feb 20, 35. *Study:* Dartmouth Col, AB, 58; Univ Mich, 58-59; Inst Fine Arts, NY Univ, 60-64. *Collections Arranged:* Berlinart (auth, catalog), 61-87; Marcel Duchamp (auth, catalog), 73, Robert Rauschenberg, 77, Jackie Winsor (auth, catalog), 79 & Joseph Cornell, (auth, catalog), 80, Mus Mod Art, New York; Andy Warhol: Aretrospective (auth, catalog), 89; and others. *Pos:* Cur painting & sculpture, Jewish Mus, New York, 65-67, acting dir, 67-68; assoc cur painting & sculpture, Mus Mod Art, New York, 68-71, cur, 71-80, sr cur, 80- *Teaching:* Asst prof art hist, Hunter Col, New York, 68-69; lectr art hist, Sch Visual Arts, New York, 69-76. *Mem:* Trustee Hopkins Ctr, Hood Mus Art, Dartmouth Col; Int Asn Art Critics; Col Art Asn; Am Asn Mus; Century Asn; and others. *Publ:* Auth, Josef Albers: Homage to the Square, 64 & Information, 70, ed & contribr, Marcel Duchamp, 73, The Natural Paradise: Painting in America 1800-1950, 76, An International Survey of Recent Painting and Sculpture, 84, Mus Mod Art, New York; Primary structures, Jewish Mus, 66. *Mailing Add:* c/o Mus Mod Art, Dept Painting & Sculpture 11 W 53rd St New York NY 10019

MCTWIGAN, MICHAEL
CRITIC, EDITOR
b Lincoln, Nebr, July 9, 48. *Study:* Lake Forest Col, Ill, BA(anthrop), 71; Columbia Univ, postgrad studies, 76-77. *Pos:* Ed asst, Craft Horizons Mag, New York, 72 & 74-78; asst ed, Art Quart, Metrop Mus, New York, 78-79; sr ed, Watson-Guptill Publ, New York, 79-81; ed, Indust Design, New York, 82-83; ed, Am Ceramics Mag, New York, 82- *Awards:* Art Critics Fel, Nat Endowment Arts, 80. *Mem:* Decorative Arts Soc of Soc Archit Historians; Col Art Asn. *Res:* Post-World War II sculpture in the new craft media of clay, glass and fiber; architecture, decorative arts and portraiture. *Publ:* Auth, Heroes and Clowns (sculpture of Robert Arneson exhib catalog), Allan Frumkin Gallery, 79; William Daley: Duality in Clay, Am Craft, 80; First things first, 82 & The fruitful mysteries of Graham Marks, 82, Am Ceramics; An interior exchanges: Cynthia Carlson and Betty Woodman, Arts Mag, 82. *Mailing Add:* 51 Prospect Pl Brooklyn NY 11217

MCVEIGH, MIRIAM LENIG
CONCEPTUAL ARTIST, PAINTER
b Wabash, Ind. *Study:* Calif Col Arts & Crafts, BFA; Acad Goetz, Paris; also with Elmer Tafflinger, Clifton Wheeler & Eugen Neuhaus. *Work:* Mus Monbart, Dijon, France; Musee des Beaux Arts de Montbard, Paris; Sweet Briar Col, Sweet Briar, Va. *Exhib:* Am Vet Soc Artists, New York, 61; one-man shows, St Petersburg Jr Col, Fla, 71 & Galerie Internationale, New York, 74; Artistes USA, Galeries Raymond Duncan, Paris, 72; Festival Int de Saint-Germain-des-pres, Paris, 73, 74 & 75. *Teaching:* Chmn, Fine Arts Dept, Shorecrest Sch, formerly; pvt classes, currently. *Awards:* Legion d'Honneur Grand Prix, Humanicaire de France, 75. *Media:* All. *Dealer:* Images East & West 7200B Gulf Blvd St Petersburg Beach St Petersburg FL 33706; Mind's Eye Gallery 239 Second Ave S St Petersburg FL 33701. *Mailing Add:* 8200 14th St N St Petersburg FL 33702

MCVEY, WILLIAM M
SCULPTOR, EDUCATOR
b Boston, Mass, July 12, 05. *Study:* Rice Univ; Cleveland Inst Art; Acad Colarossi, Acad Grande Chaumiere & Acad Scandinave, Paris, 29-31; pupil of Despiau; John Carroll Univ, Ohio, Hon DFA, 83. *Work:* Heroic head of Winston Churchill, Smithsonian Inst, Washington, DC & Chartwell, Eng; Sister Ann (hollow built ceramic), Ariana Mus, Geneva, Switz; L'Ecrivain (bronze), Houston Mus, Tex; Rumination (Ga marble) & Waiting Woman, Cleveland Mus Art, Ohio; Beached Whale (cement fondu), Lincoln Ctr, Univ Ill, Urbana. *Comn:* Jan Hus, St Olga of Russia for Washington Cathedral; Entire Churchill Porch at Nat Cathedral; George Washington at Fed Bldg, Cleveland; J Edgar Hoover for FBI Acad, Quantico, Va; Senator Harry Flood Byrd (10ft statue), capital grounds, Richmond, Va, 77; and numerous others. *Exhib:* Grand Salon; Salon d'Automne; Pa Acad Fine Arts; Tex Ann; Nat Acad Design; Nat Sculpture Soc; and others. *Pos:* Chmn, Nat Fulbright Screening Comt, four yrs; mem, Fine Arts Advisory Comt, Cleveland, Ohio. *Teaching:* Instr, Cleveland Mus, 32; instr, Houston Mus, 36-38; asst prof, Univ Tex, 39-46; instr, Ohio State Univ, summer 46; instr, Cranbrook Acad Art, 46-53; head sculpture dept, Cleveland Inst Art, 53-68; guest prof, Sch Fine Arts, Ohio State Univ, 63-64. *Awards:* Nat Syracuse Ceramic Show Award, 54; Distinguished Alumni Award, Rice Univ, 82; Purchase Awards, Everson Mus, Syracuse, NY, 51 & 52 & Butler Inst Am Art, Youngstown, Ohio, 67. *Bibliog:* Helen Borsick (auth), Story of a statue (Winston Churchill at the British Embassy in Washington), Plain Dealer Mag, 66; Sculptor for today, Ohio Mag; Animals, animal sculpture and animal sculptors, Nat Sculpture Rev, 71. *Mem:* Col Art Asn Am; fel Nat Sculpture Soc; Int Platform Asn (bd gov); assoc Nat Acad Design. *Media:* Stone, Bronze. *Mailing Add:* 18 Pepper Ridge Rd Cleveland OH 44124

MCVICKER, CHARLES TAGGART
ILLUSTRATOR, INSTRUCTOR
b Canonsburg, Pa, Aug 31, 30. *Study:* Principia Col, BA, 52; Art Ctr, Col of Design, BPA, 57. *Work:* US Capitol, US Hist Soc & US Air Force, DC; Princeton Univ; Soc Illusr, New York. *Exhib:* NJ Artists, Newark Mus, 64; NJ Ann, NJ State Mus, Trenton, 70; Illusr Ann, Soc Illusr, New York; NJ Art Dirs Ann, Newark; Am Watercolor Soc Ann, Nat Acad, New York; Nat Audubon Artists. *Teaching:* Assoc prof illus, Pratt/Phoenix, New York, 79-84; asst prof art, Trenton State Col, 85- *Awards:* Best in Show, Alumni Exhib, Art Ctr, Col Design, 75; Ralph Fabri Award, Nat Audubon Artists, 86 & Michael M Engle Award, 92, Nat Audubon Artists; Ralph Fabri Medal, NAPAC Exhib, 91. *Mem:* Soc Illusr (pres, 76-78); Artists Alliance (pres 89-92); Am Watercolor Soc; Audubon Artists, 88- *Media:* Oil, Acrylic. *Publ:* Illusr, Addie and the King of Hearts, Knopf Publ, 76; The Soccer Book, 76 & The Circus Book, 78, Random House; Guard of Honor, Franklin Libr, 78. *Mailing Add:* Dept Art Trenton State College Trenton NJ 08625

MCVICKER, J JAY
PAINTER, PRINTMAKER
b Vici, Okla, Oct 18, 11. *Study:* Okla State Univ, BA & MA. *Work:* Libr Cong, Washington, DC; Dallas Mus Fine Arts, Tex; Joslyn Art Mus, Omaha; Okla Art Ctr; Nat Mus Am Art, Washington, DC; Portland Art Mus, Ore. *Exhib:* Grand Nat Watercolor Exhib, Miss Watercolor Soc & Miss Mus Art, Jackson, 90; one-man show, Longview Mus & Arts Ctr, Tex, 77 & Exhib of Aquatints, Bethesda Art Gallery, Md, 79; retrospective exhibs, Bethesda Art Gallery, Md & Rachel W Davis Gallery, Houston, 83; Rockford International, Ill, 83. *Teaching:* Prof & chmn dept art, Okla State Univ, 41-77. *Awards:* The John Taylor Arms Award for Graphic, Audubon Artists, New York, 90. *Mem:* Audubon Artists; Soc Am Graphic Artists; Philadelphia Print Club. *Media:* Acrylic; Aquatint. *Dealer:* Bethesda Art Gallery PO Box 722 Glen Echo MD 20812; Childs Gallery 169 Newbury St Boston MA 02116. *Mailing Add:* 4212 N Washington Stillwater OK 74075

MACWEENEY, ALEN BRAZIL
PHOTOGRAPHER
b Dublin, Ireland, Sept 1, 39. *Study:* Asst to Richard Avedon and Alexey Brovovitch Design Lab, New York, 61-62. *Work:* Mus Mod Art & Metrop Mus Art, New York; Philadelphia Mus Art; Minneapolis Mus Art; Int Mus Photog, Rochester, NY. *Exhib:* Light 7, Mass Inst Technol, Cambridge, 77; Vision & Expression, Rochester Inst Technol, NY, 77; solo exhib, Pfeiffer Gallery, New York, 79; Steichen Gallery, Mus Mod Art, New York, 80 & 91; Creative Photography Gallery, Mass Inst Technol, 80; Agathe Gaillard Gallery, Paris, 80 & 92; New American Nudes, Mass Inst Technol, 84; The Making of a Collection, Minneapolis Inst Arts. *Teaching:* Instr photog, Sch Visual Arts, New York, 78-80 & 83-86, Zone IV Workshops, New York, 82-85, Maine Photo Workshops, 88. *Awards:* Art Directors Club, Andy Awards & Soc Pub Designers, 67-86. *Bibliog:* Valerie Moolman (auth), Alan MacWeeney: An Irish odyssey, Aperture #82, 79; Estelle Jussim (auth), The ethnocentric icon, The Boston Rev, 1/81; Martin Gardlin (auth), Alan MacWeeney's imperfect world, Photo District News, 5/86. *Mem:* Am Soc Mag Photogr. *Publ:* Collabr, Irish Walls, Stewart, Tibori & Chang, 86; Bloomsbury Reflections, W W Norton, New York, 90. *Mailing Add:* 171 First Ave New York NY 10003

MCWHINNIE, HAROLD JAMES
PRINTMAKER, CERAMIST
b Chicago, Ill, July 15, 29. *Study:* Art Inst Chicago, BAE; Univ Chicago, MFA; Stanford Univ, EdD. *Work:* Los Angeles Mus Art, Calif; Pasadena Art Mus, Calif; Borg-Warner Collection, Chicago; Ohio State Univ Col Fine Arts. *Comn:* Sculpture Garden, Earth Art Gallery, Ellicott City, Md. *Exhib:* Libr Cong Print Show, 55; Art League NVa, & Md Fedn Arts, 78-79; Artbarn, Washington DC, 81; 409 Gallery, Baltimore, 81; Acad Arts, Easton, Md, 81; and many other group shows & one-man exhibs. *Teaching:* Asst prof art educ, Ohio State Univ, 65-70; assoc prof ceramics, Univ Md, College Park, 70-; vis lectr, Md Inst Art, Baltimore, 82. *Awards:* Hambidge Ctr Fel, 83 & 85; Nat Arts Handicapped Grant, 83-84; IBM Grants for Computer art, 85-86; and others. *Mem:* Nat Art Educ Asn; Am Crafts Coun; Md Crafts Coun; Md Alliance Arts; and others. *Media:* Computer Drawings, Lithographs. *Publ:* Auth, Glaze Data Book, Bulletin Am Ceramics Soc, 80; Glaze Data Bank, Studio Potter, 81; A Revision of Seger glaze theory, J Nat Coun Educ Ceramic Arts, 82; and numerous glaze articles in Ceramics Monthly. *Dealer:* Earth Art Gallery Ellicott City MD. *Mailing Add:* 10111 Frederick Ave Kensington MD 20795

MAC WHINNIE, JOHN VINCENT
PAINTER, SCULPTOR
b Rockville Centre, NY, April 22, 45. *Study:* Southampton Col, NY, BA(magna cum laude), 71; studied with Fairfield Porter, Larry Rivers & Ilya Bolotowsky. *Work:* Guggenheim Mus; Brooklyn Mus; Phillips Collection; Walker Art Ctr; Parrish Art Mus. *Exhib:* Summer Loan Exhib, Metrop Mus Art, New York, 79; Art in America Since World War Two, Guggenheim Mus, 79; 24th Ann Contemp Am Painting Exhib, Lehigh Univ, 79; American Drawing in Black and White, Brooklyn Mus, 81; Am Acad & Inst Arts & Lett, New York, 81; Human Figure in Contemporary Art, New Orleans Mus Contemp Art, 82; Poets and Artists of the Region, Guild Hall, East Hampton, NY, 82. *Awards:* First Prize Painting, Parrish Mus, Southampton, NY, 71;

Excellence in Painting, Heckscher Mus, Huntington, NY, 74. *Bibliog:* David Shapiro (auth), Transcending photography, Art Int, 76. *Media:* Oil, Encaustic. *Dealer:* Marlborough Gallery New York NY. *Mailing Add:* Deerfield Rd Water Mill NY 11976

MCWHORTER, ELSIE JEAN
PAINTER, SCULPTOR
b Laurel, Miss, Apr 5, 32. *Study:* Univ Ga, BFA, 54 & MFA, 56, with Lamar Dodd, Howard Thomas, Abbott Patterson, Joseph Di Martini, Ulfert Wilkie & Dan Lutz; Brooklyn Mus Art Sch, Max Beckmann scholar, 56-57, with Reuben Tam & Yonia Fain. *Work:* Gibbes Art Gallery, Charleston, SC; Brooks Art Gallery, Memphis, Tenn; Greenville Co Mus Art, SC; Arts Comn SC, Columbia; Miss Art Asn, State Coliseum, Jackson; and others. *Comn:* Welded bronze fountain, Tom Jenkins Realty Co, Columbia, 66; mural, US Post Off, Camden, SC, 67; mural, Baker Bldg, Southern Bell Tel Co, Columbia, 68; eight historic paintings, McDonald's Restaurant, Conway, SC, 76; life-size bronze relief, Sen Rembert Dennis, Dennis Bldg, Capital Complex SC, 81; McNair Monument, SC State Capital Complex; eleven wall hangings (paintings), Keenan Chapel Trinity Cathedral, Cola, SC, 89. *Exhib:* Mid-South Exhib, Memphis, Tenn, 62; Butler Inst Am Art Ann, Youngstown, Ohio, 63; Drawing USA, St Paul 2nd Biennial Competition, St Paul Art Ctr, Minn, 63; one-woman shows, Columbia Mus Art, Fine Arts Ctr, Univ Tenn, Chattanooga, 81, Hunter Mus, Chattanooga & Laurel Rogers Libr & Mus, Laurel, Miss; and others. *Teaching:* Asst prof art, Morningside Col, 58-61; instr drawing, painting & sculpture, Richland Art Sch, Columbia Mus Art, 61-84, supvr, 78-84; instr sculpture & design, Univ SC, 66-67; vis prof, Newberry Col, 82; asst prof art, Benedict Col, 85. *Awards:* First Prize Painting, Spartanburg Art Asn Ann, SC, 74; First Prize, Dutch Fork Art Asn Exhib, Cola, SC, 74; First Prize Sculpture, Art of the Carolinas, Spring Mills Ann, Lancaster, SC, 75; and many others. *Bibliog:* Jack Morris (auth), article in Contemp SC Artist, 70. *Mem:* Guild SC Artist; Artist Guild Columbia; SC Craftmen. *Mailing Add:* 5419 Sylvan Dr Columbia SC 29206

MADAN-SHOTKIN, RHODA
PAINTER
b New York, NY. *Study:* Pratt Inst, BFA, 59; Carl Schmalz Workshops 78-79; Charles Reid Workshops, 80-85. *Work:* Discovery Mus, Bridgeport, Conn; Fairfield Art Collection, Conn; Ctr Financial Studies, Fairfield Univ, Conn. *Exhib:* Three-man show, Mus Art Sci & Indust, 81; Nat Asn Women Artists Traveling Exhib, 83-86; Ann Open Exhib, Salmagundi Club, New York, 83; Womens Art Exhib, Purdue Univ, West Lafayette, Ind, 84; 100 Years/100 Works, Fine Arts Mus South Mobile, Ala & Longview Mus Art, Tex, 89-90; Flowers & Figures, Fairfield Univ Ctr Financial Studies, 90. *Awards:* Mildred Reilly Mem, 83, Gene Alden Walker Award, 85 & Martha Reid Mem Award, 87, Nat Asn Women Artists. *Bibliog:* Thomas F Potter (auth), Art topics, Meriden Record J, 88-89; Shirley Gonzales, Watercolor's maturity, New Haven Register, 89. *Mem:* Nat Asn Women Artists; Conn Watercolor Soc; New Haven Paint & Clay Club; Westport Art Ctr. *Media:* Watercolor. *Publ:* Contribr, Pulling Your Paintings Together, Watson-Guptill, 85. *Dealer:* Greene Art Gallery 29 Whitfield St Guilford CT 06437. *Mailing Add:* Five Brookside Dr Westport CT 06880

MADDEN-WORK, BETTY I
PAINTER, HISTORIAN
b Chicago, Ill, Nov 12, 15. *Study:* Am Acad Art, Chicago; Northwestern Univ; Univ Ill, BFA; Inst Design, Chicago; with Herb Olson, Spain & Italy; John Pellew, Ireland & Eng; Tom Hill, Mex; Zornes, Vt. *Work:* Ill State Hist Libr, City Collection, Springfield; Repub China; Blue Cross-Blue Shield; Lincoln Col. *Exhib:* Midwest Watercolor Soc, 81, 86 & 89; Ill Dept of Transportation, 81 & State Fair Professional, 81, 85 & 90; Fla Celebration of Women, 84; one-man shows, Western Ill Univ, Macomb, 78 & Caterpillar Tractor Co, Peoria, 79; S Ill Med Sch, 92. *Pos:* Com artist & illusr, Consolidated Bk Publ, Chicago, 44-46; com artist, Evans, Work & Costa Advert, Springfield, Ill, 55-59; fashion illusr, S A Barker Co, Springfield, 59-61; tech asst art dept, Ill State Mus, 61-63, cur art, 63-78. *Teaching:* Instr art, Art Asn, Springfield, 78-92 & Ft Myers Beach, Fla, 85-90. *Awards:* City Purchase Award, Springfield, 83; First Prize, Fla, SW Regional, 85 & 88. *Bibliog:* Betty Madden Work: Building on a Wet-into-Wet Base, Am Artist, Watercolor 92. *Mem:* Ill Artisans; Peoria Art Guild; Springfield Art Asn; Signature mem, Midwest Watercolor Soc. *Media:* Watercolor. *Publ:* Auth, Art, Crafts and Architecture in Early Illinois, Univ Ill Press, 74. *Mailing Add:* 25 Redwood Springfield IL 62704

MADDOX, JERALD CURTIS
CURATOR, HISTORIAN
b Decatur, Ind, June 9, 33. *Study:* Ind Univ, AB, 55 & MA, 60; Harvard Univ, 60-61. *Work:* Int Mus Photog, George Eastman House, Rochester, NY. *Collections Arranged:* American Photography: The Sixties, Univ Nebr Art Galleries, 66; Creative Photography 1869-1969, Libr Cong, Washington, DC, 70. *Pos:* Asst to dir, Univ Nebr Art Galleries, 63-66; head curatorial section, Prints & Photog Div, Libr Cong, 66-78, cur photog, 66-, collections planner & coordr, 78-87; consult photog, Northern Va Community Col, 77. *Teaching:* Instr art hist, NY State Univ Col New Paltz, 62-63. *Awards:* Mus Prof Fel, Nat Endowment Arts, 74. *Mem:* Col Art Asn; Soc Photog Educ (treas, 68-73). *Res:* History and criticism of photography. *Publ:* Auth, Essay on a tintype, 1/69 & Creative photography, 1869-1969, 1/71, Quart J Libr Cong; Photography in the first decade, Art Am, 7/8/73; How much is a photograph worth, After Image, 2/75; The Pioneering Image: Celebrating 150 years of American Photography, 6/89. *Mailing Add:* 4514 Highland Ave Bethesda MD 20814

MADDOX, JERROLD WARREN
EDUCATOR, PAINTER
b Ft Wayne, Ind, Mar 6, 32. *Study:* Ind Univ, BS, 54 & MFA, 59. *Exhib:* Recent Painting USA: The Figure, Mus Mod Art, New York, 62-63; Moods of Light, Am Fedn Art, 63-64. *Teaching:* Asst prof humanities, Monteith Col, Wayne State Univ, Detroit, 60-63; lectr painting & drawing, Regional Col Art & Crafts, Hull, Eng, 64; asst prof painting & drawing, Univ Ky, Lexington, 64-66; asst prof drawing & painting, Amherst Col, Mass, 66-69; assoc prof drawing & painting, Reed Col, Portland, Ore, 69-70; assoc prof drawing & painting, Ind Univ, Bloomington, 70-74; head prof, Kans State Univ, Manhattan, 74-; dir, Pa State Univ, University Park, 80-84, prof, 84- *Mem:* Col Art Asn Am; Nat Coun Art Adminr (chmn, 82); Nat Asn Sch Art & Design. *Media:* Oil. *Publ:* Coauth, Images and Imagination: an Introduction to Art, 65. *Mailing Add:* Dept Art Pa State Univ University Park PA 16802

MADIGAN, MARTHA
PHOTOGRAPHER
b Milwaukee, Wis. *Study:* Univ Wis-Madison, BS(art educ), 72; Ariz State Univ, grad studies, 72-73; Visual Studies workshop, Rochester, NY, 76; Sch art Inst Chicago, MFA, 78. *Work:* Metrop Mus Art, New York; Philadelphia Mus Art, Pa; Art Inst Chicago, Ill; Milwaukee Art Ctr, Wis. *Exhib:* Solo Exhibs, Cranbrook Acad Art, Bloomfield Hills, Mich, 81, Colo Mountain Col, Breckenridge, Amarillo Col, Tex, 83, Notre Dame Col, Baltimore, Md, Univ Mont, Missoula, 85, Hartwick Col, Oneonta, NY, St Joseph's Univ, Philadelphia, Pa, 86 & Univ Arts, Philadelphia, Pa, 90; Philadelphia Photography Faculty, Art Inst Philadelphia, 83; Faculty Exhibition, Tyler Sch Art, Temple Univ, Philadelphia, Pa, 87; Under Construction: New Photomontage, Cranbrook Acad Art Mus, Bloomfield Hills, Mich, 88; Artists Gardens, Noyes Mus, Oceanville, NJ, 90; Photography for Children, James Danziger Gallery, New York, 91; Practicum Sponsors, Univ Arts, Philadelpia, Pa, 92; Midtown Flower Show, Midtown Payson Gallery, New York, 92. *Teaching:* Asst prof photog, Dept Art & Art Hist, Wayne State Univ, Detroit, Mich, 78-79; chairperson, Dept photog, Tyler Sch Art, Temple Univ, Dept Graphic Arts & Design, 79-85, assoc prof, 85- *Awards:* Purchase Award, Illinois Photographers 78, Ill State Mus, Springfield, 78; Individual Artists Grant Photography, Nat Endowment Arts, 80. *Bibliog:* Andy Grundberg (auth), Review, NY Times, 8/90; Robert Hirsch (auth), Exploring Color Photography, William C Brown Publ, 92. *Mem:* Soc Photographic Educ; Women's Caucus for Art. *Mailing Add:* 7933 Park Ave Elkins Park PA 19117

MADIGAN, MARY JEAN SMITH
EDITOR, WRITER
b Nanticoke, Pa. *Study:* Cornell Univ, BA; Am Univ, MA. *Collections Arranged:* Photography of Rudolf Eickemeyer (with catalog), 72; Eastlake-Influenced American Furniture (with catalog), 73; The Sculpture of Isidore Konti 1862-1938 (with catalog), 75. *Pos:* Cur Am decorative art & hist, Hudson River Mus, Yonkers, NY, 70-76, cur exhib & collections, 76-77, asst dir, 77-78; bk reviewer, Mus News, 75-; dir mus prog, Opportunity Resources Arts, 78; ed, Art & Antiques, 78-, publ, 83-; ed, Restaurant & Hotel Design, 84- *Teaching:* Lectr Am antiques, Westchester Community Col, Valhalla, NY, 75. *Awards:* Harry M Grier Scholar, Asn Art Mus Dir, 75; Jesse Neal Award Ed Excellence, Asn Bus Publ, 85. *Mem:* Am Asn Mus; Am Soc Mag Ed; Author's Guild; Author's League Am. *Res:* American decorative arts. *Publ:* Auth, Steuben Glass, Harry N Abrams, 82; ed, 19th Century Furniture, 82, Americana, 82, Early American Furniture, 83 & Prints & Photographs, 83, Watson-Guptill; auth, articles in Art & Antiques, Connoisseur, Ultra & Winterthur Portfolio; The Story of Steuben, Harry N Abrams, 82, rev ed, 83. *Mailing Add:* 565 Broadway No 6-I Hastings-on-Hudson NY 10706

MADIGAN, RICHARD ALLEN
MUSEUM DIRECTOR
b Corning, NY, Oct 29, 37. *Study:* Drew Univ, AB, 59; Univ Del; Am Univ. *Collections Arranged:* Contemporary Japanese Painting, 64; Australian Painters, 65-67; Contemporary Peruvian Painting & Sculpture, 67; Sculpture of Fumio Yoshimura, 78; The Art of Polly Hope, 79; City Images, 80; Masterpieces of Canadian Painting, 84; Edward Munch: Mirror Reflections, 86; Edward Giobbi: The Paintings, 88; Sosno Sculpture, 88. *Pos:* Dir, White Art Mus, Cornell Univ, 60-63, Mus Resources Coun, Ft Worth, Tex, 67, Brooklyn Children's Mus, 68, Norton Gallery & Sch Art, West Palm Beach, 74-89, Decorative Arts Study Ctr, San Juan Capistrano, Calif, 92-; asst dir, Corcoran Gallery Art, Washington, DC, 63-67; exec dir, Wave Hill Ctr, New York, 69-74; pres, Madigaon & Assoc (mus consult), 89-90; columnist & critic, Palm Beach Daily News, 89-90; exec dir & CEO, Atlantic Ctr Arts, New Smyrna Beach, FL, 90- *Teaching:* Inst mus studies, George Washington Univ, 65-67; instr Am art, Foreign Serv Inst, US Dept State, 65-67; instr mus studies, Lehman Col, 68-69. *Awards:* European Study Grant, NY State Coun Arts, 71. *Mem:* Am Asn Mus; Fla Art Mus Dir Asn (pres, 77-78 & 82-83); Int Coun Mus; Asn Art Mus Dirs; Palm Beach Chamber Comm. *Publ:* Contribr, Australian Painters, 71; ed, Hudson City/The Living River, 73; auth, Sculpture of Michael Schreck, 79. *Mailing Add:* Atlantic Center for the Arts 1414 Art Center Ave New Smyrna Beach FL 32168

MADONIA, ANN C
CURATOR, ADMINISTRATOR
b New York, NY. *Study:* Hunter Col, City Univ New York, AB, 72, MA, 77; Hofstra Univ, cert(appraisal), 79. *Collections Arranged:* Prairie Visions and Circus Wonders: Complete Lithographic Suite by John Stewart Curry (auth, catalog), 80; American Profile: Drawings by Norman Rockwell (auth, catalog), 80; Selected Paintings from Charles August Ficke Collection (auth, catalog), 80; Byron Burford: Recent Paintings, 1960-1980 (auth, catalog), 81; Mexican Colonial Paintings in the Davenport Art Gallery, 83; Lindley

American Collection, 84; Paul Norton Retrospective (auth, catalog), 85; Harute--Out Here: Swed Immigrant Arts Midwest Am, 85; Quad City Art Showcase (competitive exhib; auth, catalog), 86; Intent Artist (auth, catalog), 87; American Drawing Biennial (competitive exhib), 90 & 92; Spirit of the South, 92; Sculpture of Alexander Galt, 92. *Pos:* Cur collections, Davenport Mus Art, Iowa, 79-88; cur, Muscarelle Mus, Col William & Mary, Williamsburg, VA, 89- *Mem:* Am Inst Conservation Artistic & Hist Works; Am Asn Mus; Col Art Asn. *Res:* American art, particularly 19th century. *Publ:* Auth, Davenport: 1836-1936--The Centennial Mural, 80, Ralph Albert Blakelock--poet of the landscape, 80, Limners and likenesses, 81, & The Mexican Colonial Collection, 83, Bulletin, Davenport Mus Art; Early contributions by Swedish painters in America (essay), In: Harut-Out Here: Swedish Immigrant Artists in Midwest America (exhib catalog), 85; Rubens Peal still life, Thomas Hart Benton lithographs, Bulletin, Davenport Mus Art, 86; Intent of the Artist (exhib catalog), 87. *Mailing Add:* 285-55 Merrimac Trail Williamsburg VA 23185

MADSEN, LOREN WAKEFIELD
SCULPTOR
b Oakland, Calif, Mar 29, 43. *Study:* Reed Col, Portland, Ore, 61-63; Univ Calif, Los Angeles, BA, 66, MA, 70. *Work:* Walker Art Ctr, Minneapolis, Minn; Mus Mod Art, New York; Georges Pompidou Ctr, Paris; Hirshhorn Mus, Washington, DC; Israel Mus, Jerusalem,. *Comn:* Suspended Sentence, Area Two Police Ctr, Chicago, 81; Brookhollow Atrium, San Antonio, Tex, 84; Horton Plaza, San Diego, Calif, 85; Chevy Chase Metro Bldg, Chevy Chase, Md, 85; Untitled, La Guardia Community Col, NY, 91; and others. *Exhib:* Los Angeles 6, 74 & New Selections, 76, Los Angeles Co Mus Art; one man show, Mus Mod Art, New York, 75; Sculpture Made in Place, Walker Art Ctr, Minneapolis, Minn, 76; David McKee Gallery, New York, 76, 77, 82, 86 & 90; Shift LA/NY, Newport Harbor Art Asn, Newport Beach, Calif, 82; 10, Univ Mass, Amherst, 85; Univ Fla, 91; Cheryl Haines Gallery, San Francisco, 91; and others. *Teaching:* Instr painting & sculpture, Sch Visual Arts, New York, 87-88. *Awards:* New Talent Award, Mod & Contemp Art Coun, Los Angeles Co Mus Art, 75; Nat Endowment Arts Fel Grant, 76 & 80; Hon Mention, Vietnam, Veterans Mem Competition, 81. *Media:* Bronze, Steel. *Dealer:* David McKee Gallery 41 E 57th St New York NY 10022. *Mailing Add:* 428 Broome St New York NY 10013

MADSEN, METTE B
PAINTER
b New York, NY, Apr 6, 55. *Study:* Calif Col Art & Sci, BFA, 78. *Work:* Smithsonian Inst, Washington, DC. *Exhib:* Old Masters-New Master, Vox Populi Gallery, New York, 84; East Village, Ctr Contemp Art, Montreal, Can, 85; Best & Brightest from East Village & Soho, Barbara Gillman Gallery, Miami, Fla, 86; Focus New York, Moosart Gallery; Embellishment of the Statue of Liberty, Benefit for Cooper-Hewitt Mus & Smithsonian Inst, NY, 86. *Media:* Oil on Canvas. *Mailing Add:* 104 Greene St New York NY 10012

MADSEN, VIGGO HOLM
PRINTMAKER, CRAFTSMAN
b Kaas, Denmark, Apr 21, 25; US citizen. *Study:* Anderson Col, Syracuse Univ, BFA, 51, MFA, 52; New York Univ; Columbia Univ Teachers Col; Adelphi Univ; Inst Allende, San Miguel, Mex; Det Danske Selskab, Denmark. *Work:* Philadelphia Ctr Older People, Pa; Nassau Community Col, Garden City, NY; Anderson Col, Ind; C W Post Col, Brookville, NY; Nat Cintric Co, Danbury, Conn; Hunt Mfg Co; and others. *Comn:* Madsen Meets Nolde (woodcut), Gallery North, Setauket, NY, 86. *Exhib:* Nat Acad Design Show, New York, 75; Surface Design Conf Exhib, Towson Univ, Md, 77; Drawing USA II, Smithsonian Inst, 79; Functional Forms, Ore State Univ, 79; Silvermine Guild Artists Print Show, 80; Stamford Mus, Ct, 90; New York Univ Galleries, 90; solo exhib, Gallery, 84 & 90. *Pos:* Ed, Newsletter, Long Island Art Teachers Asn, 62-64,; pres, Graphic Eye Gallery, 82-83. *Teaching:* Instr art, Roslyn High Sch, NY, 60-82; prof, adj staff, Nassau Community Col, 66-; instr, Crafts Workshops, Adelphi Univ, 74-78. *Awards:* Cover design award, New York State Teacher's Asn, 81; 6th Int Miniature Prints of Binghamton, NY; and others. *Bibliog:* Jeanne Paris (auth), rev in Long Island Press, 7/71; Malcolm Preston (auth), rev in Newsday, 2/72; Dona Z Meilach (auth), chap in Creating Art with Textiles, Reilly & Lee; Helen Harrison (auth), rev 1/81 & Phyllis Braff, Review of Manhasset Library Show, 85, NY Times. *Mem:* Long Island Craftsmen's Guild; lifetime mem NY State Art Teachers' Asn; Long Island Art Teachers' Asn; NY Graphic Arts Council 83, 84, 85 & 90. *Media:* Multimedia. *Publ:* Contribr, Art in action, 61, J Nat Art Educ Asn, 63 & J Eastern Arts Asn, 64; auth & publ, three demonstration booklets: Batik, Silk screening & Woodcut prints, 70-72. *Dealer:* Graphic Eye Gallery Main St Port Washington NY 11050; Gallery 84 50 West 57th St New York NY 10019. *Mailing Add:* 5 Meldon Ave Albertson NY 11507

MADURA, JACK JOSEPH
PAINTER, INSTRUCTOR
b Chicago, Ill, Feb 6, 41. *Study:* Murray State Univ, BS(art), 64 & MA(art educ), 66; Northern Ill Univ, with Robert Kabak, MFA(painting), 70. *Work:* City Springfield Munic Collection, Ill; Kemper Insurance, Chicago, Ill; Cincinatti Bell, Ohio; Northern Ill Univ, DeKalb; Ill State Mus, Springfield; and others. *Comn:* Portrait of Ill, New State Libr, 90 & Ill State Mus, 92. *Exhib:* Chicago State Univ Flat Show, 74; Am Printmakers, London, Eng; Watercolor USA, Springfield Art Mus, Mo, 75, 77, 78, 80 & 81; Art Polish Am, St Louis, Mo; one-man show, Ill State Mus, 78; and others. *Teaching:* Instr drawing & painting, Somerset Community Col, Ky, 66-68; prof art, Lincoln Land Community Col, 70- *Awards:* Second Place for Watercolor, Ill State Fair Prof Show, 75, 76 & 77; 3rd Place & Peoples Consensus, Ill State Prof Show, 91; Mayors Award for Outstanding Visual Artist, Springfield, Ill, 91. *Bibliog:* Janet Taylor (dir), An interview with Jack Madura, Sangamon State Univ, Springfield, Ill; Jack Madura in his Studio, TV Interview, Springfield Area Arts Coun. *Mem:* Ala & Ky Watercolor Socs. *Media:* Watercolor. *Mailing Add:* Dept Art Lincoln Land Comm Col Shepherd Rd Springfield IL 62708

MAGAFAN, ETHEL
PAINTER, MURALIST
b Chicago, Ill. *Study:* Colorado Springs Fine Arts Ctr, with Frank Mechau, Boardman Robinson & Peppino Mangravite. *Work:* Metrop Mus Art, New York; Munson-Williams-Proctor Inst, Utica, NY; Butler Inst Am Art, Youngstown, Ohio; Wichita Art Mus; Evansville Mus, Ind; and others. *Comn:* Prairie Fire, Post Off Lobby, Madill, Okla, 40; Mountains in Snow (with Jenne Magafan), Dept Health Educ & Welfare, Washington, DC, 41; Horse Corral, Post Off Lobby, S Denver Br, Colo, 42; Battle of New Orleans, Recorder of Deeds Bldg, Washington, DC, 43; Grant in the Wilderness (mural), Vis Ctr, Fredericksburg Nat Mil Park, Va, 79. *Exhib:* American Painting Today, Metrop Mus Art, New York, 50; Pa Acad Design, Philadelphia, 61, 62, 64, & 69; Butler Inst Am Art, 63-66, 68-74, 78, 79 & 82; New England Exhib, Silvermine Guild Artists, 64, 78 & 79; Nat Acad Design, New York, 65-90; Munson-William-Proctor Inst, 69, 72, 77, 79 & 80; Mohawk Regional, Albany & Schenectady, 70-; Cooperstown Ann Nat, 78, 82-84; and others. *Teaching:* Artist-in-residence, Univ Ga, Athens, 73 & Syracuse Univ, 76. *Awards:* Benjamin Altman Prize, Nat Acad Design, 56, 64, 73 & 80; Childe Hassam Purchase Award, Am Acad Arts & Lett, 70; Andrew Carnegie Award, Nat Acad Design, 77. *Bibliog:* Edward Betts (auth), Masterclass in watercolor, 75 & Creative landscape painting, 78; Howard Wooden (auth), Neglected Generation of American Realistic Painters, 81; Charlotte S Rubinstein (auth), American Women Artists, 82; Marlene Park & Gerald E Markowitz (auths), Democratic vistas, post office and public art murals, 84; Eleanors Tufts (auth), American women artists, Nat Mus of Women in the Arts, 87. *Mem:* Nat Acad Design (mem coun, 72-75); Am Watercolor Soc; Audubon Artists; Woodstock Artists Asn. *Media:* Egg Tempera, Watercolor. *Publ:* Auth, Magafan & mountains, Am Artists, 12/57; Why women abstract artist can do better than men, Cosmopolitan, 10/61. *Dealer:* Midtown Payson Galleries 745 Fifth Ave New York NY 10151. *Mailing Add:* 120 Boggs Hill Woodstock NY 12498

MAGAZZINI, GENE
PAINTER
b New York, NY, Nov 5, 14. *Study:* Siena, Italy, with pvt tutors; Brooklyn Col; Art Students League, with Ivan Olinsky; studied at Leonardo da Vinci Art Sch, New York, with Ruotolo. *Work:* Sloan-Kettering Inst, New York; Nat Biscuit Co, NJ; Mary Manning Walsh pvt collection, New York; Kemper Insurance Co, Chicago; Prevention Mag, Pa. *Exhib:* Allied Artists Am, Nat Acad Design, New York; Palais Congres, Expos Intercontinentale, Monaco; Nat Arts Club & Salmagundi Club, New York; Burr Artists, Metrop Mus Art, New York, 77; Am Artists Prof League, Smithsonian Inst. *Awards:* First Prize, Salmagundi Club, 69; Best in Show & Purchase Prize, Salmagundi Club, 70; Best in Show & Gold Medal, Nat Art League, 71. *Mem:* Salmagundi Club; Artists' Fel; Nat Art League; Art Students League; Am Artists Prof League. *Media:* Oil. *Mailing Add:* 249 Euclid Ave Brooklyn NY 11208

MAGDANZ, ANDREW R
GLASS BLOWER
b River Falls, Wis, Aug 23, 51. *Study:* Univ Wis, River Falls, Univ Wis, Madison, BFA, 76, with Harvey Littleton; Calif Col Arts & Crafts, MFA, 78, with Marvin Lipofsky. *Work:* Mus Fine Arts, Boston, Mass; Oakland Mus, Calif; Corning Mus, NY. *Pos:* Studio Artist, independent. *Teaching:* Head, glass dept, Rochester Inst Technol, 79-81; instr, Alchuk Sch Glass; instr, Haystack Sch Crafts. *Awards:* Nat Endowment Arts Grants. *Mem:* Am Craft Coun (bd dirs, 88); Glass Art Soc; Soc Arts & Crafts, Boston (bd dirs). *Mailing Add:* 105 Garfield St Watertown MA 02172

MAGEE, ALAN
PAINTER
b Newton, Pa, May 26, 47. *Study:* Tyler Sch Art, 65-66; Philadelphia Col Art, 67-69. *Work:* Columbus Mus Art, Ohio; Fine Arts Mus San Francisco; Newark Mus & Rutgers Mus Art, NJ; Portland Mus Art & Farnsworth Art Mus, Maine; Norton Gallery Art, Fla. *Comn:* Illus novels, Graham Greene, Pocket Books, New York, 74, Bernard Malamud, 74, Agatha Christie, 74-78 & Patrick White, Avon Books, New York, 75; cover paintings for Time Mag, 78, 79, 81, 82 & 85; portfolio of paintings for the Atlantic: The Walls Around Us, 87. *Exhib:* One-person shows, Allport Gallery, San Francisco, Calif, 78, 81, 84 & 86, Staempfli Gallery, NY, 80, 82, 83, & 90, Schmidt Bingham Gallery, NY, 86, 89, Mekler Gallery, Los Angeles, Calif, 86, Edith Caldwell Gallery, San Francisco, Calif, 92, Kodak Ctr for Creative Imaging, 92; Found Nat des Arts Graphiques, Paris, France, 84; Smithsonian Inst, Nat Air & Space Mus, 85; Am Acad & Inst Arts & Letters, NY 87; Art and the Law (with exhib catalog), ann traveling exhib, 89, 90; traveling retrospective, Farnsworth Art Mus, Ringling Sch Art & Design, Cheekwood Ctr for the Arts, James A Michener Mus Art, 91-92; plus many others. *Awards:* Award of Excellence, Commun Arts, 77, 78, 79 & 83; Am Bk Award, 82; Leo Meissner Prize, Nat Acad Design, 90. *Bibliog:* John Canaday (auth), A dazzling new realist painter, Saturday Rev Mag, 12/80; Theodore F Wolff (auth), The emergence of a gifted artist, Christian Science Monitor, 10/26/82; John Russell (auth), article in the NY Times, 10/22/82; Edgar Allen Beem (auth), Alan Magee, Arts Mag, 10/86; plus many others. *Media:* All media. *Publ:* Stones and Other Works, Harry N Abrams; Alan Magee 1981-1991, Farnsworth Art Mus; Alan Magee, Inlets, Joan Whitney Payson Gallery Art. *Dealer:* Schmidt-Bingham Gallery 41 W 57th St New York, NY 10019; Edith Caldwell Gallery San Francisco CA. *Mailing Add:* Pleasant Point Rd Cushing ME 04563-9507

MAGEE, ALDERSON
GRAPHIC ARTIST, PAINTER
b Hartford, Conn, Oct 5, 29. *Study:* Univ Conn, BS; West Hartford Art League; also with Estelle Coniff & Walter Korder. *Work:* Leigh Yawkey Woodson Art Mus. *Comn:* Bald Eagle, United Technologies Corp, 83. *Exhib:* Conn Acad Fine Arts, Wadsworth Atheneum, Hartford, 74; Federal Duck Stamp Art, Peabody Mus, Salem, Mass, 77; Birds in Art, Leigh Yawkey Woodson Art Mus, Wausau, Wis, 84-88; Experience the West, Mus Rockies, Bozeman, Mont, 84 & 85; Northwest Rendezvous, Helena, Mont, 85; Miniature Show '86, GWS Galleries, Carmel, Calif; The Legacy Continues, Smithsonian Inst, Washington, DC, 88; Coastal Impressions II, GWS Galleries, Southport, Conn, 92; Miniature Show '92, GWS Galleries, Carmel, Calif. *Awards:* First Prize, Conn Acad Fine Arts, 74; Gold Medal, Hudson Valley Art Asn, 75 & Grand Nat Exhib, Am Artists Prof League, New York, 78. *Bibliog:* George Reiger (auth), The Wings of Dawn, 236, 80; Starting From Scratch, Midwest Art Mag, 3/87; Russell A Fink (auth), Duck Stamp Prints, rev, 92. *Mem:* Salmagundi Club; Hudson Valley Art Asn; Soc Animal Artists; Am Artists Prof League. *Media:* Scratchboard; Oils, Etching. *Publ:* Contribr, Federal Duck Stamp Design, US Govt, 76; Sporting Classics Mag, 11-12/86 & 9-10/92; Smithsonian Studies Am Art, spring 89. *Dealer:* Greenwich Workshop Galleries Carmel CA; Greenwich Workshop Galleries Southport CT. *Mailing Add:* 1940 Lakeshore Dr Sagle ID 83860

MAGEL, CATHERINE ANNE
CERAMIST, PAINTER
b La Grange, Ill, Nov 13, 56. *Study:* Kansas City Art Inst, BFA, 79; NY State Col Ceramics, Alfred, MFA, 82. *Comn:* Tile mural, Cesar Pelli & Assocs, New Haven, Conn, 83; Pritzpers, Chicago, Ill. *Exhib:* Nelson Atkins Mus Art, Kansas City, Mo 84; Introspectives, Pyramid Art Ctr, Rochester, NY, 84; solo exhib, Paul Mellon Art Ctr, Walingford, Conn, 86; group exhib, Open your Eyes, Ulrich Mus, Wichita Kans, 90. *Pos:* Artist-in-residence, Creative Arts Workshop, New Haven, Conn, 82-84 & NY State Col Ceramics, Alfred, 88; vis artist, Anderson Ranch, Showmass, Colo, 90. *Teaching:* Instr ceramics, Creative Arts Workshop, 82-84 & Trumbull Col, Yale Univ, 83-84; instr drawing, NY State Col Ceramics, 89; beginning sculpture or 3/D design, Wichita State Univ, 90. *Awards:* Fels, Nat Endowment Arts, 86 & Conn Comn Arts, 86. *Mem:* Archie Bray Found. *Mailing Add:* 1709 Washington Ave St Louis MO 63103

MAGENTA, MURIEL
SCULPTOR, VIDEO ARTIST
b New York, NY, Dec 4, 32. *Study:* Queens Col, BA, 53; Johns Hopkins Univ, MA(art hist), 62; Ariz State Univ, MFA, 65, PhD, 70. *Work:* Univ Art Collections, Ariz State Univ, Tempe; Valley Nat Bank, Phoenix; Prudential Life Insurance, Scottsdale. *Exhib:* Coiffure Carnival, video/sculpture installation, Kans City Art Inst, Mo, 91, Gallery 10, Washington, DC, 91, Madrid Int Festival of Films by Women, Spain, 91, Europ Film Festival, Osnabruck, Ger, 91, Medien Operative Berlin, Ger, 92; Coiffure Carnival Trilogy, video, CAGE, Cincinnati, Ohio; Salondoo, video, Image Union, WTTV, Chicago, Ill; and many others. *Pos:* Exec ed & designer, Hue Points Women's Caucus for Art Newsmag, 82-84; Woman Image Now: Arizona Women in Art J, Ariz State Univ, 80-90. *Teaching:* Prof inter-media art, Ariz State Univ, 69-; vis artist-in-residence studio art, Univ Wis, Madison, summer 79, St Mary's Col, Notre Dame Univ, 84. *Awards:* Ariz Siggraph Asn Award, 86; Grants for sculpture, film, video, computer arts, 74, 76, 79, 82-83, 84, 86, 88, 91 & 92; Mid-Career Achievement Award, Woman's Caucus for Art, 91. *Bibliog:* S Muchnic (auth), Here comes Magenta's bride, Los Angeles Times, 10/78; B Perlman (auth), Hiding from infinity, Artnews, 9/79; Z Dubin (auth), A stylish exhibition that's truly a wig of art, Los Angeles Times, 2/85; V Reed (auth), Playing on the power of hair, Artweek, 5/90. *Mem:* Mid-Am Col Art Asn (exec bd, 78-79); Coalition Women's Art Orgn (nat vpres, 78-80); Women's Caucus Art (nat pres, 82-84); Col Art Asn. *Media:* Video, Computer, All. *Publ:* Contribr, Women's view of art, In: Women Studies and the Arts, Whittenborn, 80; auth, Feminist art criticism: A political definition, J Theory & Criticism Visual Arts, 81; Photographic Essay, Women Artist News, Eyewitness Nairobi: United Nations World Conference of Women, Nairobi, Kenya, 86; Woman Image Now: Arizona State University, Women's Studies Quart, 87; Coiffure Carnival: Muriel Magenta, Exhib Catalog Ctr Arts, 90. *Dealer:* ARTCOM/LaMamelle 70 12th St San Francisco CA 94103. *Mailing Add:* 8322 E Virginia Scottsdale AZ 85257

MAGGS, ARNAUD (CYRIL BENVENUTI)
PHOTOGRAPHER, GRAPHIC ARTIST
b Montreal, Que, May 5, 26. *Study:* With Carl Dair, 50; Scuola Belle Arti Brera, Milan, 59; Three Schs, Toronto, 74. *Work:* Nat Gallery Can; Vancouver Art Gallery; Art Gallery Hamilton; Winnipeg Art Gallery; Can Mus Contemp Photogr; Vancouver Art Gallery; Musee d'art Contemporain de Montreal. *Comn:* Restaurant mural (photographs), Windsor Arms Hotel, Toronto, 67. *Exhib:* Solo exhibs, Photographs 1975-84, Art Gallery Hamilton & Winnipeg Art Gallery, 86, Numberworks, Macdonald Stewart Art Ctr, Guelph, 89, Neuberger Mus, Purchase, NY, 90, Saidye Bronfman Ctr, Montreal, 90, Southern Alberta Art Gallery, Lethbridge, 90, Presentation House Gallery, N Vancouver, 92; Sweet Immortality, Edmonton Art Gallery, 78; The Winnipeg Perspective, Winnipeg Art Gallery, 79; Portraits, Nat Film Bd Can, Ottawa, 81; Persona, Nickle Arts Mus, Univ Calgary, 82; Seeing People, Seeing Space, Photogr Gallery, London, Eng, 84; Responding to Photog, Art Gallery Ont, 84; Allocations, 49th Parallel, New York, 84; Numbering, Art Gallery, Hamilton, 90; Int British Print Bienalle, Brantford, Eng, 90; Spec Collections, Int Ctr Photog, Midtown, New York, 92. *Teaching:* Vis artist, Banff Ctr, Banff, Alta, 88. *Awards:* Gold Medal, Can Graphica Exhib, Montreal, 65; Can Coun Sr Arts Grants, 69, 81 & 84; Gershon Iskowitz Award, 91. *Bibliog:* John Bentley Mays (auth), The many faces of Maggs, Globe & Mail, Toronto, 1/19/86; Gary Michael Dault, (auth), The narrative and its double, C Mag, summer 89; James D Campbell (auth), Arnaud Maggs: Identification, C Mag, Spring 91. *Publ:* Arnaud Maggs, catalog, Centre Culturel Canadien, Paris, 1980; Arnaud Maggs Selected Works 1981-83, catalog, Charles H Scott Gallery, Vancouver, 84; Auth, Arnaud Maggs Photographs 1975-1984, catalog, Nickel Arts Mus, Univ Calgary, 84; Arnaud Maggs Numberworks Catalog, Macdonald Stewart Art Centre, Guelph, Ont, 89. *Dealer:* Cold City Gallery Toronto ON. *Mailing Add:* 48 Abell St Unit 103 Toronto ON M6J 3H2 Canada

MAGISTRO, CHARLES JOHN
PAINTER, PRINTMAKER
b Cleveland, Ohio, June 27, 41. *Study:* Carnegie Inst Technol, BFA, 64; Ohio State Univ, MFA, 67. *Work:* Brooklyn Mus Art; Va Mus Fine Arts, Richmond; Mint Mus Art, Charlotte, NC; Reese Mus, Tenn; Mariners Mus, Newport News, Va. *Comn:* Triptych, Gen Reinsurance Corp, New York, 78; painting, Gould Corp, Chicago, 79. *Exhib:* Juried Show, Mint Mus Art, Charlotte, NC, 70; Va Mus Art Biennial, Richmond, 71; Extraordinary Realities, Whitney Mus Art, New York, 73; 19th Nat Print Exhib, Brooklyn Mus Art, 74; one-man shows, Tibor de Nagy Gallery, New York, 80, 81 & 83, Nancy Lurie Gallery, Chicago, 80, John Davis Gallery, Akron, Ohio, 82 & 83, Passaic Co Col, 83, Lafayette Col, Easton, Pa, 86 & Ruggiero-Henis Inc, New York, 88; Constructures, Nora Haime Gallery, New York, 85; Paint, Paper and Wood, Stephen Rosenberg Gallery, New York, 85; Nat Mus Found Arts, Mead Cent Corp, Washington, DC, 86; New Spaces/New Faces, Guild Hall Mus, East Hampton, NY, 87. *Collections Arranged:* Works from the Tibor de Nagy Gallery, Tibor de Nagy, New York, 79; Current-New York (auth, catalog), Syracuse Univ, 80. *Pos:* Fac adv, Nat Student Mag, 77- *Teaching:* Assoc prof design & printmaking, Va Commonwealth Univ, 67-79; assoc prof design & drawing, William Patterson Col, NJ, 77- *Awards:* New York Arts Grant, 85. *Bibliog:* Carl Lunde (auth), Chuck Magistro, Arts Mag, 5/81; Robert Long (auth), Guild Hall picks 9 painters, 3 sculptors, Southampton Press, 7/87; Phillys Braff (auth), Guild Hall features new faces, New York Times, 7/26/87. *Publ:* Auth, Objects Altered, Kendall-Hunt, 72. *Dealer:* Tibor de Nagy Gallery 29 W 57th St New York NY 10019; John Davis Gallery Akron OH. *Mailing Add:* 52 White St No 2 New York NY 10013

MAGLEBY, FRANK (FRANCIS R)
PAINTER, EDUCATOR
b Idaho Falls, Idaho, Mar 22, 28. *Study:* Brigham Young Univ, BA & MA, 52; Art Students League; Am Art Sch, New York; Columbia Univ, EdD, 67. *Comn:* Historical paintings for various church bldgs, Mormon Church, Salt Lake City, Utah & New York, 58-59; Heleman (mural), Brigham Young Univ, 65. *Exhib:* One-man shows, Southern Vt Art Ctr, 55-59 & 71, Grand Cent Art Gallery, 57 & Brigham Young Univ, Utah, 68 & 78. *Pos:* Dir, B F Larson Gallery, Brigham Young Univ, 62-69. *Teaching:* Prof painting, Brigham Young Univ, 59- *Mem:* Am Fedn Arts; Southern Vt Art Ctr; Grand Cent Art Gallery; Western Asn Mus; Art Students League. *Media:* Oil. *Mailing Add:* 464 E 2200 N Provo UT 84604

MAGNAN, OSCAR GUSTAV
PAINTER, SCULPTOR
b Cienfuegos, Cuba, Dec 16, 37. *Study:* San Alejandro, Habana, Cuba, with Mateo Dela Torriente, MFA; Oxford Univ, Eng, Master in aribus; Sorbonne, with Dufrenne, PhD(aesthet). *Work:* Brit Mus; Libr Congress; Smithsonian Inst; RCA Corp; New York Univ; and others. *Comn:* Three panel mural, Univ Autonoma, Dom Repub, 68; bronze statue, Haina, Dom Repub, 68. *Exhib:* Salzburg Int Biennial, 64; one-man shows, Palazzo Strozzi, Florence, Italy, 66 & Galerie Motte, Paris, 70; Int Fair, Basle, Switz, 72; Inter-Kunst-Infomaturien, Dusseldorf, Ger, 72; New Jersey Selects, Squibb Corp, Princeton, NJ. *Pos:* Dir art gallery, St Peter's Col, 72-, cur mus, 73- *Teaching:* Prof aesthet-sculpture, St Peter's Col, Jersey City, NJ, 77- *Awards:* Can Coun Fel, 64; Cintas Found Inst Int Educ Fel, 66; Guggenheim Found Fel, 68; Hereward Lester Cooke Found. *Mem:* Am Abstract Artists; Artists Fel. *Media:* Acrylic, Oil; Aluminum, Bronze. *Publ:* The Art of Oscar Magnan, Ramparts, 64; Le Figaro, Litteraire, Paris, 7-20-26/70; Searching for Truth, Jersey J, 89. *Dealer:* Susan Teller Gallery 568 Broadway New York NY. *Mailing Add:* Dept Fine Arts St Peter's Col Kennedy Blvd Jersey City NJ 07306

MAGUIRE, HENRY POWNALL
HISTORIAN, WRITER
b Bath, England, May 20, 43. *Study:* Kings Col, Cambridge, BA, 65; Harvard Univ, PhD, 73. *Teaching:* Asst prof medieval art, Harvard Univ, 73-76 & Dumbarton Oaks, 76-79; asst prof, Univ Ill, Urbana-Champaign, 79-82, assoc prof, 82-88, prof, 88- *Mem:* Col Art Asn; Archaeol Inst Am; Int Ctr Medieval Art; Medieval Acad Am. *Res:* Late Roman, early Christian and Byzantine art. *Publ:* Auth, Truth and convention in Byzantine descriptions of works of art, 74 & The depiction of sorrow in middle Byzantine art, 77, Dumbarton Oaks Papers; auth, Art and Eloquence in Byzantium, Princeton, 81; auth, Earth & Ocean, The Terresterial World in Early Byzantine Art, Penn State, 87; coauth, Art & Holy Powers in Early Christian House, Univ Ill, 89. *Mailing Add:* Sch Art & Design Univ Ill 408 E Peabody Dr Champaign IL 61820

MAHAFFEY, MERRILL DEAN
PAINTER, INSTRUCTOR
b Albuquerque, NMex, Aug 12, 37. *Study:* Mesa Col, Colo; Calif Col Arts & Crafts; Sacramento State Col, BA; Ariz State Univ, MFA, 66. *Work:* Ariz State Univ; Phoenix Art Mus; Tucson Fine Arts Ctr; Mus Am Art; Colorado

Springs Fine Arts Ctr. *Exhib:* Joslyn Mus Biennial, Omaha, Nebr; Newport Art Mus, 79; Mus Am Art, Washington, DC, 79; San Francisco Mus Mod Art, 79; Sierra Nev Mus Art, 81; Fresno Art Ctr, 81; Tucson Art Mus, 82; Colorado Springs Fine Arts Ctr, 83. *Teaching:* Instr painting & art hist, Phoenix Col, 67-83; lectr & writer art hist Am West. *Media:* Acrylic, Oil. *Publ:* Auth, Merrill Mahaffey Monumental Landscapes, Northland Press, 79. *Mailing Add:* 129 W Palace Ave Sante Fe NM 87501

MAHDAVI, RAFAEL SINCLAIR
PAINTER, SCULPTOR
b Mazatlan, Mex, May 17, 46; US citizen. *Study:* Univ Rochester, NY, 63-65; Cranbrook Acad Art, Bloomfield Hills, Mich, BFA, 68. *Work:* Chicago Art Inst; Neuberger Mus, Purchase, NY; Found Cartier, Found P Stuyvesant & Fonds Nat d'Art Contemporain, Paris, France. *Comn:* Numerous theatre sets & designs. *Exhib:* Drawings, Neuberger Mus, Purchase, NY, 77; Outsider, UNESCO, Paris, France, 83; Chalmoux, Musee de Bourbon-Lancy, France, 85; History as Resistance (with catalog), Kunsthalle, Düsseldorf, Ger, traveling to Bremen & Hannover, 85; retrospective, 1980-90 (with catalog), 90, 1970-75 (with catalog), 92, Spain. *Teaching:* Prof painting, Parsons Sch Design, Paris, France, 81- *Bibliog:* M Brenson (auth), Rafael Mahdavi, Galerie Stadler, 80; G Light (auth), Rafael Mahdavi, UNESCO, 83. *Media:* Acrylic; Steel. *Dealer:* Galerie Stadler 51 Rue de Seine Paris France; Kouros Gallery 23 E 73rd St New York NY 10021. *Mailing Add:* 50 Wellesley Ave Wellesley MA 02181

MAHEY, JOHN A
MUSEUM DIRECTOR
b Du Bois, Pa, Mar 30, 32. *Study:* Columbia Col, 50-52; Pa State Univ, BA & MA(art hist). *Collections Arranged:* Sarah Miriam Peale (with catalog), Peale Mus, Baltimore, Md, 68; Master Drawings from Sacramento (auth, catalog), E B Crocker Art Gallery, Calif, 71; Native American Art at Philbrook (auth, catalog), 80 & Painter of the Humble Truth, 84, Philbrook, Tulsa, Okla; Asian Art, San Antonio Mus Art, 86; Mexican Folk Art, San Antonio Mus Art, 87; The Art of Drawing (with catalog), Flint Inst Arts, 92. *Pos:* Asst dir, Peale Mus, Baltimore, 64-69; dir, E B Crocker Art Gallery, Sacramento, 69-72, Cummer Gallery Art, Jacksonville, 72-75 & Mem Art Gallery, 75-79; chief cur, Philbrook Art Ctr, Tulsa, 79-84; dir, San Antonio Mus Art, 84- *Teaching:* Instr art hist, Sacramento State Univ, 70; adj prof, Univ Rochester, 75-79. *Awards:* Fulbright Fel, 62. *Mem:* Am Asn Mus; Asn Art Mus Dirs. *Res:* 19th century American painting; Rembrandt Peale. *Publ:* Auth, Letters of James McNeil Whistler to George Lucas, 67, The lithographs of Rembrandt Peale, 69 & The studio of Rembrandt Peale, 69; contributions to numerous exhibitions catalogs, 69-92. *Mailing Add:* c/o Flint Institute of Arts 1120 E Kearsley St Flint MI 48503

MAHLKE, ERNEST D
SCULPTOR, EDUCATOR
b Madison, Wis, Sept 15, 30. *Study:* Univ Wis, BS & MS; Inst Allende, Univ Guanajuato, Mex, MFA. *Work:* State Univ NY Oneonta; and many pvt collections. *Exhib:* Smithsonian Inst Traveling Exhibs, 55, 57 & 58; Smithsonian Inst, 55, 61 & 62; Cooperstown Art Asn Nat Ann, NY, 66-81; Artists of Cent NY Regional Ann, Munson-Williams-Proctor Inst, Utica, NY, 68-79; one-man shows, Two Rivers Gallery, Binghamton, NY, 72, The Art Ctr, Albany, NY, 76 & State Univ NY Oneonta, 80; Drawing & Small Sculpture Show, Ball State Univ Art Gallery, 75, 79 & 81; Sculpture 75 Nat, 75. *Pos:* Pres, Wis Designer Craftsmen, Milwaukee, 62; mem bd, Oneonta Art Ctr, NY, 77. *Teaching:* Assoc prof sculpture, State Univ NY Oneonta, 62-78, prof, 78- *Mem:* Am Craftsmen's Coun. *Media:* Wood, Metal. *Dealer:* Gallery 53 Cooperstown NY 13326. *Mailing Add:* Dept Art Fine Arts Bldg State Univ NY Oneonta NY 13820

MAHLMANN, JOHN JAMES
PUBLISHER, ADMINISTRATOR
b Washington, DC, Jan 21, 42. *Study:* Boston Univ, BFA, 62, MFA, 63; Univ Notre Dame, summer 62; Pa State Univ, EdD, 70. *Pos:* Asst exec secy, Nat Art Educ Asn, Washington, DC, 69-71, exec dir, 71-82; ed, Art Educ, 70-81 & Art Teacher, 71-80; exec ed, Design for Arts Educ, formerly; exec dir, Music Educators Nat Conf, 82- *Teaching:* Grad asst, Boston Univ, 62-63; grad asst & res asst, Pa State Univ, 63-64, instr, 66-67, dir gallery, Art Educ Dept, 66-67; asst prof, Tex Tech Col, 67-69. *Mem:* Music Educators Nat Conf; Rotary; Am Soc Assoc Exec. *Mailing Add:* 10703 Cross Sch Rd Reston VA 22091

MAHMOUD, BEN
PAINTER, EDUCATOR
b Charleston, WVa, Oct 6, 35. *Study:* Columbus Art Sch, Ohio, cert, 57; Ohio Univ, Athens, BFA, 58, MFA, 60. *Work:* Art Inst Chicago, Ill; Brooklyn Mus, NY; Krannert Mus, Univ Ill, Urbana; Laguna Gloria Mus, Austin, Tex; Mus Contemp Art, Chicago. *Comn:* Hapworth Med Ctr, NY, 86. *Exhib:* One-man exhibs, Lakeview Ctr Arts, Peoria, 74, Ill State Mus, Springfield, 76, Zaks Gallery, Chicago, 80, 83, 85, 86 & 90, Ill, Nardin Gallery, New York, 80 & Madison Gallery, Toronto, Can, 80; Chicago Collects Mahmoud, Northern Ill Univ, De Kalb, 81; Art Today, Indianapolis Mus, Ind, 84 & 86; Traveling Exhib, Art and the Law, 86- *Pos:* Bd mem & chmn visual arts, Ill Arts Coun, 73-77. *Teaching:* Prof art, Northern Ill Univ, 65-, presidential res. *Awards:* Creative Activity Grants, Northern Ill Univ, 65-; Painting Fel, Nat Endowment Arts, 75. *Bibliog:* David Tenuse (auth), rev, Washington Post, 4/30/77; Robert Kaupelis (auth), Experimental Drawing, Watson-Guptill, 80; Carrie Rebora (auth), Ben Mahmoud, New Art Examiner, Vol 8, 81. *Media:* Acrylic, Drawing. *Dealer:* Zaks Gallery 620 N Michigan Ave Chicago IL 60611. *Mailing Add:* Sch Art Northern Ill Univ De Kalb IL 60115

MAHON, ROBERT
PHOTOGRAPHER
b Wilmington, Del, Dec 28, 49. *Study:* Univ Del, BA, 72. *Work:* Mus Mod Art, Metrop Mus Art & New York Pub Libr, New York; Humanities Res Ctr, Austin, Tex; Philadelphia Mus Art, Pa. *Exhib:* Philadelphia Mus Art, Pa, 82; John Cage: Scores and Prints, Whitney Mus, New York, NY, 82; Am Ctr, Paris, France, 82; Kolnischer Kunstverein, Cologne, WGer, 83; Big Pictures by Contemporary Photographers, 83 & Permanent Collection Exhib, 84-86, Mus Mod Art, New York; Systems of Response, Art Inst Chicago, 85; Recent Acquisitions, NY Pub Libr, 85; Philadelphia Mus Art, 89; A Force of Repetition, NJ State Mus, 90. *Awards:* Guggenheim Grant, 85-86. *Publ:* Illusr, These Trees Stand, 81, & Between the Lions, 86, Carol Joyce; illusr, Themes and Variations, Station Hill Press, 82; auth & illusr, Tribute to Minor White, Aperture, 84; illusr, I-VI, John Cage, 90. *Mailing Add:* PO Box Q Stockton NJ 08559

MAHONEY, JOELLA JEAN
EDUCATOR, PAINTER
b Chicago, Ill, June 11, 33. *Study:* Art Inst Chicago, 51; Instituto Allende, San Miguel, Mex, 54 & 55, Northern Ariz Univ, Flagstaff, BS(art & english), 55; Claremont Grad Sch, Calif, Fel, MFA(painting), 65. *Work:* Sedona Mus Art, Ariz; Sohio Corp, Houston, Tex; Lew Coppersmith Inc, Los Angeles; Am Express Office, Phoenix, Ariz; Claremont McKenna Col, Calif. *Comn:* Painting, Mutual Life Insurance, Newport Beach, Calif, 75; painting, comn Weldon Diggs-Atty, Upland, Calif, 87; painting, Univ LaVerne, Laverne, Calif, 84. *Exhib:* Art-in-Embassies Program, US State Dept, Bhutan, Lybia & Indonesia, 70-90; Jamison Gallery, Sante Fe, NMex, 74; Laguna Beach Invitational, Laguna Beach Mus Art, Calif, 75; solo exhibs, NAU Art Gallery, Flagstaff, Ariz, 80, Austin Gallery, Scottsdale, Ariz, 84; 5 Arizona Artists, Van Buren-Hazelton Cutting Gallery, Boston, Mass, 88; Red Stone Gallery, 89 & 90. *Pos:* Bd dir, Sedona Mus Art, Ariz, 89-; docent, Mus Northern Aris, Flagstaff, 89-; art comn, City of Sedona, Ariz, 90- *Teaching:* Prof art, Univ LaVerne, LaVerne, Calif, 64- *Bibliog:* Morneen K Bratt (auth), Oil on Canvas (catalog), Northland Press, 85; Cal Poly Univ, Women's Work, Univ Press, 86. *Mem:* Sedona Arts Ctr; Coconino Ctr Arts, Flagstaff, Ariz; Mus Northern Ariz; PETA; SPCA. *Media:* Oil, Watercolor. *Res:* Paintings that honor the earth and hold up the beauty and mystery of natural SW Canyon, landforms, figurative themes, classical. *Dealer:* Lawrence S Green 310 Apple Ave Sedona Ariz 86336. *Mailing Add:* 495 Smith Rd Sedona AZ 86336

MAHONEY, MICHAEL R T
HISTORIAN, EDUCATOR
b Worcester, Mass, Jan 24, 35. *Study:* Phillips Acad, 53; Yale Univ, BA, 59; Courtauld Inst, Univ London, PhD, 65. *Pos:* Mus cur, Nat Gallery of Art, Washington, DC, 64-69, cur sculpture, 67, ed, 68-69. *Teaching:* Prof art hist, Trinity Col, Hartford, 69- *Res:* Seventeenth century art. *Publ:* Auth, Drawings of Salvator Rosa, Garland, 77. *Mailing Add:* Dept Fine Arts Trinity Col Hartford CT 06106

MAHONY, PAT
PAINTER
b Los Angeles, Calif, Dec 4, 51. *Study:* Univ Calif, Santa Barbara, BA, 73. *Work:* Carol Miller Justice Ctr, Sacramento, Calif; Permanent Collection, Springfield Art Mus, Mo. *Exhib:* 25 Years of the Artist Contemp Gallery, Crocker Art Mus, Sacramento, Calif, 83; Nat Watercolor Soc, Brea Civic Cult Ctr, Brea, Calif, 84-87 & 90; Artist Contemporary Gallery, 84-92; Art Quest 85, Calif State Univ, Long Beach, Calif, 85; Talent, Allan Stone Gallery, New York, 85-87; Watercolor USA, Springfield Art Mus, Mo, 87 & 92. *Awards:* Cash Award, 84 & Joseph A Mugnaini Award, 87, Nat Watercolor Soc; Ore Coast Coun Arts, 87; Nat Watercolor Soc, 90; Purchase Award, Springfield Art Mus, 92. *Bibliog:* Mike Ward (auth), The New Spirit of Watercolor, F&W Publ, 89; Carole Katchen (auth), Discover New Freedom with Watercolor, Artists Mag, 8/92. *Mem:* Nat Watercolor Soc. *Media:* Watercolor, Oil. *Dealer:* Artist Contemp Gallery 542 Downtown Plaza Sacramento CA 95814; Ruth Bachofner Gallery 926 Colorado Blvd Santa Monica CA. *Mailing Add:* 6915 Garden Hwy Sacramento CA 95837

MAIER, MARYANNE E
PAINTER
b Rochester, NY. *Study:* With Dana Gibson Noble, 75-77; Paier Col Art, dipl(fine arts), 77; with Charles Gruppe, 81. *Comn:* Sand Dune, Fagen's Restaurant, Stratford, Conn, 79; Harbors & Seascapes, Guenster Home Inc, Bridgeport, Conn, 82; Painting, PT Barnum, comn for mayor's off, Bridgeport, Conn, 89; Seascapes, Milford Seafood Restaurant, 90, Mechanic & Farmers Savings Bank, 90. *Exhib:* One-woman show, Milford Fine Arts Coun, Conn, 79; Audubon Artists, Nat Acad Galleries, New York, 79; Mus Art & Sci, Bridgeport, Conn, 80; Hudson Valley Art Asn, Westchester Co Ctr, White Plains, NY, 80; Seascapes of New England, Hartford State Capitol, Conn, 83. *Awards:* Salmagundi Club Prize, 79; Judge's Spec Award, Bridgeport Art League, 79; Best in Show, Conn Classic Arts, 80. *Bibliog:* Edward Meaney (auth), Family life, Lynn Item News, Mass, 76; Lynn Doherty (auth), In her eyes all the world is a canvas, Milford Citizen, 80. *Mem:* Nat League Am Pen Women; Conn Classic Arts; Milford Fine Arts; life mem Kent Art Asn; Salmagundi Club. *Media:* Oil. *Mailing Add:* 465 Gulf St Milford CT 06460

MAILMAN, CYNTHIA
PAINTER, EDUCATOR
b Bronx, NY, Dec 31, 42. *Study:* Pratt Inst, BS, 64; Art Students League; Brooklyn Mus Art Sch; Rutgers Univ, MFA, 78. *Work:* Everson Mus, Syracuse; Staten Island Mus; The Jane Voorhees, Zimmerli Art Mus, New

Brunswick, NJ; Prudential Life Ins Co, Newark, NJ; NJ State Mus, Trenton; The Port Authority NY & NJ; The Queensborough Community Col Gallery, Queens, NY. *Comn:* Mural, Citywalls Pub Arts Coun, Staten Island, NY, 77; mural, World Trade Ctr, Port Authority, New York. *Exhib:* solo exhibs, SOHO 20 Gallery, New York, 74, 76, 78, 80, 83 & 86, Everson Mus Art, Syracuse, NY, 81, Maurice M Pine Free Pub Libr, Fairlawn, NJ, 81, Fairleigh Dickinson Univ, Edward Williams Col, NJ, 82, Manhattanville Col, New York, 85, New House Gallery, Staten Island, NY, 87, Staten Island Visions, 88; Works from the Permanent Collection, Staten Island Mus, New York, 87; Open Studio Tour & Show, 87; Staten Island Invitational, Newhouse Ctr, NY, 89; Summer on Broome, SOHO 20 Gallery, New York, 89; Women Printmakers, Queensborough Community Col Gallery, 91; Women for Choice, Womans Caucus Art Int, New York, 92; Resolutions, Affirmations, Acclamations, Art Lab, Snug Harbor, Staten Island, NY, 92. *Pos:* Lectr, 77-*Teaching:* Instr art, Queensborough Community Col, 80-85, adj asst prof, 85-*Awards:* Second Prize, Staten Island Rapid Transit Mural Contest, 79; Group Studio Arts Tours Grant, Staten Island Coun Arts, 87; Individual Artists Grant, NY State Coun Arts, 87. *Bibliog:* Vivian Raynor (auth), New York Times, 5/6/89; Michael Fressola (auth), Staten Island Advance, 5/14/89; Michael Fressola (auth), Staten Island Advance, 11/16/91 & 12/8/91; Michael Fressola (auth), Newsday, 11/17/91. *Mem:* NY Womens Caucus Art. *Media:* Acrylic, Mixed Media. *Mailing Add:* 49 Broad St Staten Island NY 10304

MAIN, TIM
PAINTER
b Pa, 1960. *Study:* Carnegie-Mellon Univ, Pittsburgh, Pa, BFA(sculpture & photog), 82. *Exhib:* Nautical Interiors and Seascapes, installation, Public Image Gallery, New York, 84; The Goetz Piece, installation, 151 Ridge Space, New York, 86; Singular Visions, Art in General, New York, 87; Men's Work, Union Seminary Chapel, New York, 88; two-person show, PS 122 Gallery, New York, 89; A Dislpay at Vigah, installation, Rotunda Gallery, Brooklyn, 90; Floating Tile Mosaic, proj installation, Artpark, Lewiston, NY, 90. *Awards:* Yaddo, Saratoga Springs, NY, residency, 89; Fine Arts Work Ctr Fel, Provincetown, Mass, 89; Nat Endowment Arts Visual Artist Fel, 89. *Bibliog:* Guerilla Artist, Newsday Mag, 9/20/87; Rotunda Installation--The Phoenix, Brooklyn, NY, 5/24/90; The Main Idea, Niagara Gazette, Niagara Falls, NY, 7/6/90. *Mailing Add:* 59 Grand St Brooklyn NY 11211

MAINARDI, PATRICIA M
HISTORIAN, CRITIC
b Paterson, NJ, Nov 10, 42. *Study:* Vassar Col, AB, 63; Columbia Univ, 63-65; New York Studio Sch, 65-66; Brooklyn Col, City Univ New York, MFA, 76; Hunter Col, MA, 80; City Univ New York, MPhilos, 81, PhD, 84. *Pos:* Ed, Women & Art, 71-72; ed, Feminist Art J, 72-73, contrib ed, 73-74; contrib ed, Arts Mag, 79-; dir, Goddard MFA Visual Arts Prog, 78-81. *Teaching:* Vis lectr, Pratt Inst, Mass Col Art, 73 & 74, Brooklyn Col, 76-78, Sch Visual Arts, 77 & Goddard Col, 77-81; asst prof, Harvard Univ, 84-85; assoc prof, Brooklyn Col & Grad Sch, City Univ New York, 85- *Awards:* Chester Dale fel, Nat Gallery Art, 81-82. *Mem:* Col Art Asn; Int Asn Art Critics; Am Hist Asn. *Mailing Add:* 602 Carlton Ave Brooklyn NY 11238

MAISEL, DAVID
PHOTOGRAPHER, ENVIRONMENTAL ARTIST
b New York, NY, Apr 22, 61. *Study:* Princeton Univ, BA(visual arts, art hist), 84. *Work:* Metropo Mus Art, New York; Int Mus Photog, George Eastman House, Rochester, NY; Rose Art Mus, Brandeis Univ, Waltham, Mass; Brooklyn Mus Art, NY; Baudoin Col Art Mus, Maine. *Exhib:* Collection Visions: Twelve Contemporary Photographers, Rose Art Mus, Waltham, Mass, 86; New Acquisitions, New Work, New Directions, Int Mus Photog, George Eastman House, Rochester, 89; Selected Photographs from the Permanent Collection, Brooklyn Mus Art, NY, 89; The New American Pastoral: Landscape Photography in and Age of Questioning, Int Mus Photog, George Eastman House, Rochester, NY, 90 & Whitney Mus Am Art, Equitable Ctr, New York, 90; Landscapes of Consequence, Aldrich Mus Contemp Art, Ridgefield, Conn, 91. *Teaching:* Instr photog, Cambridge Sch Weston, Mass, 84-85, Santa Fe Photog Workshops, 91. *Awards:* Nat Endowment Arts, Visual Arts Fel, 90; Exposed Terrain exhib, OPIS Found, 91. *Mem:* Advert Photog Am. *Media:* Photographc prints. *Mailing Add:* 16 E 23rd St New York NY 10010

MAISNER, BERNARD LEWIS
PAINTER
b Paterson, NJ, June 21, 54. *Study:* Cooper Union Col Art, New York, BFA, 77. *Work:* Philadelphia Mus Art; Pierpont Morgan Libr & Philip Morris, Inc, New York. *Exhib:* Solo exhibs, Kathryn Markel Gallery, New York, 82 & 85, Stux Gallery, New York, 88; New Drawing in America, The Drawing Ctr, New York, 84; Words-Pictures, Bronx Mus Art, NY, 84; Written Imagery, Fine Arts Mus Long Island, Hempstead, NY, 84; Precious, Grey Art Gallery, New York Univ, 84; Gold Illuminators, Metrop Mus Art, New York, 85; The Shape of Abstraction, Stux Gallery, Boston, 86. *Teaching:* Guest lectr, medieval manuscript illumination technique, Cloisters Mus & Metrop Mus Art, New York, 77- & J Paul Getty Mus, Malibu, Calif, 83. *Awards:* Best in Show Award, 77 & Jurors' Award, 86, New York Univ Small Works Show. *Bibliog:* Calvin Thompkins (auth), Artists' books, New Yorker Mag, 1/25/82; Lorraine Karafel (auth), Maisner exhibition--Markel Gallery, Arts Mag, 3/83; Grace Glueck (auth), Religion makes an impact, New York Times, 4/7/85; Arlene Raven (auth), Spirited, Village Voice, 3/8/88; Judy Schwendenwein (auth), Bernard Maisner, Art News, summer 88. *Media:* Painting, All Media. *Publ:* Auth, My molding, flowing conception of image and how it affects the universe, Tracks, A Journal of Artists' Writings, spring 77. *Mailing Add:* 41 Bleecker St No 1A New York NY 10012

MAITIN, SAM (SAMUEL CALMAN)
PAINTER, SCULPTOR
b Philadelphia, Pa, Oct 26, 28. *Study:* Philadelphia Mus Sch Art, dipl, 49; Univ Pa, BA, 51; printmaking with Ezio Martinelli and painting with Paul Froelich. *Work:* Libr Cong & Nat Gallery Art, Washington, DC; Mus Mod Art, New York; Pa Acad Fine Arts; Philadelphia Mus Art; Klingspor Mus, Frankfurt, Ger; and others. *Comn:* Mural, Annenberg Sch Commun, Univ Pa, 75, expanded, 85; Ark, Tapestry, Adath-Jeshurun Synagogue, Jenkintown, Pa, 76; three-story dimensional mural, Morgan, Lewis, Bockius law firm, Miami, Fla, 87; ceiling & wall banners, Wharton Sch, Univ Pa, 88; tapestry, Adath Jeshurun Synagogue, Jenkintown, Pa, 76. *Exhib:* Yoseido Gallery, Tokyo, 67, 69 & 70; 3rd Int Graphic Biennale, Poland, 70; Samuel Fleisher Art Mem, Philadelphia Mus Art, 71; William Penn Mus, Harrisburg, Pa, 75; Bicentennial Exhib, Philadelphia Mus Art, 76; Curwen Artists, Tate Gallery, London, 77; Gallery 10, Aspen, Colo, 81, 83 & 85; Dolan/Maxwell Gallery, Philadelphia, 85; Noyes Mus, NJ, 85; Pa Acad Fine Arts, 86; and others. *Pos:* Juror, Mass Artists Found, 87; Mem, Publ Adv Comt, Univ Pa, currently. *Teaching:* Instr design, Moore Col Art, 49-51; instr printmaking & drawing, Philadelphia Col Art, 49-59; dir visual graphic commun, Annenberg Sch Commun, Univ Pa, 64-70; instr drawing & printmaking, Philadelphia Mus Art, 64-69. *Awards:* John Simon Guggenheim Found Fel graphics, 68; 50 Best Bks of Yr, Minor White, 70; Art Matters Excellence Award, Mellon Gallery, 88. *Bibliog:* Willard Randall (auth), Is Philadelphia ready for Sam Maitin?, Philadelphia Inquirer, Today Mag, 11/18/73; Walter Plata (auth), Typografen unserer Zeit, Samuel Maitin, Heft; John Corr (auth), Profile: Sam Maitin, Inquirer, 11/12/85; Jan Biberman (auth), A Portrait of Sam Maitin, The Pa Gazette, 12/87. *Media:* Graphics. *Publ:* Designer, mirrors, messages, manifestations, work of Minor White, 69 & The Appalachian photographs of Doris Ulmann, 71, Aperture; painting, Turning of the Year, 70, Gentle Thursday, 71, Holt, Rinehart & Winston; paintings, Nothing in the Word, Mushinsha Ltd, Tokyo, Japan, 72; designer, Sculpture of a City: Philadelphia's Treasure Trove in Bronze and Stone, FPAA, Walker Publ Co, 74. *Mailing Add:* 704 Pine St Philadelphia PA 19106

MAJDRAKOFF, IVAN
PAINTER, ASSEMBLAGE ARTIST
b New York, NY, June 19, 27. *Study:* Cranbrook Acad Art, with Wallace Mitchell. *Work:* Univ Minn Gallery; Minneapolis Inst Art. *Comn:* Black & white photographic collage, Bronx State Hosp, NY, 71; Masonite outdoor mural, San Francisco Art Comn. *Exhib:* Pa Acad Art, Philadelphia; Detroit Art Inst, Mich; Walker Art Ctr, Minneapolis; San Francisco Mus Art; Drawing Exhib, Mus Mod Art, New York; Mass Inst Technol, 83; one man show, Cranbrook Mus, Bloomfield Hills, Mich, 86. *Pos:* Actg dir, Univ Art Gallery, Univ Minn, 52-55; dir, Stanford Univ Gallery, 62. *Teaching:* Instr drawing & painting, San Francisco Art Inst, 57-; instr drawing, Stanford Univ, 57-58 & 68-69. *Bibliog:* Al Wong (auth), Portrait of Ivan (film), 68. *Media:* Acrylic, Ink. *Mailing Add:* Dept Drawing-Painting San Francisco Art Inst 800 Chestnut St San Francisco CA 94133

MAJESKI, THOMAS H
PRINTMAKER, EDUCATOR
b Council Bluffs, Iowa, Sept 14, 33. *Study:* Univ Omaha, BFA, 60; Univ Iowa, with Mauricio Lasansky, MFA, 63. *Work:* Philadelphia Mus Art, Pa; Sheldon Mem Art Mus, Lincoln, Nebr; Joslyn Mus, Omaha, Nebr; Mus Voor Schone Funsten, Antwerp Belg; Guangzhou Acad Fine Arts, People's Rep China. *Comn:* Opera Omaha 25th Annv Print Edition. *Exhib:* Prints, Watercolors & Drawings, Pa Acad Fine Arts, Philadelphia, 65; Brooklyn Mus, New York, 66; Philadelphia Print Club, Pa, 67; Northwest Printmakers Int Print Exhib, Seattle, Wash & Portland, Ore, 67; Art On Paper, Univ NC, Greensboro, 68; 17 State Exhib, Springfield Art Mus, Mo, 74; Colorprint USA, Tex Tech Univ, Lubbock, 74; Int Miniature Print Competition, Pratt Graphics, New York, 83. *Teaching:* Prof printmaking, Univ Nebr Omaha, 63-82, prof art, currently; Chmn art dept, Univ Nebr Omaha. *Awards:* Purchase Awards, Philadelphia Print Club, 67, Nebr Centennial, 67 & Springfield Art Mus, 74. *Mem:* Col Art Asn; Mid-Am Col Art Asn. *Media:* Monoprints. *Mailing Add:* 1730 N 106th St Omaha NE 68114

MAKI, ROBERT RICHARD
SCULPTOR, PAINTER
b Walla Walla, Wash, Sept 15, 38. *Study:* Western Wash State Col, BA, 62; Univ Washington, MFA, 66; San Francisco Art Inst Summer Workshop, 67. *Work:* Washington Univ; State Hwy Admin Bldg, Olympia, Wash; Stanford Univ; Nat Collection Am Art, Washington, DC; Seattle Art Mus. *Comn:* Evergreen State Col, Olympia, Wash; Wake Forest Univ, Winston-Salem, NC; State Revenue Bldg, Salem, Ore; co-designer, Westlake Park, Seattle, Wash. *Exhib:* West Coast Now, Portland Art Mus & De Young Mus, 68; one-man shows, Seattle Art Mus, Wash, 73, Portland Ctr Visual Arts, Ore, 74, Southeastern Ctr Contemp Art, Winston-Salem, NC, 78 & Richard Hines Gallery, Seattle, Wash, 79 & 81; Reality of Illusions, Herbert F Johnson Mus Art, Cornell Univ, 79; Images & Latitude, Mona Bismark Estate, Paris, France, 88. *Pos:* Guest lectr at many schs & mus nationwide, 70- *Teaching:* Hon lectr, Univ Wash, Seattle, 66-68; guest artist, Humboldt State Univ, Calif, 74 & Wake Forest Univ, NC, 79. *Awards:* Purchase Award, Wright Found, 80; Nat Endowment Arts Senior Drawing Fel, 85; $30,000 King Co Hon Award, 90. *Bibliog:* Peter Selz & Tom Robbins (auth), West Coast report: The Pacific Northwest today, Art Am, 11-12/68; Jan Van de Marck (auth), Robert Maki at Center for Visual Arts, Art Am, 9-10/74; Bruce Guenther (auth), 50 NW Artists, 83. *Media:* All. *Mailing Add:* 8 Florentia Seattle WA 98109

MAKI, SHEILA ANNE
PRINTMAKER, PAINTER
b Sudbury, Ont, Aug 31, 32. *Study:* North Bay Normal Sch, teacher cert, 51; Univ BC, Can, 67; Camden Arts Ctr, London, Eng. *Work:* Hamilton Art Gallery, Kitchener-Waterloo Art Gallery & Ont Inst Studies Educ, Toronto, Can; Metrop Mus & Art Ctr, Miami, Fla; Ore State Univ; Cornell Univ, Ithaca, NY; Nat Mus Civilization, Ottawa; Bell Canada; Burnaby Art Gallery. *Comn:* Circling Around, (portfolio), Merritt Publ, Toronto. *Exhib:* Printmakers '82, Art Gallery Ont, Toronto, 82; Gloucester Co Col, Sewell, NJ; Int Print Soc, New Hope, Mass; Woodstock Pub Art Gallery, Woodstock, Ont; Glenhyrst Art Gallery of Brant, Brantford, Ont, 88; WKP Kennedy Gallery, North Bay, Ont, 89; and others. *Awards:* Hon Mention, 8th Burnaby Print Exhib, Burnaby Art Gallery, 75. *Bibliog:* Elaine Sills (article), Art in a Dream, Home Decor, Canada, 81; Mary Mason (auth), Artist, Glendon Univ, 85; Franz Geierhaus (article) J of the Printworld, fall 90. *Mem:* Boston Printmakers; Heliconian Club, Toronto (exec mem, 75-80 & 83-86, secy, 86-88). *Media:* Serigraphy; Acrylic. *Mailing Add:* c/o Venturgraph Int 19-400 Esna Park Dr Markham ON L3R 3K2 Canada

MAKLER, HOPE WELSH
DEALER
b Philadelphia, Pa, Mar 24, 24. *Study:* Drexel Univ, BS; Bryn Mawr Col & Univ Pa, MA; Barnes Found. *Pos:* Owner & pres, Makler Gallery, Philadelphia, currently. *Specialty:* Twentieth century painting, sculpture and graphics; Indian and African art. *Mailing Add:* 225 S 18th St Philadelphia PA 19103-6130

MALDJIAN, VARTAVAR B
PAINTER, WEAVER
b Marash, Cilicia, July 12, 1918; US citizen. *Study:* Maristes Brothers Col; Sch of Art, Paris, grad(fine painting). *Exhib:* Nat Aleppo for Carpet Picture, 50; Int Exhib, Damascus, Carpet Picture, 56; Nat Competition of Benedictine, New York, 66; Nat for Prof Artists, New York, 68; Da Vinci Int Open Art, New York Coliseum, 70; and many others. *Awards:* Silver Medal, Gustod of Terra Sancta (carpet picture), 50; Gold Medal for Carpet Picture, Int Exhib, Damascus, 56; Award for Original Oil, Da Vinci Int, New York, 70. *Bibliog:* Rev V Hovhanessian (auth), article on carpet picture, Massis, Beirut, 49; Abdallah J Hallack (auth), Ad-Dad, Monthly Art, 52; article about Pres Kennedy's carpet picture, Newark Eve News, 11/26/63. *Mem:* Am Fedn Art, New York. *Media:* Oil, Oriental Knots. *Collection:* V B Maljian Museum, original oils and carpet pictures. *Mailing Add:* 38 Oriental St Newark NJ 07104

MALDRE, MATI
PHOTOGRAPHER, EDUCATOR
b Geestacht, Ger, Apr 3, 47; US citizen. *Study:* Univ Ill, with Joseph Jachna, BA(design), 69; Inst Design, Ill Inst Technol, with Aaron Siskind, Arthur Siegel & Charles Swedlund, Encycl Britannica grant, 70-72, MS(photog), 72; also with Paul Caponagro, Jerry Uelsmann, Nathan Lyons & Les Krims. *Work:* Kalamazoo Art Ctr, Mich; Humboldt Arts Coun, Eureka, Calif; Pasadena Mus Art, Calif; Visual Studies Workshop, Rochester, NY. *Exhib:* Int Photo Show, Chicago, 74; First Light & Light II, Humboldt Arts Coun, 75; Ill Photogr Traveling Exhibs, Ill State Mus, Springfield, 78 & 82; Freshworks 79, Va Mus Fine Arts, Richmond; Friends of Photography, Carmel, Calif, 79 & 80; Univ Wis, Green Bay, 80; and others. *Pos:* Photogr & lab technician, Encycl Britannica, Chicago, 70-74; consult photog & graphics, Chicago Urban Corps, 72- *Teaching:* Asst prof photog, Chicago State Univ, 72-78, assoc prof, 78-; instr photog, Beverly Art Ctr, Ill, 73- *Awards:* Grand Award, Photo Images '76, Springfield; Merit Award, Radius '76, Burdee Mus, Rockford, Ill; Purchase Awards, Ill Photogr, Ill State Mus, 78 & 82. *Mem:* Soc Photo Educ; Int Mus Photo, George Eastman House; Friends of Photography. *Media:* Black and White, Cibachrome. *Publ:* Illusr, Encycl Britannica & Britannica Bk of Yr, 70-74; illusr, Comptons Encycl & Comptons Yr Bk, 70-74; illusr, Great Ideas Today, 70-74; illusr, Chicago: Metropolis of the Mid-Continent, Kendel/Hunt Co. *Mailing Add:* Dept Art 9501 S King Dr Chicago State Univ Chicago IL 60628

MALENDA, JAMES WILLIAM
ENAMELIST, EDUCATOR
b Kingston, Pa, Sept 14, 46. *Study:* Miami Dade Community Col, 69; Kent State Univ, BFA, 71; State Univ NY, MFA, 75. *Work:* Roberson Ctr Arts & Sci, Binghamton, NY; Univ Ga, Athens; Nordenfjeldske Kunstridustrimuseum, Trondheim, Norway; House of Humour and Satire, Gabrovo, Bulgaria. *Comn:* Advent Wreath, St Paul's Cathedral, Peoria, Ill, 80; Crucifix, Salem Lutheran, Peoria, Ill, 80; Medallions-Putnam, Rothberg, Bradley Univ, Peoria, 85; Wall Sculpture, Reading Tube Co, Reading, Pa, 90. *Exhib:* Enameling: Art and Industry, Nat Ornamental Mus, Memphis, Tenn; Int Exhib Enameling Art in Japan, Tokyo CentMus, & Ueno Royal Mus, 81, 83 & 85; Wine, Cooper-Hewitt Mus, New York, 85; Die Kugel-Glas & Metall, Deutsche Goldschmiedehaus, Hanau, Ger, 86; Masterworks Enamel 87, Taft Mus, Cincinnati; L'Art de L'Email, 10th Biennale Int, Limoges, France, 90. *Teaching:* Instr enamel & metal, Mohave Community Col, Kingman, Ariz, 75-76; assoc prof, Bradley Univ, Peoria, Ill, 76-78 & Kutztown Univ, Pa, 87- *Awards:* Enameling Award, Thompson Enamel Co, 90; Artists Fel, Ill Arts Coun, 84 & 86; Pa State System Grant, 90. *Mem:* Distinguished mem Soc NAm Goldsmiths. *Media:* Enamel, Metal. *Publ:* Coauth, A Sculptural breakdown of static three dimensional form through multi-positioning, Leonardo, Vol 19, Issue 4, 86; auth, A breakdown of static 3-D form through multi-positioning, Glass on Metal, Vol 5, nos 2 & 3, 4-6/86. *Dealer:* Gallery 500 Church/Old York Rd Elkins Park PA 19117. *Mailing Add:* Dept Art Educ/Crafts Kutztown Univ Kutztown PA 19530

MALER, M LEOPOLDO MARIO
SCULPTOR
b Buenos Aires, Arg, Apr 2, 37. *Study:* Univ Buenos Aires, law, 60; Int Asn Comparative Law, France, 62. *Work:* Tamayo Mus, Mex; Hess Collection, Napa, Calif; Fundacion San Telmo, Buenos Aires, Arg. *Comn:* Monument, Seoul Olympic Comt, Korea, 88; monument, Mayor of Madrid, Spain, 92. *Exhib:* 1st Biennale of Latinamerican Art, Sao Paulo, Brazil, 78; Echoes & Reflections, Ctr Interamerican Relations, NY, 82; Venice Biennale, Italy, 86; Otros Diluvios, Cult Ctr, Buenos Aires, Arg, 87; Latinamerican Art, Mus OAS, Washington, DC, 90; and others. *Pos:* Prog producer, BBC World Serv, London, 62-77; dir, Napa Contemp Arts Found, 88- *Teaching:* Vis prof art, Middlesex Polytechnic, London, 71-74; dean design, Parsons Sch Design, Santo Domingo, 83-85. *Awards:* First Prize, Sao Paulo Biennale Art, 77; Guggenheim Fel, 77; Medal Art Merits, Madrid, Spain, 91. *Bibliog:* BBC's Arena (dir), Maler's Requiem (film), BBC, 79; Edward Lucie-Smith (auth), Art Now, 85; Jorge Glusberg (auth), Maler, New York Univ, 87. *Media:* Recycled Metals, Wood. *Mailing Add:* 4411 Redwood Rd Napa CA 94558

MALLARY, ROBERT W
SCULPTOR, EDUCATOR
b Toledo, Ohio, Dec 2, 17. *Study:* Escuela Artes Libro, Mexico City, 38-39; Tamarind Litho Workshop, 62. *Work:* Mus Mod Art, Whitney Mus Am Art, New York; Los Angeles Co Mus; Albright-Knox Art Gallery, Buffalo; Univ Calif, Berkeley. *Comn:* Glass and plastic mosaic (with Dale Owen), Beverly Hills Hotel, 54; NY State Pavilion, New York World's Fair, 64; welded steel mural, Albany Mall Proj, 67. *Exhib:* 16 Americans, 59 & The Art of Assemblage, 61, Mus Mod Art, New York; Carnegie Inst,Pittsburgh, Pa, 62; Ten American Sculptors, Seventh Sao Paulo Biennial, Brazil, 63; Cybernetic Serendipity, Inst Contemp Art, London, 68. *Pos:* Dir, Arstecnica: Interdisciplinary Ctr for Art & Technol, Univ Mass, 72- *Teaching:* Asst prof art, Univ NMex, 55-59; adj prof, Pratt Inst, 59-67; prof sculpture, Univ Mass, Amherst, 67- *Awards:* Tamavird Fel, 62; Guggenheim Grant, 64. *Bibliog:* Art crashes through the junk pile, Life Mag, 51 & 60-64; Collage: personalities, concepts, techniques, Janis & Plesh, 62; Harris Rothenstein (auth), Ideoloque in lotus land, Art News, 10/66. *Mem:* Computer Arts Soc. *Publ:* Auth, Self interview, Location, spring 63; The air of art is poisoned, Art News, 10/63; coauth, interview, Artforum, 1/64; auth, Computer sculpture: Six levels of cybernetics, Artforum, 5/69; Spatial, Synesthetic Art through 3-D Projection: The Requirements of a Computer-Based Supermedium, Vol 23, No 1, Leonardo, 90. *Dealer:* Allan Stone Gallery 86th St at Madison New York NY 10028. *Mailing Add:* Box 97 Conway MA 01341

MALLIN, JUDITH YOUNG
WRITER, COLLECTOR
Study: Syracuse Univ, NY, 56; NY Univ, 57 & 87. *Pos:* Lectr, Courtauld Inst, London, 91; Art Inst, Chicago, 92; Sch Visual Arts, 92. *Awards:* Who's Who in East. *Res:* Surrealism; women artists of the forties, creativity and aging. *Collection:* Surrealist, women artists of the forties. *Publ:* Auth, Muriel Streeter, Anna Howard Gallery, 90; Virgil Thomson's Swan Song, Avenue Mag, 90; Juliet Man Ray, London Ind & Quest, NY, 92; Edward James, Quest, NY, 92; View: Parade of Avant Garde 1940-47, Thunders Mouth Press, NY, 92. *Mailing Add:* 719 Greenwich St New York NY 10012

MALLORY, MARGARET
COLLECTOR, FILMMAKER
b Brooklyn, NY, Oct 30, 11. *Pos:* Former pres, Falcon Films, Inc (doc art films); trustee, Santa Barbara Mus Art; trustee, Mystic Seaport, Conn; hon life dir, art affil, Univ Calif, Santa Barbara; adv bd, Women's Nat Mus Bd, Univ Calif, Santa Barbara; trustee mem Assoc Mus Asn; adv coun, Am Mus Britain. *Collection:* American and European paintings, drawings, sculpture, predominantly 19th & 20th century. *Mailing Add:* 305 Ortega Ridge Rd Montecito CA 93108

MALLORY, NINA AYALA
EDUCATOR, HISTORIAN
b Madrid, Spain; US citizen. *Study:* Columbia Univ, BArchit, 56, MA, 62 & PhD, 65. *Teaching:* Instr art hist, Rutgers Univ, New Brunswick, NJ, 65-66; asst prof renaissance, The Cooper Union, New York, 66-68; assoc prof renaissance & baroque, State Univ NY, Stony Brook, 68-86, prof, 86- *Awards:* Fulbright Fel, US Govt, 63; Nat Endowment Humanities Grant, 84-86; S H Kress Found Grant, 84-86. *Mem:* Col Art Asn; Am Soc for Hispanic Art Hist Studies. *Res:* Seventeenth century Spanish art. *Publ:* Auth, Roman Rococo architecture from Clement XI to Benedict XIV, 1700-1758, Garland, 77; coauth, Painting in Spain 1650-1700, Princeton, 82; auth, Bartolome Esteban Murillo, Alianza, 83; El Greco to Murillo, Spanish Painting in the Golden Age: 1556-1700. *Mailing Add:* 4 Washington Sq Village New York NY 10012

MALO, TERI (THERESA A MALO-SPRAWKA)
PAINTER, PRINTMAKER
b Whitinsville, Mass, July 20, 54. *Study:* Emmanuel Col, with Michael Jacques, BA, 76; Univ Mass, Amherst, with John Townsend & Fred Becker, MFA, 78. *Work:* Philadelphia Mus Art; IBM Inc, Rose Art Mus Brandeis Univ, Waltham, Mass; De Cordova Mus, Lincoln, Mass; Newport Art Mus, RI. *Exhib:* Philadelphia Int Print Exhib, Philadelphia Mus Art, 79; solo exhib, Pucker-Safrai Gallery, Boston, 79, 80, 82 & 83-92, JRS Gallery, Providence, RI, 86, 88 & 92 & Art Collectors Gallery, New York, 81; Miami Int Print Exhib, Fla, 80; Silvermine 13th Nat Print Exhib, 80; Prints, Heritage Mus, Sandwich, Mass, 82; Jerusalem to Boston, Mitchell Mus, Mt Vernon, Ill, 83; Prints & Pots, Newport Art Mus, 85; Danforth Mus, 88 & 92. *Teaching:* Instr fine arts, Buffalo State Col, NY, 90-91. *Mem:* Fenway Studios Inc. *Media:* Oil, Watercolor; Monotype. *Mailing Add:* Malo Studio 103 30 Ipswich St Boston MA 02215

MALONE, JAMES HIRAM
PAINTER, WRITER
b Winterville, Ga, Mar 24, 30. *Study:* Morehouse Col, AA, 50; Ctr Creative Studies Col Art and Design, with Sarkis Sarkesian, AA, 59. *Work:* Atlanta Univ, Ga; Univ South Ala, Mobile; Carnegie Art Inst, Pittsburgh, Pa; Pavilion Int, Montreal, Can; Knokke-Heist Mus, Knokke-Heist, Belgium. *Comn:* Wall of Pride mural, Grace Episcopal Church, Detroit, Mich, 68; wall mural, Jim Brady Restaurant, Detroit, Mich, 71; group mural painting, Atlanta Nat Festival, Ga, 86; Malone's Atlanta Book, Atlanta newspapers, Ga, 86-88; Literacy Art Installation, Colony Sq, Atlanta, Ga, 89. *Exhib:* Nat Black Arts Festival, Atlanta, Ga, 88 & 92; Street Scenes, Nexus Gallery, Atlanta, Ga, 90; Earth Factory exhib, Atlanta Ga, 90; Nat Black Arts Festival: Vanguard meets the Thursday Night Artists, Morris Brown Col, Atlanta, Ga, 90; Ctr Creative Studies Col Art/Design Nat Juried Alumni Exhib, Detroit, Mich, 91; and others. *Pos:* Graphic designer, Northgate Advert Agency, 68-80; art dir, artist-in-residence, Contemp Studios, 59-62; graphic designer, Altanta Newspaper, 81; advertising designer, Atlanta J & Constitution, Ga, 84; publisher, Literacy Cartoon Simply Apply Yourself, Southeastern Publ, Atlanta, Ga, 90- *Awards:* George M Clapp, Carnegie Nat, George H Clapp Found, 49; Nat Newspapers Art, 34th Ann Convention, Nat Newspapers Pub Assoc, 73; 1986 Bronze Jubilee, WPBA 30 Pub TV, 86. *Bibliog:* Mary Lou Liebaert (auth), Triple Threat Artist, Impresario Mag, 72; John Hughes (auth), 1986 Bronze Jubilee, WPBA 30 Pub TV, 86; Douglas DeLoach, Mattress Factory Show, Art Papers, 87. *Mem:* Black Arts Network and Advocacy (fine arts chmn, 86); Nexus Incorp Gallery; Nat Black Arts Fest (Ad Hoc Comm) 88; Visual Vanguard Art Assn; First World Writers Group, Atlanta, Ga; and others. *Media:* Acrylics, Enamel. *Publ:* Contribr, Afro-American Artists, Boston Pub Libr, 72; illusr, Malone's Atlanta, Southway, 88; auth, Anthology of Black Writers Poetry: Word Up, Beans & Rice Publ, 90; contribr, Bankhead Highway Beat column, Atlanta News Weekly, College Park, Ga, 91; illusr/writer, No-Job Dad, Victory Press, Monterey, Calif, 92; and others. *Mailing Add:* 1796 North Ave NW Atlanta GA 30318

MALONE, NOLA LANGNER
ILLUSTRATOR, WRITER
b New York, NY, Sept 24, 30. *Study:* Bennington Col, graphics with Daniel Shapiro & painting with Paul Feeley; Summer Art Sch, graphics with Gabor Peterdi, scholar. *Pos:* Illusr & retoucher, Videocrafts Television Art Studio, New York, 54-55. *Awards:* Outstanding Book Award, New York Times Juvenile Bk Sect, 69; Boston Globe, Horn Book Award, 75. *Bibliog:* Voice of America Rafiki; Australian Broad Corp; interview for Freddy My Grandfather, WNYC. *Mem:* Author's Guild; PEN Club; Artists Equity Assoc, New York. *Media:* Pencil, Watercolor. *Publ:* Illusr, Scram, Kid, 74 & auth & illusr, Rafiki, 77, Viking Press; auth & illusr, Dusty, Coward, McCann & Geoghegan, 76; illusr, Half a Kingdom, Warne & Co, 77 & Ms Mag, anniversary ed, 77; auth & illusr, Freddy My Grandfather, 79, Prince & the Pink Blanket, 80, Four Winds Press; Man Who Played Accordian Music, Pantheon, 79; Two Ghosts on a Bench, Harper & Row, 82; By the Light of the Silvery Moon, Lothrup, Lee & Sheperd, 83; A Home, MacMillan, 88; illusr, Earrings, Atheneum, 90. *Dealer:* Jane Feder 305 E 24th St New York NY 10010. *Mailing Add:* 39 E 12th St New York NY 10003

MALONE, PATRICIA LYNN
PAINTER
b Kansas City, Mo, Dec 3, 30. *Study:* Kansas City Jr Col, 48; Kansas City Art Inst, 49-51; Univ Tulsa, 78-80. *Work:* Oklahoma Art Ctr, Oklahoma City; Transco Energy Corp, Houston, Tex; Hallmark-Crown Ctr, Kansas City, Mo; Univ Tulsa, Okla. *Comn:* Painting, Cancer Care Ctr, 88; Logsdon Woody, 89. *Exhib:* Watercolor USA, Springfield Mus, Mo, 81, 83 & 89; Tri-State Watercolor Exhib, Wichita Mus Art, Kans, 81-86; Am Watercolor Soc, Salmagundi Club & Canton Mus, NY, Ohio, 82-88; Midwest Watercolor, Neville Pub Mus, Green Bay, Wis, 83-86. *Awards:* Phyllis France Award, Midwest Watercolor Soc, 85; First Place Watercolor, 4th Ann, Phillips Petroleum, 88. *Bibliog:* Watercolor '87, Am Artist Mag, 87; Ward (auth), New Spirit of Watercolor, North Light, 89; Albert-Wolf (auth), Splash 91, North Light; & others. *Mem:* Am Watercolor Soc; Nat Watercolor Soc; Midwest Watercolor Soc; Nat Watercolor Okla. *Media:* Watercolor. *Dealer:* M A Doran Gallery 3509 S Peoria Tulsa OK; Elizabeth Weiner Gallery 101 Ocean Ave M3 Santa Monica CA 90402. *Mailing Add:* 2807 E 48th St Tulsa OK 74105

MALONE, ROBERT R
PAINTER, PRINTMAKER
b McColl, SC, Aug 8, 33. *Study:* Furman Univ; Univ NC, BA; Univ Chicago, MFA; Univ Iowa. *Work:* New York Pub Libr; Calif Palace Legion Hon, San Francisco; Philadelphia Mus Art; Smithsonian Inst & Libr Cong, Washington, DC; Art Inst Chicago; Humana Inc, Louisville, Ky; Seven-Up Co, St Louis. *Comn:* Color etching, Int Graphic Arts Soc, New York, 66; several editions of intaglio & relief prints, Ferdinand Roten Galleries, Baltimore, Md, 66-69; two editions intaglio & relief prints, De Cinque Gallery, Hollywood, Fla, 67; color etching, Ill Arts Coun, 1st Print Comn, 73; several editions of lithographs, Lakeside Studio, Lakeside, Mich, 71-80. *Exhib:* Solo exhibs, Elliot Smith Gallery, St Louis & Merida Galleries, Louisville, Ky, 85 & 87, Rapp Gallery, Louisville, 90 & 92; New Talent in Printmaking, AAA Gallery, New York, 68; Biennial Print Exhib, Calif State Col, Long Beach, 69; Bienniale Int L'Estampe 1970, Mus Mod Art, Paris, 70; 26th Ann Exhib Boston Printmakers, De Cordova Mus, 74; Currents 29: Drawing in St Louis (with catalog), St Louis Art Mus, 85. *Teaching:* Assoc prof painting & printmaking, Wesleyan Col, Macon, Ga, 61-68; assoc prof printmaking, WVa Univ, Morgantown, 68-70; assoc prof printmaking, Southern Ill Univ, Edwardsville, 70-75, prof, 75- *Awards:* Purchase Award, Colorprint USA, Tex Tech Univ, 71; Recent Am Graphics Purchase Award, Univ Wis-Madison, 75; Southern Ill Univ Sr Res Scholar Award, 75 & 84. *Mem:* Col Art Asn Am. *Media:* Oil, Acrylic; Lithography, Montotype. *Dealer:* Yvonne Rapp Gallery 2007 Frankfort Ave Louisville KY 40206; Szoke Koo Assocs 164-166 Mercer St New York NY 10012. *Mailing Add:* 600 Chapman St Edwardsville IL 62025

MALOTT, MARY
PAINTER, CRITIC
b Indianapolis, Ind. *Study:* Radcliffe Col, BA; Art Students League; Brooklyn Mus Sch; Univ Tex, MFA. *Work:* NYNEX, New York; Far East Finance Ctr, Hong Kong. *Exhib:* Laguna Gloria Mus, Austin, Tex, 79; Tex Invitational, Contemp Arts Ctr, New Orleans, 80; Image of the House in Contemporary Art, Univ Houston, 81; 4th Texas Sculpture Symposium, Univ Tex, Austin, 83; Figure as an Image of the Psyche, Sculpture Ctr, New York, 85; Bronx Mus, NY, 86; Parker/Bratton Gallery, New York, 86; Carnegie-Mellon Univ, Pittsburgh, Pa, 88; Trabia/MacAfee Gallery, New York, 88; Aging The Process, The Perception, Forum Gallery, Jamestown, NY, 90; New Am Talent, 6th ed, Tex Fine Arts Asn, Laguna Gloria Mus, Austin, Tex, 90; Food, from Pleasure to Politics, Goodard-Riverside Ctr, New York, 90; Food, Nourishment, Production, Hunger & Culture, Ceres Gallery, New York, 90; Feather, Fur & Fin, 90 & New American Talent - 6th Exhib - Tex Fine Arts Exhib, 90, Laguna Gloria Mus, Austin, Tex; Hoyt National Art Show, Hoyt Inst Fine Arts, New Castle, Pa, 90; Aging, the Process, the Perception, Forum Gallery, Jamestown, NY, 90. *Pos:* Art critic, Austin Am-Statesman, Tex, 75-78. *Teaching:* Lectr, Univ Tex, 76 & 81, San Francisco Art Inst, 79, State Univ NY, Purchase, 81, Free Univ Berlin, 81 & Univ Dallas, 82, Art Alliance, New York, 86 & Carnegie-Mellon Univ, Pittsburgh, 88. *Awards:* Second Prize, Hoyt Nat Art Show, Hoyt Inst Fine Arts, New Castle, Pa, 90. *Bibliog:* Michael Brenson (auth), Figure as an image of the psyche, New York Times, 11/8/85; Walter Thompson (auth), Mary Malot at Carnegie-Mellon University, Art Am, 5/88; Frederick Ted Castle (auth), Mary Malot, Arts, 11/88; Dennis Wepman (auth), Mary Malott's Cosmic Conflicts, Mahattan Arts, 11/89. *Mem:* Austin Visual Arts Asn; Artists Equity; Women's Caucus Art; Nat Mus Women Arts. *Media:* Oil, Acrylic, Wood. *Publ:* Auth, Janis Provisor at New Orleans Mus Art, Art Voices South, 78; Alberto Giacometti: Evolution of drawing, Artweek, 78; Robert Indiana (exhib catalog), Neuberger Mus, Purchase, NY, 78; Marina Cappelletto, Arts Mag, 11/83; Four years in New York, Art & Artists, 2/88. *Dealer:* Amos Eno Gallery 594 Broadway New York NY 10012. *Mailing Add:* 284 Lafayette St No 3D New York NY 10012

MALPASS, MICHAEL ALLEN
SCULPTOR
b Yonkers, NY, Aug 18, 46. *Study:* Pratt Inst, BFA, 69, MFA, 73, MS, 77. *Work:* Rutgers Univ; Benenson Develop Corp, New York; Hechinger Collection; Virlane Found, New Orleans, La; Educ Testing Serv, Princeton, NJ; TRW, Martin 2, Margulies. *Comn:* Sculpture, General Electric, Schenectady, NY, 84; commemorative sculpture for Pratt Inst Centennial, Ford Foundation, 86; Trammell Crow Co, Dallas, Tex, 87; NJ Inst Technol, 89. *Exhib:* Betty Parsons Gallery, 78-82; solo exhibs, Andre Zarre Gallery, NY, 83, 84, 86, 87, 88, 89 & 90, Educ Testing Serv, Princeton, NJ, 88; Cold Spring Harbor Sci Lab, NY, 87, 88, 89 & 90; Greene Gallery, Coconut Grove, 87; NJ Arts Ann, Noyes Mus, 88; Shidoni Art Gallery, Tesuque, NMex, 88; Lever, NY, 88; Nat Bldg Mus, Washington, DC; Noyes Mus, 89 & 90. *Pos:* Sculpture & welding technician, Pratt Inst, 65-70; lectr, Rutgers Univ & Pratt Instr, 89, Columbus Col Art Design, Ohio, 90. *Teaching:* Instr sculpture, Pratt Inst, 72-77, asst prof, 77-87; lectr, Georgian Ct Col, Lakewood, NJ, 87-90. *Awards:* ETS Purchase Award; Dedicated Serv Award, Pratt Inst. *Bibliog:* Grace Glueck (auth), article, New York Times, 6/11/82; Dona Meilach (auth), Decorative and Sculptural Ironwork, Crown Publ, 77; articles in Artnews Mag, 3/79 & 5/84, New York Art Rev, 5/84 & Archit Digest, 5/84 & Metropolis Mag, 10/89 & Sculpture Mag, 11/88; Eileen Watkins (auth), Newark Star Ledger, 8/88 & 8/89; Arthur Williams (auth), Sculpture, Technique, Form, Content, Davis Publ, Worchester, Mass. *Mem:* Sculptors Guild Inc; Int Sculpture Ctr; Fedn Mod Painters & Sculptors; Found for Community of Artists; Sculptors Guild (exec bd, 83-). *Media:* Welding. *Dealer:* Andre Zarre Gallery 379 W Broadway Soho NY. *Mailing Add:* 593 Parker Ave Brick NJ 08714

MALPEDE, JOHN
PERFORMANCE ARTIST
b Wichita Falls, Tex, June 29, 45. *Study:* Univ Wis, BA, 68. *Pos:* Artistic dir, Los Angeles Poverty Dept, Theater Workshop, 86- *Awards:* Adalide Kent Award, San Francisco Art Inst, 87; Visual Arts Grant, Nat Endowment Arts, 88; Bessie Creation Award, Dance Theater Workshop, Los Angeles, Calif, 89. *Mailing Add:* 2124 Elsinore Los Angeles CA 90026

MALTA, VINCENT
INSTRUCTOR, PAINTER
b Brooklyn, NY, Apr 9, 22. *Study:* Art Students League. *Work:* Univ of Minn; Philadelphia Mus; Immaculate Heart Col; Birmingham Mus Art. *Exhib:* Brooklyn Mus Biennial Print Exhib, 52; Metrop Mus Nat Exhib of Watercolors, 52; Pa Acad Fine Arts, 53; Brooklyn Mus Int Watercolor Exhib, 53; Nat Acad of Design, 53. *Teaching:* Instr fine arts, painting, Art Students League, 66- *Awards:* Emily Lowe Award, 52; Louis Comfort Tiffany Found Award, 54; Betti Salzman Award, Nat Arts Club, 77. *Bibliog:* Marlene Schiller (auth), Return of the art spirit, Am Artist Mag, 3/78; Art Showcase, Manhattan Cable TV, 5/25/83 & 10/12/83. *Mem:* Artist Equity; Artists' Fel Inc, New York. *Media:* Mixed. *Mailing Add:* 1960 60th St Brooklyn NY 11204

MALTZMAN, STANLEY
PRINTMAKER, PAINTER
b New York, NY, July 4, 21. *Study:* New York Phoenix Sch Design, degree, 48. *Work:* Schenectady Mus, New York; Readers Digest; Hudson River Mus, Yonkers, NY; Carnegie-Mellon Univ; Mus Fine Arts, Springfield, Mass. *Comn:* Steuben Glass, Corning, NY; Danbury Mint, Norwalk, Conn; Fed Land Bank & Smith & Wesson, Springfield, Mass. *Exhib:* Am Acad Arts & Lett, New York, 69; Norfolk Mus Arts & Sci, Va, 71; Smithsonian Inst Traveling Exhib, 71-72; Berkshire Mus, Pittsfield, Mass, 79; Am Watercolor Soc, NY, 80; Albany Inst Hist & Art, NY, 81; Monotypes, The Painterly Print, NY, 86 & Pastel Soc Am, 89; Nat Acad Design, New York, 90. *Collections Arranged:* Color Fields from the Evening Sky, 83; The Fine Line, 84. *Teaching:* Instr drawing, Hudson Valley Workshops, 87, 88, 89 & 90. *Awards:* First Prize, Conn Acad Fine Arts, 76; Ball State Univ Award, 81; Drawing Prize, Berkshire Mus, Pittsfield, Mass. *Bibliog:* Article, Am Artist Mag, 4/86. *Mem:* Greene Co Coun Arts, Catskill, NY (visual arts coun); Knickerbocker Artists, NY. *Media:* Graphics; Watercolor, Pastel. *Publ:* Sounds of Mystery-Sounds of a Distant Drum, Holt, Rinehart, Inc, 67; Botanical Arts & Illustration, Carnegie-Mellon Univ, 77-78; Printworld Directory, 82, 83, 84 & 85. *Dealer:* Capricorn Gallery 4849 Rugby Ave Bethesda MD 20814; The Rice Gallery 135 Washington Ave Albany NY 12210. *Mailing Add:* Rte 1 Box 158 Freehold NY 12431

MANABU, MABE
PAINTER
b Uto District Kumamoto, Japan, 1924; Brazilian citizen. *Work:* Nat Mus Art, Okaka, Japan; Mus Fine Arts, Houston; Walker Art Ctr, Minneapolis; Mus Contemp Art, Boston; Dallas Mus Fine Arts. *Exhib:* New Art of Brazil, Walker Art Ctr, Minneapolis, 62; solo exhibs, Kumamoto Mus Art, Japan, 78, Kamakura Mus Art, Japan, 78, Nat Mus Art, Osaka, Japan, 78 & Kouros Gallery, New York, 89; Mus Mod Art Latin Am, Washington, DC, 80; Realidade Galeria de Arte, Mus De Arte de Sao Paulo, Rio de Janeiro, 86; Espace Latino Americain, Paris, 88. *Awards:* Purchase Award, Dallas Mus Art, 59; Fiat Award, 30th Venice Biennial, Fiat, 1960; First Award, 1st Am Art Biennial, Cordoba, 62. *Bibliog:* Jose Gomez Silre (auth), Mabe, 86; Jayme Mauricio (auth), Mabe, Yutaka Sanematsu, 86; Theodore F Wolfe (auth), Mabe, Kouros Gallery, 89. *Mailing Add:* c/o Kouros 23 E 73rd St New York NY 10021

MANCINI, JOHN
PAINTER
b Comiso, Italy, Jan 9, 25; US citizen. *Study:* Scuola d'Arte, Comiso, Italy, dipl; Liceo & Accad di Belle Arti, Palermo, Italy, BA; Art Students League; Columbia Univ. *Work:* Galleria Della Accademia, Palermo, Italy; Bank Am & Wells Fargo Bank, San Francisco; Mus Ital Art, Stone Park, Ill; Galeria de Colecionistas, Mexico City. *Exhib:* Crocker Mus Art, Sacramento, Calif, 67; Palace of Fine Art, San Francisco, 68; Heritage Gallery, Los Angeles, Calif; Mus Ital-Am, San Francisco, Calif; Robert Dana Gallery, San Francisco, Calif. *Pos:* art dir, R W Graphics, Palo Alto, Calif, 66-70 & Mancini Design, Mountain View, Calif, 70-90; Mancini Studio, S Mateo, Calif. *Teaching:* Art teacher painting, Scuola d'Arte, Comiso, Italy, 49-51. *Awards:* Gold Medal, Ital-Am Artists in USA, 77; Environ Protection Agency, San Francisco, 80; US Embassy, Bucharest, Rumania, 90- *Bibliog:* E M Polley (auth), John Mancini, Artforum, 65; Thomas Albright (auth), John Mancini, San Francisco Chronicle, 73; R L P (auth), Los Angeles Times, 84; and others. *Media:* Oil, Acrylic. *Dealer:* Hank Baum Gallery San Francisco CA 94115; Robert Dana Gallery Inc San Francisco CA 94123. *Mailing Add:* 604 Connie Ave San Mateo CA 94402

MANCUSO, LENI
PAINTER, INSTRUCTOR
b New York, NY. *Study:* Brooklyn Mus Art Sch; Art Students League; Pratt Inst, NY. *Work:* Newberry Collection, Detroit, Mich; First Nat Bank Boston; Portland Mus Art, Maine; Kresge Gallery, Ann Arbor, Mich; Mich Bell Tel; NH State Art Bank. *Exhib:* Wadsworth Atheneum, Hartford, Conn; Masters of Watercolor, Lamont Gallery, Exeter, NH, 78; one-man shows, Currier Gallery Art, Manchester, NH, 78-81, Art Ctr Hargate, Concord, NH, 81 & Thorne-Sagendorph Gallery, Keene, NH, 81; Chapel Arts Ctr, St Anselm's Col, 84; Manchester Inst Art & Sci, NH, 86; Deer Isle Artists Asn, 86-90; Maine Coast Artists, 78, 79; Leighton Gallery, 91. *Teaching:* Instr painting & head art dept, Proctor Acad, Andover, NH, 55-60; instr painting & watercolor, Currier Gallery Art Sch, Manchester, NH, 62-70; instr painting & compos, St Paul's Sch, Concord, NH, 67-75. *Awards:* Watercolor Prize, Portland Mus Art, Maine, 61 & Currier Gallery Art, NH, 68 & 81. *Bibliog:* J Silver (auth), The shapes of memory, Concord Monitor, 2/9/84; T Rawson (auth), Leni Marcuso at Manchester Institute, Art/New Eng, 3/87. *Mem:* NH Art Asn; Deer Isle Artists' Asn; Col Art Asn; Union of Maine Visual Artists. *Media:* Watercolor, Casein. *Dealer:* Arnold Klein Gallery 4520 N Woodward Royal Oak MI 48072; Leighton Gallery Blue Hill ME. *Mailing Add:* PO Box 303 Castine ME 04421

MANDEL, DOROTHY
PRINTMAKER, GRAPHIC ARTIST
b Boston, Mass. *Study:* Boston Mus Fine Arts; Mass Sch Art; Art Students League, graphic arts with Harry Sternberg. *Work:* Museum Ein Harod, Israel; Heard Mus, McKinney, Tex; Tulsa City-Co Libr Systems, Okla; Jefferson Co Librs, Golden, Colo; Univ Kans, Lawrence. *Comn:* Illus, Colo Quart, Boulder, 79; woodcut poster, Colo Music Festival, Boulder, 81; illus & bk jacket, Tlingit Tales, Naturegraph Publ,Happy Camp, Calif, 85; woodcut design for bk jacket, Univ Ill Press, Urbana, 85. *Exhib:* Central States Exposition, Pratt Community Col Gallery, Kans, 80; 13 Printmakers, Loretta Heights Col Gallery, Littleton, Colo, 82; Wood, W Nebr Art Ctr, Scottsbluff, 84; The Great Drawing Show, Colo Gallery of Arts, Arapahoe Col, 87; 100 Years/100 Works (traveling), Nat Asn Women Artists Mus Exhib, 89. *Teaching:* Workshops on the woodcut, Oberlin Col, Ohio, 72, Anchorage Fine Arts Mus, Alaska, 77 & Univ Colo, Denver, 85. *Awards:* Purchase Prize, 6th Ann Exhib-Arts Guild, Boston, 67; Hortense Ferne Award, Nat Asn Women Artists Ann, NY, 70; Janet Turner Traditional Graphics Award, Nat Asn Women Artists Ann, 80. *Mem:* Boulder Artists Guild (secy, 70-75); Colo Found on Arts; Colo Chapt, Artists Equity (secy, 79-81); Colo Chapt, Nat Asn Women Artists (secy & publicist, 89- 90); Nat Asn Women Artists, New York, 67- *Publ:* Auth, Rediscovering angna enters, Frontiers-A Journal of Women Studies, fall 81; auth, A forgotten woman-angna enters, Daily Camera, Boulder, 11/86; auth, Uncommon Eloquence: A Biography of Angna Enters, Arden Press, Denver, 86; auth, Dame Judith Anderson-Actress of an Era (in prog). *Mailing Add:* 355 Balsam Ln Boulder CO 80304

MANDEL, HOWARD
PAINTER, SCULPTOR
b Bayside, NY, Feb 24, 17. *Study:* Pratt Inst, New York; New York Sculpture Ctr; Art Students League; Atelier Fernand Leger, Paris; Atelier Andre L Hote, Paris; Ecole Beax Arts, Sorbonne, France. *Work:* Whitney Mus Am Art, New York; Butler Inst Am Art, Youngstown, Ohio; Norfolk Mus Arts & Sci, Va; State Univ Teachers Col Mus, Oswego, NY; San Antonio Mus, Tex. *Comn:* Three-dimensional mural, Zenith Radio Corp, Woodstock, NY, 58. *Exhib:* Whitney Mus Am Art Ann, 48-59; American Painting Today 1950, Metrop Mus Art, New York, 50 & Am Watercolors, Drawings & Prints, Metrop Mus Art, New York; Nat Inst Arts & Lett, Acad Art Gallery, New York, 55 & 61; Fulbright Painters, Whitney Mus Am Art & Smithsonian Inst, Washington, DC, 59. *Pos:* Graphic artist, film design, CBS-TV Studio One, 54-57 & NBC-TV, Amahl & the Night Visitors, 55; art dir, Heath de Rochemont, D C Heath & Co, Boston, 63-68, Roemer-Young Assocs, New York, 69 & Film Group Inc, Cambridge, Mass, 71. *Awards:* Louis Comfort Tiffany Fel, 39 & 49; Hallmark Int Awards, 49, 52 & 55; Fulbright Scholar to Paris, 51-52. *Bibliog:* Herdeg & Rosner (auth), article in Graphics Ann, 55; The Art Comics & Satires of A D Reinhardt, George Wittenborn; Archives of American Art, Smithsonian Inst, Washington, DC. *Mem:* Am Watercolor Soc; Nat Soc Mural Painters; Nat Soc Painters in Casein & Acrylic; Audubon Artists; Allied Artists Am; and others. *Media:* Multi. *Mailing Add:* 285 Central Park W No 1W New York NY 10024

MANDEL, JOHN
PAINTER
b New York, NY, Dec 6, 41. *Study:* Pratt Inst, BFA, 64. *Work:* Nat Gallery Australia; Pa State Univ. *Exhib:* Whitney Mus Am Art Painting Ann, 69 & 72; The Contemporary Figure, A New Realism, Suffolk Mus & Carriage House at Stony Brook, NY, 71; In Sharp Focus, Sidney Janis Gallery, New York, 72; Indianapolis Mus Ann, Ind, 72; one-man shows, Max Hutchinson Gallery, New York, 71-73, 75 & 79. *Pos:* Assoc dean, Sch Art & Design, Calif Inst Arts. *Teaching:* Instr painting, grad & undergrad sch, Pratt Inst, 71-76; instr painting, Calif Inst Arts, 72- *Awards:* Paul Mellon Fel, 79. *Bibliog:* John Canaday (auth), Art: The figure as defined by Mandel, 11/21/71 & Art: In Mandel's Art, superb control, 4/28/73, New York Times. *Mailing Add:* c/o California Institute of Arts 24700 McBean Pkwy Valencia CA 91355

MANDEL, MIKE
EDUCATOR, PHOTOGRAPHER
b Los Angeles, Calif, Nov 24, 50. *Study:* Cal State, Northridge, BA, 72; San Francisco Art Inst, MFA, 74. *Work:* Mus Mod Art, New York; San Francisco Mus Mod Art; Bibliotech Nat, Paris, France. *Exhib:* Evidence, San Francisco Mus Mod Art, 77; New Photog 5, Mus Mod Art, New York, 89; Making Good Timé, Calif Mus Photog, Riverside, 90. *Teaching:* Instr photog, Cabrillo Col, Aptos, Calif, 83- *Awards:* Photog Fel, Nat Endowment Arts, 88; Art Pub Bldgs Prog, Calif Arts Coun, 90; James B Phelan Award, San Francisco Community Workshop, 90. *Dealer:* Douglas Drake Gallery 50 W 57th St New York NY 10019. *Mailing Add:* 235 Sunset Ave Santa Cruz CA 95060

MANDELBAUM, ELLEN
STAINED GLASS ARTIST, WRITER
b New York, NY, June 16, 38. *Study:* Ind Univ, AB, 60, MFA, 63; study with Ludwig Schaffrath, Jochem Poensgen, Albinus Elskus, Jean Dominique Fleury. *Work:* Shoreham-Wading River Libr, Long Island, NY; Living Art Found, New York; Ind Univ, Bloomington; Nishida Mus, Toyama, Japan. *Comn:* Commemorative panel for Hon Geraldine Ferraro, Queens, NY, 84; square arch, Broadcast Dept, New York, 87; landscape painted windows, comn by Dr William Wedin, Southampton, Long Island, 88; Genessee Ctr for Arts, Rochester, NY, 92. *Exhib:* Solo exhibs, Shoreham-Wading River Pub Libr, Shoreham, Long Island, 83 & 85, Port Wash Pub Libr, NY, 90; International Flatglass: 30 Women from 12 Countries, Monica Trujen Gallery, Bremen, W Ger, 88; Int Exhib, Centre Int Du Vitrail, Chartres, France, 89; Hudson River Mus, Yonkers, NY, 90; Personal visions Invitational, New Glass Workshop, NY, 91; Int Women's Exhibs, Rejkavik, Iceland, 89, Swansea, Wales, 91. *Pos:* Owner, Ellen Mandelbaum Stained Glass, 81- *Teaching:* Docent exhibs, Whitney Mus Am Art, 64-66; lectr mod painting, Hunter Col, 64-67; glass painting, Glass Crafters, Long Island, NY, 90. *Awards:* Judges Choice, Stained Glass Asn Am, Toronto, 85; Visual Art Award of Excellence, Modern Liturgy Mag, 87 & 89. *Bibliog:* Patricia Conway (auth), Art for Everyday, Clarkson N Potter Inc, New York, 90; Profile, A Brush with Freedom: The work of Ellen Mandelbaum, Professional Stained Glass, 2/90; Ellen Mandelbaum (auth), In My House there are many mansions, Faith & Form, 91. *Mem:* Prof affiliate Am Inst Archit, New York (Art & Archit Comt, 86-); Alliance Women Archit (Coord Comt, 86-87);

Glass Soc, New York (mem bd, 82-85, pres, 85); Stained Glass Asn Am. *Media:* Stained Glass. *Publ:* Dada & surrealism show at the Museum of Mod Art, Artforum, 68; contribr, Glass Art in Architecture, Thoughts & Ideas, Poensgen, Dusseldorf, 88; auth, The Vence Chapel: Matisse's Legacy in Stained Glass, New Work, 88; New Glass, The Painterly Alternative, Professional Stained Glass, 92. *Mailing Add:* 39-49 46th St Long Island City NY 11104

MANDELBAUM, LYN
PAINTER, PRINTMAKER
b New York, NY, Sept 7, 50. *Study:* Tyler Sch Art, Rome, 70-71, Philadelphia, BFA, 72, MFA, 74. *Work:* Philadelphia Mus Art; Otis Libr, Los Angeles; New York Libr; Jean Brown Arch, Tyringham, Mass. *Comn:* Mural, Byblos Dicoteque, Marigot, St Martin, 81. *Exhib:* Mus Mod Art, New York, 73; Images-Dimensional-Movable-Transferable, Akron Art Inst, Ohio, 73; Fed Reserve Bd, Washington, DC, 74; Pa State Univ Mus Art, 74; Photo-Synthesis, Johnson Mus Art, 76; two-person exhib, 14 Sculptors Gallery, New York, 80; solo exhib, Foundations Gallery, New York, 82. *Pos:* Founder & dir, Eastern Shore Press, Philadelphia, 74-76 & Street Ed Inc, New York, 79-; pres, Island Magic Inc, New York, 82- *Teaching:* Lectr printmaking, Philadelphia Col Art, 76-78; instr, Tyler Sch Art, 77-78. *Awards:* Purchase Award, Univ Del, Newark, 71. *Media:* All. *Publ:* Auth, Moderate Expectations, 78 & Anita's Revenge, 78, pvt publ; Consider Yourself Lucky, Street Ed Inc, 79; Notes: Keep a Candle Burning, pvt publ, 80; Say, Street Ed Inc, 82. *Mailing Add:* 20 Desbrosses St New York NY 10013

MANDELMAN, BEATRICE M
PAINTER
b Newark, NJ, Dec 31, 12. *Study:* Art Students League, studied with Fernand Léger, Paris, France. *Work:* NMex Mus Fine Arts; Metrop Mus, New York; Baltimore Mus. *Exhib:* One-woman shows, Balkan Series: Paintings/Collages, 78, Moontime: Small Paintings, 81, Intimate Echoes, New Gallery, Taos, NMex, 83, Jazz Suite, Harwood Found, Taos, NMex, 88 & Brazil Suite, Shidoni Gallery, Santa Fe, NMex, 89; El Paso Mus, Tex; Denver Mus; Taos Abstractionists & Taos Calendar Show, Stables Art Gallery, NMex, 89. *Teaching:* Teacher painting, Taos Valley Art Sch, 46-53. *Awards:* Oakes First Prize, Taos Art Asn Gallery, 62; Best Painting, Stables Art Gallery, 68; First Prize, Jury Show, 75. *Bibliog:* Patricia Hurst (auth), Beatrice Mandleman: The energy of stillness, Artspace Mag, 9/80; Ed Sasek (auth), Bea Mandleman: The pulse of contemporary time, Artspace Mag, spring 82. *Mem:* Taos Art Asn. *Media:* Mixed. *Publ:* Cover, Artspace Mag, fall 88. *Mailing Add:* Box 891 Taos NM 87571

MANDLE, EARL ROGER
MUSEUM DIRECTOR
b Hackensack, NJ, May 13, 41. *Study:* Williams Col, BA, 63; Art Students League; Inst Fine Arts, NY Univ, mus training cert & MA, 67; Metrop Mus Art; Victoria & Albert Mus; Univ Toledo, Hon DFA, 83; Kenyon Univ, Hon DFA, 86. *Collections Arranged:* 30 Contemporary Black Artists, 68; Catalogue of European Paintings, Minneapolis Inst Arts, 70; Dutch Masterpieces from the 18th Century, 71-72; Dutch Silver, 80; El Greco of Toledo, 82. *Pos:* Cur, Inst Fine Arts Photog Arch, New York, 67; assoc dir, Minneapolis Inst Arts, 67-71 & 72-74; assoc dir, Toledo Mus Art, 74-77, dir, 77-88; deputy dir, Nat Gallery Art, Washington, DC, 88- *Teaching:* Instr art, Phillips Acad, Andover, Mass, 63-64 & McBurney Sch, New York, 64-65; vis lectr, Univ Wis, 73; adj prof, Univ Toledo, currently. *Awards:* Andover Teaching Fel, 63; Ford Found Mus Training Fel, 66; Nat Endowment Arts Fel, 74; Ohio Gov Award, 83. *Bibliog:* J Woelm (auth), Dutch Masterpieces from the 18th century (film), Woelm-Polister Prod, 72; J Canaday (auth), Dutch masterpieces from the 18th century, New York Times, 72. *Mem:* Am Asn Mus; Am Arts Alliance; Asn Art Mus Dirs; Art Mus Asn; Col Art Asn; Nat Coun Arts; and many others. *Res:* Eighteenth century Dutch art and nineteenth century English art. *Publ:* A ceiling design by Jacob de Wit, Toledo Mus Art News, 75; Jacob de Wit's drawings of temperance, Register, Univ Kans, 2/77; Adriaen Coorte, a unique late seventeenth century Dutch still-life painter, Burlington Mag Publ Ltd; The Fine Arts and Human Values in Higher Education, Univ Toledo, 79; Lifelong Learning in the Humanities, Philadelphia, Pa, 12/79. *Mailing Add:* Nat Gallery Art 6th & Constitution Ave NW Washington DC 20565

MANDZIUK, MICHAEL DENNIS
PAINTER, SERIGRAPHER
b Detroit, Mich, Jan 14, 42. *Study:* Self taught. *Work:* Minn Mus Art, St Paul; Borg Warner Corp, Chicago; Kemper Ins Collection, Long Grove, Ill; Art Ctr Collection, Park Forest, Ill; Springfield City Collection, Ill. *Exhib:* Tex Fine Arts Asn Travel Shows, 71, 72 & 74; Boston Printmakers Nat, 72-74; Minn Mus Art Drawing Biennial, St Paul, 73; Butler Inst Am Art, Youngstown, Ohio, 73-75; one-man shows, Welna Gallery, Chicago, 74 & Ukrainian Inst Mod Art, Chicago, 75; Hunterdon Nat Print Show, 74; Okla Art Ctr Nat Print Show, 74; 22nd Art Conf, Univ Mich, 74; Mitchell Art Mus, Mt Vernon, Ill, 75; Battle Creek Art Ctr, Mich, 76. *Pos:* Artist-craftsman juror, Ann Arbor St Art Fair, 71; graphic specialist, Ford Motor Co. *Awards:* Best of Show Award; Old Capt Art Fair Award, Springfield, Ill, 73-74; Detroit Artist Market, 71-72. *Media:* Acrylic; Silk Screen. *Mailing Add:* 7191 Kolb St Allen Park MI 48101

MANERA, ENRICO ORLANDO
SCULPTOR, PAINTER
b Asmara, Italy, April 4, 47. *Study:* Liceo Artistico, Acad Fine Arts, Rome, 67. *Work:* Museo D'arte Moderna, Spoleto, Italy; Galleria D'arte Moderna Rondanini, Rome, Italy; Museo Nazionale Della Grafica, Rome, Italy; Palazzo Del Governo, Bari, Italy; Archivio Storico Della Biennale Di Venezia, Venezia, Italy. *Comn:* Sculpture, Mus Mod Art, Spoleto, Italy, 79; painting, Salzano Inst, Rome, Italy, 80 & Puglie Region, Bari, Italy, 82; sculptures (five), Valadier Inst, Rome, Italy 84; sculpture, Colaco Real Estate/Land Developer, Calif, 90. *Exhib:* Pop Art in Italy, Palazzo Collicola, 80 & Norma Jean, Mus Mod Art, 82, Spoleto, Italy; Tribute to Man Ray, Art Inst, Rome, Italy, 81; Visioni Imperiali, Cortina Inst, Rome Italy, 90; Arte Rome 90, Palazzo Del Congressi, Italy. *Awards:* Eight Premio Pittura, Martina Franca, Salvatore Basile, 80. *Bibliog:* Di Castro (auth), National Gallery, Casa Vogue, 4/79; Carmine Benincasa (auth), La Tavola Di Paro, Selecta, 6/79; Ruggero Marino (auth), Pop Art Don't Surrender, Il Tempo, 5/80. *Mailing Add:* 120 Morningside Dr San Francisco CA 94132

MANES, BELLE
PAINTER
b New York, NY. *Study:* Cooper Union, BFA, 78. *Work:* General Electric, Uminim Corp. *Exhib:* Philadelphia Mus, 47; Ann Print Show, Brooklyn Mus, 49; Albright-Knox Gallery Ann, 54; Nat Asn Women Artists Ann, Nat Acad, Fed Bldg, New York, 62-92; Hudson River Mus Ann, New York, 75-78, 90; Ann New England Show, Silvermine Gallery, Conn, 79, 81 & 91; Art of the 80's, Westport Mus, Conn, 82; Branchville Soho Gallery 82-92; Trustees Choice, Larry Aldrich Mus, Conn, 83; Pindar Gallery, New York, 86; Katonah Gallery, Conn, 88. *Teaching:* Instr art, Plainfield Community Ctr, NJ, 56-59 & privately, White Plains, NY, 62-64; mentor, Pratt Inst, 78. *Awards:* Medal Honor, Nat Asn Women Artists, 79; Top Silvermine Award, New England Show, 81. *Mem:* Nat Asn Women Artists; Hudson River Contemp Artists; Silvermine Guild. *Media:* Oil, Acrylic. *Dealer:* Branchville Soho Gallery RR Sta Rtes 7 & 102 Ridgefield CT 06829. *Mailing Add:* 1097 North St White Plains NY 10605

MANES, PAUL
PAINTER
b Austin, Tex, May 4, 48. *Study:* Lamar Univ, Beaumont, Tex, BBA, 72, BFA, 83; Sch Fine Arts Hunter Col, NY, MFA, 84. *Work:* Metrop Mus Art & Guggenheim Mus, New York; Herbert Johnson Mus Art, Cornell Univ, Ithaca, NY; Houston Mus Fine Arts, Tex; Beaumont Art Mus, Tex. *Exhib:* Jan Turner Gallery, Los Angeles, 87 & 90; Pascal de Sarthe Gallery, San Francisco, 88; Betty Moody Gallery, Houston, 88; C Grimaldis Gallery, Baltimore, 88; Marisa Del Re Gallery, NY, 92. *Bibliog:* Carter Ratcliff (auth), Paul Manes (exhib catalog), Kouros Gallery, 87; Phyllis Tuchman (auth), Paul Manes (exhib catalog), Kouros Gallery, 89. *Media:* Oil, Mixed Media. *Mailing Add:* c/o Kouros 23 E 73rd St New York NY 10021

MANETTA, EDWARD J
ADMINISTRATOR, PAINTER
b Export, Pa, Dec 26, 25. *Study:* Carnegie-Mellon Univ, BA, 53; Univ Pittsburgh; Herron Sch of Art, Ind Univ, Indianapolis, MFA, 55; Fulbright Exchange fel, Gt Brit, 58-59; John Hay Humanities fel, Williams Col, Williamstown, Mass & Bennington Col, Vt, 61; NY Univ, EdD(creative arts), 65. *Work:* Ansty Col, Eng; Marygrove Col, Detroit; Ball State Art Mus, Muncie, Ind; South Bend Art Mus, Ind; HWA Kang Mus, Taipei, Taiwan; and others. *Comn:* Paintings, Ford Motor Co, Detroit, 63; paintings, St Vincent's Priory, New York, 70; paintings, RCA Corp, New York, 70; mural, Mule Plastics Corp, Haupague, NY, 73; mural, Electrical Union Cult Ctr, New York, 75; painting, Project Liberty, Cincinnati, Ohio. *Exhib:* Butler Inst Am Art, Youngstown, Ohio, 53; Pa Acad Fine Arts, Philadelphia, 53; Cincinnati Art Mus, Ohio, 55; Nat Acad Design, New York, 56; Royal Soc Galleries, Birmingham, Eng, 59; Herron Art Mus, Indianapolis, 60; Nat Hist Mus, Taipei, 77; HWA Kang Mus, Taipei, 77. *Teaching:* Instr, Herron Sch Art, 55-61; Fulbright lectr art, Ansty Col, Sutton Coldfield, Eng, 58-59; prof, Marygrove Col, Detroit, 61-63; prof fine arts, St John's Univ, Jamaica, NY, 63-67, chmn fine arts dept, 68-, Fulbright exchange prof, Nat Taiwan Normal Univ, Taipei, spring 78. *Awards:* vis artist fel, Col Chinese Cult, Taipei, 76. *Mem:* Col Art Asn; Nat Coun Art Adminrs; Am Asn Univ Prof; Nat Soc Skull & Circle; Am Acad Art & Lett. *Media:* Oil, Acrylic. *Publ:* Contribr, Evolution of the City, 74 & illusr, Education Textbook, 77, St John's Press; illusr, Administrators Guide to New Programs for Faculty Management and Evaluation, Parker Publ Co, West Nyack, NY, 77. *Mailing Add:* 1516 Cool Creek Dr Carmel IN 46032

MANGEL, BENJAMIN
DEALER
b Philadelphia, Pa, Jan 12, 25. *Pos:* Owner, Benjamin Mangel Gallery, Philadelphia, Pa. *Specialty:* Contemporary paintings and sculpture. *Mailing Add:* Benjamin Mangel Gallery 1714 Rittenhouse Sq Philadelphia PA 19103-6110

MANGIONE, PATRICIA ANTHONY
PAINTER, MURALIST
b Seattle, Wash. *Study:* Fleisher Art Mem, Philadelphia; Barnes Found, Merion, Pa. *Work:* Inst Contemp Art, Dallas; Fleisher Art Mem, Philadelphia; Fidelity Bank, Philadelphia; Univ Pa; Noyes Mus, NJ. *Comn:* Acrylic on wood mural, Continental Bank & Trust Co, Philadelphia, 69. *Exhib:* One-man shows, Frank Rehn Gallery, 60-75 & Univ Pa, 64 & 80; Philadelphia Art Alliance, 75; Newman Galleries, Philadelphia, 78; More Gallery, Philadelphia, 82. *Pos:* Illusr, Sicilia, Ital Govt Quart, 66 & 68; bd mem, Va Ctr Creative Arts, 82- *Awards:* Six Yaddo Resident Fels, 62-79; Artistic Contrib Philadelphia, Artists Equity Asn, 82; First Prize & Medal, Philadelphia Sketch Club, 87. *Bibliog:* Burton Wasserman (auth), The Art of Patricia Mangione, Sims Press, 71; James R Mellow (auth), Mangione at Rehn Gallery, New York Times, 74; Victoria Donohoe (auth), Paintings by Pat

Mangione, Philadelphia Inquirer, 82. *Mem:* Artists Equity Asn; Philadelphia Art Alliance; Main Line Ctr Arts. *Media:* Oil, Acrylic. *Publ:* Auth, Some observations on the experience of painting, Parapsychology Found, 70; Exercise in magic, Sunday Bulletin, Philadelphia, 71. *Dealer:* Newman Gallery 1625 Walnut St Philadelphia PA 19103. *Mailing Add:* 3300 Darby Rd Apt 7315 Haverford PA 19041

MANGOLD, ROBERT PETER
PAINTER
b North Tonawanda, NY, Oct 12, 37. *Study:* Cleveland Inst Art, 56-60; Yale Univ, Fel, 59, BFA, 61, MFA, 63. *Work:* Solomon R Guggenheim Mus, Mus Mod Art & Whitney Mus Am Art, New York; Mus Fine Arts, Houston; La Jolla Mus Contemp Art, Calif; Albright-Knox Art Gallery; Art Inst Chicago; and many others. *Exhib:* Solo exhibs, Attic Series I-VI, Lisson Gallery, London, Eng, 90, New Paintings: Studies for the Attic Series, Paula Cooper Gallery, New York, 91, Daniel Weinberg Gallery, Los Angeles, 91, The Attic Series, Pace Gallery, New York, 92, Pace Eds, New York, 92, The Oberlin Window, Allen Mem Art Mus, Oberlin Col, Ohio, 92 & Le Consortium, Dijon, France, 92; The Living Object, the Art Collection of Ellen H Johnson, Allen Mem Art Mus, Oberlin Col, Ohio, 92; 15th Anniversary Exhib, Rhona Hoffman Gallery, Chicago, 92; Academy-Institute Invitational Exhib of Painting and Sculpture, Am Acad & Inst Arts & Letts, New York, 92; group show, Galerie Lelong, New York, 92; Shapes and Position, Ritter Klagenfurt, Austria, 92-93; and many other one-man & group exhibs. *Teaching:* Instr art, Sch Visual Arts, 63-, Hunter Col, 64-65, Skowhegan Summer Art Sch, Yale-Norfolk Summer Art Sch, 69 & Cornell Univ, 70. *Awards:* Nat Coun on Arts Award, 66; Guggenheim Mem Grant, 69. *Bibliog:* Judith Russi Kirshner (introd), The Refco Collection, Essays by Eleanor Heartney, Anne Rorimer & James Yood, Refco Group Ltd, Chicago, 90; Minimal Art (exhib catalog), Nat Mus Art, Osaka, 90; Geoffrey Blodgett & Elizabeth A Brown (auths), Robert Mangold: The Oberlin Window (essays), Allen Mem Art Mus, Oberlin Col, Ohio (exhib catalog), 92; Klaus Kertess (auth), Robert Mangold: The Attic Series (exhib catalog), Pace Gallery, New York, 92; Elizabeth Brown (auth), The living object, the art collection of Ellen A Johnson (exhib catalog), Allen Mem Art Mus Bull, Oberlin Col, Ohio, 92; and many others. *Dealer:* John Weber Gallery 420 W Broadway New York NY 10012. *Mailing Add:* c/o Paula Cooper Gallery 155 Wooster St New York NY 10012

MANGOLD, SYLVIA PLIMACK
PAINTER
b New York, NY, Sept 18, 38. *Study:* Cooper Union, cert, 59; Yale Univ Art Sch, BFA, 61. *Work:* Albright-Knox Art Gallery, Buffalo, NY; Yale Univ Art Gallery; Mus Mod Art, Whitney Mus Am Art, New York;; Weatherspoon Art Gallery, Greensboro, NC; Walker Art Ctr, Minneapolis, Minn; Utah Mus Fine Arts; Brooklyn Mus; Detroit Inst Art. *Exhib:* one-person shows, Young Hoffman Gallery, Chicago, 80, Nocturnal Paintings, Contemp Arts Mus, Houston, 81, Paintings, Brooke Alexander Inc, 82, 84, 86 & 89, Rhona Hoffman Gallery, 85, Tex Gallery, Houston, Brooke Alexander, New York & Fuller Goldeen Gallery, San Francisco, 87;; A Contemporary View of Nature, Aldrich Mus, Ridgefield, 86-87; 15th Anniversary, Flander's Contemp Art, Minneapolis, 87; Anne Marie Verna Galerie, Zurich, 88; 15th Anniversary, Flanders Contemp Art, Minneapolis, 87; Group Show, Annemarie Verna Galerie, Zurich, 88; Landscape Anthology, Grace Borgenicht Gallery, New York, 88; The Unnatural Landscape, Fay Gold Gallery, Atlanta, 88; The Transformative Vision; Contemporary American Landscape Painting, Three Rivers Arts Festival, Pittsburgh; Making Their Mark, Women Artists Move into the Mainstream, 1970-1985, Cincinnati Art Mus, New Orleans Mus Art, Denver Art Mus & Pa Acad Fine Art, 89; A Decade of American Drawing 1980-1989, Daniel Weinberg Gallery, Los Angeles, 89. *Teaching:* Instr drawing, Sch Visual Arts, New York, 70, instr painting, 70-71 & 74-82. *Bibliog:* Michael Florescu (auth), Sylvia Plimack Mangold, Arts Mag, 3/84; Michael Brenson (auth), Sylvia Plimack Mangold, New York Times, 11/22/85; Jeanne Silverthorne (auth), Sylvia Plimack Mangold, Brooke Alexander Gallery, Artforum, 3/86; Kenneth Baker (auth), Gestures that work or don't, San Francisco Chronicle, 5/12/87; John L Ward (auth), American realist painting, 1945-1980, UMI Research Press, Ann Arbor, Mich, 89. *Media:* Oil. *Publ:* Auth, Inches and Field, Lapp Princess Press Ltd, New York, 78; Project for Artforum, two moods, Sylvia Plimack Mangold, Artforum, 2/88. *Dealer:* Brooke Alexander Inc 59 Wooster St New York NY 10012. *Mailing Add:* 71 Bull Rd Washingtonville NY 10992

MANGOLTE, BABETTE M
FILMMAKER, PHOTOGRAPHER
b Montmorot, France, Oct 11, 41. *Study:* La Sorbonne, Paris, BA, 64; Ecole Nat Photographic & Cinematographie, Paris, 64-66. *Work:* Mus Mod Art, New York; Mus G Pompidou, Paris; New York Pub Libr; Australian Nat Libr, Canberra. *Pos:* Assoc prof, Visual Arts Dept, Univ Calif, San Diego, 89- *Awards:* Prix de la Lumiere, Toulon Film Festival, France, 75; CAPS Fel, NY, 76; Pre-production Grant, NY State Coun Arts, 86. *Mem:* Asn Independent Video & Filmmakers; Media Alliance. *Mailing Add:* 319 Greenwich St New York NY 10013

MANGUM, WILLIAM (GOODSON)
SCULPTOR, PAINTER
b Kinston, NC. *Study:* Corcoran Sch Art, Washington, DC; Art Students League; Univ NC, Chapel Hill, BA & MA. *Work:* Univ of NC, Chapel Hill; NC Mus Art, Raleigh; Salem Col, Winston-Salem, NC; Carl Sandburg Mem Mus, Flat Rock, NC. *Comn:* Lamp of Learning Monument, Dunning Industs, Greensboro, NC, 67; portrait bust of Carl Sandburg, Greensboro, NC, 68. *Exhib:* Bodley Gallery Nat, New York; Mass Mus Art, Springfield; Isaac Delgado Mus, New Orleans, La; Va Mus Fine Art Exhib; Southeastern Ctr Contemp Art, Winston-Salem, NC; Seasoned Eye #3, traveling exhib, 90; NC Mus Art, Raleigh. *Teaching:* Emer prof art hist & sculpture, Salem Col, formerly. *Awards:* Cert of distinction, Va Mus Fine Art; Isaac Delgado Mus Award; NC Mus Art Award. *Bibliog:* American Sculptors, 18th Century to the Present; article, New York Art Review, 88. *Publ:* Auth, Marino Marini as portraitist, 70. *Dealer:* Somerhill Gallery 3 Eastgate E Franklin St Chapel Hill NC 27514. *Mailing Add:* 5658 Old Rural Hall Rd Winston-Salem NC 27105

MANHART, MARCIA Y
ADMINISTRATOR, CURATOR
b Wichita, Kans, Jan 14, 43. *Study:* Univ Ariz, Tucson, with Maurice Grossman, 62; Univ Tulsa, Okla, with Duayne Hatchett, Tom Manhart & Alexandre Hogue, BA, 65, MA, 71. *Work:* Okla State Art Collection, Okla Arts Ctr, Oklahoma City; Ark Arts Ctr, Little Rock; Fred Jones Mem Mus Art, Univ Okla, Norman; Philbrook Mus Art, Tulsa; Univ Tulsa. *Exhib:* Southwestern Craftsmen Biennial, Mus Int Folk Art, Santa Fe, NMex, 65, 67, 71 & 75; Craftsmen USA '66, Dallas Mus Fine Arts, Tex, 66; Ceramic Nat, Everson Mus, Syracuse, NY, 68; Manharts, Fred Jones Mem Mus Art, Norman, Okla, 73; Ceramics Invitational, Little Gallery, Mus Contemp Crafts, New York, 74; Ann Print, Drawing & Crafts Exhib, Ark Arts Ctr, Little Rock, 74 & 76. *Collections Arranged:* Our Oklahoma Indian Heritage: The Old Ways, 76; Traders Cargo from the China Sea: The Gillert Collection of Southeast Asian Ceramics, 78; Nature's Forms--Nature's Forces: The Art of Alexandre Hogue, 84; The Eloquent Object, 87; The Sanford and Diane Besser Collection. *Pos:* Dir, Alexandre Hogue Gallery, Univ Tulsa, Okla, 67-69; dir educ, Philbrook Art Ctr, Tulsa, 72-77, asst dir, 77-83, actg dir, 83-84, exec dir, 84- *Awards:* One-man Award, Southwestern Crafts Biennial, Mus Int Folk Art, 71; George Wittenborn Mem Award; Harwelden Award, Tulsa Arts & Humanities Coun, 89. *Bibliog:* Garth Bethel (auth), Manharts, Craft Horizons, 74; Research and education, In: Your Portable Museum, Am Crafts Coun, 75; John Conrad (auth), Contemporary Ceramic Technique, Prentice-Hall, 79. *Mem:* Art Mus Asn; Asn Art Mus Dirs. *Media:* Clay, Porcelain. *Res:* Contemporary art in craft media. *Publ:* Auth, The Eloquent Object: The Evolution of American Art in Craft Media, 45; Alexandre Hogue: Nature's Forms/Nature's Forces, 84; The Search is Over Enter Janet Kardon, Art Today, 89; A Neglected History: 20th Century American Craft, 90; Objects and Drawings, The Sanford and Diane Besser Collection. *Mailing Add:* Philbrook Art Ctr PO Box 52510 Tulsa OK 74152

MANHART, THOMAS ARTHUR
EDUCATOR, CERAMIST
b Canon City, Colo, July 16, 37. *Study:* Univ Hawaii; Univ Tulsa, BA & MA. *Work:* Ark Arts Ctr, Little Rock; Fred Jones Mem Art Mus, Univ Okla, Norman; Philbrook Art Ctr, Tulsa; Okla State Art Collection, Okla Art Ctr, Oklahoma City; Tulsa Performing Arts Ctr, Okla. *Exhib:* Nat Decorative Arts Exhib, Wichita, Kans, 61, 64 & 66; Southwestern Crafts Biennial, Santa Fe, NMex, 65, 72 & 75; Craftsmen USA, Dallas & New York, 66; Regional Prints, Drawings & Crafts Exhib, Little Rock, 67 & 75; Nat Craftsmen's Exhib, Wichita, 68, 70 & 72. *Teaching:* Instr ceramics, Univ Tulsa, 61-68, asst prof ceramics, 69-73, assoc prof ceramics, 74- *Awards:* Nat Decorative Arts Exhib Medal of Honor, Wichita Art Asn, 66; Nat Merit Award, Craftsmen USA, Am Crafts Coun, 66; Okla State Art Collection, Okla Arts & Humanities Coun, 73. *Bibliog:* Gar Bethel (auth), Manharts, Craft Horizons, 74; Okla Designer Craftsmen Exhibition, Ceramics Monthly, 75. *Mem:* Am Crafts Coun (state rep, 66); Okla Designer Craftsmen; Tulsa Designer Craftsmen (pres, 68). *Media:* Clay and Fibers. *Publ:* Contribr, Profile, Am Crafts Coun, 60; contribr, Craft Horizons, 66, 68 & 74-75, Cimarron Rev, 69, Tulsa Univ Alumni Mag, 69 & Ceramics Monthly, 75. *Mailing Add:* 2115 E 27th St Tulsa OK 74114

MANHOLD, JOHN HENRY
SCULPTOR
b Rochester, NY, Aug 20, 19. *Study:* Univ Rochester, BA; Washington Univ, St Louis, MA; New Sch, with Chaim Gross & Manolo Pasqual; also with Ward Mount. *Work:* City of West Orange, NJ; Mem Sloan-Kettering Hosp, New York; Pyrofilm Corp, Whippany, NJ; A J Levera Assocs, Madison, NJ; Jacques Piccard Inst, Bern, Switz; and others. *Comn:* Bronze bust, Kallman Assocs, Jersey City, NJ; four bronze busts, Col Med & Dent NJ, Newark, 69, 70 & 78; bronze figure, Bernard Koven, 71; and others. *Exhib:* Allied Artists Am, 66; Audubon Artists Am, 67-69; Mainstreams '68 & '71, Grover M Hermann Fine Arts Ctr, Ohio, 68 & 71; Nat Sculpture Soc, 69; Am Artists Prof League, 70-72; and others. *Pos:* Dir sculpture, Ringwood Manor Asn Arts, 68-70, 1st vpres, 70-71. *Teaching:* Pvt instr, currently. *Awards:* Medal Honorfor sculpture, State of NJ, 68; First Prize, Paris Int, 70; Second Prize Patrons Award, Painters & Sculptors Soc NJ, 71; John Subkis Award, Nat Arts Club, 71; and others. *Bibliog:* David Leis (auth), pictures in Life Mag, 69; Pierre Morand (auth), La section Americaine de la Salon del'arte Francaise, La Rev Mod, 70; Ruth Ann Williams (auth), Art of the oranges, NJ Music & Art, 72. *Mem:* Acad Artists Asn; Am Artists Prof League; Painters & Sculptors Soc NJ (vpres sculpture, 74-78); Nat Arts Club; Knickerbocker Artists. *Media:* Marble, Bronze. *Mailing Add:* PO Box 9159 Treasure Island FL 33740

MANILLA, TESS
PAINTER, COLLAGE ARTIST
b Poland; US citizen. *Study:* Educ Alliance, New York, with Abbo Ostrowsky; Brooklyn Mus Art Sch, with Reuben Tam, Victor Candell, Manfred Schwartz & Louis Finkelstein; Art Students League, with Morris Kantor, Sidney Gross & Morris Davidson; Pratt Graphics Ctr, with Walter Ragolsky; Willimantic Teachers Col, Conn; Provincetown Workshop, with Leo Manzo. *Work:* Long

Island Univ; Butler Inst, Youngstown, Ohio; and many private collections throughout the US. *Exhib:* Aames Gallery, 75; one yr travelling watercolor show, Nat Asn Women Artists, Va Mus & State of Va; Nat Acad NY, 75; one-person shows, Contemp Art, New York, 66, Long Island Univ, Brooklyn, New York, Lincoln Savings Bank, 76 & Statesman's Club New York, 77. *Teaching:* Instr pvt classes, children & adults. *Awards:* Helen Hurzberger Scholar, Art Students League, 61; Nat Asn Women Artists Award, 72; Medal of Merit, League of Present Day Artists, 74; Nat Asn Women Art, 72-87. *Mem:* Nat Asn Women Artists (pub rels chmn, 73-75); Metrop Painters & Sculptors (pres, 68-83, hon pres, 84; Art Students League; League of Present Day Artists; New York Soc Women Artists; Artist Equity New York. *Media:* Oil; Graphic. *Mailing Add:* 140 Ocean Pkwy Brooklyn NY 11218

MANILOW, LEWIS
COLLECTOR, PATRON
b Chicago, Ill, Aug 11, 27. *Pos:* Pres, Mus Contemp Art Chicago, 76-81; mem of bd, Beaubourg Found, 78- *Collection:* Contemporary art, Mannerist prints and Turkish rugs. *Mailing Add:* c/o Mus Contemp Art 237 E Ontario St Chicago IL 60611

MANN, FRANK
PAINTER, DRAFTSMAN
b Washington, DC, Apr 22, 53. *Study:* George Washington Univ, Washington, DC, with painter Gene Davis, BS, 79; Pratt Inst, Brooklyn, NY, MFA, 82. *Work:* Mus Mod Art, New York; Guggenheim Mus, New York; Corcoran Gallery Art, Washington, DC; Seattle Art Mus, Wash; Parrish Art Mus, Southampton, NY. *Comn:* Window drawing, Artist's Space, New York, 89; mural, Dept Cult Affairs, New York, 90; mural, New York State Coun Arts, Binghamton, NY, 90; outdoor mural, Art Around Park, New York, 92. *Exhib:* Printmaking Today, Corcoran Gallery Art, Washington, DC; Trends in Works of Art on Paper, Brooklyn Mus, 90; Van, Jeffrey Wilkey Gallery, Seattle, Wash, 91; Summer Invitational, Charles Cowles Gallery, New York, 91; China, Ronald Feldman Gallery, New York, 91; Contemporary Sensibilities, Cie, Modern et Contemporain, Paris, France, 91; Painting Today, Mus Mod Art, Buenos Aires, Arg, 91. *Pos:* Studio asst, Dorothea Rockburne Studio, New York, 88-90; exec dir, Collab Projs, New York, 87-88; proj dir, Basic Arts Network, New York, 91-92. *Teaching:* Guest lectr, Corcoran Sch Art, Washington, DC, 78-79; guest lectr, Penn State Univ, Reading, 86-87; guest lectr, Pratt Inst, Brooklyn, 87-88. *Awards:* NY State Coun Arts, 89; Nat Endowment Arts, New Arts Prog, 89; Pollock-Krasner Found, 91. *Bibliog:* David Deitcher (auth), When worlds collide, Art Am, 2/90; Marcello Llorens (auth), Frank Mann, Mind of a Visionary, Art Al Dia, NY, 90; Mitchell Corber (dir), Frank Mann, Painter (film, 28 minutes), Public Broadcasting System, 91. *Mem:* Yr Visual Artist Comt, Am Acad Rome; New Arts Prog, Kutztown, Pa; Artists Equity, New York; Graphic Artists Guild, New York; Collab Projs, New York (prog dir, 87-88). *Media:* All. *Publ:* Illusr, Avant Garde Configurations, Judith Jacobs Gallery, New York; contribr, Works of Art on Paper with George Nelson Preston, Mus Mod Art, Buenos Aires, 90; Midnight Review, Rio Arts Proj, 91; illusr, Nerves, Domestic Press, New York, 91; contribr, Contemporary sensibilities, Cie Modern et Contemporain, Paris, France, 91. *Dealer:* Jeffrey Wilkey 1229 Park Ave Hoboken NJ 07030. *Mailing Add:* 108 Occidental Ave S Seattle WA 98104

MANN, JEAN (ADAH)
CERAMIST, SCULPTOR
b Schenectady, NY, June 27, 27. *Study:* Mannes Col Music; Hunter Col; Donald Mavros Studio, 4 yr apprenticeship, 64, Chinese Brush painting with Jongsoon Chung, Kiln Building with Gerry Williams; Glaze Chemistry with Yvonne LaFean & Louis Navias; Sculpture with Irma Rothstein. *Work:* Metrop Mus Art, New York; Smithsonian Inst Hist & Technol Dept, Washington, DC; Mus Art & Archeol, Univ Mo, Columbia; Mus Haaretz, Ceramics Mus, Tel Aviv, Israel; Everson Mus Art, Syracuse, NY; Yale Univ Art Gallery, New Haven, Conn; Martin Luther King Jr Ctr Non-Violent Social Change, Atlanta, Ga; Hammond Mus, North Salem, NY; Southern Conn, New Haven; Schenectady Mus, NY. *Exhib:* One-woman shows, Silvermine Guild, New Caanan, Conn, 76, The Galerie, Chester, Conn, 81 & 82, GWS Gallery, Southport, Conn, 87, Hammond Mus, North Salem, NY, 89, Alelier Gallery, New Milford, Conn, 89, Weslayan Potters, Middletown, Conn, 89 & Variations, Riverton, Conn, 92; Silvermine Guild, New Canaan, Conn, 76-; Mark Twain Libr Art Show, Redding, Conn, 84-91; Mendelson Gallery, Washington Depot, Conn, 87; Exhib Contemp Netsuke, Yamada Co, Tokyo, Japan, 88; Ceramics - The Oriental Influence, Farmington Valley Ctr, Fisher Gallery, 89; and others. *Teaching:* Wheel, hand methods & sculpture, Rescue: Vis Artist Prog, Dansbury & Southbury, Conn, 69; carving porcelain, Brookfield Craft Ctr, Conn, 81-82; demonstrator Netsuke carving, George Walter Vincent Smith Art Mus, Springfield, Mass, 84; Phoenix Workshop, Goffstown, NH; co-instr with Gerry Williams, The Kick Wheel Studio, New Fairfield, Conn. *Awards:* Artist Award, The Galerie, Conn Comn Arts, 81. *Bibliog:* Betty K Leavitt (auth), Netsuke-She, J Int Netsuke Collectors Soc, 83; Betty K Leavitt & C Randall (coauths), Netsuke: Superlative Pieces, Netsuke Kenkyukai Conv, 83; Diane Dowling (dir), Artist Jean Mann (film), Com Cast, 89. *Mem:* Silvermine Guild; Am Crafts Coun; Brookfield Craft Ctr; Soc Conn Crafts; New Haven Paint & Clay Club; Oriental Brush Artists Guild. *Media:* Porcelain. *Publ:* Auth, Tools for Carving Porcelain, 75 & Highfire Copper Reds on Porcelain, 79, Studio Potter; Arts of Asia, Photo & Ltr, 9-10/92. *Mailing Add:* c/o The Kick Wheel 154 Rte 39 New Fairfield CT 06812-4204

MANN, KATINKA
SCULPTOR, PHOTOGRAPHER
b New York, NY, June 28, 25. *Study:* Univ Hartford Art Sch, Conn; Pratt Graphic Arts, New York. *Work:* Brooklyn Mus, Guggenheim Mus, Mus Mod Art Study Collection, New York; Polaroid Int Corp, Boston; Williamsburg Savings Bank & Russ Togs Inc, New York; Northport Vet Hosp, NY. *Exhib:* One-man shows, Cent Hall Gallery, 74-84, Hansen Gallery, New York, 76-79, Heckscher Mus, Huntington, NY, 77 & 84; Aldrich Mus Contemp Art, 78; Ulrich Mus Art, Wichita, Kans; NJ State Mus, Trenton; Nikon, New York; Konica Gallery, Tokyo, Japan; Condeso/Lawler Gallery, New York; plus many others. *Awards:* Judith Leiber Co Purchase Award, Soc Am Graphic Artists, 69; Polaroid Corp Award, 83. *Bibliog:* Art in the World, Rinehart Press, 75; articles in New York Times, 77, 81 & 85. *Mem:* Am Abstract Artists (treas); Prof Artists Guild (vpres, 69-71, co-chmn & bd mem, 72-73); Artists Equity Asn; Prof Women Photogr, 84-92. *Dealer:* Central Hall Gallery 386 West Broadway New York NY 10012. *Mailing Add:* 294 Pidgeon Hill Rd Huntington Station NY 11746

MANN, MAYBELLE
HISTORIAN, WRITER
b Joliet, Ill, May 27, 15. *Study:* Queens Col, City Univ New York, BA(hist), 65; NY Univ, MA, 67, PhD, 72. *Exhib:* Walter Launt Palmer, Albany Inst Hist & Art, 84-85. *Collections Arranged:* Francis William Edmonds (auth, catalog), Stony Brook, NY, 75-76; The Am Art Union (auth, catalog), Whitney Mus Am Art, 77-78; St Augustine Artists (auth, catalog), H M Flagler Mus, Palm Beach, 84-85; Walter Launt Palmer (auth, catalog), Albany Inst Hist & Art, 84-85. *Pos:* Art critic, Times Herald Record, 74-83 & Jewish World, 82-85; cur, Light House Gallery, Tequesta, Fla, 87- *Teaching:* Lectr Am art, NY Univ, 74-76. *Res:* Nineteenth and early twentieth century American art. *Publ:* Articles, Antiques, Art & Antiques & Am Art J; Walter Launt Palmer: Poetic Reality, ALM Assoc, 86 & Am Art Union Revised, 88, ALM Asn; Am Art Union revised, ALM Assoc, 88. *Mailing Add:* 3264 Cove Rd Jupiter FL 33458

MANN, SALLY
PHOTOGRAPHER
b Lexington, Va, 1951. *Study:* Putney Sch, 66-69; Bennington Col, 69-71; Praestegaard Film Sch, Denmark & Aegean Sch Fine Arts, Greece (Year abroad prog) 71-72; Hollins Col (summa cum laude), BA, 74, MA, 75. *Work:* Addison Gallery Art, Andover, NH; Baltimore Mus Art, Md; Birmingham Mus Art, Ala; Boston Mus Fine Art, Mass; Corcoran Gallery Art, Hirshhorn Mus & Sculpture Garden, Nat Mus Am Art, Smithsonian Inst, Washington, DC; Metrop Mus Art & Mus Mod Art, New York; San Francisco Mus Art, Calif; Va Mus Fine Arts, Richmond. *Exhib:* Solo exhibs, Marcuse Pfeifer Gallery, New York, 86-88, Southeastern Ctr Contemp Art, Winston-Salem, NC, 88, Mus Photog Art, San Diego, Calif, 89, Cleveland Ctr Contemp Art, Ohio, 90, Houston Fotofest, Firehouse Gallery, Tex, 90, Tartt Gallery, Washington, DC, 90, Houk Gallery, Chicago, IL, 90, Md Art Place, Baltimore, 91 & Houk Friedmann, New York, 92; The Hand That Rocked the Cradle, traveling show, San Francisco Cameraworks, 89; Taboo: Controversial Art by 20 Artists, Greg Kucera Gallery, Seattle, Wash, 89; Her Family, St Olaf's Col, Northfield, Minn, 90; Flesh and Blood, Light Factory, Charlotte, NC, 90; Insect Politics, Hallwalls Contemp Arts Ctr, Buffalo, NY, 90; The Indomitable Spirit, Photographers & Friends United Against AIDS, Int Ctr Photog, New York, 90; The Awards in the Visual Arts Exhibition, New Orleans Mus Art, La, 90; Provocations: Challenging Contemporary Photographs, Robert Klein Gallery, Boston, Mass, 90; Pleasures and Terrors of Domestic Comfort, Mus Mod Art, New York, 91. *Pos:* Guest lectr, Honolulu Acad Arts, 89, Women Photog Conf, 89, Md Inst Art, 89, Bard Col, 89, San Francisco Cameraworks, 90, Photog-Retrospect/Prospect Conf 90 & many others. *Teaching:* Instr, Maine Photog Workshops, 85-89; Palm Beach Photog Workshops, 87-89; Ctr Photog Woodstock, 88 & 90; Int Ctr Photog, New York, 89; Image Found, Honolulu, Hawaii, 89; Okla Arts Found, 89; Friends Photog Workshops, 90. *Awards:* Fels, Nat Endowment Arts, 82, 88 & 89; fel, Guggenheim Found, 87; fel, Southeastern Ctr Contemp Art, 89. *Bibliog:* The world's best photographs 90 & Children, 90, Life Mag; rev, Parenting Mag, 90; rev, Wash Post, 90. *Publ:* Auth, Sally Mann, sweet silent thought (catalog), NC Ctr Creative Phot, 87; Uncommon ground (catalog), VA Mus, 88; At Twelve, Portraits of Young Women (monogr) Aperture, 88; The photographer's dialogue (catalog) Boca Mus, 89; Taken (catalog), Tartt Gallery, 89; Immediate Family, Aperture Found Inc, 92. *Dealer:* Houk Friedman New York; Houk Gallery Chicago IL. *Mailing Add:* 223 Mc Laughlin St Lexington VA 24450

MANN, WARD PALMER
PAINTER
b Detroit, Mich. *Study:* Detroit Inst Art, 33; Univ Mich, BS, 49. *Work:* Smithsonian Inst, Washington, DC; Mem Art Gallery, Rochester, NY; US Coast Guard, Washington, DC. *Comn:* Cityscape, the New Buffalo, Marsh & McLennon, Inc, Buffalo, NY, 75; Birthplace of Xerography, Xerox Corp, Webster, NY, 80; oil painting, Webster Optical Co, NY, 80; US Air, Charlotte, NC, 90. *Exhib:* Ann Shows, Salmagundi Club, New York, 75-90; Ann Nat Acad Artists, Greek Cult Ctr, Springfield, Mass, 79-91; Foothills Art Ctr, Golden, Colo, 80; 31st Ann Knickerbocker Art, Salmagundi Club, New York, 81; Mystic Int, Mystic Seaport Mus, Conn, 92. *Awards:* D Wu & Elsie Ject Key Award, Salmagundi Ann, 87; Int Soc Marine Painters Award, Rockport Art Asn, 88; Helen G Oehler Award, AAPL Grand Nat, 91. *Bibliog:* Walt Reed (ed), Ward Mann, artist, North Light Mag, 11-12/77; Artists of Rockport, Rockport Art Asn 60th Anniversary Ed, 80; 70th Anniversay Ed, 90. *Mem:* Rockport Art Asn; North Shore Arts Asn; Academic Artists Asn; Hudson Valley Art Asn; Am Artists Prof League. *Media:* Oil, Watercolor. *Dealer:* Nan Miller Gallery 3450 Winton Pl Rochester NY 14623. *Mailing Add:* 163 Stony Point Trial Webster NY 14580

MANNING, JO
PRINTMAKER, PAINTER
b Sidney, BC, Dec 11, 23. *Study:* Ont Col Art, Toronto, grad, 45, spec study printmaking, 60. *Work:* Nat Gallery Can, Ottawa; Montreal Mus Fine Art; London Libr & Art Mus, Ont; Can Coun Art Bank; Toronto Dominion Bank, Can. *Comn:* Can Cath Conf. *Exhib:* Expos Int Dessins, Rijeka, Yugoslavia, 70 & 72; Venice Biennale, 72; Prints, Gallery Pascal, 74, 77 & 80; and others. *Awards:* Second Point Biennale Award, Florence, Italy, 70; Honorable Mention, Norwegian Print Biennale, 76; Medal, Frechen, Ger, 80. *Mem:* Print & Drawing Coun Can. *Media:* Etching, Engraving; Oil on Canvas. *Publ:* Contribr, seven drawings, Canadian Catholic Conf, Sunday Missal, 76. *Mailing Add:* Box 286 Blyth ON N0M 1H0 Canada

MANO, TORU
GALLERY DIRECTOR
b Toyonaka, Osaka, Japan, Mar 23, 45. *Study:* Kyoto City Univ Arts, BA, 69. *Collections Arranged:* Kohodo: Display & Demonstration of Ancient Japanese Incense, 82; 5 Expressions from Scandinavia: New Paintings from 5 Countries, 86; Liberty: NY based artists from all nationalities, 86; Voice of Today: Current American Indian Art, 86; Constitution: Documents from the New York Hist Soc, 87. *Pos:* Coord cult affairs, Nippon Club, 81- *Publ:* Contribr, Image, Kyoto City Univ Arts, 83; ed, Directory, Nippon Club, 82-90; Nippon, NY Times, 89; You and Japan, Washington Post, 90. *Mailing Add:* c/o Imagine 60 Zamarzy Park New York NY 10010

MANOLAKAS, STANTON PETER
PAINTER
b Detroit, Mich, Jul 25, 46. *Study:* Univ Southern Calif, BA, 69. *Work:* Marriott Corp, Newton, Mass; Bechtel Industries Corp Collection, San Francisco, Calif; Datum Inc, Anaheim, Calif. *Comn:* Historic Boston Suite, Marriott Corp, 87. *Exhib:* Los Angeles Co AFL-CIO Exhib, Calif, 82-90; Calif Traditional Artists, Mus Natural Hist, San Bernadino, 83. *Awards:* First Place, Union Artist Exhibit, Los Angeles Co AFL-CIO, 89. *Bibliog:* Julia Ayres (auth), Paper the Critical Support, Watercolor 87 Am Artist, 1/87. *Media:* Watercolor. *Publ:* Auth, A Visual Odyssey Through America's Past, Watercolor 90 Am Artist, 9/90. *Dealer:* Lorentzen Gallery 1125 1/2 N Pacific Glendale CA 91202; New Masters Gallery Dolores & 7th PO Box 7009 Carmel CA 93921. *Mailing Add:* 2500 Las Flores Dr Los Angeles CA 90041

MANSARAM
PHOTOGRAPHER
b Mount Abu, India. *Study:* Sir J J Sch Art, Bombay, India, 54-59; State Acad Fine Arts, Amsterdam, fel, 63; Ryerson Polytech, Toronto, Can, cert(motion picture prod), 70. *Work:* Gemeente Mus, The Hague; Nat Gallery Mod Art, New Delhi, India; Mem Univ Gallery, St Johns, Nfld; New York Pub Libr; Art Gallery Hamilton; Air India, Electrografia Mus Int, Cuenca, Spain. *Exhib:* Solo exhibs, Gallery de Drie Hendricksen, Amsterdam, Neth, 64, Photography Gallery, Saskatoon, 86, Dhoomimal Art Gallery, New Delhi, India, 87, Toronto Image Works Gallery, 88, Burlington Cutl Ctr, 89 & Grimsby Pub Art Gallery, Ont, 90; Mini Print Int, De Cadaques, Spain, 91; Nat Ctr Performing Arts, Bombay, India, 92; Pundole Gallery, Bombay, India, 92; Habi Art Gallery, New Delhi, India, 92; BM Gallery, Islamabad, Pakistan, 92; Mus Nier Bator, Hungary, 92. *Awards:* First Prize, Bombay State Art Exhib, 59; Colour & Form Soc Award, Toronto, 75; Ont Arts Coun Grant, 90 & 91. *Mem:* Int Soc Copier Art, New York; Colour & Form Soc (pres, 78-79); Visual Arts Ont; Bombay Art Soc. *Media:* Mixed, Xerography. *Publ:* Contribr, Art-Life Mag, 2/4/86; Colour Documentation of 40th Anniversary Art Exhib of Color & Form Soc, Mississauga, 92. *Mailing Add:* 298 Gardenview Burlington ON L7T 1K6 Canada

MANSFIELD, ROBERT ADAMS
SCULPTOR, EDUCATOR
b Chicago, Ill, May 4, 42. *Study:* Minneapolis Sch Art & Design, 61-62; St Cloud State Univ, BA, 68; Univ Mass, Amherst, MFA, 70. *Work:* Univ Mass, Amherst; Smith Col Mus Art, Mass; San Diego State Univ; St Cloud State Univ, Minn. *Exhib:* Abstract Painting of 70's, DeCordova Mus, Lincoln, Mass, 71; Nat Juried Exhib, Austin Mus Art, 79; 13th Ann, Marietta Col, Ohio, 80; North Am Sculpture Exhib, Golden Col Art Ctr, Colo, 80; Corpus Christi Col Mus, Tex, 81; and others. *Collections Arranged:* New Directions, Univ Mass, 69; Twombly & Diao, Hampshire Col, 71; Arthur Hoener, San Diego State Univ, 76; Jerome Liebling Photographs, San Diego State Univ, 78. *Teaching:* Instr art, Smith Col, 70-71; asst prof art, Hampshire Col, 71-79; assoc prof art & head sculpture dept, San Diego State Univ, 76- *Awards:* Second Prize, Southern Calif Expos, Del Mar, 77; Best of Show, Marietta Col, 80. *Bibliog:* Mary Vercauteren (auth), Robert Mansfield, Holyoke Transcript, 4/12/73; Edward Silver (auth), Elliptical construction, Advocate, 12/4/75; Susan Muchnic (auth), Sculpture is alive and well, Los Angeles Times, 1/22/79. *Mailing Add:* c/o Bengert MacRae Gallery 210 Everett Ave Wyckoff NJ 07481

MANSHIP, JOHN PAUL
PAINTER, SCULPTOR
b New York, NY, Jan 16, 27. *Study:* Harvard Univ, AB, 48; with George Demetrios; Brera Acad, Milan. *Work:* Nat Collection Fine Arts, Washington, DC; Long Beach Art Mus, Calif; New Britain Mus, Conn; Hamilton Col, Clinton, NY. *Comn:* Baptism of Christ, Baptistry, St John Martyr, New York, 63; Pentecost (fresco), Chapel Sisters of St Joseph, Pawtucket, RI, 65; Stations of cross, St Clements Church, Warwick, RI, 66; Resurrection (with Margaret Cassidy), St Anthony's Church, Springfield, Mass, 71; portrait of Judge O'Connor, Worcester Co Courthouse, 72. *Exhib:* Newhouse Gallery, 82; Gallery on the Green, 88. *Pos:* Pres, Rockport Art Asn, 81-85. *Teaching:* Instr drawing & painting, Marymount Col, New York, 63; instr, Minnetonka Art Ctr, 78. *Awards:* Ranger Fund Purchase Award, Nat Acad Design, 65; Gold Medal, Burckhardt Acad, Rome, 78; Rockport Art Asn, 83; Nat Arts Club, 91. *Mem:* Am Watercolor Soc; Nat Soc Mural Painters (secy, 72-75); North Shore Art Asn (dir, 70-72); Artists Equity NY; Salmagundi Club; and others. *Media:* Oil, Watercolors; Bronze. *Publ:* Auth, Paul Claudel, Commonweal, 55; Raphael, Cath Encycl Youth, 64; Paul Manship, Abbeville, 90. *Dealer:* Gallery on the Green Lexington MA; Leonarda di Mauro Gallery New York NY. *Mailing Add:* 10 Leverett St Gloucester MA 01930

MANSION, GRACIE
ART DEALER
b Braddock, Pa, Oct 22, 46. *Study:* Clarion State Col, 64-66; Montclair State Col, BA, 79. *Exhib:* Small Works Show, 80 Wash Sq E, New York, 80; Neo York (collab with Judy Rifka), Univ Art Mus, Santa Barbara, 84. *Pos:* Dir, Gracie Mansion Gallery, 82- *Bibliog:* Peter Bach (auth), Gracie Mansion's Art Alive, Taxi Mag, 9/87; John Carlin (auth), Gracie's new mansion, Paper, 5/89; John Jost (dir), All the Vermeers in New York (film), 90 & (play & TV), 92. *Specialty:* Contemporary art. *Publ:* Articles, Gracie Mansion, New York Talk, 9/84, 10/84 & 11/84; New York Woman Mag, 7-8/87, 9/87 & 4/88; Hope Batey & Deborah Gimelson, Gracie Mansion Manhattan Catalog, Fall/Winter. *Mailing Add:* 442 E Ninth St No 4 4th Fl New York NY 10009-4940

MANSO, LEO
PAINTER, EDUCATOR
b New York, NY, Apr 15, 14. *Study:* Nat Acad Design; New Sch Social Res. *Work:* Mus Mod Art & Whitney Mus Am Art, New York; Mus Fine Arts, Boston; Worcester Mus, Mass; Corcoran Gallery Art, Washington, DC; and 40 other mus. *Comn:* Mural, Lincoln Pub Libr, Nebr, 65. *Exhib:* Nat Inst Arts & Lett, 61 & 69; Mus Mod Art, New York, 61 & 65; Whitney Mus Am Art Ann, 47-66; Pa Acad Fine Arts, Philadelphia, 68; one-man exhib Everson Mus Syracuse NY, 71; Am Masters of Collage, Montclair Mus, NJ, 79; Retrospective Exhib 25 yr, Hood Mus Dartmouth Col Hanover NY, 85; Retrospective Exhib 20 yr, Provincetown AA Assoc & Mus Provincetown MA, 87. *Teaching:* Co-founder, Provincetown Workshop, Mass, 59-; prof painting presently; artist-in-residence, Am Acad Rome, 79, Prix-de-Rome; prof painting & drawing, NY Univ, 50-; instr painting, Art Students League, NY, presently; artist-in-residence, Am Acad in Rome, 79. *Awards:* Childe Hassam Purchase Award for Juggernaut (construct), Am Acad Arts & Lett, 69; $5000 Award, Am Acad Inst Arts & Letters, 81; Guggenheim Fel Printmaking, 82; and others; Pollock-Krasner Found Grant, 88. *Mem:* Am Abstract Artists; Century Club; Nat Acad Design. *Media:* Multimedia. *Dealer:* Stuart Levy Gallery 415 W Bway New York NY; Long Point Gallery Provincetown MA 02657. *Mailing Add:* 460 Riverside Dr No 51 New York NY 10027

MANSPEIZER, SUSAN R
SCULPTURE
b New York, NY. *Study:* Art Students League, Corcoran Sch Art, 60-66; City Col New York, BA, 62, MA, 66. *Work:* Greenburgh Pub Libr, Chappaqua, NY. *Exhib:* Grass Roots, Gallery at Hastings on Hudson, NY, 78-80; John Baur-Pinder Gallery, NY, 87; Viridian Gallery, New york, 87 & 90; Ivan Karp, Gallery 54, Soho, NY, 88; New Dimensions, Hudson River Mus, Yonkers, NY, 88-90; New Members, Silvermine Guild Artists, New Canaan, Conn, 90; Hudson River Mus, Grace Glueck, Juror, Yonkers, NY, 90; Kirkland Art Ctr, Clinton, NY, 91; Southwest State Univ, Marshall, Minn, 91; Silvermine Guild of Artists, New Canaan, Conn, 92. *Teaching:* Instr drawing, Col of New Rochelle, NY, 74-75; instr collage, Art Ctr of Northern NJ, 90- *Awards:* Ivan Karp, First Place, Greenwich Art Soc, 85; Sculpture Invitational, Pelham Art Ctr; Ivan Karp, Best in Show, Soho Gallery 54, 88. *Bibliog:* New York Times Review, Vivien Raynor, 3/90 & 9/90. *Mem:* The Gallery at Hastings-on-Hudson, 79; Mamaroneck Artist Guild, 79-90; Viridian Gallery, 85-90; Art Equity, 90; Silvermine Guild Artists. *Media:* Wood, Metal. *Dealer:* Viridian Gallery 24 W 57th St New York NY 10019. *Mailing Add:* 62 Haight Cross Rd Chappaqua NY 10514

MANTER, MARGARET C
PAINTER
b Providence, RI, Feb 20, 23. *Study:* RI Sch Design, 42; Syracuse Univ, NY, BFA, 46; Workshops with Barse Miller, Ed Betts & Chen Chi, 66-72. *Work:* Col of Atlantic, Bar Harbor, Maine; Thomas Col, Waterville, Maine; Univ Maine, Machias; Eastern Maine Med Ctr, Bangor; Central Maine Power Co, Augusta. *Exhib:* Maine Coast Artists, Rockport, Maine, 88 & 89; Nat Asn Women Artists, New York, 89 & 90; Western Ill Univ, 90; Watercolor USA, Springfield, Mo, 91; Soc Experimental Artists, Bradenton, Fla, 92; and others. *Teaching:* Instr watercolor, YMCA, Bangor, Maine, 70-80; Instr design, Univ Maine, Orono, 80- *Awards:* Purchase Award, Ann Maine Heritage Exhib, Central Maine Power Co, 90. *Mem:* Nat Asn Women Artists. *Media:* Watercolor, Miscellaneous Media. *Mailing Add:* 1328 State St Veazie ME 04401

MANUEL, KATHRYN LEE
CRAFTSMAN
b Loma Linda, Calif. *Study:* San Francisco Art Inst, BFA, 59. *Work:* Richmond Art Mus, Va; Am Craft Mus, New York; M H De Young Mem Mus, San Francisco. *Exhib:* San Francisco Mus Mod Art, San Francisco, Calif, 58, 75, 76, 78 & 83; solo exhibs, Swain Sch Design, New Bedford, Mass, 73 & Calif State Univ, Hayward, Calif, 78; Folk & Craft Mus, Los Angeles, 80 & 82; Artisians Gallery, New York, 84; Phoenix Art Mus, Ariz, 86; Cleveland Ctr Contemp Art, Ohio, 87; Craft Today, USIA (Europe), 89-92. *Awards:* Nat Endowment Arts, 88. *Dealer:* Katie Gingrass Gallery Milwaukee WI 53202. *Mailing Add:* 358 Huron Ave Cambridge MA 02138

MANUELLA, FRANK R
DESIGNER, CONCEPTUAL ARTIST
b New York, NY. *Study:* Cooper Union Advan Sci & Art, BFA; Pratt Inst, MS. *Work:* NY Univ; McAllen Int Mus; Univ Tex. *Comn:* Mural, McAllen Int Mus, 83; mural, Harligen, Tex, 91; and others. *Exhib:* Plastic Show, Jewish Mus, New York, 69; one-man shows, Avanti Galleries, 70-72, Univ Tex, 88, 89, 90, 91 & 92; Director's Choice Show, Environment Gallery, New York, 71-81; McAllen Int Mus, Tex, 82-88; L'Avenir Gallery, Great Neck, NY, 86. *Pos:* Pres, F R Manuella Associates, currently. *Teaching:* Asst prof light & color, Pratt Inst, 75-82; assoc prof art, Univ Tex, 82- *Awards:* Outstanding Faculty Award, Pan Am Univ, 87; Merit Award, McAllen Int Mus, 88; Govs Award for Outstanding Serv, 89; Outstanding Faculty Award, Univ Tex, 90. *Bibliog:* Carompsun, New York Time Mag, 12/1/68; Karen Fisher (auth), Five careers, Cosmopolitan Mag, 3/69; Reviews & previews, Art News, 1/71. *Mem:* Univ Tex (fac senate, 88-92); Univ Press Univ Tex (bd mem). *Media:* Site-Specific, Mixed Media Installation. *Mailing Add:* Dept Art Univ Tex Edinburg TX 78539

MANUS, CONNIE SANDAGE See Hendrix, Connie (Connie Sandage Manus)

MANUS, JANE ELIZABETH
SCULPTOR
b New York, NY, July 3, 51. *Study:* Rollins Col, 69-71; Art Inst Boston, BFA, 73. *Work:* Butler Inst Am Art, Youngstown, Ohio; Mem Art Gallery, Univ Rochester, NY; Wichita Art Mus, Kans; Miss Mus Art, Jackson; Boca Raton Mus, Fla; Mus Art, Ft Lauderdale, Fla; Cornell Fine Arts Mus, Rollins Col, Winter Park, Fla. *Comn:* Outdoor sculptors, Searcy & Denney Sculpture Garden, W Palm Beach, Fla, 85, & Art in Pub Places, Delray Beach, Fla, 90; Am Bankers Insurance, Miami, Fla, 91. *Exhib:* One person shows, Palm Beach Comm Col Mus, 87, Ann Norton Sculpture Gardens, Palm Beach, Fla 85, 88 & 90, Cornell Fine Arts Mus, Rollins Col, Winter Park, Fla, 91; Newhouse Exhib, Flagler Mus, W Palm Beach, Fla, 87; Selected Florida Artists, Ctr Arts, Vero Beach, Fla, 88; 37th Ann All Fla, Boca Raton Mus Art, Fla, 88; Hortt Show, Ft Lauderdale Mus Art, Fla, 88; Peter Reginato & Jane Manus, Two Visions of Abstract Constructive Sculpture, Mus Art, Ft Lauderdale, Fla, 91-92. *Awards:* First Place Award, Newhouse Sculpture, Palm Beach, Fla, 87. *Bibliog:* William E Ray (auth), Portrait of the Artists, Pal Beach Co Arts Mag, 9/88; Chris Hunter (auth), The art of public places, Palm Beach Life, 2/89. *Mem:* Northwood Inst Art Advisory Bd (comt mem 87-90). *Dealer:* Margulies Taplin Gallery Gallery Center Boca Raton FL; Margulies Taplin Gallery 1401 Brickell Ave Miami FL 33131. *Mailing Add:* 2311 Embassy Dr West Palm Beach FL 33401

MANVILLE, ELSIE
PAINTER
b Philadelphia, Pa, May 11, 22. *Study:* Tyler Sch Fine Arts, Temple Univ, BFA, BS. *Work:* Temple Univ, Philadelphia; Butler Inst Am Art; Guild Hall Permanent Collection, East Hampton, NY; Univ Iowa. *Exhib:* Butler Inst Am Art, 56; Walker Art Ctr, 58; Dallas Mus, 63; 30 Year Retrospective Exhib, Snug Harbor Cultural Ctr, Staten Island, 83; The Art of Flowers, Moravian Col, 84; Focus on Realism, Glenn C Janss Collection, 85; Hermitage Found, Norfolk, Va, 85; Tyler Sch Fine Arts, Pa, 88. *Teaching:* Adj instr, Fashion Inst Technol. *Awards:* Purchase Award, Butler Inst Am Art, 78; Nat Endowment Arts Visual Artists Fel, 81 & 85; NY Fedn Arts Grant, 90. *Bibliog:* Paintings reproduced, Arts Mag, 6/75, 4/78 & 2/82, Art News, 10/78 & New York Times Art & Leisure Guide, 2/28/82. *Media:* Oil, Oil Pastel. *Mailing Add:* c/o Kraushaar Galleries 724 Fifth Ave New York NY 10019

MANZO, ANTHONY JOSEPH
PAINTER, INSTRUCTOR
b Saddle Brook, NJ. *Study:* Sch Fine Art, Nat Acad Design; Phoenix Sch Design, New York; also with Salvatore Lascari. *Work:* Losurdo Foods Collection, Hackensack, NJ. *Comn:* Landscape and still life portraits, comn by Mr & Mrs Losurdo, Saddle River, NJ, 68-79; still life portrait, comn by Mr & Mrs Perlman, Elkins Park, Pa, 68 & 70; landscape portrait, comn by Mr & Mrs J Lauren, New York, 74-79; portrait of Former Middleweight Champion Rocky Graziano, 78; still life, comn by Don & Dona Casey, Dallas, Tex, 78; portrait, comn by Dan & Margo Albright, Taos, NMex, 84; portrait, comn by Barbara Smith, Albuquerque, NMex, 92. *Exhib:* Hudson Artists Inc, 21st Ann, Jersey City Mus, 74; Salmagundi Club Summer Exhib, 75-77; Nat Miniature Art Show, 75; NJ Painter & Sculptor Soc, Nat Arts Club, 76; Hudson Valley Art Asn, 76; and others. *Teaching:* Instr life painting & drawing & oil painting composition, Renaissance Sch Art, Saddle Brook, NJ, 73- *Awards:* Oil Awards, Hudson Artist Inc, 73-74 & Am Artist Prof League, 74; Ray A Jones Mem Award, NJ Painter & Sculptor Soc, 76. *Bibliog:* Article, Southwest Art, 10/79. *Mailing Add:* c/o Collector's Gallery Box 2708 Taos NM 87571

MAPES, DORIS WILLIAMSON
PAINTER
b Russellville, Ark, June 25, 20. *Study:* Little Rock Jr Col; Hendrix Col, Ark; Ark Arts Ctr, Little Rock; Rex Brandt's Sch Painting, cert, Corona del Mar, Calif; also with George Post, Millard Sheets, John C Pellew, Louis Freund, Edgar A Whitney, Robert E Wood, John Pike & Robert Andrew Parker, 72. *Work:* Winthrop Rockefeller Gallery, Petit Jean, Ark; Ark Col Mus, Batesville; Am Found Life Ins Co, First Nat Bank & Ark Arts Ctr, Little Rock; Advan Indust, Blythville, Ark. *Exhib:* Mid-South Exhib, Brooks Mem Mus, Memphis, 68; Mid-Southern Ark Arts Ctr, 71-89; Watercolor USA, Springfield, Mo, 75; Southern Watercolor Soc, Cheekwood Mus, Jackson, Miss, 77; solo exhib, Univ Ark, Little Rock, 78; Celebrating Ark Women Artists, Russell Senate Bldg, Washington, DC, 91. *Teaching:* Oil & watercolor painting, Dansarts Sch, Little Rock, Ark, 68-86; oil painting, Bella Vista Fine Arts Ctr Ark, 71; watercolor, Miss Co Col, Blytheville, Ark, 72-73. *Awards:* Top of Show, Ark State Festival Arts, 68 & 75; First Award, Southern Artists Asn, 72; First Award, Mid-Southern Watercolorists 74 & 85; Top Award, Mid-Southern Watercolorists, 74, 84 & 85. *Bibliog:* La Revue Mod des Arts, Paris, France, 3/75; Some Remarkable Women of Arkansas, 77; Arts & Voices South, 7/79. *Mem:* Mid-Southern Watercolorists (pres, 70-72); Southwestern Watercolor Soc; assoc mem Am Watercolor Soc. *Media:* Watercolor, Acrylic. *Dealer:* Sketch Box Gallery 5606 R St Little Rock AR 72207. *Mailing Add:* 622 N Bryan Little Rock AR 72205

MARAIS
PAINTER
b New York, NY. *Study:* Acad de la Grande Chaumiere, Paris & self-taught. *Work:* J Aberbach Collection, Long Island, NY; Hugo Perls, NY Collection; Dr Milton Reder, NY; UNICEF Collection, NY; Theodora Settele Collection, New York. *Exhib:* Galerie Chantepierre, Aubonne, Switz, 72; Galerie Internationale, New York, 75; Cafe de la Paix Exhib, Paris, 79; Public TV Channel 13, 79-80; Galerie St Placide, Paris; Salon des Nations, Paris, 84. *Mem:* Visual Artists & Galleries Asn; Nat Soc Lit & Arts. *Media:* Oil. *Publ:* Art Diary, 82 & 83. *Mailing Add:* c/o Mary Rachel Brown 33 W 67th St New York NY 10023

MARAK, LOUIS BERNARD
CERAMIC SCULPTOR, EDUCATOR
b Shawnee, Okla, Sept 9, 42. *Study:* Univ Ill, Champaign-Urbana, BFA, 65; Alfred Univ, MFA, 67. *Work:* Krannert Art Mus, Univ Ill, Urbana; Western Gallery, Western Wash State Col, Bellingham; Utah Mus Fine Arts, Univ Utah, Salt Lake City; Henry Art Gallery, Univ Washington, Seattle; Los Angeles Co Mus Art, Calif. *Exhib:* San Francisco Art Inst Centennial Exhib, M H De Young Mem Mus, 71; Calif Ceramics & Glass, Great Hall, Oakland Mus, 74; Northern Calif Clay Routes: Sculpture Now, San Francisco Mus Mod Art; American Porcelain: New Expressions in an Ancient Art, Renwick Gallery, Nat Collection Fine Arts, Washington, DC, 80; Int Tea Party, Contemp Crafts Gallery, Portland, Ore, 84; Inaugural Exhib, New Am Crafts Mus, New York, 86; Ceramics from the Smits Collection, Los Angeles Co Mus Art, Calif, 87; Fired with Enthusiasm, an exhib contemp soup tureens, Campbell Mus, Camden, NJ, 87; Beyond Words: The Book as Metaphor for Art, Vol 2, Calif Crafts Mus, San Francisco, 90; 500 Years Since columbus, Triton Mus Art, Santa Clara, Calif, 92; and others. *Teaching:* Instr art, Keuka Col, New York, 67-69; prof art, Humboldt State Univ, Arcata, Calif, 69- *Awards:* Purchase Award, Utah Mus Fine Arts, 71; Award, E B Crocker Art Gallery, 75; Nat Endowment Arts Craftsmen's Fel Grant, 75. *Bibliog:* Lloyd Herman (auth), American Porcelain: New Expressions in an Ancient Art, Timber Press, 81; Paul J Smith and Edward Lucie-Smith (co-auth), Craft Today: Poetry of the Physical, Weidenfeld & Nicolson, 86; Martha Drexler Lynn (auth), Clay Today, Contemporary Ceramists & Their Work, Chronicle Books & Los Angeles Co Mus Art, 90. *Mem:* Am Craft Coun. *Media:* Ceramics. *Dealer:* Dorothy Weiss Gallery 256 Sutter St San Francisco CA 94108; Schneider-Bluhm-Loeb Gallery 230 W Superior St Chicago IL 60610. *Mailing Add:* 1110 Freshwater Rd Eureka CA 95503-9558

MARALDO, USHANNA F
FILMMAKER, PAINTER
b Osnabruck, Lower Saxony, WGer; US citizen. *Study:* Univ Mex (US Intercultural Exchange Scholar Prog); Mich State Univ, BFA (honors); Univ Osnabruck, WGer, MA; Harvard Univ, with Dr Lynn Dhority, teaching diploma, 83. *Work:* Bradley Int Airport, Los Angeles, Calif; Scripps Clinic & Res Found, La Jolla, Calif. *Comn:* Photo Mural, Warner Brothers Records, Burbank, Calif, 83; Mixed Media Triptych, La Jolla Bank & Trust, La Jolla, Calif, 84; Mural, Bible Time-Line, 43rd Church of Christ Scientist, Woodland Hills, Calif, 86. *Exhib:* Nat Drawing Exhib, San Francisco Mus Mod Art, Calif, 70 & 73; SFWA, San Francisco Mus Mod Art, Calif, 71; Calif Artists, Oakland Art Mus, Calif, 75; Solo exhib, Hand-Colored Etchings, Laguna Beach Mus Art, Calif, 76; Orig Prints, Santa Barbara Mus Art, Calif, 80. *Pos:* Producer, Media Arts Prod, San Francisco Pub Sch System, 73-75; environ designer, Sunstar Designs, 81-86; dir, Ltd Ed, LUMA Arts, Los Angeles, 82-87. *Awards:* First Prize, Nat Drawing Exhib, San Francisco Mus Mod Art, 70; First Prize, Southern Calif Artists, Century City Chamber Commerce, 79; Excel Award, Int Art, IAC, New York, 88; Exec Award, Art Horizon, NY, 88. *Bibliog:* Don Fabun (auth), Dimensions of Change, Kaiser Aluminum Corp, 73; Ann La Riviere (auth), Ushana Maraldo: Art on a Different Plane, Los Angeles Times, 76; Stephen London (ed), Ushanna Maraldo: Painting with Body & Soul, Lifestyle Mag, 87. *Mem:* Soc of Children's Book Writers. *Media:* Multi-Media. *Publ:* Magazine 2029, 91 & 92; Photographer's Forum, 92. *Mailing Add:* 535 Barker Pass Rd Santa Barbara CA 93108

MARANDER, CAROL JEAN
PAINTER, GRAPHIC ARTIST
b Minneapolis, Minn, Dec 30, 50. *Study:* Colo State Univ, BFA(with honors), 73; Col Santa Fe, Albert Handell, pastel workshop, 82. *Work:* Comlinear Corp Gallery, Fort Collins, Colo. *Comn:* Pastel paintings, Marriott Hotels, Charlotte, NC, Trumball, Conn, 90, Omaha, Nebr, 92; pastel painting, Tucson Nat Resort & Spa, Ariz, 91; pastel paintings, US Post Off, Norman, Okla, 92. *Exhib:* 12th & 13th Ann Exhib, Pastel Soc Am, New York, 84 & 85; 75th Ann Exhib, Allied Artists Am, New York, 88; Exposition Int, Societe des Pastellistes de France, Compiegne, 88; Biennial Exhib, 88, Fine Art Calendar Artists Exhib, 89, Viva l'amour Artists Invitational, 91, Loveland Mus & Gallery, Colo; one-woman show, Colorscapes, Loveland Mus & Gallery, Colo, 90. *Pos:* Graphic designer, Colo State Univ, Fort Collins, 76- *Awards:*

Ann & Richard Sauter Award, 12th Ann Exhib, Pastel Soc Am 84; First Place Other Media, Colo Artists Asn State Show, 86; Pastel Soc Am Award for Pastel, Allied Artists of Am 75th Exhib, 88. *Mem:* Pastel Soc Am; Allied Artists Am; Degas Pastel Soc; Colo Artists Asn. *Media:* Pastel. *Dealer:* Kyle Belding Gallery 1110 17th St Denver CO 80202. *Mailing Add:* 1400 Elm St Ft Collins CO 80521

MARANO, LIZBETH
SCULPTOR
Exhib: Solo shows, Baruch Col Gallery, New York & Daniel Weinberg Gallery, San Francisco, 82 & Galleria Molica, Rome, Italy, 92; Leubsdorf Gallery, Hunter Col, New York, 88; Am Acad & Inst Arts Letts, New York, 89; Molica GuidArte Gallery, New York, 90 & 91. *Awards:* Grant, Change Inc, 75; Rome Prize Fel, Sculpture, Am Acad Rome, Italy; Nat Endowment Arts, Sculpture, 78, 85 & 88-89. *Bibliog:* Paolo Balmas (auth), Entropia; Lizbeth Marano (exhib catalog), Galleria Molica, Rome, 92; Gabriella Dalesio (auth), Lizbeth Marano: Entropia, Segno, 111-112, 2-3/92; Enzo Bilardello (auth), L'Entropia di Lizbeth Marano, Corriere della Sera, 3/5/92; and others. *Mailing Add:* 108 Franklin New York NY 10013

MARASCO, ROSE
PHOTOGRAPHER, EDUCATOR
b Utica, NY, Dec 25, 48. *Study:* Syracuse Univ, BFA, 71; Goddard Col, with Todd Webb, MA, 81; Visual Studies Workshop, MFA, 91, with Nathan Lyons & Frank Gohlke. *Work:* Polaroid Int Collection; Portland Mus Art; Visual Studies Workshops, Artist Book Archive; Photogr Resource Ctr, Artist Book Archive. *Comn:* Percent for Art Grant, Harrington Elementary Sch, Me. *Exhib:* X-change, Payson Gallery, Portland, Maine, 84; Photographs from Great Britain and the McDowell Colony (solo exhib), Portland Sch Art, Maine, 86; Photokina '88, Polaroid Inst Exhib; Perspectives, Portland Mus Art, Maine, 88; Recent Aquisitions-Color Photogr, Portland Mus Art; Ritual & Community: The Maine Grange, Farnsworth Mus, Rockland, Maine, 92; Exhib Photo, Berkshire Mus, Pittsfield, Mass, 92. *Collections Arranged:* Todd Webb-Photographs, Univ Southern Maine Art Gallery, 81; Work from Five Decades-Todd Webb (auth, catalog), New Eng Found Arts, Cambridge, Mass. *Teaching:* Instr & dept head photog, Munson-Williams-Proctor Inst, 74-79; assoc prof art & dept chairperson, Univ Southern Maine, 79-; instr photog, Portland Sch Art, Maine, 81-87. *Awards:* Maine State Comn Arts & Humanities Grant, 83; MacDowell Colony Residency Fel, 85; Polaroid Materials Grant, 86; Maine Arts Comn Artists' Fel, 90; Maine Humanities Coun Major Grant, 90-91. *Bibliog:* George Bennington (auth), article, Views J, Vol 3, No 4, 82; Edgar A Beem (auth), article, Maine Times, 6/24/88 & 12/15/89; Shirley Jacks (auth), Art New Eng, 6/7-92. *Mem:* Soc Photog Educ (NE region treas, 88). *Publ:* Auth, A personal reflection based on the SPE Questionnaire: Teaching and Learning, Exposure 20:1, 3/82; How to make slides of your artwork, In: The Percent for Arts Handbook, Maine Arts Comn, 85; The silhouette craft of Kaye Housel, In: The World and I, 87; Looking at Photographs, In: 20th Century Photographs from Collection of the Bowdoin Col Mus Art (exhib catalog), 88. *Dealer:* Betsy Evans Gallery Pleasent St Portland ME. *Mailing Add:* Dept Art Univ Southern Maine Gorham ME 04038

MARAZZI, WILLIAM
PAINTER
b Paris, France, 47. *Study:* Studied at Lycee Charlemagne, France; Herbert H Lehman Col, New York; New Sch Social Res, New York. *Work:* Metrop Mus Art, Costume Inst, New York; Rutgers Univ Art Gallery, NJ; Sheldon Swope Art Gallery, Terre Haute, Ind; Musee d' Art Haitien, Port au Prince, Haiti; Guatemalan Tourism Comn, Guatemala City, Cent Am; and others. *Comn:* Mural, Lepercy residence, 83; Mural, Holman residence, 83; Mandaraji Temple, New York, 81; Mural, Lepercq residence, 83; Mural, Holman residence, 83. *Exhib:* Int Art Fair, OIA, Bologna, Italy; Anichini Gallery, New York, 80 & 81; Pelham Art Ctr, New York; Mari Galleries, Mamaroneck, NY; Musee d'Art Haitien, Port au Prince, Haiti, 82; Ctr for Peace through Culture, NJ, 82; Faculty Show, YWCA, New York, 86, 87, 88 & 89; Claire Dunphy Gallery, New York, 87; and many others. *Pos:* Graphics for Off Broadway Theater productions, 80; presentations of Painted Storie for Radio, WNYC-FM & WBAI- FM, 83; anthrop field work, Japan & China, 84. *Teaching:* Space painting workshop, East/West Ctr, Holistic Health, 78-79; art in the field, Nepal & Tibet, 86; painting workshops, Bahamas, 88. *Bibliog:* Reviews, Evansville Press, 75, Pelham Sun, 81, Le Nouveau Monde, Haiti, 82 Asahi Town News, Tokyo, Japan, 84 & New York Times, 84 & 85; TV coverage Bodley Gallery exhib, Manhattan Cable, NY, 75. *Media:* Pastel. *Publ:* Illusr, New York Mandala, Jiyusha Press, Tokyo, Japan, 86. *Mailing Add:* 188 E 75th St New York NY 10021

MARCA-RELLI, CONRAD
PAINTER, COLLAGE ARTIST
b Boston, Mass, June 5, 13. *Work:* Mus Mod Art, Whitney Mus Am Art, Solomon R Guggenheim Mus, NY; High Mus Art, Atlanta, Ga; Wadsworth Atheneum; Metrop Mus Art; Chicago Art Mus; Walker Art Ctr, Minneapolis, Minn; and others. *Exhib:* Carnegie Inst; one-man retrospective, Whitney Mus Am Art, 67; Art Inst Chicago; Am Fedn Arts, 67-68; The New American Painting & Sculpture, Mus Mod Art, 69; New Sch Social Res, 69; Am Painting 1970, Va Mus Fine Arts, Richmond, 70; one-man exhibs, Carone Gallery, Ft Lauderdale, Fla, 78, Galera Joan Prats Bracelona, Spain, 78, retrospective, Ft Lauderdale Mus Art, 79, Marlborough Gallery, New York, 79, retrospective, Ringling Mus, Sarasota, Fla, 80, Hokin Gallery, Chicago, 81, Phoenix Gallery, Washington, DC and GMB Gallery, Birmington, Mich, 82, Riva Yares Gallery, Scottsdale, Ariz, 90; plus many other group & one-man shows. *Teaching:* Former vis critic, Yale Univ, Univ Calif, Berkeley & New Col, Sarasota, Fla. *Awards:* Logan Medal & Purchase Prize, Art Inst Chicago, 54, Kohnstamm Prize, 63; Ford Found Award, 59; Purchase Prize, Detroit Inst Art, 60. *Bibliog:* Parker Tyler (auth), Marca-Relli (monogr), 60; H Harvard Arnason (auth), Marca-Relli (monogr), Abrams, 62; Gerard Miracle & Harold Rosenberg (auth), Marca-Relli, Barcelona, Spain, 75; and others. *Dealer:* Riva Yares Gallery 231 Washington Ave Santa Fe NM 87501. *Mailing Add:* 7337 Point of Rocks Rd Sarasota FL 33581

MARCHESCHI, (LOUIS) CORK
SCULPTOR, EDUCATOR
b San Mateo, Calif, Apr 5, 45. *Study:* Col San Mateo, 63-66; Calif State Col, Hayward, 66-68; Calif Col Arts & Crafts, Oakland, MFA, 70; also with Mel Ramos & Paul Harris. *Work:* Bochum Mus, WGer; Milwaukee Art Ctr; Mus Mod Art. *Comn:* environ energy sculpture, Morgan Gallery, Kansas City, Kans, 75; fluorescent & spark relief, Ulrich Mus, Wichita, Kans, 75; Citylight, Seattle, Wash, 80; neon outdoor work, Actors Theatre, St Paul, Minn, 86-91; Principle Group, Des Moines, Iowa, 91; and others. *Exhib:* One-man shows, Kunsthalle Dusseldorf, Ger, 76, Milwaukee Art Ctr, Wis, 76, Hanson-Cowles Gallery, Minneapolis, Minn, 77, Tubingen Mus, Ger, 78, Van Abbe Mus, Endhoven, Holland, 78 & Nat Gallery, Berlin, Ger, 78; New Mus, New York, 80; Rutgers Mus, 83; Paris Mus Mod Art, 84; Nat Gallery, West Berlin, 84; Braunstien Quay, San Francisco, 92; Morgan Gallery, Kansas City, Mo, 92; and others. *Teaching:* Assoc prof art & intermedia, Minneapolis Col Art & Design, 70-85 & San Francisco Art Inst, 87-92. *Awards:* Minn State Arts Coun Grant, 75; Bush Found Grant, 78; DAAD Berlin Artist Prog Grant, 78; Nat Endowment Art, 82-83. *Bibliog:* Paul Owen (auth), Energy works (16mm film), 71; Merike Weiler (auth), Art Can article, 73; Heiner Hepper (auth), Cork Marcheschi (film), Ger Pub Broadcasting, 75; George Tapley (auth), article in Arts Mag, 83. *Media:* Electricity, Found Objects. *Collection:* Art deco objects and architectural period writings. *Publ:* Auth, Objects for producing visual phenomena with high-voltage electricity, 73; Heat, light and motion, 74; Neon, 75; Energy as sculpture, Prof Kornelia V Berswordt (catalog), Mus Glaskasten, Marl, Ger, 91. *Dealer:* Modernism 236 8th St San Francisco CA 94103. *Mailing Add:* 192 Connecticut San Francisco CA 94107

MARCK, JAN VAN DER
CURATOR
b Roermond, Neth, Aug 19, 29. *Study:* Univ Nijmegen, BA, MA & PhD(hist art), 56; Univ Utrecht; Columbia Univ. *Collections Arranged:* Charles Biederman, 65 & Lucio Fontana, 66, Walker Art Ctr, Minneapolis; Pictures to be Read/Poetry to be Seen, 67, Christo: Wrap in Wrap Out, 69, Moholy-Nagy, 69 & Art by Telephone, 69, Mus Contemp Art, Chicago; American Art: Third Quarter Century, Seattle Art Mus, 73; Herbert Bayer, 77 & Acquisitions, 74-78, Dartmouth Col; In Quest of Excellence, Ctr Fine Arts, Miami, Fla, 84; Reconnecting, 87, Art in Israel Today, 91, Among Friends, 91-92, Detroit Inst Arts. *Pos:* Cur, Gemeentemuseum, Arnhem, Neth, 59-61; deputy dir fine arts, Seattle World's Fair, 61-62; cur, Walker Art Ctr, Minneapolis, 63-67; dir, Mus Contemp Art, Chicago, 67-70, Dartmouth Col Mus & Galleries, 74-80 & Ctr Fine Arts, Miami, 80-85; cent art & chief cur, Detroit Inst Arts, 86- *Teaching:* Assoc prof art hist, Univ Wash, Seattle, 72-74. *Awards:* Rockefeller Found, 57-59; CASVA, 86. *Mem:* Am Asn Mus; Int Coun Mus; Int Asn Arts Critics; CIMAM. *Publ:* Auth, Romantische Boekillustratie in Belgie, Romen, 56; Lucio Fontana, Connaissance, 74; George Segal, Abrams, 75; Arman, Abbeville, 84; Bernar Venet, Difference, 88; also articles in Art Forum, Art in Am & other journals. *Mailing Add:* Detroit Inst Arts 5200 Woodward Ave Detroit MI 48202

MARCOUX, JOHN W
DESIGNER
b Greenfield, Mass, June 13, 22. *Study:* Boston Mus Sch Fine Arts, 48-52, 55. *Work:* Boston Mus Fine Arts; Ronald Abramson, Washington, DC; Warren Ruben & Bernice Wollman, New York; Mr & Mrs Patrick Coady, Washington, DC; Fred Fiandaca, Boston, Mass. *Comn:* Garment display case, 85, Nesmin mummy case, 86 & Coptic chapel replica, 88, Mus Art, RI Sch Design. *Exhib:* NAGA Gallery, Boston, Mass, 91; Calif Crafts Mus, San Francisco, 92; Northwest Gallery Fine Woodworking, Seattle, Wash, 92; Newport Art Mus, RI, 92; and others. *Pos:* Furniture design, Boston, Mass, 56-76 & Providence, RI, 76-91. *Teaching:* RI Sch Design, 88; Peter's Valley Craft Ctr, 89; Bennington Col, 90. *Awards:* Crafts Award, 87 & 88 & Visual Arts Fel, 89, RI State Coun Arts; Visual Arts Fel, Nat Endowment Arts Fel, 90. *Media:* Furniture. *Publ:* Contribr, Mus Art Calendar, RI Sch Design, 88; Fine Woodworking Design Book IV, 88 & Book V, 89; The Guild 7, Kraus Sikes Inc, 91-92; AMBIENTE, Euro Design Guide, 91; Art New England, 4-5/92. *Mailing Add:* 283 George St Providence RI 02906

MARCUS, ANGELO P
DEALER, COLLECTOR
Study: Cairo Univ, MA. *Pos:* Pres, Eagle Art Gallery, Inc, currently. *Mem:* Nat Cowboy Hall Fame. *Specialty:* Western art. *Collection:* Olaf Wieghorst, Frank McCarthy, Robert Lougheed, William Whitaker, George Marks, John Clymer, Don Crowley, James Bama & Norman Rockwell. *Publ:* Wall Street Journal. *Mailing Add:* c/o Eagle Art Gallery 1250 Prospect La Jolla CA 92037

MARCUS, GERALD R
PAINTER, PRINTMAKER
b New York, NY, Feb 22, 46. *Study:* Art Students League, New York, with Jean Liberte, Julian Levy, Sol Wilson & Jacob Lawrence, 63-68; City Col NY, BA, 68. *Work:* Standard & Poor Inc; Am Reinsurance Co Inc; Columbia Presby Hosp. *Exhib:* Salmagundi Club Ann Exhib, New York, 75-77; Painters & Sculptors Soc NJ Ann Exhib, 77; Ann Exhib, 77 & Black & White on Paper,

82, Nat Arts Club, New York; Mus Hudson Highlands Invitational, Cornwall, NY, 82; National Drawing '83, Trenton State Col, NJ; solo exhibs, Paul Klapper Art Ctr, Queens Col, NY, 83 & Griffith Menard Gallery, Baton Rouge, La, 84; Nat Acad Design, Ann Exhib, 88 & 90; Adirondack Life, Lake Placid Art Ctr, 89 & 90. *Bibliog:* Cynthia Nadelman (auth), rev, Art News, summer 82; rev, The State Times, Baton Rouge, 11/25/84; Stephanie Rauschenbusch (auth), Finding the Catskills, Prospect Press, 11/23/86. *Mem:* Art Students League. *Media:* Oil, Watercolor; Etching. *Dealer:* Prince Street Gallery 121 Wooster St New York NY 10012. *Mailing Add:* 463 West St New York NY 10014

MARCUS, IRVING E
PAINTER, EDUCATOR
b Minneapolis, Minn, May 17, 29. *Study:* Univ Minn, BA, 50; Univ Iowa, MFA, 52. *Work:* Minneapolis Inst Art; Allen Art Mus, Oberlin Col; Crocker Art Mus, Sacramento, Calif; Reed Col, Portland, Ore; Oakland Mus Art, Calif; also in many pvt collections; M H de Young Mem Mus, San Francisco, Calif; Butler Inst Am Art, Youngstown, Ohio; Yale Univ Art Gallery, New Haven, Conn. *Exhib:* One-man shows, Zara Gallery, San Francisco, 78 & 80, Artspace, Crocker Art Mus, 78 & 88, Southeastern Ctr Contemp Art, Winston-Salem, NC, 79, Joseph Chowning Gallery, San Francisco, 85 & 91, Kathryn Sermas Gallery, 90; Vollum Gallery, Portland, Ore; Welcome to the Candy Store, Crocker Art Mus, Sacramento, Calif, 81; California Connections, The Early 1970's, Laguna Beach Art Mus, Calif, 82; The Impolite Figure: New Figurative Painting in the Bay Area, Bannam Place Exhib Space, San Francisco, 83; Seven Artists in California, Gallery Takano, Tokyo, Japan, 85; Vertigo: The Poetics of Dislocation, San Francisco Art Inst, Calif, 87; John Natsoulas Gallery, Davis, Calif, 93. *Teaching:* Instr art, Oberlin Col, 55-56, Univ Hawaii, 56-57 & Blackburn Col, 57-59; prof painting & printmaking, Sacramento State Col, retired, chmn dept art, 66-69; artist-in-residence, Wake Forest Univ, NC Sch Arts, Winston-Salem, 79. *Awards:* Prizes, Denver Mus Art, 52 & 58 & Crocker Art Mus, 63. *Bibliog:* Thomas Albright (auth), An extraordinary artist, San Francisco Chronicle, 2/11/73; Thomas Albright (auth), Bay area mythmakers, Art Gallery Mag, 11/74; various reviews in mags. *Dealer:* John Natsoulas Gallery Davis CA; Joseph Chowning Gallery 1717 17th St San Francisco CA. *Mailing Add:* 601 Shangri Lane Sacramento CA 95825

MARCUS, MARCIA
PAINTER, EDUCATOR
b New York, NY, Jan 11, 28. *Study:* NY Univ, BA, 47; Art Students League, 54, with Edwin Dickinson. *Work:* Whitney Mus Art, New York; Philadelphia Mus Art; Univ Colo, Boulder; Hirshhorn Mus; Neuberger Mus; and others. *Comn:* Private & Public Portrait Comns. *Exhib:* Young Artists, Whitney Mus Art, 60; Four Women, Kansas City, 63; Carnegie Inst, Pittsburgh, 64; Woman Choose Women, New York Cult Ctr, 73; Everson Mus, Syracuse, 75; Canton Art Inst, 84; Benton Gallery, 85; and others. *Pos:* Vis critic, Colo & Ariz, 84. *Teaching:* Adj instr painting, Cooper Union Sch Art, New York, 70-71; assoc prof painting & drawing, La State Univ, Baton Rouge, spring 72; instr, Vassar Col, 73-74; vis artist, Cornell Univ, spring 75, Syracuse Univ, 76 & Purdue Univ, 77-78; asst prof, RI Sch Design; assoc prof, Univ Iowa, 79-80; adj assoc prof, Queens Col, 81, Chio State Univ, winter 83 & Univ Calif, spring 89. *Awards:* Ingram Merrill Award, 64 & 77; artist-in-residence, RI Sch Design, Ford Found, 66; Nat Endowment Arts, 91. *Bibliog:* Paul Cummings (auth), Smithsonian Archives Interview, 75; Noel Frackman (auth), The Attic Mind of Marcia Marcus, Arts, 9/75. *Mem:* Artists Equity. *Media:* Oil, Pastel. *Mailing Add:* 80 N Moore St 32B New York NY 10013

MARCUS, ROBERT P (MRS)
COLLECTOR, PATORN
b New York, NY, July 10, 23. *Study:* Northwestern Univ; Parsons School of Design, New York. *Pos:* Bd Dir, Palm Beach Coun Arts; founder, Mus Am Folk Art, New York. *Mem:* Philharmonic Orchestra Fla; Fla Cultural Action Alliance. *Collection:* American Folk Art (exhibited in 11 museums as: Two Centuries of American Folk Art: Masterworks From the Collection of Mr & Mrs Robert Marcus) North American, Latin American & European Art. *Mailing Add:* 208 Sandpiper Dr Palm Beach FL 33480

MARCUS, STANLEY
COLLECTOR
b Dallas, Tex, Apr 20, 05. *Study:* Harvard Univ, BA, 25, Bus Sch, 26; Southern Methodist Univ, Hon HHD, 65; N Tex Univ, LHD, 83; Pratt Inst, LLD, 86. *Pos:* Dir, Dallas Symphony Soc; adv dir, Ft Worth Art Asn; trustee, Eisenhower Exchange Fel & Nat Endowment Advan Arts; Bus Comt for the Arts; pres, Dallas Art Asn, formerly; consult, Carter, Hawley Hale Stores, Inc; secy, treas & dir, Neiman Marcus, 26, merchandise mgr sport shop & apparel div, 28, exec vpres, 29, pres, 35-50, chmn bd & chief exec off, 50-72, chmn exec comt, 72-75, chmn emer, 75-; dir, Intercultura, Dallas, Tex, 90-91. *Awards:* H Neil Mallon Award, Dallas Coun World Affairs, 88. *Collection:* Paintings, contemporary art; prehistoric American Indian pottery; pre-Columbian textiles and pottery. *Publ:* Auth, Solace for the Eyes, Architectural Digest, 12/84. *Mailing Add:* 300 Crescent Ct Suite 875 Dallas TX 75201

MARDEN, BRICE
PAINTER, PRINTMAKER
b Bronxville, NY, Oct 15, 38. *Study:* Boston Univ, BFA, with Reed Kay, Arthur Hoener & Hugh Townley; Yale-Norfolk Summer Sch Music & Art, with Bernard Chaet & Jon Schueler; Sch Art & Archit, Yale Univ, MFA, with Esteban Vicente & Alex Katz. *Work:* Mus Mod Art, Whitney Mus Am Art, New York; Walker Art Ctr, Minneapolis, Minn; Ft Worth Art Ctr, Tex; Stedelijk Mus, Amsterdam; and others. *Exhib:* Whitney Mus Am Art Ann, New York, 69, 77 & 83; Modular Painting, Albright-Knox Art Gallery, Buffalo, 70; Painting--New Options, Walker Art Ctr, 72; Documenta 5, Kassel, Ger, 72; Guggenheim Mus, New York, 75; Brice Marden: Recent Paintings and Drawings, Pace Gallery, New York, 78; A New Spirit in Painting, Royal Acad Arts, London, 81; solo shows, Stedelijk Mus, Amsterdam, Holland, 81, Whitechapel Art Gallery, London, Eng, 81, Pace Gallery, New York, 82 & 84, Mizuno Gallery, Los Angeles, 82 & Daniel Weinberg Gallery, Los Angeles, 84; Affinities, Hayden Gallery, Mass Inst Technol, Cambridge, 83; Beauties and Beasts, Pratt Inst Gallery, New York, 83; Paintings, Galerie Maeght Lelong, New York, 83. *Bibliog:* N Hale (auth), Of a classic order: Brice Marden's Thira, Arts Mag, 10/80; Carter Ratcliff (auth), Mostly Monochrome, Art in Am, 4/81; Ted Castle (auth), Bouquet of mistakes, Flashart, summer 82; Maurice Poirier (auth), Color-coded mysteries, Art News, 1/85; Robert Hughes (auth), Careerism and hype admidst the image haze, Time Mag, 6/17/85. *Media:* Oil. *Dealer:* Mary Boone Gallery 417 W Broadway New York NY 10012. *Mailing Add:* 276 Bowery New York NY 10012

MARDER, DORIE
PAINTER, PRINTMAKER
b Poland; US citizen. *Study:* Sorbonne; Art Students League; New Sch Social Res; also with Harry Shoulberg & Morris Kantor. *Work:* Roberson Ctr Arts, NY; Butler Inst Am Art, Youngstown, Ohio; Seattle Art Mus; San Francisco Mus Mod Art; Nat Acad Design; British Mus; Victoria & Albert Mus, Eng; US State Dept, Washington, DC; and others. *Exhib:* Prints by Women, AAA Gallery; Audubon Artists; NJ Soc Painters & Sculptors; Palazzo Vecchio, Florence, Italy; Nat Asn Women Artists at Lever House, New York. *Awards:* Clendenen Award for Oil Painting, 61; Award for Serigraph, Montag, 65; First Prize, Village Art Ctr; Melcher Award, Nat Asn Women Artists, 87; Schweitzer Award, Nat Asn Women Artists, 89. *Bibliog:* Serigraph reproduction & commentary, Print Quart, London, Eng, 86. *Mem:* League Present Day Artists (dir, 71-72); Nat Asn Women Artists; Artists Equity Asn; Nat Serigraph Soc; Nat Asn Women Artists (exec bd, 80-84); and others. *Publ:* Serigraphy: An American Art Form on Channel 13 WNET-TV, 1/13/89. *Dealer:* Mary Ryan Gallery New York NY. *Mailing Add:* 223 W 21st St New York NY 10011

MAREE, WENDY P
PAINTER, SCULPTOR
b Windsor, Eng, Feb 10, 38. *Study:* Windsor & Maidenhead Col, Eng, 59; studied with Vasco Lazzlo, London, 59-62. *Work:* Bronze sculptures, (two) Amnesty Int, Washington, DC; prt collections of HRH Prince Faisal, Saudi Arabia, Gena Rowlands, John Cassavetes & Nicky Blairs, Los Angeles, Calif, Guilford Glazer, Beverly Hills, Calif. *Exhib:* Windsor Arts Festival, Eng, 48; Summer Viewers Delight, San Bernadino Mus, Calif, 88; one woman show, Lake Arrowhead Libr, Calif, 89; and many more. *Awards:* First Place Award, Windsor Art Festival, 48; Second Place, Nat BBC Television Show, 50; Award, San Bernardino Co Mus, Redlands, Calif, 88. *Bibliog:* Les Krantz (auth), The California Art Review, 89. *Mem:* Artist Guild of Lake Arrowhead, 88; Rowac Lake Arrowhead, 92. *Media:* Acrylic; Bronze. *Mailing Add:* PO Box 2421 Lake Arrowhead CA 92352

MARGO, BORIS
PAINTER, PRINTMAKER
b Wolotschisk, Russia, Nov 7, 02; US citizen. *Study:* Polytechnik Art, Odessa, USSR, cert; Futemas (workshop for art of the future), Moscow, USSR; Pavel Filonov Sch, Leningrad, USSR. *Work:* Metrop Mus Art & Mus Mod Art, New York; Nat Collection Fine Arts, Washington, DC; Art Inst Chicago; Sao Paulo Mus Art, Brazil. *Exhib:* Abstract and Surrealist Art in the United States, San Francisco Mus Art & others, 44; Carnegie Inst Int, Pittsburgh, 52; Japan Print Asn 30th Anniversary Int, 62; Venice Biennales, 56 & 70; Honolulu Acad Art, 73; Rutgers Univ Art Gallery, 77. *Pos:* Res assoc (on the creative process), Psychiatric Inst, Univ Md, 57-58. *Teaching:* Vis artist, Am Univ, 46-48; vis prof painting, Art Inst Chicago, 57-59; vis prof printmaking & drawing, Sch Art, Syracuse Univ, 66-67; artist in residence, Acad Art, Honolulu, 72. *Awards:* Purchase Award for oil painting, Portland Mus Art, Maine, 60; six Purchase Awards, Brooklyn Mus Print Exhibs, 47-68; Award in printmaking, Nat Endowment Arts, 74. *Bibliog:* Laurence Schmeckebier (auth), Boris Margo, Graphic Work, 1932-1968, Syracuse Univ Press, 68. *Mem:* Provincetown Art Asn; MacDowell Colony Fels; Soc Am Graphic Artists. *Publ:* Auth, Boris Margo: my theories and techniques, Mag Art, 11/47; auth, Margo: is there an American school of art?, The Tiger's Eye, 12/47; auth, Surrealism and American Art, Jeffrey Wechsler, 77. *Dealer:* Stuart Levy Gallery 415 W Broadway New York NY 10012. *Mailing Add:* Atkins-Mayo Rd Provincetown MA 02654

MARGOLIES, ETHEL POLACHECK
PAINTER, SCULPTOR
b Milwaukee, Wis, Aug 1, 07. *Study:* Smith Col, AB, 29; Silvermine Guild Artists; Umberto Romano Sch, East Gloucester, Mass; Univ Vt Summer Sch. *Work:* Burndy Libr, Norwalk, Conn; Gen Time Corp, Stamford, Conn; Springfield Mus, Mass; Int Petroleum Corp; New Haven Paint & Clay Club, Conn. *Exhib:* Silvermine Guild Artists, New Eng Exhib, New Canaan, Conn, 54-57, 60-68 & 74-75; Conn Acad Fine Arts, Hartford; Conn Watercolor Soc, Hartford; Audubon Artists, New York; H P Curtis Gallery, 87; New Canaan Libr, New Canaan, Conn. *Pos:* Gallery dir, Silvermine Guild Artists, 54-72 & Larry Aldrich Mus Contemp Art, 64-66. *Awards:* Awards for indust painting, Silvermine Guild, 54, 57, 60 & 64; Purchase Award, Springfield Mus, Mass, 57; New Haven Paint & Clay Club Award, 75. *Mem:* Artists Equity Asn New York; Silvermine Guild Artists (bd trustees, 54-75); Conn Acad Fine Arts; Conn Watercolor Soc; New Haven Paint & Clay Club. *Media:* Multimedia. *Dealer:* Sivermine Guild Artists New Canaan CT 06840. *Mailing Add:* 103 Jelliff Mill Rd New Canaan CT 06840

MARGOLIS, DAVID
PAINTER, SCULPTOR
b Voloshisk, USSR, Sept 3, 11; US citizen. *Study:* Acad Fine Arts, Odessa, USSR, BFA(equivalent), 27; Ecole de Beaux Art, Montreal, BFA(equivalent), 29; Nat Acad, New York, Art Students League New York, 32, Asst to Diego Rivera: Worked on (Progress of Man) Rockefeller Mural. *Work:* Tel Aviv Mus, Israel; Wichita Art Mus, Kans; Health & Hospital Corp, New York, 89; Nassau Co Mus, Long Island, NY. *Comn:* Modern Communications (mural), Amalgamated Broadcasting, New York, 34; History of American Music (mural), Tilden High Sch & WPA, New York, 37; Materials for Relaxation (mural), Bellevue Hosp & WPA, New York, 41; Industrial Development (mural), Design for Living, New York, 43. *Exhib:* Contemporary Sculpture, Brooklyn Col Mus, New York, 69; solo exhibs, NY Univ, 72, Wichita Art Mus, Kans, 85 & Hudson Ctr Galleries, 86; Alphabet as Art, Tragetto Gallery, Venice, Italy, 78 & Samuel Dorsky Gallery, New York, 80; Am Soc Contemp Artists, New York, 79 & 80; Contemp Artists Guild, 86; Anita Shapolsky Gallery, NY, 88 & 89; Kathazina Rich Pezlow Gallery, NY, 89. *Awards:* Pullock Krasner Found, 87; Sculpture Award Westbeth Gallery, NY, 88; Adolph & Esther Gottlieb Found, 89; and others. *Bibliog:* Francis V O'Connor (auth), American Art, Smithsonian Inst, 76; Emily Genauer (auth), New York City WPA Art, New York WPA Artists Inc, 77. *Mem:* Provincetown Art Asn; Am Soc Contemp Artists; New York WPA Artists Inc. *Media:* Mixed Media; Constructed Metal. *Mailing Add:* 505 La Quadia Pl NO 6E New York NY 10012

MARGOLIS, MARGO
PAINTER
b Lawrence, Mass, Dec 24, 47. *Study:* Skidmore Col, BS, 70; Ind Univ, MFA, 72. *Work:* Philadelphia Mus, Pa; Chemical Bank, Shearson Lehman, Chase Manhattan, IBM Corp Hq, New York; General Mills, Minneapolis, Minn; Brook Mus. *Exhib:* One-person shows, Brooke Alexander Gallery, NY, 77, 78 & 80, Conn Col, New London, 77, Miami-Dade Col, Fla, 79, Richard Greene Gallery, NY, 87, Beth Urdang Fine Art, Boston, 89; Contemporary Drawings, Pa Acad Fine Arts, Philadelphia, 78; Monoprints, Univ Maine, 88; Drawings, Lorence Monk Gallery, NY, 89; Shea Baker Gallery, NY, 89; Ground Work, Valencia Gallery, Fla, 89; Langman Gallery, Philadelphia, 90; Beth Urdang Gallery, Chicago, 91; Penzesenze, Perugia, Italy, 91. *Teaching:* Prof painting, Tyler Sch Art at Temple Univ, 88. *Awards:* CAPS Grant, NY State Coun Arts, 77-78; Nat Endowment Arts Grants, 80-81, 87-88; Nat Endowment Arts Int Fel, 87-88. *Bibliog:* John Russell (auth), New York Times, 78, 80; Lee Edwards (auth), Margo Margolis, Arts Mag, 80; Carter Ratcliffe (auth), Thick Paint, Univ Chicago, 78. *Media:* Oil, Paint. *Mailing Add:* 16 Crosby St New York NY 10013

MARGOLIS, RICHARD M
PHOTOGRAPHER, EDUCATOR
b Lorain, Ohio, June 10, 43. *Study:* Univ Americas, Mexico City, 64, Kent State Univ, BS, 69; Viusal Studies Workshop, 72; Rochester Inst Technol, MFA, 78. *Work:* Mus Mod Art, New York; Victoria & Albert Mus, London, Eng; Bibliotheque Nat, Paris, France; Int Mus Photog, Rochester, NY; Yale Univ Art Gallery, New Haven, Conn; and others. *Comn:* Treasures of Imperial Austria, currently on US tour, photographed medieval armor & armory, Landeszeughaus-Graz, Austria (exhib catalog), Mus Fine Arts, Houston, 91. *Exhib:* One-person shows, Foto, New York, 76, George Eastman House, Rochester, NY, 79, Bridges-Symbols of Progress, Rochester's Big Trees, Spectrum Gallery, Rochester, 90, Nat Acad Sci, Washington, DC, 90 & Rochester's Pub Art Dawson Gallery, 92; St Lawrence Univ, Canton, NY, 77; Carpenter Ctr, Harvard Univ, Cambridge, Mass, 78; Creative Artists Pub Serv Prog Photog Show, Whitney Mus Am Art, New York, 78; Mem Art Gallery, Rochester, NY, 79; English Landscapes, Camden Arts Ctr, London, Eng, 81; Foto, New York, 83. *Collections Arranged:* Personal Landscapes, Rochester Landscape in Various Media, Artworks Gallery, 80; Francis Murray & H Jones, Gallery 696, Rochester, 81; Photography-Art of the State (auth, catalog), State Univ NY, Brockport, 83 & NY State Mus, 83; New York Bridges, 86; Computers and Photography, Pyramid Art Center, Rochester NY, 89. *Teaching:* Instr photog, Penland Sch Crafts, 79-80, 86 & 90; adj instr photog, Nazareth Col, Rochester, NY, 79-81; asst prof photog, State Univ NY, Brockport, 81-88; vis artist, Chautauqua Inst, 83. *Awards:* New York State Coun Arts Grant, Creative Artists Public Service Program, 77-78; Agr Lift Grant, 89; Grant NY State Coun Arts, 90. *Bibliog:* Owen Edwards (auth), Raveling the knot, Saturday Rev, 4/28/79; Owen Edwards (auth), The complex complex, Am Photographer, 6/81; Contempprary Photogrophers, 82-86; A Photographer's Vision, Upstate, 90. *Mem:* Soc Photog Educ (chmn, NE region, 83 & 85); Photogr Heritage Asn, (founder & chair); Nat Trust Hist Preservation; Soc Indust Archeol. *Publ:* Bridges-Symbols of Progress Exhib Catalog, 91. *Mailing Add:* 225 Barrington St Rochester NY 14607

MARGULES, GABRIELE ELLA
ILLUSTRATOR, PAINTER
b Tachau, Czech, May 30, 27; US citizen. *Study:* Cambridge Sch Art, Eng, nat dipl fine arts; Royal Acad Schs, London; New York, studies with Hans Hofmann, Camilo Egas & Norman Carton. *Work:* Kerlan Collection, Univ Minn Res Ctr for Children's Books, Minneapolis; Forbes Collection; pvt collections, Garrison, Cold Spring & Hudson, NY, San Francisco, St Louis & Geneve, Switz. *Exhib:* New York Ctr, 54-72; Jr Coun, Mus Mod Art, 54-72; NY Artists Equity, 54-72; solo exhibs, Panoras Gallery, 57, New York Pub Libr, 60, Lieberman Studio, 69, Baronet Theatre, 70 & Garrison Art Ctr, 85; Hastings on Hudson Art Coun, 74; Garrison Art Ctr, 78-92; Barrett House, 87-92; Putnam Arts Coun, 88-92; Howland Art Ctr, 90. *Awards:* Silver Medal-First Prize for Life Drawing, Royal Acad, London, 49; Best 100 illus children's books, Am Inst Graphic Arts, 68 & 70; Best in Show, Putnam Arts Coun, 89 & 90. *Mem:* Artists Equity of New York (coun mem, 66-70); Dutchess Co Art Asn; Putnam Arts Coun; Putnam Co Hist Soc. *Media:* Sumi-e Ink, Watercolor. *Publ:* Illusr, Harper's Mag, 63; Out of the Ark, Atheneum, New York & Longman Young, London, 68; Bird Songs, Atheneum, 69. *Mailing Add:* 7 High St Cold Spring NY 10516

MARGULIES, HERMAN
PAINTER
b Boryslaw, Poland, Dec 7, 22; US citizen. *Study:* Royal Acad Fine Arts, Brussels, Belg, 47-49. *Work:* Chosen Work, Yad Vashem Mus, Holocaust Mem, Israel; Nabisco Brands USA, NJ; Pepsico, NY, Touche-Ross, NY; Conn Nat Bank, Conn Bank & Trust, Glendenning, Conn, Xerox, Conn; Marketing Corp Am, Conn; and others. *Exhib:* Middlesex Mus, NJ, 84-87; Allied Artists Am, Nat Arts Club, New York, 85-90; Audubon Artists, New York, 86-90; Canton Art Inst, Ohio, 87; Friends Art Mus, Naples, Fla, 87; and others. *Teaching:* Instr painting with pastels, Bergen Mus Art, NJ 84-85, workshop in pastels painting, Studio, Wash, Conn, 86. *Awards:* Am Artists Prof League, Pastel Award, Salmagundi Club, 87; Pastel Soc Am Award, Nat Arts Club, 87, 89 & 90; Gold Medal Honor Special Tribute, Knickerbocker Artists, NY, 91; and 90 others. *Bibliog:* Mary Beth Majeski (auth), Pastelist, interview & demo (film), Cable Vision, Conn, 5/88; Shannon Dow (auth), For Herman Margulies, barns are more than scenery, Weekly Star, Conn, 10/13/89; Eric Ruark (auth), Margulies vivid pastels, Voices, Conn, 11/29/89; and others. *Mem:* Knickerbocker Artists NY (pres, 85-90); Kent Art Asn, Conn; Allied Artists Am (dir, 88-); Salmagundi Club; Nat Arts Club; and others. *Media:* Pastel. *Publ:* Auth, Impressionistic landscape that glow (self), Artist Mag, 4/87. *Dealer:* Clapp & Tuttle Fine Art Gallery Woodbury CT; Corp Art Unlimited Westport CT. *Mailing Add:* 32 Revere Rd Washington CT 06793

MARGULIES, ISIDORE
SCULPTOR, KINETIC ARTIST
b Vienna, Austria, Apr 1, 21. *Study:* Cooper Union Art Sch, New York, 40-42; State Univ NY, Stony Brook, with Robert White and James Kleege, BA(liberal arts), 73; C W Post Col, MA, 75; with Alfred Van Loan. *Work:* Hall of Fame, State Univ NY, Stony Brook; Brookgreen Gardens, Myrtle Beach, SC; Doane Col, Fla. *Exhib:* Nat Acad Design, New York, 75, 80-81 & 86; Nat Sculpture Soc, 78-90; Joel Meisner Gallery, 77-90; R K Parker Gallery, Soho, NY, 80; Nelson Rockefeller Collection, 80-81; Art Expos, New York & Los Angeles, 90; Ambassador Gallery, Soho, NY, 90-91; Cathedral of St John the Devine, New York, 91. *Awards:* Coun Am Artists Award, Nat Sculpture Soc, 79; Gold Medal, Nat Sculpture Soc, 80; C Percival Dietsch Sculpture Prize, Nat Sculpture Soc, 83; Silver Medal, Knickerbocker Artists, 89. *Mem:* Huntington Twp Art League (chmn, 76-78); fel Nat Sculpture Soc; Knickerbocker Artists. *Media:* Bronze, Mixed. *Mailing Add:* 650 Washington Ave Plainview NY 11803

MARGULIS, MARTHA (BOYER)
PAINTER
b Jersey City, NJ, Jan 5, 28. *Study:* Syracuse Univ, NY, BFA, 49; Columbia Univ, New York, 50-51; with Rudolph Baranik, 58-61. *Work:* Herbert F Johnson Mus, Cornell Univ, Ithaca, NY; Syracuse Univ Art Collections, Lowe Gallery, Syracuse, NY; Everson Mus Art, Syracuse, NY; Smithsonian Inst; Jane Zimmerli Art Mus, Rutgers Univ, New Brunswick, NJ. *Comn:* Mural, F D Rich & Co, Inc, Stamford, Conn, 81; triptych, Bankers Trust Co, Inc, White Plains, NY, 81; mural, Summit Assocs, Edison, NJ, 82; Marriott Marquis Hotel, Atlanta, Ga, 85; Triptych, Omni Hotel, Charlotte NC, 90. *Exhib:* Works on Paper, Brooklyn Mus, NY, 75; NMex Int, Eastern NMex Univ, Clovis, 76; Hudson River Contemp Artists, Hudson River Mus, Yonkers, NY, 78; New Eng Exhib of Painting, Drawing & Sculpture, Silvermine Ctr Arts, New Canaan, Conn, 79, 81, 83 & 88; Nat Acad Design Ann, New York, 80; 44th Ann Midyear Show, Butler Inst Am Art, Youngstown, Ohio, 80; Nat Asn Women Artists: Israel & Egypt traveling exhib, 81-82; Women Artists, Sarah Lawrence Art Gallery, Sarah Lawrence Col, Yonkers, NY, 86; The Natural Image, Stamford Mus, Conn, 89; In Search of the American Experience, Mus Nat Arts Found, New York, 89; Griffith Gallery, Stephen F Austin U, Nacodoches Tex, 90. *Awards:* Condec Corp Award, New Eng Exhib, 81; Dr Maury Leibovitz Award, NY Artists Equity Asn, 85; Peabody Mem, Nat Asn Women Artists, 87. *Bibliog:* Ray Mathew (auth), Rev, Art World, 83; Carol J Everingham (auth), Art Imitates Plant Life in Natural Images, The Advocate & Greenwich Time, p D5, 4/9/89; Abraham Ilein (auth), The Delicate Balance of Emotion for Martha Margulis, Artspeak, pp 22, 23, 3/91. *Mem:* Artists Equity New York; Silvermine Guild of Art. *Media:* Acrylic on Canvas, Oil Pastel on Paper. *Dealer:* Reece Gallery 24 W 57th St New York NY 10019; The Magenta Gallery 131 Washington St Rocky Hill NJ 08553. *Mailing Add:* Valley Ridge Rd Harrison NY 10528

MARI
PAINTER, PRINTMAKER
US citizen. *Study:* Atlanta Sch Art, BFA; Butler Univ; Ga State Univ; Principia Col. *Work:* Mus Contemp Crafts, Slide Libr, New York; Vogue Fabrics Libr, Conde Nast, New York; Hunter Mus, Chattanooga, Tenn; Lily Endowment, Indianapolis, Ind. *Comn:* Batik wallhanging, Emory Univ, Atlanta, Ga; sculptured fabric wall relief, Kennedy Ctr, Tampa, Fla, 86; triptych, diptych, monoprints, Hyatt Regency, Albuquerque, NMex, 90; triptych, Dewitt Embassy, 90. *Exhib:* Midstates Painting Exhib, Evansville Mus Art, 72-74; American Fiber Art, Ball State Univ, 74; Fibers Invitational, Austin Peay State Univ, 74; Spoleto Festival, 77; The Dyers Art, Cincinnati, Ohio, 78; Southern Graphics Coun Invitational, 86. *Teaching:* Instr batik,

silkscreen & fabric painting, Ind Univ, Indianapolis, 69-72, instr painting & drawing, 72-77; instr painting, Herron Sch Art, 72. *Awards:* Objects 71, Textile Award, IMA, 71; Purchase Award, Bardstown Invitational, Ky, 73; Southeastern Arts Festival Painting Award, Atlanta, Ga, 70; Purchase Awards, Dekalb Coun for Arts Invitational, 84 & 85. *Bibliog:* Dona Meilach (auth), Contemporary Batik & Tie Dying, Crown, 73; Joanifer Gibbs (auth), Batiks Unlimited, Watson-Guptill, 74. *Mem:* Surface Design Int; Am Crafts Coun. *Media:* Oil on Canvas. *Publ:* Peachtree Papers, 85. *Mailing Add:* 2080 Bolton Rd NW Atlanta GA 30318

MARIANNE
PAINTER, DRAFTSMAN
b Austin, Tex, Aug 18, 41. *Study:* Laguna Gloria Art Mus, Austin, 52 & 53; Tex Southern Univ, with John Biggers; Fisk Univ, with Aaron Douglas, BA, 63; New York Univ, with Robert Kaupelis & John Opper, MA, 68. *Work:* First Am Nat Bank & Fisk Univ, Nashville. *Comn:* Cover illus, From these Roots (book), Austin, 70; mural, Golden Horn Music Industry, Nashville, 72. *Exhib:* Parthenon, Nashville, 69; one-woman shows, Sam Rayburn Mem Ctr, East Tex State Univ, Commerce, 70, The Parthenon, Nashville, 70 & The Carver Gallery, San Antonio, Tex, 78; Women Artists of Tex, Austin, 84; Int Women's Day Art Exhib, Austin, Tex, 88; and others. *Pos:* Designer, Golden Horn Production Co, 73-76; graphic designer, Huston-Tillotson Col, 77-80; dir mus and galleries, Fisk Univ, Nashville, Tenn, 90. *Teaching:* Instr art, Fisk Univ, 66-69 & Austin Community Col, 81-; Head, Fine Arts Dept, Austin Community Col, 88- *Bibliog:* James W Byrd (auth), Such is the South & Center shows artists work, Herald Banner, Greenville, Tex, 70; Clara Hieronymus (auth), Some gifts not wrapped, 12/18/70 & Art on deposit, 8/26/73, Tennessean. *Mem:* Nat Mus Women Arts. *Media:* Oil, Casein; Charcoal, Pencil. *Dealer:* The Home Gallery 1108 Chicon Austin TX 78702. *Mailing Add:* c/o Carl Van Vechten Gallery Fine Arts Fisk Univ Dr D B Todd Blvd & Jackson St NW Nashville TN 37203

MARINER, DONNA M
PAINTER, WRITER
b Youngsville, Pa, Aug 6, 34. *Study:* Studied with W Peterson, Edinboro Col; Ben F Stahl & John Kuller; Dr Baptist, Clarion Col, 65-75; Famous Artist Sch, Westport, Conn, 73. *Work:* Sill-House Gallery, Warren, Pa. *Comn:* paintings, Warren Co Comnrs Off, Pa, 78 & 79. *Exhib:* Clarion Art Shows, Pa, 68 & 69; Warren Art League Shows, 68-87; Bradford Art Festival, 69, 70 & 76; Int Chautauqua Art Shows, NY, 76 & 78; Am Artist Mag Nat Competition, New York, 86. *Teaching:* Instr painting, Warren Art League & Mariner's Art Studio, 76-90. *Awards:* Outstanding Achievement, World of Poetry, 90; Warren Art League, 89 & 90. *Bibliog:* Bill Bouchard (auth), Local artist has exhibit, Steppin Out Mag, 4/74; Elaine Rhodes (auth), Artist returns to work, Warren Times Observer, 6/82; E Gallenstein (auth), Artist, carver and writer, Chip Chaps Mag, 86. *Mem:* Warren Art League; Bradford Art League; Nat Woodcarvers Asn; World of Poetry. *Media:* Mixed. *Publ:* Auth, Quick tips, perfect blenders, Am Artist Mag, 12/82. *Mailing Add:* PO Box 563 Warren PA 16365-0563

MARINO, FRANK
DEALER
b Danbury, Conn, Aug 24, 42. *Study:* Parson's Sch Design, cert(environ design), 69; NY Univ, 69-70; Art Students League, 70-72. *Pos:* Owner & pres, Frank Marino Gallery, New York, currently. *Specialty:* Twentieth century & contemporary painting, sculpture and photography. *Mailing Add:* 489 Broome St New York NY 10013

MARINSKY, HARRY
SCULPTOR, PAINTER
b London, Eng, May 8, 09; US citizen. *Study:* RI Sch Design; Pratt Inst. *Work:* Metrop Mus Art, New York; Lincoln Ctr, Fordham Univ; Syracuse Univ Art Mus; York Univ Mus; Hunt Botanical Libr, Carnegie-Mellon Univ; and others. *Comn:* Large bronze bird, Scent & Touch Garden, Stamford Mus, Conn, 60; five bronze figures representing spirit of nationalism, Vet Mem Park, Norwalk, Conn, 66; St Francis, St James Episcopal Church, Danbury, Conn, 60, St Francis Col, 85 & Assisi, Italy, 86; bronze figures, Harlequin Plaza, Denver, Colo, 81. *Exhib:* Mus Mod Art, New York; Art Inst Chicago, 47; Kendall Art Gallery, Wellfleet, Mass; Hammer Galleries, New York; Shayne Galerie, Montreal; Montclair Mus, NJ, 88; Westmoreland Mus Art, Greensburg, Pa; and others. *Awards:* Silvermine Guild Sculpture Award, 56; C Percival Dietsch Prize, 85 & Henry Hering Award, 88, Nat Sculpture Soc. *Mem:* Nat Sculpture Soc, New York. *Media:* Bronze, Watercolor. *Publ:* The Sculpture of Harry Marinsky, Hammer Publ, 82; Mus of Outdoor Art, Englewood, Colo. *Dealer:* Hammer Galleries New York NY. *Mailing Add:* Villa Capriglia Via Fornace 2 Capriglia 55045 Pietrasanta (Lucca) Italy

MARIONI, PAUL
SCULPTOR, GLASS BLOWER
b Cincinnati, Ohio, July 19, 41. *Study:* Univ Cincinnati, BA, 67. *Work:* Corning Mus Glass; Hessisches Landesmuseum, Darmstadt, WGer; Oakland Mus; Yamaha Corp, Tokyo; City Seattle Portable Works Collection. *Comn:* Leaded glass windows, Stanford Univ, 78; cast glass window, Seattle Arts Comn, 80; cast glass wall, Timberline Lodge, Mt Hood, Ore, 82; cast glass sculptures, Seattle Arts Comn, 83; leaded glass windows, Wash Arts Comn, Woodinville, 83; Cast Glass Window, Seattle Arts Comn, 88. *Exhib:* Glass, Mus Contemp Crafts, New York, 78; New Glass, Corning Mus & traveling, 78-81; Contemporary Glass, Smithsonian Inst, 80; American Glass Now Traveling Exhib, Japan, 80-83; American Glass Traveling Exhib, Europe, 82-83; Pacific Glass 83, Govett-Brewster Mus, New Plymouth, NZ, 83; Vicointer 83, Cevider Mus, Valencia, Spain, 83. *Pos:* Dir, Canyon Cinema, San Francisco, 72-74; coordr glass prog, Summervail, Vail, Colo, 79-84; dir, Glass Art Soc, 84-86. *Teaching:* Lectr art, San Francisco Art Inst, 73-75; asst prof, San Francisco State Univ, 74-78; guest artist, Pilchuck Sch, Stanwood, Wash, 74-88. *Awards:* Nat Endowment Arts Grants, 75-76, 82 & 88; First Prize Archit, Fragile Art, 83. *Bibliog:* Otto Rigan (auth), New Glass, Simon & Schuster, 76; Narcissus Quagliata (auth), From Mind to Light, Mattole Press, 76; Julie Hall (auth), Tradition and Change, Dutton Press, 78. *Mem:* Glass Arts Soc; Northwest Glass Artists. *Media:* Glass. *Dealer:* Walter-White Gallery 7th & San Carlos PO Box 4834 Carmel CA 93921; Traver/Sutton 2219 Fourth Ave Seattle WA 98121. *Mailing Add:* 4136 Meridian Ave No 1 Seattle WA 98103

MARIONI, TOM
ENVIRONMENTAL ARTIST, MUSEUM DIRECTOR
b Cincinnati, Ohio, May 21, 37. *Study:* Cincinnati Art Acad, 55-59. *Work:* Oakland Mus, Calif; Student Cult Ctr, Belgrade, Yugoslavia; San Francisco Mus Art; Santa Barbara Mus Art, Calif. *Comn:* Logo, Western Asn Art Mus, 69; playground (with Jacques Overhoff), Fashion Island, Newport Beach, Calif, 67; pub sculpture, Marin Co Civic Ctr, 88. *Exhib:* Sound Sculpture As, Mus Conceptual Art, 70; De Marco Gallery, Edinburgh, Scotland, 72; White Chapel, London, Eng, 72; Student Cult Ctr, Belgrade, Yugoslavia, 74; one-man show, Foksol Gallery, Warsaw, Poland, 75, Mod Art Gallery, Vienna, Austria, 79, Pellegrino Gallery, Bologna, Italy, 79, Kunst Mus, Bern, Switz, 80, Ctr G Pompidou Mus, Paris,80. *Collections Arranged:* All Night Sculptures, Mus Conceptual Art, 73; Art Against War, San Francisco Art Inst, 84; Elegant Mineatures from San Francisco, Belca House, Kyoto, Japan. *Pos:* Cur art, Richmond Art Ctr, 68-71; dir, Mus Conceptual Art, 70-84; ed, Vision, Oakland, 75-82. *Teaching:* instr, Univ Calif, Berkeley, 79, Los Angeles, 86. *Awards:* Nat Endowment Arts, 79, 80 & 84; J S Guggemheim Grant, 80; Travel Grant, Asian Cult Coun, 86. *Bibliog:* Hilla Futterman (auth), Activity as sculpture, Art & Artists, 8/73; Bill Berkson (rev), Artforum, 5/86; David Winter (rev), Artnews, 4/86; and others. *Mem:* San Francisco Art Inst (bd dirs, 74-). *Publ:* Auth, Invisible Painting & Sculpture, 69; The Return of Abstract Expressionism, 69; The San Francisco Performance, 72; Notes & Scores for Sounds, 72; Vision (California), 75, Vision (Eastern Europe), Vision (New York City), Vision (Word of Mouth), 80 & Vision (Artist Photographs), 81. *Dealer:* Margarete Roeder 545 Broadway New York NY. *Mailing Add:* 22 Hawthorne St San Francisco CA 94105

MARISOL
SCULPTOR
b Paris, France, 1930. *Study:* Ecole Beaux Arts, 49; Art Students League, 50; New Sch, Hans Hofmann Sch, 51-54; Moore Col Art, Philadelphia, Hon DFA, 69, RI Sch Design, Providence, Hon Dr Arts, 86; State Univ NY, Buffalo, Hon DFA, 92. *Work:* Mus Mod Art, New York; Whitney Mus Am Art, New York; Albright-Knox Art Gallery, Buffalo; Mus De Arte Contemporaneo, Caracas, Venezuela; Nat Portrait Gallery, Washington, DC; Rose Art Mus, Brandeis Univ, Waltham, Mass; Hakone Open Air Mus, Japan; Art Inst Chicago; and others. *Exhib:* One-man exhibs, Sidney Janis Gallery, New York, 66, 67, 73, 75, 81, 84 & 89, Columbus Gallery Fine Arts, Ohio, 74, Makier Gallery, Philadelphia, 82, Boca Raton Mus Art, 88, Galerie Tokoro, Tokyo, 89, Hasagawa Gallery, Tokyo, 89 & Nat Portrait Gallery, Washington, 91; Forms in Wood, American Sculpture of the 1950's, Philadelphia Art Mus, 85; The Artist's Mother: Portraits & Homages, Heckscher Mus, Huntington, NY & Nat Portrait Gallery, Washington, 87; Urban Figures, Whitney Mus Am Art at Philip Morris, 88; Body Language: The Figure in the Art of Our Time, Rose Art Mus, Waltham, Mass, 90; Figures of Contemporary Sculpture (1978-1990): Images of Man, Isetan Mus Art, Tokyo, Dakimoru Mus Art, Osaka-Umeda & Hiroshima City Mus Contemp Art, 92; and many other one-man & group exhibs. *Bibliog:* Eric Gibson (auth), Marisol's sculptures offer quiet revelation, Washington Times; Paul Gardner (auth), Who is Marisol? Artnews; Robert Bernstein (auth), Marisol's self portraits: the dream and the dreamer, Arts Mag; Kay Larson (auth), Supper with Marisol, NY Mag; Theodore Wolff (auth), From fun and games to moving statement, Christian Sci Monitor, Arts/Entertainment); and many others. *Mem:* Am Acad Arts & Letters, 78. *Publ:* Contribr, Robert Bernstein & Yoshiaki Turo (auths), Marisol, Galerie Tokoro, Tokyo, 89; Carol Anne Munsun (ed), Pop Art: The Critical Dialogue, Univ Mich Res Press, Ann Arbor, 89; Contemporary American Women Artists, Cedco Publg, San Rafael, 91; Nancy Grove (auth), Magical Mixtures: Marisol Portrait Sculpture, Smithsonian Inst Press for Nat Portrait Gallery, 91; Margaret Lunn (auth), Marisol, NJ Ctr Visual Arts, Harvard Printing Co, 92; and many others. *Mailing Add:* c/o Sidney Janis Gallery 6 W 57th St New York NY 10019

MARK, BENDOR
PAINTER
b New York, NY, June 5, 12. *Study:* Cooper Union. *Work:* Denver Art Mus, Colo; Nat Collection Fine Arts, Washington, DC; Butler Inst Am Art, Youngstown, Ohio; Ga Mus Art, Athens; Los Angeles Co Mus Art. *Exhib:* American Art Today, New York World's Fair, 39; Art Inst Chicago, 40; Am Fedn Art Traveling Show, 40-41; Pepsi Cola Nat Competition, Metrop Mus, New York, 45; Am as Art Bicentennial Exhib, Nat Collection Fine Arts, Washington, DC, 76; plus others. *Awards:* Second Prize, Cooper Union, 29; Second Prize, ACA Nat Competition, 36. *Media:* All. *Mailing Add:* 5727 Chelsea Ave La Jolla CA 92037

MARK, ENID (EPSTEIN)
PRINTMAKER, PHOTOGRAPHER
b New York, NY, 32. *Study:* Art Students League; Smith Col, BA; West Chester Univ, lithography with Victor Lasuchin. *Work:* Smith Col Mus Art;

Univ Pa; Univ Del; Philadelphia Mus Art; Free Libr Philadelphia; Houghton Libr, Harvard Univ; Princeton Univ; Jewish Mus, NY; Israel Mus, Jerusalem; Toledo Mus of Art; Libr Cong. *Comn:* Germantown Friends School, Philadelphia, Pa; Two print ed, Ronbic Editions, Philadelphia, Pa; Nat Libr Can, Ottawa. *Exhib:* Solo exhibs, Swarthmore Col, Pa, 80, Shipley Sch, Bryn Mawr, Pa, 82, Smith Col, Mass, 85 & Princeton Univ Libr; Artist's Bookworks, Albright-Knox Art Gallery, Buffalo, 82; Philadelphia Bookworks, Moore Col Art, 82; Books by Printmakers, Print Club, Philadelphia, 82; Women: Self-Image, Philadelphia Art Alliance, 83; Artists of the Book, Boston Atheneum & Am Craft Mus, NY; Franz Bader Gallery, 88; Princeton Univ, 88; Contemp Philadelphia Artists, Philadelphia Mus Art, 90; Imprints, Six Philadelphia Photogrs, Old Dominion Univ, Norfolk, Va. *Pos:* Artist in residence, Springfield Sch Dist, Pa, 68-69. *Teaching:* Community Arts Ctr, Wallingford, Pa, 81-33. *Awards:* Beaver Col Purchase Award, 80; Del Art Mus Purchase Award, 81; Graphics Award, Cheltenham Arts Ctr, Pa, 83; Third Prize, Am Color Print Soc, Juried exhib, 87 & second prize, 88. *Bibliog:* Susan Teller (auth), Prints by women: A survey of graphic work, Assoc Am Artists, 86; Deborah Curtiss (auth), Introduction to Visual Literacy, Prentice-Hall, 86; Karen Fitzgerald (auth), Making reader friendly books, Ms Mag, 6/87. *Mem:* Am Color Print Soc; Cheltenham Graphics Guild, Pa; Artists Equity Asn; Southern Graphics Coun; Women's Caucus Arts. *Media:* Lithography, Drawing, Non-Silver Photographic Processes. *Publ:* Auth, Promises, 84, The Bewildering Thread, 86 & An Afternoon at Les Collettes, 88, Elm Press; Springs, 90. *Dealer:* Franz Bader Gallery 1701 Pennsylvania Ave Washington DC. *Mailing Add:* 210 Sykes Lane Wallingford PA 19086

MARK, MARILYN (SABETSKY)
PAINTER, ADMINISTRATOR
b Brooklyn, NY. *Study:* Self-taught. *Work:* Nat Art Mus Sport, Indianapolis, Ind; Du Musee des Beaux Arts Montbard, France; Nat Soccer Hall Fame, Oneonta, NY; Doane Col, Crete, Nebr; Gov Kay A Orr, The Gov's Mansion, Lincoln, Nebr; and many others. *Comn:* First Catch & Serenity, comn by Michael Nathan & Henrietta Sabetsky, 70; portraits of Ligoa Duncan & her dog Chi Chi, Paris, 75; Leur Majeste Le Roi Baudouin Et La Reine Fabiola, comn by Mr Lebon, Asn Belgo-Hispanica, Belg, 77. *Exhib:* Nat Arts Club, Metrop Mus Art, New York, 77; one-woman show, Long Island Univ, Brooklyn Ctr, 79; retrospective, 71-86, Stuhr Mus Prairie Pioneer, Grand Island, Nebr, 86; Art in Embassies Progs, Washington, DC, 92; Cannon House Rotunda, Washington, DC sponsored by Charles E Schumer, 92; Nat Soccer Hall of Fame, 92; Dahl Fine Arts Ctr, 93; Bismarck State Col, 93; and others. *Pos:* Founder, pres & global coord, Visual Individualists United, 76-; assoc trustee, Nat Art Mus Sport, 84-; rep/juror, Stuhr Mus Prairie Pioneer Nat Contemp Expo Artists Achievement, Jacob Javits Fed Bldg, New York, 86. *Teaching:* Instr, studio, 62-70. *Awards:* Gold Medal & Global Award, Acad de Ciencas Humanisticas y Relaciones & Asn Belgo-Hispanica, Belg, 77; Peter Paul Rubins Medal from Holland & Citation, 78; Grumbacher Gold Medal, NY State Pre-Biennial Nat League Am Pen Women Art Show, Lincoln Ctr, New York, 89; and others. *Bibliog:* Vyacheslav Zavalishin (auth), article, Russian Daily Newspaper, 72; Gordon Brown (auth), Arts Mag, 73; Joe Franklin (host), Women of achievement (interview), Joe Franklin Show, 4/19/88. *Mem:* Nat League Am Pen Women Inc; Metrop Painters & Sculptors; Burr Artists (mem bd, 74-); Artists Equity Asn New York, Inc; Life Mem, Life Assoc Trustee, Nat Art Mus Sport, Indianapolis, 91- *Media:* Acrylic on Belguim Linen, Mixed Media on Belguim Linen. *Publ:* Park East Newspaper, New York, 70-; World Herald, Nebr, 86; New York Art Review, 88; Daily Herald, Iowa, 88. *Dealer:* Tatem Gallery Ft Lauderdale FL; National Soccer Hall of Fame Oneonta NY. *Mailing Add:* 2261 Ocean Ave Brooklyn NY 11229

MARK, MARY ELLEN
PHOTOGRAPHER
b Philadelphia, Pa, Mar 20, 40. *Study:* Univ Pa, BFA(painting & art hist), 62; Annenberg Sch, Univ Pa, MFA(photojournalism), 64. *Work:* Bibliot Nat, Paris; Australian Nat Gallery. *Exhib:* Solo exhibs, Falkland Rd, Castelli Gallery, New York, 81 & traveling, Mother Theresa & Calcutta, Friends of Photography, Carmel, Calif, 83 & traveling, Photographs, Mus Art, Univ Okla, 87, Portraits, Photog Gallery, Santa Monica Col, 88 & Birmingham Mus Art, Ala, 89; Women of Photography, Sidney Janis Gallery, New York, 76; Am Images, Int Ctr Photog, New York, 79; Likely Stories, Castelli Graphics, New York, 80; Color as Form, Corcoran Gallery Art, Washington, DC & George Eastman House, New York, 82; Faces, United Nations 40th Anniversary Photography Exhib, Berkeley, Calif, 85; Miami Beach, Walker Art Ctr, Minneapolis, 86; Santa Barbara Contemp Arts Forum, Calif, 86; 50 Years of Modern Color Photography, Photokina, Cologne, Fed Repub Ger, 86; Ansel Adams & Friends, Scotsdale Ctr Arts, Ariz, 87; Homeless in America, Corcoran Gallery Art, Washington, DC, 88 & traveling; The Instant Likeness, Polaroid Portraits, Nat Portrait Gallery, Washington, DC, 88; and others. *Teaching:* Numerous lect series & workshops nationally & internationally. *Awards:* Nat Endowment Arts Grants, 77, 79-80 & 90; 1st Prize, Robert F Kennedy Journalism Award, 81 & 85; Photographer of Year Award, Friends of Photog, 87; World Press Award for Outstanding Body of Work Throughout the Years, 88; Art Directors Club Award, 89; Best Photojournalism Award, Life Mag, 89. *Bibliog:* Street shooter: an interview with Mary Ellen Mark, Darkroom Photog, 1-2/87; Mary Ellen Mark: shoots from the heart, New York Woman, 1-2/87; The unflinching eye, New York Times Mag, 7/12/87; article in Bomb Mag, summer 89. *Publ:* Auth, Passport, Lustrum Press, 74; coauth, The Photojournalist, Thomas Crowell, 74; Ward 81, Simon & Schuster, 79; Falkland Road, Alfred A Knopf, 81; Mother Theresa: Her Missions in Calcutta, Friends of Photog, 85; Streetwise, Univ Pa Press, 85; Homeless in America, Acropolis Books, 88; auth, Portraits, Edition Stemmle, 89; Rolling Stone - The Photographs, Simon & Schuster, 89; 25 Years, A Retrospective Book, Bulfinch Press, 92. *Dealer:* Mary Ellen Mark Library 134 Spring St New York NY 10012. *Mailing Add:* 143 Prince St New York NY 10012

MARK, PHYLLIS
SCULPTOR, ENVIRONMENTAL ARTIST
b New York, NY. *Study:* Ohio State Univ; New Sch Social Res, sculpture study with Seymour Lipton. *Work:* Dickerson-White Mus, Cornell Univ; Allentown Mus Art, Pa; RCA Collection; Corcoran Gallery Art, Washington, DC; Ft Wayne Mus Art, Ind; and others. *Comn:* Birmingham Ctr, Mich, 75; Fordham Univ, NY, 85. *Exhib:* Sculpture as Jewelry, Inst Contemp Art, Boston, 73; Works on Paper by Women Artists, Brooklyn Mus, 75; Green Scene: Outdoor Sculpture Indoors, Installation Soho 20 Gallery, 92; group show, Fed Reserve Bank Philadelphia, 92; Cast Iron Gallery, 92; Borough of Manhattan Community Col, 92; Guild Hall, East Hampton, NY, 92; and others. *Awards:* Ind Arts Comn & Nat Endowment Arts Grant, 79. *Bibliog:* Greenwich Time, Conn, 2/26/92; Ed McCormack, Artspeak, 3/92; Rose Slivka, East Hampton Star, 7/27/92; and others. *Mem:* Artist Rep Environ Art (mem bd dir & treas, currently); Women's Caucus for Art; Sculptors Guild (bd mem & vpres publs, currently). *Media:* Painted Aluminum, Stainless Steel. *Dealer:* Soho 20 Gallery 469 Broome St New York NY 10013. *Mailing Add:* 803 Greenwich St New York NY 10014

MARKARIAN, ALEXIA (MITRUS)
PAINTER
b Binghamton, NY. *Study:* Art Students League, drawing & anatomy studies with Robert Hale; Broome Community Col, State Univ NY, Binghamton, AB, 70. *Work:* Chattahoochee Valley Art Asn, La Grange, Ga. *Exhib:* Solo exhib, Free Fall, Univ St Louis, 88, Dietrich Jenny Gallery, San Diego, 89, Artists Union Gallery, Moscow, USSR, 90 & Terra Obscura, Traveling USA & Can, 91-93; San Diego Mus Art, Calif, 81 & 86; Chatauqua Inst, NY, 85; Springville Mus Art, Utah, 85-86; Riverside Mus Art, Calif, 86; National Midyear Show, Butler Inst Am Art, Youngstown, Ohio, 86-87; Five Women Artists: A Southern Californiia Perspective, traveling, USA & Can, 86-88; Fla Nat, Fla State Univ, Tallahassee, 88; On the Horizon: Emerging in California, Fresno Arts Ctr & Mus, 88; Bestiary, Women's Bldg, Los Angeles, Calif, 88; solo exhib, Free Fall, Univ St Louis, 88, Dietrich Jenny Gallery, San Diego, 89 & Artists Union Gallery, Moscow, USSR, 90; Oneiros Gallery, San Diego, 91. *Pos:* Isomata Master Class Series, painting, Idyllwild, Calif, 92. *Awards:* Bellinger Award, Gebbie Found, Chatauqua Exhib, 85; First Award, Fine Arts, Int Soc Airbrush Arts, Pasadena, Calif, 85; Permanent Collection Purchase Award, La Grange Nat, Ga, 88; Artists Fel, Calif Arts Coun, 90. *Bibliog:* Tony di Gessu (prod), interview, Channel 51-TV, San Diego, Calif, 10/26/85; Leah Ollman (auth), At the Galleries (article), Los Angeles Times, 2/12/88; Bill Van Siclen (auth), Art in Rhode Island, Providence J-Bull, 2/86; Robert L Pincus (article), San Diego Union, 10/19/89 & 6/15/90; Art in America, Rev of Exhibs, 4/90; Robert L Pincus (auth), Art Review (article), San Diego Union, 12/91; Elizabeth Kidd (auth), Outlook Mag, Vol III, issue 2, (article), Edmonton Art Gallery, 92; Gene Grey (auth), Living (article), Binghamton Press, 2/92. *Mem:* San Diego Art Inst (bd dirs, 81-82); Artists Equity (vpres, 84-86); Artists Guild San Diego Mus Art (corresp secy, 84). *Media:* Acrylic. *Publ:* Illusr, The Red Flower, Crossing Press, 88. *Mailing Add:* 4411 Alamo Way San Diego CA 92115

MARKEL, KATHRYN E
DEALER
b Richmond, Va, Oct 19, 46. *Pos:* Dir, Kathryn Markel Gallery, New York, currently. *Media:* Work on Paper. *Specialty:* Specialty work on paper by contemporary American artists. *Mailing Add:* Markel/Sears Fine Arts 560 Broadway New York NY 10012

MARKER, MARISKA PUGSLEY
PAINTER
b San Francisco, Calif. *Study:* With Leon Berkowitz, Robert Newmann, Hank Harmon, Horace Day, Daniel Greene, Albert Handell, Henry Hensche, and others. *Work:* Nat Mus Fine Arts, Valletta, Malta; The White House Artists Easter Collection, Smithsonian Inst, Washington, DC; Fed Reserve Bd Governors Collection, Washington, DC; Dulin Gallery Art, Knoxville, Tenn; Container Corp Am; and others. *Exhib:* Two-person show, Nat Mus Fine Arts, Valletta, Malta, 76; one-person shows, Fed Reserve Bd Governors, Washington, DC, 81 & 84, Va Beach Art Ctr, 83, Gilpin Gallery, The Atholl Series, 88, among others; Continuum V, Dulin Gallery Art, Knoxville, Tenn, 84; US State Dept Art in Embassies Prog, US Embassy, Muscat, Oman, 86-90; and others. *Awards:* Judged, Maine Artists, The Next Generation, Washington, DC, 90, for Maine Arts Comm & Maine State Soc. *Bibliog:* The Markers at the Museum of Fine Arts, Times Malta, 10/20/76; Teresa Annas (auth), Energetic Marker creates art with depth, 9/4/83; John Levin (auth), Illuminating images, a unique technique, 9/8/83; and others. *Mem:* Art League Alexandria, Va (bd mem, 69-70); Artists Equity. *Media:* Miscellaneous. *Res:* Max Schallinger, a rediscovered artist. *Publ:* Auth, Korean arts have a great potential, Feel of Korea, Holl M Corp, 66; also feature articles in Kansas City Star and catalogs for Northern Va Fine Arts Asn. *Mailing Add:* 9082 Belvoir Woods Pkwy Ft Belvoir VA 22060

MARKLE, GREER (WALTER GREER MARKLE)
MUSEUM DIRECTOR, HISTORIAN
b Port Arthur, Tex, Apr 12, 46. *Study:* Univ Wyoming, BFA, 68; Univ Utah, MA, 76. *Collections Arranged:* Contemp Am Prints and Drawings, UMFA Traveling, 78; Utah Wilderness Photography, traveling, 78; Potter and Prints, Sun Valley Ctr, 81; Will Martin Retrospective, Schneider Mus Art, 87; Art of the Orient: Schneider Mus Art, Zundel Col, 88. *Teaching:* Instr art hist, Univ Utah, Salt Lake City, 76-78; lectr art admin, Radcliffe Col, Cambridge, Mass, 78-82; asst prof art hist, SOre State Col, Ashland, 86- *Mem:* Col Art Asn; Ore Advocates Arts; Am Asn Mus. *Res:* Contemporary Am art and Italian Renaissance art. *Publ:* Auth, Marilyn Levine and photorealism, Ceramics Monthly, 76; Utah wilderness photography, Utah Arts Coun, 78; Potters & prints, Sun Valley Ctr, 81; Handbook for traveling exhibitions, Cambridge, Mass. *Mailing Add:* 681 S Mountain St Ashland OR 97520

MARKLE, JACK M
DEALER, SCULPTOR
b Winnipeg, Man, July 9, 39. *Study:* With Jack Markel; Ont Col Art. *Work:* Art Bank, Fed Govt, Ottawa, Ont. *Comn:* Neon chandelier, Mr & Mrs Sommerville, Toronto, Ont, 71; neon sculpture, United Trust, Toronto, 75. *Exhib:* Basel Art Fair, Switz, 73-75; IKI Art Fair, Dusseldorf & Cologne, Ger, 73-75; Art Gallery Ont, Toronto, 74; Rotterdam Cult Ctr, Holland, 75. *Pos:* The Electric Gallery, Toronto, Ont. *Awards:* Autumn Festival of the Arts Toronto, Kiwanis Club, 70. *Mem:* Prof Art Dealers Asn Can; IKI, Ger. *Media:* Miscellaneous. *Specialty:* Electric art. *Mailing Add:* 16 Cedar Forest Ct Thornhill ON L3T 2A4 Canada

MARKLE, SAM
DEALER, SCULPTOR
b Winnipeg, Man, 1933. *Study:* Self-taught. *Work:* Nat Art Bank, Ottawa; McLaughlin Mus, Oshawa. *Comn:* Neon installations (with Jack Markle), Alcan Aluminum, Head Off, Toronto, 70; United Trust, Head Off, 72, Famous Players Theatre, Four Seasons Hotel, 73, Sunoco Bldg, 73 & Concourse & Plaza, Hudson Bay Co, 73, Toronto, 74. *Exhib:* One-man shows, Pop Sign Art, Gallery Pascal, 64, Alpha 64, Four Seasons Hotel, 64 & Flower & Garden Show & Electric Gallery, Toronto, 71; New Media, Art Gallery Ont, 71; Espace V Gallery, Montreal, 74. *Pos:* Dir, Electric Gallery, Toronto. *Mem:* Prof Art Dealers Can (vpres, 75-78); Can Conf Arts. *Media:* Neon tubing. *Specialty:* Electric art exclusively. *Mailing Add:* 226 Steelcase Rd W Markham ON L3R 1B3 Canada

MARKLEY, DORIS YOCUM
PRINTMAKER, PHOTOGRAPHER
b Philadelphia, Pa, Feb 1, 21. *Study:* Philadlephia Mus Sch Indust Art, 39-43; Philadelphia Mus Art, with Martha Zelt, 72-75; Montgomery Co Community Col photography- journalism-creative writing, 85-90; study with Naomi Limont, Tony Rosati, Hobson Pitman & Douglas Skinner; Temple Univ, Tyler Sch Art, 87-88. *Work:* Friends Cent Sch, Overbrook, Pa; Sun Oil Co, Radnor, Pa; Acad Notre Dame, Villanova, Pa; Southwestern Life Insurance Co. *Exhib:* Outreach, Philadelphia Mus Art, Pa, 77; Univ Del Ann, Newark; Women in the Arts Ann, William Penn Mem Mus, Harrisburg, Pa, 79; Salmagundi Club Ann, New York, NY, 79; Allentown Art Mus Ann, Pa, 79; Hunterdon Art Ctr Nat Print Exhib, Clinton, NJ; Miami Int Print Biennial, Fla, 80; Abington Art Ctr Nat Photog Ann, Pa, 84 & 85; Nat Photog Ann, Perkins, NJ, 87-88. *Pos:* Photog asst, Montgomery County Community Col, 84-86. *Awards:* Purchase Awards, Univ Del, Newark & Rembrant Graphic Arts, Stockton, NJ; Forbes Mag Award Graphics, Salmagundi Club Ann, 79; Best of Show, Ursinus Col, 83; Louise Clearfield Award Photog, Main Line Arts, 86; Grand Prize Black & White Photog, Norristown Borough, Pa, 86, 87 & 88; Mildred Hoffman Humor Award, St David's Christian Writers Conf, 90. *Mem:* Philadelphia Watercolor Club; Am Color Print Soc. *Media:* Collagraphs. *Publ:* Auth, Pinhole Jour, NMex, 4/88; Features, Today's Post, King of Prussia, Pa, 90. *Dealer:* The Plum Gallery 195 W Lancaster Ave Paoli PA 19301. *Mailing Add:* 2325 Chestnut Ave Norristown PA 19403

MARKMAN, RONALD
PAINTER
b Bronx, NY, May 29, 31. *Study:* Yale Univ, BFA, 57 & MFA, 59. *Work:* Brooklyn Mus, New York; Art Inst of Chicago, Ill; Hirshhorn Mus & Sculpture Garden, Smithsonian Inst, Washington, DC; Metrop Mus of Art, New York; Mus of Mod Art, New York. *Comn:* Christmas Card, Mus Mod Art, 68; five murals, Riley Children's Hosp, 86. *Exhib:* Recent Acquisitions Show, Mus Mod Art, 59 & 66, Young Am, Whitney Mus Am Art, 60, Am Inst Arts & Letts, 77 & 89, New York; Young Am, Whitney Mus Am Art, 60; Chicago Biennial Print & Drawing Show, Art Inst Chicago, 64; Pa Acad Fine Arts Ann, 67, Tyler Sch Art, 76, Philadelphia; Am Painting, Butler Inst, Youngstown, Ohio, 67; Print Biennial, Brooklyn Mus, 68; Humor, Satire and Irony, New Sch for Social Res, 72; Indianapolis Mus Art, 72 & 74; Work by Students of Josef Albers, Harvard Univ, 74; one-man show, Kanegis Gallery, Boston, 59, Terry Dintenfass Gallery, New York, 65, 66, 68, 71, 76, 79, 82 & 85, Dart Gallery, Chicago, 80, & King Gallery, Indianapolis, 83 & 86. *Teaching:* Instr, Univ Fla, 59, Art Inst of Chicago, 60-64 & Indiana Univ, 64- *Awards:* Fulbright Fel, 62-63; Lilly open faculty fel, 89. *Dealer:* Terry Dintenfass Inc 50 W 57th St New York NY 10019. *Mailing Add:* 719 S Jordan Bloomington IN 47401

MARKMAN, SIDNEY DAVID
ADMINISTRATOR, HISTORIAN
b New York, NY, Oct 10, 11. *Study:* Union Col, Schenectady, NY AB, 34; Columbia Univ, MA, 36, PhD, 41. *Teaching:* Prof art hist, Univ Nac de Panama, 41-45; prof art hist, Duke Univ, 47-, actg chmn dept art, 61-62 & 75-78, prof emer, 81-; Morgan Prof, Univ Louisville, 84; distinguished vis prof, Tulane Univ, 86. *Mem:* Soc Archit Historians. *Res:* Colonial art, architecture & urbanization of Central America & Chiapas, Mexico. *Publ:* Auth, Horse in Greek Art, Johns Hopkins Univ Press, 43; San Cristobal de las Casas, Escuela de Estudios Hispano Am, Seville, Spain, 63; Colonial Architecture of Antigua Guatemala, Am Philos Soc, Philadelphia, 66; Colonial Central America, A Bibliography, Ariz State Univ Press, 77; Architecture and Urbanization in Colonial Chiapas, Mexico, Am Philos Soc Philadelphia, 83. *Mailing Add:* 919 Urban Ave Durham NC 27701

MARKOVICH, ANN MARIE
PAINTER, WRITER
b Chicago, Ill, Jan 6, 48. *Study:* Southern Ill Univ, BA, 73; Art Inst Chicago, 73; Royal Col Art, London, 78. *Work:* Satakunta Mus, Pori, Finland. *Comn:* Sports Mural, Manchester Adult-Day Ctr, Droyelsdon, United Kingdom, 78-79; Latino Community Mural, Asn House, Chicago, 76. *Exhib:* CETA Artists, Daley Civic Ctr, Chicago; Drawing Show, Guerbois Two Gallery, Chicago, 76; Abstract Landscape, Touhy Tennis Club, Skokie, Ill, 77. *Pos:* Photogr, New Art Examiner, 75-87, managing ed, 75-83; artist, Chicago CETA Proj, 75; artist-in-residence, Penlee Mus, Penzance, Eng, 79. *Teaching:* Art specialist, Model Cities, Chicago, 74-75; art therapist, Cabrini Hosp, 87-88; art teacher, Ethical Cult Sch, 88-91. *Awards:* Second Prize, Northwestern Artists, Jane Allen, 73; Outstanding Service, Latino Mural, Asn House, 76; Finlandia Found Study Grant, 90. *Bibliog:* Joshua Kind, Drawing show, New Art Examiner, 77. *Mem:* Nat Press Club; Ethical Cult Soc, New York. *Media:* Oil, Paper & Pencil. *Res:* Art criticism of contemporary, American & European art, especially study of Finnish landscape artists. *Publ:* contribr, Helsingen Sanomat, 86; Form Function Mag, Finnish Soc Crafts & Design, 88; co-auth, Marjukka Kaminen, Mus Finland, 88; Scand Rev, Am Scand Found, 89. *Mailing Add:* 146 W 73rd St 2B New York NY 10023

MARKOWITZ, MARILYN
PAINTER
b New York, NY. *Study:* Colo Col, BA, 63; Univ Colo, Boulder, MA, 71. *Work:* State of Colorado Art in Public Places, Univ Colo, Colorado Springs & Boulder. *Comn:* Painting, State of Colo, Colorado Springs, 81. *Exhib:* Solo exhibs, Brena Gallery, Denver, Colo, 75, Albatross Gallery, Boulder, Colo, 79, Carson-Sapiro Gallery, Denver, Colo, 80, Univ Colo, Colorado Springs, 82, Art Resources Gallery, Denver, 83, Western Nebr Art Ctr, Scotts Bluff & Reiss Gallery, Denver, 86; Johnson-Humrickson Mus, Coshocton, 90; Layerists, Marin Co Civic Ctr, Calif 91; WNebr Art Ctr, 92; Univ Tex, San Antonio, 92; Hassel-Haesler Gallery, Denver, 92. *Teaching:* Instr art, Dist No 11 Colorado Springs, 63-69 & Univ Colo, 70- 71. *Awards:* Award, Boulder Fine Art Ctr, 71 & 72; Nat Asn Women Artists Award, 77, 79, 85 & 86; Art in Public Places Award, State of Colo, 81. *Bibliog:* Colorado Women in the Arts; Am Artists Mag, 6/78; Very Important Women, Denver Mag. *Mem:* Rocky Mountain Watercolor Soc; Layerist Soc Am; Nat Asn Women Artists. *Media:* Acrylics, Serigraphs. *Publ:* Contribr, La Revue Moderne, Paris, France, 80; Layering, an art of time and space, Empire Mag, 91. *Dealer:* Studio 001 124 Camino Bosque Boulder CO 80302. *Mailing Add:* 124 Camino Bosque Boulder CO 80302

MARKOWSKI, EUGENE DAVID
PAINTER, SCULPTOR
b St Louis, Mo, Sept 16, 31. *Study:* Washington Univ Sch Fine Art, BFA, 60; Univ Pa Sch Fine Art, MFA, 61. *Work:* Minn Mus Art, St Paul; Lauren Rogers Mus Art, Laurel, Miss; Philip Morris Corp & First & Merchants Bank, Richmond, Va; New York Bank for Savings; Guaranty Savings & Loan, Charlottesville, Va. *Comn:* Chapel, Holy Comforter Roman Cath Church, Charlottesville, Va, 82; stained glass windows, St Mary's Roman Cath Church, Lovingston, Va, 83; sculpture (wood), St George's Roman Cath Church, Scottsville, Va, 83; painting, The Civil War Trust, Washington, DC, 92. *Exhib:* Northern Ill Univ Nat Drawing Competition, 71; Nat Drawing Competition, Minn Mus Art, 71; Int Print & Drawing Competition, Alta Col Art, 72; Regional Painting Competition, Montgomery Mus Fine Arts, 75; Novumn Gallery Ltd, Basel, Switz, 92; Frank Bustamante Gallery, New York, 91; and others. *Pos:* Art critic, Cablevision, Charlottesville, 72-; chmn, studio art dept, Univ Va, 86- *Teaching:* Asst prof painting, Univ Pa, 61-68 & Montgomery Col, Rockville, Md, 68-70; assoc prof painting, Univ Va, Charlottesville, 70-87; prof Art, Trinity Col, Washington, DC, 88- *Awards:* Drawing Award, Smithsonian Inst, 81; Sesquicentennial Associateship, Res Italy, Univ Va, 85; Fulbright Fel, research in India, Coun Int Exchange Scholars, 86. *Mem:* Col Art Asn Am. *Media:* Oil on Canvas; Wood. *Res:* Monuments and people of India, Fulbright to India, 87. *Publ:* Auth, The Art of Photography: Image and Illusion, Prentice-Hall, 84. *Dealer:* Novumn Gallery Ltd Binningerstsrasse 82-88 Basel-Alischwil Switzerland; Frank Bustamante Gallery 560 Broadway New York NY 10012. *Mailing Add:* 4703 Foxhall Crescents NW Washington DC 20007

MARKS, (MR & MRS) CEDRIC H
COLLECTOR, PATRON
Interests: Donated works to various museums and colleges in the United States and Israel. *Collection:* Far & Near Eastern, pre-Columbia medieval and classical antiquities. *Mailing Add:* 880 Fifth Ave New York NY 10021

MARKS, MATTHEW STUART
ART DEALER
b New York, NY, Nov 14, 62. *Study:* Columbia Univ 80-82, with Milton Resnick; Bennington Col, BA, 85. *Collections Arranged:* From the Collection of Matthew Marks, American Prints 1860-1960 (auth, catalog), Bennington Col, 85; British Modernist Prints 1900-1950 (auth, catalog), 85 & Je suis le cahier: The Sketchbooks of Picasso (auth, catalog), 86, Pace Gallery, New York. *Pos:* Consult, Pace Gallery, New York, 82-86; trustee, Bennington Col, Vt, 85-89; Dir, Anthony d'offay Gallery, London, 87-89; Pres, Matthew Marks, Inc, 81- *Bibliog:* Jacqueline Brody (auth), Matthew Marks: Prints at an exhibition, Print Collector's Newslett, 7/85; article, America's top young collectors, Art & Antiques Mag, 9/85; Deborah Gimelson (auth), Marks makes his Mark, Art and Auction, 4/90. *Res:* 19th and 20th century European and American art. *Publ:* Auth, Henry Farrer's early etchings of New York, Imprint, 82; Provincetown prints, Print Collector's Newlett, 84; The graphic work of Lucian Freud, Print Quart, 86. *Mailing Add:* 1018 Madison Ave New York NY 10021

MARKS, ROBERTA BARBARA
SCULPTOR, PAINTER
b Savannah, Ga. *Study:* Univ Miami, Fla, BFA, 80; Univ S Fla, MFA, 81. *Work:* Smithsonian Inst, Washington, DC; Rochester Inst Technol, NY; Notre Dame Univ, South Bend, Ind; Univ Utah Mus Art, Salt Lake City; Univ South Fla, Tampa; Victoria & Albert Mus, London, Eng; Galerie du Manoir, La Chaux-de-Fonds, Switz; AT&T Corp, Philip Johnson Bldg, New York; IBM Corp, Jacksonville, Fla. *Exhib:* Craft Multiples, Renwick Gallery, Smithsonian Inst, Washington, DC, 75; 1976 Biennial Exhib, Mint Mus Art, Charlotte, NC, 76; A Painter and a Ceramist, Galerie Du Manoir, Switz, 78; 50 National Women in Art, Edison Community Col Mus Fine Art, Ft Myers, Fla, 82; The Primal Vessel, Garth Clark Gallery, Los Angeles, 83; Southeastern Ctr for Contemp Art, Winston-Salem, NC, 85; Key West Art & Hist Soc, E Martello Mus & Gallery, 85; New Gallery, Univ Miami, Fla, 87; Katie Gingras Gallery, Milwaukee, Wis, 87; Helander Gallery, Palm Beach, Fla, 88; Galerie Scapa, Bern, Switz, 88; Deux Femmes', East Martello Mus, Key West, Fla, 90; paintings, Roberta B Marks, Biel, Switz, 90; and others. *Collections Arranged:* Lake Superior Int Craft Exhib, Tweed Mus Art, Univ Minn, 72-75 & 77. *Pos:* Mem bd dirs, Grove House Gallery, 77-79; cur, The Valley of Oaxaca: The Zapotecs, Ceramic Sculpture, Univ S Fla, Tampa, 81; cur, Two-Dimensional Key West E Martello Mus, Key West, Fla, 85. *Teaching:* Vis artist ceramics, Univ SFla, Tampa, 76; instr ceramics, Rochester Inst Technol, NY, 76, Art Inst Chicago, 77, NC State Univ, Raleigh, 81, Nat Coun Educ for Ceramic Arts, Boston Univ, Mass, 84, Brookfield Craft Ctr, Conn, 85 & Univ Wis, Milwaukee, 87. *Awards:* Best in Show, Florida Craftsmen, Ceramic Monthly Publ, 73; Purchase Award, Am Crafts Coun, Am Bankers Insurance Co, 76; Merit Award, Ceramic League, Miami, Fla, 79; Lloyd E Herman Merit Award, Smithsonian's Renwick Gallery, Washington, DC, 81; Visual Artists Fel S Fla, 90. *Bibliog:* Garth Clark (auth), A Century of Ceramics in the US, E P Dutton, 79; Leon Nigrosh (auth), Low Fire: Other Ways to Work in Clay, 80; Susan Wechsler (auth), Low-Five Ceramics, A New Direction in American Clay, Watson-Guptill, 81; The New York Art Review, Third Ed, Am References, 88; American Artists; An Illustrated Survey of Leading Contemporary Americans, Chicago, Ill, 85. *Mem:* Artists Equity Asn Inc; Am Crafts Coun; Nat Coun Educ Ceramic Arts; World Crafts Coun; Fla Craftsmen; Int Sculpture Ctr. *Media:* Assemblage. *Publ:* Contribr, Archaeology in Northwest Florida, Fla Endowment Humanities, 78; The Valley of Oaxaca: The Zapotecs (exhib catalog), Univ SFla Fine Arts Prog, 81; Auth, An artist's vision in Key West, Southern Accents Mag, Birmingham, Ala, 85; The art of Roberta B Marks, SFla Home & Gardens, Miami, 85; The Artist at Home, Fla Keys Mag, 87; Creating a new order, Zelo Mag, Winter Park, Fla, 87. *Dealer:* Garth Clark Gallery 24 W 57th St New York NY 10019. *Mailing Add:* 1800 Atlantic Blvd Apt 440 Key West FL 33040

MARKSON, EILEEN
LIBRARIAN
b New York, NY, Mar 13, 39. *Study:* Lewis & Clark Col, BA, 60; Ecole du Louvre, Institut de Phonetique, Paris, France, 62; New York Univ, MA, 64; Queens Col, MLS, 73. *Pos:* Dir lect prog, Archaeol Inst Am, 66-73, asst secy-treas, 68-73; head, Art & Archaeol Libr, Bryn Mawr Col, 73- *Mem:* Art Libr Soc N Am (exec bd, 85-86); Archaeol Inst Am. *Interests:* Classical archaeology; Dutch seventeenth century painting; Impressionism. *Publ:* Auth, Archa; Atlas of the Greek World (rev), Art Documentation, 2/82; co-auth, Archaeology resources in libraries: are they accessible?, Art Libr J, 12/87. *Mailing Add:* Art & Archaeology Libr, Thomas Libr 131 Bryn Mawr Col Bryn Mawr PA 19010

MARKUSEN, THOMAS ROY
CRAFTSMAN, SCULPTOR
b Chicago, Ill, Jan 1, 40. *Study:* Univ Wis, Madison, BS, 65, MS, 66. *Work:* Am Craft Mus, New New York; Lannan Found Art Mus, Palm Beach, Fla; Wustum Mus Fine Arts, Racine, Wis; Hand Workshop Gallery, Richmond, Va; Vatican Mus, Rome; and others. *Comn:* Sculpture Bed, Elson, Atlanta, GA, 80; Altar set, Newmen Oratory, Brockport, NY, 75-76; Altar set, First Univeralist Church, Syracuse, NY, 88. *Exhib:* Contemp Am Silversmiths & Goldsmiths, Corcoran Gallery, Washington, DC, 73; Int Goldsmiths & Weavers, Albright-Knox Art Gallery, Buffalo, NY, 74; 275 Yrs of Am Metalsmithing, Mus of Contemp Crafts, New York & Cranbrook Acad of Arts Mus, Bloomfield Hills, Mich, 75; one-man, Craft Company Sixth, Rockchester, NY, 84; 41st Int Eucharistis Exhib of Liturgical Arts, Civic Ctr, Philadelphia, 76; Solid Wrought Iron, Southern Ill Univ Mus & Art Gallery, Carbondale, 76; Arts/Objects USA, Lee Nordness Gallery & Johnson Wax Found, New York, 76; one-man, Craft Company Sixth, Rockchester, NY, 84; and others. *Pos:* Dir & organizer metal exhib, Fine Arts Gallery, State Univ NY Col, Brockport, 71-78; guest lectr metalsmithing, Univ Wash, Mont State Univ, Va Commonwealth Univ, Syracuse Univ, State Univ NY Col, New Paltz, US Embassy-Mexico & Seventh World Craft Conf, Mex, 75-77; Chairman, 85. *Teaching:* Instr crafts, Univ Wis, Madison, 65-66; asst prof metalsmithing, Radford Col, Va, 66-68; assoc prof metalsmithing, State Univ NY Col, Brockport, 68-80, prof, 80- *Awards:* Fac Res Fel, State Univ NY Res Found, 71 & 79; Craftsmen Fel, Nat Endowment for the Arts, 75; Tech Res Grant, Soc N Am Goldsmiths & Nat Endowment for the Arts, 77. *Bibliog:* Leon Nigrosh (auth), Forged iron today, Craft Horizons, 2/76; Jack O'Field (filmmaker), Hands: The Arts & Crafts of America, Raymond Lowry Int Productions, 76; Dona Z Meilach (auth), Decorative, Sculpture Ironwork, Crown, 77; Katherine Pearson (auth), American Carft, Stewart, Tabori Chang. *Mem:* World Crafts Coun; Am Craftsmen Coun; Artist & Blacksmiths Asn of N Am; Soc N Am Goldsmiths; NY State Craftsmen. *Media:* Metal, Wood. *Mailing Add:* 17218 Roosevelt Hwy Kandall NY 14476

MARLOR, CLARK STRANG
HISTORIAN, COLLECTOR
b Camden, NJ, Nov 18, 22. *Study:* Carnegie-Mellon Univ, BFA, 45; Univ Mich, MA, 46; NY Univ, DEduc, 61. *Collections Arranged:* John Barnard Whittaker (with catalog), 68 & Eleanor C Bannister (with catalog), 71, Adelphi Univ; Benjamin Eggleston, Long Island Hist Soc, 75. *Teaching:* Prof, Adelphi Univ, 56-86. *Mem:* Salmagundi Club (mem, libr comt & bicentennial comt). *Res:* 19th century American artists. *Collection:* American artists of the 19th and early 20th centuries. *Publ:* John B Whittaker, Brooklyn artist, Antiques, 11/71; A quest for independence: the SIA, Arts & Antiques, 81; The Society of Independent Artists: Exhibition Record and History, 84; Salons of America, 1922-1936, 91; Brooklyn Index of Artists, 92; and others. *Mailing Add:* 295 Sterling Pl Brooklyn NY 11238

MARLOW, AUDREY SWANSON
PAINTER, DESIGNER
b New York, NY. *Study:* Art Students League, with Robert Brackman, Robert Beverly Hale & Raphael Soyer, 51-55. *Work:* NY Univ, City Hall, New York; Middle Island Pub Libr, Long Island; Sr Citizens Complex, Newark, NJ; Little Flower Childrens Servs, Wading River, NY. *Comn:* Wallace Nye, VPres Lawrence Aviation, Port Jefferson, NY, 84; Millicent Fenwick, comn by Regency Housing Partners, Newark, NJ, 86; Harrison J Goldin, NY Comptroller, New York, 86; Monsignor John Fagan with 7 members of family, Quoque, NY, 88; Mother Katharine Drexel & 3 children, comn by Monsignor Fagan, Hanging at St Theresa of the child Jesus Convent, wading River, NY, 90. *Exhib:* Hudson Valley Artists, White Plains, NY, 79, 81, 83, 85, 88-90; Nat Acad Design, New York, 80 & 85; one-person show, Salmagundi Club, New York, 85; Parish Art Mus, Southampton, NY, 86; Pastel Invitational, Palais Rameau, Lisle, France, 88; Sumner Mus, Washington, DC, 92. *Pos:* Package designer & illus, Prince Matchabelli Perfume Co (freelance), 57-68; textile designer, RS Assocs, New York, 60-72. *Teaching:* Design, Phoenix Sch Design, 72-73; demonstrs, pastel, Catharine Lorillard Wolfe Art Club, 85 & Hudson Valley Artists, 88. *Awards:* Five Awards, Salmagundi Club Shows, 78; Gold Medal, Nat League Am Pen Women, Cork Gallery, Lincoln Ctr, 85; Pastel Soc Am, Artists Professional League, 87. *Mem:* Am Artists Prof League; Knickerbocker Artists; Hudson Valley Artists; Pastel Soc Am; Nat League Am Pen Women (pres 80-82). *Media:* Multimedia. *Publ:* Illus, Breads of Many Lands, 66 & 4 H Club Bakes Bread, J Walter Thompson Advert Agency, 66; Illustr, Anna Smith Strong and the Setauket Spy Ring, Peter Randall, 91. *Mailing Add:* 76 Northside Rd Wading River NY 11792

MARON, JEFFREY
SCULPTOR
b New York, NY, Feb 7, 49. *Study:* Washington Univ, St Louis, BA, 71; MFA, 73. *Work:* Mus Mod Art, Mexico City; Hakone Mus, Hakone, Japan; United States Embassy, Tokyo, Japan; Springfield Art Mus, MO; Sumitomo Corp, Kobe, Japan. *Comn:* Oliver Carr Corp, Washington, DC; Philadelphia Sci Ctr, Pa; Koll Corp, Calif; Hartwell Bldg, Pittsburgh, Pa. *Exhib:* Solo exhibs, Westchester Community Col, NY, 74; Minami Gallery, Tokyo, Japan, 75; United States Info Serv, Am Cult Ctrs in Nagoya, Osaka, Fukuoka & Sapporo, Japan, 75; Alexander F Milliken Gallery, New York, 77-79; Martha White Gallery, Louisville, Ky, 81; Marisa del Re Gallery, New York, 83, 84; PS1 (Inst Art & Urban Resourses), New York, 86; FIDEM Int Medalic Art, 50th Anniversary, Colo Springs, Colo, 87; Sculpture 87, Printemps des Arts, Monaco, 87; Art et Industrie, 10th Anniversary Exhib, 87; Lillian Heidenberg Gallery, New York, 88. *Awards:* Fulbright Hayes Grant to Japan, 74-75; R S Reynolds Mem Award, Reynolds Aluminum, 86; Pollock Krasner Found Award, 89. *Bibliog:* James Horwitz (auth), Olympic Tower of Power, Cosmopolitan Mag, 12/31/81; Susan A Harris (auth), Jeffrey Maron, Arts Mag, 11/84; Andrew Bill (auth), Chair Flair, Town & Country Mag, 5/87. *Mailing Add:* 248 Lafayette St New York NY 10012

MARONEY, DALTON
SCULPTOR
b Greenville, Tex, July 9, 47. *Study:* E Tex State Univ, BS, 69; Univ Okla, MFA, 72. *Work:* Arco, Dallas, Tex & Anchorage, Alaska; Prudential, Newark, NJ; IBM, Washington, DC. *Exhib:* Solo exhibs, Dallas Mus Art, Tex, 83-84, D W Gallery, Dallas, Tex, 87 & San Antonio Art Inst, Tex, 89; Excellence '86 & '87, Tex Sculpture Asn, Dallas, Tex, 86 & 87; 2D/3D Frito Lay Corp, Plano, Tex, 87; Magic & Ritual Objects, Alexander Hoague Gallery, Univ Tulsa, 87; 10th Ann Exhib, Austin Vis Arts Asn, Tex, 87; Third Coast Review: A Look at Art in Texas, traveling exhib, Aspen Art Mus, Colo, 87-88; Renwick Gallery, Nat Mus Am Art, Washington, DC, 89; The Vessel, Dallas, Tex, 90; Woodworks, Arlington Mus Art, Tex, 90. *Pos:* Asst dir, John Michael Kohler Arts Ctr, Sheboygan, Wis, 72-73. *Teaching:* Asst prof art, Morningside Col, Sioux City, Iowa, 73-76; instr, Pittsburg State Univ, Pittsburg, Kans, 76-77; asst prof, Univ Tex, Arlington, 79-84, assoc prof, 84- *Awards:* Visual Arts Fel, Nat Endowment Arts, 86-87. *Bibliog:* Jana Vander Lee (auth), article, Art Space, summer, 82; Susan Freudenheim (auth), Making art against the current, Tex Homes, 4/84 & Dalton Maroney at the Dallas Museum, Art Am, summer 84. *Dealer:* W A Graham Gallery 1431 W Alabama Houston TX. *Mailing Add:* 707 College Oaks Arlington TX 76010

MARONEY, JAMES H, JR
DEALER
b Summit, NJ, Sept 22, 43. *Study:* Columbia Univ, BA, 70. *Pos:* Dir & head Am paintings, Sotheby Parke Bernet, NY, 67-74; assoc, Hirschl & Adler, New York, 74-76. *Specialty:* American traditional paintings executed between 1812 and 1939. *Mailing Add:* c/o James Graham & Sons 1014 Madison Ave New York NY 10021

MAROZZI, ELI RAPHAEL
SCULPTOR, INSTRUCTOR
b Montegallo, Italy, Aug 13, 13; US citizen. *Study:* Univ Wash, BA; Univ Hawaii, MA; also with Mark Tobey. *Work:* St Andrew's Cathedral, Honolulu; Honolulu Leeward Community Col; Tennent Art Found. *Comn:* Stone Madonna and Child, St Philomena Church, Honolulu, 75; stone figure portrait, Vivekananda Vedanta Soc, Chicago; seven compositions in abstract in stone, Honolulu Stadium State Park, State Found Cult & Arts; Jefferson Elem Sch & Wainae High Sch, State Found Cult & Arts; Alabaster Abstract, Rimatore, 90. *Exhib:* Seattle Art Mus Ann, 47 & 48; Artists of Hawaii Ann, Honolulu Acad Arts, 50-69; Assoc Artists Hawaii, Honolulu, 52-55; Hawaii Artists League, Honolulu, 55-82; two-man show, Contemp Art Ctr. *Teaching:* Art instr, Honolulu Acad Arts, 50-55, YWCA Adult Educ, 50 & Univ Hawaii Exten, 51-53, Honolulu. *Awards:* First Prize Sculpture, Honolulu Assoc Artists, 55. *Mem:* Hawaii Artists League; hon mem Windward Artists Guild; hon mem Honolulu Assoc Artists. *Media:* Marble, Synthetic Stone. *Publ:* Contribr, Times of India Mag, 53; Essays in Philosophy, 62; Swami Vivekananda in East and West, 68; Prabuddha Bharata Mag, 69 & 73; Vedanta Kesari, 87. *Mailing Add:* 2558 Date St Apt 412 Honolulu HI 96826

MARQUIS, RICHARD
CRAFTSMAN
b Bumblebee, Ariz, 1945. *Work:* Am Craft Mus & Corning Mus Glass, New York; Art Mus, Wagga Wagga, New South Wales; Australian Arts Coun, Sydney; Australian Nat Gallery, Canberra; Craft & Folk Art Mus, Los Angeles. *Exhib:* Dowse Art Mus, Wellington, NZ, 87; Betsy Rosenfield Gallery, Chicago, Ill, 87 & 89; Kurland Summers Gallery, Los Angeles, 87, 88 & 89; Auckland Art Mus, 89; Louise Allrich Gallery, San Francisco, 89; Sandra Ainsley Gallery, Toronto, Can, 90. *Awards:* Australian Crafts Coun Grants, 74, 75 & 76; Univ Calif-Los Angeles Research Grants, 79, 80, 81 & 82; Senior Fulbright Grants - New Zealand, 81 & 88. *Mailing Add:* c/o The Seekers Collection & Gallery 2515-A Village Lane Cambria CA 93428

MARRIOTT, WILLIAM ALLEN
PAINTER, EDUCATOR
b Pontiac, Mich, July 17, 42. *Study:* Ctr Creative Studies, Col Art & Design; Wayne State Univ, BFA; Yale Univ, MFA; study with Lester Johnson, Irving Kriesberg, Nicholas Carone, Michael Goldberg, Robert Wilbert, David Mitchell, Gabor Peterdi & George Kubler. *Work:* Wayne State Univ, Detroit; The New Mus, New York. *Exhib:* Drawings USA 1975, Minn Mus Art, St Paul, 75; 5th Int Miniature Print Competition, Pratt Graphics Ctr, New York, 75; Nat Invitational Drawing Exhib, Southern Ill Univ, Carbondale, 75; 1977 Artists Biennial, New Orleans Mus Art, 77; 45th Southeastern Competition for Painting and Sculpture, Southeastern Ctr Contemp Art, 75. *Teaching:* Assoc prof painting, drawing & printmaking, Univ Ga, Athens, 67- *Awards:* Purchase Awards, Appalachian Nat Drawing Competition, Appalachian State Univ, 74 & 45th Southeastern Competition for Painting & Sculpture, Southeastern Ctr Contemp Art, 77. *Mem:* Southeastern Graphics Coun. *Media:* Oil, Charcoal. *Dealer:* Mr Dean Gillette Image South Gallery 1931 Peachtree Rd NE Atlanta GA 30309. *Mailing Add:* 588 Meigs St Athens GA 30601

MARRO, GEORGE MATTHEW
PAINTER, WRITER
b Newark, NY, Jan 12, 27. *Study:* Univ Chicago, PhB, 50; Univ Colo, teacher cert, 52; Los Angeles City Col, 58; Santa Monica City Col, 61-62. *Work:* Sen, Tim Wirth's Off, Denver; State Rep, Pat Killian's Off, Denver. *Exhib:* Artists Southern Calif, Los Angeles Co Art Mus, 60; one-man show, Newman Gallery, Venice, Calif, 66 & NCAR, Boulder, 92; Country Lines, Arvada Ctr Arts & Humanities, Colo, 87-91; Retrospective, Arvada Sr Ctr, Colo, 90; Best Artist Colo, Douglass Co Coun Arts & Humanities, 91; Colo Colors Group Show, Gallery 44, Boulder, 92; Colo Open, Foothills Art Ctr, Golden, 92. *Pos:* House organ ed, Norris-Thermador, Los Angeles, 57-58; Pub Relations, Lockheed, Los Angeles, 58-59; Publicity, Ice Capades, Los Angeles, 59-60; Probation Officer 60-63; teacher High Sch & Soc Studies, 65-68. *Teaching:* Communs asst pres, Univ NY. *Awards:* Hon Mention, County Lines, Arvada Ctr Arts & Humanities, 87; First Place, Ann Show, Arvada Fine Arts Guild, 87-88; Scholar Ceramics, Arvada Ctr Arts & Humanities, 92. *Bibliog:* Sandy Marcanto (ed), Newark native has art on exhibit, Courier, NY, 89; Shanna Wadell (art hist), NCAR Shows, George Marro, Boulder, Colo, 92; Steve Rosen (critic), George Marro paintings, rugged often likable, Denver Post, 92. *Mem:* Arvada Fine Arts Guild (vpres, 91-92); Arvada Ctr Arts & Humanities (gallery comt mem, 91-92). *Media:* Multimedia. *Res:* Impressionists, expressionists, fauves; modern art history. *Publ:* Auth, Coast People, pvt publ, 70; Beach Umbrella, pvt publ, 71; Venice Journal, pvt publ, 72; California Coast, pvt publ, 73; Beach Photos, pvt publ, 74. *Dealer:* Kitty Edwards Gallery 44 1916 13th St Boulder Co 80302. *Mailing Add:* 8525 W 53rd St No 702 Arvada CO 80002

MARRON, DONALD B
COLLECTOR
b Goshen, NY, July 21, 34. *Pos:* Trustee, Calif Int Arts, Valencia, 71-, Mus Mod Art, New York, 75- & Trust Cult Resources City New York, 76- *Collection:* Nineteenth and twentieth century American artists. *Mailing Add:* c/o Donald Marron & Paine Webber 1285 Sixth Ave 14th Fl New York NY 10019

MARRON, JOAN
PAINTER
b Custer Co, Okla, Aug 19, 34. *Study:* Univ Okla, BA(fashion art), 56; workshop study with Sergei Bongart, William Reese, Ben Konis, Don Puttman, Jon Zahourek & Bettina Steinke, Hollis Williford, Richard Schmid, Harley Brown & Michael Lynch, 80-88. *Work:* Robert S Kerr Conf Ctr, Poteau, Okla; Mercy Health Ctr, Baptist Health Ctr, Presby Health Ctr & Okla State Senate Press Ctr, Oklahoma City; Frye Mus, Seattle, Wash; Okla State Art Collection. *Comn:* Mural size paintings, Senate Rooms, Okla State Senate, Oklahoma City, 83; mural, McCauley Plaza, comn by Sisters of Mercy, Oklahoma City, 86; Mural size paintings, Mercy Birthplace Ctr, 88. *Exhib:* Solo exhibs, Ft Smith Art Ctr, Ark, 70 & Okla Mus Art, Oklahoma City, 75; Midland Stewart Haley Memorial Show, 88, 89, 91 & 92; Plein Air Painters Am, 88, 89, 90 & 92; Philbrook Mus, Tulsa, Okla, 90 & 92; Okla Soc Impressionalists Traveling Show, 90; Gilcrease Mus Show, Petroglyphs in Okla, 93; and others. *Teaching:* Prof fashion arts, Univ Okla, 60-65; instr fine art, Okla Mus Art, Oklahoma City, 65-75; instr workshops, NMex, Okla, Tex & Hawaii, 75-80. *Awards:* First Place, Scottsdale Art Sch; Best of Show, Wrass, Cheyenne, Wyo. *Bibliog:* M J Van Deventer (auth), Painter and palette, Okla Home & Garden, 83; Lorene Marvin (producer), Oklahoma Original, Educ Television, OETA, 84; M J Van Deventer (auth), Joan Marron, excited student of life, Art Gallery Mag, 85; Susan Mcgarry (auth), Southwest Art Mag, 8/89; Walter Gray, Painting on Location (film), TV-KAUT, 89. *Mem:* Fashion Group Int (secy, 60); Oklahoma City Art Guild; Soc Am Impressionists; Plein Air Painters Am; Okla Soc of Impressionists. *Media:* Oil. *Dealer:* Dodson Gallery 7660 N Western Oklahoma City OK. *Mailing Add:* 3101 Thornridge Oklahoma City OK 73120

MARROW, JAMES HENRY
HISTORIAN, EDUCATOR
b New York, NY, Mar 27, 41. *Study:* Univ Minn, BA(magna cum laude), 63; Columbia Univ, MA, 66, PhD(with distinction), 75. *Teaching:* Assoc prof hist art, State Univ NY, Binghamton, 70-76 & Yale Univ, 76-80; prof, Univ Calif, Berkeley, 80-91, Princeton Univ, 91- *Mem:* Col Art Asn Am. *Res:* Northern European art of the late Middle Ages and early Renaissance, with special interest in religious iconography, manuscript illumination and early prints. *Publ:* Coauth, The James A de Rothschild Collection at Waddesdon Manor: Illuminated Manuscripts, Office Livre, 77; coauth, Medieval and Renaissance Manuscripts at Yale: A Selection (exhib catalog), Yale Univ Press, 78; auth, Passion Iconography in Northern European Art of the Late Middle Ages and Early Renaissance, Van Ghemmert, 79; coauth, Hans Baldung Grien: Prints and Drawings (exhib catalog), Yale Univ Press, 78; auth, Simon Bening in 1521: A group of dated miniatures, Liebaers Festschrift, 84. *Mailing Add:* Art & Archeol, McCormick Hall Princeton Univ Princeton NJ 08544

MARSDEN, MICHAEL H E
PAINTER
b Providence, RI, July 16, 04. *Study:* Pratt Inst, BFA, 30. *Work:* Brooklyn Mus Art; Los Angeles Co Mus Art; Palm Spring Mus Art; San Diego Mus Fine Art. *Exhib:* New Artists, Brooklyn Mus, 31; Artists from the Permanent Collection, Palm Springs Desert Mus, 80. *Bibliog:* S E Hyman (rev), Khaki is more than a color, NY Times, 43; George Christy (auth), More than meets the eye, Town & Country, 69; Elizabeth Watts (auth), Quality is the answer, Boston Globe, 83. *Media:* Oil. *Publ:* Auth, Khaki is More Than a Color, Doubleday & Co, 43. *Mailing Add:* c/o Gallery 170 PO Box 69271 Los Angeles CA 90069-0271

MARSH, ANNE STEELE
PAINTER, PRINTMAKER
b Nutley, NJ, Sept 7, 01. *Study:* Cooper Union Art Sch; plus others. *Work:* New York Pub Libr, Brooklyn Mus, Metrop Mus Art & Mus Mod Art, New York; NJ State Mus, Trenton; plus others. *Exhib:* Metrop Mus Art; Nat Acad Design; Art Inst Chicago; Am Watercolor Soc; Soc Am Graphic Artists; plus others. *Pos:* Chmn printmaking & secy bd trustee, Hunterdon Art Ctr. *Teaching:* Instr, Newark Sch Fine & Indust Art, 46-48 & Hunterdon Art Ctr, 56-60. *Awards:* Phillips Mill, Pa, 71, 82 & 88; Pen & Brush Awards, 72-86; Soc Am Graphic Artists, 82 & 85; Audubon Artists, 86; Print Coun NJ Award, 88. *Mem:* New York Soc Women Artists; Nat Asn Women Artists; Boston, Albany & Washington Soc Printmakers; Soc Am Graphic Artists (past pres). *Mailing Add:* c/o Coryell Gallery 8 Coryell St Lambertville NJ 08530

MARSH, DAVID FOSTER
EDUCATOR, PAINTER
b Salkum, Wash, Jan 24, 26. *Study:* Cent Wash Univ, BA; Univ Ore, MS. *Work:* Westminster Col, Fulton, Mo; Inst Mexicana-N Am, Guadalajara, Mex. *Exhib:* NW Watercolor Soc Exhib, 58, 62 & 77; NW Ann, 63 & 66. *Teaching:* Prof drawing & painting, Western Wash Univ, 57-, dean, Fine and Performing Arts, 83-85. *Mem:* Col Art Asn; Nat Art Educ Asn. *Mailing Add:* Dept of Art Western Wash Univ 516 High St Bellingham WA 98225

MARSH, GEORGIA
PAINTER
b Olean, New York. *Study:* RI Sch Design, BFA, 72. *Work:* Centre Nat d'Art Contemporaine, Georges Pompidou, Paris; Metrop Life; Chemical Bank. *Exhib:* Solo exhib, Vanguard Gallery, Philadelphia, 86 & 87, Saxon-Lee Gallery, Los Angeles, 87; Lorence-Monk Gallery, New York, 86; Whitney Mus Am Art, Pa, 87; Loughelton Gallery, New York, 88. *Awards:* Fel, Nat Endowment Arts, 87. *Publ:* Contribr, David Deutsch: Interview, Bomb Mag, Spring 86; Francesco Clemente: Interview, Art Preso, 4/87. *Mailing Add:* 177 Franklin St New York NY 10013

MARSH, THOMAS A
SCULPTOR
b Cherokee, Iowa, May 7, 51. *Study:* Layton Sch Art, Milwaukee, Wis, BFA(painting), 74; Univ Southern Calif, aesthetics with John Hospers, 76-77; Calif State Univ, Long Beach, MFA, sculpture with Kenneth Glenn & Stephen Werlick, 77; also with Milton Hebald, Rome, Italy. *Work:* Univ San Francisco Rossi Libr, Calif; St Mary's Hosp Libr, San Francisco; Univ Calif Minor Hall, Berkeley; Calif State Univ, Long Beach. *Comn:* Bust, Dean Emer Meredith Morgan, Univ Calif Sch Optometry, Berkeley, 84; seven sculptured masks (costumes), Philip Glass Opera, Akhnaten, 84; archit relief panels, entrance, San Francisco, Calif, 90; bronze relief panel, exterior, San Francisco, Calif, 90; 18' bronze monument, West Cliff Dr, Santa Cruz, Calif. *Exhib:* solo exhibs, Civic Courtyard, Bracciano, Italy, 78, Alliance Francaise, San Francisco, 82 & Univ San Francisco, Calif, 85 & 87; Int Sculpture Symposium, Acad Art Gallery, San Francisco, Calif, 83; Sioux City Connection, Sioux City Art Ctr, Iowa, 84; Interfaith Religous Art, Judah L Magnes Mus, Berkeley, Calif, 86; About Faces: A Celebration of the Portrait, Walnut Creek Civic Arts Gallery, Calif, 87 & Bay Area Bronze, 88; The Goddess of Democracy, 91. *Pos:* Bd dirs, Found for Chinese Democracy, San Francisco, Calif, 82- *Teaching:* Instr sculpture, Calif State Univ, Long Beach, 78-79 & San Francisco State Univ, 79-80, Calif; instr anatomy, Acad Art Col, San Francisco, Calif, 81-, coordr MFA prog, 83-85. *Awards:* Elizabeth Greenshields Found Fel, 77. *Bibliog:* San Francisco Examiner, 1/1/91; Artweek (exhib rev), 2/21/91; San Jose Mercury News, 3/10/92. *Media:* Bronze, Wood. *Dealer:* Joslin Art Broker Five Henry Adams San Francisco CA 94103; Tamara Thomas Fine Arts Serv Inc 107 S Irving Los Angeles CA 90003. *Mailing Add:* 2377 San Jose Ave San Francisco CA 94112

MARSHALL, BRUCE
PAINTER, ILLUSTRATOR
b Athens, Tex, Dec 23, 29. *Study:* Univ Ariz, Tucson; Southern Ariz Sch of Art (full scholar). *Work:* First Cavalry Mus, Ft Hood, Tex; Confederate Res Ctr, Hill Col, Hillsboro, Tex; San Jacinto Monument, Tex; The Alamo, San Antonio; Nat Infantry Mus, Ft Benning, Ga; Inst Tex Cultures, Univ Tex, San Antonio. *Comn:* Portrait of Dick Dowling, Dowling Sch, Houston, 70, comn by Sons of Confederate Veterans; paintings, Inst Texan Cult, Univ Tex, San Antonio, 70-75; Tex Citizen Soldier (mural), Tex Nat Guard for Nat Infantry Mus, Ft Benning, Ga, 76; Ten Historic Texans (cover painting), Southwestern Bell Telephone Co, 79-80; Tom Lubbock (portrait), W Tex Mus Asn, 83; Patriots, (painting), Dallas Baptist Univ, 92. *Exhib:* Smithsonian Inst, Washington, DC, 54; Univ Ariz, 73; First Cavalry Mus, Ft Hood, 72, Llano Estacado Mus, 75; Rotunda, Tex State Capitol, Austin, 75, 76 & 84; Chamizal Nat Mem, El Paso, Tex, 77; Mus of the Big Bend, Alpine, Tex, 77; Tex Navy Exhib, Tex State Archives & Libr, 78; Star of the Repub Mus Washington State Park, Tex, 78; Le Musee de l'Historie de l'Homme, Brussels, Belg, 83; John E Conner Mus, Kingsville, Tex, 85-86. *Pos:* Auth & illusr, The Texas Star, 72-73; assoc ed, Military Hist Tex & South West, 72-88. *Awards:* Knighted by King Peter II, Yugoslavia, 66; Nat Artist, Confederate State of Am, Sons of Confederate Veterans, 76; Jefferson Davis Medal, Daughters of the Confederacy; Artist of the 65th Legislature, Tex, 77. *Bibliog:* Margaret Taylor Dry (auth), article, Austin American Statesmen, 74; Robert St Johns (auth), article in Argosy Mag, 78; Frank Woods (auth), article in Austin Mag, 80; Bess Whitehead Scott (auth), article, Austin Homes & Gardens, 80; Ned Polk (auth), article, The Westerner, 87. *Media:* Watercolor, Oil. *Publ:* Illsur, Tucson, Ariz Silhouettes, 53; Military History of Texas and the Southwest, Presidial Press, 71-78; Sabers on the Rio Grande, Presidial Press, 75; The Texas Rangers: Their First 150 Years, Encino, 75; History of Hood's Texas Brigade, Hill Jr Col, 78. *Dealer:* Westart PO Box 161616 Austin TX 78716. *Mailing Add:* PO Box 161616 Austin TX 78716-1616

MARSHALL, JAMES DUARD
PAINTER, SCULPTOR
b Springfield, Mo, Sept 29, 14. *Study:* Kansas City Art Inst, Mo, dipl painting, 40, with Thomas Hart Benton; Colo Col, BA(art), 45, with Boardman Robinson, Lawrence Barrett & Ricco Lebron; Univ Denver, MA(art), with Julio de Deigo & Ruth Reeves. *Work:* Libr of Cong, Washington, DC; Tex Fine Arts Asn, Austin. *Comn:* Murals, History of Missouri (7 ft x 30 ft), Pub Libr, comn by City of Neosho, Mo, 39; Children's Stories (500 ft long), Officer's Wives Nursery, Ft Worth, Tex, 52; Beginning of a New Day (two 4 ft x 6 ft mosaics), Jones Store, Prairie Village, Kans, 62. *Exhib:* San Francisco Mus of Art Ann, Calif, 38; Philadelphia Print Club Ann, Pa, 40, 45 & 52; one-man shows, Santa Fe Art Mus, NMex, 43 & Oklahoma City Art Ctr, 43; Carnegie Inst Int, Pittsburgh, 45; Denver Art Mus Ann, Colo, 45-47; Nat Acad of Design, New York, 46; Artists West of the Mississippi, Colorado Springs, Colo, 47. *Pos:* Chmn art dept, Ft Worth Children's Mus, Tex, 51-53; crafts dir, US Army, Ger, 54-60; asst to Thomas Hart Benton, Truman Libr & New York Power Authority Murals, 60. *Teaching:* Mem, Fed Teaching Prog, Fayetteville, Ark, 33-34; teacher summer & Saturday classes, Kansas City Art Inst, 36-40; asst prof drawing & painting, Univ Denver, Colo, 46-51; instr summer art sessions, Kansas City Univ, 63. *Awards:* Hon Mention, Denver Ann, Colo & Philadelphia Print Club, 46; Benedictine Art Awards, New York, 70-74. *Media:* Lithography, egg tempera painting; Woodcut. *Mailing Add:* 5927 Brookside Blvd Kansas City MO 64113

MARSHALL, JOHN
PAINTER, INSTRUCTOR
b St John's, Nfld, Oct 20, 57. *Study:* Univ of the South, study with Edward Carlos, 78-81; Mid Tenn State Univ, with David Le Doux, Jim Gibson, BFA, 83; Univ NC, Greensboro, with Walter Barker, MFA, 85. *Work:* Weatherspoon Art Gallery, Greensboro, NC; Meridian Mus Art, Miss. *Exhib:* Art Wave, William Carey Col Gallery Gulfport, Miss, 88; Art on Paper, Weatherspoon Art Gallery, Greensboro, NC, 89; Solo exhibs, Meridian Mus Art, Miss, 89, Miss Univ Women, Columbus, 90. *Collections Arranged:* 80's Images from North Carolina, 87, Visions of Flowers, 87, Southern Idiom: 3 Views, 88 & Stephanie Dinkins: Retro, 88, Meridian Mus Art, Miss; Jacob Drachler - Retrospective, Meridian Mus Art, 89; Homer Casteel: Early Figurative Years (essay, catalog), Meridian Community Col, 89. *Pos:* Cur asst, Weatherspoon Art Gallery, 83-85; cur, Weatherspoon Art Gallery, 86; dir, Meridian Mus Art, 86-89. *Teaching:* Cur & instr, Meridian Community Col, 86- *Awards:* Best of 3-D Design, Art Wave, 88. *Mem:* Weatherspoon Art Asn; Col Art Asn; Meridian Coun Arts. *Media:* Oil, Mixed Media. *Dealer:* Henri Gallery 11500 21st St NW Washington DC 20036. *Mailing Add:* 6008 Oakland Heights St Meridian MS 39305

MARSHALL, JOHN CARL
CRAFTSMAN
b Pittsburgh, Pa, Feb 25, 36. *Study:* Cleveland Inst Art, BFA; Syracuse Univ, MFA. *Work:* Everson Mus, Syracuse, NY; Chicago Art Inst, Ill; Am Craft Mus New; Syracuse Univ, NY; Mukhina Sch Art & Design, St Petersburg, Russia; and others. *Comn:* Gold Bowl, Hendricks Chapel, Syracuse, NY, 69; Series of 5 large silver sculptures, Patrick Lannan, 84; coffee tea service, Anne Gould Hauberg, Seattle, Wash, 87; eight flatware designs for Bloome Collection, Seattle, Wash, 88; star rose quartz sphere sculpture, White Rose Found, Calif, 91. *Exhib:* Masterworks of American Jewelry since 1950, Victoria & Albert Mus, London, 85; Hong-ik Metalcrafts Asn Exhib, Walker Hill Art Ctr Mus, Seoul, Korea, 88; Craft Today USA, premiere opening Musee Des Art Decoratifs, Paris, France & toured major Europ cities, 89; Art that Works, The Decorative Arts of the Eighties Crafted in America, toured major US cities 2 yrs, 90; one man exhib, Nat Ornamental Metals Mus, Memphis, Tenn, 91; Fortunoff Silver Competition III, Silver New Forms & Expressions, New York, NY, 91. *Teaching:* Asst prof metalworking, design & enamel, Syracuse Univ, 65-70; assoc prof, Univ Wash, 70-75, prof, 75- *Awards:* Nat Merit Award, Am Craftsmen Coun, Craftsmen USA, 66; Thomas C Thompson Prize 45th Ceramic Nat Competition, 68; Am Metalcraft Award, Nat Enamels Exhib, 70. *Bibliog:* C E Licka (auth), Sublime passages and other reflections: The work of John Marshall, Am Craft Mag, 85; John Marshall: A Conversation with Patterson Sims, Metalsmith Mag, 91. *Mem:* Am Craftsmen Coun; Soc N Am Goldsmiths; Soc Am Silversmiths. *Media:* Gold, Silver. *Mailing Add:* Dept Art Univ Wash Seattle WA 98195

MARSHALL, KERRY JAMES
DESIGNER
b Birmingham, Ala, 1955. *Study:* Otis Art Inst, Los Angeles, Calif, BFA, 78. *Work:* Studio Mus Harlem; Ark Art Ctr; Santa Monica Arts Comn; Loyola Law Sch. *Exhib:* Solo exhibs, Los Angeles Southwest Col, Calif, 81, James Turcotte Gallery, Los Angeles, 83, Pepperdine Univ, Malibu, 84, Koplin Gallery, 85 & 91, Studio Mus Harlem, 86 & Terra Incognito, Chicago Cult Ctr, 92; Only LA, Munic Art Gallery, 86; 1987 Invitational, Cerritos Col, Calif, 87; Drawingsa, Koplin Gallery, Santa Monica, 91; God's Violent World, Artists Respond Elmhurst Col, Ill, 91; Mythic Imagery, Evanston Art Ctr, 92. *Pos:* Production designer, Praise House & Hendrix Proj, 91; exhib comt mem, Randolf St Gallery, Chicago, Ill, 91- *Teaching:* Art instr, Los Angeles City Col, 80-83; art fac, Los Angeles Southwest Col, 81-85. *Awards:* Art Matters Inc Fel, 90; Nat Endowment Arts Visual Art Fel, 91; Ill Arts Coun Visual Arts Grant, 91. *Publ:* Auth, article, Visions Quart, fall 91; article, Los Angeles Times, 3/15/91. *Mailing Add:* 1649 E 50th St Chicago IL 60615

MARSHALL, MARA
PAINTER
b Nice, France, July 21, 26; US citizen. *Study:* With Rosamond Gaydash, Washington, DC; Univ Fine Arts Major, 80. *Exhib:* 25th Biennial Art Exhib, Nat League Am Pen Women, Salt Lake City, 70; one-man shows, First Fed Gallery, Chicago, 71, Nat League Am Pen Women, Washington, DC, 72 & Arts Club of Washington, 77; 41st Ann Exhib, Miniature Painters, Sculptors & Gravers Soc, Washington, DC, 74. *Awards:* State Art Exhib First Prize, 71, President's Citation, 74 & DC Br Ann Award First Prize, 75, Nat League Am Pen Women. *Bibliog:* Article in Les Editions de la Revue Moderne, 6/73. *Mem:* Nat League Am Pen Women, Inc (corresp secy, 68-70, pres, 70-72, chmn hospitality, Nat Hq, 72-74, state pres, 74-76, co-chmn, Biennial Conv, 76); Am Art League; Artists Equity Asn; Nat Soc Arts & Lett (Washington Chap pres, 78-80); Miniature Painters, Sculpture & Gravers Soc; Am Art League (bd dirs, 80-81); Nat League Am Pen Women (nat bd mem chmn, 82-84). *Media:* Oil, Acrylic. *Mailing Add:* 2929 Ellicott St NW Washington DC 20008

MARSHALL, RICHARD DONALD
HISTORIAN, CURATOR
b Los Angeles, Calif, May 5, 47. *Study:* Calif State Univ, Long Beach, BA; Univ Calif, Irvine. *Collections Arranged:* Clay (auth, catalog), 74 & Continuing Abstraction in American Art (contribr, catalog), 74, Whitney Mus Am Art; Handmade Paper: Prints & Unique Works, 76, Mus Mod Art, New York; Calder's Universe (contribr, catalogs), 76-77, Robert Irwin (ed & contribr, catalog), 77, Art About Art (coauth, catalog), 78, New Image Painting (auth, catalog), 78, Biennial Exhib (coauth, catalogs), 79, 81, 83, 85, 87, 89 & 91, Isamu Noguchi (ed & contribr, catalog), 80, Louise Nevelson: Atmospheres and Environments (contribr, catalog), 80, Developments in Recent Sculpture (auth, catalog), 81, Joel Shapiro (coauth, catalog), 82-83, American Art Since 1970 (auth, catalog), 84-85, Jonathan Borofsky (coauth, catalog), 84-85, Alex Katz (auth, catalog) 86, Robert Mapplethorpe (auth, catalog), 88, The New Sculpture: 65-75 (coauth, catalog) 89, Edward Ruscha (auth, catalog) 90, Immaterial Objects (auth, catalog) 90-91, Jean-Michel Basquiat (auth, catalog), 92-93, Whitney Mus Art. *Pos:* Consult, Art Adv

Serv, Mus Mod Art, New York, 74-76; exhib coordr, Whitney Mus Am Art, New York, 74-76, asst cur exhib, 76-78, assoc cur, 78-88, cur, 88-; art ed, Paris Rev Mag, 78- *Mailing Add:* Whitney Mus Am Art 945 Madison Ave New York NY 10021

MARSHALL, ROBERT LEROY
EDUCATOR, PAINTER
b Mesquite, Nev, Dec 15, 44. *Study:* Brigham Young Univ, BA, 66, MA, 68; studies in Europe, primarily Spain & England. *Work:* Mus of the Southwest, Midland, Tex; Brigham Young Univ, Provo, Utah; Webster Oil Co, Springfield, Mo; Springville Mus, Utah; Am Savings & Loan. *Exhib:* Watercolor West; Watercolor USA, Springfield, Mo; Utah Coun Arts, Salt Lake City; Am Watercolor Soc, New York; Butler Inst Am Art; Scottsdale Biennial, Ariz. *Teaching:* Prof painting & drawing, Brigham Young Univ, 69-, chmn dept art & design, 76-81. *Awards:* Purchase Award, Watercolor USA, Webster Oil Co. *Mem:* Nat Watercolor Soc; Nat Coun Art Adminrs; Springville Mus Art (mem bd dirs, 77-). *Media:* Watercolor, Acrylic. *Mailing Add:* Dept Art Brigham Young Univ Provo UT 84602

MARSHALL, THOMAS E
EDUCATOR, PRINTMAKER
b Rocky Mount, NC, Jan 20, 41. *Study:* Va Commonwealth Univ, BFA, 63; Univ NC, Chapel Hill, MAT, 64. *Work:* Wilson Arts Coun, NC. *Comn:* Logo, Masthead, NC Humane Fedn, Chapel Hill, 81. *Exhib:* Faculty Painters, NC State Univ, Raleigh, 69; Only Prints and Drawings, Jacksonville State Univ, Ala, 70; Fayetteville Mus Art Invitational, NC, 75. *Pos:* Ed, Crucible Mag, 74- *Teaching:* Instr painting, Rocky Mount Arts Coun, 64-65; assoc prof art, Atlantic Christian Col, 64-, chmn dept visual art, 83-88, chmn Fine art div, 88- *Mem:* Southeastern Col Art Conf; NC Art Educ Asn; Nat Art Educ Asn. *Publ:* Illusr & auth, Image Mag, Va Commonwealth Univ, 62 & 63. *Mailing Add:* Dept Art Barton Col Wilson NC 27893

MARSHALL-NADEL, NATHALIE
PAINTER, EDUCATOR
b Pittsburgh, Pa, Nov 10, 32. *Study:* Silvermine Col Art, New Canaan, Conn, AFA, 67, with Richard Lytle, Robert Gray & Nicolas Marsicano; Univ Miami, Fla, BFA, 77, MA & PhD, 82. *Work:* US Art Embassies Prog, Washington, DC; Stamford Pub Schs Collection, Conn; Brunnier Mus, Iowa State Univ, Ames; Einstein Libr, Nova Univ, Ft Lauderdale, Fla; Reno Pub Libr Art Coll, Nev; and others. *Comn:* Star Cyle (6 oil paintings), Nova Univ, Ft Lauderdale. *Exhib:* Solo exhibs, Vibrations on Revelations, Arts Unlimited, New York, 73, The Hexaemeral Image, Univ Miami, Coral Gables, 82, Mandalas and Meditations, Broward Community Col, Ft Lauderdale, 85, Bounding Line, Old Col, Reno, Nev, 86, Earth Mandala (earth works), Paiute Reservation, Nixon, Nev, 87-88, Florida Horizons, Sabal Palm Galleries, Gulfport, 92 & International Bienalle, Musee D'art Moderne, Bordeaux, France, 93; Albums, UN Conf Women, Nairobi, Kenya, 84; 4 artists, Ward-Nasse Gallery, New York, 85; Images of the Universe: The Artist's Vision, Brunnier Mus, Ames, Iowa, 86; Nat Mus Women Arts Lib, Washington, 87 & 89; Raymond James Ann Invitational, St Petersburg, Fla, 90-92; and others. *Pos:* Co-found, Conn Women Arts, 70-72; chief artist, Rockefeller Univ, 73-75; found & dir, Bakehouse Art Complex, Miami, Fla, 84-; adv bd, New World Sch Arts, Miami, 85; pres, Women's Caucus Art, Fla chap, 84-86, nat adv bd, 85-88; Advs bd, NAH YAH EE (Indian Children's Art Exhib), 87-92. *Teaching:* Instr art, Housatonic Community Col, Bridgeport, Conn, 70-72; assoc prof art & humanities, Nova Univ, 81-86; prof art & chmn arts concentration, Old Col, Reno, Nev, 86- *Awards:* Sponsor's Award, Greenwich Art Soc Ann, 67; Hon Mention, Le Juene Competition, Metrop Mus, Miami, 77; Purchase Prize, Iowa State Univ, 86. *Bibliog:* Don Webb (auth), Something on 17 (television), WLRN, Miami, 10/80 & 3/85; Marsha Cummings (auth), Art and verse are scholar's tools, 11/82 & Teresa Smith (auth), She crafts artwork of brushstrokes and words, 1/86, Miami Herald; Roger Hurlburt (auth), Star cycle, Sun Sentinel, Ft Lauderdale, 5/85; Mark Crawford (auth), Creativity unbounded in multi-media Reno artist, Gazette-J, Reno, 12/86; Corey Farley (auth), Autumnal art, 9/87 & Ingrid Evans (auth), Modern mandala mixes cultures and systems, 10/87, Gazette-J. *Mem:* Stamford Arts Soc (pres, 63); Col Art Asn; Women's Caucus Art (bd dir, 86-89). *Media:* Oil. *Publ:* Auth, The renaissance mensan, Mensa Bull, 79; auth & designer, The Firebird, Triptych Studio, Miami, 82; ed & designer, Court Theaters of Europe, Gustafson, Shangrilla Enterprises, NJ, 82; Writer-Dir, Mountain Mandala: Autumn, Mountain Mandala: Winter, KNPB, Reno, 87 & KHUT, Houston, 88; The Unexpected, On Disabililty and Creativity, 92. *Dealer:* Global Gallery Tampa Int Airport Tampa FL 33607; Sabal Palm Galleries 2814 S Beach Blvd Gulfport FL 33707. *Mailing Add:* 6213 12th Ave S St Petersburg FL 33707

MARTEL, RICHARD
CONCEPTUAL ARTIST, EDITOR
b Bagotville, Provide, Que, July 7, 50. *Study:* Univ Laval, Que, BA, 75 & Hon MA, 79. *Exhib:* Workshop Art, Dokumeusa 7- OFAJ, Kassel, 82; Casscades, Galerie Du Musée, Que, 84; Europékunstruction in Memoriam Ugorugg Maciunas, Festival, Que, 84; La Pluie Au Nicaragua, La Lieu, Centre en Art Actuel, Oue, Can, 84; So Bor Dination, Galerie Donguy, Paris, France, 85; Mohouaec, Musée Du Que, Can, 86; Defrinazione, Centro Internazionale Multimedia, Salerno, Italy, 86; Multimedia Exhib Musso del Sannio, Beneveito, Italy, 86. *Pos:* Pres, Editions Intervention, 78-; vpres, AEPOQ, 82-85. *Teaching:* Instr art, Univ Que, Chicicouimi, Can, 78-82. *Awards:* Soutien A La Création, Govt du Que, 82 & 85. *Media:* Performance Art. *Publ:* Illusr, 78-, auth, Activitiés Artisques, 1978-1982, 83 & Art Société Quebec, 1975-80, 82, Editions Intervention. *Dealer:* Le Lieu Centre Rn Art Actuel 629 St Jean Quebec PQ G1R 4P7 Canada. *Mailing Add:* 221 Lavingueur Quebec PQ G1R 1B1 Canada

MARTELL, BARBARA BENTLEY
PAINTER
b Trenton, NJ. *Study:* Philadelphia Col Art, Pa. *Work:* Mayor Watson Pharo's Collection, Borough Hall, Beach Haven, NJ; wall mural, Long Beach Island Hist Mus, Beach Haven, NJ. *Exhib:* Philadelphia Sketch Club Ann, 68-; Philadelphia Plastic Club, 71-72; Long Beach Island Found Arts & Sci; Long Beach Island Hist Mus, 79; NJ State Ann, 81 & 82. *Awards:* Second Prize for Oils, Willingboro Pa Art Alliance, 72; First & Third Awards, Manahawkin, NJ Arts Week Ann, Pine Shores Art Asn, 86. *Mem:* Ocean Co Artists Guild, Toms River, NJ. *Media:* Mixed. *Mailing Add:* 333 Kentford Ave Beach Haven NJ 08008

MARTER, JOAN
HISTORIAN, CRITIC
b Philadelphia, Pa, Aug 13, 46. *Study:* Temple Univ, BA; Univ Del, MA, PhD(art hist). *Collections Arranged:* Vanguard Am Sculpture 1913-1939 (guest cur & coauth, catalog), Rutgers Univ Art Gallery, 79; Design in America: The Cranbrook Vision 1925-1950, Detroit Inst Arts & Metrop Mus Art, 83; Beyond the Plane, American Constructions 1930-1965, NJ State Mus, 83; Alexander Archipenko Constructions (auth, catalog), Blum Art Inst, Bard Col, 85; Alexander Calder: Artist As Engineer, Mass Inst Technol, 86; Theodore Roszak: The Drawings, Elvehjem Mus Art, 92; Dorothy Dehner Retrospective, Katanoh Mus Art, 93. *Teaching:* Prof art hist, Rutgers Univ, 77- *Awards:* Charles F Montgomery Prize, Decorative Arts Soc, 84; George Wittenborn Award, Art Libr Soc, 85; John Sloan Mem Found Grant, 89; Res Coun Grants, Rutgers Univ, 92-93. *Mem:* Col Art Asn; Women's Caucus for Art; Int Asn Art Critics (mem USA sect). *Res:* 20th century art; Am Sculpture. *Publ:* Auth, Jose De Rivera Construction, Madrid, 80; articles in Am Art J, Art J, Arts Mag & Sculpture; Alexander Calder, Cambridge Univ Press, 91; Theodore Roszak Drawings, Univ Wash Press, 92. *Mailing Add:* 220 Madison Ave New York NY 10016

MARTIN, AGNES BERNICE
PAINTER
b Maklin, Sask, Can, Mar 22, 12; US citizen. *Study:* Columbia Univ; Univ NMex. *Work:* Mus Mod Art, Whitney Mus Am Art & Guggenheim Mus, New York; Tate Gallery, London, Eng; Kunstraum Munich, Ger; Stedlelijk Mus, Amsterdam; Mus Fine Arts, Canberra, Australia; Art Mus Ontario; and others. *Exhib:* Retrospective, Inst Contemp Art, 73; Mus Mod Art, prints, 73; Kumstraum Munich, Ger; Retrospective, Heyward Gallery, London, Eng, 77; Stedelijk Mus, Amsterdam, Holland, 77 & 91; Whitney Mus Am Art, 92; and others. *Mem:* Am Acad & Inst Arts & Lett. *Media:* Acrylic. *Publ:* Auth, The Perfection Underlying Life & The Untroubled Mind, 73, Univ Pa Press. *Dealer:* Pace Gallery 32 E 57th St New York NY 10022. *Mailing Add:* Lamy NM 87540

MARTIN, ALEXANDER TOEDT
EDUCATOR, PAINTER
b Kinderhook, NY, Mar 11, 31. *Study:* Albright Art Sch, cert, 52; Univ Buffalo, BFA, 57; Tulane Univ, MFA, 63. *Work:* Neuberger Mus, State Univ NY Col, Purchase; Whitney Mus Am Art, Union Carbide Corp, Salomon Brothers, New York; Schenectady Mus, NY; Continental Transport Inc, White Plains, NY; and others. *Exhib:* Albright-Knox Art Gallery, Buffalo, 59; Southeastern Exhib, Delgado Mus, New Orleans, La, 63; Wadsworth Atheneum, Hartford Conn, 66; Convocation of Arts Exhib, State Univ NY, Albany, 69; Cooperstown Ann, NY, 75; Plaza Gallery, State Univ NY Central, Albany, 82; one-man show, Barrett House, Poughkeepsie, NY, 83; The new Response, Contemp Hudson River Painters Exhib, Albany, Poughkeepsie & New York, 86; James Cox Gallery, Woodstock, NY, 91. *Teaching:* Prof painting & drawing, State Univ NY Col, New Paltz, 63- *Awards:* First Prize Painting, Schenectady Mus, 58 & Cooperstown Ann, 75. *Bibliog:* Hilton Kramer (auth), article in NY Times, 3/25/78; article, Am Artist, 5/82. *Media:* Oil, Watercolor. *Publ:* Auth, Painting the Landscape, Watson Guptill, 85. *Dealer:* Katerina Rich Perlow New York NY; James Cox Gallery Woodstock NY. *Mailing Add:* Studio Art SUNY Col at New Paltz New Paltz NY 12561

MARTIN, BERNARD MURRAY
PAINTER, EDUCATOR
b Ferrum, Va, June 21, 35. *Study:* Wake Forest Col, NC; Richmond Prof Inst, Va, BFA; Hunter Col, MA. *Work:* Va Mus Fine Arts, Richmond; Walter Rawls Mus, Courtland, Va; Chrysler Mus, Norfolk, Va; Nat Collection, Washington, DC; First & Merchants Nat Bank, Richmond, Va. *Exhib:* Nostalgia and the Contemporary Artist, Am Fedn Arts Traveling Exhib, 68; American Painting 1970, Va Mus Fine Art, 70; Friends of the Corcoran, Corcoran Gallery Art, Washington, DC, 71; one-man show, Gallery K, Washington, DC, 78 & 80; 32nd Southeastern Exhib, Gallery Contemp Art, Winston-Salem, 72. *Teaching:* Assoc prof painting, Va Commonwealth Univ, 61- *Awards:* Cert distinction, Va Artists Exhib, Va Mus Fine Arts, 64, 66, 68 & 70; First Prize, Southeastern Exhib, Gallery Contemp Art, 70 & 71. *Media:* Oil. *Dealer:* Gallery K Washington DC 20013. *Mailing Add:* Dept Painting Va Common Wealth Univ 901 W Franklin St Richmond VA 23284

MARTIN, BILL
PAINTER, SCULPTOR
b South San Francisco, Calif, Jan 22, 43. *Study:* Acad Art, San Francisco, Calif, 68; San Francisco Art Inst, MFA, 70. *Work:* San Francisco Int Airport; Neue Gallery der Stadt, Aachen, Ger; AT&T, New York; Owens Corning, Toledo, Ohio; Glenn C Janss Collection Boise Art Mus, Idaho. *Exhib:* Baja, San Francisco Mus Mod Art, 75; Ninth Biennale de Paris, Musee d'Art Modern de la Ville, Paris, France, 75; University Show, State Univ NY,

Postdam, 77; Tri-Annual Invitational of India, 78; Painting and Sculpture Today, Indianapolis Mus Art, Ind, 78; New American Painting (world traveling show), New Mus, New York, 79-80; Art in Bay Area 1945-1980, Oakland Mus, Calif, 85; American Realism, San Francisco Mus Art, 85; one-person shows, Nancy Hoffman Gallery, San Francisco, 82, 76 & 79-80, Joseph Chowning Gallery, New York, 83, 85, 87, 89 & 92, Univ Nev, 88, Chabot Col, Calif, 90, Kabutoya Gallery, Tokyo, Japan, 91, Atrium Gallery, San Francisco, 92; Art of Fantasy & Science Fiction, Del Art Mus, 89; Watercolor USA Springfield Art Mus, Mo, 89; West Coast Works on Paper, Humbolt State Univ, Calif; Exhibition 48, Southern Utah State Univ, 89; Paper in Particular, Columbia Col, Mo, 90; From the Studio Oakland Mus, Calif. *Teaching:* Instr painting, Univ Calif, San Jose, 73, Col of Marin, Kentfield, Calif, 75-78 & Col of Redwoods, Mendocino, Calif, 83- *Awards:* Grant to Artists, Louis Comfort Tiffany Found, 70; Artist's Fel. *Mem:* Mendocino Art Ctr (bd of dir); Ft Braggs Ctr Art. *Media:* Oil, Bronze; Metal Cast. *Publ:* Contribr, Visions, 77, auth, 1969-1979 Bill Martin Paintings, 79; American Realism, Abrams; Arts of the San Francisco Bay Area, Univ Calif Press; auth, Joy of Drawing, Watson-Guptill Publ. *Dealer:* Joseph Chowning Gallery 1717 17th St San Francisco CA 94103. *Mailing Add:* PO Box 511 Albion CA 95410

MARTIN, CHARLES E
DESIGNER, PAINTER
b Chelsea, Mass, Jan 12, 10. *Study:* Self taught. *Work:* Mus City New York; Metrop Mus, NY; Princeton Mus, NJ; Archives, Syracuse Univ, NY; Libr Cong. *Exhib:* One-man shows, Brooklyn Mus Art Sch, 54, Rockland Found, 56-57, Graham Gallery, 74 & Nicholls Gallery, 75; Ruth White Gallery, 60. *Pos:* Illusr, PM newspaper, 39-42; art dir, Air Drop Newspapers, New York, London, Naples & Paris, 42-45. *Teaching:* Instr watercolor painting, Brooklyn Mus Art Sch, 63-65. *Bibliog:* Monograph, Art Dept, Syracuse Univ. *Mem:* Mag Cartoonist Guild Am; Author's Guild. *Media:* All. *Publ:* Contribr, New Yorker Mag, New York Times, Playboy, Sat Rev, Life & Time Mags, 35-; illusr children's books, Bradbury Press, Random House, Western Publ & Greenwillow. *Mailing Add:* 135 Park St Portland ME 04101

MARTIN, CHRIS
PAINTER
b Washington, DC, 1954. *Study:* Yale Univ, 75. *Work:* Lannan Found; Progressive Corp. *Exhib:* Solo exhibs, Thread Bldg Gallery, New York, 80, Mary Delahoyd Gallery, New York, 85 & 87 & Philippe Briet Gallery, New York, 88, John Good Gallery, New York, 90 & Jimenez & Algus Gallery, Brooklyn, NY, 91; Penultimate Salute, A Place Apart Gallery, Brooklyn, NY, 84; Twelve from New York, Yale Sch Art, Yale Univ, New Haven, Conn, 86; Brooklyn Mus, NY, 87; Words as Symbols, Aldrich Mus, Conn, 90; Visions/Revisions: Selections from the Contemporary Collection, Denver Art Mus, 91. *Awards:* Am Acad & Inst Arts & Let, Richard & Linda Rosenthal Award, 87; Nat Endowment Arts, 90. *Bibliog:* Chris Martin, NY Times, 4/27/90; Roberta Smith (auth), Chris Martin, NY Times, 4/27/90. *Mailing Add:* c/o John Good Gallery 532 Broadway New York NY 10012

MARTIN, DIANNE L
PAINTER, GRAPHIC ARTIST
b Boston, Mass, Apr 8, 40. *Study:* RI Sch Design, BFA, 65; Univ Iowa, with Byron Burford, MA, 67. *Exhib:* Works on Paper, Brooklyn Mus, New York, 75; Juried Ann, Queens Mus, New York, 85; In search of the American Experience, Mus Nat Arts Found Nat Competition, 89. *Teaching:* Chmn, Art Dept, Spence Sch, New York, NY, 72- *Media:* Watercolor. *Dealer:* Markell Sears Fine Arts Inc 560 Broadway New York 10012. *Mailing Add:* 27-15 41st Ave Long Island City NY 11101

MARTIN, DORIS-MARIE CONSTABLE
DESIGNER, SCULPTOR
b New York, NY, July 5, 41. *Study:* Miami-Dade Community Col, S Campus, Miami, Fla, AA, 71; Univ Miami; Univ NC, Asheville, BA, 76; Penland Sch Crafts, NC; Arrowmont Sch Crafts, MA, 81; Goddard Col, MA(sculpture), 80;Univ NC, Greensborough, MFA, 89. *Work:* Miami-Dade Community Col; Durham Art Guild, M Biddle Gallery for the Blind, NC State Mus, Raleigh; Chrysler Mus, Norfolk, Va; Miami Herald, Fla; Univ NC, Asheville; and others. *Comn:* Soft sculpture, Unitarian/Universalist Church of Asheville, 78. *Exhib:* Ann Painting & Sculpture Exhib, Mint Mus, Charlotte, 73 & 76; Marietta Col Int, Grover M Hermann Fine Arts Ctr, Ohio, 76 & 77; Springs Mills Traveling Show, Ft Mill, SC, 77 & 78; one-man shows, Chrysler Mus, 73 & Beyond Craft: Fiber-Form-Fabric, Univ NC, Asheville, 75; and many others. *Teaching:* Instr soft construction sculpture, Asheville Art Mus, 76-, instr beginning printmaking, 77-, instr watercolor, drawing & painting, currently; vis artist, Western NC & Ashville sch system, 70- *Awards:* Best Sculpture, Craft Work 76, Am Crafts Coun, 76; Best Sculpture & One-Man Show, Durham Arts Guild, Inc, Allied Arts Ctr, NC, 76; Award for Sculpture, Springs Mills Traveling Show, 75 & 77. *Bibliog:* R Clermont (auth), Poloities & Expositions Diverses, Les Editions de la Revue Moderne Des Arts, Paris, France, 73; article, Miami Herald, 76. *Mem:* Am Crafts Coun; Fla Craftsmen, Miami; Western NC Fibers/Handweavers Guild (bd dirs); Handweavers Guild Am; NC Art Soc; and others. *Media:* Fiber. *Publ:* Contribr, Shuttle, Spindle & Dyepot, Handweavers Guild Am, 76. *Mailing Add:* 65 Woodland Rd Asheville NC 28804

MARTIN, DOUG
PAINTER
b Newton, Kans, Dec 10, 47. *Study:* Kans State Univ, BFA; Univ Nebr, MFA. *Exhib:* William Rockhill Nelson Gallery Art, Kansas City, 72; St Louis Art Mus, Mo, 72; Sheldon Art Gallery, Lincoln, Nebr, 75; Robert Hull Fleming Mus, Univ Vt, 81; solo exhibs, Oscarsson Hood Gallery, New York, 81 & Edward Thorp Gallery, New York, 82; Aldich Mus Contemp Art, Ridgefield, Conn, 81; Herbert Johnson Mus, Ithaca, NY, 81; Krannert Art Mus, Univ Ill, Champaign, 86; Ruschman Art Gallery, Indianapolis, 87; Sherry French Gallery, NY, 88; The Hyde Collection, Glens Falls, NY, 90. *Pos:* Vis artist, Cornell Univ, Ithaca, NY, 81-, Colo Mountain Col, Vail, 75, 76 & 78-81, Univ Ill, Champaign, 86; asst to dir, Yaddo, Saratoga Springs, NY, 84-88. *Awards:* NY Found for Arts Grant in Painting, 89. *Media:* Oil. *Mailing Add:* 457 Broome New York NY 10013

MARTIN, FRED THOMAS
PAINTER
b San Francisco, Calif, June 13, 27. *Study:* Univ Calif, Berkeley, BA, 49, MA, 52; San Francisco Art Inst, with David Park, Clifford Still & Mark Rothko. *Work:* Whitney Mus Am Art, Mus Mod Art, New York; San Francisco Mus Art; Oakland Art Mus, Calif; Fogg Art Mus, Cambridge, Mass. *Exhib:* San Francisco Mus Art Ann, 50-60; Whitney Mus Am Art, 70 & 73; one-man shows, M H DeYoung Mus, San Francisco, 54 & 64, San Francisco Art Inst, 72 & San Francisco Mus Mod Art, 58 & 73; Rena Bransten Gallery, San Francisco; and others. *Pos:* Dir, San Francisco Art Inst, 66-76, dean, 83-; contrib ed, Art Week, 77- *Teaching:* Instr art hist, San Francisco Art Inst, 79- *Awards:* Nat Found Arts Artists Grant, 70-71. *Bibliog:* Dan Tooker (auth), article, Art Int, 11/75. *Media:* Miscellaneous. *Publ:* Auth, Beulah Land, A Book of Etchings, Hansen Fuller & Crown Press, 74; A Travel Book, Arion Press, San Francisco, 77; From an Antique Land, Green Gates Press, Oakland, Calif, 79. *Dealer:* Rena Bransten 254 Sutter St San Francisco CA 94108. *Mailing Add:* 232 Monte Vista Ave Piedmont CA 94611

MARTIN, JANE
PAINTER, DRAFTSMAN
b Montreal, Que, Can, Mar 31, 43. *Study:* Bishop's Univ, Lennoxville, Que, BA, 65; Carleton Univ, Ottawa, Ont, MA, 66. *Work:* Nat Gallery, Ottawa; Can Coun Art Bank, Ottawa, Ont; City of Ottawa; Art Gallery Greater Victoria; Winnipeg Art Gallery. *Exhib:* Woman as Viewer, Winnipeg Art Gallery, 75; solo exhib, SAW Gallery, Ottawa, 77 & 85, Contact, Art Gallery Ont, 79-80, Whitewater Gallery, North Bay, 85, Berkeley Castle Works 1984-1987, Toronto, 87; Gallery 101, Ottawa, 89, Gathie's Cupboard/Emblems/Transfigurations, Gallery 101, Ottawa, 89 & Open Space, Victoria, 91; Reflecting a Rural Consciousness Traveling Show, Can, US & France, 78-79; Images of Sexuality, Symposium & Exhib, Gallery 101, Ottawa, 85; Snakes in the Garden, Artscourt, Ottawa, 88; Crossties Traveling Show, 89-91; Wrapture, Ufundi Gallery, Ottawa, 90; Nat Gallery, Ottawa, 90; and others. *Pos:* Artist-in-residence, Ont Arts Coun Project, 77; coordr, SAW Gallery, Ottawa, 78; co-founder, Can Artists' Represention Copyrights Collective, 88; founding bd, Can Reprography Collective, 88-93. *Teaching:* Lectr, UAAC Conf, Concordia Univ, Montreal, 81, Univ Ottawa, 81 & Powerhouse Gallery, Montreal, 81. *Awards:* Ont Arts Coun Grant, 75, 76, 77 & 80; Visual Arts Ont Award, 76; Can Coun Short Term Grants, 78, 79 & 83. *Bibliog:* Susan Crean (auth), Berkeley Castle Works 1984-1987, Can Art, fall 87; Lisa Rochon (auth), Portraits of suffering, Globe & Mail, 5/28/87; Joyce Nelson (auth), The Sacrement of the Flesh, Wrapture, Open Space, Victoria, 91. *Mem:* Can Artists Representation/Le Front Artistes Can (nat coun, 77-79, chairperson, Ottawa local, 81, 89-91). *Media:* Oil. *Publ:* Illusr, 77 Best Canadian Stories, Oberon, 77; auth, Who judges whom, Atlantis, 79; illusr, Stories of Quebec, Oberon, 80; auth, Woman Visual Artists on Canada Council Juries, Can Artists Representation/Le Front Artistes Can, 81; illusr, Fat Woman, General, 82. *Mailing Add:* 21 Rose Ave Toronto ON M4X 1N7 Canada

MARTIN, JOHN RUPERT
HISTORIAN, LECTURER
b Hamilton, Ont, Can, Sept 27, 16; US citizen. *Study:* McMaster Univ, BA, 38, DLitt, 76; Princeton Univ, MFA, 41, PhD, 47. *Teaching:* Instr art hist, Univ Iowa, Iowa City, 41-42; prof art hist, Princeton Univ, NJ, 47- *Mem:* Col Art Asn Am (pres, 84-86); Am Philos Soc. *Res:* Northern baroque art (Rubens, Van Dyck, Rembrandt). *Publ:* Auth, The Farnese Gallery, Princeton Univ Press, 65; Rubens Ceiling Paintings for the Jesuit Church, 68 & Rubens: Pompa Introitus Fernandi, 72, Arcade, Brussels; Rubens: The Antwerp Altarpieces, Norton, 69; Baroque, Harper & Row, 77. *Mailing Add:* Dept Art & Archeol Princeton Univ Princeton NJ 08544

MARTIN, KNOX
PAINTER, SCULPTOR
b Barranquilla, Colombia, Feb 12, 23; US citizen. *Study:* Art Students League, 4 yrs. *Work:* Corcoran Gallery Art, Washington, DC; Mus Mod Art, Whitney Mus Am Art, New York; Mus Art, Austin, Tex; Univ Calif, Berkeley; Weatherspoon Art Gallery, Greensboro, NC; Mus Art, Baltimore, Md; Art Inst, Chicago, Ill; Mus Art, Dallas, Tex. *Comn:* 19 story wall painting, City Walls, Inc, West Side Hwy, New York, 71; wall painting, Mercor, Inc, Merritt Complex, Ft Lauderdale, Fla, 72; wall painting, Houston & McDougal Streets New York, 79; wall painting, Nieman Marcus, White Plains, NY, 80; John Wayne Mural, John Wayne Sch, Brooklyn, 82. *Exhib:* Yale Univ Art Gallery, 66; Whitney Mus Am Art, New York, 72; River Gallery, Irvington, NY, 80 & 82; Nat Gallery, Yugoslavia, 81; Ingber Gallery, New York, 81; group exhib, Arras Gallery, NY, Westfield Chap Hadassah, Westfield, NJ, Art-Expo NY, 82; Int Sch Art, Italy, 90-92; Art Students League, New York, 92; Tibor De Nagy, New York, 92. *Teaching:* Asst prof drawing & painting, Yale Univ, 65-70; instr, Art Students League, 72-92; instr, Univ Minn & NY Univ. *Awards:* Nat Endowment Arts, 72; Creative Artists Pub Serv, 78; Pollack Krassner Award, 90; Goetlieb Award, 91. *Bibliog:* Knox Martin Super Creation (collage/film, color), Yale Univ Art Dept, 67; George Parrino (auth), Knox Martin, The Deadalian Work, 72; H Kramer (auth), rev, NY Times, 10/25/75; G Brown (auth), Knox Martin Retrospective, Arts, 12/75; G Henry (auth), review, Art News, 1/76. *Mem:* Visual Artists Group Asn. *Mailing Add:* 128 Ft Washington Ave New York NY 10032

MARTIN, LARRY KENNETH
PAINTER, DEALER
b Anniston, Ala, June 7, 39. *Study:* Jacksonville State Univ, BS, 61; Tulane Univ, MS, 64, PhD, 70. *Work:* Off US Cong; US Senate Corp Collection; Gov's Mansion, Montgomery, Ala; and others. *Comn:* Archaeopteryx (painting), 80, Anniston Mus Natural Hist, Ala; In Pursuit (mural), US Dept Interior, Richard Russell Bldg, Atlanta, Ga, 80. *Exhib:* Ala Zoological Soc, Birmingham, 82-84; Fernbank Sci Ctr, Atlanta, 82-83; Southern Wildfowl Festival, Point Mallard, Ala, 82-88; Oklahoma Wildlife Art Festival, Tulsa, 83-85; Southeastern Wildlife Expos, Charleston, SC, 84-88; International Exhib Wildlife, Western & American Art, Chicago, 84-85; Feature Artist, Fla-Nat Wildlife Art Show, 86; Nat Wildlife & Western Art Exhib, Minneapolis, Minn, 86- *Pos:* Co-founder/co-owner, Nance's Creek Proj: Preserv Rustic Homes (pre-1860) & Hist Structures, 70-; cur, Anniston Mus Natural Hist, 76-79; owner/founder, Wren's Nest Gallery, Jacksonville, Ala, 78- *Teaching:* Instr, Jacksonville State Univ, 82-84. *Awards:* Meritorious Serv Award, Nat Audubon Soc, 84; Painting of Bald Eagle, Southeastern Wildlife Exposition, 88- *Bibliog:* Kite (auth), cover story, Ala Purchasor, 9/82 & 10/83; Myers (auth), American characters: Eccentrics offer artist challenge and rewards, Art Bus News, 10/83. *Media:* Miscellaneous. *Mailing Add:* c/o Wren's Nest Gallery 305A Church Ave NE Jacksonville AL 36265

MARTIN, LORETTA MARSH
CARTOONIST, CALLIGRAPHER
b Plymouth, Ind, Jan 22, 33. *Study:* Art Inst Chicago, BAE, 55; Univ Notre Dame, MA, 68; Famous Artists Schs, 68(cert com art). *Work:* Many pvt collections in US & other countries. *Comn:* Calligraphy for Granaderos de Galvez, (presented to the King of Spain) 86. *Exhib:* One-woman show, First Unitarian Church, South Bend, Ind, 62; Northern Ind Artists; Alumni Asn Art Inst Chicago; Artists 70 & 71, Citrus Co, Fla; El Paso Centennial Mus. *Pos:* Asst cur, El Paso Mus Art, 74-86. *Teaching:* Instr graphic illusr, ATI Enterprises (trade sch), Hurst, Tex, 89- *Mem:* Ft Worth Calligraphers Guild; Mid-Cities Scribes; Trinity Arts Guild. *Media:* All Media. *Publ:* Graphic work included in Mangan Publ. *Mailing Add:* Martin Art Studio 1437 Simpson Hurst TX 76053

MARTIN, LUCILLE CAIAR
PAINTER, MURALIST
b Carlsbad, NMex, June 7, 18. *Study:* With La Vora Norman; Frederic Taubes Workshops, Cloudcroft & Ruidoso; Merlin Enabnit Art Sch, Chicago, dipl; workshop with Olaf Wieghorst, Puerto Vallarta, Mex, dipl, 75. *Work:* Carlsbad Libr & Mus, NMex; Houston Med Ctr, Tex; Univ Ariz, Tucson. *Comn:* Jordan River (mural), Hillcrest Baptist Church, Carlsbad, 62; Sacred River (mural), First Baptist Church, McCrory, Ark, 63; El Capitan (mural), Security Savings & Loan, Carlsbad, 64; NMex State Bird-Roadrunner, Young Democrats for Gov Off, State Capitol, Santa Fe, 64; roadrunner painting, comn by Gov Campbell for aircraft carrier constellation, 64. *Exhib:* Fla Int Art Exhib, Lakeland, 52; Nat Palo Duro Art Show, WTex State Univ, Canyon, 64; Nat Sun Carnival Art Exhib, El Paso Mus Art, 64; one-man show, NMex State Univ, Las Cruces, 65; Boulder City Art Festival, Nev, 70. *Pos:* Artist, Leanin' Tree greeting cards, reproduced by Boulder, Colo, 70- *Teaching:* Workshops, Nev & Carlsbad, NMex. *Awards:* Grand Sweepstakes, Tri-State Art Exhib, El Paso, 57; First Place, Carlsbad Area Art Asn Exhibs, 64, 65 & 66; First Place, Nat Parks Show, 73, 75 & 76. *Bibliog:* Articles in NMex Newspapers & El Paso Times, 64 & 65; Elena Montes (auth), Lucille Martin's art, NMex Mag, 4/65 & 10/88. *Mem:* Charter mem Carlsbad Area Art Asn; Tucson Art Ctr. *Publ:* Contribr, NMex Mag, 54 & 65 & Ariz Highways Mag, 3/70. *Dealer:* William Bonney Gallery Mesilla NM. *Mailing Add:* 5901 E Third St Tucson AZ 85711

MARTIN, LYS
PHOTOGRAPHER, CURATOR
b Lafayette, La, March, 3, 57. *Study:* Univ Miss, Oxford, BA(summa cum laude), 79; Art Inst Chicago, BFA, 83, MFA, 86. *Work:* Art Inst Chicago; Mus Contemp Art. *Exhib:* Solo Exhibs, Artemisia Gallery, Chicago, 86, Moming Gallery, Chicago, 87, Vanitas, Chicago Pub Libr Cult Ctr, 90 & Wade Wilson Gallery, Chicago, 90; Art Expo, 89, 90 & Selections, 90, Wade Wilson Gallery, Chicago; Personal Political: Sexuality Self-defined, Sch Art Inst Chicago, 90; Photo Projects, White Columns, New York, 90; Contrasts, John Michael Kohler Art Ctr, Sheboygan, Wis, 91; Still Alive: Contemporary Still Life, Rockford Art Col, Ill, 91; Light, Milwaukee Inst Art & Design, Wis, 92; TRINE, Parkland Col Art Gallery, Champaign, Ill, 92; Picture This, Benefit Exhib & auction, Renaissance Soc Chicago, Ill, 92; New Gallery, Houston, Tex, 92; Small Works, Hal Katzen Gallery, New York, 93. *Collections Arranged:* Polaroid & Polaroid Derived Imagery, 88, John Pluof & Howard Miller, 88 & Investigations, 90, MoMing Gallery, Chicago. *Pos:* Secy, Dept of PRints and Drawings, Art Inst Chicago, 84-87; co-cur, MoMing Gallery, 87-89; asst dir, Feigen Inc, 87-88; co-dir, Betsy Rosenfield Gallery, Chicago, 88- *Awards:* Unendowed Merit Scholar, Art Inst Chicago, 85 & 86; Spec Assistance Grant, Ill Arts Coun, 86; Community Arts Assistance Grant, Chicago Off Fine Arts, 90 & 91. *Bibliog:* Mitchell Stevens (auth0, Chicago/Lys Martin, New Art Examiner, 12/90; Buzz Spector (auth), CHicago, Art Issues, 12/90-1/91; Kathryn Hixson (auth), Chicago in review, Arts Mag, 1/91. *Media:* Photography, Mixed Media. *Publ:* Contribr, Poetry, Seams, Vol 2, No 3, 86; Artist's Pages (collab), Primer, No 3, 89; Project Pages, WhiteWalls, No 26, fall & winter 90. *Dealer:* Hal Katzen Gallery 345 W Broadway New York NY 10013. *Mailing Add:* c/o New Gallery 2639 Colquitt Houston TX 10012

MARTIN, MARGARET M
PAINTER, DESIGNER
b Buffalo, NY, Aug 15, 40. *Study:* Boston Univ, BFA; watercolor workshops with John Pike, Robert E Wood, John Pellew, Rex Brandt & Milford Zornes. *Work:* Burchfield Art Mus & Hyatt Regency Hotel, Buffalo, NY; Oklahoma Christian Col, Oklahoma City. *Comn:* Painting, Lockport Savings Bank, NY, 90; paintings, Equity Savings Bank, Oklahoma Citym 91; painting, Exchange Insurance, Buffalo, 92. *Exhib:* Am Watercolor Soc, 70-73, 78-79, 83, 86 & 88-89; Nat Arts Club, New York, 74-90; Rocky Mountain Nat Watermedia, Foothills Art Ctr, Golden, Colo, 75, 80 & 85; Midwest Watercolor Soc, 78-90; Adirondacks Nat Exhib Am Watercolors, Old Forge, NY, 83-84, 86 & 89-91; and others. *Pos:* Designer, Wagner Folding Box, Buffalo, NY, 62-64; art dir-designer, Manhardt-Alexander, Inc, Buffalo, NY, 64-77; freelance graphic designer & illusr, 77-80. *Teaching:* Watercolor classes & workshop sessions in many areas of US. *Awards:* Hardie Gramatky Mem Award, Am Watercolor Soc, 83; Catherine Lorillard-Wolfe Gold Medal Honor Watercolor, 85; Winsor & Newton Award, Adirondack Nat Exhib, 90; and others. *Bibliog:* Garden Design Mag, summer 84; Splash, F&W Publ, 90; Watercolor 90, Am Artist, spring 90. *Mem:* Am Watercolor Soc; Midwest Watercolor Soc; Nat Watercolor Soc; Nat Arts Club; Salmagundi Club; and others. *Media:* Watercolor. *Publ:* Contribr, Designers Dictionary, 74; illusr, Buffalo & Erie Co Arts Resource Directory, 74. *Mailing Add:* 78 Summer St Buffalo NY 14209

MARTIN, MARY FINCH
PAINTER, GALLERY DIRECTOR
b Glens Falls, NY, Sept 7, 16. *Study:* Pvt tutoring with Isabel La Freniere. *Exhib:* Rockport Art Asn, Mass, 71-; Hamilton-Wenham Art Show, S Hamilton, Mass, 74-; Newbury Art Asn, Mass, 75-; Gloucester & Cape Ann Exhib, Gloucester, Mass, 72; N Shore Art Asn, Gloucester, Mass. *Pos:* Art dir, Fine Arts Rockport, Mass, 71-91. *Mem:* Rockport Art Asn; N Shore Art Asn. *Media:* Oil. *Mailing Add:* 8 Clark Ave Rockport MA 01966

MARTIN, RICHARD (HARRISON)
HISTORIAN
b Bryn Mawr, Pa, Dec 4, 46. *Study:* Swarthmore Col, BA(art hist), 67; Columbia Univ, MA(art hist), 69 & MPhil(art hist), 71. *Collections Arranged:* The East Village, 86; Fashion & Surrealism, 87; Tartan, 88; Tribute to the Black Fashion Mus. *Pos:* Assoc cur art hist & archeol, Columbia Univ, 68-70; exec ed, Arts Mag, 73-74, ed, 74-88; exec dir, Shirley Goodman Resource Ctr, Fashion Inst Technol, 80-93; cur, Costume Inst, Metrop Mus Art, 93. *Teaching:* Instr art hist, William Paterson Col, 72-73; instr hist civilization & art, Fashion Inst Technol, State Univ NY, 73-76, from asst prof to assoc prof, 76-84, prof, 84-93; lectr art hist, Sch Visual Arts, 75-80; adj prof, NY Univ, 77-; critic in residence, Md Inst, 85 & 86; vis prof, Sch Art, Inst Chicago, fall 86; prof, Vt Col, 92. *Awards:* Arts & Soc Fel, Grad Ctr City Univ New York, 83. *Bibliog:* Jillian Burt (auth), Richard Martin, Bomb, winter 88; Jed Perl (auth), Sartorially Suited, Vogue, 4/89. *Mem:* Col Art Asn Am (nominating comt); Costume Soc Am (bd dirs, 83-89); Soc Archit Historians; Victorian Soc Am (bd dirs, 80-84); Art Libr Soc N AM; and others. *Res:* Contemporary art and fashion. *Publ:* Auth, articles, Arts Mag, Art & Artists, Art Educ, Dress & Art J; Fashion & Surrealism (exhib catalog), Rizzoli, 87, Jock and Nerds, 89 & The Historical Mode, 89, Rizzoli; Flair: Fashion, collected by Tina Chow, 92. *Mailing Add:* 235 E 22nd St New York NY 10010

MARTIN, ROGER
PAINTER, EDUCATOR
b Gloucester, Mass, Sept 3, 25. *Study:* Boston Mus Fine Arts Sch. *Work:* Pvt collections in New Eng, New York, the West Coast, Europe, Japan, Switz, S Africa, Boston Pub Libr, Fogg Art Mus & Harvard Univ, Cambridge, Mass. *Comn:* graphic art, D C Heath & Co, Allyn & Bacon, Beacon Press, 65-68 & United Church Teaching Pictures; designed cases & executed carvings, C B Fisk Pipe Organs, Harvard Univ & Pohick Church, Lorton, Va, 65-69; House of Hope Presby Church, St Paul, Minn, 79; Stanford Univ, 83; Presby Church, New Bern, NC, 85. *Exhib:* one-man shows, Trinity Col, Hartford, 61, Carl Siembab Gallery, Boston, 69, So Vermont Art Ctr, Manchester, 70, Rockport Art Asn, Rockport, Mass, 83, Orphanos Gallery, Boston Mass, 88, Montserrat Col Art, 90; one-man shows, Trinity Col, Hartford, 61, Carl Siembab Gallery, Boston, 69, SVt Art Ctr, Manchester, 70, Rockport Art Asn, Mass, 83, Orphanos Gallery, Boston, Mass, 88 & Montserrat Col Art, 90-92. *Teaching:* Instr design & drawing & head freshman dept, New Eng Sch Art, Boston, 67-69; instr design & painting to chmn foundation prog dept, Montserrat College of Art, Beverly, Mass, 69-90, prof emer, 91, assoc prof, 90-, mem found fac, bd trustees, 92- *Bibliog:* Article, Gloucester Daily Times, 5/83. *Media:* Oil; Prints, Woodcut. *Publ:* Contribr, illus in New Yorker Mag, Atlantic Monthly & New York Times; articles & illus in Child Life Mag & textbks; contribr, Gloucester Daily Times, Mass, 90-92; contribr, Boston Sunday Globe, Mass, 92. *Mailing Add:* 15 Penryn Way Rockport MA 01966

MARTIN, STEFAN
PRINTMAKER, COLLAGE ARTIST
b Elgin, Ill, Jan 10, 36. *Study:* Art Inst Chicago, cert(fine arts), 58. *Work:* Smithsonian Inst; Metrop Mus Art, New York; Philadelphia Mus Fine Arts; Geraldine R Dodge Found, Morristown, NJ. *Comn:* Portrait Ben Shahn, Ben Shahn Found, New York, 70; Holocaust, Coun Jewish Orgn, Windsor, NJ, 75; print landscape & bldgs, Princeton Univ, 75; prints landscape & bldg, Printmaking Coun NJ, 81 & Univ Pa Dental Col, 82. *Exhib:* Washington Printmakers, Libr Cong, 57, 59, 60 & 67; Ann Boston Printmaker Exhib, Mus Fine Ars, Boston, 59, 60 & 62; Am Acad Arts & Lett Print Exhib, New York, 59, 71 & 72; Metropolitan Young Artists, Metrop Mus Art, New York, 60; Nat Print Exhib, NJ State Mus, Trenton, 66-83; Northwest Printmakers,

Seattle Mus Fine Arts, 67; Xylon's Int, Winterthur Mus, Geneva, Switz, 69-71 & 83; Holzstiche, Hamburg Mus, Ger, 76 & 77. *Teaching:* Instr engraving, Printmaking Coun NJ, 79-, Beaver Col & Mercer Co Col. *Awards:* Tiffany Fels, 61-64; Purchase Prize, Tenth Nat Print Exhib, NJ State Mus, 66; 18th Ann Award Excellence Publ, Art Dirs Club NJ, 80. *Bibliog:* Ann Commire (auth), Something About the Author, Gale Res Co, 83. *Mem:* Visual Artists & Galleries Asn; Soc Am Graphic Artists (vpres, 72-74); Philadelphia Print Club; World Print Coun; Printmaking Coun NJ. *Media:* Engraving. *Publ:* Illusr, The Sparrow Bush: Rhymes, Horn Book Inc, 66; Small Pond, E P Dutton, 67; They Walk in the Night, W W Norton, 69; Panoramas of Literature, Random House, 69; Garrity US History, Harcourt, 82. *Dealer:* Gallery 500 Elkins Park PA 19117. *Mailing Add:* 151 Harbinson Pl Twin Rivers NJ 08520

MARTIN, THOMAS
PAINTER, INSTRUCTOR
b Amsterdam, NY, Feb 24, 43. *Study:* State Univ NY Col Buffalo, BS(art educ); Syracuse Univ, MFA(painting). *Work:* State Univ NY Col, Buffalo; Syracuse Univ. *Exhib:* Allegorical Portraits, Univ Maine, Portland-Gorham, 74; Unordinary Realities, Xerox Corp, Rochester, NY, 75; Art on Paper, Weatherspoon Ann Exhib, Univ NC, Greensboro, 76; Artists Draw, Artists Space, New York, 79; 9th St Survival Show, New York, 81; and many one-man shows. *Pos:* Cur exhibs, Mus of the Am Indian, New York, NY, 75- *Teaching:* Instr fine arts, Western Conn State Col, Danbury, 74-75; asst prof, New York Inst Technol, Metro, 80- *Bibliog:* David Pascal (auth), Comics, An American Expressionism, Graphis, Zurich, 72; rev of 77 New York exhibits, Arts Mag, 4/77; rev, Artists draw, Soho Weekly News, 1/79. *Mailing Add:* c/o Dept Fine Arts NY Inst Technol 1855 Broadway New York NY 10023

MARTINEZ, ALFRED
PAINTER
b Ennis, Tex, Dec 24, 44. *Study:* Southern Methodist Univ, Dallas, BFA, 68; Syracuse Univ, MFA, 71. *Comn:* Mr London (drawings), comn by Joe London, Dallas, 74; Coil-Fence (prints), comn by Lanny Brooks, West Hartford, Conn, 78 & Leah Rayblatt, New York, 78; Invisible-Lips (painting), comn by Gerry Dorman, New York, 81; Electric Fans (painting), comn by William Maxwell, New York, 82; Mystery (painting), comn by Gray L Cooper, Austin, Tex, 85. *Exhib:* Dallas Mus Fine Arts Ann, 63; Finger Lakes Exhib, Rochester Mus & Sci Ctr, 70; Artist-Initiate, Bronx Mus Arts, 78; Artists Books--Franklin Furnace, Walker Art Ctr, 81; History of Art Works Gallery Coop, Wadsworth Atheneum, 81; Summer Invitational, O K Harris Gallery, New York, 81; Prints Benefit, Ctr Inter-Am Arts, New York, 82; Appalachian Nat Drawing Competition, Appalachian Col, NC, 83; Movin-Light, Kamikaze Rock Club, New York, 84; Exploit/Expose, Kentler Int Drawing Space, Brooklyn, NY, 91; William Benton Mus, Storrs, Conn, 92. *Teaching:* From assoc prof art to prof, Univ Conn, West Hartford, 73-86, dir, Campus Art Gallery, 81-86. *Awards:* Traveling Artist Fel, Syracuse Univ, 69; Res Grant, Univ Conn, 74; Vis Artist Grant, Castle Gallery, Col New Rochelle, Artists Space Inc, 80. *Bibliog:* Robyn Brentano & Mark Savitt (auths), One Hundred and Twelve Workshop, 112 Green Street, NY Univ Press, 81; Roger Winter (auth), Introduction to Drawing, Prentice-Hall, 83. *Mailing Add:* 9 Chatham Sq Third Floor New York NY 10038

MARTINEZ, DANIEL J
CONCEPTUAL ARTIST
b Los Angeles, Calif, 57. *Study:* Calif Inst Arts, BFA. *Comn:* Art work in bus shelters, Los Angeles, Calif, 90; Public art work, New York, 90. *Exhib:* Centro Cultural de La Raza, San Diego, Calif, 85; Trans America Ctr Gallery, Los Angeles, Calif, 86; solo exhib, Abstraction Gallery, Los Angeles, 87; Arts Ctr, Boston, Mass, 87; performances, Barnsdall Music Mus series, Los Angeles, 88, Santa Monica Mus Art, Calif, 88, Los Angeles Festival premier, Los Angeles, 90. *Awards:* Rockefeller Found Grant Conceptual Performance, 87; Nat Endowment Arts, 89. *Mailing Add:* c/o Robert Berman/B-1 Gallery 2044 Broadway Santa Monica CA 90405

MARTINEZ, ERNESTO PEDREGON
MURALIST, ARTIST
b El Paso, Tex, Feb 26, 26. *Study:* Self-taught. *Work:* Murals, New Bowie High Sch, El Paso; St Joseph Church, Houston; Veterans Hosp, Tex; Veterans Hosp, NMex. *Comn:* Mural, War Mem Honoring Recipients of Cong Medal Honor, Vet Hosp, El Paso, Tex; murals, NMex Veteran's Ctr; mural, Desert Storm, Ft Bliss, Tex; The Resurrection, St Joseph's Church, Houston. *Exhib:* One-man shows, NMex State Univ, 74, Univ Tex, El Paso, 74, Chamizal Nat Mus, 74-75 & Officer's Clubs, Univ Colo, 75; Exhib for First Ladies of US & Mex, Chamizal Nat Mus, El Paso, 77; Wight Gallery, Univ Calif, Los Angeles; Smithsonian Art Mus, Washington, DC. *Teaching:* Art consult, Boy Scouts Am, 60-; prof Mex-Am Art, El Paso Community Col, 74-; instr free classes for underprivileged & sr citizens. *Awards:* Artist of Year, Lulac Coun, 74 & 79; City Coun Recognition, El Paso, 77; Tex Navy Admiral, Gov Tex. *Bibliog:* Interview world television, Mexico City, 78; Art Diary, 82; Commander Veterans's of Foreign Wars. *Media:* Acrylics, Watercolors. *Publ:* Auth, articles on Pre-Columbian Art, El Paso Newspaper, 85-86; art articles, El Paseno Newspaper. *Mailing Add:* 7140 Villa Hermosa El Paso TX 79912

MARTINEZ-CAÑAS, MARIA
PHOTOGRAPHER
b Havana, Cuba, May 19, 60. *Study:* Philadelphia Col Art, Pa, BFA, 82; Sch Art Inst Chicago, Ill, MFA, 84. *Work:* Int Ctr Photog, New York; Bibliotheque Nationale, Paris, France; Mus Latin Am Art Orgn Am States, Washington, DC; Los Angeles County Mus Art, Calif; Ctr Creative Photog, Tucson, Ariz; Chrysler Mus, Norfolk, Va. *Exhib:* Philadelphia Col Art, Pa, 82; World Congress Assoc UNESCO, Mayor's Palace, Sendai, Japan, 84; Grupo 12, Pan Am Festival, Olive Park, Chicago, Ill, 86; Art in Embassies Prog, Am Embassy, Madrid, Spain, 89; solo exhibs, Sol Mednick Gallery, Philadelphia, Pa, 89, Ctr Creative Photog, Tucson, Ariz, 91 & Visual Studios Workshop, Rochester, NY, 92; Fragmented Evidence, Chrysler Mus, Norfolk, Va, 92. *Awards:* Grant, Photog Fel, Nat Endowment Arts, 88-89; Cintas Fel, Cintas Found, New York, 88-89; artist-in-residence, Light Works, Syracuse, NY, 90. *Dealer:* Katherine Edelman Gallery 300 W Superior Chicago IL 60610. *Mailing Add:* PO Box 145004 Miami FL 33114

MARTINO, BABETTE
PAINTER
b Philadelphia, Pa. *Study:* L'Accademia di Belle Arti, Florence, Italy, dipl, 68; Temple Univ, Philadelphia, BA, 72; Inst Allende, Mex, MFA, 75. *Work:* Camden Co Cult & Heritage Comn, NJ; Municipal Ctr, Lawton, Okla; Mohawk Valley Community Col, Utica; Subaru of Am, NJ; Blue Cross & Blue Shield, Philadelphia, Pa; Owensboro Nat Bank, Ky; New Music West, Calif. *Exhib:* Nat Acad Design, New York; Allied Artists, New York; Butler Inst Am Art, Ohio; Suzanne Gross Gallery, Philadelphia, Pa, 85; The Martino Family: A Legacy of Excellence in Painting, Shippensburg Univ, Pa, 88; Douglass Col Rutgers Univ, New Brunswick, NJ, 90; one-woman shows, Cudahy's Gallery, New York, 90. *Teaching:* Instr painting & drawing, Munson-Williams-Proctor Inst, Utica, 78-80; instr drawing, Mohawk Valley Community Col, Utica, 78-81. *Awards:* Pa Coun on the Arts, Fel Grant; Nat Endowment Arts Fel Grant, 85; Recipient of over 45 award & honors, including: Grumbacher Gold Medal, Alled Artists Am, New York, 89; 60th Anniversary Award, Phillips Mill Art Asn, Pa, 89; Hitchcock in Sunlight Prize, Nat Acad Design, New York, 90. *Mailing Add:* 1435 Manor Ln Blue Bell PA 19422

MARTINO, EVA E
PAINTER, SCULPTOR
b Philadelphia, Pa. *Study:* Gwynedd Mercy Col; Pa Acad Fine Arts; also with Giovanni Martino, La France Art Inst; hon degree, Diploma di Maestro d'Arte, Centro Artistico e Cultrale Int Napoli, Italia, 84. *Exhib:* Pa Acad Fine Arts; Nat Acad Design, New York, 65; William Penn Mem Mus, Pa; Butler Inst Am Art, Ohio; Indiana Univ, Pa; The Martino Family, A Legacy of Excellence in Painting, Shippensburg Univ, Pa, 88. *Awards:* First Place Award, Washington & Jefferson Col, Washington, Pa,91; Equitable Life Assurance Soc Award, Milford Fine Arts Coun, Conn, 91; Renee McNeely Award, Phillips Mill Art Asn, Pa, 91; Renee McNeely Award, Phillips Mill Art Asn, Pa, 91. *Mem:* Nat Forum Prof Artists; Artists Equity Asn. *Media:* Oil; Wood. *Mailing Add:* 1435 Manor Lane Blue Bell PA 19422

MARTINO, GIOVANNI
PAINTER
b Philadelphia, Pa, May 1, 08. *Study:* Spring Garden Inst, Pa; La France Inst, Pa; Philadelphia Graphic Sketch Club. *Work:* Nat Acad Design, New York; Pa Acad Fine Arts, Philadelphia; Va Mus Fine Art; Springfield Art Mus, Mo; Butler Art Inst, Youngstown, Ohio. *Exhib:* Royal Acad Eng; Carnegie Inst Int, Pa; Whitney Mus Am Art, New York; San Francisco Int Expos; Nat Acad Design. *Teaching:* Instr painting, Lehigh Univ, 57-58. *Awards:* Hallmark Award, 72, Benjamin Altman Prize, 75 & Grumbacher Gold Medal, 87, Nat Acad Design, 87; Ward Purchase Award, Mid Am Biennial, Owensboro Mus, Ky, 86; Purchase Award, Pa Mus, Harrisburg, 87. *Mem:* Nat Acad Design; Am Watercolor Soc. *Media:* Oil, Watercolor. *Mailing Add:* 1435 Manor Lane Blue Bell PA 19422

MARTINO, NINA F
PAINTER
b Philadelphia, Pa. *Study:* Univ Florence, Italy, dipl, 68; Temple Univ, BA 72; Univ Guanajuato, Mex, 75. *Work:* Mex-NAm Inst, Mexico City; Utica Col, NY; Montgomery Col, Pa. *Comn:* Seascape (oil), Mercantil de Irapuato, Mex, 80; landscape (oil), Mercantil de Irapuato, Mex, 80. *Exhib:* Woodmere Mus, Pa; Audubon Artists, 79; Butler Inst Am Art, 79; Martino Family: A Legacy of Excellence in Painting, Mus Civic Center, Philadelphia, 80. *Teaching:* Grad instr, painting & drawing, Inst Allende, Mex, 77-80. *Awards:* Hon Mention, Phillips Mill, 84; Antonio Cirino Mem Award, Audubon Artists, 88. *Media:* Oil, Watercolor. *Mailing Add:* 1435 Manor Lane Blue Bell PA 19422

MARTINSEN, IVAR RICHARD
PAINTER, EDUCATOR
b Butte, Mont, Dec 9, 22. *Study:* Mont State Col; Univ Ore; Univ Wyo. *Exhib:* Wyo Artists Traveling Exhib, Sheridan & Laramie, Wyo; Scottsbluff, Nebr; Sheridan Inn Gallery, 75-76, 78 & 79. *Teaching:* Prof art & chmn humanities div, Sheridan Col, formerly; retired. *Awards:* Prizes, Wyo-Nebr Exhib, 58 & 59 & Wyo State Fair, 60. *Mem:* Sheridan Artist Guild; Wyo State Art Asn. *Mailing Add:* 1422 Big Horn Ave Sheridan WY 82801

MARTON, PIER
VIDEO ARTIST, EDUCATOR
b Dec 1, 50; US citizen. *Study:* Univ Calif, Los Angeles, MFA(film, video), 79; also in Paris. *Work:* Inst Contemp Arts, London, Eng; Otis Inst, Parsons Sch Design, Los Angeles; Long Beach Mus Art, Calif; Japan Victo Corp, Tokyo; Seattle Arts Comn, Wash; Mus Mod Art, New York; Beaubourg, Paris. *Exhib:* Biennale de Paris, Mus Art Mod, Paris, France, 80; Mus Mod Art, New York, 85, 86 & 91; Jewish Mus New York, 88; The Endangered Documentary & Other Species Festival at Global Village, New York, 88; Video & Language, Am Mus Moving Image, New York, 89; The Eye and the I, Whitney Mus Am Art, New York, 89; Passage de l'Image, Beaubourg, Ctr George Pompidou, Paris, 89; Video Installations, Spertus Mus, Chicago, 90

& The Art Barn, Utah Arts Coun, Salt Lake City, 91; and others. *Pos:* Dir, Found Art Resources, 81-83. *Teaching:* Asst prof film, video & photog, Occidental Col, 78-79 & 82-83; vis lectr video, Univ Calif, Los Angeles, 80-83 & Art Inst Chicago, 84; vis artist, Minneapolis Col Art & Design, 84-85; asst prof, Sch Art Inst Chicago, 85-90, chmn video area, 86-87. *Awards:* Northwest Area Found Grant, 85; Media Arts Grant, 86 & Regional Fel Award, 87, Nat Endowment Arts; Ill Arts Coun, 87 & 90; Mem Found Jewish Cult Grant Award, 89. *Bibliog:* Maria Froelke Coburn (auth), Boy talk, Chicago Reader, 12/86; Linda Frye (auth), Like men, L A Weekly, 12/86; John Russell (auth), Views of Jewish identity, emotion and healing in museum video show, New York Times, 7/29/88. *Mem:* Found Art Resources (bd dirs, 81-82). *Publ:* Auth, Ephemera No 3, U Carrion, Amsterdam, 79; Cahiers du cinema No 5, Cahiers, Paris, 81; Dreamwork No 4, Human Sci Press, 81. *Dealer:* Mus Mod Art New York NY; Electronic Arts Intermix New York NY. *Mailing Add:* 225 N Crescent Dr No 203 Beverly Hills CA 90210

MARTON, TUTZI
PAINTER, SCULPTOR
b Bucharest, Rumania, Oct 13, 36; US citizen. *Study:* Acad Journalism, Budapest, grad, 71, woodblock printing, Zhejiang Acad Fine Arts, Hangzhou, China, grad, 88. *Work:* Nat Arch, Washington, DC; Mus Art State Fla; Mus de Petit Format, Couvin, Belgique; Vatican, Rome; Mus Music & Ethnology, Haifa, Israel. *Exhib:* one-person show, Kar Gallery Fine Art, Toronto, 78; Ann Show, Mus Art, Long Beach, NY, 79 & 81; Mus Petit Format de Papier, Exposition Internationale, Couvin, Belgique, 87; 6th Ann Int Exhib Miniature Art, Toronto, Can, 91. *Pos:* Critic, 69-71. *Awards:* First Prize, Ann Show, Mus Art, Long Beach, 81; Ioan & Maria Constantinescu Grant, Fondatia Cult Neth, 81; Passatore Award of Romans, Italy, 82. *Bibliog:* Pictures on Exhibit, Pictures Publ Co, 80; Elio Bartozzi (auth), Synopsis Gallarte, Italy, 82. *Mem:* Int Asn Art, UNESCO, Paris; Artists Equity Asn; For Press Asn, NY, 81. *Media:* Mixed Media, Oil; Precious Metal. *Dealer:* Philip S Gutride 63 Avenue A Apt 16/G New York NY 10009. *Mailing Add:* 319 W 74th St New York NY 10023

MARTONE, MICHAEL
PHOTOGRAPHER
b New York, NY, Nov 8, 41. *Study:* Self-taught. *Work:* Mus Mod Art, New York; Fogg Mus, Harvard Univ; High Mus Art, Atlanta; Musee De L'Eyysee Lausanne, Switz, 90. *Comn:* AIR Light Work, Syracuse Univ, NY, 78. *Exhib:* Die Welt Ausstellung der Photographie, Akad der Kunste, Berlin, 64; New Acquisitions, Mus Mod Art, New York, 70; Multiple Image Show, Mass Inst Technol, Cambridge, 72; New Acquisitions, Fogg Mus, Harvard Univ; solo exhibs, Hirshhorn Mus, Washington, DC, 79, photographs, Print Dept, Fogg Mus, Harvard Univ, 87 & Robert Menschel Gallery, Syracuse Univ, NY, 89; Fifth Vienna Biennale Contemp Photog, Austria, 81. *Teaching:* Instr & artist in residence, Photo Dept, Tisch Sch Arts, New York Univ, 86. *Awards:* Purchase Awards, Art Festival Atlanta, 66 & 67; Photog Fel Grant, Nat Endowment Arts, 75; AIR Exhibitor & Lectr Grant for Light Work, Syracuse Univ, 78. *Bibliog:* A D Coleman (auth), Latent image, Village Voice, New York, 4/71 & article, New York Times, 3/74; Fred McDarrah (auth), Martone Show, Village Voice Rev, 85. *Publ:* Auth, Dark Light, Lustrum Press, 74; contribr, Creative Camera Mag, 74; The Grotesque in Photography, Summit Press, 78; Light Readings, Oxford Univ Press, 79; Altered photographs, Art News Mag, 81. *Mailing Add:* 342 E 15th St New York NY 10003

MARTONE, WILLIAM ROBERT
PAINTER, INSTRUCTOR
b Wilmington, Del, Nov 30, 45. *Study:* Pa Acad Fine Arts, Cressen Traveling Scholar, certif, 68; Univ Pa, BFA, 69, MFA, 91; pvt study with Morris Blackburn, 65-73, Walter Stuempfig, 66-68, Franklin C Watkins, 69-72 & Julian Levi, 77-80. *Work:* Ronald Reagan Mus, Santa Barbara, Calif; US State Dept, Gen Serv Admin; White House, Washington, DC; Vatican Art Gallery, Vatican City; also many pvt collections. *Comn:* Portrait of Fredrick Joseph Kinsman, Third Episcopal Bishop, comn by Mr & Mrs Charles Proctor, Warren, Ohio, 72; San J Caleb Boggs, comn by Sen & Mrs J Caleb Boggs, Wilmington, 73; Joe Frazier (portrait), comn by Cloverlay, Philadelphia, 74; Joe Frazier & Family, 81; Portraiture & landscape, Poet Prodns, Disney Studios/Touchstone Pictures; M Lavoisier, Lavoisier Libr, DuPont Co; Dean A J Santoro, Widener Law Sch. *Exhib:* Ann Exhib, Nat Acad Design, New York, 67 & 75; Pa Acad Fine Arts, 75 & 79; Cottage Tour, Rehoboth Art League, Del, 75; solo exhibs, Grand Opera House, Wilmington, Del, 77 & Hardcastles, Wilmington, Del, 79; Rockwood Mus, Wilmington, Del, 81; Univ Delrs; Philadelphia Art Alliance; Philadelphia Mus Art; Butler Inst Am Art, Youngstown, Ohio. *Pos:* Account exec, Southam Assocs, 87-88 & Kimble & Melody Advertising & Media Features, 89-90; William Martone & Assocs, 90. *Teaching:* Instr, Howard Pyle Studios, Wilmington, Del, 69-85; instr portraiture, Pa Acad Fine Arts, 73-81; instr art & chmn upper sch dept, Wilmington Friends Sch, 74-77; instr adv/graphic design & typography, Art Inst Philadelphia, 86; instr vis arts & literacy & dir pre-intensive prog, Arts & Educ Intensive/Urban Educ Found, 90-91. *Awards:* First Prize, Philadelphia Watercolor Club, 72; First Prize, Chestertown Arts League, Wash Col, 77, 79 & 85; First Prize Oils, Soc NJ Artists, 79; and others. *Mem:* Del Archaeol Soc; Fel Pa Acad Fine Arts; Philadelphia Watercolor Club (bd dirs, 72); Int Soc Artists; assoc Am Inst Conserv, Washington, DC. *Media:* Oil, Watercolor. *Mailing Add:* c/o Gallery Thirty-One PO Box 4578 Greenville DE 19807-4578

MARTYL (MARTYL SCHWEIG LANGSDORF)
PAINTER, MURALIST
b St Louis, Mo, Mar 16, 18. *Study:* Washington Univ, AB; Colorado Springs Fine Arts Ctr, with Arnold Blanch & Boardman Robinson. *Work:* Whitney Mus Am Art, New York; Art Inst Chicago; Colorado Springs Fine Arts Ctr; Los Angeles Co Mus; St Louis Art Mus; Hirshhorn Mus & Sculpture Garden, Fermilab, Washington, DC. *Comn:* Recorder of Deeds (mural), comn by Sect Fine Arts, Washington, DC, 43; Darkness into Light (mural), Unitarian Church, Evanston, Ill, 62; 22 projections for Pierrot Lunaire, Fine Arts Quartet, Ill, 62; portraits, James Franck, Chandrasekar, Harry Kalven, Univ Chicago. *Exhib:* American Drawing Biennial XXIV, Norfolk Mus Arts, 71; one-person shows, Art Inst Chicago, 76, Fairweather-Hardin Gallery, 77, 81, 83 & 88, Ill State Mus, 78, Lake Forest Col, 79 & Brooklyn Mus, 86; Oriental Inst Mus, Chicago, Ill, 87; Gibbes Mus, Charleston, SC, 88; Ill State Mus Art Gallery, Chicago, 90; Tokyo Expo, 90; and others. *Pos:* Art ed, Atomic Sci Bulletin, 45-72; exec comt, Artists Equity Asn Chicago, 58-69; bd dir, Arts Club & Oxbow; adv bd, Ragdale Found. *Teaching:* Instr painting, Univ Chicago, 65-70; artist in residence, Tamarind Inst, Univ NMex, 74. *Awards:* Logan Award & Medal, 50 & William Bartels Award, 57, Art Inst Chicago; Am Inst Archit Honor Award, 62. *Bibliog:* George McCue (auth), Martyl, St Louis Dispatch, 69; interview (film), WTTW Pub TV, 79; Michael Bonesteel, article, New Art Examiner, 83. *Mem:* Arts Club Chicago; Renaissance Soc (pres, 70-71); Quadrangle Club, Univ Chicago; Oxbow Sch Art. *Media:* Acrylic; Ink. *Publ:* Contribr, Methods and Techniques of Gouache Painting, 46; auth, Cliches, old and new, St Louis Post-Dispatch, 67; New Art Examiner--Fred Sweet, 68. *Dealer:* Thea Burger Assoc 223 E State St Geneva IL 60134. *Mailing Add:* Box 228 645 S Meacham Rd Schaumburg IL 60193

MARTZ, KARL
CERAMIST, EDUCATOR
b Columbus, Ohio, June 24, 12. *Study:* Ind Univ, AB, 33; Ohio State Univ, 33-34 & 39, grad study in ceramic art; sabbaticals in Kyoto, 62, & Mashiko, 71, Japan. *Work:* Nat Collection Art, Smithsonian Inst, Washington, DC; Mus Mod Art, Tokyo; Am Craft Coun Mus, New York; Mus Dec Arts, Lisbon, Portugal; Walker Art Ctr, Minneapolis. *Exhib:* 20th Int Ceramic Exhib, Syracuse Mus & Metrop Mus, New York, 59; Cult Exchange Exhib, Smithsonian Inst & many European museums, 60; Ninth Int Exhib Ceramic Art, Smithsonian Inst, Washington, DC, 63; Int Ceramic Exhib, Mus Mod Art, Tokyo, 64; Twenty Five Years of Art in Clay, USA, Scripps Col, Claremont, Calif, 69. *Teaching:* Prof ceramic art, Ind Univ, Bloomington, 45-77, emer prof, 77-; Bingham prof humanities, Allen R Hite Art Inst, Univ Louisville, 75. *Awards:* First Prize, Ind Biennial Ceramic Exhib, Herron Mus, Indianapolis, 53, 55 & 57; Third Prize, Miami Nat Ceramic Exhib, Fla, 56; Award of Merit, Nat Fiber-Clay-Metal Exhib, St Paul Gallery Fine Arts, Minn, 57. *Bibliog:* Karl Martz retrospective, Ceramics Monthly, 5/77; Paul S Donhauser (auth), Photographs of work, History of American Ceramics, The Studio Potter, Kendall/Hunt Publ Co, 78; Richard Zakin (auth), Electric Kiln Ceramics, Chilton, 81. *Mem:* Nat Coun Educ for Ceramic Arts (pres, 65-66); Am Craft Coun. *Media:* Porcelain, Stoneware. *Dealer:* The Gallery 109 E 6th St Bloomington IN 47401. *Mailing Add:* 105 N Overhill Dr Bloomington IN 47408

MARUYAMA, WENDY
DESIGNER
b La Junta, Colo, July 11, 52. *Study:* San Diego State Univ, Calif, BA, 75; Va Commonwealth Univ, 76; Penland Sch Crafts, 76; Boston Univ, Mass, 76-78; Haystack Mountain Sch Crafts, 78; Rochester Inst Technol, NY MFA, 80. *Work:* Oakland Mus Art, Calif; Univ Art Mus, Univ Ariz, Tempe. *Comn:* Linda Cohn, Phoenix, Ariz; Michael & Nina Zagaris, Modesto, Calif; Marion Lee, Portola Valley, Calif; Alice Zimmerman, Nashville, Tenn; Ronald & Anne Abramson, Washington, DC; Don Thomas & Jorge Cao, New York. *Exhib:* Solo exhibs, Snyderman Gallery, Philadelphia, Pa, 88-90, New Art Forms Expo, Joanne Raap Gallery, Chicago, 90, The Ingrained Image, Riverside Art Mus, Calif, 90, Signs of Support, John Michael Kohler Arts Ctr, Sheboygan, Wis, 90, Artists Design Furniture, Eve Mannes Gallery, Atlanta, 90, Gallery NAGA, Boston, Mass, 91 & Peter Joseph Gallery, New York, 92; Tradition & Innovation in Furniture Design, traveling exhib 89-91, Boston Mus Fine Arts, 89; Furniture Design: Three From San Francisco, Three From Boston, Gallery NAGA, Boston, 89; Functional Sculpture: Six Furniture Makers, Rena Bransten Gallery, San Francisco, 89; San Diego State Univ Alumni Exhib, Calif, 89; Signs of Support, John Michael Kohler Arts Ctr, Sheboygan, Wis, 90; The Ingrained Image, Riverside Art Mus, Calif, 90; Explorations II, Am Craft Mus, New York, 91. *Pos:* Designer & maker contemp furniture, Comns & Speculative Work, 79- *Teaching:* Instr metalworking & jewelry design, Crafts Ctr, San Diego State Univ, Calif, 73-75 & grad asst metalworking prog, 75; head, woodworking & furniture design prog, Appalachian Ctr Crafts, Tenn Technol Univ, Smithville, 80-85 & Calif Col Arts & Crafts, Oakland, 85-89; artist-in-residencies, Artpark, Lewiston, NY, 83, Carnegie-Mellon Univ, Pittsburgh, Pa, 84, Boston Univ, Mass, 84 & Ind State Univ, Evansville, 84 & San Diego State Univ, 89- *Awards:* Artists Fels, Nat Endowment Arts, 82, 84, 86, 90 & 92 & Tenn Arts Comn, 83; Leland & Carol Nance Award of Merit, 88; Metropolitan Home/Kraus Sikes Merit Award,89. *Media:* Furniture Design, Wood. *Publ:* Wendy's place, San Diego Union, 8/27/89; Crackerjack creations, Newsweek, 1/29/90; Art rev, Atlanta J & Constitution, 2/12/90; Back to the Past, Southern Accents Mag, 5/90; Contemporary Crafts for the Home, Kraus Sikes Inc, 90. *Dealer:* Peter Joseph Gallery 745 Fifth Ave New York NY 10151. *Mailing Add:* 4565 Alice St San Diego CA 92115

MARX, EVELYN
COLLAGE ARTIST, PAINTER
b Pine Bluff, Ark. *Study:* Wash Univ Sch Fine Arts; Brooklyn Acad; Univ Cincinnati; Cincinnati Art Acad. *Work:* Cincinnati Art Mus; Royal Mus, Copenhagen; Mod Art Mus, Haifa, Israel; Va Mus Art; Rochester Mem Art Ctr. *Comn:* Fabric Collage, comn by Ned Grossman, Cleveland, 80-81, Mr & Mrs Peter Miller, Lexingotn, Mass, 81, Dr & Mrs Julian Galvin, 82, Mrs Joseph Roach, 83 & Fine Arts Soc, 83, Sarasota, Fla. *Exhib:* Cincinnati Art Mus; Dayton Art Mus; Toledo Art Mus; Boston Printmakers; Libr Cong; New York Pub Libr; one-man show, Cinti Art Acad, 88. *Teaching:* Instr printmaking, Manatee Art League, Bradenton, Fla, 65-68 & Colson Sch Art, Sarasota, Fla, 68; instr art, Longboat Art Ctr, Longboat Key, Fla, 69-84. *Bibliog:* Diana Colson (dir), Fabricollage (film), Colson & Swain, 76; Meilach (auth), Soft Sculpture, Crown Publ; Cris Hassold (auth), New College; John A Michael, Handbook for Art Instr. *Media:* Fabricollage; Ink-Painting. *Dealer:* Voorhees Gallery 1315 Main St Sarasota FL 33577. *Mailing Add:* 5311 Evergreen Ridge Dr Cincinnati OH 45215

MARX, ROBERT ERNST
PAINTER
b Northeim, Ger, 1925. *Study:* Univ Ill, BFA, 51, MFA, 53; study & travel in Ger, Austria, Italy, Switz & France, 1 yr. *Work:* Mus Mod Art, New York; Philadelphia Mus Art; Dallas Mus Art, Tex; Seattle Art Mus; Hirschhorn Mus, Washington, DC; and many others. *Exhib:* Franz Bader Show, Baway Found, Vienna, Austria, 76; Art of Poetry, Nat Collection Fine Arts, Smithsonian Inst, 76; Premio Int Biella, l'Incisione, Italy, 76; Davidson Galleries, Seattle, Wash; US Embassy Gallery, Belgrade, Yugoslavia, 83; Davidson Gallery, Seattle, Wash, 87; Int Biennial Exhib Portrait Drawing, Tuzla, Yugoslavia; Int Exhib Graphic Art, Kustveilein, Zufrechen, WGer; Int Biennial Exhib Graphic Art, Ljubljana, Yugoslavia. *Pos:* Artist attached to USIA exhib in Prague & Bratislava, Czech, 65; dir, Flint Inst Art, 57; dir, Impressions Workshop, Boston, 69. *Teaching:* Instr, Univ Wis, 53; chmn dept art, Flint Jr Col, 56; instr, Sch Art, Syracuse Univ, 58; assoc prof art, State Univ NY Binghamton, 66-69; assoc prof, State Univ NY Col Brockport, 70-72, prof, 72-; lectr wkshp, Art Dept, Drake Univ, Des Moines, Iowa, 85; distinguished prof, State Univ NY, Brockport, 89, retired, 90- *Awards:* Grand Diploma Drawing, Third Int Biennial Exhib Portrait Drawings & Graphics, Tuzla, Yugoslavia, 84. *Bibliog:* Serby Jacobson (auth), article, Times-Union, 11/22/85. *Media:* Oil on Canvas. *Dealer:* Davidson Gallery 313 Occidental Ave S Seattle, WA 98104; Oxford Gallery 267 Oxford St Rochester NY 14607. *Mailing Add:* 80 Nunda Blvd Rochester NY 14610

MARZANO, ALBERT
PAINTER, DESIGNER
b Philadelphia, Pa, Aug 22, 19. *Study:* Philadelphia Graphic Sketch Club; Philadelphia Plastic Club. *Comn:* Murals, Dept Pub Health, Philadelphia, 67 & 69; portrait Riccardo Muti, Friends & Admirers Maestro Riccardo Muti, Philadelphia, 78; portrait Louis A DeSimone, Grand Lodge Pa, Order Sons Italy, Philadelphia, 81; portrait John Cardinal Krol, Archbishop Philadelphia, Grand Lodge Pa, Order Sons Italy, 84; portrait Rabbi Joshu Toledano, Congregation Mikveh Israel, 85. *Exhib:* Ann Mid-Year Show, Butler Inst Am Art, Youngstown, Ohio, 60; one-man shows, St Joseph's Col, Philadelphia, 70, La Salle Col, Philadelphia, 71, Philadelphia Sketch Club, 74, Waldron Acad, 75 & Episcopal Acad, 77; plus others. *Pos:* Designer & consult, Philadelphia Asn Blind, 53-56; art dir & consult, J Cunningham Cox Agency, Bala-Cynwyd, Pa, 58; art consult & graphic designer, Philadelphia Pub Health Dept, 58-60; art dir & consult, Benn Assocs, Philadelphia, 60. *Teaching:* Instr drawing & painting, Sons Italy in Am, Philadelphia, 65-70. *Awards:* Gold Medals, Philadelphia Art Dirs Club, 54, 55 & 56; Gold Medal, Haddonfield Art Ctr, NJ, 59; Gold Medal, Nat Soc Painters in Casein, 61. *Mem:* Watercolor Club Philadelphia; Philadelphia Art Alliance. *Media:* Mixed. *Mailing Add:* 1949 Locust St Philadelphia PA 19103-5730

MARZIO, PETER CORT
HISTORIAN, MUSEUM DIRECTOR
b New York, NY, May 8, 43. *Study:* Juniata Col, BA, 65; Univ Chicago, MA, 66 & PhD, 69. *Pos:* Historian, Smithsonian Inst, 70-72, cur of prints, 73-78; dir, Corcoran Gallery & Sch Art, 78-82 & Mus Fine Arts, Houston, 82- *Awards:* Smithsonian Fel, 68-69; Woodrow Wilson Sr Fel, Italy, 73. *Res:* Relationship of political democracy and fine art in America. *Publ:* Auth, Men and Machines of American Journalism, 73 & The Art Crusade, 76, Smithsonian Press; Rube Goldberg: His Life and Work, 75 & A Nation of Nations, 76, Harper & Rowe; The Democratic Art, David Godine, 79. *Mailing Add:* Mus Fine Arts 1001 Bissonnet PO Box 6826 Houston TX 77265

MARZOLLO, CLAUDIO
SCULPTOR
b Milan, Italy, July 13, 38; US citizen. *Study:* Columbia Col, BA. *Work:* Windsor Art Gallery, Ont; Neiman-Marcus Exec Off, Dallas, Tex; Mus Sci & Indust, Chicago; Ft Wayne Mus Art, Ind. *Comn:* Kinetic piece, ARCO Hq, Philadelphia, 74. *Exhib:* Loan Exhib, Everson Mus, Syracuse, NY, 72; one-man shows, Tafts Mus, Cincinnati, Ohio, 74, traveling exhib, Nat Acad Sci, Washington, DC, 77; Illum, Whitney Mus Am Art, New York, 74; New Acquisitions, Windsor Gallery Art, Ont, 75; The Logic & Nature of Color, Akron Art Inst, Ohio, 75; Hudson River Mus, Yonkers, NY, 76; one-man show, Virginia Beach Arts Ctr, 79. *Teaching:* Instr three-dimensional design, Sch Visual Arts, New York, 74 & Univ Bridgeport, Conn, 75-77; Mather vis scholar, Case Western Reserve Univ, Cleveland, 75; vis artist, US Military Acad, West Point, 78- *Bibliog:* Joseph Horning (dir), Metamorphoses (film), Ohio Arts Comn, 75. *Media:* Plexiglas, Aluminum. *Mailing Add:* 437 Lane Gate Rd Cold Spring NY 10516

MASBACK, DENNIS
PAINTER
Study: Wash Univ, St Louis, BFA, 71, MFA, 73. *Work:* Champion Paper Co; Fidelity Investments; Amerada Hess Co; Chemical Bank; Am Telephone & Telegraph Co. *Exhib:* Solo shows, Mark Twain Gallery, St Louis, 73, Martin Schweig Gallery, St Louis, 74, A M Sachs Gallery, New York, 76, 77 & 79, Leslie Cecil Gallery, New York, 86 & 89 & 808 Penn Modern, Pittsburgh, Pa, 92; Genovese Gallery, Boston, Mass, 91; Champion Paper Co, Stamford, Conn, 91; Victoria Munroe Gallery, New York, 91. *Awards:* Nat Endowment Art Painting Fel, 91-92. *Bibliog:* Lawrence R Levine & Janice C Oresman (auths), The Great Outdoors (exhib catalog), Chemical Gallery, Chemical Bank, 87; Ann Fitzgibbons (auth), Portraits: Here's Looking at You (exhib catalog), Anchorage Mus Hist & Art, 88; Ruth Bass (auth), rev, Art News, 4/90. *Mailing Add:* Six Varick St New York NY 10013

MASHECK, JOSEPH DANIEL CAHILL
HISTORIAN, CRITIC
b New York, NY, Jan 19, 42. *Study:* Columbia Univ, AB, 63, MA, 65, PhD, 75, study with Dorothea Nyberg, Meyer Schapiro & Rudolf Wittkower. *Collections Arranged:* Critical Perspectives, PS 1, Inst Art & Urban Resources, New York, 82; Smart Art, Carpenter Ctr Visual Arts, Harvard Univ, 85; Joseph Masheck Col Contemp Art, Rose Art Mus, Brandeis Univ, 86. *Pos:* Ed, Artforum Mag, 77-80; contrib ed, Art Am Mag, 88-; ed consult, New Observations. *Teaching:* Lectr, Maidstone (Kent) Col Art, Eng, 68-69, Harvard Univ, 83-86; preceptor art hist, Columbia Col, Columbia Univ, New York, 69-71; instr art hist, Barnard Col, 71-73, asst prof, 73-83; assoc prof, Hofstra Univ, 87- *Awards:* Art Critics' Fel, Nat Endowment Arts, 72-73, 75-76; Guggenheim Mem Found Fel, 77; Reva & David Logan Grant in Support of New Writing on Photography, Photog Resource Ctr Boston Univ, 85. *Mem:* Soc Fel Humanities Columbia Univ; Am Asn Univ Profs; Int Asn Art Critics. *Res:* Abstract painting and sculpture. *Publ:* Ed, Marcel Duchamp in Perspective & Essay, Prentice-Hall, 75; Historical Present: Essays of the Seventies, UMI Res Press, 84; Smart Art (Point, 1), Willis, Locker & Owens, 84; Abstract art since 1960, In: Walker Art Ctr: Painting and Sculpture from the Collection, Minneapolis, 90; Modernities: Art-Matters in the Present, Penn State Press, 92; and others. *Mailing Add:* 70 La Salle St (MA) New York NY 10027

MASON, ALDEN C
PAINTER, EDUCATOR
b Everett, Wash, July 14, 19. *Study:* Univ Wash, MFA. *Work:* Seattle Art Mus, Wash; San Francisco Mus Art; Denver Art Mus. *Comn:* Mural, 80 ft, Senate Chambers, State Capitol, Olympia, Wash, 81. *Exhib:* one-man shows, Portland Ctr for Visual Arts, Ore, 73, Denver Art Mus, 73 & Chas Cowles Gallery, New York, 81; Allan Stone Gallery, New York, 74 & 78; 14 Abstract Painters, Frederick Wight Art Galleries, Univ Calif, Los Angeles, 75; Univ Art Galleries, Univ NDak, Grand Forks, 78; and others. *Teaching:* Prof art, Univ Wash, 47-; retired. *Awards:* Purchase Award, 44th Northwest Ann, 63 & 54th Northwest Ann, 68, Seattle Art Mus. *Media:* Acrylic. *Dealer:* Greg Kucera Gallery 608 Second Ave Seattle WA 98104; Tortue Gallery Santa Monica CA. *Mailing Add:* c/o Greg Kucers Gallery 626 Second Ave Seattle WA 96104

MASON, FRANCIS SCARLETT, JR
ADMINISTRATOR
b Jacksonville, Fla, Sept 9, 21. *Study:* St John's Col, Annapolis, Md, BA, 43; grad study art hist with Nikolaus Pevsner; Birkbeck Col, Univ of London, 61-64. *Pos:* Cult attache & exhibs officer, US Info Agency Foreign Serv, 54-64; chief US exhibs to USSR & E Europe, US Info Agency, 65-67; pres experiments in art & technol, New York, 68; asst dir, Pierpont Morgan Libr, New York, 75-87, acting dir, 88, consult on endowment campaign, 88- *Mem:* New York Studio Sch Drawing & Sculpture (chmn, 71-74); Archit Asn, London; Gallery Asn New York (trustee, 77-). *Publ:* Ed, Steuben, Seventy Years of Glassmaking, Praeger, 74; co-auth, Balanchine's Complete Stories of the Great Ballets, Doubleday, 77; I Remember Balandrine, Doubleday, 90. *Mailing Add:* 46 Morton St New York NY 10014

MASON, FRANK HERBERT
PAINTER, INSTRUCTOR
b Cleveland, Ohio, Feb 20, 21. *Study:* Nat Acad Design, New York, with George Nelson, 36-37; Art Students League, with Frank Vincent DuMond, 37-51. *Work:* Eureka Col Mus, Ill; Butler Inst Am Art, Youngstown, Ohio; Am Embassy, London; Hall of Governors, State Capitol, Albany, NY; US War Dept, Washington, DC; Mus of the City New York, NY; Anticoli Mus, Anticoli Corrado, Italy; Westmoreland Co Mus Art, Greensburg, Pa. *Comn:* Life of St Anthony of Padua (eight large canvases), 11th Century Church of San Giovanni di Malta, Venice, Italy, 64; Resurrection, Old St Patrick's Cathedral, New York, 72; San Rocco, Church of Santa Vittoria, Anticoli Corrado, Italy; 3 murals, King Faisel Naval Acad, Jidda, Saudi Arabia, 81. *Exhib:* Expos Intercontinentale, Palais des Congres, Monaco, 68; Nat Arts Club, New York, 73; Mood Gallery, Milan, Italy, 75; John Pence Gallery, San Francisco, 77 & 79; Metrop Mus Art, New York, 79; Union League Club, 88. *Teaching:* Instr fine arts, Art Students League, New York, 50- *Awards:* Popular Prize, Assoc Artists Pittsburgh, Carnegie Inst Mus Art, 46; Figure Composition-St Anthony, Penn-National, Ligonier, 68; Prix d'Amerique du Nord, Expos Intercontinentale, Monaco, 68. *Bibliog:* Condon Riley (auth), Frank Mason, painter, Am Artist, 6/64; Alexander Eliot (auth), Frank Mason: Allegiance to the old masters, Am Artist, 12/73; David L Bell (auth), Frank Mason, Artists of the Rockies and the Golden West, fall 83. *Mem:* Art Students League; Nat Soc Mural Painters; Int Inst Conserv of Hist & Artistic Works; Academician Nat Acad Design. *Media:* Oil, Graphics. *Mailing Add:* 385 Broome St New York NY 10013

MASON, HAROLD
PRINTMAKER, PAINTER
b Springfield, Mo, Feb 1, 37. *Study:* Calif State Univ, Fresno; Art Ctr Sch Design, Pasadena, Calif, BFA. *Work:* Included in major corp collections throughout the US, including Chicago, Phoenix, Los Angeles & Seattle. *Exhib:* Gold Spike Centennial, Pac Railroad, Provost, Utah, 69; 29th Ann Soc Western Artist, de Young Mus, San Francisco, Calif, 71; Western Asn of Art Mus Traveling Exhib, 73; Watercolor Int, Dazell Hatfield Galleries, Los Angeles, 74; West Coast Watercolor Soc Exchange Exhib, Royal Watercolor Soc, London, 75. *Teaching:* Chmn art dept, Ursuline High Sch, Santa Rosa, Calif, 65-70; prof art, Santa Rosa Jr Col, 68-70. *Awards:* Best of Show, 29th Ann Soc Western Art, de Young Mus, 71; Best Watercolor, Atrium 72, Santa Rosa, 72. *Mem:* Carmel Art Asn; Fine Arts Evaluation Comt, Carmel, Calif. *Media:* Watercolor, Graphics. *Publ:* Coauth, Flight: Poems & Drawings, India House of Calif, 70; contribr, Transparent Watercolor: Ideas & Techniques, Davis Publ, 72. *Dealer:* Carmel Art Association Carmel CA 93921. *Mailing Add:* c/o Gallery Three 3819 N Third St Phoenix AZ 85012

MASON, JOHN
SCULPTOR
b Madrid, Nebr, Mar 30, 27. *Study:* Otis Art Inst, Los Angeles, 49-52; Chouinard Art Inst, Los Angeles, 53-54. *Work:* Art Inst Chicago; Los Angeles Co Mus Art; San Francisco Mus Art; Mus Contemp Crafts, New York; Nat Mus Mod Art, Kyoto, Japan; and others. *Comn:* Ceramic relief, Palm Springs Spa, Calif, 59; ceramic relief, Tishman Bldg, Los Angeles, 61; ceramic doors, Sterling Holloway, South Laguna, Calif; and others. *Exhib:* One-man shows, Pasadena Art Mus, Calif, 60 & 74; Whitney Mus Am Art, 64, 73 & 76; Retrospective, Los Angeles Co Mus Art, 66; Kompas 4, Van Addemuseum Eindhoven, Neth, 69; Nat Mus Mod Art, Kyoto, Japan, 71; and others. *Teaching:* Assoc prof art, Univ Calif, Irvine, 67-73, prof art & chmn dept studio art, 73-74; prof studio art, Hunter Col, New York, 74- *Awards:* Ford Found Award, 67th Am Exhib, Art Inst Chicago, 64; Univ Calif Award, Creative Arts Inst, 69-70; and others. *Bibliog:* John W Mills (auth), The Technique of Sculpture, Reinhold Corp, NY, 65; John Coplans (auth), John Mason--Sculpture, Los Angeles Co Mus Art, 66; Glenn C Nelson (auth), Ceramics, Holt, Rinehart & Winston, 71. *Media:* Ceramics. *Dealer:* Hansen-Fuller Gallery 228 Grant Ave San Francisco CA 94108. *Mailing Add:* 1521 S Central Ave Los Angeles CA 90021

MASON, MOLLY ANN
SCULPTOR, ENVIRONMENTAL ARTIST
Cedar Rapids, Iowa, 53. *Study:* Univ Iowa Sch Art, BFA, 73, MA, 75, MFA, 76. *Work:* Long Island Cult Ctr, Suffolk Cty, NY; City of Brisbane, Australia; Nat Sculpture Park of Hungary, Villany; Nat Sculpture Park of Yugoslavia, Kostanjevica; City of Albuquerque, NMex. *Comn:* 5 Sculptures, Spelce Collection, Austin, Tex, 84; Texaco Corp, New Orleans, La, 86; Warwick Hotel, Houston, Tex, 86; 5 Sculptures, Bright Collection Botanic Garden, New Orleans, La, 86-87; Elena Corp, New York, 91. *Exhib:* Louisiana World Expo Major Works, New Orleans, 84; Outdoor Sculpture, New Orleans Mus Art, 86-87; Forma Viva Int Sculpture Symposium, Nat Sculpture Park of Yugoslavia, Kostanjevica, 86; Villany Int Sculpture Symposium, Nat Sculpture Park of Hungary, Villany, 87; Nothing But Steel, Cold Spring Harbor Research Lab, NY, 87- 88; Int Outdoor Sculpture Exhib, Australian World Expo, Brisbane, 88; Art Space Niji & Studio Com Callery (Tachi Kichi), Koyoto, Japan, 92; Soho 20 Gallery, New York, 92. *Teaching:* Asst prof sculpture, Univ NMex, 79-82 & Tulane Univ, New Orleans, La, 82-85; State Univ NY, Stony Brook, NY, 85-92. *Awards:* Am Asn Univ Women Found Fel, 84; Fel, Lilly Found, 87-88; Fulbright Fel, Japan, 90-91. *Bibliog:* Virginia Watson-Jones (auth), Contemporary American Women Sculptors, Oryx Press, 85; Elizabeth Blair (auth), Scale, Spirit and Energy: Contemporary Sculpture thrives in Yugoslavia's Symposium, Int Sculpture Mag, 3-4/87; Jules Heller (auth), Twentieth Century North American Women Artists, Garland Press, 92. *Mem:* Col Art Asn; Int Sculpture Ctr. *Media:* Metal, Wood. *Dealer:* Soho 20 Gallery 469 Broome St New York NY 10013; Tilden-Foley Gallery 4119 Magazine St New Orleans LA 70115. *Mailing Add:* 111 Beach St Port Jefferson NY 11777

MASON, NOVEM M
SCULPTOR, DESIGNER
b North Wildwood, NJ, Nov 22, 42. *Study:* NC State Univ Sch Design, BA(archit), 68; ECarolina Univ Sch Art, MFA, 74. *Work:* Relief sculpture, ECarolina Univ. *Comn:* Sculptural screen, Southern Bank, Richmond, Va, 76; relief sculptures, Richmond Fredericksburg Petersburg Railroad, Richmond, Va, 77, Southern Univ, 80 & First Fed Savings & Loan, Lake Charles, La, 81; entrance sculpture, Mid-States Wood Preserving Inc, Simsboro, La, 82. *Exhib:* Anderson Gallery Summer Invitational, Richmond, Va, 76; Three Artists, Wyly Tower Gallery, Ruston, La, 81; Alumni Masonic Temple Studios, Anderson Gallery, Richmond, Va, 83; Canal Place/Art Place, Contemp Art Ctr, New Orleans, La, 86; Sculpture '86, Houston Mus Fine Arts, Houston, Tex, 86; The Red Clay Survey, Huntsville Mus Art, Ala, 88; Louisiana Artists, Louisiana Arts & Sci Ctr, Baton Rouge, 89; Art in Park, Lubbock, Tex, 90; Outstanding is Their Swamp, Sangle De Cristo Arts Ctr, Pueblo, Colo, 90. *Pos:* Partner, artist & designer, Design Collaborative Richmond, Va, 74-79; designer & artist, Woodsmith, Ruston, La, 79- *Teaching:* Asst prof art, Va Commonwealth Univ, Richmond, 68-79 & La Tech Univ, 79-; prof, La Tech Univ, Ruston, 79-90; prof, Univ NC, Greensboro, 90- *Awards:* Summer Res Grant, La Tech Univ, 88; Juror's Choice Award, Huntsville Mus Art, 88. *Mem:* Southern Asn Sculptors; Col Art Asn Am; Tex Sculpture Asn. *Media:* Wood; Mixed. *Mailing Add:* Dept Housing & Interior Design 239 Stone Bldg Unc-G Greensboro NC 27412-5001

MASSARO, KAREN THUESEN
CERAMIST, SCULPTOR
b Copenhagen, Denmark, Oct 23, 44; US citizen. *Study:* State Univ NY, Buffalo, BSEd, 66; Univ Mass, Amherst, 67-68; Univ Wis, Maidson, with Don Reitz, MFA, 72. *Work:* Nat Gallery Art, Washington, DC; Northern Ariz Univ, Flagstaff; Milwaukee Art Mus; Ariz State Univ, Tempe; Univ Wis, Madison; Decorative Arts Mus, Little Rock, Ark. *Exhib:* One-man shows, Kresge Art Gallery, Univ Mich, E Lansing, 79, Rochester Art Ctr, Minn, 80 & Synopsis Gallery, Winnetka, Ill, 80; American Porcelain, Renwick Gallery, Smithsonian Inst, Washington, DC, 81; Scripps Col 40th Ann Exhib, 84; Rocklands Gallery, Monterey, Calif, 84; Porcelain Today, Wita Gardiner Gallery, San Diego, Calif, 87; Massaro & Kuentzel, Viewpoint Gallery, Carmel, Calif, 89; Clay Ariz Art XV Int Conf Exhib, Northern Ariz Univ, Flagstaff; Art That Works: The Decorative Arts of the Eighties, Crafted in Am, Traveling, 15 US Mus, 90-93. *Pos:* Vis artist, Kohler Artist Ed, Kohler Co, Wis, 84- *Teaching:* Vis fac mem fine art & art hist, Beloit Col, Wis, 72-77; vis artist ceramic arts, Ohio State Univ, 77; vis fac mem, Scripps Col, Claremont, Calif, 80. *Awards:* Purchase Prize, 51st Exhib Wis Crafts, Milwaukee Art Ctr, 72; Best in Ceramics & Outstanding Wis Craftsman, Beaux-Arts Designer-Craftsman 72 & Columbus Mus Fine Arts, 72; Honorable Mention & Patron Purchase, Wichita Nat All Media Crafts Exhib, 88. *Bibliog:* Articles, Ceramic Mo, 6/87 & 4/88; articles, Am Craft, 4/82 & 12/87. *Mem:* Nat Coun Educ Ceramic Arts (exhib chmn, 78-80). *Media:* Porcelain & Low-Fire Clay. *Dealer:* Perimeter Gallery Chicago IL. *Mailing Add:* c/o Winfield Gallery 224 Crossroads Blvd Carmel CA 93923

MASSEY, ANN JAMES
GRAPHIC ARTIST, PAINTER
b Evanston, Ill, Nov 9, 51. *Study:* Univ Texas, El Paso, 70-71; Paris Am Acad, 78; Schuler Sch Fine Art, 90. *Work:* El Paso Mus Art. *Comn:* Two Portraits, comn by Peter DeWetter (former Mayor), El Paso, 90; Portraits of Student of the Week, El Paso Electric Co, 82. *Exhib:* 10th Ann September Competition, Alexandria Mus Art, La, 91; Sierra Medical Center's Ann EPAA, El Paso Mus Art, 92; Women Reflect, four-woman exhib, Carlsbad Mus & Art Ctr, NMex, 92; International Nexus 92, Trammel Crow Art Ctr, Dallas, 92; American Drawing Biennial III, Muscarelle Mus Art, Williamsburg, Va 92. *Pos:* Owner, The Montwood Gallery, El Paso, Tex, 74-78 & Massey Fine Arts, Santa Teresa, NMex, 92- *Teaching:* Pvt drawing, instr, El Paso, 75- *Awards:* Nat Arts Club Award for Graphics, Allied Artists Am 77th Ann Exhib, Nat Arts Club, 90; Silver Medal Honor in Graphics & Drawings, 40th Ann Nat Open Exhib, Knickerbocker Artists, New York, 90; Best of Show, $6500 Purchase Prize, Ann EPAA Exhib, Sierra Med Ctr & El Paso Mus Art Asn, 91. *Bibliog:* Myrna Zanetell (auth), Art columns, Westside Today, 5/30/91 & 7/4/91; Cama Duke (auth), Ann James Massey, Person of the Week, Rio Grande Gazette, 1/14/92. *Mem:* Knickerbocker Artists, New York; Am Artists Prof League; Coppini Acad Fine Arts; Women Artists West; Colored Pencil Soc Am. *Media:* Wax pencil, Oil. *Publ:* Contribr, Colored Pencil Soc Am 1992 Nat Membership Directory cover, 92; The Best of Colored Pencil, Rockport Publishing, 93. *Mailing Add:* Box 1258 Santa Teresa NM 88008

MASSEY, CHARLES WESLEY, JR
PRINTMAKER, EDUCATOR
b Lebanon, Tenn, Aug 21, 42. *Study:* Mid Tenn State Univ, BS, 64; Univ Ga, MFA(honors), 72. *Work:* Philadelphia Mus Art; Art Inst Chicago; Pushkin Mus, Moscow, USSR; Bradford City Art Gallery, Eng; Libr of Cong, Washington, DC. *Exhib:* Dulin Nat Print & Drawing Competition, 81, 82 & 86-89; Philadelphia Print Club Int Competition, 77-82 & 85; American Drawings III & IV, Smithsonian Traveling Exhib, 81-85; 1st & 2nd Int Print Exhibs, Seoul, Korea, 81-82, Taipei, Taiwan, 83-84 & 89-90 & Cortona, Italy, 79, 85, 89; Boston Printmakers Nat Print Exhib, 81-84 & 86; Colorprint USA invitational, 88; Nat Print Invitational, Univ Ala, 88; and 420 others since 1971. *Pos:* Univ prof art, Ohio State Univ, 74- & chairperson dept art, 82-88. *Teaching:* Instr art printmaking, Univ Ga, Athens, 72-74; prof printmaking, Ohio State Univ, 74- *Awards:* Ohio Arts Coun Fel Grant, 81 & 86; Purchase Awards, Philadelphia Print Club, 82 & 19th Oulin Nat, Knoxville, 87; Nat Endowment Arts Grant, 82; Nat Exhib Trenton, NJ, 88. *Bibliog:* Albert Christ-Janer (dir), Artist--Charles Massey, Jr, Printer (film), Univ Ga, 71. *Mem:* Philadelphia Print Club; Boston Printmakers; Nat Schs Art & Design; Col Art Asn; Columbus Art League (pres, 82-). *Media:* Lithography, Drawing. *Publ:* Illusr, The Complete Screenprint & Lithography, Macmillan & Free Press, 74; Sing with Understanding, Broadman Press, 80; J Higher Educ, OSU Press, 83. *Mailing Add:* 93 E Lincoln St Columbus OH 43215

MASSEY, ROBERT JOSEPH
PAINTER, EDUCATOR
b Ft Worth, Tex, May 14, 21. *Study:* Okla State Univ, with Doel Reed, BA, 47; Univ Havana, 47-48; Univ Mich, fall 48; Syracuse Univ, MFA, 52; Univ Tex, Austin, PhD, 62. *Work:* Dallas Mus Fine Art; Syracuse Univ; Soc Am Graphic Artists; El Paso Mus Art; Univ NMex; plus others. *Comn:* Enamel mosaic, State Nat Bank El Paso; applique hanging (with Sally Bishop), 69 & polyester-coated polyurethane sculpture, 69, Univ Tex, El Paso Union Bldg. *Exhib:* Nat Small Painting Exhib, Univ of the Pac, Stockton, Calif, 70; 5th Ann Gulf Coast Art Exhib, Mobile, Ala, 70; 11-State Small Painting Show, Albuquerque, NMex, 70; 12th, 13th & 14th Ann Painting Exhib, Longview, Tex, 70-72; 5-State Art Exhib, Port Arthur, Tex, 71; and others. *Teaching:* Asst, Okla State Univ, 47; instr, Inst Cult Cubano-Norte-Americano, 48; teaching fel, Univ Mich, 48-49; vis prof art, Fla State Univ, 49-50; instr, Syracuse Univ, 52-53; prof art, Univ Tex, El Paso, 53- *Awards:* Purchase Award for Painting, 6th Nat Arts Exhib, Tyler, Tex, 69; Third Award, 11 State Small Painting Show, 70. *Media:* Egg Tempera. *Publ:* Auth, Formulas

for Painters, 67 & Notes for American readers, In: Notes on the Technique of Painting, 69, Watson-Guptill; Formulas for Artists, B T Batsford, London, 68; Painting, drawing & printmaking supports, 9/70 & The artist's ideal studio, 1/71, Am Artist. *Dealer:* Two-Twenty-Two Gallery 6109 Pinehurst El Paso TX 79902. *Mailing Add:* 708 McKelligon Dr El Paso TX 79902

MASSIE, LORNA
PRINTMAKER
b Milwaukee, Wis, Dec 27, 38. *Study:* Layton Sch Art, Milwaukee; Smith Col; Univ Calif, Berkeley, BA, 61; Marshall Glazier, New York, 67; Woodstock Sch Art, 74-76; Albert Handell Sch, 77; Art Students League, 78. *Work:* Woodstock Hist Soc. *Exhib:* Mohawk Hudson Regional, Schenectady Mus, 80 & Albany Inst Hist & Art, 81, NY; Prints and Drawings, Berkshire Mus, Pittsfield, Mass, 81; Audubon Artists, Nat Arts Club, New York, 81 & 83-86; Works on Paper, Berkshire Mus, Pittsfield, Mass, 82; Salmagundi Club Exhib, New York, 82; Mus Hudson Highlands, 84, 85; Zaner Gallery, American Ann Works on Paper, 85; Allied Artists Am, 88; Knickerbocker Artists, 89, 90 & 91; Philadelphia Art Show, 90; The Print Club of Albany, 92. *Awards:* Hudson Valley Art Asn Award, 81; First Prize in Graphics, Barrett House, 85; Helen Open Oehler Award for Graphics, Allied Artists of Am, 89; Philip Isenberg Award for Graphics & Drawing, Knickerbocker Artists, NY, 91. *Mem:* Woodstock Artists Asn; Women's Studio Workshop. *Media:* Serigraphs. *Mailing Add:* 452 Whitfield Rd Accord NY 12404

MASSIN, EUGENE MAX
PAINTER, SCULPTOR
b Galveston, Tex, Apr 10, 20. *Study:* Art Inst Chicago; Univ Chicago, BFA, 48; Escuela Univ Bellas Artes, Mex, MFA, 49; first asst to David Alfara Sequeiros, Mex muralist. *Work:* Brandeis Univ, Boston; Lowe Mus, Univ Miami; Escuela Univ Bellas Artes, Mex; Ringling Mus, Fla; Norton Gallery, Palm Beach, Fla. *Comn:* Sculpture in Steel, Temple Israel, Miami, Fla, 82; Acrobats in Stainless Steel, Southern Bell, Jacksonville, Fla, 83; acrylic mural, Penn State Univ, 83; acrylic sheet/stainless steel mural, Carnival Cruise Lines, 85. *Exhib:* Metrop Mus Art, 53 & Whitney Ann, New York, 55; Art USA, 59; Am Fedn Art Traveling Exhib, 62; Southeastern Ann, Atlanta, Ga, 64. *Pos:* Pres, Artist Equity Asn, 55-58, founder, Fla Chap; adv, Arts Coun, 60-64; adv, Cafritz Found for Arts, Washington, DC, 66; juror, Nat Scholastic Art Awards, 71. *Teaching:* Instr art, Univ Wis, 49-50 & Univ SC, 52; prof art, Univ Miami, 54-85, emer prof, 85- *Awards:* Humanities Award, Univ Miami, 64 & 71; artist in residence, Univ WVa, 66; Res Award, Esso, 71. *Bibliog:* Julia Busch (auth), A painter's plastic sculpture, Art J, 70; Thelma Newman (auth), Plastics as design form, Chilton, 72; Julia Busch (auth), A Decade of Sculpture, Art Alliance Press, 74. *Media:* Acrylic Sheet; Metal. *Publ:* Contribr, Art Techniques, Reinhold, 65 & Lucite Spectrum, Du Pont Co Mag, 67-68. *Dealer:* Creative Endeavors Inc 3891 Little Ave Miami FL 33133. *Mailing Add:* 3891 Little Ave Coconut Grove FL 33133

MASTELLER, BARRY
PAINTER, CRAFTSMAN
b Los Angeles, Calif, Apr 21, 45. *Study:* Studied painting & life drawing under Walter Titus, 62-64. *Work:* Monterey Mus Art, Monterey Conf Ctr, Calif; San Jose Mus Art, Calif; Gonzaga Univ, Seattle, Wash; Syntex Corp, Palo Alto, Calif. *Comn:* Paintings, Home Fed, Los Angeles, 85, Coldwell Banker, Philadelphia, 85, Pebble Beach Corp, Calif, Stouffer Corp, Los Angeles, 86 & Hyatt Regency, Chicago, 88. *Exhib:* Solo exhib, Monterey Conf Ctr Art Comn, 79, San Jose Mus Art, 82, Monterey Mus Art, 75 & 83 & Shaklee Corp, San Francisco, 89; Exemplary Contemp, Univ Calif, Santa Cruz, 88; Newport Harbor Art Mus Invitational, 88. *Pos:* Co-dir/cur, Pacific Grove Art Ctr, Calif, 81-83; owner, Masteller/Shadow Graphics, 80-89; Claypoole-Freese Gallery, 89- *Awards:* Best of Show, Ann Monterey Peninsula Mus Art; Best of Show, Members Exhibit Pacific Grove Art Ctr; First Place Award, Monterey Co Competitive; Best of Show, Beacon House Competitive. *Bibliog:* Michael Gardner (auth), Artists taps subconcious, San Jose Mercury, 81; Richard Reilly (auth), Mastellers dreamy strokes, San Diego Union, 81; Irene Lagorio (auth), Mastellers seriocomic paintings, Monterey Herald, 83; Rick Deragon (auth), Let There Be Light, 90. *Mem:* Artists Equity; Int Inst Conservation Hist Artistic Works; Santa Cruz Art League. *Media:* Oil, Acrylic; Constructions. *Dealer:* Andrea Marquit Fine Arts 207 Newbury St Boston MA 02116. *Mailing Add:* PO Box 920 Pacific Grove CA 93950

MASTERFIELD, MAXINE
PAINTER
b Los Angeles, Calif, 1933. *Study:* Cleveland Inst Art, grad 55. *Work:* First Chicago Trust of Ariz & St Joseph Children's Ctr, Phoenix; Nat Watercolor Soc; Bancohio Nat; Ohio Savings & Loan; Laguna Beach Mus Art; Chicago Bank of Ill; 3M Corp, Minneapolis. *Exhib:* Watercolor USA, Springfield Art Mus, Mo, 68; Aqueous Open, Arts & Crafts Ctr, Pittsburgh, Pa, 76-79; Butler Midyear Exhib, Butler Inst Am Art, Youngstown, Ohio, 77; Rocky Mountain Nat Watermedia, Foothills Art Ctr, Golden, Colo, 77-79; Nat Watercolor Soc, Los Angeles, 77-79; Ky Watercolor, Owensboro Mus Fine Arts, Ky, 78 & Mid-Am Art Exhib, 79. *Teaching:* Watercolor workshops, worldwide. *Awards:* Purchase Award, Nat Watercolor Soc, 78; High Winds Medal, Am Watercolor Soc, 81; Grand Buckeye Leaf Award, Ohio Watercolor Soc, 82. *Mem:* Am Watercolor Soc; Nat Watercolor Soc; Ky Watercolor Soc. *Media:* Watercolor. *Publ:* Illusr, Watercolor Bold and Free, 80, Creative Seascape Painting, 81, auth, Painting the Spirit of Nature, Watson-Guptill; illusr, Exploring Color, North Light Bks; Auth In Harmony with Nature, 90. *Dealer:* Alan Gallery Cleveland OH; C G Rein Galleries 3646 W 70th St Edina MN 55435. *Mailing Add:* 3968 Lakeside Rd Sarasota FL 34232

MASTER-KARNIK, PAUL
MUSEUM DIRECTOR, CRITIC
b New York, NY, Nov 20, 48. *Study:* Rutgers Univ, BA, 70, MA, 71, PhD, 78; NY Univ, cert(mus studies), 79. *Collections Arranged:* Expressionism in Boston, 1945-85, DeCordova Mus, 85. *Pos:* Art critic, Staten Island Advan, Newhouse Publ, 76-81; dir, New Jersey Ctr for Visual Arts, 81-84; De Cordova Mus, 84- *Teaching:* Adj prof cult & art hist, Rutgers Univ, New Brunswick, NJ, 71-78; adj prof mus studies, New York Univ, 80-84. *Awards:* Nat Endowment Arts Critics Fel, 80-81. *Mem:* Am Asn Mus; Asn Art Mus Dirs. *Res:* Methods and styles of contemporary art criticism; social history of the art museum; contemporary American art. *Publ:* Auth, Art criticism in the suburban context, Artview, Vol 3, No 1, 79; Philip Pearlstein: Progress of a Painter (exhib catalog), 82, American Realism 1930's/1980's: A Comparative Perspective (exhib catalog), 83 & William Zorach: Sculpture and Drawings (exhib catalog), 83, NJ Ctr Visual Arts. *Mailing Add:* DeCordova Museum and Sculpture Park Sandy Pond Rd Lincoln MA 01773

MASTRANGELO, BOBBI
PRINTMAKER, SCULPTURE
b Youngstown, Ohio, May 16, 37. *Study:* State Univ NY, Buffalo, BS, 59; State Univ NY, Stony Brook, 69-79; studied printmaking with Dan Welden, John Ross, Clare Romano & Tim Ross. *Work:* Firehouse Gallery, Nassau Community Col, Garden City, NY; Mus Nat Arts Found, New York; Suffolk County Water Authority, Oakdale, NY. *Exhib:* Staller Ctr Arts, State Univ NY, Stony Brook, 92; Ward Nasse Gallery, New York, 92; Progressions in Paper, Ohio Tour, Dairy Barn Art Ctr, Athens, Ohio, 92; ARC Gallery, Chicago, Ill, 92; Transformation of Matter into Art, New York, Acad Sci, 92. *Pos:* Judge, 11th Ann Cong Art Competition, Riverhead, NY, 92. *Teaching:* Paper making, Bd Coop Servs, Suffolk Co, NY, 87-92. *Awards:* Grant, Artists Space, New York, 91; Special Opportunity Stipend, New York Found Arts, 92; Eve Helman Award, work on paper, Nat Asn Women Artists, New York, 92. *Bibliog:* Susan Howard (auth), The manhole is the message, Newsday, 12/90; Laura Muha (auth), Artists dream leads to anti-litter movement, Newsday, 1/90; Rosemary Gomez (TV reporter), Manhole Covers Fascinate St James Artist. *Mem:* Artists Space, New York; Art & Sci Collabrs Inc, Staten Island, NY; Print Club, Philadelphia, Pa; Nat Asn Women Artists; Nat Mus Women Arts. *Media:* Prints on hand-made papers, Mixed Media. *Dealer:* Burns Fine Art 568 Broadway New York NY 10012. *Mailing Add:* 12 Wexford Ct St James NY 11780

MASUROVSKY, GREGORY
DRAFTSMAN, PRINTMAKER
b Bronx, NY, Nov 26, 29. *Study:* Art Students League, New York, study with Will Barnet; Parsons Sch of Design, New York; Black Mountain Col, NC, study with Ilya Bolotowsky. *Work:* Mus Mod Art, New York; Minneapolis Inst Art, Minn; Fogg Art Mus, Cambridge, Mass; Mus Nat Art Mod, Paris; Libr Cong, Washington, DC. *Comn:* Decor, Costumes & Lighting, Ballet Theatre Contemp d'Angers, France, 75. *Exhib:* Druck Graphic, 71, Nurenberg Nat Mus, Ger, 70; Estampe Contemp, Bibliotheque Nat, Paris, 73; Third Int Biennale Nat Graphique, Kunstverein, Frechen, W Ger, 74; Minneapolis Inst Arts, Minn, 67; Mus de Pontoise, France, 82. *Pos:* Graphics monitor to Will Barnet, Art Students League, New York, 52-53. *Teaching:* Vis prof drawing, Minneapolis Col Art & Design, Minn, 66-67; prof drawing, Am Ctr, Paris, 80-87; prof drawing, Atelier Elzevir, Paris, 87-92; Int Summer Acad, Salzburg, Austria, 89. *Awards:* Critics Prize, drawing, II Biennale de Paris, 61; Int Jury Prize, Etching III Biennial de Paris, 63; Fel, Tamarind Lithography Workshop, Los Angeles, 69; Djerassi Found Grant, 87. *Bibliog:* Georges Boudaille (auth), article, Cimaise, 5/65; Michel Conil Lacoste (auth), Masurovsky, an American in Paris, Studio Int, 3/65; Michel Buter (auth), article, Opus Int, 71. *Mem:* Centre Georges Pompidou, Paris; Artists Equity Asn, New York; SPADEM, Paris. *Media:* Pen & Ink; Etching. *Publ:* Illusr, Litanie d'Eau, La Hune, Paris, 64; Western Duo, Tamarind Litho, Los Angeles, 69; Corps a Coeur, Urdla, Villeurbanne, France, 89; Ange De La Baie, J Matarasso, Nice, France, 92. *Dealer:* Galerie Daniel Varenne 15 Chemin de Sierne CH-1255 Geneva Switzerland. *Mailing Add:* 43 Rue Liancourt Paris 75014 France

MATASSA, JOHN P
PAINTER, INSTRUCTOR
b Norwich, Conn, Sept 13, 45. *Study:* Sch Mus Fine Arts, Boston, BFA, 67; Tufts Univ, with T Lux Feininger & Jan Cox, MFA, 73; Ind Study Mus Pre History, France. *Work:* Del Division of Pub Libr; Blount Collection, Ala; Logan Int Airport, Boston; Historical Soc Del; Eleutheran Mills Hagley Foundation. *Comn:* Concrete & neon wall, Eastern Airlines, Mass, 71; welded steel sculpture, Univ City Arts League, Pa, 74; sculptural relief, Del State Arts Coun, 80. *Exhib:* State Awards Wadsworth Atheneum, Conn, 63; Boston Area Show, Inst Contemp Art, Mass, 66; Traveling Scholars, Boston Mus Fine Arts, 68; one-man show, Del State Arts Coun, 80; Regional juried, Del Art Mus, 75, 78 & 81; Regional juried, Univ Del, Newark, 79 & 81; Nat Acad Design, New York, 82; Am Watercolor Soc, 82 & 83. *Pos:* Exhib dir, Club 47 Gallery, Mass, 66-68; art dir, auth & illusr, Del Steamboater Mag, Steamboat Found, 81-; chmn, Dept Visual Arts, Wilmington Friends Sch, Del, 77-; pres, John Matassa Ltd Ed, currently. *Teaching:* Grad instr painting, Sch Mus Fine Arts, Boston, 67-68; instr painting, drawing & sculpture, Wilmington Friends Sch, Del, 74- *Awards:* Grand Prize, Del Trust Co, 81; Nat Soc Painters Nauman Medal, 82; Artist of Year, Christiana Cult Arts Ctr, 84. *Bibliog:* Jean Gilmour (auth), Feature Artist, Del State Arts Coun, 80; Nancy Muhr (auth), Delaware artist, Art Voices South Mag, 80. *Mem:* Philadelphia Watercolor Club; Nat Soc Painters Casein & Acrylic; assoc Am Watercolor Soc; Rehoboth Art League. *Media:* Watercolor, Acrylic. *Publ:* Photo illusr, Seventeen Mag, 76. *Dealer:* Sporter Art Ltd Sullivan IL. *Mailing Add:* c/o 101 Sch Rd Wilmington DE 19803

MATEO, JULIO
PAINTER, PRINTMAKER
b Havana, Cuba, Apr 16, 51; US citizen. *Study:* Univ Fla, BFA, 73; Univ S Fla, MFA, 78. *Work:* New York Pub Libr; Univ S Fla, Tampa; The Printmaking Workshop, New York; Greenville Co Mus Art, SC; Chase Manhattan Bank, New York. *Exhib:* Brooklyn Mus, New York, 85; Mus Contemp Hispanic Art, New York, 86 & 88; Bronx Mus, NY, 87 & 90; PS 1, Long Island City, NY, 90; solo show, Cathedral St John the Divine, New York; and others. *Awards:* Individual Artists' Grant, Arts Coun Fla, Tallahassee, 80; Artists Grant, Nat Endowment Art, Washington, DC, 89. *Media:* Oil; Intaglio. *Publ:* Contribr, Blast, Vol 1, No 12, Colab, New York, 87; Artextreme, No 8, Philadelphia, 89; Hoopoe, No 5, New York, 90. *Mailing Add:* 281 Greene Ave Brooklyn NY 11238

MATHEWS, NANCY MOWLL
HISTORIAN, CURATOR
b Baltimore, Md, Feb 11, 47. *Study:* Goucher Col, BA, 68; Cleveland Mus Art, fel, 70-71; Case-Western Reserve Univ, MA, 72; NY Univ Inst Fine Arts, Goldwater fel, 73-74, PhD, 80. *Collections Arranged:* The World Through 19th Century Eyes, 19th Century Am Still Life & Genre Painting, 78; The Tradition of American Folk Art (auth, catalog), Am Folk Painting & Sculpture, 79; Aspects of Photorealism (auth, catalog), Photorealist Painting, 80; Abstract Art in the 80s (auth, catalog), 81; Quilts and Collages: American Art in Pieces, 82. *Pos:* Sr cur, Maiem Mus Art, Randolph-Macon Womans Col, 77-; Prendergast cur, Williams Col Mus Art, currently. *Awards:* Katherine Graves Davidson Award, 80; Smithsonian Postdoctoral Fel, 82; and others. *Mem:* Col Art Asn; Women's Caucus for Art; Am Asn Mus. *Res:* 19th century European and American painting; impressionism; Mary Cassatt, the 19th century Madonna. *Publ:* Auth, Mary Cassatt, In: Women Artists 1550-1950, Knopf, 76; Four new books on Mary Cassatt, Woman's Art J, 81; ed, Mary Cassatt and Her Circle: Selected Letters, Abbeville Press, 84; auth, Mary Cassatt, Abrams, 85. *Mailing Add:* Williams Col Mus Art Main St Williamstown MA 01267

MATHIS, BILLIE F
PAINTER, CONCEPTUAL ARTIST
b Lindale, Ga, Apr 16, 36. *Study:* Art Instruction Inc; studied with watercolorists Edgar Whitney, Ray Kinsler, Edward Betts, Robert Wood, Frank Webb & other noted watercolorists. *Work:* Contel Corp & Post Properties Inc, Atlanta, Ga; Cobb Bd of Educ Collection; Peachtree Ctr, Atlanta, Ga; also pvt collections. *Exhib:* Butler Inst Am Arts 53rd Nat, Youngstown, Ohio; Allied Artist National, New York; Okla Watercolor Soc; Georgia Watercolor Soc; Albany Univ; Visual Arts, Atlanta-Savannah Exhib; Marrietta Cobb Mus Art. *Mem:* Nat Women in Arts; Assoc Allied Artists; Assoc Georgia Watercolor Soc. *Media:* Watercolor. *Publ:* contribr, Georgia Artists, Mountain Prod, 88, Am References- Artist, 89. *Dealer:* Frame Works Gallery 26 Mill St Marietta GA 30060. *Mailing Add:* 1665 Hasty Rd Marietta GA 30062

MATHIS, EMILE HENRY, II
DEALER, COLLECTOR
b Superior, Wis, Feb 25, 46. *Study:* Dominican Col, Univ Wis, Superior, BFA, MFA. *Collections Arranged:* J A McN Whistler, (etchings & lithographs), 81; Rubber stamps by contemp Am artists, 81; 19th Century French Etching, 82; British printmakers of late 19th & early 20th century. *Pos:* Asst dir, La Porte Gallery, Racine, 70-71; dir, New Gallery One, Racine, 71-72; gallery owner, Mathis Gallery, Racine, 72-; Mem bd dirs, Wustum Mus Fine Art. *Teaching:* Instr art, Sheboygan Sch Syst, Wis, 68-69. *Mem:* Racine Urban Aesthetics. *Specialty:* Old and modern masters; contemporary graphics; paintings & fine prints. *Collection:* American nineteenth and twentieth century contemporary drawings and paintings. *Mailing Add:* 328 Main St Racine WI 53404

MATOS, JOHN See Crash (John Matos)

MATOSSE, JACKIE (JACQUELINE MALISSE MONNIER)
CONCEPTUAL ARTIST
b Neuilly-sur-Seine, France, July 12, 31; US citizen. *Exhib:* Kites: A Summer Celebration, Inst Contemp Art, London, Eng, 76; Festival d'Automne, Paris, France, 76; Artistes--Artisms, Mus des Arts Decratifs, Paris, France, 77; Flags, Banners & Kites, Allied Arts Found, Seattle, Washington, 77; Drachen, Rhein Landesmuseum, Bonn, Ger, 81; travelling exhib, Philadelphia Mus Art, 81; solo show, Fundación Miro, Barcelona, Spain, 85; Art that Flies, Dayton Art Inst, 90; Zero Gravity, 91; Les Artists Decident De Jouer, 91. *Bibliog:* Newman (auth), Kite Craft, Crown Publ Inc, 74; Jean-Michel Folon, Aquiloni, Alice Editions, Switz, 76; Suzi Gablik (auth), Cosmic kites, Art in Am, 11/80. *Publ:* Art That Flies, 91. *Dealer:* Jack Tilton Gallery 24 W 57th St New York NY 10019. *Mailing Add:* 1 Rue R Lefebvre Villiers-sovs-Grez 77760 France

MATSON, GRETA
PAINTER
b Claremont, Va. *Study:* Grand Cent Sch Art, New York; also with Jerry Farnsworth, Cape Cod; Hunter Col, BA, New York. *Work:* New Britain Mus Am Art, Conn; Va Mus Fine Arts, Richmond; Little Rock Mus, Ark; Tex Technol Col, Lubbock; Longwood Col, Farmville, Va. *Comn:* Portraits, Dean Grace Landrum, William & Mary Col, Williamsburg, Va, 46 & Mary Calcott, Calcott Sch, Norfolk, Va, 53. *Exhib:* Nat Drawing Ann, Albany Inst Hist & Art, NY, 40 & 45; Oil Nat, Carnegie Inst, Pittsburgh, 41, 44 & 45; Oil & Watercolor Nat, Art Inst Chicago, 42, 43 & 46; Oil Nat, Butler Art Inst, Youngstown, Ohio, 43, 45, 57 & 59; Oil Nat, Va Mus Fine Arts, Richmond, 53 & 57. *Awards:* Altman Figure Prize, Nat Acad Design, 45; Am Artist Mag Medal, Am Watercolor Soc, 55; Allied Artists Am Gold Medal, 62. *Mem:* Nat Asn Women Artists (pres, 61-65); Audubon Artists (corresp secy, 61-62); Allied Artists; Am Soc Contemp Artists (first vpres, 61); Am Watercolor Soc. *Media:* Oil, Watercolor. *Publ:* Auth, Painting in watercolor at the seashore, Am Artist Mag, 56. *Mailing Add:* 8750 Old Ocean View Rd Norfolk VA 23503

MATSUBARA, NAOKO
PRINTMAKER, ILLUSTRATOR
b Kyoto, Japan, Apr 5, 37. *Study:* Kyoto Acad Fine Arts, BFA, 60; Carnegie-Mellon Univ, MFA, 62; Royal Col Art, London, 63. *Work:* British Mus, London; Mus Fine Arts, Boston; Tokyo Nat Mus Mod Art; Cincinnati Mus Art; Libr Congress. *Comn:* Mural, Kyoto Univ Hosp, 59; mural, Carnegie-Mellon Univ, Pittsburgh, 62; woodcut print, Smithsonian Inst, Washington, DC, 67; woodcut print, Boston Winter Festival, 69; Solitude (portfolio), Aquarius Press, New York, 71. *Exhib:* Solo shows, Hart House Gallery, Univ Toronto, 74, Art Gallery Hamilton, Ont, 79, Hewlett Gallery, Carnegie-Mellon Univ, 80 & Wako Art Gallery, Tokyo, 81; Munakata & Matsubara Traveling Show, 76-77; The Japanese Prints Since 1900, Brit Mus, London, 83; Seoul Int Print Biennale, Korea, 83; Philadelphia Print Club, 86; Takashimaya Art Gallery, Tokyo, 87; Gairloch Art Gallery, Oakville, Can, 88; Vancouver Art Gallery, BC, 90; Hart House Gallery, Univ Toronto, 90; Oriental Mus, Durham, Eng, travelled to Ireland & Wales, 91-92. *Teaching:* Instr woodcut, Pratt Graphic Art Ctr, 65-67; instr woodcut, Univ RI, 67-68; asst prof woodcut, Univ Victoria, BC, summer 77; asst prof woodcut, Univ Guelph, Ont, 84. *Awards:* Kegon Shou, Hangain Ten, Shiko Munakata, 63; Samuel Gold Award, Soc Am Graphic Artists, 68; Soc Am Graphic Artists Awards for Excellence, 84; CBC TV Documentary Video, 90. *Bibliog:* Fritz Eichenberg (auth), The two worlds of Naoko Matsubara, Am Artist, 66; Fritz Eichenberg (auth), Naoko Matsubara, Xylon, Switz, 70; Joan Stanley-Baker (auth), The woodcuts of Munakata and Matsubara, Art Gallery Greater Victoria, 76; Franz Geirhaas (auth), The Creative Act Paths to Realization, Int Print Soc, 84; plus others. *Mem:* Soc Am Graphic Artists; Royal Can Acad Arts. *Media:* Woodcut; Watercolor. *Publ:* Auth-illusr, My woodcuts and myself, Univ Tex Quart, 63; illusr, The Tale of the Shining Princess, 66 & illusr, Kyoto Woodcuts, 78, Kodansha Int; illusr, Nantucket Woodcuts, Barre Publ, 68; In Praise of Trees (portfolio), Mosaic Press, 85; Hagoromo (porfolio), Pinetree Press, 86. *Dealer:* Gallery Tsutsui Tokyo Japan; Norman Tolman Collection Ltd Tokyo Japan. *Mailing Add:* 324 Coral Terr Oakville ON L6J 4C4 Canada

MATTERNES, JAY HOWARD
PAINTER, ILLUSTRATOR
b Corregidor, Philippines, Apr 14, 33; US citizen. *Study:* Carnegie Mellon Univ Col Fine Arts, Mellon Found scholar & BFA, 55. *Work:* Cleveland Mus Natural Sci, Ohio; Kenya Nat Mus, Nairobi; Carnegie Mus, Pittsburgh; Bedloe Island Mus Immigration, New York; Smithsonian Inst, Washington, DC. *Comn:* N Am Tertiary Murals (four), Smithsonian Natural Hist Mus, DC, 60-64, Hagerman (Idaho) Pliocene Mural, 69 & Alaska Ice Age Mural, 76; Morristown Revolutionary War Mural, Nat Park Serv, NJ, 75. *Exhib:* Art & the Animal, Royal Ont Mus, Ottawa, Can, 75; Nat Acad Western Art at Cowboy Hall of Fame, Oklahoma City, 79; Leigh Yawkey Woodson Art Mus, Wausau, Wis, 80, 81 & 83; bird art, Royal Scottish Acad, Edinburgh; Brit Mus, London, 82; Ancestors, Mus Natural Hist, New York, 84; First Western Art Classic, Minnetonka, Minn, 84; Soc Illusrs, New York, 84, 86 & 88; Commonwealth Inst, London, Eng, 85 & 86; Game Conservation Int, San Antonio, Tex, 87; Australian Mus, Sydney, 88. *Pos:* Self-employed free-lance artist, 60- *Awards:* Merit Award, 68 & Gold Medal, 82, Art Dir Club Washington; Award Merit, Soc Animal Artists, 79. *Bibliog:* Dr L B Leakey (auth), The Dawn of Man (film TV), 65 & Dr Clark Howell (auth), Man Hunters (film TV), 68, Nat Geographic Soc; John Heminway (auth), The Three Million Year Clue (film TV), Survival Anglia Ltd, 76. *Mem:* World Wildlife Found, African Wildlife; Artists Equity Asn; Game Conservation Int; Soc Animal Artists; Nat Cowboy Hall of Fame. *Media:* Oil, Acrylic; Charcoal, Pencil. *Publ:* Illusr, American Cowboy, 72 & Vanishing Wild Life of North America, 74, Nat Geographic Soc Bk Div; A New Look at Early Man in North America, World Yr Bk, 73; Lost Empires, Living Tribes, 82 & Peoples & Places of the Past, 83. *Mailing Add:* 4328 Ashford Lane Fairfax VA 22032

MATTESON, IRA
SCULPTOR, DRAFTSMAN
b Hamden, Conn, June 26, 17. *Study:* Art Students League, with Arthur Lee, 37-42, also with William Zorach, 46-51; Nat Acad, with John Flanagan, 46-47. *Work:* Akron Art Inst, Ohio; Cleveland Mus Art; Chrysler Mus, Provincetown, Mass; Norfolk Mus, Va; Case Western Reserve Univ, Cleveland, Ohio. *Comn:* Figure-Bend, Cascade Plaza, Akron, 77; Back, Case Western Reserve, Univ Cleveland, Ohio, 81. *Exhib:* Kent State Univ; Akron Univ, 88. *Pos:* Prof emer, 85. *Teaching:* Fac, Sch Art, Kent State Univ, Kent, 68-87. *Awards:* Prix de Rome, Am Acad Rome, 53-55, Louis Comfort Tiffany, 56 & 60; Ohio Arts Coun Grant, 78. *Media:* Wood, Metal. *Publ:* Dialogue, 4/88. *Mailing Add:* 621 S Depeyster Kent OH 44240

MATTHEWS, GENE (EUGENE EDWARD)
PAINTER, EDUCATOR
b Davenport, Iowa, Mar 22, 31. *Study:* Bradley Univ, 48-51; Univ Iowa, BFA, 53, MFA, 57. *Work:* Nat Mus Am Art, Washington, DC; Butler Inst Am Art, Youngstown, Ohio; Denver Art Mus, Colo; Nat Mus Poland; Chrysler Mus, Norfolk, Va. *Exhib:* Am Watercolors, Drawings & Prints, Metrop Mus Art, New York, 52; Antagonismes, Louvre, Paris, 60; one-man shows, James Yu Gallery, New York, 73 & 77, Dubins Gallery, Los Angeles, 81; Int Drawing Biennale, Middlesbrough Art Gallery, Eng, 77; American Drawings,

Smithsonian Inst, Washington, DC, 80-82; Galeria Wielka, Poznan, Poland, 82-83; Brena Gallery, Denver, Colo, 83, 86 & 88; Int Invitational, Galleria FMK, Budapest, Hungary, 85 & 87; 9th Int Exhib, Kyoto Int Art Ctr, Japan, 86 & 88. *Teaching:* Prof fine arts, Univ Colo, Boulder, 61-, assoc chmn, 85- *Awards:* Univ Colo Fac Fel for Creative Res, Boulder, 66; Quartana Purchase Award, Int Watercolor Exhib, Baton Rouge, La, 73; Purchase Award, American Drawings IV, 82. *Bibliog:* Wendon Blake (auth), Acrylic Watercolor Painting, 70 & L C Goldsmith (auth), Watercolor Bold and Free, 80, Watson-Guptill. *Mem:* fel Am Acad, Rome; Watercolor USA Hon Soc. *Media:* Acrylic, Oil. *Dealer:* Brena Gallery 313 Detroit Denver CO 80206. *Mailing Add:* 3066 Seventh St Boulder CO 80304

MATTHEWS, HARRIETT
SCULPTOR
b Kansas City, Mo, June 21, 40. *Study:* Sullins Jr Col, Briston, Va, AFA; Univ Ga, BFA & MFA; with Leonard DeLonga. *Work:* Univ Ga Art Mus; Colby Col Art Mus & Libr; Cascoe Bay Bank, Portland, Maine; Bristol K-8 Sch, Bristol, Maine. *Comn:* Designed awards for the Maine Arts & Humanities Comn, 69; outdoor sculpture, Kennebec Valley Vocational Tech Inst Per Cent for Art, 86. *Exhib:* One-person shows, Vanderbilt Univ, 74, Treat Gallery, Bates Col, Lewiston, Maine, 79, Univ Southern Maine, Gorham, 82, Montpelier Cult Arts Ctr, Laurel, Md, 83, Colby Col Art Mus, 87 & 92 & Perspectives, Portland Mus Art, Maine, 90; Payson Gallery, Westbrook Col, Portland, 85; Maine Coast Artist Gallery, 89; Dean Valentgas Gallery, Portland, Maine, 89; Anita Shapolsky Gallery, New York, 91; Frick Gallery, Belfast, Maine, 91-92; and others. *Teaching:* Vis instr sculpture, Univ Okla, 64-65; from instr to assoc prof sculpture & drawing, Colby Col, 66-85, prof, 85- *Awards:* Colby Travel Grants, 71, 76, 78, 81, 85, 87 & 90; Colby Mellon Grant, 80; Ingram Merrill Grant, 80. *Bibliog:* Virginia Watson-Jones (auth), Contemporary Women Sculptors; Arthur Williams (auth), Sculpture: Technique, Form, Content. *Mem:* Col Art Asn. *Media:* All. *Mailing Add:* Dept Art Colby Col Waterville ME 04901

MATTHEWS, WANDA MILLER
PRINTMAKER
b Barry, Ill, Sept 15, 30. *Study:* Bradley Univ, Peoria, Ill, BFA, 52; Univ Iowa, Iowa City, with Mauricio Lasansky, MFA, 57. *Work:* Libr of Cong; Philadelphia Mus Art; Los Angeles Co Mus; Boston Pub Libr; Portland Art Mus, Ore. *Exhib:* British Int Print Biennales, Bradford, Eng, 70 & 79; Int Print Biennales, Cracow, Poland, 76, 78, 80, 84 & 86; New Talent in Printmaking 1980, Assoc Am Artists, New York & Philadelphia, 80; solo exhibs, Am Ctr Gallery, US Info Agency, Belgrade & Piran, Yugoslavia, 82, A Decade of Intaglio Prints, Univ Colo, 85, House of Dreams Lost and Found, (monoprints), Jane Haslem Gallery, Washington DC, 90, The Printerly Image: Wanda Miller Matthews, 1951-1991, Arvada Ctr Arts & Humanities, Denver, Colo, 91; one-man retrospective, Prints: 1955-1982, Jane Haslem Gallery, Washington, DC, 82; 3rd Int Biennial Print Exhib, Taipei, Taiwan, 87-88; CSP Exchange Show, Brandts Klaedefabrik Mus, Odense, Denmark, 89; The Home, Wenniger Graphics, Boston, Mass, 92. *Pos:* Res assistantship printmaking, Univ Iowa, 56-57. *Awards:* Benton Spruance Prize, Print Club of Philadelphia, 71; Purchase Award, Soc Am Graphic Artists Nat Exhib, New York, 79; Stella Drabkin Award & Medallion, Am Color Print Soc Nat Exhib, Philadelphia, 81; First Place Color Prints, Ybor Nat Print Competition, Ybor City, Fla, 85; Leila Sawyer Mem Award, Nat Asn Women Artists Exhib, New York, 86. *Bibliog:* Stanley L Cuba (auth), Wanda Miller Matthews, Southwest Art Mag, 11/90. *Mem:* Soc Am Graphic Artists, New York; Boston Printmakers; Calif Soc Printmakers. *Media:* Etching, Engraving. *Dealer:* Jane Haslem Gallery 2025 Hillyer Pl NW Washington DC 20004; Szoke Koo Assocs 164 Mercer St New York NY 10012. *Mailing Add:* 3066 Seventh St Boulder CO 80304

MATTINGLY, (JAMES THOMAS)
PRINTMAKER, EDUCATOR
b Southgate, Calif, Mar 14, 34. *Study:* San Jose State Col, with Fred Spratt, Terry Frost, Ken Auvil, Jeff Bowman, Robert Collins & Robert Freemark, BA, 63, MA(art), 66. *Work:* Montreal Mus Fine Arts; Honolulu Acad Arts; State Ore Capitol Bldg, Salem; Coos Art Mus, Coos Bay, Ore; Wash State Arts Comn, Seattle; Heritage Hall, Western Ore State Col, Monmouth. *Comn:* Box (wood sculpture), comn by Glenda Milton, Salem, Ore, 80; Theatrical Heartscape (mural), comn by Mid-Valley Arts Coun, Elsinore Theatre, 84. *Exhib:* Introduction 78, R L Kidd Assoc Gallery, Birmingham, Mich, 77; 24th Nat Print Exhib, Hunterdown Art Ctr, Clinton, NJ, 80; 4th Miami Int Print Biennale, Metrop Mus Art Ctr, Miami, 80; Northwest Prints 82, Portland Art Mus, Ore, 82; Rockford Int Print & Drawing Biennale, Rockford Col, 83; Northwest Print Coun Exhib, Norske Grafikere, Osco, Norway, 84; West Region Print, Painting & Drawing Exhib, Ashland, 84, Western States Prints Invitational Exhib, Portland Mus, 85, Ore; Northwest Print Coun Manin Exhib, Hall Central of Fine Arts, Beijing, China, 86; and others. *Teaching:* Asst art, San Jose State Col, 63-66; instr, Alta Col Art, Calgary, 66-68; prof, Western Ore State Col, 68-, art dept head, 78-86 & 89-90. *Awards:* Reid Mem Award, Int Exhib Graphics, Montreal Mus Fine Arts, 71; Statewide Serv Travel Award, 74 & Visual Arts Resources Award, 77, Mus Art, Univ Ore; Faculty Honors Award, Western Ore State Col, Monmouth, 85; All Ore Juried Art Ann, Salem, 89, 90, 91. *Mem:* Salem Art Asn, Ore (mem bd dirs, 77-90); Northwest Print Coun (pres, 83-85, mem bd dirs, 82-83, 85-). *Media:* Intaglio, Acrylic. *Dealer:* Maveety Gallery Gleneden Beach Or 97388. *Mailing Add:* 15440 Strong Rd Dallas OR 97338

MATYAS, DIANE C
SCULPTOR, PRINTMAKER
b Pittsburgh, Pa, Nov 28, 61. *Study:* Cornell Univ, BFA, 84; Vermont Studio Sch, 86, Cornell, MFA, 89. *Comn:* Monkey Puzzle (sculpture), Philadelphia, Pa, 87; Water (mural, oil), Staten Island Childrens Mus, 92; Desert Pergola (sculpture), Mesa, Ariz, 93. *Exhib:* Alliance in the Park, Philadelphia, Pa, 87; New Visions Gallery, Ithaca, NY, 88; AIR Gallery, New York, 88; ARC Gallery, Chicago, Ill, 92; Columbus Circle, New York subway installation, 92. *Pos:* Artist-in-resident, Staten Island Children's Mus; prog developer/instr, Homeless Art Proj, Queens Mus, New York; instr, Studio in a School Asn, New York, 91-92; artist-in-residence & prog developer, Staten Island Childrens Mus, New York, presently. *Teaching:* instr printmaking, Cornell Univ, 89- *Awards:* Cornell Fac Medal of Art, 84; Sculpture Grant, Pa Coun Arts, 87; Grant, The Greater New York Art Develop, 88. *Bibliog:* Helen A Harrison (auth), Young artist offers works of maturity, NY Times, 3/2/86; Karin Lipson (auth), Works of young & emerging artists, Newsday, 3/86; Thomas Hine (auth), The Philadelphia Inquirer, 7/27/87. *Media:* Terra Cotta, Intaglio. *Publ:* Thoughts on Public Sculpture: The Work of Petah Coyne, 88 & The 1988 Venice Bennale, Q Mag, 88. *Mailing Add:* 1086 Bay St Staten Island NY 10305

MAUGHELLI, MARY L
PAINTER, PRINTMAKER
b Glen Lyon, Pa, Nov 20, 35. *Study:* Univ Calif, Berkeley, BA & MA; Pratt Graphic Ctr. *Work:* Fresno Art Mus, Calif; Helene Wurlitzer Found, Taos, NMex; Univ NMex Tamarind Prints, Albuquerque. *Exhib:* 85th Ann San Francisco Art Inst Exhib, San Francisco Mus Art, 66; Fac Show, Calif State Univ, Fresno, 79, 81, 83, 85, 87 & 91; Beyond New York, AIR Gallery, New York, 89-90; Atlantic Gallery, New York, 87-92; Next Wave, Fresno Art Mus, Calif, 91; Figurative Expressions, Claudia Chapline Gallery, Stinson Beach, Calif, 92; and many others. *Teaching:* Prof art, Calif State Univ, Fresno, 62-; lectr design, Univ Calif, Berkeley, summer 63. *Awards:* Fulbright Fels, Italy, 59-61; Helene Wurlitzer Found Fel, Taos, NMex, summer 76, 77, 83, 86 & 91; Humanities Res Grant, Calif State Univ, Fresno, 82 & 84; and others. *Mem:* Col Art Asn; Calif Soc Printmakers; Artists Equity; Women's Caucus for Art. *Media:* Oil; Lithography. *Dealer:* Fig Tree Gallery 1536 Fulton St Fresno CA 93721; Claudia Chapline 3445 Shorelilne Hwy Stinson Beach CA. *Mailing Add:* 1114 W Keats Ave Fresno CA 93711

MAULDIN, BILL
CARTOONIST, WRITER
b Mountain Park, NMex, Oct 29, 21. *Study:* Chicago Acad Fine Arts; Conn Wesleyan Univ, Hon MA, 46; Albion Col, Hon LittD, 70; Lincoln Col, Hon LHD, 70. *Pos:* Cartoonist, Chicago Sun-Times, 62- *Awards:* Pulitzer Prize, 44 & 58; Sigma Delta Chi Award, 64. *Mem:* Nat Cartoonists Soc. *Publ:* Auth, What's Got Your Back Up, 61 & I've Decided I Want My Seat Back, 65, Harper-Row; auth, Up Front, 68 & Brass Ring, 71, Norton; auth & illusr, articles in Life, Sat Eve Post, Sports Illus, Atlantic Monthly, New Repub & many others. *Mailing Add:* c/o Chicago Sun Times 401 N Walbash Chicago IL 60611

MAURER, EVAN MACLYN
DIRECTOR, HISTORIAN
b Newark, NJ, Aug 19, 44. *Study:* Amherst Col, BA, 66; Univ Minn, MA, 68; Univ Pa, PhD, 74. *Collections Arranged:* Fakes and Forgeries (auth, catalog), Minneapolis Inst Arts, 73; The Native American Heritage (auth, catalog), Art Inst Chicago, 77; Gerome Kamrowski Retrospective, 83; The Rising of a New Moon, 86. *Pos:* Cur & asst to dir, Minneapolis Inst Arts, 71-73; cur primitive art, Art Inst Chicago, 73-81; dir, Univ Mich Mus Art, 81-; dir & chief exec officer, Minneapolis Inst Arts, currently. *Teaching:* Vis prof primitivism & mod art, Univ Chicago, 76; lectr primitivism, mod art & mus studies, Art Inst Chicago, 78-81, assoc prof, 81; prof art hist, Univ Mich. *Mem:* Col Art Asn; Am Asn Mus; Am Asn Mus Dirs. *Publ:* Auth, Metaphysical Landscape by G de Chirico, Minneapolis Inst Arts, 73; North American Indian clothing, In: The Fabric of Culture, Mouton, 80; Dada & Surrealism, Primitivism in 20th Century Art, 85; Miro, 85; Max Ernst, 87. *Mailing Add:* 2104 Kenwood Pkwy 2400 Third Ave S Minneapolis MN 55405

MAURER, NEIL DOUGLAS
PHOTOGRAPHER
b New York, NY, Jan 12, 41. *Study:* Brown Univ, BA, 62; RI Sch Design, MFA, 75. *Work:* Mus Mod Art, New York; Corcoran Gallery Art; San Antonio Mus Art; Mus Art, RI Sch Design; Libr Cong. *Exhib:* Solo exhib, Carl Siembals Gallery, Boston, Mass, 77; Texas Photographers, Washington Proj Arts, 81; Mus Art, RI Sch Designs, Providence, 79; 12th Ann Works on Paper, Southwest Tex State Univ, 83; Museo Camilo Egas, Quito, Equador, 86; Contemporary Works Series, San Antonio Mus Art, 83; solo exhibs, Marcuse Pfeifer Gallery, New York, 88. *Teaching:* Instr, Corcoran Sch Art, 75, Dept Fine Arts, Univ Bridgeport, Conn, 77-78 & Dept Arts & Humanities, Ocean Co Community Col, 78; asst prof, Div Art & Design, Univ Tex, San Antonio, 78- *Awards:* Fulbright-Hays Grant, 75-76. *Mem:* Soc Photog Educ. *Dealer:* Marcuse Pfeifer Gallery 825 Madison Ave New York NY 10021. *Mailing Add:* 723 Woodlawn Ave San Antonio TX 78212

MAURICE, ALFRED PAUL
PAINTER, EDUCATOR
b Nashua, NH, Mar 11, 21. *Study:* Univ NH, 40-42; Mich State Univ, BA, 47, MA, 49. *Work:* Libr Cong, Washington, DC; Southern Ill Univ, Edwardsville; Anderson Art Ctr. *Comn:* Murals (with Raymond Pinet), Nat Youth Admin, Jr High Sch, Hudson, NH & Community Chest Bldg, Nashua, 39-40. *Exhib:* Butler Inst Ann, 81-83 & 90; one-man shows, Bradley Univ, 82,

Mich State Univ, 83, Chicago Pub Libr Cult Ctr, 83, Anderson Art Ctr, 83, Joy Horwich Gallery, 85 & R H Love Galleries, 88; and others. *Pos:* Dir art ctr, Kalamazoo Inst Arts, Mich, 59-65. *Teaching:* Instr printmaking, calligraphy & drawing, Macalester Col, 47-49; asst drawing, Mich State Univ, 49-50; from asst prof to assoc prof drawing, painting, printmaking & design, State Univ NY Col New Paltz, 50-57, actg chmn art dept, 55-56; exec dir, Md Inst Col Art, Baltimore, 57-59; chmn art dept, Univ Ill, Chicago Circle, 65-67, prof printmaking painting & drawing, 65-, assoc dean facs, 69-72, actg dean, Col Archit & Art, 75-77, prof emer, 88- *Awards:* Dr David Soletsky Award, Nat Soc Painters Casein & Acrylic Ann, 83; Audubon Artists Medal Hon Graphics, 84; Marion de Sola Mendes Award, Nat Soc Painters Casein & Acrylic, 85. *Mem:* Nat Soc Painters Casein & Acrylic; Pastel Soc Am. *Collection:* American prints of all periods and in all print media. *Publ:* Auth, Four Printmakers, 62; Miklos Suba, 64; Oliver Chaffee, 64. *Dealer:* R H Love Galleries 100 E Ohio Chicago IL 60611. *Mailing Add:* 1251 SE McGillivray Blvd Vancouver WA 98684

MAURICE, E(LEANOR) INGERSOLL
PAINTER, DESIGNER
b East Orange, NJ, Sept 4, 01. *Study:* Arts Student League, with F V Du Mond & Allen Tucker, 22-30; Montclair Mus, with Estelle Armstrong & Arery Johnson, 45-47. *Work:* Montclair Mus, NJ; Bloomfield Libr, NJ; Jersey City Mus, NJ; Norfolk Mus Arts & Sci, Va. *Comn:* Am Tel & Tel, NJ; Illus Ann Report, Dodge Found, 84. *Exhib:* Traveling shows, Am Watercolor Soc, New York, 63; Nat Acad Design; Audubon Artist Annuals; Allied Artist Annuals; Portland Mus, Maine; Butler Inst Annuals; one-man-shows, Bermuda Mus, Martha's Vineyard, Nantucket. *Awards:* Nat Acad Ann Award, 63; Audubon Artist Ann, 65; Butler Int Ann, 67; Ranger Prize, Am Watercolor Soc; Nat Art Club, Montclair Mus; Jersey City Mus. *Bibliog:* Norman Kent (auth), 100 Watercolor Techniques, Watson-Guptill. *Mem:* Life mem Am Watercolor Soc; life mem Art Students League; hon mem, Allied Artists of Am; Audubon Artists Am; NJ Watercolor Soc; Assoc Artist NJ. *Media:* Watercolor, Oil. *Dealer:* Chime Art Gallery 39 Maple St Summit NJ 07901. *Mailing Add:* 1412 W South Fork Dr Phoenix AZ 85044

MAUSSION, PIERRE EDUOARD See Edouard, Pierre (Pierre Edward Maussion)

MAVIGLIANO, GEORGE JEROME
ADMINISTRATOR, EDUCATOR
b Chicago, Ill, Oct 24, 41. *Study:* Western Ill Univ, BA, 64; Northern Ill Univ, MA, 67. *Pos:* Assoc Dean, Col Communications & Fine Arts, Southern Ill Univ, 86- *Teaching:* Assoc prof art hist, Southern Ill Univ, 70- *Awards:* Nat Endowment Arts Expansion Arts Grant, 77; Smithsonian Inst Fel, 81; Nat Endowment Humanities Summer Sem Award, 81 & 85. *Res:* New Deal art programs; art of the Capitol. *Publ:* Auth, A Matter of History: New Deal and the Arts (exhib catalog), 73; On Painting, Sculpture and Architecture, Stipes, 73; Fred Myers, Woodcarver, Southern Ill Univ, 80; The Federal Art Project: Holger Cahill's Program of Action, Art Education, Vol XXXVII, No 3, 5/84; The Chicago Design Workshop: 1939-1943, Journal of Decorative & Propaganda Arts, No 6, fall 87; The Federal Art Project in Illinois: 1935-43, Southern Ill Univ, 90. *Mailing Add:* Sch Art Southern Ill Univ Carbondale IL 62901

MAVROS, DONALD ODYSSEUS
CERAMIST, SCULPTOR
b New York, NY, Mar 4, 27. *Study:* Mabel Claire Brady; Cooper Union; Columbia Univ. *Work:* Everson Mus Art, Syracuse, NY; Orange Cty Community Col-Heritage Collection, Middletown, NY; Warren Wilson Col, Swannanoa, NC. *Comn:* Sculptures, City of New York, 54; portrait, Nat Republican Club, New York, 55; architectural reliefs, Lanai Restaurant, New York, 63; medallion, Theodore Roosevelt Hist Site, New York, 64; sculpture, The Bank for Savings, New York, 65; seven sculptures, Road to Mecca, production. *Exhib:* 15th & 17th Nat Exhibs, Syracuse Mus Art, NY, 50 & 52; 16th Nat Exhib (Nat Tour), Syracuse Mus Art, NY, 51; Ceramic Int, Everson Mus Art, Syracuse, NY, 58; Forms from the Earth, Mus Contemp Crafts, New York, 62; Hellenic Month, Univ Wisconsin, Madison, 77; Greek-American Artists, (sponsored by Embassy of Greece in conjunction with Search for Alexander Exhib) Grimaldis Gallery, Baltimore, Md, 81. *Pos:* Vpres, Artists-Craftsmen New York, 55-69; founder/dir, Trias Gallery, New York, 65-77; founding mem/exec bd, Empire State Crafts Alliance, New York, 80-83. *Teaching:* Dir/instr ceramics, Mavros Workshop, New York, 54-77; instr ceramics, New Sch Soc Research, New York, 60-77; dir/instr sculpture, Unionville Art Works, NY, 77- *Awards:* Sculpture Award & Pottery Award, 5th Young Americans Exhib; Sculpture Award, 3rd Young Americans Exhib, Am Crafts Coun, 52; Hon memtion, 16th Nat Ceramic Exhib, Syracuse Mus Fine Art, 51. *Bibliog:* Margot Granitsa (auth), Donald Odyesseus Mavros, John Daskalakis, 75; Louise Nevelson (auth), A Passionate Life, Summit Bks, 90. *Mem:* Artists Equity. *Media:* Clay. *Publ:* Auth, Getting Started in Ceramics, Macmillian, 70; contribr, 300th anniversary-Orange County, Publ, New York, 83; auth, Whither Mandeville, Orange Co Hist Soc, 89. *Mailing Add:* Unionville Art Works Jersey Ave Box 547 Unionville NY 10988

MAVROUDIS, DEMETRIOS
SCULPTOR
b Thasos, Greece, Nov 18, 37. *Study:* Jersey City State Col, BA; Teachers Col, Columbia Univ, MA & EdD. *Comn:* Bronze sculptures, Bus Comt for Arts, Esquire, 73-76; sculpture, Lifestyles Mag, 77; ESG Enterprises, 86; mosaic of Madonna & Child in St Constantine & Helen's Greek Cathedral, Richmond, Va, 87. *Exhib:* Albright-Knox Art Gallery, Buffalo, NY, 70 & 71; Artists-in-Residence Traveling Exhib, Del Art Mus, Wilmington, 75 & 76; Sculpture in the Fields, Storm King Art Ctr, Mountainville, NY; one-man shows, Philadelphia Art Alliance, Pa, Anchorage Hist & Fine Arts Mus, Alaska & Alaska State Mus. *Pos:* Artist-in-residence, NJ Coun Arts, 71-73. *Teaching:* Asst prof sculpture, NY Univ, New York, 69-71 & Teachers Col, Columbia Univ, 67-69 & 73-74; assoc prof sculpture & artist-in-residence, Univ Richmond, Va, 74-86. *Awards:* Dow Purchase Award, Columbia Univ, 69. *Mem:* Am Foundrymen's Soc; Nat Art Educ Asn; Col Art Asn. *Media:* Cast Metal, Wood. *Mailing Add:* 9712 Cherokee Rd Richmond VA 23235

MAX, LOPE (DIAZ)
PAINTER, EDUCATOR
b Santurce, PR, Dec 13, 43. *Study:* Univ PR, BA, 66; Hunter Col, New York, MA, 71. *Work:* Inter-Am Univ PR Art Gallery, Rio Piedras; Mus Latin Am Print, PR Inst Cult, San Juan; Carton de Venezuela, S A Graphic Collection; Glazo, RPT, Raleigh, NC; NationsBank, Charlotte, NC. *Exhib:* Solo shows, Mus Univ PR, Rio Piedras, 83 & Galeria Batello, Hato Rey, PR, 88; El Mus del Barrio, New York, 87-88; Univ PR Mus, Rio Piedras, 88; Marita Gilliam Art Gallery, Raleigh, NC, 89-90; World Gallery, Asheville, NC, 91; Peden Gallery, Raleigh, NC, 92. *Teaching:* Asst prof art, Sch Archit Univ PR, 76-88 & assoc prof, Sch Design, NC State Univ, 88- *Awards:* First Prize for Watercolor, Christmas Art Festival, Ateneo, PR, 66; First Prize for Painting, IBEC Group Show, 68; Honorary Award, Second Latin Am Graphic Biennale, Int PR Cult, 73. *Bibliog:* Manuel Perez-LIzano (auth), Arte Contemporaneo de Puerto Rico, 50-83, Univ Cent Bayamon, Ediciones Cruz Ansata, 85; Eva Sperling Cockcroft (auth), Report from Puerto Rico, Art in Am, 9/88; Max Halperen (auth), Just When He Thought it Was Safe to Hate Abstraction, Leader Mag, 7/27/89; Frank Thomson (auth), Equal Time for Multi-Cultural Art, Asheville Citizen Times, 5/5/91. *Mem:* City Gallery Contemp Art, Raleigh, NC. *Media:* Acrylic, Oil. *Publ:* Contribr, Kasimir Malevich: Revolucionario, Frente, 78. *Dealer:* Maud Duquella Gleria Botello Plaza las Americas 143 Hato Rey PR 00918; Peden Gallery II 132 E Hargett St Raleigh NC 27601. *Mailing Add:* PO Box 10012 Raleigh NC 27605

MAX, PETER
PAINTER, PRINTMAKER
b Berlin, Ger, Oct 19, 37; US citizen. *Study:* Art Students League; Pratt Inst; Sch Visual Arts. *Comn:* 12 environmental stamps, United Nations, 92; two murals (175'), Discovery, US Pavilion Expo 92; 108 portraits of Dali Lama, Hanson Gallery, 92; painting of the Nina, the Pinta & the Santa Maria, comn by Lady Pindling, 92; portrait, Gorby, comn by Mikhail Gorbachev, 92; The Better World, comn by Prince Rainier, 92; commemorative T-shirts, New York Harbor; and many others. *Exhib:* The Lady, created on the White House Lawn, 81; retrospective, Hermitage Mus, Russia, 91 & Acad Fine Arts, Moscow, 92; Flag (10' x 14'), Paints of Light Found, 92; Peter Max Paints America 92, Richmond, Va; Recent Works, Palm Beach, 92; Statue of Liberty Collage, Presidential Libr, Simi Valley, Calif, 92; Decades of the Hearts, Beverly Hills, 92; Hartmann Gallery, Munich, Ger, 92; exhib, Sporting d'Hiver, Monte Carlo, 92; and many others. *Pos:* Dir, Daly-Max Design Studio; designer, Gen Foods, Elgin Nat Industs, Takashimaya Ltd Japan, Van Heusen, UN & other major orgns. *Awards:* Celebrity Gala for Max, hosted by Don Johnson & Melanie Griffith, Aspen, Colo, 92; Official artist, Christopher Columbus Quincentenary, appointed by Congress, 92; Award, Int Poster Competition Poland; plus many others. *Bibliog:* Sal Manna (auth), Pushing it to the Max, Am Way, 6/25/85; Mark-Elliott Lugo (auth), Talent, enthusiasm hide behind Max's commercialism, 4/24/86; Maximum salute to the Statue of Liberty, 6/16/86 & Audrey Farolino (auth), Portrait of the artists-and his lady love!, 6/23/86, New York Post. *Media:* Mixed. *Publ:* Auth, Peter Max Posterbook & Peter Max Superposterbook, Crown; Peter Max Japan Book; drawings & meditations syndicated in 176 papers in US & Can, two yrs; illustr, cover for TV Guide's Super Bowl issue, 92; and many others. *Mailing Add:* Peter Max Enterprises 118 Riverside Dr New York NY 10024

MAXERA, OSCAR
PAINTER
b Argentina, Jan 12, 30. *Study:* Acad Fine Arts, Argentina, cert, 55. *Work:* Solomon R Guggenheim Mus (3 paintings), New York; Westport Mus, Conn, 77; Mus Mod Art, 82; and many more in pvt collections. *Exhib:* One-man shows, Nice Gallery, 68, 70 & 71, Ctr Cultural San Martin, 72, Lirolay Gallery, 73, Van Riel Gallery, 75, Buenos Aires, Argentina, Westport Pub Libr, 77; Mus Mod Art, Buenos Aires, 69-79; Mus Mod Art, Paraguay, 74; Solomon R Guggenheim Mus, 87. *Awards:* First Prize, Salon for Newcomers Fine Arts, 68; First Prize, Vincente Lopez Munic Salon, 70; Second Prize, San Antonio de Areco Salon, 73. *Bibliog:* Lyra Arte Sacro, Buenos Aires, 80; Fifty Years of Collections: Painting Since World War II, Guggenheim Mus, 87; Les Krantz (auth), NY Review, 90. *Media:* Acrylic. *Mailing Add:* 334 E 90th St No 3C New York NY 10128

MAXFIELD, ROBERTA MASUR
SILVERSMITH
b Chicago, Ill, Oct 30, 52. *Study:* Northern Ill Univ, with Eleanor Caldwell & Lee Peck, BFA, 74, MA, 75; Ind Univ, with Alma Eikerman, MFA, 77. *Work:* Ill State Mus, Springfield; Village Art Collection, Oak Park & River Forest High Sch, Ill. *Exhib:* Goldsmiths Show, Phoenix Art Mus, Ariz, 77; Ill Craftsmen, Ill State Mus, Springfield, 79; Everyday Metal Exhib, Nat Ornamental Mus, Memphis, Tenn, 80; Young Americans Metal, Am Crafts Mus, New York, 81; Calso, traveling, 81; Alma Eikerman Retrospective Exhib, Ind Univ Art Mus, 85; Soc Arts Crafts Pa, 85; Scent Bottle Exhibition, Signature Gallery, Mass, 85. *Awards:* Honorable Mention, Soc N Am Goldsmiths, 77; Purchase Award & Third Place, Village Art Fair, Village Art Comt, 79; Honorable Mention, Ill Crafts Exhib, Ill State Mus, 80. *Bibliog:* Craft Horizons, Am Coun Crafts, 4/77. *Mem:* Soc N Am Goldsmiths. *Media:* Sterling Silver. *Mailing Add:* 461 W Hillcrest De Kalb IL 60115

MAXIM, DAVID NICHOLAS
PAINTER, GRAPHIC ARTIST
b Los Angeles, Calif, May 11, 45. *Study:* Univ Calif Los Angeles, BA, 66, MA, 68. *Work:* Mus Moderne Kunst, Frankfurt, Ger; Carnegie Inst Art, Pittsburgh, Pa; San Francisco Mus Mod Art; Sunrise Mus, Charleston, WVa; Long Beach Mus Art, Calif. *Exhib:* Santa Barbara Selection, Santa Barbara Mus Art, Calif, 76; New Bay Area Images, Oakland Mus, Calif, 79; Bilder fur Frankfurt, Deutschen Architectur Mus, Frankfurt, Germany, 85; Ten Americans, Carnegie Inst Art, Pittsburgh, Pa, 88. *Bibliog:* Kenneth Baker (auth), David Maxim (exhib catalog), Foster Goldstrom, 90; Jan Butterfield (auth), David Maxim (exhib catalog), Galerie Sander, 91; August & Dorothy Friedman (coauths), Maxim's paint machines, Downtown, New York, 4/8/92. *Media:* Acrylic and Mixed Media on Canvas. *Dealer:* Foster Goldstrom Gallery 560 Broadway New York NY 10012. *Mailing Add:* 224 Guerrero St San Francisco CA 94103

MAXWELL, JOHN
PAINTER
b Rochester, NY. *Study:* Rochester Inst Technol; Univ Rochester; Provincetown Workshop; privately with nationally known instructors. *Work:* Philadelphia Mus Art; Nat Acad Design; Butler Inst Am Art; Wichita State Univ; Allentown Art Mus, Pa; and others. *Exhib:* Smithsonian Inst; Chicago Art Inst; Lehigh Univ; Rutgers Univ; William Penn Mus, Harrisburg, Pa; Woodmere Mus, Philadelphia; and others. *Awards:* Altman Prize, Nat Acad Design; Silver & Bronze Medals, Am Watercolor Soc; Dana Medal, Pa Acad Fine Arts; and others. *Bibliog:* Articles in Arts, Art News, Am Artist & others. *Mem:* Nat Acad Design; Am Watercolor Soc; Audubon Artists; Philadelphia Watercolor Club; Allied Artists Am; and others. *Media:* Oil, Watercolor. *Publ:* Writer on art & artists, with national magazine articles on: Giorgio Morandi, Henry C Pitz, Watercolors of John Maxwell; and others. *Dealer:* Newman & Saunders Galleries Wayne PA 19087. *Mailing Add:* 415 Holly Lane Wynnewood PA 19096

MAXWELL, PETER
DESIGNER, ART DEALER
b Easton, Pa, May 2, 30. *Pos:* Pres, Maxwell & Maxwell, 60-75, Maxwell Communications, 75-80 & Maxwell's Business, 80-; owner, Dolan-Maxwell Gallery, Philadelphia, 84- & New York, 88- *Mem:* Int Fine Print Dealers Asn; Philadelphia Art Dealers Asn. *Specialty:* Modern and contemporary art. *Publ:* Publ, Susan Rothenberg, The Prints, A Catalog Raisonne, 87; Roger Vieillard, 88; The Sculpture of Bill Freelend, 89. *Mailing Add:* 2046 Rittenhouse Sq Philadelphia PA 19103

MAXWELL, ROBERT EDWIN
PAINTER
b Mt Vernon, NY, Dec 31, 29. *Study:* Art Students League; Franklin Sch Art; Nat Acad Design, with Robert Philipp, Hallgarten travel scholarship, 51; Escuela de Bellas Artes with James Pinto, etching with Guilermo Silva Santamaria. *Work:* Galeria Moderna, Banjalvka, Yugoslavia; Inst Norteamericano de Relaciones Culturales, Mexico City; Vincent Price Collection. *Exhib:* Am Watercolor Soc, New York, 49; 14th Am Drawing Ann, Norfolk Mus, Va, 56; Nat Acad Design, 57; Acapulco Pictorial Festival, Mex, 64; Galeria Moderna, 74. *Teaching:* Instr drawing & landscape, Inst Allende, Mex, 55-56. *Awards:* Stacey Found Scholarship, 52. *Bibliog:* Image of Mexico II, Univ Tex, Austin; Crespo de la Serna (auth), Exhibit Paintings, 67 & Erasto Cortez Juarez (auth), Color and drawing, 69, Novedades, Mexico City. *Media:* Oil, Acrylic; Pastel. *Publ:* Contribr, Oil Painting-Traditional & New, 59; Painters Workshop, 69. *Mailing Add:* San Pedro 18 San Miguel de Allende Guanajuato Mexico

MAXWELL, WILLIAM C
PAINTER, PRINTMAKER
b Yonkers, NY, Sept 3, 41. *Study:* Wagner Col, Staten Island, NY, BFA, 70; Columbia Univ, New York, MA, 71, EdM, 72, EdD, 76; study with Paul Pollaro, Clare Romano & Deli Sacilotto. *Work:* Hudson River Mus, Yonkers, NY; Brooklyn Mus, NY; Arthur Wesley Dow Collection & Federico Castellon Mem Collection, Columbia Univ; Univ Mass, Amherst; State Dept of Educ, Trenton, NJ; Mus Mod Art, NJ; and others. *Exhib:* Printmakers 1973, Metrop Mus of Art, New York, 73; 19th Nat Print Exhib Traveling Show, Brooklyn Mus, 74-75; Elizabeth Weiner Galleries, New York, 79-81; Cardet Gallery, Coral Gables, Fla, 81; Brooklyn Acad Music, 82; Univ Conn, Hartford, 83; Bernice Steinbaum Gallery, New York, 83; Robert Martin Gallery, New York, 89; and others. *Pos:* Master printer, Bank St Atelier, 68-71; cur, Federico Castellon Mem Collection, Columbia Univ, New York, 75-88; master printer & vpres, Maxwell-Nova Fine Arts, Inc. *Teaching:* Vis prof art & educ, Teachers Col, Columbia Univ, New York, 71-88; prof painting & printmaking & chmn Art Dept, Col of New Rochelle, NY, 75- *Awards:* President's Award, Nat Arts Club, New York, 75; Shields Award, New York, 75; Purchase Award, Univ Dallas, Irving, Tex, 80. *Bibliog:* Edgar Bournagurio (auth), rev in Arts, 6/79; Peter Frank (auth), rev in Village Voice, 6/79; Helen Thomas (auth), rev in Arts, 10/80. *Mem:* Col Art Asn; Nat Art Educ Asn; Artist's Equity; Nat Asn Art Adminrs; and others. *Media:* Mixed Aqueous, Oil; Polymer, Oil Print. *Publ:* Contribr, Elizabeth Harris & Sue Vardin (auths), Urban Education, Open Univ, London, 74; auth, Printmaking: A Beginning Handbook, Prentice-Hall, 77. *Dealer:* Ledis-Flare Gallery 104 11th Ave Brooklyn NY; Windmueller Gallery Scarsdale NY. *Mailing Add:* 307-9 Canal St New York NY 10012

MAXWELL, WILLIAM JACKSON
SCULPTOR, ENVIRONMENTAL ARTIST
b Auburn, Calif, Feb 16, 47. *Study:* Calif State Univ, Sacramento, BA, 73; Claremont Grad Sch, MFA, 75. *Work:* San Antonio Mus Art, Citizen's First Bank, First City Bank, San Antonio, Tex; Crocker Art Mus, Sacramento, Calif; also pvt collections of Joseph & Francine Burg, Los Angeles, Mr & Mrs Rosenberg, San Rafael, Calif, Mrs Bagen Dela, San Antonio. *Comn:* sculpture, fountains & lightworks, Nev State Supreme Ct Bldg Proj, Nev State Coun Arts, Carson City, 89; Tunnel Vision, (light sculpture) New Denver Airport, Colo, 90-93; light sculpture & terrazzo floor, Dallas Conv Ctr Expansion/Veriport Proj, Dallas, 90-93; fountain & light sculpture, Univ WFla, Ctr Fine & Performing Arts, Pensacola, 90-93; fountain, Int Ctr Preserv Wild Animals Inc, Biopark, Zanesville, Ohio, 90-93; and others. *Exhib:* Summer Works, Lang Art Gallery, Scripps Col, Claremont, Calif, 76; California Lead, Peace Gallery, San Francisco, 77; Texas Select, Art League of Houston, 86; Sheppard Gallery, Univ Nev, Reno, 89; Dream Chambers, Arvada Ctr Arts & Humanities, Arvada, Colo, 90. *Teaching:* Instr sculpture & ceramics, Expos Ctr, Arts for the Handicapped, Sacramento, 78-81; instr art, Univ Tex, San Antonio, 82, San Antonio Art Inst, 83 & Southwest Craft Ctr, San Antonio, fall 85, Southside Art Ctr, Sacramento, 87-89; dept chmn, Fine Arts Prog, St Mary's Hall, San Antonio, summer, 86. *Awards:* Winning Sculpture Design for 1984 Louisiana World Expos, New Orleans, La, 83; Calif Arts Coun Artist Fel in New Genres, 88; Nat Endowment Arts, 83, 88, & 90. *Bibliog:* The shock of recognition, San Antonio Express News, 2/8/87; Simulations reflections the fragility of river life, Sacramento Bee, 6/30/89; Ingrid Evans (auth), Public art for the smallest capital, Artspace, Aug, 90. *Publ:* Auth, Carlozzi, Fifty Texas Artists, Chronicle Bks, San Francisco, 86; The Water Calendar, Artists Celebrate Nature, Global Forum, New York, 93. *Mailing Add:* 3340 Broadway St Boulder CO 80304-2242

MAY, DANIEL STRIGER
DEALER
b Decatur, Ill, Sept 5, 42. *Study:* State Univ NY, Buffalo, BA, 64, MBA, 66 & MEd, 68. *Pos:* Dir, Jackson Hole Art Gallery, 70-72; owner & dir, May Gallery, Jackson, Wyo, 72-; owner, May Gallery, Scottsdale, Ariz, 78- *Specialty:* Fine American paintings and sculpture; contemporary jewelry. *Mailing Add:* 6166 N Scottsdale Rd Scottsdale AZ 85253

MAYEN, PAUL
DESIGNER
b La Linea, Spain, May 31, 18. *Study:* Cooper Union Art Sch; Art Students League; Columbia Univ; New Sch Social Res. *Work:* Mus Mod Art. *Exhib:* Brooklyn Mus; Mus Mod Art; Nelson Gallery Art; Ann Adver Art. *Pos:* Design consult, var indust orgns; bk designer, leading publ, ads, booklets & others; art dir, Agfa, Inc, Orradio & NAm Philips Co; design coordr, Cadre Industs & Habitat, Inc; designer for exhibs, US Info Agency; staff designer, Intrex, Inc; furniture designer, Archit Suppl Inc; designer, Visitor Ctr, Fallingwater House. *Teaching:* Instr advert design, Cooper Union Art Sch; former instr advert design, Parsons Sch, New York. *Awards:* Art Dirs Club Award, NY; and others. *Publ:* Contribr, Indust Design, Interiors, Progressive Archit, Art News Ann, Progressive Archit & others. *Mailing Add:* 61 Cedar Rd Cresskill NJ 07626

MAYER, BILLY (WILLIAM ROBERT MAYER)
SCULPTOR
b St Paul, Minn, June 28, 53. *Study:* Univ Minn, BFA, 76; Pa State Univ, MFA, 78. *Work:* Frederick Weisman Collection, Los Angeles, Calif; Muskegan Art Mus, Mich; Univ Galleries, Univ Minn. *Comn:* Outdoor sculpture, Holland, Mich, 83; large-scale sculpture, Howard Miller Inc, Zeeland, Mich, 85; outdoor sculpture, Christ Community Church, Spring Lake, Mich, 88. *Exhib:* West Michigan Art Exhib, Muskegan Mus Art, 86; Signs, Times and Writing on the Wall, Detroit Inst Art, Mich, 87; Appalachian summer sculpture competition, Appalachian State Univ Gallery, Boone, NC, 88; two-person exhib, Muskegan Mus Art, Mich, 88 & Rochester Art Ctr, Minn, 90; solo exhib, Grand Rapids Art Mus, Mich, 89; SW Tex State Univ, 90. *Pos:* Chmn art dept, Hope Col, Holland, Mich, 88- *Teaching:* Instr ceramic/sculpture, Hope Col, 78-79, asst prof, 79-85 & assoc prof, 85- *Awards:* Merit Award, Whirlpool Sculpture, Krasl Art Ctr, St Joseph, Mich, 85; Merit Award, W Mich Regional, Muskegan Mus Art, 88. *Media:* Clay, Welded Metal. *Mailing Add:* Hope College Holland MI 49423

MAYER, EDWARD ALBERT
SCULPTOR, EDUCATOR
b Union, NJ, Oct 30, 42. *Study:* Brown Univ, Providence, RI, BA, 64; Univ Wis, Madison, MFA, 66. *Work:* Milwaukee Art Mus, Wis; Huntington Galleries, WVa; Rose Art Mus, Waltham, Mass; Ohio State Univ; NMex State Univ. *Comn:* Ohio Bldg Authority, Columbus, 74. *Exhib:* One-man shows, Kunsthalle Darmstadt, Ger, 78, Nassau Co Mus Fine Art, Roslyn, NY, 80, Zabriskie Gallery, New York, 80, Rose Art Mus, Waltham, Mass, 81; Architectural Sculpture, Los Angeles Inst Contemp Art, Calif, 80; Five Ohio Sculptors, Contemp Art Ctr, Cincinnati, 80; Columbus Mus, 82; Akron Art Mus, 83; Sao Paulo Bienal, 85; Zolla Lieberman, Chicago, 85; Burchfield Art Ctr, Buffalo, 88; Public Art Works, San Rafael, Calif, 89. *Teaching:* Asst prof art, Carthage Col, Kenosha, Wis, 66-70; prof sculpture, Ohio Univ, Athens, 70-83; vis sculptor, Tyler Sch Art, Rome, Italy, 73-74; prof sculpture, State Univ NY, Albany, 83- *Awards:* Nat Fel, Nat Endowment Arts, 78, 79 & 86; Ava Fel, 83; NYFA in Sculpture, 86. *Bibliog:* Ronald J Onorato (auth), review, Artforum, 12/78; Deborah Perlberg (auth), review, Artforum, 1/79; Virginia Mann (auth), Review, Arts Mag, 3/82. *Media:* All. *Mailing Add:* Dept Art State Univ NY Albany NY 12222

MAYER, GRACE M
CURATOR, COLLECTOR
b New York, NY. *Study:* Pvt schs & tutors, US & abroad. *Collections Arranged:* Currier & Ives & the New York Scene, 39, Philip Hone's New York, 40, New York Between Two Wars, 44, Stranger in Manhattan, 50, Charles Dana Gibson's New York, 50 & Currier & Ives Printmakers to the American People, 57-58, Mus of City of New York; 70 Photographers Look at New York (with Edward Steichen), 57-58, The Sense of Abstraction, 60, Steichen, The Photographer, 61 & Mus Mod Art, New York; and others. *Pos:* Cur, New York Iconography, Mus of City of New York, 31-59; spec asst to dir dept photog, Mus Mod Art, New York, 59-60, assoc cur dept photog, 61-62, cur dept photog, 62-68, cur, Edward Steichen Arch, Dept Photog, 68-72 & vol cur, 72- *Awards:* Infinity Award, Maine Photogr Bookshops. *Mem:* Print Coun Am; resident mem Cosmopolitan Club New York. *Res:* New York subjects; history of photography. *Collection:* Posters, lithographs and autographed letter signed Toulouse-Lautrec; photographs, especially those of Edward Steichen; books on photography; book on Edward Steichen, in progress. *Publ:* Auth articles, Mus of City of New York Bulletin, Mus Mod Art Bulletin & var photog mags; auth, Once Upon a City & Edward Steichen, Macmillan, 58. *Mailing Add:* 35 E 76th St New York NY 10021

MAYER, ROBERT ANTHONY
MUSEUM DIRECTOR, ADMINISTRATOR
b New York, NY, Oct 30, 33. *Study:* Fairleigh Dickinson Univ, BA(magna cum laude), 55; New York Univ, MA, 67. *Collections Arranged:* Traveling Exhibs, Photographing the American Presidency (auth, catalog), 84, Blacks in America: A Photographic Record (auth, catalog), 86 & American Writers, Int Mus Photogr. *Pos:* Exec dir, NY State Coun Arts, 76-; dir, Int Mus Photogr, George Eastman House, Rochester, NY, formerly; vpres & bd trustees, Alliance Independent Col Art, 86- *Mem:* NY State Asn Mus (pres, currently); Nat Ctr Film & Video Preserv (adv bd); Asn Art Mus Dirs; NY State Motion Picture & Television Develop (adv bd). *Publ:* Co-auth (with K C Hart), Patronage of the Arts in the United States, Funk & Wagnalls 1977 Yearbook; auth, New York: The State of Art, New York Affairs, 4/78; The Arts Debate: Elitism vs Populism, Grants Mag, 5/78. *Mailing Add:* c/o Clevland Inst Art 11141 East Blvd Cleveland OH 44106-1710

MAYER, ROSEMARY
SCULPTOR, GRAPHIC ARTIST
b Ridgewood, NY, Feb 27, 43. *Study:* State Univ Iowa, Iowa City, AB, 64; Brooklyn Mus Art Sch, 65-67; Sch Visual Arts, New York, 67-69. *Work:* Sidney Lewis Collection, Richmond, Va; Herbert Johnson Mus, Cornell Univ, Ithaca, NY; Allen Mem Art Mus, Oberlin Col, Ohio; Hartwick Col Collection, Oneonta, NY. *Comn:* Spell (temp outdoor work with weather balloons), Queens Coun Arts & Greater Jamaica Develop Coun, 77; Balloon, Rose Hill Property Assoc, New York, 78; plans for Orfeo, Soho Baroque Opera Co, New York, 82. *Exhib:* One-person shows, Whitney Mus Am Art Resources Ctr, New York, 75, 55 Mercer St, New York, 79, Cornell Univ, 80 & Locrian Mode, Interart Ctr, NY, 80; Times Square Show, NY, 80; Moontent (outdoor installation), Lansing, NY, 82; Pam Adler Gallery, New York, 85; and others. *Pos:* Art writer & reviewer, Arts Mag, 71-73 & Art Am, 74-75. *Teaching:* Vis artist painting, Art Inst Chicago, 74; vis artist painting & drawing, Hartwick Col, Oneonta, 76; Artist's Workshop Program, Nat Endowment Arts, 81-; lectr art, Baruch Col, City Univ New York, 87-; instr, Brooklyn Eng & Speech, Long Island, Univ, NY, 88- *Awards:* Creative Artists Pub Serv Grant, NY State Coun Arts, 76-77, 80-81 & 82; Nat Endowment Arts Grant, 79-80; Pollock Krasner Found, 87 & 88. *Bibliog:* Bruce Kurtz (auth), Rosemary Mayer, Art in Am, 3-4/77; Valentin Tatransky (auth), Rosemary Mayer, Arts Mag, 4/78; Ballerini & Milazzo (eds), Pontormo's Diary/Rosemary Mayer, 82; Reagan Upshaw (auth), Rosemary Mayer, Art in Am, 10/85. *Media:* Fabric, Rag Vellum; Watercolor, Pencil. *Publ:* Auth, Those, White Walls, winter 80; auth, Pontormo's Diary, Out of London Press, 82; auth, Moontent, White Walls, winter 83; auth, Beauty and Critique, TSL Ltd, 83; auth, Some of my stories, Heresies, no 23, 88. *Mailing Add:* 55 Leonard St New York NY 10013

MAYER, SONDRA
ART DEALER, PRINTMAKER
b New York, NY, July 12, 33. *Study:* Syracuse Univ, BA, 54; Columbia Univ, MA, 55; Mus Mod Art, 57-58; Pratt Inst, 68; Art Students League, 72. *Work:* Los Angeles Co Mus Art, Los Angeles; Syracuse Univ Lowe Gallery, NY; MacDowell Colony Collection, Peterborough, NH; Portland Art Mus, Ore; Crocker Nat Bank, San Francisco, Calif. *Comn:* Greeting card design, Mus Mod Art, New York, 76 & 78; design for Star & Snowflake Jewelry, Metrop Mus Art, New York 77 & 81; greeting card design, UNICEF, 79 & 81; greeting card design, Cartier, 85. *Exhib:* Philadelphia Print Club; Boston Printmakers Ann, DeCordova Mus, Lincoln, Mass, 79; Current Works, Everson Mus, Syracuse, NY, 80; Heckscher Mus, Huntington, NY, 79-82; Int Miniature Show, Seoul, Korea, 80; Queens Mus, 81; and others. *Pos:* Asst dir, Printmaking Studio Sch, 75-84; assoc gallery dir, 84-86; owner & dir, Sondra Mayer Fine Art. *Teaching:* Instr printmaking, Ruth Leaf Studio, Douglaston, NY, 76- *Awards:* MacDowell Colony fel, Peterborough, NH, 78; Leila Sawyer Mem Prize in Graphics, Nat Asn Women Artists, 79; Graphics Award, Firehouse Gallery, Garden City, New York, 81. *Mem:* Artists Equity New York; Philadelphia Print Club; MacDowell Colony Fellows. *Media:* Etching, Intaglio. *Specialty:* Contemporary and modern art in all media with a special interest in master graphics. *Publ:* Illusr, Intaglio Printmaking Techniques, Watson-Guptill, 76; contribr, Graphis Ann, Graphis Press, 78-79; and others. *Mailing Add:* 6 Wooleys Lane No 32A Great Neck NY 11023

MAYER, SUSAN MARTIN
EDUCATOR, MUSEOLOGIST
b Atlanta, Ga, Oct 25, 31. *Study:* Am Univ; Univ NC, BA(art); Univ Del; Ariz State Univ, MA(art educ); Atelier Grande Chaumier, Paris; Kans State Univ. *Exhib:* two-person show, Hanging Gardens, AIR Gallery, Austin, Tex, 87; Earthly Delights: Garden Imagery in Contemp Art, Ft Wayne Mus Art, 88; solo show, Galveston Arts Ctr, 90. *Teaching:* Coordr mus educ, Huntington Art Gallery, Univ Tex, 70- & art fac, 71- *Awards:* Mus Educators Award, Nat Art Educ Asn, 83; Distinguished Serv Award, Nat Art Educ Asn, 91. *Mem:* Nat Art Educ Asn; Tex Art Educ Asn; Tex Asn Mus; Am Asn Mus. *Media:* Oil. *Publ:* Coauth, (with B Reese), A Woman's Place, 77 Am Images, 81 & Texas, 83; coauth, (with B Reese & A Mayer), Texas, Trillium Press, 87; auth, Art Works, Holt Rinehart & Winston, 89; Museum Education: History, Theory & Practice, Nat Art Educ Asn, Reston, Va, 89. *Mailing Add:* Dept Art Univ Texas at Austin Austin TX 78712

MAYERI, BEVERLY
SCULPTOR
Study: Univ Calif, BA, 67; San Francisco State Univ, MA, 76. *Exhib:* Solo exhibs, Ivory/Kimpton Gallery, San Francisco, Calif, 81 & 83, Garth Clark Gallery, New York, 85 & 87 & San Jose Inst Contemp Art, Calif, 90; Renwick Gallery, Smithsonian Inst, Washington, DC, 81; Signet Arts Gallery, St Louis, Mo, 84; Robert L Kidd Gallery, Birmingham, Mich, 86; Fresno Arts Ctr & Mus, Calif, 87; Euphrat Gallery, De Anza Col, Cupertino, Calif, 88; Esther Saks Gallery, Chicago, 88 & 90; Dorothy Weiss Gallery, San Francisco, Calif, 90 & 92. *Awards:* Nat Endowment Arts, 82 & 88; Individual Artist Grant, Marin Arts Coun, 87; Recognition Grant, Groot Fedn, 91. *Publ:* Numerous articles in New Art Examiner, Artweek, Ceramics Mo, Am Craft, Am Ceramics, 88-90. *Mailing Add:* c/o Esther Saks Gallery 3400 N Lake Shore Dr Apt 6B Chicago IL 60657-2801

MAYES, ELAINE
PHOTOGRAPHER
b Berkeley, Calif, Oct 1, 38. *Study:* Stanford Univ, BA, 59; San Francisco Art Inst, with Paul Hassel, John Collier & Minor White. *Work:* San Francisco Art Inst; Mus Mod Art & Metrop Mus Art, New York; Minneapolis Inst Arts, Minn; Oakland Mus, Calif; and many others. *Exhib:* Mass Inst Technol, 69; New Acquisitions, 70 & Photographs of Women, 71, Mus Mod Art, New York; Landscape-Cityscape, Metrop Mus Art, New York, 74; Pratt Inst, 76 & 79; Photog & Landscape, George Eastman House, Rochester, NY, 77 & Boston Mus Fine Arts, 78; Photographs from Collection of Sam Wagstaff, Corcoran Gallery Art, DC, Grey Gallery, NY Univ, St Louis Mus, Mo, Seattle Mus Art, Wash & Berkeley Mus Art, Calif, 78-79; Ft Wayne Ind Mus Art, 88; Sandra Berler, Chevy Chase, Md, 80, 82, 84, 88 & 90; plus many others. *Teaching:* Instr photog & filmmaking, Univ Minn, 68-70; assoc prof film & photog, Hampshire Col, 71-81 & Bard Col, 82-84; assoc prof photog, Tisch Sch Art, NY Univ, 84- *Awards:* Nat Endowment Arts, 71 & 78; CAPS, 82; Guggenheim, 91 & 92. *Mem:* Soc Photog Educ. *Publ:* Auth, Chap, In, Darkroom, Lustrum Press, New York, 77; contribr, Faces: A History of Photographic Portraiture, Chanticleer Press, New York, 77; A Book of Photographs, by Sam Wagstaff, New York, 78; San Francisco Viewed, Chronicle Books, 85; The Cat in Photography, 90; and others. *Mailing Add:* 18 Mercer St New York NY 10013

MAYES, STEVEN LEE
EDUCATOR, PRINTMAKER
b Los Angeles, Calif, Nov 7, 39. *Study:* Wichita State Univ, BFA & BAE, 62, MFA, 65. *Work:* SDak Mem Art Ctr, Brookings; Sioux City Art Ctr, Iowa; Wichita Art Mus, Kans; Tamarind Inst, Univ NMex, Albuquerque; Univ NDak, Grand Forks. *Exhib:* 13th Midwest Biennial, Joslyn Mus, Omaha, Nebr, 72; Fourth Nat Print & Drawing Exhib, Minot State Col, NDak, 74; 12th Ann Paper Works, Waterloo Munic Galleries, Iowa, 76; Amarillo Art Ctr, Tex, 79 & 81; Catskill Ctr Photography, Woodstock, New York, 81; SIGGRAPH, San Francisco, Calif, 85; 15th Ann Fine Arts Competition, Greensboro Artists League, SC. *Teaching:* Prof printmaking & drawing, SDak State Univ, Brookings, 71-77; prof printmaking & design, WTex State Univ, Canyon, 77-88; prof art, Ark State Univ, Jonesboro, 88- *Awards:* Purchase Awards, Fifth NDak Ann, Univ NDak, 61, 33rd & 35th Ann Fall Show, Sioux City Art Ctr, Iowa, 71 & 73. *Media:* Multi. *Dealer:* Miriam Perlman 505 N Lakeshore Dr Chicago IL 60611; Charlton Gallery 308 N Presa San Antonio TX 78205. *Mailing Add:* 5006 S Culberhouse Jonesboro AR 72401

MAYFIELD, SIGNE S
CURATOR
Study: Univ Calif-Berkeley, BA(art hist), 65; George Washington Univ, MA Prog, Higher Education. *Collections Arranged:* From Tapestry to Vessel: Contemp Fiber Art, 90, Portraits of Literature, 90, Richard Shaw, 90, Transport, 90-91, Responsive Witness, 91, Art of the 30's in the San Francisco Bay Area, 91-92, Treasures of Old Russia, 92, Contemp Uses of Wax & Encaustic, 92 Directions in Bay Area Printmaking (auth, catalog), 92 & Palo Alto, Cult Ctr. *Pos:* Cur, Palo Alto Cult Ctr, 89- *Mem:* Graphic Arts Coun; Achenbach Found Bd Dirs. *Publ:* Coauth, Marriage in Form: Kay Sekimachi & Bob Stocksdale, Palo Alto, Cult Ctr, 93. *Mailing Add:* Palo Alto Cultural Center 1313 Newell Rd Palo Alto CA 94303

MAYHALL, DOROTHY
MUSEUM DIRECTOR, CURATOR
b Portland Ore. *Study:* Univ Nebr, Omaha, 43-45; Univ Iowa, Iowa City, BFA, 47, MFA, MA, 49; Fulbright Scholar, Paris, France, 50. *Collections Arranged:* Folk Art: Then and Now, 85, American Art; American Women, 86, Color: Pure and Simple, 87, Private Expressions, 87 & 88, American Art:

1890-1910, Stamford Mus, 85; Natural Image, 1989, John Button, 89, Cletus Johnson, 90, John Margolies, 90, Nicholas Krushenick, 92, Fiber Forms, 92. *Pos:* Dir, Aldrich Mus, Ridgefield, Conn, 65-71 & 79-84; dir, Storm King Art Ctr, 71-75; dir art, Stamford Mus & Nature Ctr, Conn, 84- *Teaching:* Instr studio arts & hist, Univ Omaha Nebr, 51-53; instr art hist survey, Univ Houston, Victoria, Tex, 76-78. *Awards:* Fulbright Scholar, Paris, France, 50-51. *Mem:* Stamford Community Arts Coun (bd mem, chairperson, gallery, CMT); Co-chmn, Mayor's Art Gallery; Stamford Public Art Comt; art adv bd, Norwalk Commun Col; bd mem, Art for Spec People, Stamford. *Res:* Contemporary & 19th century art. *Mailing Add:* 27 Middle Ridge Road Stamford CT 06903

MAYHEW, ELZA
SCULPTOR
b Victoria, BC. *Study:* Univ BC, Can, BA; Univ Ore, MFA; also with Jan Zach, Victoria, BC; Univ Victoria, Hon Dr, 89. *Work:* Univ Victoria; Art Gallery Gtr Victoria; Nat Gallery Can, Ottawa; Simon Fraser Univ, Vancouver; Meditation Ctr, Expo, Montreal. *Comn:* Coast Spirit (bronze), Univ Victoria, 67; bronze mural, Bank Can Lobby, Vancouver, 68; Concordia (bronze column), Brock Univ, Ont, 68; Column of the Sea, Confederation Ctr, Charlottetown, 73; Bronz Priestess, Univ Victoria, 88; and others. *Exhib:* Equinox Gallery, Vancouver, 80; Wallack Gallery, Ottawa, 81; EXPO 86, Vancouver; Port Angeles Fine Art Ctr, 88; Fran Willis Gallery, Victoria, 91; and others. *Pos:* Bd dirs, Nat Sculpture Ctr, Univ Kans, 68-79; BC Govt Comt for Art, 74. *Awards:* Sir Otto Beit Medal, Royal Soc Brit Sculptors, 62. *Bibliog:* Robin Skelton (auth), A language for humanity, Malahat Rev, 4/71; Univ Victoria Quart, 72; Karl Spreitz (dir), Time-Markers: Making of the Column of the Sea (film), 85; and others. *Mem:* Sculptors Soc Can, BC; Royal Can Acad Arts. *Media:* Cast Metal. *Mailing Add:* 698 Bever Lake Rd Victoria BC V8Z 5N8 Canada

MAYHEW, RICHARD
PAINTER
b Amityville, NY, Apr 3, 34. *Study:* Art Students League; Brooklyn Mus Art Sch, studied with Edwin Dickinson and Reuben Tam, 51; Columbia Univ, New York, NY. *Work:* Whitney Mus Am Art; Nat Mus Am Art, Smithsonian Inst; Brooklyn Mus; Mus Mod Art; Nat Acad Design; and many others. *Exhib:* Butler Art Inst, Youngstown, Ohio, 61; Brooklyn Mus, 61; Whitney Mus Am Art Ann; Univ Ill, 63; retrospective, Studio Mus, New York, 78; solo exhibs, San Jose Mus Art, 80, Pa State Univ Mus, 83 & Young Gallery, San Jose, 85; Midtown Galleries, New York, 82-87. *Teaching:* Instr art, Brooklyn Mus Art Sch, 63-68 & Art Students League, 65-71; instr, Smith Col, 69-70; asst prof, Hunter Col, 71-75; prof, Pa State Univ, 77- *Awards:* Benjamin Altman Award, Nat Acad Design, 70; Merit Award, Nat Acad Design, 77; Grumbacher Gold Medal, Nat Acad Design, 83. *Mem:* Nat Acad Design; MacDowell Colony Asn. *Media:* Oil, Watercolor. *Dealer:* Midtown Payson Galleries 745 Fifth Ave New York NY 10151; Braunstein/Quay Gallery 545 Sutter St San Francisco CA 94115. *Mailing Add:* PO Box 7720 Santa Cruz CA 95061-7720

MAYNARD, WILLIAM
PAINTER, EDUCATOR
b Brookline, Mass, Dec 31, 21. *Study:* Mass Col Art; Sch Mus Fine Arts, Boston, dipl, 50. *Work:* Boston Mus Fine Arts; Springfield Mus Fine Arts, Mass; Fairleigh Dickinson Univ; Fitchburg Mus Fine Arts; Tufts Univ; Mus Arts & Sci, Macon, Ga. *Exhib:* Shore Studio Galleries, Charles Childs Gallery & Vose Gallery, Boston; De Cordova Mus, Lincoln, Mass; Busche Reisinger Mus, Cambridge, Mass; J H Webb Gallery, Macon, Ga, 85. *Pos:* Chmn dept fine arts, New England Sch Art & Design, 74- *Teaching:* Instr drawing & painting, Boston Mus Fine Arts, 60-67; instr painting, New Eng Sch Art & Design, currently. *Mem:* New Eng Watercolor Soc; Provincetown Art Asn; Copley Soc; Brookline Soc Artists. *Media:* Watercolor, Acrylic. *Mailing Add:* 72A Commercial St Provincetown MA 02657

MAYO, MARGARET ELLEN
CURATOR
b Charlottesville, Va, May 18, 44. *Study:* Randolph-Macon Womans Col, AB, 66; Rutgers Univ, PhD, 73. *Collections Arranged:* Ancient Portraiture: The Sculptor's Art in Coins and Marble, 80 & The Art of South Italy: Vases From Magna Graecia (auth, catalog), 82, Va Mus; Wealth of the Ancient World: The Nelson Bunker Hunt and William Herbert Hunt Collections (coauth, catalog), 83. *Pos:* Res assoc, Iconographical Lexicon, Rutgers Univ, 73-76; dir, Summa Galleries, Beverly Hills, 76-78; cur, Ancient Art, Va Mus, 78- *Mem:* Archaeol Inst Am; Soc Promotion Hellenic Studies. *Res:* Greek art; Greek and south Italian vase-painting. *Mailing Add:* Cur Ancient Art Va Mus Fine Art 2800 Boulevard & Grove Ave Richmond VA 23221-2466

MAYO, MARTI
MUSEUM DIRECTOR, CURATOR
b Bluefield, WVa, Oct 17, 45. *Study:* Am Univ, BA, 70, MFA, 74. *Collections Arranged:* Vernon Fisher Story Paintings & Drawings (auth, catalog), 80; The New Photography (auth, catalog), 80; Placements and Performances: Works for Washington, 80; Other Realities: Installations for Performance (auth, catalog), 81; 4 Painters: Jones, Smith, Stack, Utterback (auth, catalog), 81; Robert Morris: Selected Works 1970-1980 (auth, catalog), 81; Paintings by Pat Steir (auth, catalog), 83; Michael Tracy: Requiem Para Los Olvidados (auth, catalog), 83; Southern Fictions, 83; Recent works of Robert Helm, 84; Paintings by Mark Tansey, 85; Barbara Kruger: Striking Poses, 85; Robert Rauschenberg: Work from Four Series, 86; Works of Joseph Glasco, 86; Images on Stone: Two Centuries of Artists Lithographs, 87; 6 Artists: 6 Idioms, 88; Gael Stack: A Survey 1974-1989, 89; Reinventing Reality: Five Tex Photogrs, 90. *Pos:* Coordr exhib, Corcoran Gallery Art, DC, 74-80; cur, Contemp Arts Mus, Houston, 80-86; dir, Blaffer Gallery, Univ Houston, 86- *Teaching:* Contemp art & criticism, Glassell Sch Art, Mus Fine Arts, Houston, 84-86; Art since 1960, Univ Houston, 86-91. *Mem:* Am Asn Mus; Col Art Asn. *Publ:* Auth, Robert & Morris: Selected works (exhib catalog), 81; Robert Rauschenberg: A Chronology (exhib catalog), Contemp Arts Mus, Houston, 86; Joseph Glasco: 1948-1986 (exhib catalog), Contemp Art Mus, Houston, 86; Gael Stack (exhib catalog), Univ Houston, 88; Northwest x Southwest: Painted Fictions (exhib catalog), Palm Springs Desert Mus, 90. *Mailing Add:* Sarah Campbell Blaffer Gallery 4800 Calhoun Univ Houston Houston TX 77004

MAYO, PAMELA ELIZABETH
GALLERY DIRECTOR
b Richmond, Va, June 18, 59. *Study:* Longwood Col, BFA, 81. *Collections Arranged:* Lue Osborne & Cordray Simmons, Am Regionalists (auth, catalog), 80; America, the Sporting View, Sporting Art (ed, catalog), 85; The Art of Doris Spiegel (auth, catalog). *Pos:* Dir & appraiser, Gallery Mayo, Inc, Richmond, Va, 81- *Mem:* Int Soc Appraisers. *Specialty:* Late 19th-early 20th century American art. *Mailing Add:* 5705 Grove Ave Richmond VA 23226

MAYO, ROBERT BOWERS
ART DEALER, COLLECTOR
b Phoenixville, Pa, Apr 26, 33. *Study:* Art Students League, 49; Chicago Art Inst, 51; Richmond Prof Inst (Va Commonwealth Univ), BA, 59. *Collections Arranged:* Thomas Sully & His Contemporaries, 78; Mrs Susan Waters, 19th Century Itinerant Painter, 79; American Paintings from Virginia Collectors, 81; America: The Sporting View (auth, catalog), 85. *Pos:* Cur, Jamestown Festival Park, Va, 59-61; exhibs designer, Hall Hist, Raleigh, NC, 61-66; dir, Valentine Mus, Richmond, 66-75; owner, Gallery Mayo Inc, Richmond, presently. *Teaching:* Guest lectr, NY Hist Soc, Cooperstown, summer 72; guest lectr, Longwood Col, Farmville, Va, 79. *Mem:* Am Asn Mus (nat coun, 73-77); SEastern Mus Conf Inc (pres, 74); Va Mus Fedn (pres, 72-73); Antiquarian Soc Richmond (pres, 74-75); Collector's Circle, Va Mus Fine Arts. *Interests:* Collector of early American Sporting Art - 19th & early 20th century. *Publ:* Auth, Exhibit techniques for small museums, Mus News, 73; auth, Painting collection of the Valentine Museum, Mag Antiques, 73; America: The Sporting View, 85. *Mailing Add:* 5705 Grove Ave Richmond VA 23226

MAYRS, DAVID BLAIR
PAINTER, EDUCATOR
b Winnipeg, Man, May 2, 35. *Study:* Vancouver Sch Art, dipl(hon), 57. *Work:* Vancouver Art Gallery; London Pub Libr & Art Mus, Ont; Etherington Art Ctr. *Exhib:* New Talent Show, Vancouver Art Gallery, 64; Young Contemporaries, London Art Mus, Ont, 65; Canadian Group of Painters, Montreal Mus Fine Art, 67; Nat Gallery Can Bi-Ann, 68; Young Vancouver Artists, Victoria Art Gallery, 68; H Marc Moyens Collection, Corcoran Gallery Art, 69; West Coast Artists, Sadie F Bronfman Ctr, Montreal, 75; BC Artists, Vancouver Art Gallery, 83; Mus Modern Art, Toyama, Japan, 87. *Teaching:* Instr painting & silkscreen, Emily Carr Col Art, Vancouver, 67- *Awards:* Purchase Award, Burnaby Art Gallery Print Show, 71. *Media:* Acrylic. *Mailing Add:* 440 Ellis St North Vancouver BC V7H 2G6 Canada

MAYS, VICTOR
PAINTER, ILLUSTRATOR
b New York, NY, July 2, 27. *Study:* Yale Univ, BA, 49. *Work:* De Grummond Collection of Children's Book Illus, Univ Southern Miss; Kerlan Collection, Univ Minn; Peabody Mus, Salem, Mass; Mystic Seaport Mus. *Comn:* Illus for children's bks, major US publ, 55- *Exhib:* Mystic Seaport, Conn, 79-82; Peabody Mus, 81; Mariners Mus, 85-86; Md Hist Soc, 89; Mystic Seaport Mus, 92; and others. *Awards:* Best in Show, 80, First & Second Prize Watercolor, 81 & Best in Show, 83, Mystic Int Marine Art Exhib, Mystic Seaport, Conn. *Mem:* Fel, Am Soc Marine Artists. *Media:* Watercolor. *Publ:* Auth & illusr, Fast Iron, 53, Action Starboard, 55, Dead Reckoning, 65. *Dealer:* Annapolis Marine Art Gallery Annapolis MD 21401; Mystic Maritime Gallery Mystic CT 06355. *Mailing Add:* 38 Groveway PO Box 207 Clinton CT 06413

MAYTHAM, THOMAS NORTHRUP
MUSEUM DIRECTOR, CONSULTANT
b Buffalo, NY, July 30, 31. *Study:* Williams Col, BA, 54; Yale Univ, MA, 56. *Collections Arranged:* Ernst Ludwig Kirchner Retrospective (148 works), Seattle Art Mus, Pasadena Art Mus & Boston Mus, 68-69; Great American Paintings from the Boston & Metropolitan Museum (100 paintings, with catalog), Nat Gallery Art, City Art Mus, St Louis & Seattle Art Mus, 70-71; and others. *Pos:* Asst, Wadsworth Atheneum, summer 55; res asst, Prof Carroll L V Meeks, Yale Univ, summer 56; asst in dept paintings, Mus Fine Arts, Boston, 56-57; head dept paintings, Boston Mus, 57-67, asst cur paintings, 67; assoc dir, Seattle Art Mus, 67-74; dir, Denver Art Mus, 74-83, consult, 83- *Teaching:* Lectr, mus, clubs, groups & art asns, Boston, Seattle, Denver, Nat Gallery, Wash & Portland Art Mus, Maine & Ore. *Mem:* Am Asn Mus. *Publ:* Auth, articles in Boston Mus Bulletin, Antiques & Can Art; ed, American Painting in the Boston Museum (catalog), Vols I & II, 68; auth, TV Prog for Nat Educ TV, produced by Boston Mus; Heritage Am Art (Slide/Tape); Publ Metro Mus Art, 77-present. *Mailing Add:* 1560 Fairfax Denver CO 80220

MAZUR, MICHAEL
PAINTER, PRINTMAKER
b New York, NY, Nov 2, 35. *Study:* Amherst Col, BA, 58, with Leonard Baskin; Yale Univ Sch Art & Archit, BFA, 59 & MFA, 61, with Gabor Peterdi & Bernard Chaet. *Work:* Mus Mod Art, Whitney Mus Am Art & Metrop Mus Art, New York; Boston Mus Fine Arts; Fogg Art Mus, Harvard Univ; Art Inst Chicago; Libr Cong, Washington, DC; Addison Gallery Am Art, Andover, Mass; Los Angeles Co Mus Art. *Comn:* Painting of Wassaw & Ossabaw Islands, Dept of Interior Bicentennial Exhib, 75-76; monotype murals, Mass Inst Technol, 83. *Exhib:* Painters & Sculptors as Printmakers, Mus Mod Art, 64; Young Americans, 65, American Prints: Process & Proofs, 84, Whitney Mus Am Art; Two Painters on Two Aspects of Illusion, Finch Col Mus, 71; American Landscape for Bicentennial, Corcoran Gallery, 76; American Monotype, Phillips Collection, 79; The Painterly Print & New Acquistions, 85, Metrop Mus Art; American Realism, San Francisco Mus Mod Art, 86; one-man exhibs, Albright-Knox Gallery, Buffalo, NY, 85, Beaver Col, Glenside, Pa, 86, Joe Fawbush Eds, New York, & Barbara Krakow Gallery, Boston, 87 & Fawbush Gallery, New York & Macalester Col, St Paul, Minn, 88; The Anatomy of Drawing, Hooks-Epstein Gallery, Houston, Tex, 87; The Monumental Image, Univ Art Gallery, Sonoma State Univ, Northridge, Calif, 87; 70s into 80s: Printmaking Now, Mus Fine Arts, Boston, 87 & The Unique Image, Mus Fine Arts, Boston, 90. *Pos:* Bd mem, Mass Coun on Arts & Humanities. *Teaching:* Instr prints & drawing, RI Sch Design, 61-64; asst prof prints & drawing, Brandeis Univ, 65-76; vis artist, Yale Sch Art & Archit, 71 & Harvard Univ, 76-78, 88, 90 & 92. *Awards:* Louis Comfort Tiffany Grant, 62; Nat Inst Arts & Lett Award, 64; Guggenheim Fel, 65. *Bibliog:* J Canaday (auth), rev in NY Times, 65, 66, 68 & 77; C Belz (auth), Mazur at ICA, Art Forum, 9/70; Franklyn Robinson (auth), Michael Mazur--The Vision of a Draughtsman (catalog), Brockton Art Mus, Montreal Mus Fine Arts; Grace Glueck (auth), article, NY Times, 81; William Corbett (auth), Mazur's recent work, Arts, 11-12/85. *Publ:* Auth, Prints by M Mazur, Artist Proof, 70; The Monoprints of Naum Gabo, Print Collections Newsletter; and others. *Dealer:* Barbara Krakow Gallery Boston MA 02116. *Mailing Add:* 5 Walnut Ave Cambridge MA 02140

MAZZE, IRVING
SCULPTOR, MEDALIST
b New York, NY. *Study:* With Beth Benton, 72 & Hermann Gass & Richard Hahn, 77. *Work:* Residenz Mus Munzsammlung, Munich; Cabinet Medailles, Bibliot Nat, Paris; Proust Mus, France. *Comn:* Citrine portrait, comn by Alice Whitfield, New York, 74; moonstone portrait, comn by Louise Benton, Chicago, 75; moonstone portrait Marcel Proust, comn by Mr & Mrs Milton Stern, Long Island, 75; crystal engraving, comn by James Van Aken, New York, 83; topaz engraving, comn by John Sinkankas for Smithsonian Inst, 84. *Exhib:* Fedn Int Medaille, Palazzo Ricardi, Florence, Italy, 83; Am Medallic Sculpture Asn Traveling Exhib, Am Numismatic Soc, New York, 83, Denver, 84, US Mint, San Francisco, 84, Janus Gallery, Santa Fe, 88, Helsinki Art Mus, 90, Cast Iron Gallery, New York, 92, British Mus, 92. *Pos:* Consult engraved gemstones, Dept Mineralogy, Am Mus Natural Hist, 79- *Bibliog:* Beverly Philip Mazze (auth), The making of a gem engraver, Lapidary J, 6/73. *Mem:* Am Medallic Sculpture Asn; Royal Soc Arts. *Media:* Gemstone. *Mailing Add:* 7 W 45th St New York NY 10036

MAZZOCCA, GUS (AUGUSTUS NICHOLAS)
PRINTMAKER, EDUCATOR
b Boston, Mass, Jan 2, 40. *Study:* Univ Conn, BA, 64, BFA, 65; RI Sch of Design MFA, 70. *Work:* Mus Mod Art, Munich; City Hartford Fine Arts Collection. *Exhib:* Parish Art Mus, Southampton, NY, 67; RI Col, Providence, 69; Mus of RI Sch of Design, Providence, 70; New Talent, New Eng, De Cordova Mus, Lincoln, Mass, 72; Conn Col, New London, 74. *Teaching:* Art teacher, Riverhead Cent Sch Dist, NY, 65-68; instr, RI Sch of Design, Providence, 70; assoc prof lithography & drawing, Univ Conn, Storrs, 70- *Awards:* Purchase Award, Hartford Fine Art Festival, Conn, 70; Conn Artists, Slater Mus, Norwich, 73. *Mem:* Graphic Arts Tech Found, Pittsburgh. *Media:* Charcoal, Pastel. *Mailing Add:* 333 Prospect St Willimantic CT 06226

MAZZONE, DOMENICO
SCULPTOR, PAINTER
b Rutigliano, Bari, Italy, May 16, 27. *Study:* Self taught. *Work:* Vatican Collection, Italy; UNESCO Collection, Paris, France; Resurected Christ, UN, New York; Leonardo da Vinci, Queensland Art Mus, Brisbane, Australia; Giulietta Simionato, Metrop Opera, New York. *Exhib:* one-man shows, Nechemia Glezer Gallery, New York, 68, Columbia Univ, Casa Italiana, New York, 75, Tampa Bay Art Ctr, Fla, 75, Ann Reid Art Gallery, 79, Art expo New York Coliseum, 83, Art expo Dallas Market Ctr, 83 & Waterloo Village, 84; Galleria d' arte Int, Viareggio, Italy, 72; Jacmel Gallery, New Hope, Pa, 77; Kennedy Ctr Performing Arts, Washington, DC, 79; Lever House Art Gallery, New York, 80; Columbus Ctr Gallery, Toronto, Ont, Can, 83; Gov's Exec Chamber, World Trade Ctr, New York, 85; 12th Ann Art expo, New York, 90; and many others in Italy & US. *Teaching:* Instr sculpture, UN Int Sch, New York, formerly. *Awards:* Asn Cult Artistica Vadese, 82; Gold Medal & Dipl, Accad Italia Ctr Rodino, Naples, Italy, 83; Artist of the year, Instituto D' Arte Contemporanea, Milano, Italy, 88. *Mem:* Elected mem, Nat Soc Lit & Arts, Washington, DC; diploma mem, Associazione Artistica Vadege, Italy; diploma mem, Consiglio Regionale Della Puglia, Italy; Nat Committee Arts Handicapped (bd dirs, 81); elected mem, Int Burkhardt Akademie, Rome. *Media:* Marble, Terra-cotta; Oil and Pen. *Publ:* Messanger of St Antony, Il Messaggero Padova, Italy, 87; Mazzone his art and his life, Int Ed, La Nuova Europa, Florence, Italy, 87; OGGI RCS Rizzoli Periodici, Milano, Anno; The New York Art Review, Chicago; and many other articles in publications in US & abroad. *Mailing Add:* 44 Lembeck Ave Jersey City NJ 07305

MEADER, JONATHAN GRANT See Ascian

MEADMORE, CLEMENT L
SCULPTOR
b Melbourne, Australia, Feb 9, 29; US Citizen. *Study:* Royal Melbourne Inst Technol. *Work:* Art Inst Chicago; J B Speed Mus, Ky; Atlantic Richfield Collection; Chase Manhattan Bank Collection; Metrop Mus NY; and others. *Comn:* Large outdoor sculptures, Australian Mutual Provident Soc, 68, Mexico City, 68, Columbia Univ, 68, NY State, Albany, 71, Princeton Univ, 71 & Queensland Art Gallery, 84; Tokyo Metrop Art Space, 90; and many others. *Exhib:* Guggenheim Mus, 67; Aldrich Mus, Ridgefield, Conn, 68; Rockefeller Collection, Mus Mod Art, 69 & Whitney Mus Am Art Ann, 69, New York; J B Speed Mus, 80; Columbus Mus Art, 80; Albuquerque Mus, 81; Davenport Art Gallery, 81; Amarillo Art Ctr, 81; Princeton Univ, 83; and many others. *Pos:* Instr, Studio Sch, 77-80, State Univ NY, Purchase, 83. *Awards:* Award & Citation, Am Acad Arts & Lett, 73; Guggenheim Fel, 75; Creative Artists Pub Serv Prog Grant, 76. *Bibliog:* Hughes (auth), article, Time, 4/71; Siegel (auth), Clement Meadmore: circling the square, Art News, 2/72; H H Arnason (auth), History of Modern Art, Prentice-Hall, 77. *Mem:* Am Abstr Artists, Century Club, NY. *Media:* Aluminum, Bronze. *Mailing Add:* 260 Fifth Ave New York NY 10001

MEADOWS, P B (PATRICIA)
CURATOR, PAINTER
b Amarillo, Tex, Nov 12, 38. *Study:* Univ Tex, BA, 60; additional studies with Ramon Froman, Julius Zsohar, William Henry Earle & Victor Armstrong, BA, 60. *Work:* Harlingen Court House, Tex; State Bar Tex Hq, Austin; Univ Tex Health Sci Ctr, Tyler. *Collections Arranged:* Presenting Nine (auth, catalog), Dallas, Tex, 84; Critic's Choice (auth, catalog), Dallas, Tex, 84-92; Texas Women (catalog), 88-89 & Texas: reflections, reituals (catalog), 90-91, Nat Mus Women Arts, Washington, DC. *Pos:* Co-founder & dir, D-Art Visual Art Ctr, Dallas, 81-92, pres bd dirs, 82-85; bd dirs, Arts Dist Management Asn, Dallas, Tex, 85-91, Artists Sq Design Team, 88-90; bd dirs, Tex State Comn, Nat Mus Women Arts, Tex, 86-92, Mid-Am Arts Alliance, Kansas City, Mo, 90-93; exhib dir, Texas Women, Nat Mus Women Arts, Washington, DC, 87-89; acquisition comt, Dallas Mus Art, 88-92; founder & cur, The Collectors, Dallas, Tex, 89-93; adv bd, Univ Tex, Austin, Sch Fine Arts, 90-91. *Awards:* Serv to the Arts Award, Tex Fine Arts Asn, 84 & 85 & Southwestern Watercolor Soc, 85; lora Award, 87; James K Wilson Award, 88. *Mem:* Artists & Craftsmen Asn (vpres bd dirs, 81-82, pres bd dirs, 82-83); D-Art Visual Arts Ctr, Dallas Coalition Arts, Arts Dist Friends, Dallas Mus Art; Women's Caucus Arts. *Media:* Oil, Pastel. *Mailing Add:* 2707 State St Dallas TX 75204

MECKLENBURG, VIRGINIA MCCORD
CURATOR, LECTURER
b Dallas, Tex, Nov 11, 46. *Study:* Univ Tex, Austin, BA, 68, MA, 70; Univ Md, College Park, PhD, 83. *Collections Arranged:* John R Grabach, Seventy Years an Artist (auth, catalog), 80; Across the Nation: Fine Art for Federal Buildings, 72-80; Roosevelt's America: New Deal Paintings from Nat Mus Am Art, 82; Jose de Creeft: Sculpture and Drawings (auth, catalog), 83; Modern American Realism: The Sara Roby Foundation Collection (auth, catalog); Wood Works: Constructions by Robert Indiana (auth, catalog); Special Delivery: Murals for the New Deal Era; American Abstraction, 1930-1945: the Patricia and Philip Frost Collection. *Pos:* Assoc cur 20th century painting & sculpture, Nat Mus Am Art, 79-87, cur painting & sculpture, 87-89, chief cur, 89- *Teaching:* Instr Am art, Univ Md, 79. *Mem:* Col Art Asn. *Res:* American art of the 20th century; New Deal art; theory and criticism; public art. *Publ:* Auth, The Public as Patron, A History of the Treasury Department Murals, Univ Md Art Gallery, 79; Franklin D Roosevelt: The Intimate Presidency (catalog), Smithsonian Press, 82; Advancing American Art: a Controversy of Style, In: Advancing American Art: Politics and Aesthetics in the State Department Exhibition, 1946-1948, Montgomery Mus Fine Arts, Ala, 84. *Mailing Add:* Nat Mus Am Art Washington DC 20560

MEDEARIS, ROGER
PAINTER, PRINTMAKER
b Fayette, Mo, Mar 6, 20. *Study:* Kansas City Art Inst, 38-41: study with Thomas Hart Benton & John S deMartelly. *Work:* DC Munic Ct, Washington, DC; Nat Mus Am Art; Butler Inst Am Art, Youngstown, Ohio; Hunt Inst, Carnegie-Mellon Univ; Albrecht-Kemper Mus Art, St Joseph, Mo; Nelson-Atkins Mus Art, Kansas City, Mo. *Exhib:* American Painting Today, Metrop Mus Art, New York, 50; West Coast Exhib, Frye Art Mus, Seattle, 66; Midyear Show, 69-81 & Four American Artists, 74 & Mainstream America: The Collection of Phil Desind, 87, Butler Inst Am Art, Youngstown, Ohio; one-man shows, Capricorn Galleries, Bethesda, Md, 71, 78, 81 & 84; 148th Ann, Nat Acad design, 73; Hunt Inst 5th Int, Carnegie-Mellon Univ, 83. *Bibliog:* Stephen M Doherty (auth), Roger Medearis: Turning life into art, Am Artist, 10/82; Patricia Sullivan Goss (auth), article, J Print World, fall 82; Joanna Shaw-Eagle (auth), Phil Desind: A Dealer with realist passion, Washington Mus & Arts, 7/87. *Media:* Oils, Acrylics; Lithography, Graphite. *Publ:* Auth, Giving your paintings sculptural form, 8/86 & Rejoicing in a limited palette, 3/87, Artists Mag; Student of Thomas Hart Benton, Smithsonian Studies in Am Art, Summer 90. *Dealer:* Capricorn Galleries 4849 Rugby Ave Bethesda MD 20814. *Mailing Add:* 2270 Melville Dr San Marino CA 91108

MEDEL, REBECCA ROSALIE
SCULPTOR, ENVIRONMENTAL ARTIST
b Denver, Colo, Mar 26, 47. *Study:* Ariz State Univ, Tempe, BFA (environ design), 70; Fiberworks, Ctr for Textile Arts, Berkeley, Calif, cert, 79; Univ Calif, Los Angeles, MFA, 82. *Work:* Stedelijk Mus, Amsterdam, Neth; Mus Bellerive, Zurich, Switz; Musee des Arts Decoratifs, Lausanne, Switz; Mus de

la Tapisserie, Aix-en-Provence, France. *Exhib:* Inaugural exhib, Univ Art Mus, 89; Fascinatie Textile, Mus Van Bommel-Van Dam, Venlo, Neth, 90; Contemp Fiber Art, Palo Alto Cult Ctr, Calif, 90; US/Columbia Fiber, Fla State Univ Mus & Bogota, Medellin, Calle, Colombia, 90 & 91; Transcendental Constructs, Neuberger Mus, Purchase, NY, 92; The New Narrative, NC State Univ Gallery, Raleigh, 92. *Teaching:* Asst prof fibers, Tenn Technol Univ, Smithville, 83-; Univ Calif, Los Angeles, 89-91. *Awards:* Bronze Medal, Fifth Int Triennal, Cent Mus Lodz, Poland, 85; Southern Arts Fedn Fel, 85; Nat Endowment Arts, 86 & 88. *Bibliog:* Kuniko Lucy Kato (auth), American fiber artists, Trends Mag, Tokyo, Japan, 4/84; Laurel Reuter (auth), Spotlight, Grand Forks Herald, ND, 3/9/85; Artweek, Oakland, Calif, 9/13/90. *Media:* Sized Linen & Cotton Thread. *Dealer:* Maya Behn Galerie Newmarkt 24 8001 Zurich Switz; Bellas Artes Gallery Santa Fe NM & New York, NY. *Mailing Add:* 7134 Potomac Lane Riverside CA 92504

MEDINA, ADA
DRAWER
b Carrizo Springs, Tex, June 4, 48. *Study:* Layton Sch Art & Design, BFA, 72; Univ Iowa, MA, 73, MFA, 74. *Work:* Nat Mus Am Art, Washington, DC; Equitable Life Assurance Soc, New York; Mint Mus Art, Charlotte, NC; Des Moines Art Ctr; Northwestern Bell. *Exhib:* In Homage to Ana Mendieta, Zeus-Trabia Gallery, New York, 86; Drawings From the 80's, Carnegie-Mellon Univ Art Gallery, Pittsburgh, 87; Connections Project/Conexus, Mus Contemp & Hist Art, New York, 87; Ada Medina Drawing Exhib, Janus Gallery, Santa Fe, NMex, 89; The Louise Noun Collection: Art by Women, Univ Iowa Mus Art, 90; and others. *Teaching:* Instr, Northern Ill Univ, 75-77; from instr to assoc prof, Drake Univ, 77-85; assoc prof, Carnegie-Mellon Univ, 86-89; prof, Inst Am Indian Arts, 89- *Awards:* Awards in the Visual Arts II; Nat Endowment Arts, 87; Fac Develop Grant, Carnegie-Mellon Univ, 87. *Bibliog:* Terry Ann R Nuff (ed), Awards in the Visual Arts 2 (exhib catalog), Mus Contemp Art, Chicago & Southeastern Ctr Contemp Art, Winston-Salem, NC, 83; Lee Hansley (ed), Contemporary Art Acquisitions 80-83 (exhib catalog), Equitable Life Assurance Soc, New York, 84; Jo-Ann Conklin (ed), The Louise Noun Collection (exhib catalog), Univ Iowa Mus Art, 90. *Publ:* Auth, Awards in the Visual Arts (exhib catalog), Mus Contemp Art, Chicago & Southeastern Ctr Contemp Art, Winston-Salem, NC, 83; Contemporary Art Acquisitions, 80-83 (exhib catalog), Equitable Life Assurance Soc, New York, 84; Bearing Witness/Sobreviviendo, Vol 10, No 2 & 3, 84; Saying Farewell to Ana (essay), In: Florilegia--A Retrospective, Vol 10, No 2 & 3, Calyx Books, 87; The Louise Noun Collection (exhib Catalog) Univ Iowa Mus Art, 90. *Dealer:* Janus Gallery 225 Canyon Rd Santa Fe NM 87505. *Mailing Add:* 2408 Calle Zaguan Santa Fe NM 87505

MEDOFF, EVE
PAINTER, WRITER
b Philadelphia, Pa. *Study:* Pa Acad Fine Arts; Tyler Sch Art; Pratt Graphics Ctr. *Work:* Wagner Col for Women, Staten Island, NY; Holmes Pub Sch, Mt Vernon, NY; Gestetner Corp, Yonkers; Fellowship of Reconciliation, Nyack, NY. *Exhib:* ACA Gallery, New York, 62; Riverside Mus, New York, 65; Albany Inst Art & Hist, 66; Westchester Printmakers, Fordham Univ, 67; Katonah Gallery, NY, 72. *Pos:* Ed arts page, Yonkers Rec, 66-70; ed Artslett & Interarts, Coun Arts Westchester, 68-69; contribr, Am Artist Mag, 68- *Awards:* Hudson River Mus Purchase Awards, 57 & 70; Hon Title, Mus Assoc in Art Res, Hudson River Mus, 64; Gestetner Corp Print Competition Award, 71. *Media:* Oil, Acrylic; Watercolor. *Publ:* Auth, John Moore, Joseph Solman, In: 20 Oil Painters and How They Work, 78. *Mailing Add:* 7300 Cresheim Rd Apt D9 Philadelphia PA 19119

MEDRICH, LIBBY E
SCULPTOR
b Hartford, Conn. *Study:* NY Univ, 31; Vassar Col, 49 & 54; Silvermine Col Arts, 51; Art Students League, 52-55; White Plains Co Ctr, 57 & 58; also with John Hovannes, Domenico Facci, George Koras, Harold Castor & Helen Beling. *Work:* Univ Chicago; First Church Christ, Wethersfield, Conn; Bloomsburg Univ, Pa; numerous pvt collections in US & abroad. *Exhib:* Springfield Mus Fine Art, Mass, 66; Galerie Raymond Duncan, Expo Prix de Paris, 67; Wadsworth Atheneum Mus, Hartford, Conn, 72; Metrop Mus Art, New York, 77; Hudson River Mus, Yonkers, NY, 77 & 82; Ward-Nasse Galleries, New York, 77; Silvermine Art Guild, Conn, 82; Texaco Int Hqs, Purchase, NY, 83; Nelson Rockefeller Galleries, New York, 84; Allied Artists Am, Nat Arts Club, New York, 90; and others. *Awards:* Int Women's Year Award Slide Exhib, 75-76; Am Soc Contemp Artists Sculpture Award Merit, 82; Audubon Artists Donors Sculpture Award, 82. *Bibliog:* Virginia Jones (auth), Sculptural Forms of Selected 20th Century American Women, Tex Woman's Univ, 82; Helen Harrison (auth), article, New York Times, 5/15/83; Joan Lentczner (auth), The Communigé, Bloomsburg Univ, Pa, 7/30/92. *Mem:* New York Artists Equity; Mamaroneck Artists Guild (pres, 68-70); Metrop Painters & Sculptors; Am Soc Contemp Artists; Hudson River Contemp Artists. *Media:* Bronze, Polymer Resin. *Dealer:* Ward-Nasse Gallery 178 Prince St New York NY 10012; Mag Gallery 150 Larchmont Ave Larchmont NY 10538. *Mailing Add:* 88 Carleon Ave Larchmont NY 10538

MEDVEDOW, JILL
ADMINISTRATOR, CONSULTANT
b New Haven, Conn, Oct 4, 54. *Study:* Colgate Univ, BA, 76; NY Univ, Inst Fine Arts, MA, 78. *Pos:* Prog developer, WGBH, Boston, Mass, 89-; freelance consult to museums regarding public programming; consult, Nat Endowment Arts. *Awards:* Writer in residence, Blue Mountain Ctr, NY, 84-86; Fel critical writing, Seattle Arts Comn, 85. *Mailing Add:* 80 Perry St Brookline MA 02146

MEEHAN, WILLIAM DALE
PAINTER, EDUCATOR
b Decatur, Ill, Oct 23, 30. *Study:* Art Inst Chicago, BFA; Bradley Univ, MA; Inst de Allende, Mex, MFA. *Work:* Ohio Univ; Bradley Univ; Evansville Mus Arts & Sci; DePauw Univ; Earlham Col. *Comn:* Mural design (with Richard Peeler & students), DePauw Univ Art Ctr, 72; Mem Sculpture to Chauncey Rose, Founder of Rose-Hulman Inst Technol for 100th Year of Sch, 75. *Exhib:* Works on Paper, Indianapolis Mus Art, 71; one-man shows, Ind Cent Col, 71 & 79, Galleria Pergola, San Miguelde Allende, Mex, 78, The Gallery, Bloomington, Ind, 79, Indianapolis Art League, 79, DePauw Univ, 86 & Colgate Univ, 88; The Gallery, Bloomington, Ind, 85; Hansen Galleries, Chicago, 86. *Pos:* Art dir, Southwestern Press, Ft Smith, Ark, 55-56; advert designer, Caterpillar Tractor Co, Peoria, 56-60; art dir, Nichols Advert, Decatur, summer 61; design consult, DePauw Univ, 64-; plus design consult for several industs. *Teaching:* prof design & drawing, Syracuse Univ, 60-64; prof art, DePauw Univ, 64- *Awards:* Purchase Award, Ohio Valley Oil & Watercolor Show, Athens, 59; First Prize, 22nd Ann Cent Ill Exhib, Decatur, 66; First Prize Watercolor, 62nd Ind Artists Exhib, Indianapolis, 67. *Mem:* New York Art Dir Club; Ind Art Dir Club. *Media:* Oil, Gouache. *Mailing Add:* RR 1 Greencastle IN 46135

MEEK, A J
PHOTOGRAPHER, EDUCATOR
b Beatrice, Nebr, Aug 29, 41. *Study:* Art Ctr Col Design, Los Angeles, with Todd Walker, BFA, 70; Ohio Univ, Athens, with Arnold Gassan, MFA, 72; further study with Paul Caponigro. *Work:* New Orleans Mus Art, La; Inverness Mus & Art Gallery, Scotland & Royal Comn Ancient Monuments, Edinburgh; Aberdeen City Art Gallery, Scotland; Int Mus Photo/George Eastman House; New Orleans Hist Collection. *Exhib:* Photog at Chrysler Mus, Norfolk, Va, 78; The Highlands, Inverness Mus & Art Gallery, Scotland, 79; Photog in La 1800-1980, New Orleans Mus Art, 80; Four Southeastern Photographers, Contemp Arts Ctr, New Orleans, 81; The Highlands, Aberdeen City Art Gallery, 82; Photog from the South, Janvier Gallery, Univ Del, 82; Louisiana portraits, New Orleans-Mus Art, 84; Am Photog Today, Invitational, Univ Denver, 84; Louisiana Photog 1884-1984, Corcoran Gallery Art, 85; Southern Arts Fedn, Atlanta Col Art, 88; Soc Contemp Photog Gallery, Kansas City, Mo, 90; and others. *Collections Arranged:* Spirit of Utah 1860-1976 (ed, catalog), Utah State Univ, 76. *Teaching:* Asst prof photog, Utah State Univ, Logan, 72-77; head photog film area, La State Univ, 77- *Awards:* Nat Endowment for Arts Exhib aid, 76; Louisiana State Univ Coun Research Fel, 86; Purchase Award, Soc Contemp Photog, 87; Southern Arts Fedn/Nat Endowment Arts career enhancement grant, 87. *Bibliog:* Review, Show we have seen, Popular Photography, 83; Nancy Barrett (auth), Louisiana Portraits, New Orleans Mus Art, 84; Herman Mhire (auth), A Century of Vision, Louisiana Photography 1884-1984, Univ Southwestern Louisiana Art Mus, 86. *Mem:* Soc Photog Educ; Friends of Photog. *Media:* Silver Prints, Alternative Processes. *Publ:* Contribr, The Highlands--Limited Edition Portfolio of Fine Prints, 80; AChronology of Photography, 80; New Orleans, Yesterday and Today, La State Univ Press, 83; Auth, Spirit in the Land, Vol 14, No 2, SF Camera Work, 87; monogr, Red Pepper Paradise: Avery Island, Louisiana, Audobon Park Press, 88; auth, Spirit in the Land, Vol 14, No 2, SF Camera Work, 87. *Dealer:* Gallery for Fine Photography 5423 Magazine St New Orleans LA; Afterimage Gallery the Quadrangle No 2502800 Routh St Dallas TX 75201. *Mailing Add:* 3365 Kleinert Ave Baton Rouge LA 70806-6837

MEEK, J WILLIAM, III
DEALER, CONSULTANT
b Aberdeen, Md, Nov 8, 50. *Study:* Fla Southern Col, BA, 72. *Pos:* Asst dir, Harmon Gallery, Naples, Fla, 72-77; dir-owner, Harmon-Meek Gallery, 78-; bd mem, Richard Florsheim Art Fund, Tampa, Fla. *Awards:* Paul Harris Fel, Rotary Int. *Mem:* Fel Royal Soc Arts, London; Nat Arts Club, New York; Nat Sculpture Soc, New York. *Specialty:* Paintings, drawings and sculpture by major American artists of the 20th century. *Collection:* Private collection of 20th century American art. *Mailing Add:* c/o Harmon-Meek Gallery 386 Broad Ave S Naples FL 33940

MEEKER, BARBARA MILLER
EDUCATOR, PAINTER
b Peru, Ind, Dec 31, 30. *Study:* DePauw Univ, BA; also with Jack Pellew, Ed Betts, Edgar A Whitney, Claude Croney, Charles Reid, Ed Fitzgerald, Frank Webb, Millard Sheets, Robert E Wood, Miles Batt, Dong Kingman, Glen Bradshaw & Virginia Cobb. *Work:* DePauw Univ Art Ctr Print Collection, Greencastle, Ind; Purdue Univ, Calumet & Hammond Pub Schs, Ind; Tri-State Col, Angola, Ind; Oak Park River Forest High Sch, Ill; Lake Co Pub Libr; Ind Bell Telephone; St Margaret Hosp, Hammond, Ind. *Exhib:* Ft Wayne Art Mus; Lafayette Art Mus; Artist Guild Chicago Watercolor Show, Rocky Mountain Nat Watercolor Exhib, Denver; Contemp Artists Ind, Indianapolis; Ind State Mus Invitational, Indianapolis; Nat Watercolor Oklahoma, Okla City; Watercolor USA. *Pos:* Mem Art Comn, Ind State House, 63-65; bd dir, Midwest Watercolor Soc, 83-85; coordr, Very Special Arts, Ind, 88-89, 90 & 91. *Teaching:* Emer prof freehand drawing & painting, Purdue Univ, Calumet, 65-86. *Awards:* Hon Mention, Outstanding Teacher Awards, Purdue Univ, Calumet, 71, 75, 76 & 81; Jury Prize Distinction, Indianapolis, 84; Nat Watercolor Okla, 87. *Bibliog:* Hawkins & McClarren (auth), Indiana lives, Hist Rec Asn, 67; J L Collins (auth), Women Artists in America, Les Krantz. *Mem:* Ky Watercolor Soc; Midwest Watercolor Soc; Chicago Artists Coalition; N Coast Collage Soc; San Diego Watercolor Soc. *Media:* All. *Publ:* Auth, Freehand Drawing, 72, 2nd ed, 75, 3rd ed, 80; contribr, Complete Guide to Creative Watercolor, 88. *Dealer:* Trachtenberg Gallery Merrillville IN. *Mailing Add:* 8314 Greenwood Ave Munster IN 46321

MEEKER, DEAN JACKSON
PRINTMAKER, PAINTER
b Orchard, Colo, May 18, 20. *Study:* Art Inst Chicago, BFA & MFA; Northwestern Univ; Univ Wis. *Work:* Boston Mus Fine Arts; Libr Cong, Washington, DC; Mus Mod Art, New York; Dallas Mus Fine Arts; Denver Art Mus. *Exhib:* Seattle Art Mus, 53-55; Munic Mus, The Hague, 54; Boston Mus Fine Arts, 54-56; Mus Mod Art, New York, 55; La Gravure, 59; Los Angeles Mus Art, 59; Libr Cong; Art Inst Chicago; Metrop Mus Art, New York; plus others. *Teaching:* Assoc prof art educ, Univ Wis-Madison, 46-70, prof, 70-80. *Awards:* Medal Honor, Milwaukee Art Inst, 52 & 56; Guggenheim Fel, 58. *Bibliog:* S W Hayter (auth), About Prints, Oxford Univ, 62. *Mailing Add:* Dept Art Univ Wisconsin 455 N Park St Madison WI 53706

MEGGS, PHILIP B
DESIGNER, HISTORIAN
b Newberry, SC, May 30, 42. *Study:* Univ SC, 60-61; Richmond Prof Inst, BFA, 64; Va Commonwealth Univ, MFA, 71. *Work:* Cinémathèque Française, Musée Henri Langloise; US Info Agency, Washington, DC. *Exhib:* Virginia Designers Biennial, Va Mus Fine Arts, Richmond, 80; Cinema-Festival in Posters, Inst d'Arts Visuels, Orléans, France, 83; Print Regional Design Annual, New York, 85, 88, 90 & 92; Influences, Birke Art Gallery, Huntington, WVa, 86; Am Inst Graphic Arts Commun Graphics, New York, 91. *Pos:* Senior graphic designer, Reynolds Aluminum, Richmond, Va, 65-66; art dir, A H Robins, Richmond, Va, 66-68; contrib ed, Print Mag, 88- *Teaching:* From instr graphic design to prof, Va Commonwealth Univ, Richmond, 68-, chmn dept communication arts & design, 75-86. *Awards:* Publishing Excellence Award, Asn Am Publ, 83; cert excellence, Am Inst Graphic Arts Book Show, New York, 86; Outstanding Alumni Award, Virginia Commonwealth Univ, 89;. *Mem:* Am Inst Graphic Arts; Am Printing Hist Soc; Graphic Design Educ Asn. *Media:* Graphic Design, Typography. *Publ:* Auth, A History of Graphic Design, 83, 2nd ed, 92 Type and Image, 88 & coauth, Typographic Design: Form and Communication, 85, Van Nostrand Reinhold; Typography section, in: Encyclopedia of Communications, Oxford, 88; Graphic arts section, in: Compton's Encyclopedia, Britannica, 87; The Rise and Fall of Design at a Great Corporation, Print, 92. *Mailing Add:* 10211 Windbluff Dr Richmond VA 23233

MEGHELLI, FETHI M
PRINTMAKER, PAINTER
b Algeria, Jan 9, 45; US citizen. *Study:* Nat Art Sch, Algeria, BA, 67; Ecole Nat Superieur des Beaux Arts, Paris, France, MFA, 74, with Gustave Singier. *Exhib:* Art and Culture of the American Labor Movement, Munic Art Mus, Berlin, WGer, & Europ tour, 83; Slater Mem Mus, Norwich, Conn, 83; Noyes Mus, NJ & Hunterdon Art Ctr, Clinton, NJ, 84; Shippe Gallery, New York, 85; Auburn Univ, Ala, 86; 8th Int Exhib Graphic Art (auth, catalog), Frechen, WGer, 86. *Awards:* Prize Award, Koenig Art Emporium, 83; Prize Award, Carter, Rice, Storrs & Baneut, 85. *Mem:* Print Club, Philadelphia; Arts Coun, New Haven; Int Graphic Arts Found. *Publ:* Auth, The Other America, Journeyman Press, London & New York, 85; 16th National Works on Paper, Harnett Hall Gallery, Minot State Col, NDak, 86. *Dealer:* Shippee Gallery 41 E 57th St New York NY 10022. *Mailing Add:* c/o Wave Gallery 263 College St New Haven CT 06510

MEHN, JAN (VON DER GOLZ)
PRINTMAKER
b Chicago, Ill, Aug 26, 53. *Study:* Kansas City Art Inst, Mo, Calif Col Arts & Crafts, Oakland, BFA, 79, Ariz State Univ, Tempe, MFA, 87. *Work:* Auburn Arts Ctr, Ala; Univ Tex, San Antonio; Ariz State Univ, Tempe; Kansas City Art Inst, Mo; Calif Col Arts & Crafts, Oakland. *Exhib:* 31st Ann San Francisco Art Festival, Calif, 77; 13th Nat Print Exhib, Silvermine Guild Art, New Canaan, Conn, 80; 28th Nat Print Exhib, Hunterdon Art Ctr, Clinton, NJ, 84; 6th Miami Int Print Exhib, North Miami Mus, North Miami, Fla, 84; 37th Boston Printmakers, Rose Art Mus, Waltham, Mass, 85; Prints: Washington, The Phillips Collection, DC, 88. *Pos:* Printers asst, De Soto Workshop, San Francisco, 79-80; Conserv aid, Nat Arch, Washington, DC, 88-89; preparator, Sackler Gallery Art, Smithsonian, 89-90, Washington Proj Arts, Washington, DC, 90. *Teaching:* Instr drawing & printmaking, Ariz State Univ, Tempe, 84-87; instr monotype, Arlington Arts Ctr, Va, 88 & Pyramid Atlantic, DC, 89; Virginia Mus, Richmond, 90-91; asst prof, Bradley Univ, Peoria, Ill, 91-92. *Awards:* Purchase Award, 5th Ala Works on Paper, Auburn Arts Ctr, 84; Fel, Nat Endowment Arts & Mid Atlantic Arts Found, 88; Artist's Grant, District Columbia Arts & Humanities, 89. *Bibliog:* JoAnn Lewis (auth), At the Phillips, Washington Post, 9/17/88; Daniel Barbiero (auth), Atlanta Art Papers, 1-2/89; Michael Welzenbach (auth), Washington Post, 4/7/90. *Mem:* Col Art Asn. *Mailing Add:* 4009 Jay Lane S Rolling Meadows IL 60008

MEIER, RICHARD ALAN
ARCHITECT
b Newark, NJ, Oct 12, 34. *Study:* Cornell Univ, BArch, 57. *Comn:* High Mus Art, Atlanta, Ga; Douglas House; J Paul Getty Mus & Fine Arts Ctr, comn by J Paul Getty Trust, 84; Mus Decorative Arts; Frankfurt City Hall, The Hague; Des Moines Art Ctr additions; UCLA, vis design critic, 87, 88 & 89. *Exhib:* Graham Found, Chicago, 77; 200 Yrs of Am Architectural Drawing, Art Inst Chicago & others, 78; Modernism Gallery, San Francisco, 80; Wadsworth Atheneum, Hartford, Conn, 80; High Mus Art, Atlanta, 80; Max Protetch Gallery, New York, 80; Harvard Univ, 80; Knoll Int, Tokyo, Japan, 88; October Gallery, London, Eng, 90; Royal Palace, Naples, Italy, 91; and many others. *Pos:* Resident architect, Am Acad in Rome, 73-74; mem adv coun, Col Art, Archit & Planning, Cornell Univ, Ithaca, NY, 71-; juror, Int Competition, Convention Hall, Nara, Japan, 92. *Teaching:* Adj prof, Cooper Union, 64-73; William Henry Bishop vis prof, Yale Univ, 75 & 77; Eliot Noyes vis design critic, Harvard Univ, 80 & 81; UCLA vis design critic, 87, 88 & 89. *Awards:* Bartlett, First Honor, Am Inst Architects, 65-81; Progressive Archit Design Award, 79; Medal Hon, New York Am Inst Archit, 80; Pritzker Archit Prize, 84; Royal Gold Medal, Royal Inst British Architects, 88. *Bibliog:* Richard Meier Architect, Rizzoli, 84; Wesner Blaser (auth) Richard Meier: Bldg for Art, 89; Gloria Gerace (ed), Getty Center Design Process, J Paul Getty Trust, 91. *Mem:* Nat Acad Design; fel Am Inst Architects; Int Acad Archit; Century Club New York; Am Acad & Inst Arts & Letts; hon fel Royal Inst British Architects. *Publ:* Coauth, Five Architects: Eisenman/Graves/Gwathmey/Hejduk/Meier, Wittenborn Co, 72; Richard Meier, Architect: Buildings and Projects 1966-1976, Oxford Univ Press, 76; Richard Meier, Architect, Rizzoll, 84; Richard Meir, Architect 2, Rizzoll, 91; and others. *Mailing Add:* 475 Tenth Ave New York NY 10018

MEIGS, JOHN LIGGETT
PAINTER, COLLECTOR
b Chicago, Ill, May 10, 16. *Study:* Univ Redlands; Acad Grande Chaumiere, Paris. *Work:* Roswell Mus, NMex; Univ Tex, Austin; WTex Mus, Lubbock; Mus NMex, Santa Fe; El Paso Mus Art, Tex. *Comn:* Pioneer Frescoes (with Peter Hurd), Tex Tech Univ, Lubbock, 51-54; murals, Nickson Hotel, Roswell, 51, F O Masten Farms, Tex, 60, N Jr High Sch, Abilene, Tex, 61 & Weatherford First Nat Bank, Tex, 71; and others. *Exhib:* One-man shows, Honolulu Acad Fine Arts, Calif Palace of Legion of Honor, San Francisco, Dayton Art Inst, Ohio, Mus NMex & Ball State Mus, Muncie, Ind; O S Ranch Exhib, Tex, 77-80; and others. *Bibliog:* article in New Mexico Mag, 87; Country Life, 91; Southwest Profiles, 90. *Media:* Egg Tempera, Watercolor. *Res:* American graphics, especially 1930-1950, Hurd-Wyeth Collection. *Collection:* American graphics and drawings; Peter Hurd; Henriette Wyeth; American Realists; American quilts; coverlets; books. *Publ:* Ed, Peter Hurd--the Lithographs, Baker Gallery, 70; ed, Peter Hurd--Sketchbook, 71 & ed, The Cowboy in American Prints, 72, Swallow; contribr, NMex Mag, Ford Times, Southwest Art Gallery Mag & Ariz Highways. *Mailing Add:* PO Box 107 San Patricio NM 88348

MEISEL, LOUIS KOENIG
DEALER, HISTORIAN
b Brooklyn, NY, Sept 4, 42. *Study:* Tulane Univ; Columbia Univ; New Sch Social Res. *Collections Arranged:* Photo Realism 1973, Stuart M Speiser Collection (with catalog), Smithsonian Inst; Photo-Realism, Guggenheim Mus. *Pos:* Pres, Louis K Meisel Gallery, New York, currently. *Bibliog:* Les Levine (auth), New dealer, Arts Mag, 1/74; Judy Beardsall (auth), Louis Meisel, Art Gallery Mag, 9/73. *Res:* Photo realism. *Specialty:* Photo realism; abstract illusionism. *Publ:* Auth, Nathan Wasserberger, 67; Watercolors and drawings, Am Realists, 74; American Photo Realism in New Zealand and Australia, 75; Photorealism, Harry N Abrams, 80; 15 Years of Photorealism, Horizon Mag, 11/80; Richard Estes, H N Abrams, 86; Clarice Cliff-The Bizarra Affair, H N Abrams, 88; Charels Bell, The Complete Paintings 1970-1990, H N Abrams, 91; Photo Realism Since 1980, H N Abrams, 93. *Mailing Add:* 141 Prince St New York NY 10012

MEISEL, SUSAN PEAR
PAINTER, PRINTMAKER
b New York, NY, Apr 16, 47. *Study:* Barnard, 66; Parsons Sch Design, 68; Sch Visual Arts, 70. *Work:* Larry Aldrich Mus, Richfield, Conn; Ft Wayne Mus, Ind; State Dept, Washington, DC; numerous Am Embassies world wide. *Comn:* Libr Cong, Washington, DC; Smithsonian Inst, Washington, DC; Comsat Corp Hq, Washington, DC; Independence Hall, Philadelphia, Pa. *Exhib:* 10 years of Printmaking, Ft Wayne Mus, Ind, 80; 10 years of Printmaking, Tomasulo Gallery Union Col, NJ, 81. *Teaching:* Art teacher, UN Int Sch, 90- *Bibliog:* Judy Beardsall (auth), Susan Pear Meisel, Arts Mag, 5/78; Robert Voskowitz (auth), Susan Pear Meisel(catalog), Ft Wayne Mus. *Media:* Acrylic on Canvas. *Mailing Add:* c/o Louis K Meisel Gallery 141 Prince St New York NY 10012

MEISELMAN, MARILYN NEWMARK See Newmark, Marilyn (Marilyn Newmark Meiselman)

MEISSNER, ANNE MARIE
ADMINISTATOR
Study: Oxford Univ, St Ann's Col, cert, 68; Univ Mich, Ann Arbor, MSW, 67; Univ Calif-Berkeley, BA, 79. *Pos:* Dir, San Francisco Art Comm Gallery, 87. *Mem:* Art Table (co-chair, prog comt, 91); Non-Profit Gallery Asn, San Francisco Bay Area (vpres & bd dirs); Art Span/Open Studios San Francisco. *Mailing Add:* San Francisco Arts Commission Gallery Civic Ctr 155 Grove St San Francisco CA 94102

MEISTER, MARK J
INSTITUTE DIRECTOR, ART HISTORIAN
b Baltimore, Md, June 26, 53. *Study:* Washington Univ, AB (art & archeol), 74; Univ Minn, MA (art hist & museology), 76. *Pos:* Dir, Mus Art & Hist, Port Huron, Mich, 78-79, Midwest Mus Am Art, Elkhart, Ind, 79-81 & Mus Art, Sci & Indust, Bridgeport, Conn, 86-89; exec dir, Children's Mus, St Paul, Minn, 81-86; exec dir, Archaeol Inst Am, Boston, Mass, 89- *Teaching:* Adj lectr museology, Kenyon Col, Gambier, Ohio, 77; lectr art hist, Ind Univ, South Bend, 80-81. *Awards:* Nat Endowment Humanities Museology Fel, 76-77; Kress Fel, 77; Bush Found Summer Fel, 83. *Mem:* Am Asn Mus; Am Coun Learned Socs; Archaeol Inst Am. *Publ:* Ed, Selections Art & Artifacts from the Kenyon College Collection (catalog), 77; auth, The man who painted Lake Gervais Tornado, Minn Hist Mag, 77; Midwest Photo 80 & 81, Midwest Mus Am Art; ed, American Artists Abroad (exhib catalog), 86 & Milton Avery (exhib catalog), Mus Art, Sci & Indust, 87. *Mailing Add:* Archaeological Inst of Am 675 Commonwealth Ave Boston MA 02215

MEISTER, MICHAEL WILLIAM
HISTORIAN, EDUCATOR
b West Palm Beach, Fla, Aug 20, 42. *Study:* Harvard Col, BA, 64; Harvard Univ, MA, 71, PhD, 74; Univ Pa, Hon MA, 79. *Pos:* Cur, South Asia Art Archive, 78- *Teaching:* Asst prof art hist, Univ Tex, Austin, 74-76; asst prof, Univ Pa, 76-79, assoc prof, 79-88, grad chmn hist & art dept, 78-79 & 86-90, prof, 88- *Awards:* Fulbright Scholar India, 65-68 & 76-77; Nat Endowment Humanities Award, 79-91; Smithsonian Develop Grant, 81. *Bibliog:* SARAS Bull, No 3. *Mem:* Am Comt South Asian Art (mem bd dirs, 76-79 & 83-86); Am Inst Indian Studies; Asn Asian Studies; Comt Art and Archeology. *Res:* South Asian art, particularly Hindu temple architecture, sculpture and iconology. *Publ:* Auth, Mandala and Practice in Nagara architecture, J Am Oriental Soc, 79; ed, Encyclopedia of Indian Temple Architecture, Vols 1 & 2, Princeton Univ Press, 83, 86, 88 & 91; Discourses on Siva, Univ Pa Press, 84; On the Development of a Symbolic Architecture: India, Res 12, 86; Making Things in South Asia, Univ Pa, S Asia Dept, 88. *Mailing Add:* Hist Art Dept G-29 Meyerson Hall Univ Pa Philadelphia PA 19104

MEITZLER, NEIL (HERBERT)
PAINTER, DESIGNER
b Pueblo, Colo, Sept 14, 30. *Study:* With Kenneth Callahan. *Work:* Seattle Art Mus, Wash; Memphis Acad Art, Tenn; Washington Co Mus Art, Hagerstown, Md; Henry Gallery, Univ Wash, Seattle,. *Exhib:* Art in USA, New York, 59; one-man show, Seattle Art Mus, Wash, 59; Seattle World's Fair, Wash, 62; Pac Coast Exhib, Santa Barbara Mus Art, Calif, plus five other mus, 62-63; Artists of the Northwest, Japanese World's Fair, 71; Northwest Art from Corporate Collections, Seattle, Wash, 84. *Pos:* Designer, Seattle Art Mus, 57-78. *Awards:* Katharine Baker Award, Seattle Art Mus, 58; Nat Coun Theatres Award, US Govt, 67. *Media:* Acrylic, Tempera, Watercolor. *Dealer:* Foster-White Gallery 311 1/2 Occidental Ave S Seattle WA 98104. *Mailing Add:* 637 Pleasant St Walla Walla WA 99362-3367

MEIXNER, MARY LOUISE
PAINTER, EDUCATOR
b Milwaukee, Wis, Dec 7, 16. *Study:* Milwaukee-Downer Col, BA; State Univ Iowa, MA; Art Students League, with Hale; Univ Minn & Bowling Green Univ, with Max Weber; Mills Col, with Yasuo Kuniyoshi; Am Sch, Fontainebleau, France; Carpenter Ctr Visual Arts, Harvard Univ. *Work:* Nat Am Home Econ Asn, Washington, DC; Des Moines Art Ctr, Iowa; Denison Arts Asn Gallery, Iowa; M Greeley Hosp, Ames, La. *Exhib:* Des Moines Art Ctr Ann, 54, 55 & 62; Mid Am Ann, Kansas City, Mo, 55; solo show, Nat Design Ctr, New York, 69; MacNider Mus Ann, Mason City, Iowa, 70-75; solo show, Western Ill Univ, Macomb, 79; and others. *Teaching:* Prof art hist, Milwaukee-Downer Col, 45-52; prof color, environ arts & painting, Iowa State Univ, Ames, 53-75, distinguished prof, 75-83. *Awards:* Regional exhib awards. *Mem:* Col Art Asn Am; Intersoc Color Coun; Nat League Am Pen Women. *Media:* Oil, Acrylic. *Res:* Four films: experiments in light and color with dance. *Publ:* Videotape documentary, Otto Piene's Sky Event, Iowa Star, 80; auth, Geometry of F L Wright at Richland Center, Wis Acad Rev, 82; Lowell Houser: The genesis of a mural, Palimpsest, Iowa Hist Soc, 85; Poetry, Pen Women Mag, 90; Connections: The Cultural Imperatives of Frank and Olgivanna Wright, Wisc Acad Rev, 91; Lowell Houser's Poetic Glass Mural in Des Moines, Palimpsest, Iowa Hist Soc, 92. *Mailing Add:* 2521 N 32nd St Milwaukee WI 53210

MEIZNER, PAULA
SCULPTOR
b Belchatow, Poland; US citizen. *Study:* Westchester Workshop, White Plains, NY. *Exhib:* New Eng Exhibs, Silvermine Guild Artists, New Canaan, Conn; Critics Choice, Sculpture Ctr, New York, 72; Contemporary Reflections 1972-1973, Larry Aldrich Mus, Ridgefield, Conn; Modern Maxis, New Brit Mus Am Art, Conn, 74; Sculpture in the Fields, Storm King Art Ctr, Mountainville, NY, 74-75; and others. *Teaching:* Pvt adult art classes. *Awards:* Charles N Whinston Mem Award, Nat Asn Women Artists, New York, 72, 78, 79 & 83; Silvermine-Borglum Award Sculpture, 36th Art of Northeast USA Exhibition, Silvermine, Conn, 85; Pauline Law Award for Sculpture, Nat Asn of Women Artists, New York, 4/87. *Bibliog:* National community arts program, HUD, 74. *Mem:* Audubon Artists; Silvermine Guild Artists; Nat Asn Women Artists. *Media:* Fieldstone, Aluminum. *Mailing Add:* 126 Seacord Rd New Rochelle NY 10804

MEJER, ROBERT LEE
PAINTER, EDUCATOR
b South Bend, Ind, Nov 8, 44. *Study:* South Bend Art Ctr; Ball State Univ, BS; Miami Univ, MFA; Kent State Univ, 73; Kalamazoo Art Inst, 75; Oxbow Summer Sch Art, 76-78 & 81; Notre Dame Univ, 79; Washington Univ, 80; Skidmore Col, 82-83. *Work:* Ball State Univ, Muncie, Ind; Quincy Art Ctr, Ill; Int Arts League Youth, New York; Anderson Art Ctr, Ind; Col Dupage, Ill. *Exhib:* New American Monotypes, Smithsonian Inst Traveling Exhib, 77-80; Retrospective 1969-1979, Quincy Art Ctr, 79; Krannert Art Mus, Ill, 80; Pensacola Nat Watermedia Exhib, Fla, 82; Shreveport Nat Art Biannual, La, 82; 15th Ann Washington & Jefferson Col Nat Painting Show, Pa, 83; Intermont Nat Works on Paper, Va, 83. *Collections Arranged:* Q C Alumni Invitational, 73, Middlewestern Cardscape, 74, Religious in the Arts, 77, Alps, 81, Keith Achepohl, 81 & Sylvia Solochek Waters, 82, Quincy Col; Director's Choice, Quincy Art Club, 77. *Pos:* Gallery asst, Ball State Art Gallery, 62-66 & Quincy Art Ctr, Ill, 70- *Teaching:* Instr painting & drawing, Ball State Univ, summers 66 & 67; instr drawing, Miami Univ, 66-68; prof art & gallery dir, Quincy Col, 68-; instr, John Wood Community Col, Pittsfield, 75 & Quincy, 76; vis res fac, Skidmore Col, 82-83. *Awards:* Quincy Col Fac Develop Grants, 75-83; Fel Va Ctr Creative Arts, 82; Best Show, 33rd Ann Quincy Art Ctr, 83; and others. *Bibliog:* Terrence Riddell (auth), Bob Mejer an artist, Riverword 1, 77; Richard Mammel (auth), Progressive variations of a theme: Space and Robert Lee Mejer, Quincy Art Club First Quart Bulletin, 79. *Mem:* Nat Art Educ Asn; Ill Art Educ Asn (exec coun, 70-72 & 75-77); Quincy Art Club (bd dirs, 76-80, 1st vpres, 76); Midwest Watercolor Soc; Ill Arts Coun. *Media:* Watercolor, Monotypes. *Specialty:* Contemporary artists. *Publ:* Illusr, Salt-Lick Mag, 68-71; illusr, Riverword Mag, Vols 1, 2, & 3, 77. *Dealer:* Nornberg Gallery Contemp Art St Louis MO; Prairie House IL. *Mailing Add:* 619 Meadow Lark Quincy IL 62301

MEKLER, ADAM
ART DEALER, CURATOR
b Haifa, Israel, Feb 1, 41; US citizen. *Study:* Calif State Univ, Northridge, BA, MA; Univ Southern Calif. *Collections Arranged:* Jack Zajac, Retrospective 1955-74, Fine Arts Gallery San Diego; Jack Zajac, Retrospective 1955-77, Palm Springs Desert Mus; Jack Zajac, Retrospective 1966-74, Santa Barbara Mus Art; William Dole, Retrospective 1960-75, Munic Art Gallery Los Angeles, Colorado Springs Fine Arts Ctr, Fine Arts Gallery San Diego & Santa Barbara Mus Art; Matisse and Picasso: Works on Paper, Fresno Art Ctr; David Smith, Drawings for Sculpture, Fresno Art Mus, Milwaukee Art Mus, Storm King Art Ctr, 85-87; Camille Pissarro, Works on Paper, Fresno Art Mus, 88; Milton Avery, Retrospective, Fresno Art Mus, 90; Sally Michel: Retrospective, Fresno Art Mus, 91; Invisible People: Arts of the Amazon, Fresno Art Mus, 91-92, Bowers Art Mus, Santa Ana, 93. *Pos:* Owner-dir, Mekler Gallery. *Teaching:* Mt St Mary's Col, Los Angeles, 64-71. *Specialty:* Contemporary and 20th century sculpture, paintings and works on paper. *Publ:* Invisible People: Arts of the Amazon, Fresno Art Mus. *Mailing Add:* 4313 Van Nuys Blvd Sherman Oaks CA 91403

MELAMED, HOPE See Winter, Hope Melamed

MELAMID, ALEXANDER See Komar and Melamid

MELBERG, JERALD LEIGH
ART DEALER, COLLECTOR
b Minneapolis, Minn, Aug 17, 48. *Study:* Pillsbury Col, Owatonna, Minn; Bob Jones Univ, Greenville, SC. *Collections Arranged:* 1977, 1979 & 1981 Biennial Exhibition of Piedmont Painting & Sculpture (ed, catalog), 77, 1978, 1980 & 1982 Biennial Exhibition of Piedmont Crafts (ed, catalog), 78 & Romare Bearden 1970-1980 (ed, catalog), 80, Mint Mus Art, Charlotte, NC; Seymour Lipton: Sculpture (ed, catalog), 82; Herb Jackson: Drawings (ed, catalog), 83; Ed Buonagurio: Recent Paintings (auth, catalog), 83. *Pos:* Dir, Hampton III Gallery, Ltd, Greenville, SC, 73-74; exec dir, Anderson Co Arts Coun, SC, 75-76; cur exhib, Mint Mus Art, 77-84; owner, Jerald Melberg Gallery Inc, 84- *Mem:* Int Coun Mus; Am Asn Mus; assoc Smithsonian Inst, Washington, DC. *Res:* Herb Jackson, Wolf Kahn, Romare Bearden. *Collection:* Paintings, sculpture, graphics and crafts by Southeastern United States artists, and graphics by nationally known American artists. *Publ:* Charles Basham (auth), Dialogues of Nature with Man, 89; Rick Horton (auth), Between Dusk and Daybreak, 89; Denise Lisiecki (auth), Natural Symbols and Cultural Relics, 89; Robert Peterson (auth), 91; Wolf Kahn (auth), New Landscapes, 91. *Mailing Add:* Jerald Melberg Gallery 119 E Seventh St Charlotte NC 28202

MELBY, DAVID A
PAINTER, PHOTOGRAPHER
b Wichita, Kans, June 8, 42. *Study:* Kansas City Art Inst; Wichita State Univ, BFA, 67; Univ Nebr, MFA, 70. *Work:* Am Express Corp, Salt Lake City; Hallmark Corp, Mutual Benefit Life, Kansas City, Mo; McDonald Corp, Chicago; Continental Insurance Corp, NY; Arthur Andersen, Minneapolis, Minn. *Exhib:* A Sense of Place, Joslyn Art Mus, Sheldon Mem Art Gallery, Mid-Am Arts Alliance & others, 73; Landscape, Gallery One, Bergen, Norway, 73; solo exhibs, Limassol Munic Cult Arts Ctr, Cyprus, 73 & Valdres Folk Mus, Fagernes, Norway, 77; Coos Art Mus, Coos Bay, Ore, 79; Passages, Wichita Art Mus, Kans, 79; Mid-Four, Nelson Atkins Mus, 80-83 & 87; Nat Small Works Exhib, York Univ, NY, 79, 80, 83 & 84; Gwenda Jay Gallery, Chicago, Ill, 89; American Myth, Sioux City Art Ctr, Iowa, 90. *Collections Arranged:* Artists Behind Bars, Jewish Community Ctr, Kansas City, Mo, 76; In Respect of Space, 79, Groups: A Public Face, 79 & Gold Rush: Work of Hal Parker, 80, Swan River Mus; Points of View: Six Artists, St Mary Col, 81. *Pos:* Artist in residence, US Fed Penitentiary, Leavenworth, Kans, Nat Endowment Arts, 75-76; dir exhibs, Swan River Mus, Paola, Kans, 79-80; dir, Bedyk Gallery, Kansas City, Mo, 85-86. *Teaching:* Instr drawing & painting, Iowa State Univ, Ames, 70-75; instr painting, drawing & photog, St Mary Col, Kans, 80-82; instr, Nelson Atkins Mus, Kansas City, 83-84 & Kansas City Art Inst, 90-91. *Awards:* First Prize, Kansas Two, Kans Arts Comn, 82; Award Merit, Mid-Four Exhib, Nelson Atkins Mus, 82; Fel (painting) Mid Am Arts Alliance, Nat Endowment Arts, 86. *Bibliog:* Knut Førsund (auth), article, Fotografi, 11/77; Victoria Melcher (auth), Kansas City: Dizzying directions, Art News, 10/80; David Knaus (auth), article, Art Gallery, 4-5/84. *Mem:* Kansas City Artists Coalition; Kans Grass Roots Arts Asn; Leavenworth Co Arts Coun (exec coun); and others. *Media:* Oil; Black & White Photo. *Collection:* Nineteenth and twentieth century European, American and native American art, American folk art. *Publ:* Contribr, A Sense of Place: The Artist and the American Land, Mid-Am Arts Alliance, 73; co-dir, videotape, Artist in Residence Prog, US Bur Prisons, 76; contribr, Poets on Photography, Dog Ear Press, 81; The Kansas Landscape, Kansas Dept Econ Develop, 85; New York Art Review, 88; Forum, 1-2/90. *Mailing Add:* c/o Midwestern Light PO Box 508 Leavenworth KS 66048

MELCHERT, JAMES FREDERICK
SCULPTOR, EDUCATOR
b New Bremen, Ohio, Dec 2, 30. *Study:* Princeton Univ, AB; Univ Chicago, MFA; Univ Calif, Berkeley, MA; ceramics with Peter Voulkos. *Work:* San Francisco Mus Art; Mus Mod Art, Kyoto, Japan; Victoria & Albert Mus, London; Oakland Mus Art, Calif; Stedelijk Mus, Amsterdam. *Exhib:* Abstract Expressionist Ceramics, Univ Calif, Irvine, 66; Contemporary American Sculpture, Whitney Mus Am Art, New York, 66, 68 & 70; Documenta 5, Kassel, Ger, 72; solo exhibs, Galerie Fignal, Amsterdam, 78, San Francisco Art Inst, Calif, 81 & Fuller Goldeen Gallery, San Francisco, 84 & Holly Solomon Gallery, New York; California Painting & Sculpture, San Francisco Mus Mod Art & Nat Collection Fine Arts, Washington, DC, 77; Words at Liberty, Mus Contemp Art, Chicago, 77; One Hundred Years of American Ceramics, Syracuse Mus, NY & Renwick Gallery, Washington, DC, 80; California Sculpture, San Francisco Mus Mod Art, 86; The Eloquent Object, Philbrook Mus, Tulsa, Okla; Notre Dame Col, 89; East Carolina State Univ, Greenville, SC, 89. *Pos:* Dir visual arts prog, Nat Endowment Arts, 77-81; dir, Am Acad Rome, 84-88. *Teaching:* Chmn dept ceramics, San Francisco Art Inst, 61-64; prof art, Univ Calif, Berkeley, 65-76 & 81-; vis sculptor, Univ Wis-Madison, spring 71. *Awards:* Artist Fel, Nat Endowment Arts, 73; Award of Distinction, Nat Coun Art Adminrs, 89; Hon Doctorate, San Francisco Art Inst, 84. *Mem:* Col Art Asn (bd mem); Century Asn. *Media:* Clay. *Dealer:* Holly Solomon Gallery New York NY. *Mailing Add:* 6077 Ocean View Dr Oakland CA 94618

MELIKIAN, MARY
PAINTER
b Worcester, Mass. *Study:* RI Sch Design, Providence, BFA, 55; Columbia Univ Teachers Col. *Work:* Worcester Mus Art, Mass; Mint Mus, Charlotte, NC; Yerevan Mus, Armenia; Vassar Col Art Mus; Art for US Embassies, State Dept; Centre Human Rights, UN, New York. *Exhib:* Nat Arts Club New York, 69 & 70; Galerie de Tours, San Francisco & Ankrum Gallery, Los Angeles, 70, Calif; retrospective, Centenary Col, Hackettstown, 75; one-man shows, Bodley Gallery, New York, 78 & 81, Quadrangle Gallery, Dallas, 80 & Dorsky Gallery, New York, 86; group show, Nicholas Gallery, Palm Beach, Fla, 79; Elaine Benson Gallery, Bridgehampton, NY, 91. *Pos:* Asst designer, Fuller Fabrics, NY, 56; asst dir, Grand Cent Moderns, New York, 60-61; dir pub rels, Grand Cent Art Galleries, New York, 61-67. *Teaching:* Instr art, Nutley High Sch, 57-60. *Awards:* First Prize, Kit Kat Club, 61, Armenian Student Asn, 61 & 62 & Women's Nat Repub Club, 70, 72, 73 & 75. *Bibliog:* Colette Roberts (auth), article, France-Am; N Stepanian (auth), Paintings of Mary Melikian, Voice of Am, 68; Anna Avedisian (auth), The Heart Remembers, Ararat Mag, 92. *Mem:* Parrish Art Mus, Southampton, NY; Guild Hall, Easthampton, NY; Nat Arts Club, NY. *Media:* Watercolor, Oil. *Publ:* Auth, articles, Ararat Mag. *Dealer:* Dorsky Gallery 379 W Broadway New York NY 10012. *Mailing Add:* 429 E 52nd St Rivercourt 27H New York NY 10022

MELL, ED (EDMUND PAUL JR)
PAINTER, PRINTMAKER
b Phoenix, Ariz, Sept 17, 42. *Study:* Phoenix Col, AA, 63; Art Ctr Col Design, Los Angeles, BFA(advert illus), 67. *Work:* Scottsdale Ctr Arts, Ariz. *Comn:* Oil painting, Mary Kay Cosmetics, Dallas, 80; oil murals, Empire Bank, Denver, 82, Farm Bank Ctr, Denver, 82 & Courson Oil, Perryton, Tex, 83. *Exhib:* Ariz Invitational, Scottsdale Ctr Arts, 82; Artists of Arizona, Ctr Mod Art, Guadalajara, Mex, 82; solo exhibs, Art Resources Gallery, Denver, 82, Dewey-Kofron Gallery, Santa Fe, 83 & Long Beach Mus Art, Calif, 83. *Pos:* Art dir, Kenyon & Eckhardt Advert, 68-70; artist & co-dir, Sagebrush Studio, New York, 70-73. *Teaching:* Instr art, Bacavi Community Sch, Hotevilla, Ariz, summers 71 & 73. *Bibliog:* Article, Art Voices S, 80; Ed Mell--Mesas man made, Southwest Art, 82; A portfolio of regional landscape painting, Am Artist, 84. *Media:* Oil on Canvas, Pastel; Lithography. *Mailing Add:* c/o Suzanne Brown Gallery 7160 Main St Scottsdale AZ 85251

MELLON, PAUL
COLLECTOR, ADMINISTRATOR
b Pittsburgh, Pa, June 11, 07. *Study:* Choate Sch, Wallingford, Conn, 19-25; Yale Univ, BA, 29, Hon LHD, 67; Clare Col, Cambridge Univ, BA, 31, MA, 38; Oxford Univ, DLitt, 61; Carnegie Inst Technol, LLD, 67; Cambridge Univ, Eng, LLD, 83, Royal Veterinary Col, Univ London, Hon DVM, 91. *Pos:* Trustee, Nat Gallery Art, 38-39 & 45-86, pres, 38-39 & 63-78, chmn, 79-85, hon trustee, 85-; trustee, Va Mus Fine Arts, Richmond, formerly; Old Dominion Foun, 41; trustee, Bollingen Found, 45-69, pres, 46-56, chmn, 56-69. *Awards:* Medal in Archit, Thomas Jefferson Memorial Found, 89; Hadrian Award, World Monuments Fund, 89; Benjamin Franklin Award, Am Philosophical Soc, 89; and others. *Mem:* Hon fel, Royal Inst Brit Archit; hon mem, Amer Inst Archit; Royal Acad. *Interests:* Major financial contributor to Nat Gallery Art, Va Mus Fine Arts, Yale Ctr Brit Art, & Paul Mellon Centre for Studies in British Art, London, Eng. *Collection:* (Paul Mellon) English paintings, 1700-1850; (Mr & Mrs Paul Mellon) impressionist & post-impressionist paintings. *Mailing Add:* 1729 H St NW Washington DC 20006

MELLOR, MARK ADAMS
PAINTER, ILLUSTRATOR
b Chicago, Ill, Oct, 28, 51. *Study:* Univ Bridgeport, Conn, AA, 76; Illusr Workshop, Tarrytown, NY, cert, 83. *Work:* Quaker Oats Co, Chicago, Ill; Westport Town Art Collection & Stamford Town Hall, Conn; Aetna, Hartford, Conn; Pepsico, New York; Middlebank, Middletown, Conn. *Comn:* Historic watercolor painting, Westport, Conn, 80. *Exhib:* Conn Watercolor Soc Exhib, Wadsworth Athenaeum Hartford, 76-77; 112th Am Watercolor Soc, Travelling Exhib, Frye Mus, Seattle, Wash, Tweed Mus Art, Univ Minn, Duluth, & Springfield Art Ctr, Ohio, 79-80; New Haven Paint & Clay Ann, John Shade Ely House Gallery, Conn, 86; 5th New Eng Ann, Green Art Gallery, Guilford, Conn, 86; one-man shows, Max's Art Supplies, 90 & Fairfield Libr Gallery, 91; Conn Watercolor Soc Ann, Univ Hartford, 92; Conn Acad Fine Arts, Norwich Mus, Norwich. *Pos:* Illusr asst, Fred Otnes Illusr, W Redding, Conn, 76- *Teaching:* Watercolor demonstrations, Westport Nature Ctr Ann, Fairfield Adult Educ & Fairfield Pub Libr, 90-92. *Awards:* Art Friend Prize, Conn Watercolor Soc Mem Exhib, 80; Am Watercolor Soc Award, 112th Ann Traveling Exhib, 80. *Mem:* Conn Watercolor Soc; New Haven Paint & Clay Club, 85; Conn Acad Fine Arts, 90; Conn Classic Arts, Trumball (juror awards). *Media:* Watercolor, Oils. *Publ:* Auth, The watercolor page, Am Artist Mag, 1/84. *Dealer:* Connecticut Yankee International 23 Hollow Tree Ridge Rd Darien CT 06820. *Mailing Add:* 15 Little Fox Ln Weston CT 06883

MELNICK, MYRON J
SCULPTOR, COLLAGE ARTIST
b Denver, Colo, Apr 28, 59. *Study:* Univ Colo, Boulder, BFA, 75; Univ Minn, Minneapolis, MFA, 78. *Work:* United Nations, New York; Columbus Gallery Fine Arts, Ohio. *Comn:* Cast paper wall construction, Denver Nat Bank, Colo, 80; wall relief, LA Law, NBC Studios, Burbank, Calif, 87; paper wall hanging, Pepsi Cola World Hq, New York, 88; paper wall hanging, Calvin Klein, New York, 89; paper wall hanging, Negus Design, Dallas, Tex, 90. *Exhib:* Solo exhib, Rochester Art Ctr, 77, Hamline Univ, St Paul & Studio Arts Gallery, Univ Minn, 78, Minn, Rosenbaum Fine Arts, Ft Lauderdale, Fla, 88, Tribeca Gallery, New York, 91, Laramie Community Col, Cheyenne, Wyo, 92; Paper Surface Phenomena, Shoshana Wayne Gallery, Los Angeles, Calif, 84; Colo State Art, Colo Springs Fine Art Ctr, 89; Colo 1990, Denver Art Mus, 90; Paris Gibson Square Ctr Contemp Arts, Great Falls, Mont, 91; Nat Endowment Arts Fel Winners, Farrell Collection, Washington, DC, 91; Summer Exhib 1992, Glen Green Gallery, Santa Fe, NMex, 92. *Awards:* Western States Art Fed Regional Fel, 89; Nat Endowment for the Arts Fel Grant, 90. *Media:* Hand cast paper, Monoprints. *Mailing Add:* 1366 Garfield St, #4O Denver CO 80206

MELVILLE, GREVIS WHITAKER
PAINTER, PRINTMAKER
b Damariscotta, Maine, Dec 23, 04. *Study:* Yale Sch Art & Archit; Art Students League. *Work:* William A Farnsworth Libr & Art Mus, Rockland, Maine; Pierson Col, Yale Univ, New Haven, Conn; Damariscotta Region Info Bur. *Comn:* Designed seal, co comnr, Lincoln Co, Maine, 75. *Exhib:* Pa Acad Fine Art, Philadelphia; one-man show, Smith Col Mus, Northampton, Mass; Maine State Art Festival, Augusta; Maine Artists Shows, Portland Mus Art; Bowdoin Col & Bowdoin Col Mus Art, Brunswick, Maine; Retrospective, Maine Art Gallery, 79; Maine Art Gallery, Wiscasset, juried, 82 & review, 82. *Teaching:* Artist in residence, Hackley Sch, Tarrytown, NY, 41-42. *Bibliog:* A Review: Grevis Melville & Nancy McGuire, Maine Sunday Telegram, Portland, 5/3/82. *Mem:* Maine Art Gallery (bd dirs, 68-80). *Media:* Oil, Lithography. *Publ:* Illusr, Windswept, Macmillan, 42; illusr, Maine Memories, Greene, 68. *Dealer:* Jacques Seligmann Galleries 5 E 57th St New York NY 10022; Ogunquit Gallery US Rte 1 Ogunquit ME 03907. *Mailing Add:* 38 Main St Damariscotta ME 04543

MELVIN, RONALD MCKNIGHT
MUSEUM DIRECTOR
b Regina, Sask, Oct 25, 27. *Study:* Univ British Columbia, BComm, 49. *Collections Arranged:* Important Western Art from Chicago Collections, 80; Five American Masters of Watercolor (auth, catalog), 81; American Naive Paintings from the Nat Gallery Art (auth, catalog), 82; Solitude--Inner Visions in American Art, 82; Woman, 84. *Pos:* Dir, Terra Mus Am Art, Evanston, Ill, 80-84; trustee, Berkshire Mus, 86-92. *Mailing Add:* Black Birch Norfolk Rd PO Drawer L Southfield MA 01259

MENDELSOHN, JOHN
PAINTER
b Topeka, Kans, Sept 12, 49. *Study:* Columbia Univ, BA, 71; Rutgers Univ, MFA, 74. *Work:* New Mus Contemp Art, New York. *Exhib:* Studio Program Exhib, Whitney Mus Am Art, New York, 71; US Art Now, Nordiska, Kompanient, Stockholm, Sweden, 81; Painting and Sculpture Today, Indianapolis Mus Art, Ind, 84; Paradise Lost, Paradise Regained, Venice Biennale, Italy, 84; Selections Edward R Downe Collection, Wellesley Col Mus, Mass, 86. *Awards:* Nat Endowment Arts Fel, 87. *Bibliog:* Paul Krainak (auth), Compassionate Images (catalog), Herron Sch Art, 82; Marcia Tucker (auth), Paradise Lost, Paradise Regained (catalog), New Mus Contemp Art, 84; Robert Mahoney (auth), The Alice Paintings, rev, Arts Mag, 88. *Media:* Vinyl paint on jute. *Dealer:* Michael Walls Gallery 137 Greene St New York NY 10012. *Mailing Add:* 14 Harrison St New York NY 10013

MENDELSON, HAIM
PAINTER, PRINTMAKER
b Semiatich, Builsk, Poland, Oct 15, 23; US citizen. *Study:* Am Artists Sch, 36-40; Saul Baizerman Art Sch, 40-43; pvt study with Saul Baizerman, 43-52; Educ Alliance Art Sch, 46. *Work:* Contemp Drawing Collection, Minn Mus Art, St Paul; Print Collection of New York Pub Libr; Print Collection of St Vincent Col, Latrobe, Pa; Griffiths Art Ctr of St Lawrence Univ, Canton, NY; Edwin A Ulrich Mus, Wichita State Univ, Kans; Flint Inst Fine Arts, Flint, Mich. *Exhib:* The Artist as Reporter, Mus Mod Art, New York, 40-41; Nat Acad of Design, New York, 65, 68, 75, 77 & 90; 10th Nat Exhib of Prints & Drawings, Okla Art Ctr, 68; Fedn of Mod Painters & Sculptors (traveling exhib), Gallery Asn New York, 76-78; Prints USA, Pratt Graphics Ctr Traveling Exhib, 82-85; Prominent Print Makers, Mo Western State Col, 88;

East Coast Prints, Adrian Col, Mich, 88; Artists Proof, Arts Coun Gallery, Winston-Salem, NC, 88. *Pos:* Dir, Hudson Guild Art Gallery, New York, 71-72 & 73- *Teaching:* Instr, painting and drawing, City Col New York, 61-64; Teacher, City & Country Sch, New York City, 64-91. *Awards:* First Prize, Graphics, Knickerbocker Artists Ann, New York, 64; Purchase Award, Drawings USA, St Paul Art Ctr, 66; Dr Maury Leibovitz Spec Merit Award, 87. *Bibliog:* Article, The New Yorker, 6/70. *Mem:* Fedn of Mod Painters & Sculptors (pres, 74-); The Print Consortium; Audubon Artists; Am Soc Contemp Artists. *Media:* Oil, Acrylic; Intaglio. *Publ:* Auth, Mezzotint, Prize Winning Graphics Book III, Allied Publ, Ft Lauderdale, Fla, 65. *Mailing Add:* 234 W 21st St New York NY 10011

MENDENHALL, JACK
PAINTER, INSTRUCTOR
b Ventura, Calif, Apr 7, 37. *Study:* Calif Col Arts & Crafts, BFA, 58 & MFA(painting), 70. *Work:* Univ Calif Art Mus, Berkeley; San Francisco Art Comn; Gallery Ostergren, Malmo, Sweden; Butler Inst of Am Art, Ohio; Va Mus of Fine Arts, Richmond; plus numerous pvt collections, individual & industrial, US & Europe. *Comn:* Rainbows, Waldo Tunnels, Calif Div Hwy, San Francisco, 70. *Exhib:* Amerikanske Realister, Panders Kunstmuseum, Sweden, 73; Tokyo Biennale 74, Japan, 74; New Photo Realism, Wadsworth Atheneum, Hartford, Conn, 74; one-man show, O K Harris Gallery, New York, 74, 78 & 81; Realist Painting in California, John Berggruen Gallery, San Francisco, 75; Watercolors & Drawings, American Realists, Meisel Gallery, New York, 75; plus others. *Teaching:* Assoc prof painting & drawing, Calif Col Arts & Crafts, 70- *Awards:* Purchase Award, San Francisco Art Comn, 70. *Bibliog:* William C Seitz (auth), The real and the artificial: Painting of the new environment, Art in Am, 12/72; Linda Chase (auth), Les hyperrealistes Americans, Paris, Ed Filipacchi, 73; Ellen Lubell (auth), article, Arts Mag, 2/75; and others. *Media:* Oil, Watercolor. *Dealer:* O K Harris Gallery 383 W Broadway New York NY 10012. *Mailing Add:* 5824 Florence Terr Oakland CA 94611

MENDES, BARBARA
PAINTER
b Montclair, NJ, Jan 30, 48. *Study:* Hunter Col, 67-69; Univ Calif, Riverside, BA, 80. *Work:* Beserkley Record Co, Berkeley, Calif. *Exhib:* One person shows, Speak Happiness, Factory Place Gallery, 83 & One Love Series, Theatre Art Gallery, 85, Los Angeles, Recent Work, R H Love Modern, Chicago, 88; and others. *Awards:* Weisglass Mem Award, Spring Show, Staten Island Mus, 74; Certificate of Excellence, In Art Compt, Los Angeles, 84; Third Prize, All-Cal Bienniel, Riverside, Calif, 86. *Bibliog:* Susan Threlkeld (auth), rev, KSCI TV, San Bernardino, 79; Mark Lundahl (auth), Africa woman shines on canvas, San Bernardino Sun, 80; Harold Haydon (auth), Top of the weekend, Chicago Sun Times, 3/13/81 & rev, 4/16/82; Tom Jacobs (auth), Showing her true colors, San Bernardino Sun, 11/20/83; Look of Los Angeles, Los Angeles Reader, 8/16/85. *Media:* Oil. *Publ:* Coauth, It ain't me babe, Last Gaspeco, 70; All Girl Thrills, 71 & auth, Illuminations, 72, Print Mint. *Dealer:* R H Love Modern 100 E Ohio St Chicago IL 60611. *Mailing Add:* 1308 Factory Pl Los Angeles CA 90013-2253

MENDOZA, ANTONIO G
PHOTOGRAPHER
b Havana, Cuba, July 21, 41; US citizen. *Study:* Yale Univ, BA, 63; Harvard Grad Sch Design, MA(archit), 68. *Work:* Mus Mod Art, New York; Mus Fine Arts, Boston; Fogg Art Mus; Addison Gallery Am Art. *Exhib:* Cats & Dogs, Arco Ctr Visual Art, Los Angeles, 80; Light Gallery, New York, 81; Kathleen Ewing Gallery, Washington, DC, 81; Jacksonville Art Mus, Fla, 82; New Mus, New York, 83; Los Angeles Ctr Photogr Art, 85; Mus Mod Art, NY, 85. *Teaching:* Photog, Int Ctr Photog, 82-85. *Awards:* Nat Endowment Arts Photog Grant, 81; Creative Artists Pub Serv Grant, 81; Guggenheim Fel, 85; NY State Artist Found Fel, 85. *Bibliog:* Ben Lifson (auth), Young dog, old tricks, Village Voice, 3/17/80; Owen Edwards (auth), Dog bites psyche, Saturday Rev, 6/80 & Tony Mendoza's animal farm, Am Photogr, 11/83; Andy Grundberg (auth), The modern focuses on contemporary visions, NY Times, 9/15/85. *Publ:* Auth, The Dog Observed, Knopf, 84; Ernie: A Photographer's Memoir, Capra Press, 85. *Dealer:* Virginia Miller Galleries 169 Madeira Coral Gables FL 33134; Witkin Gallery New York NY. *Mailing Add:* c/o Witkin Gallery 415 W Broadway New York NY 10012

MENEELEY, EDWARD
PAINTER, SCULPTOR
b Wilkes-Barre, Pa, Dec 18, 27. *Study:* Murray Art Sch, Wilkes-Barre, 52-56; Sch of Visual Arts, New York, 57-58; pvt study with Jack Tworkov, New York, 58-59. *Work:* Metrop Mus Art, Mus Mod Art; Whitney Mus, New York; Victoria & Albert Mus, London, Can; Tate Gallery, London; Herbert Johnson Mus, Cornell Univ; Peter Moores Found, Liverpool. *Exhib:* Recent Acquisitions, Whitney Mus, New York, 69; Machine Art, Mus Mod Art, New York, 70; Victoria & Albert Mus, London, 71; Photography into Art, Camden Arts Ctr, London, Can, 72; Printed Art, Mus Mod Art, New York, 80; one-man shows, Angela Flowers Gallery, London, 85, Col Misericondia, Dallas, Pa, 89, Craft Alliance, St Louis, 90; White Chapel Art Gallery, London, 73; and others. *Teaching:* Instr, Central Sch Art, London, 68-73; instr, Winchester Sch of Art, England, 69-; lectr, Belleville Col, St Louis, Mo, 79 & 90, Art Students League, New York, 79; Col Misericordia, Dallas, Pa, 89. *Awards:* Nat Endowment Arts Grant, Washington, DC, 71; Arts Coun Grant, London, 71; Pollack-Krasner Found Grant, New York, 86 & 90. *Bibliog:* Theodore F Wolff (auth), article, Christian Sci Monitor, 80; Carol Cleaveland (auth), Morning Call, 88; ABC-TV Doc, 89. *Mem:* Artists' Club, New York; Inst Contemp Art, London. *Media:* Miscellaneous. *Res:* Contemporary art archives; Dir Publ, ESM Doc. *Publ:* Auth, Retrospective catalog, Frank Marino Gallery, 78. *Dealer:* Angela Flowers Gallery 11 Tottenham Mews London W1P 9PJ. *Mailing Add:* The Schoolhouse 300 Franklin St Weissport PA 18235

MENIHAN, JOHN CONWAY
PAINTER, PRINTMAKER
b Rochester, NY, Feb 14, 08. *Study:* Wharton Sch, Univ Pa, 30; St John Fisher Col, LLD, 83. *Work:* Libr Cong, Washington, DC; Carnegie Inst, Pittsburgh; Mem Art Gallery, Rochester. *Comn:* Life of St Elizabeth Seton (triptych), St Thomas Apostle Church, Rochester, NY, 78; ceremonial mace, St John Fisher Col, Rochester, NY, 81, D'Youville Col, Buffalo, NY, 81 & Community Col Air Force, 81; Stations of the Cross & Alter Crucifix, Our Lady of Lourdes Roman Cath Church, Rochester, NY, 85; wall hanging, Indian theme, The Lodge at Woodcliff, Fairport, NY, 87. *Exhib:* Finger Lakes Show, Mem Art Gallery, Rochester, 30 & 71; Art Inst Chicago, 39; World's Fair, New York, 39; Nat Acad Design, 48; Am Watercolor Soc, 54, New York; retrospective, Nazareth Col, Rochester, NY, 83 & Mem Art Gallery, Rochester, 88. *Teaching:* Asst prof drawing & painting, Univ Rochester, 46-65. *Awards:* Lillian Fairchild Award, Univ Rochester, 40; Marion Stratton Gould Award, Univ Rochester Mem Art Gallery, 46; fel Rochester Mus & Sci Ctr. *Bibliog:* Norman Kent (auth), John C Menihan, lithographer, Am Artist, 45. *Mem:* Nat Acad Design; Am Watercolor Soc. *Publ:* Illusr, How Scientists Find Out, Little, 65; Historic St Mary's Church, Albany, NY, 73; St Ann's of Hornell, 76. *Mailing Add:* 208 Alpine Dr Rochester NY 14618

MENIL, GEORGES & LOIS DE
PATRON, COLLECTOR
Study: Georges de Menil: AB Harvard, PhD MIT, 62/68; Lois de Menil: AB Wellesley, 60; Univ Paris (law), 62; Harvard Univ, PhD, 72. *Pos:* Lois de Menil: vis comt, Harvard Univ Art Mus, 75-, trustee, Int Coun Mus Mod Art, New York, 75-, Nat Gallery Art, New York, vchmn trustees coun, 78-, trustee, Dia Ctr Arts, 84- & World Monuments Fund, 91- *Collection:* 20th century painting & sculpture, African Art. *Mailing Add:* 120 E 70 St New York NY 10021

MENSES, JAN
PAINTER, PRINTMAKER
b Rotterdam, Neth, Apr 28, 33; Can citizen. *Study:* Rotterdamse Kunst Akademie; hon degree, Univ Delle Arti, 81 & Accademia Bedriacense, 84. *Work:* Mus Mod Art & Guggenheim Mus, New York; Art Inst Chicago; Brooklyn Mus; Ryksmuseum, Amsterdam, Holland; Victoria & Albert Mus, London; Vatican Mus, Rome. *Comn:* Mural, Montreal Holocaust Mem Centre, Can. *Exhib:* Montreal Mus Fine Arts, 61, 65 & 76; 5th & 7th Biennial Can Painting, 63 & 68 & 1st & 2nd Biennial Can Watercolours, Drawings & Prints, 64 & 66, Nat Gallery Can, Ottawa; 20 New Acquisitions, Mus Mod Art, New York, 66; 9th & 11th Int Exhib Drawings & Engravings, Lugano, Switz, 66 & 72; Rotterdam Art Found, Neth, 74; Univ British Columbia, Vancouver, 81; Mead Art Mus, Amherst, Mass, 83; Marywood Col, Scranton, Pa, 85; and others. *Teaching:* Vis lectr, var Can univs. *Awards:* Gold Medal, Accademia Italia Delle Arte, Italy, 80; Gold Medal, Int Parliament USA, 82; Gran Premio Delle Nazioni, Italy, 83. *Bibliog:* Jan Menses--Peintre et prophete, Johathan, 82; La peinture de Jan Menses: Kaddish, Klippoth Tikkoune, Tribune Juive, Montreal, 83; Jan Menses: Exile and Redemption (film), Can Broadcasting Corp, 85. *Mem:* Royal Can Acad Arts; Soc Artistes en Arts Visuels de Que; Accademia Italia Delle Arte, Italy; Accademia D'Europa; Accademia Delle Nazione; Jewish Am Acad Arts & Sci. *Media:* Tempera, Acrylic. *Dealer:* Galerie Don Stewart 1460 Sherbrooke St W Montreal PQ H3G 1K4 Can; Michel Tetreault Art Contemporain 4260 Rue Saint Denis Montreal PQ H2J 2K8. *Mailing Add:* Blom & Dorn Gallery 164 Mercer St New York NY 10012

MENTHE, MELISSA
LIBRARIAN, PHOTOGRAPHER
b Hackensack, NJ, June 16, 48. *Study:* Montclair State Col, NJ, BA; Rutgers Univ, MLS. *Pos:* Reference librn, Art Dept, Newark Pub Libr, NJ, 71-76 & Rutgers Univ, New Brunswick, 76-82. *Awards:* Nat Endowment Arts Grant, 81. *Mem:* Art Libr Soc NAm; Asn Col & Res Libr, Am Libr Asn; Col Art Asn; Spec Libr Asn; Indust Photographers NJ. *Res:* Methodology in history of photography. *Interests:* History of photography, incunabula & fine printing, historic preservation. *Mailing Add:* PO Box 1246 Paramus NJ 07653

MERCOLINO, VERONICA FLORENCE
PAINTER, SCULPTOR
b Plainfield, NJ. *Study:* Columbus Col Art & Design, Ohio; Art Students League, New York; Colo Christian Col, DPhil. *Work:* Sheldon Swope Gallery, Ind; Museo dell Arte Contemporanea, Savona, Italy; Univ Maine, Orono; Rutgers Univ, New Brunswick, NJ. *Comn:* Portraits, Henri Nosco, late conductor NBC Symphony Orchestra, New York, Torus Shimura, pres Daido Corp, Tokyo, Japan, James Vreeland, pres Hummel Chemical Co, NJ & Hildegarde Chanteuse, New York; prog cover, Bicentennial Concert, Plainfield Symphony Orchestra, NJ, 76. *Exhib:* Chase Gallery, New York, 71; Art with Music, Washington Co Mus Fine Arts, Md, 72; Art 1972, Pebble Beach Gallery, Calif; Int Art Biennale, Mus Mod Art, Vichy, France, 75; Salon de L'Ecole Francaise, Musée Nat d'Art Mod, Paris, 76; Allied Artists Am, New York, 79; Contemporary Art, Circolo del Arte, Italy, 80. *Pos:* Dir & instr figure-portrait, Art Farm Workshop, Flemington, NJ, 70-84; owner, Mountain Gallery, Taos, NMex, 84- *Awards:* First Prize, Conv Hall, Las Vegas, Nev, 73; Gold Medal, Art Festival, Ste Germain de Pres, Brussels, 75; First Prize Oil, Bergen Community Mus Exhib, Am Artists Prof League, NJ. *Bibliog:* Lee Harbick (auth), rev, Game & Gossip, 72; R Clermont (auth),

article, La Revue Mod, Paris, 76; Vallobra (auth), article, Le Vertige du Néant, Brussels, 76. *Mem:* Taos Art Asn; Pen & Brush; Southwestern Oil Painters. *Media:* Oil, Watercolor; Clay. *Publ:* Auth, The art workshop, Am Artists, 78. *Dealer:* Mountain Gallery Taos NM; Eloise Gallery Taos NM. *Mailing Add:* Box 5166 Taos NM 87571

MEREDITH, JOHN
PAINTER
b Fergus, Ont, Can, 1933. *Work:* Agnes Etherington Art Ctr, Kingston, Ont; Art Gallery Ont, Toronto; Art Gallery Greater Victoria, BC; City Trust, Vancouver; Confederation Art Gallery and Mus, PEI. *Exhib:* One-man shows, Gallery of Contemp Art, Toronto, 58-59, Blue Barn Gallery, Ottawa, 65, Art Gallery of Ont, 74-75, Art Gallery of Greater Victoria, 80; Canada: Art d'aujour' hui, Musee Nat d'Art Moderne, Paris, 68; Nine Canadians, Inst Contemp Art, Boston, 68; Eight Artists From Canada, Tel Aviv Mus, Israel, 70; Toronto Painting, 1953-1965, Nat Gallery Can, Ottawa, 72; Modern Painting in Can, Edmonton Art Gallery, 78; Then & Now, Factory, 77 & 79; Linear Variables, Winnipeg Art Gallery, 81. *Mem:* Royal Can Acad Arts. *Media:* Oil. *Mailing Add:* c/o The Kaspar Gallery 27 Prince Arthur Ave Toronto ON M5R 1B2 Canada

MERFELD, GERALD LYDON
PAINTER
b Des Moines, Iowa, Feb 19, 36. *Study:* Am Acad Art, with William Mosby, 54-57. *Work:* Marietta Col, Ohio; McDonough Collection Am Art; US Navy Arch; John Deere & Co. *Exhib:* Hope Show, Butler Inst Am Art, 72, 74, 76, 78, 80 & 82; Okla Mus Art 14th Ann Artists Salon, 75; Allied Artists Am Ann, New York, 75-77, 80; Hudson Valley Art Asn, 75, 81, 82, 86 &90; Knickerbocker Artists, 75, 85, 86, 87 & 89; Civic Fine Arts Asn, Sioux Falls, SDak, 77; Vanishing Landmark Exhib, Springfield Art Mus, Mo, 77; Artists of the Rockies & Golden West Retrospective Exhib, Sangre de Cristo Arts Ctr, Pueblo, Colo, 83; Audubon Artists, New York, 73-90; Am Artists Prof League, New York, 89; Butler Inst Am Art, 81-83; Akron Soc Artists Grand Exhib, 91 & 92. *Pos:* Studio asst, Dean Cornwell, New York, 57-60; combat artist, US Navy, Vietnam, 69 & Mediter, 71. *Awards:* Louis E Seley Gold Medal, Salmagundi Club, 71; Okla Mus Art Award, 75; First Prize, Hope Show Butler Inst Am Art, 80; First Prize, Drawing, Butler Inst Am Art, 83; Gold Medal of Hon, Am Artist Prof League, 89. *Bibliog:* Charles Movalli (auth), Gerald Merfeld's teaching tenets, Am Artist, 12/78; Betty Harvey (auth), Gerald Merfeld, Artists of the Rockies & Golden West, fall 81; Paulette Georgantas (producer), The Merfeld Studio, video. *Media:* Oil, Pastel, watercolor. *Dealer:* The Knox Galleries Vail Village Inn Plaza No 8 100 E Meadow Dr Vail CO 81657. *Mailing Add:* 2302 Muddy Rd Westcliffe CO 81252

MERIDA, FREDERICK A
ART DEALER, PRINTMAKER
b Indianapolis, Ind, Mar 10, 36. *Study:* Kansas City Art Inst, Mo, 54-57; Brooklyn Mus Sch, NY, 57-59; New Sch Social Res, New York, 57-59. *Work:* Columbia Mus Art, SC; Libr of Congress, Wash, DC; J B Speed Mus, Louisville, Ky. *Exhib:* 11th & 13th Annual Boston Printmakers, Boston Mus Fine Arts, 58 & 60; Pasadena Art Mus, Calif, 58; 15th Annual, Pa Acad Fine Arts, Philadelphia, 61; Prints 1962, State Univ NY, Potsdam, 62; 8 State Annual, J B Speed Mus, Louisville, Ky, 85, 87. *Collections Arranged:* Melville Price Retrospective 1920-1970, 70, Rookwood: A Historical Survey, 71, Biggest Show of Little Painting, 73 & Kentuckian Painters Invitational, 75, Frame House Gallery, Louisville, Ky; Black Artists Annual, 1980-1985, Nat Black Artists, Gallery One, 1st Nat Bank, Louisville, Ky. *Pos:* dir, Frame House Gallery, Louisville, Ky, 69-75, dir bus art develop & asst to pres, 75-77; owner & dir, Merida Gallery, Louisville, Ky, 77-; cur corp art collection, Hilliard Lyons Ctr, Louisville, Ky, 88-92. *Awards:* Pennell Purchase Prize, Libr Cong, Washington, DC, 57; Purchase Awards, Nelson Gallery Art, Kansas City, Mo, 60 & J B Speed Mus, Louiville, Ky, 85, 87. *Bibliog:* Ira Simmons (auth), Art and money, Scene Mag, Louisville Times, 2/8/86. *Mem:* Am Soc Appraisers (chap pres, 85-86). *Specialty:* Contemporary art; 19th century American and European paintings. *Publ:* Ed, Art Gallery Guide of Louisville, Merida Gallery, Inc, 68-69. *Mailing Add:* Merida Galleries PO Box 53 Farmington KY 42040-0053

MERKEL, JAYNE (SILVERSTEIN)
HISTORIAN, CRITIC
b Cincinnati, Ohio, Sept 28, 42. *Study:* Simmons Col, with Wylie Sypher, BS, 64; Smith Col, with Henry-Russell Hitchcock, MA(art hist), 68; Univ Mich, with Leonard K Eaton, 66-68. *Collections Arranged:* Early Works: Alexander Calder (auth, catalog), Taft Mus, 72; Drawn by Cincinnati (auth, catalog), Collection of the Cincinnati Hist Soc, Contemp Arts Ctr, 80; 1930's Remembered, Part I, The High Style, Taft Mus, 82; In Its Place, the Architecture of Carl Strauss & Ray Roush, Contemp Arts Ctr, 85; Peter Eisenman: An Architecture of Absence, Contemp Arts Ctr, 86-87. *Pos:* cur, Contemp Arts Ctr, Cincinnati, 68-69; dir educ, Taft Mus, Cincinnati, 68-74; archit critic, Cincinnati Enquirer, 77-88; reviewer, Artforum, 80-; art & archit critic, WGUC-FM (pub radio), 83-88; contrib ed, Inland Archit, 84-. *Teaching:* Instr art hist, Art Acad Cincinnati, 73-78; vis instr art hist, Miami Univ, 78-79 & 81-82; asst prof Eng (writing), Univ Cincinnati, 88-91; actg dir, grad prog archit & design criticism, Parsons Sch Design, The New Sch, 92-. *Mem:* Soc Archit Historians; Soc Prof Journalists; Am Asn Univ Prof; Mod Language Asn; Archit League. *Res:* Contemporary American architecture, art and criticism. *Publ:* Auth, var bk reviews, Art J, 76-77 & J Aesthetics & Art Criticism, 80; articles & reviews, Am Inst Archit J, 78, Prog Archit, 80-82, 88-89, Artforum, 81-90, Inland Archit, 83-92, New Art Examiner, 83 & 88, Connoisseur, 84, Dialogue, 84-86, Amercraft 88, Art in Am, 86-92 & Competitions, 92; Michael Graves & the Riverbend Music Ctr, Contemp Arts Ctr, 86. *Mailing Add:* 60 Gramercy Park N 7B New York NY 10010

MERKIN, RICHARD MARSHALL
PAINTER, PRINTMAKER
b Brooklyn, NY, Oct, 1938. *Study:* Syracuse Univ Sch Art, BFA, 60; RI Sch Design, MFA(teaching fel), 63. *Work:* Mus Art, RI Sch Design; Mus Mod Art, New York; Am Fedn Arts, New York; Rose Art Mus, Brandeis Univ; Mass Inst Technol; Pa Acad Arts, Philadelphia; Smithsonian Inst, Washington, DC; Whitney Mus Am Art, New York. *Comn:* Seven murals, Blackstone Park Pub Sch, Boston, Mass, 75-76. *Exhib:* Whitney Mus Am Art, 67, 69 & 72; one-man exhibs, Terry Dintenfass Inc, New York, 73-74, 80-81, Eric Makler Gallery, Philadelphia, 81, 83, Karen Lennox Gallery, Chicago, 82, Susan Montezinos Gallery, Philadelphia, 84, Galleria Giulia, Rome, 84, Joe & Emily Lowe Art Gallery, Syracuse Univ, NY, 85, Foster-White Gallery, Seattle, Wash, 87, JRS Fine Art, Providence, RI, 88; Painting and Sculpture Today, Indianapolis Mus Art, 76; Alumni Artists Exhib, Syracuse Univ, 79; Nat Ann Midyear Show, Butler Inst Am Art, 79 & 82; Fiac 83, Paris, 83; I Love Paperino, Assessore alla Cultura de Commune di Roma, Rome, 84; The Music of Art, Artrain, Detroit, Mich, 85; The Grand Game of Baseball, Mus Borough Brooklyn, NY, 87; Diamonds Are Forever (traveling exhib), NY State Mus, Albany, in asn with Smithsonian Inst Traveling Exhib Serv, 87; Mod Am Realism, Sara Roby Found, Nat Mus Am Art, Washington, DC, 87; New York, New York, Helander Gallery, New York, 91. *Pos:* Contribr ed, Vanity Fair, 86-. *Teaching:* Asst prof painting, RI Sch Design, 61-70, adj prof, 70-; vis artist in residence, Syracuse Univ, 72. *Awards:* Purchase Award, Soc Washington DC Printmakers Show, Smithsonian Inst, 62; Tiffany Found Fel Painting, 62-63; Rosenthal Found Award, Nat Inst Arts & Lett, 75. *Publ:* Photog, Velvet Eden, Methuen Publ Co, 79. *Dealer:* Helander Gallery Palm Beach FL & New York NY. *Mailing Add:* 500 West End Ave New York NY 10024

MEROLA, MARIO
SCULPTOR, PAINTER
b Montreal, Que, Mar 31, 31. *Study:* Ecole des Beaux Arts de Montreal, dipl, 52; Ecole Supérieure des Arts Decoratifs de Paris, 53. *Work:* Mus d'Art Contemp & Mus Fine Arts, Montreal; Nat Gallery, Ottawa; Mus Munic, Brest, France; Brooklyn Col, NY; City Cortina Dampezzo, Italy; Won Kwang Univ, South Korea. *Comn:* Mural, Mazenod Seminary, Ottawa, 65; fountain, Expo 67, Montreal, 67; two murals, Quebec Govt, Osaka, Japan, 70; stained glass, Montreal subway, 79; Monumental Door, Nagyiatad, Hungary, 89; plus over 100 comn. *Exhib:* Solo exhibs, Luminous Reliefs, Mus Fine Arts, Montreal, 65, Mus du Quebec, 71, Constructions, 1950-1976, Mus d'Art Contemp, Montreal, 76, Mus Munic, Toulouse, France, 77, Mus Munic, Brest, France, 78, Muvezsetek Hasa, Pécs, Hungary, 91 & Ady Endre Gymnazium, Nagyatad, Hungary, 92; Affect-Effect, La Jolla Mus, Calif, 68; New Tendency, Mus d'Art Contemp, Montreal, 78; Made in Canada, Nat Libr Can, Ottawa, 84; and many other group exhibs. *Pos:* Pres, art-community integration, Soc Immobiliaire, Minn Affil Culturelles, Govt Que, 85-86. *Teaching:* Prof fine arts, Ecole des Beaux Arts, Montreal, 60-69; prof drawing, Univ Que, Montreal, 69-86. *Awards:* First Prize, murals, Can Pavilion, Brussels, 57 & Inst d'Hôtellerie, Can Govt, 73; First Prize, sculpture, Int Sculpture Meeting, St-Jean-Port-Jolie, 84; Honorary Citizen, City Iri, South Korea. *Bibliog:* Jacques de Roussan (auth), Mario Merola, Ed Lidec, 70; L Letocha (auth), Mario Merola, Formart, 72; Robert Melancon (auth), L'espace de la ville, Liberté, 82; A Metchnikov (auth), Mario Merola, Fini-Infini, 92. *Mem:* Royal Can Acad Art; Conseil de la Sculpture du Quebec; hon mem Conseil de la Peinture du Quebec; Int Sculpture Ctr. *Media:* Polymer on Wood. *Publ:* Auth, Two Projects, Mayor's Hill Park, Queen Elizabeth Driveway, Integration, Ed A L'Oree, 84. *Dealer:* Dominion Gallery 1438 Sherbrooke West Montreal PQ H3G 1K4 Canada; La Galerie D'Arts Contemporains De Montreal 2165 Crescent Montreal PQ H3G 2C1. *Mailing Add:* 216 Somerville Montreal PQ H3L 1A3 Canada

MERRILL, DAVID KENNETH
PAINTER, MURALIST
b Bridgeport, Conn, Oct 18, 35. *Comn:* Monroe Green, Town of Monroe, Conn, 72; ann report cover, William R Berkley Corp, New York, 73; IBM, Burlington, Vt, 74; 43 scenes of Southbury's past & present (mural), Southbury, Conn Town Hall Bldg Comt, 78; mural, Edmond Town Hall, Newtown, Conn, 83-85; Field Home, Yorktown Heights, New York. *Exhib:* Kent Art Asn, Conn, 69, 73 & 74; Northern Vt Artists Asn, 71-74; Mainstreams '74, Marietta, Ohio; Conn Acad Fine Art, 74; Douglas Gallery, Stamford, Conn, 74 & 75. *Teaching:* Instr art, Southbury Training Sch, Conn, 63-67. *Awards:* First Place, 72 & First & Second Place, 74, Northern Vt Artists Asn; First Prize Acrylic, Scan Art Exhib, 78 & 82. *Bibliog:* Randall E Christensen (dir), Newtown Mural (videotape). *Mem:* Kent & Washington Art Asns; Northern Vt Art Asn; New Haven Paint & Clay Club. *Media:* Acrylic. *Publ:* Auth, articles in This New England, Yankee Mag, Int Mag Marifacts, 10/78 & Connecticut's Child, 85. *Dealer:* Douglas Gallery 1117 High Ridge Rd Stamford CT 06905; Lillian Haversat Jericho VT 05465. *Mailing Add:* 195 Alpine Dr Sandy Hook CT 06482-1203

MERRILL, ROSS M
CONSERVATOR, PAINTER
b Abilene, Tex, 43. *Study:* Pa Acad Fine Arts; Oberlin Col, Ohio, MA; Intermus Conserv Asn, conserv cert. *Pos:* Admin head of conserv dept, Cleveland Mus Art, 74-81; head painting conserv, Nat Gallery Art, Washington, DC, 81-. *Teaching:* Lectr mus conserv for var mus & conserv orgns. *Mem:* Am Inst Conserv; Int Inst Conserv; Nat Conserv Adv Coun (chmn energy comt). *Media:* Oil, Watercolor. *Res:* Fifteenth century northern European painting techniques. *Interests:* Early European paintings. *Publ:* Co-auth, Honeycomb Core Construction for Supporting Panels, 72 & An Information Retrieval System for Painted Works of Art, 73, Am Inst Conserv;

auth, Juan deFlandes, a technical study, Cleveland Mus Bull, 76; co-auth, A History of Painting Forgery From 1500 to Present, 78 & auth, Technical Investigation of Cleveland Museum's Recent Forgery, St Catherine of Alexandria, 78, Am Inst Conserv. *Mailing Add:* Nat Gallery Art Washington DC 20565

MERRIN, EDWARD H
DEALER
b Brooklyn, NY, 28. *Study:* Tufts Col, BA, 50. *Pos:* Dir, Edward H Merrin Gallery, currently. *Mem:* Am Asn Dealers Ancient, Oriental & Primitive Art. *Specialty:* Classical and pre-Columbian antiquities. *Mailing Add:* Edward H Merrin Gallery 724 Fifth Ave 3rd Floor New York NY 10019

MERRITT, FRANCIS SUMNER
PAINTER, PRINTMAKER
b Danvers, Mass, Apr 8, 13. *Study:* Vesper George Sch Art; San Diego Acad Fine Art; Mass Sch Art; Boston Mus Sch; Yale Univ Sch Fine Arts; Colby Col, Hon DFA, 71; Portland Sch Art, LLD, 86. *Work:* Univ Southern Maine; William A Farnsworth Art Mus. *Comn:* Murals, Bd Educ, New London High Sch, NH, 43 & Knox Co Med Ctr, Rockland, Maine, 52. *Exhib:* Directions in American Art, Am Fedn Arts Traveling Unit, Carnegie Inst, 42; Int Watercolor Show, Art Inst Chicago, 42-43; Artists for Victory, Metrop Mus Art, 42; Butler Art Inst Ann, Youngstown, Ohio, 47; Greetings Exhib, Mus Mod Art, New York, 57; one-man show, Art Inst Pittsburgh, 78, Congress Square Gallery, Portland, Maine, 86 & Nashua NH Ctr for the Arts, 88; Mus Northern Ariz, 79; Farnsworth Print Ann, 80; one-man retrospective, Art Gallery, Univ Southern Maine, 84; Maine Biennial, 85. *Collections Arranged:* Henry R Sutter Collection, Univ Southern Maine, 85 & Farnsworth Art Mus, Rockland, 85. *Pos:* Cur, John Esther Art Gallery, Andover, Mass, 37-39; dir, Flint Inst Art, Mich, 47-51; dir, Haystack Mountain Sch Crafts, Deer Isle, Maine, 51-77, emer dir, 77- *Teaching:* Instr painting & drawing, Abbot Acad, Andover, Mass, 37-39, Colby Jr Col, New London, 40-44, Kingswood, Cranbrook, Bloomfield Hills, Mich, 46-47 & Bradford Jr Col, Mass, 53-57; instr experimental printmaking & monotype, Haystack Mountain Sch Arts, 79 & 81; instr, Penland Sch Crafts, 80-81; artist-in-residence, Univ Southern Maine, spring 84. *Bibliog:* Crafts tomorrow, standards, quality, design, Can Crafts Coun Artisan News, 9-10/79; The Haystack Tradition, Art Craft Media, Bowdoin Col Mus Art, 80; Archives of American Art Journal, Vol 20, No 1, 80; and others. *Mem:* Artists Equity (regional bd mem, 47-48); fel Am Crafts Coun (trustee, 56-62 & 80-81); fel Royal Soc Arts; Penland Sch Crafts (trustee, 80-); World Craft Coun. *Publ:* Contribr, Crafts Report, 6/88. *Mailing Add:* Centennial House RR No 1 Box 38 Deer Isle ME 04627

MERTIN, ROGER
PHOTOGRAPHER
b Bridgeport, Conn, Dec 9, 42. *Study:* Rochester Inst Technol, BFA, 65; Visual Studies Workshop, MFA, 72. *Work:* Nat Gallery Can, Ottawa; Int Mus Photog & Visual Studies Workshop, Rochester, NY; Mus Mod Art, New York; Boston Mus Fine Arts. *Exhib:* Past into Present, Seattle Art Mus, Wash, 76; Great West: Real/Ideal, Univ Colo, Boulder, 77; Mus Mod Art, New York, 78 & 81; One-of-a-Kind Am Photog, Corcoran Gallery Art, Washington, DC, 79; Photog in the 70's, Art Inst Chicago, 79; Light Gallery, New York, 80; Friends of Photog, Carmel, Calif, 81. *Teaching:* Asst prof fine arts & photog, Univ Rochester, NY, 73-81, assoc prof, 81- *Awards:* Guggenheim fel photog, 74; Nat Endowment for Arts fel photog, 76. *Publ:* Auth, Records 1976-78, Chicago Ctr Contemp Photog, 78. *Mailing Add:* Fine Arts Dept Univ Rochester Wilson Blvd Rochester NY 14627

MESA-BAINS, AMALIA
PAINTER
Study: San Jose State Univ, BA (painting), 66; San Francisco State Univ, MA, 71; Wright Inst, MA, 80, PhD, 83. *Exhib:* Solo exhib, Grotto of the Virgins, INTAR Gallery, New York, 87; Desangano - or Cafe Sphinx Moments Before the End, INTAR, New York, 87; Vida y Muerte, New Langton Arts, San Francisco, 88; LeDemon de Anges: 16 Chicano Artists from Around Los Angeles, Paris, Barcelona & Stockholm, 89; The Decade Show, Studio Mus Harlem, New York, 90. *Pos:* Panelist, Ann Coun Found Conference, Toronto, Ont, 89, Mus Mod Art, New York, 89 & Am Inst, Barcelona, Spain, 89; consult, Sci Educ Youth Found, Audubon Soc, 89 & 90 and Mt Diablo Unified Sch District, 90; consult & lectr, US Info Agency, Latin Am Inst, Univ Stockholm Acad Fine Arts, Kulturhuset, Sweden, 90; bd dirs, Galeria de la Raza, San Francisco, currently; comnr of art, City of San Francisco, currently. *Publ:* Auth, The Schartle papers-Chicana artists, Houston Mus Fine Arts, 87; The folk impulse in contemporary Chicana art - inside out, Mex Mus, 87; Contemporary Hispanic artists of New Mexico: A cultural commenary Ctr Contemp Art, 88; Cajas--containers of remembrance and belief, Mex Mus, 88; Social history through murals, San Francisco Unified Sch District, 89. *Mailing Add:* 333 Precita St San Francisco CA 94110

MESCHES, ARNOLD
PAINTER, EDUCATOR
b New York, NY, Aug 11, 23. *Study:* Art Ctr Sch; Chouinard Art Inst; Jepson Art Inst; self- taught in fine arts. *Work:* Philadelphia Mus Art; San Francisco Mus Art; Brooklyn Mus & New Mus, New York; Los Angeles Co Mus Art; Libr Cong, Washington, DC; Pa Acad Art; and others. *Comn:* Murals, Temple Isaiah, Los Angeles, 73 & Bank of Am, Beverly Hills, Calif, 75; portraits, Frederick Weisman, Los Angeles; Gordon Hampton, Los Angeles; Billie Milam, Los Angeles; Richard Weisman & Vivian Lesnick, Seattle, Wash. *Exhib:* Los Angeles Co Mus Ann, catalog, 49-58; Libr Cong Print Ann, 51; Metrop Mus Art, New York, 52; Butler Inst Ann, catalog, 60; Brooklyn Mus Invitational Print Ann, catalog, 70; The Blankfort Collection, Los Angeles Co Mus Art, Calif, 82; solo exhibs, Haines Gallery, San Francisco, 88 & 91, Carlo Lamagna Gallery, New York, 89 & 90, Robert Berman Gallery, Santa Monica, Calif, 90, East Hampton Ctr Contemp Art, NY, 90, E M Donahue Gallery, New York, 91, Galeria De Arte, Santiago, Chile, 91 & Brody's Gallery, Washington, DC, 91; Norfolk Art Mus, Va, 90; Akron Mus Art, Ohio, 90; Approach/Avoidance, Madison Art Ctr, Wis, 90; Exposed--The Figure In Jeopardy; Four Artists, Valencia Community Col Art Gallery, Orlando, Fla, 90; and others. *Pos:* Art dir, Frontier Mag, 54-60; Courtroom Artist, Walter Cronkite/CBS, 69-71. *Teaching:* Instr painting & drawing, Univ Southern Calif, summer 50; instr & dir, New Sch Art, Los Angeles, 55-58; instr, Otis Art Inst, 63-67, Otis/Parsons Art Inst, 75-84, Los Angeles; instr, Univ Calif Exten, Los Angeles, 72-77; guest prof, grad sch, Rutgers Univ, New Brunswick, NJ, 85- & vis lectr, 87-88; instr advan painting & drawing, Parsons Sch Design, New York, 86; instr grad painting & drawing, New York Univ, 88-91. *Awards:* Purchase Award, Home Savings & Loan, Los Angeles Munic Exhib, 69 & San Francisco Mus Art, 69; Nat Endowment Arts Grant, 82. *Bibliog:* Eleanor Heartney (auth), Arnold Mesches, ARTnews, 92; Janet Wilson (auth), Arnold Mesches at Brody's, Wash Post, 92; Ernest Larsen (auth), Arnold Mesches, Art in America, 92; and others. *Media:* Acrylic, Collage. *Publ:* Coauth, Selections from the 80's, Buscaglia Castellani Art gallery & Burchfield Art Ctr Catalog; coauth, Municipal Art Gallery Catalog, 83. *Mailing Add:* 254 E Seventh St No 15-16 New York NY 10009

MESEROLE, VERA STROMSTED
PAINTER, PHOTOGRAPHER
b New York, NY, Aug 10, 27. *Study:* Wellesley Col, Mass, BA(hist art, painting), with A Abbot, B Swann & E Frisch & archit with J MacAndrew; Univ Vt, Burlington, adult educ with Francis Colburn; critique with Stan Marc Wright, Vt & father, Alf Stromsted, NY & NJ. *Work:* IBM, Montpelier, Vt. *Exhib:* Northern New Eng Artists, Univ Vt, Burlington, 54; New Eng Artists, New York World's Fair, 64; Nat League Am Pen Women, Tulsa, Okla, 66 & Salt Lake City, Utah, 70; Vt Pavilion, Expo, Montreal, 70. *Pos:* Supt art, Champlain Valley Expos, Vt, 67; chmn, Ann State, Fleming Mus, Burlington, 66-73; mgr art ctr exhib, Burlington, 72-74; auth, Newsletter Northern Vt Artists Asn, 67-73. *Awards:* First Prize, Champlain Valley Expos, 60; First Prize Portraits, Nat League Am Pen Women, Vt, 66 & 70; First Prize Watercolor & Portrait, 81, & First Prize Photography, 84 & 85, Nat League Am Pen Women, Ga. *Bibliog:* Stuart Perry (auth), TV interview, WCAX, Burlington, 71; article in Burlington Free Press, 67 & 72. *Mem:* Northern Vt Artist Asn; Nat League Am Pen Women, Sarasota Fla Br; Sarasota Art Asn. *Media:* Watercolor, Macro-nature Color, Pen & Ink. *Mailing Add:* 8026 Midnight Pass Rd Sarasota FL 34242

MESIBOV, HUGH
PAINTER, PRINTMAKER
b Philadelphia, Pa, Dec 29, 16. *Study:* Fleischer Mem Art Sch, Philadelphia, 34-35; Pa Acad Fine Arts, Philadelphia, 35-37; Albert C Barnes Found, Merion, Pa, 36-40. *Work:* Metrop Mus Art & NY Univ Collection Contemp Am Art, New York; Philadelphia Mus Art; Brit Mus; Albert C Barnes Found, Merion, Pa; Whitney Mus Am Art; and others. *Comn:* Mural design, Benjamin Franklin High Sch, 37-40; mural, Work Progress Admin Art Proj, Bennet Hall, Univ Pa, 37-40; mural, Steel Indust, US Treas, US Post Off, Hubbard, Ohio, 41; paintings & color lithograph, New York Hilton Art Collection, 62; acrylic on canvas mural, Job, Temple Beth El, Spring Valley, NY, 72. *Exhib:* Pa Acad Fine Arts, 40, 43, 58 & 67; Whitney Mus Am Art, New York, 46, 56 & 59; Brooklyn Mus, 51, 53-55; Philadelphia Mus Art, 58; Corcoran Gallery Art, Washington, DC, 59; Rockland Ctr Arts, West Nyack, NY, 90; Nabisco Brands Gallery, East Hanover, NJ, 91; Graphic Excursions: American Prints, 1900-1950, Am Fedn Arts, 90-93; Ellen Sragow Gallery, New York, 91-92; Susan Teller Gallery, New York, 91; and others. *Teaching:* Art therapist, Wiltwyck Sch Boys, NY, 57-66; prof art, Rockland Community Col, Suffern, NY, 66-88, prof emer, 88. *Awards:* First Prize Oil Painting, Tappan Zee Bank, Rockland Found Award Show, 64; Thornton Oakley Mem Prize, Philadelphia Watercolor Club, 76; Rockland Co Exec Arts Award, New York, 88. *Bibliog:* Robert Delany & Richard Connely (dirs), Experience of the Artist--Hugh Mesibov (video tape), Rockland Community Col, NY; Five Artists from the 1930's and 1940's (catalog & monogr), Midtown Galleries, New York, 88; Linda Shopes (dir), audio tape & interview, Pa Hist & Mus Comn, Harrisburg, 90. *Mem:* Philadelphia Water Color Club; fel Pa Acad Fine Arts; Philadelphia Print Club; Rockland Coun Arts; Artists Equity, NY. *Media:* Acrylic, Watercolor. *Dealer:* Midtown Payson Galleries 745 Fifth Ave New York NY 10151; Sragow Gallery 73 Spring St New York NY. *Mailing Add:* 377 Saddle River Rd Monsey NY 10952

MESSER, DAVID JAMES
DIRECTOR, MUSEUM DIRECTOR
b San Diego, Calif, Aug 25, 42. *Study:* Birmingham-Southern Col, BA; Purdue Univ, MS. *Pos:* Dir dept mus studies, Vincennes Univ, Ind, 76-79; cur exhibs, Beaumont Art Mus, Tex, 79-85; dir, Mus East Tex, Lufkin, 85-87 & Bergen Mus, Paramus, NJ, 87- *Mailing Add:* Bergen Mus Art & Sci Ridgewood & Farview Aves Paramus NJ 07652

MESSER, THOMAS M
MUSEUM DIRECTOR, HISTORIAN
b Bratislava, Czech, Feb 9, 20; US citizen. *Study:* Thiele Col exchange student, Inst Int Educ, 39; Boston Univ, BA, 42; Sorbonne, Paris, France, 47; Harvard Univ, MA, 51; spec fel, Brussels, Belg, 53; Univ Mass, hon DFA, 62; Univ Arts, Philadelphia, Pa, hon DFA, 88. *Collections Arranged:* First US mus shows, Egon Schiele & New Departures: Latin America, Inst Contemp Art. *Pos:* Dir, Roswell Mus, NM, 49-52, trustee, 72-; asst dir, dir, dir exhib, Am Fedn Arts, 52-56; dir, Inst Contemp Arts, Boston, 57-61; dir, Solomon

R Guggenheim Found, 61-68 & 80-88 & dir emer, 90-; dir, Peggy Guggenheim Collection, Venice, Italy, 80-88. *Teaching:* sr fel advan studies, Wesleyan Univ Ctr Advan Studies, 66; prof, Hochschule fuer Angewandt Kunst, Vienna, Austria, 84. *Awards:* Knight First Class, Order of St Olav, Norway, 66; Officer's Cross of Order of Merit, Fed Repub Ger, 75 & Goethe Medal, 90; Officer of the Order of Leopold II, Belg, 78; Chevallier, Legion d'Honneur, France, 80, officer, 89; Cross of Honor, Science and Art, Austria, 80; Knight First Class, Order Danneborg, Denmark, 83; Order Isabella Catolica, 84. *Mem:* Asn Art Mus Dir (pres, 74-75); Am Arts Alliance; Int Coun Mus; Am Asn Mus; Arts Int. *Publ:* Auth, The Emergent Decade: Latin-American Painters and Paintings in the 60's, Thames & Hudson, 66; Edward Munch, Library of Great Painters (series), Harry N Abramn Inc, 73; Vasily Kandinsky, Egon Schiele, Paul Klee, Joseph Beuys, Henri Michaux, Julius Bissier, Jiri Kolar and many others (catalogs); articles in Art News, Art in Am, Art Int, Am Scholar, Arts, Saturday Rev, World, Studio Int, The Art Gallery, XX Siecle and others. *Mailing Add:* 303 E 57th New York NY 10022

MESSERSMITH, FRED LAWRENCE
PAINTER, EDUCATOR
b Sharon, Pa, Apr 3, 24. *Study:* Ohio Wesleyan Univ, BFA, 48, MA, 49. *Work:* Addison Gallery Am Art, Andover, Mass; Norton Gallery Art, West Palm Beach, Fla; Butler Inst Am Art, Youngstown, Ohio; Springfield Art Mus, Mo; Huntington Galleries, WVa. *Comn:* Hilton Hotel, Deland, Fla. *Exhib:* Am Watercolor Soc, 57-; Mid-Year Show, Butler Inst Am Art, 65; Yale Univ, 71; World Bk Encyclopedia; Daytona Beach Mus Art; Ringling Mus, Sarasota, Fla, 67; one man shows, Arno Gallery, Florence, Italy, 70, Old Sculpin Gallery, Edgartown, Mass, 83-86 & Michael Simpson, London, Eng, 92. *Teaching:* Chmn dept art, WVa Wesleyan Col, 49-59; chmn dept art, Stetson Univ, 59-89; instr, watercolor & drawing; artist-in-residence, Stetson Univ, 89. *Awards:* Spec Watercolor Award, Mead Packaging, Atlanta, 60; First Award, Fla State Fair, 67 & Winter Park, 75; Ala Watercolor Soc Award, 75 & 81; Gold Award, Fla Watercolor Soc, 92. *Bibliog:* Norman Kent (auth), Fred Messersmith paints on rice paper, Am Artist Mag, 12/60; Edward Feit (auth), Fred Messersmith, taking risks with watercolor, Am Artist, 9/86. *Mem:* Am Watercolor Soc; Fla Artist Group (pres, 64-66); Ala Watercolor Soc; Fla Watercolor Soc; Watercolor Hon Soc; Southern Watercolor Soc. *Media:* Watercolor, Oil. *Publ:* Auth, Pottery of Gene Bunker, 62 & Francis Chapin, 65, Am Artist Mag; contribr, Artist and Advocate, Renaissance Ed Inc, 67; 100 Watercolor Techniques, 68; Acrylic Watercolor Painting, 70; Eyewitness to Space, 71; Watercolor, Let the Medium Do It. *Dealer:* Harmon Gallery 1415 Main St Sarasota FL 33577; Galleries International 401B Park Ave Winter Park FL 32789. *Mailing Add:* Dept Art Stetson Univ De Land FL 32720

MESSERSMITH, HARRY LEE
SCULPTOR, MUSEUM DIRECTOR
b Buckhannon, WVa, Aug 7, 58. *Study:* Stetson Univ, De Land, BFA, 81; Univ Fla, Gainesville, MFA, 83. *Comn:* Life size busts (three, bronze), Stetson Univ, De Land, Fla, 87-89; life size statue (bronze), Iverson Technol, Ellburn, Ill, 89; Volusia Co Coun, De Land, 90. *Collections Arranged:* De Land Nat Sculpture Exhib, Triennial juried competition, 91. *Pos:* Artist in educ, Volusia Co Schs, Fla, 86-89; exec dir, De Land Mus Art Fla Inc, 89-. *Teaching:* Artist in educ, traveling throughout Volusia Co, Fla, 86-89. *Awards:* Best of Show Awards, Stetson Univ Homecoming, 78 & De Land Mus, 88. *Mem:* Int Sculpture Ctr; Nat Sculpture Soc; Col Art Asn; Fla Artist & Blacksmith Asn. *Media:* Cast Bronze, Metals. *Mailing Add:* 726 N Boston Ave De Land FL 32724

MESSICK, DALE
CARTOONIST
b South Bend, Ind, 1906. *Study:* Art Inst Chicago & Ray Vogue Sch. *Pos:* Designer greeting cards, Chicago; creator comic strip Brenda Starr, Reporter, Chicago Tribune-NY News Syndicate, Sunday & daily feature, 40- *Mailing Add:* c/o Tribune Media Services 64 E Concord St Orlando FL 32801

MESSINA, JOSEPH R
PAINTER
b Newark, NJ, Sept 24, 04. *Study:* Fawcett Art Sch, Newark; Nat Acad Design, New York, 20-23; Art Students League, with Bridgeman, 24. *Exhib:* Hudson Valley Art Asn, White Plains, New York, 71; Audubon Soc, Nat Acad, New York, 73; Bayberry Art Gallery, Southern Pines, NC, 77; Seventh Ann Nat Miniature Show, 81; Nat Western Small Show, Bosque Farms, NM, 81 & 83-86. *Awards:* Collectors Award, Seventh Ann Miniature Show, 81; First Prize Ivory, Nat Western Small Show, Bosque Farms, NM, 81-86; First Prize, Miniature Painters, Sculptors & Gravers Soc Washington, DC, 73, 75 & 82; 38 national awards since 1973. *Bibliog:* Spiritual qualities pervade Messina portraits of three Apollo astronauts, Montclair Times & Newark News, 8/69; Near fatal auto wreck led to bigger things for fine artist, Newark Star-Ledger, 7/24/84; The talents of Joseph Messina still growing at 81 years of age, Italian Tribune News, 10/10/85. *Mem:* Am Artist Prof League; Miniature Art Soc, NJ, Washington, DC, Fla & Mont. *Media:* Oil, Watercolor. *Mailing Add:* 71 Valley St South Orange NJ 07079

METCALF, CONGER A
PAINTER, INSTRUCTOR
b Cedar Rapids, Iowa, Apr 27, 14. *Study:* Stone City Art Colony, with Grant Wood, 31-33; Coe Col, with Marvin Cone, BMus, 36; Boston Mus Fine Arts Sch, with Alexandre Iacovleff & Karl Zerbe, 36-40; Coe Col, Hon DFA, 64, Gordon Col, Hon DFA, 78. *Work:* Boston Athenaeum, Mass; De Cordova Mus, Lincoln, Mass; Cedar Rapids Art Ctr & Coe Col, Cedar Rapids, Iowa; Phoenix Art Mus, Ariz. *Exhib:* Fifteen Years Museum Sch Alumni, Boston Mus Fine Arts, Mass, 40; Margaret Brown Mem Exhib, DeCordova Mus, Lincoln, Mass, 56; Retrospective, Brockton Art Mus, Mass, 69; Centennial Exhib, Boston Mus Fine Arts, Mass, 76; Boston Draftsmen, Boston Athenaeum, Mass, 78; Centennial Exhib, Boston Copley Soc, Mass, 79. *Teaching:* Asst to head painting & drawing dept, Boston Mus Sch, Mass, 40-41; assoc prof art drawing & painting, Boston Univ Sch Fine Arts, Mass, 56-72. *Awards:* Tiffany Found Prize, 38; Paige Travelling Scholarship, 40. *Media:* Oil, Graphite. *Mailing Add:* c/o Cornerhouse Gallery 2753 First Ave SE Cedar Rapids IA 52402

METCALFE, ERIC WILLIAM See Dr Brute (Eric William Metcalfe)

METYKO, MICHAEL JOSEPH
CONSULTANT
b Port Arthur, Tex, Feb 27, 45. *Study:* Houston Mus Fine Arts Sch; St Thomas Univ, Houston, with Dominique de Menil & Jermyne McAgy; Pratt Inst, Brooklyn; San Francisco Art Inst, MFA(printmaking). *Comn:* Tatto Parlor: Segment I (15 minute film) & Segment II (15 minute film with architect, Thomas Burke), David Gallery, Houston, 70; participation/doc event piece, Main St 76, Houston CofC, 76; installation piece, Houston Festival, 79. *Exhib:* The Bosch Show, Univ St Thomas, Houston, 76; Contemp Icons, Mus Mod Art, Houston, 76; Made in Houston, La Gallery, 78 & 79; group show, Art Ctr, Waco, Tex, 79; minatures, Univ Houston Lawndale Gallery, 79; Univ Houston Thomas Gallery, 79; and many others. *Collections Arranged:* Texas Week in San Francisco, Festival & Exhib of Texas Art & The Artist's Archives, Exhib of Materials Collected by Artists, San Francisco Art Inst, 72; Main St/Houston Festival art & video exhibitions, 78 & 79; Texas Crafts touring exhibition (ed, contribr & illusr, catalog & producer media presentation), S C Blaffer Gallery, 78; Embroidery: Houston Emb Guild, Craft & Folk Arts Adv Comt, 79, Lone Star Sampler: Works by Texas Craftsmen, 79, Art/Craft: 6 Houston Craft Guilds, 79, Selected Works: Texas Designer Craftsmen, 79 & Dimensions in Glass, 79. *Pos:* Asst to chmn, Dept of Art, Rice Univ, 66-67; cur, Grad Print & Photo Gallery, San Francisco Art Inst, 71-72; asst to dir/cur, S C Blaffer Gallery, Univ Houston, 73-78; dir crafts events, Houston Festival, 79-80. *Awards:* Tex Comn Arts exhib support grant, 78 & Cult Arts Coun Houston proj support grant, 79. *Bibliog:* Niomi Berman (auth), Interview & article in Southwestern Craftsman Mag, 76; Charlotte Moser (auth), Review of Houston Artists, Art News, 76. *Mem:* Artists Equity Asn (pres chap, Houston, 75-77); Cult Arts Coun Houston; Tex Asn Mus; Am Coun Arts; Western Asn Art Mus. *Media:* Mixed. *Publ:* Contribr & illusr, 9th Congress of European Exchange Students Journal, Int Cult Exchange Serv, 66; contribr & illusr, Conceptual Excerpts, Guano Mag, Univ Houston, 70; contribr & illusr exhib catalogues, S C Blaffer Gallery, 73-78; contribr introd, exhib catalogue for Donald Thornton, Col of the Mainland, 76; illusr, New Cultural Decision Makers in Houston, Art News, 77. *Mailing Add:* 1634 Branard St Houston TX 77006

METZ, FRANK ROBERT
PAINTER, DESIGNER
b Philadelphia, Pa, July 3, 25. *Study:* Philadelphia Mus Sch, with Ezio Martinelli; Art Students League, with Will Barnet. *Work:* Olsen Found, Guilford, Conn; Ball State Teachers Col, Muncie, Ind; Philadelphia Mus Art; Mass Inst Technol. *Exhib:* Drawing & Small Sculpture Ann, Ball State Teachers Col, 62-63 & 64-65; Am Acad Arts & Lett, Childe Hassam Fund, 66; The American Landscape-A Living Tradition, Peridot Gallery, New York, 68; one-man shows, Alonzo Gallery, 74, 77 & 79 & Haber Theodore Gallery, 84 & 85; Monhegan Artists, Allentown Mus, Pa, 74; retrospective, Gross McCleaf Gallery, 85; one-man show, Gross McCleaf Gallery, Philadelphia, Pa, 87. *Pos:* Art dir, Simon & Schuster, 50- *Awards:* Elisabeth Ball Purchase Award, Ball State Teachers Col, 64. *Bibliog:* Jules Perel (auth), Landscape drawings of Frank Metz, Am Artist, 5/62; Doreen Managan (auth), Landscape paintings of Frank Metz, Am Artists, 3/78 & Twenty Oil Painters and How They Work, Watson-Guptill, 78; Paul Bacon (auth), articles, Arts Mag, 3/84 & 4/85. *Media:* All Media. *Dealer:* Judith Selkowitz Art Advisory Services Inc 530 Park Ave New York NY 10021. *Mailing Add:* 800 West End Ave New York NY 10025

METZ, MATTHEW J
POTTER
b Kendallville, Ind, Mar 16, 61. *Study:* Ball State Univ, BA; Edinburg Univ, MFA, 86. *Work:* Erie Art Mus, Pa. *Exhib:* Swidler Gallery, 91. *Pos:* Studio potter, independent. *Awards:* Nat Endowment Arts, 91. *Dealer:* Swidler Gallery 308 W Fourth Royal Oak; Lill St Studio 1021 W Lill St Chicago IL. *Mailing Add:* 418 N Warren St Helena MT 59601

METZGER, EVELYN BORCHARD
PAINTER, SCULPTOR
b New York, NY, June 8, 11. *Study:* Vassar Col, AB, 32, with C K Chatterton; Art Students League, with George Bridgman & Rafael Soyer; also George Grosz, sculpture with Sally Farnham, Guzman de Rojas in Bolivia & Demetrio Urruchua in Arg. *Work:* Fine Arts Gallery San Diego, Balboa Park, Calif; Ariz State Mus, Tucson; Lyman Allyn Mus, New London, Conn; Univ Mo-Columbia; Butler Inst Am Art, Youngstown, Ohio; and others. *Exhib:* 19 One-man shows, including Galeria Muller, Buenos Aires, 50 & Gallerie Bellechasse, Paris, 63; Norfolk Mus Art, Va, 65; Mex-Am Cult Inst, Mexico City, 67; Van Diemen-Lilienfeld Gallery, New York, 66; Bartholet Gallery, New York, 73; Arsenal Art Gallery, New York, 83. *Pos:* Hon dir, Vassar Art Gallery. *Bibliog:* Aymel Seghers (auth), New York news (and cover), Arts Rev, 4/63; M L D'Otrange Mastai (auth), An American flowering, 5/63 & Evelyn Metzger--recent works, 12/66, The Connoisseur. *Mem:* Artists Equity Asn; Am Fedn Art; Arch Am Art. *Media:* Oil. *Mailing Add:* 815 Park Ave New York NY 10021

METZGER, ROBERT PAUL
CURATOR, EDUCATOR
b Detroit, Mich. *Study:* Wayne State Univ, BA, MA; Columbia Univ, with T Reff; Univ Calif, Los Angeles, with Fred Wight, PhD; Am Film Inst, with Jean Renoir. *Pos:* Cur, Lydia Winston Malbin Collection of Art, New York, 74-76; dir art, Stamford Mus, Conn, 76- *Teaching:* Asst prof art hist survey, Univ Detroit, Mich, 65-66; assoc prof Am art hist, Univ Bridgeport, Conn, 77- *Awards:* Univ Calif Arts Coun Traveling Grant, 69; Mich State Univ Art Hist Res Grant, 74. *Mem:* Col Art Asn Am. *Res:* Biomorphism in the 20th century, American painting and sculpture 18th through 20th century, Reuben Nakian. *Publ:* Ed, Directory of American Periodicals, Oxbridge Press, 76; auth, Karl Struss, American Cinematographer, 76, Nakian's Place in History, 77 & The Case for Pop Art as Neo-Dada, 78, Stamford Mus. *Mailing Add:* 178 Smoketown Rd Lewisburg PA 17837

METZKER, RAY K
PHOTOGRAPHER, EDUCATOR
b Milwaukee, Wis, Sept 10, 31. *Study:* Beloit Col, BA, 53; Ill Inst Technol, MS, 59, with Aaron Siskind & Harry Callahan. *Work:* Mus Mod Art, New York; Art Inst Chicago; Smithsonian Inst; Bibliot Nat, Paris; Philadelphia Mus Art. *Exhib:* My Camera and I in the Loop, Art Inst Chicago, 59; Persistence of Vision, Int Mus Photog, George Eastman House, 67; one-man shows Mus Mod Art, New York, 67, Delpire Gallery, Paris, 79, Light Gallery, 79 & 81, Pa Acad Fine Arts, 80, Marion Locks Gallery, 78 & 82, Laurence Miller Gallery, New York, 84, 85, 87, 88, 90 & 92, A New Leaf, Art Inst Chicago, 91, Landscape Photographs, Cleveland Mus Art, 91, Shadai Gallery, Tokyo Inst Polytechnics, Tokyo, 92, Turner/Krull Gallery, Los Angeles, 92; Milwaukee Art Ctr, 70; New Photog USA Traveling Exhibit, Mus Mod Art, New York, 70-72; Landscape/Cityscape, Metrop Mus Art, New York, 73; Philadelphia: Three Centuries of Am Art, Philadelphia Mus of Art, 76; The Photographer and the City, Mus Contemp Art, Chicago, 77; Venezia '79, La Fotografia, Venice, Italy, 79; Unknown Territory: Ray K Metzker (25 year retrospective), Mus Fine Arts, Houston & traveling to six other museums in the US; group shows, On the Art of Fixing a Shadow, Nat Gallery Art, Washington & Art Inst Chicago & Los Angeles Co Mus Art, 89. *Teaching:* Prof photog, Philadelphia Col of Art, 62-81; assoc prof photog, Univ NMex, 70-72; adj photog, RI Sch Design, 77, Columbia Col, Chicago, 80-83; Smith Distinguished Vis Artist, George Wash Univ, 87-88. *Awards:* Guggenheim Fel, 66 & 79; Nat Endowment Arts Fel, 74 & 88; LaNapoule Art Found, La Napoule, France, 89. *Bibliog:* Peter C Bunnell (auth), Ray Metzker, Print Collector's Newsletter, Vol IX, No 6, 79; Chuck Isaacs (auth), Ray K Metzker: An interview, Afterimage, 11/80; Andy Grundberg (auth), Ray K Metzker: form as expression, Mod Photog, 11/81; Anne W Tucker (ed), Unknown Territory; Ray K Metzker (monogr), Aperture/Mus Fine Arts, Houston, 84. *Publ:* Illusr, Razerol, Janus, 73; auth, Sand Creatures, Aperture, 79. *Dealer:* Laurence G Miller Inc 138 Spring St New York NY 10012. *Mailing Add:* S Sixth St Philadelphia PA 19147

MEW, TOMMY
PAINTER, CONCEPTUAL ARTIST
b Miami, Fla, Aug 15, 42. *Study:* Fla State Univ, BS, MA; NY Univ, PhD. *Work:* Am Tel & Tel, New York; Jacksonville Art Mus, Fla; Moderna Mus, Stockholm; McDonald's Corp Collection; Macon Mus Arts & Sci. *Exhib:* One-man shows, Montgomery Mus Fine Arts, Ala, 70 & Miss Mus Art, 79; Paintings, Mus Art, Macon, Ga, 72; Rockefeller Arts Ctr, New York; High Mus Art, Atlanta, 76; Nat Gallery Can, Ottawa, 77; Gallery 34, Kassel, Germany; and others. *Teaching:* Grad asst art, Fla State Univ, 64-65; asst prof art, Troy State Univ, Ala, 66-68 & Jacksonville Univ, Fla, 68-70; prof painting & chmn art dept, Berry Col, 70-; vis artist & lectr drawings, Nat Endowment for the Arts, 72 & Univ Tulsa, 81. *Awards:* Grant, Cowperthwaite Corp, 72 & Ga Coun Arts, 80. *Bibliog:* Annette Kuhn (auth), Scar art, Village Voice, 75; Peter Frank (auth), Auto-art-and how, Art News, 76; Alan Storey (auth), Tommy Mew, Art Voices S, 3/78. *Mem:* Col Art Asn; Southeastern Col Art Asn; Popular Cult Asn South; Nat Art Educ Asn; Am Fedn of the Arts. *Media:* Acrylic; Mixed. *Publ:* Ed & contribr, Third Floor Love Poems, 66 & auth & ed, Le Voyage, 68, Troy State Press; ed & contribr, Dramatika, New York Press, 70; ed & contribr, Scartissue, Troy State Press, 76; auth, Ray Johnson, Col Art Asn J, 77; contribr, Intermedia Mag, Can, 77. *Dealer:* Marney Rhodes 35 Huntington Rd SW Rome GA 30161. *Mailing Add:* Box 580-Art Mt Berry GA 30149

MEYER, CHARLES EDWARD
CONSULTANT, HISTORIAN
b Detroit, Mich, Sept 7, 28. *Study:* Wayne State Univ, BFA, 50 & MA, 52; Free Univ, Berlin, Ger, 52-54; Univ Wurzburg, Ger, 58-59; Univ Mich, PhD, 67. *Work:* Mus Contemp Crafts, New York; Detroit Inst Arts; Boston Mus Fine Arts; South Bend Art Ctr, Ind; Ann Arbor Potters Guild, Mich. *Exhib:* Fiber, Glass, Clay & Metal Exhib, Wichita, 52; Midwest Crafts Exhib, Ceramics, South Bend, 53 & 54; Opening Exhib, Ceramics, Mus Contemp Crafts, New York, 57. *Pos:* Bd dirs, Kalamazoo Inst Arts, 78-83, Lakeview Mus, Peoria, Ill, 85-89; visual arts, Ill Arts Comn, 85-89, art consult, 89- *Teaching:* Assoc prof art hist, head dept & dir, Div Fine Arts, Mich State Univ, 59-66; chmn dept, Western Mich Univ, 66-77, prof art hist, 66-83; dir div art, Bradley Univ, 83-90. *Awards:* Purchase Award in Ceramics, Opening Exhib, Mus Contemp Crafts, New York, 57. *Mem:* Nat Asn Schs Art (dir Div II, 72-80); Col Art Asn Am; Mid-Am Col Art Asn Am (vpres, 60-61, exec bd, 60-63, treas, 61-62); Ann Arbor Potters Guild (dir, 54-57); fel Nat Asn Schs Art & Design, 83. *Res:* European baroque architecture. *Publ:* Auth, Sebastiano Riccio, 57, A new group of ceramics, 57 & A Rodin portrait, 58, Detroit Inst Arts Bull; auth, Seymour Lipton and His Place in 20th Century Sculpture, 62. *Mailing Add:* 139 Merriweather Kalamazoo MI 49007

MEYER, EL(MER FREDERICK)
PAINTER, WRITER
b Twin Falls, Idaho, May 24, 10. *Study:* Fed Schs Com Design, diploma, 29; Calif Sch Fine Arts, 30-31 & 54; studies with Eliot O'Hara, Rex Brandt, Millard Sheets, Tom Hill, Ken Potter, Morris Shubin, Barbara Nechis & Robert E Wood. *Work:* Santa Rosa City Hall, Calif; 1st Nat Bank Ariz & Tucson Realty & Trust Co, Tucson; Arts Coun, Phoenix. *Exhib:* California Art, State Fair Galleries, Sacramento, 80; Am Watercolor Soc, Nat Acad, New York, 81; Watercolor West, Riverside Art Ctr, 82; 35th Ann Soc Western Artists, Hall Flowers, San Francisco, 85; 22nd Ann Statewide Exhib, Santa Rosa Art Guild, Veterans Mem, Calif, 85. *Teaching:* Instr watercolor, on-location workshops, Forestville, Calif, 78-85; instr watercolor, Arts Guild, Arts Sch Belvedere, Calif, 80-81; instr watercolor, Wine Country Workshops, Calistoga, Calif, 82. *Awards:* Gerry Pierce Mem, 4th Ann Southern Ariz Watercolor Guild, 71; Special Award, 31st Ann Soc Western Artists, House of Hatch Covers, 78; Neva Rall Mem, 32nd Ann Soc Western Artists, 80. *Bibliog:* Watercolor Magic (film), Calif North, KFTY chan 50, Santa Rosa, Calif, 84. *Mem:* Art Workshop Western Sonoma County; Soc Western Artists; Santa Rosa Art Guild (pres, 79-80). *Media:* Watercolor. *Publ:* Auth, Making Watercolor Work, private publ, 78; Watercolor Painting on Location, North Light Books, 84. *Dealer:* Branscomb Gallery 1588 Eastshore Rd Bodega Bay CA. *Mailing Add:* 5929 Van Keppel Rd Forestville CA 95436

MEYER, FRANK HILDBRIDGE
PAINTER, PRINTMAKER
b Fitchburg, Mass, Jan 21,23. *Study:* Am Sch Design, with Wallace Morgan; Art Students League, with Robert Brackman, Reginald Marsh, Will Barnet & George Grosz; City Univ New York, with Julius Portnoy, BA; Cent Conn State Univ, MS(art educ). *Work:* Art Students League of NY, Vale Art Gallery. *Exhib:* Bay Printmakers 1st Traveling Show, Oakland Mus Art, Calif, 55; Soc Washington Printmakers 20th Exhib, Nat Gallery, Smithsonian Inst, 56; Fundacion Ynglada-Guillet Exposition de Obras, Palacio de la Virreina, Spain, 60; 25th Ann Nat Exhib Acad Artists Asn, Mus Fine Arts, Springfield, Mass, 74; plus many others in Conn area, 75-77; Conn Chap Artists Equity Asn Ann Show, Old State House, Hartford, 80. *Pos:* Artist, framer & restorer, Morristown Fine Arts Ctr, NJ, 54-56; state art consult, Ariz Dept Educ, Phoenix, 64; lectr-demonstr cellograph printmaking, Silvermine Guild of Artists Inc & New Eng Regional Art Educ Conf, 77. *Teaching:* Instr art, Eng & jour, Penasco Independent High Sch, NMex, 62-63; head art counr, Camp Tapawingo, Sweden, Maine, 64-68; instr art, Windsor High Sch, Conn, 67-80. *Awards:* Best in Show, Fall Exhib, Springfield Art League, Mass, 52; Alice Collins Dunham Award, 69 & Sage Allen Award, 72, Conn Acad Fine Arts. *Bibliog:* Ref shows, Art News, 9/54; Junior Jottings, Monday Afternoon Club Mag, 3/56; Janet Gaston (auth), Frank Hildbridge Meyer, Rev Moderne, Paris, 4/1/61. *Mem:* Conn Art Educ Asn (regional chmn, 74-76); Art Students League; Conn Acad Fine Arts; Artists Equity Asn (founder & 1st pres Conn chap, 76-); Visual Artists & Galleries Asn Inc. *Media:* Oil, Cellograph. *Publ:* Coauth, League Mag, Art Students League, 50; Comprehensive study on facilities, physical plot and philosophy of secondary and elementary art departments, NJ Art Educ Asn, 57; New Mexican Rev, 63; illusr, Our America, Ariz Dept Educ, 65; auth, Cellographic process of printmaking, Elihu Burritt Libr, 72. *Mailing Add:* PO Box 626 Vernon FL 32462

MEYER, JERRY DON
HISTORIAN, EDUCATOR
b Carbondale, Ill, Nov 19, 39. *Study:* Southern Ill Univ, Carbondale, BS, 62, MA(art hist), 64; New York Univ, Inst Fine Arts, PhD(art hist), 73. *Teaching:* Prof art hist, Northern Ill Univ, 68-, asst chair, 85- *Mem:* Col Art Asn; Midwest Art Hist Soc. *Res:* Late 18th & 19th century English & American Art, 20th century art. *Publ:* Auth, Benjamin West's Chapel of Revealed Religion, Art Bull, 75; Benjamin West's St Stephen altar-piece, Burlington Mag, 76; Benjamin West's window designs for St George's Chapel, Am Art J, 79; The Woman Clothed with the Sun: Two Illustrations to St John's Revelation by William Blake, Studies in Iconography, Vol 12, 88. *Mailing Add:* Sch Art Northern Ill Univ De Kalb IL 60115

MEYER, MILTON E, JR
PAINTER
b St Louis, Mo, Nov 26, 22. *Study:* Washington Univ, BSBA, 43; St Louis Univ, LLB, 50; NY Univ, LLM, 53; also studied with George Carlson, 83 & Daniel E Greene, 84. *Exhib:* Mem shows, Pastel Soc W Coast, Seattle, Wash, 90 & Reno, Nev, 91; 5th Ann Open Exhib, Pastel Soc W Coast, 91 & 92, Sacramento, Calif; 19th & 20th Ann Open Exhib, Pastel Soc Am, New York, 91 & 92. *Pos:* Chmn, Denver Rotary's Artists Am, Colo, 90-92. *Awards:* First place (landscape), Pastel Soc W Coast, 91; Award Merit, 5th & 6th Ann Pastel Soc W Coast, Ferrari Color Award, 91 & 92. *Bibliog:* Starr Yelland (auth), Work of Milton Meyer, CBS (TV), Denver, 7/89; Carole Katchen (auth), A Traveller's Mood, Focus, Santa Fe, 8/92. *Mem:* Pastel Soc Am & W Coast; Cassatt Pastel Soc. *Media:* Pastels. *Publ:* Coauth, Approaching Photo Realism with Pastels, Am Artist, 11/92; contribr, Texture in Art, Quatro, Forthcoming. *Dealer:* Turner Art Gallery 301 University Blvd Denver CO 80206; Linda McAdoo Galleries 503 Canyon Rd Santa Fe NM 87501. *Mailing Add:* 5784 E Oxford Ave Englewood CO 80111

MEYER, RUTH KRUEGER
HISTORIAN, ADMINISTRATOR
b Chicago Heights, Ill, Aug 20, 40. *Study:* Univ Cincinnati, Col Design, BFA, 63; Brown Univ, MA, 68; Univ Minn, PhD, 80. *Collections Arranged:* Proposals for Sawyer Point Park, 77; Arabesque (auth, catalog), 78; Walls, 80; The Pattern Principle, 81; Inner/Urban: How the Artist Saw the City in the

70's (auth, catalog), 81; New Epiphanies: Contemporary Religious Art; David Black, An American Sculptor (auth, catalog essay) Taft Mus, Cincinnati, 85; Sandy Rosen, Vestal Vases, Taft Mus, 86. *Pos:* Cur, Contemp Arts Ctr, Cincinnati, 76-80; dir, Ohio Found Arts, Columbus, 80-83. *Awards:* Kress Found Grant for Res, 67 & 76. *Mem:* Asn Art Mus Dirs; Int Asn Art Critics; Col Art Asn; Nat Trust for Hist Preserv. *Res:* Painters of French Barbizon School, Contemporary art, monumental and environmental sculpture. *Publ:* Auth, The Tafts of Pike St, Apollo, 12/88; ed & contribr, The modern art society: the center's early years, Contemp Arts Ctr, 79; contribr, A meeting place of humanistic experience, Natur Skulptur, Kunstverein, Stuttgart, 81. *Mailing Add:* c/o Taft Museum 316 Pike St Cincinnati OH 45202

MEYER, SEYMOUR W
SCULPTOR
b Brooklyn, NY. *Study:* With Louise Nevelson. *Work:* Arlen Industs, New York; Mus Mod Art, Rio de Janeiro, Brazil; Tel-Aviv Mus & Bat-Yam Mus, Israel; Temple Beth-El, Great Neck, NY; Fine Arts Mus, Long Island; and others. *Comn:* NY Inst Technol Libr, Old Westbury, NY; Isreal Tennis Ctr, Ramat Hashiron, Israel. *Exhib:* Metrop Mus Art, New York, 76; D Justin Lester Gallery, Los Angeles, Calif, 78-80; Royal Acad, London, Eng, 79; Galeria of Sculpture, Palm Beach, Fla, 79-80; Engel Gallery, Jerusalem, 81; Exec Mansion, Albany, NY. *Mem:* Am Fedn Arts; Mus Mod Art New York; Sculptors League of NY; Guggenheim Mus; Prof Sculptors Guild. *Media:* Bronze. *Dealer:* Meisner Gallery Greene St Soho NY; Frances Aronson Gallery Atlanta GA. *Mailing Add:* 495 E Shore Rd Great Neck NY 11024

MEYER, SUSAN E
EDITOR, WRITER
b New York, NY, Apr 22, 40. *Study:* Univ Perugia, 60; Univ Wis, BA, 62. *Pos:* Managing ed, Watson-Guptill Publ, New York, 63-70; ed in chief, Am Artist, New York, 71-79, retired; ed dir, Am Art & Antiques, New York, 78-80; ed dir, Am Artist, Art & Antiques & Interiors & Residential Interiors, New York, 79-80; treas, Art Table, 81-85; founder, Roundtable Press, Inc, 81. *Teaching:* Adj prof, Empire State Col/Union Col, 76-78. *Mem:* Artists Fellowship (trustee, 78-85); Art Table (treas, 81-85). *Publ:* Will Barnet, 79; Norman Rockwell's People, 81; Treasury of the Great Children's Books Illustrators, 83; Mary Cassatt, 90; Edgar Degas, 94; Norman Rockwell's World War II, 91. *Mailing Add:* 20 E Ninth St New York NY 10003

MEYER, URSULA
SCULPTOR, PHOTOGRAPHER
b Hannover, Ger. *Study:* New Sch Social Res, BA, 60; Columbia Univ Teachers Col, MA, 62. *Work:* Brooklyn Mus; Finch Col Mus; Newark Mus; Larry Aldrich Mus; Grad Ctr, City Univ New York. *Exhib:* One-person shows, Hunter Col, 69, Lehman Col, 71 & Grad Ctr, City Univ New York, 74; Schemata 7, Finch Col Mus, 67; Listening to Pictures, Brooklyn Mus, 68; Cool Art of 1967, Larry Aldrich Mus, 68, Highlights of 1967-1968 Art Season; Cool Art, Abstractions Today, Newark Mus, 68. *Teaching:* Asst prof, Hunter Col, 66-68; assoc prof sculpture, Lehman Col, 68- *Awards:* Estelle Goodman Award for Best Sculpture, Nat Design Ctr, 66; City Univ New York Res Grant, Lehman Col, 70. *Bibliog:* Christopher Andreae (auth), Exhibition by Ursula Meyer at A M Sachs Gallery, Christian Sci Monitor, 2/26/68; Gregory Battcock (auth), Minimal Art, 68; Al Rogers (auth), Ursula Meyer, Alre-Films, 70. *Mem:* Women's Interart Ctr; Women in Arts. *Media:* Metal. *Publ:* Auth, De-objectification of the object, Arts Mag, summer 69; auth, Conceptural Art, 70 & The eruption of anti-art, In: Idea-Art, 73, Dutton; How to explain pictures to a dead hare, Art News, 1/70; Towards feminist art, Women & Art, summer-fall 72. *Mailing Add:* 52 Third St New York NY 10003

MEYEROWITZ, JOEL
PHOTOGRAPHER
b New York, NY, Mar 6, 38. *Work:* Mus Mod Art, New York; Art Inst Chicago; Boston Mus Fine Arts; Philadelphia Mus; St Louis Art Mus. *Comn:* St Louis and the Arch, St Louis Art Mus, 80; Atlanta, IBM, 89; The Nutcracker Suite, Time/Warner, 92. *Exhib:* One-man shows, Eastman House, Rochester, NY, 66, Mus Mod Art, New York, 68, Akron Art Inst, Ohio, 79 & Stedelijk Mus, Amsterdam, 80; Cape Light, Boston Mus Fine Arts, 78; St Louis Art Mus, Mo, 80; A Summer's Day, Brooklyn Mus, NY, 88. *Teaching:* Adj prof, Cooper Union, 71-78; lectr, Princeton Univ, 78 & New York Univ, 91-92. *Awards:* Guggenheim Fel, 71 & 79; Nat Endowment Arts Fel, 78; Photogr of Yr, Friends of Photog, 81. *Publ:* Auth, Cape Light, 78, St Louis and the Arch, 80 & Wild Flowers, 83, New York Graphic Soc; A Summer's Day, Times Books, 86; Redheads, Rizzoli, 91. *Dealer:* Danziger Gallery W Broadway New York NY. *Mailing Add:* 817 W End Ave New York NY 10025

MEYERS, DALE (MRS MARIO COOPER)
PAINTER, INSTRUCTOR
b Chicago, Ill. *Study:* Corcoran Gallery Sch Art; Art Students League; watercolor with Mario Cooper; graphics with Seong Moy. *Work:* Smithsonian Inst; Palace of the Legion of Honor, San Francisco; Frye Mus, Seattle, Wash; Nat Air & Space Mus, Washington, DC; Owensboro Mus Fine Art, Ky; Univ Utah, Logan; Schumacher Gallery, Capital Univ, Columbus, Ohio; Environmental Protection Agency; Nat Acad Design, New York; Arnot Mus, Elmira, NY. *Comn:* Apollo 11 Moon Flight (painting), 69 & Project Viking (landing on Mars), 75, for NASA, Nat Gallery Art, Washington, DC; ecology paintings, Environ Protection Agency, Washington, DC, 72; paintings, US Coast Guard, 84, 85 & 87. *Exhib:* Smithsonian Inst, Washington, DC, 62-63; 200 Years of Watercolor Painting in America, Metrop Mus Art, New York, 66; Nat Acad Design, 68-; Eyewitness to Space, Nat Gallery Art, 70. *Pos:* Ed newslett, Am Watercolor Soc, 62-79, chmn awards, 67-79, chmn traveling exhibs & scholarships, 78-; academician, Nat Acad Design, 79. *Teaching:* Instr watercolor, Kefauver Sch Art, Washington, DC, 61-62 & Art Students League, 79-; workshops in NMex, Calif, Maine, New York, Tex, Pa & Fla, 70-77 & 79, 81 & 88; lectr, Nat Acad & Parson's Sch Design, New York. *Awards:* Medals of Honor, Nat Art Club, 72, Knickerbocker Artists, 82 & 86; Awards, Am Watercolor Soc, 68, 72, 78, 79, 81, 83, 85, 87 & 89, Bronze Medal, 70; Samuel Finley Breese Morse Gold Medal, 73 & Adolf & Clara Obrig Awards, 76-81, Nat Acad Design; Silver Medal, Audobon Artists, 84, Allied Artists, 82, 83, 85, 86, 88, 89 & 91. *Mem:* Allied Artists Am (pres, 75-78); Miami Watercolor Soc (hon mem); dolphin fel, Am Watercolor Soc (first vpres, 85-); Soc Mex de Acuarelistas (hon mem); fel Royal Soc Arts, Gt Brit; and many others. *Media:* Watercolor. *Publ:* Auth, articles, Am Artist Mag, 69 & Today's Art Mag, 70 & 74 & Diversion Mag, 83; contribr, Eyewitness to Space, Abrams, 71; contribr, Nat Sculpture Rev, 77; contribr, Watercolor Bold & Free & Let the Medium Do It, Watson Guptill, 80; auth, The Sketchbook, Van Nostrand Reinhold, 83; contribr, Exploring Color, North Light Publ, 85. *Mailing Add:* One W 67th St New York NY 10023

MEYERS, FRANCIS JOSEPH
PAINTER, SCULPTOR
b Cleveland, Ohio, Feb 19, 21. *Study:* Fenn Col, 40; John Huntington Inst, 47; Cleveland Inst Art, BFA, 50. *Work:* Cleveland Mus Art; Akron Art Inst; Avis World Hq, Garden City, NJ; Speed Mus, Louisville, Ky; Westminster Col, New Castle, Pa. *Comn:* Prog cover, Cleveland Symphony Orchestra, 70; painting, Good Samaritan Hosp, Sandusky, Ohio, 74; sculpture, Visconsi & Sons, Cleveland; portrait, Cleveland Playhouse; bank mural, Third Fed Savings & Loan, Cleveland; mural, Cleveland Pub Libr (Sterling branch); bronze relief, Solidarity Square, Cleveland, Ohio; portrait, Cleveland Clinic. *Exhib:* One-man shows, Juried Regional, Cleveland May Show, 61, Toledo Mus Art, 65 & Westminster Col, 71; Wooster Col, Ohio, 77; Juried Nat, Butler Inst Am Art, Youngstown, Ohio; Atlanta Col Art, Ga, 78. *Pos:* Chmn dept drawing & med illus, Cleveland Inst Art, 78- *Teaching:* Prof drawing, Cleveland Inst Art, 51-80; assoc prof painting & sculpture, Notre Dame Col, 60-75. *Awards:* Second Prize, Ind State Fair; First Prize, Cleveland May Show. *Bibliog:* Katherine White (auth), Extension 18, Fine Arts Mag, 61; Paul Mooney (auth), Meyers art proves fine talent, Cleveland Press, 61; Paul B Metzler (auth), Artist showing runs the gamut, Cleveland Plain Dealer, 64. *Media:* Egg Emulsion, Acrylic; Bronze, Aluminum. *Collection:* Pre-Columbian art objects (Nyarit, Jalisco, Zapotec, Tarascan); oriental bronzes, polychrome wood, Santos and Roman glass; prints & paintings (Tamayo, Picasso, Rouault, Goya, Kolowitz, Baskin, Erni, etc). *Publ:* Auth, Drawing is the soul of art, Am Artist, 61; Charcoal Drawing (Pitman), Grosset & Dunlap, 65. *Dealer:* Ross Widen Gallery Mayfield Lyndhurst OH 44124. *Mailing Add:* 2897 Plymouth Rd Cleveland OH 44124

MEYERS, JEANNE F
CURATOR, ADMINISTRATOR
b Los Angeles, Calif, Aug 8, 44. *Study:* Univ Wis, 61-63; Univ Calif, Los Angeles, BA, 65; Univ Southern Calif, MSW, 68. *Pos:* Dir, Karl Bornstein Gallery, Santa Monica, Calif, 85-87; owner, Meyers Bloom Gallery, Santa Monica, Calif, 88-92; independent cur, 92- *Teaching:* Part time instr art, Univ Calif, Los Angeles, 85. *Mem:* Mod & Contemp Arts Coun (chair, educ); Santa Monica/Venice Art Dealers Asn; founding mem, Mus Contemp Art; Art Table (exec bd). *Specialty:* Contemporary painting, photography and sculpture. *Collection:* American & English sculpture and painting from 1970 to present. *Mailing Add:* 438 N Bowling Green Los Angeles CA 90049

MEYERS, MICHAEL K
PERFORMANCE ARTIST, PAINTER
b Chicago, Ill, Sept 28, 39. *Study:* Univ Iowa, MA (painting), 67. *Exhib:* Short Play for a Man on the Moon, Mus Mod Art, New York, 78; Reconstructing the Temple from Memory, Los Angeles Contemp Exhibs, Los Angeles, Calif, 88; Ctr for Contemp Arts, Warsaw, Poland, 91; Duke Univ Inst Arts with Performance Networks, NC, 92. *Teaching:* Assoc prof art, Art Inst Chicago, 82- *Awards:* Nat Endowment Arts Fel. *Mailing Add:* 2332 W Grand Ave Chicago IL 60612

MEYERS, RONALD G
EDUCATOR, CERAMIST
b Buffalo, NY, Nov 4, 34. *Study:* State Univ NY, Col Buffalo, BS, 56, MS, 60; Sch Am Craftsmen, Rochester Inst Technol, with Frans Wildenhain, MFA, 65. *Work:* High Mus Art, Atlanta; Lamar Dodd Art Ctr, LaGrange, Ga; SC Arts Comn, Columbia. *Exhib:* Guild Prize Winners, Columbia Mus Art, SC, 71; Southeastern Crafts, Greenville Mus Art, SC, 74; 25 Southeastern Artists, High Mus, Atlanta, 75; Artist-Craftsmen Invitational, Southeastern Ctr Contemp Art, Winston-Salem, NC, 76; Tribute to Hands, Springfield Art Asn, Ill, 78; Drinking Companions, J M Kohler Art Ctr, Sheboygan, Wis, 79. *Teaching:* Asst prof ceramics, Univ SC, Columbia, 67-72; assoc prof, Univ Ga, Athens, 72- *Awards:* Best of Show, Mid-South Ceramic & Crafts, 71 & SC Craftsmen, 71; Guild Purchase Award, Columbia Mus, 71. *Media:* Clay. *Mailing Add:* 180 Hidden Hills Ln Athens GA 30605

MHIRE, HERMAN P
MUSEUM DIRECTOR, CURATOR
b Lafayette, La, Nov 23, 47. *Collections Arranged:* Louisiana Bicentennial Exposition, Maison de Radio, France, Paris, 76; Henry Botkin: Paintings, Drawings & Collages 1928-1981 (coauth, catalog), 82 & Senegal: Narrative Paintings (coauth, catalog), 85, Univ Art Mus, Lafayette, La; A Century of Vision: Louisiana Photography 1884-1984 (auth, catalog), La State Mus, 84; Village Architecture in Jordan (contribr, catalog), Mus Anthrop, Univ Kans,

86; Baking in the Sun: Visionary Images from the South (contribr, catalog). *Pos:* Guest cur, Lafayette Natural Hist Mus, La, 75-84; dir, Gallery Sch Art & Archit, Univ Southwestern La, 77-83 & Univ Art Mus, 83-; Founder and pres, Festival Int de Louisiane, 87-89. *Teaching:* Instr drawing & printmaking, Sch Art & Archit, Univ Southwestern La, 77- *Awards:* Gold Medal Award, La Bicentennial Exposition, US Dept Com, 76. *Mem:* Am Asn Mus; Southeastern Mus Conf; La Asn Mus. *Publ:* Contribr, Contemporary Works on Paper, 84, Univ Art Mus, Lafayette, La, 84. *Mailing Add:* Univ Art Mus Drawer 42571 Univ Southwestern La Lafayette LA 70504

MICALE, ALBERT
PAINTER, SCULPTOR
b Punxsutawney, Pa. *Study:* Pratt Inst Fine & Applied Art, cert(illus). *Work:* Riveredge Found, Calgary; First Fed Savings & Loan Asn, Valley Nat Bank & Ariz Bank, Phoenix; Dartmouth Col. *Exhib:* Mountain Oyster Club Western Art Show, Tucson, Ariz, 74-79; one-man show, Lincoln Thrift Asn Pres Club, Phoenix, 75; Cody Co Art League Ann Prof Show, Wyo, 75; Western States Art Show, Cody, 75; Nebraskaland Days Western & Wildlife Art, North Platte, Nebr, 75. *Awards:* Outstanding Science Bks for Children Award, Nat Sci Teachers Asn, 76. *Bibliog:* Profile: Ariz horseman, 5/77. *Publ:* Illusr, The Sign of the Open Hand, Scribners, 62; The First Book of the Spanish American West, Franklin Watts, 63; Let's Go with Lewis and Clark, Putnam, 63; contribr, Western Horseman Mag, 72-76; illusr, Something About the Author, Gale Res Co. *Mailing Add:* 7574 N Mockingbird Lane Paradise Valley AZ 85253

MICCOLI, ARNALDO
PAINTER, COLLAGE ARTIST
Study: Istituto d'Arte G Pellegrino Lecce, Italy, 60; Acad Fine Arts, Rome, Italy, 63; Univ Social Studies, Rome, 64; Acad Tiherina, Rome. *Work:* Mus Mod Art- Republica di San Marino, Italy; Pinacoteca Provinciale, Lecce, Italy; Webb & Athey Corp, New York; Bill Evans & Son Inc, Santa Monica, Calif; Kay Home Ctr, Lodi, NJ. *Exhib:* Nona Quadriennale Nazionale, Palazzo dell'Esposizioni, Rome, Italy, 65; Arnaldo Miccoli Paintings, Bergen Community Mus, Paramus, NJ, 68; New Jersey State Museum, Trenton Mus, 71; Int Art Show, Republica di San Marina State Mus, Italy, 74; Vereniging Volksuniversiteit Mus, Rotterdam, 86; Faces, Germanow Gallery, Rochester, NY, 87. *Awards:* Gold Medal, Citta di Mentana, Mentana City, 65. *Bibliog:* Toti Carpentiery (auth), Una storia Americana, Terzocchio, 83; Carlo Munari (auth), Metropolitan Apocalypse, Nuovo Sagittario, Milan, 85; A Sala & R Barletta (coauths), Arnaldo Miccoli, Capone Editore, 89. *Media:* Oil. *Mailing Add:* c/o Clark Whitney Gallery 25 Church St Lenox MA 01240

MICHAEL, GARY
PAINTER, WRITER
b Denver, Colo, Apr 17, 37. *Study:* Denver Univ, BA; Colo Univ, MA; Syracuse Univ, with Sydney Thomas, PhD. *Work:* Denver Pub Libr Permanent Collection, Colo; Denver Art Mus; Mus Natural Hist, Denver; Colorado Springs Fine Arts Ctr, Colo; Miron Collection, Poughkeepsie, NY. *Comn:* Mural, Perlmack Corp, Regent Plaza, Denver, 75; bus panel design, Bill & Dorothy Harmsen Collection, Denver, 78 & Saks Gallery, Denver, 86. *Exhib:* one-man shows, First of Denver, Farraginous V, 76, United Bank, Denver, 75 & 76, The Fleeting Moment, Saks Gallery, Denver, 86, The Diamond and Other Wonders, Gary Michael Studio, 88 & Western Co Art Ctr, Grand Junction, Colo, 89; Northern Colo Invitational Art Exhib, 79; Pastel Soc Am, New York, 79; Faces and Places, Denver Nat Bank, 82; Of Lilies and Ladies, Kontny Studio, Englewood, Colo, 83; Group Exhib, Visual Arts Ctr, Boulder, Colo, 90; Currents & Collossi, Huntsman Gallery, Aspen, Colo, 90. *Pos:* Demonstrating artist, Spree Arts Festival, 75-; lectr & demonstr, Grumbacher, New York, 77-; contribr ed, Southwest Art, 88; fac mem, Art Students League, 91- *Teaching:* Prof humanities, Metrop State Col, Denver, 70-73; instr painting, Colo Univ, Denver, 75-76. *Awards:* Popular Vote Award, Pastel Soc Am Ann Exhib, 79; First Place, Glenwood Art Festival, Colo, 79; Merit Award, Colo State Fair, Pueblo, 79; cash award, Nat Pastel Exhib, Kans Pastel Soc. *Bibliog:* Joan Gould (auth), Academician turned artist, Southwest Art, 5/75; Irene Clurman (auth), Farraginous artist, 11/76 & Marjorie Barrett (auth), Traditional artist with a rebellious streak, 11/79, Rocky Mountain News. *Mem:* Pastel Soc Am. *Media:* Acrylic, Oil. *Publ:* Auth, Dorothy Mandel: Her woodcut magic, Am Artist, 1/79; auth, Journey to the Magi, Colo Quart, 7/79; The Art Institute of Chicago at 100, Denver Post, 8/26/79; Markings, Southwest Art, 3/81; Imagination in realist painting, Am Artist, 1/83; cover, Learning From the Pros, Watson-Guptill. *Mailing Add:* 3009 E Tenth Ave Denver CO 80206

MICHAEL, PATRICIA GORDON
ADMINISTRATOR, CURATOR
b Staten Island, NY, July 3, 40. *Study:* Notre Dame Col of Staten Island, BA, 61; Pa State Univ, 61-63. *Collections Arranged:* Full House of Fantasy: The Work of Patricia Nix (with catalog), Staten Island Inst Arts & Sci, 86; Surfaces and Forms: The Work of Pat Saab, spring 86; also arranged 2 ann juried exhibs. *Pos:* Dir, Kalamazoo Pub Mus, 78-84; exec dir, Staten Island Inst Arts & Sci, 84- *Teaching:* Guest lecturer and adjunct instructor, 78- *Mem:* Am Asn Mus; Victorian Soc Am; Am Asn State & Local Hist. *Res:* Photography, with emphasis on period 1914-1940; costume history, 1840-1940. *Mailing Add:* c/o Am Asn State & Local Hist 172 Second Ave Suite 202 Nashville TN 37201

MICHAELS, GLEN
SCULPTOR, PAINTER
b Spokane, Wash, July 21, 27. *Study:* Yale Sch Music, 50-52; Eastern Wash Col Educ, BA, 57; Cranbrook Acad Art, with Zoltan Sepeshy, MFA, 58. *Work:* Am Inst Archit, Detroit Chap; Kresge Found; Kirco Corp, Troy, Mich; Jacobson's, Birmingham, Mich; Univ Mich Alumni Ctr, Ann Arbor; and others. *Comn:* Enamel on steel, Detroit People Mover Sta, Mich, 87; fused glass pool, Mich State Mus, Archit & Libr, Mich, 90; Oakland Co Computer Ctr, Pontiac, Mich, 91; Clark Univ, Wooster, Mass, 91; Baldwin Pub Libr, Birmingham, Mich, 92; and others. *Exhib:* Thirteenth Trienale, Milan, Italy, 64; Archit League New York Gold Medal Exhib, 65; Objects: USA, 69-70; Smithsonian Plastic Exhib, 69-70; Confectioner's Art Am Craft Mus, New York, 88-89. *Teaching:* Supvr art for children, Cranbrook Acad Art, 59-65; asst prof sculpture, Wayne State Univ, 67-69 & Univ Windsor, 70-71. *Awards:* Mich Found Arts Award, 83; Kresge Grant, Detroit People Mover Station, 87; Artist of the Year Award, Mich Art Train, 90. *Bibliog:* Slivka (auth), The crafts in the modern world, Horizon, 68; Redstone (auth), Art in Architecture, McGraw, 68; Nordness (auth), Objects: USA, Viking Press, 70; The Confectioner's Art, Am Craft Coun, 89. *Media:* Bronze, Fused Glass. *Publ:* John Canady (auth), NY Times, 62; Dorothy Rodgers (auth), A Chateau the sound of music built, Look Mag, 67; Art in Archit, Am Inst Archits, 80; Archit Rec, 80-81; Am Craft Mag, 6-7/92. *Mailing Add:* 4800 Beach Rd Troy MI 48098

MICHAELS-PAQUE, J
PAINTER, SCULPTOR
b Menominee, Mich. *Study:* Layton Sch Art, Milwaukee, Wis, scholar, 55-57; Marquette Univ, 56-57; Milwaukee Inst Art & Design, 92. *Work:* Nat Mus Am Art & Nat Collection Fine Arts, Washington, DC; Univ Wis Hosp & Clinics; Objects USA, Johnson Wax Co, Racine, Wis; Wis Elec Co, Milwaukee; Univ Mus, Ill State Univ, Normal; Einhorn Assocs, Inc, Milwaukee, Wis; SCJ Insurance Serv, San Francisco; Faison Assoc, Milwaukee, Wis; St Norbert Col, De Pere, Wis. *Comn:* Sheraton, Brown Deer, Wis, 85; Comn by Dr James Englander, Milwaukee, Wis, 90; comn by The Johansens Blackhawk, Calif, 91; comn by The Einhorns, River Hills, Wis, 92; Janis Salon, Pfister Hotel, Milwaukee, Wis, 92. *Exhib:* one-man shows, Dayton Art Inst, 81, Ariel Gallery, Chicago, 83 & Univ Notre Dame, 89; Grids and Gradation, Garver Gallery, Madison, 85; R/Evolution, Univ Wis-Milwaukee & Milwaukee Art Mus & traveling, 86-87; Leader's Exhib, Albertson-Peterson Gallery, Winter Park, Fla, 87; Dynamic Dimensions, Milwaukee Art Mus, 88; Weatherspoon Art Gallery, Univ NC, Greensboro, 88; The Third Dimension Milwaukee Art Mus, 89; Antipodean Afterimages, Blatz Gallery, Milwaukee, 90; Inclinations, Godschalx Gallery, St Norbert Col, De Pere, Wis, 91. *Pos:* Adv bd, Milwaukee Art Mus, currently. *Teaching:* Vis artist, Miami Univ, Ohio, 81, Dayton Art Inst, 81, Kawashima Textile Sch, Kyoto, Japan, 83 & Bellas Artes, San Miguel de Allende, Mex, 85, Univ Queensland, St Lucia, Australia, 88, Univ Notre Dame, 89; instr art dept, Cardinal Stritch Col, 90-, workshops/seminars for Handweavers Guild Am, Amer Univ, Washington, DC, 92; vis artist, Viterbo Col, La Crosse, Wis, 92; consult corp art, currently. *Awards:* Manpower Award, Wis Art Teachers, 71; Lily Mills Award, Belding-Lily Mills, Shelby, NC, 76; Bush Found Grant, 82; Milwaukee Mag, Most Interesting Person, designee, 86. *Bibliog:* Rich Mathews (auth), Joan Michaels-Paque: An appreciation, Fiberarts, 11-12/76; Judith M Kaiser (auth), New dimensions in Wisconsin art, Exclusively Yours, 79; Peg Masterson (auth), Corporate artwork rising, Milwaukee Sentinel, 12/85; Janet De Boer (ed), Textile Fibre Forum (article), Univ Queensland, Australia, 88. *Mem:* Am Crafts Coun; Int Guild Journalists, Auths & Photogrs; Wis Painters & Sculptors; Handweavers Guild Am; Int Sculpture Ctr. *Media:* Flexible Linear Material, Mixed. *Res:* Exploring the reclamation and transformation of unpretentious materials into lightweight, large scale reliefs and sculptures; published research paper ARS Textrina, Univ Manitoba, Winnepeg, Can, 88. *Publ:* Auth, ed & illusr, Design Principles/Fiber Techniques, 73 & A Creative/Conceptual Analysis of Textiles, 79 & 85, pvt publ; auth, reviews for Textile Fibre Forum, Australian Periodical, 92. *Dealer:* Fanny Garver Gallery 230 State St Madison WI 53703; Cynthia Tilson Galleries Plaza East Suite 102 330 East Kilbourn Ave Milwaukee WI 53202. *Mailing Add:* 4455 N Frederick Ave Milwaukee WI 53211

MICHALS, DUANE
PHOTOGRAPHER
b McKeesport, Pa, Feb 18, 32. *Study:* Univ Denver, BA, 53. *Work:* Mus Mod Art, Metrop Mus Art; Nat Libr, Paris; Boston Mus Fine Arts; San Francisco Mus Mod Art; William Rockhill Nelson Gallery, Kansas City, Kans; and many others. *Exhib:* Frankfurt Kunstverein, 74; one-man shows, Galerie Watari, Tokyo, Japan, 83, Wellesley Col Art Gallery, Mass, 84, Sidney Janis Gallery, New York, 85, Studio 8 Gallery, Kalispell, Mo, 86, Art Ctr Col Design, Pasadena, Calif, 87, Ugo Ferranti, Rome, Italy, 88, Gallery for Fine Photography, New Orleans, 90; VA Mus Fine Arts, Richmond, 87 & 89; Musee d'Art Moderne, Paris, 88; Whitney Mus Am Art, 88; High Mus Art, Atlanta, Ga, 88 & 89; Fogg Mus, Cambridge, Mass, 89; Walker Art Ctr, Minneapolis, Minn, 89; Milwaukee Art Mus, Wis, 90. *Awards:* Nat Endowment Arts Grant, 76; Pa Coun Arts, 78; Carnegie Found Photog Fel, Cooper Union, 79. *Bibliog:* Carter Ratcliffe (auth), Duane Michals, Print Collector's Newslett, 9/75; Ronald H Bailey (auth), The Photographic Illusion, Alskog, 75; Stefan Mihal (auth), Take One and See Mt Fujiyama, 76; John H Lawrence (auth), Duane Michal's Recent Work, New Orleans Art Review, 1-2/90. *Publ:* The journey of the spirit after death, Winterhouse, 71; Things are queer, Wilde, Koln, 73; auth, Portraits, Twelvetrees Press, 88. *Dealer:* Sidney Janis Gallery 110 W 57th St New York NY. *Mailing Add:* 109 E 19th St New York NY 10003

MICHAUX, HENRY GASTON
EDUCATOR, SCULPTOR
b Morganton, NC, Jan 19, 34. *Study:* Tex Southern Univ, with John T Biggers, BFA, 59; Rochester Inst Technol, advanced design, 63; Pa State Univ, EdM,

60, EdD, 71. *Work:* NC State Mus, Raleigh; J B Speed Mus, Louisville, Ky; H C Taylor Gallery (A&T State Univ), Greensboro, NC. *Comn:* Ceramic Mural on Medicine, comn by Dr & Mrs Carrol, Houston,; coffee set (hand thrown), comn by John T Biggers, Houston,; welded steel gift for Graduating High School, Houston Pub Sch, Tex, 69; stainless steel award, comn by James Oxygen & Welding, Hickory, NC, 75. *Exhib:* Houston Mus Art, Tex, 56; Competitive Invitational, Henri Studio Galleries, New York, 64; Afro-American Artists, Denver Art Mus, Colo, 69; Afro-American Artists: North Carolina USA, N Mus Art, Raleigh, 80; Dimensions and Directions: Black Artists of the South, Jackson State Col Mus, Miss, 80. *Pos:* Pres, Caldwell Arts Coun, Lenoir, NC, 75-76; organizer/planner, Ann Indoor/Outdoor Sculpture Competition, Lenoir, NC, 86. *Teaching:* Prof sculpture, Tex Southern Univ, Houston, 68-70; prof ceramics, Appalachian State Univ, Boone, NC, 72-76. *Awards:* Purchace Award, 9th Ann Black Artists' Exhib, Louisville Chapter Links Inc, 88. *Bibliog:* Carolina Camera, feature story (film), WBTV Television, Charlotte, NC, 8/4/80; Biggers & Simms (coauths), Black Art in Houston, Univ Tex. *Mem:* Nat Asn Sch Art & Design; Am Crafts Coun; Nat Coun Educ Ceramic Arts; Sculpture Int; Nat Art Educ Asn. *Media:* Clay, Stainless Steel. *Publ:* Illusr, Folk Tales and Ghost Stories, Jourdan Atkinson, 57; auth, An Accommodational Esthetic: Precursor For One Legitimate Black Esthetic in African Rock Art Traditions, J Black Studies, 12/77; Black Art: Recognition, Nourishment, Celebration, Greensboro Asn Preservation Black Art, 78. *Mailing Add:* 4009 Harvey Lane NW Orangeburg SC 29115

MICHAUX, RONALD ROBERT
ART DEALER
b Springfield, Mass, Aug 8, 44. *Pos:* Dir, Rolly-Michaux Galleries, Boston. *Mem:* Newbury St Merchants League. *Specialty:* 20th century masters & contemporaries, including paintings, sculpture & graphics. *Mailing Add:* c/o Rolly-Michaux Galleries 290 Dartmouth St Boston MA 02116

MICHELS, EILEEN MANNING
EDUCATOR, ART HISTORIAN
b Fargo, NDak, Mar 27, 26. *Study:* Univ Minn, BA, 47, MA, 53, MA, 59, PhD, 71; Inst Fine Arts, NY Univ, 50-51; Sorbonne, 56-57. *Collections Arranged:* Edwin Hugh Lundie, FAIA (auth, catalog), 72. *Pos:* Free-lance cur, Minn Mus Art, 72-73, assoc dir, 73-74; free-lance cur, Minneapolis Inst Arts, 73-74. *Teaching:* Vis asst prof art hist, Stanford Univ, 72-73; assoc prof & chair dept, 78-88; prof, 89-, Univ St Thomas. *Awards:* Fulbright, Paris, 56-57. *Mem:* Soc Archit Historians (dir, 76-79, secy 82-86); Col Art Asn; Women Historians Midwest; Frank Lloyd Wright Found. *Res:* Nineteenth and twentieth century architecture; American art. *Publ:* Auth, An Architectural View: Minneapolis Society of Fine Arts 1883-1974, Minneapolis Inst Arts, 74; auth, A Landmark Reclaimed, Minn Landmarks, 77. *Mailing Add:* 2183 Hendon Ave St Paul MN 55108

MICHELSON, PHILIP L
PAINTER, PRINTMAKER
b San Francisco, Calif, July 25, 48. *Study:* Univ San Francisco, BA, 71. *Work:* Brooklyn Mus, NY; Smithsonian Inst, Washington, DC; Fine Arts Mus San Francisco; Achen Bach Found for Graphic Arts. *Exhib:* Solo exhibs, Richmond Art Ctr, 78 & Montalvo Ctr Arts, Saratoga, 82, Calif; Nat Watercolor Invitational, Cypress Col Fine Arts Gallery, Los Angeles, Calif, 80; Architectural Images, Summit Art Ctr, NJ, 82; Subjective Realities, 82 & Recent Acquisitions, 83, 85 & 91, Fine Arts Mus San Francisco, Achenbach Found, Calif; Bon A Tirer, De Saisset Mus, Univ Santa Clara, Calif, 83; Recent Acquisitions, Nat Mus Am Art, Washington, DC, 85; Rhode Island Collects Paper, Mus Art, RI Sch Design, 86; Close Focus-Points, Drawings & Photographs, Nat Mus Am Art, 87; Bay Area Drawings, Oakland Mus, 91; Silverpoint Etc, Contemp Am Metalpoint Drawings, Ark Art Ctr, 92; Directions in Bay Area Printmaking, Palo Alto Cult Ctr, 92. *Bibliog:* Lorelei Heller McDevitt (auth), Subjective realities, Designers West Mag, 7/82; Jan Ehrenworth (auth), The Cabot Corporation Collection, Boston, 84; Susan Stowens (auth), Philip Michelson: Giving a photographic appearance to imagined subjects, Am Artist Mag, 4/86. *Mem:* Artists Equity. *Media:* Watercolor; Miscellaneous. *Dealer:* Edith Caldwell Gallery 251 Post St San Francisco CA 94108. *Mailing Add:* 2627-33rd Ave San Francisco CA 94116

MICHICH, VELIZAR See Vasa, (Velizar Mihich)

MICHIE, MARY
SCULPTOR
b Ripon, Wis, Aug 8, 22. *Study:* Ripon Col, BA(cum laude), 43; Cent Sch Art, London, Eng, sculpture study, 50-52; Univ Wis, Madison, MA(art), 62. *Work:* Milwaukee Art Mus, Wis; Rahr-West Mus, Manitowoc, Wis; Madison Art Ctr, Wis. *Comn:* Bronze figure, Marshall Erdman & Assoc, Marshfield, Wis, 75; bronze figure, Tomah Pub Libr, Wis, 81; bronze chalice & tray, St Paul's Cath Ctr, Madison, Wis, 83; limestone, Citi Arts & Dane Co Cult Comt, Madison, Wis, 92. *Exhib:* Midwest Juried Exhib, Walker Art Ctr, Minneapolis, Minn, 58 & 62; Nat Drawing & Sculpture, Ball State Univ Mus, Ind, 63; Sculptors at Wingspread, Wingspread Found, Racine, Wis, 63; solo exhib, 68, 70 & TWA's Am Artists, 69, New Stanley Art Gallery, Nairobi, Kenya & Rahr-West Mus, Manitowoc, Wis, 88; XVIII Prix Internationale d'Art, Hall du Centenaire, Monte Carlo, 84; Nat April Salon, Springville Mus, Utah, 84 & 88. *Pos:* Grad asst sculpture, Univ Wis Madison, 60-61; proj asst, Univ Wis Exten Art Dept, 63-67. *Awards:* Nat Endowment Arts Grant for bronze, 83. *Bibliog:* James Auer (auth), Critical Review, Milwaukee J, 5/9/76; Virginia Watson-Jones (auth), Contemp American Women Sculptors, Oryx Press, 86. *Mem:* Wis Painters & Sculptors; Nat Asn Women Artists. *Media:* Bronze, Aluminum. *Publ:* Auth, Arts and Crafts in Kenyan Society, Univ Wis Exten, 72; Encounter with an African potter, Ceramics Monthly, 12/77; Lamu doors, Design Mag, winter 77; Search for a Kenyan craftsman, Christian Science Monitor, 11/28/78; An Artist's Eye View of Rural Wisconsin, Wis Acad Rev, 12/78. *Dealer:* Grace Chosy Gallery 218 N Henry Madison WI 53703. *Mailing Add:* 212 Bordner Dr Madison WI 53705

MICHOD, SUSAN A
PAINTER
b Toledo, Ohio, Jan 3, 45. *Study:* Smith Col; Univ Mich, BS; Pratt Inst, MFA. *Work:* Mus Contemp Art, Chicago, Ill; Ill State Mus, Springfield; Owens-Corning Fiberglass, Toledo, Ohio; Chase Manhattan Bank & Xerox Corp, New York. *Comn:* Shared Space (painted installation), Bronx Mus, NY, 83; painting with construction, Indust Trust & Savings Bank, Muncie, Ind, 84; mural, Regeneration, Rush-Pres St Luke's Hosp, Chicago, Ill, 91. *Exhib:* Painting and Sculpture Today, Indianapolis Mus Art, 76; Pattern Painting, PS1, Flushing, NY, 77; Jan Cicero Gallery, Chicago, 77-; Andre Zarre Gallery, New York, 78-79; Mus Contemp Art, Chicago, 79; Usable Art, State Univ NY, Plattsburg, 81; Susan Caldwell Gallery, New York, 81-83; The Chair Show, Thorpe Intermedia Gallery, Syracuse, NY, 82; Chicago Now, Brentwood Gallery, St Louis, Mo, 82. *Teaching:* Instr painting, Chicago Acad Fine Arts, 69-74, Columbia Col Pougealis Apprentice Prog. *Awards:* Purchase Prize, Ill State Mus, 74; Purchase Prize, Carleton Col Exhib, 75. *Bibliog:* John Russell (auth), Art, New York Times, 7/10/81; Ronny Cohen (auth), rev, Art News, Vol 81, No 9, 11/82; Judith Kirschner (auth), rev, Artforum, 3/83. *Media:* Acrylic, Watercolor. *Dealer:* Jan Cicero Gallery Chicago IL. *Mailing Add:* 2242 N Dayton Chicago IL 60614

MICKENBERG, DAVID
MUSEUM DIRECTOR, HISTORIAN
b Brooklyn, NY, Apr 29, 54. *Study:* Colgate Univ, BA, 76; Univ Wis, Milwaukee, MA(art hist), 79. *Collections Arranged:* Romantic Prints, Ind Mus Art, Indianapolis, 80; Ritual Power and Function (auth, catalog), 82, Winslow Homer: The Civil War Years, 83, Impressionism: Post-Impressionism (auth, catalog), 83 & Songs of Glory (auth, catalog), Okla Mus Art. *Pos:* Asst cur, Picker Art Gallery, Hamilton, NY, 74-76; coordr, Adult Educ Prog & asst dir, Indianapolis Mus Art, Ind, 79-81; exec dir, Okla Mus Art, Oklahoma City, 81- *Teaching:* Teaching asst, Univ Wis, 76-79. *Awards:* Dean's Scholarship, Ind Univ, 80-81. *Mem:* Col Art Asn; Am Asn Mus; Int Ctr Medieval Art. *Res:* Romanesque and Gothic architecture; contemporary prints; painting and sculpture. *Mailing Add:* Mary & Leigh Block Gallery Northwestern Univ 1967 Sheridan Rd Evanston IL 60208-2410

MICKISH, VERLE L
EDUCATOR, PAINTER
b Greeley, Colo, Sept 27, 28. *Study:* Colo State Col, BFA, 51; Univ Northern Colo, MAE, 55; Ariz State Univ, EdD, 70. *Comn:* Acrylic painting, Great Moments in Music Corp, Atlanta, Ga, 83. *Exhib:* Georgia Ann Exhib, High Mus Art, Atlanta, 83-85. *Pos:* Chmn, Int Cultural Arts, Nat Asn Partners of the Americas, 76-77; mem, Int Olympics Acad Comt, 78-80; mem, Prof Standards Comt, Nat Art Educ Asn, Reston, Va, Southeastern vpres, 86-88. *Teaching:* Art dir K-12, Boulder Valley Pub Sch, Colo, 58-71; prof art, Ga State Univ, Atlanta, 71-; presentation of over 600 workshops throughout US, Canada, Europe & Brazil since 1961. *Awards:* Nat Art Educator of the Year, Nat Art Educ Asn, 83; Distinguished Ga Educator, Ga Univ System, 83. *Mem:* Ga Art Educ Asn (pres, 79-81). *Media:* Watercolor, Acrylic. *Publ:* Auth, Creative Art-Junior High Grades, Pruett Press, 62; illusr, Corn for the Palace, Prentice-Hall, 63; The Rubáiyyát of Báhá Táhir Gryán of Hamadán, Univ Colo Press, 67. *Mailing Add:* Sch Art & Design Ga State Univ Atlanta GA 30303

MIDDAUGH, ROBERT BURTON
PAINTER
b Chicago, Ill, May 12, 35. *Study:* Univ Ill, 54-55; Art Inst Chicago, BFA, 64. *Work:* Art Inst Chicago; Boston Mus Fine Art; Los Angeles Co Mus; Phoenix Art Mus; Worcester Art Mus, Mass. *Comn:* Prehistoric Project (permanent educ display, with Martyl Langsdorf & Prof Robert Braidwood), Oriental Inst, Univ Chicago, 68. *Exhib:* Chicago & Vicinity Show, Art Inst Chicago, 64, 66 & 73-85; Ill Biennial Exhib, Krannert Art Mus, Urbana, 65; Ill Exhib, Ill State Mus, Springfield, 66, 68, 69 & 71; Am Painting Exhib, Va Mus Fine Arts, Richmond, 66; 162nd Ann Exhib, Pa Acad Fine Arts, Philadelphia, 67; and others. *Pos:* Asst cur, Art Collection First Nat Bank Chicago, 71-78, cur, 79-83. *Awards:* Purchase Prize, Am Acad Arts & Lett, 75. *Mem:* Arts Club Chicago. *Media:* All. *Publ:* Contribr, Buying Art on a Budget, Hawthorn, 68; contribr, Living World History, Scott Foresman. *Mailing Add:* 1318 W Cornelia Chicago IL 60657

MIDDLEBROOK, DAVID A
SCULPTOR, EDUCATOR
b Jackson, Mich, May 1, 44. *Study:* Albion Col, BA, 66; Univ Iowa, with Jerry Rothman, Paul Soldner & Stuart Eddie, MA, 69, with Don Reitz, Byron Burford & Hans Braeder, MFA, 70. *Work:* Univ Wash Mus Art, Seattle; Koehler Mus, Sheboygan, Wis; San Jose Mus Art, Fresno Mus, Oakland Mus Art & San Francisco Mus Art, Calif; and others. *Comn:* Earth Sample (stone & marble), Thrust IV, Inc, Mt View, Calif, 85; Black Water, Bell Savings, San Jose, Calif, 85; Time Shadow, Sacramento Light Rail, 86-87. *Exhib:* Nine Calif Artists, Everson Mus Art, Syracuse, NY, 78; A Century of Ceramics in US, Smithsonian Mus, traveling, DC, 78-80; NCCR: Sculpture Now, San Francisco Mus Mod Art, 79; Joshua Wedgwood Invitational, Philadelphia Mus Art, 80; Illusionism in Am, Los Angeles Co Mus Art, Los Angeles, 80; Reconstructions, San Jose Mus Art, 81; Klein Gallery, Chicago, 81 & 82; one-person show, Fresno Mus, 83; RAU Sculpture Court, Johannesburg, 83; Asn

Gallery, Capetown, 83; Ree Schonlau Galllery, Omaha, 85; Arvada Ctr Arts & Humanities, Colo, 85. *Teaching:* Asst prof art, Univ Ky, Lexington, 70-74; prof art, San Jose State Univ, 74-; vis prof art, Notre Dame Univ, 72 & 76, Mills Col, Oakland, Calif, 77; artist-in-residence, Darwin Community Col, Australia, 80, Shefield Polytechnic, Eng, 81; vis artist, SAfrica, 82. *Awards:* Westinghouse res award, Koehler Mus, Purdue Univ, 73; Nat Endowment for Arts artist grant, 77; Lucy Stern fel, Mills Col, 78; Environmental Improvement Award of Distinction, Assoc Landscape Contractors Am, 85. *Bibliog:* Elsbeth Wood (auth), Handbuilding, McGraw Hill, 78; Harvey Brody (auth), Low Fire Ceramics, 80; Susan Peterson (auth), Modern ceramic concerns, 81. *Mem:* Nat Conf Educ Ceramic Art; Col Art Asn; Am Crafts Coun. *Dealer:* Klein Gallery 356 Huron Chicago IL 60610. *Mailing Add:* 18404 Montevina Rd Los Gatos CA 95030

MIDDLEMAN, RAOUL F
PAINTER, MURALIST
b Baltimore, Md, Apr 3, 35. *Study:* Johns Hopkins Univ, BA, 55; Pa Acad Fine Arts, 59-61; Brooklyn Mus Art Sch, 61. *Exhib:* Solo exhibs, Landscapes & Portraits of the Ardeche, Scott- McKennis Gallery, Richmond, Va, 80, Yale Norfolk Summer Sch, 80, Boston Univ, 81, Grimaldis Gallery, Baltimore, 81-84, Water Gap Art Gallery, Walpack Ctr, NJ, 82, William Capro Gallery, New Bedford, Mass, 83 & Swanston Fine Arts, Atlanta, 88; Das Automobil in Der Kunst, Haus der Kunst, Munich, Ger, 86; Contemp Realist Gallery, San Francisco, 88; Bendann Gallery, Baltimore, 89; Ingber Gallery, New York, 89; The Landscape Revisited from Maine to Key West, Gaumann Cicchino Gallery, Ft Lauderdale, Fla, 89; The Landscape Observed, Md Inst, Baltimore, 89-90; 165th Ann Exhib, Nat Acad Design, New York, 90. *Teaching:* Chmn painting dept, Md Inst Col Art, Baltimore, 75-78; resident dir, summer landscape painting prog, Md Inst Col Art, 81-83; vis critic, Vt Studio Sch Summer Prog, 85. *Bibliog:* Gerrit Henri (auth), rev in Art News, 72; Pat Mainardi (auth), rev in Art in Am, 7/74; H O Beil (auth), Arts Mag, 5/85. *Mem:* Assoc mem Nat Acad Design, 92. *Media:* Oil, Watercolor. *Dealer:* Allan Stone Gallery 48 E 86th St New York NY. *Mailing Add:* 943 N Calvert St Baltimore MD 21217

MIDENER, WALTER
SCULPTOR, INSTRUCTOR
b Ger, Oct 11, 12; US citizen. *Study:* Vereinigten Staats Schulen Fine & Appl Art; Berlin Acad, 32-36; Wayne State Univ, MA, 50. *Work:* Whitney Mus Am Art & House Living Judaism, New York; Detroit Inst Art & Flint Inst Art, Mich. *Comn:* Justice Butzel (portrait bust), Mich Supreme Court, 62; monument, Temple Bethel Mem Park, 62; sculpture, Bundy Corp, Detroit, 63; carved wood relief, Detroit Pub Libr, 64; hammered metal screen, Pontiac Motor Div, Gen Motors Corp, 68-69. *Exhib:* Mich Artists Shows, 46-61; Modellers, Carvers, Welders, Mus Mod Art, New York, 49-50; American Sculpture, Metrop Mus, New York, 51; Pa Acad, Philadelphia, 59; Friends of Whitney Collection, Whitney Mus Am Art, 64. *Teaching:* Instr sculpture, Henry St Settlement, 39-41; head sculpture dept, Soc Arts & Crafts Art Sch, 46-66, asst dir, 58-61, actg & assoc dir, 61-67, dean fac, 67-68, dir, Ctr Creative Studies, Col Art & Design, 68-76, pres, 76-77, pres emer & prof sculpture, 77-79. *Awards:* Mus Purchase Prize, Mich Artists Show, 50; Founders Prize, Founders Soc, 52; Gold Medal, Scarab Club, 60; Mich Arts Award, Mich Found Arts, 84. *Mem:* Crooked Tree Arts Council, Petoskey, Mich; Founders Soc, Detroit Inst Arts. *Media:* Metal, Wood. *Mailing Add:* 03437 M-66 S Box 603 East Jordan MI 49727

MIECZKOWSKI, EDWIN
PAINTER
b Pittsburgh, Pa, 1929. *Study:* Cleveland Inst Art, BFA; Carnegie Inst, MFA. *Work:* Cleveland Mus Art; Robert Hull Fleming Mus, Vt. *Exhib:* One-man shows, Robert Hull Fleming Mus, 74, New Gallery, Cleveland, 74, Tyler Sch Art, Pa, 74 & Mansfield Art Ctr, Ohio, 75; All-Ohio Show, 74; Cleveland Mus Art, 75; Park Ctr Show, Cleveland, 75. *Mem:* Founding mem Anonima Group; Nat Organization Visual Artists, Cleveland. *Media:* Acrylic. *Mailing Add:* 12418 Euclid Ave Cleveland OH 44106

MIEZAJS, DAINIS
PAINTER, INSTRUCTOR
b Kaucminde, Latvia, Mar 11, 29. *Study:* Ont Col of Art, 56. *Work:* Nat Gallery of Can, Ottawa, Ont; Art Gallery of Ont, Toronto; Mus Fine Arts, Montreal, Que; Art Gallery of Winnipeg, Man; Vancouver Art Gallery, BC. *Comn:* Series of 18 paintings, Trans-Can Pipeline, Toronto, Ont, 71. *Exhib:* Ann Can Soc of Painters in Watercolors, 61-78; Can Painters in Watercolor & Am Watercolor Soc Exchange Show, 73; Can Painters in Watercolor & Watercolor Soc of Japan, 77. *Collections Arranged:* Across Canada in Watercolor, Art Gallery of Ont, 69-71. *Teaching:* Instr drawing & painting, Ont Col of Art, Toronto, 60-, chmn fine art, 83-; dir landscape, Madawaska Valley Sch Art, Maynooth, Ont, 65- *Awards:* Merit Award, Can Soc of Painters in Watercolor Ann; Purchase Awards, Can Soc of Painters in Watercolor. *Bibliog:* F Barwick (auth), Pictures from the Douglas Duncan Collection, Univ Toronto Press, 75. *Mem:* Can Painters in Watercolor (dir, 65-67); Latvia Soc Artists (vpres, 62-64). *Media:* Watercolor, Tempera. *Mailing Add:* c/o Dept Fine Arts Ont Col Art 100 McCaul St Toronto ON M5T 1W1 Canada

MIGNOSA, SANTO
CERAMIST, SCULPTOR
b Siracusa, Italy, Nov 14, 34; Can citizen. *Study:* Scuola d'Arte, Italy, Cert; Inst Statale d'Arte Firenze, Italy, Dipl: NY State Univ Alfred, MFA. *Work:* Univ Calgary Art Gallery, Can; Govt of Alta Art Found, Can; Govt of Tenn Ceramic Collection; Pall Mall of Can Art Collection; Art Centrum, Prague, Czech. *Exhib:* Int Ceramic Exhib, Ostend, Belg, 58, Prague, Czech, 61 & Gdansk, Poland, 73; Syracuse Nat, NY, 60, 62 & 66; Smithsonian Inst, Washington, DC; Faenza Int Concorso, Italy; Int Ceramic Exhib, Calgary, 73. *Collections Arranged:* Int Ceramic 73, Calgary, Can; Nat Ceramic 76, Calgary, Can. *Pos:* Co-chmn, Nat Ceramic Exhib, Calgary, Can, 75-76. *Teaching:* Instr ceramics & sculpture, Kootenay Sch of Art, Nelson, BC, 60-68; assoc prof ceramics, Univ Calgary, Alta, Can, 69-89 (retired). *Awards:* Gold Medal, Int Ceramic Exhib, Ostend, 58, Silver Medal, Prague, 61 & Second Prize Ex-Aequo, Calgary, 73, Int Acad Ceramics; Achievement Awards, Gov Alberta, 70 & 72. *Bibliog:* Al Riegger (auth), Featured Artist, Ceramic Mo, 63; article in, La Revue Mod des Arts et de la Vie, 67. *Mem:* Alta Potters' Asn (vpres, 70-71); Int Acad Ceramics, Geneva, Switz (coun mem). *Media:* Clay. *Mailing Add:* 571 N Dollarton Hwy North Vancouver BC V7G 1N3 Canada

MIHAESCO, EUGENE
PAINTER, ILLUSTRATOR
b Bucharest, Romania, Aug 24, 37, Switz citizen. *Study:* Fine Art Inst, Bucharest, BA, 59. *Work:* Cooper-Hewitt Mus, New York; Republic's Art Mus, Bucharest, Romania; Musee des Arts, Decoratifs de la Ville, Lausanne, Switz. *Exhib:* Bienal Sao Paulo, Sao-Paulo Mus, Brazil, 63; Art of the Times, Musee des Arts Decoratifs, Louvre, Paris, France; The Statue of Liberty, Ctr Pompidou, Beaubourg, Paris, France, 76. *Teaching:* Assoc prof illus, Pratt Inst, 81-82. *Awards:* Best Illus, 1977 Show, Am Inst Graphic Arts; Best Cover, News Paper Guild, 83; Gold Medal, Ann Show, Art Dirs Club, NY, 85. *Bibliog:* Deborah Phillips (auth), Eugene Mihaesco, Arts News, No 5, 81; Steven Heller (auth), Eugene Mihaesco, Arts, No 10, Vol 58, 84 & Graphis, No 238, 85. *Media:* Pastel; Pen & Ink. *Publ:* Ed artist, NY Times, 71-86; illusr, 12 covers, Time Inc, 78-86; 57 covers, New Yorker Mag, 72-86. *Mailing Add:* c/o Galerie St Etienne 24 W 57th St New York NY 10019

MIKOL, IRENE R See IRENA (Irene R Mikol),

MIKUS, ELEANORE
PAINTER, EDUCATOR
b Detroit, Mich, July 25, 27. *Study:* Art Students League; study in Cent Europe; Univ Denver, BFA & MA. *Work:* Mus Mod Art, Whitney Mus Am Art, New York; Victoria & Albert Mus, London; Los Angeles Co Mus Art; Indianapolis Mus Art, Ind; Nat Gallery Art, Washington, DC; and others. *Exhib:* One-woman shows, Pace Gallery, New York, 63, 64 & 65, O K Harris Gallery, New York, 70-74 & Mary Baskett Gallery, Cincinnati, 83-85 & 88; Mus Mod Art, New York, 74; Johnson Mus, Ithaca, 79-83; O K Harris Gallery, New York, 80-83; Mary Baskett Gallery, Cincinnati, 82-83; Twenty-five Year Tamarind Retrospective, Los Angeles City Mus Art, 84; and others. *Teaching:* Asst prof painting, Monmouth Col, 66-70; vis lectr painting, Cooper Union, 70-72; lectr painting, Cent Sch Art & Design, London, Eng, 73-77; assoc prof, Cornell Univ, 79-92, prof art, 92. *Awards:* Guggenheim Found Fel Painting, 66-67; Ford Found Tamarind Fel Lithography, 68; MacDowell Colony Fel, 69. *Bibliog:* Robert Hobbs & Judith Bernstock (auths), Eleanore Mikus, Shadows of the Real, Groton House, Univ Wash Press, Seattle & London. *Media:* Oil, Paper Folds. *Dealer:* Mary Baskett Gallery 1002 St Gregory St Cincinnati OH 45202. *Mailing Add:* PO Box 6586 Ithaca NY 14851

MILANT, JEAN ROBERT
DEALER
b Milwaukee, Wis, Dec 27, 43. *Study:* Univ Wis, Milwaukee, BA & BFA, 66; Univ NMex, Albuquerque, MA, 70; Lithography Workshop, Los Angeles. *Pos:* Dir & owner, Cirrus Ed Ltd, 70-; dir & owner, Cirrus Gallery Ltd, 70-; mem bd, Los Angeles Inst Contemp Art, 74-76; vpres, Los Angeles Visual Arts. *Awards:* Tamarind Master Printer, 69. *Specialty:* Contemporary painting, sculpture, performance, environments of Southern California artists; publisher of lithographs and screenprints of noted California artists. *Publ:* Ed, Artists/Prints 1976-1977, Contemp Art Publ Inc, 78. *Mailing Add:* 542 S Alameda St Los Angeles CA 90013

MILAZZO, RICHARD See Collins & Milazzo, (Tricia Collins & Richard Milazzo)

MILDER, JAY
PAINTER, SCULPTOR
b Omaha, Nebr, May 12, 34. *Study:* The Sorbonne; with Ossip Zadkine; with Andre L'Hote, Paris, France; Chicago Art Inst. *Work:* Tel Aviv Mus, Israel; Chrysler Mus, Norfolk, Va; Skidmore Col, NY; Mint Mus, Charlotte, NC. *Comn:* Sculpture, Sinai Temple, Los Angeles, Calif, 64; litho, Greenwich Light Opera, Conn, 70; etching, Rainbow Arts Found, NY, 77. *Exhib:* Mint Mus Art, Charlotte, NC; Joslyn Art Mus, Omaha, Nebr; Art for the Olympics, Mus Mod Art, New York; Retrospective 1958-91, (touring), Schick Art Gallery, Skidmore Col, Saratoga Springs, NY, Va Beach Ctr Arts, Va Beach, 91-92; one-man exhibs, Gallery Four, Charlotte, Va, 86, Richard Green Gallery, New York, 86, Sid Deutsch Gallery, New York, 86, Harcourts Contemp, San Francisco, 89, Missiah on the IND, Richard Green Gallery, New York, Gallery Jupiter, Little Silver, NJ, Anton Gallery, Washington, DC & Yares Gallery, Scottsdale, Ariz (catalog), 87-89; The Expanding Figurative Imagination, Anita Shapolsky Gallery, New York, 90; Horace Richter Gallery, Jaffa, Israel, 90; Private Stories (catalog), Anderson Gallery, Va Commonwealth Univ, Richmond, 91; Alitosh Kebede Fine Art, Los Angeles, Calif, 91. *Collections Arranged:* Rhino Horn Exhib, New Sch for Social Res, New York; Oakley Collection, Skidmore Col; 50 American Contemporary Drawings, Ann Arbor Mus, Mich. *Teaching:* Asst prof art, City Col, New York, 71-, assoc prof, 81- *Awards:* Gutman Award, 60; First Prizes, All Ohio

Artists, 64 & Am Figurative Artists, Bayonne, NJ, 77; Nat Endowment Art, 89-90. *Bibliog:* Leslie Judd Ahlander (auth), Miami art scene, Miami News, 11/18/88; Hilton Kramer (auth), art for art's sake show an apt finale for Ingber Gallery, NY Observer, 7/17-24/89; Barnaby Ruhe (auth), Ruhe views, Art World, summer 89. *Media:* Oil; Mixed. *Dealer:* Oscarsson Hood Gallery 41 W 57th St New York NY 10019. *Mailing Add:* 108 Wooster St New York NY 10012

MILES, CHRISTINE M
MUSEUM DIRECTOR, ADMINISTRATOR
b Madison, Ind, Mar 2, 51. *Study:* Boston Univ, BA(fine arts), 73, George Washington Univ, MA, 82, Mus Mgt Inst. *Pos:* Curatorial asst, Mus City New York, 73-75; dir, Mus Gallery, South St Seaport Mus, New York, 75-77; dir, Fraunces Tavern Mus, New York, 80-86; dir, Albany Inst Hist & Art, NY, 86- *Mem:* Am Asn Mus; Fedn Hist Serv (bd mem, 87-); Gallery Asn NY State (bd mem, 88-). *Mailing Add:* Albany Inst History & Art 125 Washington Ave Albany NY 12210

MILES, CYRIL
PAINTER, CURATOR
b Boston, Mass, June 13, 18. *Study:* Wayne State Univ, Detroit, Mich, BA, 42, MA, 43; study with Wang Chi-Yuan, cert calligraphy, 55. *Comn:* Cityscapes, Cranbrook Construction, San Francisco, Calif, 83 & 84; Mexico Santos (painting), 85 & Mexico Fiesta (painting), comn by Terry Kulka, Oakland, Calif, 81. *Exhib:* Int Watercolor Exhib, Chicago Art Mus, 41; solo shows, Inst Mex & Am Cult, Mexico City, 67 & Downey Mus Art, Downey, Calif, 68; American Flag in the Art of Our Country, Allentown Art Mus, Allentown, Pa 76. *Collections Arranged:* Universality of Indigo Blue Textiles, Northern Mich Univ, 81; Universality of Indigo Textiles and More, 81, Universal Dolls and Puppets, 84, Universal Body Adornments, 85 & Universal Symbols in Folk Art of Six Continents, 88, Int Inst, Detroit. *Pos:* Folk art cur, Int Inst, Detroit, Mich, 78-93. *Teaching:* Instr art, Highland Park Community Col, 42-85. *Awards:* Mus Purchase Award, Mich Acad Art, 62. *Bibliog:* Ellen Goodman (auth), World's wildest wall, Detroit Free Press, 10/65; Susan Heideman (auth), Art of Cyril Miles, Literary cavalcade, 5/68; Dona Z Meilach (auth), Collage and Assemblage, Crown Publ, 73. *Res:* Universality of folk art. *Publ:* Auth, Moholy Nagy, Experiment in totality, J Aesthetics, 71. *Mailing Add:* 17711 Hamilton Rd Detroit MI 48203

MILES, ELLEN GROSS
HISTORIAN, CURATOR
b New York, NY, July 28, 41. *Study:* Bryn Mawr Col, BA, 64; Winterthur Summer Inst, 67; Yale Univ Grad Sch, MPh, 70 & PhD, 76. *Pos:* Pub relations asst & registr, Corcoran Gallery Art, Washington, DC, 64-66; asst to dir, Nat Portrait Gallery, Washington, DC, 71-77, assoc cur, 77-84, cur, 84- *Mem:* Col Art Asn; Am Soc Eighteenth Century Studies; Walpole Soc London. *Res:* Eighteenth and nineteenth century British and American portrait painting and drawing; profile portraits by C B J Fevret de Saint-Memin. *Publ:* auth, The Iveagh Bequest, Kenwood, Greater London Council (England): Thomas Hudson, 1701-1779, Portrait Painter and Collector, a bicentenary exhib, 79; Saint-Memin, Valdenuit, Lemet: Federal Profiles, Am Portrait Prints, Tenth Ann Print Conf, 84; coauth (with Richard H Saunders), American Colonial Portraits: 1700-1776, Smithsonian Press, 87; auth, Saint-Memin's Portraits of American Indians, 1804-1807, Am Art J, 88; contribr, American Portraits, 1720-1920: The Taste of the People, in Three Hundred Years of American Painting, The Montclair Art Mus Collection, Hudson Hills Press, 89. *Mailing Add:* c/o Nat Portrait Gallery Eighth & F Sts Washington DC 20560

MILES, JEANNE PATTERSON
PAINTER, SCULPTOR
b Baltimore, Md, 08. *Study:* George Washington Univ, BFA; Grande Chaumiere, Paris; also with Marcel Gromaire, Paris. *Work:* Guggenheim Mus, New York; Newark Mus; Munson Williams Proctor Mus, Utica, NY; Andrew C White Mus, Cornell Univ; Santa Barbara Mus, Calif. *Comn:* Mural designs for Kentile Co, Kansas City, 60, Los Angeles, 62 & Atlanta, Ga, 63; mural symbolic design, Chicago, 64 & room divider in geometric design, NY, 65. *Exhib:* Eight exhibs, Betty Parsons Gallery, New York, 43-82; Mysticism in Art, Rome-New York Found, Rome, 57; Geometric Art, Whitney Mus Am Art, New York, 63; The Square in Art Traveling Show, Am Fedn Art, 68-69; retrospective, Three American Purists, Mus Fine Arts, Springfield, Mass, 75; solo exhib, Marilyn Pearl Gallery, New York, 88-89; Am Abstract Artists traveling exhib, Europe, 88-92. *Collections Arranged:* Purist Painting Exhib, Yale Univ, 57. *Teaching:* Docent, Mus Non Objective Art, New York, 45-50; dir art dept, Moravian Col Women, 48-51; docent, Guggenheim Mus, New York, 51-52; asst dir painting & life drawing, Oberlin Col, 52-53; instr painting, NY Inst Technol, 68-69. *Awards:* C C Ladd Study Scholar, 39-40; Am Inst Arts & Lett Emergency Grant, 69; Mark Rothko Found Grant, 71. *Bibliog:* Article in Arts Mag, 11/79; Listing as Special Event, Art Gallery Guide, 11/79; article, New York Times, 79. *Mem:* Am Abstract Artists; Fine Arts Federation, NY. *Interests:* Research into use of mandala as an art form throughout history. *Publ:* Auth, article in Arts Mag, 4/77; Three America Purists (catalog), Springfield Mass Mus, 75; Past, Present & Peculiar (catalog), Ingber Gallery, 79; Page, American Women Painters, 82; illusr, cover, Art Gallery Guide, currently. *Dealer:* Betty Parsons Gallery 24 West 57th St New York NY 10022; Marilyn Pearl Gallery 420 W Broadway New York NY 10012. *Mailing Add:* 463 West St Apt A 1103 New York NY 10014

MILES, M MARIANNE See Marianne

MILES, SHEILA LEE
PAINTER, CURATOR
b Indianapolis, Ind, Aug 10, 52. *Study:* Purdue Univ, West Lafayette, Ind, BA, 73, MA, 74; Hans Hoffman Sch Art, Provincetown, Mass (scholar), 74. *Work:* Ferdinand Roten Galleries, Baltimore, Md; Purdue Univ, West Lafayette, Ind; Yellowstone Art Ctr, Billings, Mont; Hockaday Ctr Arts, Kalispell, Mont; Deaconness Hosp, Billings, Mont. *Exhib:* Provinctwon Art Asn & Mus, Mass, 74-78; one-woman shows, Custer Co Art Ctr, Miles City, 84, Yellowstone Art Ctr (with catalog), Billings, 84, Missoula Mus Arts, 86 & Paris Gibson Sq, Great Falls, 86, Mont; Coal Tax Collections, Yellowstone Art Ctr, Billings, Mont, 86; Owings-Dewey Fine Art, Santa Fe, NMex, 86, 87 & 88. *Pos:* Gallery dir, Provincetown Art Asn & Mus, 75-77 & Mont State Univ, 85-86; artist-in-residence, Mont Arts Coun-Custer Co Art Ctr, 83-84; cur, Yellowstone Art Ctr, 86- *Teaching:* Instr drawing & painting, Eastern Mont Col, 80-82 & 85; instr painting, Mont State Univ, Bozeman, 85-86. *Awards:* Individual Artists Fel, Mont Arts Coun, 84; Purchase Award, Coal tax grant, Yellowstone Art Ctr, Mont Arts Coun, 84; Hon Mention, Western States Arts Fedn, 88. *Bibliog:* Article, Prairie Artist: Sheila Miles, Miles City News, 83; Chris Meyers (auth), Sheila Miles, Billings Gazette, 84-89; Sheila Miles, The Missoulian, Missoula, Mont, 86. *Mem:* Arts Advocacy. *Media:* Vinylic and drawing media. *Dealer:* Owings-Dewey Fine Art 74 E San Francisco St Santa Fe NM 87501; Halsted Gallery 560 N Woodward Ave Birmingham MI 48011. *Mailing Add:* 945 E 31st St Billings MT 59101

MILEY, CHUCK (CHARLES) E
PAINTER, PRINTMAKER
b Ravenna, Ohio, Sept 18, 43. *Study:* Kent State Univ, Ohio, BS, 65; Rutgers Univ, with Peter Stroud & John Goodyear, MA, 76; Pratt Graphics Ctr, with Ryo Watanabe & Anna Wong, 80-82. *Work:* Mus Mod Art, New York; Office of the Mayor, New York; Taxation Bldg, Trenton, NJ; Butler Mus, Youngstown, Ohio; Carrier Found, Belle Mead, NJ. *Comn:* Print, Hyatt Hotels, New Brunswick, NJ, 89; Print, Apollo Muses, Gladstone, NJ, 90. *Exhib:* Metro Show, City Without Walls, Newark, NJ, 86; Sullivan Cole Gallery, New York, 88; Major Marks, Santo Domingo, 88; New Abstraction, Rabbet Gallery, 92; Spontaneous Combustion, Positive, Negative, Manhattan Graphics Ctr, 89 & 91; Earthworks '90, NJ Ctr Visual Arts, 90; NJ Printmaking Coun, 89, 90 & 92; one-man shows, Noho Gallery, 87, 88, 90 & 91. *Pos:* Vpres, Noho Gallery, 83-85; art dir, NJ Printmaking Coun, Somerville, NJ, 86-88; bd dirs, NJ Printmaking Coun, 86-91; grant review comt, Somerset Co Cultural & Heritage Comn, 89-92. *Teaching:* Print instr, Summer Arts Inst, Rutgers-Livingston, 80-; prof photo-processes, Pratt Graphics Ctr, 85-88; instr painting & drawing, NJ Ctr Visual Arts, Summit, 86-92; instr photoprocess, Manhattan Graphics Ctr, New York, 88- *Awards:* Governor's Teacher Recognition Award, 86-87; Newark Star Ledger Scholars Teacher Award, 88; Master teacher, NJ Arts Found, 87. *Bibliog:* Vivien Raynor (auth), Jersey City: Work of art fellows, NY Times, 7/10/83; Murray Cahill (auth), Oversized prints, Mason Gross Sch Arts Print Rev, spring 83. *Mem:* NJ Printmaking Coun (art dir, 86); Print Club Philadelphia; Int Graphic Arts Found; Mahatten Graphics Ctr. *Media:* Miscellaneous Media; Serigraphy, Miscellaneous Media. *Mailing Add:* 36 Olcott St Somerset NJ 08873

MILEY, LES
CERAMIST, EDUCATOR
b Petersburg, Ind, Nov 1, 34. *Study:* Purdue Univ, ceramics with Bill Farrell; Ind State Univ, BA & MA; Southern Ill Univ, with Nicholas Vergette & Brent Kington, MFA. *Work:* Ceramics Monthly Collection, Columbus, Ohio; Evansville Mus Arts & Sci, Ind; Sheldon Swope Mus, Terre Haute, Int; Ind Univ-Southeast, New Albany; Univ Wis, Plateville. *Comn:* Archit ceramics, Robert L Blaffer Trust, New Harmony, Ind, 74; wall sculpture, New Harmony Inn, Ind; Citizen's Bank, Evansville, Ind, 88. *Exhib:* Salzbrand '86, Handwerkskammer Galerie, Koblenz, Ger, 86; Clay Connection, Evansville Mus Arts & Sci; solo exhibs, Sheldon Swope Mus, Terre Haute, Ind, 87, Harry Knohr Gallery, Platteville, Wis, 87 & Floyd Co Mus, New Albany, Ind, 88; Paducah Art Guild Gallery, Ky, 88; Form & Function in Clay, Evansville Mus Arts & Sci, 89; Crosscurrents, Soaper Art Gallery, Henderson, Ky, 90; Celebration of Am Art, 91; Louisville Visual Art Assoc, 91; Functional Ceramics, Wayne Ctr Arts, Wooster, Ohio, 92. *Pos:* Dir, Blafter Trust ceramic workshop, New Harmony, Ind, 67- *Teaching:* Prof art, Univ Evansville, 61-, chmn dept, 65-66 & 69-86. *Awards:* Purchase Awards, Clayfest, Ind, 84 & 44th Wabash Valley Art Exhib, Sheldon Swope Mus, 86; Phi Kappa Phi Outstanding Faculty Award, 86. *Bibliog:* Thomas Schafer (auth), Pottery Decoration, 75 & Jack Troy (auth), Salt-Glazed Ceramics, 77, Watson-Guptill; M F Baugh (auth), article Ind Arts Mag, 12/90; Phil Rogers (auth), Ash Glazes, 91. *Mem:* Nat Coun Educ Ceramic Arts. *Media:* Clay, Watercolor. *Mailing Add:* 1212 S Plaza Dr Evansville IN 47715

MILEY, MIMI CONNEEN
CURATOR
b Bryn Mawr, Pa, Aug 17, 46. *Study:* Western Col, Oxford, Ohio, BA(art hist). *Collections Arranged:* Winter Scenes by 19th Century Lithographers, 74; Pennsylvania Folk Art (auth, catalog), Allentown Art Mus, Pa, 74; Discover Texture, 75-77, Discover Color, 77-78 & Discover Design Elements, 79-80; A Salute to Walter Emerson Baum, 76; Howard Chandler Christy: Artist-Illustrator of Style (auth, catalog), 77; The Perceptive Eye: Art-Math (auth, catalog), 79; Decorative Arts in Miniature, 82. *Pos:* Cur educ, Allentown Art Mus, Pa, 70-, chief cur, 91- *Mem:* Nat Arts Club; Am & Mid Atlantic Asn Mus. *Mailing Add:* Box 388 Allentown Art Mus Allentown PA 18105-0388

MILHOAN, RANDALL BELL
ADMINISTRATOR, PAINTER
b Overton, Nebr, Feb 24, 44. *Study:* Kearney State Teachers Col, 64; Univ Nebr, Lincoln, BFA, 68; Univ Calif, Santa Barbara, Calif Regents Scholar, 70; Montana State Univ, 77; Arizona Western Col, 84-87. *Work:* Sheldon Mem Gallery, Lincoln, Nebr; Joslyn Gallery, Omaha, Nebr; San Antonio Art Inst, Tex. *Comn:* Mural, Colo Coun Arts & Humanities, Vail; murals, Vail & Beaver Creek, Colo. *Exhib:* Michael Hendrix Collection, Miami, Fla, 87; Joan Robey Gallery, Denver, Colo, 88; Cabrillo Gallery, Santa Cruz, Calif, 88; J Cotter Gallery, Vail, Colo, 88; Milhoan Studios, Vail, Colo; and others. *Collections Arranged:* Santa Fe Festival of the Arts, NMex, 81; Colo Artists, Craftsman Asn Ann, Arvada, Colo, 85; Beaver Creek Arts Festival, 92. *Pos:* Founder & dir, Summervail Workshop for Art & Critical Studies, 71-85, pres & exec dir, Summervail Workshop Found, Inc, 84-85; dean, San Antonio Art Inst, 85-86; vpres, Int Marketing & Media, 86-88; owner/designer, Milhoan Studios, Vail, Colo; exec dir, Vail Arts Coun. *Teaching:* Instr advan studies & special proj painting, Colo Mountain Col, Vail Co, 70-, 2-dimensional studies, 70-84 & dir, 71-84; instr 2-dimensional studies, San Antonio Art Inst, 85-86. *Awards:* Purchase Award, Tenth Midwest Biennial, 68. *Bibliog:* James Phelan (producer), Summervail Workshop (film), Phelan Productions, 72; Mark Huffman (auth), Milhoan's contribution to the local CMC, The Vail Trail, 2/24/84; Irene Clurman (auth), Artists, teachers, converge at Vail workshop, Rocky Mountain News, 7/29/84. *Mem:* Col Art Asn Am; Vail Valley Arts Coun; Art in Public Places Board, Vail, Colo; Adv Bd Yuma Symp. *Media:* Acrylic, Oil. *Collection:* Contemporary American fine arts and crafts; primitive toys; masks from around the world. *Dealer:* J Cotter Gallery PO Box 385 Vail CO 81658. *Mailing Add:* 483 E Gore Creek Dr Box 1114 Vail CO 81658

MILLAR, ROBERT
CONCEPTUAL ARTIST
b Los Angeles, Calif, March 6, 58. *Study:* Cal State Univ, Northridge, BA, 80. *Work:* Newport Harbor Art Mus, Newport Beach, Calif; City & Co of San Francisco; Los Angeles Co Transportation Comn. *Comn:* Grand Ave Plaza, Pacific Atlas Corp, Los Angeles, 91; Waterfront Park, City of Santa Barbara, Calif, 91; Metro-Rail Sta, Los Angeles Co Transportation Comn, 91; Muni-Metro, San Francisco Public Utility Comn, 92; Rose Theatre Site, Imry Merchant, London, Eng, 92. *Exhib:* Robert Millar, Newport Harbor Art Mus, Newport Beach, Calif, 91; Systems, Los Angeles Munic Art Gallery, 91; Breaking Boundaries, Santa Monica Mus Art, Calif, 92; Rose, Rose Theatre Site, London, Eng, 92. *Bibliog:* Colin Gardner (auth), Robert Millar, Art Forum, 91; Susan Kandel (auth), Peculiarities of Perception, Los Angeles Times, 91; Peter Frank (auth), Robert Millar, Los Angeles Weekly, 91. *Dealer:* Thomas Solomon's Garage 928 N Fairfax Ave Los Angeles CA 90046. *Mailing Add:* PO Box 515 Manhattan Beach CA 90266

MILLARD, CHARLES WARREN, III
DIRECTOR, WRITER
b Elizabeth, NJ, Dec 20, 32. *Study:* Princeton Univ, BA; Harvard Univ, MA & PhD. *Pos:* Asst dir, Dumbarton Oaks, 64-66; dir, Washington Gallery Mod Art, 66-67; cur 19th century European art, Los Angeles Co Mus Art, 71-74; art ed, Hudson Rev, 72-87; chief cur, Hirshhorn Mus & Sculpture Garden, 74-86; dir, Ackland Art Mus, NC, 86- *Teaching:* Adj prof art hist, Johns Hopkins Univ, 82-86 & Univ NC Chapel Hill, 86- *Mem:* Asn Art Mus Dir. *Res:* Nineteenth century French sculpture, particularly Degas and Preault; various topics in modern painting and sculpture. *Publ:* Auth, Sculpture of Edgar Degas, Princeton Univ, 76; and many other articles & rev in var periodicals. *Mailing Add:* Ackland Art Mus Univ NC Campus Box 3400 Chapel Hill NC 27599-3400

MILLEA, TOM (THOMAS FRANCIS)
PHOTOGRAPHER
b Bridgeport, Conn, Sept 30, 44. *Study:* Univ Western Conn, BA, 66; studied with Paul Caponigro & H Jonathon Greenwald, 67-73. *Work:* Mus Mod Art, New York; Victoria & Albert Mus, London, Eng; Ctr Creative Photog, Univ Ariz, Tucson; Oakland Mus; Philadelphia Mus Art; Australian National Gallery, Canberra; New Zealand National Mus, Wellington; and many others. *Exhib:* Solo exhibs, Friends Photog, Carmel, Calif, 78, DeSaisset Art Mus, Santa Clara, Calif, 80, Arco Ctr Arts, Los Angeles, 80, Camden Arts Ctr, London, 81, Galerie au Poisson Rouge, Praz, Switz, 81, Ctr Creative Photog, Tucson, 82 & The Malone Gallery, Rochester, NY, 86; New Orleans Mus Art, 84; Light Gallery, New York, 84; G; The Weston Gallery, Inc, Carmel, Calif, 84; Monterey Peninsula Mus Art, 85; The Platinum Print, NJ State Mus, Trenton, 86; The Western Landscape (traveling), Int Ctr Photog, New York, 86; Polaroid Int Collection Exhib, 86; and many others. *Pos:* Cinematographer, Robert Fulton Co, Danbury, Conn, 68; photographer, United Aircraft, Sikorsky, Stratford, Conn, 68-69. *Teaching:* Instructor & guest lecturer at many universities, workshops and galleries, 75-84. *Awards:* Ruttenberg Grant, 82 & Publ Workshop Grant, 83, Friends Photog; Polaroid Grant, 85. *Bibliog:* John Hafey & Tom Shillea (auths), The Platinum Print, Rochester Inst Technol, 80; interview, New Pictorialist Soc, 83; Alan Plone (auth), The Life and Work of Tom Millea, Vis Art Films Inc, 84; rev, Rochester City Newspaper & Democrat & Chronicle, Rochester, NY, 12/85. *Mem:* Friends Photog; Soc Photog Educ. *Media:* Platinum, Palladium. *Publ:* Auth, The Technique of Platinum and Palladium, Platinum Workshops, 76; Death Valley Photographs (poster), Sunlight Graphics, 83. *Dealer:* Light Gallery 724 Fifth Ave New York NY; Weston Gallery Carmel CA. *Mailing Add:* PO Box 4281 Carmel CA 93921

MILLER, ARTHUR GREEN
EDUCATOR, HISTORIAN
b New York, NY, May 19, 42. *Study:* Harvard Univ, PhD, 69. *Collections Arranged:* Maya Rulers of Time (auth catalog), Tikal Architectural Sculpture, Univ Mus, Univ Pa, 86. *Pos:* Dir, Maya Art prog, Univ Mus, Univ Pa, 79-82; dir of studies, Ecole des Hautes Etudes, Paris, 88- *Teaching:* Instr, asst prof art history, Yale Univ, 68-73; prof, Latin Am art history & archeology, Univ Maryland, Col Park, 83- *Awards:* Award, Guggenheim, 73; Grants, Nat Endowment Arts, 79, Nat Endowment Humanities 89-92. *Bibliog:* Esther Pasztory (auth), Mural painting of Teotihuacan J, Soc of Archit Hist, ArtBulletin, 74; Clemency Coggins (auth), On the Edge of the Sea, Am Antiquity, 83; William Fash (auth), Maya Rulers of Time, Am Antiquity, 88. *Mem:* Col Art Asn; Soc for Am Archeology. *Res:* Art history and archeology of pre-hispanic and early colonial Latin American; interaction between image and text communication systems. *Publ:* Auth, The Mural Painting of Teotihuacan Mexico, Dumbarton Oaks, 73; ed, The Codex Nuhall: A Picture Manuscript from Ancient Mexico, Dover Publ, 75; auth, On the Edte of the Sea, Dumbarton Oaks, 82; ed, Highland-Lowland Interaction in Mexiamerica: Interdisciplinary Approaches, Dumbarton Oaks, 83; auth, Maya Rulers of Time: Architectural Sculpture from Tikal, Guatemala, Univ Pa, 86. *Mailing Add:* 2040 Pine St Philadelphia PA 19103

MILLER, BARBARA DARLENE
PAINTER, PRINTMAKER
b Jarbidge, Nev. *Study:* Univ Wash, BA; Univ Hawaii, MEd; etching with Rudy Pozzatti & Gabor Peterdi; design with Clayton Rippey; painting with Tadashi Sato & Tseng Yu-Ho. *Work:* State Found Cult & Arts, Honolulu; Univ Hawaii Art Dept Etching Collection. *Comn:* Acrylic mural, KPOI Radio, Waikiki, Honolulu, 68; Christ with Thorns (acrylic painting), Church of Good Shepherd, Kahului, Maui, 70; Buddha (acrylic painting), Kahului Hongwanji Mission, Maui, 72; Mosaics (film), State Found & Maui Arts Coun, 72. *Exhib:* Walker Art Ctr Nat, Minneapolis, 65; Painters of Hawaii Circulating Exhib, 69; Etchings, Hawaii State Libr, 70; Regional Ethel Baldwin Mem, Wailuku, 72-81; Art Maui, Hawaii State Invitational Show, 81; plus others; Invitational Show, Honolulu Cult Plaza, 82. *Pos:* Artist, Logos Layouts, KPOI Radio, 65-67; art dir, KHVH Radio-TV, Honolulu, 67-68. *Teaching:* Art instr, Hilo High Sch, 57-60; elem art specialist, Kahului Elem Sch, 64-68; art instr & art program coordr, Maui Community Col, 68- *Awards:* Hawaii Artists Exhibs Awards & Prizes, 65-77; State Found Cult & Art Purchase Award, 72; Grand Prize, Best in Show, Hui Noeau Art Soc, 77. *Bibliog:* Eileen Webster (auth), Milady of the week--Barbara Miller, 68 & Darrell Neilson (auth), Works of Mrs Miller, 68, Maui News; Tim Mitchell (auth), Art news--Barbara Miller painter, Honolulu Mag, 69. *Mem:* Maui Arts Coun (visual arts chmn, 68-80); Hui Noeau Art Soc; Nat Art Educ Asn; Maui Mayors' Comt Cult and Art. *Media:* Acrylic, Intaglio. *Publ:* Illusr cover, Festival of Arts, 69; coauth, Grass Roots, Poetry & Art, 70; illusr cover, Our Changing Times, Univ Hawaii Div Continuing Educ, 70. *Dealer:* Village Gallery-Whalers Village Kaanapali Maui HI 96753. *Mailing Add:* Maui Community Col 310 Kaahumanu Ave Kahului HI 96732

MILLER, BRENDA
SCULPTOR, CONCEPTUAL ARTIST
b Bronx, NY. *Study:* Univ NMex, BFA, 65; Tulane Univ, MFA, 67. *Work:* Mus Boymans-Van Beuningen, Rotterdam, Holland; Haag Gemeente Mus, Holland; Hartford Atheneum, Conn; Univ Tex, Austin; Newport Harbor Art Mus, Newport Beach, Calif. *Comn:* A is for Anonymous, (pvt collection), Block Island, RI, 91. *Exhib:* solo exhib, Whitney Mus Am Art, 75; Portland Ctr Visual Art, 78; The Minimal Tradition, Aldrich Mus Contemp Art, 79; Cable Gallery, NY, 88; Dross to Art, Islip Art Mus, 89; The Fetish of Knowledge, Real Art Ways, Hartford, Conn, 91; AC Project Rm, New York, 92; Transparency, Luise Ross Gallery, New York, 92. *Teaching:* Cooper Union, 67-68 & 80; State Univ NY, Stony Brook, 72-79, Old Westbury, 75. *Awards:* Creative Artists Pub Serv Grant, 75; Fels, Guggenheim Found, 78; Nat Endowment Arts, 76, 79 & 87-88. *Bibliog:* Susan Tower (auth), The object perceived, the object apprehended, Art Forum, Vol XII, No 5, 74; Lucy Lippard (auth), Brenda Miller: Woven stamped, Art in Am, Vol 64, No 3, 76; Ted Castle (auth), About Brenda Miller & her art, Mus J, Ser 22, No 1, 77. *Mem:* Am Abstract Artists; Women's Art Coun. *Media:* All. *Publ:* Auth, Vertical Alphabet SE, pvt publ, 90; Transparent Vertical Alphabet SE (26) pvt publ, 91. *Mailing Add:* 36 W 26th St New York NY 10010

MILLER, DANIEL DAWSON
PRINTMAKER, SCULPTOR
b Pittsburgh, Pa, July 7, 28. *Study:* Lafayette Col, BA, 51; Pa State Univ, summers with Hobson Pittman; Pa Acad Fine Arts, 55-59; Univ Pa, MFA, 58. *Work:* Pa Acad Fine Arts, Philadelphia; Philadelphia Mus Art; Rutgers Mus, New Brunswick, NJ; Wilmington Soc Fine Arts, Del; Dickinson Col, Carlisle, Pa. *Exhib:* 11 Modern American Artists, Rahr Mus, Manitowoc, Wis, 63; 158th-162nd Ann Exhib, Pa Acad Fine Arts, Philadelphia, 63-67; one-man shows, Peale House, Pa Acad Fine Arts, 67, Drexel Inst, 68, Rutgers Mus, Rutgers Univ, 70, Univ Maine, 72 & Rosenfeld Gallery, Philadelphia, Pa, 81, 84 & 92. *Pos:* Asst dean faculty, Pa Acad Fine Arts, 83-86, actg dir, 84-85, head painting dept, 86- *Teaching:* Instr life painting, Pa Acad Fine Arts, 64-; instr art & head fine arts dept, Eastern Col, St Davids, Pa, 64-85; instr woodcut, Pa Acad Fine Arts, 83- *Awards:* Prize for Oil, Del Ann, Del Soc Fine Arts, 60; May Audubon Post Prize, 61, Bertha M Goldberg Mem Award, 70 & 75, Leona Karp Brauerman Prize, 76 & Percy Owens Award, 86, Fel Pa Acad Fine Arts. *Mem:* Philadelphia Watercolor Club; Am Color Print Soc. *Media:* All. *Dealer:* Rosenfeld Gallery 113 Arch St Philadelphia PA 19106. *Mailing Add:* Box 41 Christiana PA 17509

MILLER, DOLLY (ETHEL B)
PAINTER, COLLAGE ARTIST
b Johnstown, Pa, June 14, 27. *Study:* Brooklyn Col, NY, BA(chemistry); NY Univ, MA(Fr lit); art hist, The Sorbonne & the Louvre, Paris, France; studied painting with Andre Lhote, Paris; Art Students League, with Julian Levi; also with Leo Manso, NY Univ. *Work:* Johnson & Johnson, Surgico, Inc, Piscataway, NJ; The Friends Acad, Locust Valley, NY. *Exhib:* Stratton Mt Arts Festival, 81, Goddard Col, Plainfield, Wood Art Gallery, Montpelier, State House, Montpelier, Vt Studio Sch Statewide, Johnson, Vt; one-person shows, Vt Conserv Arts, 84, Culinary Inst, Montpelier, 85, N Country Hosp Gallery, Newport, 85, Vt Coun Arts Montpelier, Cornelia St Cafe, Greenwich Village, New York; Northeast Open, Worcester, Mass, 86; N Country Hosp, Newport, Vt, 88; Wickwire Gallery, Lyndon State Col, Lyndonville, Vt, 90. *Awards:* Candidates for Art Award, Am Acad Nat Inst Art, New York, 76; Salmagundi Club Award, Nat Acad Galleries, 79; Vt Studio Sch Residency Grant, 86. *Mem:* Audubon Artists, Inc; Art Students League New York; Art Resources Asn Vt. *Media:* Oil. *Mailing Add:* RFD One PO Box 448 Barton VT 05822

MILLER, DONALD
CRITIC, WRITER
b Pittsburgh, Pa, Dec 21, 34. *Collections Arranged:* Malcolm Purcell, Carnegie-Mellon Univ, 82 & Butler Inst Am Art, Youngstown, Ohio, 86. *Pos:* Art critic, Pittsburgh Post-Gazette, 66- *Teaching:* Instr 19th & 20th century art, Carnegie-Mellon Univ, 79-80; instr tiffany stained glass, Univ Pittsburgh, 90- *Awards:* Golden Quill Award, Pittsburgh Press Club, 80, 86; Forbes Gold Medal, 86. *Bibliog:* Amy Laurent-Vanderah (auth), Art surgeon, Pittsburgh Mag, 81. *Mem:* Friends Art Pittsburgh Pub Schs; hon mem Assoc Artists Pittsburgh. *Publ:* Auth, Irene Rice Pereira, 78, Eduardo Chillida, 79 & Gary Jurysta, 79, Arts Mag; co-auth, Organic Vision: Architecture of Peter Berndtson, 80; auth, A W Mellon Charitable Trust 1930-1980, Davis & Warde, 81; Malcolm Purcell: Wizard of Moon Lorn, 85. *Mailing Add:* Pittsburgh Post-Gazette Pittsburgh PA 15222

MILLER, DONALD LLOYD
PAINTER, MURALIST
b Chapleton, Jamaica, June 30, 23; US citizen. *Study:* Cooper Union, 49; Art Students League, study with Frank Riley, Isaac Muse, Edna Manley & Betty Dotson. *Work:* Smithsonian Inst, Washington, DC; Newark Mus, NJ; NJ State Mus, Trenton, Anchorage Mus. *Comn:* Portraits, Douglas Col, Rutgers Univ, New Brunswick, NJ, 80, Cornell Univ, Ithaca, NY, 85, Seton Hall Univ, South Orange, NJ, 87 & Montclair State Col, NJ, 87-89; Mural, DC Pub Libr, Washington, DC, 86. *Exhib:* Montclair Art Mus, NJ, 62-66; Newark Mus, NJ, 70; Denver Art Mus, Colo, 71; The Children of Africa, Mus Nat Hist, New York, 71; Robeson Gallery, Rutgers Univ, Newark, NJ, 84; solo exhib, The Making of the King, Newark Mus, NJ, 86, Trenton Mus, 87. *Pos:* Art dir, Chernow Agency, New York, 50-52; art dir & illusr, Black, Star & Gorham, New York, 53-57; freelance illusr, Don Miller Studio, Montclair, NJ, 57-81. *Teaching:* Instr graphics & painting, Nigerian Television Authority, Lagos, Nigeria, 81-82; instr mural painting, Newark Sch of Fine & Industrial Art, 90-91. *Awards:* Best in Show, Denver Mus, Colo, 71. *Bibliog:* Gil Noble (dir), Don Miller, Artist (film), ABC-TV, 73; Robin Longman (auth), People, places & events, Am Artist, 1/86. *Mem:* Soc Illusrs, Arts Council of Essex Area. *Media:* Oil, Watercolor. *Publ:* Illusr, Proudly We Hail, Houghton Mifflin, 69; Daniel Hale Williams, Open Heart Doctor, McGraw-Hill, 71; Between the Devil and the Sea, Harcourt Brace and Jovanovich, 72; Haji of the Elephants, McGraw-Hill, 76; Jocko, A Legend of the American Revolution, Prentice-Hall, 76. *Mailing Add:* 14 Stanford Pl Montclair NJ 07042

MILLER, ELAINE SANDRA
PAINTER, PRINTMAKER
b Philadelphia, Pa. *Study:* Drexel Univ, BS, 51; Cheltenham Ctr for Arts, with G Noble Wagner, Jimmy Leuders & Paul Gorka, 71-84. *Work:* Siemens Corp Int; Rion Corp Ltd, Tokyo, Japan. *Exhib:* Solo Exhib, Philadelphia Art Alliance, 81; Sarah Lawrence Col, NY, 92; Nat Mus Am Jewish Hist, Philadelphia, 92; Nat Soc Painters in Casein & Acrylic, NY, 92; Am Color Print Soc, St Petersburg State Mus, Russia, 93. *Teaching:* Teacher art, Forman Hebrew Day Sch, Pa, 80-82; Philadelphia Sch Sys, 81-82. *Awards:* Second Prize, Am Color Print Soc, 91; Beatrice Feldman Mem Award, Abington Art Ctr, Pa, 91; Third Prize, Philadelphia, Sketch Club, Pa, 91. *Mem:* Philadelphia Art Alliance; Nat Asn Women Artists; Am Color Print Soc; Cheltenham Ctr Arts (bd mem, 82-90); Artists Cult Exchange (pres, 87-90). *Media:* Acrylic; All Media. *Mailing Add:* 1003 Indian Creek Rd Jenkintown PA 19046

MILLER, F JOHN
PAINTER, MOSAIC ARTIST
b London, Eng, Apr 21, 29; Can citizen. *Study:* Ealing Sch Art, London, NDD, 50; Hornsey Col Art, London, ATD, 51; Emma Lake Workshops, Sask, with Clement Greenberg & Barnett Newman, 60-61. *Work:* Mus Quebec; Can Coun Art Bank, Ottawa, Ont; Concordia Univ, Montreal; Mus de Beaux Arts, Montreal. *Comn:* Mosaic murals, Govt Saskatchewan, Regina, 60-61, Catholic Church, Sask, 64 & Govt Nebr, 67. *Exhib:* Solo exhibs, Galerie Libre Montreal, 68 & Concordia Univ, 73 & 80, Espace 1428, Montreal, 88 Galerie Dan Delaney Westmount, Que, 88; Mus Art Contemp, Montreal, 67 & 69; Spring Show, Queen's Univ, Kingston, Ont, 69; Summer Show, Nat Gallery Art, Ottawa, 72. *Pos:* Dir design prog, NS Col Art, 63-65; vis prof art, Mount St Vincent Univ, NS, 63-65; prof painting, Concordia Univ, 65-, chmn dept painting & drawing, 83-85. *Awards:* Prize Winner, Sask Arts Bd, 60; Prize Winner, Art Actuel au Quebec, Govt Que, 67. *Bibliog:* Guy Robert (auth), Art Actuel au Quebec, Iconia Press, 83. *Mem:* Founding mem, Can Soc Educ Through Art, Regina, Sask; Composers Authors & Publishers Asn Can; founding mem, Can Electro-Acoustic Community. *Media:* Oil, Alkyd. *Publ:* Illusr, Gammer Glover's Grammar, Fortune Press, London, 52. *Mailing Add:* 19 Mountainview St Stanstead PQ J0B 3E0 Canada

MILLER, (RICHARD) GUY
SCULPTOR
b Pittsburgh, Pa. *Study:* City & Guilds of London Art Coun, Eng, with Ennis Fripps, 58; Art Students League, New York, with Will Barnet & Robert Hale; Pratt Inst, Brooklyn, NY, with Calvin Albert, MFA, 65. *Work:* State Univ NY Col New Paltz; Pratt Inst, Brooklyn; New Sch, New York; Bennington Col, Vt; Long Island Hall Fame, Stony Brook, NY. *Comn:* stainless steel wall sculpture, New Sch, New York, 74; free standing stainless steel dual form, Sky Island Club, Plainview, NY, 79; free standing painted steel sculpture, Atrium, Jericho, NY, 85; free standing brass sculpture, Tower Apartment, Fort Lee, NJ, 87; brass wall sculpture, New York, 88; and others. *Exhib:* Cochise Col, Douglas, Ariz, 87; Copper Village Art Mus, Anaconda, Mont, 88; Missoula Mus Art, Mont, 88; Orr's Bailey Art Asn, Orr's Island, Maine, 89-92; Maine Arts Festival, Thomas Point, Maine, 92; and many others. *Teaching:* Instr sculpture, Pratt Inst, Brooklyn, summer 64; prof art, Monmouth Col, West Long Branch, NJ, 64-65, prof sculpture, 66-69; artist-in-residence, Friends World Col, Lloyd Harbor, NY, 77-79. *Awards:* MacDowell Colony Found Fel, 68; Award, Long Island Hall Fame, Sky Island Club, 79; Award, Guild Hall Ann Exhib, East Hampton, NY 81; and others. *Bibliog:* Jeanne Paris (auth), Emotional sculpture, 8/79, Malcolm Preston (auth), Public building as a gallery, 8/81, Newsday; Sculpture Mather Hospital, NY Times, 7/82; Dictionary of American Sculptures, 84-85; Discription of Sculpture, 11/86 & Clint Hagen (auth), Miller, 9/92, Time Rec; Brian Bixler (auth), Flotsam and jetsam, Fla Today, 1/91; and others. *Mem:* Art Students League, New York; Huntington Twp Art League, NY (bd dirs, 78-81); Orrs Bailey Art Asn (chmn bd dirs). *Media:* Stainless Steel; Lucite. *Mailing Add:* PO Box 95 Orrs Island ME 04066

MILLER, INGE MORATH See Morath, Inge

MILLER, JANET
ADMINISTRATOR, BOOK DEALER
b Pittsburgh, Pa, May 28, 54. *Study:* Chatham Col, BA, 76; Am Univ, MA, 78; Columbia Univ, MS, 86. *Collections Arranged:* Celebrating Our Diversity: An Exhibit Honoring Harold Washington, 88. *Pos:* Cur visual materials, Univ Iowa, Iowa City, 79-82; nat off adminr, Women's Caucus Art, Philadelphia, 84-86; archivist & registr, dept anthrop, Field Mus, Chicago, 86- 89; Dir/Archivist, Medical Col Pa, 89- *Teaching:* Instr, Women in Medicine: 1850-1950, 89- *Awards:* New York Libr Asn-Jr Members Roundtable Grant, 85; Am Asn Univ Women Grant, 85. *Mem:* Col Art Asn; Am Asn for Hist Med; Soc Am Archivists; Oral Hist Asn; Orgn Am Historians. *Publ:* Ed, Hue Points, Women's Caucus for Art, 85-86; contibr, bk reviews, Collection Forum, 87-89; Centennial Publ, Am Asn Univ Women, Chicago, 89; Lesbian History Archives Newsletter, 90. *Mailing Add:* Medical Col Pennsylvania 3300 Henry Avenue Pittsburgh PA 19127

MILLER, JEAN JOHNSTON
LIBRARIAN, HISTORIAN
b New York, NY, Feb 19, 18. *Study:* Barnard Col, AB, 39. *Pos:* Art librn, Univ Hartford, West Hartford, Conn, 64- *Mem:* Art Libr Soc N AM. *Mailing Add:* 47 Pratt St Rocky Hill CT 06067

MILLER, JOAN L
PAINTER, COLLAGE ARTIST
b New York, NY, Nov 9, 30. *Study:* Brooklyn Mus with Gregorio Prestopino, 47; Parsons Sch Design; Tyler Sch Art Temple Univ, BFA, 52. *Work:* Butler Inst, Youngstown, Ohio; Slater Mem Mus, Norwich, Conn; Philadelphia Mus Art, Lending Libr, Pa. *Exhib:* Group drawing shows, Cocoran Gallery, Washington, DC, 53 & Brooklyn Mus, NY, 55; group womens int show, Palazzo Vecchio, Florence, Italy, 65; Nat Asn Women Artists, Nat Acad, New York, 65-80; 4-person invitational show, Port Wash Libr, NY, 70; solo exhibs, Graphic Eye Gallery, Port Wash, NY, 75 & 77 and Phoenix Art Gallery, New York, 78, 81 & 83; Benson Gallery, Bridgehampton, NY, 86, 88, 90; Books & Co, 92, Donnell Libr, New York, 92. *Awards:* Cash award, Soc Painters Casein, Nat Arts Club, 69; cash award, Ann Exhib, Nat Asn Women Artists. *Mem:* Nat Asn Women Artists (graphic jury, 85-88). *Media:* Acrylic, Collage on Paper. *Publ:* Reproduction of work in book Intaglio Printmaking Techniques by Ruth Leaf, Watson Guptill, 76. *Mailing Add:* 1192 Park Ave New York NY 10028

MILLER, JOAN VITA
MUSEUM DIRECTOR, ADMINISTRATOR
b New York, NY, Jan, 46. *Study:* Syracuse Univ, BA(art hist), MA(art hist); independent res in Italy. *Collections Arranged:* New York Eleven, 74; Louise Nevelson (auth, catalogue), 74; Gertrude Stein and Her Friends (auth, catalogue), 75; Wreck, 75; The Long Island Art Collector's Exhibit (auth, catalogue), 75; European Masters in Portraiture, 76; An Exploration of Photography 1839-1976 (auth, catalogue), 76; The Arts of China, 77; Marsden Hartley, 1877-1943, 77; Double Exposure: Alfredo Valente as Photographer and Collector, 78; The First 4000 Years: The Ratner Collection of Judaean Antiquities, 79; Realist Space, 79; African Sculpture: The Shape of Surprise, 80; Auguste Rodin, 80 & 81; Rodin: B Gerald Cantor Collection, Metrop Mus Art (auth, catalog), 86. *Pos:* Asst dir, Michael Rockefeller Arts Ctr, State Univ NY Col, Fredonia, 71-72; dir gallery & cur permanent collection, C W Post Art Gallery, C W Post Col, 73-80; dir, B G Cantor Sculpture Ctr, New York, 80-83, cur B G Cantor Collections, 83-89; mus & gallery mgr, C W Post Col, Long Island Univ, 76-80. *Mem:* Am Asn Mus; College Art Asn. *Mailing Add:* c/o Dr Gary Marotta Univ Southwestern Louisiana, VPres Office Lafayette LA 70504

MILLER, JOHN
PAINTER
b 1954. *Study:* RI Sch Design, Providence, BFA, 77; Whitney Mus Am Art Independent Study Prog, New York, 78; Calif Inst Arts, Valencia, MFA, 79. *Exhib:* 1985 Biennial, Group Material Sect, Whitney Mus Am Art, NY Metro Pictures, 85 & Biennial Exhib, 91; one-man shows, Standard Graphik, Cologne, 90, Metro Pictures, New York, 84, 85, 86, 88, 90, Roy Boyd Gallery, Santa Monica, Calif, 91, Andrea Rosen Gallery, New York, 91, DAAD, Berlin, 92, Bruno Burnnet Fine Arts, Berlin, 92 & Jablonla Galerie, Cologne, 92; Currents, Inst Contemp Art, Boston, 91; Lost Illusions, Vancouver Art Gallery, BC, 91; The Other Side, Tony Shafrazi Gallery, New York, 92; Schürmann Sammlung, Ludwig Forum für Internationale Kunst, Aachen, Ger, 92; Re: Framing Cartoons, Wexner Art Ctr, Ohio State Univ, Columbus, 92; and others. *Awards:* Fel, Nat Endowment Arts, 87. *Bibliog:* Jutta Koether (auth), John Miller in New York, Texte zur Kunst, pp 169-70, winter 91; Steve Kaplan (auth), John Miller, Etc Montreal, pp 36-38, spring 91; Catherine Liu (auth), Just Pathetic at American Fine Arts, Rock Sucks, Disco Sucks, exhib catalogue, DAAD Berlin, Artforum, pp 95-96, 4/92. *Publ:* Auth, The Death of Tragedy, Nachschub (exhib catalog), Koln, 90; Art Supplies and Utopia (exhib catalog), Ralph Wernicke, Stuttgart, 90; Formalism and Its Other, (catalog essay), Jessica Stockholder, Witte de With, Rotterdam, 91. *Mailing Add:* Metro Pictures 150 Greene St New York NY 10012

MILLER, JOHN FRANKLIN
ADMINISTRATOR
b Hagerstown, Md, June 4, 40. *Study:* St Johns Col, Annapolis, BA, 62; Yale Univ, with Edgar Munhall, 65; Univ Md, with Ruth Butler, 69-72. *Work:* Hampton Nat Historic Site, Md; Stan Hywet Hall Foundation, Ohio. *Pos:* Resident cur, Hampton Nat Historic Site, Md, 72-75, admin, 76-79; cur of educ, Stan Hywet Hall Foundation, Akron, Ohio, 79-80, exec dir, 81. *Mem:* Am Asn Mus; Nat Trust for Hist Preserv; Am Asn State and Local Hist; Intermuseum Conserv Asn (trustee, 81). *Res:* European and domestic architecture of the late 17th and early 18th centuries and its influence in America. *Mailing Add:* c/o Stan Hywet Hall & Gardens 714 Portage Path Akron OH 44303

MILLER, JOHN PAUL
JEWELER
b Huntingdon, Pa, Apr 23, 18. *Study:* Cleveland Inst Art, cert indust design; and with Baron Eric Fleming. *Work:* Cleveland Mus Art, Ohio; Mus Contemp Crafts, New York; Huntington Gallery, WVa; Minn Mus, St Paul. *Exhib:* Int Jewelry Exhib, London, 61; Objects USA Traveling Exhib, US, Europe & Japan, 69; 15 Jewelers, Schmuck-Objekte, Mus Bellevive, Zurich, 71; Masterworks of Contempory American Jewelry, Victoria & Albert Mus, London, 85; The Eloquent Object, Philbrook Mus, Tulsa, Okla, Traveling Exhib, 88; Am Craftsmen, Vatican Mus, Rome, Italy, 78. *Pos:* Gallery dir, Cleveland Inst Art, 60-81. *Teaching:* Instr design & jewelry, Cleveland Inst Art, 40-83. *Bibliog:* Von Neumann (auth), Design and Creation of Jewelry, Chilton, 61; Graham Hughes (auth), Modern Jewelry, Crown; Wolters (auth), Die Granulation, Callwey, Ger, 83; Oppi Untracht (auth), Jewelry Concepts & Technol, Doubleday, 82. *Mem:* Fel Am Craftsmen Coun; Soc N Am Goldsmiths. *Mailing Add:* 9333 Highland Dr Brecksville OH 44141

MILLER, KATHRYN
PAINTER, PRINTMAKER
b Philadelphia, Pa, June 21, 35. *Study:* Univ NC, BA, 57; Ga Southern Col, 69; Savannah Col Art & Design, Ga, 79-80. *Work:* Waycross Junior Col, Ga; Savannah Col Art & Design; Marion Co Mus, SC. *Comn:* Delta Corp, Hilton Head Island, SC, 84 & 86. *Teaching:* Instr, Armstrong State Col, Savannah, Ga, 87-88 & Trenholm Artists Guild Workshop, 88. *Awards:* Second Place, Mandarin Art Asn, 86; Award of Distinction, Tarpon Springs, 89; First Place Graphics, Atalaya Art Festival, 90 & 91. *Mem:* Ga Watercolor Soc; Southeastern Watercolor Soc; SC Crafts Asn; Savannah Art Asn; Hilton Head Art Asn. *Media:* Watercolor; Copper Etching. *Dealer:* Tatler Gallery Hilton Head Island SC 29928. *Mailing Add:* 2 Stillwood Court S Savannah GA 31419

MILLER, LARRY
PAINTER, VIDEO ARTIST
b Marshall, Mo, 1944. *Study:* Southwestern Mo State Col, BFA, 68; Rutgers Univ, MFA, 70. *Exhib:* Good Buy Supermarket, Copenhagen, Denmark, 92; Fluxus Concert, Anthology Film Archives, New York, 92; Excellent 1992, Three Stars a la carte, Judson Mem Church, New York, 92; 10 Steps, Horodner Romley Gallery, New York, 92; exhibs at var maj mus incl Mus Mod Art; and others. *Awards:* Creative Artists Prog Grant, 78; Nat Endowment Arts Artist's Fel, 79 & 89; NY State Found Arts Fel, 85. *Bibliog:* Jan van Toorn (ed), Fluxus Audio Issue, Slowscan Editions, Den Bosch, Holland, 92; Christel Schüppenhauer, Cologne, Ger, 92; Estera Milman (ed), Fluxus: A Conceptual Country, Visible Language, Vol 26, No 1/2, Providence, RI, 92; and others. *Publ:* Knives, 73; The Suitcase, 73; Discourse on All & Everything, 80; Accord, 81; Only One, 89; and others. *Dealer:* Volatile Gallery PO Box 3274 Cincinnati OH 45201. *Mailing Add:* 107 W 28th St New York NY 10001

MILLER, LAURENCE GLENN
GALLERY DIRECTOR, PHOTOGRAPHER
b New York, NY, Oct 8, 48. *Study:* Univ Wis, BS, 72, MA, 73; Univ NMex, 74. *Work:* Art Inst Chicago; Madison Art Ctr, Wis; Northwestern Univ Libr; Univ Wis, Madison; C W Post Col. *Exhib:* Photography West, Utah State Univ, Logan, 74; The Book--A New Direction for Photography, Quivira Gallery, Albuquerque, 74; Five Color Photographers, Jorgenson Gallery, Univ Conn, Storrs, 77; The Great American Foot, Contemp Crafts Mus, New York, 78; Attitudes: Photography in the 1970s, Santa Barbara Mus Art, 79; Industrial Sites, Whitney Mus, New York, 79. *Pos:* Assoc dir, Light Gallery, New York, 74-80; dir, Laurence Miller Gallery, New York, 84- *Teaching:* Instr hist photog, New Sch Social Res, 76-80; vis prof, Univ Tex, San Antonio, 80. *Awards:* Creative Artists Pub Serv Grant, 77-78. *Mem:* Asn Int Photog Art Dealers (bd dirs, 83-85). *Specialty:* Contemporary art, especially photography. *Publ:* Auth, More galleries, but the competition is keen, New York Times, 75. *Mailing Add:* 138 Spring St New York NY 10012

MILLER, LEON GORDON
PRINTMAKER
b Aug 3, 17; US citizen. *Study:* NJ State Teachers Col, BS; Newark Fine & Indust Art; Fawcett Art Sch, w Bernar Gusso w, Baldwin Wallace Col, DFA, 71; Kean Col, DFA, 73. *Work:* Libr Cong, Washington, DC; Gertrude Stein Collection; Yale Univ Comm; and others. *Comn:* Free standing bronze area sculpture, New Law Sch, Cleveland State Univ; cut & inlaid wood mosaic sculpture bas-relief, Capital Nat Bank, Cleveland, Ohio; ceramic tile murals, Mosaic Tile Co, Cleveland & New York, 6 color serigraphs for arts publication by Union Am Hebrew Congregation, 77; metal wall sculpture & free stand area, sculpture, Avis Nat Hq, NY; wall tapestries, Cuyahoga Community Col, Ohio, Relig Insts, Ga, Iowa, Ky, Mass & Omaha. *Exhib:* Close Ups, Photography, US Embassy, Cleveland, Ohio, 72; Interfaith Conf Relig Arts Exhib, Ohio, 75; 15 one-man shows, Teaching Inst Indust Design, Hollywood Art Culture Ctr, Hollywood, Fla, 84. *Pos:* Pres Leon Gordon Miller Assocs Inc, 47-80; founder, K V Design Int Ltd, 71; bd mem, Rose Art Mus, 72; US designs rep 59-74. *Awards:* Outstanding Arts Alumnus Award, Kean Col, NJ, 73; Kean Col, LHD, 74; Am Graphic Arts Award, Coun Advan Educ, 75. *Media:* Serigraphs, Watercolor. *Mailing Add:* c/o Gertrude Freeman 3192 Yattika Pl Longwood FL 32779

MILLER, MARC H
CURATOR, WRITER
b New York, NY, June 28, 46. *Study:* Univ Calif, Riverside, BA, 67; NY Univ, Inst Fine Arts, MA, 71, PhD, 79. *Collections Arranged:* Punk Art (auth, catalog) Wash Proj Arts, 78; Unforgettable Moments, ABC No Rio Gallery, 82; Television's Impact on Contemp Art (auth, catalog), Queens Mus, 86; Archit Models from the Last Decade (ed, catalog), Queens Mus, 87; Lafayette, Hero of Two Worlds (ed, catalog), Queens Mus, 89. *Pos:* Prog dir, Art-New York, Inner Tube Video, 81-85; contrib ed, East Village Eye, New York, 82-86; cur, Queens Mus, NY, 85- *Teaching:* Instr art hist, Sch Visual Arts, New York, 76-80; asst prof, St Johns Univ, NY, 82-85. *Awards:* Smithsonian Inst Fel, 74 & 76. *Res:* 19th and 20th Century art reflecting broader political and social phenomenon. *Publ:* Auth, 25 years of Space Photog, Nieuwe Revu, Holland, 82; co-ed, ABC No Rio Dinero: the Story of a Lower East Side Art Gallery, ABC No Rio, 85. *Mailing Add:* Queens Mus Art Flushing NY 11368

MILLER, MELISSA WREN
PAINTER
b Houston, Tex, Mar 3, 51. *Study:* Univ NMex, BFA, 74. *Work:* Mus Fine Arts, Houston; Mus Mod Art, NY; San Francisco Mus Mod Art; The Contemp Mus, Honolulu, Hawaii; Fort Worth Art Mus. *Exhib:* Solo exhibs, Melissa Miller: A Survey 1978-1986 (with catalog), Albright Knox Art Gallery, Buffalo, Contemp Art Mus, Houston, 81, Fort Worth Mus, Tex & Art Mus STex, Corpus Christi, 81; Whitney Biennial Exhib, Whitney Mus Am Art, 83; Biennial III, San Francisco Mus Mod Art, 84; Venice Bienniale, Italy, 84; Fresh Paint, Mus Fine Art, 85. *Pos:* Distinguished vis prof Art, SMU, 90. *Awards:* Nat Endowment Arts Grants, 79, 82 & 85; Anne Giles Kimbrough Award, Dallas Mus Fine Arts, 82. *Bibliog:* Susan Freuderheim (auth), Uniting art and allegory: The energetic paintings of Melissa Miller, Tex Homes, 82; Roni Feinstein (auth), Melissa Miller: The uses of enchantment, Arts, summer 84; Katherine Gregor (auth), Melissa Miller's Animal Kingdom, Artnews, 12/86. *Media:* Oil, Acrylic. *Mailing Add:* PO Box 5949 Austin TX 78763

MILLER, MELVIN ORVILLE, JR
PAINTER
b Baltimore, Md, May 16, 37. *Study:* Md Inst Art, dipl, 59. *Comn:* Paintings, Equitable Trust Co, Baltimore, 63-64; painting, Mercantile Bank & Trust, Baltimore, 82; AT&T Cable Ship, Long Lines (painting), Transoceanic Cable Ship Co; Baltimore City Hall, Baltimore City Coun. *Exhib:* Corcoran Gallery, Washington, DC, 58; Butler Inst Am Art, Youngstown, Ohio, 63; Am Soc Marine Artists, New York, 78-80; Greenwich Workshop Gallery, Southport, Conn, 79-83; Kirsten Gallery, Seattle, 80-83; John Pence Gallery, San Francisco, 80-83; Foxhall Gallery, 83; Art in Embassies-25th yr exhib inclusion, Sierra Leone, Africa, 89; and others. *Teaching:* Private classes. *Awards:* Second Prize, John F & Anna Lee Stacey Scholar Fund, 65. *Bibliog:* E H H Archibald (auth), Dictionary of Sea Painters, Nat Maritime Mus, London (in prep). *Mem:* Am Soc Marine Artists; Charcoal Club Baltimore. *Media:* Oil; Pen & Ink. *Dealer:* Foxhall Gallery 3301 New Mexico Ave NW Washington DC 20016; Bendann Art Galleries Towson Town Ctr 825 Dulaney Valley Rd Suite 124 Towson MD 21204. *Mailing Add:* 2001 Alto Vista Ave Baltimore MD 21207

MILLER, MICHAEL STEPHEN
PRINTMAKER, PAINTER
b Baltimore, Md, June 29, 38. *Study:* East Carolina Univ, BS, 62; Pa State Univ, MA, 64. *Work:* Art Inst Chicago, Ill; Brooklyn Mus, NY; Philadelphia Mus Art, Pa; Springfield Art Mus, Mo; Joseph Heinz Corp, Pittsburgh, Pa. *Exhib:* Extraordinary Realities, Whitney Mus, New York, 75; solo exhib, Frumkin & Struve Gallery, Chicago, Ill, 83; 19 Print Biennial, 77 & 22nd Print

Biennial, 80, Brooklyn Mus, NY; Site-Oriented Installations, Klein Gallery, Chicago, Ill, 83; Chicago Sculpture Int, Chicago Art Expo-Navy Pier, 83; Chicago Emerging Visions, Paine Art Ctr, Oshkosh, Wis, 85. *Collections Arranged:* VI Mostra De Gravura, Prints from Chicago, Curitiba, Brazil, 85. *Pos:* Chmn Grad Div & Prof Printmaking. *Teaching:* Instr printmaking, Middle Tenn State Univ, Murfreesboro, 64-67 & Southern Ill Univ, Carbondale, 68-69; asst prof printmaking, Univ Del, Newark, 69-73; prof printmaking, Art Inst Chicago, Ill, 73- *Awards:* Artists Grant, Nat Endowment Arts, 79; DeWitt Award, 74th Chicago & Vicinity Exhib, Art Inst Chicago, 82; Visual Artists Grant, Ill Arts Coun, 86. *Mailing Add:* Dept Printmaking Sch Art Inst Columbus Dr & Jackson Blvd Chicago IL 60603

MILLER, NANCY TOKAR
PAINTER
b Detroit, Mich, June 13, 41. *Study:* Chouinard Art Inst & Otis Art Inst, scholar, 56-59; Univ Calif, Los Angeles, AF, 64; Univ Ariz, MFA, 71. *Work:* Otis Elevator Co, Farmingdale, Conn; Ariz State Univ Mem Union Collection, Tempe; Valley Nat Bank, Tucson, Ariz; Pepsico, New York; and others. *Comn:* Maui International Hotel, Hawaii, 75; Int Bus Machines Corp, Tucson, Ariz, 78; Western Savings, Tucson, 81. *Exhib:* Elaine Horwitch Gallery, Scottsdale, Ariz, 80 & 83; Amarillo Art Ctr, 82; Third Western States Exhib, Brooklyn Mus, NY, 86; April Sgro-Riddle Gallery, Los Angeles, Calif, 87; and others. *Teaching:* Instr painting, drawing & design, Cambridge Ctr Adult Educ, Mass, 65-68; instr, Tucson Art Mus Sch, 72-78; vis artist, Ariz Western Col, 77. *Awards:* Purchase Award, Tucson Mus of Art, 78; Fel, Western States Arts Found, 75-76; Juror's Cash Award, Four Corners States Biennial, Phoenix Art Mus, 77. *Bibliog:* Barbara Cortright (auth), Nancy Tokar Miller, Artspace Mag, 10/81; Sarah J Moore (auth), Arts Mag, 84; Contemporary Images I, Nancy Tokar Miller (catalog essay), Tucson Mus of Art, Ariz, 84; Robert M Quinn (auth), Fusion of East and West, Nancy Tokar Miller New Paintings, Art Week, 1/19/85; and others. *Media:* Acrylic. *Dealer:* Elaine Horwitch Gallery 4200 N Marshall Way Scottsdale AZ 85251. *Mailing Add:* c/o Etherton-Stern Gallery 135 S Sixth Ave Tucson AZ 85701

MILLER, RICHARD KIDWELL
PAINTER
b Fairmont, WVa, Mar 15, 30. *Study:* Pa Acad Fine Arts; Am Univ, BA; Columbia Univ, MFA. *Work:* Phillips Collection, Washington, DC; Edward Joseph Gallagher, III Mem Collection, Univ Ariz, Tucson; Hirshhorn Mus & Sculpture Garden, Washington DC; Rochester Mus Art, NY; Albrecht Gallery, St Joseph, Mo. *Comn:* Painting, Plessey Corp, Gen Motors Bldg, New York, 71. *Exhib:* Pa Acad Fine Arts Ann, Philadelphia, 56-62; Whitney Mus Am Art Ann, New York, 60; Carnegie Inst, 62; Tokyo Int, Japan, 66; one-man shows, Baltimore Mus of Art, 52, Graham Gallery, New York, 60, 62 & 63, Albrecht Gallery of Art, St Joseph, Mo, 69, Long Island Univ, 73, Westreth Gallery, 82 & Aaron Berman Gallery, 83; Alternative Mus, New York, 81; and others. *Teaching:* Asst prof painting, Kansas City Art Inst, 68-69; adj prof painting & drawing, Westchester Community Col, 80-83. *Awards:* Gertrude Vanderbilt Whitney Scholar, Nat Inst Arts & Lett, 48-56; Washington Times-Herald Scholar, 47; Fulbright Fel, 53. *Bibliog:* Eunice Agar (auth), Richard Miller, Am Artist Mag, 88; Claude Marks (auth), Richard Miller, World Artists, 90; Theodore F Wolf (auth), Richard Miller, Christian Sci Monitor, 90. *Media:* Oil, Acrylic. *Dealer:* Glass Art Gallery Inc New York NY. *Mailing Add:* 222 W 83rd St Apt 8C New York NY 10024

MILLER, RICHARD MCDERMOTT
SCULPTOR
b New Philadelphia, Ohio, Apr 30, 22. *Study:* Cleveland Inst Art, 40-42, 49-51, grad, 51. *Work:* Sheldon Mem Art Gallery, Lincoln, Nebr; Univ Houston; Whitney Mus Am Art; Canton Art Inst, Ohio; Hirshhorn Mus, Washington, DC. *Comn:* Ashland Oil, 74; Holliday Rambler Corp, 79; Soc Medalists, 86; Trammell Crow Corp, 88; Nat Serv Indust, 90. *Exhib:* One-man shows: Feingarten Gallery, Los Angeles, 66, Alwin Gallery, London, 68, Peridot Gallery, New York, 64, 66, 67, 69, Washburn Gallery, New York, 71, 74, 75, 77, Artists' Choice Mus Retrospective, New York, 84 & FFS Gallery, New York, 87, 88, 89 & 90. *Teaching:* Prof art, Queens Col, 67- *Awards:* Gold Medals, Nat Acad Design, 74 & 81; Sculpture Award, Am Acad & Inst Arts & Lett, 78; Hakone Open-Air Mus Award, Japan, 86. *Bibliog:* Sidney Tillim (auth), Richard Miller, primary realist, Artforum, summer 67; Gabriel Laderman (auth), Unconventional realists, Artforum, 3/71; Grace Glueck (auth), A new realism in sculpture?, Art in Am, 12/71. *Mem:* Sculptors Guild; Nat Acad Design (pres, 89-); Nat Sculpture Soc. *Media:* Wax, Bronze. *Publ:* Auth, Figure Sculpture in Wax & Plaster, Watson-Guptill, 71. *Mailing Add:* 53 Mercer St New York NY 10013

MILLER, ROBERT PETER
DEALER
b Atlantic City, NJ, Apr 17, 39. *Study:* Rutgers Col, BS & MFA. *Pos:* Exec vpres, Andre Emmerich Gallery Inc, New York, 75-77; pres, Robert Miller Gallery Inc, New York, 77- *Mailing Add:* Robert Miller Gallery Inc 41 East 57th St New York NY 10022

MILLER, (MRS) ROBERT WATT
PATRON
b Oakland, Calif, July 20, 98. *Pos:* Chmn, San Francisco Opera Guild, 50-52; chmn, Ital Festival, San Francisco, 59; chmn, De Young Mem Mus Soc, 61-63. *Awards:* Ital Cross Solidarity, San Francisco, 59. *Mem:* United Bay Area Crusade (bd trustees, currently). *Interests:* Presentation of shows in museums. *Mailing Add:* 1021 California St San Francisco CA 94108

MILLER, RUTH ANN
PAINTER
b Columbia, Mo, Dec 7, 30. *Study:* Univ Mo, BA, 54; Art Students League, 55-56; studied with Esteban Vincente & Earl Kerkam, 55-58. *Work:* Dela Art Mus, Wilmington; Corcoran Gallery; Bryn Mawr Col, Philadelphia. *Exhib:* Ann-juried, Baltimore Art Mus, Md, 61; solo exhib, New York Studio Sch Gallery, 79 & 88; Vision and Tradition, Morris Mus, Morristown, NJ, 87; Colby Col Mus Art, Waterville, Maine, 88; Am Acad Inst Arts & Letts, New York, 89; Nat Acad Design, 167th Ann, New York, 92. *Teaching:* Painting-drawing, New York Studio Sch, 73-; painting-drawing, Univ Hartford, Conn, 75-78; painting & drawing, Int Sch Art, Todi, Italy, 89; painting-drawing, Parsons, Grad Painting, New York, 91- *Awards:* Ingram Merrill Grant, 81. *Bibliog:* Robert Godfrey (auth), In Praise of Space, Art Dept Westminster, 76; Hearne Pardee (auth), Vision and Tradition, NJ State Coun Arts, 88; Andrew Forge (auth), On Ruth Miller's Still Life Painting, New York Studio Sch, 88. *Mem:* Bowery Gallery, New York; Wash Art Asn, Conn. *Media:* Oil, Watercolor. *Mailing Add:* 22 Shinar Mountain Rd Washington Depot CT 06794

MILLER, SAMUEL CLIFFORD
MUSEUM DIRECTOR
b Roseburg, Ore, May 6, 30. *Study:* Stanford Univ, BA, 51; Inst Fine Arts, NY Univ, grad study; Seton Hall Univ, DFA(hon), 76; also in Japan, Europe & Mex; state Univ NJ, Rutgers, LHD, 83. *Pos:* Asst to dir, Albright-Knox Art Gallery, Buffalo, NY, 64-67; asst dir, Newark Mus Asn, 67, mus dir, 68-; art comt, Port Authority NY/NJ, currently. *Awards:* Brotherhood Award, Nat Conf Christians & Jews, 82; Katherine Coffey Award, Mid-Atlantic Asn Mus, 92. *Mem:* Am Asn Mus; Mid-Atlantic Asn Mus; Mus Coun NJ; Am Fedn Arts; Asn Art Mus Dirs. *Mailing Add:* Newark Mus Asn 49 Washington St Newark NJ 07101

MILLER, STEVE
PAINTER, CONCEPTUAL ARTIST
Work: Albright-Knox Gallery, Buffalo, NY; Birchfield Ctr, Buffalo, NY. *Exhib:* Language Drama Source Vision, New Mus, New York, 83; Between Here and Nowhere, Riverside Studios, London, 85; New York New Venue, Mint Mus, Charlotte, NC, 87; The Artist and the Computer, Bronx Mus Arts, NY, 87; Digital Visions, Everson Mus Art, Syracuse, NY, 87; Elga Wimmer Gallery, New York, 92; Int Art Exhib, Paris, France, 92; Members Gallery at Albright-Knox Mus, 92. *Awards:* Fel, Nat Endowment Arts, 87. *Bibliog:* Jerry Salz (auth), Beyond Boundaries, Alfred van der Marck, 86; Lisa Phillips (auth), New York New Venue, Mint Mus, 87; Charles Hagan (auth), Steve Miller, 2-6 Mag, 88. *Mailing Add:* c/o Elga Wimmer Gallery 560 Broadway New York NY 10012

MILLER, SUE S
PAINTER
b Henderson, Ky, Jan 30. *Study:* Memphis Col Art, BFA, 78; Memphis State Univ, MFA, 82. *Work:* Tennessee Valley Authority Collection, Knoxville. *Exhib:* American History, Atlanta Col Art, GA, 88; 32 Ann Delta Exhib, Ark Arts Ctr, Little Rock, Ark, 89; Links to the Third Theme, Mus Fine Art, Oak Ridge, Tenn, 90; CelebraTEN the Arts, Hiddenite Mus Art, NC, 91; Animal Rites and Wrongs, Memphis State Univ, Tenn, 91; West Tenn Region Nat Mus Women Arts, Memphis State Univ Gallery, 93. *Pos:* Advisory Comt Visual arts, Memphis Arts Festival Inc; chair exhib design, Arts in Park Festival, Memphis, Tenn, 91 & 92; co-moderator, Artist's Link, Memphis Aria Visual Artists, 93. *Teaching:* Asst prof basic drawing figure structure, Memphis State Univ Continuing Educ, 79-91; inst teaching artist visual art, Memphis Arts Coun, Arts Sch Inst, 90 & 91. *Awards:* Honorarium, Memphis Ctr Cont Art, 89; Honorarium, Arts in Park Inc, Memphis Art Coun, 92. *Bibliog:* Eleanor Tufts (auth), American herstory, Atlanta Col Art, 88; Caroline Weaver (auth), Complex Exhib, The Oak Ridger, Oak Ridge, Tenn, 90. *Mem:* Nat Asn Women Artists Inc, New York; Artists' Link, Memphis Area Visual Artists, Tenn (co-founder & dir, 89-92); West Tenn Chapter, Tenn Comt, Nat Mus Women Arts, Washington, DC (treas, 92); Louisville Visual Arts Asn, KY. *Media:* Arcylic, Mixed Media. *Publ:* Contrib, The Exchange Show, Memphis State Univ Press, 79; coauth, The Etruscan Coloring Book, Ginger Co, 92. *Dealer:* Cooper Street Gallery 964 S Cooper Memphis TN 38104. *Mailing Add:* 3631 Shirlwood Ave Memphis TN 38122

MILLER-CLARK, DENISE
MUSEUM DIRECTOR, CURATOR
b Chicago, Ill. *Study:* St Xavier Col, BA, 80, MBA, 86; Univ Chicago, study with Joel Snyder. *Collections Arranged:* Public-Private, Works by Contemporary Commercial and Fine Art Photographers, including Sheila Metzner, George Hurrell, Mary Ellen Mark, Victor Skrebneski, Robert Mapplethorpe, David Seidner, Burt Glinn, William Coupon & Barbara Karant, 86-87; Frank Gohlke: Landscapes from the Middle of the World--Photographs 1972-1987, 87; Contemporary Photographs from Japan, 88; Changing Chicago: Close Up, Photographic Essays on Family and Community (co-ed, catalog), 89; Fire Sites--Defense-Deterrence-Bargaining Chips--Photogrpahs by Emmet Gowin, David Graham, David Hanson, Richard Misrach, Patrick Nagatani & Barbara Norfleet, 89; Linda Connor: Spiral Journey (auth, catalog), 90; Anthony Dyrek: Poland Under Martial Law, 90. *Pos:* Dir, Mus Contemp Photog, Chicago. *Teaching:* Instr mus & curatorial practices, Columbia Col, Chicago, 85-; instr bus admin, Graham Sch Mgt, St Xavier Col, Chicago, 86. *Mem:* Am Asn Mus; Art Mus Asn Am; Col Art Asn; Lawyers for the Creative Arts; Soc Photog Educ; Int Coun Mus. *Publ:* Auth, Outside In: Public Sculpture by Richard Hunt, Columbia Col Art Gallery, 86; Frank Gohlke: Landscapes from the Middle of the World, Photographs 1972-1987, Mus Contemp Photog & Friends of Photog, San

Francisco, 88; Changing Chicago, Univ Ill Press, Champaign/Urbana, 89; auth, Linda Connor: Spiral Journey--Photographs 1967-1990, Mus Contemp Photog, Chicago, 90. *Mailing Add:* Mus Contemp Photog Columbia Col 600 S Michigan Ave Chicago IL 60605-1996

MILLETT, CAROLINE DUNLOP
ADMINISTRATOR
b Kansas City, Mo, Feb 14, 39. *Study:* Univ Edinburgh, 59-60; Univ Wis, BA, 61; Stanford Univ, MA, 63. *Collections Arranged:* Coordinator, US Contribution Sao Paulo Bienal, 73. *Pos:* Cultural attache, Brasilia, 69-70; film dir, US Information Agency, 73; asst adv arts, Dept State, 74-80; adv arts, US Int Communication Agency, 81-; vpres, Philadelphia Col Art, 84- *Teaching:* Assoc prof US cultural hist, Univ Sao Paulo, Brazil, 66-69. *Mailing Add:* 317 N 33rd St Philadelphia PA 19104

MILLIE, ELENA GONZALEZ
CURATOR
b Greenwich, Conn. *Study:* Univ NC, BA, 64. *Collections Arranged:* Travel Then & Now, 70, The Paper Weapon (auth, catalog), 76, On View, 79 & American & European Posters (auth, catalog), 80; 19th Century American Book and Magazine Posters, 89. *Pos:* Cur, Libr Cong, 65- *Publ:* Auth, Charlot, L'As des Comiques, 68, coauth, Tomorrow night, East Lynne!, 80 & auth, Posters: A collectible art form, 82, Libr Cong Quart J; College poster art, Art J, 84; Jan Sawka, a Selected Retrospective (exhib catalog), Col New Paltz, NY, 89. *Mailing Add:* Library of Congress Washington DC 20540

MILLIKEN, ALEXANDER FABBRI
DEALER
b Boston, Mass, Feb 14, 47. *Pos:* Owner, Alexander F Milliken Inc, 76- *Mem:* Skowhegan Sch Painting & Sculpture (pres bd trustees, 88-). *Specialty:* Virtuoso Art of our Time, All media, USA, Japan, Europe. *Collection:* Keith Haring, Ed Ruscha, Morris Graves, Claudio Bravo, Albert Paley, Wendell Castle, Mary Ann Currier & Steve Hawley. *Mailing Add:* 750 Camino Pinones Sante Fe NM 87501

MILLIKEN, GIBBS
PAINTER, EDUCATOR
b Houston, Tex, Dec 15, 35. *Study:* Scheiner Inst; Univ Colo; Trinity Univ, BSc; Cranbrook Acad Art, MFA. *Work:* Cranbrook Acad Art; Montgomery Mus Fine Arts, Ala; Serv League, Longview, Tex; Butler Inst Am Art. *Exhib:* San Antonio Artists, Witte Mus, 60-68; Tex Ann Painters & Sculptors, Witte Mus, Corpus Christi, Beaumont Mus & Dallas Mus Fine Arts, 62-66; Bucknell Univ, 67; Tex Fine Arts Comn, Hemisfair, San Antonio, 68; and many others. *Pos:* Asst, Univ Colo Mus, formerly; artist, photographer, asst cur, cur & head dept exhibs, Witte Mem Mus, San Antonio, formerly. *Teaching:* Instr painting & drawing, Cranbrook Acad Art, Bloomfield Hills, Mich, 64 & 65; instr art, Univ Tex, Austin, 65-69, asst prof, 69-73, assoc prof, 74-82, prof, currently. *Awards:* Grumbacher Award, Tex Watercolor Soc, Witte Mem Mus, 64, Naylor Award, 66 & Freeman Purchase Prize, 67; and many others. *Mem:* Am Fedn Arts; Am Asn Univ Prof; Men of Art Guild; Contemp Artists Group. *Mailing Add:* 434 Ridgewood Rd Austin TX 78746

MILLOFF, MARK DAVID
PAINTER, SCULPTOR
b Miami, Fla, June 19, 53. *Study:* Conn Col, New London, BA, 75; Md Inst Col Art, MFA(painting), 77. *Work:* Fogg Mus, Harvard Univ, Cambridge, Mass; Minneapolis Art Inst; Atlantic Richfield, Los Angeles; Chase Manhattan Bank, New York; Prudential Insurance Co; Berkshire Mus, Pittsfield, Mass. *Exhib:* Aviary, Mus Mod Art, New York, 82; Fellowship Winners Exhib, Rose Art Mus, Brandeis Univ, Waltham, Mass, 82; Dogs, Chicago Mus Contemp Art, 83 & Hood Mus, Dartmouth Col, Hanover, NH, 84; Drawing, Minneapolis Art Inst, 83; Inaugural Exhib, Dog Mus Am, New York, 83; Contemporary Drawing, Brockton Mus Art, Mass, 85; retrospective, Berkshire Mus, Pittsfield, Mass, 86; The Clocktower, New York, 86. *Awards:* Mass Coun Drawing Fel, 82; Nat Endowment Arts Fel Sculpture, 84. *Bibliog:* Jon Friedman (auth), Reinventing the heroic: The work of Mark David Milloff, 12/81 & Lisa Peters (auth), Mark Milloff, 5/83, Arts Mag; Christine Temin (auth), Perspective, Boston Globe, 10/10/85. *Media:* Pastels, Oils. *Dealer:* Stux Gallery 411 West Broadway New York NY. *Mailing Add:* PO Box 241 Stockbridge MA 01262

MILLS, AGNES
SCULPTOR, PRINTMAKER
b New York, NY. *Study:* Cooper Union Art Sch, dipl; Pratt Inst, BFA; NY Univ Sch Archit; Art Students League; Design Lab; studied with Raphael Soyer, Chaim Gross, Yasuo Kuniyoshi, Ruth Leaf, Harry Gottlieb, Krishna Reddy & Betty Holliday. *Work:* Libr Performing Arts, Friends Tampa Ballet; Univ Maine, Amhurst; Calif Sch Arts & Crafts, Oakland; C W Post Col; Lincoln Ctr Performing Arts. *Comn:* Mural, Wakefield Collection, Long Beach, Calif; Portraits Inc, NY; Family Portrait, Grand Collection, 92. *Exhib:* Seattle Art Mus Ann, 74; Friends Tampa Ballet, 82; Deja Vu Gallery, 90; Works in Progress, 92; Boca Raton Mus, 92; and others. *Pos:* Art dir, Mills Agency Inc. *Teaching:* Art coordr & art instr, NShore Community Art Ctr, Great Neck, NY, 57-82. *Awards:* First Prize in Printmaking, Washington Miniature Prints & Sculpture, 70; Purchase Prize, Hunterdon Co Art Mus, 72; Purchase Award, Nassau Community Col, 74; Purchase Prize, Nat Asn Women Artists, 81; Goldie Paley Award, 82. *Bibliog:* Article, Art News Mag, Oct, 81; New York Times, Mar, 81; Playbill, City Ctr Theatre, Mar, 81; Palm Beach Post, 3/91. *Mem:* Print Club; Nat Asn Women Artists; Artists Equity. *Media:* Color Etching, Cast Paper; Colograph, Monoprint. *Dealer:* Lincoln Ctr Art Gallery 65th St & Broadway New York NY 10023; Nuance Gallery Tampa FL 33609. *Mailing Add:* 8903 Glades Rd Ste L-9-144 Boca Raton FL 33434

MILLS, FREDERICK VAN FLEET
EDUCATOR, PAINTER
b Bremen Fairfield, Ohio, June 5, 25. *Study:* Ohio State Univ, BS, 49; Ind Univ, MS, 51, EdD, 56. *Pos:* Pres, Ind Art Educ Asn, 56; ed, Western Arts Bull, 58-62; consult, Latin Am Scholar Prog in Brazil, Harvard Univ, 81-82. *Teaching:* Prof art & art educ & chmn dept art educ, Ind Univ, Bloomington, 59-66; chmn dept related arts, crafts & interior design, Univ Tenn, Knoxville, 66-68; prof art & chmn dept, Ill State Univ, 68- *Awards:* Recognition Award, Ill Alliance Arts Educ, 84. *Mem:* Nat Art Educ Asn (bd dirs, 63-64); Col Art Asn Am; Western Arts Asn (pres, 62-64); Ill Art Educ Asn; Nat Coun Art Adminrs (res ed, 73-81). *Media:* Watercolor. *Publ:* Editor of various articles in Nat Coun Art Adminrs from 1976 to 1980. *Mailing Add:* RR 2 No 60 Hudson IL 61748

MILLS, LEV TIMOTHY
PRINTMAKER, DESIGNER
b Wakulla Co, Fla, Dec 11, 40. *Study:* Fla A&M Univ, BA(art educ); Univ Wis, Madison, MA & MFA; Slade Sch Fine Art, Univ London, Eng; Atelier 17, Paris, France, with Stanley W Hayter. *Work:* High Mus Art, Atlanta; Victoria & Albert Mus, London; Libr of Cong, Washington, DC; Bibliot Nat, Paris; Mus Mod Art, New York. *Comn:* Three glass mosaic designs, Ashby St Subway Sta, City of Atlanta, Metrop Atlanta Rapid Transit Authority, 78; atrium floor design, City Hall, Atlanta, 88; mixed media work, Atlanta Pub Schs, 88. *Exhib:* Slade Centenary Exhib, Royal Col Art, London, 71; Artists in Ga, High Mus Art, Atlanta, 74; 20th Century Black Artist, San Jose Mus Art, 76; Retrospective, Studio Mus in Harlem, New York, 75; Miss Mus Art, Jackson; Birmingham Mus Art, Ala; and others. *Pos:* Art consult & mem bd trustees, Art Festival of Atlanta Inc, 77- *Teaching:* Instr gen art, Everglades Jr High, Ft Lauderdale, Fla, 62-68; asst prof printmaking, Clark Col, Atlanta, 73-78; assoc prof art, Spelman Col, Atlanta, 79. *Awards:* Outstanding Postgrad Fel, Univ Wis, 69; Europ Study & Travel Fel, Ford Found, 70; Bronze Jubilee Award for Cultural Achievement, City of Atlanta, 78. *Bibliog:* Pat Gilmour (auth), Lev Mills, Arts Rev, London, 72; Lewis & Waddy (coauth), Black artists on art, Contemp Crafts Inc, Calif, 76; Samella Lewis (auth), Graphic Processes, Art: African American, Harcourt, Brace Jovanovich Inc, New York, 78. *Mem:* Nat Col Art Asn; Black Artists Atlanta. *Media:* Mixed Media. *Publ:* Auth, I Do, A Book of Etchings & Poems, Cut Chain Press, 71. *Dealer:* Assoc Am Artists 663 Fifth Ave New York NY 10022. *Mailing Add:* 3378 Ardley Rd SW Atlanta GA 30311

MILLS, PAUL CHADBOURNE
MUSEUM DIRECTOR, ART AND FLAG CONSULTANT
b Seattle, Wash, Sept 24, 24. *Study:* Reed Col, 45-48; Univ Wash, BA, 53; Univ Calif, Berkeley, MA, 61; Calif Col Arts & Crafts, Hon PhD, 71. *Pos:* Reporter, Bellevue Am, Wash, 48-51; asst cur, Henry Gallery, Univ Wash, 52-53; cur art, Oakland Mus, Calif, 53-70; vpres, Western Mus Conf, 56 & 59; dir, Santa Barbara Mus Art, 70-82; dir, New Glory Bicentennial Flag Hist & Design Proj, 74-77; exec dir, Santa Barbara Flag Proj, 77-; chmn, Herbert Bayer Sculpture Comt, currently; 2nd vpres, Santa Barbara Trust for Hist Preserv, 92-; bd dirs, Santa Barbara Coun Art Comn, 81, Santa Barbara Trust Hist Preserv, 82- & Contemp Art Forum, 83- *Awards:* Ford Found Fel, 60-61; grants from Spain, 77-79. *Mem:* Western Asn Art Mus (vpres, 56-57, treas, 71-72, trustee, 79); N Am Vexillological Asn; Heraldry Soc; Am Asn Mus; hon mem Am Asn Art Mus Dirs (trustee, 71-72, secy, 73). *Publ:* The California Missions of Edwin Deakin, 66; Colonial and Revolutionary Era Flags, 75, (with Mark Adams), 84; auth, The new figurative art of David Park, 88; art ed, O, California!, 88 & 89; auth, David Park Scroll, 89. *Mailing Add:* 314 E Figueroa St S Santa Barbara CA 93101

MILNES, ROBERT WINSTON
SCULPTOR, EDUCATOR
b Washington, DC, Apr 1, 48. *Study:* Claremont Men's Col, BA(philosophy, fine arts), 70; Univ Wash, MFA, 74; Univ Pittsburgh, PhD, 87. *Work:* Smithsonian Inst; Erie Art Mus, Pa; Seattle Arts Comn; Univ Ariz; Fed Reserve Bank, Cleveland, Ohio. *Comn:* wall-mounted sculpture, comn by Mr & Mrs Warner Bacon, Erie, Pa, 81; wall mounted sculptures, Rothenberg, Wash & Los Angeles, Calif. *Exhib:* Solo shows, Theo Portnoy Gallery, New York, 79 & 80, Erie Art Mus, Pa, 83 & Clay Place, Pittsburgh, 83; McNeese State Univ, Lake Charles, La, 90. *Teaching:* Instr ceramics, Penland Sch Crafts, NC, 72 & 79; prof, Edinboro Univ, 74-86, art dept chmn, 81-86; dir, Sch Art, La State Univ, Baton Rouge, 87-; art dept chmn, San Jose State Univ, Calif. *Awards:* Ceramic Sculpture Nat Juror Award, Stockton State Col, 74; Juror Award, Erie Art Ctr, 83; Jurors award, Louisiana Festival of the Arts, Mafur Mus, Alexandria, La, 90. *Mem:* Col Art Asn; Nat Coun Arts Adminrs; Nat Asn Sch Art & Design; Art Asn Univ Prof. *Media:* Ceramics, Copper. *Publ:* The Impact of State Governing Board Policies on Fine Arts Programs in Post-Secondary Education, (disertation), Univ of Pittsburgh, Pa. *Dealer:* Clay Place 5600 Walnut St Pittsburgh PA 15232. *Mailing Add:* 12396 Sierramar Dr San Jose CA 95118

MILONAS, HERODOTOS See Milonas, Minos

MILONAS, MINOS
PAINTER, SCULPTOR
b Heraklion, Crete, Apr 28, 36; US citizen. *Study:* Color theory with Fritz Faiss & painting with Hans Burkhardt, 68-70; studied sculpture with Everett Dupen & George Tsutakawa, 70-72; Calif State Univ, Northridge, BA, 70; Univ Wash, Seattle, MFA, 72. *Work:* Calif State Univ, Northridge; Cathedral St Demetrios, Seattle, Wash; Hellenic Cult Ctr, Long Island, NY; Cypriot Consultate, Young Broadcasting Inc, Girsberger Inc, New York. *Exhib:* 5th Ann Nat Greek Art Exhib, Springfield, Mass, 87; North Dakota Print &

Drawing Ann, Univ of NDak, Grand Forks, 87; 2nd Ann Int Miniature Art Exhib, Del Bello Gallery, Toronto, Ont, Can, 87; Paper in Particular, Columbia, Mo, 89; 35th Annual Drawing & Small Sculpture Show, Ball State Univ, Muncie, Ind, 89; and many others. *Teaching:* Teaching asst sculpture, Univ Wash, Seattle, 70-71, instr, 71-72. *Awards:* Wenatchee Arts Festival, Wash, 72; Award, Redmonds Arts Festival, Redmonds, Wash, 75; 3 Merit Awards, 5th & 7th Ann Nat Greek Art Exhib, Springfield, Mass, 87 & 89; and others. *Bibliog:* Ball State Univ Art Gallery (producer), Artists Forum Video, 89; Minos Milonas-Art is: 500 Definitions, 90; George Agelides (auth), No to the commerciality of art, Nat Herald, 90; Abraham Ilein (auth), The message is more than the medium, Art Speak, 90; George Tomko (auth), Minos Milonas emerges as a major abstract painter, Manhattan Arts, 90; and others. *Mem:* NY Artists Equity Asn Inc. *Media:* Oil; Gouache. *Publ:* The Small Caravan, collection of short stories, Athens, Greece, 62. *Mailing Add:* 790 11th Ave No 39A New York NY 10019

MILRAD, AARON M
COLLECTOR
b Toronto, Ont, Can, May 17, 35. *Study:* Univ Toronto, BA & LLB; Law Soc Upper Can, grad lawyer. *Pos:* trustee, Art Gallery Ont, 76-82; pres, Art Gallery Harborfront, Toronto, Ont, 83; pres, Koffler Art Gallery, Koffler Ctr, Toronto, 83; Comt City Toronto Pub Art; Int Bd, Tel Aviv Mus; Bd Int Found Art Res. *Teaching:* Vis prof art & the law, York Univ, Toronto, Ont, 72-; instr art & the law, art management & publ, Banff Ctr Sch Fine Arts, Alta, Can, 73-; lectr, Museology Course, Univ Toronto, 78- *Awards:* Can Coun Grant, Exploration Prog for bk on Can Art Law. *Collection:* Modern American and Canadian, 1945 to the present, primarily in the color field area, Noland, Olitski, Motherwell and others; American & International Ceramics. *Publ:* Auth, The New Cultural Property Export and Import Act of Canada, 75 & Gifts to Museums, 75, Gazette; Coauth, The Art World: Law, Business and Practice in Canada, Merritt Publ, Toronto, 79; Copyright/Canada Art & Auction, 89; Moral Rights in Canada, IFAR Reports, 90. *Mailing Add:* Six Lawn Hurst Toronto ON M6B 3C6 Canada

MILTON, PETER WINSLOW
PRINTMAKER
b Lower Merion, Pa, Apr 2, 30. *Study:* Yale Univ, with Josef Albers, BFA, 54, MFA, 62. *Work:* Mus Mod Art, Metrop Mus, New York; British Mus, London; Nat Gallery Art, Washington, DC; Tate Gallery, London. *Exhib:* Primera Bienal Americana de Artes Graficas, Mus La Tertulia, Cali, Colombia, 71; one-man shows, Corcoran Gallery Art, Washington, DC, 72 & Drawing Toward Etching, Brooklyn Mus, 80; Extraordinary Realities, Whitney Mus Am Art, 73; Norsk Internasjonal Grafikk Biennale, Gamlegyen, Norway, 74 & 92; 4th Int Exhib Original Drawings, Mus Mod Art, Rijeka, Yugoslavia, 74; Frank Kyle Gallery, London; International Exhibition Found, Traveling Retrospective. *Teaching:* Instr drawing & basic design, Md Inst Col Art, Baltimore, 61-68; instr printmaking, Yale Univ Summer Sch Music & Art, 70. *Awards:* Rockefeller Found Residency, Bellagio, Italy; Medal of Honor, Lvov, USSR; Exequo Award, Graphic Triennial, Crakow, Poland, 92; and others. *Bibliog:* Harriet Shapiro (auth), All realism is visionary: A reach into the ambiguous realm of Peter Milton, Intellectual Digest, 11/72; Piri Halasz (auth), The metaphysical games of Peter Milton, Art News, 12/74; Kneeland McKnulty (auth), Peter Milton: Complete Etchings 1960-1976, Impressions Workshop Inc, Boston, 77; Theodore F Wolff (auth), What Links Duper & Milton, The Many Masks of Modern Art, 89. *Media:* Etching, Engraving. *Dealer:* Franz Bader Gallery 2124 Pennsylvania Ave NW Washington DC 20037; Impressions Workshop 27 Stanhope St Boston MA 02116. *Mailing Add:* PO Box 137 Francestown NH 03043

MIM, ADRIENNE C (ADRIENNE CLAIRE SCHWARTZ)
SCULPTOR, PAINTER
b Brooklyn, NY, Feb 4, 31. *Study:* Brooklyn Mus Art Sch & Brooklyn Col, NY, 50; Hofstra Univ, 65. *Work:* Mus Section, Guild Hall, East Hampton, NY; Sculpturesites, Amagansette, NY. *Comn:* Murals, Southampton Col, NY, 69; Robert & Joan Tausik-Pinto, East Hampton, NY. *Exhib:* Parrish Mus, Southampton, NY, 69; Heckscher Mus, Huntington, NY, 77; Wards Island, New York, 80; Brooklyn Mus, 81 & 84; Fordham Univ, Lincoln Ctr, New York, 81; Soho 20, New York, 85-88; Benton Gallery, Southampton, NY, 86, 89 & 90; and others. *Teaching:* Asst instr painting, Parrish Art Mus, 66-67; adj prof sculpture, Southampton Col, NY, 73-74. *Awards:* Fel, MacDowell Colony, 72-74; Helen B Ellis Mem Prize, Nat Asn Women Artists, 80; Silver Medal, Audubon Artists, 80. *Bibliog:* Carrie Rickey (auth), Stalking the wild sculpture, Village Voice, 7/1/80; Vivienne Wechter (interviewer), WFUV Radio, 6/81; Alexander Russo (auth), Profiles on Women Artists, Univ Pub of Am Inc, page 181-191, 85; Phillis Braff (auth), Messages in on the edge, NY Times, 6/90. *Mem:* Fedn Mod Painters & Sculptors; Nat Asn Women Artists; Sculptors Guild; Soho 20. *Media:* Fiberglass, Steel; Oil, Mixed Media. *Publ:* Auth, Helicomodmim, pvt publ, 79; illusr, Area Sculpture: Ward Island, Artists Representing Environmental Art, 80; Sculpturesites, Roger Wilcox, 81; Appearances, Independent Publ, 12/81; illusr, Appearances, Independent Publ, 12/81. *Dealer:* Roger Wilcox Sculpturesites Box 534 Amagansette NY 11930. *Mailing Add:* 69 Skimhampton Rd East Hampton NY 11937

MIN, YONG SOON
SCULPTOR, PAINTER
b S Korea, Apr 29, 53. *Study:* Univ Calif-Berkeley, BA, MA, MFA, 79; Independent Study Prog, Whitney Mus, 81. *Comn:* Sculpture, Pub Art Fund, 88; sculpture, Creative Time Inc, 90; sculpture, Jamaica Art Ctr; sculpture, Univ Southern Maine. *Exhib:* Committed to Print, traveling, Mus Mod Art, New York, 88; Public Art Fund, City Hall Park, New York, 88; Creative Time, Art in the Anchorage, Brooklyn, NY, 90; The Decade Show, New Mus, Mus Contemp Hispanic Arts & Studio Mus Harlem, 90. *Teaching:* Instr printmaking & drawing, Univ Ohio, 81-84. *Awards:* Artist in Residence, NY State Coun Arts, 87; Artists Fel Grant, Nat Endowment Arts, 89-90; Nat Printmaking Fel, Rutgers Ctr Innovative Printmaking, 90. *Bibliog:* Geok-lin Lim (auth), The Forbidden Stitch, An Asian American Women's Anthology, Calyx books, 89; Lucy Lippard (auth), Mixed Blessings, Pantheon Books, 90; Shirley Heine (ed), Asian Americans: Comparative & Global Perspectives, Wash State Univ Press. *Mem:* Asian Am Arts Alliance (bd mem, 87-); Artist Space (bd mem, 91-); Women's Caucus for Art (bd mem, 92-). *Media:* Glass, Mirror, Photo-based Imagery, Paper. *Mailing Add:* 252 Franklin St Apt 1L Brooklyn NY 11222

MINA-MORA, RAUL JOSE
PAINTER, ILLUSTRATOR
b Santa Anna, El Salvador, Mar 13, 14; US citizen. *Study:* San Francisco Acad Advan Arts; Art Students League, with Howard Traffton; also with Daniel Green, Harte, Austria. *Work:* South Hampton High Sch, NY; Freiden Corp. *Comn:* Murals, Public Building & Numerous Private Commissions. *Exhib:* Nat Soc Casein Painters; Salmagundi Club; Parrish Art Mus, NY; Nat Acad Design; Community Gallery, Metrop Mus Art, New York, 77; Brooklyn Mus, NY; Goldsboro Mus, NC, 77; Dowling Col, Oakdale, NY 90. *Pos:* Art dir, Hanna Advert Bank Iowa Agency. *Teaching:* Archit design & visual archit, Rudolph Shapher Sch Design; instr design, San Francisco Sch Design. *Awards:* Best of Show, Am Artist Prof League Grand Nat & Washington Square Art Show, 75; Knickerbocker Award, 75, 78 & 80; Leinwand Award, First Place Watercolors, 79. *Mem:* Salmagundi Art Club; Am Artist Prof League; Nat Soc Casein & Acrylic Painters; Allied Artists Am; Audubon Artists; and others. *Media:* Watercolor, Oil. *Publ:* Illusr, Fortune Mag, Rutledge, Macmillan, Cronwell-Colliers & Holt. *Mailing Add:* 87 Central Blvd PO Box 256 Oakdale NY 11769-9427

MINEAR, BETH
CRAFTSMAN, WEAVER
b Evanston, Ill, Aug 31, 39. *Work:* Nat Inst Health, Bethesda, Md. *Comn:* Wall rug, Sulzer-Ruti Corp, Switz, 85 & 87; wall rug, Scribner, Hall & Thompson, Washington, DC, 88. *Exhib:* Philadelphia Craft Show, Pa, 87 & 89; Am Craft at the Armory, New York, 88 & 89; Washington Craft Show, DC, 88; traveling mus show, Art that Works: The Decorative Arts of the Eighties, 90-93; Fiber Focus, The Art Barn, Washington, DC, 92; and others. *Awards:* Merit Award, Guild Am Crafts Awards, 87; Grant, DC Comn Arts & Humanities, 92. *Bibliog:* Bill Henry (auth), Artist profile, Hill Rag, 88; Maryann Ondovcsik (auth), Artist profile, Matter Mag, 90. *Mem:* Potomac Craftsmen Guild, Washington, DC; Capitol Hill Art League, Washington, DC; Am Crafts Coun, New York. *Media:* Fiber. *Mailing Add:* 1115 E Capitol St SE Washington DC 20003

MINICK, ROGER
PHOTOGRAPHER, WRITER
b Ramona, Okla, July 13, 44. *Study:* Univ Calif, Berkeley, BA(hist), 69. *Work:* Mus Mod Art, Metropolitan Mus Art, New York; San Francisco Mus Mod Art; Los Angeles Co Mus Art; Houston Mus Fine Arts. *Comn:* Photo Survey, Nat Endowment Arts, 77, 78 & 80; Paramount Theater, Lancaster-Miller, Berkeley, 82. *Exhib:* Delta and Ozark Photos, Friends Photog, Carmel, Calif, 71; Sacramento Delta Photos, Int Ctr Photog, New York, 75; American Photographers and National Parks, Corcoran Gallery, 81, Amon Carter Mus, Ft Worth, 82 & Los Angeles Co Mus Art, 83; Espejo: Photographs of the Mexican-American Community, Ctr Creative Photog, Tucson, 83; Photography in California: '45 to 80, San Francisco Mus Mod Art, 84 & Ctr Georges Pompidou, Paris, 85. *Teaching:* Dir & instr photog, Assoc Students Univ Calif Studio, Berkeley, 66-75; instr, Ansel Adams Workshop, Yosemite, 74, 75, 76 & 82, Owens Valley Workshop, Sacramento Delta, Calif, 79 & 81; instr photog, Acad Art Col, San Francisco, currently. *Awards:* Am Inst Graphic Arts Award, New York, 70; Guggenheim Fel, 72; Nat Endowment Arts Grant, 80. *Bibliog:* A D Coleman (auth), Light Readings, Oxford Univ Press, 79; Hal Fischer (auth), article, Art Forum, summer 81. *Publ:* Auth, Delta West: Land and People of Sacramento-San Joaquin Delta, 69 & Hills of Home: Rural Ozarks of Arkansas, 75, Scrimshaw Press; contribr, American Photographers & the National Parks, Viking Press, 81; auth, Paramount Theater, Lancaster-Miller, 82; coauth, In the Fields, Harvest Press, 82. *Mailing Add:* c/o Academy Art Col Photog Dept 540 Powell St San Francisco CA 94108

MINISCI, BRENDA (EILEEN)
SCULPTOR, CERAMIST
b Gowanda, NY, June 15, 39. *Study:* Study in Rome, Italy, 60-61, RI Sch Design, BFA, 61; Cranbrook Acad of Art, Bloomfield Hills, Mich, MFA, 64; Provincetown Fine Arts Workshop, with Harry Hollander. *Work:* Everson Mus, Syracuse, NY; Fitchburg Art Mus, Mass; Univ Mass, Amherst; Antonio Prieto Mem Collection, Mills Col, Oakland, Calif; N Adams State Col, Mass. *Comn:* Fiberglass fountain sculpture, Murray D Lincoln Campus Ctr & clear cast polyester resin sculpture, Hampden Dining Commons, Univ Mass, Amherst; ceramic relief panels, Burnside Bldg, Worcester, Mass, 62; welded steel sculpture, Mercantile Trust Co, St Louis, Mo, 65-66; and others. *Exhib:* Wit & Whimsey in American Art, Cranbrook Art Mus, Bloomfield Hills, 63; Craftsmen of the East (traveling exhib), Mus Contemp Crafts, New York & Smithsonian Inst, Washington, DC, 64-65; Nat Ceramic Exhib, Everson Mus, Syracuse, 64 & 68; G W V Smith Mus Nat Exhib, Springfield, Mass, 70-72; Seven Sculptors, Boston City Hall Galleries, Mass, 74; and others. *Teaching:* Instr ceramics, Craft Ctr, Worcester, 61-62; instr ceramics & sculpture, Univ

Mass, Amherst, 67-71; instr ceramics & sculpture, Williston-Northampton Sch, Easthampton, Mass, 71-; instr ceramics & sculpture, Summer Grad Sch, Wesleyan Univ, Conn, 75. *Awards:* First Prize for Bronze Sculpture, 52nd Nat Exhib, G W V Smith Mus & Springfield Art League, 71; Juror's Award for Sculpture, Providence RI Art Club, 71; Purchase Prize for Sculpture, 22nd Exhib Painting & Sculpture, Berkshire Mus, N Adams Col, 73. *Mem:* Am Crafts Coun, NE Assembly (treas, 73-75); Nat Coun on Educ for the Ceramic Arts; Boston Visual Artists Union; Int Sculpture Ctr. *Media:* Multimedia. *Mailing Add:* c/o Cove Gallery Commercial St Wellfleet MA 02667

MINKOWITZ, NORMA
SCULPTOR
b New York, NY, Oct 19, 37. *Study:* Cooper Union Art Sch, 58. *Work:* Nat Mus Art/Renwick Gallery Smithsonian Inst, Washington, DC; Am Craft Mus, New York, NY; Metrop Mus Art, New York, NY; Wadsworth Antheneum, Hartford, Conn; Erie Art Mus, Pa; State Conn Comn Arts. *Exhib:* Int Textile Competition, Kyoto Int Con Hall, Kyoto, Japan, 87; The Tactile Vessel, Erie Art Mus, Erie, Pa, 88; Exploring the Figure in Sculptured Forms, Newport Art Mus, RI, 90; The Female Form in Contemporary Art, Wadsworth Atheneum, 90; one-person show, The Body As Vessel, Bellas Artes Gallery, New York; Modern Design 1880-1990, Twentieth Century Art, Metrop Mus Art, New York, 92; and others. *Awards:* Artquest First Place Fiber, Artquest 86, Nat Competition, 86; Visual Arts Fel Grant, Nat Endowment Arts, 86; Purchase Award, Conn Comn Arts, 92; and others. *Bibliog:* R Craig Miller (auth), Modern Design 1890-1990 in the Metropolitan Museum of Art; Chloe Colchester (auth), The New Textiles, Trends & Traditions, Rizzoli, 90; Norma Minkowitz (auth), The Body as Vessel, Fiberarts Mag, summer 92; and others. *Mem:* Am Crafts Coun. *Media:* Miscellaneous media. *Dealer:* Bellas Artes Gallery 301 Garcia St at Canyon Rd Santa Fe NM 87501; Bellas Artes Gallery 584 Broadway New York NY. *Mailing Add:* 25 Broadview Rd Westport CT 06880

MINNICK, ESTHER TRESS
PAINTER
b Chicago, Ill. *Study:* Art Students League; also with Edgar Whitney, Wong Suiling & Barbara Vassilioff. *Work:* Va State Col; Mem Hosp, New York; also in many pvt collections. *Exhib:* Nat Women's Republican Club, New York, 67; Nat Soc Painters Casein & Travel Exhib, New York, 68; Garden State Watercolor Soc, Princeton, NJ, 70; Princeton Art Asn, 71; two one-man exhibs, 74; plus others. *Awards:* First Award, Larchmont, 60; First & Third Prizes, Nat Women's Republican Club, 67; Princeton Bank Award, 70. *Mem:* Knickerbocker Artists; Catharine Lorillard Wolfe Art Club. *Media:* Watercolor. *Mailing Add:* Mease Manor 700 Mease Plaza Dunedin FL 34698

MINSKY, RICHARD
BOOKBINDER, CONCEPTUAL ARTIST
b New York, NY, Jan 7, 47. *Study:* Brooklyn Col, BA(cum laude), 68; New Sch Social Res, 69-71; Brown Univ, MA, 70. *Work:* Victoria & Albert Mus; Hirshhorn Mus & Sculpture Garden; New York Pub Libr Rare Book Room; Nat Gallery Art; Getty Ctr; Metrop Mus Art. *Comn:* Leather & ivory binding for The Unicorn Tapestries, Metrop Mus Art, New York, 76; binding on Sha'arei Tefiloh, Donglomur Found, Villanova, Pa, 76; Program Book, White House, Washington, DC, 77; binding for Buckminster Fuller's Tetrascroll, Universal Limited Art Ed, West Islip, NY, 77; Gracie Mansion regist, Gracie Mansion Conservancy, New York, 85; Brooklyn Mus Regist, 90. *Exhib:* Creative Arts Workshop, Ctr Book Arts, New Haven, Conn, 75; The Book as Art, Fendrick Gallery, Washington, DC, 75; The Object as Poet, Renwick Gallery, 77 & Mus Contemp Crafts, New York, 77; Crafts in the White House, Los Angeles Mus Craft & Folk Art, 77; The Artist and the Book, Dayton Arts Inst, Ohio, 78; The Open and Closed Book, Victoria & Albert Mus, 79; Int Leather Arts Exhib, Sawtooth Ctr Visual Design, Winston-Salem, NC, 84; The First Decade, New York Pub Libr, 85; Bookworks by Photographers, Watson Libr, Metrop Mus Art, New York, 86; A Survey of Bk Arts, Queens Mus, Flushing, NY, 87; The Eloquent Object, Philbrook Mus, Tulsa, Okla, 87, Chicago Pub Libr Cult Ctr, Mus Fine Arts, Boston & Oakland Mus, Calif, 88, Va Mus Fine Arts & Orlando Mus Art, 89; Invitational Exhib, Benton Gallery, Southampton, NY; Book Making: Practical & Provocative, Painted Bride, Philadelphia; 25 Year Retrospective, Hooper Collins Gallery, NY, 92. *Collections Arranged:* Book Artchitecture, Watson Libr, Metrop Mus Art, New York, 85; The Bookworks of Tom Phillips, Ctr Bk Arts, New York, 86; The Effects of Time, Bookwords: London, Jean de Gomet, Ctr Bk Arts, NY, 87; Book Arts in the USA, Ctr Bk Arts, NY & nine venues in Africa & S Am under US Info Agency sponsorship, 90-92. *Pos:* Founder, Ctr Book Arts, 74, pres, 74-78, chmn, 74-82, cur, 85-86, pres, 90- *Teaching:* Instr book arts, Sch Visual Arts, New York, 77- *Awards:* Nat Endowment Arts Fels, 77-81. *Bibliog:* Ed McCormack (auth), From neo-conceptual to bodies, Artspeak, 4/21/81; Rose Slivka (auth), Richard Minsky, Arts Mag, 5/88; Mary Ann Rossman (auth), New Medium for an urgent Message, St Paul Pioneer Press, 92. *Mem:* Ctr Bk Arts. *Media:* Books; Gold, Gems. *Publ:* Contribr, The decade: Change and continuity, Craft Horizons, 6/76. *Dealer:* Allan Stone Gallery 48 E 86th St New York NY; Zabriskie Gallery 724 5th Ave New York NY. *Mailing Add:* 15 Bleecker St New York NY 10012

MINTER, MARILYN A
PAINTER
b Shreveport, La, July 19, 48. *Study:* Univ Fla, BFA, 70; Syracuse Univ, MFA, 72. *Work:* Mus Mod Art, New York; Denver Mus, Colo; Everson Mus, Syracuse, NY; Chase Bank, New York; Deutch Bank, New York. *Exhib:* Solo shows, White Columns, New York, 88, Nicola Jacobs, London, England, 89, Max Protetch, New York, 90 & 92, Simon Watson Gallery, New York, 90, Meyers Bloom Gallery, Santa Monica, Calif, 91, Greenberg Gallery, St Louis, Mo, 91, John Stoller Gallery, Minn, 92. *Teaching:* Instr painting, Sch Vis Arts, 87- *Awards:* Grant, New York State Coun Arts, 88; Nat Endowment Arts, 89; New York State Coun Arts, 92. *Mem:* Bd mem, Whitecolumns. *Media:* Enamel on Metal. *Mailing Add:* c/o Max Protech 560 Broadway New York NY 10012

MINTICH, MARY RINGELBERG
SCULPTOR, CRAFTSMAN
b Detroit, Mich. *Study:* Albion Col; Ind Univ, BA; Queens Col; Univ Tenn; Univ NC, Greensboro, MFA. *Work:* Everson Mus Art, Syracuse, NY; Mint Mus Art, Raddisson Plaza, Charlotte, NC; R J Reynolds; St Johns Art Mus, Wilmington, NC; Nations Bank; SC State Art Collection; Am Express. *Comn:* Sculpture, NC Arts Coun, Waterworks Gallery, Salisbury, 84; Capitol Ctr, Raleigh, NC; Cent Charlotte Asn, Charlotte, NC. *Exhib:* Mint Art Mus, Charlotte, NC; McKissick Mus, Columbia, SC, 81; Greenville Mus Art, SC, 81; Southeastern Ctr Contemp Art, Winston-Salem, NC; NC Mus Art, Raleigh; Clemson Univ; Columbia Mus, SC; Atlanta Arts Festival, Ashville Mus; SC State Mus. *Teaching:* Sacred Heart Col, 67-73; Penland Sch Crafts, 72; prof sculpture, design & metals, Winthrop Col, 72- *Awards:* Purchase Awards, Ceramics Nat & 8th Regional Piedmont Crafts Exhib; Purchase Award, SC, The State of the Arts, SC Arts Comn. *Mem:* Tri-State Sculptors; Int Sculpture Ctr. *Media:* Multimedia. *Dealer:* Hodges Taylor Gallery 227 N Tryon St Charlotte NC. *Mailing Add:* PO Box 913 Belmont NC 28012

MINTZ, HARRY
PAINTER
b Sept 27, 09; US citizen. *Work:* Art Inst Chicago; New Evansville Mus, Ind; Whitney Mus Am Art, New York; Tel Aviv Mod Mus Art, Israel; Rio de Janeiro Mus Art, Brazil; and others. *Exhib:* Art Inst Chicago, 34-63; Whitney Mus Am Art, New York; Venice Biennale, Italy; Denver Art Mus, 63; Corcoran Gallery Art, Washington, DC; and many others; one-man exhib, Ruth Volid Gallery, Chicago, 86. *Teaching:* Assoc prof, Art Inst Chicago. *Awards:* Jules F Brower Prize, 52 & 54 & Silver Prize, 62, Art Inst Chicago; and many others. *Media:* Oil. *Mailing Add:* 429 W Briar Pl Chicago IL 60657

MION, PIERRE RICCARDO
ILLUSTRATOR, PAINTER
b Bryn Mawr, Pa, Dec 10, 31. *Study:* George Washington Univ; Corcoran Gallery Sch of Art, With Elliot O'Hara; also privately with Norman Rockwell. *Comn:* Solar System Evolution (mural), Smithsonian Inst, Washington, DC; team portrait of Apollo astronauts, Nat Geographic Soc; paintings of space futures, Look Mag, 69; mural, Antarctica, Nat Air & Space Mus, Washington, DC; stamp, Va Statehood & postcard, Blairhouse, US Postal Serv. *Exhib:* Nat Ann Watercolor Exhib, Smithsonian Inst, 51 & 63; Robots to the Moon, Hayden Planetarium, New York, 63; Artist & Space, Nat Gallery Art, Washington, DC, 69; Space Art, Smithsonian Inst Air & Space Mus, 71 & Hudson River Mus, Yonkers, NY, 72; one-man shows, Acad of the Arts, Easton, Md, 72 & Metropolis Bldg Asn, Washington, DC, 76; Int Space Art Show, Utrecht, Neth, 86; Nat Geographic 100 Years Show, Soc Illusrs, New York, 88. *Pos:* Art dir illus, Creative Arts Studio, Washington, DC, 57-60; vpres art-design, Northern Sci Indust Exhibs, 64-66. *Teaching:* Instr illus, Marine Corps Inst, Washington, DC, 53-54; instr watercolor, Bethesda, Md, 81-82. *Awards:* Award of Excellence, Int Edit Design Competition, 81; Award, Soc Publ Designers; Merit Award, Art Dirs Club; First Prize, Watercolor, Waterford Show, 86; Best Lodoun County Artist, Waterford, 89. *Bibliog:* Pierre Mion presents one-man show, Baltimore Sun, 72; Mary Runde (auth), Intensity brings detail to Mion's paintings, Star-Democrat, 72; Artist's cards get post office's stamp of approval, Washington Post, 89. *Mem:* Soc Illusrs. *Media:* Acrylic, Oil; Gouache, Watercolor. *Publ:* Illusr, Night driving, Popular Sci, 67; The death of a president Part III, Look Mag, 67; The squalus is down, Reader's Digest, 68; All-girl team tests the habitat, 71 & First colony in space, 76, Nat Geographic; The Titanic, 86 & Mission to Mars, 88, Nat Geographic. *Mailing Add:* Pigeon Hill Farm Rte 2 Box 72C Lovettsville VA 22080

MIOTKE, ANNE E
PAINTER, EDUCATOR
b Milwaukee, Wis, Aug 31, 43. *Study:* Mount Mary Col, Milwaukee, BA, 65; Univ Wis-Milwaukee, with John N Colt & Laurence Rathsack, MS, 70 & MFA, 73. *Work:* Wehr Corp & Joseph P Jansen Co, Milwaukee; Gilberts Commonwealth Asn, Reading, Pa; Deloitte, Haskins & Sells, Cincinnati; IBM, Los Angeles; Cent Trust Bank, Cincinnati, Scripps Howard Corp Hq, Federated Dept Stores Corp Hq, Cincinnati; Rarh-West Art Mus, Manitowoc, Wis; Bristol-Myers US Pharmaceutical & Nutritional Group, Evansville, Ind; and others. *Exhib:* J B Speed Art Mus, Louisville, 74; Watercolor USA, Springfield Art Mus, 77, 80, 82, 83 & 89; Bradley Gallery, Milwaukee, 78, 81, 83, 85, 87, 89 & 91; Contemp Art Ctr, Cincinnati, 79, 83 & 84; Cincinnati Art Mus, 75, 77 & 81; Nat Watermedia Biennial, Zaner Gallery, Rochester, NY; Realism Today, The Evansville Mus of Arts & Sci, Evansville, Ind, 86, 87, 88 & 90; Object/Image/Icon, Contemp Arts Ctr of S Australia, Parkside Adelaide, Australia, 88; Toni Birckhead Gallery, Cincinnati, 88; Int Art Expo, Chicago, 90; and others. *Pos:* Bd mem, Milwaukee Area Teachers of Art, 67-70; contrib ed, Midwest Art, 75-77. *Teaching:* Instr art, Mount Mary Col, Milwaukee, 70-72; Layton Sch Art & Design, Milwaukee, 73-74; assoc prof art, Art Acad Cincinnati, 74- *Awards:* Nat Endowment Arts Vis Specialist Grant, Milwaukee Art Mus, 75-79; Nat Endowment Arts Guest Cur Grant, John Michael Kohler Arts Ctr, Sheboygan, Wis, 79; Ohio Arts Coun Fel, 80-81 & 88-89. *Mem:* Col Art Asn Am; Am Asn Univ Prof; Phi Kappa Phi. *Media:* Watercolor, Mixed. *Dealer:* Bradley Galleries 2639 N Downer Ave Milwaukee WI 53211; Toni Birckhead Gallery Cincinnati OH. *Mailing Add:* 5639 Macey Ave No C Cincinnati OH 45227

MIOTTE, JEAN
PAINTER
b Paris, France, Sept 8, 26. *Work:* Guggenheim Mus, New York; Smithsonian Inst, Washington, DC; Mus Mod Art, Rio De Janeiro, Brazil; Mus D'Art Moderne, Paris; Wallraf-Richartz Museum, Cologne, WGer. *Exhib:* Solo exhibs, Evergreen State Col, Olympia, Wash, 82, N Mus, Singapore, 83, Striped House Mus, Tokyo, Japan, 84, Gimpel- Weitzenhofer Gallery, New York, 88. *Awards:* Ford Found Grant, 61. *Bibliog:* G Langeyine (dir), Miotte, Secret Space (film), 83; Arrabal (auth), Miotte, La Difference, Paris, 88. *Media:* Acrylic. *Dealer:* Keeser-Bohbot Gallery Hamburg Ger. *Mailing Add:* 451 Broome St New York NY 10013

MIRALDA, ANTONI
SCULPTOR
b Barcelona, Spain, Oct 2, 42. *Study:* Sch Textile Engineers, Tarrasa, 56-61; Cours de Methode Comparee des Arts Plastiques; Ctr Int d'Etudes Pedagogiques, Sovres, France, 62-64. *Work:* Moderna Museet, Stockholm; Ctr Nat Art Cult, Paris; Musee Cantini, Marseilles, France; Art Gallery of New South Wales, Australia. *Exhib:* Mus Mod Art, Paris, 66, 68 & 69; Les Assises du Siege Contemp, Musee des Arts Decoratifs, Paris, 68; one-man shows, Mus Contemp Crafts, New York, 71 & 72, Metrop Mus Art, New York, 73, Ctr Cult, Villeparsis, 75, Documenta 6, Kassel, Ger, 77 & Contemp Arts Mus, Houston, 77; and many others. *Awards:* City of Barcelona Bursary, 62-63; Laureate of 5th Bienniale de Paris, 67. *Bibliog:* Douglas Davis (auth), A new world of art, Newsweek, New York, 73; Bill Dyckes (auth), Contemproary Spanish art, Arts Mag, New York, 76; Pierre Restany (auth), Miralda artiste en tous genres, Artitudes Int, 77. *Publ:* Auth & ed, Album, pvt publ, Majorca, Spain, 73 & Food Coloring Cards, pvt publ, Paris, 75; coauth, Ceremonials, Galeria Vandres, Madrid & Centre Beaubourg, 75-78; auth, The Last Supper, Art Enlla, Barcelona, Spain, 76; coauth, Situation-color, Galeria Vandres, Madrid, 77. *Mailing Add:* Exit Art 578 Broadway New York NY 10012

MIRRA, (MIRRA TENGROTH)
PAINTER, CONCEPTUAL ARTIST
Swedish citizen. *Study:* Ecole des Beaux Arts, Paris, 75; Fine Arts Acad, Sofia, Bulgaria, MFA(with honors), 77; Stockholm Univ; Royal Acad Fine Arts, Stockholm. *Work:* Paterson Mus, NJ; Malmö Konsthall, Sweden; Beijar Collection & Reinholds AB, Stockholm, Sweden; Mus Mod Art, Sofia, Bulgaria. *Comn:* Indoor mural, Ministry of Defense, Sofia, Bulgaria, 77; outdoor mural, Reinholds AB, touring installation, Mus Mod Art/ Skadebanan, 82, murals, Teachers' Nat Convention, 83 & 84, Stockholm, Sweden. *Exhib:* 2nd Int Youth Biennial, Mus Mod Art, Sofia, Bulgaria, 79; City Mus, Kulturhuset, 80, Varsalongen, Liljevalchs Konsthall, 82, Stockholm, Sweden; 3rd Int Pictorial Art Summer, Kuopio, Finland, 80; Cell of Glass, 12th ISC, Mills Mus, Oakland, Calif, 82; Fetisch, Malmö Konsthall, Sweden, 83; Gabrielle Bryers Gallery, New York, 84; Either Side of the Mirror, documenta 8, 87 & Body-Paintings Installation, Kultur Fabrik Salzman eV, 88, Kassel, WGer. *Pos:* Chmn, Swedish Artists Asn, 79-80, cur, Mejan Gallery, 79-80, art consult, Nordiska Kompaniet AB, 84-85 & fel (art funding), Eva Bonnier Donation-Fund, 80-, Stockholm, Sweden. *Teaching:* Asst prof painting & drawing, Royal Acad Archit, Stockholm, Sweden, 79-86; prof drawing, Nat Acad Arts, Crafts & Design, Stockholm, Sweden, 86-; guest artist mural painting, Sch Visual Arts, New York, 88. *Awards:* Bulgaria's Special Prize for Outstanding Achievments in Arts, 78; Cult Scholars, City of Stockholm, 80, Swedish Inst, 81 & Alva & Gunnar Myrdal, 82; Project Grants, Swedish Arts Grants Comt & Swedish Nat Endowment Arts, 80, 81 & 87. *Bibliog:* Annelie Pohlen (auth), Der Mensch in Spiegel, General-Anzeiger, Bonn, Ger, 80; Iring Arramora (auth), On the World and on Herself, Puls, Sofia, Bulgaria, 81; Thomas Millroth (auth), On Mirra (Tengroth), Paletten 4, Göteborg, Sweden, 83. *Mem:* Media Network, New York; Stockholm Artists' Studio Asn Müchen, Sweden. *Dealer:* ArttrA Productions New York NY. *Mailing Add:* 149 W 12th St No 3 New York NY 10011

MIRTALA
SCULPTOR, WRITER
b Kharkov, USSR, Apr 29, 29; US citizen. *Study:* Boston Mus, Sch, cert(highest hon), 56; Grande Chaumiere, Paris, France, with Zadkine, 58; Ecole Arts Decoratifs, Paris, with Couturier, 58; Tufts Univ, BFA(magna cum laude), 65. *Work:* Tufts Univ; House of Ukraine, State Cult Ctr, Kiev, Ukraine; Niagara Falls Art Gallery, Can; Art Gallery, Lviv, Ukraine; Ctr Cult & Aesthetics, Kharkiv, Ukraine; and others. *Comn:* Medal, Sixth Cong, Int Soc Hemat, 56; portraits, Missionary Order Maryknoll, NY, 62; portrait of Roman Jakobson, Slavic Depts of Harvard Univ & Mass Inst Technol, 69; portrait of Pres Milton Grahm, Grahm Jr Col, Boston, 70; St Alan's Church, Troy, Mich, 83. *Exhib:* One-person shows, Attleboro Mus, Mass, 78, Cayuga Mus, Auburn, NY, 81, Bentley Col, 81, Roerich Mus, NY, 83 & Univ Mass, Boston, 83; Shevchenko Mus, Kiev, Ukraine, 91; Art Mus Kharkiv, Ukraine, 91; Art Mus Mykolayiv, Ukraine, 92; Art Mus Dnipropetrovsk, Ukraine, 92; House of Ukraine, State Cult Ctr, Kiev, Ukraine, 92. *Awards:* Second Prize Sculpture, Boston Art Festival, 56; Boston Mus Sch Albert Whitin Traveling Scholar, 57; Prize, Providence Art Club, 72. *Bibliog:* Nancy Sartin (auth), Meditation with Mandalas, Response Mag, 9/83; P M H Atwater (auth), Visionary Sculptures of Mirtala, East West Mag, 4/88; Volodymyr Voytovych & Igor Rymaruk (auth), These sculptures are like poetry, Ukraine Mag, Kiev, Ukraine, 10/91. *Media:* Bronze. *Publ:* Auth, Mandalas, sculptures & commentary, Boston, 80; Thought-Forms, sculptures & poems, second bilingual ed (Russ & Eng), Boston, 86; The Human Journey, sculpture, poetry (in Eng, Ukrainian, Russ), 90; Mandalas, sculpture, 90; Rainbow Bridge, poems & sculptures (Ukrainian), Ukrainian Writer Press, Kiev, Ukraine, 92. *Mailing Add:* 57 Fresh Pond Pl Cambridge MA 02138

MISCH, ALLENE K
PAINTER
b Utica, NY, Jan 27, 28. *Study:* Chicago Art Inst; Ind Univ; Purdue Univ; also with Tom Hill, Robert E Wood, John C Pellew & George Cherepov. *Comn:* Oil, Mem Hosp, Michigan City, Ind, 65. *Exhib:* Las Vegas Art Mus, Nev, 72-78; State Capitol, Carson City, Nev, 76; one-man shows, Green Apple Gallery, 78 & Las Vegas Art Mus, 80. *Pos:* Gallery dir, Dunes Art Found, 66-70 & Las Vegas Art Mus, 72-73; visual arts chmn, Festival: The Arts, Allied Arts Coun, Las Vegas, 77. *Teaching:* Instr oils & acrylics, Dunes Art Found, Michigan City, 65-70 & Las Vegas Art Mus, 71- *Awards:* Oils Award, Dunes Regionals, Dune Art Found, First Merchants Bank, 63, 65 & 68; Purchase Prize, Elkhart Art Festival, CofC, Ind, 65; Oil Award, Michigan Regional, South Bend Art Ctr, 67. *Bibliog:* Festival: The Arts, Las Vegas Sun, 77. *Mem:* Las Vegas Artists' Coop; Advocate for the Arts. *Media:* Acrylic, Oil; Lithograph. *Dealer:* Lewis Galleries 29835 Redwood Dr Box 4816 Canyon Lake CA 92380. *Mailing Add:* 3806 Forestcrest Dr Las Vegas NV 89121

MI SOOK, AHN
PAINTER
b Seoul, Korea, Oct 10, 59. *Study:* Univ Ill Urbana-Champaign, BFA; Tyler Sch Art, Temple Univ, MFA, 86. *Exhib:* Artemisia Gallery, Chicago, Ill, 90. *Pos:* Painter, self-employed. *Awards:* Nat Endowment Arts, 87 & 89; Ill Arts Coun Grant, 89. *Media:* Oil. *Mailing Add:* 730 S Starview Ct Anaheim Hills CA 92808

MISRACH, RICHARD LAURENCE
PHOTOGRAPHER
b Los Angeles, Calif, July 11, 49. *Study:* Univ Calif, Berkeley, BA, 71. *Work:* Victoria & Albert Mus, London; Mus Mod Art, New York; Mus Mod Art, San Francisco; Metrop Mus, New York; Los Angeles Co Mus Art; and others. *Comn:* Photography, Am Tel & Tel, Washington, DC, 78; Time Mag (cover), 7/4/88. *Exhib:* Bent Photog, Australian Ctr for Photog, Sydney, 77; Night Landscape, Oakland Mus, Calif, 77; one-man show, Desert Photographs, Ctr Georges Pompidou, Mus Art Mod, Paris, 79; Am Images, Corcoran Gallery Art & traveling, 79; Mirrors & Windows, Mus Mod Art (traveling), New York, 79-80; Beyond Color, San Francisco Mus Mod Art, 80; Whitney Biennial, Whitney Mus Am Art, New York, 81; Los Angeles Co Mus Art, 83; Honolulu Acad Arts, 84; 10-year retrospective, Friends of Photog, Carmel, 84; Bravo 20: A National Park Proposal, Traveling exhib, Friends Photog, San Francisco, 90. *Teaching:* Instr photog, Assoc Students Studio, Univ Calif, Berkeley, 71-77; vis lectr landscape archit, Univ Calif, Berkeley, 82; vis lectr, dept art, Univ Calif, Santa Barbara, 84 & Calif Arts, 91. *Awards:* Nat Endowment Arts Photog Fel, 73, 77, 84 & 92; Friends of Photog Ferguson Grant, 76; Guggenheim Found Fel, 78. *Bibliog:* David Fahey (auth), Interview with Richard Misrach, G Ray Hawkins Newsletter, 79; Carter Ratcliff (auth), Richard Misrach: Words and images, Print Collectors Newsletter, 1-2/80; Irene Borger (auth), Richard Misrach, Exposure Mag, 80. *Publ:* Auth, Richard Misrach 1979, Grapestake Gallery, 79; contribr, American Images: New Work by Twenty Contemporary Photographers, Am Tel & Tel, 79; contribr, Mirrors and Windows: American Photography Since 1960, Mus Mod Art, New York, 79; Hawaii Portfolio, 80 & Graecism Portfolio, 83, Grapestake Gallery; auth, Desert Cantos, Univ NMex Press, 87; Richard Misrach: 1975-1987, Gallery Min, Tokyo, 88; Bravo 20: The Bombing of the American West, John Hopkins Univ Press, 90. *Dealer:* Fraenkel Gallery 55 Grant Ave San Francisco CA; Fotomann Inc 42 E 76th St New York NY 10021. *Mailing Add:* 1420 45th St Emeryville CA 94608

MISS, MARY
SCULPTOR
b New York, NY, May 27, 44. *Study:* Univ Calif, Santa Barbara, BA, 66; Rinehart Sch Sculpture, Md Art Inst, Baltimore, MFA, 68. *Work:* Allen Mem Art Mus, Oberlin Col, Ohio; RI Sch Design Mus; La Jolla Mus Art; Louis Manilow Park, Governor's State Univ; Cincinnati Mus Art; Mus of Mod Art, New York; Guggenheim Mus, New York. *Comn:* Field Rotation, Governor's State Univ, Ill, 84; Laumeier Project, Laumeier Sculpture Park, Mo, 84; Study for an Entry, Danforth Mus, Framingham, Mass, 86; Southcove, Battery Park City, New York, 88; Art Ctr, Albright Col, Reading, Pa, 91; and others. *Exhib:* Sculpture Annual, Whitney Mus Am Art, NY, 70; 26 Contemporary Women Artists, Aldrich Mus Contemp Art, Ridgefield, Conn, 71; Gedok-American Women Artists, Kunsthaus, Hamburg, Ger, 72; Whitney Biennial, Whitney Mus Am Art, NY, 73; Waves, Cranbrook Acad Art, Bloomfield Hills, Mich, 73; Seven Artists, Inst Contemp Art, Boston, Mass, 74; Women in Architecture, Brooklyn Mus Art, NY, 77; Nine Artists: The Theodoran Awards, Solomon R Guggenheim Mus, NY, 77; Architectural Analogues, Whitney Mus Am Art, Downtown Br, NY, 78; The Minimal Tradition, Aldrich Mus Contemp Art, Ridgefield, Conn, 79; Drawings/Structures, Inst Contemp Art, Boston, Mass, 80; Whitney Biennial, Whitney Mus Am Art, NY, 81; solo exhibs, 55 Mercer Gallery, 71, 72; Rosa Esman Gallery, NY, 75; Salvatore Ala Gallery, Milan Italy, 75; Projects, Mus Mod Art, NY, 76; Perimeters/Pavilions/Decoys, Nassau County Mus Fine Arts, Roslyn, NY, 78; Screened Court, Minneapolis Col Art, Minn, 79; Mirror Way, Fogg Art Mus, Harvard Univ, Cambridge, Mass, 80; Metamahattan, Whitney Mus Am Art, Downtown Br, NY, 84; The Artist as Social Designer, Los Angeles County Mus Art, Los Angeles, Calif, 85; Standing Ground: Sculpture by American Women, Contemp Arts Ctr, Cincinnati, Ohio, 87; Sculpture of the Eighties, Queen's Mus, NY, 87; Vanguard Gallery, Philadelphia, Pa, 87; Making Their Mark: Women Artists Move Into the Mainstream 1970-85, Cincinnati, Ohio, New Orleans, La, Denver, Colo, Philadelphia, Pa, 89. *Pos:* Adv bd, On View (journal on pub art). *Teaching:* Sch Visual Arts, NY; Cooper Union for Advancement Sci & Art, NY; Sarah Lawrence Col, Bronxville, NY; Hunter Col, NY; Pratt Inst, Brooklyn, NY; vis lectr, Univ Rhode Island,

Kingston; resident artist, Am Acad Rome, spring 89. *Awards:* NY State Coun on Arts CAPS Grant, 73 & 76; Nat Endowment Awards, 74, 75 & 84; Brandeis Univ Creative Arts Award, 82; John Simon Guggenheim Mem Found Fel, 86. *Bibliog:* Lucy Lippard (auth), Mary Miss: An extremely clear situation, Art Am, 3-4/74; Ronald Onorato (auth), Illusive spaces: The art of Mary Miss, Artforum, 12/78; Deborah Nevins (auth), An Interview with Miss Mary Miss, Princeton, NJ, 85; Nancy Princenthal (auth), On the Lookout, Art Am, 10/86; Space exploration, Art News, 10/89; and others. *Mem:* Am Acad, Rome (bd). *Publ:* Auth, On a Redefinition of Public Sculpture, Yale Perspecta, 21, 84. *Mailing Add:* Box 304 Canal St Sta New York NY 10013

MISSAL, JOSHUA M & PEGGE
ART DEALERS, CONSULTANTS
Mr Missal, b Hartford, Conn, Apr 12, 15; Mrs Missal, b Denver, Colo, Nov 25, 23. *Study:* Mr Missal, Univ Rochester, BM, 37, MM, 38; London Inst, Hon DM, 72; Mrs Missal, N Tex State Univ, BA, 44. *Pos:* Dirs & owners, Gallery M, Farmington, Conn, 70-76 & Missal Gallery Ltd, Scottsdale, Ariz, 76-85, Missal Art Assocs, Scottsdale, Ariz, 85-88. *Teaching:* Mr Missal, assoc prof interrelated arts, Wichita State Univ, 52-70. *Mem:* Am Fedn Art; Appraisers Asn Am. *Specialty:* Consultations. *Publ:* Mrs Missal, auth, On Collecting Art, Guest Informant, 76 & An Introduction to Printmaking for the Layman, 82; Mr Missal, auth, American art--the continuing boom, Art Talk, 12/81 & articles on art collecting, World Fine Art, 82-83. *Mailing Add:* 1343 E Enrose Circle Mesa AZ 85203

MISSAL, STEPHEN J
PAINTER, INSTRUCTOR
b Albuquerque, NMex, Apr 23, 48. *Study:* Wichita State Univ, BFA, 70, MFA, 72; Marymount Col, 72. *Work:* New Britain Mus Am Art, Conn; Jefferson Federal Savings & Loan Gallery, Meriden, Conn; Ulrich Mus, Wichita, Kans; Ariz Pub Serv, Phoenix; and pvt collections. *Comn:* Packard Deli at the Borgata (mural), 89; Shakespeare Festival (mural), Scottsdale Ctr Arts, 82; Jed Nolans (mural), Scottsdale, 82. *Exhib:* 9th Ann Ark Competition, Pine Bluff, 76; Festival 8, Scottsdale Ctr Arts, Ariz, 85; Springfield Mus Art, Nat Competitive Exhib, Utah, 85; Wilde Meyer Gallery, Nat Competitive Exhib, Scottsdale, Ariz, 87; Nat Forest Serv Centennial Competitive Exhib (touring), 91; and others. *Pos:* Primary illusr, Scottsdale Progress, 79-; paintings, Raising Arizona, 20th Century Fox and others. *Teaching:* Instr, White Mountain Sch, Littleton, NH, 72-74; instr, Northeast Mo State Univ, Kirksville, Mo, 74-77; vis instr painting, drawing & design, Scottsdale Community Col, Ariz, 79-87 & Phoenix Col, 84- *Awards:* Purchase Awards, Tulsa Invitational, 72 & 14th Ann Midwest Exhib, 76; Best Drawing, Scottsdale Ctr Arts, 77; Nat Forest Serv Centennial Competition Touring Exhib, 91. *Mem:* Ariz Watercolor Soc; Ariz Artist's Guild. *Media:* Oil, Pen & Ink. *Publ:* Illusr, numerous periodicals & newspapers. *Dealer:* El Mundo Magico Gallery PO Box 186 Sedona AZ 86336. *Mailing Add:* 6255 E Earll Dr Scottsdale AZ 85251

MITCHELL, CLIFFORD
ARCHITECT, PAINTER
b Birmingham, Ala, Sept 22, 25. *Study:* Tuskegee Inst, BS, 49; Univ Hartford Art Sch, BFA, 58. *Work:* New Brit Mus Am Art; Univ Conn Sch Pharm, Storrs; Stamford Mus & Nature Ctr; Conn Gen Life Ins Co, Bloomfield; Mattatuck Mus, Waterbury, Conn; and others. *Exhib:* Silvermine Guild Artists New Eng Exhib, New Canaan, Conn, 64; Conn Pub Television, Hartford, Conn, 76; Univ Conn, Waterbury, 77; Huntsville Mus Art, Ala, 79; De Cordova Art Mus, Lincoln, Mass, 79; John Slade Ely House Gallery, New Haven, Conn, 81; Aetna Inst Art Gallery, Hartford, Conn, 84; William Benton Mus, Univ Conn, 85; Western New Eng Col, Springfield, Mass, 87; Manhattan E Gallery Fine Arts, New York, 91. *Pos:* Architect, Clifford Mitchell, Hartford, 75- *Teaching:* Instr interior design, Univ Hartford Art Sch Eve Course, 68-69. *Awards:* First Prize, New Haven Arts Festival, 59; Donald M Makie Art Ed Award, Hartford, 83; Wintonbury Art League Drawing Award, 84. *Bibliog:* Janet Gaston (auth), Aux etats-unis/a New York salon audubon, La Rev Mod, 60; J V W B (auth), Works by Mitchell at local museum, New Brit Herald, 68; Jolene Goldenthal (auth), Look at art/an architect turns artist, Hartford Courant, 71. *Mem:* Conn Acad Fine Arts; Conn Watercolor Soc (pres, 70-72); Springfield Art League (Mass). *Media:* Oil, Watercolor; Graphics. *Mailing Add:* 1024 Trout Brook Dr West Hartford CT 06119

MITCHELL, DANA COVINGTON, JR
COLLECTOR
b Bluefield, WVa, Feb 22, 18. *Study:* Univ WVa, BA & MD. *Pos:* Pres bd trustees, Columbia Mus Art, 60-61. *Collection:* Contemporary American art. *Mailing Add:* 600 Spring Lake Rd Columbia SC 29206

MITCHELL, DEAN LAMONT
PAINTER
b Pittsburgh, Pa, Jan 20, 57. *Study:* Columbus Col Art & Design, BFA, 80. *Work:* Nelson-Atkins Mus Art, Kansas City, Mo; Margaret Harwell Art Mus, Poplar Bluff, Mo; St Louis Art Mus, Mo; Miss Art Mus, Jackson; Nat Parks Found, Jackson, Wyo. *Comn:* Jazz Mural (4 ft x 140 ft) Vista/Allis Plaza Hotel, Kansas City, Mo, 84-85; five historical Kansas City scenes, Mo Art Coun, 85. *Exhib:* Miniature Invitational, Tampa Mus Art, Fla, 89; Miniature Art Soc Fla 15th Intern Exhib, St Petersburg Mus, 90; Nat Acad Design, 165th Ann, New York, 90; Arts for the Parks, Wild Life Am West Art Mus, Jackson Hole, Wyo, 90; Artist of America, Colo Hist Mus, Denver, 91-92; and others. *Teaching:* Instr, figure drawing, Kansas City Art Inst, 8-12/90. *Awards:* Hardie Gramatky Mem Award, Am Watercolor Soc, 90; Best in Show, June Baumgardner Geldart, Min Art Soc Fla, 90; Allied Artist Gold Medal, 91. *Bibliog:* James Edwards (auth), Dean Mitchell Artist, 90; Mike Smith (dir), Coming Home (film), Globalvision/Greenwich workshop, 92; Ann Saunders (auth), Coming Home, Bay Arts Alliance, 92. *Mem:* Am Watercolor Soc; Allied Artist Am; Nat Watercolor Soc; Knickerbocker Artists; Nat Soc Painters Casein & Acrylic. *Media:* Oil, Watercolors. *Publ:* Auth, article, Artist Mag, F & W Publs, 84; Am Artist, Billboard Publs, 89; US Art, Frank Sisser, 89; Southwest Art, CBH Publ, 91; Being An Artist, North Light Books, 92. *Dealer:* Strecker Gallery 332 Poyntz Manhattan KS 66502; Carol Siple Gallery 1401 17th St Denver CO 50202. *Mailing Add:* Carol Siple-Gallery 1401 17th St Denver CO 80202

MITCHELL, DIANNE (BALL)
PAINTER
b Joliet, Ill. *Study:* Univ Hartford, Conn, Art Sch, with Rudolph Franz Zallinger, 82-83. *Work:* US Coast Guard Collection. *Exhib:* Ann Exhib, Salmagundi Club, New York, 84; Nat Midyear Exhib, Butler Inst Am Art, Youngstown, Ohio, 84; 100 Nat Finalists, Grand Cent Art Galleries, New York, 85; Egg Tempera and Watercolor Exhibition, Esther Wells Collection Galleries, Laguna Beach, Calif, 86; Am Watercolor Soc, 87; one-woman shows, Lake Tahoe Visitors' Ctr, 88 & 89, & US Coast Guard Exhib, Governor's Island, NY, 90; and others. *Teaching:* Egg Tempera Workshop, King's Beach, Calif, 92; painting on safari, Kenya, Africa, 92. *Awards:* Lo Manaco Studio Award, Pastel Soc Am, 82; 1st Prize Watercolor, 2nd Prize Best of Show, Emerald City Classic, Nepenthe Mundi Soc, 86; George Gray Award, US Coast Guard, 89; 1990 Commemorative Print Competition Winner, Lake Tahoe Summer Music Festival. *Mem:* Pastel Soc Am; Nat Mus Women Arts. *Media:* Egg Tempera, Watercolor. *Publ:* Illusr, Spinning: Where to begin, Shuttle Spindle & Dyepot Mag, 85; illusr & auth, One egg, over medium, Am Artist Mag, 86; cover, Conn Transport Mag, 92. *Dealer:* Esther Wells Collection 1390 South Coast Highway Laguna Beach CA 92651; Zantman Galleries San Francisco Carmel Palm Desert CA. *Mailing Add:* 533 Worcester Dr Cambria CA 93428

MITCHELL, FRED
PAINTER
b Meridian, Miss, Nov 24, 23. *Study:* Carnegie Inst Technol, scholar, 42-43; Cranbrook Acad Art, 46-48, BFA, 48, MFA, 56; Acad Fine Arts, Rome. *Work:* Columbus Gallery of Fine Arts, Ohio; Cranbrook Acad of Art, Bloomfield Hills, Mich; Munson-Williams-Proctor Mus Art, Utica, NY. *Comn:* Cast concrete screen, Miss State Col Women. *Exhib:* Younger Am Painters, Solomon R Guggenheim Mus, New York, 54; Dallas Mus Fine Arts, Tex, 54; Vanguard 55, Walker Art Ctr, Minneapolis, Minn, 55; Painter, Sculptor & Printmaker, New York Ink Drawings, 73; Painters in Watercolor, Hunterdon Art Ctr, Clinton, NJ, 75; one-man shows, Univ Maine, Machias, 74, State Univ NY at Binghamton Art Gallery, 76 & Munson-Williams-Proctor Sch Art Gallery, 77; and many others. *Pos:* Co-founder, Tanager Gallery, New York, 52-62; founder and artist-teacher, Downtown Art Ctr, FDR Inst, Battery Park, New York, 61 & South St Seaport Mus, New York, formerly; artist-in-residence, Columbia Mus of Art, SC, 65; artist-in-residence, Aspen Sch Contemp Art, Colo, 65. *Teaching:* Prof drawing and painting, Cranbrook Acad Art, Bloomfield Hills, Mich, 55-59; vis critic, Cornell Univ, Ithaca, 68-69; vis prof art, Ithaca Col, New York, 69-70; adj assoc prof art, New York Univ, 61-71; assoc prof art, Queens Col, New York, 73-74; vis prof art, Univ Maine, Machias, 74; vis artist, Univ Oregon, Eugene, 75; prof art, NYU Grad Sch in Venice, Italy, 75; vis assoc prof art and dir, Univ Art Gallery, State Univ NY, Binghamton, 76-77; vis artist, Munson-Williams-Proctor Sch Art, Utica, NY, 77. *Awards:* Traveling Fel, Italy, 48-51; Ford Found Artist-in-Residence, Columbia Mus Art. *Media:* Watercolor, Oil. *Mailing Add:* 503 E 116th St New York NY 10029

MITCHELL, JOAN ELIZABETH See Robertson, Joan E (Joan Elizabeth Mitchell)

MITCHELL, JOHN BLAIR
PAINTER, EDUCATOR
b Brooklyn, NY, Jan 30, 21. *Study:* Pratt Inst, cert, 39-43, Pratt Inst Sch Educ, 46-47; Columbia Univ Teachers Col, BS, 48, Univ, MA, 49; Pratt Graphic Arts Ctr, 60-61, with Edmondson, Rogalski & Ponce de Leon; NY Univ Sch Educ, PhD, 63. *Work:* Metrop Mus Art, New York; Libr of Cong, Washington, DC; Silvermine Guild Artists, Conn; Baltimore Mus Art; Notre Dame Col, Baltimore; Towson State Univ, Baltimore, Md. *Comn:* Mural, Baltimore City Hosp, 72. *Exhib:* Six shows, Corcoran Gallery Art, Washington, DC, 54-63; Libr of Cong 19th Nat Exhib Prints, 63; Silvermine Guild Artists 5th Nat, 64; one-man show, Baltimore Mus Art, 64; Hochschild Kohn Md Artists Today Anniversary, 72; one-man show, Towson State Univ, 64, 77, 85 & 88. *Teaching:* Prof graphics drawing, painting & photog & coordr grad art prog, Columbia Univ Teachers Col, 49-80, instr art, summers 50, 53 & 54; chmn art dept, Towson State Col, 51-57 & 63-65; instr graphics, Baltimore Mus Art, 63-73. *Awards:* First Awards, Intercollegiate Art Exhib, Coppin State Col, 72 & Easton Acad Art, 75; Md State Arts Coun Works in Progress Grant, 80; President's Award for Distinguished Serv to the Univ, Towson State Univ, 86. *Bibliog:* Lincoln Johnson (auth), articles, Baltimore Sun, 12/71 & 2/24/77; Earl Arnett (auth), article, Baltimore Sun, 12/1/75; Marcella Sussman (auth), article, Sunday Sun Magazine, 10/12/80; Elisabeth Stevens, Baltimore Sun, 12/8/85. *Mem:* Artists Equity Asn; Baltimore Print Club. *Publ:* Auth, Art Education, 52; coauth, Art in Our Maryland Schools, State Manual, State Dept Educ, 53; auth, School Arts, 2/57; auth, Eastern Arts Quart, 1-2/63. *Mailing Add:* 9918 Finney Dr Baltimore MD 21234

MITCHELL, KATHERINE
PAINTER
b Memphis, Tenn, Oct 25, 44. *Study:* Atlanta Col Art, BFA, 68; Tyler Sch Art, Rome, 68; Ga State Univ, MVA, 77. *Work:* High Mus Art; Ga Coun Arts, Richard B Russell Fed Off Bldg, Ga State Univ, Atlanta; Ark Art Ctr, Little Rock, Ark; JB Speed Mus, Louisville, Ky. *Exhib:* Ga Artists of the 20th Century, Madison-Morgan Cult Ctr, Ga, 79; Hassam Fund Purchase Exhib, Am Acad & Inst Arts & Lett, New York, 79; Avant-Garde: 12 in Atlanta (with catalog), 79 & Artists in Georgia, 80, High Mus Art; solo exhib, Notes on the Working Process, Atlanta Col Art Gallery, 81 & The New York Series and Beyond, Chastain Gallery, Atlanta, 83, Heath Gallery (with catalog), 86 & 87, Goodwyn Gallery, Auburn Univ, Montgomery, Ala, 90; The Art of Atlanta, Southeastern Ctr Contemp Art, Winston- Salem, NC, 88; Katherine Mitchell: A Retrospective, Chastain Gallery, Atlanta, 91; Recent Work, Heath Gallery, Atlanta, 91. *Teaching:* Drawing & painting, Emory Univ, 80- *Awards:* Hassam Fund Exhib Purchase Award, Am Acad & Inst Arts & Lett, 79; Southern Arts Federation/Nat Endowment Arts Regional Fel Award, 92. *Bibliog:* John Howett (auth), Katherine Mitchell at Atlanta College of Art, Art in Am, 1/82; Katherine Mitchell: Paintings, Heath Gallery, Atlanta, Ga, 86; Amy Jinkner-Lloyd (auth), Katherine Mitchell at Chastain & Heath, Art Am, 2/92; Laura Lieberman (auth), Katherine Mitchell: A Retrospective and Recent Work, Art Papers, 2/92. *Mem:* Twentieth Century Art Soc (exec bd). *Media:* Chalks, Conte. *Publ:* Contribr, Katherine Mitchell: A Retrospectie (catalog), essay by John Howett, Atlanta, 91. *Dealer:* Heath Gallery Atlanta Ga. *Mailing Add:* 80 Stratford Place NE Atlanta GA 30342

MITCHELL, MARGARETTA K
PHOTOGRAPHER, WRITER
b Brooklyn, NY, May 27, 35. *Study:* Smith Col, BA(magna cum laude), 57; Boston Mus Sch, 58; Escuela de Bellas Artes, Madrid, Spain, 59; Univ Calif, Berkeley, MA, 85. *Work:* Int Ctr Photog, New York; Performing Arts Archive, San Francisco, Calif; Bannoft Libr, Univ Calif, Berkeley; Royal Print Collection, Windsor, Eng; Oakland Mus, Calif. *Comn:* Mural, Anixter Corp, San Francisco, Calif, 74; mural, Amax Corp, San Francisco, Calif, 74; mural, San Francisco Art Comn, Calif, 78; posters, Portal Publ, 90. *Exhib:* San Francisco Mus Mod Art, Calif, 78; Recollections: Ten Women of Photog, Int Ctr Photog, New York, 79; Marcuse Pfeifer Gallery, NY, 81 & 86; War Mem Opera House, San Francisco, 86; Dance for Life, Oakland Mus, Calif, 85; Metrop Opera House, Lincoln Ctr, New York, 86; Univ Hawaii Art Gallery, 90; Bouquet's to Art, Deyoung Mus, 91. *Collections Arranged:* Recollections: Ten Women of Photography (auth, catalog), Int Ctr Photog, 79; Dance for Life (auth, catalog), Oakland Mus, Calif, 85. *Pos:* Pres, Am, Soc Mag Photog Northern Calif, Chapter, 90-92. *Teaching:* Instr photog, Univ Calif Extension, 76-78; instr photog, City Col San Francisco, Calif, 80-81; Calif Col Arts & Crafts, Oakland, 86, Univ Calif, summer session, 86; Friends Photog, summer workshop, 87, 88; workshop, Carleton Col, April, 88; Acad Art, San Francisco, 90-92. *Awards:* Nat Endowment Arts Mus Grant, 78-79; Calif Coun Arts Grant, Berkeley Art Ctr, 81-82; Grant, L J & Mary C Skaggs Found, 81. *Bibliog:* New Photography, Prentice-Hall, 83, 209-13; Encore Mag, fall 85; Focus Mag, April, 85. *Mem:* Am Soc Mag Photog; Inst Hist Study. *Media:* Black & White, Color. *Res:* Photographers, particularly rediscoveries; Art and California history; dance. *Publ:* Co-auth, To A Cabin, Grossman Publ, 73; introduction to: After Ninety, Univ Washington Press, 77; essays for Contemp Photogr, St Martin's Press, NY, 82; Dance for Life, Elysian Editions, 85; Flowers, Elysian Editions, 91. *Dealer:* Gumps Gallery 250 Post St San Francisco CA 94108; Michael Shapiro 250 Sutter St San Francisco CA 94108. *Mailing Add:* 280 Hillcrest Rd Berkeley CA 94705

MITCHELL, N DONALD
ADMINISTRATOR, DEALER
b Mt Vernon, NY, Mar 5, 22. *Study:* Wichita State Univ; Abbe Inst, Monterey Peninsula Col, art hist, painting with George DeGroat & Fay Hopkins. *Pos:* Vpres, Universal Arts, Inc, Carmel, Calif, 60-; dir, Zantman Galleries, Ltd, Carmel, 60-; co-owner, Highlands Gallery, Carmel, 60- *Specialty:* Quality works, mostly representational, in all media, styles and techniques. *Mailing Add:* PO Box 3731 Carmel CA 93921

MITCHELL, PETER TODD
PAINTER
b New York, NY, Nov 16, 29. *Study:* Acad Bellas Artes, Mexico City, Mex, with Lozano & Galvan; Groton; Yale Art Sch. *Work:* Metrop Mus Art, New York. *Comn:* Murals, Von Wrangell, Malaga, Spain, 55 & Thomas Murphy, St Tropez, France, 70. *Exhib:* Am Painters in Philadelphia Collections, 62; Smithsonian Traveling Show Graphics, 71; London Bridge Show, Guildhall-London, 72. *Awards:* First Tiffany Found Award for Painting, 52. *Bibliog:* Berg (auth), L'oeuvre de P T Mitchell, Jardin Arts, 69. *Media:* Oil. *Dealer:* Eric Galleries 61 E 57th St New York NY 10022. *Mailing Add:* 116 E 57th St New York NY 10022

MITCHELL, ROBIN
PAINTER, EDUCATOR
b Los Angeles, Calif, Sep 29, 51. *Study:* Univ Calif at Los Angeles, 70-71; Calif Inst Arts, BFA, 72, MFA, 74. *Work:* Security/Pacific Corp Collection, Los Angeles, Calif; Flour Corp, Irvine, Calif; Kaufman/Broad-Paris Collection, France; Tuttle & Taylor Collection, Los Angeles, Calif. *Exhib:* Abstract Variations, Jan Turner Gallery, Los Angeles, 91; Drawing Show, Nomadic Site at Bliss, Pasadena, 92; Abstract Paintings, Dorothy Goldeen Gallery, Santa Monica, 92; LA Express, Art Gallery Otis Sch Art & Design, Los Angeles, 92. *Teaching:* Vis artist studio art, Claremont Grad Sch, 79 & 83; lectr, Univ Southern Calif, 81- & Univ Calif at Irvine, 87- 92. *Awards:* National Endowment Arts Grant (painting), 87. *Bibliog:* Betty Brown (auth), Arts Mag, 83; Torene Svitil (auth), State of the arts, Exposure Mag, 87; Peter Frank (auth), Signs & Apparitions, Contemporenia, 88. *Mem:* Col Art Asn. *Media:* All. *Publ:* Dialogue: Robin Mitchell & Kay Whitney, Visions Art Quarterly, Vol 6, No 1, winter, 91-92; Drawing Show (catalog), Nomadic Site at Bliss, 92; LA Express (catalog), 92. *Mailing Add:* 2614 Euclid Apt E Santa Monica CA 90405

MITCHNICK, NANCY
PAINTER, EDUCATOR
b Detroit, Mich, 47. *Study:* Wayne State Univ, BFA, 72, grad work, 72-73; Hunter Col, 74-75. *Work:* Citibank, N Am, New York; Detroit Inst Arts; Edward Duffy Co, Detroit; J B Speed Mus, Louisville, Ky; Wayne State Univ, Detroit, Mich. *Comn:* Numerous pvt portrait comns. *Exhib:* Solo exhibs, Willis Gallery, Detroit, 73, Susanne Hilberry Gallery, Birmingham, Mich, 80-84 & 91, Hirschl & Adler Mod, New York, 83 & 86 & John Berggruen Gallery, San Francisco, 85; American Still Life: 1945-83, Houston Mus Contemp Art, Buffalo Fine Arts Acad, Albright-Knox Art Gallery, Neuberger Mus, State Univ NY, Purchase, 83-84; Landscape, Hudson River Mus, Yonkers, NY, and Tucson Mus Art, Ariz, 84; Views: Interior and Exterior, Koplin Gallery, Los Angeles, 85; New Response, Albany Inst Hist Art, NY, 85; Still Life-Landscape: New Approaches to Old Tradition, Gloria Luria Gallery, Bay Harbor Island, Fla, 86; Objects Observed, Summit Art Ctr, NJ, 86; Selected Member's Gallery Works, Albright-Knox Member's Gallery, Buffalo, NY, 86; Contemporary Screens, Art Mus Asn Am, Contemp Art Ctr, Cincinnati, Ohio, Lowe Art Mus, Coral Gables, Fla, City Art Gallery, Raleigh, NC, Toledo Mus Art, Ohio, Des Moines Art Ctr, Iowa, 86-88. *Teaching:* Instr painting, Wayne State Univ, 71-73 & Bard Col, 77-86; vis artist, Calif Inst Arts, Sch Art, Valencia, 87-89 & instr, 90- *Awards:* CAPS grant, NY State Coun Arts, 76-77; Nat Endowment Arts, 86-87; Pollack Krasner Found Grant, 90; Guggenheim Fel, 90-91. *Bibliog:* Dr June Taboroff (auth), Edward W Duffy & Co, Art Auction, 10/84; New York Times, 1/24/86; Arts Mag, 3/86. *Media:* Acrylic, Oil; Gouache on paper. *Dealer:* Hirschl & Adler Modern 851 Madison Ave New York NY 10021. *Mailing Add:* c/o Susanne Hilberry Gallery 555 S Woodward Birmingham MI 48009

MITTY, LIZBETH J
PAINTER, PRINTMAKER
b New York, NY, Oct 28, 52. *Study:* State Univ NY, Stony Brook, 69-71; Univ Wis, Madison, BS, 73, MFA, 75. *Work:* Metrop Mus Art, New York; Newark Mus, NJ; Mint Mus, Charlotte, NC. *Exhib:* The Broken Surface, Tibor de Nagy, NY Gallery & Bennington Col, Vt, 81; Textured Planes, Proctor Art Ctr, Annandale-on-Hudson, 82; The Artist Celebrates New York, Bronx Mus, Jamaica Mus, City Col Mus, Long Island Univ Mus & Staten Island Mus, NY, 85; Berkshire Mus, Pittsfield, Mass 89; In Search of the Am Experience, Mus Nat Arts Found, New York, 89; Contemp Prints New York Workshops Create, Bronx Mus Emerging Collection Gallery, 89; Long Island Landscape Painting in the Twentieth Century, Mus at Stonybrook, New York, 90. *Teaching:* Instr painting & drawing, Lake Erie Col, 75-76, Ohio State Univ, 76-77 & Jewish Asn Serv Aged, NY, 81-85. *Awards:* Best of Show, Lyndon House, Athens, Ga, 78. *Bibliog:* Grace Glueck (auth), rev, NY Times, 83; Edward Lucie-Smith (auth), American art now, Morrow, Inc, 85; Ronald Pisano (auth), Long Island Landscape Painting in the Twentieth Century, Little Brown Co, 90. *Media:* Acrylic, Oil; Monoprint. *Dealer:* Pelavin Additions Print Publisher. *Mailing Add:* 165 Church St Apt 5N New York NY 10007

MIYAMOTO, WAYNE AKIRA
PAINTER, PRINTMAKER
b Honolulu, Hawaii, Sept 6, 47. *Study:* Rensselaer Polytech Inst, 65-68; Univ Hawaii, BA & BFA, 70, MFA, 74. *Work:* Fine Arts Mus, Univ Alaska, Fairbanks; Leeward Community Col, Pearl City, Hawaii; Univ Cent Fla, Orlando; Contemp Art Mus, Asilah, Morocco; Fort Hays State Univ, Kans; Portland Art Mus, Ore; The Printmaking Workshop, New York; and others. *Exhib:* Kansas 13th Nat Small Printing, Drawing & Print Exhib, 88; Silvermine Int, New Canaan, Conn, 90 & 92; 34th Nat, Clinton, NJ, 90; Pacific Prints, Pala Alto, Calif, 92; Discoveries and Voyages, Honolulu Acad Arts, 92. *Pos:* Visual art consult & acquisition comt, State Found Cult Arts, Island Hawaii, 81-; exec bd, Hawaii Alliance Arts Educ, Honolulu, 88-89; Friends of Univ Hawaii-Hilo Art, 81-, vpres, 85-88; artist-in-residence, 11th Asilah Int Cult Festival, Morocco, 88; artist-in-residence, The Printmaking Workshop, New York, 90. *Teaching:* Art Dept, Univ Hawaii, Hilo. *Awards:* Juror's Award, 9th Kans Nat Exhib, 84; Juror's Award, Print Club of Philadelphia, 88; Purchase Award, Pacific Prints, 91. *Mem:* Honolulu Printmakers Asn (mem bd & treas, 71-72); Print Club, Philadelphia; Northwest Print Coun; Southern Graphics Coun. *Media:* All. *Publ:* Auth, Unique art of Akaji, Honolulu Star Bull Advertiser, 76; Lee Chesney, 25 Years of Printmaking, Univ Presses Fla, Gainesville, 78; ed, Pacific States Regional Print Exhib (exhib catalog), Univ Hawaii, Hilo, 82; Pacific States Regional Print & Drawing Exhib, (exhib catalog), Univ Hawaii Hilo, 83, 84, 85 & 86; Pacific States Biennial Nat Print Exhib (exhib catalog), Univ Hawaii, Hilo, 88, 90 & 92. *Mailing Add:* Art Dept Univ Hawaii Hilo HI 96720

MIYASAKI, GEORGE JOJI
PRINTMAKER, PAINTER
b Kalopa, Hawaii, Mar 24, 35. *Study:* Calif Col Arts & Crafts, BFA & BAEd, 57 & MFA, 58. *Work:* San Francisco Mus Art, Calif; Brooklyn Mus Art, NY; Mus Mod Art, New York; Art Inst Chicago; Pasadena Art Mus, Calif. *Teaching:* Prof art, Univ Calif, Berkeley, 64- *Awards:* John Simon Guggenheim Fel, 63-64; Nat Endowment Arts, 80-81 & 85-86. *Bibliog:* Rudy Turk (auth), George Miyasaki, monograph, 81. *Dealer:* Stephen Wirtz Gallery 49 Geary St San Francisco CA. *Mailing Add:* Dept Art Univ Calif at Berkeley Berkeley CA 94720

MOBLEY, KAREN R
PAINTER, ADMINISTRATOR
b Cheyenne, Wyo. *Study:* Univ Wyo, BFA, 83; Univ Okla, MFA, 87. *Exhib:* Under the Western Skies, Sangre de Cristo Art Ctr, Pueblo, Colo, 89; Museo de Arte Juarez & Chihauhau, Mex, 89; Selections 89, Col Santa Fe, NMex; Vision of Excellence, Albuquerque United Artists, NMex, 90; Phoenix Triennial, Phoenix Art Mus, Ariz, 90; New Am Talent, Laguna Gloria Art Mus, Austin, Tex, 92. *Collections Arranged:* Ocho Inspiraciones, 89; Comics, 89; Painting Divergence (catalog), 90; The Computer Art Show, 91. *Pos:* Dir, Univ Art Gallery, NMex State Univ, Las Cruces, NMex, 87- *Awards:* Best show, Sangre de Cristo Art Ctr, 89. *Bibliog:* Drawings, Puerto del Sol/NMex State Univ, 88. *Mem:* Col Art Asn; NMex Mus Asn; Am Asn Mus; Mountain Plains Mus Asn; Women's Caucus for the Arts. *Media:* Charcoal. *Res:* Emphasis on painting, drawing and folk art objects. *Dealer:* Adair Margo Gallery El Paso TX; Francine Ellman Gallery Santa Monica CA. *Mailing Add:* NMex State Univ Univ Art Gallery Williams Hall Box 30001 Las Cruces NM 88003

MOCK, RICHARD BASIL
PAINTER, ILLUSTRATOR
b Long Beach, Calif, Aug 2, 44. *Study:* Univ Mich, BS(design), 65; San Francisco Art Inst, with Richard Die Benkorn, 65; New York Studio Sch, with Philip Guston, 66-67. *Work:* Metrop Mus, Mus Mod Art, New York; Ft Worth Art Mus, Tex; Brooklyn Mus; Museo de Monterrey, Mex. *Comn:* 120 portraits of athletes at the winter Olympics, Lake Placid, NY, 80. *Exhib:* Solo exhib, Houston Contemp Arts Mus, Tex, 71-77; Portraits, Otis Art Inst, Los Angeles, 78; Block Prints, Whitney Mus Am Art, 82; American Artist as Printmaker, Brooklyn Mus, 83; Bronx Mus Art, 90. *Pos:* Illusr, New York Times, 79-89 & UN Develop Forum, 91- *Awards:* Fel, Roswell Mus, NMex, 69-70; Painting Grant, Nat Endowment Arts, 73. *Media:* Block Prints; Oil, Watercolor. *Publ:* Auth, Mock of the Times, Mock Studios, 86. *Mailing Add:* c/o Souyun Yi Gallery 249 Centre St New York NY 10013

MODE, CAROL A
PAINTER, PRINTMAKER
b St Louis, Mo, Mar 27, 43. *Study:* Washington Univ, BFA, 65, Summer Art Inst, 80; Vanderbilt Univ, 81-82. *Work:* Tenn State Mus, Nashville; Hosp Corp Am, Nashville; Northern Telecom, Vanderbilt Hosp, Nashville; Nynex, Nat. *Comn:* Billboard painting, IDS, Nashville. *Exhib:* 47th Ann Nat Midyear Exhib, 83 & 50th Nat Am Midyear Show, 86, Butler Inst An Art; Critics Choice, Arrowmont Sch Art, Gatlinburg, Tenn, 84 & Tenn State Arts, 86; Clemson Nat Print & Drawing Exhib, Clemson Univ, SC, 85; solo exhibs, Transfigurations, Tenn Fine Arts Mus, Nashville, 85, Tenn Arts Community Gallery, Nashville, 88 & Leu Gallery, Belmont Univ, Nashville, Tenn, 91; 21st Bradley Nat Print & Drawing Exhib, Biennial, Bradley Univ, Peoria, Ill, 87; 6th Ann Summer Lights Exhib, Metro Arts Comn, Nashville, 89-91; and others. *Teaching:* Instr adv painting, Belmont Univ, Nashville, 81-82, instr printmaking, 83- *Media:* Acrylic, Oil; Serigraphy, Silkscreen. *Dealer:* Cumberland Gallery 2213 Bandywood Dr Nashville TN 37215. *Mailing Add:* 3811 Richland Ave Nashville TN 37205

MODEL, ELISABETH D
SCULPTOR, PAINTER
b Bayreuth, Bavaria; US citizen. *Study:* Ryksacademy, Amsterdam, with Prof Jurgens; also with Prof Walter Thor & Prof Cericioli, Munich & Moissi Kogan, Paris. *Work:* Corcoran Galleries, Washington, DC; Wadsworth Atheneum, Hartford, Conn; Jewish Mus, New York; Rose Collection, Brandeis Univ; Rykesprenten Cabinet, Amsterdam; Newark Mus, NJ; and others. *Exhib:* Mus Fine Arts, Philadelphia; Mus Fine Arts, Boston; Brooklyn Mus; Stedelyk Mus, Amsterdam, Holland; Riverside Mus, New York; plus others. *Teaching:* Pvt lessons, Amsterdam, 30-38 & New York, 42-48. *Awards:* Gold Medal of Honor, Nat Asn Women Artists, 50; plus many awards & prizes. *Bibliog:* Meilach (auth), Contemporary Sculpture & Sculpture Casting, Crown. *Mem:* Fedn Mod Sculptors & Painters. *Media:* Stone, Wood. *Mailing Add:* 340 W 72nd St New York NY 10023

MODI-VITALE, LYDIA
MUSEUM DIRECTOR, CURATOR
b New York, NY. *Study:* Scholar Award, Art Students League, New York; apprentice of Hans Hoffman, New York; internship, Museo Nac de Hist, 45-46 & Museo Nac de Antropologia, 58, Mexico City; studies in art conserv & restoration, Univ Calif, Davis, 70. *Collections Arranged:* Early American Folk Art, Nat Art Gallery, Washington, DC, 68; Art Nouveau, 68, 150 videotape exhibs, 70-78, Process Art, Wynn Bullock, 72, Six from Castelli's, 74, New Deal Art: California, 76, The Graham Nash Exhibit of Rare and Vintage Photography, 78, De Saisset Gallery, Univ Santa Clara, Calif; Bill Viola: An Instrument of Simple Sensations & The Vatican Collection with the De Young Mus, Mus Italo Americano, 83-84. *Pos:* Dir, Triton Mus, San Jose, Calif, 66-68, De Saisset Mus, Univ Santa Clara, Calif, 68-78; consult, 78-; cur, Museo Italo Americano, 83-84; asst dir, Vorpal Gallery, San Francisco, 84, consult, 87- *Awards:* Adolph's Found Grant, 74, Calif Arts Comn Grant, 74 & Nat Endowment for the Humanities Grant & exten, 74 & 75. *Mem:* Western Asn of Am Mus (exec secy, 69-71); Am Asn Art Mus; Bay Area Lawyers for the Arts; Archeoclub d'Italia (bd dirs, currently). *Publ:* Ed catalogs, Twenty Color Photographs: Light Abstractions, Wynn Bullock, 72, Fletcher Benton: Selected Works 1964-74, 74 & Scholder Collects Scholder 1965-75 Retrospective, 75, de Saisset Art Gallery & Mus; co-ed, James W McManus: Survey of Selected Works 1967-77, De Saisset Art Gallery & Mus, 77. *Mailing Add:* 100 Font Blvd Apt 3E San Francisco CA 94132

MOE, RICHARD D
ADMINISTRATOR
b Fargo, NDak, May 7, 28. *Study:* Concordia Col, Moorhead, Minn, BA, 51; Univ Colo, MEd, 53, EdD, 60. *Pos:* Dean, Sch Fine Arts, Pac Lutheran Univ, Tacoma, Wash, 68- *Mem:* Tacoma Art Mus (pres, 77-79); Pac Northwest Ballet; Int Coun Fine Arts Deans; Pantages Ctr. *Mailing Add:* Sch Arts RM ING-101 Pacific Lutheran Univ Tacoma WA 98447

MOEHL, KARL J
PAINTER, WRITER
b Oberlin, Ohio, June 24, 25. *Study:* Univ Colo, Boulder, BFA, 50; State Univ Iowa, Iowa City, MFA, 52. *Work:* Currier Mus Art, Manchester, NH; Ill State Mus, Springfield; Lakeview Mus, Peoria, Ill; Dirksen Research Libr, Pekin, Ill; Städt Bodensee-Museum, Friedrichschafen, WGer. *Exhib:* 15th Ann Int, Pa Acad Fine Arts, Philadelphia, 52; one-man shows, Lakeview Mus, Peoria, Ill, 75, Peoria Art Guild, 79, Ill Cent Col, East Peoria, 79 & Tower Park Gallery, Peoria Heights, Ill, 82; Ill Landscape Art, Lakeview Mus & traveling, 76; 31st Ill Invitational, Ill State Mus, Springfield, 79; Miss Corridor 1981, Davenport Art Gallery, Iowa, 81; two-man show with James Hansen, Bradley Univ, Peoria, Ill, 86. *Pos:* Contrib ed, New Art Asn, 80; Illnois ed, New Art Examiner, 81- *Teaching:* Instr studio, Univ NH, Durham, 53-55 & Brown Univ, Providence, RI, 56-57; prof art hist, Bradley Univ, Peoria, Ill, 57- *Awards:* Purchase Award, Springfield Art Mus, Mo, 71; Merit Award, State Mus, Ill, 81; First Prize Painting, Ill Art League, 81 & 82. *Bibliog:* Dee Kilgo (auth), Karl Moehl Recent Work, New Art Examiner, 75. *Mem:* Chicago Art Coalition; Peoria Art Guild (bd mem, 72-81); Am Asn Univ Prof. *Media:* Acrylic, Graphite. *Publ:* Auth, 200 Years of American Painting, 65 & Edward Henry Pothast, 67, Lakeview Mus; Roger Annear Mem Exhib, Peoria Art Guild, 74; Metalsmith: Enamels' 87, Soc NAm Goldsmiths, 83; The Press of Primitivism, New Art Examiner, 85; Bradley University Print & Drawing Show, J Print World, 87- 89; Dow P Mitchell, Calder Lithos, 88. *Dealer:* Peoria Art Guild 1831 N Knoxville Ave Peoria IL 61603. *Mailing Add:* Div Art Bradley Univ Peoria IL 61625

MOELLER, ROBERT CHARLES, III
CONSULTANT
b Providence, RI, Jan 22, 38. *Study:* Washington & Lee Univ, BA(hist art), 59; Harvard Univ, with John Beckwith, Dr Hanns Swarzenski, J M Delaisse & J H Plummer, MA(art hist), 63. *Collections Arranged:* Brummer Collection, Duke Univ Art Mus. *Pos:* Res assoc dept art, Duke Univ, 67-68, dir, Univ Art Mus, 68-69; asst cur dept decorative arts & sculpture, Mus Fine Arts, Boston, 70-71, cur decorative arts & sculpture, 71-80. *Teaching:* Teaching fel hist art, Harvard Univ, 64-65; instr art, Duke Univ, 68, asst prof, 68-69; instr sem medieval sculpture, Univ NC, Chapel Hill, spring 68. *Mem:* Int Coun Mus; Am Asn Mus; Am Ceramic Circle; Soc Silver Collectors; Int Ctr Medieval Art. *Res:* Study of mid-twelfth century sculpture in Burgundy concentrating on Narthex sculpture of Charlieu, seventeenth century sculpture and decorative arts. *Publ:* Contribr, The Brummer Collection at Duke University, Art J, 68; auth, foreword, The Graphic Art of Edvard Munch, Duke Univ Art Mus Exhib, 12/69; Sculpture from Brive & Sculpture from Savigny, RI Sch Design, 7/69; L'iconographie de la facade nord du narthex de Charlieu, Actes des Journees d'etudes d'histoire et d'archeologie, Charlieu, Soc Amis Arts, 73. *Mailing Add:* PO Box 20339 Jackson WY 83001

MOERSCHEL, CHIARA
PAINTER
b Trieste, Italy; US citizen. *Study:* Lindenwood Col, with Robert Hansen & Sandra Del Munch. *Work:* Mead Gallery, Amherst Col, Mass; First Northwest Bank, St Ann, Mo; Western Ill Univ; Adria Club, Trieste, Italy; Adams Mark, Houston; Johnny Mathis; TWA; Harris Hosp, Ft Worth, Tex. *Comn:* Paintings in hotels in Kansas City, Clearwater, Fla & Ft Worth Tex. *Exhib:* Span Int Pavillion, 69; one-man shows, Springfield Col, Ill, 71, Galleria Il Velocipede, Venice, Italy, 72 & Lynn Kottler Gallerie, New York, 73; Trieste, Italy, 76, 78 & 80; Sheraton Hotel, Cairo, Egypt, 84; and many others. *Teaching:* Instr workshops, US & abroad. *Awards:* Gustave Geotch Mem Prize, St Louis Artists Guild, 69; First Prize for Watercolor, Am Bar Asn, St Louis, 70; First Prize for Watercolor, Sesquicentennial Show, Northeast Mo State Col, 71; Four Grumbacher Awards, Best of Show, Downtown Gallery, Fort Worth, Tex, Springfield Art Mus, Mo, Barucci Gallery, St Louis & Finer Things Gallery, Kansas City; and over 200 other awards. *Mem:* Acad Prof Artists (mem bd, 70-75); St Charles Artists' Guild (pres, 69-75, 84-85); St Louis Artists' Guild (vchmn art sect, 70); Am Watercolor Soc; and others. *Media:* Watercolor, Oil. *Mailing Add:* 121 College Dr St Charles MO 63301

MOFFETT, KENWORTH WILLIAM
CRITIC, CURATOR
b Newark, NJ, Nov 26, 34. *Study:* Columbia Univ, BA, 58; Harvard Univ, MA, 62, PhD, 68. *Collections Arranged:* Jules Olitski, 72, Morris Louis, 73, Anthony Caro, 76, Larry Poons, 81 & Fairfield Porter, 83, Mus Fine Arts, Boston. *Pos:* Cur twentieth century art, Mus Fine Arts, Boston, 71-84; publ, Moffett's Artletter, 86-89; dir mus art, Ft Lauderdale, 89-92. *Teaching:* Prof art, Wellesley Col, 68-79. *Awards:* Ford Found Grant, 70; Award Art Criticism, Nat Endowment Arts, 72; Am Coun Learned Socs Grant, 75-76. *Mem:* Int Asn Art Critics; Am Asns Mus; Asn Art Mus Dirs; Fla Art Mus Dirs Asn. *Res:* Post-war Art. *Publ:* Auth, Meier Graefe as Art Critic, Prester Verlag, 73; Kenneth Noland, 77 & Jules Olitski, 81, Abrams; New Acrylic Painting, Giles Nérer, Paris, 92. *Mailing Add:* Mus of Art Inc Ft Lauderdale FL 33301

MOFFITT, JOHN FRANCIS
HISTORIAN, PAINTER
b San Francisco, Calif, Feb 25, 40. *Study:* Calif Col Arts & Crafts, BFA, 63; Calif State Univ, San Francisco, MA, 64; Fac Lett & Philos, Univ Madrid, PhD, 66. *Exhib:* 13th Ann NC Artists Exhib, NC State Mus Art, Raleigh, 68; 1st Biennial 5-State Exhib, Gates Gallery, Port Arthur, Tex, 71; 12th Midwest Biennial, Joslyn Art Mus, Omaha, Nebr, 72; 21st Ann Exhib, Beaumont Art Mus, Tex, 72; 50th Regional Exhib, R S Barnwell Art Ctr, Shreveport, La, 72; plus others. *Teaching:* Asst prof art, E Carolina Univ, Greenville, NC, 66-68; Sonoma State Col, Cotati, Calif, 68-69; vis prof landscape painting, Mendocino Art Ctr, Calif, 69; prof art, NMex State Univ, Las Cruces, 69-; vis assoc prof art, Fla State Univ, 78; vis prof art, Univ Valencia, Spain, 81; vis prof art hist, Univ Autonoma, Madrid, 85. *Mem:* Col Art Asn Am; Hispanic Art Hist Studies in US; Mid-Am Col Art Asn; Rocky Mountain Medieval & Renaissance Hist Asn; Hermetic Text Soc. *Media:* Acrylic, Oil. *Interests:* Field of 16th and 17th century Spanish and Modern European art. *Publ:* Who is the old man in a golden helmet, Art Bull, Vol 66, summer 84; In vino veritas! Velazquez, Baco y Perez de Moya, Boletin del Museo del Prado, 85; Painting music and poetry in Velazquez's Las Hilanderas, Konsthistorisk Tidskrift, Stockholm, 85; Occultism in Avant-Garde Art: The Case of Joseph Beuys, UMI Res Press, 88; Velazquez: Practia E Idea, Univ Málaga Press, 91; plus numerous critical reviews in Art Quart, Art J, Burlington Mag, Leonardo, etc. *Mailing Add:* 1104 Luna St Las Cruces NM 88001

MOGAVERO, MICHAEL JAMES
PAINTER
b Rochester, NY, Nov 4, 50. *Study:* Buffalo State Univ, BS, 73; Hoffberger Sch Painting, Md Inst Col Art, MFA, 75. *Work:* Rochester Mem Art Gallery, NY. *Exhib:* Md Biennial, Baltimore Mus Art, 74 & 75; Maryland Artists--A New Look, Baltimore Mus Art, 79; New Directions: Contemp Am Art from Commodities Corp Collection Traveling Exhib, 81-83; 36-18-6-1, Sarah Lawrence Col Gallery, 82; one person-exhibs, Holly Solomon Gallery, 83, Gallery Six Friedrich, Munich, Ger, 83, Gallery Corinne Hummel, Basel, Switz, 85 & Oscarsson Siegeltuck Gallery, New York, 86 & 87, Carol Getz Gallery, Miami, Fla, 88 & Ruth Siegel Gallery, New York, 89; Back to the USA Traveling Exhib, Kunstmus, Lucerne, Rheinische Landesmus, Bonn & Kunstverein, Stuttgart, 83; Made in America: 200 Years of Drawing, Minneapolis Inst Art, Minn, 83; Eaton-Schoen Gallery, San Francisco, 84; San Francisco Mus Art, 87; Siegeltuch Gallery, New York, 88; Moody Gallery, Houston, Tex, 88; Lyons Matrix Gallery, Austin, Tex, 92. *Teaching:* Asst prof, Univ Tex, Austin, 84- *Awards:* Individual Fel, NY Found Arts, 85. *Bibliog:* Ken Sofer (auth), article, Art News, 5/82; Marcia Tucker (auth), An iconography of recent figurative painting: Sex, death, violence and the apocalypse, Artforum, summer 82; Jon R Friedman (auth), Mark Milloff/ Michael Mogavero, Arts Mag, 6/83; Anette Carlozzi (auth), 50 Texas Artsits, Chronicle Books, 86, p70-71. *Media:* Acrylic, Oil on Canvas. *Dealer:* Oscarsson Siegeltuck Gallery 568 Broadway New York NY 10012. *Mailing Add:* 12 John St New York NY 10038

MOGENSEN, PAUL
PAINTER, PRINTMAKER
b Los Angeles, Calif, Dec 3, 41. *Study:* Yale Univ, 62, Univ Southern Calif, BFA, 63. *Work:* Mus Mod Art, New York; High Mus Art, Atlanta, Ga; Houston Mus Fine Arts, Tex; Wadsworth Atheneum, Hartford, Conn. *Exhib:* One-man shows, Bykert Gallery, New York, 67-69 & 75, Weinberg Gallery, San Francisco, 77 & 80 & Janus Gallery, Los Angeles, 81; Romantic Minimalism, Inst Contemp Art, Philadelphia, 67; Modular Painting, Albright-Knox Art Gallery, Buffalo, NY, 70; A View of a Decade, Mus Contemp Art, Chicago, 77; Retrospective, Houston Mus Fine Arts, 78-79; Mary Boone Gallery, New York, 78; Edward Thorp Gallery, 87 & 88; Piccalo Spoleto Festival, Charleston, SC, 92. *Collections Arranged:* Structural Art, Am Fedn of Art Traveling Exhib, 67. *Awards:* John Simon Guggenheim Mem Found Fel, 76; Nat Endowment Arts, 80; Pollock-Krasner Found Grant, 88. *Bibliog:* H Rosenstein (auth), Total and complex, Art News, 5/67; Phyllis Derfner (auth), Paul Mogensen at Bykert, Art Am, 7-8/75; Valentin Tatransky (auth), Paul Mogensen: rectangles spirals, Arts Mag, 5/79; Carter Ratcliff (auth), Paul Mogensen at Thorp, Art Am, 87. *Mailing Add:* 159 Mercer St New York NY 10012

MOHLE, BRENDA SIMONSON
CONSULTANT, ART DEALER
b Dallas, Tex, May 9, 59. *Study:* Univ Tex, Austin, BA, 80. *Pos:* Art adv, Newman Gallery, 81-84; art adv & gallery dir, Omni Art, 84-; docent, Dallas Mus Art, 85-; art consultant, Signet Art, 87- *Specialty:* Corporate work including late 19th century European work through contemporary American. *Mailing Add:* 2211 High Point Carrollton TX 75007

MOHN, CHERI (ANN)
PAINTER, INSTRUCTOR
b Akron, Ohio, Aug 12, 36. *Study:* Akron Art Inst, Ohio; Youngstown State Univ, BA. *Work:* Butler Inst Am Art; Phoenix Gallery, Philadelphia; Johnny Artcher's Ghost Town Gallery, Mogollon, NMex. *Comn:* Portrait, Dean Miller, Busn Dept, Youngstown State Univ, 79; many other comns. *Exhib:* Solo exhibs, Village Art Gallery, 76 & Gallery 732, Akron, Ohio, 85; Peter Hurd Watercolor Show, Artesia, NMex, 68; Butler Inst Am Art Midyear Show, Youngstown & Guest Artist at Studio 09, Cleveland, 70; John Young Invitational, Youngston, 72-90; Paula Insel Gallery, New York, 73; Lynn Kottler Galleries, New York, 73; Trumbull Art Guild Art Show, 79-81; Mogollon Artists Mus, El Paso, Tex, 90. *Pos:* Art columnist, Niles Times, 58; auth & illusr, articles in Pigment & Form, 67-68; asst ed, writer & illusr, Paintin' Place News Inc, 72; illusr, Village Life Inc, 72; dir, Village Art Gallery, Village Market Place, Columbiana, Ohio, 76-77; ed & illusr, Theron's Country News, 86. *Teaching:* Dir & instr fine arts, Cheri Mohn Sch Arts, Youngstown, 63-67; instr fine arts, Cheri Mohn Studio, 68-90; instr Fine Arts, Butler Inst Am Art, 86-88. *Awards:* Mademoiselle Mag Top Twenty Women Artists in USA, 60; Galerie des Champignons Purchase Award, 68; Butler Inst Am Art Purchase Prize, 70; Watercolor Awards: Women--A Celebration, 84-90; Winners Show, Youngstown State Univ, 84, 85, 87. *Bibliog:* Rakocy (auth), Artist of the month, Pigment & Form, 67; Yoder (auth), article, Paintin Place News, 74; feature in Grumbacher's Palette Talk, 86; New York Art Rev, 89. *Mem:* Copley Soc Boston; Soc NAm Artists; Friends Am Art; and others. *Media:* Oil, Watercolor. *Publ:* auth, Art Features, Niles Times, 58; auth, Art Editorials, Paintin Place News, 72. *Dealer:* Debora Altimus Gallery 2721 Heritage La Canton OH 44728. *Mailing Add:* 12691 South Ave North Lima OH 44452

MOHR, K(AREN) LEE
PAINTER, ADMINISTRATOR
b Anchorage, Alaska, Aug 13, 54. *Study:* Western Washington State Univ, BFA, Public Sculpture, studied with Lloyd Hamrol, 75; Alaska Pacific Univ/ Arts Admin, MLA, 87. *Work:* Brit Petroleum, Alaska Pacific Univ, Anchorage, Alaska. *Comn:* Painting, Alaska Pacific Univ, Anchorage, Alaska, 85. *Exhib:* Juried Exhib, Visual Arts Ctr, Anchorage, Alaska, 87, 88 & 89; Anchorage Mus Hist, Alaska, 88; Sound Art, Friesen Gallery, Seattle, 92; Making Marks Experimental Drawings, Mival Gallery, Mercer Island, Wash, 92; Christo's Umbrella Exhib, Armory Ctr, Pasadena, 92. *Pos:* Exec dir, Eagle River Arts Acad, Eagle River, 5/87-1/90. *Teaching:* Art instr, drawing & painting, Artists in Sch Gildersleave, Alaska, 88-89 & Meyers Chuck, Alaska; art instr, drawing, Kirkland Arts Ctr, Wash, 91; art instr, drawing, King Coun Parks, Seattle, 92- *Awards:* Alaska Pacific Univ, Anchorage, Alaska; British Petroleum Corp, Anchorage, Alaska; Christo's Umbrella Exhibit Int, Pasadena. *Mem:* Seattle Art Mus, 92. *Media:* Oil. *Mailing Add:* 627 9th Ave S Kirkland WA 98033

MOHR, PAULINE CATHERINE
CONSERVATOR, RESTORER
b Sheboygan, Wis, May 7, 48. *Study:* Northwestern Univ, BA; Cooperstown Grad Prog, State Univ NY, MA(cert art conserv), with Sheldon & Caroline Keck. *Pos:* Conservator, San Francisco Mus Mod Art, Calif, 76-; conservator, Western Regional Paper Conserv Lab, Calif Palace Legion Honor, San Francisco, 76- *Mem:* Int Inst Conserv Hist & Artistic Works; Am Inst Conserv Hist & Artistic Works. *Media:* Paintings, Paper. *Mailing Add:* 1809 Grant St Berkeley CA 94703

MOIR, ALFRED
HISTORIAN, CURATOR
b Minneapolis, Minn, Apr 14, 24. *Study:* Harvard Univ, AB, 48, AM, 49, PhD, 53; Univ Rome, 50-51. *Pos:* Art historian in residence, Am Acad Rome, 69-70 & 80; dir, Univ Calif Educ Abroad Prog, Italy, 78-80; chmn dept art, Univ Calif, Santa Barbara, 63-69; adj cur, Univ Art Mus. *Teaching:* From instr to assoc prof hist art, Newcomb Col, Tulane Univ, 52-62; from assoc prof to prof, Univ Calif, Santa Barbara, 62-91, prof emer, 91- *Mem:* Soc Archit Historians; Renaissance Soc; Medieval Acad Am; Southern Calif Art Historians; Soc of Fels, Acad in Rome; Ateneo Veneto, Venice (Italy). *Res:* Italian baroque art, particularly Caravaggio and his followers; drawings; Van Dyck. *Publ:* Ed, Regional Styles of Drawing in Italy 1600-1700, 77; auth, Caravaggio, 82; 89; ed, Old Master Drawings from the Feitelson Collection, 83; Old Master Drawings from the Collection of John and Alice Steiner, 86; Van Dyck's Antwerp; and others. *Mailing Add:* Dept Art Hist Univ Calif Santa Barbara CA 93106

MOJSILOV, ILENE KRUG
PAINTER
b St Paul, Minn, May 3, 52. *Study:* Univ Minn, BFA, 74, MFA, 77; Ryusei Sch, Ikebana, studied with Kosen Otsubo, lic, 84. *Work:* Maki Gallery, Tokyo. *Exhib:* Tweed Mus Art, Duluth, Minn, 76; Arizona Outlook 78, Tucson Mus Art, 78; Independent Exhibition, Keimin Gallery, Yokohama, 80; Destructive Art in Japan, Tokyo Metrop Mus, 83; Centre Nationale des Arts Plastiques, Paris, 85; Munic Gallery of Vitry, Vitry sur Seine, France, 85; 37th & 38th Salon de Jeune Peinture, Grand Palais, Paris, 85 & 86; L'Ambiente Gallery, New York, 86 & 87; No Name Gallery, Minneapolis, 88. *Pos:* Artist-in-residence, Asn Confluences, Paris, 84-85, La Vie des Formes, Chalon-sur-Saône, France, 90. *Teaching:* Instr painting, Tucson Mus Art Sch, 77-78; artist-in-residence, Minn State Arts Bd, 86-; instr, Walker Art Center, 88- *Bibliog:* Yuri Akita (auth), New painting, Ikebana Soc, 8/83; Sandra Kwock-Silve (auth), From classical to avant-garde, Paris Free Voice, 4/85. *Mem:* Univ Film Soc; Minn Citizens for Arts. *Media:* Oil, Gouache. *Publ:* Auth, Performance and the mass media, Art Network (Japan issue), spring 84. *Dealer:* No Name Gallery 100 N First St Minneapolis MN 55409. *Mailing Add:* 4130 Blaisdell Ave S Minneapolis MN 55409-1513

MOLDROSKI, AL R
PAINTER, EDUCATOR
b Terre Haute, Ind, Aug 27, 28. *Study:* Ind State Univ, BS; Mich State Univ, MA; Southern Ill Univ, grant; Md Inst Art, Post Masters. *Exhib:* Pa Acad Fine Arts; Detroit Mus Art; City Art Mus, St Louis; De Waters Art Ctr; Boston Festival Arts; and many others. *Pos:* Ill Spec Events Comn. *Teaching:* Lectr art, Southern Ill Univ, formerly; asst prof, Glenville State Col, formerly; from instr to prof art, Eastern Ill Univ, 63-; exchange prof, Portsmouth Polytech Fine Arts, Portsmouth, Eng & Wyzsza Szkola Roiniczo-Pedagogiczna w Siedlcach. *Awards:* Tiffany Found Grant; Purchase Award, Pa Acad Fine Art; Mary Richart Mem Award in Painting & Art Directors Award, Detroit Mus Art; and many others. *Media:* All. *Mailing Add:* Dept Art Eastern Ill Univ Charleston IL 61920

MOLINARI, GUIDO
PAINTER, SCULPTOR
b Montreal, Que, Oct 12, 33. *Study:* Ecole Beaux-Arts, Montreal; Sch Art & Design, Montreal Mus Fine Arts. *Work:* Kuntsmuseum, Basel, Switz; Mus Mod Art, Guggenheim Mus & Chase Manhattan Bank, New York; Nat Gallery Art, Ottawa, Ont. *Comn:* Murals, comn by Dept of Pub Works, Ottawa for Vancouver Int Airport, BC, 68 & Dept Nat Defence Hq Bldg, Ottawa, 72. *Exhib:* 4th Guggenheim Int Exhib, New York, 64; The Responsive Eye, Mus Mod Art, 65; Canada: Art Aujourdui, Rome, Paris, Lausanne, Bruxelles, 68; Venice 34th Biennial, Italy, 68; Can 101, Edinburgh, Scotland, 68; Retrospective Exhib, Nat Gallery, Ottawa, Montreal, Toronto & Vancouver, 76; 15th Anniversary Paris Biennial, Mus Mod Art, Paris & Seibu Art Mus, Tokyo, Japan, 77-78; Contemp Can Painters Exhib, Dept External Affairs World Tour, 77-78. *Pos:* Founder & pres, L'Actuelle, 55-57. *Teaching:* Head painting sect, Sir George Williams Univ, 70- *Awards:* Robertson Award, Montreal Mus Fine Arts, 65; Guggenheim Mem Found fel, 66; Bright Found Award Painting, 68. *Bibliog:* Gros Plan (film), Radio-Can, Montreal, 71. *Mem:* Academician Royal Can Acad Arts; Soc Esthetique Experimentale, Paris; Soc Color Res, Nat Coun Res (dir, 72). *Publ:* coauth, Debats sur la Peinture Quebecoise, Univ Montreal, 71. *Mailing Add:* 3288 Saint Catharine St E Montreal PQ H1W 2C6 Canada

MOLLER, HANS
PAINTER
b Wuppertal, Ger, Mar 20, 05; US citizen. *Study:* Kunstgewerbeschule Wuppertal-Barmen, 19-27; Acad Fine Arts, Berlin, 27-28. *Work:* Mus Mod Art & Whitney Mus Am Art, New York; Detroit Inst Art, Mich; Joseph Hirshhorn Mus, Washington, DC; Minneapolis Mus; and many others. *Comn:* Stained glass window, Am Fedn Arts, 53; tapestry, comn by Mr & Mrs Lawrence Buttenwieser, New York, 66; seven stained glass windows, comn by Mr & Mrs Neil Carothers, III, Washington, DC, 69. *Exhib:* Contemp Am Painting, Univ Ill, Urbana, 49-59; Third Art Int, Japan, 55; solo exhibs, Allentown Art Mus, Pa, Norfolk Mus, Va, 69 & Midtown Galleries, New York, NY, 70, 73, 76, 79, 81, 84; Contemp Painting, Sculpture & Graphics, 69. *Teaching:* Instr painting, Cooper Union Sch Art, 44-56. *Awards:* Carnegie Prize, Nat Acad, 85; Edwin Palmer Mem Prize, Nat Acad, 80 & 92; Gold Medal Prize, Audubon Artists NY, 92; and others. *Bibliog:* Abram Kampf (auth), Contemporary synagogue art, Union Am Hebrew Congregation, 66; Edward Betts (auth), Creative Landscape Painting, 78; 60 Years of Collecting American Art, Butler Inst, 79. *Mem:* Nat Acad Design. *Media:* Oil, Watercolor. *Dealer:* Midtown Payson Galleries 745 Fifth Ave New York NY 10151. *Mailing Add:* 2207 Allen St Allentown PA 18104

MOMENT, JOAN
PAINTER, EDUCATOR
b Sellersville, Pa, Aug 22, 38. *Study:* Univ Conn, BS, 60; Univ Colo, with Roland Reiss & William Wiley, MFA, 70. *Work:* E B Crocker Art Mus, Sacramento, Calif; Blue Cross of Southern Calif, Los Angeles; NY State Develop Corp, New York; Oakland Mus, Calif; Allen Mem Art Mus, Oberlin Col, Ohio; and others. *Exhib:* Contemp Am Art Biennial, Whitney Mus Am Art, New York, 73; one-person show, Whitney Mus Am Art, 74, Crocker Art Mus, Sacramento, Calif, 81 & Quay Gallery, San Francisco, Calif, 82; Touching All Things, Walnut Creek Civic Arts Gallery, Calif, 77; Crocker Kingsley, Crocker Art Mus, 78; Drawings by Painters, Long Beach Mus Art, Calif, 82; Sacramento State: The Early Seventies, Joseph Chowning Gallery, San Francisco, Calif, 82; and many others. *Teaching:* Assoc prof art, Calif State Univ, Sacramento, 70-; guest lectr, Wash State Univ & Univ Calif, Davis, 74; vis artist, Univ Colo, Boulder, 75, Ill State Mus, Bloomington, 77, Claremont Col, Calif, 80 & Long Beach State Univ, 80; vis lectr, Univ Mont, Missoula, 77 & Diablo Valley Col, Pleasant Hill, Calif, 78. *Bibliog:* Victoria Dalkey (auth), Moment in transition, Art Week, 11/79; Beverly Terwomen (auth), Two artists and the potent hit, Art Week, 4/80; Charles Shere (auth), Four exhibits by women artists, Oakland Tribune, 4/80; and many others. *Media:* Acrylic on Watercolor Board and Canvas; Painted Clothing; Gouache on Vellum. *Mailing Add:* 1424 35th St Sacramento CA 95816

MOMIYAMA, NANAE
PAINTER, EDUCATOR
b Tokyo, Japan. *Study:* Bunka Gakuin Col, Tokyo; Tokyo Women's Col; Art Students League. *Work:* Nat Mus Mod Arts, Tokyo; Metrop Mus Arts, Tokyo; City Mus Kyoto, Japan; Munic Mus Osaka, Japan; Newberger Mus, Purchase, NY. *Exhib:* Mod Arts Asn Japan, 51-81; Grand Prix Humanitaire de France, 75; one-man shows, Seibu Gallery Tokyo, 74, 77, 79, 82, 84, 87 & 90, Ligoa Duncan Gallery, New York, 75 & Galeries Raymond Duncan, Paris, 75 & 76; plus many others. *Pos:* Permanent juror, Mod Art Asn, Japan, Nat Asn Women Artists, 68-77 & 90-92 & Salone Int di Pittura, Rome, 72. *Teaching:* Instr, State Univ NY Col, Purchase, 73-80; lectr, Nat Gallery Washington, DC, Philadelphia Mus, Brooklyn Mus, Pittsfield Mus, Columbia Univ, Pratt Inst, Japan Soc, NY & numerous other institutions in US & Japan. *Awards:* Madaille d'Argent, Grand Prix Humanitaire de France, 75; Charles Woodbury Mem Prize, Nat Asn Women Artists Ann, Nat Acad, New York, 78; Gold Medal, Accademia Italia delle Arti, 79; Golden Flame Prize, Accademia Italia, 85. *Bibliog:* Takachiyo Uemura (auth), Mizue, Bijitsu Shuppan-Sha, 54 & 74; Kaoru Yamaguchi (auth), Geijitsu Shincho, Shincho-Sha. *Mem:* Mod Arts Asn Japan; Japanese Artists Asn NY (pres, 78-79); Asn Int Artists Plastiques; Japanese Artist Asn; Nat Asn Women Artists; Contemp Artist Guild. *Media:* Oil, Mixed Media. *Publ:* Auth, Sumi-e, An Introduction to Ink Painting, 67; illusr, Makura-no-Soshi of Sei Shonagon, 67; Rev Paris, 68; cover design, The Asian, 85. *Mailing Add:* PO Box 44 Glenville Sta Greenwich CT 06831

MONAGHAN, KEITH
PAINTER, EDUCATOR
b San Rafael, Calif, May 15, 21. *Study:* Univ Calif, Berkeley, BA & MA. *Work:* Wash State Univ; Seattle Art Mus; Portland Art Mus; and many corp & pvt collections. *Exhib:* San Francisco Mus, 46-48, 50 & 53; Legion of Honor Mus, San Francisco, 59; De Young Mus, San Francisco, 48, 50, 60, 62; Seattle Art Mus, 48, 50-66; 29th Ann Butler Inst Am Art, Youngstown, Ohio, 64; one-man shows, Woodside Gallery, Seattle, Wash, 82, Wash State Univ, 87, Wm Sawyer Gallery, San Francisco, 87, Tacoma Art Mus, 88; Gov Invitational, 66-70, 73-75, 79 & 81; and others. *Teaching:* Lectr art, Univ Calif, Berkeley, 46-47; prof art, Wash State Univ, 47-86, chmn dept art, 51-72, prof emer, 86- *Awards:* San Francisco Art Asn Award, 48; Seattle Art Mus Award, Northwest Watercolor Soc, 51; and others. *Media:* Acrylic on Canvas; Casein on Paper. *Mailing Add:* NE 1705 Lower Dr Pullman WA 99163

MONAGHAN, WILLIAM SCOTT
PAINTER, SCULPTOR
b Philadelphia, Pa, Nov 1, 44. *Study:* Yale Univ, BA; Harvard Grad Sch Design, MA. *Work:* Addison Gallery Am Art, Andover, Mass; Brockton Fuller Mem Art Mus, Mass; Fed Reserve Bank, Boston; Hyatt Hotel, Boston; Aldrich Mus Contemp Art, Ridgefield, Conn. *Comn:* Sculpture, Boston 200 Bicentennial Art Collection, 76. *Exhib:* Sculptors' Workshop Show, Addison Gallery Am Art, 74 & Berkshire Mus, Pittsfield, Mass, 75; one-man show, Inst Contemp Art, Boston, 75; Contemp Reflections, Aldrich Mus Contemp Art, 76; Davidson Art Mus, Wesleyan Univ, Conn, 77; two-man show, Soho Ctr for Visual Artists, New York, 77. *Mem:* Boston Visual Artists' Union. *Mailing Add:* 165 Perry St New York NY 10014

MONAHAN, GENE RITCHIE
PAINTER, PRINTMAKER
b Duluth, Minn, June 25, 08. *Study:* Duluth State Teachers Col, 29-31; Univ Minn, BS, 36, MS(art educ), 42; Nat Acad Sch Fine Art, New York, 56-59. *Work:* Columbia Presby Med Ctr, New York; Permanent, Tweed Mus Art, Duluth, Minn, 87. *Comn:* Portrait of Gov Perpich, Gov Mansion, St Paul, Minn, 79. *Exhib:* Biennial Exhib, Minneapolis Art Inst, 32; Walker Art Ctr, Minneapolis, 45; National Gallery, Smithsonian Inst, Washington, DC, 56, 60 & 62; solo exhib, Little Gallery, Minneapolis Art Inst, 64; 4th Annual Invitational, Kirby Ctr, Univ Minn, Duluth, 64; Reunion Exhib, Duluth Art Inst, 86; 50th Anniversary, Minn Artists Asn, 87. *Pos:* Dir, Summer Art Workshop, Ranier, Minn, 63-67. *Teaching:* Art supv, Faribault Pub Sch, Minn, 43-46; fel art & painting, Nat Acad Fine Art, 58-59; instr art, Univ Minn Exten, 65-68. *Awards:* First Prize Portraits, Arrowhead Regional Exhib, Duluth Art Inst, 30 & Nat League Am Pen Women Nat Exhib, Smithsonian Inst, Washington, DC. *Bibliog:* Public Broadcast System, video (studio interview), broadcast WDSE TV8, 86 & 88; articles in Academic Nurse, J Columbia Sch Nursing, fall 89 & Am J Nursing, 8/90. *Media:* Oil. *Mailing Add:* Box 63 Renier MN 56668

MONDALE, JOAN ADAMS
CRAFTSPERSON, CERAMIST
b Eugene, Ore, Aug 8, 30. *Study:* Macalester Col, St Paul, Minn, BA, 52; hon degrees from Barnard Col, 77, Macalester Col, 77, RI Sch Design, 78, Pomona Col, 79, Beloit Col, 81, Col New Rochelle, 81, San Francisco Inst Arts, 82, Corcoran Sch Art, 83, Savannah Col Art & Design, 83, Albright Col, 88, Alfred Univ, 89 & Minneapolis Col Art & Design, 90. *Work:* Boston Mus Fine Arts; Minneapolis Inst Arts; Nat Gallery Art, Washington, DC. *Exhib:* Toad Hall Potters, Art Barn, Washington, DC, 86. *Mem:* Am Crafts Coun (bd mem, 80-87); Walker Art Ctr (bd, 87); Minnesota Orchestra (bd, 87-); St Paul Chamber Orchestra (bd, 87-89); Nancy Hauser Dance Co (bd mem, 89-); and others. *Publ:* Auth, Politics in Art, Lerner, 72. *Mailing Add:* 2116 Irving Ave S Minneapolis MN 55405

MONES, ARTHUR
PHOTOGRAPHER
b New York, NY, Aug 26, 19. *Study:* NY Inst Photog, 39. *Work:* Metrop Mus Art, New York; Brooklyn Mus; Mus Art, Carnegie Inst, Pittsburgh; New Orleans Mus Art; Grey Gallery, NY Univ, New York; Columbia Univ; Kramer, Pollack Found, NY; Getty Ctr Hist Art & Humanities, Santa Monica, Calif; San Francisco Mus Mod Art; St Louis Mus Art; Mount Holyoke Col Art Mus, S Hadley, Mass; Art Inst Chicago; Noguchi Mus & Sculpture Garden, New York. *Exhib:* Solo exhibs, Crolie Variations, Edward H Merrih Gallery, New York, 79, & Zenith Gallery, Pittsburgh, 81, Artists in Photographs, Mus Art, Carnegie Inst, 81, Sicily-Legacy of a Civilization, Brooklyn Mus, 82, From NY Studios, Pace Univ, New York, 82 & Photographs, City Univ NY Grad Ctr, 82-83; Mt Holyoke Col Art Mus, South Hadley, Mass, 88-89; Sculptures in Black & White, Sculpture Ctr, New York, 89; Photographs of Sculptors, Alice Simsar Gallery, Ann Arbor, Mich, 89; Anita Shapolsky Gallery, New York, 92; Jason McCoy Gallery, New York, 92. *Bibliog:* Fred McDarrah (auth), Voice Choices, Village Voice, 5/7/79; Palmer Poroner (auth), Artists in photographs, Artspeak, 11/26/81; Natalie Canavor (auth), Books, Popular Photog, 3/82. *Publ:* Artists in Photographs by Arthur Mones, Horizon Press, 81. *Mailing Add:* 178 Prince St New York NY 10012

MONGAN, AGNES
ADMINISTRATOR, HISTORIAN
b Somerville, Mass, Jan 21, 05. *Study:* Bryn Mawr Col, AB; Smith Col, AM, Hon LHD, 41; Wheaton Col, Hon LittD, 54; Univ Mass, Hon DFA, 70; LaSalle Col, Hon DFA, 73; Colby Col, Hon DFA, 73; Univ Notre Dame, Hon DFA, 80; Boston Col, Hon DFA, 85. *Pos:* Res asst, Fogg Art Mus, Harvard Univ, 28-37, cur drawings, 37-75, assoc dir, 64-69, dir, 69-71; vis dir, Timken

Art Gallery, San Diego, Calif, 71-72; mem adv comt, I Tatti; mem, Coun of Fel of Pierpont Morgan Libr; vis dir, Metrop Mus & Art Ctr, Coral Gables, Fla, 79-80. *Teaching:* Lectr fine arts, Harvard Univ; vis lectr fine arts, Mt Holyoke Col, 66-67, Oberlin Col, 67-; vis prof, Northwestern Univ, spring, 76, Univ Louisville, Ky, fall, 76, Univ Tex, Austin, spring, 77 & 81 & Univ Calif, Santa Barbara, 79; Kress prof in residence, Nat Gallery Art, Washington, DC, 77-78. *Awards:* Palms d'Acad, Fr Govt, 47; Cavaliere, Order of Merit, Repub Italy, 71; Achievement in the Arts Medal, Signet Soc, Harvard Univ, 86. *Mem:* Col Art Asn Am; Asn Art Mus Dirs; hon fel Morgan Libr; Benjamin Franklin fel Royal Soc Arts. *Res:* Relation to drawings by the Masters, especially Tiepolo, Fragonard, Watteau, Ingres, Daumier and Degas. *Publ:* Co-auth, Drawings in the Fogg Museum, 41; Ingres Drawings, 67; Tiepolo Drawings, 70; auth, articles in Burlington Mag, Art Quart, Art News, Gazette Beaux-Arts, Master Drawings & others. *Mailing Add:* 360 Mount Auburn St Cambridge MA 02138

MONGRAIN, CLAUDE
SCULPTOR
b Shawinigan, Quebec, 1948. *Study:* Ecole des Beaux-Arts de Montreal, 66-69. *Work:* Musee des Beaux-Arts de Montreal; Can Coun Art Bank, Ottawa; Musee d'Art Contemporain de Montreal; Nat Gallery Can, Ottawa; Musee de Quebec. *Exhib:* Solo exhibs, Mongrain-Poulin, Art Gallery of Greater Victoria, BC, 80, Claude Mongrain: Oeuvres Recentes, Concordia Art Gallery, Concordia Univ, Montreal, Que, 87, Art Gallery of Windsor, Ontario, 88; Elementa Naturae, Musee d'Art Contemporain, Montreal, 87; Sans Demarcation, Sault Ste Marie, Ont, 87; Les Ouevres de la Collection Permanente du Musee, Musee du Quebec, 88; 49th Parallel Gallery, New York, 89. *Awards:* Materials Assistance Grants, Can Coun, 71, 73, 76, 85 & 86; Work Grant, 80, Bourse de Quebec, 87, Quebec Ministry Cult Affairs. *Bibliog:* Trevor Gould (auth), Claude Mongrain, No 14, C Mag, Toronto, summer 87, 65-66; Jerry McGrath (auth), Art in the Soo, Sans Demarcation, Vanguard, 2-3/88, 10-13. *Publ:* Contribr, Le Dessin Errant (catalog), Dalhousie Art Gallery, Halifax, 88. *Mailing Add:* c/o Olga Korper Gallery 17 Morrow Ave Toronto ON M6R 2H9 Canada

MONK, MEREDITH
DIRECTOR, FILMMAKER
Study: Sarah Lawrence Col, Bronxville, NY. *Comn:* Compose Opera for the Houston Grand Opera; Am Music Theater Festival; Walker Art Ctr. *Exhib:* Film-video retrospective, Whitney Mus Am Art, 84-85; Sound Installation, Whitney Mus; Performances, Am, Europe, Middle East & Far East. *Pos:* Founder, The House Found Arts, New York, 68- *Awards:* Fels, Guggenheim Found; Corp Pub Broadcasting First Prize Performance Prog, KTCA-TV, Minneapolis; Grand Prize, Turtle Dreams, Video Culture Can; Obie Awards; Bessie Award; ASCAP Awards; Am Soc Composers Auth & Publ Awards. *Mem:* ASCAP. *Mailing Add:* 131 Varick St Rm 901 New York NY 10013

MONK, NANCY
SCULPTOR, DESIGNER
b Minneapolis, Minn, Aug 1, 51. *Study:* Colo State Univ, BFA, 73; Univ Minn, MFA, 76. *Work:* Corning Mus Glass, NY; Mod Int Glaskunst, Ebeltoft, Denmark. *Exhib:* New Glass: A Worldwide Survey, Corning Mus Glass, NY, 79; Int Glas Exhib, Reria Int de Ceramica Vidrio, Valencia, Spain, 82; one-person shows, Koplin Gallery, Los Angeles, Calif, 82 & Los Angeles Junior Arts Ctr, Barnsdall Park, Calif, 84; Int Glass Exhib, Mod Int Glass Mus, Elbeltoft, Denmark, 86; Long Beach Art Mus, 88; Handmade in Pasadena, Alfred Univ, NY State Col Ceramics, 91; Some Sports I have Known, Polytechnic Sch, Pasadena, Calif, 90; and others. *Teaching:* Instr, Minneapolis Col Art & Design, 76-77; instr, Pasadena City Col, 89 & substitute teacher, 92- *Awards:* Nat Endowment Arts, 86 & 89; City of Pasadena Artist Fel, 92. *Bibliog:* Suzanne Muchnic (auth), Cheering up with collage, Los Angeles Times, 4/27/79; Clayton Lee (auth), Universal icon, Artweek, 12/25/82; K Moriyama (auth), Glassware Designed by Nancy Monk, Japan Interior Design; Suzanne K Frantz (auth), Contemporary Glass. *Media:* All Media. *Mailing Add:* 444 S Euclid Apt 9 Pasadena CA 91101

MONK, ROBERT EVAN, JR
DEALER, CURATOR
b New York, NY, Aug 20, 50. *Study:* Pratt Inst, Brooklyn, NY. *Collections Arranged:* Dimitry Merinoff, Paintings: 1950-1970, Clocktower, New York, 80. *Pos:* Cur, Merinoff Estate, Merinoff Studio, New York, 74-; dir graphics, Castelli Graphics, New York, formerly; pres, Lorence Monk Gallery, New York, 85-92; vpres & dir contemp prints, Sotheby's New York, 92- *Teaching:* Instr, Sotheby's Educ Prog. *Mem:* Int Fine Print Dealers Asn (exec vpres, 89-92). *Specialty:* Exhibitions of the graphic works of Robert Rauschenberg, Jasper Johns, Andy Warhol, Roy Lichtenstein, Ellsworth Kelly, Frank Stella, Edward Ruscha and Kenneth Noland. *Mailing Add:* c/o Sotheby's 1334 York Ave New York NY 10021

MONNIER, JACQUELINE MATISSE See Matosse, Jackie (Jacqueline Malisse Monnier)

MONORY, JACQUES
PAINTER, FILMMAKER
b Paris, France, June 25, 34. *Study:* Arts Appliques Ville de Paris; Ecole Nat Superieur des Beaux Arts, Paris. *Work:* Nat Mus Mod Art, George Pompidou Ctr, Paris, France; Stedelijk Mus, Amsterdam, Holland; La Mus, Humlebosk, Denmark; Collection Mus Ludwig, Koln, Ger; Mus Mod Art, Fukuoka, Japan. *Comn:* Sci & Indust Planetarium Villette, Paris, France, 86; RER Sta, Orsay Mus, Paris, France, 87. *Exhib:* Mythologies Quotidiennes, Mus Mod Art, Paris, 64; European Painters Today, Jewish Mus & Mus Contemp Art, Chicago, 68; one-man shows, Velvet Jungle NY, Stedelijk Mus, Amsterdam, Holland, 72, Premiers Numeros da Catalogue Mondial des Amages Incurables, Mus Mod Art, Paris, 74, Operas Glaces, Fondation Maeght, Ste Paul de Vence, France, 77, Monory 3, Lunds Konsthall Mus, Sweden, 80, Toxique, ARC Mus Mod Art, Paris, 84, NOIR, Galerie Lelong Impeobable Mus, Paris & NY, 91; Espace, Biennale de Venezia, Italy, 86. *Bibliog:* Jean Christophe Bailly (auth), Monory, Ed Aime Maeght, 79; J F Lyotard (auth), L'aksassinat de L'experience par la jeniture Monory, Castor, 84; Pierre Tilman (auth), Ed Frederk Loeb, 92. *Media:* Acrylic, Oil. *Publ:* Auth, Document Bleu, Chorus, 70; Diamondback, Christian Bourgois, 79; coauth, Vien de Bouge Assey Vite au Bord de la Mort, Thierry Bordas, 84; auth, Quick, Bloom, 85; Eldorado, Christian Bourgois, 91. *Mailing Add:* c/o Galerie Lelong 20 W 57th St New York NY 10019

MONROE, BETTY IVERSON
EDUCATOR
b Ames, Iowa, May 3, 22. *Study:* Iowa State Univ, BS, 44, MS, 50; Univ Mich, MA, 64, PhD, 73. *Collections Arranged:* Chinese Ceramics in Chicago Collections, 82-83. *Teaching:* Asst prof art hist, Wash Univ, St Louis, 66-67; asst prof, Northwestern Univ, 68-74, chmn dept, 74-78, assoc prof, 74- *Mem:* Col Art Asn; Midwest Art Hist Soc; Am Comt S Asian Art. *Res:* Asian art history; Japanese painting. *Publ:* Ed & translr, Japanese Painting in the Literati Style, Weatherhill, New York & Heibonsha, Tokyo, 74; auth, Chinese Ceramics in Chicago Collections, Northwestern Univ Press, 82. *Mailing Add:* 1416 Hinman Ave No 5 Evanston IL 60201

MONROE, EVE VALIN
PAINTER
b Collinsville, Ill, Oct 29, 20. *Study:* Studied with Max Beckman, 30 & Ben Abramowitz, 60. *Work:* Univ Md, New Educ Bldg, College Park; Gallery Selection, Rockville Civic Ctr, Md; Rogers House Mus & Gallery (collage), Ellsworth, Kans; Neill Gallery, Tucson, Ariz. *Comn:* Letter on Art & Artists, comn by Dan Millsap for Congressional Record, Washington, DC, 60; symbolic collage of Reston, comn by Alan Gallety, Va, 66; Christmas card series, comn by Michael Krepp, Tucson, Ariz, 89-92; card series, comn by Ruth N Matier, Mammoth, Ariz, 90; painting, watercolor, drawing, comn by Dr Dan T Mihaly MS, Tucson, Ariz, 92. *Exhib:* Margaret Dickey Gallery Art, Washington, DC, 60; Twentieth Century Gallery Art, Williamsburg, Va, 64; Private 8 Works, Col William & Mary, Williambsburg, Va, 64; Opening Show, Heron House Gallery, Reston, Va, 66; Projection '70, Mr Lee Bailey, New York, 70; Artists File-Art & Law-West Collection, St Paul, Minn, 87; and others. *Awards:* Huntington Hartford Found Fel, 64; Rockville Civic Ctr Gallery Selection, Md, 64. *Mem:* Copper mem Catalina Golder R Art Asn. *Media:* Mixed, Watercolor. *Mailing Add:* 5100 N Kain Tucson AZ 85705

MONROE, GERALD
PAINTER, EDUCATOR
b New York, NY, Aug 17, 26. *Study:* Art Students League; Cooper Union; NY Univ, EdD. *Work:* NY Univ Collection; NJ State Mus; Newark Mus, NJ; Port Authority NY & NJ. *Exhib:* William Paterson Col, 73; NJ State Mus, 75; Wagner Col, 76; Newark Mus, NJ, 78; Parish Art Mus, 81; Guild Hall Mus. *Pos:* Assoc prof art, Glassboro State Col, 68-86. *Awards:* Nat Endowment for Humanities Fel, 73-74, Grant, 75; Ossabaw Island Proj, 77; Va Ctr Creative Arts, 78; and others. *Media:* Oil. *Res:* Influence of left-wing politics on art; strategies for drawing instruction; artists during the Great Depression. *Publ:* Auth articles in Art J, Arch Am Art J, Studio Int & Art in Am; illusr, Am Artist. *Mailing Add:* 463 West St New York NY 10014

MONTAGUE, JAMES L
PAINTER, PRINTMAKER
b New Rochelle, NY, May 6, 06. *Study:* Dartmouth Col, AB, 28; Art Students League, with Kimon Nicolaides; also with Leger, Ozenfant & Galanis, Paris; Guy Pene du Bois, New York. *Work:* US Military Acad; Southern Vt Artists Permanent Collection; Dartmouth Col. *Comn:* Private portraits. *Exhib:* Various group shows & one-man exhibitions throughout New England states & New York. *Pos:* Dir, Sharon Art Ctr, NH, 61-63 & Southern Vt Art Ctr, 64-75. *Awards:* Fitchburg Mus Award, 62; Print Club Albany Award, 70; Award, Norwich Univ, 71. *Mem:* Art Students League; Nat Arts Club; Salmagundi Club, New York; Print Club Albany; Northern Vt Artists. *Media:* Oil; Graphics. *Mailing Add:* PO Box 926 Manchester Center VT 05255

MONTANO, LINDA (MARY)
CONCEPTUAL ARTIST, VIDEO ARTIST
b Saugerties, NY, Jan 18, 42. *Study:* Villa Schifanoia, Florence, MA(sculpture), 66; Univ Wis, Madison, MFA(sculpture), 69. *Exhib:* How to Become a Guru, Womens Bldg, Los Angeles, 75; Learning to Talk, Univ Calif, San Diego, 76; Talking About Sex: For My Father, Kitchen, New York, 80; Mitchell's Death, Mus Mod Art, New York, 81; Palm Reading, Real Art Ways, Hartford, Conn, 82; Readings: Visual Collaborations, Chicago Art Inst, 83; Seven Years of Living Art: Wearing Only One Color Each Year, Speaking in a Different Accent Each Year, Listening to One Tone Seven Hours a Day (Doing Art-Life Counseling and Reading palms at the New Mus Once A Month), 84- *Teaching:* Instr performance, San Francisco State Univ, 78-79, San Francisco Art Inst, 79-80, Womens Bldg, 81 & Chicago Art Inst, 83, Univ Tex, Austin, 91- *Awards:* Fels, Nat Endowment Arts, 77 & 85; Women's Studio Workshop Grants, 82 & 83; Fel, NY State Found Arts, 86. *Bibliog:* Moira Roth (auth), Towards a history of college performance, Arts Mag, 12/78; Marcia Tucker (auth), Not just for laughs, New Mus, 11/81; Tony Whitfield (auth), Dressing up, acting out, Live Mag, 82. *Publ:* Contribr, High Performance, 77- & auth, Art in Everyday Life, 80, Astro Artz; co-ed, Fuse Mag, Franklin Furnace, 82; auth, Before and after art-life counseling, Women's Studio Workshop, 83. *Mailing Add:* 85 Abeel St Kingston NY 12401

MONTEIRO, ISAAC
PAINTER, SCULPTOR
b Antwerp, Belg, Apr 24, 38; US citizen. *Study:* Nat Sch of Fine Arts, Rio de Janeiro, MA(hist & art), 61. *Work:* Kustmuseum, Bern, Switz; Mus Mod Art, Sao Paulo, Brazil; Check Point Charlie House (mus), Berlin, Ger; Simon Wiesenthal Holocaust Mus, Los Angeles, Calif; Mus Art, Mexico City, Mex. *Comn:* Mural, Chase Manhattan Bank, Rio De Janeiro. *Exhib:* Young Painters Biennial, Petit Palais, Paris, France, 61; Sao Paulo Biennial, Brazil, 63; Mus Mod Art, Rio de Janeiro, 63; Art Tender, Bilbao, Spain, 82; solo exhib, Mus Art, Sarajevo, Yugoslavia, travelling, US & Western Europ. *Bibliog:* Who's Who Am Art. *Media:* Oil; Wood, Plastic. *Mailing Add:* 39 Raynor St Freeport NY 11520

MONTHAN, GUY
PHOTOGRAPHER, EDUCATOR
b Tucson, Ariz, Apr 17, 25. *Study:* Syracuse Univ, BFA, 50; Calif State Univ, Los Angeles, MA, 67. *Exhib:* Los Angeles Co Mus Ann, 61; San Gabriel Valley Ann, Pasadena Art Mus, 61; Tucson Festival Art Show, 62 & 65; Southwestern Photog Exhibit, Dallas Mus Fine Arts, 73; Yuma Invitational, Ariz, 73-78; Coconino Ctr Arts Photog Show, Flagstaff, 89; 24th Southwestern Exhib, Yuma, 90. *Pos:* Advert design, Los Angeles, 50-68. *Teaching:* Assoc prof advert design, Northern Ariz Univ, Flagstaff, 68-90; Retired, 90. *Awards:* For Art and Indian Individualists, Rounce & Coffin Book Award, 76, Border Regional Libr Asn Southwest Book Award, 76, Bookbuilders W Award, 76 & For The Pueblo Storyteller, 86. *Publ:* Designer-illusr, Art and Indian Individualists, 75; designer-illusr, Nacimientos: Nativity Scenes by Southwest Indian Artisans, Northland Press, Flagstaff, 79; illusr, The Pueblo Storyteller, Univ Ariz Press, Tucson, 86. *Mailing Add:* P O Box 1698 Flagstaff AZ 86002

MONTI, JOHN
SCULPTOR
b Portland, Ore, Jan 8, 57. *Study:* Portland State Univ, Ore, BS, 80; Pratt Inst, Brooklyn, NY, MFA, 83. *Work:* Metrop Mus Art, New York; Brooklyn Mus, NY; McNag Art Mus, San Antonio, Tex; Israel Mus, Jerusalem; Chase Manhattan Bank, New York; AT&T Corp; Eli-Broad Family Found. *Exhib:* Terminal New York, Brooklyn Army Terminal, NY, 83; Printing and Sculpture Today, Indianapolis Mus Art, Ind, 84; Affiliations: Recent Sculpture, Whitney Mus, Stamford, Conn, 85; Sculpture on the Wall, Aldrich Mus, Ridgefield, Conn, 86; one-person show, Honolulu Acad Fine Arts, Hawaii, 88, Curt Marcus, New York, 88, Pence Gallery, Los Angeles, 89, Greg Kucera Gallery, Seattle, Wash, 90 & White Room, White Columns, New York, 92; Selections from the Berkus Collection, Long Beach Mus Art, Calif, 88; Drawings By Ten, Univ Calif, San Diego, 88; Norton Gallery Art, West Palm Beach, Fla, 89; Western Washington Univ, Western Gallery, Bellingham, 90; Nina Freudenheim Gallery, Buffalo, NY, 91; Univ NC, Weatherspoon Art Gallery, Greensboro, 91; Univ Akron, Univ Art Galleries, Ohio, 92; Contemporary Wood Sculpture, Brooklyn Mus, NY, 92. *Awards:* Rockefeller Found, Bellagio Italy Resident fel, 88; Yaddo Fel, 90; Triangle Artist Workshop Resident Fel, 91. *Bibliog:* Michael Brenson (auth), John Monti, NY Times, 1/22/85; Eugene Tsai (auth), John Monti, Art Mag, 4/88; Jennifer Dunning (auth), Stories Told in Movement and Talk, NY Times, 1/21/92. *Mem:* Artist Equity Asn; Found Community Artists. *Media:* Wood, Plywood; Paint. *Mailing Add:* 96 Second Pl Brooklyn NY 11231

MONTLACK, EDITH
PAINTER
b New York, NY. *Study:* Metrop Mus Art Sch, with Michael Jacobs, scholar; Nat Acad Design, with Louis Bouche; Art Students League. *Work:* Pvt collections of Shell Oil Co & Asiatic Petroleum; and others. *Comn:* Portraits of Martin Sheen; plus many others. *Exhib:* Nat Acad; Parrish Mus; Riverside Mus; Grand Central Art Gallery; Knickerbocker Artists; and many others. *Teaching:* Instruction in own studio. *Awards:* Emil Kohn Medal; St Gaudens Medal; First Prize Watercolors, Nat Asn Women Art. *Mem:* Life fel Royal Soc Art, London; Nat Asn Women Artists. *Media:* Oil. *Publ:* Auth, Paintings: A New Approach, Agni Press. *Mailing Add:* 90 Taymil Rd New Rochelle NY 10804

MONTMINY, TRACY
MURALIST, PAINTER
b Boston, Mass, 11. *Study:* Radcliffe Col, Cambridge, Mass, BA, 33; Art Students League, with Rico Lebrun, 34-35. *Work:* Selden Rodman Col, Oakland, NJ; Mus Art & Archeol, Univ Mo, Columbia. *Comn:* Mural, Post Off, Sect Fine Arts Treas Dept, Downers Grove, Ill, 41; four staircase murals, Biology Bldg, 78-80 & mural, Engineering Bldg, 81, Univ Mo, Columbia; mural, Humanities Dept, Stephens Col, Columbia, Mo, 82; murals, Boone Nat Savings & Loan Asn, Columbia, Mo, 88. *Exhib:* Corcoran Gallery, Washington, DC, 39; Am Painters in Paris, Ctr Int Paris, 75-76; Cross Country '81: Artists Who Draw, Lorretto-Hilton Gallery, St Louis, 81; Bridges, Elder Gallery, Lincoln, Nebr, 81; Painting Am: Mural Art New Deal Era, Midtown Galleries, New York, 88; group show, Still-Zinsel Fine Art, New Orleans, 90; solo show, Wartburg Col, Waverly, Iowa, 92. *Teaching:* Prof art, Univ Mo, Columbia, 48-, prof emer, currently; vis prof drawing, painting & art hist, Am Univ of Beirut, Lebanon, 63-64. *Awards:* Guggenheim Mem Found Fel Painting, 40. *Bibliog:* Charles Movalli (auth), Tracy Montminy Myth and Form, Am Artist, 3/76; K Marling (auth), Wall-to-wall America, Minneapolis Mag, 82. *Mem:* Nat Drawing Asn. *Media:* Acrylic, Oil; Conte Crayon, Pastel. *Dealer:* Still-Zinsel Fine Art 328 Julia St New Orleans LA. *Mailing Add:* 1506 Paris Rd Columbia MO 65201

MOODY, ELIZABETH C
DEALER, GALLERY DIRECTOR
b Memphis, Tenn, Nov 20, 44. *Study:* Univ Ky, Lexington, BFA, 66. *Pos:* Dir & owner, Moody Gallery, Houston, 75- *Mem:* Art Dealers Asn of Houston. *Specialty:* Contemporary American: art, paintings, sculpture, photography, original works on paper. *Mailing Add:* Moody Gallery 2815 Colquitt Houston TX 77098

MOON, JIM (JAMES MONROE)
PAINTER, PRINTMAKER
b Graham, NC, June 7, 28. *Study:* Cooper Union, 45-48; Acad Vannucci, Italy, cert, 55; Richmond Prof Inst William & Mary, BFA, 57; grad study at Mexico City Col, 57; Boston Mus Sch 58-59; Columbia Univ, 66-67. *Work:* Mus Mod Art, New York; NC Mus Art, Raleigh; Peggy Guggenheim Mus, Venice, Italy; Winston-Salem Pub Libr, NC; Northwood Inst, Midland, Mich; Hamilton Mus, Can; Duke Univ & Cent NC Univ, Durham; and others. *Exhib:* Solo exhibs, Watkins/Fair Contemp Arts, New York, 80, la Gallerie, Am Col Paris, 81, Galleria Regina Cornaro, Asolo, Italy, 81, Alber Galleries, Philadelphia, 81, Calvert Collection, Washington, DC, 83, Calvert Gallery, Palm Beach, Fla, 83 & Palm Beach Int Airport, West Palm Beach, Fla, 92. *Teaching:* Instr fine arts, Hofstra Univ, New York, 60-61; head dept visual arts, Barber Scotia Col, NC, 65-66 & NC Sch Arts, Winston-Salem, 67-71. *Bibliog:* Marion Fox (auth), Peggy's palace, Signature Mag Preferred Living, New York, 118, 5/85; William E Ray (auth), ArtScene, coming to a theatre near you!, 2-3/88 & Alice R Gray (auth), An artist for all seasons, Vol X, No 1, 1-3/92, Palm Beach Co Coun Arts, Fla; Who's Who in American Art, 1989-90, Bowker, New York, 18th ed, 742, 89; and others. *Media:* Egg Tempera, Oil; Serigraphy. *Mailing Add:* Rte 3 Box 4093 Lexington NC 27292

MOON, MARC
PAINTER, INSTRUCTOR
b Middletown, Ohio, Apr 6, 23. *Study:* Appl Art Acad. *Work:* Canton Art Inst; Masillon Mus, Ohio; Richmond Mus, Va; Springfield Mus, Mo; Taylor Mem Libr, Cuyahoga Falls, Ohio. *Comn:* Mural, Canton Hall of Fame, Canton Hist Soc, Ohio, 70; mural, Lawson Milk Co, 75; McDonalds Restaurants, Akron, Ohio, 79. *Exhib:* Am Watercolor Soc, New York, 66-70; Nat Acad Design, 74; Watercolor USA, Springfield Mus, 74; Butler Art Inst, Youngstown, Ohio, 75; Nat Soc Painters Casein & Watercolor, New York, 81. *Teaching:* Instr watercolor, Hilton Leech Art Sch, Sarasota, Fla, 68-76, Marc Moon Gallery, Cuyahoga Falls, Ohio, 82-84, Fort Meyer Branch Art Asn, 84. *Awards:* Mario Cooper Award, Am Watercolor Soc; Best in Show, Va Beach Art Asn; Purchase Award, Watercolor USA. *Bibliog:* R Fabri (auth), Medal of Merit, Todays Art, 66. *Mem:* Am Watercolor Soc; Ohio Watercolor Soc; Nat Soc Painters Casein & Acrylic; Rockport Art Asn; Allied Artist Am. *Media:* Watercolor, Acrylic. *Publ:* Auth, Watercolor page, Am Artist Mag, 74. *Mailing Add:* 198 W Portage Trail Ext Cuyahoga Falls OH 44223

MOONELIS, JUDITH C
SCULPTOR, CERAMIST
b Jackson Heights, Queens, NY, May 30, 53. *Study:* Tyler Sch Art, Temple Univ, Philadelphia, BFA, 75; NY State Col Ceramics, Alfred Univ, MFA, 78. *Work:* Pa Acad Fine Arts, Philadelphia; Heckscher Mus, Huntington, NY; NY State Col Ceramics, Alfred Univ, NY; Ill State Mus, Springfield; Everson Mus, NY; Am Craft Mus, NY. *Comn:* Sculpture, Heckscher Mus, NY, 83. *Exhib:* The Raw Edge: Ceramics of the 80's, Everson Mus, Syracuse & C W Post Col, Greenvale, NY, 83; solo exhibs, Heckscher Mus, Huntington, NY, 83 & Rena Bransten Gallery, San Francisco, Calif, 85, 88, Swarthmore Col, PA, 92, Va Commonwealth Univ, 90; Sculpture, Pa Acad Fine Arts, Philadelphia, 86; A Passionate Vision: Daniel Jacobs Collection, DeCordova Mus, Lincoln, Mass, 84; Twenty Artists, Newport Harbor Art Mus, Calif, 85; Poetry of the Physical, Am Craft Mus, New York & traveling, 86-87; The Eloquent Object, Philbrook Art Mus, OK & traveling, 87-89. *Teaching:* Vis artist & lectr, numerous schools & institutions, 80-; instr ceramic sculpture, Parsons Sch Design, New York, 84-87 & Hunter Col, New York, 86-87; vis pro, Univ Hartford, 90. *Awards:* Nat Endowment Arts Fel, 80 & 86; New York Found Arts Fel, 85; Virginia A Groot Found Grant, 91. *Bibliog:* Gnossis Nos(auth), Judy Moonelis, Am Ceramics Mag, 5/86; Edward Sozanski, Rev, Philadelphia Enquirer, 2/21/92. *Mem:* Int Sculpture Ctr Am Craft Coun. *Media:* Clay. *Dealer:* Rena Bransten Gallery 77 Geary at Grant San Francisco CA 94108. *Mailing Add:* 434 E 11th St Apt 3F New York NY 10009

MOONEY, MICHAEL J
PAINTER, ASSEMBLAGE ARTIST
b Albany, NY. *Study:* Empire State Col, Albany, BPS(arts), 80; State Univ NY, Albany, MA(painting), 82, MFA(painting), 83. *Work:* Center Galleries & State Univ, Albany; F D Rich Co, Stamford, Conn; State Univ NY, Albany; Patterson Mus, Patterson, NJ; Paco Das Artes, Sao Paulo; Museu Da Imagem Do Som, Sao Paulo. *Exhib:* Solo exhibs, Sixth Sense Gallery, 85, Bridgewater Gallery, 86, E M Donahue Gallery, 86, 88 & 89 & Landscape Antology, Grace Borgeniet Gallery, New York, 88; Nine Artists, Munson-Williams-Proctor Inst, Utica, NY, 82; East Village, NY, Galerie Knud Grothe, Copenhagen, Denmark, 83; Chicago Art Expo, Navy Pier, 84; Ruth Siegel Gallery, 83, 84, & 86; Grace Borgenicht Gallery (landscape anthology), 88. *Awards:* David Kroman Award, Discovery 78, Schenectady Art Group, 78; Albany Regional Painting Award, State Univ NY, Albany, Art Gallery, 81. *Bibliog:* Fred LeBrun (auth), Mooney at Center Gallery, Albany Times Union, 10/6/79; Peg Churchill-Wright (auth), Works Within Works, Schenectady Gazette, 10/11/79; James Lewis (auth), Art Forum, 12/89. *Media:* Oil. *Dealer:* E M Donahue Gallery 560 Broadway New York NY 10012. *Mailing Add:* 194 Warren St Brooklyn NY 11201

MOONIE, LIANA
PAINTER, INSTRUCTOR
b Trieste, Italy. *Study:* Istituto Magistrale G Carducci, Univ Trieste, BA(educ), 45; Art Student League, with Robert Brachman, 69; New York Univ; New Rochelle Col, 79 (printmaking). *Work:* State Assembly, Albany, NY; Greenburgh Libr, NY; Reference Libr, Nat Mus Arts, Washington, DC; Pepsico Inc; Credit Anstalt Bank, Verein, NY. *Exhib:* Nat Allied Artists Am , New York, 77; Nat Acad Design, New York, 78; Silvermine Artists Guild, New Canaan, Conn, 79; Hudson River Mus, NY, 79; traveling exhib, USA, 85-89; traveling exhib, India, 89. *Teaching:* Private instruction, 79-81. *Awards:* Emily Lowe Award, Allied Artists Am, 85; John Carl Georgi Award, Nat Asn Women Artists, 85; First in Mixed Media & Best in Show, Scarsdale Art Asn, 85; Elizabeth Morse Genius Found Award, 87 & Ada Cecere Award, 88, Nat Asn Women Artists. *Mem:* Mamaroneck Artists Guild (pres, 76-78); Hudson River Contemp Artists (pres, 81-83); Nat Asn Women Artists (vpres, 85-86; pres, 87-89); Silvermine Artists Guild; Greenwich Art Soc (pres, 90-91). *Media:* Watercolor, Oil. *Publ:* Contribr, article, Beaux Arts Mag, 74-76 & Philosophizing about art, 75. *Dealer:* Somerstown Studios and Gallery Route 100 Somers NY 10589; Pelham Art Center Gallery 153 Fifth Ave Pelham NY 10803. *Mailing Add:* 10 Baldwin Farms S Greenwich CT 06831

MOORE, ALAN WILLARD
ART CRITIC, PUBLISHER
b Chicago, Ill, Oct 21, 51. *Study:* Univ Calif, Riverside, BA, 74;City Univ NY Grad Ctr, PhD(candidate). *Pos:* Intern writer, Art Forum, 73-74; writer, Art-Rite, 74-75; co-founder, ABC No Rio, 80-83. *Res:* History of collaborative projects, NY. *Publ:* Coauth (with Marc Miller), ABC No Rio Dinero: Story of a LES Art Gallery, NY, 83; ed, A Day in the Life: Tales from the Lower East, Semiotexte, 91. *Mailing Add:* 73 E Houston St New York NY 10012

MOORE, ARTHUR COTTON
ARCHITECT, PAINTER
b Washington, DC, Apr 12, 35. *Study:* Princeton Univ, AB(cum laude), 58; Princeton Univ Sch Archit, MFA, 60. *Work:* Miriam & Ira D Wallach Gallery, Columbia Univ, New York. *Exhib:* Solo exhibs, Industrial Baroque, Barbara Fendrick Gallery, New York, 90, Facades, Hokin Kaufman Gallery, Chicago, 91, Covington & Burling Collection, Washington, DC, 92 & Galerie Gasnier Kamien, Paris, France, 93; Nat Bldg Mus, Washington Furniture, 90; Miriam & Ira D Wallach Art Gallery, Columbia Univ, 91. *Awards:* Award for Excellence in Design, Industrial Baroque Furniture, Archit Record Mag, 80. *Media:* Mixed Media on Canvas. *Publ:* Auth, NY Times, 6/15/89 & 3/15/90; Wash Post, 4/5/90 & 4/7/90; Trump's Mag, 6/90; Archit Record Mag, 9/90; Wash Home & Garden, 11/91; Contemporary Architectural Drawings, Donations Avery Libr, Centennial Drawings Arch, Pomegranate Artbooks, San Francisco, 91. *Mailing Add:* Hokin Kaufman Gallery 210 W Superior St Chicago IL 60610

MOORE, BENJAMIN POWELL
GLASS BLOWER, DESIGNER
b Olympia, Wash, Feb 5, 52. *Study:* Calif Col Arts and Crafts, BFA, 74; RI Sch Design, MFA, 77. *Work:* Corning Mus Glass, NY; Va Mus Mus Fine Arts, Richmond; J & L Lobmeyr Mus Collection, Vienna, Austria; Fravenau Mus, Bavaria, W Germany; Glasmusem, Ebeltoft, Denmark. *Comn:* restaurant lighting, Lola Restaurant, New York, 84; restaurant lighting, Crescent Dining Club, Dallas, Tex, 85; restaurant lighting, Bravo Pagliacci, Bellevue, Wash, 85; law office lighting, Davis, Wright, Todd, Reise & Jones, Seattle, Wash, 86; private lodge lighting, Wright Runstad & Co, Blakely Island, Wash, 87. *Exhib:* Europeans in Glass, Nat Mus Mod Art, Tokyo/Kyoto, Japan, 80; New Glass; Worldwide Survey, Victoria & Albert Mus, London, 81 & Mus des Arts Decoratifs, Paris, France, 82; Am Glass Northwest, Essener Glasgalerie, Essen, WGer, 83; Poetry of the Physical, Am Craft Mus, New York, 86; Piuchuck Glass Northwest, US Embassy, Prague, Czech, 88; one-man shows, Recent Glass, Kurland Summers Gallery, Los Angeles, Recent Glass, Benjamin Moore, Traver Sutton Gallery, Seattle, Wash, 88 & 91. *Pos:* Designer glass, Fabbrica Venini Murano, Venice, Italy, 78-79 & J & L Lobmeyr, Vienna, Austria, 80-81; designer & owner, Benjamin Moore Inc, Seattle, Wash, 85- *Teaching:* Grad instr glass, RI Sch Design, Providence, 75-77; interim prof glass, Mass Col Art, Boston, 80; admin glass, Pilchuck Glass Sch, Stanwood, Wash, 74-87. *Awards:* Young Am Award, Am Craft Mus, Am Craft Coun, NY, 78; Fragile Art Competition Award, Glass Art Mag, 83; NEA Grant, 90. *Bibliog:* Edie Lee Cohen (auth), Art Glass Lamps, Interior Design Mag, 5/85; Maureen Pickard (auth), The Light Touch, Restaurant & Hotel Design, 4/86; Lisa Hammel (auth), A Show of Hands, Metrop Home Mag, 11/88. *Mem:* Mem Am Craft Mus; Mem Glass Art Soc; Pilchuck Glass Sch (bd trustees). *Dealer:* William Traver Gallery 110 Union St Seattle WA 98101. *Mailing Add:* 1213 S King St Seattle WA 98144

MOORE, BEVERIDGE
PAINTER
b Richmond, Va, July 25, 15. *Study:* Univ Va, BA; Art Students League, with Yasuo Kuniyoshi, Morris Kantor & William Zorach. *Work:* James A Michener Art Mus, Doylestown, Pa; Fordham Univ, New York; NJ State Mus, Trenton; Evansville Mus Arts & Sci, Ind; Phoenix Art Mus, Ariz; and others. *Exhib:* Va Mus Fine Arts, Richmond, 53, 55 & 57; Art Alliance, Philadelphia, Pa, 65; Butler Inst Am Art, Youngstown, Ohio, 67; Artist of the Mo Exhibs, Continental Nat Bank, New Hope, 68, 71-76, 78, 80 & 87; one-man shows, Bodley Gallery, New York, 62-73 & Genest Gallery, Lambertville, NJ, 87; Washington & Jefferson Nat Painting Show, Washington, Pa, 85-86; Semi-Retrospective, The Artfull Eye, Lambertville, NJ, 91. *Bibliog:* Am Artists, New York Art Rev; Cathy Viksjo (auth), Beveridge Moore as Symbolist. *Media:* Oil. *Publ:* The Times, Trenton, NJ, 5/91. *Mailing Add:* 2969 River Rd New Hope PA 18938

MOORE, BRIDGET LIANE
GALLERY DIRECTOR
b York, Maine, Aug 22, 57. *Study:* Smith Col, Northampton, Mass. *Pos:* Asst dir, Ledel Gallery, New York, NY, 81-84; dir, Midtown Galleries, New York, 85-90, & Midtown-Payson Galleries, 90- *Mem:* Nat Arts Club, New York. *Specialty:* Twentieth Century and Contemp Am art. *Publ:* Maurice Freedman (auth), N Eng Views, Midtown Galleries, Introduction, 87; The Reflective Image: Am Drawings 1910-1960, Midtown Galleries, 90. *Mailing Add:* Midtown Payson Galleries 745 Fifth Ave New York NY 10151

MOORE, FAY
PAINTER, ADMINISTRATOR
b Cambridge, Mass. *Study:* Henry Hensche Sch, Provincetown; Boston Mus Sch; Phillips Gallery Sch, Washington, DC; Bennington Col, Vt, with Stephan Hirsch & Paul Feeley; Yale Grad Sch with Donald Oenslager. *Work:* NY Racing Asn; Nat Art Mus Sport, Indianapolis; Detroit Race Course, Mich; Univ Va, Charlottesville; Kentucky Derby Mus, Louisville. *Comn:* Portraits, Univ Va, Charlottesville, 67; portraits, Hockey Hall Fame, Can, 70; Portraits, New York Giants, 71; Seven Murals, Keslo Rm, NY Racing Asn, New York, 78; Murals, Rockwell Rm, Three Rivers Stadium, Pittsburgh, 76. *Exhib:* Saratoga Mus Racing, NY, 65; solo exhibs, Pittsburgh Plan Art, Pa, 69 & Nat Arts Mus Sport, New York, 70; Mus Contemp, Madrid, Spain, 72; retrospective, Headley Whitney Mus, Ky, 90; Nat Arts Club, Gregg Galleries, New York; and others. *Teaching:* Instr, Univ Kansas City, Mo, 55-57; instr, Carnegie-Mellon Univ, Pittsburgh, 57-59; instr, Yale Univ Grad Sch, New Haven, Conn, 59-60. *Awards:* Gold Medal, Nat Arts Club Ann, 75; Knickerbocker Pastel Asn, 88; Allied Artists Pastel, 89. *Bibliog:* K Hollingsworth (auth), Equine art of Fay Moore, Blood Horse Mag, 68; Creative painting with pastel, Katchen, Northlight Publ; Fay Moore - a lasting impression, Equine Images, fall 90. *Mem:* Nat Soc Mural Painters; Nat Arts Club (gov, formerly); Artists Fel (pres, emer); Nat Art Mus Sport (chair, acquisitions); Allied Artists Am (vpres); and others. *Media:* Oil, Pastel. *Dealer:* The Triangle Gallery 522 W Short Lexington KY; Frost & Reed Ltd 41 New Bond St London England. *Mailing Add:* Nat Arts Club 15 Gramercy Park S New York NY 10003

MOORE, INA MAY
PAINTER, INSTRUCTOR
b Hayden, Ariz, Feb 20, 20. *Study:* Univ Ariz, BA(educ, art & music); Ariz State Univ, MA(art educ). *Work:* First Interstate Bank, Valley Nat Bank, Ariz Bank & Thunderbird Bank, Phoenix; First Fed Savings & Loan Asn, Yuma. *Exhib:* Nat League Am Pen Women, Salt Lake City, Utah, 71; Nat Watercolor Exhib, Ctr Performing Arts, Scottsdale, Ariz, 77; Southwest Watercolor Fedn Exhib, San Diego, 83; Kerr Ctr, Scottsdale, Ariz, 83; Southwest Federation, Houston, Tex, 86. *Teaching:* Part-time instr art, Elem Pub Schs, 40-50; pvt classes, 50-64; instr watercolor, Phoenix Art Mus, 65-88; Phoenix Col, 78-; juror & watercolor workshops. *Awards:* Purchase Award, Empire Machinery Co, 77; Purchase Award, Thunderbird Bank, 79; Merit Award, Ariz Watercolor Exhibition, 85; Grumbacher Award, 86 & 88; Merit Award, Ariz Artists Guild, 86 & 89. *Mem:* Ariz Watercolor Asn (pres, 66-68); Nat League Am Pen Women; Ariz Artist's Guild. *Media:* Watercolor. *Publ:* Illusr, Junior League Calendar, 86. *Mailing Add:* 5718 N Tenth Ave Phoenix AZ 85013

MOORE, JOHN J
PAINTER, EDUCATOR
b St Louis, Mo, Apr 25, 41. *Study:* Washington Univ, Nat Found Arts & Humanities grant, Milliken foreign travel fel, BFA, 66; Yale Univ, MFA, 68. *Work:* Philadelphia Mus Art; Pa Acad Fine Arts, Philadelphia; Yale Univ Art Gallery, New Haven; Neuberger Mus, Purchase, NY; Metrop Mus Art, New York; Mus Art, RI Sch Design. *Comn:* Lincoln Ctr, New York, 80; Fabric Workshop, Philadelphia, 81; Hancock Insurance, Boston, 85; Smith, Kline, French, Philadelphia, 86; Becton-Dickinson, NJ, 88. *Exhib:* Fischbach Gallery, New York, 69, 73, 75, 78 & 80; Figure in Recent American Painting, Pa Coun Arts Traveling Exhib, 74-75; Real, Really, Super Real, San Antonio Mus Art, Tex, 81; Contemporary American Realism Since 1960, Pa Acad Fine Arts, 82; Hirschland Adler Modern, New York, 83, 86, & 90; Realism-Photorealism, Philbrook Art Ctr, Tulsa; American Realism: The Precise Image, Tokyo, Osaka, Yokohama, 86. *Teaching:* Prof painting & drawing, Tyler Sch Art, Temple Univ, 68-88 & Sch Visual Arts, Boston Univ, 88-; artist-in-residence, Yale Summer Sch, 68 & 69; fac, Skowhegan Sch Painting & Sculpture, summers, 74, 80 & 84; vis prof painting, Univ Calif, Berkeley, 81-82. *Awards:* Nat Found Arts & Humanities, 66; Hassam Award, Am Acad Arts & Lett, 73 & 87; Vis Artist Fel Painting, Nat Endowment Arts, 82 & 92. *Bibliog:* John Yau (auth), Introduction to exhib catalog, Hirschl & Adler Galleries, 83; Carol Zemel (auth), Still Life and City View, Buscaglia-Castellani Art Gallery, 83; Laura Rath (auth). *Mem:* Univ Coun, Yale Univ 85-90; CIES (sr fulbright comt, 89-92). *Media:* Oil, Watercolor. *Dealer:* Hirschl & Adler Modern 851 Madison Ave New York NY 10021. *Mailing Add:* 30 Clarendon Sr Boston MA 02116

MOORE, MARJORIE
PAINTER, ASSEMBLAGE ARTIST
b Akron, Ohio, Mar 17, 44. *Study:* Syracuse Univ, BFA, 66. *Work:* Portland Mus Art, Maine; Butler Inst Am Art; Joan Whitney Payson Gallery, Westbrook Col; Addison Gallery of Am Art, Andover, Mass; Nynex Corp, NY; Rose Art Mus; Brandeis Uni Waltham, Maine. *Comn:* Cowstructure, Artpark, Lewiston, NY, 80; Walker Art Museum Reinterpreted, Bowdoin Col, 81; Random Snapshots, One Percent For Art, Portland, Maine, 83; Toying in the Woods, Maine Festival, 86. *Exhib:* Haystack: Art in Craft Media, Rose Art Mus, Bowdoin Col, Williams Col & RI Sch Design, 81;

Selected Women Artists, Philadelphia Mus Art, 82; New Architecture, Maine Traditions, Joan Whitney Payson Gallery, Westbrook Col, 83; Sticks, Addison Gallery Am Art, 83; Elements of Landscape, Boston Univ Art Gallery, 83; Inside Outside, Bowdoin Col, Brunswick, Maine, 84; Boston Festival of the Arts, 85; Midyear Show, Butler Art Inst, Youngstown, Ohio, 86; Portland Mus Art, Maine, 90; one-woman shows, Perspectives, Portland Mus Art, Maine, 90 & Bunny Time, Howard Yezerski Gallery, Boston, Mass, 91; Interstices, Farnsworth Mus Art, Rockland, Maine, 89; On the Edge, Forty Years of Maine Painting, Maine Coast Artists, Rockport, Maine, 92. *Awards:* Fusion-Fission Regrant, Real Art Ways, Hartford, Conn; MacDowell Colony Fel, 89; New Forms Initiative Nat Endowment Arts & Rockefeller Found Regional Fel, 91; New England Found Arts, Nat Endowment Arts Regional Rel Fel, 92. *Bibliog:* Article, Boston Globe, 4/8/86; Susan Ryan (auth), 5 Political Artists in Maine: Marjorie Moore, Artists in Maine 2, spring 87; Edgar Allen Beem (auth), Maine Art Now, Dog Ear Press, 90; Francine Kosloro (auth), Marjorie Moore, Artforum, 171-72, 11/90. *Mem:* New England Found of the Arts. *Mailing Add:* 37 School St Brunswick ME 04011

MOORE, MYREEN (MYREEN MOORE NICHOLSON)
PAINTER, CONSULTANT
b Norfolk, Va, June 2, 40. *Study:* William & Mary Col, 62; Univ NC, MS, 71; with Charles Sibley, Wm Reimann & Ray Goodbred; Old Dominion Univ, MA (humanities), 92 with Linda McGreevy & others. *Work:* Old Dominion Univ, Norfolk, Va; Gibbes State Art Gallery, Charleston, SC; City of Chesapeake, Va. *Comn:* Statues, Child Study Ctr, Norfolk, 67; glass panels, Hoffler House, Virginia Beach, 88; Statute Designs, St Mark's Church, 91. *Exhib:* Working Artists' Gallery, Va Beach, Va, 89; Hampton Bay Days, City Hall, Hampton, Va, 89; Hermitage Mus, 90; Taylor Art Ctr, 91 & 92; Suffolk Mus, 91-92. *Collections Arranged:* Chrysler Mus Stud Art Show, 65; Original Art Collection, Norfolk Pub Libr Pub Lending, 72-75; W Ghent Arts Alliance Art & Literary Festival, 79; Life-Saving Mus Va Beach, 91-92; Crestar Bank, 91. *Pos:* Staff artist, William & Mary Col, 58-61; hearing reporter & secy, City of Norfolk Fine Arts Comt, 64-65; art librn & researcher, Norfolk Pub Libr, 70-80; contribr, Libr J, 73-76; ed, Poetry Soc Va, 90-93; Pres Tidewater Artists Asn, 91-92; bd dirs, Dockside Art Review, D'Art Ctr, 91-92. *Teaching:* Art teacher, Norfolk Pub Schs, 65-67; prof art, Palmer Jr Col, Charleston, SC, 67-68 & W Ghent Arts Alliance, 78-83. *Awards:* Art Scholar, William & Mary Col, 58-60; Nat Endowment Arts, 75. *Mem:* Southeastern Col Art Conf; Soc Archit Historians; Art Librs Soc; Tidewater Artists Asn (grants chmn, 90); Irene Leache Soc, 91- *Media:* All media. *Publ:* Anthology of Poems, Poems on Art in 1985, Poetry Soc Va & A Sense of Ocean and Old Trees, Road Publ, 92. *Mailing Add:* 1404 Gates Ave Norfolk VA 23507

MOORE, OLGA
PAINTER
b Chicago, Ill. *Study:* Roosevelt Univ, BA, 64; Art Inst Chicago, MFA, 69; Univ Wis, MA, 74. *Work:* Kemper Group Insurance, Chicago; US Trust Co, New York; Am Steel Foundries, Ind; Rachael Bok Seymour Collection, Philadelphia; Sony Corp Int, NJ. *Exhib:* Philadelphia Drawings, Philadelphia Mus Art, 79; solo exhibs, Jan Cicero Gallery, Chicago, 81, Newark Mus, NJ, 82, NJ State Mus, Trenton, 82 & Douglass Col, New Brunswick, NJ, 83; Eccentric Constructivists, Jan Cicero Gallery, Chicago, 82. *Teaching:* Assoc prof painting & drawing, Rutgers Univ, 78- *Awards:* NJ State Coun Fel, 82; Fulbright Fel, Morocco, 86. *Bibliog:* David Shirey (auth), article, New York Times, 7/11/82; Judy Stein (auth), article, Re-duct, 1/84. *Media:* Oil. *Dealer:* Jan Cicero Gallery 221 W Erie St Chicago IL 60610. *Mailing Add:* Fine Arts Bldg Camden Col Arts & Sci 311 N Fifth St Camden NJ 08102

MOORE, PETER
PHOTOGRAPHER, ARCHIVIST
b London, Eng, Apr 28, 32; US citizen. *Study:* Mass Inst Technol; Haverford Col. *Work:* Int Mus Photog, George Eastman House, Rochester, NY; Archiv Sohm, Ger & Archive Jean Brown, Tyringham, Mass; Dance Collection, New York Pub Libr & Mus Perform Arts, NY; Mus Contemp Art, Chicago; and others. *Exhib:* Alternative Gestures, Another View of Dance Photography, PS 1 Galleries, New York; Tangemann Gallery, Cincinnati; Four Dance Photographers, Bruce Mus, Stamford, Conn; The Judson Project, Bennington Col Mus; Gray Art Gallery; Camera Infinity, Lever House, 78, 81 & 86; Lightwork Gallery, 86; Gallery 360, Tokyo; Images of Dance, Bruce Mus; Venice Brealle, Flaxus Pavillion; Bienalle de Lyons, France. *Pos:* Artistic dir, Archives Experimental Art, New York, 62-; sr tech ed, Modern Photog Mag, formerly. *Teaching:* Instr photog, New Sch & pvt classes, New York, 74. *Awards:* Cash Grant, Finch Col Mus Art, 74. *Bibliog:* Ronald Argelander (auth), Photo-Documentation, An Interview with Peter Moore, Drama Rev, NY Univ, Sch of Arts, 9/74. *Mem:* Am Soc Mag Photogs; and others. *Res:* Experimental performance art, particularly that created by artists usually associated with the visual arts. *Publ:* Contribr, Modern Photog, Photomethods & Leica Photog. *Mailing Add:* 351 W 30th St New York NY 10001

MOORE, ROBERT ERIC
PAINTER
b Manchester, NH, Oct 13, 27. *Study:* Univ NH; New Eng Sch Art, Boston. *Work:* Farnsworth Mus, Rockland, Maine; Mus Fine Arts, Springfield, Mass; Headley Mus, Lexington, Ky; Colby Col Art Mus; Butler Mus Fine Arts, Youngtown, Ohio. *Exhib:* Centennial of Am Watercolor Soc, Metrop Mus Art, New York, 66; Maine Artists, US Embassy, Ottawa, Can, 79; Exchange Prog, Brazil, 79; Museo De La Acurela Mex, Mex City, 89; International Waters, Int Travelex, Am Watercolor Soc, 91-92; Art of Maine: A Bounty of Woods & Water, Monmouth Mus, Lincroft, NJ, 92; and others. *Awards:* Pulsifer Award, Adirondacks Nat Exhib Am Watercolor, 87; Grumbacher Gold Medallion, Audubon Artists Ann Exhib, New York, 87; Adolph & Clara Obrig Prize, Nat Acad Designs 166th Ann Exhib, 91. *Bibliog:* Ed Betts (ed), Work reproduced in Creative Landscape Painting, Watson-Guptill Publ, 78; Louis Bartlett Tracy (auth), Adventuring in Art, Pineapple Press Inc, Sarasota, Fla, 90; Robert I C Fisher (auth), The Influence of the Masters, Watercolor '90, Am Artist Mag, 90; and others. *Mem:* Am Watercolor Soc; assoc mem, Nat Acad Design, New York; Audubon Artist, New York; Allied Artists Am; Miniature Artists Am, Clearwater, Fla. *Media:* Watercolor, Acrylic. *Publ:* Auth, Creative Seascape Painting by Edward Betts, Watson & Guptill Press, 81. *Mailing Add:* 111 Cidar Hill Rd York ME 03909

MOORE, ROBERT JAMES
PAINTER, PHOTOGRAPHER
b San Jose, Calif, July 24, 22. *Study:* USAF Photo Sch, Lowry Field, Colo, grad; San Jose State Col, BA; NY Inst Fine Arts, with Salmony, Schoenberger, Panofsky & Offner; Columbia Univ Teachers Col, MFA; Art Students League, with Brackman, Miller & Will Barnet. *Work:* New York Pub Libr Print Collection. *Exhib:* Pa Acad Fine Arts, Philadelphia, 50; James D Phelan Awards Competition, San Francisco Art Mus, 51; 11 Yr Retrospective of Prizewinners, Village Art Ctr, Whitney Mus Am Art, New York, 54; NY City Ctr Gallery, 59; Audubon Artists, Nat Acad Design, New York, 62; one-man shows, Ruth Sherman Galleries, New York, 64 & Adele Bednarz Galleries, Los Angeles, 65; Berkshire Mus, Pittsfield, Mass, 66; Art Students League & Ford Found Show, New York, 75; and others. *Teaching:* Assoc prof art, Goddard Col, 54-57; instr art & photog, Battin High Sch, Elizabeth, NJ, 59-64; instr art, Julia Richman High Sch, New York, 64-90. *Awards:* Second Prize, Village Art Ctr 7th Ann Graphic Art Show, Village Art Ctr, New York, 52; Blue Ribbon, New Talent Show, Ruth Sherman Gallery, New York, 64; Berkshire Mus Award, 66. *Mem:* Artists Equity Asn of New York; life mem Art Students League; Visual Artists and Galleries Asn. *Media:* Oil, Graphics. *Mailing Add:* 246 E 51st St New York NY 10022

MOORE, RUSSELL JAMES
MUSEUM DIRECTOR, ADMINISTRATOR
b Stockton, Calif, Jan 13, 47. *Study:* Univ Calif, Davis, BA, 69, Los Angeles, MA, 72; Harvard Univ Inst in Arts Admin, 77. *Collections Arranged:* Winslow Homer's Work in Black & White (ed, catalog), 74-76, Ernest Haskell (1876-1925) A Retrospective Exhibition (auth, catalog), 76, Nancy Hemenway: Textures of Our Earth (coauth, catalog), 77-78 & Calvert Coggeshall: Paintings, 77, all circulated nationwide, Bowdoin Col. *Pos:* Asst cur, Utah Mus Fine Arts, Salt Lake City, 72-74; acting dir, Bowdoin Col Mus Art, Brunswick, Maine, 74-78; dir, Long Beach Mus Art, Calif, 78-83; exec dir, San Jose Mus Art, 83-85; owner, Allegra Gallery, San Jose, Calif, 85- *Mem:* Am Asn Mus; San Jose Art Business Asn. *Res:* American art history; early 20th century. *Specialty:* Regional California Contemporary Art: Painting, drawing and sculpting. *Mailing Add:* 1604 Sparkling Way San Jose CA 95125

MOORE, SABRA
ASSEMBLAGE ARTIST, PAINTER
b Texarkana, Tex, Jan 25, 43. *Study:* Univ Tex, Austin, BA(cum laude), 64; Brooklyn Mus Art Sch, 66; Centre WAfrican Studies Univ Birmingham, Eng, 67. *Work:* Mus Mod Art, Whitney Mus & Brooklyn Mus, Guggenheim Mus, New York; Nat Mus Women, Washington, DC. *Exhib:* All's Fair: Love & War In New Feminist Art, Ohio State Univ, Columbus, 83; Events/Heresies Collective, New Mus, New York, 83; Nat Copier Art, New York State Mus, Albany, 84; Costumes, Masks & Disguises, Clocktower, New York, 86; Connections Project/Conexus, Mus Contemp Hispanic Art, New York, 87; Committed to Print, Mus Mod Art, New York, 88; Mus de Arte Contemp, Sao Paulo, Brazil, 89. *Awards:* Fulbright Fel/Eng, 67; Helene Wurlitzer Found NMex, Artists Residency, 86 & 88. *Bibliog:* Ora Lerman (auth), Autobiographical J, Arts Mag, 5/85; Elizabeth Hess (auth), Feminist Tactics, The Village Voice, 2/10/87; Deborah Wye (auth), Catalogue statement, Committed to Print, Mus Mod Art, New York, 88. *Mem:* Women's Caucus for Art (pres, 80-82); Heresies Collective. *Media:* Wood, Paper; Oil, Cloth. *Mailing Add:* 81 Pearl St Brooklyn NY 11201

MOORE, SCOTT MARTIN
PAINTER, INSTRUCTOR
b Los Angeles, Calif, Oct 13, 49. *Study:* Calif State Univ, Long Beach, 67, 72 & 73; USMC, Hawaii, 70-72; John Pike Watercolor Sch, Woodstock, NY, 78. *Work:* Laguna Art Mus, Laguna Beach, Gibson, Dunn & Crutcher, Newport Beach, Rutaan & Tucker, Costa Mesa, Calif; Quaker Oats Co, Chicago. *Comn:* Four works oil & watercolor, Sedjwick James Insurance, 89-92. *Exhib:* Am Watercolor Soc Ann, Nat Acad, New York, 78, 80-84 & 86-87; Watercolor West, Riverside, Calif, 79-84 & 86-87; Nat Watercolor Soc, Los Angeles, 79-87; Allied Artists, Am Acad & Lett, New York, 80; Watercolor USA, 87. *Pos:* Illusr, USMC, Hawaii, 70-72; graphic designer, Scott Moore Studio, 73-78, painter, 78. *Teaching:* Instr transparent watercolor workshops, 76-92. *Awards:* First Awards, Watercolor West, 79 & 86; Walser S Greathouse Medal, 81 & Arjomari-Arches Paper Award, 86, Am Watercolor Soc. *Bibliog:* Julia P Chase (auth), Scott Moore: sheer color and light, Orange Co Illustrated, 8/79; Charles Dickens Phillips (auth), Gallery: Scott Moore, Westways Mag, 7/81; Jane Summer (auth), Familiar moments, Showcase Mag. *Mem:* Nat Watercolor Soc; Watercolor West; Am Watercolor Soc. *Media:* Transparent Watercolor, Oil. *Publ:* Auth, The drama of backlighting, The Artist's Mag, 12/84; Splash, American's Best Contemporary Watercolors, North Light Bks, 91. *Mailing Add:* 1435 Regatta Rd Laguna Beach CA 92651

MOORE, SUSAN
PAINTER
b Panama, Mar 27, 53. *Study:* Indiana Univ, BFA, 77; Univ Calif, Davis, MFA, 79. *Exhib:* One-woman shows, Timothy Burns Gallery, St Louis, 83, Univ Mich, Ann Arbor, 85, Tyler Sch Art, Temple Univ, Rome, Italy, 86, Millersville Univ, 87, Charles More Gallery, Philadelphia, 89, Pa Acad Fine Arts, Philadelphia, 90; Review/Preview, Jeffrey Fuller Fine Arts Gallery, Philadelphia, 81; 20/20/20, Univ Mo, St Louis, 83; Painterly Realism, Fontbonne Col, St Louis, 84; Little Gems, Charles More Gallery, Philadelphia, 86; Philadelphia Mus Fine Art, 90. *Teaching:* Instr, Tyler Sch Art, Philadelphia, Pa, 92- *Awards:* Nat Endowment Arts, 88 & 89; Philadelphia Coun Arts Award, 86 & 90. *Media:* Acrylic, Oil. *Dealer:* Janet Fleisher Gallery Philadelphia PA. *Mailing Add:* 210 Brown St Philadelphia PA 19123

MOORE, TODD SOMERS
PAINTER, EDUCATOR
b Oceanside, Calif, Nov 9, 52. *Study:* Evergreen State col, Olympia, Wash, BA, 75; RI Sch Design, MFA, 84. *Work:* Am Repub Insurance Co, Des Moines, Iowa; Hillhaven, Inc, Tacoma, Wash. *Comn:* Hist mural, RI State Coun Arts, E Providence, 84. *Exhib:* Wash Ann, Tacoma Art Mus, 77; Small Works, Wash Sq E Galleries, NY Univ, 80; Ann Exhib Am Art, Chautauqua Art Asn Galleries, 81 & 82; one-man show, Newport Art Mus, Newport, RI, 81; Nat Ann Show, Butler Inst Am Art, Youngstown, Ohio, 81 & 82; Untitled-without Theme, (with catalog), Alternative Mus, New York, 82; The Real Thing, N Miami Mus, 85; Art of Northeast USA, Silvermine Galleries, New Cannan, Conn, 86; 1987: A Year of the Arts, Newport Art Mus, RI, 87; two-man show, Wheeler Gallery, 91. *Teaching:* Instr 2-D design & drawing, RI Sch Design, 84- *Awards:* 2-D Grant, RI State Coun of Arts, 79; Brown Mem Prize, Am Ann at Newport, Newport Art Mus, RI, 81; Juror's Spec Mention, Nat Ann Show, Butler Inst Am Art, 82. *Bibliog:* Channing Gray (auth), rev, Providence J, 1/83 & 12/84; Helen Kohen (auth), rev, Miami Herald, 5/85; Bill van Siclien (auth), rev, Providence J, 7/88 & 9/89. *Dealer:* Helander Gallery 125 Worth Ave Palm Beach FL 33480. *Mailing Add:* 53 Lyndon St Warren RI 02885

MOORE, WAYLAND D
GRAPHIC ARTIST, PRINTMAKER
b Belton, SC, Sept 8, 35. *Study:* Pvt art study, Belton, SC, 50-54; Ringling Sch Art, Sarasota, Fla, cert, 54-57. *Work:* Headley Mus, Lexington, Ky; Nat Sports Hall Fame. *Comn:* Ky Derby, Felicie, NY, 78; Maccabian Games of Israel, Horace-Richter Galleries, Old Jaffa, 79; medallion, 100th Anniversary Madison Sq Garden; 1984 Olympics, Coca-Cola, USA, Atlanta, Ga, 84. *Exhib:* One-man exhibs, Studio 53, New York, 78, Quito, Ecuador, 78, Hermitage, La Braule, France, 80 & Gallerie Felicie, New York, 80; Cent Acad, Peking, China, 79. *Pos:* Trustee, Ringling Sch Art & Design, Sarasota, Fla, currently. *Teaching:* Instr art, Atlanta Fed Penitentiary, 70-76; instr art evening classes & spec adj lectr, Emory Univ, 83- *Awards:* Pulitzer Prize nominee, Editorial Cartooning, 67; Teaching Commendation, The White House, 74. *Mem:* Int Soc Artists; New York Soc Illusr; Am Osteopathic Acad Sports Med. *Media:* Acrylic, Serigraphy. *Mailing Add:* 2124 Azalea Cir Decatur GA 30033

MOOS, WALTER A
DEALER
b Karlsruhe, Ger, Sept 6, 26. *Study:* Ecole Superieure Com, Geneva, Switz, BA; New Sch Social Res, with Paul Zucker & Meyer Shapiro. *Pos:* Dir, Gallery Moos Ltd; vpres, Arts Mag, 77, pres, 82-83. *Mem:* Prof Art Dealers Asn Can (pres, 71-74). *Specialty:* Contemporary Canadian, European and American paintings, sculpture and graphics. *Mailing Add:* Gallery Moos Ltd 622 Richmond St W Toronto ON M5V 1Y9 Canada

MOOSE, PHILIP ANTHONY
PAINTER, ILLUSTRATOR
b Newton, NC, Jan 16, 21. *Study:* Nat Acad Design; Columbia Univ; Skowhegan Sch Painting; Taxco Sch Arts, Mex; Acad Fine Arts, Munich, Ger. *Work:* Atlanta Mus Art, Ga; Norfolk Mus, Va; NC State Mus Art, Raleigh; Colchester Mus, Eng; Mint Mus Art, Charlotte, NC. *Comn:* Mural, Montreat-Anderson Col, NC, 72. *Exhib:* Am Watercolors, Metrop Mus, New York; Corcoran Biennial, Washington, DC; Southeastern Ann, Atlanta, Ga; Fulbright Artists, WGer; Piedmont Ann, Charlotte. *Teaching:* Assoc prof art, Davidson Col, 51-53 & Queens Col, NC, 56-67. *Awards:* Pulitzer Award, 48; Tiffany Found Award, 49; Fulbright Award, 53-63. *Media:* Oil, Acrylic. *Publ:* Illusr, History of Catawba County, 52; Exploring the Mountains, 72. *Mailing Add:* Linville Rd Blowing Rock NC 28605

MOOSE, TALMADGE BOWERS
PAINTER, ILLUSTRATOR
b Albemarle, NC, June 4, 33. *Study:* Va Commonwealth Univ, BFA. *Work:* Knight Publ Co, Charlotte, NC; Campbell Univ, Buies Creek, NC; Pfeiffer Col, Misenheimer, NC. *Exhib:* 34th Semi-Ann Southeastern Print & Drawing Show, 71; Ann NC Artists Exhib, 71, 73 & 74; Art on Paper 1972, Weatherspoon Gallery, Greensboro, 72; Davidson Nat Print & Drawing Competition, 73; Retrospective Exhib, Pfeiffer Col, Misenheimer, 78. *Pos:* Pres, Gallery Uwharrie Artists, Ltd, 74-76; dir, Artists/Writers Dialogue, 75. *Teaching:* Instr drawing & painting, Stanly Tech Col, Albemarle, 72-76; Montgomery Tech Col, 80-86; Randolph Tech Col, Asheboro, NC, 85-86; Queens Col, Charlotte, NC, 89-90. *Awards:* First Prize, 34th Semi-Annual Southeastern Print & Drawing Show, 71. *Bibliog:* Clyde Burnett (auth), Limited art exhibit, Atlanta J & Constitution, 2/15/70; North Light Mag, 2-3/78; M Stephen Doherty (auth), A profitable campaign, Am Artist Mag, 2/91. *Media:* Watercolor, Oil; Pencil, Acrylics. *Publ:* Contribr, Charlotte Observer, 69; Uwharrie Rev, 74; The State Mag, 77-82; Sandlapper, 77 & Tar Heel Mag, 77-80; Exploring the Piedmont of North Carolina, 80. *Mailing Add:* 810 Lauras Lane Albemarle NC 28001

MOOZ, R PETER
MUSEUM DIRECTOR
b New York, NY, Mar 6, 40. *Study:* Wesleyan Univ, BA(with distinction; art hist); Boston Univ, MA; Univ Pa, PhD. *Collections Arranged:* Twentieth Century American Watercolors, 73; Art of American Furniture, 74; The Winslows: Pilgrims, Patrons and Portraits, 74; Painting in the South, 83. *Pos:* Teaching assoc, Winterthur Mus, Wilmington, Del, 67-73, mus coordr, Winterthur Prog, 71-73, dir, Winterthur Summer Inst, 72-73; dir, Am Painting Summer Inst, 73, Bowdoin Col Mus Art, 73-77 & Va Mus Fine Arts, 77-82; pres, Fine Arts Am, 82-83; dir, Wilton House Mus, 83-87; dir, Moody Mus, 87-88; exec dir, Mary Moody Northern Found, 88-91, Dallas Hist Soc, 91- *Teaching:* Asst prof art hist, Univ Del, 67-73; vis lectr, Univ Bath, Eng, 69; vis asst prof, Univ Vt, 71; sr lectr, Bowdoin Col, 73-; vis prof, Univ Va, 81 & Va Commonwealth Univ, 82-83. *Awards:* Kellogg Fel, 84. *Mem:* Am Asn Mus (conmr, 80-82); Col Art Asn; Soc Archit Historians; Soc Preserv New Eng Antiquities (mem adv coun, 75); Nat Trust Hist Preserv. *Res:* American art, especially colonial painting and American furniture; American painter Robert Feke. *Publ:* Auth, New clues to the art of Robert Feke, Antiques, 68; contribr, Country and Simple City Furniture, 69; auth, Smibert's Bermuda group--a re-evaluation, Art Quart, 70; contribr, American Painting to 1776: A Reappraisal, 71; coauth, The Genius of American Painting, 73; consulted, Homes of the Virginia Gentry, 88; auth, Mansions of the Virginia Gentry, Oxmoer Press, 88. *Mailing Add:* c/o Dallas Historical Soc Hall of State Fair Park PO Box 150038 Dallas TX 75315

MOQUIN, RICHARD ATTILIO
SCULPTOR
b San Francisco, Calif, July 1, 34. *Study:* City Col San Francisco, AA; San Francisco State Col, with Seymour Locks, BA & MA. *Work:* Sacramento State Col & Sacramento State Fair; Oakland Mus; Can Ceramic Int; San Francisco Mus Art. *Exhib:* 24th Ceramic Nat, Everson Mus, Syracuse, NY, 66; 23rd Scripps Col Invitational, Claremont, Calif, 67; Col Marin Invitational, Kentfield, Calif, 69; M H De Young Mus Show, San Francisco, 70; Stanford Univ Sculpture Invitational, 71 & 72; A G Gardner Gallery, 77-78. *Pos:* Vpres, Asn San Francisco Potters, 67-68. *Teaching:* Instr sculpture, City Col San Francisco, 69- *Awards:* Purchase Awards, Sacramento State Fair, 68, San Francisco Art Fair, 69 & M H De Young Mus, 70. *Bibliog:* Albright (auth), Ceramic sculpture, San Francisco Chronicle, 68 & 70; A Meisel (auth), Ceramic sculpture, Craft Horizons, 72; Charlotte Speight (auth), article in Ceramics Text Book. *Media:* Clay, Plastic. *Dealer:* H Gardner Gallery Stinson Beach CA; Michael Duneve 77 Gary St San Francisco CA 94110. *Mailing Add:* Dept Art City College San Francisco 50 Phelan Ave San Francisco CA 94112

MORALES, ARMANDO
PAINTER, PRINTMAKER
b Granada, Nicaragua, Jan 15, 27. *Study:* Sch Fine Arts, Managua, Nicaragua; Pratt Graphic Art Ctr, New York. *Work:* Mus Mod Art, Guggenheim Mus, New York; Inst Art, Detroit; Mus Art, Philadelphia; Mus Fine Arts, Houston. *Exhib:* Bienal Mod Art, Sao Paulo, Brazil, 53, 55 & 59; Carnegie Inst, Pittsburgh, 58, 64 & 67; Arte Am y Espana, Madrid, Barcelona, Rome & Berlin, 61; Guggenheim Int, New York, 60; The Emergent Decade, Cornell Univ & Guggenheim Mus, 66. *Teaching:* Instr adv painting, Cooper Union, New York, 72 & 73. *Awards:* Ernest Wolf Award, V Bienal, Sao Paulo, Brazil, 59; Award, Arte Am y Espana, Madrid, 63; J L Hudson Award, Carnegie Int, 64. *Bibliog:* Dore Ashton (auth), Visual pleasure from austerity, Studio Int, London, 2/65; Heinz Ohff (auth), Anleitnung zum optimismus: Begegnung mit Armando Morales in Berlin, Der Tagespiegel, Berlin, 6/19/65; Esperanza Brault (auth), Armando Morales, El Sol Mex, Mexico City, 10/4/68. *Mailing Add:* c/o Claude Bernard Gallery 33 E 74th St New York NY 10012

MORALES, RODOLFO
PAINTER
b Oaxaca, Mex, 1925. *Study:* Nat Sch Fine Art, San Carlos, BFA, 49, study with Rufino Tamayo. *Work:* Inst Polytecnico & Escuela Prep, Mexico City; Mus City Ocatlan, Oaxaca, Mex; Rincon de los Bosques, Bosques de las Lomas, Mex. *Exhib:* State Palace Malaga, Spain, 73; Mus Mex Art, San Francisco, Calif, 78; Mexico: The Next Generation, San Antonio Mus, Tex, 85; one-man exhib, Vorpal Gallery, New York, 85. *Teaching:* Instr art, Escuela Preparatoria No 5, 53-86. *Awards:* Medal, Oaxacan Culture House, Mexico, 86. *Bibliog:* Antonio Rodriguez (auth), Nostalgia accompanies solitude, Inst Politech Nat, Mex, 81. *Publ:* Auth, Rodolfo Morales (exhib catalog), Vorpal Gallery, New York & San Francisco, 88. *Mailing Add:* c/o Bord Street Gallery 5269 Broadway Oakland CA 94618

MORATH, INGE
PHOTOGRAPHER
b Graz, Austria, May 27, 23; US citizen. *Study:* Univ Berlin, BA, 44; asst to Henri Cartier-Bresson; Fine Arts Univ Hartford, Hon Dr Art, 84. *Work:* Metrop Mus Art, New York; Boston Mus Fine Arts, Mass; Art Inst Chicago; RI Sch Design; Bibliot Nat, Paris, France; and many others. *Exhib:* Retrospective Rupertinum Mus, Salzburg, Austria; Chicago Art Inst, 64; Univ Miami, Coral Gables, Fla, 72; Neikrug Galleries, New York, 77; one-woman show, China, Grand Rapids Art Mus, 79, Mus Mod Art, Vienna, 80; Union Photojournalists, Moscow, 88; Sala del Conal, Madrid, 88; plus many group showings. *Teaching:* Guest instr photog & compos, Cooper Union, New York;

and others. *Awards:* Photog Excellence, Stuttgart Bkwks, Bucher Publ, Switz, 11/76; Great Austrian State Prize for Photog, 92. *Bibliog:* Article, Saul Steinberg & Inge Morath, Creative Camera, 2/69; Allen Porter (auth), article, Camera Mag, 11/69; Olga Carlisle (auth), Great Photographers of Our Time--Inge Morath, Bucher, Switz, 75. *Mem:* Magnum Photos; Am Soc Mag Photogr. *Publ:* Inge Morath: Portraits, Aperture Found, 86; illustr, Saul Steinbergs Masken und andere Fotobilder, Rupertinum Mus, 88; auth, book on Russia, Aperture (in prep); Russian Journal Aperture, 91; Inge Morath Photographs 1952-1992 (monogr), Otto Mueller Publ, Salzburg, Austria. *Dealer:* Magnum Photos 72 Spring St New York NY 10012. *Mailing Add:* Tophet Rd Roxbury CT 06783

MORCOS, MAHER N
SCULPTOR, PAINTER
b Cairo, Egypt, Feb 23, 46; US citizen. *Study:* Cairo Univ, BA(archit), 69; Leonardo de Vinci, Italy, 70. *Comn:* Bust Egyptian President Nasser, Ministry of Educ, Cairo, Egypt, 62; religious paintings, Heliopolis Cathedral, Cairo, Egypt, 64; mural, Valley Nat Bank, Scottsdale, Ariz, 84. *Exhib:* Charles Russell Show, Charles Russell Mus, Great Falls, Mont, 80 & 81; Am Inst Contemp Art, San Dimas, Calif, 80 & 81; Western Artists Am, Coliseum, Reno, Nev, 80 & 81; Western Heritage Show, Arapahoe Co, Littleton, Colo, 80 & 81; George Phippen Show, CofC, Prescott, Ariz, 80 & 81. *Awards:* Gold Medal, Death Valley Show, 80; Best of Show, Western Heritage Show, Arapahoe Co Asn, 81; Best of Show, Western Artists Am, City Reno, 81. *Bibliog:* William E Freckleton (auth), Guided by imagination, Southwest Art, 4/78; Scene, Tulsa Tribune, 78; Dick Spencer (auth), Western heritage, The Western Horseman, 80. *Media:* Bronze; Oil, Watercolor. *Mailing Add:* PO Box 22659 San Diego CA 92122

MOREHOUSE, WILLIAM PAUL
PAINTER, SCULPTOR
b San Francisco, Calif, May 27, 29. *Study:* Studied with Clyfford Still, 47-50; Calif Sch of Fine Art, cert, 50; San Francisco Art Inst, BFA, 54; San Francisco State Univ, MA, 56. *Work:* San Francisco Mus Mod Art & San Francisco Art Comn Collection; Oakland Art Mus, Calif; Univ Art Mus, Berkeley, Calif; Whitney Mus Am Art, New York; Museo de Arte Moderno y Contemporaneo, Ibiza & Baleares, Spain; Archives Am Art, Smithsonian Inst, Washington, DC; and many others. *Exhib:* Younger Am Painters (with catalog), Solomon R Guggenheim Mus, New York, 56; Biennial, Whitney Mus Am Art, New York, 59; San Francisco Mus Art Ann, 55-60; Ill Biennial, Urbana & Art Inst Chicago Ann, 61; 72nd Western Painters Ann, Denver Art Mus, 66; Funk (with catalog), Univ Art Mus, Berkeley & Ctr Contemp Art, Boston, 67; Interstices, San Jose Art Mus, Calif, 75 & 77 & Cranbrook Mus, Mich, 75; Lincoln Arts Ctr, Calif, 78; American Abstraction (with monograph), Meisel Gallery, New York, 86; Berggruen Gallery, San Francisco, 92. *Teaching:* Instr art, San Francisco Art Inst, 58-67; prof, Sonoma State Univ, 67-85; retired. *Bibliog:* D M Davis (auth), Art of the Future, Praeger, New York, 73; Peter Plagens (auth), The Sunshine Muse, Praeger, New York, 74; Thomas Albright (auth), Art in the San Francisco Bay Area 1945-1980, Univ Calif Press, 85; and others. *Media:* Oil; Fiberglass. *Mailing Add:* PO Box 210 Bodega CA 94922

MORENON, ELISE
PAINTER, INSTRUCTOR
b Paris, France, June 26, 39; US citizen. *Study:* Northwestern Univ, BS, 58-61; Sch Mus Fine Arts, Boston, 62 & 63; Yale Univ Grad Sch, 64 & 65. *Comn:* Portrait, comn by A Nisula, Short Hills, NJ, 89; double portrait, comn by G Barrow, Madison, New York, 90. *Exhib:* Am Watercolor Soc, Nat Acad, New York, 75, 77, 79, 80 & 81; Midwest Watercolor Soc, Tweed Mus Art, Duluth, Minn, 78, Rahr West Mus, Manitowoc, Wis, 79 & Neville Pub Mus, Greenbay, Wis, 92; West Texas Watercolor Asn, Mus Texas Tech Univ, Lubbock, 78; Nat Asn Women Artists Traveling Exhib, Am Cult Affaire Ctr, Israel & Egypt, 81-82; Audubon Artists, Nat Art Club, New York, 82 & 91; Allied Artists Am, Nat Art Club, New York, 86, 87 & 89; Two Artists-Natural Images, Fordham Univ, New York, 89; Watercolor USA, Springfield Art Mus, Mo, 91. *Pos:* Scenic artist, designer, Berkshire Playhouse, Stockbridge, Mass, 62-64; display artist, Omega Watch Corp, New York, 66-86. *Teaching:* Instr watercolor, Sch Visual Arts, New York, 78-84; instr, Teaneck Community Educ Ctr, NJ, 91-93. *Awards:* Grumbacher Silver Medallion, 82 & 90; Elizabeth Morse Genius Found Award, Nat Asn Women Artists, 86; Nicholas Reale Mem Award, NJ Watercolor Soc, 91. *Bibliog:* Who's Who in the East, 24th ed, Marquis. *Mem:* Am Watercolor Soc; Nat Asn Women Artists; Midwest Watercolor Soc; New York Artists Equity Asn. *Media:* Watercolor. *Dealer:* Plaza Gallery Sparta NJ; Dockside Gallery Barnegat NJ. *Mailing Add:* 420 Fairview Ave Ft Lee NJ 07024

MORGAN, ARTHUR C
SCULPTOR
b Riverton Plantation, La, Aug 3, 04. *Study:* Beaux Arts Inst Design; also with Gutzon Borglum, Mario Korbel and others. *Work:* Centenary Col, Shreve Mem Libr & Civic Theater, Shreveport, La; Civic Ctr & Hist Libr, Thibodaux, La; plus numerous pvt collections. *Comn:* Heroic figure, Chief Justice Edward Douglass White, Edward Douglass White Mem Comn, US Capitol, Washington, DC, 55; Paul Geisler Mem, Comt Friends of Paul Geisler, Stadium Gounds, High Sch, Burwick, La, 65; Henry Miller Shreve Monument, City of Shreveport & Pub Subscription, River Pkwy, Shreveport, 66; A J Hodges Commemorative Bust, Trustees of Hodges Gardens, Hodges Gardens, Many, La, 72; monumental bust, Clyde E Fant, Clyde Fant Parkway, Shreveport, La, 76; Bust of Jean Despujols, Meadows Mus Art, 81; and others. *Exhib:* One-man shows, La State Univ, Baton Rouge, 27, La State Exhib Mus, Shreveport, 40 & 50; Philbrook Art Ctr, Tulsa, Okla, 52 & Centennial Mus, Corpus Christi, Tex, 57; Mem Exhib, Nat Arts Club, New York, 60-; Mem Exhib, Dartmouth House Club, London, 77. *Teaching:* Instr drawing, painting, sculpture & art hist & dir dept art, Centenary Col La, 28-34; dir sculpture & drawing, Southwestern Inst Arts, 34-74. *Awards:* Am Inst Archit Citations, 61 & 75, Shreveport Chap. *Bibliog:* Patsi Farmer (auth), Biographer in bronze, Shreveport Mag, 12/58; Mary Gray Morris Walker (auth), Portrait of an artist, NLa Hist Asn J, 7/65; Edwin Adams Davis (auth), Louisiana, the pelican state, La State Univ Press. *Mem:* Nat Arts Club; Dartmouth House Club, London, Eng. *Media:* Bronze, Marble. *Mailing Add:* 657 Jordan St Shreveport LA 71101

MORGAN, BARBARA BROOKS
PHOTOGRAPHER
b July 8, 1900. *Study:* Univ Calif, Los Angeles, 19-23; Marquette Univ, Hon DFA, 78. *Work:* Nat Gallery of Can, Ottawa; Marquette Univ; Fotografiska Museet, Stockholm; Univ Calif Los Angeles Libr; Mus Fine Arts, St Petersburg, Fla. *Exhib:* Ohio Univ, Athens, 79; Baldwin Street Gallery, Toronto, 79; George Eastman House/Int Mus Photog, 79-80, traveling US, 80-81; Recollections Exhibit, Int Ctr Photog, 79, touring US, 80-81; one-person exhibs, Vision Gallery, Boston, 80 & Photomontages et Danses, Galerie Zabriskie, Paris, 81; and others. *Teaching:* Instr art, Univ Calif, Los Angeles, 25-30. *Awards:* Fel, Philadelphia Mus Art, 70; Soc Photog Educ Plaque, 79. *Bibliog:* Cecil Beaton & Gail Buckland (auths), The Magic Image, London & Boston, 75; Ruth Spencer (auth), article, Brit J Photog, London, 6/13/75; Petr Tausk, Photography in the 20th Century, Cologne, 77 & London, 80. *Publ:* Auth, photogr & designer, Summer's Children: A Photographic Cycle of Life at Camp, 51; ed, photogr & designer, Barbara Morgan (monogr), 72; photogr, Barbara Morgan Dance Portfolio, Morgan & Morgan, 77; contribr, Recollections: Ten Women of Photography, Viking, 79; photogr, auth & designer, Barbara Morgan: Photomontage, Morgan & Morgan, 80. *Mailing Add:* 120 High Point Rd Scarsdale NY 10583

MORGAN, CLARENCE (EDWARD)
PAINTER, EDUCATOR
b Philadelphia, Pa, May 21, 50. *Study:* Pa Acad Fine Arts, cert, 75; Sch Fine Arts, Univ Pa, MFA, 78; Temple Univ, summer 78. *Work:* Equitable Life Assurance Soc US, Washington, DC; Prudential Insurance Co Am, Jacksonville, Fla; Pa Acad Fine Arts, Philadelphia; Mem Union Gallery, Ariz State Univ, Tempe; General Mills Corp, Minneapolis, Minn. *Comn:* Large scale painting, comn by NC Gen Assembly, Raleigh, 83 & St Thomas Celebration Arts, Wilmington, 86, NC. *Exhib:* Seven Contemporary American Artists, Cleveland Mus Art, Ohio, 83; Portrait of the South, Palazzo Venezia, Rome, Italy, 84; Recent Works, Wake Forest Univ, Winston-Salem, NC, 84; Paradoxical Behavior, Hodges Taylor Gallery, Charlotte, NC, 85; Drawings & Paintings, Carleton Col, Northfield, Minn, 85; Southern Exposure, Alternative Mus, New York, 85; solo exhib, Harris Brown Gallery, Boston, Mass, 86. *Teaching:* Assoc prof painting & drawing, Sch Art, East Carolina Univ, 78-; artist-in-residence, Minneapolis Col Art & Design, 84-85. *Awards:* Fac Res Grant, East Carolina Univ, 79; Merit Award Painting, Fayetteville Mus Art, 82; Visual Arts Fel, NC Arts Coun, 82. *Bibliog:* Rubel Romero (auth), Universal language, Spectator, 84; Mason Riddle (auth), Midwest reviews, New Art Examiner, 84; Richard Maschal (auth), Abstractionist uses religous imagery, Charlotte Observer, 85. *Mem:* Col Art Asn Am. *Dealer:* Elizabeth Harris-Harris Brown Gallery 476 Columbus Ave Boston MA 02118; Dot Hodges-Hodges Taylor Gallery 227 N Tryon St Charlotte NC 28202. *Mailing Add:* c/o Marita Gilliam Gallery 126 Glenwood Ave Raleigh NC 27603-1704

MORGAN, JAMES L
PAINTER
b Aug 7, 47. *Study:* Utah State Univ, BFA, 70. *Work:* Utah State Univ, Logan; Crecent Cardboard Co, Chicago; Leigh Yawkey Woodson Art Mus. *Comn:* 36 Paintings, Texaco, Washington, Iowa, 83-85; Merril Lynch, Salt Lake City, Utah, 87. *Exhib:* Birds in Art, Leigh Yawkey Woodson Mus, 82-83 & 86-92; Easton Waterfowl Exhib, Tidewater Inn, Md, 83-86; Soc Animal Artists Exhib, 86; Bateman Selects, Nicolay Sen Art Mus, Casper, Wyo, 86; Arts for the Parks Competition, Birds Art Nat Tour, 88-91; and others. *Awards:* Merit Award, Soc Animal Artists Ann Exhib, 83 & Nat Art Exhib of Alaska Wildlife, 85; Purchase Award, Festival Am West, Pepperidge Farm Inc, 84; Nat Ducks Unlimited Artist, 85-87. *Mem:* Soc Animal Artists; Northwest Rendezvous Group. *Media:* Oil, Watercolor. *Publ:* Ducks Unlimited Mag, 76; Cache Mag, Herald J, 85; Fishes of the Great Basin, Univ Nev Press, 86; Art of the West Mag, 92; Southwest Art Mag, 92; and others. *Mailing Add:* PO Box 331 Mendon UT 84325

MORGAN, MARITZA LESKOVAR
PAINTER, ILLUSTRATOR
b Zagreb, Yugoslavia, Nov 20, 21; US citizen. *Study:* Cornell Univ, 42; Art Students League, 43; Westminister Col, Hon DFA. *Work:* Wilson Mus, Dartmouth Col, Hanover, NH; All Souls Unitarian Church, Tulsa, Okla; First Presby Church, Warren, Pa; St Luke's Chapel & Hurlbut Mem Church, Chautauqua, NY. *Comn:* Murals, Smith-Wilkes Mem Libr, Chautauqua Inst, 70; East Liberty Presby Church, Pittsburgh. *Exhib:* Nat Jury Show, Chautauqua, 66; Festival Arts Northwest Pa, 72; Gallery 100, Princeton, NJ, 75; Deson-Zaks Gallery, Chicago, 75; Lighthouse Gallery, Tequesta, Fla, 75; Mural, Vanguard and Victory, Battle of the Nice, Vanguard Group, Valley Forge, Pa, 92. *Pos:* Artist in residence, Chautauqua Inst, 66- & Pittsburgh Theological Seminary, currently. *Media:* Miscellaneous. *Publ:* Illusr, The Chautauqua Cookbook for the Elegant Eighties; co-translr, Rudolph Tesnohlidek's The Cunning Little Vixen, Farrar Straus & Giroux; illus, Chatauqua, I Love You. *Mailing Add:* Box 168 Chautauqua NY 14722

MORGAN, MYRA J
ART DEALER
b Birmingham, Ala, Jan 26, 38. *Study:* Univ Ala, BA. *Pos:* Owner, Morgan Gallery, Kansas City, Mo, 69- *Specialty:* Fine contemporary art including painting, sculpture, drawings and prints; photography; major representation of established artists, primarily American. *Mailing Add:* c/o Morgan Gallery 412 Delaware St No A Kansas City MO 64105-1218

MORGAN, NORMA GLORIA
PAINTER, ENGRAVER
b New Haven, Conn. *Study:* Art Students League, with Julian Levi; Hans Hofmann Sch Fine Art, New York; Atelier 17, New York, with Stanley W Hayter. *Work:* Nat Gallery Art & Pennell Collection, Libr of Cong, Washington, DC; Mus Mod Art, New York; Victoria & Albert Mus, London; Philadelphia Mus Art; Metrop Mus Art, New York; Art Inst Chicago; Lynd Ward Mem Collection, Portland, Ore Art Mus, 92. *Comn:* Engraving, Woodstock Artists Asn, 83; Moorland Sanctuary (oil mural), Old White Lion Inn, Haworth, Eng, 63; Grand Canyon (acrylic mural), Mary Ellen Pettee Collection, Salisbury, Conn, 80; Elk Lake (acrylic painting 7'x3 1/2') Adirondack Mountains, 92; Elk Lake (engraving), Adirondack Mountains, 92. *Exhib:* one-man show ann exhibs with Audubon Artists, New York, Watermark/Cargo Gallery, Kingston, NY, 89; Moor Lodge engraving, Woodstock Artists' Show, Asn Am Galleries, New York, 87; Old Bergen Art Guild, 88; Audubon Artist, 90; group shows, Idillwood Mus, Long Island, 92 & Audubon Artists Ann, New York, 92; and others. *Teaching:* Pvt lessons in drawing. *Awards:* Gold Medal for Graphics, Painters & Sculptors Soc NJ 26th Ann, 67; Blue Ribbon-First Prize for Graphics, Composers, Authors & Artists Conv, 69; Medal Honor-Gold Medal, Audobon Artists, New York, 76 & 90. *Bibliog:* Fritz Eichenberg (auth), The Art of the Print, Abrams Publ, 76. *Mem:* Soc Am Graphic Artists (coun mem, 74-75); Audubon Artists, New York; Assoc Am Artists; Woodstock Artists Asn. *Media:* Acrylic, Watercolor; Copper. *Mailing Add:* 595 Columbus Ave New York NY 10024

MORGAN, ROBERT COOLIDGE
PAINTER, CRITIC
b Boston, Mass, July 10, 43. *Study:* Univ Redlands, BA, 64; Northeastern Univ, EdM, 68; Univ Mass, Amherst, MFA, 75; NY Univ, PhD, 78. *Work:* Mus Mod Art, New York; Clark Art Inst, Williamstown, Mass; New York Pub Libr; Chase Manhattan Bank Collection; Commodities Corp Collection, NJ; and many pvt collections. *Comn:* Painted Forms on Steel, Mayor's Off Cult Affairs, Boston, 72; Curved Curbs, Mass Coun on Arts, Boston, 74. *Exhib:* Interventions in Landscape, Hayden Gallery, Mass Inst Technol, Cambridge, Mass, 74; Performances: 4 Evenings, 4 Days, Whitney Mus Am Art, New York, 76; Artists & Bks, Ulrich Mus Art, Wichita State Univ, 79; Judson Mem Church, 84; White Columns, 87; Erik Stark Gallery, 92; Daniel Newburg Gallery, 92; Galerie A B, Paris, 92; and others. *Pos:* Bd adv, Art Omi, appt, 92. *Teaching:* Instr mod art hist, NY Univ, 76; prof art hist, Rochester Inst Technol, NY, 81-; instr, Sch Visual Arts, Columbia Univ, NY, 90 & Barnard Col, 91-92; vis prof, Pratt Inst, 91-93. *Awards:* Nat Endowment Humanities Fel, 80 & 87 & 88. *Bibliog:* David Carven (auth), article, Arts Mag, 9/83; Collins and Milazzo (coauth), article, New Observations, 87; Gary Nickark (auth), article, CEPA Quarterly, 87. *Mem:* Col Art Asn Am; Int Asn Art Critics; Am Soc Aesthetics. *Res:* Role of documentation in conceptual art; structural interactions, literal time and progressive sequence, often manifested in appropriation of swim images & TV images, recent photos of tondo paintings. *Publ:* Auth, The making of Wit: Joseph Kosuth and the Feudian Palimsest, Arts, 1/88; Oskar de Mejo, Abrams, 92; Duchamp, Androgyhy, etc, Editions Antoine Candou, Paris, 90; After the Deluge: The Return of the Inner-Directed Artist, Arts, 3/2. *Mailing Add:* Col Fine & Appl Arts Rochester Inst Technol Rochester NY 14623

MORGAN, SUSAN
PAINTER, INSTRUCTOR
b Queens, NY, June 3, 53. *Study:* Art Students League, New York, 73-77. *Exhib:* International Multimedia Exhib, univ Sao Paolo, Brazil, 79; Tree Guards, Foundations Gallery, 82 & The Arsenal, 85, New York; Cloudworks, Stuart Neill Gallery, New York, 82; Ann Exhib, Queens Mus, Flushing, NY, 83; solo exhib, South-Dade Libr, Miami, 84, Silpakorn Univ, Bangkok, US Info Serv, Chiang Mai, Thailand, 90; Off the Wall, Kamikaze Gallery, New York, 86; Second Ann Women's Exhib, Bangkok, Thailand. *Collections Arranged:* Community Cultural Center Annual Exhibitions, Brookings, SDak, 80. *Pos:* Co-owner, Nobe Gallery, New York, 77-79; asst to Jeanne-Claude Christo, New York, 82-84; co-owner, The Five & Dime, New York, 84-86. *Teaching:* Vis lectr, Silpakorn Univ, Bangkok, 90, Chaing Mai Informal Group, 92, Thaiand; vis artist, Chaing Mai Univ, 90. *Bibliog:* Helen L Kohen (auth), article, Miami Herald, 84; Artists in the city, by Jenny Dixon, WNYC radio broadcast, 84; Ban Suan mag & several Thai newspaper articles, 90. *Media:* Oil Paint, Oil Pastel. *Publ:* Coauth, Tree Guards, with Holly O'Grady, silk screen edition, 80, Morgan/O'Grady publ, 82; For a Lahu Girl (video), 89. *Mailing Add:* 450 W 50th St New York NY 10019

MORGAN, SYBIL ANDREWS See Andrews, Sybil (Sybil Andrews Morgan)

MORGAN, THEODORA (THEODORA MORGAN OLSEN)
WRITER
b Brooklyn, NY. *Study:* Packer Collegiate Inst, Brooklyn; NY Univ. *Pos:* Bd dir, Nat Arts Club, New York, formerly; pub relations dir, Crayon, Watercolor & Craft Inst, 57-60; exec ed, Sculpture Review, 56-92; co-dir, Sculpture Libr Bk Club, Mt Vernon, NY, 79-83. *Mem:* Nat Sculpture Soc. *Res:* Figuralive sculpture, American and worldwide. *Mailing Add:* c/o Nat Sculpture Review 15 E 26th St New York NY 10010

MORGAN, WILLIAM
HISTORIAN, WRITER
b Princeton, NJ, June 13, 44. *Study:* Dartmouth Col, AB; Columbia Univ, MA & cert in restoration & preservation hist archit; Univ Del, PhD. *Work:* Portland Mus; Miami Univ; Univ Louisville. *Exhib:* J B Speed Mus, Louisville, Ky, 88. *Pos:* Chmn, Ky Hist Preservation Rev Bd, 75-90; archit critic, Courier-J, 75-80; bk rev ed, Landscape Archit Mag, 76-78. *Teaching:* Lectr art & archaeol, Princeton Univ, 71-74; asst prof fine arts, Allen R Hite Art Inst, Univ Louisville, 74-76, assoc prof, 76-81, prof, 81- *Awards:* Nat Collection Fine Arts Vis Res Fel, Smithsonian Inst, 71; Nat Endowment Humanities Res Fel, 84-85. *Mem:* Soc Archit Historians; Nat Trust Gr Brit & Northern Ireland; and others. *Media:* Photographer. *Res:* American art and architecture; Gothic revival. *Publ:* Coauth, Bucks County photographs of early architecture, Horizon, 74; Old Louisville: The Victorian era, Courier-J, 75; auth, Louisville--Architecture and the Urban Environment, Bauhan, 79; Portals: Photographs by William Morgan, Bauhan, 81; The Almighty Wall: Architecture of Henry Vaughan, Archit Hist Found, 83; Collegiate Gothic: Architecture Rhodes Col, Mo, 89. *Mailing Add:* Dept Fine Arts Univ Louisville Louisville KY 40292

MORGANSTERN, ANNE MCGEE
HISTORIAN, EDUCATOR
b Morgan, Ga, Feb 5, 36. *Study:* Wesleyan Col, Ga, BFA, 58; Inst Fine Arts, NY Univ, MA, 61, PhD, 70. *Teaching:* Instr art hist, Vassar Col, Poughkeepsie, NY, 65-66; lectr art hist, Univ Wis, Milwaukee, 70-73; from asst prof to assoc prof, Ohio State Univ, 73- *Mem:* Historians Netherlandish Art; Medieval Acad Am; Col Art Asn; Int Ctr medieval Art (domestic adv, 83-86). *Res:* Gothic Sculpture in NEurope; Flemish painting of the 15th century. *Publ:* Auth, The La Grange tomb and choir, Speculum, 73; Pierre Morel, master of works in Avignon, 76 & The rest of Bosch's Ship of Fools, 84, Art Bull; The pawns in Bosch's Death & the Miser, Studies Hist Art, 82; coauth, Gothic splendor in Paris: A review, Gesta, 83. *Mailing Add:* 70 Webster Park Columbus OH 43214

MORGANSTERN, JAMES
HISTORIAN, EDUCATOR
b Pittsburgh, Pa, Oct 16, 36. *Study:* Williams Col, BA, 58; NY Univ, MA, 64, PhD, 73. *Teaching:* Asst prof hist art, Univ Wis, Milwaukee, 70-73; asst prof, Ohio State Univ, Columbus, 73-80, assoc prof, 80- *Mem:* Col Art Asn; Soc Archit Historians; Archaeol Inst Am; Medieval Acad; Int Ctr Medieval Art. *Res:* Byzantine art, architecture and archaeology; western medieval architecture. *Publ:* Auth, The church at Dereagzi: A preliminary report, Vol 22, 68 & The church at Dereagzi: A preliminary report on the mosaics of the Diaconicon, Vols 23 & 24, 69 & 70, Dumbarton Oaks Papers; The church at Dereagzi: Its date and its place in the history of Byzantine architecture, Actes, XIV Congres Int Etudes Byzantines, 76; coauth, The settlement at Dereagzi: A preliminary report on the 1974 and 1975 seasons, Turk Arkeoloji Dergisi 25, 79; auth, The Byzantine Church at Dereagzi and its Decoration, Ernst Warmuth, 83. *Mailing Add:* Dept Hist Art Ohio State Univ Columbus OH 43210

MORGENLANDER, ELLA KRAMER
PAINTER, INSTRUCTOR
b Bronx, NY, Aug 7, 31. *Study:* Brooklyn Col, 53; Brooklyn Mus Art Sch, with Reuben Tam, 60-70; New York Univ, 62; Barnes Found, Merion, Pa, 74-76; Art Students League, with Will Barnett, 78-79. *Exhib:* Ann Nat Asn Women Artists, Nat Acad Arts Gallery, New York, 71-81; Brooklyn Mus, NY, 76; one-woman show, Nicholas Roerich Mus, New York, 76; Artists Depicting the Humanities, Henry St Settlement, New York, 82. *Teaching:* Instr art, St George's Pre-Sch NY, 62-67; instr, Ethical Culture Sch, Brooklyn, NY, 63-66; instr art, Bank St Sch Childhood Educ, 68-72. *Awards:* Adelle M Schiff Award, 73; Ziuta & Joseph James Akston Found, 88th Ann Nat Asn Women Artists; Lillian Cotton Mem Award, 90; Hon Mention Award, Nat Asn Women Artists, 92. *Mem:* Artists Equity Asn, NY; Nat Asn Women Artists; Contemp Artists New York. *Media:* Oil, Watercolor. *Dealer:* Brooklyn Mus Community Gallery File 188 Eastern Parkway Brooklyn NY. *Mailing Add:* 210 Park Pl Apt 2C Brooklyn NY 11238

MORIN, FRANCE
CURATOR, ART DEALER
b Montreal, Que. *Study:* Montreal Univ, BA(art hist & film), 75. *Collections Arranged:* Canada-New York: From the Studios of Canadian Artists Living in New York, 84 & Icarus: The Vision of Angels, 86, 49th Parallel, Ctr Contemp Can Art, New York. *Pos:* Cofounder & co-ed, Parachute (contemp art mag), 75-80; dir, Galerie France Morin, 80-83; dir & cur, 49th Parallel Ctr Contemp Can Art, 83-89; sr cur, New Mus Contemp Art, 89- *Teaching:* Teacher art hist, grad prog, Concordia Univ, Montreal, 81-83. *Mailing Add:* New Museum of Contemporary Art 583 Broadway New York NY 10012

MORIN, JAMES CORCORAN
CARTOONIST, EDITOR
b Washington, DC, Jan 30, 53. *Study:* Syracuse Univ Sch Art, BFA, 75. *Work:* Mus Cartoon Art, Portchester, NY; Emerson Col, Boston, Mass; Ohio State Univ, Columbus. *Pos:* Ed cartoonist, Beaumont Enterprise & J, 76-77, Richmond Times Dispatch, 77-78 & Miami Herald, 78- *Awards:* Overseas Press Club Award, Foreign Affairs Cartoons, 79 & Hon Mention, 81; SDX Green Eyeshade Award, 86. *Bibliog:* Dick Comer (auth), A baker's dozen questions for one of America's brightest young cartoonists, Cartoonist Profiles, 9/79; David Finkel (auth), Etching political, Miami Mag, 8/79. *Mem:* Asn Am Ed Cartoonists; Nat Cartoonists Soc; Newspapers Features Coun. *Media:* All Media. *Publ:* Contribr, Best Editorial Cartoons of the Year,

Pelican, 78 & 79; America's Political System, Random House, 79; Famous Cats, William Morrow, 82; auth, Jim Morin's Field Guide to Birds, William Morrow, 85; auth, James Morin's Line of Fire, Fla Univ Press, 92. *Mailing Add:* One Herald Plaza Miami FL 33132

MORIN, THOMAS EDWARD
SCULPTOR, EDUCATOR
b Malone, NY; Sept 22, 34. *Study:* Mass Col Art, BS(educ), 56; Cranbrook Acad Art, MFA, 57; Brown Univ, cert(basic metal), 66, cert(plastics technol), 67. *Work:* Richmond Mus Art, Va; Brown Univ, Providence, RI; Barn Gallery Assoc, Ogunquit, Maine; NY Univ, Oneonta. *Comn:* Cast aluminum high relief, Brown Univ, 64; bronze sculpture & bronze screen, Am Tube, 72. *Exhib:* Inst Contemp Art Invitational, Boston, 60; Whitney Mus Am Art Ann, New York, 61; 11 New Eng Sculptors, Wadsworth Atheneum, Hartford, Conn, 63; Contemp Box & Wall Sculpture Invitational, RI Sch Design Mus Art, 65; Univ Conn Mus Art, Storrs, 70. *Teaching:* Head dept sculpture, Silvermine Guild Artists Col Art, 58-60; assoc prof sculpture & head sculpture grad prog, RI Sch Design, 61- *Awards:* First Prize & Best in Show, Silvermine Guild Artists, 60; First Prize, RI Art Festival, 63; First Prize, New Haven Art Festival, 66. *Mem:* Union Independent Cols Art; Am Foundrymens Soc. *Mailing Add:* 15015 Woods Edge Hopkins MN 55345

MORIN-MILLER, CARMEN A
AUTHOR, CURATOR
b Montreal, Que, Can. *Study:* Pvt studie, art & art history, 47-50 & 65-78. *Pos:* Writer, 55-74; dir & cur, Morin-Miller Galleries, 86- *Publ:* Auth, Conspiration, Intrinseque, 77; Lumiere, Minerve, 88. *Mailing Add:* 233 Greenwood Ave Collegeville PA 19426-2707

MORISHITA, JOYCE CHIZUKO
HISTORIAN, PAINTER
b Newell, Calif, Aug 22, 44. *Study:* Northwestern Univ, Evanston, Ill, BA(painting), 64, MA(painting), 65, PhD(art hist), 79. *Work:* Michael Reese Hosp & Med Ctr, Chicago, Ill. *Comn:* Oil-vaporous nudes, Michael Reese Hosp & Med Ctr, 72. *Exhib:* Mid-America Biennial Nat Exhib, Owensboro Mus Fine Arts, Ky, 82; 4/4 Invitational, ARC Gallery, Chicago, 82; Chicago/Chicago Artists, Hayes Gallery, 83; Ill Artists, Springfield, 83 & 85; Rockford & Vicinity, Ill, 83 & 85-86; Int Art Expo, Chicago, 83; 5/5 Beacon St Gallery, Chicago, 85; Campanile Gallery, Chicago, 86; Art Achievement Award Exhib, Artists' Soc; Int Gallery, San Francisco, 87; Ill Prof Art Exhib, Springfield, 87; Ill Painters, Springfield, 88; Her Works, Art Ctr, Sound Bend, IN, 89; Women Artists, Artemesea Gallery, Chicago, 90; New Horizons in Art, Evanston, IL, 90. *Collections Arranged:* Third World Art Exhib, Gov State Univ, 76 & 77. *Pos:* Mem adv comt, Renovation of Chicago Pub Libr, 73; bd trustees, Third World Conf Found, Chicago, 82- *Teaching:* Prof art, painting & art hist, Gov State Univ, Park Forest South, Ill, 73- *Awards:* Artists & Lectrs Grant, 74 & Craftsman in Residence Grant, 75, Nat Endowment Arts; Acquisition Prog Grant, 76, Artist Grant, 84, Ill Art Coun. *Mem:* Col Art Asn Am; Chicago Artist Coalition; Turner Soc, London. *Media:* Oil, Mixed. *Res:* Study of J M W Turner at Petworth, 1802-1837. *Mailing Add:* Box 128 1448 E 52nd St Chicago IL 60615

MORITA, JOHN TAKAMI
PRINTMAKER, PHOTOGRPHER
b Honolulu, Hawaii, Apr 10, 43. *Study:* Chaminade Col, BA, 65; San Francisco Art Inst, BFA(photography), 74; San Francisco State Univ, MA(printmaking), 76. *Work:* Philadelphia Mus Art, Pa; San Francisco Mus Mod Art, Calif; Honolulu Acad Art, Hawaii; Cabo Frio Int Print Biennial, Brazil; Intergrafix, E Berlin, Ger. *Comn:* State of Hawaii's Comn on the Columbian Quincentennial Observance, 92. *Exhib:* Honolulu Acad Arts, Hawaii, 77; San Francisco Mus Mod Art, 79; Recent Prints, Alternative Mus, New York, 87; Photo Etchings, Print Club, Philadelphia, 90; Radierungen USA, Intergrafik 90, Berlin, Ger. *Teaching:* Lectr, Univ Hawaii, 82-84. *Awards:* Nat Endowment Arts Fel for Printmaking, 86; First Prize, Intergrafik '87, Ger; Selection Award, Print Club, 88. *Mem:* Honolulu Printmakers (vpres, 89); Los Angeles Printmaking Soc; Northwest Print Coun. *Media:* Drypoint. *Dealer:* Gallery EAS 1426 Makaloa Honolulu Hawaii 96814. *Mailing Add:* 1640 Ahihi St Honolulu HI 96819

MORLEY, MALCOLM
PAINTER, SCULPTOR
b London, Eng, 1931. *Study:* Camberwell Sch Arts & Craft, 53; Royal Col Art, Assoc degree, 57. *Work:* Whitney Mus, Mus Mod Art & Metrop Mus Mod Art, New York; Wadsworth Atheneum, Hartford, Conn; Hirshhorn Mus Sculpture Garden, Washington, DC; Musee Nat d'Art Moderne, Paris; Victoria & Albert Mus, London; La Mus, Humlebaek, Denmark. *Exhib:* Contemp Am Painting, Whitney Mus, New York, 72; Documenta V, Kassel, 72, Projeckt & Cologne, 74, Ger; retrospective exhib, Whitechapel Art Gallery, London, Kunsthalle Basel, Boymansvan Beuningen, Rotterdam, Cocoran Art Gallery, Washington DC, Mus Contemp Art, Chicago, Brooklyn Mus, New York, 83-84; one-man shows, Akron Art Mus, Ohio, 81-82, Print and Process, Pace Prints, NY, 86-87, Recent Drawings, Lithographs and watercolors, Temperance Hall Gallery, Bellport, 88, New Work, Pace Gallery, NY, 88-89, Paintings, Sculpture and Watercolors, Anthony d'Offay Gallery, London 90, Recent Paintings and Sculptures, Pace Gallery, New York, 91 & Watercolors, Tate Gallery, Liverpool, 91-92; Portraits on Paper, Robert Miller, New York, 91. *Teaching:* Assoc prof, Ohio State Univ, 65-66, State Univ NY, Stony Brook, 72-74; instr, Sch Visual Art, NY, 67-69. *Awards:* First Ann Turner Prize, Tate Gallery, London, 84. *Bibliog:* John Russell (auth), Art: 20th Century Works in Royal Academy Show, 1/13/87 & Morley's careful frenzy, NY Times, 12/9/88; Susan Gill (auth), Malcolm Morley, Art News, Vol 86, no 3, 3/87; K Levin (auth), Malcolm Morley: Post style illusionism, Arts Mag, New York, 2/73. *Media:* Oil, watercolor. *Dealer:* Pace Gallery 32 E 57th St New York NY 10022. *Mailing Add:* c/o Pace Gallery 32 E 57th St New York NY 10022

MOROLES, JESÚS BAUTISTA
SCULPTOR
b Corpus Christi, Tex, Sept 22, 50. *Study:* El Centro Col, Dallas, AA, 75; NTex State Univ, Denton, BFA, 78. *Work:* Albuquerque Mus, NMex; Mus Fine Arts, Santa Fe; Old Jail Art Ctr, Albany, Tex; Univ Houston, Tex; Mint Mus, Charlotte, NC; Dallas Mus Art, Tex; Nat Mus Am Art, Smithsonian, Washington, DC. *Comn:* Lapstrake, Tex Commerce Bank, Dallas, 83; Inner Column Towers, Riata Develop, Houston, 84; Zig Zag Inner Column, Siena Sq, Boulder, Colo, 85; Interlocking, Nat Health Insurance Co, Dallas, 86; Zig Zag Inner Column, IBM, Raleigh, NC, 86. *Exhib:* One-person exhibs, Davis-McClain Gallery, Houston, Tex, 82, 84, 86, 88, 90 & 92, Janus Gallery, Santa Fe, NMex, 84, 85, 86, 89, 90 & 92, Marilyn Butler Gallery, Scottsdale, Ariz, 86 & 89, Richard Green Gallery, Los Angeles, 89 & 91, New York, 89, Santa Monica, 90, Chicago Int Art Expos, Klein Art Works, Chicago, 91 & Mus SE Tex, Beaumont, 92; Group Sculpture Show, Wirtz Gallery, San Francisco, Calif, 90; Escultura 1991, Expositum, Polanco, Mex, 91; Adams-Middleton Gallery, Dallas, Tex, 92; Carl Schlosberg Fine Art, Sherman Oaks, Calif, 92. *Pos:* Bd dirs, Int Sculpture Ctr, Washington, DC. *Teaching:* Instr, Nat Mus Am Art Symposium, 92. *Awards:* Visual Art Fel, Southeastern Ctr Contemp Art, Winston-Salem, NC, 82; Matching Grant, Nat Endowment Arts, Birmingham Botanical Gardens, Ala, 84; President's Citation Award, Univ NTex, 92. *Bibliog:* Dorothy Chaplik (auth), review, Latin Am Art, fall 91; Joseph Cunniff (auth), review, Inside Lincoln Park, 6/24/91; Rafael Longorla (auth), A Conversation With Jesus Bautista Moroles, Cite Mag, spring 91. *Mem:* Tex Sculpture Asn, Houston. *Media:* Granite. *Publ:* Auth, Granite Sculpture, Meriden Gravure Co, Conn, 84. *Dealer:* Davis McClain Gallery 2627 Colquitt Houston TX 77098. *Mailing Add:* 404 W Sixth St Rockport TX 78382

MORONI, ALDO LEONARD, JR
SCULPTOR, PAINTER
b Chicago, Ill, July 9, 53. *Study:* Minneapolis Col Art & Design, BFA, 76. *Work:* State Off Bldg Minn State Capitol, St Paul; Fredrich Weisman Collection; Lorring Park, Minneapolis; Walker Art Ctr, Minneapolis; First Bank Minneapolis; State of Minn; Nat City Bank, Minneapolis, Minn; Repub Bank, Houston, Tex; General Mills. *Comn:* Encaustic mural, Minn Mutual Life Insurance, 82; encaustic mural, Opus Corp, Minnetonka, 82; two encaustic murals, Repub Bank, Houston, Tex, 83; six wall relief bronze, Minn Percentage for Arts Fund, St Paul, 85; wall relief cast resin, Nat City Bank, Minneapolis, 86; Beta West, Minneapolis, 88. *Exhib:* Walker Art Ctr, Minneapolis, 77; Art Park (auth, catalog), Lewiston, NY, 78; solo exhib, Minn Mus Art, St Paul, 82 & L'Ambiante, New York; Art Ctr Minn, Minnetonka, 83; Minneapolis Inst Arts, 86; Vessels, Rochester Art Ctr, Minn, 86. *Pos:* Mem adv panel, Art Paper, Minneapolis, 84-86. *Teaching:* Lectr, Univ of Minn. *Awards:* McKnight Fel, Daytons Corp, 82, 85 & 88; First Prize Painting, Art Ctr Minn, 82; Assoc Comn Award, Minneapolis Col Art & Design, 83. *Bibliog:* Lisa Lyons (auth), Scale and Environment, Walker Art Ctr, 77; Mason Riddle (auth), Monoprints, Forcast Publ, 84; Eleanor Heartney (auth), Aldo Moroni, Minneapolis Art Inst Arts Mag, 85. *Dealer:* Fromer Fine Arts New York NY; Merrillchase Chicago IL. *Mailing Add:* c/o 21 Spinning Wheel Rd Hinsdale IL 60521

MOROSAN, RON
PAINTER
b Detroit, Mich, Mar 25, 47. *Study:* Wayne State Univ, Mich, BFA, 71; Univ Iowa, Iowa City, MA & MFA, 73; Univ Mich, Ann Arbor, 74-75. *Work:* Univ Iowa Mus, Iowa City; Mus Contemp Art, Chicago; Detroit Inst Arts; The New Mus, New York. *Exhib:* Solo exhibs, Feigenson-Rosenstein Gallery, Detroit, 77 & 81, Robert Freidus Gallery, New York, 78 & Sheldon Ross Gallery, Birmingham, Mich, 90; Memory Show, C Space, New York, 77; The Language of Outdoor Sculpture, Colgate Univ, NY, 80; Selection, 81 & Hundreds of Drawings, 83, Artists Space, New York; Paradise Lost-Paradise Regained, Venice Biennale, 84; Relative Meaning, Hallwalls, Buffalo, NY, 85; Deaoconotation, Connotation, Implication, Eisner Gallery, City Col New York, 88; Snug Harbor Sculpture Festival, Staten Island, NY, 89. *Teaching:* Vis lectr, Frostburg State Col, Md, 77, Ill State Univ, Normal, 79 & Univ NC, Greensboro, 80; instr & head, sculpture dept, Sch of the Worcester Mus, Mass, 80-81. *Awards:* Nat Endowment Arts Grant, 74; Grant in Sculpture, Louis Comfort Tiffany Found, 77; Ariana Found Grant, 83; Artists Fellowship Grant, 85; Residency: Bemis Found, Omaha, Nebr. *Bibliog:* Statements, Detroit Artists Monthly, 12/78; Peter Frank (auth), article, Village Voice, 5/79; New York Terminal Show, EVillage Eye, 83. *Mem:* Col Art Asn. *Mailing Add:* 510 Broadway New York NY 10013

MOROZ, MYCHAJLO
PAINTER
b Ukraine, July 7, 04; US citizen. *Study:* Art Sch, Lviv, Ukraine; Conservatoire National des Arts et Metiers, Paris & Acad Julian, Paris, 28-29; additional study, var mus, Italy, 32. *Work:* State Mus, Lvov & Kiev, Ukraine; State Mus, Moscow; St Sergii et Vacci Mus, Rome; Ukrainian Inst Am, New York; White House, Washington, DC; plus many others. *Exhib:* Ukrainian Artists from all European Countries Exhib, Lviv, 34; Artists Exhib, Moscow, 40-41; Exhib, Regensburg & Munich, Ger, 47-48; Int Group Exhib, Locust Valley, NY, 58; one-man shows, Panoras Gallery, New York, 59-63 & W & W Art Gallery, Toronto, 64-65; Ukrainian Inst Am, New York, 81. *Teaching:* Asst prof drawing & painting, Ukrainian Art Sch, Lviv, 30-35; also pvt lessons,

Europe & US, 50- *Awards:* Silver Cap Second Award, Dem Club, Locust Valley, NY, 58; Prix de Paris, Galeries Raymond Duncan, 61; Most Artistic Christmas Card Prize, Onondaga Bank, Syracuse, NY, 62; Gold Medal, Accademica Italia delle Arti, 80. *Bibliog:* Max M Rhoude (auth), M Moroz, Mittelbayerische Zeitung, Regensburg, Ger, 47 & 48; Prof J Leschko (auth), Mychajlo Moroz--an appreciation, Ukrainian Weekly, JC, 6/81; plus many articles in US, Ukrainian , Russian & French papers. *Mem:* Orgn Ukrainian Artists Am; Accademia Italia delle Arti. *Media:* Oil, Pastel. *Mailing Add:* 76 Coursen Pl Staten Island NY 10304

MORPHESIS, JIM (JAMES GEORGE)
PAINTER
b Philadelphia, Pa, Aug 26, 48. *Study:* Tyler Sch Art, with Stephen Greene, BFA, 70; Calif Inst Arts, with Paul Brach, Miriam Schapirow & Allan Kaprow, MFA, 72. *Work:* Los Angeles Co Mus Art; San Diego Mus Art; San Francisco Mus Mod Art; Oakland Mus; Loyola Law Sch, Los Angeles. *Comn:* The Fall of Icarus (mural), Loyola Sch Law, Los Angeles, 83-84; painting, John Wayne Airport, Costa Mesa, Calif, 90. *Exhib:* Los Angeles Artists, 76, Eight Artists, 76, Young Talent Awards: 1963-1983, 83, Los Angeles Co Mus Art; solo exhib, Tortue Gallery, Santa Monica, Calif, 83, 84, 86, 87, 90 & 92, Los Angeles Co Mus Art, Calif, 87, Deson/Saunders Gallery, Chicago, Ill, 87, 90 & 93 & Littlejohn/Sternau Gallery, New York, 92; Concerning the Spiritual, San Francisco Art Inst, 85; group exhib, Ancient Currents, Fisher Gallery, Univ Calif, Los Angeles, 86; Avant-Garde in the Eighties, Los Angeles Co Mus Art, Calif, 87; Abstract Expressionism & After, San Francisco Mus Mod Art, Calif, 87; Images of Death in Contemp Art, Haggerty Mus, Milwaukee, Wis, 90; Cruciformed: Images of the Cross Since 1980, Cleveland Ctr Contemp Art, Ohio, 92; Sanctuaries: Recovering the Holy in Contemp Art, Mus Contemp, Relig Art, St Louis, Mo, 93. *Teaching:* Instr painting, Calif Inst Arts, Valencia, 72-73, Los Angeles City Col, 74-83 & Otis Art Inst, Parsons Sch Design, 77-83. *Awards:* Nathan Margolis Mem Award Painting, Tyler Sch Art, 70; Los Angeles Co Mus Art Young Talent Purchase Award, 83; Louis Comfort Tiffany Found Grant Award, 85. *Bibliog:* Suzanne Muchnic (auth), article, Arts Mag, 9/79; Peter Clothier (auth), article, Art in Am, summer 82; Robert L Pincus (auth), Art as Artifact, Flash Art, summer 85. *Mem:* Col Art Asn Am; Am Hellenic Inst. *Media:* Oil, Mixed Media. *Publ:* Justin Spring (monogr), Jim Morphesis: Paintings, 91-92. *Dealer:* Tortue Gallery 2917 Santa Monica Blvd Santa Monica CA 90404; Littlejohn/Sternau Gallery 41 E 57th St New York NY 10022. *Mailing Add:* 21 E 22nd St Apt 8H New York NY 10010-5335

MORRELL, WAYNE (BEAM)
PAINTER
b Clementon, NJ, Dec 24, 23. *Study:* Philadelphia Sch Indust Art; Drexel Inst-Famous Artist Sch. *Work:* Sloan Kettering Cancer Res Ctr, New York; Clark Mus, Carversville, Pa; Lahey/Clinic, Burlington, Mass. *Exhib:* Expos Intercontinentale, Monoco, France; one-man shows, Washington Co Mus, Hagerstown, 73, Bliech Gallery Carmel, Calif, 82 & Golden Web, Santa Fe, NMex; Grand Cent Gallery, NY; Mont Crest Gallery, Chattanoga, Tenn; Dassin Gallery, Los Angeles; Newman Gallery, Philadelphia; many others. *Pos:* Art dir, John Oldham Studios, Conn, 55-61; owner & dir, Wayne Morrell Gallery, currently; designer, Paris & Brussel-World Fairs, currently. *Awards:* Jane Peterson Prize, 69 & 74 & Coun Am Art Socs Award, 71, Allied Artist Am; Gold Medal, 70, Mariboe Award, 80 & Harriet-Mattson Award, 80, Rockport Art Asn. *Bibliog:* R Kolby (auth), A stand for nature, Am Artist, 3/72. *Mem:* Allied Artist Am; Springfield Acad Artist (coun, 60-61); Hudson Valley-Am Soc Veteran Artists; Rockport Art Asn. *Media:* Oil, Watercolor. *Publ:* Illusr, Readers Digest, 67; Yankee Magazine, 8/80. *Dealer:* Newman Galleries 1625 Walnut Philadelphia PA 19103; Grand Central Galleries 24 W 57th Ave New York NY 10017. *Mailing Add:* One Squam Hollow Rockport MA 01966

MORRIN, PETER PATRICK
CURATOR, HISTORIAN
b St Louis, Mo, Oct 31, 45. *Study:* Harvard Univ, AB, 68; Princeton Univ, MFA, 72. *Pos:* Dir, Vassar Col Art Gallery, 74-78; cur 20th century art, High Mus, 79-86; dir, Speed Museum of Louisville, currently. *Teaching:* Instr art hist, Vassar Col, 74-78, Emory Univ, 80-86 & Univ Louisville, 87- *Awards:* Nat Collection Fine Arts Res Fel, Smithsonian Inst, 73-74. *Res:* Modern and American art. *Publ:* Coauth (with Dr Eric M Zafran), Drawings from Georgia Collections: 19th and 20th Centuries (catalog), 81, auth, J J Haverty: The Taste of a Southern Collector (catalog), 81, 20th Century Paintings from the Collection of the Museum of Modern Art: A Viewer's Guide (catalog), 82, Chase Manhattan: The First Ten Years of Collecting, 1959-1969 (catalog), 82 & Content in Abstraction: The Uses of Nature (catalog), 83, High Mus Art, Atlanta; Advent of Modernism: Post Impressionism and North American Art (catalog), High Mus, 86. *Mailing Add:* Speed Mus of Louisville 2035 S Third St Louisville KY 40208

MORRIS, CARL
PAINTER
b Calif, 1911. *Study:* Art Inst Chicago; Kunstgewerbeschule, Vienna; Akad Bildenden Kuenste, Vienna. *Work:* Guggenheim Mus, Metrop Mus, Mus Mod Art & Whitney Mus Am Art, New York; Nat Gallery Art & Joseph Hirshhorn Collection, Washington, DC; Ore Health Sci Univ; Portland Art Mus, Ore. *Comn:* Murals, US Treas Dept, Post Off Bldg, Eugene, Ore, 41; murals, Ore Centennial Comn, Hall of Relig Hist, 59. *Exhib:* Carnegie Int, Pittsburgh; Rome-New York Art Found Exhib; Pittsburgh Int; San Francisco Mus Art; Art USA Int; Acad Arts & Letters, NY; Art Inst Chicago; Corcoran Gallery, Washington, DC; Nat Mus Art, Osaka, Japan. *Awards:* Ford Found Award, Retrospective Exhib, 60-62; Purchase Award, Ford Found, 60 & Nat Inst Arts & Lett; Distinguished Service Award, Ore Health Sci Univ, 87. *Bibliog:* G L M Morley (auth), article for Ford Found, 60; David Wagoner (auth), The journey of Carl Morris, Malahat Rev, 10/74; Robin Skelton (auth), Encore Mag of Arts, 78; Intersecting Light, Ore Health Sci Univ; Bruce Guenther (auth), 50 Northwest Artists. *Media:* Oil, Acrylic. *Publ:* illusr cover & drawings, Five Poets of the Pacific Northwest, Univ Wash, 64; auth & illusr, Sketch Book: Carl Morris, Reed Col, Ore, 85. *Dealer:* Laura Russo Gallery 805 NW 21st Ave Portland OR 97209; Foster/White Gallery 311 1/2 Occidental Ave South Seattle WA 98104. *Mailing Add:* 919 NW Skyline Blvd Portland OR 97229

MORRIS, DONALD FISCHER
DEALER
b Detroit, Mich, Apr 12, 25. *Pos:* Owner & dir, Donald Morris Gallery Inc, Birmingham, Mich, currently. *Mem:* Art Dealers Asn Am; Mich Coun Arts; Detroit Art Dealers Asn (pres, 71-). *Specialty:* Twentieth Century American and European painting and sculpture; African art. *Mailing Add:* Gallery Inc 105 Townsend Birmingham MI 48011

MORRIS, FLORENCE MARIE
DEALER
b Detroit, Mich, Apr 30, 28. *Study:* Wayne State Univ, BS. *Pos:* Dir, Donald Morris Gallery, Detroit, 58- *Mem:* Art Dealers Asn Am; New Detroit (mem visual arts comt, 77-); Detroit Art Dealers Asn. *Specialty:* 20th century painting, sculpture and drawings; African sculpture. *Mailing Add:* 105 Townsend Birmingham MI 48011

MORRIS, GREGG
PAINTER
b Ann Arbor, Mich, Jan 21, 51. *Study:* Vanderbilt Univ, 68-69; Md Inst, BFA, 75; Syracuse Univ, MFA, 85. *Comn:* Sculpture, Nat Icee Corp, 90. *Exhib:* Solo Ctr Visual Art, 82; Smallworks 83, Univ Mass, 83; Rochester Finger Lakes Exhib, Rochester, NY, 84; 47th Ann Artists of Central NY, Muson-Williams-Procton Inst; Utica, NY, 84; Everson Biennial, Everson Mus Syracuse, NY, 84; Spectrum: The Generic Figure, Cororan Gallery Art, Washington, DC, 86; McIntosh/Drysdale Gallery, Washington, DC, 86; Case Gallery, Kennett Sq, Pa, 91. *Awards:* MacDowell Colony Grant, 79; Artists Fel Grant, Nat Endowment Arts, 87. *Mailing Add:* 60 Calvary Rd Elkton MD 21921

MORRIS, JACK AUSTIN, JR
MUSEUM DIRECTOR, ART DEALER
b Macon, Ga, Sept 29, 39. *Study:* Univ SC, AB, with Edmund Yaghjian, Augusta Wittkowski & Catherine Rembert; Univ SC; Harvard Univ Inst Arts Admin. *Collections Arranged:* Arnold H Maremont Collection (20th Century American & European Painting & Sculpture), 65; Ida Kohlmeyer (one-man exhib), 67; Jasper Johns Prints (with catalog), Harbor Town Mus, Hilton Head Island, SC, 71; Andrew Wyeth in Southern Collections, 78; Select Works by Andrew Wyeth: The Arthur and Holly Magill Collection, 79; Complete Serigraphs of Jasper Johns, 80; The John B Connally Collection, 88. *Pos:* Curatorial assoc, Columbia Mus Art, 62-63, asst to dir, 63-65; exec dir, Greenville Co Mus Art, 65-80 & Greenville Co Art Asn, 75-80; mem exec bd, Metrop Arts Coun, 78-80; exec dir, Period Gallery West, 80-81; owner, Morris Fine Arts, 81-83; exec dir, Connally, Altermann & Morris Art Gallery, 83-87; co-owner, Altermann & Morris Galleries, Dallas & Houston, 87-; bd trustees, Mus Art Am West, Houston, 88; bd dirs, Houston Art Dealers Asn, 90. *Teaching:* Lectr, Kress Collection, Columbia Mus Art, SC, 62-65; instr drawing & painting, Richland Art Sch, Columbia, 64-65. *Mem:* Guild SC Artists (pres, 68); founder, SC Fedn Mus (vpres, 71-72, pres, 73-74); SC Arts Comn (chmn exec comt, 72-73); SC Arts Found (pres, 75-80); Houston Art Dealers Asn (vpres, 91); and others. *Res:* Contemporary American art; Art of the American West. *Specialty:* 19th & 20th Century American Art; Western and wild life, sporting art. *Publ:* Auth, Contemporary Artists of South Carolina (catalog), 70; William M Halsey: Retrospective (catalog), 72; Western Collectors, 84-92; American Art Classic, 86-92; Texas Renaissance, 89-92; and others. *Mailing Add:* 8960 Chatsworth Pl Houston TX 77024

MORRIS, ROBERT
SCULPTOR
b Kansas City, Mo, Feb 9, 31. *Study:* Kansas City Jr Col; Kansas City Art Inst, 48-50; Univ Kansas City; San Francisco Art Inst; Reed Col, 53-55; Hunter Col, MA, 66. *Work:* Modern Museet, Stockholm, Sweden; Dallas Mus Fine Arts, Tex; Whitney Mus Am Art, New York; Tate Gallery, London, Eng; Wadsworth Atheneum; Detroit Art Inst; Nat Gallery Can, Ottawa; Nat Gallery Victoria, Melbourne, Australia; Walker Arts Ctr, Minneapolis, Minn; Pasadena Art Mus, Calif; Milwaukee Art Ctr. *Comn:* Earth Proj, Nat Planning Comn, Ottawa; Steam Piece, Western Wash Univ, Bellingham, 69; Grand Rapids Proj, City of Grand Rapids, Mich, 74; Observatory, Sonsbeek Unlimited, Oost-Flevoland, Holland, 77. *Exhib:* Guggenheim Int, Solomon R Guggenheim Mus, 67; The Art of the Real, Mus Mod Art, 68; one-man shows, Galerie Ileana Sonnabend, Paris, 71, Inst Contemp Art, Univ Pa, Philadelphia, 74, Mirror Works & Drawings, Wright State Univ, Dayton, Ohio, 79, Selected Works 1970-1981, Contemp Arts Mus, Houston, 81, Recent Felt Pieces, Galerie Nordenhake, Malmo, Sweden, 84, Sonnabend Gallery, New York, 85, Works of the Eighties, Mus Contemp Art, Chicago, 86 & Sonnabend Gallery, New York, 92; Whitney Mus Am Art, 72, 73, 75 & 76; Art Inst Chicago, 74, 76 & 77; Some Recent American Art, Mus Mod Art, New York & traveling, 74; Galerie Ricke, Cologne, Ger, 74; Sculpture, Am Directions 1945-1975, Nat Collection Fine Arts, Smithsonian Inst, Washington, DC, 75; High Mus Art, Atlanta, Ga; NY State Mus, Albany, 77; Madison Art Ctr, Wis, 77; New Gallery Contemp Art, Cleveland, Ohio, 77;

Kansas City Art Inst, Mo, 78; Mus Contemp Art, La Jolla, Calif, 78; A View from the Sixties: Selections from the Leo Castelli Collection and the Michael and Ileana Sonnabend Collection, Guild Hall Mus, East Hampton, New York, 91; Dessins d'Ameriques, Frac Picardie, Amiens, France, 92; plus many others. *Teaching:* Instr, Hunter Col, 67- *Awards:* Prize, Guggenheim Mus, 67; Guggenheim Found Fel, 69; Sculpture Award, Soc Four Arts, 75. *Bibliog:* Annette Michelson (auth), Three notes on an exhibition as a work, Artforum, 6/70; Jack Burnham (auth), Robert Morris: Retrospective in Detroit, Artforum, 3/70 & Voices from the gate, Arts Mag, Vol 46 summer 72; Jeremy Gilbert-Rolfe (auth), Robert Morris: The complication of exhaustion, Artforum, 9/74. *Publ:* Auth, The art of existence, 1/71, Some splashes in the ebb tide, 2/73 & Aligned with Nazca, 10/75, Artforum; auth, The present tense of space, Art in Am, 1-2/78. *Dealer:* Leo Castelli Gallery 420 W Broadway New York NY 10012. *Mailing Add:* c/o Leo Castelli 420 W Broadway New York NY 10012-3764

MORRIS, ROBERT CLARKE
PAINTER, EDUCATOR
b New York, Apr 2, 31. *Study:* Yale Univ, with Josef Albers, BFA; Univ Tex, MFA. *Work:* Allentown Art Mus, Pa; Okla Art Ctr, Oklahoma City; Mus Fine Arts Houston, Tex; Beaumont Art Mus, Tex. *Exhib:* One-man shows, Washburn Gallery, New York, 76 & 79, Artist's Postcards-Drawing Ctr, New York, 77 & Conn Painting, Drawing & Sculpture, 78; New Eng Ann, Silvermine Guild, 78 & 79; Award Candidates, Am Acad Inst Arts & Letters, New York, 81; and others. *Collections Arranged:* Out of the Ordinary, Contemp Arts Mus, Houston, 58, Tenth St, 58 & Architectural Graphics, 59. *Pos:* Dir, Contemp Art Mus, Houston, 58-60; vis design cur, Univ Tex Art Mus, Austin, 68-69. *Teaching:* Instr painting, Univ Houston, 57-59; instr painting & drawing, Mus Sch, Mus Fine Arts Houston, 58-59; prof art, Univ Bridgeport, 61-; vis critic, Columbia Univ, 81. *Mem:* Am Asn Univ Prof. *Media:* Multimedia. *Dealer:* Dianne David 1900 Rockmoor Ave Austin TX 78703. *Mailing Add:* 10 Sturtevant Pl Bridgeport CT 06610

MORRIS, ROGER DALE
PAINTER
b Huntington, WVa, Feb 23, 47. *Study:* Art instruction schools, illustrating, 68; workshop, with Albert Handell, 87. *Exhib:* Kentucky Revisited, Sate Cap Mus, Frankfort, KY, 83; Kentucky Artists Painting in a Southern Tradition, JB Speed Mus, Louisville, Ky, 84; Montana Miniature Art Soc, Castle Gallery, Billings, Mont, 84; Kentucky Artists Postcard Series, Barren River Arts Coun, KY, 85; Oil Pastel Assoc Am, Pen & Brush Gallery, New York, 86; Miniature Painters, Sculptors, Gravers Soc, Arts Club, Washington, DC, 87; Pastel Soc Am, Nat Arts Club, New York, 87. *Awards:* Northlight Award, Oil Pastel Assoc Am, Northlight Books, 86; Marie Devor Award, Pastel Soc Am, 87; Dow Corning Wright Award, Cent S Art Exhib, Nashville, 90. *Bibliog:* Betty Lowry MC (auth), The Art Scene, Murray Cable TV Network, 88. *Media:* Acrylic, Pastel. *Mailing Add:* 1007 First St Carrsville KY 42081

MORRIS, WRIGHT
WRITER, PHOTOGRAPHER
b Central City, Nebr, Jan 6, 10. *Study:* Pomona Col, 30-33; Westminster Col, Dr Lit, 68; Univ Nebr, Lincoln, Dr Lit, 68; Pomona Col, Dr Lit, 73. *Work:* Mus Mod Art, New York; Sheldon Mem Art Gallery, Univ Nebr, Lincoln; San Francisco Mus Art; Corcoran Gallery Art. *Exhib:* Solo exhibs, Sheldon Mem Art Gallery, Univ Nebr, Lincoln, 75, Corcoran Gallery Art, 83 & San Francisco Mus Mod Art, 92. *Teaching:* Prof lit, San Francisco State Univ, 62-74. *Awards:* Nat Book Award, 56; Am Book Award, 80; Commonwealth Award Lit, 82. *Bibliog:* David Madden (auth), Wright Morris, Wayne Publ, 64; Leon Howard (auth), Wright Morris, Univ Minn, 68; Robert Knoll (ed), Conversations with Wright Morris, Univ Nebr Press, 77. *Publ:* Auth, The Inhabitants, 46 & The Home Place, 48, Charles Scribner; Photographs and Words, Friends Photog, 82; Wright Morris: Origin of a Species, San Francisco Mus Mod Art, 92. *Mailing Add:* Harper Collins Publs Trade Div 10 E 53rd St New York NY 10022

MORRISON, BEE (BERENICE G)
WEAVER
b Florence, Italy, Jan 16, 08. *Study:* Self taught, also with Porfirio Lopez & Ted Hallman. *Work:* State Collection Found Cult & Arts, Honolulu, Hawaii. *Exhib:* Volcano Art Ctr, Volcanoes Nat Park, 74-75 & 79; Queen Emma Gallery, Honolulu, 81; Hawaii Women Artists, 82; Fiber Artists Hawaii, 82; Consortium Hawaii, 82. *Teaching:* Instr floorloom & offloom weaving, free design knitting & crochet, Volcano Art Ctr, Kalani Honua, currently. *Mem:* Hawaii Craftsmen; Honolulu Weavers Hui; Kiluea Weavers Guild (pres, 74); Fibers Hui of Hawaii (pres 76-79, bd, 79-). *Mailing Add:* PO Box 335 Volcano HI 96785

MORRISON, BOONE M
ARCHITECT, PHOTOGRAPHER
b Berkeley, Calif, Jan 28, 41. *Study:* Stanford Univ, BA(archit), 62, BA(commun), 63; Yosemite Photog Workshops, with Ansel Adams, 71-73. *Work:* Honolulu Acad Art & Bishop Mus, Honolulu, Hawaii; State of Hawaii Collection; US Nat Park Serv; Nat Gallery Art, Washington, DC. *Comn:* Mural photographs, Kauai Mus, 71 & C Brewer & Co, 73; interior wall mural, State of Hawaii, Ka'u Hosp, 75. *Exhib:* Artists of Hawaii, 71-75; Mountains and the Shore, Honolulu Acad Traveling Exhib; Milolii, A Most Hawaiian Place Traveling Exhib, 75; Time on the Land Traveling Exhib, 76-77 & American Photographers and the National Parks, 81-83, Nat Park Serv. *Pos:* Owner-founder, The Foundry Gallery, Honolulu, 69-71; dir, Hawaii Photog Workshops, 71-; dir & founder, Volcano Art Ctr, Hawaii; pres & publ, Summit Press; principle & pres, Boone Morrison Archit, Inc, 88- *Teaching:* Instr photog, Univ Hawaii, Manoa Campus, 69-71, instr archit, 70-72; instr photog, Hawaii Photog Workshops, 71-, State Hawaii Artists Schs, 74 & Kauai Community Col, 84; lectr, Univ Hawaii Ford Found, 80 & Art Dept, Univ Hawaii, Hilo, 82-84. *Awards:* Purchase Awards, Hawaii State Found Cult & Arts, 70-75; Gold Medals For "Song of South Kona" San Francisco Int Film Festival, Houston Int Film Festival. *Bibliog:* Joan Murray (auth), Photography in Hawaii, Art Week, 73; Portfolio, 1979 Popular Photog Ann; The Photographers Eye (film), Hawaii, 80. *Mem:* Image Continuum Group; Am Inst Architects. *Publ:* Auth, Journal of a Pioneer Builder, Hawaii Nat Hist Asn, 77; Images of the Hula, Summit Press, 83; Song of South Kona (video), KHET Television & Hawaiian Air, 86; Legacy of Lia (video), 88; Mainstreet Hawaii (video), 88. *Mailing Add:* PO Box 131 Volcano HI 96785

MORRISON, DORIS
PAINTER, ADMINISTRATOR
b Alameda, Calif. *Study:* Calif Sch Fine Arts; Cleveland Inst Art, BFA, 49; Col of Marin, 61-62; printmaking with Ron Roberton, Santa Barbara City Col, 80-82; enameling with Floy Meyers, 82-86; City Col. *Work:* Cleveland Mus Art; Womens City Club of Cleveland; Ross Valley Hosp, Calif; Oak Knoll Naval Hosp, Oakland, Calif; Univ Calif Santa Barbara; and many others. *Exhib:* De Young Mus, San Francisco Mus Art, Cleveland Mus Art Annuals & Butler Inst Am Art Annuals & Nationals; San Francisco Art Inst Traveling & Ann Exhib; East Bay Artists Asn Traveling Exhib; Invitationals, Jack London Sq, Oakland, Calif; Arts Coun Ann Exhibs, 78, 79 & 80 & four-person show, 84, Mus Natural Hist Galleries, Santa Barbara; one-person show, Astra Gallery, Santa Barbara, 88; The Santa Barbara Scene, 89. *Collections Arranged:* Still Life, Cabillo Arts Ctr, 84. *Pos:* Co-founder Santa Barbara Mus Art Rental Gallery, 71; Co-op Gallery 113, 73; co-dir Art Coun Gallery, Santa Barbara, Calif, 85-86, Cabrillo Arts Ctr, currently. *Teaching:* Instr color, design & drawing, Dominican Col, 56. *Awards:* San Francisco Women Artists Award, 68; 12 awards, Santa Barbara Art Asn, 70-79; Univ Calif Santa Barbara, Women's Ctr. *Mem:* Life mem, Marin Soc Artists; life mem, Santa Barbara Art Asn; Contemp Art Forum (dir, 78); Arts Coun, Santa Barbara Chap (co-dir, 83-87); Artist Equity, Santa Barbara, (vpres, 83-84, mem bd, 85-86). *Media:* Enamel on Metal. *Mailing Add:* 333 Old Mill Rd 204 Santa Barbara CA 93110

MORRISON, FRITZI MOHRENSTECHER
PAINTER, LECTURER
b Quincy, Ill. *Study:* Art Inst Chicago; Univ Chicago, with Edmund Giesbert, also with Charles W Hawthorne, Anthony Thieme, Karl Knaths, watercolor with Eliot O'Hara, John Pike & Dyke Remuller. *Work:* St Louis Art Mus, Mo; Western Ill Univ Art Mus, Macomb, Ill; Dartmouth Col Art Gallery, Hanover, NH; Whatcom Mus Hist & Art, Bellingham, Wash; Quincy Art Center, 6 watercolors, Ill; City Hall, Quincy, Mass; Am Savings; Huber Indust; Quincy Pub Libr; Blessing Hosp, Quincy, Ill. *Comn:* Expedition Artist-Tuckish Village, Anatolis, Turkey, 62. *Exhib:* Pa Acad Fine Arts 50th Int Exhib Watercolors, Prints & Drawings (traveling), Am Fedn Arts, Washington, DC; Sesquicentennial Ohio Valley Oil & Watercolor Show Invitational, Ohio Univ; Western Art, Denver Mus, Colo; Mid-South Ann Brooks Mem Gallery, Tenn; Krannert Art Mus Irwin Collection, Univ Ill, Champaign; 3rd Ann Invitational Central Ill Arts Consortium; Am Watercolor Soc & Philadelphia Watercolor Club (traveling); solo-shows (51), including Lighthouse Gallery, Tequesta, Fla, 87, Western Ill Univ Macomb, 80 & 89, Elizabeth Sinnock Gallery Art Center, Quincy, Ill, 81 & 88, Quincy Soc Fine Arts, Ill, 92. *Pos:* Former resident artist & vpres, Quincy Art Club, Ill. *Teaching:* Inst, Watercolor Classes, Quincy Art Club, Quincy Col, Hannibal, Mo Art Club & other regional workshops. *Awards:* Hon Mention, Ill Watercolor Soc, 89; Quincy Art Club Awards: 5 first, in watercolor & 4 Best-in-Show; Purchase Grant, Ill Arts Coun. *Bibliog:* Krannert Mus Univ, Ill (auth), The George M Irwin Collection, 80; featured artist, Arts/Quincy, 12/84; Significant Architecture in Quincy, Ill from 1835-1915 (monogr), 85. *Mem:* Sig mem Am Watercolor Soc; Philadelphia Watercolor Club; Midwest, Great River, Mississippi & Pa Watercolor Soc(s). *Media:* Transparent Watercolor. *Publ:* Contribr, Facets of a Sparkling Medium, Palette Talk #46, 3/80. *Mailing Add:* 1845 Jersey St Quincy IL 62301

MORRISON, GEORGE
PAINTER
b Grand Marais, Minn, Sept 30, 19. *Study:* Minneapolis Sch Art, MFA (hon), 69; Art Students League; Univ Aix-Marseille, Aix-en-Provence, France. *Work:* Whitney Mus Am Art, New York; Art Inst Chicago; Va Mus Fine Arts, Richmond; Heard Mus, Phoenix, Ariz; Amon Carter Mus, Ft Worth, Tex; and others. *Comn:* Cedar wood mural, Minneapolis Regional Native Am Ctr, 75; redwood mural, City Seattle, Daybreak Star Art Ctr, 77; found wood collage, Hennepin County Med Ctr, Minneapolis, 77. *Exhib:* Corcoran Biennial, Washington, DC, 50; Whitney Mus Am Art Ann, New York, 52; Joslyn Art Mus, Omaha, Nebr, 55; Los Angeles Co Mus Art, 58; Dallas Mus Fine Arts, 58; Brooklyn Mus, 61; RI Sch Design Mus Art, Providence, 68; Mus Am Indian, New York, 71. *Collections Arranged:* Morrison Drawings Traveling Exhib, Walker Art Ctr, Minneapolis, 73, Heard Mus, Phoenix, 73, Mus STex, Corpus Christie, 73 & Amon Carter Mus, Ft Worth, 74. *Teaching:* Vis prof, Cornell Univ, 62 & Pa State Univ, 63; assoc prof painting & drawing, RI Sch Design, Providence, 63-70; prof painting & drawing, Univ Minn, Minneapolis, 70-83; retired. *Awards:* Fulbright Scholarship, 51; J H Whitney Fel, 53. *Bibliog:* Dragos Kostich (auth), George Morrison: The Story of an American Indian, Dillon Press, 76; Encounter with Artists: George Morrison (film), KTCA-TV, Minn Educ TV, 77. *Mem:* Audubon Artists; Fedn Mod Painters & Sculptors; Minneapolis Soc Fine Arts (trustee, 78-82). *Media:* Oil, Weathered Wood. *Mailing Add:* Box 150 Grand Portage MN 55605

MORRISON, KEITH ANTHONY
PAINTER, EDUCATOR
b Jamaica, West Indies, May 20, 42; US citizen. *Study:* Art Inst Chicago, BFA, 63, MFA, 65; Univ Ill; DePaul Univ; Loyola Univ. *Work:* Art Inst Chicago; Nat Mus Am Art, Washington, DC; Corcoran Gallery Art, Washington, DC; Philadelphia Acad Art. *Comn:* Painting for Liberian Govt, 64 & Dusable Mus Afro-Am Hist, 71; mural commissioned by Phyllis Kind Gallery for Main Bank, Chicago, 72; and others. *Exhib:* Biennial Chicago & Vicinity, Art Inst Chicago, 71; Corcoran Gallery Art, 83; Brody's Gallery, Washington, DC, 87; Calif Afro-Am Mus, Los Angeles, 89; Bronx Mus, 90; Alternative Mus, New York, 90; Alternative Mus, New York, 90; Cavin-Morris Gallery, New York, 92; and others. *Collections Arranged:* Toussaint L'ouverture (paintings of Jacob Lawrence, with catalog), DePaul Univ, Chicago, 69; Black Experiences in Art (exhib of painting & sculpture, with catalog), Bergman Gallery Univ Chicago, 71; Afro-Am Artists, Washington Proj Arts, 79; Wisconsin 80, Univ Wis, 80; Brandywine Workshop, 88; Smithsonian Inst, 89. *Pos:* Chmn art dept, DePaul Univ, Chicago, 69-71; assoc dean, Col Art & Archit, Univ Ill, Chicago, 71-75; prof & chmn, art dept, Univ Md Col Park, 88-92; dean, San Francisco Art Inst, 93- *Teaching:* Instr art, Hyde Park Art Ctr, Chicago, 65-67; asst prof drawing, Fisk Univ, Nashville, Tenn, 67-68; assoc prof printmaking & chmn dept, DePaul Univ, 68-71; assoc prof, Univ Ill, Chicago Circle, 71-79; prof, Univ Md, College Park, 79- *Awards:* Prize, Jamaica Inst, 59; Bicentennial Award Painting, City Chicago, 76; Int Painting Award, Orgn African Unity, Liberia, 79. *Bibliog:* Robin Glauber (auth), Keith Morrison at Black Hawk, Skyline, 9/70; Harold Hayden (auth), article, Chicago Sun-Times, 10/79; Paul Richard (auth), article, Washington Post, 83. *Mem:* Col Art Asn; Nat Conf Artists; Int Asn Art Critics. *Media:* Oil, Watercolor. *Res:* Role of black institutions in modern art of Washington, DC, 1940-1970; contemporary black artists in America. *Publ:* Auth, art criticism: A Pan-American point of view, 79, guest ed, Afro-American Art, 81 & auth, Kitai: The sword of Don Quixote, 81, New Art Examiner; auth, 200 Years of Afro-American Women Art: A Critic's View, Ill State Univ, 80; auth, Poetic objects, New Art Examiner, 82. *Dealer:* Jan Cicero Gallery 437 N Clark St Chicago IL 60610. *Mailing Add:* 3556 13th St NW Washington DC 20010

MORRISON, ROBERT CLIFTON
PRINTMAKER, CALLIGRAPHER
b Billings, Mont, Aug 13, 24. *Study:* Carleton Col, BA; Univ NMex, MA. *Work:* Harvard Univ Libr Print Collection, Cambridge; Ministry Art & Culture, Ghana; Rocky Mt Col, Billings; Int Col Copenhagen, Denmark; Centre Medieval Studies, Oxford, Eng. *Comn:* Mosaic murals, Mont State Unemployment Comn, Helena, 61 & Lucerne Pub Schs Wyo; mural, Lockwood Pub Schs, Billings; Bicentennial mural, Yellowstone Co Courthouse, Billings; mural, Rocky Mountain Col, Billings. *Pos:* Ed, Rocky Mt Rev, 63-69; pres bd dirs, Yellowstone Art Ctr, Billings, 64-65. *Teaching:* Dir art educ, Billings Pub Schs, 57-67; prof art, Rocky Mt Col, 67-90; artist in residence, Herning Folk Skole, Denmark, 83. *Awards:* Mont Artist-Teacher of Yr, Am Artists Prof League, 64. *Media:* Wood. *Publ:* Translr & illusr, Maxims of LaRochefoucauld, 67. *Mailing Add:* 2815 Woody Dr Billings MT 59102

MORRISON, ROBERT J
SCULPTOR
Study: Calif State Univ Fresno, BA(art); Stanford Univ, MA(art); Univ Calif, Davis, postgrad. *Exhib:* Stremmel Gallery, Reno, Nev, 91; Sheppard Gallery, Reno, Nev, 91; XS Gallery, Carson City, Nev, 91; solo exhib, Foster Goldstrom Gallery, New York, 92. *Awards:* Educational Enhancement Grant, Univ Nev, Reno, 90; Grant, Sierra Arts, Reno, Nev, 90; Nat Endowment Art Fel, 90. *Bibliog:* Oasis, San Francisco Chronicle, 1/7/88; Electric oasis, 1/15/88 & O Coeur, 10/17/89, Artweek; Electric 34 oasis, High Performance, 4/88. *Mailing Add:* 2650 Erminia Rd Reno NV 89523

MORRISS, MARY RACHEL
PAINTER
b Memphis, Tenn. *Study:* Memphis State Univ, BS, 27; Univ Colo, Boulder, Grad Sch, 31, 34, 37 & 40; Maxine Masterfield, cert, 81, workshop, 83 & workshop with George Cress, 87. *Work:* Parkway Village Branch, First Tenn Bank, Memphis; Memphis Eastwood Hosp; TVA Sequoyah Nuclear Plant; and others. *Exhib:* one-woman show Pathenon Art Gallery, Nashville, Tenn, 71; Central South, Parthenon, Nashville, Tenn, 76, 78-79 & 84, 86, 87, 88, 89; Tenn Ann Watercolor Soc Traveling Exhib, 80-82, 84-85, 88 & 90; Southern Watercolor Soc Exhib, 82, 86, 89 & 90; J J White Mem Juried Show, Helena, Ark, 87, 88, 90, 91 &92; Nine State Watercolor Soc Classic, 88; Delta Ann, Little Rock, Ark; Soc Experimental Artists, Fla, 92; and others. *Teaching:* Instr art, Memphis City Sch System, Bellevue, 36-66; pvt classes, 66- *Awards:* Dr & Mrs Randolph Burton Purchase Award, Tenth Watercolor Soc Show; Daochin of Madison Award, 19th Cent S Pantheon, Nashville, Tenn; First Prize in Collage, Mid-South Fair, 88; Prize, J J White Mem, 87; Merit Award, S Watercolor Soc, 89. *Mem:* Tenn Watercolor Soc; Memphis Watercolor Group; Southern Watercolor Soc (signature mem); Tenn Art League; Soc Experimental Artists. *Media:* Watercolor, Acrylic. *Dealer:* Paul Edelstein Gallery 519 N Highland St Memphis TN 38122 38117. *Mailing Add:* 4819 Parkside Ave Memphis TN 38117

MORRISSEY, LEO
PAINTER, SCULPTOR
b Philadelphia, Pa, Aug 22, 58. *Study:* Marietta Col, Ohio; Univ Fla, BFA, 83; Mason Gross Sch Arts, Rutgers Univ, MFA, 85. *Work:* Jane Voorhees Zimmerli Mus, New Brunswick, NJ; King Stephen Mus, Hungary; Glasmuseum, Ebeltoff, Denmark; Can Postal Mus, Ottawa. *Exhib:* Solo exhibs, J Wayne Reitz Union Gallery, Gainseville, Fla, 83, Mason Gross Sch Arts, Rutgers Univ, New Brunswick, NJ, 85 & Esta Robinson Contemp Art Gallery, New York, 86; Art By Instruction, Ecole Nat d'Art, Paris, France, 84; Jane Voorhees Zimmerli Art Mus, New Brunswick, 85; Experimental Art, Yamanashi Mus Art, Japan, 86; Sculpture Six, Bronx Mus Arts, NY, 86; Ninth Ann Outdoor Light Exhib, Austin, Tex, 87; Metro Show, City Without Walls, Newark, NJ, 87; Visual Poetry, Cult Ctr Sao Paulo, Brazil, 88; Arf Art (with catalog), Trabia MacAfee Gallery, New York, 88; A & A Gallery, Yale Univ, New Haven, Conn, 89; New Yorkers in Spain, Togo Brunnes Gallery, Barcelona, 90; Gallery Vincent Bernat, Barcelona, Spain, 91; Z Gallery, New York, 91; Russell Sage Gallery, Troy, NY, 92; Artlink Gallery, Ft Wayne, Ind, 92. *Awards:* Pollock-Krasner Found Grant, 87. *Bibliog:* John Froonjian (auth), Noyes marks a year, 6/84 & Marjorie Donchey (auth), Morrissey self-portrait, 3/85, The Press, Atlantic City, NJ; Janson Kaufman, Watercolors and sculpture, Daily Tarqum, New Brunswick, NJ, 2/85. *Media:* All Media. *Publ:* Contribr, Books Build Bridges, Artist Bk, 86; The Search for Accidental Significance, Money for Food Press, 87. *Mailing Add:* PO Box 1794 New Brunswick NJ 08903

MORROW, ROBERT EARL
DESIGNER, MURALIST
b Milan, Ohio, Mar 21, 17. *Study:* Cleveland Inst of Art, Ohio; Ohio State Univ, Columbus. *Work:* Cleveland Mus of Art; Butler Inst of Am Art, Youngstown, Ohio; Akron Art Inst, Ohio; Canton Art Inst, Ohio; Massillon Mus, Ohio. *Comn:* Hanging banners, Kent State Univ, Ohio, 62; murals (tile mosaic), Firestone High Sch, Akron, 63; murals (sgraffito), Temple Univ, Philadelphia, Pa, 66; mural (polyester resin, polychrome), Akron Pub Libr, 69; mural (portland cement sgraffito), II Cascade Plaza, Akron, 70. *Exhib:* Cleveland Mus of Art Ann Regional; Butler Inst of Am Art, Youngstown. *Teaching:* Prof drawing & painting, Kent State Univ, 46-87; vis prof mural design, Tyler Sch of Art, Temple Univ, Philadelphia, 64-66. *Awards:* Second Award/Painting, Army Art Show, Nat Gallery, Washington, DC, 44; Purchase Awards, Cleveland Mus of Art, 64; Second Award, Butler Inst of Am Art, Youngstown, 50. *Media:* Concrete; Constructions. *Publ:* Illusr, Orchestra Mice, Reilly & Lee, Chicago, 70. *Mailing Add:* 141 E Crain Ave Kent OH 44240

MORROW, TERRY
DRAFTSMAN, PRINTMAKER
b Austin, Tex, Oct 1, 39. *Study:* Univ Tex, BFA; Univ Wis; Ind Univ, MS, study with Rudy Pozzatti. *Work:* Univ Tex, Austin; Tex Christian Univ, Ft Worth; Western Tex Col, Snyder; Odessa Col, Tex. *Exhib:* Appalachian Nat Drawing Competition, Boone, NC, 78 & 79; two-person exhibs, Sch Galleries, Houston Mus Fine Arts, 71 & Art Dept Teaching Gallery, Univ Tenn, Knoxville, 77; one-person exhib, Clara M Eagle Gallery, Price Doyle Fine Art Ctr, Murray State Univ, 73; and many others. *Pos:* Consult in litho printing, Tex Christian Univ, Ft Worth, 69, Western Tex Col, Snyder, 74 & San Angelo Col, Tex, 78; guest artist, ETex State Univ, Commerce, 79. *Teaching:* Instr painting & printmaking, Univ Pa, Philadelphia, 65-66; asst prof drawing & printmaking, Univ Chattanooga, Tenn, 67-68; assoc prof drawing, printmaking, Tex Tech Univ, Lubbock, 68-, prof art, currently. *Awards:* Cash awards, 16th Ann Drawing and Small Sculpture exhib, 70 & Tri-State Art Exhib, 76; 12th Ann Del Mar Drawing & Small Sculpture, 78. *Media:* Pen and Ink; Intaglio. *Mailing Add:* Dept Art Box 4281 Tex Tech Univ Lubbock TX 79409-2081

MORSE, BART J
PAINTER, PRINTMAKER
b Salt Lake City, Utah, Aug 16, 38. *Study:* Brigham Young Univ, BS, 62; Univ Wash Sch Art, MFA, 64. *Work:* Latter Day Saints Mus Church Hist & Art, Salt Lake Co, Univ Utah, Salt Lake City; Wells Fargo Corp, Los Angeles; Provident Mutual Life Insurance Co, Philadelphia; Laguna Gloria Art Mus, Austin, Tex; US Forest Serv, Williams, Ariz. *Comn:* I'm Going West to Go East, Col Fine Arts Grant Columbus Print, Univ Ariz, 92. *Exhib:* National Print Show, Moravian Col, Bethlehem, Pa & Hunterdon Art Mus, NJ, 81; Bradley National Drawing & Print Show, Peoria, Ill, 83; National Show, E Ky State Univ Mus, Richmond, 85; New Art in the West, Vorpal Gallery, San Francisco, 85; Contemp SW Art, Roland Gibison Gallery, New York; The First National Printmaking/Video Exchange, Denver College, 90. *Teaching:* Assoc prof studio art, Univ Ariz, Tucson, 70-, assoc prof & dir of painting, drawing; vis assoc prof studio art, Univ Del, Newark, 83-84. *Media:* Watercolor, Woodcuts. *Publ:* Illusr, Dialogue: A Journal of Mormon Thought, Vol VII, No 2, Los Angeles, summer 72; auth, articles, The Ariz Daily Star, Tucson, Ariz, 75 & 81; articles, Salt Lake Tribune, Utah, 81 & 85; illusr, Brigham Young Univ Arts, Vol I, Brigham Young Univ Press, Provo, Utah, 77; auth, article, The Eastern Progress, Richmond, Ky, 85. *Dealer:* Phillips Gallery 444 E 2 South Salt Lake City UT 84111; Rosequist Galleries Tucson Az. *Mailing Add:* 4530 N Soldier Tucson AZ 85748

MORSE, MARCIA ROBERTS
PRINTMAKER, WRITER
b Detroit, Mich, Mar 14, 44. *Study:* Radcliffe Col, BA(cum laude), 66; Stanford Univ, MFA, 74; with S W Hayter, Misch Kohn, Adela Akers, Leonore Tawney, Walter Nottingham & Ed Rossbach. *Work:* Honolulu Acad Arts & Contemp Arts Ctr, Honolulu, Hawaii; Smithsonian Inst, Div Graphic Arts, Washington, DC; Int Paper Co, New York; Greenville Co Mus Art, SC. *Comn:* Ann gift print, Honolulu Printmakers, Hawaii, 77; prints, Hawaii State Found Culture & Arts, Honolulu, 78. *Exhib:* Collectors' Choice, Joslyn Art Mus, Omaha, Nebr, 68; New Am Graphics, Madison Art Ctr, Wis, 75; one-woman show, Contemp Arts Ctr, Honolulu, Hawaii, 78; Textures, Contemp Artisans Gallery, San Francisco, Calif, 81; Nat Crafts, Greenville Co Mus Art,

SC, 81; First Int Shoebox Sculpture, Univ Hawaii Art Gallery, Honolulu, 82. *Pos:* Freelance art writer, Artweek, 78-; art columnist, Honolulu Star Bulletin, Hawaii, 79- *Teaching:* Instr printmaking, Univ Calif, Santa Cruz, 69-74; lectr printmaking & textiles, Univ Hawaii, 79-; instr papermaking, Honolulu Acad Arts, Hawaii, 80- *Awards:* Craftsmen's Fel, Nat Endowment Arts, 81-82. *Mem:* Honolulu Printmakers (pres, 76-79, bd mem, 75-80); Hawaii Craftsmen (secy, 78); Surface Design Asn; Nat Soc Arts & Letters; Am Crafts Coun. *Media:* Handmade Paper. *Res:* Contemporary craft art; Japanese art both historical and contemporary. *Publ:* Illusr, Writing from the Inside, Addison-Wesley, 73; illusr, The Eight Rainbows of Umi, Topgallant Press, 76; auth, Nature distilled and distorted, 78 & auth, Language of materials, 81, Artweek; auth, Filaments of the imagination, Fiberarts, 81. *Dealer:* The Source Gallery Folsom St San Francisco CA; Art Loft Honolulu HI. *Mailing Add:* Dept Humanities Honolulu Community Col 874 Dillingham Blvd Honolulu HI 96817

MORSE, MITCHELL IAN
DEALER, CONSULTANT
b Brooklyn, NY, Mar 10, 26. *Study:* Himeji Univ, 45-46; City Col New York, BBA, 47. *Pos:* Pres, Mann-Morse Graphics 68-69, Mitch Morse Gallery, Inc, 69-, M Morse Graphics, Inc, 69-91, Graphic Source I, 71-73; Pres, Morse-Sun Art Assoc Inc, 72-75, Art Spectrum, 79-, China Spectrum Inc, 81-86, Art St Regis, 87-88, Whitney Morse Art Group, Inc, 88-; chief exec off, Morse Harris Art Group, Inc, presently. *Awards:* Designer Official Seal, Village Lawrence, 67. *Mem:* Am Soc Interior Designers; Prof Picture Framers Asn. *Specialty:* Artists agents, publishers of limited edition, original graphics; distributor painting, serigraphs on porcelain, sculpture. *Publ:* Auth, Graphics as an original art form, Designer, 8/73. *Mailing Add:* Mitch Morse Gallery Inc 425 East 58th St New York NY 10022

MORSE, PETER
HISTORIAN, COLLECTOR
b Chicago, Ill, Oct 29, 35. *Study:* Yale Univ, BA, 57. *Pos:* Assoc cur graphic arts, Smithsonian Inst, Washington, DC, 65-67; res assoc, Honolulu Acad Arts, 67-; consult, Charlot Collection, Univ Hawaii Libr, Honolulu, 81-85 & Hokusai's Prints, Nat Endowment Humanities proj, 85-92. *Awards:* Uchiyama Prize, Japan Ukiyoe Soc, 90. *Bibliog:* Katsushika Hokusai Ten, Tokyo, 88. *Mem:* Appraisers Asn Am; Tamarind Inst; Editorial Bd. *Res:* Prints and printmaking; Hokusai; Daumier; American, Mexican and French art of the 20th century. *Publ:* Jean Charlot's Prints, Univ Press Hawaii, 76; Coauth, Netherlandish Artists, Vol 2, 77 & Antoni Waterloo, 92, Abaris Press; auth, Popular Art, Capra Press, 78; Daumier's early lithographs, Print Review 11, 80; Hokusai: One Hundred Poets, Braziller, New York, 89; and others. *Mailing Add:* PO Box 22759 Honolulu HI 96822

MORTELLITO, DOMENICO
PAINTER, SCULPTOR
b Newark, NJ, Sept 1, 06. *Study:* Newark Sch Fine Arts, cert, 21; Pratt Inst, BA, 26; Harvard Univ Bus Sch, cert, 42. *Work:* Mus Mod Art, New York; Newark Mus, NJ; Univ Del, Newark; Freedom Bell, Berlin, Ger; DuPont Co, Wilmington, Del. *Comn:* Exterior murals, B Altman & Co, New York, 38; murals, 8 pavilions, NY World's Fair, New York, 39; white Teflon sculpture, DuPont Co, Houston, 60; Crucifix & Altar, St Joseph on the Brandywine, Wilmington, Del, 76; Space Sculpture polycarbonate, Radnor Corp, Philadelphia, 87. *Exhib:* Plastic as Plastic, Mus Contemp Crafts, New York, 69; Wilmington Savings Fund Soc, Del, 75; Bicentennial Exhib, Philadelphia Mem Hall, 76; Am Freedom Caravan, Southern Vt Art Ctr, Manchester, 76; Ann Exhib, Nat Sculpture Soc, New York, 77, 78 & 79; and other group & one-man shows. *Pos:* Master designer, Mack, Jenny & Tyler, Archit Decor, New York, 26-31; creative dir, Mortellito Studio, New York, 31-42; dir graphic presentation, US Army Air Force, DC, 42-45; mgr design sect & chmn color coun, E I du Pont de Nemours & Co, Inc, Wilmington, Del, 45-77, Mobay Chemical Corp, 45-77. *Awards:* Creative Printing Award, Graphic Arts Rev, 66. *Bibliog:* Ernest Watson (auth), New mediums, Am Artist Mag, 38, 42 & 65; Time-Life ed, New medium in art, Life-Sci Libr, 66; Howard L Slater (auth), Cromalin, new art medium, Leonardo Mag, Paris, 76. *Mem:* Nat Soc Mural Painters; Am Artists Prof League; Artists Equity Asn; Inter-Soc Color Coun; Nat Sculpture Soc. *Media:* Oil; New Synthetics, Stone. *Publ:* Auth, Symbology and the corporate image, 59 & Graphics in a three-dimensional setting, 60, Print Mag; coauth, New medium for modern art, DuPont Mag, 63; auth, Sculpture overboard, Indust Design, 68; How to produce cromal in art, Graphic Arts Mo, 73. *Mailing Add:* 716 W Matson Run Pkwy Wilmington DE 19802

MORTENSEN, GORDON LOUIS
PRINTMAKER, PAINTER
b Arnegard, NDak, Apr 27, 38. *Study:* Minneapolis Col of Art & Design, BFA; Univ Minn. *Work:* Nat Mus Am Art, Washington, DC; Honolulu Acad Art; Minn Mus Art, St Paul; Philadelphia Mus Art; Walker Art Ctr, Minneapolis; and others. *Exhib:* Brooklyn Print Show, Brooklyn Mus, 76 & Eight West Coast Printmakers, 78; Plains Art Mus, Moorhead, Minn, 76 & 78; Boston Printmakers Nat Exhib, De Cordova Mus, 77, 79 & 83; Tokyo Cent Mus Art, Japan, 78; Ten West Coast Printmakers, RI Sch Design Mus; Rockford Int, Ill, 81; and others. *Awards:* Juror's Award, Rockford Int, Ill, 81; Purchase Award, Boston Printmakers 35th Nat Print Exhib, 83; Donna Jenssen Award, 21st Nat Print & Drawing Exhib, Bradley Univ, Peoria, Ill, 87; plus others. *Bibliog:* Robert McDonald (auth), Four West Coast woodcut artists, Graphics, 8-9/79; Karen Haber (auth), Gordon Mortensen, Southwest Art, 11/86 & Am Artist, 4/88. *Mem:* Boston Printmakers; Philadelphia Print Club; World Print Coun; Artist Equity. *Media:* Woodcut; Oil, Watercolor. *Dealer:* Mary Ryan Gallery 452 Columbus Ave New York NY 10024; C G Rein Galleries 949 Sibley Memorial Hwy MN 55118-3698. *Mailing Add:* 4153 Crest Rd Pebble Beach CA 93953

MORTON, RICHARD H
PAINTER, GRAPHIC ARTIST
b Dallas Tex, Aug 8, 21. *Study:* Pratt Inst, cert, 42; Oklahoma City Univ, BA, 51; Univ Tulsa, MA, 57; Inst Allende, Mexico, MFA, 69. *Work:* Okla Art Ctr, Oklahoma City; Univ Tulsa, Okla; Northeast Mo State Univ, Kirksville; Permanent Collection Pratt Inst. *Exhib:* Watercolor USA, Springfield Art Mus, Mo; Eight State Exhib, Okla Art Ctr; Okla Bicentennial Competition, State Capitol, Oklahoma City; Bicentennial Competition Selections, Kennedy Ctr, Washington, DC. *Pos:* Illusr, US Army, Ft Sill, Okla, 76-79, graphic artist, 79-81; self-employed artist, Aberdeen, Md, 81- *Teaching:* Instr art, Southern Ill Univ, Carbondale, 55-59; asst dean, Columbus Col Art & Design, Ohio, 59-60; asst prof art, Cent State Univ, 61-65; assoc prof painting, Northeast Mo State Univ, Kirksville, 65-72. *Awards:* John Marin Mem Award, Watercolor USA, 74; Award of Excellence, Okla Bicentennial Competition, State Capitol, Oklahoma City, 76; and others. *Mem:* Assoc mem Baltimore Watercolor Soc. *Media:* Watercolor; Ink, Pencil. *Dealer:* Arnold White Winner's Circle 12659 Moorpark Circle Suite No 1 Studio City CA 91604-2238. *Mailing Add:* 623 W Bel Air Ave Aberdeen MD 21001

MORTON, ROBERT ALAN
PUBLISHER, WRITER
b Jersey City, NJ, May 20, 34. *Study:* Dartmouth Col, BA, 55. *Pos:* Series ed, Time-Life Libr of Art, New York, 66-70; ed dir, New York Graphic Soc, Inc, 70-73; ed in chief, Harry N Abrams, Inc, 76-78, dir spec proj, 78- *Teaching:* Western Conn State Col, 80-81; Int Ctr Photography, 82-83. *Res:* American decorative arts; photography. *Publ:* Auth, Southern Antiques and Folk Art, Oxmoor House, 76. *Mailing Add:* Box 16 Redding Ridge CT 00876

MOSBY, DEWEY FRANKLIN
MUSEUM DIRECTOR, HISTORIAN
b San Augustine, Tex, Jan 2, 42. *Study:* Lamar Univ, BS, 63; Univ Calif, Los Angeles, MA, 69; Harvard Univ, PhD, 74. *Collections Arranged:* French Painting 1774-1830: The Age of Revolution, 75; Cinco Siglos de Obras maestras de la pintura en colecciones norteamericanas cedidas en prestamo a Costa Rica, 78; The Second Empire: Art in France under Napoleon III, 1852-1870, Detroit, 79; Gods, Saints & Heroes: Dutch Paintings in the Age of Rembrandt, Detroit, 81; The Fodor Collection: Nineteenth Century French Drawing and Watercolors from Amsterdam's Historisch Museum, Hamilton, NY, 85; Abstraction, Non-objectivity and Realism: Twentieth-Century Painting from the Solomon R Guggenheim Museum, Hamilton, NY, 87. *Pos:* Cur European art, Detroit Inst Arts, 74-81; dir, Picker Art Gallery, Colgate Univ, Hamilton, NY, 81- *Teaching:* Asst prof art hist, State Univ NY Buffalo, 73-74; asst prof art hist, Harvard Univ, summer 74. *Awards:* Chevalier, Ordre des Arts et des Lettres, 79; Silver Medal of Merit, Order of Costantiniano Di S Giorgio, 81. *Mem:* Col Art Asn Am; Am Asn Mus; Soc de l'Histoire de l'art Francaise. *Res:* 18th and 19th century art with an emphasis on Alexandre-Gabriel Decamps (1803-60). *Publ:* articles in Arts Mag, 9/75 & 9/83; Alexandre-Gabriel Decamps 1803-1860, 2 Vols, New York, 77; The Figure in Nineteenth-Century French Painting, Detroit, 79; Impressionist and Post-Impressionist Works from a British Collection, Hamilton, NY, 86; Henry Ossawa Tanner, New York, Rizzoli, 91. *Mailing Add:* Picker Art Gallery Colgate Univ Hamilton NY 13346

MOSCA, AUGUST
PAINTER, PRINTMAKER
b Naples, Italy, Aug 19, 07; US citizen. *Study:* Yale Sch Fine Arts; Pratt Inst; Art Students League; Grand Cent Art Sch. *Work:* Libr Cong, Washington, DC; Brooklyn Mus; Forham Univ; New York Pub Libr; Grey Collection, NY Univ; Fordham Univ; and others. *Comn:* Portrait of Heywood Brown, Newspaper Guild of New York, 55 & Newspaper Guild of Am, Washington, DC, 57. *Exhib:* Brooklyn Mus Watercolor Int Ann, 59; Mus Mod Art, New York, 61; Butler Inst Am Art, Youngstown, Ohio, 62; The Fine Line, Drawing with Silver Exhib, Norton Gallery & Sch Art, West Palm Beach, Fla, 85; Selected Drawings in Silver, Leslie Cecil Gallery, New York, 88; Impressionists and Post-Impressionists, Grand Central Art Galleries, New York, 88; A Fifty Year Retrospective, Grand Central Art Galleries, NY, 90; Silverpoint Etcetera: Contemporary Metalpoint Drawings, ACA Galleries, NY, Newark Mus, NJ, Montclair Mus, NY, Tobey C Moss Gallery, Los Angeles, Calif; and others. *Teaching:* Instr art & drawing, Pratt Inst, Brooklyn, NY, 55; instr art & painting, Tuxedo Park Sch, NY, 68-72; instr art, drawing & painting, pvt studio. *Awards:* Calif Palace of the Legion of Honor Silver Medal, 45; Audubon Artists Presidents Award, 76; Soc Am Graphic Artists Purchase Award, 77; Cert of Merit Award, Audubon Artists, 84. *Bibliog:* George A Perret (auth), August Mosca, New York Cult Ctr, 73; Impressionism and Post-Impressionism, 1900-1950, Grand Central Gallery, NYC. *Mem:* Audubon Artists. *Media:* Oil Painting; Lithography. *Publ:* Auth, Art of Post-Impressism, M Grumbacher, 76; Lecture on Art Materials, Color and Conservation, Eastend Arts & Humanities Coun, 86; Auth, The Art and History of Silverpoint Drawing, TV interview on closed channel. *Mailing Add:* Shelter Island NY 11964

MOSCATT, PAUL N
PAINTER, INSTRUCTOR
b Brooklyn, NY, July 9, 31. *Study:* Cooper Union Art Sch; Yale Univ Sch Fine Arts, BFA & MFA. *Work:* Univ Bridgeport, Conn; Yale Univ Art Gallery; Earlham Col, Richmond, Ind; Cincinnati Art Mus; Peale Mus, Baltimore, Md. *Comn:* portrait, comn by Joseph Romano, 89; portrait, comn by Frank Toto, 89; portrait, comn by Fred Lazarus, 89; portrait, comn by Richard Kim Frank, 90; portrait, comn by S Reinholt; and others. *Exhib:* One-man shows, Portrait Drawings of the American Indian, Md Inst Col Art, 73, Interiors & Nudes, C Grimaldis Gallery, Baltimore, Md, 78, Heads, Faces & Portraits, Blue

Mountain Gallery, New York, 90 & Studio Nudes, Blue Mountain Gallery, 92; Hassam Exhib, Am Acad Arts & Lett, 79. *Teaching:* Instr painting & drawing, Univ Bridgeport, 62-64; instr painting & drawing, Art Acad Cincinnati, 64-66; prof painting & drawing, Md Inst Col Art, 67-, chmn, painting dept, 77-79, acting chmn, 90-92. *Awards:* Mellon Fac Enrichment Grant, 84; Int Asn Art Critics Grant, 86. *Mem:* Artists Equity Asn. *Media:* Oil, Acrylic. *Publ:* Bernard Chaet (auth), The Art of Drawing. *Mailing Add:* Md Inst Col Art 1300 Mt Royal Ave Baltimore MD 21217

MOSENTHAL, CHARLOTTE DEMBO
PAINTER, PRINTMAKER
b Cleveland, Ohio. *Study:* Case Western Reserve Univ, BA; Cleveland Inst Art, studied with Donald Stacy, Mus Mod Art; Gregorio Prestopino, New Sch, New York. *Work:* Exxon Inc, Florham Park, NJ. *Comn:* Poster Designs, Gallery 9, Chatham, NJ 82, 84 & 86. *Exhib:* Nat Asn Women Artists, 89-92, Nat Soc Painters in Casein & Acrylic, Nat Arts Club, New York, 92; Mus Southwest, Midland, Tex, 91; Anna Howard Gallery, Wash, Conn, 92; Kimball Art Ctr, Park City, Utah, 92. *Collections Arranged:* West Side Printmakers, Broadway Mall Gallery, NY, 89. *Pos:* Ed, Newsletter, Westside Arts Coalition, New York, 86-91; chmn, traveling paintings, Nat Asn Women Artists, 90-92; serials libr technician, Cooper-Hewitt Mus, New York, 90- *Awards:* Elaine & Jas Hewitt Mem Award, Audubon Artists, New York, 89; Best in Show, Visual Individualists, New York, 89; First Prize Prints, Housatonic Art League, Conn, 90. *Mem:* Nat Assoc Women Artists; Nat Soc Painters in Casein & Acrylic; Audubon Artists Assoc; Burr Artists, NY (rec sec, 70-81); NY Artists Equity Asn. *Media:* Acrylic; Woodcut, Colograph. *Dealer:* Gallery 9 215 Main St Chatham NJ 07928. *Mailing Add:* 322 W 57 St, Apt 10L New York NY 10019

MOSER, BARRY
GRAPHIC ARTIST, PRINTMAKER
b Chattanooga, Tenn, Oct 15, 40. *Study:* Auburn Univ; Univ Tenn Chattanooga, with George Cress; also studied with Leonard Baskin & Jack Coughlin. *Work:* Brit Mus, London, Eng; Boston Athenaeum, Mass; Nat Gallery Art, Spec Collections, Washington, DC; Grolier Club, New York; Mus Fine Arts, Springfield, Mass; Newberry Libr, Chicago, Ill. *Exhib:* Boston Printmakers, Waltham, Mass, 72; one-man shows, Berkshire Mus, Pittsfield, Mass, 73 & Boston Athenaeum, Mass, 76; Los Angeles Nat Print Show, Calif, 74; Libr Cong Nat Print Exhib, Washington, DC, 75-76; History of Printed Books, San Francisco Pub Libr, Calif, 76; 4th Int Exhibit of Botanical Art, Hunt Inst, Carnegie-Mellon Univ, Pittsburgh, Pa, 77-78; R Michelson Galleries, Northhampton, Mass, 85-92. *Collections Arranged:* New York Pub Libr; Swarthmore Col, Pa; Harvard Univ, Cambridge, Mass; Univ Iowa, Ames (collection of illus bks); Smith Col, 76. *Teaching:* Head studio art, Williston Northampton Sch, Easthampton, Mass, 67-82 & RI Sch Design, 90- *Awards:* Second Prize, Cape Cod Ann, 71; Award of Merit, New Hampshire Int, 74; Am Bk Award. *Bibliog:* Worcester Sunday Telegram, 11/86; American Traditions in Watercolor, Abbeville Press, 87; The Art of Seeing, Prentice-Hall, 88. *Mem:* Am Printing Hist Asn. *Media:* Ink; Wood. *Publ:* Contribr, The Tinderbox, Little, Brown, 90; The Guild Shakespeare, Doubleday Bk Club, 90; The Holy Bible, Oxford/Doubleday, 90; Appalachia, HBJ, 90; Messiah, HarperCollins (in Prep); and others. *Mailing Add:* R Michelson Galleries 132 Main St Northampton MA 01060

MOSER, JOANN
CURATOR, HISTORIAN
b Chicago, Ill. *Study:* Smith Col, BA(art hist), 69; Univ Wis, Madison, MA(art hist), 72, PhD(art hist), 76. *Collections Arranged:* Atelier 17 (50 yr retrospective traveling exhib to five mus; auth, catalog), 77-78; Jean Metzinger in Retrospect, 85; Modernist Abstraction in American Prints, 89; The Drawings of Joseph Stella, 90. *Pos:* Cur of collections, Univ Iowa Mus Art, 76-86, actg dir, 80-83; head cur graphic arts, Nat Mus Am Art, Washington, 86- *Awards:* Ford Fel, Dept Art Hist, Univ Wis, 71-73; Kress Fel, Nat Gallery Art, Washington, DC, 75-76. *Mem:* Iowa Mus Asn; Col Art Asn; Midwest Art Hist Soc; Am Assoc Mus. *Res:* Prints and twentieth century art. *Publ:* contribr, Mauricio Lasansky and Intaglio Printmaking (catalog), Univ Iowa Mus Art, 76; The Graphic Art of Emil Ganso, 80; auth, The impact of Stanley William Hayter on Post-war American art, Archives Am Art J, Vol 18, No 1; auth, Jiri Anderle, 84; Visual Poetry: The Drawings of Joseph Stella, 88. *Mailing Add:* 5203 Benton Ave Bethesda MD 20814

MOSES, BETTE J
PAINTER
b Blackwell, Okla. *Study:* Northwestern State Univ, Alva, Okla, BFA, 46; Inst Allende San Miguel, Guanajuato, Mex, with James Pinto, 74-75. *Exhib:* Smoky Hill, Ft Hays Univ, Kans, 74 & Women Aware Show, 75; Am Painters in Paris, Centre Int de Paris, France, 75-76; Kans I, Hutchinson Art Asn, Kans, 78; Kans Pub TV, Wichita, 78; Wichita Art Mus, 80; Kans Tri-state Watercolor Show, 84. *Collections Arranged:* Soc Prof Painters, West, State Capitol, Topeka, Kans, 78-80 & Wichita Art Mus, Kans, 79-81. *Pos:* Founder, Art Inc, Barton Co Community & Col, 70, pres, 71-72 & bd adv, 78-81. *Awards:* First & Second Prizes Mixed Media, Art Inc, Barton Community Col, 71-85; First Prize Prof Painters, Russell Original Art Revue, 73; Holliday Prize, Kans Tri-state Watercolor, 85. *Mem:* Kans Soc Prof Painters, West; Kans Watercolor Soc. *Media:* Mixed. *Mailing Add:* 20810 Desert Sands Dr Sun City West AZ 85375

MOSES, ED
PAINTER
b Long Beach, Calif, April 9, 26. *Study:* Univ Calif, Los Angeles, BA, 55, MA, 58. *Work:* Art Inst Chicago; Mus Mod Art & Whitney Mus Am Art, New York; Albright-Knox Mus, Buffalo; Walker Art Ctr, Minneapolis, Minn; San Francisco Mus Art; Philadelphia Mus, Pa; Smithsonian Inst, Washington, DC; Mus Contemp Art, Los Angeles, Calif. *Exhib:* Annual, Los Angelas County Mus Art, Calif, 53, 54, 59; Annual, San Francisco Mus Art, Calif, 58, 62; Fifty California Artists, Whitney Mus Am Art, NY, Walker Art Ctr, Minneapolis, Minn, Albright-Knox Art Gallery, Buffalo, NY & Des Moines Art Ctr, Iowa, 62; The Late Fifties at Ferus, Los Angeles County Mus Art, Calif, 68; 32nd Biennial Exhibition of Contemporary American Painting, Corcoran Gallery Art, Washington, DC, 71; American Art, 1948-1973, Seattle Art Mus, Wash, 73; Robert Arneson and Edward Moses, San Francisco Mus Art, Calif, 74; 34th Biennial of Contemporary American Painting, Corcoran Gallery Art, Washington, DC, 75; Thirty Years of American Painting, Mus Mod Art, New York, 76; Painting and sculpture in California, The Modern Era, San Francisco Mus Art, Calif, 76; Selections from the Frederick Weisman Company Collections of California Art, Corcoran Gallery of Art, Washington, DC, 79; History of California Arts, San Francisco Mus Art, Calif, 80; Abstraction, San Francisco Art Inst, Calif, 81; Exchange Between Artists, Mus Mod Art, Paris, France & Lodz, Poland, 82; The Folding Image, Nat Gallery Art, Washington, DC, 84; Visions of Inner Space, Wright Art Gallery, Univ Calif, Los Angeles & Nat Gallery Mod Art, New Delhi, India, 88; solo exhibs, Galerie Georges Lavrov, Paris, France, 89; Gallery Kukje, Seoul, Korea, 89; Louver Gallery, Ny, 89; Ed Moses: Prints, Santa Monica Heritage Mus, Calif, 90; L A Louver Gallery, Venice, Calif, 90 & 91, Tex Gallery, Houston, 92, Zola Lieberman Gallery, Chicago, 92; L A Louver Gallery, Venice, Calif, 89, New York, 91; Galeria Joan Prats, NY, 89; Abstraction: John Altoon, Sam Francis, Craig Kauffman, John McLaughlin and Ed Moses, Nagoya City Art Mus, Mus Mod Art, Shiga, Hora Mus ARC, Japan, 90; Achenbach Found, San Francisco, 91. *Teaching:* Instr art, Univ Calif, Los Angeles, 68-72 & 75-76, Skowhegan Sch Painting & Sculpture, 83; Calif State Col, Long Beach, 85-86. *Awards:* Fel, Tamarind Lithography Workshop, Los Angeles, 68; Nat Endowment Arts Grant, 76; Guggenheim Fel, 80. *Bibliog:* George Rosalind (auth), review, The Outlook, 6/5/87; Winston Conrad (auth), Los Angeles: The New Mecca, Horizon XXX/I, 1-2/87, 17-30; Kenneth Baker (auth) Industrial-Strength Beauty (article), San Francisco Chronicle, 3/16/88. *Mem:* Nat Soc Literature & Arts Biographical Record. *Dealer:* Leslie Rubin. *Mailing Add:* 1233 Palms Blvd Venice CA 90291

MOSES, FORREST (LEE), JR
PAINTER, PRINTMAKER
b Danville, Va, May, 1934. *Study:* Washington & Lee Univ, BA, 56; Pratt Inst, 60-62. *Work:* Huntington Gallery, Univ Tex, Austin; Ill State Univ, Normal; Mus Fine Arts, Santa Fe, NMex; Citibank, New York, NY; W R Grace & Co, Dallas; Mint Mus, Charlotte; Chicago Hilton, Ill; Roswell Mus, NMex. *Exhib:* Contemporary Landscape Painting, Okla Art Ctr, Oklahoma City, 75; solo exhibs, Tratson/de Nagy Gallery, 82 & 84, Marvin Seline Gallery, Austin, Tex, 85, Munson Gallery, 86, 87 & 89, Peregrine Press, Dallas, Tex, 86, Sheldon Mem Mus Gallery, Lincoln, Nebr, 86, Watson Gallery, Houston, Tex, 86 & Gumps Gallery, San Francisco, Calif, 89; American Artists as Print Makers, 23rd Nat Print Exhib, Brooklyn Mus, NY, 83; Contemporary Western Landscape, Mus Art Am West, Houston, Tex, 84; Egypt, Munson Gallery, Santa Fe, NMex, 85; James Fisher Gallery, Denver, Colo, 85; Monotypes, James Robischon Gallery, Denver, Colo, 85; Contemporary American Monotypes, Chrysler Mus, Norfolk, Va, 85. *Teaching:* Instr drawing, Pratt Inst, 61-62; instr drawing & watercolor, Univ Houston, 69. *Awards:* Selected Juror's Award & Museum Purchase, Mus NMex Biennial, 74. *Media:* Oil; Lithography. *Dealer:* Munson Gallery 225 Canyon Rd Santa Fe NM 87501. *Mailing Add:* 837 El Caminito Santa Fe NM 87501

MOSKOWITZ, IRA
PAINTER, PRINTMAKER
b Turka, Poland, March 15, 12; US citizen. *Study:* Art Students League, 30-33. *Work:* Metrop Mus Art & Whitney Mus Am Art, New York; Nat Gallery Art, Washington, DC; Biblioteque Nationale, Paris. *Exhib:* One-man shows, Bernhard Crystal Galleries, New York, 67, Waddington Galleries, Montreal, Can, 69, traveling show, Paris, Scotland, Ireland, 74 & Weintraub Gallery, New York, 79; Drawings of Ira Moskowitz, Haifa Mus, Israel, 69; 45 Yrs of Graphics (retrospective), Brooks Mem Art Gallery, Memphis, 75; John Davis Hatch Collection, Nat Gallery Art, Washington, DC, 79. *Pos:* Ed Fine Arts Books, Shorewood Publ, New York, 55-62; dir publs, Am Art Collections Ltd, 83. *Awards:* Am at War, prize for Lithograph, 44; Libr Congress Award, Pennell Show, 45; fel creative art, Guggenheim, 43. *Bibliog:* John Davis Hatch (auth), The Drawings of Ira Moskowitz, Shorewood Publ, 66; Isaac Bashevis Singer (auth), Reaches of Heaven, Landmark Publ & Ferrar, Strauss & Giroux, 80; Joseph S Czestochowski (auth), 55 Years of Drawings of Ira Moskowitz, Alpine Fine Arts Collections Ltd, 84. *Media:* All Media. *Publ:* Coauth, La Mythe de Pygmalion, Mourlot, Paris, 66; ed, Great Drawings of All Time, Am, German, English, Italian, Swedish, Japanese, 62 & 75; coauth, Hasidim, Crown Publ, 73; A Little Boy in Search of God, Doubleday, 76; (with Isaac Bashevis Singer), Satan In Goray, Sweetwater Eds, 82. *Dealer:* Brewster Gallery 41 W 57th St New York NY 10019; J N Bartfield Galleries 30 W 57th St New York NY 10019. *Mailing Add:* 390 W End Ave New York NY 10024

MOSKOWITZ, ROBERT S
PAINTER
b New York, NY, June 20, 35. *Work:* Mus Mod Art & Whitney Mus Am Art, New York; Albright-Knox Art Gallery, Buffalo; Rose Art Mus, Brandeis Univ, Waltham, Mass; Wadsworth Atheneum, Hartford, Conn; Joslyn Art Mus, Omaha, Nebr; Kitakyushu Munic Mus, Japan; Philadelphia Mus Art; La Jolla Mus Contemp Art, Calif. *Exhib:* Art of Assemblage, Mus Mod Art,

New York, 61; Whitney Mus Am Art Ann, 69 & New Image Painting, 78; Painting the 80's, Grey Art Gallery, New York, 79; one-man shows, Daniel Weinberg Gallery, San Francisco, 79, Margo Levin Gallery, Los Angeles, 79 & La Jolla Mus Contemp Art, Calif, 79; Painting and Sculpture Today, Indianapolis Mus Art, 80; Great Big Drawings, Hayden Gallery, Mass Inst Technol, Cambridge, 82; Season's Greetings, Daniel Weinberg Gallery, Los Angeles, 83; Content: A Contemporary Focus: 1974-1984, Hirshhorn Mus & Sculpture Garden, Washington, DC, 84; Drawings and Sculpture, Manhattan Art Inc, New York, 85; Mus Mod Art, New York, 89. *Awards:* Guggenheim Fel, 67; Award, NY State Coun Arts, 73; Award, Nat Endowment Arts, 75. *Bibliog:* Michael Compton (auth), Art and responsbility, Flashart, summer 80; Nan Freeman (auth), The magnitude of drawing, Art New Eng, 4/82; Ellen Schwartz (auth), What's New in Nueva York?, Artnews, 4/84; Robert Taylor (auth), Images endowed with layers of meaning at MIT, Boston Sunday Globe, 6/2/85. *Mailing Add:* 81 Leonard St New York NY 10013

MOSKOWITZ, SHIRLEY (MRS JACOB W GRUBER)
PAINTER, COLLAGE ARTIST
b Houston, Tex, Aug 4, 20. *Study:* Mus Sch Art, Houston; Rice Univ, BA, 41; Oberlin Col, MA, 42; Philadelphia Col Art, 74-76; also with Morris Davidson, New York. *Work:* Allen Mus Art, Oberlin, Ohio; Museo Roma, Italy; Free Libr of Philadelphia; William Penn Mus, Harrisburg, Pa; Philadelphia Mus Art. *Exhib:* Juried shows of Pa Acad of Fine Arts, 53, 58, 61, 63 & 65; one-man shows, Paley Libr, Temple Univ, Philadelphia, 70, Nocara; William Penn Mem Mus, 74-75; Univ Pa, Philadelphia, 81; Mus of Philadelphia Civic Ctr; Port of Hist Mus, Philadelphia; Philadelphia Art Alliance; Mus of Fine Arts, Houston, TX; Nat Acad of Design, NY; Nat Mus, Wellington, New Zealand; Contemp Philadelphia, Artists, Philadelphia Mus of Art, 90. *Teaching:* Instr art hist, Univ Tex, Austin, spring 43; lectr art, Houston Pub Schs, 43-46; dir art, Oberlin Pub Schs, 46-47. *Awards:* IBM Painting Prize, Expressions, Earth Art III, Philadelphia Civic Ctr, 79; Mid-Atlantic Regional Collage Show Prize, Univ Del, 79; Watercolor Prize, Artists Equity Triennial, Philadelphia, 81; and others. *Bibliog:* Gerald F Brommer (auth), The Art of Collage 1978, Print World, 81, 82. *Mem:* Philadelphia Watercolor Club (secy, 68-70); Print Club; Am Color Print Soc; Philadelphia Chap Artists Equity (sec, 80-82); and others. *Media:* Watercolor, Acrylic; Ink, Intaglio. *Dealer:* Philadelphia Print Club Gallery; Dolan/Maxwell Gallery 2046 W Rittenhouse Sq Philadelphia PA 19103. *Mailing Add:* 1530 Locust #14 C Philadelphia PA 19102

MOSLEY, ZACK T
ILLUSTRATOR, CARTOONIST
b Hickory, Okla, Dec 12, 06. *Study:* Chicago Acad Fine Arts, 26-27; Art Inst Chicago, 27-28. *Pos:* Creator syndicated comic strip, Smilin' Jack, Chicago Tribune-New York News, 33-73. *Mem:* Nat Cartoonists Soc. *Publ:* Auth & illusr, Brave Coward Zack, 76, Hot Rock Glide, 79 & De-Icers Galore, 80. *Mailing Add:* 262 SE Edgewood Dr Stuart FL 34996

MOSS, IRENE
PAINTER
b Eperjes, Hungary; US citizen. *Study:* Brooklyn Mus Sch Art; also with Moses Soyer & Dmitri Romanofsky, New York. *Work:* Akron Art Inst, Ohio; Rose Art Mus, Brandeis Univ, Mass; New Brit Mus Am Art, Conn; Norfolk Mus, Va. *Exhib:* Ft Worth Art Ctr, Tex, 68; Rochester Mem Art Gallery, NY, 68; one-woman show, Suffolk Mus, Stony Brook, NY, 71; Stamford Mus, Conn, 72; Philadelphia Civic Ctr Mus, 74. *Pos:* Co-ed, Feminist Art J, 72-73. *Bibliog:* John Gruen (auth), Friday tour of art, World J Tribune, 66; Jacqueline Barnitz (auth), Images, 68 & Gordon Brown (auth), Irene Moss & the repetition of the natural image, 3/74, Arts Mag; Ed McCormack (auth), Re-invented realities of Irene Moss, Artspeak, 4/90. *Media:* Oil. *Publ:* Contribr, Sunstorm Arts Publ Co, Long Island, NY, 85-86; cover Social Psychology, Baron & Byrne, 87; cover Exploring Social Psychology, Baron, Byrne, Suls, 88. *Dealer:* Reece Galleries 24 W 57th St New York NY 10019. *Mailing Add:* 45 W 60th St New York NY 10023

MOSS, JACQUELINE
HISTORIAN, EDUCATOR
b New York, NY. *Study:* Univ Bridgeport, Conn; New York Univ; Cooper Union, New York, cert, 50, BFA, 75; Queen's Col, New York, MA(art hist), 80. *Collections Arranged:* American Women Painters (auth, catalog), Housatonic Community Col, 76. *Pos:* Cur educ, Aldrich Mus Contemp Art, Ridgefield, Conn, 66-80; art critic & spec corresp, The Advocate, Stamford, Conn, 81-84 & Greenwich Time, Conn, currently. *Teaching:* Chairperson, Dept Art, Daycroft Sch, Greenwich, Conn, 60-75; instr art hist, Univ Bridgeport, Conn, 69, 80-82 & 85, Housatonic Community Col, Bridgeport, Conn, 72-73; instr design, Norwalk Community Col, 85. *Awards:* Conn Comn Arts Grant, 78. *Mem:* Col Art Asn. *Res:* Modernist; concentration on geometric abstraction and constructivism of the 1930s and 1940s and its connection with the contemporary period (post World War II); contemporary art outside the United States; the women's movement. *Publ:* Auth, Anatomy of a brushstroke, Christian Sci Mon, 74; contribr, Sculpture 76, Greenwich Arts Coun, 76; auth, Subjects and objects, Conn Comn Arts, 78; Gertrude Greene: Constructions of 1930s and 1940s, Arts Mag, 81; contribr, Abstract Painting and Sculpture in America: 1927-1944, 83; American Art: American Women, 1965-1985, 85. *Mailing Add:* 131 Davenport Ridge Lane Stamford CT 06903

MOSS, JOE (FRANCIS)
SCULPTOR, PAINTER
b Kincheloe, WVa, Jan 26, 33. *Study:* WVa Univ, AB, 51, MA, 60. *Work:* Del Art Mus, Wilmington; Johnson Mus, Ithaca, NY; St Louis Art Mus, St Louis, Mo; and others. *Comn:* Sound sculpture, Martin Fine Villa, Miami, Fla, 80; and others. *Exhib:* Members Exhib, Mus Mod Art, New York, 65; one-man shows, J B Speed Mus, Louisville, Ky, 77 & Madison Square Park, New York, 80; Leading Contemp Sculptors Exhib, Sculpture Now, New York, 79; Beginnings Exhib, Laumeier Int Sculpture Park, St Louis, Mo, 79; Soundings, Neuberger Mus, Purchase, New York; Sculpture on Shoreline Sites, Wards Island, New York, 82; and other group & one-man shows. *Pos:* Vis res fel, Ctr Advan Visual Studies, Mass Inst Technol, Cambridge, 73, 85 & 87-88. *Teaching:* Assoc prof art, WVa Univ, 60-70; vis prof, Univ Md, summer 67; prof, Univ Del, 70- *Awards:* Prize for Environ Design, Three Rivers Arts Festival, Pittsburgh, 68; Sculpture Award, Appalachian Corridors Exhib, Charleston, 70. *Bibliog:* Alan Gerstle (auth), Joe Moss, Arts Mag; James Kelly (auth), The Sculptural Idea, Third Ed; Quintessence, Alternative Spaces Residency Prog, Dayton, Ohio & Wright State Univ. *Media:* Multi-Media. *Dealer:* Max Hutchinson Gallery 138 Greene St New York NY 10012. *Mailing Add:* Dept Art Univ Del Newark DE 19716

MOSS, KAREN CANNER
PAINTER, EDUCATOR
b Boston, Mass, May 2, 44. *Study:* RI Sch Design, BFA, 66; Tufts Univ, Boston Mus Sch, MFA, 74. *Work:* Boston Mus Fine Arts, Mass; Addison Gallery Am Art, Andover, Mass; Vassar Col Art Gallery, Poughkeepsie, NY; Rose Art Mus, Brandeis Univ, Waltham, Mass; Bristol Community Col, Fall River, Mass. *Comn:* Outdoor mural, Mass Bay Transportation Authority, Boston, Mass, 77; ceramic tile mural, First Nat Bank Boston, 83. *Exhib:* Edinburgh Festival, Queens Col, Scotland, 74; Works on Paper, Fogg Mus, Harvard Univ, Cambridge, Mass, 74; Primitive Presence in the '70's, Vassar Col, Poughkeepsie, NY, 75; Boston Watercolor Today, Boston Mus Fine Arts, 76; one-woman show, Addison Gallery Am Art, Andover, Mass, 76; Contemp Issues: Works on Paper by Women, traveling show to Los Angeles, Salt Lake City & Houston, 77; Prints & Drawings, Mus Mod Art, New York, 78; one-woman show, Kathryn Markel Gallery, New York, 83; and others; Ceramic File Art, Boston Design Ctr; 12th annual drawing show. *Pos:* Artist, trustee & rep, Boston Visual Artists Union, Inst Contemp Art, Boston, Mass, 71-73. *Teaching:* Instr drawing, Boston Mus Fine Arts Sch, 83. *Awards:* Blanche E Coleman Award, 72; First Prize for Watercolor, Silvermine Art Guild, 73; Finalist in State, Mass Arts & Humanities Found, 76-77. *Bibliog:* Wolf Kahn (auth), The subject matter in new realism, Am Artist, 11/79; Pam Allara (auth), Boston: shedding its inferiority complex, Art News, 11/79; Sarah McFadden (auth), Report from Boston, Art Am, 5/83. *Mem:* Boston Visual Artists Union. *Media:* Painting. *Dealer:* Kathryn Markel Fine Art 50 W 57th St New York NY 10019. *Mailing Add:* 14 Elm St Brookline MA 02146

MOSS, TOBEY C
ART DEALER, HISTORIAN
b Chicago, Ill, June 1, 28. *Study:* Univ Ill, Champaign-Urbana; Univ Calif, Los Angeles, AA, 47. *Collections Arranged:* Helen Lundeberg Since 1970, Palm Springs Mus, 83; Colorforms (auth, catalog), Gallery-Security Pacific, 85; Helen Lundeberg, Sesnon Art Gallery, Univ Calif, Santa Cruz, 88. *Pos:* Dir, Tobey C Moss Gallery, Los Angeles, currently. *Mem:* Col Art Asn; Art Table; Women's Caucus Art; Los Angeles County Mus Art Graphics Art Coun; Docent Coun; Int Fine Print Dealer Asn. *Res:* Modernist Californian artists working 1920-1960. *Specialty:* Modernism, Post-Surrealism, Hard-Edge; Lorser Feitelson, Helen Lundeberg, Peter Krasnow, Knud Merrild, Oskar Fischinger, S M Wright, Dorr Bothwell. *Publ:* Gallery Catalog of Essays. *Mailing Add:* Tobey C Moss Gallery 7321 Beverly Blvd Los Angeles CA 90036

MOSS-VREELAND, PATRICIA
PAINTER, DRAFTSMAN
b New York, NY, July 26, 51. *Study:* Philadelphia Col Art, BFA, 73; Tyler Sch Art, Philadelphia, 73. *Work:* Philadelphia Mus Art; Norton Gallery Art, W Palm Beach; Beaver Col, Glenside, Pa; Atlantic Richfield Co, Los Angeles; Bell Tel Labs, NJ; Fed Reserve, Philadelphia, Pa. *Comn:* Numerous private portrait commissions; mural, Philadelphia Mus Art, 89; handpainted ceramic mural, pvt residence, 91. *Exhib:* Philadelphia-Houston Exchange (with catalog), Inst Contemp Art, Philadelphia and Houston, 75; Contemporary Drawings (with catalog), Philadelphia Acad Fine Arts & Philadelphia Mus Art, 79; Made in Philadelphia III, Inst Contemp Art, Philadelphia, 80; American Drawings: Black & White, Brooklyn Mus, 80; New Acquisitions, Philadelphia Mus Art, 86; Nat Group Invitational, Pindar Gallery, New York, NY, 89; Contemp Women Artists Int Juried Exhib, Brussels, Belgium, 89; Julius Bloch Mem Exhib, Pertaining to Philadelphia, Philadelphia Mus Art, Pa, 92. *Awards:* Drucker Painting Award, Cheltenham Ann Painting Exhib, Pa, 77; Purchase Award, Ann Juried Exhib, Beaver Col, Pa, 86; Philadelphia Mus Art Award, Ann Juried Show, Cheltenham Art Ctr, 86. *Bibliog:* Articles in The Philadelphia Inquirer, 75, 77, 86 & 88; On tour in Philadelphia, Am Artist, 80. *Mem:* Col Art Asn. *Media:* Pencil, Oil. *Mailing Add:* 2229 Bainbridge St Philadelphia PA 19146

MOSZYNSKI, ANDREW
PAINTER
b Eye, Suffolk, Eng. *Study:* Univ Nat de Buenos Aires, Argentina. *Work:* Metrop Mus Art, New York. *Exhib:* Solo exhibs, C Space, 80, J Walter Thompson Gallery, 83, Mission Gallery, 86, New York; Tweed Gallery, NJ, 82; Galeria Alberto Elia, Buenos Aires, Argentina, 83; PS1, Long Island City, NY, 84; Alternative Mus, New York, 85; Leonardo di Mauro Gallery, New York, 87. *Teaching:* Prof art & design, Fashion Inst of Technol, New York, 82- *Awards:* Nat Endowment of Arts Grant, 85. *Bibliog:* Susana Torruella Leval (auth), Painting from under the volcano, Art News, 3/85; Elaine Louie (auth), Flat tops, NY Times, 4/90; John Howell White (auth), article, Artforum, 5/90. *Mailing Add:* 181 Mott St New York NY 10012

MOTY, ELEANOR H
JEWELER
Study: Univ Ill, Urbana, BFA, 68; Tyler Sch Art, Temple Univ, Philadelphia, Pa, MFA, 71. *Work:* Minn Mus Art, St Paul; Tyler Sch Art, Philadelphia, Pa; Lannon Found, Palm Beach, Fla; Ga State Univ, Atlanta. *Exhib:* Contemporary Jewelery, Mus Mod Art, Tokyo & Kyoto, Japan, 84; Contemporary Artists Jewelery, Philbrook Art Ctr, Tulsa, Okla, 85; Craft Today: Poetry of the Physical, Am Craft Mus & traveling, New York, 86-88; Perimeter Gallery, Chicago, Ill, 88; 100 Years of Wisconsin Art, Milwaukee Art Mus, 88; Korean-American Metalworks Exhibition, Walker Hill Art Ctr Mus, Seoul, Korea, 88; Artful Objects: Recent Am Crafts, Fort Wayne Mus, Ind, 89; Crafts Today USA, traveling exhib, Paris, Helsinki, Frankfurt, Warsaw, Lausanne, Moscow, 89-90. *Pos:* Haystack Mountain Sch, Deer Isle, Maine, (bd trustees 82- & pres, 89-). *Teaching:* Prof metalsmith, Univ Wis, Madison, 81- *Awards:* Craftsman Fel, Nat Endowment Arts, 75; H I Romnes Fel, Univ Wis, 80. *Bibliog:* Barbara Cartlidge (auth), 20th Century Jewelry, 85; feature article and cover, Am Craft, 6-7/87; Barbara Mayer (auth), Contemp Am Craft Art: A Collector's Guide, 88. *Mem:* Distinguished Mem, Soc NAm Goldsmiths; Am Craft Coun. *Mailing Add:* c/o Perimeter Gallery 750 N Orleans Chicago IL 60610

MOULTON, ROSALIND KIMBALL
PHOTOGRAPHER, COLLAGE ARTIST
b Buffalo, NY, Nov 25, 41. *Study:* Photog with Minor White, 66; Art Inst Chicago, BFA(Anna Louise Raymond Traveling Fel), 71; State Univ NY, Buffalo, MFA, 76; numerous photog workshops. *Work:* St Louis Art Mus; Ga Southern Col, Statesboro; Buffalo Found, State Univ NY; Hallmark Cards Photog Collection; Springfield Art Mus, Mo. *Exhib:* Four Photographers, Eppink Art Gallery, Emporia State Univ, Kans, 91; one-person show, Rosalind Kimball Moulton, Exhib USA, Mid-Am Arts Alliance, 91-92; Creating Ourselves, Miles Mus, Eastern NMex, Portales, 92; Midwest Invitational VII, Univ Wis, Green Bay, traveling show, 92-93; Fine Art Competition, Breckenridge Fine Art Ctr, Tex, 92; and others. *Teaching:* Vis instr photog, Purdue Univ, West Lafayette, Ind, 71; instr photog, Empire State Col, Buffalo, 75, State Univ NY, Buffalo, 76 & Stephens Col, 76-; vis artist, Univ Mo, Columbia, 81. *Awards:* Stephens Grants, 78 & 82; Grant, Mo Humanities Coun/Nat Endowment Humanities, 87-88; Distinguished Teacher, Stephens Col, 90. *Bibliog:* Nancy Weckly (auth), Rosalind-Kimball Moulton (exhib catalog), Burchfield Art Ctr, 90. *Mem:* Col Art Asn; Soc Photog Educ; Ctr Creative Studies, Ariz; Friends Photog. *Publ:* Contribr, Photography for Collectors Vol II: The Midwest, 84; Menchenim Wasser, Eine Fotografische Bildgeschichte 1853-1986, 87; New York Art Rev, 88; Photoalbums: images of time and reflection of Self, Qualitative Sociology Mag, 8/89; Percy Land, an entrepreneur of vision, View Camera Mag, 1/90. *Mailing Add:* 4600 Rte E Columbia MO 65202

MOULTON, SUSAN GENE
HISTORIAN, PAINTER
b Long Beach, Calif, June 7, 44. *Study:* Univ Calif, Davis, study with Wayne Thiebaud, BA(art), 66; Univ Padua, Italy, 64-65; Accad, Venice, Italy, with Prof Balest, 64; Stanford Univ, MA(art hist; Carnegie Found Fel), 69, PhD(art hist), 77. *Comn:* Glenn Ellen Winery. *Teaching:* Prof Renaissance & mod art, Sonoma State Univ, 71-, chairperson dept art, 75-79 & 81-83. *Awards:* Nat Endowment Humanities, 76-78. *Mem:* Col Art Asn; Women's Caucus Art; San Francisco Mus Soc; Nat Asn Schs Art & Design. *Media:* Watercolor, Drawing. *Res:* Sixteenth century Venetian painting, specifically Titian and the evolution of donor portraiture in Venice; 20th century American art, Aesthetics and Ecology. *Publ:* Contribr, From Frontier to Fire, Univ Calif, Davis, 64; auth, Interdisciplinary Women's Studies Courses, Women's Caucus Art, 77; Titian and the Evolution of Donor Portraiture, Stanford Univ, 77; auth, Four From California, Edinburg, Scotland, 81; Works in Bronze; A Modern Survey, Sonoma State Univ, Calif, 85. *Mailing Add:* Dept Art Sonoma State Univ 1801 E Cotati Ave Rohnert Park CA 94928

MOUNT, MARSHALL WARD
HISTORIAN, ADMINISTRATOR
b Jersey City, NJ, Dec 25, 27. *Study:* Columbia Col, AB, 48; Columbia Univ, MA, 52, PhD, 66. *Pos:* Leader art study tours to Mali, Cameroun, India, Explorer Tours, Montreal, 69-77; dir art hist prog, Finch Col, San Marino, Italy, 73-75; cataloguer, Zim Collection of African Art, Children's Mus, Brooklyn, NY, 77 & 79; dir, L Kahan Gallery African Art, New York, 81-82. *Teaching:* Prof & chmn art hist dept, Finch Col, New York, 58-75; vis prof, Univ Iowa, Iowa City, summer 70 & Parsons Sch of Design, New York, 70-72; vis assoc prof, Hunter Col, New York, 72-73; prof and chmn creative arts dept, Univ Benin, Nigeria, 77-80; adj asst prof art hist, Fashion Inst Technol, New York, 82-; vis asst prof, Rutgers Univ, 87-88. *Awards:* Rockefeller Found Fel, 61, 62 & 68; Fac Scholar Int Studies, Columbia, 66-67; Am Coun Learned Soc Grant, 73. *Mem:* Col Art Asn; fel African Studies Asn; Ctr for African Art. *Res:* Traditional and contemporary art of sub-Saharan Africa. *Publ:* Auth, African Art: The Years Since 1920, Ind Univ Press, 73, DaCapro Press, 89; African Art from New Jersey Collections, Montclair Art Mus, 83. *Mailing Add:* 74 Sherman Pl Jersey City NJ 07307

MOUNT, WARD
PAINTER, SCULPTOR
b Batavia, NY. *Study:* Art Students League; NY Univ; also with Albert P Lucas & Joseph P Pollia. *Work:* Jersey City Mus; Roosevelt Mus, Hyde Park, NY; Delgado Mus; Mus of Mod Art; Hudson River Mus. *Comn:* Bronze medal, Painters & Sculptors Soc, Jersey City Mus; holiday card for 1971 (casein), Am Heart Asn, 71; and others. *Exhib:* Audubon Artists, New York, 40-42, Nat Acad Design, 44 & Nat Sculpture Soc, 45-48; Pa Acad Fine Arts, Philadelphia, 49; Smithsonian Inst, Washington, DC, 51; New York Hist Soc; Allied Artists Am; Mus Mod Art, New York; Delgado Mus; Hudson River Mus; Riverside Mus. *Pos:* Former founder & head painting & sculpture, Jersey City Med Ctr, NJ; dir, Ward Mount Art Classes, Jersey City, 39-; charter mem, Nat Mus Women in Arts. *Teaching:* Head dept painting & sculpture, NJ State Teachers Col, 41-45. *Awards:* First Prize Sculpture, Kearney Mus, 47, Art Fair, New York, 50; Gold Medal, Jersey J Woman of Achievement, 71; Artist of the Yr, Hudson Artists, 85. *Bibliog:* Peyton Boswell (auth), article in Arts Digest; articles in Cue Mag, Saturday Eve Post & Rev Mod Francaise; and others. *Mem:* Founding mem Artists Equity Asn; Painters & Sculptors Soc NJ (founder & pres); fel Royal Soc Art; founding mem Audubon Artists; Acad Italy. *Mailing Add:* 74 Sherman Pl Jersey City NJ 07307

MOVALLI, CHARLES JOSEPH
PAINTER, WRITER
b Gloucester, Mass, Aug 20, 45. *Study:* Clark Univ, BA; Univ Conn, MA & PhD; spec study with Emile Gruppe, Roger Curtis, Zygmund Jankowski & Betty L Schlemm. *Work:* General Mills; High Voltage Engr; Hilton Hotel, Altamonte Springs; Exel Technol; Virginia Slims Collection; and others. *Pos:* Contributing ed, Am Artist Mag, 76- *Teaching:* Painting workshops in USA, Can, Mex & Europe. *Awards:* Gold Medal, 82 & Silver Medal, 89, Rockport Art Asn; Gold Medal, Salmagundi Club, 85. *Bibliog:* Numerous articles in American Artist Mag. *Mem:* Acad Artists; Guild of Boston Artists; Rockport Art Asn; N Shore Arts Asn. *Media:* Oil. *Res:* Contemporary and older painters working in plein-air tradition. *Publ:* Ed & coauth, Gruppe on Painting, 76; Brushwork, 77, Color in Outdoor Painting, 77 & Painting with Light, 78 & Art of Landscape Painting, 79, Watson-Guptill; auth, Croney on Watercolor, North Light, 82. *Mailing Add:* 237 Western Ave Gloucester MA 01930

MOXEY, PATRICIO KEITH FLEMING
ART HISTORIAN
b Buenos Aires, Arg, Jan 4, 43; Brit & Arg citizen. *Study:* Univ Edinburgh, MA, 65; Univ Chicago, MA, 68, PhD, 74. *Teaching:* From instr to asst prof art hist, Tufts Univ, 71-74; from asst prof to assoc prof art hist, Univ Va, 74-86, prof, 86-, chmn art hist, 76-79 & actg chmn, 81-82; prof art hist, Barnard Col, 88-, chair art hist, 89-; prof art hist, Columbia Univ, 88- *Awards:* Nat Endowment Humanities Fel, 78-79; sen fel, Ctr Advan Study Visual Arts, Nat Gallery Art, 80-81; Humboldt Found Fel, 82-83; scholar, J Paul Getty Ctr Hist Art & Humanities, 91 & 92. *Mem:* Col Art Asn; Renaissance Soc; Hist Netherlandish Art; Sixteenth Century Soc. *Res:* Late medieval and Renaissance art in Northern Europe; critical theory & historiography. *Publ:* Auth, Peasants, Warriors & Wives, Popular Imagery in the Reformation, Chicago, 89; co-ed, Visual Theory: Painting & Interpretation, Polity, 91; Semiotics & the Social History of Art, New Lit Hist 22, 91; The Social History of Art in the Age of Deconstruction, Hist Human Sci, 5/92. *Mailing Add:* Columbia Univ Barnard Col New York NY 10027

MOY, HENRY
MUSEUM DIRECTOR, MUSEOLOGIST
b Chicago, Ill, Dec 8, 55. *Study:* Univ Chicago; Beloit Col, BA, 77, MA, 78. *Pos:* Cur col exhib, Lakeview Mus, Peoria, Ill, 81-84; dir mus, Beloit Col, Wis, 85- *Teaching:* Adj asst prof mus studies, Beloit Col, Wis, 85- *Mailing Add:* 700 College Beloit WI 53511

MOY, MAY (WONG)
PAINTER, INSTRUCTOR
b New York, NY, Dec 2, 13. *Study:* Parsons Sch Fine & Appl Arts, NY; Montclair Teacher's Col; Oriental Artists Sch. *Exhib:* Show Castle '79, Sands Point, NY, 79; 16th Ann Exhib Sumi-e Soc Am, Am Inst Architects, DC, 79; Sumi-e Soc Am, Meridian House Int, Washington, DC, 83; Salmagundi Club, 85; The Artist's Book, 91; and others. *Teaching:* Lectr & demonstr Chinese brush painting, Sr Citizens Groups, Huntington Schs, 71-; lectr Oriental brush painting, Artisan House, Northport, NY, 72-74 & Huntington Hist Soc, NY, 74- *Awards:* Zen, 63, Bamboo, 69 & Heart of Winter, 75, Sumi-e Soc Am. *Bibliog:* Sally Miller (auth), May W Moy exhibits Chinese painting, Half Hollow Hills Community Libr, 72; Hedda Friedman (auth), May Moy Chinese exhibition, Long Islander Newspaper, 72; Rhoda Amon (auth), Long Island Sumi-e style, Newsday, 74. *Mem:* Sumi-e Soc Am, New York; Suffolk Co Porcelain Artists; Nat Mus Women Arts. *Media:* Ink, Watercolor. *Dealer:* Islip Art Mus Brookwood Hall Irish Lane East Islip NY 11730. *Mailing Add:* 27 Maryland St Dix Hills NY 11746

MOY, SEONG
PAINTER, PRINTMAKER
b Canton, China, April 12, 21; US citizen. *Study:* St Paul Sch Art, with Cameron Booth, 36-40; Art Students League, with Vaclav Vytacil, 41-42; Hofmann Sch, with Hans Hofmann, 41-42; Atelier 17, New York, 48-50. *Work:* Mus Mod Art; Brooklyn Mus; Metrop Mus Art; Pa Acad Fine Arts; NY Pub Libr; plus others. *Comn:* Three ed, Int Graphic Arts Soc; New York Hilton Hotel. *Exhib:* Metrop Mus Art, 50; Whitney Mus Am Art, 50; Univ Ill, 51, 53 & 54; Carnegie Inst, 52 & 55; New York World's Fair, 64-65; plus many other group & one-man shows. *Pos:* Dir, Seong Moy Sch Painting & Graphic Arts, Provincetown, Mass, summers 54- *Teaching:* Instr, Univ Minn, 51, Ind Univ, 52-53, Smith Col, 54-55, Univ Ark, 55, Vassar Col, 55, Cooper Union Art Sch, 57-70, Columbia Univ, 59-70 & Art Students League, 63-; prof, City Col New York, 70-90. *Awards:* John Hay Whitney Found Grant, 50-51; Guggenheim Fel, 55-56. *Bibliog:* Saff & Sacilatto (auths), Printmaking--History and Process, Holt-Reinhart Winston Publ, 70. *Mem:* Art Students League; Am Fedn Arts; Artists Equity Asn; Col Art Asn Am; Fedn Mod Painters & Sculptors. *Mailing Add:* 100 La Salle St New York NY 10027

MOYA SOTO, ROBERTO
PAINTER, PRINTMAKER
b San Juan, PR, Oct 15, 35. *Study:* Eastern NMex Univ, 51-53; Pratt Graphics Art Ctr, 60-62, USC with Harry Sternberg, 80-82. *Work:* Mus Fine Art, Ft Lauderdale, Fla; Rutgers Univ; Jane Voorhees Zimmerli Art Mus; Rutgers Univ, Printmaking Studios; Duke Univ, Schaefer House, Raleigh, NC; and others. *Comn:* Schaefer House, Duke Univ, comm by Mr & Mrs Norb Schaefer. *Exhib:* I Encuentro Ibero, Palacio del Instituto de Cultura Hispanica, Madrid, 88; one-man exhib, Series-Large Scale Paintings, Pratt Inst, New York, 89; Contemp Am Printmakers 1960 to the present, Newark Pub Libr, Newark Art Div; 45 Anos de Grafica Puertorriquena, Seville, Spain, 92-93; Selected by the US Dept State, Art in Embassies Prog (oil on canvas), on tour two years, 500 Anos de Arte en Puerto Rico traveling exhib, 93; and others. *Pos:* Founder & pres, Galeria Palomas, 78-88. *Teaching:* Artist in residence, computer generated studies, Univ PR, 89- *Bibliog:* Homines, Revista de Ciencias Sociales, PR, 83; E Ruiz de la Mata (auth), Roberto Moya Painter as Computer Whiz, 6/30/91; E Ruiz de la Mata (auth), 3 by Homar 2 by Moya, 3/29/92; and ohters. *Mailing Add:* PO Box 4642 Old San Juan PR 00904

MOYER, MARINA PAVLOVA
ADMINISTRATOR, SCULPTURE
b Gottingen, WGer, Sept 29, 52; US citizen. *Study:* Rutgers Univ; Broward Community Col; Fla Atlantic Univ, BFA, 83; Univ Miami (scholar). *Work:* Discovery Ctr Mus, Ft Lauderdale, Fla. *Collections Arranged:* Ann Exhib (with catalog), 85-90; Human Image Exhib, 85-90; Membership Exhib (with catalog), 85-90; Riverwalk Art Festival (with catalog), 87-90; Salon des Refuse (with catalog), 87-90. *Pos:* Exec dir, Broward Art Guild, Ft Lauderdale, Fla, 85; community adv bd, WXEL; pres, Fla Asn Nonprofit Organizations Inc, currently. *Teaching:* Artist in residence weaving, Discovery Ctr Mus, 78-86, Univ Miami, 86-87 & Broward Community Col, 90-93. *Awards:* Moretti Award, Community Achievement Comt, 88 & 89; Outstanding Community Service, Junior League, Ft Lauderdale, 88. *Mem:* Broward Co Teachers Art Guild; Women's Caucus Art; Coalition Women's Art Orgn (vpres corresp S states, 91-93). *Media:* Mixed Media. *Mailing Add:* 5750 SW 16th Court 207 S Andrews Ave Plantation FL 33317

MOYER, ROY
PAINTER, ADMINISTRATOR
b Allentown, Pa, Aug 20, 21. *Study:* Columbia Col, BA, Columbia Univ, MA. *Work:* Rochester Mem Art Gallery, NY; Brandeis Univ Art Gallery, Waltham, Mass; Wichita Art Mus, Kans; Nat Mus Am Art, Washington, DC; Fordham Univ, Lincoln Ctr, NY. *Exhib:* Nat Acad Design, New York, 77; Sneed Gallery, 79; Carl Battaglia Gallery, 80; Fordham Univ, 81; Rolly-Michaux Gallery, Boston, 81; and others. *Collections Arranged:* Inverse Illusionism, traveling exhib; numerous others for Am Fedn Arts. *Pos:* Dir, Am Fedn Arts, 63-72; chief art & design, UNICEF, 72-86. *Teaching:* Lectr art hist, Univ Toronto, 53-55. *Awards:* First Prize, Butler Inst Am Art, 73 & Nat Acad Design, 77. *Bibliog:* An American Bestiary, Abrams, 78; Modern American Realism, Smithsonian Inst, 87. *Mem:* Nat Coun Arts (exec comt, 65-72); Am Soc Contemp Artists (pres). *Media:* Oil. *Res:* Byzantine art and architecture; sixteenth century painting and sculpture. *Publ:* Auth, Dogancay, 86; Nineteen films on visual perception with Rudolf Arnheim; editorials in Artspeak Mag, 88- *Dealer:* Keen Gallery 423 Broome New York NY 10013. *Mailing Add:* 440 Riverside Dr New York NY 10027

MOYERS, WILLIAM
PAINTER, SCULPTOR
b Atlanta, Ga, Dec 11, 16. *Study:* Adams State Col, major fine arts; Otis Art Inst. *Work:* Gilcrease Inst, Tulsa, Okla; Nat Cowboy Fame, Oklahoma City; Adams State Col; Albuquerque Mus; Sangre Cristo Arts Ctr, Pueblo, Colo; Cowboy Artists Am Mus, Kerrville, Tex. *Comn:* Wind & Rain (life size sculpture), Albuquerque Mus, NMex & Adams State Col. *Exhib:* Cowboy Artist of Am Shows, Cowboy Hall of Fame & Phoenix Art Mus, since 68; one-man shows, Adams State Col, Alamosa, Colo, 71 & Nat Cowboy Hall of Fame, Oklahoma City, 73; group show, Mont Hist Soc, Helena, 72 & 73. *Awards:* Silver Medal sculpture, Cowboy Artists Am 1979 Exhib, Phoenix Art Mus, 79 & 80; Gold Medal-Sculpture, Cowboy Artists Am Exhib, 84; Silver Medal-Watercolor, Cowboy Artists Am Show, 89 & 91; and others. *Bibliog:* Ainsworth (auth), Cowboy in Art, World Publ, 68; Harmsen (auth), Western America, Northland, 71; Broder (auth), Bronzes of the American West, Abrams, 74. *Mem:* Cowboy Artists Am (vpres, 82-83, pres, 83-84 & 88-89). *Media:* Oil, Watercolor; Bronze. *Publ:* Illusr bks for nat publ, 45-62. *Dealer:* Taos Art Gallery Inc PO Box 1007 Taos NM 87571; Trailside Galleries 7330 Scottsdale Mall Scottsdale AZ 85251. *Mailing Add:* 1407 Morningside Dr NE Albuquerque NM 87110

MOZLEY, ANITA VENTURA
HISTORIAN, CRITIC
b Washington, DC, Aug 29, 28. *Study:* Northwestern Univ, Evanston, Ill, BA; Art Students League, with Morris Kantor. *Collections Arranged:* Ansel Adams: The Portfolios, Stanford Univ Mus Art, Calif, 72; Eadweard Muybridge: The Stanford Years, 1872-1882 (ed & co-auth, catalog), 72; Mrs Cameron's Photographs from the Life (auth, catalog), 74; Monsen Collection of American Photography (auth, catalog), Seattle Art Mus, Wash, 76; Nadar: Portraits and Catacombs, 78; The Grand Tour: Mid-19th Century Photographs from the Leonard-Peil Collection, 79; Paintings by Joseph Raphael (1869-1950), 80; Ansel Adams: Ski Experience, 83; Images of Hope and Despair: Robert Frank's Photographs, 85; Peter Stackpole, A photojournalist in Retrospect, 86. *Pos:* Reviewer, managing ed & West Coast corresp, Arts Mag, New York, 55-64; poster designer, Leo Castelli Gallery, New York, 55-62; film librn, Sextant, Inc, New York, 60-61; cur asst & ed, SEA Letter, San Francisco Maritime Mus, 62-67; registr, Stanford Univ Mus Art, Calif, 70-78; cur photog, 71-86. *Teaching:* Hist photogr, Stanford Univ, spring 81. *Awards:* Faricy Art Award, Nev, 49; Out-of-Town Scholar, Art Students League, 50. *Bibliog:* Reviews (monogr), Arts Mag, Studio International, 55-63, New York, 63-85, Photograph, Image, Afterimage, Print Collector's Newsletter; Design: All posters, Leo Castell Gallery, 6/55-63. *Mem:* Phi Beta Kappa. *Res:* Nineteenth and twentieth century photographers, particularly the works of Eadweard Muybridge, Julia Margaret Cameron, Thomas Annan, Imogen Cunningham, Joe Deal & Lorie Novak. *Publ:* Auth, Thomas Annan, Photographs of the Old Closes and Streets of Glasgow, Dover, 77; Mybridges's Complete Human and Animal Locomotion, Dover, 79; Harry Smith's Magic Moments, White, 81; The Fault Zone, Joe Deal's Portfolio, 81; The Man and the Bridge, The Bridge Builders, Pomegranate, 84; The Stanfords and Photography, Mus Builders in the West, Stanford, 86; Leo Holub's Photographs of Artists in the Collection of Mr and Mrs H W Anderson, Vol I, Atherton, Calif, 89; Joel Leivick's Photographs of Carrara (exhib catalog), Stanford, 90; contribr, Catalogue of the Drawing Collection, Stanford Mus, 92. *Mailing Add:* 601 Laurel Ave Menlo Park CA 94025

MUCCIOLI, ANNA MARIA
PAINTER, SCULPTOR
b Detroit, Mich, Apr 23, 22. *Study:* Soc Art & Crafts; with Sarkis Sarkisian, Charles Culver & Jay Holland. *Exhib:* Ford Motor Co Art Exhib, 61-79; Mich State Fair Art Exhib, 68-78; Butler Inst Am Art, Youngstown, Ohio, 69; Nat Acad Galleries, New York, 71; Nat Small Painting Exhib, traveling, 72-78; Birmingham Mus Arts, 74; one-man show, Univ Liggett Sch, Grosse Point, Mich, 74; Mich Watercolor Soc, Detroit Inst Arts, 76; Art Ctr Fibers Exhib, Mt Clemens, 77; Retrospective Watercolors, Lawrence Inst Technol, Mich, 86. *Pos:* Owner, Muccioli Studio Gallery. *Awards:* Third Place, Scarab Club, 71, Hon Mention, Silver Medal Exhib, 76 & 79; Second Place, Ford Motor Co Art Exhib, 76, First Place, 77, & Second Place, 79. *Bibliog:* Am Artists: An Illustrated Survey of Leading Contemporary Americans, 85. *Mem:* Founders Soc Detroit Inst Arts; Friends Mod Art; Arts Crafts Ctr Studies Alumni, Col Art & Design, Detroit, Mich, 91. *Media:* Watercolor; Bronze, Stone. *Mailing Add:* c/o Muccioli Studio Gallery 511 Beaubien Detroit MI 48266

MUCHNIC, SUZANNE
CRITIC, INSTRUCTOR
b Kearney, Nebr. *Study:* Scripps Col, BA, 62; Claremont Grad Sch, MA, 63. *Pos:* Ed, Artweek, Los Angeles, 77-78, contrib ed, 78-80; art critic & staff writer, Los Angeles Times, 78- *Teaching:* Instr art hist, Los Angeles City Col, 74-82; instr art criticism, Univ Southern Calif, 81 & Claremont Grad Sch, 83. *Awards:* Distinguished Alumna Award, Claremont Grad Sch, 82; Distinguished Alumna Award, Scripps Col, 87. *Mem:* Int Asn Art Critics; Art Table. *Res:* Contemporary art. *Publ:* Auth, exhibition catalogue essays on Tim Nordin, Martha Alf, Mark Lere, Paul Darrow & Barbara Strassen. *Mailing Add:* c/o Los Angeles Times Times Mirror Square Los Angeles CA 90053

MUDFORD, GRANT LEIGHTON
PHOTOGRAPHER
b Sydney, Australia, Mar 21, 44. *Study:* Univ New South Wales, Australia, 63-64. *Work:* Mus Mod Art, New York; Int Mus Photog, George Eastman House, Rochester, NY; Victoria & Albert Mus; Australian Nat Gallery, Canberra; Nat Mus Am Art, Washington, DC. *Comn:* Ten photog prints, Calif State Univ, Long Beach, 80 & CSR Ltd, Sydney, 81; Parliament House, Lewis comn, Canberra (under construct); Comprehensive Cancer Center Cedars-Sinai Medical Ctr, Los Angelas (under construction). *Exhib:* The Land: 20th Century Landscape Photographs, Victoria & Albert Mus, 75-76; solo exhib, Hirshhorn Mus & Sculpture Garden, 79; Long Beach: A Photographic Survey, Art Mus & Galleries, Calif State Univ, Long Beach, 80; Biennial Exhib, Whitney Mus Am Art, 81; Double Take: A Comparative Look at Photographs, Int Ctr Photography, New York, 81; Photography: A Sense of Order, Inst Contemp Art, Univ Pa, 81. *Teaching:* Instr, Art Ctr Sch Art & Design, Pasadena & Calif Inst Arts, Valencia. *Awards:* Nat Endowment Arts Photogr Fel, 80. *Bibliog:* Photographs by Grant Mudford, Interview Mag, 6/79; Celebrating the seldom-noticed, Los Angeles Times, 3/6/83; article, Artforum, summer 83; Availible Light, Mus Contemp Art, Los Angeles; Grant Mudford (auth), catalogue, Gallery Min, 86; California Photographers; catalogue, Gallery Min, 86. *Dealer:* Rosamund Felsen Gallery 669 N La Cienega Blvd Los Angeles CA 90069. *Mailing Add:* 5619 W Fourth St No 2 Los Angeles CA 90036

MUEHLEMANN, KATHY
PAINTER
b Feb 9, 50. *Study:* State Univ NY, BFA, 79. *Work:* Ackland Art Mus, Univ NC, Chapel Hill; Cleveland Mus, Ohio; Contemp Mus Art, Honolulu, Hawaii; Lannan Found, Los Angeles, Calif; Nelson-Atkins Mus Art, Kansas City, Mo. *Exhib:* Solo exhibs, Oscarsson Hood Gallery, New York, 84, Oscarsson Gallery, New York, 86 & Lannan Mus, Lake Worth, Fla, 88, Zabriski Gallery, New York, 89 & Nelson-Atkins Mus Art, Kansas City, Mo, 91, Contemp Mus Art, Honolulu, Hawaii, 91 & Pamela Auchincloss Gallery, New York, 91; Inspiration Comes from Nature, Jack Tilton Gallery, New York, 86; Works on Paper, Paul Cara Gallery, Philadelphia, Pa, 86; Stalking the Light, Noyes Mus, Oceanville, NJ, 87; The New Rigor, John Good Gallery, New York, 87; Am exhib, Am Acad Rome, Rome, Italy, 88; Prints from the Garner Tullis Workshop, Auchincloss Gallery, New York, 88; Black, Gray and White, Henry Feiwel, New York, 88; New Acquisitions, Cleveland Mus Art, Ohio, 89; Three Painters, Nina Freudenheim Gallery, Buffalo, NY, 90; New Generations, New York, Carnegie Mellon Art Gallery, Pittsburgh, Pa, 91;

Intimate Universe, Michael Walls Gallery, New York, 92; Contemporary Surfaces, Pamela Auchincloss Gallery, New York, 92. *Awards:* Prix De Rome, 87-88; Nat Endowment Arts Grant, 87-88. *Bibliog:* Stephen Westfall & Bonnie Clearwater (auths), Kathy Muehlemann (exhib catalog), 88; Peggy Moorman (auth), Starry nights, Kathy Muchlemann, Artnews, 11/90; Deborah Emont Scott (auth), Kathy Muehlemann (exhib catalog), Nelson-Atkins Mus Art, 91. *Mem:* Fel Am Acad, Rome. *Media:* Oil. *Dealer:* Pamela Auchincloss Gallery 558 Broadway 2nd Floor New York NY 10012. *Mailing Add:* 13-15 Laight St 6th Fl New York NY 10013

MUELLER, HENRIETTA WATERS
PAINTER, PRINTMAKER
b Pittsburgh, Pa, Apr 13, 15. *Study:* Art Inst Chicago, with Helen Gardner, BFA, 38, Univ Wyo, 49, Art Students League, with Will Barnet; Univ Colo, Boulder, with Wendell Black; Univ Wyo, with Ad Reinhardt & Ilya Bolotowsky; Santa Fe, NMex, Masters Art Prog, with Helen Frankenthaler, 90. *Work:* Joslyn Mus, Omaha, Nebr; New York Pub Libr, NY; William Rockhill Nelson Gallery, Kansas City, Mo; Mills Col Collection, New York; Univ Wash, Seattle. *Comn:* Stainless steel monument, Commemorative Wyo Women's Rights 1890-1970, Laramie, Wyo, 72. *Exhib:* Six shows, Print Club Philadelphia, Philadelphia Mus Art, 52-61; Western Art Ann, Denver Art Mus, 52-55; 22nd Drawing & Print Ann, San Francisco Mus Art, 58; Metrop Mus Art, New York, 60 & 61; Own Your Own Exhibs, Denver Art Mus, 67; 11th Art Ann, Pioneer Mus, Stockton, Calif, 71; solo exhib, Handworks, Boulder, Colo, 87, 88, 89 & 90. *Pos:* Lectr art hist, San Joaquin Delta Col, Stockton, Calif, 70-71. *Teaching:* Asst prof art & design, Univ Wyo, 50-61; asst prof art, Univ Nebr, 56-57; asst prof art, Univ Pac, Stockton, Calif, 70-71. *Awards:* Int Textile Exhib Award, Univ NC, Greensboro, 48; Wilson Daly Prize, 50 Ind Prints, John Herron Art Inst, Indianapolis, 52; Purchase Award, Univ Wyo Art Mus, 72 & 73; First prize painting, Ninth Ann Miniature Show, Laramie, Wyo, 84. *Mem:* Wyo Artists' Asn; Boulder Art Asn, Boulder, Colo, 89-90. *Media:* Oil, Watermedia. *Dealer:* Hassel-Haeseler Gallery Denver CO; One West Contemp Art Ctr Ft Collins CO. *Mailing Add:* 1309 Steele St Laramie WY 82070

MUELLER, (SISTER) M GERARDINE OP
CALLIGRAPHER, STAINED GLASS ARTIST
b Newark, NJ. *Study:* Caldwell Col, BA; Univ Notre Dame, MA & MFA, with A Lauck, W Otto, Berlin & Albinas Elskus; Inst Cult, Guadalajara, Mex; Fordham Univ; Columbia Univ. *Work:* Illumination, Newark Pub Libr. *Comn:* windows, Sisters Chapel, Caldwell, 62; six-panel mosaic mural, Caldwell Col, NJ, 70; windows, Puyo Cathedral, Ecuador, 77; Caldwell Col Chapel Windows, 82; Wall mural & glass panel, Dominican Sisters, Caldwell, NJ, 86; windows, extended care facility, Newark, 87; stained glass stations, 89, life-size sculptures, 90 & 92, Dominican Sisters, Caldwell. *Exhib:* Old Bergen Art Guild Tour, 79-86; NAm Calligraphers, Dallas, Tex, 74, Nat Miniature Art Soc, Fla, 75; Art by US Relig Women, Indianapolis, 81; Contemp Relig Art, Newark, 83-88; Barron Arts Ctr, Woodbridge, NJ, 86. *Pos:* mem, Archdiocese Comn Div Worship (art & archit), 74-77; dir art & design, Liturgy Convention, 81; ed bd, Word on Worship, currently. *Teaching:* Lectr lettering & crafts, Fordham Univ, 61; prof art, Caldwell Col, 63-, chmn art dept, 63-79, adj prof art, currently. *Awards:* Nat Cath Educ Asn Award (glass), 86. *Bibliog:* Articles in The New York Times, 11/77, New Jersey Music & Arts 12/77, Today's Art, 1/81, Newark Advocate, 10/81, Newark Star-Ledger, 11/81 & 1/86, Jersey J, 5/86, Suburban Life, 4/86 & New Community, Newark, 5/87. *Media:* Stained Glass, Illuminator. *Publ:* Auth, Yearbook production, Photolith Mag, 61; Art in Latin America & Art in Indian Mission of US, Cath Youth Encycl, McGraw-Hill, 62; New mosaic evolvement, Cath Fine Arts Soc, 68; contribr, Stained Glass Quart, summer 78. *Mailing Add:* Dept Art Caldwell Col Caldwell NJ 07006

MUELLER, TRUDE
SCULPTOR
Study: County Art Ctr, White Plains; Greenwich House, New York; New Sch Social Res, New York; with H Beling, Lu Duble, M Pascual & P Graussman, Montoya, Fla. *Work:* Palm Springs Desert Mus, Calif; Ben-Gurion Univ, Israel. *Exhib:* NY Univ, 68; Allied Artists Am, Nat Acad Gallery, New York, 68; Aritst-Craftsmen Am, Lever House, New York, 68-72 & 73; Bruce Mus, Conn, 74; Petits Formats des Maitres Contemporains, Chantilly, 75. *Pos:* Art therapist, Child Sch, New York, 73. *Bibliog:* Meditation, Beaux Arts, 65; R Stevens (auth), Aux Etats-Unis, La Revue Mod, Paris, 69; K Beals (auth), articles in Daily Times, Westchester. *Media:* Wood, Clay, Bronze. *Mailing Add:* 1200 S Flagler Dr West Palm Beach FL 33401

MUENCH, JOHN
PAINTER, PRINTMAKER
b Medford, Mass, Oct 15, 14. *Study:* Art Students League; Acad Julian, Paris; studied with Julian Levi. *Work:* Metrop Mus Art, New York; Victoria & Albert Mus, London; Bibliot Nat, Paris; Nat Collection & Smithsonian Inst, Washington, DC; Nat Mus, Jerusalem; and others. *Exhib:* One-man shows, Smithsonian Inst, Nat Collection Fine Arts, Philadelphia Art Alliance, Assoc Am Artists, New York, Rochester Mem Gallery, Bouidoin Col, Portland Mus Art, Payson Gallery Art & Farnsworth Mus, and many others; retrospective, Westbrook Col, Portland, Maine, 92; Included in over one hundred group shows including those at the Metrop Mus Art, NY, Am Acad & Nat Inst Arts & Letters, NY, Petit Palais, Paris, Bibliotheque Nationale, Paris, as well as shows in the Near East, Japan & numerous AFA Traveling Exhibs & Art for US Embassies. *Teaching:* Dir, Portland Sch Fine & Appl Arts, Maine, 58-65; assoc prof art, RI Sch Design, 65-77; artist-in-residence, Westbrook Col, Portland, Maine; dir, Maine Printmaking Workshop. *Awards:* John Taylor Arms Award, Nat Acad Design, 74; Special Award, Audubon Artists, 80; Leavin Award, Nat Acad Design, 83; and others. *Bibliog:* Clinton Adams (auth), American Lithographers, 1900-1960, The Artists and Their Printers, Univ NMex Press, 83; Susan Teller (auth), interview, 7/24/84; John Muench: Paintings & Prints 1950-1990, Maquoit Press, Freeport, Maine, 91. *Mem:* Soc Am Graphic Artists; Audubon Artists; Nat Acad Design. *Media:* Multimedia. *Publ:* Auth, The painter's guide to lithography, Northlight Press-Writers Digest, 83. *Dealer:* Assoc Am Artists 663 Fifth Ave New York NY 10019. *Mailing Add:* Box 262 South Freeport ME 04078

MUGAR, MARTIN GIENANDT
PAINTER
b Boston, Mass, Jan 23, 49. *Study:* Yale Univ, with William Bailey & Bernard Chaet, BA(cum laude), 71, with Al Held & Lester Johnson, MFA, 74. *Work:* Mass Inst Technol Mus, Cambridge; Boston Pub Libr, Mass; Fuller Mus, Brockton, Mass; Weatherspoon Art Gallery, Univ NC, Greensboro; Tufts Univ Mus, Medford, Mass. *Exhib:* Five Armenian American Artists, Mus Mod Art, Erevan, Armenia, 86; Southeastern Figurative Painters, Univ Hawaii Hilo, 86; one-man shows, Mass Inst Technol, Cambridge, 87, Hood Mus, Dartmouth, Hanover, NH, 88 & Bowery Gallery, New York, 91; Vision and Tradition, Morris Mus, Morristown, NJ, 87 & Colby Col, Waterville, Maine, 88; Contemporary Landscapes, Art Inst Boston, 91. *Teaching:* Asst prof painting, Univ NC, Greensboro, 80-86, Univ NH, Durham, 86-87, Dartmouth Col, Hanover, NH, 87-88 & Art Inst Boston, 88-92. *Awards:* John Courtney Murray Fel, Yale Univ, 71. *Bibliog:* Robert Taylor (auth), A lot to see at MIT, Boston Globe, 6/87; Charles Giuliano (auth), Rev, Art New Eng, 7/90; Philip Bragdon (auth), Mugar's new painting, Voice Am, 6/90. *Media:* All. *Mailing Add:* 97 Goodwin Rd Eliot ME 03903

MUHLBERGER, RICHARD CHARLES
WRITER, EDUCATOR
b Englewood, NJ, Jan 20, 38. *Study:* Calif Concordia Col, AA, 58; Wayne State Univ, BA(art hist), 64; Johns Hopkins Univ, Baltimore, MA(art hist), 67. *Pos:* Cur mus educ, Worcester Art Mus, Mass, 66-72; chmn educ, Detroit Inst Arts, 72-75; dir, Mus Fine Arts & George Walter Vincent Smith Art Mus, Springfield, Mass, 76-87; vice dir educ, Met Mus Art, 87-90; dir, Knoxville Mus Art, Tenn, 90-91. *Teaching:* Western New Eng Col, Springfield, Mass, 91- *Awards:* Woodrow Wilson Nat Fel, 65-67. *Mem:* Am Asn Mus; Asn Art Mus Dirs; New Eng Mus Asn (pres, 85-). *Res:* Dutch seventeenth century bird painters. *Publ:* The Bible in Art, The New Testament, 90 & The Bible in Art, The Old Testament, 91, Crown, New York; The Christmas Story, Harcourt Brace Javanowich, New York, 90; What Makes a Monet a Monet, et al (6 titles), Metrop Mus Art, NY, 92. *Mailing Add:* 49 Chestnut St Springfield MA 01103

MUHLERT, CHRISTOPHER LAYTON
PAINTER
b Brooklyn, NY, Mar 24, 33. *Study:* Case Western Reserve, BA, 64; Oberlin Col, MA, 66; Pratt Inst; Union Col; Cleveland Inst Art. *Work:* Cleveland Mus Art; Allen Mem Art Mus, Oberlin, Ohio; Phillip Morris Corp, Estate Joseph Hirshhorn, Washington, DC; Prudential Insurance Co, Merrillville, Ind; Brenton Bank of Cedar Rapids, Iowa; Alcon Lab, Fort Worth, Texas. *Exhib:* Black and White, Smithsonian Inst, 70-72; 19th Area Exhib, Corcoran Gallery Art, 74; two-person show, Barbara Fiedler Gallery, Washington, DC, 76; one-man shows, Davenport Munic Art Gallery, Iowa, 77, Barbara Fiedler Gallery, Washington, DC, 78, Carlin Gallery, Ft Worth, 83 & Graham Gallery, Houston, Tex, 84, Moudy Art Gallery, Texas Christian Univ, 87, William Campbell Contemp Art, 87-90. *Pos:* Preparator, Cleveland Mus Art, 60-64. *Teaching:* Instr design & painting, Oberlin Col, 66-68; instr found, Corcoran Sch Art, 70, asst prof drawing & design, 71-75. *Media:* Acrylic, Miscellaneous. *Dealer:* William Campbell Contemporary Art Ft Worth TX. *Mailing Add:* 3825 Clarke Ft Worth TX 76107

MUHLERT, JAN KEENE
MUSEUM DIRECTOR, HISTORIAN
b Oak Park, Ill, Oct 4, 42. *Study:* Neuchatel Univ; Inst European Studies, Paris; Sorbonne, with Andre Chastel; Inst de Phonetique; Acad Grande Chaumiere, 62-63; Albion Col, BA, 64; Oberlin Col, with Ellen H Johnson & Wolfgang Stechow, MA, 67. *Collections Arranged:* H Lyman Sayen (with catalog), Nat Collection Fine Arts, 70, Romaine Brooks, Thief of Souls (with catalog), 71 & William H Johnson 1901-1970 (with catalog), 71; The Ninth Level: Funerary Art from Ancient Meso America (with catalog), 78 & African Sculpture, The Stanley Collection (with catalog), 79, Mus of Art Univ Iowa. *Pos:* Asst cur collections, Allen Mem Art Mus, Oberlin Col, 66-68; asst cur contemp art, Nat Col Fine Arts, 68-73, assoc cur 20th century paintings & sculpture, 74-75; dir, Mus Art, Univ Iowa, 75-79; dir, Amon Carter Mus, Ft Worth, Tex, 80- *Awards:* Grant, Asn Art Mus Dir, 79. *Mem:* Asn Art Mus Dir; Am Asn Mus; Am Arts Alliance. *Res:* Charcoal drawings, 1900-1940; Arthur G Dove, 1880-1946. *Publ:* Contribr, An Exhibition of Paintings, Bozzetti and Drawings by Baciccio (catalog), Oberlin Col, 67; coauth, Tribute to Mark Tobey (catalog), Nat Collection Fine Arts, 74; contrib, Mauricio Lasansky, A Retrospective Exhibition, Univ Iowa, 76; contrib, American Paintings Selections from the Amon Carter Mus, 86. *Mailing Add:* Amon Carter Mus PO Box 2365 Ft Worth TX 76113

MUIR, EMILY LANSINGH
PAINTER, SCULPTOR
b Chicago, Ill. *Study:* Art Students League, with Richard Lahey & Leo Lentelli; Univ Maine, LHD, 69. *Work:* Brooklyn Mus; Univ Maine; Margaret Chase Smith Libr. *Comn:* Designs & contracting of contemp summer & year round homes, mosaics & interior design, portraits and portrait busts for pvt owners. *Exhib:* Int Watercolor Soc; Maine Art Gallery; Univ Maine;

Farnsworth Mus Art. *Pos:* appointee, Nat Comn Fine Arts, 55-59. *Teaching:* Lectr art, Asn Am Cols, 50-60. *Awards:* Outstanding Achievement in Commercial Venture, Contrib to Visual Arts, Maine Comt Skowhegan Sch, 72; Design Int Woman of Yr; Award in Archit, Maine Women in the Arts; Maine Woman of Yr, Westbrook Col. *Bibliog:* Martin Dibner (auth), People of the Maine Coast, Doubleday; William Caldwell (auth), article in Portland Press Herald; J R Wiggins (auth), article in Bangor Daily News; and others. *Mem:* Deer Isle Artists. *Media:* Oil, Mosaic; Clay, Wood. *Publ:* Auth, Small Potatoes, Scribner, 40. *Mailing Add:* Muir Studios Stonington ME 04681

MULCAHY, KATHLEEN
GLASS ARTIST, SCULPTOR
b Newark, NJ, June 23, 50. *Study:* Kean Col NJ, Union, BA, 72; Alfred Univ, NY, MFA, 74. *Work:* Corning Mus Glass, NY; pvt collections, Westmoreland Co Mus Art, Pa. *Comn:* Illuminated Glass Wall: Light Rail Transit, City Pittsburgh, 85 & Honor Room, RODEF, Shalom Congregation, 91. *Exhib:* Corning Mus Glass Int Rev, 83 & 87; Glass Nat, Heller Gallery, New York, 83; New American Glass: Focus 2 West Virginia, Huntington Galleries, 86; one-person exhib, Snyderman Gallery, Philadelphia, Pa, 86 & Kimzey Miller, 90; Clifford Gallery, Pittsburgh Ctr Arts, 88; Crafts Today/USA traveling exhib, Am Crafts Coun, 89-92; Ruth Volid Gallery, Chicago, 89; Vesperman Galleries, Atlanta, 92; Glass Gallery, Bethesda, Md, 93; and others. *Teaching:* Dir & assoc prof art, Glass Sculpture Prog, Carnegie-Mellon Univ, Pittsburgh, 76-89; artist-in-residence, Haystack Mt Sch Crafts, summer, 79 & 83, Artpark, Lewiston, NY, summer, 80; lectr, Portcon Glass Conf, 82 & 83. *Awards:* Visual Arts Fel, Pa Coun Arts, 81, 83; Lusk Fel, Fulbright, 84; Artist of the Year, Pittsburgh Ctr Arts, 92; and others. *Bibliog:* Donald Miller (auth), A touch of glass, Pittsburgh Post Gazette, 91; Jack Etzel (dir), Artist of the Year, Channel 11, 92; Patricia Lowry (auth), Artist of the Year Gives New Twist to Glass, Pittsburgh Press, 92; Donald Miller (auth), Mulcahy's 'Vapors' a breath of artistry, Pittsburgh Post Gazette, 92; Harry Schwalb (auth), Center stage, Pittsburgh Mag, 92; and many others. *Mem:* Glass Art Soc (bd dirs, 86-90); Am Crafts Coun; Chartiers Valley Arts Coun, (bd dirs, 90). *Media:* Glass, Sculpture; Mixed Media. *Publ:* Profile, Glass Studio Mag, 11/81. *Mailing Add:* RD#3, Box 3AD, Whittental Oakdale PA 15213

MULHERN, MICHAEL
PAINTER
b Paisley, Scotland. *Study:* Newark Sch Fine & Indus Arts, Newark, NJ; Brooklyn Mus Sch, NY; Sch of Visual Arts, New York. *Exhib:* Group shows, Brata Gallery, 61, Duane Street Gallery, 70, Alan Stone Gallery, 81, Allan Frumkin Gallery, 83, YU/USA Cork Gallery, 84 & Merrill Hall Gallery, New York, 85, Klein Gallery, Chicago, 86, Sorkin Gallery, New York, 87, The Drawing Center, New York, 88, Pratt-Manhattan Gallery, New York, 89, Art in General, New York, 89; one-person shows, Duane Street Gallery, 70, Adam Gimbel Gallery, 81, Exit Art Gallery, 85 & Stephen Rosenberg Gallery, New York, 88 & 90. *Awards:* Fel Grant, Nat Endowment Arts, 87; Painting Grant, Pollock-Krasner Found Inc, 89. *Bibliog:* Claude LeSeur (auth), An inter-continental melange of talents, Artspeak, 3/84; Grace Glueck (auth), Outline, cutout, silhouette, New York Times, 7/19/85; Elaine King (auth), Abstraction/abstraction, Dialogue: An Art Journal, 3/86; Barry Schwabsky (auth), Abstraction & Its Double: Transformations within the Constructive Mode, Arts, 9/86; Mary Sherman (auth), Is Abstract Coming Back?, Chicago Reader, 7/86. *Media:* Acrylic, Oil. *Mailing Add:* 125 Cedar St 9N New York NY 10006

MULLARKEY, MAUREEN
PAINTER, CRITIC
b New York, NY, Nov 10, 42. *Study:* Col of New Rochelle, BA, 64; Boston Univ, MFA, 68; Art Student League with Gabriel Laderman, 74-75. *Work:* Markston Investments, New York; many pvt collections. *Comn:* Pencil drawings, Parnassus: Poetry in Review, spring/summer 86; portrait, comn by Mr & Mrs John Gallagher, Bradford, NY, 87. *Exhib:* Mus of Hudson Highlands, 84; Ninth Ann Small Works, NY Univ, 85; Costumes-Masks & Disquises, Clock Tower, New York, 86; Working in Brooklyn, Brooklyn Mus, NY, 87; Works on Paper, Trenton City Mus, NJ, 89; Biannual Exhib, Nat Acad Design, New York, 90. *Pos:* Art critic & ed, Hudson Review, NY, 86-87; arts commentator, Nation, NY Times, Commonwealth, Hudson Review, J of Artists Choice Mus & Women's Art J, 80- *Bibliog:* Jack Newfield (auth), A case of censorship, Village Voice, 10/29/85. *Mem:* Col Art Asn; Nat Asn Women Artist. *Media:* Oil on Canvas, Pencil. *Publ:* Auth, Nude: politics & sensibility, New York Times, 8/29/85; Tuesday at the Met, summer 87, The figure and how it fared, winter 87, Hudson Review; Review of women art & power, Nation, 88; Analysis of Lois Dodd, Arts Mag, 90. *Dealer:* First Street Gallery 560 Broadway New York NY 10012. *Mailing Add:* c/o First Street Gallery 580 Broadway No 402 New York NY 10012

MULLEN, JAMES MARTIN
EDUCATOR, PRINTMAKER
b Altoona, Pa, May 14, 35. *Study:* Pa State Univ, BA, 57, MA, 63. *Work:* NJ State Mus, Trenton; Portsmouth Va Mus; Everson Mus, Syracuse, NY; Pa State Univ, Univ Park; Pushkin Mus, USSR. *Exhib:* Am Drawings III, Portsmouth Arts Ctr, Va, 80; World Print III, San Francisco Mus Mod Art, 80; 5th Nat Print, Honolulu Acad Art, Hawaii, 80; Small Works, Wash Square Gallery, New York Univ, 80; Silvermine Guild Prints, New Cannann, Conn, 80. *Pos:* Gallery dir, State Univ Col, Oneonta, NY, 76- *Teaching:* Prof art, State Univ Col, Oneonta, NY, 63- *Awards:* Chancellor's Award for Teaching Excellence, State Univ NY, 73; Chaning Hare Award, Soc Four Arts, Palm Beach, Fla. *Mem:* Soc Am Graphic Artist; Am Color Print Soc; Cooperstown Art Asn. *Publ:* Auth, Subject matter, 66 & Student work, 69, Sch Arts Mag. *Dealer:* Miriam Perlman Inc Lake Point Tower Suite 1902 505 N Lakeshore Dr Chicago IL 60611. *Mailing Add:* Dept Art SUNY Col at Oneonta Oneonta NY 13820

MULLEN, JO (STAUFFER)
PAINTER, PRINTMAKER
b Philadelphia, Pa, April 26, 08. *Study:* Art Students League, 47-50; Wellesley Col, BA 29. *Work:* Metrop Mus Print Col, New York; Cleveland Mus Print Col, Ohio; Philadelphia Mus Art, Pa. *Exhib:* Art Students League 75th, Nat Acad, New York, 50; Pa Acad Ann, Philadelphia, Pa, 53; invitational solo show, Philadelphia Art Alliance, 56; Conn Acad Annuals, Wadsworth Atheneum, Hartford, 62 & 63; Salute to Seniors, Chester Co Art Asn, West Chester, Pa, 88-92; 8th Ann Invitational, Chester Co Art Asn, 92. *Awards:* Jill Jones Prize for Graphics, Chester Co Art Asn, 86 & 92. *Mem:* Del Ctr Contemp Arts; Nat Asn Women Artists; Chester Co Art Asn. *Media:* Oil. *Dealer:* Artworks 121 E State St Kennett Square Pa 19348. *Mailing Add:* 123 Kendal Kennett Square PA 19348

MULLEN, PHILIP EDWARD
PAINTER, EDUCATOR
b Akron, Ohio, Oct 10, 42. *Study:* Univ Minn, BA; Univ NDak, MA; Ohio Univ, PhD. *Work:* Guggenheim Mus, New York; Brooklyn Mus; Palm Springs Desert Mus; Denver Mus. *Exhib:* Biennial, Contemporary Am Art, Whitney Mus Am Art, New York, 75; Smithsonian Inst Traveling Exhib; and many others. *Teaching:* Prof, Univ SC, currently. *Bibliog:* Arts Mag, 2/76, 11/78, 3/82, 10/83 & 9/85; Art Voices S, 4/80; Art Am, 1/84; Artist's Mag, 4/85, 12/89, 5/90 & 6/91. *Media:* Acrylic. *Dealer:* David Findlay Galleries 984 Madison Ave New York NY 10021; Dubins Gallery 11948 San Vicente Blvd Los Angeles CA 90049. *Mailing Add:* Dept Art Univ SC Columbia SC 29208

MULLER, HELEN B
PAINTER, GALLERY DIRECTOR
b Mansfield, Ohio, June 28, 22. *Study:* Ohio State Univ, BFA, 44; Univ Mich; Adelphi Univ, NY Univ, MA, 65. *Work:* Southampton Hosp, NY. *Exhib:* Biblical Batik Genesison, De Andreis Gallery, St Johns Univ & Leidy Gallery Guild Hall Mus, East Hampton, 74; solo shows, Firehouse Gallery, Nassau Community Col, 79, Biblical Batik, Cathedral Church St Paul, Burlington, Vt, 79, People, Elaine Benson Gallery, 79 & Gallery 84, New York, 83, 85, 87 88, 91 & 93. *Pos:* Gallery dir, Firehouse Gallery, Nassau Community Col, 63-84. *Teaching:* Prof Art, Nassau Community Col, 63-84. *Mem:* Aquarelle (pres, 63); Nassau Co Coun Art Mus (pres, 73); Nat Sculpture Soc (bd mem, 92-); Parrish Art Mus, Southampton, NY (trustee, 89-). *Media:* Batik Painting, Watercolor Wax Resist. *Mailing Add:* Paul's Lane PO Box 455 Bridgehampton NY 11932

MULLER, JEROME KENNETH
COLLECTOR, PAINTER
b Amityville, NY, July 18, 34. *Study:* NY Univ; Marquette Univ, BS; Layton Sch Art; Brandt Painting Workshop; Calif State Univ, Fullerton; Nat Univ, MA; Newport Psychoanalytic Inst. *Exhib:* Souk Gallery, Newport Beach, Calif, 70; Gallery 2, Santa Ana, 71; Cannery Gallery, Newport Beach, Calif, 74; Mus Graphics Gallery, Costa Mesa, Calif, 92. *Collections Arranged:* Cartoon Show, Original Works by 100 Outstanding American Cartoonists, Laguna Beach Mus Art, Calif, 72, Bowers Mus, Santa Ana, Calif, 76, E B Crocker Art Gallery, Sacramento, Calif, 77, Indianapolis Mus Art, Ind, 77, Tweed Mus Art, Duluth, Minn, 78, Everson Mus Art, Syracuse, NY, 78, Montgomery Mus Fine Arts, Ala, 78, South Bend Art Ctr, Ind, 79, Mem Art Gallery, Univ Rochester, 79, Neville Pub Mus, Wis, 79; Mickey Mouse: 1928-1978 (cur), Bowers Mus, 78; The Moving Image, art used in animated films, San Jose Mus Art, Calif, 80, Cooper-Hewitt Mus, New York, 81 & Nelson Gallery Art, Kansas City, 81; The Engravings of William Hogarth, Bowers Mus, 81; The American Comic Strip, Univ Tex, Arlington, 81, Univ Chicago, 83, Wichita Art Mus, Kans, 84 & Monterey Peninsula Mus Art, Calif, 85. *Pos:* Photogr, New York, 53-56; art dir, Orange Co Illustrated, 62-68, art ed, 70-79; dir, Mus Graphics, 79- *Teaching:* Instr photog, Lindenhurst High Sch, NY, 53-54; instr, The Cartoon & the Comic Strip in Am, Univ Calif, Irvine, 79. *Awards:* Two Silver Medals, 20th Ann Exhib of Advert & Ed Art in the West, Los Angeles Art Dir Club, 64; Award of Merit, Illustration West, Los Angeles Illusr Club, 72-74. *Bibliog:* Steven Parker (auth), Comics are collectible, Acquire Mag, 7/77; and others. *Mem:* Int Animated Film Soc; Art Mus Asn. *Media:* Oil. *Collection:* Cartoons, comic art and original animation art, exhibited regularly in major museums throughout America. *Publ:* Auth, It's Rex Brandt, 10/73 & The comics: worth a second look, 11/73, SW Art; contribr, Mark Rothko, 74 & The Artist as Collector, 75, Newport Harbor Art Mus, Newport Beach, Calif; Arts of Oceania, Shells of Oceania, Bowers Mus, 75. *Mailing Add:* Box 10743 Costa Mesa CA 92627

MULLER, MAX PAUL
PAINTER, ART DEALER
b Dover, NJ, Sept 26, 35. *Study:* WVa Wesleyan, BA, 57; studied with Frank Webb, Valfred Thëlin & Fred Messersmith. *Comn:* Six paintings, comn by Dr Jack Corn, Sarasota, Fla, 89; two paintings, Handicapped Children's Ctr, Sarasota, 90. *Exhib:* NJ Watercolor Soc, Morris Mus, Morristown, 75; Orange Co Arts Coun, Trotter Mus, Goshen, NY, 78; Southwest Watercolorists V, DeLand Mus, Fla, 88; Fla Watercolor Soc, Rollins Col Mus, Winter Park, 89; Grand Nat Watercolor Exhib, Miss Mus Art, Jackson, 90. *Pos:* Pres, M P Muller Gallery, Sarasota, Fla, 89- & Art Uptown Gallery, Sarasota, 90-; mem bd dirs & exhib chmn, Sarasota Art Asn, Fla, 90. *Teaching:* Instr watercolor, Sarasota Art Asn, 90-91, Leach Studios, Sarasota, Fla, 91-; instr, Ringling Sch Art, currently. *Awards:* Best of Show, WVa Wesleyan Art Exhib, 57; Award of Merit, Orange Co Arts Coun, 78; Grumbacher Silver Medal, Sarasota Art Asn, 89. *Bibliog:* Joan Altabe (rev), article, Sarasota Herald Tribune, 89; Srotff (auth), Profile, Sarasota Mag, 90; article, Artists Fla Mag, Vol II, Mountain Productions Inc, 90. *Mem:* Am Watercolor Soc; Fla Watercolor Soc; Miami Watercolor Soc; Fla Artists Group; Int Soc Marine Painters. *Media:* Watercolor, Oil. *Specialty:* Original art; contemporary American artists. *Mailing Add:* 6902 Stetson St Circle Sarasota FL 34243

MULLER, PRISCILLA ELKOW
ART HISTORIAN, CURATOR
b New York, NY, Feb 15, 30. *Study:* Brooklyn Col, BA, 50; New York Univ, Inst Fine Arts, MA, 59, PhD, 63. *Pos:* Asst cur, Hispanic Soc Am, 64-68, cur paintings & metalwork, 68-, cur mus, 70-; consult, Time-Life Bks, 68-69, Tree Publ, 81-82; adv bd, Archivo Espanol de Arte. *Teaching:* Lectr, Brooklyn Col, 66. *Awards:* Fel Nat Endowment Arts, 77; Hispanic Soc Am; Real Acad de Ciencias, Bellas Letras y Nobles Artes de Cordoba; and others. *Mem:* Am Soc Hispanic Art Hist Studies; Int Comt Fine Arts; Int Coun Mus; Soc Jewelry Historians; Int Found Art Res; and others. *Res:* Spanish and Hispanic fine arts, 15th-20th centuries. *Publ:* Auth, The Drawings of Antonio del Castillo y Saavedra, Ann Arbor, 64; contribr, Francisco Goya's Portraits in Paintings, Prints and Drawings, Richmond, 72; auth, Jewels in Spain 1500-1800, New York, 72; Goya's Black Paintings, Truth and Reason in Light and Liberty, New York, 84; and numerous articles in art-hist periodicals. *Mailing Add:* Hispanic Soc Am Mus Broadway & 155th St New York NY 10032

MULLICAN, LEE
PAINTER, EDUCATOR
b Chickasha, Okla, Dec 2, 19. *Study:* Abilene Christian Col; Univ Okla; Kansas City Art Inst, with Fletcher Martin, dipl; San Francisco Art Inst, study with Stanley Hayter. *Work:* San Francisco Mus Art; Phillips Mem Gallery, Washington, DC; Santa Fe Art Mus, NMex; Santa Barbara Mus Art, Calif; Mus Mod Art, New York; Oklahoma Art Ctr, Oklahoma City; Univ Calif, Los Angeles; New Orleans Mus Art, La. *Exhib:* Pa Acad Fine Arts, Philadelphia, 68; one-man shows, Museo Nac Bellas Artes, Santiago, Chile, 68, UCLA Art Galleries, 69, Santa Barbara Mus Art, 73 & 76, Herbert Palmer Gallery, Los Angeles, 85 & 89 & Santa Monica Heritage Mus, 89; The Artists Collects, Newport Harbor Mus Art, 75; Five Footnotes to Art History, Los Angeles Co Mus Art, 77; retrospective exhib, Municipal Art Gallery, Barnsdale Park, Los Angeles, 80; Herbert Palmer Gallery, Los Angeles, 85; Surrealism in California, Fischer Gallery, Univ Southern Calif, 85; Moderns in Mind (with G Onslow & Gerome Kamrowski), Artists Space, New York, 86; Fenix Gallery, Taos, NMex; Johnson Gallery, Univ Mus, Albuquerque, 89; Turning the Tide, Laguna Art Mus, Calif, 90. *Collections Arranged:* Los Angeles Collects Folk Art, Craft & Folk Art Mus, Los Angeles, 77; Neo-Tantra Exhib Contemp Art from India, Wight Art Galleries, Univ Calif, Los Angeles; Visions of Inner Space, Contemporary American Painting, Wight Art Galleryies, Univ Calif, Los Angeles, 87 & Nat Gallery Mod Art, New Delhi, India, 88; Assemblage, Corcoran Gallery, Santa Monica, 88. *Teaching:* Prof painting & drawing, Univ Calif, Los Angeles, 62-86. *Awards:* Guggenheim Fel, 59; Award, Inst Creative Arts, Univ Calif, 63; Tamarind Fel, 64-65. *Bibliog:* Wolfgang Paalen & G Onslow Ford (auth), Dynaton, San Francisco Mus Art, 51; Langsner (auth), Mullican paints a picture, Art News, 52; Fink Tuchman (auth), Three Footnotes to California Art History, Los Angeles Co Art Mus, 77. *Media:* Oil. *Dealer:* Herbert Palmer Gallery 802 N La Cienega Blvd Los Angeles CA 90069. *Mailing Add:* 370 Mesa Rd Santa Monica CA 90402

MUNCE, JAMES CHARLES
PRINTMAKER, DRAFTSMAN
b Sioux Falls, SDak, Aug 24, 38. *Study:* Minneapolis Sch Art, BFA, 66; Ind Univ, MFA, 71. *Work:* Brooklyn Mus, NY; Palace Legion Honor, San Francisco, Calif; Boston Printmakers, Mass; Univ Louisville, Ky; Mitsubishi Corp, Tokyo, Japan. *Exhib:* 38th Boston Printmakers, De Cordova Mus, Lincoln, Mass, 86; 39th Boston Printmakers, Danforth Mus, Framingham, Mass, 87; Nat Works on Paper, Univ Miss, 90; 5th Int Print Biennial, Taipei, Taiwan, 91; 35th Chautauqua Nat Exhib, NY, 92. *Teaching:* Instr prints, drawing, Univ Hawaii, Honolulu, 71-72; assoc prof prints, drawing, Kans State Univ, Manhattan, Kansas, 72- *Awards:* Van Derlip Award, Minneapolis Sch Art, 66; Prints & Drawing Fel, Mid Am Arts Alliance, 84; Purchase award, Boston Printmakers, 86; Chautauqua Inst Award, 92. *Bibliog:* Artists-A Kansas Collection, Rowley & Harper Artists Registry Inc. *Media:* Intaglio. *Dealer:* Strecker Gallery 332 Poyntz Manhattan KS 66502. *Mailing Add:* 1738 Fairchild Manhattan KS 66502

MUNDT, ERNEST KARL
SCULPTOR, EDUCATOR
b Bleicherode, Ger, Oct 30, 05; US citizen. *Study:* Berlin Inst Technol, dipl archit, 30; Univ Calif, PhD, 61. *Work:* San Francisco Mus Art. *Comn:* Steel sculpture, Westmoor High Sch, Daly City, Calif. *Exhib:* Detroit Inst Art, 44; San Francisco Mus Art, 46; Calif Palace of Legion of Honor, 49; Metrop Mus Art, 50; Whitney Mus Am Art, 51; plus others. *Pos:* Chmn dept art, Calif State Univ, San Francisco, 58-61. *Teaching:* Asst prof, Univ Mich, 41-44; instr, Brooklyn Col, 45-46; instr, Calif Sch Fine Art, 47-50, dir, 50-55; from asst prof to prof art, Calif State Univ, San Francisco, 55-76, emer prof, 76- *Awards:* Gold Medal Honor, Am Inst Archit, 56. *Media:* All. *Publ:* Auth & illusr, A Primer of Visual Art, 50; Art, Form, & Civilization, 52; Birth of a Cook, 56; contribr, Arts & Archit, Col Art J, Art Quart & J Aesthet Mags; and others. *Mailing Add:* 574 Congo St San Francisco CA 94131

MUNIOT, BARBARA KING
COLLECTOR
b New Orleans, La. *Study:* Sullins Col, Bristol, Va, art degree; Newcomb Col, spec study with Prof Franklin Adams. *Pos:* Asst dir, Orleans Gallery, 68-70, dir, 70-73; asst dir, Galerie Simonne Stern, 73-75, dir, 75-83. *Specialty:* Contemporary art. *Collection:* Paintings, drawings, prints, photographs & African art. *Mailing Add:* 3532 Laurel New Orleans LA 70115

MUNO, RICHARD CARL
SCULPTOR, DIRECTOR
b Arapaho, Okla, July 2, 39. *Study:* Okla State Univ Sch Tech Training, cert com art. *Work:* Diamond M Mus, Snyder, Tex. *Comn:* Sculpture of Cavalry Man and Horse, Winchester Firearms, Hartford, Conn, 68; Western Heritage Awards Wrangler Trophy, Nat Cowboy Hall Fame, Oklahoma City, 68; Sculpture of a Lawman, Colt Firearms, Hartford, 73; Sculpture of Cowboy Branding Calf, Oklahoma City CofC, 75; Lifesize Sculpture of Pioneer Man, Bicentennial Comn of Clinton, Okla, 75; Promenade (sq dancers), Oklahoma City Fairgrounds, 89; Memorial (figures & fountains), Edmond Post Off, Okla, 89; Young at Heart (Johnny Kelley figures), Boston Athletic Assoc, Newton, MA, 93. *Exhib:* Philbrook Mus Art Exhib, Tulsa, Okla, 67; Sci & Arts Found Exhib, Oklahoma City, 68; Oklahoma City Zoological Exhib, 68; Okla Mus Art Five State Salon, Oklahoma City, 71-72; Solon Borglum Mem Sculpture Exhib, Nat Cowboy Hall of Fame, Oklahoma City, 75. *Pos:* Preparator, Gilcrease Inst Am Hist & Art, Tulsa, 60-64; cur, Nat Cowboy Hall Fame, Oklahoma City, 65-69, art dir, 70-77, dep dir, 77-78, managing dir, 78-85. *Awards:* Numerous ribbons in various art shows. *Bibliog:* Marcia Preston(auth), Orbit Mag, Okla Publ Co, 68; Dean Krakel (auth), End of the Trail, Okla Univ Press, 73. *Media:* Bronze, Wood. *Collection:* Nat Acad Western Art Ann Exhibs, 73-75. *Publ:* Contribr, Persimmon Hill Mag, 72-75. *Mailing Add:* 6300 E Danforth Edmond OK 73034

MUÑOZ, CELIA ALVAREZ
PHOTOGRAPHER
b Aug 15, 37. *Study:* Univ Tex, El Paso, BA, 64; NTex State Univ, Denton, MFA, 82. *Work:* NMex State Univ, Las Cruces; Fed Reserve Bank, Dallas, Tex; Atlantic Richfield Co, Arco Ctr, Dallas, Tex; Sackner Archives, Los Angeles, Calif; Ctr Book Arts Archives, New York. *Exhib:* Solo exhibs, 30th Ann Invitational, Longview Mus & Arts Ctr, Postales, Bridge Ctr Contemp Arts, El Paso, 89, Rompiendo La Liga, Ctr Res Contemp Arts, Univ Tex, Arlington, 89 & New Langton Arts, San Francisco, Calif, 90, Celia Munoz, Mod Dallas Art & Paper Dolls and Patron Saints, Adair Margo Gallery, El Paso, 90, Abriendo Tierra, Breaking Ground, Dallas Mus Art & El Limite, San Diego Mus Contemp Art, La Jolla, 91 & Ctr Fine Arts, Miami, Fla, 92; Volumination: The Book as Art Object, Edwin A Ulrich Mus Art, Wichita State Univ, 92; Slouching Toward 2000: The Politics of Gender, Women & Their Work, Austin, Tex, 92; Gender: Fact or Fiction, Laguna Gloria Art Mus, Austin, Tex, 92; Si Colon Supiera--11 instalaciones efimeras, Museo de Monterrey, Mex, 92; The Return of the Cadavre Exquis, Drawing Ctr, New York, 93. *Teaching:* Visiting lectr, Sch Art Inst Chicago, Ill, 92. *Awards:* Grant, Nat Endowment Arts, 91-92. *Bibliog:* Lucy Lippard (auth), Slouching Towards 2000: The Politics of Gender, Women & Their Work, Austin, 92; Helen L Kohen (auth), rev, Miami Herald, 4/19/92; Janey Tyson (auth), rev, Ft Worth Star Telegram, 7/25/92. *Mailing Add:* 5815 Arbor Valley Dr Arlington TX 76016

MUNOZ, RIE
PAINTER, PRINTMAKER
b Los Angeles, Calif. *Study:* Washington & Lee Univ; Univ of Alaska; pvt lessons. *Work:* Alaska State Mus; Anchorage Hist & Fine Arts Mus; Gov Off, Alaska; Frye Mus, Seattle, Wash. *Comn:* Alaska Coun Churches Mural, Univ Alaska Libr, Fairbanks, 67; Reindeer Round-Up, Reindeer Serv Bur Indian Affairs, 68; Ethnic People of Alaska Mural, Alaska State Libr, Juneau, 69. *Exhib:* Anchorage Mus Fine Arts, 71 & 78; Alaska State Mus, Juneau, 71 & 76; Ketchikan Mus, Alaska, 72; Charles & Emma Frye Mus, Seattle, Wash, 73, 75 & 81; Contemp Art from Alaska, Smithsonian Inst, Washington, DC, 78. *Pos:* Political cartoonist, SE Alaska Empire, 52-67; cur exhib, Alaska State Mus, Juneau, 68-72. *Awards:* Outstanding Alaska Artist, Anchorage Fine Arts Mus Asn, 77. *Bibliog:* Article, Artist in Juneau captures Alaska, Alaska Log, 73; Yvonne Mozee (auth), An interview with Rie Munoz, Alaska J, 74; Yvonne Mozee (auth), Rie Munoz--the artist from Juneau who gets around, Alaska Woman, 77; Rie Munoz, Alaskan Artist, Alaska Northwest Publ Co, 84. *Media:* Water-Base Colors; Silkscreen and Stone Lithography. *Publ:* Illusr, Juneau & its development, Alaska Develop Bd, 56; Alaska Camp Cook Book, Alaska Northwest, 62; Alaska Mag, 62-67; auth & illusr, Nursing in Alaska 1867-1967, Alaska Nurses Asn, 67; illusr, Kahtatah, Alaska Northwest Publ, 76; Goodbye My Island, 83 & King Island Christmas, 85, Greenwillow Bks. *Mailing Add:* c/oFrame Design & Sunbird Gallery 916 NW Wall St Bend OR 97701

MUNRO, ELEANOR
WRITER, LECTURER
b Brooklyn, NY, Mar 28, 28. *Study:* Smith Col, BA, 49; Columbia Univ, MA, 65; Sorbonne, Paris. *Pos:* Assoc ed, Art News, New York, 53-59; managing ed, Art News Ann, New York, 54-59. *Teaching:* Multiple vis-lectureships at Am Schs & Cols, 89- *Awards:* Yaddo Fel, 84; Arts Prize, Cleveland, Ohio, 88; Woodrow Wilson Vis Fel, 89- *Mem:* Am Asn Art Critics; Int Asn Art Critics; Authors Guild; Women's Caucus Art; PEN Am; Art Table, Inc. *Res:* American women artists; imagination and the creative process in the visual arts; pilgrimage in myth and art. *Publ:* Auth, Encyclop Art, Western Printing, 61; Originals: American Women Artists, Simon & Schuster, 79 & Touchstone Press, 82; On Glory Roads, Thames & Hudson, 87; Memoir of a Modernist's Daughter, Viking, 88; Art in America: Essays by contemp Soviet and Am writers, Univ Wash Press, 90; and auth of essays, articles & reviews in collections, national magazines & newspapers. *Mailing Add:* 1095 Park Ave New York NY 10028

MUNRO, JANET ANDREA
PAINTER
b North Reading, Mass, Dec 8, 49. *Study:* Self-taught artist. *Work:* The White House & Smithsonian Inst, Washington, DC; Am Mus, Bath, Eng; Jay Johnson Am Folk Heritage Gallery, New York; and others. *Exhib:* One-woman shows, Country Art Gallery, Locust Valley, NY, 80, Fowler Mills Galleries, Santa Monica, Calif, 80, Art World Gallery, Acton, Mass, 80-81 & Americas Folk Heritage Gallery, New York, 81; Easter Egg Roll, White House, Washington, DC, 81; and others. *Bibliog:* Carolyn Norwood (auth), Mrs Munro paints for the White House, Islander Weekly, 81; Kevin Dean (auth), Mrs Munro, Art Voices, 11-12/81; Contemporary primitives, Colonial Homes Mag, 1-2/82. *Media:* Oil, Egg Tempera. *Mailing Add:* c/o Gallery 53 Artworks 118 Main St Cooperstown NY 13326

MUNSTERBERG, HUGO
HISTORIAN, EDUCATOR
b Berlin, Ger, Sept 13, 16; US citizen. *Study:* Harvard Col, AB, 38, Harvard Univ, PhD, 41. *Pos:* Art critic, Arts Mag, 57-60. *Teaching:* Asst prof fine arts, Mich State Univ, 46-49, assoc prof, 49-52; prof art hist, Int Christian Univ, Tokyo, 52-56; prof art hist, State Univ NY Col New Paltz, 58-78, chmn dept, 68-78; vis lectr, Bard Col & Parsons Sch Design, 79-91. *Mem:* Oriental Ceramic Soc London; Japan Soc. *Res:* Oriental art, China and Japan. *Collection:* Oriental art, especially ceramics. *Publ:* Auth, The Sculpture of the Orient, Dover, 72; auth, A History of Women Artists, 75; auth, The Modern Art of Japan, 78; contribr, Dictionary of Chinese and Japanese Art, 81; auth, Japanese Prints, 82; and others. *Mailing Add:* 48 Elting Ave New Paltz NY 12561

MUNZNER, ARIBERT
PAINTER, EDUCATOR
b Mannheim, Ger, Jan 9, 30. *Study:* Syracuse Univ, BFA; Cranbrook Acad Art, MFA. *Exhib:* Nat & regional shows, 53-63. *Teaching:* Instr painting & design, Minneapolis Sch Art, 55-68, assoc prof painting, Div Fine Arts, 68- *Mailing Add:* 2749 Bryant Ave S Minneapolis MN 55408

MURAKISHI, STEVE
PRINTMAKING, SCULPTOR
b Honolulu, Hawaii, 1949. *Study:* Mich State Univ, E Lansing, BFA(sculpture), 72; Cent Mich Univ, Mt Pleasant, MA(printmaking),79; Univ Mich, Ann Arbor, MFA(printmaking), 81. *Work:* Mint Mus, Charlotte, NC; Brooklyn Mus, NY; Va Mus Fine Art, Richmond; Detroit Inst Art, Mich; Newport Harbor Mus Art, Newport Beach, Calif. *Exhib:* Assembled Object, Mich Coun Arts Gallery, Detroit, 89; Engines of Perception, Slusser Art Gallery, Univ Mich, Ann Arbor, 90; Cranbrook Acad Art Mus, Bloomfield Hills, Mich, 90; L'Amour Fou, Banff Ctr, Alberta, Can; A Question of Purity, Hoffman Gallery, Ore Sch Arts & Crafts, Portland, 92. *Pos:* Head printmaking dept, Cranbrook Acad Art, Bloomfield Hills, Mich, 82- *Teaching:* Instr, Toledo Mus Art Sch, Ohio, 81; instr, Univ Mich, Ann Arbor, 84, Mich State Univ, E Lansing, 90. *Awards:* Visual Artists Fel Grant, Workson Paper, Nat Endowment Arts, 89. *Mailing Add:* c/o Cranbrook Acad Arts 500 Lone Pine Rd, Box 801 Bloomfield Hills MI 48303-0801

MURANAKA, HIDEO
PAINTER, PRINTMAKER
b Mitaka-shi, Tokyo, Japan, Feb 4, 46, nat US. *Study:* Tokyo Nat Univ Fine Arts & Music, BFA, 70, MFA, 72, cert, 74. *Work:* Brooklyn Mus; Achenbach Found, Calif Palace Legion Hon. *Exhib:* One Hundred New Acquisitions, Brooklyn Mus, 78; Pacific Coast States Collection From the Vice President's House, Nat Mus Am Art, 81; IEEE Centennial Art Contest, New York, 83; Am Drawing Biennial, Muscarelle Mus Art, 88; Grand Prix de France Int, Chapelle de la Sorbonne, Paris Mus, France, 90. *Teaching:* Instr sumie, Acad Art Col, San Francisco, 74-75 & 84; teacher sumie & calligraphy, Acad Muranaka, San Francisco, 76-79. *Awards:* Purchase Prizes, Wesleyan Int Exhib Prints & Drawings, 80, Mid-Am Biennial, Owensboro Mus Fine Art, 82; Second Prize, Museo Hosio, Capranica-Viterbo, Italy, 84, first prize, 88; Hon Mention, San Bernardino County Mus, Redland, Calif, 85. *Bibliog:* Tom Kent (auth), Visuals, City, 5/14/75; Thomas Albright (auth), Art, San Francisco Chronicle, 5/14/75. *Media:* All. *Mailing Add:* 179 Oak St No W San Francisco CA 94102

MURASHIMA, KUMIKO
EDUCATOR, TAPESTRY ARTIST
b Nishinomiya, Japan. *Study:* Women's Col Fine Arts, Tokyo, BFA(textiles), 63; Serizawa Dyed Paper Inst, Tokyo, 63-67; Ind Univ, Bloomington, MFA(textiles), 70. *Work:* Evansville Mus Arts & Sci, Ind; Wills Eye Hosp, Philadelphia; Flour Corp Hq, Irvine, Calif; Hackensack Med Ctr, NJ; North Am Re-Insurance Co, New York; Chubb Insurance Corp Hq, NJ; Caxton Commodities, Princeton, NJ; AT&T Telecommuns, NJ; Marck, Sharpe & Dorne, Penn. *Comn:* Metrop design, Properties Inc, Birmingham, Ala; mural (woven tapestry), Disneyland Hotel Convention Ctr, Anaheim, Calif. *Exhib:* NJ State Mus, 78; Artists Equity Triennial Juried Exhib, Mus Philadelphia, Civic Ctr, 81; Oriental Influence in Contemp Am Crafts, The Craftman's Gallery, Scarsdale, NY, 81; Fairmount Inst, Philadelphia, 82; Henry Chauncey Conf Ctr, ETS, Princeton, NJ, 86; Pavillion Galleries, Mt Holly, NJ. *Pos:* Freelance fiber artist, Izumi Archit Design, Co, Tokyo, 65-67 & Saphier, Lerner, Schindler, Inc, Environetics, Chicago, Ill, 7-71. *Teaching:* Instr fiber art, Glassboro State Col, 71-75, asst prof, 75-82, assoc prof, 82- *Awards:* Purchase Award, Mid-States Crafts Show, Malcolm Koch Mus, 69; Mr & Mrs Paul Arnold Merit Award, Mid-States Crafts Show, 70. *Bibliog:* Dona Meilach (auth), Art Fabric: Form/Design, Crown Publ, 77; Eva Balassa (auth), article, Fibre Arts, 1-2/79; Burton Wasserman (auth), article, Artcrafts Mag, 8-9/80. *Mem:* Am Crafts Coun; Handweaver's Guilds Am; Am Asn Univ Women; Surface Design Asn; NJ Designer-Craftsmen Inc. *Publ:* Contribr, Pamela Scheiman's American Crafts, Am Crafts Coun, 78; Courier Post, Gloucester Times, Philadelphia Inquirer & Philadelphia Bull. *Dealer:* Dumont-Landis Fine Arts New Brunswick NJ; Faviana-Olivie-Galleria Manhattan Beach CA. *Mailing Add:* PO Box 515 Williamstown NJ 08094

MURATA, HIROSHI
PAINTER, PRINTMAKER
b Tokyo, Japan, Jan 18, 41. *Study:* RI Sch Design, BFA, 64; Yale Univ Sch Art, MFA, 66. *Work:* Larry Aldrich Mus Contemp Art, Ridgefield, Conn; Tokyo Univ Col Art; Nat Mus Mod Art, Kyoto; Nat Mus Mod Art, Tokyo; Kamakura Mus Mod Art, Japan. *Exhib:* Made with Paper Exhib, Mus Contemp Crafts, NY, 67; 17th Nat Print Exhib, Brooklyn Mus, 70; Contemporary Reflections, 71-72; Aldrich Mus, 72; Japanese Artists in the Americas, Nat Mus Mod Art, Tokyo & Kyoto, 73-74; Biennial Contemp Am Art, Whitney Mus, 75. *Teaching:* Asst prof art, Western Mich Univ, 66-70; from asst prof to assoc prof art, Trenton State Col, 72- *Awards:* Creative Arts Artists Pub Serv Grant, NY State Coun Arts, 72-73; Nat Endowment Arts Grant, 75-76. *Media:* Acrylic on Canvas; Silkscreen, Lithography. *Publ:* Illusr, Asahi J, 69 & Shincho-Sha Publ, 70. *Dealer:* Donna Schneier Inc E 71st St New York NY 10021. *Mailing Add:* c/o Rabbet Gallery 120 Georges St New Brunswick NJ 08901

MURCH, ANNA VALENTINA
CONCEPTUAL ARTIST, ENVIRONMENTAL ARTIST
b Dunbarton, Scotland, Dec 7, 48. *Study:* Leicester Polytech, BA, 71; Royal Col Art, London, MA, 73; Archit Asn, London, dipl, 74. *Comn:* If Wishes Were Fishes We Would All Cast Nets (suspended light sculpture Ferrucci Junior High Sch) Puyallup, Wash State Arts Comn, 87; Chaotic Chains, Exploratorium, San Francisco, 89; Railway Suite, outside waiting room, Cal Train Sta Santa Clara, Calif Arts Coun, 90; Everett Arbour (sculptural installation), Everett Community Col, Wash State Arts Comn, 92. *Exhib:* Holiday Exhib, San Francisco Mus Mod Art, Calif, 78; Staged Garden, San Francisco Mus Mod Art, 87; Voyages, San Francisco Mus Mod Art, 87; Memory Station, Art Park, Lewiston, New York, 88; On the Horizon: Emerging in California, Fresno Arts Ctr & Mus, 89; Art from the Exploratorium, World Trade Ctr, NY, 90; All for One Earth San Francisco-Leningrad Ecological Arts Project SOMAR, San Francisco, 90; and others. *Teaching:* Lectr, Cal Polly Archit Dept, San Luis Obispo, 83, vis artist, 83-85; vis lectr, introd to sculpture, Univ Calif Berkeley, 84-86; vis lectr clay sculpture, San Mateo Community Col, 85; vis artist, East Carolina Univ, 87; vis lectr, San Francisco Art Inst, 87-89; vis artist, Mills Col, 91-92 & asst prof art, 92- *Awards:* Pro Arts, 83; SECA Award, San Francisco Mus Mod Art, 87; Artist Fel, Calif Arts Coun, 92; and others. *Bibliog:* Francis Butler (auth), Shadow in the visual arts, installation by Murch, Berkeley Monthly, 9/87; A Study in Light & Shadow Landscape Archit, 1/88; Dorothy Burkart (auth), Three who broke barriers, cover story, San Jose Mercury News. *Mem:* San Francisco Art Inst (Artist Comt). *Media:* Multimedia, Sculpture. *Mailing Add:* 499 Alabama St Studio 306 San Francisco CA 94110

MURCHIE, DONALD JOHN
LIBRARIAN, WRITER
b Plainfield, NJ, Nov 23, 43. *Study:* Univ Colo, BA; Dalhousie Univ, MLS. *Pos:* Libr dir, NS Col Art & Design, Halifax, 72-90. *Mem:* Art Libr Soc/NAm (mem exec bd, 75-78, chmn, 76). *Media:* Mixed. *Res:* Contemporary art; Canadian art history. *Publ:* Auth, Lines, Eye Level Gallery, 79; A Quiet Evening, 79; Opeing, Open, Closed, Eye Level Gallery, 80; An Invitation; or One-Way Ticket, 83. *Mailing Add:* RR 2 5163 Duke St Sackville NB E0A 3C0 Canada

MURDOCK, GREG
SCULPTOR
b Saskatoon, Sask, Can, Jan 8, 54. *Study:* Univ Sask, BFA, 75-77; Inst Allende, San Miguel De Allende, Mex, 77-78; Emily Carr Col of Art & Design, 79-81. *Work:* Osler-Hoskin, McMillan-Binch, Guaranty Trust, Midland-Doherty, Abols & Posthumous & Conwest Exploration Ltd, Toronto, Ont; Air Canada & Maison Alcan Inc, Montreal, Que; Ring House Gallery, Edmonton, Alta; First City Trust, Vancouver, BC; Dept External Affairs, Ottawa. *Exhib:* Solo exhibs, 49th Parallel Center for Contemporary Canadian Art (with catalog), New York, 85, Equinox Gallery, Vancouver, BC, 86 & 88, Tableaux (with catalog), Southern Alberta Art Gallery, Lethbridge, 87, Littlejohn-Smith Gallery, New York, 87; Ten plus One, Surrey Art Gallery, BC, 86; traveling exhib, Vancouver Now/Vancouver '86: Insertion, Walter Phillips Gallery, Banff, Alta, Optica Gallery, Montreal, Que, London Regional Art Gallery, Ont, 86; Tables Turned: Aspects of Furniture as Visual Art (with catalog), Whyte Mus Can Rockies, Banff, Alta, 87. *Bibliog:* Elizabeth Godley (auth), review, Vancouver Sun, 9/14/88; Art Perry (auth), review, Province, Vancouver, 9/12/88; Monico Forestall (auth), review, Can Art Mag, spring 88. *Mailing Add:* c/o Olga Korper Gallery 17 Morrow Ave Toronto ON M6R 2H9 Canada

MURDOCK, ROBERT MEAD
CURATOR
b New York, NY, Dec 18, 41. *Study:* Trinity Col, BA, 63; Yale Univ, MA(hist art), 65. *Pos:* Ford Found Mus Curatorial Training Prog interne, Walker Art Ctr, Minneapolis, 65-67; cur, Albright-Knox Art Gallery, Buffalo, 67-70; cur contemp art, Dallas Mus Fine Arts, 70-78; dir, Grand Rapids Art Mus, 78-83; chief cur, Walker Art Ctr, 83-85; program dir, IBM Gallery Sci & Art, New York, 85-87; dir exhib, Am Fedn Arts, New York, 88- *Awards:* Nat Endowment for the Arts Fels for Mus Prof, 73. *Res:* 20th century, especially

constructivism, and recent American painting and sculpture. *Publ:* Auth, Today's half-century in Buffalo, Arts Mag, 3/68; Berlin/Hanover: The 1920s, Dallas Mus Fine Arts, 77; Pioneers: Early 20th Century Art from Midwestern Mus, Grand Rapids Art Mus, 81; Public passages: David Novros, Art in Am, 1/85; Variations on Geometry in Tyler Graphics: The Extended Image, 87. *Mailing Add:* 261 W 11th St No 4 New York NY 10014

MURPHY, CATHERINE E
PAINTER
b Cambridge, Mass, Jan 22, 46. *Study:* Pratt Inst, BFA, 67; Skowhegan Sch Painting & Sculpture, with Elmar Bichoff, summer 66. *Work:* Metrop Mus Art & Whitney Mus Art, New York; Hirshhorn Mus & Sculpture Garden & Phillips Collection, Washington, DC. *Exhib:* Whitney Mus Am Art Ann, New York, 71; Am Fedn Arts Group Traveling Landscape Show, 71-72; Whitney Mus, New York, 73; Storm King Arts Ctr, New York, 73; Indianapolis Mus, Ind, 74; Smithsonian Inst traveling exhib, 74-76; Mus Contemp Art, Chicago, 77; Am Acad Inst Arts & Lett, New York, 79, 87, 89, 90; retrospective, Phillips Collection, Washington, DC; and others. *Teaching:* Senior critic, Yale Univ, 89-90. *Awards:* Purchase Award, Am Fedn Arts, 71; Nat Endowment Arts, 79 & 89; Guggenheim Fel, 82; Ingram Merrill Found Grant, 86. *Bibliog:* Hilton Kramer (auth), An uncommon painter of the commonplace, NY Times, 3/75; John Gruen (auth), Catherine Murphy: The rise of a cult figure, ARTnews, 12/78; Wendy Becket (auth), Contemporary Women Artists, New York: Universe, 88. *Media:* Oil. *Mailing Add:* Lennon, Weinberg Inc 580 Broadway Second Fl New York NY 10012

MURPHY, CHESTER GLENN
PAINTER
b Harper, Kans, May 28, 07. *Study:* With Clyde Keller, Portland, Ore. *Comn:* Mural, Little World's Fair, Damascus, Ore, 62; two murals, Lake Oswego Shopping Ctr, Ore, 67; Ore scene in oil, USS Sperry, 69; two Ore scenes in oil, Western Elec, Vancouver, Wash, 72; George Fox Col, Newberg, Ore, 75. *Exhib:* Maryhill Mus Fine Arts, Wash, 60; Dedication, Anna Hyatt Huntington Statue, Lincoln City, Ore, 65; Coun Am Artist Soc, 66; Vis Exhib of Ore Art, NMex State Capitol Bldg, 69; Am Artists Prof League Grand Nat, 71-77. *Teaching:* Instr oil painting, Willamette View Manor, 69-78 & summer workshops, Ore; instr, Ore Soc Artists, 87; guest lectr oil painting, Ore & Wash Pub Schs. *Awards:* First Prize, Lake Oswego Ann Arts & Flowers Festival; First in Prof Div, All-Ore Art Show, State Fair; Best of Show, Oak Grove Ann, 75. *Mem:* Fel Am Artists Prof League (pres, Ore Chap, 71); Ore Soc Artists; Coun Am Artist Soc; Oregon Soc Artists, (pres, 89). *Media:* Oil. *Publ:* Contribr, Art is For Everybody, 60; co-auth, An Artist Paints the Northwest, 71. *Mailing Add:* 18675 Midhill Circle West Linn OR 97068

MURPHY, DUDLEY C
EDUCATOR, GRAPHIC DESIGNER
b Danville, Ky, Apr 16, 40. *Study:* Univ Tulsa, BA, 65, MA, 69; Univ Okla, MFA, 71. *Exhib:* Okla Art Ctr, Oklahoma City, 70; Contemp Int Landscape Sculpture, traveling, Mo Arts Coun, 72; Nelson Gallery Art, St Louis, Mo, 74; Joslyn Art Mus, Omaha, Nebr, 74; SDak Art Ctr, Brookings, 75; Pittsburg State Univ, Kans, 79; and others. *Pos:* Design & layout artist, Litho Art Serv, Tulsa, Okla, 66-68; design & layout artist, Pub Relations Int Ltd, 68-69; owner & creative dir, Adworks, Springfield, Md, currently; ed, designer & publ, Nat Fishing Lure Collectors Mag, currently. *Teaching:* Instr design, SW Mo State Univ, Springfield, 69-70; cur educ, Springfield Art Mus, Mo, 71-78; assoc prof, Drury Col, Springfield, Mo, 78- *Awards:* First Place, 80 & Merit Award, 82, Springfield Ad Club; Merit Awards, Springfield Ad Club, 89, 90 & 91. *Bibliog:* Edgar A Albin (auth), Dudley Murphy, Artcraft Mag, 80. *Mem:* Springfield Ad Club; Nat Coun Ceramic Arts. *Publ:* Auth, Straw, pvt publ, 71. *Mailing Add:* Dept Art Drury Col Springfield MO 65802

MURPHY, HASS
SCULPTOR, DRAFTSMAN
b Boston, Mass, Nov 1, 50. *Study:* Pratt Inst. *Exhib:* Romantic Abstraction, Brandeis Univ, Waltham, Mass, 71; Works on Paper, Logic Transformations, Contemp Arts Gallery, New York, 74; Biennial Exhib, Whitney Mus Am Art, New York, 75; New Drawings, New York, Grapestake Gallery, San Francisco, 75; Spare, Cent Hall Gallery, New York, 75. *Bibliog:* Interview, Seven Painters, Artrite, spring 75; Judy Rifka & Willy Lenski (dirs), Ten Studios (film), Basel Art Fair, 75. *Media:* Steel, Limestone. *Dealer:* Nancy Lurie Gallery 1632 N La Salle Chicago IL 60614; Nancy Lurie Gallery 230 E Ohio St Chicago IL 60611. *Mailing Add:* 399 Washington St New York NY 10013

MURPHY, HERBERT A
ARCHITECT, PAINTER
b Fall River, Mass, June 13, 11. *Study:* RI Sch Design, 32. *Exhib:* Rockport Art Asn; NShore Art Asn; Providence Art Club; Providence Watercolor Club; RI Sch Design; and others. *Pos:* Registered architect, pvt practice, 41-83. *Awards:* Gold Medal for Distinguished Serv, Rockport Art Asn, 84. *Mem:* Rockport Art Asn (vpres, 60-62, pres, 63-65); Providence Watercolor Club. *Media:* Oil, Watercolor. *Mailing Add:* 17 King St Rockport MA 01966

MURPHY, MARILYN L
PAINTER, EDUCATOR
b Tulsa, Okla, Sept 22, 50. *Study:* Okla State Univ, BFA, 72; Univ Okla, MFA, 78. *Work:* Okla State Collection, Oklahoma City; State Univ NY, Potsdam; Vanderbilt Univ; Northern Telecom, Nashville; Kemper Collection. *Comn:* Shelter (color drawing), Prudential, Chicago; graphite drawing, Carroll Corp-Citi Corp, Nashville; Night Theatre, WDCN-PBS TV, Nashville; color drawing, Third Nat Corp, Nashville; Home (graphite drawing), Tenn Humanities Comn, Nashville. *Exhib:* solo exhibs, Judy Caden Gallery, New York, 82, Cheekwood Fine Arts Ctr, Nashville, 83 & 87, Cumberland Gallery, Nashville, 84 & 88 & Smith Col Fine Arts, Mass, 86; Auburn Univ, Ala, 87; Jan Cicero Gallery, Chicago, 87; 10 in Tenn, Dulin Gallery Art, Knoxville & Brooks Mus, Memphis; Drawing Ctr, New York; Realism Today, Evansville Mus Art, Ind, 89; Rutgers Nat, Stedman Art Gallery, Camden, NJ, 90; Humor? Cudahy Gallery, New York, 90. *Collections Arranged:* Film as an Art Form, Sarratt Cinema, 81-, The Music City Biennial, 81, 83 & 85, Dangerous Works, 82, Cohen Art Gallery, Microwave-Small Works, Fine Arts Gallery, 85, Vanderbilt Univ, Nashville, Tenn; The Home Show, Tenn Arts Comn Invitational, 86; Four x Four, Fine Arts Gallery, Vanderbilt Univ, Nashville. *Pos:* Drafter Geophysical Archit Drafting Rm, Oklahoma City, Okla, 74-76; geological drafter, John A Taylor Petrol Exploration, Oklahoma City, 76-77. *Teaching:* instr drawing & prints, Univ Okla, Norman, 78-80; assoc prof painting & drawing, Vanderbilt Univ, 80- *Awards:* Fel, Southern Arts Fed, 90; fel, Tennessee Arts Comn; Merit Award, New Harmony Gallery Contemp Art. *Bibliog:* Portfolio: Profiling an Artist Marilyn Murphy (film), WDCN-PBS TV, Nashville, 82; Dorothy Habel (auth), Marilyn Murphy-metropolis, Art Papers, 12/84; Susan Knowles (auth) Southern realism, New Art Examiner, summer 85. *Mem:* Sinking Creek Film Festival (vpres, bd dirs, 90). *Media:* Graphite; Oil. *Dealer:* Jan Cicero Gallery 221 W Erie Chicago Ill. *Mailing Add:* c/o Cumberland Gallery 4107 Hillsboro Circle Nashville TN 37215

MURPHY, SUSAN (SUSAN AVIS MURPHY COLOMBINI)
PAINTER
b New London, Conn, Sept 18, 50. *Study:* Col New Rochelle, with William Maxwell, 78-79. *Work:* General Motors, US Gypsum, Int Harvester, Quaker Oats, Beatrice. *Exhib:* Southern Watercolor Soc, La Tech Univ, 81-86 & 90; Allied Artists Am, Nat Arts Club, New York, 81 & 82; Am Watercolor Soc, Nat Acad Design, New York, 82; Butler Inst Am Art Midyear Show, 82-88; Midwest Watercolor Soc, Davenport, Iowa, 83. *Pos:* Mgr, Falling Acorns Editions, 86- *Teaching:* Instr watercolor, Falling Acorns Studio, Sandy Spring, Md, 86- *Awards:* Gold Medal, Catharine Lorillard Wolfe Art Club 87th Ann, 79; Matching Funds Award, Allied Artists Am, 82; Gold Medal, Baltimore Watercolor Soc Mid-Atlantic Exhib, 86. *Bibliog:* The Watercolor Page: Susan Murphy, Am Artist Mag, 3/86; Dream Studio, Am Artist Mag, 5/91. *Mem:* Watercolor Soc, Southern, Baltimore & Midwest. *Media:* Watercolor. *Publ:* Orange Marmalade, Falling Acorns Editions, 91; Carnations and Lace & Dear Diary, Front Line Graphics, 92. *Dealer:* Artshowcase 336 N Charles St Baltimore MD; Miriam Perlman Inc Lake Point Tower Suite 5410 Chicago IL. *Mailing Add:* 17520 Dr Bird Rd Sandy Spring MD 20860

MURRAY, EILEEN M
DIRECTOR, CURATOR
b Elizebeth, NJ, Aug 7, 59. *Study:* Upsala Col, BA(art), 81; Univ Chicago, MA(art hist), 82; Northwestern Univ, MM(mktg & non-profit), 90. *Collections Arranged:* Are You Serious?, Group show, 92; Faculty Exhib, 92. *Pos:* Exec Dir, Hyde Park Art Ctr, 91- *Mem:* Chicago Artists Coalition; Ill Arts Alliance. *Mailing Add:* Hyde Park Art Center 1701 E 53rd St Chicago IL 60615

MURRAY, ELIZABETH
PAINTER
b Chicago, Ill, 1940. *Study:* Art Inst Chicago, BFA, 62; Mills Col, MFA, 64. *Work:* Detroit Inst Arts; Guggenheim Mus, New York; Hirshhorn Mus, Washington, DC; McCrory Corp, New York. *Exhib:* One-person exhibs, Paula Cooper Gallery, New York, 88 & 89, Mayor Rowen Gallery, London, 89, Gerg Kucera Gallery, Seattle, 89, Barbara Krakow Gallery, Boston, 90, Gallery Mukai, Tokyo, 90, Paula Cooper Annex, NY, 90 & John Berggruen Gallery, San Francisco, 90; Cleveland State Univ, 90; Univ Wis, Milwaukee, 90; Ark Art Ctr, Little Rock, 90; Rose Art Mus, Brandeis Univ, Waltham, Mass; Large Scale Works on Paper, John Berggruen Gallery, San Francisco, 91; and many other one-man & group exhibs. *Teaching:* Instr painting, Bard Col, 74-75 & 76-77; vis prof painting, Calif Inst Arts, Valencia, 75-76; instr, Princeton Univ, NJ, 77, Yale Univ, New Haven, Conn, 78-79 & Sch Visual Arts, New York, 78-80; Lectr, NY Studio Sch Drawing, Painting & Sculpture, New York, 87. *Awards:* Walter M Campana Award, Art Inst Chicago, 82; Am Acad & Inst Arts & Letts, 84; Skowhegan Prize Painting, 86. *Bibliog:* Donald Kuspit (auth), Elizabeth Murray's dandyish abstraction, Artforum, 2/78; Jeff Perone (auth), rev in Artforum, 1/79; John Russell (auth), Elizabeth Murray's shaped canvases, New York Times, 6/9/81; Robert Storr (auth), Added dimension, Parkett, No 8, 86. *Media:* Oil on Canvas. *Mailing Add:* c/o Paula Cooper 155 Wooster New York NY 10012

MURRAY, FLORETTA MAY
ADMINISTRATOR, PAINTER
b Minn. *Study:* Winona State Univ, BEd; Univ Minn, MA & PhD; Minneapolis Col Art & Design; Univ Chicago; also in France, Belg & Italy. *Work:* Watkins Retirement Home; Univ Chicago; private collections of Benjamin & Abbey Grey, Dr & Mrs Truman Porter, Charles B Sweatt, Joseph Leioht, Mr & Mrs William White and others. *Comn:* History of Winona County (mural), Winona Co Hist Mus; pres medallion, Winona State Univ. *Exhib:* St Paul Gallery Art, 60; Northrup Gallery, Univ Minn, 62; Nat League Am Pen Women, 68; Smithsonian Inst, 69; Minn Mus Art, 71-74; one-artist show, Jewish Community Ctr, St Paul, Minn, 76; Col St Teresa, Grand Central; Minneapolis Art Inst. *Teaching:* Prof art & chmn dept, Winona State Univ, 38-76; prof art & actg head dept, Bemidji State Col, 49-50; prof, Col St Teresa, Winona, 55-58; instr painting, Univ Minn, Minneapolis, 58; lectr, St Mary's Col (Minn), 70. *Awards:* Merit Award, Minn State Fair, 38 &

Rochester Art Ctr; Purchase Prize, Minn Mus Art, St Paul. *Mem:* Am Asn Univ Prof (secy-treas, 69-71); Nat Art Educ Asn; Am Asn Univ Women; Col Art Asn Am; Int Platform Asn; plus others. *Media:* Watercolor, Oil. *Mailing Add:* 65 West Lake Blvd Winona MN 55987

MURRAY, FRANCES
PHOTOGRAPHER
Work: Fine Arts Mus, Houston, Tex; Int Mus Photog at George Eastman House, Rochester, NY; Ctr for Creative Photog, Tucson, Ariz; Santa Barbara Mus Art, Calif; Okla Mus Art. *Exhib:* One-person exhibs, Univ Wis, Superior, 82, Etherton Gallery, Tucson, Ariz, 83, Neikrug Photographica Gallery, New York, 85, Univ Mo, St Louis, 87, Dinnerware Artists Coop Gallery, Tucson, Ariz, 89, Zeit Foto Gallery, Tokyo, Japan, 89, Temple Gallery/Etherton Stern, Tucson, Ariz, 92; Dinnerware Artists Coop Gallery, 85, 87, 89 & 90, Ctr for Creative Photog, Snell & Wilmer Collection, 90, New Acquisitions, Tucson, Ariz, 90, Tucson Mus Art/Fine Art for Fine Causes, 91. *Awards:* Nat Endowment Visual Artists, 86; Nat Endowment Arts US/Japan Exchange Fel, 87; Tucson Pima Arts Coun Visual Fel, 91. *Bibliog:* Photograhy for the Art Market, Watson Guphill Publ, 90. *Mailing Add:* 420 E Fourth St Tucson AZ 85715

MURRAY, IAN STEWART
SCULPTOR, CONCEPTUAL ARTIST
b Pictou, NS, Nov 4, 51. *Study:* NS Col Art & Design, BFA(fine art), 72. *Work:* Art Gallery Ont; Can Coun Art Bank, Ottawa; Nat Gallery Can; Banff Ctr Walter Phillips Gallery; Trinity Square Video, Toronto. *Comn:* Changing Channels (3 color monos), Projections: Positions- Point of View (audio/video collage) & NOVA BOETIA-Another World, Halifax, Dartmouth & Sackville Community TV Stas, NS, 76; Tutorial: Radio by Artists, Fine Arts Broadcast Serv, Toronto, Ont, 80; DIET: Television by Artists, Fine Arts Broadcast Serv, Toronto, Ont, 80; The Lunatic of One Idea, Public Access Videowall series, Mississauga, Ont, 88. *Exhib:* Record as Art, Royal Col Art, London, 73; Audio Scene, Mod Art Galerie, Wein, Austria, 79; Books by Artists, 80-82; Biennale of Sydney, Australia, 82; Second Link, Banff Mus Art & traveling, 83; From Sea to Shining Sea, The Power Plant, Toronto, 88; solo exhib, Vancouver Art Gallery, Vancouver, BC, 88. *Collections Arranged:* Attitudes Toward Photography (auth, catalog), Ann Leonowens Gallery, 72; Video From Eastern Canada, Forest City Art Gallery, 76; Radio by Artists (auth, catalog), Fine Art Broadcast Serv, 80. *Pos:* Mem, Bd Governors, Planning & Priority Comt & Chmn, Film/Photog/video Comt, Toronto Arts Coun, currently. *Teaching:* Instr, Media Arts Film & Video Courses & Film Tech Studies, The Ryerson Polytech Inst, Toronto, 86-87. *Awards:* Can Coun Awards, 73, 76, 79 & 81. *Bibliog:* Phillip Monk (auth), Television by artists, Can Forum, 81; Mary-Beth Laviolette (auth), Audio by artists, Vanguard Mag, 4/83; Jill Pollack (auth), Work rich in meaning, metaphor, The Vancouver Courier, BC, 88. *Mem:* Nightingale Arts Coun (vchair, 80-81); Artists Union; Trinity Square Video. *Media:* Multimedia; Collage. *Publ:* Auth, Twenty Waves in a Row, Straw Books, 71. *Dealer:* V/Tapes Toronto Canada; Art Metropole Toronto Canada. *Mailing Add:* 5 Boustead Ave Suite 3 Toronto ON M6R 2N5 Canada

MURRAY, JOAN
CRITIC, PHOTOGRAPHER
b Annapolis, Md, Mar 6, 27. *Study:* Calif Col Arts & Crafts, San Francisco Art Inst; Ruth Bernard Insight Studio; Univ Calif Exten; also studied with Wynn Bullock. *Work:* Int Mus Photog, Eastman House, Rochester, NY; San Francisco Mus Mod Art; Oakland Mus, Calif. *Exhib:* Male Nudes--One Man, Mind's Eye Gallery, Vancouver, BC, 73; 7 Visions, Heller Gallery, Berkeley, 89 & self protrait, 91; Children of Our Times, Steven Wirtz Gallery, San Francisco, 87; Joan Murray, Retrospective 1967-1992, Vision Gallery, San Francisco, 92; The Oakland Fire, Robert Koch Gallery, 92; and others. *Pos:* Photog ed, Artweek, 69-; WCoast critic, Popular Photog, 75-77; contrib ed, Am Photogr, 78-81; consult, Photog Dept, Getty Mus, 86; mgr assoc, Art Studio, Univ Calif, 87- *Teaching:* Instr photog, Univ Calif Exten, 70-82; instr photog, City Col San Francisco, 75-82; Friends of Photog Workshops, 90. *Awards:* Nat Endowment Arts Grant Art Criticism, 78. *Mem:* Int Asn Art Critics; Soc Encouragement Contemp Art San Francisco Mus Art; San Francisco Mus Mod Art Foto Forum. *Dealer:* Vision Gallery 1155 Mission St San Francisco CA 94103. *Mailing Add:* 120 Blair Ave Piedmont CA 94611

MURRAY, JOHN MICHAEL
PAINTER
b Tampa, Fla, May 28, 31. *Study:* Univ Tampa, BA, 63; Ohio Univ, MFA, 65. *Work:* Staten Island Mus, NY; Bundy Art Mus, Waitsfield, Vt; NS Col Art, Halifax; NJ Mus. *Exhib:* Int Print Exhib, Crakow, 75; Langsam Gallery, Melbourne, Australia, 75; 19 Nat Print Exhib, Brooklyn Mus, 75; one-man shows, Dorsky Gallery, New York, 72, Halifax, 72, Blue Parrot, New York, 74 & Am Ctr, Belgrade, 81. *Teaching:* Chmn dept fine arts, New York Inst Technol, 66- *Awards:* First Prize in Painting, Fla State Ann, 63. *Mem:* Am Asn Univ Prof; Col Art Teachers. *Publ:* Contribr, Art Work--No Commercial Value, Grossman, 72; Pratt Graphics Reprint, 74. *Dealer:* James Yu Gallery 393 W Broadway New York NY 10012. *Mailing Add:* 124 W Houston St No 4 New York NY 10012

MURRAY, JUDITH
PAINTER
b New York, NY, Feb 22, 41. *Study:* Pratt Inst, Brooklyn, NY, BFA, 62, MFA, 64; Acad Fine Arts, Madrid, Spain, 63. *Work:* Brooklyn Mus, New York Pub Libr & Chase Manhattan Bank, New York; Libr Cong; Nat Mus Am Art, Washington, DC; Mus Modern Art, New York; British Mus. *Comn:* Poster & print, Mostly Mozart Festival, Avery Fisher Hall, Lincoln Ctr, New York, 81 & 86; poster & print, Mozart Bicentennial, Loncoln Ctr, 91 & 92. *Exhib:* Print Exhib, Brooklyn Mus, New York, 62; A Painting Show & Works (traveling in ten countries), PS I, Project Space One, New York, 77; solo exhibs, The ClockTower, Inst Art & Urban Resources, New York, 78, Dallas Mus Fine Arts, 82 & Bronx Mus Arts, 86; New York/a Selection from the Last Ten Yrs, Otis Art Inst, Los Angeles, 79; 1979 Biennial Exhib, Whitney Mus Am Art, New York, 79; Art in Our Time, traveling exhib, 80-82; traveling exhibs, Art in Our Time, 80-82, A Living Tradition; Selections from Am Art Asn (Eur, Can, near east), 86 & 100 Lines of Vision - Drawings by Contemporary Women (US & Eur), 89-91. *Awards:* Artist Fel Grant-Painting, Nat Endowment Arts, 83-84. *Bibliog:* William Zimmer (auth), Murray mint, Soho Weekly News, 1/2/80; Judy Collischan Van Wagner (auth), Judith Murray: Interview, Long Island Univ Catalog, 11/85; Gail Stavitsky (auth), Three aspects of abstraction, Arts Mag, 4/86. *Mem:* Am Abstract Artists. *Media:* Oil. *Mailing Add:* 429 W Broadway New York NY 10012

MURRAY, REUBEN
ADMINISTRATOR
Study: Univ NMex, BFA(theatre), 85, Univ Phoenix, MA, 91. *Pos:* Exec dir, SArk Arts Ctr, El Dorado, 91- *Mailing Add:* South Arkansas Arts Center 110 E Fifth St El Dorado AR 71730

MURRAY, RICHARD NEWTON
MUSEUM DIRECTOR, CURATOR
b Bartlesville, Okla, Aug 7, 42. *Study:* San Jose State Univ, Calif, BA, 68; Univ Chicago, MA, 70. *Collections Arranged:* Art for Architecture: Washington DC 1895-1925 (auth, catalog), Nat Collection Fine Arts, Smithsonian Press, 75; America as Art, 76; Elihu Vedder (auth, catalog), 78; American Renaissance: 1876-1917 (auth, catalog), Brooklyn Mus, 79. *Pos:* Asst to dir, Nat Collection Fine Arts, Washington, DC, 76-79; dir, Birmingham Mus Art, Ala, 79-83 & Arch Am Art, Smithsonian Inst, 83-; cur, Nat Mus Am Art, Smithsonian Inst, 88- *Publ:* Auth, The drawings of Kenyon Cox, Drawing Mag, 80; Art of the American West, Birmingham Mus Art, 82; Murals of the American Renaissance, Influence on Am Art, 89; John Norton Mural Painter, In: John Norton, Ill Univ Press, 92. *Mailing Add:* 11300 Palisades Ct Kensington MD 20895

MURRAY, ROBERT (GRAY)
SCULPTOR, PAINTER
b Vancouver, BC, Mar 2, 36. *Study:* Univ Sask Sch Art, 55-58; Mex, 59; Emma Lake Artist's Workshops. *Work:* Whitney Mus Am Art, Metrop Mus Art, New York; Walker Art Ctr, Minn; Everson Mus, Syracuse; Hirshhorn Mus, Washington, DC; Chase Manhattan Collection, NY; Detroit Mus Fine Arts, Mich; Univ Toronto, Ont, Can; Del Art Mus; and many others. *Comn:* Sculpture, Dept External Affairs, Ottawa, 72, Wayne State Univ, Detroit, 74, Univ Mass, Amherst, 75, Alaska Court Bldg, Juneau, 78, Honeywell Inc, Minn, 79 & Univ Toronto, 83; direct purchases as well as numerous commissions. *Exhib:* Columbus Mus; Art Gallery Greater Victoria; Nothing But Steel, The Lab, Cold Springs Harbor, LI, 87; The Opening Exhib, Nat Gallery Can, Ottawa, 88; Working Models & Other Sculpture, Del Art Mus, 90; Frank Martin Gallery, Muhlenberg Col, Allentown, 91; and others. *Teaching:* Lectr, cols throughout US; instr, Sch Visual Arts, currently. *Awards:* Can Coun Bursary, 60 & Sr Grant, 69 & 83; Second Prize, X Sao Paulo Biennial, Brazil, 69; Nat Endowment Arts Grant, 69; Royal Archit Inst Can Allied Arts Medal, 77. *Bibliog:* Krainin-Sage (auth), ArtIs (film), NY State Coun Arts, 71; Neil Marshall (auth), Robert Murray sculpture, Dayton Art Inst, 79; G Bellerby (auth), Robert Murray: Sculpture & Working Models, Art Gallery Greater Victoria, 83; Kim Rich (auth), Culture Shock (article), Anchorage Daily News, 10/9/88. *Media:* Steel, Aluminum. *Mailing Add:* 66 Grand St New York NY 10012

MURRAY, TIM(OTHY DOUGLAS GORDON)
SCULPTOR, DIRECTOR
b Reading, Eng, Oct 28, 38; US citizen. *Study:* Univ NC at Chapel Hill, BA, 61, MA(creative arts), 66. *Work:* Asheville Mus, NC; Greenville Mus, SC; Northern Telecom Corp, Research Triangle, NC; Governor's Mansion Western NC, Asheville. *Comn:* Three faceted glass sactuary windows, font, confessional stained glass, 88, Stations of the Cross (wood), 90, Sacared Heart Catholic Church, Brevard, NC. *Exhib:* Piedmont Graphics, 13th, 15th & 17th Ann Exhib, Greenville Mus, SC, 76, 78 & 81; Tri-State Sculptors', 16 Galleries Sawtooth Ctr, Winston-Salem, NC, 84, 88; Architecture & Artist, Greenville Ctr for NC Art, Greensboro, 84; Drawing Eden-Murray-Welsh, Asheville Mus, NC, 84; The Written Word, Southeastern Ctr for Contemp Art, Winston-Salem, NC, 86 & 87; Urban Landscape, 88; Landmarks, Stratmore House, Rockville, Md, 90. *Collections Arranged:* Nat Sculpture 1980 (with catalog), Southern Asn Sculptors, Univ SC, Columbus & traveling; The Last Nat Sculpture Show, Southern Asn Sculptors, Univ Ga, at Athens, 82. *Pos:* Bd dir, Southern Asn Sculptors, 80-83; adv, Asheville Mus Consortium, 85-; NC representative for Tri-State Sculpture; bd trustees, Ashville Art Mus, 89. *Teaching:* Dir, Sims Art Ctr, Brevard Col, NC, 69-, prof art, 71-; vis artist, Clemson Univ, 82, Ind State, 82; vis scholar, Univ NC, Charleston, 89; vis artist, Cleveland State 91 & Pa Acad, 92. *Awards:* Honor, Piedmont Graphic, 17th Ann Exhib, Greenville Mus, 81; Purchase Awards, NC Sculpture Exhib, Northern Telecom Corp, 82 & Southern Asn Sculptors Exchange Competition, Bernhart Industries, 84. *Mem:* Tri-State Sculptors; Southeast Col Art Asn. *Media:* Wood; Mixed. *Mailing Add:* Rte 1 PO Box 3 Brevard NC 28712

MURRELL, CARLTON D
PAINTER
b Bridgetown, Barbados, WI, July 17, 45; nat US. *Study:* Art Student's League, 70; Pels Art Sch, 74. *Work:* Ctr Art Cult Bedford-Styvesant, Brooklyn; Barbados Mus, Bridgetown; Howard Univ, Washington, DC; Barbados Cent Bank. *Exhib:* West Indian Artist, Brooklyn Mus, 76; Caribbean Connection, Nat Afro Am Mus Cult Ctr, Ohio Hist Soc, 86. *Teaching:* Instr drawing & painting, Brooklyn Truth Ctr & Fort Greene Sr Citizen Ctr, 88- *Awards:* Second Prize, Flushing Art League; Fulton Art Fair Award, 82 & 87. *Bibliog:* David Shirey (auth), Realism stands out in show by blacks, New York Times, 81; Will Grant (auth), To a Bajan beat, Art Speak, 88; Jude Schwendenwien (auth), Appealing, informative West Indian-American art exhibit, Hartford Courant, 88. *Mem:* Brooklyn Watercolor Soc. *Media:* Oil, Watercolor. *Mailing Add:* 543 E 21st St Brooklyn NY 11226

MURRILL, GWYNN
SCULPTOR
b Ann Arbor, Mich, June 15, 42. *Study:* Univ Calif, Los Angeles, BA, 68, MA, 70, MFA, 72. *Work:* Bankers Life Co, Des Moines, Iowa; Bank Denver, Colo; Los Angeles Co Art Mus; Trans America, San Francisco, Calif; Security Pacific Bank, Los Angeles, Calif. *Comn:* California State Bldg, Los Angeles; Plaza Park Towers, Sacramento, Calif. *Exhib:* Los Angeles Eight, Painting & Sculpture, 76 & 20 Years of Talent Winners, Los Angeles Co Art Mus, Calif; Contemporary Californians VIII, Laguna Beach Art Mus, Calif, 82; Wood Renditions, Security Pac Bank, Los Angeles, 84; Asher/Faure Gallery, Los Angeles, 87; John Berggruen Gallery, San Francisco; Gail Swerin Gallery, Ketchum, Idaho; and others. *Awards:* Prix Di Rome, Am Acad, Italy, 79; Nat Endowment Art Fel, 84 & Guggenheim Fel, 86. *Media:* All. *Dealer:* Asher Faure Gallery 612 N Almont Los Angeles CA 90069; John Berggruen Gallery San Francisco CA. *Mailing Add:* 29012 Crest Dr Agoura CA 91301

MUSGRAVE, SHIRLEY H
EDUCATOR, PHOTOGRAPHER
b Lexington, Ky, Nov 28, 35. *Study:* Miss State Col Women, BFA, 57; Colorado Springs Fine Arts Ctr, summer 56; Univ Kans, scholar, 57-58, MS, 63; Univ Ark, 64-65; Univ Iowa, 66-67; Fla State Univ, PhD(fel), 70. *Exhib:* One-artist photog exhib, Iowa City Civic Ctr, 65, Univ Ala-Huntsville, 72, Athens Col, Ala, 73 & Lambuth Col, Tenn, 74; Professional Women Artists of Florida, Lowe Art Mus, Miami, 76; Photograph, Huntsville Art League & Mus Asn Ann, Huntsville Art Mus, 79; and others. *Teaching:* Art supvr, Linwood Pub Schs, Kans, 58-60; assoc prof art educ, Memphis State Univ, 70-72 & Fla Int Univ; prof art educ & chairperson dept, Univ Ala, 78. *Awards:* Ark Artists Ann First Prize in Graphics, Little Rock Mus Fine Arts, 56; Fla Int Univ Found Grant, 76. *Mem:* Nat Art Educ Asn; Southeastern Col Art Conf; Ala Alliance Arts Educ; Ala Art Educ Asn. *Publ:* Coauth, Experiences in the Arts, 77; coauth, Annotated sources for Afro-American arts and the ancestral African background, Art Teacher, spring 80. *Mailing Add:* 306 Garland Box 870231 Tuscaloosa AL 35487-0231

MUSGROVE, STEPHEN WARD
ADMINISTRATOR, CURATOR
b Pittsfield, Mass, Mar 28, 49. *Study:* Lenoir-Rhyne Col, BA(hist), 73; State Univ NY, Oneonta, 73-74, Cooperstown Grad Progs, MA(mus studies). *Pos:* Dir, Catawba Sci Ctr, Hickory, NC, 74-75; asst dir, Mint Mus of Art, Charlotte, NC, 75- *Mem:* Am Asn Mus; Am Asn for State & Local Hist; Southeastern Mus Conf; NC Mus Coun. *Publ:* Auth & illusr, Making exhib labels: a mechanical lettering system, 76 & Electrifying exhibits: low voltage techniques, 78, Hist News; The alamanac: neglected witness of the American experience, 79 & For the fun of it, 80, Southeastern Mus Conf J. *Mailing Add:* Mint Mus Art 2730 Randolph Rd Charlotte NC 28207

MUSSELMAN, DARWIN B
PAINTER
b Selma, Calif, Feb 16, 16. *Study:* Fresno State Col, AB, 38; Art Ctr Col Design, Los Angeles, 38-39; Calif Col Arts & Crafts, MFA, 50; Univ Calif, Berkeley, MA, 52; also with Lyonel Feininger, 37 & Yasuo Kuniyoshi, 49. *Work:* Oakland Art Mus, Calif; Fresno Arts Ctr, Calif; Sloan-Kettering Hosp, New York; Harvey Mudd Col. *Comn:* Mural of cotton indust, Prod Cotton Oil Co, Fresno, 54; portrait of former President, Calif State Univ, Fresno, 82. *Exhib:* 3rd Ann Legion of Honor Exhib, San Francisco, 48; Calif Artists Exhib, Los Angeles Mus, 49; Denver Mus Ann, Colo, 54; Butler Inst Am Art, Youngstown, Ohio, 56; Fresno Arts Ctr, 82; Wichita Art Asn, 82; and others. *Pos:* Artist & art dir, Thomas Advert, Fresno, 39-41 & 45-46. *Teaching:* Assoc prof painting & art educ, Calif Col Arts & Crafts, 48-53; prof painting & commercial art, Fresno State Univ, 53-78. *Awards:* First Prize Painting, San Joaquin Valley Art Contest, Rouze Gallery, Fresno, 47, Northern Calif Arts, Crocker Gallery, Sacramento, Calif, 56 & Ann Show, Fresno Arts Ctr, 61. *Bibliog:* Emil Kosa, Jr (auth), California painters, Am Artist Mag, 3/50; Barbara Cott (auth), Darwin Musselman, Fresno Arts Ctr, 62; Gordon T McClelland (auth), The California Style, 85; Directory of American Portrait Artists, Am Portrait Soc, 85. *Mem:* Am Watercolor Soc; Calif Nat Watercolor Soc; Am Portrait Soc; Am Soc Portrait Artists. *Media:* Oil, Egg Tempera. *Publ:* Illusr, Valley of the Yokuts, 40. *Dealer:* Hunter Gallery Carmel CA; Ratliff Gallery Ft Worth Texas. *Mailing Add:* 2550 Pecho Valley Rd Los Osos CA 93402

MUSSMANN, LINDA L
DIRECTOR, WRITER
b Gary, Ind, Apr 20, 47. *Study:* Purdue Univ, BA, 69. *Exhib:* Door, Cooper Hewitt Mus, New York, 80; Harbors Wait, Mus Mod Art, New York, 85; Silent When Loaded, Yale Univ Art Gallery, New Haven, 85; Whitney (Equitable Branch), Mary Sarratt, 88; Whitney (Philip Morris), Lincoln Speak, 88; Whitney (Equitable Branch), Danton's Death, 90. *Pos:* Art dir, Time & Space Ltd, New York, 71-86; publ, TSL Press, 80-90. *Awards:* New York Foundation for the Arts Fellowship, 87. *Bibliog:* Richard Kostelenetz (auth), Scenarios, Assembling Press, 80 & Wilson, Forman, Mussmann, NY Arts J, 81; Jack Anderson (auth), Mixed-Media: A Door, 3/11/80 & Jennifer Dunning (auth), Dance: Mussmann's Harbors Wait, 8/2/85, New York Times; Harmony Hammond (auth), Performance, Heresies, 84; Ernestine Stodelle (auth), Secret ingredient of time & space is craftmanship, New Haven Regist, 11/17/85. *Media:* Installation; Performance. *Res:* Writer of performance texts. *Publ:* Auth, Room-Raum, 81 & Beauty & Critique, 82, TSL Press; Pies & Cakes, Hersies, 83; auth, L Mussmann, Cross-way Cross, Women & Performance, 88. *Mailing Add:* 139 W 22nd St New York NY 10011

MYATT, GREELY
SCULPTOR
b Aberdeen, Miss, Mar 17, 52. *Study:* Delta State Univ, Cleveland, Miss, BFA, 75; Univ Miss, Oxford, MFA, 80. *Work:* Masur Mus Art, Monroe, La; Univ Miss, Oxford; Miss Mus Art & Miss Craftsmen's Guild, Jackson; Ringling Sch Art & Design, Sarasota, Fla; Franklin Furnace Archives, New York, NY. *Comn:* Wood sculpture, Triangle Cult Ctr, Yazoo City, Miss, 79; wood sculpture, Prudential Insurance, Memphis, Tenn, 80; on site installation, Arts Festival Atlanta, 83 & 86. *Exhib:* Solo exhibs, Southeastern Ctr Contemp Art, Winston-Salem, NC, 84 & Kansas City Artists' Coalition, Kansas City, Mo, 88; solo installation, ARC/Raw Space, Chicago, Ill, 87, Memphis Ctr for Contemp Art, Memphis, Tenn, 88; window installation, Franklin Furnace, New York, NY, 88; Galveston Art Ctr, Tex, 89; Robinson Willis Gallery, Nashville, Tenn, 89; Memphis State Univ, Tenn, 90. *Teaching:* Instr art, Itawamba Jr Col, Fulton, Miss, 80-85; asst prof art, Ark State Univ, Jonesboro, 85-88, assoc prof, 88-89; asst prof art, Memphis State Univ, Tenn, 89. *Awards:* Merit Awards, Miss Exhib, Miss Mus Art, Jackson, 78, Gertrude Herbert Mem Art Inst Competition, Augusta, Ga, 83 & September Competition, Alexandria Mus, La, 85; Individual Artist Grant, Art Space, New York, 88; Installation Grant, Alexander Mus Art, La, 89; Site Grant, Arts in the Park, Memphis, Tenn, 89. *Mem:* Int Sculpture Ctr. *Media:* Mixed. *Dealer:* Robinson Willis Gallery Nashville TN. *Mailing Add:* 1985 Walker Ave Memphis TN 38104-5636

MYER, PETER LIVINGSTON
KINETIC ARTIST, EDUCATOR
b Ozone Park, NY, Sept 19, 34. *Study:* Brigham Young Univ, BA, 56; Univ Utah, MFA, 59; summers with Harry Sternberg & Joseph Hirsch. *Work:* Colorado Springs Fine Arts Ctr; Univ Nev, Las Vegas; Phoenix Art Mus, Ariz; Salt Lake City Art Ctr; Denver Art Mus. *Exhib:* One man shows, Salt Lake Art Ctr, 80, Kimball Art Ctr, Park City, Utah, 85 & Las Vegas Art Mus, 86; Light, Motion, Space, Walker Art Ctr, Minneapolis, 67; Some More Beginnings, Brooklyn Mus, 68; Art & Technology, High Mus Art, Atlanta, Ga, 69; Art of the 60's, Denver Art Mus, 70; Kinetic Light Show, Phoenix Art Mus, Ariz, 73; Utah Valley Sculptors Invitational Exhib, Springville Art Mus, 77; retrospective, Springville Art Mus, Utah, 79; and others. *Teaching:* Assoc prof art & chmn dept, Univ Nev, Las Vegas, 62-72; art gallery dir, Brigham Young Univ, 72-78, prof art, 72- *Awards:* Best in Show for Ars Moriendi, Spring Art Roundup, 65; Purchase Award, Utah Biennial/Salt Lake City Art Ctr, 75; First Prize, Eccles Art Ctr Statewide Competition, Ogden, Utah, 85. *Bibliog:* Kranz (auth), Science and Technology and the Arts, Rheinhold, 74. *Mem:* Western Asn Art Mus; Am Asn Art Mus; Utah Mus Asn (mem adv comt, 77). *Media:* Kinetic Light Art, Pastels. *Mailing Add:* Dept Art Harris Fine Arts Ctr Brigham Young Univ Provo UT 84602

MYERS, C STOWE
DESIGNER, PAINTER
b Altoona, Pa, Dec 7, 06. *Study:* Univ Pa, BFA; Grand Cent Sch Art, New York; Chouinard Sch Art, Los Angeles, Calif. *Exhib:* Int Exhib Indust Design, Mus Mod Art, Buenos Aires, Arg, 63; Int Exhib Indust Design, Salle Arts Decoratif, Louvre, Paris, 64; var design exhibs, USA & Abroad, 64-80; Art Inst Chicago, Sales & Rental Gallery, 81-86. *Pos:* Designer, Norman Bel Geddes, 33-35; partner, Walter Dorwin Teague, 35-49; assoc, Raymond Loewy, 49-53; owner, Stowe Myers Design, 54-72; owner, Design Planning Group/Chicago, Ill, 72-74, consult, 74-77; retired, 78; partic artist, US Air Force Art Prog, 79- *Teaching:* Lectr design, Sch Design, Ill Inst Technol. *Mem:* Indust Designers Soc Am; Munic Art League of Chicago; Artists Guild Chicago; La Watercolor Soc; and others. *Mailing Add:* 3601 Behrman Place Apt 323 New Orleans LA 70114

MYERS, CAROLE See Myers, Carole Ann

MYERS, CAROLE ANN
PAINTER, INSTRUCTOR
b Shawnee, Okla, Dec 28, 34. *Study:* Instituto Allende, San Miguel de Allende, Mexico, 71; Univ Okla, Extension Div Colima, Mexico with Milford Zornes, 75-76; with Edgar Whitney, Robert E Wood & Tom Nicholas, 77-79. *Work:* Monsanto World Hq, Brown Group, St Louis, Mo; Sinclair Research, Tulsa, Okla; Ft Smith Art Ctr, Ark; US Nat Bank, Omaha, Nebr; Price Waterhouse, Mich. *Comn:* Painting, Store Planning & Design Off, Famous-Barr, St Louis, Mo. *Exhib:* Am Watercolor Soc 112th Ann, Nat Acad Galleries, 79 & 122nd & 124th Ann, Salmagundi Club, New York, 89 & 91; Open Watercolor Exhib, Nat Arts Club, New York, 81 & 83; San Diego Watercolor Soc Int Exhib, 83, 86 & 87 & 91; Nat Acad Design 159th & 167th Ann Exhib, New York, 84 & 92; First, Second, Third & Fourth Ann N Coast Collage Soc Exhib, Ohio, 85-88; Nat Watercolor Soc 65th Ann Exhib, Brea

Civic Cult Ctr, Los Angeles, Calif, 86 & 66th Ann Exhib, Muckenthaler Cult Ctr, Fullerton, Calif, 87; solo show, Barucci's Gallery, St Louis, Mo, 87 & 89; Watercolor USA, Springfield Art Mus, Mo, 88; Adirondacks Nat Exhib Am Watercolors, Old Forge, NY, 92. *Collections Arranged:* Christian Art by St Louisans, Bellefontaine United Methodist Church, Mo, 75. *Pos:* Regional Rep, Nat Watercolor Soc, Southern Watercolor Soc. *Teaching:* Instr watercolor, Private Workshops, Ciudad Valles, Mex, 79- 81, & watercolor/collage, Oaxaca, 81 & 83, Dillman's Sand Lake Lodge, Lac Du Flambeau, Wis, 84-86, Tallahassee Watercolor Soc, Fla, 85 & Fort Myers Beach Art Asn, 86; Vero Beach Art Club & Ctr Arts, Fla, 87, Acapulco, Mex, 88, 89 & 90, Hilton Leach Studio, Sarasota, Fla, 90, Grand Strand WC XVI, Myrtle Beach, SC; and many others, 92- *Awards:* John Young-Hunter Mem, 112th Ann Am Watercolor Soc, 79; Elizabeth Erlanger Mem Award, 26th Ann, 79; Marion de Sola Mendez Award, 29th Ann, 82; AES Peterson Mem Award, Nat Soc Painters Casein & Acrylic 33rd Ann, 86; Elizabeth Morse Genius Found Award, Nat Asn Women Artists, New York, 87; High Winds Medal, Am Watercolor Soc, 122nd Ann Exhibit, New York, 89; Belle Cramer Mem Award, Nat Asn Women Artists, New York, 90. *Bibliog:* Chrystal Jackson (dir), Painting with Carole Myers (film), 87; Nita Leland (auth), The Creative Artists, North Light Publ; American artists: An illustrated survey of leading contemporaries, New York Art Rev. *Mem:* Signature mem Am Watercolor Soc; Signature mem, Nat Watercolor Soc; Nat Asn Women Artists; North Coast Collage Soc; Invited mem, Nat Soc Painters in Casein & Acrylic. *Media:* Watercolor, Acrylic-Collage. *Dealer:* Barucci's Gallery 8121 Maryland St Louis Mo 63131; Joan Hodgell Gallery 16 S Palm Ave Sarasota FL 34236. *Mailing Add:* 12870 Ellsinore Bridgeton MO 63044

MYERS, DOROTHY ROATZ
PAINTER, LECTURER
b Detroit, Mich, March 24, 21. *Study:* Study with Yashuoe Kuniyoshi & Terrence Coyle; Antioch Col, Corcoran Gallery Art Sch; Art Students League. *Work:* US Coast Guard Collection, Washington, DC. *Comn:* Painting, Texas Rose, Hess Oil Corp; painting, Main Course, Seafood Leader. *Exhib:* Salon des Nations, Paris, 83; Grand Prix Universal du Centenaire de la Cote d' Azure, 88; Grand Prix European du Biniellenaire de Strausbourg, 89; Mini Print Int, Cadaques-Taller Galeria Fort, Barcelona, Spain, Salmagundi Mus, Hellenic Inst, Athens, Greece, Tangentl, Liechtenstein; Festival Int, Paris, 88, Osaka, Japan, 89; Phoebus II, Athens, Greece, 90; Cornel Med Ctr, 92; Brookdale Col, 92. *Pos:* Bk rev ed, Artists' Proof, NY Artists Equity, 85-, ed, new products column, 88-; publicity, Montserrat Gallery. *Teaching:* Pvt critiques & art lecture programs. *Awards:* Artist of the Year 1978, Citizens Coun Arts, New York; Diplome de Medaille d'Honneur Ligue d'Enseignement et Education Sociale, 87; Medialle Bronze Societe Academique d'education et d'encouragement (Paris) Arts, Sciences, Lettres, 88; 2 medals, Festival Int 89, Osaka, Japan. *Bibliog:* Anne Vanoli (auth), Roatz, La Cote des Arts, 10/84; feature article, Manhattan Arts Mag, 90. *Mem:* Life mem, Art Students League; NY Artists' Equity (dir); Salmagundi Club (mus dir, 88); Fine Arts Fedn New York; Am Fedn Art. *Media:* Oil, Watercolor; Monoprints. *Publ:* Various syndicated newspaper articles. *Mailing Add:* Box 204 FDR Sta New York NY 10150-0204

MYERS, FORREST WARDEN
SCULPTOR
b Long Beach, Calif, Feb 14, 41. *Study:* San Francisco Art Inst. *Work:* Whitney Mus Am Art, New York; Hirshhorn Mus, Washington, DC; Storm King Art Ctr, NY; Walker Art Ctr, Minneapolis; Aldrich Mus Contemp Art, Ridgefield, Conn; and others. *Exhib:* Philadelphia Mus Art, 68; Los Angeles Co Mus, 68; Whitney Mus Am Art, 68, 70 & 73; Middleheim Mus, Antwerp, Belg, 71; Unlimited Possibilities of Structure, Gallery 91, New York, 86; one-man show, Art et Industry Gallery, New York, 88-90; Katonah Mus, New York, 90; Brutus Gallery, Japan, 90; and many others. *Teaching:* Instr sculpture, San Francisco Art Inst, 67; instr, Sch Visual Art, NY, 68; instr sculpture, Kent State Univ, 78. *Awards:* Guggenheim Fel, 73; Creative Artists Pub Serv Prog Grant, 77; Nat Endowment Arts Grant, 78; Design 100 Award, Metrop Home, 90. *Bibliog:* article, NY Times Home Section, 1/2/86; article, Now Art That You Can Sit On, NY Times Business Section, 1/30/89; article, Furniture Design by Artists, Bomb Mag, Fall 89. *Mailing Add:* 120 N Sixth St Brooklyn NY 11211

MYERS, FRANCES
PRINTMAKER
b Racine, Wis, Apr 16, 38. *Study:* Univ Wis, MFA; San Francisco Art Inst. *Work:* Libr Cong & Nat Collection Fine Arts, Washington, DC; Victoria & Albert Mus, London; Metrop Mus Art, New York; Art Inst Chicago; Boston Mus Fine Arts; Brooklyn Mus. *Comn:* Limited ed print, & Madison Print Club, 79; ed of prints, Frank Lloyd Wright Portfolio, Perimeter Press, 80 & Gov Wis Arts Awards, 81. *Exhib:* 20th, 22nd & 24th Print Biennale, Brooklyn Mus, 76, 81 & 86; Madison Art Ctr, Wis, 81; Am Biennial Graphic Arts, Cali, Colombia, 81; 14th & 16th Int Biennial Graphic Arts, Ljubljana, Yugoslavia, 81 & 85; Perimeter Gallery, Chicago, 86, 88, 91 & 93; Amerikahaus, Cologne, Ger, 91; Presswork: The Art of Women Printmakers, travelling exhib, Lang Communs Corp Collection; and others. *Pos:* Cur, Printed by Women Exhib, Port Hist, Penn's Landing, Philadelphia, 83. *Teaching:* Distinguished prof art, Mills Col, Oakland, Calif, 79; vis lectr, art dept, Univ Calif, Berkeley, 82; asst prof, Univ Wis, Madison, 86-88, assoc prof, 88- *Awards:* H Lester Cooke Found Fel, 77; Wis Arts Bd Grant, 77-78; Romnes Fel, 91-92. *Media:* Xerox, Etching. *Dealer:* Perimeter Gallery Chicago IL. *Mailing Add:* Hollandale WI 53544

MYERS, JACK FREDRICK
PAINTER,
b Lima, Ohio, Feb 17, 27. *Study:* Cleveland Art Inst, Ohio; Kent State Univ, MFA. *Work:* Butler Inst Am Art. *Exhib:* May Show, Cleveland Mus of Art, 49-54, 76-81; Freedson Gallery, Lakewood, Ohio, 69; Mid-Year Show, Butler Inst of Am Art, Youngstown, Ohio, 76, 78, 79 & 82; Nat Print Competition, San Diego State Univ, Calif, 80; Birke Art Gallery, Marshall Univ, Huntington, WVa, 81; Colorprint USA, Mus Tex Tech Univ, Lubbock, 83. *Pos:* Art dir, Premier Industrial Corp, 56-70. *Teaching:* Instr graphics & film, Cooper Sch Art, Cleveland, 70-80; prof art & dir commercial design, Univ Dayton, 82-87. *Awards:* First Prize (one minute animated film), ASIFA Festival, New York, 74; Purchase Prize, Mid-Year Show, Butler Inst of Am Art, 79; Special Mention, May Show, Cleveland Mus Art, 79 & 80; and others. *Media:* Oil, Screen Print. *Publ:* The Language of Visual Art: Perception as a Basis for Design, Holt, Rinehart & Winston, 89. *Dealer:* Miller Gallery 2722 Erie Ave Cincinnati OH 45208. *Mailing Add:* 4420 Woodner Rd Kettering OH 45440

MYERS, JOEL PHILIP
ARTIST IN GLASS, EDUCATOR
b Paterson, NJ, Jan 29, 34. *Study:* Parsons Sch Design, NY, grad with honors, 54; NY State Col Ceramics, Alfred Univ, BFA, 62, MFA, 67. *Work:* Corning Mus Glass, NY; Ill State Mus, Springfield; Mus du Verre, Liege, Belg; Mus Stadt Dusseldorf, WGer; Mint Mus, Charlotte, NC; Chicago Art Inst. *Exhib:* One-man shows, George Walter Vincent Smith Art Mus, Springfield, Mass, 72, Columbia Col Gallery, Chicago, 79, Habatat Gallery, Dearborn, Mich, 79, Sandra Ainsley Gallery, Toronto, Ont, Can, 91, Habatat Galleries, Boca Raton, Fla, 91, Riley-Hawk Galleries, Cleveland, Ohio, 92 & Kurland/Summers Gallery, Los Angeles, 92; Glas Heute, Mus Bellerive, Zurich, Switz, 72; Enmansglas, Rosska Konstlojdsmuseet, Sweden, 74; The 9th Stockholm Art Fair, Sweden, 89; Expos Internationale de Verre Contemporain, Counseil Regional De Haute Normandie, Rouen, France, 91-92; 2nd Masterworks of Contemp Glass Benefit Auction, Christie's New York, New York Experimental Glass Workshop, 91; Illinois Glass: Univ Ill & Ill State Univ Perspective, Marx Gallery, Chicago, 91; Glass from Ancient Craft to Contemp Art: 1962-1992 & Beyond, Morris Mus, NJ, 92. *Pos:* Dir design, Blenke Glass Co, Milton, WVa, 63-70. *Teaching:* Prof art, ceramics & glass, Ill State Univ, Normal, 70- *Awards:* Fed Glass Award, Columbus Gallery Fine Arts, 73; Craftsmen's Fel, Nat Endowment Arts, 76-77 & 84; Purchase Award, Evansville Mus Arts & Sci, 79. *Bibliog:* Dan Klein (auth), Glass: A Contemporary Art, Rizzoli Pub, 89; Susanne K Frantz (auth), Contemp Glass, 89; Glasswork, No 6, Kyoto, Japan, 8/90. *Mem:* Glass Art Soc. *Media:* Glass. *Mailing Add:* Dept Art Illinois State Univ Normal IL 61761

MYERS, LEGH
SCULPTOR
b Ventnor, NJ, Nov 11, 16. *Study:* Pa State Univ, 35-36; Lehigh Univ, 36-39; also with J Wallace Kelly, 52-54. *Work:* Numerous pvt collections in Tokyo, Japan & throughout US; G E Corp Collection; New York Botanical Garden; Diversified Economic Servs, New York. *Exhib:* 13 shows, Knickerbocker Artists Ann, Nat Arts Club, New York, 57-81; 17 shows, Audubon Artists Ann, Nat Acad Design, New York, 60-84 & Allied Artists Ann, 61 & 62; Sculptors Guild Ann Mem Show, Lever House, New York, 71-88; plus four one-man shows in New York. *Awards:* Audubon Artists Medal Creative Sculpture, 28th Ann Exhib, 70 & Margaret Hirsch Levine Mem Prize Sculpture, 30th Ann Audubon Artists Exhib, 72, Nat Acad Design. *Bibliog:* Anthony Padovano (auth), The Process of Sculpture. *Mem:* Sculptors Guild (dir & secy, 72-); Audubon Artists; Knickerbocker Artists; Artists Equity Asn of New York. *Media:* Marble, Wood. *Publ:* Auth, articles, Artnews, 10/60 & 5/65, Arts Mag, 10/60, 1/70, 12/70 & 2/77, Herald Tribune, Charlotte Lichtblau, 4/10/65. *Mailing Add:* 101 E Devonshire Ave Linwood NJ 08221

MYERS, MALCOLM HAYNIE
PRINTMAKER, PAINTER
b Lucerne, Mo, June 19, 17. *Study:* Wichita State Univ, BFA; Univ Iowa, MA & MFA. *Work:* Libr Cong, Washington, DC; St Louis Art Mus; Walker Art Ctr, Minneapolis; Seattle Art Mus; Brooklyn Art Mus. *Exhib:* Ford Found, USA, 57; Am Prints Today, Print Coun; New York World's Fair Art Exhib; retrospective, Mr Possum and Friends, 1940-1983, Mus Art, Univ Minn, 82; one-person exhib, Walking the Dog, Dolly Fiterman Fine Art Gallery, Minneapolis, 82; A Spectrum of Inovation: Color in American Printmaking, 1890-1960, Amon Carter Mus, Fort Worth Tex, Nelson Atkins Mus Art, Kansas City, Samuel P Harn Mus Univ Fla, Gainseville, Worcester Art Mus, Worcester, Mass; and others. *Teaching:* Instr art, Univ Iowa, 45-47; prof art, Univ Minn, Minneapolis, 48-, chmn dept art, 65-70. *Awards:* Guggenheim Fels, 50-51 & 54-55; John Simon Guggenheim Fel, Paris, France, 50-51, Mexico City, Mexico, 54-55; Alumni Achievement Award, Wichita State Univ, Kans, 73. *Bibliog:* Article in Artists Proof, 60; Kenneth Campbell (dir), Malcolm Myers (film), Wis State Univ-Eau Claire, 69. *Mem:* Artists Equity Asn (pres Twin City chap, 53-55). *Dealer:* Dolly Fiterman Fine Art Gallery Minneapolis MN. *Mailing Add:* Dept of Studio Arts Univ Minn Minneapolis MN 55455

MYERS, MARTIN
SCULPTOR, PAINTER
b Syracuse, NY, April 21, 51. *Study:* Va Commonwealth Univ, BFA, 73; Calif Col Arts & Crafts, MFA, 74. *Work:* Oakland Mus; San Francisco Mus Mod Art; Univ Art Mus, Berkeley, Calif; Newport Harbor Art Mus. *Comn:* Sculpture, IBM, 85. *Exhib:* Virginia Artists--1973, Va Mus Fine Arts, 73; Cityscapes, Fine Arts Mus San Francisco, 77; 35th Biennial Contemp Painting, Corcoran Gallery Art, 77; A Sense of Scale, Oakland Mus, 77;

Viewpoint/77--Options in Painting, Cranbrook Mus, 77-78; Sculpture in California, 1975-1980, San Diego Mus, 80; New Bay Area Painting & Sculpture, Calif State Univ, Northridge, 82 & San Francisco Art Inst, 83; Constructions: Between Sculpture and Architecture, Sculpture Ctr, New York, 88; Redding Mus, Calif, 90. *Bibliog:* Judith Dunham (auth), Sculpture as painting as sculpture, Artweek, 77; Morris Yarowsky (auth), article, Art in Am, 79; Richard Armstrong (auth), catalog, Modernism, 81. *Media:* All Media; Acrylic, Oil. *Dealer:* Modernism Gallery San Francisco CA. *Mailing Add:* 376 President St Brooklyn NY 11231

MYERS, RITA
VIDEO ARTIST
b Hammonton, NJ, Dec 10, 47. *Study:* Douglass Col, Rutgers Univ, New Brunswick, NJ, BA, 69; Hunter Col, City Univ New York, MA, 74. *Exhib:* Solo exhibs, Gate, Anderson Gallery, Va Commonwealth Univ, Richmond, 85, Rift/Rise, Mass Col Art, Boston, 86, Alternative Mus, NY, 87, R H Love Mod, Chicago, 88, In The Drowning Pool, Long Beach Mus Art, Calif, 89, Berkshire Mus, Pittsfield, mass, 90 & Phantom Cities, Univ Gallery, Univ Mass, Amherst, 90; Video and Ritual, Mus Mod Art, NY, 84; American Landscape Video, Carnegie Mus Art, Pittsburgh, Pa, San Francisco Mus Mod Art, Calif, 88 & Newport Harbor Art Mus, Newport Beach, Calif, 89; Making Their Mark: Women Artists Move into the Mainstream, 1970-1985, Cincinnati Art Mus, Ohio, 89; Video-Sculptur Retrospektiv und Aktuell 1963-1989, Neuer Berliner Kunstverein, Berlin, 89 & Kolnischer Kunstverein, Koln, 89; Madison Art Ctr, Wis, 91; Carnegie Mus Art, Pittsburgh, Pa, 92; Tenth Worldwide Video Festival, Kijkhuis, Hague, Neth, 92; and other one-man & group exhibs. *Pos:* Panel, Creative Artists Pub Serv Prog (CAPS), 77, New York State Coun Arts, 85-88 & New York City Film/Video Prog, Jerome Found, 88-; film/video artists panel, MacDowell Colony, 92- *Teaching:* Var lectures & screenings, 76-92. *Awards:* Nat Endowment for Arts, Inter Arts Grant, 84, Media Arts Grant, 87 & Visual Artist's Fel, 76, 80 & 87; Art Matters, Inc, 88; Checkerboard Found, 89. *Bibliog:* Shelley Rice, Mythic Space, The Video Installations of Rita Myers, Afterimage, 1/82; John G Hanhardt, The Allure of the Real (catalog), Rita Myers-Rift Arise, Alternative Mus, New York, 9/26-11/7/87; John T Paoletti, Rita Myers and Deep Time, Arts Mag, 2/88. *Mem:* Parabola Arts Found, NY; Col Art Asn Media Alliance. *Publ:* Auth, Directions/Questions: Approaching A Future Mythology, Illuminating Video; An Essential Guide to Video Art, Aperture with Bavc, 91. *Mailing Add:* 131 Spring St No 4EF New York NY 10012

MYERS, TERRY R
CRITIC, HISTORIAN
b Ft Wayne, Ind, Jan 25, 65. *Study:* Depauw Univ, Greencastle, Ind, BA, 87. *Pos:* Libr asst, Mus Mod Art, New York, 87-90; catalogue coord, Roy Lichtenstein Catalogue Raisonne, New York, 90- *Teaching:* Vis instr art criticism, Pratt Inst, New York, 90. *Mem:* Int Asn Art Critics; Col Art Asn. *Res:* Criticism & chronicling of contemporary art & its context. *Publ:* Auth, Controlled substance: Marilyn Lerner's recent paintings, 89, Pressing pleasures: the urgent sculptures of Rona Pondick, From the junk aesthetic to the junk mentality, 90, Hard copy: the sincerely fraudulent photographs of Larry Johnson, 91 & coauth, White boy as Abstraction: do we really need another New York school, 92, Arts Mag, 92. *Mailing Add:* Nine Stanton St 2D New York NY 10002

MYERS, VIRGINIA ANNE
PRINTMAKER, PAINTER
b Greencastle, Ind, May 8, 27. *Study:* Corcoran Sch Art & George Washington Univ, Washington, DC, BA, 49; Calif Col Arts & Crafts, MFA, 51; Univ Ill, Champaign; Univ Iowa, Iowa City, printmaking with Mauricio Lasansky; Atelier 17, Paris, printmaking with Stanley William Hayter. *Work:* San Francisco Art Mus; Nelson-Atkins Mus, Kansas City, Kans; Toledo Mus Art, Ohio; Nat Collection Women's Art, Washington, DC; US State Dept. *Exhib:* One hundred and nine one-woman shows, 53-86; Engravings America 1974, Albrecht Art Gallery, St Joseph, Mo, 74; West '79/The Law Exhibition, Minn Mus Art, St Paul; Nat Invitational Exhib, Univ Hawaii, Hilo, 82; Artists in the Trenches, Univ Minn, 84; and others. *Teaching:* Instr printmaking, Univ Iowa, Iowa City, 62-68, asst prof, 68-71, assoc prof, 71-80, prof, 81- *Awards:* Fulbright Grant to Paris, 61; Develop Leave Award, Univ Iowa, 73, 78, 84 & 89; Arts Endowment Grants, State Iowa Arts Coun & Nat Endowment Arts, 74, 77, 82 & 85; Old Gold Summer Fel, Univ Iowa, 84 & 90. *Bibliog:* Denis O'Brien Van (auth), Iowan seeks perfections in art, teaching, Des Moines Register, 8/29/72; Joan Liffring & John Zug (coauth), Virginia Myers, printmaker, Iowan Mag, winter 81. *Media:* Copper Plates; Oil on Canvas. *Publ:* Creator, A Time of Malfeasance (21 engravings & drypoints), 77; Views from Tenacre: The Seasons (66 paintings & drawings on landscape themes); contribr, Handmade ink: A primer of basic principles, Printnews, 4-5/79; creator, Landscape in Iowa (36 drawings, paintings & prints), 85; and others. *Mailing Add:* 4244 NE 200 Tenth St Solon IA 52333

MYFORD, JAMES C
SCULPTOR, EDUCATOR
b Brackenridge, Pa, Aug 9, 40. *Study:* Edinboro Univ Pa, BS(art educ), 62; Ind Univ Pa, MEd(art educ), 66, MA(sculpture), 78. *Work:* Westmoreland Co Mus Art, Greensburg, Pa; Carnegie Libr, Pittsburgh, Pa. *Comn:* Outdoor aluminum sculptures, Aluminum Co Am, Pittsburgh, Pa, 75, First Nat Bank Pa, Erie, 78, Bloomsburg Univ, 80 & Manufacturing Data Systems Inc, Ann Arbor, Mich, 81; sculpture (stone & aluminum), City Pittsburgh, Pa, 83. *Exhib:* Assoc Artists Pittsburgh, Mus Art, Carnegie Inst, 70-83; 25th Ann Ball State Exhib, 79; Aluminum Sculpture, William Penn Mem Mus, Harrisburg, Pa, 79, Westmoreland Co Mus Art, Greensburg, Pa, 79 & Butler Inst Am Art, 83; Cast Aluminum Sculpture, Mus Art, Carnegie Inst, Pittsburgh, Pa, 80; Art Gallery Ont, 83; Sculptors Who Teach, Gov Mansion, Harrisburg, Pa, 83. *Teaching:* Assoc prof art, Slippery Rock Univ, 68- *Awards:* Alcoa Award, Assoc Artist Pittsburgh, 78; Jurors Award, Pittsburgh Soc Sculptors, 80; Second Prize Sculpture, Great Lakes Art Exhib, 82. *Bibliog:* Richard Sutphen (producer), Preparation for Museum Show (videotape), 81; Marilyn Evert (auth), Discovering Pittsburgh's Sculpture, Univ Pittsburgh Press, 83. *Mem:* Int Sculpture Ctr; Pittsburgh Soc Sculptors (bd mem, 80-82); Assoc Artists Pittsburgh. *Media:* Aluminum. *Mailing Add:* c/o Brubaker Gallery 415 St Armands Circle St Armands Key Sarasota FL 34236

MYRON, ROBERT
HISTORIAN
b Brooklyn, NY, Mar 15, 28. *Study:* NY Univ, BA, 49, MA, 50; Ohio State Univ, PhD(fel), 53. *Teaching:* Prof art hist & art appraisal, Hofstra Univ, Hempstead, NY, 54- *Awards:* Belgium-Am Found Awards, 53. *Mem:* Am Soc Appraisers; Appraisers Asn Am (bd dirs). *Res:* Tribal arts; American-Asian and Western art. *Publ:* Auth, Prehistoric Art, 59 & Italian Renaissance, 61, Pitman; auth, Mounds, Towns, Totems, 63 & Two Faces of Asia: India, China, 65, World; auth, American Art, 2 vols, Crowell-Collier, 70. *Mailing Add:* 401 Garden Blvd Garden City NY 11530

N

NAAR, HARRY I
PAINTER, EDUCATOR
b New Brunswick, NJ, July 28, 46. *Study:* Philadelphia Col Art, BFA, 68; Ind Univ, MFA, 70. *Work:* Jane Voorhees Zimmerli Art Mus, Rutgers Univ; NJ State Mus, Trenton; Continental Life Insurance Corp, Piscataway, Ingersoll Publ Co, Princeton, NJ & Rider Col, Lawrenceville, NJ; Johnson & Johnson Corp, NJ; Bristol Myers Squibb Corp, Plainsboro, NJ; and others. *Exhib:* Nat Drawing Exhib, Indianapolis Mus Art, 70, Corcoran Gallery Art, 70, High Mus Art, 70 & Trenton State Col, 83; USSR Artists Union Gallery, Moscow; Trenton City Mus, 91; ALJIRA, Ctr Contemp Art, NJ, 91; Paintings: New Jersey, William Paterson Col, NJ, Ben Shahn Galleries, 92; Nat Inst Health, Bethesda, Md, 92; and others. *Collections Arranged:* Down to Earth: Landscape in Print, 83, NJ Print Coun, 83; WPA, Then/Now, Leon Bibel, 83; Graphite: A Collector's Choice, a Selection of Drawings from the Collections of Ronald Abramson, 84; Color in Space, Paintings & Collages of Prich Matthews, 84; Larry Day, Paintings & Drawings, 85; Humanistic Show Portraits in Contemp Am Art, Boris Putterman, cur, 86; Old Man Mad About Drawing, Retrospective by Jacob Landau of Drawings - Youth to Present, 88; Water Darby Bannard, Paintings the Barcelona Run Series, 89; Jonathan Shahn, Sculpture and Drawings, 90; Robert Godfrey Paintings about Drawings, Drawings about Paintings, 90; Robert Birmelin, On Being an Observer, 91; Ruth Fine, California Landscapes, 91; Peter Paone, Drawings, 91; Elias Friedensohn, Narratives of Place and Timeless Being, 92; Lois Dodd, Paintings--Views of Windows and Doors, 92; Anthony Dubovsky, The Land of Polin, 92; Edith Neff, Paintings and Drawings, 92. *Teaching:* Instr painting & drawing, Beaver Col, Pa, 75-78 & Rutgers Univ, 78-80; assoc prof painting, drawing, printmaking & design, Rider Col, NJ, 80-; vis artist, Philadelphia Col Art, 84. *Awards:* Rider Col Summer Res Grant, 82-88; Res Grant, Rider Col Summer, 82 & 88; Dorothy Malloy Mem Award, Trenton City Mus, 92. *Bibliog:* Rachel Mullen (auth), Strength from nature, Bernardsville News, 4/77; Doris Brown (auth), Focus on still life, Sunday Home News, NJ, 1/7/79; Estelle Sinclaire (auth), Harry Naar's art talks about communication, Princeton Packet, NJ, 5/86; Rachael Mullen (auth), Harry Naar, still life's glow with color and light, Bernardsville News-Observer Tribune, NJ, 85; Robert Godfrey (auth), Naar's art influenced by French, Arts Ashville Citizen-Times, NC, 89; Zolton Buki (auth), Harry I Naar drawings & watercolors (one-person catalog), Chelsa Gallery, WCarolina Univ, Cullowhee, NC, 89; Robert Godfrey, Jon Jecha, James E Smith, Gene Thornton (auths), Drawing, points of view; John Perreault (auth), Decade of the Eighties, Belk Art Gallery, WCarolina Univ, Cullowhee, NC, 89; Elizabeth Vogt (auth), Still life's paintings and drawings by Harry I Naar (catalog), Rabbet Gallery, New Brunswick, NJ, 90; Cathy Viksjo (auth), Harry Naar, art is not a fluff thing, its thinking, Sun, Trenton Times, NJ, 90. *Mem:* Col Art Asn Am; Printmaking Coun NJ (bd mem, 83). *Media:* Oil, Acrylic, Watercolor. *Publ:* Auth, Prich Matthews Color in Space, NJ State Mus, 82; contribr, Graphite: A Collector's Choice, An Idea About Contemporary Drawing, Montgomery Col, 83; auth, Enjoyable to Sense, Beautiful to See, Ericson Gallery, 83; A natural thing, Jean Helion's representational paintings, Arts Mag, 4/84; Reginald Neal (auth), Works from 1958 to the present, NJ, State Mus, Trenton, NJ, 89. *Dealer:* Rabbet Gallery 120 Georges Rd New Brunswick NJ 08901; Riverside Studio Pottersville NJ. *Mailing Add:* c/o Rabbet Gallery 120 Georges Rd New Brunswick NJ 08901

NADALINI, (LOUIS ERNEST)
PAINTER
b San Francisco, Calif, Jan 21, 27. *Study:* City Col San Francisco; Art Students League, with George Grosz; also with Martin Baer, San Francisco, 58-60; San Francisco Art Inst, Hon MA, 70. *Work:* Oakland Art Mus, Univ Calif, Berkeley, San Francisco Pub Sch & Wells Fargo Bank, San Francisco, Calif; Veterans Admin Hosp, Seattle, Wash. *Exhib:* One-man shows, Village Art Ctr, New York, 53 & Am Student & Artist Ctr, Paris, 54; San Francisco Mus Art Painting Ann, 57-59 & 66; Calif Palace Legion Honor, San Francisco, 63-67; Pa Acad Fine Arts 161st Ann, 66; Oakland Art Mus

Painting Ann, 66-69; La Galerie Mouffe, Paris, France; Minami Gallery, Tokyo, Japan; El Crito Gallery, Caracas, Venezuela. *Teaching:* Instr art, San Francisco Pub Sch, 69-70. *Awards:* James D Phelan Award, Calif Palace Legion Honor, 65 & 67; Salon Int Diploma, D Honneur, Paris, France, 81; Merit Award Art, London, Eng, 80; Gold Medal, Acad Italy, 80; First Palce, Salute to the Arts, Seattle, Wash, 86. *Bibliog:* A Fried (auth), article, San Francisco Examiner, 58; A Frankenstein (auth), article, San Francisco Chronicle, 66; W Ramsey (auth), Paintings, KPIX-TV, San Francisco, 1/66; Robert Henkes (auth), The Crucifixion in American Paintings, 80; Thomas Albright (critic), Art in the San Francisco Bay Area, 1945-1980, 80. *Mem:* Artists Equity Asn (vpres Seattle chap, currently). *Media:* Oil, Acrylic. *Publ:* Auth, Catalogue of the Art Bank, San Francisco Art Inst Sch, 59-60; From the West, San Francisco Art Inst, 64; articles & rev in Artforum, 3/66 & 5/71 & San Francisco Arts, 6/67. *Dealer:* La Galerie Mouffe 67 Rue Mouffetard 75005 Paris France. *Mailing Add:* 1726 15th Ave No 10 Seattle WA 98122

NADEL, ANN HONIG
SCULPTOR
b San Francisco, Calif, May 9, 40. *Study:* Univ Calif, Berkeley, 58-59; San Francisco State Univ, BA, 62, MA, 70. *Work:* VPres House, Washington, DC; Frederick Weisman Found Art, Los Angeles; Hewlett-Packard Co. *Comn:* Stoneware plate, comn by Joan Mondale, Washington, DC, 78; Rocky Mountain High, stoneware, comn by Carl Djerassi, Palo Alto, Calif, 83; Paint-Stiks-Stoneware, Fireman Fund Insurance, San Marin Co, 83; Eden, bronze, Hewlett Packard Co, Palto Alto, 86; Kimono 88, bronze, comn by Marcia Weisman, Beverly Hills, Calif, 88; Kimono, comn by Pac-Tel, 92. *Exhib:* Northern Calif Craft Exhib, Mindocino Art Ctr, 82; One-woman shows, Kimonos, Bluxome Gallery, San Francisco, 83-85, sculpture, Gallery 454 North, Los Angeles, Temple Emanu-El, San Francisco, 88, Graduate Theological Union, Flora Lamson Hewlett Libr, Berkeley, Calif, 88 & Earl McGarth Gallery, Los Angeles, 90 & 92; Jewish Themes, Northern Calif, Judah L Magnes Mus, Berkeley, 87; Order and Diversity, Flora Lamson Hewlett Libr, Berkely, 88. *Bibliog:* News and Retrospect, Ceramic Monthly, 9/83; Galleries, Los Angeles Times, 2/5/88. *Media:* Bronze, Clay. *Dealer:* Earl McGrath Gallery 454 N Robertson Los Angeles CA 90048; Earl McGrath Gallery New York NY 10021. *Mailing Add:* 6 Starboard Ct Mill Valley CA 94941

NADOLSKI, STEPHANIE LUCILLE
PAINTER, PRINTMAKER
b Sacramento, Calif, Feb 21, 45. *Study:* San Jose State Col, 62-68; Sch Art, Bellevue, Nebr, 72; with Edgar Whitney, Robert E Wood & Glen Bradshaw, 78-83. *Work:* Univ Miss Libr, Oxford; Tex Commerce Bank, Scurlock Towers, Arthur Anderson & Co & Mus Art Am West, Houston; Bowne Corp, Detroit Mich and Chicago Ill. *Comn:* Painting & offset lithographs, LeClub Condominiums, Galveston, Tex, 84; Mixed media painting, ACA Corp, Streamwood, Ill, 89; Handcast Paper wall relief, S McAllister, Palatine, Ill, 89; Paper wall relief, Unique Coupon Corp, Lake Barrington Shores, Ill, 91; Abstr monoprints, three, comn by Mr & Mrs Dilworth, Kenilworth, Ill, 92. *Exhib:* Kentucky Highlands: Small Painting Nat, Highlands Mus Art, Ashland, 87 & 88; N Coast Collage Soc Ann Exhib, Beachwood Mus, Ohio, 89; one person shows: Schaumburg Prairie Ctr Arts, Ill, 87; Barrington Area Arts Coun, 89, O'Kane Gallery, Univ Houston, Tex, 88; Nat juried exhib: 12th Annual Print & Drawing, Harper Col, Palatine, Ill, 88; Nat Art Competition, Northeast Mo State Univ, Kirksville, 89; Watermedia, Mont Watercolor Soc, Helena, 89; Paper in Particular, Columbia Col, Mo, 89; Soc of Layerists in Multi-Media, Coshocton, Ohio, 90; Hats, Helmets & Headgear, Textile Arts Ctr, Chicago Ill, 89. *Pos:* Dir, Archway Gallery Houston, 76-87; dir, Barrington Area Arts Coun, 87-89; adv bd, Barrington Area Arts Coun, 89. *Teaching:* Instr watercolor, North Harris Co Col, 84-86; Papermaking - mixed media monotypes, free lance workshops, 87-92; Artist in residence, Virginia Lake Elem, Palatine, Ill, 90; Willow Grove Sch, Buffalo Grove, Ill, 93. *Awards:* First Ann Flo Bash Award, Barrington Area Arts Coun, 89; First Award, Glenview Outdoor Art Fair, Glenview Art League, 90; Award of Excellence, Crystal Lake Com Arts Coun, 91. *Bibliog:* Kirk Birginal (auth), Artful Pursuit, Barrington Courier Pioneer Press, 87; Sandra Dybal (auth), Portrait of an Artist, Daily Herald Paddock Publs, 87 & Chicago Art Rev, 89; American References. *Mem:* Houston Art Dealers Asn (dir, 83-85); Watercolor Art Soc, Houston (pres elect, 86); Northwest Cult Coun, (bd dir); Barrington Area Arts Coun, (adv bd); assoc, Chicago Artists Coalition (bd dirs); assoc, Allied Artists Am. *Media:* Watercolor, Acrylic; Monoprint, Handmade paper. *Publ:* Coauth, Mixed Media Gallery, Crafts Report, 84 & Shuttle, Spindle & Dyepot, 84; auth, Paintings, monotypes & paper, Town Mag, 85. *Dealer:* Art Independent Gallery 623 Main St Lake Geneva WI 53147; Janis Craig Gallery Eight N Dunton Ave Arlington Heights ILL 60005. *Mailing Add:* 25287 Barsumain Dr Barrington IL 60010

NAEGLE, MONTANA
PAINTER
b April 21, 40. *Study:* Univ Wyo, BFA. *Work:* First Interstate Bank Ariz, Tucson; Miller & Blau, Casper, Wyo; Fred Dowd & Co, Casper, Wyo; Hines Indust, Albuquerque, NMex; Williams, Porter & Day, Casper, Wyo; and others. *Exhib:* NMex Inter, Clovis, 85; solo exhib, Wyo State Art Mus, Cheyenne, 79, Nicolaysen Art Mus, Casper, 79 & 84, Casper Col Visual Art Ctr, 88; Watercolor USA, Springfield, Miss, 88; Univ NMex, Albuquerque, 88; Contemporary Art in Cowboy State, Nicolaysen Mus, 9/88; and others. *Teaching:* Watercolor instr, Casper Col, Wyo, 83-84. *Bibliog:* Mary Carrol Nelson (auth), article, Southwest Art, 84; Montana Naegle-Report to Wyo, News Special, KTWO. *Media:* Watercolor. *Mailing Add:* 1540 Linda Vista Casper WY 82609

NAEVE, MILO M
ADMINISTRATOR, HISTORIAN
b Ness Co, Kans, Oct 9, 31. *Study:* Univ Colo, BFA; Univ Del, Winterthur Prog Am Studies & MA. *Pos:* Mem staff, Winterthur Mus, Del & Colonial Williamsburg, Va; dir, Colorado Springs Fine Arts Ctr, Colo; Art Inst Chicago; ed bd, Am Art J; trustee, Showhegan Sch Painting & Sculpture, 91. *Awards:* Field McCormick Curator Emeritus Am Art, Art Inst Chicago, 91; Ill Acad Fine Arts Lifetime Achievement Award, 91. *Mem:* Brit Mus Asn; Royal Soc Arts; Am Asn Mus; Nat Trust for Hist Preservation; Victorian Soc Am; and others. *Res:* American painting, sculpture, architecture, and decorative arts from the seventeenth to the twentieth century. *Publ:* Contribr, art mags & prof jour; ed, Winterthur Portfolio, Vol I-III & auth, The Classical Presence in American Art, Art Inst Chicago, 78; Identifying American Furniture: A Pictorial Guide to Styles and Terms, Am Asn State & Local Hist, 81, 2nd ed, 90; auth, John Lewis Krimmel: An Artist in Federal America, Univ Del Press, 87; and others. *Mailing Add:* 24 Ingleton Circle Kennett Square PA 19348

NAFTULIN, ROSE
PAINTER
b Philadelphia, Pa. *Study:* Philadelphia Col Art, 43-45; Barnes Found, 62-64. *Work:* Woodmere Art Mus, Philadelphia; Philadelphia Free Libr, Pa; Burlington Indust, NY; Johnson & Johnson, NJ; Fidelity Bank, Pa; Prescott Forbes, EI Dupont de Nemours & Co; Provident Bank; Fed Nat Mortgage Asn; State Mus NJ; State Mus Pa; Bryn Mawr Col; Bryn Mawr Hosp. *Exhib:* Philadelphia Mus Art, Pa, 58; Nat Watercolor Exhib, Pa Acad Fine Art, Philadelphia, 67; Cheltenham Art Ctr Ann Award Show, Pa, 59-81; Allied Artists Am, Nat Acad Design, New York, 76; Nat Acad Design Ann Exhib, New York, 76 & 80; Juried Ann, Allentown Art Mus, Pa, 80; solo show, Gross McCleaf, 81, 83, 85, 87, 91; Kornbluth Gallery, Fairlawn, NJ, 89-90 & 92; Pandion Gallery, Fishers Island, New York, 89, 90 & 92. *Teaching:* Instr painting, Cheltenham Art Ctr, 64-80; instr painting, Woodmere Art Mus, 77-81. *Awards:* David Humphreys Prize, Nat Acad Design, 76; Cert of Merit, Nat Acad Design, 80; Blumenthal Award, Cheltenham Art Ctr, Pa, 83. *Media:* Oil, Watercolor. *Publ:* Contr Painting Flowers, Watson-Guetill Publ; Color Strategies for the Painters, Prentice Hall. *Mailing Add:* c/o Gross McCleaf Gallery 127 S 16th St Philadelphia PA 19102

NAGANO, PAUL TATSUMI
PAINTER, DESIGNER
b Honolulu, Hawaii, May 21, 38. *Study:* Columbia Col, BA, 60; Pa Acad Fine Arts, Philadelphia, 63-67. *Work:* Hawaii State Found of Cult & the Arts, Honolulu; William Rockhill Nelson Gallery, Kansas City, Mo; New Brit Mus Am Art, Conn; Boston Public Libr. *Comn:* Lilac Sunday (watercolor), The Arnold Arboretum, Harvard Univ, 86; Sheraton Kauai Hotel, Hawaii, 90. *Exhib:* Pa Acad Fine Arts 75th Ann Fel Exhib, 72; Japanese Artist in Hawaii, 78-81; Fine Art of Business, Boston, 81; Duxbury Art Complex Mus, Mass, 82; Honolulu Acad Arts, 88; Ctr Strategic & Int Studies, Jakarta, Indonesia, 90; Two Visions, Neka Mus, Ubud, Bali, 92; and others. *Pos:* Art dir, Pucker-Safrai Gallery, Boston, 67-89. *Awards:* First Prize Landscape with Figures, Popular Photog, 63; Packard Prize Drawing, 64 & Lewis S Ware Traveling Scholar, 67, Pa Acad Fine Arts. *Mem:* Fel Pa Acad Fine Arts. *Media:* Watercolor. *Publ:* Contribr, Am Artist, 3/85. *Mailing Add:* Fenway Studio 406 30 Ipswich St Boston MA 02215-3616

NAGANO, SHOZO
PAINTER
b Kanazawa, Japan. *Study:* Kanazawa Fine Arts Univ, AB; Art Students League, with Julian Levi; Pratt Inst, New York. *Work:* Allentown Art Mus, Pa; Berkshire Mus, Pittsfield, Mass; Citicorp, New York; Hudson River Mus, Yonkers, NY; State Univ NY Albany. *Comn:* It is Finished (painting), comn by Richard Hirsch, cur James Michener Collection, 71. *Exhib:* Nat Inst Arts & Lett, 72; Brooklyn Mus, 75, 77 & 78; one-man show, Squibb Art Ctr, 76; Japan Today, 79; Sindin Gallery, 82; Newark Mus, 83; and others. *Teaching:* Instr painting, Seibu Gakuen, Tokyo, 60-65. *Bibliog:* Alvin Smith (auth), article in Art Int, 5/72; David Shirey (auth), articles in New York Times, 9/75 & 3/76. *Mem:* Japanese Artists Asn NY (pres, 75). *Media:* Acrylic. *Publ:* Illusr, Kiristo-Kyo-Hoiku, 61-72; contribr, Haha no Hikari, 69-72. *Mailing Add:* c/o Moran 39 Race St Jim Thorpe PA 18229

NAGENGAST, WILLIAM JOSEPH
PAINTER, DESIGNER
b Newark, NJ, May 28, 34. *Study:* Newark Sch Fine & Indust Arts, cert, 53; studied with Hans Weingartner & H Gasser, 54-60; with James Carlin & John Grabach, 55-57. *Work:* Advert Marketing Corp, Sparta, NJ. *Comn:* Abstract painting, Spinello Construction Co, Morristown, NJ, 76; Shaw Plastic Corp, Berkeley Heights, NJ, 79; painting, Advert Marketing Corp, Sparta, NJ, 80. *Exhib:* Ocean City Mus, NJ, 73; one-man show, Kean Col, NJ, 74; Am Bicentennial Exhib, Paris, France, 75; Newark Pub Libr, 75, Montclair Art Mus & Newark Mus, NJ; and others. *Pos:* Illusr/art consult, Advert Marketing Corp, Sparta, NJ, 75-; spec effects coordr, Chicksilva, New York, 78-79; spec effects coordr, Peter Runfolo Asn NJ, 80-81. *Teaching:* Instr, Newark Sch Fine & Indust Arts, 60-72. *Awards:* Grand Prizes, Atlantic City 12th Ann Nat, NJ, 75, South Orange Nat Art Show, 80 & Irvington State Nat Art Show, NJ, 80. *Bibliog:* Ruth Ann Williams (auth), article, NJ Music & Arts, spring 73; Eileen Watkins (auth), New Jersey artist, Newark Star Ledger, 75. *Mem:* Irvington Art Assocs NJ (bd dirs, 76-78, pres, 77-79); Nat Soc Painters Casein & Acrylics (bd dirs, 75-76). *Publ:* Illusr, contribr, Out of our past, Am Graphic Inc, 74; and others. *Dealer:* Offices Unlimited Gallery Morristown NJ. *Mailing Add:* 159 Park Pl Irvington NJ 07111

NAGIN, MARY D
PAINTER, EDUCATOR
b Amityville, NY, Dec 28, 53. *Study:* State Univ Col Plattsburgh, NY, BA, 75; Adelphi Univ, Garden City, NY, MA, 83, with Jeffrey R Webb. *Exhib:* Selections from the NDA, Hermitage Found Mus, Norfolk, Va, 88; Wichita Small Oil Competition, Wichita Art Asn, Kans, 88; Works on Paper Nat Exhib, Firehouse Gallery, NCC, Garden City, NY, 89; Allied Artists Ann, Nat Arts Club, New York, 90; Pastel Invitational, Mill Pond House STAC, St James, NY, 92; and others. *Pos:* Exhib chmn, Nat Drawing Asn, 88-89; cur gallery, Nassau Community Col, 89-90; art comt, Salmagundi Club, 90; exhib chmn, pastel div, Pen & Brush Club, 92. *Teaching:* instr drawing & painting, Huntington Township Art League, 83-; instr watercolor, St John's Univ, New York, 91. *Awards:* Beatrice Vare Award, Ann Pastels Only, Pastel Soc Am, 90; Philip Isenberg Award, Ann Pastel Exhib, Pen & Brush, 92. *Bibliog:* Phyllis Braff (auth), Show mixes the unusual and the traditional, NY Times, 1/22/86; NF Karlins (auth), Pastels front & center, Westsider, New York, 9/92. *Mem:* Huntington Township Art League (fac mem, 83); Pastel Soc Am, New York, 88-; Salmagundi Club, New York (art comt, 90-); Pen & Brush, New York (exhib chmn, pastel div, 92). *Media:* Oil, Pastel. *Dealer:* Robley Gallery 1356 Old Northern Blvd Roslyn NY 11576. *Mailing Add:* 270 Lowndes Ave Apt 117 Huntington Station NY 11746

NAGLE, RON
CERAMIST
b San Francisco, Calif, 39. *Study:* San Francisco State Col, BFA, 61. *Work:* Everson Mus Art, Syracuse, NY; Oakland Mus, Calif; Philadelphia Mus Art; San Francisco Mus Mod Art; St Louis Mus Art. *Exhib:* One-person exhibs, Currents 4, St Louis Art Mus, Mo, 79, Charles Cowles Gallery, New York, 81, 83, 85 & 89, Quay Gallery, San Francisco, Calif, 82 & 84, Greenberg Gallery, St Louis, Mo, 82, Delahunty Gallery, Dallas, Tex, 83, Betsy Rosenfield Gallery, Chicago, Ill, 84, Ron Nagle: Big Work, Rena Bransten Gallery, San Francisco, Calif, 88; Clay Revisions: Plate, Cup, Vase, Seattle Art Mus, Wash, 87; Ceramics for the Marer Collection, Pasadena City Col Art Gallery, Calif, 90; Building with Clay, Hoffman Gallery, Oregon Sch Arts & Crafts, Portland, 90; Vessels: From Use to Symbol, Am Craft Mus, NY, 90; Rituals of Tea XI, Garth Clark Gallery, Los Angeles, Calif, 90. *Teaching:* San Francisco Art Inst, Calif, 61-65, 76-78; Univ Calif, Berkeley, 62-73; Univ Calif Exten, San Francisco, 73-75; Calif Col Arts & Crafts, Oakland, 73-75; Calif State Univ, Hayward, 75; Univ Calif, Irvine, 75; Mills Col, Oakland, Calif, 78-. *Awards:* Fel, Nat Endowment Arts, 74, 79, 86; Adaline Kent Award, 78; Mellon Grant, 81 & 83. *Mailing Add:* c/o Charles Cowles Gallery 420 W Broadway New York NY 10012

NAHAS, DOMINIQUE FRANÇOIS
MUSEUM DIRECTOR, CURATOR
b Sallanches, France, Dec 27, 51; US citizen. *Study:* Univ Wis Madison, BA, 74; Sch Visual Arts, New York, BFA, 80; Inst Fine Arts, New York, MA, 85. *Collections Arranged:* Nancy Spero-Works since 1950, Everson Mus, traveled to Mus Contemp Art, Chicago & New Mus, New York, 87; Public Mind: Les Levine's Media Sculpture and Mass Ad Campaigns, 1969-1990, Everson Mus, traveled to Stedjek, Muka, Amsterdam, 90. *Pos:* Chief Cur Contemp Art, Everson Mus, Syracuse, NY, 85-89; dir, Neuberger Mus, State Univ NY, 90. *Teaching:* Vis fac, computer arts, Sch Visual Arts, New York, 89-90; Ed Dept, Metrop Mus Art, New York (lectr 90-). *Awards:* Grant, Luso Am Found, 89. *Mem:* Am Asn Mus, 85-92. *Publ:* Auth, Sacred Spaces, 87, coauth, Figures Form & Fiction, 88, Nancy Spero, works since 1950-Retrospective, 87 & auth, Public Mind: Les Levine's Media Sculpture & Mass Ad Campaigns, 69-90, Everson Mus; auth, Site: the recent work of Michel Gerard, Sculpture Mag, 5-6/92. *Mailing Add:* PO Box 1491 New York NY 10009

NAIMAN, LEE
DEALER, CONSULTANT
b Baltimore, Md. *Study:* Goucher Col, BA; Sorbonne, Paris; Johns Hopkins Univ; NY Univ. *Work:* IBM, AT&T, MCI Corps; Philadelphia Nat Bank; Equitable Life Insurance; Consolidado Int Bank, NY. *Comn:* Etched glass, comn by B Gilsoul, NJ Supreme Ct; Hillsborough Int Airport, Tampa; Lincoln Hosp, New York; Amwerst Subway Sta, Buffalo; Johnson & Johnson, NY. *Exhib:* Baltimore Mus Art; Manhattanville Col, Purchase, NY; Davison Art Ctr, Weslayan Univ. *Collections Arranged:* Etchings of Gunter Grass, A G Becker Inc, New York; Equitable Life Insurance Co. *Pos:* Owner, Naiman Fine Art, 70-. *Teaching:* Instr, workshops, New Sch Social Res, NY & Glassboro Col. *Mem:* Women's Adv Coun; New York Coun Econ Develop Admin. *Specialty:* Corporate collections, public sculpture. *Mailing Add:* 300 Central Park W New York NY 10024

NAKAMURA, KAZUO
PAINTER
b Vancouver, BC, Oct 13, 26. *Study:* Cent Tech Sch, Toronto. *Work:* Nat Gallery Can, Ottawa; Art Gallery Ont, Toronto; Mus Mod Art, New York; Hirshhorn Mus, Washington, DC; Musee d'Art Contemporain, Montreal. *Comn:* Two sculptures, Toronto Int Airport, 63; mural panel, Queen's Park Complex, Toronto. *Exhib:* 2nd Bienniale Mus Art Mod, Paris, 61; Recent Acquisitions, Mus Mod Art, New York, 63; Can Artists 68, Art Gallery Ont, Toronto, 68; Nakamura 1951-1974, R McLaughlin Art Gallery, Can tour, 74-75; Ont Heritage Found Firestone Collection European Tour, 83-84; Grand Opening Exhib, Nat Gallery Can, Ottawa, 88. *Awards:* Prizewinner, 4th Int Exhib Drawings & Engravings, Lugano, Switz, 56. *Bibliog:* Andrew Bell (auth), The Art of Nakamura, Can Art, 8/59; J M Careless (ed), The Canadians, Macmillan Co, Can, 67; The Canadian Encyclopedia Hurtig Publ, 85 & 88. *Media:* Oil, Watercolor. *Mailing Add:* 3 Langmuir Crescent Toronto ON M6S 2A6 Canada

NAKAZATO, HITOSHI
PAINTER, PRINTMAKER
b Tokyo, Japan, Mar 15, 36. *Study:* Tama Col Art, Tokyo, BFA(painting), 60, with Shosuke Oksawa; Univ Wis, MS(art, printmaking),64; Univ Pa, MFA(painting), with Piero Dorazio, 66. *Work:* Mus Mod Art, New York; Philadelphia Mus Art; Nat Mus Mod Art, Kyoto, Japan; Pa Acad Fine Arts, Philadelphia; Brooklyn Mus, New York. *Comn:* Mural, Furukawa Pavilion, Expo 70, Osaka, Japan. *Exhib:* Artists in Americas, Nat Mus Mod Art, Kyoto, 74; Three Hundred Years of American Art, Philadelphia Mus, 76; Contemporary Japanese Painting, Japan Art Festival 10th Anniversary, Tokyo, 77; Prints in Series: Idea into Image, Brooklyn Mus, New York, 77; one-man shows, Mercer Col, 78, West Chester Col, 79, Pa Acad Fine Arts, 79 Contemporary Drawings: Philadelphia II, Philadelphia Mus Art, 79, One Eleven One, Tokyo Gallery, 89, Yaseido Gallery, Tokyo, 91, Gallery Kuranuki, Osaka, Japan, 92; Yokohama '92, First Int Contemp Art Fair, Japan, 92. *Teaching:* Asst prof painting, Tama Col Art, Tokyo, 68-71; asst prof printmaking, Grad Sch of Fine Arts, Univ of Pa, Philadelphia, 73-79, assoc prof, 79-. *Awards:* John D Rockefeller 3rd Grant, 66-67; Creative Artists Public Service Grant, 74-75. *Bibliog:* Joseph Love (auth), Tokyo Letter, Art Int, 3-12/71; Ruth Lehrer (auth), Three Hundred Years of American Art: Philadelphia, Philadelphia Mus, 76; Teruazu Suenage (auth), Art 78, Bijutsu Techo, 1/78. *Mem:* Am Color Print Soc. *Media:* Acrylic, Oil; All Media. *Mailing Add:* 361 W 36th St New York NY 10018

NAKONECZNY, MICHAEL
PAINTER
b Detroit, Mich, Oct 30, 52. *Study:* Cleveland State Univ, Ohio, BFA, 79; Univ Cincinnati, MFA, 81. *Exhib:* 39th Corcoran Biennial Exhis Am Painting, Corcoran Gallery Art, Washington, DC (and toured US), 85; Made in America: The Great Lakes States, Alternative Mus, New York, NY, 86; solo exhib, Landscapes of the Mind, Cleveland Ctr Contemp Art, Ohio, 86; Awards in Visual Arts, Los Angeles Co Mus, 88; Zolla/Lieberman Gallery, Chicago, 92; Tamarind Inst, Albuquerque, NMex, 92; Bemis Found, Omaha, Nebr, 92; and others. *Teaching:* Instr, Herron Sch Art, Univ Ind. *Awards:* Fel, Awards in Visual Arts, 87; Artist-in-Residence, PS 1 Long Island City, NY, 86; Individual Artist Fel, Ohio Arts Coun, 90. *Mem:* Chicago Artist Collection. *Dealer:* Zolla/Lieberman Gallery 2010 Wesley Evanston IL. *Mailing Add:* c/o Zolla/Lieberman Gallery 325 W Huron Chicago IL 60610

NAMA, GEORGE ALLEN
PRINTMAKER, SCULPTOR
b Pittsburgh, Pa, Feb 23, 39. *Study:* Carnegie-Mellon Univ, BFA & MFA; Atelier 17, Paris, with Stanley William Hayter. *Work:* Philadelphia Mus Art; Smithsonian Inst, Libr Cong, Washington, DC; Brooklyn Mus; Butler Inst Am Art, Youngstown, Ohio; Carnegie Inst Mus Art; Biblioteque Nationale, Paris. *Comn:* Gulf Oil Co, Pittsburgh. *Exhib:* Original Prints, Calif Palace of Legion of Honor, San Francisco, 64; Pratt Graphic Art Ctr Serigraph Exhib, 65; Northwest Printmakers Int Exhib, 65-67; Contemp Am Prints, Gt Brit, 69-71; US Info Agency Exhibs, Japan Expo, 70; Nat Acad Design, 80-86. *Teaching:* Instr, Pratt Inst, 76-86, Sch Visual Arts, 79, The New Sch, 85-86 & Nat Acad Design, 80-86. *Awards:* David Berger Mem Prize, Mus Fine Arts, Boston, 67; Stuart M Egnal Prize, Philadelphia Print Club, 68; Stella Drabkin Mem Award, Am Color Print Soc, 71; Cannon Prize, Nat Acad Design, 85. *Bibliog:* Leonard Slatkes (auth), Printmakers on Exhibit, Art Scene, 68; Richard Shelton (auth), Journal of Return, Kayak, 69; S Hazo (auth), Poets & Prints, Artist Proof Mag, 71. *Mem:* Asn Nat Acad Design. *Media:* Intaglio, Casting. *Publ:* Monuments, 71; Seascript, 71; Origin of Language, Nine Etchings, 79; Desert Water, 81; Grapes of Zeuxis, 87; and others. *Mailing Add:* RFD 1 Box 72 Montauk NY 11954

NAMINGHA, DAN
PAINTER, PRINTMAKER
b Polacca, Ariz, May 1, 50. *Study:* Univ Kans, Lawrence, 67; Inst Am Indian Arts, Santa Fe, NMex, 67-69; Am Acad Art, Chicago, Ill, 69. *Work:* US Dept Interior Arts Collection, Washington, DC; Mus Am Indian Arts and Culture, Chicago, Ill; Mus Northern Ariz, Flagstaff; Heard Mus, Phoenix, Ariz; Mus Fine Art, Santa Fe, NMex; US Embassy, Brazilia; Montclair Art Mus, NJ. *Comn:* View from Walpi (mural), City Phoenix, Ariz, 79. *Exhib:* Mus Northern Ariz, Flagstaff, 77; one-man show, Orange Coast Col, Costa Mesa, Calif, 77; Extensions of the Nampeyo Creative Spirit, Calif; Contemp Am Indian Painting, Chile, Bolivia, Peru, Columbia, Ecuaador, South Am, 79; Hopi Kachina Spirit of Life, Calif Acad Sci, San Francisco, Calif, 80-82; Carnegie Mus, Pittsburgh; Am Mus Natural Hist, New York; Smithsonian Inst, Washington, DC; Field Mus, Chicago, Ill; Am Indian Art in the 1980's, Native Am Ctr Living Arts, Niagara Falls, 80; Nat Acad Sciences, Washington, DC. *Bibliog:* Mary Carroll Nelson (auth), Dan Namingha--the migration of a Hopi artist, Am Artist Mag, 79; Jamake Highwater (auth), The Sweet Grass Lives On, Lippincott and Crowell, 80; Jack Peterson (dir), Am Indian Artist II (film series), Native Am Public Broadcasting Consortium, Inc, 82; Dan Namingha, CBS Sunday Morning, Bob Pierpoint, Charles Kuralt. *Dealer:* Niman Fine Art 125 Lincoln Ave Ste 116 Santa Fe NM 87501. *Mailing Add:* c/o Niman Fine Art 125 Lincoln Ave Suite 115 Santa Fe NM 87501

NAPOLES, VERONICA KLEEMAN
GRAPHIC ARTIST
b New York, NY, July 9, 51. *Study:* Univ Miami, BA, 72; Univ Calif Berkeley, BArch, 79. *Pos:* Designer, Mus Anthrop, San Francisco, 77-79 & Napoles Design Group, 79-. *Teaching:* Teacher dynamic graphics, Educ Found, San Francisco, 84-; Univ Calif, Berkeley, 80-86; Sonoma State Univ, 81-85. *Awards:* Print Design Award, 88; NY Art Dir Club Award, 89; Print Design,

90; Creativity NY, 89 & 90; Am Corp Identity, 89 & 90. *Mem:* Am Inst Graphic Arts; Women in Commun. *Publ:* Corporate Identity Design, Van, Nostrand, Reinhold, NY, 83. *Mailing Add:* 47 N Knoll Rd No 201 Mill Valley CA 94941

NAPONIC, TONY (ANTHONY GEORGE)
PAINTER, CONSULTANT
b Adamsburg, Pa, Jan 16, 54. *Study:* Univ Pittsburgh, 73; Kansas City Art Inst, BFA, 74. *Work:* Kansas City Art Inst, Kemper Mus Art & Design, Wilcox Corp, Mutual Benefit Life, Kansas City, Mo; Art Inst Chicago, Ill; Madison Art Ctr, Wis; Lake Forest Col Mus, Lake Forest, Ill; Mus Towers, New York; and others. *Exhib:* One-person shows, Kemper Gallery, Kansas City Art Inst, Mo, 80, Zolla/Lieberman, Chicago, Ill, 80 & 83 & Douglas Drake, 88, 90 & 91; Dreams & Dislocations, Douglas Drake Gallery, New York, Kansas City, Kans, 82; Visions '83, traveling exhib, sponsored by Mid-Am Arts Alliance, at major mus in Okla, Kans, Ark, Nebr & Mo, 83; Highlights of the First 100 Years at Kansas City Art Inst, Nelson-Atkins Mus, Kansas City, Mo, 85; Situations, traveling exhib, organized by Mus Mod Art, New York, 88. *Pos:* Art consult, Continental Corp, New York. *Teaching:* Printmaking technician, Kansas City Art Inst, 75-76, vis artist, 87. *Awards:* Grant, Mid-Am Arts Alliance; Emerging Artist Grant, Nat Endowment Arts, 83. *Bibliog:* Elizabeth Kirsch (auth), Artists and Their Spaces, Kansas City Mag, 7/83; Peter Franz Von Ziegesar (reporter-critic), Public Radio, 4/85; Ellen Goheen (critic), Kansas City Bus J, 5/85. *Mem:* Artist's Space, New York; Mid-Am Arts Alliance, Kansas City, Mo. *Media:* Acrylics, Oil. *Dealer:* Douglas Drake Gallery 50 W 57 St New York NY 10019; Concept Art Gallery 1031 S Braddock Ave Pittsburgh PA 15218. *Mailing Add:* 106 Suffolk St Apt 5A New York NY 10002

NARANJO, MICHAEL ALFRED
SCULPTOR
b Santa Fe, NMex, Aug 28, 44. *Study:* Wayland Col, Plainview, Tex; Highland Univ. *Work:* Indian Pueblo Cult Ctr, Albuquerque, NMex; Heard Mus, Phoenix, Ariz; Albuquerque Mus, NMex; Colo Springs Fine Arts Ctr, Colo; Mus Fine Arts, Santa Fe, NMex. *Comn:* Kokopelli, Indian Springs Estates, Chatsworth, Calif, 85; sculpture, Found Exceptional Children, 88; The Dancer, six ft bronze, Albuquerque Mus. *Exhib:* Contemp North Am Indian Art, Smithsonian Inst, Washington, DC, 83; San Diego Mus of Man, 85; 16th World Cong Rehabilitation Int, Tokyo, Japan, 88; San Diego Mus Men, 89; Santa Barbara Mus Art, Calif, 91; Eiteljorg Mus Am Indian & Western Art, 92; and others. *Pos:* Bd mem, NMex Arts Comn, 71-73, NMex Very Special Arts Festival, 83-, Access to Art, proj of Mus Am Folk Art, 87. *Awards:* NMex Veteran Yr, Daughters Am Revolution, 86; Distinguished Achievement Award, Am Indian Resources Inst, 90; Clinton King Purchase Award, Mus Fine Arts, Santa Fe, NMex, 91; and others. *Bibliog:* Guy & Doris Monthan (coauth), Art & Indian Individualists, Northland Press, 75; Peggy & Harold Samuels (coauths), Contemporary Western Artists, Southwest Art Publ; Bodywatching, CBS Special produced by New Screen Concepts, 88; Jerry & Lois E Jacka (auths), Beyond Tradition: Contemporary Indian Art and Its Evolution, Northland Press, 88. *Media:* Bronze, Stone. *Publ:* Auth, Arizona highways, Ariz Dept Transportation, 5/86; Southwest Art Mag, 10/89; Colores, Pub Broadcast System documentary, 92. *Dealer:* Four Winds Gallery Inc Pittsburgh PA; Michael Naranjo Studio Espanola NM. *Mailing Add:* PO Box 747 Espanola NM 87532

NARDI, DANN
SCULPTOR
b Shelbyville, Ill, June 22, 50. *Study:* Ill State Univ, Normal, BS(art), 76, MS(painting), 78. *Work:* US Equities Inc, Chicago; State of Ill collection, State of Ill Bldg, Chicago; William Rainey Harper Col, Palatine, Ill; Ill State Univ, Normal; Coca Cola Corp Collection, Atlanta, Ga. *Comn:* Outdoor site-specific sculptures, City of Mattoon, Ill, 82, State of Ill, Edwardsville, 85, Coe Col, Cedar Rapids, Iowa, 88-89 & Secy State, Springfield, Ill, 88-89; Indoor site specific environ, State of Ill, Champaign, 88-89; Rhone-Poulenc Rorer Inc, Philadelphia, Pa, 92; Eastern Ill Univ, Charleston, 92. *Exhib:* Abstract Art in Chicago, Lakeview Mus, 85; one-man shows, Roy Boyd Gallery, Chicago, 85, 88, 90 & 92, Fay Gold Gallery, Atlanta, Ga, 89, Dann Nardi, Merwin Gallery, Ill Wesleyan Univ, Bloomington, Ill, 90; Interior/Exterior, Rockford Mus Fine Art, Ill, 86; Sculptors Drawings, Sonoma State Univ, Ronhert Park, Calif, 87; Chicago Cult Ctr, 88; Faculty & Alumni, Ill State Univ, Chicago, 88; Sculpture in the Landscape, Paine Art Center & Arboretum, Oshkosh, Wis, 88; Monuments and Memorials, State of Ill Gallery, 90. *Teaching:* Instr sculpture, Ill State Univ, Normal, 86-88. *Awards:* Grant, Ill Arts Coun, 83, 86 & 87; Fel, Nat Endowment Arts, 86 & 88. *Bibliog:* Alan Artner (auth), review, Chicago Tribune, 2/22/85; Claire Downey (auth), review, Artpapers, 12/86; Buzz Spector (auth), catalog essay, Dept Cult Affairs, 10/88. *Mem:* Int Sculpture Ctr. *Dealer:* Roy Boyd Gallery 739 N Wells Chicago IL 60610. *Mailing Add:* 1701 E Taylor Bloomington IL 61701

NARDIN, MARIO
COLLECTOR, SCULPTOR
b Venice, Italy, Mar 17, 40. *Study:* Acad Belle Arti, Venice, with Guido Manarin. *Work:* Hudson River Mus, Yonkers, NY; Fordham Univ; also in pvt collections. *Exhib:* One-man shows, Fordham Univ, 69, Lesnick Gallery, 70, Sindin Galleries, 77, Village Gallery at Gallimafry, Croton-on-Hudson, NY, 78 & Soho Gallery-Herald Ctr, NY, 86; State Univ Plattsburgh, NY, 71; and others. *Pos:* Asst to Jacques Lipchitz, 64-71; asst mgr, Avent-Shaw Art Foundry, 64-75. *Awards:* New Rochelle Art Asn Award, 67; Greenburgh Arts & Cult Comt Award, 71 & 72; Mamaroneck Artist Guild Award, 73. *Bibliog:* Noel Frankman (auth), Nardin at the Hudson River Museum, Arts Mag, 3/72; Successo a Nuova York di uno scultore Veneziano, Gazzetino Venice, 72; David L Shirey (auth), Sculptor as master builder, New York Times, 3/78. *Mem:* Am Soc Contemp Artists; Sculptors League; Yonkers Art Asn; Artists Equity Asn. *Media:* Bronze. *Mailing Add:* 184 Warburton Ave Hastings-on-Hudson NY 10706

NARDONE, VINCENT JOSEPH
PAINTER, COLLECTOR
b South Orange, NJ, Oct 19, 37. *Study:* Montclair State Col, NJ, BA, 61; Univ Southern Calif, Los Angeles, MFA, 66; Paris Am Acad Ecole De Beaux-Arts France, 78; Villa Schifandia Grad Sch Art, Florene, Italy, 81, with Genieve Secord, Joseph Domareki, Isa Petrozzani, Mildred Taylor, Paul Harris & Arnauld D'Hauterives. *Work:* Newark Mus & Newark Pub Libr, Newark, NJ; Rome Daily Am News, Italy; Isadora & Raymond Duncan Mus, Paris; Relais et Chateaux Inn, Lake Saranac, NY. *Comn:* Western pastel mural, Bonanza Restaurant, Bloomfield, NJ, 68; exterior stone carving, Music & Art Corp, NJ, 70; original litho insert, NJ Music & Arts Mag, 72; relig watercolor painting, Christ the King Parish, Ploughe, Sardinia, 72. *Exhib:* Ligoa Duncan Gallery, New York, 76-79; IL Centro Artistico San Niccolo, Florence, Italy, 81; NJ Corp Art Consults Traveling Exhib, 81-82; Whistler's Daughter Gallery, NJ, 82-86; Seoul Int Arts Exhib Tour, Korea, 84-85; Int Art & Fashion Exhib, Val-de-Grace, Paris, 85; ITT Worldwide Communications Inc, NJ, 88; Seagirt Art Gallery, NJ, 90; Robin Hutchins Gallery, Maplewood, NY, 92-93. *Pos:* Illusr & art consult, NJ Music & Art Mag, Chatham, 69-73; art adminr, Essex County, NJ, 73; art collector, 70- *Teaching:* Elem art specialist, South Orange/Maplewood Sch Dist, NJ, 61-89; instr painting adult sch, Maplewood, NJ, 66-70; adj instr art educ, Seton Hall Univ, South Orange, NJ, 68-74. *Awards:* Raymond Duncan Medal, Prix de Paris, 78, Painting Award, Le Salon, Grand Palais, Paris, 78; Queen Fabiola, Prix Rubens Medal, Belgium, 78; Silver Medallion, Seoul Int Arts Competition, 84. *Bibliog:* Francois Perche (auth), critique, La Revue Moderne des Arts, Paris, 78; Viaczeslau Zaualiszin, Art Critic/Novoye Russkoye Slovo, 78; Dorothy Hall (auth), critique, Park East, 11/78; Nardone the artist, NJ Art Form Mag, 8-9/82; Beth Fand (auth), Major Auction Review News Record of S Orange, Maplewood 8/91. *Mem:* Artistique Les Surindependants, Paris; Allied Artists Am; Art Gallery of South Orange, Maplewood, NJ. *Media:* Multi, watercolor. *Publ:* Auth, Panning for Federal Funds, 12/71; auth & illusr, Graven images, NJ Music & Arts Mag, 4/72; Ecological Genesis (portfolio), Rubicon Graphics, 72. *Dealer:* Robin Hutchins Gallery 179 Maplewood Ave Maplewood NJ 07040. *Mailing Add:* 75 Essex Ave Maplewood NJ 07040

NAROTZKY, NORMAN DAVID
PAINTER, PRINTMAKER
b Brooklyn, NY, Mar 14, 28. *Study:* Brooklyn Col, BA(cum laude), 49; Art Students League, 45-49; Cooper Union, 52, BFA, 79; Atelier 17, Paris, 54-56; Kunstakademie, Munich, 56-57; New York Univ, Inst Fine Arts, 57-58; study with Moses Soyer, Ad Reinhardt, S W Hayter, Morris Kantor. *Work:* James A Michener Collection of 20th Century Am Painting, Univ Tex Art Mus, Austin; Philadelphia Mus Art; Mus Contemp Art, Madrid, Spain; Mills Col Art Gallery, Oakland, Calif; Museo Popular de Arte Contemporaneo de Villafames, Spain. *Comn:* Mural, Banco de Guipuzcoa, San Sebastian, 63; ltd ed lithograph, Collectors Guild Ltd, 69 & Fine Arts 260, 72 & 76; ltd ed etchings, Galeria Fort, Barcelona, 75 & 83; Miquel Plana (ltd ed etching), Olot, 90. *Exhib:* VI Bienal Sao Paulo, Brazil, 61; Mus Mod Art, 62; Whitney Mus Am Art Ann, New York, 62; Arte Am y Espana, traveling Europe, 63-64; San Francisco Mus Art, 68; Grosse Kunstler Ausstellung, Haus der Kunst, Munich, 71; Fundacion Joan Miro, Barcelona, 84, 85 & 86; Bienal d'Art, Barcelona, 85 & 87; L'Informalisme a Catalunya, Barcelona, 90; and 41 one-man shows. *Pos:* Staff, Collector's Guild Inc, 69-71 & Fine Arts 260, 71-80; dir art gallery, Cadaques, 73; dir painting workshop, Northern Mich Univ, summer 79. *Teaching:* Pvt studio, Cadaques, Spain, 59-69, Barcelona, 76-; Northern Mich Univ, summer, 79. *Awards:* French Govt Fel, Paris, 55-56; Fulbright Fel, Ger, 57-58; Painting Grant, Generalitat de Catalunya, Spain, 83; Grand Prize, II Bienal d'Art, Barcelona, 87. *Bibliog:* Jose M, Moreno Galvan (auth), Spanish painting, the latest avant-garde, NY Graphic Soc, 69; Meilach & Ten Hoor (auth), Collage & Assemblage, Crown Publ, 73; Lourdes Cirlot (auth), La Pintura Informal en Cataluna, 1951-1970, Anthropos, 83. *Mem:* Art Students League; Cercle Artistic de Sant Lluc, Barcelona. *Media:* Acrylic, Oil; Etching, Lithography. *Publ:* Auth, Spain: a disenchantment with materia, 9-10/65, Conversation with Cuixart, 3/66 & The Venice Biennale: pease porridge in the pot nine days old, 9-10/66, Arts Mag; auth, Ibiza--from art refuge to art center, Art Voices, fall 65;; auth, Form & communication in my art work, Leonardo Mag, 7/69. *Dealer:* Anita Shapolsky 99 Spring St New York NY 10012; Manhattan E Gallery of Fine Arts 202 E 76 St New York NY 10021. *Mailing Add:* Corcega 198-6 Barcelona 08036 Spain

NASGAARD, ROALD
CURATOR, HISTORIAN
b Denmark, Oct 14, 41; Can citizen. *Study:* Univ BC, BA, MA, 67; Can Coun Fels, 67-71; NY Univ Inst Fine Arts, PhD, 73. *Pos:* Cur contemp art, 75-78, chief cur & cur int contemp art, 78-, Art Gallery Ont; deputy dir and chief cur, 90- *Teaching:* Asst prof art hist, Univ Guelph, Ont, 71-75; vis lectr, York Univ, Toronto, 76-78; vis lectr, Univ Toronto, 83- *Mem:* Col Art Asn; Univ Art Asn Can; Int Art Critics Asn (Canadian secy-gen, 76-78); Toronto Pub Art Comn, 86-88; Gersiton Iskowitz Found (trustee, 91-). *Res:* Late 19th century to contemporary art. *Publ:* Auth, Structures for Behaviour, New Sculptures by Robert Morris, David Rabinowitch, Richard Serra and George Trakas, 78, Gary Neill Kennedy: Recent Works, 78, Yves Gaucher: Fifteen Year Perspective, 79 & 10 Canadian Artists in the 1970's, 80, Art Gallery Ont; The Mystic North: Symbolist Landscape Painting in Northern Europe and North America, 1890-1940, Art Gallery Ont, Univ Toronto Press, 84;

Gerhard Richter: paintings, Thames & Hudson, London, Eng, 88; Individualtés: 14 contemporary Artists from France, 91 & Free Worlds: Metaphods and Realities in Contemporary Hungarian Art, 91, Art Gallery Ont, Toronto, 91. *Mailing Add:* c/o Art Gallery Ontario 317 Dundas St W Toronto ON M5T 1G4 Canada

NASH, ALICE LOUISE
CONSULTANT
b Mattoon, Ill, June 21, 15. *Study:* James Millikin Univ, Decatur, Ill, 35-36; Heatherleys Sch Fine Art, London, Eng, 47-48; Atelier Zadkine, with Ossip Zadkine, Paris, France, 48-49; Chelsea Col Art, London Univ, with Henry Moore & Bernard Meadows, 49-51; Anglo-French Art Sch, London, 52. *Pos:* Exec secy, Edward MacDowell Assocs, 57-60; asst dir, Contemporaries Gallery, New York, 60-62; dir, Osgood Gallery, New York, 62-63; dir, Alice Nash Gallery, New York, 63-65; staff mem for exhibs & librn, Am Acad & Inst Art & Lett, New York, 65-72; assoc, Harmon Gallery, Naples, Fla, 78-84; dir, Friends of Art Mus Gallery, Naples, Fla, 84-89; assoc cur & registrar, Philharmonic Ctr for the Arts, Naples, Fla, 89-, actg cur, 91- *Mem:* Fel Royal Soc Arts, Eng; Naples Art Asn (bd mem 78-). *Specialty:* Contemporary American and European paintings and sculpture. *Publ:* Auth, Collectors Handbook, Harmon-Meek Gallery, 82. *Mailing Add:* 6101 Pelican Bay Blvd Apt 302 Naples FL 33963

NASH, MARY
PAINTER, LECTURER
b Washington, DC, May 8, 51. *Study:* George Washington Univ, BA, 73; Wash State Univ, Pullman, MFA, 76. *Work:* Dimock Gallery, George Washington Univ; Erie Art Mus, Pa; Wash State Arts Comn, Olympia; San Antonio Mus Mod Art, Tex; Mus Contemp Art, Chicago, Ill; Whitney Mus Am Art, New York. *Exhib:* Knoxville Mus Art, Tenn, 89; Charles Allis Art Mus, Milwaukee, Wis, 91; Neville Pub Mus, Green Bay, Wis, 91; Corcoran Gallery Art, Washington, DC, 92; Asheville Art Mus, NC, 92; and others. *Pos:* Guest lectr, Mus Art, Wash State Univ, 76-, Second St Gallery, Charlottesville, Va, 78-, Univ Ala, Tuscaloosa, 81-, Southeastern Women's Studies Asn Conf, Univ Va, Charlotteville, 83 & Arlington Arts Ctr, Va, 85 & 86; artist-in-residence, alkyd painting, Va Mus Fine Arts, 84-85. *Awards:* MacDowell Colony Fel, 77; Honorable Mention, Southeastern Ctr Contemp Art, 79; Purchase Award, Wash State Arts Comn, Olympia, 82. *Bibliog:* Janet Isaacs Ashford (auth), Mary H Nash, Whole Birth Catalog, 83; Colleen Heninger (auth), Secret Truths, The Gazette, 4/29/87; Artists' book beat, Print Collector's Newsletter, 5-6/88. *Media:* Oil, Alkyd. *Publ:* Auth, Skulls are Forever, Ichthys Books, 86. *Mailing Add:* 8536 Aponi Rd Vienna VA 22180

NASH, PAUL
WRITER, EDUCATOR
b Newcastle Upon Tyne, UK, Sept 2, 24; US citizen. *Study:* London Sch Econs, BSC(econs), 49; Univ Toronto, MEd, 55; Harvard Univ, EdD, 59. *Pos:* Vpres, RI Sch Design, Providence, 84-91. *Teaching:* Prof educ, McGill Univ, Montreal, 59-62, Boston Univ, 62-84 & Tufts Univ, Medford, Mass, 89-92. *Mem:* Nat Asn Schs Art & Design (future comt mem, 88-91). *Media:* Photography, Ceramics. *Res:* The sources of creativity; the education of the artist. *Publ:* Auth, Authority & Freedom in Education, 66 & Models of Man, 68, Wiley; Culture and the State, Columbia Univ, 68; History and Education, Random House, 70; The Consultants Handbook, Nat Endowment Humanities, 71. *Mailing Add:* Rhode Island School of Design 123 Park St Newton MA 02158

NASH, STEVEN ALAN
HISTORIAN, CURATOR
b Wadsworth, Ohio, Apr 8, 44. *Study:* Dartmouth Col, BA; Stanford Univ, PhD. *Pos:* Res cur, Albright-Knox Art Gallery, Buffalo, 73-77, chief cur, 77-80; asst dir & chief cur, Dallas Mus Fine Arts, 80-88; assoc dir & chief cur, Fine Arts Mus San Francisco, 88- *Teaching:* Adj prof, State Univ NY, Buffalo, 73-80. *Awards:* Mabel McCloud Lewis Found Fel, 71; Fr Govt Res Grant, 71; Prof Grant, Nat Endowment Arts, 81. *Mem:* Archives Am Art (adv panel); Am Asn Mus. *Publ:* Auth, Ben Nicholson: Fifty years of His Art, Buffalo Acad, 78; Albright-Knox Collection (catalog), 79; Naum Gabo: 60 Years of Constructivism, 85 & A Century of Modern Sculpture: The Nasher Collection, 87, Dallas Mus Art. *Mailing Add:* M H De Young Mem Mus and Calif Palace of The Legion Of Honor San Francisco CA 94121

NASHER, RAYMOND DONALD
COLLECTOR, PATRON
b Boston, Mass, Oct 26, 21. *Study:* Boston Pub Latin Sch, 39; Duke Univ, BA, 43; Boston Univ, MA, 50; Southern Methodist Univ, LHD, 73. *Work:* Dallas Mus Art, Tex; Nelson-Atkins Mus Art, Kansas City, Mo; Nat Gallery Art, Washington, DC. *Exhib:* Sir Anthony Caro Retrospective, Trajan Market Pl, Rome, Italy, 92; TransForm, Kunstmuseum Basel, Switz, 92; Still Lifes by Picasso, Cleveland Mus Art, Philadelphia Mus Art, Pa & Musée Picasso, Paris, France, 92; and others. *Pos:* Ambassador cult affairs, City of Dallas, 88-92; bd dir/secy, Bus Comt Arts Inc,88-92; chmn, Dallas Bus Comt Arts, 88-92. *Awards:* Bus Arts, 76 & 87. *Bibliog:* Margaret Robinette (auth), Interview: Raymond and Patsy Nasher, Sculpture, 3-4/87; Joan Chatfield-Taylor (auth), The collectors: a passion for sculpture, Archit Dig, 10/87; Claire Frankel (auth), Collecting patterns, Art & Auction, 6/90. *Mem:* Pres Comt Arts & Humanities, 90-92; Dallas Mus Art (bd dirs, acquisitions comt, 88-92); Nat Gallery Art (trustees coun, 88-91); InterCultura (bd trustees, 89-92). *Interests:* Modern & contemporary art. *Collection:* Modern & contemporary sculpture, paintings & prints; Pre- Columbian art; Guatemalan textiles; Indonesian gold. *Mailing Add:* PO Box 829007 Dallas TX 75382-9007

NASISSE, ANDY S
SCULPTOR, WRITER
b Pueblo, Colo, Nov 1, 46. *Study:* Inst Allende, Mex, 69; Univ Colo, MFA, 73. *Work:* High Mus Art. *Comn:* Four Walls, City Altanta, 81. *Exhib:* Southeast Ctr Contemp Arts Exhib, Winston-Salem, NC, 79; Ga Artists, High Mus, 79, 80 & 83; More than Land or Sky, Nat Mus Am Art, 82; Southern Fervor, Anderson Gallery, Richmond, Va, 83; Birmingham Mus Biennial, 83; New Epiphanies, Univ Colo Mus, 83; New Talent, Nexus Space, Atlanta, 83; solo exhib, La Mar Dodd Ctr, La Grange, Ga, 84. *Teaching:* Assoc prof, Univ Ga, Athens, 76-, gallery dir, 82-83. *Awards:* Nat Endowment Arts Grant, 79; Creative Res Award, Univ Ga, 82; Ga Coun Grant, 84. *Media:* Ceramic. *Res:* Folk art. *Dealer:* Fay Gold Gallery 3221 Cains Hill Pl Atlanta GA 30305. *Mailing Add:* 256 Georgia Dr Athens GA 30605

NATHANS, RHODA R
PHOTOGRAPHER
b Detroit, Mich, May 29, 40. *Study:* Wayne State Univ, BS; NY Univ Sch Continuing Educ, photog under Dr Roman Vishniac. *Exhib:* Neidrug Gallery, New York UN Woman's Yr, 74; one-woman exhibs, Avanti Gallery, New York, 74 & Nikon House, Rockefeller Ctr, New York, 78; Mus City New York, 74. *Publ:* Contribr, Time, Fortune, Newsweek & Print Mag, 9/75; contribr, Camera 35, 12/75. *Dealer:* Mrs Frances Wynshaw 157 E 72nd St New York NY 10022. *Mailing Add:* 141 E 89th St New York NY 10028

NATKIN, ROBERT
PAINTER
b Chicago, Ill, Nov 7, 30. *Study:* Kansas City Art Inst, Mo, BFA, 70; Univ Calif, Davis, MFA, 73. *Work:* Hewitt Mus, Everson Mus Art, New York; Carnegie Mus Art, Pittsburgh, Pa; Crocker Art Mus, Sacramento; Honolulu Acad Arts; Kunstindustrimuseet, Oslo, Norway; Los Angeles Co Mus Art; Mus Fine Arts, Houston, Tex; Smithsonian Inst, Washington, DC; and many others. *Exhib:* Whitney Mus Am Art, 60, 66 & 68; Carnegie Inst, 63; Int Biennale, Japan, 63; Mus Fine Arts, Houston, 63; retrospective, San Francisco Mus Art, 69; one-man exhibs, Strong Tea: Richard Natkin & the Yixing Tradition, Seattle Art Mus & traveling, 90, Garth Clark Gallery, New York, 85, 87, 88 & 91, Garth Clark Gallery, Los Angeles, 84, 88, 90 & 92. *Teaching:* Vis/asst prof, Univ Utah, Salt Lake City, 75; vis instr & actg chairperson, Md Inst Col Art, Baltimore, 77; adj asst prof, Mont State Univ, Bozeman, 81; vis artist & lectr, Ohio State Univ, Columbus, 82; vis artist, Kans City Art Inst, 84; Bezalel Acad Art & Design, Jerusalem, Israel, 90. *Awards:* Emerging Artist Fel, 79 & Visual Artists Fel, 81 & 88, Nat Endowment Arts; Fel in Sculpture, John Simon Guggenheim Mem Found, 90; Fel, Louis Comfort Tiffany Found, 91; and others. *Bibliog:* Jan & Karen McCready (coauths), Porcelain: Traditions & New Visions, Watson-Guptil, 81; Susan & Kim Zumwalt (coauths), Artists at Work, Alaska Northwest Bks, 90. *Dealer:* Gimpel Fils London; Klonaridis Toronto. *Mailing Add:* 24 Mark Twain Lane West Redding CT 06896

NATSOULAS, ANTHONY
SCULPTOR
b Ann Arbor, Mich, Jan 16, 59. *Study:* Univ Calif, Davis, BA, 82, Grad Res Grant, 84, MFA, 85; Md Inst Col Art, 82-83; Skowhegan Sch Painting & Sculpture, Scholar, 83. *Work:* Ceramic figures, Oakland Mus, Calif; three life size ceramic figures, Kidd Corp, Davis, Calif; ceramic figure, DiRosa Found, Napa, Calif. *Comn:* Joggers (two full size bronze figures), City of Davis, Calif, 86; Neptune (ceramic figure & fountain), comn by Mr & Mrs Day, Turlock, Calif, 87; This is Not a Game (life size bronze figure & fountain), City of Sacramento, Calif, 88; Simultaneous Melodies (three life size ceramic figures), Kidd Corp, Davis, Calif, 90. *Exhib:* Diamonds Are Forever, Oakland Mus, Calif, 89; Nat Mus Ceramic Art, Baltimore, Md, 90; Figures in Ceramics, La State Univ, Baton Rouge, 90; Blues Show, San Francisco Mus Mod Art Rental Gallery, Calif, 90. *Teaching:* Lectr ceramic sculpture & mod art hist, Calif State Univ-Stanislaus, 85-87; vis artist ceramic sculpture & poetry, Ohio State Univ, Columbus, 87; instr ceramics, Butte Col, Oroville, Calif, 89. *Bibliog:* Article, Contemporary American Craft Art/A Collectors Guide, Pereguine Smith Bks, 88; Elaine Levine (auth), Contemporary Ceramics: The Artist of TB9 (exhib catalog), 89. *Mem:* Col Art Asn. *Media:* Clay, Cast Metal. *Dealer:* Rena Bransten Gallery 77 Geary St San Francisco CA 94108. *Mailing Add:* c/o John Natsoulas Gallery 140 F St Davis CA 95616

NATZLER, OTTO
CERAMIST, SCULPTOR
b Vienna, Austria, Jan 31, 08; US citizen. *Work:* Mus Mod Art & Metrop Mus Art, New York; Art Inst Chicago; Mus Bellerive, Zurich, Switz; Victoria & Albert Mus, London; Nat Mus Am Art, Washington, DC; and others. *Exhib:* One-man exhibs, Art Inst Chicago, 63 & San Francisco Mus Art, 63; retrospective exhibs, Los Angeles Co Mus Art, 66, M H De Young Mem Mus, San Francisco 71 & Renwick Gallery, Smithsonian Inst, Washington, DC, 73 (coauth all catalogs). *Bibliog:* Article, Natzler exhibition, Ceramics Monthly, 5/78; Sarah Booth Conroy (auth), article, Washington Post, 9/20/81; Florence Rubenfeld (auth), Otto Natzler--solo, Am Craft, 2-3/82. *Media:* Multimedia. *Dealer:* Louis Newman Galleries 322 N Beverly Dr Beverly Hills CA 90210; Susan Conway Gallery 1058 Thomas Jefferson St NW Washington DC 20007. *Mailing Add:* c/o Lewis Newman 322 N Beverly Dr Beverly Hills CA 90210

NATZMER, CHERYL LYNN
DEALER, HISTORIAN
b Detroit, Mich, May 14, 47. *Study:* Mich State Univ, BA, 69. *Collections Arranged:* Zuniga, Drawings, Graphics & Sculpture, 78; Sebastian-Geometric Transformables, steel sculpture, 79; A Tribute to Rufino Tamayo, Recent

Works, 79; Dibujos/Drawings, survey of Latin Am drawings, 79; The New World and the Beast, Animal Imagery in Latin Am Art, 79; Tamayo's Mexico, 80; The Imaginary Surface, paintings by Manuel Felguerez, 81; El Zodiaco--Sculpture by Sebastian Traveling Exhib, 82-83; Images From Dream Myth and the Subconscious, 88; Artists choose Artists, 89; First Ann Muraling Festival, 90. *Pos:* Dir & pres, Gryphon Galleries, Ltd, Denver, 71-78; dir & bd dirs, Rutherford Barnes Collection, Ltd, Denver, Colo, 78-; adv Mex art, Denver, 82-; cur, Centerspace, Lansing, Mich, 88-90. *Mem:* Family Arts Network. *Res:* Public art in Mexico today. *Specialty:* Twentieth century Mexican and Latin American art; works of the Masters Tamayo and Cuevas. *Publ:* Co-producer, Columbian Art in the 80's (video). *Mailing Add:* 6112 Columbia Haslett MI 48840

NAUMAN, BRUCE
SCULPTOR
b Ft Wayne, Ind, Dec 6, 41. *Study:* Univ Wis, Madison, with Italo Scanga, BS, 64; Univ Calif, Davis, with William Wiley, Robert Arneson, Frank Owen & Stephen Kaltenbach, MFA, 66. *Work:* Whitney Mus, New York; Wallraf-Richartz-Mus, Cologne, Ger; Kunstverein, Aachen, Ger; Mus Mod Art, New York; Los Angeles Co Mus Art, Calif; Fogg Art Mus, Cambridge, Mass; Australian Nat Gallery, Canberra, Australia; and numerous pvt collections. *Exhib:* One-man exhibs, Nicholas Wilder Gallery, Los Angeles, 66, Leo Castelli Gallery, New York, 68 & 81, Art in Progress, Munich, Ger, 74, Minneapolis Inst Arts Col Gallery, Minn, 78, Hester van Royer Gallery, London, Eng, 79, Carol Taylor Art, Dallas, Tex, 83 , Kunsthalle, Basel, Switz, 86, Drawings 1965-1986 , travelling exhib to Europe & US, 86 & Sperone Westwater Gallery, New York, 88; Am Sculpture of the Sixties, Los Angeles Co Mus Art, Calif, 67; Corcoran Gallery Art, Washington, DC, 69; Anti-Illusion: Procedures/Materials, Whitney Mus Art, New York, 69; Solomon R Guggenheim Mus, New York, 69; Information, Mus Mod Art, New York, 71; Art & Image in Recent Art, Art Inst Chicago, 74; Mus Mod Art, New York, 75, 87 & 88; Whitney Mus Am Art, New York, 76, 87 & 88; Los Angeles Co Mus Art (also traveling), 82; Fogg Art Mus, Cambridge, Mass; one-man exhibs, Biennial Exhib, Whitney Mus Am Art, New York, 91, Mus Boymans-van Beuningen, Rotterdam, Neth, 91, Fundacio Espai Poblenou, Barcelona, Spain, 91-92, Use Me (Graphics, Multiples, Videos and Installations), Inst Contemp Arts, London, Eng, 91-92, Neons, Anthony d'offay Gallery, London, Eng, 92 & Ydessa Hendeles Found, Toronto, Ont, Can, 92; retrospective, Galerie Hummel, Vienna, Austria, 91; Documenta IX, Kassel, Ger, 92; Transform BildObjektSkulptur im 20, Jahrhundert, Kunsthalle Basel, Switz, 92; Szenenwechsel, Mus Moderne Kunst, Frankfurt am Main, Ger, 92; Re: Framing Cartoons, Wexner Ctr, Ohio State Univ, Columbus, Ohio, 92; Cross Section, Battery Park City & the Worlds Financial Ctr, New York, 92; Both Art and Life: Gemini at 25, Newport Harbor Art Mus, Newport Beach, Calif, 92; var exhibs at maj mus incl Whitney Mus Am Art, Mus Mod Art, Milwaukee Art Mus and others. *Teaching:* Instr, San Francisco Art Inst, 66-68; instr sculpture, Univ Calif, Irvine, 70. *Awards:* Nat Endowment Grant, Washington, DC, 68; Aspen Inst for Humanistic Studies Grant, Colo, 70. *Bibliog:* Robert Pincus-Witten (auth), Bruce Nauman: Another kind of reasoning, Artforum, 2/72; Jurgen Harten (auth), T for technics, B for body, Art & Artists, London, 11/73; J Minton (auth), Bruce Nauman: Gunslinger, Artweek, 6/74. *Publ:* Auth, Pictures of Sculptures in a Room, Davis, Calif, 66; Clear Sky, San Francisco, 68; Burning Small Fires, San Francisco, 68; LA Air, Los Angeles, 70; Body Works, Interfunktionen, Cologne, Ger, 9/71. *Mailing Add:* c/o Leo Castelli Gallery 420 W Broadway New York NY 10012

NAUMANN, FRANCIS M
HISTORIAN, WRITER
b Albany, NY, Apr 25, 48. *Study:* State Univ NY, Buffalo, BA, 70; Sch Art Inst Chicago, MFA, 73; City Univ New York, PhD, 88. *Pos:* Dir, Parsons Summer Prog Italy, 81-84. *Teaching:* Instr art hist, Sch Art Inst Chicago, 72-73; adj prof, Queens Col, City Univ New York, 74-75; prof, Parsons Sch Design, 77-90. *Awards:* Nat Endowment Humanities Fel, 91-92. *Mem:* Col Art Asn Am. *Res:* Dada and surrealism in Europe and America. *Publ:* Auth, Affecteusement Marcel: ten letters from Marcel Duchamp to Suzanne Duchamp and Jean Crotti, Arch Am Art J, 83; The Mary and William Sister Collection, Mus Mod Art, 84; coauth, Adolf Wolff: poet, sculptor and revolutionist, Art Bull, 85; Man Ray and the Ferrer Center: Art and Anarchy in the Pre-Dada Period, Dada-Surrealism, 85; co-ed, Marcel Duchamp: Artist of the Century, MIT Press, 89. *Mailing Add:* 14 E Fourth St Apt 1112 New York NY 10012

NAUMER, HELMUTH
PAINTER
b Ger, Sept 1, 07; US citizen. *Study:* Frank Wiggins Art Sch; Otis Art Inst, Los Angeles. *Work:* NMex State Art Mus; Bandelier Nat Monument; Univ Wyo; Univ NMex; Mus Sci & Hist, Ft Worth, Tex; NMex State Art Mus Archives; Smithsonian Archives. *Exhib:* Am Asn Mus & Can Mus Asn Meeting, Toronto, 67. *Bibliog:* Articles in Am Ger Rev, NMex Mag & El Palacio. *Media:* Oil, Pastel, Watercolor. *Mailing Add:* Rancho de San Sebastian Rte 3 Box 98A Santa Fe NM 87501

NAVARETTA, CYNTHIA
LECTURER, EDITOR
b New York. *Study:* Univ Wis; NY Univ; Columbia Univ, BA, 46, MA, 48. *Collections Arranged:* Women Choose Women (auth, catalog), Cult Ctr, New York, 73; Artists of Long Island (contribr, catalog), Guild Hall, East Hampton, NY, 79; Int Festival Women Artists, Copenhagen, 80; A Lifetime of Art: Six Women of Distinction, Women's Caucus Art, New York, 82; American Women in Art; Works on Paper Africa & Europe (auth, catalog), 85. *Pos:* Ed, Women Artists News, Midmarch Arts Press, 75-; dir corp archit, 50-86. *Awards:* Nat Orgn Women, 80. *Mem:* Coalition of Women's Art Orgns (chmn, 77-78); Nat Women's Caucus for Art (bd mem, 78-81); Found for Community of Artists (bd mem, 75-89); Women Artists Filmmakers (bd mem, 78-88); Artists Talk on Art (bd mem, 76-90). *Res:* Women artists; women's art groups; art and politics. *Publ:* Auth, Guide to Women's Art Organizations, 79; ed, Voices: Three on Three on Three, Midmarch Arts Press, 80; Women Artists of the World, 85; Whole Arts Dir, 86; Artists and their Cats, 90. *Mailing Add:* 300 Riverside Dr No 8A New York NY 10025

NAVRAT, DEN(NIS EDWARD)
ADMINISTRATOR, PAINTER
b Marion, Kans, May 15, 42. *Study:* Kans State Univ, Manhattan, BA, 64; Wichita State Univ, Kans, MFA, 66; Univ Iowa, Iowa City, 69, with Virginia Myers; Photographer's Place, Derbyshire, Eng, 77, with Paul Hill & Ralph Gibson; Anderson Ranch Arts Ctr, Aspen, 83, with Catherine Reeve, Marilyn Sward, Bernie Vinzani, Katie McGregor and Terry Allen, Emma Lake, Sask, Can, 86, with Peter Bradley and John Link. *Work:* Mus of Fine Art, Houston, Tex; Atkinson Art Gallery, Metrop Bur of Sefton, Eng; Plains Art Mus, Moorhead, Minn; Univ Iowa Gallery, Iowa City; ND Heritage Ctr, Bismarck. *Exhib:* Eighth Colorprint USA, Tex Tech Univ, 78; Images on Exchange traveling exhib (illusr, catalog), 78-80; 10th Ann Nat Invitational Drawing Exhib, Eppink Art Gallery, Emporia State Univ, Kans, 86; Eighth Ann Nat Print Exhib, Artlink Contemp Artspace, Ft Wayne, Ind, 88; Eighteenth Nat Works on Paper, Minot State Univ, Minot, NDak, 88; Minot Art Gallery, NDak, 88; NDak Centennial Art Exhib, Bismark, NDak, 88-89; 48th, 49th & 51st Ann Exhib, Sioux City Art Ctr, Iowa, 89, 90 & 92; Invitational Handmade Paper Show, Artlink Contemp Artspace, 89; Drake Invitational Works on Paper Exhib, Drake Univ, Des Moines, Iowa, 89; Nat Invitational Exhib, Sarah Spurgeon Gallery, Ellensburg, Wash, 91; solo exhib, Paper Press, Chicago, Ill, 91. *Pos:* Visual consult, ASAAUM, Minneapolis, 81; COMPAS Artist Group, St Paul, Minn, 82; Visual Consult, Arts Midwest, Minneapolis/ Des Moines, Iowa, 88. *Teaching:* Instr, Inst of Logopedics, Wichita, Kans, 65-66; from instr to asst prof art, Dickinson State Univ, 66-71, assoc prof art & chmn art dept, 72-79, prof art, 79-89; Fulbright-Hays Exchange prof art, Southport Col of Art, Eng, 76-77; prof of art & chmn, Univ South Dakota, 89- *Awards:* Merit Award, Eleventh Ann Nat Exhib, Minot Art Gallery, NDak, 88; Merit Award, NDak Centennial Art Exhib, Bismark, NDak, 88-89; Dakota Visions 1991 Juried Touring Exhib, 91 & 93. *Bibliog:* Sally Prince Davis (auth), The Fine Artist's Guide to Showing and Selling Your Work, North Light Bks, Cincinatti, Ohio, 89; Catharine Reeve (auth), Darkroom Photog Mag, 12/90. *Mem:* Fulbright Alumni Asn. *Media:* Mixed Media. *Publ:* Auth, Images on Exchange, Mind's Eye Gallery, 78. *Dealer:* Neville-Sargent Gallery 215 W Superior St Chicago IL 60610. *Mailing Add:* 2308 E Cherry St Vermillion SD 57069

NAVRATIL, AMY (AMY NAVRATIL CICCONE) See Ciccone, Amy Navratil

NAWARA, JIM
PAINTER, EDUCATOR
b Chicago, Ill, Jan 25, 45. *Study:* Sch Art Inst Chicago, BFA, 67; Univ Ill, Champaign, MFA, 69. *Work:* Boston Mus Fine Arts; Detroit Inst Arts; Bradford City Art Gallery, Eng; Cleveland Mus Art; Nat Mus, Warsaw, Poland; Toledo Mus Art, Ohio; Butler Inst Am Art; and others. *Comn:* Screenprints, Western Mich Univ, Kalamazoo, 74; etchings, Mich Workshop Fine Prints, 75; wall drawing, Dept Recreation, 78; billboard, First Fed Savings, Detroit, 80. *Exhib:* Butler Inst Am Art, Youngstown, Ohio, 72, 73 & 75; Brooklyn Mus, 76; Victoria & Albert Mus, London, 79; Cranbrook Acad, Bloomfield Hills, Mich, 80; Franklin Inst, Philadelphia, 84; Nat Air & Space Mus-Smithsonian Inst, Washington, DC, 86; Impact Int Art Festival, Kyoto City Mus, Japan, 86; Recent Acquisitions: Modern Graphic Arts, Toledo Mus Art, Ohio, 92; American Drawing Biennial III, Muscarelle Mus Art, Col William & Mary, Williamsburg, Va, 92; and others. *Pos:* Acting chmn, dept art & art hist, Wayne State Univ, 88-89. *Teaching:* Prof drawing & painting, Wayne State Univ, 69- *Awards:* Purchase Awards, Butler Inst Am Art Mid-Yr, 72 & Mich Printmakers, Detroit Inst Arts, 77; Res Awards, Wayne State Univ, 77, 81, 84, 87-88 & 90-92; Creative Artist Grants, Mich Coun Arts, 81, 85 & 89. *Bibliog:* Simon Zalkind (auth), 30 yrs of American printmaking, Arts Mag, 2/77; Elizabeth Glassman & Marilyn Symmes (coauth), Cliche Verre: Hand-Drawn, Light-Printed, A survey of the medium from 1839 to the present, Detroit Inst Arts, 80; Gottfried Jäger (auth), Bildgebende Fotografie, Fotografik-Lichtgrafik-Lichtmalerei, Dumont Buchverlag Köln, 88. *Media:* Oil, Drawing. *Mailing Add:* 13343 Kingston Huntington Woods MI 48070

NAWARA, LUCILLE PROCTER
PAINTER, LECTURER
b Oklahoma City, Okla, June 26, 41. *Study:* Smith Col, with Leonard Baskin, BA, 62; Boston Univ, Sch Fine & Applied Arts, with Walter Murch & Arthur Polonsky, BFA, 67; Univ Ill, Champaign, MFA, 69. *Work:* Mich Coun Arts & Detroit Inst Arts, Detroit; Springfield Col, Mass; Nat Endowment Arts, Washington, DC; Univ Mich Art Mus, Ann Arbor; Kalamazoo Art Inst. *Comn:* Sea Squirts (intaglio), Oxbow Portfolio, Mich Coun Arts, Detroit, 73; Prisms (intaglio), Women's Portfolio, Nat Educ Asn & Mich Workshop Fine Prints, Detroit, 76; Mural, Broken Symmetries, Fraser High Sch, Mich Coun Arts, 86. *Exhib:* San Francisco Mus Art, 70; Watercolor USA, Springfield Art Mus, Mo, 71; Los Angeles Printmaking Soc, Otis Art Inst, 74; Mid-Yr Ann, Butler Inst Am Art, Youngstown, Ohio, 75; Krannert Art Mus, Champaign, Ill, 76; 2 man show, Pontiac Art Ctr, 87; Midwest Landscape Part II, 89 & New Work, 90, Joy Emery Gallery, Grosse Pointe Farms, Mich; and others.

Pos: Exhib coordr, Detroit Focus Gallery, 80; Artist-in-the-Schools Residency, Mich Coun Arts, Fraser Pub Schs, 83-86; dir, Nawara Gallery, Walled Lake, Mich, 86-88; co-pres bd, Detroit Focus Gallery, 91-92. *Teaching:* Asst prof drawing, Wayne State Univ, Detroit, 69-76; instr drawing, Macomb Co Community Col, 77-82, Henry Ford Community Col, 82 & Ctr Creative Studies, 82-83; vis artist painting, Cranbrook Acad Art, Bloomfield Hills, Mich, 92; painting & design, Macomb Community Col, Mt Clemens, Mich. *Awards:* First Prizes, Art Ctr, Mt Clemens, Mich, 77; Visual Artists Grants landscape painting, Mich Coun Arts, 81 & 83; Cash Award, Mich Watercolor Soc, 43rd Ann Exhib, Univ Mich, 89. *Mem:* Mich Watercolor Soc; Detroit Focus Gallery. *Media:* Oil, Watercolor. *Dealer:* Joy Emery Gallery 131 Kercheval Ave Grosse Pointe Farms MI 48236. *Mailing Add:* 13343 Kingston Huntington Woods MI 48070

NAWROCKI, THOMAS DENNIS
PRINTMAKER, EDUCATOR
b Milwaukee, Wis, June 26, 42. *Study:* Univ Wis-Milwaukee, BFA, 64, MA, 65, MFA, 67. *Work:* Univ Wis-Madison; Northern Ill Univ; Brand Libr Art Galleries, Glendale, Calif; Montgomery Mus Art, Ala; Miss Art Asn, Jackson; Dulin Gallery Art, Knoxville, Tenn; Hunterdon Art Ctr, NJ; Univ Miss, Oxford. *Exhib:* Seattle Int Print Exhib, Seattle Art Mus, 68 & 71; Hawaii Nat Print Exhibs, Honolulu Acad Arts, 73, 75, 79, 82 & 84; World Print Competition, San Francisco Mus Mod Art, 77; Int Print Bienniale, Krakow, Poland, 78, 80, 84, 86 & 88; Wesleyan Int Exhib, 80; Rockford Int, Ill, 81 & 82; Bradley Univ Nat Exhib, Peoria, Ill, 81, 85 & 89; 57th Ann Int, Print Club, Philadelphia, 81 & 83; Soc Am Graphic Artists, New York, 88 & 89; Boston Printmakers, 90; and many others. *Teaching:* Instr printmaking, Southwest Tex State Univ, 67-70; from asst prof printmaking & drawing to assoc prof, Miss Univ Women, 70-83, prof, 83- *Awards:* Dixie Annual Print Competition Award, Montgomery Mus Art, 74; Purchase Award, Nat Print Competition, Edinboro State Col, Pa, 79; Okla Nat Print Award, Okla Art Ctr, 82; Purchase Award & Top Graphics Award, Nat Arts Festival, Tupelo, Miss, 83; Purchase Award, Dulin Nat Works on Paper Competition, Dulin Gallery Art, 85. *Mem:* World Print Coun; Southern Graphics Coun; Los Angeles Printmaking Soc; Am Color Print Soc, Philadelphia; Print Club, Philadelphia; Society of Am Graphic Artists, New York City. *Media:* Printmaking, Textiles. *Publ:* contrib, Artists proof, Vol VI, no 9-10, Pratt Graphic Art Ctr, New York, 67; 1st National Invitational Color-Blend Print Exhibition, Univ Miss Press. *Mailing Add:* 147 Shane Circle Columbus MS 39702

NAY, MARY SPENCER
PAINTER, EDUCATOR
b Crestwood, Ky, May 13, 13. *Study:* Art Ctr Asn Sch, Louisville, Ky, 34-40; Cincinnati Art Acad, 41; Univ Louisville, BA, 41; Art Students League, 42; with Boris Margo, Provincetown, Mass, 50-51; Univ Louisville, MA, 60. *Work:* Speed Art Mus & Univ Louisville, Louisville; Ky Wesleyan Col, Owensboro; Ohio Univ, Athens. *Comn:* Mural for children's room, Louisville Pub Libr, Fed Art Proj, 34. *Exhib:* IBM Exhib, New York World's Fair, 40; Artists for Victory, Metrop Mus Art, 41; Contemp Color Lithography Int Biennials, 50, 52 & 54; 60th Ann Am Exhib, Art Inst Chicago, 51; Terry Nat Exhib, Miami, Fla, 52. *Pos:* Supvr, Puppet Proj, Nat Youth Admin, 37-39. *Teaching:* Instr painting & printmaking, Art Ctr Asn Sch, 40-59, dir, 44-49; prof art educ & painting, Univ Louisville, 59-71, distinguished prof art educ, 71-, Marcia S Hite prof painting, 75-79. *Awards:* Ashland Oil Co Purchase Awards, Art Ctr Asn Regional, 45, 50 & 58; Evansville Mus Purchase Awards, Tri-State Ann, 52, 56 & 58; Ky State Fair Bd Purchase Awards, 54, 56 & 58. *Mem:* Ky Arts & Crafts Guild (bd dirs, 67-70); Art Ctr Asn (librn & bd dirs, 71-72); J B Speed Art Mus; Provincetown Art Asn; Ky Art Educ Asn. *Media:* Acrylic, Oil. *Mailing Add:* Atkins Mayo Rd Provincetown MA 02657

NAYLON, BETSY ZIMMERMANN
PRINTMAKER, PAINTER
b Buffalo, NY, Jan 27, 34. *Study:* Rosary Hill Col, BA, 55; Daeman Col, 76; tutorial with William Paden, New York, 86. *Work:* Albright-Knox Members Gallery, Buffalo, 81-90; Blue Cross of Western NY, 88. *Comn:* Indust Presentation Paintings, CECOS Int Inc, 81, Browning Ferris Industs, Niagara Falls, NY, 82; two paintings, Mader Corp, Buffalo, NY, 83; portrait & two plaques, Snyder Tank Co, Int Harvester Co, Ohio, 85; On an Updraft (mural), Peller & Mure Co, Buffalo, NY, 85; Award design, Carborundum Abrasives, Niagara Falls, NY, Ohio & Virginia, 84; Wood engraving frontispiece, Bantam, Doubleday, Dell Publishing Co; Woodcut & drawing for play Men Should Weep, Studio Arena Theater, Buffalo, NY. *Exhib:* 38th Western NY Exhib, Albright-Knox Gallery, Buffalo, 80; Art of the Printmaker, Burchfield Art Ctr, State Univ NY, Col Buffalo, 81; Eight American Artists, O'Keefe Ctr, Toronto, Can, 82; Nat All on Paper Exhib, AAO Galleries, Buffalo, NY, 84; solo exhibs, Postcards from Italy, E W Brydges Pub Libr, Niagara Falls, 84, Woodcuts and Drawings, Chautauqua Inst Art Gallery, Chautauqua, NY, 84 & Woodcut Prints and Woods, Capen Hall, State Univ NY, Buffalo, 86, Paintings & Wood Cut Prints (94 works, 30 poems), Kans Ctr, Lockport, NY, 12/89; Nat Asn Women Artists, Jacob K Javits Fed Bldg, New York, NY, 86-90; Nat League of Am Pen Women, Inc, New York, 85-90; paintings & woodcut prints & drawings, P C Chelsea Art Gallery, Buffalo, NY, 88; Buscaglia-Castellani Art Gallery, 85-90; Nat Asn Women Artists Traveling Printmaking Show, Woodcut Print, 87-89; Response '87, Emerging Vision, Univ Wis Nat Art Exhib, 87; Nat Asn Women Artists Traveling Show to India, 89. *Teaching:* Instr drawing, Daeman Col, Buffalo, 69-70; instr drawing & painting, State Univ NY, Buffalo, 74-79; Art Park, Lewiston, NY, 76, instr figure drawing, Adult Educ, Niagara Univ, 81-83. *Bibliog:* D Stary (auth), Born on Paper, Cut in Wood, Niagara Gazette, 83; Kathleen M DeLaney (auth), Updraft Sweeps You Away, Niagara Gazette, 6/24/86; E Comerford (auth) Niagara Gazette, 12/30/88, 12/8/89. *Mem:* Nat Asn Women Artists; Nat League Am Penwomen; Niagara Coun Arts (bd mem, 83-84); Niagara Frontier Watercolor Soc; Nat Mus Women in the Arts; National Women's Caucus for Art. *Media:* Woodcut; Acrylic, Oil. *Publ:* Contribr, A Room of Our Own, State Univ NY Buffalo, 87; Special Editions, The Catalogue of Regional & Nat Art; Artistic Objective (poem), Pen Women Nat Mag, 88; Related Possibilities (video, slides); Quadrant J, 9/90. *Mailing Add:* 4116 Washington St Niagara Falls NY 14305

NAYLOR, JOHN GEOFFREY
SCULPTOR, EDUCATOR
b Morecambe, Eng, Aug 28, 28; US citizen. *Study:* Leeds Col Art, nat dipl design; Hornsey Col Art, ATD; Univ Ill, MFA. *Comn:* Smithsonian Inst & Nat Collection Art, Washington, DC; Pub Libr, Chattanooga, Tenn; Columbis Mus Art, Ohio; Lincoln Ctr, Dallas, Tex; Daytran Bldg, Miami, Fla. *Exhib:* Gallery Contemp Art, Winston-Salem, NC, 74; Hirshhorn Mus & Sculpture Gardens, Washington, DC, 77; Univ Ariz, Tucson. *Pos:* Cur, Ft Wayne Art Mus, Ind, 65-66. *Teaching:* Prof sculpture, Univ Fla, 69- *Awards:* Fulbright Travel Grant, 54; Nat Found Arts Award, 67; Fine Art Grant, State of Fla, 80. *Media:* Mixed. *Dealer:* Art Sources Jacksonville FL 32207. *Mailing Add:* c/o Art Sources Inc 1253 Southshore Dr Orange Park FL 32073

NAZA (MARIA NAZARETH MCFARREN)
PAINTER, INSTRUCTOR
b Santa Cruz do Piaui, Piaui, Brazil, Apr 19, 55; US citizen. *Work:* Fayetteville Mus Art, NC; Mus The State of Piaui-Brazil, Teresina, Piaui. *Comn:* Bandepe, Bank of the State of Pernambuco, 77; portrait, comn by General M Antonio Noriega, Panama, 86; Mr Ganen Abbas (portrait), comn by Ms Huda Aduraham, Washington, DC, 89. *Exhib:* Pirelli Prize of Young Artist, Sao Paulo Mus Art, Spain, 83; NAZA - Back to the Origins, Mus The State of Piaui-Teresina, Piaui, 90; Salon de Peinture et D'Estampe de Montreal, Galerie Art-Jeuness, Montreal, Que, 90; Emerging Artist Grant, Fayetteville Arts Coun, NC, 91; Competition for North Carolina Artists, Fayetteville Mus Art, NC, 91. *Teaching:* Instr drawing, Fayetteville Tech Community Col, 91-92; instr oil portraits, figure & landscape drawing, Fort Bragg Arts & Crafts Ctr, 92. *Awards:* Best show, MSA Art Show, Southern Comand, Panama, 87; Emerging Artists Grant, Fayetteville Arts Coun, 91; Merit Award, NC Artists Competition, Fayetteville Mus Art, 91. *Bibliog:* Marcelo X Mendonca (auth), Brasileira foi Retratista, Folha de Sao Paulo, 1/90; Mary Gabriel (auth), Power Portraits, Mus & Arts Mag, Washington, DC, 3/90; Karen Jawers (auth), Extra Demensions to Portraits, Army Times, 6/90. *Mem:* Wash Project for the Arts; Wake Visual Arts Asn; Fayetteville Art Guild. *Media:* Oil. *Publ:* Auth, Art Diary Int, Giancarlo Politi Editore, 91. *Mailing Add:* 5900 Moorgate Circle Fayetteville NC 28304

NAZARENKO, BONNIE COE
PAINTER
b San Jose, Calif, Oct 26, 33. *Study:* San Jose State Col; Carmel Art Inst, under John Cunningham. *Work:* Mint Mus, Charlotte, NC. *Exhib:* Soc Animal Artists, Grand Cent Art Gallery, New York, 72, 74 & 75; Game Conservation Int, San Antonio, Tex, 80; Int Fish & Wildlife Expo, NY, 86; Soc Animal Artists, Daytona Beach, Fla, 90 & Mus Natural Hist, Cleveland, 91; and others. *Awards:* Beaufort Art Festival Award, SC, 66; Mint Mus Purchase Award, 68. *Mem:* Soc Animal Artists; Am Artists Prof League. *Media:* Oil. *Mailing Add:* 8314 Pocahontas St W Tampa FL 33615

NEAL, ANN PARKER See Parker, Ann

NEAL, (MINOR) AVON
WRITER, PRINTMAKER
b Indiana, July 16, 22. *Study:* Long Beach Col; Escuela Bellas Artes, Mex, with Siquieros, MFA. *Work:* Metrop Mus Art, New York; Libr Cong & Smithsonian Inst, Washington, DC; Abby Aldrich Rockefeller Mus Am Folk Art, Williamsburg, Va; Winterthur Mus, Wilmington, Del. *Comn:* 500 original rubbings, 70, 250 original rubbings, 71 & ed 350 original rubbings, 74, Am Heritage; ed 100 original rubbings, 70 & ed 70 original rubbings, 74, for Arton Assocs (all with Ann Parker); ed 100 original rubbings, Mead Art Gallery, Amherst Col, 76; ed 475 original rubbings, Sweetwater Editions, New York, NY, 82. *Exhib:* New Eng Gravestone Rubbings, Mead Art Gallery, 76; Gravestone Art, William Benton Mus Art, Univ Conn, 76; Molas, Art of the Cuna Indians, Alternative Ctr Int Arts, New York, 76; and others. *Pos:* Founder & pres, Thistle Hill Press, 78- *Awards:* Ford Found Grants, 62-63 & 63-64; Harriette Merrifield Forbes Award, Asn Gravestone Studies, 84. *Bibliog:* M J Gladstone (auth), New art from early American sculpture, Collector's Quart Report, 63 & Pedestrian art, Art in Am, 4/64; Stephen Chodorov (auth), Know Ye the Hour, Camera Three, CBS-TV, 11/68. *Mem:* The Artists Found, Mass Artists Fel Prog, 79. *Interests:* Stone rubbing and folk art. *Publ:* co-auth, Molas, Folk Art of the Cunas Indians, Barre, 77; auth, Scarecrows, Barre, 78; auth, Pigs & Eagles, Thistle Hill Press, ltd ed, 78; coauth, Early American Stone Sculpture, Sweetwater Editions, 82; auth, Los Ambulantes, the Itinerant Photographers of Guatemala, MIT Press, 82. *Dealer:* Gallery of Graphic Arts 1603 York Ave New York NY 10028. *Mailing Add:* 126 School St North Brookfield MA 01535

NEAL, IRENE
PAINTER, SCULPTOR
b Greensburg, Pa, May 14, 36. *Study:* Wilson Col, BA, 58; Sch Visual Arts, Rio de Janeiro, Cert, 76-77; Triangle Art Workshop. *Work:* Planetarium, Rio de Janerio, Brazil; Westmoreland Mus Art, Greensburg, Pa; Newport Harbor Art Mus, Calif; Hoover Inst, Stanford Univ, Calif; Columbia Univ, New York. *Exhib:* State Ten, NJ State Mus, Newark, 75; New Directions in Abstraction,

Shippee Gallery, New York, 86; State of the Artist, Aldrich Mus Contemp Art, Ridgefield, Conn, 87; Eight Winners Exhib, Stamford Mus, Conn, 89; Outside New York, Univ Alta, Can, 90. *Awards:* Special Mention of Honor, Brazilian Acad Arts & Letters, 77; Bronze Medal, Secy Brazilian Navy, 77. *Bibliog:* Kenworth Moffett (auth), articles in Moffetts Artletter, 86, 87 & 88; Valentin Tatransky (auth), Irene Neal (monogr), 86; Andi Rierden (auth), Junk to jewelry, NY Times, 4/8/90. *Media:* Acrylic on Canvas; Miscellaneous Media. *Dealer:* Michael Stone Collection 1055 Thomas Jefferson St NW Washington DC 20007. *Mailing Add:* 108 N Mailon Rd Broomall PA 19008

NEALS, OTTO
PAINTER, PRINTMAKER
b Lake City, SC, Dec 11, 30. *Study:* Basically self-taught, studied briefly at Brooklyn Mus Art Sch with Isaac Soyer; Printmaking Workshop, studied with Bob Blackburn, Robert DeLamonica & Krishna Reddy. *Work:* Ghana Nat Mus, Accra; Prime Minister Forbes Burnham, Guyana Statehouse; Columbia Mus, SC; Medgar Evers Col. *Comn:* Earl Graves Publ Co. *Exhib:* Resurrection, Studio Mus, NY, 71; Millenium, Philadelphia Mus Art, Pa, 73; Selections 73, 74, Brooklyn Mus, 74; 14 Black Artists, Pratt Inst Gallery, Brooklyn, 76; Migrations, Museo De Arte Moderno, Cali, Colombia, S Am, 76 & Caracas, Venezuela, 77. *Bibliog:* Peter Bailey (auth), Ten Black artists depict Christ, Ebony Mag, 4/71; Diane Weathers (auth), Black artists taking care of business, New York Times, 8/19/73; Elton Fax (auth), Black Artists of the New Generation, Dodd/Mead & Co, 77. *Mem:* Nat Conf Artists; Asn Caribbean Am Artists. *Media:* Oil, Acrylic; Wood, Stone. *Publ:* Illusr, African Heritage Cookbook, Macmillan, 71; The Adventures of Tony David & Marc, Exposition Press, 76. *Dealer:* Dorsey's Gallery 553 Rogers Ave Brooklyn NY 11225. *Mailing Add:* 138 Sullivan Pl Brooklyn NY 11225

NECHIS, BARBARA
PAINTER, LECTURER
b Mt Vernon, NY, Sept 25, 37. *Study:* Univ Rochester, BA, 58; Alfred Univ, MS, 59; Parsons Sch Design. *Work:* Butler Inst Am Art; Slater Mem Mus, Conn; Banco de Crefisul, Sao Paulo, Brazil. *Comn:* Citicorp, New York; Int Bus Machines, New York; Westinghouse; New York Graphic Soc. *Exhib:* Am Watercolor Soc Exhib, Nat Acad Design, New York, 70-86; Mainstreams, Marietta Col, Ohio; Nat Acad Design Ann; Hudson River Mus; Tweed Mus, Minn; and others. *Teaching:* Fac mem, Parsons Sch Design, Univ Alaska, 83-87; quest lectr, Can Soc Painters Watercolor; lectr workshops, currently. *Awards:* Lena Newcastle Award, Am Watercolor Soc, 85. *Mem:* Am Watercolor Soc; Artists Equity. *Media:* Watercolor, Mixed. *Publ:* Illusr, American Artists Group Reproduction, 73; auth, Watercolor, The Creative Experience, North Light/Van Nostrand Reinhold, 79; North Light, 6/79-92. *Dealer:* The Artful Eye Calistoga CA 94515; F Dorian San Francisco CA. *Mailing Add:* 1085 Dunaweal Lane Calistoga CA 94515

NECHVATAL, JOSEPH JAMES
PRINTMAKER, DRAFTSMAN
b Chicago, Ill, Jan 15, 51. *Study:* Southern Ill Univ, Carbondale, BFA, 75; Cornell Univ, 76; Columbia Univ, 77. *Work:* Chase Manhattan Bank, New York; Beijer Collection, Stockholm, Sweden. *Comn:* XS: The Opera, Mass Coun Arts, Boston, 86. *Exhib:* Whitney Mus Am Art Biennial, New York, 85. *Awards:* Painting Award, 85, Opera Award, 85 & Inter Arts Award, 86, Nat Endowment Arts; Painting Award, NY State Coun Arts, 88. *Bibliog:* Donald Kuspit (auth), rev, Artforum, 12/84; Collins & Millazo (coauths), Tropical codes, Kunstforum, 5/86. *Media:* Acrylic, Computer-assisted. *Publ:* Auth, Joseph Nechvatal, Machine Language Books, 86. *Mailing Add:* c/o Brooke Alexander Inc 59 Wooster St New York NY 10012

NEDDEAU, DONALD FREDERICK PRICE
PAINTER, DESIGNER
b Toronto, Ont, Jan 28, 13. *Study:* Ont Col Art; also with J W Beatty, Franklin Carmichael & Archibald Barnes. *Work:* The Royal Collection of Drawing and Watercolour, Windsor Castle, Eng; Sunny Brook Hosp Mem Collection, Toronto. *Exhib:* 11 shows, Royal Can Acad, 36-61; 20 shows, 42-65 & traveling exhibs, 44-48 & 51-65, Ont Soc Artists; group shows, 43 & 48-65 & traveling exhibs, 49-65, Can Soc Painters in Watercolor; Can Soc Painters in Water Colour & Calif Watercolor Exhib, 50-75; Can Group Painters, 55, 56, 58 & 61; plus others. *Teaching:* Head dept art & art summer sch, Cent Tech Sch, Toronto, Ont, 48-78, emer, 78- *Awards:* Scholar, 36 & Rous & Mann Award, 36, Ont Col Art. *Mem:* Fel Int Inst Arts & Lett; Can Soc Painters Watercolour (past pres); Can Guild Potters; Arts & Lett Club, Toronto; Royal Can Acad of Arts; and others. *Mailing Add:* 609 Avenue Rd Toronto ON M4V 2K3 Canada

NEEDLER, MABEL GLIDDEN See Howard, Linda

NEES, LAWRENCE
EDUCATOR, HISTORIAN
b Chicago, Ill, Aug 9, 49. *Study:* Univ Chicago, BA, 70; Harvard Univ, MA, 73, PhD, 77. *Teaching:* Vis lectr, Univ Victoria, BC, 76-77; lectr, Univ Mass, Boston, 77-78; from asst to prof, Univ Del, Newark, 78- *Mem:* Int Ctr Medieval Art; Byzantine Studies Asn; Medieval Acad Am; Majestas; Medieval Acad Ireland. *Res:* Medieval manuscript illumination; Carolingian art. *Publ:* Auth, Two illuminated Syriac manuscripts, Cahiers Archeol, 81; The iconographic program of decorated chancel barriers, Zeitschrift Kunstgeschichte, 83; The colophon drawing in the book of Mulling, Cambridge Medieval Celtic Studies, 83; From Justinian to Charlemagne, G K Hall, 85; The Gundohinus Gospels at Autun, Medieval Acad Am, 87. *Mailing Add:* Dept Art Hist Univ Del Newark DE 19716

NEFF, EDITH
PAINTER, INSTRUCTOR
b Philadelphia, Pa, Aug 27, 43. *Study:* Philadelphia Col Art, BFA, 65. *Work:* Philadelphia Mus of Art; Pa Acad of Fine Arts; Minn Mus of Art, St Paul; Washington & Jefferson Col; Allentown Mus of Art; Villanova Univ, Pa; Del Art Mus, Wilmington, Del; Asheville Art Mus, NC; Southern Alleghenies Mus Art, Loretto, Pa. *Comn:* Lobby mural, Univ City Sci Ctr, Philadelphia, 74; Four pastels, Cooper Hosp, Camden, NJ, 92. *Exhib:* one-woman show, Pa Acad Fine Arts, Philadelphia, 77, More Gallery, Philadelphia, 88, Southern Alleghenies Mus Art, Loretto, Pa, 89, & Sch Gallery, Pa Acad Fine Arts, 89, Western Carolina Univ (catalog), Cullowhee, NC, 90 & Rider Col (catalog), Lawrenceville, NJ, 92; Contemp Philadelphia Drawing, Philadelphia Mus Art, 79; Ten Pa Artists, Allentown Art Mus, 79; American Realism Since 1960, Pa Acad Fine Arts, Richmond Mus Art, Oakland Mus & Europe, 81-82; Painters of the Pennsylvania Landscape, Southern Mus Alleghenies, Loretto, Pa, 83; The Artist's Studio in American Art, Allentown Art Mus, 83; Realism Today, selections from the Rita Rich Collection, Nat Acad of Design, Butler Inst, 88; New Am Talent, Laguna Gloria Art Mus, Austin, Tex, 89; Artists Choose Artists (senior artist), Inst Contemp Art, Philadelphia, 91. *Pos:* Guest lectr, Pa Acad Fine Arts, 80-81. *Teaching:* vis prof, Western Carolina Univ; adj assoc prof, Univ Arts, 71-86; vis artist, Brandywine Workshop, Philadelphia, 92-93. *Awards:* Philadelphia Art Alliance Exhib Award, 79; Artists Fel, Pa Coun Arts, 82; Faculty Venture Award, Philadelphia Col Art, 83 & 86; Winner, Philadelphia Art NOW Competition, 88. *Bibliog:* Patricia Stewart (auth), article, Art Am, 11/88; Edward Sozanski (auth), rev, Philadelphia Inquirer, 7/6/89; Michael Allison (auth), Edith Neff Pastels, Chronicle Higher Educ, 7/12/89; Carole Katchen (auth), Creative Painting with Pastels, Northlight, 90. *Media:* Oil, Pastel. *Mailing Add:* 730 Kater St Philadelphia PA 10147

NEFF, JOHN A
PAINTER, DESIGNER
b Lebanon, Pa, May 5, 26. *Study:* Whitney Sch Art, New Haven, Conn, cert; Paier Col Art, Hamden, Conn, with Herbert Gute. *Work:* New Brit Mus Am Art, Gtr Hartford Arts Coun & Mus Art, Sci & Indust, Bridgeport, Conn; Mus Fine Arts, Springfield, Mass; First Nat Bank Boston. *Exhib:* Landscape I, De Cordova Mus, 70 & New England in Winter, Lincoln, Mass, 78; Am Watercolor Soc, New York, 75; Watercolor USA, Springfield, Mo, 75; Hudson Valley Nat Exhib, White Plains, NY, 90; Allied Artists, New York, 91. *Pos:* Sr graphic designer, Muirson Label Co, North Haven, Conn, 50-71; owner, Crossmark Assocs, Wallingford, Conn, 72-87. *Teaching:* Watercolor, privately. *Awards:* Wm Church Osborne Award, Am Watercolor Soc, 75; Best Show, US Coast Guard Acad, 82; Strathmore Award, New Eng Watercolor Soc, 86. *Bibliog:* T F Potter (auth), A proxy visit, Meriden Rec-J, Conn, 69. *Mem:* Am Watercolor Soc; Allied Artists Am; NEng Watercolor Soc; Hudson Valley Art Asn; Conn Watercolor Soc (bd dirs, 71-72). *Media:* Transparent Watercolor. *Mailing Add:* 17 Parkview Rd Wallingford CT 06492

NEFF, JOHN HALLMARK
ART HISTORIAN, MUSEUM DIRECTOR
b Miami, Fla, Mar 28, 44. *Study:* Wesleyan Univ, Middletown, Conn, BA, 66; Harvard Univ, MA, 68, PhD, 74. *Collections Arranged:* 180 Beacon Collection (auth, catalog), Boston, Mass, 67; Great Ideas Prog, Container Corp, 78-80; First Nat Bank Chicago, 84-; Am Medical Asn, 89. *Pos:* David E Finley fel, Nat Gallery Art, Washington, DC, 69-72; asst cur, Sterling & Francine Clark Art Inst, Williamstown, Mass, 72-73; cur mod art, Detroit Inst Arts, 74-78; dir, Mus Contemp Art, Chicago, 78-83; mem, adv comt for exhibs, Am Fedn of the Arts, 81-; mem, Nat Adv Comt, Art in Pub Places, Dade Co, Fla, 82-90; dir, art prog-art adv, First Nat Bank Chicago, 83-; mem adv comt, Art & Ideas Prog, Sch Art Inst Chicago, 85- *Teaching:* Teaching fel 19th & 20th century art hist, Harvard Univ, 67-69; asst prof 19th & 20th century art, Williams Col, Williamstown, Mass, 72-74, vis lectr, grad prog, 73-74. *Bibliog:* Hilton Kramer (auth), Rediscovering the genius of Henri Matisse, New York Times, 7/27/75; Robert Pincus-Witten (auth), Detroit notes, Arts Mag, 78. *Mem:* Arts Club, Chicago; Col Art Asn; Midwest Adv Bd, Am Found Blind; Am Fedn Arts, Exhib Adv Comt. *Res:* Matisse scholar, currently working on book about Max Newhaus, sound artist; catalogs on nineteenth and twentieth century art. *Publ:* Auth, Matisse and Decoration: The Schukin Panels, Art Am, 75; coauth, Henri Matisse: Paper Cut-Outs, Abrams, 77; coauth & ed, Charles Simonds, Mus Contemp Art, Chicago, 81; auth, Contemporary Art from the Netherlands, 82; Peter Joseph (catalog), 83; Anselm Kiefer: Bruch und Einung, Marian Goodman, New York, 88. *Mailing Add:* Art Prog, First Nat Bank Chicago First Nat Plaza Suite 0523 Chicago IL 60670

NEFFSON, ROBERT
PAINTER
b New York, NY, Dec 28, 49. *Study:* Art Students League, 64-67; Skowhegan Sch Painting, 69; Boston Univ, BFA(cum laude), 71, MFA, 73. *Work:* Roswell Mus, NMex; Boston Univ; Bristol Col, Mass; Charlestown Savings Bank, Boston. *Exhib:* Butler Inst Am Art 45th Ann Midyear Show, 81; The Realist Vision, Joanna Dean Gallery, New York, 82; Nocturnes, First St Gallery, New York, 82; solo exhibs, Capricorn Gallery, Bethesda, Md, 83, Summer Remembered, Squibb Gallery, Princeton, NJ, 84 & Gallery Henoch, New York, 90 & 92; New Faculty, Pa State Univ Mus Art, 83; Artists Studio 1840-1983, Allentown Mus, Pa, 83-84. *Pos:* Artist in residence, Roswell Mus, NMex, 77-78. *Teaching:* Asst prof art, Ariz State Univ, 81-82 & Pa State Univ, 82-88. *Awards:* Fulbright-Hays Fel, Rome, 76-77; Mass Coun Arts Grant, 76; Pa Coun Arts Visual Artists Grant, 83. *Bibliog:* Article, Survey of contemporary still lifes, Am Artist Mag, 2/86. *Mem:* Col Art Asn. *Media:* Oil. *Dealer:* Gallery Henoch 80 Wooster St New York NY 10012. *Mailing Add:* 35 Sidney Place Brooklyn NY 11201

NEGRI, ROCCO ANTONIO
ILLUSTRATOR, PAINTER
b Reggio Calabria, Italy, June 26, 32; US citizen. *Study:* Aurel Kessler Acad, Arg, BsAs; Art Students League; Sch of Visual Arts, New York; Pratt Graphic Ctr, New York. *Work:* Univ Minn, Minneapolis; Cedar Rapids Pub Libr, Iowa; Univ Tokyo, Japan; Fed Home Loan Bank, New York; Albert Einstein Sch, Bronx, NY. *Exhib:* Painter's Mill Gallery, Rochester, NY, 74; one-man shows, Ratafia Gallery, Ft Lauderdale, Fla, 75 & Mainstream Gallery, Westhampton, NY, 75; Studio Gallery, Greenport, NY, 76; Reece Galleries Inc, New York, 76. *Teaching:* Instr pvt & group classes, currently. *Awards:* Sixth Place, WSOAE, Kiwanis Club, 72; Excellence Award, Long Beach Art Asn, NY, 74; Merit Award, Coconut Grove Merchants Asn, Miami, Fla, 76. *Bibliog:* June Dixon (auth), Fantasy of a better place, Chattanooga Times, 6/69; A critic's choice of the year's best, New York Times, 12/70; Picture books, Hornbook, 2/71. *Media:* Collages, Acrylics. *Publ:* Illusr, Journey Outside, 69 & Fee, Fi, Fo, Fum, 69, Viking; The One Bad Thing About Father, Harper & Row, 70; The Magic Pumpkin, Four Winds, 71; The Son of the Leopard, Crown, 74. *Dealer:* Carroll-Condit Galleries 210 Mamaroneck Ave White Plains NY 10601. *Mailing Add:* 7747 79th St Flushing NY 11385

NEGROPONTE, GEORGE
PAINTER
b New York, NY, Feb 11, 53. *Study:* Skowhegan Sch of Painting & Sculpture, 73; Yale Univ, BA, 75. *Work:* Chemical Bank, New York, NY; Bank of Am, San Francisco, Calif; Reader's Digest Asn, New York, NY; Metrop Mus Art, NY; Mus Art, Andros, Greece. *Comn:* Paintings, Olympia & York, 81 & TWA, 86, New York; IBM, New York. *Exhib:* Solo exhibs, Brooke Alexander Inc, New York, 81, 83 & 85, John Good Gallery, New York, 87-88, Real Art Inc, New York, 90 & Jason McCoy, 90-91; New Drawing in America, Mus Mod Art Ca'Pesaro, Venice, Italy, 83; An International Survey of Painting & Sculpture, Mus Mod Art, New York, 84 New York, 87 & 88; Recent Acquistions, Metrop Mus Art, 89. *Pos:* Consult, Drawing Ctr, New York, 82-84; visual arts panelist, NY State Coun Arts, 85-89, appeals panel, currently. *Teaching:* Instr, Studio Sch, NY, 90- *Awards:* Individual Artists Award, NY State Coun Arts, 88. *Bibliog:* Charles Hagen (auth), Art Forum, 10/87; Robet Edelman (auth), Art Am, 1/89; Jed Perl (auth), New Criterion, 3/89. *Media:* Oil. *Dealer:* Jason McCoy Inc New York NY. *Mailing Add:* 59 Wooster St New York NY 10012

NEHER, FRED
CARTOONIST
b Nappanee, Ind, Sept 29, 03. *Study:* Chicago Acad Fine Arts. *Work:* Syracuse Univ; Butler Inst Am Art; Albright Col, Reading, Pa; Ohio State Univ, Columbus; Univ of Colo, Boulder. *Exhib:* Humor Festival, World Cartoon Exhib, Knokke, Heist, Belg, 70 & 71. *Pos:* Cartoonist, Life's Like That, 34-77. *Teaching:* Instr cartooning, Univ Colo, Boulder, 64- *Awards:* US Treas Dept Red Cross. *Mem:* Nat Cartoonist Soc; Soc Illusr. *Mailing Add:* One Neher Lane Boulder CO 80304

NEHER, ROSS JAMES
PAINTER, WRITER
b Kingston, NY, June 5, 49. *Study:* Art Students League with Henry Billings & Fletcher Martin, 64-67; Sch Fine Arts, Wash Univ, BFA, 71; Pratt Inst, NY, MFA, 75. *Work:* Brooklyn Mus, NY; Mint Mus, Charlotte, NC; Sidney Lewis, Richmond, Va; Commonwealth Co, Lincoln, Nebr; Binney & Smith, Easton, Pa; Chase Manhattan Bank & Chemical Bank, New York, NY. *Exhib:* Recent Abstract Painting, State Univ NY, Brockport, 76; The New Spiritualism, Robert Hull Fleming Mus, Burlington, 81; GRP Exhib, Albright Knox, Buffalo, 82; Newcastle Salutes New York, Newcastle-upon-Tyne Gallery, Eng, 83; 2 Smart Art Too, 55 Mercer, New York, 85; New Work, New York, Harvard Univ, Cambridge, 85; The New Response, Contemporary Painters of the Hudson River, Albany Inst Art, New York, 86. *Teaching:* Prof grad painting, Pratt Inst, 80- *Awards:* Tiffany Award, Tiffany Found, 86; Cité Des Arts, Paris Residency, Wash Univ, 86. *Bibliog:* Adrian Goddard (auth), Ross Neher: Painting Behavior, Artforum, 12/79; April Kingsley (auth), The New Spiritualism, Oscarrson Hood, 81. *Media:* Oil, Canvas. *Publ:* Auth, Bathysiderodromophobia, The Fox, 76; Dennis Masback's Paintings, 78 & Mentalism Versus Painting, 79, Artforum; The Death of Perception, Issue No 1, 84 & The Legacy of Picasso, Issue No 2, 85. *Dealer:* David Beitzel 113 Greene St New York NY 10012. *Mailing Add:* 545 Broadway New York NY 10012

NEIDHARDT, CARL RICHARD
PAINTER, SCULPTOR
b Chattanooga, Tenn, May 4, 21. *Study:* Ga Sch Tech, 39-41; Univ Tenn, Chattanooga, BA, 49; Univ Fla, MFA, 52; Rijksacademie, Amsterdam, Netherlands, 53-54; Ohio State Univ, PhD, 61. *Work:* Atlantic Richfield Oil Co. *Exhib:* Fifty Florida Artists, Ringling Mus, Sarasota, 60; Artist Teachers in Southeastern Univs, Jacksonville Mus, 60; Ark Art Ctr Mus, Little Rock, 61-63 & 69; Dallas Mus Fine Arts, Tex, 63; Okla Art Ctr Mus, Oklahoma City, 64-69; Hunter Mus Art, Chattanooga, Tenn, 80; Mus Art, Sci & Indust, Bridgeport, Conn, 81; Univ Dallas, Tex, 88; Tex Woman's Univ, Denton, 89; Univ N Tex, Denton, 90; Art Mus SE Tex, Beaumont, 91. *Pos:* Chmn dept art, Hardin-Simmons Univ, Abilene, Tex, 60-65; dir dept art, Angelo State Univ, San Angelo, Tex, 65-66; chmn dept art, Austin Col, Sherman, Tex, 66-86, emer prof art, 86- *Awards:* Fulbright Award to Netherlands, 53-54; Danforth Grant Res Painting, 58-59; Cullen Grant, 73; Richardson Grant, 75 & 82. *Media:* Acrylic on Canvas; Bronze. *Mailing Add:* 321 N Grand Ave Sherman TX 75090

NEIKRUG, MARJORIE
ART DEALER
b New Rochelle, NY. *Study:* Sarah Lawrence Col. *Pos:* Owner & dir, Neikrug Photograhica Ltd; appraiser & consult, fine art photog. *Teaching:* Instr, The Photographer's Eye (class), NY Univ, four yrs. *Awards:* Copley Award, Smithsonian Inst, 88. *Mem:* Am Soc Appraisers (pres & sr mem, 80-81, dep state dir, 82); Am Arbitration Soc; Am Soc Mag Photogr; Am Soc Picture Professionals; Photog Adminr Inc; Appraisers Asn Am (bd mem). *Specialty:* Contemporary photography; photographica; rare books; portfolios; daguerreotypes; important historical photographs. *Mailing Add:* 224 E 68th St New York NY 10021

NEIL, J M
MUSEUM DIRECTOR, ADMINISTRATOR
b Boise, Idaho, June 2, 37. *Study:* Yale Col, AB, 59; Univ Wis, MS, 63; Wash State Univ, PhD, 66. *Collections Arranged:* Will James: The Spirit of the Cowboy (ed, catalog), 85-86 & Historic Ranches of Wyoming (with catalog), 86 & traveling, Nicolaysen Art Mus, Casper, Wyo. *Pos:* Dir, Idaho Bicentennial Comn, Boise, 72-76 & Nicolaysen Art Mus, Casper, Wyo, 83-89; city conservator, Seattle, Wash, 78-81. *Teaching:* Asst assoc prof Am studies, Univ Hawaii, 67-72; vis lectr art hist, Univ Victoria, BC, 76-77. *Mem:* Wyo Coun Arts (bd mem, 85-89); Natrona Co Pub Libr (bd mem, 88-89). *Res:* Primarily in the history of American environmental design--architecture, landscape design, urban planning and others. *Publ:* Auth, Toward a National Taste: America's Quest for Aesthetic Independence, Univ Press Hawaii, 75; Saints & Oddfellows: A Bicentennial Sampler of Idaho Architecture, Boise Gallery Art, 76; The impact of the Armory Show, S Atlantic Quart, 80; Paris or New York? The shaping of downtown Seattle, 1903-1914, Pac NW Quart, 84. *Mailing Add:* PO Box 911 McCall ID 83638

NEILL, BEN E
PAINTER
b Quincy, Mass, Dec 11, 14. *Study:* Sch Practical Art, Boston, Mass, 33; Mass Col Art, Boston, 34. *Comn:* 3 Major Pieces, State of Md, 83-84; Sand Glass Mus, Mass, 85; Sandwich Pub Libr, Mass, 87; Yarmouth Town Hall, Mass, 88; Mural, Nantucket Isle, 90. *Exhib:* Am Soc Marine Artists, Grand Cent Art Galleries, Inc, New York, 80 & 82; Int Maritime, Gallery-Mystic Seaport; Contemp Marine Art, Peabody Mus, Salem, Mass, 81; Of Ships & the Sea, Greenwich Workshop Gallery, Southport, Conn, 81-83; Annapolis Marine Art Gallery Ltd, 82-84; and others. *Pos:* Editorial artist, Boston Herald Traveler, Mass, 46-73. *Awards:* Award of Excellence, Mystic Int, 89. *Bibliog:* John S Carter (auth), Contemporary Marine, Nimrod Press, 81. *Mem:* Am Soc Marine Artists; Int Soc Marine Painters. *Media:* Acrylic. *Publ:* Auth, The Cape Cod Compass, Quarterdeck Communication, Inc, Mass, 85; Time Out, Cape Cod Times, Hyannis, Mass, 86. *Mailing Add:* c/o Misty Marsh Studio 88 Wood Ave Rd 1 Sandwich MA 02563

NEILL, JOE
SCULPTOR
b New Eagle, Pa, Aug 29, 44. *Study:* Westminster Col, BA, 66; Bowling Green State Univ, MFA, 68. *Work:* Mem Art Gallery, Rochester, NY; Tyler Mus, Tex; Everson Mus; Phillip Morris, McCrory Corp, New York. *Exhib:* Solo exhibs, Robert Freidus Gallery, New York, 77, 79 & 80, Vanderwoude Tananbaum Gallery, New York, 82 & Butler Inst Am Art, 84; Current New York, Lowe Gallery, Syracuse Univ, 80; Works on Paper, Weatherspoon Art Gallery, Greensboro, NC, 82-83; Suspended Object, Berkshire Mus, Pittsfield, Mass, 83. *Bibliog:* Jean Feinberg (auth), article, 79 & Margaret Sheffield (auth), Joe Neill--the kinetic and the indeterminate, 82, Arts Mag. *Media:* Wood, Plastics. *Mailing Add:* 392 Broadway New York NY 10013

NEIMAN, LEROY
PAINTER, PRINTMAKER
b St Paul, Minn, June 8, 27. *Study:* Art Inst Chicago; Univ Chicago; Univ Ill; Franklin Pierce Col, Rindge, NH, LHD, 76; St Johns Univ, NY, Hon DFA; Iona Col, DFA, 85. *Work:* Ill State Mus; Joslyn Art Mus; Wodham Col, Oxford, Eng; Hermitage, Leningrad, USSR; Art Inst Chicago; Museo de Bellas Artes, Caracas. *Comn:* America's Cup, New York Yacht Club; Newport Jazz Festival; New York Marathon; Theater Collection Mus City of New York; Univ Tex, Ind & Ky. *Exhib:* American Exhibition of Oil Painting, Corcoran Gallery Am Art, Washington, DC, 57; Chicago American Exhibit of Painting & Sculpture, Art Inst Chicago, 60; Chicago Artists & Vicinity Show, 50-60; Hammer Gallery, 63-86, 89 & 92; Knoedler Gallery, London, 76; Retrospective, Minn Mus Art, 76, Oklahoma City Mus Art, 81; Neiman-Warhol, Los Angeles Inst Contemp Art, 81; New State Tretyakov Mus, 88; Butler Institute, Youngstown, Ohio, 90. *Pos:* Computer artist, Superbowl 78, CBS Sports Spectacular, 79, Good Will Games, Moscow, 86. *Teaching:* Instr figure drawing, Art Inst Chicago, 50-60; instr painting, Winston-Salem Art Ctr, 64 & Atlanta Poverty Art Prog, 67-68. *Awards:* Hamilton-Graham Ball State Col, 58; Gold Medal, Salon d'Art Mod, Paris, 61; Municipal Prize, Chicago Show, 58. *Bibliog:* LeRoy Neiman Art & Life Style, Felicie Press, 74; Prints of LeRoy Neiman, Knoedler Publ, 80-90 & 91. *Media:* Oil, Enamel; Serigraphy, Etching. *Publ:* Auth, Horses, 79 & Winners, 83, Harry N Abrams Inc, Carnaval, Knoedler Publ, 81; Monte Carlo Chase, Van Der Marck Editions, 88; Big Time Golf, Harry N Abrams Inc, 92. *Dealer:* Hammer Galleries 33 W 57th St New York NY 10022; Knoedler Publ Co 19 E 70th St New York NY 10021. *Mailing Add:* 1 W 67th St New York NY 10023

NEIMANAS, JOYCE
PHOTOGRAPHER
Study: Art Inst Chicago, MFA, 69. *Work:* Mus Contemp Art, Chicago, Ill; San Francisco Mus Mod Art, Calif; Art Inst Chicago. *Exhib:* Solo exhib, Ctr

Creative Photog, Tucson, Ariz, 84; Art & Photog in Interaction, Sala Arcs Gallery, Barcelona, Spain, 90; Past, Present, Mus Fine Arts, Houston, Tex, 92. *Teaching:* Prof photog, Art Inst Chicago, 77- *Awards:* Visual Arts Fel, Nat Endowment Arts, 78, 83 & 90; Artist Grant, Ill Arts Coun, 87. *Mailing Add:* 10300 Viretta Lane Los Angeles CA 90077

NELLIS, JENNIFRED GENE
SCULPTURE
b Lincoln, Nebr. *Study:* Univ Nebr, Lincoln, BFA, 70; Univ Iowa, Iowa City, MA, 76, MFA, 77. *Work:* Masur Mus, Monroe, La; Fine Arts Gallery, Univ Minn, Morris; Sprague Art Gallery, Joliet Jr Col. *Exhib:* Dahl Fine Arts Ctr, Rapid City, SDak, 89; three-person exhib, WARM Gallery, Minneapolis, Minn, 89; Icons made in Minnesota, AIR Gallery, New York, 89; WARM Kansas City Artists Coalition, 90; Artemisia Gallery, Chicago, 90; plus many other group & solo shows. *Teaching:* Assoc prof sculpture, drawing, basic studio & ceramics, Univ Minn, Morris, 78-86, assoc prof, 86- *Awards:* Sculpture Award, 29th Ann Iowa Artists, 77; Purchase Award, Monroe Nat, 79; Second Prize Award, Pyramid Art Ctr, Rochester, NY, 84. *Bibliog:* Mellissa Stang (auth), New Art Examiner, 5/87; Norita Dittberner (auth) Warm Journal, Vol 8, No 2, 87; Nancy Cohen (auth), Warming Up, Vinyl Arts, 1/12/88. *Mem:* Women's Art Registry Minn; Col Art Asn; Women's Caucus for Art. *Media:* Mixed Media. *Publ:* Auth, Geographies-Geologies, Milkweed Chronicle, winter 83; 1984 Calender, Women in Art, 84. *Dealer:* Anderson & Anderson Gallery Minneapolis MN; Hamilton Frame & Gallery Independence MO. *Mailing Add:* Dept Art Univ Minn Morris MN 56267

NELSON, BASHA RUTH See Nelson, Ruth Basha (Basha Ruth Nelson)

NELSON, CAREY BOONE
SCULPTOR
b Lexington, Mo. *Study:* Wellesley Col, BA; Univ Mo; Wagner Col, MSEd; Art Students League, with John Hovannes, Arturo Lorenzani & John Terken; Nat Acad Design. *Work:* Wright-Patterson Air Force Mus, Dayton, Ohio; Sheldon Swope Mus, Terre Haute, Ind; Durban Art Mus, SAfrica; Victoria Libr, Melbourne, Australia; Deaf Oral Sch, Louisville, Ky. *Comn:* George Balanchine, Nat League Am Pen Women, Washington, DC; Gen Jimmie Doolittle, USAF, 89; Douglas A Munro, Coast Guard Training Ctr, Cape May, NJ, 89; Col G Vaughn, Col Aeronautics, LaGuardia Airport, New York; James Madison, Montpelier, Va, 92; and others. *Exhib:* Int Art Exchange, Monte Carlo, Monaco, Paris & Cannes; Salmagundi Club, New York, 75-90; Am Artists Prof League Grand Nat; Rockefeller Plaza, NY, 85-; Federal Hall, NY, 86; solo exhib: Epiphany Libr, New York, 92; over 300 other group shows & fourteen one-man shows, New York. *Teaching:* Instr sculpture seminars, Snug Harbor Cult Ctr, 82 & 83, demonstr art groups, 84-92; pvt lectr, 84-92. *Awards:* Award of Excellence, Nat League Am Pen Women, 86; Achievment Award, Nat League Am Pen Women, 88; Lifetime Hon Artist Mem, Catharine Lorillard Wolfe Art Club, 89; and others. *Bibliog:* Nat Collection Fine Arts, Smithsonian Inst, Washington, DC; What Happens at the Foundry (video), 90; Birth of a Bronze (from day to medal) video, 90. *Mem:* Nat League Am Pen Women (pres, Manhattan, New York branch, 82-86, 90-92, 92-); life fel Am Artists Prof League; Life Mem, Nat Arts Club; Soc Illusr; fel Royal Soc Arts (Eng). *Media:* Bronze, Marble. *Mailing Add:* 282 Douglas Rd Staten Island NY 10304

NELSON, DONA RAE
PAINTER
b Grand Island, Nebr, Aug 2, 47. *Study:* Ohio State Univ, BFA, 68; Independent Study Program, Whitney Mus Am Art, 68. *Work:* Metrop Mus Art, Guggenheim Mus, New York. *Exhib:* Twenty-Six Contemporary Woman Artists, Larry Aldrich Mus Contemp Art, Conn, 70; 10 Young Artists: Theodoran Artists, Solomon R Guggenheim Mus, New York, 71; Personal Visions: Places and Spaces, Bronx Mus Art, NY, 78; Body Language: Recent Figuration, Mass Inst Technol, Cambridge, 81; Ripe Fruit, PS 1, Long Island City, NY, 85; 4 Artists, Artist Space, 85. *Teaching:* Vis artist, Chicago Art Inst, 82, Va Commonwealth Univ, Richmond, 83, Tyler Sch Art, Philadelphia, 84, Ohio State Univ, Columbus, 85, La State Univ, Baton Rouge, 86 & Univ Calif, Berkeley, 87-88. *Awards:* Theodoran Purchase Award, Guggenheim Mus, 71; Creative Artists Pub Serv Prog Grant, 78-79; Nat Endowment Arts Grants, 79 & 87. *Bibliog:* Paul Mattick (auth), Arts Mag, fall 90; Lisa Liebmann (auth), Dona Nelson's Time Pieces, Artform, 3/89. *Mem:* Found Community Artists. *Media:* Acrylic, Cloth Collage. *Publ:* Contribr, Body Language: Recent Figuration, MIT Press, 81; Contemporary Painting/Figuration, Univ Calif, 81; The Painterly Figure, Parrish Art Mus, Southampton, NY, 83. *Mailing Add:* 110 Duane St New York NY 10007

NELSON, HAROLD B
DIRECTOR
b Providence, RI, May 14, 47. *Study:* Bowdoin Col, AB, 69; Univ Del, MA, 72. *Collections Arranged:* Sounding the Depths: 150 Years of American Seascape, Am Fedn of Arts, 90-91. *Pos:* Cur mus art & archaeology, Univ Mo, 77-79; registrar, Solomon R Guggenheim Mus, 79-83; chief admin for exhibs, Am Fedn Arts, 83-89; dir, Long Beach Mus Art, 89- *Awards:* Fel, Smithsonian Research, Nat Mus Am Art, 76. *Mem:* Col Art Asn; Am Asn Mus; Coalition for the Freedom of Expression. *Publ:* Auth, Sounding the Depths: 150 Years of American Seascape (catalog), Chronicle Books, 89. *Mailing Add:* Long Beach Mus Art 2300 E Ocean Blvd Long Beach CA 90803

NELSON, JACK D
SCULPTOR, GRAPHIC ARTIST
b Chicago, Ill, Jan 26, 29. *Study:* Art Inst Chicago, dipl, 54; Goodman Theatre. *Work:* Mus Mod Art, Stockholm, Sweden; Everson Mus, Syracuse; also in pvt collections of Joseph H Hirshhorn, Malcolm S Forbes & Yves Tanquey, Kay Sage Estate. *Comn:* Sculptural wall, Philips Electronics Corp, Lidingo, Sweden, 63; kinetic clock sculpture, Halprin Assoc for City of Minneapolis, 66. *Exhib:* International Movement in Art Show, Stockholm, Paris & Amsterdam, 61; Nat Aspect '61 Show, Stockholm, 61; Retrospective Show, Everson Mus, 72; Circuit Existential Videotape Exhib, Cologne, Ger, Boston & Los Angeles, 74-75. *Pos:* Asst art dir, Visualscope, Inc, New York, 56-59; dir & designer children's TV show, G K Films Studio, Swedish TV-Radio, Stockholm, 60-63. *Teaching:* Assoc prof sculpture & film video, Col Visual & Performing Arts, Syracuse Univ, 66-78, emer prof, 78- *Bibliog:* Gunnar Berefelts (auth), Ord och bild, Sartrvck, Stockholm, 62; article, Time Mag, 65; Lawrence Halprin (auth), The RSVP Cycles, Braziller, 69. *Media:* Vacuum Formed Plastic, Stretched Muslin Membrane; Videotape, Film. *Dealer:* Krasner Gallery 1043 Madison Ave New York NY 13210. *Mailing Add:* 819 Comstock Ave Syracuse NY 13210

NELSON, JAMES P
PAINTER
b Boston, Mass, 1949. *Study:* Carnegie-Mellon Univ, BFA, 71. *Work:* The Carnegie Mus Art; Pittsburgh Nat Bank; Western Pa Hosp. *Exhib:* The New American Still Life, Westmoreland Mus Art, Greensburg, Pa, 79; one-man shows, Hewlett Gallery, Carnegie-Mellon Univ, Pittsburgh, 81, Blue Sky Gallery, Pittsburgh, 86, Common's Room Gallery Pittsburgh Ctr for the Arts, 88, UP Gallery, Univ Pittsburgh, 89 & Carson Street Gallery, Pittsburgh, 90; Unlimited Horizons, Carnegie-Mellon Art Gallery, Pittsburgh, 87; Ruth Siegel Gallery, New York, 89; Pittsburgh in Chicago, Deson-Saunders Gallery, Chicago, 90. *Awards:* Purchase Award & Juror's Award, Carnegie Mus Art, Pittsburgh, 87; Festival Award & Highlight Award, Three Rivers Arts Festival, Pittsburgh, 87; Nat Endowment Arts, 89. *Bibliog:* Patricia Lowry (auth), City is the Subject, What is the Object, Pittsburgh Press, 11/8/87; Cheryl Regan (auth), James P Nelson, Dialogue Mag, 36, 1-2/88; William Homisak (auth), Nelson's Pittsburgh: Moody City on the Mon, Tribune Rev, 4/21/89. *Mailing Add:* 5100 Liberty Ave Pittsburgh PA 15224

NELSON, JANE GRAY
CURATOR
b Kankakee, Ill, Oct 10, 28. *Study:* Univ Calif, Berkeley, MLS, 63, MA(classical archeol), 71. *Pos:* Librn, Fine Arts Mus, San Francisco, 71-89, asst cur, Dept Ancient Art, 74-76 & 89- *Mem:* Am Inst Archeol; Soc Promotion Hellenic Studies; Brontë Soc; Jane Austen Soc; Calif Classical Asn. *Res:* Gnathia ware. *Publ:* Contribr, Three Centuries of French Art, 73, Claude Monet, 73, Africa, Ancient Mexican Art: The Loran Collection, 74, Two Early Hittite Theriomorphic Vessels of the Karum-Period, 82, Inside Wuthering Heights, 84 & Xylophones on Gnathia Vases, 86. *Mailing Add:* Fine Arts Mus Golden Gate Park San Francisco CA 94118

NELSON, JOAN
PAINTER
b Torrance, Calif, 58. *Study:* Washington Univ, St Louis, Mo, BFA, 81; Brooklyn Mus Sch, Max Beckman Mem Scholar, 81-82. *Work:* Mus Mod Art, Solomon R Guggenheim Mus, New York; Los Angeles Co Mus Art; Hirshhorn Mus & Sculpture Garden, Nat Mus Women Arts, Washington. *Exhib:* Solo exhibs, Contemp Arts Mus, Houston, Tex, 88 & Freedman Gallery, Albright Col, Reading, Pa, 91; Currents 39, St Louis Arts Mus, 89; 1989 Biennial, Whitney Mus Am Art, New York, 89; American Realism & Figurative Art, Miyagi Mus, Japan, 91-92; New Viewpoints, Seville World Expo, Spain, 92; Earth and Sky, Hodd Mus Art, Dartmouth Col, NH, 92; Quotations, Aldrich Mus Art, Ridgefield, Conn, 92; Robert Miller Gallery, (with catalog), New York, 90 & 91. *Bibliog:* Michael Brenson (auth), Straightened Landscapes of a Post-Modern Era, New York Times, 1/13/89; Kay Larson (auth), Back to Nature, New York, 4/90; Michael Boodro (auth), Joan Nelson: Second Nature, Artnews, 9/90. *Media:* Oil, Wax on Wood. *Publ:* Auth Donald Kuspit, Joan Nelson, Robert Miller Gallery, 90 & 91. *Mailing Add:* c/o Robert Miller Gallery 41 E 57th St New York NY 10022

NELSON, JON ALLEN
CURATOR, HISTORIAN
b Omaha, Nebr, July 9, 36. *Study:* Univ Nebr, Lincoln, BFA, 59; museology, Univ Minn. *Collections Arranged:* Etchings of J Alden Weir (auth, catalog), 67, Thomas Coleman, Printmaker (auth, catalog), 72 & Sigmund Abeles: The First Twenty Years (auth, catalog), 79, Sheldon Mem Art Gallery, Univ Nebr, Lincoln; Great Plains 1930-1939 (auth, catalog), Ctr in Greater Plains Studies, Univ Nebr, 85. *Pos:* Pres, Nebr Mus Conf, 73; cur, Ctr Great Plains Studies Art Collection, Univ Nebr, formerly. *Publ:* Auth, Art of Printmaking, Univ Nebr, Lincoln, 66. *Mailing Add:* 1323 C St Lincoln NE 68502

NELSON, LEONARD
PAINTER, SCULPTOR
b Camden, NJ, Mar 5, 12. *Study:* Pa Acad Fine Arts, 36-40; Barnes Found, 36-41; Philadelphia Col Art, BFA, 52. *Work:* Mus Mod Art; Philadelphia Mus Art; Dallas Mus Mod Art; Walker Mus Art; Portland Mus; plus many others. *Exhib:* Sixty two-man shows, New York & Philadelphia; many exhibs, Pa Acad Fine Art; Mus Mod Art; Art Inst Chicago; Maj Retrospective Exhib, Moore Col of Art, Philadelphia, 78. *Teaching:* Prof printmaking, Moore Col Art, 52-83, head dept, 69-80, prof emer, 83- *Awards:* European Fel, Bd Fine Art, 39; Nat Wood Block Award, 42. *Mem:* Print Club (mem bd trustees, 52-57). *Media:* Oil; Metal. *Mailing Add:* 65 Bodine Rd Berwyn PA 19312-1236

NELSON, MARY CARROLL
WRITER, PAINTER
b Bryan, Tex, Apr 24, 29. *Study:* Barnard Col, BA(fine arts), 50, art hist with Julius Held & painting with Peppino Mangravite & Dong Kingman; Univ NMex, MA(art educ), 63, painting with Kenneth M Adams; art educ with Alexander Masley; grad studies art hist with John Tatschl, 69-70. *Exhib:* retrospective, 25th Ann NMex Arts & Crafts Fair, 86; New Mexico '87, NMex Mus Fine Arts, 87; Layering, Level to Level, Ohio, 90; The Artist as Shaman, Ohio, 90; Layering: A Gathering of Voices, Calif, 91; Art is for Healing, Tex, 92. *Collections Arranged:* Layering: An Art of Time & Space, (auth, catalog), Albuquerque Mus, 85; Shrines & Sacred Places, NMex A & CF, Albuquerque, 88. *Pos:* cur, Layering, An Art of Time & Space, Albuquerque Mus, 85 & Something About the Author, Vol XXIII, 81. *Bibliog:* Speaking from experience, Am Artist, 10/87. *Mem:* NMex Press Women; Soc Layerists Multi-Media (founder, 82, pres, 82-84, secy, 84-89). *Media:* Mixed Media. *Res:* American, Native American & Southwest artists; the relationship of artists' philosophy and their technique. *Publ:* Coauth (with Robert E Wood), Watercolor Workshop, 74, coauth (with R Kelley), Ramon Kelley Paints Portraits, Figures, 77, Legendary Artists of Taos, 80 & auth, Masters of Western Art, 82, Watson-Guptill; The Driscoll Collection of American Western Art (exhib catalog) Beijing, 81; auth, Connecting, the art of Beth Ames Swartz, Northland Press, 84; and others. *Mailing Add:* 1408 Georgia NE Albuquerque NM 87110

NELSON, PAMELA HUDSON
ASSEMBLAGE ARTIST, SCULPTOR
b Oklahoma City, Okla, Mar 25, 47. *Study:* Southern Methodist Univ, Dallas, Tex, BFA, 74. *Work:* MTV Collection, New York; Steak & Ale Collection, Dallas, Tex. *Comn:* Relief Animals, Dallas Zoo, Tex; Cotton Crown, County Govt, Blytheville, Ark; Parkland Hosp, Dallas. *Exhib:* Tex Exhib, Nat Mus Women, Washington, DC, 88; Handmade in Texas, LTV Ctr, Dallas, Tex, 87; Tex Ann, Laguna Gloria Mus, Austin, Tex, 87. *Pos:* Design Artist, Dallas Light Rail System. *Teaching:* Arlington Art Mus, Tex. *Awards:* Ron Gleason Award, Excellence 88, Tex Sculpture Asn, 88; Billboard Winner, Outdoor Art, Patrick Media Group, 88. *Bibliog:* Judy Kelly (dir), Artseye (TV prog), KERA-Pub Television, Dallas, 87; Paul Nathan (auth), Texas Collects, Taylor Publ Co, 88; Sylvia Moore (auth), No Bluebonnets, No Yellow Roses, Midmarch Arts, 88. *Mem:* Tex Sculpture Asn. *Media:* Wood, Mixed Media. *Dealer:* Peregrine Gallery at the Crescent 2200 Cedar Springs Rd Dallas Tex 75201. *Mailing Add:* 2801 Westminister Dallas TX 75205

NELSON, RUTH BASHA (BASHA RUTH NELSON)
SCULPTURE, PAINTER
b New York NY, July 1, 39. *Study:* Hunter Col, BA, 60; New York Univ, MA, 76. *Work:* Woodstock Hist Soc, NY; Inst Arts, Nassau, Bahamas; US Embassy, Nassau, Bahamas. *Exhib:* Recent Work, 60 Washington Sq E, New York, 76; Edges & Insights, US Embassy, Nassau, Bahamas, 78; Watercolors, Norton Gallery & Mus, Palm Beach, Fla, 80; Postcard exhib, New York Carlsberg Glyptotek Mus, Copenhagen, Denmark, 80; Recent Work, Manhattanville Col, Purchase, NY, 90; group exhib, Art & Cult Ctr, Hollywood, Fla, 82; Women in Art, N Miami Mu & Art Ctr, Fla, 82; Hudson Valley Artist, Mid Hudson Arts & Sci Ctr, Poughkeepsie, NY, 87. *Pos:* Dir, Summerwood Art Ctr, Lake Hill, NY, 85-87; arts coodr, Ulster Co BOCES, New Paltz, NY, 85-90. *Teaching:* Asst instr drawing, Metrop Mus Art, NY, 74-76; instr art, Col of Bahamas, Nassau, 78-80; adj instr art appreciation, Marist Col, Poughkeepsie, NY, 85-88. *Awards:* Welfred McGibbon, Norton Gallery & Mus, 80; Green Co Coun on Arts, The Artist at Play, 86. *Bibliog:* Brent Malone (auth), Edges-Insights: Cultural Shock, Nassau Guardian, 12/6/78; Tram Combs (auth), Basha Nelson's boxed colors, Woodstock Times, 6/25/87; New York Gallery Guide, Art Now, 5/88. *Mem:* Artists Equity; Woodstock Artists Asn. *Dealer:* Noho Gallery 168 Mercer St New York, NY 10012. *Mailing Add:* PO Box 86 Lake Hill NY 12448

NELSON, SIGNE (SIGNE NELSON STUART)
PAINTER
b New London, Conn, Dec 3, 37. *Study:* Univ Conn, BA, 59; Yale-Norfolk Summer Art Sch, 59; Univ NMex, MA, 60; Univ Ore, sem with Ad Reinhardt, 63. *Work:* Tacoma Art Mus, Wash; Roswell Mus & Art Ctr, NMex; SDak Art Mus; Plains Art Mus, Minn; Sheldon Mem Art Gallery, Lincoln, Nebr; and others. *Comn:* Landwave (mural), Five Seasons Ctr, Cedar Rapids, Iowa, 77 & 78-79; Dakotaloft (painted relief), Convention Ctr, Aberdeen, SDak. *Exhib:* Solo exhibs, Sheldon Mem Art Gallery, 72, Montgomery Mus Art, 77, Plains Mus Art, 89, Civic Fine Art Ctr, Sioux Falls, SDak, 89, NDak Mus Art, 90 & Kans State Univ, 91; Jan Cicero Gallery, Chicago, 81, 83, 87 & 92; Vessels and Paper, Minneapolis Art Inst, 82; 11th Nat Drawing Exhib, Eppink Art Gallery, Kans, 88; Art for a New Century, SDak Art Mus, 89; Midlands Invitational, Joslyn Art Mus, 90; and others. *Teaching:* prof, Visual Arts Dept, SDak State Univ, 80- *Awards:* SDak Artist Fel, 86; Nat Endowment Arts Art Pub Places, 78-79; U-Cross Found, residency, 90; and others. *Bibliog:* Jan Vander Marck (auth), The chromatic waves of Signe Nelson, Artscanada, 71; Mosaic: Interview with Signe Stuart (TV film), SDPTV, 77 & 86; Laurel Reuter (auth, essay), Signe Stuart (exhib catalog), Civic Fine Art Ctr, Sioux Falls, SDAk, 89. *Mem:* Col Art Asn; Women's Caucus for Art. *Media:* Acrylic on Canvas Constructions. *Mailing Add:* 719 Eighth St Brookings SD 57006

NEMEC, NANCY
PRINTMAKER, PAINTER
b Pinehurst, NC, Nov 30, 23. *Study:* Colby-Sawyer Col, New London, NH; Vesper George Sch Art, Boston, grad 44; Columbia Univ Sch Gen Studies, 48. *Work:* Libr Cong; New York Pub Libr; Philadelphia Free Libr; Hudson River Mus; Ga Mus Art; plus others. *Comn:* Print ed, Collectors Am Art, Silvermine Guild Artists, Hudson River Mus, Print Club Albany & New York Graphic Soc. *Exhib:* One-man shows, Hudson River Mus, 59, 62 & 65; Albany Inst Hist & Art, 62 & 63; Silvermine Guild Artists; Westfield Atheneum, Jasper Rand Mus & Fremont Found; plus many others. *Pos:* Secy, Cent Regional Planning Comn, NH, 88- *Teaching:* Instr, Westchester Art Workshop, White Plains, NY, Hudson River Mus & Manhattanville Col, formerly. *Awards:* Knickerbocker Artists, New York, 60, 65, 71, 80 & 85; Acad Artists Asn Award, 65-67, 73-74, 76-78 & 80; Miniature Art Soc NJ, 71-72, 78, 85, 90 & 92; plus others. *Mem:* Am Color Print Soc; Nat Asn Women Artists; Miniature Painters & Gravers Soc; Acad Artists Asn; League NH Craftsmen. *Publ:* Opinion columns, Concord Monitor, Concord, NH, 89. *Mailing Add:* Kearsarge Mountain Rd RFD 2 Box 155 Warner NH 03278

NEMEC, VERNITA MCCLISH
CONCEPTUAL ARTIST, PAINTER
b Painesville, Ohio, Nov 30, 42. *Study:* Ohio Univ, BFA, 64; New York Univ, MA, 66; Naropa Inst, 78; with Simone Forti, 80. *Work:* Savaria Mus; Group Junij; Asian American Arts Centre; Fairfax Hosp. *Exhib:* solo exhibs, Fiatal Muveszek Klubja, Budapest, 80, I Stood Without Moving, 10 on 8, 84, Private Places, Women's Bldg, Los Angeles & Franklin Furnace, New York, 85 & Surface Tensions, Experimental Intermedia Found, 86; Copycat Show, Franklin Furnace, 82 & The Autumn of Her Descent (performance), AIR Gallery, 83, New York; Ritual & Rhythm, Kenkeleba House, 82; Snug Harbor Cult Ctr, NY, 87; Casa del Lago, Mexico City, 88; The Stories Exhib, Henry St Abrons Art Ctr, New York, 92; and others. *Pos:* exhib coordr, Mus, A Project for Living Artists, New York, 69-70; contrib ed, Womanart, New York, 76-77; co-dir, Whitney Counterweight, New York, 77-81; pres & exec dir, Artists Talk on Art; dir, Floating Performance, 86-; bd dirs, Found New Ideas, 86- *Teaching:* Prof art, City Univ New York, 73-79; vis artist, Univ Calif, Santa Barbara, 83; Studios in a Sch, New York, 86-87; slide cur, Baruch Col, NY, 90-92. *Awards:* Exhib Grant, Artists Space, 79, 83, 85 & 86; Artist in Residence, Millay Colony Arts, 81; Jerome Found Grant, 88. *Bibliog:* Janet Heit & Linda Burnham (auths), High Performance, spring-summer 82 & summer 85; Michael Fressola (auth), Staten Island Advance, 7/31/87; Kathleen Becket (auth), NY Times, 3/17/91. *Mem:* Women's Caucus Art; Orgn Independent Artists; Dance Theatre Wkshp. *Media:* Mixed; Performance Art. *Publ:* Auth, Unmaled, private pub, 78; contribr, Re-View: Artists on art, Vered Lieb, 78; Tenth assembling, Richard Kostelanetz, 80; auth, Private Thoughts, Private Places, pvt publ, 84. *Mailing Add:* 361 Canal St New York NY 10013

NEMSER, CINDY
CRITIC, WRITER
b Brooklyn, NY, Mar 26, 37. *Study:* Brooklyn Col, BA, 58, MA, 64; Inst Fine Arts, NY Univ, with Walter Friedlander, Charles Sterling & Donald Posner, MA(art hist). *Pos:* Curatorial intern, NY State Coun Arts, Mus Mod Art, 67; contrib ed, Arts Mag, 71-; ed, Feminist Art J, 72-77; theatre critic, New York Law J, 90- *Teaching:* Guest lectr, Pratt Inst, Md Inst, RI Univ, NY Univ; and others. *Awards:* Art Critics Fel, Nat Endowment Arts, 76; Commencement Speaker, Minneapolis Col Art, 77; semi-finalist, L Arnold Weisberger Playwrighting Competition, New Dramatists, 90. *Bibliog:* Judy K Collischan Van Wagner (auth), Women Shaping Art, NY Praeger, 84; Marilyn Horne: Queen of Rossini, Opera Monthly, 6/92; Profile: on being Marilyn Horne, Arts & Entertainment Mag & Program Guide, 12/91; and others. *Mem:* Founding mem Women Arts; Pen Am Ctr; Poets & Writers; Dramists Guild; Women's Cacus Art (adv bd mem, 75-78). *Res:* Position of women in the art world. *Publ:* Auth, Art Talk Conversations with 12 Women Artists, Scribners, 75; Eve's Delight, Pinnacle Books, 82; Ben Cunningham Monograph, 86. *Mailing Add:* 41 Montgomery Pl Brooklyn NY 11215

NERBURN, KENT MICHAEL
SCULPTOR, CRITIC
b Minneapolis, Minn, July 3, 46. *Study:* Univ Minn, BA(summa cum laude), 68; Stanford Univ, 70; Grad Theological Union, PhD(with distinction), 80; training in wood technique, Marburg, WGer, 71; life drawing with Helmut Schmitt, 74-76; stone sculpture technique, Pietrasanta, Italy, 76; anatomy study with Herbert Shrebnik, Univ Calif, Berkeley, 76. *Work:* Greek Orthodox Diocese, San Francisco; Christ United Methodist Church, St Paul, Minn; Hiroshima Peace Memorial Hall, Japan. *Comn:* Wood sculpture: pvt commissions, San Francisco, 74, Taylors Falls, Minn, 75 & Big Sur, Calif, 76; wood sculpture, Westminster Benedictine Abbey, Mission, BC, 80; bronze sculpture, New World Libr, San Rafael, Calif, 85; Humane Soc Hennepin County, Minn, 91. *Exhib:* Spring Invitational Exhib, United Theological Seminary, New Brighton, Minn, 82; Religious Art, Lutheran Brotherhood Int Hq, Minneapolis, 83; Spiritual Forms, Hennepin Avenue Methodist Church, Minneapolis, 83; Religious Artifacts, Wesley United Methodist Church, Minneapolis, 85; Elegy-an installation in memory of victims of the holocaust, Bemidji State Univ, Bemidji, Minn, 88. *Pos:* Visual Arts Critic, St Paul Pioneer Press & Dispatch, 86, 87; sculpture writer, Art Mag, 86, 87, 88; founder & visual arts critic, Northern Arts Reviewers, Bemidji, Minn, 88; art criticism specialist, Minn Discipline - Based Art Educ Consortium, Minneapolis, 88- *Teaching:* Instr, Grad Theological Union, 77-79 & Minneapolis Inst Arts, 85 & 86; J Paul Getty Found lect art criticism, Robbinsdale Sch Dist, 87, 88; Minn Humanities Comn visiting prof in Humanities & visual arts, Bemidji State Univ, Minn, 88. *Bibliog:* Adelheid Fischer (auth), The art of Kent Nerburn, Minn Monthly, 5/83. *Mem:* Soc Art, Religion & Cult; Soc Values in Higher Educ. *Media:* Wood. *Publ:* Auth, The age of bronze, Arts Mag, 86; Tribal masks evoke spirits of culture & Artists focus on Minnesota, St Paul Pioneer Press, 86; Peerless Perfection Polykleitos' Doryphoros, Arts Mag, 87; Henry Moore's Warrior with Shield, Arts Mag, 88; numerous reviews, critical articles & commentaries, currently. *Mailing Add:* PO Box 1204 Bemidji MN 56601

NERDRUM, ODD
PAINTER
Study: Art Acad, Oslo; study with Joseph Beuys, Dusseldorf. *Work:* Nat Gallery & Riksgalleriet, Oslo; Walker Art Ctr, Minneapolis; Hessisches Landes Mus, Darmstadt, WGer; Norsk Kultarrad, Norway. *Exhib:* Solo exhibs, Kunstnerforbundet, Oslo, 64, 67, 70, 73, 76 & 80, Gallery Tanum, Norway, 77 & 83, Martina Hamilton Gallery, New York, 84-87, Del Art Mus, Wilmington, 85 & Germans Van Eck Gallery, New York, 86; The Classic Tradition in Painting and Sculpture, Aldrich Mus, Conn, 85; Neo-Neoclassicism, Edith Blum Inst, Bard Col, Annandale, NY, 86; Second Sight: Biennial IV, San Francisco Mus Mod Art, San Francisco, 86; The Here and Now, Greenville Co Mus, SC, 86; Morality Tales: History Painting in the 1980s, Grey Art Gallery, New York Univ, 87; Univ Art Mus, Long Beach, Calif, 88; Mus Contemp Art, Chicago, 88; Madison Art Ctr, Wis, 88; Edward Thorp Gallery, New York, 88; Nelson-Atkins Mus, Kansas City, 89. *Bibliog:* Donald Kuspit (auth), Odd Nerdrum: The Aging of the Immediate, Arts Mag, 9/84; Eleanor Heartney (auth), Apocalyptic visions, arcadian dreams, Art News, 1/86; John Russell (auth), rev, in: New York Times, 5/16/86; Charles Jencks (auth), Postmodernism; and other art criticism. *Mailing Add:* c/o Martina Hamilton Gallery 1623 Third New York NY 10128

NERI, MANUEL
SCULPTOR
b Sanger, Calif, Apr 12, 30. *Study:* San Francisco City Col, 49-50; Univ Calif, Calif Col Arts & Crafts, 52-57; Calif Sch Fine Arts, 57-59. *Work:* Oakland Mus, Calif; San Francisco Mus Mod Art; Sheldon Mem Art Gallery, Lincoln, Nebr; Seattle Art Mus; Des Moines Art Ctr; Memphis Brooks Mus, Tenn. *Comn:* Marble sculpture, State Calif Gen Serv Admin, Bateson Bldg, Sacramento, 81-82 & Fed Bldg, Portland, Ore, 88. *Exhib:* Solo exhibs, San Francisco Mus Mod Art, 71 & 89, Oakland Mus, Calif, 76, Seattle Art Mus, 81 & Western Asn Art Mus travelling exhib, 81-83, Charles Cowles Gallery, NY, 81, 82, 86 & 90, John Berggruen Gallery, San Francisco, 81-90, Gimpel-Hanover & Emmerich Galerien, Zurich, Switz, 84; Drawings since 1974, Hirshhorn Mus, Washington, DC, 84; Bay Area Figurative Art (travel thru US), San Francisco Mus Art, 89-90; Queens Mus, New York, 90; Corcoran Gallery, Washington, DC. *Teaching:* Instr, Calif Sch Fine Arts, 59-64; prof art, Univ Calif, Davis, 64- *Awards:* Guggenheim Fel, 79; Nat Endowment Arts Fel, 80; Am Acad & Inst Arts & Lett Award, 82. *Bibliog:* Joanne Dickson (auth), Manuel Neri, Seattle Art Mus, 81; Pierre Restany (auth), Manuel Neri, John Berggruen Gallery, Charles Cowles Gallery & Gimpel-Hanover Galerie, 84; Thomas Albright (auth), Manuel Neri, Bay Area Figurative Art, 89; Carolyn Jones (auth), Manuel Neri Plasters, Bay Area Figurative Art, 89. *Dealer:* John Berggruen Gallery 228 Grant Ave San Francisco CA 94108; Charles Cowles Gallery 420 W Broadway New York NY 10012. *Mailing Add:* 251 Post St No 540 San Francisco CA 94108

NESBITT, ALEXANDER JOHN
EDUCATOR, CALLIGRAPHER
b Paterson, NJ, Nov 14, 01. *Study:* Art Students League; Cooper Union; study with Harry Wickey; Southeastern Mass Univ, Hon DFA, 79. *Work:* Cooper Union Mus; Houghton Libr, Boston; Providence Pub Libr; Klingspor Mus, Offenbach am Main, Ger; Deutche Bucherei, Leipzig. *Comn:* Mem tablet, comn by Col Truman Smith, St John's Church, Stamford, Conn, 52; mem tablet, comn by John D Skilton, Trinity Chapel, Southport, Conn, 56; mem doc, Pilgrim John Howland Soc, presented to Lady Churchill, 66; designs for four gravestones, comn by John D Skilton, Monroeville, Ohio, 66; genealogical chart of Sherman family, comn by Mrs Gilbert H Sherman, 72. *Exhib:* Calligraphy & Handwriting, Peabody Inst, 63, 2000 Years Calligraphy, 65; Alexander Nesbitt--Lettering, Calligraphy, Typographic Design, Crapo Gallery, New Bedford, 66; Int Buchkunst-Ausstellung, Leipzig, 71; Work of the Third & Elm Press, Redwood Libr, Newport, RI, 77 & Alexander Nesbitt--Writing & Lettering, 79; Pensacola Nat Calligraphy Exhib, Tallahassee, Clearwater, Fla, 85. *Collections Arranged:* Working Calligrapher & Lettering Artist, Brown Univ, 61. *Pos:* Tech art dir, Jordanoff Aviation Co, 42-44; art dir, Technographic Publ, 44-45; owner, Third & Elm Press, 65- *Teaching:* Instr typography & lettering, Cooper Union, 50-57; assoc prof graphic design & chmn dept, RI Sch Design, 57-65; prof design, Southeastern Mass Univ, 65-74, emer prof, 74- *Awards:* Travel & Study Grant, 59; Bronze Medal, Int Buchkunst-Ausstellung, 71. *Bibliog:* Leo Joachim (auth), Nesbitt reviews recent European graphics safari, Printing News, 3/5/60; Leona G Rubin (auth), Nesbitt calligraphy exhibit praised, New Bedford Standard Times, 2/20/66; Walter Plata (auth), Alexander Nesbitt, Polygraph, 72; Walter Plata (auth), The Third & Elm Press, Philobiblon, Heft Four, 85. *Mem:* Soc Printers, Boston; Type Dirs Club New York; Am Printing Hist Asn; Newport Art Asn; Goethe Soc New Eng. *Publ:* Auth, Lettering--the History and Technique of Lettering as Design, 50; ed, Decorative Alphabets and Initials, 59; ed, 200 Decorative Title-Pages, 64; coauth, Weathercocks and Weathercreatures, 70; translr, The Typefoundry in Silhouette, 82. *Mailing Add:* 29 Elm St Newport RI 02840

NESBITT, ILSE BUCHERT
PRINTMAKER, ILLUSTRATOR
b Frankfurt-Main, Ger, Sept 6, 32. *Study:* Univ Frankfurt, 53-54; Art Acad Hamburg, 54-56, with Richard von Sichowsky, 57-59; Art Acad Berlin, 56-57. *Work:* Deutsche Staatsbibliothek, Leipzig, EGer; Klingspor Mus, Offenbach, WGer; Hunt Botanical Libr, Pittsburgh; Houghton Libr, Harvard Univ, Cambridge, Mass; Newberry Libr, Chicago; State & Univ Libr, Hamburg, Ger. *Comn:* Woodblock prints, Redwood Libr, Newport, RI, 90. *Exhib:* Int Book Exhib, Leipzig, EGer, 65 & 71; 20th Century Botanical Illustration, Hunt Botanical Libr, Pittsburgh, Pa, 68-69; solo exhibs, Brown Univ Libr, Providence, 83, Rutgers Univ Libr, New Brunswick, NJ, 84 & Trinity Col, Burlington, Vt, 86, State & Univ Libr, Hamburg, Ger, 88. *Pos:* Designer, illusr & printer, Third & Elm Press, Newport, RI, 65- *Teaching:* Asst, typography & book design, RI Sch Design, Providence, 60-65. *Awards:* Hon Mention, Int Book Exhib, Leipzig, EGer, 65, Bronze Medal, 71; First Prize, Print, Newport Art Mus, RI, 83. *Bibliog:* Kiki Scotti (auth), Ilse Nesbitt, tradition of lady printers in Newport, Providence J, 67; William Flanagan (auth), The Third and Elm Press, Yankee Mag, 77; Walter Plata (auth), The Third and Elm Press, Philobiblon Quart, 85. *Mem:* Boston Soc Printers; Newport Art Asn & Mus. *Media:* Woodcut; Book Design. *Publ:* Coauth & illusr, Weathercocks and Weathercreatures, 70, illusr, The Wren and the Bear, 71, coauth & illusr, Sandy's Newport, 75, ed & illusr, The Best Tailor in the World, 83, auth & illusr, My Garden, 88, Third & Elm Press. *Mailing Add:* c/o Third & Elm Press 29 Elm St Newport RI 02840

NESBITT, LOWELL (BLAIR)
PAINTER, SCULPTOR
b Baltimore, Md, Oct 4, 33. *Study:* Tyler Sch Fine Arts, Temple Univ, BFA; Royal Col Art, London, Eng. *Work:* Nat Collection Fine Arts, Smithsonian Inst, Nat Gallery Art, NASA, Washington, DC; Mus Mod Art, New York; Auchenbach Found, San Francisco, Calif; Philadelphia Mus; Nat Art Gallery, Wellington, New Zealand; Bibliog Nat, Paris, France; Fogg Art Mus, Cambridge, Mass; and many others. *Comn:* Posters, List Found, New York City Ctr, 68, Lincoln Ctr, 78 & Jewish Mus, 79; Apollo 9 & 13 (oils), NASA, 69 & 70; poster of Renwick Mus, Smithsonian Inst, 71; Clearing Sky 72 (oil), Environ Protection Agency, Washington, DC, 72. *Exhib:* Whitney Mus Am Art, New York, 67; Kent State Univ, Ohio, 78 & 80; Inst Contemp Art, Philadelphia, Pa, 83; Tyler Alumni Gallery, Temple Univ, Philadelphia, Pa, 85; Hillwood Art Gallery, Long Island Univ, New York, 85; American Realism, 20th Century Drawings and Watercolors, San Francisco Mus Mod Art, Calif, 85-; one-artist exhibs, RH Love Galleries, Chicago, 87, Wally Findlay Galleries, Palm Beach, 87, Louis Newman Galleries, Beverly Hills, 87, Joy Tash Gallery, Scottsdale, Ariz, 87-89, Di Laurenti Gallery, New York, 88, Larsen Dulman Gallery, New Hope, Pa, 88 & Dyansen Galleries, San Francisco, Lahaina, Maui, Hawaii, San Diego, Beverly Hills, 88 & 89; Digital Visions, IBM Gallery, 88. *Pos:* Asst set designer, Ogunquit Playhouse, Maine, 53 & 54; art dir TV, Walter Reed Med Ctr, 56-60; cur, Humanist Icon, Bayly Mus, Charlottesville, Va, New York Acad Art, & Ulrich Mus, Wichita, Kans. *Teaching:* Instr printmaking, Towson State Col, 66-67; instr printmaking, Baltimore Mus Art, 67-68; honorarium lectr, Univ Miami, Univ Richmond & Baltimore Mus Art, 68, 69 & 71; instr painting, Sch Visual Arts, 70-71. *Awards:* Purchase Awards for Oils & Prints, Baltimore Mus Art, 56; Award for Ben Berns Studio (oil), Nat Collection Fine Arts, 69, Baker Brush Co (drawing), 71. *Bibliog:* American Realism Twentieth Century Drawings and Watercolors, San Francisco Mus Mod Art, 85; Rick Bard & Lowell Nesbitt (auths), Lowell Nesbitt, Manhattan, 86; Lowell Nesbitt Dream Gardens, Wally Findlay Galleries, Palm Beach, 86; The 1986 Artnews Directory of Corporate Art Collections, 86; Cynthia Goodman (auth), Digital Visions Computer & Art, 87; and many others. *Mem:* Nat Arts Club, New York. *Media:* Oil on Canvas. *Dealer:* Images Gallery Toledo OH 43606. *Mailing Add:* 69 Wooster St New York NY 10012

NESBITT, PERRY LOREN
GALLERY DIRECTOR, CURATOR
b New York, NY, June 12, 47. *Study:* Univ Wis, Madison, BS, 75, MFA, 80. *Exhib:* Portrait of America (travelling), Smithsonian Inst, Washington, DC, 75; Paintings & Fibers, Ripon Col Art Gallery, Wis, 79; Wis Biennale, Madison Art Ctr, Wis, 80; Dane Co Arts Coun, Madison, Wis, 81; Artists in Central NY, Munson-Williams-Proctor Inst, Utica, 82. *Pos:* Dir, Dowd Art Ctr, State Univ NY, Cortland, 82-84; dir, Univ Galleries, Univ Akron, Ohio, 84-85; dir, Gray Art Gallery, East Carolina Univ, Greenville, 85-89; dir, Kamerick Art Gallery, Univ Northern Iowa, Cedar Falls, 89-91; dir, Freedman Gallery, Albright Col, Reading, Pa, 91- *Awards:* Series Award, Camera Concepts, Meuer Art House, 75; Best in Show, Wis Women Arts, Madison Art Ctr, 77. *Bibliog:* Michael Bonesteel (auth), Perry Nesbitts Linens & Wires, WHA Radio, Madison, Wis, 5/15/79; Rob Fixmer (auth), Can't Go Wrong Art Show, Capitol Times, 3/22/80; Ellen Rulseh (auth), Madison-Los Angeles Success Express, Isthmus, 8/14/81. *Mem:* Col Art Asn; Asn Univ Women; Am Asn Mus; Asn Col & Univ Mus (mem chmnm, 89-90). *Media:* Mixed. *Publ:* Coauth, Structures of Illumination: Lamplight, 87, Enigmatic Inquiry: The Search for Meaning, 88, Art of Tibet, 89 & Fiber: Fabrication/Revelation, 90, East Carolina Univ. *Mailing Add:* c/o Freedman Gallery Albright College Box 15234 Reading PA 19612

NESLAGE, OLIVER JOHN, JR
ART DEALER
b Joplin, Mo, Mar 8, 25. *Study:* Univ Pittsburgh, AB, 50, Grad Sch, 51-52, Sch Law, 52-53; Oxford Univ, 51. *Pos:* Pres & managing dir, Venable Neslage Galleries, Washington, DC, 63-; pres, Neslage McDuff Assocs, Washington, DC, 68- *Mem:* Prof Picture Frames Asn; Army/Navy Club. *Specialty:* Contemporary European and American artists in oil, graphics and drawings featuring artist-in-residence Frederick McDuff. *Mailing Add:* 1803 Connecticut Ave NW Washington DC 20009

NESS, (ALBERT) KENNETH
PAINTER, DESIGNER
b Saint Ignace, Mich, June 21, 03. *Study:* Univ Detroit, 23-24; Detroit Sch Appl Art, 24-26; Wicker Sch Fine Art, 26-28; Art Inst Chicago, with Boris Anisfeldt, dipl, 32. *Work:* NC State Art Mus, Raleigh; R J Reynolds Collection, Winston-Salem, NC; Ackland Art Ctr, Chapel Hill, NC; Duke Univ Mus Art. *Exhib:* Int Watercolor Exhibs, 34-39 & Am Painting Ann, 35 & 37 Art Inst Chicago; Golden Gate Int Expos, San Francisco, 39; Am

Painting Ann, Butler Inst Am Art, Youngstown, Ohio, 51; Pa Acad Fine Arts Ann, 53 & 54. *Pos:* Dir, War Art Ctr, Univ NC, Chapel Hill, 42-44, actg head dept art & actg dir, Person Hall Art Gallery, 44-45, 55, 57-58. *Teaching:* Resident artist, Univ NC, Chapel Hill, 41-73, from assoc prof to prof art, 43-73, emer prof art, 73- *Awards:* Purchase Awards, NC State Mus Ann, 54 & R J Reynolds Competition, 77; NC Award, 73; and others. *Mem:* Hon assoc NC Chap Am Inst Architects; life fel Int Inst Arts & Lett. *Media:* Oil, Tempera. *Publ:* Ed, Student Art at the University of North Carolina, Chapel Hill, 64; producer, Mona Lisa Rides Again (film), 69; Art is Where You Mind It (film), 71-72. *Dealer:* Optique Gallery 28 N Union St Lambertville NJ 08530; Ross-Constantine Gallery 65 Prince St New York NY 10012. *Mailing Add:* PO Box 14 Chapel Hill NC 27514

NESSIM, BARBARA
PAINTER
b Bronx, NY, Mar 30, 39. *Study:* Pratt Inst, BFA. *Work:* Smithsonian Inst, Washington, DC; World Trade Ctr, New York, NY; Libr Cong, Washington. *Comn:* 52nd Street Fair banner, City of New York, 78. *Exhib:* First Int Erotic Art Exhib, Lunds Kronstall, Lund, Sweden, 68; Pushpin Graphic Exhib, The Louvre, Paris, France, 70; Color, Whitney Mus Am Art, 74, Random Access Memories, Rempire Gallery, New York, 91; The Statue of Liberty, NY State Mus, Albany, 87; Computer Art, Mass Inst Technol Mus, Cambridge, 87; Underground Art, Cooper-Hewitt Mus, New York, 87; Art in the Computer Age, Everson Mus, Syracuse, NY, 87. *Teaching:* adj prof visual concepts, Sch Visual Arts, New York, 67-87, adj prof computer art, 87-92; adj prof, Pratt Inst, Brooklyn, NY, 74-84; chairperson illus dept, Parsons Sch Design, New York, 92. *Bibliog:* Elinor Craig (auth), Barbara Nessim, Macweek, 5/88; Carol Olsen Day (auth), The art of Barbara Nessim, PC Computing, 10/88. *Mem:* Nat Computer Graphics Asn (bd mem & treas, Arts Sect, 87-); Asn Computer Art & Design Educ; Graphic Artists Guild (treas, 88-); Siggraph. *Publ:* Auth, Barbara Nessim Sketchbook, private publ, 75; contribr, Living with Art, Alfred A Knopf, 87; Digital Visions, 87 & Varieties of Visual Experience, 87, Harry Abrams. *Mailing Add:* 63 Greene St New York NY 10012

NESTOR, LULA B
PAINTER, ADMINISTRATOR
b Weirton, WVa. *Study:* WVa Univ, 55-56; West Liberty State Col, WVa, BAE; Eastern Mich Univ, MA(art), 73. *Work:* Pittsburgh Plate & Glass Co; Mt Lebonen Greek Orthodox Church, Pittsburgh; WVa Univ; Mich Educ Asn, State Collection Art; Ins Com & Galleries, Michalsons Gallery, Washington, DC. *Exhib:* Butler Inst Art, Butler Mus, Youngstown, Ohio, 73 & 75; Nat Soc Painter in Casien, Nat Gallery of Acad, NY, 76; Audubon Artist 35th Ann Exhib, Nat Acad Gallery, New York, 76; Nat Watercolor Soc 57th Ann, Calif State Univ, 77; one-woman exhibs, Univ Mich, 75, Univ WVa, Morgantown, 75, Constantine Grimaldis Gallery, 80 & 81 & Bowling Green State Univ, Ohio, 83. *Pos:* Dir, Hartland Regional Fine Arts Festival, 68-77; past pres & trustee mem, Hartland Art Show, Mich. *Teaching:* Instr, Richie Jr High Sch, Wheeling, WVa, 57-58, Elida High Sch, Elida, Ohio, 58-59 & South Lima Jr High Sch, Lima, Ohio, 60-62; art instr & dir art dept, Hartland High Sch, Mich, 68-81; instr adult educ classes, Hartland Consolidated Schs. *Awards:* First Place, Nat Pittsburgh Watercolor Aqueous Open Competition, 74 & 76; Int Artist in Watercolor Competition, London, 82; Award, Nat Watercolor Soc Ann, 82. *Mem:* Mich Watercolor Soc (mem bd); Midwest Watercolor Asn, Minn; Nat Watercolor Soc. *Media:* Watercolor; Casien. *Mailing Add:* 9865 Edwards Dr Brighton MI 48116

NEUBERGER, ROY R
COLLECTOR, PATRON
b Bridgeport, Conn, July 21, 03. *Study:* NY Univ; Univ Sorbonne; State Univ NY, Purchase, DFA, 82; Parson's Sch Design, New Sch Social Res, LHD, 85; Bar-Ilan Univ, Israel, DHL, 87. *Pos:* Bd dir, City Ctr Music & Drama, Inc, 57-74, finance chmn, 71-74, trustee, 74-; chmn adv coun arts, New York City Housing Authority, 60-68; trustee, Whitney Mus Am Art, 61-68, emer trustee, 69-; fine arts gifts comt, Nat Cult Ctr, 62-68; adv comt art, Mt Holyoke Col, 63-78; fine arts adv comt, Amherst Col, 63-70; hon trustee, Metrop Mus Art, 68-; pres coun, Mus City New York, 71- *Teaching:* Lectr art, Wadsworth Atheneum, Vassar Col, Brooklyn Mus, Detroit Inst Art, Mass Inst Technol Alumni Assocs, State Univ NY, Purchase. *Awards:* Gary Melchers Medal, Artist's Fel, Inc, New York, 84; Arts Award Coun for in Arts Westchester, NY, 85; State Univ NY Purchase Award, Neuberger Mus Art; and others. *Mem:* life fel Nat Acad Design; Benjamin Franklin Soc Arts; New Sch Social Res (trustee & mem exec comt, 67-78); Nat Gallery Art, Washington, DC (trustee, mem collector's comt, 78); Purchase Col Found (trustee, 71-85, chmn, 74-85); and others. *Collection:* Primarily American art. *Publ:* Contribr, Art in Am & var other art catalogs. *Mailing Add:* 522 Fifth Ave New York NY 10036

NEUBERT, GEORGE WALTER
SCULPTOR, CURATOR
b Minneapolis, Minn, Oct 24, 42. *Study:* Hardin-Simmons Univ, BS, 65; San Francisco Art Inst, 67; Mills Col, MFA(Trefethen Found Fel), 69. *Work:* Oakland Mus, Calif; Richmond Art Ctr, Calif; San Francisco Fine Arts Mus; Achenbach Found; Santa Cruz Mus Art, Calif. *Exhib:* Bay Area Sculptors under Thirty-Five, Michael Walls Gallery, San Francisco, 69; Paris-Dusseldorf Art Fairs, 76; Paper on Paper, San Francisco Mus Mod Art, 79; Art of Collage Today, Impressions Gallery, Boston, 79; Pacific Coast Museum Collections, Mus Am Art, Washington, DC, 81; Elegant Miniatures, San Francisco & Kyoto, Japan, 83; Univ SDak, 86. *Collections Arranged:* Thomas Hill: The Grand View (with catalog), 80, Paul Wonner: Abstract Realist (with catalog), 81, Fresh Paint: 15 California Painters (with catalog), 82 & Stella Survey: 1959-1982 (with catalog), 83, San Francisco Mus Mod Art; San Francisco Bay Area Paintings (with catalog), 84 & Contemporary Bronze: Six in the Figurative Tradition (with catalog), 86, Sheldon Mem Art Gallery, Univ Nebr-Lincoln; R Diebenkorn: An Intimate View (with catalog) Diebenkorn: Small Paintings from Ocean Park), 86; A Calder: An American Invention (with catalog), 86, Sheldon Sampler: loo American Masterworks (with catalog), 87. *Pos:* Cur art, Oakland Art Mus, Calif, 70-80; assoc dir, San Francisco Mus Mod Art, 80-83; dir, Sheldon Mem Art Gallery, Univ Nebr-Lincoln, 83- *Awards:* Nat Endowment Arts Grant, 80. *Bibliog:* D McCann (auth), Six, six, six, 6/71 & J Dunham (auth), article, 4/73, Artweek; article, Washington Post, 3/13/75; plus others. *Mem:* Am Asn Mus; Western Asn Art Mus; Asn Art Mus Dir; fel Ctr Gt Plains Study; Nebr Mus Roundtable; Art Mus Asn Am (bd mem). *Media:* Steel, Collage. *Publ:* Ed, Tropical, 71; Xavier Martinez, 74; Public Sculpture-Urban Environment, 74. *Mailing Add:* 3009 Jackson Dr Lincoln NE 68502

NEUHAUS, MAX
SCULPTOR, LECTURER
b Beaumont, Tex, Aug 9, 39. *Exhib:* Solo shows, River Grove, Roaring Fork River, Aspen Col, 88, A Bell for St Cacilien, Kolnischer, Kunstverein, Cologne, 89, Two Sides of the Same Room, Dallas Mus Art, Tex, 90; Two Identical Rooms, Deichtorlallen, Hamburg, 90; Three to One, Documenta IX, Kassel, Ger, 92. *Mailing Add:* 350 Fifth Ave, Suite 3304 New York NY 10118

NEUMAN, ROBERT S
PAINTER
b Kellogg, Idaho, Sept 9, 26. *Study:* Calif Col Arts & Crafts; Calif Sch Fine Arts; Univ Idaho; Mills Col; also in Stuttgart, Ger. *Work:* San Francisco Mus Art; Boston Mus Fine Arts; Worcester Mus Art, Mass; Mus Mod Art, New York; Addison Gallery Am Art, Andover, Mass; plus others. *Exhib:* De Cordova & Dana Mus, 60-65; New England Art Today, 63 & 65; Mus Mod Art, 64; Pace Gallery, Boston, 65; Allan Stone Gallery, New York; Sunne Savage Gallery, Boston. *Teaching:* Instr, Calif Cols Arts & Crafts, 51-53, Brown Univ, 61-63 & Carpenter Ctr Visual Arts, Harvard Univ, 64-65; prof art & chmn dept, Keene State Col, NH, 72-77. *Awards:* Fulbright Grant, 53-54; Prize, San Francisco Mus Art; Guggenheim Fel, 56-57; and others. *Publ:* Auth, Artists Book: Ship of Fools/Ship to Paradise, High Loft Press, Seal Harbor, Maine. *Mailing Add:* 135 Cambridge St Winchester MA 01890

NEUSTEIN, JOSHUA
PAINTER, CONCEPTUAL ARTIST
b Danzig, Poland, Oct 16, 40; US citizen. *Study:* City Col New York, 57-61, BA, 61; Art Students League, 59-61; Pratt Inst, Brooklyn, NY, 60-63. *Work:* Mus Mod Art, Whitney Mus Am Art, New York; Jerusalem Mus of Israel; Tel Aviv Mus of Art, Israel; Louisiana Mus, Copenhagen, Denmark. *Exhib:* Travel Art, Mus Mod Art, Oxford, Eng, 71; Documenta V, Kassel, Ger, 72; Photog in Art Camden Art Ctr, London, 72; Photog Triennale, Israel Mus, Jerusalem, 76; One-man shows, Mus Art, Wocester, Mass, 75 & Neutein-Ten Years, Tel Aviv Mus, Israel,; With Paper About Paper, Albright-Knox Gallery, Buffalo, 80; Henri Onstad Art Ctr (catalog), Norway, 81; and many other solo & group exhibs. *Awards:* Willem Sandberg Prize, Jerusalem, 74; Guggenheim Fel, 87. *Bibliog:* R Pincus-Witten (auth), Sons of Light, 9/75, Six propositions, 12/75 & Neustein papers, 10/77, Arts Mag; Steven Kasher (auth), The substance of paper, 3/78 & Seven Artists of Israel, summer 79, Artforum Mag; Joseph Masheck (auth), Nothing not nothing something, Artforum Mag, 11/79 & Marking & Disclosure, H Johnson Mus, 83; Donald Kuspit (auth), Art with a moral mission, Flash Art, 87; Robert Morgan (auth), Neustein, Flash Art, 88; and many others. *Media:* Environment, Photo. *Res:* Art criticism. *Dealer:* Mary Boone 420 W Broadway New York NY 10012; B Urdang 23 E 74th St New York NY 10021. *Mailing Add:* 7 Mercer St New York NY 10013

NEVELSON, MIKE
SCULPTOR
b New York, NY, Feb 23, 22. *Work:* Colby Col; Wadsworth Atheneum; Whitney Mus Am Art; Strater Mus; Stratford Col. *Exhib:* Staempfli Gallery; Whitney Mus; Grand Cent Moderns; Amel Gallery; Expo 68, Montreal; plus others. *Media:* All. *Mailing Add:* PO Box N New Fairfield CT 06812

NEVIA, (JOSEPH SHEPPERD ROGERS)
PAINTER
b Washington, DC. *Study:* Longfellow Sch with Theodora Kane and Berthold Schmutzart, 63; Greensboro Col, with Irene Cullis and Callie Braswell, BA, 67; Univ NC, Greensboro, with Will Insley, Peter Agostini, Walter Barker, Andrew Martin, Gilbert Carpenter & Stephen Antonagis, MFA, 69. *Work:* Maryland Collection, Univ Md. *Comn:* Mural, Bishop O'Connell Sch, Arlington, Va, 79; also pvt comns. *Exhib:* Artists of the 80's, Dallas, Tex, 85; Shelters '85, Zenith Gallery, Washington, DC, 85; The Art of Fantasy, Artspace, Raleigh, NC, 87; The Artful Chair, Target Gallery, Alexandria, Va, 90; Dream House, Peninsula Fine Arts Ctr, Newport News, Va, 92; and others. *Pos:* Dir, Garfinckle's Art Gallery, Washington, DC, 72-74, Porcelaine Galleries, Baltimore, 74-75. *Teaching:* Instr art, Prince George Co Bd Educ, Upper Marlboro, Md, 69-70, Corcoran Sch Art & Col Inst Art, Columbia, Md, 70-71. *Bibliog:* Klim Caviness (auth), Renaissance and Joe Rogers, Alexandria Port Packet, Va, 84; Doris Miller (interviewer), Artist Nevia, Channel 10 Cable Station, Alexandria, Va, 84; Ann M Augherton (auth), Nevia's shadow boxes, Alexandria Gazette, Va, 84; and others. *Mem:* Am Asn Mus; Soc Archit Hist; and others. *Media:* Oil, Acrylic. *Mailing Add:* Beall's Pleasure PO Box 1268 Landover MD 20785

NEW, LLOYD H (LLOYD KIVA NEW)
EDUCATOR
Study: Sch Arts Inst, Chicago, BAE, 38; Harvard Univ, 73; Okla State Univ; Univ NMex; Univ Chicago. *Pos:* Co-dir, R & D Prog, Rockefeller Found; formerly arts dir, pres, Inst Am Indian Arts, 66-78, retired; interim pres, Inst Am Arts, Santa Fe, NMex, 89; sr adv, Nat Mus Am Indian, Smithsonian Inst, NY & Washington, DC. *Mem:* Indian Arts & Crafts Bd (comnr, chmn); Heard Mus of Anthropology & Primitive Art, Phoenix, Ariz (founding trustee, Nat Adv bd); Mus Am Indian, Heye Found, New York, Plains Indian Mus & Buffalo Bill Hist Soc, Cody, Wyo (Nat adv bd); Am Inst Interior Designers (hon mem); Am Crafts Coun (hon fel). *Mailing Add:* 706 Calle Vibora Santa Fe NM 87501

NEW, LLOYD KIVA See New, Lloyd H (Lloyd Kiva New)

NEWER, THESIS
PAINTER
b New York, NY. *Study:* Acad Delle Belle Arte, Florence, Italy, 4 yrs; Pratt Inst Interior Design, grad. *Exhib:* Allied Artists Am; Knickerbocker Artists; Jersey City Mus; Hudson Valley Art Asn. *Awards:* Best in Show, Catherine Lorillard Wolfe Art Club, 68; Top Award for Polymer, Am Artists Prof League, 68; Nat Art League Gold Medal, Nat Arts Club, 69 & First Prizes, 72 & 75. *Bibliog:* Articles, La Rev Mod, Paris, 70-71. *Mem:* Am Artists Prof League; Catherine Lorillard Wolfe Art Club; Nat Art League; Allied Artists Am. *Media:* Oil. *Dealer:* Thomson Gallery 19 E 75th St New York NY 10021. *Mailing Add:* 876 Adams Ave Franklin Square NY 11010

NEWICK, CRAIG D
ARCHITECT
b Feb 14, 60. *Study:* Lehigh Univ, Bethlehem, Pa, BA, 82; Yale Univ, New Haven, Conn, MA, 87. *Comn:* Gallery Jazz, design for art gallery, New Haven, 85-86; interior renovation & exterior rehab, residence, 85-88; exhib display cabinet, Artspace, Inc, New Haven, 87; interior renovation & addition, residence, Florham Park, NJ, 88. *Exhib:* Camera Obscura: The Camera as Physical Space, John Slade Ely House, 88; A House for the Jersey Meadows, Aetna Gallery, Hartford, Conn, 91; Small Works Invitational, Artspace, New Haven, Conn, 92; 1692 Salem Witch Trials: 1991 Competition Designs for a Permanent Memorial, Essex Inst, Salem, Mass, 92; The New England Holocaust Memorial Competition: An American Process, Gund Gallery Harvard Grad Sch Design, Cambridge, Mass, 92. *Pos:* Designer/draftsman, The Architectural Studio, Easton, Pa, 81 & 83-84; designer/draftsman, Centerbrook Architects, Centerbrook, 86; job captain/proj designer, P B Svigals & Assocs, 87-88 & job captain/proj designer; Allan Dehar & Assoc, 88-90. *Awards:* Ann Design Review Award, ID Mag, 91; Archit League New York, 91; Proj grant, New Eng Found Arts, 92. *Bibliog:* Jude Schwendenwien (auth), Wesleyan exhibit explores reading as a public act, Hartford Courant, 5/20/90; Mildred F Schmertz (auth), A decade of young architects, Archit, 7/91; Annual Design Review, ID Int Design Mag, 7-8/90 & 7-8/91. *Mem:* Archit League New York. *Mailing Add:* 219 Livingston St New Haven CT 06511

NEWLAND, JOSEPH NELSON
EDITOR, WRITER
b Knoxville, Tenn, July 7, 53. *Study:* Univ NC, Chapel Hill, BA(hons), 75; Univ Wash, MA, 78. *Pos:* Asst dir, Diane Gilson Gallery, Seattle, 78-79; publ ed, Henry Art Gallery, Univ Wash, Seattle, 79-88; ed, Los Angeles County Mus Art, 88- *Teaching:* Calif State Univ, Northridge, 89- *Mem:* Am Asn Mus; Col Art Asn. *Interests:* East Asian influence on American art & culture. *Publ:* coauth & ed, Henry Art Gallery, Univ Washington, 1927-1986, Henry Art Gallery, Univ Wash, 86; ed, Mind Landscapes: The Paintings of C C Wang, Henry Art Gallery, Univ Wash, 88; American Art: The Los Angeles County Museum of Art Collection, LACMA, 91; West Coast Duchamp, Grassfield, 91; Indian Painting: The Los Angeles County Museum of Art Collection, Vol 1, LACMA/Mapin/Abrams, 93. *Mailing Add:* c/o Los Angeles City Mus Art 5905 Wilshire Blvd Los Angeles CA 90036

NEWMAN, ARNOLD
PHOTOGRAPHER
b New York, NY, Mar 3, 18. *Study:* Univ Miami, Hon DFA; Art Ctr Col Design, Pasadena, LHD, 85; Univ Bradford, Eng, hon degree, 89; New Sch Social Research, New York, DFA, 90. *Work:* Metrop Mus Art & Mus Mod Art, New York; Art Inst Chicago; Nat Portrait Gallery, London; Israel Mus, Jerusalem; Moderna Museet, Stockholm; Nat Gallery Can, Ottawa; Victoria & Albert Mus, London; Australia Nat Gallery, Canberra; Tel Aviv Mus, Israel; and other galleris, universities, public and private collections. *Exhib:* One-man shows, Art Inst Chicago, 53, 4th Int Biennale Fotografia, Venice, Italy, 63, George Eastman House, Rochester, 72, Galerie Fiolet, Amsterdam, 77, Israel Mus, Jerusalem & Tel Aviv, 78, Moderna Musset, Fotografiska Musset, Stockholm, 78, Clarence St Lighthouse, Melbourne, Australia, 82, Daniel Wolfe Gallery, New York, 83, Gallery Octant, Paris, France, 84 & New Gallery, Univ Miami, Coral Gables, Fla, 85; Faces in Am Art, Metrop Mus Art, 57, & Counterparts and Affinities, 82; Camera & Human Facade, Smithsonian Inst, 70; Portraits of Artists, Sidney Janis Gallery, New York, 76; The Great Great Brit, Nat Portrait Gallery, London, 79; Photo Gallery Int, Tokyo, 81; The Portrait in Photog, Rheinischres Landemuseum, Bonn, 82; Artists, Iwaki Munic Art Mus, Japan, 84; La Grande Parade, Stedelijk Mus, Amsterdam, 85; Am Images-Photog 1945-1980, Barbican Art Gallery, London, 85-86; Arnold Newman: Five Decades (with catalog), Mus Photog Arts, San Diego, 86; Frankfurter Kunstverein, Ger, 91; Arnold Newman's Americans, Nat Portrait Gallery, Washington, DC, 92; and many others. *Pos:* Adv, photog dept, Israel Mus, Jerusalem, 67- *Teaching:* Instr, Maine Photography WorkShops, Rockport. *Awards:* Newhouse Citation, Syracuse Univ, 61; Gold Medal, 4th Biennale Int Fotografia, 63; Life Achievement in Photography Award, Am Soc Mag Photogr, 75; plus others. *Bibliog:* The Encyclopedia of Photography, Hawthorn, 64; Peter Pollack (auth), Arnold Newman, In: The Picture History of Photography, Abrams, 69; Helen Gee (auth), Photography of the Fifties: An American Perspective, Univ Ariz, 80; Barbaralee Diamonstein (auth), Visions and Images: American Photographers on Photography, Rizzoli Int Publ, 81; The International Center of Photography Encyclopedia, Crown Publ, 84; plus others. *Mem:* Am Soc Mag Photogr. *Media:* Multi-Media. *Publ:* Auth, Faces USA, Amphoto, 78; The Great British, Weidenfeld & Nicholson, London & New York Graphic Soc, Boston, 79; Artists: Portraits from Four Decades, New York Graphic Soc, Boston, 80; contrib, In: World Photography: 25 Contemporary Masters Write About Their Work, Techniques and Equipment, Hamlyn Publ Group, London, 81; auth, I Grandi Fotographi: Arnold Newman, Gruppo Editoriale, Milan, 83, Ital, Sp, Eng & Am eds; Arnold Newman: Five Decades, Harcourt Brace Jovanovich, 86; and others. *Dealer:* Sidney Janis Gallery New York; Commerce Graphic Ltd Inc 160 E Union St East Rutherford NJ 07073. *Mailing Add:* 33 W 67th St New York NY 10023

NEWMAN, ELIZABETH H
SCULPTOR
Study: Mich State Univ, BFA, 78; Sch Art Inst Chicago, MFA, 84. *Exhib:* One-man shows, Superior St Gallery, Chicago, 84, Brookens Gallery, Sangamon State Univ, Springfield, Ill, 85, Marianne Deson Gallery, Chicago, 86, Galerie Eric Franck, Geneva, Switz, 89, Galerie Lelong, New York, 92 & Inst Contemp Art, Boston, Mass, Mus Contemp Art, Chicago, Ill, 92; CompassRose Gallery, Chicago, 89; Focus, 13th Ann Chicago Int Art Expos, Univ Chicago, 92; Art at the Armory: Occupied Territory, Mus Contemp Art, Chicago, Ill, 92-93. *Awards:* Nat Endowment Arts, 88; Ill Art Coun, 86, 87 & 89. *Bibliog:* 'Places with a past' opens in Charleston, J Art, 6-8/91; Jenifer P Borum (auth), Elizabeth Newman, Artforum, 5/92; Holland Cotter (auth), Elizabeth Newman, NY Times, 2/7/92. *Mailing Add:* c/o Galerie Lelong 20 W 57th St 5th Floor New York NY 10019

NEWMAN, JOHN See Newman, John Beatty

NEWMAN, JOHN BEATTY
PAINTER, DRAFTSMAN
b Toronto, Ont, Canada, Apr 6, 33. *Study:* Ontario Col Art; Art Acad Cincinnati, scholarship. *Work:* Art Gallery Hamilton, Ont; Canadian Embassy, Washington, DC; Montreal Mus Fine Art; Art Bank, Can Coun; and others. *Exhib:* Royal Acad, London, Eng, 72; Tokyo Metrop Gallery, Japan, 76; Art Gallery Ont, Toronto, Can, 76; Art Gallery of Hamilton, Ont, 76; Soc Int Beaux Arts, Grand Palais, Paris, France, 77; Palazzo Strozzi, Firenze, Italia, 77; Sichuan Fine Art Inst, Chongging, People's Repub China, 89; Seoul Watercolours Int, Seoul, Korea, 91; Centro Culturale Canadese in Roma, Italia, 92. *Pos:* Exhib designer, Royal Ont Mus, Toronto, 58-63; mem gov coun, Ont Col Art, 73-76 & 79-81, chmn fine arts dept, 79-83. *Teaching:* Instr figure painting, Ont Col Art, 63- *Awards:* Int Painting Competition First Prize, Can Soc Graphic Art, 56, John Alfsen Award for Drawing, 73; Honor Award, Can Soc Painters Watercolor, 74; and others. *Bibliog:* Kay Kritzwiser (auth), A tender look at little girls, Globe & Mail, Toronto, 73; Peter Bell (auth), The transition to maturity, Evening Telegram, St John's, Nfld, 74; Deborah Godin (auth), Seven Portrait Painters a Personal Choice, Arts West, Calgary, Alta, 81. *Mem:* Royal Can Acad; Can Soc Painters Watercolor. *Media:* Oil, Watercolor. *Dealer:* Kinsman Robinson Galleries 112 Scollard St Toronto Can M5R 1G2; Galerie Walter Klinkoff 1200 West Ave Sherbrooke Montreal Can H3A1H6. *Mailing Add:* Ont Col Art 100 McCaul St Toronto ON M5T 1W1 Canada

NEWMAN, LIBBY
PAINTER, PRINTMAKER
b Rockland, Del. *Study:* Univ Arts, BFA. *Work:* Nat Mus Belgrade, Yugoslavia; Philadelphia Mus Art; Mus Philadelphia Civic Ctr; Mus Mod Art, Buenos Aires, Arg; Glassboro State Col. *Comn:* Smith, Kline & French Labs; Univ Pa Law Sch; Sichuan Fine Arts Inst, China; Tianjin Fine Arts Col, China. *Exhib:* Nat Watercolor & Drawing Exhib, Pa Acad Fine Arts, 64; Eastern Cent Drawing Exhib, Philadelphia Mus Art, 65; solo exhibs, Mangel Gallery, Philadelphia, 70-88 & Philadelphia Art Alliance, 81; Twenty-Five Pa Women Artists, Southern Alleghenies Mus Art, Loretto, Pa, 79; Am Colorprint Soc Exhib, 79; Gov Thornburgh's Inaugural Art Comt--Cur of Contemp Sculpture Exhib, 79; and others. *Pos:* Cur exhibs, Univ City Sci Ctr, currently. *Awards:* Best Picture of Year Award, Philadelphia Art Alliance, 65; National Print Award, Cheltenham Art Ctr, Pa, 70; Carl Zigrosser Award, Am Color Print Soc, 81. *Bibliog:* Victoria Donohoe (auth), article, Philadelphia Inquirer, 72; Sheila Reid (auth), exhib catalog, Mus de Grand Palais. *Mem:* Artists Equity Asn (pres, Philadelphia Chap, 68-70, nat vpres, 71-75); Philadelphia Art Alliance; Am Color Print Soc; Philadelphia Watercolor Soc; and others. *Media:* Acrylic; Woodcut. *Publ:* Auth, Obtaining art grants, Artists Equity Nat Newslett, 74; A City Sketched, a Guide to the Art & History of Philadelphia. *Dealer:* Mangel Gallery 1714 Rittenhouse Sq Philadelphia PA 19103. *Mailing Add:* 327 Meeting House Lane Merion Station PA 19066

NEWMAN, LOUIS
ART DEALER, COLLECTOR
b June 21, 47, US citizen. *Study:* Ariz State Univ, BA, 70; Univ Southern Calif, Los Angeles, MA, 74. *Pos:* Art dealer, Beverly Hills. *Bibliog:* Gerald Brommer & Joseph Gatto (co-auth), Careers in art, 84; Les Krantz (auth), American Art Galleries, 85; article, Los Angeles Mag, 4/85. *Mem:* Art

Dealers Asn Calif (bd mem). *Specialty:* Contemporary and early twentieth century paintings, prints, drawings and sculpture. *Publ:* Paul Cadmus: Selected Works on Paper and Canvas, 86; Elie Nadelman: Selected Drawings, 87; Kurt Schwitters: Collages and Other Works on Paper, 88; Edward Hopper: Selected Drawings, 89; Reginald Marsh: Selected Works on Paper, 90; Thomas Hart Benton: Paintings and Drawings, 90. *Mailing Add:* Louis Newman Galleries 322 N Beverly Dr Beverly Hills CA 90210

NEWMAN, RICHARD CHARLES
SCULPTOR, PHOTOGRAPHER
b North Tonawanda, NY, Dec 29, 38. *Study:* Cleveland Inst Art, dipl painting, 60; Cranbrook Acad Art, BFA, 62; Cornell Univ, MFA, 64. *Work:* Addison Gallery Am Art, Phillips Acad, Andover, Mass; Middle Tenn State Univ, Murfreesboro; Herbert F Johnson Mus Art, Ithaca, NY; Univ Ore Mus Art, Eugene. *Exhib:* The Last National Sculpture Show, Univ Ga, Athens, 82; Sculpture Invitational, Fla State Univ, Tallahassee, Fla, 86; 37th New England Exhib, Silvermine Gallery Art, New Canaan, Conn, 86; Clark Whitney Gallery, Lenox, Mass, 86; one person shows, 10 yr Retrospective, Bradford Col, Mass, 81, Gov Dummer Acad, So Byfield, Mass, 82, Goeth Inst, Boston, Mass, 82; Multicultural Art Ctr, Cambridge, Mass, 89; Cape Cod Community Col, West Barnstable, Mass, 91; New Art of the West, Eiteljorg Mus, Indianapolis, Ind, 92; Just Plain Screwy, Wustum Mus Fine Arts, Racine, Wis, 92; and others. *Pos:* Juror, Marblehead Art Asn, Mass, 78: Ann Spring Art Exhib, Newton Art Asn, Mass, 80, Boston Globe Scholastic Art Awards, State Finals, Mass, 87, 88 & 89; guest speaker, Artists on Art (lectr ser), Addison Gallery/Phillips Acad, Andover, Mass, 78, Artists Series, Boston Visual Artists Union, Mass, 80; panelist, T W MacKesey Seminar Ser, Col Archit, Art & Planning, Cornell Univ, Ithaca, NY, 82; cur, Sculpture As Monument Exhib, Boston Visual Artists Union Gallery, Mass, 84; showcase artist, Jubilee Celebration, City of Hartford, Window Proj, Conn, 86; keynote speaker, Reflection of Life & Death: The Arts and Thanatology Symp, Found Thanatology, New York, 89; speaker, Art and Healing Conf, New Harmony, Ind, 90; pres, Soc Layerist in Multi-Media, 86-90. *Teaching:* Instr art, Univ Wash, Seattle, 64-65; asst, Sch Archit, Cornell Univ, 63-64; prof, Bradford Col, 65- *Awards:* Finalist in Sculpture, Mass Artists Found Grant, 77; Showcase Artist, Jubilee Celebration, City of Hartford, Conn, 86. *Bibliog:* Nicholas Roukes (auth), Design Synectics, Davis Publ, Worcester, Mass, 89; Arthur Williams (auth), Sculpture: Technique-Form-Content, Davis Publ, Worcester, Mass, 89; Les Krantz (auth), Am Artists, Am References Publ, Chicago, Ill, 90. *Mem:* Soc of Layerists in Multi-Media, Albuquerque, NMex (pres, 86-92); Boston Mus Fine Arts, Mass; Pythagorean Press, Bradford, Mass. *Publ:* Contribr, Collage: Critical Views, Univ Mich Press, 89; Am Craft Mag, 8-9/90 & 4/91; Golden Relationship Ser, Paragon Press, 92; and others. *Mailing Add:* PO Box 5162 Bradford MA 01830

NEWMAN, SOPHIE
PAINTER, SCULPTOR
b Brooklyn, NY, Mar 4, 25. *Study:* Kreloff Art Sch, Brooklyn, 66-69; Brooklyn Mus Art Sch, NY, 69-71; Brooklyn Mus, NY, 71-72 & 79; Women's Interart Ctr, New York, 73; Creative Women's Collective, New York, 74. *Exhib:* Contemp Reflections, Aldrich Mus Contemp Art, Ridgefield, Conn, 74; Brooklyn Mus, 77; Paperworks, Hudson River Mus, Yonkers, NY, 80; Cichinelli Gallery, New York, 80; Am State Arts Gallery, New York, 80; Hudson River Mus, Yonkers, 81; Belt Buckle Gallery, Los Angeles, Calif, 81; Survival Show, Am State Arts Gallery, New York, 81; 12 Women Artists, Downtown Cult Ctr, Brooklyn, NY, 82; one-woman show, Brooklyn Col, 82; and others. *Teaching:* Instr painting & crafts, Jewish Asn Services Aged, 75- *Awards:* Curator's Choice, Brooklyn Mus Art Sch, 72; First Prize Oils, Int Pen Women's Club, 74. *Mem:* Women's Caucus Art; Creative Women's Collective (bd mem, 73-); Women in the Arts (bd mem, 74); Artists League Brooklyn (vpres, 73). *Mailing Add:* 2680 E 29th St Brooklyn NY 11235

NEWMAN, WALTER ANDREWS, JR
ART DEALER, GALLERY DIRECTOR
b Philadelphia, Pa, May 16, 30. *Pos:* Pres, Newman Galleries, Philadelphia & Bryn Mawr, Pa, 69- *Specialty:* Early 20th century impressionists; Pennsylvania landscape school. *Mailing Add:* 1625 Walnut St Philadelphia PA 19103

NEWMAN-RICE, NANCY
PAINTER, CRITIC
b New York, NY, Mar 28, 50. *Study:* Cornell Univ; Washington Univ, BFA, 72, MFA, 74. *Exhib:* Drawing & Sculpture, Ball State Univ, Ind, 76; St Louis Artists, Cervantes Convention Ctr, St Louis, 78; Painting Invitational, Salisbury State Univ, Md, 79; Mississippi Corridor, Davenport Art Gallery, Iowa, 80; Works On-Of Paper, Bixby Gallery, Washington Univ, Landscapes 88 BZ Wagman, 80; solo exhibs, Currents 2, St Louis Art Mus, 79 & Brentwood Gallery, St Louis, 85 & 86, Sazama/Braver Gallery, Chicago, 87 & 89. *Pos:* Ed in chief, St Louis Seen, Newspaper for Visual Arts, 75-77; St Louis ed & critic, New Art Examiner, 78-; Critic, St Louis Post Dispatch. *Teaching:* Asst painting, Washington Univ, 72-74; assoc prof, Maryville Col, 74- *Awards:* Midwest Art Alliance-Nat Endowment Arts Grant. *Bibliog:* Sidra Stitch (auth), Nancy Rice & Yvette Woods, New Art Examiner, 79; Mary King (auth), Rice's floating lattice spheres, St Louis Post Dispatch, 80; P Desmer (auth), Nancy Rice's work dazzles, St Louis Post Dispatch; Herb Gralnick (auth), Nancy Rice, St Louis Globe Democrat; Betsy Goldman (auth), Nancy Rice, New Art Examiner. *Mem:* Col Art Asn; Midwest Col Art Asn; Women's Caucus for Art (bd dirs, 76-77). *Media:* Acrylic, Oil. *Dealer:* Sazama/Braver Gallery 361 West Superior Chicago Ill 60610; BZ Wagman Gallery, Galleris St Louis Mo 63117. *Mailing Add:* Maryville Col Dept Art 13550 Conway Rd St Louis MO 63141

NEWMARK, MARILYN (MARILYN NEWMARK MEISELMAN)
SCULPTOR
b New York, NY, July 20, 28. *Study:* Adelphi Col; Alfred Univ; also with Paul Brown, Garden City, NY. *Work:* Nat Mus of Racing, Saratoga, NY; Nat Art Mus of Sport, Indianapolis, Ind; Am Saddle Horse Mus, Lexington, Ky; Int Mus Horse, Ky Horse Park, Lexington, Ky. *Comn:* Majestic Light, comn by Ogden Phipps, 76; Man o' War, comn by Franklin Mint, 77; Will Shriver, comn by Broomley Farm, 79; Affirmed, comn by Thoroughbred Racing Asn, 79; Ruffian & Genuine Risk, Int Mus Horse; and others. *Exhib:* Nat Acad Design, New York, 71-72, 74-82 & 86-91; Calif Acad Sci, 86; Ky Derby Mus, 86-91; Cleveland Mus Natural Hist, Ohio, 84; Invitational Modern Masters, 92; and others. *Awards:* Gold Medal, Allied-Artist Am, 81; Artist Fund Award, Nat Acad Design, 82; Bronze Medal, Nat Sculpture Soc, 86; plus others. *Bibliog:* The Horse in Bronze, Horsemans J, 76; Horsewoman & Artist Extraordinaire, Horse of Course, 77; The Horse in Bronze, Saddle & Bridle, 79. *Mem:* Nat Acad Design; Nat Sculpture Soc; Allied Artists Am; Soc Animal Artists; Pen & Brush. *Media:* Bronze. *Publ:* Contribr, Equine Sculpture, A Mixed Medium, Morning Telegraph, 8/9/71; Equine Sculpture, Chronicle of the Horse, 9/10/71; Horse in sculpture, Am Horseman, 12/72; From the love of horses, Catasus, spring 89. *Dealer:* Arthur Ackermann Gallery 50 E 57th St New York NY 10022. *Mailing Add:* Woodhollow Rd East Hill NY 11577

NEWSOM, BARBARA YLVISAKER
ADMINISTRATOR, WRITER
b Madison, Wis, July 14, 26. *Study:* Bethany Lutheran Col, Mankato, Minn, AA; Univ Minn, BA; Hunter Col, MA. *Pos:* Pub affairs consult to 100th Anniversary Comt, Metrop Mus Art, New York, 67-70, consult to vdir for educ, 70-71; study dir, Coun Mus Educ, 71-73; proj dir, Coun Mus & Educ in Visual Arts, New York & Cleveland, Ohio, 73-78; staff assoc, Rockefeller Brothers Fund, 73-80, consult, 80- *Mem:* Am Asn Mus (coun mem, 75-78). *Res:* Art museum education and urban aesthetics. *Publ:* Auth, The museum as the city's aesthetic conscience, Metrop Mus Bull, 68; The Metropolitan Museum as an Educational Institution, 70; ed, The Art Museum as Educator, 78. *Mailing Add:* PO Box 235 Holderness NH 03245

NEWTON, DOUGLAS
ADMINISTRATOR, MUSEUM DIRECTOR
b Malacca, Malaysia, Sept 22, 20. *Collections Arranged:* Art Styles of the Papuan Gulf, (with catalog), 61; Art of the Massim Area, New Guinea, 64; Art of Africa, Oceania and the Americas, Metrop Mus Art, 69. *Pos:* Dir & trustee, Mus Primitive Art, currently; chmn dept primitive art, Metrop Mus Art, New York, currently. *Res:* Relationships of art and oral traditions in New Guinea. *Publ:* Auth, New Guinea Art in the Museum of Primitive Art, 67; auth, Crocodile and Cassowary, 72; auth, Art of the Massim Area, 72. *Mailing Add:* Metrop Mus Art Fifth Ave at 82nd St New York NY 10028

NEWTON, EARLE WILLIAMS
ADMINISTRATOR, EDUCATOR
b Cortland, NY, Apr 10, 17. *Study:* Amherst Col, AB; Columbia Univ, MA, Walden Univ, PhD. *Collections Arranged:* British Painting 17th-18th Centuries, 57, 62, 69 & 70; Jacob Eicholtz: Pennsylvania Painter, 58; Hogarth & His School, 59, 87; Fielding, Gay & Hogarth, 90. *Pos:* Ed, Vermont Life, 46-50; ed, Am Heritage, 49-54; dir, Inst Archival Admin (Harvard & Radcliffe), 54-56, Pa State Mus, 56-59, Mus Art Sci & Indust, Conn, 59-62 & St Augustine & Pensacola Hist Preserv Bd, 60-68, 89-; pres, Col Am, 72-; dir, Mus of the Americas, 84- *Teaching:* Vis prof, Univ London, 55-56; lectr, Univ Upsala, Sweden, 56; adj prof, Norwich Univ, 79-87. *Awards:* Award of Merit, Am Inst Graphic Arts, 50-52; comdr, Order of Isabel la Catolica, Spain, 65; Order of Merit, Spain, 68. *Mem:* Am Asn State & Local Hist (secy-treas, 47-53); Soc Am Historians (secy, 48-50); New Eng Mus Asn; Am Asn Mus; Nat Trust Hist Preserv; and others. *Res:* Anglo-American art. *Collection:* Anglo-American art of the 17th & 18th centuries; pre-Columbian art; Latin American folk art; American maps; Americana. *Publ:* Auth, Before Pearl Harbor, 42; ed, Gulf Coast Conf Proc, 70-72; The Vermont Story, 1749-1949, rev ed 83. *Mailing Add:* Rt 14 Brookfield VT 05036

NEWTON, JOHN NEIL
PHOTOGRAPHER, PRINTMAKER
b Montreal, Que, Can, Oct 30, 33. *Study:* St Martins Sch Art, London, England, 53-55; Open Studio, 72-73; Visual Studies Workshop, Rochester, NY, with Nathan Lyons, 73. *Work:* Nat Gallery Can; Nat Film Bd Can, Can Coun Art Bank, Pub Arch Can, Ottawa; Mod Mus, Stockholm. *Exhib:* Solo exhib, Shaw Rimmington Gallery, Toronto, 74; Exposure--Canadian Contemporary Photography, Art Gallery Ont, 75; Photographs From the Permanent Collection, Nat Gallery Can, 75; 1001 Photographs, Mod Mus, Stockholm, 78; retrospective, Can House Exhib Ctr, London, England, 80; Academic Images, Can Ctr Photog, Toronto, 82; Art Forms, Kitchener-Waterloo Art Gallery, Ont, 83. *Pos:* Founding dir, Photog Gallery, Bowmanville, Ont, 71-78 & Newcastle Visual Arts Ctr, Bowmanville, Ont, 74-76. *Teaching:* Lectr photog, York Univ, Toronto, 70-72 & Ryerson Polytech Inst, Toronto, 77-78. *Bibliog:* Annette Snowdon (auth), Holdouts, Can Mag, 7/22/78; Joan Murray (auth), Neil Newton Retrospective (exhib catalog), Robert McLaughlin Gallery, Oshawa, 4/78. *Mem:* Royal Can Acad Arts (coun mem, 83-85); Visual Arts Ont; Can Artists Rep. *Media:* Silver and Non-Silver Printmaking. *Mailing Add:* 9738 Willow St Box 748 Chemaines BC V0R 1K0 Canada

NEWTON, RICHARD EDWARD
CONCEPTUAL ARTIST, FILMMAKER
b Oakland, Calif, Feb 29, 48. *Study:* Univ Calif, Irvine, study with Ed Moses, John Mason, Vija Celmins, Tony Delap, Barbara Rose & Phillip Leider, MFA, 73. *Comn:* Mural, comn by John Mason, Los Angeles, 72; mural, comn by Mark Finkelstein, Corona del Mar, 74; theater piece, Los Angeles Theatre Ctr, 86. *Exhib:* California Suite, Los Angeles County Mus Art, 77; Re: Pages travelling exhib, New Eng, 81; Space Invaders, PS 1, NY, 82; 26th Chicago Int Film Festival, 90; Anthology Film Archives, New York, 91; ARCO '91 & ARCO '92, Exhib of Experimental Cinema, Madrid, Spain, 91 & 92; Melbourne Int Film Festival, Australia, 91; 20th Int Festival of Short Films, Huesca, Spain, 92. *Pos:* Assoc ed & designer, High Performance, Los Angeles, 77-80. *Awards:* Best First Film & Runner-up as best film in festival, 19th Festival Int de Cinema, Portugal, 90; Third Prize, Exhib of Experimental Cinema, Spain, 91; First Prize, Cetamen Int de Cine Ciutat D'Igualada, Spain, 91. *Bibliog:* Jorge Castilho (auth), Richard Newton: um underground com bisavo portugues, J de Coimbra, 9/90; Manohla Dargis (auth), National Obsessions, Village Voice, 1/91; David E Williams (auth), underground, Film Threat, 10/92. *Media:* Live Performance. *Mailing Add:* 444 N Martel Ave Los Angeles CA 90036

NGUYEN, LONG
PAINTER, SCULPTOR
b Nha-Trang, Vietnam, December 23, 58. *Study:* Christian Brothers Col, BS, 80; San Jose State Univ, MFA, 85. *Exhib:* Solo shows, Miller/Brown Gallery, Calif, 87-89, D P Fong/Spratt Gallery, Calif, 90 & 92 & San Francisco Art Comn Gallery, Calif, 92; Triton Mus, Calif, 87; Oakland Mus, Calif, 90; Galleria Civica D'Arte Contemporana, Marsala, Italy, 91; Michael Walls Gallery, New York, 91. *Teaching:* Part-time lectr painting & drawing, San Jose State, 88-91, Univ Calif, Berkeley, 89-90 & Univ Calif, Davis, 91-92. *Awards:* Nat Endowment Arts, 89. *Bibliog:* Dorothy Burkhart (auth), Images from the deep, San Jose Mercury News, 2/28/92; Casey Fitzsimons (auth), Long Nguyen, Artweek, 3/19/92; Harry Roche (auth), Critics choice, Bay Guardian, 7/15/92. *Dealer:* D P Fong/Spratt Gallery 383 S First St San Jose CA 95113. *Mailing Add:* 1050 47th Ave, Suite 2 Oakland CA 94601

NIBLETT, GARY LAWRENCE
PAINTER
b Carlsbad, NMex, Jan 9, 43. *Study:* Art Instruction Inc, Minneapolis, Minn; Eastern NMex Univ, Portales; Art Ctr Col of Design, Los Angeles, Calif. *Comn:* Albuquerque Munic Airport, 88; Carlsbad Mus Fine Art, NMex, 88; Sunwest Bank Hist Collection, Santa Fe, NMex; NMex State Capitol Bldg; calendar artist, NMex Mag, 90; and others. *Exhib:* One-man show, Tex Art Gallery, Dallas, 75 & 76; Cowboy Artists Am, Phoenix Art Mus, Ariz, 77-91; Artists of America, Colo Hist Mus, Denver, 82-91; Hubbard Mus, Ruidoso, NMex, 90-91; A New Mexico Tradition: Southwestern Realism, Taiwan Mus Art, Taichung, 91; and others. *Teaching:* Cowboy Artist Am Mus, 86 & 88. *Awards:* Silver Medals, Cowboy Artists Am Show, Phoenix Art Mus, 77, 82, 83 & 86; Artist of the Year, Tucson Festival Soc, 86; Hubbard Award Excellence, Hubbard Mus, Ruidoso, NMex, 90-91; and others. *Bibliog:* Vicki Stavig (auth), Art of the West, 9-10/89; Mary Terrence McKay (auth), Gary Niblett: A New Look at the Old West, Actian Press, 90; Neirdra Jane Almjer (auth), A new look at the old west, Int Fine Art Collector, 8/91. *Mem:* Cowboy Artist Am; charter mem Santa Fe Watercolor Soc. *Media:* Oil. *Publ:* Cowboy Artist of Am, Desert Hawk Publ, El Paso, Tex, 88. *Mailing Add:* 308 Vistoso Pl Santa Fe NM 87501

NIBLOCK, PHILL
FILMMAKER, VIDEOMAKER
b Anderson, Ind, Oct 2, 33. *Study:* Ind Univ, BA, 56. *Work:* Carpenter Ctr Visual Arts, Harvard Univ. *Comn:* New Works Prog, Mass Coun Arts, 88; New York Found Arts, 87. *Exhib:* Cineprobe, Films and Music, Mus Mod Art, New York, 73; Sur, Wadsworth Atheneum, Hartford, Conn; Trabajando, Herbert F Johnson Mus, Cornell Univ, 76; Carpenter Ctr Visual Arts, Harvard Univ; Inst Contemp Arts, London; Contemp Arts Forum, Santa Barbara, Calif; and others. *Pos:* Dir, Experimental Intermedia Found, New York, 70- *Teaching:* Prof film, video, photog, Col Staten Island, City Univ New York, 71- *Awards:* NY State Coun Arts Grant, Kirkland Art Ctr, 70, Exp Intermedia Found, 72-74; Nat Endowment Arts Pub Media Prog, 75-76; Guggenheim Fel; and others. *Bibliog:* Tom Johnson (auth), Music reviews, Village Voice, 72, 73 & 74; John Rockwell (auth), What's new, High Fidelity/ Musical Am, 5/74; Abigail Nelson (auth), Who's Who in Film, Sight Lines, winter 74. *Mem:* Experimental Intermedia Found. *Mailing Add:* 224 Centre St New York NY 10013

NICE, DON
PAINTER
b Visalia, Calif, June 26, 32. *Study:* Univ Southern Calif, BFA, 54; Yale Univ, MFA, 64. *Work:* Del Art Mus, Wilmington; Minneapolis Inst Art; Mus Mod Art, New York; Walker Art Ctr; Whitney Mus Am Art; Julius Bar Bank, Zurich, Switz; Art Gallery Ont, Can; Arnhems Mus, Holland; and many others. *Comn:* Wall murals, Nat Fine Arts Comn, Lake Placid, NY; Art in Archit Prog, Vets Admin, White River Junction, NY; participant bicentennial exhib, America, 1976, US Dept Interior; Mostly Mozart Festival, Lincoln Ctr Posters, 78; 18th Annual Holiday Festival, Lincoln Ctr Posters, 88. *Exhib:* Solo exhibs, Lake Placid Ctr Arts, New York, 87, Recent Watercolors, John Berggruen Gallery, San Francisco, 87, Recent Works, John Berggruen Gallery, 89, Recent Paintings, Frederick Gallery, Washington, DC, 89, New Watercolors, Sun Valley Ctr Arts & Humanities, Idaho, 90, Images Gallery, Toledo, 91 & Hudson River Journey, Albany Inst Art, NY, 92; Monumental Drawings, John Berggruen Gallery, San Francisco, 91; Common Objects, Pfizer Inc Loan, Art Adv Servs, Mus Mod Art, New York, 91; To Grant or Not to Grant, Sherry French Gallery, New York, 91; The Unique Print, Pace Prints, New York, 91; The Art of Advocacy, Aldrich Mus Contemp Art, Ridgefield, Conn, 91; and many other one-man & group exhibs; A Feast for the Eyes, Mus Mod Art, 84; The New Expressive Landscape, Sordoni Art Gallery, Wilkes Barre, Pa, 85. *Teaching:* Instr, Minneapolis Sch Art, 60-62; instr, Sch Visual Arts, New York, 63-, dean, 64-66; artist-in-residence, Dartmouth Col, New Hampshire, 82- *Awards:* Ford Found Purchase Award, 63. *Bibliog:* Todd Strasser (auth), interview, Ocular, fall 79; Suzanne Muchnic (auth), Really big show in Newport, Los Angeles Times, 80; Donald B Kuspit (auth), What's real in realism, Art in Am, 81. *Mailing Add:* c/o John Berggruen Gallery 228 Grant Ave San Francisco CA 94108

NICHOLAS, DONNA LEE
CERAMIST, SCULPTOR
b South Pasadena, Calif, Mar 30, 38. *Study:* Pomona Col, BA(cum laude), 59; apprentice with Hiroaki Morino, Kyoto, Japan, 60-62; Claremont Grad Sch & Univ Ctr, with Paul Soldner & MFA, 64-66. *Work:* Flint Inst Arts, Mich; Edinboro Univ, Pa; Lowe Gallery, Miami; Calif Polytechnic Univ; Plains Art Mus, Moorhead, Minn; St Petersburg Univ Art, Russia; Erie Art Mus. *Exhib:* Salt Glaze Ceramics, Mus Contemp Crafts, New York, 72; Object as Poet, Renwick Gallery, Smithsonian Inst, Washington, DC & Mus Contemp Crafts, New York, 76; Clay, Fiber, Metal, Women Artists, Bronx Mus, NY, 78; A Century of Ceramics in the US 1879-1979, Everson Mus, Syracuse, NY, 79; one woman exhib, Canton Art Inst, Canton, OH, 88; Fragile Blossoms, Enduring Earth, Everson Mus Art Syracuse, NY, 89; AC Delegates Exhib, Scottish Gallery, Edinburgh, Scotland, 90; and other group & one-woman shows. *Teaching:* Instr ceramics, Mott Community Col, Flint, 66-69; prof ceramics, Edinboro Univ, 69-; vis artist-instr, Penland Sch Crafts, NC, 71, Scripps Col, 74 & Moore Col Art, Philadelphia, 75. *Awards:* Outstanding Educators Am Award, 75; Distinguished Teaching Chair, Commonwealth of Pa Teachers, 81. *Bibliog:* Susan Wechsler (auth), Low Fire Ceramics, Watson-Guptill, 81; Elsbeth Woody (auth), Handbuilding Ceramic Forms, Farrar Strauss & Giroux, 78; John Byrum (auth), New Art Examiner, 88; Richard Zakin (auth), Ceramics, Mastering the Craft, Chilton, 90. *Mem:* Am Craftsmen's Coun (Pa rep to NE Assembly, 75-78); Northwest Pa Artists Asn; Assoc Artists of Pittsburgh; Nat Coun Educ Ceramic Arts; Am Crafts Coun. *Media:* Clay. *Publ:* Auth, 27th Syracuse Nat, Craft Horizons, 12/72; Nat Coun on Educ for Ceramic Arts J, Vol 9, No 1, fall 88. *Mailing Add:* 19 Valley View Dr Edinboro PA 16412

NICHOLAS, THOMAS ANDREW
PAINTER
b Middletown, Conn, Sept 26, 34. *Study:* Studied with Ernest Lohrmann, Mariden, Conn, 50-53; Sch Visual Arts, NY, scholar, 53-55. *Work:* Butler Inst Am Art, Youngstown, Ohio; Ga Mus, Athens; Farnesworth Mus, Rockland, Maine; Adelphi Univ; Greenshields Mus, Montreal; and others. *Comn:* Four ten-colored lithographs, Franklin Mint, 77. *Exhib:* Major exhibs, New York, New Eng, Washington, DC, 59- & Calif, 80- *Teaching:* Instr, Famous Artists Schs, Westport, Conn, 58-61, summer workshops, Rockport, Mass, 62-65, etc, Jade Fon Watercolor Workshop, Carmel, Calif, 78- *Awards:* Elizabeth T Greenshields Mem Found Grants, 61 & 62; Gold Medal Honor, Allied Artists Am, 68; Gold Medal Honor, Am Watercolor Soc, 69; and many others. *Bibliog:* Articles in Am Artist, 3/60 & 8/72; article in North Light Mag, fall 70; John L Cooley (auth), article in The Old Watercolor Soc, Eng, 71; plus others. *Mem:* Nat Acad Design; Am Watercolor Soc; Allied Artists Am; New Eng Watercolor Soc; Knickerbocker Artists; and others. *Media:* Oil, Watercolor. *Publ:* Auth, article, SW Art, 12/82. *Dealer:* Grand Central Galleries 24 W 57th St New York NY 10019; Tom Nicholas Gallery 73 Main St Rockport MA 01966. *Mailing Add:* 7 Wildon Heights Rockport MA 01966

NICHOLS, EDWARD EDSON
PAINTER
b Chicago, Ill, Nov 6, 29. *Study:* Univ Kans, BFA, 57, MFA, 59. *Work:* Miss Art Asn, Jackson; Tex Instruments Collection, Dallas; McAllen Int Mus, Tex. *Comn:* Painting, Hidalgo Co Hist Mus, 92. *Exhib:* Tenth Washington Area Show, Corcoran Gallery Am Art, 56; 22nd Ann, Butler Inst Am Art, 57; 154th Ann, Pa Acad Fine Arts, 59; Third Ann Delta Exhib, Ark Arts Ctr, Little Rock, 60; 23rd Am Drawing Biennial, Norfolk Mus Art, Va, 65; Art Mus STex Ann, Corpus Christi, 70; Tex Painting & Sculpture, Dallas Mus Fine Art, 71; Tex Watercolor Soc Travel Award Exhib, San Antonio, 80. *Teaching:* Assoc prof art, Univ Tex Pan-Am, Edinburg, Tex, 65- *Awards:* Winsor Newton Award, Tex Watercolor Soc Exhib, 80; Del Mar College Drawing Award, Ann Nat Drawing Competition, 84; Juror's Choice Award, Tip o' Texas Exhib, 91. *Mem:* Tex Watercolor Soc. *Media:* Watercolor, Oil. *Publ:* Riversedge, Univ Tex Pan-Am, Edinburg, Tex, 92. *Mailing Add:* 2018 Shary Rd Mission TX 78572

NICHOLS, FRANCIS N, II
PRINTMAKER, EDUCATOR
Study: Wichita State Univ, MFA; also with David Bernard & Robert Kiskadden. *Work:* Anderson Fine Art Ctr, Ind; Univ Miss; Wichita State Univ. *Exhib:* Kans 17th Ann Small Painting, Drawing & Print Exhib, 91; Print Types Consortium Exhib, Ind Univ, 91; Cimarron Nat Works on Paper, Okla State Univ, 91; 8th Ann Nat Works on Paper, Berkeley, Calif, 92; and others. *Teaching:* Fel, Wichita State Univ, 65-67; prof printmaking, Ft Hays State Univ, 67- *Awards:* Merit & Purchase Award, Anderson Winter Show, Ind, 89; Best of Show, 15th Ann Prairie Art Exhib, Sterling, Kans, 89; First Place, Carrier Found Nat Competition, Belle Meade, NJ, 91. *Mem:* Kans Art Educ Asn; Print Consortium; Nat Educ Asn; Nat Art Educ Asn; Kans Art Educ Asn. *Media:* Intaglio, Lithography. *Dealer:* Rueben Saunders Gallery Wichita KS. *Mailing Add:* 1100 Amhurst Hays KS 67601

NICHOLS, JAMES WILLIAM
PAINTER
b Pasadena, Calif, Nov 22, 28. *Study:* Univ Calif, Los Angeles, BA, 50; Univ Calif, Berkeley, with Worth Ryder & Estaben Vicente, MA, 54. *Work:* Mus Mod Art, New York; Long Beach Mus Art, Calif; Aldrich Mus Contemp Art, Ridgefield, Conn; Westmoreland Co Mus Art, Greensburg, Pa; Wichita Art Mus. *Comn:* Eight collage paintings, Henkel Factory, Dusseldorf, Ger, 66-67; two collage constructions, Singer Co, New York, 67; metal mural painting, Lombard Wall, New York, 71; four panel screen & new logo, Long Beach Mus Art, 73; metal mural painting, Gotham Audio, New York, 75. *Exhib:* Jim Nichols' Metal Collage Constructions, New York Cult Ctr, 74, Long Beach Mus Art, 75, Wichita Art Mus, 75, Scottsdale Ctr Arts & Civic Ctr Gallery, 75 & Everson Mus Art, Syracuse, NY, 75. *Publ:* Illusr, About the House, London, 3/65; Art & artists, London, Vol 2, No 7 & Vol 3, No 8; Works, New York, Vol 1, No 3; illusr & contribr, Mag 4, New York, 69. *Mailing Add:* 215 Bowery No 4 New York NY 10002

NICHOLS, MAXINE MCCLENDON See McClendon, Maxine (Maxine McClendon Nichols)

NICHOLS, WARD H
PAINTER
b Welch, WVa, July 5, 30. *Study:* WVa Univ. *Work:* Integon Corp & R J Reynolds Co, Winston-Salem, NC; Gutenberg Mus, Mainz, WGer; Huntington Gallery Art, WVa; Springfield Mus Art, Mass; Lowes Corp, North Wilkesboro, NY; NC Nat Bank, Charlotte, NC. *Comn:* Oil painting, Integon Corp, Winston Salem, NC, 75; oil painting, Printing Indust Carolina, Charlotte, NC, 81, 83 & 92; oil painting, NC State Beekeepers Asn, Raleigh, 82. *Exhib:* Allied Artist Exhib, Nat Acad Galleries, New York; El Paso Mus Art, Tex; Russell Centenary Exhib, Nottingham, Eng; NC Mus Art, Raleigh; Mainstreams, Fine Arts Ctr, Marietta Col, Ohio; and others. *Pos:* Artist in residence, Univ Ind, Terre Haute, Ind, Greenbrier, White Sulphur Springs, WVa & W Liberty Col, West Liberty, WVa. *Teaching:* Guest lectr, many cols in eastern US. *Awards:* Grumbacher Award Merit, El Paso Mus Art, 70; Jurors Merit Award, Miss Mus Art, 71; PICA Award, Printing Indust Carolinas, 75-90. *Bibliog:* Article, Pace Mag, Piedmont Airlines, 78; article, Todays Art, 80; Invitation to a Country Walk (film), Assoc Images, 80. *Mem:* Wilkes Art Guild; Assoc Artists. *Media:* Oil. *Publ:* Contemp Graphic Artists, 87; New York Art Rev, 90; Dict Int Bio, 91; Country J, 2/92; Who's Who in the South & Southwest, 92. *Dealer:* Top Drawer 209 W Third St Winston-Salem NC 27101. *Mailing Add:* 318 Elm St Beaumont Wilkesboro NC 28659

NICHOLS, WILLIAM ALLYN
PAINTER, EDUCATOR
b Chicago, Ill, Apr 1, 42. *Study:* Art Inst Chicago, BFA(painting & drawing), 66; Univ Ill, Urbana, MFA(painting), 68; Slade Sch Art, Univ Col, London, Fulbright Grant, 68-69. *Comn:* Earth (acrylic landscape painting), Third Nat Bank & Trust Co, Dayton, Ohio, 79. *Exhib:* One man exhibs, O K Harris Gallery, 79, 81 & 83; Watercolors 1980, Frumkin-Struve Gallery, Chicago, 80; Contemporary American Landscape, Taft Mus, Cincinnati, Ohio, 81; Contemporary American Realism Since 1960, Pa Acad Fine Arts, Philadelphia & traveling in US & Europe, 81-82; Painterly Realism, Rahr-West Mus, Manitowoc, Wis, 82; Watercolor USA, Springfield Art Mus, Mo, 83. *Teaching:* Assoc prof art, Univ Wis-Milwaukee, 70- *Bibliog:* Carter Radcliff (auth), article, Art Int Mag, 5/6/77; Catherine LaMagna (auth), article, Arts Mag, 79; Frank H Goodyear, Jr (auth), Contemporary American Realism Since 1960, NY Graphic Soc, 81. *Media:* Acrylic, Watercolor. *Dealer:* O K Harris Works of Art 383 W Broadway New York NY 10012. *Mailing Add:* c/o Michael H Lord Gallery 420 E Wisconsin Ave Manitowoc WI 53202

NICHOLSON, MYREEN MOORE See Moore, Myreen (Myreen Moore Nicholson)

NICHOLSON, NATASHA
ASSEMBLAGE ARTIST, SCULPTOR
b St Louis, Mo, May 29, 45. *Study:* Ringling Sch Art, 64-65. *Work:* Oakland Mus Art, Calif; Addison Gallery Am Art, Phillips Acad, Andover, Mass; Los Angeles Co Mus Art; Madison Art Ctr, Wis. *Comn:* Sculpture, Rayovac Corp, Madison, Wis, 86. *Exhib:* Solo exhibs, Addison Gallery Am Art, 74, Asher-Faure Gallery, Los Angeles, 81 & 83 & Perimeter Gallery, Chicago, 83; Collage and Assemblage in Southern California, Los Angeles Inst Contemp Art, 75; A Sense of Space, Oakland Mus Art, 77; Global Space Invasions, San Francisco Mus Mod Art, 78; Our Own Artists: Art in Orange County, Newport Harbor Art Mus, 79; Tableau, Middendorf-Lane Gallery, Washington, DC, 80; Forgotten Dimension: A Survey of Small Sculpture in California Now, Fresno Art Ctr, traveling, 82; Chicago & Vicinity Exhib, Chicago Art Inst, 84; and others. *Collections Arranged:* The Other Things That Artists Make, San Francisco Mus Mod Art, 76; Useable Art, Decorative Arts, Quay Gallery, San Francisco, 77; Decorative Arts of Dane County, Madison Art Ctr, Wis, 82. *Pos:* Dir, Natasha Nicholson/works of Art, Madison, Wis, 87-90. *Awards:* Individual Artist Grant, Nat Endowment Arts, 77; Artists Fel, 83 & Proj Grant, 83, Wis Arts Bd. *Bibliog:* Alfred Frankenstein (auth), For the magical love of oddities, San Francisco Chronicle, 77; Melinda Wortz (auth), Los Angeles, Art News Mag, 12/79; Vivien Raynor (auth), Anxious interiors, NY Times, 9/85. *Media:* Mixed. *Mailing Add:* 1962 Atwood Ave PO Box 3493 Madison WI 53704

NICHOLSON, ROY WILLIAM
PAINTER, PRINTMAKER
b Cambridge, Eng, Mar 21, 43. *Study:* Hornsey Col Art, London, Eng, with John Hoyland, NDD, 65; Brooklyn Mus Sch Art, Max Beckman Mem Scholar, 66. *Work:* Guild Hall Mus; State Univ Stony Brook; Heckscher Mus, Huntington, NY; Royal Col Heralds & Abbot Hall Art Gallery Mus, Eng. *Exhib:* 28th Ann, Parrish Art Mus, Southampton, NY, 81-82; Winterscape, Guild Hall Mus, East Hampton, NY, 81-82; Condeso/Lawler Gallery, New York, 85; Am Consulates, Brazil, 87; Katharina Rich Perlon Gallery, New York, 91; and others. *Collections Arranged:* The Art of Claude Lorrain, Newcastle & London, 69; The Art of Paul Nash, Newcastle, 71; Alan Davie/David Hockney: Watercolors & Drawings, touring, 71; The Craftsman's Art, Victoria & Albert Mus, London, 73; Watercolor & Pencil Drawings by Paul Cezanne, Hayward Gallery, London & Newcastle, 73; many one person & group exhibs organized at Long Island Univ, Southampton Fine Arts Gallery, 86-, including photography of Peristroika, 91 & Betty Parson, 92. *Pos:* Asst dir, Brook Street Gallery, London, 66-68; visual arts officer, Northern Arts, Newcastle, Eng, 68-74; bd gov, Lancaster Col Art, Eng, 72-74; dir, art gallery, Long Island Univ Southampton Campus, 86- *Teaching:* Vis artist, State Univ NY, Stony Brook, 78-79; adj assoc prof art, Long Island Univ Southampton Campus, 81-86, asst prof art, 86-92 & assoc prof Art 92-, Victor C'Amico Art Inst, Easthampton, NY, 83- *Bibliog:* Kenny Mann (auth), article, Sunstorm; several articles, reviews, New York Times between 83 & 87; Ronald Pisano (auth), Long Island Landscape Painting, The Twentieth Century. *Media:* Oil, Alkyd; Lithography, Etching. *Dealer:* Katharina Rich Perlon Gallery 560 Broadway New York NY 10012. *Mailing Add:* Rd 3 Box 487 Sag Harbor NY 11963

NICK, GEORGE
PAINTER, EDUCATOR
b Rochester, NY, Mar 28, 27. *Study:* Cleveland Inst Art, with Frank Wilcox; Brooklyn Mus Art Sch; Art Students League, with Edwin Dickinson; Yale Univ, BFA & MFA. *Work:* Hirshhorn Mus, Washington, DC; Boston Mus Fine Arts; Joslyn Art Mus, Omaha, Nebr; Rose Art Gallery, Brandeis Univ, Waltham, Mass; Metro Mus, New York. *Exhib:* Md Artists Ann Exhib, Baltimore, 66; Pa Artists Ann, Philadelphia Acad Fine Arts, 67. *Teaching:* Assoc prof drawing, Carnegie-Mellon Inst, 64-65; assoc prof painting, Univ Pa, 66-69; assoc prof painting, Mass Col Art, Boston, formerly, prof two-dimensional art, currently. *Awards:* Mass Coun Arts Grant, 74; Nat Endowment Arts Award, 76; Am Acad Arts & Lett Award, 76. *Media:* Oil. *Mailing Add:* c/o Levinson Kane Gallery 14 Newbury St Boston MA 02116

NICKARD, GARY LAURENCE
PHOTOGRAPHER, CURATOR
b Toronto, Ont, June 14, 54. *Study:* State Univ NY, Buffalo, BFA, 78, MA, 82, MFA, 86. *Work:* Albright-Knox Art Gallery, Buffalo; Burchfield Art Ctr, Buffalo; Capen Gallery, State Univ NY, Buffalo. *Exhib:* Mod Sci, CEPA Gallery, Buffalo, 82; 40th Western NY Exhib, Albright-Knox Art Gallery, Buffalo, 84; Alien Art, Artists Gallery, Buffalo, 85; Insidious Protocols, Artmart, Buffalo, 86; Insidious Protocols, Dana Art Ctr, Colgate Univ, 87; Soc Studies, YYZ Gallery, Toronto, 87; Dislocations, Alternative Mus, New York, 87; 42nd Western NY Exhib, Albright-Knox Art Gallery, Buffalo, 88; Science as Spectacle, Burchfield Art Ctr, Buffalo, 91. *Collections Arranged:* Riding First Class on the Titanic, Nathan Lyons (catalog), 87, Crocodile Tears, Douglas Huebler (catalog), Albright-Knox Art Gallery, 85; Sharp Rocks, Edgar Heap of Birds (catalog), 86, Tableau Morte, Akin/Ludwig, 87, Stereo Views, Jim Pomeroy (catalog), 88, On Britain's Doorstep, Stephen Shortt, 88, CEPA Gallery; Belfast/Beirut, Alternative Mus, 90; Photostroika: New Soviet Phtography, Aperture Burden Gallery, 90 & 91; Light Images, Chrysler Mus, 90. *Pos:* Exec dir & cur, CEPA Gallery, Buffalo, 82-88; consult, Nat Endowment Arts, 84-89 (panelist, 88-90); NY State Coun Arts, 88-90 & NJ State Arts Coun, 90; assoc cur, Alternative Mus, NY, 88-90; dir & cur, Aperture Burden Gallery, NY, 90- *Teaching:* Instr photog, State Univ NY, Buffalo, 85-88. *Awards:* Grant, NY State Coun Arts. *Bibliog:* Anthony Bannon (auth), Romantic era lives in photos, 2/19/84, Welch Everman (auth), Group exhibition offers four perspectives, 5/21/85 & Richard Huntington (auth), Gary Nickard's weird science, 5/2/86, Buffalo News; Robert C Morgan (auth), Gary Nickard, 1/88, Arts Mag. *Mem:* Soc Photog Educ; Arts Coun Buffalo & Erie Co; Nat Asn Artists Orgns. *Media:* Installation. *Res:* Orientalism and photography; postmodern photography; science as spectacle. *Publ:* Contribr, Buffalo Arts Rev, Center Quart (Catskill Ctr Photog) & Cepa Quart, 86; High performance, Buffalo News, 88. *Mailing Add:* c/o Burohfield Art Ctr 1300 Elmwood Ave Buffalo NY 14222

NICKERSON, JOHN HENRY
GLASS BLOWER, SCULPTOR
b Minneapolis, Minn, May 15, 39. *Study:* Mont State Univ, BA, 64; Soc Arts & Crafts, Detroit, 65-66, Alfred Univ, NY, MFA, 69. *Work:* Colo Springs Fine Arts Ctr; Corning Mus Glass, NY; Del Art Mus, Wilmington; Denver Art Mus; Musée des Arts Décoratifs, Lausanne, Switz. *Comn:* Liturgical appointments, Light of the World Cath Church, Littleton, Colo. *Exhib:* Colorado Crafts: Seventeen Views, Denver Art Mus, 79; New Glass/Glass '79, Corning Mus Glass, NY, 79; Nat Invitational Glass Exhib, Renwick Gallery, Washington, DC, 79; National Crafts '81, Greenville County Mus Art, SC, 81; Emergence, Art in Glass, Bowling Green State Univ, Ohio, 81; Americans in Glass, Leigh Yawkey Woodson Mus Art, Wausau, Wis, 84; Studio Glass, Redding Mus Art, Calif, 85; New American Glass: Focus 2 West Virginia, Huntington Galleries, WVa, 86. *Teaching:* Asst prof ceramics & design, Colo State Univ, Ft Collins, 69-70; assoc master, ceramics, glass & design, Georgian Col Appl Art & Technol, Barrie, Ont, 74-75. *Awards:* Nat Endowment Arts Craftsman's Fel Grant, 81-82. *Bibliog:* Suzanne Foley (auth), The measure of success, Am Craft, 11/84; Grace Glueck (auth), article, Glass Art Soc J, 85. *Mem:* Glass Art Soc; Int Sculpture Ctr. *Mailing Add:* PO Box 457 Sedalia CO 80135

NICKERSON, RUTH (MRS EDMUND GREACEN JR)
SCULPTOR, INSTRUCTOR
b Appleton, Wis, Nov 23, 05. *Study:* Simcoe Col Inst, Ont; Nat Acad Design; also with Ahron Ben-Smuel, New York. *Work:* Brooklyn Pub Libr; Cedar Rapids Mus Art, Iowa; Montclair Art Mus, NJ; Interchurch Ctr, New York; Mitchel Wolfson Mus, Miami, Fla. *Comn:* Many portrait comns for pvt collectors, 32-; Learning (stone group), Fed Art Proj, Brooklyn, 34; Tympanum, Fed Govt, New Brunswick Post Off, NJ, 36; Am Oriental Rug Weaving (ceramic mural), Fed Art Proj, Eden Post Off, NC; mem plaque, New Rochelle Art Comt for City Hall, 60. *Exhib:* Nat Acad Design Ann, New York, 32-; Whitney Mus Am Art, New York, 34; Mus Mod Art, New York, 39; Artists for Victory, Metrop Mus Art, New York, 42; Pa Acad Fine Arts, Philadelphia, 48; Audubon Artists, 81. *Pos:* Charter mem & secy pro tem, White Plains Civic Art Comn, 48-60. *Teaching:* Instr sculpture, Roerich Mus, New York, 34-35 & Westchester Art Workshop, 45-69; instr modeling & sculpture, Nat Acad Design Sch, New York, 80 & 81. *Awards:* Guggenheim Fel, 46-47; Vincent Glinsky Award, 81; Therese Richard Prize, Allied Artists, 82; Dietsch Prize, Nat Sculpture Soc, 83. *Bibliog:* Jacques Schneir (auth), Art in Modern America. *Mem:* Nat Sculpture Soc; Nat Acad Design; Audubon Artists. *Media:* Stone Carving. *Publ:* Contribr, Marlene Park & G E Markowitz's Democratic Vistas; Clark Marlor's Independant Artists; Nat Sculpture Review. *Mailing Add:* 30 Lake St Apt 8K White Plains NY 10603-4020

NICKFORD, JUAN
SCULPTOR, EDUCATOR
b Havana, Cuba, Aug 8, 25; US citizen. *Study:* Acad Art, Havana, MFA, 46; Sch Archit, Univ Havana. *Work:* Smith Col Mus Art; Spaeth Found, New York; also in collections of Roy Neuberger, New York & Phil Berg, Los Angeles. *Comn:* Welded metal sculptures, Socony Oil Bldg, New York, 56; metal mural, Trade Show Bldg, New York, 56; free standing group, Philco Corp Trade Mart, Chicago, Ill, 57; screens, Grace Line, SS Santa Rosa, 60; outdoor sculpture, Tappan Town Soc, NY, 72. *Exhib:* Whitney Mus Am Art Ann, 50-57; Jr Coun, Mus Mod Art, New York, 61; Man Came This Way, Los Angeles Co Mus Art, 71; one-man exhibs, Manhattanville Col, Purchase, NY, 75, Emanuel Col, Boston, 77, The Sculpture Gallery, Palo Alto, Calif, 81, James Gallery, Summit, NJ, 81 & Sculptor's Guild, New York, 81; Sculpture Ctr, New York, 84; The Glass Art Gallery, Toronto, 85; Hoppe House Gallery, Nyack, NY, 86. *Pos:* Trustee, Sculpture Ctr New York, 70-84; mem exec comt, City Col New York, 75-83. *Teaching:* Vis artist, Univ Hartford, 65-66 Smith Col, 66-69; asst prof sculpture, City Col New York, 70-75, assoc prof art, 75-80, prof, 80-91, prof emeritus 91- *Awards:* Bronze Medal, NY State Expos, 64; Inst Int Educ Grant for Creative Sculpture, Cintas Found, 71; Grant, Res Found, City Univ New York, 83. *Bibliog:* Meilach & Seiden (auth), Direct Metal Sculpture, George Allen & Unwin, Ltd, London, 66; Nathan Cabot Hale (auth), Welded Sculpture, Watson-Guptill, 68; Wayne Andersen (auth), American Sculpture in Process: 1930/1970, NY Graphic Soc, 75. *Mem:* Sculptor's Guild; Rockland Found Art. *Media:* Metal, Mixed. *Dealer:* Ann Leonard 63 Tinker St Woodstock NY 12498. *Mailing Add:* 161 Old Tappan Rd Tappan NY 10983

NICKSON, GRAHAM G
PAINTER, EDUCATOR
b Knowle Green, Lancashire, Eng, 1946. *Study:* Camberwell Sch Arts & Crafts, London, BA, 69; Royal Col Art, London, MA, 72; Prix de Rome (scholarship) RS, 72-74. *Work:* Metro Mus Art, New York; Neuburger Mus, Purchase, NY; Albright-Knox Gallery & Mus, Buffalo, NY; La Jolla Mus Contemp Art, Calif; William Benton Mus Art, Univ Conn. *Comn:* Painting, Skidmore Owings & Merrill, San Francisco, 85. *Exhib:* One-man exhib, William Benton Mus, Storrs, Conn, 82, Northern Ctr Contemp Art, Sunderland, Eng, 88, Warwick Arts Ctr, Mead Mus, Eng, 89 & Weatherspoon Art Gallery, Univ NC, Greensboro; 30 Painters: New Acquisitions, Metro Mus Art, New York, 82; New Drawing in America, Drawing Ctr, New York, 82; Motion-Arrested Motion, Chrysler Mus, Norfolk, Va, 87; London-Glasgow-New York, Metro Mus Art, New York, 88. *Pos:* Dean, New York Studio Sch Drawing Painting & Sculpture, 88- *Awards:* Harkness Fel, Commonwealth Fund, 76; Howard Found Fel, Brown Univ, 80; Guggenheim Fel, 89. *Bibliog:* Jack Flam (auth), Graham Nickson: Drawing into color, William Benton Mus, 82; John Russell (auth), Painter of beach life, Nickson's Beaches, NY Times, 82; Andrew Forge/Jack Flam/Bob McDaniel (coauths), Graham Nickson paintings & drawings, Northern Ctr Contemp Art, 88. *Media:* Oil, Acrylic. *Dealer:* Salander-O'Reilly Galleries Inc 20 E 79th St New York NY 10021. *Mailing Add:* PO Box 318 Canal St Sta New York NY 10013

NICODEMUS, CHESTER ROLAND
SCULPTOR, DESIGNER
b Barberton, Ohio, Aug 17, 01. *Study:* Cleveland Sch Art, grad, 25; Univ Dayton; Ohio State Univ. *Work:* Dayton Art Inst; Columbus Gallery Fine Arts, Ohio; Capital Univ. *Comn:* Wright Bros Tablet, Wilbur Wright High Sch, Dayton, 28; Francis C Sessions Tablet, Columbus Gallery Fine Arts, 32; Columbus Art League Medal, 47; Edward Orton Tablet, Unitarian Church, Columbus, 63; Butler Inst Am Art Medal, Youngstown, Ohio, 72. *Exhib:* Ceramic Nat, Syracuse, NY, 54; Ceramic Int, 58; Columbus Art League, 63; Butler Inst Am Art, 65. *Pos:* Designer & producer, Ferro-Stone Ceramics, 43- *Teaching:* Instr sculpture, Dayton Art Inst, 25-30; instr sculpture, Columbus Art Sch, 30-43, dean, 31-32. *Mem:* Nat Sculpture Soc; Columbus Art League (pres, 33-36). *Media:* Ceramics, Bronze. *Mailing Add:* 447 Clinton Heights Ave Columbus OH 43202

NICOTRA, JOSEPH CHARLES
PAINTER
b Corona, NY, Aug 9, 31. *Study:* Art Students League (Bernay Scholarship), 55-60; Am Art Sch, 60-61. *Work:* An American on Nov 22, Nat Archives, JFK Libr, Washington, DC. *Comn:* Mayor O'Dwyer, Disabled Am Vet Orgn, Woodside, NY, 55; Portrait Bishop Richard Allen, African Methodist Escopalin Church, Flushing, NY, 77; mural, Queens Mus, Flushing, NY, 81; Long Island Symphony Orchestra, Huntington, NY, 78. *Exhib:* Academia Italia Invitational, 80; Long Beach Mus Ann, NY, 80; Unversita del Art, Italy, 82; Flushing Coun Cult & Arts Ann, Flushing Gallery, NY, 86. *Teaching:* Lectr, Queens Mus, Flushing, NY, 72. *Mem:* Life mem Art Students League; Flushing Coun Culture & Arts; Orgn Independent Artists. *Media:* Oil. *Mailing Add:* 59-32 156 St Flushing NY 11355

NIEDERER, CARL
PAINTER
b Portland, Ore, Mar 14, 27. *Study:* Univ Ore, Eugene, with Jack Wilkinson, BS, 49; Atelier Fernand Leger, Paris, France, 51; New Sch, New York, with Alexi Brodovitch, 53. *Work:* Univ San Francisco Collection & City of San Francisco Collection, Calif. *Comn:* Bronze facia frieze, Bank Calif Hq, San Francisco, 63; polychrome ceiling stabile, Univ Calif, Berkeley, 74; enamel entryway panels, Pac Bell, San Francisco, Calif, 75; elevator door murals, Standard Oil, 75 & AT&T, 77, San Francisco, Calif. *Exhib:* Pac Int, Perc Tucker Gallery, Townsville, Australia, 82; Australian Observations, Nicolaysen Art Mus, Casper, Wyo, 82; Wyo Biennial, traveling exhib, Cheyenne, 86 & 88; Wyo Fel Show, 88; Australian Watercolors, City Corp Plaza, Los Angeles, Calif, 91; and others. *Pos:* Prof emer, Univ Wyo, Laramie, 91. *Teaching:* Assoc prof design, Univ Ore, Eugene, 68-70; head dept painting, Univ Wyo, Laramie, 77-82, prof art & watercolor, 82-89. *Awards:* Purchase Award, San Francisco Arts Festival, 64; Second Prize, Laramie Art Guild Show, 86; Best of Show, Wyo Watercolor Soc Show, 87; Wyo Coun Arts Fel, 88. *Bibliog:* Francis H Hoover (auth), San Francisco Gallery Guide, 75. *Mem:* Laramie Art Guild; Wyo Watercolor Soc. *Media:* Watercolor, Acrylic. *Mailing Add:* PO Box 2833 Florence OR 47439-0163

NIEDZIALEK, TERRY
SCULPTOR, ENVIRONMENTAL ARTIST
b July 10, 56. *Study:* Univ Colo, Boulder, 78-80; NY Inst Technol, Old Westbury, NY, BFA, 81. *Work:* Galerie Alain Oudin, Paris; NY Inst Technol, Old Westbury; Galerie Il Diaframma, Milan, Italy. *Exhib:* Long Island's Alternative Spaces, Islip Mus, New York, 85; Fashion & Surrealism, Fashion Inst, New York, 87 & Victoria & Albert Mus, London, 88; The Political Landscape, Hillwood Art Mus, Greenvale, NY, 90; Hair Sculpture & Its Roots, Lehigh Univ Mus, Bethlehem, Pa, 91; and others. *Teaching:* Fac sculpture, Pa Govs Sch Arts, Erie, 92. *Awards:* Nat Endowment Arts Grant, 88; Individual Artists Award, Pollock-Krasner, 89; Cross Disciplinary Award, Performance, Pa Counc Arts, 91. *Bibliog:* Julius Vitali (auth), Hair Sculpture, Domus, Italy, 85; Andrienne Redd (auth), Hair Sculpture & Its Roots, Lehigh Univ Mus, 91; Dan Friedman (auth), Terry Niedzialek Hair Sculpture, Fiber Arts, 91. *Media:* Miscellaneous Media. *Publ:* Illus, Italian Vogue, 86; Epoca, Mondadori, Italy, 86; New look, Filipachi, France, 86; contribr, The Costume Maker's Art, Lark Bks, 92; Earth Journal, Buzzworm Bks, 92. *Mailing Add:* PO Box 75 Flicksville PA 18050

NIELSEN, NINA I M
DEALER
b Riverdale, NY, Nov 5, 40. *Study:* Bucknell Univ, BA, 62; Univ Vienna. *Pos:* Owner, Nielsen Gallery, Boston, currently; vis comt mem, Boston Mus Sch, 79-80. *Specialty:* Modern and contemporary paintings, drawings and sculpture. *Mailing Add:* c/o Nielsen Gallery 179 Newbury St Boston MA 02116

NIEMANN, EDMUND E
PAINTER, SCULPTOR
b New York, NY. *Study:* Nat Acad Design; Art Students League. *Work:* Slater Mus, Norwich, Conn; Butler Inst Am Art, Youngstown, Ohio; Storm King Art Mus, Mountainville, NY; Syracuse Univ Art Mus; Swarthmore Col. *Exhib:* Directions of American Painting, Carnegie Inst, Pa, 41; Nat Acad Design Ann, 62-68; Pa Acad Fine Arts Watercolor & Drawing Ann, 64; Butler Inst Am Art Painting Nat, 68, 74, 77 & 80; Watercolor USA, 72. *Awards:* New Eng Ann Lyon Award, 77; Audubon Artist Ann Hirsch Mem Award, 78; Young-Hunter Mem Award, Allied Artists, 80; and others. *Mem:* Audubon Artists; Am Watercolor Soc; Allied Artists Am; Nat Soc Painters Acrylic & Casein. *Publ:* Contribr, Todays Art, 7/68 & 8/73; auth, Drawing with unusual tool, Am Artists, 1/70. *Mailing Add:* 38-15 208th St Bayside NY 11361

NIEMEYER, ARNOLD MATTHEW
COLLECTOR, PATRON
b St Paul, Minn, Mar 7, 13. *Pos:* Trustee, Minn Mus Art. *Collection:* All media, especially fine graphics. *Mailing Add:* 1186 St Clair Ave St Paul MN 55105

NIERMAN, LEONARDO M
PAINTER, SCULPTOR
b Mexico City, Mex, Nov 1, 32. *Study:* Nat Univ Mex, BA. *Work:* Ft Worth Art Mus, Tex; Mus Arte Mod, Mexico City; The Wave, Detroit Inst of Arts; Bird in Flight, Acad Fine Arts, Honolulu; Genesis, Israel Mus, Jerusalem; and others. *Comn:* Murals Sch Com, Univ City, Mex, 56; mural, Golden West Savings, San Francisco, 65; stained glass windows, two temples, Mexico City, 66-67; Cosmic Meditation (mural), Physics Bldg, Princeton Univ, NJ, 68;

Eagle (bronze sculpture), Toronto, Can, 72. *Exhib:* Paris Biennale, Mus Mod Art, France, 61; Marlborough-Gerson Gallery, New York, 64; Pittsburgh Int, Carnegie Inst, Pa, 64 & 67; El Paso Mus Art, Tex, 64 & 71; Mus Arte Mod, 72; and many one-man shows. *Awards:* First Prize, Art Inst Mex, 64; Palm D'Or Beaux Arts, Monaco, 69; Gold Medal, Tomasso Campanella Found, Italy, 72. *Bibliog:* Enrique Gual (auth), Leonardo Nierman, Ed Monterrey, 64; Jose Gomez Sicre (auth), Nierman, Artes Mex, 71; Julio Cortazar & Max Pol Fouchet (auth), Leonardo Nierman, A Capell & A Elmayan Ed, Paris, 75. *Mem:* Royal Soc Arts, London; Int Biog Asn: UK; Int Arts Guild, Monte Carlo; Salon Plastica, Mex. *Media:* Acrylic; Onyx, Bronze. *Mailing Add:* Lublin Graphics 95 E Putnam Ave Greenwich CT 06830

NIESE, HENRY ERNST
ENVIRONMENTAL ARTIST, PAINTER
b Jersey City, NJ, Oct 11, 24. *Study:* Cooper Union, cert, with Robert Gwathmey & Morris Kantor; Acad Grande Chaumiere, cert, with Othon Friesz; Columbia Univ, BFA, with Leo Manso, John Heliker & Meyer Schapiro. *Work:* Whitney Mus Am Art, New York; Corcoran Gallery, DC; Albright-Knox Mus; Nat Mus Am Art, Washington, DC; Filmkundliches Arkiv, Cologne, WGer; Chrysler Mus, Norfolk; and others. *Exhib:* Young American, Whitney Mus Am Art, 62 & 40 Artists Under 40, 64; 4th Int Exp Film Festival, Brussels, Belg, 69; New York Avant Garde Festivals, 69-78; Six Nations Mus, NY & Corcoran Gallery, 76; Foundry Gallery, DC, 80; also numerous on-site ceremonial structures and performances in New York City, Mass, Vt, Md & SDak since 1978. *Pos:* Dir, Eagle Voice Ctr, Glenelg, Md, currently. *Teaching:* Spec lectr grad humanities, NY Univ, 65-69; asst prof studio art, Ohio State Univ, 66-69; assoc prof studio art, Univ Md, 69-; guest fel, Yale Univ, 79; vis artist, Univ Calif, Santa Barbara, 75. *Awards:* Pulitzer Found Traveling Fel, 55; Int Cinema Prize, Mus Arte Mod, Vitoria, Brasil, 69; Creative & Performing Arts Grant, Univ Md, 71 & 73. *Media:* Multimedia. *Dealer:* Foundry Gallery 2121 P St Washington DC 20037. *Mailing Add:* Folly Quarter Rd Glenelg MD 21737

NIETO, JOHN W
PAINTER, SCULPTOR
b Denver, Colo, Aug 6, 36. *Study:* Pan Am Univ, 55-56; Southern Methodist Univ, 57-59; Dallas Mus Fine Arts, 60. *Work:* Heard Mus, Phoenix, Ariz; Smithsonian Inst, Washington, DC; NMex Mus Fine Arts, Santa Fe; Wagner Corp Collection, Austin, Tex; Goldwaters Pvt Collection; The White House, Washington, DC; Marine Corp Mus. *Comn:* Murals, Lakewood State Bank, Dallas, 61; bronze bust of chmn of bd, Tex Power & Light, Dallas, 80; portrait of Barry Goldwater, Goldwaters, Phoenix, Ariz, 83; Plains Prayer (poster), comn by ABC. *Exhib:* 20th Century American Indian Artist, Kimball Art Mus, Park City, Utah, 81; American Indian Contemporary Art, Smithsonian Inst, Washington, DC, 82; Night of the First American, John F Kennedy Ctr, Washington, DC, 82; Salon d'Automne, Grand Palais, Paris, 82; one-man shows, US Embassy, Barbados, 82 & Wheelwright Mus, Santa Fe, 86; Images of Ranchos de Taos Church, NMex Fine Arts Mus, Santa Fe, 83; Native American Works, Pensacola Mus Art, Fla; The Art of the Native American, Owensboro Mus Fine Art, Ky; Le Salon Des Nations A Paris, Centre Int D'Art Contemporain, 86. *Pos:* Bd dir, Wheelwright Mus, Santa Fe, NMex, 84. *Teaching:* Art, NTex State Univ, Denton, 64-65 & Southern Methodist Univ, Dallas, 74-75. *Awards:* Blue Ribbon Award, Arts & Crafts Show, Heard Mus, Phoenix, 81; Artist of Year, Santa Fean Mag, 82; Featured Artist, Festival Arts & Pageant of Masters, Laguna Beach, Calif; Feather Dancer Poster Piece, 65th Inter-Tribal Indian Ceremonial, Gallup, NMex, 86. *Bibliog:* Erica Benis (auth), John Nieto Artist, Voice Am, US Int Commun Agency, 81; Ms Goldman (auth), Artist in Santa Fe, Nat Pub Radio, Washington, DC, 82; William Carpenter (auth), Profile of John Nieto, Carpenter & Assoc, 83. *Media:* Oil, Watercolor; Clay. *Dealer:* Enthios Gallery 1111 Paseo de Peralta Santa Fe NM 87501; Western Images Ltd 560 Broadway New York NY 10012. *Mailing Add:* c/o J Cacciola Galleries 125 Wooster St New York NY 10012-3106

NIGROSH, LEON ISAAC
CERAMIST, INSTRUCTOR
b Cambridge, Mass, Aug 7, 40. *Study:* Carnegie Inst Technol, 58-59; RI Sch Design, BFA, 63; Rochester Inst Technol, MFA, 65. *Comn:* Five ceramic fountains, Group One Inc, New Seabury, Mass, 73; ceramic sculpture, Temple Shalom Emeth, Burlington, Mass, 83; porcelain wall panel, comn by Mr & Mrs Joseph Epstein, Carlsbad, Calif, 83; porcelain signature wall, Holden District Hosp, Barre, Mass, 84; porcelain mural, Worcester Historical Mus, Mass, 86. *Exhib:* Artworks, Worcester, Mass, 81; Peters Valley Gallery, Layton, NJ, 82; Mirage Collectables, Miami, Fla, 82; Ely Art Gallery, Westfield, Mass, 83; Benchmarks Gallery, Washington, DC, 84; Signature, Boston, 85; Grove St Gallery, Worcester, Mass, 86; Cambridge Gallery, Worcester, 88. *Pos:* Comnr, Worcester Cult Comn, 86- *Teaching:* Instr ceramics, Auburn Community Col, 64-65; instr ceramics & studio mgr, Greenwich House Pottery Sch, New York, 65-66; instr ceramics & head dept, Craft Ctr, Worcester, 67-78; vis prof, RI Col, 78-79; lectr art, Clark Univ, Worcester, Mass, 81- *Awards:* Mass Arts Lottery Coun Grant, 82 & 84; Third Prize, Arts Worcester, 85. *Bibliog:* Articles, Moment Mag, 84 & Worcester Mag, 85. *Mem:* Worcester Cult Comn (bd dirs, 86-); Am Crafts Coun; Nat Asn Educ in Ceramic Arts; Worcester Cult Assembly (bd dirs, 81-). *Media:* Ceramic. *Publ:* Contribr, Craft Horizons, 71-78; auth, Claywork, 75 & Low Fire, 80, Davis; five articles in Sch Arts, 76-77; Claywork, second ed, 86; Ten Treasures of the Musee d'Orsay (monogr), 88. *Mailing Add:* 11 Chatanika Ave Worcester MA 01602

NIIZUMA, MINORU
SCULPTOR
b Tokyo, Japan, Sept 29, 30. *Study:* Tokyo Univ Arts, BFA. *Work:* Mus Mod Art & Guggenheim Mus, New York; Nat Mus Mod Art & Am Embassy, Tokyo; Gulbenkian Mus, Lisbon, Port; Nat Mus Contemp Art, Korea; and others as well as pvt collections including Mrs John D Rockefeller III. *Comn:* Stone monuments, Metrop Tokyo, 56, Asia House, Tokyo, 58; Int Sculpture Symp, Vt, 68, St Margarethen, Austria, 69 & New York, 71. *Exhib:* 2nd Henry Moore Grand Prize Exhib, Hakone, Open-Air Mus, Japan, 81; The 1960's - A Decade of Change in Contemp Japanese Art, Nata Mus Mod Art, Tokyo & Kyoto, 81; World Stone Sculpture, Kunsthaus Zug, Switz, 82; Soloman R Guggenheim Mus Art, New York, 83-84 & 87-88; Mekler Gallery, Los Angeles, 83; Neuberger Mus, Purchase, NY, 83-84; solo exhibs, Centro Cult S Laurenco, Almansil, Port, 86, Mekler Gallery, Los Angeles 86 & 89, Galeria Quadrom, Lisbon, 88, Blue Hill Cult Ctr, New York, 88-89, Galerie Nichido, Tokyo, 89 & Fandation Veranneman, Belg, 89; and many others. *Teaching:* Instr sculpture, Brooklyn Mus Art Sch, 64-69; adj prof, Columbia Univ, 72-84. *Mem:* Sculptors Guild. *Media:* Marble, Granite. *Mailing Add:* c/o Gremillion & Co Fine Art Inc 2501 Sunset Blvd Houston TX 77005

NIKKAL, NANCY EGOL
COLLAGE ARTIST
b New York, NY, 44. *Study:* Syracuse Univ Sch Fine Arts, 62-64; Hunter Col, City Univ New York, 73; Pratt Graphics, Manhattan, 80. *Work:* Exec offs, Sun Chemical, New York; exec offs, Dainippon Ink & Chemical, Tokyo, Japan; Kawamura, Mus Mod Art, Tokyo, Japan; exec offs, St Paul Reinsurance Mgt, NY; Cong Off, Cong Dioguard, Washington, DC. *Exhib:* 9th Small Works Exhib, Wash Sq Galleries, New York, 85; New Art USA, Isis Gallery, Long Island, NY, 86; Ann Exhibs, Bergen Mus Arts Sci, Paramus, NJ, 87 & 89; Metro Show, City Without Walls Gallery, Newark, NJ, 88; Other Realities, Jadite Gallery, New York, 88; solo exhib, William Carlos Williams Ctr Performing Arts, Rutherford, NJ, 88; Centennial Exhib, Jehangir Gallery, Bombay, India, 89. *Awards:* Fourth Prize, New Art USA, Isis Gallery, 86; Irwin Z Lowe Mem, Fed Plaza, Nat Asn Women Artists, New York, 88; Contemporary Art/Painting Award, Westbeth Galleries, Am Soc Contemp Artists, 90. *Bibliog:* Helen A Harrison (auth), Winners in a juried show whose novelty is in its concept, NY Times, 4/13/86; John Zeaman (auth) A clearer picture at Bergen Museum, Record, 1/3/88; Jerry Tallmer (auth), Art's sexism gets a good once-over, NY Post, 8/4/89. *Mem:* Am Soc Contemp Artists; NJ Women's Caucus Art; Nat Asn Women Artists (foreign exchange co-chmn, 88-89); Salute Women Arts (regional, pres, 90-92). *Media:* Collage, monoprint, mixed media. *Mailing Add:* 115 Dwight Place Englewood NJ 07631

NILSSON, GLADYS
PAINTER
b Chicago, Ill, May 6, 40. *Study:* Art Inst Chicago, dipl, 62. *Work:* Mus Mod Art, New York; Whitney Mus Am Art; Mus Contemp Art, Chicago; Art Inst Chicago; Mus Mod Kunst, Vienna. *Exhib:* The Hairy Who, Dupont Ctr, Corcoran Gallery Art, 69; Poetic Fantasy, San Francisco Mus Art, 71; Chicago Imagist Art, Mus Contemp Art, Chicago, 72; one-person exhib, Whitney Mus Am Art, 73; The Koffler Foundation Chicago Currents, Smithsonian Inst, 79; Parallel Vision: Modern Artists and Outsider Art, Los Angeles Co Mus (traveling exhib), 92-93. *Media:* Watercolor. *Mailing Add:* 1035 Greenwood Ave Wilmette IL 60091

NIND, JEAN
PAINTER, PRINTMAKER
b Miri, Sarawak, Borneo, June 17, 30; Can citizen. *Study:* Chelsea Art Sch, London, Eng; Univ Sask, Can, studied with Otto Rogers & Eli Bornstein. *Work:* Sask Power Corp, Regina; Esso Can Ltd, Vancouver, BC; Trent Univ, Peterborough, Ont; Volvo Corp, Halifax, NS; Sir Sandford Fleming Col, Peterborough, Ont. *Comn:* Symphony (oil), comn by mem bd, Saskatoon Symphony, Sask, 64; five serigraphs (for presentation to guest speakers), Trent Univ, Peterborough, Ont, 69. *Exhib:* Ont Soc Artists 99th & 101st Ann Juried Exhib, Toronto; Kingston Spring Exhibs, Agnes Etherington Art Ctr, Ont, 69; one-person shows, Artspace, Ont, 75, 77, 78 & 88, Bau-xi Gallery, Toronto & Vancouver, 78 & 79 & Williamson House Gallery, Peterborough, Ont, 88 & 90; Art Gallery Peterborough, 81 & 89; Lindsey Gallery, Ont, 89; Magic Image Gallery, Pickering Village, On, 92; and others. *Teaching:* Instr child art classes, Mendel Art Gallery, Saskatoon, Sask, 65-66; instr early childhood art, Sir Sandford Fleming Col, Peterborough, Ont, 69-71, instr painting, 73-77; instr painting, Trent Univ, Peterborough, Ont, 73-77. *Awards:* Prize Winner, Sask Exhib, Sask Arts Coun, 65; Purchase Award, Sir Sandford Fleming Col, Peterborough, Ont, 75; Merit Award, Ont Arts Coun, 74, 75, 89 & 90; Award Winner, Juried Show, The Lindsay Gallery, 87. *Bibliog:* Harry Underwood (auth), Spirit in the Art of Jean Nind, Globe & Mail, Toronto, 76; Colin Macdoneld (ed), Dictionary of Canadian Artists, Vol 5, Can Paperbacks, Ottawa, 77; Hennie Wolff (auth), The index of Ontario artists, 77; Printworld Inc, Bala Cynwyd, Pa, 87; Marketa Newman (auth), Biographical Dictionary of Saskatchewan Artists, Women, 90. *Mem:* Art Gallery Peterborough (mem bd, 72-78); Artspace, Peterborough, Ont (mem steering comt, 75); Visual Arts Ont; Art Gallery Ont, Toronto. *Media:* Oil on Canvas; Serigraphy. *Dealer:* Williamson House Gallery Peterborough ON. *Mailing Add:* 29 Merino Rd Peterborough ON K9J 6M8 Canada

NISULA, LARRY
PAINTER, SCULPTOR
b Phoenix, Ariz, Oct 10, 60. *Study:* Glendale Community Col, 83; self-taught painting. *Work:* Valley Nat Bank Corp Collection, Phoenix; Tavan Sch Masterpiece Collection, Phoenix; Nott Corp, Irving, Tex. *Comn:* Abstract

painting, comn by John Gibney Med Ctr, Scottsdale; sculpture, comn by Mr & Mrs Augustus Boss, Ramada Corp, Scottsdale. *Exhib:* Glendale Community Col Art Exhib, Glendale Community Col Mus, Ariz, 82; Mesa Sunburst Show, Mesa Mus, 83; Galeria Mesa, Mesa Mus, 85, 86; solo exhib, Phoenix Col, 85; Bell-Ross Gallery, Memphis, Tenn, 87; Fagen-Peterson Fine Art, Scottsdale, 87. *Awards:* Third Place Sculpture, Glendale Festival of Art, 82 & 84, First Place, 83. *Media:* Acrylic; Steel. *Publ:* Barbara Cortright (auth), Profile Larry Nisula, Zone Mag, spring 91. *Dealer:* Bell-Ross Gallery 1080 Brookfield Rd Memphis TN 38119; Fagen-Peterson Fine Art 7077 E Main St Scottsdale AZ 85251. *Mailing Add:* 1506 W Fillmore Phoenix AZ 85007

NIX, PATRICIA (LEA)
SCULPTOR, PAINTER
US citizen. *Study:* NY Univ, BA; New Sch Soc Res, with Anthony Toney; Art Students League. *Work:* Nat Mus Am Art, Smithsonian Inst, Washington, DC; Heckscher Mus, Huntington, NY; Univ Windsor, Can; Staten Island Mus, NY; Newport Harbor Mus, Calif; Credit Svisse, NY; and others. *Exhib:* One-woman show, New York Univ Contemp Arts Gallery, 80; Bodies & Souls, Artists Choice Mus, 83; New Acquisitions, Smithsonian Inst, 83; Staten Island Mus, NY; Galarie Zum Glass Haus, Switz; Virginia Lust Gallery, NY. *Awards:* Salzman Prize, Nat Arts Club Ann, 78 & 88 & 1st Prize 86; Cert of Hon for Oil Painting, Nat Acad Design, 87. *Mem:* Nat Acad Design Club; New York Artists Equity; Nat Arts Club. *Media:* Oil, Found Objects; Mixed. *Dealer:* Nerlino Gallery 96 Breene St New York NY 10012. *Mailing Add:* 15 Gramercy Park S New York NY 10003

NIXON, NICHOLS
PHOTOGRAPHER
b Detroit, Mich, 47. *Work:* Mus Mod Art, New York; Fogg Art Mus, Harvard Univ, Mass; Australian Nat Gallery, Canberra; San Francisco Mus Mod Art; Detroit Art Inst, Mich; Philadelphia Mus Art, Pa. *Exhib:* One-man exhibs, Inst Contemp Art, Boston, 82, Corcoran Gallery, Washington, DC, 83, Fraenkel Gallery, San Francisco, 84, Art Inst Chicago, 85, Pace-MacGill Gallery, New York, 86, Detroit Inst Arts, 89 & San Francisco Mus Mod Art, 89; American Photography in the 70's, Chicago Art Inst, 80; The Contact Print, Friends Photog, Carmel, Calif, 83; Santa Barbara Mus Art, Calif, 86; Photographs from the Last Decade, San Francisco Mus Mod Art, 87; Twelve Photographers Look at US, Philadelphia Mus Art, 87. *Awards:* Photog Fels, Nat Endowment Arts, 76, 80 & 87; Fels, Guggenheim Mem Found, 77 & 86; New Works Grant, Mass Coun Arts, 82. *Bibliog:* Renato Danese (ed), American Images, McGraw-Hill, 79; Ruth Silverman (auth), The Dog Observed, Knopf, 84; John Szarkowski (auth), 20th Century Photographs from the Museum of Modern Art, New York, 84; Peter Galessi (auth), Nicholas Nixon: Pictures of People, Mus Mod Art, New York, 88. *Mailing Add:* c/o Fraenkel Gallery 55 Grant Ave San Francisco CA 94108

NOBLE, HELEN (HARPER)
PRINTMAKER, PAINTER
b Northville, Mich, Mar 27, 22. *Study:* Wayne State Univ, 39-41; Western Reserve Univ, 42-43; Santa Barbara Art Inst, 70-72. *Exhib:* Nat Competition Watercolor Soc Ala, Birmingham Mus, 77, 79 & 81; Small Works National 81, Rochester, NY; Second Nat Print Exhib, Springfield, Ill, 82; 24th Ann Exhib Prints & Drawings, Oklahoma City, 82; Third Women in Art Exhib, Springfield, Ill, 83; Arts Festival, Santa Barbara, Calif, 85. *Awards:* Eight Awards, Santa Barbara Art Asn, 71-79;; Third Place, 41st Ann Minature Art Soc, Washington, DC, 74; Hon Mention Seventh Annual Exhib Miniature Art Soc, NJ, 77. *Mem:* Int Graphic Art Found; Contemp Arts Forum Santa Barbara. *Media:* Oil, Wood. *Dealer:* Fay Gold Gallery 247 Buckhead Ave Atlanta GA 30305; Yvonne Rapp Gallery 2007-C Frankfort Ave Louisville KY 40206. *Mailing Add:* 1702 Cliff Dr Santa Barbara CA 93109

NOBLE, JOHN A
PRINTMAKER, PAINTER
b Paris, France, Mar 17, 13; US citizen. *Study:* Nat Acad Design; also with father, John Noble. *Work:* Metrop Art Mus, New York; Carnegie Inst Int, Pittsburgh; New Britain Mus, Conn; South Street Seaport Mus, New York; Penobscot Marine Mus, Penobscot; and others. *Comn:* Lithograph commemorating Bayonne NY Centennial, 69; lithograph commemorating New York Diamond Jubilee, Staten Island CofC, 73; and others. *Exhib:* Ann Exhib, Nat Acad Design, 52-83; Comprehensive Exhib Oils & Print Mariner Mus, 65; Audubon Artists Ann; Am Soc Graphic Artists Ann; S St Seaport Gallery Exhib Oils & Lithographs, 75; Libr Cong, Nat Print Exhib. *Awards:* Five Purchase Prizes, Libr Cong, 50-; Audubon Artists Medal Honor, 56; Cannon Prize, 72 & Samuel Findley Breese Morse Medal of Honor, 75, Nat Acad Design. *Mem:* Academician Nat Acad Design; Audubon Artists; SAGA; Calif Printmakers; Print Club Albany. *Media:* Lithography; Acrylic, Oil. *Mailing Add:* 270 Richmond Terr Staten Island NY 10301

NOBLE, JOSEPH VEACH
MUSEUM DIRECTOR, MUSEOLOGIST
b Philadelphia, Pa, Apr 3, 20. *Study:* Univ Pa. *Collections Arranged:* Drug Scene, 71; Cityrama, 72; Revolution, 75; The Big Apple, 79. *Pos:* Vdir, Metrop Mus Art, 56-70; trustee, Corning Mus Glass, 69-; dir, Mus City of NY, 70-85; chmn, Brookgreen Gardens, 76-; exec dir, Soc Medalists, 85- *Teaching:* Instr filmmaking, City Col NY, 46-49. *Awards:* Medal, Nat Acad Design, 76; Medal, Nat Sculpture Soc, 78; Am Watercolor Soc Award, 82; Medal, Am Asn of Mus, 91. *Mem:* Archeol Inst Am (treas, 63-70); NY State Asn Mus (pres, 70-72); NY State Hist Trust (chmn, 72-75); Am Asn Mus (pres, 75-78). *Publ:* Auth, The Historical Murals of Maplewood, 61; coauth, An Inquiry into the Forgery of the Etruscan Terra-cotta Warriors, 61; auth, The Techniques of Painted Attic Pottery, 65. *Mailing Add:* 107 Durand Rd Maplewood NJ 07040

NOBLE, KEVIN
PAINTER
b Brooklyn, NY, 52. *Study:* State Univ Col, Buffalo, NY, BA, 75; State Univ NY, Buffalo, MFA, 78. *Exhib:* Solo exhibs, Artists' Space, New York & Cepa Gallery, Buffalo, 80, The Kitchen, New York, 81, White Columns, 86, Mednick Gallery, Philadelphia, 87, Frank Bernaducci Gallery, New York, 87 & Panopticon, Irish Art Ctr, New York, 91; A Decade of New Art, Artists' Space, New York, 84; Photo-Syntheseis, Frank Bernaducci Gallery, New York, 87; Belfast/Beirut, A Tale of Two Cities, Alternative Mus, New York, 89; Images of War, El Bohio, New York, 91; Bloody Sunday Show, Irish Arts Ctr, New York, 92. *Awards:* Artists Fel, Nat Endowment Arts, 79 & 87. *Mailing Add:* 51 Murray St New York NY 10007

NOCHLIN, LINDA (POMMER)
HISTORIAN, EDUCATOR
b New York, NY, Jan 30, 31. *Study:* Vassar Col, BA; Inst Fine Arts, NY Univ, PhD. *Teaching:* Mary Conover Mellon prof art, Vassar Col, 63-80; distinguished prof art hist, City Univ New York Grad Ctr, 80-90; prof art hist, Yale Univ, 90- *Awards:* Kingsley Porter Prize Best Article in Art Bulletin, 67; E Harris Harbison Award Gifted Teaching, 72; Am Coun Learned Soc Fel, 72-73; Frank Jewett Mather Prize Critical Writing, 77; Hon Dr, Colgate Univ, 87. *Res:* Painting and sculpture of 19th and 20th century. *Publ:* Auth, Mathis at Colmar, Red Dust, 63; Realism and Tradition in Art, 1848-1900, 66 & Impressionism and Post-Impressionism, 1874-1904, 66, Prentice-Hall; Realism, Penguin, 72; Gustave Courbet: A Study of Style & Society, 76; contribr, Art Bull, Art News, Art News Ann & Artforum; Woman Artists: 1550-1950, Alfred Knopf, 76; ed, Art & Architecture in the Service of Politics, MIT Press, 78; Courbet Reconsidered, Yale Univ Press, 88; Women, Art, Power & Other Essays, Harper & Row, 88. *Mailing Add:* 875 West End Ave New York NY 10025

NODA, TAKAYO
GRAPHIC ARTIST, PRINTMAKER
b Tokyo, Japan. *Study:* Art Students League, studied printmaking with Michael Ponce de Leon and Seong Moy, 79-83. *Work:* Honolulu Acad Arts, Hawaii; NJ State Coun Arts, Trenton; Educ Testing Serv, Princeton, NJ; Taller de Artistas Graficos Asociados, Caracas, Venezuela; Portland Art Mus, Ore. *Exhib:* Nat Print Exhib, Honolulu Acad Arts, Hawaii, 85; 16th Ann Exhib Boston Printmakers, Art Complex Mus, Duxbury, Mass, 88; Int Biennial Prints, Roopankar Mus Fine Arts, Bhalat Bhavav, India, 89; Silvermine Prints Int, Silvermine Guild Arts Ctr, New Canaan, Conn, 90; 165th Ann Exhib, Nat Acad Galleries, New York, 90; Nat Print Exhib, Alexandria Mus Art, La, 91; Nat Asn Women Artists, Bergen Mus Art & Sci, Paramar, NJ, 91; Silvermine Print Int, Silvermine Guild Arts Ctr, New Canaan, Conn, 92. *Awards:* First Prize, Nat Print Exhib, Silvermine Guild Ctr Arts, 83; Purchase Prize, Hawaii Nat Print Exhib, Honolulu Acad Arts, 85; Silver Medal Graphics, 47th Ann Exhib, Audubon Artists, 89; Eilzabeth Morse Genius Award, 102nd Ann Exhib of Nat Asn Women Artists; Gold Medal Honor, 50th Ann Exhib Audubon Artists, 92. *Bibliog:* Geraldine E Rhoads (ed), It's all in a woman's day, Woman's Day Mag, Fawcett Publ, 3/70. *Mem:* Silvermine Guild Ctr Arts; Boston Printmakers; Soc Am Graphic Artists; Audubon Artists; Pen Brush. *Media:* Graphics, collage-relief. *Dealer:* Galerie Select Ltd Manfred E Huffman 56 Univ Place New York NY 10003; Reece Gallery 24 W 57th St New York NY 10019. *Mailing Add:* Five Charles St New York NY 10014

NODINE, JANE ALLEN
PAINTER, DESIGNER
b Spartanburg, SC, Mar 14, 54. *Study:* Western Carolina Univ, Cullowhee, 72-73; Univ SC, Columbia, BFA, 76, MFA, 79; Kent State Univ, 78. *Work:* Bankers Trust of SC & Fed Reserve Bank Richmond, Charlotte, NC; Palmetto Bank & Trust, SC; two Stouffers Hotels, NC; Capital South Inc, SC; Buyers Communs Systems, Atlanta, Ga; and others. *Exhib:* S E Juried Exhibition, Famos Mus, Mobile, Ala, 90; Ky Exhib of SC Artists, Owensboro Mus, 91; This Year's Model, Greenville Mus Art, SC, 91; SC Expressions, Columbia Mus Art, 92; SC Triennial, SC State Mus Art, 92; Southern Exposure, New York, 92; and many others. *Teaching:* Instr, Greenville Mus, SC, 79-80, Presby Col, Clinton, SC, 80-, Wofford Col, Spartanburg, SC, 81 & 83 & Sacred Heart Col, Belmont, NC, 82-; Converse Col, Spartanburg, SC, 90; Univ SC, Spartanburg, 90-92. *Awards:* Best in Show, Spoleto Competition, Charleston, SC, 83; SC Art; Spartanburg Arts Coun Grant, 89; and others. *Mem:* Col Art Asn; Am Crafts Coun. *Media:* Acrylic; Metal. *Dealer:* Mary Praytor Gallery 26 Main St Greenville SC. *Mailing Add:* 113 Rockwood Dr Spartanburg SC 29301

NOE, JERRY LEE
SCULPTOR, EDUCATOR
b Harlan Co, Ky, Sept 27, 40. *Study:* Univ Ky, BA; Art Inst Chicago, Ford Found Scholar, MFA. *Exhib:* Sculpture 70, Art Inst Chicago, 70; Forty Years of American Landscape, Gimpel-Wietzenhoffer Gallery, New York, 73; Nat Sculpture Traveling Exhib, 73-75; Contemporary Reflections, 1973-74, Aldrich Mus Art, Ridgefield, Conn, 74; Southeast 7, Southeastern Ctr Contemp Art, Winston-Salem, NC, 77; one-man shows, Henri Gallery, 77 & Mercer Gallery, 77. *Teaching:* Sculptor, Young Artists Studio, Art Inst Chicago, 69-71; vis lectr sculpture, Wis State Univ, Whitewater, 70-71; assoc prof art, Univ NC, Chapel Hill, 71- *Awards:* John Quincy Adams Traveling Fel, 71; First Place, 73 & Third Place, 75, Southern Asn Sculptors; Nat Endowment Arts Grant, 77; and others. *Bibliog:* B J Ott (auth), Artist builds bridge, Buffalo Courier Newspaper, 75; Fun & games at art park, New York Times Sunday Ed, 75; and others. *Mem:* Southern Asn Sculptors (mem bd dirs, 74-75, conf chmn, 75, exhib chmn, 75); Col Art Asn; Southeastern Col

Art Conf; Southeastern Ctr Contemp Art. *Media:* Neon, Mixed. *Publ:* Coauth, Neon--The Artist (film), Res Coun, Univ, NC, 75. *Dealer:* Henri Gallery 1500 21st St NW Washington DC 20036. *Mailing Add:* 2008 Ridgewood Rd Chapel Hill NC 27516

NOEL, DONALD CLAUDE
SCULPTOR
b Blue Island, Ill, Aug 2, 30. *Study:* St Norbert Col, De Pere, Wis, BA(philos), 57; Univ Wis, Madison, MA(libr sci), 63; Rosary Col, Grad Sch Fine Arts: Villa Schifanoia, Florence, Italy, MFA(sculpture), 83. *Work:* Inter Sculpture Garden, Marusici, (Istria) Croatia. *Comn:* Norbert of Xanten, St Norbert Col, DePere, Wis, 84; James Kenneth Allen (7' bronze), Morris, Ill, 88; The De Pere History Walk, De Pere Hist Walk Trust, Wis, Forthcoming. *Exhib:* One man show, Galeri ja di Villa Schifanoia, Florence; Ten Pietrasanta Pieces, The Tree Studios, Chicago, Ill, 83; Matter Over Mind, Fermi Lab Nat Atomic Accelorater, Batavia, Ill, 91. *Pos:* Sculptor & Owner, The Open Sea Sculpture Studio, Green Bay, Wis, 83- *Mem:* Inter Sculpture Ctr, Washington, DC; assoc mem Nat Sculpture Soc, New York; Chicago Artists Coalition. *Mailing Add:* 1406 Main St Green Bay WI 54302

NOEL, GEORGES
PAINTER, SCULPTOR
b Beziers, France, Dec 25, 24. *Study:* Studied in France. *Work:* Albright-Knox Art Gallery, Buffalo, NY; Chase Manhattan Bank, New York; Aldrich Mus of Contemp Art, Ridgefield, Conn; Centre Nat d'Art, Contemporain, Paris; Mus Mod Art, New York; Schlumberger Co, Paris; Guggenheim Mus, New York; National Galerie, Berlin. *Comn:* Painting, Cité de la Musique, Paris. *Exhib:* Galerie Municipale d'Art Contemporain, Saint-Priest, Musee de Brou, Bourg en Bresse-Centre National des Arts Plastiques, Paris/New York, Arnold Herstand Co, 88 & 90; Galerie Nothelfer, Berlin, Ger, 89 & 92; Arnold Herstand Co, New York, 88 & 90; Denis Hotz Fine Art Ltd, London, 90; Lorenzelli Arte, Milan, Italy, 90; Galerie Sander, Darmstadt, Ger & Zurich, Switz, 91; Galerie Baumgarten, Freiburg, Ger, 91; Base Gallery, Tokyo, 91 & 92. *Teaching:* Instr, Minneapolis Sch Arts, 68-69. *Media:* Multi. *Dealer:* Arnold Herstand 24 W 57th St New York NY 10019. *Mailing Add:* 16 Greene St New York NY 10013

NOEL, JEAN
SCULPTOR
b Montreal, Que, Can, 1940. *Study:* Assumption Col, Worcester, Mass, 60; Ecole des Beaux-Arts, Montreal, Que, 63. *Work:* Assumption Col, Worcester, Mass; Musée des Beaux-Arts, Montreal; Musée d'Art Contemporain, Montreal; Galerie Nationale du Can, Ottawa; Musée nat D'Art Moderne, Paris. *Exhib:* One-man shows, Musée du Que, 81, Centre Cult Can, Paris, 83 & Galerie Gabrielle Maubrie, Paris, 83 & 84; Musée de Toulon, France, 82; Art Bank, Can Coun, Montreal & Vancouver, 82; Photosequences, Art Gallery Peterborough, Ont, 83; Avec Plastiques et Plasticiens, Musée de Martiques, Centre Georges Pompidou, Paris, 84; Galerie Krief, Paris, 87-89; plus many other one-man & group shows. *Teaching:* Instr, Parsons Sch Design, Paris, France, 82-88. *Mailing Add:* 4 Rue Git-le-Coeur Paris 75006 France

NOESTHEDEN, JOHN
SCULPTOR
b Amsterdam, Holland, 1945. *Study:* Univ Windsor, BA, 72, Tulane Univ, New Orleans, La, MFA, 75. *Work:* Mint Mus Art, Charlotte, NC; General Foods, Toronto, Ont; Dept External Affairs, Ottawa, Ont; Cineplex Odeon, Houston, Tex; Can Coun Art Bank, Ottawa. *Exhib:* Solo exhibs, Brampton Pub Libr & Art Gallery, Ont, 84, Durham Art Gallery, Ont, 87; Second Anniversary Exhib, Mississauga Civic Centre Art Gallery, Ont, 89; traveling exhib, McLarin Art Centre, Barrie, Ont, Art Gallery of Hamilton, Ont & Koffler Centre Gallery, Toronto, 90; Extension (with catalog), Print & Drawing Gallery of Can, Toronto, 90. *Bibliog:* John Bentley Mays (auth), John Noestheden, Olga Korper Gallery, Globe & Mail, Toronto, 1/8/87; Jean Marc Boileau (auth), Noestheden, Shuebrook, Andrews, Liason St Louis, Montreal, 4/29/87; Jim Algie (auth), Nature Becomes Art, Sun Times, Owen Sound, 5/21/88. *Mailing Add:* c/o Olga Korper Gallery 17 Morrow Ave Toronto ON M6R 2H9 Canada

NOFER, FRANK
PAINTER, GRAPHIC ARTIST
b Philadelphia, Pa, Nov 5, 29. *Study:* Univ Arts, Univ Pa; Charles Morris Price Sch; pvt study with Maurice Molarsky. *Work:* Am Col; Ametek Inc; Mc Neil Pharmaceuticals Inc. *Comn:* City logotypes of Philadelphia, 74, New York, 75, Boston, 76, San Diego, 77, New Orleans, 78, Chicago, 79 & San Antonio, 80. *Exhib:* One-man shows, Newman Galleries, Ris Galleries, Philadelphia Cricket Club, Hahn Chestnut Hill Gallery, Philadelphia. *Awards:* Ralph Pallen Coleman Award; First W Emerton Heitland Memorial Award; Dawson Mem; Harrison Morris Prize; Four John Geiszel Mem Awards; Am Watercolor Soc Walser S Greathouse Medal, 86; Woodmere Mus Ann Watercolor Prize, 87. *Bibliog:* Art Matters, Exhib Review, 11/88. *Mem:* Philadelphia Art Dir Club (vpres); Artist's Guild of Delaware (graphics chmn); Whitemarsh Community Art Ctr (pres); Philadelphia Watercolor Club (bd mem); Am Watercolor Soc (full mem, 91); Woodmere Art Mus. *Media:* Watercolor, Acrylic; All Media. *Publ:* contrib ed, The Artist's Mag, 1/87; auth, How to Make Watercolor Work for You, Northlight Publ. *Dealer:* Newman Galleries 1625 Walnut Street Philadelphia Pa 19103; Ris Galleries Stone Harbor NJ. *Mailing Add:* 501 Dogwood Lane Conshohocken PA 19428

NOFFKE, GARY L
GOLDSMITH
b Decator, Ill, Aug 27, 43. *Study:* Southern Ill Univ, MFA, 69. *Work:* Am Craft Mus, New York; Mint Mus, Charlotte, NC; Nat Ornamental Metal Mus, Memphis, Tenn; Melbourne State Col, Victoria, Australia; McDougal Art Gallery, Christ Church, NZ. *Exhib:* Masters in Am Metalsmithing, Nat Ornamental Metal Mus, Memphis, 89; Silver-Now Forns & Expressions, Fortunoff's Silver Co, New York, 90; Vessels: From Use to Symbol, Am Craft Mus, New York, 90; retrospective, Kohler Arts Ctr, Sheboygan, Wis, 91. *Teaching:* Prof artt, Univ Ga-Athens, 71- *Mailing Add:* PO Box 776 Farmington GA 30608

NOGGLE, ANNE
PHOTOGRAPHER, EDUCATOR
b Evanston, Ill, June 12, 22. *Study:* Univ NMex, BFA(art hist), MA(art), with Van Deren Coke, hon DFA, 91. *Work:* San Francisco Mus Mod Art; Mus Mod Art, New York; Nat Gallery Can; Bibliot Nat, France; Denver Art Mus; plus others. *Exhib:* Solo exhibs, San Francisco Mus Modern Art, 80, Mus Contemp Photog, Chicago, 84, Camerawork, San Francisco, 85, Photogs Gallery, London, 88, Gallery Fine Photog, New Orleans, 89, Derby, Eng, 90, Ashton-Under-Lyne Mus, Eng, 90 & Amon Carter Mus, 91; Jonson Gallery, Univ NMex, 89; Stables Gallery, Taos, NMex, 89; Fine Arts Mus NMex, Santa Fe, 90; Ind Univ Art Mus, 90; The Forum Gallery, Jamestown Community Col, NY, 90; and others. *Collections Arranged:* Laura Gilpin Retrospective (with catalog), 74; Women of Photography: A Historical Survey (catalog, with Margery Mann). *Pos:* Cur photog, Mus Fine Art, Santa Fe, NMex, 70-76. *Teaching:* Adj prof art, Univ NMex, currently. *Awards:* Guggenheim Fel Grant, 82; Nat Endowment Arts (fel photog, 75, 78 & 88). *Bibliog:* J Z Grover (auth), Anne Noggle's insightful images, Artweek, 10/76; Self-Portrayal: the Photographers Image, Friends of Photog, Carmel, Calif, 78; Van Deren Coke (auth), History of Photography in New Mexico, Univ NMex Press, 79; plus others. *Mem:* Soc Photog Educ; All Russia Art Photogs Union. *Res:* Three years research on Soviet airwomen in World War II, 90-92. *Publ:* Auth, Prestidigitation, eyesight & hindsight, Album Mag, 70; auth, The long skinny photography of Captain Anne Noggle, Camera 35, 73; photographs, Silver Lining, Univ NMex Press, 84; auth, For God, Country & the Thrill of It: Women Airforce Service Pilots in WWII (photogs & text), Tex A & M Univ Press, 90; A Dance with Death: Personal memoirs of Soviet Airwomen in WWII (text & photogs), Tex A & M Univ Press (in press). *Mailing Add:* 1204 Espanola NE Albuquerque NM 87110

NOLAN, MARGARET PATTERSON
LIBRARIAN
b New York, NY. *Study:* Col Mt St Vincent, BA(magna cum laude); Columbia Univ, MA. *Pos:* Asst librn photog & slides, Metrop Mus Art, New York, 58-61, chief photog & slide libr, 61-68, chief librn photog & slide libr, 68- *Teaching:* Vis lectr, Queens Col City Univ New York, 74-75. *Mem:* Asn Am Mus; Col Art Asn; Art Libr Soc North Am. *Res:* Color film: its properties and conservation; organization of collections of visual resources for art history. *Interests:* Western decorative arts, particularly 19th and 20th century American. *Mailing Add:* 530 E 90th St New York NY 10128

NOLAND, KENNETH
PAINTER, PRINTMAKER
b Asheville, NC, Apr 10, 1924. *Study:* Black Mountain Col, 46-48 & 50; also with Ossip Zadkine, Paris, 48-49. *Work:* Guggenheim Mus, Mus Mod Art, Metrop Mus Art & Whitney Mus Am Art, New York; Mus Fine Arts, Boston; Art Inst Chicago; Los Angeles Co Mus Art; Nat Gallery Art, Washington, DC; Teatre Mus, London, Eng; Australian Nat Gallery, Canberra. *Exhib:* Masters of the Fifties: American Abstract Painting from Pollack to Stella, Marisa del Re Gallery, NY, 85; New York/New Art Now 85 ARCA Marseille, ARCA Centre d'Art Contemporairi, France, 85; Contemporary American Monotypes, Chrysler Mus, Norfolk, Va, 85; An American Renaissance: Painting and Sculpture Since 1940, Mus Art, Ft Lauderdale, Fla, 86; one-person exhibs, Gallery One, Toronto, Can, 88, Hokin Gallery, Bay Harbor Islands, Fla, 89, Heath Gallery, Atlanta, Ga, 89, Salander-O'reilly Galleries Inc, NY, 89; Helander Gallery, Palm Beach, Fla, 90; Salander-O'Reilly Galleries Inc, Beverly Hills, Calif, 90; Edmonton Art Gallery, Alberta, Can, 90-91; Albright-Knox Art Gallery, NY; Art Inst Chicago, Ill; Baltimore Mus Art, Md; Corcoran Gallery Art, Washington, DC; Solomon R Guggenheim Mus, NY; Los Angeles County Mus Art; Metrop Mus Art, NY; Mus Mod Art, NY; Nat Gallery Art, Washington, DC; Walker Art Ctr, Minneapolis, Minn; Whitney Mus Am Art, NY. *Pos:* Bd of trustees, Bennington Col, 85- *Teaching:* Inst Contemp Art, Washington, 49-51; Cath Univ, Washington, 51-60; Washington Workshop Ctr for Arts, 52-56; Milton Avery Prof Arts, Bard Col, Annandale-on-Hudson, NY, 85; First Artist in Residence, Computer Video Arts, Pratt Inst, NY, 86-87. *Bibliog:* Contemporary American Monotypes (exhib catalog), Chrysler Mus, Norfolk, Va, 85; Gene A Mittler (auth), Art in Focus, Bennett & McKnight Publ Co, Peoria, Ill, 86; New York New Art Now 85, ARCA Marseille (exhib catalog), ARCA Centre d'Art Contemporain, 7/9-8/31/85. *Dealer:* Salander-O'Reilly Galleries Inc 20 E 79th St New York NY 10021. *Mailing Add:* 125A Kitchawan Rd South Salem NY 10590

NOLAND, WILLIAM
SCULPTOR
b Washington, DC, May 13, 54. *Study:* Hampshire Col, with Gary Hudson & Leonard Delonga, 72-74; Sarah Lawrence Col, with Lou Sgroi & Mary Miss, BA, 77. *Exhib:* Solo exhib, Va Polytechnic Inst Art Gallery, 81; New Works in Clay III, Everson Mus Art, 81; Sculpture Invitational, Tibor de Nagy Gallery, New York, 81; Contemporary Art in Detroit Collections,

Detroit Inst Arts, 82; Five American Artists, Galeria Joan Prats, New York, 83. *Bibliog:* Gene Baro (auth), article, Art Int, 8-9/81; Jo Ann Lewis (auth), article, Washington Post, 11/5/81; Valentin Tatransky (auth), article, Arts, 1/84. *Media:* Metal. *Mailing Add:* c/o Galeria Joan Prats 24 W 57th St New York NY 10019

NOLD, CARL R
MUSEUM DIRECTOR, HISTORIAN
b Mineola, NY, Nov 26, 55. *Study:* St Johns Univ, Jamaica, NY, BA(hist), 77; Cooperstown Grad Prog, MA(mus studies), 82. *Pos:* Registr, NY State Hist Asn, Cooperstown, 78-80; dir, Gadsby's Tavern Mus, Alexandria, Va, 80-84 & State Mus Pa, 84- *Mem:* Am Asn Mus; Am Asn State & Local Hist; Mid Atlantic Asn Mus (bd mem, 87-88); Cooperstown Grad Asn (bd mem, 85-88). *Publ:* Auth, Co-op docents: Volunteer management, Hist News, Am Asn State & Local Hist, 84; coauth, Gadsby's Tavern Museum Interpretive Master Plan, Alexandria, Va, 85. *Mailing Add:* c/o The State Mus Pa Box 1026 Harrisburg PA 17108-1026

NOLTE, GUNTER
SCULPTOR, DRAFTSMAN
b Gottingen, Ger, Jan 28, 38; Can citizen. *Study:* Sir George Williams Univ, BA, 70; Concordia Univ, Montreal, MFA, 76. *Work:* Winnipeg Art Gallery; Mus des Beaux Arts & Mus d'Art Contemp, Montreal; Art Bank Collection, Ministry External Affairs Ottawa & Lavalin Collection. *Comn:* Five kinetic fiberglass sculptures, North West Mall, Calgary, Alta, 70-71. *Exhib:* Quebec Sculpture, 1945-1970, Mus Rodin, Paris, 70; Installation, NS Col Art & Design, Halifax, 73; Mus d'Art Contemp (with catalog), Montreal, 78; Galerie Optica, Montreal, 78; solo exhibs, Etherington Art Ctr (with catalog), Kingston, 83, Can Cult Ctr (with catalog), Paris, 84; Architectural Marquettes, Sch Archit, Univ Waterloo, Ont, 85; Fountain Competition, Fac Archit, Univ Toronto, Ont, 85. *Teaching:* Assoc prof art hist, drawing & sculpture, Univ Ottawa, 77- *Awards:* First Prize, Sculpture, 11th Winnipeg Show, Winnipeg Art Gallery, 68; Arts Bursaries, Can Coun, 71-73; Project Cost Grant, Ont Arts Coun, 80. *Media:* Wood, Steel; Metallic Paints, Papers. *Dealer:* Art 45 2155 rue McKay Montreal PQ H3G 2J2 Canada. *Mailing Add:* Fournier Ottawa ON K0B 1G0 Canada

NONAS, RICHARD
SCULPTOR
b New York, NY 36. *Work:* Mus Contemp Art, Los Angeles, Calif; Mus Mod Art, New York; Moderna Museet,Stockholm, Sweden. *Exhib:* One-man exhibs, Ink, Zurich, Switz, 79, Oil & Steel Gallery, NY, 80, Hudson River Mus, Yonkers, NY, 81 & Univ Mass, Amherst, 82; Drawing, Hal Bromm Gallery, 79; Sculpture at the Coliseum, Inst Art & Urban Resources, Long Island City, NY, 80; Studio La Citta, Verona, Italy, 81; Construction and Process, Lodz, Poland, 82; Hoshour Gallery, Albuquerque, NMex, 83-84; Galeria Zapiecek, Warsaw, Poland, 84-85; Pori Art Mus, Finland, 86; Mus Mod Art, Wakayama, Japan, 87; Anders Tomberg Gallery, Lund, Sweden, 90. *Bibliog:* Jonathan Crary (auth), Richard Nonas: Boundary works, Artforum, 4/78; Donald Kupsit (auth), rev, Art in Am, 3/81; Grace Glueck (auth), An art blackout in Poland, 1/24/82. *Publ:* Auth, Summer 1906, 73, My Life on the Floor, 75 & Lost in Spoleto, 76, Buffalo Press; Hotel, 80, Boiling Coffee, 80 & Goats Itch (sound tape), 82, Tanam Press; auth, Richard Nonari Sculpture 1970-1988, Ace Contemp Exhibits, 88. *Dealer:* Ace Contemporary Exhibitions 5514 Wilshire Blvd Los Angeles CA 90036. *Mailing Add:* 14 Harrison St New York NY 10003

NONG
PAINTER, SCULPTOR
b Seoul, Korea, Oct 10, 30; US citizen. *Study:* Self-taught. *Work:* Nat Mus Hist, Taipei, Taiwan; Musee Nat Beaux-Arts, Monte Carlo, Monaco; Nat Gallery Mod Art, New Delhi, India; Asian Art Mus San Francisco; Nat Mus Mod Art, Seoul, Korea; and others. *Exhib:* Nat Collection Fine Arts, Smithsonian Inst, 61; Denver Art Mus, 65; Oakland Art Mus, 71; one-man exhibs, Nat Mus Hist, Taipei, Taiwan, 71, Nat Mus Mod Art, Seoul, Korea, 75 & Consulate Gen Repub Korea, New York, 83; San Francisco Mus Art, 72; and many others including Salons in Paris. *Awards:* Lett Appreciation Achievement Art, Minister Cult & Info, Repub Korea, 71; Cert Distinguished Achievement, State Calif, 82; Proclamation, City & Co San Francisco, 82. *Media:* Multimedia. *Publ:* Auth, Nong Questions, 82. *Mailing Add:* 345 Stockton St San Francisco CA 94108

NORDHAUSEN, A HENRY
PAINTER
b Hoboken, NJ, Jan 25, 01. *Study:* NY Sch Fine & Appl Art; Royal Acad Fine Art, Munich, Ger; Kunst Geverve Schule, Munich; Mass Inst Technol; New Sch Social Res. *Work:* Cleveland Mus Fine Art; Columbus Art Mus, Ga; New Brit Mus, Conn; Syracuse Univ; Pentagon, Washington, DC; and others. *Comn:* Several portraits, Syracuse Univ, Pentagon, Royal Crown Cola Co, Columbus, Ga, Ga Inst Technol, Atlanta & Ga Power Co, plus many others. *Exhib:* Metrop Mus Art; Nat Acad Design, New York; Glass Palace, Munich; Art Inst Chicago; Corcoran Gallery, Washington, DC; and others. *Pos:* Lectr, Metrop Mus Art & Brooklyn Mus Art. *Teaching:* Instr portraits, Roerich Mus; instr art, New York High Schs; instr art, Musemont, Columbus. *Awards:* MacDowell Colony Fel; Trask Found Fel; Tiffany Found Fel; and others. *Mem:* Am Watercolor Soc; Salmagundi Club; Artist Fel (vpres); Dutch Treat Club; Explorers Club; plus others. *Media:* Oil, Watercolor. *Dealer:* Grand Cent Art Gallery Biltmore Hotel Madison Ave E & 43rd New York NY 10017; Capricorn Gallery 8003 Woodmont Ave Bethesda MD 20014. *Mailing Add:* 1108 16th Ave Columbus GA 31906

NORDIN, PHYLLIS E
SCULPTOR, DESIGNER
b Chicago, Ill. *Study:* Beloit Col & Wayne State Univ, 54-56; Univ Toledo, BS, 62, BA(cum laude), 74; Toledo Mus Art, grad, 74, Univ Toledo, Minneapolis, 92. *Work:* Sylvania Chamber Commerce, Ohio; Town Ctr Mall, Port Charlotte, Fla; Univ Toledo; Beloit Col, Wis; Lucas Co Main Libr, Toledo, Ohio; Fort Defiance Park, Defiance, Ohio. *Comn:* Playmates (bronze), Treasure Coast Mall, Stuart, Fla; Beloved Son (bronze), Christ Presby Church, Toledo; Time Out (bronze), Ore, Ohio Branch Libr; Discovery (bronze), Port Clinton, Ohio Libr; Spiritus (ferro-cement), Flower Hosp, Sylvania, Ohio; and others. *Exhib:* Ann Sculpture & Ceramic Show, Butler Inst Am Art, 68-78; Liturgical Arts Nat, McFall Gallery, Bowling Green State Univ, 81 & 83; Liturgical Art Guild Ohio Ann, Schumacher Gallery, Capital Univ, 81 & 83; Allied Artists Am Ann, Nat Acad Galleries, NY, 84; N Am Sculpture Exhib, Far Hills Gallery, Golden, Colo, 84; Audubon Artists Ann Exhib, Nat Arts Club, New York, 87; and others. *Teaching:* Instr, Lourdes Col, Sylvania, Ohio, University of Toledo; instr, ceramics & sculpture, home studio. *Awards:* First Prize, 43rd Ann Nat Art Exhib, Cooperstown Art Asn, NY, 78; Alpha Award, Best of Show, Energy Art Nat Exhib, Foothills Art Ctr, Golden, Colo, 83. *Bibliog:* Louise Bruner (auth), Toledo, city of sculptures, Blade, 80; M Biedron (ed), On the cover, Radio Listener, WGTE Pub Radio, 80; J Hayes (auth), Contemporary sculpture alive, Columbus Dispatch, 82. *Mem:* Nat Asn Women Artists; Ohio Designer Craftsmen; Interfaith Forum Religion, Art & Archit; Liturgical Art Guild Ohio; Toledo Arts Comn (bd mem); Toledo Mod Art Group (trustee); Catharine Lorillard Wolfe Art Club. *Media:* Bronze, Welded Steel. *Publ:* Auth, Downtown churches house treasures, Accent Arts, 80; contribr, Centennial Mall's crowning jewel, Alumnus, Univ Toledo, 80; Auxiliary presents sculpture, Toledo Hosp News, 81; Gallerie Women Artists, 90; Liturgical Art Guild Ohio, newsletter, 92. *Mailing Add:* 4035 Tantara Rd Toledo OH 43623

NORDLAND, GERALD JOHN
GALLERY DIRECTOR, CRITIC
b Los Angeles, Calif. *Study:* Univ Southern Calif, AB & JD. *Collections Arranged:* Gaston Lachaise (with catalog), Los Angeles Co Mus Art & Whitney Mus Am Art, 63-64; Richard Diebenkorn Retrospective, 64, Josef Albers, 65, Washington Color Painters, 65, Washington Gallery Mod Art, Washington, DC; John Altoon, Julius Bissier (with Guggenheim Mus), Robert Natkin, Al Held, Fritz Glarner, Paul Jenkins, Peter Voulkos Bronzes, and others, San Francisco Mus Art; Gaston Lachaise Retrospective (with Cornell Univ; catalog), 74, Alberto Burri (with Guggenheim Mus; catalog), 77, and others, Frederick S Wight Art Gallery, Univ Calif, Los Angeles; Richard DeVore 1972-1982, 83, Controversial Public Art (with catalog), 83, and others, Milwaukee Art Mus. *Pos:* Dean, Chouinard Art Sch, Calif Inst Arts, 60-64; dir, Washington Gallery Mod Art, 64-66, San Francisco Mus Art, 66-72, Frederick S Wight Galleries, Univ Calif, Los Angeles, 73-77 & Milwaukee Art Mus, 77-85; art consult, Chicago, 86- *Awards:* Lachaise Found Grant, 73; Guggenheim Found Fel, 85-86. *Res:* More than forty museum publications on twentieth century artists and movements, emphasizing American painting, sculpture and photography. *Publ:* Auth, Gaston Lachaise: The Man and His Work, Braziller, 74; ed, Richard Diebenkorn, Rizzoli Int, 87, Frank Lloyd Wright: In the Realm of Ideas, SIU Press, 88. *Mailing Add:* 645 W Sheridan Rd No 3FL-2 Chicago IL 60613-3316

NORDSTRAND, NATHALIE JOHNSON
PAINTER
b Woburn, Mass. *Study:* Bradford Jr Col; Barnard Col; Columbia Univ; also with Jay Connaway, Roger Curtis, Paul Strisik & Don Stone. *Work:* First Nat Bank Boston & Commercial/Union Assurance Co, Boston; A T & T & IBM , New York; Peabody Mus, Salem, Mass; and others. *Exhib:* Acad Artists Am, 67-92; Am Watercolor Soc Ann, 69-82; Allied Artists Am, 69-92; Salmagundi Club, New York, 73-90; Peabody Mus Permanent Collection, Salem, Mass; De Cordova Mus, Lincoln, Mass; Butler Inst of Am Art, Youngstown, Ohio; and others. *Pos:* Owner, Nordstrand Gallery, Rockport, Mass, 70-92; dir, North Shore Art Asn, 85-90. *Awards:* Bronze Medal, Catharine Lorillard Wolfe Art Club, 70; Gold Medal, Am Artists Prof League, 71 & 75; Louis E Seely Purchase Prize, 84 & Joseph Hartley Award, 89, Salmagundi Club; and over 165 other awards. *Bibliog:* Robert Kolbe (auth), Nathalie J Nordstrand poetry of the sea, Am Artist Mag, 9/72. *Mem:* Am Watercolor Soc; Allied Artists Am; Am Artists Prof League; Copley Soc (Copley Master); Guild Boston Artists (secy 82-83, bd dirs 88-92); and others. *Media:* Watercolor, Oil. *Publ:* Contribr, La Rev Mod, Paris, 72; auth, The salt wind and I, Palette Talk, winter 73 & 74; Palette Talk, Grumbacher Publ, 86. *Mailing Add:* 384 Franklin St Reading MA 01867

NORELLI, MARTINA ROUDABUSH
CURATOR
b Washington, DC, Oct 2, 42. *Study:* Mary Washington Col, Fredericksburg, Va, 60-62; George Washington Univ, DC, BA(art hist), 69, MA(museology), 72. *Collections Arranged:* Artist-Naturalists: Observations in the Americas (auth, catalog), 72, Birds (auth, catalog), 80, An American Perspective: Selections from the Bequest of Frank McClure (auth, catalog), 81, Werner Drews, Sixty-five Years of Printmaking (auth, catalog), 84, Art, Design and the Modern Corporation (auth, catalog), 85, Symbols and Ceremonies: Pueblo Indian Watercolors, 86, Figure Prints: Washington Print Club 11th Biennial Members' Exhibition (auth, catlog), 86, Close Focus: Prints, Drawings, & Photographs, 87, Nat Mus Am Art, Smithsonian Inst, Washington, DC; East Meets West: Chen Chi Watercolors (auth, catalog), Columbus Mus Art, Ga, 89; Naturally Drawn: Drawings from the Collection (auth, catalog), Leigh Yawkey Woodson Art Mus, Wausau, Wis, 92. *Pos:* Curatorial asst, Dimock

Gallery, George Washington Univ, DC, 68-69; secy, Dept Graphic Arts, Nat Mus Am Art, Smithsonian Inst, DC, 70-71, mus technician, 71-74, asst cur, 74-78, assoc cur, 78-91; independent curator, 91- *Awards:* Serv Award, Leigh Yawkey Woodson Art Mus, Wausau, Wis, 86; David Lloyd Kreeger Prize in Art History, George Washington Univ, DC, 88; Univ Fel, George Washington Univ, DC, 88-92. *Mem:* Print Coun Am; Am Asn Advancement Slavic Studies; Asn Advancement Baltic Studies; Col Art Asn. *Res:* American prints and drawings; Estonian 19th & 20th art; Wildlife art; German expressionism. *Publ:* Auth, American Wildlife Painting, Watson-Guptill, 75, Galahad Bks, 83; Hermitage, Leningrad, USSR, sv World Art Mus: Greenwood Press, 87; The Watercolors of Antoine-Louis Barye, In: Antoine-Louis Barye, The Corcoran Collection, Washington, DC, 88; John James Audubon, John Woodhouse Audubon & Vincent Gifford Audubon, SV, Allgemeineo Künstlerlexikon, Vol 5, Saur Verlag, Leipzig, 92; Drawing on Nature, Geelong Art Gallery, Melbourne, Australia, 92. *Mailing Add:* 11219 S Shore Rd Reston VA 22090

NORFLEET, BARBARA PUGH
CURATOR, EDUCATOR
b Lakewood, NJ. *Study:* Swarthmore, BA, 47; Harvard-Radcliffe, MA, 50 & PhD, 51. *Work:* Mus of Mod Art, New York City; Harvard Univ, Cambridge, Mass; Mus Fine Arts, Boston; Corcoran Gallery Art. *Exhib:* Boston Mus Fine Arts Arch, 83; Inst Contemp Art, Boston, 83; Mass Col Art, Boston, 85; Mus Art, Eugene, Ore, 86; Int Ctr Photography, New York, 87; Philadelphia Mus Art, Philadelphia, 87; Mus Mod Art, New York, 87. *Collections Arranged:* The Photography Archive on the Photographic Social History of the US; The Social Question: Social Reform at the Turn of the Century, Harvard & Mus Mod Art, 73. *Pos:* Cur, Harvard Univ, 72-; consult on art, numerous orgns, 73- *Teaching:* Sr lectr photog, Harvard Univ, Cambridge, 70-78. *Awards:* Nat Endowment Arts, 75, 79, 81, 83 & 84; MA Artists Fel, 82; Nat Endowment Arts Fel, 82; John Simon Guggenheim Fel, 84; MA Artists Fel in Photog, 87. *Media:* Photog. *Res:* Have compiled an archive of over 30,000 negatives and prints on the social history of the US from 1900-1970. *Publ:* Auth, Wedding, Simon & Schuster, 76 & 77; The Head and the Heart, Harvard Press, 78; The Champion Pig, 79 & Killing Time, Godine, 83; All the Right People, New York Graphic-Little Brown, 86; Manscape with Beasts, New York, Harry Abrams, 90. *Mailing Add:* Carpenter Ctr for the Visual Arts Harvard Univ Cambridge MA 02138

NORMAN, DOROTHY (S)
WRITER, PHOTOGRAPHER
b Philadelphia, Pa, Mar 28, 05. *Study:* Smith Col; Univ Pa. *Work:* Philadelphia Mus Art; Mus Mod Art, New York; San Francisco Mus Art; Boston Mus Fine Arts; Getty Mus, Los Angeles; Houston Mus Fine Arts; Amon Carter Mus, Ft Worth, Tex; San Antonio Mus; Int Ctr Photog, New York. *Exhib:* 60 Photographs & New Workers, Mus Mod Art; Selections from Dorothy Norman Collection, Philadelphia Mus Art, 68; A Sense of the Sacred, Cathedral of St John the Divine, 83; Beyond a Portrait (auth, catalog), Philadelphia Mus Art, 84; The Intimate Eye, Guild Hall, Southampton, NY, 86; Intimate Visions, Int Ctr Photog, 93; Intimate Visions: The Photographs of Dorothy Norman (catalog), 93; The Great Round (catalog), 93; and others. *Pos:* Assoc cur photog, New Orleans Mus Art, 77-79, sr cur, 79-83, consult, 82-85. *Bibliog:* William Wasserstrom (auth), Introd in Civil Liberties and the Arts, Syracuse Univ Press, 64. *Collection:* Contemporary and ancient symbolical art. *Publ:* Co-ed, America and Alfred Steiglitz, 34, rev ed, 79; ed, Selected Writings of John Marin, 49; auth, Alfred Stieglitz-An American Seer, 60; The Hero: Myth/Image/Symbol, 69; Alfred Steiglitz, an American Seer, winter 73; Indira Gandhi, Letters to an American Friend, Harcourt Brace, 85; Encounters: A Memoir, Harcourt Brace, 87; Essay, Aperture's Masters of Photography--Alfred Stieglitz, 89; Intro, The Hero Anchor NY, 90. *Mailing Add:* 124 E 70th St New York NY 10021

NORRIS, ANDREA SPAULDING
HISTORIAN, MUSEUM DIRECTOR
b Madison, Wis, Apr 2, 45. *Study:* Wellesley Col, BA, 67; NY Univ, MA, 69, cert(mus training), 70, PhD, 77; Mus Mgt Inst, Univ Calif, Berkeley, 80. *Exhib:* The Sforza Court, Milan in the Renaissance, 1450-1535, 88-89. *Pos:* Asst to dir, Yale Univ Art Gallery, 77-80; chief cur, Archer M Huntington Art Gallery, Univ Tex, Austin, 80-88; dir, Spencer Mus of Art, Univ Kans, Lawrence, 88- *Teaching:* Lectr art hist, Queens Col, City Univ New York, 73-74, Yale Univ, 78-79 & Univ Tex, Austin, 84-88; adj instr art hist, NY Univ, 76-77; adj prof art hist, Univ Kans, Lawrence, 88- *Awards:* Ford Found Mus Training Grant, 69-72. *Mem:* Col Art Asn Am; Renaissance Soc Am; Asn Art Mus Dirs. *Res:* Italian Renaissance painting and sculpture; medals; Gian Cristoforo Romano; Lombard Renaissance sculpture; art patronage in America. *Publ:* Coauth, Medals and Plaquettes from the Molinari Collection at Bowdoin Col, 76; contribr, Dizionario Biografico degli Italiani, Treccani, 77-81; auth, New-Found Works and Pollock's Career, In: Jackson Pollock: New-Found Works, Yale Univ Art Gallery, 78; Gian Cristoforo Romano: The courtier as medallist, In: Studies in the History of Art, 88; The Sforza of Milan, In: Schifanoia, 91. *Mailing Add:* Spencer Mus Art Univ Kans Lawrence KS 66045

NORRIS, (ROBERT) BEN
PAINTER
b Redlands, Calif, Sept 6, 10. *Study:* Pomona Col; Harvard Univ; Inst Art & Archeol, Sorbonne, Paris; also with Stanton MacDonald Wright, Jean Charlot, Max Ernst & Josef Albers. *Work:* Honolulu Acad Arts, Hawaii; Nat Collection Fine Arts, Washington, DC; Am Fedn Arts Mus Collection; Weatherspoon Mus, Greensboro, NC; Hawaii State Comn Cult & Arts; McNay Art Inst, San Antonio, Tex. *Comn:* Murals, First Hawaiian Bank, Honolulu, Royal Hawaiian Hotel, Honolulu & Royal Lahaina Hotel, Maui. *Exhib:* Six one-man shows, Honolulu Acad Arts, 36-58 & The Early Watercolors of Ben Norris 1932-1953, 93; Metrop Mus Mid-Century Exhib, 51; Whitney Mus, 61; Pacific Heritage, West Coast Mus & Berlin, Ger, 65; A M Sachs Gallery, New York, 79, 80 & 83; Belanthi Gallery, Brooklyn, 87-92; Encounters with Paradise (1778-1941), Honolulu Acad Arts. *Teaching:* From instr to prof art, Univ Hawaii, 37-76. *Awards:* Mary S Litt Medal, Am Watercolor Soc, 82. *Media:* Oil, Watercolor. *Mailing Add:* 231 Bedford Ave Brooklyn NY 11211

NORRIS, LEONARD MATHESON
CARTOONIST, ILLUSTRATOR
b London, Eng, Dec 1, 13; Can citizen. *Study:* Ont Col Art; Univ Windsor, Hon LLD, 74. *Work:* Nat Libr Can; Univ Mo; Pavilion of Humor, Montreal, Que; Winnipeg Art Gallery, Man; Vancouver Arch, BC Prov Arch & munic W Vancouver Arch. *Comn:* Can Pavilion Caricature, Nat Arch, 90. *Pos:* Art dir, Maclean Hunter, Toronto, Ont, 45-50; ed cartoonist, Vancouver Sun, 50- *Awards:* Nat Newspaper Award, Can Newspapers, Toronto, 62; Can News Hall of Fame, 79; Mem Order Brit Empire Military. *Bibliog:* Nat Film Bd, The Hecklers, Cartoon History of Can, 75; articles, Time Mag, Punch & Macleans. *Mem:* Asn Am Ed Cartoonists; Royal Can Acad Art. *Publ:* Illusr, Johan's Gift to Christmas, Scrivner US MacIntyre Douglas Can, 75. *Mailing Add:* 25 Chartwell Green 8737 212th St Langley BC V1M 3E8 Canada

NORRIS, MERRY
CONSULTANT, COLLECTOR
Study: Univ Calif, Berkeley, AA, 59; Univ Calif Los Angeles, 80. *Pos:* Co-founder, Mus Contemp Art, 80; consult, City Santa Monica Arts Comn, 83; mem bd dirs, Southern Calif Inst Arch, currently; pres, Cult Affairs Comn, Los Angeles, 84-90; mem bd dirs, Los Angeles Munic Art Gallery; exec comt, Los Angeles Task Force on Arts, 86-89. *Teaching:* Vis lectr, Calif State Univ, Fullerton, 79, Claremont Grad Sch Fine Arts, 81 & 88; Art Ctr Col Design, 90. *Awards:* Vesta Award; hon mem, AIA, Los Angeles. *Bibliog:* A new museum has an instant impact, The NY Times, 11/27/83; Cultural commission casts wary eye on the design of public architecture, Los Angeles Bus J, 2/8/88; Beauty from the bureaucracy, Los Angeles Times, 3/12/88; Los Angeles in search of stylish face 7/5/88, Angeles Mag, 90. *Mem:* Art Table. *Publ:* Auth, Daniel Weinberg, 12/89-1/90. *Mailing Add:* 1473 Oriole Dr Los Angeles CA 90069

NORRIS, WILLIAM A
COLLECTOR
b Turtle Creek, Pa, Aug 30, 27. *Study:* Princeton Univ, BA, 51; Stanford Univ, JD, 54. *Pos:* Founding pres, 79-82 & mem bd trustees, Mus Contemp Art, Los Angeles, 79; trustee, Craft & Folk Art Mus, Los Angeles, 79-87; circuit judge, US Ct Appeals, 9th circuit, Los Angeles, currently. *Collection:* Contemporary California paintings and sculpture. *Mailing Add:* Hon Ct of Appeals Ninth Circuit 17th Floor 312 N Spring St Los Angeles CA 90012

NORTH, JUDY
PAINTER
b Los Angeles, Calif, June 24, 37. *Study:* Los Angeles Art Inst; San Francisco Art Inst. *Work:* Los Angeles Co Mus, Security Pac Bank, Los Angeleseles; Mus Contemp Art, Chicago; Oakland Mus, Calif; Opera Plaza Restaurant, San Francisco, Calif; Boise Art Mus, Idaho; Madison Art Ctr, Wis. *Comn:* Stained Glass, Northbrae Community Church, 59; stained glass, Holy Name Jesus Christ, 63; stained glass, Salvation Army, 72; Portrait of Dean of Law Sch, Stanford Univ, 77. *Exhib:* Middle, East, West, South, Corcoran Gallery of Art, Washington, DC, Ft Worth Art Mus, Tex & La Jolla Mus of Contemp Art, Calif, 75; Other Work, San Francisco Mus Art, 76; one-woman shows, Quay Gallery, San Francisco, 76 & Purdue Univ, 79; Recent Acquisitions, Oakland Mus, 77; Fuller-Goldeen, 84 & 86; Pilchuck Fac Exhib, Seattle, Wash, 85; Am Realism, 20th Century Drawings & Watercolors, 85; Prichard Gallery, Idaho, 86; Monumental Image, Springfield, Mo, 86; and others. *Pos:* Staff designer, Actors Workshop, 60-64 & Cummings Stained Glass Studio, 63-65; designer, Bennington Col, 66-69. *Teaching:* Instr theatre design & stained glass, Bennington Col, 66-69; instr theatre design, Actors Workshop, San Francisco, 60-64; instr, Univ Calif, Davis, 83-86, Acad Art, San Francisco, 85 & Pilchuck Glass Sch, 85-88. *Awards:* L C Tiffany, Stained Glass, 66. *Bibliog:* Otto Regan (auth), New Glass, San Francisco Book Co, 77; Giacopetti (auth), Native Funk and Flash, Scrimshaw Press, 74 & Craze for quilts, Life Mag, 5/5/72. *Media:* Watercolor; Mixed. *Dealer:* Marion Parmenteer San Francisco Mus Gallery Ft Mason San Francisco CA. *Mailing Add:* 3 Tamarack Rd San Geronimo CA 94963

NORTON, MARY JOYCE
PAINTER, JEWELER
b Tampa, Fla. *Study:* Akron Univ; Ariz State Univ; color theory with Dorothy Fratt. *Work:* Honeywell Corp, Minneapolis, Minn; First Nat Bank, Phoenix; Houston Oil & Mineral Corp, Tex; IBM, Endicott, NY; Drexel, Burnham, Lambert, Scottsdale, Ariz. *Comn:* Gateway Hotel, Phoenix, 85. *Exhib:* Watercolor Biennial, Phoenix Art Mus, 70-72, Four-Corners Biennial, 71-73; 8 West Biennial, Colo Ctr Arts, 72-74; Southwestern Fine Arts Biennial, Mus NMex, 72-74; Joslyn Mus, Omaha, Nebr, 74; and others. *Awards:* Southwestern Purchase Prize, Yuma Fine Arts Ctr, 67 & 73; 19th Nat Sun Carnival Exhib, El Paso Mus Art, 77; Ariz Painting Nat Competition, Scottsdale Ctr Arts, Ariz, 77. *Bibliog:* Barbara Cortright (auth), Meet the circle, Phoenix Mag, 2/75 & The look of nature, the flow of paint, Artweek, 5/75; Rosemary Holusha (auth), Mary Joyce Norton, Art Voices S, 5-6/79. *Mem:* Nat Women's Caucus Art. *Media:* Acrylic; Mixed. *Mailing Add:* 10648 N 100th St Scottsdale AZ 85260

NORTON, PAUL FOOTE
HISTORIAN, EDUCATOR
b Newton, Mass, Jan 23, 17. *Study:* Oberlin Col, BA, 38; Princeton Univ, MFA, 47, PhD, 52. *Pos:* Mass State Hist Comn, 80-83; asst nat dir, Census Stained Glass Am, currently. *Teaching:* From asst prof to assoc prof hist art, Pa State Univ, University Park, 47-58; from assoc prof to prof hist art, Univ Mass, Amherst, 58-, chmn art dept, 58-71, Chmn Art History, 82-85 & 89-93. *Awards:* Fel, Am Coun Learned Socs, 51-52; Fulbright Sr Res Fel, 53-54; Nat Endowment Humanities Sr Fel, 71-72; and others. *Mem:* Soc Archit Historians (dir & ed jour, 59-64); Soc Archit Historians Gr Brit; Soc Francaise Archeol; Archeol Inst Am; Soc Preserv N Eng Antiquities; and others. *Res:* History of architecture; England and America in the 18th and 19th centuries; census of stained glass windows in America. *Publ:* Co-auth, Arts in America: the Nineteenth Century, 69; Amherst: A Guide to its Architecture, 75; Latrobe, Jefferson and the National Capitol, 77; ed, The Papers of Samuel McIntire, Architect, Salem, Mass, 78; auth, articles in J Soc Archit Historians, Art Bull, Britannica Encycl Am Art & Encycl World Biog; and others. *Mailing Add:* Dept of Art Univ of Mass Amherst Campus Amherst MA 01003

NORVELL, PATSY
SCULPTOR, ENVIRONMENTAL ARTIST
b Greenville, SC, July 13, 42. *Study:* Bennington Col, Vt, BA; study with David Smith; San Francisco Art Inst; Hunter Col, MA. *Comn:* Cooperheads, outdoor sculpture, Fed Courthouse, Bridgeport, Conn, Gen Serv Admin, 83-84;; Glass Jungle, environ glass installation, 4600 East-West Hwy, 84-88; Glass Passage, environ glass installation, Home Savings Am Tower, 87-88; New York Newstand, collab with Frances Halstand, AIA Pub Art Fund, 88, installation, New York, 93; renovation & art installation, Metrop Transportation Authority, Beverly & Courtelyou Subway Sta, 92-94; and others. *Exhib:* Solo exhibs, AIR Gallery, New York, 73, 75, 78, 80, 82, 87 & Matthew Hamilton Gallery, 84; Retrospective Exhib, Barrett House & Vassar Col Art Mus, 79; The Folding Image, Nat Gallery Art, Washington, DC & Yale Univ Art Gallery, 84; Gallery Artists, Max Protetel Gallery, New York, 87-88; Gardens Real and Imagined, Nat Mus Tour, 90-93; Artists Gardens, Noyes Mus, NJ, 90; Midtown Flower Show, Midtown-Payson Gallery, 92; Am Artist's Ode to Gardens & Flowers, Nassau Ctr Mus, 92; and many others. *Teaching:* Instr sculpture & drawing, Rutgers Univ, Newark, NJ, 69-70; instr materials & printmaking, Montclair State Col, Upper Montclair, NJ, 70-74; panelist, lectr & instr workshops, Nassau Co Mus, Aldrich Mus, Sarah Lawrence Col, City Univ New York, Skidmore Col, Mt Holyoke Col, Grad Sch Sculpture, Yale Univ & Wooster Col, Ohio, 71-79; assoc in sculpture, Columbia Univ, New York, 77; adj instr sculpture, Queens Col, NY, 77-78; adj & vis asst prof sculpture & drawing, Hunter Col, NY, 78-; vis artist & lectr, pub art, Okla Arts Inst, 91. *Awards:* Nat Endowment for the Arts Grant, 76-77; vis artist, Experimental Glass Workshop, New York, 80, 83 & 84. *Bibliog:* Paul Tschinkel (dir), video interview, Manhattan Cable TV, 78; Michael Komanecki & Virginia Fabri Butera (auths), The Folding Image, Nat Gallery Art & Yale Univ (catalog), 84; Grace Glueck (auth), The screen comes into its own, New York Times, 9/19/82. *Media:* Glass, Natural & Man-made Materials. *Publ:* Contribr, Six Years, Lucy Lippard, Praeger, 69; Glass Art Soc J, 84; auth, Patsy Norvell, Artists Discuss Their Work, Glass Art Soc J, pp 55-57, 84-85. *Mailing Add:* 78 Greene St New York NY 10012

NORWOOD, MALCOLM MARK
PAINTER, EDUCATOR
b Drew, Miss, Jan 21, 28. *Study:* Miss Col, BA & MEd; Univ Ala, MA; Univ Colo, painting with Mark Rothko. *Work:* Miss Mus Art, Jackson; Miss Collection, First Nat Bank, Jackson; Miss Col; Belhaven Col; Jackson Country Club. *Comn:* Landscapes & watercolors, First Nat Bank, Cleveland, Miss, 64 & 66; Rosalie (painting), comn by Daughters Am Revolution for USS Miss, 78; 5 Mile Run, comn by Gov's Coun on Physical Fitness, 81; and others. *Exhib:* Southern Methodist Univ Invitational, Ft Worth, Tex, 62; Washington Watercolor Asn, Smithsonian Inst, 63; Contemp Southern Art Exhib, Weatherspoon Art Gallery, Univ NC, 66; Artists Registry Exhib, Brooks Art Gallery, Memphis, Tenn, 69; La State Art Comn, Baton Rouge, 69. *Pos:* Bd dirs, Miss Mus Art, Jackson; dir festival, Grosstie Arts Coun, 70-75, pres 79-80; mem bd dir, Miss Arts Comn, 80-85. *Teaching:* Prof & chmn dept art, Delta State Univ, 62- *Awards:* First Prize, Nat Oil Exhib, Miss Power & Light Co, 63; Painting Award, Holiday Inns Am Arts Festival, 69; First Prize in Drawing, Edgewater Merchants Asn Ann, 71. *Mem:* Miss Art Asn; Cross-Tie Arts Couns. *Media:* Watercolor, Oil. *Publ:* Auth, article in Jackson Daily News/Clarion Ledger, 64; illusr, 64 & cover, 68, Delta Rev; coauth, The Art of Marie Hull, 75; auth, Guide to the Roberts Library Art Collection, 77. *Mailing Add:* 600 Canal Ave Cleveland MS 38732

NOTARBARTOLO, ALBERT
PAINTER, ENVIRONMENTAL ARTIST
b New York, NY. *Study:* Nat Acad Fine Arts, scholar, 50; apprenticeship to mural painter Ignacio La Russa, 51-53. *Work:* Ft Bragg, NC; Aldrich Mus Contemp Art, Ridgefield, Conn; Nat Gallery Art, Washington, DC. *Comn:* Series of paintings, comn by Larry Aldrich, New York, 67; painting, Radio Corp Am, New York, 71; drawing, Newsweek, 72; tapestry, Aubusson, France. *Exhib:* Corcoran Gallery Art, Washington, DC, 68; Mus Mod Art, New York, 68-70; 21 Am Artists, Del Art Mus, 70; Aldrich Mus Contemp Art, 72; Aubusson Tapestry Exhib, Norton Gallery Mus, Fla; Nat Gallery Art, Washington, DC, 76; plus others. *Awards:* First Prize, New York Intercult Soc, 53; Dept Housing & Urban Develop Nat Community Art Competition Award, Washington, DC, 73; Nat Award, New Glory Bicentennial Flag Design Competition (for flag for first lunar colony), Santa Barbara Mus of Art, 76. *Mem:* Nat Soc Lit & Arts. *Media:* Acrylic, Mixed. *Publ:* Contribr, Art Workers News, 4/74; Leonardo Mag, spring 75; Art-World newspaper, 1-2/78. *Mailing Add:* 215 W 98th St New York NY 10025

NOTESTINE, DOROTHY J
INSTRUCTOR, PAINTER
b Udall, Kans, Dec 3, 21. *Study:* Univ Houston, 62-63; study with John Pike, Zolten Szabo, Edgar Whitney and others, 76-85. *Exhib:* Ann Art Show, Hill Country Arts Found, Ingram, Tex, 77; Art of Dorothy/Tom Notestine, Univ Tex Sci Ctr, San Antonio, 79; Carrizo Art Inst Show, Ruidoso, NMex, 85 & 86; Artists of Tex, Dallas Creative Arts Bldg, 86; Art of Travel, Love Gallery, Int Airport, San Antonio, 88. *Collections Arranged:* Watercolors of the World (with catalog), Northside Bank, San Antonio, 76; Collection Int Known Artists (with catalog), Kerrville, Tex, 77. *Pos:* Bd mem, Coppini Acad Fine Arts, San Antonio, 80-82; co-ed, monthly pub, San Antonio Watercolor Group, 76-78. *Teaching:* Instr watercolor, Carrizo Art Ctr, Ruidoso, NMex, 85-86, Artists of SW Cruise Art, 86, San Antonio Col, 70-86; art instr, S S Star Princess cruising Mediterranean & Europe, 92. *Bibliog:* Pat Breedlove (auth), Artists of Texas, Mountain Productions Inc, 86; Carla Tam (auth), Carrizo Art Mag, 86; Skip Singleton (auth), Ruidoso Life Style, Sunrise Productions, 87. *Mem:* San Antonio Watercolor Group (co-founder); River Arts of San Antonio; Colonial Hills Watercolor Artist Asn. *Media:* Watercolor. *Publ:* Coauth, Oklahoma Artists of Distinction, Paint Spree Publ, 89; many articles in daily and monthly publ. *Dealer:* River RR Arts Gallery 510 De la Villita San Antonio TX 78216. *Mailing Add:* 358 Ave Maria San Antonio TX 78216

NOTESTINE, TOM W
LECTURER, INSTRUCTOR
b Oxford, Kans, Dec 1, 19. *Study:* Southwestern Col, Winfield, Kans, 38-40; Univ Houston, 48-50; John Pike Watercolor Sch, summer 75 & 76; also with Millard Sheets, Robert E Wood, Edgar Whitney & others. *Comn:* Mural, San Antonio Bd Realtors, Tex, 76. *Exhib:* Coppini Acad Fine Arts, San Antonio, Tex, 75-85; Int Art Show, Brownsville Art Mus, Tex, 77; World Wide Air Force Show, San Francisco, Calif, 77; one-man shows, Dahl Fine Arts Mus, Rapid City, SDak, 78, Int Art Mus, McAllen, Tex, 79; and others. *Pos:* Ed, San Antonio Watercolor Slurp, 75-76; dir to pres, Coppini Acad Fine Arts, San Antonio, 77-86. *Teaching:* Instr watercolor & oil, numerous art workshops, 76-89; instr, Carrizo Lodge Art Sch, Ruidoso, NMex, 83-84; instr watercolor, S S Rotterdam, Holland Am Line, 84, S S Southward, NCL line, 88 & S S Star Princess, Mediterranean, 92. *Awards:* Best of Show & 1st Place Watercolor, Int Art Show, Brownsville Art League & Mus, 77; 1st Place, World Wide Air Force Show, 77. *Bibliog:* Pamela Bell (auth), Artists take step into history, Alamo Artist, 76; Judy Veach (auth), Famous artist workshop, Sand Dollar Watch, 77; The pro's nest, Palette Talk No 40, 79; Artists of Texas, Mountain Productions, Inc, 86. *Mem:* San Antonio Watercolor Group (chmn, 75-76); Coppini Acad Fine Arts, San Antonio. *Media:* Watercolor, Oil. *Publ:* Auth, Placing people in paintings, Carrizo Lodge Art Sch Mag, 85; co-auth & publ, Oklahoma Artists of Distinction, 89. *Mailing Add:* 358 Ave Maria San Antonio TX 78216

NOTKIN, RICHARD T
SCULPTOR, CERAMIST
b Chicago, Ill, Oct 26, 48. *Study:* Kansas City Art Inst, with Dale Eldred & Ken Ferguson, BFA, 70; Univ Calif, Davis, with Robert Arneson, MFA, 73. *Work:* Stedelijk Mus, Amsterdam, Holland; Nat Collection Fine Arts, Smithsonian Inst, Washington DC; Los Angeles Co Mus Art; Everson Mus Art, Syracuse, NY; Victoria & Albert Mus, London, Eng; Seattle Art Mus, Wash; Nelson-Atkins Mus Art, Kansas City, Mo. *Exhib:* One-man shows, Frumkin Gallery, New York, 75, Quay Gallery, San Francisco, 81, Mus Art, Univ Ore, Eugene, 81, Garth Clark Gallery, Los Angeles, 84 & 88, Garth Clark Gallery, New York, 85, 87, 88 & 89 & Esther Saks Gallery, Chicago, 87; Echoes ... Historical References in Contemporary Ceramics, Atkins Mus Art, Kansas City, Mo, 83; and others; American Potters Today, Victoria & Albert Mus, London, 86; American Ceramics Now: 27th Ceramic Nat Exhib, Everson Mus Art, 87; East-West Contemp Ceramic Exhib, Korean Cult & Arts Found, Seoul, 88; Functional Ceramics & Beyond: Inspiration from the Vessel Aesthetic, Union Art Gallery, La State Univ, Baton Rouge, 88; Contemporary Ceramics: The Artists of TB-9, Visual Arts Ctr, Calif State Univ, Fullerton, 89; Surrealist Ceramics, John Michael Kohler Arts Ctr, Sheboygan, Wis, 89; Kansas City Collects Contemporary Ceramics, Nelson-Atkins Mus Art, Mo, 89; Clay, Color, Content: The 28th Ceramic, Nat Exhib, Everson Mus Art, Syracuse, NY, 90. *Pos:* Artist-in-residence, Kohler Co, Wis, 76 & 78; artist-in-residence, Archie Bray Found, Helena, Mont, 81. *Teaching:* Vis asst prof sculpture & ceramics, Univ Utah, Salt Lake City, 75; acting chmn & vis lectr ceramics, Md Inst Col Art, Baltimore, 77; vis artist/lectr, Ohio State Univ, 82; vis artist, Found Dept, Kansas City Art Inst, 84. *Awards:* Western States Art Found Fel, 76; Nat Endowment Arts Fel, 79, 81 & 88; Ore Arts Comn Individual Artists Fel, 85; Guggenheim Found Fel Sculpture, 90. *Bibliog:* Lynn Eder (auth), Ceramics Monthly, 11/82; Michael Dunas & Sarah Bodine (auths), article, Am Ceramic, 11/3/87. *Mem:* Nat Coun Educ Ceramic Arts; Am Crafts Coun. *Media:* Ceramics, Mixed. *Dealer:* Garth Clark Gallery 24 W 57th St New York NY 10019; Garth Clark Gallery 170 S La Brea Los Angeles CA 90036. *Mailing Add:* HC-85, Box 145-C Myrtle Point OR 97458

NOVAK, BARBARA (MRS BRIAN O'DOHERTY)
HISTORIAN, EDUCATOR
b New York, NY. *Study:* Barnard Col, Columbia Univ, BA, 51; Radcliffe Col, MA, 53, PhD, 57. *Teaching:* Altschul prof art hist, Barnard Col, Columbia Univ, New York, 58-; vis Mellon prof, Univ Pittsburgh, fall 78. *Awards:* Belg-Am Educ Found Fel, 53; Fulbright Award to Belg, 53-54; Guggenheim Award, 74; Life Fel, Philadelphia Athenaeum. *Mem:* Col Art Asn Am; Am Antiqn Soc; Soc Am Historians; PEN. *Res:* Nineteenth century American painting. *Publ:* Auth, American Painting of the Nineteenth Century, Praeger, 69; contribr, Metropolitan Museum Symposium on 19th Century American

Art, 72; auth, Nature and Culture: American Landscape and Painting 1825-75, Oxford Univ Press, 80; ed, Next to Nature, Harper & Row, 80; auth, Nineteenth Century American Painting in the Thyssen- Bomemisya Collection, 86; Alice's Neck, 87; Thr Ape and the Whale (play), 87; Dreams and Shadows: Thomas H Hotchkins in Nineteenth Century Italy, 92; contribr to numerous art hist periodicals. *Mailing Add:* 15 W 67th St New York NY 10023

NOVINSKI, LYLE FRANK
PAINTER, EDUCATOR
b Montfort, Wis, June 23, 32. *Study:* Wis State Univ, BA; Univ Wis, MS & MFA; Marquette Univ. *Comn:* Major leather wall construct, Amarillo & Dallas, Tex, 77; chapel, Holy Trinity Sem, 79; Chapel of the Incarnation, Univ Dallas, 85; and others. *Exhib:* Tex Gen, 64 & 72; Okla Eight State Exhib, 68; Okla Invitational, 70; Ft Worth Art Ctr, 71; Nat Interfaith Conf on Relig & Archit, 75; and others. *Teaching:* Prof art & dir dept art, Univ Dallas, 60-; fel, Dallas Inst Humanities & Cult, 80- *Awards:* Purchase Award, Okla Eight State, 68; Top Award, Tex Gen, 72. *Bibliog:* Articles, Christian Arts, 68, Liturgical Arts, 70 & Art Gallery, 71-72. *Mem:* Interfaith Forum Relig, Art & Archit; Col Art Asn Am. *Media:* Leather, Oil. *Dealer:* Valley House Gallery 6616 Spring Valley Rd Dallas TX 75240. *Mailing Add:* Dept Art Univ Dallas Box 466 Irving TX 75061

NOVOTNY, ELMER LADISLAW
PAINTER, EDUCATOR
b Cleveland, Ohio, July 27, 09. *Study:* Cleveland Sch Art, dipl; Case Western Reserve Univ, BA; Kent State Univ, MA; Slade Sch, Univ London; Acad Zagreb, Yugoslavia; Yale Univ. *Work:* Cleveland Mus Art, Cleveland Hist Mus, Cleveland Sch, Ohio; Butler Inst Am Art, Youngstown, Ohio, North Eastern Ohio Mus Art; Akron Art Mus; Canton Art Inst; Cleveland Munic Collection, Cleveland Historical Mus, Ohio; Johnson-Humerick House Mus, Coshocton, Ohio. *Comn:* Mural for game room, comn by John Sherwin, Jr, Waite Hill Village, Ohio, 37; History of Kent (mural), Portage Nat Bank, Ohio, 49; portrait of Gov Martin L Davey, comn by family, Kent, 50; portrait of Robert Carr, Oberlin Col, 70; portrait of James A Michener for Michener Libr, Univ Northern Colo, 71. *Exhib:* Cleveland Mus Ann May Show, 29-84; Butler Inst Am Art Ann Nat, 35-82; Canton Art Inst Ann Show, 37-65; Akron Art Inst Ann May Show, 37-71; Directions in American Painting, Carnegie Mus, Pittsburgh, 42; 50-year retrospective show, Canton Art Inst, Ohio, 76. *Teaching:* Instr portraiture, Cleveland Inst Art, 33-43; prof painting & drawing, Kent State Univ, 36-46, dir sch art, 46-74, prof emer & dir, 74- *Awards:* First prize & Third Prize (Portraiture) & First Prize Still Life Painting, Cleveland Mus Art; President's Medal for Meritorious Serv; Kent State Univ, Kent, 60; Jurors Award for Chateaux, Akron Art Inst, 69; Purchase Award, Butler Inst Am Art, Youngstown, Ohio. *Mem:* Hon life mem Akron Soc Artists; life fel Int Inst Arts & Lett; Cleveland Soc Artists. *Media:* Oil, Watercolor. *Publ:* Auth, Byways of Southern Europe, Kent State Univ, 69. *Mailing Add:* 2620 Saklan Indian Dr, No 4 Walnut Creek CA 94595

NOVROS, DAVID
PAINTER
b Los Angeles, Calif, 41. *Study:* Univ Southern Calif, BFA, 63. *Work:* Miami Fed Ct House, Fla; Mus Mod Art, New York; Whitney Mus Am Art, New York; Univ Tex Health Sci Ctr, Dallas; Atlantic Tower (Philip Johnson Bldg), Ga; Doumani House, Marina Del Ray, Calif; Menil Found Collection, Houston; Lafrenz Collection, on loan to Nat Gallery, Dublin, Ireland & Bremin, Ger, 91. *Exhib:* Systemic Painting, Solomon R Guggenheim Mus, New York, 66; Sound, Light & Silence, William Rockhill Nelson Gallery of Art, Kansas City, Mo, 66; Whitney Mus Am Art, 67, 69 & 73; The Structure of Color, Whitney Mus Am Art, 71; Corcoran Biennial, Washington, DC, 71; White on White, Mus Contemp Art, Chicago, Ill, 71-72; Art Inst of Chicago, 72; Five Artists: A Logic of Vision, Mus Contemp Art, 74; one-man exhibs, Sperone Westwater Fischer Inc, New York, 76 & 78, Picollo Spoleto, Charleston, SC, 92, Int Mus Mod Art, Dublin, Ireland, 92; Opening Exhib, Menil Found, Houston, Tex, 87; Hoffman Borman Gallery, Santa Monica, Calif, 88; Abstraction Geometry painting, Albright-Knox Art Gallery, Buffalo, NY, 90; Inaugural Exhib, Mus Contemp Art, Dublin, Ireland, 91; Casien on canvas, Charleston, Col, SC, 92. *Awards:* Fel, Guggenheim Found. *Bibliog:* Frances Colpitt (auth), The Shape of Painting in the Sixties, Art J, Vol 50, No 1, spring 91; Loic Malle (auth), Virginia Dwan Art Minimal-Art Conceptuel Earthwork, Gallerie Montaigne, 92; Michael Phillip's, Painting Self Evident, 92. *Mailing Add:* 433 Broome St New York NY 10013

NOWACK, WAYNE KENYON
PAINTER, GRAPHIC ARTIST
b Des Moines, Iowa, May 7, 23. *Study:* Drake Univ, 43-45; State Univ Iowa, BA(summa cum laude), 47, MA, 48, MFA, 50. *Work:* Joseph H Hirshhorn Found, Greenwich, Conn; Yale Univ Art Gallery, New Haven, Conn; Des Moines Art Ctr, Iowa; Williams Col, Williamstown, Mass; Ft Worth Art Mus, Tex. *Exhib:* Gallery Mod Art, Washington, DC, 63; Albright-Knox Art Gallery, Buffalo, NY, 63 & 71; Recent Am Drawings, Rose Art Mus, Brandeis Univ, 64; one-man shows, Allan Stone Gallery, New York, 67, 70 & 74; Human Concern, Whitney Mus Am Art, New York, 69; Unordinary Realities, Xerox Sq Exhib Ctr, Rochester, NY, 75; Am Drawings: 1927-1977, Minn Mus Art, St Paul, 77; Thirty Years of Box Construction, Sunne Savage Gallery, Boston, 79; The Private Eye, Neuberger Mus, State Univ NY, Purchase, 84. *Teaching:* Assoc prof art hist & painting, Union Col, Schenectady, NY, 57-65. *Awards:* Danforth Found Grant, 63-64; Nat Endowment Arts Painting Grant, 73-74. *Media:* Oil, Pastel. *Mailing Add:* RD 1 346 Spencer NY 14883

NOWAK, LEO
ILLUSTRATOR, CARTOONIST
b Elizabeth, NJ, Dec 24, 07. *Study:* Cleveland Sch Art, Ohio; John Huntington Sch Art, Cleveland. *Comn:* Mural (105 ft long), Brotherhood of Locomotive Engineers' Bldg, Cleveland, 34; many portraits comn by pvt parties & collectors. *Exhib:* May Show, Cleveland Mus Art, Cleveland, 30-36; Traveling Show, US, 36; Traveling Show, US Navy, Australia, NZ & US, 44-45; Art Festival, Laguna Beach Art Asn, Calif, 50-53; Los Angeles Co Mus Art, 51-52. *Pos:* Illusr, children's bks, Nat Illustrating Studios, World Syndicate, 29-34; illusr, Superman Cartoon, Action Comics, 41-43; chief illusr, Stamps-Conhaim Newspaper Serv, Los Angeles, 47-73; illusr/cartoonist, Ridgecrest Daily Independent, Calif, 76- *Awards:* Second Award-Figure, Laguna Beach Art Asn, 52; Presidential Award, Calif Art Club, 68; and many others. *Bibliog:* Western paintings, 5/76 & cover painting, 1/77, Desert Mag. *Mem:* Calif Art Club (vpres, 63-65); Valley Artists' Guild (vpres, 62-66); Desert Art League. *Media:* Oil, Walercolor; Pen. *Mailing Add:* 7960 Walden Ave Inyokern CA 93527

NOWYTSKI, (SLAVKO) SVIATOSLAV
FILMMAKER, PHOTOGRAPHER
b Oct 19, 34; Can citizen. *Study:* Pasadena Playhouse Col Theatre Arts, BA(theatre), 58; Columbia Univ, MFA(motion pictures), 64. *Work:* Educ Film Libr Asn, New York; Libr Cong; Dept Tourism, Recreation & Cult Affairs, Govt Man; Fedn Assoc Arts, Man; Ont Ministry Educ, Toronto. *Comn:* Reflections of the Past (film), Ukrainian Cult & Educ Ctr, Winnipeg, 74; Last of the Jacks (film), Minn Hist Soc, 76; Immortal Image (film), Filmart Prod, 78; Grass on the Roof (film), Underground Space Ctr, Univ Minn, 79; The Helm of Destiny (film), UNA, NJ, 81; Harvest of Despair (film), UFRC, Can, 84; We're Not Robots, You Know (video), Synergenesis Corp, 88. *Exhib:* Sheep in Wood (film), Am Film Festival, New York, 71; Reflections of the Past (film), Can Film Awards, Niagara on the Lake, Ont, 75 & 11th Int Chicago Film Festival, Ill, 75; Pysanka: The Ukrainian Easter Egg (film), Chicago Int Film Festival, 76. *Pos:* Ed, Ukrainian, Polish & Russian Sect, Cinema & TV Digest, 63-; pres, Filmart Prod, St Paul, Minn, 71-82. *Awards:* Blue Ribbon Award for Sheep in Wood, Am Film Festival, 71; Gold Hugo for Pysanka: The Ukrainian Easter Egg, Chicago Int Film Festival, 76 & Silver Venus Medal, Virgin Islands Int Film Festival, 77; Bronze Medal for Immortal Image, Int Film & TV Festival, NY, 78. *Mem:* Minn Soc Fine Arts; Twin Cities Metrop Arts Alliance; Intermedia Arts. *Mailing Add:* 77 Sixth Ave Minneapolis MN 55413

NOYES, SANDY
PHOTOGRAPHER
b New York, NY, Dec 18, 41. *Study:* Yale Univ, with Bud Leak, BA, 63; workshop with Paul Caponigro, 73 & Minor White, 74; New Sch Soc Res, with George Tice, 74. *Work:* Metrop Mus Art, New York; Bibliot Nat, Paris; Addison Gallery Am Art; High Mus Art; Int Mus Photog at George Eastman House, Rochester, NY. *Exhib:* NJ State Mus, Trenton, 79; Contemporary Platinotype, Rochester Inst Technol, NY, 79; Intervals, 22 Wooster St Gallery, New York, 82; Nikon House, New York, 84; Albany Inst Hist & Art, 89. *Teaching:* Instr, Int Ctr Photog, New York, 76-81. *Awards:* Proj Grant (co-recipient), Seven Photogrs, Del Valley, Nat Endowment Arts, 77; Ossabaw Island Proj Fel, Ga, 79; Creative Artists Prog Serv Grant, NY, 83. *Mem:* Albany/Schnectady League Arts. *Mailing Add:* RD 1, Box 183 Chatham NY 12037

NUGENT, BOB L
PAINTER, SCULPTOR
b Santa Monica, Calif, Aug 15, 47. *Study:* Col Creative Studies, Univ Calif, BFA, 69; Univ Calif, Santa Barbara, MFA(Regents Grant), 71. *Work:* Bank Am Headquarters, San Francisco, Calif; Washington State Art in Public Places, Spokane; Indianapolis Mus Art, Ind; Ariz State Univ, Tempe; Brooklyn Mus, NY. *Exhib:* One-man shows, Antiscope, Brussels, Belgium, 79, Kathryn Markel Fine Arts, New York, 80, Los Angeles Munic Art Gallery, Calif, 80 & Tucson Mus Art, Ariz, 81; Paper Art, Smithsonian Inst, Washington DC, 80; Painting & Sculpture Today, Indianapolis Mus Art, Ind, 80. *Collections Arranged:* California Collage (auth, catalog), 81; California Clay (auth, catalog), 81; Sculpture 82 (auth, catalog); Chicago Abstract Painting (auth, catalog). *Pos:* Dir art gallery, Sonoma State Univ, Calif, 81- *Teaching:* Prof art painting, Pepperdine Univ, Calif, 73; prof art painting, Col Siskiyavs, Calif, 73-81; prof art, Sonoma State Univ, Rohnert Park, Calif, currently. *Awards:* Individual Artists Fel, Nat Endowment Arts, 79; Fulbright Travel Grant to Brazil, 86; Fel, Calif Arts Coun Artist, 90. *Media:* Mixed. *Publ:* Contribr, Paper Art, E B Crocker Art Mus, 80. *Mailing Add:* c/o Magnolia Editions 2527 Magnolia St Salinas CA 98901

NUNNELLEY, ROBERT B
PAINTER, EDUCATOR
b Birmingham, Ala, Sept 5, 29. *Study:* Univ Ark, BA(art), 51, with David Smith, MFA(painting), 56; Boston Mus Sch, with Karl Zerbe & David Aronson, 51-53; Colorado Springs Fine Arts Ctr, with Robert Motherwell, 54. *Work:* Rockhill Nelson Gallery, Kansas City, Mo; Des Moines Art Ctr, Iowa. *Exhib:* Solo exhibs, Hudson River Mus, Yonkers, 67 & Schenectady Mus, NY, 79; Focus on the Arts, Bergen Community Mus, Paramus, NJ, 82; Nat Competion 2 Dimensional Work, Bowery Gallery, New York, 91; Nat Drawing, Trenton State Col, NJ, 92; and others. *Pos:* Dir, Maples Gallery, Farleigh Dickinson Univ, Teaneck, NJ, 82-87. *Teaching:* Prof painting-drawing-design, Fairleigh Dickinson Univ, Rutherford, NJ, 66- *Awards:* Purchase Award, Mid-Am Col Art Asn, 55; Research Grant, Fairleigh Dickinson Univ, 73. *Mem:* Nat Asn Sch of Art & Design; Col Art Asn. *Media:* Oil. *Mailing Add:* RD 2 Box 168 Greenwich NY 12834

NUSE, OLIVER WILLIAM
PAINTER, PHOTOGRAPHER
b Oberlin, Ohio, Jan 20, 14. *Study:* Pa Acad Fine Art, BFA, 38 & MFA, 41; Univ Pa. *Work:* Philadelphia Watercolor Club in Philadelphia Mus Art, Samuel Fleischer Art Mem, Del Co Mus & Wm Penn Charter Sch, Philadelphia, Pa. *Comn:* Ten Sculptors, Pa Acac Fine Arts, Philadelphia, 70; Chinese Calligraphy, Philadelphia Mus Art, Pa, 71; Moving Sculpture, comn by sculptor Hortense Baer, Philadelphia, Pa, 72. *Exhib:* Ann Butler Art Inst, Youngstown, Ohio, 59; Oil, Drawing, Watercolor, Philadelphia Art Alliance, Pa, 59 & 64; Allied Artists, Nat Acad Design, New York, 61; Ann Pa Acad Oil & Sculpture, Pa Acad Fine Arts, Philadelphia, 61; Am Watercolor Soc, Nat Acad Design, New York, 62; Bi-Annuals Print & Watercolor, Pa Acad Fine Arts, Philadelphia, 62-67; Artists Equity Regional, Philadelphia Mus Art, Pa, 66; Painters of Maine, Carnegie Gallery, Univ Maine, Orono, 76; Artfellows, Belfast, Maine; Farnstworth Mus, Maine. *Teaching:* Chmn art dept studio & art hist, Wm Penn Charter Sch, 41-74; instr painting, Samuel Fleischer Art Mem, 58-65; instr filmmaking, Philadelphia Mus Art, 70-71. *Awards:* Hon Mention Watercolor, Audubon Artists, New York, 57; Philadelphia Watercolor Prize, Philadelphia Watercolor Club, 64; Harrison S Morrison Prize, 66. *Mem:* Artist Equity Asn (pres, 63-64); Philadelphia Watercolor Club (pres, 64-67); Union of Maine visual artists. *Media:* Acrylic, Pastel. *Mailing Add:* RR 1 No 17 Stockton Springs ME 04981

NUSHAWG, MICHAEL ALLAN
PRINTMAKER, EDUCATOR
b Dayton, Ohio, Oct 31, 44. *Study:* Miami Univ, Ohio, BFA, 66; Ohio Univ; Univ Iowa, MFA, 70. *Work:* Honolulu Acad Arts; Joslyn Art Mus, Nebr; Dulin Gallery Art, Tenn; Midwest Mus Am Art, Ind; Des Moines Art Ctr, Iowa. *Exhib:* 21st Nat Print Exhib, Brooklyn Mus, NY, 78; 31st Nat Exhib, Boston Printmakers, Mass, 79, 82 & 83; Mus Mod Art, Parana, Brazil; World Print III, World Print Coun, Calif, 80; Smithsonian Inst Traveling Exhib, 80; 15th Nat Print Exhib, Univ NY, Potsdam, 80; one-person exhib, Miriam Perlman Gallery, Chicago. *Teaching:* Assoc prof printmaking, Univ Nebr, Lincoln, 72-83. *Awards:* Sunday Times Award, 79; Purchase Awards, 6th Hawaii Nat, Honolulu & Rockford Int, Ill. *Bibliog:* Janice McCullagh (auth), Six prints by Michael Nushawg, Kans Quart, Vol 14, 82. *Media:* Etching, Miscellaneous. *Dealer:* Jane Haslem 2121 P St NW Washington DC 20037; Miriam Perlman 505 N Lake Shore Dr Chicago IL 60611. *Mailing Add:* 248 S Marion No 104 Oak Park IL 60302

NUSSBAUM, SHEILA FORD
ART DEALER, CONSULTANT
b Philadelphia, Pa, Mar 9, 40. *Study:* Univ Pa; New York Univ; New Sch Social Res, New York. *Pos:* Owner, Sheila Nussbaum Gallery, Millburn, NJ, currently. *Awards:* 1987 Woman of the Year, Bus & Prof Women Millburn-Short Hills, Inc;; Bus Watch Award, Business J, NJ, 88. *Bibliog:* Patricia Malarcher (auth), New luster for Essex, New York Times, 11/7/82; Yolanda Cifarelli (auth), New Jersey gallery targets--, Crafts Report, 1/85; Katherine Kaye (auth), Sheila Nussbaum: At Home with Art, Star Ledger, 11/17/89. *Mem:* Am Craft Coun; Assoc Am Craft Mus. *Specialty:* Contemporary Art Am crafts & art jewelry; young emerging artists. *Mailing Add:* Sheila Nussbaum Gallery 358 Millburn Ave Millburn NJ 07041

NUTT, CRAIG
CRAFTSMAN, SCULPTOR
b Belmond, Iowa, Apr 13, 50. *Study:* Univ Ala, BA, 72. *Work:* Birmingham Mus Art; Fine Arts Mus of the South; High Mus Art. *Comn:* Many comns for pvt collections. *Exhib:* First Int Shoebox Sculpture Exhib, Univ Hawaii & int tour, 82-84; Nat Furniture Invitational, Tupelo Artist Guild Gallery, 85; Innocence & Experience, Greenville Co Mus Art, SC, 85; New Wood-New Ways, Clara M Eagle Gallery, Murray State Univ, 86-87; Wood & Glass Invitational, Southeastern Ctr Contemp Art, Winston-Salem, NC, 86; Political Statements, Saratt Gallery, Vanderbilt Univ, 86-87; one-man show, Dinosaurs & Flying Vegetables, Kentuck Mus, Northport, Ala, 87, Huntsville Mus Art, Ala, 89; Red Clay Survey, Huntsville Mus Art, 88; Nat Objects Invitational, Ark Arts Ctr, Little Rock, 89; Focus: Four Alabama Artists, Birmingham Mus Art, 90; Signs of Support: Furniture Forms in Contemporary American Art, Kohler Arts Ctr, Sheboygan, Wis, 90; Contemporary Works in Wood, Southern Style, Huntsville Mus Art, 90; Artists, Archits & Designers: Furniture of our Century High Mus Art, Atlanta, Ga, 92; Seeds of Change, Smithsonian Inst, 91. *Awards:* Gov Art Award, Ala State Coun Arts, 85, fel, 88; Nat Endow Arts Fel, 89. *Bibliog:* Craig Nutt (auth), article in Am Craft, 87 & From furniture to flying vegetables, Southern Accents Mag, 88; Craig Nutt: Combining Humor and a Bit of Cayenne, Fine Woodworking, 91. *Mem:* Ala Crafts Coun (trustee, 80-86); Am Crafts Coun (bd dir, 82-88). *Media:* Wood. *Publ:* Auth, Lathe turned, woodturners gather at Arrowmont, Am Craft, 86; A partnership, The Guild, 87; Ed, Spotlight 88, SE/SW Crafts Exhib Catalog, Am Craft Coun, SE Region, 88. *Dealer:* Connell Gallery 333 Buckhead Ave Atlanta GA 30305. *Mailing Add:* 2014 Fifth St Northport AL 35476

NUTT, JIM (JAMES TUREMAN)
PAINTER, DRAFTSMAN
b Pittsfield, Mass, Nov 28, 38. *Study:* Wash Univ, St Louis, 58-59; Art Inst Chicgo, with Whitney Halstead & Dominic DiMeo, dipl, 65. *Work:* Whitney Mus Am Art, Mus Mod Art, Metrop Mus Art, New York; Mus Contemp Art, Chicago; Mus Mod Kunst, Vienna; High Mus, Atlanta, Ga; Philadelphia Mus Art; Scotish Nat Mus, Glasgow; Weatherspoon Gallery, Univ NC, Greensboro; Mem Art Gallery, Univ Rochester, NY. *Exhib:* Pictures to be Read, Poetry to be Seen, Mus Contemp Art, Chicago, 67; Am Exhib, Art Inst Chicago, 72 & 76; Who Chicago?, Sunderland Arts Ctr, Eng, 80; solo exhib, Rotterdamse Kunststichting, Holland, 80, Phyllis Kind Gallery, Chicago, 70, 72, 75, 77, 79, 82, 85 & 91, Phyllis Kind Gallery, New York, 76, 77, 80, 84, 88, 91 & Galerie Bonnier, Geneva, Switz, 92; American Painting 1930-1980, Haus Kunst, Munich, Ger, 81; Intoxication, Monique Knowlton Gallery, New York, 83; Contemporary Focus: 1974-1984, Hirshhorn Mus & Sculpture Garden, Washington, DC, 84-85; Morgan Gallery, Kansas City, Mo; 39th Biennial Exhib Contemp Am Painting, Corcoran Gallery Art, Washington, DC, 85; Word As Image: American Art 1960-1990, Milwaukee Art Mus, Wis & traveling to Oklahoma City Art Mus & Contemp Arts Mus, Houston, Tex, 90-91; Parallel Visions: Modern Artists & Outsider Art, Los Angeles Co Mus Art traveling to Kunsthalle Basel, Centro de Arte Reina Sofia, Madrid, Spain & Setagaya Art Mus, Tokyo, Japan, 92-93; From America's Studio: Twelve Contempory Masters, Art Inst Chicago, 92. *Teaching:* Assoc prof painting & drawing, Calif State Univ, Sacramento, 68-75. *Bibliog:* Whitney Halstead (auth), Jim Nutt, (exhib catalog), Mus Contemp Arts Chicago, 74; Russel Bowman (auth), Jim Nutt, (exhib catalog), Rotterdam Kunststichting Lijnbaan Centrum, 80; John Yau (auth), Jim Nutt: Recent Works, Mazon Gallery, London, Eng. *Dealer:* Phyllis Kind Gallery 313 W Superior Chicago IL 60610. *Mailing Add:* 1035 Greenwood Ave Wilmette IL 60091

NUTZLE, FUTZIE (BRUCE JOHN KLEINSMITH)
ARTIST, CARTOONIST
b Lakewood, Ohio, Feb 21, 42. *Study:* Self-taught. *Work:* Mus Mod Art, New York; San Francisco Mus Mod Art; Oakland Mus, Calif; Santa Cruz City Mus, Calif; Whitney Mus Am Art, New York. *Comn:* Mural, with Art Decker, Gilroy, Calif, 92. *Exhib:* Corresp Sch Art, Whitney Mus, New York, 70; Empty Canoes, Lithographs, San Francisco Mus Mod Art, 72; Opening, Santa Cruz Artists' Mus Proj, 73; Twin Rocker Paper Exhib, Indianapolis Mus Art, Ind, 75; Laica, Los Angeles, 78; one-man shows, Santa Barbara Mus Art, 80; Univ Col Santa Cruz, Retrospective, 90; Prague Eco-Fair, 91. *Teaching:* Artist-in-residence, Victor Valley Col, 83; instr, adult classes, cartooning & drawing, Art Sch Santa Cruz, fall, 88. *Bibliog:* My art belongs to Dada, Esquire Mag, 8/74; feature article in Quest, 6/79. *Media:* Pen and Ink, Wash on Paper; Oil on Canvas. *Publ:* Contribr, Balloon Newspaper, 68-72, Rolling Stone, 75-80, Quarry West, 77 & San Francisco Bay Guardian, 81-83; Japan Times/current; auth, Modern Loafer (cartoons & drawings) Thames & Hudson, Inc, 81; auth & illusr, Futzie Nutzle, Jazz Press, 83; Run the World: 50 cents, Chronicle Bks, 91; Howard McCord (auth), The Duke of Chemical Birds, Bloody Twin, Stout, Ohio; Bob Brozman, Devil's Slide, Rounder Records; Twenty-Fifth Int Salon of Cartoons, 88; Int Pavilion of Humour, Man and His World, Montreal, Can. *Mailing Add:* Eloise Pickard Smith Gallery Univ of Calif Santa Cruz CA 95064

NYDORF, ROY HERMAN
PAINTER, PRINTMAKER
b Port Washington, New York, Oct 1, 52. *Study:* Art Students League of New York, 69; State Univ NY, Brockport, with Robert Marx, BA, 74; Yale Univ Sch Art, with Peterdi, Bailey & Johnson, MFA, 76. *Work:* Hirshhorn Mus & Sculpture Garden & Nat Mus Am Art, Washington, DC; Honolulu Mus Am Art, Hawaii; Weatherspoon Art Gallery, Greensboro, NC; Yale Art Gallery, New Haven, Conn; Nelson Atkins Mus Art, Kansas City, Mo. *Comn:* Wall mural, comn by Garret Trudeau, New Haven, Conn, 77; portrait pres, Guilford Col, Greensboro, NC, 81. *Exhib:* 6th Hawaii Nat Print Exhib, Honolulu Acad Arts, Hawaii, 83; Art on Paper, Weatherspoon Art Gallery, Univ NC, Greensboro, 84 & 89; Small Works National, Zaner Gallery, Rochester Gallery, Rochester, NY, 85; Neo-Espressionism, SECCA, Winston-Salem, NC, 89; Landscape/Cityscape, Franz Bader Gallery, Washington, DC, 88; Saints & Religious Heroes, Weatherspoon Art Gallery, Univ NC, Greensboro, 91; Large Paintings, Raleigh Contemp Galleries, NC, 91; solo exhib, New Paintings, Danville Mus Fine Arts & Hist, Va, 92; Pacific States Biennial Nat Print Exhib, Univ Hawaii, Hilo, 92. *Teaching:* Instr design, Univ New Haven, Conn, 77; asst prof art & art hist, Guilford Col, Greensboro, NC, 78-86, assoc prof, 86- *Awards:* Purchase Award, 6th Hawaii Nat Print Exhib, Honolulu Acad Arts, 83; MAC TAC Award, Henley Southeastern Spectrum, Sawtooth Ctr Visual Arts, 84; Juror's Award, Southern Graphics Coun Exhib, Atlanta Col Art, 86; Merit Award, Bradley Nat Print & Drawing Exhib, Bradley Univ, Peoria, Ill, 91. *Mem:* Southeastern Ctr Contemp Art; Green Hill Ctr NC Art; Southern Graphics Coun. *Media:* Oils, Gouache; Ink. *Dealer:* Somerhill Gallery 5504 Chapel Hill Blvd Durham NC 27707. *Mailing Add:* 1815 Oak Ridge Rd Oak Ridge NC 27310

NYE, MOLLY HARDING
ART DEALER, GALLERY DIRECTOR
Study: Wells Col, Aurora, NY, BA(art hist), 61. *Pos:* Dir, Gallery on the Green, Lexington, Mass, currently. *Teaching:* Docent, American art, Corcoran Gallery Art, Washington, DC, 77-79. *Mem:* Lexington Arts & Crafts Soc (pres, 76-77); Lexington Coun Arts (co-chmn, 80-82); Lexington Bus Women, 87- *Specialty:* Contemporary art, such as by T Lux Feininger, Trefonides, George Rhoads, Lissa Hunter, Austine Wood Comarow & Verina Warren. *Mailing Add:* Gallery on the Green 1837 Massachusetts Ave Lexington MA 02173

NYERGES, ALEXANDER LEE
MUSEUM DIRECTOR, HISTORIAN
b Rochester, NY, Feb 27, 57. *Study:* George Washington Univ, BA(Am studies & anthrop), 79, MA(mus studies), 81. *Collections Arranged:* Southeastern Watercolorist I-III (auth, catalogs), 83-85 & Piranesi: 18th Century Etchings (ed, catalog), 84, DeLand Mus Art, Fla; Collector's Choice 1985 & French and American Impressionism 1855-1912, 85, The American Landscape 1850-1910, 86, Miss Mus Art, Jackson; Norman Rockwell: The Great American Story teller, 88. *Pos:* Exec dir, Deland Mus Art, Fla, 81-85

& Miss Mus Art, Jackson, 85-92; southeast regional rep, non-print media comt, Am Asn Mus, 83-85, legislative comt, 86-; dir, Dayton Art Inst, Ohio, 92- *Awards:* Phi Beta Kappa, 79. *Mem:* Miss Inst Arts & Letts (bd trustee); Southeast Mus Conf (bd trustee); Art Mus Asn Am (regional rep); Am Asn Mus; Asn Am Govt Affairs Comt; Asn Art Mus Dirs. *Res:* American painting 19th century; South American, Pre-Columbian Art. *Publ:* Auth, Museums and the videodisc revolution, Videodisc-Videotex, Vol II, fall 82; The Ages of Mexico (exhib catalog), DeLand Mus Art, No 4, 83; The Black artist as artist, Epoch Mag, 82; Norman Rockwell, 88. *Mailing Add:* Mississippi Mus Art 201 E Pascagoula St Jackson MS 39201

NYGREN, JOHN FERGUS
GLASS ARTIST
b Big Springs, Nebr, Oct 8, 40. *Study:* Univ Nebr, BFA, 65; Cranbrook Acad Art, Bloomfield Hills, Mich, MFA(ceramics), 67; Penland Sch of Crafts, spec study in glass, 68 & 88. *Work:* Corning Mus of Glass, NY; Sheldon Art Gallery, Lincoln, Nebr; Chrysler Mus, Norfolk, Va; Mint Mus Art, Charlotte, NC; Smithsonian Inst. *Exhib:* Nat Artist Exhib Works in Glass, Craft Alliance, St Louis, Mo, 87; Am Contemp Glass from the Corning Glass Collection, Spaso House, Moscow, USSR, 88; Am Glass, Naples Art Gallery, Naples, Fla, 89; Heller Gallery, New York, 90; Glass Am, 90; NC Glass, Western Carolina Univ, Collowhee, NC, 90; and others. *Teaching:* Instr, Univ NC, Wilmington, 67-69. *Awards:* Vreeland Award, Univ Nebr, 64; Nat Merit Award, Craftsmen USA 66, Am Crafts Coun, 66; Purchase Award, NC Glass 76, NC Nat Bank, 76. *Bibliog:* B Mayer (auth), Contemporary American Craft Art, 88; S Frantz (auth), Contemporary Glass: A World Survey from the Corning Mus of Glass, 89; J Byrd (auth), North Carolina Glass 90, Western Carolina Univ, 90. *Mem:* Am Crafts Coun; Glass Art Soc; Piedmont Crafts, Inc; Hon Admiral, the Great Navy of the State of Nebr. *Dealer:* Heller Gallery 71 Greene St New York NY 10012. *Mailing Add:* c/o Heller Gallery 71 Greene St New York NY 10012

NYMAN, GEORGIANNA BEATRICE
PAINTER
b Arlington, Mass, June 11, 30. *Study:* Boston Mus Fine Arts Sch, study with David Aronson & Karl Zerbe, dipl, 52, cert, 54. *Work:* Rose Art Mus, Brandeis Univ, Waltham, Mass. *Comn:* Portrait (chief of surgery), Brookline Hosp, 83; portrait (chief Critical Care Inst), Sch Med, Univ Pittsburgh, 84; portrait, D Blair McClosky Voice Studios, Boston, 85; portrait, Sandra Day O'Connor, Justice US Supreme Court, 91; portrait, Headmaster & Wife, Milton Acad, Mass, 92. *Exhib:* Boston Arts Festival And Juried Exhibs, 54 & 61; Shore Studio Galleries, Boston, 63; Group Show, Lee Nordness Galleries, New York, 65; Nat Acad Design, New York, 90; solo exhib, Nancy Lincoln Gallery, Chestnut Hill, Mass, 90. *Teaching:* Instr drawing & painting, Boston Ctr Adult Educ, 52-54; instr painting, Boston Univ Sch Continuing Educ, 58-59. *Awards:* Boit Prize, Boston Mus Sch, 51; Kate Morse Prize, Boston Mus Fine Arts, 53; Cert Merit, Nat Acad Design, New York, 92. *Bibliog:* Who's Who East, 23rd ed & Who's Who Am Women, Marquis. *Media:* Acrylic, Oil. *Publ:* Contribr, Native Island (Gerta Kennedy), Houghton-Mifflin, 56; Art of Karl Zerbe (film), 88. *Mailing Add:* 137 Brimstone Lane Sudbury MA 01776

O

OAKES, JOHN WARREN
EDUCATOR, PHOTOGRAPHER
b Bowling Green, Ky, Feb 26, 41. *Study:* Art Instr Sch Minneapolis; Art Students League, New York, Albert Dorne Scholar; Western Area Voc Sch; Western Ky Univ, AB, 64; Univ Iowa, MA, 66, MFA, 73; Harvard Univ, cert arts admin, 75. *Work:* Numerous works in pub and pvt collections in Ala, Fla, Ga, Ind, Iowa, Ky, Mass, NY, NH, Miss, Tenn & Tex. *Exhib:* Twenty-nine solo exhibs. *Pos:* Gallery dir, Western Ky Univ Gallery, 66-85, staff asst, off dean, Potter Col Arts & Humanities, 73-75, asst dean admin, 75-85. *Teaching:* Instr art, Western Ky Univ, 66-71, asst prof art, 71-76, assoc prof art, 76-87, prof art, 87- *Bibliog:* Joseph G Rosa (auth), The West of Wild Bill Hickok, Daily News 6/82 & Univ Okla Press, 83. *Mem:* Ky Arts Admin (pres, 82-83); Ky Citizens for Arts; Southern Ky Photog Soc (pres, 86-89); Kappa Pi. *Media:* Photography, Computer Graphics. *Res:* Influences of Pablo Picasso's work that have been overlooked; minimum aperture photography. *Publ:* Auth, Computer graphics for artists, AMIGA World Mag, 86; Camera Blending, Instant Projects, Polaroid Corp Publ, 86; Photography Using Pinhole Cameras, Univ Press of Am, 86; Action Amiga: Computer Graphics, Animation and Video Production, Univ Press of Am, 88; Art by Computer, Acorn Press, 90. *Dealer:* J B Speed Mus Louisville KY 40208. *Mailing Add:* 2722 Utah Dr Bowling Green KY 42104

OAKES, WILLIAM LARRY
PAINTER, SCULPTOR
b Richmond, Va, Apr 16, 44. *Study:* Univ Md, 69-70; Cornish Sch Allied Art, 64-65; Burnly Sch Art, 65-67; Univ Mass, MA, 84-88. *Work:* US Navy Fine Art Collection, US Info Agency & Libr Cong, Washington, DC; Franklin Mint, New York; US Naval Acad, Annapolis, Md. *Comn:* Portrait, Secy of Navy, US Naval Mus, Washington, DC, 69; Court Art, Watergate Hearings, Washington Post, ABC News, Nat Geographic & Christian Sci Monitor, Washington, DC & Boston, 74. *Exhib:* Imaginations, Corcoran Gallery Art, DC, 71; Naval Hist, Navy Mus, DC, 71; Illusr 13, traveled, New York, 72 & Art Dirs' Show 50, 72; Combat Art, Salmagundi Gallery, New York, 72; Painter as Illusr, Old Town Hall Gallery, Salem, Mass, 79-80; The Power of a Tiny Light, Newburyport Cult Ctr, 92. *Teaching:* Instr art, Comt for Community Improvement, Washington, DC, 68-71; instr drawing & painting, pvt classes, Washington, DC & Boston, 71-76; dean freshman found & illus, New Eng Sch Art & Design, 76-80; instr, Art Inst Boston, 80- *Awards:* Scholar Award, Salmagundi Club, New York, 70; Award of Merit, Soc Illusr, New York, 71; Award of Excellence, Art Dirs Club, New York, 71. *Bibliog:* Peggy Thompson (auth), Pick a dot, Am Mag, 72; David Windor (auth), Morocco: A visual documentary by Bill Oakes, Christian Sci Monitor, 78; David Wiegand, (auth), Bill Oakes, Illustrator Extraordinaire, Divisions, 79. *Mem:* Soc Children's Bk Writers. *Media:* All. *Publ:* Auth, The Lesson Sketcher, 78, Imagination 2, Cowleybinder, 80 & Art by Design, 81, Acorn Press; illusr, Sound and the Fury, by Faulkner, 77 & The Plays of Shakespeare, 78-79, Franklin Libr; Numblers, 88, Dial Books 88 & 89, Puzzlers, 89 & Once Upon Another Dial Books, 90. *Dealer:* Intuit Art Gallery 861 Lafayette Rd Hampton NH 03842. *Mailing Add:* 277 South Rd Kensington NH 03827

O'BANION, NANCE
ASSEMBLAGE ARTIST
b Oakland, Calif, June 7, 49. *Study:* Univ Calif, Berkeley, BA, 71, MA, 73. *Work:* Seattle Art Mus; Mus Arts Decoratifs Ville Lausanne, Switz; Am Craft Mus, NY; City & Co San Francisco; Cleveland Art Mus; Oakland Mus. *Comn:* Large wall construction (paper & bamboo), Sheraton Hotel, Tokyo, Japan, 87; painting (paper & bamboo), Bishop Ranch, Calif, 87; construction (paper & bamboo), Cranston Securities; well construction, pair (paper & bamboo), Ballston, Va, 88. *Exhib:* Making Paper, Am Craft Mus, New York, 82; Papier, Mus Arts Decoratifs Ville Lausanne, Switz, 83; On and Off the Wall: Shaped and Colored, (with catalog), Oakland Mus, 83; Papier: Un Nouveau Langage Artistique, Mus Bellerive, Zurich, 83; one-woman shows, Gallery Coco, Kyoto, Japan, 83, Kauffman Galleries, Houston, 83, Hestkobgaard-Birkerod, Denmark, 84 & B Z Wagman Gallery, St Louis, 84, Allrich Gallery, 80-85 & 87-88; Monterey Art Mus, Calif, 89; Fiber Art, Musee des Decoratif, Paris, France, 85; Recent Twentieth Century Acquisitions, Oakland Mus, Calif, 89; Craft Today USA, Musee des Decoratifs, Paris, France, 89; Works on Paper: the Craft Artist as Draftsman, Renwick Gallery Nat Mus Am Art, Washington, DC, 92; Craft Today USA, Zappeion Mus, Athens, Greece, 92. *Teaching:* Instr, Univ Calif, Davis, 72-79; assoc prof, Calif Col Arts & Crafts, 74-; vis artist & lectr, Hestkobgaard-Birkerod, Denmark & Carnegie Mellon Inst, Pittsburgh, Pa, 84; Chicago Art Inst, 87, San Francisco Craft Folk Art Mus & San Luis Obispo Art Asn, 89 & many others. *Awards:* Nat Endowment Arts, Vis Art, 82-83 & 88-89; Nat Endowment Arts Fels, 79 & 82-83. *Bibliog:* Kenneth Baker (auth), O'Banion shows how to make decorativeness work, San Francisco Chronicle, 4/3/87; Charles Talley (auth), Nance O'Banion: lines of energy, Artweek, 11/15/88; Robert Atkins (auth), Artspeak: A Guide to Contemporary Ideas, Movements and Buzzwords, Abbeville Press, New York, 69; Claire Campbell Park (auth), Finding the Link Between Fiber and Mixed Media: Nance O'Banion, Fiber Arts, summer 91. *Media:* Handmade Paper and Bamboo. *Publ:* Coauth, Fiberfinder: A Guide to Bay Area Sources, Fiberworks, 77; Contribr, Handcrafted investments, US News World Report, 1/18/88; Bay area artists, Horizon, 3/88; Contemporary American Craft Art: a Collector's Guide, Peregrine Bks, 88. *Mailing Add:* c/o Allrich Gallery 251 Post St San Francisco CA 94108

O'BEIL, HEDY
PAINTER, CRITIC
b New York, NY. *Study:* Art Students League, 53; Brooklyn Mus Art Sch, 58 & 59; Skowhegan Sch Art, 59; Empire State Col, State Univ NY, BS, 77; Goddard Col, MFA, 79. *Work:* Guild Hall, Easthampton, NY; also pvt collections of Eva Gatling, Ruth Solomon & Mr & Mrs Jack Lang; and others. *Exhib:* One-person exhibs, Guild Hall, Easthampton, NY, 70, Heckscher Mus, Huntington, NY, 72, Landmark Gallery, 79 & Barbara Ingber Gallery, 83; Contemporary Art, Philadelphia Mus Art, 82 & 83; Katherina Rich Perlow Gallery, 85 & 86; The Clocktower Gallery, 86; Barbara Ingber Gallery, 86; Pleiades Gallery, 90; Woodstock Artists Asn, 92; and others. *Collections Arranged:* The Symbolic View, Soho 20 Gallery, 82; Revelations, Pleiades Gallery, 84; Costumes, Masks & Disguises, The Clocktower Gallery, 86. *Pos:* Critic, Arts Mag, 76-86, Manhattan Arts Mag, 89- *Teaching:* Instr art, Nassau Community Col, 74; lectr, Art Ctr Northern NJ, 76-; lectr art hist, 92nd St Y, New York, 81-82. *Awards:* First Award, Long Island Artists, Hofstra Univ, 65; First Award, Long Island Painters, Guild Hall, Easthampton, NY, 69; Heckscher Mus, 69. *Bibliog:* William Zimmer (auth), article, Soho News, 79; Elaine Wechsler (auth), article, Arts Mag, 83; Jennifer Dunning (auth), article, New York Times, 86; Diana Roberts (auth), Manhattan Arts, 90; Artspeak, 90; and others. *Mem:* Women's Caucus Art; Cummington Community Arts; Yaddo; Woodstock Artists Asn, 91-92; Am Soc Contemp Artists, 92; and others. *Media:* Oil. *Res:* Classical and modern art history with emphasis on surrealism; Mihoan civilization and art. *Publ:* Contribr, Beaux Arts, 70-75; Arts, 76-; Artspeak, 82; Art Express, 83; Manhattan Arts, 90-92. *Dealer:* Paul Cohen New York NY. *Mailing Add:* 45 W 86 St New York NY 10024

OBLER, GERI
PRINTMAKER, COLLAGE ARTIST
b New York, NY, May 1, 42. *Study:* Pratt Inst, with Richard Lindner & Fritz Bultman, BFA, 63; Hunter Col, with Ron Gorchov, MA, 66; Columbia Univ, with Peter Golfinopolis, EdD(fine arts & fine arts educ), 74. *Work:* Berkshire Mus, Pittsfield, Mass; Univ Wyo Art Mus, Laramie; US Embassy, Nairobi, Kenya; Conf Bd, Scottish Develop Agency, New York. *Exhib:* Nat Asn Women Artists, New York Dept Cult Affairs, 81 & Traveling Graphics Exhib, 92; 67th Hudson River Mus Ann, Yonkers, NY, 82; Jesse Besser Mus,

Alpena, Mich, 83; Pratt Graphics Ctr Ann, New York, 83; Hunterdon 27th Nat Print Exhib, Wallingford Art Ctr, Pa, 83; Sarah Lawrence Col, Bronxville, NY, 92; and others. *Bibliog:* Malcolm Preston (auth), Three printmakers on display, Newsday, 6/18/79; Helen Harrison (auth), Many shades of white, New York Times, 1/11/81; Jeanne Paris (auth), A showing of Long Island's best graphics, Newsday, 10/6/81; Phyllis Braff (auth), Bending Paper into a Complex Modern Medium, New York Times, 3/16/86. *Mem:* Nat Asn Women Artists; Philadelphia Print Club; Graphic Eye Artists (pres, 78-80, bd dirs, 81). *Dealer:* Henry Howels Gallery 164 Thompson St New York, NY 10012. *Mailing Add:* 26 Brokaw Lane Great Neck NY 11023

OBUCK, JOHN FRANCIS
PAINTER
b Detroit, Mich, Aug 20, 46. *Study:* Wayne State Univ, BFA, 68; Sch of Art Inst Chicago, MFA, 72. *Work:* Mus Contemp Art, Chicago; Cincinnati Mus Art; Chase Manhattan Bank. *Exhib:* Chicago and Vicinity Show, Art Inst Chicago, 80; New Abstraction, Milwaukee Art Ctr, 85; The Persistence of Abstraction, Edwin A Ulrich Mus, Wichita State Univ, Kans; Weights and Balances, Annina Nosei Gallery, New York, 88; Am Acad Rome, Italy, 89; Jack Hanley Gallery, San Francisco, 91; Feigenson-Preston Gallery, Birmingham, Mich, 92. *Teaching:* Instr, Univ NC, 87, Univ Tex, Austin, 87, 90-91, Tyler Sch Art, Philadelphia, 92 & Princeton Univ, NJ, 92-93. *Awards:* NY State Coun on the Arts, 88; Rome Prize Fel Painting, 88-89; Pollock-Krasner Grant, 92. *Bibliog:* Judith Kirshner (auth), rev, Art Forum, 83; Grace Glueck (auth), NY Times, 11/16/84; Kim Levin (auth), rev, Village Voice, 85. *Mem:* Am Abstract Artists. *Media:* Oil Paint, Watercolor. *Dealer:* Feigenson-Preston Gallery 796 N Woodward Birmingham MI; Dart Gallery 712 N Carpenter Chicago IL. *Mailing Add:* PO Box 1148 Church St Sta New York NY 10008

OCAMPO, MIGUEL
PAINTER
b Buenos Aires, Arg, Nov 29, 22. *Study:* Archit. *Work:* Albright-Knox Collection, Buffalo; Mus Mod Art, New York; State Collection, France; Mus Fine Arts, Montevideo, Uruguay; Mus Fine Arts, Buenos Aires. *Exhib:* Stedelijk Mus, Amsterdam, 53; one-man shows, Mus Mod Art, Rio de Janeiro, 59, Galeria Aele, Madrid, 74 & Jacques Kaplan Gallery, NY, 75; Mus d'Art Mod, Paris, 73. *Media:* Acrylic, Oil. *Dealer:* Jacques Kaplan 19 E 71st St New York NY 10021. *Mailing Add:* 135 Hudson St New York NY 10013

OCEPEK, LOU (LOUIS DAVID)
PRINTMAKER, PAINTER
b Detroit, Mich, Aug 27, 42. *Study:* Wayne State Univ, BFA, 64; Univ Iowa, Iowa City, with Lasansky, MA, 67. *Work:* Portland Art Mus, Ore; Portland State Univ, Ore; San Diego State Univ; State Univ NY, Oswego; Western Mich Univ, Kalamazoo. *Comn:* Paintings, Metrop Arts Comn, Portland, Ore, 78 & Art Advocates Inc, Portland, Ore, 78; prints, Clairmont Hotel Collection, Berkeley, 78, Seattle Arts Comn, 80 & Wash Arts Comn, Olympia, 81. *Exhib:* Northwest Printmakers Int, Seattle Art Mus, 70; Testimony to a Process, 74 & Constructions, Drawings and Prints, 76, Portland Art Mus; 12 Northwest Artists, 77 & A Directors Choice, 81, Portland Ctr Visual Arts, 81. *Teaching:* Prof design & printmaking, Portland State Univ, 71-83; prof design & illus, Mont State Univ, Bozeman, 83-. *Awards:* Purchase Awards, The Artist Teacher Today, State Univ NY, 68, San Diego State Print Exhib, 69 & Multiples USA, Western Mich Univ, 70. *Bibliog:* David Stewart (producer), Lou Ocepek, artist, teacher, eckist, ECK World News, 78. *Mem:* Northwest Print Coun (bd dirs, 83). *Media:* Silkscreen; Gouache, Acrylic. *Mailing Add:* Dept Art NMex State Univ Dept 3372 Box 30003 Las Cruces NM 88003

OCHI, F DENIS
ART DEALER, CONSULTANT
b Idaho Falls, Idaho, Feb 11, 46. *Study:* Univ Calif, Los Angeles, BA, 68, MA, 70, MFA, 71, studied with Richard Diebenkorn, Anthony Berlant, Arman, Lynn Foulkes, R B Kitaj & Lee Mullican. *Work:* Long Beach Mus, Calif; Boise Gallery Art, Idaho; Frederick Wright Galleries & Univ Calif, Los Angeles. *Exhib:* Southern Calif Ann, Long Beach Art Mus, Calif, 71; 74th Western Ann, Denver Art Mus, Colo, 74. *Pos:* Dir, Boise State Univ Mus Art, Idaho, 80-84, Ochi Gallery, Boise & Sun Valley, Idaho, currently. *Teaching:* Assoc prof art, Boise State Univ, Idaho, 71-84. *Specialty:* Contemporary paintings, drawings and prints. *Mailing Add:* Ochi Fine Art & Art Services 1322 Main St Boise ID 83702

OCHS, ROBERT DAVID
COLLECTOR, PATRON
b Bloomington, Ill, Mar 27, 15. *Study:* Ill Wesleyan Univ, AB, 36; Univ Ill, MA, 37, PhD, 39. *Pos:* Trustee, Columbia Mus Art, 66-69 & 74-77, acquisition comt, 86-; chmn mus comt, Univ SC, Columbia, 74-76. *Interests:* Contemporary art. *Collection:* Contemporary paintings, prints and sculpture, including Johns, Rauschenberg and Twombly. *Publ:* Co-ed, The Columbia Art Association 1915-1975, The Columbia Museum of Art 1950-1975, A History, Columbia Mus Art, 75. *Mailing Add:* 100 Sunset Blvd No 401 West Columbia SC 29169

OCKENGA, STARR
PHOTOGRAPHER, EDUCATOR
b Boston, Mass, June 14, 38. *Study:* Wheaton Col, Ill, BA, 60; RI Sch Design, with Harry Callahan & Aaron Siskind, MFA, 74. *Work:* Sheldon Art Gallery, Univ Nebr; Bibliot Nat, Paris; Mus Mod Art, New York; Addison Gallery of Am Art, Andover, Mass; Albert O Kuhn Gallery, Univ Md; Polaroid Collection, Cambridge, Mass; Univ Md, Baltimore. *Exhib:* Univ Bridgeport, Conn, 83; Ga State Univ, Atlanta, 83; Currents, Inst Contemp Art, Boston & Baskerville & Watson, New York, 84; Boston Now, Inst Contemp Art, Boston & Contemp Arts Ctr, New Orleans, 85; Catskill Ctr Photog, Woodstock, NY, 86; Albert O Kuhn Gallery, Univ Md, 87; The Ark in the Attic, Children's Mus Boston, Mass, 87; Starr Ockenga, Film in the Cities, St Paul, Minn, 87; Mothers & Daughters, Aperature Found, New York, 87; Photog: A Child's World, Michael Shapiro Gallery, San Francisco, Calif, 88; Am Color, Slatell Art Gallery, Los Cruces, NMex, 88. *Pos:* Dir, Creative Photog Lab, Mass Inst Technol, 76-82; owner, Starr Ockenga Studio, currently. *Teaching:* Assoc prof photog, Mass Inst Technol, 76-82; vis prof, Bennington Col, 84. *Awards:* Nat Endowment Arts Photog Fel, 81; Mass Artist Photog Fel, 83. *Bibliog:* Parish Dobson (auth), Views, PRC Boston, Vol 2 & 3, 81; article, Mass Rev, Vol XXIV, No 1; Kelly Wise (auth), Boston Globe review, 2/27/84; John Dorsey (auth), Baltimore Sun review, 3/9/87; Steve Purchase (auth), Baltimore Sun review, 3/26/87. *Mem:* Soc Photog Educ. *Media:* Polaroid & Fresson Prints. *Publ:* Auth, Mirror After Mirror, Amphoto, 75; Dressup, Addison House, 78; The Ark in the Attic, Godine, 87; World of Wonders, Houghton Miffin, 88; coauth, A World of Wonders, A Trip Thru Numbers, 89 & Then & Now, a Book of Days, 90, Houghton & Mifflin. *Mailing Add:* 68 Laight St New York NY 10013

OCKERSE, THOMAS
DESIGNER, EDUCATOR
b Holland, Apr 12, 40; US citizen. *Study:* Ohio State Univ, BFA, 63; Yale Univ, MFA, 65; with Norman Ives, Herbert Matter, Walker Evans, Paul Rand & Alvin Eisenman. *Work:* Mus Mod Art, New York; Stedelijk Mus, Amsterdam; Jean Brown Arch; Richard Demarco Gallery, Edinburg, Scotland; Indianapolis Mus Art. *Exhib:* Solo exhibs, Gallery Sch Art, Sheffield Polytechnic, Sheffield, Eng, 75, Richard Demarco Gallery Ltd, Edinburgh, Scotland, 75, Wheeler Gallery, Providence, 75, Lit Gallery, Md Writers' Coun, Baltimore, 76, other Bks & So Gallery, Amsterdam, Neth, 77, Swain Sch Design Gallery, New Bedford, Mass, 79 & Feren's Art Gallery, Hull, Eng, 81; Faculty Biennial, RI Sch Design Mus, 88; Decade of the Eighties, Belk Bldg Art Gallery, Western Carolina Univ, Cullowhee, NC, 88; Kopie Als Origineel, Mus Photogr, Antwerp, Belg, 88; Universal/Unique, Rosenwald-Wolf Gallery, Univ Arts, Philadelphia, 88; Artist's Books: An Investigation of Time/Sequence Manipulation, Western Carolina Univ, Bell Gallery, 90; and many other one-man & group exhibs. *Pos:* Vpres bd, Am Inst Graphic Arts, 80-85, chmn educ comt, currently; consult graphic design, United Nations Development prog, 86; expert graphic design, Nat Inst Design, Ahmedabad, India, 86. *Teaching:* Asst prof graphic design, Ind Univ, Bloomington, 67-71; assoc prof graphic design, RI Sch Design, Providence, 71-, head graphic design dept, 73- *Awards:* Fac Develop Fund Grant, RI Sch Design, 85; Nominated, John Frazier Award Excellence in teaching, RI Sch Design, 85-; Educ Award, Am Ctr Design, Chicago, 91; and many others. *Bibliog:* J Bowles (auth), This Book is a Movie, Dell, 71; Kostelanetz (auth), Breakthrough Fictioneers, Something Else Press, 72; Camera Three (NY TV prog), 74. *Mem:* Semiotic Soc Am; Am Inst Graphic Arts; Indust Designers Soc Am; Soc Typographic Arts; Am Ctr Design; and others. *Publ:* Auth, Professional degrees for graphic design, proposed progs, RI Sch Design, 81; Aperture 93, Aperture Inc, Millerton, NY, 83; Design education theory vs practice, Am Inst Graphic Arts J, Vol 2, No 4, 84; De-sign/super-sign, Semotica 52-3/4, Mouton Publ, 84; Chaoni CE (or chance/choice), Providence, RI, 88; and many others. *Mailing Add:* 37 Woodbury St Providence RI 02906

O'CONNELL, ANN BROWN
PRINTMAKER, COLLECTOR
b Worcester, Mass, June 3, 31. *Study:* Bradford Col, AA; Boston Univ Exten; George Mason Univ, BA(art hist); Sumi-e with Evalyn Aaron, Port Washington, NY; Chinese brush painting with Audrey Nossal, Potomac, Md; also with Roddy McLean, Annandale, Va; etching, monotype, watercolor, Art League Sch, Alexandria, Va. *Exhib:* Sumi-e Soc Am Inc Ann Exhibs; Sixth Ann Exhib, Bank of Tokyo Trust Co, New York, 69; 7th Ann Exhib, Nippon Club, New York, 70; Am Inst Architects, 79 & 80; Open Ann Art Exhib Anthenaecen, Mid-Atlantic Regio, 92. *Awards:* President's Prize, Sumi-e Soc Am, Inc, 69. *Mem:* Sumi-e Soc Am, Inc (mem secy, 71-73, founder, Wash Chap, 72, nat vpres, 72-73, nat pres, 74-78); Washington, DC Print Club. *Collection:* Print collection specializing in early 20th century American printmakers; 19th and early 20th American and European paintings. *Publ:* Coauth (with Brian O'Connell), Volunteers in Action, Found Press, New York, 89. *Mailing Add:* 1341 Woodside Dr McLean VA 22101

O'CONNELL, DANIEL MOYLAN
PAINTER, ADMINISTRATOR
b Springfield, Mass, Aug 24, 49. *Study:* Univ Iowa, Iowa City, BFA, 72, MA, 75. *Work:* Berkshire, Pittsfield, Mass; Univ Iowa; Air Gold, New York; City of Pittsfield, Mass; Canyon Ranch of the Berkshires, Lenox, Mass. *Comn:* Mural, Berkshire Housing Authority, Pittsfield, Mass, 86; mural, Brenner Investments, Pittsfield, Mass, 87; mural, Nichols Brothers Inc, 87; Vietnam Vets Mem Mural, 90 & 91; mural, Capitol Theatre, Pittsfield, Mass, 92-93. *Exhib:* Graduate Exhib, Univ Iowa Mus, Iowa City, 75; Alumni Exhib, Berkshire Community Col, Pittsfield, Mass, 76; Abstract Landscapes, Berkshire Artisans, Pittsfield, Mass, 76; Berkshire Art Asn Exhib, Berkshire Mus, Pittsfield, 80 & 81; Artists Living in the Berkshires, Clark Whitney Gallery, Lenox, Mass, 86. *Collections Arranged:* Arts and the Handicapped, Univ Mass-Northeast Artist Festival, 80; Arts and Mental Illness, Boston Univ, 90. *Pos:* Comnr Cult Affairs, Pittsfield, Mass, 76-; regional consult, Nat Endowment Arts, 80-82. *Teaching:* Prof watercolor, Berkshire Artisans, 78-80, 81- , mural painting 86- *Awards:* Gov's Award, Design in Mass, 82; Arts Inter-Arts Grant, Nat Endowment, 85; City of Pittsfield Ann Report Award.

Bibliog: Rosalyn Wilder (auth), Arts and Older Americans, Harcourt Press, 82. *Mem:* Consortium of Local Arts Agencies in Mass; Berkshire Arts Alliance; Nat Alliance Local Arts Agencies; Lichtenstein Found Music & Art (assoc dir, 82-88); Pittsfield Cult Comn (assoc dir, 85-86, Comnr 87-). *Mailing Add:* Berkshire Artisans Community Arts Ctr 28 Renne Ave Pittsfield MA 01201

O'CONNELL, EDWARD E
PHOTOGRAPHER, PRINTMAKER
b New York, NY. *Study:* Hofstra Univ, BS; Pratt Inst, MFA. *Work:* Metrop Mus Art, New York; Brooklyn Mus, NY; Philadelphia Free Libr, Pa; Univ Mass, Amherst; Univ Tenn, Knoxville; plus others. *Exhib:* Photography into Sculpture, Mus Mod Art, New York, 70; 17th Nat Print, Brooklyn Mus, 70; US Pavilion, World's Fair, Osaka, Japan, 70; New Talent in Printmaking, Am Artists, New York, 70; Oversize Prints, Whitney Mus, New York, 71. *Teaching:* Asst prof photog & graphics, Montclair Sch Visual Arts, New York, 69-71; asst prof photog & printmaking, Fordham Univ, 70- *Awards:* Found Grant in Printmaking, Louis Comfort Tiffany Found, 66; Purchase Award, Brooklyn Mus, 70. *Bibliog:* James R Mellow (auth), Contemporary prints, the medium is not the message, New York Times, 6/28/70. *Mem:* Col Art Asn Am. *Media:* Silkscreen; Acrylic. *Dealer:* Assoc Am Artists Gallery 663 Fifth Ave New York NY 10022. *Mailing Add:* 119 Spring St New York NY 10021

O'CONNELL, GEORGE D
PRINTMAKER, EDUCATOR
b Madison, Wis, Oct 16, 26. *Study:* Univ Wis, BS, 50, MS, 51; Ohio State Univ; Rijksakademie Van Beeldende Kunsten, Amsterdam, Netherlands, Fulbright fel, 59-60. *Work:* Baltimore Mus Art; Smithsonian Inst, Washington, DC; Libr Cong, Washington, DC; Gemeentemuseum Van Schone Kunsten, The Hague, Netherlands; Brit Mus, London, Eng; and others. *Comn:* Volunteer artist prog, Dept Hist Army, 71; presentation print ed, Rochester Print Club, 83. *Exhib:* Am Embassy, Dublin, Ireland; Baltimore Mus; John & Mabel Ringling Mus Art; Contemporary American Graphic Art, Corcoran Gallery Art, Washington, DC; US Info Agency Traveling Exhib Contemp Prints; Miriam Perlman Gallery, Chicago, 84; one man show, The Jazz Series, Oswego Art Guild, NY, 88; Retrospective, All that Jazz, 54-92, SUNY Oswego, Tyler Gallery, NY, 92. *Pos:* Dir, Master Printer, Grey Heron Press, Oswego, NY. *Teaching:* Assoc prof printmaking, Univ Md, 61-68; prof printmaking, State Univ New York Col, Oswego, 69-91, prof emer, 91-; vis artist, Tamarind Inst, Univ NMex, 79. *Awards:* Creative Art Award, State Univ NY, Oswego, 86; Soc Am Graphic Artists Award, 89; Juror's Commendation, Boston Printmakers, Mem Exhib, 92. *Mem:* Boston Printmakers; Print Club, Philadelphia; Soc Am Graphic Artists; Int Soc Graphic Artists. *Media:* Relief, Lithography. *Mailing Add:* 39 Baylis St Oswego NY 13126

O'CONNELL, KENNETH ROBERT
FILMMAKER, ADMINISTRATOR
b Ogden, Utah, Jan 22, 45. *Study:* Univ Ore, BS, 66, MFA, 72. *Work:* Sinking Creek Film Collection, Nashville; Univ Ore Film Libr, Eugene; Uncross Found Collection, Wyo; Northwest Film Study Ctr, Portland; Charles Samu Int Prod, New York; Int Animation Libr, Tokyo, Japan. *Exhib:* USA Film Festival, Cult Ctr Hall, Dallas, 80; Athens Int Festival, Univ Theater, Athens, Ohio, 81; Hong Kong Film Festival, Exhib Hall, Hong Kong, 81; Oregon Biennial, Portland Art Mus, 83 & 87; New York Film Festival Exposition, Metrop Mus Art, New York, 85; Bumbershoot '85, Seattle Art Comn, 85; Hiroshima '85, Peace Park, Japan, 85; Zagreb '86 World Animation Festival, Yugoslavia, 86; Stuttgart '90 Animation Festival, Int Festival of Children's Films, Chicago, 90; Medicine Wheel Animation Festival, Groton, Mass. *Collections Arranged:* Computers in the Creative Process (traveling exhib), Univ Ore Mus Art, 86-89; Computers in the Creative Process II, 89-91; Jack Wilkinson; Artist, Philosopher 1914-1973, Univ Ore Mus Art, 90. *Pos:* Co-dir, Comput Graphics Conf, Univ Ore, Eugene, 81-82; steering comt mem, Pac NW Comput Graphics Conf, Eugene, Ore, 82-90; Electronic Theather Comt, ACM/SIGGRAPH, Chicago, Ill. *Teaching:* Prof film & visual thinking, Univ Ore, Eugene, 78-83, assoc prof comput art & head dept, 83-; adj prof slides & film, Goddard Col, Vt, 80-81. *Awards:* Cash Award, Ann Arbor Film Festival, 80; Third Place, USA Film Festival, 80; Selection Award, New York Film Expos, 85; First Place, Eugene Celebration Film & Video Festival. *Bibliog:* Cathy Goethals (auth), Painting at the Speed of Thought, Venture, 84. *Mem:* Col Art Asn; Found Art, Theory & Educ; Soc Animation Studies (SAS); Assoc Computer Machinery (ACM-SIGGRAPH). *Media:* Computer Graphics, Drawing. *Publ:* Auth various articles in Sch Arts Mag, 84-92. *Dealer:* Film Distributor: Picture Start 221 E Cullerton 6th Fl Chicago IL 60616; Chicago Filmmakers 1229 W Belmont Chicago IL 60657. *Mailing Add:* Dept Fine & Applied Arts Univ Ore Eugene OR 97403

O'CONNOR, FRANCIS VALENTINE
HISTORIAN, LECTURER
b Brooklyn, NY, Feb 14, 37. *Study:* Manhattan Col, New York, BA, 59; Johns Hopkins Univ, MA, 60, PhD(art hist), 65. *Pos:* Sr vis res assoc, Nat Collection of Fine Arts, Smithsonian Inst, Washington, DC, 70-72; ed & publ, Fed Art Patronage Notes, 74-86; dir, Raphael Res Enterprises, 79- *Teaching:* Lectr art hist, Univ Md, 64-66, asst prof, 66-70; Robert Sterling Clark, vis prof art hist, Williams Col, 90. *Awards:* Grant, Nat Endowment Arts, 67-68; fel, US Capitol Hist Soc, 87; Independent Scholars Fel, Nat Endowment Humanities, 87-88; Rockefeller Resident Fel, Inst Med Humanities, Univ Tex, Med Br, Galveston, 91. *Mem:* Soc fro the Arts, Relig & Contemp Cult (mem bd, 74-80); Col Art Asn; Founder Asn Independent Hist Art (pres, 83-87). *Res:* Twentieth century American art; New Deal Art Projects; abstract expressionism; projected history of American mural; psychodymanics of creativity. *Publ:* Auth, Jackson Pollock, Mus of Mod Art, NY, 67; Federal Support for the Visual Arts: The New Deal and Now, NY Graphic Soc, 69; 000577570ew Deal Art Projects: An Anthology of Memoirs, Smithsonian Press, 72; Art for the Millions, NY Graphic Soc, 73; coauth & co-ed (with Eugene V Thaw), Jackson Pollock: A catalogue raisonne of paintings, drawings and other works, Yale Univ, 78. *Mailing Add:* 250 E 73rd St 11C New York NY 10021

O'CONNOR, JOHN ARTHUR
PAINTER, ADMINISTRATOR
b Twin Falls, Idaho, Jan 23, 40. *Study:* Univ Calif, Davis, AB(with hon & scholar), 61, with Wayne Thiebaud & William T Wiley, MAA, 63; San Francisco Art Inst(scholar), with James Weeks, 61. *Work:* Ringling Mus Art, Sarasota, Fla; State Calif Collection, Sacramento; Bates Gallery, Edinboro State Col, Pa; Kemper Gallery, Kansas City Art Inst, Mo. *Comn:* Carr Van Anda Award for New York Times, Ohio Univ, 68; triptych, comn by Mr & Mrs George Varian, Palo Alto, Calif, 71. *Exhib:* 20th Ann Nat Exhib of Prints & Drawings, Okla Art Ctr, Oklahoma City, 78; 46th Southeastern Competition: Drawing, Photog & Printmaking, Southeastern Ctr Contemp Art, Winston-Salem, NC, 78; Southern Realism, Miss Mus Art, Jackson, 79 & traveling; Personal Statements: Drawing, Southeastern Ctr Contemp Art, 79; Reality of Illusion, Denver Art Mus & traveling; State Univ Syst Painting Fac, Visual Arts Gallery, Fla Int Univ, Miami, 80; Ann Exhib Am Painting, Butler Inst Am Art, Youngstown, Ohio (honorable mention), 82; Mainstream America, The Collection of Phil Desind, Butler Inst Am Art, Youngstown, Ohio, 87; 52nd Ann Nat Exhib Contemp Paintings, Soc Four Arts, Palm Beach, Fla, 90; 1991 Cheekwood Nat Painting Exhib, Nashville, Tenn, 91; and many other group & one-man shows. *Pos:* Dir, Art Gallery, Univ Calif, Davis, 62-63, Art Gallery, Ohio Univ, 67-68 & Appalachian Ctr Crafts, Smithville, Tenn, 81-; sr investr, Ctr Creative & Optimal Design, Univ Fla, 72-, dir dept art gallery, 79-80, dir, MBA degree prog arts admin, 91-; artist-in-residence, Col Creative Studies, Univ Calif, Santa Barbara, 74; fac prog consult, Bd Regents, State Univ System, Fla, 83- *Teaching:* Inst painting & drawing, Univ Calif, Santa Barbara, 63-64 & Ohio Univ, 65-69; prof painting, drawing & contemp art hist, Univ Fla, 69- *Awards:* Modular Systems Theory & Design Analysis Award, Air Force Off Sci Res, 74; State of Fla Individual Artist's Fel, 91 & 92; Southern Arts Fedn, Nat Endowment Arts Regional Fel, 92. *Bibliog:* Hariette von Breton (auth), O'Connor show, Artforum Mag, 64; Betty Rubenstein (auth), Tallahassee Democrat, 10/14/88; Erin Birx (auth), Gainsville Sun Scene, 7/3/92. *Mem:* Col Art Asn Am; Fla Cult Action Alliance. *Media:* Acrylic, Watercolor. *Publ:* Ed, Graphics 1968-Ultimate Concerns, 68; coauth, Unbottle Your Creative Ideas-A Cooperative Venture of Engineering and Art, 72; contribr, A Pictorial History of the World, 75; Florida Arts Celebration and the Art in Public Places Initiative, Int Conf Sculpture, Dublin, Ireland, 89; auth, The public art process in Gainesville: a case history, J Arts Mgt, Law & Soc, fall 92. *Dealer:* Capricorn Galleries 4849 Rugby Ave Bethesda MD 20814-3077. *Mailing Add:* c/o Dept Art 302 Fac Univ Fla Gainesville FL 32611

O'CONNOR, STANLEY JAMES
HISTORIAN, EDUCATOR
Study: Cornell Univ, BA, 51, PhD, 64; Univ Va, MA, 54. *Pos:* Dir, Southeast Asia Program, Cornell Univ, 79-84. *Teaching:* Prof art hist, Cornell Univ, 64- *Mem:* Asn Asian Studies (SE Asia Coun, 78-81); Borneo Res Soc; Malaysian Br, Royal Asiatic Soc; Am Comt South Asian Art; Siam Soc. *Res:* Early trade of Southeast Asia; Buddhist and Hindu art. *Publ:* Auth, Hindu Gods of Peninsular Siam, Artibus Asiae, 72; contribr, Buddhist Votive Tablest & Caves in Peninsular Siam, Nat Mus Bangkok, 74; contribr, Iron working as spiritual inquiry in Indonesia, Hist of Relig, 75; contribr, Tambralinga and the Khmer Empire, Siam Soc J, 75; coauth, Dyer's Art, Weaver's Hand: Textiles from the Indonesian Archipelago, 85. *Mailing Add:* Dept of Art Hist Goldwin Smith Hall Cornell Univ Ithaca NY 14853

O'CONNOR, THOM
PRINTMAKER
b Detroit, Mich, June 26, 37. *Study:* Fla State Univ, BA; Cranbrook Acad Art, MFA; Tamarind Printery Fel, 64; State Univ NY Res Found Fel, 65 & 72. *Work:* Mus Mod Art, Whitney Mus Am Art, New York; Brooklyn Mus; Philadelphia Mus Art; Puskin Mus, Moscow. *Comn:* Witches of Salem (suite), State Coun Arts, NY, 72. *Exhib:* Brooklyn Print Ann, 68; San Diego Print Invitational, 72. *Teaching:* Prof lithography, Univ Albany, 62-; vis artist, Swedish Acad Fine Arts, 78 & Cranbrook Acad Art, 81. *Awards:* Rissanen Prize, Kuopio, Finland, 83. *Dealer:* Hanna-Kent Gallery, New York NY. *Mailing Add:* Moss Rd Voorheesville NY 12186

OCVIRK, OTTO G
SCULPTOR, PRINTMAKER
b Detroit, Mich, Nov 13, 22. *Study:* State Univ Iowa, BFA & MFA. *Work:* Dayton Art Inst, Ohio; Detroit Inst Art; Dayton Co, Minneapolis. *Exhib:* Walker Art Ctr, Minneapolis, 47-49; Brooklyn Nat Print, NY, 49; Northwest Printmakers, Seattle, Wash, 49; San Francisco Ann Print & Drawing, 49-50; Libr Cong Nat Print Show, Washington, DC, 50. *Teaching:* Prof emer art, Bowling Green State Univ, 50- *Awards:* Sculpture Exhib, Walker Art Ctr, Minneapolis, 47; Mich Artist Exhib, Hal H Smith, Detroit, 50; Broadcast Media Award, WBGU-TV, 19th Ann Broadcasters, San Francisco. *Media:* Stone; Intaglio. *Publ:* Coauth, Art Fundamentals, Theory and Practice, Brown, 60, 68, 75, 81, 85 & 90. *Mailing Add:* 231 Haskins St Bowling Green OH 43402

ODA, MASAYUKI
SCULPTOR
b Tokyo, Japan, Jan 27, 50. *Study:* Cranbrook Acad Art, Mich, 76; Univ Calif Los Angeles, MA, 78, MFA, 79. *Work:* Univ Calif Los Angeles Career Planning & Replacement Ctr, Security Pac Bank, Keye/Donna/Pearlstein Inc, Robert Ross Inc, Yasuda Bank and Trust, & Kajima Int, Los Angeles, Calif; Citizen Corp, Santa Monica, Calif; Detroit Art Inst, Mich; Merchant Bank of Beverly Hills, Calif; Cranbrook Acad Art, Bloomfield Hills, Mich. *Comn:* Sculpture plaza, Mazda, Flatrock, Mich, 87-87, comn by Frederick Weisman Virginia Beach, 90; environ sculpture, Osaka Expo, Japan, 90. *Exhib:* Solo exhibs, Yaw Gallery, Birmingham, Mich, 75, 80, Art Asia Gallery, Cambridge, Mass, 75, Recreation Ctr Univ Calif Los Angeles, 76, Mizuno Gallery , Calif, 83, Hunsaker/Schlesinger Gallery, Calif, 85, Krygier/ Landau Contemp Art, Calif, 86, Virginia Beach Ctr for Arts, 90; Imagine There's a Future, Japanese Am Cult & Community Ctr, Los Angeles, Calif, 85; Japan-America, Long Beach Mus Art, Calif, 86; sculpture, Krygier/ Landau Contemp Art, Calif, 89; Int Environ Art Exhib, Osaka, Japan, 90. *Awards:* Travel Grant, Ford Found, 78; Grant, Nat Endowment Arts, 88; First Prize, Int Environ Art Competition, Osaka, Japan, 90. *Dealer:* James Corcoran Gallery Santa Monica CA. *Mailing Add:* 441 N Croft Ave Los Angeles CA 90048

ODA, MAYUMI
PAINTER, PRINTMAKER
b Tokyo, Japan, June 2, 41. *Study:* Tokyo Univ Fine Art, BA, 66. *Work:* Mus Mod Art, New York; Mus Fine Arts, Boston; Libr Cong, Washington, DC; Honolulu Acad Art; Cincinnati Art Mus; Cleveland Mus; Portland Art Mus. *Comn:* Poster, Rainbow Art Found, New York, 77; Goddess of Hawaii, East West Ctr, Honolulu, 85; poster, Hawaiian Int Film Festival, Honolulu, 85. *Exhib:* Mus Mod Art, Tokoyo, 70; 22nd Nat Exhib Prints, Libr Cong, Washington, DC, 71; Bradford City Gallery, Eng, 72; Mus Mod Art, Ljubljana, Yugoslavia, 73; solo exhibs, Goddesses: Visions of Women, Univ Hawaii, Honolulu, Tucson Art Mus, Ariz, 82 & Expression of Yin, Mills Col, Oakland, Calif, 86, Expression of Yin, Mills Col, Oakland, Calif, 86; retrospective, East West Ctr, Honolulu, 85; Honolulu Acad Art 87; Cathedral St John the Divine, NY. *Teaching:* Artist-in-residence, Inst Cult & Communication, East West Ctr, Honolulu, 85-86. *Bibliog:* Martha Gressing (producer), Women Artists, KQED-TV, San Francisco, 78; Mary & Norman Tolman (auths), People who make Japanese prints, Sobunsha, 83; Pauline Sugino (auth), Goddesses, vision of women, Bridge Mag, 84; Connecting Conversations, Eucalyptus Press; Womens Culture, Bettina Aptheker Gallerie, 88; Mary Ann Lutzker (auth), Goddess Banners, Orientation, 2/90. *Publ:* Collabr, Goddesses, Lancaster Miller, 84; Song of Vegetables, Koguma Sha, Tokyo, 86; Goodesses, Volcano Press, 88; Happy Veggies, Parallex Press, 88. *Mailing Add:* 1709 Shore Line Hwy PO Box Sausalito CA 94965

ODATE, TOSHIO
CONCEPTUAL ARTIST, INSTRUCTOR
b Tokyo, Japan, July 9, 30. *Study:* Art Sch, Tokyo, 50-54; Nat Chiba Univ, 57-58. *Work:* Rochester Mem Art Gallery, NY; Bundy Art Gallery, Waitsfield, Vt; Great Southwest Atlanta Corp, Atlanta, Ga; Brooklyn Mus, NY. *Exhib:* Waning Moos and Rising Sun--Japanese Artists, Houston Mus Art, Tex, 59; Joseph H Hirshhorn Collection, Solomon R Guggenheim Mus, New York, 63; The Artists Reality, New Sch Social Res, New York, 64; Whitney Mus Am Art Sculpture Ann, 65-66; Attitudes, Brooklyn Mus, 70. *Teaching:* Instr sculpture, Brooklyn Mus Art Sch, 61- & Pratt Inst, 68-82; guest lectr, Denver Mus Art, 67, Univ Wis, Wausau, 68 & Univ Ky, 69. *Publ:* Contribr, Modern sculpture from the Joseph H Hirshhorn Collection, 62; Modern American sculpture, 67. *Mailing Add:* Dept Fine Arts South Hall Pratt Inst 200 Willougby Ave Brooklyn NY 11205

O'DELL, ERIN (ANNE)
PAINTER, DESIGNER
b Phoenix, Ariz, Dec 7, 38. *Study:* Moore Col Art, BFA(textile design); Ariz State Univ; also with John Pike in Mex, Jamaica, Ireland, Italy & Guatemala. *Work:* Ariz Bank, Phoenix; Colo Nat Bank, Colorado Springs; First Nat Bank, Mesa, Ariz; Valley Nat Bank, Scottsdale & Mesa, Ariz. *Exhib:* Two Flags Festival Arts, Douglas, Ariz, 73-79; Laramie Nat Miniature Show, 78 & 79; Ariz State Fair, 81; La Galeria Group Show, Casa Grande, 85; Solo exhibs, Scottsdale Methodist Church, Ariz, 86 & Phoenix Women's Club, 88; and others. *Pos:* Designer, Henry Cantor, Inc, Philadelphia, Pa, 61-64; freelance designer, C A Reed Co, Williamsport, Pa & Beach Prod, Kalamazoo, Mich, 64-75; artist, Modern Color Printing, Mesa, 69-74. *Teaching:* Instr hist textiles, Moore Col Art, 63-65. *Awards:* Mesa Artist of the Year, Mesa Art League, 73 & 79; Watercolor Award, Douglas Art Asn, 73; Artist of the Year, Ariz Saguaro Artists League, 77. *Mem:* Southwestern Watercolor Soc; Scottsdale Artists League; Midwest Watercolor Soc; Ariz Artists Guild; Watercolor West. *Media:* Watercolor. *Mailing Add:* 1310 E Grandview Mesa AZ 85203

O DONOHUE, TEIGE ROS
PAINTER, PRINTMAKER
b New York, NY, Apr 15, 42; US & Irish citizen. *Study:* City Univ New York, with Arun Bose, BFA(cum laude), MFA(summa cum laude). *Work:* Art Inst Chicago; Brooklyn Mus; Hugh Lane Munic Gallery, Dublin, Ireland; Nat Collection Fine Arts, Washington, DC; Tate Gallery, London. *Exhib:* Nat Arts Club, New York, 76; Hudson River Mus, Yonkers, NY, 77; Magic Realism, Utah Mus Fine Art, traveling, 79-81; Gallery Mod Art, Ljubljana, Yugoslavia, 79 & 81; Art Inst Chicago, 80-81. *Bibliog:* William Zimmer (auth), article, Arts Mag, 2/76. *Media:* Oil, Mixed Media; Etching, Aquatint. *Mailing Add:* c/o Lublin Graphics 95 E Putnam Ave Greenwich CT 06830

O'DOWD, ROBERT See Dowd, Robert (O'Dowd Robert)

OECHSLI, KELLY
ILLUSTRATOR
b Butte, Mont, Feb 23, 18. *Study:* Cornish Sch of Art, Seattle, Washington, cert. *Pos:* Trustee, Mt Pleasant Pub Libr, Pleasantville, NY. *Awards:* Ann Children's Picture Storybook Award, Univ Ga, 83. *Media:* Multimedia. *Publ:* Illusr, Too Many Monkeys, Western Publ, 80; Herbie's Troubles, Dutton, 80; auth & illusr, Home Sweet Home, Carnival Press, 83; illusr, In My Garden , Macmillan, 85; auth & illusr, Mice at Bat, Harper & Row, 86. *Mailing Add:* 115 Sherman Ave Hawthorne NY 10532

OEHLSCHLAEGER, FRANK J
DEALER
b Paducah, Ky, Sept 8, 10. *Study:* Cornell Univ, grad, 33. *Pos:* Dir, Chicago Galleries of Assoc Am Artists, 45-47; dir, Marshall Fields & Co Art Gallery, Chicago, 47-49; dir & owner, Oehlschlaeger Gallery, Chicago, 49-, Sarasota, Fla, 62- *Specialty:* Contemporary American and European art. *Mailing Add:* c/o Oehlschlaeger 285 Blvd of the Presidents Sarasota FL 33577

OESTERLE, LEONHARD FRIEDRICH
SCULPTOR, INSTRUCTOR
b Bietigheim, Ger, Mar 3, 15; Can citizen. *Study:* With Fritz Wotruba, Otto Muller & Hans Aeschbacher, Kunst Gewerbeschule, Zurich, Switz. *Work:* Württembergischer Kunstverein, Staats Gallery, Stuttgart, Ger; Nat Gallery, Ottawa, Can; London Art Gallery, Ont; Kitchener Waterloo Art Gallery, Can. *Comn:* Four figure group in bronze, Col McLaughlin Collegiate, Oshawa, 63; bronze statuary, St Augustin Chapel, Scarborough, Can, 64; wall sculpture & mural, Cent Labs, Toronto, 67; sculpture in lobby, Can Trust Bldg, London, Ont, 69; large sculpture for park, Sarnia, Ont, 79. *Exhib:* Young Sculptor's Exhib, Helmhaus, Zurich, 49; Schwebische Maler und Bildhauer, Zurich, 51. *Teaching:* Instr sculpture, Ont Col Art. *Awards:* Ont Soc Artists Spec Award, 68. *Bibliog:* John Sommer (auth), Leonhard Oesterle, Peter Shore, 11/71. *Mem:* Sculptor's Soc Can (vpres, 58 & 70-72); Ont Soc Artists; Royal Can Acad Arts. *Media:* Stone, Diverse Metals. *Dealer:* Sussex Gallery 515 Sussex Dr Ottawa ON Can; Del Bello Gallery 307 Queen St W Toronto ON Canada M5V 2A4. *Mailing Add:* 27 Alcina Ave Toronto ON M6T 2E7 Canada

OESTREICH, JEFFREY
CERAMIST
b St Paul, Minn, 1947. *Study:* Univ Minn, studied with Warren MacKenzie, 67; Bemidji State Univ, BA; studied with Bernard Leach, Eng, 69-71. *Work:* Everson Mus Art, Syracuse; Victoria & Albert Mus, London; Taipei Fine Arts Mus, Taiwan; Kansas City Art Inst; Smithsonian Mus; and others. *Exhib:* Garth Clark Gallery, New York, 91; Pro-Art, St Louis, Mo, 92. *Awards:* Fel, Nat Endowment Arts, 86; Minn State Arts Board Fel Grant, 90; Double Award of Merit, Fletcher Challenge Ceramics Award, Auckland, New Zealand, 91. *Dealer:* Pro-Art 5595 Pershing St Louis MO 63112. *Mailing Add:* 36835 Pottery Trail Taylors Falls MN 55084

OFFNER, ELLIOT
SCULPTOR, PRINTMAKER
b Brooklyn, NY, July 12, 31. *Study:* Cooper Union; Yale Univ, with Josef Albers & Rico Lebrun, BFA & MFA. *Work:* Brooklyn Mus; De Cordova Mus, Lincoln, Mass; Lowe Art Mus, Syracuse Univ; Smith Col; Joseph Hirshhorn Mus. *Comn:* Bronze Plaques (12), Veda Corp, Alexandria, Va; Cockerell, bronze, Springfield, Mass; three bronze sculptures, Nat Asn Letter Carriers, Milwaukee, Wis, 89; The Welcoming, bronze, Children's Inn, Nat Inst Health, Bethesda, Md, 90; Fountain and Sculptures (granite & bronze, 20' x 30' x 17'), Downtown Minneapolis. *Exhib:* One-man shows, Forum Gallery, New York, 64, 67, 72, 79 & 84, Int Fine Arts Galleries, Washington, DC, 68, 73 & 79, Slater Mem Mus, Norwich, Conn, 76, Boston Atheneum, 79, Jorgensen Gallery, Univ Conn, 80 & Springfield Mus Fine Arts, 84 & Franz Bader Gallery, Washington, DC, 86 & 92; and other one-man and group shows. *Pos:* Dir, Rosemary Press, 67-; printer, Smith Col, 75- *Teaching:* Instr art, Univ Mass, 59-60; prof art, Smith Col, 60-74, Andrew W Mellon prof humanities, 74-; vis lectr, Royal Col Art; Yale Univ, others. *Awards:* Vis fel, Wolfson Col, Cambridge Univ, 89; Mary Amelia Cummins Harvey Fel, Girton Col, Cambridge Univ, 90; Gold Medal, Nat Sculpture Soc, 92. *Bibliog:* Cathedral's death camp sculpture, One World, 9/78; The sculpture of Elliot Offner, Hampshire Life, 5/26/79; The Fowl of the Air, the Fish of the Sea & the Beasts of the Field: The Animal Sculptures of Elliot Offner, Mus Fine Arts, Springfield, Mass, 84. *Mem:* Printing Hist Soc; William Morris Soc; Am Printing Hist Asn; Bibliog Soc; Sculptors' Guild; Hon Fel, Nat Sculpture Soc. *Media:* Wood, Bronze; Mixed. *Publ:* Auth & illusr, The Granjon Arabesque, Rosemary Press, 69. *Dealer:* Forum Gallery 1018 Madison Ave New York NY 10021. *Mailing Add:* 74 Washington Ave Northampton MA 01060

OGINZ, RICHARD
SCULPTOR, INSTRUCTOR
b Philadelphia, Pa, Feb 7, 44. *Study:* Tyler Sch Art, Temple Univ, BFA, 66; Univ Wis-Madison, MA, MFA, 68. *Work:* Los Angeles Co Mus Art, Security Pac Bank & Wells Fargo Bank, Los Angeles; Arts Coun Gt Brit, London; Bradford Mus, Yorkshire. *Exhib:* Ellie Blankfort Gallery, Los Angeles, 77, Molly Barnes Gallery, 80, Arco Ctr Visual Art, 80, Art Space Gallery, 85, The Figure, Security Pacific Bank Gallery, 87, Koslow Gallery, Los Angeles; Edge Gallery, Fullerton, Calif, 83-84; Concrete, Paulo Salvador Gallery, New York, 86; Artists Liaison, Evanston Art Ctr, Ill, 88; Table as Art, Gallery Functional Art, Santa Monica, Calif, 88. *Teaching:* Principal lectr sculpture, Middlesex Polytech, London, 74-76; sculpture fac, Otis Art Inst Parsons Sch Design, Los Angeles, 76- *Awards:* Gregory Fel, Leeds Univ, Yorkshire, Eng, 70-73; New Talent Award, Los Angeles Co Mus Art, 79; Ford Found Grant,

79. *Bibliog:* Susan Geer (auth), Richard Oginz, Robert Miller, Images & Issues, 3/84; Pamela Hammond (auth), Narratives of isolation, Artweek, 11/10/84; Peter Plagens (auth), Bee-Bop Da Reebok in LA, Art in Am, 4/85. *Media:* Mixed. *Mailing Add:* c/o Ruth Bachfner Gallery 926 Colorado Ave Santa Monica CA 90401

O'GORMAN, JAMES FRANCIS
EDUCATOR, WRITER
b St Louis, Mo, Sept 19, 33. *Study:* Washington Univ, Mo, BA(arch); Univ Ill, Urbana, MA(arch); Harvard Univ, PhD. *Teaching:* Grace Slack McNeil Prof of Am Art, Wellesley Col, 75- *Awards:* NEH fel, 88-89. *Mem:* Soc of Archit Historians (pres, 70-72); Col Art Asn; life fel Philadelphia Athenaeum. *Res:* American art and architecture. *Publ:* Auth, The Architecture of the Monastic Library in Italy, New York Univ Press, 72; coauth, The Architecture of Frank Furness, Philadelphia Mus of Art, 73; auth, H H Richardson and His Office: Selected Drawings, Harvard Col, 74; This Other Gloucester, pvt publ, 76; H H Richardson, Architectural Forms for an American Society, Univ Chicago Press, 87; Three American Architects: Richardson, Sullivan and Wright, 1865-1915, Univ Chicago Press, 91. *Mailing Add:* Dept of Art Wellesley Col Wellesley MA 02181

O'HAGAN, DESMOND BRIAN
PAINTER
b Wiesbaden, Ger, July 17, 59; US citizen. *Study:* Univ NMex 77-79; Colo Inst Art, AA, 82. *Work:* Denver Pub Libr Art Collection, Colo. *Exhib:* Cancer League Colo Ann Benefit, Hyatt Regency Hotel, Denver, 86-92; 100 Years of Colorado Artists, Hirschfeld Bldg, Denver, 88; Pastel Soc Am Ann Exhib, Nat Arts Club, Landmark Bldg, New York, 87 & 88; Celebration of the Arts-A Fine Art Show, Highlands Ranch Mansion, Colo, 91. *Bibliog:* Stanley L Cuba (auth), Introductions-Desmond O'Hagan, Southwest Art, 11/87; M Stephen Doherty (auth), Stirring the viewer's imagination, Am Artist, 12/89; Donna Michaels (auth), Artists worth watching, Art-Talk, 6- 7/90. *Mem:* Pastel Soc Am. *Media:* Pastels, Oils. *Mailing Add:* 121 S Holly St Denver CO 80222

O'HARA, MORGAN
PAINTER, CONCEPTUAL ARTIST
b Los Angeles, Calif, Jan 7, 41. *Study:* Immaculate Heart Col, Los Angeles, Calif, BA(art), 69; Calif State Univ, Los Angeles, MA(art), 71. *Work:* Stedelijk Mus, Amsterdam, Holland. *Comn:* Frieze (175 Ft), comn by Eugene Burgur Corp, Larkspur, Calif, 83. *Exhib:* Solo exhibs, Musée Cantonal des Beaux Arts, Lausanne, Switz, 80 & Univ Calif, Berkeley, 82; Elegant Miniatures from San Francisco & Kyoto, San Francisco Mus Mod Art, Calif, 83; Earsight-Sound and Image in the Contemporary Arts, Southern Alleghenies Mus, Johnstown, Pa, 85; Alles und Noch Viel Mehr, Kunsthalle, Bern, Switz, 85; Choices-Making an Art of Everyday Life (with catalog), New Mus Contemp Art, New York, 86. *Teaching:* Instr, San Francisco Art Inst & Ecole des Beaux Arts. *Awards:* Interarts Grants, Nat Endowment Arts, 85, Echoes from the Moon, Mobius, Boston, 86 & Time-Geography Studies, Fessenden Found, 86. *Bibliog:* Kristie Stiles (auth), Introduction to the Art of Morgan O'Hara, Musée Catonal des Beaux Arts, Lausanne, Switz, 80; Ron Gagnon (auth), Six Portraits, Action Image, 84. *Media:* Ideas, Time & Space. *Publ:* Auth, Zeit und Raumbilder, Feministisches Studien, Weinheim, Ger, 82; coauth, Formal records of time and movement through space: A conceptual & visual series of artworks, Leonardo J, 83; Interviews with Artists, 86; auth, Geographical self portraits, Corona 4, 86; Time out of mind, The Act, New York, 86. *Mailing Add:* 106 MacDougal St New York NY 10012

O'HARA, SHEILA MARY
TAPESTRY ARTIST, WEAVER
b Kobe, Japan, Dec 29, 53; US citizen. *Study:* Philadelphia Col Art, Pa, fall 74; Calif Col Arts & Crafts, Oakland, with Trudi Guermonprez & Kay Sekimachi, BFA(with distinction), 76. *Work:* Oakland Mus, Calif; Bank Am, San Francisco; Am Craft Mus, NY; Smithsonian's Cooper-Hewitt, NY; Minneapolis Inst Art. *Comn:* AT&T Commun Planning Ctr, San Francisco; Lloyds Bank Int Ltd, New York, NY; Konnatsu Store Co, Ltd Tokyo, Japan; Edward Ricci & Assoc, West Palm Beach, Fla. *Exhib:* Solo show, Modern Master Tapestries, New York, 82 & 85, Elaine Potter Gallery, San Francisco, 88, Ctr Tapestry Arts, New York, 90; touring show, Art & Industry: The Jacquard Project; Nurnberg Mus Cult Indust, Calif Crafts Mus, San Francisco; Tex Woman's Univ, NDak Mus Art, 91-92; Fiber Arts, Manchester Inst Arts & Sci, NH, 92; and others. *Teaching:* Instr, Workshops, Univ Col SQueensland, Toowoomba, Australia, 91, Nurnberg Acad Fine Arts, Ger, 91, Ecole Atelier Construct Textiles, Montreal, Can, 91 & Convergence 92, Washington, DC; instr, Fiberworks, Ctr Textile Arts. *Awards:* First Place, Calif State Expos, 80; Bay Area Craftsperson of the Year, Oakland Mus, Calif, 85. *Bibliog:* Betty Park (auth), Sheila O'Hara, Wry humor and virtuoso weaving, Fiberarts, 1-2/83; Joanne Mattera (auth), Tapestries, Metropolis Mag, 1-2/85; Bobbi Miller (auth), Tapestries in a New Light, Shuttle, Spindle & Dyepot, winter 90/91. *Mem:* Calif Contemp Crafts Asn, Calif; Calif Crafts Mus, San Francisco, Calif; Am Crafts Coun, NY; San Francisco Craft & Folkart Mus, Calif. *Media:* Wool. *Publ:* Auth, You Are Now Weaving Oakland, Arts Textrina, Univ Winnipeg, Can, 86; Back to the Future, Textilforum, Hannover, Ger, 9/88 & Weaver's Mag, 4th Q, 90; Art & Industry: The Jacquard Project, Shuttle, Spindle & Dyepot, winter 91/92. *Dealer:* Suzy Locke & Assocs 201 Estates Piedmont CA 94610. *Mailing Add:* 2562 26th Ave San Francisco CA 94116

OHE, KATIE (MINNA)
SCULPTOR, INSTRUCTOR
b Peers, Alta, Can, Feb 18, 37. *Study:* Alta Col Art, dipl(fine arts); Montreal Sch Art & Design, with Dr Lismer; Sculpture Ctr, New York, with Sahl Swarz & Dorothy Denslow. *Work:* Can Coun Art Banks, Ottawa, Ont Alta Art Found, Edmonton; Visual Arts, Cult Activities, Edmonton; Shell Can Art Collection, Calgary; Alta Col of Art. *Comn:* Michael the Archangel (cast stone sculpture relief), Church, Calgary, Alta, 64; chromed steel sculpture, Univ Calgary, 67 & 75; cast stone sculpture relief, Fed Western Regional Bldg, Calgary, 67; bronze sculpture, Sch Bd, City of Calgary, 75; Esso: Imperial Oil, Res Ctr, Calgary, 90. *Exhib:* Sculpture Ctr, New York, 62-70; Brit Int Print Show, London, Eng, 71; Venice Biennial, Italy, 72; Alta Art Found Traveling Exhib, Can House Gallery, London, Brussels, Paris & New York, 75-76; Changes: 11 Artists Working on the Prairies Traveling Exhib, 75-76; retrospective, Alta Col Art, Calgary, 91. *Teaching:* Instr sculpture, Mt Royal Col, Calgary, 70-, Alta Col Art, Calgary, 70-90 & Univ Calgary, 79. *Awards:* Nat Gallery Study Grant, 58; Can Coun Grants, New York, 63, Europe, 68 & Verona, Italy, 74; Allied Arts Award Medal, Royal Archt Inst of Can, 84. *Bibliog:* Clement Greenburg (auth), View of art on the prairies, Can Art, 63; Anita Aarons (auth), Allied Art Catalogue, Vol 2, Arts and Architecture, Royal Archit Inst Can, 68; Barb Kwasney (auth), Canadian Golden West, Western Artist, Spring 76. *Mem:* Royal Can Acad Arts; Alta Soc Artists. *Media:* Multimedia. *Mailing Add:* Alberta Col Arts 1407 14th Ave NW Calgary AB T2M 4R3 Canada

OHLAU, JUERGEN UWE
GALLERY DIRECTOR
b Freiburg, WGer, Dec 24, 40. *Study:* Erlangen, Ger, PhD(hist & German lit). *Pos:* Dir, Goethe House New York, 86- *Mailing Add:* Goethe House New York 666 Third Ave, 19th floor New York NY 10017

OHLSON, DOUGLAS DEAN
PAINTER, EDUCATOR
b Cherokee, Iowa, Nov 18, 36. *Study:* Univ Minn, BA, 61. *Work:* Corcoran Gallery Art, Washington, DC; Mus Purchase Fund Collection, Am Fedn Arts; Minneapolis Inst Art; Dallas Mus Fine Art; Metrop Mus Art, New York; Mus Mod Kunst, Frankfurt, Ger; Brooklyn Mus, NY; and others. *Exhib:* Art of the Real: USA 1948-1968, Mus Mod Art, New York, 68-69; Structure of Color, Whitney Mus Am Art, New York, 71; American Art Since 1960, Art Mus, Princeton Univ, 70; The Way of Color, 33rd Biennial Exhib, Corcoran Gallery Art, Washington, DC, 73; 14 Abstract Painters, Wight Gallery, Univ Calif, Los Angeles, 75; and others. *Teaching:* Prof art, Hunter Col, 64- *Awards:* Guggenheim Fel, 68; Nat Endowment Arts, 76. *Bibliog:* G Battcock (ed), Minimal Art (critical anthology), Dutton, 68; Britannica Encyl Am Art, Simon & Schuster, 73; Carter Ratcliff (auth), Doug Ohlson's color condensations, Art in Am, 5-6/78; and others. *Media:* Acrylic, Oil. *Dealer:* Andre Zarre 154 Wooster St New York NY 10012. *Mailing Add:* 35 Bond St New York NY 10012

OHNO, MITSUGI
GLASSBLOWER
b Tochigi, Japan, June 28, 26; US citizen. *Work:* US Capitol replica, Smithsonian Inst, Washington, DC; Independence Hall, White House, 72; US Capitol, 75; Anderson Hall, Kans State Univ, 77; Dwight D Eisenhower Libr; Chemistry Bldg, Tokyo Univ, Japan; Royal carriage & harp replica (given to Crown Prince of Japan), 87. *Comn:* Ohno Klein Bottle, Smithsonian Inst, Washington DC, 75, given to Emperor of Japan, 79; Nikko Toshogu Shrine, 86 & 88, Tochigi Prefecture, Japan. *Pos:* Full-time technician, Kans State Univ. *Awards:* Yoshikawa-Eiji Prize for Cult Merit, Tokyo, Japan, 79; Walter E Morrison Award, Kans State Univ, 79. *Media:* Glass. *Mailing Add:* 2808 Nevada St Manhattan KS 66502

OI, MOTOI
PAINTER, INSTRUCTOR
b Osaka, Japan, Nov 3, 10; US citizen. *Study:* Pac Fine Art Col, Tokyo, dipl, 28. *Work:* Metrop Mus Art, New York; Nat Gallery Art, Washington, DC; Philadelphia Mus Art; Cincinnati Art Mus; Nagaoka Mus Mod Art, Japan. *Comn:* Indust map mural, Foreign Dept of Govt, Tokyo, 50; indust map mural, Yokohama Expo, Japan, 51. *Exhib:* Nippon Bijutsuten, Japanese Govt, 36-38 & 50; Int Exhib, Educ Dept of Govt, Japan, 38; Ann exhib, Lincoln Ctr Plaza, New York, 82, 83, 84, 85, 86, 87, 88 & 89. *Pos:* Founder & chmn, The Japan-Am Sumi-e Club Inc. *Teaching:* Instr painting, Queens Col, City Univ New York, 60-74; Brooklyn Inst Art & Sci, 67-90. *Awards:* Rising Sun, Emperor Japan, 81. *Bibliog:* Fusetsu Nakamura (auth), Upset hat, Educ Art, Japan, 38. *Media:* Sumi-e Ink. *Publ:* Auth, Sumi-e Painting & Life, 58; Step by Step in Sumi-e Painting (7 vols), 58-62; Brush Strokes in Sumi-e Painting, 63-; Work by Motoi Oi, 65; Suiboku Landscape, 68; Encyclopedia of Sumi-E, 86; and others. *Mailing Add:* 24-50 95th St East Elmhurst NY 11369

OJI, HELEN SHIZUKO
PAINTER
b Sacramento, Calif, Aug 27, 50. *Study:* Yuba Col, AA, 70; Calif State Univ, Sacramento, BA, 72, MA, 75. *Work:* Jacksonville Art Mus, Fla; Gen Elec Corp, Fairfield, Conn; Prudential Insurance Co Am, Newark, NJ; Kidder, Peabody & Co, Inc, New York; Chemical Bank, New York, NY. *Comn:* Calendar-poster, Asian Cinevision, New York, 84; Monoprint etching, The Jane Voorhees Zimmerli Art Mus, New Burnswick, 85. *Exhib:* New Imagists, the Alternative Mus, New York, 80; New Art II: Surfaces & Textures, Mus Mod Art, New York, 81; A New Bestiary, Inst Contemp Art of Va Mus, Richmond, 81; Monique Knowlton Gallery, 81, 82; Collector's Choice, Miss Mus Art, Jackson, 82; End of the World, New Mus Contemp Art, New York,

83; Lifeline, Greenville Co Art Mus, SC, 85; Intar Gallery, New York, 86; New Sensations, Jay Gallery, NY, 86; New York Now works on paper, Nordjyllands Kunst Mus, Aalorg, Denmark; Committed Print, Mus Mod Art, New York, 88; Visual Impact, Salena Gallery & Long Island Univ, Brooklyn, NY, 88. *Awards:* Graphics Fel, Creative Artists Pub Serv Prog, 82-83; Ariana Found Arts Inc Mixed Media Grant, 84. *Bibliog:* William Zimmer (auth), Art Breakers New York's Emerging Artists, Soho News, Vol 7, No 51, 80; Ronny H Cohen (auth), Helen Oji, Artforum, Vol 21, No 5, 83; Marsha Tajima (auth), Helen Oji, Bridge Mag, Vol 10, No 1, 85. *Media:* Painting. *Mailing Add:* 284 Lafayette St Apt 5D New York NY 10012

OKAMURA, ARTHUR
PAINTER
b Long Beach, Calif, Feb 24, 32. *Study:* Art Inst Chicago(scholar), 50-54; Univ Chicago, 51 & 53; Yale Univ Summer Art Sem, 54; Edward L Ryerson Travel Fel, 54; Univ Chicago, 57. *Work:* Corcoran Gallery Art, Washington, DC; Nat Collection Fine Arts, Smithsonian Inst; Nat Inst Arts & Lett; Hirshhorn Mus, Washington, DC; San Francisco Mus Art, Calif; and others. *Exhib:* Painters Behind Painters, Calif Palace Legion Honor, San Francisco, 67; one-man shows, San Francisco Mus Art, 68, Calif Col Arts & Crafts, 72, Southern Idaho Col, 72, Kent State Univ, Ohio, 73 & Honolulu Acad Arts, 73; Takashima 1970 Expos, Osaka, Tokyo, Japan, 70; Asian Artists, Oakland Mus, 71; and others. *Pos:* Dir, San Francisco Studio Art, 58. *Teaching:* Instr, Cent YMCA Col, Chicago & Evanston Art Ctr, Ill, 56-57, Art Inst Chicago, N Shore Art League, Winnetka, Ill & Acad Art, San Francisco, 57, Saugatuck Summer Art Sch, Mich, 59 & 62; prof, Calif Col Arts & Crafts, 58-59 & 66-92; guest lectr, Univ Utah, 64 & 75. *Awards:* Schwabacher-Frey Award, 79th Ann, San Francisco Mus, 60; Neysa McMein Purchase Award, Whitney Mus Am Art, 60; Purchase Award, Nat Soc Arts & Lett; plus many others. *Bibliog:* Lee Nordness (ed), Art: USA: Now, C J Bucher, 62; Art Trek Watercolor Workshop, Univ Calif, 89 & 92. *Mem:* Am Fedn Arts. *Dealer:* Ruth Braunstein Gallery 254 Sutter St San Francisco CA 94108. *Mailing Add:* 210 Kale St Bolinas CA 94924

OKOSHI, E SUMIYE
PAINTER, COLLAGE ARTIST
b Seattle, Wash. *Study:* St Margaret & Futaba Col, Tokyo; Seattle Univ, with Fay Chang & Nicholas Damascus; Henry Frye Mus Sch & New Sch Workshop. *Work:* Miami Mus Mod Art; Lowe Gallery, Univ Miami; Nat Women Educ Ctr, Japan; Nat Acad Sci, Washington, DC; Nikko Hotel, Atlanta. *Exhib:* Metrop Mus Art, New York, 77; Tokyo-To Nat Mus, Japan, 79; Newark Mus, NJ, 83; Bergen Mus Art & Sci, NJ, 83; Nat Acad Sci, Washington, DC; Port Washington Pub Libr; Viridian Gallery, NY; and others. *Awards:* Belle Cramer Mem Award; Ziuta & Akston Found Award. *Bibliog:* Articles in Wash Post, NY Times & OCS News, NY. *Mem:* Nat Asn Women Artists. *Media:* Acrylic; Etching. *Publ:* Contribr, Int Economy Mag, Yomiuri News & Manhattan Art. *Mailing Add:* Westbeth Studio G226 463 West St New York NY 10014

OKUHARA, TETSU
PHOTOGRAPHER
b Los Angeles, Calif, Mar 3, 40. *Study:* Univ Chicago, 58-61; Cooper Union, New York, 70. *Work:* Metro Mus Art & Mus Mod Art, New York; Art Inst Chicago; Wight Art Gallery, Los Angeles; Nat Gallery of Australia, Melbourne. *Comn:* B&W photo Tryptch, Greater Hartford Comm Col, Conn, 82; Photographic mural, Automated Data Processing, Chicago, 88; March of Dimes, New York, 90. *Exhib:* Mirrors & Windows, Mus Mod Art, New York, 78; Twentieth Century Photographs from the Mus Mod Art, Sebu, Tokyo, Japan, 83; Big Pictures, Mus Mod Art, New York, 84; Grupa Junij 85, Belgrade Hilton, Yugoslavia, 85; Art In Gen, New York, 90; AAAC, New York, 91; Chicago Art Inst Ill, 91-92. *Awards:* Fel Guggenheim Found, 75; NY Found for Arts, New York State, 87-88; Nat Endowment Arts, 88-89. *Bibliog:* Marjorie Bevlin (auth), Design Through Discovery, HR&W, 77; Ralph Gibson (auth), Contact: Theory, Lustrum Press, 80. *Publ:* Auth, Foto, Sweden, 88; Nueva Luz, 88; New York Mag, 88; 100 Nudes, Sun Mag, Tokyo, Japan, 91; Intuitive Eye, Chicago Art Inst, 92. *Mailing Add:* 202 E 42nd St New York NY 10017

OKULICK, JOHN A
SCULPTOR
b New York, NY, Mar, 1947. *Study:* Univ Calif, Santa Barbara, BA, 69; Univ Calif, Irvine, MFA, 74. *Work:* Hawaii Mus Contemp Art, Honolulu; Fogg Art Mus, Harvard Univ, Cambridge, Mass; Smithsonian Inst, Washington, DC; Va Mus Fine Arts, Richmond; Power Gallery, Contemp Art, Univ Sydney, Australia; Phoenix Mus Art; and many others. *Comn:* Los Angeles State Office Bldg, Van Nuys; Ronald Reagan State Office Bldg, Los Angeles, 90; Port of Los Angeles, Harbor Con Multiuse Bldg, San Pedro, Calif, 92; City of Reno, Nev, 92. *Exhib:* Solo exhibs, Asher/Faure Gallery, Los Angeles, 85 & 87, Palm Springs Mus Art, Calif, 91, Del Art Mus, Wilmington, 91 & Fay Gold Gallery, Atlanta, Ga, 92; Lower Manhattan Revisited: Soho, Noho & Tribeca, Maier Mus Art, Randolph-Macon Women's Col, Lynchburg, Va, 87; Art in Pub Bldgs, Phebe Conley Gallery, Calif State Univ, Fresno, 88; Trompe l'oeil, The Magic of Deception, Muckenthaler Cult Ctr, Fullerton, Calif, 88; Alice Through the Looking Glass, Bernice Steinbaum Gallery, New York, 88; Eastside-Westside, Helander Gallery, Palm Beach, Fla, 88; Images of Am Pop Cult Today III, La Foret Mus, Tokyo, 89; The Vessel: Studies in Form & Media, Craft & Fold Art Mus, Los Angeles, 89; Collected Sculptures, Contemp Mus, Honolulu, Hawaii, 90; John Okulick/Alan Siegel, Ann Jaffe Gallery, Bay Harbor Islands, Fla, 91. *Bibliog:* Michele Hunevan (auth), A way with wood, Angeles Mag, 3/89; Alan G Arther (auth), Chicago Tribune, 3/89; Michael Webb (auth), Concrete dreams, LA Style Mag, 7/89. *Dealer:* Nancy Hoffman 429 W Broadway New York NY 10012; Richard Gray Gallery 620 N Michigan Chicago IL 60611. *Mailing Add:* 604 Hampton Dr Venice CA 90291

OKUMURA, LYDIA
PAINTER
b Sao Paulo, Brazil. *Study:* Fac Plastic Arts, Armando Alvares Penteado Found, Sao Paulo, Brazil, BFA, 73; Pratt Graphics Ctr, New York, 74-77. *Work:* Metrop Mus Art, New York; Hara Mus Contemp Art, Tokyo; Pinacotheca of State & Mus Mod Art, Sao Paulo, Brazil; Mus Mod Art, Bogota, Colombia. *Exhib:* Solo exhibs in Sao Paulo, Tokyo, Osaka & New York, 68-84; Sao Paulo Biennial, Brazil, 73, 77, 79 & 83; Graphic Biennials, Europe, 76-82; Recent Acquisitions, Metrop Mus Art, New York, 79; Cranbrook Acad Art Mus, Bloomfield Hills, Mich, 79; Biennial Art, Medellin, Colombia, 81; Atlantic Capital Corp, NY, 81; Nat Mus Osaka, Japan, 81; and others. *Awards:* Creative Artists Pub Serv Prog Graphic Grant, 78; Japan Found Fel, 79; Norway Graphic Biennial, 80. *Bibliog:* Barbara Rose (auth), Environmental art, Vogue, 4/79; L G Redstone (auth), Public Art, New Directions, McGraw-Hill, 80; Deborah Phillips (auth), article, Art News, 82; Lydia Okumura (catalog), Galeria Sao Paulo, Brazil, 4/84; Today's Art of Brazil (catalog), Hara Mus Contemp Art, Tokyo, Japan, 11/85. *Publ:* Coauth, Dialogue with the contemporary, Mizue Mag, No 904, Tokyo, 80. *Dealer:* Condeso & Lawler Gallery 79 Greene St New York NY 10012. *Mailing Add:* 32 Union Square W New York NY 10003

OKUN, BARBARA J
CONSULTANT, ART DEALER
b New Rochelle, NY, July 29, 32. *Study:* Mt Holyoke Col, S Hadley, Mass, BA, 54; Lindenwood Col, St Charles, Mo, 86. *Collections Arranged:* Ceramics & Social Commentary (auth, catalog), Laumeier Sculpture Park Gallery, 85. *Pos:* Owner, Okun Gallery, Sante Fe, NMex, currently; friends bd, St Louis Art Mus, Mo, 84-86; trustee, Laumeier Sculpture Park, St Louis, Mo, 84-86 & Am Craft Coun, New York, 86-89; Santa Fe Inst Fine Art, NMex, 89. *Teaching:* Inst, Educ Ctr, Longboat Key, Fla, 91. *Mem:* Am Soc Appraisers (mem valuation sci comt, 86); Am Craft Coun; Collectors Circle; Mod Art Coun; Contemp Art Soc. *Specialty:* 20th Century American art & craft and The Art of the Basketmaker. *Publ:* Auth, Five Colorado Potters, Colo Art, summer 83; Auction house activities; The secondary market for contemporary art, Am Soc Appraisers Personal Property News, spring & summer, 86. *Mailing Add:* PO Box 665 Tesuque NM 87574

OLDENBURG, CLAES THURE
SCULPTOR
b Stockholm, Sweden, Jan 28, 29. *Study:* Yale Univ, BA, 51; Art Inst Chicago, 52-54. *Work:* Albright-Knox Art Gallery, Buffalo; Mus Mod Art, Whitney Mus Am Art, Guggenheim Mus, New York; Art Gallery Ont, Toronto; Art Inst Chicago; Walker Art Ctr; plus many others. *Comn:* Sculptures, Oberlin Col, Ohio, 70, City St Louis, Mo, 71, Morse Col, Yale Univ, 74, Walker Art Ctr, Minneapolis, 74 & Hirshhorn Mus, Washington, DC, 75; Mistos, Match Cover, Olympic Village, Barcelona, 92; plus others. *Exhib:* Guggenheim Mus, New York; Metrop Mus Art, New York, 69; Retrospective, Mus Mod Art, New York, 69, Pasadena Art Mus, Calif, 71, Walker Art Ctr, 75 & Kunsthalle, Tubingen, WGer, 75; Los Angeles Co Mus Art, 71; Expo 70, Osaka, Japan; Documenta, Kassel, WGer, 72; Seattle Art Mus, Wash, 73; Am Pop Art, Whitney Mus Am Art, 74; Newport Art Mus, RI, 74; Kestner-Gesellschaft, Hanover, 76; Centre Georges Pompidou, Musee Nat d'Art Contemporain, Paris, 77 & 89; Chicago Int Art Expos, Ill, 86; Inst Contemp Art, London, Eng, 87; Mus Mod Art, New York, 87, 88, 90 & 91; Whitney Mus Am Art, 88; solo-exhib, Walker Art Ctr, Minneapolis, 91; Solomon R Guggenheim Mus, NY, 92; and many others. *Awards:* First Prize Sculpture, 72nd Ann Exhib, Art Inst Chicago, 76; Wilhelm-Lehmbrück Sculpture Award, Ger, 89; Wolf Found Prize Visual Arts, Israel, 89. *Bibliog:* Ellen Johnson (auth), Claes Oldenburg, Penguin, 71; articles in Art in Am, 5/74 & 9/74; Monuments and Monoliths (catalog), New York, 78. *Mem:* Am Acad Inst Arts & Lett; Am Acad Arts & Sci. *Publ:* Auth, Store Days, Something Else Press, 68; auth, Notes in Hand, Dutton & Petersburg, 71; auth, Object into monument, Pasadena Art Mus, 71; Raw Notes, Nova Scotia Col Art & Design Press, 73; coauth (with Coosje van Bruggen), Sketches and Blottings Toward the European Desk Top, Milan and Turin: Galleria Christian Stein; and Florence: Hopeful Monster, 90. *Dealer:* Pace Gallery 32 E 57th St New York NY 10022. *Mailing Add:* 556 Broome St New York NY 10013

OLDENBURG, RICHARD ERIK
MUSEUM DIRECTOR
b Stockholm, Sweden, Sept 21, 33; US citizen. *Study:* Harvard Col, AB, 54. *Pos:* Dir publ, Mus Mod Art, New York, 69-72, dir mus, 72- *Mailing Add:* 11 W 53rd St New York NY 10019

OLENDORF, WILLIAM CARR
PAINTER, PRINTMAKER
b Deerfield, Ill, Apr 18, 24. *Study:* Washington & Lee Univ, 41; Harvard Univ, 43; Art Inst Chicago Summer Sch. *Work:* US Airforce Collection, Washington, DC; The White House, Washington, DC; State of Ill, Springfield. *Comn:* The Childhood Homes of Ronald & Nancy Reagan (paintings), comn by State Ill, Gov Thompson, Washington, DC, 81; Pres Bush, Pres Ford, Pres Nixon Collections. *Exhib:* Galerie Marcel, Bernheim, Paris, 61, 73, 90; Chicago Artists Show, Art Inst Chicago, Ill, 65; Art USA, New York, 70; American Artists Show, Marshall Field Gallery, Chicago, 78; US Airforce Show, Pentagon, Washington, DC, 80-89; Olendorf Gallery, Chicago, 91 & 92. *Awards:* Rockefeller Found Grant, 63. *Mem:* US Airforce Artists Group. *Media:* Oils, Black & White Sketches. *Publ:* Auth, Addison Mizner Architecture Affluent, A Sketch Book, 81, Gale Pub Co; Chicago Sketchbook 88 & Palm Beach Sketchbook 88, Olendorf Graphics Publ; Paris Sketchbook, 90; London Sketchbook, 92. *Mailing Add:* 9 E Ontario Chicago IL 60611

OLENICK, DAVID CHARLES
ADMINISTRATOR, DEALER
b Rockville Centre, NY, Apr 21, 47. *Study:* NY Univ; Hofstra Univ; New Sch Social Res; State Univ NY. *Pos:* Co-dir, Mansight Educ, Full Circle Assocs, 68-69; owner & dir, Park Gallery, Brooklyn, 69-71; ed consult & field prog coordr, Proj Am Develop, US AID State Dept, 69-70; asst dir, Brooklyn Mus Art Sch, 74-77, admin head, 77-81, adminr educ & prog develop, 78-81; gallery dir, Adam L Gimbel Gallery, New York, 81-83; cur contemp art, Saks Fifth Ave, New York, 81-83; owner & dir, David Olenick Fine Art, New York, 85- *Specialty:* Contemporary paintings and sculpture. *Mailing Add:* 120 Park Pl Brooklyn NY 11217

OLESZKO, PATRICIA
VISUAL ARTIST, PERFORMANCE ARTIST
b May 19, 47. *Study:* Univ Mich, BFA, 70. *Exhib:* Performances, Revel Without a Claus, Whitney Mus, Phillip Morris, New York, 88; Humor's the Oddity, Hallways, Buffalo, New York, 89; Nora's Art, Md Art Place, Baltimore, 90; Bluebeard's Hassle, Pub Sch 122, New York, 90; Forefront: Pat Oleszko, Nat Mus Women Arts, Washington, DC, 92. *Awards:* NY State Coun Arts Grant, 73, 80, 87 & 91; Nat Endowment Arts Fel, 78, 85 & 87; Mass Coun Arts, New Works, 88; Guggenheim Fel, 90; NY Dance & Performance Award (Bessie). *Bibliog:* Articles in Art Am, 82 & 91, Art Express, 82, Portfolio, 83, High Performance, 83 & 84, Arts & Antiques, 84 & Artforum, 86, New Yorker, 90. *Publ:* Films, Not a Pretty Sight: The Wurst is Yet to Come, 86; Little Red Writing: The Free Little Pig. *Mailing Add:* 190 Duane St New York NY 10013

OLIN, FERRIS
HISTORIAN, ADMINISTRATOR
US citizen. *Study:* Douglass Col, BA, 70; Rutgers Univ, MLS, 72, MA, 75, ABD(art hist), 90. *Work:* Hopewell Mus, NJ. *Collections Arranged:* Architecture of New Brunswick and its Environs, 79; Women in the Community, series exhibs, 82; Artists Books: From the Traditional to the Avant-Garde, 82; Women's Spheres (co-ed, catalog), 83; Baroness Hyde de Neuville, Sketches of America, 1807-22, 83; Representative Works and Focused Fragments, 84; Past and Promise: Lives of New Jersey Women, 90. *Pos:* Dir, Rutgers Art Libr, 76-85; res-consult, New York Feminist Art Inst, 77-78; bk reviewer, Leonardo, 77-82; ed prof lit column, Art Libr Soc NAm Newslett, 80-84; exec officer, Inst Res on Women, Rutgers & Laurie NJ Chair in Women's Studies, 85- *Teaching:* Dir & art librn, Rutgers Univ, New Brunswick, 76-85, assoc prof, 80- *Awards:* Rhoda Freeman Recognition Award, NJC & UCWE, 88. *Mem:* Womens Caucus for Art; Col Art Asn; Nat Women's Studies Asn. *Res:* Contributions of women artists to art history; issues facing art librarians; regional history and material culture. *Interests:* 19th & 20th Century Europ & Am art & archit; women's art history. *Publ:* Ed, Representative Works and Focused Fragments, Rutgers & Nat Women's Studies Asn, 84; Baroness Hyde de Neuville, Sketches of America 1807-1822, New York Hist Soc, 84; contrib, Dictionary of Women Artists Born Before 1900, G K Hall, 85; coauth, Making Their Mark: Women Artists, 1970-85, 89; co-ed & auth, The New Jersey Project: Integrating the New Scholarship on Gender, 1986-90, 90. *Mailing Add:* Three Dead Tree Run Rd Belle Mead NJ 08502

OLIPHANT, PATRICK
POLITICAL CARTOONIST
b Adelaide, Australia, July 24, 35; US citizen. *Study:* Dartmouth Col, DHL. *Exhib:* Nat Portrait Gallery, Smithsonian Inst, Washington, DC, 90. *Pos:* Copyboy, press artist, Adelaide Advertiser, 53-55, ed cartoonist, 55-64; ed cartoonist, Denver Post, 64-75, Washington Star, 75-81; syndicated cartoonist, Los Angeles Times Syndicate, 65-79 & Universal Press Syndicate, 79- *Awards:* Pulitzer Prize for Editorial Cartooning, 67; Reuben Award, Nat Cartoonist soc, 68 & 72; Nat Headliner Asn Award, 79; and others. *Mem:* Int Salon Cartoons (jury chmn). *Publ:* Auth, Oliphant An Informal Gathering, 78, Oliphant, 80, the Jelly Bean Society, 81, Ban This Book, But Seriously Folks, 83, The Year of Living Dangerously, 84 & Make My Day, 85, Andrews & McMeel, Between Rock and a Hard Place, 86, Up to Here in Alligators, 87, Nothing Basically Wrong, 88, What Those People Need Is a Puppy, 89, Oliphant's Presidents, (exhib catalog), 90. *Mailing Add:* c/o Cocoran Gallery Art 17th St & New York Ave NW New York NY 20006

OLITSKI, JULES
PAINTER, SCULPTOR
b Snovsk, Russia, Mar 27, 22. *Study:* Nat Acad Design, New York, 39-42; Beaux Arts Inst, New York, 40-42; Acad Grande Chaumiere, Paris, France, 49-50; NY Univ, BS & MA, 52-54. *Work:* Art Inst Chicago; Corcoran Gallery Art, & Nat Gallery, Washington, DC; Whitney Mus Am Art, Mus Mod Art, New York; Guggenheim Mus, Metrop Mus, New York; Nat Gallery Australia, Canberra; Israel Mus, Jerusalem; Art Collection of Nordrhein-Wastfallen, Dusseldorf, Ger. *Comn:* Welded steel sculpture, Gallaudet Col for the Deaf, Washington, DC, 79. *Exhib:* Retrospective, Fondation du Chateau de Jau, Perpignan, France, 84 & Buschlen-Mowatt Gallery, Vancouver, BC, 90; Arte Contemporaneo Norteamericano, Coleccion David Mirvish, Am Embassy, Madrid, 84; An American Renaissance-Painting and Sculpture, Mus Art, Ft Lauderdale, Fla, 86; The Painter and the Printmaker, Asn Am Artists, New York, 89; solo shows, Gallery One, Toronto, 90 & 91 & Salander O'Reilly Galleries, Berlin, Ger, 92; Strategies for the Next Painting, Wolff Gallery, New York, 91; Gallery Selections, Salander-O'Reilly Galleries Inc, New York, 91; Inaugural Exhibition, Salander-O'Reilly Galleries Inc, Berlin, Ger, 91. *Teaching:* Asst prof, State Univ NY Col New Paltz, 54-55; prof & chmn dept fine arts, C W Post Col, Long Island Univ, 56-63; instr art, Bennington Col, 63-67. *Awards:* Corcoran Gold Medal, 30th Int Biennial Exhib Art, US Pavilion, Venice, Italy, 66; First Prize for Painting, Corcoran Gallery Art, 67; Milton & Sally Avery Distinguished Professorship, Bard Col, 87. *Bibliog:* Valentin Tatransky (auth), Jules Olitski, Arts Mag, 5/85; Jules Olitski (auth), The Courage to Grow Old, Balentine Books, New York, 89; John Gruen (auth), Abstract pursuits in New Hampshire, Archit Digest, p 56, 60, 64, 6/91. *Publ:* Auth, First Chapter (a short story), Partisan Rev, Vol II, 78; The Courage of Conviction, Dodd Mead & Co, Ballantine Books, 86; How I Got My First New York Show, Partisan Rev, 1/89. *Mailing Add:* 22 E 80th St New York NY 10021

OLIVEIRA, NATHAN
PAINTER
b Oakland, Calif, Dec 19, 28. *Study:* Mills Col, 50; Calif Col Arts & Crafts, MFA, 52, DFA, 68. *Work:* Hirshhorn Mus & Sculpture Garden, Smithsonian Inst, Washington, DC; Mus Mod Art, New York; San Francisco Mus Mod Art; Solomon R Guggenheim Mus, New York; Acad Art, Honolulu; and many others. *Exhib:* The Contemporary Monotypes, Edith C Blum Art Inst, Annandale-on-Hudson, NY, 85; John Berggruen Gallery, San Francisco, 85; Recent Acquisitions, John Berggruen Gallery, 85; Contemporary Monotypes: Six Masters, De Saisset Mus, Santa Clara Univ, Calif, 85; solo exhibs, Sites and Related Works, 1957-86, Stanford Univ Art Gallery, Palo Alto, Calif, 86, Italian Sites, Monotypes, Richard Gray Gallery, Chicago, 86, John Berggruen Gallery, San Francisco, 87, 89, 90 & 93, Nathan Oliveira, 1957-1977, Campbell-Thiebaud Gallery, 91, Paintings and Works on Paper, 1959-1991, Salander-O'Reilly Galleries, 91 & New Mexican Sites: Hand Painted Monotypes executed at Hand Graphics, Santa Fe, John Berggruen Gallery, 91; Large Scale Works on Paper, John Berggruen Gallery, San Francisco, 91; and many other one-man & group exhibs. *Teaching:* Prof art, San Francisco Art Inst, Calif Col Arts & Crafts, 55-56, Univ Ill, 61-62, Univ Calif Los Angeles, 63-64, Cornell Univ, 64, Stanford Univ, 64-, Univ Colo, 65, Univ Hawaii, 71, Cranbrook Acad Art, Bloomfield Hills, Mich, 72, Baltimore Art Inst, 72, John Herron Art Inst, Indianapolis, Ind 72 & Kent State Univ, 73; artist-in-residence, Univ Ill, Urbana, 61-62, Univ Calif, Los Angeles, 63, Santa Rosa Jr Col, Calif 78 & Harvard Univ, Cambridge, Mass, 78; vis artist, San Antonio Art Inst, Tex, 61-62, Univ Colo, Boulder, summer 65, Univ Hawaii, Honolulu, 71, Cranbrook Acad Arts, Bloomfield Hills, Mich, 72, Fullerton Col, Calif, 72, Herron Sch Art, Indianapolis, Ind, 72, Md Inst Col Art, Baltimore, 72, Kent State Univ, Ohio, 72, Ft Wright Col, Wash, 73, Wichita State Univ, Kans, 76, Centrum, Port Townsend, Wash, summer, 77. *Awards:* Grant, Nat Endowment Arts, 74; Award, Am Acad & Inst Arts & Lett, NY, 84; Academician, Graphic Arts, Nat Acad Design, NY, 85. *Mem:* Nat Acad Design, New York, 82. *Mailing Add:* c/o Salander-O'Reilly Galleries Inc 20 E 79th St New York NY 10021

OLIVER, BOBBIE
PAINTER
b Canada, June 17, 49. *Study:* Ctr Creative Studies, Detroit, 66-68; St Albans Sch Art, Eng, 68. *Work:* Robert McLaughlin Gallery, Oshawa, Can; Nuffield Found, Eng; Can Coun Art Bank, Can; Glenbow Mus, Alta, Can. *Exhib:* Art Gallery Ont, Toronto, 78; solo exhibs, Art Gallery of S Alta, 79, Freidus Ordover, New York, 84, Wolff Gallery, New York, 85 & Olga Korper Gallery, Toronto, 86, 87, 88, 91. *Teaching:* Instr, RI Sch Design, Princeton Univ, Sch Visual Arts, New York & Banff Sch Fine Arts, Can. *Awards:* Ont Arts Coun Grant, 80; Pollock-Krasner Grant, 86; Can Coun Arts Grants, 80, 83, 85; and others. *Bibliog:* J Zinsser (auth), Bobbie Oliver at Wolff, East Village Eye, 5/85; John Bentley Mays (auth), Invoking a sense of place, Globe & Mail, 3/89. *Media:* Oil. *Mailing Add:* 140 W Broadway New York NY 10013

OLIVER, MARVIN E
CRAFTSMAN
Study: San Francisco State Univ, BA, 70; Univ Wash, MFA, 73. *Comn:* Eagle & Killer Whale, World Fair Expos, Spokane, 74; Glass Casting, Pratt Fine Arts Ctr, 90; wood & cast glass sculpture, Transition, Seattle Opera House, 91; bronze, glass & concrete sculpture, Spirit of Washington, 92; 40 ft bronze sculpture, Spirit of Our Youth, 92-93. *Exhib:* Evolution of a Heritage, State Capitol Mus, Olympia, Wash, 78, A Showing of Birds, 90; Native Am Art - Past Into Present, Denver Art Mus, 78; many invitational exhibs, 78- *Pos:* Bd pres, Inst Am Indian Arts, 83-87; artists, Elders Forum, 86; comt mem, Wash State Centennial, 89; instr, Pratt Fine Arts Ctr, 91; lect, Seattle Art Mus, 92. *Awards:* Nat Endowment Arts, 88; Fel Glass Casting, Pratt Fine Arts Ctr, 90. *Bibliog:* Pat Baillargeon (auth), Arts Interview; Marvin Oliver, Puget Soundings, 4/77. *Mem:* Asn Nat Humanities Fac, 78-88; pres, Inst Am Indian Arts, 84-86. *Mailing Add:* 3725 Wallingford Ave N Seattle WA 98103

OLIVER, SANDI See Oliver, Sandra (Sandi)

OLIVER, SANDRA (SANDI)
ART DEALER, PAINTER
b Bronxville, NY, April 2, 41. *Study:* Marymount Col, Tarrytown, BA, BFA, 63. *Work:* Hammer Mus Gallery, Conn; Lilco Gallery, Long Island; McKlean-Grove Mus, Greenwich. *Comn:* Productions & prom, ABC & NBC TV, 80; USA space production, United Tech-Norden, 80. *Exhib:* Westport Merchants Show, Conn, 78, 86, 87 & 92; Waveny Barn Mus, New Canaan, 85, 86 & 87; Westport Art Ctr Mus, 86 & 87; Wilton Historical, Soc Am Craftsmanship Show, Conn, 91 & 92. *Pos:* Commercial artist rep, Sandi Oliver Inc, Weston, 79-84; pres, Sandi Oliver Fine Art Inc, 82-; dir, Sandi Oliver, 91- *Teaching:* Art & art hist teacher, New York City Sch System, 63-65 & Westchester Diocese Cath Sch, 64-67. *Awards:* First Prize, Christmas Show, Pelham Chamber of Com, 60; Revlon Bravo Award, Revlon Corp, 80; First Prize, Casa D'Oliver Garden Show, Conn, 91. *Bibliog:* Contribr, Vision of

flowers (article), Your Family, 3/90. *Mem:* NEAA; AAA Inc; AFA. *Media:* Oil. *Specialty:* American impressionist painting & sculpture. *Publ:* Auth, American Impressionist Paul Alan Williams His Garden & His Oil Paintings, 91, 92 & 93. *Mailing Add:* PO Box 1203 Weston CT 06883

OLKINETZKY, SAM
COLLAGE ARTIST, CONSULTANT
b New York, NY, Nov 22, 19. *Study:* Brooklyn Col; Inst Fine Arts, NY Univ. *Work:* Philbrook Art Ctr, Tulsa, Okla; Okla Art Ctr, Oklahoma City; Mus Art, Univ Okla, Norman; Sch Bus, Okla State Univ, Stillwater; Lawton Munic Collection, Okla. *Exhib:* Philbrook Art Ctr Ann, 50-70; Int Painting & Sculpture Exhib, Mus Non-Objective Art, New York, 51-52; Recent Drawings, USA, Mus Mod Art, New York, 55; Momentum Midcontinental, Chicago Inst Design, 55; Southwestern Painting and Sculpture Ann, Okla Art Ctr, 60-70; Artsplace II, Oklahoma City, 79; 50 Yr Retrospective 1942-1992, Norick Art Ctr, Oklahoma City, 92. *Pos:* Art consult, Kerr-McGee Indust, 64-; dir, Mus Art, Univ Okla, 59-; art consult, Okla Art Ctr, 72- *Teaching:* Asst prof art, Okla State Univ, 47-57; prof art, Univ Okla, 57-; vis prof art & humanities, Univ Ark, 62-67; lectr humanities, Langston Univ, 69-70. *Awards:* St Gaudens Medal for Draughtsmanship, City New York, 37; Purchase Award for Painting, Philbrook Art Ctr, 51; Purchase Award for Drawing, Okla Art Ctr, 65; Gov's Art Award, 81. *Mem:* Am Asn Mus; Okla Mus Asn; Art Mus Asn. *Media:* Collage, Drawing. *Publ:* Auth, Oklahoma Designer Craftsman Exhibition, Craft Horizons, 71; contribr, The Art of Douglas Warner (catalog essay), 80. *Mailing Add:* Rte 1 Box 151 A Norman OK 73072

OLLMAN, ARTHUR L
PHOTOGRAPHER, CURATOR
b Milwaukee, Wis, Mar 6, 47. *Study:* Univ Wis-Madison, BA, 69; Visual Studies Workshop, Rochester, 72; San Francisco Art Inst, 74; Lone Mountain Col, MFA, 77. *Work:* Mus Mod Art, New York; Bibliot Nat, Centre Georges Pompidou, Mus Nat d'Art, Paris, France; Mus Mod Art, San Francisco; Mus Fine Arts, Houston; Tokyo Inst Polytech. *Exhib:* Contemp Am & Can Photog, Monas Hieroglyphics, Milan, Italy, 78; Mirrors & Windows, Mus Mod Art, New York, 78; Grapestake Gallery, San Francisco, 79; Beyond Color, San Francisco Mus Mod Art, 80; Biennial, Whitney Mus, New York, 81; one-man shows, Contemp Art Ctr, New Orleans, 80, Photography Gallery, New York, 81; Centre Georges Pompidou, Mus Nat d'Art, Paris, France. *Pos:* Dir, Mus Photog Arts, San Diego, 83- *Awards:* Special Proj Award, Calif Arts Coun, 77; Nat Endowment Arts Fel, 79. *Bibliog:* Charles Whitin (auth), Arthur Ollman, Am Photog Image Nation, 11/78; Arnaud Claass (auth), Arthur Ollman, Zoom/Publicness, 6/79; Arthur Ollman, Time-Life Photog Yr, 79. *Mem:* Soc for Photog Educ; Friends of Photog. *Media:* Photography; Videotape. *Publ:* Images of India, Photographs Samuel Bourne, Friends of Photog, 83; Arnold Newman, Decades, Harcourt Brace Javanovich, 86; Other Images, Other Realities, Rice Univ Press, 89; Revelaciones, Art of Manuel Alvarez Bravo, Mus Photog Arts, 90. *Mailing Add:* 4310 Goldfinch St San Diego CA 92103

OLMSTED, SUZANNE M
PHOTOGRAPHER, PRINTMAKER
b Palo Alto, Calif, April 15, 56. *Study:* Univ Calif, Santa Cruz, BA, 79; Southern Ill Univ, MFA, 82. *Work:* Ariz State Univ, Yellowstone Art Ctr. *Exhib:* Invitational Auction, Yellowstone Art Ctr, 83; Recent Works, Castle Gallery, Billings, Mont, 83; Recent Brownprints, Montalvo Ctr Arts, Saratoga, Calif, 83; Experimental Photo, Pac Grove Art Ctr, Calif, 84; Air-Gallery, New York, 87 & 88; and others. *Pos:* Dir, Artlink, 91. *Teaching:* Instr photog, Eastern Mont Col, 82-87. *Awards:* Eben Demarest Award, 87. *Mem:* Col Art Asn. *Media:* Non-Silver Photography, Photo-Printmaking Techniques. *Publ:* Contribr, Photogr Forum, 81; Northern Lights, 86, 87 & 89. *Mailing Add:* 800 W Pkwy Eastern Mont Col Tempe AZ 85281

OLPIN, ROBERT SPENCER
HISTORIAN, ADMINISTRATOR
b Palo Alto, Calif, Aug 30, 40. *Study:* Univ Utah, BS, 63; Boston Univ, AM, 65, PhD, 71. *Work:* Utah Mus Fine Arts, Univ Utah. *Collections Arranged:* Alexander Helwig Wyant, 1836-1892 (with catalog), 68, Mainstreams of American Architecture-Reflections on Salt Lake City (with catalog), 73 & Am Painting Around 1850, 76, Utah Mus Fine Arts; Contemporary Utah Artists Exhibition, Billboard Art, Tracy Collins Bank (with catalog), 74 & The Art Life of Utah, 1776-1976 (with catalog), 76, Salt Lake Art Ctr; A Retrospective of Utah Art (with catalog), Utah Arts Coun, Utah Mus Fine Arts, 81; Waldo Midgley Retrospective (with catalog), Utah State Univ, Univ Utah & Springville Mus Art, 83; Salt Lake County Fine Art Collection (with catalog), 87; Jos A F Everett (1883-1945), Springville Mus Art & Salt Lake Art Ctr, 89; George Dibble Paintings, 1928-1988, Utah Mus Fine Arts, 89. *Pos:* Chmn art hist prog, Univ Utah, 68-71 & 82-87, actg chmn dept art dept, 76-82; Consult cur Am art, Utah Mus Fine As, Univ Utah, 73-; dean, Col Fine Arts, 87- *Teaching:* Lectr art hist, Boston Univ, 65-67; from asst prof to assoc prof art hist, Univ Utah, 67-77, prof, 77- *Awards:* Utah Hist Media Award, Utah State Hist Soc, 92. *Mem:* Col Art Asn Am; Utah Acad Sci, Arts & Lett; Salt Lake Art Ctr (bd advisors). *Res:* Nineteenth and 20th century American art, with special emphasis on 19th century American landscape painting and the regional art and architecture of Utah. *Collection:* Eighteenth and 19th century European and American prints. *Publ:* Dictionary of Utah Art, Salt Lake Art Ctr, 80; coauth, Portrait of a portraitist, Univ Utah, Col Fine Arts, 81; auth, intro and notes & ed, A Basket of Chips: An Autobiography of James Taylor Harwood, 86; Signs and Symbols in Early, and Sometimes Much Later, Utah Art, 88; coauth, Utah Art, Peregrine Smith, 91. *Mailing Add:* Art & Archit Ctr 161 Univ Utah Salt Lake City UT 84112

OLSEN, ERNEST MORAN
DESIGNER, PAINTER
b Pittsfield, Mass, May 5, 10. *Study:* Pratt Inst, pictorial illus; portraiture with Ivan Moschowitz; Boothbay Harbor Summer Sch Art, landscape study with Frank Allen. *Work:* Berkshire Mus, Pittsfield, Mass; Fine Arts Mus, Asbury Park, NJ. *Exhib:* Int Print Exhib, Chicago World's Fair, 30; Pittsfield Art League, Berkshire Mus, 31-36; Stockbridge Art Exhib, Berkshire Playhouse, Mass, 35-38; Williams Col, Williamstown, Mass, 37; Yonkers Mus Exhib, NY, 55. *Collections Arranged:* Fine Arts Mus, Asbury Park, NJ, 77. *Pos:* Art dir, Leica (house organ), Pallard Corp, 45-50, Copper & Brass Res Asn, 45-65, Bolex (house organ), E Leitz Corp, 50-55, Maxwell House Messenger, Gen Foods, 60-76 & Sculpture Mag Nat Sculpture Rev, Nat Sculpture Soc, 62-92; designer, Union Carbide Corp, New York, 52-82. *Awards:* Cert of Merit, Folmer Graflex Corp, 40 & Printing Indust of Metrop New York, 65-74. *Mem:* Art Dir Club of New York; fel Am Artists Prof League. *Media:* Oil, Wash. *Mailing Add:* 465 Westchester Ave Mt Vernon NY 10552

OLSEN, FREDERICK L
CERAMAIST, SCULPTOR
b Seattle, Wash, Feb 25, 38. *Study:* Univ Redlands, BA; Univ Southern Calif, MFA; Kyoto City Col Fine Art, Japan; also apprenticeship with Tomimoto Kenkichi & Kondo Yuzo, Kyoto, 3 yrs. *Work:* Gallery New South Wales, Sydney, Australia; Contemp Craft Mus, Denmark; Sturt Collection, Mittigong, Australia; Palm Springs Desert Mus, Calif; Bowan Collection, San Marcos, Calif; Bakersfield Col Collection. *Exhib:* One-man exhibs, Sydney, 63, 64 & 69, Melbourne, 63 & 69, Adelaide, 69, Copenhagen, 65, Seattle, 71 & 73, Portland, Ore, 71, Los Angeles, 71, 73 & 74 & Palm Springs Art Mus, 77 & 80; Mt Jacinto Col Gallery, Jacinto, Calif, 81; Bowman Gallery, San Marcos, Calif, 82; Bakersfield Col Gallery, Calif, 84; Living Desert Invitational, 82-85, Focus Clay Invitational, Elaine Horowitz Gallery, 88, Palm Springs; Sierra Nevada Art Mus Invitational, Reno, Nev, 87 & 88; Scripps Ceramic Ann, 88; Anagama Wood Fire Ceramics Exhib, Saddleback Community Col, Mission Viejo, Calif, 89; two man exhib, M O A Gallery, Los Angeles, Calif, 90. *Pos:* Owner, Pinyon Crest Pottery & Olsen Kiln Kit Co, 67- *Teaching:* Lectr kiln bldg, Univ Southern Calif, 66-68; asst prof, Univ Puget Sound, summer 71 & 73; prof, Mt San Jacinto Col, Calif, 82-83. *Awards:* Nat Endowment Grant Arts, 76; Mino Ceramic Int Exhib Award, Tajimi, Japan, 87. *Bibliog:* American Potter in Japan, Asahi TV Corp, 63. *Media:* Clay. *Publ:* Auth, The Kiln Book, Chilton Books, 2d ed 81. *Mailing Add:* Pinyon Crest Box 205 Mountain Center CA 92361

OLSEN, THEODORA MORGAN See Morgan, Theodora (Theodora Morgan Olsen)

OLSEN BERGMAN, CIEL
PAINTER, EDUCATOR
b Berkeley, Calif, Sept 11, 38. *Study:* San Francisco Art Inst, MFA(with honors); Univ Calif, Berkeley with Fred Martin, Bob Hudson, Harold Paris & Peter Plagens. *Work:* Univ Mus, Univ Calif, Berkeley; Arts Coun Gt Brit; Oakland Mus; San Francisco Mus Mod Art; Metrop Mus Art, New York. *Comn:* 1990 136' ceramic form, Gildea Ctr, Paseo Nuevo, 87. *Exhib:* Nat Drawing Exhib, Potsdam, NY, 73; Davidson Nat Print & Drawing, NC, 73; Women From Permanent Collection, Univ Mus, Berkeley, 73; Biennial, Whitney Mus Am Art, New York, 75; San Francisco Mus Art, 75; 18 Bay Area Artists, Los Angeles Inst Contemp Art, 76; New Work, Oakland Mus, 76; Hamilton Gallery Contemp Art, New York, 79; Ruth Schaffner Gallery, Los Angeles, 79; Ian Birksted, London; Fresh Paint--15 Calif Artists (auth, catalog), San Francisco Mus Mod Art, 82; Revelations, The Transformative Impulse in Recent Art, Aspen Art Mus, (catalog), 89. *Teaching:* Lectr painting, Calif State Univ, Hayward, 75; vis lectr painting, Univ Calif, Berkeley, 75-79; assoc prof painting & drawing, Univ Calif, Santa Barbara, 79, prof 80- *Awards:* Tamarind Lithographic Inst Fel, 72; SECA Award, Soc Creative Arts, San Francisco, 75; Louis Comfort Tiffany Award, 80. *Bibliog:* Mary Stofflet (auth), Three Bay Area Artists, UC Riverside; Charles Shere (auth), Cheryl Bowers (catalog), Kirk deGooyer Gallery, 83; Alfred Jan (auth), Images/Issues, 11-12/83; T Albright (auth), Art in the San Francisco Bay Area, 45-80; Sylvia Moore (auth), Yesterday & Tomorrow Calif Woman Artists; Dr Elinor Gaddon (auth), The Once & Future Goddess; Henry Hopkins (auth), rev, California Painters. *Mem:* Santa Barbara Contemp Art & Art Forum, New Mus, New York. *Media:* Oil, Watercolor; Lithography, Etching. *Mailing Add:* Dept Art Univ Calif Santa Barbara CA 93106

OLSHAN, BERNARD
PAINTER, PRINTMAKER
b New York, NY, Jan 31, 21. *Study:* Am Artists Sch, New York, 37-40; Ozenfant Sch Fine Arts, New York, 47; Academie de la Grande Chaumiere, Paris, 48-51. *Work:* Emily Lowe Mus, Coral Gables, Fla; New York City Community Col & Health & Hosp Corp, New York. *Comn:* Mural, Theodore Roosevelt High Sch & WPA, New York, 39-40. *Exhib:* Camp Maxey Art Exhib, Dallas Mus Fine Arts, 43; Whitney Mus Am Art, New York, 48; Art USA, Madison Sq Garden, New York, 58; 144th Ann Exhib, Nat Acad Design, New York, 69; Hudson River Mus, New York, 71; Seven Bronx Artists, Herbert H Lehman Col, New York, 74; GCCA Mountain Top Gallery, Windham, Vt, 84; Bronx Mus Arts, 86; Lehman Col Art Gallery, 86. *Pos:* Chmn visual arts comt, Amalgamated Houses, New York, 80- *Teaching:* Instr, Crafts Students League, 53 & New York City Community Col, 65-69; teacher & dir, Cult Arts Dept, Mosholu-Montefiore Community Ctr, New York, 66-79. *Awards:* Inter-city Mural Award, Theodore Roosevelt High Sch & Works Progress Admin, 39-40; Emily Lowe Award 1st Prize, 2nd Ann, 50; Ralph Mayer Mem Award, 84. *Bibliog:* Dr Lawrence J Hatterer (auth), The Artist in Society, Grove Press, New York, 65; Barry Schwartz (auth), The

New Humanism in Time of Change, Prager Publ, 74; articles in New York Times, Art News, Herald Tribune, Art Digest & others. *Mem:* New York Artists Equity Asn; Am Soc Contemp Artists (treas); Bronx Soc Sci & Lett. *Mailing Add:* 3965 Sedgwick Ave Bronx NY 10463

OLSON, BETTYE JOHNSON
PAINTER, INSTRUCTOR
b Minneapolis, Minn, Jan 16, 23. *Study:* Univ Minn, BS(art educ), 45, MEd, 49; Univ NMex, Taos, 47; Cranbrook Acad Art, Mich, 48. *Work:* Vaxjo, Sweden; Pillsbury World Hq, Minneapolis; Augsburg Col; Luther Col, Decorah, Iowa; St Paul Co's; and many others. *Comn:* Radisson Hotel, Fla, 83. *Exhib:* Minneapolis Art Inst Biennial, 47, Walker Art Ctr Biennial, 47; Metamorphose One, Minn Mus Art, St Paul, 76; Mid Year Show Ann, Butler Inst Am Art, Youngstown, Ohio, 77; Watercolor USA, Springfield Art Ctr, Mo, 77; Women Invite Women, Warm Gallery, Minneapolis, 77; Minn Artists Selected for Kuopio, Finland, Univ Minn Gallery, 81; Looking Back: Minn Mus Art, St Paul, 88; solo exhibs, St Olaf Col, 77, Augsburg Col, 79, Luther Col, Decorah, Iowa, 80, Am Swedish Inst, Minneapolis & Smaland Mus, Vaxjo, Sweden, 82, Westlake Gallery, Minn, 64-82, Lutheran Brotherhood Co, 83; Mento-Protogee Show, Macalester Col, 92; and many others. *Pos:* Art fac Lutheran Cols, Concordia Col, 78 & Augsburg Col, 89; Juried Women, Warm Gallery, Minneapolis, 90 & Mentor Prog Warm, 91-92. *Teaching:* Instr, Summit Sch Girls, 45-47 & Univ Minn, 47-49; artist in residence, Holden Village Lutheran Retreat Ctr, Chelan, Wash, 67-79 & 86-88; instr, Painting & Design, Concordia Col, St Paul, 75-78, 83-84 & Augsburg Col, summer, 84-86 & 87-88; instr painting & printmaking, Augsburg Col, Minneapolis, 87-88. *Awards:* Merit Award, Twin City Show, Minn Mus Art, 61; 3rd Prize, Merit Award, Minn State Fair, 76 & 77; Grand Prize, Purchase Award, Northern Lights Show, White Bear Arts Coun, Lakewood Col, 77; Am Asn Col Women Arts Award, St Paul, 85. *Mem:* Delta Phi Delta (pres, 46); Artists Equity Asn (secy, 74); WARM, Women's Orgn. *Media:* Watercolor, Acrylic. *Publ:* Crisp Pine, Poetry Sketches, AAUW Press, St Paul, 90; Grand River Rev, 82-83. *Mailing Add:* 2370 Lexington Ave, Apt 109 St Paul MN 55120

OLSON, DOUGLAS JOHN
PHOTOGRAPHER, EDUCATOR
b Wausau, Wis, Aug 26, 34. *Study:* Layton Sch Art, BFA; Univ Cincinnati, MFA. *Work:* Montgomery Mus of Fine Arts, Ala; Pope & Quint Corp; Gallery S; First Nat Bank of Ala; South Central Bell, Birmingham, Ala; and others. *Exhib:* Alabama Landscape Photography, Huntsville Mus Art, Montgomery Mus Fine Arts, Anniston Mus Natural Hist, Fine Arts Mus of South, Mobile, Ala, 89; Tennessee Valley Photography Exhibit, Tenn Valley Art Ctr, Tuscumbia, Ala, 90; one-man show, N Ga Col, 91, St Johns Col, Santa Fe, New Mexico, 92; Fall Photo Exhib, Bradley Galleries, Milwaukee, Wis, 92; Of Life's Beauty, Fuller Lodge Art Ctr, Los Alamos, NMex, 93. *Teaching:* Instr drawing, Univ Cincinnati, 67-68; prof drawing, design & photog, Auburn Univ, 68- *Awards:* Mary Houghton Mem Award, 78 & First Prize, 80, Montgomery Mus Fine Arts; Best of Show, LaGrange Nat X, Chattahoochee Valley Art Gallery, 85; Res Awards, Auburn Univ, 85-90; and others. *Media:* Black & White Photography. *Mailing Add:* 302 E Thach Ave Auburn AL 36830

OLSON, GENE RUSSEL
SCULPTOR
b Lake City, Minn, Mar 1, 49. *Study:* Univ Minn, 67-72. *Work:* Pac Gas & Elec, San Francisco, Calif. *Comn:* Steel Painted Welded Kinetic, Childrens Mus, Minneapolis, Minn, 83; Cast Bronze, City of Minneapolis, Minn, 85 & Minneapolis Pub Libr, 87; Woven Bronze & Copper, Jostens Inc, Minneapolis, 86; Anodized Aluminum, Univ Wis, River Falls, 88-89; Woven Copper wall relief, Fountains Country Club, Lake Worth, Fla, 90. *Exhib:* A Feast of Function, Gallery Functional Art, Santa Monica, Calif, 88. *Awards:* Second Honor, 74th Fine Arts Show, Minn State Fair, 85; Cover Background Artist, The Guild, Kraus Sikes, 88. *Bibliog:* Robert T Smith (auth), column, Minneapolis Start Tribune, 81; Gary Gillson, TV review interview, KTCA Channel 2, Minneapolis/St Paul, 83. *Mem:* Int Sculpture Ctr. *Media:* Bronze. *Mailing Add:* c/o The Mettle Works 8600 NE Odean Elk River MN 55330

OLSON, JOSEPH OLAF
DESIGNER, PAINTER
Study: Tadama Art Sch, Seattle, Wash; Nat Acad, New York; Art Students League. *Work:* Brooklyn Mus; also in pvt collections of Whitney, Pratt, Morgan, Harriman, Frick & Dupont families. *Exhib:* One-man shows, Corcoran Gallery, Washington, DC; Carnegie Inst, Pittsburgh; Chicago Art Inst. *Pos:* Stained glass designer, Rambusch Decorating Co, New York, 45-69. *Awards:* Isidor Prize, Salmagundi Club. *Media:* Oil, Watercolor. *Mailing Add:* RFD 1 Box 149 Mystic CT 06355

OLSON, MAXINE
PAINTER, EDUCATOR
b Kingsburg, Calif, June 29, 31. *Study:* Otis Art Inst, Los Angeles, Calif, 71 & 72; Inst Allende, San Miguel, Mex, 73; Calif State Univ, Fresno, BA, 73, MA, 75; Univ Calif, Santa Barbara. *Exhib:* Norten Gallery Invitational, West Palm Beach, Fla, 77; Oakland Mus Invitational, Calif, 81; West As Art 1800-1982 (with catalog), Palm Springs Desert Mus, Calif, 82; 25th Anniversary , Nat Mus Sport, NJ, 84; American Realism, William Sawyer Gallery, San Francisco, Calif, 85; Palazzo Vagnotti, Cortona, Italy, 87; Nexus Contemp Gallery, Atlanta, Ga, 88 & 90; Soho 20 Gallery, New York, Palazzo Casali, Cortona, Italy; Church of San Stae, Venice, Italy, 89. *Collections Arranged:* About Women, Orange Co Ctr Contemp Art, 82; Symposium on Portuguese Traditions, Univ Calif, Los Angeles, 85; Fresno Arts Mus, 85. *Teaching:* Instr painting & drawing, Fresno City Colo, 73-90 & Calif State Univ, 76-85; asst prof painting & drawing, Univ Ga, Athens, 86-89; asst prof, Univ Ga Studies Abroad Prog, Cortona, Italy, 86-87. *Bibliog:* Robert Ewing (auth), Sociological considerations, Artweek, Los Angeles, 82; Nicholas Treadwell (auth), Sex: Female, Occupation: Artist, Kent, Eng, 84. *Mem:* Col Art Asn; Nat Women's Caucus Arts; Fresno Art Mus; Nat Women's Mus Art, Washington, DC. *Media:* Oil, Pencil. *Mailing Add:* 1555 Lincoln St Kingsburg CA 93631

OLSON, RICHARD W
PAINTER, EDUCATOR
b Rockford, Ill, Aug 14, 38. *Study:* Univ Wis-Madison, BS & with R Knipschild, Leo Steppat & Italo Scanga, 60, MS(studio art-painting & graphics) 61 & MFA with Warrington Colescott, 62. *Work:* Mus Contemp Art, Chicago; Nat Gallery; Albright-Knox Gallery; Walker Art Ctr; Mus Mod Art, New York; and others. *Exhib:* 25th Print Nat, Intaglio, Nat Collection Fine Arts Div, Smithsonian Inst, Washington, DC, 64; Book as Object, Visual Studies Workshop, 79; Artists Books Permanent Collection, 82 & Artists Books & Recordings, 85, Mus Contemp Art, Chicago; Less is More, Pratt Manhattan Ctr, New York, 83; Artifacts at the End of a Decade, Franklin Furnace, New York, 83; Artists Books, Univ of Ore, Eugene, 88; Arts of the Book, Philadelphia Col Art & Design, 88. *Pos:* Cur prints & drawings, Wright Art Mus, Beloit Col, currently. *Teaching:* From asst prof to assoc prof, Beloit Col, Wis, 63-77, chmn art dept, 69-76, prof art drawing, printmaking, painting & sem, 77-, chmn dept art, 80-82, 84-85, 87-88. *Awards:* Gimbels Award, Wis Painters & Sculptors, Gimbels-Milwaukee, 62; Gimbels-Schusters Award, Wis Salon Art, Gimbels-Schusters, 68; Cullister Awards, 78-85; Hewlitt Mellon Award, 83; Wis Artists Biennal Cash Award, 87. *Bibliog:* Books in an expanded context, Artweek, 7/81; Fluxus and friends, Milwaukee J, 11/84. *Publ:* Illusr covers, Beloit Poetry J, 64 & 69; Artifacts at the End Decade, Ed Watson & Heubner, 81. *Dealer:* Printed Matter 7 Lispenrod St New York NY 10013. *Mailing Add:* Dept Art Beloit Col Beloit WI 53511

OLSON, RICK
PAINTER
b Mayville, NDak, Mar 15, 50. *Study:* Moorhead State Univ, Minn, 68-72. *Work:* Mus Art, Ft Lauderdale, Fla; Boca Raton Mus Art, Boca Raton, Fla; Canton Art Inst, Canton, Ohio; Nat Portrait Gallery, Smithsonian Inst, Washington, DC; Butler Inst Am Art, Youngstown, Ohio. *Comn:* Five portraits, Joseph H Hirshhorn, Washington, DC, 79. *Exhib:* Butler Inst Am Art, Youngstown, Ohio. *Media:* Pastels, Colored Pencils. *Dealer:* Harmon-Meek Gallery 386 Broad Ave S Naples FL 33940. *Mailing Add:* 732 Eighth Ave S Naples FL 33940

OLSON, ROBERTA JEANNE MARIE
HISTORIAN, CURATOR
b Shawano, Wis, June 1, 47. *Study:* St Olaf Col, BA, 69; Univ Iowa, MA, 71; Princeton Univ, MFA, 73, PhD(Kress Fel, 73-74, Whiting Fel, 74-75), 76. *Collections Arranged:* An Album, Italian 19th Century Drawings & Watercolors (auth, catalog), Shepherd Gallery, New York; Sixty Italian 19th Century Drawings (auth, catalog), San Jose Art Mus, 76; Italian Drawings 1780-1890 (auth, catalog), Nat Gallery, Washington, DC, 80-81; Disegni di Tommaso Minardi (auth, catalog), Galleria Nazionale d'Arte Moderna, Rome, 82-83; Fire & Ice: A History of Comets in Art (auth, catalog), Nat Air & Space Mus-Smithsonian Inst, 85-86; Thomas Jefferson Bryan Gallery: Changing Attributions, NY Hist Soc, 90-; Ottocento: Romanticism and Revolution in Nineteenth Century Italian Painting, Walters Art Gallery, Baltimore, 92. *Pos:* Contrib ed, Arts Mag, 73-75; art news ed, Soho Weekly News, 76-78; bd dirs, The Drawing Soc, 84- *Teaching:* Prof art hist & A Howard Meneely Prof, Wheaton Col, Mass, 75-, chair, Art Dept, 87-89, 92- *Awards:* Nat Endowment Humanities Fel, 82-83 & 88; Am Philosophical Soc Grant, 89; Am Coun Learned Soc Grant, 90-91. *Mem:* Col Art Asn Am; Drawing Soc. *Res:* Italian renaissance; 19th century Italian painting, sculpture and drawings aimed at illuminating cultural backgrounds and interconnections across disciplines; astronomical images in art. *Publ:* Auth, Pelagio Palagi's works on the theme of Charles VIII and Gian Galeazzo Sforza at Pavia, Antonlogia di Bell Artk, 90; Donati's Comet, Burlington Mag, 90; Historical Comets Over Bavaria: The Nuremberg Chronicle and Broadsides, Comets in the Post-Halley Era, 91; 1816 solar eclipes and comet 1811I in John Linnell's astronomical album, J Hist Astronomy, 92; Italian Renaissance Sculpture, Thames & Hudson, 92; and others. *Mailing Add:* 1220 Path Ave New York NY 10128

OMAR, MARGIT
PAINTER, EDUCATOR
b Berlin, Ger, May 17, 41; US citizen. *Study:* Univ Colo, Boulder, MFA, 71. *Work:* Los Angeles Co Mus Art, Mus Contemp Art & Polygram Pictures, Los Angeles; Atlantic Richfield Co, Denver; Turtle Creek Mansion, Dallas; and others. *Comn:* Aerojet Gen, La Jolla, Calif, 82; Robinson's, Newport Beach & Santa Monica, Calif, 82. *Exhib:* New Abstract Painting in Los Angeles, Los Angeles Co Mus Art, 76; solo exhibs, Janus Gallery, Venice, Calif, 77, 78, 80, 82 & 84, Univ Southern Calif, Los Angeles, 86 & Calif State Univ, Long Beach, 87; Fresh Paint, San Francisco Mus Mod Art, 82; Drawings by Painters, Oakland Mus Art, 83; Young Talent Awards 1963-1983, Los Angeles Co Mus Art, 83. *Teaching:* Assoc prof graduate studies & painting, Univ Southern Calif, Los Angeles, 73- *Awards:* Young Talent Award, Los Angeles Co Mus Art & Contemp Art Coun, 77; Individual Artists' Grant, Nat Endowment Arts, 80. *Bibliog:* Susan C Larsen (auth), Margit Omar's California Suite, Arts Mag, 9/78; Water Gabrielson (auth), Pasadena pluralism: The painting Seventies, Art Am, 5/81; Ruth Weisberg (auth), Margit Omar at Janus, Images & Issues, 10/82. *Mem:* Los Angeles Contemp Exhibs. *Media:* Acrylic; Mixed Media. *Mailing Add:* Univ Southern Calif Los Angeles CA 90089

O'MEALLIE, KITTY (KATE CHAMNESS JOHNSON)
PAINTER, GRAPHIC ARTIST
b Bennettsville, SC, Oct 24, 16. *Study:* Newcomb Art Sch, with Xavier Gonzales and Will Stevens, BFA(design), 37, advan painting with Pat Trivigno, George Rickey, John Taylor & Edward Corbett, 54-59. *Work:* New Orleans Mus Art & Tulane Univ, New Orleans; Meridian Mus Art, Miss; Masur Mus Art, Monroe, La; Wake Forest Univ, Winston-Salem, NC. *Comn:* Oil painting, Sellers & Sanders Clinic, New Orleans, 60; oil painting, Eustis Engineering Co, New Orleans, 67; acrylic painting, New Orleans Pub Libr, 77; mixed media painting, Houston Athletic Ctr, 81; and other pvt comns. *Exhib:* Southeastern Ctr Contemp Art, Winston-Salem, NC, 71; New Orleans Mus Art, 73; Contemp Arts Ctr, New Orleans, 77; solo exhibs, Masur Mus Art, Monroe, La, 79 & Meridian Mus Art, Miss, 81 & 85; New Orleans Women's Caucus Art Honorary Invitational, 86; and many others. *Awards:* Hon Mention, 5th Monroe Ann, Masur Mus Art, 68; Award Merit, 51st Regional, R S Barnwell Ctr, 73; Ann Art Auction Award, WYES Pub TV, New Orleans, 79. *Bibliog:* Keith Marshall (auth), A fresh look at art in the city that care forgot, Art Voices South Mag, 3/78; George Jordan (auth), A portrait of three artists, Merci Mag, 9/80; New Orleans Art: Three Attitudes (film), WYES Pub TV, 80. *Mem:* Nat Women's Caucus Art; New Orleans Women's Caucus Art. *Media:* Acrylic, Oil; Miscellaneous Media. *Publ:* Illusr, A time to die, a time to mourn, St Charles Ave Presby Church, 78. *Dealer:* Galerie Melancon 241 W Sallier St Lake Charles LA 70601; Van Gogh's Other Bar The Island Shops Hwy 17 Pawleys Island SC 29585. *Mailing Add:* 211 Fairway Dr New Orleans LA 70124

OMWAKE, EO, JR
PAINTER, SCULPTOR
b New Rochelle, NY, June 14, 46. *Study:* Pa Acad Fine Arts, 64-68. *Work:* Whitney Mus Am Art, New York; Philadelphia Mus Art, Pa Acad Fine Arts, Philadelphia. *Exhib:* Philadelphia Mus Art, 70; Whitney Ann Am Painting, New York, 72; Cheltenham Ann Painting Exhib, 72; one-man show, Marian Locks Gallery, 72; Marcel Duchamp Retrospective, Philadelphia Mus Art, 74; Tehran, Iran, 76; Dusseldorf, Ger, 76; Austin, Tex, 77; plus others. *Teaching:* Instr painting, Pa Acad Fine Art, Cheltenham Art Ctr, Pa & Chaddsford Art Sch, formerly. *Media:* Mixed. *Mailing Add:* Dept Painting Pa Acad Fine Arts Broad & Cherry Sts Philadelphia PA 19102

O'NEAL, ROLAND LENARD
ILLUSTRATOR, GRAPHIC ARTIST
b Meridian, Miss, Feb 1, 48. *Study:* Meridian Mus Art, Miss, 68; Jackson State Univ, BS(art educ), 72, studied with Hale Woodruff, New York, 76. *Work:* Wyo Univ Art Mus, Laramie; Idaho Univ Art Mus, Moscow; Sch Archit, Univ Southern Calif; Family Serv Ctr, W A Reed Jr Vocational & Tech Bldg, Meridian Community Col, Meridian, Miss; Retired Sr Vol Prog, Meridian; and others. *Exhib:* Ball State Univ Drawing & Sculpture Exhib, 74; Colo Print & Drawing Exhib, Sch Art, Univ Colo, Boulder, 75; Wind River Nat, Wind River Artist Guild, Ladner, Wyo, 76; Meridian Pub Libr, 77; Afro-Am Art Show, Ala A&M Univ, 78; NC Arts Coun, Raleigh. *Teaching:* Volunteer arts & crafts, Miss Action Progress, Meridian, 72-79; substitute teacher art educ, Meridian pub schs, Miss, 72-80. *Mem:* Wind River Valley Artist Guild; Athenian Art Club, Jackson State Univ. *Media:* Pencil, Charcoal; Watercolor, Mixed Media. *Mailing Add:* Apt G No 9 Highway Village Meridian MS 39301

O'NEIL, BRUCE WILLIAM
PAINTER, INSTRUCTOR
b Winnipeg, Man, Can, July 14, 42. *Study:* Alta Col of Art, dipl(fine art painting), 59-64; Instituto Allende, San Miguel De Allende, Mex, 65. *Work:* Can Coun Art Bank, Ottawa, Ont, Can; Edmonton Art Gallery, Alta; Glenbow Alta Inst, Calgary; Alta Culture (Alta govt); Mem Univ, St Johns Nfld; and others. *Exhib:* Abstraction West, Emma Lake & After, Nat Gallery of Can, 76; 14 Can, A Critics Choice: Hirschhorn Mus and Sculpture Garden, Washington, DC, 77; New Abstract Art, Edmonton Art Gallery, 77; one-man shows, Layola Col, Montreal, 68; Bruce O'Neil, 1973-76, traveling, Univ of Sask, Southern Alta Art Gallery, Lethbridge, Edmonton Art Gallery, 75, Mira Godard Gallery, Toronto, 77 & 80, Montreal, 78 & Calgary, 80 & Can Art Galleries, Calgary, 77-78. *Pos:* Chmn, Alta Soc Artists, Calgary, Alta, 72-73. *Teaching:* Instr painting, Alta Col Art, 68-80; guest instr, painting, Mount Allison Univ, Sackville, New Brunswick, 76; guest instr painting, Emma Lake Artists Workshop, Emma Lake, Sask, 76; instr, Banff Ctr, Alta, 78; instr, Univ Calgary, currently. *Awards:* Instituto Allende, Post Grad Exhib, Instituto Allende, Mex, 64; Can Coun Arts Grant, 75, 78 & 80. *Bibliog:* Dale McConathy (auth), The Can Cultural Revolution, Art Can Art Mag, 75; Karen Wilkin (auth), Bruce O'Neil, Art Mag, 77; Mike Hepburn (producer), Alberta Character-Bruce O'Neil-Artist, Can Broadcasting Corp, 78. *Mem:* Alta Soc Artists (Calgary chmn, 72-73); Can Artists Represenatives. *Media:* Acrylic on Canvas. *Dealer:* Paul Kuhn Fine Arts 722 11 Ave SW Calgary AB Canada. *Mailing Add:* 904 Memorial Dr NW No 6 Calgary AB T2N 3C9 Canada

O'NEIL, JOHN
PAINTER, EDUCATOR
b Kansas City, Mo, June 16, 15. *Study:* Univ Okla, BFA & MFA; Colo Springs Arts Ctr, with Boardman Robinson, Paul Burlin & Henry Varnum Poor; Taos Sch Art, with Emil Bisttram; Studio Hinna, Rome, Italy. *Work:* Denver Art Mus; Dallas Mus Fine Arts; Libr Cong, Washington, DC; Univ Mich Mus Art; Seattle Art Mus. *Exhib:* Directions in American Painting, Carnegie Inst, Pittsburgh; Abstract & Surrealist Art, Art Inst Chicago; Contemporary American Painting, Univ Ill; Mid-Am Ann, Nelson-Atkins Gallery, Kansas City, Mo; Watercolor USA, Springfield Art Mus, Mo; SW Am Art, Kyoto Mus, Japan; Main St II Exhib, Contemp Arts Mus, Houston, Tex; Troisieme Salon Int des Realites Nouvelles, Paris, France; M-59 Exhib, Copenhagen, Denmark. *Pos:* Dir, Sewall Art Gallery, Houston, 71-77. *Teaching:* Dir sch of art, Univ Okla, 51-65; prof painting, Univ Okla, 39-65; Rice Univ, 65-83, chmn art dept, 65-70, prof emer, 80. *Awards:* 23 awards in regional & nat exhib. *Bibliog:* Art in America, 2/55. *Mem:* Col Art Asn Am. *Media:* Acrylic, Watercolor. *Publ:* Contribr, Oklahoma: A guide to the Sooner State, Art & Archit, 57; Thoughts on Light, Kunst, 63; On color, Cimarron Rev, 72. *Mailing Add:* 2224 Wroxton Rd Houston TX 77005

O'NEIL, JOHN JOSEPH
ADMINISTRATOR, DESIGNER
b Brooklyn, NY, Apr 20, 32. *Study:* State Univ NY, Brooklyn, BA; State Univ NY, Buffalo, BS; Columbia Univ, MA, prof dipl & EdD. *Work:* Florence Mus, SC; Furman Mus, Greenville, SC; Beaufort Mus, SC; SC Arts Comn. *Exhib:* Piedmont Ann Crafts, 68 & Ann Graphics Exhib, 69-71, Mint Mus Art, Charlotte, NC; 24th Ann Southeastern Exhib, High Mus Art, Atlanta, Ga; 37th Southeastern, Gallery Contemp Art, 72. *Pos:* Mem, Panel Fed Graphics Prog, Nat Endowment Arts, currently; bd trustees, Columbia Mus Art & Sci, currently. *Teaching:* Prof graphic design, Univ SC, 63-, assoc head dept art, 65-75, head dept art, 75- *Mem:* SC Craftsman; Southeastern Art Conf; Columbia Artists Guild (vpres, 67, treas, 73-74); Guild SC Artist; Southeastern Print Coun. *Mailing Add:* 1830 Greene St Columbia SC 29201

O'NEILL, JOHN PATTON
PAINTER, CURATOR
b Houston, Tex, Apr 12, 42. *Study:* Univ Okla, Norman, BS; La State Univ, Baton Rouge, MS & PhD. *Exhib:* Nat Wildlife Fedn; Brit Mus Natural Hist; Leigh Yawkey Woodson Art Mus, 85. *Pos:* Curatorial asst, La State Univ Mus Zoology, Baton Rouge, 74-76, cur higher vertabrates, 76-78 & dir & cur, 78-82, coordinator field studies, 82- *Teaching:* Grad asst gen zoology, La State Univ, 64-73, asst prof ornithology, 78. *Bibliog:* Jonathan Fisher (auth), John O'Neill doesn't just paint birds, Int Wildlife, 77; Painting of John O'Neill, Cornell Lab Ornithology, 77; Frank Graham (auth), Outpacing Extinction, Audubon Mag. *Media:* Watercolor, Gouache. *Publ:* Illusr, Finding the Birds in Western Mexico, Univ Ariz Press, 69; illusr, Grouse and Quails of North America, Univ Nebr Press, 73; var illus for Encycl Britannica, 76; A Guide to the Birds of Trinidad and Tobago, Harrowood Bks, 77; National Geographic Field Guide to the Birds of North America. *Dealer:* Mill Pond Press Inc 204 S Nassau St Venice FL 33595. *Mailing Add:* 569 Maxine Dr Baton Rouge LA 70808

O'NEILL-CONTINI, ANITA See Contini, Anita

ONLEY, TONI
PAINTER, PRINTMAKER
b Douglas, Isle of Man, Eng, Nov 20, 28. *Study:* Douglas Sch Art; Inst Allende, Mex. *Work:* Tate Gallery, London; Nat Gallery Can; Victoria & Albert Mus, London; Mus Mod Art, New York; Seattle Mus, Wash; Libr Congress, Washington, DC; Vancouver Art Gallery, BC; Leeds Art Gallery, Eng. *Comn:* Oil mural, Queen Elizabeth Playhouse, Vancouver, BC, 62. *Exhib:* Seattle World's Fair, 62; Contemporary Canadian Art, Nat Gallery Can & Africa, 62-63; Fifteen Canadian Artists, Mus Mod Art & traveling in US, 63-64; Two Canadians, Commonwealth Inst, London, 64; 36th Venice Biennale, Italy, 72. *Teaching:* Asst prof fine arts, Univ BC, 67-76. *Awards:* Jessie Dow Award, Montreal Spring Exhib, 60; Sam & Ayala Zacks Award, 83rd Ann, Royal Can Acad, 63; Sr Can Coun Fel, 63. *Bibliog:* Honesty & Ostentation, Vanguard, 4/81; Articles, Design, 12/83 & 3/84; Only Onley (video), 89 BC TV. *Mem:* Royal Can Acad Arts. *Media:* Watercolor, Oil. *Publ:* Auth, Onley's Arctic, Douglas E McIntyre Publ; Walls of India, Onley-Woodcock, Lester & Orpen Dennys Publ; Toni Onley a Silent Taunder, Cerebrus, Prentice Hall. *Dealer:* Heffel Gallery 2247 Granville St Vancouver BC Canada. *Mailing Add:* 4279 Yuculta Crescent Beach BC V6N 4A9 Canada

ONO, YOKO
CONCEPTUAL ARTIST
b Tokyo, Japan, Feb 18, 33; US citizen. *Study:* Peers' Sch, Gakushuin Univ, Tokyo; Sarah Lawrence Col, New York; Harvard Univ, Cambridge, Mass. *Exhib:* Solo exhibs, Alchemical Wedding, Albert Hall London, 67, Evening with Yoko Ono, Birmingham, 68, Event, Univ Wales, 69, & Everson Mus, Syracuse, NY, 71; Fluxshoe, Sch Art, Falmouth, Cornwall, England, 72; and many others. *Bibliog:* P Devlin (auth), Yoko Ono, Vogue, New York, 12/71; Michael Benedikt (auth), Yoko notes, Art & Artists, London, 1/72; E Wasserman (auth), This is not here: Yoko Ono at Syracuse, Artforum, New York, 1/72. *Publ:* Auth, Six Film Scripts, Tokyo, 64; Thirteen Film Score Scores, London, 67; John & Yoko Calendar, New York, 70; Grapefruit, London, 70 & A Hole to See the Sky Through, New York, 71. *Mailing Add:* c/o Studio One 1 W 72nd St New York NY 10023

ONORATO, RONALD JOSEPH
HISTORIAN, CURATOR
b Jersey City, NJ, Jan 26, 49. *Study:* Rutgers Col, AB, 70; Brown Univ, MA, 73, PhD(Kress Found Grant), 77. *Collections Arranged:* Labyrinths, 75; Watson Gallery, Wheaton Col, 75-77; Mary Miss Interior Works, 82; Sailing Design Today, 86; Vito Acconci Domestic Trapping, 87; The Art of Douglas Huebler, 88. *Pos:* Asst cur, New York Cult Ctr, 73-74; dir exhib, Univ RI, 77-82; sr cur, La Jolla Mus Contemp Art, 85-88; trustee, Newport Hist Soc, 92-; trustee, Newport Art Mus, 92- *Teaching:* Vis lectr art hist, Wheaton Col, 75-77; chmn & prof art hist, Univ RI, 77-; adj prof criticism & art hist, RI Sch Design, 81- *Awards:* Visiting Specialist Grant, Nat Endowment Arts, 78; Nat

Endowment Humanities Grant, 83; Nat Endowment Arts Exhib Grants, 86 & 87; Sea Grant, 90; Champlin Found Grant, 92. *Res:* Nineteenth century American art, and architecture; contemporary art criticism; public sculpture. *Publ:* Auth, The modern maze, Art Int, 75; Photography and teaching: Eakins at the academy, Am Art Rev, 76; Illusive spaces: The art of Mary Miss, Arforum, 78; Dan Graham: Laumeier Bridge (catalog) & Ursula Von Rydingsvand: Laumeier Project (catalog), 90; coauth, Sitings: Aycock, Fleischner, Miss, Trakas (catalog) & Being There, Context, Perception and Art in the Conditional Tense (catalog), Mus Contemp Art, Los Angeles, 86; auth, Vito Acconci: Domestic Trappings, 87; auth, Douglas Huebler, 88; Richard Fleischner's St Louis Project (catalog), 90; selections; permanent collection, San Diego Mus Comtemp Art, 90. *Mailing Add:* Dept of Art Univ RI Kingston RI 02881

ONSLOW FORD, GORDON M
PAINTER
b Wendover, Eng, Dec 26, 12; US citizen. *Study:* Surrealist Group, 38-43. *Work:* Tate Gallery, London; Solomon R Guggenheim Mus, New York; Whitney Mus Am Art, New York; San Francisco Mus Mod Art; Fogg Art Mus, Cambridge; and others. *Exhib:* Karl Nierendorf Gallery, New York, 46; Retrospective, 48, Drawings and Watercolors, 64 & Large Paintings, 71, San Francisco Mus Mod Art; Rabow Gallery, 56-73; Paintings 1950-1962, M H de Young Mem Mus, San Francisco, 62; Gallery Art, Victoria, BC, 71; Pyramid Galleries Ltd, Washington, DC, 75; Retrospective of 100 paintings, Oakland Mus, 77; Galerie Samy Kinge, Paris, 85; Artists Space, NY, 86. *Teaching:* Lectr surrealist painting, New Sch Social Res, NY, 40; lectr mod art, Calif Col Arts & Crafts, Oakland, 58-59, Blaisdell Inst Conf, 79. *Awards:* Award of Honor, Arts Comn San Francisco, 86. *Bibliog:* Madeline Tourtelot (contribr), Island Time (20 minute film), Oakland Mus, 66. *Publ:* Auth Painting in the Instant, Thames & Hudson, London & Harry Abrams, New York, 64; co-auth, The Dynaton 25 Years Later (catalogue), Los Angeles Co Mus, 77; auth, Creation, Schreiner Galerie, Basel, Switz, 78; Tanguy and Automatism, Bishop Pine Press, 84; Insights, Lapis Press, 91. *Mailing Add:* PO Box 129 Inverness CA 94937

OOSTEROM, RICHARD H
ART DEALER, CONSULTANT
b New York, NY, Apr 5, 55. *Study:* Moravian Col, McCoy Scholar, BA(art hist), 77. *Collections Arranged:* Black American Folk Art, Moravian Col, 83. *Pos:* Cur asst, Allentown Mus Art, Pa, 76-77; asst, Terry Dintenfass Gallery, New York, 77-78; dir, R H Oosterom, Inc, 78-80; partner, Gallery Casas Toledo Oosterom, New York, 85-87; pvt consult, currently. *Res:* Black American folk art, Hispanic American folk art. *Specialty:* Contemporary art; American folk art. *Mailing Add:* 24 Fifth Ave New York NY 10011

OPIE, JOHN MART
PAINTER
b Sandusky, Ohio, Dec 10, 36. *Study:* Kent State Univ, BFA, MA. *Work:* Allentown Art Mus, Pa; Akron Art Inst, Ohio; Fordham Univ, NY; New Orleans Art Mus, La; St Lawrence Univ, NY. *Exhib:* Art Now, Philadelphia Mus Art, 90; Personal Visions, Places, Spaces, Bronx Mus, 78; one-man shows, New Orleans Art Mus, 68, Galerie Simonne Stern, New Orleans, 69, 70, 72, 75, 80 & 83, Bowery Gallery, New York, 73, 76 & 79 & Allentown Art Mus, Pa, 84; The More Gallery Inc, Philadelphia, 81, 82, 87-89; Award Winning Artists, Witte Mem Mus, San Antonio, Tex. *Teaching:* Instr painting, Pasadena City Col, Calif, 63-65; assoc prof painting, La State Univ, Baton Rouge, 65-70. *Awards:* Nat Endowment Arts Award, 67; Best of Show, 21st Ann Juried Exhib, State Mus Pa, 88. *Bibliog:* Leonard Edmondson (auth), Etching, Van Nostrand Reinhold, 73. *Media:* Acrylic on Paper, Oil on Canvas. *Dealer:* Charles More Gallery 1630 Walnut Philadelphia PA 19103. *Mailing Add:* c/o More Gallery Inc 1630 Walnut St Philadelphia PA 19103

OPPENHEIM, DENNIS A
SCULPTOR
b Mason City, Wash, Sept 6, 38. *Study:* Calif Col Arts & Crafts, BA; Univ Hawaii; Stanford Univ, MFA. *Work:* Mus Mod Art, Whitney Mus Am Art, New York; Stedelijk Mus, Amsterdam, Neth; Centre Georges Pompideau, Paris; Kunsthaus, Zurich, Switz; Detroit Art Inst, Cranbrook Acad Art, Bloomfield Hills, Mich; Everson Mus Art, Syracuse; plus many others. *Comn:* Sculpture, Cranbrook Acad Art, Bloomfield Hills, Mich, 81; sculpture, Rijksmuseum Kroller-Muller, Otterlo, Holland, 82; sculpture, Fattoria di Celle, Pistoia, Italy, 83; sculpture, Olympic Park, Seoul, Rep Korea, 88. *Exhib:* One-man exhibs, Whitney Mus Am Art, New York, 84, Seattle Art Mus, Wash, 84, Visual Arts Ctr, Alaska, 84, La Jolla Mus Contemp Art, Calif, 84, Grand Rapids Art Mus, Mich & Anne Plumb Gallery, New York, 88; Whitney Mus Am Art, New York, 86; Yvon Lambert, Paris, France; Pierides Mus, Athens, Greece, 90; Le Chanjour, Nice, France, 90; Berndt & Krips, Kolin, Ger, 90; Blum Helman Gallery, New York. *Teaching:* Guest artist sculpture, Yale Univ, 69; guest artist, Pratt Inst Art, Brooklyn, 69; guest artist, Calif Col Arts & Crafts, 70; guest artist, RI Col Design, 70; guest artist, Univ Wis-Whitewater, 70; guest artist sculpture, Art Inst Chicago, 71-72; guest artist sculpture, NS Col Art, 71-72. *Awards:* Newhouse Found Grant, Stanford Univ, 65; John Simon Guggenheim Found Fel, 71-72; Nat Endowment Arts, Grant, 74 & 81. *Dealer:* Sonnabend Gallery New York NY. *Mailing Add:* 54 Franklin St New York NY 10013

OPPER, JOHN
PAINTER
b Chicago, Ill, Oct 29, 08. *Study:* Cleveland Sch Art; Case Western Reserve Univ, BS; Columbia Univ, MA & EdD; also with Hans Hofmann. *Work:* Mus Mod Art, New York; James Michener Found Mus, Austin, Tex; Milwaukee Art Ctr, Wis; NY Univ Metrop New York Collection; Montclair Mus Art, NJ; Whitney Mus; Nat Mus Am Art, Smithsonian; Gen Elec, Dansbury. *Exhib:* Int Watercolor Exhib, Art Inst Chicago, 60; Int Watercolor Exhib, Brooklyn Mus; Int Exhib Paintings, Carnegie Inst, Pittsburgh, 61; American Drawings, Moore Inst, 68; Recent Acquisitions, Mus Mod Art, New York; Corcoran Gallery Art, 78; and others. *Teaching:* Assoc prof art, Univ NC, 52-57; prof art, NY Univ, 57-74, emer prof, 74- *Awards:* Nat Endowment Arts Grant Painting, 74; Spaeth Award, Guild Hall Mus, East Hampton, NY, 89; Distinguished Alumnus, Retrospective Exhib, Cleveland, Ohio, 90; and others. *Media:* Oil, Watercolor. *Dealer:* Borgenicht Gallery 724 Fifth Ave New York NY 10019. *Mailing Add:* PO Box 347 Amagansett NY 11930

ORDER, TRUDY
PAINTER
b Munich, Ger, Nov 22, 44; US citizen. *Study:* Akad Malkunst, Munich; Scoula di Pictura, Ancona, Italy; Nat Acad Design, New York, with Maxwell Starr & Umberto Romano. *Work:* Columbia Mus Art, SC; Mt St Vincent Col; Ft Tyron Jewish Ctr, New York; Holy Rood Episcopal Church, New York. *Comn:* The Gift (oil), comn by Mme Trau, Antwerp, Belg, 70; Bar Mitzwa (oil), comn by Signora Cagli, Ancona, 72; Bar Mitzwa (graphic), comn by Mme Tilli le Brewster, Paris, 73; In the Park (oil), comn by Ernest Raaschou, St Thomas, VI, 73. *Exhib:* Audubon Artists, New York, 61; Allied Artists, New York, 62; Knickerbocker Artists, New York, 64; one-man shows, Mt St Vincent Col, 66-74 & Pietrantonio Gallery, New York, 68; Metrop Mus Art, New York, 79. *Awards:* First Prize for Oil, Twilight Park Artists, 63, Second Prize for Pastel, 63 & First Prize for Watercolor, 63. *Bibliog:* Peggy London (auth), Trudy Order, Nat Soc Arts & Lett, 64. *Mem:* Nat Soc Arts & Lett; Kappa Pi; fel Royal Soc Arts. *Media:* Oil, Watercolor. *Dealer:* Town Gallery 1036 Lexington Ave New York NY 10021. *Mailing Add:* 250 Cabrini Blvd New York NY 10033

ORDUNO, ROBERT DANIEL
PAINTER, SCULPTOR
b Ventura, Calif, Sept 5, 33. *Study:* Los Angeles Art Ctr, 60. *Work:* Buffalo Bill Hist Ctr, Cody, Wyo; Red Cloud Indian Sch, The Heritage Ctr, Inc, Pine Ridge, SDak. *Comn:* Lewis & Clark, mural, City of Great Falls, Mont, 83. *Exhib:* Red Cloud Indian Art Exhib, Heritage Ctr, Pine Ridge, SDak, 85, 86 & 87; Ann Native Am Art Exhib, Great Falls, Mont, 85-88; Contemp Native Am Exhib, 86 & Invitational Shows, 86-87, C M Russel Mus, Great Falls; Plains Indian Art Exhib, Cody Mus, Wyo, 87; Nat Native Indian Artists Symp, Univ Lethbridge, Alta, Can, 87; Colo Indian Market, Denver, 87; Mont Indian Nations Art Rendezvous, Gov's Residence, Helena, 87. *Awards:* 1st & 2nd place, graphics, 85 & 86, Red Cloud Indian Sch, SDak, 85; James Bama Award, Best Painting & Best of Show, Buffalo Bill Hist Ctr, 87; Best oil painting, Seventh Ann Colo Indian Market, Denver, 87; 5th Ann Native Am Art exhib, artists choice, best painting, merit award, Great Falls, Mont, 87. *Bibliog:* Shirley Edam-Diaz (auth), Inspiration come from farm & ranch life, Aurora, spring 88; International Fine Art Collector Magazine, Featured Artist & Cover Image, 2/92; Shaman's Dram, Featured Artist, winter 92. *Media:* Oil; Cast Metal. *Publ:* Southwest Art Mag, 6/90. *Mailing Add:* 153 Calle Don Jose Santa Fe NM 87501

O'REILLY, JOHN B
PHOTOGRAPHER, COLLAGE ARTIST
b Orange, NJ, Feb 22, 30. *Study:* Syracuse Univ, BFA, 52; Art Inst Chicago, MFA, 56. *Work:* Mus Mod Art, New York; Addison Gallery Am Art, Andover, Mass; Bowdoin Col Mus, Brunswick, Maine; Worcester Art Mus, Worcester, Mass; Mus Fine Arts, Boston, Mass. *Exhib:* 4 Rooms-4 Artists, Addison Gallery Am Art, Andover, Mass, 83; The Photographers Persona 1840-1985, Mus Mod Art, New York, 85; Legacy of Light, Int Ctr Photog, New York, 87; Photographic Truth, Bruce Mus, Greenwich, Conn, 88; 3 Referees, North Carolina Mus Art, Raleigh, 90; Assembled, Wright State Univ Art Gallery, Dayton, Ohio, 91; Cannibal Eyes, Mass Inst Technol, List Visual Arts Ctr, Cambridge, 92. *Awards:* Fel Mass Art Fdn, 86; Fel Nat Endowment Arts, 88. *Media:* Photographic collage. *Dealer:* Howard Yezerski Gallery 186 South St Boston MA 02111. *Mailing Add:* 1168 Grafton St Worcester MA 01604

ORENS, ELAINE FRANCES
GRAPHIC ARTIST, PRINTMAKER
b New York, NY, July 18, 29. *Study:* Studied with Don G Kingman, Ruth Leaf Workshop & Stephen Czoka, 47-48; Hunter Col, BA, 51; Long Island Univ, MA, 78. *Work:* Adelphi Univ Gallery, Garden City, NY; Queensboro Community Col Gallery, Queens, NY; Hunter Col, New York. *Exhib:* Parrish Mus Open Exhib, Southampton, NY; Nassau County Fine Arts Mus First Open Exhib, Roslyn, NY, 88; 100 Years/100 Works, Nat Asn Women Artists, Islip Art Mus, East Islip, NY, 89; Nat Asn Women Artists Traveling Exhib, Palazzo Vecchio, Florence, Italy; Guild Hall Members Exhib, Guild Hall Mus, Easthampton, NY; Miniatures (prints), A A Gallery, New York; Hunterdon Museum Open Exhib, NJ. *Teaching:* Dir pvt printmaking workshops, Great neck, NY, 78-; instr serigraphy, Adelphi Univ, Garden City, NY, 79-82. *Awards:* Silver Medal, Audubon Artists, 76; Medal Honor, Nat Asn Women Artists Ann Printmaking Exhib, 82; Visual Art Alliance of Long Island Bronze Award, Nassau Co Mus Fine Arts, 88. *Bibliog:* Ruth Leaf (auth), Intalio Printmaking, Wattson-Guptil, 76; Helen Harrison (auth), Large prints, NY Times, 79 & 90. *Mem:* Nat Asn Women Artists (printmaking jury); Audubon Artist Asn; Hempstead Harbor Artists (exhib comt). *Media:* All Media. *Mailing Add:* 121 Shoreward Dr Great Neck NY 11021

ORENSANZ, ANGEL L
SCULPTOR, CERAMIST
b Larues, Spain, Feb 11, 41. *Study:* San Jorge Royal Fine Arts Sch, Barcelona, MA(fine arts), 64; Ecole Nat Beaux Arts, Paris, dipl(advan studies), 67; Royal Sch Fine Arts, London, dipl(advan studies), 68. *Work:* Calif Mus Sci & Indust, Los Angeles; Mus Art Mod Ville Paris; Mus Arte Contemp, Madrid, Spain; Univ Madrid, Spain; Univ Bunka Gakuin, Tokyo, 90. *Comn:* Refractory Facade, Dean & Mgt, Barcelona, Spain, 78; Metal Environment, Mgt Defense, Paris, 80; American Landscapes, IBM Corp, Boca Raton, Fla, 81; Purple Environment, comn by Martin Gelber, Los Angeles, 82; South Music, Atlanta, 85; Sun Screen & Sea Island, Ga, 86; World Fair, Seville, Spain, 92. *Exhib:* Dau al Set, Barcelona, 79; solo exhib, Flying Sculpture, Calif Mus Sci & Indust, Los Angeles, 81; Sculpture Today, Mus Luxemburg, Paris, 83; Roppongy Park, Heartland Gallery, Tokyo, 90-91; Bridges, Red Sq, Moscow, 91; Tallinn Arts Ctr, Etonia, 91; Metrop Mus Art, Tokyo, 92; Estacio de France, Barcelona, 92. *Awards:* Prix Everitube, Int Exhib, City Everitube, 75; Gold Medal, City Saragossa Bienale, 76; Arts, Sci, Lett, City Paris, 77. *Bibliog:* James Sweeney (auth), Orensanz's sculpture, 81 & Pierre Restany (auth), The great interplay, 81, Sculpture & Environment; Mario A Marrodan (auth), Escultoevaluacion de Angel Orensanz, 90. *Mem:* Royal Acad St Louis, Saragossa; Asn Artists & Ecrivains, Paris; Artists Social Responsibility, New York. *Mailing Add:* 172 Norfolk St New York NY 10002

ORENSTEIN, GLORIA FEMAN
EDUCATOR, HISTORIAN
b New York, NY, Mar 8, 38. *Study:* Brandeis Univ, BA(romance lang & lit), 59; Radcliffe Col, MA(Slavic lang & lit), 61; NY Univ(Danforth Grad Fel for Women), 66-71, PhD(comp lit), 71. *Pos:* Contrib ed, Womanart, Chrysalis Mag & Feminist Art J; co-founder, The Woman's Salon; dir, cultural prog for hon students & fac-in-residence, Pac Apartments, Univ Southern Calif, 81-85; coord & dir, UN End of Decade Conf on Women, Nairobi, 85. *Teaching:* Lectr women of surrealism, Cornell Univ, 73, Pa State Univ, 74, Inst 20th Century Studies, Univ Wis, 75, Sheridan Col, 75 & Artists Space, New York, 75; asst prof women in contemp arts, Douglass Col, 74-, asst prof Eng, 75-, chairperson women's studies prog, 76-78; dir, Rutgers Jr Yr in France, 78-79; assoc prof comparative lit & prog for study of women & men in soc, Univ Southern Calif, Los Angeles, 81-82. *Bibliog:* Article in Female Artists: Past & Present, Women's Hist Res Ctr, 74; coordr panel, Women Artists: Preparing for Changing our Future, Centre Cult Am, Paris, 79; articles in: WomanArt, Feminist Art J, Fireweed , Chry Salis, Heresies, and others. *Mem:* Mod Lang Asn; Jewish Women Fac Group; Nat Women's Studies Asn; Int Comparative Lit Asn; Int Asn Study Dada & Surrealism. *Res:* Surrealism; women's art history; women in the arts; re-emergence of the goddess in contemporary art and literature. *Publ:* Auth, A renaissance of goddess-culture art, Fireweed: A Woman's Lit & Cult J, No 1, 78; coauth (with Miriam Brumer), Americans in Paris revisited, Women Artists News, 79; The goddess in art by contemporary women, Women's Resource & Res Ctr, London, Eng, 79; Reclaiming the great mother: A feminist journey to madness and back in search of a goddess heritage, Symposium, spring 82; Towards a bifocal vision in surrealist aesthetics, Trivia, fall 83; A World in words, in: Women Artists of the World, Midmarch Arts, NY, 85. *Mailing Add:* Dept Comp Lit & Sociology Univ Southern Calif University Park Los Angeles CA 90089

ORENTLICHER, JOHN
VIDEO ARTIST, SCULPTOR
b Roanoke, Va, June 7, 43. *Study:* Goddard Col, BA, 68; Art Inst Chicago, MFA, 70. *Work:* Everson Mus, Syracuse, NY; Video Collection, Long Beach Mus, Calif; V-tapes, Toronto, Ont; Montevideo, Amsterdam; London Video Arts, London. *Exhib:* Outrageous Film, Whitney Mus Am Art, New York, 74; Everson Video Revue, Everson Mus & traveling, Syracuse, NY, 79-80; one person exhibs, Art Metropole, Toronto, 82, Ctr Art Tapes, Halifax, NS & Hallwalls (video), Buffalo, NY, 82; Basil Art Fair, Basil, Switz; Athens Int Film & Video Festival, Ohio, 82; Sixth Annual Tokyo Video Festival, Japan, 84; SONY Home Video Festival AFI, Los Angeles, 88; II Bienal Int Video Festival, Mus Mod Art, Medellin, Colombia, 88. *Pos:* Peace Corps, Chile, 64-66; bd trustees, Synapse Video, Syracuse, NY, 78- *Teaching:* Prof video, Col Visual & Performing Arts, Syracuse Univ, 76-81, chmn dept experimental studios, 81-85, chmn art media studies, 83-85 & 87-89; Fulbright lectr video, Bogota, Colombia, 85; chmn, Art Media Studies, 81-85 & 87-89. *Awards:* Rockefeller, 88; United States Information Agency, 88; Nat Endowment Arts, 88. *Bibliog:* Sarah McFadden (auth), Detroit, Art in Am, 79; Victor Anconia (auth), Ithaca video, Videography, 79; Sherry Chayat (auth), America on video, Syracuse Herald Am, 9/4/88. *Mem:* Media Alliance, New York. *Media:* Video. *Mailing Add:* Art Media Studies Syracuse Univ 223 Smith Hall Syracuse NY 13210

ORLAND, TED N
PHOTOGRAPHER, WRITER
b San Francisco, Calif. *Study:* Univ Southern Calif, BS(industrial design), 63; San Francisco State Univ, Calif, MA(interdisciplinary arts), 74. *Work:* Corcoran Gallery Art, Washington, DC; San Francisco Mus Mod Art, Calif; Amon Carter Mus, Tex; Boston Mus Fine Art, Mass; Univ Ariz Ctr Creative Photog, Tucson. *Exhib:* Polaroid Images, Franklin Inst, Philadelphia, Pa, 78; The Mechanical Eye, Oakland Mus, Calif, 80; New Acquisitions, Corcoran Gallery Art, Washington, DC, 81; Am Photog & Nat Parks, national tour, 81-83; Univ Ore Art Mus, Eugene, 82; Monterey Art Mus, Calif, 86; Nat Mus Mod Art, Kyoto, Japan, 87; Crocker Art Mus, Sacramento, Calif, 90. *Pos:* Apprentice, Saul Marks, Los Angeles, Calif, 62-63; asst, Charles Eames, Venice, Calif, 68-71; asst, Ansel Adams, Carmel, Calif, 72-75; ed, Image Continuum Press, 74- *Teaching:* Asst prof & dir undergrad and grad prog, Univ Ore, 81-84; dir, Ansel Adam's Gallery Photog Workshops, 84-86; resident fac, Maine Photog Workshops, 85-90; Roy Acuff Chair of Excellence in the Creative Arts, Austin Peay State Univ, Tenn, 89. *Awards:* Artist-in-Residency, Volcanoes Nat Park, Volcano Arts Ctr, Hawaii, 76; Grant to pursue creative work, The Polaroid Corp, 77-78 & Walnut Creek Civic Arts Gallery, 78-79; Individual Artist's Fel, Ore Arts Comn, 82. *Bibliog:* Joel Pickford (auth), Ansel Adams & Ted Orland: A critical comparison, Image Continuum J, 79; David Robertson (auth), The Art & Literature of Yosemite, Yosemite Nat Hist Asn, 82. *Mem:* Ctr Photog Art, Carmel, Calif. *Media:* Hand-colored Silverbase Prints, Electronic Imaging. *Publ:* Illusr, Yosemite Reflections, Flying Spur Press, 77; contribr, Other Realities, Jerry Uelsmann, 81; auth, T Orland's Compendium of Photographic Truths, Image Continuum Press, 81; Man and Yosemite: A Photographer's View of the Early Years, Image Continuum Press, 85; Scenes of Wonder & Curiosity: The Photographs and Writings of Ted Orland, David R Godine Publ, 88. *Dealer:* Ansel Adams Gallery PO Box 455 Yosemite CA 95389. *Mailing Add:* 1017 Seabright Ave Santa Cruz CA 95062

ORLOWSKY, LILLIAN
PAINTER, COLLAGE ARTIST
b New York, NY, Oct 14, 14. *Study:* Educ Alliance Art Sch, 32; Am Art Sch, with Raphael-Moses Soyer & Anton Refregier, 32-35; Hans Hofmann Sch Fine Art, New York, 37-47 & Provincetown, Mass, 38. *Work:* Chrysler Mus Art, Provincetown, Mass & Norfolk, Va; Archives Smithsonian Inst, Washington, DC; Provincetown Art Asn & Mus, Mass; Metrop Mus Art, New York; Baltimore Mus Fine Arts, Md, 92-; Cape Mus Fine Arts, Dennis, Mass, Purchase, 92; Fine Arts Mus Prague, Czech, 92. *Exhib:* Provincetown: A Painter's Place (with catalog), Everson Mus, Syracuse, NY, 76; Works Progress Administration: Then & Now (with catalog), Parsons Sch Design, New York, 77; Hans Hofmann & His Students, Metrop Mus Art, New York, 78; Recent Acquisition, Provincetown Art Asn & Mus, Mass, 79; one-man show, Goddard Col, Vt, 80; Ingber Gallery, New York, 81; WPA Artist's 50th Anniversary, City Gallery, New York, 84; Nat Coun Aging, Washington, DC, 85; The Provocative Years--Hans Hofmann & His Students in Provincetown, 35-45 (with catalog), Provincetown Art Asn & Mus, 90; Recent Purchase, Cape Mus Fine Arts, Dennis, Mass, 92. *Collections Arranged:* Dir, James Gallery, 59-62. *Pos:* Instr painting & drawing, Bronx House, NY, 63-77; cur, Provincetown Art Asn & Mus, 90. *Awards:* Richard A Florsheim Found Art Fund, 92. *Bibliog:* Norma Holt (auth), Faces of the Artists, Nat Coun Aging, 80; interview, Voice of Am, Washington, DC, 84; plus many others. *Mem:* Artists Equity; Provincetown Art Ctr & Mus. *Media:* Ink, Oil. *Publ:* Interview with Cynthia Goodman, 78; Provincetown Advocate Extra, 86; Why Study Art?, Interview with Kathy Shorri, 86; Interview-Debbie Forman, Works by Hofmann's Ambassadors, Cape Cod Times, mag sect, 8/31/90; Interview with Jeffrey Vand de Visse, Radio Sta WOMR, Provincetown, 92. *Mailing Add:* 530 W 113th St Apt 3A New York NY 10025-8018

ORLYK, HARRY V
PAINTER
b Troy, NY, Jan 8, 47. *Study:* New York State Univ Col, New Paltz, BS, 70; Univ Nebr, Lincoln, MFA, 74. *Work:* Springfield Mo Art Mus; Albany Inst Hist & Art, NY; Sheldon Art Mus, Lincoln, Nebr. *Exhib:* Candidates for Art Awards, Am Acad & Inst Arts & Lett, NY, 87; Contemp Landscape Photographs & Paintings, Mem Art Gallery, Univ Rochester, 88; Artists of the Mohawk-Hudson Regional Invitational, Ctr Galleries, Albany, NY, 90; Truth & Beauty, Loyola Marymount Univ, Los Angeles, Calif, 92; Under the Influence, Tatistchiff, Santa Monica, Calif, 92; Venable/Neslage Gallery, Washington, DC, 92. *Awards:* L A Sawyer, Mohawk-Hudson Regional, 89; Albany Inst Purchase Award, 89; Purchase Award, Albany Inst Hist & art, 92. *Bibliog:* Thomas Bolt (auth), Harry Orlyk, Arts Mag, 11/86; Margaret Mathews Berenson (auth), Am Artist, 7/87; Timonthy Cahill (auth), Working the Land, Metroland, 12/88. *Dealer:* Tatistcheff 50 W St New York NY 10019. *Mailing Add:* Bind Buck Rd Salem NY 12865

ORNSTEIN, JUDITH
PAINTER
b Newark, NJ, May 4, 51. *Study:* Wimbledon Sch Art, Eng, 70-71, Philadelphia Col Art, BFA, 73, Yale Univ, MFA, 75. *Work:* Albright Knox Mus, Buffalo, NY; Cooper Hewitt Mus, New York; Vassar Col Mus, Poughkeepsie, NY. *Exhib:* one-person shows, Willard Gallery, New York, 77, 79, Cirruss Gallery, Los Angeles, 83, V Levy Fine Arts, New York, 84. *Awards:* Nat Endowment Arts Fel. *Mailing Add:* 28 Tiffany Place Brooklyn NY 11231

OROPALLO, DEBORAH
ARTIST
b Hackensack, NJ, Nov 29, 54. *Study:* Leo Marchutz Sch Drawing & Painting, Aix-en-Provence, France, 75; Alfred Univ, New York, BFA, 79; Univ Calif, Berkeley, MA, 82, MFA, 83. *Work:* Baltimore Mus Art, Md; Bank Am, San Francisco; La Jolla Mus Contemp Art, Calif; Weatherspoon Art Gallery, Greensboro, NC; Lang Communications, New York. *Exhib:* Currents/Deborah Oropallo, Inst Contemp Art, Boston, Mass, 90, Stephen Wirtz Gallery, 90, Artspace, San Francisco, Calif,90, Greenville Co Mus Art, SC, 91, Weatherspoon Gallery, Univ NC, Greensboro, 92, Raab Gallery, London, Eng, 92, Ann Jaffee Gallery, Bay Harbor Island, Fla, 92; Susan Cummins Gallery, Mill Valley, Calif, 92; Aspen Art Mus, Colo, 92; Germmans Van Eck Gallery, New York, 92; Krakow Gallery, Katie Block Fine Art, Boston, Mass, 92; Directions in Bay Area Printmaking, Palo Alto, Calif, 93. *Teaching:* San Francisco Art Acad Col, Calif, 86 & 87. *Awards:* Art Space Grant, San Francisco, Calif, 90; Calif Arts Coun Grant, 90; Nat Endowment Arts Award, 91. *Bibliog:* Elisa Turner (auth), Deborah Oropallo, Artnews, summer 92; Chiori Santiago (auth), The fine art of apprehension, Oakland Tribune, 2/17/92; Kenneth Baker (auth), Why, paintings in Mill Valley, San Francisco Chronicle, 3/14/92. *Mailing Add:* c/o Stephen Wirtz Gallery 49 Geary 3rd Fl San Francisco CA 94108

ORR, ARTHUR (LESLIE)
PAINTER, GRAPHIC ARTIST
b Rockport, Mass, Nov 12, 38. *Study:* Mass Col Art, BFA, 63; Univ Ill, Urbana, MFA, 65. *Work:* Tenn Fine Arts Collection, Opryland Hotel, Nashville; High Mus; Bridgestone Tire, US Hq, Nashville; Colonial Corp Am, New York. *Comn:* Paintings, Bass & Assoc & Commerce Union Bank, Nashville, 76; Interior Design Servs, Billboard Art Series, 84. *Exhib:* Southeastern Ann, High Mus, 68; Whitney Mus Art Ann, 70; Southeastern Ctr Contemp Art Invitational, Winston-Salem, NC, 79; Tenn Valley Invitational, Washington, DC, 79; solo exhibs, Parallel Realities, Tenn Botanical Ctr, Nashville, 79, Recent Works, Fisk Univ, 81 & Systems & Cutouts, Tenn Fine Arts Ctr, Nashville, 83; Tenn Arts Comn Gallery, Nashville, 87; Memphis Ctr Contemp Art, Inaugural Exhib, Memphis, Tenn, 88. *Pos:* Vis lectr, Art Inst Chicago, 70, Vanderbilt Univ, 81, Tenn Fine Arts Ctr, 83 & Nashville Artists Guild, 88. *Teaching:* Instr fine arts, Mass Col Art, 65-66; asst prof, Moore Col Art, 66-67 & Peabody Col, 67-72, Fisk Univ, 77, Middle Tenn State Univ, 80; prof, Tenn State Univ, 85-86. *Awards:* Jury Awards, Hunter Mus Ann, 69 & Mazur Mus Ann, Monroe, La, 69; Purchase Award, Century III Fine Art Exhib, Nashville, 80; Tenn Valley Authority Purchase Award, 85-86 & 88; WDCN-PBS TV 10th Anniversity Poster & Print, Gavel Award. *Bibliog:* Charles Jansen (auth), Arthur Lorr, Art Voices, 1/78-2/78. *Media:* Acrylic. *Dealer:* Bell Ross Gallery 1080 Brookfield Rd Memphis TN. *Mailing Add:* c/o Studio L'Atelier 3 Maryland Farms Brentwood TN 37027

ORR, ELLIOT
PAINTER
b Flushing, New York, June 26, 04. *Study:* Grand Cent Art Sch, with George Luks & Charles W Hawthorne. *Work:* Whitney Mus Am Art & Brooklyn Mus, New York; Butler Inst Am Art, Youngstown, Ohio; Boca Raton Mus, Fla; William A Farnsworth Art Mus, Rockland, Maine; Heritage Plantation, Sandwich, Mass; Midwest Mus Art, Elkhart, Ind; Phillips Mem Gallery, Washington, DC; and others. *Exhib:* Romantic Painting in America, Mus Mod Art, New York, 43; American Painting Today, 50 & American Watercolors, Drawings & Prints, 52, Metrop Mus Art, New York; Golden Anniversary, Provincetown Art Asn, 64; By the People, For the People: New England, De Cordova Mus, Lincoln, Mass, 77; Retrospective, 1924-1983 (auth, catalog), Harmon-Meek Gallery, Naples, Fla, 83; American Art of the 1930's & 1940's, Mitchell Mus, Mt Vernon, Ill, 83; American Painting of the 1930's (with catalog), Boca Raton Mus, Fla, 89-90; and others. *Awards:* Joseph Lewis Weyrich Mem Prize, Baltimore Mus, 30; Crossett First Prize, Cape Cod Art Asn, 48. *Bibliog:* F F Sherman (auth), Notes on Elliot Orr, Art in Am, 40; Rosamund Frost (auth), Contemporary Art, Crown, 42; John I H Baur (auth), Revolution and Tradition in Modern American Art, Harvard Univ, 51. *Mem:* Life mem Provincetown Art Asn. *Media:* All. *Dealer:* Harmon-Meek Gallery 1258 Third St S Naples FL 33940. *Mailing Add:* 442 Broad Ave S Naples FL 33940

ORR, JOSEPH CHARLES
PAINTER
b Tokyo, Japan, Oct 31, 49; US citizen. *Study:* With Anthony Allison, 71; Univ Mo, Columbia, with Frank Stack, 77-78. *Work:* State Mo Hist Soc, Columbia; Nat Collegiate Athletic Asn, Kansas City, Mo; Osage Co Hist Soc, Linn, Mo; Dunnegan Mus Art, Bolivar, Mo; Fed Reserve Bank, Kansas City, Mo. *Comn:* Paintings, Community Fed Savings, Mexico, Mo, 80 & Mercantile Bank, Eldon, Mo, 81; centennial painting, City Eldon, Mo, 82. *Exhib:* Salmagundi Club Exhib, NY, 88, 89, 91 & 92; Contemp Art Exhib, Mo Athletic Club, 88 & 89; Exhib 91 & 92, Nat Oil & Acrylic Painters' Soc, Osage Beach, Mo; solo exhib, Culver Gallery, St Louis Pub Libr, Mo, 88; 4th Ann Arts for Parks Competition, Jackson Hole, Wyo, 90; and others. *Awards:* First Prize, Beverly Art Ctr, Chicago, 83; First Prize, Nat Wildlife Collectors Soc Ann Exhib, Minneapolis, Minn, 84; Winsor & Newton Award, 14th Salmagundi Club Exhib, NY, 91. *Bibliog:* Rita Mathews-Orr (auth), My husband the artist, Mo Life, 75; Hope Matthews (auth), Rural scenes with an Ozark Flavor, Midwest Art, 10/84; article, Families of artists coping with day-to-day problems, Am Artist, 10/87. *Mem:* Nat Soc Painters Casein & Acrylic; co-founder, Nat Oil & Acrylic Painters' Soc, Osage Beach, Mo. *Media:* Acrylic on Masonite, Watercolor. *Publ:* Auth, Painting in acrylic, Am Artist, 3/86. *Dealer:* Union Hill Galleries 3013 Main Kansas City MO 64108; E S Lawrence Galleries 132 E Kit Carson Rd Taos NM 87571. *Mailing Add:* Rt 1, Box 1229 Osage Beach MO 65065

ORR-CAHALL, ANONA CHRISTINA
CURATOR, HISTORIAN
Study: Mt Holyoke Col, BA; Oxford Univ; Ecole du Louvre; Yale Univ, MA, MPhil, PhD. *Collections Arranged:* Am Drawing 1970-1973, Yale Univ Art Gallery, 73; Addison Mizner Architect of Dreams and Realities and Contemp Views of the Am Family, Norton Gallery Art, 77; Charles Griffin Farr: A Retrospective, 84 & Gordon Cook: A Restropective, 87, Oakland Mus. *Pos:* Chief cur art, Oakland Mus, formerly; dir, Corcoran Gallery Art, Washington, DC, formerly. *Teaching:* Asst prof art hist & mus studies, Calif Polytech State Univ, San Luis Obispo, 78-81. *Res:* California art 1925-present. *Mailing Add:* Norton Gallery 1451 S Olive Ave West Palm Beach FL 33401

ORTIZ, CARLOS See Sueños, Carlos

ORTIZ, RAPHAEL MONTANEZ
CONCEPTUAL ARTIST, EDUCATOR
b New York, NY, Jan 30, 34. *Study:* Brooklyn Mus Art Sch; Art Students League; Pratt Inst, BS & MFA; Columbia Univ, EdD, 82. *Work:* Whitney Mus Am Art, Finch Mus, Mus Mod Art, New York & Museo del Barrio, New York; Syracuse Mus Contemp Art, NY,; Ludwig Mus, Cologne, Ger; Mus Mod Art, Brussels, Belg; Friedricheshof Mus, Zurndorf, Austria; and many others. *Exhib:* Traveling Assemblage Exhib, Mus Mod Art, New York, 63; Young America Exhibition, Whitney Mus Am Art, New York, 65; retrospective, sculpture, performance, computer-laser-video, Museo del Barrio, New York, 88; Computer-Laser-Video, Selected Works, Berlin Video & Film Festival, Ger, 91; performance, Rites of Spring, Alternative Mus, Soho, NY, 92; exhib, Artists of Conscience, Alternative Mus, Soho, NY, 92; performance, Ritual and Installation, Kunst, Vienna, Austria, 92; performance, Utilizing Video Conference System Between Kõln & Kassel Germany, Documenta, Electronic Cafe, 92; plus numerous one-man & group shows & performances. *Pos:* Founder, dir & cur, Museo del Barrio, New York, 69-; comt mem, Ghetto Arts Panel, NY State Coun Arts, 70-71; vchmn, Planning Corp Arts, New York, 71; chmn bd, Fondo Del Sol, Washington, DC, 79-81; founder & pres, Mus Computer Art, NJ, 84. *Teaching:* Full prof visual arts, grad & undergrad fac, Mason Gross Sch Arts, Rutgers Univ, 72- *Awards:* John Hay Whitney Fel Grant, 65; Nat Endowment Arts Grant, 72; NJ Coun Arts, 87. *Bibliog:* Dr Kristine Stiles (auth), Work discussed in Out of Control, ARS Electronea, Duke Univ, 91; Dr Kristine Stiles (auth), Survival ethos and destruction art (discourse), J Theoretical Studies Media & Culture, Duke Univ, spring 92. *Mem:* Col Art Asn of Am; Mus Computer Art (founder & pres, 84); Hispanic Asn Higher Educ, NJ; Asn Res & Enlightenment. *Media:* Mixed Media, Technology. *Publ:* Auth, Disassemblage, Art & Artists, 66; ed & auth, Ritual theatre, Aspen Mag, 69; auth, Culture and the people, Art in Am, 71; Towards an Authenticating Art, Univ Mich, Dissertation Serv, Ann Arbor, 82. *Mailing Add:* Rutgers Univ Visual Arts Dept 125 New St New Brunswick NJ 08901

ORTLIEB, ROBERT EUGENE
SCULPTOR, GRAPHIC ARTIST
b San Diego, Calif, July 4, 25. *Study:* Univ Southern Calif, with Merrell Gage, Francis de Erdely & Glen Lucens, BFA & MFA; independent study, Europe, Mex & SAm; San Francisco State Col. *Work:* Calif Palace Legion Honor Mus, San Francisco; Laguna Beach Art Mus; Univ Calif, Riverside; Riverside Community Col; Loma Linda Univ; Palm Springs Desert Mus, Calif. *Comn:* Community Church, Palos Verde, Calif, 68; Apothecaries (bronze), Dr MacFarlane, Univ Southern Calif, 75; Genesis (bronze), Lobby of Lawson Products Corp Hq, Des Plaines, Ill, 80; Mother & Child (bronze) in Fountain, Community Ctr, Costa Mesa, Calif, 82; Emergence (bronze) Inst Beauty Surgery Med Group, Beverly Hills, Calif, 83; and others. *Exhib:* Int Graphic Exhib, Cincinnati, Ohio, 53; Los Angeles Co Mus Calif; Denver Art Mus; one-man shows, Ill State Mus, Springfield, 64 & Dean Mus, Cherry Valley, Calif, 75; Dallas Mus Fine Arts; Oakland Art Mus, Calif; Palm Springs Desert Mus, Calif, 81; and others. *Teaching:* Instr sculpture, Riverside Art Ctr, Univ Calif, 62-75 & Univ Southern Calif, Idyllwild, 64-76; inst prof de Stato per l'Industria de l'Artigianato del Marmo in, Carrara, Italy, 72; Village Ctr for the Creative Arts, Palm Springs, Calif, 68- *Awards:* First Awards, Calif State Fair & Expos, 48 & 57, Long Beach Art Mus, 57 & 77 & 50th Nat Orange Show, San Bernardino, 65. *Bibliog:* Robert Ortlieb, La Rev Mod, Paris, France, 62; Janice Lovoos & Felice Paramore (co-auth), Wood carving and wood mosaic, In: Modern Mosaic Techniques, Watson-Guptill, 65; Betje Howell (auth), Twelve California artists, Am Artist, R Riedinger, 68; Janice Lovoos (auth), Robert Ortlieb Sculpture, Artist of the Rockies & Golden West, J Manson, 85 & The many faces of Robert Ortlieb, Am Artist, G Heffernan, 86; article, Cailf Art Review, Am References, Inc, 89. *Mem:* Hon life mem Inglewood Art Asn, Calif. *Media:* Stone, Wood Carving. *Dealer:* Galleries Miranda Hotel Laguna 417 S Coast Hwy Laguna Beach Calif 92651. *Mailing Add:* 11111 Jerry Lane Garden Grove CA 92640

ORTLIP, MARY KRUEGER
PAINTER
b Scranton, Pa. *Study:* NY Sch Social Res, studied with Emil Lindenfield; Montclair Mus Art Sch, studied with Paul D Ortlip; Houghton Col, Hon DFA, 88. *Work:* Mus Parc Rocheteau, Revin, France; Palais des Artes, Marseille, France. *Comn:* Oil paintings, comn by Colette Nomura, Paris, Frances B Harrison, Sr, Stephen Pistner, New York, Maria T G Douglas, Spain, Milton Spahn, Riverdale, NY. *Exhib:* 13th Int Salon, Mus Parc Rocheteau, Revin, France; Salon D'Aquitaine, Mouleon-Soule, France, 86; Seigneurs de l'Art, Salon Int, Palais des Art, Marseille, 87; one-woman shows, Les Amis des Arts, Aix-en-Provence, France, 87 & The Ardennes as Seen By an American, Revin, France, 90; Salon Int de Seigneurs de l'Art, Plais des Arts, Parc Chanot, France, 87; Salon Int des Beaux-Arts, Club Int de Peinture, France, 89; James Hunt Barker Galleries & Salmagundi Club, New York. *Awards:* Medal, Artist of Yr, Salon D'Aquitaine, 86; Gold Medal & Dipl, Festival des Artes en Ardennes, France-Belg, 87; Medal of Hon, Aix-en-Provence, France, 87; Cup & Grant Prize, Salon Int des Beaux Arte, Salon de Peinture, 87. *Bibliog:* Paul Keifer (auth), NY Art Speak, 83; Donatelle Micault (auth), A painter- her work, La Press Francaise, 84; Gene Brislin (auth), European art world honors Mary Krueger Ortlip ambassadress, Scranton Tribune, 88. *Mem:* Salmagundi Club; Acad Italia; Inst d'Arte Contemp; Nat Soc Arts & Letts. *Media:* Oil. *Dealer:* Curzon Gallery 501 E Camino Real Boca Raton FL 33487. *Mailing Add:* 2917 S Ocean Blvd Apt 703 Highland Beach FL 33487

ORTLIP, PAUL DANIEL
PAINTER
b Englewood, NJ, May 21, 26. *Study:* Houghton Acad; Art Students League; with Louis Bouche, 47, Reginald Marsh, 48, Robert Brackman & Edwin Dickinson, 49; Acad Grande Chaumiere, 50; Houghton Col, Hon DFA, 88. *Work:* US Navy Art Collection, Pentagon, Washington, DC; Bergen Community Mus, Paramus, NJ; Air & Space Mus, Smithsonian Inst,

Washington, DC; Am Col Clin Pharmacology, NY Acad of Med, New York; Fairleigh Dickinson Univ; and others. *Comn:* Mem portrait of JFK, Fairleigh Dickinson Univ Libr, 64; Gemini 5 Astronauts, Off Info, USN, 65, Vietnam (painting), 67, Apollo 12 Astronauts, 69 & Apollo 17 Astronauts, 72; and others. *Exhib:* Salon L'Art Libre Ann, Paris, France, 50; Allied Artists Am Ann, 60-71; Collection of Fine Arts, Smithsonian Inst, Washington, DC; Galerie Vallombreuse, Biarritz, France, 74; La Galerie Mouffe, Paris, 75; James Hunt Barker Galleries, New York, Palm Beach & Nantucket, 83. *Pos:* Off US Navy artist, Off Info, Washington, DC, 63-; art cur, Fairleigh Dickinson Univ, 67-70. *Teaching:* Instr painting, Montclair Acad, NJ, 57-58; artist in residence, Fairleigh Dickinson Univ, 57-67; instr painting, Montclair Mus, 58-59 & 76-80. *Awards:* First Prize, US Armed Forces Exhib, Far East, 46; First Prize, Am Artist Prof League, State Exhib, NJ Chapter, 60; Outstanding Achievement Award, Oil Painting, USN, 68; Artist of Year Award, Hudson Artists, Jersey City Mus, NJ, 70. *Bibliog:* Marg Dulac (auth), Odyssey of an artist, NJ Mus & Arts, 5/71; Luc Elysēē Serraf (auth), Paul Ortlip, Artiste American, La Cote des Arts, cover Marseil, France; M Stephen Doherty (auth), Paul Ortlip, His Heritage and His Art, Phoenix Pub, 83. *Mem:* Life mem Art Students League New York; Allied Artists Am; Salmagundi Club; Nat Soc Mural Painters; Artists Fel, Inc. *Media:* Mixed. *Dealer:* The Curzon Gallery 501 E Camino Real Boca Raton FL 33432. *Mailing Add:* 588 Summit Ave Hackensack NJ 07601

ORTMAN, GEORGE EARL
PAINTER, SCULPTOR
b Oakland, Calif, Oct 17, 26. *Study:* Ariz State Univ; Calif Col Arts & Crafts; Atelier 17, New York; Acad Andre Lhote, Paris; Hans Hofmann Sch, New York. *Work:* Guggenheim Mus & Mus Mod Art, New York; Walker Art Ctr, Minneapolis, Minn; Albright-Knox Art Gallery, Buffalo; Milwaukee Art Ctr; Nat Gallery Art; and others. *Comn:* Mural, comn by Bd Educ, PS 192, New York, 67; Reredo, Unitarian Church, Princeton, NJ, 68; banners, Ind Univ Opera House, 71; Oracle (three panels), Mfrs Hanover Trust, 71; Albert Kahn & Assoc Inc, 81; Wharton Ctr Performing Arts, Mich State Univ. *Exhib:* Carnegie Inst Int, Pittsburgh, 60, 64 & 70; Toward a New Abstraction, Jewish Mus, New York, 63; Tokyo Biennial, Japan, 64; 100 Years of Amerian Art, 64 & Two Decades of Geometric Abstraction, 65, Whitney Mus Am Art. *Teaching:* Sr fel painting, Princeton Univ, 66-69; head painting dept, Cranbrook Acad Art, 70- *Awards:* Guggenheim Fel, 65; First Prize Religion Art, Birmingham Mus Art, 66; First Prize, NJ State Mus Second Ann, 67. *Bibliog:* J Borgzingler (auth), Analytical art, Time Mag, 4/64; Martin Friedman (auth), Symbols, Art News, 10/65. *Media:* Oil, Mixed Media. *Dealer:* Hill Gallery 163 Townsend Birmingham MI 48009. *Mailing Add:* PO Box 144 Bloomfield Hills MI 48013-0801

ORZE, JOSEPH JOHN
ADMINISTRATOR, SCULPTOR
b Exeter, Pa, Dec 11, 32. *Study:* Syracuse Univ, BFA(magna cum laude), 55, MS, 56; George Peabody Col, EdD, 70. *Work:* Munson, Williams, Proctor Inst, Utica, NY; Sch Benedictine Fathers, Rome, Italy; Mass Maritime Acad, Buzzards Bay. *Exhib:* One-man & two-man shows, J B Speed Art Mus, Louisville, Ky, 65, Dana Arts Ctr, Colgate Univ, Hamilton, NY, 69; Brooks Mem Gallery, Memphis; Hunter Gallery, Univ Chattanooga; Syracuse Univ, NY; Conn Acad Fine Arts, Wadsworth Atheneum, Hartford; Everson Mus Fine Art, Syracuse; and others. *Pos:* Vpres & dir, Southern Asn Sculptors, 64-66; chmn, Conn Col Coun Arts, 67-69; vpres & dir, Marion Art Ctr, Mass, 73-75; dir & treas, Pub Art Proj, Inc, New Bedford, Mass, 74- *Teaching:* Instr art & educ, Syracuse Univ, 56-59; assoc prof sculpture & art educ, State Univ NY Col New Paltz, 59-61; assoc prof art & head dept, Middle Tenn State Univ, 61-66; prof art & chmn dept, Southern Conn State Col, 66-69; dean, Col Fine & Applied Arts, Southeastern Mass Univ, 69-75; pres, Worcester State Col, 75-, Northwestern La State Univ, currently. *Awards:* Purchase Award for Sculpture, Munson, Williams, Proctor Inst, 58; R A Rathbone Best in Show Award, New Haven Print & Clay Club, 66; First Prize in Sculpture, New Eng Arts Festival, Waterbury, Conn, 67 & 68. *Mem:* Col Art Asn; Nat Art Educ Asn. *Publ:* Auth, Understanding children's art, Instr Mag, 5/64; Enigma of modern art, Peabody Reflector, 5/66; Role of the Fine Arts in the University, Middle Tenn State Univ, 69; Visual arts in higher education, Mass Art Educ Asn, 70; co-auth, Art From Scrap, Davis, 2nd ed, 73. *Mailing Add:* 26 Towle Fram Rd No 13 Hampton NH 03842

OSBORN, ELODIE C (MRS ROBERT OSBORN)
DIRECTOR, ADMINISTRATOR
b Brooklyn, NY, Dec 6, 11. *Study:* Packer Col Inst; Wellesley Col, BA; Sch Fine Arts, NY Univ; Sorbonne, cert, 35. *Collections Arranged:* Many exhibs at Mus Mod Art, New York, and touring to other mus, cols & schs; Klee Mem Exhib, Mus Mod Art, New York, 41; Seven Decades of MacDowell Artists, 76. *Pos:* Dir traveling exhibs, Mus Mod Art, New York, 33-48; dir, Salisbury Film Soc, 51-81. *Awards:* Film Fel, MacDowell Colony, 84. *Mem:* Am Fedn Arts; Mus Mod Art; Int Film Seminars (bd trustees, 68-80); MacDowell Colony (mem bd dirs, 70-87, secy bd, 72-, vpres, 73-75, pres, 75-77, dir emer, 87-); Am Fedn Film Socs (vpres, 57-58). *Publ:* Auth, Modern Sculpture (portfolio), 51; Manual of Traveling Exhibitions, UNESCO, 53; contribr, Art in Am, 66; Film Quart, 68; Film Libr Quart, 72; auth, program notes for Modern Arts and Artists Traveling Exhib of Films, 79. *Mailing Add:* 392 Taconic Rd Salisbury CT 06068

OSBORN, KEVIN RUSSELL
BOOK ARTIST, PRINTMAKER
b Boston, Mass, July 3, 51. *Study:* Ecole Nat Arts Decoratifs, Nice, France, 71-72; Univ Vt, Burlington, BA(cum laude), 73; Visual Studies Workshop, State Univ NY, Buffalo, MFA, 77. *Work:* Mus Mod Art, New York; Mus Nat Art Mod, Paris; Whitney Mus; Art Inst Chicago; DeYoung Mus, San Francisco. *Comn:* Parallel (artist book), Ga State Arts Coun, Atlanta, 80. *Exhib:* Words and Images, Philadelphia Art Alliance, 80; solo exhib, Washington Proj Arts, 80; Ex Libris, Traction Gallery, Los Angeles, 81; Re/pages, New England Found Arts Touring Exhib, 81-82; Cent Livres d'Ailleurs, Ed Jean-Michel Pl, Paris, 82; 12th Biennale Paris, Mus Mod Art, Paris, 82. *Pos:* Dir, Bookworks Prog, Writer's Ctr, Bethesda, Md, 77- *Teaching:* Instr workshops, Calif Col Arts & Crafts, 80, Va Commonwealth Univ, 83 & State Univ NY, Purchase, 83. *Awards:* Grant Vector Rev (artist book), Found Todays Art, 83; Va Mus Fel, 83; Nat Endowment Arts Fel, 84. *Bibliog:* Clive Phillpot (auth), Real lush, Artforum, 5/82; Paul Zelevansky (auth), Visual literature, Am Book Rev, spring 83; Nancy Solomon (auth), The layered look, Afterimage, summer 83. *Media:* Artists Books; Experimental Offset. *Mailing Add:* 3411 15th St N Arlington VA 22201

OSBORN, ROBERT
ILLUSTRATOR, PAINTER
b Oshkosh, Wis, Oct 26, 04. *Study:* Yale Univ; Brit Acad, Rome; Acad Scandinav, Paris; also with Friesz, Varoquier & Despiau; Md Inst Art, Hon DFA, 63. *Work:* Mus Mod Art, New York; Addison Gallery Art, Andover, Mass; Paine Art Mus, Oshkosh, Wis; Corcoran Gallery Art, Washington, DC; Wadsworth Atheneum, Hartford, Conn. *Comn:* Mural, Quinta da Bacalhoa Azeitao, Port, 38-39; mural, Am Mus Natural Hist, New York, 55; mural, comn by Stonoroff for Planning Comn Philadelphia, 56; two murals for Puerto Rico Planning Comn, 70 & three murals for Smithsonian Exhib on Productivity, 72, comn by Ivan Chermayeff; three murals, comn by Ivan Chermayeff for Smithsonian Exhib on Productivity, 72. *Exhib:* Wartime Posters, Art Inst Chicago, 46; Va Mus Fine Arts, Richmond, 52; Wadsworth Atheneum, 58; Whitney Mus Am Art, New York, 60; Brooklyn Mus, 61; Live From Conn, Whitney Mus, Stamford, Conn; Nuclear Conflict, Carpenter Ctr, Harvard Univ, 84. *Pos:* Presented first show of Edward Weston in the East, Hotchkiss Sch, 31. *Teaching:* Founder & head dept art, Hotchkiss Sch, Lakeville, Conn, 29-35; chmn Yale Coun, Sch Art & Archit, Yale Univ, 60-65, alumni exec coun, 70- *Awards:* Gov Medal, Wis; Distinguished Pub Serv Award, Legion of Merit; Yale Art Assocs Albers Medal. *Bibliog:* Leo Lionni (auth), Osborn, Print, Vol 5; Russell Lynes (auth), Osborn's Americans, Horizon, 9/60; Fritz Eichenberg (auth), Osborn, Am Graphic Artist, 65; Drawings Robert Osborn, Houghton Mifflin (in prep); plus others. *Mem:* Elizabethan Club; Century Asn. *Media:* Pen, Crayon; Watercolor. *Collection:* Despiau, Miros, Klees, Calders, Marinni, MacIver, Hartley, Picasso, Dubuffet, Friedman, Shahn and others. *Publ:* Auth, Osborn on Osborn, Ticknor & Fields, Houghton Mifflin, 82; and others. *Mailing Add:* Salisbury CT 06068

OSBORNE, CYNTHIA A
PRINTMAKER, EDUCATOR
b New Milford, Conn, Dec 13, 47. *Study:* Conn Col, New London, BA, 69; Univ Wis-Madison, MFA, 73. *Work:* Bradley Univ, Peoria, Ill; Davidson Col, NC; Security Pac Nat Banks, Calif; State Univ NY Buffalo; US Info Agency, Selected US Embassies. *Exhib:* Miami Graphics Biennial, Metrop Mus, Fla, 76 & 80; Current Directions in Southern Calif Art, Los Angeles Inst Contemp Art, 77 & 78; Nat Print Exhib, Soc Am Graphic Artists, New York, 77 & 79; Drawings & Prints, Space, Los Angeles, 79; Paper in Particular, Columbia Col, Mo, 80; and many others. *Pos:* Vis artist, Nat Print Symp, Cranbrook Acad Art, Detroit, spring 80. *Teaching:* Assoc prof printmaking, Calif State Univ, Long Beach, 75-82, assoc prof art, currently; lectr printmaking, Otis Art Inst, Los Angeles, 77. *Awards:* Purchase Awards, Griffin Press Co, Oakland, Calif, 75 & Los Angeles Printmakers Nat Exhib, Graphic Chemical, Chicago, 77. *Mem:* Los Angeles Printmaking Soc (bd mem, 77); Soc Am Graphic Artists; World Print Coun, San Francisco. *Media:* Printmaking; Lithography. *Mailing Add:* Dept Art Calif State & Long Beach 1250 Bellflower Blvd Long Beach CA 90840

OSBORNE, ELIZABETH
PAINTER, INSTRUCTOR
b Philadelphia, Pa, June 5, 36. *Study:* Pa Acad Fine Arts, cert(Schiedt Traveling Scholarship), 58; Univ Pa, BFA(with hons), 59. *Work:* Chase Manhattan Bank, New York; Philadelphia Mus Art, Pa; Pa Acad Fine Arts, Philadelphia; Del Art Mus, Wilmington; McNay Art Mus, San Antonio, Tex. *Comn:* Etching Edition 100 Prints, Philadelphia Print Club, Pa, 81; Lithograph Ed 125 Prints, Friends of the Philadelphia Mus Art, Pa, 79. *Exhib:* Philadelphia: Three Centuries of Am Art, Philadelphia Mus Art, Pa, 76; Painting & Sculpture Today, 1978, Indianapolis Mus Art, 78; The New American Still Life, Westmoreland Co Mus, Pa, 79; Contemporary American Realism Since 1960, Pa Acad Fine Arts, 81; Collectors Gallery, McNay Art Inst, San Antonio, Tex, 82; Realist Watercolors Fla, Univ Miami, 83; Mainstream America, Butler Art Inst, 87; Janss Collection, Boise Art Mus, 88; Utopian Visions, Mus of Mod Art, New York, 88. *Pos:* Critic & chairperson, Pa Acad Fine Art, Philadelphia, 61- *Awards:* Fulbright Scholar, Paris, 63; Rosenthal Found Award, Nat Inst Arts & Lett, 71; MacDowell Fel, Pa Acad of Arts, 83. *Bibliog:* Eve Medoff (auth), article, Am Artist, 77; Christine Hopf (dir), In Praise of Women Artists (film), Bo-Tree Productions, 79; Frank Goodyear (auth), Contemporary Realism Since 1960; Charles LeClair (auth), The Art of Watercolor; M Martin (auth), American Realism: 20th Century Drawings and Watercolors from the Janss Collection. *Mem:* Philadelphia Print Club. *Media:* Watercolor, Oil. *Dealer:* Locks Gallery 600 Washington Sq S Philadelphia PA 19106. *Mailing Add:* 2125 Cypress St Philadelphia PA 19103

OSBORNE, JOHN PHILLIP
PAINTER, INSTRUCTOR
b Paterson, NJ, July 9, 51. *Study:* Pratt Inst, cum laude BFA(art educ & environ design), 73. *Work:* NY Life; Union Labor Life, Washington, DC; Metrop Life, New York; First Common Wealth Saving Bank, Washington, DC. *Comn:* Seascape, comn by pvt collector, Rogue Bluffs, Maine, 74; 4 Landscapes of each season, comn by pvt collector, Kinnelon, NJ, 85-86; Still Life, comn by pvt collector, Wyckoff, NJ, 87; Portrait, comn by pvt collector, Saddle River, NJ 92. *Exhib:* Invitational Exhib, Nat Arts Club, New York, 88; Invitational Exhib, US Embassy, Moscow, 91-93 & Harare, Zimbabwe, 92-94; Invitational Exhib, pvt gallery, Taiwan, 92; Nat Juried Exhib, Am Artist Prof League, New York, 92. *Pos:* Illustr, Rudolph, Russell & Fluery Assoc, New York, 72; art restorer & conserv of oil paintings, Frank Moratz, Wyckoff, NJ, 79-84; gallery partner, Albert, Schlenz & Osborne Studio-Gallery, Midland Park, NJ, 81; pres & owner, Artists on Location-J P Osborne, Inc, Ringwood, NJ, 85- *Teaching:* Dir oil painting, Artists on Location-J P Osborne Inc, Ringwood, NJ, 85-; sr instr oil painting, Ridgewood Art Inst, NJ, 86-; instr oil painting, Scottsdale Artists' Sch, Ariz, 93- *Awards:* 7 Best in Show Awards, East Coast Exhibs, 73-92; Gold Medal Honor, Hudson Valley Art Asn, 86; Nat Achievement Award, Teacher Oil Painting, Am Artist Mag, 92. *Mem:* Ridgewood Art Inst (trustee, 87-); Am Artists Prof League; Allied Artists Am; Hudson Valley Art Asn; Knickerbocker Artists, New York. *Media:* Oil. *Publ:* Auth, Romancing the Light, Am Artist, Don Frost, 91; Critical Initial Lay-In, Palette Talk, Grumbacher, 91; contribr, Stroke of Genius, NJ Monthly, Tomlinson Enterprises, 92. *Dealer:* The Gallery at Four India at 4 India St Nantucket MA 02554. *Mailing Add:* 325 Lakeview Ave Ringwood NJ 07456

OSBORNE, ROBERT LEE
PAINTER, EDUCATOR
b Chandler, Ind, June 24, 28. *Study:* Ind Univ, with Pickens, Marx, Engel, Ballinger & Hope, MA; Univ Iowa, with Lechay, Hecksher, Longman, Ludens & Tomasini, MA. *Exhib:* Fac Shows, Ringling Sch Art, Sarasota, Fla; Venice Art League, Fla; one-man shows, Beaux Arts Gallery, St Petersberg, Hilton Leech Gallery, Sarasota, South Fla Col, Lakeland & Manatee Art League, Bradenton, Fla. *Pos:* Designer, Olszewski Art Glass Co, St Louis, formerly; dir, Manatee Art League, Bradenton, 71-72; dean fac, Ringling Sch Art, currently. *Teaching:* Lectr, Evansville Mus; asst prof art & head dept, Evansville Col; instr, Evansville Mus; instr, Ringling Sch Art, currently. *Awards:* Gold Key Award, Evansville, Ind, 46; Prize, Ind Univ, 52. *Mem:* Tri-State Art Guild (pres, 58-66); Fla Artists Group. *Media:* Oil, Acrylic. *Publ:* Illusr, Organization Aquatic Clubs, 55; var illus in Image Mag. *Mailing Add:* Ringling Sch Art 2700 N Tamiami Trail Sarasota FL 34234

OSBY, LARISSA GEISS
PAINTER
b Artemowsk, Russia, June 7, 28; US citizen. *Study:* Lyceum & Univ Goettingen, Ger; Univ Munich; Acad Fine Arts, Munich, Ger. *Work:* Carnegie Inst, Pittsburgh; Alcoa Collection; US Steel Collection; Westinghouse Elec Co Collection; plus others. *Comn:* Am for Democratic Action, 69; Koppers Co & First Fed Savings & Loan Asn, Pittsburgh, 72; United Steelworkers of Am, 73; Nat Steel Corp, 77. *Exhib:* One-man shows, Carnegie Inst Mus of Art, 72 & Pa State Unit, New Kensington, 73; Young Art, Ger, 51; Walker Art Ctr Biennial, Minneapolis, 66; Assoc Artists Ann, 55-; Mid-Yr Nat, Butler Inst Am Art, Youngstown, Ohio, 58, 59 & 79; Guest of Hon Exhib, Birmingham Arts Festival, Mich, 61; Drawings USA, St Paul Art Ctr, Minn, 63; Chautaugua Art Ctr Ann, NY, 64; Am Artists in France, Palais des Congres, Paris, 75-76; Dunfermline, Scotland, 84; solo exhib, Pittsburgh Ctr Arts, 83- *Teaching:* Instr art, Pittsburgh High Sch Creative & Performing Arts & Pittsburgh Ctr Arts. *Awards:* Jury Award of Distinction, Mainstreams Int, 68 & Assoc Artists Pittsburgh Ann, 58-59, 60-61 & 69; Pittsburgh Artist of the Year, 83; and others. *Mem:* Assoc Artists Pittsburgh. *Media:* Oil, Collage. *Mailing Add:* 4218 Maple Lane Allison Park PA 15101

OSCARSSON, VICTORIA CONSTANCE GUNHILD
ART DEALER
b Stamford, Conn, Dec 18, 51. *Study:* The Sorbonne; Trinity Col, Hartford, Conn, BA(art hist & languages), 73; Sotheby's Works of Art Course, London, 74. *Pos:* Researcher, Guggenheim Mus, New York, 73; asst, Richard Nathanson, pvt dealer, London, 74-76; dir, Noonday Graphics, London, 76-77; Landmark Gallery, New York, 77-80; art consult, Boston Mutual Life Insurance Co, 78-79; dir, Oscarsson-Hood Gallery, New York, 80-86, Oscarsson-Siegeltuch & Co, 86-87; pres, Oscarsson Mod & Contemp, 87- *Mem:* Art Table; Drawing Soc. *Specialty:* Modern and contemporary art, American and European, all media. *Mailing Add:* Schreyrogelgasse 3/12 Vienna 1010 Austria

OSGOOD, JERE
CRAFTSMAN
b Staten Island, New York, 36. *Study:* Univ Ill, 55-57; Rochester Inst Technol, Sch Am Craftsmen, BFA, 60. *Work:* Mus Contemp Crafts; Rochester Inst Technol; Mus Fine Arts, Boston. *Exhib:* American Chairs, Kohler Arts Ctr, 78; Wood Traditions & Motivations, Kagain Gallery, Philadelphia, 78; New Hampshire Furniture, Mus Contemp Crafts, 79; Brockton Mus Show, 81; Studio Craft Furniture at Work, Pritam & Eames Gallery, Easthampton, New York, 83; Brentwood Today, RI Sch Design, 84; Elegant Wit, Gallery Naga, Boston, 85. *Teaching:* Instr woodworking & furniture design, Craft Students League, New York, 62-70; Philadelphia Col of Art, 70-72; Rochester Inst Technol Sch Am Craftsmen, 72-75; lectr, RI Sch Design, Va Commonwealth Univ, 75-77; workshop, NH League of Craftsmen, 77; assoc prof, Prog in Artisanry, Boston Univ, 75-85; adj prof, woodworking & furniture design, Swain Sch Design, 85- *Awards:* Nat Endowment Arts, 80. *Bibliog:* Dona Meilach (auth), Creating Modern Furniture. *Mailing Add:* c/o Snyderman Gallery 317-319 South St Philadelphia PA 19147

O'SHEA, TERRENCE PATRICK
PAINTER, SCULPTOR
b Los Angeles, Calif, Sept 8, 41. *Study:* Holy Cross Col; Boston Mus Sch; Chouinard Art Inst. *Work:* Los Angeles Co Mus Art; Patrick Lannan Mus, Palm Beach, Fla; AT&T Collections, Chicago; Metromedia Collection; Laquna Mus Art, Laquna, Calif. *Exhib:* A Plastic Presence, Jewish Mus, New York, 69-70; Permutation, Light & Color, Mus Contemp Art, Chicago, 70; Pierres de Fantaisie, Oakland Mus, 70; Temple Street, Long Beach Mus, 71; First Int Biennial Small Sculpture Show, Budapest, Hungary, 71. *Teaching:* Instr, Otis Art Inst, Los Angeles, 76 & Art Ctr Col Design, Pasadena, 80-81. *Awards:* Contemp Art Coun Purchase Award, Los Angeles Co Mus Art, 65. *Bibliog:* Jerry Rosen (auth), Terry O'Shea (video taped interview), 74. *Mem:* Artist Equity Asn (bd dir, 80-81). *Media:* All. *Mailing Add:* 11365 Sound Ave Mattituck NY 11952

OSHIMA, MARI
SCULPTOR
Study: Giovanni Cusa Art Inst, Nuoro, Italy, 80; State Univ NY, Albany, BA(fine arts), 83; Empire State Col, New York, Studio Prog, 86; NY Univ, 88; Parsons Sch Design, New York, MFA(sculpture), 88. *Exhib:* Solo exhibs, Losing of Home, installation, NY Univ, 86, Buddha's Birthday, installation on 13th St, New York, 87, Keiko Space, New York, 89, Baca Downtown, Brooklyn, NY, 90, Soho 20, New York, 90, Gallery Shimada, Yamaguchi, Japan, 90 & 92; Keyaki Hall, Tanto, Hyogo, Japan, 90 & 92; JAA at Consulate Gen of Japan, New York, 91; Pelham Art Ctr, NY, 92; Pacifico Yokohama Plaza, Japan, 92. *Teaching:* Lectr, Ako Pub Sch, Hyogo, Japan, 89, Global Study, Japan, 89, Vis Arts Prog, State Univ NY, Albany, 91. *Awards:* Artists Grant, Artist Space, New York, 88-89, 89-90 & 90-91; Visual Arts Fel, Nat Endowment Arts, 90; Artist Grant, NY Found Arts, 91. *Bibliog:* Randolph Williams (auth), The Trend Gallery, Brooklyn Trend, 11/87; Mikio Takada (auth), Contemp Art Info, No 15, 1/91. *Mailing Add:* 231 Smith St, Apt 8 Brooklyn NY 11231

OSHITA, KAZUMA
SCULPTOR
b Hiroshima, Japan, Oct 17, 49. *Study:* Nat Tokyo Univ Arts Grad Sch, 74. *Work:* Am Express Co, New York; J B Speed Mus, Louisville, Ky. *Exhib:* Solo exhibs, Kanuma Gallery, Tokyo, 76, the Art of Metal Hammering, Alexander F Milliken Inc, New York, 83 & 87, Hokin Kaufman Gallery, Chicago, 89 & 92, Alexander F Milliken Inc, 90 & Gallery Art Point, Tokyo, Japan; Innerspace, Liberty Nat Bank, Louisville, Ky, 88; New Art Forms, Int Expo, Navy Pier, Chicago, 88 & 90; On the Floor and More, Arden Gllery, Boston, 88; Fall Exhibition-Gallery Artists, Alexander F Milliken Inc, 88; On Paper, Hokin Kaufman Gallery, Chicago, 90; and many others. *Awards:* Salon de Printemps Prize, Nat Tokyo Univ Arts, 72; Fel, Nat Endowment Arts, 86-87. *Bibliog:* Art Perry (auth), Japanese art follows American hype, The Province, Vancouver, Can, 11/22/74; Lynn Nesmith (auth), The arts - metal fragments of reality, Archit, 11/84. *Media:* Hammered Metal. *Mailing Add:* c/o Hokin Kaufman Gallery 210 W Superior St Chicago IL 60610

O'SICKEY, JOSEPH BENJAMIN
PAINTER, EDUCATOR
b Detroit, Mich, Nov 9, 18. *Study:* Cleveland Sch Art, with Paul Travis, Henry G Keller, Carl Gaertner, Frank N Wilcox & Hoyt L Sherman, cert. *Work:* Cleveland Mus Art; Pepsi Cola, New York; Cleveland Arts Asn; Canton Art Inst, Ohio; Westmoreland Art Mus. *Exhib:* Two-person show, Butler Inst Am Art; Pa Acad Fine Art, Philadelphia; one-man shows, Akron Art Inst, Canton Art Inst, Butler Inst Am Art, Youngstown, Ohio, seven shows, Jacques Seligman Galleries, New York, 64-78, Cleveland Inst Art, 82; and others. *Pos:* Art dir & graphic designer, pvt co, 49-64. *Teaching:* Instr art, Ohio State Univ, 46-47 & Akron Art Inst, 49-52; lectr art, Case Western Reserve Univ, 56-64; prof art, Kent State Univ, 64-, coordr painting & sculpture, 68-73. *Awards:* Cleveland Arts Cash Prize for Outstanding Achievement in the Arts, 74; Medal, Cash Award & Purchase Award, Butler Inst Am Art, Ohio, 74; First Prize Cash Awards, All-Ohio Exhibs, 74 & 77 & Best in Show Cash Prize, 74; Purchase Award, Am Acad and Inst Art and Letters, 11/88. *Media:* Oil, Watercolor. *Mailing Add:* 7308 SR 43 Kent OH 44240

OSTENDORF, (ARTHUR) LLOYD, JR
PAINTER, INSTRUCTOR
b Dayton, Ohio, June 23, 21. *Study:* Dayton Art Inst; Lincoln Mem Univ, Lincoln Dipl Hon, 66, hon ArtD, 74; Lincoln Col (Ill), LittD, 68. *Work:* Gov William Lee De Ewing (oil portrait) & Speaker W Robert Blair (oil portrait), Ill State Capitol, Springfield; Msgr Harry Ansbury (oil portrait), Parish Recreation House, Corpus Christi; Msgr Joseph D McFarland (oil portrait), Holy Angels Sch, Dayton, Ohio; Dr Herbert Y Livesay (oil portrait), Lincoln Mem Univ; Gen George Rogers Clark (oil), Restored Gov Mansion, Springfield. *Comn:* The Jesuit Martyrs (oil), Jesuit Retreat Chapel, Milford, Ohio, 49; six religious oil paintings, Hoyne Funeral Chapel, Dayton, 55. *Exhib:* Dayton Art Inst, 41. *Pos:* Art ed, Lincoln Herald, 57- *Teaching:* Instr com art & painting & dir, Ostendorf Art Acad, 69- *Awards:* Winner in Design for Chicago Lincoln (statue), Lincoln Sq C of C, 58. *Mem:* Montgomery Co Hist Soc (vpres, 56); Civil War Round Table of Dayton (pres, 55-56 & 58-59). *Media:* Watercolor, Oil. *Publ:* Auth, Mr Lincoln Came to Dayton, 59; auth & illusr, A Picture Story of Abraham Lincoln, 62; co-auth, Lincoln in Photographs, An Album of Every Known Pose, 63; auth, The Photographs of Mary Todd Lincoln, 69. *Mailing Add:* 225 Lookout Dr Dayton OH 45419

OSTER, GERALD
PAINTER, KINETIC ARTIST
b Providence, RI, Mar 24, 18. *Study:* Brown Univ, BS, 40; Cornell Univ, PhD, 43. *Work:* Milwaukee Art Ctr; San Francisco Mus Art; Tel Aviv Mus. *Exhib:* Mus Mod Art, 64; Walker Art Ctr, Minneapolis, 67; Milwaukee Art Ctr, 68; Inst Contemp Art, Chicago, 68; Tel Aviv Mus, 71; and others. *Pos:* Res assoc, Mass Inst Technol, 43-44, Princeton Univ, 44-45, Rockefeller Inst, 45-49; assoc, Birkbeck Col, London, 49-50; Rockefeller Fel, Royal Inst, London, 50-51; vis scientist, Sorbonne, Paris, 51. *Teaching:* Prof, Poly Inst Brooklyn, 51-69; prof biophysics, Mt Sinai Sch Medicine, New York, 69-89. *Publ:* Auth, Physical Techniques in Biological Research, 56; auth, The Science of Moire Patterns, 64 & 69; contribr, Art Int & Sci Am. *Mailing Add:* 241 W 11th St New York NY 10014

OSTERWEIL-WEBER, SUZANNE
PAINTER, PRINTMAKER
b Brooklyn, NY, June 22, 40. *Study:* Pratt Inst, BS, 61, MFA, 64, with Richard Lindner, Jacob Landau, Fritz Eichenberg, Federico Castellon & Philip Pearlstein; Pratt Graphic Ctr, with Vasilios Toulis; NY Univ, with Lawrence Alloway. *Work:* US Info Agency (prints); Nat Art Mus Sport. *Comn:* Loral Corp, comn by Bernard Schwartz, New York, 75; Cent Rigging Corp, comn by Monroe Myerson, New York, 77; US Info Agency, Washington, DC, 78. *Exhib:* Printmakers USA, Brooklyn Mus, NY, 73; 25th Anniversary, Nat Art Mus Sport, New Haven, Conn, 84; Salute to Liberty, Dyansen Gallery, New York, 86; 25 Yr Retrospective, Presidents Gallery, Pratt Inst, New York; Wagner Col Gallery, 92. *Pos:* Graphics juror, Nat Asn Women Artists, 68-; Bd Trustees, Nat Art Mus Sport; interviewer, Bennington Rev. *Teaching:* Instr painting, Brooklyn Mus, NY (formerly); asst principal art, High Sch Art & Design, New York, 79-90; principal, Port Richmond High Sch, Staten Island, NY, 90- *Awards:* Janet E Turner Prize, 74 & Dorothy Seligson Prize, 80, Nat Asn Women Artists; Leadership in Art Educ, NYCATA/UFT, 85; Fac Appreciation Award, HS of Art & Design, 90. *Bibliog:* Statue of Liberty, Am Heritage Houghton Mifflin, 85; Robert Henkes (auth), Sport and Art, Prentice-Hall, 86; Design Dimensions, Prentice-Hall, 90. *Mem:* Nat Asn Women Artists Inc; Nat Art Mus Sport. *Media:* Acrylics on Canvas; Serigraphy. *Publ:* Interviewer & auth, Bennington Rev, 77-79. *Dealer:* Eileen Michels Owl Gallery 1074 Broadway Woodmere NY 11598. *Mailing Add:* 479 Broome St New York NY 10013

OSTIGUY, JEAN-RENE
PAINTER, ART HISTORIAN
b Marieville, PQ, Aug 14, 25. *Study:* Univ Montreal, BA; Ecole des Beaux-Arts, Montreal; Sch Art & Design, Montreal, dipl. *Work:* Carleton Univ, Ottawa; Ottawa Univ. *Exhib:* Montreal Spring Exhib, 51 & 52. *Collections Arranged:* Leon Bellefleur, 68, Adrien Hebert, 71 & Ozias Leduc, 74, Nat Gallery Can. *Pos:* Cur Can art, Nat Gallery Can, 64-85. *Teaching:* Prof, Ecole des Beaux-Arts, Montreal, 53-55; prof Can art, Ottawa Univ, 66-71; vis prof Can art, Laval Univ, 71-72. *Awards:* Chriss Award, 62. *Mem:* Can Mus Asn (councillor, 63-65); Int Comt Mus. *Res:* Nineteenth and early twentieth century Canadian art. *Mailing Add:* 21 Rue Thibault Hull PQ J9A 1H4 Canada

OSTROW, STEPHEN EDWARD
ADMINISTRATOR, LIBRARIAN
b New York, NY, May 7, 32. *Study:* Oberlin Col, BA, 54; NY Univ Inst Fine Arts, MA, 59, PhD, 66. *Collections Arranged:* Baroque Painting: Italy and Her Influence (with catalog), 68; Visions and Revisions (with catalog), 68; Raid the Icebox I, with Andy Warhol, (with catalog), 69-70. *Pos:* Cur collections, Herron Mus Art, 66-67; chief cur, Mus Art, RI Sch Design, 67-71, dir, 71-78; dean Sch Fine Arts, Univ Southern Calif, 78-, dir mus studies prog, 79-82; exec dir, Portland Art Asn, 82-84; chief, Prints & Photog div, Libr Congress, 84- *Teaching:* asst prof art hist, Univ Mo-Columbia, 62-66; vis lectr art hist, Brown Univ, 70, 71, 74, 76 & 77; prof art hist, Univ Southern Calif, 78-82. *Mem:* Print Coun Am (exec bd, 86-89). *Publ:* Auth, Annibale Carracci and the Jason frescoes: Toward an internal chronology, Art Bull, 64; Diana or Bacchus in the Palazzo Riario, Marsyas, 65; A drawing by Annibale Carracci for the Jason frescoes and the S Gregorio baptism, Master Drawings, 70; prefaces and introductions, In: The Selection Series & Classical Collection (10 catalogs), Mus Art RI Sch Design, 72-77. *Mailing Add:* Prints & Photog Div Libr Congress Washington DC 20540

O'SULLIVAN, DANIEL JOSEPH
PAINTER, INSTRUCTOR
b Brooklyn, NY, Aug 18, 40. *Study:* Fordham Col; Brooklyn Mus Art Sch; Pratt Graphics Ctr. *Work:* Commerce Trust Co, Kansas City, Mo; Wichita Art Mus; Mus of Albuquerque, NMex; also in pvt collections of Hirshhorn, Neuberger & West; Tobin Collection, San Antonio, Tex. *Comn:* Portraits, Brooklyn Bar Asn & Pace Univ, Adelphi Univ & Cox Enterprises. *Exhib:* New Talent Exhib, Kraushaar Galleries, New York, 73; Kalamazoo Inst Art, Mich, 74; US Dept State Art in Embassies Prog, Korea, 75; Am Acad Arts & Lett, New York, 75 & 76; one-man show, Kraushaar Galleries, New York, 75 & 79, 82 & 86; Food, Bronx Mus Art, New York, 87; Narrative Art, Fla Int Univ, Miami, 88; Newspapers, Amherst Col Mus, 88. *Awards:* Purchase Award, Am Acad Arts & Lett, New York, 76; Art & Law Purchase Award, West Publ Co, 76. *Media:* Oil, Acrylic. *Mailing Add:* c/o Kraushaar Galleries 724 Fifth Ave New York NY 10019

O'SULLIVAN, JUDITH ROBERTA
CURATOR, MUSEUM DIRECTOR
b Pittsburgh, Pa, Jan 6, 42. *Study:* Carlow Col, BA, 63; Univ Md, MA, 67, PhD, 76. *Pos:* Deputy asst dir, Smithsonian Inst, Nat Mus Am Art, 84-89; pres & CEO, Mus Stony Brook, NY, 89- *Mem:* Asn Art Mus Dir; Am Asn Mus; Mid Atlantic Mus Conf; Smithsonian Women's Coun (chair, 88-89). *Publ:* Auth, The Art of the Comic Strip, 71 & Workers and Allies, 75, Smithsonian; ed, Am Film Inst Catalog, R R Bowker, 76; coauth, The Complete Prints of Leonard Baskin, 84 & auth, The Great American Comic Strip, 90, Little Brown. *Mailing Add:* 50 Main St Stony Brook NY 11790

OSVER, ARTHUR
PAINTER
b Chicago, Ill, July 26, 12. *Study:* Northwestern Univ, 30-31; Art Inst Chicago, with Boris Anisfeld, 31-36. *Work:* Mus Mod Art; Whitney Mus Am Art; Metrop Mus Art, New York; Peabody Mus, Salem, Mass; plus many others. *Comn:* Cover, Fortune Mag, 60. *Exhib:* Solo exhibs, St Louis Art Mus, 73, Nelson Gallery-Atkins Mus, Kansas City, 73, Terry Moore Gallery, St Louis, 75 & 77, Timothy Burns Gallery, St Louis, 81 & 84, Art Expo 85, Navy Pier, Chicago, 85 & BZ Wagman Gallery, St Louis, 87; Am Acad & Inst Arts & Letts; Art Inst Chicago; Corcoran Gallery; Galeria Naz Roma; Gallery Mod Art, Tokyo; Mus Mod Art, Rio de Janeiro; Venice Biennale; and others. *Teaching:* Instr painting, Brooklyn Mus Art Sch, 49-51; instr, Columbia Univ, 52 & Univ Fla, 54-55; instr painting, Cooper Union Art Sch, 55 & 58; vis critic painting, Yale Univ, 56-57; painter in residence, Am Acad Rome, 57-58; instr, Washington Univ, 60-, prof emer, 81- *Awards:* Medal, Art Dirs Club, Chicago, 61; J Henry Schiedt Mem Prize, Pa Acad Fine Arts, 66; Sabbatical Grant, Nat Endowment Arts, Washington, DC, 66; plus many others. *Bibliog:* Ray Bethers (auth), How Paintings Happen, Norton, 51; Lee Nordness (ed), Art: USA: Now, C J Bucher, 62. *Mailing Add:* 465 Foote Ave St Louis MO 63119

OSYCZKA, BOHDAN DANNY
PAINTER, ILLUSTRATOR
b Herkimer, NY. *Study:* Vesper George Sch Art; Col Fine Arts, Syracuse Univ, BFA; Art Students League. *Work:* Syracuse Univ, NY; Prudential Insurance Co Am, Mass; Hoffman-La Roche, Nutley, NJ; AT&T & IBM, Gen Food & Corp Hq, Rockfeller Found, Manufacturers Trust, New York. *Comn:* Religious murals, St Peter & Paul Ukranian Orthodox Church, Utica, 48; Painting (watercolor), Pepsico World Hq, Purchase, NY, 71. *Exhib:* Am Watercolor Soc, 68 & 70; one-man shows, Katonah Gallery, NY, 71, 76 & 82, Silvermine Guild Artists, New Canaan, Conn, 71 & 78 & Nicolaysen Art Mus, Casper, Wyo, 79; Hudson River Mus, Yonkers, NY, 74 & 76; New England Ann, Silvermine Guild, Conn, 71, 73, 76, 80, 89- 91; Temple Univ, Philadelphia, Pa, 81; De Cardova Mus Corp Exhib, Fed Reserve Bank, Boston, Mass, 81; Katonah Mus Art, NY, 92. *Pos:* Inst, Parson Sch Design, 70-; lectr-demonstr, Katonah Gallery, 71-84, Kirkland Col, Clinton, NY, 74 & Hudson River Mus, Yonkers, NY, 74; juror of selection, 86, juror of awards, 89, Cooperstown Art Asn. *Teaching:* Instr, Parsons Sch Design, NY, 75-; lectr, Katonah Gallery, 71-83, Kirkland Col, 74-, Hudson River Mus, 74. *Awards:* Augusta Hazard Fel, Syracuse Univ, NY, 43; Watercolor Award, Westchester Art Soc, 67-70; Sindin Harris Gallery Award, 71 & Mus Purchase Award, 76, Hudson River Mus. *Bibliog:* Joan Hanauer (auth), Osyczka watercolors are a Maine event, NY J Am, 3/6/65; Noel Frackman (auth), Process: Earthy and oozing, Patent Trader, 4/1/71; Bella O'Hara (auth), World of arts, Stamford Advocate, 9/23/71. *Mem:* Silvermine Guild Artists; Artist Equity Asn, New York; Hudson River Contemp Artists; Soc Illusr. *Publ:* Contribr, Am Artist, 9/65; New York Art Rev, 88 & 89. *Mailing Add:* 1450 Summit Ave Peekskill NY 10566

OSZE, ANDREW E
SCULPTOR
b Nagykanizsa, Hungary, Jan 14, 09; US citizen. *Study:* Acad Art, Budapest; Acad D'Ungheria, Rome, fel, 47-49. *Work:* Denver Art Mus; Hanley Collection, Pa; Mus Budapest; and numerous others. *Comn:* fountain, Rome, 48; T S Eliot Relief, St Louis, 80; Dezso Kosztolanyi, Budapest, 86; TeljesÖröm Nagy Kanizsa, 86; Spiritual Dance, Vero Beach, Fla, 88. *Exhib:* Montclair Art Mus, 61; Far Gallery, New York, 64 & 70; De Young Mus, San Francisco, 73; Denver Art Mus, 75. *Teaching:* Prof sculpture, Fra Angelico Art Sch, 59-60; prof sculpture & dir, Acad Mus Arte, Lima, 63-64; prof sculpture, Cath Univ, Peru, 63-64. *Awards:* Grant, France & Greece, 67; Fel Roma, 47-49; Fel Italy, Hungarian Govt. *Bibliog:* George Szabo (auth), A Osze, New Horizons, 70; I Soter (auth), Osze, Jelenkor, 80; G Tuskes (auth), Figures of rhythm, New Hamparian Quart, 83. *Mem:* Col Art Asn Am. *Media:* Stone, Bronze. *Publ:* Auth, Universal Thought and the Arts in Modern Time, Philos Question Series 10, Learned Publ, Inc, New York. *Mailing Add:* 855 Dahlia Ln Apt 7 Vero Beach FL 32963

OTANI, JUNE
ILLUSTRATOR, PRINTMAKER
b Santa Paula, Calif, July 7, 34. *Study:* Pasadena City Col, Calif, AA, 54; Art Ctr Col Des, BFA, 56; Pratt Graphic Ctr, 76-85. *Exhib:* Solo exhib, Palisades Gallery of Hudson River Mus, Yonkers, NY, 87. *Awards:* Printmaking Award, Gallery at Hastings-on-Hudson, 78; Mamaroneck Artist Guild Award, ann show, 80; Dr & Mrs I C Gaynor Award, Nat Asn Women Artists, ann show, 87. *Mem:* Nat Asn Women Artists; Silvermine Guild. *Media:* Etching, Oils. *Publ:* Illusr, The Poodle Who Barked at the Wind, 87, Ten Potatoes in a Pit, 90 & Oh Snow, 91, HarperCollins; Peach Boy, Bantam, 92; If You Lived in Colonial Times, Scholastic, 92. *Mailing Add:* 47 Calumet Ave Hastings-on-Hudson NY 10706

OTT, JERRY
PAINTER
b Albert Lea, Minn, July 31, 47. *Study:* Mankato State Col, 65-70; Univ Minn, 71. *Work:* Walker Art Ctr, Minneapolis; Smithsonian Inst; Mus Contemp Art,

Tokyo, Japan; Univ Kans Mus; Metrop Mus, New York; and others. *Exhib:* One-man shows, Louis K Meisel Gallery, New York, 73, 75 & 79, Smith Fine Art Gallery, Monte Carlo, Monaco, 74 & Morgan Gallery, Kansas City, Mo, 77 & 79; Tokyo Biennale, 74; Three Centuries of American Nudes, New York Cult Ctr, 75. *Teaching:* Artist in residence, St Cloud State Univ, 79. *Media:* Airbrush, Acrylic. *Dealer:* Morgan Gallery 5006 State Line Rd Shawnee Mission KS 66205. *Mailing Add:* c/o Thomson Gallery 321 Second Ave N Minneapolis MN 55401

OTT, MICHAEL E
PAINTER
b Bartlesville, Okla, Dec 8, 45. *Study:* Univ Colo, Boulder, BFA, 67; Univ Calif, Berkeley, MA, 69. *Work:* Hughes Corp Collection, Los Angeles, Calif; Hallmark Corp Collection, Kansas City, Mo; Koch Industs, Wichita, Kans; Lotus Develop, Cambridge, Mass; Student Loan Marketing Asn, Lawrence, Kans. *Pos:* Bd mem, Lawrence Arts Ctr, 80-85; panelist, Educ Testing Serv, Princeton, NJ, 86- *Teaching:* Prof art, Univ Kans, Lawrence, 69- *Awards:* Purchase Awards, Kans Watercolor Soc, Koch Industs, 87; Percent for Arts, Lawrence, Kans, 87; Hays Art Ctr, Hodley Regional Med Ctr, 87. *Bibliog:* Chuck Twardy (auth), Shirt People, Lawrence, Jour-World, 85; Jackie White (auth), Looking smart, Kansas City Star, 86; Ruthie Thompson (auth), Non-wearable by Michael Ott, Screen Printing Mag, 86; Don Lambert (auth), Art That's Just Hanging Around, watercolor, spring 90. *Mem:* Kans Grassroots Arts Asn. *Media:* Watercolor. *Dealer:* Capricorn Gallery Bethesda MD; Alpha Gallery Denver CO. *Mailing Add:* 1520 Crescent Rd Lawrence KS 66044

OTT, ROBERT WILLIAM
EDUCATOR, MUSEOLOGIST
b Sharon, Pa, Mar 14, 34. *Study:* Pa State Univ, BS, 56, MEd, 63, DEd, 73; Univ London, Eng, 75. *Pos:* Past ed, The Museologist; past pres, Pa Art Educ Asn; exec dir, Very Spec Arts, Pa; bd dir, Pa Alliance Arts Educ. *Teaching:* Instr art educ, Pa State Univ, 68-73, asst prof, 73-77, assoc prof art & mus educ, 77-84, prof art educ, 84-; vis prof, Univ Toronto, 93-94. *Awards:* Art Educ of Year, Nat Art Educ Asn, 92. *Mem:* Am Asn Mus; Mid-Atlantic Mus; Nat Art Educ Asn; fel Royal Soc Arts, London, 76; fel Int Asn Advan Educ, Belgium, 78. *Publ:* Auth, Museum Education and Society: Relevance Today, Concordia Univ, 81; Interdisciplines in the Art Museum, Int Coun Mus, Sweden, 82; Museums: The Encyclopedia of Education Research, Am Soc Educ Res, 82; ed, Art in Education: An International Perspective, Pa State Press, 84; Teaching Criticism in Mus, Nat Art Educ Asn, 89. *Mailing Add:* Sch Visual Arts Pa State Univ Main Campus University Park PA 16802

OTT, SABINA
PAINTER
b New York, NY, 1955. *Study:* San Francisco Art Inst, Calif, BFA, 79, MFA, 81. *Work:* Metropolitan Mus Art, New York; Southland Corp, Dallas, Tex; Los Angeles Co Mus Art; Dayton Hudson Found, Minneapolis; Chase Manhattan Bank, New York; The Banker's Life, Des Moines, Iowa. *Exhib:* Solo shows, Los Angeles Inst Contemp Art, 83, Attack Gallery, Los Angeles, 85, Davies/Long Gallery, 85, 86 & 87, Galerie am Moritzplatz, Berlin, WGer, 87, Betsy Rosenfield Gallery, Chicago, 87 & 88 & Pence Gallery, Santa Monica, 88; plus others; group shows, Third Western States Exhibition (with catalog), Brooklyn Mus and travelled, 86; Avant-Garde in the Eighties, Los Angeles County Mus Art, 87; Contemporary Diptychs: Divided Visions, Whitney Mus Am Art, Equitable Ctr, NY, 87; On the Horizon: Emerging in Calif, Fresno Arts Ctr & Mus, Calif, 87; New Works by Gallery Artists, Charles Cowles Gallery, 87-88; and others. *Mailing Add:* c/o Experimental Workshop Pier 46B PO Box 77504 San Francisco CA 94107

OTT, WENDELL LORENZ
MUSEUM DIRECTOR, PAINTER
b McCloud, Calif, Sept 17, 42. *Study:* San Francisco Art Inst, 60-61; Trinity Univ, San Antonio, Tex, BA, 68; Univ Ariz, Tucson, MFA, 70. *Work:* Witte Mem Mus, San Antonio, Tex. *Exhib:* Tex Painting & Sculpture, Dallas Mus Fine Arts, 66; 11th Ariz Ann, Phoenix Art Mus, 69; Yuma Fine Arts Asn, Ariz, 69; Juarez Mus Art, Mex, 73; one-man shows, George Walter Vincent Smith Art Mus, Springfield, Mass, 73 & Eastern NMex Univ, Portales, 74. *Pos:* Dir, Roswell Mus & Art Ctr, NMex, 70-86; dir, Tacoma Art Mus, Tacoma, Wash, 87-92; pres, Wash Art Consortuim, 89-90; pres, Mus Southwest, 92. *Teaching:* Instr painting, NMex Mil Inst, Roswell, 74-80. *Awards:* Onerdonk Award, Witte Mem Mus Ann, 68; Purchase Award, 11th Ariz Ann, Phoenix Art Mus, 69; Nat Mus Act Travel Grant, 73. *Mem:* Am Asn Mus; NMex Asn Mus (chmn, 73-75). *Media:* Oil. *Mailing Add:* c/o Tacoma Art Museum 12th & Pacific Aves Tacoma WA 98402

OTTIANO, JOHN WILLIAM
JEWELER, SCULPTOR
b Medford, Mass, July 23, 26. *Study:* Mass Col Art, BS, 54; Boston Univ, MFA, 60; Pa State Univ, DEd, 63. *Work:* Viktor Lowenfeld Mem, Pa State Univ; Univ Western Ill; Gloucester Co Col; Glassboro State Col. *Comn:* Mimosa & The Age of Miracles (murals) & two other large exterior murals, Glassboro State Col, 67, sculpture, 74; Art Educator Award, Sculpture, NJ Art Educ Asn, 69. *Exhib:* Pa Acad Fine Arts, Philadelphia, 64; Nat Acad Galleries, New York, 65; Art From NJ, NJ State Mus, 66-70; Sculpture in the Park, Van Suan Park, Paramus, NJ, 71; Artists Equity, Philadelphia Civic Ctr, 72. *Teaching:* Instr three-dimensional design & jewelry, Boston Univ, 54-60; asst prof, Mass Col Art, 61-62; prof, Pa State Univ, University Park, 62-63; prof, Glassboro State Col, 63- *Awards:* First for Sculpture, NJ Tercenternary, 64; Award for Sculpture, Somerset Art Asn, 73. *Bibliog:* Artist/Educator, Sch Arts, 2/66; article in La Rev Mod, 3/1/66. *Mem:* Am Asn Univ Prof; NJ Art Educ Asn (pres, 70-); NJ Designer-Craftsmen Asn (Pres, 70-72, NJ state pres, 75-); Artists Equity Asn; Nat Art Educ Asn (NJ state rep, 63-). *Media:* Bronze, Gold, Silver. *Res:* The relationship between surface texture preference, personality characteristics and three-dimensional art performance. *Mailing Add:* 1115 Glen Lake Blvd Pittman NJ 08071

OTTMANN, KLAUS
CURATOR, CRITIC
b Nuremburg, Ger, 1954. *Study:* Free Univ Berlin, Ger, MA(philos, art hist), 80. *Pos:* Cur, Ezra & Cecile Zilkha Gallery, Wesleyan Univ, Middletown, Conn, 88-; ed, J Contemp Art, 90- *Mem:* Am Asn Mus; Int Asn Art Critics. *Res:* Twentieth century art. *Publ:* Auth, Painting in the age of anxiety, Flash Art Mag, 84; The re-invention of painting, Arts Mag, 89; The new spiritual, Arts, 90; L'activite fractale, Art Press, Paris, 90; Heidegger, Bevys & the consequences, Flash Art, 10/90. *Mailing Add:* c/o Ezra & Cecile Zilkha Gallery Center for the Arts Wesleyan Univ Middletown CT 06459-0442

OUBRE, HAYWARD LOUIS
SCULPTOR, PAINTER
b New Orleans, La. *Study:* Dillard Univ, BA; Univ Iowa, MFA; also with Hale Woodruff, Nancy E Prophet, James Lechay, Mauricio Lasansky & Humbert Albrizio. *Work:* Univ Iowa Gallery, Iowa City; Atlanta Univ Gallery, Ga. *Comn:* Ram (wire sculpture), Winston-Salem State Univ Libr, 65; two paintings, Bakker Auction, Cambridge, Mass, 5/92. *Exhib:* Six States Exhib, Joslyn Mem Mus, Omaha, Nebr, 47; Northwest Printmakers, Seattle Art Mus, Wash, 48; John & Mable Ringling Mus, Sarasota, Fla, 48; Ball State Ann Exhib, Muncie, Ind, 60-62; Madison Gallery Exhib, New York, 62; Lenexa Nat Three-Dimensional Art Show, Kans, 85. *Collections Arranged:* Installed Dr Selma Burke's Art collection, Selma Burke Gallery, Winston-Salem State Univ, 83. *Pos:* Arranger & cur, Selma Burke Gallery, Winston-Salem State Univ, NC, 83-84, cur, 84-90. *Teaching:* Chmn painting & sculpture, Fla A&M Univ, Tallahassee, 48-49; chmn drawing & painting, Ala State Univ, Montgomery, 49-65 & Winston-Salem State Univ, 65-81. *Awards:* First Prize for Trailerview (oil), Iowa State Fair, 47; First Prize for Crown of Thorns (wire), 58 & Second Prize for Equivocal Fox (painting), 68, Atlanta Univ; and many others. *Bibliog:* Art of wire sculpture, Design Mag, 62, 68 & 71. *Mem:* Southeastern Art Asn; Nat Conf Artists. *Media:* All; Acrylic. *Res:* Designed & copyrighted Colorwheel with Four Intensity Bands, 62 & Colorchart with Three Intensity Bands, 66; corrected color triangle devised by Johann Wolfgang Von Goethe, 75; designed Four Intensity Bank Color Wheel, 77. *Publ:* Auth, Directions of modern art, Art Rev Mag, 66. *Mailing Add:* 2422 Pickford Ct Winston-Salem NC 27101

OURSLER, TONY
VIDEO ARTIST
b New York, NY, May 19, 57. *Study:* Calif Inst Arts, BFA, 79. *Comn:* L-7, L-5, The Kitchen, New York, 84; EVOL, CAT Fund, Boston, Mass, 84; Spheres of Influence, Centre Georges Pompidou, Paris, France, 85-86; Constellation: Intermission, Serious Fun Festival, New York, 88. *Exhib:* Video Viewpoints, Mus Mod Art, New York, 81; Binational, Inst Contemp Art, Boston, Mass, 88; Film Video Arts--17 years, Mus Mod Art, New York, 88; 1989 Biennial Exhibition, Whitney Mus Am Art, New York, 89; The Technological Muse, Katonah Mus Art, Katonah, New York, 90; solo shows, Diane Brown Gallery, New York, 90, Hallwalls, Buffalo, New York, 90, Diane Brown Gallery, New York, 91, Dummies, Hex Signs, Watercolors, Living Room, San Francisco, Calif, 91, F/X Plotter, 2 Way Hex, Kijkhuis, The Hague, Holland, 92 & Station Project (with James Casebere), Kortrijk train sta, Belg, 92; New York Time Festival, Ghent, Belg, 91. *Teaching:* Vis lectr art, Art Inst Chicago, 82; Univ Calif, San Diego, 85; asst prof art, Mass Col Art, 88- *Awards:* Fel, Nat Endowment Arts, 84; Production Grant, NY State Coun Arts, 84; Video Fel, NY Found Arts, 87. *Bibliog:* C Carr (auth), Relatives, Artforum, 5/89; Caryn James (auth), Critics notebook: avant garde films struggle to stay avant, NY Times, 6/29/89; Andy Grundberg (auth), article, NY Times, 6/8/90; David Joselit (auth) Mind over matter: Tony Oursler and Erick Beckman master the politics of art, The Boston Phoenix, 9/7/90; John Miller (auth), Tony Oursler - Diane Brown Gallery, Artforum, 10/90. *Publ:* Auth, Vampire, Communications Video, 88; contribr, Illuminating Video: An Essential Guide to Video Art, Apterture Found (in prep). *Mailing Add:* c/o Diane Brown Gallery 560 Broadway 2nd fl New York NY 10012

OUTLAND, WENDY HELEN
ADMINISTRATOR, GALLERY DIRECTOR
b St Petersburg, Fla, Jan 9, 53. *Study:* Ringling Sch Art & Design, Cert, 79, BFA, 84. *Collections Arranged:* Images of the Everglades, Gov office, Tallahassee & traveling, 86; Maggie Davis, 87, The Ten: Women in Art, 88, Akiko Sugiyama, 89, selected exhibs from Capitol Complex Exhib Prog, Tallahasee; The Three Graces: Janet Mauney, Dawn McMillan & Yvonne Tucker, 90. *Pos:* Cur asst & asst registr, Ringling Mus Art, Sarasota, Fla, 81-85; arts adminstr, Fla Arts Coun, Tallahasee, formerly. *Awards:* Fla dept of State Service Award, 89. *Mem:* Am Asn Mus; Nat Trust for Historic Preservation. *Publ:* Asst Ed, Ringling Mus of Art J, Ringling Mus Art, 82; contribr, Art museums of the world, Greenwood Press, 87. *Mailing Add:* PO Box 394 Swannanoa NC 28778

OUTTERBRIDGE, JOHN WILFRED
SCULPTOR, ADMINISTRATOR
b Greenville, NC, Mar 12, 33. *Study:* Agr & Tech Univ, Greensboro, NC; Am Art Acad, Chicago, with Vernon Stakey. *Work:* Oakland Mus, Mills Col, Oakland, Calif; Calif State Col, San Jose; Compton Community Col, Calif; Med Facility, Watts, Univ Southern Calif, Los Angeles. *Comn:* Mural collages

(mixed-media), Communicative Arts Acad, Compton, 70; Ethnic Heritage Doll Ser (five units), Studio Watts Endowment Fund, 77. *Exhib:* Oakland Mus, 67; 6th & 9th Southern Calif Ann, Long Beach Mus Art, 68 & 70; Los Angeles Co Mus Art, Los Angeles, 69; Dimensions in Black Art, La Jolla Mus Contemp Art, Calif, 70; St Art by Black Am, Merabash Mus, Willingboro, NJ, 75; W Coast Artists, Studio Mus of Harlem, New York, 77. *Pos:* Painter/designer, Art Craft, Div Traid Corp, Burbank, 64-68; artistic dir, Communicative Arts Acad, Compton, 69-75, mem bd dir, presently; dir, Watts Towers Arts Ctr, Cult Affairs Dept, Los Angeles, 75- *Teaching:* Instr assemblage & sculpture, Pasadena Art Mus, 67-70; lectr art hist, Calif State Col, Dominguez Hills, 67-71. *Awards:* First Place/Sculpture, Westwood Art Asn, 67; Our Auth Study Club Award, Los Angeles Area Artists, 67; Nat Conf Artists Award, 75; Nat Art Educators Asn, 87; Fulbright Fel, New Zealand, 87. *Bibliog:* Samella Lewis (auth), John Outterbridge/Black Artist (film), Contemp Crafts Inc, 68; article, Wilson Libr Bull, 4/69; Elton C Fax (auth), Black Artists of the New Generation, Dodd, Mead & Co, 77. *Mem:* Calif Confedn of Arts, Los Angeles; Advocates for the Arts; Mus African Am Art; Nat Conf Artists, Va Commonwealth Univ. *Media:* Welded Metal, Wood. *Mailing Add:* c/o Watts Tower Art Ctr 1727 E 107th St Los Angeles CA 90002

OVERLAND, CARLTON EDWARD
CURATOR, HISTORIAN
b Stoughton, Wis, Feb 28, 42. *Study:* St Olaf Col, BA; Univ Wis-Madison, MA. *Collections Arranged:* 20th Century Graphics: The Hollaender Collection, 74. *Pos:* Cur prints & drawings, Elvehjem Art Ctr, Madison, Wis, 72-77, cur collections, 77- *Teaching:* Instr art hist, Univ Northern Iowa, Cedar Falls, 68-70. *Mem:* Am Asn Mus. *Mailing Add:* 5113 Sherwood Rd 800 University Ave Madison WI 53711

OWEN, FRANK (FRANKLIN CHARLES)
PAINTER
b Kalispell, Mont, May 13, 39. *Study:* Antioch Col; Calif State Univ Sacramento; Univ Calif, Davis, BA & MA. *Work:* Corcoran Gallery of Art, Washington, DC; Albright-Knox Art Gallery, Buffalo, NY; St Louis Art Mus, Mo; Des Moines Art Ctr, Iowa; Madison Art Ctr, Wis; plus others. *Exhib:* 32nd Corcoran Biennial, Washington, DC, 71; Madison Art Ctr Exhib, 73; 15th Nat Exhib of Contemp Am Painting & Sculpture, Univ Ill, 74; 71st Ann Exhib, Art Inst Chicago, 74; Soho in Berlin, Berlin Kunstmuseum, WGer, 76; one-man shows, Leo Castelli Gallery, 72, 75 & Sable-Castelli Gallery, Toronto, 77. *Teaching:* Instr painting, Calif State Univ, Sacramento, 67-68; instr fine arts, Sch Visual Arts, New York, 70- *Bibliog:* Peter Schedjahl (auth), Six painters of the 70s, Ackland Art Ctr, NC, 73; Douglas Davis (auth), Painter's painters, Newsweek, 5/13/74. *Mailing Add:* c/o Nancy Hoffman Gallery 429 W Broadway New York NY 10012

OWENS, GWENDOLYN JANE
MUSEUM DIRECTOR, CURATOR
b Baltimore, Md, July 8, 54. *Study:* Tufts Univ, BA, 76; Williams Col, MA, 79. *Collections Arranged:* Watercolors by Maurice Prendergast from New England Collections (auth, catalog), 78 & Master Drawings from the Collection of Ingrid and Julius Held (co-auth, catalog), 79, The Dr and Mrs Milton Lurie Kramer Collection (auth, catalog), 81; Golden Day, Silver Night, Perceptions of Nature in American Art, 1850-1910 (coauth, catalog), 82; The Watercolors of David Milne (auth catalog), 84; Nature Transcribed: The Landscapes and Still Lifes of David Johnson, 1827-1908 (auth, catalog), 88. *Pos:* Ed asst, Am Asn Mus, Washington, DC, 76-77; registr, Williams Col Mus Art, Mass, 78-79; asst cur, Herbert F Johnson Mus, Cornell Univ, Ithaca, NY, 79-81, assoc cur, 81-85, cur, 85-86; Prendergast Fel, Williams Col Mus Art, 86-88; dir, The Art Gallery, Univ Md, 88-; affiliated fac, 88- *Teaching:* Affiliated fac, Univ Md, dept art hist. *Mem:* Col Art Asn; Am Asn of Mus. *Res:* 19th and 20th century American art and architecture. *Publ:* Contribr, Harvard Honors Lafayette, Fogg Art Mus, 75; Pioneers in American Museums: Bryson Burroughs, Mus News, 79; H Siddons Mowbray, Easel Painter, Art & Antiques, 80; Alive, Well and Prospering, Cooperative Conservation Centers Come of Age, Mus New, 82; Coauth, Maurice & Charles Pendergust: A Catalogue Raisonne, Prestel, 90. *Mailing Add:* c/o The Art Gallery Univ Md College Park MD 20742

OWENS, MARY (MARY LOUISE SCHNORE)
PAINTER, SCULPTOR
b Des Moines, Iowa, Dec 4, 35. *Study:* State Univ NY, Buffalo, BS, 57; Albright-Knox Art Sch, with Sam Amato, Buffalo, 53-54. *Work:* Los Angeles Water & Power Credit Union Corp Hq; Citybank Int, San Francisco; Fluor Corp Hq, Irvine, Calif; State Univ NY, Buffalo. *Exhib:* Watercolor Calif Ann Exhib of Artists, Los Angeles Co Mus Art, 61; Watercolor Ann, Brand Art Galleries, Glendale, Calif, 72, 79-82 & 87-88; Watercolor USA, Springville Art Mus, Mo, 77; Ann Nat Art Exhib, Springville Mus Art, Utah, 77 & 78; Rocky Mountain Nat Water Media Exhib, Golden, Colo, 77 & 82; one-person shows, Pac Basin Ser, Janus Gallery, Los Angeles, Calif, 76 & Watercolor Exhib, Brand Libr Art Galleries, Glendale, Calif, 77 & Ashley Gallery, Sherman Oaks, Calif, 89; Nat Watercolor Soc Exhib, Laguna Beach Mus Art, Laguna Beach, Calif, 76, Calif State Univ, Northbridge, Calif, 81; Nat Watercolor Travel Exhib, 77-79, 81-82, 84-87 & 90-91; Am Watercolor Soc 112th Ann Exhib, Nat Acad Galleries, New York, 79; Mt San Jacinto Open, 83; Art Asn Springfield, Ill, 84; and others. *Awards:* Golden CofC Award, Rocky Mt Watermedia Exhib, 77; Cash Award, Mt San Jacinto Open, 83. *Mem:* Nat Watercolor Soc. *Media:* Watercolor, Oil; Clay, Metal. *Mailing Add:* 813 Glenview Rd Glendale CA 91202

OWENS, TENNYS BOWERS
DEALER
b Washington, NC, June 25, 40. *Study:* St Mary's Jr Col, Raleigh, NC; Univ NC. *Pos:* Pres & owner, Artique Ltd, 71- *Specialty:* General art merchandise, prints, paintings, sculpture and pottery, traditional and contemporary. *Mailing Add:* c/o Artique Ltd 314 G St Anchorage AK 99501

OWENS, WALLACE, JR
ADMINISTRATOR, PAINTER
b Muskogee, Okla. *Study:* Langston Univ, BA(art educ), 59; Cent State Univ, Edmond, Okla, Masters(teaching), 65; Inst Allende, San Miguel de Allende, Mex, MFA(painting), 66. *Work:* Okla State Permanent Collection, Oklahoma City; Gainesville Col, Ga; Okla Univ. *Exhib:* Cent State Univ, Edmond, 65; Univ Okla, Norman, 69. *Teaching:* Dept chmn visual arts, Langston Univ, Okla, 66-; dept of art, Cent State Univ, Edmond, Okla, 80-87, Retired, 87. *Awards:* Fulbright Scholar Italy, Univ Rome, 70; Study Tour Award, African Am Inst, New York, 74. *Mem:* Okla Art Ed Asn; Nat Conf Artist (charter mem, 60). *Media:* Acrylic. *Collection:* Contemporary paintings in acrylic and oil; fine prints in lithography woodcuts and etching; some metal sculpture. *Mailing Add:* Rte 6 Box 782 Guthrie OK 73044

OWSLEY, DAVID THOMAS
CONSULTANT
b Dallas, Tex, Aug 20, 29. *Study:* Harvard Col, AB, 51; Inst Fine Arts, NY Univ, MFA, 64. *Collections Arranged:* Decorative Arts Collection & Ailsa Mellon Bruce Collection, Carnegie Inst Mus Art. *Pos:* Fel, Am Wing, Metrop Mus Art; asst cur decorative arts & sculpture, Mus Fine Arts, Boston; visitor, Victoria & Albert Mus, London, Eng; cur antiquities, Oriental & decorative arts, Carnegie Inst Mus Art. *Teaching:* Decorative arts, Univ Pittsburgh Ext. *Awards:* Cert Appreciation, Am Soc Appraisers, 83. *Mem:* Sr mem Am Soc Appraisers; Knickerbocker Club. *Publ:* Auth, article, Antiques, 12/72 & 4/73 & Apollo, 8/73; coauth, Wendy and Emery Reves Collection (exhib catalog), Dallas Mus Art, 85. *Mailing Add:* 116 E 68th St New York NY 10021

OX, JACK
PAINTER, CONCEPTUAL ARTIST
b Denver, Colo, Feb 4, 48. *Study:* San Francisco Art Inst, BFA, 69; Univ Calif, San Diego, MFA, 77. *Work:* Univ Iowa Collections, Iowa City; Atlantic Richfield Corp, Dallas, Tex; Gen Electric Corp, Ridgefield, Conn; Hood Mus Art, Dartmouth Col, Hanover, NH; Nordstern Versicherung, Cologne. *Exhib:* Sound: Scores & Notations, Inst Art & Urban Resources, PS 1, Long Island City, NY, 79; Sonorita Prospettiche, Comune Di Rimini, Italy, 82; solo exhibs, Brooklyn Acad Music, NY, 82, Contemp Arts Ctr, New Orleans, La, 83 & Univ Calif, Irvine, 88; Music to My Eyes, Pyramid Gallery, Rochester, NY, 84; On the Wall, On the Air, Hayden Gallery, Mass Inst Technol, Cambridge, 84; Vom Klang Der Bilder, Staatgalerie Stuttgart, WGer, 85; Capriccio, Palais des Beaux-Arts, Brussels, Belgium, 86. *Teaching:* Vis assoc prof, Univ Calif, Irvine, 86. *Awards:* Juror's Choice Award, The Moment Redefined Exhib, 82. *Bibliog:* Carter Ratcliff (auth), Looking at sound, Art Am, 4/80; Hearne Pardee (auth), The New American landscape, Arts Mag, 5/84; Grace Glueck (auth), article, New York Times, 5/3/85; Laura Tuchman (auth), Painter puts art to music of Bruchner, Orange County Register, 10/2/88; Cathy Curtis (auth), For Jack Ox much is found in music-to-act transliteration, LA Times, 10/3/88. *Mem:* Col Art Asn Am. *Media:* Oil, Drawing. *Publ:* Coauth, The systematic translation of musical compositions into paintings, Leonardo Mag, fall 84. *Dealer:* Meyers/Bloom Gallery 2112 Broadway Santa Monica CA 90404. *Mailing Add:* 712 Broadway No 5 New York NY 10003-9507

OXMAN, KATJA
PRINTMAKER
b Munich, Ger; US citizen. *Study:* Pa Acad Fine Arts, Philadelphia, cert, 65; Acad Munich, 65-66; Royal Col Art, London, Eng, cert, 67. *Work:* Philadelphia Mus; NJ State Mus, Trenton; Smithsonian Inst, Washington, DC; Clemson Archit Found Collection, SC; Pa Acad Fine Arts; Southern Alleghenies Mus Art. *Exhib:* Solo exhibs, Jane Haslem Gallery, Washington, DC, 81, Assoc Artists, New York & Philadelphia, 83, The Print Club, 86 & David Adamson Gallery, 87, 89 & 92, Marcus Gordon, Pittsburgh, Pa, 89, Randal Beck Gallery, Boston, Mass, 90; Boston Printmakers Nat Exhibs, Boston, Mass, 82-88; Print Club Ann Int Competition, Philadelphia, 83-86; NDak Prints & Drawing Ann, 83, 84 & 87; Auburn Works on Paper Touring Exhib, Ala, 87; The Art Complex Mus, Duxbury, Mass, 91; Eastern Ill Univ, Charleston, 91; Nat Mus Women Arts, Washington, DC, 91; Large Scale American Prints, Dusseldorf, Ger, 92. *Teaching:* Adj prof printmaking, Am Univ, 76-85; vis lectr, Univ Mass, 75. *Awards:* Purchase Prize, Univ Del, 85 & Auburn Works on Paper, 87; Materials Award, Boston Printmakers, 87 & 88; Purchase Award, 22nd Bradley Nat, 89. *Bibliog:* Jill Wexler (auth), Etching her environment, Am Artist, 7/82; Florence Gilboard (auth), review, Museums & Arts, 11-12/87; Jo Ann Lewis (auth), The cool hues of summer's end, Washington Post, 8/27/88; Clare Romano (auth), The Complete Printmaker, 89. *Mem:* Boston Printmakers; The Print Club of Philadelphia. *Media:* Etching, Aquatint. *Dealer:* Orion Editions 270 Lafayette St New York NY 10012. *Mailing Add:* 620 Gist Ave Silver Spring MD 20910

OXMAN, MARK
SCULPTOR, EDUCATOR
b New York, NY, Mar 9, 40. *Study:* Adelphi Univ, Long Island, NY, 58-61; Pa Acad Fine Arts, Philadelphia, 61-65; Showhegan Sch, summer 65; City & Guilds London, 65; Art Sch, London, 67. *Comn:* Large sculpture relief, Bellmore Mem Libr, Long Island, NY, 73; large sculpture relief, Queens Plaza Complex, New York, 76. *Exhib:* One-man shows, Washington Co Mus Fine

Arts, Hagerstown, Md, 88, Fountains & Figures, Am Univ, 90, Western Md Col, 92, Mary Baldwin Col, Va, 92, Salisbury State Univ, Md, 93, Arts Alive, Montgomery, Md, 93, Washington Col,Md, 94; 21st Area Show Sculpture, Corcoran Mus, Washington, DC, 78; Int Monetary Fund, Washington, DC, 78. *Pos:* Dean students, Skowhecan Sch, 69 & 72. *Teaching:* Lectr art, Haverford Col, Pa, 67-70; asst prof art, Amherst Col, Mass, 70-76; assoc prof sculpture, Am Univ, Washington, DC, 76- *Media:* Bronze, Plastic. *Mailing Add:* Dept Art American Univ 4400 Massachusetts Ave NW Washington DC 20016

OZONOFF, IDA
PAINTER, COLLAGE ARTIST
b La Crosse, Wis, July 27, 04. *Study:* State Teachers Col, Milwaukee, grad, 24; Milwaukee Downer Col, 58 & 59; Univ Wis-Milwaukee, 60-64 & 69-70. *Work:* Print Div, Smithsonian Inst, Washington, DC; Milwaukee Pub Schs; Univ Wis, Fond du Lac Campus; Abilene Fine Arts Mus, Tex; Carleton Col, Northfield, Minn. *Exhib:* Nat Acad Design Exhib, New York, 68 & 69; Allied Artists Am Exhib, New York, 70; West Bend Gallery Fine Arts, Wis, 76 & 77; Univ Wis Alumni Exhib, 78; Kohler Art Ctr, Sheboygan, WI, 88-90. *Awards:* Purchase Award, Western Publ, 66; Benjamin Altman First Prize, Nat Acad Design, 68; Carleton Col Purchase Award, Charles E Merrill Trust Fund, 75. *Bibliog:* Gerald F Brommer (auth), The Art of Collage, 78; Wis Acad Rev (spec ed), Wis Painters & Printmakers, 3/83; and others. *Mem:* Wis Arts Coun. *Media:* Acrylic, Oil. *Dealer:* Bradley Galleries 2639 N Downer Milwaukee WI 53211. *Mailing Add:* 500 W Bradley Rd C216 Milwaukee WI 53217

P

PABLO
PAINTER, EDUCATOR
b Moulton, Iowa, Feb 18, 34. *Study:* Iowa Wesleyan Col, with S Carl Fracassini, BA, 55; Wichita State Univ, with Robert Kiskadden, MA, 59. *Work:* Iowa Wesleyan Col Art Dept; Wichita State Univ Art Dept & Wichita Art Mus, Kans; Citizens Libr, Washington, Pa. *Comn:* Mosaic mural, Halstead Hosp Lobby, 59; mural, Tosco Mining Co, Washington, Pa, 78. *Exhib:* Ann Nat Graphics Art Show, Wichita Art Asn, 60; Ann Juror's Award Show, Huntington Gallery, WVa, 65; Ann Nat Decorative Arts Show, Wichita Art Asn, 66; Max 24, Nat Small Painting Show, Purdue Univ, 66; 2nd Nat Polymer Exhib, Eastern Mich Univ, 68. *Collections Arranged:* Washington & Jefferson Col Nat Painting Show, 67-86; L Evans Parcell-Retrospective, Olin Art Gallery, 85. *Pos:* Co-dir, Bottega Art Gallery, Wichita, 60-62; pres, Wichita Artists Guild, 61-62; dir, Gallery 319, Wichita, 62-63. *Teaching:* Instr ceramics, Wichita State Univ, summer 62; asst prof sculpture & ceramics, WLiberty State Col, 63-66; prof art & chmn art dept, Washington & Jefferson Col, 66- *Awards:* E D Caldwell Award First Prize, Bethany Col Ann, 64; First Prize, Oglebay Inst Summer Show, 64; Juror's Best of Show Award, Huntington Gallery, 65. *Mem:* Arts Coun Washington Co (pres & founding mem, 69-73); Am Asn Univ Prof; Am Coun Art Admninrs. *Media:* Acrylic, Oil. *Publ:* Illusr, Nonverbal Communication, Vol 5, In: Commun Sci & Technol Ser, Marcel Dekker, Inc, 74. *Mailing Add:* 65 Dewey Washington PA 15301

PACE, JAMES ROBERT
PAINTER, PRINTMAKER
b Tahlequah, Okla, Feb 19, 58. *Study:* Univ Okla, BFA, 81; Ariz State Univ, MFA, 84. *Work:* State Okla; Amoco Collection, Denver, Colo; Ariz Western Col, Yuma; Lamar Dodd Art Ctr, LaGrange, Ga. *Exhib:* 21st Invitational Exhib, Plains Art Mus, Moorehead, Minn, 80; 15th Works on Paper Exhib, Southwest Tex State Univ, San Marcos, 85; 19th Southwestern Invitational, Yuma Fine Arts Ctr, Ariz, 85; New Am Talent Exhib, Austin, Tex; Fla Nat, Tallahassee; and many others. *Teaching:* Grad asst drawing, Ariz State Univ, Tempe, 82-83; art instr drawing & design, SMt Community Col, Phoenix, Ariz, 85; assoc prof drawing & printmaking, Univ Tex, Tyler, 85- *Awards:* H L Gully Res Award, Ariz State Univ, 84; Juror's Choice Award, New Art: Painting from NY, Calif & Tex; Nat Endowment Arts, 92; and many others. *Mem:* Col Art Asn. *Media:* Mixed; Drawing. *Mailing Add:* 2300 Pine Crest Tyler TX 75701

PACE, MARGARET BOSSHARDT See Willson, Margaret (Bosshardt) Pace

PACE, STEPHEN S
PAINTER, PRINTMAKER
b Charleston, Mo, Dec 12, 18. *Study:* Inst Arte, San Miguel Allende, Mex; Acad Grande Chaumiere, Paris; Inst Arte Statale, Florence, Italy; Art Students League, with Cameron Booth & Morris Cantor; Hans Hofmann Sch. *Work:* Metrop Mus Art & Whitney Mus Am Art, New York; Univ Calif, Berkeley; James Michener Found, Univ Tex, Austin; Walker Art Ctr, Minneapolis; and others. *Exhib:* Int Watercolor Exhib, Brooklyn Mus, 53 & 55; Whitney Ann, 53-54, 57-58 & 61; Int Biennial, Japan, Selected by Mus Mod Art, New York, 57; one-man shows, Howard Wise Gallery, New York, 60-61 & 63-64 & A M Sachs Gallery, New York, 74, 76 & 78-79, 81, 83 & 85; Walker Art Ctr, 62; Abstract Watercolors by 14 Americans, Mus Mod Art, tour of Europe, Asia & Australia, 64-66; 10-Yr Retrospective, Des Moines Art Ctr, 70; Univ Tex Art Mus, 70; Katharina Rich Perlow Gallery, New York, 87, 89 & 91; Vanderwoude Tananbaum, New York, 91. *Teaching:* Artist-in-residence, Washington Univ, spring-summer 59; instr art, Pratt Inst, 61-68; instr art sem, Univ Calif, Berkeley, spring, 68; prof art, Am Univ, 75-83. *Awards:* Dolia Lorian Award, 54; Hallmark Co Purchase Award, 61; Guggenheim Fel, 80-81; and others. *Bibliog:* Hubert Crehan (auth), A change of pace, Art News, 4/64; Russell Arnold (auth), Paintings by Stephen Pace, Crucible, fall 65; Denver Lindley (auth), In a landscape (film), 69-71; Martica Sawin (auth), Stephen Pace: Action Painting in Two Modes, Arts, 4/87. *Mem:* Nat Acad Design. *Media:* Oil, Watercolor; Monotype, Prints. *Mailing Add:* 164 11th Ave New York NY 10011

PACHNER, WILLIAM
PAINTER
b Brtnice, Czech, Apr 7, 15; US citizen. *Study:* Acad Arts & Crafts, Vienna, Austria; Univ Tampa, DFA AC, 81. *Work:* Whitney Mus Am Art, New York; Butler Inst Am Art, Youngstown, Ohio; Ft Worth Art Ctr, Tex; Iowa State Teacher's Col; Rose Gallery, Brandeis Univ; Hirshorn Mus, Washington, DC; also pvt collections of Lee A Ault and Walter P Chrysler. *Exhib:* Carnegie Inst Int, Pittsburgh; Whitney Mus Am Art Ann; Corcoran Gallery Art Biennial, Washington, DC; Pa Acad Fine Arts, Philadelphia; US Fine Arts Pavilion, New York World's Fair, 65; Gallery Mod Art, New York, 69; Univ Tampa, 81; Detroit Inst Fine Arts; one-man show, Pachner Landscapes (with catalog), Mus Fine Arts, St Petersburg, Fla, 83; more than twelve one-man shows in New York; Affirmations--1936-1986, 50 year retrospective (with catalog), Tampa Mus Art, Fla, 86; black & white drawings, Univ S Fla, 86 & Art Ctr, St Petersburg, Fla, 87. *Teaching:* Instr painting & drawing, Art Students League, 69-70. *Awards:* Am Acad Arts & Lett Award, 49; Ford Found Awards, 59-64; Guggenheim Fel, 60. *Media:* Oil, Watercolor. *Mailing Add:* 962 Ohayo Mountain Rd Woodstock NY 12498

PADOVANO, ANTHONY JOHN
SCULPTOR, DRAFTSMAN
b Brooklyn, NY, July 19, 33. *Study:* Carnegie Inst Technol; Pratt Inst; Columbia Univ, with Oronzio Maldarelli; Hunter Col, MA, 80. *Work:* Whitney Mus Am Art; Nat Collection Fine Arts, Washington, DC; Univ Ill; John Herron Art Inst; Storm King Art Ctr, NY. *Comn:* Sculpture In The Park, Parks Dept, New York, 68; design, NY State Art Awards, NY State Coun Arts, 69; sculpture, World Trade Ctr, Port Authority NY & NJ, 70; three arcs, donated by Trammel & Crow Co for City of Dallas, 72; sculpture, Nebr Bicentennial Sculpture Corp, 76. *Exhib:* 3rd Mostra Arte Figurative Int, Rome, Italy, 61; Young Am, Whitney Mus Am Art, 65; Am Sculpture, Mus Mod Art, 66; Am Express Pavilion, New York World's Fair, 66; Inauguration of Nat Collection Fine Arts, Washington, DC, 67. *Pos:* Adv mem, NJ State Coun Arts, 65-67. *Teaching:* Asst prof sculpture, Columbia Univ, Univ Conn, 72 & Kingsborough Community Col, 83; adj asst prof sculpture, Queens Col, City Univ New York, 72; instr, Dept Art, Art Students League, New York; assoc prof, Kingsborough Community Col, 88. *Awards:* Guggenheim Found Fel, 64; Ford Found Purchase Award, 66; Inst Arts & Lett Award, 76; Prix de Rome, 60 & 61. *Bibliog:* Young talent, Art Am, 65; James Mellow (auth), article in New York Times Sun Rev, 4/70. *Mem:* Sculptors Guild (vpres, 68-69); Silvermine Guild Artists. *Media:* Metal, Stone. *Publ:* auth, Process of Sculpture, Doubleday Co, 81. *Dealer:* Vorpal Gallery 411 W Broadway New York NY 10012. *Mailing Add:* Dept Art Art Student League 215 W 57th St New York NY 10019

PADULA, FRED DAVID
FILMMAKER, PHOTOGRAPHER
b Santa Barbara, Calif, Oct 25, 37. *Study:* Univ Calif, Santa Barbara; Calif State Univ, San Francisco, BA(music), with Jack Welpott, Don Worth & Wynn Bullock, MA(art). *Work:* George Eastman House, Rochester, NY; San Francisco Mus Art; Oakland Mus Art; Kalamazoo Art Ctr, Mich; Crocker Mus Art, Sacramento, Calif; and many pvt collections. *Comn:* Children's Letters to God (film), Lee Mendelson, San Francisco, 68; Navaho (film), Pub Broadcast Lab, KQED-TV, San Francisco, 68; S F Mix (film), Ford Found, 70; film, Am Film Inst. *Exhib:* 30 Photographers Nat Exhib, Buffalo, NY, 64; one-man shows, San Francisco Mus, 64, George Eastman House, 68 & DeYoung Mus, San Francisco, 69; Mus Mod Art, New York, 67; completion & premiere showing of El Capitan (film), San Francisco Mus of Mod Art, 78; and others. *Pos:* Mem Selection comt, US Art in the Embassies, 68; mem bd dirs, Canyon Cinema Coop, 71- *Teaching:* Lectr photo & film making, San Francisco State Univ, 63- & Univ Calif, San Francisco, 66-71; resident artist, Univ Minn, Minneapolis, 70. *Awards:* Awards for film El Capitan: Grand Prize, Banff Festival Mountain Films, Can, 79, Gold Medal, Festival Int Film Alpin, Les Diablertets, Switz, 79 & Silver Medal, Int Bergfilm Munchen, Munich, Ger, 79; and others. *Bibliog:* Callenbach (auth), Ephesus, Film Quart, Univ Calif, winter 66-67; Winston (auth), American film maker, Melbourne Art Rev, fall 68; Hoffmann (auth), Ephesus, Weg Zum Nachbarn, Oberhausen, Ger, 68. *Dealer:* Canyon Cinema Coop San Francisco, CA. *Mailing Add:* 47 Shell Rd Mill Valley CA 94941

PAGE, JEAN JEPSON
COLLECTOR, HISTORIAN
b Minneapolis, Minn, Aug 22, 24. *Study:* With Walter S Baum; Minneapolis Inst Arts; San Francisco Inst; Smith Col, BA, 46. *Pos:* Comnr, Dist Columbia Comn Arts & Humanities, 76-80. *Res:* American painting, particularly 19th century; political aspects of art patronage; Frank Mayer. *Collection:* American paintings, prints and drawings, primarily representational; books illustrated by painters. *Publ:* Auth, Francis Blackwell Mayer, Antiques, 2/76; Frank Blackwell Mayer: Painter of the Minnesota Indian, Minn Hist, 78; Notes on the contributions of Francis Blackwell Mayer and his family to the cultural history of Maryland, Md Hist Mag, 81; James McNeill Whistler, Baltimorean, and the white girl, Md Hist Mag, 89. *Mailing Add:* 3219 Chesapeake St NW Washington DC 20008

PAGE, JOHN HENRY, JR
PRINTMAKER, EDUCATOR
b Ann Arbor, Mich, Jan 18, 23. *Study:* Minneapolis Sch Art; Art Students League; Univ Mich, BDesign; Univ Iowa, MFA. *Work:* Libr Cong, Washington, DC; Walker Art Ctr, Minneapolis; Des Moines Art Ctr, Iowa; Joslyn Art Mus, Omaha, Nebr; Carnegie Inst, Pittsburgh. *Comn:* Memberships Print, Des Moines Art Ctr, 69. *Exhib:* One-man retrospective, Hearst Ctr Arts, Cedar Falls, Iowa, 38-55, Waterloo Mus Art, Iowa, 56-71 & Gallery Art, Univ Northern Iowa, Cedar Falls, Iowa, 72-91; Young Am Printmakers, Mus Mod Art, New York, 53; 10th Nat Print Show, Brooklyn Mus, 56; Midwest Printmaker Invitational, Walker Art Ctr, Minneapolis, 73; one-person exhib, Muskegon Mus Art, Mich, 83; and others. *Teaching:* Prof printmaking, Univ Northern Iowa, 54-87, actg head art dept, 84-85; chmn dept art, Univ Omaha, 60-61. *Awards:* Younker Prize for Prints, Des Moines Art Ctr, 71; Nat Endowment Arts, Individual Artist Fel, 74; Purchase Prize & Cash Award, Fourth Ann Midwestern Printmaking & Drawing Competition, Tulsa, Okla, 77; plus others. *Media:* All. *Dealer:* Percival Galleries Inc Walnut at 6th Des Moines IA 50309; Quinlan Gallery 1906 N Halsted Chicago IL 60614. *Mailing Add:* 1615 Tremont Cedar Falls IA 50613

PAIGE, WAYNE LEO
PAINTER, DRAFTSMAN
b Chicago, Ill, Mar 5, 44. *Study:* Univ Ill, Urbana, BFA, 68; George Washington Univ, MFA, 71. *Exhib:* Solo exhibs, Gallery K, Washington, DC, 78, 82 & 84, Washington Co Mus, Hagerstown, Md, 85 & Zaks Gallery, Chicago, 85; Works on Paper, Corcoran Gallery, Washington, DC, 80; Southern Fervor, Anderson Art Gallery, Richmond, Va, 83; Emergency, Md Art Place, Baltimore, 83. *Teaching:* Instr drafting, Eastern High Sch, Washington, DC, Md Drafting Inst, 79- *Bibliog:* David Tannous (auth), Wayne Paige at Gallery K, Art in Am, 3/79; Jo Ann Lewis (auth), Galleries: Paintings by Wayne Paige, Washington Post, 2/13/82; Judith Cox (auth), East Coast Review: Wayne Paige, New Art Examiner, 4/82. *Media:* Miscellaneous. *Dealer:* Gallery K 2010 R St NW Washington DC 20009; Zaks Gallery 600 N Michigan Ave, Chicago IL 60611. *Mailing Add:* c/o Gallery K 201G R St NW Washington DC 20009

PAIK, NAM JUNE
VIDEO ARTIST
b Seoul, Korea, 1932. *Study:* Univ Tokyo, BA, 56. *Exhib:* Fluxus Festival, Mus Wiesbaden, WGer, 62; Cybernetic Serendipity, Inst Contemp Arts, London, Eng, 68; The Machine as Seen at the End of the Mechanical Age, Mus Mod Art, New York, 68; Vision & Television, Rose Art Mus, Brandeis Univ, Waltham, Mass, 69; St Jude Video Int, de Saisset Art Gallery & Mus, Univ Santa Clara, Calif, 71;; solo exhibs, Mus Mod Art, New York, 71 & 77, The Kitchen, New York, 73 & 76, Everson Mus Art, Syracuse, NY, 74, Whitney Mus Am Art, New York, 80 & 82, Tokyo Metrop Art Mus, 84 & Holly Solomon Gallery, New York, 86, 88, 89 & 90, San Francisco Mus Mod Art, Calif, 89 & Seville World Expo, Korean Pavilion, 92; Circuit: a Video Invitational, Everson Mus Art, Syracuse, NY, 73; Open Circuits: The Future of Television, Mus Mod Art, New York, 74; Chicago Int Art Expos, 86; Computers & Art, Everson Art Mus, Syracuse, 87; Biennial Exhib, 87 & Video Art: Expanded Forms, 88, Whitney Mus Am Art, New York, 88; The Arts for Television, Mus Mod Art, New York, 89; Whitney Mus Art, Stamford, Conn, 89; ARCO, Madrid, 91 & 92; CIAE 92, Chicago Art Fair, Ill. *Teaching:* Artist-in-residence, WGBH-TV, Boston, 69 & GNET-TV, New York, 71. *Bibliog:* Patricia Sloane Discusses the Work of Nam June Paik, Art & Artists, London, 3/72; C Carr (auth), Beam me up, Nam June, Village Voice, 10/14/86; Walter Robinson (auth), Nam June Paik at Holly Solomon, Art Am, 6/87; David Deitcher (auth), When Worlds Collide, Art Am, 90, vol 78. *Mailing Add:* Holly Solomon Gallery 724 Fifth Ave New York NY 10019

PAIKOWSKY, SANDRA R
CURATOR, HISTORIAN
b St John, NB, Can, Dec 29, 45. *Study:* Sir George Williams Univ, BA(art hist), 67; Univ Toronto, MA(art hist), 70. *Collections Arranged:* Eric Fischl: Painting (auth, catalog), 83, The Non-Figurative Artist's Association of Montreal (auth, catalog), 83, Goodridge Roberts: The Figure Works (auth, catalog), 84, Betty Goodwin: Passage (auth, catalog), 86, Ron Shuebrook: Recent Work (auth, catalog), 86, David Craven: Recent Work (auth, catalog), 86, Concordia Art Gallery, Montreal, Que; Rita Letendre: The Montreal Years (auth, catalog), 89. *Pos:* Cur, Concordia Univ Art Gallery, Montreal, Que, 81- *Teaching:* Assoc prof art hist, Concordia Univ, 69- *Publ:* Publ & co ed, The Journal of Canadian Art History, Owl's Head Press, 76. *Mailing Add:* Concordia Univ Art Gallery 1455 W Blvd de Maisonneuve Montreal PQ H3G 1M8 Canada

PAL, PRATAPADITYA
CURATOR, HISTORIAN
b Sylhet, Bangladesh, Sept 1, 35. *Study:* Delhi Univ, BA(hons), 56; Calcutta Univ, MA, 58, DPhil, 62; Cambridge Univ, PhD, 65. *Collections Arranged:* The Sensuous Line (with catalog), 76; The Sensuous Immortals (with catalog), 77; The Divine Presence (with catalog), 78; The Classical Tradition in Rajput Painting (with catalog), 78; The Ideal Image (with catalog), 78; Elephants and Ivories (catalog), 81; Light of Asia (with catalog), 84; From Merchants to Emperors (with catalog), 86; Romance of the Taj Mahal, 89. *Pos:* Sr res assoc, Am Acad Benares, 66-67; keeper of Indian collections, Mus Fine Arts, Boston, 67-69; curator Indian & Southeast Asian art, Los Angeles Co Mus Art, 70- *Teaching:* Lectr Indian art, Harvard Univ, 68-69; lectr Nepali art, Univ Calif, Los Angeles, 70; adj prof SE Asian art, Univ Southern Calif, 70-89. *Awards:* Most Distinguished Indian (fine arts award), Fed Indian Asn NAm, 80. *Mem:* Asiatic Soc; Am Acad of Religion; Asia Soc, Calcutta. *Res:* Arts, architecture and cultural history of India, Islamic countries, Nepal, Tibet & Southeast Asia. *Publ:* Auth, Bronzes of Kashmir, 75; The Ideal Image, 78; The Classical Tradition in Rajput Painting, 78; A Buddhist Paradise: The Murals of Alchi, 82; Court Painting in India, 83; Indian Sculpture, vol 1, 86; Indian Sculpture, Vol II, 88; Buddhist Book Illuminations, 88. *Mailing Add:* Los Angeles Co Mus Art 5905 Wilshire Blvd Los Angeles CA 90036

PALAIA, FRANC (DOMINIC)
PAINTER, PHOTOGRAPHER
b New Rochelle, NY, Sept 18, 49. *Study:* Newark State Col, Union, NJ, BA(fine arts), 71; Univ Cincinnati, Ohio, MFA(scholar, teaching asst), 73. *Work:* Newark Mus, NJ; Stedelijk Mus, Holland; McDonald Corp; White House, Washington, DC; Polaroid Corp; and others. *Comn:* Painting, comn by Richard Ekstract, NY. *Exhib:* Alternative Mus, New York, 81; Fashion Moda, NY, 84; Metrop Mus Art, New York, 84; New Mus, NY, 85; Hal Bromm Gallery, NY, 85; Sidney Janis Gallery, New York, 88; and others. *Teaching:* Instr art hist, Essex Co Col, Newark, NJ, 76-77; instr sculpture, Upsala Col, East Orange, NJ, 76; instr painting, Kean Col, NJ, 78-82. *Awards:* Grant, Louis Tiffany Found, New York, NY, 84; Rome Prize (Painting), Am Acad in Rome, Italy, 85; Sponsorships, Polaroid Corp, Boston, Mass, 86 & 87. *Bibliog:* Peter Frank (auth), article, Village Voice, 78; John Caldwell (auth), review, New York Sunday Times, 81; Precious, Grey Art Gallery, Art in Am, 85. *Media:* All. *Publ:* Contribr, Art Am, Appearances Mag, Umbrella Mag, NJ, Monthly Mag, 83, New Look Mag, 85 & Street Art, Dial Press, 85; Great Walls of China, Eastview Eds, 74. *Mailing Add:* 371 Fourth St Jersey City NJ 07302

PALAU, MARTA
SCULPTOR
b Albesa, Lerida, Spain, July 17, 34; Mexican citizen. *Study:* La Esmeralda, Inst Nat Bellas Artes, Mex; San Diego State Univ, Calif; Barcelona Escuela Artes Oficios. *Work:* Secretaria Relaciones Exteriores, Mexico City; Mus Mod Art, Mexico City; Mus Mod Art Latinamerica, Washington, DC; Tamayo Mus, Mexico City; Mus Mod Art, Univ Sao Paulo, Brazil. *Comn:* Mural, Ctr Mod Art, Guadalajara, 71; tapestry mural, Hotel El Cid, Mazatlan, Sin Mex, 80; mural tapestry, Hotel Sheraton, Cancun, Mex, 80; metal sculpture, Chapultepec Park, Mexico City, 81; metal sculpture, Univ Metropolitana, Xochimilco, DF Mex, 81; ambiental tapestry, First & Second Int Festival Poetry, Morelia, Michoacan, Mex, 83; metal sculpture, Hotel Morelia, Michoacan, Mex. *Exhib:* One woman show, La Jolla Art Mus, Calif, 64, Mod Art Mus, Mexico City, 78 & Sala Nac, Fine Arts Pal; Mod Art Mus, Tokyo & Mod Art Mus, Kyoto, Japan, 77; Eighth Biennial Int de la Tapisserie, Lausanne, Switz, 78; 19 Biennial of Sao Paulo, Brasil, 87; and others. *Teaching:* Artist in Residence, Casa Americas & Inst Superior de Arte, Havana, Cuba. *Awards:* Installation Award, II Biennial Havana, Cuba, 86; Visitors Award, 5 Triennale Fellbach Kleinplastik, Fellbach, Ger, 92. *Bibliog:* Juan Acha (auth), Fiber Works, Americas-Japan, Mus Mod Art, Kyoto, Japan, 78; Rita Edes (auth), Marta Palau, La Intuicioin y la Tecnica, CEGM, 85; Margaret Sayers Peden (auth), Out of the Vacano, Smithsonian Inst Press, 91. *Publ:* Auth, Lo Mas Antiguo y Lo Mas Moderno en el Arte de Marta Palau, Antonio Rodriguez, 73. *Dealer:* Galeria de Arte Mexicano Gob Rafael Rebollar 43 Mexico 11850 DF. *Mailing Add:* Galileo 16-6 Mexico DF 11560 Mexico

PALAZZOLO, CARL
PAINTER
b Torrington, Conn, 45. *Study:* Boston Mus Sch, 65-69; Tufts Univ Mus Sch Prog, 66-68; Boston Mus Sch (independent grad prog), 69-70. *Exhib:* Biennial, Whitney Mus Am Art, New York, 75; Bicentennial Travelling Exhib, Inst Contemp Art, Boston, 75; solo exhibs, Harcus Gallery, 75, 78, 83 & 88, D Clayton & Co, 80, Hadler-Rodriguez Galleries, Houston, 83 & 85, Bette Stoler Gallery, New York, 84 & 86, New Paintings, Lennon, Weinberg Inc, New York, 90 & 92, Drawings, Thomas Babeor Gallery, La Jolla, Calif, 92; American Graffiti Gallery, Amsterdam, Neth, 80; On the Edge: Forty Years of Maine Painting, Maine Coast Artists, Rockport, 92; Painting, Self Evident: Abstraction 1992, Gibbs Mus Art, Charleston, SC, 92. *Bibliog:* Douglas MacCash (auth), Abstraction: Carl Palazzolo & Gregory Amenoff, New Orleans Art Rev, 11-12/91; Robert L Pincus (auth), Visual Arts: Critics Choice, San Diego Union-Tribune, 3/12/92; Jonathan Saville (auth), Hovering at the Edge of Meaning, San Diego's Weekly Reader, 2/20/92. *Dealer:* THe Harcus Gallery 210 South St Boston Mass 02111. *Mailing Add:* c/o Harcus Gallery 210 South St Boston MA 02111

PALEY, ALBERT RAYMOND
GOLDSMITH, DESIGNER
b Philadelphia, Pa, Mar 28, 44. *Study:* Tyler Sch Art, Temple Univ, BFA, 66, with Stanley Lechtzin, goldsmithing, MFA, 69; Univ Rochester, Hon Dr, 89. *Work:* Minn Mus Art, St Paul; Wilmington Soc Fine Arts, Del; Metrop Mus Art, New York; Mus Fine Arts, Houston, Tex; Va Mus Fine Arts, Richmond. *Comn:* Wrought iron portal gates, Renwick Gallery, Smithsonian Inst, Washington, DC, 74; Sculpture, Willard Bldg, Washington, DC, 85; Stairway sculptures & door pulls, Wortham Theatre Ctr, Houston, Tex, 87; bridge railings, Rochester, NY, 89. *Exhib:* one-man shows, Walter Gallery, San Monica, Calif, 88, Barbara Fendrick Gallery, New York & Washington, DC, 89; Archit Art: Affirming the Design Relationship, Am Craft Mus, NY, 88; Craft Today in Am, traveling to 12 Erop mus, 89; Art That Works, touring 12 mus, 89. *Pos:* pres, founder, Paley Studios Limited, Rochester, NY, 72. *Teaching:* prof, State Univ NY Col, Brockport, 72-84; prof & artist in residence, Sch Am Craftmen, Rochester Inst, 84- *Awards:* Award of Excellence, Am Inst Architects, 82; Visual Artists' Fel Grant, Nat Endowment Arts, 84; Silver Medal, Int Teaching Ctr Metal Design, 86.

Bibliog: Robert Bishop & Patricia Coblents (coauth), American Decorative Arts: 360 Years of Creative Design, 82; Barbaralee Diamondstein (auth), Handmade in America, 83; Marian Campbell, An Introduction to Ironwork, 85. *Mem:* Soc NAm Goldsmiths; Am Crafts Coun. *Media:* Forged and Fabricated Mild Steel. *Mailing Add:* c/o Snyderman Gallery 317 South St Philadelphia PA 19147

PALLADINO-CRAIG, ALLYS
DIRECTOR, CURATOR
b Pontiac, Mich, Mar 23, 47. *Study:* Fla State Univ, BA, 67, MFA, 78; Univ Toronto, 68-69; Univ Va, 75-76. *Pos:* Dir, Contemp Art, Four Arts Ctr, Tallahassee, 73-82; dir, Fla State Univ Gallery & Mus, Tallahasse, 82. *Awards:* Individual Artist Fel, Fla Arts Coun, 79. *Mem:* FAMDA; FAM. *Publ:* Auth, Copyright: The Works of Don Wright (catalog), Fla State Univ, 82; Harvey K Littleton: Glass Sculpture (catalog), Fla State Univ, 83; New directions: Southern studio glass (catalog), Kingsport Tenn Art Ctr, 85; contribr, Nocturnes/Nightmares: Comtemporary Figuartive American Painting (catalog), Fla State Univ, 87; Monochrome/Polychrome: Contemporary Realist Drawing, Fla State Univ Gallery & Mus, 90. *Mailing Add:* 1410 Grape St Tallahassee FL 32303

PALLER, GARY
PAINTER, PRINTMAKER
b Los Angeles, Calif, Feb 8, 53. *Study:* Univ Calif, Los Angeles, BA, 74, MFA, 77. *Exhib:* One-man shows, Galerija Equrna, Lugljana, Yugoslavia, 88 & 90, Galerie Wolf, Dusseldorf, Germ 88, Lasorda-Iri Gallery, Los Angeles, Calif, 89, Market Street Gallery, Venice, Calif, 90, Gallery Indeco, Seoul, Korea, 91 & Lorenzelli Arte, Milano, Italy, 91; Maloney Gallery, SAnta Monica, 88. *Awards:* Penelope Rigby Fel, 75 & Anna Bing Arnold Fel, 76, Univ Calif Los Angeles Art Coun. *Media:* Oil on Canvas. *Mailing Add:* 3025 Barry Ave Los Angeles CA 90066

PALMER, A LAURE
SCULPTOR, WRITER
b Albany, NY. *Study:* Williams Col, BA(eng & art), 81; Art Inst Chicago, MFA(art), 88. *Work:* Artists Books Collection, Mus Contemp Art, Chicago. *Comn:* Outdoor sculpture, Krasl Art Ctr, St Joseph, Mich, 92. *Exhib:* Occupied Territory: Art at the Armory, Mus Contemp Art, Chicago, 92; Collection of Wilhelm Shurman, Ludwig Forum, Aachen, Ger, 92; Young Curators Group Show, Magasin, Grenoble, France, 92; Porgetto Cuspide Sardegna, ASPIS, Caglian-Pirri, Italy, 92; Hothouse: The Orchid Room, Hewett Gallery, Carnegie Mellon Univ, Pittsburgh, Pa, 92. *Teaching:* Asst prof sculpture, Univ Calif, Santa Barbara, 89-90; asst prof sculpture, Carnegie Mellon Univ, 91-92. *Awards:* Art Matters Fel, 89; Arts Midwest, Nat Endowment Arts Fel, 89; Ill Arts Coun Artists Fel, 90. *Res:* Contemporary art and sculpture installation. *Publ:* Contribr, Artforum, 89-91; Jeanne Dunning (catalog), Ill State Univ, 91. *Mailing Add:* PO Box 1139 Evanston IL 60204-1139

PALMER, HERBERT BEARL
DEALER, COLLECTOR
b New York, NY, June 23, 15. *Study:* NY Univ Inst Fine Arts, with A P McMahon, BA(Carnegie Scholar), MA(Michael Friedsam Scholar, Charles Hayden Scholar); Univ Southern Calif; Univ Calif, Los Angeles. *Collections Arranged:* The Film and Modern Art (auth, catalog), Los Angeles Munic Art Gallery, 69; Tantric Art, Twentieth Century Masters & many solo exhibs incl Bridget Riley, Allen Jones & George Grosz, Herbert Palmer Gallery; Calder, Red Grooms, Henry Moore. *Pos:* Western ed, Minicam Photogr, Cincinnati, 46-50; mgr, Feigen Palmer Gallery, Los Angeles, 63-68; owner & pvt art dealer, Herbert B Palmer & Co, Los Angeles, 68-75 & 81- & Beverly Hills, 75-81. *Teaching:* Lectr collecting & investing in art, Univ Calif, Los Angeles Exten. *Mem:* Am Asn Mus; Col Art Asn; Ethnic Arts Coun Los Angeles (bd dirs, 69-71); Int Coun Mus; Art & Antique Dealers League Am. *Specialty:* Modern and contemporary painting, sculpture and drawings. *Collection:* Twentieth century abstract American painting. *Publ:* Auth, Art museums face crisis of identity, Los Angeles Times; Anti-educational influence of pictorial communication, J Sec Educ; Perspective and optical illusions, Design; The mollusk in art, Nature Mag; and others. *Mailing Add:* 802 N La Cienega Blvd Los Angeles CA 90069

PALMER, LUCIE MACKAY
PAINTER, LECTURER
b St Louis, Mo, May 23, 13. *Study:* Boston Mus Fine Arts Sch; St Louis Sch Fine Arts, Washington Univ; Art Students League, with Rapheal Soyer, J N Newell & Robert Brackman. *Exhib:* One-man show, Akari Gallery, Cuernavaca, 76, Barbizon Gallery, Arvin Gallery & Am Mus Nat Hist, New York, Field Mus, Chicago, Acad Sci, San Francisco, McAllen Int Mus, Tex, Borda Gallery & Plastica de Morelos Gallery, Cuernavaca, Mex; McAllen Int Mus, Tex, 79; spec group show for Pres of Mex Portillo, Plastica de Morelos Gallery, Cuernavaca, 78; Borda Gallery, Cuernavaca, 81; Univ Morelos, 81; and other group & one-man shows. *Pos:* Staff artist, expeditions Sulu Sea, S Philiphines, Caribbean & Pacific Coasts of Mex. *Teaching:* Elderhostel instr, See It & Sketch It, Isles of Shoals, NH, 9/91 & 9/92. *Awards:* Cooper Prize, Nat Asn Women Artists, 44; Governor's Award for Best Landscape, Morelos State Art Exhib, 77. *Mem:* Nat Asn Women Artists; St Louis Art Guild; Orlando Art Asn; (life mem), Art Students League; St Louis Artist's Guild; NH Art Asn. *Media:* Oil. *Res:* Underwater painting. *Mailing Add:* 31 Atlantic Ave North Hampton NH 03862

PALMER, MABEL (EVELYN)
PAINTER
b Denver, Colo, Oct 19, 03. *Study:* With Richard Yip, Warren Brandon, Vernon Nye & Michael Green. *Work:* Revue Studios Hollywood; Nat Cowgirl Hall of Fame, Hereford, Tex; City Santa Rosa, Calif; Bank Am Regional Off, Santa Rosa, Calif; and others. *Comn:* First Telegraph Line, Union Pac Gold Spike Centennial, Calif & Nev, 69. *Exhib:* M H de Young Mem Mus, San Francisco, 65-66, 68-69 & 71; Watercolor USA, Springfield, Mo, 69; 141st Ann Exhib, Nat Acad Design, New York, 66; Am Watercolor Soc, 62, 72 & 77; Calif State Fair, 72; Los Angeles Mus of Sci & Indust, 76; Trails West Secy State, Calif, 76; Nat Cowgirl Hall of Fame, Tex, 77; Charles and Emma Frye Mus, Wash, 77; Saddle Back, Los Angeles, 78; Mus Mountain Men, Pinedale, Wyo, 87-89. *Pos:* Dir, Occidental Art Gallery, Calif, 68-89; listed state judge, N Calif Fairs & Soc Western Artist Ann. *Awards:* Best of Show & First Award, All Western Art Show, Ellensburg, Wash, 72; Best in Show, Las Vegas Art Mus, 79; Bronze Medal & 1st Award, Women Artists of the West Int Exhib, Visalia, Calif, 91; and many others. *Mem:* Soc Western Artists; Women Artists Am West (historian, emer); Santa Rosa Art Guild. *Media:* Acrylic, Transparent Watercolor. *Publ:* Illusr, La Revue Mod, 66, Southwest Art, 79, 82 & 83 & Artwest, 81, 85 & 86. *Dealer:* Occidental Fine Art Gallery 10395 Barnett Valley Rd Sebastopol CA 95472. *Mailing Add:* c/o Occidental Fine Arts Gallery 10395 Barnett Valley Rd Sebastopol CA 95472

PALMER, MEREDITH ANN
ART DEALER, GALLERY DIRECTOR
b Los Angeles, Calif, July 7, 51. *Study:* Radcliffe Col, Harvard Univ, with Rudolf Arnheim, BA, 73; Harvard Bus Sch, Owner/Pres Prog, 84. *Collections Arranged:* Chinese Arched Exhib, US Dept State, 74-75; Print Publishing in America (overseas exhibs), US Info Agency, 79-80; Sam Francis: Works on Paper, 80-81; American Paintings from the Boston Mus Fine Arts in China, 81; The New American Realism 1960-80, 82; Bunka-Viewing: Sculptors & Their Drawings from Japan (auth, catalog), 90; Shoichi Ida, 86 & 89; Figurative European Moderns, 87; and others. *Pos:* Foreign serv reserve officer (art specialist), US Dept State, 73-76 & US Info Agency, 76-82; dir & partner, Herbert Palmer Gallery, Los Angeles, Calif, 82-91; pres, Meredith Palmer Gallery Ltd, New York, 91- *Awards:* Grant, Nat Endowment Arts, 73. *Bibliog:* Susan Bidel (auth), Like Father, Like Daughter, Success: The Next Generation, Angeles Mag, 6/91. *Mem:* Am Asn Mus; Col Art Asn; Art Table, Inc; and others. *Res:* Influence of traditional Asian arts on contemporary American and European art. *Specialty:* 20th century Modern masters and Contemporary art, painting, sculpture and drawings, includes American, European and emerging Asian artists. *Publ:* Auth, The Plundered Past, J Int Law, 4/74; China Premiers Art, US Dept State Exchange Mag, spring 75; Bunka-Viewing: Sculptors & Their Drawings from Japan, 90 (exhib catalog, Herbert Palmer Gallery, LA); Monet to Matisse Exhibition: A look at its positive elements, Los Angeles Times, 8/26/91. *Mailing Add:* c/o Meredith Palmer Gallery Ltd 30 E 85th St Suite 4H New York NY 10028

PALMER, MICHAEL ANDREW
PAINTER, ART DEALER
b Mt Sterling, Ky, Dec 8, 42. *Study:* Univ Ky; Univ Hawaii; Univ NH, BA, 70. *Work:* Ogunquit Mus Art, Maine; DeCordova Mus Art, Lincoln, Mass; Colby Col Mus, Waterville, Maine; Elliott Mus Art, Stuart, Fla; Univ Maine, Orono. *Comn:* Auburn (portrait of city), Scammon & Gould, Inc, Maine, 78. *Exhib:* Nat Drawing & Small Sculpture, Ball State Col, Muncie, Ind, 72; Artists of Our Time, Ogunquit Mus Art, Maine, 75, 76 & 78; Am Artists Paris, State Dept, France, 76; one-man shows, Hobe Sound Galleries, Fla, 73, 74 & 81, Bates Col, Lewiston, Maine, 78, Elliot Mus, Stuart, Fla, 80, Elsa London, Montreal, Can, 80, 83 & 85, Art Ctr, Spartanburg, SC, 85 & Lane Gallery, Key West, Fla, 90-92; Arts Exclusive, Simsbury, Conn, 85-92. *Pos:* Dir, Bray-Hampton Gallery, Atlanta, Ga, 65-67; co-owner & dir, PS Galleries, Ogunquit, Maine, 78- & Dallas, Tex, 81-86. *Awards:* Dr Morton M Shur Mem Award, Nat Soc Painters Casein & Acrylic, 75; Purchase Award, DeCordova Mus, 76; First Prize, Bankers Int Collection, Orlando, Fla, 78. *Bibliog:* A young artist in Georgia, Southern Living, 68; Kathleen Hawk (auth), Michael A Palmer in Dallas, Art Voices, 81; Betty Joyce (auth), Maine in Transition, Phoenix Press, Kennebunk, Maine, 92. *Mem:* Nat Soc Painters Casein & Acrylic; Ogunquit Art Asn (pres, 74-77). *Media:* Ink, Acrylic. *Specialty:* Primarily representational contemporary artists as well as late 19th and early 20th century American artists. *Dealer:* PS Galleries Rte 1 Ogonquit ME 03907. *Mailing Add:* PO Box 1559 Ogunquit ME 03907

PALMGREN, DONALD GENE
PAINTER, PHOTOGRAPHER
b Moline, Ill, Nov 22, 38. *Study:* Augustana Col, BA; Lutheran Sch Theol, Chicago, MDiv; Detroit Soc Arts & Crafts; Cranbrook Acad Art, with George Ortman, MFA. *Work:* St John's Univ; Anoka-Ramsey Col; Gustavus Adolphus Col; 3 M Corp. *Exhib:* Drawings USA, 73; Appalachian Nat Drawing Competition, Appalachian State Univ, Boone, NC, 77; Rutgers Nat Drawing, 79; Talent at Allan Stone Gallery, New York, 89; Hamline Univ, 89; Mankato State Univ, 89; plus many others. *Teaching:* Vis asst prof drawing & design, Murray State Univ, 72; assoc prof drawing & photog, Gustavus Adolphus Col, 72- *Awards:* Res grants, Gustavus Adolphus Col, 73, 75 & 76. *Media:* Charcoal, Pastel Oil; Black & White Film. *Publ:* Auth, Space Upon Space: The Liberal Connection, Art and Academe, spring 89. *Dealer:* Jane Haslem Gallery Washington DC; Groveland Gallery Minneapolis MN. *Mailing Add:* 1619 S Third St No 5 St Peter MN 56082

PALUMBO, JACQUES
PAINTER, SCULPTOR
b Philippeville, Algeria, Sept 16, 39; Can citizen. *Study:* Sch Fine Arts, Algiers, Algeria, BA, 60; Sch Fine Arts, Paris, France, MA, 65; Educ Technols Univ Montreal, PhD, 87. *Work:* Mus Contemp Art, Mus Fine Arts, Montreal, Que; Nat Gallery, Ottawa, Ont; Sincron Cult Ctr, Brescia, Italy; Found IDC, Zoetermeer, Neth. *Comn:* Monumental sculpture, City Hall, Trois-Rivieres, 92. *Exhib:* Konkret Acht, Kunsthaus, Nürnberg, Nuremberg, 88; Systematic & Constructive Art, Villa de Madrid, Spain, 88; Europa 90, Sincron Cult Ctr, Brescia, Italy, 90; De L'Abstraction Géométrique, Mus Fine Arts, Montreal, 91; Propos D'Art Contemp, Mus Contemp Art, Montreal, 91; and others. *Teaching:* Prof art, Ahuntsic Col, Montreal, 68-92. *Bibliog:* Peter Perrin (auth), Icon and Numbers, Arts Canada, 78; Gianguido Fucito (auth), Dualità, catalogue, 89; Leo Rosshandler (auth), Vers un Art Exact, Vie Des Arts, 90. *Mem:* Soc des Artistes Profs du Que, Montreal, 71; Conseil de la Peinture, Montreal, 91. *Media:* Acrylic, Oil; Metal, Cast. *Dealer:* Gianguido Fucito Arteka Cabinet Conseil 4200 Rue Hollinger CP 2078 Rawdon Que J0K 1S0 Canada. *Mailing Add:* 467 Ave Wiseman Montreal PQ H2V 3J9 Canada

PAN, THEODORE (ION)
SCULPTOR, INSTRUCTOR
Study: Leonardo DeVinci Art Sch; studied with George Demitriades; Art Students League. *Work:* Am Col, Greece. *Comn:* Portrait busts, comn by Utah Symphony, BillBoard, Armor Artists Soc, New York, Metrop Mus Art, Govt Dept, Harvard Univ, & Michael Mordkin Ballet; Statues, Am Col Athens, Greece, Rest Resort, Atlanta, Ga, Rose Bros, Real Estate Corp, George Firgis, Salt Lake City, Am Dance Machine, Texaco & Patriarch Athenagoras. *Exhib:* Nat Acad Design; Phillips Gallery, Utah; Pa Acad Fine Arts; Soc Independent Artists; Hudson Valley Art Asn; NJ Painters & Sculptors Asn. *Teaching:* Horace Mann Sch, 41 yrs. *Awards:* Hudson Valley Artists, 47; NJ Painters & Sculptors Award, 51. *Mailing Add:* Horace Mann Sch 231 W 246th St Bronx NY 10471

PANCZENKO, RUSSELL
MUSEUM DIRECTOR
b Frille, Ger, Mar 23, 47. *Study:* Fairfield Univ, BA, 69; Universita degli Studi di Firenze, Italy, Dottore in Lettere, 79. *Pos:* Asst dir, Williams Col Mus Art, 80-84; dir, Elvehjem Mus Art, Univ Wis, Madison, 84- *Teaching:* Mus studies & connoiseurship. *Awards:* Mus Fel, Nat Endowment Arts. *Mem:* Asn Art Mus Dirs; Am Asn Mus; Col Art Asn; Int Coun Mus; Wis Fedn Mus. *Res:* Early Italian Renaissance; late 19th Century and 20th Century Art. *Publ:* Auth, Gentile da Fabriano and classical antiquity, 80 & Umanesimo di Gentile da Fabriano, 83, Artibus et Historiae; Florence in Italian Paintings, 1850-1910, Clark Inst, Williamstown, Mass, 82; Richard Artschwager: PUBLIC/public (exhib catalog), 91. *Mailing Add:* Elvehjem Mus Art 800 University Ave Madison WI 53706

PANDOZY, RAFFAELE MARTINI
CONCEPTUAL ARTIST, LECTURER
Study: Accademia Belle Arti Roma, 63; Univ Dallas, Tex, MA (sculpture), 74; New York Univ, NY, PhD, 85. *Work:* Dallas Mus Fine Arts, Tex; Ft Worth Mus Mod Art, Tex; San Francisco Mus Art, Calif. *Comn:* Pubsculpture, Eastfield Col, Dallas, Tex; indoor sculpture, Univ Tex, Dallas. *Exhib:* Tarrant Co Exhib, Ft Worth Mus, Tex, 72; Dallas Artist, Dallas Mus Fine Arts, Tex, 75; Twelve Texas, Mus Contemp Art, Houston, Tex, 76; 25 Contemps, Ft Worth Mus, Tex, 76; Texas Art, Univ Tex Campus, Dallas, 78; Dallas-San Francisco Exchange, San Francisco Mus Art, Calif, 78; Epigraphs, Hunter Col Gallery, New York, 80. *Awards:* Campbell Found Award for Sculpture, 75; First Place Award, Dallas City Hall, 78. *Bibliog:* Janet Kunter (auth), The art of hole making, Art News, 76; Janet Kunter (auth), Phenomenology, Dallas Morning News, 81. *Mem:* Col Art Assn; Nat Art Educ Asn; Nat Comt Hist Art; Am Soc Aesthetics; Int Asn Philos & Lit. *Media:* Earth Pigment. *Dealer:* Art for the 90's 65 S 11th St Brooklyn NY 11211. *Mailing Add:* PO Box 168 New York NY 10012

PANTELL, RICHARD KEITH
PAINTER, PRINTMAKER
b Bronx, NY, May 2, 51. *Study:* Univ Bridgeport, Conn, 69-71; Art Students League, with David Leffel, Frank Mason & Earl Mayan, 74-75. *Work:* Butler Inst Am Art, Youngstown, Ohio; Wichita Art Mus, Kans; New York Pub Libr; Jewish Mus, Stokholm, Sweden; Portland Art Mus, Ore. *Exhib:* Butler Inst Am Art, 81-83; Ann Allied Artists Exhib, Nat Arts Club, New York, 83, 85, 87, 89, 90 & 91; solo exhibs, Gallery Roundout, Kingston, NY, 83 & Gallery Luciano, Uppsala, Sweden; Bernard & S Dean Levy Gallery, New York, 84; Soc Am Graphic Artists, New York, 86, 89 & 91; Old Print Shop, New York; and others. *Teaching:* Instr painting & drawing, Continuing Educ, Univ Uppsala, Sweden, 76-77 & Woodstock Sch Art, NY, 79-; instr printmaking, State Univ NY, Col New Paltz, 89-91. *Awards:* Julius Hallgarten First Prize, 157th Ann Exhib, Nat Acad Design, 82; Ben & Beatrice Goldstein Found Purchase Prize, Soc Am Graphic Artists, NY Pub Libr, 86; NY State Found Grant, 92. *Bibliog:* Palmer Paroner (auth), The art of Richard Pantell, 7/23/81 & A transplanted New Yorker, 7/7/83, Artspeak; Tram Combs (auth), Pantell's luminous urbanities, Woodstock Times, 7/21/83; Fridolph Johnson (auth), Richard Pantell, Am Artist, 2/87. *Mem:* Allied Artists Am; Art Students League, NY; Woodstock Artists Asn (mem bd dirs, 79-80 & 82-83); Soc Am Graphic Artists (coun mem, 89-). *Media:* Oil; Etching. *Dealer:* Old Print Shop 150 Lexington Ave New York NY. *Mailing Add:* Bearsville NY 12409

PANTER, GARY
SET DESIGNER, PAINTER
b Durant, Okla, 1950. *Study:* E Tex State Univ, BFA. *Work:* Pensacola Mus Art, Fla. *Exhib:* Solo exhibs, Post Pop, Fiorucci, Los Angeles, 78, Gary Panter Square (a video bar), Hagoya, Japan, 85, Tilden-Foley Gallery, New Orleans, La, 86, La Luz de Jesus Gallery, Los Angeles, 87, Pensacola Mus Art, Fla, 88; plus others; Los Angeles Inst Contemporary Art, 79; Graphic Art, Inst Contemp Art, London, Eng, 82; Comic Art Show, Whitney Mus Am Art, New York, 83; Strip Language, Gimpel Fils, London, 85; Art for Arts's Sake, Contemp Art Ctr, 85; American Comic Art, Culturhussett, Stockholm, Sweden, 88; Pop Apocalypse, Gracie Mansion Gallery, New York, 88; Res Nova Gallery, New Orleans, La, 88. *Pos:* Set designer, Pee Wee Herman (CBS-TV), formerly. *Publ:* Invasion of the Elvis Zombies, Raw Books & Graphics, New York, 85; Road Kills, Forced Exposure, Boston, Mass, 86; Jimbo: Adventures in Paradise, Pantheon Books, NY, 88. *Dealer:* Res Nova Gallery New York NY. *Mailing Add:* 505 Court St, N7J Brooklyn NY 11231

PAONE, PETER
PAINTER, PRINTMAKER
b Philadelphia, Pa, Oct 2, 36. *Study:* Philadelphia Col Art, BFA, 58. *Work:* Libr Cong; Philadelphia Mus Art; Mus Mod Art; Art Inst Chicago; Victoria & Albert Mus, London, Eng; and others. *Exhib:* Brooklyn Mus, 62 & 64; Butler Inst Am Art, 65; Forum Gallery New York; Otis Art Inst, Los Angeles, 64 & 66; one-man shows, Contemp Art Mus, Houston, 76, Roswell Mus, NMex, 77 & Hooks-Epstein Galleries, Houston, 78-88; Pa Acad Fine Arts, 83; and many others. *Teaching:* Instr, Philadelphia Col Art, 59 & Pratt Inst, 59-66; instr art hist, Positano Art Sch, Italy, 61; instr drawing & chmn graphics dept, Pa Acad Fine Arts, 78- *Awards:* Purchase Prize, Syracuse Univ, 64; Guggenheim Fel, 65-66; Print Club Award of Merit, Philadelphia, 83; and others. *Bibliog:* Selden Rodman (auth), The Insiders, La State Univ, 60. *Mem:* Soc Am Graphic Artists; assoc mem Nat Acad Design, New York. *Media:* All. *Publ:* Auth & illusr, Paone's Zoo, 61, Five Insane Dolls, 66 & My Father, 68; auth, Kachina--Paone, 76; and others. *Mailing Add:* 1027 Westview St Philadelphia PA 19119

PAPAGEORGE, TOD
PHOTOGRAPHER
b Portsmouth, NH, Aug 1, 40. *Study:* Univ NH, BA; Yale Univ, Hon MA. *Work:* Mus Mod Art; Art Inst Chicago; Bibliot Nat, Paris; Boston Mus Fine Arts; Seagrams Inc, New York. *Comn:* The American Courthouse Bicentennial Doc, Seagrams, Inc, 75; American Images, AT&T, 78; The Acropolis, Warner Commun Inc, 83. *Exhib:* Recent Acquisitions, Mus Mod Art, 71, 73, 74 & 79, Pub Landscapes, 74 & Mean Streets, 91; 14 Am Photogr, Baltimore Mus of Art, 75; Ten Am Photogr, Galerie Zabriskie, Paris, France, 77 & 87; Mirrors & Windows, Mus Mod Art, 78; one-man exhibs, Light Gallery, New York, 73 & 79, Art Inst Chicago, 78, Galerie Zabriskie, Paris, 80, Daniel Wolf Gallery, New York, 81 & Akron Art Mus, 81; Daniel Wolf Gallery, New York, 85. *Teaching:* Prof photog, & dir grad studies, Yale Univ, 78- *Awards:* Guggenheim Found Fel Photog, 70 & 77; Nat Endowment Arts Fel Photog, 73 & 75. *Bibliog:* Leo Rubinfien (auth), Love-hate relations, Artforum, summer 78; Ben Lifson (auth), Clothed in possibilities, Village Voice, 12/12/79; Maren Stange (auth), Tod Papageorge, In: Contemporary Photographers, St Martin's Press, 82. *Publ:* Contribr, articles, Aperture, Vol 19, No 1 & No 85, 81; auth & ed, Public Relations, The Photographs of Garry Winogrand, Mus Mod Art, 77; auth, Walker Evans and Robert Frank: An Essay on Influence (catalog), Yale Art Gallery, 81; and others. *Mailing Add:* Six Varick St No 9A New York NY 10013

PAPIER, MAURICE ANTHONY
EDUCATOR, PAINTER
b Ft Wayne, Ind, Apr 14, 40. *Study:* Ball State Univ, Muncie, Ind, BS, 63; St Francis Col, Ft Wayne, Ind, MS, 67; Bowling Green State Univ, Ohio, MA, 78. *Work:* Lincoln Life Insurance Co; Gen Tele Co; First Nat Bank; North Am Van Lines; Warner Commun, New York. *Exhib:* Ball State Drawing & Small Sculpture, Ball State Univ, Muncie, Ind, 68; Northwestern Indiana Artists, Hammond Mus, Ind, 76; Paper Chase, Artlink Gallery, Ft Wayne, Ind, 83; Tri-Kappa Regional Artists, Ft Wayne Mus Art, Ind, 83; Rental Gallery, Ft Wayne Mus Art, Ind, 83. *Teaching:* Instr art, Ft Wayne Community Sch, 63-72; dept head art, St Francis Col, 72- *Awards:* Third Prize Sculpture, Van Wert Regional, 70; Tri-Kappa Regional Artists Exhib, several awards; Outstanding Professor of Year, St Francis Col, 92. *Mem:* Artlink Alternative Artists' Space (panel mem); Mayor's comt Pub Art Works; Col Art Asn. *Media:* Acrylic, Collage. *Dealer:* Sharon Eisbart 3601 N Washington Rd Ft Wayne IN 46808. *Mailing Add:* Dept Art St Francis Col 2701 Spring St Ft Wayne IN 46808

PAPO, ISO
PAINTER
b Sarajevo, Yugoslavia, May 2, 25; US citizen. *Study:* Polytech Milan; Brera Acad Fine Arts, Milan, Italy, grad, 51; Boston Mus Sch; also with Carlo Carra. *Work:* Boston Pub Libr. *Comn:* Paintings for films & posters, United Church of Christ, 64-65. *Exhib:* Inst Contemp Art, Boston, 68; Brockton Art Ctr, 70; Tanglewood, 71; one-man shows, Boston Athenaeum, 73 & Boston Psychoanal Soc & Inst, 75 & 86; Boston Visual Artists Union, 78; Helen Bumpus Gallery, Duxbury, 80; Hess Gallery, 86 & 88. *Teaching:* Instr art, Kirkland House & Quincy House, Harvard Univ, 64-69; assoc prof painting, Boston Univ, 67-75; assoc prof & chmn, Arts and Commun Div, Pine Manor Col, 68- 89. *Awards:* Nat Scholastic Competition First Prize, Govt Italy, 50; Camargo Found Fel, 86. *Mem:* Boston Visual Artists Union. *Media:* Watercolor, Oil. *Publ:* Illusr, The Art of Responsive Drawing & Figure Drawing, Prentice-Hall; Artistic Anatomy and Figure Drawing, Van Nostrand Reinhold. *Mailing Add:* 212 Aspinwall Ave Brookline MA 02146

PAPPAS, GEORGE
PAINTER
b Boston, Mass, Jan 25, 29. *Study:* Mass Col of Art, BS, 52; Harvard Univ, MA, 53; Mass Inst of Technol, with Gyorgy Kepes, 52-53; Pa State Univ, PhD(educ), 57. *Work:* De Cordova Mus, Lincoln, Mass; St Paul Gallery of Art, Minn; Tampa Bay Art Ctr, Fla; Pa State Univ, Univ Park; Nat Gallery Art, Washington, DC; First Fla Bank, Tampa, Fl; McDonald Corp, Chicago, Il. *Exhib:* Corcoran Biennial, Washington, DC; De Cordova Mus Art, Lincoln, Mass; Ringling Mus Art, Sarasota, Fla; Detroit Inst of Art, Mich; Boston Mus Fine Arts, Mass; Kanegis Gallery, Boston; Nordness Gallery, New York; Stein Gallery, Tampa, Fla; Fla Gulf Coast Art Ctr, Fla; Univ S Fla Mus. *Teaching:* Asst prof painting & art educ, Pa State Univ, 55-56; chmn dept art, Univ S Fla, 66-83, prof art, 66- *Awards:* Purchase Awards, Drawing USA, St Paul Gallery of Art, Chautaqua Nat, Chautaqua Art Asn & Tampa Bay Art Ctr, Fla. *Mem:* Col Art Asn; Nat Conf of Art Adminr; Nat Art Educ Asn. *Media:* Oil. *Publ:* Co-auth, Design, It's Form and Function, Pa State Univ, 65; Concepts in Art & Education, Macmillan, 70. *Dealer:* Stein Gallery Tampa FL; Gillman Gallery Miami FL. *Mailing Add:* Dept of Art Univ S Fla Tampa FL 33620

PAPPENHEIMER, WILL D
PAINTER, GLASS BLOWER
b Boston, Mass, July 27, 54. *Study:* Harvard Col, BA, 77. *Work:* Am Craft Mus, New York; Detroit Inst Arts, Mich. *Exhib:* New American Glass: Focus 2 West Virginia, Huntington Mus Art, WVa, 86; Boston Now: Glass and Clay, Inst Contemp Art, Mass, 89; Shaping the Tradition, New Directions in Glass, Stedman Art Gallery, Camden, NJ, 91; The David Jacob Chordorcoff Collection, Detroit Inst Arts, Mich, 91; Glass from Ancient Craft to Contemporary Art: 1962-1992 and Beyond, Morris Mus, NJ, 92. *Teaching:* Vis lectr glass, Inst Contemp Art, 89 & Mass Col Art, 89-92; vis critic drawing, Harvard Col, Visual & Environ Class Workshop, 90-91. *Awards:* Masterworks Sessions, Creative Glass Ctr Am, 89; Fel, Nat Endowment Arts, 90; Artist in Residence, New York Experimental Glass Workshop, 90. *Bibliog:* Michael Lamar (auth), Will Pappenheimer, New Work Mag, spring 89. *Media:* Glass. *Mailing Add:* 36 Newbury St Somerville MA 02144

PARADISE, PHIL (HERSCHEL)
PAINTER, SCULPTOR
b Ontario, Ore, Aug 26, 05. *Study:* Chouinard Art Inst, grad; also with F Tolles Chamberlain, Rico Lebrun & Leon Kroll. *Work:* Libr Cong, Washington, DC; Philadelphia Watercolor Club; San Diego Fine Arts Soc. *Exhib:* Los Angeles Co Mus Art, 40; San Francisco Art Asn, 41; Art Inst Chicago, 43; Carnegie Inst Int, Pittsburgh, 43-44; Whitney Mus Am Art, New York, 45. *Pos:* Art dir & prod designer, Sol Lesser Prod, Paramount Studios, 41-48; dir, Greystone Galleries, 62-75. *Teaching:* Prof painting, Chouinard Art Inst, 31-40, dir fine arts, 36-40; lectr painting & drawing, Univ Tex, El Paso, 52; lectr painting & drawing, Scripps Col, 56-57. *Awards:* Purchase Award for Goleta, Philadelphia Watercolor Club, 39; Purchase Award for Landscape, San Francisco Int Exhib, 41; Dana Medal for Suburban Supper, Philadelphia Watercolor Club, 43. *Bibliog:* Janice Lovos (auth), Guatemela journey, Am Artist Mag, 50; Beverly Johnson (auth), Phil Paradise and his works, Los Angeles Times Home Mag, 67; Janice Lovos (auth), Phil Paradise serigraphs, Am Artist Mag, 69. *Mem:* Assoc Nat Acad Design. *Media:* Graphics. *Publ:* Illusr, Fortune Mag, Westways Mag, True Mag & others, 40-60. *Mailing Add:* c/o Bakersfield Mus Art 1930 R St Bakersfield CA 93301

PARCHER, JOAN ANN
JEWELER
b Pittsburgh, Pa, 56. *Study:* Kent State Univ, Ohio, BFA, 79; RI Sch Design, Providence, MFA, 86. *Exhib:* Int New Art Forms Exhib, Chicago, Ill, 91; Hand & Spirit, Scottsdale, Ariz, 92; Int Jewelry Exhib, Munich, Ger, 92; Pritam & Eames, East Hampton, NY, 92; and others. *Awards:* Nat Endowment Arts, 90; Second Place, Spec Exhib, Int New Art Forms Exhib, Chicago, Ill, 91. *Bibliog:* Stephen Luecking (auth), FunctionNonFunction, New Art Examiner, 39, 1/90; Catherine Jacobi (auth), FunctionNonFunction, 47, spring 90, Edward S Cooke Jr (auth), Jewelries/Epiphanies, 52, 53, spring 91 & Myra Mimlitsch Gray(auth), Joan Parcher, 43, spring 91, Metalsmith; James S Ackerman (auth), Jewelry, art, society, (introd exhib catalog), Artists Found Boston, Mass, 9/90 & Mus Decorative Arts, Prague, Czech, 2/91. *Mailing Add:* 52 Barnes St Providence RI 02906

PARDEE, WILLIAM HEARNE
PAINTER, EDUCATOR
b Pittsburgh, Pa, Aug 25, 46. *Study:* Yale Univ, with Sewell Sillman, BA, 69; New York Studio Sch, with Philip Guston, George McNeil & Leland Bell, 69-73; Columbia Univ, with Meyer Schapiro, MFA, 75. *Work:* Maine Savings Bank. *Exhib:* Bowery Gallery, 85 & 86; Jersey City Mus, NJ, 86; Maine Coast Artists, Rockport, 87; Bowery Gallery, 89 & 92; Congress Square Gallery, Maine, 92; and others. *Collections Arranged:* Linens, Wall-Clothing and Straw Sculpture, sculptures by Maureen Connor, 82; Aspects of Abstraction, sculpture by Deborah de Moulpied, Gerald DiGiusto & Lawrence Fane, 83; Landscape and Abstract Art: A Continuing Dialogue, 85, Inner Images, 86 & Clear Perceptions, 88, Colby Mus Art, Maine; Meyer Schapiro's Semiotics of Painting, New York Studio Sch, 89. *Pos:* Consult contemp art, Colby Col Mus Art, Maine, 82-88; asst prof painting & design, Colby Col, Maine, 82-90. *Teaching:* vis asst prof, Col William & Mary, 83; asst prof painting & design, Colby Col, Maine, 82-90; painting & drawing, Univ of Va, 92. *Awards:* Residency, Djerassi Found, 86. *Bibliog:* Gerard Haggerty (auth), Hearne Pardee: Paintings and cut-ups, Art New Eng, 4/82; Edgar Allen Beem (auth), Approaching landscape from two directions, Maine Times, 2/18/83; Jennifer Dunning (auth), Where to get off the beaten track, NY Times, 1/18/85. *Mem:* Col Art Asn Am. *Media:* Oil, Collage. *Publ:* Auth, Proust's visual imagery, Yale French Studies, 65; A reading of Marsden Hartley, 83, Six painters at the Hudson River Museum, 83, Landscape and the language of abstraction, 9/85, Inner Images, 11/86 & Peter Campus, 11/88, Arts Mag; short reviews, Artnews, 87-90. *Dealer:* Bowery Gallery 121 Wooster St New York NY 10012; Congress Square Gallery 42 Exchange St Portland ME 04101. *Mailing Add:* 549 W 123rd St No 15A New York NY 10027

PARDINGTON, RALPH ARTHUR
CERAMIST, SCULPTOR
b Highland Park, Mich, June 14, 38. *Study:* Albion Col, BFA, 60; Alfred Col Ceramics, summers 61 & 65; Cranbrook Acad Art, MFA, 62; with Hal Reiger & Palo Soleri, 64 & Dominic Labino, 67. *Work:* Inst Contemp Arts, Washington, DC; Mus Int Folk Art, Santa Fe; Mus Fine Arts, Div Mus NMex, Santa Fe; Mus Albuquerque; Mus Fine Art, Univ Okla. *Comn:* Bas-relief wall sculpture of patron saint, 69, holy water fountain, 69, Christ Desert Monastery, Albuquerque; sculpture, comn by Fritz Scholder, Galisteo, NMex, 70; outdoor planters, comn by A J O'Brien, Harbor Springs, Mich, 73; two large punch bowls, Int Folk Art Mus, Santa Fe, 73. *Exhib:* 25th Ceramic National, Syracuse, NY, 68; Object Makers, Univ Utah, 71; Inst Am Indian Arts Fac Exhib, Smithsonian Inst, Washington, DC, 73; Christmas Exhib, ACC Gallery, New York, 74; NMex Exhib, Univ Albuquerque, 74; and others. *Teaching:* Prof emer, Inst Am Indian Arts, 62-90; instr ceramics, Penland Sch Crafts, summers 67 & 69. *Awards:* First Prize, Int Folk Art, 68; Outstanding Work Award, Mus Albuquerque, 70; Commission Prize, Mus NMex, 71. *Bibliog:* Article in NMex Mag, winter 71. *Mem:* NMex Potters Asn; Am Crafts Coun; NMex Designer Craftsmen (pres, Santa Fe Chap, 64-65, state pres & vpres, 65-66). *Media:* Clay, Wood. *Publ:* Auth, 30-minute demonstration prog, KNME TV, 66. *Mailing Add:* One Elk Circle Santa Fe NM 87501

PARE, RICHARD
PHOTOGRAPHER, CURATOR
b Portsmouth, Eng, Jan 20, 48; US citizen. *Study:* Brighton Col, Eng, 60-65, Winchester Sch Art, Eng, 66-67, Ravensbourne Col Art & Design, Eng, BFA, 70, Art Inst Chicago, MFA, 73. *Work:* Mus Mod Art, New York; Stedelijk Mus, Amsterdam, Neth; Victoria & Albert Mus, London; Art Inst, Chicago; Mus Fine Arts, Houston. *Comn:* Casa Pilaltos, comn by Duque de Segorbe, Seville, Spain, 83; Japanese Gardens, Can Ctr Archit, Montreal, 86-; Musee du Nouveau Monde, La Rochelle, France, 80. *Exhib:* Court House, travelling exhib in US & Eng (cur & ed catalog), Mus Mod Art, New York, Art Inst, Chicago, San Francisco Art Inst, Atlanta Hist Soc, Ctr Creative Photog, Tucson, Old Court House, St Louis, Mo, 76-80; solo exhibs, Art Inst, Chicago, 81 & 85 & Corcoran Gallery Art, Washington, DC, 87. *Collections Arranged:* Robert Macpherson, 1811-1872 (auth catalog), Can Ctr Archit, 82-84; Photography & Architecture, 1839-1939 (auth catalog), Can Ctr Archit, 82-84. *Pos:* Cur photog, Can Ctr Archit, Montreal, 74-90; consult cur, Seagram Collection, 74-90. *Teaching:* Prof photog & photog hist, Columbia Col, Chicago, 73-75; Mellon Found vis lectr photog hist, Cooper Union, New York, 77. *Awards:* Photo Kina Award, Photog and Archit Exhib, 83; Fel, John Simon Guggenheim Mem Found, 87. *Publ:* Auth, Egypt: Reflections on Continuity, Timken Publ, 90. *Dealer:* Brent Sikkema Fine Art 155 Spring St New York NY 10012. *Mailing Add:* 174 Park St Montclair NJ 07042

PARELLA, ALBERT LUCIAN
PAINTER, INSTRUCTOR
b Youngstown, Ohio, Mar 21, 09. *Study:* Cleveland Sch Art, dipl art; Am Acad, Chicago. *Work:* Butler Inst Am Art; Hoyt Inst; The Owens-Illinois Co; West Reserve Health Care Systems Inc, Ohio. *Comn:* Set designs, Youngstown Playhouse, 33; emblem design, Youngstown YMCA, 60; emblem design, Youngstown Symphony Soc, 70; plague design, Choffin Voc Sch, 73; medal design, Butler Inst Am Art, 73. *Exhib:* Am Vet Art Soc, 74; Nat Acad, 74; Am Watercolor Soc, 74; Audubon Artists, 75; Soc Painters Casein, 75; Retrospective Show Winners of Prizes, Nat Arts Gallery, 78; one-man retrospective Butler Inst Am Art, 88. *Pos:* Cartoonist, Youngstown Telegram, 32-34; art dir, Wearstler Adv, Youngstown, Ohio, 34-45; adv dir, Century Foods, Youngstown, 45-50; art dir, WKBN TV, Youngstown, 50- *Teaching:* Instr art, Butler Inst Am Art, 46-48; instr art, Youngstown State Univ, 65-67. *Awards:* Gold Medal, Butler Inst Am Art, 73; President's Award, Audubon Artists, 74; Strathmore Watercolor Award, 77. *Mem:* Am Watercolor Soc; Audubon Artists; Artists in Casein & Acrylic; Knickerbocker Artists; Ohio Watercolor Soc. *Media:* Casein, Watercolor. *Publ:* Auth, Art in television, Today's Art, 73. *Mailing Add:* 208 Evergreen Dr Poland OH 44514

PARFENOFF, MICHAEL S
EDUCATOR, LITHOGRAPHER
b Gary, Ind, Aug 8, 26. *Study:* Art Inst Chicago, with Boris Anisfeld & Max Kahn, BFA & MFA. *Exhib:* Print Exhib, Libr Cong, Washington, DC; Momentum, Art Inst Chicago; Philadelphia Print Club. *Pos:* Pres, Blackhawk Mountain Sch Art, 63- *Teaching:* Instr lithography, Art Inst Chicago, 58-65; prof art, Chicago City Col, 58- *Mem:* Am Asn Univ Prof; Ill Art Educators. *Media:* Stone. *Mailing Add:* 453 W Roslyn Pl Chicago IL 60614

PARIS, JEANNE C
CRITIC, CONSULTANT
b Newark, NJ. *Study:* Newark Sch Fine Arts; Tyler Sch Art, Temple Univ; Columbia Univ; NY Univ. *Collections Arranged:* Organized & directed The Artist of the Month, providing lecturers & demonstrators in all the arts for organizations & schools; organized exhibs of American art for Latin America,

Italy & USA. *Pos:* Assoc dir, Valente Gallery, New York, currently; art critic, Long Island Press, 63-; art critic, Newsday, 77- *Teaching:* Lectr art, univs, cols, art leagues, women's clubs, mus asns, radio & NBC-TV series, You're a Part of Art. *Mem:* Glen Cove Pub Libr; Coun Arts North Shore; New York Reporters Asn; Newspaper Women's Club; and others. *Collection:* Twentieth century painting & sculpture. *Publ:* Auth articles for Weekly Newspaper Chain, Record Pilot & Newsday; article, Cue Mag, 7/72. *Mailing Add:* 21 Whitney Circle Glen Cove NY 11542

PARIS, LUCILLE M
PAINTER, PRINTMAKER
b Cleveland, Ohio, Apr 8, 28. *Study:* Univ Calif, Berkeley, BA(Taussig Traveling Fel), 51, MA(McEnerney Grad Fel), 52; Atelier 17, Paris; Columbia Univ, EdD, 59. *Work:* Butterfield Collection; NJ State Mus Contemp Art; Newark Mus Collection Contemp Art. *Exhib:* Oakland Mus, Calif, 52-54; San Francisco Mus Art, 50-51, 53-55, 61-62 & SFW Ann, 52-53 & 56-58; one-person shows, Aegis Gallery, New York, 65, NJ State Mus, Trenton, 73, Bronx Mus Art, 76 & Vodra Gallery, Jersey City State Col, 85; Robeson Gallery, 81 & Walters Gallery, 82, & Habel S Douglas, 82, Rutgers Univ; Educ Testing Serv, Princeton, 84; American Abstraction, Schering-Plough, NJ State Mus, 85; Chubb World Hq Gallery, 85; and others. *Teaching:* Prof painting & graphics, Ball State Univ, 55-57; prof art, William Paterson Col, 59- *Mailing Add:* Dept Art William Paterson Col Wayne NJ 07470

PARIZEK, JARO
DEALER, COLLECTOR
b Prague, Czech, Mar 16, 34; US citizen. *Study:* Art & Tech Col Vienna, 56; Art Students League, with Brackman, 66-69. *Pos:* Art dealer-mgr, Wally Findlay Galleries Inc, New York, 70-75; art dealer-owner, Jaro Art Galleries, New York, 75- *Mem:* Am Artists Asn. *Res:* History of the Yugoslav Naive School of Art. *Specialty:* Yugoslav naive art and American contemporary primitives. *Collection:* Yugoslav naive art, to be eventually shown in different museums throughout the country. *Mailing Add:* Jaro Art Galleries 955 Madison Ave New York NY 10021

PARKE, WALTER SIMPSON
PAINTER, PRINTMAKER
b Little Rock, Ark, Dec 30, 09. *Study:* Art Inst Chicago; Am Acad Art; also with Wellington Reynolds. *Work:* Univ Ill Col Dentistry; Union League Civic & Arts Found; plus others in pvt collections. *Exhib:* Union League Club Art Show, Chicago; Allied Artists Am 52nd Ann, New York; Munic Art League, Chicago; Am Artists Prof League, New York; Denver Art Mus; plus many others. *Teaching:* Instr portrait painting, Palette & Chisel Acad. *Awards:* Six Purchase Awards, Union League Club Exhib, 55-78; Gold Medal, Munic Art League, 71; Gold Medal, Diamond Medal & Silver Medal, Palette & Chisel Acad, 76-79. *Mem:* Brown Co Art Guild; Palette & Chisel Acad; Munic Art League; Oak Park Art League; Union League Civic & Arts Found. *Media:* Oil, Watercolor; Etching. *Mailing Add:* 30 W 225 Argyll Ln Naperville IL 60563

PARKER, ANN
PHOTOGRAPHER, WRITER
b London, Eng, Mar 6, 34; US citizen. *Study:* RI Sch of Design; Yale Univ, BFA. *Work:* Metrop Mus Art, New York; Smithsonian Inst, Washington, DC; Mus Mod Art, New York; Boston Pub Libr, Mass; Ctr Creative Photog, Tucson, Ariz. *Comn:* Arton Assoc, 70 & 74; Mead Art Gallery, Amherst, Mass, 76; Sweetwater Eds, 82; Thistle Hill Press, 83-85. *Exhib:* One-man exhibs, Nat Mus Art, La Paz, Bolivia, 85, Princton Univ Libr, NJ, 86, Inst Dominicano de Cultura Hispanica, Santo Dominican Republic, 87, Maxwell Mus, Univ NMex, Albuquerque, 88. *Awards:* Ford Found Grant in Arts & Humanities, 62-64; First Prize in Photog, Americana Bicentennial Photog Contest, 76 & Mass Open, 77. *Bibliog:* Stephen Chodorov (producer), Know Ye the Hour, Camera Three, CBS-TV, 11/68; Vicki Goldberg (auth), Am Photogr, 1/83; Lois Parkinson Zamora (auth), Spot, Houston Ctr Photog, fall 89. *Mem:* Friends of Photog; Photog Resource Ctr, Boston Mass; Asn Gravestone Studies. *Media:* Cibachrome, Silver Prints; Non Fiction. *Publ:* Photogr, Ephemeral Folk Figures, Clarkson Potter, New York, 69; Molas Folk Art of the Cuna Indians, Barre Publ, New York, 77; Scarecrows, Barre Publ, New York, 78; Early American Stone Sculpture, Sweetwater Eds; photogr, Los Ambulantes, the itinerant photographers of Guatemala, MIT, Cambridge, 82. *Dealer:* Gallery of Graphic Arts 1603 York Ave New York NY 10028. *Mailing Add:* 7 Tory Rd Shrewsbury MA 01545

PARKER, CAROLYN JOHNSON
PAINTER
b Cleveland, Ohio, Nov 22, 42. *Study:* Skidmore Col, BA(art hist), 65. *Work:* Berkshire Mus, Pittsfield, Mass; Needham, Harper, Steers Advert, Chicago; Am J Psychiatry, Washington, DC; Sybil & Stephen Stone Collection, Brocton Mus, Mass; Art in Embassies, Washington, DC. *Exhib:* 100 Years, 100 Artists, Nat Asn Women Artists, NY & Franz Bader, Washington, DC, 89; Int Art Exhib, Ariel Gallery, NY, 90; Earth, Sea, Sky, Adelphi Univ, Long Island, NY, Peel Gallery, Danby, Vt, Ariel Gallery, New York & Franz Bader, Washington, DC, 91. *Awards:* Michael Engel Award, Nat Soc Painters in Acrylic & Casein; Runner Up Govesnors Award, Md; 1st & 2nd Mural Awards, Sign of the times, Int Competition. *Mem:* Copley Soc Boston, Mass; Nat Soc Painters Acrylic & Casein, NY; Nat Soc Women Artists, NY. *Media:* Acrylic. *Publ:* Contemporary Women Artists Calendar, Washington DC Recreation Register. *Dealer:* Franz Bader Washington DC; Peel Gallery Danby VT. *Mailing Add:* 239 Dill Ave Frederick MD 21701

PARKER, HARRY S, III
MUSEUM DIRECTOR
b St Petersburg, Fla, Dec 23, 39. *Study:* Harvard Univ, BA; Inst Fine Arts, NY Univ, MA. *Pos:* Asst to dir, Metrop Mus Art, New York, 63-67, vdir educ, 68-73; dir, Dallas Mus Art, 74-87; dir, Fine Arts Mus San Francisco, 87- *Teaching:* Lectr mus educ. *Mem:* Am Asn Mus; Am Fedn Arts; Int Coun Mus; Asn Art Mus Dirs. *Mailing Add:* c/o Fine Arts Mus Lincoln Park San Francisco CA 94121

PARKER, JAMES VARNER
DESIGNER
b Senath, Mo, June 27, 25. *Study:* Phoenix Community Col, AA; Ariz State Univ, BFA & MA. *Work:* Southeast State Teachers Col; City of Phoenix Civic Art Collection; Malaysian Embassy, Washington, DC; Scottsdale Art Collection; Pres Ronald Reagan. *Comn:* Carl Hayden High Sch Student Body, Phoenix, 60; Greater Ariz Savings Bank, Tucson; Heard Mus; Cape Girardeau Pub Libr. *Exhib:* Tucson Art Ctr, 66; Phoenix Art Mus, 66; Stanford Res Inst, Palo Alto, Calif, 66; Yuma Art Asn, Ariz, 70; plus others. *Collections Arranged:* Indian Art Collection, 68 & 72; African Art, Heard Mus, 6/72 & 9/72; Indian Art of the Americas; Missouri Mills, 77; Beckwith Collection, 77; William Faulkner, 80. *Pos:* Cur educ, Heard Mus, 58-68, illusr, 58 & 71, cur art, 68-75; consult adminr, Phoenix Mus Hist, 75-77; mus dir, Southeast Mo State Univ Mus, 77-90, retired. *Teaching:* Instr art, Phoenix Col, 68-70; instr art, Glendale Community Col, 71-72; instr, Southeast Mo State Univ, 76-90. *Awards:* Nat Vet Award, Santa Monica Recreation Dept, 53; O'Brien Art Award, Ariz State Fair, 60; UNICEF Award, 68. *Bibliog:* Design-Crafts-Education (film), KAET TV, Ariz State Univ, 60. *Mem:* Ariz Watercolor Asn (found & pres, 59); Ariz Art Asn (pres & secy, 60); Nat Art Educ Asn; Am Mus Asn. *Publ:* Illusr, The Story of Navaho Weaving, 61; Pima Basketry, 65; The Dennis Collection, Egyptian Antiquities, 79; The Art of Collage, 79. *Mailing Add:* 445 Marie Cape Girardeau MO 63701

PARKER, NANCY WINSLOW
ILLUSTRATOR, WRITER
b Maplewood, NJ, Oct 18, 30. *Study:* Mills Col, Calif, BA, 52; Art Students League & Sch Visual Arts, New York. *Exhib:* Audubon Artists 29th Ann Exhib, New York, 71; Webb & Parsons, Bedford Village, NY, 76; Master-Eagle Gallery, NY, 80, 83, 85 & 87; Webb & Parsons, New Canaan, Conn, 83; Jane Vorhees Zimmerli Art Mus, Rutgers Univ, NJ, 86. *Pos:* Art dir, Appleton, Century, Crofts, New York, 68-70; graphic designer, Holt Rinehart & Winston, New York, 70-72. *Awards:* My Mom Travels A Lot, New York Times Ten Best Illustrated Books, 81; Chistopher Award, 76 & 81; AIGA Book Show, 76 & 81. *Mem:* Authors Guild. *Media:* Watercolor, Wood. *Publ:* Coauth & illusr, Frogs-Toads-Lizards & Salamanders, Greenwillow, 90; The President's Cabinet (rev), Crowell, 91; Barbara Frietchie (Whittier), 92, Working Frog, 92, The Dress I'll Never Wear to the Party (Neitzel), 92 & Sheridan's Ride (Read), 93, Greenwillow; and others. *Mailing Add:* 51 E 74th St New York NY 10021

PARKER, OLIVIA
PHOTOGRAPHER
b Boston, Mass, June 10, 41. *Study:* Wellesley Col, BA, 63. *Work:* Victoria & Albert Mus, London; Boston Mus Fine Arts; Mus Mod Art, New York; Art Inst Chicago; Int Mus Photog, Eastman House, Rochester; and others. *Comn:* Photographic Resource Ctr, Boston, 81. *Exhib:* 14 New Eng Photogr, Boston Mus Fine Arts, 78; Loans to the Collection, Art Inst Chicago, 78; One of a Kind Traveling Exhib, Mus Fine Arts, Houston; 20 x 24, Light Gallery, New York, 79; one-person shows, Friends Photog, Carmel, Calif, 79 & 81, Eastman House, Rochester, 81, Mus Art, Univ Ore, 82, Catskill Ctr Photog, Woodstock, 82 & Art Inst Chicago, 82; and others. *Awards:* Artists Found fel, 78; Cert of Excellence, Am Inst of Graphic Arts Bk Show, 79; Ferguson Grant, 81. *Bibliog:* Owen Edwards (auth), The clear Yankee eye, Saturday Rev, 79; Vicki Goldberg (auth), Signs of (still)life, Am Photogr, 79; David Featherstone (auth), Olivia Parker, Mod Photog, 80. *Mem:* Soc for Photog Educ; Friends Photog. *Media:* Photography. *Publ:* Auth, Signs of Life, 78 & contribr, One of a Kind, 79, David Godine; contribr, Darkroom Dynamics, Curtin & London, 79; auth, Under the Looking Glass, New York Graphic Soc, 83. *Mailing Add:* Photography West Gallery Delores at Ocean Ave PO Box 4829 Carmel CA 93921

PARKER, ROBERT ANDREW
PAINTER
b Norfolk, Va, May 14, 27. *Study:* Art Inst Chicago, BAE, 52; Skowhegan Sch Painting & Sculpture; Atelier 17, New York, 52-53. *Work:* Los Angeles Co Mus; Metrop Mus Art; Morgan Libr, New York; Mus Mod Art; Whitney Mus Am Art; plus others. *Comn:* Designer sets, William Shuman Opera, Mus Mod Art, 61. *Exhib:* Brooklyn Mus, 55; Mus Mod Art, 57; Laon Mus, Aisne, France, 56; New Sch Social Res, 65; Sch Visual Arts, NY, 65; and many others. *Teaching:* Instr, Parson Sch Design, 80-85, RI Sch Design, 84 & Pratt Inst, Brooklyn, NY, 85. *Awards:* Rosenthal Found Grant, Nat Inst Arts & Lett, 62; Tamarind Lithography Workshop Fel, 67; Guggenheim Fel, 69-70; plus others. *Media:* Watercolor, Etching. *Publ:* Illusr, hand-colored ltd ed poems, Mus Mod Art, 62; illusr poetry, The days of Wilfred Owen (film), 66. *Mailing Add:* c/o Terry Dintenfass Gallery 50 W 57th St New York NY 10019

PARKER, SAMUEL MURRAY
PAINTER
b Madison, Wis, Aug 6, 36. *Study:* Wis State Univ, Eau Claire, BA(art), 63; Univ Wis, MS(painting & drawing, 64, MFA(painting), 65. *Work:* Springfield Mus; Playboy Club; Laura Musser Mus, Muscatine, Iowa; Container Corp

Am. *Comn:* Serigraphy, Ill Print Comn, Ill Arts Coun, 73. *Exhib:* Univ Pac Nat Small Painting Show, 71; 3rd Nat Drawing Show, Oshkosh, Wis, 71; New Talent: Midwest USA, Gallery 1640, Montreal, Que, 72; Dong a Ibo Korean Int Print Show, Seoul, 72; Nat Print Invitational, Artists Contemp Gallery, Sacramento, Calif, 73. *Teaching:* Assoc prof painting & drawing, Western Ill Univ, 65-78, prof, 78- *Awards:* First Prize for Painting, Ill State Fair Show, 72, 25th Ill Invitational, Ill State Mus, 72 & Laura Musser Mus, 73. *Media:* Acrylic Polymer. *Mailing Add:* 216 E Jefferson St Macomb IL 61455

PARKER, WILL (WILLIAM CRAWFORD)
GRAPHIC ARTIST, PAINTER
b Augusta, Ga, Sept 24, 44. *Study:* Clemson Univ, drawing with Robert Hunter, 61-63; Univ SC, Columbia, pvt criticism with J Bardin & painting with Edmund Yaghjian, AB, 65; Sch Boston Mus Fine Arts, printmaking with Ture Bengtz, advan study, 65-67; Imageworks Sch Photog, Cambridge, Mass, with Ron MacNeil, 73. *Work:* SC Chap Am Inst Architects, Columbia, SC. *Exhib:* 9th, 10th & 11th Ann Piedmont Graphics Show, Mint Mus Art, Charlotte, NC, 72, 73 & 74; NH Art Asn Ann, Currier Gallery Art, Manchester, 78 & 80-84; one-man show, Recent & Other Works on Paper, Sharon Arts Ctr Juried, Peterborough, NH, 77-79, 83, 84, 86 & 88 & Nashua Arts & Sci Ctr, NH, 79; 30th Ann Exhib, Guild SC Artists, Gibbs Art Gallery, Charleston, SC, 80; 2nd NH Arts Biennial, Manchester Inst Arts & Sci, 81; Third Ann Invitational, Plymouth State Col Art Gallery, NH, 84. *Pos:* Graphic designer, NH & Mass, 81-91. *Teaching:* Instr drawing & printmaking & actg head dept art, Nathaniel Hawthorne Col, Antrim, NH, 75-78; instr drawing & design, Sharon Arts Ctr, Peterborough, NH, 76-81 & Arts & Sci Ctr, Nashua, NH, 76-83. *Awards:* Selection for Traveling Show, Springs Mill, Inc, Lancaster, SC, 72; First Prize Drawing, 34th Ann Exhib, 81 & Merchants Nat Bank Drawing Award, 38th Ann Exhib, 84, NH Art Asn, Currier Gallery Art, Manchester, NH; First Prize for Drawing, 7th, 10th & 11th Ann Exhib, Sharon Arts Ctr, Peterborough, NH, 83, 86 & 88. *Bibliog:* Barbara Center (auth), Amherst artist explores painting, drawing, printmaking, Milford Cabinet, 5/8/86; Artist etches 3-way career, Nashua Telegraph, 12/13/83; Chris Chinlund (auth), Artists plotting strategy for change, Boston Globe, 10/9/83. *Mem:* NH Art Asn. *Media:* Prismacolor, Pencil; Miscellaneous Media. *Mailing Add:* 32 Ramsgate Ridge Nashua NH 03063

PARKER, WILMA (WILMA PARKER DE PAVLOFF)
PAINTER
b Springfield, Mass, May 15, 41. *Study:* RI Sch Design, BFA, 63; Art Inst Chicago, MFA, 66. *Work:* de Saisett Mus; Laguna Gloria Mus Austin, Tex; Mesa Southwest Mus, Mesa, Ariz; Kaiser Permanente, San Francisco; Mass Gen Hosp, Boston; and others. *Comn:* IBM, Tucson, 81; IBM, Poughkeepsie, NY, 85; Sonora Cafe, Los Angeles, 86; Presidental Suite, Fairmont Hotel, Calif, 88; Launch of the Springfield, US Navy, 92. *Exhib:* Nat Air & Mus, Smithsonian Inst, Washington, DC, 86; Mus Hudson Highlands, Cornwell, 89; Springfield Mus Fine Arts, 81 & 92; Shalilee Corp, San Francisco, 91; Gump's, San Francisco, 92; Lyman Allyn Mus, New London, 92; Nautlus Mus, Groton, Conn, 92. *Bibliog:* Art Talk, Scottsdale, Ariz, 10/89; Calif Art Rev, 91; Am Artists, Am Ref Publ Group, 91. *Mem:* COGAP; Salmagundi Club, New York; Am Soc Marine Artists. *Media:* All. *Publ:* Auth, Wilma Parker, an interchange in life, Southwest Art Mag, 81; Mono No Sono, SF Tea Poetics Soc, 91. *Dealer:* Lisa Dubins Gallery San Vincente Blvd Los Angeles CA; Gump's Gallery San Francisco CA. *Mailing Add:* 222 Clara St San Francisco CA 94107

PARKHURST, CHARLES
EDUCATOR, CURATOR
b Columbus, Ohio, Jan 23, 13. *Study:* Williams Col, BA, 35; Oberlin Col, MA, 38; Princeton Univ, MFA, 41. *Pos:* Asst to dir, Albright Art Gallery, Buffalo, 45-47; dir, Allen Mem Art Mus, Oberlin Col, 49-62; dir, Baltimore Mus Art, 62-70; asst dir & chief curator, Nat Gallery Art, 71-83; co-dir, Williams Col Mus Art, 83-84, dir, Graduate Prog Hist Art, 86-87; interim dir, Smith Col Mus Art, 91-92 (dir emer); retired. *Teaching:* Asst prof art & archaeol, Princeton Univ, 47-49; prof hist & art appreciation & head dept art, Oberlin Col, 49-62; vis lectr, Univ Minn, Univ Calif, Los Angeles & Johns Hopkins Univ; vis prof & lectr, Williams Col, 85-92; lectr, Univ Wis. *Awards:* Chevalier, Legion of Honor, Fr Govt, 47; Ford Found Fel, 52-53; Fulbright Res Fel, Univ Utrecht, 56-57; plus others. *Bibliog:* H Matile (auth), Die Farbenlehre P D Runges, Munich, 79; A Ziggelaar (auth), Francois de Aguilon - Scientist & Architect, Inst Historicum, Roma, 83; M Kemp (auth), The science of art, Yale Univ Press, London, 90. *Mem:* Col Art Asn Am (past pres); Intermus Conserv Asn (co-founder & past pres); Asn Art Mus Dirs (vpres); Am Asn Mus (pres). *Res:* History of scientific color theories and their relationship to visual arts. *Publ:* auth, Aquilonius' Optics and Ruben's Color, Nederlands Kunsthistorisch Jaarboek, 61; coauth (with R L Feller), Who invented the color wheel?, Color Res & Application, 82; Alberti's Place in the History of Color Schemes, J J Augustin, Locust Valley, NY, 87; Roger Bacon on Color: Sources, Theories and Influence; Essays in Honor, W S Heckscher, Italica Press, NY, 90. *Mailing Add:* 33 Dana Pl Amherst MA 01002

PARKINSON, ELIZABETH BLISS (MRS HENRY IVES COBB)
PATRON, COLLECTOR
b New York, NY, Sept 25, 07. *Pos:* Trustee, Mus Mod Art, New York, 39-, pres int coun, 57-65, pres mus, 65-68, vchmn, 69-; mem art comt, Addison Gallery, Phillips Acad, Andover, Mass, 55-72, trustee, Archives Am Art, 69-80. *Collection:* Twentieth century American paintings and drawings. *Mailing Add:* 215 E 72nd St No 15E New York NY 10021

PARKS, CARRIE ANNE
CERAMIST, EDUCATOR
b Chattanooga, Tenn, June 9, 55. *Study:* Wesleyan Col, BFA, 76; apprentice to Takeo Sudo, Mashiko, Japan, 77-78; Va Commonwealth Univ, Richmond, MFA, 81. *Work:* Clemson Univ, Clemson, SC; Rutgers Univ, Camden, NJ; Auburn Univ, Ala; Austin Peay State Univ, Clarksville, Tenn; Saginaw Valley State Univ, University Center, Mich. *Comn:* Ceramic tile murals, Alma Col, Alma, Mich, 87. *Exhib:* Rutgers Nat Works on Paper, Rutgers Univ, Camden, NJ, 88 & 92; Figurative Clay: Nat Juried Exhib, Ga State Univ, Atlanta, 91; Works in Clay VII, Wichita Falls Mus, Tex, 91; 5th Ann Great Lakes Show, Lill Street Gallery, Chicago, 91; 7th Ann San Angelo Nat Ceramic Competition, San Angelo Mus Fine Arts, Tex, 92. *Teaching:* Adj fac ceramics, Va Commonwealth Univ, Richmond, Va, 81; assoc prof art, Alma Col, Mich, 82. *Awards:* Purchase Award, Rutgers Univ, 88; Second Place, Lill Street Gallery, 91; First Place, Wichita Falls Mus, 91. *Bibliog:* Margaret Hawkins (auth), Trends in Clay Show Fit Mold, Chicago Sun Times, 5/16/86; Paula Blume Leonard (auth), Figurative Clay: a National Juried Exhibition, The Art papers, Nov/Dec, 91; Amy Brower Gleason (auth), 7th Wichita Falls National, Ceramics Monthly, Vol 40, 92. *Mem:* Col Art Asn; Nat Coun for Educ in Ceramic Arts; Am Crafts Coun; Mich Potters Asn. *Media:* Clay, Pencil. *Dealer:* Objects Gallery 230 W Huron Chicago IL 60610. *Mailing Add:* 9667 Van Buren Rd Riverdale MI 48877-9707

PARKS, CHARLES CROPPER
SCULPTOR
b Va, June 27, 22. *Study:* Pa Acad Fine Arts, 47-51; Wemys Found Travel Grant, Greece, 65-66, Widener Univ, LHD, 88. *Work:* Del Art Mus, Wilmington; Brookgreen Gardens, Murrells Inlet, SC; Mystic Seaport, Mystic, Conn; Blount Corp, Montgomery, Ala; Amway Corp, Ada, Mich. *Comn:* Boy & Dogs, H B du Pont, Wilmington, Del, 69; James F Byrnes, Byrnes Found, Columbia, SC, 70; Boy with Hawk, Brandywine River Mus, 73; Boy with Gulls, Mystic Seaport Mus, 75; Sunflowers, Brookgreen Gardens, SC, 85. *Exhib:* Nat Sculpture Soc Ann, 62-77; Nat Acad Design, 65-77; six-city tour, Equitable Life Assurance Soc, 76-77. *Pos:* Mem adv comt, John F Kennedy Ctr, 68- *Awards:* Am Artists Prof League Gold Medal, 70; Nat Sculpture Soc Gold Medal, 71; Watrous Gold Medal, Nat Acad Design, 80; Watrous Gold Medal, Nat Acad Design, 80. *Bibliog:* Nancy Mohr (auth), The Parks Family, Del Today Mag, 72. *Mem:* Fel Nat Sculpture Soc (pres, 76-78); Pa Acad Fine Arts; Del Ctr for Contemp Arts, Artists' Fel; Pa Acad Fine Arts. *Media:* Cast Bronze, Welded Steel. *Publ:* Contribr, Sights and Sounds of Easter, TV film produced by Wilmington Coun Churches, 64. *Mailing Add:* 44-A Bancroft Mills Wilmington DE 19806

PARMAKELIS, JOHN
SCULPTOR
b Greece, 32. *Study:* Sch Fine Arts, with John Pappas, Ecole Des Beaux Arts, Paris, with Zadtkine & Kouturier, 61-64. *Work:* Com Bank Greece. *Comn:* Democracy in Silver (six medals), Commemorative Collection. *Exhib:* Int Exhib Mod Sculpture, Paris, 66; Biennale, Budapest, 71; one-man show, Pagani Gallery, Milan, 73; Greek Art Now, Tower Athens, Greece, 74; China-Greece, Hellenic Found, Rodi Karkazis Gallery, 84. *Mailing Add:* c/o Rodi Karkazis Gallery 168 N Michigan Ave No 300 Chicago IL 60601

PARNESS, CHARLES
PAINTER
b Staten Island, New York, Jan 1, 45. *Study:* Parsons Sch Design, 65; New York Univ, Sch Educ, BS, 66; Pratt Inst Grad Sch, MFA, 69. *Work:* Oakleigh Collection, Boston; Reader's Digest, Westchester, NY; Butler Inst, Youngstown, Ohio. *Exhib:* Two man show, Mercer Union, Toronto, Can, 82; Portrait show, PS1, Long Island City, NY, 84; Self Portraits Message/ Material, Hofstra Mus, Hempstead, NY, 87; Concept of Self, Asian Art Inst, New York, 87; Positive ID, Southern Alleghenies Mus, Lovetto, Pa, 89; one man show, Butler Inst, Youngstown, Ohio, 90. *Teaching:* Vis artist painting, Marie Walsh Sharp Found 89-92; Vt Studio Sch, 91 & 93. *Awards:* Vis Artist Fel, Brandywine Workshop, Philadelphia, Pa, 88. *Bibliog:* Louise Hamlin (auth), Review of one man show, Cover Mag, 10/87; Edmund Leites (auth), Review of one man show, Art in Am, 11/87; John Arthur (auth), We're talking serious comedy, Am Artist, 7/90. *Mem:* Artist Equity. *Media:* Oil. *Dealer:* G W Einstein 591 Broadway New York NY 10012. *Mailing Add:* 68 Greene St New York NY 10012

PARRA, CARMEN
PAINTER, PRINTMAKER
b Mexico City, Mex, Nov 12, 44. *Study:* Escuela Nac Antropologia e Hist, Mexico City, BA, 64; Acad Belles Artes, Rome, BFA, 67; Esmeralda, 67; Royal Col Art, London, 70. *Work:* Mus de Arte Mod, Mexico City; Univ Nac Autonoma Mex. *Comn:* XIV Anniversary of Tabamex Libr, 84-; Mural Libr of Justice Dept, Mexico City. *Exhib:* Decima Bienal Paris, Mus D'Art Mod, France, 77; Las Ventanas, Mus Art Mod, Mexico City, 79; Mexico de Manana, Mus Bibliot Pape, Monetove, Coahuila, 79; La Creacion Femenina, Kunstler Haus Bethanien, Berlin, 80; Musica y Angeles, Metrop Cathedral Mex, Mexico City, 83; La Catedral de Mexico, Temps Captif, Orangerie in the Sully Hotel, Paris, France; Hojas Transfiguradas, Palacio de Minieria of the Nat Univ Mex, Mexico City, 86; Eternidad de lo Efimero, Mus de Arte Mod, Mexico City, 87; Museo Nacional de la Estampa, 91. *Pos:* Stage & wardrobe designer; film art dir, Frida, Naturaleza Viva, 88. *Awards:* Fiesta Primavera Otono, Mexico City, 81. *Bibliog:* Imagenes (Videotape) Carton y Papel de Mex, 82; La Mujer Mex en el Arte, ed Bacreser, 87. *Mem:* Soc Amigos del Centro Hist de la Ciudad de Mexico; Soc Amigos de la Catedral Metropolitana. *Media:* Acrylic, Oil; Lithography. *Publ:* Illusr, La Grafostatica u Oda a Eiffel, Talleres Graficos Nacion, 78; Tiempo Cautivo, La Cathedral

de Mexico, Ed Arvil, 80; De la Pluma al Angel, Ed Nayaqui, 83; Templo Mayor, Ed Multiarte, 83; La Eternidad to lo Efimero, Miquel Angel Porrua, 83; Via Crucis, Multiarte, 91. *Dealer:* Lourdes Chumacero Gallery Estocolmo 34 Mexico DF Mex 06600; Sloane Arcotta Gallery. *Mailing Add:* Primera Cerrada de Galeana 13 San Angel Mexico DF 01000 Mexico

PARRINO, GEORGE
PAINTER, ADMINISTRATOR
b New York, NY, Sept 25, 42. *Study:* Cooper Union Art Sch, BFA, 64; Yale Univ Art Sch, MFA, 70; Acad Fine Art, India, Fulbright Res Fel Painting, 71-72. *Work:* Metrop Mus Art & Guggenheim Mus, New York; Brooklyn Mus, NY; Marion Koogler McNay Art Mus, San Antonio, Tex. *Exhib:* Solo exhibs, Ingber Gallery, New York, 74 & 76, Univ Tex, San Antonio, 79; Fac Exhib, Brooklyn Mus, NY, 73; Fulbright Artists, Inst Int Educ, New York, 77; Cubist Syntax in the 70's, Ingber Gallery, 78; Artists' Kites, Danforth Mus, Conn, 78; and others. *Teaching:* Instr painting, Brooklyn Mus Art Sch, NY, 73; asst prof humanities, St John's Univ, New York, 74-75; lectr painting, N Tex State Univ, Denton, 77-78; lectr painting, Univ Tex, San Antonio, 78-79; dean, San Antonio Art Inst, 78-85; pres, Kansas City Art Inst, 85-87; prof & dean, div Vis Arts, State Univ NY, Purchase, 87- *Awards:* Residence fels, Yaddo, 75 & 76. *Bibliog:* Phyllis Derfner (auth), New York letter, Art Int, 1/75; Modris Ramans (auth), George Parrino, Arts Mag, 11/76; Lawrence Alloway (auth), Cubist syntax in the 70's, Nation, 78. *Mem:* Col Arts Asn; Nat Coun Art Adminr; Nat Asn Sch Art & Design; Tex Arts Alliance (bd mem). *Media:* Acrylic. *Mailing Add:* Vis Arts Div State Univ 735 Anderson Hill Rd Purchase NY 10577-1400

PARRIS, NINA GUMPERT
CURATOR, EDUCATOR
b Berlin, Ger, Sept 11, 27; US citizen. *Study:* Bryn Mawr Col, BA(art hist; Woodrow Wilson Fel), 68; Univ Pa, MA(art hist), 69, PhD(art hist), 79. *Collections Arranged:* Prints & Paintings in Permanent Collection (auth, catalog), Robert Hull Fleming Mus, 71. *Pos:* Cur, Robert Hall Fleming Mus, Univ Vt, 71-79; chief cur, Columbia Mus Art, 79-90; fac residence art hist, Vermont Col. *Teaching:* Lectr art hist, Philadelphia Col Art, 70-71; lectr mus studies, Univ SC, Columbia, 72- *Mem:* Am Asn Mus; Int Coun Mus; SC Crafts Guild (bd mem, 81-82). *Res:* Late 19th and 20th century art including contemporary art. *Publ:* Auth, Van de Velde, Obrist, Hölzel: The Basic Course at the Bauhaus, McMaster Colloquium, 81; The South Carolina Collection, Columbia Mus Art, 86; numerous exhib catalogs. *Mailing Add:* 17 S Union St Burlington VT 05401

PARRISH, DAVID BUCHANAN
PAINTER
b Birmingham, Ala, June 19, 39. *Study:* Univ Ala, with Melville Price & Richard Brough, BFA. *Work:* Brooks Mem Art Gallery, Memphis; Wadsworth Atheneum, Hartford, Conn; Parthenon, Nashville; Monsanto Chem Co, Decatur, Ala. *Exhib:* One-man shows, Galerie Francois Petit, Paris, 73 & Sidney Janis Gallery, 75; Sharp Focus Realism, Sidney Janis Gallery, New York, 72 & 75; Painting & Sculpture Today, Indianapolis Mus Art, 72; Phases of New Realism, Lowe Mus, Coral Gables, 72; Realists Revival, Am Fedn Arts Traveling Show, 72-73; New/Photo Realism, Wadsworth Atheneum, Hartford, Conn, 74; Super Realism, Baltimore Mus Art, 75. *Awards:* Award of Merit, 23rd Southeastern Ann Exhib, High Mus, Atlanta, 68; Top Award, 61st Ann Exhib, Birmingham Mus Art, 69; Top Award, Mid-South Ann, Brooks Mem Art Gallery, 70. *Media:* Oil. *Dealer:* Nancy Hoffman Gallery New York NY 10012. *Mailing Add:* 700 Cleermont Dr SE Huntsville AL 35801

PARRISH, JEAN
PAINTER
b Plainfield, NH, June 26, 11. *Study:* with father, Maxfield Parrish, 25-35. *Work:* Mus NMex, Santa Fe; W ex Mus, Lubbock; NMex State Fair Permanent Collection Art Gallery, Albuquerque. *Exhib:* Cracker Barrel Bazaar, Newberry, Vt, 59; Paintings & Sculpture, Okla City Junior League, Okla, 66; Margaret Jamison Presents, Sweeney Auditorium, Sante Fe, NMex, 80 & 81; Sante Fe Festival of the Arts, Sweeney Auditorium, Sante Fe, NMex, 82; Artists of Am Invitational, Denver, Colo, 84, 85, 86 & 87; and others. *Awards:* Grand Award, NMex State Fair, 55; First Prize, NMex State Fair, 55; Purchase Prize, NMex State Fair, 55. *Bibliog:* Margaret I Meaders (auth), The art of Jean Parrish, Empire Mag & Denver Post, 69; Susan E Meyer (ed), 20 Landscape Painters & How they Work, Watson-Guptill Publ, 80; Mary Carroll Nelson (auth), Masters of Western Painting, 82. *Mem:* Am Artists Prof League, New York. *Media:* Acrylic, Oil. *Dealer:* Woodrow Wilson Fine Arts 319 Read St Sante Fe NM 87501. *Mailing Add:* 4814 Guadalupe Tr NW Albuquerque NM 87107

PARRY, ELLWOOD COMLY, III
HISTORIAN
b Abington, Pa, Aug 9, 41. *Study:* Harvard Univ, AB, 64; Univ Calif, Los Angeles, MA, 66; Yale Univ, PhD, 70. *Teaching:* Asst prof, Dept Art Hist & Archaeol, Columbia Univ, 69-75; assoc prof, Sch Art & Art Hist, Univ Iowa, 76-81; prof, Dept Art, Univ Ariz, Tucson, 81- *Awards:* Nat Endowment Humanities Fel, 75-76; Huntington Libr Fel, 88. *Mem:* Col Art Asn; Asn Historians Am Art. *Res:* Iconography of American art and the interaction between 19th-century painting, the popular arts, photography, and science. *Publ:* Auth, The Image of the Indian and the Black Man in American Art, 1590-1900, George Braziller, 74; coauth, Reflections of 1776: The Colonies Revisited, Viking Studio, 74; auth, Thomas Eakins's "Naked Series" reconsidered: another look at the standing nude photographs made for the use of Eakins's students, Am Art Journal, vol 20, no 2, 88; The Art of Thomas Cole: Ambition and Imagination, Univ Del Press, 88. *Mailing Add:* Dept Art Univ Ariz Tucson AZ 85721

PARRY, MARIAN
ILLUSTRATOR, PRINTMAKER
b San Francisco, Calif, Jan 28, 24. *Study:* Univ Calif, BA, 46; Contemporaries Gallery, etching & lithography with Michael Ponce de Leon, stone engraving with Ben Shahn. *Work:* Houghton Libr, Harvard Univ, Cambridge, Mass; Metrop Mus Art Print Collection, New York; Smith Col Rare Bk Collection; Wellesley Col Rare Bk Collection; Univ Mass Rare Bk Collection, Northampton; Boston Mus Fine Arts Rare Bk Collection. *Exhib:* Boston Visual Artists Union, 74; Cambridge Art Asn; one-man show, Smith Col Rare Bk Rm, 77 & Wendell St Gallery, Cambridge; Los Angeles Inst of Contemp Art, 78. *Teaching:* Lectr, Radcliffe Sem Prog, 74- & Emmanuel Col, 74- *Awards:* Scholar, Radcliffe Inst, 65-67; Best Illus Bk Award for Birds of Basel, New York Times Bk Panel, 69; One of 50 Bks of the Yr (Birds of Basel), Am Inst of Graphic Arts, 69. *Mem:* Soc Children's Bk Writers; New England Authors & Illusrs Children's Bks; New England Poetry Soc. *Media:* Pen and Ink, Watercolor; Printmaking with Linoleum, Xerox Watercolor. *Publ:* Auth & illusr, Birds of Basel, Pharos Verlag, 67 & Knopf, 69; auth & illusr, Roger & the Devil, Knopf, 72; auth & illusr, King of the Fish, MacMillan, 77; auth & illusr, I Am a Big Help, Greenwillow, 80; illusr, The Education of a Mouse, Countryman Press, 83; and others. *Dealer:* Wendell Street Gallery 17 Wendell St Cambridge MA 02138; Galerie Caroline Corre 14 rue Guenegaud 75006 Paris France. *Mailing Add:* 60 Martin St Cambridge MA 02138

PARRY, PAMELA JEFFCOTT
LIBRARIAN, ADMINISTRATOR
b New York, NY, Mar 6, 48. *Study:* Univ Ariz, BA, 69; Columbia Univ, MA(art hist & archaeol), 71, MLS, 73. *Pos:* Asst fine arts librn, Columbia Univ, New York, 72-76; ed, Art Reference Collection, 78-82 & Art Doc, 82, 85-86; ed, Art Libr Soc NAm, 78-81, exec secy, 80-83, exec dir 83-; librn, Int Dada Arch, Univ Iowa, 79-81. *Mem:* Visual Resources Asn; Soc Am Archivists; Am Soc Assoc Execs; and others. *Publ:* Contribr, From Realism to Symbolism: Whistler and His World, Columbia Univ/Philadelphia Mus Art, 71; auth, Contemporary Art and Artists, 78, Photography Index, 79 & Print Index, 83, Greenwood Press. *Mailing Add:* 3775 Bear Creek Circle Tucson AZ 85749

PARSLEY, JACQUE (CARTER)
ASSEMBLAGE ARTIST, CURATOR
b Memphis, Tenn, Jan 10, 47. *Study:* Louisville Sch Art, BFA, 80; Univ Louisville, MA, 90. *Work:* Evansville Mus Arts & Sci, Ind; Alabama Power & Light, Huntsville; US Office Comptroller of Currency, Cincinnati, Ohio; Hillard Lyons Kentucky Art Collection, Louisville; Owensboro Mus Fine Art, Ky. *Comn:* Collage Assemblage, Home of the Innocents, Louisville, 88; many private commissions. *Exhib:* Eight State Ann, Speed Mus, Louisville, 77 & 85; Thread & Fiber, Alexandria Mus, La, 81; Soft as Silk, Wadsworth Antheneum, Hartford, Conn, 82; The Garden: New Form, New Function, Arrowment Sch Arts & Crafts, Tenn, 84; The Regionalists, Owensboro Mus, Ky, 85 & 89; Under a Foot, Galeria Mesa, Ariz, 88; Exhib 280 Works on Walls, Hunting Mus Art, WVa. *Collections Arranged:* 50 Local & Regional shows, Liberty Gallery, 80-92; Flowers & Gardens, Louisville Visual Art Asn, 83; Kentucky Baskets, Louisville Craftsman Guild, Kentucky Art & Craft Fedn, 85; Scholastic Art Awards, 85, 86, 87 & 90. *Pos:* Dir, Liberty Gallery, 80-, WHAS Gallery, 80-81. *Teaching:* Louisville Visual Art Asn, Water Tower. *Awards:* Merit Award, Water Tower Ann, Louisville Visual Art Asn, 84 & 89; Purchase Award, Mid-State Craft exhib, Evansville Mus, 88; First Place, Small Works National, Amos Eno Gallery, New York, 90; First Place, National Art Competition, 90. *Bibliog:* Jan Arnow (auth), Shared vision, Fiberarts Mag, 7-8/81; FMassie Meloy (auth), A new direction, Fiberarts Mag, 9/85. *Mem:* Kentucky Art & Craft Asn (bd dirs, 82-88); Louisville Visual Art Asn (bd dirs, 84-87); Am Crafts Coun, Ky (rep SE Region 86-); Surface Design Asn (Ky rep). *Media:* Collage, Mixed Media. *Publ:* Auth, Avalon Series, Fiberarts Mag, 82; Exposure, Surface Design J, winter 87; Art Papers, McGrath Art Gallery, 7-8/92. *Dealer:* Gayle Willson Gallery 16 Jobs Lane Southampton NY; Kentucky Art & Craft Gallery Louisville KY. *Mailing Add:* Liberty Gallery Liberty National Bank 416 W Jefferson Ave Louisville KY 40206

PARSONS, DAVID GOODE
SCULPTOR, EDUCATOR
b Gary, Ind, Mar 2, 11. *Study:* Chicago Art Inst, 30; Univ Wis, Experimental Col, BS, 34 & MS(art & art hist), 37. *Comn:* Birdforms, Moody Nat Bank, Galveston, Tex, 62-63; patterned brick for biology, geology & space sci bldgs, Rice Univ, 57-66; Large Cellist, Rice Univ, 74-75; Quartet, Rice Univ, 83; Ernest Bel Fay Mem, Houston, Tex, 88. *Exhib:* Am Sculpture, Carnegie Inst Int, 39; Am Exhib, Art Inst Chicago, 38-40; Six State Sculpture Exhib, Walker Art Ctr, Minneapolis, 45; Pa Acad Fine Arts Ann Exhib, 45; The Artist & His World, Denver Art Mus, Colo, 49; Houston Mus Fine Arts Ann, 53, 54 & 58; 11th Ann Midwest Exhib, Joslyn Art Mus, Omaha, Nebr, 67; one-man shows, Beaumont Mus, Tex, 53-67 & Witte Mus, 56; 50 Yr Retrospective Show, Bellaire City Hall, Tex, 82. *Pos:* Sculptor, Pub Works Art, 33-34, Fed Art Proj, Milwaukee, Wis, 38-42; sculptor & visual educ aid designer, US Army, Camp Lee, Va, 24-44; surgical artist asst in plastic surgery, Civil Serv US Army Valley Forge Gen Hospital, 44-47. *Teaching:* Dir mus sch, Denver Mus Art, Colo, 47-49; asst prof sculpture, drawing & ceramics, Bradley Univ, Peoria, Ill, 49-52; assoc prof sculpture, drawing & art educ, McNeese State Univ, Lake Charles, La, 52-53; prof sculpture & drawing, Rice Univ, Houston, 53-81, emer prof, 81- *Awards:* First in Sculpture, Va Biennial, Va Mus Art, Richmond, 42; Sculptor Award, Houston Mus Art Ann, 54; Mus Dir Award, Beaumont Regional, Beaumont Mus Art, Tex, 70. *Mem:* Col Art Asn Am; Tex Soc Sculptors (pres, Gulf Coast Sect, 75-76); Artists Fedn of Wis (pres, 40-42); Houston Munic Art Comn. *Media:* All Media. *Mailing Add:* 645 Mulberry Ln Bellaire TX 77401

PARSONS, MERRIBELL MADDUX
MUSEUM DIRECTOR, CURATOR
b San Antonio, Tex. *Study:* Newcomb Col, BFA; Ecole du Louvre, cert; Inst Fine Arts, NY Univ, MA; Metrop Mus & Inst Fine Arts, dipl (mus training). *Pos:* Bell Mem cur decorative arts, Minn Inst of Arts, 69-74, chief cur & cur sculpture & decorative arts, 74-79; chmn & curatorial liaison for educ, Metrop Mus Art, 79-80, vice dir, 80-87; dir, Columbus Mus Art, 87- *Teaching:* Adj prof, Inst Fine Arts, NY Univ, 80-87; adj prof, Ohio State Univ, 88- *Awards:* Longhi Fel; Ford Found Fel; Nat Endowment Arts Fel. *Mem:* Am Asn Mus; Asn Art Mus Dirs. *Res:* European sculpture, 1600-1900. *Publ:* Auth, Sculpture in the David Daniels Collection, Minn Inst Arts Bulletin, 69-74. *Mailing Add:* Columbus Mus of Art 480 E Broad St Columbus OH 43215

PARTIN, ROBERT
PAINTER, EDUCATOR
b Los Angeles, Calif, June 22, 27. *Study:* Univ Calif, Los Angeles, with Clinton Adams, Gordon Nunes & S Macdonald-Wright, BA, 50; Yale-Norfolk Art Sch, fel & study with Conrad Marca-Relli, 55; Columbia Univ, with Andre Racz, John Heliker, Meyer Shapiro, Paul Tillich, MFA, 56; Tamarind Lithography Workshop, Herron Art Sch, fel & study with Garo Antreasion, 63. *Work:* Solomon R Guggenheim Mus Art, New York; Jonson Gallery, Univ NMex; Weatherspoon Art Gallery, Univ NC. *Exhib:* Whitney Mus Am Art Ann, New York, 63; San Francisco Art Asn Centennial Exhib, De Young Mus, 71; Visual Poetics/Abstract Space, Calif State Univ, Los Angeles, 79; Stage One Gallery, Orange, Calif, 80; one-man show, Sherman Oaks, Calif, 81; Perceptions on Paper/A Visual Dialogue, Long Beach Gallery, Calif, 81; and others. *Teaching:* Assoc prof art, Univ NC, Greensboro, 57-66; vis assoc prof art, Univ NMex, 63-64; prof art, Calif State Univ, Fullerton, 66- *Awards:* Ford Found Purchase Prize, Whitney Mus Am Art Ann, 63; Purchase Prize, NC Mus Art Ann, 64 & 65; Purchase Award, Viewpoints Five, Colgate Univ, 71. *Bibliog:* Van Deren Coke (auth), Robert Partin, The Painter and The Photograph, 65; Robert Ewing (auth), Reticence clarified, Artweek, 4/80; Suzanne Muchnic (auth), The valley, Los Angeles Times, 1/81; and others. *Media:* Mixed. *Dealer:* Stage One Gallery 420 W Chapman Ave Orange CA 92666; Orlando Gallery 14553 Ventura Blvd Sherman Oaks CA 91403. *Mailing Add:* 380 Shasta Ave Morro Bay CA 93442

PARTON, NIKÉ
ENVIRONMENTAL ARTIST, PAINTER
b New York, NY, June 23, 22. *Study:* Ringling Sch Art, fine art cert; also sculpture with Lesley Posey & painting with Jay Connaway. *Work:* Univ Fla; Stetson Univ; S Fla Mus, Bradenton. *Exhib:* One-man shows, Sarasota Art Asn, 69; Art League of Manatee Co, 73; Beaux Arts Gallery, Pinellas Park, Fla, 80; Friends Art & Sci, Sarasota, Fla, 86; Golden Apple Gallery, Sarasota, Fla, 91; and others. *Teaching:* Instr painting, Art League Manatee Co, 54-74; instr pvt studio, 63- *Awards:* Second Prize, Fla Suncoast Watercolor Soc, 87; Second Prize Figure Show, Art League of Manatee Co, 87; Equal Award, Longboat Art Ctrs, 92. *Mem:* Fla Artist Group; Sarasota Art Asn; Art League of Manatee Co; Fla Suncoast Watercolor Soc; Longboat Key Art Ctrs, Fla. *Media:* Watercolor, All Media. *Dealer:* Art Uptown Inc 1367 Main St Sarasota FL 34236. *Mailing Add:* 840 Edgemere Lane Sarasota FL 34242

PARTON, RALF
SCULPTOR, EDUCATOR
b New York, NY, July 2, 32. *Study:* Albright Art Sch, Buffalo, dipl, 53; NY Univ Col Buffalo, BS(art educ), 54; Columbia Univ, MA(art), 55. *Work:* Civic Ctr, Turlock, Calif; City Hall, Turlock, Calif; Northwestern Mich Col Gallery, Traverse City, Mich; Our Lady of Fatima, Modesto, Calif. *Comn:* Tree of Life (steel sculpture), Beth Shalom Synagogue, Modesto, Calif, 79; and many pvt commissions. *Exhib:* one man show, Galerie de la Maison des Beaux-Arts, Paris, 82, Artists Forum, Los Angeles, Calif, 85; San Francisco Mus Art, San Francisco, Calif, 72; Art Fac Exhib, Calif State Col Stanislaus, Turlock, Calif, 73; Calif State Col Stanislaus Art Fac Exhib, Univ of the Pac, Calif, 76; McKissick Mus, Columbia, SC, 88. *Teaching:* Chmn dept painting & sculpture, Northwestern Mich Col, 58-62; prof sculpture, Calif State Univ, Stanislaus, 63-, chmn dept art, 63-70. *Awards:* Horohoe Prize Originality Sculpture, Sisti Gallery, Buffalo, NY, 57; Reynolds Prize Sculpture, Stockton Art Show, Calif, 66. *Bibliog:* David Otth (auth), Monoliths to miniatures, Toy Train Operating Soc Bulletin, Vol 2, No 2; Dr H Werness (auth), Calif Landscapes, catalog, 86. *Media:* Bronze, Vacuum Formed Styrene. *Mailing Add:* Dept Art Calif State-Stanislaus 800 W Monte Vista Ave Turlock CA 95380

PARTRIDGE, DAVID GERRY
PAINTER, SCULPTOR
b Akron, Ohio, Oct 5, 19; Can citizen. *Study:* Univ Toronto, BA; Queen's Univ, Kingston, Ont; Art Students League; Slade Sch, London; Atelier 17, Paris, with W S Hayter. *Work:* Tate Gallery, London; Nat Gallery Can, Ottawa; Libr Cong, Washington, DC; Art Gallery Ont, Toronto; Gallery NSW, Sydney, Australia. *Comn:* Nail murals, York Univ, Toronto, 70, Westminster Cathedral, London, 71 & foyer, Toronto City Hall, 77, Bell Trinity, Toronto, 83 & Can Capital Cong Ctr, Ottawa, 83; and others. *Exhib:* Montreal Mus Spring Show, 62; Int Print Exhib, Cincinnati, 62; Art of the Americas & Spain, Madrid & Barcelona, 63; Carnegie Int, Pittsburgh, 65; Sculpture '67, Toronto; Art Gallery Windsor, 79. *Teaching:* Art master, Ridley Col, St Catharines, Ont, 46-56; instr art, Queens Univ, Ont, summers 56-60 & Ont Col Art, 74-75. *Awards:* Brit Coun Scholar to Slade Sch, 50-51; Sculpture Prize & Purchase Award, Montreal Mus Fine Arts, 62. *Bibliog:* Alan Jarvis (auth), Configurations, Can Art, autumn 60; Charles S Spencer (auth), David Partridge's Nail Mosaics, Studio Int, 7/65; Kenneth Coutts-Smith (auth), David Partridge, Quadrum, 65. *Mem:* Fel Royal Soc Arts; Royal Can Acad. *Media:* Acrylic on Canvas; Wood, Nails. *Dealer:* Nancy Poole Studio 16 Hazleton Ave Toronto Ont Can. *Mailing Add:* 77 Seaton St Toronto ON M5A 2T2 Canada

PARTZ, FELIX (RON GABE)
PAINTER
b Winnipeg, Man, 45. *Study:* Univ Man Sch Fine Arts, 63-67. *Work:* Can Coun Art Bank & Nat Gallery Can, Ottawa; Ctr d'Art Contemporain, Geneva, Switz; Lucio Amelio Gallery, Naples, Italy; Mod Art Gallery, Vienna, Austria; Musée d'Art Contemporain, Montreal; Art Gallery Ont, Toronto. *Comn:* Ursa Major and Taurus: Pavilion Fragments from the Starry Vault, Toronto Stock Exchange, 83; Ottawa Courthouse, 86. *Exhib:* Nat Gallery Can, Ottawa, 88; 1988: The World of Art Today, Milwaukee Art Mus, 88; The Young and the Restless, Baltimore Mus Art, Md, 90; Language in Art, Aldrich Mus Contemp Art, Ridgefield, Conn, 90; The Art of Advocacy, Aldrich Mus Contemp Art, Ridgefield, Conn, 91; solo exhibs, Green (Permanent) Placebo, Galerie Daniel Buchholz, Cologne, Ger & Blanc Blanc Blanc, Kõlnischer Kunstverein, Cologne, Ger, 91, Blue (Cobalt) Placebo, Galerie Montenay, Paris, France, Magic Bullet, Stux Gallery, New York, Generic (Helium), Taormina Arte, Italy & Eldorado (Marscaibo), Galeria Fucares, Madrid, Spain, 92 & Fin dessiècle, touring Can, USA & Spain, 92-93; S L Simpson Gallery, Toronto, Can, 92; Wiener Fest Wochen, Vienna, Austria, 92; Transform, Kunsthalle Basel, Switz, 92; Stampa, Stampa Gallery, Basel, Switz, 92; From Media to Metaphor: Art About AIDS, travelling exhib, Can & US, 92-93; and others. *Awards:* Can Coun Grants, 68-92; Toronto Arts Award, 89. *Bibliog:* Norbert Messler (auth), General idea, Daniel Buchholz, Art forum, New York, 131, 2/92; Jutta Koether (auth), Exit art, Artscribe, London, 78-79, 3/92; Todd Roulette (auth), Ideal generals, QW, New York, 38-39, 5/17/92; and others. *Media:* Miscellaneous. *Publ:* Contribr, General Idea, 1968-1984, Stedelijk Van Abbemuseum, Eindhoven, 84; General Idea's Fin de siècle, 1992, Wurttembergischer Kunstverein, Stuttgart, Kunstverein Hamburg & Power Plant, Toronto. *Dealer:* Stux Gallery 163 Mercer St New York NY 10012. *Mailing Add:* S L Simpson Gallery 515 Queen St W Toronto ON M5V 2B4 Canada

PAS, GERARD PETER
PAINTER, SCULPTOR
b Valkenswaard, North Brabant, Neth; Can citizen. *Study:* H B Beal Tech Sch, London, Can, Spec Art, 73-74; assisted artist-inventor Murray Favro in Art Fabrication, independent study, 74; L'Abri, Eck En Wiel, Neth, independent study, 75-81. *Work:* De Appel, Amsterdam, Neth; Middelburg Archieven, Rotterdam, Neth; McIntosh Gallery, Univ Western Ont, London, Can; Ont Arts Coun, Toronto, Can; London Regional Art Gallery, Can. *Comn:* The Public Crutch in the Private House, Filmworks Inc, London, Can, 87. *Exhib:* This Is Information, Gallery T'Venster, Rotterdam, Neth, 80; Solo shows, Päs Plus-Päs Moins, Walter Phillip Gallery, Banff Ctr Arts, Can, 88 & Red-Blue Works, Mercer Union Ctr Contemp Arts, Toronto, 89; Hommage-Demontage, group show, Neve Galerie-Sammlung Ludwig, Aachen, Ger, 88-89; Hommage-Demontage, travelling exhib, Wilheim Hack Mus, Ludwigs Hafen, Ger, 88-89 & Mus Moderner Kunst, Vienna, Austria, 88-89; The Place of Work, travelling exhib, Royal Archit Inst Can, Winnipeg, 89-90. *Pos:* Mem bd dirs, Forest City Art Gallery, London, Can, 75-79 & Embassy Cult House, London, Can, 89-91; writer & critic, Art Zien Mag, Amsterdam, Neth, 78-79. *Teaching:* Lectr performance art, Academisch Kunst Institute, Enschede, Neth, 79; instr drawing figure, London Regional Art Gallery, Can, 86-88; prof drawing & painting, Redeemer Col, Ancaster, Can, 89- *Awards:* Travel Award, Ministry Cult Neth, 79; B Grant Award, Can Coun, 90; Proj Grant, Ont Arts Coun, 79. *Bibliog:* Dr Uli Bohnen (auth), Pas: Less & More-More of Less, McIntosh Gallery, V W O, Can, 87; Linda Genereux (auth), Toronto-Gerard Pas, Art Forum, New York, 89; Dr Graham Birtwistle (auth), Pas: The Modular Ambulant, Ctr Art Gallery-Calvin Col, 91. *Media:* Mixed. *Publ:* Contribr, L'Arte Di Gerard P Päs, Domus Mag, 88; The Living Meridian, Visual Aids London Life/AIDS Comt, 88; Typographie, Rotis Inst, Druckhaus Mack, 88; A Re-invented Object, Can Art, 90; Untitled Legs, Banner Publ, 91. *Mailing Add:* 631 Wallace St London ON N5Y 3R8 Canada

PASCAL, DAVID
PAINTER, CARTOONIST
b New York, NY, Aug 16, 18. *Study:* Am Artists Sch, with John Groth. *Work:* Swann collection; ITT: Sammlung Karikaturen & Cartoons, Basel, Switz. *Exhib:* One-man shows, Mus Art, Sao Paulo, Brazil, Mus Mod Art, Rio de Janeiro, Brazil, Graham Gallery, New York, 73, Man and His World, Montreal, 74 & Mus Art, Angouleme, France, 83; First Int Davos Cartoon Biennale, Davos, Switz. *Pos:* Ed, Graphis Mag, 72; artistic counr, bd dirs, Int Comics Cong, Lucca, Italy, 76; US rep, Fr Int Comics Cong, Angouleme, France; Secy Foreign Affairs, Nat Cartoonists Soc. *Teaching:* Instr graphic journalism, Sch Visual Arts, 55-58. *Awards:* Dattero D'Oro, Salone Int dell Umorismo, Italy, 63; Award for Illus Excellence, Nat Cartoonists Soc, 69 & 77, Silver T-Square, 72. *Bibliog:* Sergio Trinchero (auth), Visit to funland, Sgt Kirk Mag, 68; Rinaldo Traini (auth), Incontro con David Pascal (slide prog), Immagine, 3/15/69; Claude Moliterni (auth), David Pascal, Phoenix Mag, 70. *Mem:* Nat Cartoonists Soc; Cartoonists Asn; Int Comics Orgn. *Media:* Acrylic, Oil; Ink. *Publ:* Illusr, Fifteen Fables of Krylov, 65; auth & illusr, The Silly Knight, 67; ed & auth, comics: The Art of the Comic Strip, Graphis Press, Switz, 72; Goofus, Paris, 75; auth & illusr, Perspectives, Paris, 85. *Dealer:* Graham Gallery 1014 Madison Ave New York NY 10024. *Mailing Add:* 133 Wooster St New York NY 10012

PASCHALL, JO ANNE
PRINTMAKER, LIBRARIAN
b Murray, Ky, Mar 9, 49. *Study:* Memphis State Univ, BFA, 71; Univ GA, MFA, 74; Art Studies Abroad, Cortona, Italy, Dodd-Carnegie scholar, 73-74; Univ Ala, 76-77; Atlanta Univ, MLS, 81. *Work:* Huntsville Mus Art, Ala; Memphis State Univ Collection; Univ Ga Collection. *Exhib:* Eleven Printmakers, Southeastern Ctr Contemp Art, Winston-Salem, NC; Invitational Exhib, Atlanta Artworkers Coalition Gallery, Ga; Invitational Print Exhib, Huntsville Mus Art, Ala; one-person exhib, Memorabilia, Univ Ala Gallery, Huntsville; Inst Prof Femminnile di Stato Gino Severini, da Cortona, Italy. *Pos:* Grad asst printmaking, Univ Ga Art Dept, 73-74; intern, Art for Exceptional Children, Ga Retardation Ctr, 77; cur, Visual Collections, Atlanta Col Art Libr, 78-79, head librn, 79-86; orgn consult, High Mus Art, 83-85; asst dir, Nexus Press, 86- *Teaching:* Assoc instr printmaking, Art Studies Abroad, Cortona, Italy, 74; div head printmaking dept, Univ Ala, Huntsville, 75-77 & Atlanta Col Art, 80-85. *Awards:* Third Place, painting, Tenn All-Artists Exhib, Nashville, 71; Special Purchase Award, Inst Prof Femminnile di Stato Gino Severini da Cortona, Italy, 74. *Mem:* Art Libr Soc NAm; Anarchist Librns Group Am. *Media:* All Media. *Interests:* 20th century; contemporary issues; artists books and publications, bookworks; developed the Atlanta Col Art artists books collection. *Publ:* Contribr, Macmillan Encycl Archits, Macmillan Publ Co, 82. *Dealer:* Heath Gallery 416 E Paces Ferry Atlanta GA 30305. *Mailing Add:* 733 Sherwood Rd Atlanta GA 30324

PASCHKE, EDWARD F (ED)
PAINTER
b Chicago, Ill, June 22, 39. *Study:* Art Inst Chicago, BFA(Raymond Fel), 61 & MFA(Ponte del Arte Fel), 70. *Work:* Art Inst Chicago; Mus Contemp Art, Chicago; Mus Boymans, Rotterdam; Musee d'Art Moderne Nationale, Paris; Baltimore Art Mus, Md; and many others. *Exhib:* Soc for Contemp Art, Art Inst Chicago, 70-72; Whitney Annuals, Whitney Mus Am Art, New York, 72-74 & Biennial Contemp Am Art, 73; Made in Chicago, Mus Contemp Art, Chicago, Mexico City & Washington, DC, 74 & 75 & View of a Decade, 77; Am Show, Art Inst Chicago, 74; Nat Collection of Fine Arts, Washington, DC, 75; Ed Paschke Retrospective, Contemp Art Ctr, Cincinnati, Ohio, 75; one-man shows, Whitney Mus Am Art, Brooklyn Mus, Metrop Mus Art, New York, 86 & Ripon Col, Caestecker Gallery, Ripon, Wis, 92; Focus on Ed Paschke, Turman Gallery, Indiana State Univ, Terre Haute, 91; From America's Studio: Twelve Contemporary Masters, Art Inst Chicago, 92. *Teaching:* Instr painting, Art Inst Chicago, 74-76; instr painting, Columbia Col, Chicago, Ill, 76-78; prof drawing, Northwestern Univ, Evanston, Ill, 77- *Awards:* Cassandra Grant, Cassandra Found, 72; Logan Medal, Art Inst Chicago, 73. *Bibliog:* Barry Schwartz (auth), Humanism in 20th Century American Art, Praeger, 72; Sheldon Williams (auth), Made in Chicago, Art & Artists, 75; Peter Schjeldahl (auth), Letter from Chicago, Art in Am, 76; and others. *Media:* Oil; Pencil. *Dealer:* Phyllis Kind Gallery 226 E Ontario Chicago IL 60611. *Mailing Add:* 6129 N Killburn Chicago IL 60646

PASHGIAN, M HELEN
PAINTER, SCULPTOR
b Pasadena, Calif. *Study:* Pomona Col, BA; Columbia Univ; Boston Univ, MA(fine arts). *Work:* Andrew Dickson White Mus Art, Cornell Univ; Security Pac Bank, Los Angeles & Singapore; Seattle First Nat Bank, Wash; Atlantic Richfield Co, Dallas, Tex. *Comn:* painting, Home Savings & Loan World Hq, Irwindale, Calif, 88. *Exhib:* Solo exhibs, Kornblee Gallery, New York, 69-72, Univ Calif, Irvine, 76, Stella Polaris Gallery, Los Angeles, 81, Kaufman Galleries, Houston, 82, Modernism Gallery, San Francisco, 83, The Works Gallery, Long Beach, Calif, 87-88 & The Works Gallery South, Costa Mesa, Calif, 90; San Francisco Mus Art, 69-70; A Plastici Presence, Milwaukee Art Ctr, 69-70; Welton Beckett, Architects, 84; Selections from Security Pacific Bank Collection, Laguna Art Mus, 87; Town Hall, Paris, France, 88; Hotel de Ville Mus, Paris, France, 89; and others. *Pos:* Trustee, Pomona Col, Claremont, Calif, life-term. *Awards:* Fel, Nat Endowment Arts, 86. *Bibliog:* Mueller, Gaye Ann (auth), Cast Resin Sculpture: Five Los Angeles Artists, 1965-1972, Calif State Univ, 79; Melinda Wortz (auth), Blowing in the wind, Art News, 3/82; Merle Schipper (auth), Light/energy/radiance: the epoxy paintings of Helen Pashgian, Images & Issues, spring 82; and others. *Media:* Miscellaneous Media; Plastic. *Mailing Add:* c/o Charles J Pollyea & Assoc 445 S Beverly Dr Beverly Hills CA 90212

PASINSKI, IRENE
PAINTER, SCULPTOR
b Pittsburgh, Pa, Oct 14, 23. *Study:* Carnegie-Mellon Univ, BFA, 45; Ecole du Louvre & Inst d'Art Applique a l'Industrie, cert, 51. *Work:* Chase Manhattan Bank, New York; WVa Univ Collection, Morgantown; Pittsburgh Bd Educ, Univ Pittsburgh, Nat Steel Co & Westinghouse Corp, Pittsburgh. *Comn:* Scene design & costume, Steel City Symphony, Pittsburgh Ballet Co, 76; poster, Poetry on the Buses, Pa Coun on Arts, 76; plexiglass wall mural, Westinghouse Credit Corp, Pittsburgh, 79; mall sculptures, Youngstown, Ohio, 81 & Melbourne & Miami Fla, 83; scene design, Don Juan, 86. *Exhib:* Carnegie Inst, 44-79; Albright-Knox Gallery, 57; Inst Contemp Crafts, New York, 57; Butler Inst Am Art, 62 & 77; Silvermine Guild Ann, New Canaan, Conn, 63; Westmoreland Co Mus Art, 64-78; New Glass, Corning Mus, NY, 79. *Pos:* Indust designer 7 head, Irene Pasinski Assoc, currently. *Teaching:* Instr fundamentals of design, Carnegie-Mellon Inst, Pittsburgh, 68-73. *Awards:* Outstanding Work, Assoc Artists of Pittsburgh, 47-50, 70 & 72; Purchase Award, Erie Art Ctr Ann, 69; Best of Show, Pa Sculpture Exhib, Southern Alleghenies Mus Art, Loretto, Pa, 77. *Mem:* Assoc Artists Pittsburgh; Western Pa Soc Sculptors; Indust Designers Soc Am; Pittsburgh Art Comn. *Media:* Mixed. *Mailing Add:* 6026 Penn Circle S Pittsburgh PA 15206

PASKEWITZ, BILL, JR
PAINTER, EDUCATOR
b Brooklyn, NY, Aug 5, 53. *Study:* Cooper Union, with Deborah Remington, BFA, 75; Queens Col, City Univ, New York, with Louis Finkelstein, MFA, 78. *Work:* KUB Res, Irvine, Calif; also pvt collections of Mr & Mrs Herbert Brownell, Laguna Beach, Calif, Mr James Rush, New York, NY, Dr & Mrs Michael Moses, Newport Beach & Mr Jules Marine, Newport Beach, Calif. *Comn:* Mural, comn by Henry Seger Strom, Costa Mesa, Calif, 86. *Exhib:* Solo exhibs, Contemp Art Gallery, New York, 72, Jacques Seligmann, New York, 78, West Coast Gallery, Newport, Calif, 80, James Turcotte Gallery, Los Angeles, 84 & Orange Coast Col, Costa Mesa, Calif, 87; New York Painters, Columbus Mus Art, Ohio, 78; Art in Orange County, Newport Harbor, Newport Beach, Calif, 79. *Pos:* Dir, Art Squad, Bayside, NY, 73-75. *Teaching:* Instr printmaking, Newport Harbor Art Mus, 79-81; instr painting, Irvine Valley Col, Irvine, Calif, 79-; adj lectr fine arts, Golden West Col, Huntington Beach, 80-; Visual Arts Dept coord & instr painting, drawing, art hist & art appreciation, Las Positas Col, Livermore, Calif, currently. *Awards:* Harvey Medal, 71, Sch Art League; Gold Metal Scholastic Award in Printmaking, 72; Anna E Meltzer Soc Award for Creativity in Painting, 75. *Bibliog:* Barbara Cavaliere (auth), Newcomers, 9/77 & Bill Paskewitz, 9/78, Arts Mag; Ralph Bond (auth), Texture image diversity, Artweek, 81. *Mem:* Col Art Asn Am. *Media:* Acrylic, Pastel. *Publ:* Auth, Art connections, Orange County Arts Comn, 74; Art in Orange County, Newport Harbor Art Mus, 79; Carving out an artistic lifestyle, Branding Iron, 4/12/84; The why and how of making your own pastels, Inksmith, 9/85. *Dealer:* The Barlett Gallery 163 W Neal St Pleasanton CA 94566. *Mailing Add:* 1715 Freeport Court Oakley CA 94561

PASQUINE, RUTH
CURATOR
b Newark, NJ, Jan 21, 48. *Study:* Franconia Col, BA; Clark Art Inst, MA, Grad Ctr City Univ NY. *Pos:* Res asst, Nat Acad Design, New York, 86-89; cur educ, Norton Art Gallery, West Palm Beach, 89-91; cur collections, Ark Arts Ctr Little Rock, 91- *Mem:* Am Asn Mus; CAA. *Res:* American art, 20th century. *Mailing Add:* c/o The Arkansas Arts Ctr PO Box 2137 Little Rock AR 72203

PASSANTINO, GEORGE CHRISTOPHER
PAINTER, INSTRUCTOR
b New York, NY. *Study:* Art Students League, 48-53. *Work:* Adelphi Univ, Garden City, NY. *Exhib:* Conn Acad Fine Arts, Wadsworth Antheneum, Hartford, 75-76; Audubon Artists, Nat Acad, New York, 76; 49th Ann Exhib, Hudson Valley Art Asn, White Plains, NY, 77. *Teaching:* Instr drawing, painting & compos, Famous Artists Sch, Westport, Conn, 57-63, supervisor, 63-74; instr, Univ Bridgeport, Conn, 74-75; instr drawing & painting, Art Students League, 78- *Awards:* Charles Noel Flagg Mem Prize, Conn Acad Fine Arts, 76. *Mem:* Life mem Art Students League; Allied Artists Am. *Media:* Oil, Watercolor. *Publ:* Coauth, Six artists paint a portrait, Northlight, 74; The Portrait and Figure Painting Book, Watson-Guptill, 79. *Dealer:* Portraits Inc 985 Park Ave New York NY 10022; Portrait Brokers of America 36B Church St Birmingham, Al. *Mailing Add:* 30 Rising Ridge Rd Ridgefield CT 06877

PASSLOF, PAT
PAINTER, EDUCATOR
b Brunswick, Ga. *Study:* Queens Col, 46-48, Black Mountain Col, 48; studied with Willem de Kooning, 48-50; Cranbrook Acad Art, BFA, 52. *Work:* Milwaukee Art Ctr & Mus; Corcoran Mus, Washington, DC; Ciba Geigy Collection, Ardsley, NY; Birla Mus, Calcutta, India; Mrs Harry Lynde Bradley Collection. *Exhib:* Art USA, New York Coliseum, 57; Carnegie Int, Pittsburgh, 58; This Is Not Here, Everson Mus, Syracuse, 73; Women in the Arts, NY Cultural Ctr, 73; Works on Paper-WIA, Brooklyn Mus, 75; Abstract Painting 1960-1969, PS 1, Long Island City, NY, 83; The Gathering of the Avant-Garde, Kenkeleba Gallery, New York, 85; Naked Paint, New House Gallery, Snug Harbor Cultural Ctr, Staten Island, NY, 85; Jack Tilton Gallery, New York, 89. *Teaching:* Prof art, Col Staten Island, City Univ New York, 72- & State Univ NY, New Paltz, 73-74. *Bibliog:* Donald Judd (auth), Complete Writings 1959-75, New York Univ Press, 11/75; Al Brunelle (auth), Pat Passlof, Art in Am, 12/78. *Media:* Oil on Canvas. *Publ:* Auth, Artist's statement, Artforum, 9/75; Gretna Campbell, 4/76 & Claire Moore, 12/78, Arts; Nostalgia, Issue 5, winter 86. *Dealer:* Tilton Gallery 24 W 57th St New York NY. *Mailing Add:* 80 Forsyth St New York NY 10002

PASSUNTINO, PETER ZACCARIA
PAINTER, PRINTMAKER
b Chicago, Ill, Feb 18, 36. *Study:* Art Inst Chicago, scholar, 54-58; Oxbow Sch Painting, Mich, summer 58; Inst Art Archeol, Paris, 63-65. *Work:* Walter P Chrysler Mus; Hirshhorn Mus, Washington, DC; Norfolk Mus, Va; Titan Steel Corp; Provincetown Art Asn & Mus; also pvt collections of Joseph H Hirshborn, Walter P Chrysler, Henry Geldzahler and others. *Exhib:* Art Inst Chicago, Ill, 57; Corcoran Gallery Art, Washington, DC, 74; one-man exhibs, Gallery K, Washington, DC, 77, Art Latitude, New York, 79, The White Room, Belg, 81, Yvonne Séguy Gallery, New York, 82 & 84, Fordham Univ at Lincoln Ctr, New York, 86, Terne Gallery, New York, 86 & Pike Street Art Ctr, Pt Jervis, NY, 91; AIR Invitational Exhib, New York, 83-84; Trisolini Gallery, Ohio Univ, Athens, 84; Expressionism an American Beginning, Provincetown Art Asn & Mus, RI, 85; Kisker Gallery, Scottsdale, Ariz, 86; Daedal Fine Arts, Fallstown, Md, 88; Frankel Estate, Mus Contemp Art, Chicago, Ill, 88. *Pos:* Chmn, Momentum, Chicago, 57-58. *Teaching:* Instr Rutgers-Livingston Col, Bayonne Jewish Community Ctr, NJ & Greenwich Art Soc, Conn. *Awards:* Fulbright Fel, 63-64; Guggenheim Fel in Graphics,

71; Nat Endowment Arts Grant, 83. *Bibliog:* Articles in Art News, summer 76 & 9/84, Art in America, 5/75 & 9/84, Soho News, 4/76 & 3/79, Arts Mag, 3/76 & 6/76. *Dealer:* Terne Gallery 38 E 57th St New York. *Mailing Add:* 530 La Guardia Pl New York NY 10012

PATERNOSTO, CESAR PEDRO
PAINTER
b La Plata, Buenos Aires, Arg, Nov 29, 31; US citizen. *Study:* Nat Univ La Plata, Sch Fine Arts, 57-59, Inst Philos, 61. *Work:* Mus Mod Art, New York; Nat Fine Arts Mus, Buenos Aires; Plastic Arts Mus, La Plata; Albright-Knox Gallery, Buffalo; Hirshhorn Mus, Washington, DC; and others. *Exhib:* Latin American Art Since Independence, Yale Univ, Conn, 65; 3rd Biennial Am Art, Cordoba, Arg, 66; The 1960's, Mus Mod Art, New York, 67; 2nd Biennial Coltejer, Medellin, Colombia, 70; one-man shows, Dusseldorf, WGer, 72, New York, 73, Paris, 74 & Tokyo, 82; and others. *Awards:* First Prize, 3rd Biennial Am Art, Cordoba, 66; Acquisition Award, 15th Exhib, Mar Del Plata, Arg, 66; Guggenheim Fel Painting, 72. *Bibliog:* Sam Hunter (auth), The Cordoba biennial, Art Am, 4/67; J R Mellow (auth), New York letter, Art Int, 11/68; Lucy R Lippard, Overlay, 83. *Media:* Acrylic & Oil on Canvas. *Publ:* Auth, Piedra Abstracta, Mexico-Buenos Aires, 89. *Mailing Add:* 135 Hudson St New York NY 10013

PATERSON, ANTHONY R
SCULPTOR, EDUCATOR
b Albany, NY, Dec 17, 34. *Study:* Sch of Mus Fine Arts, Boston, dipl & grad dipl; study with Harold Tovish, Ernest Morenon, Peter Abate; La Grande Chaumiere Sch Drawing, Paris; Mass Inst Technol, welding; Univ Guadalajara, Mex. *Work:* Rose Art Mus, Brandeis Univ, Waltham, Mass; Univ Art Gallery, Univ Pittsburgh, Pa; State Univ NY, Buffalo; San Bernardino Fine Arts Mus, Calif. *Comn:* Portrait of Seymour H Knox (bronze torso), comn by Buffalo Found, 78-79; life-size portrait of Charles Darwin, Centennial Conf on Darwin, 82. *Exhib:* NAm Sculpture Exhib, Denver, Colo, 86, 88 & 90; Dimensions 88--3D Art Show, Lenexa Ann Nat, Kans, 86, 88 & 90; 63rd Ann Nat Exhib, Nat Acad Design, New York, 88; solo exhib, Andrews Gallery, William & Mary Col, Williamsburg, Va, 88; Metal Media, Sawtooth Ctr Visual Arts, Winston-Salem, NC, 90; and others. *Teaching:* Instr sculpture, Sch Mus Fine Arts, Boston, 62-65 & Mt Ida Jr Col, Newton, Mass, 64-68; assoc prof sculpture, State Univ NY, Buffalo, 68-86. *Awards:* Festival Award, Three Rivers Art Nat Festival, 89 & 90; Elliot Lisken Award for Sculpture, Audubon Artists Nat Soc, 89; Acad Artist Asn Nat Award, Springfield, Mass, 90. *Mem:* Artists Comt, Buffalo. *Media:* Metal, Cast. *Mailing Add:* 530 Norwood Ave Buffalo NY 14222

PATKIN, IZHAR
PAINTER, SCULPTOR
b Israel, 1955, US citizen. *Study:* Corcoran Sch Art, Washington, DC, BFA, 79; Whitney Independent Study Prog, New York. *Work:* Mus Mod Art, New York; Contemp Mus, Honolulu, HI; Brooklyn Mus, New York; Whitney Mus, NY; Palais Liechtenstein, Vienna. *Comn:* Don Quixote (monument), VMS, New York, 88. *Exhib:* Back to USA (travelling exhib), Kunstverein, Stuttgart, Rheinche Landmuseum, Bonn, Kunst Mus, Lucern, 84; Whitney Biennial 1987, Whitney Mus, New York, 87; Art Space, San Francisco; Yokohama Mus Art, Japan, 89; solo exhibs, Holly Solomon Gallery, New York, 83-85, 87 & 89-90, Winnipeg Art Mus, Manitoba, Can, 88, John & Mable Ringling Mus Art, Sarasota, Fla, 89, Stedelijk Mus, Amsterdam, 90 & Venice Bianale, 90. *Teaching:* Sch Visual Arts, New York. *Awards:* Fel, Nat Endowment Arts, 87. *Bibliog:* Herbert Muschamp (auth), Narrative Painting, Limbo, New York, 86; Pedro Cuperman (auth), Go East by Going West, Carla Sozzan: Editore, Milan, 90; Izhar Patkin (auth), Stedelijk Mus Catalog, 90. *Media:* Acrylic, Oil; All. *Dealer:* Holly Solomon 724 Fifth Ave New York NY 10019. *Mailing Add:* 154-156 Ludlow St New York NY 10002

PATMAGRIAN, ETHELIA M
SCULPTOR, PAINTER
Study: Art Inst Chicago, 44-54. *Work:* Stone Piece, Mitchell Col, New London, Conn, 89. *Comn:* John Lodge Bust (bronze), Alderson Broaddus Col, Philippi, WVa, 87; Commemorative piece (stone), First Congregational United Church of Christ, Sarasota, Fla, 88; Font Sculpture (bronze), St Vincent de Paul Church, Holiday, Fla, 88; Sarasota Opera House (bronze), Fla, 90; exterior archet/concrete piece, Sarasota Opera, 91; and others. *Exhib:* Spring Invitational, Longboat Key Art Ctr, Sarasota, 82; one-woman show, Voorhees Gallery, Sarasota, Fla; Contemp Women Artists, Brinewater Art Ctr, Rosendale, New York. *Teaching:* Owner & instr painting & sculpture, Chicago Fine Arts Ctr, 60-68; chmn basic studies & instr advan sculpture, Ringling Sch Art & Design, Sarasota, 70-90, instr figure painting, 90- *Media:* Bronze, Stone, Steel. *Dealer:* Voorhes Gallery 1359 Main St Sarasota FL 33577; Florida Global Gallery Airport Tampa FL. *Mailing Add:* 3181 Hatton St Sarasota FL 33577

PATNODE, J SCOTT
EDUCATOR, GALLERY DIRECTOR
b Seattle, Wash, Oct 19, 45. *Study:* Gonzaga Univ, AB, 68; Pratt Inst, fel, 68, MFA, 70; also with George McNeil, Walter Rogalski & Clare Romano. *Work:* Cheney Cowles Mem Mus, Spokane; Kalamazoo Inst Arts, Mich; Evergreen State Col, Olympia, Wash; Pac Nat Bank of Wash, Seattle; Honolulu Acad Art, Hawaii. *Exhib:* Hawaii Nat Print Exhib, Honolulu Acad Art, 71 & 73; CCAC World Print Competition, San Francisco Art Mus, 73; New Generation Drawings Exhib, circulated by Western Asn Art Mus, 73-75; 59th Ann Exhib Northwest Artists, Seattle Art Mus, 74; Gov Invitational, 78; Northwest Juried Art, 83; Cheney Cowles Mem Mus, Spokane, Wash, 83. *Pos:* Dir, Ad Art Gallery, Gonzaga Univ, 71- *Teaching:* Prof art, Gonzaga Univ, 70-, chmn dept art, 79-82. *Awards:* Print Purchase Award, Honolulu Acad Art, 71; Fremont Lane South Award for Painting, Spokane Art Mus, 72. *Mem:* Am Asn Mus. *Mailing Add:* Dept Art Gonzaga Univ East 502 Boone Ave Spokane WA 99258-0001

PATRICK, ALAN K
CERAMIST, PAINTER
b Richmond, Ind, June 16, 42. *Study:* Ball State Univ, with Byron Temple, BS, 64, MA, 66. *Work:* Ball State Univ Art Gallery; Earlham Col & Richmond Art Asn Gallery, Richmond, Ind; Minnetrista Cul Ctr, Muncie, Ind; City of Muncie, Ind. *Exhib:* Functional Pottery, Wooster Col, Ohio, 87; The Gallery, Bloomington, Ind, 88; Minnetrista Ann, Muncie, Ind, 90, 91 & 92; Art Forms 90, Lafayette, Ind; Ball State Univ Art Gallery, 90; Hoosier Salon, Indianapolis, Ind, 90, 91 & 92; Ind Artist Club Juried Exhib, Indianapolis, 92. *Awards:* Best of Show, Hoosier Salon, Indianapolis, Ind, 91-; 2nd Place, Minnetrista Regional Exhib, Muncie, Ind, 91-; Best Landscape, Hoosier Salon, Indianapolis, Ind, 92- *Bibliog:* Ruth Chin (auth), Bethel Pike Potters, Ceramics Mo, 74; Kathleen R Postle (auth), Bethel Pike Pottery, Spinning Wheel, 6/79; Gerry Williams (auth), Conversations with Indiana Potters, Studio Potter 19:2, 6/91. *Mem:* Ind Artist-Craftsmen; Ind Potters Guild; Ind Artists Club. *Media:* Stoneware, Porcelain; Oil. *Mailing Add:* Rt 1 Box 80-B Albany IN 47320

PATRICK, CHARLES WILLIAM
CONCEPTUAL ARTIST, WRITER
b Indianapolis, Ind, Feb 20, 37. *Study:* Purdue Univ, BA; Art Students League, New York; John Herron Art Inst, Indianapolis; Sch Visual Arts, New York, 53-59; Harvard Univ, MBA, 57; Univ Geneva, Switz, PhD, 66. *Work:* Carnegie Endowment Int Peace, New York; Rutgers Univ, New Brunswick; New York Univ; Univ PR, San Juan; George Washington Univ, DC. *Comn:* Performance with Color Poems (film), Nat Endowment Arts, Washington, DC, 79; Art in America (film), Nat Film Inst, Washington, DC, 83. *Exhib:* Group shows, Walker St Gallery, Craftmans Gallery & Azuma Gallery, New York, 74; Aames Gallery, New York, 75 & 76; Letter Poem, New York Univ, New York, 76; Words & Images, Smithsonian Inst, DC, 76-77; Learning to Read Through the Arts, Guggenheim Mus, New York, 77. *Pos:* Consult, Nat Endowment Arts, 77-79; fel, Ctr for Advan Visual Studies, Smithsonian Inst/Mass Inst Technol Centerbeam Proj, 78; consult, Am Inst Architects Found, 78 & Washington DC Slide Registry for the Visual Arts, 78-79. *Teaching:* Lectr art in Am, Harvard Univ Club, New York, Am Univ & others, 77-83; lectr visual arts & poetry, Va Poetry Soc, Univ Va, Rutgers Univ, Harvard Club & others, 77-83. *Awards:* Nat Endowment Arts Special Proj Grant, Performances with Color Poems, 79. *Bibliog:* Leslie Jacobson (auth, text) & Pat Mollela (auth, film), Color Poems in the Dramatic Arts, Nat Endowment Arts, 80. *Mem:* Artists Equity Asn; Cult Alliance Washington DC. *Media:* Acrylic, Collage. *Publ:* Auth, Art in America--The Great Happening, pvt publ, 78; New Forms of Poetry in the Visual Arts, George Washington Univ, 79; Public Poem About America, Libr Cong, 80. *Mailing Add:* 1214 Lyndale Dr Alexandria VA 22308

PATRICK, DARRYL L
HISTORIAN
b Havre, Mont, Oct 5, 36. *Study:* Northern Mont Col, BS, 62; Univ Wash, MA, 70; N Tex State Univ, PhD, 78. *Teaching:* Instr art hist, Factory of Visual Arts, Seattle, Wash, 69-71; Assoc prof, Sam Houston State Univ, Huntsville, Tex, 71-79, dir dept art, 78-84, asst prof, 79-80 & prof, 91- *Mem:* Col Art Asn; Nat Coun Art Adminr. *Res:* Late 19th Century Europe, 19th & 20th Century Am Art. *Publ:* Auth, Pop Art, In: Popular Culture & Libr, Scarecrow Publ, 85. *Mailing Add:* Dept Art Sam Houston State Univ Huntsville TX 77340

PATRICK, GENIE HUDSON
PAINTER, INSTRUCTOR
b Fayetteville, Ark, Nov 25, 38. *Study:* Miss State Col Women, 56-58; Univ Ga, BFA, 60; Univ Ill, Urbana-Champaign, 60-61; Univ Colo, MA, 62. *Exhib:* Walker Ann, Minneapolis, 66; Mid-Miss Invitational, Davenport Munic Art Gallery, 79; two-man exhib, Drawing & Painting, Coe Col Galleries, Cedar Rapids, Iowa, 71, Laura Musser Mus, Muscatine, Iowa, 72 & 77, Fine Art Ctr, Univ Mo-Columbia, 75 & Myers Fine Art Gallery, State Univ NY, Plattsburgh, 76; and others. *Pos:* Fel-in-Residence, Huntington Hartford Found, Pacific Palisades, Calif, summer 64. *Teaching:* Instr art, Northeast Miss Jr Col, Booneville, 62-64; instr art, Radford Col, Va, 64-65; instr children's art classes, Cedar Rapids Art Ctr, Iowa, 65-70; instr drawing & painting, Univ Iowa Exten, 74-, instr drawing, Sch Art & Art Hist, Univ Iowa, Iowa City, 74 & 80. *Media:* Oil, Drawing. *Mailing Add:* 1190 E Court St Iowa City IA 52240

PATRICK, JOSEPH ALEXANDER
PAINTER, EDUCATOR
b Chester, SC, Feb 10, 38. *Study:* Univ Ga, BFA, 60; Univ Colo, Boulder, MFA, 62. *Work:* Keokuk Art Asn, Iowa; Luther Col, Iowa; SDak Mem Art Ctr, Brookings; Laura Musser Mus, Muscatine, Iowa; Univ Mo Alumni Collection, Columbia. *Exhib:* One-man shows, Augustana Col, SDak, 72, Univ Iowa Mus Art, 73, Iowa State Univ Design Ctr, Ames, 74, Kans State Univ, Manhattan, 75, Northwest Mo State Univ, Maryville, 77 & Friends Gallery, Minneapolis Inst Arts, Minn, 77; and others. *Pos:* Mus asst, Univ Ga Mus Art, Athens, 58-60. *Teaching:* Asst art, Univ Colo, Boulder, 60-62, instr drawing & painting, 61-62; instr & head dept, Northeast Miss Jr Col, Booneville, 62-64; instr, Radford Col, 64-65; instr, Univ Iowa, 65-68, asst prof drawing & painting, 68-71, assoc prof drawing, 71, head dept drawing, 79- *Awards:* Residence Fel, Huntington Hartford Found, 64; Summer Fac Fel, 69 & Fac Grants, 73, 77 & 78-79, Univ Iowa Found. *Mem:* Mid-Am Art Asn; Col Art Asn Am. *Media:* Oil, Watercolor. *Mailing Add:* Dept Art & Art Hist Rm W205 AB Univ Iowa Iowa City IA 52242

PATTERSON, CLAYTON IAN
SCULPTOR, VIDEO ARTIST
b Calgary, Alta, Can, Oct 9, 48. *Study:* Univ Alta, BEd, 73; Nova Scotia Col Art, BFA, 77. *Work:* Brooklyn Mus, NY; New York Pub Libr; Libr Cong, Washington, DC; Rutgers Mus, New Brunswick, NJ; Flint Mus, Mich; Matt Dillon, also pvt collections of Mick Jagger & Jack Nicholson. *Exhib:* Staff Show, Atla Col Art, 78; Sacred Artifacts and Objects of Devotion, Alternative Mus, New York, 82; Works on Paper, NC Mus, Greenville, 84; Australian Invitational Traveling Print Show, 84-85; Works on Paper, Bronx Mus, 85; Tiffany Collection, Brooklyn Mus, 85; Beauty and the Beast, Pratt Inst, NY, 85; Am Collections Private and Public, Brooklyn Mus, 86. *Pos:* Tattoo Soc New York (pres). *Teaching:* Instr art, Alta Col Art, 78. *Awards:* Philadelphia Print Club, 84; Justice Orgn Award, 92; Manhattan Cable Access Awards, 92. *Bibliog:* Eric Shawn (auth), Blow up!, Fame Mag, 89; Richard Merkin (auth), The discreet charm of the baseball cap, Gentleman's Quart, 89; Mark Rose (auth), Top hat, New York Press, 91. *Media:* All. *Publ:* Lower East Side, New York (video), 87-88; Tompkin Square Park Police Riot (video), 88. *Dealer:* Arborite Art 161 Essex St New York NY 10002. *Mailing Add:* PO Box 103 Prince St Sta New York NY 10012-0103

PATTERSON, CURTIS RAY
SCULPTOR, INSTRUCTOR
b Shreveport, La, Nov 11, 44. *Study:* Grambling State Univ, BS, 67; Ga State Univ, MVA, 75. *Comn:* Coretin steel, Bur Cult & Int Affairs, 77; mild steel, Atlanta Rapid Transit Authority, 78. *Exhib:* Thirty-five Artists in the SE (contribr, catalog), High Mus Art, Atlanta, Ga, 76; 35 Artists in the SE Traveling Show, 77-78; Festival of Arts & Cult, Lagos, Nigeria, 77; Fourteen Sculptors, High Mus Art, Atlanta, 77. *Pos:* Vpres, Thirteen Minus One, 76-77. *Teaching:* Teacher sculpture & pottery, Therrell High Sch, Atlanta, 70-76; instr sculpture, Atlanta Col of Art, 76- *Awards:* Bronze Jubilee Award Visual Arts, WETV, Channel 30, Atlanta, Ga, 79. *Mem:* Black Artist of Atlanta; Thirteen Minus One. *Media:* Metal, Clay. *Mailing Add:* c/o Nexus Contemp Art Ctr 535 Means St Atlanta GA 30315

PATTERSON, PATRICIA
FILM CRITIC, PAINTER
b Jersey City, NJ, Mar 17, 41. *Study:* Parson's Sch of Design, grad cert. *Exhib:* Houston Mus Contemp Art, Tex, 77; La Jolla Mus Contemp Arts, Calif, 78; Inst for Art & Urban Resources, PS 1, New York, 78; Cleveland Mus Art, Ohio, 78; Fine Arts Gallery, Univ Calif, Irvine, 78; and others. *Pos:* Contrib writer, Film Comment Mag, New York, 75- *Teaching:* Asst prof painting, drawing & art criticism, Univ Calif, San Diego, 76- *Media:* Casein, Enamel; Watercolor. *Publ:* Coauth, Werner Herzog, The cinema of Fata Morgana, 75 & The new breed of filmmakers: A multiplication of myths, 75, City Mag; auth, Fassbinder, 75 & coauth, Gun crazy--Part II, 76 & Beyond the new wave: I (Kitchen without Kitsch), 77, Film Comment; auth, Aran kitchen, aran sweaters, Heresies, 78. *Dealer:* Ellie Blankfort Gallery 2341 Ronda Vista Dr Los Angeles CA 90027. *Mailing Add:* c/o znewspace 5241 Melrose Ave Los Angeles CA 90038

PATTERSON, SHIRLEY ABBOTT
PAINTER, INSTRUCTOR
b Buffalo, NY, Dec 13, 23. *Study:* Albright Sch Fine Art, Buffalo, NY, dipl, 44; New York State Univ, Buffalo, BS(art educ), 45. *Work:* E I Dupont deNemours & Co, Del Trust Co, Sun Oil Co & Blue Cross-Blue Shield, Wilmington, Del; Widener Col Mus, Chester, Pa; State Del Div Libr, Dover. *Exhib:* Regional Art Echib, Univ Del, Newark, 75-77, 79 & 81; Regional Art Exhib, Del Art Mus, Wilmington, 75, 78-79 & 81; Am Watercolor Soc, Nat Acad Galleries, New York, 79; Pa Soc Watercolor Painters, Harrisburg, 79 & 85; Ky Watercolor Soc, Louisville Water Tower Mus, 80-81; Mattatuck Mus, Waterbury, Conn, 90, 91; Connecticut Women Artists, New Haven, Conn, 91. *Collections Arranged:* Mid-Atlantic Regional Exhib Collage, Univ Del, 79; Charter Oak Temple Annual Exhib, Hartford, Conn, 91. *Pos:* Juror, Delaware Camera Club, 86, 87, 88; Radio Talks, WXDR, 86, 87, 88; WDEL, 76, 79, 81. *Teaching:* Instr art, Griffith Inst Cent Sch, Springville, NY, 45-46; critic instr art, Kenmore Pub Sch, NY, 46-49; instr art, privately, 58-70. *Awards:* Artist of the Year, Hotel DuPont, Wilmington Christmas Comt, 76; First Prize, Del State Biennial, Nat League Am Pen Women, 77, 79, 81, 83 & 85. *Bibliog:* Lise Monty (auth), feature in Sunday News J, 4/8/79; article in Artists register, Del Artline, 7/79; Delaware Artists Series (slides), Univ Del, 83, 86. *Mem:* Nat League Am Pen Women, Diamond State Branch (pres, 78-80); Studio Group Inc, Wilmington, Del (pres, 78-80); Pa Watercolor Soc; Ky Watercolor Soc. *Media:* Watercolor, Mixed Media. *Mailing Add:* 15 Wedgewood Lane South Windsor CT 06074

PATTERSON, WILLIAM JOSEPH
PAINTER, PRINTMAKER
b Albany, NY, Mar 16, 41. *Study:* Hartford Art Sch, BFA, 65; Am Acad Rome, Abbey Found Fel, 65-67; Syracuse Univ, MFA, 69. *Work:* Libr Cong; Honolulu Acad Art; New Britain Mus; State Univ NY Col Potsdam; Northern Ill Univ. *Comn:* Five drawings, Third Nat Bank, Springfield, 75; ed of prints, Mass Bar Asn. *Exhib:* One-man shows, Nat Acad Design, New York, 68 & New Britain Mus, 81; Assoc Am Artists, New York, 70 & 72; NY State Univ, 72; 23rd Nat Exhib Prints, Libr of Cong & Nat Col Fine Arts, 73. *Teaching:* Instr printmaking, Hartford Art Sch, Univ Hartford, 69-71; assoc prof printmaking & drawing, Univ Mass, Amherst, 71- *Awards:* Mass Coun Arts Fel, 75; Purdue Univ Award, 80; New Britain Mus, Conn, 81. *Bibliog:* Florence Berlman (auth), Prints of Patterson, Hartford Courant, 7/71; Tom Hart (auth), Bank commissions painting, Springfield Daily News, 75. *Mem:* Boston Printmakers. *Media:* Intaglio; Watercolor, Tempera. *Publ:* Young Man, 71, Four Artists, 72, After Rembrandt, 73 & Daumier, 75, Assoc Am Artists; Self Portrait Near a Window, 74. *Dealer:* Assoc Am Artists 663 Fifth Ave New York NY 10021. *Mailing Add:* 24 Applewool Lane Amherst MA 01002

PATTI, TOM
SCULPTOR
b Pittsfield, Mass, 43. *Study:* Pratt Inst Sch Art & Design, BID, 67, Grad Sch Art & Design, MID, 69; New Sch Social Res, with Rudolph Arheim, 69. *Work:* Metrop Mus Art & Mus Mod Art, New York; Toledo Mus Art, Ohio; Kunstmuseum Dusseldorf, WGer; Victoria & Albert Mus, London. *Comn:* Plastics Technol Ctr, Gen Elec Plastics Genic Doron Divider (atrium), 84; Gen Elec Co, Plastics Group Awards Comn, 86. *Exhib:* Art & Relig, Vatican Mus, Rome; Mex-NAm Cult Inst, Mexico City, 82; Recent Aquisitions: Archit & Design, Mus Mod Art, New York, 79; New Glass: A Worldwide Survey, Corning Mus Glass, 79. *Awards:* Nat Endowment Arts, 79; 1st Prize, Glaskunst 81, Kassel, WGer. *Media:* Glass. *Publ:* Auth, articles, Neues Glas, 3/81 & Art News, summer 81. *Mailing Add:* c/o Signature Gallery 10 Steeple St PO Box 207 Mashpee MA 02649

PATTISON, ABBOTT
SCULPTOR, PAINTER
b Chicago, Ill, May 15, 16. *Study:* Yale Col, BA, 37, Yale Sch Fine Arts, BFA, 39. *Work:* Whitney Mus Am Art; Israel State Mus, Jerusalem; San Francisco Mus; Buckingham Palace, London; Art Inst Chicago; and others. *Comn:* Sculpture, Cent Nat Bank, Cleveland; Ill State Capitol, Springfield; Lincoln Libr, Springfield; Chicago State Univ; US State Dept; and others. *Exhib:* Art Inst Chicago, 40-69; Metrop Mus Art, 51 & 52; four shows, Whitney Mus Am Art, 53-59; one-man shows, Holbrook Mus, Univ Ga, 54 & Sculpture Ctr, NY, 56; Pa Acad Fine Arts, Philadelphia; Calif Palace Legion of Honor, San Francisco; and many others. *Teaching:* Instr, Art Inst Chicago, 46-52; sculptor-in-residence, Univ Ga, 54; instr, Skowhegan Sch Art, 55-56. *Awards:* First Logan Prize, Art Inst Chicago, 42; Prize, Metrop Mus Art, New York, 50; Prize, Bundy Mus, Vt, 67. *Mem:* Chicago Art Club. *Mailing Add:* c/o Fairweather Hardin Fine Art PO Box 129 Plano IL 60545

PATTISON, BILLY DEE
PAINTER, GRAPHIC ARTIST
b Marion, Ind, July 3, 50. *Study:* Wash Sch Art, Lasalle Inst, Portland; Ind Wesleyan Univ, Marion. *Work:* Hellenic Fine Arts Ctr, Athens, Greece. *Comn:* Portrait of Ind Univ, Basketball Coach, Bob Knight, pvt collector, Marion, Ind, 81; portrait of Notre Dame Football Coach Gerry Faust, pvt collector, South Bend, Ind, 85; portrait, Ind High Sch Basketball Champs, Hoosier Reproduction, Marion, 86; mag cover, House of White Birches, Berne, Ind, 88; portraits of generals, Ind Nat Guard, Indianapolis, 92. *Exhib:* Ohio Valley Art Exhib, Madison, Ind, 87; Va Highlands Fine Art Festival, Vinton, 88; Phoebus Touring Artists, Hellenic Fine Arts Ctr, Athens, Greece, 90; Monseratt Art Exhib, Monseratt Art Gallery, New York, 91; 3rd Ann Art Showcase, Prestige Gallery, Toronto, 91; and others. *Pos:* Pres, Grant Co Art Asn, Marion, Ind, 82-87; bd dirs, Hellenic Arts Inst, New York, 91- *Awards:* First Place, Nat league Pen Women, 86; Award Excellence, Ohio Valley Art Exhib, 87; Merit Award, Va Highlands Fine Arts Festival, 88. *Bibliog:* Angel Johansen (auth), Artists Profile, Collector's Mart, 90; Constance Franklin (auth), Encyclopedia of Living Artists, Art Network Press, 90; Diane Roberts (auth), Artists in the 1990's, Manhattan Arts, NY, 91. *Mem:* Hellenic Arts Inst (bd dirs, 91-); Am Soc Artists; Traditional Artists Am. *Media:* Graphite, Oil. *Publ:* Illusr, Christmas Stories, House of White Birches, 88. *Dealer:* Artistic Expressions PO Box 40994 Indianapolis IN 46240. *Mailing Add:* 2025 E 80th St Indianapolis IN 46240

PATTON, ANDY (ANDREW JOHN)
PAINTER
b Winnipeg, Man, Can, Feb 25, 52. *Study:* Univ Man, BA, 72. *Work:* Nat Gallery Can, Ottawa; Art Gallery Ont, Toronto; Univ Lethbridge, Alta. *Exhib:* International Projects: Canada, Artists Space, New York, 83; Fifth Bienniale Sydney (with catalog), Art Gallery New SWales, Australia, 84; Toronto Painting 84 (with catalog) & Art Gallery Ont, 85, Toronto; Cover-Double-Doppelganger, Aorta, Amsterdam, 85; Fire & Ice (with catalog), Gallery Walcheturm, Zurich, 85; Late Capitalism (with catalog), Harbourfront, Toronto, 85; Allegorical Image (with catalog), Agnes Etherington Arts Ctr, Kingston, Ont, 85; Songs of Experience (with catalog), Nat Gallery Can, Ottawa, 86. *Awards:* Canada Coun B Grants, 84 & 85. *Mem:* YYZ Artists Outlet (bd mem, 82-); Independent Artists Union. *Media:* Oil on Canvas, Oil on Linen. *Publ:* Auth, Poems and Quotations, Four Humours Press, 75; The Real Glasses I Wear, A Space, Toronto, 81; Civil space, Parachute Mag, Montreal, 83; Buchloh's history, C Mag, Toronto, 85; coauth, The Interpretation of Architecture (exhib catalog), YYZ, Toronto, 86. *Dealer:* S L Simpson Gallery 515 Queen St W Toronto ON M5V 2B4 Canada. *Mailing Add:* 243 Macdonell Ave Unit 2 Toronto ON M6R 2A9 Canada

PATTON, KAREN ANN
PAINTER
Work: Watercolor Olympus Corp of Am. *Comn:* Watercolor, Am Automobile Asn, Garden City, NY, 85. *Exhib:* HTAL Open Juried Show, Heckscher Mus, Huntington, NY, 81 & 85; Nassau Co Mus Fine Arts, Roslyn, NY, 88. *Teaching:* Instr watercolor, Five Towns Music & Art Found,. *Awards:* Award of Excellence, Malverne Artists of Long Island, 83, Art League Nassau Co, 85; Grumbacher Silver Medal, Tri-Co, 88. *Bibliog:* Malcolm Preston (auth), articles in Newsday, 83 & 85. *Mem:* Nat Asn Women Artists; National Art League; Thirty Artists Inc. *Media:* Watercolor, miscellaneous Media. *Mailing Add:* 3 Carol St Lynbrook NY 11563

PATTON, TOM
PHOTOGRAPHER, CURATOR
b Sacramento, Calif, May 17, 54. *Study:* San Francisco Art Inst, BFA, 76; Univ NMex, MA, 77, MFA, 82. *Work:* San Francisco Mus Mod Art;

Australian Nat Gallery Art, Canberra; St Louis Art Mus; Oakland Mus, Calif; Art Mus, Univ NMex, Albuquerque. *Exhib:* History of Photography in NMex traveling exhib, (with catalog), Art Mus, NMex, 79; Recent Acquisitions, San Francisco Mus Mod Art, 79; New Acquisitions, Hallmark Photog Collection, Nelson Atkins Mus Art, Kansas City, 83; solo exhib (with monogr), Brockton Art Mus, Mass, 84; Highlights: Aspects of the Collection, Mus Photog Art, San Diego, 85; The Isolation & Intrusion Series, Developed Image, Adelaide, Australia, 85; New Landscapes (auth, catalog), Tasmanian Sch Art & Australian Ctr Photog, Hobart, Sydney, Australia, 85; Night Light: A survey of 20th century night photography (traveling exhib), Nelson-Atkins Mus Art, Kansas City, Evansville Mus Art, Ind, Lowe Art Mus, Coral Gables, Fla, 89. *Collections Arranged:* New Views: Landscape Photographs From Two Continents, Univ Mo, St Louis, 86. *Teaching:* Instr photog, Skidmore Col, Saratoga Springs, NY, 82-83; assoc prof photog, Univ Mo, St Louis, 83-, dept chair, dir, Gallery 210, 84-86; vis lectr, Univ Tasmania, Australia, 85. *Awards:* Visual Artists Fell, Nat Endowment Arts, 90-91. *Bibliog:* James Jacobs (auth), Prelude 1976, Artweek Mag, 1/31/76; Joan Murray (auth), Books: The individual and history receive recognition, Artweek, 9/15/79; Michael Costello (auth), Space invaders, Afterimage (visual studies workshop), Rochester, NY, 4/9/80. *Mem:* Soc Photog Educ. *Mailing Add:* Art Dept Univ Mo 8001 Natural Bridge Rd St Louis MO 63121

PAUL, ARTHUR
DESIGNER, PAINTER
b Chicago, Ill, Jan 18, 25. *Study:* Art Inst Chicago, 41-43; Inst Design, Chicago, 46-50. *Exhib:* Kunstverein Munchen, Munich, WGer, 72, musee des Art Decoratifs, Lausanne, Switz, 72, Lowe Mus Art, Coral Gables, Fla, 73, Munic Art Gallery, Los Angeles, 74, New York Cult Ctr, 74, Columbia Col, 81 & Bowling Green Univ, 88; traveling exhibs, Beyond Illus-the Art of Playboy, Royal Col Art, London, 71, The Art of Playboy-the First 25 Yrs, Chicago Cult Ctr, 78; Chicago Art Inst, Betty Rymer Gallery, 92. *Pos:* Self-employed freelance designer, 50-53; art dir, Playboy Mag, 53-82, vpres corp art & graphics dir, Playboy Enterprises, Inc, 78-82. *Teaching:* Guest lectr mag design & illus, Art Inst Chicago, 78, Syracuse Univ, NY, 79, summer designers course 83 & hon teacher, Tokyo Design Sch, Japan, 81, Art Center, Pasadena, 86 & Univ of Ill, Chicago, 87. *Awards:* Trademark, Soc Typographic Arts, 64; Gold Medal, City Milan, Italy, 72; Polycube Award, Art Dirs Club Philadelphia, 75; Gold Medal, Poster Design, NY Acad Club, 80; Art Directors Hall of Fame, 86. *Bibliog:* Sarah Bodine (auth), Contemporary Designers, 90; Mark Hawkins-Dady (auth), Contemporary Master Work, 91; Koichiro Inagaki (auth), Visual Identity in Chicago, 91. *Mem:* Alliance Graphique Int; Mus Contemp Art (bd trustees, 71-86); Am Ctr Design; NY Art Dir Club. *Media:* Acrylic, Mixed. *Publ:* Auth, Problems of art direction, Comment 200, 60; The high art of low art, Print Mag, 72; The world of work: An artists-design view, In: National Art Education Association Carrer Education Handbook, Purdue Univ; Vision, Art Paul, Japan Publ, 81; The Art of Playboy, Alfred Van Dermark Publ, 85. *Mailing Add:* 175 E Delaware Pl Chicago IL 60611

PAUL, KEN (HUGH)
PRINTMAKER, PAINTER
b Ogden, Utah, Apr 24, 38. *Study:* Univ Utah, 58-59; Univ Wyo, BA(with honors), 61, MA, 65. *Work:* Art Gallery SAustralia, Adelaide; Art Gallery Tasmania, Hobart, Australia; Univ Ore Mus of Art, Eugene; Portland Art Mus, Ore. *Comn:* Translucent painting, Adelaide Arts Festival, 67; ceiling panel restoration, Sacred Heart Chapel, Geelong, Australia. *Exhib:* First Springfield Col Nat Print Exhib, Mass, 65; Denver Art Mus Nat Show, 65; Calif Soc Printmakers Ann, Richmond, 71; Seattle Print Int, 71; Ore Artists Ann, Portland, 72-73 & 75; one-man show, Cheney Cowles Mus, Spokane, 79. *Teaching:* Lectr art, Gordon Inst Technol, Geelong, 66-67; lectr printmaking, SAustralian Sch Art, Adelaide, 67-69; assoc prof printmaking, Univ Ore, 70-; vis instr, M I Kerns Art Ctr, Eugene, Ore, summer 71; vis instr, Pac Northwest Graphics Workshop, Cheshire, Ore, 74. *Awards:* Printmakers Ore Exhib First Prize, M I Kerns Art Ctr, 72; Prize for Painting, Ore Col Educ, Monmouth, 72; Graduate School Summer Res Grant, Univ Ore, 73. *Mem:* Contemp Art Soc SAustralia (vpres, 68-69). *Media:* Lithography, Silkscreen; Oil, Acrylic. *Mailing Add:* 3837 Potter St Eugene OR 97405

PAUL, RICK W
SCULPTOR
b 1945. *Study:* Univ Fla, Gainesville, BFA, 67; Pa State Univ, Univ Park, MFA, 69. *Work:* Crocker Nat Bank, San Francisco, Calif; Blakley Corp, Browning Investments Inc, Ind Arts Comn, Indianapolis Art League, Ind State Mus, Indianapolis, Ind; Greater Lafayette Mus Art, Ind; Miami Univ, Oxford, Ohio; Univ Fla, Gainesville. *Exhib:* Solo exhibs, Ft Wayne Mus Art, Ind, 89 & 92, Shepherd Col, Shepherdstown, WVa, 89, Portland Sch Art, Ore, 89, Patrick King Contemp Art, Indianapolis, Ind, 90, Miami Univ Art Gallery, Oxford, Ohio, 94; American Art Clay Company's Indiana Artists Vase Exhibits, Patrick King Contemp Art, Indianapolis, Ind, 88 & 90; Ann Marie LeBlanc and Rick Paul, Eastern Ky Univ, Richmond, Ky, 89. *Teaching:* Asst prof art, Eastern Ky Univ, Richmond, 69-74; assoc prof art & design, Purdue Univ, W Lafayette, Ind, 74- *Awards:* Creative Endeavors Fel, Purdue Univ, 85; Individual Artist Fel, Ind Arts Coun, 87; Individual Artist Fel, Nat Endowment Arts, 90. *Bibliog:* James Yood (auth), Midwestern Art, Arts & Antiques, 89; Geoff Gephart (auth), Arts Indiana, Indianapolis, Ind, 90; Dell Ford (auth), Journal-Gazette, Ft Wayne, Ind, 90. *Dealer:* Patrick King Contemp Art Inc 427 Massachusetts Ave Indianapolis IN 46220-1610. *Mailing Add:* 900 S 10th St Lafayette IN 47905

PAUL, WILLIAM D, JR
PAINTER, PHOTOGRAPHER
b Wadley, Ga, Sept 26, 34. *Study:* Atlanta Col of Art, BFA; Univ Ga, AB & MFA; Emory Univ; Ga State Col; Univ Rome, Italy. *Work:* General Mills, Inc, Minneapolis; Hallmark Cards, Kansas City, Mo; Little Rock Art Ctr, Ark; Univ Ga, Ga Mus Art, Athens; and others. *Exhib:* Southeastern Ann, Atlanta; Va Intermont Col, Bristol; Birmingham Ann, Ala; Corcoran Gallery Art, Washington, DC; Art of Two Cities, Nat Traveling Exhib, Am Fedn Arts; USA-Volti del Sud, Palazzo Venezia, Rome, Italy; and many others. *Collections Arranged:* Sixty small original exhibs, Charlotte Crosby Kemper Gallery, Kansas City Art Inst, 61-65; Art of Two Cities, Am Fedn Arts Traveling Exhib, 65; The Visual Assault, 67, Drawings by Richard Diebenkorn, Selections: The Downtown Gallery, Drawing and Watercolors by Raphael Soyer, Recent Collages by Samuel Adler, 20th Anniversary Exhibition & Art of Ancient Peru, The Paul Clifford Collection, Ga Mus Art; American Painting: the 1940's, 68; American Painting, the 1950's, 68; American Painting: the 1960's, 69; Philip Pearlstein, Retrospective Exhibition (auth, catalog), 70; Alice Neel, Retrospective Exhib (auth, catalog), 75; and many others. *Pos:* Dir exhibs & cur study collections, Kansas City Art Inst, 61-65; cur, Ga Mus Art, 67-69; dir, Ga Mus Art, 69-80. *Teaching:* Instr art & art hist, Kansas City Art Inst, 59-64; asst prof, Univ Ga, 65-69, assoc prof, 69- *Awards:* Macy's Ann, Kansas City, 59, 61, 63 & 64; Atlanta Paper Co Ann, 61; Hallmark Award, Mid-Am Ann, 62; and others. *Mem:* Am Fedn Arts (trustee, 69-80); Col Art Asn; Southeastern Mus Conf; Am Asn Mus; Arts Festival Atlanta (vpres, 82-85). *Media:* Watercolor, Collage. *Publ:* Auth foreword, Alice Neel, Harry N Abrams, 83. *Mailing Add:* 150 Bar H Ct RR 3 Athens GA 30605

PAULIN, RICHARD CALKINS
MUSEUM DIRECTOR, CRAFTSMAN
b Chicago, Ill, Oct 25, 28. *Study:* DePaul Univ, BA,51; Univ Denver, MA, 58; Inst Fine Arts, NY Univ; also in Guadalajara, Mex. *Exhib:* Univ Ill, 60; Rockford Art Asn, 61; Beloit Col, 61-63 & 65; two-man show, Nat Col Educ, Evanston, Ill, 64; Oregon Folk Art, Mus Art Univ Ore, 86. *Collections Arranged:* Teachers Who Paint, 59; Chicago Painters, 60; Six Chicago Painters, 61; Picasso Preview, 62; George Rouault-His Aqua Tints and Wood Engravings, 63; Collectors Showcase, 64; 30 Contemporary Living American Painters, 64; First National Invitational Painting Exhibition: Fifty States of Art, 65; Swedish Handcraft, 61. *Pos:* Dir, Harry & Della Burpee Art Gallery, Rockford, Ill, formerly; dir mus art & asst prof art hist, Univ Ore, 67-88; Emeritus, Univ Oregon Mus Art. *Teaching:* Instr arts & crafts, Roosevelt Jr High Sch, Rockford, Ill; former instr basic & intermediate art courses, Rockford Art Asn; prof art, Mus Art Univ Ore, 68-88; lectr art hist, Univ Oregon. *Awards:* Canfield Award, Rockford Art Asn, 61. *Mem:* Nat Educ Asn; Nat Coun Art Educ; Mus Dirs Asn N Am; Western Art Asn; Mid-Western Mus Dirs Asn; plus others. *Mailing Add:* 1080 Patterson St No 802 Eugene OR 97401

PAULSEN, BRIAN OLIVER
PAINTER, PRINTMAKER
b Seattle, Wash, Mar 29, 41. *Study:* Univ Wash, BA, 63; Wash State Univ, MFA, 66. *Work:* Springfield Art Mus; Amoco Oil Co, Denver; Rothmans Art Gallery, Stratford, Ont; Western Ill Univ; S S Kresge Inc, Detroit, Mich; Wesleyan Univ, Lincoln, Nebr. *Comn:* 3 Wall murals, Nat Endowment Arts, 77. *Exhib:* San Francisco Art Int Centennial Exhib, San Francisco Mus Art, 70; Extraordinary Realities, Whitney Mus Am Art, New York, 73; Touring exhib, 5 Atlantic Provincial Can Mus, 74; Artrain Traveling Art Exhib, Cent US, 75; Smithsonian Traveling Drawing Exhib, 79-80; solo exhib, Rochester Art Ctr, Minn, 80; New American Graphics 82-83, Butler Inst Am Art, 82; Shelby, NC, 87; Colorprint USA, 88. *Teaching:* Asst prof printmaking & drawing, Calif State Univ, Chico, 66-71; asst prof painting & drawing, Univ Calgary, 71-73; prof, Univ NDak, 73- *Awards:* Purchase Awards, Lagrange, Ga, 78, Owensboro Mus, Ky, 79 & Masur Mus, La, 79; Watercolor USA, 77, 80-85; Nat Endowment Arts Fel, 81-82; SWTSU San Marcos, 85; Print Club, 85; Hoyt Inst, 87. *Bibliog:* Article, Art Express Mag, 1-2/82. *Mem:* Print Club Philadelphia; Soc Am Graphic Artists, New York; Boston Printmakers. *Media:* Watercolor; Engraving. *Mailing Add:* 320 N 16th St Grand Forks ND 58203

PAVLOFF, WILMA DE See Parker, Wilma (Wilma Parker de Pavloff)

PAYNE, JOHN D
SCULPTOR, EDUCATOR
b Pontotoc, Miss, Sept 17, 34. *Study:* Beloit Col, BA, studied with Franklin Boggs, O V Shaffer & A D Popinsky; Univ Wis-Madison, MS, studied with Dean Meeker, W Colescott, A Sessler & others, MFA, Danforth Study Grant; Univ Kans, Lawrence, studied with Elden Teft & Sheldon Cary. *Work:* Univ Wis Union Collection, Madison; Beloit State Bank, Adams Collection, Wis; Atlanta Univ, Ga; Loyola Univ, New Orleans; Chicago Hilton & Towers Collections, Chicago, 87; and others. *Comn:* The Sculptor, The Campus & The Prairie (three steel works), Govs State Univ, Park Forest South, Ill, 70-76; Kellogg Co, Battle Creek, Mich, 87; steel sculpture, comn by Western Mich Univ, Kalamazoo, Mich, 89; Lakeview Mus, Peoria, Ill, 81; Univ Ind, Gary, 81; Gruen Gillman Gallery, Chicago, 84; Kalamazoo Art Inst, 89; Buckham Fine Arts, Flint, Mich, 89; and others. *Exhib:* Lakeview Mus, Peoria, Ill, 81; Univ Ind, Gary, 81; Gruen Gillman Gallery, Chicago, 84; Kalamazoo Art Inst, 89; Buckham Fine Arts, Flint, Mich, 89; and others. *Teaching:* Chmn dept art, Langston Univ, Okla, 61-63; assoc prof sculpture & 3-D design, Southern Univ & La Inst Interior Design, 63-71; prof art, Southern Univ, New Orleans, La, 63-65 & Southern Univ, Baton Rouge, 66-71; sculptor-in-residence, chmn dept art & coordr art, music & theatre, Gov State Univ, 71-

82, prof sculpture & ceramics, formerly, prof & sculptor-in-residence, currently; chmn art dept, Western Mich Univ, Kalamazoo, 88-89. *Awards:* Top Award, State Fair, Milwaukee, Wis, 61; All Wis Exhib, 61; Danforth Grant (full year), 68-69; Second Award, Atlanta Univ Ann, Ga, 64, 65 & 66; Visiting prof, Western Mich, Kalamazoo, 88-89. *Bibliog:* American Printmaker, Graphic Group, Calif, 74; Afro-American Artist 1800 to Present, Boston Univ Libr, Mass, 75; Art: African American, Harcourt Brace Jovanovich, Inc, 78; Richard Love (auth), Art Forum, Chicago, Ill, 87-88. *Mem:* Col Art Asn; Nat Coun Art Adminr; Int Sculpture Ctr. *Media:* Metal, Wood. *Publ:* Auth, American References: Chicago Art Review, 89, Am Artist Rev, 90. *Mailing Add:* 25645 Western Park Forest IL 60466

PAYSON, JOHN WHITNEY
ART DEALER, COLLECTOR
b New York, NY, Aug 7, 40. *Study:* Pepperdine Univ, BA, 66. *Pos:* Founder, Joan Whitney Payson Gallery Art, Westbrook Col, Portland, Maine; bd trustees, Skowhegan Sch Painting & Sculpture, currently; mem, bd trustees, St Gaudens Mem, Cornish, NH, currently; pres, Payson Enterprises, Inc; pres, Hobe Sound Galleries & Hobe Sound Galleries, North; pres, Midtown Galleries, Inc; bd mem, Spoleto, 87. *Awards:* Maine Patrons Award, Skowhegan Sch Painting & Sculpture, 77. *Bibliog:* David Patillo (auth), The real Hobe Sound, Palm Beach Life Mag, 7/86. *Mem:* Martin County Coun Arts (mem, adv bd); fel Portland Mus Art; Salmagundi Club, New York; Barn Gallery Assocs; Penobscot Marine Mus. *Specialty:* Contemporary American art. *Publ:* Auth, forward to catalog, Expressions from Maine, 76; forward to catalog, From Goya to Wyeth, The Joan Whitney Payson Collection, 80; forward to catalog, Bernard Langlais, The Middle Years, 86; forward to catalog of the permanant collection, Joan Whitney Payson Gallery Art, Westbrook Col, Portland, Maine. *Mailing Add:* Midtown Payson Galleries Exec Offices 11870 SE Dixie Hwy Hobe Sound FL 33455

PEACE, BERNIE (KINZEL)
PAINTER, PRINTMAKER
b Williamsburg, Ky, Oct 20, 33. *Study:* Berea Col, AB(art), 54; Ind Univ, MFA(painting), 57. *Work:* Fed Reserve Bank, Richmond, Va; Ind Univ; WVa Univ; State WVa, Charleston; Washington & Jefferson Col; and others. *Comn:* Painting, WVa Arts & Humanities Coun, Charleston, 72. *Exhib:* 11th Ann Piedmont Painting & Sculpture Exhib, Mint Mus, Charlotte, NC, 71; 42nd Ann Exhib Contemp Am Paintings, Palm Beach, Fla, 80; 12th Nat Painting Show, Washington & Jefferson Col, Pa, 80; retrospective exhib, Delf Norona Mus, WVa, 80; 14th Ann Nat, Marietta Col, Ohio, 81; W & J Nat Painting Show, 87 & 91; solo exhibs, Northeast Mo State Univ, Kirksville, 87, WVa juried exhib 87, 89, Oak Ridge Mus of Fine Art, Tenn, 88, Art Store Gallery, Charleston, WVA, 92; Retrospective (catalog essays) Charleston Art Mus, WVa, 78; and others. *Teaching:* Prof drawing & painting, West Liberty State Col, 60- *Awards:* Merit Awards, 43rd Ann Upper Ohio Valley Art Show, Wheeling, WVa, 81 & Bethany Col Fall Ann, 81; Best of Show, Upper Ohio Valley Art Show, Wheeling, WVa, 82; Award of Excellence, Allied Artists of WVa, 90; Grumbacher Medal of Merit, 89, 92; Best of Show, Bethany Col, Fall, 91; and others. *Mem:* Allied Artists WVa. *Media:* Acrylic; Woodcuts. *Dealer:* Gallery G 211 Ninth St Pittsburgh PA; The Art Store Charleston WV. *Mailing Add:* Dept Art West Liberty State Col West Liberty WV 26074

PEACOCK, CLIFFTON
PAINTER
b Chicago, Ill, Oct 21, 53. *Study:* Boston Sch Fine Arts, Boston Univ, BFA, 75, MFA, 77, with Paul Guston. *Work:* Mus Fine Arts, Boston; Hood Mus, Dartmouth Col, Dartmouth, NH. *Exhib:* Boston Now: Figuration, Inst Contemp Art, Boston, 82, 83; Boston Invitational, Thomas Segal Gallery, Boston, 82; Solo exhibs, Thomas Segal Gallery, Boston, 83, 86 & 90, Germans Van Eck, New York, 89 & 90, Jan Baum Gallery, Los Angeles, 91, William Halsey Gallery, Col Charleston, SC, 91, Greenville Co Mus Art, SC, 91, Southeastern Ctr Contemp Art, NC, 92, Germans van Eck Gallery, New York, 93; Personal Imagery, Danforth Mus, Framingham, Mass, 85; Currents, Inst Contemp Art, Boston, 85; Gallery Artists and Friends, Germans van Eck Gallery, New York, 92; Thomas Segal Gallery, Boston, Mass, 92. *Awards:* Award in the Visual Arts VI, 88; Louis Comfort Tiffany Grant, 89; Mass Artist Fel, Finalist in Painting, 90. *Bibliog:* Robert Taylor (auth), Currents/Endgame, Contrast Nicely at ICA, Sunday Boston Globe, 9/28/86; Christine Temin (auth), Basement artists on Newbury Street, Boston Globe, 12/15/83, 99, 103; William Wilson (auth), article, Los Angeles Times, 6/5/88. *Mailing Add:* c/o Germans Van Eck 420 W Broadway New York NY 10012

PEAK, ELIZABETH JAYNE
PRINTMAKER, EDUCATOR
b Ft Belvoir, Va, May 19, 52. *Study:* Univ Calif, Santa Barbara, BA, 74; Brandeis Univ, Waltham, Mass, with Michael Mazur, 75; Yale Univ, New Haven, Conn, with Gabor Peterdi, MFA, 77. *Work:* Yale Univ Mus Art, New Haven, Conn; Kent State Univ Gallery, Ohio; Smithsonian Inst and Libr Cong, Washington, DC; Brigham Young Univ, Logan, Utah; Bowdoin Col; and others. *Comn:* Catalog frontpiece, Bowdoin Col Mus, Brunswick, Maine, 81; monotype, Michael Cleary, Washington, DC, 81. *Exhib:* 25th Nat Print Show, Smithsonian Inst, Washington, DC, 77; 10th Ann Works on Paper, SW Texas State Univ, San Marcos, 80; Va Mus, Richmond, 81; 8th Int Miniature Print Exhib, Pratt Graphics, New York, 81; one-person shows, Jane Haslem Gallery, Washington, DC, 81 & Bowdoin Col Mus Art, Brunswick, Maine, 82. *Teaching:* Asst prof drawing, Kent State Univ, Ohio, 79-80; asst prof, Bowdoin Col, Brunswick, Maine, 80-82, Col Holy Cross, 83- *Awards:* Helen G Wintermitz Award, Yale Univ, 77. *Mem:* Intaglio Relief Soc; Col Art Asn; Los Angeles Printmaking Soc. *Media:* Intaglio; Oil Monotype. *Mailing Add:* 306 N Oak St Falls Church VA 22046

PEARL, MARILYN
DEALER
b Akron, Ohio. *Study:* Hunter Col, BA; Columbia Univ, MA. *Pos:* Dir & pres, Marilyn Pearl Gallery, 76- *Teaching:* Asst prof hist, New York Inst Technol, New York & Old Westbury, NY, 68-74. *Mem:* Art Dealers Asn. *Specialty:* Contemporary American painting, sculpture, drawing. *Mailing Add:* Marilyn Pearl Gallery 420 W Broadway New York NY 10012-3764

PEARLMAN, ETTA S
PAINTER
b New York, NY, Mar 30. *Study:* Brooklyn Col, BA, 60; Brooklyn Mus Art Sch. *Work:* Power Gallery Contemp Art, Univ Sydney, Australia; Brooklyn Mus; Temple Univ, Pa. *Exhib:* One-woman shows, Brooklyn Mus Little Gallery Series, 73 & 74 & Pleiades Gallery, 75-76, 78-80 & 82; Gallery 91, Brooklyn, 75; Brooklyn Mus Art Sales & Rental Gallery, 75. *Media:* Multimedia. *Publ:* The Art of Collaging, G F Brommer, Davis Publ, 78. *Dealer:* Pleiades Gallery 164 Mercer St New York NY 10012. *Mailing Add:* 2934 Clubhouse Rd Merrick NY 11566

PEARLSTEIN, ALIX
SCULPTOR
Study: Cornell Univ, BS, 83; SUNY Purchase, MFA, 88. *Exhib:* One-man shows, White Columns, New York, 88 & Laurie Rubin Gallery, New York, 90; Climate 89 & Sculpture, Laurie Rubin Gallery, 89; Work on Paper, Paula Allen Gallery, New York, 90; All Quiet on the Western Front?, Antoine Candau Gallery, Paris, 90; Total Metal, Simon Watson Gallery, New York, 90. *Teaching:* Instr, Sculpture for Non-Majors, State Univ NY, Purchase, 87; instr sculpture, Community Col, 90. *Awards:* Nat Endowment Arts, 89; Maximal Grant, Cornell Coun Creative & Performing Arts, 83. *Bibliog:* Jennifer P Borum (auth), New York Reviews, Alix Pearlstein at Laurie Rubin Gallery, Artforum, 4/90. *Mailing Add:* 152 Mercer New York NY 10012

PEARLSTEIN, PHILIP
PAINTER, EDUCATOR
b Pittsburgh, Pa, May 24, 24. *Study:* Carnegie Inst, with Sam Rosenberg, Robert Lepper & Balcomb Greene, BFA, 49; Inst Fine Arts, New York Univ, MA, 55. *Work:* Whitney Mus Am Art; Metrop Mus Art, New York; Corcoran Gallery Art, Washington, DC; Hirshhorn Collection, Brooklyn Mus; Art Inst Chicago; also in pvt collections. *Exhib:* Solo exhibs, Carnegie-Mellon Univ, 79, Reed Col Art Mus, Portland, Ore, 79 and others; retrospective, Milwaukee Art Mus, The Brooklyn Mus, The Pa Acad, Philadelphia, The Toledo Mus Art & Mus Art, Carnegie Inst, Pittsburgh, 83-84; The Opposite Sex: A Realistic Viewpoint, traveling exhib, Univ Mo-Kansas City, 79; The Figure of Five, Western Asn Art Mus, travel through western US, 79-80; Biennial Exhib, Whitney Mus Am Art, New York, 79; Figurative/Realist Art, Artists' Choice Mus, 79; An American Renaissance in Art: Painting & Sculpture Since 1940, Ft Lauderdale Mus Art, 86; and many others. *Teaching:* Instr, Pratt Inst, 59-63; from asst prof to prof art, Brooklyn Col, 63-87, distinguished prof art emer, currently. *Awards:* Fulbright Fel to Italy, 58-59; Nat Endowment Arts Grant, 69; Guggenheim Fel, 71 & 72. *Bibliog:* Jerome Viola (auth), The Paintings and Teachings of Philip Pearlstein, Watson & Guptill, 82; Mark Strand (ed), Art of the Real: Nine American Figurative Painters, Clarkson N Potter, Inc, 83; Russell Bowman (auth), Philip Pearlstein: The Complete Paintings, Alpine Fine Arts Collection, 83; Philip Pearlstein draws the artist's model, Interactive laserbeam videodisc or videocassette, Interactive Media Corp, New York, 85; John Perreault (auth), Philip Pearlstein Drawings and Watercolors, Harry N Abrams Inc, 88. *Mem:* Am Acad & Nat Inst Arts & Lett. *Publ:* Auth, Figure paintings are not made in heaven, Art News, 62; Whose painting is it anyway? Arts Yearbook 7, 64; A Concept of New Realism: Real, Really Real, Superreal, San Antonio Mus Asn, 81; When paintings were made in heaven, Art in Am, 2/82. *Dealer:* Hirsch & Adler Modern 851 Madison Ave New York NY 10021. *Mailing Add:* 361 W 36th St New York NY 10018

PEARLSTEIN, SEYMOUR
PAINTER, EDUCATOR
b Brooklyn, NY, Oct 14, 23. *Study:* Pratt Inst; Art Students League; also pvt study with Jack Potter, New York. *Work:* Mus NMex, Santa Fe; Mint Mus Art, Charlotte, NC; Nat Acad Design & Queens Mus, New York; Fine Arts Gallery San Diego, Calif; Munson-Williams-Proctor Inst, Utica, NY. *Exhib:* Butler Inst Am Art, Youngstown, Ohio, 75; US Dept State Art in Embassies Prog, 76-78; Am Watercolor Soc, New York, 77; Nat Arts Club 78 & 90, Nat Acad Design 78 & 90 & Queens Mus, New York 78; New York Hist Soc, 81; Colo Heritage Ctr Mus, Denver, 81; and many one-man shows. *Teaching:* Prof & chmn, dept art & advert design, New York City Tech Col, City Univ, Brooklyn, 70- *Awards:* Childe Hassam Purchase Award, 77 & Grant, 75, Am Acad of Arts & Lett; Henry Ward Ranger Purchase Award, Nat Acad of Design, 82 & W H Leavin Prize, 85; George Tweed Mem Award-Allied Artists of Am, 89. *Bibliog:* Malcolm Preston (auth), Seymour Pearlstein Newsday, 5/4/79; David L Shirey (auth), Seymour Pearlstein, New York Times, 5/13/79. *Mem:* Alliance of Figurative Artists (chmn, 76-77); Allied Artists of Am (dir, 76-78); Am Watercolor Soc (dir, 78-80); Audubon Artists (dir, 90-93); Nat Acad of Design (bd dirs, 80-84). *Media:* All. *Publ:* Auth, Acrylics, Am Artist Mag, 2/79. *Mailing Add:* Dept Art NY Col Tech Col 300 Jay St Brooklyn NY 11201

PEARMAN, SARA JANE
HISTORIAN, LIBRARIAN
b Dallas, Tex, Sept 6, 40. *Study:* Univ Wichita, BAE; Univ Kans, MA(art hist); Case-Western Reserve Univ, PhD(art hist). *Collections Arranged:* Glass Collection of the University of Kansas (auth, catalog); The Fine Art of

Graphic Design, 85 & The Fine Art of Graphic Design (auth, catalog), 86, Beck Fine Arts Ctr, Cleveland Mus Art. *Pos:* Slide librn, Cleveland Mus Art; Bk reviewer, Art Documentation, 80- & Visual Resources, 85. *Teaching:* Instr art hist, Kearney State Col, 64-66; lectr, Akron State Univ, 68-, Cleveland State Univ, 77- & Kent State Univ, currently. *Mem:* Col Art Asn; Midwest Art Hist Asn; Cleveland Medieval Soc; Art Libr Soc NAm; Mid-Am Col Art Asn; Visual Resources Asn; Hist Netherlandish Art. *Res:* Iconography of all periods; Late Medieval and northern Renaissance wood sculpture; slide classification systems and visual resources; history of graphic design. *Publ:* Auth, Mirror of Art, Ralph, Vol 4, 77; Otto Dix, A Self Portrait (exhib catalog), Univ Kans; A Netherlandish Saint Andrew from Cleves, Bull Cleveland Mus Art, 12/80. *Mailing Add:* 2120 Hampstead Rd Cleveland Heights OH 44118

PEARSON, CLIFTON
SCULPTOR, INSTRUCTOR
b Birmingham, Ala, June 24, 48. *Study:* Ala A&M Univ, BS, 70; Ill State Univ, MS, 71, EdD, 74; also with Joel Myers, Timothy Mather, Ruddy Audio, Thomas Malone, Max Rennels, M M Chambers. *Work:* Illinois State Mus; Fisk Univ, Nashville, Tenn; United Way. *Comn:* Salt glaze sculptures, comn by Dr & Mus E W Womack, Huntsville, Ala & Wayman AME Church, Bloomington, Ill; Celebrated Lady (mural), comn by Mrs Jane Rhinehart, Huntsville; Slavery Chains (ceramic bust), Ala A&M Univ, Normal. *Exhib:* Black Artists-South, Huntsville Mus Art, 79; Ala Craftsmen Invitational, Birmingham Mus Art, 79; Black Artists of the South: Dimensions & Directions, Miss Mus Art, 79; and many others. *Collections Arranged:* Twenty-one exhibs, Ala A&M Univ Gallery Art. *Teaching:* Asst ceramics & art educ, Ill State Univ, 71-73; asst prof ceramics, drawing & art educ, Ala A&M Univ, 73-74, prof, 74- *Awards:* Purchase Award, Ill State Mus, Springfield, 73; Southern Fel Grant, 74; House of Bamboo Award Sculpture, Tenn Art League, 75. *Bibliog:* C Pearson (auth), 60 programs on ceramics, Educ TV-Ala A&M Univ TV Commun, 8/75. *Mem:* Nat Conf Artists; Am Crafts Coun; Nat Art Educ Asn; Ala Craftsmen Coun (trustee, 75). *Media:* Clay Stoneware, Glass. *Mailing Add:* Art Ed Ala A&M Univ PO Box 285 Normal AL 35762

PEARSON, HENRY C
PAINTER, INSTRUCTOR
b Kinston, NC, Oct 8, 14. *Study:* Univ NC, BA, 35; Yale Univ, MFA, 38; Art Students League, 53-56. *Work:* Mus Mod Art, Metrop Mus Art & Whitney Mus Am Art, New York; Albright-Knox Art Gallery, Buffalo; NC Mus Art, Raleigh. *Comn:* World University Service (poster), List Art Posters, 65; 6th New York Film Festival--Lincoln Center (poster), List Art Posters, 68;. *Exhib:* The Responsive Eye, Mus Mod Art, New York, 65; 29th Biennial Exhib, Corcoran Gallery Art, Washington, DC, 65; Drawings USA, Minn Mus Art, St Paul, 71-73; Art Students League Centennial Exhib, 75; Truman Gallery, New York, 76-79; Marilyn Pearl Gallery, New York, 79-; Dissent: The Issue of Modern Art, Inst Contemp Art, Boston, Mass, 86; Retrospective, Columbia Mus Art, SC, 88; and others. *Teaching:* Instr painting, New Sch Social Res. *Awards:* Kreeger Purchase Prize, Corcoran Gallery Art, 65; J Henry Scheidt Award, Pa Acad Fine Arts, 69; NC Governor's Gold Medal Achievement Fine Arts, Raleigh, 70. *Bibliog:* Lippard (auth), Henry Pearson, Art Int, 65. *Mem:* Am Abstract Artists; Century Asn. *Media:* Oil, Watercolor. *Publ:* Illusr, Five Psalms, Brandeis Univ, 69; illusr, Poems an da Memoir (auth, Seamus Heaney), The Limited Editions Club, New York, 81; illusr, Sweeney Praises the Trees (auth, Seamus Heaney), Kelly/winterton Press, New York, 81. *Dealer:* Marilyn Pearl Gallery 420 W Broadway New York NY 10012. *Mailing Add:* 58 W 58th St New York NY 10019

PEARSON, JAMES EUGENE
INSTRUCTOR, SCULPTOR
b Woodstock, Ill, Dec 12, 39. *Study:* Northern Ill Univ, BS(educ), 61, MS(educ), MFA, 64; Tyler Sch Art, Temple Univ; Ithaca Col. *Work:* Northern Ill Univ, DeKalb; Palais des Beaux Arts, Charleroi, Belg; Taft Field Campus, Northern Ill Univ, Oregon; Dixon State Sch, Ill; Sch Dist 15, McHenry, Ill. *Comn:* Lorado Taft, Taft Field Campus, Northern Ill Univ, 67; Vicki Unis, Sarasota, Fla, 69; Mae Stinespring, Harry Stinespring, McHenry, Ill, 69; portraits in oils of Mr & Mrs Francis Hightower, comn by Mrs Nancy Langdon, Woodstock, Ill, 71. *Exhib:* 21st Am Drawing Biennial, Norfolk Mus Arts & Sci, Va, 65; 54th Ann Exhib, Art Asn Newport, RI, 65; 2 eme Salon Int de Charleroi, Palais des Beaux Arts, Belg, 69; 5th Int Grand Prix Painting & Etching, Palais de la Scala, Monte Carlo, Monaco, 69; one-man show sculpture, Mitchell Art Mus, Mt Vernon, Ill, 75. *Teaching:* Instr art, Woodstock High Sch, Ill, 61-; instr art, McHenry Co Col, Crystal Lake, Ill, 70- *Awards:* Best of Show Award, William Boyd Andrews, 61; Purchase Prize, Mr & Mrs Allen Leibsohn, 63; Mary E Just Art Award, Waukegan News-Sun, 69. *Bibliog:* F Tramier (auth), James E Pearson, La Rev Mod, 65; Sally Wagner (auth), Volume tells McHenry history, Chicago Tribune, 69. *Mem:* Col Art Asn Am; Ill Art Educ Asn; Ill Craftsmen's Coun; Am Fedn Arts; Centro Studi E Scambi Internazionali, Rome. *Publ:* Illusr, McHenry County 1832-1968, 68; auth, A dream never realized, 69 & Eagle's nest colony, 70, Outdoor Ill; Perspective: outdoor education from an artists point of view, J Outdoor Educ, 71; illusr, The rectangle, 72. *Mailing Add:* 5117 Barnard Mill Rd Ringwood IL 60072

PEARSON, JOHN
PAINTER, EDUCATOR
b Boroughbridge, Yorkshire, England, Jan 31, 40. *Study:* Harrogate Col Art, Yorkshire, nat dipl design, 60; Royal Acad Schs, London, cert, 63; Northern Ill Univ, MFA, 66. *Work:* Mus Mod Art, New York; Bochumer Mus, Stuttgart, WGer; Pasadena Mus Fine Art, Calif; Kleye Collection, Doertmund, WGer; Kunstverien, Hanover, WGer; Art Inst Chicago; Cleveland Mus Art. *Exhib:* American Drawing 1963-73, Whitney Mus Am Art, New York; one-man shows, Gray Gallery, Chicago, 67, 68 & 82, Paley & Lowe Gallery, 71, Fischbach Gallery, 74 & 76, New York & Akron Art Mus, 83. *Teaching:* Instr painting, Univ NMex, 66-68; assoc prof painting & head dept, NS Col Art & Design, Halifax, 68-70; int artist-in-residence, Cleveland Inst Art, Ohio, 70-72; prof art & chmn dept art, Oberlin Col, 72- *Awards:* Can Coun Grant, 70; Cleveland Arts Prize, 75; Nat Endowment Arts, 76. *Bibliog:* Jock Wittet (auth), Editorial, Studio Int, 3/68; Harry Borden (auth), John Pearson, Artforum, 2/72; James R Mellon (auth), article, New York Times, 2/3/75; Edward Henning (auth), The art of John Pearson: an analogy of works of art & general systems, Art Int, 4-5/77. *Publ:* Contribr, Art: The measure of man, Directions 66/67; contribr, article in Mus Educ J, 66. *Dealer:* Bertha Urdang Gallery 23 W 74th St New York NY 10021; Richard Gray Gallery 620 N Michigan Ave Chicago IL 60611. *Mailing Add:* 290 Elm St Oberlin OH 44074

PEART, JERRY LINN
SCULPTOR
b Winslow, Ariz, Feb 26, 48. *Study:* Ariz State Univ, BFA(sculpture); Southern Ill Univ, Carbondale, MFA(sculpture). *Work:* Mus Contemp Art, Chicago; Palm Springs Desert Mus, Calif; Ill State Mus, Springfield; Mus NMex, Santa Fe. *Comn:* Sculpture, Col Du Page, Glen Ellen, Ill, 83; sculpture, City Albuquerque, 84; sculpture, City Toledo, Ohio, 84; 39' sculpture, Triangle Plaza, Chicago, 85; Ill Ctr, 86; City of Aurora, Ill, 87. *Exhib:* Am Eight, Interpace Corp, Parsipanny, NJ, 81; Citywide Contemp Sculpture Exhib, Toledo Art Mus, 84; New Traditions in Sculpture, Hyde Park Art Ctr, Chicago, 85; one-man show, Maquettes, Eve Mannes Gallery, Atlanta, 85. *Teaching:* vis prof sculpture, Ariz State Univ, spring, 84. *Awards:* Jeannette Sacks Art Achievement Medal, Ariz State Univ, 70; First Chicago Art Awards for Best Body of Work Over the Yr, Chicago Art Asn, 76-77. *Mem:* Sculpture Chicago (comt mem, 85-); City of Chicago, Percent for Art (mem pub art comt, 86-). *Dealer:* Richard Gray Gallery 620 N Michigan Chicago IL 60611. *Mailing Add:* 1544 N Sedgwick St Chicago IL 60610

PEASE, DAVID G
ADMINISTRATOR, PAINTER
b Bloomington, Ill, June 2, 32. *Study:* Univ Wis-Madison, BS, 54, MS, 55, MFA, 58. *Work:* Whitney Mus Am Art, New York; Philadelphia Mus Art; Pa Acad Fine Arts, Philadelphia; Power Gallery, Univ Sydney, Australia; Des Moines Art Ctr, Iowa. *Exhib:* Carnegie Int Exhib Painting & Sculpture, Carnegie Inst, Pittsburgh, 61; Corcoran Biennial Painting, Corcoran Gallery Art, Washington, DC, 61 & 63; Whitney Ann Exhib Painting, Whitney Mus Am Art, New York, 63; Nat Drawing Exhib, San Francisco Mus Art, Calif, 69; Drawings USA, Minn Mus Art, St Paul, 71, 73 & 75. *Pos:* Dean, Tyler Sch Art of Temple Univ, 77-83; dean, Sch Art, Yale Univ, 83- *Teaching:* Prof painting dept painting & sculpture, Tyler Sch Art, Temple Univ, 60-83; prof painting, Yale Univ, 83- *Awards:* William A Clark Award, Corcoran Gallery Art, 63; Guggenheim Fel, 65-66; Childe Hassam Fund Purchase Award, Am Acad Arts & Lett, 70. *Mem:* Col Art Asn Am; Nat Coun Arts Adminr (bd dirs, 88); Nat Asn Sch Art & Design; Alliance of Indep Cols Art (bd dirs, 88); Louis Comfort Tiffany Found (bd trustees, 88-). *Media:* Acrylic, Gouache. *Mailing Add:* Sch Art Yale Univ 180 York St New Haven CT 06520

PECCHENINO, J RONALD
PAINTER, EDUCATOR
b Murphy, Calif, Apr 3, 32. *Study:* Col Pac, BA, 56; Calif Col Arts & Crafts, MFA, 69. *Work:* Univ Calif, Chico; Univ Pac. *Comn:* Acrylic lacquer paintings, Hilton Hotel, Stockton, Calif, 81; Sheraton Hotel, Boston, 83; Cruise Ships, MS Skyward, 85 & Song of Norway, 86. *Exhib:* Third Ann Art Invitational, Pleasant Hill, Calif, 69; Northern Calif Arts Exhib, Crocker Mus Art, Sacramento, 72; solo exhib, Lyon Art Gallery, San Francisco, 79 & 81. *Pos:* Mem, Art Adv Panel, Calif State Comn, 71-80. *Teaching:* Instr art, Manteca Unified Sch Dist, Calif, 56-70; prof painting, Univ Pac, 70-, chmn art, 83- *Awards:* Purchase Awards, Lodi Ann Exhib, M Neufield & Sons, 68, Third Ann Art Invitational, City Pleasant Hill, 69 & Northern Calif Arts Exhib, Crocker Art Gallery, 72. *Media:* Acrylic Lacquer, Air Brush. *Dealer:* Contract Art Inc Falls River Offices PO Box 520 Essex CT 06426. *Mailing Add:* Dept Art Univ of the Pacific 3601 Pacific Ave Stockton CA 95211

PECHE, DALE C
PAINTER
b Long Beach, Calif, Nov 28, 28. *Study:* Long Beach City Col, BPA; Art Ctr Col Design, Los Angeles; also with Reckless, Tyler, Legakes, Feitelson, Polifka, Williamaoski & Kramer. *Comn:* California City, 73 & Off Highway One, 75, Glendale Fed Savings & Loan Permanent Collection; Wild Blackberries & Hay Barn, McCleary-Cummings, Artists Am Collection, 74. *Exhib:* One-man shows, Challis Galleries, Laguna Beach, Calif, 72, 73 & 74; 149th Nat Acad Design, New York, 74; 206th & 207th Summer Exhib, Royal Acad Arts, London, 74 & 75; 61st Ann Exhib, Allied Artists Am, New York, 74. *Awards:* Two awards, Los Angeles Art Dirs Show, 63 & 70; Pageant of the Oaks Award, 74; Brea Art Asn Award, 75. *Mem:* Nat Watercolor Soc; Allied Artists Am; Royal Soc Arts. *Media:* Acrylics. *Mailing Add:* c/o Conacher Galleries 134 Maiden Lane San Francisco CA 94108

PECK, JAMES EDWARD
PAINTER, DESIGNER
b Pittsburgh, Pa, Nov 7, 07. *Study:* Cleveland Inst Art, cert. *Work:* Cleveland Mus Art, Ohio; US Govt, Carville, La; Dayton Art Inst, Ohio; Am Acad Arts & Lett, New York; Seattle Art Mus, Wash. *Exhib:* Am Watercolor Soc, New York; Seattle Art Mus Northwest Ann; Pepsi-Cola Drawing & Watercolor

Exhib, Metrop Mus Art, New York; Dayton Art Inst; Watercolor Invitational, Bellevue Art Mus, Seattle, Wash, 90. *Pos:* Illusr, Fawn Art Studios, Cleveland, 36-46; art dir, Miller, McKay, Hoeck & Hartung, Seattle, 54-60, graphic designer, 60-66; graphic designer, Boeing Co, 66-70. *Teaching:* Head dept art, Cornish Sch, Seattle, 47-52; instr painting & graphic design, Burnley Sch Art, Seattle, 66-76. *Awards:* Awards for watercolors, Dayton Art Inst, 42-45; award for painting, Guggenheim Found, 42 & 46; Seattle Art Mus Awards, var shows & yrs. *Mem:* Puget Sound Group Northwest Painters (past pres). *Media:* Watercolor, Enamel. *Publ:* Illusr, Ford Times Mag & Am Artist Mag. *Mailing Add:* 19155 130th Ave NE Bothell WA 98011

PECK, JUDITH
SCULPTOR, WRITER
b New York, NY, Dec 31, 30. *Study:* Adelphi Col, BA; Art Students League; Sculpture Ctr, New York; Columbia Univ, MA & EdM; New York Univ, EdD. *Work:* Yale Univ; Ghetto Fighters Mus, Acco, Israel. *Comn:* Monuments, Temple Beth El, Spring Valley, NY, 71, James Richard Elster Mem Courtyard, Tenafly High Sch, NJ, 72 & Temple Oheb Sholom, Baltimore, Md, 75; Annual Partners Award Sculpture, Art Coun Rockland, 83,84, 85; Rockland Ctr Holocaust Studies, Spring Valley, NY, 88; North Shore Synagogue, Syosset, NY, 92. *Exhib:* solo sculpture shows, Unicorn Gallery, New York, 75 & 76, NJ Statte Mus, Trenton, 78, Col Misericordia, Dallas, Pa, 85 & Lincoln Ctr Campus, Fordham Univ, New York, 90; Blue Hill Cult Ctr, Pearl River, NY, 84-85; Edward Hopper House, Nyack, NY, 84; Montclair State Coll, 92; Adelphi Univ, 92; and others. *Teaching:* Prof art, Ramapo Col, NJ, 71- *Awards:* Grants, Art on the Outside, NJ Dept Higher Educ, Title I, 75, 76 & 77; Distinguished Service Award, Rockland County legislature, 88. *Media:* Bronze, Fiberglass. *Publ:* Auth, Leap to the Sun: Learning through Dynamic Play, Prentice-Hall, 79; Sculpture as Experience: Working with Clay, Wire, Wax, Plaster, Foil and Found Objects, Chilton Publ, 89; Art & Interaction, Ramapo Col, 90. *Mailing Add:* PO Box 5 Sterling Forest NY 10979

PECK, LEE BARNES
JEWELER, EDUCATOR
b Battle Creek, Mich, Sept 21, 42. *Study:* Kellogg Community Col, AA, 63; Western Mich Univ, BS(art educ), 65; Univ Wis, MFA(art metal), 69. *Work:* Johnson Wax Co. *Exhib:* The Goldsmith, Renwick Gallery, Smithsonian Inst, Washington, DC, 74; Am Goldsmiths Now, Washington Univ, St Louis, 78; Sangree De Cristo Art Ctr, Pueblo, Colo, 78; Northeast Mo State Univ, Kirksville, 78; Visual Arts Ctr Alaska, Anchorage, 78; one-man show, Mich Tech Univ, Houghton, 78; Objects 79, Western Colo Arts, 79; and many others. *Teaching:* Assoc prof jewelry & metalwork, Northern Ill Univ, 70-82, prof art, currently; lectr in jewelry, Rosary Col, 72- *Awards:* Lakefront Festival Art Prize, Milwaukee Art Ctr, 75; The Metalsmith Award, Phoenix Art Mus, Ariz, 77; First Prize in Metal, Cooperstown Art Asn, NY, 77. *Mem:* Am Crafts Coun (Ill rep, 72-74); Wis Designer Craftsman; Soc NAm Goldsmiths. *Media:* Precious Metals. *Publ:* Auth & illusr, Jewelry Making, Vol 3, In: Illustrated Libr of Arts & Crafts, 74. *Mailing Add:* Nothern Ill Univ De Kalb IL 60115

PECK, WILLIAM HENRY
CURATOR, HISTORIAN
b Savannah, Ga, Oct 2, 32. *Study:* Ohio State Univ, 50-53; Wayne State Univ, BFA, 60, MA, 61. *Collections Arranged:* Mummy Portraits from Roman Egypt (with catalog), 67, Detroit Collects: Antiquities, 73 & Akhenaten and Nefertiti, 73-74, Detroit Inst Arts; Cleopatra's Egypt, 89; plus many others. *Pos:* Jr cur educ, Detroit Inst Arts, 60-62, asst cur educ, 62-64, assoc cur, 64-68, cur ancient art, 68-, sr cur, 88-; mem, Brooklyn Mus Theban Exped, 78-, assoc field dir, 80- *Teaching:* Lectr art hist, Cranbrook Acad Art, 63-65; adj prof art hist, Wayne State Univ, 66-; vis lectr classics, Univ Mich, 70. *Awards:* Travel Grant, Ford Motor Co, Eng, 62; Am Res Ctr Egypt Fel, 71; Travel Grant, Smithsonian Inst, 75; Arts Achievement Award, Dept Art & Art Hist, Wayne State Univ. *Mem:* Soc Study Egyptian Antiques; fel Am Res Ctr Egypt; Cranbrook Acad Art (mem bd gov, 74-); Archaeol Inst Am; Int Asn Egyptologists. *Res:* Ancient Near East and classical world with a particular specialty in Egyptian art and archaeology. *Publ:* Auth, The present state of Egyptian art in Detroit, 12/70 & The arts of the Ancient Near East in Detroit, 7/73, Connoisseur; A seated statue of Amun, J Egyptian Archaeol, 71; Drawings From Ancient Egypt, Thames & Hudson, 78, German transl, 79, French transl, 80, Arabic transl, 87; The constant lure, chapter In: Ancient Egypt: Discovering its splendors, Nat Geogrpahic, 78; The Detroit Institute of Arts: A Brief History, 91. *Mailing Add:* Detroit Inst of Arts 5200 Woodward Ave Detroit MI 48202

PECKHAM, NICHOLAS
ARCHITECT, EDUCATOR
b Teaneck, NJ, Apr 11, 40. *Study:* US Merchant Marine Acad, BS, 62; Univ Calif, Berkeley, 63; Univ Pa, BArch, 67, MArch, 73, with Louis Kahn, PhD cand with R Buckminster Fuller. *Pos:* Pres, Peckham & Wright Architects, Columbia. *Teaching:* Prof design, Stephens Col, Columbia, 75- *Awards:* Cycle-4 Solar Award & Passive Cycle Award, Dept Housing & Urban Develop; Com Solar Award, Dept Energy. *Mem:* Construct Specifications Inst; Am Inst Architects; Int Solar Energy Soc. *Res:* Optimization in architecture. *Publ:* Auth, Evolution in architecture, Pass-Age, summer 75. *Mailing Add:* 3151 W Rte K Columbia MO 65203

PEDEN, DONALEE
PAINTER
b Syracuse, NY, Apr 1, 52. *Study:* Syracuse Univ, BFA, 76, MFA, 92. *Work:* Everson Mus, Syracuse, NY; Munson-Williams-Proctor Mus, Utica, NY. *Exhib:* Solo exhibs, Munson-Williams-Proctor Inst, Utica, NY, 86, Gertrude Thomas Chapman Art Gallery, Cazenovia Col, NY, 86 & 87, Colgate Univ, Hamilton, NY, 88 & Tyler Art Gallery, Oswego, NY, 90; Oneonta Univ, NY, 87; Oswego Art Guild, NY, 88; New Visions Gallery, Ithaca, NY, 88; group shows, NY Women Artists, NY State Mus, Albany, 89-90, Burchfield Art Ctr, Buffalo, NY, 90, Ariel Gallery, New York, 90, Syracuse State, 90, Gertrude Thomas Chapman Art Gallery, Cazenovia Col, NY, 90-91 & Colgate Univ, Hamilton, NY, 91. *Teaching:* Instr watercolor & figure drawing, Syracuse Univ, 83-, material & techniques, 89, 90 & 91; instr drawing, Cazenovia Col, 86-87 & Hamilton Col, 89. *Awards:* Ford Found Awards, 76, 77 & 78; New York Found Arts Fel, Drawing, 86; Nat Endowment Arts Grant, Drawing, 87; Jacob Javits Fel, 90. *Mailing Add:* 1639 Valley Dr Syracuse NY 13207

PEDERSEN, CAROLYN H
PAINTER
b Dec 12, 42; US citizen. *Study:* Syracuse Univ, BS, 64; Rockland Ctr for Arts, W Nyack, NY, studied printmaking with Roberta De Lamonica, 86-, studied watercolor with Edgar A Whitney. *Work:* Art Pub Places, Rockland Co, New City, NY; Gallery Mus Hebrew Home for Aged, Riverdale, NY; Community Savings Bank, Holyoke, Mass; Pub Serv Elect & Gas, NJ; Katz Commun, San Francisco, Calif. *Exhib:* Watercolor USA, Springfield Mus, Mo, 85; Am Watercolor Soc, Salmagundi Club, New York, 84; Nat Watercolor Soc, Los Angeles, Calif, 84, 85, 87; Audubon Artists Annual, Nat Arts Club, New York, 85, 86, 88. *Pos:* Pres Art Craft Assoc Rockland Co, NY, 79-80; mem chmn, Northeast Watercolor Soc, NY, 87-; exhib comt mem, Rockland Ctr Arts, NY, 88-; asst treas, Catharine Lorillard Wolfe Arts Club, 90- *Teaching:* Instr watercolor (workshops & demonstrations) Rockland Ctr Arts, West Nyack, NY, 85- *Awards:* Am Watercolor Soc Travelling Award, 84; travel award, Ky Watercolor Soc, Aqueous 86, 86. *Bibliog:* Adam Pfeffer (auth), On the arts, Spotlight Mag, 2/88. *Mem:* Nat Watercolor Soc; Nat Asn Women Artists; Audubon Artists; Catherine Lorillard Wolfe Arts Club; Artists Equity. *Media:* Watercolor. *Publ:* Auth, Splash, watercolor book, Northlight, 90. *Mailing Add:* 119 Birch Lane New City NY 10956

PEEPLES, MAIJA (MAIJA GEGERIS ZACK WOOF)
PAINTER
b Riga, Latvia, Nov 21, 42. *Study:* Univ Calif, Davis, BA, 64, MA, 65; also with William T Wiley, Robert Arneson & Wayne Thiebaud. *Work:* Crocker Art Gallery, Sacramento, Calif; La Jolla Mus Art, Calif; Matthews Art Ctr, Tempe, Ariz; San Francisco Mus Art; Norman MacKenzie Art Gallery, Regina, Sask. *Comn:* Beast rainbow painting, City San Francisco, Civic Ctr, 67; rainbow house, pvt party, San Francisco, 67-68; ceiling murals, Rainbow House, San Francisco, 67-68; crocheted, woven & sewn beast curtains, Univ Calif Art Bldg, Davis, 71. *Exhib:* San Francisco Art Mus, 73-75; Rainbow Show, De Young Mus, San Francsico, 74-75; Welcome to the Candy Store, Crocker Art Mus, 81; Maija's World, San Jose, Calif, 84; The Candy Store, Redding Mus, Redding Calif, 89; one woman show, Iris Upon a Star, J'Nette Gardens, Oakland, Calif, 87-88, Maija's Flowers, Candy Store Gallery, Folsom, Calif, 90, Life Is Just a Bowl of Terriers, Nev Mus Art, Reno, 91; All Creatures Great & Small, Natsoulas Gallery, Davis, Calif, 92; and many other group and solo shows. *Collections Arranged:* The Nut Show, for Kaiser-Aetna, Tahoe Verdes, Calif, 72. *Teaching:* Instr art, Laney Col, Oakland, 68-69, Univ Calif, Davis, 71-72 & Sierra Col, Rocklin, Calif, 71-73. *Awards:* Award, Ceramics Excellence, Calif State Fair, 74. *Bibliog:* Jane Goldman (auth), Peeples' animals bring smiles, Sacramento Union, 79; Jane Goldman (auth), Enough to make you smile, Sacramento Mag, 8/80; Ellen Schlesinger (auth), As fate would have it, Peeples is an artist, Sacramento Bee, 7/4/82; Ronnie Cohen (auth), Maija's Zoo, Neighbors Mag, 2/84. *Media:* Multi. *Dealer:* Adeliza McHugh 2249 Columbia St Palo Alto CA 94306. *Mailing Add:* 2586 King Richard Dr El Dorado Hills CA 95762

PEEPS, CLAIRE
CURATOR, PAINTER
b Vancouver, BC, Oct, 24, 56. *Study:* Stanford Univ, MFA, 78; Univ NMex, MA, 82. *Exhib:* Houston Art Ctr, Tex, 83; San Francisco Camera Works, Calif, 84. *Pos:* Assoc art dir, cur performing & visual arts, Los Angeles Arts Festival, Calif, 89- *Awards:* Purchase Award, Univ Ariz, 82. *Mem:* 18th St Arts Complex (bd mem, 88-); Arts Inc (bd mem, 89-). *Mailing Add:* 725 N Ogden Dr Los Angeles CA 90046

PEI, I M (IEOH MING)
ARCHITECT, DESIGNER
b Canton, China, Apr 26, 17; US citizen. *Study:* Mass Inst Technol, BArch, 40; Harvard Univ, MArch, 46; Hon DFA degrees from New York Univ, Univ Pa, Rensselaer Polytechnic Inst, Brown Univ, Carnegie-Mellon Univ, Northeastern Univ, Dartmouth & Univ Rochester; DHL degrees from Columbia Univ, Univ Hong Kong, Am Univ Paris & Univ Colo; Chinese Univ, Hong Kong & Pace Univ, DL. *Comn:* JFK Library, Boston, 79; West Wing, Mus Fine Arts, Boston, 81; Fragrant Hill Hotel, Beijing, China, 82; New York Expos & Conv Ctr, NY, 86; Grand Louvre, Paris, 89 & 93; Bank China, Hong Kong, 89; Dallas Symphony Hall, 89; and others. *Pos:* Head Archit division, Webb & Knapp Inc, New York, 48-55; archit, New York, 55-; mem, Nat Coun Humanities, 66-70; mem, Urban Design Coun, New York, 67-72. *Teaching:* Instr, Harvard Grad Sch Design, 45-48. *Awards:* Gold Medal, Univ Calif, Los Angeles, 90; First Award for Excellence, Colbert Found, 91; Excellence 2000 Award, 91; and many others. *Bibliog:* Bruno Suner (auth), Ieon Ming Pei, Hazan, Paris, 88; Carter Wiseman (auth), I M Pei, A Profile in American Architecture, Abrams, New York, 90. *Mem:* Royal Inst Brit Archit; fel Am Inst Architects; Am Acad Arts & Lett (chancellor, 78-80); hon fel Am Soc Interior Designers; Am Acad Arts & Sci; Nat Coun Arts; and others. *Mailing Add:* c/o I M Pei & Partners 600 Madison Ave New York NY 10022

PEII, AHMAD OSNI
SCULPTOR, DESIGNER
b Palembang, Indonesia, Sept 7, 30; US citizen. *Study:* Craft Students League; New Sch Social Res, scholar, 66; Haystack Mountain Sch Arts; Fairfield Univ; Pac Western Univ, BFA, DFA. *Work:* Spring Mills, Inc, New York; Univ Conn Libr, Storrs; Bernhard Garretz, St Moritz, Switzerland; Int Rotary Club, Toronto; Oppenheimer Fund, World Trade Ctr, New York. *Comn:* Johnson & Wales Col, Providence, RI; L Goldfein, Westport, Conn; Jes Design Assocs Inc & Roberts & Holland, New York; E Bernstein, Rye, NY. *Exhib:* Int Art Exhib, Minneapolis/St Paul, 72; American Craft Coun Gallery, New York, 73; Brooklyn Mus, 73; Silvermine Guild, Conn, 74; Wadsworth Antheneum, Hartford, Conn, 78; Schulman Sculpture Garden, White Plains, NY, 86; Hudson River Mus, NY, 88. *Pos:* Exhib chmn, Sculptors Guild, NY, 72; art juror, Artist-Craftsmen, New York, 76; display consult, Johnson & Wales Col, 79- *Teaching:* Instr sculpture, Craft Students League, New York, 76-77, Johnson & Wales Col, Providence, 79- & New Sch Soc Res, 80; N Eng Ctr Contemp Arts, Conn, 77-78. *Awards:* grant, Conn Comn on Arts, 78; Groton Arts Comt Award, Conn, 79; World of Poetry, 86-89. *Bibliog:* Steven Slosberg (auth), Penumbra, New London Day, Conn, 79; Ruth Lamp Ross (auth), Profile, Norwalk News, Conn, 82; Larry Hartstein (auth), Uplifting Forms, Stamford Advocate, Conn, 92. *Mem:* Int Sculpture Ctr; Sculptors Guild, Inc. *Media:* Bronze, Fiberglass. *Publ:* Auth, Should the public get the art it likes?, Norwich Bulletin, 6/17/79; Art as an elevation of life, Norwalk News, 3/11/82; The Denomination of an Artwork Amidst the Confusing Diversity of Mannerism & Movement in Contemporary Arts, Toth-Maathian Rev, Lubbock, Tex, 85. *Dealer:* Renate Shapiro 60 Sutton Pl New York NY 10022. *Mailing Add:* PO Box 613 New Canaan CT 06840-0613

PEIPERL, ADAM
KINETIC ARTIST, VIDEO ARTIST
b Sosnowiec, Poland, June 4, 35; US citizen. *Study:* George Washington Univ, BS, 57; Pa State Univ, 57-59. *Work:* Nat Mus Am Hist, Nat Mus Am Art & John F Kennedy Ctr Performing Arts, Washington DC; Pa Acad Fine Arts, Philadelphia; Boymans-Van Beuningen Mus, Rotterdam, Holland. *Comn:* Video shorts, WETA TV Channel 26, Washington, DC, 84; dance video collaboration, George Washington Univ, 87. *Exhib:* Corcoran Gallery Art, 68; one-man shows, Baltimore Mus Art, 69, Pa Acad Fine Arts, 69, Nat Mus Am Hist, 72-73, Philadelphia Art Alliance, 78, Nat Mus Am Art, 81; Kent State Univ, 69; Mem Art Gallery, Univ Rochester, 78; Pa Acad Fine Arts, 86. *Awards:* Int Platform Asn Art Show Silver Medal, 83, Gold Medal, 84. *Bibliog:* Frank Getlein (auth), He defied tradition and made it work, Sun Star, 7/21/68; Diane Chichura & Thelma Stevens (auths), Super Sculpture, Van Nostrand-Reinhold, 74; Victoria Donohoe (auth), Kinetic art lives on, Philadelphia Inquirer, 10/27/78. *Media:* Miscellaneous. *Publ:* Cover, Applied Optics, 90; poster image, Elektra Entertainment, 90; cover, Grauer's Cobol, Vols 1 & 2, Prentice-Hall, 91; cover, Benjafield's Cognition, Prentice-Hall, 92; cover, Cobb's Adolescence, Mayfield, 92. *Dealer:* Artworks Gallery Santa Barbara CA. *Mailing Add:* 1135 Loxford Terr Silver Spring MD 20901

PEKAR, RONALD WALTER
PAINTER, SCULPTOR
b Cleveland, Ohio, Oct 9, 42. *Study:* Cleveland Inst Art; Wash Univ, BFA, fel, 66-67, MFA. *Work:* Memphis Brooks Mus Art; Mississippi Mus Art; Carroll Reece Mus, Tenn; Cheekwood Mus Art, Tenn; St Jude Children's Res Hosp; painting series, Federal Express Corp. *Comn:* Mural series, Memphis Convention Ctr Complex; sculptural environments, Holiday Inns, Inc (nationwide); illuminated painting, Gen Pub Utilities, Pa; two 3-story illuminated sculptures, Lemoyne-Owen Col. *Exhib:* Solo shows: Memphis Brooks Mus, Miss Mus Art, Rhodes Col, Univ Tenn, Memphis Col Art & Ark State Univ; 10 in Tennessee, Statewide-Traveling Bicentennial Exhib; Mid South Artists Traveling Exhib; Memphis Pink Palace Mus Commemorative Painting; Spirit of the River (audio-visual environment), Memphis Brooks Mus, 77-81. *Pos:* Found div chair, Memphis Col Art, currently; Lectr & critic, Univ Tenn, ETex State Univ, Ark State Univ. *Teaching:* Prof, 2-D and 3-D design, drawing and painting, Inst Parsons Sch Design & Calif State Univ, Northridge. *Awards:* Cult Contribution Award, State of Tenn; Tenn Valley Authority Monumental Sculpture Award. *Bibliog:* Man of steel and crayon, Mid South Mag Commercial Appeal; profile, Memphis Mag. *Media:* Acrylic, Oil, All. *Publ:* Illusr, Air poster, Memphis Acad Arts, 69; illusr rec label, Ardent Rec, 72; ed & illusr, Homage to the Land and Sky, 73; illusr rec label, Privilege Rec, 74. *Mailing Add:* 1426 Highland Ave Glendale CA 91202

PEKARSKY, MEL (MELVIN HIRSCH)
PAINTER, EDUCATOR
b Chicago, Ill, Sept 18, 34. *Study:* Art Inst Chicago; Northwestern Univ, BA, MA. *Work:* Yale Univ Mus Fine Arts; Corcoran Gallery Art, Washington, DC; Minneapolis Inst Arts; Cleveland Mus; Weatherspoon Mus, Univ NC. *Comn:* Exterior mural, City Walls Inc: Kaplan Fund, 70; exterior mural, Nat Endowment Arts, 72; exterior mural, US Dept Housing & Urban Develop, 74. *Exhib:* Oversize Prints, Whitney Mus Am Art, New York, 71; Am Prints, Brooklyn Mus, NY, 74-75 & San Diego Fine Arts Gallery, Calif, 75; New Editions 74-75 & New York Cult Ctr, 75; Drawings by Seven Am Artists, Cleveland Mus, 78; one-man shows, G W Einstein, New York, 75, 77-78, 80-81, 84, 86, 88 & 91, Gallery 112 Greene St, New York, 80 & Butler Inst Am Art, 90; The American Landscape: Recent Developments, Whitney Mus Am Art, New York, 81. *Pos:* Founding mem & mem bd, City Walls, Inc, 69-75, vpres, 70-75. *Teaching:* From asst to assoc dean art, Sch Visual Arts, New York, 67-69; prof art, State Univ NY, Stony Brook, 75-, chmn, 76-78 & 84-89, dir studio progs, 75-78. *Bibliog:* Lawrence Alloway (ed), Landscape Views, Montclair State Col, NJ, 79; Ann Lockhart (auth), Mel Pekarsky, Arts Mag, 3/78; Ronny Cohen (auth), Mel Pekarsky, Arts, 10/82; Donald Kuspit (auth), Mel Pekarsky, catalog, 10/84 & Pekarsky's Desert Tundra, catalogue, 10/88; Robert G Edelman (auth), The Transformative Vision: Contemporary Am Landscape Painting, Pittsburgh Carnegie Mus, 89. *Mem:* Col Art Asn. *Media:* Oil, Mixed Media. *Publ:* Illusr, The Curious Cow, 60, Little Quack, 61, The Three Goats, 63 & The Little Red Hen, 63, Follett; Handbook of Gestures, Mouton, The Hague, 72. *Dealer:* G W Einstein Co Inc Fine Art 591 Broadway New York NY 10012. *Mailing Add:* Box CH Stony Brook NY 11790

PELADEAU, MARIUS BEAUDOIN
WRITER, MUSEUM DIRECTOR
b Boston, Mass, Jan 27, 35. *Study:* St Michael's Col, Winooski Park, Vt, BA(cum laude), 56; Boston Univ, Mass, MS, 57; Georgetown Univ, Washington, DC, MA(fel), 61. *Pos:* Dir, Maine League of Hist Soc & Mus, 72-76; dir, William A Farnsworth Libr & Art Mus, 76-87, consult & writer, 87- *Mem:* Fel, Vt Hist Soc, Co Military Historians. *Res:* American art and the decorative arts. *Publ:* Ed, The Verse of Royall Tyler, Univ Va Press, 68; The Prose of Royall Tyler, Vt Hist Soc, 72; auth, Chansonetta: The Photographs of Chansonetta Stanley Emmons, 1858-1937, Morgan & Morgan, 77; Stephen R Deane: Early Maine Folk Calligrapher, Kennebec River Press, 84. *Mailing Add:* RFD 1 Box 599A Redfield ME 04355

PELLETTIERI, MICHAEL JOSEPH
PRINTMAKER, PAINTER
b New York, NY, Nov 25, 43. *Study:* Art Students League New York, with Robert B Hale, Edwin Dickinson, Harry Sternberg & Joseph Hirsch, 63-66; City Col New York, BA, 65; City Univ New York, MA, 69. *Work:* De Cordova Mus, Lincoln, Mass; Taz Gallery & Co, Boston; Newark Art Libr, NJ; Ben Goldstein Collection, New York; Columbia Mus Art, SC; New York Pub Libr; and others. *Exhib:* Boston Printmakers 32nd Nat, DeCordova Mus, Lincoln, Mass, 79; Hunterdon Art Ctr 23rd & 25th, Newark Art Libr, NJ, 79 & 81; Nat Acad & Inst Arts & Letts, 80; Charlotte Printmakers, NC, 81; Columbia Univ, New York, 87; Landmark Gallery, Kingston, NY, 88; New Renaissance Gallery, New York, 91. *Teaching:* Instr lithography, Art Students League New York, 77-79, instr graphics, 79-, instr intaglio, Summit Art Ctr, 82-88; instr printmaking, Columbia Univ, Teachers Col, 87- *Awards:* Mitchell Fund Award, 86; Mac Dowell Colony Fel, 88; Purchase Prize, Nat Works Paper, Univ Miss, 91; and others. *Bibliog:* Garry Simpson (auth), Currier & Ives (film for television), Univ Vt, 76. *Mem:* Artist Equity New York; Art Students League New York (bd control, 65, treas, 66-67). *Media:* Intaglio, Lithography; Oil. *Publ:* Contribr, Print Review Ten, Pratt Graphic Art Ctr, 79. *Dealer:* Gallery Graphic Art 1601 York Ave New York NY 10028; Miriam Pearlman Inc Suite 5410 505 N Lake Shore Dr Chicago IL 60611. *Mailing Add:* 325 W 77th St New York NY 10024

PELLEW, JOHN CLIFFORD
PAINTER
b Heamoor, Eng, Apr 9, 03; US citizen. *Study:* Penzance Sch Art, Eng. *Work:* Metrop Mus Art, New York; Butler Inst Am Art, Youngstown, Ohio; Ga Mus Fine Arts, Athens; Adelphi Col, NY; New Brit Mus Am Art, Conn; and others. *Exhib:* Nat Acad Design, New York, 48-72; Butler Inst Am Art, Youngstown, Ohio, 64; 200 Years of Watercolor Painting in America, Metrop Mus Art, New York, 67; Landscape 1, De Cordova & Dana Mus, Lincoln, Mass, 70; Am Watercolor Soc Exchange Exhib, Can, 72. *Awards:* Adolph & Clara Obrig Prize, Nat Acad Design, 61; First Award Watercolor, Butler Inst Am Art, 64; Silver Medal, Am Watercolor Soc, 70. *Bibliog:* Norman Kent (auth), Watercolor Methods, Watson-Guptill, 55; Wendon Blake (auth), Complete Guide to Acrylic Painting, Watson-Guptill, 71. *Mem:* Nat Acad Design; Am Watercolor Soc; Southwestern Watercolor Soc. *Media:* Watercolor, Oil. *Publ:* Auth, Acrylic Landscape Painting, 68; Painting in Watercolor, 69; Oil Painting Outdoors, 71; Painting Maritime Landscapes, 73. *Dealer:* Baker Gallery Fine Art PO Box 1920 Lubbock TX 79408. *Mailing Add:* 123 Murray St Norwalk CT 06851

PELLI, CESAR
ARCHITECT
b Tucuman, Arg, Oct 12, 26; US citizen. *Study:* Univ Tucuman, Dipl in Archit(cum laude), 49; Univ Ill, MS(archit), 54. *Comn:* Mus Mod Art, New York; World Financial Ctr, New York, 81; Herring Hall, Rice Univ, Houston, Tex, 82; Norwest Ctr, Minneapolis, 83. *Exhib:* Houses for Sale, Castelli Galleries, New York, 80; Late Entries, Chicago Tribune Competition, Ill, 80; Art & Archit Exhib, New York, 80; Lingotto-Fiat Proposal, Turin, Italy, 83. *Pos:* Designer, Eero Saarinen & Assoc, 54-64; dir & vpres design, Daniel Mann, Johnson & Mendenhall, 64-68; partner in charge of design, Gruen Assoc, Los Angeles & New York, 68-77; partner, Cesar Pelli & Assoc, New Haven, 77- *Teaching:* Dean, Sch Archit, Yale Univ, 77-84, vis lectr, currently. *Awards:* First Prize, Int Archit Competition, United Nations City, Repub of Austria, City of Vienna, 69; Honor Award, Pac Design Ctr, 76; AIA Honor Award, Cleveland Clinic; 86, Herring Hall, Rice Univ, 86; CSA/AIA Unbuilt Project Award, 88. *Bibliog:* John Pastier (auth), Cesar Pelli, Whitney Libr Design, 82; Cesar Pelli Special Ed at U Mag, 7/85; Michael Crosbie (auth), Profile - Cesar Pelli & Associates, Archit, 2/89; Cesar Pelli: 1965-1948, Rizzoli Int Publs, 90. *Mem:* Fel Am Inst Archit; Am Acad & Inst Arts & Lett; Perspecta Archit Mag (bd gov mem); trustee, Wadsworth Atheneum. *Publ:* Auth, Architectural Form & the Tradition of Building, VIA, 83; Skyscrapers, Perspecta No 19, 81; Pieces of the City, Archit Digest, Aug, 88; Cesar Pelli: The Megabuilding in Context, Archit Design, 11/12/88; Statement, A&U Mag, 2/90. *Mailing Add:* c/o Cesar Pelli & Assoc Inc 1056 Chapel St New Haven CT 06510

PELLICONE, WILLIAM
PAINTER, SCULPTOR
b Philadelphia, Pa, Apr 12, 15. *Study:* Pa Acad Fine Arts, Philadelphia; Barnes Found, Merion, Pa. *Work:* Boston Mus, Mass; Smithsonian Inst, Washington, DC; Am Broadcasting Co, New York; Iowa City Mus, Bayonne Mus, NJ. *Comn:* Murals, Abraham & Strauss, Brooklyn, NY, 69 & 70. *Exhib:* Pa Acad Fine Arts, 39; Nat Acad Design, New York, 39; Woodmere Art Gallery & Art Alliance, Philadelphia; Baltimore Mus, 71; Parrish Mus, Southampton, NY, 85. *Pos:* Prof advan painting, Univ Iowa, 74. *Awards:* Barnes Found, Pa, 40; Pa Acad Fine Arts, Philadelphia, 40; Scholarship, Greece, 73. *Bibliog:* Article, ArtSpeak Publ, New York, 83. *Mem:* Pa Acad Fine Arts, Philadelphia. *Media:* Oil, Acrylic. *Publ:* Auth, reviews & critiques for ArtSpeak Publ, New York & Dan's Papers, Bridgehampton, NY, Southampton Press, NY. *Dealer:* d p Fong/Spratt Galleries 383 S 1st St San Jose CA 95113; Goodman Gallery 53 North Sea Rd Southampton NY 11968. *Mailing Add:* 1856 North Sea Rd Southampton NY 11968

PELS, ALBERT
PAINTER, ADMINISTRATOR
b Cincinnati, Ohio, May 7, 10. *Study:* Art Acad Cincinnati; Univ Cincinnati; Beaux Arts Sch; Art Students League, six scholarships; also with Thomas Hart Benton, Kenneth Hayes Miller & Bridgeman. *Work:* Butler Inst Am Art; NY State Mus Art; Smithsonian Inst, Washington, DC; West Moreland Mus Art, Greensburg, Pa; Martin Luther King Fund Collection. *Comn:* The Landing of the Swedes, Courthouse, Wilmington, Del, 42; Early History of Normal, Ill, in post off; Africa scene for ship, North African Line, 50; History of Norfolk, Va, for naval base; gen hist of Anniston, Ala area, YMCA. *Exhib:* Whitney Mus Am Art Ann, 40-50; Carnegie Int Exhib, 42-48; Nat Acad Design, 45-52; Butler Inst Am Art Ann, 45-55; Chicago Ann, 49; Cincinnati Mus world tour; one-man-show, Wigmore Galleries, New York, NY, 88; NY State Mus, Albany. *Pos:* Dir & owner, Albert Pels Sch Art Inc, 72-; demonstr oil painting on educ TV. *Teaching:* Instr art, Jones Mem Sch & Hessian Hills Sch; instr fine art, Albert Pels Sch Art, Inc, 46-82. *Awards:* First Prize for Sea Disaster, Butler Inst Am Art, 46; Schackenberg Scholar, 49. *Mem:* Life mem Art Students League. *Media:* Mixed, Acrylic, Oil. *Publ:* Contribr, Art News, 46; illusr, Easy puppets, 52 & Water pets, 56. *Dealer:* Gorwit Galleries Roslyn NY 11576; Rainone Art Galleries 1212 Park Row Arlington TX 76013. *Mailing Add:* 2109 Broadway New York NY 10023

PELUSO, MARTA E
PHOTOGRAPHER, GALLERY DIRECTOR
b New Brighton, Pa, Apr 30, 51. *Study:* Allegheny Col, Meadville, Pa, BA, 73; Panopticon Photo Workshop with Garry Winogrand, Greece, 77; Univ Calif, Davis, MFA, 82. *Work:* Univ Calif, Davis/Nelson Gallery; Mercyhurst Col Libr, Erie, Pa. *Exhib:* Solo Exhib, Photographs, Pittsburgh Filmmakers Gallery, Pa, 81; The Guiding Light, Eye Gallery, San Francisco, Calif, 90 & Santa Barbara Contemp Arts Forum, Calif, 91; Scarred Texts/Sacred Territories, Scarlet Palette, Cambria, Calif, 92. *Pos:* Photograph proj coord, Ethnic Impressions, Erie, Pa, 75-79; Gallery dir, Cuesta Col, San Luis Obispo, Calif, 86- *Teaching:* Lectr photog, Cal Polytech State Univ, San Luis Obispo, 83-87; instr studio art, Cuesta Col, San Luis Obispo, Calif, 86- *Bibliog:* Les Krantz (auth), California art review, Am References, 89. *Mem:* Soc Photog Educ (W Region chmn, 89); Friends of Photog; Visual Studies Workshop; Black Photographers; San Luis Obispo Co Arts Coun (bd mem, 90-93). *Media:* Photography, Video. *Mailing Add:* 348 S Court Los Osos CA 93402

PENA, AMADO MAURILIO, JR
PAINTER, ILLUSTRATOR
b Laredo, Tex, Oct 1, 43. *Study:* Tex A&I Univ, BA(art), 65, MA, 71. *Work:* Tex A&I Univ; Dept For Lang, Univ Ky; Univ Tex, Austin; Juarez-Lincoln Univ, Austin; Los Pinos, Pres Palace, Mexico. *Comn:* Mural, Laredo Independent Sch Dist, Serv Ctr, 70; mural, City Hall, Crystal City, 72; painting, City Coun Crystal City, 72; centenial poster, Univ Tex, Austin, 83; Amarille Art Ctr, Tex, 83; and others. *Exhib:* Chicago Art Exhib, Nat Lulac Conf, Washington, DC, 73 & Univ Tex Student Ctr, 74; Chicano Artists of the Southwest, Inst Mex Cult, San Antonio, 75; one-man retrospectives, Mus Nuevo Santander, Laredo, Tex, 83 & Laguna Gloria Art Mus, Austin, Tex, 83; and others. *Teaching:* Teacher art, Laredo Independent Sch Dist, 65-71, Crystal City Independent Sch Dist, 71-73 & L C Anderson High Sch, Austin, 73- *Awards:* Citation Award, Laguna Gloria Art Mus, 68; Corpus Christi Art Found Award, 69; Rio Grande Art Festival Award, Laredo Art Asn, 71, 72 & 74. *Bibliog:* Kelly Fearing (auth), Art & the Creative Teacher, Univ Tex, 69; Jacinto Quirarte (auth), The Art of Mexican Americans, The Humble Way, Exxon Oil Co, 69 & Mexican American Artists, Univ Tex, 72. *Mem:* Laredo Art Asn (pres, 68-69); Austin Art Teachers Asn (treas, 74-75). *Media:* Serigraphy; Watercolor. *Publ:* Contribr & auth, Chicano Art of the Southwest, Chicano Slide Collection, 73; contribr, Tejidos, Magazin & Calendario Chicano; illusr, Cuenots, 75. *Dealer:* El Taller Gallery 723 E Sixth St Austin TX 78701; Gallery Mack Seattle WA. *Mailing Add:* c/o El Taller Inc 1221 W Sixth St Austin TX 78703

PENCE, JOHN GERALD
DEALER, PATRON
b Ft Wayne, Ind, Feb 8, 36. *Study:* Wabash Col, BA, 58; Am Univ, MA, 63. *Collections Arranged:* Douglas Fenn Wilson, Worcester Mus, Dartmouth Col, Janus Gallery, Santa Fe, San Francisco Mus, Hibernia Bank, San Francisco & Deloitee, Haskins & Sells, New York; Michael Bergt, Pence Gallery, San Francisco & San Francisco Mus; Frank Mason, Clorox Co & Pence Gallery, San Francisco; Robert Maione, Pence Gallery, San Francisco, Clorox Co, Standard Oil of Calif, Hering & Assoc, Portland & Allen-Pacific Co, San Francisco; Gillian Wiles, Pence Gallery, San Francisco & URS Corp, Dallas; Donald Davis, Cellocon Inc, San Francisco, Deloitee, Haskins, Sells, New York & James Malott Architects; Will Wilson, Buckeye Petroleum, NJ & Butler Inst Am Art. *Interests:* American contemporary realists--advance support prior to initial presentations. *Publ:* Auth, Will Wilson, Am Artist Mag, 5/83. *Mailing Add:* Pence Gallery 750 Post St San Francisco CA 94109

PENCZNER, PAUL JOSEPH
PAINTER
b Hungary, Sept 17, 16; US citizen. *Study:* In Hungary. *Work:* Vatican, Rome; Capitol Bldg, Jefferson City; Univ Tenn, Memphis; Univ Mo, Cape Girardeau; Fla State Univ, Tallahassee. *Exhib:* Pa Acad Fine Arts, Philadelphia; Brooks Mem Art Gallery, Memphis; Jersey City Mus; Smithsonian Inst, Washington, DC; El Delgado Mus, New Orleans; Tenn Botanical Gardens & Fine Art Ctr, Nashville. *Pos:* Owner Penczner's Fine Art Studio & Gallery, Memphis, Tenn. *Awards:* Distinguished Achievement Award, Modern Maturity, 86. *Mem:* Nat Soc Painters Casein; Tenn Watercolor Soc; Am Artist Prof League; Southern Watercolor Soc. *Media:* Multimedia. *Dealer:* Laurelwood Gallery 404 Perkins Ext Memphis TN 38117. *Mailing Add:* 273 Strathmore Circle Memphis TN 38104

PENDERGRAFT, NORMAN ELVEIS
MUSEUM DIRECTOR, HISTORIAN
b Durham, NC, Mar 4, 34. *Study:* Univ NC, Chapel Hill; Conservatorio di Musica G Rossini, Pesaro, Italy, with Maestra Raggi-Valentini; Ohio Univ, Athens; Mus Mgt Inst, Univ Calif, Berkeley; Nat Endowment Humanities Sem, Rome, Italy. *Pos:* Dir art mus, NC Cent Univ, Durham, 76- *Teaching:* Prof art hist, NC Cent Univ, Durham, 66- *Awards:* Outstanding contribution to Art Educ Award, NC Art Educ Asn, 84. *Bibliog:* O M Foushee (auth), Art in North Carolina: Episodes & Developments, Chapel Hill, NC, 72; L M Igoe (auth), 250 yrs of Afro-Amer Art: An Annotated Bibliography, R R Bowker, 81. *Mem:* Am Asn Mus; Southeastern Mus Coun; Col Art Asn; Am Asn Univ Prof; NC Mus Coun. *Res:* Italian Renaissance, Afro-American and American art. *Publ:* Auth, Heralds of Life: Artis, Bearden & Burke, 77 & Duncanson: A British American Connection, 84 & Geoffrey Holder: Painter, 86, & Gullah Life Reflections, 88, NC Cent Univ Mus Art; Tracing the rise of Afro-American art in North Carolina, & other articles in Art Voices-South; On tour in Winston-Salem North Carolina, Am Artist, 10/81. *Mailing Add:* 208 Watts St Durham NC 27701

PENDLETON, MARY CAROLINE
HANDWEAVER, WRITER
b Rochester, Ind. *Study:* Dayton Art Inst, Ohio; Cranbrook Acad Art; also with Lili Blumenau & Mary Meigs Atwater. *Comn:* Over the years, many pieces for pvt homes, bus & churches such as drapery fabrics, upholstery, dividers & paraments. *Exhib:* Int Textile Exhib, Woman Col, Univ NC, 52 & 54; Ann Women's Int Expos, New York, 59 & 60; Crafts Western US, Southern Calif Expos, Del Mar, 61; one-man show, Charles W Bowers Mem Mus, Santa Ana, 65; two-man show, Stanford Med & Res Inst, 63; Six Craftsmen Exhib, Heard Mus, Phoenix, Ariz, 63. *Pos:* Mem bd dirs, Handweavers Guild Am, 70; auth & ed, The Looming Arts, Nat Handweavers. *Teaching:* Teacher handweaving, Pendleton Fabric Craft Sch, 58-; weaving instr, Northern Ariz Univ, Flagstaff, 76-81; teach workshops all over the country. *Awards:* Int Textile Exhib, Women's Col, Univ NC, 52; Contemporary Craftsmen Far West, Mus Contemp Crafts, 62; Ariz State Fair, 62. *Bibliog:* Isabel Stroud (auth), Couple finds weaving and full-time career, Christian Sci Monitor, 1/6/75; articles, Handwoven Mag, 5-6/90. *Mem:* Nat League Am Pen Women; Ariz Designer Craftsmen. *Publ:* Auth, Navajo & Hopi Weaving Techniques, Macmillan, 74; Double Weave Series, 74 & Overshot Weave Series, 77. *Mailing Add:* c/o Interweave Press 201 E Fourth St Loveland CO 80537

PENKOFF, RONALD PETER
EDUCATOR, PAINTER
b Toledo, Ohio, May 18, 32. *Study:* Bowling Green State Univ, BFA, 54; Ohio State Univ, MA, 56; Stanley William Hayter's Atelier 17, Paris, 65-66; Univ of Kansas, 80 & 81. *Work:* Libr Cong, Washington, DC; Columbus Gallery Art, Ohio; Munson-Williams-Proctor Inst, Utica, NY; Montclair Mus, NJ; Ball State Art Gallery, Muncie, Ind. *Exhib:* Pennell Int Exhib Prints, Libr Cong, Washington, DC, 55-57; Notre Dame Mus, 70; Skylight Gallery, 73; Madison Art Ctr, 75; Alvehjem Mus, 77 & 83; Milwaukee Art Mus, 78; Crossman Gallery, Univ Wis, Whitewater, 90. *Teaching:* Asst prof art, State Univ NY Col, Oneonta, 56-59; asst prof, Ball State Univ, 59-67; vis prof, Bath Acad Art, Corsham, England, summer 66; prof, Univ Wis, Waukesha, 67-87, Richland Ctr, 87-, chmn, Ctr Syst Art Dept, 70-89. *Awards:* Munson-Williams-Proctor Inst Award, Cent NY Artists, 58-59; First Award Painting, Eastern Ind Artists, 64; Nat Endowment Humanities Grant, 78. *Bibliog:* W Fabricki (auth), Prints and drawings of Ronald Penkoff, Quartet, 63; M E Young (auth), Profile, Wis Acad Rev, 69; Donald Key (auth), Color printing is an elusive endeavor, Milwaukee J, 71. *Mem:* Col Art Asn. *Media:* Intaglio. *Publ:* Auth, The eye and the object, Forum, 62; Roots of the Ukiyo-E, 65; Sign, Signal, Symbol, 70; The Japanese Print & the Grounding of Frank Lloyd Wrights' Architecture, 90. *Mailing Add:* Dept Art Univ Wis Richland Center WI 53581

PENN, IRVING
PHOTOGRAPHER
b NJ, 1917. *Study:* Philadelphia Mus Sch Indust Art, 34-38. *Work:* Mus Mod Art & Metrop Mus Art, New York; Art Inst Chicago; Victoria & Albert Mus, London; Nat Portrait Gallery, Nat Mus Am Art & Smithsonian Inst, Washington, DC. *Exhib:* One-man shows, Mus Mod Art, New York, 75 & 84, Galleria Civica D'Arte Moderna, Torino, 75 & Metrop Mus Art, New York,

77. *Bibliog:* John Szarkowski (auth), Irving Penn, New York, 84. *Publ:* Auth, Moments Preserved, 60; Worlds in a Small Room, 74; Inventive Paris clothes, 1909-1939, 77; Flowers, 80; Passage, 91. *Mailing Add:* c/o Irving Penn Studios 89 Fifth Ave New York NY 10003

PENNEY, CHARLES RAND
COLLECTOR, PATRON
b Buffalo, NY, July 26, 23. *Study:* Yale Univ, BA; Univ Va, LLB & JD. *Collections Arranged:* Prints from the Charles Rand Penney Found, traveling NY & Tex, 64-75; Selections from the Charles R Penney Collection, Lakeview Gallery, NY, 70; Prints From the Charles Rand Penney Foundation, Niagara Co Community Col Mus, 71 & 77; Staffordshire Pottery Portrait Figures, Niagara Co Hist Soc, 72; 44 Charles Burchfield Drawings & two paintings, Charles Burchfield Ctr, Buffalo, 73; Decade, Graphics in the Sixties, 74; NY State Photographers, 74; Victorian Staffordshire Figurines, Carborundum Mus of Ceramics, Niagara Falls, 74 & Columbus Gallery of Fine Arts, Ohio, 76; Charles Burchfield: The Charles Rand Penney Collection, traveling throughout US, 78-81; The Graphic Art of Emil Ganso, Univ Iowa Mus Art, 79; The Charles Rand Penney Collection: Twentieth Century Art, traveling throughout US, 83-88; The Charles Rand Penney Collection of Western New York Art, Burchfield Art Ctr, 92-93. *Awards:* Distinguished Service to Culture Award, State Univ NY Col Potsdam, 83; President's Distinguished Serv Award, Buffalo State Col, 91. *Mem:* Smithsonian Inst, Washington, DC; Am Ceramic Circle; hon life mem Rochester Art Club; hon trustee Buffalo Soc Artist; and many others. *Collection:* International contemporary art; works of Charles E Burchfield and Emil Ganso; Western New York artists; Spanish-American Santos and Retablos; Victorian Staffordshire pottery portrait figures; American antique historic glass and textiles; American antique pressed glass; international primitive art; US World's Fairs & Expositions. *Mailing Add:* 538 Bewley Bldg Lockport NY 14094

PENNEY, JACQUELINE
PAINTER, INSTRUCTOR
b Roslyn, NY, Mar 26, 30. *Study:* Phoenix Sch Design, New York, 48; Black Mountain Col, 49; Inst Design, Chicago, 50, with Tom Hill, Carl Molno, Charles Reid, Frank Webb, Robert E Wood & Christopher Schink. *Work:* Port Authority, World Trade Ctr, New York; Stony Brook Sch, NY; Eastern Long Island Hosp, Greenport, NY; Unitarian Universalist Church Oak Park, Ill; Banca Commerce Italiana, Italy; Southold Savings Bank, Southold, NY. *Comn:* Cutchogue Pub Libr, Cutchogue, NY. *Exhib:* White Containers, Guild Hall Mus, East Hampton, NY, 86; What Comes After Winter, Audubon Artists Juried Exhib, 86; Nat Asn Women Artists Traveling Show, 88, 89; Monhegan Backyard, San Diego WC So Int, 89; Earth, Sea & Ski, Nat Asn Women Artists, Aldelphi Univ, New York, 91; Dancing in the Light, Salmagundi Club, New York, 92. *Teaching:* Art classes all media, 77- *Awards:* ER Langer-Seligson Mem Award, Nat Asn Women Artists, 89; Langnickel Award, Nat League Am Pen Women, 90; Landscape Award, Mid-Atlantic Regional Watercolor Exhib, 90; William Meyerowitz Mem Prize, Nat Asn Women Artists, 86. *Bibliog:* Kathleen Sullivan (auth), Scream painting, Sun Newspaper, 1/28/82; Paul Demery (auth), An artist dreams in Cutchogue, Long Island Traveler-Watchman, 3/17/83; Manhattan Arts Mag, 4-5/91. *Mem:* Artist Equity New York; Nat Asn Women Artists; Salmagundi Club, New York, 92; Nat Asn Am Penwomen, 92. *Media:* Acrylic, Watercolor. *Publ:* Auth, A painting in progress--from far to near, Palette Talk Mag, 81. *Dealer:* Gallery East 257 Pantigo Rd East Hampton NY 11937; Elaine Benson Gallery Bridgehampton NY 11932. *Mailing Add:* 270 North St Box 959 Cutchogue NY 11935

PENNINGTON, ESTILL CURTIS
MUSEUM DIRECTOR, HISTORIAN
b Paris, Ky, Oct 3, 50. *Study:* Univ Ky, BA, 72; Univ Ga, MA, 75; George Washington Univ. *Collections Arranged:* A New Quarter: Contemporary New Orleans Artists, 83; Birney Imes III: An exhib of photographs, 84; Storytime: Art as Episode, 85; William Edward West (1788-1857): Kentucky Painter (auth, catalog), 85; Reveries & Mississippi Memories, 86. *Pos:* Guest cur & asst registrar, Nat Portrait Gallery, 77-78; art historian, Archives Am Art, 78-83; mus dir, Lauren Rogers Mus Art, Laurel, Miss, 83- *Mem:* Miss Inst Arts & Letts (pres, 85-); Am Asn Mus; Victorian Soc Am. *Res:* American painting and portraiture. *Publ:* Auth, Joseph Cornell: Dimestore Connoisseur, 83 & Painting Lord Byron: An Account of William Edward West, 84, Archives Am Art J; The Climate of Taste in the Old South, Southern Quart, 85; collabr, The South on Paper: Line, Color & Light, Robert Hicklin, Inc, 85. *Mailing Add:* c/o New Orleans Mus of Art Lelong Ave & City Park New Orleans LA 70119

PENNINGTON, MARY ANNE
MUSEUM DIRECTOR, LECTURER
b Franklin, Va, Apr 12, 43. *Study:* Va Commonwealth Univ, BFA, 65, MFA, 66; Univ NC, Chapel-Hill, dipl(art mgt), 80. *Collections Arranged:* Work Prog Admin Graphics Collection, 82; For the Sake of a Single Verse, 84. *Pos:* Coord visual arts & humanities prog, Ludwigsberg, Ger, 74-76; exec dir, Greenville Mus Art, 80-87; speaker, NC Dept Corrections, 80-87; columnist, Pitt-Greenville Times, 81-; prog coordr, Pitt-Greenville Leadership Inst, 85-; field reviewer, Inst Mus Servs, 86; Lauren Rodgers Mus Art, Laurel, Miss, 87-; coord cult arts prog, Jones Co Leadership Inst, 89-90, participant, 90-91, chmn curriculum comt, 91-92 & chmn bd dirs, 92- *Teaching:* Guest lectr art, Converse Col, Spartansburg, SC, 66; inst art, Presby Col, Clinton, SC, 66-69, Pitt Co, 70-71, Greenville City, NC, Sch Systems, 71-73 & Pitt Community Col 72-73; vis artist-in-residence, Salt Pond Art Ctr, Blacksburg, Va, summer 78; asst prof art, Pembroke State Univ, 76-80. *Awards:* NC Arts Coun Scholar Grant Award, 80 & 87; Volunteer Award, NC Gov, 81; NC Distinguished Women Award, 86. *Mem:* Am Asn Mus (accreditation surveyor, 90-, map reviewer, 90- & map surveyor, 91-); Southeastern Mus Conf Inc (steering comt, 90-91; Miss Arts Comn (proj support grants panel, 90-, bd dirs, 90-, adv bd dirs, 90-, vpres, 92-); Jones Co Competitive Community Prog Team (chmn educ task force, 91-92); Miss Inst Arts & Letts (bd govs, 90-, chmn Visual Arts Awards, 91, vpres, 92-). *Publ:* Auth, Art in eastern NC, Carolina Arts, summer 81; A Visit to Greenville Museum Art, 86; Handbook to the Collection of the Lauren Rogers Mus Art, 89; Mus in the Schools Education Program, 92; weekly columns for Laurel Leader Call, 90- *Mailing Add:* c/o Lauren Rogers Mus of Art Fifth Ave & Seventh St PO Box 1108 Laurel MS 39441

PENNINGTON, SALLY
PAINTER
b Seattle, Wash, 53. *Study:* Mills Col, MFA(painting), 83. *Exhib:* Pro Arts Ann, Oakland, 85; Introduction Show, Triangle Gallery, San Francisco, 86; Connected by Nature, Pro Arts, Oakland, 86; Gallery Artists, Triangle Gallery, 86; Six East Bay Artists, Mills Col Art Gallery, Oakland, Calif, 89. *Teaching:* instr, Diablo Valley Col, Calif, 83-87. *Awards:* Catherine Morgan Trefethew Fel in Art, 82; Visual Artists Fel Grant, Nat Endowment Arts, 87. *Dealer:* Triangle Gallery 95 Minna St San Francisco CA 94105. *Mailing Add:* 23216 SE 31st St Issaguah WA 98027

PENNUTO, JAMES WILLIAM
CONCEPTUAL ARTIST, CONSERVATOR
b Joliet, Ill, June 15, 36. *Study:* Art Students League. *Work:* Oakland Mus, Calif; San Francisco Mus Mod Art. *Exhib:* Butler Inst Am Art, Youngstown, Ohio, 66-67; Oakland Mus, 69-70; Mus Mod Art, New York, 70; St John's Univ, New York, 70; Joslyn Art Mus, Omaha, Nebr, 70; San Francisco Mus Mod Art, 71. *Bibliog:* Palmer French (auth), San Francisco, Artforum, 2/70; New dimensions, Time, 4/13/70; Carter Ratcliff (auth), Report from San Francisco, Art in Am, 5-6/77. *Mem:* Am Inst Conserv. *Media:* Miscellaneous. *Mailing Add:* 1717 17th St San Francisco CA 94103

PENNY, AUBREY JOHN ROBERT
PAINTER, SCULPTOR
b London, Eng, July 30, 17; US citizen. *Study:* Univ Calif, Los Angeles, BA(art & art hist), 53, MA(art), 55. *Work:* Contemp Art Soc, London; Edward Dean Mus, Cherry Valley, Calif; Mt San Jacinto Col Gallery Art; Phillips Collection, Washington, DC, 85. *Exhib:* Corcoran Gallery Art, Washington, DC, 57; Am Watercolor Soc, New York, 57-58; two-man shows, Madison Gallery, New York, 63 & Int De Deauville, France, 72; one-man shows, Mt San Jacinto Col, Calif, 72 & 82 & Talmadge House Exhib, Los Angeles, 85; Los Angeles Inst Contemp Art, 81; Galerie Salammbo, Paris, France, 88. *Pos:* Owner, Aubrey Penny Fine Art, Los Angeles, 55-; mem art coun, Univ Calif, Los Angeles, 55- *Awards:* Merit Award, Nat Watercolor Soc, 55; Gold Seal Award, Los Angeles Inst Contemp Art, 81. *Bibliog:* Article, Art Voices S, 1-2/80. *Mem:* Contemp Art Soc, London; Victoria Inst, London; Am Soc Aesthetics & Art Criticism. *Media:* Acrylic, Wood. *Publ:* Auth, The Mind-Line Approach of Aubrey Penny, 76; Sculpture-Halcyon Series, 79, Geneva Series, 80 & Amor Series, 87; filmmaker, Towards a richer synthesis, 84; The Power of the Non-Objective, 91. *Mailing Add:* Aubrey Penny MA PO Box 7796 Van Nuys CA 91409

PENNY, DONALD CHARLES
CRAFTSMAN, SCULPTOR
b Atlanta, Ga, Oct 5, 35. *Study:* Ga Inst Technol, 57-58; Ga State Univ, with Joe Perrin & Joe Almyda, BBA, 61; Fla State Univ, with Karl Zerbe & Ralph Hurst, MS, 63. *Work:* Middle Tenn State Univ, Murfreesboro; Metrop Mus Art, Miami; Ahmadu Bello Univ, Zaria, Nigeria. *Comn:* Ga Coun Arts & Humanities, Valdosta, 81-82; Emory Univ, Atlanta, Ga, 81-82. *Exhib:* Mint Mus Art, Charlotte, NC, 67, 69 & 70; Smithsonian Inst, Washington, DC, 70; solo exhibs, Metrop Mus & Art Ctr, Miami, Fla, 70, Brenau Col, Gainesville, Ga, 89; Greenville Co Mus, SC, 74; Furman Univ-R J Reynolds, Winston-Salem, NC, 77; Mus Arts & Sci, Macon, Ga, 82 & 89; Fla Sch Art, 89; Broward Community Col, 92; and others. *Teaching:* Instr, Palm Beach Jr Col, West Palm Beach, Fla, 61-63; prof art, Valdosta State Col, Ga, 63-91; sr lectr, Ahmadu Bello Univ, Zaria, Nigeria, 72-73; prof emeritus art, Valdosta State Col, Ga, 92. *Awards:* Best Show, Columbus Mus Arts & Crafts, Ga, 69; First Prize, St Augustine Festival, Fla, 70; Purchase Award, High Mus Art, Atlanta, Ga, 71; Purchase Award, Macon Mus Arts & Sci. *Bibliog:* Barclay F Gordon (auth), Record houses: 1978, Archit Record Mag, 5/78; The connection, Atlanta Impressions Mag, summer 81; Alexandra Mettler (auth), Emory's Cannon Chapel: Master touches, Atlanta Mag, 12/81. *Mem:* Am Crafts Coun (trustee, 80-84); Ga Designer Craftsman (vpres, 68); founding mem Ga Crafts Prof; Nat Coun Educ Ceramic Arts; World Crafts Coun. *Media:* Clay. *Publ:* Auth, Nigerian Crafts, Nat Coun Educ Communication Arts. *Dealer:* Creative Mark Madison Ga. *Mailing Add:* 2005 Bay Tree Rd Valdosta GA 31602

PENNYPACKER, JAMES S
DESIGNER, PUBLISHER
b Sellersville, Pa, Oct 11, 51. *Study:* Va Polytechnic Inst & State Univ, 69-72; Temple Univ, with Joseph Margolis, BA(magna cum laude), 78, fel, 78-80; Ariz State Univ, with Beth Luey, 83-84. *Comn:* Mural, Shelly's Hardware Inc, Perkasie, Pa, 71; logos, Emil's Diner, Sellersville, Pa, 72 & Interlude, Philadelphia, 77; posters, Nat Endowment Humanities Summer Inst, Phoenix, 83. *Pos:* Dir, Ctr Study Normative Futures, Philadelphia, 80-82, ed & designer, Crotonan Times, 82; publ designer, Pecksnipp's Ed Serv, Tempe, Ariz, 82-84; newspaper designer, Gentle Strength Food Coop, Tempe, Ariz,

82-84; publ & designer, Wizard Press, Philadelphia, 84- *Teaching:* Asst, Temple Univ, 79-80; lectr, Univ Colo, Boulder, 82. *Mem:* Writers Guild; World Future Soc Philadelphia (bd dirs, 80-82). *Media:* Pen and Ink, Colored Pencils. *Res:* The future of culture. *Publ:* Designer, Rudyard Kipling's Plain Tales From the Hills, 84, Stephen Crane's Last Words, 84 & Winston Churchill's The River War, 84, Renaissant Books; lead ed, Who's Who in American Art, R R Bowker, 84; designer, Deborah Weiss's Monsters and Ogres, Wizard Press (in prep). *Mailing Add:* Show Mgt Co North Point Off Ctr 200 Gibraltar Rd Suite 100 Horsham PA 19044

PENTAK, STEPHEN
PAINTER, EDUCATOR
b Denver, Colo, Aug 24, 51. *Study:* Union Col, NY, BA, 73; Tyler Sch Art, with Stephen Greene, MFA, 78. *Work:* Schenectady Mus, NY; Free Libr Philadelphia; Columbus Mus Art. *Exhib:* New Drawing in America, Drawing Ctr, New York, 82; Selected Works, Sutton Place, London, 82 & Gallerie D'Arte Mod Ca'Pesaro, Venice, 83; solo exhib, Jan Cicero Gallery, Chicago, 83 & Noel Butcher Gallery, Philadelphia, 83, Univ Akron, 87, J Rosenthal, Chicago & Wexner Ctr Arts, Columbus, 92; Landscape Anthology, Grace Borgenicht Gallery, New York, 88; Ohio Selections IX, Cleveland Ctr Contemp Arts, 90. *Teaching:* Vis asst prof, Art Inst Chicago, 81-82; assoc prof, Ohio State Univ, Columbus, 83- *Awards:* Ohio Arts Coun Individual Artists Fel, 85, 89. *Bibliog:* Edward Sozanski (auth), review, Philadelphia Inquirer, 6/8/83; Leslie Constable (auth), Review, Columbus Dispatch, 1/92; Lorraine Padden (auth), Columbus Art, 1/92. *Media:* Oil on Panel and Paper. *Publ:* Auth, Gregory Amenoff's new pictures, 81 & Daryl Hughto, 81, Arts Mag. *Dealer:* Toni Birckhead Gallery Cincinnati OH. *Mailing Add:* 211 Greenglade Ave Worthington OH 43085-2264

PENTELOVITCH, ROBERT ALAN
PAINTER
b Minneapolis, Minn, Oct 13, 55. *Study:* Minneapolis Col Art & Design, BFA, 78; San Francisco Art Inst, MFA, 80. *Work:* Walker Art Ctr & Regis Corp, Minneapolis, Minn; Chicago Inst Arts; Martin Marietta Corp, New York; Maslon, Kaplan, Borman & Brand, Minneapolis; Robin Farkas, New York; Gen Electric Group, New York. *Exhib:* Concours Auto Art Show, Oakland Univ, Troy, Mich, 85; solo exhibs, Trumbull Art Guild, Warren, Ohio, 85 & Arras Gallery, New York, NY, 86; Zumbach Gallery, New York, 88 & 89; Greenleaf Gallery, Nags Head, NC, 92; Animal Imagery, Juried, Madison, NJ, 92; and others. *Awards:* First Place, Minneapolis Col Art & Design, 77; Award of Excellence, Concours Auto Art, Oakland Univ, Troy, Mich, 85; Fel, John Simon Guggenheim Mem Found, 91. *Mem:* Artists Equity Asn. *Media:* Acrylic. *Publ:* Contribr, Edsel Owners News, 79 & 80, & Automotive Showcase, 1/82. *Mailing Add:* 340 W 55th St Apt 2D New York NY 10019

PENTZ, DONALD ROBERT
PAINTER, PRINTMAKER
b Bridgewater, NS, Can, Sept 18, 40. *Study:* Mt Allison Univ, Sackville, NB, BFA, 66; Univ Regina, Sask, MFA, 79; Banff Sch Fine Art, Alta, 79. *Work:* Art Gallery NS, NS Art Bank, Halifax; Can Coun Art Bank, Ottawa; Confederation Ctr Art Gallery, Charlottetown, PEI; Imperial Oil, Calgary, Alta. *Comn:* Selected Birds, Parks Can, Newfoundland, 82. *Exhib:* Young Artists of the Prairies, Walter Phillips Gallery, Banff, Alta, 79; Force Field Series, Art Gallery NS, Halifax, 79; RCA Centennial Exhib, CNE Bldg, Toronto, 80; Emerging Canadian Artists, Muttart Gallery, Calgary, Alta, 81; Atlantic Artists, Shell Can, Calgary, Alta, 81. *Teaching:* Instr art, privately, 70-72, Univ Regina, Sask, 77-79 & Mt St Vincent Univ, Halifax, NS, 80. *Awards:* Prof Artists Award, 75 & NS Talent Trust, 78, NS Govt; Can Coun Grant, 80. *Bibliog:* Janet Smith (producer), D Pentz--Wildlife Artist, CBC-TV, 83. *Mem:* Visual Arts NS; Royal Can Acad. *Media:* Acrylic, Pen and Ink. *Dealer:* Studio 21 5435 Spring Garden Rd Halifax NS Can B3J 1G1; La Galerie Continentale 1450 Rue Drummond Montreal Que Can H3G 1V9. *Mailing Add:* RR1 Pleasantville Lunenburg County NS B0R 1G0 Canada

PEPICH, BRUCE WALTER
MUSEUM DIRECTOR, CURATOR
b Elmhurst, Ill, June 5, 52. *Study:* Northern Ill Univ, De Kalb, BA(art hist), 74. *Collections Arranged:* Ruth Kao: Silk Tapestries, Wustum Mus, 84, Robert Burkert: 30 Years, 85, Claire Prussian, 85, Fiber Individualists, 86, Lee Weiss: 25 Years in Wisconsin, 87 & Wis Craft Masters, 88; For the Birds: Artists Examine Aviary Abodes, 90; Artists and the American Yard: Lawn Gnomes, Pink Flamingoes and Bathtub Grottos, 91; Craft: The Discerning Eye, 91; Walter Samuel Hamady: Handmade Books, Collages and Sculptures, 91; Watercolor Wisconsin: Celebrating 25 Years, 91; Just Plane Screwy: Metaphysical and Metaphorical Tools by Artists, 92. *Pos:* Cur, Univ Art Collection, Northern Ill Univ, 71-74; art dir, Charles A Wustum Mus Fine Arts, 74-80, dir, 81- *Awards:* Endowment Arts Avan Program, Overview Panel, 6/92. *Mem:* Am Craft Coun; Am Asn Mus; Am Film Inst. *Mailing Add:* Charles A Wustum Mus Fine Arts 2519 Northwestern Ave Racine WI 53402

PEPPARD, BLAYLOCK A
PAINTER
b Burlington, Vt, Dec 28, 52. *Study:* St Lawrence Univ, Canton, NY, BA(art honors), 75; Maryland Inst Col Art, Hoffberger Sch Painting, study with Grace Hardigan, Sal Scarpitta & Robert Moskowicz, MFA, 79. *Work:* Lewis & Clarke Mus, Portland, Ore; St Lawrence Univ, Canton, NY; Hagstromer Col, Stockholm, Sweden; Best Products, Ashland, Va; Berger Col, New York. *Exhib:* Pace Gallery, Philadelphia, 80; Art Fair, Stockholm Mus, Sweden, 81; solo show, Concord Gallery, New York, 82 & 83; Everson Biennial, Everson Mus, Syracuse, NY, 84; Art Quest, Shardin Mus, Kutetown Univ, Pa, 86; Proj Studio Installation, PS 1, Long Island City, NY, 86. *Pos:* Tech Etching, Parker Etching Studio, New York, 83-84; installation technician, Queens Mus, Flushing, NY, 83-85; Exhibs coordr, Jewish Mus, New York, 85-86. *Teaching:* Painting instr, New York Univ, 82-83; vis lectr, St Lawrence Univ, Canton, NY, 83. *Awards:* Painting Fel, Nat Endowment Arts, 90. *Bibliog:* Sylvia Falcon (auth), Blaylock Pepperd, Arts Mag, 83; Katherine Howe (auth), Blaylock Pepperd, Images & Issues Mag, 83; Art Quest '86, Film/Artquest/Slabey, 86. *Mem:* Col Art Asn; Orgn Independent Artists. *Media:* Archival Board, Oil. *Mailing Add:* 231 W 29th St 12A-8 New York NY 10001

PEPPER, BEVERLY
SCULPTOR, PAINTER
b Brooklyn, NY, Dec 20, 24. *Study:* Pratt Inst; Art Students League; also with Fernand Leger & Andre L'hote, Paris; Pratt Inst, Hon PhD, 82; Md Inst, Hon PhD, 83. *Work:* Albright-Knox Art Gallery, Buffalo, NY; Mass Inst Technol, Boston; Fogg Art Mus, Cambridge, Mass; Walker Art Ctr, Minneapolis; Metrop Mus Art, New York; and others. *Comn:* Excalibur (painted Steel), San Diego Fed Courthouse, 74; Amphisculpture (site sculpture), Bedminster, NJ, 75; Thel (site sculpture), Dartmouth Col, Hanover, NH, 77; Nat Endowment Arts, Toledo City Hall, 79; Janus Agri Altar, Iowa State Univ, Ames, 86; Sol y Ombra Park, City Barcelona, 86-92; Villa Cella Sculpture Park, Pistoia, Italy, 90-92; and many others. *Exhib:* Plus by Minus, Today's Half Century, Albright Knox Art Gallery, Buffalo, 68; San Francisco Mus Mod Art, 76; Seattle Mus Contemporary Art, 77; Princeton Art Mus, 78; Earthworks & Land Reclamation, Seattle Mus, 79; Int Sculpture Conf, Washington, DC, 80; Nat Collection Arts, Smithsonian Inst, Washington, DC, 80; Laumeier Int Sculpture Park, St Louis, 82; Sculpture in Place, Albright Knox Art Gallery, traveling exhib, 86; and many others. *Pos:* Artist-in-residence, Am Acad, Rome, 86. *Teaching:* Santa Fe Inst Fine Arts, 89-90. *Awards:* Best Art in Steel, Iron & Steel Inst, 70; Nat Endowment Arts Grant, 75 & 79; Gen Serv Admin Grant, 75. *Bibliog:* Wayne Andersen (auth), Sculpture Today, MIT Press, 70; Vittorio Armentano (auth), B P Making Sculpture (film), G Ungaretti, narrator, 70; Amphisculpture (film), Barbara Rose & Beverly Pepper, narrators, 77; Rosalind Krauss (auth), Beverly Pepper-Sculpture in Place, Abbeville Press, 86; and others. *Media:* Cast Iron, Earthwork. *Dealer:* Andre Emmerich Gallery 41 E 57th St New York NY 10022. *Mailing Add:* Torre Gentile Di Todi (PG) Italy

PEPPER, KATHLEEN DALY See Daly, Kathleen (Kathleen Daly Pepper)

PERA, ISABELLA
SCULPTOR
b Trivero, Italy, Sept 24, 45. *Study:* State Univ NY Cortland, BA, 73; Univ Ill Urbana-Champaign, MFA, 77. *Work:* Sheldon Swope Art Mus, Terre Haute, Ind; Del Mar Col, John Seaman Collection, Corpus Christi, Tex; Kirkland Fine Arts Ctr, Millikin Univ, Decatur, Ill; Almidones Mejicanos Bldg, Guadalajara, Mex; Italian Cultural Ctr, Chicago. *Exhib:* One-woman shows, Gilman Galleries, Chicago, 77, Freeport Art Mus, Ill, 79, Sheldon Swope Art Mus, Terre Haute, 80 & 88, Italian Cult Ctr, Chicago, 80 & Burpee Art Mus, Rockford, Ill, 81; 30th & 31st Ann Mid-States Art Exhib, Evansville Mus Art & Sci, Ind, 77-78; Art Expo, NY, 84 & 85; and others. *Collections Arranged:* 7th Ann Mid-States Traveling Art Show, Evansville Mus Art & Sci, 77-78. *Awards:* Art Casting of Colo Award, Foothills Art Ctr, 79; First Prize Sculpture, La Junta Fine Arts League, 79; First Prize Sculpture, Italian Cultural Ctr, Chicago, 81; and others. *Bibliog:* Janelle Hirchert (auth), Artistry in bronze wins recognition, News Gazette, 76; Harold Haydon (auth), Art, Sun Times, Chicago, 77; Nina Rubel (auth), Relief in bronze, Heartland Beat, Kerning Arts Press, 81. *Mem:* Int Sculpture Ctr. *Media:* Bronze; Epoxy. *Mailing Add:* 1303 Belmeade Dr Champaign IL 61821

PERANTEAU, MICHAEL
CURATOR
b Houston, Tex, July 16, 51. *Study:* Univ Houston, 70-74; Univ St Thomas, 77-78. *Collections Arranged:* Mexico Hoy/Mexico Today: A Look at Sixteen Contemporary Mexican Artists; Forrest Prince: A Retrospective; Big Pictures: Recent Work by Jean Dibble and Richard Thompson. *Pos:* Vpres bd dirs, Nat Asn Artist Orgns, 86-89; panelist, Visual Arts Prog & Inter-Arts Prog, Nat Endowment Arts, Cult Arts Coun of Houston & Mass Art Coun; co-dir, DiverseWorks Artspace, Houston, currently. *Mem:* Houston Coalition Visual Arts; Houston Arts Task Force; Cult Arts Coun Houston (bd mem); Nat Endowment Arts. *Mailing Add:* Diverse Works 1117 E Freeway Houston TX 77002

PERCY, ANN BUCHANAN
CURATOR, HISTORIAN
b Lynchburg, Va, Nov 13, 40. *Study:* Sweet Briar Col, BA, 62; Pa State Univ, MA, 65; Courtauld Inst Art, Univ London, with Anthony Blunt, PhD, 74. *Collections Arranged:* Giovanni Benedetto Castiglione: Master Draughtsman of the Italian Baroque (auth, catalog), Philadelphia Mus Art, 71; A Scholar Collects: Selections from the Anthony Morris Clark Bequest (co-ed, catalog), Philadelphia Mus Art, 80; New Art on Paper (coauth, catalog), Philadelphia Mus Art, 88; Pietro Testa, 1612-1650: Prints & Drawings, Philadelphia & Cambridge, Mass, 88-89; Francesco Clemente: Three Worlds (coauth, catalog), Philadelphia Mus Art, 90. *Pos:* Art hist ed, Pa State Univ Press, 69-72; asst cur drawings, Philadelphia Mus Art, 72-74, assoc cur drawings, 74-84, acting cur drawings, 81-84, cur, 84- *Mem:* Print Coun Am. *Res:* Seventeenth and eighteenth century Italian drawings and paintings; contemporary drawings. *Publ:* Auth, Castiglione's chronology: Some documentary notes, Burlington Mag, 67; coauth, Philadelphia: Three Centuries of American Art, Philadelphia Mus Art, 76; coauth, Bernardo Cavallino of Naples, 1616-1656; catalogs, Cleveland Mus Art, Kimbell Art Mus, Ft Worth & Museo Pignatelli Cortes, Naples, 84-85. *Mailing Add:* Philadelphia Mus Art PO Box 7646 Philadelphia PA 19101

PEREGRIN, MAGDA ELIZABETH
PAINTER, INSTRUCTOR
b Budapest, Hungary, Jan 2, 23. *Study:* John Huntington Polytech Sch, cert, 44; Pasadena City Col, cert, 52. *Work:* Smithsonian Inst, Washington, DC; Arcadia Meth Hosp, Arcadia, Calif; City of Hope, Duarte, Calif; Home Saving & Loan; Hillcrest Congregational Church, Whittier, Calif. *Comn:* Painting, Unical, Los Angeles, Calif, 75. *Exhib:* Edward Dean Mus Invitational, Cherry Valley, Calif, 79; Brand Library Art Gallery, Glendale, Calif, 80, 81 & 83; Nat Watercolor Soc Ann, Calif, 81; Watercolor West Ann, Riverside, Calif, 84, 86, 87 & 88, 90; Pasadena Soc Artists Ann, San Bernadino Co Mus, Calif, 84-88; Invitational, Mus Hist & Art, Ontario, Calif, 85; Yosemite Renaissance Nat Exhib, Fresno, Calif, 86; San Diego Int, San Diego Watercolor Soc, 86, 87 & 88; Padsadena Arts Alliance, 89; Downey Mus Art, 90; Brea Cult Ctr, 90; Calif Watercolor West, 90, 91. *Pos:* Staff artist, Am Greetings, Cleveland, Ohio, 44-50. *Teaching:* Instr watercolor, Foothill Creativ Arts Group, Sierra Madre, Calif, 82- & Yosemite Art & Activity Ctr, Calif, 82- *Awards:* Windsor & Newton Award, 81 & Challis Gallery Award, 82, Watercolor West Ann; Purchase Award, Hillcrest Invitational, 89, 90, 91, 92. *Mem:* Watercolor West (bd mem, 77-79); Pasadena Soc Artists; Mid-Valley Arts League Inc (bd mem, 75-76 & 78); Creative Arts Group. *Media:* Transparent Watecolor. *Mailing Add:* 8517 Ravendale Rd San Gabriel CA 91775

PEREHUDOFF, WILLIAM W
PAINTER
b Saskatoon, Sask, Apr 21, 19. *Study:* Colorado Springs Fine Arts Ctr; Ozenfant Sch Art, New York; Univ Sask, Emma Lake, workshops with Cherry, Noland & Greenberg. *Work:* Glenbow Mus, Calgary, Alta; Mendel Art Gallery, Saskatoon; Edmonton Art Gallery; London Art Gallery, Ont; Nat Gallery Can, Ottawa, Ont. *Comn:* Mural, Toronto Dominion Bank, Regina, 75. *Exhib:* Solo exhibs, Mendel Art Gallery, Saskatoon, Sask, 65, Edmonton Art Gallery, Alta, 72-73, Glenbow Alta Inst (with catalog), Calgary, 77-78, Theo Waddington Gallery, London, Eng, 79, Waddington Galleries, New York, 82, Eva Cohon Gallery Ltd, Chicago, Ill, 88, Waddington Gorce Inc, Montreal, Que, 90, Mirium Shiell Fine Art Ltd, Toronto, Ont, 90; Modern Painting in Canada (with catalog), Edmonton Art Gallery, 78; Seven Prairie Painters (with catalog), Art Gallery Ont, 78-79; Aspects of Canadian Painting in the Seventies (with catalog), Glenbow Mus, Calgary, Alta, 80; The Heritage of Jack Bush, A Tribute, The Robert McLaughlin Gallery, Oshawa, Ont, 81; The Flatside of the Landscape, The Emma Lake Workshop, Mendel Art Gallery, Sask, 89; and others. *Teaching:* Instr, Emma Lake Art Workshop, Emma Lake, Sask, 88. *Awards:* Nat Award Painting, Univ Alta. *Bibliog:* Clement Greenberg (auth), Painting and Sculpture in Canada, Can Art, 63; Karen Wilkin (auth), William Perehudoff, Art Int, 77; Joan Murray (auth), The Best Contemporary Canadian Art, Hurtig Publ, Edmonton, 87. *Mem:* Royal Can Acad Art. *Media:* Acrylic on Canvas. *Mailing Add:* 1131 Second St E Saskatoon SK S7H 1R4 Canada

PERESS, GILLES
PHOTOGRAPHER
b Neuilly-sur-Seine, France, Dec 29, 46. *Study:* Inst d'Etudes Politiques, dipl, 68; Univ Vincennes, dipl, 71. *Work:* Art Inst Chicago; Mus Fine Arts, Houston; Minneapolis Inst Art; Mus Mod Art & Metrop Mus Art, New York; Arts Coun-Great Britian, Bibliotheque Nationale, Paris. *Comn:* Double Diary of the Twin Cities, First Banks Minnesota, Minneapolis, 86. *Exhib:* Photo Politic, PS 1/Inst Art & Urban Resources, New York, 80; Paris: Magnum, Palais du Luxembourg, Paris & traveling, 81; Photographie Français d'Aujourd'hui, Mus d'Art Mod, Paris, & traveling, 84; Telex: Iran, PS 1/Inst Art & Urban Resources, New York, 84; Magnum: Concert, Mus d'Art, Fribourg, Switz, 85; The Indelible Image, Corcoran Gallery, Washington, DC & traveling, 85; On the Line: New Color Photojournalism, Walker Art Inst, Minneapolis & traveling, 86; Power in the Blood: The North of Ireland, Art Inst of Chicago, 92; one-man show, Palais de Tokyo, Paris, 93. *Pos:* Exec, Magnum Photos, Inc, currently. *Teaching:* Lectr photog, Int Ctr Photog, New York, 80-86, RI Sch Design, 82, Harvard Univ, 86-87. *Awards:* Nat Endowment Art Grants, 79 & 84; Bourse de la Photog, Found Nat Photog, Paris, 83; W Eugene Smith Found Award, 84; Gahan Photog Fel, Harvard Univ, 86-87. *Bibliog:* Charles Hanson (auth), Iran: Another view, Afterimage, fall 82; Michel Maingois (auth), L'Iran de Peress, Photo Mag, Paris, 5/84; Pete Hamill (auth), Prey for the dead, Am Photog, 8/84. *Mem:* Am Soc Mag Photogrs (vpres, 84-85, pres, 86-). *Publ:* Telex: Iran, Aperture/Contrejour, 84; contribr, Identities, Exposition Palais du Tokyo, Paris (exhib catalog), Editions du Chêne, 85; Men's Lives, Random House, 86; auth, An Eye for an Eye: Northern Ireland 1970-1986, Aperture, 87; Power in the Blood: The North of Ireland, Jonathan Cape, Eng, Parkett, Zurich, 93. *Mailing Add:* 304 Bowery New York NY 10012

PEREZ, BETTY WEISS
PAINTER
b Chicago, Ill. *Study:* Hunter Col, BA. *Work:* Islip Mus; Queensborough Community Col; State Univ NY, Albany. *Exhib:* Queens Mus, Flushing, NY, 81, 82, 87 & 89; Islip Mus, 87; Butler Inst Am Art, Youngstown, Ohio, 87; solo shows, Galerie Leif Stahle, Paris, France, 87 & 88, Queensboro Community Col, Gallery 89. *Awards:* Purchase Prize, Queensborough Community Col, 89; Grant, New York Found For The Arts, 90. *Media:* Acrylic, Works on Paper. *Mailing Add:* 10-34 49 Ave Long Island City NY 11101

PEREZ, CELIS
PAINTER, SCULPTOR
b Buenos Aires, Argentina, Jan 15, 39. *Study:* Fine Arts Sch, Art Master, 64; Orden del Sol, Peru, Comendador, 85. *Work:* Mus Modern Art, New York; Museo de Arte Moderno, Buenos Aires; Mus Contemp Latin & Am Art, Washington; Museo de Bellas Artes, Caracas, Venezuala; Museo de la Universidad de Rio Piedras, Puerto Rico. *Comn:* Murak Ezeyzn Airport, 74, Buenos Aires Airport, 79, Argentinian Airlines, Paris, 82, Government; sculpture, government, Rosario, 88. *Exhib:* V Bienal of Art, Museo Bellas Artes, Tokyo, Japan, 66; Biennal of Jeunes Artists, Museo Gran Palais, Paris, 71; Perez Celis, Museo de Bellas Artes, Caracas, 79, Nat Ctr Arts, Ohawa, Canada, 86; Perez Celis antos yahora, Centro Cultural, Buenos Aires, 85; Contemp Abstract, Kiserlet Mus, Budapest, 85; Perez Celis, Galeria de Art Moderno, San Jose , Costa Rica, 88; Mira Show, 7 USA Mus, 88. *Teaching:* Instr, Abstract Art, Parson Sch-Altos de Chovon,80; lectr, Abstract Art, Mus Visual Arts, Detroit, Mus Contemp Art, Washington. *Awards:* III Award, Salon Nacional, 70; Alba Award, Salon Nacional, Museo Edwardo Sivori, 72; Prix du Jury, Contemp Art, Grand Prixde Monaco, 80. *Bibliog:* Gaston Dielh (auth), Perez Celis, Goglianone Publ, 83; F Ted Castle-Peter Frank (coauths), Perez Celis, Shapolvsky Publ, 88; IBM (auth), Perez Celis, Adin visual-video, 90. *Media:* Oil, Mixed Media. *Dealer:* Anita Shapolsky Galleries 99 Spring St New York NY 10012. *Mailing Add:* c/o Anita Shapolsky Galleries 99 Spring St New York NY 10012

PEREZ, VINCENT
PAINTER, ILLUSTRATOR
b Jersey City, NJ, July 17, 38. *Study:* Pratt Inst, BFA; Univ Am, Mex; Calif Col Arts & Crafts, MFA. *Work:* Mus Art, Calif Palace Legion Hon, San Francisco; Oakland Art Mus, Calif; Playboy Enterprises, Chicago; Time Inc, New York; and many others. *Comn:* Mural, Arleigh Gallery, San Francisco, 69; portrait of State Supreme Court Judge Peters, comn by Clerks of Supreme Court for Univ Calif, Berkeley Law Sch, 74; woodcuts, Civic Arts Asn, Walnut Creek, Calif, 74. *Exhib:* One-man shows, Calif Col Arts & Crafts, 77 & Hoover Gallery, 80; 12 Artists, Calif Col Arts & Crafts, 78; Human Form, Walnut Creek Col, 78; Palo Alto Cult Ctr, 80; Ctr Visual Arts, 86. *Teaching:* Prof drawing & art for artists, Calif Col Arts & Crafts, 66- *Awards:* Union Independent Col Art Res Grant, 70; Best of Show, Tech Writers Convention, Los Angeles, 72; Gold Medal, Acad Italy, 80; Gertrude B Murphy Award, 84. *Bibliog:* Fred Martin (auth), San Francisco letter, Art Int, 66; Cecille McCann (auth), Vincent Perez, FMb Fine Arts, 69; Palmer French (auth), San Francisco artists, Artforum, 69. *Mem:* Bohemian Club; San Francisco Soc Illurs; Union Independent Col Art. *Media:* Mixed. *Publ:* Illusr cover, Time Mag, 69; illusr, Art & Tools, 72; Archives of Institutional Change Humanizing Technology, 73; Psychol Today, 73; Playboy, 74. *Mailing Add:* Fine Arts Calif Col Arts & Crafts 5212 Broadway Oakland CA 94618

PERHAM, ROY GATES
PAINTER
b Paterson, NJ, Apr 18, 16. *Study:* Grand Cent Art Sch; also with Frank V Dumond & Frank J Reilly. *Work:* Americana Mus, Univ SC; Plymouth Plantation, Mass; Salisbury Pub Libr, Md; Maywood Pub Libr, NJ. *Comn:* portrait of Dr Arthur Armitage, S Jersey Col, Rutgers Univ, 61; portrait of Dr Milton Hoffman, Cent Col, Iowa, 66; portrait of H Bruce Palmer, Conf Bd, New York, 71; portrait of former Secretary of State Edmund S Muskie, Dept State, Washington, DC, 86; portrait of Franklin Delano Roosevelt, Jr, Roosevelt Campobello Int Park, Campobello Island, NB, Canada, 89. *Exhib:* Allied Artists Am, New York, 66; Fairleigh Dickinson Univ, NJ, 67; Fair Lawn Art Asn, NJ, 68; Bergen Mall Exhib, Paramus, NJ, 70. *Awards:* Purchase Prize, Bergen Mall, 64. *Mem:* Hackensack Art Club. *Media:* Oil. *Mailing Add:* 269 Raymond St Hasbrouck Heights NJ 07604

PERINE, ROBERT HEATH
PAINTER, WRITER
b Los Angeles, Calif, Nov 30, 22. *Study:* Univ Southern Calif; Chouinard Art Inst, cert. *Work:* Butler Inst Am Art, Youngstown, Ohio; Univ Mass, Amherst; Brigham Young Univ; Utah State Univ; San Diego Mus Art. *Exhib:* Nat Watercolor Soc Ann, 49-53 & 71-77; San Diego Art Inst Ann, 71-; Butler Inst Ann, 72; Pierce Col, Los Angeles, 77; Laguna Beach Mus, 77; San Diego Mus, 80. *Teaching:* Instr, Univ Ala, Tuscaloosa, 51, Chouinard Art Inst, Los Angeles, 52-53 & Mira Costa Col, San Diego, 83 & 85. *Awards:* First Place & Purchase Award, 58th Ann Nat Orange Show, San Bernardino, 73; First Place in Watercolors & Purchase Award, 21st Ann San Diego Art Inst Show, 74; Purchase Award, 13th Ann Riverside Art Ctr Show, 75. *Bibliog:* Donovan Maley (auth), The delicate balance, San Diego Mag, 2/73 & A one-man renaissance for watercolor, Southwest Art Mag, summer 73; Fran Preisman (auth), Robert Perine's Geoglyphica revisited, Artweek, 4/75. *Mem:* Nat Watercolor Soc; San Diego Art Guild. *Media:* Watercolor. *Publ:* Auth, Chouinard: An Art Vision Betrayed, 86, The California Romantics: Harbingers of Watercolorism, 87 & San Diego Artists, 88, ARTRA Publ Inc, Encinitas, Calif. *Mailing Add:* 628 San Dieguito Dr Encinitas CA 92024

PERKINS, A ALAN
CERAMIST, ENAMELIST
b Toronto, Ont, Nov 30, 15. *Study:* Danforth Tech Sch, Toronto, dipl; Ont Col Art, Toronto, scholar; Brookfield Craft Ctr, Conn, with Margaret Seeler & Francis Felton. *Work:* Ont Inst of Studies, Toronto; Ont Craft Coun Permanent Collection, Toronto, Confedn Centre Gallery & Mus, Charlottetown, PEI, Can; Chalmers Collectors Col Mus of Civilization, Ottawa, Can. *Comn:* Mural, Cochran Murray Co, Toronto, 69; modular assemblage, Cadillac Develop Corp, Toronto, 72, Crown Life Insurance Head Off, Toronto, & George Brown Col, Toronto, Can, 90; and others. *Exhib:* First World Craft Exhib, Ont Sci Centre, Don Mills, 74; Ont Craft Coun Traveling Exhib, 77-78; Biennale International, Limoges, France, 88; Kunstverein Coborg, WGer: 3rd Salon; International Del Esmalte, Madrid Spain. *Pos:* Tread bd dirs, Ont Craft Found, Toronto, 68-69. *Teaching:* Instr enameling

& jewelry arts, George Brown Col, Toronto, 68-; instr glazes on metal, Toronto Bd Educ, 68-87. *Awards:* Adelaide Merriot Award of Excellence, Can Nat Exhib, 70; Award of Excellence, MAKE Exhib, Ont Can Guild of Crafts, 71; Best in Show, Graphics, Aviva Art Show, 81; and others. *Bibliog:* Una Abrahamson (auth), Crafts Canada, The Useful Arts, Clarke Irwin & Co Ltd, Toronto, 74; David Piper (ed), Canadian Interiors, Maclean Hunter Publ, 74; J Hartley Newman (auth), Wire Art, Crown Publ, New York, 75; Glass on metal, Enamelist Soc Int, Vol 5, No 2, 4/86. *Mem:* Soc Can Artists (chmn exhib comt, 76-77); Ont Soc Artists; Ont Crafts Coun (secy-treas bd dirs, 68-70); Metal Arts Guild, Ont; assoc mem, Soc NAm Goldsmiths. *Media:* Multimedia. *Dealer:* Harbinger Gallery Waterloo ON Can; Gallery House Sol Georgetown ON Can. *Mailing Add:* 29 Glen Davis Toronto ON M4E 1X6 Canada

PERKINS, ANN
HISTORIAN, EDUCATOR
b Chicago, Ill, Apr 18, 15. *Study:* Univ Chicago, AB, 35, AM, 36, PhD, 40. *Teaching:* Res assoc ancient art, Yale Univ, 55-65; assoc prof ancient art, Univ Ill, Urbana, 65-69, prof ancient art, 69-78, emer prof, 78- *Awards:* Guggenheim Fel, 54-55. *Mem:* Archaeol Inst Am. *Res:* Greek and Roman art. *Publ:* Auth, The Art of Dura-Europos, 73. *Mailing Add:* 1905 S Harding Dr Urbana IL 61801

PERKINS, G HOLMES
ARCHITECT, EDUCATOR
b Cambridge, Mass, Oct 10, 04. *Study:* Harvard Univ, AB, 26, MArch, 29, LLD, 72. *Pos:* Ed, J Am Inst Planners, 50-52; chancellor col fels, Am Inst Architects, 64-66; chmn, Philadelphia City Planning Commission, 58-68. *Teaching:* Chmn dept archit & dean grad sch fine arts, Univ Pa, 51-71, chmn grad prog archit & prof archit & urbanism, 71-80. *Mem:* Fel Am Inst Architects; hon corresp mem Royal Inst Architects Can. *Mailing Add:* Dept of Archit Univ Pa Philadelphia PA 19104-6311

PERKINS, LOIS BOUTHILLIER
PAINTER, EDUCATOR
b Asbestos, Que, June 23, 37; US citizen. *Study:* Fla Atlantic Univ, BFA, 81, independent study, Beijing PR of China, 88, London, Paris, Rome, 89. *Work:* Barrington Mus, Delray, Fla; Pompano Beach Pub Libr, Fla; Broward Co Court House, Ft Lauderdale, Fla; Chende Teachers Col, People's Repub China; Private Collections, Sam Sneed & Dr Brent Bracco. *Exhib:* Sch Exhib, Boston Mus Fine Art, Mass, 60-61; 36th All-Fla Juried Exhib, Boca Raton Art Mus, 87; Soc Four Arts, Palm Beach, Fla, 88 & 91; Curzon Gallery, Boca Raton Hotel & Club, Fla, 89. *Teaching:* Instr, pottery & painting, Broward Co Sch System, Fla, 75-; instr, painting, Broward Co Community Col, 88; youth prog, Fla Atlantic Univ, 92. *Bibliog:* Dorothy Anne Flor (auth), feature article, Ft Lauderdale News & Sun Sentinel, 4/17/83; Pat Curry (auth), feature article, Ft Lauderdale News & Sun Sentinal, 3/4/90; Tamara Kerrill (auth), feature article, Ft Lauderdale News & Sun Sentinal, 6/19/92. *Mem:* Fla Arts Ed; Fla Prof Artists Inc; Coral Springs Artists Guild Inc. *Media:* All Media; Bronze Metalic Powders. *Mailing Add:* 436 NE 25th Ave Pompano Beach FL 33062

PERKINS, ROBERT EUGENE
ADMINISTRATOR
b Pittsfield, Mass, Oct 20, 31. *Study:* Sioux Falls Col, BA, 56; Columbia Univ, MA, 57; Univ SDak; Sioux Falls Col, LHD, 74. *Pos:* Asst prin, Canton High Sch, SDak, 59-61; dir admis, Sioux Falls Col, 61-63, dean students, 63-70; pres, Ringling Sch Art, Sarasota, Fla, 71-81; exec dir, William G Selby Found, currently. *Publ:* Coauth, Profile of the South Dakota High School Graduate of 1968, 69; auth, The Maestro, 70; auth, 50 Year History, Ringling School of Art and Design, 81. *Mailing Add:* 3424 S Lockwood Ridge Rd Sarasota FL 34239

PERLESS, ROBERT
SCULPTOR
b New York, NY, Apr 23, 38. *Study:* Univ Miami, Coral Gables, Fla. *Work:* Aldrich Mus Contemp Art, Ridgefield, Conn; Chrysler Mus, Norfolk, Va; Phoenix Art Mus, Ariz; Stamford Mus, Conn; Whitney Mus Am Art, New York. *Comn:* Mobil Oil, Fairfax, Va, 81; Space Ctr Tysons, Tysons Corner, Va, 88; Benerofe Properties, Pub Park, Port Chester, NY, 88; Fuji Film Bldg, Elmsford, NY, 89; Deloitte Touche, Wilton, Conn, 90; City of Palm Desert, Calif, 92. *Exhib:* Recent Acquisitions, Whitney Mus Art, New York, 70; Recent Sculpture, Taft Mus, Cincinnati, Ohio, 80; group shows, Aldrich Mus Contemp Art, Ridgefield, Conn, 87 & Stamford Mus Art, Conn, 88; Connecticut Biennial, Bruce Mus, Greenwich, Conn, 89; André Emmerich Top Gallant Farm, Pawling, NY, 91 & 92. *Bibliog:* Harbinger of village renaissance: Perless' kinetic sculpture, Greenwich Time, 6/15/87; Shaping the art of motion, Stamford Advocate & Greenwich Time, 6/23/89; 22 artists participate in Bruce's biennial, New York Times, 8/6/89. *Media:* Aluminum, Stainless Steel. *Mailing Add:* 37 Langhorne Lane Greenwich CT 06831

PERLIN, BERNARD
PAINTER, ILLUSTRATOR
b Richmond, Va, Nov 21, 18. *Study:* Nat Acad Design, with Leon Kroll, 36-37; Art Students League, with Isabel Bishop, William Palmer & Harry Sternberg, 36-37; also in Poland. *Work:* Tate Gallery, London; Nat Collection Fine Art, Smithsonian Inst; Mus Mod Art & Whitney Mus Am Art, New York; Va Mus Fine Arts; and others. *Comn:* US Post Off Dept, 40. *Exhib:* Brussels World's Fair, 58; Detroit Inst Art, 60; Pa Acad Fine Arts, 60; retrospective, Univ Bridgeport, 69; and many other group & one-man shows. *Teaching:* Instr, Wooster Community Art Ctr, Danbury, Conn, 67-69. *Awards:* Fulbright Fel, 50; Guggenheim Fels, 54-55 & 59; Nat Inst Arts & Lett Award, 64; and others. *Bibliog:* Lloyd Goodrich & John I H Baur (auths), American Art of Our Century, Whitney Mus Am Art, 61; Daniel M Mendelowitz (auth), A History of American Art, Holt, 61; Selden Rodman (auth), Conversations with Artists, Capricorn Press, 61; and others. *Publ:* Illusr, Life & Fortune Mags. *Mailing Add:* 56 Shadow Lake Rd Ridgefield CT 06877

PERLIN, RAE
PAINTER
b St John's, Nfld. *Study:* With Samuel Brecher, 41, 42 & 46 & Hans Hofmann, 47 & 48, New York; Acad Graande Chaumiere, Paris. *Work:* Mem Univ Nfld Permanent Collection, Can. *Exhib:* Mem Univ Nfld Art Gallery, 71; solo retrospective, Mem Univ Nfld, 82. *Pos:* Art critic, St John's Daily News, 60-71; art critic, St John's Eve Telegram, 64-67. *Awards:* Arts & Lett, Nfld Govt, 56 & 62-67; Can Coun Grant, 70. *Bibliog:* Marian Frances White (compiled & ed), Not a Still Life, the Art and Writings of Rae Perlin, Killick Press, St John's, Nfld, 91. *Mem:* Canadian Artist Representation. *Media:* Miscellaneous Media, Watercolor. *Publ:* Illusr, Spindrift and morning light, 68. *Mailing Add:* 11A Monkstown Rd St John's NF A1C 3T1 Canada

PERLIN, RUTH RUDOLPH
EDUCATOR, HISTORIAN
b Washington, DC. *Study:* Wellesley Col, BA, 57; Metrop Mus Art, Inst Fine Arts, 61-62; New York Univ Inst Fine Arts, MA, 64. *Pos:* Chief, mus educ, Baltimore Mus Art, 69-72; cur dept exten progs, Nat Gallery Art, Washington, DC, 74-80, chair ed bd, 76-82, head cur-in-charge, dept exten progs, 80-89, head educ resources, 90-; officer bd, Mus Educ Roundtable, 78-81; contrib ed, Sch Arts Mag, 78-82. *Teaching:* Head docent training art hist, Baltimore Mus Art, 65-69; instr art hist, Towson State Col, Md, 67-69. *Awards:* Cine Golden Eagle, 83-86 & 88- 90. *Mem:* Am Asn Mus; Nat Art Educ Asn, Mus Educ Div (eastern region dir-elect); Prof Mats Comt; Mus Educ Roundtable; Extended Productions Non Print Mats (chair). *Res:* Collections, exhibitions of National Gallery; 19th & 20th century painting; 19th century American art. *Publ:* Auth, The Far North, 76, Index of American Design: Pottery, Textiles and Furniture, 77 & auth & ed, Thomas Jefferson: Art and Reason, 78, Nat Gallery Art, Washington, DC; proj dir, laserdisc, 83 & producer, laserdisc, Am Art, Nat Gallery Art, Washington, DC, 92; producer, Impt Info Inside, Peto, 84, Audubon, 85, Winslow Homer, 86, Wm Merritt Chase Shinnecock, 88 & Frederick E Church Landscapes, 89, Nat Gallery Art, Washington, DC. *Mailing Add:* c/o Nat Gallery Art EB 503 Washington DC 20565

PERLMAN, BENNARD BLOCH
PAINTER, CRITIC
b Baltimore, Md, June 19, 28. *Study:* Carnegie-Mellon Univ, BFA, 49; Univ Pittsburgh, MA, 50. *Work:* Libr Cong, Washington, DC; Peale Mus & Baltimore Mus Art, Baltimore, Md; Univ Ariz, Tucson; Univ Md, College Park. *Comn:* Mural, 66 & History of Gardenville (oil), 80, City Baltimore. *Exhib:* Baltimore Mus Art; Corcoran Gallery Art, Washington, DC; Carnegie Mus, Pittsburgh; Pa Acad Fine Arts, Philadelphia. *Pos:* Art critic, The Daily Record, Baltimore, 84- *Teaching:* Prof & chmn dept art, Community Col Baltimore, 54-86; vis lectr, Oxford Univ, Eng, 75 & Dartmouth Col, 81. *Awards:* Freeland Art Award, Md Artists Exhib, Baltimore Mus Art; First Prize & Mus Purchase, Peale Mus Ann. *Mem:* Artists Equity Asn (nat vpres, 69-71 & 77-79); Baltimore Mus Art Artists Comt (chmn, 59-61 & 69-70); Greater Baltimore Arts Coun (pres, 64-66). *Media:* Oils, Ink. *Res:* American art; Robert Henri and the Eight. *Publ:* Auth, The Golden Age of American Illustration, 78 & The Immortal Eight: American Painting from Eakins to the Armory Show, rev ed 79, North Light; The Eight and Its Influence (exhib catalog), Art Students League New York, 83; 75th Anniversary of The Eight (exhib catalog), Whitney Mus Am Art, 83; Arthur B Davies: Drawings and Watercolors (exhib catalog), Baltimore Mus Art, 87; Robert Henri: His Life and Art, 91. *Mailing Add:* 6603 Baythorne Rd Baltimore MD 21209

PERLMAN, HIRSCH
PAINTER
b 1960. *Study:* Yale Univ, BA, 82. *Exhib:* Randolph St Gallery, Chicago, Ill, 86; solo exhibs, Cable, New York, NY, 87, Galerie Claire Burrus, Paris, France, 88, Shodhalle, Zurich, Switz, 90 & Galerie Hufkens, Brussels, Belg, 90; Wolff Gallery, New York, NY, 87; Whitney Mus Am Art, New York, NY, 89; Galerie Max Hetzler, Cologne, W Ger, 90; Carnegie Mellon Art Gallery, Pittsburgh, Pa, 90; one-man shows, Shedhalle (with catalog), Zurich, Switz, 90, Halle Sud, Geneva, Switz, 90, Galerie Hufkens, Brussels, Belg, 90, Feature, New York, 90 & 92, Donald Young Gallery, Chicago, Ill, 90, Galerie Claire Burrus, Paris, France, 91, Interim Art, London, Eng, 91; Dirty Data (with catalog), Ludwig Forum, Ger, 92; Génériques le Visuel & l'écrit, Hotel de arts, Paris, France, 92. *Awards:* Nat Endowment Arts, 89 & 91; Louis Comfort Tiffany Found Grant, 91. *Bibliog:* Kate Bush (auth), Exhibit 'A', 15-16 (repro), Art Monthly, 5/92; Jose Lebrero Stals (auth), review (repro), Flash Art, 136, 1-2/92; Doris von Drathen, Hirsch Perlman Ästhetik des Fehlers (repro), Kunstforum, 9-10/91. *Publ:* Contribr, Artists Writings: Twice-Told Tales, Art J, fall 89; auth, Contingency, Iron & Solidarity, Artforum, 12/89; coauth (with Jeanne Dunning), Introduction to the Relationship Between Art & Pervision, DU, 6/91; coauth (with Jeanne Dunning), Getting to Know the Law or Make Things Mean What I Want Them to Mean or A Collection of Quotes I Like, Dirty Data (catalog), Ludwig Mus, Aachen, Ger; auth, Exhibit Z 1 (Judicial), Framework, vol 5, issued 2 & 3, 92. *Mailing Add:* c/o Feature 484 Broome St New York NY 10013

PERLMAN, JOEL LEONARD
SCULPTOR, INSTRUCTOR
b New York, NY, June 12, 43. *Study:* Cornell Univ, BFA, 65; Cent Sch of Art & Design, London; Univ Calif, Berkeley, MA, 68. *Work:* Larry Aldrich Mus Contemp Art, Ridgefield, Conn; Storm King Art Ctr, Mountainville, NY; Johnson Mus, Cornell Univ; Hirshhorn Mus & Sculpture Garden; Metrop Mus Art, New York; Los Angeles County Mus. *Comn:* Outdoor sculpture, RTKL Inc, Baltimore, 71; Night Traveler (outdoor sculpture), Storm King Art Ctr, 77; High Peaks, 80 Winter Olympics, Lake Placid; Big Square Tilt, IBM Inc, Northwood, NY. *Exhib:* Axiom Gallery, London, 69; Bennington Col, Vt, 70; Whitney Mus Am Art Biennial, 73; Contemp Reflections, Aldrich Mus Contemp Art, 73; Andre Emmerich Gallery, New York, 73, 76, 78, 80, 82, 85 & 87 & Zurich, 77; Storm King Art Ctr, 74 & 75; Roy Boyd Gallery, Chicago & Los Angeles, 78, 80, 81, 83, 86 & 88; Gloria Luria Gallery, Fla, 83. *Teaching:* Instr sculpture, Sch Visual Arts, 73-; Sarah Lawrence Col, 88- *Awards:* Guggenheim Found Fel Sculpture, 74; Nat Endowment Arts Grant, 79; Reynolds Aluminum Award, 87. *Bibliog:* Barbara Zucker (auth), article, Artnews, summer 76; Jon Cauman (auth), article, summer 76 & Gene Kaplan (auth), Joel Perlman's new sculpture, 10/82, Arts Mag; Lisa Mintz Messenger (auth, catalog), article, Arts Mag, 5/85; Will Ameringer (auth, catalog), Andre Emmerich Gallery, 10/87. *Mem:* Sculptors Guild. *Media:* Welded Steel, Cast Bronze. *Mailing Add:* c/o Gloria Luria Gallery 1033 Kane Concourse Bay Harbor Islands Miami FL 33154

PERLMAN, MARK A
PAINTER
b Pittsburgh, Pa, Mar 23, 50. *Study:* Clarion Univ, 68-70; Eastern Mich Univ, BFA, 74; WVa Univ, MFA, 78. *Work:* Hirshhorn Mus & Spanish Embassy, Washington, DC; Ashland Oil Co, Ky; Univ Notre Dame, S Bend, Ind; Minneapolis Mus; Univ Tex, El Paso. *Exhib:* Solo exhib, Hoyt Mus Art, New Castle, Pa, 82; Norona Art Mus, WVa, 80; Re-Encounter-US-Mexico, Imperial Palace, Mexico, 85; Brainerd National, Potsdam, NY, 85; Texas Annual, Laguna Gloria Mus, Austin, 85; ArtQuest 86, Los Angeles, Calif; Artists Liaison 86, Los Angeles Design Ctr. *Teaching:* Vis artist workshop, Univ Notre Dame, S Bend, Ind, 79; asst prof painting, Thiel Col, Greenville, Pa, 80-83 & Univ Tex, El Paso, 83- *Awards:* Best in Show, Bethany Col 10th Juried Exhib, 80; Best in Show, Images 85, Warren Hadler, 85; Merit Award, Tex A&M Univ, 85. *Bibliog:* Joseph Gregory (auth), Postmodern self-hood, Artspace, 85. *Mem:* Col Art Asn. *Media:* Oil Paint. *Dealer:* Kron-Reck Albuquerque NM; Udinotti Scottsdale AZ. *Mailing Add:* c/o Michael Dunev Gallery 77 Geary St San Francisco CA 94108

PERLMUTTER, JACK
PAINTER, PRINTMAKER
b New York, NY, Jan 23, 20. *Work:* Nat Gallery Art, Phillips Collection & Corcoran Gallery Art, Washington, DC; Metrop Mus Art, New York; Nat Mus Mod Art, Tokyo. *Comn:* First Saturn Moon Rocket Launching (painting), 67 & Saturn V, Apollo 6 (painting), 68, NASA, Kennedy Space Ctr, Fla; Woodcuts for Apollo 16, Mission Control Ctr, Houston, Tex, 72; Columbia Space Shuttle (painting), NASA, 81; Voyager II (painting), NASA, 81. *Exhib:* Four Corcoran Gallery Art Am Biennials, 49-61; American Prints Today, Print Coun Am, exhibited in ten cities, 59-60; 3rd & 4th Expos Gravure, Ljubljana, Yugoslavia, 59 & 61; 3rd Nat Exhib Printmaking, Univ Wis, 71; 2nd Nat Print Show, Fine Arts Gallery, San Diego, 71. *Pos:* Dir, Dickey Gallery Art, DC Teachers Col, 56-68; contrib ed, Art Voices. *Teaching:* Chmn dept graphics, Corcoran Sch Art, 60-82; vis prof, Univ Costa Rica, 83. *Awards:* Fulbright Grant in art & printmaking to Tokyo, 59-60; Print Prize, 1st Int Exhib Fine Arts Saigon, 62; also numerous purchase awards. *Bibliog:* Reproduction, Art Today, Holt, Rinehart & Winston, 4th ed; Eyewitness to Space, Abrams, 72; The Art of the Print, Abrams, 76. *Mem:* Soc Am Graphic Artists; Cosmos Club (art comt, 63-). *Media:* Acrylic, Oil; Lithography. *Publ:* Contribr, Transactions of 5th International Conference of Orientalists (Toho Gakkai), Japanese Prints Today, 7/60; auth, Western art influences in Japan, Today's Japan Orient/West, 8/60; Painting in a land of transition (with reproductions), Inst Int Educ Mag, 1/61. *Mailing Add:* 2511 Cliffbourne Pl NW Washington DC 20009

PERLMUTTER, LINDA M
PAINTER, INSTRUCTOR
b New York, NY, Mar 1, 43. *Study:* Hunter Col, BA, 63, MA, 67; Art Student's League, with Mario Cooper, 71-81. *Work:* Gabelli Funds Inc, Rye, NY; Powell Duffryn Inc, Bayonne, NJ; Yonkers Bd Educ, NY; Blue Cross Blue Shield Md, Baltimore; Ernst & Young, Stamford, Conn. *Comn:* Marriott Corp, comn by Baird Eaton, Tarrytown, NY, 85. *Exhib:* Filth, Hudson River Mus, Yonkers, NY, 71; Beaux Arts, State Univ NY, Purchase, 78; Nat Asn Women Arts, traveling, Sarah Lawrence Col, Bronxville, NY, 85, Jesse Besser Mus, Alpena, Mich, 86, Schenectady Mus, NY, 86 & Adelphi Univ Mus, Garden City, NJ, 87. *Pos:* Art dir, N Tarrytown Art in the Park, 86-90. *Teaching:* Fine arts, New York City Bd Educ, 66-69 & art supervisor, 68-69; Instr Creative Use Art Media, State Univ NY, 69. *Awards:* Best in Show, Ossnuing Women's Club, 78; Nat Asn Women Artists Travelling Exhib, 85; Ada Cecere Mem Award, Nat Asn Women Artists Ann, 89. *Bibliog:* Harriett Edelson (auth), Genius Culled from Natural Phenomena, Gannett, 77; Helen Brooks (auth), A singular woman, McCall's Mag, 79; Phyllis Riffel (auth), Organization and Creativity Makes Artists' Life Productive, 83; Valerie Bohigian (auth), Lady-Bucks, Dodd Mead & Co, 87. *Mem:* Nat Asn Women Artists (bd mem, 82); Katonah Mus Artist's Asn. *Media:* Watercolor. *Publ:* H George Caspari Inc as notecards, 1980-present. *Dealer:* River Gallery Main St Irvington NY 10533. *Mailing Add:* 470 Bellwood Ave North Tarrytown NY 10591

PERLMUTTER, MERLE
PRINTMAKER
b London, England, Apr 16, 36; US citizen. *Study:* Art Students League, with Ethel Katz; Pratt Inst, Brooklyn, NY; Ruth Leaf Graphic Workshop, Douglaston, NY. *Work:* Rufino Tamayo Mus Chapultepec, Mexico City; DeCordova Mus, Mass; Portland Mus Art, Wash; Musee de Petit Format, Couvin, Belgium; New York City Pub Libr, 42nd St Branch Print Collection. *Exhib:* Eleven one-person shows, Soc Am Graphic Artists, Taiwan, China, 84 & Silvermine Gallery, Conn, 85, Hudson River Mus, 88; Boston Printmakers Nat Competition, Mass, 74, 76, 79, 80 & 83; Pratt Int Miniature Graphics Exhib, 75, 77, 81, 83, 85 & 87; Premio Internazionale Biella Por L'Incisione, Italy, 76 & 80; Miami Int Biennial, Metrop Mus & Art Ctr, Fla, 77 & 80; Martha Jackson Gallery, New York, 79; NY State Mus, Albany, 81; Third & Fourth Int Biennial, 87-89; Taipei Fine Arts Mus, Taiwan, China; Tucson Mus Art, Ariz; Biennial graphic Art, Mus Mod Art, Ljublyana, Yugoslovia; Mus Mod Art, Wakayama, Japan, 88; Rufino Tamayo Mus, Chapultepec, Mex; Noyes Mus, NJ, 90. *Teaching:* Instr etching & printmaking, Ruth Leaf Graphic workshop, Douglaston, NY, 76-; guest printmaker prints & techniques, Grey Art Gallery & Study Ctr, NY Univ, New York, 76. *Awards:* Two Gold Medals & Silver Medal, Audubon Artist Nat Competition, New York, 75, 77, 80, 84 & 88; Creative Artist Pub Serv Prog Fel, 76; Soc Am Graphic Artists Award, 78, 80 & 83; and many others. *Bibliog:* Ruth Leaf (auth), Intaglio Printmaking Techniques, Watson-Guptill, 77; Jacquline Brody (auth), Prints Published, Print Collectors News Lett, 9-10/78; Phyllis Braff (auth), articles, New York Times, 11/4/84 & 9/15/85; Carol Wax Abrams (auth), The Mezzotint, 90. *Mem:* Boston Printmakers, Mass; The Print Club, Philadelphia, Pa; Audubon Artists; Soc Am Graphic Artists. *Media:* Intaglio, Etching. *Mailing Add:* 20 Cherry Ave New Rochelle NY 10801

PERLOFF, MARJORIE G
CRITIC, HISTORIAN
b Vienna, Austria, Sept 28, 31; US citizen. *Study:* Barnard Col, AB, 53; Catholic Univ, MA, 56, PhD, 65. *Teaching:* Prof English, comparative literature & art literature, Univ Southern Calif, 77-86, Stanford Univ, 86-; Sadie D Padek chair humanities, 91- *Res:* Modern and postmodern poetry and painting; artists books; intermedia. *Publ:* Auth, The Poetics of Indeterminacy: Rimbaud to Cage, Princeton, 81, Northwestern, 83; The Dance of the Intellect, Cambridge Univ Press, 85; The Futurist Moment, Univ Chicago Press, 86; Poetic License, Studies in Modernist & Postmodernist Lyric, Northwestern, 90; Radical Artifice, 92. *Mailing Add:* 1467 Amalfi Dr Pacific Palisades CA 90272

PERLOW, KATHARINA RICH
DEALER, GALLERY DIRECTOR
b Vienna, Austria; US citizen. *Study:* Hunter Col (art hist), 75-77. *Pos:* Dir, Jack Gallery, New York, formerly; partner, A M Sachs Art Gallery, 83-85; pres & dir, Katharina Rich Perlow Gallery, New York, 85- *Mem:* Mus Mod Art, New York; Metrop Mus Art, New York; Whitney Mus Am Art. *Specialty:* Contemporary art, 20th century, John Ferren, Douglas Maguire, Stephen Pace, Jon Schueler, Ian Hornak, Brian Yoshimi Isobe, Michael Harnett, Sheppard Craige, Scott Kahn, John Gundelfinger, Steven Katz, Balcomb Greene, Selina Trieff, Bessie Boris, Anne Lloyd, Mark Metcalf, Ray Ciarrochi & Woody Gwyn. *Mailing Add:* Katharina Rich Perlow Gallery 560 Broadway No 301 New York NY 10012

PERLS, KLAUS G
DEALER
b Berlin, Ger, Jan 15, 12; US citizen. *Study:* Univ Basel, Switz, PhD, 33. *Pos:* Partner, Perls Galleries, 37-; trustee, Metrop Mus, New York, 92. *Mem:* Art Dealers Asn Am. *Specialty:* Modern masters. *Publ:* Auth, Complete works of Jean Fouquet, 40; Maurice de Vlaminck, 41. *Mailing Add:* 1016 Madison Ave New York NY 10021

PERNOTTO, JAMES ANGELO
PAINTER, SCULPTOR
b Youngstown, Ohio, Oct 20, 50. *Study:* Ohio State Univ, BFA(cum laude), 73; Univ Wis, MFA, 75. *Work:* Chicago Art Inst; Univ Dallas; Indianapolis Mus Art; Madison Art Ctr; Butler Inst Am Art. *Comn:* King Toot, Traveling Children's Mus, Madison Art Ctr, 78; Worlds of TSR, Javitts Conv Ctr, New York, 87; Paradiso, Ohio State Univ, Lima Campus, 88; Insight/On Site, Cleveland Mus Art 75th Anniversary Celebration. *Exhib:* Solo exhib, Love Hurts, Butler Inst Am Art, 81, Walking the Line Between Heaven and Hell, Fendrick Gallery, Washington, DC, 81, Entropy, Spaces, Cleveland, Ohio, 85 & Personal Odysseys, Ohio Art Coun, Gund Gallery, Columbus, 86 & Sunrise- Sunset, Madison Art Ctr, 90; Dynamix, Cincinnati Contemp Mus, 82; Nat & Int Studio Artists, The Clocktower, New York, 87; The New Frontier, Kaufman-Astoria Studies, Astoria, NY, 87; Open Studios, Inst Art & Urban Resources, NY, 87; Coming of Age, Madison Art Ctr, Wis, 90; and others. *Pos:* Cur prints, Butler Inst Am Art. *Awards:* First Award, Wis Bienalle, Madison Art Ctr, 78 & Midyear Show, Butler Inst Am Art, 81. *Bibliog:* Jules Heller (auth), Papermaking, Watson-Guptill, 78; Jo Ann Lewis (auth), Steelyard stories, Washington Post, 10/8/81; David Tannous (auth), James Pernotto at Fendrick, Art in Am, 2/82; Dr Louis A Zona (auth), Play as art, Dialogue Mag, 2/86; Gregory Conniff (auth), James Pernotto, Art Muscle Mag, 5/90. *Mem:* Int Asn Hand Papermakers & Paper Artists. *Media:* Multi. *Mailing Add:* 27 1/2 Federal Plaza W Youngstown OH 44503

PERRAULT, PIERRE
PHOTOGRAPHER
b Montreal, Can, Jan 25, 57. *Comn:* Hand colored photographs, Integration of Art in Architecture, Ministry Cult Affairs, Que, 83. *Exhib:* One-man shows, Photogramme Gallery, Montreal, 81; Los Angeles Photog Ctr, 82; Berkshire Mus, Pittsfield, Mass, 83; L'Alliance de France, Fr Consulate, San Francisco, 84; mois de la Photo, Mus Art Mod, Liege, Belg, 86. *Awards:* 3 First Prizes, Jobo Int Photo Contest, Lisle-Kelco Ltd, Can, 87. *Bibliog:* Colorifiction, Editons Carni Lte, 86. *Mem:* Can Asn Photographers & Illusrs. *Mailing Add:* CP 104 Succ M Montreal PQ H1V 3L6 Canada

PERREAULT, JOHN
CRITIC, CURATOR
b New York, NY, Aug 26, 37. *Exhib:* Pattern Painting, PS 1, New York, 77; Usable Art, 81 & Streamline Design, 84, Queens Mus, NY. *Pos:* Art critic, Village Voice, New York, 66-74 & 87-; sr art critic, Soho News, New York, 75-82; cur, Everson Mus, 83-84; dir visual arts, Snug Harbor Cult Ctr, Staten Island, NY, 85-88; sr cur, Am Craft Mus, 90- *Teaching:* Vis prof, Univ Calif, San Diego, 76; prof art criticism, Univ Ariz, Tucson, 79 & State Univ NY, Binghamton, 81. *Awards:* Art Criticism Fels, Nat Endowment Arts, 73 & 79. *Bibliog:* Alex Gildzen (ed), John Perreault issue, Serif, Kent State Univ Libr, Ohio, Vol XI, fall 74. *Mem:* Am Sect Int Asn Art Critics (pres, 78-81); Col Art Asn; Am Asn Mus; Nat Coun Educ Ceramic Arts; Nat Writers Union. *Res:* Contemporary art, American ceramic art and design and crafts. *Publ:* Auth, articles in Artforum, Art Am, Arts, Artscanada, Art Int; Auth, Drawings & Watercolors of Philip Pearlstein, Abrams, 88; Philip Pearlstein; Drawing & Watercolors, Abrams; and many others. *Mailing Add:* 54 E 7th St New York NY 10003

PERRET, DONNA C
ART DEALER
b Jackson, Miss, June 23, 49. *Study:* Miss State Col Women, BS, 72. *Pos:* Dir, Galerie Simonne Stern, New Orleans; curator, Joseph C Canizaro Interests, Art Consult. *Awards:* Times Picayune Woman to Watch 90. *Mem:* Contemp Arts Ctr (vpres fundraising); Warehouse Gallery Asn New Orleans; New Orleans Mus Art-Friends of Cont Art. *Specialty:* Contemporary fine art. *Mailing Add:* Galerie Simonne Stern 518 Julia St New Orleans LA 70130

PERRIN, C ROBERT
PAINTER, ILLUSTRATOR
b Medford, Mass, July 13, 15. *Study:* Sch Practical Art, scholar, also with John Wharf & Lester Stevens, four yrs. *Work:* Ford Motor Co Collection Am Watercolors; Lyman Allyn Mus, New London, Conn. *Comn:* Four Seasons of the Island (watercolor murals), Tomkin's of Nantucket, Mass, 77; Historic Asn, Nantucket, Mass (in prep). *Exhib:* Mus Fine Arts, Boston, 52; Am Watercolor Soc, 58-; US Info Agency World Tour, 59; Boston Watercolor Soc, 60-; One-man show, Reno Art Asn, Nev, 60; Nat Acad Design. *Pos:* Freelance illusr, Boston, 39-42 & 46-68. *Teaching:* Artist, lectr & demonstr, Boston & Nantucket Island, Mass, 50. *Awards:* Richard Mitton Mem Award, 32nd Ann Exhib Painting by Contemp New Eng Artists, 61; First Award, Copley Soc, 65; six First Prizes, Artist Asn Nantucket, 73-82. *Bibliog:* James S Geggis (auth), Art studio on wheels, United Press, 47; Patricia Boyd Wilson (auth), The home forum, Christian Sci Monitor, 66; Norman Kent (auth), 100 Watercolor Techniques, Watson-Guptill, 68. *Mem:* Am Watercolor Soc; New Eng Watercolor Soc; Artist Asn Nantucket; Guild Boston Artists. *Publ:* Coauth, Watercolor page, 59 & Making a rug mural, 66, Am Artist Mag; contribr, The Folk Arts and Crafts of New England, 65 & Creating Art From Anything, 68. *Mailing Add:* 91 Washington St PO Box 1335 Nantucket MA 02554

PERRONE, JEFF
CERAMIST
b Atwater, Calif, 1953. *Exhib:* Univ Art Gallery, Calif State Univ and travelled, 83; White Columns, New York, 84; Bernice Steinbaum Gallery, New York, 86; What's New?, American Ceramics Since 1980: The Alfred and Mary Shands Collection, J B Speed Mus, Louisville, Ky, 87; Charles Cowles Gallery, New York, 87; plus others. *Teaching:* Instr, Sch Visual Arts, New York, 77-83, Univ Tex, San Antonio, 84 & Brown Univ, Providence, RI, 86. *Awards:* Nat Endowment Arts, 78. *Bibliog:* J Kozloff (auth), Like a dense curry with coconut milk, Am Ceramics, 5/4/87. *Mailing Add:* c/o Nancy Margolis Gallery 367 Fore St Portland ME 04101

PERROT, PAUL N
ADMINISTRATOR, LECTURER
b Paris, France, July 28, 26; US citizen. *Study:* Inst Fine Arts, NY Univ, 46-52. *Collections Arranged:* Three Great Centuries of Venetian Glass, 58; most exhibs shown at The Corning Mus Glass, 60-72. *Pos:* Asst, The Cloisters, Metrop Mus Art, 48-52; asst to dir, Corning Mus Glass, 52-55, asst dir, 55-60, dir, 60-72; ed, J Glass Studies, 59-72; asst secy mus progs, Smithsonian Inst, 72-84; dir, Va Mus Fine Arts, formerly. *Teaching:* Instr glass hist, Corning Community Col & Alfred Univ. *Awards:* Chevalier Ordre des Arts et Lettres, France. *Mem:* Am Asn Mus; US Int Coun Mus; Int Coun Mus Found; Int Asn Hist Glass; Int Ctr Study Preserv & Restoration Cult Property; and others. *Publ:* Auth, Three great centuries of Venetian glass, 58; articles, Antiques, Apollo, Arts Va, col Art J and others. *Mailing Add:* Santa Barbara Mus of Art 1130 State St Santa Barbara CA 93101

PERROTTI, BARBARA
PAINTER, INSTRUCTOR
b Akron, Ohio. *Study:* Paier Sch Art, New Haven, Conn, 67-73; Madison Sch Art, with Robert Brackman, Conn, 74; with Burt Silverman, Cinnaminson, NJ, 89. *Work:* Plainville Pub Libr, Conn; Doan Col, Rall Gallery, Crete, Nebr. *Comn:* Kent Cottage (mural), Stuart Treatment Ctr, Daytona Beach, Fla, 86; mural, Family Study Ctr, Ormond Beach, Fla, 87; oil painting, Walt Disney-Epcot, 92; portrait of Chapman S Root Mus Arts & Scis, Daytona Beach, Fla (in progress). *Exhib:* Of the Figure II, Ctr Arts, Vero Beach, Fla, 90; one-woman show, Poetry in Pose, Casements Cult Ctr, Ormond, Fla, 90; Art Three by Three, Maitland Art Ctr, Fla, 91; Juried Members Show, Deland Mus Art, Fla, 91; Mixed Media, Arts Park, Lakeland, Fla, 91; and others. *Teaching:* Oil Painting, Casements Cult Ctr, Ormond Beach, Fla, 80-92; creative portrait, Art League Daytona Beach, Fla, 80-92. *Awards:* Second Place, Pen Women Spring Fiesta, Daytona Beach, 83; Lillian Gitner Portrait Award, Juried Mem Show, Art League Daytona, 89; Equal Merit, Juried Mem Show, Beaux Art of Vol, 89. *Mem:* Art League Daytona Beach (pres, 82-84); endowment mem Mus Arts Scis; Fla Pastel Asn; Deland Mus Art; Nat League Am Pen Women, Daytona Branch. *Media:* Oil, Acrylic. *Mailing Add:* 1411 N Beach St Ormond Beach FL 32174

PERRY, CHARLES O
SCULPTOR
b Helena, Mont, Oct 18, 29. *Study:* Yale Univ, MA(archit). *Work:* Art Inst Chicago; Oakland Mus, Calif; San Francisco Mus Art, Calif; Mus Mod Art, New York; de Young Mus, San Francisco. *Comn:* Hyatt Regency Hotel, San Francisco, Calif, 73; Gen Elec Hq, Conn, 74; Ministry of Defense, Riyadh, Saudi Arabia, 75; Nat Air & Space Mus, Washington, DC, 76; City of Miami Beach, Fla, 78; Barnett Plaza, Tampa, Fla, 86; Shell Oil, Melbourne, Australia. *Exhib:* Fed Reserve Bank, Minneapolis, Minn, 73; Whitney Mus Am Art, New York, 64 & 66; Venice Bienale, 70; Quadriennale di Roma, Italy, 77; one-man shows, Alpha Gallery, 70, Hopkins Art Ctr, Dartmouth, 72 & Arts Club of Chicago, 72; and others. *Pos:* Sculptor in residence, Am Acad Rome, 68 & Hopkins Art Ctr, Dartmouth, 72. *Awards:* Prix de Rome in Archit, 64-66; Am Inst Steel Design Award, 68 & 70; Nat Acad Design, New York, 87. *Mem:* Century Asn, New York; Sculptor's Guild, New York; Silvermine Guild, Conn; Nat Acad Design, New York; Katonah Gallery, NY. *Media:* Metal. *Mailing Add:* Shorehaven Rd Norwalk CT 06855

PERRY, DONALD DEAN
PAINTER, EDUCATOR
b Hutchinson, Kans, Sept 29, 39. *Study:* Pittsburg State Univ, BFA, 62; Kans State Univ, MS, 67; Univ Wis-Madison, MFA, 67. *Work:* IBM Corp, United Telecommun Systems Inc, AT&T Corp, Kansas City, Mo; Software AG NAm, Chicago. *Comn:* Wildlife Panorama, Marshfield Libr, Wis, 70. *Exhib:* Nat Print Exhib, State Univ NY, Potsdam, 67; Miami Graphics Biennial Int, Metrop Mus, Fla, 74; Nat Print & Drawing Exhib, Univ NDak, Minot, 76; Ann Printmaking West, Logan, Utah, 78; Ann Nat Drawing & Small Sculpture Show, Ball State Univ, Ind, 80; Telec III Int Exhib, Art Res Ctr, Kansas, City, Mo, 85; Abstract Paper (three-person exhib), Batz-Lawrence Gallery, Kansas City, 86; Hypergraphics Int VIII Exhib, Bannister Gallery, RI Col, Providence, 87; Dakotas 100 Int Works on Paper Exhib, Dickinson State Univ, NDak & Univ SDak, Vermillion, 88; and many others. *Pos:* Mem bd dirs, Community Arts Inc, Emporia, 73-74; dir, Univ Art Galleries, Emporia State Univ, 79- *Teaching:* Instr drawing & printmaking, Univ Wis, Marshfield, 67-72; prof art, Emporia State Univ, Kans, 72-, chmn art dept, 77-84. *Awards:* Purchase Award, Miami Graphics Biennial, 74. *Mem:* Emporia Arts Coun, Kans. *Media:* Screenprint; Acrylic. *Mailing Add:* 1908 Coronado Ave Emporia KS 66801

PERRY, EDWARD (TED) SAMUEL
ADMINISTRATOR
b New Orleans, La, June 4, 37. *Study:* Baylor Univ, BA, 61; Univ Iowa, MA, 66, PhD, 68. *Pos:* Dir film dept, Mus Mod Arts, New York, 75-78. *Teaching:* Prof cinema & chmn dept, Univ Iowa, Univ Tex & NY Univ, 69-75; Luce vis prof cinema, Harvard Univ, spring 75; Middlebury Col, 78-; Am Film Inst Ctr for Advanced Film Study, 81-87. *Mem:* Soc Cinema Studies; Speech Commun Asn (mem res bd, 74-). *Publ:* Ed, Performing Arts Resources, 75; coauth, New Film Index, Dutton, 75; auth, Filmguide to 8-1/2, Ind Univ, 75; The passenger, Film Comment, Vol 2, No 4; Formal strategies as an index to the evolution of film history, Cinema J, 75. *Mailing Add:* 49 South St Middlebury VT 05753

PERRY, FRANK
SCULPTOR
b Vancouver, BC, Jan 15, 23. *Study:* Univ BC, BA, 49; Cent Sch Arts & Crafts, London, Eng; Regent Poly, Chelsea Sch Art, London. *Work:* Granite carving, Burnaby Art Gallery, BC, 58; Vancouver Art Gallery; Univ BC Sch Archit; Art Gallery Greater Victoria, BC; Univ Victoria; London Art Gallery, Ont. *Comn:* Bronze fountain, Crescent Apts, West Vancouver, 61; cor-ten welded, Fed Govt Bldg, Victoria, 66; bronze cast, Playhouse Theatre, Vancouver, 67 & BC Govt for Prov Bldgs, 73. *Exhib:* Montreal Mus Fine Arts, 58; Winnipeg Show, 58; BC Centennial Outdoor Show, 58; BC Centennial Outdoor Sculpture Show, 67; Burnaby Art Gallery, 77. *Pos:* Pres, Northwest Inst Sculpture, 59-60. *Awards:* First Prizes, Montreal Mus Fine Arts, Winnipeg Show & BC Centennial Outdoor Show, 68; Grand Prize, BC Centennial Outdoor Sculpture Show, 67; Rothman Award, 67. *Mem:* Sculptor's Soc Can; Sculptor's Soc BC; Royal Can Acad Art. *Media:* Bronze, Welded Steel. *Mailing Add:* 3526 Everglade Pl North Vancouver BC V7N 3T9 Canada

PERRY, KATHRYN POWERS
GRAPHIC ARTIST, PAINTER
b Chico, Calif, Mar 13, 48. *Study:* Concordia Col, seminar in Italy with Barbara Glasrud, 69, with Cy Running, BA(art, Eng), 70; Stanford Univ, 68; Art Students League, with Will Barnet, Earl Mayan, Knox Martin & Gregory

d'Alessio, 71-74, Emily Ferrier-Spear scholarship, 73-74; Sch of Visual Arts, 78-79. *Exhib:* Solo exhib, Aames Gallery, New York, 76; Berg Art Ctr, Moorhead, Minn, 77; Ore Independent Artists, Arte Fiera, Bologna, Italy, 78; Marietta Nat, Ohio, 79; Ligoa Duncan Gallery, New York, 79; and others. *Pos:* Asst art dir, Metrop Opera Guild, 81-83, art dir, 83-89. *Awards:* ECHO Leader Award for an Educational Brochure Design, 86. *Bibliog:* Review of four Concordia College artists, Fargo Forum, 5/70; Rob Edelman (auth), Three Brooklyn artists probe their role in society, Courier-Life, 7/74; New York Challenges Artists, Concordia, winter 78. *Mem:* Life-member, Art Students' League; Charter mem, Nat Mus Women Arts. *Media:* Charcoal, Pencil; Acrylic, Watercolor. *Mailing Add:* PO Box 311 Ft Meade SD 57741

PERRY, LALLAH MILES
PAINTER, EDUCATOR
b Auburn, Ala, July 15, 26. *Study:* Alabama Polytechnic Inst, Auburn, BA, 46; Delta State Univ, MEd, 72; Univ Ala, Univ Tenn (postgrad). *Work:* Miss Mus Art, First Nat Bank & Peat/Marwick Collection, Jackson, MS; Montgomery Mus Art, Ala; Miss Power & Light; Miss Collection, Deposit Guarantee Bank. *Comn:* Fabric collage, comn by Nancy Gilbert, Jackson, Miss, 85; drawing, for Christmas card, comn by US Rep G B Montgomery, 87; watercolor, landscape, Meridian Community Col, Miss, 88; Invitation & Billboard design, Azalea Ball, Asthma Found. *Exhib:* Louisiana World's Fair, New Orleans; Art in the Embassies, Am Embassy, Rabbat, Morocco, 70-80; Washington Watercolor Soc Exhib, Smithsonian Inst; Salute to Belgium, Birmingham Mus Art, Al. *Pos:* Exec dir, Miss Art Colony; exhib chmn, Crosstie Arts Coun, 76-78; bd dirs, Meridian Mus Art, Miss, 87- *Teaching:* From instr to asst prof art, Delta State Univ, 72-87; spec instr, Governor's Sch Gifted Children, 84; prof, Meridian Community Col, Miss, 87- *Awards:* Purchase awards, 6th Dixie Ann, Montgomery Mus Art, Ala, Frontal Images & Nat Watercolor Competitive Exhib, Miss Art Asn. *Bibliog:* Louis Dollarhide (auth), Of Art and Artists, Univ Press Miss, 81. *Mem:* Miss Watercolor Soc; Craftsmen Guild Miss; Miss Inst Arts & Lett; Miss Art Asn; Miss Art Colony. *Media:* Mixed Media. *Publ:* Illusr, Flower Place Plant Farm, Barton/Lowery, 88. *Dealer:* Gulf S Gallery Astin Ave McComb Miss. *Mailing Add:* 3250 Poplar Spring Dr Meridian MS 39305

PERRY, LINCOLN FREDERICK
PAINTER
b New York, NY, May 28, 49. *Study:* Columbia Univ, BA, 71; Queens Col, MFA, 75. *Work:* Bayly Mus, Charlottesville. *Comn:* Work & Leisure (murals), John Hancock, Inc, Boston, 84; triptych, Solomon Brothers, New York, 86; MetLife (murals) St Louis, Mo, 88; Mural for 1700 Pennsylvania Ave, Washington, DC, 90. *Exhib:* Tatistcheff Gallery, New York, 80, 82, 84, 86, 88 & 90; Contemporary Realism, NY Coun Arts Mus, New York, 82; Bodies and Souls, Artists Choice Mus, New York, 83; New Talent-New York, Sioux City Art Museum, 84. *Teaching:* Asst prof painting & drawing, Univ NH, Durham, 75-80, Univ Ark Fayetteville, 83-84 & Univ Va, 85. *Awards:* Nat Endowment Arts Grant, 84. *Bibliog:* James Cooper (auth), rev, News World, 81 & 82; Eunice Agar (auth), Lincoln Perry, Am Artist, 84; Liebemann Butler (auth), intro to catalog, Sioux City Art, 84. *Mailing Add:* c/o Tatistcheff & Co 50 W 57th St 8th Fl New York NY 10019

PERRY, REGENIA ALFREDA
HISTORIAN
b Virgilina, Va, Mar 30, 41. *Study:* Va State Col, BS, 61; Case Western Reserve Univ, MA(Va Mus Fine Arts Out of State Fel), 62; Univ Pa, 63-64, PhD(art hist), 66; Yale Univ, 70-71. *Pos:* Spec res asst, Cleveland Mus Art, 64-65; vis scholar, Piedmont Univ Ctr, Winston-Salem, 71-72. *Teaching:* Asst prof art hist, Howard Univ, 65-66; asst prof art hist, Ind State Univ, Terre Haute, 66-67; prof art hist, Va Commonwealth Univ, 67- *Awards:* Danforth Found Post-Doctoral Fel, 70-71. *Mem:* Col Art Asn Am; Am Asn Mus; Soc Archit Historians; Am Asn Univ Prof. *Publ:* auth, James Van Derzee--Photographer, 73; Auth, A History of Afro-American Art 1619-1976, 78. *Mailing Add:* c/o Art Dept Va Commonwealth Univ 922 W Franklin St Richmond VA 23284

PERSHAN, MARION
PAINTER, TEACHER
b New York, NY. *Study:* Hunter Col, with William Starkweather, BA, 38; Nat Acad Fine Arts, with Louis Bouche, 53; Art Students League, with Edwin Dickinson & Frank Mason, 54. *Work:* Dow Chemical Corp, Midland, Mich; Cardiology Assoc, Westport, Conn. *Exhib:* Brooklyn Artists Biennial, Brooklyn Mus, NY, 53; Metrop Mus of Art, 76 & 77; Catherine Lorillard Wolfe Arts Club, Nat Arts Club, New York, 76-83 & 90; Allied Arts Am, Nat Acad Design, New York, 78, 82 & 84; Hudson Valley Art Asn, NY, 78-86; Salmagundi Club, New York, 81; 157th Ann, 82 & 159th Ann, 84, Nat Acad Design, New York; Knickerbocker Artists, 85-87. *Collections Arranged:* Brooklyn Comes to the Met, Metrop Mus of Art, 76 & 77. *Pos:* Art dir, Camp Roselake, Honesdale, Pa, 54-55; Art dir, Camp Racquette Lake, NY, 57. *Teaching:* Instr & coordr art, New York City Public Sch, 60-77. *Awards:* Gold Medal of Honor, Catherine Lorillard Wolfe Club Inc, 79 & Silver Medallion, 82; First Award, Nat Arts Club, 82; Second Prize Watercolor, Knickerbocker Artists, 82 & Gold Medal, 85; Cynthia Goodgal Mem Award, 83. *Bibliog:* Walter Cruickshank (auth), Art Rev, Flatbush Life, 5/8/71; Claude Leseur (auth), article, Artspeak, 83. *Mem:* Catherine Lorillard Wolfe Art Club Inc; Knickerbocker Artists; Hudson Valley Art Asn; Asn Am Watercolor Soc. *Media:* Watercolor. *Publ:* Auth, Language Arts in the Art Curriculum, Fac News Asn, 4/72; illusr, Career Opportunities Exposition, Am Educ Asn, 10/73. *Dealer:* Grand Central Art Galleries New York NY. *Mailing Add:* 209-25 18th Ave Bayside New York NY 11360

PERSKY, ROBERT S
WRITER, PUBLISHER
b Jersey City, NY, Jan 5, 30. *Study:* NY Univ, 49; Harvard Law Sch, JD, 52. *Pos:* ed, Photograph Collectors Newsletter, 80-; publ, Photograph Collectors Resource Directory & The Photographic Art Market: Auction Price Series, currently. *Mem:* Soc Photog Educ; Am Photog Hist Soc. *Publ:* Auth, The Artist's Guide to Getting & Having a Successful Exhibition, Consul Press; ed & publ, The Photographic Art Market, Vol III, IV & V; Guide to Tax Benefits: For Collectors, Dealers & Investors, second ed, Consultant Press, 91. *Mailing Add:* c/o The Photograph Collector 163 Amsterdam Ave New York NY 10023

PERUO, MARSHA
PAINTER, PRINTMAKER
b Brooklyn, N Y, March 21, 51. *Study:* Queens Col, BA, 71; Pratt Inst, MFA, 80. *Exhib:* Mont Miniature Art Soc 12th Ann Int Show, Billings, 90; Ga Miniature Art Soc 5th Ann Int Miniature Art Show, Marietta, 90; Laramie Art Guild 16th Ann Am Nat Miniature Show, Wyo, 91; Miniature Painters, Sculptors & Gravers Soc Washington 58th Ann Int Exhib, DC, 91; Am Soc Contemp Artists Ann Exhib, Broome St Gallery, New York, 92. *Awards:* Dorothy Fiegen Mem Award for Graphics, 62nd Ann, Am Soc Contemp Artists, 80. *Mem:* Am Soc Contemp Artists (awards chmn, 80-81, corresp secy, 81-83, dir, 83-85, 1st vpres, 85-87); NY Artists Equity Asn; Colored Pencil Soc Am. *Media:* Mixed Media. *Mailing Add:* 55 W 14th St New York NY 10011

PESNER, CAROLE MANISHIN
DEALER
b Boston, Mass, Aug 5, 37. *Study:* Ecole du Louvre, Inst d'Art et d'Archit, Paris, 58; Smith Col, Northampton, Mass, BA, 59. *Pos:* Dir, Kraushaar Galleries, New York, currently. *Specialty:* 20th century American art. *Publ:* Auth & coauth, Kraushaar Gallery Publ & Catalogs. *Mailing Add:* Kraushaar Galleries 724 Fifth Ave New York NY 10019

PETER, FRIEDRICH GUNTHER
DESIGNER, GRAPHIC ARTIST
b Dresden, Ger, Feb 23, 33. *Study:* Hochschule fuer Bildende Kuenste, W Berlin, Ger, 50-56; Meisterschueler Dipl in lettering & graphic design, 56-57. *Comn:* Postage stamp designs, Can Post Off, 70, 79-80, 82 & 90; calligraphy, Expo 86, Invitation to the World Expo 86, Vancouver, BC; 100 dollar gold coin, 82 & 20 dollar silver Olympics coin, 88, One dollar special issue coin, 93, Royal Can Mint; official sports medal design, XV Olympic Winter Games, Calgary, Alta, 88; murals: 90 ft for World Coun Churches 6th Assembly, 83 & 30 ft for Lutheran Church in Can Bi-Ann Convention, 89. *Exhib:* Royal Can Acad Arts Exhib, Spectrum 76, Olympics, Montreal, 76; Royal Can Acad Exhib, Toronto, 81; Calligraphy Today, New York, NY, 80; one-man show, Lettering paintings, 89, Landscape and Lettering Paintings, Lookout Gallery, Regent Col, Univ, 92; 3:16, Int Traveling Calligraphy Exhib, 90; group show, The Art of the Coin, Royal Canadian Mint, Roy Thompson Hall, Toronto, Ont, 92; two one-man shows, Following Higher Orders, Gulf War Drawings at Gallery Alpha and Lookout Gallery, UBC, Vancouver, BC, 91. *Collections Arranged:* 26 Letters (traveling exhib), Fine Arts Gallery, Univ BC, Vancouver. *Teaching:* Instr graphic design, Vancouver Sch Art, BC, 59-78, chmn dept, 76; instr graphic design, Emily Carr Col Art & Design, Vancouver, BC, 76- *Awards:* Second Prize for Magnificat Typeface, Int Typeface Design Competition, Letraset Corp, 72; First Prize in Latin Category, Sanbika typeface, Morisawa Int Typeface Design Competition, Japan, 87; Prize Winner, Latin Category, Shinko Typeface, Morisawa Int Typeface Design Competition, Japan, 90. *Mem:* Royal Can Acad; Graphic Designers Can; Can Postage Stamp Adv Comt, 82-85. *Media:* Lettering, Graphic Design; Painting, Drawing. *Publ:* Auth & ed, Idea Mag, No 110, Yoshinobu Kawasaki, 72; auth & ed, Novum education Vancouver School of Art, Novum/Gebrauchsgraphik Mag, 3/75; illusr, Der Turm, Ulrich Schaffer (auth), Oncken, Ger, 79; bk illusr, Wenn Mauern Fallen, U Schaffer (auth), Kreuz Verlag (publ), Ger, 90. *Mailing Add:* 193 E St James Rd North Vancouver BC V7N 1L1 Canada

PETER, GEORGE
PAINTER, INSTRUCTOR
b New York, NY, 1922. *Study:* Brooklyn Mus Art Sch, with Reuben Tam, Abraham Rattner & Gabor Peterdi. *Work:* Butler Inst Am Art, Ohio; Ga Mus Art; Norfolk Mus Art & Sci, Va; Telfair Acad Arts & Sci, Ga; Univ Mass; Hobart & William Smith Cols. *Comn:* Paintings, Broadway Maintenance, 68 & Winslow Construct Corp, 75, New York; Curry Corp; IBM; NYNEX; Reichold Chemical Corp. *Exhib:* Am Embassy, Athens, Greece; 6th & 7th Ann Print, Brooklyn Mus, NY; Berkshire Mus, Mass; New York World's Fair, 65; Silvermine Guild, Union Carbide Corp Bldg, 74. *Pos:* Founder, George Peter Sch Art. *Teaching:* Adj prof painting & drawing, Westchester Art Workshop, White Plains, NY, 69-; lectr & demonstr contemp painting, many cols & schs. *Media:* Oil, Acrylic. *Mailing Add:* 8 Kingwood Rd Scarsdale NY 10583

PETERDI, GABOR F
PAINTER, PRINTMAKER
b Pestujhely, Hungary, Sept 17, 15; US citizen. *Study:* Hungarian Acad, Budapest; Acad Julien, Paris; Atelier 17, Paris, with Hayter. *Work:* Whitney Mus Am Art, Mus Mod Art & Metrop Mus Art, New York; Art Inst Chicago; Boston Mus Fine Arts; and others. *Exhib:* Retrospectives, Brooklyn Mus, 59, Cleveland Mus, 62, Corcoran Gallery Art & Yale Univ Art Gallery, 64 & Honolulu Acad Arts, 68; Suzanne Brown Gallery, Scottsdale, Ariz, 81; Jacques Baruch Gallery, Chicago, 81; Conn Fine Arts, Westport, 81; over 100

solo exhibits and 22 retrospectives. *Teaching:* Instr, Brooklyn Mus Art Sch, 48-52; assoc prof, Hunter Col, 52-59; prof art, Yale Univ, 60- *Awards:* Prix du Rome, 30; Mus Western Art, Tokyo, 64; Guggenheim Fel, 64-65. *Bibliog:* V Johnson (auth), Graphic Work 1934-69, Touchstone, 69. *Mem:* Silvermine Guild Artists; Florentine Acad Design; Nat Drawing Soc. *Media:* Oil, Intaglio. *Publ:* Auth, Printmaking, 59 & Great Prints of the World, 69, Macmillan; auth, Printmaking, Encycl Britannica. *Dealer:* Grace Borgenicht Gallery 1018 Madison Ave New York NY 10021. *Mailing Add:* 108 Highland Ave Norwalk CT 06853

PETERS, ANDREA JEAN
PAINTER
b Boston, Mass, Dec 27, 47. *Study:* Vesper George Sch Art, Boston, 65-66; Mass Col Art, Boston, 66-68; Roger Curtis, Gloucester, 78-83. *Work:* Hoyt Inst Fine Art, New Castle, Pa; NE Tel Corp Off, Boston. *Exhib:* The '86 Hoyt Nat, Hoyt Inst Fine Art, New Castle, Pa; 15th, 16th & 17th Ann Pastel Soc Am, New York; 45th Nat Audubon Artists Asn, New York; 17th Nat Works on Paper, Harnett Hall Gallery, Minot State, NDak. *Awards:* Daniel B Hoye Mem Award, 86 Hoyt Nat, 86; Pearl Paint Award, 15th Ann Pastel Soc Am, 87; J Giffuni Scher Award, 16th Ann Pastel Soc Am, 88. *Mem:* Am Artists Prof League, NY; Pastel Soc Am, NY (master pastelist); North Shore Arts Asn, Mass; Copley Soc Boston, Mass (copley artist); Depot Square Artists, Mass. *Media:* Oil, Pastel. *Mailing Add:* Four Furguson Rd Wilmington MA 01887

PETERS, DIANE (PECK)
PAINTER, COLLAGE ARTIST
b Corpus Christi, Tex, May 14, 40. *Study:* Univ Okla Art Workshop, with Milford Zornes, 75; Class with Chen Chi, 76, Master Class in Watercolor, with Edward Betts, 78 & 84; La Tech Univ, with Douglas Walton, 78. *Work:* Corpus Christi Mus, Tex; McAllen State Bank, McAllen, Tex. *Comn:* Seascape mural, Dr & Mrs William Roof; Lake wildlife mural, John Peters Mem, 86; The Cooking Habit, 87; Jungle Fantasy & Tropical Flowers mural, Mr & Mrs J M Smith. *Exhib:* 39th Watercolor Soc of Ala Ann Nat Competition, Birmingham Mus Art, Ala; Southern Watercolor Soc 2nd Ann Exhib, Columbus Mus Arts & Sci, Ga; Allied Artists Am 65th Ann Exhib, Nat Acad Galleries, New York; Salmagundi Club 2nd & 3rd Ann Non-member Exhib, Salmagundi Galleries, New York; Southwestern Watercolor Soc Ann Membership Exhib, Dallas; Tex Watercolor Soc Exhib, 84. *Awards:* John Herweck Award, John Herweck Co, 77; Purchase Award, Tex Watercolor Soc, 84; Best of Show Award, Art Community Ctr Exhib, 89. *Bibliog:* Lee Dodds (auth), Tonkaland a winner, Corpus Christi Times, 6/79; Spotlight Ed (auth), Local artist has show in New York, Corpus Christi Times, 12/79; Local Artist Honored, Corpus Christi Caller Times, 5/90. *Mem:* Assoc Allied Artists Am; assoc Am Watercolor Soc; Southwestern Watercolor Soc; Ky Watercolor Soc. *Media:* Watercolor, Acrylic; Collage. *Publ:* Illusr, cover, Star to Star, 1/72; cover, Giving (catalog), 85; cover, The Cooking Habit, 87; paintings featured, The Artist Mag, 5/88; paintings featured, The New Spirit of Watercolor, North Light Books, 4/89. *Dealer:* Sundial II Gallery 508 S Austin St Rockport TX 78382. *Mailing Add:* HCR2 Box 6546 Sandia TX 78383-9405

PETERS, LARRY DEAN
CURATOR, ADMINISTRATOR
b Manhattan, Kans, July 15, 38. *Study:* Washburn Univ, BFA, 62; Southern Ill Univ, with Nicholas Vergette, MFA, 65. *Work:* Afghanistan Embassy, Kabul; Singapore Embassy. *Exhib:* 16th Mid-Am Exhib, William Rockhill Nelson Gallery, Kansas City, Mo, 66; North Coast Col Soc Ann Exhib, Ohio, 86. *Collections Arranged:* Artists of the American West, 74, Topeka Competition 1-14, 77-90, Recent Acquisitions, 78, Ukiyo-E, Pictures of the Floating World (The Japanese Woodblock Print), 78, Precolumbian Figurative Clay, Carpets of the Caucasus, Robert Motherwell's a la pintura & The Age of Art Nouveau, Gallery Fine Arts, Topeka Pub Libr. *Pos:* Readers adv, Dept Fine Arts, Topeka Pub Libr, 65-73, gallery dir, Gallery Fine Arts, 73- *Teaching:* Instr pottery, Washburn Univ Topeka, Kans, 69-70. *Awards:* Kansas Governor's Arts Award for Arts Advocacy, 90. *Mem:* Am Asn Mus; Mountain Plain Mus Asn; Kans Mus Asn (bd mem, 79-); Kans Art Comn; Kans Artist Craftsmen Asn (sec, 69-71, pres, 71-73); Mulvane Art Ctr (pres, 89-90). *Mailing Add:* c/o Gallery of Fine Arts 1515 W Tenth Topeka KS 66604

PETERSEN, FRANKLIN G
PAINTER
b Staten Island, NY, July 19, 1940. *Study:* Art Students League, 69-73. *Comn:* Portraits, Admiral A B Durek, US Navy, Washington, DC, former Gov Malcom Wilson, NY, former Atty Gen Louis J Lefkowitz, New York, Fed Judge Irving R Kaufman & Very Rev James Fewhagen, pres, General Theological Seminary NY for Allin Collection, Fordham Law Sch, New York. *Exhib:* Salmagundi Club, New York, 72-78; Nat Arts Club, New York, 73-76; Staten Island Mus Annual, 74-75; Allied Artists, Nat Acad, New York, 74-75; Pentagon Exhib, Washington, DC, 75; Nacal Artists Exhib, US Navy War Mus, Washington, DC, 75; New York Press Club, 78; and others. *Awards:* Greenshields Found Grant, 73; Stacey Mem Grant, 74; Pouch Award, Staten Island Mus, 75. *Mem:* Life mem Art Students League (secy, 72). *Media:* Oil. *Dealer:* Portraits Inc 985 Park Ave New York NY 10028; Portraits South 4008 Barret Dr Suite 106 Raleigh NC 27609. *Mailing Add:* 201 Seguine Ave Staten Island NY 10309

PETERSEN, ROLAND CONRAD
PAINTER, PRINTMAKER
b Endelave, Denmark, Mar 31, 26; US citizen. *Study:* Univ Calif, Berkeley, AB, 49 & MA, 50; San Francisco Art Inst, 51; Calif Col Arts & Crafts, summer 54; Atelier 17, Paris, with Stanley W Hayter, 50, 63 & 70; Islington Studio, London, 77; The Print Workshop, London, 80. *Work:* Mus Mod Art & Whitney Mus Am Art, New York; Philadelphia Mus Art, Pa; Nat Collection Fine Arts, Washington, DC; Univ Reading, Eng; San Francisco Mus Mod Art. *Comn:* Dams of the West (portfolio of 25 color prints), US Dept Interior, Bur Reclamation, Washington, DC, 70. *Exhib:* Carnegie Inst Int, Pittsburgh, 64; 25th Ann Exhib Contemp Art, Art Inst Chicago, 65; one-man shows, Staempfli Gallery, New York, 63, 65 & 67, Phoenix Art Mus, Ariz, 72, Santa Barbara Mus, Calif, 73 & Rorick Gallery, San Francisco, 81-85; Vanderwoude/Tananbaum Gallery, New York, 87-89; Harcourts Gallery, San Francisco, 89-91. *Pos:* Mem educ process, Col Lett & Sci, Univ Calif, Davis, 65, mem exec comt, 65-66. *Teaching:* Instr painting, Wash State Univ, 52-56; prof painting & printmaking, Univ Calif, Davis, 56-91; instr printmaking, Univ Calif, Berkeley, 65. *Awards:* Guggenheim Fel, 63; appointee, Inst Creative Arts, Univ Calif, 67 & 70; Fulbright Travel Award, 70. *Bibliog:* Andree Marchal-Workman (auth), article, Artweek, 81; Kenneth Baker (auth), article, San Francisco Chronical, 89; Bruce Nixon (auth), Art of Calif, 91. *Mem:* Intercontinental Biog Asn; Calif Soc Etchers. *Dealer:* Harcourts Gallery 460 Bush St San Francisco CA 94108. *Mailing Add:* Art Dept Univ Calif Davis CA 95616

PETERSEN, TONI
LIBRARIAN, DIRECTOR
b New York, NY, May 13, 33. *Study:* Pratt Inst, 50-53; Brooklyn Col, BA, 56; Simmons Col Libr Sch, MLS, 63. *Pos:* Exec ed, Int Repertory of Lit of Art, Williamstown, Mass, 72-80; dir, Bennington Col Libr, Bennington, Vt, 80-86; Art & Archit Thesaurus, Getty Art Hist Info Prog, Williamston, Mass, 83- *Mem:* Art Libr Soc NAm (vice charirperson, 84-85, chairperson, 85-86); Nat Info Standards Orgn, Subcommittee to Revise the ANSI Standard on Thesaurus Construction, 89-90; Am Libr Asn, 88-91. *Res:* Helped develop projects in art information and documentation. *Publ:* auth, The AAT in the Online Catalog Environment, Art Documentation, 82; The AAT: A model for the restructuring of LCSH, J Acad Librarianship, 83; Multiple Authorities in Library Systems, Art Libr Soc NAm, 86, Symposium proceedings; Subject Control in Visual Collections, Art Documentation, 88; Beyond the Book; Extending MARC for Subject Access, G K Hall, 90. *Mailing Add:* 51 Bulkley St Williamstown MA 01267

PETERSEN, WILL
PAINTER, PRINTMAKER
b Chicago, Ill, Dec 9, 28. *Study:* Mich State Univ, BA, 51, MA, 52; Calif Col Arts & Crafts, MFA, 56; Kawamura Noh Theatre, Kyoto, Japan, 57-65. *Work:* Philadelphia Mus Art; Victoria & Albert Mus, London, Eng; Portland Art Mus, Ore; San Francisco Palace Legion Honor & Achenbach Found, San Francisco; Oakland Mus, Calif. *Comn:* Six etching steel, Inland Steel, 91; paintings world premier. *Exhib:* Ten Years Am Prints, Brooklyn Mus Art, NY, 56; The Figure: Continuing Tradition, Fairweather-Hardin Gallery, 83; Eastern Influence on Western Artists, Fairweather-Hardin Gallery, 84; Contemporary Chicago Lithography, Ill State Mus; Art Inst Chicago Ann, 85; Int Biennial Print Exhib, Mus Art, Taipei, Taiwan, 87; Chicago Int New Art Forms Expo, 88; and others. *Pos:* Founder, Bay Printmakers Soc, Oakland, Calif, 55; ed, Plucked Chicken Journal, Morgantown, WVa, 77-79; Dir, Plucked Chicken Press, Evanston, Ill, currently. *Teaching:* Assoc prof, Kyoto, Japan, 57-65, Ohio State Univ, 65-69 & WVa Univ, 70-77, Western Mich Univ, 87-88. *Awards:* Maimichi Newspaper: Best-of-the-Yr, 63; Suda Prize: Painting, Kyoto Fine Arts Mus, 65; Provost's Purchase Bradley Nat Print & drawing Exhib; and others. *Bibliog:* Nancy Wilson Ross (ed), The World of Zen, Random House, 60; A Caterpillar Anthology, Anchor Bks, 71; and others. *Media:* Oil, Mixed Media; Lithography. *Publ:* Translr, Akutagawa's A Fool's Life, Eridanos Press, 88; Zeami's Noh: Yashima, Mushinsha, 77; Space: Moby Dick as Noh, Japan and America, Vol I, 84; auth, September Ridge, Gary Snyder, Dimensions of a Life, Sierra Club Press & Random House, 91; translr, The Fictives, Tsutsui, Lapis Press, 92. *Dealer:* Plucked Chicken 1604 Greenleaf Evanston IL 60202. *Mailing Add:* Plucked Chicken Press 1604 Greenleaf Evanston IL 60202

PETERSON, DAVID WINFIELD
PAINTER
b Chicago, Ill, Feb 7, 13. *Study:* Northwestern Univ & Univ Wis, BS, 35; with David R Peterson, Carroll Berry, Edmond J Fitzgerald, Emile A Gruppe & S E Oppenheim. *Work:* Brevard Art Mus, Melbourne, Fla; Gold Room, Easton, Md; Salmagundi Club, New York; City Hall, Naples, Fla. *Comn:* Venetian Villas (painting), comn by B A Blackmer, 84. *Exhib:* Am Art Prof League; Gold Room, Waterfowl Festival, 81-83; Mariner's Mus, Newport News, Va; Bradley Mus Gallery, Naples, Fla, 90; R J Schaefer Mus, Mystic Seaport, Conn; and others. *Teaching:* Pvt classes. *Awards:* Award, Ft Myers Beach Art Asn, Elizabeth Niven, 78; Rowland Award, Fla Artists Group. *Mem:* Int Soc Marine Painters; Salmagundi Club; Naples Art Asn (bd dirs, 76-81); Artists Fel; Am Artists Prof League; and others. *Media:* Oil, Watercolor. *Publ:* Illusr, Hunting is for the birds, Naples Calender & Naples Now Mag, Naples Printing Co, 81. *Dealer:* Darvish Fine Art Gallery 1199 Third St S Naples FL 33940; Arnold Art 210 Thomas St Newport RI 02840. *Mailing Add:* 2036 View Point Dr Naples FL 33963

PETERSON, DOROTHY (HAWKINS)
PAINTER, EDUCATOR
b Albuquerque, NMex, Mar 14, 32. *Study:* Univ NMex, Albuquerque, BSEd, 53; Dallas Mus Sch, studied painting with Otis Dozier, 63-64; Univ Tex, Permian Basin, Odessa, MA, 79. *Work:* First Nat Bank Chicago Collection, Ill; Eastern NMex Univ, Roswell; Immaculata Hosp, Westlock, Alta, Can; Mus Southwest, Midland; Odessa Col, Tex. *Comn:* Library Windows, Jal, NMex Jr High Sch; murals, Tarahumara Sch, Creel, Chi, Mex. *Exhib:* Solo exhibs, Carlsbad Mus, NMex, 85, Mus Southwest, Midland, Tex, 85 & Thompson Gallery, Univ NMex, Albuquerque, 86; Eastern NMex Univ, Portales, 88;; Centennial Gallery, Univ NMex, 89. *Pos:* Comnr, NMex Arts Comn, Santa Fe, 83-; artist rep, NMex Arts & Crafts Fair, Albuquerque, 84-86. *Teaching:* Instr painting, Midland Col, Tex, 71-75, Roswell Mus, 81-83; prof art hist, Eastern NMex Univ, Roswell, 89-; painting instr, NMex Military Inst, Roswell, 92- *Awards:* Spec Award Transparency Watercolor & Herwecks Award, Tex Watercolor Soc, 77; Second Award, NMex Watercolor Soc, 81 & Bd Dir Award, 90; Award of Merit, NMex Arts & Crafts Fair, 86; San Diego Watercolor Soc Award, 88; First Place Award Prof Watercolor, NMex State Fair, 88. *Bibliog:* NMex Mag, 5/89. *Mem:* NMex Watercolor Soc. *Media:* Acrylic, Oil, Watercolor. *Publ:* Savoring the Southwest, RSG Pub, 83;; Artists of NMex, Mtn Pub, 89. *Dealer:* Pinon Tree Gallery 400 San Felipe NW D1 & 2 Albuquerque NM. *Mailing Add:* PO Box 915 Roswell NM 88201

PETERSON, GWEN ENTZ
PRINTMAKER
b Newton, Kans, Mar 8, 38. *Study:* Northern Colo Univ, BFA, 59; Goshen Col, Florence, Italy, 77; Univ NMex, 77-79. *Work:* Golden Collection, Eastern NMex Univ; Int Bus Machines; AT&T; Albuquerque Nat Bank; Jonson Collection, Univ NMex. *Comn:* Frame Work, Wright Edge Advert Agency. *Exhib:* Solo exhibs, Jonson Gallery, Univ NMex, 75, 77, 79 & 81; retrospective, Thompson Gallery, Univ NMex, 84. *Teaching:* Instr pub sch, Colby, Kans, 59-61, Denver, Colo, 61-62 & Lake Bluff, Ill, 65-66. *Awards:* Prof Competition Award, NMex State Fair, 78, 80, 82 & 83; Poster Award, NMex Arts & Crafts Fair, 82; Purchase Award, Art in Pub Places, Fairbanks, Alaska, 86. *Bibliog:* Jean Blackmon (auth), Gwen Peterson, Southwest Profile, 9-10/84. *Media:* Serigraphy. *Dealer:* John Cacciatore 206 Dartmouth NE Albuquerque NM 87106. *Mailing Add:* 3717 General Patch NE Albuquerque NM 87111

PETERSON, HAROLD PATRICK
LIBRARIAN, EDITOR
b Chicago, Ill, Aug 27, 35. *Study:* Harvard Col, AB; Univ Wis, MA. *Pos:* Ed-in-chief, Minneapolis Inst Arts, 72-82, art librn, 72- *Mem:* Art Libr Soc NAm; Col Art Asn; Midwest Art Hist Asn. *Interests:* Decorative arts, history of printing, illustration of books. *Publ:* Ed, Victorian High Renaissance, 78, New Treasures at the Institute, 78, Millet's Gleaners, 78 & Treasures of the Hermitage Museum of Leningrad, 79, Minneapolis Inst Arts; Chinese Jades: Archaic & Modern, Tuttle, 77; and many others. *Mailing Add:* Minneapolis Inst Arts 2400 Third Ave S Minneapolis MN 55404

PETERSON, JOHN DOUGLAS
ADMINISTRATOR, MUSEUM DIRECTOR
b Peshtigo, Wis, July 9, 39. *Study:* Univ Wis, 58; Layton Sch Art, cert indust design, BFA, 62; Cranbrook Acad Art, 62-64, MFA, 66; Oakland Univ, 64-65. *Exhib:* Made of Plastic, Bloomfield Art Asn, 70; Detroit Artists, Mkt, 71; James Yaw Gallery, 71; Bloomfield Art Asn, 71. *Collections Arranged:* Dr & Mrs Hilbert De Lawter-African Collection, 67; Miaja Grottel Retrospective-Ceramics, 71; Wallace Mitchell Retrospective-Painting, Memorial--Painting 77; Concept and Manufacture of Decorative Arts, 78; Survey of Illinois Fiber, 78; Survey of Illinois Photography, 78. *Pos:* Pres, Romaine Gallery, 64-65; asst dir, Cranbrook Acad Art/Mus, 68-70, assoc dir, 70-71, dean students, Acad, 72-74, dir mus, 71-77; pres, VCI Inc, 77-; dir, Lakeview Mus Arts & Sci, 77-82; exec dir, Morris Mus, 82- *Teaching:* Instr exhib design, Cranbrook Acad Art, 70-72. *Mem:* Mid-Atlantic Asn Mus; NJ Asn Mus; NJ Art Pride; Am Coun Arts; Am Asn Mus; and others. *Mailing Add:* 29 Decker Basking Ridge NJ 07920

PETERSON, KRISTIN
SCULPTOR, ASSEMBLAGE ARTIST
b Urbana, Ill, May 17, 54. *Study:* Kansas City Art Inst, BFA, 78; Univ Calif, Davis, MFA, 82. *Exhib:* One woman shows, Performance Project, Diablo Valley Community Col Art Gallery, Pleasant Hill, Calif, 81, Master of Fine Arts Exhibit, Mem Union Art Gallery, Univ Calif Davis, 82, Joseph Chowning Gallery, San Francisco, Calif, 87 & 89, Diablo Valley Community Col Art Gallery, Pleasant Hill, Calif, 92; A Selection of Kansas City's Pride, Molgan Gallery, Mo, 89; Tools: Instruments, Implements, Utensils, San Francisco Int Airport, Calif, 89; Rags: Clothing as Allegory, San Francisco Arts Comn Gallery, Calif, 89; Functional Fantasy, Transamerica Pyramid Lobby, San Francisco, 90; Couturier Gallery, Los Angeles, Calif, 92; Sun Gallery, Hayward, Calif, 92. *Awards:* Humanities Grant, Univ Calif, Davis, 81; First Prize & Hon Mention, Calif State Fair, Cal Expo, Sacramento, 85; Nat Endowment Arts Grant, 86. *Bibliog:* Charles Shere (auth), Artscene, Oakland Tribune, 7/87; Therese Poletti (auth), Introducing Art's New Breed, The Sutter Post, 7/87; Jamie Brunson (auth), Sensual Surfaces, Disparate Forms, Art Week, 4/88. *Media:* Mixed Media. *Dealer:* Joseph Chowning Gallery 1717 17th St San Francisco CA 94103. *Mailing Add:* 1420 45th St No 48 Emeryville CA 94608

PETERSON, LARRY D
PAINTER, EDUCATOR
b Holdrege, Nebr, Jan 1, 35. *Study:* Kearney State Col, BA, 58; Northern Colo Univ, MA, 62; Univ Kans, EdD, 75. *Work:* Univ Minn; US Nat Bank, Omaha; Kearney State Col; Nebr Art Collection; 512 works in pvt collections; Sheldon Art Gallery, Lincoln, Nebr. *Comn:* Acrylic & oil paintings, First Methodist Church, Kearney, 72; watercolor paintings, Kearney state Bank, 80. *Exhib:* 13th Midwest Biennial, 74 & Nebraska '75 Exhib, Joslyn Art Mus, 75, Omaha; Ann Am Nat Miniature Exhib, Laramie, Wyo, 77 & 80-81; Augustana Col, Sioux Falls, SDak, 80; Col St Mary, Omaha, 80; Landworthy Watercolor Exhib, Seward, 85-90; Six-State Competitive, McCook Col, 88; Nebr Art Mus, 89. *Pos:* Dir, Mus Nebr Art. *Teaching:* Instr art, North Platte Pub Schs, 58-65; North Platte Col, 66-67; prof art, Kearney State Col, 67-; grad asst, Univ Kans, Lawrence, 70-71. *Awards:* Gov Art Award, State Nebr, 81; Nebr Art Educator Year, 83; Coun of Deans Award, Kearney State Col, 84; Gold Medal Award, Calvatone, Italy, 85; Pratt-Heins Award, Kearney State Col, 87. *Bibliog:* Nancy Kalis (auth), article, Art Rev, 68; Reva Remy (auth), one-man rev in Rev Mod Art, Paris, 68 & 72; Tom Norwood (auth), Contemporary Nebraska Art and Artists, Univ Nebr, 78; Nebraska Art Asn, Sheldon Art Gallery, Lincoln, 88. *Mem:* Nat Art Educ Asn (nat comt, 83-84); Nebr Art Teachers Asn (past pres); Asn Nebr Art Clubs (past pres); Kappa Pi (past pres, Beta Beta Chap). *Media:* Watercolor, Acrylic. *Publ:* Coauth, Nebraska Art Guide K-6, Elem Art Curric, State Nebr, 66; Nebraska Art Collection, Rural Artreach Catalog, 81-83. *Dealer:* Studio 44 Four Seminole Lane Kearney NE 68847; Art Ctr 4844 St Paul St Lincoln NE 68504. *Mailing Add:* 4 Seminole Lane Kearney NE 68847

PETERSON, ROGER TORY
ILLUSTRATOR, WRITER
b Jamestown, NY, Aug 28, 08. *Study:* Art Students League; Nat Acad Design; DSc Degrees from Franklin & Marshall Col, 52, Ohio State Univ, 62, Fairfield Univ, 67, Allegheny Col, 67, Wesleyan Univ, 70, Colby Col, 74 & Gustavus Adolphus Col, 78, Conn Col, 85, Univ Conn, 87, Mem Univ, Nfdl, 87, Hamilton Col, Hon PhD(Humanities), 76; LHD Degrees, Amherst Col, 77 & Skidmore Col, 81; Univ Hartford, Hon DFA, 81, and many others. *Work:* New Britain Mus Am Art, Conn; Am Mus Natural Hist, Metrop Mus Art, New York; Calif Acad Arts & Sci, San Francisco; Carnegie Mus Natural Hist, Pittsburgh, Pa; Smithsonian Inst, Washington, DC; Rochester Mus & Sci Ctr, NY. *Exhib:* Leigh Yawkey Woodson Art Mus, Wausau, Wis, 76, 78 & 81; Smithsonian Inst, 79; Mass Audubon Soc, 81; Univ Conn, Storrs, 81; Univ Hartford, Conn, 81; Calif Acad Sci, San Francisco, 81-82; Mo Botanical Gardens, St Louis, 84; La Fish & Wildlife Serv, Baton Rouge, 84; Halley & Steele Galleries, Boston, 84; Thames Sci Ctr, New London, Conn, 85; Legislative Bldg, Albany, NY, 87. *Pos:* Art ed, Audubon Mag, 34-43; art dir, Nat Wildlife Fedn, 46-75; ed, Houghton Mifflin Co, Am Naturalist Series, 65-; spec consult, Nat Audubon Soc, 70-; roving reporter, Int Wildlife Mag, 70; mem, Galapagos Int Sci Proj, 64. *Teaching:* Instr art & sci, Rivers Sch, Brookline, Mass, 31-34; educ dir, Nat Audubon Soc, 34-43; lectr, Audubon Screen Tour, Nat Audubon Soc, 46-72; fel, Davenport Col, Yale Univ, 66- *Awards:* Presidential Medal of Freedom, 80; Ludlow Griscom Award, 80; Bradford Washburn Award, Boston Mus Sci, 81; Nominated for Nobel Peace Prize, 83; Eugene Eisenmann Medal, Linnaean Soc, New York, 86. *Bibliog:* Jerry Bowles (auth), Artist profile: Roger Tory Peterson, Acquire, 76; Sevlin/Naismith (auth), The world of Roger Tory Peterson, Times Bks, 77; John Diffily (auth), A field guide to Roger Tory Peterson, Am Artist, 77. *Mem:* Soc Animal Artists; Soc Wildlife Artists, Eng (vpres, currently); Nat Audubon Soc (bd dirs, 58-60, 65-67 & 68-70); patron Am Ornithologists Union (1st vpres, 62-63); Int Comt Bird Protection (chmn, 65-70); and others. *Publ:* Ed, A Field Guide to Southwestern and Texas Wildflowers, Houghton Mifflin, 84; intro to Kay McCrackens The Bird Lady of Texas, Tex A & M Univ Press, 85; James Bretts The Mountain and the Migration, 86; foreword, Looking for the Wild, Doubleday, 86; auth, articles and photographs in Life, Nat Geographic, New York Times Mag, Readers Digest and numerous other mags. *Dealer:* Mill Pond Press Inc 204 S Nassau St Venice FL 33595. *Mailing Add:* Neck Rd Old Lyme CT 06371

PETERSON, SUSAN HARNLY
EDUCATOR, CERAMIC ARTIST
b McPherson, Kans, July 21, 25. *Study:* Monticello Col, Alton, Ill, AA, 44; Mills Col, Oakland, Calif, AB, 46; New York State Col Ceramics, Alfred Univ, NY, MFA, 50. *Work:* Mus Art, Oakland, Calif; Mus Art, Long Beach, Calif; Mus Art, Lausanne, Switz; Smithsonian Inst, Washington, DC; Mengeikan Mus, Tokyo, Japan. *Comn:* Television: Wheels Kilns and Clay, 54 Halfhours for CBS- KNXT, 70. *Exhib:* Nat Decorative Arts & Ceramic, Wichita Art Asn Mus, 47-62; Ceramic Art of the 60s, Los Angeles Co Mus Art; Smithsonian Exhib Ceramics; Am Ceramic Soc; Int Ceramic, Brussels Worlds' Fair; World Craft Coun, Lima, Peru; Mus Contemp Craft, New York; and others. *Collections Arranged:* Indian Artists: Five Matriarchs (auth, catalog), ACA Gallery, New York, 80; Maria Martinez: Five Generations of Potters (auth, catalog), Smithsonian Inst, Renwick Gallery, Washington, DC, 78. *Teaching:* Instr ceramics, Wichita Art Asn Sch, Kans, 47-49; instr & chmn ceramics, Chouinard Art Inst, Los Angeles, 52-55; assoc prof ceramics, Univ Southern Calif, Los Angeles, 55-72; prof studio art, Hunter Col, New York, 72- *Awards:* Wrangler Award for Best Western Art Book, Nat Cowboy Hall Fame, 79; Nat Endowment Arts Critics Fel, 80; Fel, Am Craft Coun, 84; Pres Award for Excellence, Hunter Col, 86. *Bibliog:* F Carlton Ball (auth), Terra-sigilatta of Susan Peterson, Ceramics Monthly, 56; Garth Clark (auth), History of Ceramics in the USA, Abbeyville Press, 88; Elaine Levin (auth), The History of American Ceramics, Abrams, 88. *Mem:* Nat Coun Ceramic Educ; World Craft Coun; Am Craft Coun; Southern Calif Design Div Am Ceramic Soc (pres, 66). *Media:* Ceramic Art. *Res:* Glaze technology and

indigenous folk art. *Publ:* Auth, Wheels, Kilns, and Clay, Univ Southern Calif, Press, 69; auth, Shoji Hamada: A Potter's Way and Work, 74, The Living Legend of Maria Martinez, 77 & Lucy M Lewis: American Indian Potter, 84, Kodansha Intl; contribr, Studio Potter, Am Craft, Ceramics Monthly & Craft Int; Craft and Art Clay, Prentice Hall, 92. *Mailing Add:* Dept Studio Art c/o Hunter Col 695 Park Ave New York NY 10021

PETHEO, BELA FRANCIS
PRINTMAKER, PAINTER
b Budapest, Hungary, May 14, 34; US citizen. *Study:* Univ Budapest, MA, 56; Acad Fine Arts, Vienna, with A P Guetersloh, 57-59; Univ Vienna, 58-69; Univ Chicago, MFA, 63. *Work:* Hungarian State Mus Fine Arts, Budapest; Kunstmus, Bern, Switz; Boston Public Libr; Tweed Mus, Duluth, Minn; Plains Art Mus, Moorhead, Minn; Minn Mus Art, St Paul; and others. *Comn:* Kindliche Untugenden (mural), Asn Austrian Boyscouts, Vienna, 58; The History of Handwriting (exhib panel), comn by Noble & Noble Publ for Hall of Educ, New York World's Fair, 64; plus others. *Exhib:* Hamline Univ, 66; Coffman Gallery, Univ Minn, 68; Moorhead State Col, 69; Biennale Wis Printmakers, 71; Duluth: A Painterly Essay, Tweed Mus Art, Minn, 75; B P Themes: 1953-1983, CSB Gallery, St Joseph, Minn, 83; and others. *Teaching:* Instr art, Univ Northern Iowa, 64-66; assoc prof art & artist-in-residence, St John's Univ, 66-80, prof 80- *Awards:* Graphic Prize, Univ Chicago, 62; Purchase Award, Pillsbury Invitational, 81; Burlington-Northern Fac Excellence Award, 92; and others. *Bibliog:* J Gray Sweeney (auth), Bela Petheo: Painter of the Center in an Age of Extremes (monogr), St John's Univ Publ, 85; Arts Salutes Bela Petheo, Arts, Minneapolis, 12/87. *Mem:* Col Art Asn Am. *Media:* Oil, Acrylics; Lithography. *Publ:* Auth, Polymer-coated lithographic transfer paper, In: Five artists--their printmaking methods, Artists Proof, 68; The college art gallery, Art J, summer 71; Lithography: an introduction, traveling exhib, 78; Kokoschka Remembered, Arts(Minneapolis), 12/87; Mission and Commissions: Oskar Kokoschka in Minnesota, 1949-1957 (monogr), SJU Press, 91; and others. *Dealer:* Groveland Gallery 25 Groveland Terrace Minneapolis MN 55403; Probst Gallery 620 N Michigan Ave Chicago IL 60611. *Mailing Add:* 400 NE Riverside Dr St Cloud MN 56301

PETLIN, IRVING
PAINTER
b Chicago, Ill, Dec 17, 34. *Study:* Art Inst of Chicago, BFA, 52-56; Yale Univ, MFA, with Josef Albers, 59. *Work:* Art Inst Chicago; Jewish Mus, New York; Mus Mod Art, New York; Mus d'Art Mod, Paris, France; Metrop Mus, New York; Hirshhorn Mus. Washington, DC; Pa Acad, Philadelphia; Penn Acad, Philadelphia, Pa. *Exhib:* Art Inst of Chicago, 53, 56 & 72; Mus d'Art Mod, Paris, 61-66; Chicago Imagist Art, Mus Contemp Art, Chicago, 72; Whitney Mus Am Art, New York, 73; Retrospective, Palais des Beaux-Arts, Brussels, Belg, 65; Neuberger Mus, State Univ NY Col, Purchase, 78; Arts Club Chicago, 78; Wiessewald, Kent Fine Art, New York, NY, 86; 25 yr Retrospective Pastels, Kent Fine Art, New York, NY, 88; The World of Bruno Schulze, Krugier, Geneva, 92. *Teaching:* Vis artist, Univ Calif, Los Angeles, 63-66; artist-in-residence, Dartmouth Col, fall 83; vis prof, Cooper Union, New York, 77-89; vis prof, Pa Acad, grad prog, 90-92. *Awards:* Ryerson Fel, 56; Copley Found Grant, 61; Guggenheim Found Fel, 71. *Bibliog:* Michel Butor (auth), Spiral, 65; R B Kitaj (auth), Irving Petlin: Rubbings, 78; Edward Fry (auth), Irving Petlin: Kent, 87. *Media:* Oil on Canvas; Pastel on Paper. *Publ:* Coauth (with M Palmer), A Song for Sarah; Auth, Irving Petlin: 25 Yrs of Pastels, Paul Cummings, 88. *Dealer:* Kent Fine Art 47 E 63rd St New York NY 10019; Krugier-Ditesheim 29-31 Grand-Rue Geneve 1204. *Mailing Add:* 71 Rue du Cardinal Lemoine Paris 75005 France

PETRIE, FERDINAND RALPH
PAINTER, ILLUSTRATOR
b Hackensack, NJ, Sept 17, 25. *Study:* Parsons Sch Design, New York, cert advert, 49; Art Students League, with Frank Reilly; Famous Artists Course Illus, cert, 59. *Work:* Nat Collection Fine Art, Smithsonian Inst, Washington, DC; Indianapolis Mus Art; J F Kennedy Libr, Boston; US Navy Combat Art Gallery, Washington, DC; US Coast Guard, Washington, DC. *Comn:* Salvation Army Nat Hq, New York. *Exhib:* Am Artists Prof League Grand Nat, New York, 71-79; Am Watercolor Soc Travel Exhib, 73, 75-78. *Pos:* Illusr, J Gans Assoc Studio, New York, 50-69, Salvation Army, 75-86. *Teaching:* Pvt instr watercolor, 72-78; instr, DuCret Sch Art, 75-77, Ridgewood Art Inst, 80-85. *Awards:* Salmagundi Club Awards, 70-83; US Navy Gold Medal for Watercolor, 74; Gold Medal, Hudson Valley Art Asn, 76. *Mem:* NJ Watercolor Soc; Artists Fel; Rockport Art Asn; Am Watercolor Soc. *Media:* Watercolor, Oil. *Publ:* illusr, Reader's Digest covers, 77 & 79; auth, Drawing Landscapes in Pencil, Watson-Guptill, 79, The Color Book, 81, The Alkyd Book, 82 & Watercolorists Guide Series, 83-85. *Dealer:* Petrie Gallery 57 Main St Rockport MA 01966; Grand Central Galleries New York NY 10017. *Mailing Add:* 51 Vreeland Ave Rutherford NJ 07070

PETRIE, SYLVIA SPENCER
PRINTMAKER, PAINTER
b Wooster, Ohio, June 15, 31. *Study:* Col Wooster, BA; State Univ Iowa, with Mauricio Lasansky & Eugene Ludens; Univ RI. *Work:* Art Ctr Mus, Wooster Col; RI Group Health Asn, Providence; Providence Public Libr; Boston Pub Libr; Mus Art, RI Sch Design. *Exhib:* 9th Nat Print Exhib, Silvermine Guild, New Canaan, Conn, 72; Images on Paper, Springfield Art Asn, Ill, 73; 64th & 66th Am Annuals, Art Asn Newport, RI, 75 & 77; 16th Bradley Nat Print & Drawing Exhib, Peoria, Ill, 77; 19 on Paper, Soviet Hall of Art, Moscow, USSR, 88; Springfield Art Mus, Mo, 90; and others. *Pos:* Vis artist, Title III Prog, Coventry Elem Schs, RI, 75-77. *Awards:* Netta Strain Scott Prize Art, Wooster Col, 53; First Prize & Purchase Award, Fantle's, 56; First Prize Graphics, Westerly Art Festival, 75; and many others. *Bibliog:* Elizabeth Findley (auth), Petrie prints and pastels depend on point of view, Eve Bulletin, Providence, 10/15/77; Edward Sozanski (auth), Print forms offer intriguing tones, Providence Sunday J, 10/15/78; Arline Fleming (auth), Variety of Interest Reflected in Work of Peace Dale Artist, Providence Jr Bull, 3/4/87. *Mem:* Print Consortium, St Joseph, Mo; Artists Guild & Gallery; Nineteen on Paper, Providence, RI; South County Art Asn. *Media:* Intaglio, Collagraph; Oil, Pastel. *Publ:* Illusr, From under the Hill of Night, Vanderbilt Univ, 69; The Idol, 73 & Time Songs, 79, Biscuit City Press. *Dealer:* Wenniger Graphics 174 Newbury St Boston MA 02116. *Mailing Add:* 200 Pendron Rd Peace Dale RI 02879

PETRO, JOE, III
PRINTMAKER, PAINTER
b Lexington, Ky, May 3, 56. *Study:* Univ Tenn. *Comn:* Silkscreen, Ed, IBM, New York, 88; Silkscreened painting, IAMS Co, Dayton, Ohio, 89; Silkscreened ed & poster, Greenpeace, Washington, DC, 90; Silkscreened ed & poster, Nature Conservancy, Arlington, Va, 91; Sculpture TV, State Ky, Lexington, 92. *Media:* Silkscreen. *Dealer:* John Cavaliero Fine Arts 41 E 57th St New York NY 10022. *Mailing Add:* PO Box 2104 Lexington KY 40594

PETRO, JOSEPH (VICTOR), JR
PAINTER, ILLUSTRATOR
b Lexington, Ky, Nov 4, 32. *Study:* Transylvania Col, with Victor Hammer; grad sch, Cincinnati Med Sch, art as appl to med. *Work:* Hermitage Mus, Leningrad, USSR. *Comn:* series of paintings of all Triple Crown winners for Oaklawn Park, 73-77; mural, Hardin Mem Hospital, 82; commemorative mural, St Johns Hosp, Anderson, Ind, 90; life size series of portraits of judges, Fayette Courthouse & US Fed Bldg, Lexington, Ky, 90; designer of 1992 Ky bicentennial postage stamp for the US Postal Serv, Washington, DC, 92; and many others. *Pos:* Publ, series ltd number collector prints, 54-79; consult, Spindletop Res, Inc, Lexington, 65-68; head, Dept Appl Art, Loyola Univ of Chicago, Rome Ctr, Italy, 69-77; cult adv, US Info Serv, Am Embassy, Rome, Italy, 73-77; designer, Franklin Mint, Franklin Ctr, Pa, 80- *Teaching:* Vis prof art, John Cabot Int Col, Rome, Italy, 75-76; prof art, Transylvania Univ, Lexington, Ky, 78- & artist-in-residence, 82-; consult, adv, Dept Army, Nat Endowment Arts, Washington, DC, 86- *Awards:* Morrison Medallion, Transylvania Univ, 83. *Mem:* Soc Illusr; Southeastern Ctr Contemp Art; Artists Equity, Washington, DC; Nat Soc Arts & Letts, Washington, DC. *Media:* Acrylic, Oil. *Publ:* Illusr, var publ including Thoroughbred Rec, Nat Geog, Holiday, Better Homes & Gardens & others. *Mailing Add:* 357 Henry Clay Blvd Lexington KY 40502

PETTIBONE, JOHN WOLCOTT
CURATOR, GRAPHIC ARTIST
b Springfield, Ohio, Jan 30, 42. *Study:* Wittenberg Univ, 62-63; Cleveland Inst Art, 63-65, Ford grant, 64. *Work:* Am Red Cross, Washington, DC; Town of Rockport, Mass. *Exhib:* Rockport Art Asn, 71-; Am Fortnight Exhibition, Hong Kong, 73. *Pos:* Dir marketing, Hammond Castle Mus, Gloucester, Mass, 83-85, cur, 85-; instr drawing, Rockport Pub Schs, 73-78, Endicott Col, 85; Registrar, Higgins Armory Mus, Worcester, Mass, 78-83. *Teaching:* Instr drawing, Lakewood Pub Schs, Ohio, 59, Springfieid Art Asn, Ohio, 61-63, Rockport Pub Schs, 73-78 & Endicott Col, 85-86. *Mem:* Rockport Art Asn; Arms & Armour Soc, London; Japanese Sword Soc USA; Co Mil Historians, Washington, DC. *Media:* Conte Crayon, Silverpoint. *Dealer:* Rockport Art Asn 12 Main St Rockport MA 01966. *Mailing Add:* 509 Washington St Gloucester MA 01930-1749

PETTIBONE, RICHARD H
PAINTER, SCULPTOR
b Los Angeles, Calif, Jan 5, 38. *Study:* Pasadena City Col, AA, 59; Otis Art Inst, MFA, 62. *Work:* Israel Mus, Jerusalem; Lowe Art Ctr, Syracuse, NY; De Mennil Found, Houston; Rose Art Mus, Brandeis Univ; Art Mus, Princeton Univ, NJ; Mus Mod Art; Laguna Art Mus, Calif. *Exhib:* Small Objects, 77, Art About Art, 78, Whitney Mus, New York; Art Against AIDS, Nature Morte, New York, 87; Aspects De L'Art Du XXe Siecle L'oeuvre re produite, Abbay Ste Andre Ctr Contemp Art (catalog), France, 91; Art Apropriates Art (catalog), Calif State, Fullerton, 91; Quotations, Aldrich Mus Contemp Art, 92. *Awards:* Nat Endowment Arts Grant, Sculpture, 88. *Media:* Oil on Canvas, Silkscreen on Canvas; Wood. *Dealer:* Curt Marcus 578 Broadway New York NY 10012. *Mailing Add:* Star Route Charlotteville NY 12036

PEVEN, MICHAEL DAVID
PHOTOGRAPHER, EDUCATOR
b Chicago, Ill, Apr 12, 49. *Study:* Univ Ill, Chicago, AB, 71; Sch Art Inst Chicago, MFA, 77. *Work:* Ctr Creative Photog, Tucson; Humanities Res Ctr, Austin; Mus Contemp Art, Chicago; Ark Arts Ctr, Little Rock; Mus Mod Art, New York. *Exhib:* Visions 83, 82-83 & Fellowship Winners (with catalog), 85-86 Mid-Am Art Alliance, Kansas City; Alternative Image II, Kohler Art Ctr, Sheboygan, 84; Offset: Survey of Artists Books (with catalog), Hera Found, Wakefield, RI, 84; one-man shows, Ark Arts Ctr, Little Rock, 85, Artists Book Works, Chicago, 88; Photographic Book Art in the United States, (Photo Book Art in US), 91, travel, 94; and other one-man shows, 77-90. *Teaching:* Assoc prof art, Univ Ark, Fayetteville, 77- *Awards:* Artists Fel, 82 & Photographers Fel, 83, Mid-Am Art Alliance; Photographers Fel, Ark Art Coun, 86 & 90. *Mem:* Soc Photog Educ; Friends of Photog. *Media:* Still Video, Book Arts. *Publ:* Auth, Snatches--or Man Made Wonders, Verb: Print, 79; Prophesy Panorama, 82, The Marriage of Heaven & Hell, Part 1, 86 Global Family, 90, Primitive Press; Too Scents Worth, pvt publ, 87. *Mailing Add:* 514 N Mission Blvd Fayetteville AK 72701-5115

PEZZATI, PIETRO (PETER S)
PAINTER
b Boston, Mass, Sept 18, 02. *Study:* Child-Walker Sch Art; also with Charles Hopkinson; in Europe. *Work:* Med Sch & Bus Sch, Harvard Univ; Sch Med & Sch Educ, Univ Pa; Children's Hosp Medical Ctr, Boston; Yale Sch Med; Mass Hist Soc; and others. *Exhib:* Exhibited regionally and nationally in group and one-man shows. *Teaching:* Instr, schs and pvt classes & demonstr techniques. *Media:* All. *Mailing Add:* c/o Fenway Studios 30 Ipswich St Boston MA 02215

PFAFF, JUDY
SCULPTOR, EDUCATOR
b London, Eng, 1946. *Study:* Washington Univ, St Louis, BFA, 71; Yale Univ, MFA, 73. *Work:* Whitney Mus, New York; Albright Knox Mus, Buffalo, NY. *Comn:* special installation, Wacoal Ctr, Tokyo, Japan, 85 & Spokane, Wash. *Exhib:* Whitney Biennial, Dragon Group, Whitney Mus Am Art, Columbus, Ohio, 75; Rorschach, Ringling Mus, Sarasota, Fla, 81; Solo exhib, Rock-Paper-Scissors, Albright Knox Mus, Buffalo, NY, 82; Either War, Venice Biennale, Italy, 82; Int Survey of Recent Painting & Sculpture, Mus of Modern Art, New York, 84; An American Renaissance, Painting & Sculpture since 1940, Mus of Art, Ft Lauderdale, Fla, 85; Holly Solomon Gallery, New York, 85; Daniel Weinberg Gallery, Calif, 85; Recent Aquisitions, Whitney Mus, New York, 86. *Teaching:* Instr sculpture, Yale Univ & Skowhegan Sch of Painting, currently. *Awards:* Creative Artists Public Serv, 76; Nat Endowment for the Arts Fel, 79 & 86; Guggenheim Fel, 83; Bessie Award, 84. *Bibliog:* Roberta Smith (auth), Judy Pfaff: undone: done, Village Voice, 2/83; Wade Saunders (auth), Talking Objects, interviews with 10 younger sculptors, Art in Am, 10/85; John Russel (auth), Bright young talents: 6 artists with a future, New York Times, 5/16/86. *Media:* All. *Mailing Add:* 319 Greenwich Street No 5FL New York NY 10013

PFAFFMAN, WILLIAM SCOTT
SCULPTOR, DRAFTSMAN
b Albany, Ga, July 10, 54. *Study:* Auburn Univ, BFA, 74; Hunter Col, City Univ, New York, MA, 78. *Work:* John F Kennedy High Sch, Bronx, NY; Dept Gen Serv, Brooklyn, NY. *Comn:* Artpark Proj Comn, Natural Heritage Trust, Lewiston, NY, 84; Sculpture Chicago, Burnham Park Planning Bd, Chicago, Ill, 85; Sculpture, NY State Coun Arts, Bronx, NY, 87; Brooklyn Bears Greenthumb Project, NYC Dept Gen Serv, 88. *Exhib:* American Pantheon, City Univ New York Grad Ctr, 82 & Art on the Beach, Battery Park City, New York, 82; Spec Proj Exhib, Proj Studios One, Queens, NY, 83. *Pos:* Artist-in-residence, Athena Found. *Awards:* Annual Award, Am Acad Arts & Lett, 85; Artist Fel, Pollack-Krasner Found, 86. *Bibliog:* Martignioni (auth), Socrates Sculpture Park, Athena Found, 86; Allen Rokach (auth), article, Sculpture Mag, Int Sculpture (tr, 87). *Mem:* Brooklyn Waterfront Artists Coalition (vpres); Found Community of Artists; Am Coun Arts; Kentler Int Drawing Space, sec. *Media:* All. *Publ:* Auth, Five years of outdoor sculpture, Brooklyn Waterfront Artists Coalition, 87. *Mailing Add:* 223 Water St Brooklyn NY 11201

PFAHL, CHARLES ALTON, III
PAINTER
b Akron, Ohio, May 15, 46. *Study:* With Robert Brackman, Madison, Conn, John Koch, New York & Jack Richard, Cuyahoga Falls, Ohio. *Exhib:* Audubon Artist Ann, 70-72; Butler Inst Am Art Ann, Youngstown, Ohio, 72-74; FAR Gallery, New York, 73 & 78; Three Centuries of American Nude Traveling Exhib, 75; Westmorland Co Mus, 79; retrospective, Grand Central Galleries, 80; and others. *Teaching:* Instr painting, Art Students League, New York, 81- *Awards:* Halgarten Awards, Nat Acad Design, 76 & 81; Andrew Carnegie Prize, Nat Acad Design, 78; Isaac N Maynard Prize, Nat Acad Design, 80; plus others. *Bibliog:* Article, Am Artist Mag, 3/73; J Singer (auth), Charles Pfahl: Artist at Work, Watson-Gutptill, 77; articles, After Dark, 3/81 & Studio Int Mag, 85. *Mem:* Allied Artists Am; Audubon Artists; Salmagundi Club. *Media:* Pastel, Oil. *Dealer:* Grand Central Art Galleries 24 W 57th St New York NY. *Mailing Add:* 525 W 45th St New York NY 10036

PFAHL, JOHN
PHOTOGRAPHER
b New York, NY, Feb 17, 39. *Study:* Syracuse Univ, BFA, 61, MA, 68; Niagara Univ, Hon Dr Fine Art, 90. *Work:* George Eastman House, Rochester, NY; Albright-Knox Art Gallery, Buffalo, NY; Art Inst Chicago; San Francisco Mus Mod Art; Los Angeles Co Art Mus. *Exhib:* Color As Form? A History of Color Photography, Corcoran Gallery Art, Washington, DC, 82; Photography? A Facet of Modernism, San Francisco Mus Mod Art, 86; On the Art of Fixing a Shadow, Nat Gallery Art, Washington, DC, 89; The New American Pastoral, George Eastman House, Rochester, NY, 90; one-man shows, Albright-Knox Art Gallery, Buffalo, NY, 90, Chicago Art Inst, 91, High Mus, Atlanta, Ga, 92 & Los Angeles Co Mus Art, 93. *Teaching:* Prof photog, Rochester Inst Technol, NY, 68-82. *Awards:* Nat Endowment Arts Photog Fel, 77 & 90; NY State Creative Artists Prog Serv Photog Grant, 79. *Bibliog:* Peter Bunnell (auth), Altered Landscapes, Friends Photog, 81; Estelle Jussim & Anthony Bannon (coauths), Arcadia Revisited, Castellani Art Mus, 88; Estelle Jussim (auth), A Distanced Land, Albright-Knox Art Gallery, 90. *Publ:* Contribr, New Color/New Work, 84 & Photography and Art: Interactions Since 1946, 87, Abbeville Press; On the Art of Fixing a Shadow, Bullfinch Press, 89; Aperture No 120: Beyond Wilderness, Aperture Found, 90; auth, Tainted Prospects, Castellani Mus, 91. *Dealer:* Janet Borden Inc 560 Broadway New York NY 10012. *Mailing Add:* 797 Potomac Ave Buffalo NY 14209

PFEIFER, MARCUSE
DEALER, GALLERY DIRECTOR
b Little Rock, Ark, Nov 4, 36. *Study:* Sarah Lawrence Col, AB, 58. *Collections Arranged:* Gravure, 74; American Indian Photographs from the 19th & Early 20th Century, 74; Cyanotype, 75; The Male Nude (auth, catalog), Marcuse Pfeifer Gallery, 78; The Dividing Line, Screens by Nine Photograhers & Thirteen New Americans, Arles, France, 86; Photos of Heinrich Harrer from early 40's Tibet, Am Mus Nat Hist, 91-92. *Pos:* Asst to dir, New Sch Art Ctr, New York, 66-70; dir photog art, Robert Schoelkopf Gallery, New York, 70-76; gallery owner, Marcuse Pfeifer Gallery, New York, 76-91. *Awards:* American Photographers Award, 83; Invited Colloquium Speaker, Sorborne, 88 & Harvard, 90. *Bibliog:* Article in Am Photogr, 5th Anniversary Issue, 83. *Mem:* Asn Int Photography Art Dealers (pres, 80-82); Art Table. *Specialty:* Photography. *Publ:* Auth, Thank Heaven for Little Girls-Lewis Carroll, Bk Forum, 79; coauth, On Collecting Photographs, Asn Int Photog Art Dealers. *Mailing Add:* 6 Hornbeck Lane Accord NY 12404

PFEIFFER, WERNER BERNHARD
SCULPTOR, PRINTMAKER
b Stuttgart, Ger, Oct 1, 37; US citizen. *Study:* Graphic Arts Sch, Stuttgart, Ger, dipl, 57; Acad Fine Arts, Stuttgart, dipl, 61; Pratt Inst, 62. *Work:* Bibliotheque Nat, Paris, France; Libr Cong, Washington, DC; Mus Modern Art, New York; Nat Mus, Stockholm, Sweden; City Mus, Stuttgart, Ger. *Comn:* Sculpture, State of Niedersachsen, Ger, 80; sculpture, Fed Govt Ger, 81; sculpture, Conn Comn Arts, 85; sculpture, Mass Comn Arts, 85; wall relief, Travenol Labs, Deerfield, Ill, 86. *Exhib:* Letter Forms, Mus Modern Art, New York, 69; Beartling, Fahlstrom & Pfeiffer, Norrköpings Mus, Sweden, 69; Biennal Santiago, Chile, 70; Young Artist's 1973, New York, 73; solo exhibs, Ostgotlands Mus, Linkoping, Sweden, 74, City Mus & Gallery, Stuttgart, Ger, 80 & Mattatuck Mus, Waterbury, Conn, 84; Found Objects, Marisa del Re Gallery, New York, 84. *Teaching:* Prof printmaking, Pratt Inst, 67-75, adj prof, 75- *Awards:* Purchase Award, Soc Am Graphic Artists, 69 & 10th Ann Nat Print Exhib, Silvermine Guild, Conn, 74; Special Paper Award, Soc Am Graphic Artists, Special Papers, Inc, 73. *Bibliog:* TV interview, Today Show, NBC-TV, 76; Ryna Segal (auth), Dimensional prints, Print Review No 17, 83; David Boraus (auth), Werner Pfeiffer Li-bra-ry, Sunday Republican, 84. *Media:* Metal, Welded; All. *Publ:* Auth, Liber Mobile, Pratt Adlib Press, 65. *Mailing Add:* Flat Rock Rd Cornwall Bridge CT 06754

PFISTER, HAROLD FRANCIS
ADMINISTRATOR
Evanston, Ill, Dec, 25, 47. *Study:* Harvard Col, BA, 69; Univ Del, MA, 74; Harvard Law Sch, JD, 92. *Collections Arranged:* Facing the Light: Historic American Portrait Daguerreotypes, 78; American Portrait Drawings (with Marvin S Sadik), 80. *Pos:* Asst dir, Nat Portrait Gallery, Washington, DC, 80-82, actg dir, 81-82; asst dir, Cooper-Hewitt Mus, New York, 82-89. *Res:* American architectural history; portraiture. *Publ:* Auth, Burlingtonian architectural theory in England & America, Winterthur Portfolio II, 76; Facing the Light: Historic American Portrait Daguerreotypes, 78 & coauth, American Portrait Drawings, 80, Smithsonian Press. *Mailing Add:* 33 Union Park Apt 3 Boston MA 02118

PFRIEM, BERNARD
PAINTER, DIRECTOR
b Cleveland, Ohio, Sept 7, 14. *Study:* John Huntington Polytech Inst, 34-36; Cleveland Inst Art, 36-40; Europ study, 50-52. *Work:* Mus Mod Art, Chase Manhattan Bank, Metrop Mus Art, New York; Brooklyn Mus; Columbia Banking, Savings & Loan Asn, Rochester, NY. *Comn:* Murals, Guerrero & Mexico City, Mex. *Exhib:* Six shows, Iolas Gallery, NY, 49-63; Whitney Mus Am Art, 52 & 65; retrospective, Cleveland Inst Art, 63; Richard Feigen Gallery, Chicago, 67; Am Drawing Soc, 70; Cleveland Inst Art, 73; Pa State Univ, 74; plus others. *Pos:* Dir, studio arts sessions in Southern France, Cleveland Inst Art. *Teaching:* Instr drawing & painting, Peoples Art Ctr, Mus Mod Art, 46-51; instr drawing, Cooper Union Sch Art & Archit, 63-71; instr, Sarah Lawrence Col, 69-76. *Awards:* Mary Ranney Traveling Scholar, Western Reserve Univ; Copley Award Painting, 59; Prize Drawing, Norfolk Mus Arts & Sci. *Bibliog:* Patrick Waldberg (auth), Bernard Pfriem (monogr), William & Noma Copley Found, 61 & Main et marvielles, Mercure, France, 61; Patricia Allen Dreyfus (auth), The inward journey (monogr), Am Artist, 9/72. *Media:* All. *Mailing Add:* 115 Spring St New York NY 10012

PHARIS, MARK
CERAMIST
b Minneapolis, Minn, 47. *Study:* Univ Minn, 67-71 with Warren Mackenzie and Curt Hoard. *Work:* Victoria & Albert Mus, London, Eng; Univ Colo; Univ Wis, River Falls; State Col Ceramics, New York; also pvt collections of Robert Pfannebecker, Joan Mannheimer, Daniel & Caroline Anderson, Dr & Mrs Edward Okun, Betty & George Woodman and many others. *Exhib:* Solo exhib, Hadler Rodriguez, New York, Pro Art, St Louis, 86 & 89, Garth Clark, Los Angeles, 87; Rhode Island Sch Design, Providence, RI; Marion Art Ctr, Lancaster, Pa; Minneapolis Art Inst, Minn; Victoria & Albert Mus, London, Eng; Univ Minn, St Paul. *Teaching:* Assoc prof, Univ Minn, currently. *Awards:* Fel, Nat Endowment Arts, 86; Two Nat Endowment Grants for Individual Craftsmen; Minn State Art Coun Grant. *Media:* Clay. *Dealer:* Pro Art Gallery 5595 Pershing St Louis Mo, 63112. *Mailing Add:* c/o Pro-Art Gallery 5595 Pershing St Louis MO 63112

PHELAN, ELLEN DENISE
PAINTER
b Detroit, Mich, Nov 3, 43. *Study:* Wayne State Univ, BFA, 69, MFA, 71. *Work:* Detroit Inst Arts; Mus Mod Art, New York; Whitney Mus Am Art; Walker Art Ctr. *Exhib:* New Art for the New Year, Mus Mod Art, New York, 78; Drawings, Albright-Knox Art Gallery, Buffalo, NY, 79; American Abstraction Now, Inst Contemp Art, Va Mus, Richmond, 82; Out of Square, Cranbrook Acad Art, Bloomingfield Hills, Mich, 84; The New Romantic Landscape, Whitney Mus Am Art, Stamford, Conn, 87; Recent Drawings, Whitney Mus Am Art, New York, 88; Contemporary Environment, Mus Mod Art, 89; The 80's in Review: Selections from the Permanent Collection, Whitney Mus Am Art, Fairfield Co, Conn, 89; Drawings of the Eighties from the Collection of the Mus Mod Art, New York, 89; solo exhibs, Asher/Faure, Los Angeles, 89 & 92, Baltimore Mus Art, 89, Susanne Hilberry Gallery, Birmingham, Mich, 90, Barbara Toll Fine Arts, New York, 90, Member's Gallery, Albright-Knox Art Gallery, Buffalo, NY, 91 & Univ Art Gallery, Univ Mass, Amherst, 92, traveling, 93; and others. *Teaching:* Instr painting, Calif Inst Arts, 78-79 & 83; instr painting & drawing, Sch Visual Arts, 81-83; instr, Calif Inst Arts, 83. *Awards:* Nat Endowment Arts Grant, 78-79; Arts Achievement Award, Wayne State Univ, 88. *Bibliog:* Margaret Moorman (auth), Ellen Phelan-shapechanger, ARTnews, Vol 91, No 2, 2/92; Peter Schjeldahl (auth), Drawing blood, Village Voice, 3/3/92; Benjamin Weissman (auth), Ellen Phelan: Asher/Faure, Artforum, Vol XXX, No 7, 115, 3/92; and others. *Media:* Oil, Gouache. *Dealer:* Barbara Toll Fine Arts 146 Greene St New York NY 10012. *Mailing Add:* 284 Lafayette St New York NY 10012

PHILBRICK, MARGARET ELDER
PRINTMAKER, PAINTER
b Northampton, Mass, July 4, 14. *Study:* Mass Col Art, grad; De Cordova Mus Workshop, with Donald Stoltenberg. *Work:* Libr Cong, Washington, DC; Wiggin Collection, Boston Pub Libr & First Nat Bank, Boston; Nat Bezalel Mus, Jerusalem; Philadelphia Mus Art, Pa; New Britain Mus, Conn; Brooklyn Mus, NY. *Exhib:* 2nd Int Miniature Print Exhib, Pratt Graphic Art Ctr, New York, 66; Soc Am Graphic Artists 51st Nat, Kennedy Galleries, New York, 71; 50-Yr Retrospective Exhib of Graphics & Paintings, Westenhook Gallery, Sheffield, Mass, 85; Boston Printmakers 38th Nat Exhib, De Cordova Mus, Lincoln, Mass, 86; Centennial Exhibition, New Eng Watercolor Soc, Fed Reserve Bank Gallery, Boston, 86; and others. *Pos:* Artist & designer, Wedgwood Commemorative Plates, 44-55. *Awards:* John Taylor Arms Mem Prize, Nat Acad Design, 72; Ralph Fabri Award, Nat Acad Design, 77; Acad Artists Graphics Award, 86; and 60 others. *Bibliog:* Am Prints, Libr Congress. *Mem:* Boston Printmakers (exec bd, 50-); New England Watercolor Soc (exec bd, 75-77); Nat Acad Design; Academic Artists Asn; Miniature Art Socs Fla, NJ & Washington, DC. *Media:* Intaglio, Oil. *Publ:* Illusr, On Gardening, 64 & In Praise of Vegetables, 66, Scribners; Natural Flower Arrangements, Doubleday, 72; Sheffield: Frontier Town, 76; illusr, Robert Frost's Spring Pools, Lime Rock Press, 83. *Dealer:* Westenhook Gallery 690 North Main St Sheffield MA 01257. *Mailing Add:* Box 714 Sheffield MA 01257

PHILLIPS, ALICE JANE
PAINTER
b New York, NY, Aug 30, 47. *Study:* NY Univ, with Chuck Close & John Opper, BS, 70, MA, 72. *Work:* Aldrich Mus Contemp Art, Conn; Mus City New York, Brooklyn Mus, Chase Manhattan Bank, Shearson Lehman Hutton, New York. *Exhib:* Solo exhib, David Findlay Galleries, New York, 82, Van Straaten Gallery, Chicago, 83, Dubins Gallery, Los Angeles, 83, 84, 86 & 88, Gallery 500, Philadelphia, 88 & 91; Works on Paper--Women Artists, Brooklyn Mus, 75; Contemporary Reflections, Aldrich Mus, Conn, 77; Fifteen New Talents, Aldrich Mus, Conn, 79; Contemporary Views '84, Queens Mus, NY, 84; 45th Annual, Woodmere Mus, Philadelphia, 85; Art of the 1970s & 1980s, Aldrich Mus, Conn, 85; American Art-American Women, Stamford Mus, Conn, 85; Natural Image, Stamford Mus, Conn, 89; Salute to Women, Nat Mus Women Arts, Washington, DC, 91; and others. *Teaching:* Adj asst prof art & drawing, NY Univ, 81-82. *Bibliog:* Mary Vaughn (auth), article in Arts Mag, 1/82; Grace Glueck (auth), article in New York Times, 1/27/84; Victoria Donahue (auth), article, Philadelphia Inquirer, 8/5/88. *Mem:* Women in Arts Found (exec coordr, 78-80, secy, 80-82); Women's Caucus Art. *Media:* Acrylic, Pastel. *Dealer:* Gallery 500 Church & Old York Rds Elkins Park PA 19117. *Mailing Add:* 32 Greene St New York NY 10013

PHILLIPS, BERTRAND D
PAINTER, PHOTOGRAPHER
b Chicago, Ill, Nov 19, 38. *Study:* Art Inst Chicago, with Paul Wieghardt & Leroy Neiman, BFA; Northwestern Univ, MFA. *Work:* Governors State Univ, Park Forest South, Ill; David & Alfred Smart Gallery, Univ Chicago, Ill; Du Sable Mus African Am Hist, Chicago; Art Inst Chicago; Erie Art Ctr, Pa; and others. *Exhib:* Art Inst Chicago, 78-80; Ill State Mus, 78 & 80; Nat Mus Haitian Art, 79-80; Cult Ctr Guyana, 79-80; NAME Gallery, Chicago, 81; Mid-America Biennial Nat Exhib, Owensboro Mus Fine Arts, Ky, 82; and many others. *Teaching:* Instr drawing & painting, Elmhurst Col, 70-72; asst prof drawing & painting, Northwestern Univ, 72-79; vis artist, Sch Art Inst Chicago, 81- *Awards:* George D Brown Foreign Traveling Fel, Art Inst Chicago, 61; Governor's Purchase Award, State Ill. *Bibliog:* Elton Fax (auth), Black Artists of the New Generation, Dodd Mead & Co, 77; and others. *Media:* Oils, Acrylic. *Mailing Add:* 6617 S Perry Ave Chicago IL 60621

PHILLIPS, BONNIE
DEALER, PAINTER
b Salt Lake City, Utah, July 8, 42. *Study:* Univ Utah, BA. *Work:* Salt Lake Art Ctr, Utah; Utah Mus Fine Arts, Salt Lake City; Braithwaite Gallery, Southern Utah State Col, Cedar City. *Exhib:* Intermountain Biennial, Salt Lake Art Ctr, 66-77; Utah State Ann Exhib, 81-84; Women Artists of Utah, Springville Mus Art, 84; Nat Mus, Taipei, Taiwan, 85; two-person show, Collett Art Gallery, Weber State Col, Ogden, Utah, 86. *Pos:* Co-owner, Phillips Gallery, Salt Lake City, currently. *Awards:* Purchase Prize, Utah 81; Award of Merit, Utah '84; Best of Show, Utah Watercolor Soc, 86. *Mem:* Utah Watercolor Soc. *Media:* Watercolor, Gouache. *Mailing Add:* Phillips Gallery 444 E Second S Salt Lake City UT 84111

PHILLIPS, DICK (RICHARD CORTEZ)
PAINTER, INSTRUCTOR
b Ft Worth, Tex, May 6, 33. *Study:* Texas A & M Univ, BBA, 55; with Milford Zornes, 73; also with Robert E Wood, 74, 77-88. *Work:* City of Himeji, Japan; Old Jail Art Ctr, Albany, Tex; Desert Cabaleeros Mus, Wickenburg, Ariz; City Scottsdale, Ariz; Chandler Ctr Arts, Ariz. *Comn:* Int Paper Corp, Memphis, Tenn; Phoenix Mutual Life Insurance Co, Hartford, Conn; paintings, Lewis & Roca, Phoenix, 87. *Exhib:* Watercolor Exhib, US State Dept, toured Taiwan, 75; Rocky Mountain Nat, Golden, Colo, 78; Am Watercolor Soc Ann, Nat Acad Design, New York, 78 & 86; Watercolor Biennial, Ctr Arts, Scottsdale, Ariz, 78 & 80; Nat Watercolor Exhib, 85 & 92; and others. *Teaching:* Pvt lessons, Phoenix, Ariz, 72-; instr, Sch Int Training, Univ Okla, 77 & 78. *Awards:* Merit Awards, Western Fedn Watercolor Anns, 75, 79, 80 & 83; Best of Show, Southwest Watercolor Soc, 77; First Place, Watercolor West, 82 & Am Watercolor Soc Traveling Exhib, 86. *Bibliog:* Paul Perry (auth), One artist's metamorphosis, Southwest Art, 78; Barbara Pearlman (auth), Making changes, Ariz Arts & Lifestyle, 81. *Mem:* Scottsdale Artists League; Ariz Watercolor Soc (bd dirs, 73-77); Nat Watercolor Soc; Watercolor West. *Media:* Watercolor, Acrylic. *Publ:* Illusr, Si! Si! Mrs Crusoe, Franklin Publ, 70; Highways Mag (inside backcover), 90; Vitality Mag (cover), 90. *Dealer:* Suzanne Brown Galleries 7156 Main St Scottsdale AZ 85251. *Mailing Add:* 7829 E Hubbell Scottsdale AZ 85257

PHILLIPS, DUTCH (JAMES O), JR
GALLERY DIRECTOR, DEALER
b Ft Worth, Tex, Mar 29, 44. *Study:* Univ Tex, Austin, BA, 67. *Pos:* Dir, Ft Worth Gallery, currently. *Specialty:* Contemporary painting and sculpture; Pre-Columbian and African art. *Mailing Add:* Ft Worth Gallery 901 Boland Ft Worth TX 76107

PHILLIPS, GIFFORD
COLLECTOR, WRITER
b Washington, DC, June 30, 18. *Study:* Stanford Univ, 36-38; Yale Univ, BA, 42. *Mem:* Trustee Mus Mod Art, New York; trustee Phillips Collection, Washington, DC; trustee Rothko Found, New York; trustee Pasadena Art Mus (pres, 73-74, secy-treas, 75-76); Mus Mod Art Int Coun (bd dirs); Los Angeles Co Mus Art Contemp Art Coun. *Collection:* Contemporary American painting and sculpture. *Publ:* Auth, Arts in a Democratic Society, 66; auth, articles, Art News, Artforum & Art Am. *Mailing Add:* 3881 Old Santa Fe Trail Santa Fe NM 87505

PHILLIPS, HELEN (ELIZABETH)
SCULPTOR, GRAPHIC ARTIST
b Fresno, Calif, Mar 3, 13. *Study:* Calif Sch Fine Arts, San Francisco, with Ralph Stackpole, 32-36. *Work:* Mus Mod Art, Bank Am World Hq, San Francisco; De Young Mus; Victoria & Albert Mus, London; Dallas Mus Contemp Art; Albright-Knox Mus, Buffalo, NY. *Comn:* Fountain of all Nations (sculpture), San Francisco World's Fair, 39. *Exhib:* San Francisco Art Asn Ann, San Francisco Mus Mod Art, 36, 48 & 60; Salon de Mai, Mus Art Mod, Paris, 51-74; II Int Bianalle Sculpture, Middleheim, Belg, 53; Women's Int Art Club, New Burlington Gallery, London, 55; Int Biannalle Sculpture, Mus Rodin, Paris, 56, 61 & 65; Formes Francaises, Mus Art Mod, Zurich, 57; 14 Americaines En France, Smithsonian Traveling Exhib, 60-62; Salon de Mai en Holland, Stedleck Mus, Amsterdam, 61. *Teaching:* Instr sculpture, Calif Art Inst, 48 & 60. *Awards:* Phelan Traveling Award Sculpture, San Francisco Art Asn, 36 & 48; Copley Found Int Sculpture Prize, 58; French Prize, Tate Gallery, London. *Bibliog:* Carola G Walker (auth), Modern Sculpture; Film, Monitar Prog, Brit Broadcasting Co. *Publ:* Contribr, Ides of March, Tigers Eye Mag, 49. *Mailing Add:* 737 Washington St New York NY 10014

PHILLIPS, IRVING W
CARTOONIST, ILLUSTRATOR
b Wilton, Wis, Nov 29, 05. *Study:* Chicago Acad Fine Arts. *Work:* Smithsonian Inst. *Comn:* Stage play adaptations, One Foot in Heaven, Gown of Glory, Mother was a Bachelor & Rumple, Alvin Theatre, New York, 55; and others. *Exhib:* Nat Cartoonist Soc; New York World's Fair; one-man shows, Comedy in Art, Ariz State Univ & El Prado Gallery, Sedona, Ariz. *Pos:* Cartoon humor ed, Esquire Mag, 37-39; cartoon staff, Chicago Sun-Times Syndicate, 40-52; motion picture assignments with Warner Bros, RKO, Charles Rodgers Prod & United Artists, formerly; auth & illusr, syndicated strip appearing int in 180 papers in 22 countries, The strange world of Mr Mum, formerly; Syndicated Allied Feature syndicate, Barnaby Bungle, 79. *Teaching:* Instr cartooning & humor writing, Maricopa Tech & Phoenix Col, Phoenix, formerly. *Awards:* Int First Prize & Cup, Salone dell'Umorismo of Bordighera, Italy, 69. *Mem:* Writers Guild Am; Dramatists Guild; Nat Cartoonists Soc; Mag Cartoonists Guild; Newspaper Cartoon Coun; and others. *Publ:* Auth & illusr, The Strange World of Mr Mum, 65; auth, The Twin Witches of Fingle Fu, 69; No Comment by Mr Mum, Popular Libr, 71; auth & co-auth, 260 TV scripts; contribr, scripts & animation to ABC-TV children's prog, Curiosity Shop; and many others. *Mailing Add:* 2807 E Sylvia St Phoenix AZ 85032

PHILLIPS, JAMES M
MUSEUM DIRECTOR, COLLECTOR
b Philadelphia, Pa, July 18, 46. *Study:* Glassboro State Col, BA, 75. *Work:* Antietam Nat Mus, Sharpsburg, Md; and others. *Comn:* Sculpture-medallion, Spec Forces Regiment, 91. *Exhib:* Washington County Mus Fine Arts, 86. *Pos:* Dir, Antietam Nat Mus, 68-; Bladesmiths Soc, 86-; bd dirs, Am Mus Comt, 92. *Teaching:* Lectr, Univ Wyo, 83; Armed Forces Inst Pathology, 88; O P Gator, 88. *Awards:* Best of Show Award, Connie Kalitta Service Inc, 85. *Mem:* Co of Military Historians; Am Bladesmiths' Soc; Asn Former Intelligence Officers; Spec Forces Asn. *Res:* Clandestine weapons and equipment, subminiature cameras-photo devices, US elite Forces. *Collection:* Artifacts of soldiers who fought in the Civil War through the Viet Nam Wars; uniforms, weapons, photographs, paintings, documents and writings of participants; espionage and intelligence literature and related material. *Publ:* Auth, The Devil's Bodyguard, 86; Stand In The Door, 88; coauth, Bowie Knives, 92; contribr, The Microcol, 92; Subminature Photography, 92. *Mailing Add:* PO Box 168 Williamstown NJ 08094

PHILLIPS, LAUGHLIN
MUSEUM DIRECTOR
b Washington, DC, Oct 20, 24. *Study:* Yale Univ, 42-43; Univ Chicago, MA(philos), 49. *Pos:* Pres & trustee, Phillips Collection, Washington, DC, 67-, dir, 72-92. *Mem:* Am Asn Mus Dirs. *Mailing Add:* c/o Phillips Collection Washington DC 20009

PHILLIPS, MATT
PAINTER, EDUCATOR
b New York, NY. *Study:* Univ Chicago, MA; Stanford Univ; Barnes Found. *Work:* Nat Collection Fine Art in Pub Libr, Whitney Mus Am Art, Metrop Mus Art, New York; Nat Gallery Art; Philadelphia Mus Art. *Exhib:* Retrospective, Baltimore Mus Art, 61-75; Princeton Gallery Fine Art, 71; Smithsonian Inst Traveling Exhib, 72; William Zierler Gallery, New York, 72-73; Retrospective, Phillips Collection, Washington, DC, 76-77; Middendorf/Lane, Washington, DC, 78; Donald Morris Gallery, Birmingham, Mich; and others. *Teaching:* Prof & head dept art, Bard Col, 64-. *Publ:* Auth, Maurice Prendergast: The Monotypes (catalog), 67 & Milton Avery: Works on Paper (catalog), 71, Bard Col; auth, The monotype today, Artist's Proof, 69; auth, The Monotype: An Edition of One, Smithsonian Inst Traveling Exhib, 72. *Dealer:* Marilyn Pearl 29 W 57th St New York NY 10019. *Mailing Add:* c/o Marsha Mateyka Gallery 2012 R St NW Washington DC 20009

PHILLIPS, MICHAEL
PAINTER, SCULPTOR
b New York, NY, Feb 22, 37. *Study:* Inst Fine Arts, New York, with H W Janson & Robert Goldwater, MA, 62. *Work:* Inst Contemp Art, Boston. *Comn:* Mural, Inst Contemp Art, Boston, 70; sculpture, City of Boston, 70; painting, Sonesta Hotel, Amsterdam, Holland, 83. *Exhib:* One-man shows, Inst Contemp Art, Boston, 70, Frank Marino Gallery, New York, 82, Mu Gallery, Boston, 92; Oscarsson-Hood Gallery, New York, 85; Greenville Mus, SC, 86; 12 Americans, Moma, Buenos Aires, Argentina, 87-88; Recent Guggenheim Paintings, Boston, Mass, 90; Abstraction Per Se, Pratt Inst, NY, 92; and others. *Teaching:* Vis artist painting, Univ SC, Columbia, 81; assoc prof painting, Col Charleston, SC, 84-; vis artist Am Acad Rome, 87; vis artist, Cardift Col Art, Wales, 88-89. *Awards:* Nat Endowment Arts Grant Painting, 80-81; Painting Grant, SC Arts Comm, 85-86; Guggenheim fel, 89-90. *Bibliog:* John Chandler (auth), Collaboration: A Boston issue, Art Gallery Mag, 6/69; John Koethe (auth), Boston is here now, Arts News, 9/69; Hilton Kramer (auth), Art in Boston kindles hope for cities, NY Times, 6/9/70; Mary Sherman (auth), Three galleries invite closer look, Boston Globe, 5/30/90; Cate McQuaid (auth), Light shows, Southend News, Boston, Mass, 5/10/90. *Mem:* Col Art Asn. *Media:* All. *Publ:* Auth, New Options in Painterly Abstration, OIA, New York, 79; Painting Self Evident: Evolutions in Abstraction, Gibbes Mus, Charleston, SC, 92. *Dealer:* Joan Sonnabend/ Obelisk Gallery Boston MA 02108. *Mailing Add:* Sears Rd Goshen MA 01032

PHILLIPS, ROBERT J
FILMMAKER, PHOTOGRAPHER
b Montclair, NJ, Feb 28, 46. *Study:* Jersey City State Col, BA(art educ), 68: New York Univ Grad Sch Arts, MFA(phogog, film & TV), 72; Found for Mind Res, Pomona NY, creative actualization with Dr Jean Houston, Res & Teaching Assoc, 75-l Farleigh Dickinson Univ, EdD, 88. *Exhib:* Faculty Show, Caldwell Coll, 86 & 90. *Pos:* Designer of high sch film educ prog, identified as exemplary model curriculum site by Am Film Inst, DC, 68-70; coordr, Film Festival, 19th Congress Int Soc for Educ Through Art, 69; asst proj dir, NJ State Coun on Arts, Inner City Arts Proj, Hoboken, NJ, 70; proj dir, Summer Arts Workshop for Mentally Handicapped, Title VI grant, East Orange, NJ, 71; chmn, Comt for Creative Actualization, New Ways of Being Inst Conf, Minneapolis, Dallas, Los Angeles & NJ, 78-79. *Teaching:* Instr art, Photog & film, Woodbridge Sr High Sch, NJ; educator-at-large, master classes & teacher-in-service training in creative actualization, camera arts & fine arts, schs, communities & cols throughout the east, 72-; adj instr, creative actualization & camera arts, Caldwell Col, NJ, 72-; art dir/designer, creative dir & dir mktg communications, WLMW & Assocs, Bozell Inc, FDS/Merrill Lynch. *Awards:* Bronze Phoenix Award for outstanding creative achievement in filmmaking, Atlanta Int Film Festival, Ga, 74; Award for Outstanding Achievement in film direction, in graphic design, Int Creativity Ann, Art Direction Mag, 74; Cert Excellence, filmmaking, NJ Art Dir's Club, 75; plus others. *Media:* Video Tape, Multi Media. *Publ:* Filmmaker & photog, Qualify (film), Net Channel 13, New York, 71; Choice Not Chance (film), 74 & Daydreams and Indecision, 79, NJ State Dept Educ; Asbury Park--A Renaissance, Asbury Park Dept Community Affairs, 79; Art and Multi-Sensory Learning (filmstrip), Educ Frontiers Assocs, 80-90. *Mailing Add:* 446 Westgate Dr Edison NJ 08820

PHILLIPS, TONY
PAINTER, DRAFTSMAN
b Miami Beach, Fla, Sept 16, 37. *Study:* Trinity Col, Hartford, BA, 60; Sch Art, Yale Univ, BFA, 62, MFA, 63. *Work:* Art Inst Chicago; Mus Contemp Art, Chicago. *Exhib:* Painting & Sculpture Today, Indianapolis Mus Art, 82; Traveling Exhib to seven mus, Mus Contemp Art, Chicago, 84; Artists Choosing Artists, Artist's Choice Mus, New York, 85; Chicago Vicinity, Art Inst Chicago, 85; one-man shows, Marianne Deson Gallery, Chicago, 82, 86; Deutsch-Am Inst, Regensburg Munic Gallery, Regensburg, WGer, 88, 89; American Art Since World War II: Prints & Drawings, Art Inst Chicago, 89; The Chicago Show, Chicago CultCtr, 90. *Teaching:* Instr painting & design, Sch Visual Arts, New York, 65-68; prof painting & drawing, Sch Art Inst Chicago, 68- *Awards:* Nat Endowment Art Fels, 78 & 85; Ill Arts Coun Grant, 84, 88- *Bibliog:* Alan Artner (auth), rev, Chicago Tribune, 4/25/86; Robert Berlind (auth), rev, Art in Am, 7/86. *Media:* Oil, Pastel. *Publ:* Auth, Leon Golub: Portraits of political power, New Art Examiner, 1/78; Essay on Drawing, Whitewalls, spring 86. *Dealer:* Dart Gallery 750 N Orleans Chicago IL 60610. *Mailing Add:* 807 W 16th St Chicago IL 60608

PHILLIS, MARILYN HUGHEY
PAINTER, INSTRUCTOR
b Kent, Ohio, Feb 1, 27. *Study:* Ohio State Univ, BS, 49; Toledo Mus Art Sch Design, 61; studied with Fred Leach, Jeanne Dobie, Edward Betts & Glenn Bradshaw. *Work:* Springfield Mus Art, Springfield, Ohio; E F McDonald Co, Gem Savings, Dayton; Rolls Royce Ltd, Palmyra, NY; Neumann Indust, Cleveland; Dean Witter Reynolds Inc, Jackson, Miss; Holiday Inns, Memphis, Tenn; On Line Computer Libr Ctr, Dublin, Ohio. *Comn:* Harpischord decorative design, comn by Rosalyn Schneider, 84; abstr painting, Dr & Mrs Eugene Schmiedl, 88. *Exhib:* Allied Artists Am, Nat Acad & Nat Arts Galleries, New York, 74-77, 80, 81, 85 & 87; Am Watercolor Soc, Nat Acad Gallery, New York & traveling, 74, 76, 78, 79, 82, 89 & 91; Nat Watercolor Soc, Laguna Beach Mus & Palm Springs Mus, Calif, 74, 80, 83 & 89; solo exhib, Columbus Mus Art, Ohio, 81; Watermedia Exhib, Springfield Art Ctr, Ohio, 81 & 83; Ohio Northern Univ, 84; Davis & Elkins Univ, Elkins, WVa, 86; Zanesville Art Ctr, Ohio, 87. *Pos:* Illusr, Western Reserve Mag, 74-78. *Teaching:* Instr art, Edison State Community Col, 76; instr watercolor, Springfield Art Ctr, Ohio, 76-84; guest lectr painting throughout US; juror nat painting and all media exhibs. *Awards:* William Church Osborne Award, Am Watercolor Soc, 74; Nat Arts Club Award, Allied Artists Am Exhib, 87; First Award, Watercolor West, 90; First Award, WVa Watercolor Soc, 92. *Bibliog:* Fred Kalister (auth), Directions in watercolor dialogue, Ohio Arts J, 1-2/81; Jacqueline Hall (auth), Phillis art works offer poetic look at nature, Columbus Dispatch, 5/2/82; Maxine Masterfield (auth), Painting the Spirit of Nature, Watson-Guptill, 84; Prof Yong Xian-Rang (auth), article, Meiyuan (Chinese art mag), pages 44-45, 85; Mike Ward (auth), The New Spirit of Watercolor, North Light, 89; Nita Leland (auth), The Creative Artist, North Light, 90. *Mem:* Nat Watercolor Soc; Allied Artists Am; Watercolor West; Ohio Watercolor Soc (rec secy, 79-82, vpres, 82-89 & pres, 90-94); Soc Layerists Multimedia (vpres, 88-93); Am Watercolor Soc (bd dir, 91-93 & newsletter ed). *Media:* Watermedia, Collage. *Publ:* Illusr, Historic Piqua: An Architectural Survey, Piqua Br, Am Asn Univ Women, 76; auth, Painting from the imagination, The Artists Mag, 1/85; auth, Watermedia techniques for releasing the creative spirit, Watson Guptill Pub, 92. *Dealer:* Windon Gallery 17 Aldrich Ave Columbus OH. *Mailing Add:* 72 Stamm Circle Wheeling WV 26003

PHILLPOT, CLIVE JAMES
LIBRARIAN, WRITER
b Thornton Heath, Eng, June 26, 38. *Study:* Polytech of N London, ALA, 67; Univ London, Dipl HA(with distinction), 74; Fel Lib Asn UK, 90. *Collections Arranged:* Artists' Books (auth, catalog), Inst Contemp Arts, London, 76; The Art Press (auth, catalog), Victoria & Albert Mus, London, 76 & Art Gallery of Ontario, Toronto, 79; The Page as Alternative Space, Franklin Furnace, New York, 80; What Are You Waiting For? (auth, catalog), Seattle, 84; Fluxus: Selections from the Silverman Collection (auth, catalog), Mus Mod Art, New York, 88. *Pos:* Librn, Chelsea Sch Art, London, 70-77; dir libr, Mus Mod Art, New York, 77-; pres bd dirs, Printed Matter, Inc. *Mem:* Art Libr Soc NAm (pres, 89-90); Col Art Asn; Int Asn Art Critics; Arch Am Art (adv comt). *Res:* Visual language; marginal art. *Interests:* Contemporary art. *Publ:* Guest ed, Art J, summer 82; Artists Books - A Critical Anthology, Visual Studies Workshop Press, 85; Reader in Art Librarianship, Saur, 85; Adrian Piper: Reflections, Alternative Mus, 87; Move Works by Ray Johnson, Moove Col, 91. *Mailing Add:* Mus Mod Art 11 W 53rd St New York NY 10019

PIASECKI, JANE B
ADMINISTRATOR
b Brooklyn, NY, Jan 21, 53. *Study:* Brooklyn Mus Art Sch, 72-75; City Univ New York-Col Staten Island, AS(liberal arts), 78, BS(econ, 82; City Univ New York-Baruch Col, MBA, 85. *Pos:* Accounting asst, Brooklyn Botanic Gardens, 73-76; asst mgr finance & personnel, Brooklyn Mus, 76-80; bus & personnel mgr, NY Hall Sci, 80-85; assoc dir, Newport Harbor Art Mus, 85-. *Mem:* Art Pub Places (comt, 88-92); Int Coun Mus (mgt comt, 92-92); Am Asn Mus, Finance & Admin Comt (treas, 92-93); Calif Asn Mus (treas, 92-93). *Mailing Add:* Newport Harbor Art Museum 850 San Clemente Dr Newport Beach CA 92660

PIATEK, FRANCIS JOHN
PAINTER, INSTRUCTOR
b Chicago, Ill, Dec 9, 44. *Study:* Sch Art Inst Chicago, BFA & MFA. *Work:* Art Inst Chicago; Ill State Mus; First Nat Bank Chicago; Kemper Insurance Bong Warren Corp. *Comn:* Mural, Main State Bank Chicago, 72. *Exhib:* Whitney Mus Am Art Ann Exhib Contemp Am Painting, 68; one-man shows, Hyde Park Art Ctr, 69, Phyllis Kind Gallery, 72, NAME Gallery, Chicago, 75 & Roy Boyd Gallery, 84-87; Chicago Art Inst Soc Contemp Art; Surface, 2 Decades of painting in Chicago Terra Mus Am Art, 87; Selection from the Dennis Adrain Collection of Contemp Art, Chicago. *Teaching:* Instr painting, Art Inst Chicago, 70-71 & 75-; instr painting, Washington Univ, St Louis, 73-74. *Awards:* Art Inst Traveling Fel, Francis Ryerson, 67; Pauline Potter Palmer Award, 68 & John G Curtis Prize, 69, Chicago & Vicinity Shows; Nat Endowment Arts, Visual Arts Fel, 85. *Bibliog:* Franz Schulze (auth), Frantastic Images: Chicago Art since 1945, Follett Publ Co, 72; Franz Schulze (auth), Artists the Critics Are Watching Art News, 5/81; Mary Mathews Gedo (auth), Abstraction As Metaphor: The Evacative Imagery of William Conger, Miyoko Ito, Richard Loving & Frank Piatek, Art Mag, 10/82. *Media:* Oil, Multi Media. *Dealer:* Roy Boyd Gallery Chicago Ill. *Mailing Add:* Sch Art Inst Chicago Chicago IL 60603

PICCIANO, LANA (LANA PATRICIA PICCIANO)
PAINTER, PRINTMAKER
b Evanston, Ill. *Study:* Bloomfield Col, BA, 69; Art Students League, with Vaclav Vytlacil, scholar, 70-72 & with Theodoras Stamos, Scholar, 71-72; Provincetown Workshop, with Leo Manso & Victor Candell, 74. *Work:* Int Monetary Fund, Washington, DC; Bell Laboratories, Holmdell & Parsippany, NJ; Integrated Resources, Inc, New York; Wertheim Schroder & Co, Equitable Ctr, New York; Morrison and Foerester, New York. *Comn:* Painting, Bell Laboratories, Holmdell, NJ, 80; painting, Lutz and Carr, New York, NY, 87; painting, Jad Corporation of Am Col Point, NY, 89; painting, comn by Mr & Mrs Martin Gottlieb, Boca Raton, Fla, 89. *Exhib:* First Ann Brandeis Show, Washington, DC, 82; Contemporary Artists, Islip Art Mus, East Islip, NY, 88; 100 Years/100 Works, Women Artists Today Salute Their Centennial, Islip Art Mus, East Islip, NY, 89, Fine Arts Mus of South Mobile, Ala, 89 & Chattanooga Regional Hist Mus, Tenn, 89; The New Romanticism, 8th Plaiedes Gallery, New York, 90. *Bibliog:* First Place in Oils, Framingham Ann Competition, 74; Best in DC Slide Registry & Best of DC Artists, D Christensen, 82. *Mem:* Artists Equity NJ (pub relations dir, 79-81); Nat Asn Women Artists (financial relations dir, 86-88); Artist Equity NY. *Media:* Oil on Canvas. *Publ:* Auth, An Illustrated Survey of Leading Contemporaries, Am Artists, 90; New York Art Review, Les Krantz, 90. *Mailing Add:* 8 Porpoise Dr Centereach NY 11720

PICCILLO, JOSEPH
PAINTER
b Buffalo, NY, Jan 9, 41. *Study:* State Univ NY Col Buffalo, MFA, 64, fel, 68, 69 & 72. *Work:* Mus Mod Art, New York; Brooklyn Mus; Art Inst Chicago; Butler Inst Am Art, Youngstown, Ohio; Minn Mus Art, Minneapolis; Metrop Mus, NY. *Exhib:* One-man show, Albright-Knox Art Gallery, Buffalo, 69; Smithsonian Inst Traveling Drawing Exhib, 71; Monique Knowlton Gallery, 80, 81 & 83; Betsy Rosenfield Gallery, 80, 83; one man shows, Monique Knowlton, New York, 84, Betsy Rosenfield, Chicago, 80, 85, 86, 88 & 91, Elliot Smith Gallery, St Louis, Mo, 86 & 88, Barbara Fendrick Gallery, NY, 88, Brendan Walter Gallery, Los Angeles, Calif, 90 & 92. *Pos:* Consult, NY State Coun Arts, 75-77. *Teaching:* Prof art, State Univ NY Col Buffalo, 67- *Awards:* Childe Hassam Purchase Award, Am Acad Arts & Lett, 68; Nat Endowment for Arts fel, 79. *Bibliog:* Diane Cochrane (auth), J Piccillo's game structures, Am Artist, 12/73. *Publ:* Illusr (covers), Poverty in America, 5/17/68 & Black vs Jew-A tragic confrontation, 1/31/69, Time Mag; contribr (cover), Art Gallery Int, 90. *Mailing Add:* Dept Art Education, SUNY Buffalo 1300 Elmwood Ave Buffalo NY 14222

PICCOLO, RICHARD
PAINTER
b Hartford, Conn, Sept 17, 43. *Study:* Pratt Inst, 66; Art Students League, 66; Brooklyn Col, MFA, 68. *Work:* Crown Am Corp, Johnstown, Pa; Grosvenor Int, Sacramento, Calif; also pvt collections of Lillian Cole, Sherman Oaks, Calif, Mr & Mrs Robert Emery, San Francisco, Graham Gund, Boston, Robert Gutterman, San Francisco, Dr & Mrs Joseph Jennings, San Francisco and others. *Comn:* Mural, Crown Am Corp, Johnstown, Pa; mural, Lobby Park Plaza Tower, Grosvenor Int, Sacramento, 91- *Exhib:* Solo exhibs, Robert Schoelkopf Gallery, New York, 75, 79, 83 & 89, Suffolk Community Col, Long Island, 76, Am Acad, Rome, Italy, 77, Galleria Temple, Rome, Italy, 79, Galleria il Gabbiano, Rome, Italy, 85 & Contemp Realist Gallery, San Francisco, 89; The Italian Tradition in Contemporary American Landscape Painting, Gibbes Mus Art, Charleston, SC with Spoleto Exhib, 90; The Italian Landscape, Contemp Realist Gallery, San Francisco, 90; Figure, Contemp Realist Gallery, Calif, 90; Paintings from Contemporary Realist Gallery, NY Acad Art, 91-92; New American Figure Painting, Contemp Realist Gallery, San Francisco, 92; and others. *Teaching:* Instr, Pratt Inst, New York & Pratt Inst, Tyler Sch Art, Rome, Italy. *Awards:* E A Abbey mem Scholar, 73-75; Nat Endowment Arts Grant, 89. *Bibliog:* Steve Jenkins (auth), Back to the future, Artweek, 11/89; Karen Stein (auth), Graresian Images, Archit Rec 2/90; John Hollander (auth), Landscape Painting 1960-1990, Gibbes Mus Art, Charleston, SC & Bayly Mus Art, Charlottesville, Va, 90; Alfred Kay (auth), Grand Canvas, Sacramento Bee, 4/92; Thomas Bolt (auth), New American Figure Painting, Contemp Realist Gallery, San Francisco, 92; and others. *Mailing Add:* c/o Contemporary Realist Gallery 506 Hayes St San Francisco CA 94102

PICHER, CLAUDE
PAINTER, CURATOR
b Quebec City, Que, Can, May 30, 27. *Study:* Que Fine Arts Sch, 45-46; New Sch Social Res, New York, with Julian Levi, 48; Ecole du Louvre, Paris, with Jean Cassou, 48-49; Ecole Nat Superieure des Beaux-Arts de Paris, with Demeter Galanis. *Work:* Nat Gallery Can, Ottawa; Art Gallery Ont, Toronto; Lord Beaverbrook Art Gallery, Fredericton, NB; Agnes Etherington Art Gallery, Kingston, Ont. *Comn:* Mural of Old Que, Hall of the Claridge, Quebec City, 67. *Exhib:* Montreal Mus Fine Arts, 58 & 64; 2nd Int Biennial, Mus Mod Art, Paris, France, 61; Lord Beaverbrook Art Gallery, 62; Que Mus, Quebec City, 67. *Pos:* Eastern rep, Nat Gallery Can, 58-61; assoc dir, Que Mus, 63-64. *Awards:* Jessie Dow Found Award, 73rd Spring Exhib, Montreal Mus Fine Arts, 56; Acquisition Prize, Nat Gallery Can, Govt of Can, 57 & Lord Beaverbrook Art Gallery, Can Art Coun, 62. *Bibliog:* Robert Fulford (auth), Twenty-four young Canadian artists, Can Art Mag, 61; Guy Viau (auth), La peinture au Canada-Francais, Ministere des Affaires Culturelles, 64; Guy Robert (auth), La peinture au Quebec depuis 1940, Ed La Presse, 73. *Mem:* Royal Can Acad Arts. *Media:* Oil. *Interests:* Pre-1920 art work. *Mailing Add:* Saint-Leandre Matane County PQ G0J 2V0 Canada

PICKETT, KERI L
PHOTOGRAPHER
Exhib: Photo Eye 91, AIGA Juried Show, Dayton's Gallery 12, Minneapolis, Minn, 91; Five Jerome Artists, Minn Col Art & Design Gallery, Minneapolis, 91; Picturing Hennepin, Minn Hist Soc, Minneapolis, 92; Celebrate Freedom, Los Angeles Photo Ctr, 92; solo shows, Kids Coping with Illness, Studio 13 Gallery, Minneapolis, 89, Photographs from Africa & India, Studio 13 Gallery, 89. *Teaching:* Ms Found Nat Girls Initiative Photog Proj, 91; Youth Photog Prog, Film in the Cities, St Paul, Minn, 91; collabr audio visual, Earth Survival Sch, 92. *Awards:* Photog Fel, Nat Endowment Arts, 90; McKnight Found Fel, Film in the Cities, 92; Bush Found Artists Fel, 92. *Mem:* Panelist, Minn State Arts Bd Photog. *Mailing Add:* 17 Greenway Gables Minneapolis MN 55403

PICKFORD, ROLLIN, JR
PAINTER
b Fresno, Calif. *Study:* Calif State Univ; Stanford Univ, BA; also with Alexander Nepote, Ralph DuCasse, James Weeks & Joseph Mugnaini. *Work:* Springfield Art Mus, Mo; State of Calif Collection, Sacramento; Ford Motor Co, Dearborn, Mich; City of Santa Paula, Calif; Monterey Peninsula Mus Art; and others. *Comn:* UNICEF Card (UN painting), comn by United Nations, New York. *Exhib:* Watercolor USA, Springfield, MO, 62, 65 & 66; Mainstreams Marietta, Ohio, 68; Austrian-Am Exchange Exhib, Linz, Salzburg & Vienna, Austria, 72; Taiwan-Am Exchange Exhib, 73; Royal Watercolor Soc, London-WCoast Watercolor Soc Exchange Exhib, 75-76; Fresno Art Mus Residency, 89; and others. *Teaching:* Instr art, Fresno State Col, 48-62. *Awards:* Best of Show, All-California Exhib, 60; First Prize & Purchase Award, Watercolor USA, 62; First Prize & Purchase Award, Calif State Fair, 63. *Mem:* West Coast Watercolor Soc; Watercolor USA Honor Soc; Carmel Art Asn; and others. *Media:* Multimedia. *Publ:* Illusr, stories by William Saroyan, Lincoln-Mercury Times & Ford Times, 50s; auth, A Philosophical Approach to Watercolor, 69 & The California Style, 85, Am Artist. *Mailing Add:* 930 E Sierra Madre Fresno CA 93704

PICKHARDT, CARL
PAINTER, PRINTMAKER
b Westwood, Mass, May 28, 08. *Study:* Harvard Univ, AB, 31; study with Harold Zimmerman, 30-35. *Work:* Mus Mod Art, New York; Mus Fine Arts, Boston; Newark Art Mus, NJ; Libr Cong, Washington, DC; Brooklyn Art Mus, NY. *Exhib:* Mus Mod Art, NY, 40, 63 & 64; Carnegie Inst Int, 52; Int Exhib, Japan, 52; Am Drawing Biennial, Norfolk, Va, 66; Pa Acad Fine Arts, Philadelphia, 68; Radcliffe Col, 83; Fitchburg Art Mus, 91. *Teaching:* Instr printmaking, Worcester Mus Art Sch, 49-50 & Arts Students League, 51; instr painting, Fitchburg Art Mus, 51-62. *Awards:* Shope Prize, Nat Acad Design, 42. *Bibliog:* Parker Tyler (auth), Carl Pickhardt, Horizon, 72; and others. *Mailing Add:* 66 Forest St Sherborn MA 01770

PICOT, PIERRE
PAINTER
b Tours, France, Jan 11, 48. *Study:* Calif Inst Art, MFA, 73. *Work:* Los Angeles Co Mus Art, Calif; Security Pac Bank, Los Angeles, Calif; Patrick J Lannan Found, Los Angeles, Calif. *Exhib:* Hirshhorn Mus Art, Washington, DC, 84. *Teaching:* Instr, Art Ctr Col Design, Los Angeles, Calif, 85- *Awards:* Art Fel, Nat Endowment Arts, 88. *Mailing Add:* 3516 Crestmont Ave Los Angeles CA 90026

PIEHL, WALTER JASON, JR
PAINTER, EDUCATOR
b Marion, NDak, Aug 1, 42. *Study:* Concordia Col, BA, 64; Univ NDak, MA, 66; Univ Minn, 69. *Work:* Pillsbury Co, St Paul, Minn; Fed Reserve Bank Minneapolis; NDak Governor's Collection, Bismarck; Plains Art Mus, Moorhead, NDak. *Comn:* Mosaic mural, Devils Lake Sioux Tribe, NDak, 71; Univ NDak Mobile Art Gallery Graphic, Art Gallery Asn, NDak statewide tour, 79. *Exhib:* 19th Ann Drawing, Ball State Mus, Muncie, Ind, 73; Ann Images, Anoka Ramsey Col Gallery, Minn, 73; Midwestern Graphics, Tulsa City Libr Mus, Okla, 74; 15th Ann Nat Graphics, Okla Art Ctr, Oklahoma City, 74; one-man shows, Dynamics of Rodeo & Landscape, Univ Art Galleries, Grand Forks, NDak, 75 & 81 & Rodeo Imagery, Plains Art Mus, Moorhead, Minn, 66, 69, 70 & 76. *Collections Arranged:* Great Plains Traveling Exhib, 70-71; Northwest Biennial Invitation (auth, catalog), 71; Artrain (traveled), 75; Dakota Made, Mobile Gallery, 79; Nat Watercolor

Invitation (auth, catalog), 79-80. *Teaching:* Instr art, Valley City State Col, NDak, 67-68; from asst prof to assoc prof art, Minot State Col, NDak, 69-. *Awards:* Purchase Awards, Nat Graphics, Univ NDak, 72 & Northwestern Bak Corp, 74 & Drawing USA, Minn Mus Art, 73. *Bibliog:* Nancy Edmonds Hanson (auth), Contemporary artists of the west, NDak Horizons, 75; article, Art Voices South, 81. *Mem:* NDak Art Gallery Asn (vpres, 79-80); NDak Coun on Arts. *Media:* Mixed. *Dealer:* Wildine Gallery 903 Rio Grande Blvd NW Albuquerque NMex 87104. *Mailing Add:* Art Dept 500 Univ Ave W Minot State Univ Minot ND 58707

PIENE, OTTO
SCULPTOR, PAINTER
b Laasphe, Westphalia, Ger, Apr 18, 28. *Study:* Blocherer Art Sch & Acad of Fine Arts, Munich, 48-50; Dusseldorf Art Acad, WGer, 50-53; Univ Cologne, WGer, 53-57. *Work:* Albright-Knox Art Gallery, Buffalo, NY; Mus Mod Art, New York; Carnegie Inst Int Mus Art, Pittsburgh, Pa; Nat Gallery of Can, Ottawa, Ont; Stedelijk Mus, Amsterdam, Holland; Nat Gallary, Berlin;; and others. *Comn:* Olympic Rainbow, Munich, 72. *Exhib:* Sixteen German Artists, Corcoran Gallery of Art, Washington, DC, 62; Mus am Ostwall, Dortmund, WGer retrospective, 67; Earth, Air, Fire, Water: Elements of Art, Mus Fine Arts, Boston, Mass, 71; Westphalian Art, Westfalisches Land Mus, Munster, Ger, 73; Documenta 6, Ctr Advan Visual Studies, Mass Inst Technol, 77, Kassel, Ger; one-man shows, Trumbull Col, Yale Univ, New Haven, Conn, 69, Centro de Arte y Communicacion, Buenos Aires, Art, 72 & Kolnischer Kunstverein, Cologne, 73; Hayden Gallery, Mass Inst Technol, Cambridge, Mass, 75; Fitchburg Art Mus, Mass, 77; and many others. *Pos:* Dir, Ctr Adv Visual Studies, Mass Inst Technol, Cambridge, currently. *Teaching:* Prof environmental art, Sch Archit & Planning, Mass Inst Technol, 72. *Awards:* Konrad von Soest Prize, Munster, 68; Tamarind Fel, Los Angeles, Calif, 69; Prize, Tokyo Graphics Biennale, Mus Mod Art, Tokyo, Japan, 72. *Bibliog:* Dietrich Mahlow, et al (auth), Otto Piene--Werkverzeichnis der Druckgrafik 1960-76, Karlsruhe, WGer, 77;; Heiner Stachelhaus & Jurgen Claus (auth), Otto Piene, Essen, Ger, 83; Manfred Schneckenburger, et al (auth), Otto Piene und das cavs, Karlsruhe, Germany, 88. *Media:* Multimedia. *Publ:* Auth, Rainbows, 71, More Sky, 73 & co-auth, Zero, 73, Cambridge, Mass; coauth & co-ed, Sky Art (conference catalogs), Cambridge, Mass, 81, 82 & 83; and others. *Mailing Add:* c/o Mass Inst Technol 40 Massachusetts Ave Cambridge MA 02139

PIEPENBURG, ROBERT
SCULPTOR
b Detroit, Mich, Oct 28, 41. *Study:* Eastern Mich Univ, BS, 64, MA, 65, MFA, 73. *Work:* Detroit Inst Arts; Smithsonian Inst. *Comn:* Sculpture, Cadillac City Co Bldg, Mich, 79; mural, Liberty State Bank, Clinton, Mich, 81; sculpture, Fed Mogul World Hq, Southfield, Mich, 82; fountain, Sheraton Hotel, Novi, Mich, 82; wall relief, Delta Airlines Terminal, Orlando, Fla, 90. *Exhib:* Solo exhib, Robert Kidd Gallery, Birmingham, Mich, 80; Wichita Art Mus, Kans, 81; Duluth Art Inst, Minn, 81; Eastern Ill Univ, 82; Ceramic League of Miami, 88; Univ Mich, Ann Arbor, 90. *Teaching:* Instr ceramics, Oakland Community Col, Ill, 69-, Vancouver Sch Art, 76 & Tyler Sch Art, 77. *Awards:* Nat Endowment Arts Fel, 80; Mich Coun Arts Creative Artist Grant, 81, 86 & 90. *Bibliog:* Steve Branfman (auth), Rako, A Practice Appr, Chilton, 91. *Mem:* Nat Coun Educ Ceramic Arts. *Media:* Ceramics, Welded Steel. *Publ:* Auth, Raku Pottery, Pebble Press, 91. *Mailing Add:* Dept Humanities Oakland Comm Col Orchard Lake Farmington Hills MI 48018

PIERCE, ANN TRUCKSESS
PAINTER, EDUCATOR
b Boulder, Colo, Aug 28, 31. *Study:* Univ Colo, Boulder, BFA, 53, MFA, 55; Yale Univ summer sch, fel, 53; study with Bernard Chaet, Gabor Peterdi, Jimmy Ernst, N Marsicano; workshops with Harold Gretzner, Robert E Wood, Morris Shubin, Jade Fon, George Post, Tom Hill, Tom Nicholas & Millard Sheets. *Work:* Tri-Counties Bank, Mangrove; Pillsbury Branches, Chico, Calif; Yale Univ, New Haven, Conn; Forum Gallery, New York; Calif State Univ, Chico; Univ Colo, Boulder. *Comn:* Oil painting, Colo State Univ, Fort Collins. *Exhib:* Rocky Mt Nat Watermedia Exhib, Foothills Art Ctr, Golden, Colo, 74, 77-79, 81-83, 85, 88 & 89; San Diego Watercolor Soc Nat, Cent Fed Tower Plaza Gallery, 76-78 & 80-84; Scottsdale Watercolor Biennial, Scottsdale Ctr for Arts, Ariz, 78 & 80; Ann Exhib Watercolor Soc Ala, Birmingham Mus Art, 78 & 79; Watercolor West, Riverside Art Ctr, Calif, 79, 81-83, 87 & 88; Nat Watercolor Soc, Desert Mus, Palm Springs, Calif, 79-81 & traveling exhib, 79, 80, 82 & 88; Watercolor USA, 80 & 88; Watercolor Now, 87 & 89-90. *Teaching:* Grad asst drawing & watercolor, Univ Colo, Boulder, 53-54, instr, summers, 59 & 62; prof drawing & watercolor, Calif State Univ, Chico, 64-, chmn art dept, 80-83, numberous workshops, 90-92. *Awards:* Springfield Art Mus Award, Watercolor USA, 80; Purchase Awards, Joyce Media, Nat Watercolor Soc, 80 & Hutchings, Watercolor West, 81; First & Second Prize, Calif State Fair, 82; Award of Excellence & Purchase Award, Lodi Ann, 83. *Bibliog:* Brommer-Kinne (auth), Exploring Painting, Davis Publ, 88; Watercolor 89, Am Artist Mag Publ, 89; Greg Albert (auth), Splash, North Light Bks, 91. *Mem:* Nat Watercolor Soc; West Coast Watercolor Soc; Watercolor West; Rocky Mountain Nat Watermedia Soc; Nat Asn Women Artists; Watercolor USA. *Media:* Watercolor. *Mailing Add:* 545 W Shasta Ave Chico CA 95926

PIERCE, CHARLES ELIOT, JR
ADMINISTRATOR, DIRECTOR
b Springfield, Mass, Dec 25, 41. *Study:* Harvard Col, BA, 64; Harvard Univ, PhD, 70. *Pos:* Dir, Pierpont Morgan Libr, New York. *Mailing Add:* Pierpont Morgan Library 29 E 36th St New York NY 10016

PIERCE, DANNY P
SCULPTOR, PAINTER
b Woodlake, Calif. *Study:* Schouinard Inst Art, Los Angeles; Am Art Sch, New York; Brooklyn Mus Art Sch; Univ Alaska. *Work:* Mus Mod Art, New York; Nat Libr, Paris; Nat Mus Sweden, Stockholm; Huntington Libr, San Marino, Calif. *Comn:* Eskimo scene panels, 62, abstract design in concrete for cafeteria bldg, 63, Univ Alaska; Logging (diorama), White River Hist Soc Mus; 3 murals, Kent, Wash. *Exhib:* Traveling Exhib Prints, Europe, Eurasia, 59-62; Northwest Printmakers Int, Seattle Art Mus, 68; Washington Art, Worlds Fair, Osaka, Japan, 70; Edge of the Sea, Bradley Gallery, Milwaukee, 73, 75, 77, 79 & 81; one-man show, Small Bronzes, 74 & Oostduinkerke, Belgium, 80. *Pos:* Artist-in-residence, Univ Alaska, 59-63. *Teaching:* Assoc prof art, Univ Wis, Milwaukee, formerly, emer prof, formerly, retired full prof & prof emer, 84. *Awards:* Green Memorial Award for Best Oil, Conn Acad Art, 49; Purchase Award, Libr Cong, 52, 53 & 58; Northwest Printmakers International Award, Seattle Art Mus, 68. *Media:* All. *Publ:* Auth & illusr, Cattle Drive, 76, 77, Shepherdess of Monument Valley, 79, Man, Horse, Sea, 80, Sea Wreck, 81 & Birds, 81; Golden Seas, Horse Logging; Sugaring Fever, 89; Irish Vignettes, 92. *Dealer:* Jube Gallery 243 First Ave Kent WA; Martin-Zambito 721 Pike Seattle WA. *Mailing Add:* 330 Summit Ave Kent WA 98031-4714

PIERCE, DIANE (DIANE PIERCE-HUXTABLE)
ILLUSTRATOR, PAINTER
b Lakewood, Ohio, Mar 6, 39. *Study:* Cleveland Inst Art, Ohio, dipl, 61; Western Reserve Univ, BA, 62. *Work:* Ward Found Mus, Salisbury, Md; Heard Mus, McKinney, Tex; Ind State Mus, Indianapolis; Prime Minister Indira Ghandi, New Delhi, India; Fla Nature Conservancy, Winter Park; Fla Audubon Soc, Maitland. *Comn:* warbler calendar, Nat Wildlife Fedn, 79-81; postal stamp design, Govt India, 82; Ding Darling Guide, Dept of Interior, 86; Wekiva River Guide, 88; First Forax at Dawn, Fla Chap Ducks Unlimited. *Exhib:* Game Coin Int, San Antonio, Tex, 79; NAm Wild Animal Art Exhib, Cowboy Hall of Fame, Oklahoma City, Okla, 79; Fla State Mus, Gainesville, 86; Fla State Capital, 87; Ann Conf Nature Conservancy, Orlando, Fla, 88; and others. *Awards:* First Place, Ind Duck Stamp Contest, 79; First Place, Long Island Duck Stamp Contest, 80. *Bibliog:* Midwest Art, 88; US Art, 89, 90; Fla Naturalist, 90. *Mem:* Save our Creeks; Fla Native Plant Soc; Fla Chap Nature Conservancy; Sea Shepherd Conservation Soc; Fund Wild Nature. *Media:* Watercolor, Oil; Scratchboard, Pen and Ink. *Publ:* Contribr, The Living Bird, Cornell Univ Lab Ornithology, 72-83; illusr, An Introduction to Ornithology, Macmillan, 75; contribr (illus), Children's Sci Mag, 77; illusr, Endangered Birds/Temple, Wis Press, 78; illusr, Nat Geographic Field Guide to the Birds of North America, 83; Fla Chap News/The Nature Conservancy. *Mailing Add:* c/o Edge of the Wild Spring Creek Dr Bonita Springs FL 33923

PIERCE, DONALD (BENJAMIN)
PAINTER, INSTRUCTOR
b Toms River, NJ, Jan 23, 16. *Study:* Pratt Inst, cert, 37; Grand Cent Sch Art, 38-40; with Edgar Whitney & Frederic Taubes, 47-48. *Work:* San Diego Mus Art; Rutgers Univ; Slater Mem Mus, Norwich, Conn; Celanese Corp Am, New York; Butler Inst Am Art; MMT Sales Inc, New York; Pratt Inst, Brooklyn, NY. *Exhib:* Small Works, NY Univ, 82; Pratt Faculty Show, Pratt Inst Gallery, New York, 79; solo exhibs, Westbeth Galleries, New York, 81 & 89, Dome Gallery, New York, 92 & Am Scene Gallery, Sarasota, Fla, 92; Am Soc Contemp Artists Ann, New York, 75-93; Westbeth Artists, 87-90; and others. *Pos:* Co-chair, Westbeth Art Comm 88-89; vpres, Am Soc Contemp Arts, 90-93; bd dirs, NY Artists Equity Asn, 92-93. *Teaching:* Instr painting, Donald Pierce Sch Painting, Provincetown, Mass, 55-78 & Plateau Cirque, Bronxville, NY, 58-93; instr life drawing, Pratt Inst, New York, 74-79. *Awards:* Ranger Fund Purchase Award, Audubon Artists Ann, 68 & 75; Doris Krindler Mem Award, Am Soc Contemp Artists, 88; Elizabeth Erlanger Mem Award, 89, Theresa Lindler Mem Award, 90, Am Soc Contemp Artists. *Bibliog:* Norman Kent (auth), Seascapes and Landscapes in Watercolor, 56 & Ernest W Watson (auth), Composition in Landscape Still Life, 59, Watson-Guptill; Frederic Taubes (auth), A Guide to Traditional and Modern Painting Methods, Viking Press, 63. *Mem:* Audubon Artists Am; NY Artists Equity Assn Inc; Am Soc Contemp Artists. *Media:* Oil, Watercolor. *Publ:* Auth, Watercolor Series, Am Artist, 54. *Mailing Add:* 463 West St D-806 New York NY 10014

PIERCE, PATRICIA JOBE
DEALER, HISTORIAN
b Seattle, Wash, May 18, 43. *Study:* Univ Conn, 64; Boston Univ Sch Fine & Appl Arts, BFA, 65, Harvard Univ, 89-90. *Comn:* Art video, comn by Finlay Holiday Film Corp, 90; Republican Conv Art, Houston, 92. *Exhib:* Design Ctr, Boston, 92; Bridgewater State Col, Anderson Gallery, Mass, 92; Daniel Reni, Boston, 92; Gallery, Nantucket, 92. *Pos:* Pres, Pierce Galleries, Inc, Hingham, Mass, 66-; owner, Pierce Galleries Publ Co, 80-; exclusive agent, Kahlil Gibran & Giovanni DeCunto (1931) estate; prof mgr, World Champion Tae Kwon Do Martial Artists, 82. *Awards:* Golden Poet Award, Calif, 88, 89 & 90; Citation for Patriotism & Coverage, Pres Bush's Task Force, 89; Presidential Comn, Washington, DC, 92; and others. *Mem:* Patron Brockton Art Ctr; Nat Writer's Club; Nat Writer's Union; Int Platform Asn; Presidential Task Force, 92; and many others. *Res:* The life & work of Edward Henry Potthast, JAM Whistler & the rock band Aerosmith; Cape Ann painters; surrealism. *Specialty:* Nineteenth to twentieth century American painting, specializing in American & French impresionism; supports & promotes Boston living painters & musicians & their work; agent for Samuel Rose, Dale Malner, J W S Cox, W S Barrett, Kahli Gibran, Roy Thompsen and E Joseph Fontaine. *Collection:* Nineteenth century American & French impressionists, William S Barrett, Jane Peterson, E C Tarbell, J W S Cox, J

J Enneking & Walter Granville Smith, super realism of Samuel Rose; sculpture by Kahlil Gibran. *Publ:* The Prophetic Odessey of Richard Thompson, Am Impressionist, 82; The Watercolored World of J W S Cox, 81; Edward Henry Potthast: More than One Man, 90; The Master's Touch, 90; Elvis: The Gospel Truth-The History of Rock 'N' Roll, 92; and others. *Mailing Add:* c/o Pierce Galleries Inc 721 Main St Rte 228 Hingham MA 02043

PIERCE-HUXTABLE, DIANE See Pierce, Diane (Diane Pierce-Huxtable)

PIERRE-NOEL, VERGNIAUD
DESIGNER, GRAPHIC ARTIST
b Port-au-Prince, Haiti, Aug 2, 10; US citizen. *Study:* Cent Sch Damien, Univ Haiti, dipl; Columbia Univ, cert; Casa de Moneda, Buenos Aires, cert. *Work:* Nat Mus Haiti, Port-au-Prince; Am Mus Nat Hist, New York; UN, New York; Pan Am Health Orgn, Washington, DC; Wingspread Collection, Racine, Wis. *Comn:* Insects of Haiti, Serv Tech Damien, 33; Caribbean Cong commemorative stamp designs, Govt Haiti, 40; bicentennial commemorative stamp designs 1749-1949, Haiti Postal Admin, 49; World Health Orgn commemorative poster design, Washington, DC, 68. *Exhib:* Am Mus Natural Hist Staff Artists Exhib, New York, 36; Mil Club Haiti, Port-au-Prince, 40; Women Club Arg, Buenos Aires, 48; Nat Asn Indust Artists, Washington, DC, 65; Washington Tech Inst, DC, 68. *Pos:* Graphic designer, Dept Educ, Haiti, 30-34, Am Mus Natural Hist, 35-40, Haiti Postal Admin, 40-54 & Pan Am Health Orgn, 56-75. *Awards:* Gold Medal Award for Bicentennial of City of Port-au-Prince, 49; First Award for UN Postage Stamp Design, 65; First Award, Nat Asn Indust Artists, 65. *Bibliog:* Albert F Kunze (auth), V Pierre-Noel, creator of stamp designs for Haiti, Linn's Weekly Stamp News, 10/52; Belmont Faries (auth), Philatelic news, Washington Star, 2/62. *Mem:* Indust Graphics Int; Washington Tech Inst Advert Design. *Media:* Pen & Ink. *Publ:* Contribr illus, Am Mus Natural Hist, New York, 31, Entom Soc Am, 31, Haiti Postal Admin, 40, UN Postal Admin, 65 & Pan Am Health Orgn, 75. *Mailing Add:* 4706 17th St NW Washington DC 20011

PIET, JOHN FRANCES
SCULPTOR, INSTRUCTOR
b Detroit, Mich, Feb 23, 46. *Study:* Detroit Soc Arts & Crafts, BFA, 73; Wayne State Univ, MFA, 75. *Comn:* Detroit Bank & Trust, Mich, 72; Pingree City Park, Detroit, Mich, 73; Grand Circus Park, Mich Coun Arts, 75; sculpture, KMart Courtyard, KMart Int, Troy, Mich, 79; Oakland Univ, Rochester, Mich, 81. *Exhib:* Tradition & Invention, Kresge Art Gallery, Mich State Univ, East Lansing, Mich, 77; Kick Out the Jams, Detroit Inst Arts, 80 & Mus Contemp Art, Chicago, 81; Detroit Artists, Cranbrook Acad Art, West Bloomfield, Mich, 80; Meadowbrook Invitational, Oakland Univ, Rochester, Mich, 81; and others. *Awards:* Nat Endowment Arts Grant, Oakland Univ Festival, 81. *Bibliog:* Robert Pincus-Witten (auth), Islands in the blight, Arts Mag, 1/78; Mary S Smyka (auth), Dreams in steel, Detroit Monthly Mag, 80; Dennis A Nawrocki (auth), Art in Detroit public places, Wayne State Press, 80. *Media:* Steel. *Dealer:* Cantor-Lemberg Gallery 538 N Woodward Ave Birmingham MI 48010. *Mailing Add:* Humanities Macomb Community Col Ctr Campus 44575 Garfield Rd Clinton Township MI 48038

PIJANOWSKI, EUGENE M
EDUCATOR, CRAFTSMAN
b Detroit, Mich, Oct 5, 38. *Study:* Wayne State Univ, BFA, 65, MA, 67; Cranbrook Acad Art, Bloomfield Hills, Mich, MFA, 69; Tokyo Univ Art, 69-71. *Work:* The Art Gallery of Western Australia, Perth; Nat Mus Mod Art, Kyoto; Worshipful Co of Goldsmiths Hall, London; Cranbrook Art Mus, Bloomfield Hills, Mich; Vienna Mus Appl Arts; Am Crafts Mus, New York. *Exhib:* 211 in the US, Japan, Eng, Ger, Neth and other countries, 69-86; International Jewelry 1900-1980, Kunstlerhaus, Vienna, 80; Contemporary Jewelry, Nat Mus Mod Art, Kyoto & Tokyo, 84 & traveling Asia, 85-87; 20th Century Jewelry, Electrum Gallery, London, 85; International Goldsmithing, Ulm, WGer, 85; Flux, Galerie Dusseldorf, Perth, Australia, 86; Craft Today-Poetry of the Physical, Am Craft Mus, New York, 86; Century Jewelry, Geije, Yogosivaiz, 87; Contemporary Metalcraft, Seoul, Korea, 88; Fourth Internat Non Arts Forays Exposition, Navy Pier, Chicago, 88, 89, & 90; Crafts Today-USA traveling exhib (15 countries), 89-93. *Pos:* Assoc dean, Sch Art, Univ Mich, Ann Arbor, currently. *Teaching:* Instr metalwork, jewelry & crafts design, San Diego State Univ, Calif, 72-73; lectr Japanese metalworking, over 84 workshops throughout the US, Europe, Japan and Australia; assoc prof metalwork, jewelry & three-dimensional design, Purdue Univ, West Lafayette, 73-81; prof, Sch Art, Univ Mich, Ann Arbor, 81-92. *Awards:* Fulbright Fel, Vienna Inst Appl Arts, Austria, 85; Herbert Hofman Prize Schmuck gene, 87; Best of Show, The Wichita Nat, 87. *Bibliog:* Mokume-Gane (film), Oberon Films, 81. *Mem:* Distinguished mem, Soc NAm Goldsmiths. *Media:* Non-ferrous Metals. *Publ:* Contribr to 26 books on metalwork, 73-92; coauth, 15 articles on Lamination of nonferrous metals by diffusion: Adaptations of the traditional Japanese technique of Mokume-Gane, Goldsmiths J, 77; Mokume-Gane, Craft Horizons, 78; Chong Hap design: Korea, Goldschneide Zeitung, 81; Refractory metals, Jewel, Japan, 82; Update II: Mokume-Gane, Metalsmith, 83. *Mailing Add:* Sch Art Univ Mich Ann Arbor MI 48105

PIKE, JOYCE LEE
PAINTER, WRITER
b San Fernando, Calif, July 25, 29. *Study:* Sergei Bongart Sch Art, 55-57; Los Angeles Valley Col, 58-62; Art League Los Angeles, 60-63. *Work:* Fort Hays State Univ, Kans; Brandes Art Inst, Northridge, Calif; Scottsdale Artists Sch, Ariz. *Comn:* Pico Adobe San Fernando Hist Soc, Calif, 72; Ralph Liebman, Los Angeles, Calif, 82; A J Diani Corp, Santa Maria, Calif, 83. *Exhib:* One person shows, Brand Libr, Glendale Calif, 73, English Gallery, Beverly Hills, Calif, 84 & Americana Gallery Carmel by the Sea, Calif, 85; Women Artists of the American West, Nat, 83-88. *Pos:* Vpres, San Fernando Valley Art Club, Calif, 68-72; dir, Pikes School Workshops, Pacific Grove, Calif, 72-88; consult, Art Video Prod, 83-88. *Teaching:* Instr Fine Arts, Art League Los Angeles, Calif 57-88; instr editing, Los Angeles Valley Col, Calif 61-78; instr fine arts, Art Students League, Northridge, Calif, 78-88, Scottsdale Artists Sch, Ariz, 87- *Awards:* Spec Merit Award, Artists of the Southwest, Southern Calif Arts Coun, 70; Best of Show, Catalina Festival of Arts, Calif, 72; Best of Show, Pasadena Festival of Arts, Calif, 81; Artists Prof League Award for Floral. *Mem:* Woman Artists Am West; Am Inst Fine Arts; Calif Coun Arts; San Gabriel Fine Arts Inc; Calif Art Club. *Media:* Oils. *Res:* Reference art material. *Publ:* Auth & illusr, Painting Floral Still Lifes, Northlight Publ Co, 83; Oil Painting, A Direct Approach, Writer's Digest, 88. *Mailing Add:* 2536 Bay Vista Lane Los Osos CA 93402

PILAVIN, SELMA F
COLLECTOR, PATRON
b Providence, RI, Sept 20, 08. *Pos:* Bd dirs, Mus Art, RI Sch of Design, 68-; trustee, RI Sch of Design, 74- *Awards:* Providence Art Club Medal, Providence Art Club, 71; Hon PhD (fine arts), 79. *Bibliog:* The Albert Pilavin. *Mem:* Providence Art Club. *Interests:* 20th century American. *Collection:* Twentieth Century, Am Art, Vol I, 69, Vol II, 73; article in The Connoisseur, 2/70. *Mailing Add:* 601 Elmgrove Ave Providence RI 02906

PILDES, SARA
PAINTER, COLLAGE ARTIST
b New York, NY. *Study:* Maxwell Sch Teachers, Pratt Inst; Col City of NY, with Doris Cross, BS, 53; Brooklyn Mus with Harold Baumbach. *Work:* Doane Col Mus, Crete, Nebr. *Exhib:* Stuhr Mus, Grand Island, Nebr; Governor's Mansion, Lincoln, Nebr; Raymond Duncan Gallery, Paris, France; Galerie Int, New York; Loeb Ctr, NY Univ; and others. *Pos:* treas, Metrop Painters & Sculptors, 82- *Mem:* Nat Asn Women Artists; Artists Equity; Metrop Painters & Sculptors; Burr Artists. *Media:* Acrylic. *Mailing Add:* Logan Square E Two Franklin Town Blvd Philadelphia PA 19103

PILE, JAMES
PAINTER
b Pueblo, Colo, Nov 7, 43. *Study:* Univ Nebr, BFA, 65, MFA(Woods Fel), 71; Univ Sonora, Mex, hon dipl, 72. *Work:* Int Bus Machines, Tucson; Sioux City Art Ctr, Iowa; Krasdale Foods Inc, Bronx, NY; Kalicow Corp, New York; West Publ Co, St Paul, Minn. *Exhib:* Solo exhib, P M & Stein Gallery, 82 & Bernice Steinbaum Gallery, 84, 86 & 89, New York; Time Out-Sports & Leisure in America, Tampa Mus, Fla, 83; Cowboys & Indians-Common Ground, Boca Raton Mus & Lock Haven Art Ctr, Orlando, Fla, 85; The City Observed-Point of View, Bronx Mus Arts, NY, 86; Annual Hassam & Speicher Purchase Exhib, Am Acad Arts & Lett, New York, 87 & 88; West Art & the Law, St Paul, Minn, 88 & 89. *Teaching:* Prof painting & drawing, Ariz State Univ, Tempe, 71- *Awards:* Visual Artists Fel, Nat Endowment Arts, 87. *Bibliog:* Peter Schwepker (auth), Summer's scattered rewards, Artspeak, Vol III, No 25, 6/24/82; Donald Locke (auth), Jim Pile: New icons for the southwest, Artspace, spring 82; Renee Phillips (auth), James Pile at Bernice Steinbaum, Manhattan Arts & Entertainment, 84. *Media:* Acrylic. *Mailing Add:* 954 W 16th St Tempe AZ 85281

PILGRIM, DIANNE HAUSERMAN
MUSEUM DIRECTOR, HISTORIAN
b Cleveland, Ohio, July 8, 41. *Study:* Pa State Univ, University Park, BA(art hist), 63; New York Univ, Inst Fine Arts, MA, 65; City Univ New York Grad Ctr, 71. *Collections Arranged:* American Impressionist and Realist Paintings and Drawings from the Collection of Mr & Mrs Raymond J Horowitz (auth, catalog), Metrop Mus Art, New York, 73; American Renaissance 1876-1917 (auth, catalog), traveling, Brooklyn Mus, Nat Collection Fine Arts, DC, Fine Arts Mus San Francisco, Denver Art Mus, 79-80; Renovation of 21 Period Rooms at the Brooklyn Mus, 80-84; The Machine in America 1918-1941 (auth, catalog), Brooklyn Mus, Mus Art Carnegie Inst, Pittsburgh, Los Angeles County Art Mus & High Mus, Atlanta. *Pos:* Asst to dir, Pyramid Galleries, Ltd, DC, 69-71; researcher, Metrop Mus Art, New York, spring, 71 & res consult, 72-73; asst to dir, Finch Col Mus Art, New York, summer, 71; chmn, Decorative Arts, Brooklyn Mus, 73-88; dir, Cooper-Hewitt Mus, 88- *Teaching:* Adj asst prof museological problems: the period rooms, Columbia Univ Sch Archit & Planning, 76-78. *Awards:* Chester Dale Fel, Metrop Mus Art, 66-68; Alumni Achievement Award, Pa State Univ, 90. *Mem:* Decorative Arts Soc; Soc Archit Hist; Friends of Clermont; Victorian Soc in Am. *Res:* American 19th and 20th century decorative arts and paintings. *Publ:* Auth, Alexander Roux, his plain and artistic furniture, 2/68 & Reopening of the period rooms at the Brooklyn Museum, 10/84, Antiques; Inherited from the past: the American period room, 5/78 & The revival of pastels in nineteenth century America: the Society of Painters in Pastel, 10/78, Am Art J; Eighteenth century American interiors, Apollo, 4/82; The American Renaissance 1876-1914, 79 & The Machine Age in America 1918-1941, 85, Brooklyn Mus, New York. *Mailing Add:* Cooper-Hewitt Mus 2 E 91st St New York NY 10128

PILGRIM, JAMES F
CURATOR, ADMINISTRATOR
b Richmond, Ind, Feb 19, 41. *Collections Arranged:* American Impressionist Paintings, Corcoran Gallery, 68; John Storrs Retrospective, 69; Robert Morris (coauth, catalog), 69; Alexander Liberman (coauth, catalog), 70; The Vincent Melzac Collection, 70; Paintings from the Metrop, 71. *Pos:* Cur Am art, Corcoran Gallery Art, 68-70, chief cur, 70-71; assoc cur Am painting, Metrop

Mus Art, 71, asst cur-in-chief, 71-74, coordr mus art exhibs, 73-, deputy vdir curatorial affairs, 74-79, deputy dir, 79- *Teaching:* Asst prof mus studies, George Washington Univ, 70-71. *Awards:* Ford Found Fel Mus Training, NY Univ, 64-66; Clawson Mills Fel, Metrop Mus Art, 67-68. *Mem:* Am Inst Conserv; Col Art Asn; Am Asn Mus; Int Coun Mus. *Res:* Late 19th & 20th century art. *Publ:* Contribr, J William Middendorf Collection (catalog), 67; auth, Recent Paintings of Leon Berkowitz, 68; auth, H Marc Moyens Collection (catalog), 70. *Mailing Add:* 501 Overhill Rd Baltimore MD 21210

PILLSBURY, EDMUND P
MUSEUM DIRECTOR
b San Francisco, Calif, Apr 28, 43. *Study:* Yale Univ, BA(hist art), 65; Univ London, Courtauld Inst Art, MA, 67, PhD, 73. *Collections Arranged:* Florence and the Arts: Five Centuries of Patronage, Cleveland Mus Art, 71; Sixteenth-Century Italian Drawings: Form and Function, Yale Univ Art Gallery, 74; The Graphic Work of Federico Barocci: Selected Drawings and Prints, Yale Univ Gallery & Cleveland Mus Art, 78. *Pos:* Cur of Europ Art, 72-76 & asst dir, 75-76, Yale Univ Art Gallery; dir, Yale Ctr Brit Art, Yale Univ; dir, Kimbell Art Mus; vpres, Kimball Art Found, 80- *Teaching:* Lectr art hist, Yale Univ, 72-76, adj prof, 76-80. *Awards:* Travel Grant Mus Prof, Nat Endowment Arts, 74; Morse Fel, Yale Univ, 75; Decorated Chevalier dans l'Ordre des Arts et des Lettres, 85; and others. *Mem:* Burlington Mag Found (trustee, 87-); Master Drawings Asn, NY (bd dirs, 87-); Yale Univ Art Gallery (bd govs, 90-). *Publ:* Contribr, The Cabinet Paintings of Jacopo Zucchi: Their Meaning and Function; Monuments et Mémoires: Foundation Eugéne Piot, LXIII, 80; auth, The rebirth of Venus: Titian and Picasso, Art News, 4/83; Chuck Close and the art of anti-portraiture, Perspectives, Vol 3, No 11, Contemp Art Mus, Houston, Tex, 85; Paul Mellon as Collector and Patron of British Art, Selected Acquisitions 1976-1980, In Honor of Paul Mellon, Collector and Benefactor: Essays, John Wilmerding (ed), Wash Nat Gallery Art, 86; foreword, In Pursuit of Quality, The Kimbell Art Museum, An Illustrated History of the Art and Architecture, 87. *Mailing Add:* Kimbell Art Mus 3333 Camp Bowie Blvd Ft Worth TX 76107

PIMENTEL, DAVID DELBERT
GOLDSMITH, EDUCATOR
b Plymouth, Mass, June 29, 43. *Study:* Mass Col Art, BS(art educ), 65; Sch Am Craftsmen, Rochester Inst Technol, MFA, 72. *Comn:* Three holloware pieces, Hawaii State Found Cult & Arts, Honolulu, 72; Mace (pres chain off), Ariz State Univ, 81. *Exhib:* The Goldsmiths '74, Renwick Gallery, Smithsonian Inst, DC, 74; Contemp Crafts Americas, Colo State Univ, Ft Collins, 75; The Metalsmith, Phoenix Art Mus, 77; Soc NAm Goldsmiths, Minn Mus Art, St Paul, 79-80; Europ Exhib, Schmuck Mus, Pforzheim, Ger & others; Viewpoint '80 Art in Craft Media, Mus Tex Tech Univ, Lubbock, 80. *Teaching:* Asst prof jewelry metalworking, Ariz State Univ, 73- *Awards:* Cash Award, Scottsdale Ctr Arts, 76; Pat Mutterer Award, Tucson Mus Art, 77. *Mem:* Soc NAm Goldsmiths; Am Crafts Coun; World Crafts Coun. *Media:* Jewelry, Metal. *Mailing Add:* Dept Art Ariz State Univ Tempe AZ 85287

PINARDI, ENRICO VITTORIO
SCULPTOR, PAINTER
b Cambridge, Mass, Feb 11, 34. *Study:* Apprentice with Pelligrini & Cascieri, five yrs; Boston Archit Ctr; Sch Mus Fine Arts, Boston; Mass Col Art, BS(educ); RI Sch Design, MFA. *Work:* Worcester Art Mus, De Cordova Mus, Lincoln & Boston Inst Contemp Art, Mass; Chase Manhattan Bank, New York. *Exhib:* New England Art Part IV Sculpture, 64 & Surrealism, 70, De Cordova Mus; 21 Sculptors & Painters, Boston Univ, 64; New England Art Today, Northeastern Univ, 65; 10 Sculptors, Nashua, NH, 68. *Teaching:* Instr sculpture, Worcester Art Mus Sch, 63-67; prof RI Col, 78. *Media:* Wood. *Dealer:* Pucker Safrai Gallery 171 Newbury Boston MA 02116; Vorpal Gallery 465 W Broadway New York NY 10012. *Mailing Add:* Dept Art Rhode Island Col 600 Mt Pleasant Providence RI 02908

PINCHBECK, PETER G
PAINTER
b London, Eng, Dec 9, 40; US citizen. *Study:* Twickenham Col Art, Eng, 57-58; Polytechnic Art Sch, London, Eng, 58-59. *Work:* Corcoran Mus, Washington, DC; Mutual Benefit Insurance Co, Newark, NJ. *Exhib:* Primary Structures, Jewish Mus, New York, 66; American Painting: The Eighties, Grey Art Gallery, New York, Contemp Arts Mus, Houston, Am Cult Ctr, Paris & touring Europe & Japan, 80-; Painting Up Front, Johnson Mus, Cornell Univ, Ithaca, NY, 81; solo exhibs, June Kelly Gallery, New York, 87 & 89. *Teaching:* Instr, Manhattan Community Col, 68- *Awards:* Nat Endowment Arts Fel, 81; Albee Found, 80-82; Gottlieb Found, 92. *Bibliog:* Anita Feldman (auth), Space and subjectivity, Art Forum Mag, 79; Claudia Rowe (auth), Mass of field, Cover Mag, 89. *Mem:* Artists Equity Asn. *Media:* Oil. *Publ:* Auth, Structures of reality in word and image, Arts Mag, 72; Believing is seeing, Artextreme, summer, 82. *Mailing Add:* 69 Greene St New York NY 10012

PINCKNEY, STANLEY
PAINTER, TAPESTRY ARTIST
b Boston, Mass, Sept 30, 40. *Study:* Famous Artist Sch, Westport, Conn, 57-61; Mus Sch Fine Arts, Boston, Mass, 67. *Work:* Nat Ctr African-Am Art, Roxbury, Mass; Mus Dynamique, Dakar, Senegal, W Africa; Palace de l'Pres, Dakar. *Comn:* tapestry, Mus Sch Fine Arts, Boston, 75. *Exhib:* A Century of the Mus Sch, Boston Mus Fine Arts, 77;; African-Am Master Artists-in-Residency Prog Exhib, Dodge Libr Gallery, Northwestern Univ, 78 & Univ Lowell, 79; Recent Tapestries, Mus Sch Fine Arts Gallery & Boston Mus Fine Arts, 78; Resist-Dyed Tapestries, Stanley McCormick Gallery, Boston Archit Ctr, 79; Traveling Scholarship Exhib, Mus Fine Arts, Boston, 81; Object of the Month, Mus Fine Arts, Boston, 84; Art in Craft Media, Newton Arts Ctr, Newtonville, Mass, 88; and others. *Collections Arranged:* Twelve Black Artists, Rose Art Mus, Brandeis Univ, 69; Osubamba (auth, catalog), Boston Ctr for the Arts, 76 & Cyclorama Gallery, Boston, 76; A Century of the Museum School (auth, catalog), Boston Mus Fine Arts, 77. *Teaching:* Instr African & traditional arts, Mus Sch Fine Art, Boston, 72- *Awards:* 19th Albert H Whitin Fel, Boston Mus Fine Arts, 69; Ford Found Fac Enrichment-Artist Grant, Mus Sch Fine Art, 78; Blance E Colman Fel, 78; Mellon Found, Fac Enrichment Grant, Mus Sch Fine Arts, 87; and others. *Media:* Watercolor. *Publ:* Beyond Tradition (exhib catalogue), New England Fiber Collective, 83; auth, article, Am Crafts Mag, 86. *Mailing Add:* Dept African Arts 230 Fenway Boston MA 02115

PINCUS, DAVID N
COLLECTOR
b Philadelphia, Pa. *Pos:* Trustee, Philadelphia Mus Art, 74-, Fairmount Park Art Asn, 76- & Pa Acad Fine Arts, 79- *Collection:* Contemporary sculpture; New York school of abstract expressionists; major contemporary European artists. *Mailing Add:* 1319 Remington Rd Wynnewood PA 19096

PINCUS, LAURIE JANE
PAINTER, SCULPTOR
b New York, NY, Dec 14, 51. *Study:* Bard Col, with Murray Reich, Matt Phillips; Sarah Lawrence Col, with Richard Povsette-Darte, BA, 75. *Work:* Los Angeles Co Mus Art; Univ Calif Los Angeles; LA Foret Mus. *Comn:* Tom & Betty (sculpture), Takashimaya Dept Store, Osaka, Japan, 85-90; spec art proj, Fuji Television, Tokyo, Japan, 90, Hollywood Roosevelt Hotel, Hollywood, Calif. *Exhib:* Calif Contemp Artists, Laguna Art Mus, Calif, 87; Guest Artist, Orange Co Ctr Continuing Art, Santa Ana, Calif, 89; 10 Year Survey Show, LaBand Art Gallery, Loyola Marymount Univ, Los Angeles, 89; America Pop Culture Today III, LA Foret Mus, Tokyo, Japan, 89; External Fantasies, Internal Realities, Security Pac Corp, Gallery at Plaza, Los Angeles, 91; and others. *Bibliog:* Marva Marrow (auth), Inside The LA Artist, Penegrine Smith Books, 88; Betty Brown (auth), Exposures: Women & Their Art, New Sage Press, 89; Kei Nagashima (auth), America Pop Culture Today, Vol 3, Seibundo Shinkosha, 90. *Mem:* Westside Arts Ctr, Santa Monica (bd dirs, currently); Friends Jr Arts Ctr, Los Angeles (bd dirs & Joanna Cotsen fel comt); Artists Equity. *Media:* Paper, Canvas; Wood. *Dealer:* Jan Baum Gallery 170 S La Brea Los Angeles CA. *Mailing Add:* 1118 Chautauqua Pacific Palisades CA 90272

PINCUS, ROBERT L(AWRENCE)
CRITIC, HISTORIAN
b Bridgeport, Conn, June 5, 53. *Study:* Univ Calif, Irvine, BA, 76; Univ Southern Calif, MA, 80, PhD, 87. *Pos:* Contrib reviewer, Artweek, 79; art critic, Los Angeles Times, 81-85, San Diego Union-Tribune, 85-; corresp ed, Art in Am, 87- *Teaching:* Instr writing & Am studies, Univ Southern Calif, 79-83; vis prof art hist, San Diego State Univ, 85 & 92. *Awards:* Ring of Truth Prizes, Best Art Story, 86, 87 & 88; San Diego Press Club Award for Criticism, 91. *Mem:* Mod Language Asn; Col Art Asn; Int Asn Art Critics, Am Sect. *Res:* 20th century American art history with emphasis on west coast. *Publ:* Auth, On a Scale that Competes with the world: The Assemblages of Edward Kienholz & Nancy Reddin Kienholz, Univ Calif Press, 81. *Mailing Add:* San Diego Union-Tribune P O Box 191 San Diego CA 92112

PINCUS-WITTEN, ROBERT A
EDUCATOR, WRITER
b New York, NY, Apr 5, 35. *Study:* Cooper Union, Emil Schweinburg Grant, 56; Univ Chicago, MA(dept fel), 60, PhD(dept fel), 68; Univ Paris, Sorbonne, exchange fel, 63-64. *Pos:* Assoc ed, Arts Mag, 63-90; ed, Artforum Mag, 66-76; dir, Gagosian Gallery, New York, 90- *Teaching:* Prof art hist, Queens Col & Grad Ctr, City Univ New York, currently. *Res:* Symbolism; the history of contemporary art and photography. *Publ:* Auth, Occult Symbolism in France, Josephin Peladan and the Salons de la Rose-Croix, Garland Press, 76; Post-Minimalism, Art of the Decade, 77 & Entries (Maximalism), Art at the Turn of the Decade, 83, Out of London Press; Eye Contact, Twenty Years of Art Criticism, UMI Res Press, 84; and others. *Mailing Add:* c/o Gagosian Gallery 980 Madison Ave New York NY 10021

PINDELL, HOWARDENA DOREEN
PAINTER, EDUCATOR
b Philadelphia, Pa, Apr 14, 43. *Study:* Boston Univ Sch Fine & Applied Arts, BFA, 65; Cumminton Sch Arts, 63; Sch Art & Archit, Yale Univ, MFA, 67. *Work:* Mus Contemp Art, Chicago; Fogg Art Mus, Harvard Univ; Whitney Mus Am Art, Mus Mod Art, Metrop Mus Art, New York; Philadelphia Mus of Art; Chase Manhattan Bank, New York & Tokyo. *Comn:* Comn by IBM, 85; comn by GSA, 87; Metrop Mus Art, 91; Lehman Col, Bronx, NY, 93. *Exhib:* One-woman shows, Grove Gallery, SUNY, Albany, NY, 91, David Heath Gallery, Atlanta, Ga, 91, George N'Namdi Gallery, Birmingham, Mich, 91, Traveling exhib, Roland Gibson Gallery, SUNY, Potsdam, NY, Bevier Gallery, Rochester Inst Technol, Rose Art Mus, Brandeis Univ, Kenkeleba House Gallery, New York, Alternative Mus, New York, SUNY at New Platz, Hillwood Art Gallery, C W Post, Davison Art Gallery, Wesleyan Univ, Picker Art Gallery, Collgate Univ, fall 92-95; New Am Graphic Art, Fogg Art Mus, Cambridge, Mass, 73; Painting & Sculpture Today, Indianapolis Mus, Ind & Taft Mus, Cincinnati, 74; Five Americans in Paris, Gerald Piltzer Gallery, Paris, 75; 9th Paris Biennale, Mus Mod Art, Paris, 75; H Pindell: Video Drawings, Sonja Heine Onstad Found, Oslo, Norway, 76; Vassar Col Art Gallery, 77; Birmingham Mus, Ala, 85; Grand Rapids Art Mus, Mich, 86; Wadsworth Athenium, Hartford, Conn, 89; 43

Ann Acad Purchase Exhib, Am Acad, NY, 91; African Am Artists, Philadelphia Mus, 92; Twentieth Year Representative Invitational Show, Rutgers Univ, Univ Wis, Milwaukee, 92; This Sporting Life, 1878-1991, High Mus Art, Atlanta, Ga, 92. *Collections Arranged:* Pop Art Prints, Drawings and Multiples, 70, California Prints, 72 & tour, 73, Projects: Chuck Close and Liliana Porter, 73, Published in Germany (co-dir), 74, Printed, Cut, Folded and Torn, 74, Felix Vallotton (co-dir), 74, Points of View, 75, Projects: John Walker, 75, Projects: Mary Miss and Charles Simonds, 76, Narrative Prints, 76 & Abstraction-Creation, 77, Mus Mod Art, New York; The War Show, Ann McCoy, 83; Michael Singer: Ritual Series, Retellings, 87; Poetic Liscence, 90. *Pos:* Exhib asst, Mus Mod Art, New York, 67-69, cur asst, 69-71 & asst cur, prints & illus books, 71-77, assoc cur, 77-79. *Teaching:* Assoc prof, State Univ NY, Stony Brook, 79-84, prof, 84- *Awards:* Painting Award, Nat Endowment for Arts, 72-73 & 83-84; Distinguished Alumni Award, Boston Univ, 83; Guggenheim, 87-88; Col Art Asn Award for Distinguished Body of Work, 90. *Bibliog:* Nancy Heller (auth), Women Artists, An Illustrated History, Ableville Press, New York, 91; Clarence White (auth), Howardena Pindell, Art Papers, 7-8/91; Charles Hagen (auth), Who's on first?, NY Times, 8/2/91. *Mem:* Col Art Asn; Int Art Critics Asn. *Media:* Acrylic on Canvas. *Res:* Twentieth century prints. *Publ:* Auth, Mary Quinn Sullivan, Notable American Women, Harvard Univ, 72; California Prints, Arts Mag, New York, 5/72; Ed Ruscha: Words, Print Collectors Newsletter, 1/73; Robert Rauschenberg: Link, Mus Mod Art, 10/75; Alan Shields: Tales of Brave Ulysses, 1/75 & Artists' Periodicals: Alternative Space, 9/77, Print Collector's Newsletter; Convenant of Silence: Defacto Censorship, 10/90 & 11/90; New Art Examiner, 3rd text, 9/90. *Mailing Add:* Dept Art State Univ NY Stony Brook NY 11794-5400

PINEDA, MARIANNA
SCULPTOR
b Evanston, Ill, May 10, 25. *Study:* Cranbrook Acad with Carl Milles, Mich, 42; Univ Calif, Berkeley, with Raymond Puccinelli, 43-45; Columbia Univ, New York with Oronzio Maldarelli, 45-46; Ossip Zadkine Sch Sculpture, Paris, France, 49-50. *Work:* Walker Art Ctr, Minneapolis, Minn; Wadsworth Atheneum, Hartford, Conn; Ratcliffe Col, Cambridge, Mass; Dartmouth Col, NH; Muscarelle Mus Art, Williamsburg, Va; and others. *Comn:* Bronze medallion, Jan Veen Dance Libr, Boston Conservatory Music, 65; bronze relief, Newton Col Sacred Heart, class of 74, Mass, 75; Twirling (bronze figures), Boston Redevelop Authority, 76; Queen Lili'uokalani (bronze), State Hawaii, Honolulu, 82. *Exhib:* American Sculpture, Metrop Mus Art, New York, 51; one-man shows, Walker Art Ctr, Alpha Gallery, Boston, 72, Twenty years of Sculpture, Newtown Col, Mass, 72, Search for the Queen, Contemp Arts Ctr, Honolulu, 82, Sculpture and Drawings, Pine Manor Col, Chestnut Hill, Mass, 84, The Eve Celebrant Series, Judi Rosenberg Gallery, Boston, 90 & Four Decades of Drawing, Andrews Gallery, Col William & Mary, Va, 92; Sculpture Biennials, Whitney Mus Am Art, New York, 53, 55, 57 & 59; Recent Sculpture, Mus Mod Art, New York, 59-60; 64th Exhib, Art Inst Chicago, 61; Silver Anniversary of the State Foundation on Culture and the Arts Collection, Contemp Mus, Honolulu, 90; Ann & Juried Exhib, Nat Acad Design, New York, 92; Int Sculpture Convention, Sculptors Guild, Philadelphia, 92; Juried Exhib, Nat Sculpture Soc, New York, 92; and others. *Pos:* Ed bd, Sculpture Rev, Nat Sculpture Soc,New York. *Teaching:* Instr sculpture, Newton Col Sacred Heart, 72-86; adj prof, Boston Univ, Mass, 74-78, 82-84 & 89-92; instr, Boston Col, Mass, 76-77; Sch Mus Fine Arts, Boston, 91. *Awards:* Fel, Am Acad Design, New York, 86; Lampston Prize, 86, Gold Medal, 89 & Taillex Award, 91, Nat Sculpture Soc, New York; Gold Medal, 87 & Artists Award, 88, Nat Acad Design, New York; and others. *Bibliog:* American Women Sculptors, G K Hall, Boston, 90. *Mem:* Sculptors Guild New York; Boston Visual Artists Union; Artists Equity; Nat Acad Design; Int Sculpture Ctr; and others. *Media:* All. *Mailing Add:* 380 Marlborough St Boston MA 02115

PINKEL, SHEILA MAE
PHOTOGRAPHER, SCULPTOR
b Newport News, Va, Aug 21, 41. *Study:* Univ Calif, Berkeley, BA, 63, MFA, 77; Univ Calif, Los Angeles, with Robert Heinecken. *Work:* Walker Art Ctr, Minn; Los Angeles Co Mus, Calif; Ctr Creative Photog, Tucson; Mus Mod Art & Int Mus Photog, George Eastman House, New York. *Comn:* Cyanotype mural, Park La Brea Towers, Los Angeles, Calif, 76. *Exhib:* Photo Fusions, Pratt Inst, Brooklyn, NY, 81; G Ray Hawkins Gallery, Calif, 82; The Artist & the Computer, Long Beach Mus, Calif, 83; two-women show, Santa Barbara Mus Art, Calif, 83; Lensless Photography, Franklin Inst, Philadelphia, 83; Thermonuclear Garden Installation, Visual Studies Workshop, NY, 85; Critical Messages, Artemia Gallery, Chicago, Ill, 85; Light from Illumination to Pure Radiance, San Francisco Mus Mod Art, 85; Nuclear Vision, Ariz State Univ, Tempe, 85; Artists & Social Comment, Md Inst, Baltimore, 86; Univ Barcelona Biennial, 88; Borderline: Photography in the 150th Year, Art Space, New Haven, Conn, 89; Missing: El Salvador, Exec Coordinator, Los Angeles Ctr Photo Studies, 90; Smog: A Matter of Life & Breath, Calif Mus Photog, Riverside, 92. *Collections Arranged:* Multicultural Focus (auth, catalog), Cross Cultural Photog Exhib. *Teaching:* Instr photog, Univ Calif Exten, Los Angeles, 76-83, Otis Parsons Art Inst, 81-83, Sch Art Inst Chicago, 83 & Calif Inst Arts, 84-86; assoc prof, Pomona Col, 86; Friends Photo Workshops, 87 & 88. *Awards:* Nat Endowment Arts Emerging Artist Grant, 79 & 82; Sloan Found Grant, 87-88 & 90. *Bibliog:* Sylvia Moore (auth), Yesterday and Tomorrow: Collection Women Artists, Midmarch Press, NY, 89; George M Craven (auth), Object & Image, Prentice-Hall, 89; Robert Hirsh (auth), Photographic Possibilities, Focol Press, 91. *Mem:* Los Angeles Ctr Photog Studies (vpres, 78-83); Soc Photog Educ (nat bd mem, 86-90). *Media:* Black & White, Xeroradiography. *Publ:* Auth, Multicultural Focus, 81 & contribr, Obscura, 82, Los Angeles Ctr Photog; contribr, Afterimage, Visual Studies Workshop, 5/81; contribr, Leonardo, summer 82 & fall 86; contribr, High Performance, spring 87; contribr, Frame/work, fall 87, spring 91; contribr, Heresies, summer 90. *Mailing Add:* 620 Moulton Ave, No 109 Los Angeles CA 90031

PINKERTON, CLAYTON (DAVID)
PAINTER
b San Francisco, Calif, Mar 6, 31. *Study:* Calif Col Arts & Crafts, BAEd & MFA; Harwood Found, Univ NMex, Univ Paris. *Work:* De Young Mus & Calif Palace Legion of Honor, San Francisco; Ill Bell Tel, Chicago; Crocker Art Mus, Sacramento; MacDonald Corp, Calif; also numerous pvt collections. *Exhib:* Recent Paintings USA: The Figure, Mus Mod Art, New York, 63; one-man shows, Esther Robles Gallery, Los Angeles, 68, Arleigh Gallery, San Francisco, 70, Cent Calif Biennial, Pac Grove Art Ctr, 83, Univ Pac, 88, Calif State Univ, Chico, 88 Himovitz-Salomon Gallery, Sacramento, 91 & 93 & Am Cult Ctr, Brussels, 91; Contemp Am Painting & Sculpture, Univ Ill, 67 & 69; Three Centuries of American Painting, Calif Palace Legion of Honor, 71; Whitney Mus Art, 71; Monterey Peninsula Mus Art, 88; 500 Years Since Colombus, Triton Mus, San Jose, 92; and others. *Teaching:* Prof fine arts, Calif Col Arts & Crafts, 58- *Awards:* Fulbright Scholar, 57-58; James Phelan Award, 57 & 61; San Francisco Art Asn Award in Painting, De Young Mus, 60. *Bibliog:* Joan Mondale (auth), Politics in art, Lerner, 77; NY Art Rev, 88 & Calif Art Rev, Am References. *Media:* Acrylic, Oil. *Dealer:* Michael Himovitz Gallery 1020 Tenth St Sacramento CA. *Mailing Add:* PO Box 77 Amador City CA 95601

PINKNEY, HELEN LOUISE
CURATOR, LIBRARIAN
b Decatur, Ill. *Study:* Dayton Art Inst Sch, grad. *Collections Arranged:* The Camera, the Paper and I, Collection of Photographs by Jane Reece, 52; The Wonderful World of Photography, Jane Reece Mem Exhib, 63; Oriental & Europe Textiles Exhib, 72; Am Indian Textiles & Baskets, 73; Hidden Treasures: Textiles from the Dayton Art Institute Collection, 83; Webster-Titsch Collection of Quilts and Coverlets, 88; Fire-Water-Earth & Air: Navajo Blankets, Collection of Dayton Art Inst, 90 & 92; Chinese Silk Shawls and Their Forerunners, 91. *Pos:* Registr of collections, Dayton Art Inst, 36-45, cur, 45-59, librn, 45-86, assoc cur textiles, 59-, librn emer, 86-, cur textiles, 86- *Awards:* Pres Award, Ohio Mus Asn, 84; Ohio Arts Coun Award, 85; Helen Pinkney Libr Endowment Fund for 50 yrs DAI Librn, 86. *Mem:* Art Libr Soc/NAm; Am Asn Mus; Spec Libr Asn, Mus Div. *Res:* Jane Reece Photographic Collection; textiles; bibliographies. *Publ:* Auth, articles and catalogues on Jane Reece Collection in Dayton Art Inst Bulletin, 52 & 63. *Mailing Add:* 37 Stoddard Ave Dayton OH 45405

PINKNEY, JERRY
ILLUSTRATOR
b Philadelphia, Pa, Dec 22, 39. *Study:* Philadelphia Mus Col Art, 58-60. *Work:* Mus Am Illus, New York; H C Taylor Art Gallery, NC A & T State Univ; Miami-Dade Pub Libr; Afro-Am Hist & Cult Mus, Philadelphia; Air & Space Mus, Washington, DC. *Comn:* 10 US Postal Stamps, US Postal Serv, Washington, DC, 77-86; limited edition poster, Negro Ensemble, New York, 82; limited edition books, Franklin Libr, New York; NASA Art Team (painting), NASA, 82; Cover & interior illus, Nat Geog Mag, Washington, DC, 84. *Exhib:* Through American Eyes; Moscow Int Bk Fair, USSR, 89; Biennale Illustrations, Bratislave, Chechoslovakia, 89; Soc Illustrators, 86-90; solo exhibs, Schomburg Ctr for Res, New York, 90. *Pos:* Mem, comts at US Postal Serv, Washington, DC, 82- *Teaching:* Vis critic illus, RI Sch Design, 69-70, adj prof, 70-71; assoc prof illus, Pratt Inst, Brooklyn, NY, 86-; Distinguished vis prof, Univ Del, Newark, 86-87, assoc prof, 88- *Awards:* Randolph Caldecott Medal of Hon (bk), Mirandy and Brother Wind, 89; Coretta Scott King Award (bk), Mirandy and Brother Wind, 89; Award, Libr of Congress Books for Children (bk), More Tales of Uncle Remus, 89; award, The Year's Best Illustrated Book for Children, New York Times, 89; award, The Year's Twelve Outstanding Works for Children, Time Mag, 89; First Place, New York Bk Show; Randolph Caldecott Medal of Hon (bk), The Talking Eggs. *Bibliog:* Donald Stermer (auth), Jerry Pinkney, Communication Art Mag, 5-6/75; Nick Meglin (auth), The strength of weakness, Am Artist Mag, 1/82; Jerry Pinkney, Idea Mag, Japan, 82. *Mem:* Soc Illusrs. *Media:* Watercolor. *Publ:* Illusr, The Tales of Uncle Remus, 88; More Tales of Uncle Remus, 89; Home Place, MacMillan, 90; Further Tales of Uncle Remus, 90; Pretend You're Cat, 90. *Mailing Add:* 41 Furnace Dock Rd Croton-on-Hudson NY 10520

PINSKER, ESSIE
SCULPTOR
b New York. *Study:* Brooklyn Col, BA; Art Students League, New York Univ (with Vincent Glinsky); Mus Mod Art; New Sch Soc Res (with Leo Manso); Cambridge Univ, Eng; Oxford Univ, Eng. *Work:* Aldrich Mus Contemp Art, Ridgefield, Conn; Nat Portrait Gallery, Washington, DC; Everson Mus Art, Syracuse, NY; Vassar Mus, Poughkeepsie, NY; Okla Art Ctr, Oklahoma City; Minn Mus Art, St Paul, Minn; and others. *Comn:* marble sculpture, Marriott Hotels, USA, 88; bronze sculpture, Granard Comm Ltd, 89; steel sculpture, Tauck Tours, Westport, Conn, 90; Queensboro Steel, Wilmington, NC; Jos P Day Realty, New York, NY. *Exhib:* N Shore Arts Ctr, Manhasset, NY, 80; Lever Bros, New York, 81; Lincoln Ctr Fordham Univ, New York, 81; Pace Univ, New York, 81; Eureka Col, Eureka, Ill, 81; Mus Arts & Sci, Daytona Beach, 87; Konstmasson Int Art Fair, Stockholm, Sweden, 88; Arco Int Art Fair, Madrid, Spain, 88; Rutgers Art Collection, Camden, NJ, 88; Mus Mod Art, Warsaw, Poland, 89. *Awards:* Sculpture Award, Knickerbocker Artists 24th Ann Exhib, 74; Sculpture Award, Metrop Life Ann Exhib. *Bibliog:* Palmer Poroner (auth), Sculpture in stone and steel, Artspeak, 81; David J

Shapiro (auth), The Art of Essie Pinsker, brochure for Vorpal Show, 87; Joseph Merkel (auth), Essie Pinsker poses a Gordian knot, Artspeak, 87. *Mem:* Artists Equity, New York. *Media:* Stone, Bronze. *Mailing Add:* Eight Peter Cooper Rd New York NY 10010

PINTO, ANGELO RAPHAEL
PAINTER, PRINTMAKER
b Casal Velino, Italy, Sept 27, 08; US citizen. *Study:* Pa Mus & Sch Indust Arts, Philadelphia; Barnes Found, Merion, Pa, Europ Study Scholar, 31-33. *Work:* Pa Acad Fine Arts, Philadelphia; Metrop Mus Art, New York; Libr Cong, Washington, DC; Boston Pub Libr; Chrysler Mus, Norfolk, Va; and others. *Comn:* Ballets & costumes, Philadelphia Ballet Co, 37. *Exhib:* One-man shows, Bignou Gallery, Paris, France, 33, Valentine Gallery, New York, 34, Mellon Galleries, Philadelphia, 35, Makler Gallery, Philadelphia, 60, Medici II Gallery, Miami, Fla, 70 & 74 & Marion Locks Gallery, Philadelphia, 83; and others. *Teaching:* Fac mem, Barnes Found, 35- *Awards:* First Prize American Painters, Four Arts Club, Palm Beach, 38; Silver Medal, Da Vinci Alliance, Philadelphia, 40. *Bibliog:* Helen McCloy (auth), Art of Pinto Brothers, Parnassus, 35; Mildred Lee-Ward (auth), Reverse Paintings on Glass, Spencer Mus Art; Violette De Mazia (auth), Barnes Foundation Journal. *Mem:* Art Alliance, Philadelphia; United Scenic Artists, New York. *Dealer:* Marion Locks Gallery Philadelphia PA; Child Gallery New York NY. *Mailing Add:* 28 W 69th St New York NY 10023

PINTO, JODY
ENVIRONMENTAL ARTIST, SCULPTOR
b New York, NY, Apr 8, 42. *Study:* Pa Acad Fine Arts, Cresson fel, 67, 68; Philadelphia Col Art, BFA, 73. *Work:* Philadelphia Mus Art & Pa Acad Fine Arts, Philadelphia; Newberger Mus, Purchase, NY; Whitney Mus Am Art, New York; Des Moines Art Ctr, Des Moines, Iowa; Guggenheim Mus, New York. *Comn:* Fingerspan Bridge, Fairmont Park, Philadelphia, Pa, 87; East/West Arbor & Gift Gardens, Spokane, Wash, 91; Papago Park/City Boundary and South Ave Streetscape/Patrick Park Plaza, Phoenix, Ariz, 92; and others. *Exhib:* Hal Bromm Gallery, 78-87; 1979 Biennial, Whitney Mus Am Art, New York, 79 & 81; Venice Biennial 1980, Italy; Calif State Univ, North Ridge, 80; Tel-Hai 80 Conference, Israel; Inst Contemp Art, Philadelphia, 84; Roger Ramsay Gallery, Chicago, 84; Landmarks, Bard Col, NY, 84; and many other solo and group exhibitions. *Teaching:* Pa Acad Fine Arts, 78-; RI Sch Design, 80-83. *Awards:* Design Honor Award, Am Soc Landscape Archit, 92; Environ Excellence Award, 92; Fleisher Mem Award, Exellence Arts, 92. *Bibliog:* Grace Glueck (auth), New York Times, 12/24/81; Lucy Lippard (auth), Overlay, Pantheon Bks, 83; Michael Brenson (auth), article, New York Times, 12/15/85; Patricia Phillips (auth), rev, Artforum, 1/86; and others. *Mem:* Women Caucus Art. *Media:* Natural & Industrial Materials. *Publ:* Auth, Excavations and Constructions: Notes for the Body/Land, Marian Locks Gallery, 79. *Mailing Add:* 124 Chambers St New York NY 10007

PINZARRONE, PAUL
PAINTER
b Grand Rapids, Mich, Nov 19, 51. *Study:* Univ Ill, BFA(painting), 73. *Work:* Butler Inst Am Art, Youngstown, Ohio; Ill State Mus, Springfield; Kemper Insurance, St Xavier Col & Union League, Chicago. *Exhib:* New Horizons in Art, Chicago, 75, 76 & 80; 28th Ill Exhib, Springfield, 75; 39th & 40th Midyear Exhibs, Butler Inst, 75 & 76; Mainstreams 75-, Marietta Int, Ohio, 75; one-man shows, Joy Horwich Gallery, Chicago, Ill, 76, 77, 80 & 83, Rockford Arts Coun, 88, Rockford Arts Coun, 89 & Univ Wis, 90. *Teaching:* Instr art, Rock Valley Col, Rockford, Ill, 75-76 & 78, Rockford Col, 76; guest lectr, Univ Miami, 77, Gloria Luria Gallery, Miami, 77, Regent Art Asn, 78, St Xavier Col, Chicago, 80 & Highland Col, 81. *Awards:* First Prize, New Orleans Int, 75; First Prize, Ill State Fair Prof, 75; First Prize, Art Inst Juried, Chicago, 84. *Bibliog:* Article, New Art Examiner, Chicago, 12/80; Carrie Rebora & Laura Cottingham (auths), article in The Chicago Art Review, 81. *Mailing Add:* 103 Paris Ave Rockford IL 61107

PIONK, RICHARD C
PAINTER
b Moose Lake, Minn, Apr 26, 38. *Study:* with Daniel E Greene, 76-77; David A Leffel, 77-78; Art Students League, New York, cert, 83. *Work:* Pastel Soc Gallery & Salmagundi Club, New York. *Comn:* Completed over 35 portrait commissions in the past 10 years. *Exhib:* Pastel Soc Am Exhib, Queens Mus, Flushing, NY, 82, Hermitage Found Mus, Norfolk, Va, 83-85 & Pastels, Monmouth Mus, Lincroft, NJ, 85; Curators Choice of Salmagundi Members, Fordham Gallery, New York, 83; Soc Impressionists Exhib, St Louis Athletic Club Gallery, Mo, 84; The Still Life, Hermitage Found Mus, Norfolk, Va, 85; Commoisseur Gallery, NY, 87, 88, 89, 90, 91 & 92. *Pos:* Exhib chmn & 2nd vpres, Pastel Soc Am, New York, 78-; instr pastel-still life, Pastel Soc Am Studio, Nat Arts Club, New York, 82-; adminr-cur comt, Salmagundi Club, New York, 82-; control bd, Allied Artists Am, New York, 88, treas, 84-86; bd dirs, Artists Fel, New York, 84-; instr pastel-portraiture, Summit Art Ctr, NJ, 84-85; control bd, Art Students League, New York, 84-88. *Teaching:* Art Students League & Pastel Soc Sch, NY. *Awards:* Grumbacher Gold Medal, 84; Henry Gasser Mem Found, 85; Newington Award, Hudson Valley Art Asn, 86; over 100 awards for oils & pastels from all art organizations. *Bibliog:* Artists Mag, Keys to classical still lifes, 4/88; Carole Katchen (auth), Creative Paintings with Pastel, North Light, 91; Carole Katchen (auth), Unlock the Potential of Pastel, Artist's Mag, 6/91. *Mem:* Knickerbocker Artists; Allied Artists; Pastel Soc Am; Audubon Artists; Nat Arts Club. *Media:* Pastel, Oil. *Dealer:* Wind-Borne Gallery Ltd 559 Post Rd Darien CT 06820; Connoisseur Gallery Rhinebeck NY 12572. *Mailing Add:* 1349 Lexington Ave Apt 8B New York NY 10128

PIRKL, JAMES JOSEPH
DESIGNER, EDUCATOR
b Nyack, NY, Dec 27, 30. *Study:* Pratt Inst, cert adv design, 51 & BID, 58; Wayne State Univ; Syracuse Univ; Univ Monterrey, Hon diploma, Mexico, 81. *Pos:* Jr designer, General Motors Design staff, 58-59, designer, 59-60, sr designer, 61-64 & asst chief designer, 64-65; principal, James J Pirkl/Design, Cazenovia, NY, 65- *Teaching:* Instr, Ctr for Creative Studies, Detroit, Mich, 63-65; asst prof indust design, dept of design, Syracuse Univ, 65-68, assoc prof, 69-73, prof, 74-, prof in charge, Indust Design Prog, 79- 85, chmn, dept of design, 85- *Awards:* Fel, Indust Designers Soc Am, 85. *Mem:* Indust Designers Soc Am (chmn cent NY chap, 77-79, vpres, mid-east region, 80-82, dir, 86-88); Human Factors Soc; Am Asn Univ Prof; Nat Asn of Sch of Art & Design. *Publ:* Co-ed, State of the Art and Science of Design, 71; auth, Design is seen entering a new humane stage, Industrial Design, 7-8/78; auth, A focus on form, Indust Designers Am Papers, 7/81; Transgenerational design: an instructional project to prepare designers, Innovation-The jour of the Indust Designers Soc Am, Summer 87; Humane design Accommodation: A future imperative, Design News: Mag for Indust Design, Japan, 88; coauth with Anna Babic, Guidelines and Strategies for designing Transgenerational Products, Copley, 88. *Mailing Add:* Rd 5 Meadow Hill Rd Cazenovia NY 13035

PISANI, JOSEPH
MURALIST, PAINTER
b New Rochelle, NY, Oct l, 38. *Study:* San Francisco Art Inst; Calif Col Arts & Crafts, with George Post, Richard Diebenkorn, Nathan Oliveira & Ralph Borge, BFA. *Work:* Dept of Defense, The Pentagon, Arlington, Va; The White House, Washington, DC, 81; Hq Dept of the Army, Pentagon. *Comn:* Mondavi Tomb, Caesar Mondavi Family, St Helina, Calif, 62; General Marshall Mem Corridor, comn by Secy of the Army, Pentagon, 75; Army Bicentennial Murals, comn by Secy of Defense, 75-76; Gen Pershing mural, comn by Gen Yerks, Ft Myer, Va, 77-78; Gen MacArthur Mem, 81, Anzus Mem Corridor, 82, Military Womens Corridor, 83, Eisenhower Corridor, 85, Military Intelligence Corridor, 86 & Gen Mark Clark Display, 86, comn by Secy of Defense Weinberger, Pentagon, 90, Portrait Comm King Fahd, Saudi Arabia. *Exhib:* Army Wide Art Exhib, Pentagon, 63, 65; Corcoran Washington Area Show, 69; Artist Equity Group Shows, Washington, DC, 72 & 73; Va Beach Art Shows, 73 & 75. *Pos:* Chief graphic arts, Chief of Staff (Personnel), Pentagon, 67-73; graphic designer, Dept of Defense, 73-75; art dir, US Army Hq, 75-88; dir, Art Gallery 101-Ltd. *Awards:* Outstanding Achievement in Art, Bank of Am, 61; Scholar to Study Fine Arts, Scholastic Mag, 62; First Prize for Painting, Art League Va, 70; and many other awards. *Bibliog:* Article, Art Voices/South, 5-6/78. *Mem:* Art League of Va; League of Reston Artist; Art Guild of Woodbridge, Va. *Media:* Mixed; Watercolor. *Publ:* Illusr, Yorktown 1781-1981 Poster, 81; 1980 & 1981 Army Weapon Systems Covers; and others. *Dealer:* Art Gallery 101 10640 Main St Fairfax VA 22030. *Mailing Add:* 2658 Quincy Adams Dr Herndon VA 22071

PISANO, RONALD GEORGE
HISTORIAN, CONSULTANT
b New York, NY, Dec 19, 48. *Study:* Adelphi Univ, Garden City, NY, BA; Univ Del. *Collections Arranged:* An American Place (auth, catalog), 81, The Long Island Landscape, 1865-1914: The Halycon Years (auth, catalog), 81 & The Long Island Landscape, 1914-1946: The Transitional Years (auth, catalog), 82, Parrish Art Mus, Southampton, NY; American Paintings from the Parrish Museum, (auth, catalog), Coe-Kerr Gallery, New York, 82; A Leading Spirit in American Art: William Merritt Chase, 1849-1916, Henry Art Gallery & Metrop Mus Art (auth, book), 83-84; Heckscher Mus, 87; The Art Students League Traveling Exhib: Selections from the Permanent Collection (auth, catalog), Nassau Co Mus of Fine Arts, 88; Centenial Celebration Nat Asn Women Artists (auth cat). *Pos:* Dir exhib, Baruch Col, New York, 74-76; consult cur of Am art, Heckscher Mus, Huntington, NY, 75-77; guest cur, Mus of Stony Brook, NY, 77, 78, 85 & 90; assoc cur, Parrish Art Mus, Southampton, NY, 77-79, dir, 79-81, pvt art consult, 81- *Awards:* A Conger Goodyear Award, Adelphi Univ, 71; Stebbins Family Res Grant, Heckscher Mus, 72-73; Distinguished Art Historian Award, Grand Cent Art Gallery, 79. *Mem:* Col Art Asn. *Res:* Late 19th and early 20th century American art; William Merritt Chase; artists of Long Island. *Publ:* Auth, Catalog of the Heckscher Museum, Part I: American Art, Heckscher Mus, 78; William Merritt Chase, Watson Guptill, 79; Long Island Landscape Painting, 1820-1920, Little Brown, 85; Idle Hours: Americans at Leisure, 1865-1914, Little Brown, 89;; Long Island Landscape Painting in the 20th Century, Little Brown, 90. *Mailing Add:* 375 Riverside Dr New York NY 10025

PISKOTI, JAMES
PRINTMAKER, PAINTER
b Logan, WVa, July 5, 44. *Study:* Univ Mich, Ann Arbor, BS(design), 67; Yale Univ, MFA, 69. *Work:* Detroit Inst Arts; Bradley Univ; City of Stockton, Calif; Minot State Col. *Exhib:* San Francisco Art Inst Centennial Exhib, San Francisco Mus Art, 71; 10-5 from California, Thomas Ctr Gallery, Gainesville, Fla & Contemp Art Ctr Gallery, Univ City, MO, 87; California Works, Calif State Fair, Sacramento, Calif, 77, 79, 80, 81, 83 & 87; Crocker Kingsley Exhibs of Northern Calif Art, Crocker Mus, Sacramento, 76, 77, 80, 84, 87 & 88; Western Regional Printmaking Exhib, Tarbox Gallery, San Diego, Calif, 5/90-6/90. *Teaching:* Lab asst Intaglio Printmaking Studio, Univ Mich, 65-67; teaching asst printmaking, Yale Univ, 68-69; vis lectr printmaking, Southern Conn State Col, spring 69; prof fine art, Calif State Univ Stanislaus, Turlick, 69- *Awards:* Award of Excellence, Calif State Fair, 1987, Sacramento, 87; Cash Merit Award, University Mus, Miss, 1/90-3/90; Pacific Art League Serigraphy Award & Timothy Duran Purchase Award, Pacific Art League, Palo Alto, Calif, 5/90-6/90. *Bibliog:* Peter Fierz (auth),

Young American Painter, Der Kunst, 69; Gabor Peterdi (auth), Four prints, Eye-Mag of Yale Arts Asn, 69. *Mem:* Los Angeles Printmaking Soc. *Media:* Acrylics; Color Intaglio. *Mailing Add:* Dept Art Calif State Univ Stanislaus 801 W Monte Vista Ave Turlock CA 95380

PITCHER, JOHN CHARLES
PAINTER, ILLUSTRATOR
b Kalamazoo, Mich, Aug 6, 49. *Study:* Self taught. *Work:* Anchorage Mus Hist & Art, Alaska; Nat Wildlife Fedn, Washington, DC; Univ Alaska Mus; Leigh Yawkey Woodson Art Mus, Wausau, Wis; Juneau Empire, Alaska. *Exhib:* Charles & Emma Frye Art Mus, Wash, 75; Leigh Yawkey Wooden Art Mus, 78-89; Royal Scottish Acad, Edinburgh, Scotland, 82; British Mus Nat Hist, London, 82; Alaska's Artists in Washington, DC, Capitol Rotunda Rm, 83; solo shows, Antique Ltd, Alaska, 76-84; Alaska State Mus, 84-85; Calif Acad Sci, 85-86; Beijing Natural Hist Mus, China, 86; group shows, Soc Animal Artists Ann Exhib, 76, 79, 86, 87-92, miniatures, Minn, 84-92; Original Art Showcase, Can, 89-92. *Teaching:* Leads workshops & gives slide/lectures on drawing & painting wildlife for Ultima art & media programs. *Awards:* First Place, Nat Exhib Wildlife Art, Anchorage Audubon Soc, 83; one of the featured artists, First Ann Pac Rim Wildlife Art Show, 88, 91-92; Keynote speaker, workshop presenter Alaska Loon Festival, Anchorage, 90. *Bibliog:* Elaine Rhode (auth), John Pitcher: In perspective with nature, Alaska J, autumn 79; Sandy Preston (auth), John Pitcher, perfect squares, Midwest Art (Now US Art), 88; Patricia Black Bailey (auth), John C Pitcher, Southwest Art, 3/92. *Mem:* Soc Animal Artists Inc. *Media:* Watercolor; Oil, Acrylic. *Publ:* Illusr, A Guide to the Birds of Alaska, Alaska NW Publ Co, 80; Contribr-illusr, bird sect rev, World Bk Encycl, 81; illusr, Field Guide Birds of NAm, Nat Geographic Soc, 83; illusr, Birds of the Seward Peninsula, Alaska, brina Kessel, Univ Alaska Press, 89. *Dealer:* Mill Pond Press 310 Center Ct Venice FL 34292. *Mailing Add:* 115 McKinley Ave Randle WA 98377

PITT, SUZAN (LEE)
PAINTER, FILMMAKER
b Kansas City, Mo. *Study:* Cranbrook Acad Art, BFA, 65. *Work:* Mus Mod Art, New York; Walker Art Ctr; Whitney Mus Am Art. *Comn:* Damnation of Faust, an opera by Berlioz (stage designs, costumes & animated film) State Opera Theatre, Hamburg, Ger, 90; Animated video, Brooklyn Acad Music, New York, 90. *Exhib:* Solo exhib, Holly Solomon Gallery, New York, 79, Whitney Mus Am Art, 79, Galerie Denise-Rene Hansmayer, Düsseldorf, 81 & Delahunty Gallery, New York, 82, Cantor/Lemberg Gallery, Detroit, MI, 84, Gallozzi-LaPlaca Gallery, New York, 86;; Comic Iconoclasm, Inst Contemp Art, London, England, 88; Pop Apocalypse, Gracie Mansion Gallery, New York, 88. *Teaching:* Prof art, Psychopolis Vrije Akad Haag Holland, 74-75; guest lectr film animation, Harvard Univ, 75-76, assoc film animation, 87. *Awards:* Production of Year Award, Opera World Ann, Wiesbaden, Ger, 83; Hoops Faculty teaching Prize, Harvard Univ, 88; Media Arts Filmmaker Grant, Nat Endowment Arts, 88; Howard Fdn Del, Brown Univ, 90. *Bibliog:* Marsha Miro (auth), article, Detroit Free Press, 10/29/84; Joy Hakanson-Colby (auth), "Suzan Pitt/Ideas That Go Bump", Detroit News, 10/21/84; Kim Levin (auth), "Suzan Pitt", Village Voice, New York, 84. *Mem:* Int Asn Film Animation, (publ comt, 89-). *Dealer:* Hans Mayer Dusseldorf Germany. *Mailing Add:* 112 Washington St Fountain City WI 54629

PITTMAN, IRENE K
SCULPTOR, DESIGNER
b Tampa, Fla, Aug 16, 38. *Study:* Univ Ala, Tuscaloosa, BA, 60. *Work:* Art in Archit Prog, Dade Co, Miami, 80; Fla State, Talahassee, 83 & 88. *Comn:* Weaving, HI Develop Corp, Miami, 87; hanging mobile, Opus Corp, Tampa, 87; fabric kite mobile, St Joseph Diagnostic Ctr, Tampa, 88; umbrella silk mobile, Hyatt Regency Hotel Group, Miami, 88; hanging silk banners, Donald Trump, Nassau, Bahamas, 88; design of fabrics/wallpaper for Miami Intl Airport Hotel, 92. *Exhib:* Ars Electronica, Mass Inst Tech, Cambridge & Linz, Austria, 80; Int Textile Show, Brucknerhaus, Linz, 81 & Kuntzlerhaus, Austria, 81; Sky Art Conf, Mass Inst Tech, 81 & Munich, Ger, 83. *Mem:* Am Crafts Coun. *Media:* Fabric. *Mailing Add:* c/o Artist Studio 115 S Lincoln Tampa FL 33609

PITTMAN, LARI
PAINTER
b Los Angeles, Calif, 1952. *Study:* Univ Calif, Los Angeles, 70-73, Calif Inst Arts, Valencia, BFA, 74, MFA, 76. *Exhib:* Solo exhibs, Newport Harbor Art Mus, Newport Beach, Calif, 82-83, Rosamund Felsen Gallery, Los Angeles, 83, 84, 85, 87, 88, 89, 90 & 91; Meanwhile, Back at the Ranch, Kuhlenschmidt-Simon Gallery, Los Angeles, 86; Biennial Exhib, Whitney Mus Am Art, New York, 87; Cal Arts: Skeptical Belief(s), Renaissance Soc, Univ Chicago & Newport Harbor Art Mus, 87-88; Westerns States Biennial, Phoenix Art Mus (with catalog), Ariz, 87; Striking Distance, Mus Contemp Art, Los Angeles & travelling, Triton Mus, Santa Clara, Calif, Fresno Arts Ctr & Mus, Calif, 87-88; Victoria, Pence Gallery, Santa Monica, Calif, 89; Cultural Fetish, Pasadena City Col Art Gallery, Calif, 89; Constructing a History: A Focus on Mus Contemp Art's Permanent Collection, Los Angeles, 90; Helter Skelter, Mus Contemp Art, Los Angeles, 92; Jay Gorney Mod Art, 92; Studio Guenzani, Milan, Italy, 92; 42nd Biennial Exhib Contemp Am Painting, Corcoran Gallery Art, Washington, DC. *Awards:* Art Matters Grant, 86; Fel, Nat Endowment Arts, 87 & 89. *Bibliog:* Hunter Drohojowska (auth), Lari Pittman at Rosamund Felsen Gallery, Los Angeles Herald Examiner, 10/26/84 & Lari Pittman, Artnews, 2/86; Constance Mallinson (auth), Lari Pittman at Rosamund Felsen, Art in Am, 2/85; Colin Gardner (auth), Cal Arts: Skeptical Belief(s), review, Artforum, 4/88; James Scarborough (auth), Carving Out a Niche, Artweek, 5/17/90; Donald Britton (auth), cover, Art Issues, 5/90. *Mem:* Los Angeles Contemp Exhibs (bd dirs, 86-91). *Mailing Add:* c/o Rosamund Felsen Gallery 8525 Santa Monica Blvd Los Angeles CA 90069

PITTORE, CARLO
PAINTER, MURALIST
b New York, NY, May 14, 43. *Study:* Tufts Col, BA, 66. *Work:* Mus Mod Art Libr, New York; Sackner Archive, Miami, Fla; J Paul Getty Inst Art Hist & Humanities, Los Angeles, Calif; Sohm Arch; Sonia Henie Mus, Carlo Pittore Archive Int Mail Art, Oslo. *Comn:* Fedn of Handicapped, New York. *Exhib:* Mod Realism Gallery, Dallas, 83; No Se No, New York, 85; NAME Gallery, Chicago, 86; Gallery 127, Portland, Maine, 90. *Collections Arranged:* Bern Porter Retrospective, Franklin Furnace & travelling, 79. *Pos:* Ed, Me Mag, 80-; Cult Coun, Fdn CETA Artists Proj, New York. *Teaching:* Instr, Acad Carlo Pittore, Bowdoinham, Maine; Univ Maine, Augusta. *Awards:* Max Beckmann Scholar, 77; Portland Sch Art Award, 83. *Bibliog:* Articles, Art News, 12/81, Rubber Stamp Madness, 7/82 & Nat Stampographic, 7/83, Artforum 9/84, New Art Examiner 4/85,. *Mem:* Union Maine Visual Artists (pres). *Publ:* Ed, Colleagues, 80 & illusr, The Adventures of Carlo Pittore, 80, Pittore Euforico; illusr, Boxers, 82 & The Man With an Egg, 83, Bern Porter. *Mailing Add:* Acad Carlo Pittore Bowdoinham ME 04008-0182

PITTS, RICHARD G
PAINTER, PRINTMAKER
b Ft Monmouth, NJ, Oct 15, 40. *Study:* Newark Sch Fine Arts, 61; Pratt Inst, BFA, 68; New York Studio Sch, Paris, 72. *Work:* Anot Mus Art, Elmira, NY; General Electric Co, New York; Port Authority of New York; Continental Insurance Co, New Brunswick, NJ; Univ Va Mus, Charlottesville, Va. *Comn:* Mural, Chelsea Health & Fitness, 91-92. *Exhib:* Solo exhib, David Findlay Jr, 83 & 85, Randolf Manchon, Ashland, Va, 84, Rutherin Gallery, Columbus, Ohio, 85; Bodies and Souls, Marborough Gallery, New York, 83; Contemporary Images, Mendik Gallery, New York, 86; First Street Gallery Invitational, 86; Shirley Goodman Resource Ctr, F I T Galleries, 87; Cedar Art Ctr, Corning, NY, 92; and others. *Pos:* Chmn, Artist Bd, Artist Choice Mus, currently. *Teaching:* Assoc prof painting, Kansas City Art Inst, 70-73 & Fashion Inst Technol, 73- *Bibliog:* David Tully (auth), Richard Pitts One Man Show, Arts Mag, 2/85; Jacqueline Hall (auth), Landscapes, Columbus Dispatch, 5/85; Animal Life at One Penn Plaza, Art World, 11/87; David Matlock (auth), Nature and Art, Art World, 4/88; Abigail Wender (auth), Paintings by Richard Pitts, Diversion Mag, 8/88. *Media:* Oil on Canvas. *Dealer:* David Findlay Jr Inc 41 E 57 St New York NY 10022; Carola Van der Houten 390 West End New York NY 10024. *Mailing Add:* 233 W 18th St New York NY 10011

PITTS, TERENCE RANDOLPH
DIRECTOR, CURATOR
b St Louis, Mo, Feb 05, 50. *Study:* Univ Ill, Champagne-Urbana, BA, 72, MLS, 74; Univ Ariz, MA, 86. *Collections Arranged:* Contemporary Photography in Mexico, 78; Edward Weston: Color Photography, 86; One Hundred Years of Photography in the American West, 87; Photography in the American Grain, 88; 4 Spanish Photographers, 88. *Pos:* Cur, Ctr for Creative Photog, Tucson, Ariz, 78-89, dir, 89- *Awards:* Mus Fel, Nat Endowment for Arts. *Mem:* Am Asn of Mus. *Publ:* Auth, 100 Years of Photography in the American West, Phoenix Art Mus, 87; auth, Edward Weston: Color Photography, Ctr for Creative Photog, 86; auth, Photography in the American Grain, Ctr for Creative Photog, 88; Auth, Public places/private spaces: American photography 1960-70, decade by decade, Little Brown, 89. *Mailing Add:* 6291 N Camino Katrina Tucson AZ 85718

PITYNSKI, ANDRZEJ P
SCULPTOR
b Ulanow, Poland, March 15, 47; US citizen. *Study:* Acad Fine Arts in Cracow, Poland, MFA(sculpture), 74; Art Students League, New York, 75. *Work:* Portrait bust M Curie (bronze on granite, 7'), Bayonne, NJ; Sculpture Partisans (aluminum, 3'), Polish Am Mus, Port Washington, NY. *Comn:* Partisans (aluminum, 24' x 36' x 12'), Johnson Atelier of NJ, Boston, 83; Father Jerzy Popieluszko (bronze on granite, 12'), St Hedwig's Church, Trenton, 87; Avenger (bronze on granite, 36'), Polish-Am Veterans US, Doylestown, PA, 87; Katyn-1940 (bronze on granite, 38'), Katyn Memorial Fund, Comt Jersey City, 91; Pope John Paul II (bronze on granite, 12'), Polish Am Cong, New York, 91. *Exhib:* Contemporary Artists Guild Exhib, Lever House, New York, 91; Zacheta International Exhib, Zacheta Nat Art Gallery, Warsaw, Poland, 91; Federation Internationale De La Medaille-23rd Congress, British Mus, London, Eng, 92; American Medallic Sculpture Association Exhib, Cast Iron Gallery-Soho, New York, 92; Johnson Atelier Sculpture Exhib, Alternate Extension Gallery, Philadelphia, 92. *Pos:* Asst to sculptor Alexander Ettl, Sculpture House, New York 75-79; supv modeling, enlarging, resins & moldmakings, Johnson Atelier Tech Inst Sculpture, Mercerville, NJ 79- *Teaching:* Instr Sculpture, Rider Col, Trenton, NJ, 92. *Awards:* Silver Medal Honor, 72nd Ann Exhib, 85 & Elliot Liskin Memorial Award, 76th Ann Exhib, 89, Allied Artists Am, New York; Cultural Achievement Award, Am Coun Polish Culture, Washington, DC, 92. *Bibliog:* Theodora Morgan (ed), cover story, A Pitynski - for our freedom and yours, Sculpture Rev, Nat Sculpture Soc, 85; J Kondracka (producer), A Pitynski - Sculptor (1-hr film), Polish TV, 91; Steve Di Lauro (auth), Spirit in bronze, Downtown Art Mag, New York, 88. *Mem:* Contemp Artists Guild, New York; Audubon Artists, New York; Allied Artists Am, New York; fel mem Nat Sculpture Soc, New York; Am Medallic Sculpture Asn, New York. *Mailing Add:* 90 Dupont St Brooklyn NY 11222

PIZZAT, JOSEPH
EDUCATOR, COLLAGE ARTIST
b Creekside, Pa, Nov 4, 26. *Study:* Kalamazoo Col, Mich, BA, 49, MA, 50; Columbia Univ Teachers Col, New York, EdD, 55; vis scholar, Pa State Univ, 59 Pratt Inst, New York, 61. *Work:* Sioux Falls Art Mus; Normandale Jr Col. *Exhib:* One-man shows, Taping, Gannon Col, Erie, 75, Tapings 1975, Ivy Sch Prof Art, Pittsburgh, Americana, 76, T is for Taping, Grafika Gallery, Erie, Pa, 81, Taping Retrospective 1974-1984, Mercyhurst Col, Erie, Pa, 84, Collage works: An Art Journey, Schuster Gallery, Gannon Univ, Erie, Pa, 91; Liturgical Arts, Newman Ctr, Bowling Green State Univ, Ohio, 79; Ind Univ Pa Exhib, 83; Westwood Racquet Club, 88; Faculty Exhib, Mercy Hurst Col, Erie, Pa, 71- *Teaching:* Prof art & chmn art prog, SW Minn State Col, Marshall, 67-71; prof art, Mercyhurst Col, Erie, Pa, 71-, chmn, creative arts div, 71-78. *Awards:* Outstanding Art Educator Award, Pa Art Educ Asn, 81. *Mem:* Artists' Equity Asn; Am Art Therapy Asn; Pa Art Educ Asn; Nat Art Educ Asn. *Media:* Adhesive, Contact. *Res:* Pressure sensitive art, a visual-tactile art system using self-adhesive & pressure sensitive materials as primary art media. *Publ:* I'm a right brained person, why me God?, Nat Art Educ Asn Art Educ J, 79; Artmaking with tape, Arts & Activities Mag, 85; The Book, A Learning Experience, 86; T & T Art, 5/88, What's Up? Art's Up-that's what!, 6/90, Kites: An art flight of fantasy, 10/91, Arts & Activities. *Mailing Add:* 2046 Charleston Ave Erie PA 16509

PLACE, BRADLEY EUGENE
EDUCATOR, GRAPHIC ARTIST
b Rule, Tex, Nov 4, 20. *Study:* Tex A&M Univ, 38-40; NTex Univ, with Carlos Merida & Ivan Johnson, BS, 42. *Pos:* Mem visual arts adv panel, Okla Arts & Humanities Coun, 72-; mem selection comt, Art for Pub Places, Tulsa, 75- *Teaching:* From asst prof to prof lettering & typography, Univ Tulsa, 47-86, chmn dept art, 64-86, emer prof art, 86. *Awards:* Brad Trust Scholar, 73. *Bibliog:* Jenk Jones, Jr (auth), Honor roll for May, Tulsa Tribune, 71; Connie Cronley (auth), Profile of a teacher of artists, Tulsa, 6/14/73; Myrna Smart (auth), Dilemma of penal reform, Arts & Humanities Coun Tulsa & KTEW-TV, 5/74. *Mem:* Tulsa Advert Fedn; Tulsa Art Dir Club (exec bd, 70-75, 77 & 81-, pres, 74-75); Tulsa Arts & Humanities (mem bd, Chmn Mayor's Arts Comn, 77). *Mailing Add:* 2156 S Fulton Pl Tulsa OK 74114-2250

PLACZEK, ADOLF KURT
LIBRARIAN, HISTORIAN
b Vienna, Austria, Mar 9, 13; US citizen. *Study:* Univ Vienna, 31-38; Inst Art History, 34-38; Sch Libr Serv, Columbia Univ, 41-42. *Pos:* Asst librn, Avery Archit & Fine Arts Libr, Columbia Univ, 48-60, librn, 60-80, librn emer, 80-; comnr, Landmarks Preservation Comn, New York, 84- *Teaching:* Adj prof archit hist, Columbia Univ, 65-80, prof emer, 80- *Awards:* Award Merit,79 & Inst Honor, 86, Inst Archit, New York Chap; Munic Art Soc, 81. *Mem:* Soc Archit Hist (pres, 78-80). *Res:* Eighteenth century European and nineteenth century American architecture. *Publ:* Ed, Avery Index to Architectural Periodicals, 63 & Catalog of the Avery Architectural Library, 68, G K Hall Press; contribr, Palladio, The Four Books of Architecture, Dover Press, 65; coauth, Piranesi, Drawings & Etchings, Sackler Found, 75; contribr, Hitchcock, American Architectural Books, DaCapo Press, 76; ed, Macmillan Encyclopedia of Architects, 82. *Mailing Add:* 176 W 87th St New York NY 10024

PLAGENS, PETER
PAINTER, CRITIC
b Dayton, Ohio, Mar 1, 41. *Study:* Univ Southern Calif, BFA, 62; Syracuse Univ, MFA, 64. *Work:* Baltimore Mus Art; Albright-Knox Gallery, Buffalo, NY; Hirshhorn Mus, Washington, DC; Santa Fe Mus Art, N Mex; Tawaraya, Kyoto; Denver Art Mus, Co. *Exhib:* solo exhibs, Baun-Silverman Gallery, Los Angeles, Calif, 80, Nancy Hoffman Gallery, New York, 81, 84, 87, 90 & 92, Lincoln Ctr Art Gallery, New York, 83, SECCA, Winston-Salem, NC, 84, Univ Art Mus, Calif State Univ, Long Beach, 85, Jan Cicero Gallery, Chicago, Ill, 85, Jan Baum Gallery, Los Angeles, 88; San Francisco Mus Art, 77; Collectors Gallery XXI, Marion Koogler McNay Art Mus, San Antonio, Tx, 87; Nancy Hoffman Gallery, New York, 88-91; Hofstra Mus, Hempstead, NY, 89; Working on Paper: contemporary American Drawing, Hugh Mus Art Atlanta, 90; 79th Ann Exhib, Randolph-Macon Woman's Col, Maier Mus Art, Lynchburg, Va, 90. *Pos:* Contrib ed, Artforum, 66-76; Chmn, bd dirs, Los Angeles Inst Contemp Art, 77-79; Art Critic, Newsweek Mag, 89- *Teaching:* Assoc prof art, Calif State Univ, Northridge, 69-78, Univ Southern Calif, 78-80; chmn, dept art, Univ NC at Chapel Hill, 80-83, prof, 80-84; prof, Hofstra Univ, Hempstead, NY, 85- *Awards:* John Simon Guggenheim Fel in Painting, 72-73; Nat Endowment Arts, Grant in Art Criticism, 73-74, Fel in painting, 77-78. *Bibliog:* Carrie Rickey (auth), Peter's Principles, Village Voice, 1/28/80; Jane Bell (auth), rev, Art News, 1/85; Gerrit Henry (auth), rev, Art in Am, 1/85. *Publ:* Auth, Ecology of evil, 12/72, Peter and the pressure cooker, 6/74 & None dare call it BoHo, 9/75, Artforum; Sunshine Muse: Contemporary Art on the West Coast, Praeger Publ, 74; Moonlight Blues: An Artist's Art Criticism, UMI Research Press, 86. *Dealer:* Jan Cicero Gallery, Chicago IL. *Mailing Add:* c/o Nancy Hoffman Gallery 429 W Broadway New York NY 10012

PLASTER, ALICE MARIE
PAINTER, INSTRUCTOR
b Hickory, NC. *Study:* Md Inst, Col Art, BFA, 77. *Work:* George Washington House Mus, Bladensburg, Md. *Comn:* Mural, Md Nat Capital Park & Planning Comn, Riverdale, 79. *Exhib:* Nat Soc Arts & Letters, Washington DC, 73-76; Md Inst Printmaking Exhib, Baltimore, 77; Urban Landscapes, 3rd Ann Juried Visual Arts Exhib, Strathmore, Hall Arts Ctr, Rockville, Md, 88. *Pos:* Graphic artist, Prince George's Co Mem Libr System, Hyattsville, Md, 80- *Teaching:* Instr painting, Md Nat Capital Park & Planning Comn Montpelier Cult Arts Ctr, 86-92. *Awards:* Cash Award, Nat Soc Arts & Letters, 73; and others. *Bibliog:* Richard Carter (auth), Spectrum, The Post, 9/15/78; Joanne Hoover (auth), The arts, Washington Post, 3/22/79; William N Swetcharnik (auth), The view from my easel, The Post, 11/19/80; Maryland Weekly, The Washington Post, 2/27/86; The Prince Georgian, (Publ Cover Artist), Washington Post, 6/17/88. *Media:* Oil, Pencil. *Mailing Add:* 3925 Winchester Ln Bowie MD 20715

PLATH, IONA
WRITER, WEAVER
b Dodge Center, Minn, May 24, 07. *Study:* Westmoreland Col; Art Students League; Art Inst Chicago. *Teaching:* Instr art & design, 30-; instr handweaving, 65- *Mem:* Handweavers Guild Am; STex Fiver Arts Guild; Byliners. *Publ:* Auth & illusr, Decorative Arts of Sweden, Scribner's, 48 & Dover, 65; Hand Weaving, 64 & The Craft of Handweaving, 72, Scribner's; auth, The Handweaver's Pattern Book, Dover, 81. *Mailing Add:* 523 Airline Rd Corpus Christi TX 78412

PLATTNER, PHYLLIS
PAINTER
b New York, NY, Apr 25, 40. *Study:* Bennington Col, BA, 60; Brooklyn Mus Sch, 59; Claremont Grad Sch, Calif, MFA, 62. *Work:* St Louis Art Mus; Springfield Art Mus, Mo; The Kemper Group, Chicago; Xerox Corp, Stamford, Conn. *Comn:* Three-panel watercolor, Coinco, St Louis, 84; five-panel curved watercolor, IBM Bus Machines, Rochester, Minn, 85. *Exhib:* New Acquisitions, St Louis Art Mus, 83; Solo exhibs, B Z Wagman Gallery, St Louis, 85 & 86, Fendrick Gallery, Washington, DC, 86 & 89, Esther Saks Gallery, Chicago, Ill, 87 Locus, St Louis, Mo, 89, Steven Scott Gallery, Baltimore, Md, 89 Brody's Gallery, Washington, DC, 91-92 & Elliot Smith Gallery, St Louis, Mo, 92; Contemporary Works on Paper, Frumkin & Struve Gallery, Chicago, 85; Watercolor USA: The Monumental Image, Springfield Art Mus, 86; and other one-man exhibs. *Teaching:* Vis assoc prof painting, Washington Univ, St Louis, 81-85 & 91-93, vis assoc prof watercolor, 85-87; instr, Md Inst Col Art, Baltimore, Md, 87- *Awards:* Mayor's Award for the Arts, St Louis, 84; Mid-Atlantic States Nat Endowment Arts, 88. *Bibliog:* Robert Duffy (auth), It's a jungle in there, St Louis Post Dispatch, 84; Betsy Goldman (auth), Phyllis Plattner, Am Artist Mag, 85. *Media:* Oil, Watercolor; Oil Pastels. *Dealer:* Brody's Gallery 1706 21 St NW Washington DC 20009; Elliot Smith Gallery 4727 McPherson Ave St Louis MO 63108. *Mailing Add:* 6204 Redwing Rd Bethesda MD 20817

PLAUT, JAMES S
ART ADMINISTRATOR, WRITER
b Cincinnati, Ohio, Feb 1, 12. *Study:* Harvard Univ, AB, 33, AM, 35; Wheaton Col, hon DFA, 74. *Collections Arranged:* In charge of all exhib planning, US Pavilion, Brussels World's Fair, 58, New York World's Fair, 64, Montreal, 67 & Osaka, 70; First World Crafts Exhib, Ont Sci Ctr, Toronto, 74. *Pos:* Asst cur paintings, Mus Fine Arts, Boston, 35-39; dir, Inst Contemp Art, Boston, 39-56; vpres, Old Sturbridge Village, Mass, 59-62; secy gen, World Crafts Coun, 67-76; adv, NJ State Mus & Pac Northwest Arts Ctr; pres, Aid to Artisans Inc, 76-; planning consult, New York Pub Libr, 76-; mem vis comt, Prog in Artisanry, Boston Univ, 75- *Teaching:* Lectr hist art, Harvard Univ, 34-35, 37-38; lectr hist art, New Eng Conserv Music, 38-39. *Awards:* Off, Royal Order St Olav, Norway, 50; Comdr, Royal Order of Leopold, Belg Govt, 58. *Mem:* Art Vis Comt of Wheaton Col (chmn); MacDowell Colony; Coun Arts, Mass Inst Technol. *Publ:* Auth, Oskar Kokoschka, 48; Steuben glass, 48, 51 & 72; Assignment in Israel, 60; In Praise of Hands (with Octavio Paz), 74. *Mailing Add:* 64 Fairgreen Pl Chestnut Hill MA 02167

PLEAR, SCOTT
PAINTER
b Vancouver, BC, Mar 26, 52. *Study:* Univ BC, BFA, 76; Univ Sask, with Emma Lake, 77, 80, 84, 85 & 88; Triangle Artists Workshop, Pine Plains, NY, 82. *Work:* Edmonton Art Gallery, Alta; The Art Bank; Burnaby Art Gallery, BC; Art Gallery Greater Victoria, BC. *Exhib:* Ninth Burnaby Biennial Print Show, Burnaby Art Gallery, BC, 77; Malaspina Printmakers Fifth Ann, Presentation House, NVancouver, BC, 79; The West Face, Charles H Scott Gallery, Emily Carr Col Art, Vancouver, BC, 81; BC Currents, Sarnia Art Gallery, Ont, 81; Royal Can Acad Invitational, Kenneth G Heffel Gallery, Vancouver, BC, 81; The Current Generation, Edmonton Art Gallery, 83; Dealing with Colour, Richmond Art Gallery, BC, 83; The Joy of Form, Burnaby Art Gallery, BC, 86; solo travel exhib, Scott Plear: Recent Paintings, Edmonton Art Gallery, Alta, Grand Forks Art Gallery, BC & Burnaby Art Gallery, 87; North of the Border, Whatcom Mus Hist & Art, Bellingham, Wash, 90. *Teaching:* Instr, Univ BC, 78-79; asst prof, Univ Alta, 83; fac mem & dept chmn, Vancouver Community Col, Langara Campus, 86. *Bibliog:* Kenworth Moffett (auth), Moffett's Artletter, Vol 1 No 10, 12/86; Boulet Roger H (auth), Scott Plear, Recent Paintings, The Edmonton Art Gallery, 87; Robert Amos (auth), Victoria Times Colonist, 92. *Media:* Acrylic. *Dealer:* Art Placement Inc 228 Third Ave S Saskatoon Sask; Fran Willis North Park Gallery 200-1619 Store St Victoria BC. *Mailing Add:* 1947 Adanac St Vancouver BC V5L 2E5 Canada

PLETCHER, GERRY
PAINTER, PRINTMAKER
Study: Edinboro State Univ, BS; Pa State Univ, MA(fine arts); also with Montenegro, Carol Summers, Harold Altman, Nelson Sandgren & Shobaken; Vanderbilt Univ, Nashville, PhD. *Work:* Evansville Mus Arts & Sci, Ind; Fisk Univ, Tenn; Jacksonville State Univ, Ala; Tenn Arts Comn; Tenn Botanical Gardens; First Am Bank, Nashville; and others. *Exhib:* Cent South Art Exhib,

Nashville; Nat Acad Design 145th Ann, New York; Wonderworks Four, Nat Print Show, Nashville; Springfield Nat Exhib, Ill; Brooks Mem Gallery, Memphis; Gallery Contemp Art, NC; and others. *Teaching:* Prof art, Tenn State Univ, currently. *Awards:* Graphics Purchase Award, 22nd Ann Mid-States Art Exhib, Evansville Mus Arts & Sci; seven Purchase Prizes, Tenn Arts Comn; Purchase Award, 13th Ann Tenn All-State; Purchase Award, Jacksonville Nat, Ala; and others. *Bibliog:* Artists USA, 1972-73; Am Printmakers, 74; Who's Who Am Art, 83-92. *Media:* Acrylic, Oil; Etchings, Woodcuts. *Mailing Add:* Dept Art Tenn State Univ 3500 Jr A Merritt Blvd Nashville TN 37203

PLETKA, PAUL
PAINTER, PRINTMAKER
b San Diego, Calif, 1946. *Study:* Ariz State Univ, Tempe; Colo State Univ, Ft Collins. *Work:* San Antonio Mus Art, Tex; Milwaukee Fine Arts Ctr, Wis; St Louis Art Mus, Mo; Minneapolis Inst Art, Minn; Phoenix Art Mus, Ariz; and others. *Comn:* Ghost Dancer (lithograph), Phoenix Art Mus, Ariz, 77; Those Living at the Sunrise (lithograph), Heard Mus, Phoenix, Ariz, 79; Papageno (poster), St Louis Opera Theater, Mo, 80. *Exhib:* Four Corners Biennial, Phoenix Art Mus, Ariz, 77; one-man show, El Paso Mus Art, Tex, 78; A Sense of Space, Univ NMex Art Mus, 79; Eiteljorg Collection, Indianapolis Mus Art, 79; Here and Now, Albuquerque Art Mus, NMex, 80. *Awards:* Certificate of Excellence, Chicago, 76; Nat Watercolor Soc Award, Watercolor USA, 77. *Bibliog:* Edna Gundersen (auth), Pletka bares Indian souls on canvas, El Paso Times, 5/13/78; Ed Montini (auth), Unmasking a dedicated artist, The Ariz Republic, 3/22/81; Edna Gundersori (auth), Pletka, Northland Press, 83. *Media:* Acrylic, Watercolor. *Mailing Add:* c/o Susan Duval Gallery 525 E Cooper Ave Aspen CO 81611

PLETSCHER, JOSEPHINE MARIE
LIBRARIAN, PRINTMAKER
b Muscatine, Iowa. *Study:* Immaculate Heart Col, BA, 62, MA, 64; Univ Calif, Los Angeles. *Comn:* Feel Free (poster), Wilson Libr Bulletin, Bronx, NY, 69. *Exhib:* Iowa Artists 4th Ann Exhib, Des Moines Art Ctr, 52 & 11th Ann Iowa Artists Exhib, 59; Calif State Fair, Sacramento, 62. *Collections Arranged:* Mexican Festival--Arts and Crafts, Pasadena Pub Libr, 72. *Pos:* Fine arts coordr, Pasadena Pub Libr, Pasadena, 64-82; reference librn, Rio Hondo Col Libr, Whittier, Calif, 83- *Awards:* Watercolor Hon Award, Des Moines Art Ctr, 59 & State Calif, 62; Recognition Award, Pasadena Pub Libr, 68. *Bibliog:* Larry Palmer (auth), Local art and artists, Pasadena Star News, 7/13/69; Jack Birkinshaw (auth), Joy of children painting is captured on librarian's film, Los Angeles Times, 9/4/69; Arthur Plotnik (auth), This is a library feel free, Wilson Libr Bulletin, 11/69. *Mem:* Art Libr Soc NAm; Hollywood Art Coun; and others. *Media:* Serigraphy. *Interests:* Architecture, graphics, printmaking and rare art objects. *Publ:* Illusr, Immaculate Heart College--Announcement of Courses, Immaculate Heart Col, 63-64; illusr & contribr, Painting from the heart, Business: Pasadena CofC, 5/69; Illusr, Learning By Heart, Bantan, 92. *Mailing Add:* 1917 Rodney Dr No 216 Los Angeles CA 90027

PLOCHMANN, CAROLYN GASSAN
PAINTER, GRAPHIC ARTIST
b Toledo, Ohio, May 4, 26. *Study:* Toledo Mus Art Sch Design, 43-47; Univ Toledo, BA, 47; State Univ Iowa, MFA, 49; with Alfeo Faggi, 50; Southern Ill Univ, 51-52. *Work:* Evansville Mus Arts & Sci, Ind; Fleischmann Found Collection, Cincinnati, Ohio; Butler Inst Am Art, Youngstown, Ohio; pvt collection of Mr & Mrs Arthur Magill, Greenville, SC; The West Collection, St Paul, Minn. *Exhib:* One-man shows, Witte Mus, San Antonio, Tex, 68, Toledo Mus Art, 65 & Kennedy Galleries, New York, 73, 81, 83, 87 & 89; 164th Prints & Drawings Ann, Pa Acad Fine Arts, Philadelphia, 69; Evansville Mus Arts & Sci, 62, 68, 79. *Awards:* George W Stevens Fel, Toledo Mus Art, 47-49; Tupperware Art Fund First Award, 53; Emily Lowe Found Competition Award, 58; First Award, Art and the Law, West Collection, 85. *Bibliog:* Thomas Hoving (auth), article, Connoisseur, 83; Ilene Susan Fort, article, Arts Mag, 83; Matthew Daub (auth), Carolyn Plochmann: A Charmed Vision, Evansville Mus Arts & Sci, 90. *Mem:* Philadelphia Watercolor Club. *Media:* Oil, Acrylic; Graphics. *Publ:* Auth, University Portrait: Nine Paintings by Carolyn Gassan Plochmann, Southern Ill Univ Press, 59. *Dealer:* Kennedy Galleries 40 W 57th St New York NY 10019. *Mailing Add:* Rte 9 Box 104 Carbondale IL 62901

PLOSSU, BERNARD
PHOTOGRAPHER
b Dalat, S Vietnam, Feb 26, 45. *Work:* Bibliotheque Nat, Paris; Amon Carter Mus, Ft Worth, Tex; George Eastman House, Rochester, NY; Ctr Creative Photography, Tucson, Ariz; Niepce Mus, Chalon, France; Mus Fine Arts, Santa Fe, NMex; Albuquerque Mus, NMex. *Exhib:* Plossu by Atelier Fresson, Eaton-Shoen Gallery, San Francisco, 82; solo exhib, Etherton Gallery, Tucson, Ariz, 82; The Spirit of Travelling, Arles Photo Fest, Arles, France, 82; In Place, Albuquerque Mus, NMex, 82; two-person show, Hoshour Gallery, Albuquerque, NMex, 83; The Mexican Voyage, Eaton-Schoen Gallery, San Francisco, 84. *Teaching:* Photography workshops, Okla Summer Arts Inst, 83. *Bibliog:* Gilles Mora (auth), La rupture creatrice du Voyage Mexicain, Cahiers Photo, 81; L Sherman & S Parks (auths), I photograph the weather, Artlines, 81; M Foley (auth), Bernard Plossu, Artspace, 81; Gilles Mora (auth), Bernard Plossu, Camera, 86. *Publ:* Photogr, Surbanalism, Chene, France, 72; Go West, Chene, France, 72; Le Voyage Mexicain, Contrejour, France, 79; Egypte, Photoeil, France, 79; New Mexico Revisited, Univ NMex Press, 83. *Mailing Add:* c/o Ernesto Mayans Galleries 601 Canyon Rd Santa Fe NM 87501

PLOTEK, LEOPOLD
PAINTER
b Moscow, USSR, 1948. *Study:* McGill Univ, Montreal; Sir George Williams Univ, Montreal, BFA, 70; study with Roy Kioyooka & Yves Gaucher; Slade Sch Art, London, Eng, study with William Townsend, 70-71. *Work:* Montreal Mus Fine Arts; Musee d'Art Contemporain; Concordia Univ; Can Coun Artbank; Alcan Aluminum. *Exhib:* Solo exhibs, Univ Col London Gallery, England, 71, Vehicule Art, Montreal, 72 & 74, Weissman Gallery, Concordia, Quebec, 75, Galerie Yajima, Montreal, 76, 79, 81 & 83; traveling exhib, Selections from the Westburne Collection (with catalog), Nickle Arts Mus, Calgary, BC, Rodman Hall Arts Centre, St Catherines, Dalhousie Univ Art Gallery, Halifax, Oakville Galleries, Owens Art Gallery, Sackville, NB, Sir George Williams Art Galleries, Montreal, 83; Abstraction X 4 (with catalog), Canada House Cult Ctr Gallery, London, Eng, 85. *Awards:* Alfred Pinsky Medal in Fine Arts; Four Can Coun Arts Coun; two travel grants to Italy. *Mailing Add:* c/o Olga Korper Gallery 17 Morrow Ave Toronto ON M6R 2H9 Canada

PLOTKIN, LINDA
PAINTER, PRINTMAKER
b Milwaukee, Wis, Dec 21, 38. *Study:* Univ Wis, Milwaukee, BA, 61; Pratt Inst, Brooklyn, NY, MFA, 62. *Work:* Metrop Mus Art & Mus Mod Art, New York; Bibliotheque Nationale, Paris, France; Libr Cong, Washington, DC; Brooklyn Mus. *Exhib:* 30 Years of American Printmaking, Brooklyn Mus, NY, 76; 10th Ann Tokyo International Print Biennial, Tokyo, Japan, 77; 30 American Printmakers, Ohio State Univ, Columbus, 81; International Print Exhib, Taipei Mus, Taiwan, 84; Va Mus Print Invitational, Va Mus Art, Richmond, 86. *Teaching:* Asst prof art, Pa State Univ, State Col Pa, 62-77; artist in residence, St Mary's Col, Notre Dame, Ind, 85; State Univ NY, Purchase, 86- *Awards:* MacDowell Fel, 76, 78 & 79; Ossabaw Island Fel, 78; Camargo Found Fel, 81. *Bibliog:* Judd Tully (auth), Linda Plotkin, Arts Mag, 5/19/84; James Watrous (auth), A Century of American Printmaking, 84. *Mem:* Soc Am Graphic Artists (bd mem, 83-); Int Graphic Artists Found; Artists Equity. *Publ:* Contribr, In Praise of Women Artists (calendar), Bo-Tree Prods, 85. *Dealer:* G W Einstein Inc 591 Broadway New York NY. *Mailing Add:* 55 Perry St New York NY 10014

PLOTKIN, LYNN
ART DEALER, CURATOR
b St Louis, Mo, Apr 17, 45. *Study:* Centenary Col for Women, AA, 65; Finch Col, 65-66. *Pos:* Dir & owner, Brentwood Gallery, 82- *Mem:* Contemp Art Soc & Decorative Art Soc, St Louis Art Mus. *Specialty:* Contemporary American furniture, paintings, drawings, ceramics, sculpture and wearables. *Publ:* Contribr, Miriam Shapiro, Brentwood Gallery, 85. *Mailing Add:* 25 Dromara Rd St Louis MO 63124

PLOTKIN, SYLVIA
ADMINISTRATOR, MUSEUM DIRECTOR
US citizen. *Study:* Univ Washington, BS, 46; Univ Ariz, 56. *Awards:* Tunisian Legacy Belle Latchman for Outstanding Community Service, 85 & 88. *Mem:* Am Asn Mus; Western Mus Asn; Cent Ariz Mus Asn (vpres, 82); Coun Am Jewish Mus. *Mailing Add:* Plotkin Judaica Museum of Greater Phoenix at Temple Beth Israel 3310 N Tenth Ave Phoenix AZ 85013

PLOTT, PAULA (PAULA PLOTT AMOS)
PAINTER, SCULPTOR
b Wichita, Kans, Sept 22, 46. *Study:* Wichita State Univ, BFA (cum laude), 68; Univ Ore, MFA (summa cum laude), 70. *Work:* Wichita Art Mus, Kans. *Comn:* Carved reception desk & 12 paintings, J P Weigand & Sons Real Estate, Wichita, 76-77; Day in the Life of an Aztec (paintings), Taco Tico, Inc, 78-84; Symphony Calendar, Wichita Symphony, 79-80; panel designs, Trinity Methodist Church, Hutchinson, Kans, 80-81; Herbal Calendar, 87 & Wildflowers Calendar, 88, 89, 90 & 91 Wildlife Fedn; Lipton Herbal Tea Calendar, 89 & 90, Commemorative Cup, 90, Lipton Tea Co; Wichita Art Mus Commemorative Christmas Ornament, 89. *Exhib:* One-woman shows, Mus Fine Art, Los Gatos, 75, Wichita Gallery Fine Art, 78, Wichita Art Asn, 82 & Birger Sandzen Gallery Art, 83; Kansas Watercolor Tri State Show, 81, Seasons Greetings Invitational, 81, Facets in Wood, 84, Woods Worthy Christmas, 85, Wichita Art Mus; Plott Toy Shop, 86, 87, 88, 89 & 90. *Collections Arranged:* Historic Cowtown, Religion in 1863, 82-83. *Pos:* Designer & graphic coordr, US Govt, Stuttgart, WGer, 71-73; tech adv, Chabot Galleries, 75-76; lectr religious symbolism, Methodist Church, 79-82; League artist pub relations, Jr League Wichita, 84-86; artist, Propellor Mag, currently. *Teaching:* Guest lectr Western art, Kurisini Inst Int, Dar Es Salaam, Tanzania, 67; teaching asst painting, Univ Ore, Eugene, 69-70. *Awards:* First place & Grand Prize, Religion Art Festival, Congregational Church, 82. *Bibliog:* E O'Hara (auth), A woman for all seasons: Religious symbolism, The Wichitan City Mag, 82; Wonder of wood, Colonial Homes, 12/88. *Mem:* Wichita Artists Guild; Kans Watercolor Soc; Nat League Am Pen Women (treas, 85-86). *Media:* Watercolor; Woodcarving, Relief. *Publ:* Illusr, Diagnostic & therapeutic implications of schizophenic Art, J Arts & Psychotherapy, 84; Country Wildlife, Hammond Publ, 85; auth, Seasons of Inspiration, 86 & Paula Plott's Herbal, 87, Hammond Publ; Wild Flowers, 89, 90 & 91. *Dealer:* Wichita Gallery Fine Arts 4th Financial Ctr Wichita KS 67201. *Mailing Add:* 350 S Fountain St Wichita KS 67218

PLOUS, PHYLLIS
CURATOR
b Green Bay, Wis. *Study:* Univ Wis, with Oskar von Hagen & James Watrous, BA, 47; Univ London; Univ Calif, Santa Barbara. *Collections Arranged:* Ralph A Blakelock retrospective & tour (coauth, catalog); Charles Demuth

retrospective & tour (coauth, catalog); 19 Sculptors of the 40's; Sculptors in the 50's, catalog & tour; Jack Tworkov Recent Paintings, catalog; Sculptural Perspectives in the 70's catalog; Richard Diebenkorn, Intaglio Prints 1961-1978, catalog; Dark/Light: Extensions of Photography, catalog and tour; New York, Report on a Phenomenon, catalog; Terry Winters, Painting & Drawings, catalog & tour; Abstract Options, catalog & tour. *Pos:* Asst to dir, Santa Barbara Mus Art, 54-56; asst to dir, Univ Art Mus, Univ Calif, Santa Barbara, 63-72, cur, 72- *Awards:* Nat Endowment Arts Fel, Mus Professionals, 80. *Mem:* Am Asn Art Mus; Col Art Asn Am; Southern Calif Art Writers Asn; Int Coun Mus. *Mailing Add:* 375 Toro Canyon Rd Carpinteria CA 93013

PLOWDEN, DAVID
PHOTOGRAPHER, WRITER
b Boston, Mass, Oct 9, 32. *Study:* Yale Univ, BA, 55; pvt study with Minor White, 59-60. *Work:* Smithsonian Inst & Libr Cong, Washington, DC; Art Inst Chicago; Ctr Creative Photog, Tucson, Ariz; Calif Mus Photog, Riverside. *Comn:* Design resources photog study, Dept Transportation, Washington, DC, 66; Bridges of NAm, photog study, Smithsonian Inst, Washington, DC, 69-72; Railroad men, photog study, Smithsonian Inst, Washington, DC,, 76; Chicago industry, photog study, Chicago Hist Soc, 80-85; State Hist Soc Iowa, 87; Iowa Humanities Bd & Nat Endowment Humanities, 87-88. *Exhib:* Solo exhibs, American Vernacular, Int Ctr Photog, Washington, DC, 76, An American Chronology, Chicago Ctr Creative Photog, 82, Calif Mus Photog, Riverside, 82 & 83 & Federal Hall Mus, New York, 82; Metrop Mus Art, New York, 67; Whitney Mus, New York, 79; Art Inst Chicago, Ill, 83; State Univ New York, 86; Ctr Col Danville, Kentucky, 86; Ill State Univ, 87; Kunst Mus, Luzern, Switz, 87; Witkin Gallery, New York, 88; Smithsonian Inst, 71, 75, 76, & 89; Mid-Am Arts Alliance, Exhibs USA, 90. *Teaching:* Assoc prof photog, Inst Design, Ill Inst Technol, Chicago, 78-84; lectr, Univ Iowa, Iowa City, 85-87; prof, Grand Valley State Univ, Allendale, Mich, 88-89; vis prof, Univ Baltimore, Inst for Publ Design, 90. *Awards:* Guggenheim Found Fel, 68; Wilson Hicks Award, Univ Miami, 77; Seymour & Knox Found, 87. *Mem:* Am Soc Mag Photogr. *Publ:* Auth, Floor of the Sky, Sierra Club, 72; Bridges: The Spans of North America, Viking, 74, republ, Norton, 84; An American Chronology, Viking, 82; Industrial Landscape, Norton, 85; A Time of Trains, Norton, 87; A Sense of Place, Norton, 88. *Dealer:* Witkin Gallery 415 W Broadway New York NY 10012; Catherine Edelman Gallery 300 W Superior St Chicago Ill 60610. *Mailing Add:* 609 Cherry St Winnetka IL 60093

PLUMB, JAMES DOUGLAS
PAINTER, CURATOR
b New Haven, Conn, Dec 20, 41. *Study:* Univ Va; Philadelphia Col Art, BFA. *Work:* Acad Arts, Easton, Md. *Exhib:* Ann Md Show, Acad Arts, Easton, Md, 74, 78, 79 & 81; Art Asn Newport Ann Show, RI, 75; Conn Acad Arts Ann Show, Wadsworth Atheneum, 75; Five From the Eastern Shore, 76 & Md Biennial, 78, Baltimore Mus Art. *Collections Arranged:* Collection of the Academy of the Arts, 175 Works (auth, catalog), 79; College Show (auth, catalog), Contemporary Maryland Photographers (auth, catalog), 79; Eight Artists' Invitational Shows (auth, catalog), 79; Contemporary Works on Paper, 80. *Pos:* Cur, Acad Arts, Easton, Md, formerly. *Teaching:* Instr painting & drawing, Acad Arts, Easton, MD, 71-76; lectr art hist, State Extension Home Economics & Improvement, Univ Md, 73-76. *Awards:* Acad Arts Ann Show Awards, 74, 78 & 80; Best in Show, Easton Lions' Club Show, 75. *Media:* Oil on Canvas, Pencil on Paper. *Mailing Add:* PO Box 1088 Easton MD 21601

PLUMMER, CARLTON B
PAINTER, INSTRUCTOR
b Brunswick, Maine. *Study:* Vesper George Sch Art, dipl, 48-51; Mass Col Art, BS, 55-58; Boston Univ, MFA, 61-64. *Work:* Mus Military Art, Washington, DC; First Nat Bank Boston, Mass; Mus Fine Arts, Springfield, Mass; Aetna Insurance Co, Hartford, Conn. *Exhib:* Boston Watercolor Soc, Boston, 69 & Springfield, 70, Mus Fine Arts, Mass; 40 New England Watercolorists, 70 & Landscape I, 73, De Cordova Mus, Lincoln, Mass; Am Watercolor Soc Traveling Exhib, Frye Mus, Seattle, Wash, 76-77 & 79-81; Maine Artists, Farnsworth Mus, Rockland, 77; Boston's Jubilee 350, Copley Soc Boston, Mass, 80; Nat Acad Design Ann, Nat Acad Galleries, New York, 82, 84 & 86. *Pos:* Free-lance illusr, own pvt studio, Summerville, Mass, 53-58; art coodr, Chelmsford Sch System, Mass, 58-64; instr watercolor, own pvt workshop studio, Boothbay, Maine, 78-; vpres, New Eng Watercolor Soc, 79-82, pres, 82-84. *Teaching:* Prof art, drawing & painting, Univ Lowell, Mass, 64-86; watercolor workshops in Boothbay, Maine, and throughout US. *Awards:* Wash Sch Award, Am Watercolor Soc Ann, 79; Gold Medal Hon, Am Artists Prof League, 83; Grumbacher Gold Medal, Allied Artists Am, 83. *Bibliog:* Nita Leland (auth), Exploring Watercolor, North Light Publ, 85; Watercolor Demo (film), Chelmsford Cable TV, 86. *Mem:* Am Watercolor Soc; Allied Artists Am; Guild Boston Artists; Rocky Mountain Nat Watermedia Soc. *Media:* Watercolor, Oil. *Publ:* Auth, Carlton Plummer on the rocks, Palette Talk, 73; Using diagonal compositions in watercolor, 82 & Capturing the essence of a scene, 84, Am Artist; Exploring Watercolor, Northlight Publ, 85. *Dealer:* Peel Gallery Box 1 Peel Gallery Rd Danby VT 05739. *Mailing Add:* 10 Monument Hill Rd Chelmsford MA 01824

POCHMANN, VIRGINIA
PAINTER, DRAFTSMAN
b Starkville, Miss, Mar 13, 38. *Study:* Univ Wis, Madison, BS, 59; Am Acad Art, Chicago, Ill, 66-68; De Burgos Sch Art, Washington, DC, 68-70. *Work:* City of Sunnyvale Permanent Collection. *Exhib:* Am Watercolor Soc Ann, New York, NY, 82; Rocky Mountain Nat Watermedia Exhib, Golden, Colo, 82, 84 & 86; Watercolor USA, Springfield Art Mus, Mo, 83; 15th Ann Watercolor West, Harrison Mus Art, Logan, Utah, 83; Watercolor West Ann, Riverside, Calif, 83, 85 & 86; West Coast Watercolor Soc, Monterey Peninsula Mus Art, Calif, 84; San Diego Watercolor Soc Int Exhib, Calif, 84; one-person shows, Fireside Gallery, Carmel, Calif, 84 & 85; 65th Ann, Nat Watercolor Soc, Brea, Calif, 85; Bernard Galleries, Walnut Creek, Calif, 88; Foliage and Flowers, Sunnyvale, Calif, 88. *Awards:* Purchase Award, La Watercolor Soc Exhib, Pontchartrain Clinic, 85; Cash Award, WTex Watercolor Soc Nat Exhib, Mus Tex Tech, 85; First Award, Northern Calif Watercolor Competition, Pacific Art League, Palo Alto, 85. *Mem:* Nat Watercolor Soc; Artists Equity; WCoast Watercolor Soc (treas, 84-85). *Media:* Watercolor. *Publ:* Contribr, Gerald Brommer, Watercolor & Collage Workshop, Watson-Guptill, 86; Contemp Women Artists, (calender), Pomegranate Publ Co, Petaluma, Calif, 89; Contribr, Exploring Painting, Davis Publ Co, 87. *Dealer:* Bernard Galleries 1489 E Newell Ave Walnut Creek CA 94596. *Mailing Add:* 235 Oak Rd Danville CA 94526

PODUSKA, T F
LECTURER, PAINTER
b Cedar Falls, Iowa, Dec 6, 25. *Study:* Univ Northern Iowa, BA(art educ). *Work:* Denver Art Mus, Contemp Collection; Atlantic Richfield Corp; Amoco; Int Bus Machines; Exeter; and others. *Exhib:* Colo Womens Col, 79; Aspen Inst, 79; Univ Wyo, 80; Watercolor USA, Springfield, Mo, 80; Carson-Sapiro Gallery, Denver, 82; and others. *Pos:* Lectr, consult & proj asst, Colo Coun Arts & Humanities, 73. *Teaching:* Bus skills workshops, 75. *Awards:* Colo Governor's Award for Arts & Humanities, 77; Merit Award, Nat Acad of Design, 77. *Mem:* Alliance Contemp Art; Asian Art Asn. *Media:* Water Media, Paper. *Publ:* Coauth, Insuring the artist's work, Am Artist Bus Lett, suppl, 74; coauth, Business Practices for Artists, Artists Equity Asn, 75. *Mailing Add:* 10233 W Powers Ave Littleton CO 80127

POEHLMANN, JOANNA
ILLUSTRATOR, PRINTMAKER
b Milwaukee, Wis, Sept 5, 32. *Study:* Layton Sch Art, four-year dipl, 54; Kansas City Art Inst, 55; Marquette Univ, 58; Univ Wis, Milwaukee, 65 & 85. *Work:* Milwaukee Art Mus; Victoria & Albert Mus, London; Ruth & Marvin Sackner Archive Concrete & Visual Poetry, Miami Beach, Fla; Int Print Biennial, Embragel, Cabo Frio, Brazil; New York Pub Libr, New York; Mus Kunsthandwerk, Frankfurt, Ger; Istran Kiraly Muzeum-Szekasfechevar, Budapest, Hungary; and others. *Comn:* animal note cards, Recycled Paper Co, Chicago, 81-83; Edition of Hand Colored Lithograph, Quad/Graphics Inc, Pewaukee, Wis, 87; Poster Design, Charles Allis Art Mus, Milwaukee, 88; 50th Anniversary card design, Wustum Mus Art, Racine, Wis, 91; Artist Book Retirement Gift, Midwest Express Airlines, Milwaukee, Wis. *Exhib:* Retrospective, Drawings, Collages, Mindscapes, Milwaukee Art Mus, 66; Wisconsin Directions I & II, Milwaukee Art Mus, 75 & 78; Works on Paper, Art Inst Chicago, 78; Prints, Multiples, Art Inst Chicago, 81 & Nat Mus Am Art, 82; 10 Year Retrospective, Charles Allis Art Mus, Milwaukee, Wis, 91; Verbal Text/Non-Verbal Context: Handmade Books, Milwaukee Art Mus, 92; Cross Section World Financial Ctr, New York, 92; Artists Books in the USA, Galerie Druck & Buch, Tübingen, Ger; Retrospective, Wis Acad Art, Sci & Lett, 92; Book Arts in the USA, Ctr Bk Arts, New York, 90 (Touring Africa through 92); and others. *Awards:* Purchase Awards, 20th Bradley Nat Print & Drawings Exhib, Bradley Univ, Peoria, Ill, 85, 22nd Nat Works on Paper Biennial, Univ of Del, Newark, 86, 10th Print Nat, Univ Dallas, Irving, Tex, 88 & Univ NDak Print & Drawing Ann, Grand Forks, 88; Sacajawea Awards Competition, Milwaukee, Wis. *Bibliog:* James Auer (auth), Independent Artists of Wisconsin, Wis Acad Rev, 3/83; Laura Murphy (auth), Art in Wisconsin, 4/87; Printworld Directory/87-88, 91-92. *Mem:* Print Club Philadelphia; Printforum Milwaukee Art Mus; Ctr Bk Arts, New York; Artist Bookworks, Chicagl, Ill. *Media:* Watercolor, Collage; Lithography, Stone Hand Color Lithography. *Publ:* The chimp who went fishing, Int Wildlife Mag, 78; auth & illusr, The Day Before Christmas, Western Publ Co, 79; illusr, A Nutrition Monograph for Taking Off Pounds Sensibly, Tops Club, 80; auth & illusr, So have a Canary, self publ, 87; Love Letters, Food for Thought & Cancelling Out, Abbeville Press, Inc, 91. *Dealer:* Bradley Galleries 2565 N Downer Ave Milwaukee WI 53211; Tony Zwicker 15 Gramercy Park New York NY 10003. *Mailing Add:* 1231 N Prospect Ave Milwaukee WI 53211

POGACH, GERALD
PAINTER, SCULPTOR
b Philadelphia, Pa. *Study:* Pa State Univ, Univ Park Pa, BA, 52; Temple Univ, Philadelphia, Grad Study; St Joseph's Univ, Philadelphia, Grad Study, Univ Paris, doctorate, summa cum laude, 61. *Work:* City of Philadelphia, Pa; City of Atlantic City, NJ; State of NJ, Atlantic City, NJ; Blue Cross Greater Philadelphia, Pa; Noyes Mus, Oceanville, NJ. *Exhib:* One-man show, Noyes Mus, Oceanville, NJ, 85, Univ NC, Chapel Hill, 85, Univ City Sci Ctr, Philadelphia, 87; Tenth Int Sculpture Conf, Sculpture Park, Toronto, Can, 78; Sculpture Outdoors, Temple Univ, Ambler, Pa, 79-81; Ann Exhib, Woodmere Art Mus, Philadelphia, 87; Del State Mus, 90. *Pos:* Creative adminr & coordr, Philadelphia Art '79, 79-80; exec dir exhib, Philadelphia Olde City Arts Collaborative, 76-80; first vpres, Artist Equity Philadelphia, 82-83. *Awards:* First Prize in Sculpture, Atlantic City Ann, 75-76; Prix Meir Asn, Swiss-Am Exchange, 76; Best of Show, New York Coun Arts, 78. *Bibliog:* Abraham A Davidson (auth), Gerald Pogach, Noyes Mus, 85; WVHY Staff (dir), Pogach At Work, WVHX-Public TV, 82; Lillian Bregman (auth), Paris Artist in Philadelphia, Philadelphia Mus, 85. *Mem:* Philadelphia Art Alliance; Pa Acad Fine Arts; Inst Contemp Art. *Media:* Acrylic, Oil; All Media. *Mailing Add:* 709 Corinthian Ave Philadelphia PA 19130

POGANY, MIKLOS
PAINTER, PRINTMAKER
b Budapest, Hungary, Feb 4, 45. *Study:* St Procopins Col, BA, 65; Univ Chicago, MA, 65, PhD, 72. *Work:* Metrop Mus Art, New York, NY; Philadelphia Mus Art, Pa; Phillips Collection, Washington, DC; Victoria & Albert Mus, London, Eng; Nat Mus Am Art, Washington. *Exhib:* The American Artist as Printmaker, Brooklyn Mus, NY, 83; Contemp Am monotypes, Chrysler Mus, Norfolk, Va, 85; 1987 Invitational, New Britain Mus Am Art, Conn, 87; Contemp Art Exhib, Spencer Mus, Lawrence, Kans, 87. *Awards:* SECA Award Painting, San Francisco Mus Mod Art, 77; Grant for Printmaking, Conn Comn Arts, 80; Louis Comfort Tiffany Found Award, 81. *Dealer:* Victoria Munroe Gallery 415 W Broadway New York NY 10012. *Mailing Add:* Four St Ronan Terr New Haven CT 06511

POINDEXTER, ELINOR FULLER
DEALER
b Montreal, Can; US citizen. *Pos:* Dir, Poindexter Gallery, currently. *Mem:* Art Dealers Asn Am. *Specialty:* Contemporary painting and sculpture, especially American. *Mailing Add:* 1160 Fifth Ave No 202 New York NY 10029

POINIER, ARTHUR BEST
EDITORIAL CARTOONIST
b Oak Park, Ill, Feb 9, 11. *Study:* Drake Univ, 34; Ohio Wesleyan Univ, AB, LHD, 55. *Pos:* Sports cartoonist, Columbus Dispatch, Ohio, 29-32; cartoonist, Des Moines Register & Tribune, Iowa, 34-36; cartoonist comic strip, Jitter, 36-43; political cartoonist, Detroit Free Press, 40-51 & Detroit News, 51-76; mem, Bell-McClure Syndicate & United Features Syndicate, 50- *Mem:* Asn Am Ed Cartoonists. *Mailing Add:* 2174 Spruceway Ln Ann Arbor MI 48103

POLAN, ANNETTE
PAINTER, DRAFTSMAN
b Huntington, WVa, Dec 8, 44. *Study:* Hollins Col, BA, 63-67; Ecole du Louvre, 64-65. *Work:* Washington Post, Washington, DC; Huntington Mus, Huntington, WVa; WVa Coun Arts & Humanities, Charleston, WVa; Nat Drug Abuse Coun, Washington, DC; Columbia Hosp Women, Washington, DC. *Comn:* Portraits: Am Pharmaceutical Asn, Washington, DC, 90; Honorable Sandra Day OConnor, US Supreme Court; Bergen Brunswig Corp, Orange, Calif, 90. *Exhib:* New Washington Women, Anderson Gallery, Richmond, Va, 75; Am Genius, Corcoran Gallery, Washington, DC, 76; Am Drawing Biennial, Muscarelle Mus, Williamsburg, Va, 88; Self Portraits/ Images of Woman, Mus Contemp Art, Marywood Col, Scranton, Pa, 89. *Pos:* Artist-in-residence, Art Therapy Italia, Vignale, Italy, 86; vis artist, Landscape Painting Prog, La Napoule, France, 87; dir Corcoran Summer Prog, La Napoule, 88; lectr Contemp Am Portraiture, China, and Japan, 89; admin artists in residence, La Napoule, 90. *Teaching:* Asst prof fine art, Corcoran Sch Art, Washington, DC, 74- *Awards:* DC Comn Arts & Humanities Grants in Aid, 85. *Mem:* Corcoran Fac Asn (pres, 88-89). *Media:* Painting, Drawing. *Publ:* Illusr, Say What I Am Called, Selected Riddles from the Exeter Book, Sibyl-Child Press, 88. *Dealer:* J Gibson Edwards 1320 19th St NW Washington DC 20036. *Mailing Add:* 641 E St SE Washington DC 20003

POLAN, LINCOLN M
COLLECTOR, PATRON
b Wheeling, WVa, Feb 12, 09. *Study:* NY Univ; Univ Va; Ohio State Univ. *Pos:* Mem bd dirs, Huntington Galleries, WVa; trustee, Ctr for the Arts, Vero Beach, Fla. *Mem:* Mus of Mod Art; Metrop Mus Art. *Collection:* Line and wash drawings by Rodin; drawings by French impressionists; American paintings, predominantly of the Ash Can School; Renaissance portraits of men; Renaissance prints and engravings; Collections exhibited at Huntington Galleries Art Museum, Charleston Art Gallery, University of West Virginia Art Museum, Museum of Fine Arts, Houston, Texas, Phoenix Art Museum, Arizona and NY Pub Libr. *Mailing Add:* 2 Prospect Dr Huntington WV 25701

POLAN, NANCY MOORE
PAINTER
b Newark, Ohio. *Study:* Marshall Univ, AB; Huntington Mus Art, with Fletcher Martin, Hilton Leech, Paul Puzinas & Robert Friemark; Al Schmidt, Fla. *Work:* Huntington Mus Art; OVAR Mus, Portugal; Cabell Huntington Hospital; Templari, Roma, Italia. *Exhib:* Pa Acad Fine Arts, 61; Nat Arts Club, New York, 62-87 & 89-92; Joan Miro Graphics, Barcelona, 70 & Travel Exhib, 70-71; 21st Contemp Art, La Scala, Florence, Italy, 71 & 77; one-woman show, New York World's Fair, 65; Am Watercolor Framed Traveling Exhib, 72-73; and many group & one-woman shows. *Pos:* Mem, Art Comn Int Platform Asn, 68-83 & 91; hon vpres, Centro Studi e Scambi Internazionali, Rome, Italy, 78-88; fel, Intercontinental Biog Asn, 75-91. *Awards:* Grumbacher Watercolor Award, Pen & Brush, 75 & 78; Gold Medal, Acad Italy, 79, 84 & 86; Gold Medal Best of Show, Int Platform Asn, 91. *Bibliog:* The First Five Hundred, Melrose Press Ltd, Cambridge, England, 85; Who's Who in America, Marquis, current. *Mem:* Nat Arts Club; Pen & Brush, Inc; Accademia Italia; Allied Artists WVa; WVa Watercolor Soc (charter mem). *Media:* Watercolor, Oil. *Publ:* Contribr, cover, La Rev Mod, 61 & 66; spec issue, WVa Hillbilly, 73; Contemporary European Artists, 80; The New York Art Review, Les Krantz, 88. *Mailing Add:* 2 Prospect Dr Huntington WV 25701

POLANSKY, LOIS B
PRINTMAKER, COLLAGE ARTIST
b New York, NY, Dec 20, 39. *Study:* Queens Col, NY, with Miller & Ferren, BA, 60, MA, 67; Pratt Graphics Ctr, Sch Visual Arts & Bennington Col, 65-75. *Work:* Hunter Mus Art, Chattanooga, Tenn; Int Paper Co, New York; Sackner Archives, Fla; Prudential Insurance Co, New York; Bob Leslie Paper Mus, Beersheba, Israel. *Exhib:* The New Explosion: Paper Art, Fine Arts Mus of Long Island, Hempstead, NY, 82; Making Paper, Am Craft Mus, New York, 82; Sacred Artifacts, Objects of Devotion, Alternative Mus, New York, 83; Artists Books, Cleveland Mus, Ohio, 85; solo exhib, Metropolitan Opera House Lincoln Ctr, New York, 85-86; Seibu Mus, Tokyo; Beyond Words; Mem Art Gallery, Univ Rochester, NY; Regalia, Henry Street Arts Living Ctr, New York. *Pos:* Prog chair, Graphic Eye Gallery, 73-75; news ed, Central Hall Coop Gallery, Pt Washington, NY, 75-80. *Teaching:* Instr printmaking & papermaking, Adelphi Univ, 79-86. *Awards:* Nat Endowment Arts Visual Arts Fel Grant, 83-84. *Bibliog:* William Zimmer (auth), Lois Polansky, Arts Mag, 5/82; Dora Valler (auth), Le livre objet, L'Oeil Mag, Paris, 4/83; Marion Muller (auth), The metamorphosis of a book, Upper & Lower Case, 2/85. *Mem:* Col Art Asn Am; Soc Graphic Artists. *Dealer:* Alexander F Milliken Inc 98 Prince St New York NY 10012. *Mailing Add:* Dept Art Adelphi Univ Garden City NY 11530

POLCARI, STEPHEN
HISTORIAN, ADMINISTRATOR
b Boston, Mass, Jan 22, 45. *Study:* Columbia Col, BA, 67; Columbia Univ, MA, 71; Univ Calif, Santa Barbara, PhD, 80. *Pos:* Cur, DeCordova Mus, Lincoln, Mass, 76. *Teaching:* Asst prof mod art, Univ Ill, Urbana, 79-83; State Univ NY, Stony Brook, 83-90. *Awards:* Rubinstein Mus Fel, Whitney Mus Art, 77; Nat Endowment Humanities, 82; Inst Advan Study, Princeton, 82; Nat Mus Am Art, 91. *Mem:* Col Art Asn; Alumni of the Inst Advanced Studies. *Res:* Intellectual, cultural & political history and the development of modern art, especially abstract expressionism, moderne and American Art, the Depression and War, 1930-1950s. *Publ:* Abstract Expressionism, New & Improved, 88; Abstract Expressionism and the Modern Experience, Cambridge Univ Press, 91; Martha Graham & Abstract Expressionism, Smithsonian Studies in Am Art, 90; Orozco & Pollock: Epic Transfigurations, Am Art, 92. *Mailing Add:* Dir NY Archives Am Art 1285 Sixth Ave New York NY 10019

POLESKIE, STEPHEN FRANCIS
ENVIRONMENTAL ARTIST, PRINTMAKER
b Pringle, Pa, June 3, 38. *Study:* Wilkes Col, BA, 59; New Sch Social Res, 61. *Work:* Whitney Mus Art, Metrop Mus Art & Mus Mod Art, New York; Victoria & Albert Mus; Tate Gallery, London. *Comn:* Aerial theatre, Toledo, Ohio, 84 & Richmond, Va, 85; Int Video Festival, Locarno, Switz, 85; Zone Art Ctr, Springfield, Mass, 88. *Exhib:* Word & Image-Posters and Typography (1879-1967), Mus Mod Art, New York, 68; Recent Acquisitions: Prints and Drawings, Metrop Mus Art, 69; Oversize Prints, Whitney Mus Am Art, 71; Louis K Meisel Gallery, New York, 78 & 80; Int Commun Agency tour of USSR, 79; one-man exhib, Palace of Cult & Sci, Warsaw, Poland & Gallery of Mod Art, Gdansk, 79; Sky Art Conference, Mass Inst Technol, 81; Int Biennial Graphic Art, Ljubljana, Yugoslavia, 81 & 83; Anderson Gallery, Va Commonwealth Univ, 83; Studio D'Ars, Milano, 84; Stadt Mus, Kassel, WGer, 86; John Hansard Gallery, Southampton, Eng, 89; Lee Art Gallery, Clemson Univ, SC, 90. *Teaching:* Instr, Sch Visual Arts, New York, 66-68; assoc prof silk-screen & contemp art issues, Cornell Univ, 68-81, prof, 81-; vis prof, Univ Calif, Berkeley, 76. *Awards:* Am Fedn Arts, 65; New York State Coun Arts, 73. *Bibliog:* Pierre Restany (auth), Christo and Poleskie, D'Ars, Milano, 83; Peter Frank (auth), Flights of Fancy, catalog essay, Richmond, Va, 85; Enrico Crispolti (auth), catalog essay, Rome, 87. *Media:* Aerial Theatre Performance, Etching. *Publ:* Auth, Dell'arte e del Volo, Dars Milano, 84; Art and Flight: Historical Origins to Contemporary Works, Leonardo, 85. *Dealer:* Apogee Airway 306 Stone Quarry Rd Ithaca NY 14850; New Acquisitions Gallery 120 E Washington St Syracuse NY 13202. *Mailing Add:* 306 Stone Quarry Rd Ithaca NY 14850

POLING, CLARK V
HISTORIAN
US citizen. *Study:* Yale Univ, BA, 62; Columbia Univ, MA, 66, PhD, 73. *Collections Arranged:* Bauhaus Color, 76, Contemporary Art in Atlanta Collections, 76 & Contemporary Art in Southern California, 80, High Mus Art; Kandinsky: Russian and Bauhaus Years, 1915-1933, Guggenheim Mus, 83; Henry Hornbostel-Michael Graves, Emory Univ Mus, 85. *Teaching:* Asst prof mod art, Emory Univ, 73-79, assoc prof, 79-88, prof, 88- , dir, 88-86, chmn Mus Art & Archeol, 87- *Awards:* Kress Found Fel, 64-65; Deutscher Akad Austauschdienst Grant, 77 & 81; Nat Endowment Humanities Stipend, 78. *Mem:* Col Art Asn; Twentieth Century Art Soc (bd dirs, 88-). *Res:* Early 20th century European art and theory, especially surrealism: contemporary American art. *Publ:* Auth, Geometric abstraction: A new generation, Inst Contemp Art, Boston, 81; Kandinsky's Teaching at the Bauhaus, Rizzoli, NY, 87; The City and Modernity: Art in Berlin in the First World War and Its Aftermath, Art in Berlin 1815-1989, High Mus Art, Atlanta, 89. *Mailing Add:* c/o Art Hist Dept Carlos Hall Emory Univ Atlanta GA 30322

POLK, FRANK FREDRICK
SCULPTOR
b Louisville, Ky, Sept 1, 08. *Study:* With Hughlette Wheeler, George Phippen & J R Williams. *Work:* Colorado Springs Fine Arts Ctr; John Ascuaga's Nuggett, Sparks, Nev & pvt collection Ezra Brooks. *Exhib:* Cowboy Artists Am Ann Show, Cowboy Hall Fame, Oklahoma City, 68-72 & Phoenix Art Mus, Ariz, 73-75; Matthews Traveling Exhib to eastern mus & galleries,

including the Kennedy Gallery, New York, 71. *Awards:* Golden Spur Award, Bronze, Nat Rodeo Cowboy's Asn, 68; Silver Medal, George Phippen Mem Ann Art Show, Prescott, Ariz, 76. *Bibliog:* Anne Grose (auth), Cowpoke sculptor, Quarter Horse J, 1/68; Patricia Broder (auth), Bronzes of the American West, Abrams, 74; Ten Years with the Cowboy Artists of America, Northland Press, 76. *Mem:* Cowboy Artists Am. *Publ:* Auth, F-F-F-Frank Polk: An Uncommonly Frank Autobiography, Northland Press, 78. *Dealer:* Texas Trails Gallery 255 Losoya San Antonio TX 78205. *Mailing Add:* Box 126 Mayer AZ 86333

POLLACK, REGINALD MURRAY
PAINTER, SCULPTOR
b Middle Village, NY, July 29, 24. *Study:* Apprentice to Moses Soyer, 41; study with Wallace Harrison, 46-47; Acad Grande Chaumiere, Paris, 48-52. *Work:* Whitney Mus Am Art & Mus Mod Art, New York; Tel Aviv Mus, Jerusalem Mus & Haifa Mus, Israel; Nat Mus Am Art & Hirshhorn Mus & Sculpture Garden, Washington, DC; Brooklyn Mus; Rockefeller Inst. *Comn:* Peace (greeting card), Jewish Mus, New York, 61; painting for Great Thoughts of Western Man series, Container Corp Am, 64; cover for State of NY Dir, Bell Tel Co, 68-69; Chinese animal destiny calendar, Colgate-Palmolive Co, 72; Jacob's Dream (103' painting), Washington Cathedral, 74; Touche Ross New Perspective Awards, 79. *Exhib:* 63 one-man shows, 12 at Peridot Gallery, New York, 49-69, Felix Landau Gallery, Los Angeles, Washington Project for Arts: Retrospective, 77 & Jack Rasmussen Gallery, Washington, DC, 78-82; Summit Gallery, New York, 83; The Tartt Gallery, Washington, DC, 86; Denise Cade Gallery, NY, 86; Arctic Images Gallery, Colo, 87; The Gallery, Leesburg, Va, 92. *Pos:* Mem bd trustees, Washington Proj for the Arts, DC, 75-80; dir, The Gallery, Leesburg, Va, 92- *Teaching:* Vis critic art, Yale Univ, 62-63; instr art, Cooper Union, 63-64; staff mem, Human Rels Training Ctr, Univ Calif, Los Angeles, at Lake Arrowhead, 66; pvt art classes, 67-69; instr, Quaker Half-Way House, Los Angeles, 68; vis artist, Mat Res Lab, Pa State Univ, 77 & 78. *Awards:* Prix Othon Friesz-V, Paris, 56; Prix des Peintres Etrangers - Laureate, Paris, 58; Ingram-Merrill Found Grants in painting, 64 & 70-71. *Media:* Oil; Bronze, Wood. *Publ:* Auth & illusr, The Magician and the Child, Atheneum, 71; illusr, Ctr for Dem Insts Mag, 3/72; auth, To artists with love & Brancusi's sculpture versus his home, Art News; illusr, Sounds Freedomring, Martin, Holt-Rinehart & Winston; Ted Knight (auth), Oedipus, 73; O is for Overkill, Viking, Pollack; The Enjoyment of Music, Machlis, Norton. *Mailing Add:* Rte 1 Box 955 Waterford VA 22910

POLLAK, THERESA
PAINTER, DRAFTSMAN
b Richmond, Va, Aug 13, 1899. *Study:* Westhampton Col, Univ Richmond, BS; Art Students League; Fogg Mus, Harvard Univ, Carnegie Fel; with Hans Hofmann, Provincetown, Mass; Univ Richmond, Hon DFA, 73; Va Commonwealth Univ, Hon DH, 78. *Work:* Va Commonwealth Univ, Richmond; Va Mus Fine Arts, Richmond; Chrysler Mus Norfolk, Va; Univ Va, Charlottesville; Westhampton Col, Univ Richmond, Va. *Exhib:* 12th Biennial Exhib Contemp Am Painting, Corcoran Gallery Art, Washington, DC, 30; 1st Biennial Contemp Am Painting, Whitney Mus Am Art, New York, 32; New Eng Soc Contemp Art, Boston Mus Fine Arts, 33; Oakland Art Gallery, Calif, 41, 42 & 43; Butler Inst Am Art, Youngstown, Ohio, 47; 19th Irene Leache Mem Regional Painting Exhib, Chrysler Mus Norfolk, 68; Virginia Artists 1971, Va Mus Fine Arts, Richmond, 71; one-person show, Reynolds/Minor Gallery, Richmond, Va, 83, 86 & 88; retrospective, Anderson Galley, Va Commonwealth Univ, 86; Westhampton Artists, Marsh Gallery, Univ Richmond, Va, 90. *Teaching:* Instr drawing & painting, Va Commonwealth Univ, 28-35, prof drawing & painting, 35-69, fac chmn, 42-50, emer prof, 69-; instr drawing & painting, Westhampton Col, Univ Richmond, 30-35. *Awards:* Cert Distinction, Va Mus Fine Arts, 71; Theresa Pollak Bldg of Fine Arts, Va Commonwealth Univ, 71; First Laureate Award, Peer Eminent in art, Va Cult Laureate Ctr, 77. *Bibliog:* Portrait of a very special woman, Va Commonwealth Mag, 2/80. *Mem:* hon mem Richmond Artists Asn; life mem Art Students League, New York. *Media:* Oil; Miscellaneous Media. *Publ:* Contribr, art criticisms in Richmond Newsleader & Richmond Times Dispatch, 31-49; auth, An Art School--Some Reminiscences, Va Commonwealth Univ, 69. *Mailing Add:* Reynolds Gallery 1514 W Main St Richmond VA 23221

POLLARD, DONALD PENCE
DESIGNER, PAINTER
b Bronxville, NY, Sept 13, 24. *Study:* Pvt study with Harriet Lumis; RI Sch Design, BFA; Brown Univ. *Work:* Eisenhower Mus; Kennedy Collection; Govt of Can, Ottawa, Ont; also in pvt collections in the US, Europe, Asia & the Far East. *Comn:* Design of the Great Ring of Canada (with Alexander Seidel); other comns as assigned by Steuben Glass. *Exhib:* Conn Nat Acad, 42; all major Steuben Exhibs, 53-; Phillips Mall Ann, 72. *Pos:* Sr designer, Steuben Glass, formerly. *Media:* Crystal, Oil. *Mailing Add:* 3704 N Ocean Blvd Myrtle Beach SC 29577

POLLARO, PAUL
PAINTER
b Brooklyn, NY. *Study:* Flatiron Sch Art, New York; Art Students League, Pratt Graphic Ctr. *Work:* Currier Mus Art; Jan Perry Mayer Collection; Chrysler Mus; Orlando Mus Art, Fla; Notre Dame Univ Mus Art, South Bend, Ind. *Exhib:* Ann, Pa Acad Fine Arts, Philadelphia, 64; Am Acad Arts & Lett, 66 & 72; Nat Inst Arts & Lett, 69 & 72; Artists of the 20th Century, Mus Mod Art, New York, 70; Artists at Work, Finch Col Mus, 71; Babcock Gallery, New York, 73; Louis Newman Gallery, Beverly Hills, Calif; L K Meisel Gallery, New York; one man exhib, Chrysler Mus, 91. *Pos:* Assoc dir, The MacDowell Colony, 73-77. *Teaching:* Instr painting, New Sch Social Res, 64-69; asst prof painting, Wagner Col, 69-72; vis artist, Notre Dame Univ, summers 65 & 67. *Awards:* Second Prize, Jersey City Mus, 62; MacDowell Colony Fels, 66, 68 & 71; Tiffany Found Grant, 67. *Media:* Acrylic, Oil. *Publ:* articles in: Art in America, Art News, Arts, NY Times, Art Space, Art New Eng, Art Int. *Mailing Add:* Norway Hill Hancock NH 03449

POLLEI, DANE F
MUSEUM DIRECTOR, ADMINISTRATOR
b Fond du Lac, Wis. *Study:* Beloit Col, BA. *Collections Arranged:* Wayang Puppets: Art of Indonesia, Logan Mus Anthropology, 84; German Expressionism, Wright Mus Art, 85; Beloit and Vicinity, Wright Mus Art, 86; Franklin Boggs and V O Schaffer: Art and Architecture, Freeport Art Mus, Ill, 88; Scenes of Madagascar: Ethnographic Portraits 1890-1930, Freeport Art Mus, Ill, 88; The Art of Persuasion: Posters from the World Wars, Kenosha Hist Mus, 90. *Pos:* Asst cur, Logan Mus Anthropology, 83-85; asst to dir, Wright Mus Art, 85-86; dir, Freeport Art Mus, Ill, 87-89. *Teaching:* Instr, mus studies, Univ Wis, Oshkosh, 87; instr, Am Indian art, Highland Community Col, 88-89; exec dir, Kenosha Co Hist Soc Mus, Wis. *Mem:* Am Asn Mus; Ill Arts Alliance; Wis Art Educ Asn. *Mailing Add:* 5946 Fifth Ave Kenosha WI 53140-1570

POLLITT, JEROME JORDAN
HISTORIAN, EDUCATOR
b Fair Lawn, NJ, Nov 26, 34. *Study:* Yale Univ, New Haven, Conn, BA, 57; Columbia Univ, New York, PhD, 63. *Pos:* Ed-in-chief, Am J Archeol, 74-78. *Teaching:* Prof classic art & archeol, Yale Univ, 62- *Publ:* Auth, The Art of Greece: Sources and Documents, 64 & The Art of Rome: Sources and Documents, 65, Prentice-Hall & Cambridge Univ Press, 83 & 90; Art and Experience in Classical Greece, Cambridge Univ Press, 72; The Ancient View of Greek Art, Yale Univ Press, 75; Art in the Hellenistic Age, Cambridge Univ Press, 86. *Mailing Add:* Dept of Classics 1967 Yale Station New Haven CT 06520

POLLOCK, BRUCE
PAINTER, SCULPTOR
b Painesville, Ohio, July 7, 51. *Study:* Carnegie-Mellon Univ, 70; Cleveland Inst Art, BFA, 76; Tyler Sch Art, MFA, 78. *Work:* Philadelphia Mus Art; Prudential Insurance Co. *Comn:* 12th Walnut brick-walk, Redevelop Authority Philadelphia. *Exhib:* Solo exhibs, Alan Stone Gallery, New York, 82, Karen Lennox Gallery, Chicago, Ill, 82, Laurence Miller Gallery, New York, 84, Jeffrey Fuller, Philadelphia, 84, Cavin-Morris Gallery, New York, 86, Janet Fleisher Gallery, Philadelphia, 87-90, Pa Acad Fine Art, Philadelphia, 90; May Show, Cleveland Mus Art, Ohio, 73, 81 & 88; Pertaining to Philadelphia, Philadelphia Mus Art, 83; An Inside Place, 85 & Stalking the Light, 87, Noyes Mus, Oceaville, NJ; An Inside Place, Noyes Mus, Oceanville, NJ, 85; Made in Philadelphia No 7, Inst Contemp Arty, Pa, 87; Perspectives Pa, Carnegie-Mellon Univ Gallery, 88; Contemp Philadelphia Artists, Philadelphia Mus Art, 90. *Awards:* Fel, Macdowell Colony, Peterborough, NH, 87; Distinguished Artist Award, Contemp Philadelphia Artists, Philadelphia Mus Art, 90. *Bibliog:* Reviews in Artforum, 10/79, Art in America, 10/82, New Art Examiner, 10/82, 3/83 & 3/88. *Media:* Acrylic, Oil. *Publ:* Illusr, Metapsychology Mag, Vol I No II, autumn, 85. *Dealer:* Janet Fleisher S 17th St Philadelphia PA. *Mailing Add:* c/o Janet Fleisher Gallery 211 S 17th St Philadelphia PA 19103

POLLOCK, MERLIN F
PAINTER, EDUCATOR
b Manitowoc, Wis, Jan 3, 05. *Study:* Art Inst Chicago, BFA & MFA; Ecole Beaux Arts, Paris; Sch Fine Arts, Fontainebleau, France. *Work:* Syracuse Univ; Munson-Williams-Proctor Inst, Utica; Everson Mus, Syracuse; State Univ NY Col Environ Sci & Forestry, Syracuse; Archives Am Art, Smithsonian Inst. *Comn:* Steel (fresco), Tildon Tech High Sch, Chicago; mural, O'Fallon Ill Post Off, comn by US Treas Dept. *Exhib:* 125 Years of New York State Painting & Sculpture, NY State Fair, 66; one-man shows, Mich State Univ, East Lansing, 59, Everson Mus, Syracuse, 66 & 82, Lubin House, New York, NY, 70 & Lowe Art Ctr, Syracuse Univ, 71; and others. *Pos:* Supvr mural painting, Ill Art Proj, Works Proj Admin, 40-43; chmn grad prog, Sch Art, Syracuse Univ, 47-71, actg dean, Sch Art, 60-61, 67-68 & 69-70. *Teaching:* Instr mural painting, fresco & drawing, Art Inst Chicago, 35-43; prof painting, Syracuse Univ, 46-71. *Awards:* James Nelson Raymond Fel, Art Inst Chicago, 30; Syracuse Ann, Everson Mus, 47, 54-56, 60 & 64-66; Finger Lakes Ann, Rochester Mem Mus, 56-58 & 60; Centennial Medal, 70 & Chancellor's Citation, 79, Syracuse Univ. *Media:* Multimedia. *Mailing Add:* 120 Wellwood Dr Fayetteville NY 13066

POLONSKY, ARTHUR
PAINTER, EDUCATOR
b Lynn, Mass, June 6, 25. *Study:* Boston Mus Sch, with Karl Zerbe, dipl (with highest honors), 48; Europ Traveling Fel, 48-50. *Work:* Fogg Mus, Harvard Univ, Cambridge; Mus Fine Arts, Boston; Addison Gallery Am Art, Andover; Walker Art Ctr; Stedelijk Mus, Amsterdam, Holland. *Comn:* Stone with the Angel (portfolio of ten original lithographs), Impressions Workshop, Inc, Boston, 69. *Exhib:* Art Today-50, Metrop Mus Art, New York, 50; twenty-four one-man exhibs in Boston, New York & Washington, 51-92; Boston Arts Festival, Boston, 85; Starr Gallery, Boston, 87; Fitchburg Art Mus, Mass, 90; Boston Public Libr, 90. *Pos:* Founding mem & dir, Artists' Equity Asn, 48-67. *Teaching:* Instr painting, Boston Mus Sch, 50-60; asst prof painting, drawing & design, Brandeis Univ, 54-65; assoc prof painting, drawing & design, Boston Univ, Sch for the Arts, 65-90, prof emer, 90. *Awards:* Tiffany Found Grant for Painting, 51-52; First Prize, Boston Arts Festival, 54; Purchase Award,

Drawings '74, Wheaton Nat Exhib, Wheaton Col, 74. *Bibliog:* Article, Life Mag, 12/48; reviews of exhibs in Art News, Arts Mag, NY Times, Time Mag, New Yorker Mag & others, 48-81; Archives Am Art, Smithsonian Inst, 72; Nathan Goldstein (auth), The Art of Responsive Drawing, Prentice Hall, 73, 77 & 84; Nathan Goldstein (auth), Figure Drawing, Prentice-Hall, 76. *Media:* All. *Publ:* Illusr, Sexual Decisions, Little, Brown & Co, 80; Poetry in Motion, Sundance Publ, 87;; Leo Bronstein (auth), Kabbalah And Art, Brandeis Univ Press, 78;; Richard Jones (auth), The Dream Poet, Schenkman Books, 81; Sadie, Remember, Sundance Publ, 92; and others. *Mailing Add:* 364 Cabot St Newtonville MA 02160

POLSKY, CYNTHIA HAZEN
MUSEUM TRUSTEE, COLLECTOR
b New York, NY, Feb 16, 39. *Study:* Art Students League; New Sch Social Res; Marymount Manhattan Col, BA; Fordham Univ, MBA. *Work:* Corcoran Gallery Am Art, Washington, DC; Israel Mus, Jerusalem; Ulrich Mus of Art, Wichita, Kans; Fogg Art Mus, Cambridge, Mass; American Embassy, London, Eng; and others. *Exhib:* One-woman shows, Benson Gallery, Bridgehampton, Long Island, NY, 68, Comara Gallery, Los Angeles, 69, Artisan Gallery, Houston, Tex, 70, Palm Springs Desert Mus, 72-73 & Crispo Gallery, New York, 73 & 74; Ulrich Mus of Art, Wichita, Kans, 77. *Pos:* Trustee, Metrop Mus Art, mem acquistions comt, adv comt publishing merchandise, adv comt asian art, chmn, adv comt membership & develop visiting comt for 20th century art, currently; vpres & trustee, Storm King Art Ctr, Mountainville, NY, mem exec comt, chmn, acquisitions comt; chmn, President's Coun, Asia Soc, New York, currently; vchmn, Coun Fel, Pierpont Morgan Libr, New York, currently. *Bibliog:* Judith Denham (auth), article, in: Art Week, 73; Alfred Frankenstein (auth), article, in: San Francisco Chronicle, 73. *Media:* Acrylic, Watercolor. *Publ:* Auth, Indian Paintings from the Polsky Collection, The Art Mus, Princeton Univ, 82; Cynthia Polsky, Paintings 1973-1974, 90. *Mailing Add:* 50 E 79th St New York NY 10021

POLZER, JOSEPH
HISTORIAN
b Vienna, Austria, May 7, 29; US citizen. *Study:* Univ Iowa, BA(art), 50, MA(art hist), 52; Inst Fine Arts, NY Univ, PhD(art hist), 63. *Teaching:* Instr, Univ Kans, 57-58; lectr, Univ Buffalo, 58-62; from asst prof to prof, Univ Louisville, 62-73; prof art, Queen's Univ, Kingston, formerly, Univ Calgary, Alberta, Can, currently. *Res:* Late Rome, Renaissance. *Publ:* Auth, articles in Late Antique & Renaissance Art. *Mailing Add:* Dept of Art Univ Calgary 2500 Univ Dr Calgary AB T2N 1N4 Canada

POMEROY, FREDERICK GEORGE
PAINTER
b Oakland, Calif, Aug 30, 24. *Study:* Calif Col Arts & Crafts, Oakland, AB(scholar), 53; Ecole de Beaux Arts, Fontainebleau, France, with Lucien Fontanarosa, cert, 51; La Grande Chaumiere, Paris, France, cert, 51; Centre Universitaire de la Mediterrane, Nice, France, cert, 65. *Comn:* Murals commissioned privately in Pebble Beach, Calif, 58 & Carmel Valley, Calif, 58; Restorations, Beeches Gallery, Carmel, Calif, 86- *Exhib:* James Phelan Competition, San Francisco Mus Art, 50; Artist of Monterey County, Monterey Mus Art, Calif, 81; Watercolor Work, Seaside City Hall, Calif, 83; Recent Paintings, Marjory Evans Gallery, Carmel, Calif, 86; Local Color, Sangre de Cristo Arts Ctr, Pueblo, Colo, 89. *Teaching:* Instr art, Robert Luis Stevenson Sch, Pebble Beach, Calif, 54. *Awards:* French Government Cultural Relations Prize, 51; Kiwanis of Pacific Grove First Prize in Watercolor, 5th Ann Competition, 69; First Prize, Pacific Grove Mus 13th Ann Competition, 77. *Bibliog:* Lyman Pitman (auth), Natures detail--, Chieftain, Pueblo, Colo, 3/12/89. *Mem:* Monterey Peninsula Watercolor Soc. *Media:* Oil, Watercolor. *Publ:* Illusr, Trees of the San Francisco Bay Area, Univ Calif Press, 59; The Poetry Shell, Mag of Verse, fall 77 & spring 78. *Dealer:* Maison Val du Soleil El Caminito Rd Carmel Valley CA 93924; Beech's Gallery Seventh & San Carlos Carmel CA 93921. *Mailing Add:* 88 Boronda Rd Carmel Valley CA 93924

POMEROY, LYNDON FAYNE
SCULPTOR
b Sidney, Mont, Mar 9, 25. *Study:* Mont State Univ, BS, 52, MAA, 60. *Work:* Yellowstone Art Ctr, Billings, Mont; Mont State Hist Mus, Helena. *Comn:* Loggers, Savings & Loan, Green Bay, Wis, 80; Ditch Builder, Hist Centennial Co, Worland, Wyo, 89. *Exhib:* Nat Religious Art Exhib, Detroit, Mich, 64. *Teaching:* Asst prof, Northern Mont Col, 53-58; Eastern Mont Col, 58-61. *Awards:* Mont State Gov's Arts Award Visual Arts, 91. *Mem:* Growth Thru Art for Disabled Adults (bd dir, 90); Stillwater Soc. *Media:* Steel. *Mailing Add:* 5000 Rimstock Rd Billings MT 59102

POMEROY, MARY BARNAS (MRS F G POMEROY)
PAINTER, ILLUSTRATOR
b Frankfurt a/Main, Ger, Mar 3, 21; US citizen. *Study:* Studied with Carl Barnas, Quito Eduador, 38-46; Pa Acad Fine Arts, with Daniel Garber, Roy Nuse, Franklin Watkins & Henry Pitz, 46-48. *Work:* Univ Calif Dept of Botany, Berkeley; Hunt Inst Botanical Doc, Carnegie-Mellon Univ, Pittsburgh, Pa. *Comn:* Geological Illustrations, comn by Dr Sauer, Univ Cent, Quito, Ecuador, 40; Fruits & Vegetables (paintings), comn by Mrs Foote, Carmel Valley, Calif, 74; Flowering Trees of America (Plate design), Franklin Mint Corp, Pa, 79; Restorations, Beeches Gallery, Carmel, 87-; Wildflowers of the Asilomar Dunes (poster), Asilomar Operating Corp & Dept Parks, Pacific Grove, Calif, 89-90. *Exhib:* Solo exhib, Wildflowers of Ecuador, Universidad Cent, Quito, Ecuador, 40, Ecuadorian Wildflowers & Fungi, Acad Nat Sci, Philadelphia, Pa, 46 & Acad Sci, Golden Gate Park, San Francisco, Calif, 48 & Jungle Flowers, Mus of Mo Botanical Gardens Traveling Show, Mo, 74; Int Exhib of Botanical Art & Illus, Hunt Inst, Pittsburgh, Pa, 64, 72 & 77; Exhib Contemp Botanical Artists & Illusr, Cleveland Mus Art, Ohio, 66; California Land & Seascapes, Portraits, Florals, Marjorie Evans Gallery, Carmel, Calif, 81-86; Natural Color, Sangre de Cristo Art & Conf Ctr, Pueblo, Colo, 89. *Pos:* Illusr, Fossil Foraminifera & Shells, Int Petroleum Co, Guayaquil, Ecuador, 43-44; botanical illusr, Univ Calif Berkeley for H Mason & others, 47-53; free-lance painter & illusr, 53- *Teaching:* Pvt lessons in watercolor & botanical illust, Berkeley, Calif, 50; pvt workshops in outdoor landscape in watercolor, Carmel, Calif, 66, 67 & 69. *Awards:* Pa Acad Fine Arts, First Prize in Anatomy & Animal Drawing, Students Work Acad Gallery, Philadelphia, 47; Mus Nat Hist Best Monterey County Subject, 14th Ann Watercolor Competition, 78 & Best Small Painting, 18th Ann Watercolor Competition, 82, Pacific Grove. *Bibliog:* Pat Griffith (auth), Carmel Valley's nature artist M B Pomeroy, Carmel Valley Outlook, 10/12/72; art ed, A calendar full of birthday flowers, Carmel Pinecone, 10/27/83; Lyman Pittman (auth), Nature's details, colors, inspire California couple, Pueblo Chieftain, 3/12/89. *Mem:* Monterey Peninsula Watercolor Soc. *Media:* Watercolor, Pen & Ink. *Publ:* Illusr, Las Plantas, Publicaciones de las Univ Cent, Quito, Ecuador, 39; A Flora of the Marshes of California & Native Trees of the San Francisco Bay Region, Univ Calif Berkeley Press, 59; Saloya, 67 & Eduador's edible jewels, 69, America's Mag, Pan-Am Union Publ. *Dealer:* Beeches Gallery PO Box 4092 Carmel CA 93921; Maison Val Du Soleil Gallery PO Box 696 Carmel Valley CA 93924. *Mailing Add:* 88 Boronda Rd Carmel Valley CA 93924

PONCE DE LEON, MICHAEL
PRINTMAKER, PAINTER
b Miami, Fla, July 4, 22. *Study:* Univ Mex, BA; Art Students League; Nat Acad Design; Brooklyn Mus Art Sch; also in Europe. *Work:* Mus Mod Art & Metrop Mus Art, New York; Nat Gallery Art & Smithsonian Inst, Washington, DC; Brooklyn Mus; and others. *Comn:* Many print editions, 60-; ten prints, US State Dept, 66; glass sculpture, Steuben Glass, 71; 100 prints, Pioneer Moss, Inc, annually, 68-83. *Exhib:* Mus Arte Mod, Paris; Victoria & Albert Mus, London; Venice Bienale, 70; Mus Mod Art & Metrop Mus, New York; Smithsonian Inst, Washington, DC; and others. *Pos:* Int Cult Exchange, US State Dept, teaching, lect & travel, Yugoslavia, 65, India & Pakistan, 67-68, Spain, 71 & SAmerica. *Teaching:* Instr printmaking, Hunter Col, 59-66; prof, New York Univ, 77 & Pratt Inst, 78; instr printmaking, Art Students League, 78-, Berkeley Univ, Calif, Univ Calif, Los Angeles, and others. *Awards:* More than 65 medals & awards, incl Tiffany Found Grants, 54 & 55; Fulbright Grants, 56 & 57; Guggenheim Found Grant, 67. *Bibliog:* G Peterdi (auth), Printmaking, Macmillan, 72; F Eichenberg (auth), The Art of the Print, Abrams, 77; D Saff (auth), Printmaking History and Process, Holt, Rinehart & Winston, 78. *Mem:* Soc Am Graphic Artists (treas, 68); Asn Am Univ Prof. *Publ:* Contribr, Experiments in three dimensions, Art Am, 68; auth, The collage intaglio, 72; The collage-intaglios of Michael Ponce de Leon, Am Artist, 8/74; History of an Art, Skira (in 4 languages), 81; History of International Art, Academia Italia (in 4 languages), 81. *Dealer:* Jane Haslem Gallery 2121 P St NW Washington DC 20036; AAA Gallery 663 Fifth Ave New York NY. *Mailing Add:* Dept Art Art Students League 215 W 57th St New York NY 10019

POND, CLAYTON
PAINTER, PRINTMAKER
b Long Island, NY, June 10, 41. *Study:* Carnegie Inst Technol, BFA, 64; Pratt Inst, MFA, 66. *Work:* Smithsonian Nat Air & Space Mus, Nat Gallery Art & Nat Collection Fine Arts, Washington, DC; Mus Mod Art, New York; Boston Mus Fine Arts; Philadelphia Mus Art; Art Inst Chicago; and many others. *Comn:* Large painted construction, 1985-86 Fly-by of Halley's Comet, Nat Air & Space Mus, Washington, DC; serigraph, Sailing Canoe, Madison Print Club, Wis; large painted sculpture & study painting, Printing Press, Motter Printing Press Co, York, Pa, 88; serigraph, Adirondack Window, Albany Print Club, NY, 90; large painted sculpture & study painting, The Intimidator, Anderson Gallery, Buffalo, NY, 91. *Exhib:* Whitney Mus Am Art Ann, New York, 67; Int Exhib Colored Graphics, Mus Mod Art, Paris, 70; New Am Prints Traveling Exhib, US Info Agency, Vienna, 71; 23rd Libr Cong Exhib, Nat Collection Fine Arts, Smithsonian Inst, 73; Linden Gallery, New York, 81; one-man shows, Sheldon Mem Art Gallery, Univ Nebr, Lincoln, 74, Phoenix Mus Art, Ariz, 74, Yumi Gallery, Tokyo, Japan, 75, Linden Gallery, New York, 81, St Mary's Col, Md, 83, Schenectady Mus Art, NY, 86, Elvejhem Mus, Madison, Wis, 86, Hammer Galleries, New York, 91; Overview, De Graaf Fine Arts, Chicago, IL; Sylvia Cordish Gallery, Baltimore, Md, 88; Retrospective Vision of Flight, 1988-1992, travelling NASA art collection. *Teaching:* Instr photog & printmaking, C W Post Col, Long Island Univ, 66-68; adj instr serigraphy, Sch Visual Arts, New York, 68-70; guest lectr, Univ Wis-Madison, spring 72; vis prof, St John's Univ, Queens, NY, 90-91. *Awards:* State Dept Grant, Smithsonian Inst Int Art Prog & Abby Gray Found, 67; Ford Found Grant, 70; Nat Endowment Arts Grant, 73. *Bibliog:* Dorothy Spencer (auth), The Colorful World of Clayton Pond, Am Artist Mag, Billboard Publ Inc, New York, 3/81; James Watrous (auth), Century of American Printmaking 1880-1980, Univ Wis Press, Madison, 84; Elevator World Mag, Mobile, Ala, Vol XXXVI, No 7, 7/85. *Mem:* Am Color Print Soc; Print Coun Am; Boston Printmakers; Philadelphia Print Club. *Publ:* Articles in Artist's Proof, Pratt Graphic Art Ctr, New York, 66 & 68. *Dealer:* Jack Gallery 138 Prince St New York NY 10012; De Graaf Fine Arts 300 W Superior St Chicago IL 60610. *Mailing Add:* 130 Greene St New York NY 10012

PONSOT, CLAUDE F
EDUCATOR, PAINTER
b Rabat, Morocco, May 29, 27; US citizen. *Study:* Atelier Perrier/Jaudon, 47-50; Atelier Andre L'hote, 48-50; Atelier Fernand Leger, 49-50. *Work:* Associated Metals & Minerals Corp, New York; also pvt collections. *Comn:* Graphics, LaGuardia Community Col, NY, 79-80 & St John's Univ, 81; South Oaks Hospital, Amityville, 81; and others. *Exhib:* One-man show, Galerie Maitre Albert, Paris, 76; Cabinet des Estampes, Biblioteque Nat, Paris, 78; Brand X, Glendale, Calif, 80; In the Best Tradition, Heckscher Mus, Huntington, 81; Firehouse Gallery, Nassau Community Col, NY, 82 & 83; and others. *Teaching:* Prof art, St John's Univ, New York, formerly. *Awards:* Pat Lambert Award, Shreveport Art Guild; Purchase Award, Images-Shapes 76, Plattsburgh; Patron Purchase Award, Watercolor USA, Springfield Mus, 77. *Bibliog:* Jean Parris (auth), articles, Newsday, 79-81. *Mem:* Nat Drawing Asn. *Media:* Oil, Watercolor. *Dealer:* Ruth Solomon Art Connections Unlimited. *Mailing Add:* 83-29 169th St Jamaica NY 11432

PONTYNEN, ARTHUR
EDUCATOR, HISTORIAN
b Brooklyn, NY, Mar 23, 50. *Study:* Univ Iowa, Iowa City, PhD, 83. *Teaching:* Asst prof art hist, Stephen F Austin State Univ, 85- *Awards:* Fel, Smithsonian Inst, Washington, DC, 79-80. *Mem:* Col Art Asn. *Res:* Art theory and philosophy. *Publ:* Auth, The deification of Laozi in Chinese history and Art, 80 & The dual nature of Laozi, 80, Oriental Art Mag Ltd; Philosophia perennis ars Orientalis I-II, Oriental Art, 82-83; A winter landscape: Reflections on the theory and practice of art history, Art Bull, Col Art Asn, 86. *Mailing Add:* Univ Wis 800 Algoma Blvd Oshkosh WI 54901

POOLE, LESLIE DONALD
PAINTER, PRINTMAKER
b Halifax, NS, May 3, 42. *Study:* Prince of Wales Col, Charlottetown, PEI, 60; Univ Alta, Edmonton, BFA, 67; Yale Univ, MFA, 70. *Work:* Can Coun Art Bank, Ottawa; Beaverbrook Art Gallery, Fredericton, NB; Confederation Ctr Art Gallery, Charlottetown, PEI; Hyatt Hotel, Chicago, Ill; Ring House Gallery, Univ Alta, Edmonton. *Comn:* Portrait lieutenant gov, Prov Alta, 73; mural, Minto Suite Hotel, Ottowa, ON, 89. *Exhib:* Solo exhib, Confederation Ctr Art Gallery, Charlottetown, PEI, 73 & Edmonton Art Gallery, 74; Alberta Artists, Can House, Paris, Brussels, London, New York & Montreal, 76; Confessions, Vancouver Art Gallery, 79; Vancouver: Art and Artists, Vancouver Art Gallery, 83; Drawing retrospective, Scott Gallery, Vancouver, 84, touring, 86-87; Dualities: A Retrospective, 1974-1989, Art Gallery S Okanagan, 89; After Yale: 1970-1976, Simon Fraser Univ Art Gallery, Vancouver, 90. *Teaching:* Lectr design, Univ Alta, Edmonton, 71-72; instr painting, Banff Sch Fine Arts, 73; lectr drawing, Vancouver Community Col, 75-87. *Awards:* Can Coun Arts Grants, 72, 74, 75 & 80. *Bibliog:* Glenn Howarth (auth), An ecumenical intent, Vanguard Mag, Vancouver, 78; David Watmough (auth), Not exactly limpid Pooles, Interface, Alta, 81; Capilano Rev, No 34, 85. *Media:* Acrylic; Lithography. *Dealer:* Madison Gallery Toronto Ont Can. *Mailing Add:* 526 Fourth St New Westminster BC V3L 2V6 Canada

POOLE, NANCY GEDDES
GALLERY DIRECTOR
b London, Ont, May 10, 30. *Study:* MacDonald Col, McGill Univ, dipl, 49; Univ Western Ont, BA, 55; Univ Western Ont, LLD, 90. *Collections Arranged:* SW18-London, Rothman Gallery, Stratford, Eng, 69; Canadian Printmakers, 70 & Jack Chambers, 79, Canada House Gallery; British Printmakers, Ont galleries tour, 71; Victorian Artists, London Regional Art Gallery, 86. *Pos:* Dir & owner, Nancy Poole's Studio, 69-78; chmn governing coun, Ont Col Art, 73-74; gov, Univ Western Ont, 74-85; interim dir, London Regional Art Gallery, 81, exec dir, London Regional Art & Hist Mus, 85- *Awards:* Mayor's New Year's Honours List, 84; Women of Distinction Award, 84; Award of Merit, Univ Western Ont, 85. *Mem:* Hardy Geddes House (bd dir); London Health Asn (bd dir); London Social Planning Coun (vice-chmn). *Specialty:* Living Canadian aritsts with emphasis on London painters. *Publ:* Auth, Jack Chambers, pvt publ, 78; The Art of London: 1830-1980, Blackpool Press, 84. *Mailing Add:* London Regional Art Gallery 421 Ridout St N London ON N6A 5H4 Canada

POON, YI-CHONG SARINA CHOW
PAINTER, CALLIGRAPHER
b Canton, China; Jan 26, 44. *Study:* Sir Robert Black Col of Educ, Hong Kong; Hwa Kui Col; Studio of Chinese Art. *Work:* Univ Toronto, Canada; Mus Miami, Fla; Int Y's Men's Club, Osaka, Japan; Sir Robert Black Col Educ. *Exhib:* Asia Mod Art Exhib, Art Gallery Tokyo, Japan; Mus Hist, Taiwan; Art Mus of Korea; Hong Kong Art's Festival. *Teaching:* Pres, Int Studio Chinese Art, 67-88; prof, dept extramural studies, Chinese Univ, Hong Kong, 79-80; principal, Kei Yam Sch, 70-85; Kei Ho Sch, 85-88. *Mem:* Chinese Art Asn, Hong Kong; Kwong Ngar Calligraphy Soc; Asia Artist Asn. *Mailing Add:* 15221 SW 89th Ave Miami FL 33157

POONS, LARRY
PAINTER
b Tokyo, Japan, Oct 1, 37. *Study:* Boston Mus Fine Arts Sch, 59. *Work:* Mus Mod Art, Metrop Mus Art, Solomon R Guggenheim Mus, Whitney Mus Am Art, New York; Albright-Knox Art Gallery; Stedelijk Mus, Holland; Woodward Found, Washington, DC; Mus Fine Arts, Boston, MA; Philadelphia Mus Art, PA; Tate Gallery, London, Eng. *Exhib:* Art Inst Chicago, 66; Corcoran Gallery Art, 67; Carnegie Inst, 67; Documenta IV, Kassel, Ger, 68; Whitney Mus Am Art Ann, 68 & 72 & Whitney Biennial, 73; Albright-Knox Art Gallery, Buffalo, NY, 68 & 70; Pasadena Art Mus, Calif, 69; retrospective, Boston Mus Fine Arts, 80; Solo Exhib, Andre Emmerick Gallery, New York, 80, 82, 83, 85 & 86, Gallery One, Toronto, Can, 80, 82, 84 & 86, Meredith Long & Co, Houston, TX, 82 & 91, Galerie Montaigne, Paris, France, 89-90, Helander Gallery, Palm Beach, FL, 90, Salander-O'Reilly Galleries, New York, 90; Mus Fine Arts, Boston, MA 82; Fort Worth Art Mus, TX, 85; Galleria Chisel, Milan, Italy, 86; Hokin Gallery, Bay Harbor, FL, 87; Meadow Brook Art Gallery, Rochester, MI, 88; Daniel Newburg Gallery, New York, 89-90; Salander-O'Reilly Galleries, Inc, New York, 90; and many others. *Teaching:* Vis fac, NY Studio Sch, 67, Bennington Col. *Awards:* Francis J Greenburger Found Award, 88. *Bibliog:* Catherine Barnett (auth), Beyond Recognition, Art & Antiques, 5/88, p56-61; John Zinsser (auth), Larry Poons Interview, Journal of Contemp Art, Fall/Winter 89, p28-38; Phillipe Dagen (auth), Poons le meconnu, Le Monde, 1/90; and others. *Publ:* Auth, The Structure of Color, 71. *Dealer:* Andre Emmerich Gallery Inc 41 E 57th St New York NY 10022. *Mailing Add:* 831 Broadway New York NY 10003

POOR, ANNE
PAINTER
b New York, NY, Jan 2, 18. *Study:* Bennington Col; Art Students League, with Alexander Brook, William Zorach & Yasuo Kuniyoshi; Acad Julian, Paris, painting with Jean Lurcat & Abraham Rattner. *Work:* Whitney Mus Am Art; Brooklyn Mus; Art Inst Chicago; Wichita Mus; Des Moines Art Ctr. *Comn:* Murals, Pub Works Admin, 37; murals, Skowhegan Sch Painting & Sculpture, 54, South Solon Free Meeting House, Maine, 57. *Exhib:* Artists for Victory, Metrop Mus Art, 42; Am Brit Art Ctr, New York, 44, 45 & 48; Maynard Walker Gallery, New York, 50; seven shows, Graham Gallery, New York, 57-79; plus others. *Teaching:* Mem fac painting & dir, Skowhegan Sch Painting & Sculpture, 47-61, gov & trustee, 63- *Awards:* Edwin Austin Abbey Mem Fel for Mural Painting, 48 & First Prize for Landscape Painting, 70, Nat Acad Design; Nat Inst Arts & Lett Grant in Art, 57. *Bibliog:* Alan Gussow (auth), A sense of place, Friends of Earth, Sat Rev Press, 72. *Mem:* Artists Equity Asn. *Media:* Oil, Watercolor. *Publ:* Illusr, Greece, Viking Press, 64. *Dealer:* Graham Gallery 1014 Madison Ave New York NY 10021. *Mailing Add:* 92 S Mountain Rd New City NY 10956

POOR, ROBERT JOHN
HISTORIAN
b Rockport, Ill, July 10, 31. *Study:* Boston Univ, BA, 53 & MA, 57; Univ Chicago, with Ludwig Bachhofer, PhD(art hist), 61. *Collections Arranged:* Art of India (exhib catalog), 69 & Far Eastern Art in Minnesota Collections (exhib catalog), 70, Univ Minn Gallery; Hanga, The Modern Japanese Print (exhib catalog), Minn Mus Art, St Paul, 72. *Pos:* Consult Asian art, Minneapolis Inst Art, formerly; cur Asian art, Minn Mus Art, St Paul, formerly. *Teaching:* Asst prof Asian art, Dartmouth Col, 61-65; from assoc prof Asian art to prof art hist, Univ Minn, Minneapolis, 65- *Res:* Chinese bronzes. *Publ:* Auth, Notes on the Sung archaeological catalogs, 65 & auth, Some remarkable examples of I-Hsing ware, 66-67, Arch of Chinese Art Soc Am; auth, Ancient Chinese Bronzes, Inter-Cult Arts Press, 68; auth, Evolution of a secular vesseltype, 68 & On the Mo-tzu-Yu, 70, Oriental Art. *Mailing Add:* Dept Art Hist Univ Minn Minneapolis MN 55455

POPE, MARY ANN IRWIN
PAINTER
b Louisville, Ky, Mar 8, 32. *Study:* Art Ctr, Louisville; Univ Louisville; Cooper Union. *Work:* IBM, Robinson Humphrey, Sonat Inc; Mint Mus, Charlotte, NC; Huntsville Mus of Art; Fine Arts Mus S, Mobile, Ala; Zerox. *Comn:* Boy Scouts Am. *Exhib:* Palos Altos Mus, Calif, 75; Watercolor USA, 1982, 83, 87, 88 & 89; Birmingham Biennial, 83 & 85; Art Quest, 85; Nat Biennial Invitational, Watercolor USA, 89; and others. *Awards:* Birmingham Biennial, 85; Art Quest, 85; Watercolor USA, 89. *Bibliog:* Watercolor, fall 92. *Mem:* Kentucky Watercolor Soc; Ala Watercolor Soc; Nat Honor Soc-Watercolor USA; Ala Art League. *Media:* Oil, Watercolor. *Mailing Add:* 1705 Greenwyche Rd SE Huntsville AL 35801

POPINSKY, ARNOLD DAVE
SCULPTOR, CERAMIST
b Bronx, NY, Aug 21, 30. *Study:* Albright Art Sch, State Univ NY, Buffalo, BS; Univ Wis-Madison, MS; Alfred Univ. *Comn:* Metal sculpture, Wright Art Ctr, Beloit, Wis, 64; 3 cast iron plaques, 64 & aluminum sculpture, 68, Beloit Col, Wis. *Exhib:* Colt & Popinsky, Wright Art Ctr, Beloit, Wis, 67; one-man shows, Lang Art Ctr, Claremont, Calif, 69, Univ WFla, Pensacola, 73 & Fishey Whale Gallery, Milwaukee, Wis, 75; Wis Designer-Craftsman, Milwaukee Art Ctr, 73. *Pos:* Artist-in-residence, Inst Artes Plasticas, Univ Guadalajara, Mex, 64-65; vis sculptor, Scripps Col & Claremont Grad Sch, Calif, 68-69; artist-in-residence, Univ WFla, Pensacola, 72-73; owner, Clarksville Pottery & Am Crafts Gallery, Austin, Tex, 76-; Clarksville Pottery Studio Inc, 91. *Teaching:* Prof sculpture & ceramics, Beloit Col, Wis, 57-76. *Mem:* Col Art Asn; Am Craft Coun; Austin Contemp Visual Arts Asn (mem bd dirs, 78); Rock Prairie Arts Coun. *Media:* Clay, Metal. *Mailing Add:* 1004 Eason Austin TX 78703

POPKIN, ELSIE DINSMORE
GRAPHIC ARTIST
b Abingdon, Pa, Jan 11, 37. *Study:* Cornell Univ, Col Archit, Art & Planning, BFA, 58; New York Univ, studied with Leo Manso, 60-68. *Work:* Cornell Univ Sch Hotel Admin, Ithaca, NY; RJR Nabisco, New York; Chrysler Corp, Detroit, Mich; Weatherspoon Gallery, Univ NC, Greensboro; Duke Med Ctr, Durham, NC. *Exhib:* Piedmont Painting & Sculpture, Mint Mus Charlotte, NC, 81; Women's Invitational Project 1, Converse Col, travelling exhib, 85-89; one-woman show, Herbert F Johnson Mus, Ithaca, NY, 88; Artist of

Yr, Milton Rhodes Gallery, Winston-Salem, NC, 89; Uptown Gallery, New York, 86, 89 & 91; Cardozo School of Law, New York, 90. *Pos:* Artist-in-residence, Reynolds Mus Am Art, Winston-Salem, 75-78; courtroom artist, WXII-TV & Winston-Salem J, 77-78; bd mem, NC Volunteer Lawyers for the Arts, 86- *Awards:* Hon mention, Southeastern Ctr Contemp Art, 78; Cash award Southern Spectrum, Henley Paper Co, 84; Best in Show, NC Artists Competition, 85; Fel, Va Ctr Creative Arts, 83-85; Yaddo Fel, 85. *Bibliog:* Profile, Art Voices South, 5-6/79; Artist comes home for rare exhibition, Reading Eagle, 11/2/86; Elsie Popkin's Paintings Glow with Color, Light, Winston Salem J, 2/28/89. *Mem:* Artist Equity Asn; Assoc Artists Winston-Salem. *Media:* Pastel, Charcoal. *Publ:* Illusr, Lincoln Ctr Stagebill, 8/81 & 8/86; Music abroad 83, NY Times, 5/8/83; The Crescent Rev, spring 84 & fall, 90; Contemporary women artists address book and calendar, Bo-Tree Productions, 87; Women in art calendar, Am Asn Univ Women, 89; Carole Katchen (auth), Creative Painting with Pastel, North Light. *Dealer:* Uptown Gallery 1194 Madison Ave New York NY 10128. *Mailing Add:* 740 Arbor Rd Winston-Salem NC 27104

POPOVAC, GWYNN
PAINTER, GRAPHIC ARTIST
Wilmington, Dela, Dec 1, 48. *Study:* Univ Calif, Los Angeles, Eng lit, honors, 66-71. *Exhib:* Behind the Disguise, Olive Hyde, Fremont City Gallery, Calif, 89; The Art of the Mask, Hearst Gallery, Moraga, Calif, 91. *Pos:* Designer/creator of masks for Kabuki play, The Dream of Kitamura, Sierra Repertory Theatre, 92. *Bibliog:* Knight Time-Popovac (film), David Knight Productions, 3/89; Liz Winter (auth), Behind the disguise, Monitor, Fremont, Calif, 10/25/89; Gary Linehan (auth), Working in the bugs, Union Democrat, Sonora, Calif, 4/3/92. *Media:* Mixed Media, Oil, Fibers. *Publ:* Auth, Ripe plums, Ms Mag, 7/84; Wet Paint, Houghton Mifflin & Ballantine, 86; illusr, Wet Paint (dust jacket for hardback ed), Houghton Mifflin & Ballantine, 86; Trappers (play poster & progs), 88 & The Dream of Kitamura (play poster & progs), 92, Sierra Repertory Theatre. *Dealer:* Wellspring Gallery 120 Broadway Suite 105 Santa Monica CA 90401-2385. *Mailing Add:* 17270 Robin Ridge Sonora CA 95370

POPPITZ, JAMES
PAINTER, PERFORMER
b Rolla, Mo, Nov 27, 57. *Study:* Univ Colo, Boulder, MFA, 85. *Work:* Chase Manhattan Bank, New York; Denver Mus Art, Colo; Mus Mod Art, New York; Smithsonian Mus; Bass Mus Art. *Comn:* White Mans Burden (performance), Ctr Idea Art, Denver, Colo; Defeated Meanings, Denver Mus Art, Colo; Fiorruci, New York, 85; Ronald Feldman Gallery, 86; Flaming Colossus, Los Angeles, 88, Memphis Brewery, 92. *Exhib:* Many group and one-man exhibs, performances, events. *Collections Arranged:* Traveling Exhib, Of the Street, 84-86. *Pos:* Exec dir, Fashion Moda, 85-88; found, Fourth World, 89, Fish Head Soup Folk Art Studio. *Bibliog:* Art in America, Art Forum, LA Times, NY Times, etc; Denver Post, San Francisco Chronicle, Memphis Times Picayone Television Appearances, Radio. *Mem:* Fish Head Soup. *Media:* Living materials. *Publ:* Publ, Fashion Moda portfolio of limited fine art prints & auth, vol of poetry. *Mailing Add:* 201 S Santa Fe, 200 Los Angeles CA 90012

PORADA, EDITH
HISTORIAN
b Vienna, Austria, Aug 22, 12; US citizen. *Study:* Univ Vienna, PhD, 35; Smith Col, DLitt, 67. *Work:* Pierpont Morgan Libr, New York. *Pos:* Hon cur seals & tablets, Pierpont Morgan Libr, 55- *Teaching:* Instr art hist, Queens Col, NY, 49-55, asst prof, 50-58; asst prof art hist & archaeol, Columbia Univ, 58-62, assoc prof, 62-64, prof, 64-73, Arthur Lehman prof, 73-84, Arthur Lehman prof emer, 84-; chmn, Columbia Univ Sem Archaeol Eastern Mediterranean, Eastern Europ & Near E, 66- *Awards:* Guggenheim Found Fel, 50 & 83-84; Award Distinguished Archaeol Achievement, Archaeol Inst Am, 77. *Mem:* Fel Am Acad Arts & Lett; Am Philos Soc. *Publ:* Auth, Seal Impressions of Nuzi, Am Schs Orient Res; auth, Corpus of Ancient Near Eastern Seals in North American Collections, Bollingen, 48; auth, Alt-Iran, Holle, 62; auth, Art of Ancient Iran, Crown, 65; auth, Tchoga Zanbil IV: La Glyptique, Mem Deleg Arch Iran, 70. *Mailing Add:* 757 Schermerhorn Hall Columbia Univ New York NY 10027

PORTA, SIENA GILLANN
SCULPTOR
b New York, NY, Nov 5, 51. *Study:* Art Students League, 69-70; Brooklyn Col, NY, BS(studio arts), 77; Pa State Univ, Pa, MFA (sculpture), 79. *Work:* Fulbright Comn, Reykjavik, Iceland; Bergen Co Community Col, Paramus, NJ; Am Cult Ctr, Reykjavik. *Comn:* Co Rockland, NY. *Exhib:* Solo exhibs, Dominican Col, Blauvelt, NY, 80 & Mari Galleries, Ltd, Mamaroneck, NY, 85, Rabbits Among Us, New York, 14 Sculptors Gallery, 11/90, Mid Hudson Arts & Sci Ctr, Poughkeepsie, NY; Big and Small, Terrain Gallery, New York, 84; Body Memories, BACA Cult Coun, Brooklyn, 84; Sculpture and Drawings, Seraphim Gallery, Englewood, NJ, 88; Am Cult Ctr, Reykjavik, Iceland, 88; Notre Dame Univ, Isis Gallery, S Bend, Ind, 90; Columns, Lehigh Univ, Bethlehem, Pa, 91; Lorraine Kessler Gallery, Poughkeepsie, NY, 92; Barbara Gibson Gallery, Nyack, NY, 92. *Pos:* Scenic artist, Saturday Night Live, 86-89 & Metrop Opera, New York, 87-; vpres, 14 Sculptors Gallery, 87-89, pres, 89-91. *Awards:* Artist-in-Residence, Vriesland West Hudson Arts Ctr, Pearl River, NY, 80-81; NY State Coun Arts Grant, 86; US Info Agency Grant, Partners of the Americas, 92. *Bibliog:* John Arthur Shanks (auth), article, Women Artists News, vol 9, no 4, 84; Franz Vila (prod), Siena Porta (video), VIA Productions, 89; Aspects of the Arts, Siena Porta, Sculptor (video), TKR Channel 30, 91. *Mem:* Women's Caucus Art; Artists Equity; Col Art Asn, 75- *Media:* Cast & Sprayed Metal, Plastics. *Publ:* Illusr, Southern Ocean Atlas, Columbia Univ Press, 82. *Dealer:* 14 Sculptors Gallery 164 Mercer St New York NY. *Mailing Add:* PO Box 46 Palisades NY 10964

PORTER, ALBERT WRIGHT
EDUCATOR, PAINTER
b Brooklyn, NY, Nov 25, 23. *Study:* Ecole Des Beaux-Arts, Paris; Chouinard Art Inst; Univ of Calif, Los Angeles, BA; Calif State Univ, Los Angeles, MA; Otis Art Inst. *Work:* Los Angeles City Art Comn; Utah State Univ. *Exhib:* Nat Watercolor Soc, Laguna Beach, Calif, 69; Southern Calif Expo, Del Mar, 72; Watercolor West, Riverside Art Mus, Calif, 74; Nat Watercolor Soc, Northridge, Calif, 77; Nat Watercolor Soc, Palm Springs, 83; Nat Watercolor Soc, Whittier, Calif, 86. *Pos:* Art supervisor, Los Angeles City Schs, 58-71. *Teaching:* Prof art, Calif State Univ, Fullerton, 71-89. *Awards:* Cash Award, Nat Watercolor Soc, Del Mar Col, 72. *Mem:* Nat Watercolor Soc (1st vpres, 77); Watercolor West; Calif Art Educ Asn; Nat Art Educ Soc. *Media:* Watercolor, Drawing Media. *Publ:* Auth, Shape and Form: Design Elements, 74, Pattern: A Design Principle, 75, The Art of Sketching, 77, Exploring Visual Design, 78 & Expressive Watercolor Techniques, 82, Davis Publ. *Mailing Add:* 8554 Day St Sunland CA 91040

PORTER, (EDWIN) DAVID
PAINTER, SCULPTOR
b Chicago, Ill, May 18, 12. *Work:* Whitney Mus Am Art; Miami Mus Mod Art; Chrysler Art Mus; Norfolk Mus Arts & Sci; Parish Art Mus, Southampton. *Exhib:* Solo exhib, Am Inst Archit, NY Chap, 69 & Guild Hall, East Hampton, 70; Outdoor Sculpture, Artists of the Region, Guild Hall, NY, 70; Artists at Dartmouth Retrospective, City Hall, Boston, 71; Artists of Suffolk County, Part V, New Directions, Heckscher Mus, Huntington, NY, 71. *Teaching:* Artist-in-residence, Dartmouth Col, 64-65 & Cooper Union, 67-68; lectr art, Corcoran Gallery Art, Washington, DC, 68 & 69; instr painting, Guild Hall, East Hampton, 75-78; lectr painting techniques, Wainscoth, NY, 76. *Awards:* Gold Medal of Pres Gronchi of Italy, Sassoferrato, Italy, 61; Beaux Arts Award in Painting, Beaux Arts Club, 69; Nat Inst Arts & Lett Grant, 70. *Bibliog:* Today's living, New York Herald Tribune, 56; The Making of a Construction (TV film interview), Voice Am, 57; maj articles on work publ in newspapers in Norway & Sweden, 60. *Publ:* Auth, Why I ran away, Am Weekly, 7/10/60. *Mailing Add:* PO Box 71 Wainscott NY 11975

PORTER, ELMER JOHNSON
EDUCATOR, PAINTER
b Richmond, Ind, May 5, 07. *Study:* Art Inst Chicago, BAE; Ohio State Univ, MA; Earlham Col; Univ Cincinnati; Univ Colo; Butler Univ; San Carlos Univ, Guatemala. *Work:* Earlham Col; Ind State Univ; Richmond Ind High Sch; Richmond Art Asn, Ind. *Exhib:* Hoosier Salon, Chicago; Art League, Columbus, Ohio; Art Asn Richmond, Ind; also in Cincinnati & New York. *Teaching:* Instr art, McKinley High Sch, Cedar Rapids, Iowa, 30-37; instr art, Hughes High Sch, Cincinnati, 38-46; prof art, Ind State Univ, Terre Haute, 46-73, emer prof, 73- *Awards:* Appl Arts Prize, Indianapolis Art Asn, 29; Watercolor Award, Art League, Columbus, 38; Bonsib Purchase Prize, Hoosier Salon, 39. *Mem:* Art Educ Asn Ind (pres, 52-53, secy-treas, 54-67); Kappa Pi (int secy, 70-); Nat Art Educ Asn; Am Soc Bookplate Collectors & Designers; Pen & Brush Club. *Media:* Watercolor. *Publ:* Auth, Bookplates of Ernest Haskel, Bookplate Ann, 51. *Mailing Add:* 3115 Margaret Ave Terre Haute IN 47802

PORTER, JEANNE CHENAULT
EDUCATOR, HISTORIAN
b New York, NY, Mar 18, 44. *Study:* Barnard Col, Columbia Univ, BA, 65; Univ Mich, Ann Arbor, MA, 66 & PhD(Ford Found Graduate Fel), 71; Univ Florence, Rome & Ghent. *Collections Arranged:* Bradley Tomlin: A Retrospective View, traveling exhib (auth, catalog), Hofstra Univ, 75-76. *Teaching:* Assoc prof, Finch Col, New York, 72-74 & Pa State Univ, 74- *Awards:* Fulbright Grant to Rome, 68-69; Belgian Govt Grant, 68. *Mem:* Col Art Asn Am. *Res:* Abstract Expressionism (American), and Spanish, French and Italian Baroque Painting. *Publ:* Auth, Bradley Walker Tomlin: Early paintings & intimations, Archives Am Art J, 74; auth, Bradley Walker Tomlin: A painter's painter, Arts Mag, 75; Painting and Sculpture in the Samuel Gallu Collection (catalog), 80 & Works on Paper: Henry Varnum Poor (catalog), 83, Pa State Press; Tomlin (catalog), Munson-Williams-Proctor Inst, Utica, NY, 89. *Mailing Add:* PO Box 249 Lemont PA 16851

PORTER, LILIANA
PAINTER, PRINTMAKER
b Buenos Aires, Arg, Oct 6, 41; US citizen. *Study:* Sch of Fine Arts, Buenos Aires; printmaking, Iberoamerican Univ & La Ciudadela, Mexico City & Pratt Graphic Art Ctr, New York. *Work:* Mus of Mod Art, New York; Mus of Fine Arts, Philadelphia; Museo de Bellas Artes, Caracas, Venezuela & Santiago, Chile; La Bibliot Nat, Paris. *Exhib:* Museo de Bellas Artes, Caracas, 69; Museo de Bellas Artes, Santiago, 69 & 90-91; Info, Mus Mod Art, 70, Proj Ser, Mus Mod Art, 73, Barbara Toll, 79, 82 & 84, New York; Museo de Arte Moderno, Bogota, Colombia, 74; Biennial of Paris, 75; The Space, Boston, 88; Syracuse Univ, NY, 90; Fundacion San Telmo, Buenos Aires, Argentina, 90; Museo Nacional De Artes Plasticas, Montevideo, Uruguay, 90. *Pos:* Co-dir, Studio Porter-Wiener, 79- *Teaching:* Instr etching, New York Graphic Workshop, 65-68; adj lectr graphics, State Univ NY, Purchase, 87; instr, printmaking workshop, New York, 88; Assoc Prof, Art Dept, Queens Col, NY, 91. *Awards:* Guggenheim Fel, 80; Grand Prix, XI Int Print Biennial, Cracow, Poland, 86; First Prize, Latin Am Graphic Arts Biennial, Mocha, New York, 86; First Prize, VIII Latin Am Print Biennial, San Juan, PR, 86; and others. *Bibliog:* James Collins (auth), articles in Artforum, 73 & Arts Mag, 5/77. *Publ:* Contribr, Wrinkle, 68, Nail, 73 & String, 73, New York Graphic Workshop. *Dealer:* Bernice Steinbaum Gallery 132 Greene St New York NY 10012. *Mailing Add:* 178 Franklin St 5th Fl New York NY 10013

PORTER, RICHARD JAMES
CONSULTANT, COLLECTOR
b Bellefonte, Pa, Jan 2, 50. *Study:* Pa State Univ, BA, 71, MA, 73, PhD, 83. *Collections Arranged:* Sidney Goodman: Paintings, Drawings & Graphics 1959-1979 (coauth, catalog), Mus Art, Pa State Univ, Queens Mus, Columbus Mus Art & Del Art Mus, 80-81; Henry Varnum Poor (coauth, catalog), Mus Art, Pa State Univ, Burchfield Ctr, Everson Mus & Nat Acad Design, 83-84. *Pos:* Registrar & cur Am art, Mus Art, Pa State Univ, Pa 78-85; dir, Joe & Emily Lowe Art Gallery, 85-86; chmn, Grad prog in Mus Studies, Syracuse Univ, 85-86; sales assoc, Villager Realty, 86-87 & Assoc Realty, 87-90; assoc broker, Assoc Realty, 90-92; broker/partner ReMax Ctr Realty, 92. *Teaching:* Instr art hist, Middle Tenn State Univ, 73-76; adj assoc prof art hist, Juniata Col, 84. *Mem:* Am Asn Mus; Mid Atlantic Asn of Mus; Asn Col Univ Mus Galleries; Col Art Asn. *Res:* American and European art, 17th century to present, particularly American 18th-20th centuries. *Collection:* 20th Century American Paintings, Watercolor and Drawings. *Publ:* Auth, A newly discovered painting by Ammi Phillips, Conn Hist Soc Bull, 79; Introduction, selected works from the collection of Samuel Gallu, Pa State Univ, 80; Jerome Witkin, A Decade of Work (exhib catalog), 82; Henry Varnum Poor, 1887-1970 (exhib catalog), 83; The oil paintings of Henry Varnum Poor, Arts Mag, 85. *Mailing Add:* PO Box 249 Lemont PA 16851

PORTER, SHIRLEY
PAINTER
b Tallahassee, Fla. *Study:* Fla State Univ, BS(educ), 62; Univ SFla, MA(educ), 69. *Work:* Tweed Mus, Duluth, Minn; Montgomery Co Dept Parks, Rockville, Md; Utah State Univ. *Exhib:* Am Watercolor Soc, Nat Acad Gallery, New York, 75-77 & 79; Allied Artists, Nat Acad Gallery, 75-77; Nat Acad Design, Nat Acad Gallery, 77-81; Rocky Mountain Nat Watermedia, Foothills Art Ctr, Golden, Colo, 78, 80 & 81; Watercolor USA, Springfield Art Mus, Mo, 79. *Awards:* David Soloway Mem Award, 77 & Gold Medal, 78, Allied Artists; Silver Medal, 80 & Gold Medal, 81, Baltimore Watercolor Soc. *Mem:* Am Watercolor Soc; Allied Artists Am; Audubon Artists; Nat Watercolor Soc; Midwest Watercolor Soc; and others. *Media:* Watercolor. *Dealer:* Prince Royal Gallery Alexandria VA 22313. *Mailing Add:* 14315 Woodcrest Dr Rockville MD 20853

PORTMAN, BRIAN
PRINTMAKER
b Woonsocket, RI, 1960. *Study:* RI Sch Design, BFA, 83. *Work:* Centro Cultural del Arte Contemporaneo, Mexico City, Mex; Mus Fine Art, Houston, Tex; Southwestern Bell Corp, St Louis, Mo. *Exhib:* Solo exhibs, List Art Ctr, Brown Univ, Providence, RI, 83 & Hiram Butler Gallery, Houston, Tex, 88, 90 & 92; Gallery Yves Arman, New York, 84; DiverseWorks, Houston, 86 & 87; Contemp Art Mus, Houston, 88; Janice C Lee Gallery, Houston, 89. *Awards:* Nat Endowment Arts, 89-90. *Mailing Add:* c/o Hiram Butler Gallery 4520 Blossom Houston TX 77007

PORTNOW, MARJORIE ANNE
PAINTER
b New York, NY. *Study:* Western Reserve Univ, with Dr Sherman E Lee, BA(art hist), 64; Skowhegan Sch Painting, with Lenart Anderson, A Leslie & A Katz, 65; Brooklyn Col, with P Pearlstein & G Laderman, MFA(painting), 72. *Work:* Metrop Mus Art, Chase Manhattan Bank, New York, NY; Sheldon Art Mus, Lincoln, Nebr; Commerce Bank Shares, Kansas City, Mo; Albany Inst Art, NY; Citibank Corp of NAm. *Exhib:* A Sense of Place, travelling, 73-74; Chicago Biennial Contemporary Art, Chicago Art Inst, 75; Painting/Sculpture for Awards, Am Acad & Inst Arts & Lett, New York, NY, 80, 90 & 92; Recent Developments in American Landscape, Whitney Mus, Stamford, Conn; Graham Gund Collection, Mus Fine Arts Boston, 82; Skowhegan Fac Show, Portland Mus Art, 89; The Italian Tradition on Contemporary Landscape Painting, Gibbs Mus, Charleston, SC; 1990 Invitational Exhib Paintings & Sculpture, Am Acad & Inst Arts & Lett; The Landscape in 20th Century American Art: Selections from the Metrop Mus Art, 91. *Teaching:* Fac, Vt Studio Sch, 87-93, Univ Pa (Grad Sch), 88-91, Pa Acad Art, 88-91, Skowhegan Sch, 89 & Univ Calif, Santa Cruz, 92-93. *Awards:* Ingram Merrill Grant, 76; Nat Endowment Arts Grant, 80; NY Found Arts Award, 86; Hassam Purchase Prize, Am Acad & Inst Arts & Lett, 90. *Bibliog:* James R Mellow (auth), Five young painters, 5/27/73 & Vivien Raynor (auth), New paintings on 57th Street, 11/27/81, New York Times; Allan Ellenzweig (auth), Marjorie Portnow, Arts, 11/74; John Arthur (auth), Spirit of Place: Contemporary Landscape Painting; Laurie Hururtz (auth), Contemporary Masters: Marjorie Portnow, Am Artist, 9/90; R Rosenblum (auth), The Landscape in 20th Century American Art: Selections from the Metrop Mus, 91. *Mem:* NY Artists Equity Asn. *Media:* Acrylic, Oil. *Dealer:* Fischbach Gallery 29 W 57th St New York NY 10019. *Mailing Add:* 67 Vestry St New York NY 10013

PORTNOY, THEODORA PREISS
DEALER
b New York, NY. *Study:* Manhattanville Col; Sarah Lawrence Col, BA. *Pos:* Dir, Theo Portnoy Gallery, currently. *Specialty:* Sculpture with emphasis on work that has evolved from craft media, clay, glass, wood and forged steel. *Mailing Add:* 204 Mamaroneck Rd Scarsdale NY 10583

POSEN, STEPHEN
PAINTER
b St Louis, Mo, Sept 27, 39. *Study:* Washington Univ, St Louis, Mo, BFA, 62; Yale Univ, New Haven, Conn, MFA, 64. *Work:* Va Mus Fine Arts; Chase Manhattan Collection; Pa Acad Fine Arts; Guggenheim Mus, New York; JB Speed Art Mus, Louisville, Ky. *Exhib:* Highlight of the 1971 Season, Aldrich Mus Contemp Art, Ridgefield, Conn, 71; The New Realists, Chicago Mus Contemp Art, 71; solo exhibs, OK Harris Gallery, 71, 74, Robert Miller Gallery, 78, Jason McCoy, Inc, New York, 86; Whitney Mus Am Art Ann, New York, 72; Chicago Art Inst, 74; Taft Mus, 75; Canberra Nat, 77-78; Pa Acad Fine Arts, 77; American Realism: Twentieth-Century Drawings & Watercolors, traveling exhib, 85; More Than Meets the Eye: The Art of Tompe l'oeil, Columbus Mus Art, Ohio, traveling, 86; Two Generations of Creativity, 80 Wash Sq E, New York, 89. *Teaching:* Asst prof painting, Cooper Union. *Awards:* Fulbright Brant, 66; Creative Artists Pub Serv Grant, 72; Guggenheim Fel, 87. *Bibliog:* A Mackie (auth), Dialectic in modernism: The paintings of Stephen Posen, Art Int, 1/80; John Arthur (auth), Realism/Photorealism, Philbrook Art Ctr, 80; John L Ward (auth), American Realism: 1945-1980, UMI Res Press, 89. *Dealer:* Jason McCoy Gallery 41 E 57th St New York NY. *Mailing Add:* 116 Spring St New York NY 10012

POSES, (MR & MRS) JACK I
COLLECTORS
Mr Poses, b Russia, Dec 28, 1899; US citizen; Mrs Poses, b New York, NY, June 5, 08. *Study:* Mr Poses, NY Univ, BCS, 23 & MBA, 24; Brandeis Univ, LLD, 68; Mrs Poses, Hunter Col, BA, 27; Bryn Mawr Col, (Susan B Anthony Fel), 28; Sch Law, NY Univ, LLB, 30. *Pos:* Mr Poses, vchmn, New York Bd Higher Educ, 63-; mem bd trustees, mem educ & budget comts, founder Poses Inst Fine Arts & chmn coun fine arts, Brandeis Univ; founder, Einstein Med Sch; Mrs Poses, mem & secy, New York City Charter Rev Comn, 61; mem bd visitors, Grad Ctr, City Univ New York, 77-78; practicing attorney, New York, currently. *Awards:* Mr Poses, Chevalier, Legion of Honor, 58; Citation Distinguished & Exceptional Serv to City New York, Mayor Lindsay, 67; and others. *Interests:* Established numerous scholarships at many leading universities, as well as devoting active support to major art museums. *Collection:* French and American. *Mailing Add:* 1107 Fifth Ave No 6 New York NY 10128

POSEY, ERNEST NOEL
PAINTER, EDUCATOR
b New Orleans, La, Dec 25, 37. *Study:* Tulane Univ, Art Ctr Col; La State Univ, BFA. *Work:* San Francisco Mus Art; Santa Barbara Mus Art; New Orleans Mus of Art; Brooklyn Mus; Oakland Mus; San Jose Mus Art; The Achenbach Collection; plus others. *Exhib:* New Accessions, San Francisco Mus Art, 73; Achenbach Found, Calif Palace of the Legion of Hon, 77; Aesthetics of Graffiti, San Francisco Mus Mod Art, 78; solo exhibs, Palace of the Legion Of Honor, 71, Bank of Am Concourse, San Francisco, 77, Nuage Gallery, Los Angeles, 78, Walnut Creek Civic Arts Gallery, 78, Palo Alto Cult Ctr, 79 & Allrich Gallery, San Francisco, 80; The Artist & the Airbrush, San Jose State. *Pos:* Bus mgr, Calif Fedn of Art Teachers, 77-. *Teaching:* Instr painting & design, San Francisco Acad Art, 72-83. *Mem:* Arts Arbitration Mediation Serv. *Media:* Acrylic, Airbrush. *Mailing Add:* 42350 Covelo Rd Willits CA 95490

POSKAS, PETER EDWARD
PAINTER
b Waterbury, Conn, Oct 29, 39. *Study:* Univ Conn, 57-60; Paier Sch Art, 60-62; Univ Hartford, BS, 62-65. *Work:* Mattatuck Mus, Waterbury, Conn; Exxon Corp, New York; Mint Mus, Charlotte, NC; Gen Foods Corp, White Plains, NY; FMC Corp, Chicago. *Comn:* Landscape, Metropolitan Life, New York, 89. *Exhib:* Solo exhibs, Mazur Mus, Monroe, La, 72, Mattatuck Mus, Waterbury, Conn, 74 & Hunter Mus Art, Chattanooga, Tenn, 84; Hassam Speicher, Am Acad & Inst Arts & Lett, New York, NY, 77; Butler Inst, Youngstown, Ohio, 77; Artists of Am, Colo Heritage Ctr, Denver, 82-83; The Connecticut View, P P William Benton Mus Art, Storrs, Conn, 84; The Recognizable Image, Bruce Mus, Greenwich, Conn, 85; Acts of Season, Southern Alleghenies Mus Art, Loretto, Pa, 86. *Bibliog:* John Arthur (auth), Peter Poskas, Arts Mag, 83; Theodore Wolf (auth), Mondrian would have liked it, Christian Sci Monitor, 84; Michael Brenson (auth), Peter Poskas, NY Times, 84. *Media:* Oil, Pastel. *Publ:* Coauth, Peter Poskas, Watson-Guptill, 87 & 92. *Dealer:* Schmidt-Bingham Gallery 41 W 57th St New York NY. *Mailing Add:* Nettleton Hollow Rd Washington CT 06793

POSNER, DONALD
HISTORIAN, EDUCATOR
b New York, NY, Aug 30, 31. *Study:* Queens Col, AB, 56; Harvard Univ, AM, 57; NY Univ, PhD, 62. *Pos:* Art historian in residence, Am Acad Rome, 68-69; ed-in-chief, Art Bull, 68-71; deputy dir, NY Univ Inst Fine Arts, 83-. *Teaching:* Instr art hist, Queens Col, 57; asst prof art hist, Columbia Univ, 61-62; Ailsa Mellon Bruce prof art hist, NY Univ Inst Fine Arts, 62-; Robert Sterling Clark vis prof, Williams Col, 73; William R Kenan Jr vis prof, Univ Va, 76-77; vis prof, Univ Wash, Seattle, 91. *Awards:* Phi Beta Kappa Award, 56; Rome Prize Fel, Am Acad Rome, 59-61; C R Morey Bk Award, 72. *Mem:* Col Art Asn Am (dir, 70-74); Am Soc 18th Century Studies. *Res:* Italian painting of 16th through 18th century; French painting of 17th & 18th century. *Publ:* Auth, Annibale Carracci, 71; coauth, 17th & 18th Century Art, 72; auth, Watteau's Lady at her Toilet, 73; Antoine Watteau, 84; auth, Mme de Pompadour as a Patron of the Visual Arts, Art Bull, 90. *Mailing Add:* NY Univ Inst Fine Arts 1 E 78th St New York NY 10021

POSNER, HELAINE J
GALLERY DIRECTOR, CURATOR
b New York, NY, Nov 17, 53. *Study:* Georgetown Univ, BA(art hist), 75; George Washington Univ, MA, 78. *Collections Arranged:* Jasper Johns Prints: Three Themes (coauth, catalog), Whitney Mus Am Art, 78; Selection from the Chase Manhattan Bank Art Collection (auth, catalog), 81, Martin Puryear Sculpture (coauth, catalog), 83 & Anish Kapoor, 86, University

Gallery, Univ Mass, Amherst. *Pos:* Cur asst to dir, Chase Manhattan Bank Art Prog, New York, NY, 78-81; chief cur, Nat Mus of Women in the Arts, Washington, DC, 88-90; cur, MIT, List Visual Arts Ctr, Cambridge, 90- *Teaching:* Asst prof, dept art, Univ Mass, Amherst, 81-88, cur collections & educ, University Gallery, 81-84, dir, 84-88. *Mem:* Am Asn Mus; New Eng Mus Asn. *Res:* Modern and contemporary art. *Specialty:* Development of permanent collection of 20th century works on paper. *Mailing Add:* MIT List Visual Arts Ctr Weisner Bldg 20 Ames St Cambridge MA 02139

POSNER, JUDITH L
DEALER, PUBLISHER
b Milwaukee, Wis, Sept 22, 41. *Study:* Univ Wis, BFA. *Pos:* Dir & pres, Judith L Posner & Assocs, Inc, currently; pres, Milwaukee Art Dealers Asn. *Teaching:* Instr, Comprehensive Employment & Training Act, Milwaukee, currently. *Bibliog:* Curtis Casewitt (auth), Making a Living in the Fine Arts, Macmillan. *Mem:* Indust Found Am Soc Interior Designers; Prof Tempo, Milwaukee Art Dealers Asn; Int Soc Appraisers; Picture Framers Asn. *Specialty:* Nineteenth and twentieth century American and European painting, sculpture and graphics. *Publ:* Publisher of posters & prints. *Mailing Add:* 207 N Milwaukee St Milwaukee WI 53202

POSNER, RICHARD
SCULPTOR
b Los Angeles, Calif, Aug 16, 48. *Study:* Calif State Univ-Chico, BA, 73; Calif Col Arts & Crafts, Oakland, MFA, 76. *Work:* Am Embassy, Stockholm, Swed; Victoria & Albert Mus, London; Corning Mus Glass, NY; Smithsonian Inst, Washington, DC; Metrop Mus Art, New York; numerous pvt collections in the US, Europe, Mex, Scand & Japan. *Comn:* Barton Garden, Md Nat Capital Parks & Planning, 91; Alcherny Park, Wallace, Roberts & Todd, Landscape Architects, San Diego, 91-92; Westchester Green Line Metro Sta, Los Angeles Co Transportation Comn, Design Team Artist with Escudero-Fribourg Architects, 91-94; Descarguen Sus Dudas, Robert Mueller Airport, Austin, Tex, 92; Hope Diamond, Univ SCalif, Los Angeles, 92. *Exhib:* Solo exhibs, Fowl Music, Galleri Mornier, Stockholm, Swed, 79, Viking Symbol Mystery, Theo Portney Gallery, New York, 80, Drawings and Sculptures; 1975-85, Ctr Contemp Art, Seattle, Wash, 85, Kitschina Mus, Greg Kuccra Gallery, Seattle, Wash & Coping Saws, Univ Colo Arts Ctr, Boulder, 86, CO2, Wash Projects Arts, Washington, DC & ProAmerican Bandstand, Painted Bride Arts Ctr, Philadelphia, Pa, 87, Poor Richard's Almanac, Minneapolis Col Art & Design, Minn, 88; New Sculpture, Univ Hawaii, Honolulu, 87; Monument and Memorial, New Langton Arts, San Francisco, 88-90; The Eloquent Object, Mus Fine Arts, Boston, 88-90; A Different War (traveling), Whatcom Mus, Bellingham, Wash, DeCordova Mus, Boston, Mass, Akron Art Mus, Ohio & Frederick White Gallery, Univ Calif-Los Angeles, 89-92; Twenty-Seven Chairs, Daniel Saxon Gallery, Los Angeles, 91. *Teaching:* Guest instr, Konstfaekskolan, Stockholm, Swed, 90; vis asst prof, Univ SCalif, Los Angeles, 91-92. *Awards:* Nat Endowment Arts Design Fel, 89; Jerome/Dayton-Hudson Found Travel Grant to the Soviet Union, 90; McKnight Found Visual Artist Fel, Minneapolis, Minn, 91. *Mailing Add:* PO Box 1151 Culver City CA 90232

POST, ANNE B
SCULPTOR, GRAPHIC ARTIST
b St Louis, Mo. *Study:* Bennington Col, BA(fine arts); study with Simon Moselsio, Stephen Hirsch & Edwin Park; study in Europe. *Work:* Israel Mus, Jerusalem; Maison Francaise; Cooper Union Mus Gallery; Norfolk Mus; Va Bennington Visual Arts Mus. *Exhib:* St Louis Mus Art; Univ NJ Mus; benefit exhib, Acad Medicine, New York; Bennington Mus Art; Bennington Col Visual Arts Mus; AIR Gallery, New York; and others. *Teaching:* Drawing & sculpture, Army Hosps, WVa, Tex, Mo & Settlement House, St Louis, 42-46. *Bibliog:* Gunter Klotz (auth), Zcichnunsen und skulpturen der Anne Post, Klotz-Makowckie, 65. *Mem:* Artists Equity. *Media:* Wood, Stone. *Mailing Add:* 29 Washington Sq W New York NY 10011

POST, GEORGE (BOOTH)
PAINTER
b Oakland, Calif, Sept 29, 06. *Study:* Calif Sch Fine Arts. *Work:* San Francisco Mus Art; Seattle Art Mus; Calif Palace of Legion of Honor; San Diego Fine Arts Soc; Metrop Mus Art; and many others. *Exhib:* Metrop Mus Art; San Francisco Mus Art; DeYoung Mem Mus; Seattle Art Mus; San Diego Fine Arts Gallery; California Palace Legion of Honor; and others. *Teaching:* Instr, Stanford Univ, 40; prof fine arts, Calif Col Arts & Crafts, 47-73; instr, San Jose Col, 51-52; class workshops conducted internationally, 74- *Awards:* Purchase Awards, Watercolor USA, Springfield Mus Art, Mo, 66 & Jack London Square Art Festival, 68; First Award, Zellerbach Show, 75; and others. *Mem:* Am Watercolor Soc; San Francisco Art Asn; Calif Nat Watercolor Soc; Int Inst Arts & Lett; Southwest Watercolor Soc. *Publ:* Contribr illus in Fortune, Calif Arts & Archit, Art Digest, Am Artist & Ford Times Mags. *Mailing Add:* 327 Cumberland St San Francisco CA 94114

POST, MARION (MARION POST WOLCOTT)
PHOTOGRAPHER
b Montclair, NJ, June 7, 10. *Study:* NY Univ; Univ Vienna, BA, 34; with Ralph Steiner, 35-36. *Work:* Metrop Mus Art, Mus Mod Art, New York; Nat Gallery Can; San Francisco Mus Contemp Art; J Paul Getty Mus, Malibu, Calif; Creative Photog, Tucson, Ariz. *Exhib:* FSA Anniversary Show, Brooklyn Mus, 55; The Bitter Years, Mus Mod Art, New York, 62; Women Look at Women, Libr Cong Traveling Exhib, 77; Everson Mus Art, 78; solo exhib, Univ Calif Mus Art, Berkeley, 78; Image de l'Amerique en Crise: Photos de la FSA, Ctr George Pompidou, Paris, 79; American Photography and Social Conscience, Victoria, Australia, 80; Santa Barbara Mus Art, 88; photogs, Int Ctr Photog, New York 90. *Pos:* Press staff photogr, Philadelphia Evening Bulletin; staff photogr, Farm Security Admin, Wash, DC. *Awards:* Vesta Award, Woman's Bldg, Los Angeles, Calif, 88; Sprague Award, Press Photogrs Asn, 90; Distinguished Photojournalist, Univ Calif, Riverside, 88; and others. *Bibliog:* Hal Fischer (auth), MPW's spectrum of the depression, Artweek, 5/27/78; Joan Murray (auth), FSA veteran gets back to work, Am Photogr, 3/80; Paul Hendrickson (auth), Double Exposure, Washington Post Mag, 88; F Jack Hurley (auth), Marion Post Wolcott, A Photographic Journey. *Mem:* Friends Photog; Friends Imogen Cunningham. *Publ:* Contrib, Portrait of a Decade, La State Univ Press, 72; In This Proud Land, New York Graphic Soc, 73; Marion Post Wolcott, FSA Photographs, Friends of Photography, (monogr), 83; Marion Post Wolcott, A Photgraphic Journey; Paul Hendrickson, Looking for the Light, 92; and others. *Dealer:* Witkin Gallery New York; Halsted Gallery Birmingham Mich. *Mailing Add:* 400 E Pedregosa St-G Santa Barbara CA 93103

POSTER, JUNE
ADMINISTRATOR
b New York, NY. *Study:* State Univ NY, Buffalo, BFA, 70; Univ Calif, Berkeley, MA, 75. *Pos:* Dir, Grapestake Gallery, San Francisco, 80-81; exec dir, San Francisco Camerawork, Calif, 81-84; dir develop, Meredith Monk, The House Found Arts, New York, 84-87; dir finance, Cunningham Dance Found, 87-90; managing dir, David Gordon/Pick Up Co, 91- *Mailing Add:* 253 W 72nd St Apt 2106 New York NY 10023

POSTIGLIONE, COREY M
PAINTER, EDUCATOR
b Chicago, Ill, July 35, 43. *Study:* Univ Ill, Circle Campus, BFA; also with Martin Hurtig & Roland Ginzel. *Exhib:* One-man shows, Evanston Art Ctr, Ill, 72 & Jan Cicero Gallery, Chicago, 76, 78 & 83; Cool Abstraction, Richard Gray Gallery, Chicago, 76; Works on Paper, Chicago & Vicinity Show, Art Inst Chicago, 78; Ill State Mus, Springfield, 83; and many others. *Pos:* Contribr ed, New Art Examiner, New Art Asn, 75-76 & illusr the little artist cartoon, 75-76; asst dir, Jan Cicero Gallery, Chicago, 77- *Teaching:* Instr painting, Evanston Art Ctr, Ill, 71-79, Ill Inst Technol, 75-83, Columbia Col, Chicago, 79-, Art Inst Chicago, 81-83 & Univ Ill, Chicago, summer 83; Art Inst Chicago, 81- *Awards:* 3rd Prize, Italian American Exhib. *Bibliog:* Franz Schultz (auth), Jan Cicero Group Show, Chicago Daily News, 77; C L Morrison (auth), One-person show Jan Cicero Gallery, Artforum, 79; Alan G Artner (auth), article, Chicago Tribune, 83. *Media:* Multimedia. *Publ:* Auth, Interview with five abstract painters, New Art Examiner, 76. *Mailing Add:* 1645 W Summerdale Ave Chicago IL 60640

POTOTSCHNIK, JOHN MICHAEL
PAINTER, INSTRUCTOR
b St Ives, Cornwall, Eng, Nov 14, 45; US citizen. *Study:* Wichita State Univ, BFA, 68; Art Ctr Col Design, 69-71. *Work:* Wichita Sedgwick Co Hist Mus, Kans; City of McKinney (Collin Co Courthouse), Tex; City of Carrollton (City Hall), Tex; Wichita Ctr Arts, Kans; Ponca City Art Asn, Okla. *Exhib:* 5th Ann Nat Small Oil Painting Show, Wichita Ctr Arts, Kans, 85; Midwest Gathering of Artists, Art Central, Carthage, Mo, 85-92; The Director's Invitational, Wichita Ctr Arts, Wichita, Kans, 86; American Art in Miniature, Thomas Gilcrease Mus, Tulsa, Okla, 92; Miniatures 92, Albuquerque Mus, NMex, 92. *Pos:* Newsletter ed, Artists & Craftsman Assoc, 83-85, first vpres, 85-86, pres, 86-88. *Teaching:* Art instr painting, Plano Art Asn, 90- *Awards:* George Washington Honor Medal, Freedom's Found Valley Forge, 84, 86; Best of Show, 5th Ann Nat Small Oil Painting Exhib, Wichita Ctr Arts, 85; John Steven Jones Fel, Bosque County Conservatory of Fine Arts, Roland & Joyce Jones, 92. *Bibliog:* Peter Anderson (auth), Introductions, Southwest Art Mag, 87. *Publ:* Illusr, First Mag, Bauer Publ, 90; contribr, Am Artist, BFI Communs, 90. *Mailing Add:* 6944 Taylor Lane Wylie TX 75098

POTTER, (GEORGE) KENNETH
PAINTER, PRINTMAKER
b Bakersfield, Calif, Feb 26, 26. *Study:* Acad Art, San Francisco, 47 & 48; Acad Frochot, Paris, with Metzinger, 50-52; Inst Statale Belli Arte, Florence, Italy, summer 51; study in Sicily, 53; San Francisco State Univ, BA, 74. *Work:* Admiral's Conference Room, USS Enterprise; Univ San Francisco Collection; Fed Housing & Urban Development, Regional Off, San Francisco; City of San Francisco Art Comn. *Comn:* Dome (stained glass & resin), Soc Calif Pioneers, Hale Mem Gallery, Civic Ctr, San Francisco, 74; acrylic mural, Coliseum Off, Dept Motor Vehicles, Oakland, Calif, 75; triptych (stained glass & resin windows), Univ Calif, San Francisco, Moffitt Hosp, San Francisco, 76; hist mural (ink & acrylic on canvas), Corte Madera Town Hall. *Exhib:* Phelan Awards Exhib, San Francisco Mus Art, 49, Calif Palace Legion Hon, San Francisco, 58 & 60; Soc of Western Artists, M H De Young Mus, San Francisco, 56-64; Cult Exchange Exhib, Fukuoka, Japan, 64; Watercolor USA, Springfield Art Mus, Mo, 73 & 74; Watercolor West, Riverside Mus, Calif, 74; Royal Watercolor Soc Galleries Invitational, London, England, 75; California The Urban Tempo, Palos Verdes Art Ctr, Rancho Palos Verdes, Calif, 91, also invitational travelling to var mus in Calif; and many others. *Pos:* Art dir, McCann-Erikson Inc Advert, Rio de Janeiro, 54-55, Johnson & Lewis Advert, San Francisco, 57 & Michelson Advert, Palo Alto, 59-60; artist demonstr, Grumbacher Inc, New York, 78-79. *Teaching:* Instr watercolor, Civic Art Ctr, Walnut Creek, Calif, 68-70, Acad Art, San Francisco, 70, San Francisco State Univ, 74 & 75 & Richmond Art Ctr, Calif, 78-79. *Awards:* Non-Purchase Award for Watercolor, Calif State Fair & Expos, 58 & 72; First Award Watercolor, Alameda Co Fair Statewide Competition, 74, 79 & 85; San Francisco Art Comn Festival Exhib Award, 75; Best of Show, Calif Arts League Sixth Ann Nat Open, 88. *Bibliog:* Harold Rogers (auth), Color out of the West, Christian Sci Monitor, 2/26/49; Milton Goldring (auth), O pintor

Americano Kenneth Potter, Correio da Manha, Rio de Janeiro, 6/2/55; The California Style, McClelland & Last Hillcrest Press, Inc, Beverly Hills, Calif, 85. *Mem:* West Coast Watercolor Soc (pres, 68-70). *Media:* Watercolor, Miscellaneous Media. *Publ:* Contribr, Golden Gate Bridge, 5/27/62, A walk in Chinatown, 6/10/62 & A walk in the art world, 9/29/63, Bonanza, San Francisco Chronicle; Mission San Antonio, Calif Automobile Asn, 9/67; Marin portfolio, Image Mag, 10/67; Toward Diversity California Post War Watercolors, Gordon McClelland (auth), Antiques & Fine Art 1-2/91; Review of California The Urban Tempo, Charlotte Berney (auth), Antiques & Fine Art, 3-4/91. *Dealer:* Holloway Howard 20th Century American Art 59 Grant Ave San Francisco CA 94108; Joanne Chappell Gallery 625 Second Street 4th Floor San Francisco CA 94107. *Mailing Add:* 4824 Skyway Dr Fair Oaks CA 95628

POTTER, KENNETH See Potter, (George) Kenneth

POTTER, TED
PAINTER, ADMINISTRATOR
b Springhill, Kans, Dec 6, 33. *Study:* Northwestern Univ; Univ Kans; Baker Univ, BFA; Univ Calif, Berkeley; Calif Col Arts & Crafts, MFA. *Work:* Calif Col Arts & Crafts, Oakland; Univ Kans Art Gallery, Lawrence; Wake Forest Univ, Winston-Salem; Vanderbilt Univ, Nashville; Glaxo Inc, RTP, NC; and many pvt collections. *Exhib:* Solo exhibs, State Univ, Salem Col, Winston-Salem, Barbara Fiedler Gallery, Washington, DC, Morehead Galleries, Greensboro, NC & Marita Gilliam Gallery, Raleigh, NC, 89; New Orleans Acad Fine Art, 84. *Pos:* Dir art, Glide Found, 65-67; dir, Southeastern Ctr Contemp Art, Winston-Salem, 68-; dir, Awards Visual Arts, Nat Artist Fel Prog, Atlanta Ctr Arts, New Smyrna Beach, Fla. *Mem:* NC State Arts Soc (adv coun, 69-72); NC State Arts Coun. *Dealer:* Estelle Dodge Associates New York, NY; Barbara Fiedler Galleries Washington DC. *Mailing Add:* c/o Gilliam & Pedeh Gallery 126 Glenwood Ave Raleigh NC 27603

POULIN, ROLAND
SCULPTOR
Study: Ecole des Beaux-Arts de Montreal, 64-69, Atelier Mario Merola, 69-70, Univ Laral, PhD, 80. *Work:* Musee d'Art Contemporain, Montreal, PQ; Musee du Quebec; Nat Gallery, Ottawa, Ont; Musee des Beaux-Arts de Montreal; Art Gallery Ont, Toronto. *Exhib:* Solo exhibs, Mus van Hedendaagse Kunst, Ghent, Belg, 87, Galerie Chantel Boulanger, Montreal, 88, Centre Culturel Canadien, Paris, France, 89, Macdonald Stewart Art Ctr, Guelph, Ont, 90, Canada House, London, Eng, 90; Quebec '88--A Selection, Art Gallery Toronto Art Rental, 88; Historical Rouse: Art in Montreal, Power Plant, Toronto, 88; 49th Parallel, New York, 89; Cologne Art Fair, Ger. *Pos:* Instr sculpture, Univ du Quebec a Montreal, 71-72; instr composition, Col du Vieux-Montreal, 72-74, Col Brebeuf, 75-76; instr sculpture, Univ Laval, Quebec, 73-81, Concordia Univ, Montreal, 82-83, Univ Ottawa, 87- *Bibliog:* Gilles Daignault (auth), La nouvelle sculpture de Roland Poulin, Le Devoir, Montreal, 5/17/86; Norman Theriault (auth), L'oeuvre d'art prend le pas sur l'histoire, Forces, No 84, Montreal, winter 89; Chantal Pontbriand (auth), Roland Poulin, No 53, Parachute, Montreal, 89. *Mailing Add:* c/o Olga Korper 17 Morrow Ave Toronto ON M6R 2H9 Canada

POULOS, BASILIOS NICHOLAS
PAINTER, EDUCATOR
b Columbia, SC, Dec 15, 41. *Study:* Atlanta Sch Art, BFA; Tulane Univ, MFA; Univ SC. *Work:* Houston Mus Fine Arts; Chase Manhattan Bank, New York; Voores Mus, Athens; Tulane Univ, New Orleans, La; New Orleans Mus Art; and others. *Exhib:* One-man exhibs, High Mus Art, Atlanta, Ga, 65, Columbia Mus Art, SC, 67 & 84, Simonne Stern Gallery, New Orleans, La, 73, 74, 76 & 78, Greenville Co Mus Art, SC, 79; Watson de Nagy & Co, Houston, Tex, 75, 76 & 79; Tibor De Nagy Gallery, New York, 80; 35th Biennial, Corcoran Gallery Art, Washington, DC, 77; McIntosh-Drysdale Gallery, Washington DC, 85 & 86; Harris Gallery, Houston, 86. *Teaching:* Assoc prof painting, Rice Univ, 75- *Awards:* Fine Arts Found Grant, Atlanta, Ga, 65; French Govt Grant, 65-66; Guggenheim Found Fel, 73-74. *Bibliog:* Mimi Crossley (auth), Poulos at Watson De Nagy, Art in Am, 77. *Media:* Acrylic on Canvas, Wood. *Dealer:* Heath Gallery 416 E Paces Perry Rd Atlanta GA 30305; Harris Gallery 1100 Bissonnet Houston TX 77005. *Mailing Add:* 1430 W 23rd St Houston TX 77008

POUNIAN, ALBERT KACHOUNI
PAINTER, CURATOR
b Chicago, Ill, Mar 7, 24. *Study:* Art Inst Chicago, BFA, 48 & MFA, 49. *Work:* Borg-Warner Corp, Chicago; Ill Bell Tel, Chicago; Harper Col, Palatine, Ill; Barat Col, Lake Forest, Ill. *Exhib:* Chicago & Vicinity, Art Inst Chicago; Ringling Mus, Sarasota, Fla; Northwest Territory, Springfield, Ill; Violence in Contemp Am Art, Mus Contemp Art, Chicago, 68. *Pos:* Consult & contribr, Am Educ Encycl; coordr, Nat Upward Bound Exhib, Off Econ Opportunity, 66 & consult, 67-68; corp art cur, Continental Ill Nat Bank & Trust Co, Chicago, 79-89; founding chmn, Asn Corp Art Curators, Chicago, 80; consult, Nixon Assoc, Chicago, 89- *Teaching:* Instr, painting & drawing, Art Inst Chicago, 48-56; lectr art hist, Lake Forest Col, 50-65; prof painting & drawing, Barat Col Lake Forest, 49-79 & chmn art dept, 70-74; Fulbright-Hays Exchange Prof, Sch Fine Arts, Ulster Col, Northern Ireland Polytechnic, Belfast, Northern Ireland. *Mem:* Am Asn Univ Prof. *Media:* Acrylic, Pen & Ink. *Publ:* Auth, articles, Am Educ Encycl. *Mailing Add:* 46 N Washington Circle Lake Forest IL 60045

POUPENEY, MOLLIE
CERAMIST, WRITER
b Oregon; US citizen. *Study:* Univ Calif, BA, 69. *Work:* Oakland Mus, Calif; Saks Fifth Ave Am Craft Collection, San Francisco, Calif; US State Dept. *Exhib:* Solo exhibs, Valley Arts Gallery, Walnut Creek, Calif, 68, 70, Scott Gallery, Orinda, Calif, 78, Antonio Prieto Gallery, Mills Col, Oakland, 81 & Oakland Mus, Calif, 82; Calif Artists, Oakland Mus, Calif, 81; Invitational 1984, Craftsman's Gallery, Scarsdale, NY, 84; Five Western Artists, Artisans Am Fine Crafts, Tex, 86; Los Angeles Int Art Show, Barclay Simpson Fine Arts, Calif, 87; Jewel Savadelis Collection, Triton Mus, Santa Clara, Calif, 88; Renwick Gallery, Smithsonian, Wash, DC, 88. *Mem:* Asn Calif Ceramic Artists; Baulines Crafts Guild, Sausalito. *Media:* Clay, Paint. *Publ:* Auth, articles, Ceramics Monthly. *Mailing Add:* 3669 MT Diaslo Blvd Lafayette CA 94549

POUSETTE-DART, JOANNA
PAINTER
b New York, NY, 1947. *Study:* Bennington Col, BA, 68. *Work:* Mus Mod Art, Solomon R Guggenheim Mus, Citibank, Fox Glynn & Melamed, Lehman Brothers, McCrory Corp, Wells Rich & Greene, Brooklyn Mus, New York; Indianapolis Mus, Ind; Portland Art Mus, Ore; Coopers & Lybrand, Houston, Tex; Security Pacific Nat Bank, Calif. *Comn:* Doumani House (mosaics & architect), comn by Robert Graha, Los Angeles. *Exhib:* Solo exhibs, Susan Caldwell Gallery, New York, 76, 78, 79 & 83, Janus Gallery, Los Angeles, Calif, 81 & Schmidt-Dean Gallery, Philadelphia, Pa, 88; Painting and Sculpture Today 1980, Indianapolis Mus Art, Ind, 80; Collectors Gallery XVI, Marion Koogler McNay Art Inst, San Antonio, Tex, 82; Recent Acquisition: Paintings & Sculpture, 83 & Contrasts of Form: Geometric Painting 1960-1980, 85-86, Mod Mus Art, New York; Drawings, Gallery 201, traveling, 86; Abstractions Self-Evident, Piccalo Spaleto, Charleston, SC, 91. *Teaching:* Instr, Ramapo Col, NJ, 72-76 & Hunter Col, 86- *Awards:* John Simon Guggenheim Memorial Fel, 81; Nat Endowment Arts Grants, 89-90. *Bibliog:* Lenore Malen (auth), New York Reviews, ARTnews, 10/88; Vered Leib (auth), Joanna Pousette-Davis: Exploring the Possiblities of Dialogue, Arts, 4/88. *Mailing Add:* 433 Broome St New York NY 10013

POWELL, DAN T
PHOTOGRAPHER
b Richland, Wash, July 12, 50. *Study:* Cent Wash Univ, with Jim Sahlstrand, BA, 73, MA(art), 77; Univ Ill, with Art Sinsabaugh & Luther Smith, MFA(art), 80. *Work:* Hallmark Collection, Kansas City, Mo; Calif Inst Arts; Art Inst Chicago, Ill; Midwest Mus Am Art, Elkhart, Ind; Ill State Univ, Normal. *Exhib:* Summer Light, Light Gallery, New York, 82; Group exhib, Fifth Vienna Int Biennial, Austria, 82, Chicago Art Inst, 88, San Francisco Mus Mod Art, 88; four-person exhib, San Francisco Camerawork, 83; Susan Spiritus Gallery, Los Angeles, 83. *Teaching:* Asst prof, Univ Northern Iowa, 80-; asst prof, Univ Ore, 87- *Awards:* Second Award, Contemp Photoworks, Univ NMex, 80; Best of Show, Midwest Photo 80, Midwest Mus Am Art, 80; Best of Prints & Drawings, Iowa Artists, Des Moines Art Ctr, 82. *Bibliog:* Joan Murray (auth), rev of New Photographics, 79 & Diane Neumaier (auth), Visual & Verbal Language, 80, Artweek; Barbara Westerfield (auth), Constructed Realities, Art News, 86. *Mem:* Soc Photog Educ; Soc Contemp Photog, Kansas City, Mo. *Dealer:* Ledel Gallery 168 Mercer St New York NY; Thom Barry Fine Arts Minneapolis MN. *Mailing Add:* Thomas Barry Fine Arts 400 First Ave N Suite 304 Minneapolis MN 55401

POWELL, EARL ALEXANDER, III
DIRECTOR, HISTORIAN
b Spartanburg, SC, Oct 24, 43. *Study:* Williams Col, BA, 66; Harvard Univ, MA, 70, PhD, 74. *Pos:* Cur Michener Collection, Univ Tex, Austin, 74-76; mus cur & asst to asst dir, Nat Gallery of Art, Washington, DC, 76-78, exec cur, 79-80; dir, Los Angeles Co Mus Art, 80-92. *Teaching:* Asst prof Am art, Univ Tex, Austin, 74-76; teaching fel fine arts, Harvard Univ, 70-74. *Awards:* King Olav Medal, Norway; Chevalier of Arts & Lett Award, France. *Mem:* Col Art Asn; Commission for the Preservation of the White House; Am Asn Mus Dirs; Fed Coun Arts & Human; Fine Arts Adv Panel, Fed Reserve Bd. *Res:* English influences in the art of Thomas Cole. *Publ:* Coauth, American Art at Harvard (catalog), 73; auth, Catalogue Raisonne of the Michener Collection, 78; plus article & catalogue essay on Am art. *Mailing Add:* Los Angeles Co Mus Arts 5905 Wilshire Blvd Los Angeles CA 90036

POWELL, GORDON
SCULPTOR
b Decatur, Ill, May 4, 47. *Study:* Sch Art Inst, Chicago, BFA, 75; Univ Ill, MFA, 80. *Work:* Cresap, McCormick and Paget, Chicago; Levy Organization, Chicago; Prudential Insurance; Saks Fifth Ave, Portland, Ore; State Ill Collection, Springfield. *Exhib:* New Horizons in Art, Cult Ctr, Chicago, 84; 81st Exhib Artists of Chicago & Vicinity, Art Inst Chicago, 85; Fetish Show-Obsessive Expressions, Rockford Art Mus, 86; Extended Boundaries, Cult Ctr, Chicago, 86; Columnar, Hudson River Mus, Yonkers, 88; Body Fragments, Shea and Beker Gallery, New York, 89; The Chicago Show, Chicago Cult Ctr, Ill, 90; Summer 1990, Rosa Esman Gallery, New York, 90; one-person exhibs, Roy Boyd Galleries, Chicago, 82, 83, 85, 86 & 89, Santa Monica, Calif, 87 & Vaughan & Vaughan, Minneapolis, Minn, 90. *Awards:* Artist-in-Residence, ArtPark, Lewiston, NY, 85; Fel Nat Endowment Arts, 86; Prix de Rome, Am Acad Rome, 87-88. *Bibliog:* Emerging Sculptor Show, The New York Times, 12/11/87; reviews, Chicago Tribune, 7/16/82, Los Angeles Times, 11/17/87. *Media:* Wood. *Dealer:* Gordon Powell Studio 1117 W Lake St Chicago IL 60607. *Mailing Add:* 319 N Thatcher River Forest IL 60305

POWELSON, ROSEMARY A
PAINTER, PRINTMAKER
b La Junta, Colo. *Study:* Univ Nebr, Lincoln, BFA, 71; Mich State Univ, East Lansing, MFA, 74. *Work:* Art Inst Chicago; Cranbrook Acad Art, Bloomfield Hills, Mich; Hackley Art Mus, Muskegon, Mich; Kalamazoo Inst Art, Mich; Sioux City Art Ctr, Iowa; Lower Columbia Col, Longview, Wash. *Comn:* Mich bicentennial portfolio prints in collotype, Nat Endowment Arts, Alma, Mich, 76; Prints 83 (portfolio), Lower Columbia Col Found, Longview, Wash, 83. *Exhib:* One-woman show, Alma Col, Mich, 78; Kans 5th Nat Small Paintings & Drawings, Art Gallery, Ft Hayes State Univ, 81; Wash Women Art, Art Gallery, Eastern Wash Univ, Cheney, 81; Print Exhib, Fort Steilacoom Community Col, Tacoma, Wash, 83; Print Exhib, Ore State Univ, Corvallis, Ore, 84; Invitational Group Show, Clatsop Community Col, Astoria, Ore, 85. *Pos:* Humanities consult, Wash Humanities Project, Olympia, 81- *Teaching:* Instr painting & drawing, Alma Col, Mich, 75-78; instr design & drawing, Ft Steilacoom Community Col, Tacoma, Wash, 78-79; instr art hist & design, Lower Columbia Col, Longview, Wash, 79- *Awards:* Purchase Award, 33rd Ann Fall Show, 71; Merit Award, Saginaw Ann Area Art Exhib, 77. *Media:* All Media. *Publ:* Producer, Women in Art (film), Wash State Humanities Project, Olympia, 81. *Mailing Add:* Art Dept PO Box 3010 Lower Columbia Col Longview WA 98632

POWER, MARK
PHOTOGRAPHER, EDUCATOR
b Washington, DC, Mar 6, 37. *Study:* Bowdoin Col; Art Ctr Col. *Work:* Bibliotheque Nat, Paris; Libr Cong, Corcoran Gallery Art, Smithsonian Inst, Washington, DC; New Orleans Mus Art, La; Baltimore Mus Art. *Exhib:* One-man shows; Corcoran Gallery, Washington, DC, 70 & 74; Rita Hayworth series, Diane Brown Gallery, Washington, DC, 77, Ewing Gallery, Washington, DC, 79 & 85; Mexican Photographs, Jefferson Place Gallery, Washington, DC, 74; Color Work, Galerie Chambre Clair, Paris, 83; Palladium Work, Contrasts Gallery, London, 80; and others. *Collections Arranged:* Marcel Bardon Photographs, 74 & Wright Morris: Words and Pictures (contribr, catalog), 82, Corcoran Gallery. *Pos:* Photog critic, Washington Post, 74-75 & 86-87; Washington Correspondent, After Image, 76, Photog Rev, 86-; contrib ed, Washington Review. *Teaching:* Assoc prof photog, Corcoran Sch Art, Washington, DC, 70-, prof, 90-; vis prof art, Univ Tex, San Antonio, 82. *Awards:* Grant-in-Aid Fel, Washington Gallery Mod Art Fund, 70-72; Materials Grant, Polaroid Corp, 72-75. *Bibliog:* David Tannous (auth), Art America, 12/77-1/78; Paul Richard (auth), Beasts of Beauty, Washington Post, 10/6/79; John Brumfield (auth), Washington's strongest, Artweek, 7/83. *Publ:* Photographs, Camera Mag, Switz, 67, 69, 74, 78 & 79; photographs, Creative Camera, Great Britain, 5/70; auth, introd, George Krause-1, 72; introd, Nancy Rexroth, Iowa, 77. *Dealer:* Kathleen Ewing Gallery 3243 P St NW Washington DC 20007. *Mailing Add:* c/o Corcoran Sch Art 500 17th & NY Ave NW Washington DC 20006

POWER, S BRENDA JOAN
SCULPTOR, PAINTER
b New York, NY, May 12, 41. *Study:* St Johns Univ, BS, 62; Pratt Inst, with Calvin Albert, George McNeil & Walter Rogalski, MFA(sculpture), 77. *Exhib:* Brooklyn 77, Brooklyn Mus, 77; Audubon Artists Ann Exhib, Nat Acad Galleries, New York, 77; Brighton Beach Maquettes & Ethnifest, Downtown Cult Ctr, Brooklyn, 81; Salmagundi Gallery, 81 & 82; Images and Symbols, Cork Gallery, New York, 82; The Rotunda Gallery, New York, 84; Gallery 1199, New York, 85. *Pos:* Dir art gallery, Harriman Col, 77-80. *Teaching:* Asst prof art hist, St Johns Univ, Jamaica, NY, 83- & Mercy Col, Dobbs Ferry, NY, 83- *Awards:* Ford Found Award Sculpture, 76; Long Beach Mus Art Creativity Award, 76. *Bibliog:* Alternative spaces--some highlights, 1/21/82, Claude Lesuer (auth), Brenda Power: Drawing in space & beyond, 1/6/83, Will Grant (auth), Belanthi, growing & maturing, 10/16/83 & Palmer Poroner (auth), S Brenda Power: Unifying the abstract message, 1/11/86, Art Speak. *Mem:* Am Soc Contemp Artists; Metrop Painters & Sculptors (pres, currently); New York Artists Equity; Found Community Artists; Col Art Asn. *Media:* Polychromed Sculpture. *Mailing Add:* c/o Belanthi Gallery 142 Court St Brooklyn NY 11201

POWERS, DONALD T
PAINTER
b Madison, Tenn, May 20, 50. *Study:* Tenn Technol Univ, 69-70; David Lipscomb Col, 70-72. *Work:* Smithsonian Inst Nat Portrait Gallery, Washington, DC; Butler Inst Am Art, Youngstown, Ohio; Ga Mus Art, Univ Ga, Athens; Am Acad & Inst Arts & Lett, New York, NY; Mus Mod Art, Haifa, Israel. *Comn:* Portrait of Jimmy Carter, Friends of the President, Washington, DC, 85; portrait of His Holiness the Dalai Lama, 90. *Exhib:* Jimmy Carter in Plains, Hunter Mus Art, Chattanooga, Tenn, 86; Art and the Law, Minn Mus Art, St Paul, Minn & Moscarelle Mus, Col William & Mary, Williamsburg, Va, 87; The Eternal Landscape, Southeastern Ctr for Contemp Art, Winston-Salem, NC, 91. *Awards:* Lyndhurst Prize, Lyndhurst Found, 84-86; Purchase Award, West Publ Co, 87. *Media:* Egg Tempera, Oil. *Mailing Add:* 217 Edgewood Dr PO Box 3295 Thomasville GA 31799

POWERS, W ALEX
PAINTER
b St Charles, Va, Apr 25, 40. *Study:* Emory & Henry Col, Emory, Va, BA, 62; Eliot McMurrough Sch Art, Indialantic, Fla, 67-69; Art Students League, Woodstock, NY, 69. *Work:* SC State Art Collection, Columbia; Trammel Crowe Co, Charlotte, NC; Waccamaw Art & Crafts Guild, Myrtle Beach, SC; Coca Cola, Charlotte, NC. *Exhib:* Am Watercolor Soc, New York, NY, 76, 88, 90 & 92; Nat Watercolor Soc, Los Angeles, 84-86; San Diego Watercolor Soc Int Exhib, 85-86 & 91-92; Rocky Mountain Nat, Golden, Colo, 90; Watercolor USA, Springfield, Mo, 91. *Teaching:* Self-employed teacher, watercolor workshops throughout US, Canada & Abroad, 72- *Awards:* Best-of-Show, Rocky Mountain Nat Watermedia Exhib, Golden, Colo, 85; Best-of-Show, Southeastern Watercolorists III, Deland, Fla, 85; Best-of-Show, Okla Patrons Gala Watercolor Exhib, 86. *Bibliog:* Carole Katchen (auth), Faces and Figures, Watson-Guptill, 86; Nita Leland (auth), The Creative Artist, Northlight Publ, 90; Everything You Always Wanted to Know About Watercolor, Watson-Guptill, 92. *Mem:* Nat Watercolor Soc; Southern Watercolor Soc; Waccamaw Arts & Crafts Guild, SC (pres, 76, vpres, 86); SC Watercolor Soc. *Media:* Watercolor, Drawing. *Publ:* Am Artist Mag, 2/85; Artist's Mag, 2/85; auth, Painting People in Watercolor, Watson-Guptill Publ, 89. *Mailing Add:* 401-72nd Ave N Apt 1 Myrtle Beach SC 29577

POWLEY, DONALD
PAINTER
b St Louis, Mo, 55. *Study:* Wash Univ, St Louis, Mo, BFA, 79. *Work:* Chase Manhattan Bank, New York. *Exhib:* Selections 23, Drawing Ctr, New York, 83; Joe Fawbush, New York, 88; solo exhibs, Cash/Newhouse, New York, 86 & 87, Julian Pretto, New York, 88 & 89, White Columns, New York, 90; Borgenicht Gallery, New York, 88; New Romantic Landscape, Whitney Mus Fairfield Co, Conn, 87; Michael Kohn Gallery, Los Angeles, 88; Painting and Sculpture, Julian Pretto, New York, 89; Empire State Biennial, Emerson Mus, Syracuse, NY, 90; Curt Marcus Gallery, New York, 91; Strategies for the Next Painting, Wolff Gallery, New York, 91; Cotextures & Constructures, Rubenstein/Diacomo Gallery, New York, 92; How It Is, Tony Scafrazi Gallery, New York, 92. *Awards:* Visual Arts Fel, Painting, Nat Endowment Arts, 87. *Bibliog:* Gary Indiana (auth), Vice picks, Village Voice, 7/9/85 & 3/25/86; Rosetta Brooks (auth), Space Fictions, Flash Art, 12/86; Michael Brenson (auth), Are the Whitney's satellites out of orbit?, New York Times, 8/9/87. *Dealer:* Rubenstein/Diacomo Gallery 130 Prince St New York NY 10012. *Mailing Add:* 153 Rutland Rd Brooklyn NY 11225-5314

POZZATTI, RUDY O
PRINTMAKER, PAINTER
b Telluride, Colo, Jan 14, 25. *Study:* Univ Colo, BFA & MFA; Hon LHD, Univ Colo, 73; also with Wendell H Black, Max Beckman & Ben Shahn. *Work:* Mus Mod Art, New York; Libr Cong, Washington, DC; Art Inst Chicago, Ill; Sheldon Mem Art Mus, Lincoln, Nebr; Cleveland Mus Art, Ohio. *Comn:* Spec Print Eds, Cleveland Print Club, Cleveland Mus Art, 54; Int Graphic Arts Soc, New York, 58-61 & 63; Conrad Hilton Hotel, New York, 61; Clairol, Inc, comn for New York World's Fair, 63; Ferdinand Roten Galleries, Baltimore, Md, 67 & 68. *Exhib:* Young Americans, Whitney Mus Am Arts, New York, 61; Stampe di Due Mondi: Prints of Two Worlds, Tyler Sch Art, Rome, Italy, 67; 20 Year Retrospective, Sheldon Mem Art Gallery, Univ Nebr, 69; Artists Abroad, Inst Int Educ, Am Fedn Arts, New York, 69; Int Cultural Conf, Budapest, Hungary, 85; Rudy Pozzatti, Four Decades of Printmaking (82 works with catalog), Mitchell Mus, Mt Vernon, Ill, Travelling Show, 92-93; and others. *Pos:* US State Dept Cult Exchange Proj, USSR, 61, Yugoslavia, 65 & Brazil, 74; artist-in-residence, Roswell Mus & Art Ctr, 79. *Teaching:* Asst prof printmaking & painting, Univ Nebr, 50-56; prof printmaking, Ind Univ, 56-72, distinguished prof, 72- *Awards:* Guggenheim Fel, 63-64; George Norlin Silver Medal, Assoc Alumni of Univ Colo, 72. *Bibliog:* Norman Geske (auth), Rudy Pozzatti; American Printmaker, Univ Kans, 71; Richard Taylor (auth), Pozzatti (film), Artists in America, NETV, 71; Nancy Carroll (auth), A visit with Rudy Pozzatti, North Shore Art League, 72. *Mem:* Soc Am Graphic Artists; Am Color Print Soc; Col Art Asn, New York (bd dirs). *Media:* All Media. *Dealer:* Neville-Sargent Gallery 215 W Superior St Chicago IL 60610; The Gallery, 109 E Sixth St Bloomington IN 47401. *Mailing Add:* 117 S Meadowbrook Ave Bloomington IN 47401

POZZI, LUCIO
PAINTER, PRINTMAKER
b Milano, Italy, Nov 29, 35; US citizen. *Study:* Sculpture with Michael Noble. *Work:* Mus Modern Art, New York; Mus Contemp Art, Chicago; Detroit Art Inst; Neuberger Mus, Purchase, NY. *Exhib:* DIA Ctr for the Arts, New York, 91; Paula Cooper, 91; Holly Solomon, New York, 92; Bargenidst, New York, 92; John Weber, New York, 93. *Pos:* Art writer & critic various art publications. *Teaching:* Asst prof art & art hist, Cooper Union, 69-75; vis prof art, Princeton Univ, 75; instr art, Sch Visual Arts, 78-; sr critic, Yale Univ grad sculpture prog, 90. *Awards:* Nat Endowment Arts Fel, 83. *Bibliog:* David Shapiro (auth), An interview with Lucio Pozzi, NY Art J, 11/79; J Van Der Marck (auth), Reconnecting (exib catalog), Detroit Art Inst, 87. *Mem:* Am Abstract Artists. *Media:* Acrylic, Oil; All Media. *Res:* Modern movement. *Publ:* Auth, Five Stories, 75 & 78. *Mailing Add:* 142 Greene St New York NY 10012

PRACKO, BERNARD F, II
PAINTER, SCULPTOR
b Ada, Okla, Jan 17, 45. *Study:* NMex Military Inst, AA, 65; Univ Colo, BA, 70; Ariz State Univ Sch Fine Art, 92. *Work:* Sun Cities Art Mus, Ariz; Ariz State Univ Sch Art, Tempe; Univ Colo Govs Collection, Boulder. *Comn:* Man in the Cosmos, SCI, Scottsdale, Ariz, 91; Jack Healy (portrait), Amnesty Int, Washington, DC, 92. *Exhib:* For Amnesty Int, Sena Gallery Invitational, Santa Fe, NMex, 91; Sacred Spaces, Long Island, 91; Roaring Fork Ann, Aspen Art Mus, Colo, 92; Art Plates-A Gala, Nelson Fine Art Mus, Tempe, Ariz, 92; Egyptian Echoes, Sun Cities Art Mus, Ariz, 93. *Bibliog:* Lynn Pyne (auth), Sounds move artist, Phoenix Gazette, 7/92; Ann Bonnano (dir), Pracko - His Art (film), Video Media Productions, 7/92. *Media:* Acrylic on Canvas; Metal, Stone. *Publ:* Contribr, Amnesty Int Calendar, 90. *Dealer:* Marcelle Fine Art 996 Madison Ave New York NY 10021; ACA Gallery 41 E 57th St New York NY 10022. *Mailing Add:* 6991 E Camelback Rd Suite B111 Scottsdale AZ 85251

PRACZUKOWSKI, EDWARD LEON
PAINTER, EDUCATOR
b Norwich, Conn, May 25, 30. *Study:* Norwich Art Sch, fine arts dipl, 50; Sch Mus Boston, cert with hons in painting, 56, Clarrisa Bartlett travel fel & grad cert, 59; Tufts Univ, BS(art educ), 58; Cranbrook Acad, MFA, 65. *Work:* Slater Mem Mus, Norwich, Conn, 81; City of Seattle, Wash. *Exhib:* Drawing USA, St Paul Art Ctr, Minn, 66 & 69; Nat Polymer Exhib, EMich Univ, 67 & 68; 11th Ann Nat Drawing Exhib, Oklahoma Art Ctr, 69; one-man shows, Greenwood Gallery, Seattle, Wash, 81 & 83; Living With the Volcano, The Artists of Mt St Helens, Mus Art, Wash State Univ, 83. *Teaching:* Assoc prof drawing & painting, Univ Wash, 65- *Awards:* First Prize Painting, Int Arts Festival, Detroit, 65; MacDowell Colony Grants, 66 & 69; Wash Water Power Award, Spokane Ann, 81. *Mem:* Edward MacDowell Colony, New York; Allied Artists, Seattle, Wash. *Media:* Oil, Acrylic. *Mailing Add:* Univ Washington Seattle WA 98105

PRAEGER, FREDERICK A
COLLECTOR, PUBLISHER
b Vienna, Austria, Sept 16, 15; US citizen. *Study:* Univ Vienna; Univ Denver, LHD. *Pos:* Pres, Frederick A Praeger Publ, New York, 50-68; chmn, Phaidon Publ, Ltd, London, 67-68; gen mgr, Ed Praeger, Munich, 69-74; Vchmn & publ, Westview Press, Boulder, 75- *Teaching:* Adj prof, Grad Sch Librarianship, Univ Denver, Colo. *Mem:* Cosmos Club. *Collection:* Contemporary art; Gothic and Baroque sculpture; African Mexican art. *Mailing Add:* 1402 Old Tale Rd Boulder CO 80303

PRAGER, DAVID A
COLLECTOR
b Long Branch, NJ, July 25, 13. *Study:* Columbia Univ, BA & LLD; also with Jack Tworkov. *Pos:* Asst secy, Friends of Whitney Mus Am Art, New York, 59-63, secy, 63-67; mem acquisitions comt, Whitney Mus Am Art, 60-61, 67-68 & 70-71; bd trustees, Am Fedn Arts, 67-82, treas, 69-79; treas, Munic Art Soc, 67-69, bd dirs, 69-, pres, 72-74, vpres, 74-; bd dirs, Mark Rothko Found, 77- *Mem:* Century Asn. *Collection:* Contemporary American painting. *Mailing Add:* 14 E 90th St No 11A New York NY 10128

PRAKAPAS, DOROTHY
DIRECTOR
b New York, NY, May 13, 28. *Study:* Hunter Col, New York, BA(art), 49; Fashion Inst Technol, BS(drafting & design), 51; Parson's Sch Design, with Hananiah Harari, 52; Sch Visual Arts, Advert Design, 54. *Pos:* Animator, Lee Blair Film Graphics, 52-54; stylist, Playtex, 55-62; fashion design, Mercantile, 62-76; dir, Prakapas Gallery, 76- *Mem:* Art Dealer's Asn Am; Asn Int Photog Art Dealers. *Specialty:* Twentieth century modernism with special emphasis on photography. *Mailing Add:* Box 272 Canal St Sta New York NY 10013

PRAKAPAS, EUGENE JOSEPH
ART DEALER, EDITOR
b Lowell, Mass, July 29, 32. *Study:* Yale Univ, BA, 53; Oxford Univ, Eng, with Balliol, MA, 59. *Pos:* Vis cur, San Francisco Mus Mod Art, 86; dir, Prakapas Gallery, New York, currently. *Mem:* Art Dealers Asn Am; Asn Int Photog Art Dealers. *Specialty:* Twentieth century modernism, with special emphasis on photography. *Publ:* Auth, Bauhaus Photography, Mass Inst Technol Press, 85. *Mailing Add:* 800 Prospect SE Apt 3C La Jolla CA 92037-4204

PRAMUK, EDWARD RICHARD
PAINTER
b Akron, Ohio, Feb 14, 36. *Study:* Kent State Univ, BFA, MA; Queens Col, grad study; Akron Art Inst; also with John Ferren, James Brooks & Louis Finkelstein. *Work:* New Orleans Mus Art; Cornell Univ; Pan Am Life Corp; Banc Texas, Houston. *Comn:* Paintings, James Talcott Inc, New York, 74. *Exhib:* Pelham-Von Stoffler Gallery, Houston, Tex, 78; Edinboro State Univ, Edinboro, NY, 78; one-man shows, Contemp Art Ctr, New Orleans, 80 & First St Gallery, New York, 83 & 85; Landscape, Cityscape, Seascape, Contemp Art Ctr, New Orleans, 86; Louisiana Landscape, Downtown Gallery, New Orleans, 90; Sylvia Schmidt Gallery, New Orleans, 91; and others. *Teaching:* Prof art, La State Univ, 64- *Awards:* Award, La Prof Artists, Baton Rouge, 71; Purchase Award, 7th Nat Drawing & Sculpture Show, 73; Purchase Award, New Orleans Mus Art, 74. *Media:* Acrylic. *Publ:* Contribr, two colorplates, How to Make an Oil Painting, Watson-Guptill, 90. *Mailing Add:* Univ Baton Rouge Dept Fine Arts Baton Rouge LA 70808

PRANGE, SALLY BOWEN
CERAMIST, SCULPTOR
b Valparaiso, Ind, Aug 11, 27. *Study:* Univ Mich, Ann Arbor, BA. *Work:* Victoria & Albert Mus, London, Eng; William Hayes Ackland Mem Art Ctr, Univ NC, Chapel Hill; NC Mus Art, Raleigh; Smithsonian Inst, Washington, DC; Mus Art, Pa State Univ, University Park; Mus Int Ceramics, Faenza, Italy; J Patrick Lannan Found Cont Art, Palm Beach, Fla; Everson Mus Art, Syracuse, NY; Hickory Mus Art, Hickory, NC; NC Mus Hist, Raleigh, 89; Southern Prog Corp, Birmingham, Ala, 90. *Comn:* Booke & Co, Winston-Salem, NC; Wachovia Bank, Winston-Salem, NC. *Exhib:* Am Ceramic & Sculpture Show, Butler Inst Am Art, Youngstown, Ohio, 67-68 & 71; Horace Williams House Art Ctr, Chapel Hill, NC; Greater Reston Arts Ctr, Va, 90; Tri-State Sculptors Guild, Flossie Martin Gallery & Radford Univ, Radford, Va, 90; Tyndall Galleries, Durham, NC, 92; Durham Art Guild, NC, 93; and others. *Teaching:* Instr ceramic pottery, Univ NC, Chapel Hill, 65-66; instr, Arrowmont, Gatlinburg, Tenn, 79 & 80, Penland Sch Crafts, NC, 81, NC State Univ Crafts Ctr, Raleigh, 82, Univ Calif, San Diego Craft Ctr, 82 & Greenwich House Pottery, New York, 83; instr, Penland Sch Crafts, NC, 81; guest lectr, Brit Craftsmen Potters Asn, London, 80, Int Mus Ceramics, Faenza, Italy, 80, Octagon Ctr, Ames, Iowa, 84, Kansas City Inst, Mo, 85 & Greenhill Ctr NC Arts, 85. *Bibliog:* Lloyd Herman (auth), American Porcelain: New Expressions in an Ancient Art, 80; Katherine Pearson (auth), Am Crafts, 83; Peter Lane (auth), articles, Studio Potter, 81 & Studio Ceramics, 85. *Mem:* Tri-State Sculptors Guild; Am Crafts Coun; World Crafts Coun; Carolina Designer Craftsmen; Nat Coun Educ Ceramic Art. *Media:* Clay. *Publ:* Ceramic Form: Shape & Decoration, 88; Hist of Am Ceramics, Elaine Levin, 89; Clays the Way, Gene Kleinsmith, 89; New York Art Rev, Third Ed, Les Krantz Publ, 89. *Mailing Add:* 6421 Heartwood Dr Chapel Hill NC 27514

PRATT, DALLAS
PATRON, COLLECTOR
b New York, NY, Aug 21, 14. *Study:* Yale Univ, BA; Columbia Univ, MD. *Pos:* Ed, Columbia Libr Columns, 51-80; co-founder & trustee, Am Mus Britain, 59-; ed, Am in Britain, 63-64; founder, John Judkyn Mem, Bath, Eng, 64-; vchmn, Council Friends Columbia Univ Libr, 87; donor, Am Mus Brit, Dallas Pratt Collection Hist Maps, 88. *Bibliog:* Rodney W Shirley (auth), The Dallas Pratt Collection of Maps at the Ammerican Museum, Bath, Map Collector, summer 92. *Collection:* Renaissance maps and manuscripts. *Publ:* Auth, Discovery of a world-early maps of America, Antiques Mag, 12/69 & 1/70; Angel-motors, Columbia Libr Columns, 5/72; The Best Books, Col Libr Columns, 5/74; This stone and these flowers, Am Brit, XVII, 1/79; Historical Maps at the Am Mus in Brit, Imprint, vol 15, 1/90. *Mailing Add:* 228 E 49th St New York NY 10017

PRATT, FRANCES (FRANCES ELIZABETH USUI)
PAINTER, ILLUSTRATOR
b Glen Ridge, NJ, May 25, 13. *Study:* New York Sch Appl Design for Women; Art Students League, with Richard Lahey; Hans Hofmann Sch Art. *Work:* Brooklyn Mus, NY; Va Mus Fine Arts, Richmond. *Exhib:* Denver Art Mus Ann, 42; Addison Gallery, 45; Cleveland Mus Art, 47; Brooklyn Mus Watercolor Int, 47, 49 & 51; Corcoran Gallery Art Biennial, 49; Ceramic Figures of Ancient Mexico (260 original drawings), Edward H Merrin Gallery, New York, 86; Stubbs Books & Prints, New York, 87; Archit Sardonica Watercolors. *Collections Arranged:* Ancient Mexico in Miniature, Am Fedn Arts, 64-66; Guerrero, Stone Sculpture from the State of Guerrero, Mex, Finch Col Mus Art, 65. *Teaching:* Instr painting, Ballard Sch New York, 42-59; instr painting, Parsons Sch Design, 48-51. *Awards:* Anne Payne Robertson Prize, 46 & Prize for Oil, 50, Nat Asn Women Artists Ann; Audubon Prize for Crayon Mixed Media, Audubon Artists Ann, 52. *Res:* Pre-classic cultures of Mexico (1600 BC-300 AD). *Publ:* Illusr, Mezcala Stone Sculpture: The Human Figure, Mus Primitive Art, 67; Chalcacingo, 71 & Ceramic Figures of Ancient Mexico (260 illus), 79, Akad Druck--U Verlagsanstalt, Graz, Austria; Paleolithic & Megalithic Traits in the Olmec Tradition of Mexico, Inst Canarium, Hallein, Austria, 72; coauth, illusr (169 drawings) Mezcala, Ancient Stone Sculpture from Guerrero, Mexico, Balsas Publ, Geneve, Switz, 92. *Mailing Add:* 33 W 12th St New York NY 10011

PRATT, VERNON GAITHER
PAINTER, EDUCATOR
b Durham, NC, Dec 9, 40. *Study:* Phillips Acad, Andover, Mass; Duke Univ; Univ NC; San Francisco Art Inst with James Weeks & Richard Diebenkorn, hon BFA, 62, MFA, 64. *Work:* Duke Univ Mus of Art; San Francisco Art Asn; R J Reynolds World Hq, Winston-Salem, NC; NC Mus Art; Phillip Morris, Inc; and others. *Comn:* Paintings, Brainstorm, MGM production, 81; Outdoor sculpture garden, granite, (25000 lbs), Durham Arts Ctr, 87; Education Wall (32' x 96' granite wall, 8 stone benches, sandblasted and colored), NC Pub Educ Bldg, Raleigh, 92. *Exhib:* O K Harris Gallery, New York, 73; DeGestlo Gallery, Hamburg, Ger, 73; Basel Int Art Fair, Switz, 73; New Orleans Mus, La, 77; John Weber Gallery, 80; Alternative Mus, New York, 84; NC Mus Art, 85; Southeastern Ctr Creative Arts, Winston-Salem, NC, 86; and others. *Collections Arranged:* Real Cool-Cool Real, Duke Univ Mus of Art, 73. *Pos:* Dir, Duke Univ-New York Arts Program, 82-85. *Teaching:* Assoc prof art, Duke Univ, 64- *Awards:* Nealie Sullivan Award for Drawing, San Francisco Art Inst, 62; First Purchase Award, NC Mus of Art, NC Art Soc, 72; Duke Univ Outstanding Professor, 73. *Bibliog:* John Russell (auth), article, New York Times, 7/80. *Media:* All Media. *Dealer:* Tyndall Gallery Durham NC; John Weber Galley New York NY. *Mailing Add:* 3300 Marywood Dr Durham NC 27712

PRAVDA, MURIEL
INSTRUCTOR, SCULPTOR
b Brooklyn, NY. *Study:* Brooklyn Col Journalism, AA, 47; Traphagan Sch Fashion (cert), 47; S Fla Art Inst, certification, 75-92, Bruno Luchese Seminars, 80-91, certificatioin; Atterbury Sch Sculpture, certification. *Work:* N Miami Mus, Fla; Int Boat Show, Miami Beach; Hollywood Art Guild, Fla; Community Art Alliance, Hollywood, Fla. *Comn:* John Kennedy, pvt comn, Dallas, Tex, 89. *Exhib:* One-woman show, S Fla Art Inst, Miami, 87; Sculpture Show, Gallery Turnberry, N Miami Beach, 89; Faculty Show, Discovery Ctr, Ft Lauderdale, 89; Miniature Show, Del Bello Gallery, Toronto, Can, 90; Leonard Art Gallery, Ft Lauderdale, 90; and others. *Pos:* Restorer paintings, Lang Gallery, Jamaica Estates, NY, 70-80, asst sales, 70-80. *Teaching:* Instr clay sculpture, S Fla Art Inst, 80-, lectr sculpture workshop, 82-84. *Awards:* Second Place Sculpture, Fresh Meadows, Merchants, 78; First Place Sculpture, 81 & Merit Award Sculpture, 82, Miami Art League; Silver Poet, Writer's Lullaby, 90 & Gold Poet, Song of the World, 91, World of Poetry. *Bibliog:* M L Pesora (auth), Art show sizzles, Hollywood Sun, 91; Cindy Stauger (auth), News item, Sun Sentinal, 89; Florence Gould (auth), Inside Art (Hallandale) Sculpture, Hallandale Press, 87. *Mem:* Community Art Alliance; charter mem, Nat Mus Women Arts; assoc mem, Nt Sculpture Soc; Int Sculpture Soc. *Media:* Clay. *Publ:* Sculptures, Friends and Neighbors Column, 88, Hallandale Press; Poem, The Survivors, Miami Herald, 9/92. *Mailing Add:* 1655 NE 115th St North Miami FL 33181

PREEDE, NYDIA
PAINTER, ILLUSTRATOR
b Manhattan, NY, Nov 7, 26. *Study:* Art Students League; Pratt Inst, 45-46; Columbia Univ, 49; Monmouth Col, BA, 62, MA, 73. *Exhib:* Butterfly, Sanmagundi Club, New York, 89; Shaped Pieces, Fed Plaza, New York, 89; 56th Ann Exhib, Miniature Painters/Sculptors/Gravers, Washington, DC, 89; Congruity, life/death, 26 Fed Plaza, New York, 90; Squirrel Habitat, Salmagundi Club, New York, 90; Art/Space/Life, New Yorker Show, Barcelona, Spain, 90; and many others. *Pos:* Art coord, Monarts Found Gallery, 83-84. *Awards:* M S Jameson Award, Landscape, 85; Charles Horman Mem Prize, 88; and others. *Bibliog:* Contemporary Images (exhib catalog), Triangle Gallery, Washington, DC, 86; Frances Molinaro (auth), Complex Artists Themes Done in Various Styles, Asbury Park Press, 87; and others. *Mem:* Nat Asn Women Artists (juror, 90-92); Artist Equity. *Media:* Acrylic, All Media. *Mailing Add:* PO Box 344 Eatontown NJ 07724

PREIS, ALFRED
ARCHITECT, ADMINISTRATOR
b Vienna, Austria, Feb 2, 11; US citizen. *Study:* Vienna Inst Technol, Archit. *Work:* USS Ariz Mem, Pearl Harbor, Hawaii; Honolulu Zoo Entrance Bldg; First United Methodist Church, Honolulu; Laupahoehoe High & Elementary Sch, Hawaii; Wahiawa Intermediate Sch, Oahu. *Pos:* Designer, Dahl & Conrad, 39-41; designer, Hart Wood, 42-43; principal archit, Alfred Preis, 43-63; state planning coordr, Dept Planning & Econ Develop, 63-67; exec dir, State Found Cult & the Arts, 67-80. *Awards:* Am Church Archit Award, 56; Honor Awards, Am Inst Archit, Hawaii, 52-63. *Mem:* Fel Am Inst Archit (pres, Hawaii Br, 51). *Mailing Add:* 3233 Melemele Pl Honolulu HI 96022

PREISS, ALEXANDRU PETRE
DESIGNER
b Bucharest, Romania, Oct 4, 52. *Study:* N Grigorescu Fine Arts Inst, Bucharest, BA & dipl, 76 cert, 77; Purdue Univ, MA, 81. *Work:* Greater Lafayette Mus Art, Ind. *Comn:* Homage: The Soldier (environmental sculpture), Greater Lafayette Mus Art, Ind, 82. *Exhib:* Smithsonian Inst Travelling Exhib, 82; Summer Invitational Show, Pleiades Gallery, New York, 83; one-man show, Second Street Gallery, Charlottesville, Va, 84; 11th Biennial Graphic Design, Brno, Czech, 84; Great Ann Int Exhib, Ctr Int D'Art Contemporain, Paris, France, 86; and others. *Pos:* owner, Kennedy & Preiss Design, Honolulu, HI, 86- *Teaching:* Asst prof graphic design, Purdue Univ, W Lafayette, Ind, 81-86 & Univ Hawaii at Manoa, Honolulu, 86-88. *Awards:* Silver Medal, 11th Biennial Graphic Design, Brno, Czech, 84; Pele Award of Excellence in Illus, AAF Hawaii, 89; Award of Excellence, IABC, Hawaii, 89. *Bibliog:* Marion Garmel (auth), Purdue designer creates superb homage, Indianapolis News, 82. *Mem:* Am Inst Graphic Art. *Media:* Mixed. *Publ:* Contribr, American Illustration 2, Am Illus Inc, New York, 83; illusr, Season Mosaics of Roman North Africa by David Parrish, Series Archeological Giorgio Bretschneider, Rome, Italy, 84; Ethnic foods, Cincinnati Enquirer, 85; The Broken Window-Beckett's Dramatic Perspective by Dane Alison Hale, Purdue Univ Press, 86. *Mailing Add:* 2118 Kuhio Ave #701 Honolulu HI 96815

PREKOP, MARTIN DENNIS
PAINTER, SCULPTOR
b Toledo, Ohio, July 2, 40. *Study:* Cleveland Inst Art; Cranbrook Acad Art, MFA; RI Sch Design, MFA; Slade Sch Art, London, Eng. *Work:* Univ Ill, Edwardsville. *Exhib:* Roof Works, Mus Contemp Art, 72; Art Inst Chicago, 74 & 75; one-man shows, Photographs, Yale Univ, 75, Name Gallery, Chicago, 75; Jan Cicero Gallery, Chicago, 79 & 84; LYC Gallery, Cumbria, Eng, 81. *Pos:* Dean, Art Inst Chicago, 88. *Teaching:* Prof & grad prog chmn painting, sculpture & photog, Art Inst Chicago, 66-, chmn Freshman Found, 70-73 & chmn grad div, 73-77, chmn painting dept, 78-, chmn undergrad div, 82- *Awards:* Fulbright Fel, US State Dept, 65; Artists grant, Ill Arts Coun, 85; Fel, Nat Endowment Arts, 87. *Bibliog:* Jan Vendermark (auth), Roof Works Rev, Artforum, 72. *Media:* All. *Mailing Add:* c/o Art Inst Chicago S Michigan Ave & E Adams Chicago IL 60603

PRENT, MARK
ENVIRONMENTAL ARTIST, SCULPTOR
b Montreal, Que, Dec 23, 47. *Study:* Sir George Williams Univ, Montreal, 66-70, BFA, 70, study with John Ivor Smith. *Work:* Art Gallery of Ont, Toronto; Art Bank of Can; Sir George Williams Art Galleries; Musee Du Quebec, Que. *Comn:* Le Festin Chez la Comtesse Fritouille, staged by Suzanne Lantagne, Espace Libre, Montreal, 87. *Exhib:* Eighth Biennale de Paris, Nat Mus Mod Art, France, 73; one-man shows, Akademie der Kunste (auth, catalog), Berlin, Ger, 75-76, Kunsthalle Nuremberg, Ger, 76, Stedelijk Mus (auth, catalog), Amsterdam, Holland, 78, Mus d'Art Contemporain (auth, catalog), Montreal, 79 & Galerie Esperanza, Montreal, 86; Birmingham Festival Arts, Ala, 79; 11th Int Sculpture Conf, Dupont Ctr, Cochran Gallery, Washington, DC, 80; Maison Cult Rennes, France, 80-81; Issacs Gallery, Toronto, 81; Art Against Repression Traveling Exhib, 82-83; East West Visual Arts Encounter, Bombay, India, 85; one-man show, Power Plant (catalog), Toronto, Ont, 87, Chaffee Gallery, Rutland, Vt, Galerie Esperanza, Montreal, Que, 88, Isaacs Gallery, Toronto, 90. *Awards:* Guggenheim Mem Found Fel, 77; Can Coun Sr Arts Award, 78-81 & 85-88; Art Matters Inc, 87 & 88. *Bibliog:* Joyce Zeemans (auth), Freedom and the artist, Can Forum, 8/74; Werner Rhode (auth), Mark Prents macabre manipulation, Mag Kunst, No 3, 75; Hartmut Kraft (auth), Antiasthetica 1978, Helmut Braun Kg, Koln, WGer, 78; and others. *Mem:* Can Artists Representatives; Royal Can Acad; Int Sculpture Asn. *Media:* Polyester Resin, Fiberglass. *Mailing Add:* 35 Bank St St Albans VT 05478

PRENTICE, DAVID RAMAGE
PAINTER, PRINTMAKER
b Hartford, Conn, Dec 22, 43. *Study:* Hartford Art Sch. *Work:* Wadsworth Atheneum, Hartford; Yale Univ, New Haven, Conn; Mus Mod Art, New York; Corcoran Gallery Art, Nat Gallery, Washington, DC; Aldrich Mus, Ridgefield, Conn. *Exhib:* One-man shows, Livingstone-Learmonth Gallery, 75, New York & Genesis Gallery, New York, 78; Other Ideas, Detroit Inst Fine Arts, Mich, 69; Prospect, Dusseldorf, Ger, 69; Whitney Mus Am Art Ann, New York, 70; From Los Angeles & other places, Silverman Gallery, Los Angeles, 78. *Teaching:* Guest instr painting, Hartford Art Sch, Univ Hartford, fall 70. *Media:* Acrylic. *Mailing Add:* 654 Broadway New York NY 10012

PRESCOTT, KENNETH WADE
MUSEUM DIRECTOR, ADMINISTRATOR
b Jackson, Mich, Aug 9, 20. *Study:* Western Mich Univ, BS; Univ Del, EdM; Univ Mich, MA & PhD. *Collections Arranged:* Ben Shahn Retrospective Exhib, Nat Mus Mod Art, Tokyo & other Japanese mus (with catalog), 70 & 91; Jack Levine Retrospective Exhib, Jewish Mus, New York, 79-80; Burgoyne Diller Exhibs, Meredith Long & Andre Emmerich & Harcourts Gallery, 79-92. *Pos:* Dir, Kansas City Mus, Mo, 54-58; managing dir, Acad Nat Sci, Philadelphia, 58-63; dir, NJ State Mus, Trenton, 63-71; prog officer, Div Arts & Humanities, Ford Found, New York, 71-74; prof art & chmn art dept, Univ Tex, Austin, 74-84. *Teaching:* Adj prof changing perspectives in the humanities, Grad Sch, Temple Univ, 60-70. *Mem:* Tex Asn Schs Art; Am Color Print Soc (hon vpres, 68-71); Col Art Asn Am; Nat Coun Art Adminr (chmn, 79-80); Am Fedn Arts. *Res:* Preparation for exhibitions and Catalogue Raisonne on contemporary American artists (Shahn, Levine, Diller, Hunt, de Creelt, Lorrie Goulet, James Chapen, Hunt Slonem & others). *Collection:* Works of contemporary American artists. *Publ:* Auth, Ben Shahn: A Retrospective (catalog), 76-77; auth, Jack Levine: A Retrospective (catalog), 78; auth, Burgoyne Diller 1938-1962, Paintings, Drawings and Collages (catalog), 79; auth, The Prints and Poster of Ben Shahn, 82; auth, The Prints and Posters of Jack Levine, 83. *Mailing Add:* Tanglewood Trail Austin TX 78703

PRESSER, ELENA
ASSEMBLAGE ARTIST
b Buenos Aires, Nov 3, 40; US citizen. *Study:* Dade Community, AA, 75. *Work:* Florida Capitol, Dept Nat Resources & Art Pub Places, Fla; Ala Power Co, Birmingham, Ala; IBM, Gaithersburg, Md. *Comn:* Anna Magdalena Bach Notebook, Ruth & Marvin Sackner Arch, Miami Beach, Fla, 85; Italian Concerto-J S Bach, comn by Dr & Mrs Roley Kohen, Miami Beach, Fla, 87. *Exhib:* Solo exhibs, Elena Presser: Bach's Goldberg Variations, Frances Wolfson Art Gallery, Miami, Fla, 85, Meadows Mus & Gallery, Dallas, Tex, 87, Mus Contemp Hispanic Art, NY, 87 & Elena Presser: Transpositions, Moore Col Art, Philadelphia, Pa, 88; group shows, Calligraffitti, Leila Taghinia Micani Gallery, NY, 84, Collage: The State of the Art, Bergen Mus, Paramus, NJ, 85, Southern Abstraction, City Gallery Contemp Art, Raleigh, NC, 87 & Expresiones Hispanas, Ctr Fine Arts, Miami, Fla, 89. *Awards:* Purchase Award, House of Repr, 79; Purchase Award, Fla Dept State, 81; Artist-in-Residence Fel, D Jerassi Gounf, 85. *Bibliog:* John & Joan Digby (auth), The Collage Handbook, Thames & Hudson Inc, 85; Marvin Sackner (auth), Ruth & Marvin Sackner Arch Concrete & Visual Poetry, Ruth & Marvin Sackner, 86. *Mem:* Women's Caucus For Art, Miami Chap, (bd dir 83-85); Lowe Art Mus, 78-88; Ctr Fine Arts, 88; Bass Mus, 84-88; Soc Layerists Multi-Media, 87-88. *Media:* Wall Relief Assemblage. *Mailing Add:* 7020 SW 100th St Miami FL 33156

PRESSLY, NANCY LEE
CURATOR, ADMINISTRATOR
b Suffern, NY, Feb 11, 41. *Study:* Goucher Col, BA, 62; Columbia Univ, with T Reff, L Hawes & O Brendel, MA, 69; Inst Fine Arts, with W Rubin, R Rosenblum & G Schiff, 69-71. *Collections Arranged:* The Pursuit of Happiness: A View of Life in Georgian England (auth, catalog), 77 & The Fuseli: Circle in Rome: Early Romantic Art of 1770s (auth, catalog), 79, Yale Ctr Brit Art; A Birthday Celebration: Recent Gifts and Acquisitions, 1981 (auth, catalog), 82, Salome: La belle dame sans merci (auth, catalog), 83 & Revealed Religion: Benjamin West's Commissions for Windsor Castle and Fonthill Abbey (auth, catalog), 83, San Antonio Mus Art. *Pos:* Cataloger Am art, Metrop Mus Art, New York, 69-71; assoc res & asst cur, Yale Ctr Brit Art, 71-79; chief cur, San Antonio Mus Art, 81-84; asst dir, Mus Prog, Nat Endowment Arts, Washington, DC, 84- *Awards:* Paul Mellon Vis Sr Fel, Nat Gift & Art Asn, fall 92. *Bibliog:* Hilton Kramer (auth), Henry Fuseli: A leader in Romanticism, Sunday New York Times, 9/16/79; John Ashbery (auth), Dark satanic mills, New York Mag, 10/6/79; Gert Schiff (auth), article, Arts Mag, 12/79. *Mem:* Col Art Asn; Am Asn Mus; Soc 18th Century Studies. *Publ:* Auth, Whistler in America: An album of early drawings, Metrop Mus J, 72; James Jefferys and the master of the giants, Burlington Mag, 4/77; Guy Head and his echo flying from Narcissus: A British artist in Rome in the 1790s, Bull Detroit Inst Arts, 82. *Mailing Add:* 6135 31St St NW Washington DC 20015

PRESSLY, WILLIAM LAURENS
HISTORIAN, EDUCATOR
b Chattanooga, Tenn, Apr 1, 44. *Study:* Princeton Univ, BA, 66; Inst Fine Arts, New York Univ, PhD, 73. *Teaching:* Assoc prof 17th-19th century European art, Yale Univ, 73-82; sr lectr, Univ Tex, Austin, 82-83; assoc prof, Duke Univ, 85-87; assoc prof, Univ Md, 87- *Awards:* Morse Fel, Yale Univ, 75-76; Guggenheim Mem Fel, 83-84. *Mem:* Fel Royal Soc Arts, London; The Am Soc for Eighteenth Century Studies; Col Art Asn; Walpole Soc, London.

Publ: Auth, The praying mantis in surrealist art, Art Bull, 12/73; The Life and Art of James Barry, Yale Univ Press, 81; James Barry: The Artist as Hero, Tate Gallery, London, 83; Gilbert Stuart's The Skater: An essay in romantic melancholy, Am Art J, Vol XVIII, 86; A Catalogue of Paintings in the Folger Shakespeare Libr, Yale Univ Press, 93. *Mailing Add:* 6135 31st St NW Washington DC 20015

PRESTINI, JAMES LIBERO
SCULPTOR, DESIGNER
b Waterford, Conn, Jan 13, 08. *Study:* Yale Univ, BS, 30, Sch Educ, 32; Univ Stockholm, with Carl Malmsten, 38; Inst Design, Chicago, with L Moholy-Nagy, 39; also study in Italy, 53-56. *Work:* Nat Collection Fine Arts, Smithsonian Inst, Washington, DC; San Francisco Mus Art, Calif; Brooklyn Mus Art, New York; Metrop Mus Art, Mus Mod Art & Cooper--Hewitt Mus, New York; Boston Mus Fine Arts, Mass; Berlin Bauhaus Archiv; Georges Pompidou Ctr, Paris, France; Chicago Art Inst. *Comn:* Aluminum sculpture, R S Reynolds Mem Sculpture Award, Richmond, Va, 72. *Exhib:* James Prestini, Sculpture from Structural Steel Elements, San Francisco Mus Art, 69; James Prestini, Art Inst Chicago, 69; Excellence: Art from the University, Univ Calif, Berkeley, 70; International Collection of 20th Century Design, Mus Mod Art, New York, 72; Twentieth Century Accessions 1967-1974, Metrop Mus Art, New York, 74; Philadelphia Mus Art, 79; Mus Fine Arts, Boston, 80; Brooklyn Mus, 81. *Pos:* Co-founder, Creators Equity Found, Berkeley, Calif, 82- *Teaching:* Instr design, Lake Forest Acad, 33-42 & Inst Design, Chicago, 39-46 & 52-53; assoc prof design, NTex State Univ, 42-43; prof design, Univ Calif, Berkeley, 56-, res prof, Creative Arts Inst, 67-68 & Bauhaus-Archiv, WBerlin, 77. *Awards:* Guggenheim Fel for Sculpture, 72-73; Univ Calif Berkeley Award, 75; Elected Am Asn Woodturners Hall of Fame, 92. *Bibliog:* Edgar Kaufmann (auth), Prestini's Art in Wood, Pantheon, 50; Gerald Nordland (auth), James Prestini, Sculpture from Structural Steel Elements, San Francisco Mus Art, 69; George Staempfli (auth), James Prestini, Recent Sculpture, Staempfli Gallery, 71 & 74. *Mem:* Life fel Metrop Mus Art. *Media:* Steel, Aluminum. *Publ:* Co-auth, The Place of Scientific Research in Design, 48; co-auth, Research in Low-cost Seating for Homes, 48; co-auth, Survey on Construction Materials Demonstration & Training Center, 51; auth, Survey of Italian Furniture Industry (Milan), 54; auth, Proposed policy statement on architectural research for the College of Architecture of the University of California, Berkeley, 58. *Mailing Add:* 2324 Blake St Berkeley CA 94704

PRESTON, ANN L
SCULPTOR
b Seattle, Wash, 42. *Study:* Swarth Col, Pa, 59-61; Sch Mus Fine Arts, Boston, 62-66; Tufts Univ, Boston, BFA, 68; Calif Inst Arts, Valencia, BFA, 80. *Work:* Chase Manhattan Bank, NA, New York; Carnation Corp, Los Angeles; Phoenix Art Mus, Ariz. *Comn:* Los Angeles Cent Publ Libr; Los Angeles Transportation Comn, Willow Sta. *Exhib:* Solo exhibs, Atlantic Richfield Co, Ctr Visual Arts, Los Angeles, Calif, 81, Pence Gallery, Santa Monica, Calif, 86-91, Barbara Toll Fine Arts, New York, 87, 88 & 91, Los Angeles Contemp Exhibs, 88 & Guggenheim Gallery, Chapman Univ, Orange, Calif, 92; Phoenix Triennial, Phoenix Art Mus, Ariz, 90; Selections from the Carnation Company Collection, Armory Ctr Arts, Pasadena, Calif, 90; In Her Image, Barbara Toll Fine Arts, New York, 90; The Lick of the Eye, Shoshana Wayne Gallery, Santa Monica, Calif, 91; From Studio to Station: Public Art on the Metro Blueline, FHP Hippodrome Gallery, Long Beach, Calif, 92; and others. *Awards:* Nat Endowment Arts, 88. *Bibliog:* Jennifer Anderson (auth), Art: 1990 Phoenix Triennial, State Press Mag, 9/13/90; Jerome Du Bois (auth), Art: Fright Gallery, New Times, 9/19-25/92; Going down to the crossroads: Ann Preston at Pence Gallery, LA Times, 12/7/90. *Mailing Add:* 24618 Gulfview Dr Valencia CA 91355

PRESTON, GEORGE NELSON
HISTORIAN, EDUCATOR
b Dec 14, 38; US citizen. *Study:* City Col New York, BA, 62; Columbia Univ, MA, 68, PhD, 73. *Collections Arranged:* African Art: Rare and Familiar Forms (auth, catalog), State Univ New York Art Gallery, Potsdam, 76; The Innovative African Artist (auth, catalog), Ithaca Col Mus Art; Permanent Installation, African Hall, Brooklyn Mus, 68-78; Ancient Terracottas of Ghana and Mali (with catalog), 81-82. *Pos:* Spec consult, Brooklyn Mus, 68. *Teaching:* Asst prof art, Rutgers Univ, Livingston Col, 70-72; asst prof art, City Col, City Univ New York, 72-80, assoc prof, 81- *Awards:* Fels, Ford Found, 68-70 & 72 & Kress Found, 69; Res Award, Res Found City Univ New York, 81-82. *Mem:* Columbia Univ Seminar Primitive & Pre-Columbian Art; Washington Hq Asn, New York (bd dirs, 79-); Int Asn Art Critics. *Res:* Conceptual and culture historical aspects of African art; contemporary American artists whose styles are outside the definition of the most popular isms. *Publ:* Auth, Dynamic/Static, African Art as Philosophy, Interbook, New York, 74; auth, Jay Milder: Painter of discovery, resolution and rediscovery, 11/76 & auth, Against the grain: The paintings of Ann Tabachnik, 2/79, Arts Mag; auth, Reading the Art of Benin, Images of Power: Royal Court Art of Benin, New York Univ, 81. *Mailing Add:* c/o Art Dept City Col City Univ NY Convent Ave & 138th St New York NY 10031

PRESTON, MALCOLM H
CRITIC, PAINTER
b West New York, NJ, May 25, 20. *Study:* Univ Wis, BA; Columbia Univ, MA & PhD. *Work:* Hofstra Univ Collection; Dayton Art Inst; Guild Hall Mus, East Hampton, NY; Portland Mus; Living Arts Found & Queens Mus, New York. *Exhib:* Kendall Gallery; Tower Gallery; Linden Gallery; Himelfarb Gallery; Benson Gallery; Mourlot Galerie. *Pos:* Dir, Inst Arts, Hofstra Univ, 60-64; art critic, Newsday, 68- & Boston Herald Traveler, 70-72. *Teaching:* Asst instr fine arts, New Sch Social Res, 40-41; instr fine arts, Adelphi Univ, 47-48; prof fine arts, Hofstra Univ, 49-74. *Awards:* Joe & Emily Lowe Found Educ Res Grant, 50; Ford Found Grant, 56 & 57; Shell Oil Res Grant, 64. *Media:* Oil. *Publ:* Contribr, Christian Sci Monitor, Arts Mag, Boston Globe & other mag & newspapers; writer, producer & principal performer, Arts Around Us & American Art Today (Ford Found-sponsored nat educ television series), 55-56. *Dealer:* Galerie Mourlot 119 Newbury St Boston MA 02116-2907; International Images 30 Cooper Sq New York NY. *Mailing Add:* Box 182 Truro MA 02666

PREUSS, ROGER
PAINTER, WRITER
b Waterville, Minn, Jan 29, 22. *Study:* Minneapolis Col Art & Design, BFA. *Work:* Nat Wildlife Gallery & Smithsonian Hall Philately, Washington, DC; US Fed Bldg & Minn State Capitol & Minn Mus Art, St Paul; Blauvelt Art Mus, Oradell, NJ; Weisman Art Mus & Univ Art Mus, Univ Minn, Minneapolis; Roger Preuss Art Collection, Ctr Western Studies, Sioux Fall, SDak & Kraus-Hartig Post, Minneapolis; and others. *Comn:* 150 paintings of wildlife, Thos D Murphy Co, Red Oak, Iowa, 54; Commemorative Centennial Pheasant Stamp Design, 81; Gold Waterfowl Medallion Franklin, Mint, 83; Gold Wildlife Medallion, Wildlife Mint, 88; 40th Commemorative Fed Duck Etching, 89. *Exhib:* Wildlife Artists of the World Exhib, Bend, Ore, 84; Univ Minn Art Mus, 90; Blauvelt Art Mus, Oradell, NJ, 90; Rochester Art Ctr, 91; Minn Hist Soc-Hill House, 92; and others. *Pos:* Vpres & chmn, Fine-Arts Bd, Wildlife Artists of the World; critic, Wildlife Art News. *Teaching:* Sem lectr wildlife painting, Minneapolis Col Art; speaker's bur, Minneapolis Inst Arts. *Awards:* Fed Duck Stamp Design Award, US Fish & Wildlife Serv, 49; named US Bicentennial Artist Am Heritage Asn, 76; Knight of Mark Twain, Mark Twain Soc, 78; named Dean of Wildfowl Artists, Int Inst Arts, 81. *Bibliog:* Jeff Benson (auth), Preuss puts nature on canvas, Waseca Herald News, 4/23/85; B Hildebrant (auth), Preuss leads world fine art group, Waterville Region Life, 11/13/86; Your BFA-Care and Maintenance by Union of Independent Colleges of Art (film), 88. *Mem:* Emer Soc Animal Artists; fel Int Inst Arts; Minn Artists Asn (dir & vpres, 53-56); found charter mem Wildlife Artists World. *Media:* Oil, Watercolor. *Publ:* Auth & illusr, The official wildlife of America calendar, 53-; Outdoor Horizons, 57; American game birds, 64; illusr, Twilight over the wilderness, 71; contribr/illusr, Nat Wildlife, Country Gentleman, Contemp Western Artists, Wildlife Art News, Art West, Art Impressions (Can), Today's Art & many other nat periodicals & ltd ed prints by Wildlife Am; auth, Is wildlife art recognized fine art?, 86. *Dealer:* Wildlife of America Box 580004-WA Minneapolis MN 55458. *Mailing Add:* 2224 Grand Ave Minneapolis MN 55458

PREUSSER, ROBERT ORMEROD
PAINTER, EDUCATOR
b Houston, Tex, Nov 13, 19. *Study:* Pvt study with McNeill Davidson, Houston, 30-39; Inst Design, Chicago, 39-40 & 41-42; Newcomb Sch Art, Tulane Univ, 40-41; Art Ctr Sch, Los Angeles, 46-47. *Work:* Mus Fine Arts, Houston; Contemp Arts Mus, Houston; Tex Christian Univ, Ft Worth; Addison Gallery Am Art, Andover, Mass; Witte Mem Mus, San Antonio, Tex. *Exhib:* Int Watercolor Exhib, 42, Abstract & Surrealist Am Exhib, 47 & Am Artists Ann, 51, Art Inst of Chicago; Contemp American Artists Ann, 46 & 47; Gulf-Caribbean Exhib, Houston Mus of Fine Arts Circulating Exhib, 56-57; Survey of American Painting, Am Fedn Arts Circulating Exhib, 57-58; Texas Painting & Sculpture--the 20th Century, Owens Arts Ctr Circulating Exhib, Dallas, 71-72; Transco Gallery, Houston, 90; Parkerson Gallery, Houston, 90; MIT Mus, Cambridge, 91; and others. *Pos:* Art ed, Tex Cancer Bull, 48-50; co-dir, Contemp Arts Mus, Houston, 49-51; stage set designer, Tex Stage, Houston, 50-51; assoc cur educ, Mus Fine Arts, Houston, 52-54; dir educ, Ctr Advan Visual Studies, Mass Inst Technol, 74-85; co-ed, Leonardo, 74-88; corp bd, Cambridge Multicultural Arts Ctr, 78-88. *Teaching:* Instr painting, Houston Mus Fine Arts Sch, 47-54 & Univ Houston, 51-54; prof visual design, Mass Inst Technol, 54-85; instr drawing, Harvard Univ Grad Sch Design, 55-56. *Awards:* Purchase Prize, 16th Ann Houston Artists Exhib, Mus Fine Arts, Houston, 40; Purchase Prize, 27th Ann Houston Artists Exhib, Contemp Arts Mus, 52. *Bibliog:* Ralph M Pearson (auth), Chap 3, In: The Modern Renaissance in American Art, Harper & Row, 54; Vision in engineering (interview), Int Sci & Technol, 10/65. *Media:* Mixed Media, Oil. *Publ:* Auth, Visual education for science & engineering students, In: Education of Vision, Braziller, 65, Fr & Ger ed, 67; Art & the engineer, Mech Eng, 12/67; Relation of art to science and technology: an educational experiment at MIT, Leonardo, Vol 6, No 3, 73; Revitalizing art & humanizing technology: an educational challenge, Impact, Vol 24, No 1, 74; Coloured illumination and the environment, in: Colour for Architecture, Studio Vista, 76. *Mailing Add:* 2 Willard St Ct Cambridge MA 02138

PREZIOSI, DONALD A
HISTORIAN, CRITIC
b New York, NY, Jan 12, 41. *Study:* Fairfield Col, BA, 62; Harvard Univ, MA, 63, PhD, 68. *Teaching:* Asst prof art hist, Yale Univ, 67-73 & Mass Inst Technol, 73-77; assoc prof, State Univ NY, Binghamton, 78-86; prof, Univ Calif Los Angeles, 86- *Awards:* Fels, Nat Endowment Humanities, 73-74, Ctr Advan Study Visual Arts, Nat Gallery, 81-82 & Ctr Advan Study, Stanford Univ, 83-84; Am Coun Learned Soc, 89-90. *Mem:* Col Art Asn Am; Archaeol Inst Am; Semiotic Soc Am (vpres, 83-84, pres, 84-85). *Res:* Ancient art and architecture; contemporary theory and criticism. *Publ:* Auth, The Semiotics of the Built Environment, Ind Univ Press, 79; Architecture, Language and Meaning, 79 & Minoan Architectural Design, 83, Mouton; Constructing the origins of art, Art J, 83; Rethinking Art Hist, Yale Univ Press, 89. *Mailing Add:* Dept Art Hist 3209 Dickson Univ Calif Los Angeles 405 Hilgard Ave Los Angeles CA 90024

PRIBBLE, EASTON
PAINTER, INSTRUCTOR
b Falmouth, Ky, July 31, 17. *Study:* Univ Cincinnati. *Work:* Whitney Mus Am Art, New York; Munson-Williams-Proctor Inst, Utica; Hirshhorn Mus, Washington, DC; Parrish Mus, Southampton, NY; State Univ NY. *Comn:* Painted wood relief mural, Munson-Williams-Proctor Inst Sch Art, 61; painted wood relief mural, Oneida Co Off Bldg, NY, 69. *Exhib:* Whitney Ann Am Painting, Whitney Mus Am Art, 50, 54 & 55; Univ Nebr Ann, Lincoln, 56; Everson Mus, Syracuse, 63; Retrospective Exhib, Munson-Williams-Proctor Inst Mus Art, 76; one-man exhib, Munson-Williams-Proctor Inst Mus, 82; Kirkland Art Ctr, Clinton, NY, 88; Rome Art Ctr, Rome, NY, 90. *Teaching:* Instr painting, Munson-Williams-Proctor Inst Sch Art, 57-; instr hist art, Utica Col, 60-73. *Awards:* Painting Award, Everson Mus, 60 & 64; Painting Award, Munson-Williams-Proctor Inst, 63. *Media:* Oil, Acrylic. *Publ:* Contribr, Contemporary American culture, Chicago Rev, 54; New talent in America, Art Am, 56. *Mailing Add:* Munson-Williams-Proctor Inst 310 Genesee St Utica NY 13502

PRICE, ANNE KIRKENDALL
CRITIC
b Birch Tree, Mo, June 14, 22. *Study:* Univ Mo, Columbia, BJ; Univ Ga, Athens, art seminars; Southern Regional Educ Bd workshop for art critics. *Pos:* Art critic, Morning Advocate, Baton Rouge, La, 60- *Awards:* Award for Arts Coverage, La Coun Music & Performing Art, 74; Communicator of the Yr Award, Pub Relations Soc La, 78; Humanities Coun Award for Serv to the Arts, Greater Baton Rouge Arts, 86. *Mem:* Capitol Corresp (pres, 68); Baton Rouge Arts Coun; Baton Rouge Little Theater (bd mem). *Mailing Add:* c/o Morning Advocate 525 Lafayette Baton Rouge LA 70802

PRICE, BARBARA GILLETTE
ADMINISTRATOR, PAINTER
b Philadelphia, Pa, June 26, 38. *Study:* Univ Ala, BFA, 66, MA, 68. *Work:* Univ Ala, Tuscaloosa; Dept Health, Educ & Welfare N Portal Bldg, Washington, DC; Ferris State Col, Mich. *Exhib:* One-woman shows, Foundry Gallery, Washington, DC, 76, Spiritscapes, Cranbrook Acad Art Mus, Bloomfield Hills, Mich, 80, Landscapes of the Mind, Ferris State, Big Rapids, Mich, 81, Md Inst, Col of Art, Baltimore, 82, Schweyer Galdo Galleries, Birmingham, Mich, 82, Notre Dame Col, Baltimore, 85, Columbia Asn Ctr for Arts, Md, 89; Faculty Show, Md Inst Col of Art, 83 & 85-92; Artscape, Baltimore, 86; Art in the Bell Tower, Baltimore, 88; Intimate Works, Morris Mechanic Theatre Gallery, 89; one-person show, Le Ninfee, Loyola Col, Baltimore, Md, 91; group exhib, Members Only Premiere, Artshowcase, Baltimore, Md, 90, Reverberations: 4 Voices, Barbara Price, Nancy K Roeder, Jann Rosen-Queralt and Jo Smail, Roper Gallery, Frostburg State Univ, 91, Media-Mix, Artshowcase, Baltimore, Md, 91; Finding Beauty in the Ordinary, John Dorsey, Baltimore Sun, 91. *Pos:* Dean, Cranbrook Acad Art, 78-82; vpres, Acad Affairs, Maryland Inst, Col Art, 82- *Teaching:* Asst prof art, Corcoran Sch Art, DC, 70-78, dir summer prog, 75-78. *Bibliog:* Marsha Miro (auth), Celebration of legacy, Detroit Free Press, 2/21/82; Jeanne Heifeitz (auth), Price landscapes explore territory of Psyche, Jewish Times, 83; Mike Guliano (auth), Barbara Price at the Columbia Art Center, Columbia Flyer, 89. *Mem:* Nat Coun Art Adminr; Col Art Asn; NASAD; Am Asn of Higher Educ. *Media:* Oil, Acrylics. *Publ:* Ed, Sculpture at Cranbrook (catalog), Cranbrook Acad Art Mus, 79; Spiritscapes (catalog), Ferris State Col, 81. *Mailing Add:* Md Inst Col Art 1300 Mt Royal Ave Baltimore MD 21217

PRICE, DIANE MILLER
PAPERMAKER
b Paterson, NJ, Sept 13, 43. *Study:* RI Sch Design, 61-63; Parsons Sch Design, New York, 63-64; Monclair State Col, NJ, papermaking as art form with Anne Chapman, BA, 84. *Exhib:* Small Impressions, Montclair Art Mus, NJ, 87; 100 Years/100 Works, Nat Asn Women Artists, Islip Art Mus, NY, 89; Reflections on Art, Scanticon Ctr, Princeton, NJ, 91; The Tree-An Artists Gift, Bergen Mus Arts & Sci, Paramus, NJ, 91; Printmaking Coun of NJ Mems Show, Newark Mus, 92; and others. *Awards:* Fel Grant, NJ State Coun, 86-87; Honorable Mention, Int Show, NJ Ctr Visual Arts, 89; Eve Helman Award, 102nd Ann Mems Show, Nat Asn Women Artists, 90. *Mem:* Nat Asn Women Artists (asst awards chair, 86-); Womens Caucus for Art; Printmaking Coun NJ; NJ Ctr Visual Arts. *Media:* Handmade Paper. *Mailing Add:* 49 N Baums' Court Livingston NJ 07039

PRICE, DORIS C
PAINTER, PRINTMAKER
b Millsboro, Del. *Study:* Temple Univ, 47-50; Empire State Col (SUNY), Old Westbury, BS(Painting & Writing), 74. *Work:* Nassau Co Mus, Roslyn, Long Island, NY; York Col (CUNY), Queens, NY; Medgar Evans Col (CUNY), Brooklyn, NY; Nanticoke Indian Mus, Millsboro, Del; Apex Mus, Atlanta, Ga. *Exhib:* Touching Base with Ancient Egypt, Am Int Col, Springfield, Mass, 80 & Fordham Univ, New York, 84; New Prints, North East, Print Club, Philadelphia, Pa, 85; OPA 3rd Int Exhib, Pen & Brush Gallery, New York, 86; Ann Juried Exhib, Knickerbocker Artists, New York, 86; NYNEX Corp, White Plains, NY, 92; Readers Digest, Pleasantville, NY, 92. *Pos:* Treas, Roosevelt Island Artists' Asn, 83-84. *Awards:* First Prize for Mixed Media, Washington Sq Outdoor Art Exhib, 80; Honorable Mention, Anthropology in Art, Queens Col (CUNY), 87 & 90. *Bibliog:* Lila Kain (auth), American International College recalls ancient Egypt, Daily News, Springfield, Mass, 3/12/80; Mel Tapley (auth), Painters Price & Coppedge pick flowers, NY Amsterdam News, 3/8/87 & Spiral Gallery presents two unique artists, 10/10/87. *Mem:* Jamaica Arts Ctr Co-op; Knickerbocker Artists. *Media:* Acrylic, Miscellaneous Media; Etching. *Publ:* Illusr, Madonna on cloud nine, Response, United Methodist Church, 85. *Dealer:* Savacou Gallery 240 E 13th St New York NY 10003; Apercu Objets D'Art 27 Smith St Brooklyn NY 11201. *Mailing Add:* 531 Main St No 109 New York NY 10044

PRICE, GEORGE
CARTOONIST
b Coytesville, NJ, June 9, 01. *Pos:* Cartoonist & bk illusr. *Publ:* Auth of 10 books & illusr of 24 books; illusr, Life, Vogue, New York Times, Forbes, Business Week, The New Yorker and others. *Mailing Add:* 81 Westervelt Ave Tenafly NJ 07670

PRICE, JOAN WEBSTER
ENVIRONMENTAL ARTIST, SCULPTOR
b Camden, NJ, Jan 8, 31. *Study:* Tyler Sch Art, Temple Univ, BFA, 54; Columbia Univ, MA, 58, EdD, 71. *Work:* Brooklyn Mus; Bronx Mus Arts; Mus Mod Art; British Mus, London; NJ State Mus; Solomon R Guggenheim Mus, New York. *Exhib:* Abstraction in Action, Am Abstract Artists, City Gallery, 82; On and Off the Wall, Women's Caucus Art NJ, Newark Mus, 82; Am Abstract Artists Exhib, Weatherspoon Gallery, Greensboro, NC, 83; Am Abstract Artists Exhib, Art Gallery, Univ Ala, 83; Modern Mythology, Fordham Univ, 83-85; In A Sense, 27 NJ Artists (with catalog), Bergen Mus Art & Sci, Paramus, NJ, 84; Public Visions/Public Monuments, Women's Caucus Art, NY, 86; 50th Anniversary Celebration, Bronx Mus Arts, NY, 86; American Abstract Artists 50th Anniversary Print Portfolio Exhib, City Gallery, New York & James Howe Gallery, Kean Col, NJ, 87; RISE Exhib, Johnson Atelier Gallery, 87, 88; Geometric Abstraction & the Modern Spirit, Neuberger Mus, New York, 89; Am Abstract Artist Persistence of Abstraction, Ulrueh Mus Art, Kans, 92. *Collections Arranged:* University Artists-Teachers (auth, catalog), Bronx Mus Art, 76; Women Artists 78, City Univ New York Grad Ctr, 78; Works on Paper Am Abstract Artists, Betty Parsons Gallery, 79; Ageless Perceptions I & II: Forms of Figuration, SoHo 20, New York, 88 & 89. *Pos:* Vpres & bd gov, Inst Study Art in Educ, 76-78; co-vpres, Higher Educ, NYCATA, 83-84. *Teaching:* Asst prof painting & design, Suffolk Community Col, NY, 65-67; lectr art educ, Queens Col, NY, 67-68; prof environ art, newform-intermedia, City Col New York, 68. *Awards:* Fel, Va Ctr Creative Arts, 84; Art Educator Award, Art Works, 85. *Bibliog:* Stephen P Breslow (auth), Art: Price show has its own energy, Staten Island Advance, 9/24/81; Palmer Paromer (auth), article, Artspeak, 1/12/82; Irene Rousseau (auth), Abstraction in action, American abstract artists, Arts Mag, 5/82; Joseph Merkel (auth), Sculpture throws a curve, Artspeak, 11/1/84; William Zimmer (auth), American Abstract Artists look back at 50 year history, NY Times, 3/30/86. *Mem:* Am Abstract Artists; Women's Caucus Art; Int Soc Arts, Sci & Technol; Univ Coun Art Educ; New York City Art Teachers Asn. *Media:* All. *Publ:* Auth, A Response for an Environmental Response Center, NY State Arts & Humanities, 71; auth, VTR: The Observed and the Observer, NY State Publ, 75; auth, Light Boxes, NY State Art Teachers, 75; coauth, Sun altar, Landscape Archit, 11/80. *Mailing Add:* 35 Ridgewood Terr Maplewood NJ 07040

PRICE, JOE (ALLEN)
SERIGRAPHER, INSTRUCTOR
b Ferriday, La, Feb 6, 35. *Study:* Northwestern Univ, Evanston, Ill, BS, 57; Art Ctr Col Design, Los Angeles, with Glenn Vilppu, 67-68; Stanford Univ, Calif, MA, 70. *Work:* Philadelphia Mus Art, Pa; Nat Mus Am Art, Washington, DC; Libr Congress, Washington, DC; Achenbach Found Graphic Art, Legion Honor, San Francisco; San Francisco Mus Mod Art; Mus Int Contemp Graphic Art, Fredrikstad, Norway. *Comn:* Print, Int Graphic Arts Found, Darien, Conn. *Exhib:* One-man shows, Tahir Gallery, New Orleans, 82, New Talent in Printmaking, Asn Am Artists, New York & Philadelphia, 84, Triton Mus Art, Santa Clara, 86, Ankrum Gallery, Los Angeles, Calif, 86, Huntsville Mus Art, Ala, 87 & Gallery 30, San Mateo, Calif, 88 & 91; Miniprint Int traveling exhib, Spain, 87-89; Sixth Int Exhib Botanical Art, Hunt Inst, Carnegie-Mellon Univ, Pa, 88; Interprint '90, Lviv Mus, USSR; Fourth Int Biennial Print Exhib '89, Taipei Fine Arts Mus, Taiwan, Rep of China; Norwegian Int Print Biennial, Fredrikstad, Norway, 84 & 86. *Pos:* Chmn art dept, Col San Mateo, Calif. *Teaching:* Prof studio drawing, Col San Mateo, Calif, 70- *Awards:* Louis Lozowick Mem Award, Audubon Artists 36th Ann, 78; Lessing J Rosenwald Prize, Philadelphia Print Club Int, 79; Ture Bengtz Mem Purchase Award, 39th NAm Print Exhib, New York, 86; Creative Achievment Award, Calif State Legislature, 89; Audubon Artists Silver Medal Honor in Graphics, 91. *Bibliog:* Duane Wakeham (auth), Joe Price: Serigraphs in light and tone, Am Artist, 10/77; Tom Cervenak (auth), Bay area printmakers, Visual Dialog, spring 78; Prints Charming, Pol, Sydney, Australia, 1/80; Mary Ann & Mace Wenniger (coauths), Secrets of Buying Art, 10/90. *Mem:* Calif Soc Printmakers; Los Angeles Printmaking Soc; Boston Printmakers; Am Color Print Soc; Audubon Artists; Print Club, Philadelphia. *Media:* Serigraphy. *Dealer:* Jane Haslem Gallery 2025 Hillyer Pl NW Washington DC 20009; Gallery 30 311-315 Primrose Road Burlingame CA 94010. *Mailing Add:* PO Box 3305 Sonora CA 95370

PRICE, KENNETH
PRINTMAKER, SCULPTOR
b Los Angeles, Calif, 1935. *Study:* Chounard Art Inst; Los Angeles, County Art Inst; Univ Southern Calif, BFA, 56; State Univ NY at Alfred, MFA, 59. *Work:* Los Angeles Co Mus Art; Albright-Knox Art Gallery; Dallas Art Mus; Mus Modern Art, New York; Philadelphia Mus Art; San Francisco Mus Modern Art; Seattle Art Mus; Art Inst Chicago; St Louis Art Mus; Victoria & Albert Mus; Whitney Mus Am Art. *Exhib:* One-man exhibs, Visual Arts Mus, NY, 80, Texas Gallery, Houston, 80 & 84, Betsy Rosenfield Gallery, Chicago, 80, Willard Gallery, NY, 82, 85 & 86, James Corcoran Gallery, Los Angeles, 82, Leo Castelli Gallery, NY, 83, La Palme Restaurant at Newporter, Newport Beach, Calif, 83, Sena West Gallery, Santa Fe, 90, James Corcoran Gallery, Los Angeles, 91, Charles Cowles Gallery, New York, 92; Fifty California Artists, Whitney Mus Am Art, NY, 62; Robert Irwin/

Kenneth Price, Los Angeles County Mus Art, 66; Ten from Los Angeles, Seattle Art Mus, 66; Recent Acquistions, Whitney Mus Am Art, NY, 66; American Sculpture of the Sixties, Los Angeles County Mus Art, 67; Tamarind: Homage of Lithography, Mus Mod Art, NY, 69; Nine Print Portfolios, Mus Mod Art, NY, 70; Nine Print Portfolios, Mus Mod Art, NY, 71; Silkscreen, A Historical Review, Philadelphia Mus Art, PA, 72; Clay Whitney Mus Am Art, NY, 74; 200 Years of American Sculpture, (catalog), Whitney Mus Am Art, NY, 76; 30 Years of American Printmaking, Brooklyn Mus, 76; 1979 Biennial Exhibition (catalog), Whitney Mus Am Art, 79; Contemporary Sculpture, Mus Mod Art, NY, 79; Los Angeles Prints, 1883-1980 (catalog), Los Angeles Mus Art, 80; 1981 Biennial Exhibition (catalog), Whitney Mus Mod Art, NY, 81; Art in Los Angeles, 17 Artists in the Sixties (catalog), Los Angeles County Mus Art, 81; Ceramic Sculpture: Six Artists (catalog), Whitney Mus Am Art & San Francisco Mus Mod Art, 81; An International Survey of Recent Painting and Sculpture (catalog), Mus Mod Art, NY, 84; Clay Revisions: Plate, Cup, Vase, Seattle Art Mus, WA, 87; L A Hot & Cool: Pioneers, Bank of Boston Gallery, Mass, 87; Big/Little Sculpture, Williams Col Mus Art, 87; History of American Ceramics: 1950 to the Present, Helen Druitt Gallery, New York, 89; California Finish Fetish, Univ Southern Calif, Los Angeles, 91; Selections from Permanent Collection, Mus Contemp Art, Los Angeles, 91; Shigariki Mus Ceramic Art, Tokyo, 91. *Awards:* Tamarind Fel, 68-69. *Bibliog:* Thomas Hess (auth), Art, New York Mag, 12/74; Judith Tannenbaum (auth), Kenneth Price--Willard, Arts Mag, 2/75; Kenneth Price at Willard, Art in Am, 5-6/75. *Dealer:* Willard Gallery 14 E 17th St New York NY 10021. *Mailing Add:* c/o Charles Cowles Gallery 420 W Broadway New York NY 10012

PRICE, LESLIE KENNETH
PAINTER, EDUCATOR
b New York, NY. *Study:* Sch Visual Arts, NY, 63-64; Pratt Inst, with James Gahagan, Ernest Briggs, G Laderman, BFA, 69; Mills Col, Oakland, Calif, MFA, 71. *Work:* Oakland Mus, Calif; Johnson Publ Co, Chicago. *Exhib:* Blacks USA, New York Cult Ctr, 73; New Directions in Afro-Am Art, Cornell Univ, Ithaca, NY, 74; Berkeley Art Ctr, Calif, 76; San Jose Mus, Calif, 76; Studio Mus in Harlem, NY, 77. *Teaching:* From assoc prof painting to prof art, Humboldt State Univ, Arcata, Calif, 72- *Awards:* Painting Award, Pratt Inst, 68; Award of Merit, Calif Palace Legion Honor, 73; Honorarium, Cornell Univ, 74. *Bibliog:* Alfred Frankenstein (auth), article, San Francisco Chronicle, 11/77. *Mem:* Nat Conf of Artists. *Media:* Acrylic, Graphite. *Publ:* Contribr, Black Artists on Art, Vol II, Contemporary Crafts, 72; Existence Black, Southern Ill Univ, 72; contribr, Directions in Afro-American Art, Cornell Univ, 74. *Mailing Add:* Dept Art Humboldt State Univ Arcata CA 95521

PRICE, MICHAEL BENJAMIN
SCULPTOR, EDUCATOR
b Chicago, Ill, Oct 21, 40. *Study:* Univ Ill, Urbana-Champaign, with Frank Gallo, AB, 63, MA, 64; Tulane Univ, MFA(sculpture). *Work:* Berman Mus, Ursinus Col, Collegeville, Pa; Carleton Col Permanent Collection, Northfield, Minn; Art Gallery Mus, Mobile, Ala; Hamline Univ, Permanent Collection, St Paul, Minn; Governor's Mansion, St Paul, Minn; and others. *Comn:* Allentown Fire Dept, Allentown, Pa; St Mary's Church, Esconoldo, Calif; Sacred Heart Church, Oscoda, Mich; Albright Col, Reading, Pa; Moravian Col, Bethlehem, Pa. *Exhib:* One-man shows, Vincent Price Gallery, Chicago, 69, Krasner Gallery, New York, 73-74, 76-77 & 80, Imprimatur, St Paul, Minn, 84, Waterloo Munic Art Gallery, Iowa, Mussavi Art Ctr, New York, 87 & Berman Mus, Collegeville, Pa, 88; C G Rein Gallery, Scottsdale, Ariz, 79; Imprimatur Gallery, St Paul, Minn, 84; Int Juried Art Competition, New York, 85; Mussavi Art Ctr, New York, 85; and others. *Teaching:* Instr sculpture, Univ Ala, Huntsville, 66; prof sculpture, drawing & art hist, Hamline Univ, 70-, chmn art dept, 80- *Awards:* Purchase Prize, Gulf Coast Art Exhib, 68. *Mem:* Col Art Asn Am. *Media:* Cast Bronze. *Mailing Add:* 1954 Laurel Ave St Paul MN 55104

PRICE, MORGAN SAMUEL (MARGARET MORGAN PRICE)
PAINTER, INSTRUCTOR
b Cleveland, Ohio, Feb 9, 47. *Study:* Ringling Sch Art, Cert, 68, with Loran Wilford, 66-68 & Carl Cogar, 76. *Work:* Goddard Art Ctr, Ardmore, Okla; Libr Cong, Washington, DC; Kirchman Corp Gallery, Orlando, Fla. *Comn:* Oil painting, St Mary's Catholic Church, Annapolis, Md, 68, Walker Oil, 73, painting, comn by Mr & Mrs Norman Yodi, 78, 79, 80 & 81, Gant Oil Co, 78, Woodruff Oil Co, 80, Ardmore, Okla, Law Offices of Tanya Plant 78, Law Offices of Mort Rosenblum 75-80, Orlando, Fla. *Exhib:* Salmagundi Club, New York, 88, 90-91; 78th Ann Exhib, Allied Artists Am, New York, 89 & 91 & 92; Brevard Cult Alliance, Savannahs, Merritt Island, Fla, 90; Quintuple Galerie, Argenteuil, France, 91; one-woman show, State of Fla, Capitol Bldg, Tallahassee, 91, McDonald Douglas Corp, Kennedy Space Ctr, 91 & Brevard Mus Art, Melbourne, Fla, 92, Marie Ferrer Gallery, 92; The Cloisters, Sea Island, Ga, 91; Arts of the Park (Top 100), Nat Park Acad, Jackson Hole, Wyo, 92; Pastel Soc Am, New York, 92. *Pos:* Vpres, Knickerbocker Artists, New York, 91-92. *Teaching:* Instr oil painting, Goddard Art Ctr & Mus (oil, watercolor & pastel), Ardmore, Okla, 72-; workshops, oil, painting, watercolor & pastel, Throughout US & Europe, 72- *Awards:* Joseph Hartley Award, Ann Open Show, Salmagundi Club, 90; Leon Stacks Mem, 78th Ann Exhib, Allied Artists, 91; Salmagundi Club, New York, New York, Antonio Cirino Award for a Pastel 1991; New Mems Show Oil Award Copley Soc Boston, Mass, 91; and many others. *Bibliog:* Dorothy Michaels (auth), Knowing How to Determine Value and Intensity, Am Artists, 6/91. *Mem:* Salmagundi Club; Copley Soc Boston; Am Artists Prof League; Pastel Soc Am; Knickerbocker Artists, New York (vpres, 91-92); Allied Artists Assoc, New York; Audobon Artists Asso, New York. *Media:* Oil, Watercolor. *Mailing Add:* PO Box 362598 Eau Gallie FL 32936-2598

PRICE, RITA F
PAINTER, PRINTMAKER
b Bronx, NY. *Study:* Art Inst Chicago, BFA, 82; Univ Ill, Chicago, 83. *Work:* Carter Presidential Libr & Policy Ctr Mus, Atlanta, Ga; Int Mineral & Chemical Corp, Northbrook, Ill; Schiff, Hardin & Waite, Chicago, Ill; Ctr Prof Advan, E Brunswick, NJ. *Comn:* A Place Where a Dreamer Goes, comn by Mr & Mrs Marshall Field, Chicago, 88; Cheries Garden, comn by Cherie Melchiorre, Chicago. *Exhib:* Curs Choice Collectibles, Prints & Drawings, Art Inst Chicago, 86; Ill Regional Print Show, Dittmar Gallery, Northwestern Univ, Evanston, Ill, 87; Ann Exhib, Am Jewish Arts Club, Spertus Mus, Chicago, 87, 88, & 89; 100 Years/100 Artists Traveling Exhib, 89; Nat V Print Exhib, Haggin Mus, Stockton, Calif, 90; Traveling Print Exhib, India, 90-91; and others. *Pos:* Asst dir admis, Art Inst Chicago, 83-85, asst dir, non-degree progs, 85-88 & dir alumni affairs, 88- *Teaching:* Instr experimental printmaking N Shore Art League, Winnetka, Ill, 84-; instr printmaking, Sch Art Inst, Chicago, 88; instr printmaking, Ox-Bow, Saugatuck, Mich, 88. *Awards:* Award of Excellence, N Shore Art League, Ann Exhib, 82, Am Jewish Arts Club, 86, 87 & 88, Munic Art League, Chicago, 89 & Old Orchard Art Festival, 91. *Bibliog:* Les Krantz (auth), The Chicago Art Rev, Am Reference Inc, 89; Louise Dunn Yochim (auth), Harvest of Freedom, Am Reference Inc, 89; Who's Who Am Art, 93-94. *Mem:* Nat Asn Women Artists; N Shore Art League (bd dir, 73-); Chicago Soc Artists; Chicago Arts Coalition; Evanston Art Ctr (bd trustees, 92-); and others. *Media:* Acrylic, Oil; All Media. *Dealer:* Chicago Ctr for Print Ltd 1509 W Fullerton Chicago IL 60614; Ruth Volid Gallery Chicago IL 60610. *Mailing Add:* 1665 Dartmouth Lane Deerfield IL 60015

PRICE, ROSALIE PETTUS
PAINTER
b Birmingham, Ala. *Study:* Birmingham-Southern Col, AB; Univ Ala, MA. *Work:* Birmingham Mus Art, South Trust Bank, Bell South, Spain Ctr Collection, Univ Ala, Birmingham; Springfield Art Mus, Mo. *Exhib:* Nat Watercolor Soc Ann, 45-48 & 70; Am Watercolor Soc, Nat Acad Design, New York, 47, 74; Watercolor & Print Exhib, Pa Acad Fine Arts, Philadelphia, 48; solo shows, Birmingham Mus Art, Ala, 66, 73 & 82-83; 35th Ann Midyear Show, Butler Inst Am Art, Youngstown, Ohio, 70; Ann Drawing & Small Sculpture Show, Ball State Univ, Muncie, Ind, 72, 74 & 78-82; Rocky Mountain Nat, Golden, Colo, 74 & 80; Audubon Artists Ann, New York, 81; Watercolor Now, Springfield Art Mus, Springfield, Mo, 87, Houston, Tex, 89; and others. *Awards:* W Alden Brown Mem Prize, Nat Soc Painters in Casein, 70; Purchase Award, Watercolor USA, 72; Joseph A Cain Mem Prize, Nat Soc Painters Casein & Acrylic, 83. *Mem:* Nat Watercolor Soc; Watercolor Soc Ala (secy, 48-49); Watercolor USA Hon Soc; Birmingham Art Asn (pres, 47-49); Nat Soc Painters Casein & Acrylic. *Media:* Acrylic, Oil. *Mailing Add:* 2132 20th Ave S Birmingham AL 35223

PRICE, SARA J
PAINTER, PHOTOGRAPHER
Study: Pratt Inst, BFA, 76; New Sch Soc Res, 77-80; study with Burt Silverman, William Katavolos & Don Stacy. *Exhib:* Nat Exhib, Heckscher Mus, Huntington, NY, 85 & 86; Talent, Allan Stone Gallery, New York, 86 & 88-91; Giannetta Gallery, Philadelphia, Pa, 89; Nat Asn Women Artists, traveling exhib, Washington Cty Mus Fine Arts, Hagerstown, Md, 88, Greenville Mus Art, NC, 89, Butler Inst Am Art, Youngstown, Ohio, 89, Jesse Besser Mus, Alpena, Mich, 90 & Sansker Kendra Mus, Ahmedebad, India, 89-90; Mus Southwest, Midland, Tex, 91; Richmond Art Mus, Ind, 92. *Pos:* Freelance photogr, Tomlin Art Co, 77-92. *Awards:* Silver Medal/Printmaking, Int Art Competition, 84; Award of Excellence, Huntington Township Art League, 85; Purchase Award, Hoyt Inst Fine Arts, 86. *Mem:* Nat Asn Women Artists (exec bd 90-); NY Artists Equity Asn; Asn Flatbush Artists. *Media:* Oil on Paper, Watercolor. *Mailing Add:* 59 Sullivan St New York NY 10012

PRICE, VINCENT
COLLECTOR, DEALER
b St Louis, Mo, May 27, 11. *Study:* Yale Univ, BA, 33; Univ London, Courtauld Inst, 34-35; Ohio Wesleyan, Hon LLD; Calif Col Arts & Crafts, Hon DFA; Columbia Col, Hon DFA. *Pos:* Founder, Mod Inst Art, 45; former pres, Univ Calif, Los Angeles Art Coun; dir, Vincent Price Art Gallery; former mem bd, Archives Am Art; mem, Whitney Mus Friends Am Art; mem, US Indian Arts & Crafts Bd; former mem fine arts comt, White House; bd dir, Ctr Arts of Indian Affairs; adv comt, Friends of Art, Univ Southern Calif; art consult, Sears Roebuck & Co. *Mem:* Royal Soc Art; Indian Arts & Crafts Bd, Dept Interior (chmn, 68-72). *Publ:* Auth, Vincent Price on art, syndicated column, Chicago Tribune, 3 yrs; auth, I Like What I Know, The Book of Joe & Treasury of American Art; co-ed (with Ferdinand V Delacroix), Drawings of Delacroix; auth, many articles on art in nat mags & newspapers. *Mailing Add:* c/o Paul Kohner Inc 9169 Sunset Blvd Los Angeles CA 90069

PRIEST, HARTWELL WYSE
PAINTER, PRINTMAKER
b Brantford, Ont, Jan 1, 01; US citizen. *Study:* Smith Col, 24; Paris-Atelier, with Andre L'Hote; also with Hans Hofmann, New York. *Work:* Libr Congress; Newark Pub Libr; Smith Col Art Mus Pvt Collection; Univ Maine; Hunt Botanical Libr, Richmond Mus Fine Art. *Comn:* Murals, Children's Ward, Univ Va Hosp, Charlottesville, 55; flowers & woodland scene for ann report, Hunt Botanical Libr, Pittsburgh, 71. *Exhib:* Award Winners Exhib, Pen & Brush, New York, 91; Nat Print Show, SAGA, 91; Ann Print Show, NAWA, 92; NAWA Traveling Show, US, 92; invited by NAWA, Carlyce Furniture Showroom, New York, 92; and others. *Teaching:* Instr, Va Art Inst, 69-75. *Awards:* Purchase Award, Va Mus, Richmond, 72; Edna Stauffer Mem

Prize for Etching, 77; First Painting Award, 79 & First Graphics Award, 82, Blue Ridge Sch An Exhib; First Graphic Award, Blue Ridge Sch, 86; and many other New York print awards. *Mem:* Nat Asn Women Artists; Soc Am Graphic Artists; Washington Printmakers; Pen & Brush (voted mem, 92). *Media:* Acrylic, oil; Etching. *Mailing Add:* 41 Old Farm Rd Charlottesville VA 22901

PRIEST, T (THERESA KHOURY STRUCKUS)
PAINTER
b Worcester, Mass, Jan 20, 28. *Study:* Worcester Art Mus Sch, Mass, 47-48; Quinsigamond Community Col, Worcester, 72 & 73; Univ Mass, Amherst, BFA(painting), 75, MFA(painting), 77. *Work:* Worcester Art Mus, Mass; Aldrich Mus Contemp Art, Ridgefield, Conn; DeCordova Mus, Lincoln, Mass; Bundy Art Ctr, Waitsfield, Vt; Brockton Art Mus. *Comn:* Three color serigraph, Worcester Art Mus, 77; ltd ed print, Holy Cross Col, Worcester, 81; and others. *Exhib:* New Eng Women, DeCordova Mus, Lincoln, 75; Painting Invitational, Brockton Art Ctr, Mass, 75; one-person shows, Drawings, Worcester Art Mus, Mass, 76 & Washington World Gallery, Washington, DC, 81; Paperworks, Hudson River Mus, New York, 80; and others. *Pos:* Instr, Hampshire Col, Amherst, Mass, 75; vis cur, Col Art Gallery Prog, Worcester Art Mus, 79. *Teaching:* Assoc prof intermediate painting, visual design & color, Col Holy Cross, Worcester, currently. *Awards:* Kinnicutt Travel Award, Worcester Art Mus, 74; Charles & Roseanna Batchelor Summer Fel, Holy Cross Col, Worcester, 81; Res & Publ Award, Holy Cross Col, 82, 84 & 86. *Bibliog:* Nina Kaiden & Bartlett Hayes (auth), Artist and Advocate, Renaissance, 67. *Mem:* Boston Visual Artists Union; Col Art Asn; Worcester Art Mus. *Media:* Oil; Pastel. *Dealer:* Howard Yezerski Gallery Boston MA 02109; Thronja Art Gallery Springfield MA. *Mailing Add:* 5 Pratt St Worcester MA 01609

PRINA, STEPHEN JAMES
CONCEPTUAL ARTIST, EDUCATOR
b Galesburg, Ill, Nov 3, 54. *Study:* Carl Sandburg Col, Galesburg, Ill, AA, 74; Northern Ill Univ, Dekalb, Ill, BFA, 77; Calif Inst Art, Valencia, Calif, MFA, 80. *Work:* Mus Contemp Art, Los Angeles, Calif. *Exhib:* Investigations: Probe, Structure, Analysis, New Mus Contemp Art, New York, 80 & The Art of Memory/The Loss of History, 85-86; 74th Am Exhib, Art Inst Chicago, Ill, 82; Striking Distance, Mus Contemp Art, Los Angeles, Calif, 88; BiNational: Am Art of the Late 80's, Inst Contemp Art, Boston, Mass, 89-90; solo exhibs, Galerie Gisela Capitain, Koln, 90, Luhring Augustine Gallery, New York, 90 & 92, Robbin Lockett Gallery, Chicago, 90 & Galerie Fricke, Dusseldorf, Ger, 91; 51st Carnegie Int, Carnegie Mus Art, Pittsburgh, 91; Allegories of Modernism: Contemporary Drawing, Mus Mod Art, New York, 92. *Teaching:* Instr, Art Ctr Col Design, 80-; Calif Inst Arts, 87. *Awards:* Individual Artist Fel, Nat Endowment Arts, 88; Englehard Found Award, Englehard Found, Boston, 88. *Bibliog:* Susan Kandel (auth), Skewering institutional myths, Los Angeles Times, 1/24/92; Collette Chattopadhyay (auth), An ordered past: Stephen Prina at Luhring Augustine Hetzler, Artweek, 2/92; Michael Kimmelman (auth), Just what is a drawing? definitions, definitions, NY Times, 2/21/92. *Publ:* Coauth (with Christopher Williams), A Conversation with Shelia Mc Laughlin & Lynne Tillman, LAICA Journal, 85; auth, The Twenty-Six Inch Experience, TV Guides, 85; coauth (with Christopher Williams), By These Walls (exhib catalog), Cal Arts: Skeptical Beliefs, 88. *Dealer:* Luhring Augustine & Hodes Gallery 41 E 57th St New York NY 10022. *Mailing Add:* 5017 Institute Pl No 6 Los Angeles CA 90029

PRINCE, ARNOLD
SCULPTOR, EDUCATOR
b Basseterre, West Indies, Apr 17, 25. *Study:* Brit Coun with John Harrison, Jose DeCreeft, William Zorach & John Hovvannes; Art Students League. *Work:* First Vest Pocket Park, New York; Art Students League. *Comn:* Concrete sculpture, City North Adams, Mass, 68; gate post sculpture, Spruces Residential Park, 72; concrete sculpture, comn by Robert Potrin, Stamford, Vt, 73. *Exhib:* St Marks on the Bowery, 64; Sculptors Guild Exhib, Mus RI Sch Design, 69-75; Slide Show Collection of Afro-Am Artists, Univ Ala, 71; Boston Pub Libr, 73; group show RI Sch Design, 75. *Teaching:* Dir sculpture educ, Fed Govt Poverty Proj Harlem, HARYOU, 64-67; adj prof sculpture, North Adams State Col, 70-72; asst prof fine arts & sculpture, RI Sch Design, 72-82. *Bibliog:* Article in Village Voice, 12/65; article in NAdams Transcript, 66-71. *Mem:* Sculptors Guild NY. *Media:* Wood, Stone. *Publ:* Auth, Carving Wood and Stone, Prentice Hall, 80. *Dealer:* Sculptors Guild Inc 75 Rockefeller Plaza New York NY 10020. *Mailing Add:* 19 Academy Ave Providence RI 02908

PRINCE, RICHARD EDMUND
SCULPTOR, EDUCATOR
b Comox, BC, Apr 6, 49. *Study:* Univ BC, BA(art hist), 71 & study, 72-73; Emma Lake Artists Workshop, Sask, with Ron Kitaj, 70. *Work:* Nat Gallery Can, Ottawa; Vancouver Art Gallery, BC; Govt of BC, Victoria Art Collection; Can Coun Art Bank, Ottawa; Vancouver Art Collection, Can; and others. *Comn:* Can Pavillion, Expo 86, Vancouver, Can. *Exhib:* One-man shows, Issacs Gallery, Toronto, 78 & 82 & Figure Structures, Burnaby Art Gallery, BC, 79, Hamilton Art Gallery, Ont, 84; Canadian Cultural Ctr, Rome, Italy, 87; 49th Parallel Gallery, New York, 89; A New Decade: Vancouver, Alta Col Art Gallery, Calgary, 79; Vancouver Heritage, Vancouver Art Gallery, 83; and others. *Teaching:* Instr sculpture, Vancouver Community Col, BC, 74-75; instr fine arts & sculpture, Univ BC, 75-; vis lectr sculpture, Univ of BC, 77-78, asst prof sculpture, 78-83, assoc prof, 83-. *Awards:* Art Vancouver for 74 Award, City of Vancouver, 74; Can Coun Arts Grant, Govt Can, 75; Can Coun Arts Grant, 77-78. *Bibliog:* Joan Lowndes (auth), Richard Prince: bringing the outdoors in, Artscanada, Toronto, 10-11/78; Arthur Perry (auth), Richard Prince: figure structures, Vanguard Vancouver, BC, 11/79; Joel Kaplan (auth), Richard Prince, Parachute, Montreal, Que, summer 85; Stephen Godfrey (auth), Focus on Richard Prince, Can Art, fall 88; J P Borum (auth), Richard E Prince, Artforum, New York, 1/90. *Mem:* Life mem Royal Can Acad; Univ Art Asn Can. *Media:* Multimedia. *Dealer:* Equinox Gallery 2321 Granville St Vancouver BC Can V6H 3G3. *Mailing Add:* 285 W 18th Ave Vancouver BC V5Y 2A8 Canada

PRINDIVILLE, JIM
PAINTER
b Chicago, Ill, Feb 12, 41. *Study:* Am Acad Art; Ill Inst Design; Sch Art Inst Chicago. *Work:* Ill State Mus, Springfield; Univ Wyo, Laramie; Borg-Warner Corp, Chicago; US Air Force, Washington, DC; Park Forest Art Ctr, Ill. *Comn:* Painting (acrylic), FMC Corp, Houston, Tex, 78; paintings (acrylic), Chicago White Metal Casting Inc, Bensenville, Ill, 85. *Exhib:* Am Watercolor Soc, Nat Acad Gallerie, New York, 68-71 & Charles & Emma Frye Mus, Seattle, Wash, 68; 23rd Ill Invitational, Ill State Univ, Springfield, 70; Watercolor Exhib, Chico State Col, Calif, 71; one-man show, Northwestern Univ Gallery, Evanston, Ill, 78; Ill Inst Technol, Chicago, 79; Invitational Watercolor Exhib, Edward Dean Mus, Cherry Valley, Calif, 81; Watercolor Invitational, Mitchell Mus, Mt Vernon, Ill, 83. *Pos:* Dir, Munic Art League Chicago, 82-84. *Awards:* Best of Show, Artist Guild Chicago, 67; First Prize, Ill State Fair Prof Exhib, 69. *Bibliog:* Barbara Haddad (auth), The fine arts, Denver Post, 11/10/68; Jerry Klein (auth), Arts, criticism, Journal Star, Peoria, 10/2/77; Maggie Wilson (auth), Gallery, Ariz Repub, 12/19/79. *Mem:* Am Watercolor Soc; Air Force Art Prog; hon life mem Ariz Watercolor Asn; hon mem Union League Civic & Arts Found, Chicago. *Media:* Watercolor, Acrylic & Serigraph. *Publ:* Illusr, Shifting Anchors, Reading Program Basic Series, Rand McNally & Co, 72; The Young America, Basic Reading Program, Lyons & Carnahan, 72; auth & illusr, The Joy of Painting, Hunt Manufacturing, 80. *Mailing Add:* c/o Cogswell Gallery 223 E Gore Creek Dr Vail CO 81657

PRINTZ, BONNIE ALLEN
PAINTER, PHOTOGRAPHER
b Luray, Va. *Study:* Va Commonwealth Univ, Richmond, BFA, 68; Hunter Col, New York, MA, 70. *Work:* Baltimore Mus Art; Corcoran Gallery Art, Washington, DC. *Exhib:* Open Space Gallery, Victoria, BC, 78; Blue Sky Gallery, Portland, Ore, 79; one-person exhib show, Baltimore Mus Art, 79; Corcoran Gallery Art, Washington, DC, 79, 82 & 88; William Penn Mem Mus, Harrisburg, Pa, 79-80 & 82; Va Mus Fine Arts, Richmond, 80 & 83; Baltimore Mus Art, 80, 83 & 86; McIntosh/Drysdale Gallery, Washington, DC, 87; Galerie Des Saints Peres, Paris, France, 92. *Pos:* Tech asst spec collections, Mus Mod Art, New York, 68-70. *Teaching:* Instr fine arts, Md Inst, Col Art, Baltimore, 72-73, 76 & 79- *Awards:* Va Mus Fine Arts Fel, 79-80; First Place, Women Arts, Pa, 82; Mellon Grant, Md Inst, Col Art, 85; Alliance Independent Col Art Grant, 85; Yaddo Fel, 88. *Bibliog:* Allan Ripp (auth), Polaroid photos allow artists to develop their talents, News Am, Baltimore, 12/31/78. *Media:* Acrylic, Oil. *Publ:* Illusr, Frank Young's Visual Studies: A Foundation Course for the Visual Arts, Minneapolis Col Art & Design, 85. *Mailing Add:* 1104 Regester Ave Baltimore MD 21239

PRIP, JANET
CRAFTSMAN, SCULPTOR
b Hornell, NY, June 17, 50. *Study:* Moore Col Art, 68-70; RI Sch Design, BFA, 74. *Work:* RI Sch of Design Mus, Providence; Boston Mus Fine Arts. *Exhib:* Poetry of the Physical, ACC Mus, New York, NY, 86; Today's Artisan: The Art of Craft, Newport Art Mus, RI, 88; Craft Today in America, traveling exhib to Europe, 89-91; Arts That Work: The Decorative Arts of the 80's Crafted in America (traveling in US), Craft & Folk Art Mus, Los Angeles, Calif, 90-93; Am Jewellery & Metalwork, Art Gallery of Western Australia, Perth, 92. *Awards:* Fel, Nat Endowment Arts, 86. *Bibliog:* Jamie Bennet (auth), American Holloware: Changing Criteria, Metalsmith, summer 84; Sarah Bodine (auth), Janet Prip, Metalsmith, fall 88. *Media:* Bronze, Pewter. *Dealer:* Pritam & Eames 27 Race Lane East Hampton NY. *Mailing Add:* 163 Arnold Ave Cranston RI 02905

PRIP, JOHN A
SILVERSMITH, SCULPTURE
b New York, NY, July 2, 22. *Study:* Apprentice to Evald Nielsen, 37-42; Copenhagen Tech Col, grad, 42; RI Sch Design, Hon Doc, 89. *Work:* Chicago Art Inst, Ill; Am Craft Mus, New York; Minn Mus Art, St Paul, Minn; Yale Univ, New Haven, Conn; Mus Art, RI Sch Design, Providence, 87; Renwick Gallery, Smithsonian Inst, Washington, DC. *Exhib:* Retrospective, Mus Art, RI Sch Design, Providence, 87; retrospective, Am Craft Mus, New York, 88; Gimpel Weitzenhoffer, New York, 88; and others. *Teaching:* Inst, Alfred Univ, NY, Rochester Inst Technol, NY, Mus Fine Arts, Boston & RI Sch Design. *Awards:* Nat Endowment Arts Fel, 86; Governor's Art Award, State of RI, 90; Gold Medal, Am Craft Coun, 90. *Media:* Meta, Paper. *Mailing Add:* 101 Perryville Rd Rehoboth MA 02769

PRITZLAFF, (MR & MRS) JOHN, JR
COLLECTORS
Mr Pritzlaff, b Milwaukee, Wis, May 10, 25; Mrs Pritzlaff, b St Louis, Mo. *Study:* Mr Pritzlaff, Princeton Univ, BA, 49; Mrs Pritzlaff, Briarcliff Col. *Pos:* Mr Pritzlaff, US Ambassador to Malta, 69-72; Ariz State Sen, formerly; mem bd dirs, Heard Mus, Phoenix, Ariz, 76-77; Mrs Pritzlaff, pres, bd dirs, Phoenix Art Mus. *Mailing Add:* 7352 E McLellan Blvd Scottsdale AZ 85250

PROCHOWNIK, WALTER A
EDUCATOR, PAINTER
b Buffalo, NY, Dec 12, 23. *Study:* Art Inst of Buffalo; Art Students League. *Work:* Albright-Knox Art Gallery, Buffalo, NY; Norfolk Mus Arts & Sci, Va; Minn Mus Arts, St Paul; Burchfield Ctr, State Univ NY, Buffalo; Ball State Univ Art Gallery, Muncie, Ind. *Comn:* You the People (mural), Co of Erie, Rath Off Bldg, Buffalo, 74; mural, Blue Cross Bldg, Buffalo, NY, 88. *Exhib:* One-man shows, Member's Gallery, Albright-Knox Art Gallery, Buffalo, 64, Col of Wooster, Ohio, 66, Chautauqua Art Asn Gallery, NY, 68 & Burchfield Ctr, Buffalo, 75 & 89; Smithsonian travel tour, 68-69. *Teaching:* Lectr art, State Univ NY, Buffalo, 63-81, adj prof, 81- *Awards:* First Oil Award, Chautauqua Art Asn, 58; Purchase Prize, Drawings USA, 63 & 66; Perkin-Elmer Corp Award, Silvermine Guild, 69. *Mem:* Patteran Artists. *Media:* Oil, Multimedia. *Dealer:* Barbara Schuller Gallery 345 Franklin St Buffalo NY 14202. *Mailing Add:* c/o Barbara Schallen Gallery 345 Franklin St Buffalo NY 14202

PROHASKA, ELENA ANASTASIA
CONSULTANT, CURATOR
b Southampton, NY, Sept 3, 46. *Study:* NY Univ, Washington Sq Col, BA, 70; Univ Va, Charlottesville, with William Seitz, MA, 72; New Sch; NY Univ. *Work:* Investment Counrs, New York. *Collections Arranged:* Monthly exhibs, (auth, catalogs), Upstairs Gallery, East Hampton, NY, 72-74; Twelve Americans: Masters of Collage, Crispo Gallery, New York, 77; Artists of the Springs, East Hampton, NY, 81; East Hampton Hist Soc Invitational, 86; Consult & Appraiser, Artists of the Hamptons, Quernsey's Auctioneers, 92. *Pos:* Owner, Elena Prohaska Fine Arts; cur, Art Collection, E M Warburg, Pincus, New York & Los Angeles. *Teaching:* Docent & art lectr, Guggenheim Mus, New York, 74-76; instr art, The Town Sch, New York, 74-77. *Mem:* Appraisers Asn Am, New York. *Specialty:* Contemporary paintings, sculpture and photographs; also specialize in advising private and corporate clients on art acquisitions. *Mailing Add:* 41 Central Park W New York NY 10023

PROKOPOFF, STEPHEN
MUSEUM DIRECTOR, HISTORIAN
b Chicago, Ill, Dec 24, 29. *Study:* Univ Calif, Berkeley, BA & MA; NY Univ, PhD. *Collections Arranged:* Romantic Minimalism, 67; Spirit of the Comics, 68; Highway, 69; Two Generations of Color Painting, 70; Against Order, 71; White on White, 72; Post-Mondrian Abstraction in America, 73; Logic of Vision, 74; Made in Chicago, 75; Prinzhorn Collection, 85; and others. *Pos:* Dir, Hathorn Gallery, Skidmore Col, 66-67, Inst Contemp Art, Univ Pa, 67-71, Mus Contemp Art, Chicago, 71-77, Inst Contemp Art, Boston, 78-82 & Krannert Art Mus, Univ Ill, 82-92, Univ Art Mus, Univ Iowa, 92- *Teaching:* Inst art, Rutgers State Univ, Newark, NJ, 59, Lake Erie Col, Painsville, Ohio, 59-61; vis asst prof, Univ Wash, Seattle, 64-65; asst prof, Skidmore Col, 61-67, Univ Pa, 67-71; Robert B Mayer prof hist art, Univ Chicago, 75; prof, Univ Ill at Chicago Circle, 74, Boston Univ, 78-82, Univ Ill, Urbana-Champaign, 82-92, Univ Iowa, 92- *Awards:* Nat Endowment Arts; Award, Am Inst Archit, 76; Travel Grant, Am Coun Ger, 80 & 83. *Mem:* Am Asn Mus Dirs; Am Asn Mus; Col Art Asn Am. *Publ:* Coauth, 19th Century Architecture of Saratoga Springs, NY, 72; The Modern Dutch Poster: 1890 to 1940, 86. *Mailing Add:* Krannert Art Museum 500 E Peabody Champaign IL 61820

PROMUTICO, JEAN
PAINTER
b Baltimore, Md, Nov 23, 36. *Study:* Md Inst Art, with Lila Katzen & Jon Schueler, BFA(painting & drawing), 66; Univ NMex, Albuquerque, with John Kacere, MA(painting & art hist), 68. *Work:* Fine Arts Mus NMex, Santa Fe; Univ Art Mus, Univ NMex, Albuquerque; Mus Albuquerque, Roswell Mus & Art Ctr, NMex; Lynn Mahew Gallery, Ohio Wesleyan Univ, Delaware; Amoco, Houston, Tex; Roanoke Mus Fine Arts, Va. *Exhib:* Women Am West, Bruce Mus, Greenwich, Conn, 85; Marymount- Manhattan Col, New York, 87; NJ Center Visual Arts, Summit, 88; Mus Fine Arts NMex, Santa Fe, 89; E Mont Col, Billings; and many others. *Awards:* Nat Endowment Arts Grant, 74; Artist-in-Residence Grant, Roswell Mus & Art Ctr, 78-79 & 90-91; Nat Studio Program Grant, Inst Art & Urban Resources, New York, 81. *Bibliog:* William Peterson (auth), article, Artspace, spring 79; Gerrit Henry (auth), article, Art News, 9/81; William Peterson (auth), article, Artspace, fall 83. *Media:* Miscellaneous Media, Oil. *Mailing Add:* 104 W 17th St 3S New York NY 10011

PROPERSI, AUGUST J
ADMINISTRATOR, PAINTER
b Bronx, NY, Apr 3, 26. *Study:* Sch Art Studies, with Isaac Soyer & Sol Wilson, 46-47; Sch Visual Arts, with Jack Sheridan, Ben Dale & Francis Criss, grad, 50; Conference Conservation of Paintings, Brooklyn, Mus, 62. *Work:* Veterans Administration Hospital, Montrose, NY. *Exhib:* Artists USA, Bohman Gallery, Stockholm, Sweden, 68; 50 State Competition, Duncan Galleries, Paris, France, 68; Am Artists, Propersi Gallery D'Arte, Scarsdale, NY, 68 & 80; Propersi Galleries, Greenwich, Conn, 77-84. *Pos:* Founder & dir, The Little Studio and Art Gallery Art Sch, 59-68; founder and dir, Propersi Galleria D'Art, Scarsdale, NY, 68-70; founder & pres, Propersi Galleries & Sch Art Inc, 70-84. *Teaching:* Dir & instr life drawing, The Little Studio, Pelham, NY, 59-68; dir & instr fine arts, Propersi Gallerie D'Arte, 68-70; chmn fine and commercial art, Propersi Sch Art, Inc, 70-84. *Awards:* Prix d'Paris, 50 States Competition, Raymond Duncan Galleries, 68. *Bibliog:* Kathie Beals (auth), Dealer bullish on American art, Gannett Westchester Newspaper, 6/13/75; Dorothy Friedman (auth), Personal attention key to success, Greenwich Time Newspaper, 10/13/75; John Branca & Steve Acunto, Profiles, WVOX-WFAS Radio Westchester, 76-77. *Mem:* Artist Guild (bd dirs, 53); Am Veterans Soc Artists (bd dirs, 68). *Media:* Pastels, Oils. *Specialty:* Listed American painters and European painters--19th & 20th centuries. *Mailing Add:* 225 Magnolia Ave Mt Vernon NY 10552

PROSS, LESTER FRED
EDUCATOR, PAINTER
b Bristol, Conn, Aug 14, 24. *Study:* Oberlin Col, BA, 45, MA, 46; Ohio Univ, with Ben Shahn, summer 52; Skowhegan Sch Painting & Sculpture, summer 53; with Simon, Zorach, Levine, Hebald & Bocour; Univ Colo Kyoto Sem, Japan, 75-76; study painting with Kono Shuson. *Exhib:* Midstates Ann, Evansville, 64; Face of Kentucky I & II Traveling Exhib, 68-70; Appalachian Corridors II Traveling Exhib, 70-71; Morehead State Univ, 73; Ky Bicentennial, 74; More than Land or Sky: Art from Appalachia, Nat Mus Am Art, Smithsonian Inst, Washington DC, 81-82, Traveling Exhib, 82-84; Headley-Whitney Mus, Lexington, Ky, 83, 89, Kentucky to Ecuador, 89-90; one-person shows, Ky Guild Gallery, 88, Prestonsburg Col, 90; retrospective, Doris Ulmann Galleries, Berea Col, 90; group show, Yeiser Art Ctr, Paducah, 92. *Pos:* Bd dirs, Doris Ulmann Found, 60-84; chmn adv bd, Appalachian Mus, Berea Col, 69-84. *Teaching:* Prof art, Berea Col, 46-91, chmn dept, 50-84; Fulbright lectr painting & art hist, Univ Panjab, Pakistan, 57-58; vis assoc prof art educ & hist, Union Col, summer 61; vis prof art, Am Univ Cairo, 67-68; Bryant Drake guest prof art, Kobe Col, Japan, 84-85. *Awards:* Haskell Traveling Fel, Oberlin Col, 57-58; Ky Guild of Artists & Craftsmen Fel; Merit Award, UK Appalachian Ctr, 87. *Mem:* Col Art Asn Am; Am Comt SAsian Art; Ky Guild Artists & Craftsmen (pres, 61-63); Asn Asian Studies; Asia Soc. *Media:* Oil, Watercolor. *Publ:* Auth, Five Expressionists, Allen Mem Art Mus, Oberlin, Ohio, 46; Celebration, Berea Col, Ky, 78; illusr, The Passion, Mountain Life & Work, Berea, 51. *Mailing Add:* 1287 CPO Berea KY 40404

PROVDER, CARL
PAINTER, INSTRUCTOR
b Brooklyn, NY, Feb 7, 33. *Study:* Pratt Inst, BFA; Columbia Univ, MA, prof dipl; Inst Allende, MFA; Educ Alliance Art Sch; Art Students League; NY Univ; Acad Belli Arti, Perugia; also with Samuel Adler. *Exhib:* Contemp Artists of Brooklyn, Brooklyn Mus, 72; Painters & Sculptors Soc, Jersey City Mus, NJ, 72; La Jolla Mus, 74 & 75; San Diego Mus, 75 & 79; Laguna Beach Mus, Calif, 77; and others. *Pos:* Mem, San Diego Mus Art & La Jolla Mus Contemp Art. *Teaching:* Instr fine arts, Bd Educ, New York, 64-73 & San Diego Community Col, 74-83; instr, Mira Costa Col, 76-77 & Mendocino Art Ctr, 80-81. *Awards:* First Prize-Mixed Media, Southern Calif Expo, Del Mar, 77 & Third Prize Mixed Media, 79; Purchase Award, Small Image Art Show, San Diego, 78-80; First Prize Painting, San Diego Art Inst Ann, 80 & Hon Mention, 81; Second Prize Painting, 82; Third Prize Painting, 83. *Bibliog:* Denise Draper (auth), An exhibit that passes the test, Coast Dispatch, 1/21/78; Richard Reilly (auth), Artist's work is from within, 1/22/78 & Joan Levine (auth), Art on a cul-de-sac, 10/19/78, San Diego Union. *Mem:* Artists Equity Asn (vpres, 76-79); San Diego Artists Guild; Soc Layerists in Multi-Media. *Publ:* Auth, A colorists approach to abstract painting, Today's Art, Vol 26, No 11, 78. *Mailing Add:* 1416 Elva Terr Encinitas CA 92024

PROVISOR, JANIS
ARCHITECT
b Brooklyn, NY, 1946. *Study:* Univ Mich, Sch archit & Design, 66; Univ Cincinnati, Col Design, Art & Archit, 68; San Francisco Art Inst, BFA, 69, MFA, 71. *Work:* Albright-Knox Art Mus, Buffalo, NY; The Annex, Tucson, Ariz; Ludwig Mus, Aachen, Ger; Univ Art Mus, Berkeley, Calif; Oakland Art Mus, Calif. *Comn:* Times Square Project, Proskauer Rose Goetz & Mendelsohn, New York. *Exhib:* One-person exhibs, Gloria Luria Gallery, Miami, Fla, 90, Lisa Sette Gallery, Scottsdale, Ariz, 90, Dorothy Goldeen Gallery, Santa Monica, Calif, 90, Eugene Binder Gallery, Cologne, Ger, 91, San Francisco Art Inst, Calif, 91, Barbara Toll, New York, 92, Timothy Brown Fine Art, Aspen, Colo, 92; Contemporary Prints, Gallery 44, 90, 20th Anniversary Visiting Artist Program, Univ Art Gallery, Colo Univ, Boulder, 92; Post Earthquake Prints, Crown Point Press, San Francisco, Calif, 90; The Common Wealth Exhibition, Roanoke Mus Fine Art, Va, 90; Woodcuts, Crown Point Press, 90, The Tree, Elysium Art Gallery, 91, Sheh Zand Proj, New York, 92; Works on Paper, Timothy Brown Fine Arts, Aspen, Colo, 91; Presswork: The Art of Women Printmakers, Nat Mus Women in the Arts, Washington, DC, 91; Vital Forces, Hecksher Mus, Huntington, NY, 91; Miniatures, Lisa Sette Gallery, Scottsdale, Ariz, 92; Big Ideas, Tucson Mus Art, Ariz, 92; Abstract Paintings, Dorothy Goldeen Gallery, Santa Monica, Calif, 92. *Teaching:* Vis artist, Anderson Ranch Arts Ctr, Snowmass, Colo, 90 & 92, State Univ NY, Purchase, 92. *Awards:* Ford Found Grant, Univ Tex, 78; Nat Endowment Arts, Individual Artist's Fel, 80, 85 & 91; Colo Coun Arts & Humanities Fel, 88. *Bibliog:* John Rapko (auth), Glitter & Ti-Dye, Artweek, 4/91; Allan Schwartzman (auth), Landscapes of the Mind, Aspen Mag, midsummer 92; Jane Wilson (auth), Artist Comes 'Home' with New Work, Aspen Times, 8/8/92. *Mailing Add:* c/o Dorothy Goldeen Gallery 1547 Ninth St Santa Monica CA 90401

PROWN, JULES DAVID
HISTORIAN
b Freehold, NJ, Mar 14, 30. *Study:* Lafayette Col, AB, 51; Harvard Univ, AM(fine arts), 53; Univ Del, AM(early Am cult), 56; Harvard Univ, PhD(fine arts), 61; Lafayette Col, Hon DFA, 79. *Collections Arranged:* John Singleton Copley Traveling Exhib (auth, catalog), 65-66 & American Art from Alumni Collections, 68, Yale Univ Art Gallery; travelling exhib), 65-66 & American Art from Alumni Collections, 68, Yale Univ Art Gallery. *Pos:* Asst to dir, William Hayes Fogg Art Mus, Harvard Univ, 59-61; cur, Garvan & Related Collections of Am Art, Yale Univ, New Haven, 63-68; dir, Yale Brit Art Ctr, New Haven, 68-76; assoc dir, Nat Humanities Inst, New Haven, 77. *Teaching:* Fel art hist, Harvard Univ, Cambridge, Mass, 56-57; from instr to prof, Yale Univ, 61-86, Paul Mellon prof hist of art, 86- *Awards:* Guggenheim Fel, 64-65; Blanche Elizabeth MacLeish Billings Award, Yale Univ, 66; Robert C Smith Award, Soc Arch Historians, 83; George Washington Kidd

Award, Lafayette Col, 86. *Mem:* Am Soc 18th Century Studies (exec bd mem, 73-76); Col Art Asn (bd dir, 75-79); Benjamin Franklin fel Royal Soc Arts; Am Antiquarian Soc (mem coun, 77-). *Res:* American and English art; John Singleton Copley; Benjamin West; Winslow Homer; material culture. *Publ:* The Architecture of the Yale Center for British Art, Yale Ctr for Brit Art, 77; Style as Evidence, 80 & Mind in Matter, 82, Portfolio; Thomas Eakins' Baby at Play, Studies in the History of Art, Nat Gallery Art, Washington, Vol 18, 121-7, 85; Benjamin West's Family Picture: A Nativity in Hammersmith, in John Wilmerding, ed, Essays in Honor of Paul Mellon, Washington, DC, 269-81, 86; Charles Willson Peale in London, Charles Willson Peale: New Perspectives, A 250th Anniversary Celebration, Univ Pittsburgh Press, 91; and others. *Mailing Add:* Dept Art Hist Box 2009 Yale Univ New Haven CT 06520

PRUITT, LYNN
SCULPTOR, ASSEMBLAGE ARTIST
b Washington, DC, May 24, 37. *Work:* Marlboro Hall, Prince George Com Col, Largo, Md. *Comn:* Sculptured canvas wall relief, Naval Acad, Annapolis, Md, 76. *Exhib:* Corcoran Gallery Art, Washington, DC, 65 & 72; one-person shows, Md Artists Today, East Coast Univ Tour, Baltimore Mus, 75 & 76, Nat Audubon Soc, Chevy Chase, Md, 77 & Nourse Gallery, Washington, DC, 80; Am Chairs, Form, Function & Fantasy, John Michael Kohler Arts Ctr, Sheboygan, Wis, 78; Washington Proj for the Arts, DC, 80; and others. *Pos:* Juror, Prince George's Community Col, 72-75, Nat Inst Health, 73-75, Md Col Art, 76 & Scholastic Art Awards, Washington, DC, Md & Va, 77-78; dir & consult, Holden Gallery, Inc, Kensington, Md, 76- *Teaching:* Instr basic art, Jewish Community Ctr, Rockville, Md, 74- *Awards:* First in Painting, 68, 69 & 70, Best in Show, 68, 69 & 70 & First in Sculpture, 70, 71, 73 & 74, Nat Inst Health, Bethesda, Md. *Mem:* Washington Womens Arts Ctr; Am Crafts Coun. *Media:* Plaster. *Dealer:* Nourse Gallery Washington DC 20013. *Mailing Add:* 12806 Poplar Ave Silver Spring MD 20904

PRUNEDA, MAX
SCULPTOR
b Laredo, Tex, 48. *Study:* Univ Tex, Austin, BFA, 73. *Exhib:* One-person shows, Brigitte Schluger Gallery, Denver, Colo, 89 & 91, Gallery Elena, Taos, NMex, 89, 90 & 91, Quintana Gallery, Portland, Ore, 89, 90, 91 & 92; Marianne Partlow Gallery, Olympia, Wash, 92; Ralph Green Gallery, Albuquerque, NMex, 92; Gallery Elena, Taos, NMex, 92; and others. *Awards:* Nat Endowment Arts Fel, 88; Cult Arts Coun Houston Grant, 89. *Mailing Add:* 2323 Krogh Ct NW Albuquerque NM 87104

PUCKER, BERNARD H
ART DEALER
b Kansas City, Mo, Oct 19, 37. *Study:* Columbia Univ, BA, 59; Hebrew Univ, Jerusalem, 60; Brandeis Univ, MA, 66. *Pos:* Dir, Pucker Gallery, Boston, currently. *Specialty:* Contemporary artists; Chagall graphics; Israeli artist Bak, Sharir; New England artists such as Ali and Jim Schantz; fantastic realist artists like Shigeru Matsuzaki; Antique African carvings; bronzes by David Aronson, Igor Galanin, Jim Ritchie & David Chamberlain, porcelains by Brother Thomas. *Mailing Add:* 171 Newbury St Boston MA 02116

PUETT, GARNETT G
SCULPTOR
b Hahira, Ga, 1959. *Study:* Pratt Inst, MFA, 83. *Exhib:* Solo exhibs, Univ Wash, Seattle, Wash, 81 & 83, Laumier Sculpture Park, St Louis, Mo, 87, Glenn/Dask Gallery, Los Angeles, Calif, 89 & Pittsburgh Ctr Arts, 90; Galerie Georges Verney, Carron, Villeurbanne, France, 89; Lead and Wax, Stephen Wirtz Gallery, San Francisco, Calif, 90; Curt Marcus Gallery, New York, 91; Assemblage, Southeastern Ctr Contemp Art, NC, 92; and others. *Awards:* Nat Endowment Arts Fel, 88. *Bibliog:* Ingrid Schaffner (auth), Flash Art Int, 1-2/89; Eric Gibson (auth), Decade in review, Sculpture, 5-6/89; The Sciences, 3-4/92; and others. *Mailing Add:* c/o Curt Marcus Gallery 578 Broadway 10th fl New York NY 10012

PUFAHL, JOHN K
EDUCATOR, PRINTMAKER
b Urbana, Ill, Nov 6, 42. *Study:* Wesleyan Univ, Ill, BFA(hon), 65; Northern Ill Univ, MA & MFA, studied with David F Driesbach, 67. *Work:* Univ Wis, Platteville; Art Gallery of Windsor, Ont; Bd Educ, Windsor, Ont. *Exhib:* Chicago & Vicinity Exhib, Art Inst Chicago, 66; 162nd Ann Exhib, Philadelphia Acad Fine Arts, 67; Can Print Exhib, Windsor, Ont, 74; Calgary Int Drawing Exhib, Alta, 74; Imprint 76 (in conjunction with Olympic Games), Montreal, Que, 76; Fourth Biennale Int de l'Image, Epinal & Paris, France, 77 & 78. *Collections Arranged:* Can Printmakers, Art Gallery Toronto, Ont, 70; Imprint 76, Art Gallery Ont, 76-77. *Pos:* Pres, Pufahl & Krassov Ltd, Press Manufacturers, 74-; actg dir, Sch Fine Arts, Univ Windsor, Ont, 76-77; artist-in-residence, Sch of Art, Yeovil Col, Somerset, Eng, 78. *Teaching:* Asst instr intaglio, Ill Wesleyan Univ, Bloomington, 64-65; assoc prof intaglio & drawing, Univ Windsor, Ont, 67- *Awards:* Can Coun Grant, Adaptation of Stainless Steel to Intaglio Printmaking, 77. *Mem:* Can Univ Art Asn; Print & Drawing Coun Can; Royal Soc Arts, London, Eng. *Media:* Intaglio, Wood Engraving. *Publ:* Contribr, Canadian print workshops, Art Mag, 77. *Mailing Add:* Dept Visual Arts Univ Windsor Windsor ON N9B 3P4 Canada

PUGH, GRACE HUNTLEY
PAINTER, ART HISTORIAN
b Schenectady, NY, Sept 25, 12. *Study:* Wellesley Col, 30-32; Barnard Col, BA(fine arts), 34; Nat Acad Design, with Leon Kroll, Charles Hinton & Ivan Olinsky, 34-36; with Samantha Littlefield Huntley, 34-38; Parsons Sch Design, summer 37; Art Students League, with Reginald Marsh, summer 38. *Work:* Barnard Col; 100 Friends of Pittsburgh & Montefiore Hosp, Pittsburgh; Mamaroneck Free Libr, NY; Westchester Co Art in Pub Places, White Plains, NY. *Comn:* Harbor mural, St Thomas Episcopal Church, Mamaroneck, 63-66; paintings, Mamaroneck Harbor, Dime Savings Bank, Mamaroneck, 75, Mill Stream, Harrison, NY, 76 & Scarsdale Summer, Scarsdale, NY, 77. *Exhib:* Artist Equity Exhib, Whitney Mus Am Art, New York, 51 & Riverside Mus, New York, 53; Ann, Nat Acad Design, New York, 57 & Am Watercolor Soc Ann, 57, 59 & 61; NY State Painters, NY State Bldg-World's Fair, Flushing, 65 & Butler Art Inst, Pa; one-woman shows, Sails, Wildcliff Mus, New Rochelle, NY, 75 & Rockport Art Asn, Mass, 76 & 80; Franklin & Marshall Col, 74, Pa; Gloucester Sawyer Libr, 78, Mass. *Pos:* Chmn art, Mamaroneck Free Libr, 50-87; artist-in-residence & adv fine arts, Village of Mamaroneck, 77-; first chmn, Mamaroneck Hist Preserv Adv Comt, archit art, 82. *Teaching:* Artist-in-residence & head dept art, Briarcliff Jr Col, Briarcliff Manor, NY, 36-40; art instr, Westchester Co Workshop, White Plains, 61-63. *Awards:* Grace Huntley Pugh Day, Village Mamaroneck, with commendation from Pres Bush, 10/17/82 & 6/14/91; First Prize, New Rochelle Art Asn, 51; First Prize, Beaux Art, Westchester Co Womens Clubs, 54, 57 & 64. *Bibliog:* Jim Kinter (auth), Show mirrors artist's strong moods, Intel J Newspaper, 74; Herb Rosoff (auth), The pro's nest meet with Grace Huntley Pugh, Palette Talk Mag, 77. *Mem:* Am Watercolor Soc; Rockport Art Asn; Mamaroneck Artists Guild (pres, 53-55, 61-63, dir, 53-80); Artists Equity. *Media:* Oil, Watercolor. *Publ:* auth, Buoy 16, Mamaroneck Harbor, Village of Mamaroneck; ed & designer, Mamaroneck Hist Soc Newsletter, 80; contribr, Portfolio '78, Howard Publ Co, 77; illusr, Archaeology Inst Am-Westchester Soc Newslett, 77-80; and others. *Mailing Add:* 823 Stuart Ave Mamaroneck NY 10543

PUJOL, ELLIOTT
EDUCATOR, MEDALIST
b Memphis, Tenn, June 4, 43. *Study:* Southern Ill Univ, BS(theatre), 68, with Brent Kington, MFA(art), 71; Penland Sch, with Arline Fisch, 70. *Work:* Minn Mus Art, St Paul; Sheldon Mem Art Gallery, Lincoln, Nebr; Topeka Public Libr; Wichita Art Mus; Louisiana Sch Visually Impaired. *Comn:* Pendulum (sculpture), Kansas State Univ Col Eng, 83. *Exhib:* Visual Arts Ctr Alaska, Anchorage, 80; Brookfield Craft Ctr, Conn, 80; Basketry: Tradition in New Form, Traveling Exhib, Inst Contemp Art, Boston, Mass, Cooper-Hewitt Mus, NY & Greenville Co Mus Art, NC, 83; The New Basket: A Vessel for the Future, Traveling Exhib, New York State Mus, Albany & Rochester & Brainerd Art Gallery, 84; The New American Basket, Traveling Exhib, Africa, US Info Agency, 87-88; Super Bowls - Gallery Eight, La Jolla, Calif, 88; American Craft at the Armory, New York, 88; Univ of Ore Mus of Art Traveling Metals Exhib, 88-89; Fiber/Metal Invitational USA 1992, Craft Alliance Gallery, St Louis. *Collections Arranged:* First Blacksmith Conference, Carbondale, Ill, 70; Third National Student Metal International (auth, catalog), Tyler Sch Art, 72; Summer Vail Metal Symposium, Colo, 74; American Metal Work (auth, catalog), Sheldon Mem Art Gallery, 76; First National Ring Show, Athens, Ga & Manhattan, Kans, 77. *Pos:* Guest artist, Penland Sch, NC, 71, 73, 76, 79 & 89, Arrowmont Sch, Gatlinburg, Tenn, 73, 79 & 86, Brookfield Craft Sch, Conn, 73, 76 & 79, Summer Vail, Colo, 74-84 & 47th Ann Conf Mid Am Col Art Asn, St Louis. *Teaching:* Instr jewelry & silversmithing, Tyler Sch Art, Philadelphia, 71-73; prof metalsmithing, Kans State Univ, Manhattan, 73- *Awards:* First Place, Mus Contemp Crafts, Copper Develop Asn, 71; 50 Outstanding Craftsmen, Penland Sch, Nat Endowment for Arts, 71; Purchase Award, Renwick Gallery, DC, 74. *Bibliog:* Philip Morton (auth), Contemporary Jewelry, Holt, Rinehart, Winston, 70; Oppi Untracht (auth), Jewelry Concepts and Techniques, Doubleday, 71; plus var newspaper articles. *Mem:* Am Crafts Coun; Artist Blacksmith Asn NAm; Kans Artist Craftsmen Asn (pres, 76-78); Soc NAm Goldsmiths. *Media:* All. *Dealer:* J Cotter Gallery Vail CO 81657; Signature Shop Atlanta GA 30305. *Mailing Add:* 1609 Leavenworth Manhattan KS 66502

PULOS, ARTHUR JON
DESIGNER, HISTORIAN
b Vandergrift, Pa, Feb 3, 17. *Study:* Carnegie Inst Technol, BFA, 39; Univ Ore, MFA, 43. *Work:* Walker Art Ctr, Minn; Newark Mus Fine Arts, NJ; Detroit Inst Art, Mich; Mus Mod Art, New York; Chicago Art Inst. *Comn:* Indus Design for Dictaphone, Rockwell International, Piper Aircraft & others; silverware & jewelry. *Exhib:* Brussels World Fair, 58; Metrop Mus, 66; Smithsonian Inst, 66; Louvre, Paris, 66; US Info Agency Exhib, 66. *Pos:* Pres, Pulos Design Assoc, Inc, 58- *Teaching:* Prof indust design, Univ Ill, 46-55; prof indust design & chmn dept, Syracuse Univ, 55-82, prof emer, 82- *Awards:* Distinguished Designer Fel, NEA; Worldesign Award, 88; First Design Educ Award, IDSA, 88; Bronze Apple Award, Ind Designers Soc Am, New York, 83; Design fel, Nat Endowment Arts, 84; First Dist Educ Award; Worldesign Conf Worldesign Award, 88. *Bibliog:* Contemporary Designers, McMillan, 84. *Mem:* Fel Indust Designers Soc Am (pres, 73-75, chmn bd, 75-77); Int Coun Soc Indust Design (pres, 80-81, senate pres, 81-84, senator 85-); hon mem Mexican Acad Design. *Media:* Industrial Design, Silversmithing. *Publ:* Auth, Careers in Industrial Design, Nat Textbk Co, 70 & 78; American Design Ethic, 83 & American Design Adventure, 88, Mass Inst Tech Press, 83; Contact-Selling Design Services, Off Design, Can Govt, 85; auth, articles on design, Am & foreign publ. *Mailing Add:* No 3 The Orchard Fayetteville NY 13066

PUNIA, CONSTANCE EDITH
PAINTER
b Brooklyn, NY. *Study:* Brooklyn Mus Art Sch; oil with Edwin Dickinson & Yonia Fain; oil and sumi-e with Murray Hantman. *Exhib:* Les Surindependants, Paris, 75; Grand Prix Humanitaire de France, Paris, 75; Des

Artistes Francais, Grand Palais, Paris, France, 76 & 77; Sun Yat Sen Ctr of Asian Studies at St John's Univ, Jamaica, NY, 76; Nat A Arts Club, New York, NY, 77; Meridien House Int, Washington, DC, 86. *Awards:* Silver Medal & Laureate of Honor, Grand Prix Humanitaire de France, 75; Bronze Medal, Akad Raymond Duncan, 75; Order of Merit Medal, Acad of Sci & Human Rels, Dominican Repub; Palme D'Or. *Mem:* Nat League Am Pen Women; Sumi-E Soc Am. *Media:* Oil, Sumi-e. *Mailing Add:* 519 Magnolia Ave Brielle NJ 08730

PUNIELLO, FRANÇOISE SARA
LIBRARIAN
b Boston, Mass, June 3, 47. *Study:* RI Col, BA, 69; Rutgers State Univ NJ, MLS, 70, MA(art history), 77. *Pos:* Assoc dir pub service, Douglass Lib, 85-88; dir, Mabel Smith Douglass Libr, 88- *Mem:* Art Librarian Asn NAm (chmn, NJ chapter, 90); Am Libr Asn (art section). *Res:* Women artists and how to research their lives and works. *Interests:* Women artists. *Publ:* Auth, Elsie Driggs in Past and Promise: Lives of New Jersey Women, Scarecrow, 90; Women Painters born after 1900 in Women Artists in the United States, G K Hall, 90. *Mailing Add:* 302 Harrison Ave Highland Park NJ 08904

PURA, WILLIAM PAUL
PRINTMAKER, PAINTER
b Winnipeg, Man, Dec 19, 48. *Study:* Sch Art, Univ Man, BFA, 70; Ind Univ, Bloomington, MFA, 73. *Work:* Art Bank, Can Coun, Ottawa, Ont; Miller Brewing Co, Milwaukee, Wis; Prudential Life Insurance Co, Minneapolis; Gallery III, Univ Man, Winnipeg; Wilfred Laurier Univ, Kitchener, Ont. *Exhib:* Solo exhibs, Gallery III, Univ Man, Winnipeg, 80, Ukrainian Inst Mod Art, Chicago, 84 & Winnipeg Art Gallery, 85; Virginia Beach Art Ctr, Va, 79; Charlotte Printmakers, NC, 79; Contemp Can Printmaking, Australia, 85-86. *Teaching:* Assoc prof, Sch Art, Univ Man, 73- *Awards:* Print & Drawing Coun Can, Opus Frames Ltd, Vancouver, 80; Art Ventures Grant, Man Arts Coun, 85; Explorations Grant, Can Coun, 86. *Mem:* Man Printmakers Asn; Can Artists Representation. *Media:* Lithography; Acrylic, Oil. *Publ:* Auth, A quiet in the land, Arts Manitoba, spring 85; George Flynn interview, Border Crossings, winter, 88. *Dealer:* Can Art Galleries 801 Tenta Ave SW Calgary AB T2R 0B4; Van Straaten Gallery 361 W Superior St Chicago IL 60610. *Mailing Add:* Dept Art Univ Man Winnipeg MB R3T 2N2 Canada

PURCELL, ANN
PAINTER
b Arlington, Va, Nov 18, 41. *Study:* Corcoran Sch Art, DC; George Washington Univ, BA(fine arts), 73. *Work:* Corcoran Gallery Art, DC; Phillips Collection, DC; Albright-Knox Mus, Buffalo, NY; AT&T; Milwaukee Art Mus; and others. *Exhib:* 19th Area Exhib, Corcoran Gallery Art, DC, 74,; one-woman show, 5 Washington Artists, 76 & Corcoran Fac Exhib, 76; Group Show, Selected, Southern Alleghenies Mus Art, Loretto, Pa, 78; 5 Artists, Mus Fine Arts, St Petersburg, Fla, 78; Selected Works from Tibor de Nagy, Mint Mus, Charlotte, NC, 79; plus many others. *Teaching:* Instr painting & drawing, Smithsonian Inst, DC, 74-78, Corcoran Sch Art, 74-79, Parsons Sch Art & Design, 83- *Bibliog:* Jane Livingston (auth), Five Washington Artists, Garamond Press, 76; article, Arts, 11/83. *Mem:* New York Artists Equity Asn. *Media:* Acrylic. *Dealer:* Tibor de Nagy Gallery 29 W 57th St New York NY 10019; Osuna Gallery 2121 P St NW Washington DC 20037. *Mailing Add:* 155 Henry St 8F Brooklyn NY 11201

PURCELL, HUGH D
PAINTER
b Los Angeles, Calif, Apr 26, 15. *Study:* Univ Wash, Seattle, 34-38; Art Ctr, Los Angeles, 38-39; Otis Art Inst, Los Angeles, with Joe Magnani, 51. *Exhib:* Northwest Printmakers, Henry Art Mus, Seattle, 33; E Ala Art Exhib, 64; 34th Nat Spring Exhib, Art League Long Island, 64; Jack Carr Gallery, Pasadena, Calif, 72; 12th Ann Fine Arts Exhib, Goldsboro, NC, 91. *Pos:* Free-lance, oil & watercolor artist, 32- *Media:* Oil, Watercolor. *Dealer:* Village Gallery & Frame E Valley Rd Montecito CA 93108. *Mailing Add:* 17310 Kingsbury Granada Hills CA 91344

PURDUM, REBECCA
PAINTER
b Idaho Falls, Idaho, June 16, 59. *Study:* St Martins Sch Art, London, Eng 80; Skowhegan Sch Painting & Sculpture, Maine, 81; Syracuse Univ, NY, BFA, 81. *Work:* Munson Williams-Proctor Inst, Utica, NY; List Visual Arts Ctr, Mass Inst Technol, Cambridge, Mass; Mus Mod Art, Ft Worth, Tex. *Exhib:* 10 plus 10: Contemporary Soviet & American Painters, Mod Art Mus Ft Worth, traveling exhib, San Francisco Mus Art, Albright-Knox Gallery, Corcoran Gallery, Moscow, Tbilisi & Leningrad, 89-90; Jack Tilton Gallery, New York, 89 & 91; List Visual Arts Ctr, Mass Inst Technol, 90; Whitney Biennial, New York, 91. *Awards:* Eugene M McDermitt Award, Mass Inst Technol. *Bibliog:* Jonathon Seliger (auth), Effect that paint produces: new paintings by Rebecca Purdum, Art Am, 87; Margaret Mooman (auth), The mysterious light, Art News, 88; Dana Erus-Hansen (auth), Painting Aether, List Visual Arts Ctr, Mass Inst Technol, 90. *Media:* Oil. *Dealer:* Jack Tilton Gallery 611 Broadway Suite 808 New York NY 10012. *Mailing Add:* 45 W 11th St 2D New York NY 10011

PURDY, DONALD R
PAINTER
b Conn, Apr 10, 24. *Study:* Univ Conn, BA; Boston Univ, MA. *Work:* New Britain Mus; Colby Col; Chase Manhattan Bank Collection; Univ Kans; Chrysler Mus; Butler Inst, Ohio. *Exhib:* USA Int Show; Silvermine Guild Artists; Audubon Artists; Allied Artists Am; Hudson Valley Exhib, 85. *Awards:* Gold Medal, Allied Artists Am; First Prize, Silvermine Guild Artists; Jane Peterson Award, Audubon Artists; Hudson Valley Award. *Bibliog:* F Whitaker (auth), article, Am Artist. *Mem:* Am Fedn Arts; Allied Artists Am; Silvermine Guild Artists. *Media:* Oil. *Collection:* American and Barbizon; Impressionist. *Dealer:* Hammer Gallery E 57th St New York NY 10022; Flemington Art Gallery Main St Flemington NJ 08822. *Mailing Add:* 70 Poverty Hollow Rd Newtown CT 06470-1822

PURDY, HENRY CARL
PAINTER, EDUCATOR
b Wolfville, NS, Nov 6, 37. *Study:* NS Col Art, Halifax, assoc, 58. *Work:* Confederation Ctr Arts, Island Art Collection, Charlottetown, PEI; Dofasco Steel, Hamilton, Ont; NB Mus, St John; Art Ctr Gallery, Univ NB, Fredericton. *Comn:* Steel sculpture, Fathers of Confederation Trust, Charlottetown, NB, 73; steel fountain sculpture, Parkdale, PEI, 73; acrylic painted mural, Univ PEI, Charlottetown, 79; stained glass windows, St Dunstan's Basilica, Charlottetown, 81; carved wooden mural, Can Coast Guard Col, Sydney, NS, 81. *Exhib:* Ars Sacra Int, St Mary's Art Gallery, Halifax, 79; Maritime Art Asn, Eptek Exhib Ctr, Summerside, PEI, 79; Royal Can Acad Arts Ann, Toronto Exhib Ctr, 80; Between Two Islands, Visby Art Gallery, Sweden, 81; solo exhib, St John City Hall Gallery, NB, 83; and others. *Collections Arranged:* Arts East '79 (maritime art work), PEI, 79; Arts East '80 (work from Atlantic provs), Memracook, NB, 80; Island Visual Artists, 82 & 83. *Teaching:* Instr commercial design, Holland Col, 69-77, dir art & crafts, Sch Visual Arts, 77- *Awards:* Centennial Awards, Gold Medal Sculpture, 63 & Gold Arts Medal, 73, Prov PEI; Silver Medal for Contrib to Art in Atlantic Can, Royal Soc Arts, 81. *Bibliog:* Robert Percival (auth), Purdy in the Maritimes, Art Mag, 74; Pat Murphy (auth), Look out! Here comes Henry Purdy, Axiom Mag, 3/76; Rich Smith (dir), Henry Purdy--Artist (video), Confederation Ctr Arts, 78. *Mem:* Royal Can Acad Art (vpres Atlantic region, 78-); Can Soc Educ Through Art; Can Artists Rep; Royal Soc Arts; PEI Coun Arts (chmn bd, 78-83). *Media:* Acrylic, Welded Steel. *Publ:* Auth, Me Too!, Holland Press, 74; illusr, Icons of Poverty & Riches, 81 & Francis, 83, A Arsenault; contribr, Sand Patterns--A Commemorative Issue, Sand Patterns Group, 83. *Mailing Add:* 6 St Peters Rd Charlottetown PE C1A 5H2 Canada

PURTLE, CAROL JEAN
HISTORIAN, EDUCATOR
b St Louis, Mo, Feb 20, 39. *Study:* Maryville Col, St Louis, BA(magna cum laude), 60; Manhattanville Col, MA, 66; Washington Univ, St Louis, PhD, 76. *Teaching:* Instr art hist, Washington Univ, St Louis, 70-76; assoc prof art & coordr art hist, Memphis State Univ, 77- *Awards:* Advan Res Fel, Belgian-Am Educ Found, 74-75; Nat Endowment Humanities Summer Fel, 82 & 88; Coolidge Fel, 85. *Mem:* Historians Netherlandish Art (nat pres, 83-85); Col Art Asn Am; Southeastern Col Art Conf; Midwest Art Hist Soc; Centre european d etudes bourguignonnes. *Res:* Painting of Jan van Eyck; 15th century devotional images; relationship between word and image in church-related art. *Publ:* Auth, The Marian Paintings of Jan van Eyck, Princeton Univ Press, 82; ed & contribr, 600 Years of Netherlandish Art: Selected Symposium Lectures, Memphis State Univ, 82; auth, Structuring the Jewish-Christian Reality in Early Flemish Painting, Religion and Intellectual Life, fall 87; Iconography of Prayer, Jean de Berry and the Origin of the Annunciation in a Church, Simiolus, 90-91. *Mailing Add:* 777 Mt Moriah #6 Memphis TN 38117

PURYEAR, MARTIN
SCULPTOR
b Chicago, Ill, May 23, 41. *Study:* Cath Univ Am, Washington, DC, BA, 63; Yale Univ, MFA, 71. *Work:* Mus Mod Art & Whitney Mus Am Art, New York; Art Inst Chicago; Walker Art Ctr, Minneapolis, Minn; Los Angeles Co Mus. *Comn:* Bodark Arc (sculpture), Nathan Manilow Sculpture Park, Governors State Univ, University Park, Ill, 82; Sentinel (sculpture), Gettysburg Col, Pa, 82; Knoll (sculpture), Nat Oceanographic & Atmospheric Admin, Seattle, Wash, 83; sculpture, Chevy Chase Garden Plaza, Md, 85; sculpture, City of Chicago, River Rd Sta, Chicago Transit Authority, 85. *Exhib:* Solo exhibs, Corcoran Gallery Art, 77, Joslyn Art Mus, 80, Univ Art Mus Berkeley, Calif, 85, Brooklyn Mus, 88; The Presence of Nature, 78, 1979 Whitney Biennial Exhib, 79, 1981 Whitney Biennial Exhib, Enclosing the Void: Eight Contemp Sculptors, 88, 1989 Whitney Biennial Exhib, 89, Whitney Mus Am Art, New York; Young American Artists, 78, Transformations in Sculpture: Four Decades in American & European Art, 85, Emerging Artists 1978-1986: Selection from Exxon Series, 87, Solomon R Guggenheim Mus, New York; An Int Survey of Recent Painting & Sculpture, Mus Mod Art, New York, 84; Ten-year survey travelling exhib: Univ Gallery, Univ Mass, Amhurst, Berkshire Mus, Pittsfield, Mass, New Mus Contemp Art, New York, La Jolla Mus Contemp Art, Calif, 84; New Sculpture/Six Artists, St Louis Art Mus, 88; Sculpture Inside Outside, Walker Art Ctr, Minneapolis, Minn, 88; Traveling retrospective exhib, Art Inst Chicago, Hirshhorn Mus & Sculpture Garden, Washington, DC, & Mus Contemp Art, Los Angeles, 91-92; Documenta IX, Kassel, Ger, 92; and many others. *Teaching:* Prof art, Univ Ill, Chicago, 70 & 78-88. *Awards:* Brandeis Creative Arts Award for Sculpture, Brandeis Univ, 89; Sao Paulo Biennal grand prize for best artist, Brazil, 89; Skowhegan Medal for Sculpture, Skowhegan Sch Painting & Sculpture, New York, 90. *Media:* All Media. *Dealer:* Donald Young Gallery 2107 Third Ave Seattle WA 98121. *Mailing Add:* c/o Donald Young Gallery 352 W Huron St Chicago IL 60610

PUTNAM, NOL (OLIVER DE MONTALANT)
SCULPTOR
b Boston, Mass, May 12, 34. *Study:* Trinity Col, Conn, AB, 59; Univ Mass, MEd, 72. *Work:* Alice Dike Barney House, Smithsonian Inst, Washington,

DC. *Comn:* Processional cross, Episcopal Church, Delaplane, Va, 84; mem gate, Nat Cathedral, Washington, DC, 87 & 92. *Awards:* Allied Prof Award, Va Soc Am Architects, 83. *Mem:* Artists Blacksmiths Asn NAm (bd dir, 87-90); Piedmont Craftsman. *Media:* Wrought Iron. *Mailing Add:* c/o White Oak Forge Ltd PO Box 341 The Plains VA 22171

PUTTERMAN, FLORENCE GRACE
PAINTER, EDUCATOR
b Brooklyn, NY, Apr 14, 27. *Study:* New York Univ, BS; Bucknell Univ; Pa State Univ, MFA, 73. *Work:* Metrop Mus Art, Everson Mus, Brooklyn Mus, New York; Art Inst Chicago; Nat Mus Women Arts, Washington, DC; Philadelphia Mus, Pa; NJ State Mus, Trenton; and others. *Comn:* Harris Saving Bank, Harrisburg, Pa, 80. *Exhib:* State Mus Pa, 86; Mus Art, Univ Ariz, Tucson, 88; Contemporary Collections, Mus Fine Arts, St Petersburg, Fla, 88; Artist Choose Artists, Tampa Mus, Fla; Owensburg Mus Art, Ky; and many others. *Pos:* Founder & pres, Arts Unlimited, Selinsgrove, Pa, 65-78; cur, Milton Shoe Co Print Collection, Pa, 70-; bd dirs, Art Gallery, Bucknell Univ, Lewisburg, Pa. *Teaching:* Artist in residence, Fed Title III Prog, 67-68 & 69-70; instr, Lycoming Col, Williamsport, Pa, 73-75; instr, Susquehanna Univ, 84-; instr, Monotype Workshop, Bennington Col, Vt, 89. *Awards:* Gold Medal of Honor, Audubon Artists, 79; Nat Endowment Arts, 79-80; Va Ctr Creative Arts Fel; Distinguished Alumni Award, Sch Arts & Archit, Pa State Univ. *Bibliog:* New American Monotypes, 79-80; articles, Am Artist, 7/79 & 2/81; The Nation, Art News, 1/83; New Art Examiner, 90. *Mem:* Boston Printmakers; Nat Asn Women Artists; Soc Am Graphic Artists (vpres); Nat Colorprint Soc; Audubon Artists. *Media:* Oil, Acrylic. *Publ:* Southwest Art, 6/88. *Mailing Add:* 3 Fairway Dr Selinsgrove PA 17870

Q

QUACKENBUSH, ROBERT
ILLUSTRATOR, WRITER
b Hollywood, Calif, July 23, 29. *Study:* Art Ctr Col Design, Pasadena, Calif, BA, 56; Pratt Graphic Art Ctr, with John Ross & Clare Romano, 61. *Work:* Whitney Mus, New York, NY; Smithsonian Inst, Washington, DC; Mazza Collection Gallery, Findlay Col, Ohio; Lena Y de Grummond Collection, Univ Southern Miss; Kerlen Collection, St Paul, Minn. *Comn:* Paintings, US Dept Interior, 68 & US Air Force Mus, 69, Washington, DC. *Exhib:* Audubon Artists Ann, Nat Acad Art Galleries, 60; Continental American Print Show, Whitney Mus, 62; Nat Acad Arts Ann, 66; Soc Illustrators Ann, Soc Illustrators Gallery, 68, 70 & 84; New Acquistions, Mus Am Illus, 84, New York, NY. *Teaching:* Instr painting & bk illus, Sch Visual Arts, 68-73; instr painting & illus, Robert Quackenbush Studio-Gallery, 68-; guest lectr, nationwide tours to universities, schools and libraries, 68- *Awards:* Citation, 50 Best Books Exhib, Am Inst Graphic Arts, 62; Edgar Allen Poe Special Award for Best Juvenile Mystery, Mystery Writers Am, 82; Citations (2), Best Children's Books of 1992, Soc Illustrs, 92. *Bibliog:* The art of Robert Quackenbush, Am Artist Mag, 65; Morton Schindel (dir), Signature Collection, Weston Woods Studio, 76; Something about the author, Gale Research Inc, Vol 7, 89. *Media:* All Media. *Publ:* Illusr, The Pilot (by James Fenimore Cooper), 68 & The Life of Washington (by Rev Mason L Weems), 74, Ltd Ed Club; The Scarlet Letter (by Nathaniel Hawthorne), Reader's Digest Bks, 84; auth & illusr, Robert Quackenbush's Treasury of Humor, Doubleday, 90; Evil Under the Sea, Pippin Press, 92. *Mailing Add:* 460 E 79th St New York NY 10021

QUAGLIATA, NARCISSUS
STAINED GLASS ARTIST, PAINTER
b Rome, Italy, May, 42; US citizen. *Study:* San Francisco Art Inst, BFA, 66 & MFA, 68. *Work:* Metrop Mus Art, NY; Oakland Mus, Calif; Corning Mus Glass, Corning, NY; many pvt collections. *Comn:* Glass mural, Pankow Devt Inc, Oakland, Calif; Reels (glass mural), Screen Actors Guild, Burbank, Calif; two glass murals, Nat Advan Systems, Santa Clara, Calif. *Exhib:* Forms of Faith, Judah L Magnes Mus, Berkeley, Calif, 86; Thirty Years of New Glass, Corning Mus Glass, 87; Crossroads, Washington Square, Washington, DC, 88; Eloquent Object, Oakland Mus, Calif, 89; Forty Oakland Artists, Oakland Mus, 90. *Teaching:* Taught and lectured on art and glass throughout US and abroad. *Awards:* Fel, Nat Endow Arts, 76 & 86. *Bibliog:* Suzanne Frantz (auth), Contemporary Glass, Harry Abrams, NY, 89; Andrew Moore (auth), Architectural Glass, Whitney Library Design, 89. *Publ:* Auth, Stained Glass from Mind to Light, Mattole Press, 76; The design process (series of articles), Professional Stained Glass, 88-89; Glass art: A collaborative effort, Glass Mag, 88. *Mailing Add:* 1520 Third St Oakland CA 94607

QUANDT, ELIZABETH (ELIZABETH QUANDT)
PRINTMAKER, PAINTER
b Oxfordshire, Eng, July 13, 22; US citizen. *Study:* San Francisco Art Inst, BFA, MFA. *Work:* Bibliot Nat, Paris; Stanford Univ Art Mus; Libr Cong, Washington, DC; Achenbach Found, San Francisco; Kaiser Hosps, Santa Rosa & Petaluma, Calif; New York Pub Libr. *Comn:* Ed of 20 Prints, City of San Francisco, 74. *Exhib:* One-woman exhib, Monoprint Drawings, Achenbach Found, Calif Palace Legion Honor, 75 & Five Printmakers, San Francisco Mus Mod Art, 71, Graystone Gallery, San Francisco, 86, J Noblett Gallery, Sonoma, 91, Santa Rosa Jr Col Art Gallery, Santa Rosa, Calif, 88; World Print Competition, 77; and others. *Teaching:* Instr printmaking & drawing, Santa Rosa Jr Col, Calif, 70-86. *Awards:* Djerassi Found Fel, 85, & 86. *Mem:* Calif Soc Printmakers; San Francisco Mus Mod Art. *Media:* Drawing, Watercolor. *Publ:* Illusr, Ten Poems of Frances Ponge, Greenwood Press, 83. *Dealer:* Graystone Gallery Sutter St San Francisco CA; J Noblett Gallery 22 Boyes Blvd Boyes Hot Springs CA. *Mailing Add:* 920 McDonald Ave Santa Rosa CA 95404

QUASIUS, SHARRON G
SCULPTOR
b Sheboygan, Wis, Dec 15, 48. *Study:* Univ Wis, BFA, 72; Univ Okla, MFA, 75. *Work:* Metrop Mus Art, New York; Mus Art, Tampa, Fla; Martin Marguilies, Coconut Grove, Fla; Long Ridge Mall, Rye, NY; Ctr For Arts, Vero Beach, Fla. *Comn:* Members Only (fabric sculpture), New York, 88. *Exhib:* Solo exhib, Queens Mus, Flushing, NY, 81, A Fabricated History, Ctr Arts, Vero Beach, Fla, 90 & Soft and Hard Margulies (sculpture), Tapian Gallery, Miami, Fla, 90; Homage, Danforth Mus, Mass, 81; Return of the Narrative, Palm Springs Desert Mus, 84; The Classic Tradition in Recent Painting and Sculpture, Aldrich Mus Contemp Art, Conn, 85; The Hot Center: Contemporary Art selected by Ivan Karp, Norton Ctr Arts, Ctr Col, Danville, Ky, 87; A Sigh of Relief, Wilson Arts Ctr, Hartley Sch, Rochester, NY, 87; Figure It Out: Visual Body Language, Helander Gallery, Palm Beach, Fla, 88; Fabrics, Gallery Henoch, New York, 88. *Awards:* Nat Endowment Arts Fel, 76; Wis Arts Bd Fel, 76 & 79. *Bibliog:* Jack Burnham (auth), Sharron Howlett at NAME, Art in Am, 80; Vivien Raynor (auth) A return to classicism in Ridgefield, 85 & Grace Glueck (auth), When today's artists raid the past, 85, New York Times; Edward Lucie Smith (auth), Am Art Now, 85; Tony Towle (auth), Sharon Quasies at O K Harris, Art Am, 9/87; Charles Jencks (auth), Post Modernism: The New Classicism in Art & Architecture, Rizzoli, 88; Robert Mahoney (auth), Arts Mag, 2/89. *Media:* All. *Dealer:* O K Harris Works of Art New York NY; Hokin Gallery Palm Beach FL. *Mailing Add:* c/o Hokin Gallery 245 Worth Ave Palm Beach FL 33480

QUAT, HELEN S
PRINTMAKER, PAINTER
b Brooklyn, NY, Oct 2, 18. *Study:* Skidmore Col; Columbia Univ; Art Students League; also with Raphael Soyer, Joseph Solman, Leo Manso, Ruth Leaf & Krishna Reddy; CW Post, Long Island Univ, MFA; Queens Col, MA, candidate Art Hist. *Work:* Univ Mass, Amherst; NJ State Mus, Trenton; Nassau Community Col; Butler Inst Am Art, Youngstown, Ohio; Slater Mus, Norwich, Conn. *Exhib:* Pratt Graphics Ctr Third Int Miniature Print Exhib, 68; 164th Ann, Pa Acad Fine Arts, 69; Int Exhib Women Artists, Ont & France, 69; State Univ NY Potsdam 10th Print Ann, 69-70; Nat Exhib Prints & Drawings, Okla Art Ctr, 69-72; Brooklyn Mus. *Teaching:* Art Appreciation, Roslyn Schs, Long Island, 89. *Awards:* Vadley Art Co Award for Graphics, Catharine Lorillard Wolfe Art Club, 67; Purchase Prize, Hunterdon Art Ctr, NJ, 70; Mr & Mrs Benjamin Ganeles Prize, Nat Asn Women Artists, 71. *Mem:* Nat Asn Women Artists; Soc of Am Graphic Artists; fel MacDowell Colony. *Media:* Mixed. *Mailing Add:* 16 Elliot Rd Great Neck NY 11021

QUAYTMAN, HARVEY
PAINTER
b Far Rockaway, NY, Apr 20, 37. *Study:* Syracuse Univ; Tufts Univ; Boston Mus Fine Arts Sch, BFA. *Work:* Tate Gallery, London; Whitney Mus Am Art & Mus Mod Art, New York; Israel Mus, Jerusalem; Carnegie Inst of Technol, Pittsburgh, Pa; and others. *Exhib:* Solo exhibs, Paula Cooper Gallery, 69 & 71, David McKee Gallery, NY, 75, 77, 78, 80, 82, 84, 86, 87, 88 & 90, Galerie Nordenhake, Malmo, Sweden, 82, 86, 87 & 90, Nielsen Gallery, Boston, Mass, 76, 78, 80, 83, 86 & 89, Hoffman/Borman Gallery, Los Angeles, 88, Persons Lindell Gallery, Helsinki, 90, Gilbert Brownstone Gallery, Paris, 90, Tony Oliver Gallery, Melbourne, Australia, 90 & Gallery NSW, Sydney, Australia, 90; Corcoran Biennale, Corcoran Gallery Art, Washington, DC, 87; Generations of Geometry, Whitney Mus Am Art, Equitable Ctr, NY, 87; Mus Mod Art, NY, 87-88; Germans Van Eck Gallery, NY, 89; 1989 Ljubljana Bienale 18, Int Centre Craphic Art, Yugoslavia, 89; 50 Years Collecting: Art at IBM, IBM Gallery Sci & Art, NY, 89; Abstraction in the Eighties, Rose Art Mus, Brandeis Univ, Waltham, Mass, 90; and others. *Teaching:* Former instr, Boston Mus Fine Arts Sch, Middlebury Col, Essex Col Art, Colchester, Eng & Sch Visual Arts, New York; instr, Cooper Union, Parsons Sch Design, New York; vis lectr, Harvard Univ, 82 & 83; adj asst prof, Hunter Col, 83. *Awards:* Artist Fel, Nat Endowment Arts; Guggenheim Fel, 79 & 85. *Bibliog:* Peter Clothier (auth), Harvey Quaytman, Artnews, 5/88; Charles Hagan (auth), Harvey Quaytman, Artforum, 12/88; Ellen Handy (auth), Harvey Quaytman, Arts, 1/89. *Media:* Miscellaneous Media. *Mailing Add:* 231 Bowery New York NY 10002

QUENTEL, HOLT
PAINTER
b Milwaukee, Wis, 1961. *Study:* Lawrence Univ, 79-83; Sch Art Inst Chicago, 84-85; Princeton Univ, 86-87. *Work:* Milwaukee Art Mus. *Exhib:* Trends, Milwaukee Art Mus, 85; Self Portraits, Then & Now, ARC Gallery, Chicago, 86; The New Poverty, John Gibson Gallery, New York, 87; Art at the End of the Social, Rooseum, Malmö, Sweden, 88; Baltimore Sales & Rental Gallery, Baltimore, 90; one-woman shows, Stux Gallery, New York, 90 & Busche Gallery, Cologne, Ger, 90. *Awards:* Elizabeth Richarson Award, 83; Smith Merit Scholar, Sch Art Inst Chicago, 84-86; Nat Endowment Arts, 89. *Bibliog:* Nancy Stapen (auth), Holt Quentel, Artforum, 12/87; Kay Larson (auth), Holt Quentel is the Standout in Two Group Shows, New York Mag, 2/8/88. *Mailing Add:* 58 Gansevoort St New York NY 10014

QUEST, CHARLES FRANCIS
PAINTER, EDUCATOR
b Troy, NY, June 6, 04. *Study:* Washington Univ Sch Fine Arts, St Louis, Mo, 24-29; advan study in Paris, 29; summer study, Spain, France & England, 60.

Work: Brit Mus & Victoria & Albert Mus, London; Nat Mus, Stockholm; Bibliot Nat, Paris; Mus Mod Art & Metrop Mus Art, New York; plus 45 mus & many pvt collections worldwide. *Comn:* Altar painting, St Mary's Church, Helena, Ark, 34; baptistry murals, St Michael & St George Episcopal Church, St Louis, Mo, 34; altar painting, Trinity Episcopal Church, St Louis, 35; altar painting, Old Cathedral, St Louis, 59-60. *Exhib:* Soc Am Graphic Artists Ann, New York, 46-; Les Peintres Graveurs Actuels Aux Etats-Uni, Bibliot Nat, Paris, 51; Am Watercolor, Drawings & Prints Exhib, Metrop Mus Art, New York, 52; Art in the Embassies Prog, Dept of State, Washington, DC, 67; one-man show, Mint Mus, NC, 79, Bethesda Art Gallery, Md, 83, Jerald Melberg Gallery, Charlotte, NC, 84 & Hampton III Gallery, Greenville, SC, 92; plus 109 group & one-man exhibs in mus & galleries throughout world. *Teaching:* Instr art, St Louis Pub Schs, Mo, 29-44; prof art, Washington Univ Sch Fine Arts, 44-71, emer prof, 71- *Awards:* Recipient of 53 prizes and awards. *Bibliog:* Article, St Louis Post Dispatch, 60; Art in St Louis, KMOX-TV, St Louis, 68; article, Greenville News, SC, 72; and others. *Mem:* St Louis Club; Soc Am Graphic Artists, New York; Philadelphia Color Print Soc; St Louis Artists Guild; Print Club Philadelphia. *Media:* Oil. *Dealer:* Hampton III Gallery Taylors SC 29678; Bethesda Art Gallery 7950 Norfolk Ave Bethesda MD 20814. *Mailing Add:* 200 Hillswick Rd Tryon NC 28782

QUEST, DOROTHY (JOHNSON)
PAINTER, EDUCATOR
b St Louis, Mo, Feb 28, 09. *Study:* Washington Univ Sch Fine Arts, St Louis, Mo, 28-33; study in Europe, 29; Columbia Univ, summer 37. *Work:* Erskine Col, Due West, SC; St Luke's Hospital, Columbus, NC; Washington & Lee Univ, Va; Bob Jones Univ, Greenville, SC; Univ Eastern Ill, Charleston; Washington Univ (Umrath Hall), St Louis, Mo. *Comn:* Portrait of Dr John S Bradshaw, Dr Wm R Bosien, Dr John Preston & Dr Roy Morgan, comn by St Luke's Hosp, Columbus, NC, 79; portrait, J Fred Buzhardt, Pres Nixon's atty, 79; portrait, Dr Iranaeus McCane, Erskine Col, 80; portrait, Ralph H Cuthbertson, pres Stevens Beechcraft, Greenville Airport, 80; portraits of Mr & Mrs Arthur Farwell, Lanier Libr, Tryon, NC; plus over 650 other portraits, 31- *Exhib:* One-man shows, St Louis Club, Pierre Laclede Bldg, Clayton, Mo, 64, Tryon Fine Arts Ctr, NC, 72 & Fine Arts Ctr, Anderson, SC, 75; Southern Vt Artists Asn; Tryon Fine Arts Ctr, NC; Anderson Art Ctr, SC; Hampton III Gallery, Taylors, SC; and many others. *Pos:* Lectr painting, St Louis City Art Mus, radio sta KMOX & KSD. *Teaching:* Instr art, Community Sch, St Louis, 36-38; head art dept, Acad Sacred Heart, St Louis, 39-41 & Maryville Col, St Louis, 44-45; instr art, Tryon Fine Arts Ctr, 71-78. *Bibliog:* Walter Orthwein (auth), article, 67 & Lynn Hawkins (auth), articles, 69 & 82, St Louis Globe Democrat; feature article in Spartanburg Herald, SC, 10/4/79. *Mem:* Tryon Painters & Sculptors, Inc; St Louis Post Dispatch; St Louis Artists Guild. *Media:* Oil. *Dealer:* Hampton III Gallery Taylors SC 29678. *Mailing Add:* 200 Hillswick Rd Tryon NC 28782

QUICK, EDWARD RAYMOND
MUSEUM DIRECTOR, DIRECTOR
b Los Angeles, Calif, Mar 22, 43. *Study:* Univ Calif, Santa Barbara, with Dr Herbert Cole, BA, 72, MA, 77. *Collections Arranged:* Art Inc, 79; George Sugarman, 81; Views of a Vanishing Frontier, 84; Johann Berthelsen, 88; Swope Art Mus Collections, 87. *Pos:* Asst cur, Santa Barbara Mus Art, Calif, 77-78; dir registration, Joslyn Art Mus, Omaha, Nebr, 80-85; dir, Sheldon Swope Art Mus, Terre Haute, Ind, 86- *Teaching:* Mus Mgt, Ind State Univ, Terre Haute, 89- *Mem:* Am Asn Mus (map surveyor, 85-; Inst Coun Mus; Arts Illiana (bd pres, 86, secy, 88); Asn Ind Mus (bd, 88-); Midwest Mus Conf. *Publ:* Contribr, Regional styles of drawing in Italy: 1600-1700, Univ Calif, Santa Barbara, 77; contribr, Registrars on Record: essays on museum collections management, Am Asn Mus, 88; ed, Johann Berthelsen: An American master painter, Swope Art Mus, 88. *Mailing Add:* Sheldon Swope Art Mus 25 S Seventh St Terre Haute IN 47807

QUIGLEY, MICHAEL ALLEN
ADMINISTRATOR
b Buffalo, NY, Oct 28, 50. *Study:* Univ Pa, BA(art hist), 71. *Collections Arranged:* Joan Jonas/Stage Sets, 76, Material Pleasures/The Fabric Workshop, 79 & Art Materialized, 81, Independent Curators Inc, Inst Contemp Art, Univ Pa. *Pos:* Mus asst, Nat Collection of Fine Arts, Smithsonian Inst, Washington, DC, summer 1971; curatorial asst, Inst of Contemp Art, Univ Pa, 71-75, asst dir, 75-79; assoc dir, The Fabric Workshop, Philadelphia, 79-80, dir, 80- *Mailing Add:* 2238 Bainbridge St Philadelphia PA 19146

QUIGLEY, ROBIN L
JEWELER, METALSMITH
b New York, NY, 47. *Study:* Tyler Sch Art, Elkins Park, Pa, BFA, 74; RI Sch Design, Providence, MFA, 76. *Exhib:* Craft Today USA, Musee Des Arts Decoratifs, Paris, France, 89; Function--Non-Function, Rezac Gallery, Chicago, Ill, 89; New Bronze Age, Soc Art Crafts, Pittsburgh, Pa, 91; Neoteric Jewelry, Snug Harbor Cult Ctr, Staten Island, NY, 91; American Jewellery & Metalwork, Art Gallery Western Australia, Perth, 92; and others. *Teaching:* Prof, Philadelphia Col Art, 76-78; asst prof, RI Sch Design, 81- *Awards:* Craftsman Fel, Nat Endowment Arts, 79 & 86. *Media:* Precious Metals, Bronze. *Mailing Add:* c/o CDK Gallery 24 W 57th St New York NY 10019

QUILLER, STEPHEN FREDERICK
PAINTER, PRINTMAKER
b Osmond, Nebr, Aug 15, 46. *Study:* Colo State Univ, BA, 68. *Work:* City Medford Art Collection, Ore; Petro-Lewis Corp Gallery, Colo Coun Arts, United Bank Denver Pub Collection & Cent Bank Denver, Colo; Colorado Springs Fine Arts Ctr. *Comn:* Gov's Export Award (painting), Colo Coun Arts, Denver, 79; City of Creede (mural), Colo Coun Arts. *Exhib:* One-man show, Foothills Art Ctr, Golden, Colo, 73; Am Watercolor Soc, 73 & 76 & Nat Soc Painters Casein & Acrylic, 74 & 76-78, Nat Acad Design, New York; Rocky Mountain Nat, Foothills Art Ctr, Golden, Colo, 74-75, 77-79 & 81; Watercolor USA, Springfield Art Mus, Mo, 77; American & Italian Printmakers, Sangre de Cristo Art Ctr, Pueblo, Colo, 80; and others. *Teaching:* Instr art, SW Watercolor Soc, Dallas, spring 76; instr art, NMex Watercolor Soc, Albuquerque, spring 79; guest artist-in-res intaglio, Adams State Col, Alamosa, Colo, fall 81; instr painting & printmaking, Adams State Col, 81-89. *Awards:* John Wegner Mem Award, Nat Soc Painters Casein & Acrylic, 76; Alta Woodcarvers Award, Rocky Mountain Nat Watermedia, 78; Gov's Award, Colo Coun Arts, 79. *Bibliog:* Web Allison (auth), Steve Quiller: Creede's artist in residence, Colo Country Life, San Luis Valley, 11/72; G A Minshew (auth), Spotlight on the artist, Scene, SW Watercolor Soc, 4/75; Susan Meyer (auth), 40 Watercolorists And How They Work, Watson-Guptill, 78. *Mem:* Rocky Mountain Nat Watermedia; Nat Soc Painters Casein & Acrylic; Watercolor West; Artists Equity Asn; Watercolor Asn Ala; and others. *Media:* Watercolor, Casein; Intaglio. *Publ:* Auth, Watercolor Page, Am Artist Mag, 5/75; coauth, Watermedia, Watson-Guptill, 5/83; Water Media: Processes & Possibilities, 5/86 & auth, Color Choices, 9/89, Watson-Guptill; Water Media: Watercolor & Gouache (video), Water Media: Acrylic & Casein (video), Color Concepts (video) & Color for the Painter (video), Chrysal Productions. *Mailing Add:* Arts Adams State Col Alamosa CO 81102

QUINN, BRIAN GRANT
SCULPTOR, PAINTER
b Wahoo, Nebr, Oct 21, 50. *Study:* Nebr Wesleyan Univ, with Maynard Whitney, BAE; Ariz State Univ, with Ben Goo, MFA. *Work:* Weber State Col, Odgen, Utah; Ariz State Univ, Tempe; Tucson Art Mus, Ariz; Univ NMex; and others. *Comn:* Sculpture, Blue Ribbon Food, Phoenix, Ariz, 81; sculpture, Median Inst, Pittsburgh, Pa, 83; sculpture, Northern Ariz Univ, 83; sculpture, Nebr Wesleyen Univ, 87; sculpture, Lincoln Nebr Pub Sch, 87; sculpture, Glendale Community Col, 90. *Exhib:* Jewelry/Small Sculpture Invitational Exhib, Weber State Col, Ogden, Utah, 77 & 81; Fac Exhib, Ariz State Univ, 80; 14th & 16th Southwest Invitational, Yuma Arts Ctr, 80 & 82; Ariz Biennial, Tucson Art Mus, 80-84; 1st & 2nd Northern Ariz Univ Sculpture Invitational, 80 & 81; 13th-18th Midwestern Invitationals, O'Rourke Gallery, Moorhead, Minn, 81-86; 17th Annual National Drawing & Small Sculpture Show, Del Mar Col, Tex, 83; and others. *Pos:* Preparator, Phoenix Art Mus, 75; artist-in-residence, Nat Endowment Art, 75-76; asst to Fritz Scholder, 75-82. *Teaching:* Vis instr sculpture, Glendale Community Col, 76-90; lectr sculpture, Ariz State Univ, Tempe, 80 & 81; prof sculpture & jewelry, Glendale Community Col, 90-, cur art collection, 90- *Awards:* Fred Wells Purchase Award, Small Sculpture and Drawing Exhib, Nebr Wesleyan Univ, 76; Jurors Award, First & Third Ariz Wood-in-Art Exhib, 77-79, Ariz State Univ; Jurors Award, Galeria Mesa, 85. *Bibliog:* James Mills (auth), Quinn works express beauty, lyricism yet remain lighthearted, Roundup, Denver Post, 10/9/77; Barbara Cortright (auth), Brian Quinn, Artspace, winter 82-83; Kelly Walton (auth), Sculptor, painter? Always an artist, City Life, Phoenix Gazette, 12/21/83; Barbara Cortright (auth), Brian Quinn at Northern Arizona Univ and the University of New Mexico, Artspace, spring 84. *Mem:* Southern Asn of Sculptors; Japanese Sword Soc of the US. *Dealer:* Fagen-Peterson Fine Art 7077 Main St Scottsdale AZ 85251 2; Ann Jacob Gallery Phipps Plaza 3500 Peachtree Rd NE Atlanta GA 30326. *Mailing Add:* 6132 E Lincoln Dr Paradise Valley AZ 85253

QUINN, HENRIETTA REIST
COLLECTOR, PATRON
b Lancaster, Pa, Dec 11, 18. *Study:* Edgewood Park Jr Col. *Collection:* American primitive paintings; eighteenth century porcelain; eighteenth century miniature memoribilia; eighteenth century American and English furniture. *Mailing Add:* Rollings Meadows Cornwall PA 17016

QUINN, NOEL JOSEPH
PAINTER, INSTRUCTOR
b Pawtucket, RI, Dec 25, 15. *Study:* RI Sch Design, grad, 36, Hon BFA, 90, fel, Paris; Parsons Sch Fine & Appl Arts, Paris & Italy, cert dipl; Ecole Beaux Arts; also with Andre L'hote & Andre Cassandre; Nat Gallery & Kaiser Frederick Mus, Berlin, Ger. *Work:* Butler Art Inst, Youngstown, Ohio; Air Force Acad, Denver; Pentagon, Libr of Cong & House of Rep, Washington, DC; and others. *Comn:* Thoroughbred Racing (portfolio of paintings), Los Angeles Turf Club, 60. *Exhib:* American Paintings & Prints, Metrop Mus Art, New York, 52; Hallmark Int Show, Wildenstein Galleries, New York, 53; Southwest Watercolor Soc Show, Southern Methodist Univ, Dallas, 69; one-man show, Yoseido Gallery, Tokyo, 55; plus many others. *Teaching:* Instr watercolor, Otis Art Inst, 53-75; guest instr, Palo Verdes Art Ctr, 76-77. *Awards:* Cert of Esteem for work in Korea & Japan, Secy Defense Charles E Wilson, 55; Watercolor USA Award, Springfield Art Mus, 64; Alumni of the Year Award, RI Sch Design, 81; and others. *Bibliog:* Norman Kent (auth), 100 American Watercolorists, Watson-Guptill, 69; feature article, Today's Art Mag, 2/80; California Watercolorists 1930-1960, Hillcrest, 84. *Mem:* Nat Watercolor Soc (pres, 63); Soc Motion Picture illusr (pres, 65-68); fel Int Inst Arts & Lett. *Media:* Watercolor. *Interests:* Creator of new language of symbols for color and value in bas-relief for education of the blind. *Publ:* Auth, article, Am Artist Mag, 5/63; Scene, Southwestern Watercolor Soc Mag; The California Style, 85. *Mailing Add:* 3946 San Rafael Ave Los Angeles CA 90065

QUINN, THOMAS PATRICK, JR
PAINTER
b Honolulu, Hawaii, June 5, 38. *Study:* Col of Marin, Kentfield, Calif, 56-58, Art Ctr Col Design, Pasedena, Calif, BA, 58-63. *Work:* Leigh Yawkey Woodson Art Mus, Wasau, Wis; Wildlife Am West Mus (permanent collection), Jackson, Wyo. *Comn:* Painting, Monterey Bay Aquarium, Calif, 84. *Exhib:* Nat Exhib Alaskan Wildlife, Alaskan Mus Art, Anchorage, 82; The Nature of the Best, Southern Alleghenies Mus Art, Loretto, Pa, 86; solo exhib, Frederic Remington Art Mus, Ogdensburg, NY, 88; NY Mus Natural Hist; Alexander Koenig Mus, Bonn, Ger; Frederic Remington Art Mus, Ogdensburg, NY; Wildlife Am West Mus, Jackson, Wyo; Gilcrease Mus, Tulsa, Okla, 92; 25 Artists Nature Exhib, Zeist, Holland, 92. *Bibliog:* Thomas Fox (auth), The elusive quality of a wild thing, Southwest Art, 83; Tom Davis (auth), Influencing the eye, Wildlife Art News, 87; M Stephen Doherty (auth), Thomas Quinn, Am Artist, 88. *Mem:* Soc Animal Artists; Trumpeter Swan Soc. *Media:* Mixed Media. *Publ:* Auth, First Person, Sports Illus, 83; The Working Retrievers, E P Dutton, 83; contribr, Wildlife Painting Techniques of Modern Masters, Watson Guptill, 85; Wildfowl Art, Ward Found, 86; Auth, R Riviere, Thomas Quinn on Art: Illustration and Inspiration, Art Today, 87; Wind, Wad & Waterverf (Dutch), 91. *Dealer:* Thomas Beckett Gallery Ltd 142 James St S Hamilton Ont L8P 3A2 Canada. *Mailing Add:* 175 Third St Pt Reyes Station CA 94956

QUINN, WILLIAM
PAINTER
b St Louis, Mo, Sept 5, 29. *Study:* Washington Univ, BFA, study with Paul Burlin & Carl Holty; Univ Ill, MFA, 57. *Work:* Butler Inst of Am Art, Youngstown, Ohio; Brooks Mem Art Gallery, Memphis, Tenn; Nelson-Atkins Gallery, Kansas City, Mo; St Louis Art Mus; Weatherspoon Art Gallery, Univ NC; High Mus Art, Mo; and others. *Comn:* High Mus, Atlanta, Ga; Mulvane Art Ctr, Topeka, Kans; Univ Mo, Columbia; Mus Art, Ft Lauderdale, Fla; Mexican-Am Cult Inst, Mexico City; and many others. *Exhib:* Twenty-two one-man shows. *Teaching:* Prof painting & drawing, Washington Univ, 58- *Awards:* Miliken Travel Scholar, Washington Univ, 58; Cité Des Arts Fel, Paris, France, 82; Painting Fel, Nat Endowment Art, 86; and over 30 other awards in regional museums & galleries. *Media:* Oil, Gouache. *Mailing Add:* Sch of Fine Arts Washington Univ St Louis MO 63130

QUINSAC, ANNIE-PAULE
HISTORIAN, WRITER
b Bouches du Rhone, France, Aug 2, 45. *Study:* Univ Montpellier, 59-61; Paris, DES, 63; Sorbonne, Paris, PhD, 68. *Collections Arranged:* Ottocento Painting in Am Collections (auth, catalog), NY Cult Ctr, Columbia Mus Arts & Mass Inst Technol, 72-73; Exhib Segantini: Japan 1978, Japan, 78; Millet Corot and the Sch of Barbizon (auth, catalog), Japan, 82; An Anthology of Occidental Landscape (auth, catalog), Japan, 83-84. *Pos:* Mitarbeiter, Inst Kunstwissenshaft, Zurich, 74-75. *Teaching:* Prof art history, Univ SC, 70- *Awards:* Mellon Fel, Univ Pittsburgh, 69-70. *Mem:* Nat Soc Lit & Arts; Col Art Asn Am; Arte Lombarda Milan; Soc Amis de Segantini. *Res:* 19th century Italian studies; currently working on Rosa Boneur and Giuseppe Pellizza da Volpedo. *Publ:* Auth, Peinture Divisionniste Italienne: Origines et premiers developpements, Klincksieck, 72; auth, Catalogue raisonne of Giovanni Segantini, Electa Editcice, Milan, 82; auth, Vent'anni di vita artistica europea nei cartegi inediti de Giovanni Segantini e suoi mecenati a cura di Annie-Paule Quinsa, Milan (in press). *Mailing Add:* Dept Art Univ SC Main Campus Columbia SC 29208

QUIRARTE, JACINTO
HISTORIAN, ADMINISTRATOR
b Jerome, Ariz, Aug 17, 31. *Study:* San Francisco State Col, BA, 54, MA, 58; Nat Univ Mex, PhD, 64. *Pos:* Dir cult affairs, Ctr Venezolano Am, Caracas, 64-66; bd mem & vpres, San Antonio Arts Coun, 73-77; mem visual arts & humanities panel, Tex Comn on the Arts & Humanities, 76-80. *Teaching:* Art instr, Colegio Americano, Mexico City, 59-61; asst to Alberto Ruz Lhuillier, Seminario de Cultura Maya, Nat Univ Mex, 61-62; dir cult affairs, Centro Venezolano Americano, Caracas, 64-66; vis prof hist contemp art Latin Am & pre-Columbian art, Yale Univ, New Haven, Conn, 67; prof hist pre-Columbian, Colonial & contemp art of Mex & Guatemala, Univ Tex, Austin, 67-72; vis prof hist pre-Colombia art of Mesoamerica & Colonial art of Latin Am, Univ NMex, 71; dean, Col of Fine & Applied Arts, Univ of Tex, San Antonio, 72-78; dir & prof art hist, Research Ctr Arts & Humanities, 77- *Mem:* Mid-Am Col Art Asn; Soc for Am Archaeol; Int Cong of Americanists; Int Cong of the Hist of Art; Int Cong of Ethnology & Anthrop. *Publ:* Auth, El estilo artistico de Izapa, Cuadernos de Historia del Arte, No 3, Instituto de Investigaciones Esteticas, Univ Nac Autonoma de Mexico, 73; auth, Izapan style art--a study of its form and meaning, Studies in Pre-Columbian Art & Archaeology, No 10, Dumbarton Oaks, Washington, DC, 73; auth, Mexican American Artists, 73 & Maya Vase, (in prep), Univ Tex Press, Austin. *Mailing Add:* Dept Art Design Univ of Tex San Antonio TX 78285

QUIRK, THOMAS CHARLES, JR
PAINTER
b Pittsburgh, Pa, Dec 31, 22. *Study:* Edinboro State Col, BS, 48; Univ Pittsburgh, MEd, 64. *Work:* Butler Inst Am Art, Youngstown, Ohio; Chatham Col, Pittsburgh; Pittsburgh Pub Schs; Millersville State Col, Pa; Rutgers Univ, Camden, NJ. *Exhib:* Pa Acad Fine Arts Ann, Philadelphia, 69; Drawing & Small Sculpture Ann, Ball State Univ, 71; Nat Acad Design Ann, New York, 74; Philadelphia Watercolor Club Ann, 74 & 79; Philadelphia Watercolor Club, 76; Ann Nat Soc of Painters in Casein & Acrylic, New York, 76 & 79; and others. *Pos:* Artist-in-residence, Everhart Mus, Scranton, Pa, 72- *Teaching:* Emeritus Prof Art, Kutztown Unov of Pa, 66-89. *Awards:* Dawson Mem Prize, Philadelphia Watercolor Club, 74. *Mem:* Soc Painters in Casein & Acrylic; Philadelphia Watercolor Club; Guild of Natural Sci Illustr. *Media:* Multimedia. *Publ:* Auth, Reptiles and Amphibians, Dover Publs; Fishes of the Western Atlantic, Dover Publs. *Mailing Add:* 310 E Main St Kutztown PA 19530

QUISGARD, LIZ WHITNEY
PAINTER, SCULPTOR
b Philadelphia, Pa, Oct 23, 29. *Study:* Md Inst Col Art, dipl, 49, BFA(summa cum laude), 66; studied with Morris Louis, 57-60; Rinehart Sch Sculpture, MFA, 66. *Work:* Univ Baltimore; Johns Hopkins Univ; Libyan Mission UN, Englewood, NJ, Can Imperial Bank Com, New York, Great Northern Nekoosa Corp, Norwalk, Conn, Quality Inns, Newark, NJ, Datalogy Corp, Valhalla, NY, Rosenberg Diamond Corp, New York, Ctr Club, Baltimore, Md; Fordham Univ, New York; Miss Mus, Jackson; and others. *Comn:* Mural painting, William Fell Sch, Baltimore, 78; mural painting, Urban Wall, Atlanta, Ga, 90; floor painting, Vets Stadium, Philadelphia, 92. *Exhib:* Corcoran Biennial Am Painting, 63; Univ Colo Show, 63; Am Painting & Sculpture Ann, Pa Acad Fine Arts, 64; Art Inst Chicago Ann, 65; solo exhibs, Henri Gallery, Washington, DC, 87, Savannah Col Art & Design, Savannah, Ga, 87, Three Financial Plaza, Chicago, 88, Franz Bader Gallery, Washington, DC, 89, Fairleigh Dickinson Univ, Hackensack, NJ, 90, Herr-Chambliss Gallery, Hot Springs, Ark, 90 Retrospective Gallery, La Jolla, Calif, 90; Fordham Univ, New York, 85; Huntington Col, Ind, 91; Broadway Windows, New York, 92; and others. *Pos:* Theatre designer, Goucher Col, Theatre Hopkins & Ctr Stage, Baltimore, 66-; art critic, Baltimore Sun, 69 & 70; area reviewer, Craft Horizons Mag, 69- *Teaching:* Instr painting & design, Baltimore Hebrew Congregation, 62-; instr painting & color theory, Md Inst, Baltimore, 65-80; lectr design, Goucher Col, 66-69; lectr art hist, Univ Md, Catonsville, 69-70; instr painting, Baltimore Jewish Community Ctr, 74. *Awards:* Rinehart Fel, Md Inst, 64-66; Best in Show, Loyola Col, 66; Florsheim Art Fund Grant, 91; and others. *Bibliog:* B Rose (auth), article, Art Int, 11/62; articles, Arts Mag, 11/62 & Art News, 11/62, Baltimore Sun, 4/78 & 10/88, Artspeak, 11/84 & 9/85, Manhatten Arts, 3/84, New Art Examiner, 3/89, NY Times, 2/90 & 7/92. *Media:* Oil, Watercolor; All media. *Publ:* Auth, Baltimore's top twelve, Baltimore Mag, 5/69; auth & illusr, An artist's travel log, Baltimore News Am, 71; illusr, Shore Writers' Sampler, Friendly Harbor Press, 87. *Mailing Add:* 145 Reade St New York NY 10013

R

RAAB, GAIL B
COLLAGE ARTIST, PAINTER
b New York, NY, Jan 15, 34. *Study:* Univ Colo with Louis Shanker, 53; Univ Mex, 54; Tyler Sch Fine Arts, BFA, 55; Queens Col. *Work:* Philadelphia Mus; Seventeen Mag, New York; Scherling-Plough Corp, NJ; CBS Recordings, New York. *Comn:* Paintings, Columbia Broadcasting, New York, 86; wall assemblage, Schering-Plough Corp, NJ, 88; wall collages, Haines, Lundberg Waehler, New York, 89. *Exhib:* Solo-exhibs, Viridian Gallery, New York, 80, 82, Whitney-Clark Gallery, Lenox, Mass, 88 & Bachelier, Cardonsky, Kent, Conn, 90; Paper Show, Philadelphia, 88 & 89; Paper Works, Berkshire, Pittsfield, Mass, 88 & 89 & Nassau Co, New York, 88 & 89; Nat Asn Women Artists Juried Show, Nat Acad Design, New York, 88 & 89; Marabella Gallery, Bks & Co, New York, 90. *Pos:* Art Reach dir, Whitney Mus, New York, 89-90. *Awards:* Medal of Honor, 80 & C Winston Mem Prize, 88, Nat Asn Women Artists; Martha Reed Mem Award. *Bibliog:* Jeanne Paris (auth), The artists inspiration, Newsday, 6/2/78; Jerry Tallmer (rev), New York Post, 6/3/78; Margaret Pomfret (rev), Arts Mag, 1/80. *Mem:* Nat Asn Women Artists (exec bd); Long Island Craftsman Guild. *Media:* Mixed Media, Acrylic. *Mailing Add:* 300 E 74th St New York NY 10021

RABB, (MR & MRS) IRVING W
COLLECTORS
Study: Mr Rabb, Harvard Univ, AB, Harvard Bus Sch; Mrs Rabb, Smith Col, AB; Radcliffe Col, AM. *Mem:* Trustee, Mus Fine Arts & Inst Contemp Art, Boston. *Collection:* Twentieth century sculpture, including Henry Moore, Giacometti, Maillot, Arp, Lipshitz, Calder, Rickey, Nevelson, Kirk and Laurens; twentieth century drawings and collages, with emphasis on Cubism and sculpture drawings. *Mailing Add:* 1010 Memorial Dr Cambridge MA 02138

RABB, JEANNETTE See Solomon, (Mrs) Sidney L

RABB, MADELINE M
ADMINISTRATOR, PAINTER
Study: Univ Md, College Park, 61-63; Md Inst Col Art, Baltimore, BFA(painting), 66; Ill Inst Technol, Inst Design, MS(visual design), 75. *Exhib:* In Our Own Image: Works by Woman, Capital East Graphics, Washington, DC, 80; The Chicago Exchange Group, Chicago State Univ Gallery, 81; The Young Collector's Sale, Renaissance Soc Invitational, Univ Chicago, 82; Jazzonia Gallery, Detroit, Mich, 83; Members Show, Arts Club Chicago, 84-85. *Pos:* Asst dir art & production, Tuesday Publs, Chicago, 66-68; vpres-bus manager, Myra Everett Designs Inc, Chicago, 77-78; account exec, Corporate Concierge, Chicago, 78-79; owner, Madeline Murphy Rabb Studio, Chicago, 79-83; exec dir, Chicago Office Fine Arts, 83-90; pres, Murphy Rabb Inc, Chicago, 83-90. *Awards:* Numerous Awards

for work and service to publ. *Bibliog:* Big City Cultural Bosses (article), Ebony Mag, 88. *Mem:* Arts Club Chicago; Nat Conf Artists; Chicago Artists Coalition; Art Table Inc; Ill Arts Alliance. *Publ:* Auth, Removing Cultural Viaducts: Initiatives for Traditionally Underserved Audiences, Connections Quarterly, 86; Chicago: An Artistic Renaissance Under Way, Am Visions mag, 87. *Mailing Add:* 161 E Chicago Ave Chicago IL 60611

RABBIT, RUNNING See Red Star, Kevin

RABINOVICH, RAQUEL
PAINTER, SCULPTOR
b Buenos Aires, Arg, Mar 30, 29. *Study:* Univ Cordoba, Arg; Univ Edinburgh; Atelier Andre LHote, Paris. *Work:* World Bank Fine Art Collection, Washington, DC; Univ Art Mus, Austin, Tex; Container Corp Am; Frances & Sidney Lewis Collection; Walker Art Ctr; Cincinnati Art Mus. *Comn:* Homage to R C Murphy (outdoor sculpture); indoor sculpture, Banco Provincia Buenos Aires, New York; and others. *Exhib:* Hecksher Mus, Huntington, NY, 74; Susan Caldwell Gallery, New York, 75; City Univ New York Grad Ctr, 78; Jewish Mus, New York, 79; PS 1, New York, 79; Kouros Gallery, New York, 83; Ctr Int-Am Relations, NY, 83; Sculpture on the Square, Robert Moses Plaza, Fordham Univ Lincoln Ctr, New York, 85; Sculpture installation and Drawings, The Bronx Mus Arts, New York, 86-87; Am Soc, NY, 90. *Teaching:* Lectr, Whitney Mus, 83-86 & Marymount Manhattan Col, 84-90, New York. *Bibliog:* John Gruen (auth), article, Soho Weekly News, 75; Grace Glueck (auth), article, NY Times, 79; Bill Zimmer (auth), catalog essay, 81; John Stringer (auth), article, Arte Informa, 83; George Collins (auth), article, Arts, 83; Barry Schwabsky (auth), catalog essay, 86-87; Michael Kimmelman (auth), Art Rev, NY Times, 90; Fatima Bercht (auth), catalog essay, 90. *Mem:* Abstract Am Artists. *Media:* Oil; Glass. *Mailing Add:* 141 Lomoree Rd Rhinebeck NY 12572

RABINOVICH, RHEA SANDERS See Sanders, Rhea (Rhea Sanders Rabinovich)

RABINOVITCH, WILLIAM AVRUM
PAINTER, SCULPTOR
b New London, Conn, Sept 16, 36. *Study:* Worcester Polytech Inst, BSME; Boston Mus Sch Fine Arts; San Francisco Art Inst, MFA; Whitney Mus, independent study prog, 73. *Work:* US Post Office, Canal St, New York; Monterey Conf Ctr, Calif; Fairmont Hotel, San Francisco & New Orleans; Mercedes Benz Show Room, San Rafael, Calif. *Comn:* Mural, Fairmont Hotel, 74; US Post Off, Canal St, New York, 87. *Exhib:* One-man shows, Worcester Polytech Inst, 83 & Ingrid Cusson Gallery, New York, 88; Moscow USSR, 91, Gallerie Illuminati, Santa Monica, Calif, 90, Barbara Mendes, Los Angeles, 90, Pacific Grove Art Ctr, Calif, 91; Whitney Counterweight, Soho Gallery, New York, 77, 79, 81 & 83; Allentown Art Mus, Pa, 86; San Francisco Art Inst, 87; plus many others. *Pos:* Dir, Whitney Counterweight, 77, 79 & 81; moderator, American Expressionism Panel Artist Talk on Art, New York, 89. *Teaching:* Instr, Gallatin Prog, New York Univ, 82. *Awards:* First Prize, Monterey Peninsula Mus Art, 65; Nat Endowment Arts Grant, 77; Grant, Artists Space, New York, 83. *Bibliog:* Barnaby Tulte (auth), Art World, 3/87 & 2/89; David Howard (dir), video documentary, San Francisco, 89; articles in New York and Am Art Revs, 89 & 90; 4 page article, Worcester Polytech Inst J, Worcester, Mass, winter 90. *Mem:* AMISA Computer Graphics Asn. *Media:* Multi. *Publ:* Cover artist, Jacob Boehme & Gregory of Nyssa: The Life of Moses, Paulist Press, 78. *Mailing Add:* PO Box 403 Canal St Station New York NY 10013

RABINOWITCH, DAVID
SCULPTOR
b Toronto, Ont, Mar 6, 43. *Work:* Mus Mod Art, New York; Mus Contemp Art, Los Angeles; Nat Gallery Can, Ottawa; Art Gallery, Ont, Toronto, Can; Mus Fine Arts, Montreal, Can; Musée de Que, Can; and others. *Comn:* Clocktower and PS 1, New York, 76; Forum Metall, City of Linz, Austria, 77; Documenta VI-VIII, Kassel, Ger, 77, 82 & 87; Situation Kunst, Ruhr Univ, Bochum, Ger, 86-90; Muzeum Historii Miasta, Lodz, Poland, 90. *Exhib:* One-man shows, Pollock Gallery, Toronto, 68, Carmen Lamanna, Toronto, 69-84, Helman Gallery, St Louis, 71, Rolf Ricke, Cologne, Ger 72 & 74, Bykert Gallery, New York, 73 & 75, Daniel Weinberg, San Francisco, 74-78, Annemarie Verna, Zürich, Switz, 77-92, Galerie m Bochum, Ger, 77-92, Richard Bellamy/Oil & Steel, New York, 78-92, Mus van Hedendaagse Kunst, Gent, Belg, 78, Mus Haus Lange, Krefeld, Ger, 78, Galerie Mailhot, Montreal, 79, Haus Ester, Krefeld, Ger, 87, Kunsthalle Tübigen, Ger, 87, Kunsthalle Bielefeld, Ger, 88, Kunstmuseum Düsseldorf, Ger, 88, Flynn, New York, 89-92, Galerie nächst St Stephan, Vienna, 90 & Kunsthalle Baden-Baden, 92; Art Gallery Ont, Toronto, 68-; Nat Gallery Can, Ottawa, 68-; Mus Mod Art, Paris, 72, 77, 82 & 91; Mus Mod Art, New York, 77 & 79; Zeitlos, Berlin, Ger, 88; Kroller-Muller Mus, Otterlo, Holland, 88; Einleuchten, Hamburg, Ger, 89-90; Kunstmuseum Winterthur, Switz, 92; Kaiser-Wilhelm Mus, Krefeld, Ger, 92; and others. *Awards:* Guggenheim Fel, 75; Can Coun Lynch Staunton Award, 77; Nat Endowment Arts, 86. *Bibliog:* David Carrier (auth), Arts, 91; Philippe Dagen (auth), Le Monde, 91; Barbara MacAdam (auth), Art News, 92. *Media:* All. *Publ:* Auth, article, Artforum, 91; article, Parkett, 91; article, Blast, 91; article, David Rabinowitch, Kunsthalle Baden-Baden; article, Drawings of a Beech Tree, Düsseldorf, 92. *Mailing Add:* 49 E First St New York NY 10003

RABINOWITCH, ROYDEN LESLIE
SCULPTOR
b Toronto, Ont, Mar 6, 43. *Study:* Self taught. *Work:* Mus Ludwig, Cologne, Ger; Mus Contemp Art, Gent, Belgium; Mönchengladbach Mus, Ger; Ulster Mus, Belfast, NIreland; Nat Gallery Australia, Canberra. *Comn:* Eloges de Fontenalle, Toronto Convention Ctr, Ont; Bell, Mus Contemp Art, Gent, Belg. *Exhib:* 10th Paris Biennial, Mus d'Art Mod, France, 77; Brooklyn Mus, 80; Mus Contemp Art, Gent, Belgium, 83 & 84; Lodz Mus, Poland, 84; Mönchengladbach Mus, Ger, 84; Künsthaus, Zurich, Switz, 85; and others. *Teaching:* Vis assoc, Clare Col, Cambridge Univ, Gt Brit, 84, vis fel, 85 & life assoc, 86- *Awards:* Can Coun Arts Bursary, 67-69 & 71-72 & Sr Arts Grant, 74, 76-77 & 79-80; Staunton Award, Can Coun, 86. *Bibliog:* David Bellman (auth), The Barrel Constructions of Royden Rabinowitch: Their Meaning and Effect, Orchard Press, Londonderry, NIreland, 83; Jan Holt (auth), Sculptures in Collection, Mus Contemp Art, Gent, Belg, 85; Johannes Claddess (auth), Royden Rabinowitch, Mus Mönchengladbach, Ger, 85. *Media:* Mixed. *Publ:* Auth, Development of the Early Sculpture Leading to the Most Recent Sculpture, Orchard Press, 83; auth, Notes on the handed - limited - numbered, developed manifold, In: Sculptors' Drawings, The Seagram Collection, 83. *Mailing Add:* Jan Ver Speyenstraat 15 Gent B-9000 Belgium

RABKIN, LEO
SCULPTOR, PAINTER
b Cincinnati, Ohio, July 21, 19. *Study:* Univ Cincinnati; NY Univ. *Work:* Mus Mod Art, Whitney Mus Am Art, Guggenheim Mus, New York; Smithsonian Inst; LaJolla Mus Contemp Art, Calif; Brooklyn Mus, NY; NC Mus, Raleigh; Newburger Mus, Purchase, NY. *Exhib:* Seven Painting & Sculpture Biennials, Whitney Mus Am Art, 59-69 & Drawings & Watercolor, 74 & 75; A Plastic Presence, San Francisco Mus Art, Milwaukee Art Ctr & Jewish Mus, 70; Storm King Art Ctr, Mountainville, NY, 70; one-man shows, La Jolla Mus Contemp Art, 81 & Marilyn Pearl Gallery, New York, 83, 85-86 & 90-91; Art Concrete, Nuremberg, WGer, 83; Persistence of Abstraction, Wichita, Kans, 92; and others. *Pos:* Hon vpres, Fine Arts Fed, New York. *Awards:* Ford Found Award for Watercolor, 61; First Prize for Watercolor, Silvermine Guild Artists, 61; Award Sculpture, First Ann Westchester, 67. *Mem:* Am Abstr Artists (pres, 64-78); US Comn Int Asn Art (secy, 68-70); Fine Arts Fedn New York (mem bd dirs, 70-), (hon vpres, 89-). *Media:* Box Constructions; Watercolor. *Collection:* Whirligigs; outsiders art; 20th Century American Art (outsider), Shaker Artifacts & Furniture; Glyptic (Sumerian); Primitive American Folk Art. *Publ:* Ed, American Abstract Artists, 1936-1966. *Dealer:* Maryland Pearl 420 W Broadway New York NY. *Mailing Add:* 218 W 20th St New York NY 10011

RACITI, CHERIE
PAINTER, SCULPTOR
b Chicago, Ill, June 17, 42. *Study:* Univ Ill, Urbana, 60-61; Memphis Col Arts, Tenn, 63-65; San Francisco State Univ, BA, 68; Mills Col, Oakland, MFA, 79. *Work:* San Francisco Mus of Mod Art, Calif; Mills Col, Oakland. *Exhib:* Whitney Mus Am Art Biennial, New York, 75; Los Angeles Inst Contemp Art, Calif, 76 & 78; one-woman shows, Adaline Kent Award Exhib, San Francisco Art Inst, 77, Fuller-Goldeen Gallery, San Francisco, 79 & Marianne Deson, Chicago, 80, Long Beach Mus, Calif, 82; Clocktower, 85, Artists Space, 88, New York; Angles Gallery & Fresno Mus, 87; Reese Bullen Gallery, Humboldt State Univ, Arcadia, Calif, 90; Terrain, San Francisco, Calif, 92; and others. *Teaching:* Lectr, Calif State Univ, Hayward, 74; lectr, San Francisco State Univ, Calif, 77-80, asst prof art, 80-84, assoc prof art, 84-89, prof art, 89-; instr, San Francisco Art Inst, Calif, 78. *Awards:* Adaline Kent Award, 76; Trefethen Fel, Mills Col, 79; Eureka Fel, Fleishhacker Found, 88. *Bibliog:* Lynn Hershman (auth), Resin painters, Artweek, 9/23/72; Claudia King (auth), 5 Women Artists in Las Vegas, Univ Nev, 3/75; Phillip Linhares (auth), interview, Currant, 4-5/75; Thomas Albright (auth), Art in the San Francisco Bay Area, 1945-1980, Univ Calif Press, 85; Moira Roth (ed), Connecting Conversations: Interviews with 28 Bay Area Woman Artists, Eucalyptus Press, 88. *Mem:* San Francisco Art Inst Artist Comt (mem, 74-85); New Langton Arts (bd mem, 88-). *Media:* Mixed Media. *Mailing Add:* 1045 17th St San Francisco CA 94107

RACKUS, GEORGE (KEISTUS)
PAINTER, PRINTMAKER
b Lithuania, May 29, 27; Can citizen. *Study:* Wayne Univ, 48-50; Ont Col Art, 50-52; with Andre L'Hote, 52-55; Ecole des Beaux Arts, Paris, 52-55. *Work:* Victoria & Albert Mus, London; New York Cent Libr; Nat Gallery Can; NB Mus, St John; Contemp Mus, Sao Paulo, Brazil; Lithuanian TSR Art Mus, Vilnius; R McLaughlin Gallery, Can; Art Gallery Ont, Can; and others. *Comn:* Murals (anodized aluminum), Howoco, Brussels, 69, Alcan Aluminum Ltd, Toronto, 70, Shell Can, Oakville, Ont, 70, Univ Western Ont, London, 71 & Dental Arts Bldg, Dunnville, Ont, 75. *Exhib:* Solo exhib, Galerie Foyer des Artists, Paris, 54-59, Anodized Aluminum Works, Commonwealth Inst, London, 70 & Anodized Aluminum Works & Prints, NB Mus, St John, 73; Agnes LeFort Galerie, Montreal, 60; Picture Loan Soc - Gallery, Toronto, 60, 63, 65, 66, 69 & 71; Gallery Moos, Toronto, 62; Fifth Ann Exhib Can Art, Montreal Mus, 62; Can Nat Art Gallery Tour for Australia, Nat Art Gallery, Victoria, 67, Nat Gallery, S Australia, Adelaide, 67 & Art Gallery New S Wales, Sydney, 68; Vilnius Contemp Mus, Lithuania, 79, 87 & 88; Brand Libr Art Gallery, Glendale, Calif, 81; Grimsby Art Gallery, Can, 86; Peel Region Art Gallery, Brampton, Can, 87; Goethe Inst, Toronto, 87; traveling exhibs, Lithuania Mus Tour, 88 & art exhib, Dum Polonii, Warsaw & Paltusky, Poland, 89-90. *Pos:* Admin & Cur, Glenhyrst Arts Coun, Brantford, Can, 62-63; admin, Colour & Form Soc, Can, 85-89, admin, 89- *Teaching:* Instr art, Dundas Valley Art Sch, Ont, 65-66, McMaster Univ, Hamilton, Ont, 68-69 & Brock Univ, St Catharines, Ont, 77-78. *Awards:* Print of Year, Soc Can Painter-Etchers & Engravers, 71; Graphic Award, Baltic Roots, Baltic Studies Asn, 78; First Prize Anodized Aluminum Work, Colour & Form Exhib, 81. *Bibliog:* Robert Ayre (auth), article, Montreal Star, 62; Robert Percival (cur),

doc, The New Brunswick Mus; Paul Duval (auth), doc, 88. *Mem:* Ont Soc Artists Can (pres, 86-88); Colour & Form Soc Can (pres, 74-76 & 79-84); The Print Consortium, USA. *Media:* Anodized Aluminum, Lithography. *Publ:* Auth, British sculpture at Montreal Museum, Weekly, 61; A painter speaks up, Globe & Mail, 62; Anodized aluminum as an art media, 71 & Exploring new media, Vol II, 71, Arts Mag, Can. *Mailing Add:* 1998 Lakeshore Rd W Mississauga ON L5J 1J8 Canada

RACZ, ANDRE
PAINTER, PRINTMAKER
b Cluj, Romania, Nov 21, 16; US citizen. *Study:* Univ Bucharest, BA, 35. *Work:* Mus Mod Art, Whitney Mus Am Art & New York Pub Libr, New York; Libr Cong, Washington, DC; Bibliot Nat, Paris. *Exhib:* 50 Yrs Am Art, Mus Mod Art, Paris, London, Belgrade & Barcelona, 55; Int Watercolor Biennial, Brooklyn Mus, 61; Nat Inst Arts & Lett, New York, 68; 50 Yrs American Printmaking, Mus Mod Art, 74; Surrealism & American Art 1931-1947, Rutgers Univ, 77; 50th Anniversary Retrospective, Atelier 17, Univ Wis, 77; Columbia Univ, 83; and others. *Teaching:* Prof painting, Columbia Univ, 51-, chmn div painting & sculpture, 64-73 & 75-77, prof emer painting, 83. *Awards:* Guggenheim Fel Printmaking, 56; Fulbright Res Scholar, Chile, 57; Ford Found Award, 62; Bankroft Award for Distinguished Teacher, Columbia Univ, 83. *Bibliog:* Carmen Valle (auth), Poets on painters & sculptors, Tiger's Eye, 49; Rosamel del Valle (auth), Una tarde con el pintor Andre Racz, Nacion, 49; Antonio Romera (auth), Andre Racz pintor y grabador, Ed Pacifico, 50. *Mem:* Am Asn Univ Prof. *Publ:* Auth, The Reign of Claws, 45, XII Prophets of Aleijadinho, 47, Via Crucis, 48, Mother & Child, 49 & Canciones Negras, 53. *Mailing Add:* PO Box 43 Demarest NJ 07627

RADAN, GEORGE TIVADAR
ADMINISTRATOR, HISTORIAN
b Budapest, Hungary, Dec 31, 23; US citizen. *Study:* Univ Budapest, MA, 46 PhD, 48, with Peter Pazmany; Ecole de Louvre, Paris AEM, 67. *Work:* Nat Maritime Mus, Haifa, Israel. *Collections Arranged:* Ships through the Ages (with catalog), Nat Maritime Mus, 55. *Pos:* Dir archeol, Ky State Univ & Wayne State Univ, 70-76; dir archeol excavations, Siena, 84. *Teaching:* Prof art hist, Villanova Univ, Pa, 60-, chmn dept art, 63-; prof art hist, Am Col in Paris, 66-67. *Awards:* Am Coun Learned Soc Scholarship to Hungary Acad Sci, 73 & 75; Outstanding Fac Publ Award, 85. *Mem:* Col Art Asn; Asn Ancient Historians. *Res:* Art historian dealing with ancient art and archeology. *Publ:* Auth, An Introduction to Ancient Art and Architecture, 67, Del Villanova Press; Coauth, The Archeology of Roman Pannonia, Univ Ky Press, 80; The Villanova University Art Collection: A Guide, Villanova Press, 86; and others. *Mailing Add:* Villanova Univ Dept Art Villanova PA 19085

RADECKI, MARTIN JOHN
ADMINISTRATOR, CONSERVATOR
b South Bend, Ind, Jan 4, 48. *Study:* Ind Univ, AB, 70; Intermuseum Conserv Lab (internship), 74-75. *Exhib:* Forgery: The Steele/Forsyth Controversy, 89. *Collections Arranged:* Conservation of Indiana Governors Portraits, Indianapolis Mus Art, 78. *Pos:* Apprentice conservator, Indianapolis Mus Art, 71-73, asst conservator, 73-74, actg chief conservator, 75-; conserv intern, Intermuseums Conserv Lab, 74-75, chief conservator, 75- *Mem:* fel Am Inst Conserv Historic & Artistic Works; Int Inst Conserv Historic & Artistic Works. *Res:* Treatment of blanched paintings; methods of forgery detection, specifically on late 14th-early 20th century American paintings. *Mailing Add:* 9029 Chestnut Ct Indianapolis IN 46260

RADES, WILLIAM L
PAINTER, SCULPTOR
b Milwaukee, Wis, Aug 13, 43. *Study:* Univ Wis, Milwaukee, BFA, 65, MFA, 68; San Francisco Art Inst, with Ron Nagle & Jack Jefferson, 66. *Work:* Santa Barbara Mus Art, Calif; Am Telephone & Telegraph, New York; Minneapolis Inst Art, Minn; Georgia Pacific Corp, Portland, Ore; Eastern Wash Univ, Cheney. *Comn:* Drawing on paper, Wash State Arts Comn & Evergreen State Col, Olympia, 79; Painting on paper, Wash State Arts Comn, Olympia, 80; Painted wood relief, Wash State Arts Comn, Spokane, 82. *Exhib:* Oregon Artists Under 35, Portland Art Mus, 74 & 77; Drawing USA, Minn Mus Art, 77; Washington Painting, Tacoma Art Mus, 77, 79 & 81; 21st Nat Chautauqua Exhib Am Art, New York, 78; Illusionism: Handmade, Henry Art Gallery, Univ Wash, Seattle, 81; Northwest Perspectives, traveling exhib in US, 82-84. *Teaching:* Instr drawing, Univ Wis, Milwaukee, 65-68; asst instr ceramics, San Francisco Art Inst, 66; vis asst prof drawing, Ore State Univ, 72-74. *Awards:* Purchase Awards, Pensacola Nat Drawing Competition, Visual Arts Gallery, 76, Drawing USA, Minn Mus Art, 77 & Fourth LaGrange Nat Competition, CVAA Gallery, 78. *Bibliog:* Bill Rades paintings, Artweek, 74; Mus interview, KTRS Pub TV, 82; Harvey West (auth), The Washington Year, Univ Wash Press, 82. *Mem:* Col Art Asn. *Mailing Add:* 12709 Lake City Blvd SW Tacoma WA 98498

RADICE, ANNE-IMELDA MARINO
HISTORIAN, CURATOR
b Buffalo, NY, Feb 29, 48. *Study:* Wheaton Col, Norton, Mass, AB, 69; Villa Schifanoia, Florence, Italy, MA, 71; Univ NC, Chapel Hill, PhD, 76. *Collections Arranged:* Two on Two at the Octagon (auth, catalog), Drawings from the Collection of the Architect of the Capitol, US Capitol, 80. *Pos:* Asst cur & staff lectr, Nat Gallery Art, 72-76; archit historian for the architect, US Capitol, 76-80, cur, 80- *Res:* Italian renaissance architecture, architecture of Thomas Jefferson and US Capitol. *Publ:* Auth, Il Cronaca: Fifteenth Century Florentyne Architect, Univ Microfilms, 76; ed, ann reports of architect of Capitol, 76- & contribr, The Capitol, Govt Printing Off, 80; auth, US Capitol, Art J, fall 80, The Original Libr Congress, 81. *Mailing Add:* 2311 Connecticut Ave NW No 102 Washington DC 20008

RADIN, DAN
PAINTER, INSTRUCTOR
b New York, NY, May 12, 29. *Study:* Queens Col; Cranbrook Acad Art, BFA & MFA. *Work:* Cranbrook Mus, Bloomfield Hills, Mich; Detroit Inst Arts, Mich; Butler Inst Am Art, Youngstown, Ohio. *Exhib:* Butler Inst Am Art 26th Ann, 61; Painting Part II, 63 & Landscape II, 71, De Cordova Mus; Am Acad Ann, Rome, 64; Contemp Surv, J B Speed Mus, Louisville, Ky, 66; The Figure Today, Slater Mus, Norwich, Conn, 77; Invitational, Slater Mus, Norwich, Conn, 80; 25th Ann Regional Exhib, Mystic Art Asn, Conn, 81. *Teaching:* Instr painting, Swain Sch Design, New Bedford, Mass, 64-71; instr painting & drawing, Univ Conn, 72; instr drawing, RI Sch Design, 72. *Awards:* Louis Comfort Tiffany Found Awards in Painting, 62 & 64; Second Purchase Award, Lowe Gallery, 63. *Media:* Oil, Acrylic. *Mailing Add:* Rte 6 Norwich CT 06360

RADJAI, ABBAS
PAINTER, CONSERVATOR
b Shiraz, Iran, Feb 18, 50; US citizen. *Study:* Lincoln Univ, Jefferson City, Mo, BA, 78; Chicago Art Inst, MFA, 80; Art Inst, Tehran, Iran, Hon DA, 85. *Comn:* American Landscape, comn by Dr Jafar Shah Mirang, Glenview, Ill, 91. *Exhib:* Exhibition by Abbas Radjai, Jefferson City Art Inst, Mo, 76; Contemporary Arts of Abbas Radjai, Capital City Univ, Tehran, Iran, 78; Presenting Abbas Radjai, Royal Acad Fine Arts, London, Eng, 79; Painting by Abbas Radjai, Chicago Art Inst, Ill, 80. *Teaching:* Pvt art lessons, Jefferson City, Mo, 74-78; pvt classes, Chicago Park Dist, 86 & 88. *Awards:* First Prize, 76 & best of show, 78, Jefferson City Art Inst, Mo. *Media:* Oil. *Dealer:* De Bouver Fine Arts Inc 15-109 Merchandise Mart Chicago IL 60654. *Mailing Add:* 5710 N Hermitage Chicago !L 60660

RADOCZY, ALBERT
PAINTER
b Stamford, Conn, Oct 24, 14. *Study:* Parsons Sch Design; Cooper Union, grad. *Work:* Brooklyn Mus, NY; Ball State Teachers Col, Ind; Lyman Allyn Mus, Conn; Sloan-Kettering Mem. *Comn:* Tapestry murals, Allegheny Col, Meadville, Pa, 66. *Exhib:* NJ State Mus Ann, Trenton, 61; Whitney Mus Am Art Ann, New York, 62; Brooklyn Mus Nat Print Exhib, NY, 62; Mus Mod Art Lending Collection, 65; Bergen Community Mus, 73; The Figure in Drawing, Univ of Bridgeport, 77. *Teaching:* Lectr drawing, Cooper Union, 50-55; prof design, City Col New York, 55- *Awards:* Purchase Award, Ball State Teachers Col, 59. *Media:* Oil. *Dealer:* Barbara Walter Gallery 1015 Madison Ave New York NY 10021. *Mailing Add:* 61 Cedar St Cresskill NJ 07626

RADOVICH, DONALD
PAINTER, EDUCATOR
b Nazareth, Pa, Jan 3, 32. *Study:* Univ NMex, BFA, 56, with Randall Davey & Kenneth Adams, MA, 60; also in San Miquel Allende, Mex, 70. *Work:* Univ NMex Mus, Albuquerque; State Capitol, Santa Fe, NMex; Nat Wildlife Fedn, Washington, DC. *Exhib:* Wave Hill Mus, Bronx, NY, 82; Ark Wildlife Fedn Traveling Exhib, 85; Colo Ctr Arts, Grand Junction, 86; one-man exhib, Nat Wildlife Fedn, Washington, 88. *Teaching:* Prof painting, Western State Col, Gunnison, Colo, 64-88, emer prof, 88-; instr, Nat Wildlife Fedn, Washington, DC & Estes Park, Colo, 78-85; Keynote Address, Guild of Natural Science Illustrators 1992, Rocky Mountain Biological Laboratory, 90-92. *Awards:* Gold Medal, Nat Exhib, Tubac, Ariz, 65; Purchase Award, Nat Exhib, Cedar City, Utah, 68. *Bibliog:* J W Campbell (auth), Donald Radovich: Artist, naturalist, teacher, Southwestern Art, Vol IV, No 4, 74. *Mem:* Kappa Pi (sponsor, 65-). *Media:* Oil, Watercolor. *Publ:* Illusr, Birds of New Mexico: Where To Find Them, Univ NMex Press, 63; Birds of Colorado's Gunnison Country, Western State Found Press, 80; stamp designs, stamp sheet, Nat Wildlife Fedn, 86-; illusr, Reader's Digest Book of North American Birds, 90-; illusr, Pennsylvania Breeding Bird Atlas, in prep; Colorado Birds, Denver Mus Nat Hist, 92. *Mailing Add:* 720 N Spruce St Gunnison CO 81230

RADY, ELSA
CERAMIST, SCULPTOR
b New York, NY, July 29, 43. *Study:* Chouinard Art Sch, 62-66. *Work:* Smithsonian Inst, Renwick Gallery, Washington, DC; Boston Mus Fine Arts; Victoria & Albert Mus Art, London, England; Brooklyn Mus, NY; Los Angeles Co Mus Art; Metrop Mus Art; NYNEX Corp, White Plains, NY; Chase Manhattan Bank, NY; General Motors, NY; Am Med Int Inc, Beverly Hills, Calif; Denver Art Mus; and many others. *Comn:* Sculptures, Jules Stein Eye Inst, Univ Calif, Los Angeles, 66 & Disneyland, 67. *Exhib:* Craftsmen USA '66, Los Angeles Co Mus Art, 66; Am Porcelain, Renwick Gallery, Smithsonian Inst, Washington, DC, 80; Pacific Connections, Los Angeles Co Mus Art, 85; solo exhibs: Garth Clark Gallery, NY, 85, Jan Turner Gallery, Los Angeles, 87 & 88, Holly Solomon Gallery, NY, 87 & Lily (catalogue), 90, Ochi Gallery, Suny Valley, Idaho, 90 & Still Life (catalogue), Isetan Fine Arts Inc, Tokyo, Japan, 91; American Potters Today, Victoria & Albert Mus, London, England, 86; World War II Holdings, Metrop Mus Art, New York, 89; Selections from the Joyce & Jay Cooper Collection of Contemporary Ceramics, Nelson Fine Arts Ctr, Ariz State Univ Art Mus, 89-90; Building a Permanent Collection: A Perspective on the 1980s, Am Craft Mus, New York, 90; 28th Ann Ceramic Exhib (catalogue), Everson Mus Art, Syracuse, NY, 90; Southeast Bank Collects, A Corporation Views Contemporary Art, Harn Mus Art, Univ Fla, West Palm Beach. *Awards:* Nat Endowment Fel, 81; Calif State Arts Comn Grant, 83. *Bibliog:* William Wilson (auth), California ceramics: shape of things to come, Los Angeles Times, 8/9/84; Mac McCloud (auth), Elsa Rady: porcelain vessels, Am Ceramics, Vol III, No 4, 85; Gerrit Henry (auth), Elsa Rady, Art News, Vol 85, No 2, 86; and others. *Media:* Ceramics; Porcelain. *Publ:* Ornaments aand Surfaces on Cermics,

Kunst & Handwerk, 77; Studio Porcelain, Chilton Book Co, 80; Porcelain: Tradtions and New Visions, Watson-Guptill, 81; Ceramics of the 20th Century, Rizzoli, 82; American Crafts: A Source Book for the Home, Stewart, Tabori, Chang, 83. *Mailing Add:* 1500 Andalusia Ave Venice CA 90291

RADYCKI, J(OSEPHINE) DIANE
HISTORIAN, EDUCATOR
b Chicago, Ill, Dec 4, 46. *Study:* Univ Ill, Chicago Circle, BA, 69; Hunter Col, City Univ NY, MA, 76; Harvard Univ, MA, 83, PhD research ongoing. *Collections Arranged:* The Legacy of Raphael, Fogg Art Mus, 83; Works by Women Artists, Fogg Art Mus, 87. *Pos:* Staff aid, New York City Dept Cult Affairs, 80; res assoc, Metrop Mus Art, 80-81; intern, Busch-Reisinger Mus, 84-85. *Teaching:* Teaching fel mod art, Harvard Univ, 84- *Mem:* Col Art Asn; Women's Caucus Art; Mod Lang Asn. *Res:* Nineteenth and twentieth century European and American art. *Publ:* Coauth, Voices of women: Three critics, three poets, three heroines, Midmarch Assoc, 80; ed, The Letters and Journals of Paula Modersohn-Becker, Scarecrow Press, 80; auth, The life of lady art students: changing art education at the turn of the century, Art J, 82; auth, Jahrhundertwende, In: Deutsche Kunst des 20 Jahrhunderts aus dem Busch-Reisinger Museum, Harvard University, USA, Städtische Galerie im Städelschen Kunstinstitut Frankfurt am Main, 82; ed, Poussin: The Early Years in Rome, 88. *Mailing Add:* Harvard Univ Fogg Museum Cambridge MA 02138

RAFFAEL, JOSEPH
PAINTER, PRINTMAKER
b Brooklyn, NY, Feb 22, 33. *Study:* Cooper Union, 53-54, Yale Sch Fine Arts, BFA, 56, studied with Josef Albers. *Work:* Metrop Mus Art, Whitney Mus Am Art, New York; San Francisco Mus of Mod Art; Libr of Cong, Hirshhorn Mus & Smithsonian Inst, Washington, DC; Oakland Mus, Calif; Mint Mus, Charlotte, NC; and many others. *Exhib:* Human Concern, Personal Torment, Whitney Mus Am Art, New York, 70; solo exhibs, Nancy Hoffman Gallery, New York, 83, 84, 86, 87, 89, 90 & 92, Woltjen/Udell Gallery, Edmonton, Can, Richard Gray Gallery, Chicago & John Berggruen Gallery, San Francisco, 86, A Dream Remembered, 86, In France, The Lannis Series, Part I, 87 & Lannis in Sieste, 89, Nancy Hoffman Gallery, New York, Secret Silence: Art of Joseph Raffael, Davenport Mus Art, Iowa, 87-88; Smithsonian Inst, Washington, DC, 87; The Natural Image, Stamford Mus & Nature Ctr, Conn, 89; Summer Pleasures: Water, Nancy Hoffman Gallery, New York, 89; Butler Inst Am Art, Youngstown, Ohio, 90; Miyagi Mus Art, Japan, 91-92; Hunter Mus Art, Chatanooga, Tenn, 92. *Teaching:* Instr art, Sch Visual Arts, 66-69; assoc prof art, Univ Calif, Berkeley, 69; prof art, Sacramento State Univ, 69-74. *Awards:* L C Tiffany Found Fel, 60; First Prize, Tokyo Biennial Figure Art, 74; First Prize & Purchase Award, Oakland Mus, Calif, 75. *Bibliog:* Gloria Smith (auth), The Eyes Have It: Joseph Raffael (film), NBC-TV, 72; Wm S Wilson (auth), The paintings of Jos Raffael, Studio Int, 5/74; Jerome Tarshis (auth), Nature upclose, Horizon, 9/78. *Media:* Oil, Watercolor; Lithography. *Dealer:* Nancy Hoffman Gallery 429 W Broadway New York NY 10012. *Mailing Add:* c/o Nancy Hoffman Gallery 429 W Broadway New York NY 10012

RAFFAEL, JUDITH K See North, Judy

RAFFERTY, JOANNE MILLER
PAINTER
b Morristown, NJ, May 31, 48. *Study:* Daemen Col, NY, with James Kuo & Jay Jodway, BS(art educ), 70; State Univ NY, Buffalo, 75. *Work:* Albright Knox Art Gallery, Buffalo, NY; Master Charge Int, New York; Bankers Trust, New York; Equitable Life Insurance, Atlanta, Ga; Dun & Bradstreet, New York. *Comn:* offices, City Fed Savings Bank, C S Schulte Fine Art, NJ, 86; Swanke, Hayden & Connell, Reece Galleries NY, Bermuda, 87; lobby, Int Bus Machines, comn by Armand Avakian, architect, Harrison, NY, 89; lobby, Bayside Hospital, Va Beach, comn by Christian Brydon Gallery, Va, 92. *Exhib:* NJ Group Traveling Exhib, Hickory Art Mus, Cayuga Mus Art, Walter Elwood Mus, 86-88; Abstract Impressions, Reece Galleries, New York, 87 & 90; Fiftieth Ann NJ Watercolor Soc, Montclair Mus, Noyes Mus, Monmouth Mus, 88; 99th Ann Exhib Nat Asn Women Artists, Javits Fed Bldg, New York, 88; solo exhib, Aquamedia, Christian Brydon Gallery, Richmond, Va, 89-92, Broden Gallery, Madison, Wis, 91, Sienna Galleries, San Mateo, Calif, 91; People's Choice Exhib, Long Beach Island Fdn Arts & Sciences, Loveladies, NJ, 90. *Teaching:* Instr art, Middleport Central Schs, NY, 70-71; Amherst Central Schs, NY, 71-76. *Awards:* NJ Watercolor Soc Award, 89; Winsor & Newton Award of Achievement, NJ Watercolor Soc Found 45th Anniversary Show, 92. *Bibliog:* Robert Merritt (auth), Rafferty Paintings, Richmond Times Dispatch, 5/92; Susan Fields (auth), Publishers Refine Lines and Grow, Art Business News, 4/89. *Mem:* Nat Asn Women Artists; NJ Watercolor Soc; New York Artists Equity. *Media:* Oil; watercolor. *Dealer:* The Reece Galleries 24 West 57 St New York NY 10019. *Mailing Add:* 27 S Crescent Maplewood NJ 07040

RAFFO, STEVE
PAINTER, DRAFTSMAN
b Hoboken, NJ, Aug 21, 12. *Study:* Cooper Union Sch Art, New York, 2 certs, 33 & 37. *Work:* Delgado Mus, New Orleans, La; Fla Gulf Coast Art Ctr, Clearwater; Pa Acad Fine Arts, Philadelphia; Legal Aid Offices, New York. *Exhib:* Whitney Mus Am Art, New York, 47-49 & 51; Corcoran Gallery, Washington, DC, 47 & 51; Pa Acad, Philadelphia, 48, 49, 53, 61, 62 & 69; Carnegie Inst, Pa, 49; Am Acad Inst Arts, New York, 51, 58 & 60; Art Inst Chicago, 52 & 61; 4 Young Americans Exhib, RI Mus Art, 55; Nat Acad Design, New York, 60, 67, 69, 75, 76 & 88. *Teaching:* Instr painting, Cooper Union, 39-43 & 47-50 & Parsons Sch Design, 56-63, New York. *Awards:* Scheidt Mem Prize, Pa Acad, 48; Guggenheim Fel, 50 & 51; Prix de Rome, 52-55. *Bibliog:* Emily Genauer (auth), Art review, NY World Telegram, 4/25/49; David Friend (auth), Case History--Raffo--Composition, 75; John Corry (auth), East Harlem artist, NY Times, 9/8/80. *Media:* Oil; Pen & Ink. *Publ:* Contribr, How Paintings Happen, Norton, 51; Composition--A Painters Guide, Watson-Guptill, 75-; New York Art Rev - Am References, 88 & 90. *Mailing Add:* 332 E 116th St New York NY 10029

RAFSKY, JESSICA C
COLLECTOR
b New York NY, Sept 18, 24. *Study:* George Washington Univ; NY Univ. *Mem:* Whitney Mus; sustaining mem Mus Mod Art; assoc Metrop Mus Art; assoc Am Fedn Arts. *Interests:* Benefactor of Foundation Maeght and friend of Tate Gallery, British Mus, & Victoria & Albert Mus, London. *Collection:* Contemporary art. *Mailing Add:* 200 E 62nd St New York NY 10021

RAGGIO, OLGA
HISTORIAN, CURATOR
Study: Liceo E O Visconti, Rome, BA(with hon), 44; Lycee Chateaubriand, Rome, Baccalaureat I, 45; Vatican Libr, dipl, 47; Sch Art Hist & Archaeol & Sch Mod Lang, Univ Rome, PhD(cum laude), 49; Inst Fine Arts, 51-53. *Collections Arranged:* Patterns of Collecting: Selected Acquisitions 1965-1975 (coauth & ed, catalog), 75, Highlights from the Untermeyer Collection, 77-78, The Splendor of Dresden, 78-79, Treasures from the Kremlin, 79, & The Vatican Collections: The Papacy and Art, 83, Cent Europ Decorative Arts, 89, Europ Sculpture Ct Galleries, 90 & Metro Mus Art, New York. *Pos:* Cur asst, Dept of European Sculpture & Decorative Arts, 52-54, asst cur, 54-63, assoc res cur, 63-68, cur, 68-71, chmn dept, 71-, Metrop Mus Art, New York. *Teaching:* Adj asst prof fine arts, Inst Fine Arts, NY Univ, 64-67, adj assoc prof fine arts, 67-68, adj prof fine arts, 68- *Awards:* Metrop Mus Trustee Fel, 69; Am Coun of Learned Socs Grant-in-aid, 76-77; Res Fel, Am Acad, Rome, '83. *Mem:* Col Art Asn Am; Am Mus Asn; Int Coun Mus Orgn; The Renaissance Soc of Am. *Publ:* Auth, The Velez Blanco Patio, Metrop Mus Art Bulletin, Vol XXIII, pages 141-176, 64-65; A Algardi egli stucchi di Villa Pamphili, Paragone, Vol 251, pages 3-38, 71; Bernini and the Collection of Cardinal Flavio Chigi, Apollo, 5/83; Tiziano Aspetti's Reliefs with scenes of the Martydom of St Daniel of Padua, Metrop Mus J Vol 16, 82; co-auth, Liechtenstein: The Princely Collections, New York, Metrop Mus Art, 85. *Mailing Add:* c/o Dept of Europ Sculpture & Decorative Arts Metrop Mus Art Fifth Ave at 82nd St New York NY 10028

RAGINSKY, NINA
PAINTER, PHOTOGRAPHER
b Montreal, Que. *Study:* Rutgers Univ, BA, 62. *Work:* Nat Film Bd Can; Edmonton Art Gallery; George Eastman House; Nat Gallery Can. *Exhib:* International Photo Show, Nat Gallery Can, 68; Vision and Expression, George Eastman House, Rochester, NY, 69; solo exhibs, San Francisco Mus Art, 75 & Art Gallery Ont, 79; Between Friends, Field Mus, Chicago, 76. *Teaching:* Instr photog, Emily Carr Col Art, Vancouver, 72-81; workshops, Univ Ottawa, Univ Victoria & Banff Sch Fine Arts. *Awards:* Can Coun Grant, 76. *Bibliog:* Geoffrey James (auth), An inquiry into the aesthetics of photography, Arts Can, 12/74. *Mem:* Royal Can Acad Art; Officer, Order of Can, 85. *Media:* Oils. *Publ:* Vision & Expression, Horizon Press, 69; An Inquiry into the Aesthetics of Photography, Arts Can, 75; Bonff Purchase, Wiley, 79; Aperture 88, Aperture, 82; Between Friends; Nat Film Board Image Series, 1, 2, 3, 5, 6. *Mailing Add:* RR #2 Beddos Rd Compartment 7 Ganges BC V0S 1E0 Canada

RAGLAND, BOB
PAINTER, SCULPTOR
b Cleveland, Ohio, Dec 11, 38. *Study:* Rocky Mountain Sch Art, Denver, Colo; study with Phil Steele. *Work:* Denver Pub Libr; Karamu House, Cleveland; Irving St Ctr, Cult Arts Prog, Denver. *Comn:* Logo, Metro State Col Black Student Union, 74; art print, Big Sisters of Colo, 75. *Exhib:* 16th Ann Drawing Exhib, Dallas Mus Fine Art Traveling Exhib, 67; one-man show, Cleveland State Univ, 68, Denver Nat Bank, Colo, 80-81, Century Bank Cherry Creek, Denver, Colo, 80-81; Juried Jewish Community Ctr Collector's Mart, 80; Group Exhib, Boston, Mass Tubman Gallery, 81. *Pos:* Chmn, Arts & Humanities Comt, 68-69; founding fac mem, Auraria Campus, Community Col, Denver, 70-72; lectr Afro-American art of the 60's & 70's; visual arts coordr, City Spirit Proj, 78. *Teaching:* Instr painting & drawing, Denver Pub Libr, 69-71 & Eastside Action Ctr, Denver, 69-71; artist-in-residence, Model Cities Cult Arts Ctr Workshop, 71-73; artist/teacher, KRMA-TV; instr, Gove Community Sch, 79-; instr, Metrop State Col, Denver, Colo; instr, Arapahoe Community Col, Littleton, Colo. *Awards:* Recognition Award, KCNC-TV & Denver Ctr Performing Arts, 86. *Bibliog:* Arlynn Nellhaus (auth), Ragland turns out survival tips for artists, Denver Post, 1/81; Diane Wengler (auth), Bob Ragland--He's learned to survive by using his wits and considerable talent, Gazette-Telegraph, Colo Springs, 4/81; Alexandra King (auth), article, Street Talk Mag, Denver, 10/81; Bonnie McCune (auth), What to do until rich & famous, This Week in Denver, 11/22/82; Carson Reed (auth), Denver artist is more method than madness, Up the Creek Newspaper, 1/25/85. *Mem:* Colo Black Umbrella. *Media:* All Media; Metal, Welded. *Res:* Oral history project with Colorado artists over the age of fifty. *Collection:* Traditional renderings of the figure and landscape in all mediums. *Publ:* Auth, The Artists Survival Handbook or What to do till you're rich and famous, 80; publ, Colorado Gallery Guide, 78-; contribr, Black Umbrella/Black Artists Denver. *Mailing Add:* 1723 E 25th Ave Denver CO 80205

RAGLAND, JACK WHITNEY
PAINTER, PRINTMAKER
b El Monte, Calif, Feb 25, 38. *Study:* Ariz State Univ, BA & MA, with Dr Harry Wood, Arthur Jacobson & Ben Goo; Univ Calif, Los Angeles, with Dr Lester Longman, Sam Amato & William Brice; Akad Angewandte Kunst; Akad Bildenden Kunste; Graphische Bundes-Lehrund Versuchsanstalt, Vienna. *Work:* Albertina Mus, Vienna, Austria; Phoenix Art Mus, Ariz; Bibliotheque Nat, Paris; Kuns Mus, Basel, Switz; Los Angeles Co Mus, Calif. *Comn:* Portrait, Henry Nollen, Equitable Life Insurance, 73; stained glass windows, Methodist Church, Derry, Iowa, 74. *Exhib:* Ariz Ann Exhib, Phoenix, 61; Exhib Nat Recognized Artists, Seattle, 63 & Ft Lauderdale, Fla, 64, 65; Iowa Ann Exhib, Des Moines, 70 & 72; Artists Fedn Traveling Exhib, Eight Midwest States, 75; Southern Calif Exhib, Del Mar, Calif, 81, 83-92. *Teaching:* Grad asst drawing & painting, Univ Calif, Los Angeles, 61-64; instr drawing & painting, Ariz State Univ, summer 63; art dept head & assoc prof art hist, drawing, printmaking & painting, Simpson Col, 64-76. *Awards:* Grand Purchase Prize, Ariz Ann, Phoenix Art Mus, 61; Painting Selected for Prize Winning Paintings, Book II, Allied Publ, 62; First Prize, Prints & Graphics, Iowa State Fair, 74; First Prize, Acrylic Painting, Southern Calif Exhib, Del Mar, 84. *Bibliog:* Applause, NY Mag of Arts, 11/3/71; New woman, Fla Mag, 11-12/74. *Media:* Acrylic, Oils; Serigraphy. *Dealer:* A Albert Allen Fine Art Gallery Palm Desert CA; Tarbox Gallery San Diego CA. *Mailing Add:* 5490 Rainbow Heights Rd Fallbrook CA 92028

RAGUIN, VIRGINIA C
HISTORIAN, CONSULTANT
b New York, NY, Feb 24, 41. *Study:* Marymount Col, Tarrytown, NY, BA(magna cum laude), 63; Univ Toulouse, France, cert, 64; Yale Univ, with Summer McK Crosby, PhD, 74. *Collections Arranged:* Col Gallery Prog, Worcester Art Mus, 75-84; Northern Renaissance Stained Glass (with catalog), Cantor Gallery, Holy Cross, 87. *Pos:* Dir, Census Stained Glass Windows Am, 82-; hist res consult, Stained Glass Mag, 83-; consult, Mem Hall Restoration, Harvard Univ, 85- *Teaching:* Prof art hist, Col Holy Cross, 74- *Awards:* Fulbright Scholar, 64; Woodrow Wilson Fel, 64; Nat Endowment Humanities Educ Proj Grant, 77-80. *Mem:* Int Ctr Medieval Art; Col Art Asn; Soc Archit Historians; Société Francaise d'Archéologie. *Res:* Medieval Renaissance and Modern stained glass; Medieval iconography. *Publ:* Auth, Isaiah master of the Sainte-Chapelle in Burgundy, Art Bull, 77; Stained Glass in Thirteenth-Century Burgundy, Princeton, 82; Worcester's Tradition of Stained glass, Worcester Art Mus J, 83; coauth, Stained Glass Before 1700 in American Collections, Nat Gallery, 85-88; auth, Revivals Revivalists and Architectural Stained Glass, Soc Archit Historians J, 90. *Mailing Add:* 280 Boston Ave Medford MA 02155

RAGUSA, ISA
HISTORIAN
b Rome, Italy, Dec 30, 26; US citizen. *Study:* New York Univ, BA(magna cum laude), 47, Inst Fine Arts, MA, 51, PhD, 66. *Pos:* Reader & acting dir, Index Christian Art, formerly; res art hist, Princeton Univ, formerly. *Teaching:* Vis scholar, Inst Fine Arts, NY Univ, 83-84; vis prof, Univ Cattolica del Sacro Cuore, Milan, 92-93. *Mem:* Medieval Acad Am; Col Art Asn; Renaissance Soc; Int Ctr Medieval Art. *Publ:* Coauth (with R B Green), Meditations on the Life of Christ, Princeton Univ Press, 61 & 77; auth, Porta patet vitae Sponsus vocat Intro venite and the Inscriptions of the lost Portal of the Cathedral of Esztergom, Zeitschrift fur Kunstgeschichte, 43, 77; Il manoscritto ambrosiano L 58 Sup: L'infanzia de Cristo e le fonti apocrife, Arte Lombarda, 83, 87; The iconography of the Abgar Cycle in Paris, Ms lat 2688 and its Relationship to Byzantine Cycles, Miniature, 2, 89; Mandylion-Sudarium: the 'Translation' of a Byzantine Relic to Rome, Arte Medievale, V, 91. *Mailing Add:* 30 W 12th St New York NY 10011

RAHILL, MARGARET FISH
CURATOR, CRITIC
b Milwaukee, Wis, Feb 21, 19. *Study:* Univ Wis, Milwaukee. *Collections Arranged:* Karl Priebe Retrospective (with catalog), 68, Marc Chagall Painting and Prints from Milwaukee Collections (with catalog), 70, Eskimo Sculptures and Stone Prints from Baffin Island, Canada (with catalog), 70, Wisconsin Art of the 1920's and 1930's (with catalog), 75 & American Plains Indians, Paintings and Drawings (with catalog), 76, Charles Allis Mus. *Pos:* Art ed & critic, Milwaukee Sentinal, contribr reviewer, Milwaukee Art J & art critic, Wis Archit, 46-61; pub relations, Milwaukee Art Ctr, 62; pub relations & exhibs, Layton Sch of Art, 62-68; cur, Charles Allis Mus, 68-; vpres, City Milwaukee Art Comn, 81-83, pres, 84-85, mem, 86- *Awards:* Four Milwaukee Press Club Ann Awards for articles on art, museums, art education, 55-60; Milwaukee Art Comn Award for Excellence, 76; Bookfellows Award for outstanding serv to Allis Mus, Milwaukee Pub Libr,78; Commendation Award, Milwaukee Co Hist Soc, 82. *Mem:* Hon mem Wis Painters & Sculptors Inc; hon mem Wis Designer-Craftsman Inc; Wis Women in Art; Wis Acad Sci, Arts & Lett(counr-at-large, 82-86); Milwaukee Press Club. *Res:* American 19th century landscapists; Wisconsin art and artists. *Publ:* Auth, Richard Lorenz, Milwaukee Art Ctr, 65; Aaron Bohrod, Allis Mus, 84. *Mailing Add:* 1014 Sheffield Ct Columbia MO 65203

RAHJA, VIRGINIA HELGA
PAINTER, ADMINISTRATOR
b Aurora, Minn, Apr 21, 21. *Study:* Hamline Univ, BA, 44; Sch Assoc Arts, DFA, 66. *Exhib:* Walker Art Ctr; Minn State Fair, Minn Art Inst; Hamline Galleries; Sch Assoc Arts, Univ Minn; plus many other exhibs & ann. *Pos:* Asst supt fine arts, Minn State Fair, 44-48. *Teaching:* Assoc prof painting, Hamline Univ, 43-48 & dir, Hamline Galleries, 45-48; prof painting, Sch Assoc Arts, St Paul, 48-65, dean, 48-73, dir, 73-, pres, 75-86. *Mem:* Col Art Asn Am; Am Asn Univ Women; Midwest Col Art Conf; Am Fedn Arts. *Media:* Oil. *Mailing Add:* 550 Summit Ave St Paul MN 55102

RAIMONDI, JOHN
SCULPTOR
b Boston, Mass, May 29, 48. *Study:* Mass Col Art, BFA, 73. *Work:* Nat Mus Am Art, Smithsonian Inst, Washington, DC; Milwaukee Art Mus, Wis; Mus Fine Arts, Boston; Newark Mus, NJ; Okla Mus Art, Oklahoma City. *Comn:* Lupus, Cabot, Cabot & Forbes, Lotus Corp, Cambridge, Mass, 85; Aquila, Lincoln Prop Co, Miami, Fla, 86; Dance of the Cranes, Omaha Airport Auth, Nebr, 88; Artorius, Stanhope PLC Stockley Park Ltd, London, Eng, 89; Athleta, Univ Nebr, Kearney, 90. *Exhib:* C Grimaldis Gallery, Baltimore, 90; Helander Gallery, Palm Beach, Fla, 91; Stars in Florida, Mus Art, Ft Lauderdale, 92; Romantic Abstraction: A 20-Year Survey of Works by John Raimondi, traveling exhib (catalog), Stuart & Vero Beach, Fla, 92; The Hyde Collection, Glens Falls, NY, 92; and others. *Teaching:* Artist-in-residence, Portland Regional Vocational Tech Ctr, Maine, 75, San Angelo Independent Sch Dist, Tex, 79 & Univ Nebr, Kearney, 89. *Awards:* MacDowell Colony Fel, 82. *Bibliog:* John Raimondi: Artist-in Residence, Nat Endowment Arts, Guggenheim Productions, Washington, DC, 75; Harry Rand (auth), cover story, Arts Mag, 4/83; Dance of the Cranes, Pub Broadcasting System Documentary (film), 89. *Mem:* Mass Coun Arts & Humanities. *Media:* Bronze, Steel. *Mailing Add:* 1420 N Ocean Blvd Palm Beach FL 33480

RAISELIS, RICHARD
PAINTER, EDUCATOR
b Bridgeport, Conn, July 15, 51. *Study:* Skowhegan Sch painting & sculpture, 72; Yale Univ, BA, 73; Tyler Sch Art of Temple Univ, MFA, 76. *Work:* Chemical Bank, New York; Exxon Corp; pvt collection of Glenn C Janss; Michigan Bell, Detroit; Univ Iowa. *Exhib:* Collectors Gallery XVIII, McNay Art Inst, San Antonio, Tex, 84; Am Realism: 20th drawings & watercolors, San Francisco Mus Mod Art, 85; Directors Choice, Ark Art Ctr, Little Rock, 87; Direct Responses: Contemp Landscape Painting, Rochester Mem Art Gallery, 89; Invitational Exhib Painting & Sculpture, Am Acad & Inst of Arts & Letters, New York, 90; Robert Schoelkopf Gallery, New York, 91. *Collections Arranged:* Pittura Figurativa Americana, Temple Univ, Rome, Italy, 88. *Teaching:* Asst prof painting & drawing, Univ Mich Sch Art, 83-89, Temple Univ, Rome, Italy, 86-88, Boston Univ Sch Visual Art, 89- *Bibliog:* Alvin Martin (auth), American Realism, San Francisco Mus Fine Arts, 86; Shara Wasserman (auth), Four Americans in Rome, Next: Trimestrale di Arte e Cultura, 3-5/88; Judith Reynolds (auth), Out in the Open, Rochester City Newspaper, 6/89. *Media:* Oil. *Publ:* Auth, Don Shields, Detroit Focus Quarterly Vol 3 No 3, 9/84. *Mailing Add:* 1284 Beacon St Apt 520 Brookline MA 01246-3718

RAKOCY, WILLIAM (JOSEPH)
PAINTER, MURALIST
b Youngstown, Ohio, Apr 14, 24. *Study:* Butler Inst Am Art, with Clyde Singer, 39-41; Am Acad Art, 44; Kansas City Art Inst, with Ross Braught, Ed Lanning & Bruce Mitchell, MFA, 51. *Work:* US Naval Training Sta, Great Lakes, Ill; YMCA, Youngstown; Butler Inst Am Art; El Paso Mus Art, Tex. *Comn:* Mural, Woodrow Wilson High Sch, Youngstown, 46; four murals (with Robert Sonoga & Chet Kwiecinski), McSorleys Colonial Rest, Pittsburgh, Pa, 55; three murals, YMCA, Youngstown; three murals, Mesa Inn, El Paso, Tex, 75; fourteen dioramas, Cavalry Mus & Wilderness Park Mus, El Paso, Tex, 78. *Exhib:* Butler Inst Am Art Ann, 55; One-man show, Juarez, Mex, 79 & 81, El Paso Mus Art, 86. *Pos:* Installation cur, Wilderness Park Mus, 77; founder, Bill Rakocy Sch Art, El Paso, Tex. *Teaching:* Instr painting & drawing, Mohn Sch Art, 54-56; asst prof painting & drawing, Col Artesia, 66-67, assoc prof, 67-71; vis prof, Sul Ross State Univ, Alpine, Tex, currently. *Awards:* Art Travel Grant to Study in Italy, Ital Businessmen, Kansas City, Mo, 53; Area Award in Watercolor, Butler Inst Am Art, 56-60. *Mem:* Kansas City Area Artists Asn; El Paso Art Asn; founder Rio Bravo Watercolorists; Western Asn Art Schs & Univ Mus; El Paso Hist Soc; Am Soc Appaisers. *Media:* Oil, Watercolor. *Interests:* Promote art auctions to assist artists via sales and scholarships; publisher of art and history books; founder and manager of Raks Art and History Museum, Ruidoso, New Mexico. *Publ:* Auth, A Western Portfolio, 65; Art Reporter, 72; Sketches & Observations, 72; Images, Paso del Norte, 79 & Villa Raids 80, Col of NMex; Mogollon Diary No 2, Great Western Publ. *Mailing Add:* 4210 Emory Way El Paso TX 79922

RAKOVAN, LAWRENCE FRANCIS
PRINTMAKER, PAINTER
b Eleria, Ohio, Oct 26, 39. *Study:* Detroit Soc Arts & Crafts; Wayne State Univ, BS; RI Sch Design, MA. *Work:* Brooklyn Mus, NY; Colby Col; Calif Col Arts & Crafts, Oakland; Bowdoin Col Mus Art; Univ Maine, Orono. *Comn:* 14 Stations of the Cross & exterior monumental cross with stoneware reliefs of The Four Evangelists, St Charles Borromeo Church, Brunswick, Maine, 75. *Exhib:* Two-man show, St Peter's Ctr, New York, 73; Maine 75, Bowdoin Col, 75; Sculpture in Wood, Maine Festival of Arts, Bowdoin Col, 77; one-man shows, Treat Gallery, Bates Col, 76, Univ Southern Maine, 84 & Merrill Art Gallery, Nichols Col, Dudley, Mass, 85; juried competitions, Mamaroneck Artist Guild, Nat Exhib, 85, Chautauqua Nat Exhib Am Art, Chautauqua Inst, NY, 85, Fine Arts Inst, San Bernardino Co Mus, Redlands, Calif, 85, 13th Int Dogwood Arts Fest, Atlanta, Ga, 86, Springfield Art League 67th Nat, Mus Art, Mass, 86, & Arts Asn Harrisburg, Pa, 86. *Pos:* Dir, Chocolate Church Art Gallery Ctr Arts, Bath, Maine, 84- 91. *Teaching:* Assoc prof painting & printmaking, Univ Southern Maine, 67-; vis prof art, Univ Maine, Augusta, 79-80. *Awards:* State of Maine Res Grant, 73. *Mem:* Copley Soc, Boston, Mass; Skowhegan Sch Painting & Sculpture. *Media:* Oil, Stone Lithography. *Dealer:* Barridoff Gallery Portland ME. *Mailing Add:* Upper Maine St Brunswick ME 04011

RALEIGH, HENRY PATRICK
PAINTER, WRITER
b New York, NY, Feb 5, 31. *Study:* Pratt Inst, BS, 56 & MS, 59; New York Univ, PhD, 63. *Exhib:* Ten Artists Under Thirty, Riverside Mus, New York, 64; Artists of the Mid-Hudson Valley, Albany Inst of Art, NY, 70-75 & 82; First Street Gallery, New York, 83-85; Sacks Gallery, New York, 85; The New Response, 86; Mus Hudson Highlands, 87; Rice Gallery, Albany, NY, 87; Woodstock Sch Art, 88. *Teaching:* Chmn art dept, Pratt Inst Art Sch, 61-68; prof film hist, art criticism & aesthet, State Univ NY, New Paltz, 68-, chmn studio art & art hist, 68-74 & co-dean fac fine & performing art, 71-73. *Awards:* Travel Grant, 7th Int Am Coun Learned Soc, Cong, Rumania, 72; Prize Winner, 4th Nat Painting Exhib, Woodstock, NY. *Media:* Oils. *Res:* Application of value study to examinations of contemporary art and art criticism. *Publ:* Auth, Exhaustion thresholds of painting, Bucknell Rev, 72; Revival of aesthetic symbolism, 74 & Aesthethic of chance, 75, J Aesthet & Art Criticism; Art and the public, 79 & The Ambiguous Art (film), 82, J Aesthetic Educ; Post Modernism in the Visual Arts, Hofstra Univ, 86; auth, Art Times (film). *Mailing Add:* State Univ NY New Paltz NY 12561

RALEY, ROBERT L
COLLECTORS
b Baltimore, Md, Aug 22, 24. *Study:* Univ Pa, MArch, with Louis Kahn; Univ Del, MA. *Pos:* Mem bd dir, Del Art Mus; mem Am art comt, Philadelphia Mus Art; state adv, Nat Trust for Hist Preserv; bd trustees, Hist Soc Del; mem, State Rev Bd Hist Preserv, Del. *Mem:* Am Inst Architects; Am Asn Mus (mem trustees comt). *Collection:* Twentieth century European and American paintings and drawings and contemporary sculpture. *Mailing Add:* 800 Center Mill Rd Greenville DE 19807

RAMANAUSKAS, DALIA IRENA
PAINTER, DRAFTSMAN
b Kaunas, Lithuania, Jan 10, 36; US citizen. *Study:* Southern Conn Col, BS(art educ). *Work:* Prudential Insurance Co; Smithsonian Inst, Washington, DC; Va Mus, Richmond; Chase Manhattan Bank; Calif Palace, Legion Hon. *Exhib:* Am Drawing 1927-1977, Minn Mus Art, St Paul; solo shows, O K Harris Gallery, New York, 77-79, Capricorn Gallery, Washington, DC, 77, 82, 85, 90 & 93, Stockholm Int Art Expo, 81 & Payson Weisberg, New York, 84; Chicago Expo, 82; Mainstream America, Butler Inst, Ohio, 87; 41st Ann Art Northeast USA, Silvermine, Conn, 90; Earth Art, Tokyo, Japan, 90; Irving Galleries, Palm Beach, Fla, 91-92; and others. *Awards:* Am Drawing 20th Ann Purchase Award, Norfolk Mus Arts & Sci, 63; Purchase Award American Drawing, Minn Mus Art, St Paul. *Bibliog:* Rev, Artforum, 4/74; M L D'Otrange Mastai (auth), Illusionism in Art, Abaris, 76; Watercolor, fall 92. *Media:* Color Inks, Watercolor. *Dealer:* Capricorn Gallery Washington DC. *Mailing Add:* PO Box 264 Main St Ivoryton CT 06442

RAMBERG, CHRISTINA
PAINTER
b Camp Campbell, Ky, Aug 21, 46. *Study:* Art Inst Chicago, BFA, 68, MFA, 72. *Work:* Art Inst Chicago; Whitney Mus Am Art, New York; Nat Collection Fine Art, DC; 20th Century Mus, Vienna, Austria; Mus Contemp Art, Chicago. *Exhib:* Spirit of the Comic in the 50's & 60's, Univ Pa, Philadelphia, 69; False Image II, Hyde Park Art Ctr, Chicago, 69; Whitney Ann, Whitney Mus Am Art, New York, 72, 73 & 79; Made in Chicago, Sao Paulo Biennial, Brazil, 73; one-person shows, Phyllis Kind Galleries, 75 & 77; Who Chicago, 80-81, traveling to London, Sunderland, Glasgow, Edinburgh, Belfast & Boston; mid-career retrospective, Renaissance Soc, Chicago, 88. *Teaching:* Vis artist-instr painting, Univ Colo, Boulder, 72; assoc prof & chmn painting, Sch Art Inst Chicago, 75-; vis artist drawing & painting, Northwestern Univ, Evanston, 79-80. *Awards:* Nat Endowment for Humanities, 78 & 83. *Media:* Acrylic, Masonite. *Dealer:* Phyllis Kind Gallery 313 W Superior St Chicago IL 60611. *Mailing Add:* c/o Phyllis Kind Gallery 313 W Superior St Chicago IL 60611

RAMES, STANLEY DODSON
PAINTER, EDUCATOR
b Woodson, Ark, Aug 11, 23. *Study:* Chicago Art Inst, cert, 45-49; also with Edgar Whitney, Robert E Wood, Henri Casselli, Bud Shackelford, Tom Hill & Rex Brandt. *Work:* Ark Bank and Trust; First Nat Bank Hot Springs, Hot Springs Art Ctr Col. *Comn:* Mural, 375th Fighter Squadron, England, 44; mural, In Home for the Incurables, New Orleans, 75. *Exhib:* New Orleans Art Asn, Delgado Mus, La, 55; Southern Watercolor, Tenn Fine Arts Ctr Cheekwood, Nashville, 77; Southern Watercolor, Columbus Mus Art, Ga, 78; Southern Watercolor, Columbia Mus Art, SC, 80. *Pos:* Set designer, NBC-TV, Chicago, 49-54; art dir, WDSU-TV, New Orleans, La, 54-72. *Teaching:* Instr art, Tulane Univ Col, New Orleans, La, 72-79; Painting workshops & show judging in Columbus Ga, 80 & 82; Watercolor workshop, Montgomery, Ala, 90. *Awards:* Watercolor Award, Southern Watercolor Ann, La Watercolor Soc; Best of Show, Southern Artists, Hot Springs Art Ctr, 81; Best of Show, Hot Springs Art Crt, 90. *Bibliog:* Article, Wayne King sets, Popular Mechanics, 53. *Mem:* Southern Watercolor Soc; Southern Artists Asn; Ky Watercolor Soc. *Media:* Watercolor, Oil. *Dealer:* Revolutionary Art Gallery 201 Broadway Hot Springs National Park AR 71901. *Mailing Add:* 311 Glen St Hot Springs National Park AR 71901

RAMIREZ, JOEL TITO
PAINTER, CALLIGRAPHER
b Albuquerque, NMex, June 3, 23. *Study:* Univ NMex, with Randall Davey, Kenneth M Adams & Ralph Douglass; also with Enrique Montenegro & Raymond Jonson. *Work:* Mus NMex, Santa Fe; Univ Albuquerque; NMex State Univ; Univ NMex. *Comn:* La Hacienda, Ford Motor Co, Dearborn, Mich, 73; Keep New Mexico Beautiful, Kennecott Copper Corp, 74; Tex Int Airlines; Paramont Pictures; Arthritis Found. *Exhib:* War with Japan, 47; Fiesta Show, Mus NMex, 62; Art Intimates, Galerie de Paris, New York, 65; Museo Ibariano Arte De Norte America, Madrid, Spain, 85-86; and others. *Pos:* First vpres, NMex Art League, 58-59; assoc ed & art dir, El Clarin; art dir, Quijotes De America. *Teaching:* Teacher oil painting, Ramirez Art Studio, 65-73. *Awards:* Anitiqua, Fine Arts Mus, Santa Fe, James T Forrest, 62; Los Trampas, Fiesta Show, Bernique Longley, 63; Nat Contest Columbus & the New World First Prize, Art Studio League, Denver, 91 & 92. *Bibliog:* Jacinto Quirate (auth), Southwest Artists, Exxon Oil Co, 73 & Mexican-American Artists, Univ Tex, Austin, 74; Frank Duane (auth), Pilgrims to the West, KLRN-TV, San Antonio, Tex, 73. *Mem:* Int Soc Artists. *Media:* All Media, Oil. *Publ:* Contribr, After Cortez, 73; illusr, Juan Diego and the Virgin of Guadalupe, 75; St Bernadette of Lourdes, 75; Across America, McDougal, Littell & C0, 86; text books for 8th grade literature 87-88 & art work studies, 88-89; Insignia, for 98th Bombardment Gr, Freedom Force, 90. *Mailing Add:* 10305 Santa Paula NE Albuquerque NM 87111

RAMOS, JULIANNE
ADMINISTRATOR, CONSULTANT
b New York, NY. *Study:* Dominican Col, BA, 75; Columbia Univ, MFA, 91. *Pos:* Exec dir, Rockland Ctr Arts, 84- *Teaching:* Adj prof, Marketing the Arts, New York Univ, spring 93. *Mailing Add:* 5 Old Farm Ct West Nyack NY 10994

RAMOS, (MEL) MELVIN JOHN
PAINTER, EDUCATOR
b Sacramento, Calif, July 24, 35. *Study:* Sacramento Jr Col, with Wayne Thiebaud, 54; San Jose State Col, 55; Sacramento State Col, BA, 57 & MA, 58. *Work:* Mus Mod Art, New York; Neue Galerie, Aachen, Ger; Oakland Art Mus & San Francisco Art Mus, Calif; Guggenheim Mus; Indianapolis Mus; Nat Gallery, Washington, DC. *Comn:* Paintings, Time Inc, New York, 68 & Syracuse Univ, NY, 70. *Exhib:* Pop Art USA, Oakland Mus & Six More, Los Angeles Co Mus, Calif, 63; Human Concern, Personal Torment, Whitney Mus Am Art, New York, 69; Pop Art Revisited, Hayward Gallery, London, 69; Looking West, Joslyn Art Mus, Omaha, Nebr, 70; Am Pop Art, Whitney Mus Am Art, 74; Krannert Mus, Univ Ill, Champaign, 74; Cornell Univ, Ithaca, NY, 74; Retrospective, Mus Havs Lange, Krefeld, WGer, 75; solo exhib, Schaufenstergalerie, Frankfurt, Ger, 91, Louis K Meisel Gallery, New York, 91, ARTAX, Düsseldorf, Ger, 92 & Galerie B Haasner, Wiesbaden, Ger, 92; Hand-Painted Pop: American Art in Transition, 1955-62 (catalog), Mus Contemp Art, Los Angeles, 92; and others. *Teaching:* Assoc prof painting, Calif State Univ, Hayward, 66-92, prof art, 80- *Awards:* Nat Endowment Artist Fel, 86; US-France Exchange Fel, 86. *Bibliog:* Liz Claridge (auth), Mel Ramos, Mathews Miller Dunbar, London, 75; Mel Ramos--Watercolors, Lancaster-Miller, 79; Claudia Betti & Teel Sale (auths), Drawing: A Contemporary Approach, Chicago, 245,246, 92. *Media:* Oil, Watercolor. *Publ:* Contribr, History of Modern Art, 69, Erotic Art 2, 70, Art Now/New Age, 71, The High Art of Cooking, 72 & Art as Image & Idea, 72. *Dealer:* Louis K Meisel Gallery 141 Prince St New York NY 10012. *Mailing Add:* 5941 Ocean View Dr Oakland CA 94618

RAMOS, THEODORE
PAINTER, ILLUSTRATOR
b Oporto, Portugal, Oct 30, 28; British citizen. *Study:* Royal Acad Schs, London, Eng, RAS Dipl, 54. *Work:* Nat Portrait Gallery, London; Guildhall Chamber, Windsor, Berks, Eng; Royal Acad Arts, London; Government House, Perth, W Australia. *Comn:* H M Queen Elizabeth the Queen Mother, Irish Guards, 78; The Transfiguration, Distillers Company, London, 79; H R H the Duke of Edinburgh Grenddier Guards, 89; H M Queen Elizabeth II, Grenadier Guards, 91. *Exhib:* Bicentenary Exhib, Royal Acad Arts, London, 68; 20th Century Portraits, Nat Portrait Gallery, London, 80 & 89. *Teaching:* vis lectr fine art, Brighton Col Art, Eng, 59-65; Harrow Sch Art, Eng, 64-67; Royal Acad Arts, London, 60-84. *Awards:* Silver Medal, Royal Acad Schs, 54. *Media:* Oil on Canvas. *Publ:* Illustr, Chinese Art, Pelican & Thames & Hudson, 55; Monumental Brasses, Penguin Books, 57. *Dealer:* Portraits Inc 985 Park Ave New York NY 10028. *Mailing Add:* Studio 3 Chelsea Farm House Milmans St London SW10 OBY England United Kingdom

RAMSAUER, JOSEPH FRANCIS
PAINTER
b Chicago, Ill, Aug 12, 43. *Study:* Southern Ill Univ, Carbondale, BA, 67, MFA, 69; also with David Slivka. *Work:* Univ Galleries, Southern Ill Univ; Louisville Arts Club; AMOCO Corp of Chicago; McDonald Corp Indianapolis; Augustana Col. *Comn:* Saukenuk Indian Mem, Ill State Bicentennial Comn, Black Hawk Col, Ill, 76. *Exhib:* Mid-Am Two, City Art Mus of St Louis, 69; Mid-Miss Valley Ann, Davenport Art Gallery, Iowa, 70, 74-77, 80 & 81; 19th Mid-South Biennial, Brooks Mem Art Gallery, Memphis, 75; Washington & Jefferson Nat, Washington & Jefferson Col, Washington, Pa, 76; Am Painters in Paris, Paris Convention Ctr, France, 76; Ann Seven State Competition, Univ Wis, Platteville, 77; 41st Nat Ann Midyear Show, Butler Inst of Am Art, Youngstown, Ohio, 77; 69th Ann Jury Exhib, Birmingham Mus of Art, Ala, 77; Tex Fine Arts Asn Traveling Exhib, 78. *Collections Arranged:* Spectrum Invitational, Davenport Art Gallery, Iowa, 72; Black Hawk Col & Ill Cent Col Art Fac Exhib, 74; 31st Ill Invitational, Ill State Mus, 79; Two Midwest Artists, Sangamon State Univ, Springfield, Ill, 81. *Teaching:* Prof art, Black Hawk Col, 69-87, chmn art dept, 71-83. *Awards:* Best of Show, Ann Seven State Competition, Univ Wis, 77; First Place in Acrylic Division & The Judges Award, Pilot Club of Golden Sands Int Fine Arts Exhib, 77; First Place in Painting, Boston Mills Art Festival, Peninsula, Ohio, 84 & 87. *Mem:* Chicago Artists Coalition; Deaf Artists of Am Inc. *Media:* Acrylic on Canvas. *Mailing Add:* PO Box 375 Viola IL 61436-0375

RAMSEY, DOROTHY J
PAINTER, WRITER
b Northampton, Mass, May 1, 35. *Study:* Northampton Commercial Col, 54; Smith Col, 75-76; pvt study with Helen Van Wyk, Roger Curtis & Michael Stoffa. *Work:* New England Telephone. *Exhib:* Burr Artists Ann Exhibs, New York, 82-85; Salmagundi Club Ann Exhibs, New York, 82-87 & 90-; North Shore Arts Asn, Gloucester, Mass, 82-; Rockport Art Asn, Mass, 84- *Pos:* Dir & instr oil painting, Ramsey Art Studio, 77-80; co-owner & operator, Michael Stoffa Gallery, Rockport, Mass, 80- *Awards:* Grumbacher Award, North Shore Arts Asn, 88; Distinguished Serv Award, North Shore Arts Asn, 90; Roger Clarke Popular Award, Rockport Art Asn, 91. *Mem:* Rockport Art Asn; North Shore Arts Asn, Gloucester, Mass (secy, 80-84, mem bd, 80-90); Salmagundi Club, New York; Artist Fel, New York. *Media:* Oil. *Mailing Add:* 49A Main St Rockport MA 01966

RANALLI, DANIEL
ARTIST, EDUCATOR
b New Haven, Conn, Oct 17, 46. *Study:* Clark Univ, Worcester, Mass, BA, 68; Boston Univ, MA, 71. *Work:* Polaroid Europa Collection; Boston Mus Fine Arts; San Francisco Mus Mod Art; Worcester Art Mus, Mass; Mus Mod Art, New York; Baltimore Mus Fine Arts; St Petersburg Mus Fine Art, Fla; and others. *Comn:* New Works, Mass Council Arts, Photographic Resource Ctr, 81. *Exhib:* One-man shows, Mass Inst of Technol Photog Gallery, 77, Foto Gallery, New York, 78, Carl Siembab Gallery, Boston, 78, 79 & 82 & Vision Gallery, Boston; Inst Contemp Art, Boston, 81; Boston Mus Fine Arts, 81; San Francisco Mus Mod Art; Baltimore Mus Fine Arts; and others. *Collections Arranged:* Elements of Landscape, Boston Univ Art Gallery, 83 & Earthworks, 89. *Pos:* Prog dir, The Artists Found, 75-79; exec dir, Truro Ctr Arts, 79-81; actg dir, Boston Univ Art Gallery, 82-83; dir, Arts Admin Prog, Lesley Col Grad Sch, Cambridge, Mass, 84-92, Boston Univ, 92. *Teaching:* Prof, Lesley Col Grad Sch, Cambridge, 84-92; assoc prof art hist dept, Boston Univ, currently. *Awards:* Individual Artist Fel, Nat Endowment Arts, 81; Mass Arts Lottery Grant, 83. *Bibliog:* Candida Finkel (auth), Light lines, Afterimage, Rochester, NY, 6/77; article, Camera Arts, 5/83; C Temin (auth), Mingling scientific detachment & personal passion, Boston Globe, 12/7/89. *Mem:* Mass Alliance Art Educ (bd trustees, 76-79); Photog Resource Ctr, Boston; Boston Visual Artists Union (vpres, 77); Am Asn Mus. *Publ:* Auth, Forum (monthly column), Art New Eng, 82; coauth, Darkroom Dynamics, Curtin & London, 78; contrib ed, Provincetown Arts, Mass. *Dealer:* Zoe Gallery 207 Newbury St Boston MA. *Mailing Add:* 76 Sumner St Newton MA 02159

RAND, ARCHIE
PAINTER, MURALIST
b New York, NY, Aug 13, 49. *Study:* City Col New York, 65-66; Art Students League NY, 67-68; Pratt Inst, Brooklyn, BFA, 70. *Work:* Brooklyn Mus, Pratt Inst, NY Public Libr, Jewish Mus, New York; Israel Mus, Jerusalem; Mint Mus Art, Charlotte, NC; Carnegie Inst; Art Inst Chicago; Chicago & Speruts Mus; Victoria & Albert Mus, London. *Comn:* Mural wall panels, Yeshivah of Flatbush, New York, 73-77; murals on stone, Congregation B'nai Yosef, New York, 75-77 & fresco & mosaic interior, 78-79; 12 stained glass windows, Anshe Emet Synagogue, Chicago, 80; three stained glass windows, Temple Sholom, Chicago, 83; exterior murals, Michlalah Col, Jerusalem, 83; murals, Eresco, Hebrew Home Greator Washington, 87, Chapters, Freyer Found, NY, 88. *Exhib:* One-man shows, Tibor de Nagy Gallery, New York, 72, 74, 78, 79, 80, 82 & 84 & Dart Gallery, Chicago, 80, Cincinnati Contemp Art Ctr, 84, Phyllis Kind Gallery, 86-88, Jewish Mus Art, 86-88, Mem Art Gallery, Rochester, 89 & Scott Hanson Gallery, 89 & 90 Exit Art, 90; Selected Works from Tibor de Nagy Gallery, Mint Mus Art, Charlotte, NC, 78; New York Collection, Albright-Knox Art Gallery, Buffalo, NY, 78-79 & 79-80; Artists Choice Mus, New York, 79 & 83; Bibliotheque National de France, 90; Victoria & Albert Mus, London, 90; Scott Hanson Gallery, New York, 89 & 90; Exit Art, New York, 91; Philadelphia Mus Art, 92; Feigensen-Preston Gallery, Detroit, Mich, 91 & 92. *Pos:* Designer, Rambusch Stained Glass Studios, 83, Edward Fields Tapestries Inc 83-84 & Xicon Animation Inc, 87; US rep, UNICEF Art Coun, 85-; acting dir, Hoffberger Grad Sch Painting, Md Inst, 89-90; co-chair, Studio Arts Prog, Col Art Asn, 92-94, chair, 94-; acq comt, George Mus, New York, 92- *Teaching:* Vis prof, State Univ Ill, Normal, 84, Va Commonwealth Univ, 85, Columbia Univ, RI Sch Design, State Univ NY, Albany, Brooklyn Col, 90 Univ Syracuse, 91; grad faculty, Bard Col, 86-91, Sch Visual Arts, 88-91; assoc dir grad prog, Md Inst Col Art, 89-; prof art, Columbia Univ, 92-93; artist-in-residence, Hoffberger Grad Sch Painting & Mt Royal Grad Sch Art, Md Inst, Col Art, 92-93; grad fac, Sch Vis Arts, 93- *Awards:* Creative Artists Pub Serv Prog, NY State Coun Arts, 75; Clayworks Residency, Nat Endowments Arts, 83; Engelhard Award, 85; awards, Visual Arts, 87; NY Found Arts Fel, 90. *Bibliog:* Ross Feld (auth), On the hook: The work of Archie Rand, Arts, 12/77; John Ashbery (auth), A joyful noise, New York Mag, 6/79; John R Lane (auth), Archie Rand, the consistency of choice, Arts, 11/79; Barry Schwabsky (auth), Archie Rand Connections, Art Mag, 6/84; John Yau (auth), Archie Rand, Art Forum, 86; Barry Schwabsky (auth), What is painting about--a conversation with Archie Rand, ARTS Mag, 4/87. *Mem:* Nat Soc of Mural Painters (bd mem); Int Soc Film Animators; IFRAA Am Inst Architects. *Media:* Acrylic on Canvas; Stained Glass, Fresco. *Publ:* Auth, The victory of the futile, ARTS Mag, 11/88; illusr, Two or Three Things, Collectif Generation, 90; auth, Trevor Winkfield's goon show, Arts, 9/89; coauth (with Malcolm Morley), Sensation without memory, Tema Celeste, Autumn 91, No 32-3. *Mailing Add:* 326 55th St Brooklyn NY 11220

RAND, HARRY
HISTORIAN, EDUCATOR
b New York, NY, Jan 10, 47. *Study:* City Col New York, BA, 69; Harvard Univ, AM, 71, PhD, 74. *Pos:* Contrib ed, Arts Mag, New York, 75-; cur 20th century painting & sculpture, Nat Mus Am Art, DC, 79-; hon ed, Leonardo, Berkeley, 83-; consult, Nat Acad Sci, 84; consult, Consanti Found, 89- *Teaching:* Asst prof mod art & methodology, State Univ NY Buffalo, 74-78. *Awards:* Rockefeller Found Develop Grant, 83; Smithsonian Inst Res Opportunities Grant, 85; US Patent Holder, 89. *Bibliog:* Hilton Kramer (auth), The pictures in the paintings, 6/21/81 & A true museum of record, 2/14/82, New York Times. *Mem:* Explorers Club, New York. *Res:* History of modern art; problems of methodology and implications. *Publ:* Auth, The Beginning of Things, Dryad Press, 83; Manet's Contemplation at the Gare St Lazare, UCal Press, 87; Paul Manship, Smithsonian Press, 89; Hundertwassen, Taschen, 91; Julian Stanczak, State Univ NY, 92. *Mailing Add:* 5511 Greystone St Chevy Chase MD 20815

RAND, PAUL
DESIGNER
b New York, NY, Aug 15, 14. *Study:* Pratt Inst; Art Students League, with George Grosz; Parsons Sch Design; Philadelphia Col Art, Hon DFA, 79; Kutztown Univ, LHD; Yale Univ, Hon MA. *Work:* Mus Mod Art; Libr Cong, Washington, DC; and many mus in US, Japan & Europe. *Exhib:* One-man shows, Composing Room, 47, Am Inst Graphic Arts Gallery, 58 & IBM Gallery, 71; Pratt Inst, 72; many shows, Art Dirs Club New York. *Pos:* Art dir, Esquire Apparel Arts, 37-41; art dir, Weintraub Advert Agency, 41-54; design consult, IBM Corp, 56, Westinghouse Elec Corp, 60-81 & Cummins Engine Co, 63- *Teaching:* Instr design, Cooper Union, 42; instr graphic design, Pratt Inst, 46-47; prof graphic design, Yale Univ, 56-69 & 74-89, prof emer graphic design, currently; Yale summer sch prog, Brissago, Switz, 77- *Awards:* Gold Medal, Am Inst Graphic Arts, 66; Art Dirs Hall of Fame, 72; First Florence Prize for Visual Commun, 87. *Bibliog:* Georgine Oeri (auth), article, Graphis Mag, 47; Y Kamekura (auth), The work of Paul Rand, Zokeisha, Tokyo & Knopf, NY, Yale Univ Press, fall 85; article in Am Artist, 70. *Mem:* Art Dirs Club New York; Am Inst Graphic Arts; Alliance Graphique Int, Paris; Benjamin Franklin fel, Royal Soc Arts & Sci, London. *Publ:* Auth, Thoughts on design, Wittenborn, 47 & Van Nostrand Reinhold, 70; illusr, I Know a Lot of Things, 56, Sparkle & Spin, 57, Little 1, 62 & Listen, Listen, 70, Harcourt; auth, Paul Rand: A Designer's Art, Yale Univ Press, fall 85. *Mailing Add:* 87 Goodhill Rd Weston CT 06883

RAND, STEVEN JAY
SCULPTOR
b Yonkers, NY. *Study:* State Univ NY, Buffalo, BFA, 75; Univ Ariz, MFA, 77. *Work:* Phoenix Art Mus; Tucson Mus Art; Colorado Springs Fine Arts Ctr; Plains Art Mus, Moorhead, Minn; City Palo Alto, Calif. *Comn:* Sculptures, City Scottsdale, 79, City Phoenix, 81 & City Casa Grande, 82. *Exhib:* Six Artists Invitational, Tucson Mus Art, 79; Okla Arts Ctr Ann Competition, 81; solo exhibs, Scottsdale Ctr Arts, Ariz, 82 & Plains Art Mus, Moorhead, Minn, 83; Sept Competition, Alexandria Mus, La, 83; Coos Mus Ann, Coos Bay, Ore, 83. *Mem:* Artists Equity Asn. *Media:* Metal. *Mailing Add:* Ten Warren St New York NY 10007

RANDALL, LILIAN M C
CURATOR
b Berlin, Ger, Feb 1, 31. *Study:* Mt Holyoke Col, BA, 50; Radcliffe Col, MA, 51, PhD, 55; Hon degree, Towson State Univ, 93. *Work:* Walters Art Gallery, Baltimore, Md. *Collections Arranged:* Armenian Manuscripts, Walter Art Gallery, Baltimore, Md, 74; Printed Books before 1500, Walters Art Gallery, 77; Splendor in Books, Grolier Club, New York, 77-78; An American Art Agent in Paris, George A Lucas (1857-1909), Walters Art Gallery, 78-79; Illuminated Manuscripts: Masterpieces in Miniature, Highlights from the Collection of the Walters Art Gallery. *Pos:* Asst dir, Md Arts Coun, 72-73; cur manuscripts & rare books, Walters Art Gallery, 74. *Teaching:* Vis lectr medieval illumination, Johns Hopkins Univ, 64-68. *Awards:* Sesquicentennial Award, Mount Holyoke Col, 87. *Mem:* Medieval Acad Am; Col Art Asn; Int Ctr Medieval Art (bd dirs, 78-82); Baltimore Bibliophiles (pres, 81-83). *Res:* Medieval European illumination. *Publ:* Auth, Exempla and their influence on Gothic marginal art, Art Bull, 57; auth, Images in the margins of Gothic manuscripts, Univ Calif, 66; co-ed & contribr, Gatherings in honor of Dorothy Miner, Walters Art Gallery, 74; auth, The Diary of George A Lucas: An American Art Agent in Paris, (2 vols), Princeton Univ Press, 79; auth, A Nineteenth-Century Medieval Prayerbook Woven in Lyon, In: Art the Ape of Nature: Studies in Honor of H W Janson, Harry N Abrams, 81; auth & ed, Medieval and Renaissance Manuscripts in the Walters Art Gallery: France, 875-1420, 89 & 1420-1540, 92, Johns Hopkins Univ Press. *Mailing Add:* c/o Walters Art Gallery 600 N Charles St Baltimore MD 21201-5185

RANDALL, RICHARD HARDING, JR
CURATOR, HISTORIAN
b Baltimore, Md, Jan 31, 26. *Study:* Princeton Univ, AB(archit); Harvard Univ, MA(fine arts). *Collections Arranged:* American Furniture in the MFA (with catalog), Mus Fine Arts, Boston, 64; reinstallation of the entire collection of the Walters Art Gallery, 74. *Pos:* Assoc cur, Cloisters, Metrop Mus Art, New York, 53-59; asst cur, Mus Fine Arts, Boston, Mass, 59-64; asst dir, Walters Art Gallery, Baltimore, 64-65, dir, 65-81, cur, medieval art, 81-84. *Res:* American furniture, medieval art, arms and armour. *Publ:* Auth, Bestiary of the Cloisters, 59; Masterpieces of Ivory, 85. *Mailing Add:* 301 Kendall Rd Baltimore MD 21210

RANDLETT, MARY WILLIS
PHOTOGRAPHER
b Seattle, Wash, May 5, 24. *Study:* Whitman Col, BA, 47; photog with Hans Jorgensen, Seattle, 48. *Work:* Dept Photog & Prints, Metrop Mus Art, New York; Arch Am Art, Nat Collection Fine Arts, Nat Portrait Gallery, Washington, DC; Manuscripts Div & Spec Collections, Univ Wash Collections, Seattle; Wash State Capitol Mus, Olympia, Wash; Western Wash State Univ, Bellingham. *Comn:* Wash State Artists (photog), Wash State Libr, Olympia, 68; doc ser (photogs), Noguchi Skyviewing sculpture, Western Wash Univ, Bellingham, 70, Tony Angell's of raven, Pacific NW Bell, Seattle, 78, Artists, Everett, 80, 4 artists for Kingdome, King County Arts Comn, Seattle, 78-80, Wash. *Exhib:* One-woman shows, Action/Better City, Am Inst Architects, Seattle Art Mus, 68, Artists of Pac Northwest, Seattle Art Mus Pavillion, 71, Seattle Sci Ctr, 71, Northwest Portfolio: The photog of Mary Randlett, Off of the Gov, Olympia, Wash, 91 & Stonington Gallery, Seattle, Wash, 92; Infinity 70, 25th Anniversary Exhib, Am Soc Mag Photogrs, New York 70; Wash St Photog Exchange of Sickuan Prov, China, Charles 7 Emma Fry Mus, Seattle, Wash, 84; 100 Years of Washington Photography, Tacoma Art Mus, Wash, 89; In Retrospect: 25 Years, Gov Invitational Art Exhib, Wash St Capital Mus, Olympia, 89. *Awards:* Gov Award, Wash, 83; Individual Artists Award, King County Arts Comn, Seattle, 89; GAP Award, Artists Trust, 89. *Bibliog:* In Retrospect: Twenty Five Years, Gov Invitational Art Exhib Sept/Nov 1989, Seattle Times, 7/13/89; Whitman, Mag Whitman Col, summer, 90. *Mem:* Am Soc Mag Photogr. *Publ:* Photogr, Openings, Univ Wash Press, Seattle, 90; Auth, Dancing on the Rim of the World, Univ Ariz Press, Tuscon, 90; George Tsutakawa, 90, The Natural History of Puget Sound Country, 91, The Wright Space, 91 & Art in Seattle's Public Places, Univ Washington Press, Seattle, 92. *Mailing Add:* Box 10536 Bainbridge Island WA 98110

RANDOLPH, LYNN MOORE
PAINTER
b New York, NY, Dec 19, 38. *Study:* Univ Tex, Austin, BFA, 61. *Work:* San Antonio Mus Art; Mus Arts, Houston; The Merry Ingraham Bunting Inst, Radcliffe/Howard. *Exhib:* Ten Houston Artists in Dallas, 500 Exposition Gallery, 80; Thirteen Artists: A Look at Houston, Ga State Univ Gallery, Atlanta, 82; solo exhib, Contemp Arts Mus, Houston, 78, Graham Gallery, 84, 86 & 91, The Texas Landscape 1900-1986, Mus Fine Arts, Houston, 86, Bunting Inst, Radcliffe Col, 90 & Everyday Miracles: Retablos, Ex Votos and Contemp Texas Artists, Contemp Art Mus, Houston, Tex, 90; Texas Artists, Contemp Arts Ctr, New Orleans, 80; Third Coast Review: A Look at Art in Texas, Aspen Art Mus, Aspen, Colo, 87; Act of Faith: Politics & the Spirit, Cleveland State Univ, Ohio, 88; Houston '88, Houston Art Dealers Asn, Cullen Ctr, Tex, 88; Evidence: Contemporary Narrative Art of the Southwest, San Antonio Mus Art, 89; Slouching Towards 2000: The Politics of Gender, Women & Their Work, Austin, 92. *Awards:* Residency at Yaddo, June 87; Fel, The Bunting Inst, Radcliffe Col, 89-90. *Bibliog:* Suzanne Bloom, Ed Hill, review, Artforum, 3/87; Robert Hobbs, No Blue Bonnets, No Yellow Roses: Essays on Texas Women in the Arts, Midmord Press, 88; Andy Sparks (auth), review, Dialogue, 7-8/88; Thomas Frick (auth), Art in Americas, 12/90; Donna Haraway (auth), Cultural Studies, 91; David Connelly (auth), Arts Papers 1-2/92. *Mem:* Nat Women's Caucus Art (regional vpres, 82-86); Houston Women's Caucus Art (pres, 79-80). *Media:* Oil. *Publ:* Auth, Beyond political and economic equality, Women Artists' News, 83. *Dealer:* Bill Graham 1431 N Alabama Houston TX 77098. *Mailing Add:* 1803 Banks Houston TX 77098

RANES, CHRIS
PAINTER
b Warsaw, Poland; US citizen. *Study:* Pratt Inst, New York, Art Cert; Univ Santa Clara, BA & MA. *Work:* Arco Ctr Visual Arts, Los Angeles; Bank Am & Crown Zellerbach, San Francisco; Triton Mus Art, de Saisset Mus, Santa Clara Univ, Santa Clara, Calif; Nev Mus Art; Hewlett-Packard Corp; and others. *Exhib:* Solo shows, De Saisset Mus, Calif, 78, La Galerie Bleue, Grenoble, France, 80, Ivory-Kimpton Gallery, San Francisco, 83, La Galerie d'Art UNA, Geneva, Switz, 80 & Fine Arts Mus, Alexandria, Egypt, 83; Stanford Univ Gallery, Calif, 86; J J Brookings Gallery, San Jose, 88; Leo Kamen Gallery, Toronto, Canada, 88; Galerie Suisse de Paris, Paris, France, 89; Sharon Park Gallery, Menlo Park, Calif, 90; Quantum Corp, Milpitis, Calif, 92; and others. *Pos:* Textile designer & stylist, Riverdale Fabrics, Blanc Studios, New York, 51-55; bd mem, De Saisset Mus, Santa Clara, Calif, currently. *Teaching:* Lectr painting & graphic printmaking, Univ Santa Clara, Calif, 68-73, lectr French, 72-73. *Awards:* Second Prize, Calif State Competition, 66 & Nat Award of Merit, Nat Biennial, 66, Nat League Am Pen Women. *Bibliog:* Ada Garfinkel (auth), Oils are distinctive, Independent J of Marin, Calif, 78; Premiere Exposition Europeenne de Chris Ranes, Le Dauphine Libere, Grenoble, France; F Cebulski (auth), The adequate symbol, Artweek, 7/82; Stefano Benedetti (auth), Chris Ranes, Firenze Nazione, Florence, Italy, 84; Dorothy Burkhart (auth), Critic's choice, San Jose Mercury News, 10/21/88. *Media:* Oil. *Dealer:* J J Brookings Gallery 330 Commercial St San Jose CA 95108. *Mailing Add:* 3973 Bibbits Dr Palo Alto CA 94303

RANKAITIS, SUSAN
PAINTER, PHOTOGRAPHER
b Cambridge, Mass, Sept 10, 49. *Study:* Univ Ill, Champaign, BFA(painting), 71; Univ Southern Calif, Los Angeles, MFA(painting & photography), 77. *Work:* Ctr Creative Photog, Tucson, Ariz; San Francisco Mus Mod Art, Calif; Los Angeles Co Mus Art, Calif; Nat Mus Am Art; Int Mus Photog George Eastman House; and others. *Exhib:* Solo exhibs, Los Angeles Co Mus Art, 83, Int Mus Photog at George Eastman House, 83, Min Gallery, Tokyo, Japan, 88, Meyers/Bloom, Santa Monica, Calif, 89 & 90, Schneider Mus, 90, Ctr Creative Photog, 91, Roth Bloom Gallery, Santa Monica, 92; Fresno Mus, 87; San Francisco Mus Mod Art, 87 & 89; Santa Fe Art Mus, 87; Axiom Ctr Arts, Eng, 87-88; Los Angeles Co Mus Art, 88; Nat Mus Am Art, 89; and others. *Teaching:* Fletcher Jones chair in art (prof), Scripps Col. *Awards:* Nat Endowment Arts Fels, 80 & 88; US/France Fel, LaNapoule Art Found, 90; Agnes Bourne Fel in painting & photog, Djerassi Found, 90. *Bibliog:* Merle Shipper (coauth with) Marjorie Perloff, Susan Rankaitis, Gallery Min, Tokyo, 88; Andy Grundberg & Kathleen Gauss (auths), Photography and Arts Interactions Since 1946, Abeville Press; Susan Kendell (auth), Susan Rankaitis, Meyers/Bloom Gallery, 90. *Mem:* Col Art Asn; Los Angeles Ctr Photog Studies; Los Angeles Contemp Exhibs (bd trustees); Women's Action Coalition. *Media:* Miscellaneous Media. *Dealer:* Ruth Bloom Gallery 2112 Broadway Santa Monica CA 90404. *Mailing Add:* 3117 Lansbury Claremont CA 91711

RANKIN, DON
PAINTER, PRINTMAKER
Study: Famous Artists' Sch; also with Bill Yeager; Samford Univ, BA(fine art & psychol). *Comn:* Birmingham Centennial Commemorative Coins, Arlington Shrine, 70, Univ Ala Med Complex, 71 & Birmingham-Jefferson Civic Ctr, 71; prints, First Nat Bank, Tuskaloosa, 74-76; painting, Country Club Birmingham, 79; Watercolor & print, comn by Air War Col, class of 90, Maxwell AFB, Montgomery, Ala; and others. *Exhib:* One-man show, Birmingham Mus Art, 74 & 79; First Ann Juried Exhib, Southern Watercolor Soc, Cheekwood, Tenn, 77; Second Ann Juried Exhib, Southern Watercolor Soc, Columbus Mus Arts & Sci, 78; The Am Barn & Its Translation in Watercolor, Chautauqua Art Asn Exhib Am Art, NY, 79; 3rd Ann Exhib Southern Watercolor Soc, N Tex State Univ Galleries, Denton, 79; Southern Connections - a Nat Invitational, Blount Collection, Montgomery, Ala, 86; Invitational Exhib, Southern Watercolor Painters, Takarazuka, Japan, 90. *Teaching:* National & international watercolor workshops for various art associations; instr, Samford Univ. *Bibliog:* Featured artist, watercolor page, Am Artist, 3/80; Elizabeth Leonard (auth), Painting the Landscape, Watson-Guptill; Watercolor 89, Am Artist; reviews, NY Art Rev, 89, Am Artist (video), 6/90 & Artist's Mag (video), 7/90. *Mem:* Ala Watercolor Soc; charter mem La Watercolor Soc; Southern Watercolor Soc. *Media:* Watercolor, Egg Tempera. *Publ:* Auth, Mastering Glazing Techniques in Watercolor, Watson-Guptill, 86; Painting from Sketches, Photographs and Imagination, Watson-Guptill, 87; Fifty Most Asked Questions About Watercolor Glazing Techniques, Watson-Guptill, 91. *Mailing Add:* 3412 Wellford Circle Birmingham AL 35226

RANSOM, BRIAN
CERAMIST
Study: Univ Puget Sound, Tacoma, Wash, 72-73; RI Sch Design, Providence, 73-74; NY State Col Ceramics at Alfred Univ, New York, BFA(art), 76-78; Universidad de San Marcos (res in Pre-Columbian musical instruments), Lima, Peru, 78-79; Univ Tulsa Okla, MA(ceramics, anthropologh), 83-84; Claremont Grad Sch, Calif, MFA(sculpture), 84-85. *Work:* Everson Mus Ceramics, Syracuse, NY; NY State Col Ceramics Mus, Alfred, NY; also pvt collections of Edward Judd, Lynn Bonyhadi-Scheicher, Pat & Darrel Maveety and others. *Exhib:* Solo exhibs, Cera Cossa Col, Ridgecrest, Calif, 89, Sounding Clay & Activated Clay, 92, Couturier Gallery, Los Angeles, 89, Univ Col Redlands Calif, 89; group shows, East Meets West, Ore Sch Arts & Crafts, Portland, 88; Collectors Exhib, Wita Gardner Gallery, San Diego, 88; Faith Nightingale Gallery, San Diego, 90; performance of the ceramic ensemble, Art Prk, Mus Contemp Art, Second Stage Theatre, Hollywood, Calif; and many other performances. *Teaching:* Numerous lectrs & workshops, Music & Sculpture, 79-90; Art teacher, Univ Calif-Los Angeles extension, Chino Inst Men, Calif, 9; ceramics & glaze calculation instr, Chaffey Col, Calif, 90. *Awards:* Res Fel for Sound Research, Claremont Grad Sch, Calif, 85; Res Fel, Univ Tulsa, Okla, 85; Visual Artist Fel Sculpture, Nat Endowment Arts, 86. *Bibliog:* Jenny Cashman (auth), Ransom Sculpts Special Sounds with Art, Music, Idylwild Town Crier, p 15, 9/17/89; Mario Caseta (auth), interview KPFK Pacifica Radio, Los Angeles, 10/3/90; and others. *Publ:* Auth, The Enigma of the Peruvian Whistling Water Vessel, Univ Mo, Columbus, Ohio, 85; contribr (with patrick O'Hearn), music sound track for film "The Destroyer" released by MGM, 87; auth, Sounding Clay, Ceramics Monthly, vol 36, no 8, p 30-34, 88; Sounding Clay (music), Hubba Hubba Studio, Hubbard, Ore, 90. *Mailing Add:* c/o Couturier Gallery 166 N La Brea Ave Los Angeles CA 90036

RANSOM, HENRY CLEVELAND, JR
PAINTER
b Chattanooga, Tenn, Aug 19, 42. *Study:* Univ Ga, BFA, 64, MFA, 72. *Work:* Montgomery Mus Fine Art, Ala; Mint Mus Art, Charlotte, NC; Hunter Mus Art, Chattanooga, Tenn; Columbus Mus Art, Ohio. *Exhib:* one-man shows, Mint Mus Art, 76, Hunter Mus Art, Chattanooga, 76, Montgomery Mus Fine Art, 76 & Far Gallery, New York, 78; Southern Realism, Miss Mus Art, Jackson, 79; New Am Still Life, Westmoreland Co Mus Art, Greenburg, Pa, 79; Henry W Ranger Exhib, Nat Acad Design, New York, 80; 46th Ann Nat Midyear Show, Butler Inst Am Art, Youngstown, Ohio, 82; 45th Ann Exhib, Soc Four Arts, Palm Beach, Fla, 83. *Awards:* Atwater Kent Award, 39th Ann Exhib, Soc Four Arts, Palm Beach Fla, 77; Purchase Award, Mint Mus Art Biennial, 77; Julius Hallgarten Prize, 155th Ann Exhib, Nat Acad Design, New York, 80. *Media:* Oil, Pencil. *Publ:* Contribr, Ga Rev, Univ Ga Press, 76. *Mailing Add:* PO Box 25 Good Hope GA 30641

RANSON, NANCY SUSSMAN
PAINTER, PRINTMAKER
b New York, NY, Sept 13, 05. *Study:* Pratt Inst Sch Art & Design, BFA; Art Students League; Brooklyn Mus Art Sch; also with Alexander Brook; Robert Laurent & Jean Charlot. *Work:* Butler Inst Am Art, Youngstown, Ohio; Smithsonian Inst; New York Mus; Nat Art Gallery, Sydney, Australia; Nat Mus Mod Art, New Delhi, India; and others. *Exhib:* Brooklyn Mus, 50, 54 & 56; Whitney Mus Am Art, New York, 51; Pa Acad Fine Arts, 57; Color Prints of Americas, NJ State Mus, 70; Nat Soc Painters in Casein & Acrylics, Am Inst & Acad Arts & Lett, 79; solo shows, George Binet Gallery, New York, 48-50, Brooklyn Pub Libr Main Br, 51 & Univ of Maine, Orono, 64-78; traveling exhibs in Israel & Egypt, 81. *Awards:* MacDowell Found Fel, 64; First Prize in Graphics, Am Soc Contemp Artists, 70-84; Best Silk Screen, Audubon Artists, 82. *Mem:* Nat Asn Women Artists (chmn foreign exhibs, 63-67, chmn admis, 69-71, chmn nomination, 75-77, mem adv bd, 77-80 & chm graphics, 80-82); Am Soc Contemp Artists (pres, 69-71, permanent bd mem, 71-); Audubon Artists (dir graphics, 70-73, 75-78); hon mem Nat Soc Painters, 90. *Media:* Oil, Acrylic; Serigraphy. *Mailing Add:* 400 Rugby Rd Brooklyn NY 11226

RAPOPORT, SONYA
CONCEPTUAL ARTIST
b Boston, Mass. *Study:* Mass Col Art; New York Univ, BA; Univ Calif, Berkeley, MA. *Work:* Stedelijk Mus, Amsterdam, Holland; Grey Art Gallery, New York Univ; Indianapolis Mus Art, Ind; Oakland Art Mus, Calif; Crocker Art Mus, Sacramento, Calif. *Comn:* Abstract painting (acrylic/canvas), Hall of Justice, Hayward, Calif, 76. *Exhib:* One-person shows, Calif Palace Legion Honor & Crocker Art Mus, 64 & 74, Peabody Mus, Harvard Univ, Cambridge, Mass, 76 & Kuopio Mus, Finland, 92; Art Scene, San Francisco Mus Mod Art & Baltimore Mus Art, 65 & 73; Survey of Contemp Artists Books, Art Alliance Mus Pa, 81; Book Arts III, Nat Mus Women, Washington, DC, 90; Artists Books, Anchorage Mus Hist & Art, Alaska, 90; Books as Metaphor for Art: Beyond Words, vol 1 & 2, Crafts & Folk Art Mus & Calif Craft Mus, San Francisco, 90. *Pos:* Reviewer, Leonardo Mag. *Teaching:* San Francisco Art Inst, 74; New Sch Social Res, New York, 81; Sarah Lawrence Col, Bronxville, NY, 84; Univ Calif, Berkeley, 88; Ohio State Univ, 92. *Awards:* Vera Adams Davis Mem Award, 63 & Rhea Keller Mem Prizes, 65, San Francisco Mus Art; Individual Juror's Award, Richmond Art Ctr Ann, Calif, 66; Eyes & Ears Found Grant, 82; Calif Art Coun Grant for Telecommun, 88. *Bibliog:* Stephen Moore (auth), Sonya Rapoport--An Aesthetic Response, Union Gallery, San Jose State Univ, 78 Rapoport, Ctr Visual Arts, 79; Edgar Buonagurio (auth), Interaction art & science, Truman Gallery review, Arts Mag, 4/79; Patricia Zimmerman (auth), Metaphysical or Virtual Reality, Soma Mag, vol 18, spring 92; and others in LAICA J, 82 High Performance, 83, 88 & Heresies, 86. *Mem:* Womens Caucus Art; Pacific Ctr Book Arts; Ylem. *Media:* Scanning, Copy Images; Computer interactive. *Publ:* Auth, About Me, 79, Surface, 80, Chelate, 80 & The Remainder, 80, The Animated Soul-Gateway To Your Ka, pvt publ. *Mailing Add:* 6 Hillcrest Court Berkeley CA 94705

RAPP, LOIS
PAINTER, EDUCATOR
Study: Philadelphia Col Art, dipl(teacher's training) & cert(illus), 29; also with Earl Horter. *Work:* Woodmere Mus, Philadelphia; Valley Forge Mem Chapel, Pa; Gwynedd-Mercy Col, Gwynedd Valley, Pa; Norristown Pub Libr, Pa; Montgomery Hosp, Norristown; and others. *Exhib:* Am Drawing Ann XV, Norfolk, Va, 57; Am Watercolor Soc 91st Ann, New York, 58; Regional Exhib, Philadelphia Mus Art, 59; Philadelphia Watercolor Club, 71; Woodmere Mus, 72. *Teaching:* Instr art, Mater Misericordiae Acad, Merion, Pa, 33-45, Collegeville-Trappe Pub Schs, Pa, 35-48, Conshocken Art League, Pa, 35-37 & Greater Norristown Art League, 73-81. *Awards:* Gold Medal for Along the Schuylkill River, Lansdale Art League, 52; Awards for Meeting House Interior, 60 & Falls of the Potomac, 63, Woodmere Art Gallery. *Mem:* Am Watercolor Soc. *Media:* Watercolor, Oil. *Publ:* Auth, Past Tense, Plates Sun Lines, pvt publ, 83. *Mailing Add:* 116 Haws Ave Norristown PA 19401

RASCOE, STEPHEN THOMAS
PAINTER, EDUCATOR
b Uvalde, Tex, May 8, 24. *Study:* Univ Tex, Austin; Art Inst Chicago, BFA & MFA. *Work:* Dallas Mus Fine Arts; Southern Methodist Univ, Dallas; Ford Motor Co, Dearborn, Mich; Ling-Temco-Vought Res Ctr, Grand Prairie, Tex. *Comn:* Rancho Seco Land & Cattle Co, Corpus Christi, Tex, 67; Tex Instruments Corp, Dallas, 67; Arlington Bank & Trust Co, Tex, 69; First Nat Bank, 69 & Lakewood Bank, 71, Dallas. *Exhib:* Longview Ann, Tex, 57-86; Artists West of the Mississippi, Denver, 67; San Antonio Hemisphere, Tex, 68. *Teaching:* Assoc prof art, Univ Tex, Arlington, 64- *Awards:* Houston Mus Fine Arts Purchase Award, Tex Show, 56; First Prize, Tex Painting & Sculpture Show, Dallas Mus, 57; D D Feldman Award, 58. *Bibliog:* Texas Painting and Sculpture: 20th Century, 71. *Mem:* Dallas Art Asn; Ft Worth Art Asn; STex Art League (pres, 60-61); Arlington Art Asn (pres, 67-68). *Media:* Oil. *Publ:* Auth, Pecos to Rio Grande, Tex A&M Press, 83. *Dealer:* The Upstairs Gallery 1036 W Abram St Arlington TX. *Mailing Add:* Dept Art Univ Tex Arlington TX 76019

RASCON, ARMANDO
PAINTER, CURATOR
b Calexico, Calif, 1956. *Study:* Col Creative Studies, Univ Calif, Santa Barbara, Calif, BA, 79. *Exhib:* What's Happening: Contemp Art from Calif, Ore & Wash, Alternative Mus, New York, NY, 84; Mexian/American Art, Salon de Actos de la Loteria Nacional, Mexico City, 87; The AIDS Time line, Univ Art Mus, Berkeley, 89; Tattoo Collection, Jennifer Flay Galerie, Paris, France, 92; Existential Monochrome, Southern Exposure, San Francisco, Randolph St Gallery, Chicago, 92; Mis/Taken Identities, Univ Art Mus, Santa Barbarba, 92. *Pos:* Art dealer, conceptual artist, cur, educator, painter. *Teaching:* Univ Calif, Davis, 88; Calif Col Arts & Crafts, Oakland, Calif, 91. *Awards:* Fel, Nat Endowment Arts, 87. *Bibliog:* Suzaan Boettger (auth), The impolite figure, Art forum, 10/83; Judith Christensen (auth), Business as usual, Artweek, 12/12/87; Lydia Natthews (auth), Armando Rasan at Souhern Exposure, Visions, spring 92. *Publ:* Ed, The Multicultural Reading Room at Randolph Street Gallery, Artpapers. *Mailing Add:* 1539 A Falsom St San Francisco CA 94103-3728

RASH, NANCY
HISTORIAN, WRITER
b Louisville, Ky, Nov 19, 40. *Study:* Radcliffe Col, BA(magna cum laude), 62; Bryn Mawr Col, MA, 65, with Charles Mitchell, PhD, 71. *Teaching:* Prof art hist, Conn Col, 72-, chmn dept, 79-84, 87- *Mem:* Col Art Asn; Renaissance Soc Am; Int Ctr Medieval Art; Medieval Acad; Asn Historians Am Art. *Res:* Apulian Romanesque art; Florentine Renaissance art; George Caleb Bingham. *Publ:* Auth, A Note on the Stanza della Segnatura, Gazette des Beaux Arts, 79; auth, The months at Lentini, J Warburg & Courtauld Inst, 79; coauth, Orcagna's tabernacle in Orsanmichele in context, Art Bulletin, 81; auth, George Caleb Bingham's Lighter Relieving a Steamboat Aground, Smithsonian Studies in Am Art, 88; article, The Painting and Politics of George Caleb Bingham, Yale Univ Press, 91. *Mailing Add:* Dept Art Hist Conn Col New London CT 06320

RASKIND, PHILIS
SCULPTOR, INSTRUCTOR
b New York, NY. *Study:* Art Students League; Nat Acad Sch Fine Arts, cert, 73. *Work:* Elizabeth T Greenshields Mem Found, Montreal, Can. *Comn:* Peace Medal US & N Vietnam, pvt comn, New York, 73; theatre masks for New York City Opera, Conn Opera Co, 73-75; bust: Pompidou, Waxworks, Can, 74; miniature series, Quantum Arts, New York, 78-79; life-size figure for WAM Satta, 82; portrait bust, Sculpture Group, New Am Libr, 84. *Exhib:* Catharine Lorillard Wolfe Art Club, Nat Arts Club, New York, 72-79; Nat Sculpture Soc, New York, 72-80; Pen & Brush Club, New York, 75, 76, 78 & 79; Nat Acad Fine Arts Exhib, Nat Acad Fine Arts, 76-78; Salmagundi Club, New York, 79. *Pos:* Ed newsletter, Catharine Lorillard Wolfe Art Club, 75-78. *Teaching:* Instr sculpture, Manhattan Community for Psychotherapy, 73-75; instr sculpture, Am Telegraph & Telephone Adult Educ Prog, New York, 73-74; instr, Fashion Inst Technol, New York, 85-87. *Awards:* Gold Medal, Pen & Brush Club, 78; Bronze Medal, Catharine Lorillard Wolfe Art Club, 77; Kalos Kagathos Found Award, Nat Sculpture Soc, 82; and others. *Mem:* Catharine Lorillard Wolfe Art Club (sculpture chmn, 75-78); Nat Art League; Vis Artists & Galeri Galleries Asn; Int Soc Artists; Artists Equity Asn. *Media:* Clay; Wood. *Dealer:* Belanthi Gallery 142 Court St Brooklyn NY. *Mailing Add:* 330 Third Ave No 15G New York NY 10010

RASMUSSEN, ANTON JESSE
PAINTER, ADMINISTRATOR
b Salt Lake City, Utah, Nov 12, 42. *Study:* Univ Utah, BFA, 67, MFA, 74. *Work:* Utah Mus Fine Arts, Eccles Health Sci Libr, Univ Utah, Salt Lake City; Davis Co Libr, Farmington, Utah. *Comn:* Oil paintig, Bountiful, 76 & three panels, Clearfield, 77, Davis Co Libr, Utah; oil painting, four panels (4 ft x 5 ft), Salt Lake Int Airport, Utah. *Exhib:* Utah Painting 75, Utah Mus Fine Arts, Salt Lake City, 75; one-man exhibs, Davis Co Libr, S Davis Br, Bountiful, Utah, 76, N Davis Br, Clearfield, Utah, 76 & Eccles Health Sci Libr, Univ Utah, Salt Lake City, 76; Two Utah Artists, Boise State Univ, Idaho, 77. *Pos:* Dir, Bountiful Art Ctr, Univ Utah Exten, Bountiful, 74-84; asst dir, Prog for Higher Educ, Davis Co/Univ Utah, Bountiful, 75-84. *Teaching:* Adj asst prof art, Univ Utah, Salt Lake City, 74-84. *Bibliog:* Claudia Sisemore (producer, color film), Anton J Rasmussen--painter of abstractions from nature, pvt publ, 77. *Media:* Oil. *Mailing Add:* 1308 E Yale Ave Salt Lake City UT 84105

RASMUSSEN, ROBERT NORMAN See Redd Ekks (Robert Norman Rasmussen)

RATCLIFF, CARTER
CRITIC, WRITER
b Seattle, Wash, Aug 20, 41. *Study:* Univ Chicago, BA, 63. *Pos:* Assoc ed, Art News, 69-72; adv ed, Art Int, 70-75; contrib ed, Art in Am, 76-, Saturday Rev, 80-82. *Teaching:* Workshop dir, Poetry Proj, St Mark's Church, New York, 69-70; vis prof, Hunter Col, New York, 85-86; lect at numerous insts & univs. *Awards:* Poets Found Grant, 69; Nat Endowment Arts Fels, 72 & 78; Guggenheim Mem Found Fel, 76; Mather Award, 87. *Res:* Post-war American art. *Publ:* Auth, John Singer Sargent, Abbeville, New York, 82; Andy Warhol, Abbeville Press, New York, 83; Dramatis Personae (5 parts), Art in Am, 85-86; Robert Longo, Rizzoli, New York, 85; Komar and Melamid, Abbeville Press, New York, 89; and others. *Mailing Add:* 26 Beaver St New York NY 10004

RATH, ALAN T
SCULPTOR
b Cincinnati, Ohio, 59. *Study:* Mass Inst Technol, BSEE, 82. *Work:* San Diego Mus Contemp Art; Denver Mus Art; Walker Art Ctr Minneapolis. *Exhib:* Bay Area Media, San Francisco Mus Art, 90; 1991 Biennial Exhib, Whitney Mus Mod Art, New York, 91; solo shows, San Jose Mus Art, Calif, 90, Art Ctr, travelled, Minneapolis, Minn, 91 & Dorothy Goldeen Gallery, Santa Monica, Calif, 92. *Teaching:* Lectr, Sch Creative Arts, San Francisco State Univ, 86; vis artist, Summer Arts Prog, Cal-Poly State Univ, San Luis Obispo, Calif, 87. *Awards:* Individual Artist Grant, Coun for the Arts, Mass Inst Technol, 82;

Small Project Award, InterArts of Marin, 85; Nat Endowment Arts, 88. *Bibliog:* Christopher Knight (auth), review, Los Angeles Times, 11/23/90; Peter Boswell (auth), Alan Rath (brochure), Walker Art Ctr, Minneapolis, Minn, 91; Alan Rath (catalog), Gallery 210, Univ Mo, St Louis, 92. *Dealer:* Carl Solway Gallery 314 W Fourth St Cincinnati OH 45202; Dorothy Goldeen Gallery 1547 9th St Santa Monica LA 90401. *Mailing Add:* c/o Dorothy Goldeen Gallery 1547 Ninth St Santa Monica CA 90401

RATH, HILDEGARD
PAINTER, LECTURER
b Freudenstadt, Black Forest, Ger; US citizen. *Study:* Atelier House, Stuttgart, Ger, with Adolf Senglaub; Kunstgewerbe Sch, Stuttgart; Akad Bildenden Kunste, Berlin, Ger; also with Otto Manigk, Berlin; Cambridge, England, IBC dipl, 76. *Work:* Württembergisches Kultministerium, Stuttgart; Metrop Mus Art, Pub Libr, New York; Brooklyn Mus, NY; Libr Cong, Washington, DC; over 800 works in mus & pvt collections. *Comn:* Oil paintings, portraits & landscapes, comn by Willi Eiselen, Ulm, Donau, Ger, 32; portraits, landscapes & still lifes, comn by Walter Freudenberg, Baden, Ger, 46; Triplets, comn by Mrs Sig Buchmeyer, Paris, 48; Mrs Siegtraut Gauss-Glock, Württemberg, Ger, 54; Madonna, comn by Klaus Heuck, Frankfurt, Ger, 59. *Exhib:* Allied Artists Am, Nat Acad Design, New York, 51; Artists Equity Bldg Fund Exhib, Whitney Mus Am Art, 51; 15th Nat Print Exhib, Libr Cong, 57; murals, traveling exhibs, throughout US, 57-84; Salon des Nations, Paris, 83; 260 nat & int one-man shows in Stuttgart, Paris, New York, Washington, DC; and others. *Teaching:* Dir painting, Europ Sch Fine Art, NY, 49-54; lectr hist art, Great Neck Pub Schs, formerly; lectr serigraphy, NShore Art Ctr, formerly. *Awards:* Prix de Paris, 63; Cert Merit for Distinguished Serv to the Community, Cambridge, Eng, 76; Gold Medal, Accad Italia, 80. *Bibliog:* Hennemann-Bayer (auth), Zur Ausstellung, Schwarzwalder Bote Stuttgart, 59; Dannecker (auth), Von werker, Stuttgarter Nachrichten, 59; P H Buhner (auth), Hildegard Rath im Kunsthaus Schaller, Stuttgarter Zeitung, 59. *Mem:* Württembergischer Künstverein, Stuttgart; Landesverband Würtemburg Künstler Tübingen, Ger; Nat Asn of Adult Educators; Nat Soc of Mural Painters; and others. *Media:* Mixed. *Publ:* Auth articles in Art Digest, 52, Schwarzwald Zeitung, 59 & Am Artist, 63; contribr, Enciclopedia Int Degli Artisti, 70-71; Artisti Contemporaney, Accad Italia, 80. *Dealer:* Southern Vermont Art Center Manchester VT 05255. *Mailing Add:* PO Box 298 Manchester Center VT 05255

RATHBONE, PERRY TOWNSEND
MUSEUM DIRECTOR
b Germantown, Pa, July 3, 11. *Study:* Harvard Col, AB, 33, Harvard Univ, 33-34; Wash Univ, Hon DFA, 58; Northeastern Univ, Hon DHL, 60; Bates Col, Hon DFA, 64; Suffolk Univ, Hon DHL, 69; Williams Col, Hon DHL, 70; Boston Col, Hon DFA, 70; RI Sch Design, Hon DFA, 72. *Pos:* Cur, Detroit Inst Art, 36-40; secy & dir masterpieces of art, New York World's Fair, 39; dir, City Art Mus St Louis, 40-55; dir, Boston Mus Fine Arts, 54-72; dir, Christie's USA, 73-, sr vpres, 77-85, consult, 85- *Awards:* Chevalier, Legion of Honor. *Mem:* Am Asn Mus (vpres, 60-); Asn Art Mus Dirs (pres, 59-60 & 69-70); Benjamin Franklin fel Royal Soc Arts, London; Fogg Art Mus. *Publ:* Auth, Max Beckmann, 48, Mississippi Panorama, 49, Westward the Way, 54, Lee Gatch, 60 & Handbook for the Forsyth Wickes Collection, 68; contribr art mags & mus bulletins. *Mailing Add:* c/o Christie's International 502 Park Ave New York NY 10022

RATHBUN, WILLIAM JAY
CURATOR
b Sioux City, Iowa, June 19, 31. *Study:* Univ Wash, BA, 54, MA(art hist), 66. *Collections Arranged:* Song of the Brush: Japanese Paintings from Sanso Collection (auth, catalog), 79, Treasures of Asian Art from the Idemitsu Collection (auth, catalog), 81, Yo no Bi: The Beauty of Japanese Folk Art (auth, catalog), 83 & 50 Years: A Legacy of Asian Art, 83, Seattle Art Mus. *Pos:* Asst cur, Seattle Art Mus, 73-76, assoc cur Asian painting, 76-78, cur Japanese art, 78- *Teaching:* Asst art hist, Univ Wash, Seattle, 66-67; asst prof, Portland State Univ, 70-71. *Awards:* Governor's Writers' Award, 84. *Mem:* Oriental Ceramic Soc, London; Japan Soc. *Publ:* Coauth, Asiatic Art in the Seattle Art Museum, Seattle Art Mus, 73; contribr, A Myriad of Autumn Leaves, New Orleans Mus Art, 83; Asian Art Collection (catalog), Seattle Art Mus (in prep). *Mailing Add:* Seattle Art Mus Volunteer Park Seattle WA 98112

RATHLE, HENRI (AMIN)
PAINTER
b Cairo, Egypt, Nov 4, 11; US citizen. *Study:* Self-taught; Royal Palace, with El Hawawini, 29-30; also studied with Henry Gasser, 70. *Work:* Phoenix Fire Mus & Mus of City, Mobile, Ala. *Comn:* President Nixon, Washington, DC, 69; Oakley and Southern Belle, Emperor Clocks, WGer, 73; President Charles deGaulle, comn by J F Bezou, New Orleans, La. *Exhib:* One-man shows, Percy Whiting Art Ctr, Fairhope, Ala, 68, Biloxi Municipal Art Gallery, Miss, 68, Jackson Co Col, Gautier, Miss, 68 & Fine Arts Mus South, Mobile, Ala, 72. *Awards:* Purchase Award, Bellingrath Gardens, Mobile, Ala, 70; Purchase Award, Fine Arts Mus South, Mobile, Ala. *Bibliog:* John Fay (auth), Masculinity found in art, Mobile Register, 3/67; J F Bezou (auth), Exposition à Biloxi, France-Amerique, 2/68; German & Swedish Monographs, 78. *Mem:* Mobile Art Asn; Easte. *Media:* Oil, Acrylic. *Mailing Add:* 756 Sullivan Ave Mobile AL 36606

RATKAI, GEORGE
PAINTER, SCULPTOR
b Budapest, Hungary, Dec 24, 07. *Work:* Tel-Aviv Mus, Israel; Abbott Labs Collection; Univ Ill; Butler Inst Am Art; Univ Nebr; Worcester Art Mus. *Exhib:* Pa Acad, Philadelphia, 48-53 & 61; Carnegie Inst, Pittsburgh, Pa, 49; Whitney Mus Ann, New York, 49, 50 & 56; Mint Mus, Charlotte, NC; Metrop Mus Ann, New York, 50; Univ Ill, Urbana, 51, 53, 55 & 57; Dayton Art Inst, Ohio, 56; Recent Drawing Show, Mus Mod Art, Spoleto, Italy, 61; Butler Inst Art, Youngstown, Ohio, 62; Provincetown Art Asn Golden Anniv, 64; Nat Acad Art & Letters; and many others. *Awards:* Gold Medals, 53 & 65 & Mem Medal, 56, Audubon Artists; Childe Hassam Award, 59. *Mem:* Artists Equity Asn; Audubon Artists; fel Int Inst Arts & Lett; Am Fedn Arts; Nat Soc Painters in Casein; and others. *Mailing Add:* 350 W 57th St New York NY 10019

RATNER, DAVID M
PAINTER, EDUCATOR
b Minneapolis, Minn, June 14, 22. *Study:* Minneapolis Sch Art; Skowhegan Sch of Painting & Sculpture; Acad de la Grande Chaumiere. *Work:* Walker Art Ctr, Minneapolis; Minneapolis Art Inst. *Comn:* Illus for Mathematics Presentation Project, Nat Sci Found, 61-63; Diorama, Am Mus Immigration, New York, 71. *Exhib:* Painting Biennial, Walker Art Ctr, Minneapolis, 56 & 58; solo exhibs, Minneapolis Inst Art, 61 & Carl Siembab Gallery, Boston, 68; Boston Arts Festival, Boston, 63 & 64; The Skowhegan Sch, Inst Contemp Art, Boston, 76; Cont Still-Life, Newport Art Asn, Newport, RI, 78; Helen Bumbus Gallery, Duxbury, Mass, 82. *Teaching:* Instr painting & drawing, Minneapolis Sch Art, 53-62; prof art, Boston Univ, 62-; prof emeritus, 87. *Awards:* Minn State Fair, 55-57; Purchase Award, Walker Art Ctr, 58; Esther Conant Memorial Prize, Helen Bumbus Gallery, 82. *Media:* Oil; Gouche. *Dealer:* The Elon Gallery Brookline MA. *Mailing Add:* 22 Richard Rd Natick MA 01760

RAUF, BARBARA CLAIRE
INSTRUCTOR, PAINTER
b Covington, Ky, Mar 13, 44. *Study:* Thomas More Col, AB, 68; Univ Cincinnati, BFA, 74; Univ Pa, MFA, 77. *Work:* Atkins & Pearce Manfacturing, Co, Cincinnati, Ohio; Saint Clair Med Ctr, Morehead, Ky; Admin Bldg, Sci Wing & Chancellors Room, Thomas More Col, Crestview Hills, Ky. *Comn:* Amy (portrait), comn by Mr & Mrs George Deitmaring, Ft Mitchell, Ky, 80; Asa (portrait), Atkins & Pearce Co, Cincinnati, 81; pres series & chancellor series (portraits), Thomas More Col, 84-86; Pat (portrait), comn by Dr & Mrs Forrest Calico, Ft Mitchell, Ky, 85. *Exhib:* Inst Contemp Art, Philadelphia, 75, 76 & 77; solo exhibs, CCA Gallery, Cincinnati, 84, Carnegie Art Ctr, Covington, Ky, 84 & City Hall, Cincinnati, 85. *Pos:* Dir, Thomas More Gallery, Thomas More Col, 78- *Teaching:* Asst prof art & dept chair, Thomas More Col, 77-83, assoc prof, 83- *Awards:* Advan Inst Development Grants, US Govt; KY Found Women, 90. *Bibliog:* B Wheatley (auth), Carnegie Center today, Kenton County Recorder, 84; Mary McCarty (auth), Portrait painter, Cincinnati Mag, 85. *Mem:* Contemp Art Ctr, Cincinnati; Col Art Asn; Carnegie Art Ctr. *Media:* Oil, Pencil. *Mailing Add:* 715 Willard St Covington KY 44011

RAUSCHENBERG, ROBERT
PAINTER, PHOTOGRAPHER
b Port Arthur, Tex, Oct 22, 25. *Study:* Kansas City Art Inst & Sch Design, 46-47; Acad Julian, Paris, 47; Black Mt Col, with Josef Albers, 48-49; Art Students League, with Vaclav Vytlacil & Morris Kantor, 49-50. *Work:* Albright-Knox Art Gallery; Whitney Mus Am Art; Wadsworth Atheneum; Tate Gallery, London; Mus Mod Art, New York; Neue Galerie, Aachen, Ger; Moderna Museet, Stockholm, Sweden; Hirshhorn Mus, Washington, DC. *Exhib:* Solo Exhibs Galerie Mathilde,Amsterdam, 79, Espace Nicois d'Art et de Culture, Nice, France, 86, Museo Nacional, Havana, Cuba, 88, Galerie Alfred Kren, Cologne, Ger, 88 & 89, Central House Culture, Tretyakov Gallery, Moscow, Russia, 89, Nat Art Gallery, Kuala Lumpur, Malaysia, 90, The Silk Screen Paintings 1962-1964, 90-91, Whitney Mus Am Art, New York, 90, ROCI, Nat Gallery Art, Washington, DC, The Early 1950's, Guggeheim Mus, 92 & many others; Retrospective, Nat Collection Fine Arts, Washington, DC, Mus Mod Art, New York, San Francisco Mus Mod Art, Albright-Knox Art Gallery, Buffalo, NY & Art Inst Chicago, 77-78; Guggenheim Mus, New York, 85 & 88; Sogetsu Art Mus, Jaspan, 88; Mus Mod Art, New York, 88; Whitney Mus Am Art, Stamford, Conn, 88 & 89; Galerie Kaj Forsblom, Helsinki, Finland, 88; Corcoran Gallery Art, Washington, DC, 88; Whitney Mus Am Art, New York, 88; Brooklyn Mus, NY, 89; Nat Gallery Art, Washington, DC, 89 & 90; Heland Wetterling Gallery, Stockholm, Sweden, 90; Milwaukee Art Mus, Wis, 90; Art Gallery of Ontario, Canada, 90; Makuhari Messe, Japan, 90; LA Louvre, Venice, Calif, 90. *Awards:* Grand Prix D'Honneur, 13th Int Exhib Graphic Art, Ljubljana, Yu; Gold Medal, Oslo, Norway; Officier, Ordre des Arts et Lettres, Ministry Culture & Commun, France; Grand Prize, Venice Biennale, 64; Symposium: Art Science & Spirituality in a Changing Economy, Amsterdam, The Netherlands, 90. *Bibliog:* Rauschenber: Modern Masters '89, Viikonvaihde, Helsinki, Finland, 6/3/89; Nava Semel (auth), Robert Rauschenberg, Studio Art Mag (in Hebrew), Israel, 12/89; Henry Kamm (auth), Rauschenberg Show Heralds Union of the Arts in Berlin, New York Times, 3/10/90; Daniel Waterman (auth), Rauschenberg's Bandages, ArtNews, 5/90. *Mailing Add:* c/o M Knoedler & Co Inc 19 E 70th St New York NY 10021

RAUTBORD, DOROTHY H
COLLECTOR, PATRON
b Winamac, Ind, Aug 13, 06. *Study:* Univ Ill; self-taught. *Mem:* Arts Club, Chicago. *Collection:* Post impressionism. *Mailing Add:* 44 Cocoanut Row Palm Beach FL 33480

RAVARRA, PATRICIA
SCULPTOR
b San Francisco, Calif, Aug 19, 47. *Study:* San Francisco State Univ with Francis Coehlo & Wes Chamberlain, BA, 71, with Margarey Livingston & Candace Crocket, MA, 76; State Col Art, Poznan, Poland with Magdalena Abakanowicz, 79. *Work:* Danish Mus Applied Arts, Copenhagen, Denmark. *Exhib:* Solo Exhib Color & Light, Danish Mus Applied Arts, Wroclaw Pol, 90; group exhib, 32nd Ann Design Frontiers, Richmond Art Ctr, 85; 5th Omt Triennale & Extiles, Textiles Mus, Kodz, Poland, 85; 8th Ann Nat Black Art Exhib & Competition & Comtemp Art Exhib, Nat Black Arts Festival, Atlanta, 88. *Teaching:* Instr fiber art, Apprentice Alliance, San Francisco, 85-90; instr visual arts, San Jose State Univ, Calif, 90. *Awards:* Fulbright-Hays Travel Study Grant, Inst Int Educ, 77-79. *Bibliog:* Chiora Santiago (auth), Building a life structure, winter 85; Jonna Dwinger (auth), Vaever med lys og farver, Politiken, Copenhagen, 10/26/89. *Mem:* Artists Equity (bd mem, 85-87); Bay Area Consortium Visual Arts (coordr, 87-89); Calif Confederation Arts (bd mem, 87-90). *Media:* Fiber. *Publ:* Auth, 5th International Kodz Triennale, Fiberarts, 86. *Mailing Add:* 1045 Leavenworth St Apt 5 San Francisco CA 94109

RAVEN, ARLENE
WRITER, HISTORIAN
b Baltimore, Md, July 12, 44. *Study:* Hood Col, BA, 65, HHD, 79; Univ Madrid; Md Inst Col Art; George Washington Univ, MFA, 67; Johns Hopkins Univ, NDEA, Kress & Gilman fels, 69-73, MA, 71; Int Col, PhD, 75. *Pos:* Co-founder, Ctr Feminist Art Hist Studies, 73-79; vpres, Women's Community Inc, Los Angeles, 73-83; co-founder & dir, Woman's Bldg, Los Angeles, 73-83; founding ed, Chrysalis Mag, cur innovative exhibs, Los Angeles, 80 & Artemisia Gallery, Chicago, 80; freelance critic for Arts, New Art, Examiner, Women's Review of Books, Village Voice and others. *Teaching:* Tutor, Calif Inst Arts, 72-74, Otis Art Inst Parsons Sch Design, 81-83 & New Sch Soc Res, 83-88. *Awards:* Nat Endowment Arts Critic Fel, 79 & 84-85; Vesta Award, Woman's Bldg, 83; Calif Coun Humanities Grant, 83-84; and others. *Bibliog:* Shirley Koploy (auth), Art: the woman's building, MS Mag, 10/74; Focus, KNBC-TV, 74; Angry artist speaks out, spring 86 & Phillis Rossei (auth), Feminism & art: A lecture by Arlene Raven, fall 83, Women Artist News. *Mem:* Col Art Asn Am; Women's Caucus Art (bd dirs, 74-78); bd dir Feminist Art Inst; Art Critics Int. *Res:* Washington color school; contemporary art and art theory; abstract expressionist men's and women's art; Georgia O'Keeffe and Romaine Brooks; public art. *Publ:* Crossing Over: Feminism and Art of Social Concern, UMI Res Press, Ann Arbor, 88; co-ed, Feminist Art Criticism: An Anthology, UMI, 88; auth, Exposures: Women and their Art, New Sage Press, 89; Art in the Public Interest, UMI, 89; Nancy Grossman, Hillwood Art Mus, 91; and others. *Mailing Add:* 105 Eldridge St New York NY 10002

RAVETT, ABRAHAM
FILMMAKER, PHOTOGRAPHER
b Poland, Aug 2, 47; US citizen. *Study:* Brooklyn Col, BA, 68; Mass Col Art, BFA(film-photog), 75; Syracuse Univ, MFA(filmmaking), 78. *Exhib:* Cineprobe, Mus Mod Art, New York, 86; New Eng Film Festival, Boston, Mass, 86 & 90; Image Forum, Tokyo, 87; Anthology Film Archives, New York, 89; Collective for Living Cinema, New York, 90; Mus Mod Art, New York, 91; Edison Black Maria, 91. *Pos:* Artist-in-residence, The Artist Found, Boston, 79. *Teaching:* Assoc prof film-photog, Hampshire Col, Amherst, Mass, 79- *Awards:* Andrew Mellon Found Grant, 81, 87, & 90; Artist Found Fel, Boston, 83; Nat Endowment Arts Grant, 85, 87 & 92; Japan-US Friendship Comn Grants, 83, 85, 87 & 90; Mass Productions, 88-89. *Mailing Add:* 193 Nonotuck St Florence MA 01060

RAWLINSON, JONLANE FREDERICK
PAINTER, INSTRUCTOR
b Memphis, Tenn, Feb 12, 40. *Study:* Memphis State Univ, 58-59; Memphis Acad Arts, BFA, 63; Syracuse Univ, MFA, 75. *Work:* Parthenon, Nashville, Tenn; Watkins Collection of Tenn Art; Fall Creek Falls Collection of Tenn Art; Memphis Acad Art Collection. *Comn:* Mississippi River Bridge (painting), comn by Young Republican Party, US House of Rep, 73; paintings of farm, Pin Oak Farms, Versailles, Ky, 75. *Exhib:* Mid-South Exhib, Memphis, 71; Tenn All-State Competition, 71-73; Cent South Exhib, Nashville, 72-73; Tenn Watercolor Soc, 72-75; Watercolor USA, Springfield, Mo, 75. *Teaching:* Graphic art instr, Univ Tenn, 65-75; instr art, Memphis Acad Arts, 72-92. *Awards:* Second Purchase Prize for Mixed Media, Tenn All-State Competition, 71; Art Dirs Club Memphis First Prize, Art South, 72; First Award & Gold Medal of Merit, Tenn Watercolor Soc, 75. *Mem:* Tenn Watercolor Soc (vpres, 75). *Media:* Watercolor. *Mailing Add:* 628 Rue Toulouse New Orleans LA 70130

RAY, CHARLES
SCULPTOR
b Chicago, Ill, 1953. *Study:* Univ Iowa, Iowa City, BFA(cum laude), 75; Mason Gross Sch Art, Rutgers, MFA, 79. *Work:* Whitney Mus Am Art, New York; Newport Harbor Art Mus. *Exhib:* Contemp Arts Ctr, New Orleans, La, 80; Cape Gallery, New Orleans, La, 81; one-man shows, 64 Market St, Venice, Calif, 83, Mercer Union, Toronto, 85, Feature, Chicago, 87, New York, 89, 90, 91 & 92, Burnett Miller, Los Angeles, 88, The Mattress Factory, Pittsburgh, 89, Galerie Claire Burrus, Paris, 90, Feature, New York, 90, Donald Young Gallery, Seattle, Wash, 92; Recent Drawings, Whitney Mus Am Art, New York, 90; Documenta IX, Kassel, Ger, 92; Helter Skelter: LA Art in the 1990's (with catalog), Mus Contemp Art, Calif, 92. *Awards:* NJ Coun on the Arts Grant, 80; Nat Endowment Arts, 85 & 88. *Bibliog:* Christopher Knight (auth), An Art of Darkness at MOCA, Los Angeles Times, F1, F4-F5 (reproduction), 1/28/92; Susan Kandel (auth), LA in Review, Arts, 98-99, 4/92; Hunter Drohojowska (auth), LA Raw, Artnews, 78-81, 4/92. *Mailing Add:* c/o Burnett Miller Gallery 964 N LaBrea Ave Los Angeles CA 90038

RAY, CHRISTOPHER T
SCULPTOR, CRAFTSMAN
b Albany, NY, May 7, 37. *Study:* Pa Acad Fine Arts, 60. *Work:* Mus Am Jewish Hist & Port of Hist Mus, Philadelphia; Pa State Mus, Harrisburg. *Comn:* Sculptured gates, Penn's Landing Sq, Philadelphia, 73; pub sculpture, Scheie Eye Inst, Philadelphia, 75, First Pa Bank, Philadelphia, 76 & Great Valley Corp Ctr, Malvern, Pa, 79; sculptured gate/bas-relief, Chestnut St Park, Philadelphia, 79. *Exhib:* Figure & Fantasy, 75 & Animal Art, 81, Smithsonian Inst, Washington, DC; Am Craft Show, Philadelphia Mus Art, 77; Sculpture Outdoors, Temple Univ, Ambler, Pa, 79; Mod Wrought Ironwork & Sculpture Int Exhib, Lindau, Ger, 81; Ornamentalism, Hudson River Mus, Yonkers, NY, 83; and others. *Pos:* Pres/founder, GENUS Collab, Philadelphia, 77- *Bibliog:* Donna Z Meilach (auth), Decorative & Sculptural Ironwork, Crown Publ; R Jensen & P Conway (coauth), Ornamentalism, Potter, Inc; B Brolin & J Richards (coauth), Architectural Ornament, Van Nostrand Rheinhold Co, 82. *Mem:* Artists' Equity Asn (vpres, 76-78); fel Pa Acad Fine Arts; Artists-Blacksmiths Asn NAm; Am Crafts Coun. *Media:* Forged Iron, Carved Wood. *Mailing Add:* 315 E Wister PO Box 44128 Philadelphia PA 19144

RAY, DEBORAH See Kogan, Deborah

RAY, ROBERT (DONALD)
PAINTER, SCULPTOR
b Denver, Colo, Oct 2, 24. *Study:* Univ Southern Calif, BFA(cum laude); Centro Estudios Universitarios, Mexico City, MA(magna cum laude). *Work:* Baltimore Mus Art, Md; Brooklyn Mus Art, NY; Denver Art Mus, Colo; Mus NMex, Santa Fe; Columbia Mus Art, SC. *Exhib:* Denver Art Mus, 53-; 13th Nat Exhib Prints, Libr Cong, Washington, DC, 55; Taos Now, San Diego Mus Fine Arts, Calif, 60; Art & The Atom, Calif Palace of Legion of Honor, 65; The West--80 Contemporaries, Univ Ariz Art Gallery, Tucson, 67; one-man show, Mus NMex, Santa Fe, 59 & 67 & Colorado Springs Fine Arts Ctr, Colo, 68; Three Cultures--Three Dimensions, 69 & Southwestern Artists Biennial, 70, Mus NMex; 73rd Ann Exhib Western Art, Denver Art Mus, 71; and many others. *Awards:* Purchase Award, Ball State Teachers Col, 59; First Prize for Sculpture, Mus NMex, 69; Graphics Award, Taos Art Asn, NMex, 72. *Bibliog:* Fels (auth), Compression & expansion in the works of Blackburn & Ray, 72; Harmsen (auth), Harmsen's Western Americana, Northland, 72. *Mem:* Taos Art Asn. *Media:* Oil; Wood. *Mailing Add:* 115 Los Cordovas Rte Taos NM 87571

RAYBURN (DALE), BOYD
PAINTER, PRINTMAKER
b Carriere, Miss, May 12, 42. *Study:* Univ Southern Miss, BS, 64; Univ Miss, MFA, 70. *Work:* DeCordova Mus, Lincoln, Mass; High Mus, Atlanta; Mint Mus, Charlotte, NC; Southeastern Ctr Contemp Art, Winston-Salem, NC; Yale Univ Art Gallery. *Exhib:* 20th Southeastern Exhib, High Mus, Atlanta, 65; Piedmont Painting & Sculpture, Mint Mus, Charlotte, NC, 71; Audubon Artist Ann, Nat Acad Gallery, New York, 73; two-person show, Mint Mus, Charlotte, NC, 74 & Miss Mus Art, Jackson, 77; Hunterdon Print Exhib, Hunterdon Art Ctr, Clinton, NJ, 78. *Teaching:* Instr art, Univ Miss, 69-70; instr printmaking, Ga Southwestern Col, 72-73; asst prof, La State Univ, Shreveport, 80-82. *Awards:* Purchase Award, DeCordova Mus, 77 & Southeastern Ctr Contemp Art, 78; Rembrandt Graphic Award, Boston Printmakers Exhib, 90. *Mem:* Boston Printmakers; Southeastern Printmakers Asn. *Media:* Etching, Monotype. *Dealer:* Lagerquist Gallery 3235 Paces Ferry Place NW Atlanta GA 30305. *Mailing Add:* 3295 Lynhurst Marietta GA 30062

RAYDON, ALEXANDER R
DEALER, COLLECTOR
Study: Tech Univ Munich, grad. *Pos:* Dir, Raydon Gallery. *Res:* American art of the nineteenth and early twentieth centuries. *Specialty:* Paintings, sculpture, prints and drawings from the Renaissance to the present, with emphasis on the nineteenth and early twentieth centuries. *Publ:* Ed, Americans Abroad, 72; Charles Burchfield--Master Doodler, 72; American Scene--American Artists Abroad, 75-77; Masters in European Portraiture, 76; Am Watercolor Painting, 80. *Mailing Add:* 1091 Madison Ave New York NY 10028

RAYEN, JAMES WILSON
PAINTER, EDUCATOR
b Youngstown, Ohio, Apr 9, 35. *Study:* Yale Univ, BA, BFA & MFA; with Josef Albers, Seawell Sillman & Rico Lebrun. *Work:* Addison Gallery Am Art, Andover, Mass; Yale Univ, New Haven, Conn; Wellesley Col, Mass; First Nat Bank, Boston; Mint Mus, NC; Harvard Univ, Cambridge, Mass. *Comn:* Marriott Hotel Corp; Hyatt Hotel Corp. *Exhib:* One-man shows, Durlacher Brothers Gallery, New York, 66 & Eleanor Rigelhaupt Gallery, Boston, 68; Landscape II, De Cordova Mus, Lincoln, Mass, 71; 10 Year Retrospective, Brockton Art Ctr, Mass, 73; Recent & Revised, Wellesley Col Mus, 78; Chapel Gallery, Boston, 84; and others. *Teaching:* Prof, Wellesley Col, 61-, Elizabeth Christy Kopf chair in studio art, 83. *Awards:* Ital Govt Grant in Painting, 59-60; Ford Found Grant in the Humanities, 69-70; Wellesley Col Fac Grant, summer 75, spring 84 & 85. *Bibliog:* Robert Taylor (auth), Boston Globe, 73; Christine Temon (auth), Boston Globe, 83, 90. *Mem:* Boston Visual Artists Union. *Media:* Acrylic, Watercolor; Monotype, Oil. *Dealer:* Ginzburg-Hallowell Boston; Gallery on the Green Lexington MA. *Mailing Add:* Wellesley Col Wellesley MA 02181

RAYMOND, EVELYN L
SCULPTOR
b Duluth, Minn, Mar 20, 08. *Study:* Minneapolis Sch Art, 28-30; St Paul Sch Art, 28-30; Art Students League, 32. *Comn:* Maria L Sanford Statue, Minn Statehood Centennial Comn, installed US Capitol Rotunda, Washington, DC, 58; Bierman Bust, Univ Minn, Minneapolis, 75; Legacy, Fairview Hosp, Minneapolis, 82; Newport Ladies, Minn Mus Art, St Paul, 88. *Exhib:* Ann Regional Sculpture Exhib, Walker Art Ctr, Minneapolis, 44-47; For Common Learnings, Minneapolis Inst Arts, 49; Encounter with Artists (2 person exhib), Minn Mus Art, St Paul, 73. *Pos:* Dir sculpture dept, Walker Art Ctr Sch, 38-51. *Bibliog:* Sylvia Paine (auth), Evelyn Raymond, WARM Jour, 82; Virginia Watson-Jones (auth), Contemporary American Woman Sculptors, Oryx Press, 86. *Mem:* Minn Sculpture Soc. *Media:* Metal. *Mailing Add:* 3730 Monteray Dr Minneapolis MN 55416

RAYMOND, LILO
PHOTOGRAPHER
b Frankfurt, Ger, June 23, 22; US citizen. *Study:* Photog Sem, with David Vestal, 61-63. *Work:* Sheldon Mus Art Gallery, Mus Mod Art & Metrop Mus, New York; High Mus, Atlanta; New Orleans Mus Art. *Exhib:* Still Life in Photog, Helios Gallery, New York, 76; Contrasts Gallery, London, Eng, 80; Woodman Gallery, Morristown, NJ, 81; Photo West, Carmel, 82; Baker Gallery, Kans, 82; and many one-woman shows. *Teaching:* Mem sem photog, Sch Visual Arts, New York, 78-, Maine Photog Workshop, Rockport, summer 79 & Int Ctr Photog, New York, winter 79. *Awards:* Creative Artists Pub Serv Prog Grant, 78. *Bibliog:* Sir Cecil Beaton (auth), The Magic Image, Little Brown & Co, 75; Alicia Wille (auth), Lilo Raymond, gravure portfolio, Popular Photog, 77; Richard Blodgett (auth), A Collectors Guide, Ballatine Bks, 79. *Publ:* Photogr, Classic County Inns of America, Knapp Press & Holt, Rinehart & Winston, 78. *Dealer:* Marcuse Pfeifer 825 Madison Ave New York NY 10021. *Mailing Add:* 212 E 14th St New York NY 10003

RAYNER, GORDON
PAINTER
b Toronto, Ont, 1935. *Work:* Philadelphia Mus Art; Mus Mod Art, New York; Can Coun, Ottawa, Ont; Hirshhorn Collection, Nat Gallery Can, Ottawa. *Comn:* Wall Mural, Bank of Montreal, Toronto, 70; building facade & canopy, Ontario Hydro/Ont Place, Toronto, 71; outdoor wall mural, Benson & Hedges Tobacco Co, Toronto, 71; Tempo (ceramic tile mural), Toronto Transit Comn, 77. *Exhib:* Sixth Biennale of Can Painting, Nat Gallery Can, Ottawa, 65; Mus Mod Art, New York, 67; Coughtry/Rayner/Markle, Nat Gallery Can (traveling), Ottawa, 68; Toronto Painting 1953-1965, Nat Gallery Can, 72; Artists Jazz Band, Mus d'Art Contemporian, Montreal, 74-75; Survey Can Painting, Art Gallery Ont, Toronto, 75; Artists Jazz Band, Beaubourg Centre, Can, Paris, France, 78; Paradise, The Isaacs Gallery, 79. *Teaching:* Painting, Three Schs Art, Toronto, 68-77; teacher painting & founder, For Art's Sake Inc, Toronto, 77-80. *Awards:* First Prize, Graphics 12th Winnipeg Art Show, 70; Can Coun Sr Arts grant, 73 & 75. *Bibliog:* Barrie Hale (auth), Gordon Rayner: The first decade, 2/70 & Theodore Heinrich (auth), Edging up to paradise, 5/6/79, Artscanada. *Media:* Acrylic, Collage. *Mailing Add:* 1493 Dupont St Toronto ON M6P 3S2 Canada

RE, MARISA DEL
DEALER
b Rieta, Italy; US citizen. *Study:* Univ Naples, graduate. *Pos:* Owner, Marisa del Re Gallery, New York, currently. *Specialty:* European and American paintings, sculptures and drawings by contemporary masters. *Mailing Add:* c/o Marisa del Re Gallery 41 East 57th St New York NY 10022

READ, DAVE (DAVID DOLLOFF)
PHOTOGRAPHER, EDUCATOR
b Belfast, Maine, July 14, 38. *Study:* Ohio Univ, BFA, 63, MFA, 65. *Work:* Mus Mod Art, New York; Libr Cong, Washington, DC; Mus Fine Arts, St Petersburg, Fla; Univ Mich, East Lansing; Univ Louisville, Ky. *Exhib:* Photog Fine Arts, Metrop Mus Art, New York, 67; Photog Art Form, Ringling Mus, Sarasota, 77; Dave Read Photog, Mich State Univ, 77 & Light Factory, Charlotte, NC, 78; Dave Read: 1st Mid-west Photogs, Sheldon Art Gallery, Lincoln, Nebr, 80; Photographs by Dave Read, Friends Photog, Carmel, Calif, 83. *Collections Arranged:* Flash (photog by Mertin, Hume, Cohen & Bishop, auth, catalog), Miami Dade Community Col, 76. *Teaching:* Instr photog, Univ NMex, Albuquerque, 65-66; assoc prof photog, Miami-Dade Community Col, Fla, 69-77; prof photog, Univ Nebr, Lincoln, 78- *Awards:* Artist's Fel, Mid-Am Arts Alliance & Nat Endowment Arts, 83. *Mem:* Soc Photog Educ; Friends of Photog. *Media:* Silver Prints. *Publ:* Contribr, Afterimage, Visual Studies Workshop, 81; Electronic Flash Photography, Van Nostrand Reinhold, 80; contribr, Exposure, 79. *Mailing Add:* 6716 Francis St Lincoln NE 68505

REARDON, MARY A
PAINTER, MURALIST
b Quincy, Mass. *Study:* Radcliffe Col, AB; Yale Univ Sch Fine Arts, BFA; also with Eliot O'Hara, Eugene Savage, Jean Charlot & David Siqueiros. *Work:* Mural drawings, De Cordova Mus, Lincoln, Mass; Radcliffe Col, Cambridge, Mass; archives of mural work, St Louis Cathedral, St Louis Univ. *Comn:* Creation & Last Judgement (mosaic ceilings), Nat Shrine Immaculate Conception, Washington, DC, 73; Chapel of the Patrons, St Mary's Cathedral, San Francisco, Calif; portraits, Judge Edmund Dewing, 78, Cardinal Humberto Medeiros, 80 & Judge Francis Murphy, 87; stained glass window, First Church, Weymouth, Mass, 81; Resurrection & Holy Spirit (mosaic domes), St Louis Cathedral, Mo, 81-88; altar painting, Church of St Martin de Porres, Montserrat, BWI, 92. *Exhib:* Int Exhibs Relig Art, Trieste, Italy, 61 & 66; 7th Centennial Exhib, Basilica St Anthony, Padua, Italy, 63; one-man exhib, Trieste, 71; additional exhibs in Boston, New York & Richmond, Va. *Pos:* Design consult, San Francisco Cathedral, 74- *Teaching:* Instr adult educ, Boston Mus Fine Arts; assoc prof studio courses, Emmanuel Col, Boston, 51-70. *Awards:* President's Medal, 2nd Int Exhib Relig Art, 66; Spec Award, S Shore Arts Festival, 90. *Bibliog:* Frank De Frederico (auth), The Mosaics of the National Shrine of Immaculate Conception, Decatur House Press, 81. *Mem:* Nat Soc Mural Painters; Cambridge Art Asn; Harvard Club of Boston; South Shore Arts Asn; Copley Soc. *Media:* Oil, Watercolor; Mosaic. *Publ:* Auth, Pope Pius XII, Rock of Peace, E P Dutton. *Dealer:* South Shore Art Centre Cohasset MA; Hingham Galleries MA. *Mailing Add:* 12 Martin's Lane Hingham MA 02043

REBBECK, LESTER JAMES, JR
PAINTER, SCULPTOR
b Chicago, Ill, June 25, 29. *Study:* Art Inst Chicago & Univ Chicago, hist with K Blackshear, BAEd, MAEd, 59; also painting with Wieghardt, drawing with Isoble McKinnon. *Comn:* Paintings & prints, comn by William Fischer, 69. *Exhib:* Sculptors Gallery, St Louis, 67; Ball State Teachers Col, 75; Mus Sci & Industry, Chicago, 83; Ill State Mus, Springfield, 83; Peace Mus, Chicago, 83; Fort Wayne Mus Art, Indiana Ex, 89-90; and others. *Pos:* Gallery dir, Countryside Art Gallery, Arlington Heights, Ill, 63-68; gallery dir, Chicago Soc of Artists Gallery, 67-68. *Teaching:* Asst prof art appreciation & painting, Harper Col, 67-71. *Awards:* GI Show Medal Award, Art Inst Chicago, 53; First Place Oils, McHenry Art Fair, 60, Best of Show, 62. *Bibliog:* Louise D Yochim (auth), Role and impact, Chicago Soc Artists; Nicolo Pan Epinto & Calo Géro Pan Epinto (coauths), Tendenze E Testimonianze Del Arte Contemporanea, Accademia Italia, 83; Lis Krantz (auth), American Artists, Facts on File Publs, New York/Oxford, Eng, 85. *Mem:* Col Art Asn Am. *Media:* Oil on Canvas; Wood Sculpture. *Dealer:* Aardvark Gallery 150 N Brainard Ave La Grange IL 60525. *Mailing Add:* 2041 Vermont St Rolling Meadows IL 60008

REBER, MICK
SCULPTOR, PAINTER
b St George, Utah, June 6, 42. *Study:* Brigham Young Univ, BFA & MFA; independent studies in San Francisco, Chicago, Montreal, New York & Paris. *Work:* Springville Art Mus; Brigham Young Univ, Utah; Southern Utah State Col. *Comn:* Hilton Hotel Corp, Nev; paintings, 20th Century Fox, 73; Don Rey Advert, Nev. *Exhib:* Mainstreams Exhib, Marietta Col, Ohio, 74; Western State Art Found Traveling Exhib, San Francisco Mus of Mod Art, Denver Art Mus & Seattle Art Mus, 78; one-man shows, Gallery Sloan, Scottsdale, Ariz, 90, Byrne-Getz Gallery, Aspen, Colo, 90 & Presden Gallery, Santa Fe, NMex, 90; and others. *Teaching:* Prof advan painting & sculpture, Ft Lewis Col, Durango, Colo. *Awards:* Painting Award, Springville Nat, Springville Mus of Art, Utah, 70; First Cash Award, Four Corners Biennial, Phoenix Art Mus, 73. *Bibliog:* H Lester Cooke (auth), A Biennial of Painting & Sculpture (catalog); Arthur Williams (auth), Sculpture (cover story), Santa Fean Mag. *Media:* All Media. *Mailing Add:* c/o The Durango Arts Center 835 Main Ave No 210 Durango CO 81301

REBHUN, PEARL G
PAINTER, PRINTMAKER
b New York, NY, Feb 20, 24. *Study:* Studied with Isaac Soyer, Leo Manso, Shirley Gorelik, Jerry Okomoto & Jerry Samuels. *Work:* Nassau Mus Fine Art, Roslyn, NY; Trinity Col, Hartford; Public Serv Gas & Elec Utility, NJ; Martha Lincoln Gallery, Vero Beach, Fla; Isis Gallery, Port Washington, NY. *Comn:* Oppenheim, Appel Dixon & Co, New York, 78; Brookhaven Bursing Corp, Nassua Co, 79; Fleischmanns Distilling Corp, New Hyde Park, 80; Forest Elec Corp, New York, 87; Dr & Mrs Harold Klein, Boca Raton, 92. *Exhib:* Palazzo Vecchio, Florence, Italy, 83; Mencul Ctr Arts, Cairo, Egypt, 83; Parrish Mus Art, Southampton, NY, 83; Hecksher Mus Art Ann, Huntington, NY, 85; Ft Lauderdale Mus Art, 90-91; and others. *Awards:* Grumbacher Award for Outstanding Contrib to the Arts, 76; Elizabeth Erlanger Award of Merit, Nat Asn Women Artists, 79; Chase Manhattan Bank Purchase Award, Nassau Mus Fine Art, 85. *Mem:* Nat Asn Women, New York (bd mem 80-91); Old Sch Square Cult Arts Ctr, Delray, Fla, 91-92; Boca Raton Mus Art, 92. *Mailing Add:* 7826 Wind Key Dr Boca Raton FL 33434

RECANATI, DINA
SCULPTOR
b Cairo, Egypt. *Study:* Art Students League, with Jose de Creft, 59-62. *Work:* Israel Mus, Jerusalem; Tel Aviv Mus; Ben Gurion Airport, Tel Aviv; Tel Aviv Univ, Israel; Jewish Mus, New York; Herrzliah Mus, Continental Grain Collection, New York. *Comn:* Gate (bronze), Ministry of Transportation, Israel, 74; Gates (spec bronze ed), Am-Israel Cult Found, New York, 76; Israel Chancellery, Washington, DC, 80; President's Garden Collection, Jerusalem; Weizmann Inst Sci, Rehovot, Israel. *Exhib:* July M Gallery, Tel-Aviv, 81-84; Jewish Mus Sculpture Garden, New York, 81-84; Mus Contemp Art (with catalog), Ramat Gan, Israel, 89; Barbican Art Gallery, London, Eng, 90; Installation Ben Gurion Airport, 92; and others. *Bibliog:* Amnon Barzel (auth), Pillars and Parchments, 86; Prof M Omer (auth), Transformation from Within, Cimaise, 87 & Signs of Survival in the Culture of Decay, 89; Gil Goldfine (auth), Through the Trees, Jerusalem Post, 89; and others. *Media:* Bronze, Wood. *Publ:* Contribr, The Artist's Notebook, Gordon Galleries, Israel, 75. *Dealer:* E P Gurewitsch Works of Art 55 E 74th St New York, NY 10021; Julie M Gallery Tel Aviv Israel. *Mailing Add:* 136 Grand St New York NY 10013

RECKLINGHAUSEN, MARIANNE VON
PAINTER, SCULPTOR
b Munich, Ger, Jan 24, 29; US citizen. *Study:* Self taught. *Work:* Smithsonian Inst. *Exhib:* One-woman shows, Hudson River Mus, Yonkers, 63 & 84 & Katonah Mus Art, 82, NY, Islip Mus Art, 87, NY, Univ Mass, Lowell, 90; 19th Area Exhib, Corcoran Gallery Art, Washington, DC, 74; The Animal Image, Renwick Gallery, Smithsonian Inst, Washington, DC, 81; Assemblage & Collage Traveling Exhib, Miss Mus Art, Jackson, 81-83; Germans in New England, Goethe House, Boston, 83; Catholic Univ Art Gallery, Washington, DC, 83. *Teaching:* Lectr, Katonah Gallery, 82 & 86, Univ Lowell, Mass, 83 & 90. *Awards:* Painting Award, Charles of the Ritz Found, New York & 16th Ann New England Exhib, 65; First in Painting Award, Westchester Art Soc, 65-66; First in Painting Award, Lowman Mem Award, Art of the Northeast, 34th Ann Exhib, Silvermine, 83. *Bibliog:* Les Krantz (auth), American Artists; an illustrated survey of leading contemporary americans, Facts on File, New York & Oxford, England, 85; Virginia Watson-Jones (auth), Contemporary American Women Sculptors, Oryx Press, 86; Miles Under (auth), Darkness and Light Visible: Recklinghousen's Works, The Boston Globe, 12/90. *Mem:* Artists Equity; Silvermine Guild. *Media:* Acrylic on Wood; Sequential Painted Contructions. *Publ:* Dir, Mark Sadan & Lawrence Miller (film makers) Legends From life: 12 Constructions from Paradiso (film), Film & Video Workshop, NY, 86. *Mailing Add:* c/o Uptown Gallery 1194 Madison Ave New York NY 10128

REDD, RICHARD JAMES
PRINTMAKER, EDUCATOR
b Toledo, Ohio, Oct 22, 31. *Study:* Toledo Mus Sch; Univ Toledo, BEd, 53; Univ Iowa, MFA, 58, study with Eugene Ludins & Mauricio Lasansky. *Work:* Allentown Art Mus, Pa; Lehigh Univ, Bethlehem, Pa; Philip & Muriel Berman Collection, Allentown; Kutztown Univ, Pa; East Stroudsburg Univ, Pa. *Exhib:* One-man shows, Allentown Art Mus, 61, Kemerer Mus, Bethlehem, Pa, 80 & Zhejiang Art Acad, Hangzhou, China, 89; Jiangsu Art Gallery, Nanjing, China 92; Mushroom Magic, Reading Mus, 82; Breaking with Tradition, Int Quit Exhib, 83; 30 yr Print Retrospective, Lehigh Univ, 88; and others. *Teaching:* Prof, Lehigh Univ, 58-; chmn dept fine art, 70-77; cur, Masks: Other Faces, Kemerer Mus, 88; lectr in China, 89 & 92. *Awards:* Garth Howland Award, Lehigh Art Alliance, 63, 75; Print Award, Lehigh Art Alliance, 88 & Phillips Mill 88; First Award, Mid-Atlantic Regional Col, Univ Del, 79. *Mem:* Lehigh Art Alliance (bd dir, 72-75, 86-92, pres, 75-77); Printmaking Coun NJ; Print Club Philadelphia; Kemerer Mus, Bethlehem (bd dirs, 78-88). *Media:* Intaglio, Collagraph. *Mailing Add:* 174 Stonesthrow Rd Bethlehem PA 18015

REDD EKKS (ROBERT NORMAN RASMUSSEN)
SCULPTOR, CERAMIST
b Oslo, Norway, Feb 11, 37. *Study:* San Francisco Art Inst, BFA, 59; Calif Col Arts & Crafts, MFA, 70. *Work:* San Francisco Mus Mod Art, San Francisco; Los Angeles Co Mus Art, Los Angeles; Mills Col Art Gallery, Oakland. *Exhib:* Mix, San Francisco Mus Art, 73; Ceramic Sculpture, San Francisco Art Inst, 74; Newport Harbor Art Mus, Newport Beach, Calif, 81; New Mus, New York, 81; Artists Space, New York, 82; Joseph Chowning Gallery, San Francisco, 83; Joseph Chowning Gallery, San Francisco, 86; Ten Years Later, Calif State Univ Fullerton, Fullerton, Calif, 87; New Langton Arts, San Francisco, 87; and others. *Teaching:* Instr ceramics, San Francisco Art Inst, 71-; instr ceramics, Univ Wis-Madison, summer, 75. *Awards:* Nat Endowment Arts, 81. *Mailing Add:* c/o San Francisco Art Inst 800 Chestnut St San Francisco CA 94133

REDDINGTON, CHARLES LEONARD
PAINTER, EDUCATOR
b Chicago, Ill, Mar 22, 29. *Study:* Art Inst Chicago, with Paul Wieghardt, dipl, 54, BFA, 58; Southern Ill Univ, MFA, 70. *Work:* Commonwealth Govt Collection, Canberra, Australia; Art Gallery NSW, Sydney; Nat Gallery Victoria, Melbourne; Western Australian Art Gallery, Perth; Southern Ill Univ, Carbondale. *Comn:* Harold Mertz Pub Collection, New York, 63; Four Color Lithographs, Nat Gallery Victoria, Melbourne, 64. *Exhib:* Australian Painting Today, 64; Young Contemporaries of Australia, Japan, 65; Travel Exhib of Art, Ind, 71; one-man show, Swope Art Gallery, Terre Haute, Ind, 73; G Bablo, Acad D'Arts, Rivera dei Fiori, Bordighera, Italy; and many others. *Pos:* Dir educ abroad, Ind State Univ, Terre Haute, 75- *Teaching:* Lectr drawing & painting, NSW Univ, Sydney, 63-66; prof painting, Ind State Univ, Terre Haute, 70- *Awards:* Willis Painting Award, H O Willis Corp, Inc, Sydney, 65; Louis Comfort Tiffany Grant, 70; Works on Paper Prize, Indianapolis Mus, 72; and many others. *Bibliog:* Robert Hughes (auth), Art in Australia, Pelican Books, 70; James Gleeson (auth), Modern Painters, Landsdowne Press, 71; Alan McCulloch (auth), Encyclopedia of Australian Art, Hutchinson & Co. *Mem:* Col Art Conf; Art Inst Chicago Alumnae; Int Inst Conserv Historic & Artistic Works; Ind Arts Comn. *Media:* Acrylic, Oil. *Mailing Add:* Dept Art Ind State Univ Main Campus Terre Haute IN 47809

REDDIX, ROSCOE CHESTER
PAINTER, EDUCATOR
b New Orleans, La, Nov 15, 33. *Study:* Southern Univ, BA; Univ New Orleans; Ind Univ, Bloomington, MS(art educ); Univ Southern Miss; also with Dr Eddie Jordan; Vanderbuilt Univ, Nashville, Tenn, PhD. *Comn:* Pastic painting, Southern Univ New Orleans; painting, Superdome, New Orleans, La. *Exhib:* Expo 72, La Artist Exhib, Ill State Univ; NJ State Mus; Black Artist, Ind Univ; one-man shows, Ala State Univ, Southern Univ New Orleans & DeWitt Hist Soc, Ithaca, NY. *Pos:* Bd dir, New Orleans Mus Art. *Teaching:* Instr art, Shreveport, La & New Orleans, La; from asst prof to assoc prof art, Southern Univ New Orleans, 74- *Bibliog:* Samella S Lewis & Ruth Waddy (auth), Black Artist on Art, Contemp Crafts. *Mem:* Nat Conf Artist (state dir, 73); Col Art Asn; Creative Artists Alliance New Orleans. *Media:* Oil. *Publ:* Contribr, Black Artist on Art, Vol 2, 71. *Mailing Add:* 1330 Cambronne St New Orleans LA 70118

REDDY, KRISHNA N
PRINTMAKER, SCULPTOR
b Chittoor, Andhra State, India, July 15, 25. *Study:* Int Univ Santiniketan, India, dipl(fine arts), 47; Univ London Slade Sch Fine Arts, cert(fine arts), 52; Acad Grande Chaumiere, Paris, with Zadkine, cert(fine arts), 55; Atelier 17, Int Ctr Gravure, Paris, 55; Academie DiBelle Arti DiBrera, Milan, with Marino Marini, cert(fine arts), 57. *Work:* Mus Mod Art, New York & Paris; Libr Cong, Nat Galleries, Smithsonian Inst, Washington, DC; and others. *Comn:* Monumental sculpture in marble, Int Sculpture Symposium, St Margarethan, Austria, 62 & Montreal, 64. *Exhib:* one-man shows, Madison Art Ctr, 73, Assoc Am Artists, New York, 74, Univ Calif Gallery, Santa Cruz, 75 & Galerie Vivant, Tokyo, 78; retrospectives: Bronx Mus Arts, New York, 81; Lalitkala Akademi, New Delhi, 84; Museo del Palacio de Bellas Artes, 88. *Pos:* Dir art dept, Col Fine Arts, Kalakshetra, Madras, 47-49. *Teaching:* Prof & co-dir printmaking, Atelier 17, Int Ctr Graphics, Paris, 57-76; prof & dir graphics, printmaking prog, Dept Art & Art Educ, NY Univ, 77- *Awards:* Padma Shree, Pres India, 72. *Bibliog:* S W Hayter (auth), About Prints, 64 & New Ways of Gravure, 66, Oxford Univ Press, London; Gabor Peterdi (auth), Printmaking, MacMillan Co, New York, 71; The Great Clown, Gallerie Borjeson, Malmo, Sweden, 85. *Media:* Engraving, Etching; Stone. *Publ:* Auth, Intaglio Simultaneous Color Printmaking, State Univ New York Press, Albany, 88. *Dealer:* Sylvan Cole Gallery 200 W 57th St New York NY 10019; Weintraub Gallery 992 Madison Ave New York NY 10021. *Mailing Add:* 80 Wooster St New York NY 10012

REDGRAVE, FELICITY
PAINTER, VIDEO ARTIST
b UK, 1920; Can citizen. *Study:* Sheridan Col, Oakville, Ont, dipl(hon; graphic design), 70; Univ Guelph, Ont, BA(hon; fine arts), 73; Univ Toronto, BEd(art), 75. *Work:* Can Art Bank, Ottawa; Esso Resources Ltd, Calgary, Alta; Lavalin Inc, Montreal; Teleglobe, Montreal; Telesat, Ottawa. *Exhib:* Solo exhib, Images of Nova Scotia & Newfoundland, Harbour Front, Toronto, 77, Art Gallery of Nova Scotia, 78, Confederation Ctr, Charlottetown, PEI, 80, Night-Spaces, St Mary's Univ, Halifax, NS, 84 & Moncton Univ, 86; Night Radio, Galerie Sans Nom, Moncton, 87. *Pos:* Contrib ed, Art magazine, 78-82; art crtic, Discussion Concordia Univ, Montreal, 80; contrib writer, arts Atlantic, 81. *Teaching:* Vis artist, Univ Toronto, York Univ, 77 & Univ Waterloo, 79 & 81; lectr, Owens Art Gallery, Mt Allison Univ, NS, 85. *Awards:* Can Coun B Grant, 83-84; Intermedia Group & video Grants, 87-88. *Bibliog:* Susan Gibson (auth), article, Vangard Mag Review,85. *Mem:* Visual Arts NS; Can Artists Representation; Prof Artists NS. *Media:* Acrylic, Oil. *Publ:* Auth, Tom Forrestal, Arts Atlantic, 79; Marlene Creates and Pat Martin Bates at Mt St Vincent's Art Gallery, 85; Brian Porter at Dalhousie Art Gallery, 85; John Neville, Art Gallery NS, 88. *Dealer:* Ineke Graham Studio 21 Bank of Montreal Bldg Cobury Rd Halifax NS. *Mailing Add:* 1725 Beach Dr Apt 206 Victoria BC V8R 6H9 Canada

REDINGER, WALTER FRED
SCULPTOR, MURALIST
b Wallacetown, Ont, Jan 6, 42. *Study:* Beal-Spec Art, London, Ont; Meinsinger Sch Art, Detroit; Ont Col Art, Toronto. *Work:* Nat Art Gallery, Ottawa; Art Gallery Ont, Toronto; Can Coun, Ottawa; Univ Western Ont; Univ Sask. *Comn:* Caucasian totems (set of 5), Rothman's, Stratford, 72; caucasian totems (set of 4), Samuel Bronfman, Can Jewish Cong, 73; Xabis (monument, 6 units), Ct House, London, Ont, 74; Montagne (monument), Pinetree Develop, Toronto, 75; Umbria (monuments, 3 units), Univ Guelph, 75. *Exhib:* Survey, Montreal Mus Fine Arts, 68; Plastic Presence, Jewish Mus, New York, Milwaukee Art Ctr, 70; Venice Biennale, 72; Owens Art Gallery, Mt Allison, NB, 75; Birmingham Festival Arts, Ala, 79; Harbourfront Art Gallery-Toronto, 82. *Pos:* Resident artist, Univ Western Ont. *Awards:* Sculpture Prize, Montreal Mus, 69; Can Coun Jr Awards, 68-71, Sr Awards, 73-74; Victor Lynch-Stauton Award, 77. *Bibliog:* Robert Arn (auth), Rebirth of humanism, Arts Can, 74; Document Venice Biennale (film), Educ TV Toronto, 74; film, Can Broadcasting Co, 74. *Mem:* Royal Can Acad Arts. *Media:* Fiberglass, Steel. *Mailing Add:* Rte 3 West Lorne ON N0L 2P0 Canada

REDMOND, ROZZE (ROSEMARY)
PAINTER, PRINTMAKER
b Anchorage, Alaska, Mar 16, 52. *Study:* Univ Alaska, BFA, 82; Pratt Inst, grant & fel, MFA, 85. *Work:* Univ Alaska, Anchorage. *Exhib:* Nat, current visions, Germanow Gallery, Rochester, NY, 86; Nat, New American Talent, traveling, Tex Fine Arts Assoc, Austin, 89; solo exhib, On the Kvichak, Visual Arts Ctr Alaska, Anchorage, 91. *Awards:* Yaddo Fel, Yaddo Corp, 89; Grants, Artists Space, New York, 90 & 91. *Bibliog:* Nancy Jordan (auth), Abstract Artist with Anchorage Times, 5/6/90; Martin Parsons (auth), Redmond's Stunning Debut, Artspeak, 4/91; Jan Ingram (auth), solo exhib combine for Strong Show, Anchorage Daily News, 11/17/91. *Mem:* Col Art Asn, 86-; Visual Arts Ctr Alaska, 90- *Media:* Oil on Canvas. *Publ:* Auth, An Eskimo in Touch with Two Cultures, Alaska Mag, 11/79. *Dealer:* Stonington Gallery 415 F St Anchorage Alaska 99501. *Mailing Add:* PO Box 202634 Anchorage AK 99520-2634

RED STAR, KEVIN
PAINTER, PRINTMAKER
b Lodge Grass, Mont, Oct 9, 43. *Study:* Inst Am Indian Art, Santa Fe, NMex, 62-65; San Francisco Art Inst, 65-67; Mont State Univ, 68-69; Eastern Mont Col, Billings, BA, 72. *Work:* Heard Mus, Phoenix, Ariz; Northern Plains Mus, Browning, Mont; Inst Am Indian Art Mus, Santa Fe, NMex; Denver Art Mus, Colo; Shenyang Nat Art Mus, Liaoning, China; and others. *Comn:* Mural, Crow Tribal Office, Crow Agency, Mont. *Exhib:* Wheelwright Contemp Indian Artist Show, Wheelwright Ceremonial Art Mus, Santa Fe, 78; 100 years of Native American Painting, Okla Mus Art, 78; Indian Images '80, Natural History Mus, Denver; Peking Exhibit of American Western Art, China, 81; Lublin Collection, New York, 86 & Greenwich, Conn, 87; and others. *Collections Arranged:* 77 West Coast Experience (auth, catalog), Tokyo, Japan; American Indian Art Exhibition, Espace Pierre Cardin, Paris, 79; The Real People, Havana, Cuba, 79; Santa Fe Festival of the Arts, 78-81; American Indian Art in the 80's, Native Am Ctr Living Arts Mus (auth, catalog), Niagara Falls, NY, 81. *Teaching:* Instr art, Lodge Grass, Mont, 73-74, Inst Am Indian Art, Santa Fe, 75-76. *Awards:* Governor's Trophy, Scottsdale Nat Indian Art Exhib, 65; First Place, Cent Wash State Col Art Exhib, Ellensburg, Wash, 74. *Bibliog:* Scott E Dial (auth), Visual portrayals of Kevin Red Star, Southwest Art, 2/76; Penny Cox (auth), Red Star: Modern mystic and on the move, Santa Fe Profile Mag, 12/79; Jamake Highwater, The Sweet Grass Lives On, Harper & Row, 79-80. *Media:* Acrylic, Oil; Lithography, Etchings. *Mailing Add:* c/o Lublin Graphics 90 E Putnam Ave Greenwich CA 06830

REDSTONE, LOUIS GORDON
ARCHITECT, WRITER
b Grodno, Poland, Mar 16, 03; US citizen. *Study:* Univ Mich, BS(archit), 29; Cranbrook Acad Art, MArch & Urban Design, 48. *Comn:* Brick mural, Jewish Community Ctr, West Bloomfield, Mich, 75 & First Federal Savings & Loan of Detroit, Operations Ctr, Troy, Mich, 76; Tapestries (woven in Mex by Mr Delgado), Manufacturers Bank & 333 W Fort Off Bldg, Detroit, Mich, 78. *Exhib:* Ann Mich Artists Water Color Exhib, Detroit, 28 & 42; The Levant Fair, Israeli Artists Inst Exhib, Tel Aviv, Israel, 34; Watercolor USA, 69; Mich Watercolor Soc, 72; and others. *Awards:* Robert F Hastings Award for Outstanding Achievement, Mich Soc Archit. *Bibliog:* William Tall (auth), L G R: Minor Miracles in Watercolors, 11/22/69 & Marsha Miro (auth), Art in Architecture, 2/22/77, Detroit Free Press; Joy Hakanson (auth), Louis G Redstone: Fighting His Own War on Ugliness, Detroit News, 72. *Mem:* patron Mich Foundation Arts, 77 (bd mem, 78); Mich Gov Spec Comn on Art in State Bldg; hon fel Royal Acad Fine Art, The Hague; corresponding acad Royal Acad Fine Arts, San Fernando, Spain; Mich Soc Archit. *Media:* Watercolor. *Interests:* Support of Michigan Society of Ceramic Artists. *Collection:* Pre-Columbian Art, Aztec, Inca. *Publ:* Auth, New Dimensions in Shopping Centers and Stores, 73, The New Downtowns, 76 & 80 & Public Art-New Directions, 81, McGraw-Hill; contribr, Art in Public Places in the US, Bowling Green Univ, 75; contrib, Masonry in Architecture, 84; and others. *Mailing Add:* c/o The Art Ctr 125 Macomb Place Mt Clemens MI 48043

REECE, MAYNARD
PAINTER, ILLUSTRATOR
b Arnolds Park, Iowa, Apr 26, 20. *Work:* Cent Nat Bank, Des Moines, Iowa; Norwest Bank, Des Moines; Leigh Yawkey Woodson Art Mus, Wausau, Wis. *Comn:* Designs for postage stamps, Govt of Bermuda, 65; First Iowa Duck Stamp, State Conserv Comn, 72; Marshlander Mallards, Ducks Unlimited Inc, 73; Canada Geese & Mallards, Winnebego Indust; Canada Geese, Remington Arms, Bridgeport, Conn, 76; Am Artist Collection, 85. *Exhib:* Various mus throughout the US & Can. *Awards:* Five Time Winner, Fed Duck Stamp Competition; Ark Duck Stamp Award, 82; Tex Duck Stamp Award, 83; Master Artist, Leigh Yaukey Woodson Art Mus, Wausau, Wis. *Bibliog:* John Diffely (auth), Maynard Reece: Wildlife artist, Am Artist, 78; Chuck Wechsler (auth), I've been there with Maynard Reece, Wildlife Art News, 84; M Stephen Doherty (auth), Am Artist, 85; Mark E Stegmaier (auth), Maynard Reece: Celebrator of the marsh, Midwest Art, 85. *Mem:* Grand Cent Art Galleries New York; hon trustee Ducks Unlimited Inc; Soc Animal Artists; Nat Audubon Soc; Outdoor Writers Asn Am (past bd mem). *Media:* Oil, Watercolor; Stone Lithography. *Publ:* Illusr, Life, Outdoor Life, Sports Afield & others; auth & illusr, Fish & Fishing, Meredith, 63; illusr, Waterfowl in Iowa & Iowa Fish & Fishing, Iowa Conserv Comn; auth & illusr, Waterfowl Art of Maynard Reece, Abrams, 85. *Dealer:* Mill Pond Press Inc 310 Center Court Venice FL 34292. *Mailing Add:* 5315 Robertson Dr Des Moines IA 50312

REED, CLEOTA
HISTORIAN, LECTURER
b Chicago, Ill. *Study:* Syracuse Univ, BFA, 75, MA, 76. *Awards:* Am Philos Soc Grant, 76; Nat Endowment Humanities Fel, 80 & 91; Merit Award, NY Regional Coun Hist Agencies, 85. *Res:* American ceramic tiles; arts and crafts movement; John Gough Nichols and the Gothic revival. *Publ:* Auth, The Arts & Crafts Ideal: The Ward House, Syracuse: IDEA, 78; Irene Sargent: A Comprehensive Bibliography, Syracuse Univ: Courier, 81; William Ittner & H Mercer: Art & Architecture, Erie Co Hist Soc, 82; ed, Henry Keck Stained Glass Studio 1913-1974, Syracuse Univ Press, 85; auth, Henry Chapman Mercer and the Moravian Tile Works, Univ Pa Press, 87. *Mailing Add:* 329 Westcott St Syracuse NY 13210

REED, DAVID
PAINTER
b San Diego, Calif, Jan 20, 46. *Study:* Reed Col, BA; New York Studio Sch; Skowhegan Sch Painting & Sculpture. *Work:* Metrop Mus Art, New York; La Jolla Mus Contemp Art, Calif; Musee Nat d'Art Moderne, Centre George Pompidou, Paris. *Exhib:* One-man shows, Max Protetch Gallery, 77, 79, 83, 85, 86, 88, 89, 91 & 92, Galerie Rolf Ricke, Cologne, Ger, 91 & San Francisco Art Inst, Calif, 92; Asher/Faure Gallery, Los Angeles, 88; Biennial Exhib, Whitney Mus Am Art, New York, 89; Galerie Nachst St Stephan, Vienna, Austria, 92; Galerie Rolf Ricke, Cologne, Ger, 92. *Teaching:* Cooper-Union Sch, 91. *Awards:* Rockefeller Found Grant, 66; Fel, Guggenheim Found, 88; Nat Endowment Arts, 91. *Bibliog:* Daniel Wheeler (auth), Art Since Mid-Century, 1945 to the Present, Vendome Press, NY; Charles Hagen (auth), The Anatomy of Autonomy, Artforum, 11/90; David Reed (interview), ART Press, William Bartman Found, 90; and others. *Media:* Oil on Canvas. *Publ:* Interview with David Reed, J Contemp Art, spring 88; auth, Memories of Rome, New Observations, #68, 6/89; Reflected Light; in Siena with Beccafumi, Arts Mag, pgs 52-53, 3/91; Two Bedrooms in San Francisco (essay, exhib catalog), San Francisco Art Inst, 92. *Dealer:* Max Protetch Gallery 560 Broadway New York NY 10012; Asher/Faure Gallery 612 N Almont Dr Los Angeles CA 90069. *Mailing Add:* 315 Broadway New York NY 10007

REED, DENNIS JAMES
CURATOR, DESIGNER
b Culver City, Calif, Oct 30, 46. *Study:* Calif State Univ, Fullerton, BA, 69, MA, 71; MMI, Univ Calif, Berkeley, 83. *Collections Arranged:* Japanese Photography in Los Angeles, 1920-1945 (auth, catalog), 82 & The Furniture of Gustav Stickley, 83, Art Gallery, Los Angeles Valley Col; Japanese Photography in America 1920-1940 (auth, catalog), Japanese-Am Cult Ctr, 86; Travel Exhib 88-89: Oakland Mus, Rahr-West Art Mus; Whitney Mus Am Art, Corcoran Gallery Art; and other exhibitions. *Pos:* Dir, Conejo Valley Art Mus, 78-80 & Art Gallery, Los Angeles Valley Col, 80-91, assoc dean, 91. *Teaching:* Assoc prof art, Los Angeles Valley Col, 80- *Awards:* Award of Excellence, Am Fed of the Arts; Award, Parallels and Contrasts, Am Inst Graphic Arts, 89. *Res:* Pictorial photography. *Publ:* Auth, Japanese Photograph in Am 1920-1940, 86; Richard Pettibone, Forty Years of California Assemblage, Wight Art Gallery, Univ Calif-Los Angeles, 89. *Mailing Add:* 3937 Northland St Newbury Park CA 91320

REED, FLINT WINTER
PAINTER, PRINTMAKER
b Bastrop, La, Oct 4, 33. *Study:* Kansas City Art Inst, with Julius Schmidt, 56-57; Sch Fine Art, Madrid, Spain, with Julio Moises, 60-61; Univ Calif, Santa Cruz, BFA, 77. *Work:* Convent Mus/Gallery, Pollenca, Mallorca, Spain; Silver Sands Hotel, St George's, Grenada; Martin Segal & Assocs, New York; Eckert Cold Storage, Manteca, Calif; Valley Packing Ser, Watsonville, Calif. *Exhib:* Int Art Festival, Convent Mus, Pollensa, Mallorca, 64; A View of Island Life, Careenage Mus, St George's, Grenada, 69; Art Festival, Galveston, Tex, 89; San Diego Fair, Del Mar, Calif, 89 & 90; many others in Europe, West Indies & the US. *Media:* Acrylic, Oils; Etching. *Dealer:* Crimson Shadows Gallery 450 N Highway 89A Sedona AZ 86336. *Mailing Add:* 5 Blue Anchor Coronado CA 86336

REED, HAL
PAINTER, MEDALIST
b Frederick, Okla, Feb 22, 21. *Study:* Trade Tech Col Los Angeles; Art Ctr Col Design; Art League San Francisco; also with Nicolai Fechin & Burt Proctor. *Work:* Los Angeles City Hall Permanent Collection; and other pub & pvt collections. *Comn:* Albert Einstein Bust, Permanent Collection, Los Angeles Co Mus Sci & Indust, 79; Bicentennial bronze medals, US Navy & US Marine Corps, US Mint; bronze plaque of Jesse Owens, Los Angeles Coliseum; two portrait bronzes, St Mary's Hosp, Long Beach, Calif; 45 coins, Hutt River Province, Australia; and others. *Exhib:* Nat Open, Miniature Painters, Sculptors & Gravers Soc, Washington, DC, 72; Nat Open, Miniature Art Soc NJ, 72; Am Artists Prof League, New York, 72; plus many others. *Teaching:* Instr art, 124 programs on video tapes, Art Video Productions Inc. *Awards:* Best in Sculpture & Col King Award, Miniature Painters & Sculptors Soc Washington, DC, 72; selected NACAL artist, US Navy, 74; Award of Highest Merit, Miniature Art Soc of NJ, 74; and many others. *Mem:* Coun Traditional Artists Soc (pres, 71-72); fel Am Artists Prof League; fel Am Inst Fine Arts. *Media:* Oil, Acrylic. *Publ:* Auth, How to Compose Pictures & Achieve Color Harmony, Walter Foster Publ, 69; Art instruction videotapes, Art Video Productions Inc. *Mailing Add:* 6225 Shoup Ave No 106 Woodland Hills CA 91367

REED, HAROLD
DEALER
b Newark, NJ, Jan 11, 37. *Study:* Stanford Univ, BA; Art Students League. *Pos:* Dir, Harold Reed Gallery, New York, currently. *Teaching:* Instr, New York Univ Sch Continuing Educ, 84-86. *Mem:* Art Dealers Asn Am. *Mailing Add:* Harold Reed Gallery 120 E 78th St New York NY 10021

REED, JESSE FLOYD
PAINTER, PRINTMAKER
b Belington, WVa, July 25, 20. *Study:* Grand Cent Sch Art, 39-42; Art Students League, 45-47; Davis & Elkins Col, BA; WVa Univ, MA. *Work:* Huntington Galleries, WVa; Charleston Art Galleries, WVa; Rosenberg Libr, Galveston, Tex. *Exhib:* Print Show, Brooklyn Mus, 49; Libr Cong, 55; Print Club Albany Ann; Soc Washington Printmakers Ann; Boston Printmakers Ann. *Teaching:* Prof art & hist, Davis & Elkins Col, 49- *Awards:* Purchase

Award, Print Club Albany, 74; Merit Award & Purchase Award, Charleston Art Gallery, WVa, 75; Merit Award, Cult Ctr, WVa, 79. *Mem:* Salmagundi Club; Boston Printmakers; WVa Watercolor Soc; Print Club Albany. *Media:* Watercolor; Aquatint Etching. *Mailing Add:* PO Box 650 Elkins WV 26241

REED, PAUL ALLEN
PAINTER
b Washington, DC, Mar 28, 19. *Study:* San Diego State Col, Calif; Corcoran Sch Art, Washington, DC. *Work:* In over 50 pub collections, including: San Francisco Mus Art; Hirshhorn Mus, Washington, DC; Corcoran Gallery Art & Nat Mus Am Art, Washington, DC; Detroit Inst Art; Walker Art Ctr, Minneapolis; Phillips Collection, Washington, DC. *Exhib:* 25th Ann Soc Am Art, Art Inst Chicago, 65; Washington Color Painters, Washington, DC, Tex, Calif, Mass & Minn, 65-66; 250 Years American Art, Corcoran Gallery Art, 66; Jackson Pollock to the Present, Steinberg Gallery, Washington Univ, St Louis, 69; Inaugural Exhib, Wadsworth Atheneum, Hartford, Conn, 69; Washington 20 Years, Baltimore Mus Art, 70; one-man exhib, Phoenix Art Mus, 77. *Teaching:* Instr painting, Art League Northern Va, 71-74; asst prof & coordr first yr core prog, Corcoran Sch Art, 71-80. *Bibliog:* Barbara Rose (auth), The primacy of color, 5/64 & Legrace Benson (auth), Washington Scene, 69, Art Int; Walter Hopps (auth), The Vincent Melzac Collection, Corcoran Gallery Art, 71. *Media:* Acrylic, Gouache. *Mailing Add:* 3541 N Utah St Arlington VA 22207

REED, WALT ARNOLD
HISTORIAN, DEALER
b Big Spring, Tex, July 21, 17. *Study:* Pratt Inst; NY-Phoenix Sch Design; also with Franklin Booth. *Comn:* Designer US postage stamp series, 50 state flags, US Postal Serv, 76. *Pos:* Art dir, CARE, New York, 52-55; ed, North Light Publ, Westport, 72-78; proprietor, Illus House, 75- *Teaching:* Art instr, Famous Artists Sch, Westport, Conn, 57-66, asst to dir, 66-72. *Awards:* Wrangler Award for Best Western Art Book, Cowboy Hall Fame & Western Heritage Ctr, 72. *Mem:* Appraisers Asn Am Inc; New York Soc Illusr; Sanford Low Mem Collection Am Illus, New Brit Mus Am Art. *Res:* American illustrations, 1880 to the present. *Publ:* Auth, Harold Von Schmidt Draws and Paints the Old West, 72 & John Clymer, 76, Northland; The magic pen of Joseph Clement Coll, North Light, 78; Fifty Great American Illustrators, Artabras, 79; The Illustrator in America 1880-1980, Madison Sq Press, 84. *Dealer:* Illustration House Inc 96 Spring St (7th fl) New York NY 10012. *Mailing Add:* Seven Belaire Dr Westport CT 06880

REEDY, MITSUNO ISHII (MITSUNO ISHII HACKLER)
PAINTER
b Osaka, Prefecture, Japan, Jan 18, 41; US citizen. *Study:* Laguna Gloria Art Mus Sch, 76; Elizabeth Ney Mus Sch, 77-79; Scottsdale Art Sch, 92. *Work:* State Capitol Rotunda, Oklahoma City, Okla; Univ Okla, Sch Law Courtroom Portrait Gallery, Norman. *Exhib:* Pastel Soc Am Ann, Nat Arts Club, New York, 91. *Media:* Pastel. *Mailing Add:* 437 Sundown Dr Norman OK 73069

REEP, EDWARD ARNOLD
PAINTER, EDUCATOR
b Brooklyn, NY, May 10, 18. *Study:* Art Ctr Col Design, cert, 41; also with E J Bisttram, Stanley Reckless & Willard Nash. *Work:* Los Angeles Co Mus, Calif; 66 works, US War Dept, Pentagon; Grunwald Graphic Arts Collection, Univ Calif, Los Angeles; Lytton Collection, Los Angeles; State of Calif Collection, Sacramento; Nat Mus Am Art, Smithsonian Inst, Washington, DC. *Comn:* Three panels of early conquests in Calif, SAm & US (with Gordon Mellor), USA Private's Club, Ft Ord, Calif, 41; Painter's Impression of International Airports (10 pages in full color), Life Mag, 6/56; Impressions of the Berlin Wall, Ger, US Govt, 71. *Exhib:* Whitney Mus Am Art Ann, New York, 46-48; Los Angeles Co Mus Ann, 46-60; Corcoran Gallery Art Biennial, Washington, DC, 49; Nat Acad Design, New York; Nat Gallery Art, Washington, DC. *Pos:* Coord art chmn, Los Angeles City Art Festival Exhibs, 51; official war artist & corresp, World War II. *Teaching:* Instr painting & drawing, Art Ctr Col Design, Los Angeles, 46-50; instr painting & drawing & chmn, Dept Painting, Chouinard Art Inst, Los Angeles, 50-69; prof painting, artist in residence, E Carolina Univ, 70-85, prof emer, currently. *Awards:* Guggenheim Fel Creative Painting, 45-56; First Prize in Oil Painting, Los Angeles All City Ann, 63; Nat Endowment Arts Grant, 75; and others. *Bibliog:* Schaad (auth), Realm of Contemporary Still-life, 62 & Mugnaini (auth), Drawing, a Search for Form, 65, Van Nostrand Reinhold; James Jones (auth), World War II, Grosset & Dunlap, 75. *Mem:* Nat Watercolor Soc (pres, 57-58). *Media:* Oil, Watercolor. *Publ:* Auth, The Content of Watercolor, Van Nostrand Reinhold, 83; A Combat Artist in World War II, Univ Press Ky, 87. *Mailing Add:* 9021 Crowninshield Dr Bakersfield CA 93311

REESE, MARCIA MITCHELL
SCULPTOR
b Cleveland, Ohio. *Study:* Case Western Reserve Univ, BA, 51. *Work:* Hofstra Mus, Hofstra Univ, Hempstead, NY; MONY Financial Services World Headquarters, New York. *Exhib:* Stone Sculpture Soc New York, 83-91; Nat Asn Women Artists, New York, 84-91; Solo shows, CAPA Rotational Art Exhib, 80, Bloomingdale's, Model Room #3, New York, 81, Chemical Bank, North Shore Towers, 82, Port Washington Libr Gallery, 82, Bryant Libr Gallery, 86, Gallery Lincoln Ctr, 86, Plandome Gallery, 91; Guild Hall Mus, East Hampton, NY 87-90; Elaine Benson Gallery, Bridgehampton, NY, 83. *Pos:* Who's Who in the East. *Awards:* Cleo Hartwig Mem Award, Nat Asn Woman Artists, 89; Dr Max Ellenberg Award, Nat Asn Woman Artists, 91; Nassau Co Mus Art, 92. *Mem:* Nat Asn Women Artists; Sculptors Inc (pres); Stone Sculpture Soc New York; Artists Network Great Neck (archivist, 88-90); Archeol Inst Am, LI Soc (vpres). *Media:* Stone. *Mailing Add:* PO Box 1318 Great Neck NY 11023

REESE, THOMAS FORD
HISTORIAN, ADMINISTRATOR
b New Orleans, La, Oct 9, 43. *Study:* Fac Filosofia y Letras, Univ de Madrid, 63-64; Tulane Univ, BA, 65; Yale Univ, MA, 69, PhD, 73. *Pos:* Assoc dir, Getty Ctr Hist Art & Humanities, 86-92, actg dir, 92- *Teaching:* Asst prof art hist, Univ Tex, Austin, 70-76, assoc prof art hist, 76-83, prof, 83-86. *Awards:* John Simon Guggenheim Mem Found Fel, 76-77; Academico correspondiente, Real Academia de Bellas Artes de San Fernando, Madrid, 77; Samuel H Kress Sr Fel, Ctr Advan Study in Visual Arts, Nat Gallery Art, Washington, DC, 83. *Mem:* Col Art Asn Am; Soc of Archit Historians; Am Soc for Hispanic Art Hist Studies; Asn for Latin Am Art; Asn of Res Insts in Art Hist. *Res:* History of the arts of Spain and Portugal; Latin American Colonial Art; European architecture since 1400. *Publ:* Auth, The Architecture of Ventura Rodriguez, Garland Publ Inc, 76; intro to Libro de diferentes pensamientos unos imbentados y otros delineados por Diego de Villanueva, Real Academia de Bellas Artes de San Fernando, 80; ed, Studies in Ancient American and European Art--The Collected Essays of George Kubler, Yale Univ Press, 85; introd to La configuracion del tiempo--Observaciones sobre la historia de las cosas, Editorial Nerea, Madrid, Spain, 88; coauth, Boehm, Gehry, Hollein and Stirling in Los Angeles--The Competition Entries for the Walt Disney Concert Hall, Zodiac 2, Milan, Italy, 9/89. *Mailing Add:* Getty Ctr 401 Wilshire Blvd Suite 400 Santa Monica CA 90401-1455

REESE, WILLIAM FOSTER
PAINTER
b Pierre, SDak, July 10, 38. *Study:* Wash State Univ; Orange Coast Col; Los Angeles Trade Tech Sch; Art Ctr Sch Design, Los Angeles. *Work:* Frye Art Mus, Seattle, Wash. *Comn:* Painting, Walter Lommell Hosp, Woodburn, Ore, 72; paintings, St Francis Hotel, San Francisco, 72. *Exhib:* Rocky Mountain Nat, Golden, Colo, 75, 76 & 77; Am Watercolor Soc Show, 76; Pastel Soc Show, 76-77; NAWA Show, Cowboy Hall of Fame, Oklahoma City, 77; one-man show, Frye Art Mus, 77; and others. *Awards:* Leon Augustine Hermitte Award, Puget Sound Exhib, Frye Mus, 75 & 77; House of Heydenryk Award, Nat Arts Club, 77; Best Show, Mus Great Plains, 78. *Bibliog:* Mary N Balcomb (auth), William F Reese: Form follows function, Am Artist Mag, 12/78; Laurel Andrews (auth), The visual poetry of William F Reese, Art West Mag, fall 79; Mary N Balcomb (auth), The art of painting, Southwest Art Mag, 10/82. *Mem:* Puget Sound Group Northwest Painters (secy, 70-71, treas, 71-72); Nat Acad Western Art; Whiskey Painters Am; Pastel Soc Am; Soc Animal Artists. *Media:* Oil, Watercolor. *Mailing Add:* c/o Wichita Gallery Fine Art 100 Broadway Wichita KS 67202

REESER, ROBERT D
EDUCATOR, ADMINISTRATOR
b Orangeville, Ill, Mar 4, 31. *Study:* Northern Ill Univ, BS, 53; Univ Denver, MA(art), 59; Ohio State Univ, PhD(art educ), 74. *Work:* Burpee Art Gallery, Rockford, Ill. *Pos:* Assoc dean, Sch Arts & Letters, Calif Southern Univ, Los Angeles, 87- *Teaching:* Prof art, Calif State Univ, Los Angeles, 71- *Mem:* Calif Art Educ Asn (pres, 76-78); Nat Art Educ Asn; Artists Equity Asn; Int Soc Educ Art. *Res:* Teaching of secondary school art; aesthetics, art criticism and art history. *Mailing Add:* Dept Art Calif State Univ Los Angeles CA 90032

REEVE, JAMES KEY
HISTORIAN, CONSULTANT
b Lewistown, Mont. *Study:* Univ Tulsa, Okla, BA, 50; NY Univ Inst Fine Arts, MA, 54; Univ London Courtauld Inst, postgrad, 61-63. *Collections Arranged:* Masters of the Landscape: 1650-1900 (auth, catalog), 77, 100 Years of Native American Painting, 78, Oklahoma Sculpture Today (auth, catalog), 78 & Masters of the Portrait (auth, catalog), 79, Okla Mus Art. *Pos:* Cur, Univ Notre Dame Art Gallery, 58-61; cur-dir, Anglo-Am Art Mus, La State Univ, Baton Rouge, 63-67; cur Am art, Toledo Mus Art, Ohio, 67-72; cur art, Philbrook Art Ctr, Tulsa, Okla, 72-74; dir, Okla Mus Art, Oklahoma City, 75-81; art consult, Oklahoma City, 81-83; independent art & mus consult, Tulsa, 83- *Teaching:* Asst prof art hist, Univ Notre Dame, Ind, 58-61; asst prof art hist & museology, La State Univ, Baton Rouge, 63-67; adj prof art hist, Univ Tulsa, Okla, 72-74; adj prof, Oklahoma City Univ, 77-80; vis assoc prof, Univ Okla, 81-82. *Mem:* Am Asn Mus; Okla Mus Asn (coun mem, 79-81); Int Coun Mus. *Res:* American and English art and architecture, eighteenth century to present; museology; art installation techniques. *Publ:* Coauth, Nineteenth century religious architecture in Toledo, Ohio, Northwest Ohio Hist Soc Quart, 71; The Art of Showing Art, Riverrun Press & Council Oak Bks, Tulsa, 86, rev ed 92. *Mailing Add:* 4913 E 27th St Tulsa OK 74114

REEVES, DANIEL MCDONOUGH
VIDEO ARTIST, INSTALLATION ARTIST
Study: Ithaca Col, BS, 76. *Exhib:* High Mus Contemp Art, Atlanta, Ga; Mus Mod Art & Whitney Mus Am Art, New York; Tate Gallery, UK; Pearce Inst, Glasgow, Scotland; Long Beach Mus Art, Calif; Nat Video Festival/Am Film Inst, Los Angeles, Calif; and others. *Pos:* Exec Dir, Shakti Productions, Greenwich Village, New York & Tarbert, Scotland, UK. *Awards:* Fel & Grant Nat Endowment Arts, 80-92; NY State Coun on the Arts Prodn Grants, 80-92; Fel, John S Guggenheim Found, 83-84; NY Found Arts Fel, 87; Scottish Arts Council Grants, 90-92. *Publ:* Single channel video tapes, Smothering Dreams, Nat Video Festival Blue Ribbon Winner, 82; Mosaic for the Kali Yuga, 85; Sabda, Nat Video Festival Blue Ribbon Winner, 85; Ganapati/A Spirit in the Bush, 86; Sombra a Sombra, 88; video installations, The Well of Patience, 89, Eingang/The Way In, 90 & Jizo Garden, 92. *Mailing Add:* 799 Greenwich St Suite 6 South New York NY 10014-1843

REEVES, ESTHER MAY
PAINTER
b Riverside, Calif, Oct 12, 37. *Study:* Calif State Univ-Fullerton, MA, 86, MFA, 88; studied with H Ralph Love. *Work:* United First Methodist Church, Riverside, Calif; Truth Consciousness-Poona Ashram, India. *Comn:* Angel of Light (mural), Truth Consciousness, Boulder, Colo, 81; Fallopian Tissue & Dermal Pore, Riverside City Col-Life Sci Dept, Calif, 83 & 84; Landscape with Ducks, comn by Jones, Riverside, Calif, 83; portrait, comn by Headman, Orange, Calif, 88; portrait, comn by Bavaresco, Sacramento, Calif, 92. *Exhib:* Solo shows, Progressive Creativity, Inland Empire Gallery, 83 & Arising from Scripture, Riverside Art Mus, Calif, 92; Images 87, Bowers Mus, Santa Ana, Calif, 87; Grace Street Artists, Corona Gallery Ltd, Calif, 87; In Praise of Maleness, Piret's Gallery, Costa Mesa, 87; Celebration, Grand Hotel, Anaheim, 87; The Art of Love, Riverside Art Mus, 90; Wildlife Art, San Bernardino Art Mus, Calif, 90. *Pos:* Illusr & secy, Riverside Unified Sch Dist, 60-61; instr, Calif State Univ-Fullerton, 88-89. *Awards:* Best of Show, Grumacher Award, M Grumbacher Inc, 89; Best of Show, Ann Exhib, Clarks, 90. *Bibliog:* Melody Rogers (host), Two on the Town (CBS-TV), Joel Tator, 87; Joey Bavaresco (host), The World of Joey Bavaresco (TV), Ron Gallup, 92. *Media:* Oil on Canvas. *Dealer:* The Olive Branch Gallery 2890 Grand Ave Los Olivos CA 93441; A Albert Allen Gallery 73-200 El Paseo Dr Palm Desert CA 92260. *Mailing Add:* 4033 Rosewood Pl Riverside CA 92506

REEVES, JAMES FRANKLIN
HISTORIAN, COLLECTOR
b Huntsville, Ala, July 4, 46. *Study:* Univ Ala, Huntsville, BA(art hist), 72; Vanderbilt Univ, Nashville, Tenn, MA(art hist), 75. *Collections Arranged:* Gilbert Gaul, (with catalog), Tenn Fine Arts Ctr, Nashville & Huntsville Mus Art, 75. *Pos:* Asst, P L Hay House Mus, Macon, Ga, 66-67; asst to dir, 73-75, cur Huntsville Mus Art, 75-77. *Mem:* Col Art Asn Am; Southeastern Col Art Conf; Kappa Pi (pres local chapter, 71-72). *Res:* Gilbert Gaul, 1855-1919; Huntsville architecture, 1820-1975. *Collection:* 19th and 20th century American paintings; 18th and 19th century American decorative arts; 19th century European paintings; Oriental porcelains and sculpture. *Mailing Add:* 2005 Kildare St Huntsville AL 35811

REEVES, JOHN ALEXANDER
PHOTOGRAPHER
b Burlington, Ont, Can, Apr 24, 38. *Study:* Sir George Williams Art Sch, Montreal, 56-57; Ont Col Art, Toronto, 57-61, AOCA. *Work:* Nat Film Bd Can, Ottawa; Archives Canada; Dept Indian & Northern Affairs, Ottawa; Can Mus Contemp Photog, Ottawa; Nat Libr Can, Ottawa. *Exhib:* One-man shows, 30 Portraits of Women, Deja Vue Gallery, Toronto, 77, The Magic Word, Nat Archives Can, 81, Inuit Art World, Can Ctr Photog, Toronto, 82, Corkin Gallery, Toronto, 83, Can Cult Ctr, Rome, 91, About Face (travelling exhib), Cambridge, Simcoe & Brantford Art Galleries, Ont, 92 & Exile's Exiles, Bystriansky Gallery, Toronto, 92; Academic Images, Can Ctr Photog, 82; Creative Canadians (travelling exhib), Dept External Affairs, Ottawa, 82; Authors, Harbourfront Gallery, Toronto, 83; and others. *Pos:* Critic, host, Toronto Rev, Can Broadcasting Corp, Radio, 68- 71. *Teaching:* Instr photog, Ontario Col Art. *Awards:* Am Inst Graphic Arts Award, 63 & 68; Award of Merit, Art Dir Club, Toronto, 71, 72, 76 & 77; Int Asn Printing House Craftsmen, 77. *Bibliog:* Charles Oberdorf (auth), articles, 11/72 & 6/77 & Gunter Ott (auth), Sand on the beach, 87, Camera Can Mag; Gary Michael Dault (auth), article, Toronto Star, 6/77; Gary Michael Dault (auth), Inuit Art World Catalogue, 82. *Mem:* Royal Can Acad Art; Can Asn Photogs & Illusrs Communs. *Publ:* Auth, John Fillion--Thoughts About My Sculpture, Martlet Press, 68; God's Big Acre--Life in 401 Country, Methuen, Can, 86; About Face, 90 & Exile's Exile, 92, Exile Eds, Toronto; Jazz Lives, McClelland & Stewart, Toronto, 92. *Dealer:* Jane Corkin Gallery 144 Front St W Toronto ON Can. *Mailing Add:* 33 St Paul St Toronto ON M5A 3H2 Canada

REFF, THEODORE
HISTORIAN
b New York, NY, Aug 18, 30. *Study:* Columbia Col, BA, 52; Harvard Univ, MA, 53, PhD, 58. *Collections Arranged:* Cezanne Watercolors (ed, catalog), M Knoedler & Co, New York, 63; Degas in the Metropolitan, Metrop Mus, New York, 77; Cezanne: the Late Work, Mus Mod Art, New York, 77; Manet and Modern Paris, Nat Gallery, Washington, DC, 82-83. *Teaching:* Prof art hist & mod art, Columbia Univ, 57-; vis prof, Univ Mich, Princeton Univ, NY Univ; Slade prof, Johns Hopkins Univ, Cambridge Univ; plus others. *Awards:* Chevalier, Ordre des Palmes Academiques, 87. *Mem:* Col Art Asn Am (dir, 77-81); Int Found Art Res (dir, 80-); Swann Found Caricature (dir, 82-89); Psychoanalytic Perspectives Art (dir, 84-). *Res:* 19th and 20th century art; relations between art and literature. *Publ:* Ed, Unpublished Correspondence of Toulouse-Lautrec, Phaidon Press, 69; auth, The Notebooks of Edgar Degas, Clarendon Press, 76; Degas: the Artist's Mind, Harper & Row, 76; Manet: Olympia, Penguin, 76; ed, Modern Art in Paris, 1850-1900, Garland, 81; auth, Manet and Modern Paris, Univ Chicago Press, 83. *Mailing Add:* Dept of Art Hist Columbia Univ New York NY 10027

REGAT, JEAN-JACQUES ALBERT
SCULPTOR, MURALIST
b Paris, France, Sept 12, 45. *Study:* Univ Alaska, BA; Soc Beaux Arts, France. *Work:* Sheik Zayed Ben Sultan Al-Nahyan, Pres of United Arab Emirates, Abu Dabi; Fairbanks North Star Borough Pub Libr, Alaska; Soroptimist Int of Anchorage; RCA Alascom, Anchorage; Kobuk Valley Jade Co, Alyeska. *Comn:* The Man Who Became Caribou (bas relief wood), Noatak Artic Sch Dist, 81; Miners of the Yukon (tryptic bas relief wood), Yukon Off Supplies Co, 82; Delta Pastoral (bas relief wood), Delta Greely Sch Dist, 82; The Resolution (bronze & bas relief wood), Carr-Gottstein Ltd; St Joseph & St Francis, St Anthony Cath Church Anchorage, 83. *Exhib:* One-man show, Artique Ltd, Anchorage, 72-77; Heritage Northwest Gallery, Juneau, 73-74; House of Wood, Fairbanks, 74-80; Erdon Gallery, Houston, Tex; Rendezvous Gallery, Anchorage. *Bibliog:* Judy Shuler (auth), Jacques & Mary Regat, Alaska J autumn 77; Nancy Cain Schmitt (auth), Ancient legend of Sedna is captured in bronze, Anchorage Times, 5/20/79; Mary Sawyer-Albert (auth), Stories carved in wood and stone, Jacques and Mary Regat, Southwest Art, 8/79; plus others. *Media:* Stone, Wood. *Dealer:* House of Wood 529 Fourth Fairbanks AK 99701. *Mailing Add:* Jacques & Mary Regat Galleries 518 Pearl Dr Anchorage AK 99518

REGAT, MARY E
SCULPTOR, MURALIST
b Duluth, Minn, Nov 12, 43. *Study:* Univ Alaska. *Work:* Anchorage Fine Arts Mus, Alaska; Soroptimist Int of Anchorage; Kobuk Valley Jade Co, Alyeska, Alaska; Fairbanks North Star Borough Pub Libr; RCA-Alascom, Anchorage. *Comn:* Trail of 98 (bas relief wood), Pioneers Asn Alaska, 79; Creek Woman (bas relief wood & bronze), Kokanok, Peninsula Sch Dist, 80; Huskies (bronze), Kotzebue Artic Sch Dist, 82; Dance of the Oomialik (sculpture), Gottstein Inc, 82; High, Wild and Free (sculpture), Greyling, Iditarod Sch Dist, 83. *Exhib:* One-woman show, Artique Ltd, Anchorage, 72-77; House of Wood, Fairbanks, 74-80; Erdon Gallery, Houston, Tex; Boreal Traditions Gallery, Anchorage; plus others. *Awards:* Sculpture Award, Design I, 71; Purchase Award, Anchorage Fine Arts Mus, 71. *Bibliog:* Judy Schuler (auth), Jacques and Mary Regat, Alaska J, autumn, 77; Nancy Cain Schmitt (auth), Ancient legend of Sedna is captured in bronze, Anchorage Times, 5/20/79; Mary Sawyer-Albert (auth), Stories carved in wood and stone, Jacques and Mary Regat, Southwest Art, 8/79; plus others. *Mem:* Artist Guild; Anchorage Fine Arts Mus Asn. *Media:* Wood, Bronze. *Dealer:* Boreal Traditions 939 W 5th Ave Suite J Anchorage AK 99501; New Horizons 519 1st Ave Fairbanks AK 99701. *Mailing Add:* Jacques & Mary Regat Galleries 518 Pearl Dr Anchorage AK 99518

REGENSTEINER, ELSE (FRIEDSAM)
DESIGNER, WEAVER
b Munich, Ger, Apr 21, 06; US citizen. *Study:* Univ Munich; Inst Design, Chicago; Black Mountain Col, with Moholy-Nagy, Marli Ehrman & Anni & Josef Albers. *Work:* Cooper-Hewitt Mus, New York; Art Inst Chicago; Ill State Univ; Univ Houston. *Exhib:* Designer-Craftsmen USA, Smithsonian Inst, 53; Designer-Craftsmen Ill, Ill State Mus, Springfield, 66; Decorative Arts Nat, Wichita, Kans, 70; Textiles for Collectors, Art Inst Chicago, 71; Fabrications, Cranbrook Acad Art, 72; Am Crafts, Philadelphia Mus Art, 77; Midwest Constructed Fiber, 80. *Pos:* Ed bd, The Working Craftsman, Northbrook, Ill, 75-78. *Teaching:* Instr weaving, Hull House, Chicago, 41-45; instr weaving, Inst Design, Chicago, 42-46; prof weaving, Art Inst Chicago, 45-71 & prof emer, 71-; workshops & lect throughout US, Can & Greece, 71-; consult, Am Farm Sch, Thessaloniki, Greece, 72-78. *Awards:* five Citations of Merit, Am Inst Interior Design, 47, 48 & 51; Hon Mention, State Mus Art, Springfield, 66; Regensteiner Award, Midwest Weavers Asn, 80. *Bibliog:* Naomi Whiting Towner (auth), Interview: Else Regensteiner, Shuttle, Spindle & Dyepot, spring 79; Louise Bradley & Ann Walker Budd (auths), Profiles: Else Regensteiner - Handwoven, 90; Philis Alvic (auth), article profile, Else Regensteiner, Shuttle, Spindle & Dyepot, fall 91. *Mem:* Fel Am Craft Coun; Handweavers Guild Am (bd dir, 71-78). *Publ:* Auth articles in Handweaver & Craftsman, 65 & 69; articles, Shuttle, Spindle & Dyepot, 71-80; Weaving Sourcebook, Ideas and Techniques, Weaver's Study Course, 83, rev ed, 86, Schiffer Publ Ltd; Geometric Design in Weaving, 86 & The Art of Weaving, rev ed 86, Schiffer Publ Ltd; Die Kunst zu Weben (Ger ed), Munich, 87. *Mailing Add:* 1416 E 55th St Chicago IL 60615

REGER, LAWRENCE L
ADMINISTRATOR
b Lincoln Nebr, June 23, 39. *Study:* Univ Nebr; Vanderbilt Univ, JD, 64. *Pos:* Dir prog develop & coord, Nat Endowment Arts, DC, 71-78; dir, Am Asn Mus, DC, 78-86; pres, Nat Inst for the Conserv of Cult Property, 86. *Mailing Add:* 2400 Virginia Ave NW Washington DC 20037

REGINATO, PETER
SCULPTOR
b Dallas, Tex, Aug 19, 45. *Study:* San Francisco Art Inst, 63-66. *Work:* Metrop Mus Art, Chase Manhattan Bank, New York; Houston Mus of Fine Arts; Mint Mus Art, Charlotte, NC; Brown Univ, RI; Boston Mus Fine Arts, Mass; Corcoran Gallery Art, Washington, DC; Storm King ARt Ctr, Mountainville, NY; Univ Fla, Gainesville. *Comn:* High Plains Drifter (large sculpture), Allen Ctr, Houston, Tex; Outdoor Sculpture Exhib, Rutgers State Univ, Camden, NJ, 78; sculpture, Glick Orgn, Promenade Bldg, New York. *Exhib:* Whitney Mus of Am Art Biennial, 70; Highlights of the Season, Aldrich Mus Contemp Art, Ridgefield, Conn, 71; solo exhibs, 112 Greene St, 85, 87 & 89, 57th Street West Gallery, New York, 86 & Brunnier Gallery & Mus, Ames, Iowa, 88; Sculpture with Color, Gimpel & Weitzenhoffer Gallery, New York, 89; Significant Surface, Philadelphia Art Alliance, Pa, 90; USX Tower Steel Works, Pittsburgh, Pa, 90; 30 Years & Growing, Acad Arts, Eastland, Md, 90; Alberto Magnani, Jaffey-Baker Gallery, Boca Raton, Fla, 91; contemp sculpture, Va Mus Fine Arts, Richmond, 91; Peter Reginato/ Jane Manus: Two Visions of Abstract Construction, Mus Art, Ft Lauderdale, Fla, 91; Adelson Galleries, New York, 92. *Teaching:* Adj lectr sculpture, Hunter Col, 71-73. *Awards:* John Simon Guggenheim Mem Found Fel, 76; Purchase Award, Hirshhorn Mus, Washington, DC, 79; Clayworks Residency, Nat Endowment Arts, 84. *Bibliog:* Jean Lawlor Cohen (auth), Sculpture thrives in Washington law firms, Washington Lawyer, Vols 2 & 3, 1-2/88; Margo Guralnick (auth), Timely Obsessions, House & Gordon, 9/89; Carter Ratcliff (auth), Reginato's improvisations, Art in Am, No 12, 12/89; plus others. *Media:* Painted Welded Steel, Clay. *Mailing Add:* 60 Greene St New York NY 10012

REHBERGER, GUSTAV
PAINTER, DRAFTSMAN
b Riedlingsdorf, Austria, Oct 20, 10; US citizen. *Study:* Art Inst Chicago, scholar; Art Instr Schs, Minneapolis, scholar. *Work:* Lyman Allyn Mus, New London, Conn; St Johns Univ, NY; Sports Hall, Peking, China; numerous pvt collections in US, Can, Mex, Europe, Saudi Arabia & China. *Comn:* Two World War II murals, Union Sta, Chicago, 42; mural, St Paul's Evangelical Lutheran Church, Chicago, 43; portrait of Beethoven, Beethoven Soc, 79. *Exhib:* One-man shows, Soc Illusrs, New York, 57 & 65, Nat Arts Club: Expo '67, Montreal, 67, Wickersham Gallery, New York, 71 & Jacques Seligman Gallery, New York, 77; Oldfield Gallery, Pittsburgh, Pa, 83; Abelle Gallery, Princeton, NJ, 85; Snug Harbor Cult Ctr, 91; Pompeii Museum: Monica North Gallaries, Saratoga Springs, NY, 92; A Painting Performance Gala to Benefit the Mus, Carnegie Hall, 92. *Teaching:* Instr & lectr, Art Students League, 72- *Awards:* Awards, Art Directors Club of New York, 54 & 55; Award, Allied Artists of Am, 74; Awards, Pastel Soc of Am, 76, 79, 81, 82 & 84; elected honoree to Hall of Fame, 88; and others. *Bibliog:* Dale Denmark (auth), The art of rock, Newsweek, 2/22/71; Julie Charles (auth), The American who captured Odysseus: Gustav Rehberger, Atlantis, 4/72; David Eskes (auth), Beethoven powers sweep of inspired artist's brush, 1/11/84. *Media:* Oil, Gouche; Pen & Ink, Pencil. *Mailing Add:* Carnegie Hall Studio 1206 881 Seventh Ave New York NY 10019

REIBACK, EARL M
SCULPTOR, KINETIC ARTIST
b New York, NY, May 30, 48. *Study:* Lehigh Univ, BA & BS; Mass Inst Technol, MS. *Work:* Whitney Mus Am Art, New York; Philadelphia Mus Art; Milwaukee Art Ctr; New Orleans Mus Art; Wichita Art Mus, Kans. *Exhib:* Experiments in Light & Technology, Brooklyn Mus, NY, 68 & 69; Milwaukee Art Ctr, Wis, 69; Metrop Mus Art, New York, 69; Philadelphia Mus Art; Albright-Knox Art Gallery, Buffalo, NY; New Orleans Mus Art, La; Long Beach Mus Contemp Art, Calif; Aldrich Mus Contemp Art, Ridgefield, Conn; Mus d'Art Contemporain, Montreal, Que; Am Ctr, Beirut, Lebanon; US Cult Ctr, Tel Aviv, Israel; Fine Arts Gallery, Ankara, Turkey; and others. *Publ:* Auth, articles, House & Garden, 1/69 & Electronics Age, spring 70. *Mailing Add:* 20 E Ninth St New York NY 10003

REIBEL, BERTRAM
SCULPTOR, GRAPHIC ARTIST
b New York, NY, June 14, 01. *Study:* Art Inst Chicago; also with Alexander Archipenko. *Exhib:* Metrop Mus Art & Nat Acad Design, New York; Pa Acad Fine Arts, Philadelphia; Northwest Printmakers; Libr Cong, Washington, DC; plus many others, incl one-man shows at Univ d'El Salvador, San Salvador, Korean Design Ctr, Seoul, Merrick Art Gallery, New Brighton, Pa & La Casa Cultura, Pueblo, Mex. *Pos:* Dir packaging & design, Revlon Inc & Revlon Int, 47-62; Chmn, Young Designors Competition. *Mem:* Artists Equity Asn; Asn Int Arts Plastiques. *Media:* Wood, Bronze. *Mailing Add:* 1127 Hardscrabble Rd Chappaqua NY 10514

REICH, NATHANIEL E
PAINTER, COLLAGE ARTIST
b Brooklyn, NY. *Study:* Art Students League; Pratt Inst; Brooklyn Mus. *Work:* Huntington Hartford Collection, Gallery Mod Art, New York; Joe & Emily Lowe Mus, Univ Miami; Washington Co Mus Fine Arts, Hagerstown, Md; Evansville Mus Arts & Sci, Ind; New York Heart Asn; and others. *Exhib:* Eighth Serv Command Competition USA, 44; 4th Har Zion Temple Art Show, Philadelphia, 66; Prospect Park Centennial, 66; Mus Mod Art, Paris, 70; Boston Inst Fine Arts, 71; two retrospectives, NY Univ; Long Island Univ; 13 solo exhibitions; and others. *Awards:* St Gaudens Medal, 23; First Prize, Eighth Serv Command Competition, USA, 44. *Mem:* Artists Equity Asn. *Media:* Oil. *Mailing Add:* 1620 Ave I Brooklyn NY 11230

REICH, OLIVE B
PAINTER
b Brooklyn, NY, Mar 1, 35. *Study:* Mt Holyoke Col, South Hadley, Mass, BA, 56; Art Students League, 66-67; Craft Students League; Parsons Sch Design. *Work:* Mt Holyoke Col Art Mus; Lutheran Med Ctr, NY; Brooklyn Botanic Garden/Nature Conser, NY; Brooklyn Union Gas Co, NY. *Comn:* Series of drawings, comn by Union Chapel Grove, Shelter Island, NY, 76-86; Centennial Celebration (painting), comn by Fox River Paper Co, Appleton, Wis, 84. *Exhib:* Brooklyn Watercolor Soc Exhib, Metrop Mus Art, New York, 77; solo exhibs, Present Day Club, Princeton, NJ, 78 & Brooklyn Botanic Garden, NY, 86, Ward-Nasse Gallery, NY, 88; Brooklyn 80 & Award Winners, 82, Brooklyn Mus, NY; Energy Art, Foothills Art Ctr, Golden, Colo, 82; Visual Artists, Pa State Univ, State Col; Elaine Benson Gallery, Bridgehampton, NY 90 & 92; Monmouth Mus, Lincroft, NJ, 90; Adelphi Univ, NY, 90. *Pos:* Instr watercolor, YWCA, 74-77, own studio, 78-, Brooklyn, NY & Aquarelle Studio, Shelter Island, NY, 83-88. *Awards:* Outstanding Work, Salmagundi Club, 88, 90 & 91; Halpern Mem Award, Nat Asn Women Artists, 88; Catharine Lorillard Wolfe Art Club Award, 92; and others. *Bibliog:* William Pellicone (auth), Four Soloists at Keane-Mason, 83 & Palmer Paroner (auth), A Flower Grows in Brooklyn; Barbara Dunne (auth), Reich exhibts watercolor, Shelter Island Reporter, 84. *Mem:* Nat Asn Women Artists; Salmagundi Club; Artists Equity; Contemp Artist Guild (corresp secy, 80-); Catharine Lorillard Wolfe Art Club (exec bd, 85-88). *Media:* Watercolor. *Publ:* Illusr, God's Summer Cottage, Shelter Island Hist Soc, 80; Chronicle of Shelter Island churches, MIT Graphics, 83; Shelter Island Yacht Club-A History, Mad Printers, 86. *Dealer:* Nahas Gallery Brooklyn NY 11209; Whale's Folly Gallery Sheeter Island NY 11965. *Mailing Add:* 36-79th St Brooklyn NY 11209

REICH, SHELDON
HISTORIAN, LECTURER
b Brooklyn, NY, Sept 5, 31. *Study:* Univ of Miami, BA, 54; New York Univ, MA, 57; Univ of Iowa, PhD, 66. *Pos:* Prof of art hist, Univ of Ariz, Tucson, 60-68; dept head of art hist, Univ of Cincinnati, 68-72; prof of art hist, Univ Ariz, 72- *Awards:* Arch Am Art Res Grant, 63; Sr Res Fel, Nat Mus Art, Smithsonian Inst, 71-72. *Mem:* Col Art Assoc; Am Asn of Univ Prof; Mid-Am Col Art Asn. *Res:* Specialize in early 20th century American painting. *Publ:* Auth, John Marin: A Stylistic Analysis and a Catalogue Raisonne, Univ Ariz, 70; A H Maurer, Smithsonian, 73; Isabel Bishop, Univ Ariz, 74; Graphic Styles of the American Eight, Univ Utah, 76; Francisco Zuniga, Sculptor, Univ Ariz, 80. *Mailing Add:* Dept Art Univ Ariz Tucson AZ 85721

REICHEK, ELAINE
CONCEPTUAL ARTIST
b New York, NY, Apr 30, 43. *Study:* Brooklyn Col, BA, 63; Yale Univ Sch Art & Archit, BFA, 64. *Work:* Norton Gallery Art, West Palm Beach, Fla; Portland Art Mus, Ore; Arthur Anderson & Assoc; AT&T; New Sch Social Res. *Exhib:* Solo exhibs, Philadelphia Col Art & Design, Pa, 87, Revenge of the Cocoanuts: A Curiosity Room, 56 Bleecker, New York, 88, Desert Song, Barbara Braathen Gallery, New York, 88, Visitations, Carlo Lamagna Gallery, New York, 89, Fatal Passage, Everson Mus Art, Syracuse, NY, 89, The War Room, Carlo Lamagna Gallery, New York, 90, Braunstein-Guay Gallery, San Francisco, Calif, 90, Akron Art Mus, Ohio, 92, Irish Mus Mod Art, Dublin, Ireland, 93; Landscape/Mindscape, Carlo Lamagne Gallery, New York, 90; Words and Images with a Message, Women's Studio Workshop, Rosendale, NY, 90; 6th Int Triennale of Tapestry, Lodz, Poland, 88; American Art Today: Clothing as Metaphor, Art Mus, Fla Int Univ, Miami, 93; Empty Dress: Clothing as Metaphor, Independent Curs Inc, New York & traveling. *Teaching:* Guest lectr, Bryn Mawr, Pa, 89, Kent State Univ, Ohio, 89, Hobart-William Smith Col, Geneva, NY, 89, Everson Mus, Syracuse, NY, 90, Syracuse Univ, NY, 90, Art of the Middle Ages: Recent Work by Mid-Career Feminists, Women's Caucus Art, New York, 90, Ethnicity/Ethnography: The Uses and Misuses of Traditional Aesthetics by Contemporary Artists, Col Art Asn, New York, 90. *Awards:* Creative Artists Pub Serv Grant, NY State Coun Arts, 83; New York Found Grant, 88. *Bibliog:* Mary Haus (auth), ArtNews, (review), 9/90; Susan Hapgood (auth), Art in America (review), 6/90, 176-177; Nancy Princenthal, Elaine Reichek's 'Native Intelligence', Print Collector's Newsletter, 7-8/92, 94-95. *Mem:* Women's Caucus Art. *Publ:* Auth, Liberals at War (article, book review), Artforum, 1/90, 23-24. *Dealer:* Michael Klein Inc 594 Broadway New York NY 10012; AIR Gallery 63 Crosby St New York NY 10013. *Mailing Add:* 140 Riverside Dr New York NY 10024

REICHEK, JESSE
PAINTER, EDUCATOR
b Brooklyn, NY, Aug 16, 16. *Study:* Inst Design, Chicago, 41-42; Acad Julian, Paris, 47-51. *Work:* Amon Carter Mus Western Art, Ft Worth, Tex; Art Inst Chicago; Bibliot Nat, Paris; Los Angeles Co Mus Art, Los Angeles; Mus Mod Art, New York; and others. *Exhib:* Mus Mod Art, 62, 65 & 69; one-man shows, Am Cult Ctr, Florence, Italy, 64 & Univ NMex Mus, 66; retrospective, Univ Southern Calif Art Mus, 67; San Francisco Mus Art, 69; and others. *Teaching:* Assoc prof design, Univ Calif, Berkeley, 58-60, prof, 60-; artist in residence, Tamarind Lithography Workshop, Los Angeles, 66; res prof, Creative Arts Inst, Univ Calif, 66-67. *Awards:* Co-partic, Graham Found Grant, 62; Res Travel Grant, Creative Arts Inst, Univ Calif, summer 63; Tamarind Fel, 66. *Publ:* Auth, Jesse Reichek-Dessins, Ed Cahiers Art, Paris, 60; auth, La Montee de la Nuit, 61 & Fontis, 61, P A Benoit, Alex; auth, Etcetera, New Directions, 65; auth, The Architect & the City, Mass Inst Technol, 66; plus many others. *Dealer:* Betty Parsons Gallery 24 W 57th St New York NY 10019. *Mailing Add:* 5925 Red Hill Rd Petaluma CA 94952

REICHEL, MYRA
TAPESTRY ARTIST, WEAVER
b Philadelphia, Pa, June 19, 51. *Study:* Philadelphia Col Art, 69-71, apprenticed with Nora Johnson, 81-82, study workshops with Mary Lane, 88-89. *Work:* Hercules Corp, Wilmington, Del; Fox Co, Chesterbrook, Pa; Educ Testing Serv, Princeton, NJ; Wolf Block Schorr Solis, Cohen, Philadelphia, Pa; Dupont Corp, Wilmington, Del. *Comn:* Colorado Mountains (tapestry), comn by Dr Richard Small, Reading, Pa, 80; Spring Dreams (tapestry), comn by George & Toni Wiswessler, Reading, Pa, 81; Miroian Dream (tapestry), comn by Helene & Walter Sencer, New York, 85; Night tales (tapestry), comn by Arthur Gershkoff, Merion, Pa, 88; Star Flower (tapestry), comn by Jean Bradley, Philadelphia, Pa, 88; Daybreak, Lee Nedlhem, 89. *Exhib:* Craftsmen 78, Philadelphia Civic Ctr, Pa, 78; one-person show, Hudson River Mus, Yonkers, NY, 85, Del Ctr Contemp Arts, Wilmington, 85, Henry Chauncy Conf Ctr Ets, Princeton, NJ, 87; Biannial Art/Craft Exhib, Del Art Mus, Wilmington, 89; Philadelphia Build of Handweavers, Swedish Mus, Pa, 92. *Teaching:* Philadelphia Guild of Handweavers, 84-92; Community Arts Ctr, Wallingford, Pa, 91. *Awards:* Judges Choice Award, Handweavers for Univ Am; First Prize Hangings, Philadelphia Guild Handweavers & Second Prize Hangings; Jeffrey Bruce Mem Award, 89; Cert Excellance, Soho Art Competition #8, 89; Katherine Wellman Memorial Award, 92. *Mem:* Am Tapestry Alliance; Philadelphia Guild of Handweavers; Am Crafts Coun. *Publ:* Contribr, Handmade Charter Issue, FiberArts, 81. *Dealer:* Studio in Swarthmore. *Mailing Add:* 121 E Sixth St Media PA 19063

REICHERT, DONALD KARL
PAINTER, EDUCATOR
b Libau, Man, Jan 11, 32. *Study:* Univ Man Sch Art, with Robert A Nelson & George Swinton, BFA, 56; Inst Allende, Mex, with James Pinto; Emma Lake Artist's Workshops, with Jules Olitzki, Stepan Wolpe, Lawrence Alloway, John Cage & Frank Stella. *Work:* Nat Gallery Can; Art Gallery Ont; Winnipeg Art Gallery; Mt Allison Univ; Montreal Mus Fine Arts. *Exhib:* Winnipeg Show Nat Biennial; Montreal Spring Show Nat; Nat Gallery Biennial; Visua '67, Nat Exhib; Midwest Painters. *Teaching:* Artist in residence, Univ NB, 61-62; prof painting, Univ Man Sch Art, 64-; retired. *Awards:* Can Coun Bursary, 62 & Sr Nat Awards, 67 & 74. *Mem:* Royal Can Acad Arts. *Media:* Acrylic, Oil. *Mailing Add:* 228 Glenwood Crecent Winnipeg MB R2L 1J9 Canada

REICHERT, MARILYN F
MUSEUM DIRECTOR
b Cincinnati, Ohio. *Study:* Bryn Mawr Col, BA, 58; Xavier Univ, MEd, 78. *Mem:* Am Asn Mus; Asn Col & Univ Mus; Ohio Mus Asn. *Mailing Add:* Hebrew Union College-Jewish Institute of Religion, Skirball Museum, Cincinnati Branch 3101 Clifton Ave Cincinnati OH 45220

REICHMAN, FRED
PAINTER
b Bellingham, Wash, Jan 28, 25. *Study:* Univ Calif, Berkeley, BA(cum laude) & MA; San Francisco Art Inst. *Work:* San Francisco Mus Mod Art; Oakland Mus Art, Calif; Nat Mus Am Art, Washington, DC; Edwin A Ulrich Mus Art, Wichita, Kans; Milwaukee Art Mus, Wis; and others. *Comn:* Murals, Stanford Univ Med Sch, Palo Alto, Calif, 61 & San Francisco Art Festival, Civic Ctr, 68. *Exhib:* One-man shows, San Francisco Mus Mod Art, 56 & 69 & Santa Barbara Mus Art, 74; 50 Calif Artists, Whitney Mus Am Art, New York, 62; Gallery Paule Anglim San Francisco, 78 & 80; Chikyudo Gallery, Tokyo, 80; Miyagi Mus Art, Sendai, Japan, 82; Forum Gallery, New York, 84; Charles Campbell Gallery, San Francisco, 84 & 86; David Barnett Gallery, Milwaukee, 85 & 89; Smith Andersen Gallery, Palo Alto, 87; Mekler Gallery, Los Angeles, Calif, 88; Iannetti Lanzone Gallery, San Francisco, Calif, 89; Galerie B Haasner, Wiesbaden, Ger, 90 & 92; Mary Porteer, Sesnon Art Gallery, Univ Calif, Santa Cruz, 91; Ruth Siegel Gallery, New York; Harcourts Mod & Contemp Art, 92. *Teaching:* Instr art, Univ Calif Exten, San Francisco, 66- *Awards:* Purchase Award, San Francisco Art Festival, 64; Award of Merit, Art Festival City & Co San Francisco, 68. *Bibliog:* Judy Stone (auth), interview, San Francisco Chronicle, 10/15/63; Mimi Jacobs (auth), interview, Pac Sun, 1/16/75; Henry Hopkins (auth), 50 West Coast Artists, 81; Ichiro Haryu (auth), The Myth of Everyday Living, Poetry & Thought, Tokyo, 82; Thomas Albright (auth), Art in San Francisco Bay Area 1945-80, 85. *Media:* Acrylic, Alkyd. *Dealer:* Harcourts Modern and Contemporary Art San Francisco; David Barnett Gallery Milwaukee. *Mailing Add:* 1235 Stanyan St San Francisco CA 94117

REICHMAN, LEAH CAROL
PAINTER
b Kansas City, Mo, Aug 9, 51. *Study:* Oxbow Summer Sch Painting Saugatuck, Mich, 70; Univ Wis, Madison, BS, 73; Whitney Mus Independent Study Prog, New York, NY, 73, 74; Hunter Col, New York, MA, 80. *Work:* Mus Mod Art, New York; Mus Bilboa, Spain; Archives Am Art, New York; Univ Wis, Madison; De Warande, Belgium; Best Products Co Inc, Richmond, Va. *Exhib:* A Piece of Cake, 75 & The Object and the Viewer, 78, 3 Mercer St Store, New York; Art Now 2-3, Woman Art Gallery, New York, 77; Pie in the Sky, Soho Art Fair, New York, 78; $100 Gallery, New York, 78; The Emerging Collector, New York, 91; and others. *Mem:* Nat Asn Female Execs. *Media:* Oil, Watercolor. *Publ:* Auth, Robert Indiana and the Psychological Aspects of his Art, Hunter, 80. *Mailing Add:* 249 Sixth Ave Parlor Brooklyn NY 11215-2104

REID, CHARLES
WRITER, PAINTER
b Cambridge, NY, Aug 12, 37. *Study:* S Kent Sch; Univ of Vt; Art Students League, study with Frank Reiley. *Work:* Yellowstone Art Ctr, Billings, Mont; Brigham Young Univ, Salt Lake City, Utah; Smith Col Mus, South Hampton, Mass. *Comn:* US Postage Stamp to Commemorate Family Planning, US Postal Dept. *Exhib:* Nat Acad of Design, Am Watercolor Soc & Am Inst of Arts & Letters, New York; Far Gallery, New York; Munson Gallery, Mass & NMex. *Awards:* Salmagundi Award, Allied Artists, 75; Silver Medal, Soc Illustrs, 83; Adolph & Clara O'Brig Prize, Nat Acad, 87 & 92. *Mem:* Academician Nat Acad of Design. *Media:* Watercolor; Oil. *Publ:* Auth & illusr, Figure Painting in Watercolor, 72, Portrait Painting in Watercolor, 73, Flower Painting in Oil, 76 & Flower Painting in Watercolor, 79, Watson-Guptil; Painting What You Want To See, 83; Pulling Your Paintings Together, 85; Painting by Design, 88. *Dealer:* Munson Gallery Chatham MA. *Mailing Add:* c/o Munson Gallery 800 Main St Chatham MA 02633

REID, LESLIE
PAINTER, PRINTMAKER
b Ottawa, Ont, Feb 8, 47. *Study:* Queen's Univ, Kingston, Ont, BA(art hist), 67; Byam Shaw Sch Art, London, Eng, LCAD, 70; Chelsea Sch Art, London, Eng, 71; Slade Sch Art, London, Eng, 77. *Work:* Nat Gallery Can, Ottawa; Can Coun Art Bank, Ottawa; Agnes Etherington Art Ctr; Montreal Mus Fine Arts; Musee d'Art Contemporain, Montreal; and others. *Exhib:* Nat Gallery Can, Ottawa, 75, 78 & 84; one-man shows, Mira Godard Gallery, Toronto, 78, 81 & 84, Can Cult Ctr, Paris, 80, Can House Gallery, London, 80 & Galerie Jolliet, Montreal, 82; Arts Ctr, Ottawa, 90; Univ Calif, Santa Cruz & Davis, 91; Meridian Gallery, San Francisco, 91; Augusta Col, Ga, 92; and others. *Teaching:* Assoc prof painting & printmaking, Univ Ottawa, Ont, 72-, chmn art dept, 80-81, 85-86 & 87-88. *Awards:* Ed Award, First Can Biennial Prints & Drawings, Ont Arts Coun, 78; Ont Arts Coun Grant, 83, 84 & 89; Arts Abroad Grant, 91; and others. *Bibliog:* Robert Swain (auth), Leslie Reid, Agnes Etherington Art Centre, Kingston, 84; Anna Babinska (auth), Leslie Reid, Arts Ct, Ottawa, 90; Rolando Castellon (auth), Leslie Reid, Meridian Gallery, San Francisco, 91; and others. *Mem:* Royal Can Acad; Can Artist Representation (Ottawa exec, 77); Univ Art Asn Can. *Media:* Oil; Lithography, Etching. *Dealer:* Galerie L'Autre Equivoque 333 Cumberland St Ottawa K1N 7J3 Canada; Gallery One 121 Scollard St Toronto M5R 1G4 Canada. *Mailing Add:* Dept Visual Arts Univ Ottawa Ottawa ON K1N 6N5 Canada

REID, ROBERT DENNIS
PAINTER, INSTRUCTOR
b Atlanta, Ga, 1924. *Study:* Clark Col, 41-43; Art Inst Chicago, 43-46; Parson Sch Design, New York, 48-50. *Work:* Myers Col, Birmingham, Ala; Studio Mus Harlem; Cornell Univ, Ithaca, NY; Montclair Art Mus, NJ; Mus et Galerie des Beaux-Arts, Bordeaux, France; Md Savings & Loan, Baltimore, Md; Baltimore Gas & Electric Co; Price Waterhouse Co, Boston, Mass; US State Dept, Cairo, Egypt; Morgan Guaranty Trust Co, NY. *Exhib:* US Info Serv Tour, Paris, Brest, Vannes & Tours, 71; Black Artists: Two Generations, 71 & Recent Acquisitions, 71, Newark Mus; Black Artists Am, Whitney Mus Am Art, 71; Artists Postcards, Drawing Ctr, New York & Smithsonian Inst-sponsored tour, 78-79; one-man shows, Alonzo Gallery, 72, Leslie Rankow Gallery, New York, 74-75, Lenore Gray Gallery, Providence, RI, 77 & George Ciscle Gallery, Baltimore, Md, 87 & 88; Liz Harris Gallery, Boston, Mass, 87; and many others. *Teaching:* Instr painting, State Univ NY Col Purchase, summer 75; vis instr, Parsons Sch Design, New York, 77 & Drew Univ, Madison, NJ, 78; retired. *Awards:* Childe Hassam Purchase Award, Am Acad Arts & Lett, 69; Fel, MacDowell Colony, Peterborough, NH. *Media:* Oil, Watercolor. *Mailing Add:* 309 Mott St New York NY 10012

REIF, (F) DAVID
SCULPTOR, EDUCATOR
b Cincinnati, Dec 14, 41. *Study:* Univ Cincinnati, 60-63; Sch Art Inst Chicago, BFA, 68; Yale Univ, with J Tworkov, J Rosati, R Serra, R Morris & A Held, B Rose, et al, MFA, 70. *Work:* Weatherspoon Art Gallery, Univ NC, Greensboro; Univ Wyo Art Mus, Laramie; Asheville Art Mus, NC; Wichita Art Mus, Kans; Renwick Gallery, Smithsonian Inst, Washington, DC. *Exhib:* Joslyn Art Mus, Omaha, Nebr, 78 & 79; Springville Art Mus, Utah, 79; one-man shows, Slusser Gallery, Univ Mich, Ann Arbor, 80 & Dorsky Gallery, New York, 80; Miss Mus Art Traveling Show, 81-; Flatworks, Washington Project Arts, Washington, DC, 83-84; Univ Northern Ariz Art Mus; La Sculpture Tour, (La Coun Arts); Wyo Biennials, (touring West, US). *Pos:* Juror, Uccross Artists Residency Prog, Wyo; vis artist, Univ Mich, Univ Wis, Madison, Univ Houston, Northern Ariz, Univ Colo State Univ & Centenary Col. *Teaching:* Assoc prof, Univ Wyo, Laramie, 70-80, prof, 81-; assoc prof, Univ Mich, Ann Arbor, 80-81. *Awards:* Best Sculpture Award, Joslyn Art Mus, Omaha, 78; Emerging Artist Grant, Nat Endowment Arts, 79-80; Creative Res Grants, Univ Wyo, 73, 83, 86 & 87. *Bibliog:* George P Tomko (auth), Regionalism, Seven Views, Joslyn Art Mus, 7-8/79; Martha Keller (auth), Art, a catalyst to thought and dialog, Ann Arbor News, Mich, 8/16/81; Joanna Frueh (auth), The Voice of the Bleeding Heart (catalog0, La Sculpture Tour, Centenary Col. *Mem:* Col Art Asn; Int Sculpture Ctr, Washington, DC. *Media:* Mixed Media. *Publ:* Auth, Contemporary art on the Wyoming frontier: 1978, Wyo News Mag, 8/78. *Dealer:* Peter Stremmel Galleries 1400 S Virginia St Reno NV. *Mailing Add:* 3340 Aspen Lane Laramie WY 82070

REILAND, LOWELL KEITH
SCULPTOR
b Wahpeton, NDak, May 11, 48. *Study:* NDak State Univ, Fargo, 66-68; Moorhead State Univ, with Lyle Laske, BA, BS, 71; Cornell Univ, (fel, 72-74) with Jack Squire & Jason Seley, dipl, 74. *Work:* Claire M Eagle Mus, Murray, Ky; Palace of the Sultan Brunei; Aldrich Mus Contemp Art, Ridgefield, Conn. *Comn:* Sculptures, Moorhead State Univ, 78 & City Fargo, NDak, 78; Sumitono Corp, New York, 88; Richard Brown Baker, New York, 89; Melvin Stark, New York, 88 & 90. *Exhib:* Soho Ctr for Visual Artists, New York, 78 & 87; DiLaurenti Gallery, New York, 87; Todd Capp Gallery, New York, 87 & 88; Aldrich Mus Contemp Art, Ridgefield, Conn, 88; one-person exhib, Plains Art Mus, Moorhead, Minn, 88, Bayly Mus, Univ Va, Charlottesville; traveling New York Acad Art & Edwin A Ulrich Mus, Wichita, 90. *Teaching:* lectr C W Post Univ, Greenvale, NY, 76; lectr Moorehead State Univ, 75-78, artist-in-residence, 78; lectr, Conn Psychiatric Asn Ann Meeting, New Haven, 76; new sch, mus, galleries & studios, New York, 86 & 88; NDak State Univ, Fargo, 87 & 88. *Awards:* Individual Artist's Grant, Comn on the Arts, Hartford, Conn, 75; Grant, Artist's Space, New York, 85; Am Acad & Inst Arts & Letters Award, New York, 86; Pollock/Krasner Found Grant, NY, 87-88; Change Inc, Grant, NY, 89. *Bibliog:* Barbara Flannagan (auth), column item, Minneapolis Star Tribune, 7/15/88; Kathy Freise (auth), Art From The Soil, NDak Horizons, Vol 18, No 4, fall 88; Roger Sherman (cur), Lowell Reiland, Copper & Asphalt Series, 77-87, Plains Art Mus, Moorehead, Minn, 11/88, 1/22/89 (catalog). *Media:* Copper, Asphalt. *Dealer:* Knoedler & Co 19 E 70th St New York NY 10021. *Mailing Add:* 83 Grand St New York NY 10013

REILLY, BERNARD FRANCIS
HISTORIAN, CURATOR
b Philadelphia, Pa, June 7, 50. *Study:* Villanova Univ, BA, 72; Bryn Mawr Col, with Arthur Marks, MA(hist art), 74. *Exhib:* Caricature Since 1870, Libr

Cong, Washington, DC, 79. *Collections Arranged:* American Political Prints (cataloged), Libr Cong, 78; Applied Graphic Art, Libr Cong; Photographs from 1845 to 1876 (cataloged), Libr Co Philadelphia. *Pos:* Cur prints & drawing, Libr Co Philadelphia, 74-77; cur popular & applied graphic art, Prints & Photographs Div, Libr Cong, 78-87; head cur, Prints & Photog Div, Libr Congress. *Teaching:* Am political art, Humanities Prog, Georgetown Univ, 81. *Mem:* Print Coun Am; Am Print Conf; Asn Historians of Am Art. *Res:* History of 19th century painting, graphic art and photography, particularly landscape; history of political art from Renaissance to current times with emphasis on theory of expression. *Publ:* Auth, Drawings of Nature and Circumstance, Caricature since 1870, contribr, Posada's Mexico, Libr Cong, 79; auth, American Political Prints in the Library of Congress, GK Hall, 89. *Mailing Add:* Prints & Photographs Div Libr of Cong Washington DC 20540

REILLY, JACK
PAINTER, VIDEO ARTIST
b Pittsburgh, Pa, Nov 4, 50. *Study:* Fla State Univ, BFA, 76, MFA, 77. *Work:* Oakland Mus Art, Calif; Matthews Ctr Mus, Ariz State Univ, Tempe; Arco Ctr Visual Arts, Am Airlines, Los Angeles, Calif; Fresno Metrop Mus, Calif. *Comn:* Pub Art Comn, Co San Diego; Painting Am Airlines. *Exhib:* Reality of Illusion, Denver Art Mus, Colo, Oakland Mus Art, Calif & Toledo Art Mus, Ohio; Am Painters in Paris, Ctr Int, Paris, France, 75; New Floridians, Jacksonville Art Mus, 77; Eyes and Ears, Calif Mus Sci, Los Angeles, 78; one-man show, Matthews Ctr Mus, Ariz State Univ, Tempe, 80; Laguna Beach Mus Art, Calif; Downtown LA, Palm Springs Mus, Calif. *Teaching:* Adj instr painting, Fla State Univ, 78; vis prof painting, Ariz Western Col, Yuma, 80-81; assoc prof, Calif State Univ, Northridge, 87-; instr, Otis-Parsons Art Inst, Los Angeles, 85-86. *Awards:* Painting Award, Marietta Nat, Marietta Col, Ohio, 78; Best of Show, Belleair, Fla Nat, 78; Exhib Travel Grant, Nat Endowment Arts & Ariz Commission Arts, 81. *Bibliog:* Linda Jacobson (auth), article, 12/81, Arts Mag; Edward Lucie-Smith (auth), article, Am Art Now, 85; Morrow Marva (auth), Inside the Los Angeles, Artist, 88; Shauna Snow (author), Article, The Fugue A Public Art Commission, Los Angeles Times, 10/90. *Mem:* Col Art Asn Am; Los Angeles Contemp Exhibs. *Media:* Acrylic, Oil. *Publ:* Auth, Shelia Ruth, A Discourse on Flowers Rev, 1/85 & Ed Paschike, Exhib Rev, Artweek, 12/90. *Dealer:* Nemiruff/Deutch Gallery 2444 Wilshire Blvd Santa Monica CA 90403. *Mailing Add:* Calif State Univ Northridge 18111 Nordhoff St Northridge CA 91330

REILLY, NANCY
PAINTER
b Bryn Mawr, Pa, Mar 29, 27. *Study:* Portraiture with Samuel E Brown, Westport, Conn & Mimi Jennewein, New York. *Exhib:* Allied Artists Am, Nat Acad Design, New York; Allied Artists Am, Am Acad Arts & Lett, New York; Wadsworth Atheneum, Conn Acad Fine Arts, Hartford, 81; Am Artists Prof League, Salmagundi Club, New York, 85; Salmagundi Club, New York, 89; Nat Arts Club, New York, 92. *Awards:* Jane Peterson Award, Allied Artists Am; Silver Medal, Nat Arts Club; Charles Noel Flagg Award, Conn Acad Fine Arts. *Mem:* Allied Artists Am Inc (bd dirs, 91-92); Nat Arts Club; Pastel Soc Am; Acad Artists Asn New England; Hudson Valley Art Asn. *Media:* Oil. *Mailing Add:* Nine Marilane Rd Westport CT 06880

REILLY, RICHARD
DIRECTOR, HISTORIAN
b New York, NY, Mar 13, 26. *Pos:* Dir, James S Copley Libr & Art Collection, La Jolla; fine arts adv, James S Copley Found. *Mem:* Manuscript Soc; Soc Am Archivists. *Res:* French artist-illustrator Robert Kastor project, circa 1900. *Publ:* Auth, A Promise Kept, 83; reviewer, Copley Newspapers. *Mailing Add:* PO Box 1530 La Jolla CA 92037

REIMANN, ARLINE
PRINTMAKER, PAINTER
b St Louis, Mo, Nov 25, 37. *Study:* Rutgers Univ, BA, 74; Montclair State Col, NJ, MA, 80. *Work:* Newark Pub Libr Fine Print Collection, NJ; Montclair State Col, Upper Montclair, NJ. *Exhib:* Hunterdon Nat Print Exhib, Hunterdon Art Ctr, Clinton, NJ, 82; Celebration of Women's Week, Galeria San Jeronimo, San Juan, PR, 87; Audubon Artists Ann Exhib, Nat Arts Club, New York, 88; Celebration 89, Interchurch Ctr, New York; Nat Asn Women Artists Traveling Printmaking Exhib, Butler Inst Am Art, Youngstown, Ohio, 89. *Awards:* Best in Show, Lincoln Ctr, 81. *Mem:* Nat Asn Women Artists (chmn travel printmaking exhib, 84-86 & 87-89 & printmaking jury 87-89); Audubon Artists (recording secy, 91-93); Nat Soc Painters Casein & Acrylic. *Media:* Intaglio-Etching. *Mailing Add:* Eight Rande Dr Wayne NJ 07470

REIMANN, WILLIAM P
SCULPTOR, EDUCATOR
b Minneapolis, Minn, Nov 29, 35. *Study:* Yale Univ, BA, 57, BFA, 59, MFA, 61; with Josef Albers, Rico Lebrun, Robert M Engman, James Rosati, Gilbert Franklin, Seymour Lipton, Gabor Peterdi, Neil Welliver & Bernard Chaet. *Work:* Mus Mod Art, Whitney Mus Am Art & Rockefeller Univ, New York; Boston Mus Fine Arts; Nat Gallery Art, Washington, DC. *Comn:* Relief-mural, First Church of Christ, Boston, Mass, 81; suspended sculpture, Shell Oil Corp, Houston, Tex, 81 & Southwestern Bell Telephone Co, 86; Designated Artist, Radnor Twp, Pa, Blue Route Enhancement Proj, 89-90; Sandblasted Relief, Boston Red Sox Baseball Club, Fenway Park, Mass, 90. *Exhib:* Structured Sculpture, Galerie Chalette, New York, 61-68; Sculpture Ann, 64-65 & Young Americans, 65, Whitney Mus Am Art; Int Exhib Contemp Painting & Sculpture, Carnegie Inst, Pittsburgh, 67-68. *Teaching:* Asst prof art, Old Dom Col, 61-64; lectr visual & environ studies, Harvard Univ, 64-, Carpenter Ctr Visual Arts, spring 71, sr preceptor visual & environ studies, 75-, head tutor dept visualstudies, 86- *Media:* Plexiglas, Stone. *Dealer:* Galerie Chalette 9 E 88th St New York NY 10028; Estelle Dodge Associates 301 East 47th St New York NY 10017. *Mailing Add:* One Gerry's Landing Cambridge MA 02138

REINER, GLADYS & JULES
COLLECTORS, PATRONS
Mr Reiner, b New York, NY, Mar 3, 18. *Study:* Mr Reiner, St Johns Univ, LLB; Mrs Reiner, NY Univ, BA. *Mem:* Friends Whitney Mus Am Art; assoc Guggenheim Mus; Mus Mod Art; Metrop Mus Art; Friends Hofstra Univ Mus. *Collection:* Late nineteenth century art; twentieth century art. *Mailing Add:* 295 Madison Ave New York NY 10017

REINERTSON, LISA
SCULPTOR
b Washington, DC, May 15, 55. *Study:* Univ Calif, Davis, BA, 82, MFA, 84; Skowhegan Sch Painting & Sculpture, Scholar, 83. *Work:* Martin Luther King (bronze bust), Calif State Univ, Chico; ceramic, Davis Art Ctr, Calif. *Comn:* Martin Luther King Jr (terra cotta portrait), King Law Sch, Univ Calif, Davis, 87; portrait, George Washington HS, San Francisco, Calif, 89; Martin Luther King Jr (full size bronze), City of Kalamazoo, Mich, 89. *Exhib:* Fifty-ninth Ann Crocker-Kingsley Exhib, Crocker Art Mus, Sacramento, Calif, 84; City of Savona, Italy; Introductions, Dorothy Weiss Gallery, San Francisco, 89; Reynolds Gallery, Univ Pac, Stockton, Calif, 90; Figures in Ceramics, La State Univ, Baton Rouge, 90. *Teaching:* Vis artist & instr ceramics, La State Univ, Baton Rouge, 84; lectr ceramics & drawing, Calif State Univ-Stanislaus, 86-87; asst prof ceramics, Calif State Univ, Chico, 87- *Awards:* Grand Central Gallery Educational Asn Award, New York, 85; Research Award, Calif State Univ, Chico, 89. *Bibliog:* Saunthy Singh (auth), Lively ceramic sculpture, Artweek, 10/86; Craig Thomas (auth), Kalamazoo Gazette, 89; Elaine Levin (auth), Contemporary Ceramics: The Artists of TB9 (exhib catalog), 89. *Mem:* Col Art Asn. *Media:* Clay. *Dealer:* Natsoulas/Novelozo Gallery Davis CA 95616. *Mailing Add:* 177 E Fourth Ave Chico CA 95926

REINHART, MARGARET EMILY
PAINTER
b De Pere, Wis, May 19, 08. *Study:* Fontbonne Col, AB; Univ of Mo, MA; studied with Jean Charlot, Walter Quirt, Boris Margo, Ben Cunningham & Gaell Lindstrom. *Work:* Green Bay Wis Pub Sch Collection; Avila Col Collection; K C Plaza Pub Libr; Cardinal Ritter Inst, St Louis. *Comn:* Calligraphic design for Pope Pius XII, comn by Bishop Edwin O'Hara, 49; calligraphic design for Bishop Marling, comn by Kansas City Diocesan Confraternity, 50; fresco mural, O'Shaughnessy Hall, work with Jean Charlot, comn by Notre Dame, 55; Stations of the Cross in metal, comn by S Dallavis, Foyle Chapel, Kansas City, 64. *Exhib:* One-woman shows, Neville Art Mus, Green Bay, 47 & Blue Springs City Hall, Mo, 75; Jr League Voters, Kansas City, Mo, 68 & 69; Am Assoc Univ Women, Kansas City, 74; Avila Col, 80, 84 & 87. *Collections Arranged:* Women Religious of the Congregation of St Joseph at Avila Col, 70; Faculty of Cols, Kansas City Regional Coun for Higher Educ, 75. *Pos:* Art supervisor, St Louis & St Joseph parochial schs, 38-39. *Teaching:* Instr painting & design, St Teresa Acad, Kansas City, 45-50; asst prof painting, art hist & humanities, Avila Col, 50-65, chmn dept fine arts, 63-64, prof painting & art educ, 65-67, coordr art, 69-76, artist in residence, 76-; art inst, Vita Int Col Tour, Europe, 68-69 & 77; Orient, 85. *Awards:* Medal of Honor, Pres Dallavis, Avila Col, 63; Grant for Study in New York, Kansas City Regional Coun for Higher Educ, 70; Service Award, Dean Richard Scott, Avila Col, 75, 87. *Mem:* Nat Art Educ Assoc; Fed Religious Artists. *Media:* Oil, Watercolor. *Mailing Add:* Art Dept Avila Col 11901 Wornall Rd Kansas City MO 64145

REININGHAUS, RUTH (RUTH REININGHAUS SMITH)
PAINTER
b New York, NY, Oct 4, 22. *Study:* Nat Acad Design, with Morton Roberts, 62; Frank Reilly Sch Art, with Frank Reilly, 63; Art Student's League, with Robert Philip & Robert Beverly Hale, 68; New York Univ; studied with Bob Maione & Rudy Colao, 57-62. *Exhib:* Allied Artists Am Ann, Nat Acad Design, New York, 72 & 87; Salmagundi Club Ann, New York, 74-; Catherine Lorillard Wolfe Art Club Ann, New York, 78-; Pastel Soc of Am, 88-; Knickerbocker Artists, 85-; solo exhib, Petrucci Gallery, 88; Ashland Area Gallery, Ky, 89; Heidi Neuhoff Gallery Inc, New York, 90; and others. *Pos:* Freelance tech illusr, 60's. *Teaching:* Instr oil painting, Bankers Trust, New York, 71- & Kittredge Club for Women, 72-77. *Awards:* Best of Show, Anna Hyatt Huntington Award, Catharine Lorillard Wolfe Art Club Ann, 88; J Giffuni Purchase Award, Pastel Soc Am Ann, 88; Medal Honor, Salmagundi Club, 89; and others. *Bibliog:* Lucien Mandose (auth), 58th Ann Allied Artists Am Exhib, La Rev Mod, Paris, 72; Profile, Art Times, 8/89; Jennifer McGhee Siler (alumnae ed), New York artist pursues international following, Adelphean, summer 91. *Mem:* Salmagundi Club (dir at large, 74-77, chmn admiss, 81-83, pres, 83-87 & cur, 89-); fel Am Artist's Professional League; Catherine Lorillard Wolfe Club (bd dirs, 87-); Hudson Valley Art Asn; Pastel Asn Am; and others. *Media:* Oils, Pastels. *Dealer:* Petrucci Gallery 25 Garden Circle Rte 9W Saugerties NY 12477. *Mailing Add:* 222 E 93rd St Apt 26A New York NY 10128

REIRING, JANELLE
DIRECTOR
b Los Angeles, Calif, Jan 3, 46. *Study:* Berkeley Col, Calif, BA, 67. *Pos:* Dir, Metro Pictures, New York, currently. *Mailing Add:* Metro Pictures 150 Greene St New York NY 10012

REIS, MARIO
PAINTER
b Weingarten, Ger, 1953. *Study:* Dusseldorf Art Acad, 73-78; study with Prof Gunther Vecker, 78-79. *Work:* Ministerium fur Wissenschaft und Kunst des Landes; Baden-Wurttemberg; Stadische Galerie Ludenscheid; Mus der Stadt Gelsenkirchen; Ulmer Mus. *Exhib:* One-man shows, Unge Kunstneres Samfund, Oslo, Norway, 86, Galerie Vayhinger, Radolfzell, 86, Fenderesky Art Gallery, Belfast, Ireland, 86, Galerie Dorothea van der Koelen (with catalog), Mainz, 86, Galerie Monochrom, Aachen, 87, Gallery Carla Fuehr, Munchen, 88, Salon des Modernes Mus, Belgrad, Yugoslavia, 88; Stadisches Bodenses-Mus (with catalog), Freidrichshafen, 86; Nur Rost---? (with catalog), Skulpturenmuseum Glaskastn, Marl, 86; Kunstmuseum Karlsruhe, 88; Kunstmuseum Dusseldorf, 88. *Media:* Watercolor. *Mailing Add:* c/o Olga Korper Gallery 17 Morrow Ave Toronto ON M6R 2H9 Canada

REISS, ROLAND
SCULPTOR, EDUCATOR
b Chicago Ill, May 15, 29. *Study:* Univ Calif, Los Angeles, BA, 55, MA, 57; also at Am Acad Art, Chicago. *Work:* Los Angeles Co Mus Art; Laguna Art Mus, Laguna Beach, Calif; Oakland Mus, Calif; Hallmark Inc; Newport Harbor Art Mus, Newport Beach, Calif. *Exhib:* Biennial, Whitney Mus Am Art, New York, 75; one-person exhib, Los Angeles Co Mus Art, 77; Documenta 7, Kassel, Ger, 82; 20 American Artists, Mus Mod Art, San Francisco, 82; Currents, Inst Contemp Art, Boston, 83; Boxes, Mus Tamayo, Mexico, 85; Avant Garde in the 80s, Los Angeles Co Mus Art, 87; Contemporary California, Taipei Fine Arts Mus, Taiwan, 87; Ace Contemp Exhibs, 87, 88 & 89; solo exhib, Ace Contemp Exhibs, Los Angeles, 88; Montgomery Art Gallery, Claremont, Calif, 90; Barnsdall Munic Art Gallery, Los Angeles, 91; Univ Ariz Mus Art, Tucson, 92; Neuberger Mus Art, State Univ NY, Purchase, 92; Palm Springs Desert Mus, 92. *Teaching:* Asst prof art, Univ Calif, Los Angeles, 57; from asst to assoc prof, Univ Colo, Boulder, 57-61; chmn & prof, Claremont Grad Sch, 71- *Awards:* Visual Arts Fel, Nat Endowment Arts, 71, 77, 80 & 87. *Publ:* Auth, Roland Reiss, A Seventeen Year Survey, Fels Contemp Art. *Mailing Add:* Dept Art Claremont Grad Sch 251 E Tenth St Claremont CA 91711

REITZENSTEIN, REINHARD
SCULPTOR
b Uelzen, Ger, May 27, 49; Can citizen. *Study:* Ont Col Art. *Work:* Art Gallery of Ont; Can Coun Art Bank; Nat Gallery Can; Mem Univ Art Gallery; Government of Ont. *Comn:* Wall relief, Govt of Ont, Can, 85; outdoor sculpture, Mem Univ Art Gallery, St John's Newfoundland, 85. *Exhib:* Nat Gallery Can, 74 & 77; Landscape Canada Traveling Exhib, Art Gallery Ont & Edmonton, 76; 17 Can Artists: A Protean View, Vancouver Art Gallery, 76; Carmen Lamanna Gallery, Bologne Art Fair, Italy, 77; one-man shows, Carmen Lamanna Gallery, Toronto, 75-88, London Art Gallery & Art Gallery of Ont, 81-82, Can; Nat Film Bd Can, Ottawa, 81; Royal Botanical Gardens, Sculpture Symposium, 83; Outdoor Sculpture Symposiums, 86, 87 & 88. *Teaching:* Instr, Univ Guelph, 80-88, Univ Waterloo, 83. *Awards:* Can Coun Proj Cost Grants, 74 & 76-84 & Art Grants, 78-88. *Bibliog:* John Bentley Mays (auth), Reinhard Reitzenstein, Globe & Mail, Toronto, 11/80; Jeanne Randolphe (auth), Reinhard Reitzenstein, Artforum, 9/82; Jerry McGrath (auth), Reinhard Reitzenstein, Vanguard, 5/83 & Sans Demarcation, 3/88; Carol Corbel (auth), article, Globe & Mail, Toronto, 3/86. *Media:* Mixed Media. *Publ:* Auth, Natural Areas Divisions Charter, 75; According (record album), 80. *Dealer:* Carmen Lamanna Gallery 788 King St W Toronto Can. *Mailing Add:* 146 Ridge Rd W RR 1 Grimsby ON L3M 4E7 Canada

REKER, LES
PAINTER, EDUCATOR
b Indianapolis, Ind, Aug 7, 51. *Study:* Ind Univ, Bloomington, BFA, 73; Queens Col, MFA, 75; study with Robert Birmelin & Gabriel Laderman. *Work:* Reading Mus, Reading, Pa. *Comn:* Landscape paintings, Hawk Mountain Sanctuary, Kempton, Pa, 82 & Republic Bank, Dallas, 84. *Exhib:* In Praise of Space, Westminster Col, New Wilmington, Pa, Gross-McCleaf Gallery, Philadelphia, Pa & Parsons Sch Design, New York, NY, 77-78; Christmas Invitational, Allentown Art Mus, Allentown, Pa, 77 & 78; Co-op Invitational, Philadelphia Art Mus, 81; Queens Alumnus, Godwin-Ternbach Mus, Flushing, NY, 82; Sherry French Gallery, New York, 83-86; Art of Our Time, Temple Emanuel, Woodcliff-Lake, New York, 84; Emerging Realists: Sherry French Gallery, New York, 84; Emerging Realists: East Meets South, Col Mainland, Texas City, Tex, 86. *Collections Arranged:* Contemporary Narrative Figure Painting (auth, catalog), 85 & Landscapes of the Hudson River Sch (auth, catalog), 86, Payne Gallery, Moravian Col; Artificial Light: Paintings by William Haney (auth, catalog), 85; Robert Arneson (auth catalog), 87; Clarence Carter. *Pos:* Dir & cur, Payne Gallery, Moravian Col, Bethlehem, Pa, 84-; asst prof art, Moravian Col, Bethlehem, Pa, 84. *Teaching:* Instr art hist, Leigh County Community Col, Schnecksville, Pa, 78-83; asst prof drawing, Kutztown Univ, Kutztown, Pa, 83-84; asst prof studio & art hist, Moravian Col, 84- *Bibliog:* Hedy O'Beil (auth), reviews, Arts Mag, 6/78 & 1/84; Freddie Kaplin (auth), Landscape painting in America, Am Artist, 2/84. *Mem:* Assoc Col & Univ Gallery & Mus; Am Assoc Mus. *Media:* Oil on canvas. *Dealer:* Sherry French Gallery 41 W 57th St New York NY 10019. *Mailing Add:* Moravian College Bethlehem PA 18018

REMBERT, VIRGINIA PITTS
EDUCATOR, HISTORIAN
b Birmingham, Ala, Nov 15, 21. *Study:* Univ Montevallo, BA, 42; Columbia Univ, MA, 44, univ traveling fel, 67, Am Asn Univ Women fel, 67, PhD, 70; Univ Wis, MA, 59. *Work:* NC State Mus, Raleigh. *Exhib:* Ala State Exhib, Birmingham, 43; NC State Exhib, Raleigh, 48 & 49; Ala Watercolor Soc, Birmingham, 62 & 86. *Pos:* Pres, Birmingham Art Asn, 70-71 & Ala Watercolor Soc, 62-63; chmn, comt to study baccalaureate degree, Univ Ark, Little Rock, 85-86. *Teaching:* Instr art, Beloit Col, 53-55; asst prof art hist, Mass Col Art, 56-60; from asst prof to prof art & chmn dept, Birmingham Southern Col, 60-73; prof art & chmn dept, Univ Ala, Birmingham, 74-75, Univ Ala, Tuscaloosa, 81-90 & prof emer, 90, head, fine arts area, Col Educ, 84-86; Donaghey Distinguished prof art & art hist, Univ Ark, Little Rock, 75-81; lectr, Fine Arts Club, Vanderbilt Univ, 79, Birmingham Mus Art, 82-88, Montgomery Mus Art, 83; Columbia Mus Art, 88. *Awards:* Silver Bowl Award, Birmingham Area Chamber of Com, 70; Pres Award, Univ Montevallo, 81; Cert Merit, Southeastern Col Art Asn. *Mem:* Col Art Asn; Southeastern Col Art Asn (bd dirs, 74-76, 88-91, pres, 77-78, chmn ann meeting, 86). *Media:* Drawing, Photography. *Res:* Rondrian's life, work and influence in America; Bolotowsky, Von Wiegand, Baber & Gillespie; modernism & post-modernism in art and architecture. *Publ:* Column, Birmingham News, 66-73; contribr, Mass Col Art Alumni Bulletin, 58 & Southeastern Col Art Asn Rev, 68-78; Arts Mag, 76-83; Woman's Art Journal, 84-86. *Mailing Add:* 310 Riverside Dr New York NY 10025

REMBSKI, STANISLAV
PAINTER, WRITER
b Sochaczew, Poland. *Study:* Technol Inst, Warsaw, Poland; Ecole Beaux Arts, Paris; Royal Acad Fine Arts, Berlin, Ger. *Work:* Woodrow Wilson House, Washington, DC; Franklin D Roosevelt Mem Libr, Hyde Park, NY; Archbishop's House, Baltimore; Hist Soc, Madison, Wis; Nat Acad Design, New York. *Comn:* Conversion of William Duke of Acquitaine, Trustees of St Barnard's Sch, Gladstone, NJ, 31; I Am the Life, Mem Episcopal Church, 62; Jefferson & the Four Maryland Signers of the Declaration of Independence (large hist painting), 76-77; Brigham Young, Mormon Church, Salt Lake City, Utah. *Exhib:* One-man shows, Dudensing Galleries, New York, 27, Carnegie Hall Gallery, New York, 34, Arthur U Newton Galleries, New York, 35, Baltimore Mus Art, 47; Baltimore Inst Art, Md, 50; Engineering Ctr, Baltimore, Md, 81. *Pos:* Vis critic, Md Inst Art, 52-55. *Mem:* Salmagundi Club; Allied Artists Am; Nat Soc Mural Painters; Am Artists Prof League. *Media:* Oil, Crayon. *Publ:* Auth, Mysticism in Art, Leonardo da Vinci Forum, 36; Freedom, New Age, 72. *Mailing Add:* 1404 Park Ave Baltimore MD 21217

REMENICK, SEYMOUR
PAINTER, INSTRUCTOR
b Detroit, Mich, Apr 3, 23. *Study:* Tyler Sch Fine Arts, 40-42; Hans Hofmann Sch, 46-48. *Work:* Philadelphia Mus; Pa Acad Fine Arts; RI Sch Design; Phoenix Art Mus; Dallas Mus Contemp Art. *Exhib:* Am Painting, Rome, Italy, 55; Four Young Americans, RI Sch Design, 56; 11 Contemp Am Painters, Paris, France, 56; Art Inst Chicago Ann, 61; Drawing Show, Philadelphia Mus, 65. *Teaching:* Instr painting & drawing, Pa Acad Fine Arts, 77- *Awards:* Louis Comfort Tiffany Found Grant, 55; Benjamin Altman Landscape Prize, Nat Acad Design, 60; Hallmark Purchase Award, 60. *Mem:* Nat Acad Design, New York. *Media:* Oil, Watercolor. *Mailing Add:* 812 Catharine St Philadelphia PA 19147

REMINGTON, DEBORAH WILLIAMS
PAINTER
b Haddonfield, NJ, June 25, 35. *Study:* San Francisco Art Inst, BFA, 57; studies in Asia, 57-59. *Work:* Whitney Mus Am Art, New York; Mus Boymans von Beuningen, Rotterdam, Holland; Centre d'Art et de Cult George Pompidou, Paris; Nat Mus Am Art; Art Inst Chicago. *Comn:* Cleveland Print Club, 90. *Exhib:* One-person shows, Bykert Gallery, New York, 67, 69, 72 & 74, Galerie Darthea Speyer, Paris, 68, 71, 73 & 92, Hamilton Gallery, New York, 77, Jack Shainman Gallery, New York, 87; Shoshana Wayne Gallery, Los Angeles, Calif, 89; Whitney Mus Ann Exhib, 65, 67 & 72; 71st Am Exhib, Art Inst Chicago, 74; Painting Endures, Inst Contemp Art, Boston, 75; 20 Year Retrospective, Newport Harbor Art Mus, Calif, 83; 20 Year Retrospective, Oakland Mus Art, Calif, 84. *Teaching:* Cooper Union, New York, 73- *Awards:* Fel, Tamarind Inst, Albuquerque, 73; Nat Endowment Fel, 79-80; Guggenheim Fel, 84. *Bibliog:* R C Kenedy (auth), Deborah Remington, Art Int, summer 74; Donald B Kuspit (auth), Deborah Remington: Autonomy and absences in the visual koan, Art Int, summer, 79; Dore Ashton (auth), Deborah Remington, A 20 Year Survey, (catalogue exhib), Newport Harbor Art Mus, 84. *Media:* Oil; Lithography. *Dealer:* Galerie Darthea Speyer 6 Rue Jacques Callot Paris 75006. *Mailing Add:* 309 W Broadway New York NY 10013

REMSEN, JOHN
PAINTER, CONSULTANT
b Glen Cove, NY, Apr 21, 39. *Study:* Pratt Inst, BFA; NY Univ, MA(art educ). *Exhib:* One-man shows, State Univ NY, Stony Brook, 77, James Hunt Baker Galleries, Palm Beach, Fla, 80, Burlington Bookshop, New York, 80, Canios Bookshop, Sag Harbor, NY, 90 & Gallery Authentique, Roslyn, NY, 92; HTAL First Ann Fall Invitational, Hutchins Gallery, Long Island Univ, C W Post Campus, Brookville, NY, 89; Artist Choice I, Northport Galleries, Huntington, NY, 90; Fifteen Artists Invitational, Smithtown Township Arts Coun, Chase Manhattan Bank, Smithaven Mall, Lake Grove, NY, 91; Works on Paper, Discovery Art Gallery, Glen Cove, NY, 91; Spring Invitational 92, HTAL Hutchins Gallery, Long Island Univ, C W Post, Brookville, NY, 92; and others. *Pos:* Sales & print inventory, Harbor Galleries, New York, 85; dir, Nora Galleries, Great Neck, NY, 85; lect, slide discussion & drawing class, Smithtown Township Arts Coun Inc, Mill Pond House, St James, NY, 86; artist rep, corps, architects & design firms, 87; art reviewer, Rec Newspapers, Port Jefferson Station, NY, 88; sales, Northport Galleries, 88, cur & gallery

rep, 89; sales dir/opening gallery, Artstar, Los Angeles, 91; recreational dir, Brookhaven Township Adult Ctrs, Mastic & New Village, Suffolk Co, New York. *Teaching:* Painting, drawing & collage, Brookhaven Adult Ctrs, Mastic & New Village, Suffolk Co, NY, 92. *Media:* Acrylic, Oil. *Specialty:* Nineteenth-twentieth century American painting and graphic arts. *Mailing Add:* 77 Main St PO Box 2803 Setauket NY 11733

REMSING, (JOSEPH) GARY
PAINTER, SCULPTOR
b Spokane, Wash, Sept 18, 46. *Study:* San Jose State Univ, BA & MA. *Work:* De Saisset Mus, Univ Santa Clara; Oakland Mus. *Comn:* Maj sculptural comn, State of Calif, 78. *Exhib:* One man exhibs, Willima Sawyer Gallery, San Francisco, 71, 73, & 74; Project Proposals: Art in Public Buildings, Sacramento Community Arts Gallery, Calif, 78; Int Sculpture Competition, State of NJ, traveling, 79-80; Calif Invitational, House of Rep, Washington, DC, 82; Djurovich Gallery, Sacramento, Calif, 85; Palo Alto Cult Ctr, 85; Chuck Levitan Gallery, New York, 86; Lighting Collabarative, New York, 87. *Teaching:* Instr, Modesto Jr Col, 71- *Awards:* Award, Maryville Col, Tenn, 70; Award, Calif Arts Comn, 70. *Bibliog:* Articles in San Francisco Chronicle, 9/8/69 & 5/7/71, Artforum, 11/69 & Art Wk, 5/71, 4/72 & 6/74; and others. *Mailing Add:* 2437 Topeka St Riverbank CA 95367

RENDL, M(ILDRED MARCUS)
PAINTER, WRITER
b New York, NY, May 30, 28. *Study:* New York Univ, BS, 48, MBA, 50; Radcliffe-Harvard, PhD, 54. *Exhib:* Faber Birren Color Award Show, Stamford Art Asn, Conn, 85; Art of the Northeast, Silvermine Guild Ctr Arts, New Canaan, 86; Phoenix Gallery, New York, 89; Lever House Gallery, New York, 90; Cork Gallery, New York, 90; Greater Hartford Archit Conservancy, Conn, 91. *Pos:* Art Econ Consult. *Mem:* Women's Caucus Arts, Miami, San Antonio; Artists Equity Asn; Southwest Soc Economists; Western Economics Asn; Women Arts Found, New York (ed bd). *Media:* Oil, Acrylic; Ink. *Res:* Economics of art; complex art appraisals and pricing art; art as investment or money substitute; art as consumer durable good and valuation. *Publ:* Auth, Economics of the fine arts: Fad, fashion and value, Eastern Community Col Asn, 84; Pricing contemporary art & Economic issues in the arts, Women Arts Found, 86-90. *Mailing Add:* Art Complex PO Box 814 New Canaan CT 06840

RENEE, LISABETH
SCULPTOR, ASSEMBLAGE ARTIST
b Brooklyn, NY, July 28, 52. *Study:* Univ Puget Sound, Tacoma, Wash, 72-73; State Univ NY, Buffalo, BA, 77; Art Students League, New York, studied drawing with Marshall Glasier & Anthony Palumbo, sculpture with Jose Decreeft & Sidney Simon, painting with Knox Martin & Theodoros Stamos, 78-80; New Sch Social Res, New York, with Dorothy Gillespie & Alice Baber, 79; Long Island Univ, MFA, 82; Rollins Col, Winter Park, Fla, teaching cert, 84; Univ Cent Fla, Orlando, ABD, 90. *Comn:* Mural (8ft X 11ft), State Univ NY, Buffalo, 76; Peaches on the Roof (mural), comn by Dr Michael Reeves, Montgomery, Ala, 84; Jet (floor installation), McCoy Elementary Sch, Orlando, Fla, 85. *Exhib:* Solo exhibs, The Painted Box, Ctr Arts, Vero Beach, Fla, 86 & Harris, Atlantic Ctr Arts, New Smyrna Beach, Fla, 92; Spaces, three-woman show, Fla Ctr Contemp Art, Tampa, 87; Inside Out, Atlantic Ctr Arts, New Smyrna Beach, 89; Small Works Exhib, Valencia Community,Col, 89; Nat Art Educ Asn Exhib, Kansas City, 90 & Atlanta, Ga, 91; Nat Art Educ Asn Exhib, Atlanta, Ga, 91; and others. *Pos:* Dir, Southern Artists' Registry, Winter Park, Fla, 84-87; Juror, Riverfront Fine Arts Festival, Seminole Community Col, 90 & Ponce Inlet Art Festival, 92. *Teaching:* Instr studio art, Long Island Univ, Greenvale, NY, 80-82, Orange Co Pub Schs, Fla, 83-86 & Seminole Co Pub Schs, Fla, 86-; adj fac drawing, Rollins Col, Winter Park, Fla, 83. *Awards:* Sculptural Excellence Award, Ann East Meadow Exhib, Long Island Pub Libr, 79; Teacher Merit Award, Walt Disney World Co, 90; FACTS Grant, 91. *Bibliog:* Heidi Barszcz (auth), Sexuality in the visual arts, Imprint, fall 77; Art Rev, Tampa Art Today, Channel 8, Tampa, Fla, 10/85; Teacher excels in art fields, Wings, spring 88. *Mem:* Women's Caucus Art; Col Art Asn; Int Sculpture Ctr; Nat Art Educ Asn; Fla Art Educ Asn, (central Fla regional rep). *Media:* Mixed. *Publ:* Cooperative Art, The ARTISTeacher, 91. *Mailing Add:* 20 Cobblestone Way Casselberry FL 32707

RENEE, PAULA
PAINTER, TAPESTRY ARTIST
b Hackensack, NJ. *Study:* Empire Col, Nyack, NY; Fairleigh Dickenson Univ, Teaneck, NJ, 73-77; Rockland Community Col, Suffern, NY, 70-71; Ramapo State Col, Mahwah, NJ, 73; Thomas A Edison Col, Princeton, NJ, 78; Empire State Col (State Univ NY), Hartsdale, NY, 88-; Empire Col, AS, 90. *Work:* Nat Inst Design, Ahmedabad, India; The Wood Sch, New York. *Comn:* Tapestries, Biomatrix, Inc, Ridgefield, NJ, 86; tapestry, Admiral Royale Hotel, Egg Harbor, NJ, 87; tapestry, Sheraton Hotel, Chicago, Ill, 88; handwoven Moroccan bldgs, Stouffers' Resort, Indian Wells, Calif, 89; Our Lady of Peace Mausoleum at St Nicholas Cemetery, Lodi, NJ, 91. *Exhib:* Creative Arts Workshop, New Haven, Conn, 89; Trenton City Mus, Trenton, NJ, 91; PanAm Gallery, New York, 91; Pennswood Art Gallery, Philadelphia, Pa, 91; Edward Hopper Found, Nyack, NY, 92; and others. *Pos:* Artist-in-residence, Bergen Community Col, Paramus, NJ, Studio/Gallery-Hackensack, NJ, 78-79. *Teaching:* Artist-in-residence, Bergen Community Col, Paramus, & Studio Gallery, Hackensack, NJ, 78-79. *Bibliog:* June Avignon (auth), Colorful masks can't disguise her whimsical art, North Jersey Suburbanite, 2/1/84; Edith Sobel (auth), Artist fabricates symbolic tapestry, Federation News, 8/85. *Mem:* Rockland Ctr for the Arts; Edward Hopper Found. *Media:* Gouache, Oil; Loom-woven Fiber. *Publ:* Illusr, Photo Cover, Dyepot Mag (Handweavers Guild of Am), 81; auth, Shuttle, Spindle & Dyepot (mag, cover), Handweavers Guild Am, Bloomfield, Conn, 86; photograph and article, Fiberarts, Ashville, NC, 11/86 & 12/86; Creative thought, Religious Sci Int, Spokane, Wash, 6/90; mag cover, Sci of Mind Mag, Sci of Mind Communications, Div Church Relig Sci, Los Angeles, Calif, 7/90 & 4/91. *Mailing Add:* 103 Gedney St Rivercrest No 1H Nyack NY 10960

RENK, MERRY
GOLDSMITH, PAINTER
b Trenton, NJ, July 8, 21. *Study:* Sch Indust Arts, Trenton, NJ; Inst Design, Chicago. *Work:* Boston Mus Art; San Francisco Art Comn; Am Craft Mus, New York; Oakland Mus Art, Calif; Calif Craft Mus, San Francisco. *Comn:* Wedding crown, comn by Johnson Wax, Objects, USA; copper sculpture, Contra Costa Jr Col Dist, Martinez, Calif; iron sculpture, Walnut Creek Pub Libr, Calif. *Exhib:* One-woman show, De Young Mem Mus, San Francisco, 71 & Mus Hist & Technol, Smithsonian Inst, 71-72; Objects USA Traveling Exhib, US & Europe, 70-72; retrospective, Calif Craft Mus, San Francisco, 81; Le Trou Gallery, San Francisco, Watercolors, 86, 88 & 90. *Teaching:* Instr enamel for jewelry, Haystack Mt Sch Crafts, Deer Isle, Maine; instr design, Univ Calif, Berkeley. *Awards:* San Francisco Art Comn Awards, 54, 57, 59, 60 & 70; San Francisco Women Artists Award, 65; Oakland Mus Art, Calif, 69; Craftsman Grant, Nat Endowment Arts, 74; San Francisco Comn Awards Honor, 86- *Bibliog:* C McCann (auth), Three fine craftsmen, Artweek, 2/71; A Fried (auth), article in San Francisco Examiner, 3/71; Joan Watkins (auth), article, Am Crafts Mag, 4/81; and others. *Mem:* Metal Arts Guild (pres, 53); distinguished mem Soc NAm Goldsmiths. *Media:* Watercolor. *Publ:* Auth, Design Autobiography, Goldsmith J, summer 80. *Mailing Add:* 17 Saturn St San Francisco CA 94114

RENNER, ERIC
PAINTER, PHOTOGRAPHER
b Philadelphia, Pa, Nov 6, 41. *Study:* Univ Cincinnati, BS, 64; Cranbrook Acad Art, MFA, 68. *Work:* Mus Mod Art, New York; Nat Gallery Can, Ottawa; Mus Mod Art, Mexico City; Mus Art Sao Paulo, Brazil; Inst Contemp Art, Chicago. *Comn:* Photographs, State Ohio, State Off Tower, 74. *Exhib:* Nat Gallery Can, 71, 73 & 75; solo exhib, Mus Mod Art, Mexico City, 71 & Mus Sao Paulo, Brazil, 78; The Great West, Univ Colo, Denver, 79; The Extended Frame, Visual Studies Workshop, Rochester, NY, 80; Handmade Cameras, Tyler Sch Art, Temple Univ, 82; The Panoramic Image, Univ Southampton, England, 82; The Pinhole Image, Va Mus, Richmond, 83. *Teaching:* Asst prof design, State Univ NY, Alfred, 68-71; adj prof photog, Visual Studies Workshop, 75; dir, Pinhole Resource Ctr & ed, Pinhole J, currently. *Awards:* Nat Endowment Arts Fel, 76 & 79-80. *Mem:* Soc Photog Educ. *Publ:* Auth, From the Stars, the Sun, and the Air for Laurie, 75 & The Horsefetter, 77, Visual Studies Worhshop. *Dealer:* Jeffrey Fuller Fine Art 2108 Spruce St Philadelphia PA. *Mailing Add:* Star Rte 15 Box 1355 San Lorenzo NM 88041

RENNINGER, KATHARINE STEELE
PAINTER
b Philadelphia, Pa, Feb 26, 25. *Study:* Moore Col Art, Philadelphia, BFA, 46; Univ Pa, with Paul Domville, 48. *Work:* William Penn Mem Mus, Harrisburg, Pa; Rutgers Univ Mus, New Brunswick, NJ; SmithKline Beckman Corp, Philadelphia, Pa; Devecchi Collection, Bucks Co Educ Serv, Doylestown, Pa; Woodmere Mus, Chestnut Hill, Pa; Blue Cross of Greater Philadelphia, Pa; James A Michener Art Mus, Doulestown, Pa. *Exhib:* Butler Inst Am Art, Youngstown, Ohio, 63, 68 & 74; traveling exhib, Nat Drawing Soc, New York, 65; Childe Hassam Purchase Mem, Am Acad Arts & Lett, New York, 69, 75 & 78; Nat Acad Design, New York, 69, 74-75 & 80; Allied Artists Am, New York, 70-92; Allentown Mus, Pa, 79-85; and others. *Awards:* Grumbacher/Kreidler, Ann Exhib, Nat Soc Painters Casein & Acrylic, 73, 74 & 82; Hassam Mem Purchase Award, Am Acad Arts & Lett, 79; Salmagundi Award, 82, Everitt Award, 85, B Janson, 89 Allied Artists Am. *Mem:* Allied Artists Am; Nat Soc Painters Casein & Acrylic; Philadelphia Watercolor Club; Bucks Co Coun Arts (chmn, 74-75 & 78); James A Michener Art Mus (secy bd, 88-92). *Media:* Casein. *Publ:* Auth, Watercolor page, Am Artist, 77. *Dealer:* Mickelson Gallery 707 G St Washington DC 20001; Newman Galleries 1625 Walnut St Philadelphia PA 19103. *Mailing Add:* 148 N State St Newtown PA 18940

RENOUF, EDDA
PAINTER
b Mexico City, Mex, June 17, 43; US citizen. *Study:* Academie Julian, Paris, 63-64; Sch Art, Columbia Univ, MFA, 71; Academie der Bildende Künste, Munich, 69-70; Columbia Univ, Paris, France, painting fel, 71-72. *Work:* Art Inst Chicago, Ill; Dallas Mus Fine Arts, Tex; Metrop Mus Art, NY; Mus Mod Art, NY; Whitney Mus Am Art, NY; Australian Nat Gallery, Camberra, Australia; Tel Aviv Mus, Tel Aviv, Israel. *Exhib:* Mus Mod Art, New York, 73, 77 & 90; Whitney Mus Am Art, New York, 78, 79, 85; solo exhibs, Blum Helman Gallery, New York, 82, 85, 87 & 89, Francoise Lambert, Milan, 83, Yvon Lambert, Paris, 84, Martina Hamilton Gallery, 85, 86, Galerie Liesbeth Lips, Amsterdam, 87, Cairn Gallery, Gloucestershire, Eng, 90, Gallery S65, Aalst, Belg, 91; Metrop Mus Art, NY, 82, 83, 87; Edda Renouf: Prints, Greene Gallery, Coral Gables, Fla, 89; Lines of Vision: Drawings by Contemporary Women (traveling exhib), Hillwood Art Gallery, Long Island Univ Brooksville, NY, 89; Group Show, Francis Lambert Gallery, Milan, 89; Künstler der Galerie, Galerie Mühlenbusch, Düsseldorf, Gier, 89; Matrix 36, Wadsworth Atheneum, Hartford, Conn, 78; Contemp Drawing-New York, Univ Calif, Santa Barbara, 78; Biennial Exhib, Whitney Mus of Am Art, 79; New Works of Contemp Art & Music, Fruit Market Gallery & Graeme Murray, Edinburgh, Scotland, 89; Drawing Acquisitions 1981-1985, Whitney Mus Am Art, 85; 20th Century Art, Metrop Mus of Art, New York, NY 87;

A Sleep of Reason, Mus Fridericianum, Cassel, Ger, 88; Recent Drawings, Blum-Helman Gallery, New York, NY, 88 & 89; Gisele Linder Gallery, Basel, Switz, 91. *Awards:* Pollock-Krasner Found Inc Grant, 90. *Bibliog:* Wehlte-Höschell (auth), Die Moderne träunt von sich, Frankfurter Allgemeine Nr 86, 4/13/88, Seite 27; unsigned (auth), Wach mit, Schlafe der Vernunft, Der Spiegol, 88, 192; Elisa Turner (auth), Artists grid for new approaches, Miami Herald, 2/15/89, 8D. *Mem:* Art Students League, NY, 67-68. *Media:* Acrylic, Oil; Pastel Chalk, Oil Pastels. *Publ:* Auth, Lines, Edizione Flash Art, Milan, 74; Lines and Non-Lines, Lapp Princess Press & Printed Matter Inc, New York, 77; Echoes, Graeme Murray Gallery, Scotland, 79; Lines of Vision-Drawings by Contemporary Women, Hudson Hills Press, NY, 89. *Dealer:* Blum-Helman Gallery 20 W 57th St New York NY 10019; Yvon Lambert Gallery 5 Rue Grenier-St-Lazare 75003 Paris France. *Mailing Add:* 10 East St Washington CT 06793

RENOUF, EDWARD
PAINTER, SCULPTOR
b Hsiku, China, Nov 23, 06; US citizen. *Study:* Phillips Andover Acad, 24; Harvard Univ, 28; Columbia Univ, 36-40; also drawing & painting with Carlos Merida, Mex, 41. *Comn:* Steel sculpture, 65 & mural painting, 67, Horace Mann Sch, Riverdale, NY. *Exhib:* Whitney Mus Am Art Sculpture Ann, 60 & 64; Conn Acad Show, Wadsworth Atheneum, Hartford, 61; Pa Acad Fine Arts 161st Ann, Philadelphia, 66; one-man shows, Allan Stone Gallery, New York, 73, 78, 80, 82 & 86; Sculptors Guild Ann; Fedn Mod Painters & Sculptors Ann; and others. *Teaching:* Vis artist painting, Akad Bildenden Kunste, Munich, Ger, 70. *Awards:* Second Prize Sculpture, Sharon Creative Arts Found, 64. *Bibliog:* Gordon Brown (auth), article, 5/78, John Deckert (auth), article, 5/78 & Mathew Licht (auth), article, 11/82, Arts; plus others. *Media:* Multimedia. *Publ:* Contribr, Dyn, Mex, 42. *Dealer:* Allan Stone Gallery 48 E 86th St New York NY 10028. *Mailing Add:* 26 Juniper Meadow Rd Washington Depot CT 06794

RENSCH, ROSLYN
HISTORIAN, WRITER
b Detroit, Mich. *Study:* Northwestern Univ, BM & MM; Univ Ill, MA(art hist); Univ Wis-Madison, PhD(art hist), 64. *Pos:* Bd dirs, Sheldon Swope Art Gallery, Terre Haute, Ind, 77-82, World Harp Congress, 83- *Teaching:* Lectr art hist & humanities & chmn div humanities, Nat Col Educ, 62-65; prof art hist & humanities, Ind State Univ, 65-87. *Mem:* Col Art Asn Am; Midwest Art Hist Soc; Int Ctr Medieval Art; life mem Art Inst Chicago. *Res:* Pre-Romanesque stone carving in the British Isles; representations of the harp in art monuments; American landscape painting. *Publ:* Auth, Harp, its History, Technique & Repertoire, Praeger, 69 & Duckworth, 69; auth, Development of the medieval harp: A re-examination of the evidence of the Utrecht Psalter and its progeny, Gesta, Vol 11, No 2; auth, Harp carvings on the Irish crosses, Am Harp J, winter 74; auth, Landscape painting in America to c 1900, Ind State Univ, 75; Harps & Harpists, Duckworth, 89 & Ind Univ Press, 89. *Mailing Add:* Captains Walk No 17 798 Mallory Street St Simmons Island GA 31522

REPLINGER, DOT (DOROTHY THIELE)
WEAVER, DESIGNER
b Chicago, Ill, Jan 30, 24. *Study:* Sch Art Inst Chicago, BA(educ), study with Carolyn Howlett & Else Regensteiner. *Work:* Amerinvesco, Chicago; Caterpillar Int, Peoria, Ill; Haskins & Sells, Stand Oil Bldg, Chicago; State of Ill Bldg, Chicago; Waterfront Place, Seattle, Wash. *Comn:* Ark curtain, Sinai Temple, Champaign, Ill, 76; wall piece, Friends of Champaign Pub Libr, Ill, 78; Citizens Bank, Ind. *Exhib:* Craft Multiples, Renwick Gallery, Smithsonian Inst, Washington, DC, 75; Marietta Crafts Nat, Ohio, 75 & 77; Clay & Fiber--15 Viewpoints, Wustum Mus Fine Arts, Racine, Wis, 78. *Awards:* Craftsmen's Fel, Nat Endowment Arts, 76-77; Creativity Award, Miss River Craft Show, Brooks Mem Art Gallery, Memphis, Tenn, 76; Purchase Award, Mid-States Craft Exhib, Evansville, Ind, 77. *Mem:* Am Crafts Coun (state rep, 70-76); Handweavers Guild Am; Midwest Weavers Cong. *Media:* Fiber. *Mailing Add:* 4 Burnett Circle Urbana IL 61801

RESEK, KATE FRANCES
PAINTER
b Cleveland, Ohio. *Study:* Univ Wis, Madison, BS(fine arts); Columbia Univ, MFA, 69. *Work:* Aldrich Mus of Contemp Art, Ridgefield, Conn; Neuberger Mus, Purchase, NY; Housatonic Mus, Bridgeport, Conn; Columbia Univ. *Exhib:* One-man shows, Soho 20, New York, 74 & 76, Noyes, Van Cline & Davenport, New York, 77 & Bertha Urdang Gallery, New York, 77; Contemporary Reflections 1974-1975, Aldrich Mus of Contemp Art, 75; 40th Ann Show, Butler Inst of Am Art, Youngstown, Ohio, 76; New Acquisitions, Neuberger Mus, 76; New Acquisitions, Aldrich Mus of Contemp Art, 78; Penthouse Show, Mus Mod Art, 80-81; Adam Gimbel Gallery, New York, 81; and others. *Teaching:* Instr drawing/painting, State Univ NY, Purchase, 75-76, Fairleigh Dickinson Univ, Teaneck, NJ, 78-82, Brooklyn Mus, 83. *Awards:* Silver Hill Award/Painting, & Inez Leon Greenberg Award/Drawing, Silvermine 22nd New Eng Exhib; Yaddo Fel, 78 & 82; NJ State Coun Arts Grant, 83. *Bibliog:* Ellen Lubell (auth), Kate Resek, Arts Mag, 12/76; Holland Cotter (auth), article in NY Arts J, 9/77; Carrie Rickey (auth), Village Voice, 10/82. *Mem:* Women's Caucus of Art; Women in the Arts; Col Art Asn. *Media:* Pastel on Canvas. *Dealer:* Adam Gimbel Gallery 17 E 49th St New York NY. *Mailing Add:* 354 Bowery No 2 New York NY 10012

RESIKA, PAUL
PAINTER
b New York, NY, Aug 15, 28. *Study:* With S Wilson, 40-44 & Hans Hofmann, 45-47, New York; also in Venice & Rome, 50-54. *Work:* Indianapolis Mus Art; Metrop Mus Art, New York; Neuberger Mus, State Univ NY, Purchase; Sheldon Mem Gallery, Univ Nebr-Lincoln; Roby Collection, Nat Mus Amer Art; Univ Wyo, Laramie, Wyo; and many others. *Exhib:* Solo exhibs, Graham Modern, New York, 85-88 & 90, Artist's Choice Mus, New York, 85, Crane Calman Gallery, London with Robert De Niro, 86, Kornbluth Gallery, Fairlawn, NJ, 86, Meredith Long Gallery, Houston, 86, Long Point Gallery, Provincetown, 88 & Mead Art Mus, Amherst Col, Mass, 91; Hommage a Bernard Pfriem, Found Mona Bismarck, Paris, France, 91; Gallery Selections, Salender-O'Reilly Galleries, Beverly Hills, 92; Three American Master, Kornbluth Gallery, Fairlawn, NJ, 92; Seven Artists, Seven Media on Paper, Katharina Rich Perlow Gallery, New York, 92; Color as a Subject, Artists' Mus with Tibor de Nagg Gallery & Staempfli Gallery, New York, 92; and many other one-man & group exhibs. *Pos:* Artist in residence, Dartmouth Col, 72; chmn masters prog, Parsons Sch Design, NY 78-90. *Teaching:* Adj prof painting & drawing, Cooper Union, 66-78; instr painting, Art Students' League, 68-69; instr, Skowhegan Sch Painting, 73 & 76; instr Grad Sch, Univ Pa, 74 & 79. *Awards:* Fel, Guggenheim Mem Found, 84; Purchase Awards, Hassam Fund & Speicher Fund, Am Acad & Inst Arts & Letts, 86, 88 & 91; Benjamin Altman Landscape Prize, Nat Acad Design, 91; and many others. *Bibliog:* Jacek Gulla (auth), Resika at Graham Modern: a leap of pure painting, Artworld, 3/90; Hilton Kramer (auth), Some shows that deliver what they promise, NY Observer, 12/90; New England, Nat Geographic Bks, 90; Christopher Busa (auth), Long Point Gallery: Thirteen Ways of Looking at an Artist, Provincetown Arts, Vol 7, 91; Henry Gerrit (auth), Paul Resika at Salander-O'Reilly, Art Am, 91; and many others. *Mem:* Nat Acad Design; Century Asn, NY. *Dealer:* Salander-O'Reilly Gallery 20 E 79th St New York NY. *Mailing Add:* 114 E 84th St New York NY 10028

RESNICK, DON
PAINTER
b New York, NY, May 19, 28. *Study:* Hobart Col, BA, 49; Int Acad of Fine Art, Salzburg, Austria, Cert, 57, studied with Oskar Kokoschka, Raphael Soyer, Seymour Lipton, 58-59. *Work:* Dartmouth Col Mus; Currier Gallery of Art; Williams Col Mus Art; Portland Mus Art, Portland, Maine; Sheldon Mem Art Gallery, Univ Nebr-Lincoln. *Exhib:* Solo exhibs, Hofstra Univ, 78, Adelphi Univ, 79; Land, Sea, Sky, Gallery North, Setauket, 88; Sky, Sea & In between, Elaine Benson Gallery, Bridgehampton, 89; Long Island Artists, Nassau County Mus Fine Art, Roslyn, New York, 89; Figurative Abstraction, Andrea Marquis Fine Arts, Boston, 89. *Awards:* First Prize, Long Island Artists, 58; Nominated, Am Acad & Inst of Arts & Lett, 82, 86; Millay Colony Found Arts, 89; and others. *Bibliog:* Phyllis Braff (auth), Celebrating land and sea, 1/5/83 & Mixed graphics and Long Island scenes, 1/27/85, NY Times; Malcolm Preston (auth), Land & sea revisited, Newsday, 6/7/83. *Mem:* Artist's Equity. *Media:* Oil, Watercolor. *Dealer:* Gallery North 90 N Country Rd Setauket NY 11733; Rubiner Gallery 7001 Orchard Lake Rd Suite 430 West Bloomfield MI 48322. *Mailing Add:* 15 Revere St Rockville Centre NY 11570

RESNICK, MARCIA AYLENE
PHOTOGRAPHER, CONCEPTUAL ARTIST
b New York, NY, Nov 21, 50. *Study:* NY Univ, 67-69; Cooper Union, BFA, 72; Calif Inst Arts, MFA, 73. *Work:* Metrop Mus Art & Mus Mod Art, New York; George Eastman House, Int Mus Photog; Contemp Arts Mus, Houston; San Francisco Mus. *Exhib:* Photography Unlimited, Fogg Mus, Harvard Univ, 74; Women of Photography, San Francisco Mus & Traveling Show, 75; two-person show, Chicago Ctr Contemp Photog, 78; Punk Art, Washington Proj Arts, 78; Book Art, Art Inst Chicago, 78; Kunst als Photographie 1879-1979, Tiroler Landesmuseum Ferdinandeum, Innsbruck, Austria, 79; Galerie Wilde, Cologne, 81; John Belushi, Univ Dallas, Tex, 87; Gallery Mod Objects, Los Angeles,Calif, 87; Suzan Cooper Gallery, New York, 87 & 88; Tuchong Gallery, New York, 88; New Photographs, Old Friends, Oregon Sch Arts & Crafts, Portland, Ore, 89; Photographic Collection of Robert Olden, Arles, France, 90. *Teaching:* Instr photog, Queens Col, Cooper Union, Int Ctr of Photog, Staten Island Col, City Univ NY & La Guardia Community Col, New York, 87-88. *Awards:* Nat Endowment Arts Photography Grants, 75 & 78; Creative Artists Pub Serv Prog Grant, 77. *Bibliog:* Pop up people, Time-Life Yearbk, 74; Layered eye, Camera 35 Mag, 7/74; Peter Frank (auth), Picture books, Soho Weekly News, 7/17/75. *Mem:* Soc Photog Educ. *Publ:* Auth, Landscape; See; & Tahitian Eve, 75; Re-visions; & Landscape-Loftscape, 78. *Dealer:* Suzan Cooper Pikes Rd PO Box 1299 Woodstock NY 12498. *Mailing Add:* 2 Grove St 1F New York NY 10013

RESNICK, MILTON
PAINTER
b Bratslav, Russia, Jan 7, 17; US citizen. *Study:* Paris & New York. *Work:* Calif Mus Fine Arts, Berkeley; Metrop Mus Art, Mus Mod Art, New York; Honolulu Acad Arts, Hiawaii; Nat Gallery Can, Ottawa, Ontario; Fort Worth Art Mus, Tex; Nat Gallery, Washington, DC; Cleveland Mus, Ohio; Guggenheim Mus; also many others including pvt collections. *Exhib:* One man shows, Ft Worth Art Ctr Mus, 71, Milwaukee Art Ctr, Wis, 71, Gallery Urban, Nagoya, Japan, 86, Robert Miller Gallery, New York, 85, 86, 88, 91 & 92, Mus Contemp Art, Houston, Tex, 85, Galerie Montenay-Delsol, Paris, France, 87, Daniel Weinberg Gallery, Los Angeles, Calif, 88; Four shows, Whitney Mus Am Art, 57-67 & Whitney Biennial, 73; San Francisco Mus Art, 63; Mus Mod Art, New York, 69; The Gestural Impulse, Whitney Mus Am Art, 89; Aldrich Mus Contemp Art, Ridgefield, Conn; Am Acad Inst Arts & Letts, 89 & 90; The Image of Abstract Painting in the 1980's, Rose Art Mus,

Waltham, Mass, 90; The Figure in the 20th Century, Meredith Long & Co, Houston, Tex, 90; Manny Silverman Gallery, Los Angeles, 92; plus many others. *Teaching:* Instr, Pratt Inst, Brooklyn; vis lectr & critic, var schs, including RI Sch Design, Yale Summer Sch, Wagner Col & Silvermine; vis prof, Univ Calif, Berkeley, 55-56; instr, NY Univ, 64-68; vis lectr & critic, NY Studio Sch, 65-70; vis prof, Univ Wis-Madison, 66-67; vis artist, Barnard Col, 74-83. *Awards:* Jimmy Ernst Art Award, Am Acad & Inst Arts & Letters, NY, 90. *Bibliog:* Linda Cathcart (auth), Milton Resnick: Paintings from 1945-1985, Mus Fine Art, Houston, Tex, 85; Stephen Westfall (auth), Milton Resnick Paintings 1957-60 from the Collection of Howard & Barbara Wise, Robert Miller Gallery, New York, 88. *Mem:* Am Acad & Inst Arts & Letts, New York. *Media:* Oil. *Dealer:* Robert Miller Gallery 41 E 57th St New York NY 10022. *Mailing Add:* 87 Eldridge St New York NY 10002

RETZER, HOWARD EARL
PAINTER
b Rochester, Pa, Jan 31, 25. *Study:* Geneva Col, Pa; Univ Colo, BA; Temple Univ Sch of Med, MD; study for ten years with Pawel A Kontny & five years with John Jellico. *Work:* Anchorage Hist & Fine Arts Mus, 88. *Exhib:* Fur Rendezvous, Anchorage, Alaska, 75; Zang Mus, Denver, Colo, 77-78; Heritage Mus, Anchorage; one-man show, Residence of Gov Wm Sheffield, Anchorage, 88. *Awards:* First Prize Oil-Scenery & Div Champion Oil-all categories, Fur Rendezvous, 88. *Bibliog:* John Jellico (auth), Howard Retzer, Southwestern Art, 77. *Media:* Multi, Oil. *Collection:* Many works of Kontny, as well as Fechin, Frank Hoffman, Timmermans, Frank Tenny Johnson & others. *Dealer:* O'Briens Art Emporium 7122 Stetson Dr Scottsdale AZ 85251; Gallery 20-Dimond Ctr 800 E Dimond Blvd Anchorage AK. *Mailing Add:* c/o Elk Mountain Ranch PO Box 340 Parshall CO 80468

REUTER, LAUREL J
MUSEUM DIRECTOR
b Devils Lake, NDak, Oct 17, 43. *Study:* Univ NDak, MA, 74; interned at Minneapolis Inst Arts. *Collections Arranged:* Frontiers in Fiber, US Info Agency tour to Asia, 88-90; Shields of the American Indian and others. *Pos:* Founder & dir, NDak Mus Art, 70-; reviewer, Inst Mus Servs, Wash, 90, 91; USIA Int Progs, 91, Nat Endowment Arts, 91; vis specialist, Nat Mus Jakarta, 90; vis critic, Univ Hawaii, 92; served on numerous panels & as juror for founds & art groups including the MacArthur Found, Chicago. *Teaching:* Lectured and conducted workshops at 13 nat mus in Pacific Rim countries & China. *Awards:* Mus Internship Fel, Minneapolis Inst Arts, 72; Nat Endowment Arts Mus Prof Fel, 73, 90. *Mem:* Am Asn Mus. *Publ:* Auth, Walls: Gerhardt Knodel Installation, Am Craft, Oct/Nov, 91; exhib catalog essay for Chinese artist Xu Bing, summer, 92; critical essay for exhib catalog on contemp basketry, Univ Hawaii, spring, 93; coauth, Whole Cloth, MIT Press, 93; numerous mag articles & exhib catalogs with essays. *Mailing Add:* 321 Princeton Grand Forks ND 58202

REVINGTON BURDICK, BETTY
COLLECTOR
Collection: Modern American painting and sculpture exhibited at major museums throughout the United States. *Mailing Add:* 3000 Woodkirk Dr Columbia MO 65203

REVOR, REMY
DESIGNER, EDUCATOR
b Chippewa Falls, Wis, Sept 17, 14. *Study:* Mt Mary Col, BA; Sch Art Inst Chicago, BFA & MFA. *Work:* Milwaukee Art Ctr; St Paul Art Ctr, Minn; Mus Tex Tech Univ; Sheldon Art Gallery. *Comn:* Col Notre Dame Maryland, Baltimore. *Exhib:* Wis Designer Craftsmen Ann, 53-72; Mus Contemp Crafts, New York, 62, 63 & 66-68; Wichita Art Asn, 64; Chicago Pub Libr, 64 & 74. *Teaching:* Prof textile design, Mt Mary Col, 52-70, prof, 70-; instr textile design, Arrowmont Sch Arts & Crafts, Gatlinburg, Tenn, summers 69-88; vis lectr, Univ Tenn, Knoxville, 73-74; instr, Sch Am Craftsmen, Rochester Inst Technol, NY, summer 79; Notre Dame Women's Col, Kyoto, Japan, 80. *Awards:* Louis Comfort Tiffany Found Award Textiles, 62; Am Inst Architects Gold Medal Award Craftsmanship, 67; Fulbright Award Res Textile Design, Finland, 69-70. *Mem:* Wis Designer Craftsmen (publ chmn, 66-68); Col Art Asn Am; Am Craft Coun. *Mailing Add:* Mt Mary Col Milwaukee WI 53222

REXROTH, NANCY LOUISE
PHOTOGRAPHER
b Washington, DC, June 27, 46. *Study:* Marietta Col, Ohio, 64-65; Am Univ, BFA, 65-69; Ohio Univ, MFA(photog), 69-71. *Work:* Mus Mod Art, New York; Smithsonian Inst & Libr Cong, Wash, DC; Biblioteque Nat, Paris, France; Ctr Creative Photog, Tucson, Ariz; Houston Mus Fine Arts. *Exhib:* One-person shows, Corcoran Gallery Art, Washington, DC, 73, Light Gallery, 75, 77 & 80, Grapestake Gallery, San Francisco, 78 & Ctr Creative Photog, Tucson, 82; Baltimore Mus Art, Md, 73; Smithsonian Inst, Washington, DC, 73; Halstead 381 Gallery, Birmingham, Mich, 77; Int Ctr Photog, New York, 78; Nat Mus Am Art, Washington, DC, 84. *Teaching:* Instr beginning-advan photog, Antioch Col, Yellow Springs, Ohio, 77-79 & Wright State Univ, 79-82. *Awards:* Nat Endoment for the Arts Award, 72; Ohio Arts Coun Grant, 81. *Bibliog:* Janis Crystal Lipzin (dir), Trepanations (film). *Mem:* Soc Photog Educ; Am Asn Univ Women. *Media:* Photography. *Publ:* Auth, IOWA, 76 & The Platintotype 1977, 76, Violet Press; contribr, The Diana and the Nikon, Godine, 79; contribr, The Platinum Print, Graphic Arts Res Ctr-RIT, 80; and others. *Mailing Add:* 1228 South 24th St Arlington VA 22202

REYNARD, CAROLYN COLE
PAINTER, INSTRUCTOR
b Wichita, Kans, Aug 6, 34. *Study:* Wichita State Univ, BFA; Ohio Univ, MFA. *Work:* Wichita State Univ; State Univ NY Col Oswego. *Exhib:* Exhibition 80, Huntington Galleries, WVa, 57-59; Santa Barbara Art Mus, Calif, 60; Artists of Santa Barbara, Faulkner Gallery, Santa Barbara, 60-62; Artists of Central New York, Munson-Williams-Proctor Inst Mus Art, Utica, NY, 64-65 & 67; Mid-Hudson Armory Show, 90-91. *Teaching:* Instr art, Ohio Univ, 58-59; asst prof art, State Univ NY, Col Oswego, 63-69; instr art, Wappingers Cent Sch Dist, NY, 69-, adminr/coordr fine arts dept, 78-79. *Mem:* NY State Art Teachers Asn; Dutchess Co Art Asn. *Media:* Acrylic. *Publ:* Auth, I can't draw, 71 & Getting it all together, 74, Sch Arts. *Mailing Add:* 110 College Ave Poughkeepsie NY 12603

REYNOLDS, JAMES ELWOOD
PAINTER
b Taft, Calif, Nov 9, 26. *Study:* Kann Inst Art, Beverly Hills, Calif; Sch Allied Arts, Glendale, Calif. *Work:* Phoenix Art Mus, Ariz; Cowboy Hall Fame, Oklahoma City; Mus Southwest, Midland, Tex. *Comn:* Design gold & silver medals Cowboy Artists Am 8th Ann Exhib & future competitions, Cowboy Artists Am & Franklin Mint, 73; painting used by Marlboro for spec Christmas advert, Philip Morris Co, 7 & 85; plus many others paintings. *Exhib:* Cowboy Hall Fame, Oklahoma City, 69-73; Ann Cowboy Artists Am Show, Phoenix Art Mus, 73-75; Texas Art Gallery; Settlers West Gallery; O'Briens Gallery; Main Trail Gallery. *Teaching:* Instr, Scottsdale Artist's Sch, 83 & 84. *Awards:* Gold Medal First Prize, Cowboy Hall Fame, 71 & 78; Most Outstanding Western Painter, 74-75; Artist of the Yr, Tucson Festival of Arts, Ariz, 77; plus others. *Mem:* Cowboy Artists Am (secy, 72-73, vpres, 74-75, pres, 75-76); Western Art Asn, Phoenix; Ariz Artists in Action. *Media:* Oil. *Publ:* Contribr, Cowboy in Art, 68; West & Walter Bisom, Univ Ariz, 71; American cowboy in life & legend, Nat Geographic, 72; Renaissance of Western Art, Franklin Mint, 74; Western Painting Today, Watson-Guptill, 75. *Mailing Add:* c/o O'Brien's Art Emporium 7122 Stetson Dr Scottsdale AZ 85251

REYNOLDS, JOCK
DIRECTOR, WRITER
Study: Harvard Univ, AB, 66, MAT, 67. *Work:* Center Gallery, Bucknell Univ, Lewisburg, Pa; Freedman Gallery, Albright Col, Reading, Pa; Anderson Gallery, Va Commonwealth Univ, Richmond; Washington Project for Arts, Washington, DC. *Collections Arranged:* The First Texas Triennial, 88, Works From a Decade (with catalog), 88, The Border/La Frontera, 89, Everyday Miracles, 90 & Happy Families (with catalog), 90, Contemp Arts Mus, Houston, Tex. *Teaching:* Asst prof art hist, Bucknell Univ, Lewisburg, Pa, 74-77, Albright Col, Reading, Pa, 77-81 & Va Commonwealth Univ, 81-86. *Res:* Contemporary art with sepecial interest in social and political content. *Publ:* Auth & ed, Sue Coe: Police State, 87 & Hunt Slonem: Baroque Beatitudes, 87, Va Commonwealth Univ; Belchite/South Bronx, Univ Mass, 88; Bill Viola: Works From a Decade, 88 & Ida Applebrong: Happy Families, 90, Contemp Art Mus, Houston. *Mailing Add:* c/o Phillips Acad Addison Gallery Am Art Andover MA 01810

REYNOLDS, PATRICIA ELLEN
PAINTER
b Portchester, NY, April 6, 34. *Study:* State Univ NY; studied with Mario Cooper, 79, Barbara Necchia, 81 & Jeanne Dobie, 82. *Work:* Temple Univ; State Vt, Montpelier; IBM Corp, Burlington, Vt; Gen Electric Corp, Schenectady, NY; Int Trade & Commerce, Montreal, Que & Waitsfield, Vt; and others. *Comn:* Acrylic collage mural, Pizzagalli Construction Corp, Burlington, Vt, 79. *Exhib:* Solo exhib, US Nat Tour Univs, 82-84; Mid-West Watercolor Soc, Davenport Art Gallery, Iowa, 83, 89 & 92; Allied Artists Exhib, 87 & 91; State Univ NY; Hyde Collection; Cayuga Mus; Remington Mus; Headley-Whitney Mus, 90-91; and many others. *Pos:* Treas, Adirondack Art Asn, 62-65, dir gallery, 66-77; consult, Coun Arts (Essex & Clinton Co). *Awards:* Award, Midwest Watercolor Soc, 92; Award, State Univ New York Multi-Focus, 92; Award, Adirondack Park Centennial Exhib, 92; and many others. *Bibliog:* Peg Byrne (auth), Patricia Reynolds experiments, Adirondack Life Mag, 71; JoAnn Taylor (producer), Patricia Reynolds Work, Educ TV, 79-81; Mal Boright (interviewer), Good Morning Am, 81; NY Art Rev, 88; Morning Line (radio interview). *Mem:* Mid-West Watercolor Soc; Watercolor Soc, Cent NY, Asn Am & Nat; assoc Allied Artists Am. *Media:* All Media. *Dealer:* Hobe Sound Galleries Hobe Sound FL & Brunswick ME; Hales Gallery Glens Falls NY. *Mailing Add:* East Side Studio Point Rd Willsboro NY 12996

REYNOLDS, RICHARD (HENRY)
SCULPTOR, PAINTER
b New York, NY, May 16, 13. *Study:* San Bernardino Valley Col, AA, 33; Univ Calif, Berkeley, BA, 36, Life General Secondary teaching cert, 39; Univ Calif, Los Angeles, 39; Mills Col, with Moholy-Nagy, 40; Univ Pac, Calif, MA, 42; Rudolph Schaefer Sch; Ore State Univ, Shell grant; Morningside Col, Sioux City, Iowa, Hon DFA, 76. *Comn:* Steel Viking symbol, Edison High Sch, Stockton, Calif, 64; life-size metal Bengal tiger & bronze relief, Univ Pac, 65; cast stone buffalo, Manteca Union High Sch, Calif, 65; bronze relief, New Wing, Stockton Rec Bldg, 66 & Swenson Golf Course, Stockton, 66; bronze relief, San Joaquin Gen Hosp, 86. *Exhib:* Northern Calif Arts Painting Open, Sacramento, 70, 80-81 & 83; Stockton Art League Ann Exhib, Haggin Mus, 74-88; Crocker-Kingsley 57th Ann Exhib, Sacramento, 80 & 82; 21st Ann Lodi Exhib, 81-84; Am Nat Miniature Show, 84-86. *Teaching:* Instr art & asst chmn div arts & lett, Stockton Col, 39-48; prof art, Univ Pac, Calif, 48-80, chmn dept art, 48-73, sr prof, 73-80; guest prof art educ, Univ Idaho, summer

54; guest lectr, Alaska Methodist Univ, 62; retired, 80; columnist, Golden Palette, Senior Spectrum newspaper, San Joaquin Valley edition, 90-92. *Awards:* Sculpture Prizes, Crocker-Kingsley Exhib, Sacramento, 80 & 82; Purchase Awards, Lodi Acampo Shows, 80-82; Second Prize Painting, Unitarian Ann Art Fest. *Mem:* Life fel Int Inst Arts & Lett; hon mem Stockton Art League (pres, 52-53 & 80-82). *Media:* Wood, Stone; Mixed Media. *Publ:* Contribr, Arts & Archit, 1/48; auth, A plea for wider distribution of art values, Col Art J, winter 51-52; A buffalo sculpture for a California high school, Am Artist, 1/66; Auto paint art, Design, spring 73; contribr poster design, fall 74 & cover design, 83, Pythian Mag; and others. *Mailing Add:* 1656 W Longview Ave Stockton CA 95207

REYNOLDS, ROBERT
PAINTER, EDUCATOR
b San Luis Obispo, Calif, Mar 7, 36. *Study:* Art Ctr Col of Design, Los Angeles, Calif, BPA; Calif Polytech State Univ, San Luis Obispo, MA; also with Lorser Fettelson, Harry Carmean, Robert Clark, Arne Nybak & Joe Henninger. *Work:* San Luis Obispo Co, Calif; Mus Nat Hist, Morro Bay, Calif; Mus Nat Hist, Santa Barbara, Calif; Calif Polytechnic Univ, San Luis Obispo; over 1200 pvt collections. *Comn:* large mural, Mus Natural Hist, Morro Bay, Calif, 82; ltd ed print, Natural Hist Asn Central Coast, Calif, 82; painting & prints, Mozart Festival, San Luis Obispo, Calif, 88; paintings & serigraphs, San Luis Obispo Co Symphony, 88; post card stamp design, US Postal Serv, 88. *Exhib:* Int Wildlife Art Show, Safari Club Int, Las Vegas, Nev, 75-78; solo exhibs, retrospective, Art Ctr, San Luis Obispo, 75, Allan Hancock Col, Santa Maria, 80, Clark Galleries, Bakersfield, 88, Hutchins Gallery, Cambria, 88 & 90, Calif Polytechnic Univ Union Galeria: Sierra Suite, 89 & Vision Art Gallery, Morro Bay, Calif, 91; traveling exhib, Ford Motor Co, Dearborn, Mich, 77-78; Cunningham Art Mus Watercolor Exhib, Bakersfield, Calif, 78; and many other group & one-man shows. *Pos:* Pres, Art Asn, San Luis Obispo, Calif, 68-69; mem design & review bd, City of San Luis Obispo, 68-73; mem bd of trustees, San Luis Obispo Art Ctr, 69-78; founding mem, Cent Coast Watercolor Soc, Calif, 77-, pres, 80-81. *Teaching:* Prof art, drawing & painting, Dept Art, Calif Polytech State Univ, 64-, actg dept head, 82-83, chmn, dept art & design, 84-86; art instr drawing & painting, Evening Div, Cuesta Community Col, 72-76. *Awards:* Award, Calif Survey Drawing & Watercolork Humboldt Cult Ctr, Eureka, Calif, 83; Distinguished Teaching Award, Calif Polytech Univ, 88-89. *Bibliog:* Watercolor Page, Am Artist, 3/88; Mary Ann Travathan (auth), An artist whose time has come, San Luis Rev, 3/88; cover/feature article, the Artist's Mag, 90. *Mem:* Artist's Equity. *Media:* Multimedia. *Publ:* Illusr, VEP Productions, Calif Polytechnic State Univ, 64-74; illusr, Vocational Report, Vocational Div State of Calif, 67; contribr, WestCoast Graphics, WestArt, 70; illusr, Disappearing windmill, 74 & California Mendocino Coast, 77, Ford Times, Ford Motor Co. *Mailing Add:* 958 Skyline Dr San Luis Obispo CA 93401

REYNOLDS, STEPHEN FRANCIS
PAINTER, SCULPTOR
b Royal Oak, Mich, Aug 24, 50. *Study:* Univ Mich, BFA, 72; Univ Art Inst Chicago, MFA, 77. *Work:* Prudential, NJ; McDonalds, NY. *Exhib:* Chicago Art Perspective: Chicago Area Invitational Navy Pier, 80; Collection Artists Select: State Ill Gallery, Chicago, 85; Emerging: Renaissance Soc Invitational, State Ill Gallery, Chicago, 85. *Pos:* Recording secy, bd mem, Exhibs comt, Randolph St Gallery, Chicago, 85-86. *Awards:* Nat Endowment Arts Grant, 87. *Bibliog:* James Yood (auth), An emerging, New Art Examiner, 85; Deven Golden (auth), review, New Art Examiner, 86; Barbara Glass (auth), Tastemakers accent, Inside Chicago Mag, 89. *Mem:* Art Inst Chicago. *Media:* Oil; All Media. *Publ:* L J Douglas (ed), Chicago Art Write (essay), 88. *Mailing Add:* 1101 N Paulina Chicago IL 60622

REYNOLDS, VALRAE
CURATOR
b San Francisco, Calif, Dec 18, 44. *Study:* Univ Calif, Davis, BA, 66; New York Univ, MA, 68, cert mus training, 69. *Collections Arranged:* Chinese Art from the Newark Museum, China Inst, 80; Tibet, A Lost World (auth, catalog), 81-82 & Japan, The Enduring Heritage, 83, Newark Mus; 16 permanent galleries of Asian Art, Newark Mus, 89. *Pos:* Ford Fel arms & armor dept, Metrop Mus Art, New York, fall 68; Ford Fel Islamic ceramics, Asian Art Mus, San Francisco, spring 69; asst cur Oriental collection, Newark Mus, 69-70, cur Oriental collection, 70- *Awards:* Nat Endowment Humanities Grant Film Production, 72-74; Nat Endowment Arts Grant Publ, 82-83 & 85-86; J Paul Getty Grant Publ, 86, 88-91; Nat Endowment Arts Special Artistic Initiative Grant galleries & programs, 88; Asian Cult Coun grants, travel, 89; Nat Endowment Humanities galleries & progs, 90-91. *Mem:* Comt SAsian Art; Asia Soc; Japan Soc; China Inst Am; Tibet Soc. *Res:* Arts of Tibet, India and Himalayas. *Publ:* Auth, Journey to Tibet: Dr Albert L Shelton, Newark Mus, spring-summer 72; Tibet, A Lost World, Ind Univ Press, 79; Chinese Art from the Newark Museum, China Inst, 80; The Newark Museum Tibetan Collection, Vol I, 83 & Vol III, 86; Japan, the enduring heritage, Newark Mus Quart, 83. *Mailing Add:* Newark Mus 43 Washington St Newark NJ 07101

REYNOLDS, WADE
PAINTER
b Jasper, NY, 1929. *Study:* Self-taught. *Work:* Santa Barbara Mus Art, Calif; Cleveland Mus Art, Ohio; Miami Inst Fine Art, Fla; Times-Mirror Corp, Los Angeles. *Comn:* Official Portrait Gov Deukmejian, State of Calif, 89. *Exhib:* Solo Exhib, Realism, Calif Palace Legion Honor, 67-68 & California Visions, Santa Barbara Mus, Calif, 77; Prints, Miami Inst Art, 79; Retrospective, Pioneer Mus, Stockton, Calif, 82; Selections from Ellen & Jerome Westheimer Collection, Okla Art Ctr, 88. *Awards:* Best Show, Madonna Festival, San Luis Obispo, Calif, 77 & Miami Print Biennial, 79. *Bibliog:* Frankenstein (auth), New realists, San Francisco Chronicle, 67; Stowens (auth), Intense realism, Am Artist, 1/81; Pincus (auth), Los Angeles Times, 6/25/82. *Media:* Oil, Acrylic. *Publ:* Auth, Painting Faces and Figures, Carole Katchen/Watson-Guptil, 86. *Dealer:* Gallery Henoch 80 Wooster St New York NY 10012; Louis Newman Galleries 322 N Beverly Dr Beverly Hills CA 90210. *Mailing Add:* 14844 Mission Glen Lane Sylmar CA 91342

REZAC, RICHARD
CONCEPTUAL ARTIST
b Lincoln, Nebr, 1952. *Study:* Pacific Northwest Col Art, Portland, Ore, BFA, 74; Md Inst, Col Art, Baltimore, MFA, 82. *Exhib:* Solo exhib, Sculpture Chicago, 86, Susanne Hilberry Gallery, Birmingham, Mich, 87 & 89, Feature, Chicago, 87 & Loughelton Gallery, New York, 88 & 89 & Mus Contemp Art, Chicago, 90, Susanne Hilberry Gallery, Birmingham, Mich, 92, Feature, New York, 92; Sculptors' Drawings, Sculpt Ctr, New York, 88; Tenth Anniversary Exhib, Blackfish Gallery, Portland, Ore, 89; Function-Non-Function, Rezac Gallery, Chicago, Ill, 89; Apfelbaum, Rezac, Smith, Ctr Contemp Art, Chicago, 89; Grounded: Sculpture on the Floor, Univ Mich Mus Art, Ann Arbor, 90; New Generations: Chicago, Carnegie Mellon Univ Art Gallery, Pittsburgh, Pa, 90; Feigen Inc, Chicago, Ill, 91; Northern Ill Univ Art Mus, DeKalb, 92; Chicago Artists, Feigen Inc, Chicago, Ill, 92. *Pos:* Gallery dir, Pacific Northwest Col Art, Portland, Ore, 77-80. *Teaching:* Instr painting & Design, Mt Hood Community Col, Creshaw, Ore, 79-80 & Portland State Univ, Ore, 82-83; instr drawing & design, Pacific Northwest Col Art, Portland, 82-84; instr drawing & three-dimensional design, Sch Art Inst Chicago, Ill, 85-; vis artist, Univ Chicago, 86, 88 & 90, adj faculty, 91. *Awards:* Visual Artist Fel Grants, Nat Endowment Arts, 76 & 86 & Ore Arts Comn, 83; Art in Public Places Grant, Metrop Arts Comn, Portland, Ore, 77; Prof Grants, Art Matters Inc, New York, 87 & Chicago Artists Abroad, Ill, 88; fel grant, John Simon Guggenheim Mem Found, 89. *Bibliog:* Peter Frank (auth), Art Pick of the Week, LA Weekly, 125, 2/15 & 2/21/91; Alan Artner (auth), Rezac's Uncanny Take on Japanese Sources Stand Out (reproduction), Chicago Tribune, 9/20/91; Susan Snodgrass (auth), review, Sculpture, 57, 1-2/92. *Mailing Add:* 2251 W Thomas St Chicago IL 60622

RHODEN, JOHN W
SCULPTOR
b Birmingham, Ala, 1918. *Study:* With Richmond Barthe, 38; Columbia Univ Sch Painting & Sculpture, with Oronzio Maldarelli, Hugo Robus & William Zorach. *Work:* Stockholm Mus; Carl Milles Collection; Heinz Collection, Pittsburgh; Steinberg Colletion, St Louis, Mo; Del Mus, Wilmington; and many others. *Comn:* monumental bronze, Harlem Hosp, New York; bronze & jewel glass monumental sculpture, Pub Sch 223, Queens, NY; monumental bronze, Frederick Douglass, 89; monumental bronze, Rev Fred L Shuttleworth, Birmingham, Ala; and others. *Exhib:* Metrop Mus Art; Audubon Ann; Pa Acad Fine Arts; Nat Acad Design; Am Acad Arts; retrospective, Ala Mus, Birmingham, 85. *Pos:* Specialist, US Dept State Tour Iceland, Europe & NAfrica, 55-56; mem artist deleg, US Dept State Tour USSR, Poland & Yugoslavia, 59 & Asia, 60; consult, Seni-Rupa Inst Teknol, Bandung, Indonesia, 62; mem, Nat Screening Comt, Fulbright-Hays Inst, 83-85; art comn, City New York, 92-95. *Teaching:* Artist-in-residence, Albany State Col, Ga, 86 & Montclair State Col, NJ. *Awards:* Distinguished Serv Award, Inst Int Educ, 86; Rosenwald Fel; Fulbright Fel, Prix de Rome, Am Acad Rome. *Mem:* Life mem Munic Art Soc; Am Soc Contemp Artists. *Media:* Mixed. *Mailing Add:* 23 Cranberry St Brooklyn NY 11201

RHODES, CURTIS A
PAINTER, PRINTMAKER
b Butler, Mo, Nov 5, 39. *Study:* Univ Kans, BFA, 62; Ohio Univ, MFA, 66. *Work:* Univ Kans Art Mus, Lawrence; Flint Inst Art, Mich; Grand Rapids Art Mus, Mich; Kalamazoo Art Ctr, Mich; Trisolini Gallery, Ohio Univ. *Comn:* Multi-color lithograph, Oxbox Sch Art, Sagituck, Mich, 73; multi-color photo-etching, Detroit Print Workshop, Mich, 76; five multicolor lithographs, comn by Terry Allen, 81; four multicolor lithographs, comn by Ed Paschke, 85. *Exhib:* Butler Ann, Butler Inst Art, Youngstown, Ohio, 60; And Another, Western Mich Univ, Kalamazoo, 66; Nat Painting & Sculpture Invitational, Flint Inst Art, Mich, 66-67 & 70; Paper as Medium, Smithsonian Invitational & Traveling Exhib, Washington, DC, 79-81. *Collections Arranged:* 3rd Nat Drawing-Prints (auth, catalog), Juried Drawing-Prints, 68; Multiples USA (auth, catalog), Nat Juried Invitational Exhib of Prints, 70; Markings, Major Int Exhib of Prints, 75; Strike/Restrike-The Revitalized Print (with catalog), traveling exhib, 83-86. *Pos:* Visual arts adv, Mich Coun Arts, 75-78. *Teaching:* Prof, Western Mich Univ, Kalamazoo, 66- *Awards:* Nat Endowment Arts Fel, 74-75; Ford Found Awards, 77-82; Mich Coun Arts Fel, 84-85. *Bibliog:* Kathy Clark (auth), Twinrocker: Collaboration in Custom Papermaking, Fine Print, 77 & Pigments and Dyes in Hand Papermaking, Tamarind Tech Papers, 78. *Media:* Color Lithography. *Publ:* Mayan Legends/Replies, Limited Ed, Twinrocker Paper Mill, 81. *Mailing Add:* Dept Art Western Mich Univ Kalamazoo MI 49008

RHODES, JAMES MELVIN
GLASS BLOWER, SCULPTOR
b Gorman, Tex, Dec 1, 38. *Study:* Univ Wis, Mechanical eng; Univ Hawaii, BA. *Work:* State Found on Cult & the Arts, Hawaii. *Comn:* Glass mural, Steven B Dixon, 83. *Exhib:* Honolulu Acad Arts, Hawaii, 72; two-man shows, The Foundry, Honolulu, Hawaii, 72 & 74, Metes & Bounds, Sausalito, Calif, 74, Hand & Eye, Honolulu, 74, Downtown Gallery, Honolulu, Hawaii, 77 & Sculptore, Hawaii, 80; VAC Hawaii, 87. *Pos:* Chmn, Easter Art Festival, Hawaii, 76; vpres, Big Island Artists Guild, Hawaii, 76. *Teaching:* Instr arts & crafts, Schofield Arts & Crafts, Wahiawa, Hawaii, 70-74; instr off hand glass

blowing, The Foundry, Honolulu, Hawaii, 70-74. *Awards:* Am Fac Award, Hawaii Craftsmen Show, 73; Campus Ctr Bd Award, Univ Hawaii Show, Univ Hawaii, 74. *Mem:* Hawaii Concert Soc; E Hawaii Cult Coun. *Media:* Blown glass. *Mailing Add:* Box 1131 Keaau HI 96749

RHODES, REILLY PATRICK
MUSEUM DIRECTOR
b Bloomington, Ill, Mar 28, 41. *Study:* Kansas City Art Inst, BFA, 66; Wichita State Univ, MFA, 68; Sterling Inst, Boston, art gallery mgt, 69; Syracuse Univ, mus mgt, 70; Univ Mo-Columbia, 70. *Pos:* Dir, Albrecht Gallery, St Joseph, Mo, 68-71; dir, Canton Art Inst, Ohio, 71-73 & Charles W Bowers Mem Mus, Santa Ana, Calif, 73-82; dir, Centennial Detroit Inst Arts, MI, 82-83; cur, Mexico, EPCOT Ctr, Walt Disney World, Orlando, Fla, 82-87; exec dir, Nat Art Mus Sport, Indianapolis, Ind, 89- *Mem:* Int Coun Mus; Am Asn Mus; Western Asn Art Mus; Am Fedn Arts; Art Mus Develop Dirs Asn. *Publ:* Auth, Public Relations Catalogue, Albrecht Gallery; auth introd to var catalogs, including L E Shafer Bronzes, An Exhibition of Sculpture & Drawings by O V Shaffer, Moses Soyer: A Selection of Paintings 1960-1970, The Art of Irving Ramsey Wiles (1861-1948) & All Ohio (Canton Art Inst Ann); and others. *Mailing Add:* Nat Art Mus of Sport Bank One Center/Tower Indianapolis IN 46204

RHYNE, CHARLES SYLVANUS
HISTORIAN
b Philadelphia, Pa, Mar 29, 32. *Study:* Wittenberg Col, AB, 54; Univ Chicago, MA, 56, advan study, 56-60; Fulbright fels, Courtauld Inst, Univ London, 62-64. *Work:* Mr & Mrs Paul Mellon; Yale Ctr British Art. *Collections Arranged:* Lee Kelly: Outdoor Pub Sculpture in the Northwest, 10/76, Miriam Schapiro: Anatomy of a Kimono, 4/78 & Francise Grossen: Fiber as Sculpture, 8/78, Reed Col Art Gallery; and others. *Pos:* Chief reader, Advan Placement Prog, Art Hist of Art Educ Testing Serv, Princeton, NJ, 70-75; bd dirs, Portland Ctr for the Visual Arts, 73-80; dir art gallery, Reed Col, 74-80; mem long-range planning comt, Portland Art Mus, 75-77. *Teaching:* Instr art hist & humanities, Reed Col, 60-62, from asst prof to assoc prof art hist, 62-68, prof, 68-; vis teacher art hist, Mus Art Sch, Portland, 74-75. *Awards:* Sr Fel, Ctr Advan Study Visual Arts, Nat Gallery Art; Younger Humanities Fel, Nat Endowment Humanities, 72-73; Resident fel, Yale Ctr for Brit Art, 78; and others. *Mem:* Col Art Asn; sr fel Ctr Adv Study Visual Arts; Soc Archit Historians; Soc of Indust Archaeol; res fel Yale Ctr British Art; Am Inst for Conservation; Int Inst for Conservation. *Res:* History and interpretation of landscape painting: John Constable (preparing catalogue raisonne); architecture of bridges; philosophy and practice of conservation (preparing handbook). *Publ:* Auth, Lionel Constable's East Berlin Sketchbook, Art News, 78; Constable Drawings and Watercolors in the Collections of Mr & Mrs Paul Mellon at the Yale Ctr for Brit Art, Part I, Authentic Works, Part II, reattributed works, Master Drawings, Vol XIX, No 2, 4/81, Discoveries in the Exhibition, Salander-O'Reilly Galleries, New York, 88, Constable's First Two Six-Foot Landscapes, Studies in the History of Art, Nat Gallery Art, Washington, DC, Vol XXIV, 90; John Constable: Toward a Complete Chronology, 90. *Mailing Add:* Reed Col Portland OR 97202

RICCI, JERRI
PAINTER
b Perth Amboy, NJ. *Study:* New York Sch Appl Design for Women, 35; Art Students League, with Scott Williams, George Bridgman, Mahonri Young & others, 35-38. *Work:* Fairleigh Dickinson Col; Parrish Mus, Southampton, NY; Am Acad Arts & Lett; Butler Art Inst, Clark Univ; Addison Gallery Am Art, Andover, Mass; and others. *Exhib:* Toledo Mus Art; Pa Acad Fine Arts; Art Inst Chicago; Dayton Art Inst; Addison Gallery Am Art; and others. *Awards:* Silver Medal, Catharine Lorillard Wolfe Art Club, 54; Clara Obrig Award, Nat Acad Design; Gold Medal, Audubon Artists, 55; and others. *Mem:* Am Watercolor Soc; Allied Artists Am; Assoc Nat Acad Design; Philadelphia Watercolor Club; Audubon Artists; and others. *Mailing Add:* 25 Old Farm Rd Needham MA 03192

RICE, ANTHONY HOPKINS
SCULPTOR, PAINTER
b Angeles Pampanga, Philippine Islands, July 21, 48. *Study:* Va Commonwealth Univ, Richmond, BFA, 70; Univ NC, Chapel Hill, MFA, 72. *Work:* New York Public Libr, New York, NY; Nat Mus Am Art, Smithsonian Inst, Washington, DC. *Comn:* Indoor environmental sculpture, Sarasota Sq Mall, Sarasota, Fla, 89. *Exhib:* New Sculpture, Washington, Baltimore, Richmond, Corcoran Gallery, Washington, DC, 70; Translucent and Transparent Art, St Petersburg Mus Art, Fla, 71; Renwick Gallery, Smithsonian Inst, Washington, DC, 81; Brooklyn Mus Art, New York, 88; Nat Sculpture '89, Libr Congress, Washington, DC, 89; Gallery Camina Real, Boca Raton, Fla, 90; one-man shows, Mary Ryan Gallery, New York, 89, Kathy Albers Gallery, Memphis, Tenn, 90, 92, McIntosh Gallery, Atlanta, Ga, 92. *Teaching:* Chmn, Dept Fine Arts, Ringling Sch Art & Design, Sarasota, Fla, 85-88, fac mem, 85- *Awards:* Visual Arts Fel Award in Painting, Nat Endowment for the Arts. *Bibliog:* Greg Thielew (auth), article, Art Voices, 3/81. *Mem:* Col Art Asn; Am Asn Univ Prof. *Media:* Steel, Wood. *Dealer:* Mary Ryan Gallery New York NY. *Mailing Add:* c/o McIntosh Gallery One Virginia Hill, 587 Virginia Ave Atlanta GA 30306

RICE, EDWARD
PAINTER
b Augusta, Ga, Feb 24, 53. *Study:* Freeman Schoolcraft, 72-80. *Work:* Gibbes Mus Art, Charleston, SC; Morris Mus Art, Augusta, GA; NationsBank, Charlotte, NC; State SC, Columbia; Springs Industries, NY. *Exhib:* Mid America Biennial, Owensboro Mus Art, Ky, 86; South Carolina Realism, Greenville County Mus Art, SC, 87; Mint Museum Biennial, Charlotte, NC, 88; Southern Arts Fedn/Nat Endowment for Arts Regional Fel Exhib, Atlanta Col Art Gallery, 89 & Louisianna Arts & Science Center, Baton Rouge, 90; SC Arts Commission Fel Retrospective, SC State Mus, Columbia, 90; solo exhib, Tree Paintings, Heath Gallery, Atlanta, 90. *Awards:* Merit Award, Mint Mus Biennial, Charlotte, NC, 88; SC Arts Commission Visual Arts Fel, 88; Nat Endowment for Arts Regional Fel, Southern Arts Fedn, 88. *Bibliog:* Charles A Twady (auth), Paint it contemporary, The State, 3/89; Catherine Fox (auth), Fellowship winners show individualism, Atlanta J-Constitution, 6/14/89; David Houston (auth), Edward Rice, New Art Examiner, 10/89; James Rosen (auth), Tree paintings, Art Papers, 6/90; Jeffrey Day (auth), Resurrecting the mundane, The State, 3/1/92. *Dealer:* Heath Gallery Inc 416 E Paces Ferry Rd Atlanta GA 30305; Hodges Taylor Gallery 227 N Tryon St Charlotte NC 28202. *Mailing Add:* 502 Lucerne Ave North Augusta SC 29841

RICE, M ROBERT & BARBARA MENEN
DEALERS, COLLECTORS
b New York, NY. *Pos:* Owners, Robert Rice Gallery, Houston. *Specialty:* Nineteenth and twentieth century American/French traditional. *Collection:* Hassem, Potthast, Carlson, Martha Walter, W M Chase, A Bierstadt, Boldini, Jean Bernaud, F Freiseke, F Church, T Cole, M Luce and K Von Dongen. *Publ:* Ed, C K Chatterton, 77 & ed, Emil Carlson, NA, 78, Graphics Houston; ed, William S Horton, Fox Press, 79; ed, Gallery Collection, 82; ed, Thomas Cole and Frederick Church, 83; and others. *Mailing Add:* 2627 Kipling Houston TX 77098

RICE, NANCY NEWMAN See Newman-Rice, Nancy

RICE, NORMAN LEWIS
PAINTER, EDUCATOR
b Aurora, Ill, July 22, 05. *Study:* Univ Ill, BA, 26; Art Inst Chicago, 26-30. *Pos:* From asst dean to dean, Art Inst Chicago, 30-43; dir, Sch Art, Syracuse Univ, 46-54; dean, Col Fine Arts, Carnegie-Mellon Univ, 54-72, emer dean, 72- *Teaching:* Instr drawing & design, Art Inst Chicago, 28-43; prof painting, Syracuse Univ, 46-54; prof painting & hist art, Carnegie-Mellon Univ, 54-73; dean, prof emeritus, Col Fine Arts, 73. *Mem:* Fel Nat Asn Schs Art & Design; fel Am Coun Arts in Educ; plus others. *Media:* Paint, Print. *Mailing Add:* 201 East End Ave (1) Pittsburgh PA 15221

RICE, SHELLEY ENID
CRITIC, HISTORIAN
b Bronx, NY, Aug 20, 50. *Study:* Smith Col, 68-69; State Univ NY, Stony Brook, BA(summa cum laude), 72; Inst Fine Arts, New York Univ, MA, 75; Princeton Univ. *Pos:* Photog critic, Village Voice, 76-77; columnist, SoHo Weekly News, 78-79; freelance curator, 78-; staff writer, Artforum Mag, 80-82. *Teaching:* Instr art hist, Brooklyn Col, NY, 72-77; mem fac photog hist & criticism, Sch of Visual Arts, New York, 75-78 & 81-; instr art hist & criticism, Tyler Sch Art, Temple Univ, 78-80; adj asst prof photog, New York Univ, 82- *Awards:* Nat Endowment Arts Art Critics Fel, 80; NY State Coun Arts Video Writing Grants, 82 & 83; Nat Endowment Humanities Travel to Collections Grant, 85. *Mem:* Womens Caucus Art; Col Art Asn; Am Sect Int Asn Art Critics. *Res:* Historical and contemporary photography; contemporary multi-media art. *Publ:* Auth, Essential differences: A comparison of the portraits of Lisette Model and Diane Arbus, Artforum, 5/80; Deconstruction-Reconstruction (catalog), New Mus, New York, 7/80; Schemes: A Decade of Installation Drawings (catalog), Elise Meyer Gallery, New York, 6/81; Fields of Vision (exhib catalog), Landmarks, Bard Col, 84. *Mailing Add:* Sch Visual Arts New York NY 10010

RICH, FRANCES L
SCULPTOR, DRAFTSMAN
b Spokane, Wash, Jan 8, 10. *Study:* Smith Col, BA, 31; sculpture with Malvina Hoffman, drawing & frescoes with Angel Zarraga, Paris, France, 33-35; Beaux Art Acad; Boston Mus Sch, with Alexander Iacovleff, 35-36; Cranbrook Acad Art, sculpture with Carl Milles, 37-40; Claremont Col, with Millard Sheets, 46; Columbia Univ, 47. *Work:* Palm Springs Desert Mus, Calif; Santa Catalina Sch, Monterey, Calif; bronze portrait head, Virgil Thomson, Thomson Rm, NY Univ; also pvt collection of Father Edward Boyle, Holy Trinity Church, Bremerton, Wash; Bronze Portrait Head, Virgil Thomson, Thomson Rm, NY Univ. *Comn:* Christ of the Sacred Heart, St Sebastian's Church, West Los Angeles, 74; bronze plaque honoring Dr Mario Gonzalez Ulloa, 77; 15 bronze flying birds, Aviary Wall, Living Desert Reserve, Palm Desert, Calif, 78; nine bronzes, Cranbrook Acad Art Mus, 81; and others. *Exhib:* One-man shows, Santa Barbara Mus Art, 52, Calif Palace Legion Hon, 55, Palm Springs Desert Mus, 69 & 77; Calif Relig Artists, De Young Mem, 52; Lenten Exhib Liturgical Arts, Denver Art Mus, 55; Smith Col Mus Art, 81. *Bibliog:* Articles in Liturgical Arts Quart; Sculpture of Frances Rich, Manzanita Press, 74; and others. *Mem:* Archit League New York; Alumna Cranbrook Acad Art. *Media:* Bronze, Stone. *Mailing Add:* 1208 E Bolivar St Payson AZ 85541

RICH, GARRY LORENCE
PAINTER
b Newton Co, Mo, Nov 11, 43. *Study:* Kansas City Art Inst, BFA; New York Univ, MA. *Work:* Whitney Mus Am Art, New York, NY; Aldrich Mus Contemp Art, Ridgefield, Conn; Phoenix Art Mus, Ariz; Nelson Gallery Art, Kansas City, Mo; Miami Art Ctr, Fla. *Exhib:* Whitney Mus Am Art Ann, 71; Highlights of the Season, Aldrich Mus Contemp Art, Ridgefield, 71; one-man shows, Max Hutchinson Gallery, New York, 71-72, 74, 77, 79, 81, 83 & 85, Henri Gallery, Washington, DC, 72 & Gallery A, Sydney, Australia, 72. *Teaching:* Asst prof painting, New York Univ, 65-71, Hofstra Univ, 71-72 &

Bard Col, 72. *Awards:* Max Beckman fel, Brooklyn Mus, 66; Nat Coun Arts Award, 67; Nat Endowment Art, 74. *Bibliog:* Domingo (auth), Color abstractionism, 12/70 & Bowling (auth), Color & recent painting, 72, Arts Mag; Ratcliff (auth), Young New York painters, Art News, 70. *Mailing Add:* 167 Crosby St New York NY 10012

RICHARD, JACK
PAINTER, RESTORER
b Akron, Ohio, Mar 7, 22. *Study:* Chicago Prof Sch Art, scholar; Univ Ohio, Athens; Kent Univ; Akron Univ; also with R Brackman, A Bohrod, Y Kunioshi, B Shahn, J Carroll & many others. *Work:* Canton Art Inst, Ohio; Umbaugh Pole Bldg Collection, Ravenna, Ohio; Woodrum Ins Collection, Stow, Ohio. *Comn:* President & Mrs Eisenhower, Tupperware Int, Orlando, Fla; murals, Central Christian Church Kettering, Dayton; Valley Savings & Loan, Cuyahoga Falls; mural, First United Church of Christ, Akron; portraits, comn by Bing & Cathrine Crosby, Byron Nelson, Juan Rodrigues, President Gerald Ford, Bob Hope, Dinah Shore, Arnold Palmer & Nancy Lopez. *Exhib:* Retrospective, Ambassador Col, Pasadena, 70; City Ctr Gallery, New York; Fifty Am Artists, Gallerie Int & Salmagundi Club, New York; Butler Inst Am Art Nat, Youngstown, Ohio. *Pos:* Illusr, Stevens-Gross Studios, Chicago. *Teaching:* Instr painting & design & dir, Cuyahoga Valley Art Ctr, Cuyahoga Falls, 53-63; instr, Woman's City Club, Akron, Ohio, 60-; instr painting & design & dir, Almond Tea Galleries, Cuyahoga Falls, 63-; instr, Madison Sch Art, Conn, 81. *Awards:* Purchase Award & Second Award Painting, Canton Art Inst; Best in Show Award, Akron Art Inst, 48; Huntington Hartford Fel, 58. *Bibliog:* Six Rotos, Beacon J, Knight Newspapers; M M (auth), Jack Richard Al Lavoro, Il Pungold Verde, Italy, 74. *Mem:* Artists, Ohio; Ohio Arts & Crafts Guild; Tri-County Art Soc, Ohio; Akron Soc Artists; Cuyahoga Valley Art Ctr. *Media:* Acrylic, Oil. *Interests:* Assisting in training of young artists and rehabilitation use of arts. *Collection:* R Brackman, L Grell, R Skemp, G Eluegren, D Cornwell, Ball, Japanese Prints, A Loomis & 60 others. *Publ:* Illusr, Staley J, Ind, 43-45; The Helm Mag; Ohio Edison Ann Report, 60; Ohio Story, TV prog, Ohio Bell Tel. *Mailing Add:* c/o Almond Tea Galleries 2250 Front St Cuyahoga Falls OH 44221

RICHARD, PAUL
CRITIC
b Chicago, Ill, Nov, 22, 39. *Study:* Harvard Col, BA, 61; Univ Pa Grad Sch Fine Arts. *Pos:* Art critic, Washington Post, DC, 67- *Mailing Add:* 1673 Columbia Rd NW Washington DC 20009

RICHARDS, BILL
PAINTER
b Grantsville, WVa, July 15, 36. *Study:* Ohio Univ, with Dwight Mutchler, BFA; Ind Univ, with Leon Golub & James McGarrell, MFA; Skowhegan Sch Painting & Sculpture. *Work:* Philadelphia Mus Art; Brooklyn Mus & Guggenheim Mus, New York; NJ State Mus Art, Trenton; Westinghouse Corp, Pittsburgh; and others. *Comn:* Diptych painting & performance, The Travelers Corp, Commercial, 86. *Exhib:* Friends Collect 20th Century, Philadelphia Mus Art, 67; Pa Acad Fine Arts Ann, 68; Whitney Mus Am Art Biennial, 75; one-man shows, Marian Locks Gallery, Philadelphia, 75, Olympia Galleries Ltd, Philadelphia, 76 & Ohio Univ, Athens, 79; 19 Artists--Emergent Americans, Exxon Nat Exhib, Guggenheim Mus, 81; Westinghouse Collection, Loch Haven Art Ctr, Orlando, Fla, 83; New York Painting Today, Three Rivers Arts Festival, Pittsburgh, 83; Pa Acad Fine Arts, 85; Traveling Exhib, US & Canada, Independent Curators, Inc, 85-87; Painting, Beyond the Death of Painting, Kuznetsky Most Exhib Hall, Moscow, USSR, 89. *Pos:* Originator & dir Harlem Horizon Art Studio, Harlem Hosp Ctr, New York, 88- *Teaching:* Assoc prof, Moore Col Art, 67-81, prof, 81-82. *Bibliog:* Victoria Donohoe (auth), rev in Philadelphia Inquirer, 5/75; Ann Jarmusch (auth), article, Art News 1/77; Peter Frank (auth), article, Art Am, 3/77. *Media:* Acrylic. *Mailing Add:* 40 W 24th St New York NY 10010

RICHARDS, BILL (WILLIAM A)
DRAFTSMAN
b Brooklyn, NY, Sept 19, 44. *Study:* Pratt Inst, BFA, 66; Univ Iowa, MA, 68; Univ NMex, MFA, 70. *Work:* Chase Manhattan Bank, New York; Ill Bell Tel, Chicago; Asheville Art Mus, NC. *Exhib:* On Paper, Va Mus Fine Arts, 80; The American Landscape: Recent Developments, Whitney Mus Am Art Fairfield Co Br, Stamford, Conn, 81; Contemporary American Realism Since 1960, Pa Acad Fine Arts, Va Mus Fine Arts, Oakland Mus Art & mus in Europe, 81-83; Nature Transformed, Anderson Gallery, Va Commonwealth Univ, 82; solo exhibs, Hite Art Inst, Univ Louisville, 83 & Moravian Col, Bethleham, Pa, 85; American Realism, Twentieth Century Drawings and Watercolors, San Francisco Mus Mod Art, 85; Tomasulo Gallery, Union Col, Cranford, NJ, 86; Divergent Styles: Contemporary American Drawing, Univ Gal, Univ Fla, Gainsville, 90. *Teaching:* Asst adj prof drawing, State Univ NY, Purchase, 77-78; instr, Sch Visual Arts, 77-79 & Parsons Sch Design, 85- *Awards:* Creative Artists Pub Serv Grant, 75-76; Nat Endowment Arts Fel, 77-78. *Bibliog:* Vivian Raynor (auth), Art: A tranquil show of American landscape, New York Times, 5/15/82; Ronny Cohen (auth), Drawing the meticulous realist way, Drawing, 3-4/82; Antony Nicoli: (auth), Bill Richards, Arts, summer 85. *Dealer:* Nancy Hoffman Gallery 429 W Broadway New York NY 10012. *Mailing Add:* 77 Seventh Ave Apt 8P New York NY 10011

RICHARDS, EUGENE
PHOTOGRAPHER, LECTURER
b Dorchester, Mass, Apr 25, 44. *Study:* Northeastern Univ, Boston, BA(Eng), 67; Mass Inst Technol, grad level study with Minor White. *Work:* Mus Mod Art, New York; Mus Fine Arts, Boston; Addison Gallery Am Art, Andover, Mass; J B Speed Art Mus, Louisville, Ky; Everson Mus, Syracuse, NY. *Comn:* Art in Public Places, Mass Artists Found, Boston, 78. *Exhib:* We the People, Smithsonian Inst, DC, 75; Photogs, J B Speed Art Mus, Louisville, Ky, 76; Recent Acquisitions, Mus Fine Arts, Boston, 76 & Fourteen New Eng Photogrs, 78; Recent Acquisition Show, Addison Gallery Am Art, Andover, Mass, 77; one-man show, Photogs, Folkwang Mus, Essen, WGer, 79; Mass Art Found Winners, Worcester Art Mus, Mass, 80. *Pos:* Artist-in-residence, Maine Photo Workshop, Rockport, 77-78 & Int Ctr Photog, New York, 78-79; nominee mem, Magnum Photos, New York, 78- *Teaching:* Instr photog, Art Inst Boston, 74-76 & Union Col, Schenectady, NY, 77. *Awards:* Nat Endowment for Arts grant, photog, 74 & 83; Mass Artists Found, 78 & fel, 79; Guggenheim fel, photog, 80. *Bibliog:* Lou Stettner (auth), A look at forgotten books, Camera 35, 3/78; Vickie Goldberg (auth), Half dirty realities, Am Photogr, 78; Julia Scully (auth), Dorchester days, Mod Photog, 6/79. *Mem:* Photog Resource Ctr. *Publ:* Auth, Few Comforts or Surprises: The Arkansas Delta, Mass Inst Technol, 73; Contribr- Photographer's Choice, Addison House, 76; contribr, Family of Children, 77 & contribr, Family of Women, 78, Ridge Press; auth, Dorchester Days, Many Voices Press, Wollaston, Mass, 78. *Mailing Add:* c/o Magnum Phots 72 Spring St New York NY 10012

RICHARDS, GLENORA
PAINTER
b New London, Ohio, Feb 18, 09. *Study:* Cleveland Sch Art, with Rolf Stohl. *Work:* Philadelphia Mus Art; Waterbury Mus Collection, Mattatuck Hist Soc, Conn; Nat Collection Fine Arts, Smithsonian Inst; US Post Off. *Exhib:* Philadelphia Watercolor Soc Show, 47; Nat Asn Women Artists, Nat Acad, New York, 53-74; Royal Soc Miniature Painters Exhib, London, 58; Smithsonian Mus Traveling Show, 66. *Awards:* Best of Show, Fla Miniature Int Show, 88; First in Portraiture, Miniature Painters Sculptors & Gravers Soc Washington, DC, 91; First in Portraiture, Miniature Art Soc Fla, 92. *Bibliog:* Frederick Whitaker (auth), The art of painting portraits in miniature, Am Artist Mag, 58. *Mem:* Miniature Painters, Sculptors & Gravers Washington, DC; Whiskey Painters Am; Soc Miniature Painters, NJ & Fla. *Media:* Watercolor on Ivory. *Publ:* Auth, Good things come in small packages, North Light, 72; auth, The magic of miniatures, Dynamic Maturity, 76; auth, North Light Collection II, 79. *Mailing Add:* 87 Oak St New Canaan CT 06840

RICHARDS, JEANNE HERRON
PRINTMAKER, PAINTER
b Aurora, Ill. *Study:* Univ Iowa, with Mauricio Lasansky, BFA, 52, MFA, 54; Atelier 17, Fulbright grant, 54-55, with Stanley William Hayter. *Work:* Lessing J Rosenwald Collection, Nat Gallery Art; Prints & Photographs, Libr Cong, Washington, DC; Nat Mus Am Art, Washington, DC; Sheldon Mem Art Galleries, Univ Nebr-Lincoln; British Mus, London, Eng. *Exhib:* NW Printmakers, Seattle Art Mus, 53 & 61; Bay Printmakers, Oakland Mus Art, Calif, 56-59; Boston Printmakers, Boston Mus Fine Arts, 56-57, 59 & 61; Prints From Brooklyn Mus Nat, Am Fedn Arts US Tour, 56; Intaglio Prints USA, US Info Agency Tour S Am, 59; Nat Print & Drawing, Dulin Gallery of Art, Knoxville, Tenn, 68; one-man show, Univ Ill, Champaign, 69; Sheldon Mem Art Galleries, Univ Nebr, Lincoln, 70; 19th Area Exhib, Corcoran Gallery Art, Washington, DC, 74; plus others. *Teaching:* Asst instr drawing, Univ Iowa, 55-56; asst prof prints & drawing, Univ Nebr-Lincoln, 57-63. *Awards:* Purchase Award, Corcoran Gallery Art, 57; Purchase Award, Print Club Albany 13th Nat, 69; SW Printmakers Purchase Prize to Philadelphia Mus of Art in hon of Carl Zigrosser, 76. *Bibliog:* Archives of American Art, Smithsonian, 83. *Media:* Etching. *Mailing Add:* 9526 Liptonshire Dallas TX 75238

RICHARDS, JOSEPH EDWARD
PAINTER
b Des Moines, Iowa, Oct 10, 21. *Study:* Am Acad Art, Chicago, 46-49; Chicago Art Inst, 49-50; Pa Acad Fine Arts, Philadelphia, 50-52. *Work:* American Republic Insurance Co, Des Moines, Iowa; Mobil Oil Co; United Airlines; Am Oil Co; Siemens Int; and pvt collections in US and Europe. *Exhib:* Audubon Artists Ann, Nat Acad Design, New York, 75, 77 & 78; Ann Midyear Exhib, Butler Inst Am Art, Youngstown, Ohio, 76, 77, 78 & 81; Tex Fine Arts Asn 66th Ann, Laguna Gloria Mus, Austin, 77; Fel Exhib, Pa Acad Fine Arts, Philadelphia, 78 & 80; Nat Acad Design Ann, New York, 78; New Eng Exhib, Silvermine Guild Artists, New Canaan, Conn, 78 & 79; Va Artists 27th Biennial, Va Mus Fine Art, Richmond, 79; O K Harris West, Scottsdale, Ariz, 81 & 82 & O K Harris South, Miami, Fla, 86; New Realism, Robert Kidd Galleries, Birmingham, Mich, 84; Soghor, Leonard & Assocs, New York, 85; Tortue Gallery, Santa Monica, Calif, 88; Art Expo-Tokyo, Tokyo, Japan, 90; Amerkansk Foto Realism, Art Now Gallery, Gothenburg, Sweden, 90; Perspectives on Realism 1950-1991, Louis Stern Gallery, Beverly Hills, Calif, 91; O K Harris Works of Art, New York, 82, 89 & 92. *Awards:* Distinguished Artist, Va Mus Fine Arts, Richmond, 79. *Mem:* Fel Pa Acad Fine Arts. *Media:* Oil. *Dealer:* O K Harris Works of Art New York NY. *Mailing Add:* PO Box 374 Hillsdale NY 12529

RICHARDS, SABRA
PRINTMAKER, PAINTER
b Utica, NY. *Study:* Syracuse Univ BFA(cum laude), 58; Bennington Col & Parsons Sch Design, 83-86. *Work:* Mus Arts & Sci, Daytona Beach, Fla; Mem Art Gallery, Univ Rochester, NY; Syracuse Univ Fine Arts Collection, NY; NY State Fine Arts Collection, Albany; City of Ann Arbor Fine Arts Collection, Mich. *Comn:* Six Works, IBM, Atlanta, Ga, 84; 4 ft x 5 1/2 ft piece, Humana Hosp, Louisville, Ky, 85; 12 pieces, Temple Univ, Philadelphia, 86; 2 pieces, IBM lobby installation, San Francisco, 87; 4 ft X

9 ft piece, Ann Arbor Pub Libr. *Exhib:* Hunterdon Nat Print Show, travelling exhib, 79-83; Nat Asn Painters Acrylic, travelling exhib, 80-82; solo exhibs, Visions of the Sea, Krasl Mus Art, St Joseph, Mich, 85 & State Univ NY, Rockefeller Ctr Art, Fredonia, NY, 86; Six Artists, Rochester Inst Technol, NY, 87; Collages, Neville Sargent Gallery, Chicago, 88; Hand Made Paper, Rubiner Gallery, Detroit, 88. *Teaching:* Instr, painting, St John Fisher Col, Rochester, NY, 78-82; Artist-in-residence, Artpark, Lewiston, NY, 81. *Awards:* Miller Mem Award, Nat Asn Women Artists; 1st Prize painting, Syracuse Univ, 73; 1st Prize graphics, World Orchid Show, Am Orchid Soc, 84. *Bibliog:* Karen Wenger (auth), Not just hand painted, Screen Printing, 85; Sebby Jacobson (auth), Sabra Richards, Rochester Times-Union, 86; Jan Serasky (auth), Sabra Richards, Artist Mag, spring 89. *Mem:* Nat Asn Women Artists; Arena Group (treas, 88, vpres, 90)), Rochester, NY; Ohio Designer Craftsmen. *Media:* Collage; Handmade Paper. *Mailing Add:* 478 Hoffman Rd Rochester NY 14622

RICHARDS, TALLY
DEALER, WRITER
b Clarkston, Ga. *Pos:* Dir, Tally Richards Gallery, Taos, 69-91, Tally Richards Gallery, Palm Desert, 83-85. *Mem:* Taos Art Asn; Soc Muse Southwest. *Specialty:* Contemporary art by Southwest artists. *Publ:* Auth, Scholder, Darthmouth: Renewed commitments, Southwest Art Mag, 74; auth, Lary Bell, 75; Indian in Paris, Am Indian Art Mag, 77; Tally 13, collected stories, 80; Three AM, Puerto Del Sol, 82; auth, The Paintings of D H Lawrence, Visions of NM Mag, 88. *Mailing Add:* 203 Ledoux Taos NM 87571

RICHARDS, WALTER DUBOIS
PAINTER, PRINTMAKER
b Penfield, Ohio, Sept 18, 07. *Study:* Cleveland Sch Art, grad, 30. *Work:* Cleveland Mus Art; Whitney Mus Am Art, New York; New Britain Mus Am Art, Conn; Johnson Mus, Tex; William A Farnsworth Libr & Art Mus. *Comn:* American Trees (four stamps), 78, 100th Anniversary Nat Park Serv stamp design, Cape Hatteras, 72 & American Architecture (16 stamps), 79-82, US Postal Serv; James Hoban Stamp, White House painting, 81; and others. *Exhib:* Int Watercolor Exhib, Art Inst Chicago, 38; 12th Biennial, Brooklyn Mus Art, 43; Royal Soc Painters in Watercolor, London, 62; Am Prints Around the World, various nations, 63; 200 Years of Watercolor Painting, Metrop Mus Art, New York, 66; Mystic Int, Mystic Maritime Gallery, Conn, 83. *Pos:* Illusr, Tranquillini Studios, Cleveland, 31-36 & Charles E Cooper Studios, New York, 36-50. *Teaching:* Instr pvt classes drawing & watercolor, 68- *Awards:* Lily Saportas Award, Am Watercolor Soc, 62; First Graphics, Hudson Valley Art Asn, 75; Environ Improvement Award, Conn Soc Archit, 83. *Bibliog:* Howard Munce (auth), One artist: one subject: endless variations, N Light Mag, 11/12/72; Susan E Meyer (auth), On location with Fairfield Watercolor Group, Am Artist, 7/72; 200 Years of American Illustration, NY Hist Soc Mus, 77. *Mem:* Am Watercolor Soc (recording secy, 60-61, vpres, 62-70); assoc Nat Acad Design; Conn Watercolor Soc; Soc Illusr; Fairfield Watercolor Group (pres, 48-). *Media:* Watercolor; Lithography. *Publ:* Illusr, Divided South searches its soul, 56 & The age of psychology in the US, 57, Life Mag; illusr, Readers Digest, Colliers, Am Legion & Fortune Mag; auth, 200 Years of American Illustration, NY Hist Soc Mus, 77. *Mailing Add:* 87 Oak St PO Box 1134 New Canaan CT 06840

RICHARDSON, BRENDA
MUSEUM CURATOR
b Howell, Mich, July 15, 42. *Study:* Univ Mich, Ann Arbor, BA, 64; Univ Calif, Berkeley, MA, 66. *Collections Arranged:* Eighties, 70, William T Wiley (with catalog), 71, Eight New York Painters, 72, Terry Fox (with catalog), 73, Joan Brown (with catalog), 74 & Stephen A Davis, Howard Fried, Steven J Kaltenbach, 74, Univ Art Mus, Berkeley; Fourteen Artists, 75 & Andy Warhol, 75, Baltimore Mus Art; Mel Bochner (with catalog), 76; Frank Stella Black Paintings (with catalog), 76; Barnett Newman Complete Drawings (with catalog), 79; Mondrian Drawings, 81; Bruce Nauman Neons (with catalog), 82; Gilbert & George (with catalog), 84; Oskar Schlemmer (with catalog), 86; Scott Burton (with catalog), 86; and many others. *Pos:* Cur exhib, Univ Art Mus, Berkeley, 66-72, asst curatorial dir, 72-74; cur painting & sculpture, Baltimore Mus Art, Md, 75-77, asst dir art, 77- *Awards:* Distinguished Alumni Lectureship, Univ Calif, Berkeley, 73. *Publ:* Auth, Howard Fried: Paradox of approach-avoidance, summer 71 & Nancy Graves: A new way of seeing, 4/72, Arts Mag; plus many others. *Mailing Add:* 4300 N Charles Baltimore MD 21218

RICHARDSON, CONSTANCE (COLEMAN)
PAINTER
b Indianapolis, Ind, Jan 18, 05. *Study:* Pa Acad Fine Arts. *Work:* Indianapolis Art Inst; Detroit Inst Arts; Santa Barbara Mus Art; Mrs John D Rockefeller III Collection; Columbus Gallery Fine Arts; Pa Acad Fine Arts, Philadelphia. *Comn:* This Land is Ours (painting), Omaha Nat Bank, 66. *Exhib:* Am Painting Today, Metrop Mus Art, New York, 50; Am Landscape, A Changing Frontier, Nat Collection Fine Arts, Washington, DC, 66; Fifty Artists from Fifty States Circulating Exhib, Am Fedn Arts, 67-68; Am Paintings of Ports & Harbors, 1774-1968, Jacksonville-Norfolk, 69; Remnants of Things Past, Jacksonville-St Petersburg, 71. *Bibliog:* Louise Bruner (auth), Constance Richardson, Am Artist, 1/61; Alan Gussow (auth), A sense of place: the artist & the American land, Sat Rev, 71. *Media:* Oil. *Mailing Add:* c/o Kennedy Galleries 40 West 57th St New York NY 10019

RICHARDSON, FRANK, JR
MURALIST
b Baltimore, Md, Jan 14, 50. *Study:* Community Col Baltimore, AA; Md Inst Col Art, BFA; Towson State Col; Riverside Art Ctr with Jacob Laurence, Romare Bearden. *Work:* ILE-IFE Mus Afro-American Cult, Philadelphia; ThirdWorld Mus, 111 & Assoc, Baltimore; Merabash Mus, Inc, Willingboro, NJ; Old Slave Mart Mus, Charleston, SC; Nat Ctr Afro-American Artists, Inc, Dorchester, Mass. *Comn:* Mural for film Amazing Grace, 74; mural, Enoch Pratt Free Libr, Baltimore, 74; Black Art (murals), FAN: Baltimore Arts Tower, 74; Amen America, (murals with Berkeley S Thompson), Asn Black Arts/East, Nat Endowment Arts, 75. *Exhib:* First and Second Wide-Regional, Black Art Show, Baltimore; Black Mural Painter, Inst Art Ctr, Lima, Peru, 75; Mural Painter, Univ Pretoria, Repub South Africa, 75. *Collections Arranged:* An Evening With the Links, 74; Awards Extravaganza 74. *Teaching:* Dir graphics, Sinai Druid Camp, Baltimore, 71-72; dir, Mus Prep Sch, 72-; instr printing, Career Opportunities Inc, Baltimore, 71- *Awards:* Best Black Art Work in Show, Black Cult Endowment, 69; Children's Hour Prog, Md Art Coun, 74; Third World Prep Sch, Nat Endowment Arts, 75. *Bibliog:* Averil Jordan-Kadis (auth), Colorful mural, Baltimore Sun, 67; Priscilla Coger (auth), Mr Richardson's beautiful wall, Baltimore Afro-American, 72; James Kelmartin (auth), Museum unit to expand, News American, 75. *Mem:* Asn Black Arts/East. *Media:* Paint. *Mailing Add:* 3016 Baker St Baltimore MD 21216

RICHARDSON, JEAN
PAINTER, PRINTMAKER
b Hollis, Okla, Feb 10, 40. *Study:* Weslayan Col, Macon, Ga, BFA, 62, Arts Student League, New York, 78. *Work:* Phillips Petroleum Corp, Marriott Hotels Corp, Washington, DC; Arthur Anderson Cos, St Charles, Ill; State Collection of Okla, Oklahoma City; US State Dept, Copenhagen, Denmark. *Comn:* Murals, State Capitol Okla, Okla House of Reps, Oklahoma City, 76; mural, Co Courthouse, Okla Co, Oklahoma City, 92. *Exhib:* Okla Ann, Philbrook Mus, Tulsa, 75; Ann Exhib, Nat Acad Design, New York, 78; West 80 Exhib, Minn Mus Art, Minneapolis, 80; Okla Artist Showcase, Goddard Mus Arts, Ardmore, 81; Arts Place Exhib, Okla Art Mus, Oklahoma City, 91. *Bibliog:* Joy Waldron Murphy (auth), Jean Richardson, artist, painting the horse as symbol, Santa Fean, 11/87; Joan Carpenter (auth), Plains Myths & Other Tales, John Szoke Graphics, 88; Sandy Clarke (auth), Jean Richardson, A certain mystique, Equine Images, summer 90. *Mem:* Nat Women Arts; Okla Visual Artists Coalition. *Media:* Acrylic on Canvas. *Publ:* Santa Fean Mag, 84 & 87; Southwest Profile Mag, 85; Art Gallery Mag, 85; Western Art Digest, 86. *Dealer:* John Szoke Graphics Inc 164 Mercer St New York NY 10012. *Mailing Add:* 1106 NW 50th Oklahoma City OK 73118

RICHARDSON, JOHN ADKINS
HISTORIAN, EDUCATOR
b Gillette, Wyo, Oct 24, 29. *Study:* Eastern Wash State Univ, BA, 51; Columbia Univ, New York, MA, 52, EdD, 58. *Teaching:* Asst prof art hist, State Univ NY, 57-58; asst prof art hist, Fresno State Col, Calif, 58-59; prof art hist, Southern Ill Univ, Edwardsville, 59- *Mem:* Col Art Asn; Am Soc Aesthetics. *Res:* Art as intellectual-cultural history in late nineteenth and earlier twentieth centuries. *Publ:* Auth, Art: The Way It Is, Abrams/Prentice-Hall, 74, rev ed, 80, 86 & 92; contribr, Technology as Institutionally Related to Human Values, Acropolis Books, 74; auth, The Complete Book of Cartooning, Prentice-Hall, 76; Design: Systems, Elements, Applications, Prentice-Hall, 83; contribr, Cultural Literacy & Arts Education, Univ Ill Press, 91; and others. *Mailing Add:* 802 W High St Edwardsville IL 62025

RICHARDSON, SAM
SCULPTOR, EDUCATOR
b Oakland, Calif, July 19, 34. *Study:* Calif Col Arts & Crafts, BA, 56 & MFA, 60. *Work:* Dallas Mus Fine Art, Tex; Denver Art Mus; M H De Young Mem Mus, San Francisco; Milwaukee Art Ctr; Nat Mus Am Art, Smithsonian Inst, Washington, DC. *Exhib:* Plastic as Plastic, 63 & Creative Casting, 73, Mus Contemp Crafts, New York; New Media, New Methods, Mus Mod Art, New York, 69; Whitney Mus Am Art, 68-69; Stanford Univ, Calif, 72; Vassar Col, 72; Rutgers Univ, 75; Vpres US Home, Artists Pac Coast States, 80; and others. *Teaching:* Instr art, Oakland City Col, 60-61; art dir, Mus Contemp Crafts, New York, 61-63; asst prof art, San Jose State Univ, 63-66, assoc prof art, 67-72, prof art, 72- *Dealer:* Martha Jackson Gallery 521 W 57th St New York NY 10019; Hansen Fuller Goldeen Gallery 228 Grant Ave San Francisco CA 94108. *Mailing Add:* Dept Art San Jose State Univ San Jose CA 95192

RICHARDSON, W C
PAINTER, EDUCATOR
b San Diego, Calif, May 15, 53. *Study:* Univ NC, Chapel Hill, BFA, 75; Wash Univ, St Louis, MFA, 77. *Work:* Hirshhorn Mus & Sculpure Garden, Washington, DC; Ackland Art Ctr, Chapel Hill, NC. *Comn:* Two paintings, Reston Town Ctr, Va, 90. *Exhib:* Md Biennial, Baltimore Mus Art, 80, 83; one-person shows, Osuna Gallery, Washington, DC, 82, 85, 87 & Baumgartner Galleries Inc, Washington, DC, 89, 91 & 93; Washington Show, Corcoran Gallery Art, Washington, DC, 85; two-person show, Va Mus Fine Arts, Richmond, 86; Washington/Moscow Art Exchange, Tretyakoff State Mus, Russia, 90; Abstract Icons, Roanoke Mus Fine Arts, Va, 92; WPA at the Hemicycle, Corcoran Gallery Art, Washington, DC, 92. *Teaching:* Assoc prof painting & drawing, Univ Md, College Park, 78- *Awards:* First Prize, Md Biennial, Baltimore Mus Art, 83; Artist's Fel, Md State Arts Coun, 81, 87. *Bibliog:* Alice Thorson (auth), W C Richardson, Wash Times, 4/17/89; Michael Welzenbach (auth), W C Richardson, Wash Post, 4/13/91; J W Mahoney (auth), DC Dreaming, Art Am, 10/91. *Mem:* Wash Proj Arts. *Media:* Acrylic, Oil. *Dealer:* Baumgartner Galleries Inc 2021 R St NW Washington DC 20009. *Mailing Add:* 4309 Sheridan St University Park MD 20782

RICHENBURG, ROBERT BARTLETT
PAINTER, SCULPTOR
b Boston, Mass, July 14, 17. *Study:* George Washington Univ; Boston Univ; Corcoran Sch Art; Art Students League, With Reginald Mard & George Grosz, Ozenfant Sch Art; Hans Hofmann Sch Fine Art. *Work:* Hirshhorn Mus, Washington, DC; Pasadena Art Mus, Calif; Philadelphia Mus Art, Pa; Whitney Mus Am Art & Mus Mod Art, New York; Norfolk Mus Arts & Sci, Va; plus other pub & pvt collections. *Exhib:* One-person exhibs, Chrysler Art Mus, Provincetown, Mass, 58, RI Sch Design, Providence, 60, Santa Barbara Mus, Calif, 61, Upstairs Gallery, Ithaca, 76 & 81 & Benton Gallery, Southampton, NY, 86; Baltimore Mus Art, 61; Solomon R Guggenheim Mus, 61, Whitney Mus Am Art, 61, 63 & 68, NY; Inter Selection Contemp Painting & Sculpture, Dayton Art Inst, Ohio, 62; Cocoran Mus Art, Washington, DC, 63; Emerging Decade, Seattle Art Mus, 65; Hilles Collection of Paintings & Sculpture, Mus Fine Arts, Boston, 66; Kunstverein Wolfsburg, Galerie Für Mod Für Kunst, Golar, Ger, 83; Guild Hall Mus, East Hampton, NY, 83-84; plus many other one-man & group shows. *Teaching:* Lectr, Pratt Inst, Cooper Union, 51-64, New York Univ, 60-61, Cornell Univ, 64-67, Hunter Col, 67-70 & Ithaca Col, NY, 70-83. *Bibliog:* Dorothy Seckler (auth), Artists In America: Victims of the cultural boom? 12/63 & Fifty-six painters and sculptors, 8/64, Art in Am; Donald Judd (auth), articles in Arts, 4/62 & 4/63; Dore Ashton (auth), Art USA 1962, 3/62 & article, 2/65, Studio Mag; James A Michener (auth), James A Michener on Richenburg, 11/62, Art Voices. *Mem:* Artists Alliance, East Hampton; life mem Art Students League. *Mailing Add:* 1006 Springs Fireplace Rd East Hampton NY 11937

RICHMOND, REBEKAH
PRINTMAKER
b Ashland, Ky. *Study:* Ringling Sch Art; Univ Ky, Lexington; Art Inst Pittsburgh. *Work:* Coos Art Mus, Coos Bay, Ore; Albany Inst Hist & Art; Nat Arts Club, New York. *Comn:* Presentation Print, Print Club Albany, 76-77. *Exhib:* Ann Artists Salon, Okla Mus Fine Art, 75 & 77; solo exhib, Albany Inst Hist & Art, 77; April Salon, Springville Mus Art, Utah, 77, 78, 80 & 82; Colorprint USA, Tex Tech Univ, 80; Audubon Artists Ann, Nat Arts Club, New York, 81. *Awards:* Gold Medal Hon, Acad Artists Asn, Mass, 78 & 79; Anna Hyatt Huntington Bronze Medal, Catharine Lorillard Wolfe Art Club, 79; Mrs John Newington Award, Hudson Valley Art Asn Ann, 82. *Mem:* Salmagundi Club; Hudson Valley Art Asn; Catharine Lorillard Wolfe Art Club; Print Club Albany; Acad Artists Asn. *Media:* Etching, Oils. *Dealer:* Kerwin Galleries 1107 California Dr Burlingame CA 94010. *Mailing Add:* Box 878 Estes Park CO 80517

RICHTER, HANK
PAINTER, SCULPTOR
b Cleveland, Ohio, Oct 10, 28. *Study:* Philadelphia Mus Sch of Art. *Work:* DeGrazia-Gonzales Cult Ctr & Mus, Casa Grande, Ariz; Valley Nat Bank Collection, Phoenix; First Nat Bank Collection, Tucson, Ariz; Read Mullan's Gallery Western Art, Ariz State Univ; Principia Col, Elsah, Ill. *Comn:* Ted DeGrazia portrait (ltd edition pewter bas-relief plate) & Tracks Across America (series of six ltd edition pewter bas-relief sculptures), comn by Richard Smith, Century Reproductions, Inc, Wilmington, Mass, 77; three 50 year commemorative belt buckle sculptures, Western Savings & Loan, Phoenix. *Exhib:* Mountain Oyster Invitational Show, Tucson, 74-79; Charles M Russell Invitational Art Auction, Great Falls, Mont, 76-79; Ann San Dimas Am Indian & Cowboy Artists Soc Show, Calif, 77-88; First Fed Savings & Loan Traveling Exhib; Western Gallery, 1st Interstate Bank, Tucson, Az. *Teaching:* Student instr anat, Philadelphia Mus Sch Art, 49-50; instr creative design, Kachina Sch Art, Phoenix, 54-56; sculpture instr & drawing instr, Principia Col, Elsah, Ill; instr pvt classes, currently. *Awards:* Gold Medal, Atlanta Film Festival, 69; Golden Eagle, CINE/USA, 69. *Bibliog:* The West & Walter Bimson, Univ Ariz Press, 72; Pat Broder (auth), Bronzes of the American West, Abrams, 75; Lil Rhodes (auth), A man and his art, Southwest Art, 78. *Mem:* Am Indian & Cowboy Artists Soc (past pres); Art Group 12, Payson, Ariz. *Media:* Oil, Watercolor; Bronze. *Dealer:* American West Galleries Main St Scottsdale AZ; Rosequist Galleries 1615 E Ft Lowell Rd Tucson AZ. *Mailing Add:* 219 W Montebello Phoenix AZ 85013

RICHTER, SCOTT
SCULPTOR
b Atlanta, Ga, 1943. *Study:* The New Sch, BFA. *Exhib:* 20th Century Three Dimensional Portraits, Cleveland Ctr Contemp Art, Ohio, 84; Affiliations: Recent Sculpture and Its Antecedents, Whitney Mus, Stamford, Conn, 85; Sculpture on the Wall, Aldrich Mus, Ridgefield, Conn, 86; Avant-Garde the Eighties, Los Angeles Co Mus Art, 87; Figures Form and Fiction, Everson Mus Art, Syracuse, NY, 88; Nina Freudenheim Gallery, Buffalo, NY, 89; solo exhibs, PS1, Long Island, New York, 83, Zabriski Gallery, New York, 85, Curt Marcus Gallery, 87 & 89, Univ Mass, Amherest, 88, Fuller Gross Gallery, San Francisco, Calif, 89 & 92, Beth Urdang Fine Art, Boston, Mass, 90. *Teaching:* Inst, State Univ New York, 78-84; Cooper Union, NY, 83-92. *Awards:* Grants, Nat Endowment Arts, 84 & 86; Engelhard Grants, 85; NY Found Arts, 86. *Bibliog:* Kathryn Kramer (auth), Lifesigns, Arts Mag, 2/84; Michael Brenson (auth), Sculpture breaks the mold of minimalism, New York Times, 11/23/86; Kenneth Baker (auth), Minimalism and runaway wits, San Francisco Chronicle, 7/11/87; Nancy Princenthal (auth), Art Am, 9/92. *Mailing Add:* c/o Curt Marcus Gallery 578 Broadway New York NY 10012

RICKEY, GEORGE W
SCULPTOR
b South Bend, Ind, June 6, 07. *Study:* Glenalmond Sch, Scotland; Balliol Col, Oxford Univ, BA, 29, MA, 41; Ruskin Sch Drawing, Oxford; Acad Lhote & Acad Mod, Paris; Inst Fine Arts, New York Univ; State Univ Iowa, 47; Inst Design, Chicago, 48-49; Eight honorary degrees. *Work:* Mus Mod Art, New York; Neue Nationalgalerie, Berlin, Ger; Tate Gallery, London; Nat Mem Mus Expo, Japan; Joseph H Hirshhorn Mus & Sculpture Garden, Washington, DC; Storm King Art Ctr, NY; Nat Gallery Art, Washington, DC; La Mus; Rijksmuseum Kröller-Muller, Holland. *Comn:* Laumeier Sculpture Park, St Louis, 86; Golden Gate North, San Francisco, 87; Parliament Bldg, Dusseldorf, WGer, 88; Olympic Ctr, Seoul, Korea, 88; New Theatre, Rotterdam, Holland, 89; Fukutake Publ, Okayama, Japan, 90; Tokyo City Hall, Japan, 91; Musée de Grenoble, France, 91. *Exhib:* Mus Mod Art, New York, 59; Guggenheim Mus, 67 & 79; Albright-Knox Art Gallery, 68; Kestner-Gesellschaft, Hanover, Ger, 73; Staedel Mus, Frankfurt, Ger, 77; Bauhaus Arch, Berlin, Ger, 84; Josef Albers Mus, Bottrop, Ger, 84; Veranneman Found, Belgium, 86; Neuberger Mus, 87; Neuer Berliner Kunstverein, W Berlin, 88; Gallery Kasahara, Osaka, Japan, 88; Mus Boymans-van Beuningen, Rotterdam, Holland, 89; Artcurial, Paris, France, 90; Katonah Mus Art, NY, 91; Berlinische Galerie (permanent exhib), Berlin, Ger, 92; and others. *Awards:* Guggenheim Fel, 60 & 61; Am Inst Arts & Letters, 74; Akademie der Künste, Ger, 87. *Bibliog:* Peter Riedl (auth), George Rickey: Kinetische Objekte, Philipp Reclam J, Stuttgart, 70; Nan Rosenthal (auth), George Rickey, Abrams, New York, 77; Seth Schneidman (auth), George Rickey: Portrait of the Artist (film), New York, 87. *Mem:* Century Asn; Nat Inst Arts & Lett. *Media:* Stainless Steel. *Publ:* Auth, Constructivism: Origins & Evolution, Braziller, 67; Origins of Kinetic Art, Studio Int, London, 67; All good art is public, Educ Perspectives, Vol 16, No 3, 77; Naum Gabo 1890-1977, Artforum, 11/77. *Mailing Add:* Rd 2 Box 235 East Chatham NY 12060

RIDDLE, JOHN THOMAS, JR
SCULPTOR, PAINTER
b Los Angeles, Calif, Mar 18, 33. *Study:* Los Angeles City Col, AA, 60; Los Angeles State Col, BA, 66; Calif State Univ, MA, 73. *Work:* High Mus Art, Atlanta, Ga; Golden State Mutual Life Inst Co, Calif State Univ, Los Angeles; Oakland Mus, Calif; Albany Mus Art, Ga. *Comn:* Murals, Bank of Am (2 br), Los Angeles, 70; The Operation (welded steel), Los Angeles Co Mental Health Clinic, 72; relig murals, Shrine of Black Madonna, Atlanta, 74; Expelled Because of Their Color (bronze), State of Ga, Atlanta, 77; Spirit Bench 1, City of Atlanta, 78; Painted, Welded, Sculpture Walls, Mid-Town Marta Sta, Atlanta, Ga. *Exhib:* Black Artists, Oakland Mus, Calif, 73; Calif Artists, Calif State Univ, Sacramento, 74; Artists in Ga, High Mus Art, Atlanta, 75-80; Calif Artists, the Black Experience, State Capitol, Sacramento, Calif, 76; Black Artists S, Huntsville Mus Art, Ala, 78; 8th Ann Art Festival, Martinique, WI, Port de France, 79; Calif African-Am Mus, Los Angeles, 89; William Grant Still Gallery, Los Angeles, Calif, 92. *Pos:* Dir, Neighborhood Arts Ctr, Inc, Atlanta, 75-81. *Teaching:* Instr ceramics & sculpture, Pub Schs, Los Angeles & Beverly Hills, Calif, 66-73; asst prof painting, Spelman Col, Atlanta, 79-80; asst dir, Atlanta Civic Ctr, 84-92. *Awards:* Emmy Award, TV Acad Arts & Sci, 71; Ga Gov Award Visual Art, 81. *Bibliog:* Lewis Productions, Three artists, Lewis, Riddle, Pajaud, 68; Larry Stuart (auth), Renaissance in black, KNBC, 10/71; Lewis & Waddy (coauth), Black Artists on Art, 2 vols, Contemp Crafts, 72. *Mem:* Black Artists Atlanta; Ga Coun for Arts; Gov Artist-in-Schs; Atlanta Urban Design Comn, 90-91. *Publ:* Contribr, Prints by American Negro Artists, Cult Exchange Ctr, 67; Black Artists on Art, 2 vols, Contemp Crafts, 71; Art: African American, Harcourt-Brace, 78. *Dealer:* Camille Love 3230 Kingsdale Dr SW Atlanta GA 30311. *Mailing Add:* 3034 Rebecca Dr SW Atlanta GA 30311

RIDLEY, GREGORY D, JR
PAINTER, SCULPTOR
b Smyrna, Tenn, July 18, 25. *Study:* Fisk Univ, with Aaron Douglas, 45-49; Tenn State Univ, with Frances Thompson, BS, 51; Univ Louisville, Ky, with Ulfret Wilke, Justus Bier, Creighton Gilbert, Walter Creese, 54-55 & Hayward Oubre, 51. *Work:* Fisk Univ; Univ Louisville; Grambling Col; Mt Zion Baptist Church, Smyrna, Tenn; Fisk Univ; Tenn State Univ; Reed Sch, Long Island, NY; Atlanta Univ Collections, Ga; Toledo Mus Art, Ohio; Tenn State Mus. *Comn:* Directed mural, Harlem Hosp Ctr & High Sch Music & Art, 70; St Jaquims, Queens, NY, 71; Carver Savings Bank, New York, 74; Meharry Med Col, 83. *Exhib:* Fisk Univ Traveling Shows, throughout US, 51-; South Cent Show, Nashville, Tenn, 67-71; Two Centuries Black American Art Traveling Exhib, Brooklyn Mus, 71-75; Amstad II, 75; Nashville Artist Guild, 67-92. *Pos:* Cult coordr, Harlem Backstreet Youth Inc, 67; consult, African-Am Mus, Nashville, 83. *Teaching:* Asst prof art, Ala State Col, 51-58, Grambling Col, 58-62, Elizabeth City State, 62-64 & Tenn State Univ, 66-71 & 75-78; adj prof, Brooklyn Col, summers 66-75, Lehman Col, summers 71-74 & Medgar Evers Col, summers 71-75; asst prof, Fisk Univ, 66-71, assoc prof, 81-; instr, Central Islip Sch Dist, 85-86; art consult, 89-91 & acting curator, 90-91, Fisk Univ; adj prof art, Tenn State Univ, Nashville, retired. *Awards:* Six Prizes, Atlanta Univ Ann, 51-65; Battle of Gettysburg First Prize Gold Medal, Am Soc Vet, 65; First prize, relief sculpture, Washington Sq Outdoor Ann Exhib, NY, 73; Teacher of the Year, Tenn State Univ, 78. *Bibliog:* Cedric Dover (auth), American Negro Art, 61; Ralph Hudson (auth), Black Artist South, 79. *Mem:* Nat Conf Artist (vchmn, 62); Am Asn Univ Prof; Nat Educ Asn; Long Island Black Artists Asn. *Media:* Stone, Metal. *Res:* Great battles of the Civil War; Two Hundred & Fifty Years of Afro-American Art, Igoe. *Collection:* African masks, textiles, prints & paintings. *Publ:* Contribr, Great Negroes Past and Present, 65 & Decision for Destiny, 74; auth, Two Centuries of Black American Art, Driskell, 77. *Mailing Add:* Fisk Univ Art Gallery Box 2 Nashville TN 37208

RIDLON, JAMES A
SCULPTOR, ASSEMBLAGE ARTIST
b Nyack, NY, July 11, 36. *Study:* Syracuse Univ, BA, 57, MFA, 65; San Francisco State Col, 58-59. *Work:* Munson-Williams-Proctor Inst, Utica, NY; Julliard Sch, New York; Rochester Mem Gallery, NY; Everson Mus, Syracuse, NY; Smithsonian Inst, Washington, DC; and others. *Comn:* Assemblage, ABC, New York, NY, 58; Outland Trophy, Football Writers Asn Am, 88. *Exhib:* New Paintings, Everson Mus Art, 74; one-man retrospective, Logan Alexander Ctr Creative Arts, Concord Col, 75; Lubin House Gallery, New York, 77; Herbert F Johnson Mus, Cornell Univ, Ithaca, NY, 77; Alan Brown Gallery, Hartsdale, NY, 81; Canton Art Inst, Canton, Ohio, 89; and others. *Pos:* Dir, NY State Summer Sch Arts Sch of Visual Arts. *Teaching:* Assoc prof sculpture & studio arts, 68-74, Syracuse Univ, prof sculpture & synaesthetic educ, 74-81, prof & chmn, CORE dept, 82- *Awards:* Purchase Prize, 32nd Ann Exhib, Munson-Williams-Proctor Inst, 68; First Prize in Sculpture, 10th Ann Westchester Art Soc Exhib, 70; First Prize Sculpture, NY State Fair, 92; and others. *Publ:* Contribr, Synaesthetic Education, Syracuse Univ, 71; auth, Synaesthetic education as a basis for symbolic expression, Humanities J, 5/73; co-producer & dir, Icons and Eclecticism (film), Syracuse Univ, 81; producer & dir, Artist-Athlete (film), Syracuse Univ, 82; co-producer & dir, The Wonder of Friction (film), Syracuse Univ, 83. *Dealer:* Oxford Gallery 267 Oxford Rochester NY 14607; Alan Brown Gallery 60 E Hartsdale Ave Hartsdale NY 10530. *Mailing Add:* Fire House 20 Dept Art Syracuse Univ Syracuse NY 13210

RIEBER, RUTH B
PRINTMAKER, PAINTER
b New York, NY, Mar 9, 24. *Study:* New York Univ, BS, 45; Art Students League, 47; Columbia Univ, MFA, 48. *Work:* Trenton State Col, NJ; Westinghouse Electric, Pittsburg, Pa; Pub Serv Electric & Gas Co, Newark, NJ; State NJ Dept Treasury, Trenton; Newark Teachers Union, NJ. *Exhib:* Art from NJ 8, NJ State Mus, Trenton, 73; Nat Acad Art Exhibs 153, 154, 161, 163 & 165, New York, 78-79, 86, 88-90; NJ Invitational Graphics, Morris Mus Art & Sci, 80; Nat Asn Women Artists Centennial Celebration (juried, travel), India, 89; solo exhibs, Insights, Saint Peters Church Gallery, New York, 87, Relief Print, Johnson and Johnson World Hq, New Brunswick, NJ, 90 & Works on Paper, Int Church Ctr, New York, 91; Hudson River Open 91, Hudson River Mus, Yonkers, NY, 91. *Teaching:* Teacher art, Bd Educ, New York, 46-49; art therapist, Teaneck Sch System Spec Educ, NJ, 68-74; printmaker specialist, Project Impact Arts in Educ Found, NJ, 85-92. *Awards:* Medal of Honor, Catherine Lorillard Wolfe Art Club, 83; Graphics Award, Nat Asn Women Artists, Janet Turner, 84; Purchase Award, Nat Print 86 Exhib, Trenton State Col, 86. *Bibliog:* Dori Halasz (auth), A Show in Trenton Survey's States Art, NY Sunday Times, 4/1/73; Eileen Watkins (auth), Shedding Artistic Light on Women's Issues, The Star Ledger, 3/5/88; Vivian Raynor(auth), Well Known Artists Join the Crowd at NY Art Gallery Auction, NY Times, 6/21/92. *Mem:* Nat Asn Women Artists; Print Coun NJ; Painting Affiliates, NJ; Audobon Artists; Catherine Lorillard Wolfe Art Club. *Mailing Add:* 407 Warwick Ave Teaneck NJ 07666

RIEGEL, MICHAEL BYRON
METALSMITH
b Hannibal, Mo, Nov 21, 46. *Study:* Eastern Ill Univ, Charleston, BSEd, 68, MA, 72; Southern Ill Univ, Carbondale, with Brent Kington, MFA, 74. *Work:* Ark Art Ctr, Little Rock; Ill State Mus, Springfield. *Exhib:* Biennial Lake Superior Nat Craft Exhib, Tweed Mus Art, Univ Minn, Duluth, 72; 7th Biennial Beaux Arts Designer Craftsmen Exhib, Columbus Gallery Fine Arts, Ohio, 73; Miss River Craft Exhib, Brooks Mem Art Gallery, Memphis, Tenn, 73 & 75; Baroque 74, Forms in Metal, 75 & Homage to the Bag, 75, Mus Contemp Crafts, New York; Craft Multiples, Renwick Gallery, Smithsonian Inst, Washington, DC, 75; Goldsmiths, Phoenix Art Mus, Ariz, 77. *Teaching:* Instr design & 2-D design, Southeast Mo State Univ, Cape Girardeau, 75 & instr metalsmithing, 76; instr art metals & drawing, Calif State Univ, Sacramento, 76-81, asst prof art, 81-82, assoc prof, currently. *Awards:* Exhib Award, Goldsmiths, Renwick Gallery, 74, Design in Steel Award Prog, 74-75, Steel Indust, 75 & Miss River Craft Show, Brooks Mem Art Gallery, 76. *Mem:* Artists Blacksmiths Asn of N Am; Calif Blacksmiths Asn. *Media:* Steel. *Mailing Add:* Dept Art Cal State Univ 6000 J St Sacramento CA 95819

RIEGLE, ROBERT MACK
ART DEALER, COLLECTOR
b Sedan, Kans, Nov 11, 24. *Study:* Tex A&M Univ, College Station, 43; Univ Kans, Lawrence, BS(archit), 50. *Pos:* Dir, Wichita Gallery Fine Art, currently. *Specialty:* Original fine paintings and sculpture; realism, impressionism and expressionism. *Collection:* Contemporary realists and impressionists of the southwest; The Taos Six; oils, watercolors and pastels; bronze sculpture. *Mailing Add:* Wichita Gallery Fine Art Fourth Financial Ctr 100 N Broadway Wichita KS 67202

RIES, MARTIN
PAINTER, PRINTMAKER
b Washington, DC, Dec 26, 26. *Study:* Corcoran Gallery Art, 40-44; Am Univ, with William Calfee, Jack Tworkov & Leo Steppat, BA, 50; Hunter Col, MA, 68, with Leo Steinberg, William Rubin, Ad Reinhardt & E C Goossen. *Work:* Pace Univ Mus; Riverside Mus Collection, Rose Art Mus, Brandeis Univ; Inst Cult Hisp, Madrid, Spain; New York Pub Libr Print Collection; Netherlands Consulate. *Exhib:* Corcoran Gallery Art, 52; Inst Cult Hisp, Univ Madrid, 55; Mus Mod Art, 56; Paul Gallery, Tokyo, Japan, 68; Verfeil, France, 73; Stamford Mus, Conn, 87; Inst Contemp Art, London, 88; Raja Idris Gallery, Melbourne, Australia, 89. *Pos:* Asst dir pub rels, Nat Cong Comt, 51; asst dir, Hudson River Mus, Yonkers, NY, 57-67; adv, Westchester Cult Ctr, 65-67; contrib ed, Arts Mag; art ed, Greenwich Village News; bd dir, Artists Representing Environmental Art, currently. *Teaching:* Instr medieval art hist, Marymount Col, 59; instr mod art hist, Hunter Col, 63-67; prof hist art, color theory, printmaking, drawing & painting, Long Island Univ, 68- *Awards:* Honorable Mention, 52nd Nat Soc Arts & Lett Award, Corcoran Gallery Art; Critics Choice, Whyte Gallery, 57; Yaddo Fel; Research-Time Award, Long Island Univ. *Bibliog:* Masters & Houston, Psychedelic Art, Grove Press, NY, 68; C Dantzic (auth), Design Dimensions, Prentice-Hall, NJ. *Mem:* Asn Int des Critques d'Art, Am Sect; Artists Equity Asn; Am Soc Contemp Artists. *Media:* Acrylic, Silk Screen Printing. *Res:* Braque's Atelier and the Symbolic Bird; Abstract-Perspectivism of John Hultberg; Andre Masson: Surrealism and its Discontents; Willem de Kooning's Asheville. *Publ:* Auth, Elusive Goya, New Repub, 57; monthly articles, Hudson River Mus Bull, 57-67; Endowments for Great Society, Art Voices Mag, 65 & New Art: Anthology, Dutton, 66; Picasso and the Myth of the Minotaur, Art J, winter 72-73, portion reprinted in: Picasso in Perspective, Prentice Hall, 75; Environmental Art: Working with Elements, video produced by AREA. *Dealer:* Glass Gallery 315 Central Park West New York NY 10025. *Mailing Add:* 36 Livingston Rd Scarsdale NY 10583

RIESE, BEATRICE
PAINTER
b The Hague, Neth; US citizen. *Study:* Ecole d'Art et de Dessin de la Ville de Paris, 36-40; Commonwealth Univ, Richmond, Va, with Clifford Still, 43-45; study with Will Barnet, 56-66. *Work:* Va Mus Fine Arts, Richmond; Mint Mus Art, Charlotte, NC; Hunter Mus Art, Chattanooga, Tenn; Huntsville Mus Art, Ala; Snite Mus Art, Notre Dame, Ind. *Exhib:* Solo exhibs, 55 Mercer St Gallery, 75 West Broadway Gallery, 76, 78, 80 & 81, Hudson Gallery, 86, New York & Danville Mus Fine Arts & Hist, Va, 88; Recent Trends in Works on Paper, Museo de Ark Moderno, Buenos Aires, Arg, 90; American Abstract Art 1930 to the Present, NJ State Mus, Trenton, 91; American Abstract Artists: Persistence of Abstraction, Edwin A Ulrich Mus, Wichita, Kans, 92; America 500, Centro Cult Recoleta, Buenos Aires, Arg, 92. *Bibliog:* Hedy O'Beil (auth), Beatrice Riese, Arts Mag, 80; Joanne Bojinoff (auth), Beatrice Riese-Painter, Women Artist News, 83; Marcelo Llorens (auth), Beatrice Riese, Arle Al Dia, 91. *Mem:* Adv Coun, Snite Mus Art, Notre Dame, Ind, 87-93; Am Abstract Artists (pres, 90-93). *Media:* Oil on linen, Gouache on Paper. *Dealer:* Pleiades Gallery 164 Mercer St New York NY 10012. *Mailing Add:* 470 West End Ave New York NY 10024

RIESS, LORE
PAINTER, PRINTMAKER
b Berlin, Ger; US citizen. *Study:* Art Acad, Contempora (Bauhaus Sch), Berlin; Sumi Drawing & Calligraphy, Tokyo; Art Students League. *Work:* Corcoran Gallery Art, Washington, DC; Tel Aviv Mus & Israel Mus, Jerusalem; US Embassy, Japan & Korea; pvt collections in US, Japan, Belg, Eng & Israel; AT&T; and others. *Comn:* Ed of etchings, Mickelson Gallery, Washington, DC, 71. *Exhib:* One-man shows, Old Jaffa Gallery, Israel, 70, 73, 75 & 79, Nora Art Gallery, Jerusalem, 71, 74 & 82, Jeanne Frank Gallery, New York, 78 & Park Village West, London, 79 & 80; Linden Galleries, New York, 81, Artist Studio, New York, 82, 85 & 90, Park West Gallery, London, England, 83, Lillian Heidenberg Gallery, New York, 84, Zack Schuster Gallery, Boca Raton, Fla, 85, 86 & 89. *Awards:* William McNulty Merit Award, Art Students League, 64; M J Kaplan Prize, Nat Asn Women Artists, 69; Gallery of Graphic Art Award, Int Miniature Print Exhib, 71. *Bibliog:* T Ichinose (auth), Colorful abstract oils by Lore Riess, Mainichi Daily News, 65; articles in Jerusalem Post, 7/70 & 3/71. *Media:* Acrylic, Pastel. *Dealer:* Margaret Lipworth, FL; Adler Arts Int Washington DC. *Mailing Add:* 1200 Broadway New York NY 10001

RIFKIND, ROBERT GORE
COLLECTOR
b Beverly Hills, Calif, July 12, 28. *Study:* Univ Calif, Los Angeles, AB, 50; Harvard Univ, LLB, 54. *Awards:* Order of Merit, First Class, Fed Repub Ger. *Collection:* Largest private collection of German Expressionist graphic arts in US; more than 6,000 graphics and 3,500 volumes. *Publ:* Contribr, German Expressionist Woodcuts, de Saisset Art Gallery & Mus, Santa Clara, 80; contribr, The Human Image in German Expressionist Graphic Art, Berkeley Univ Art Mus, 81; contribr, An Alle Kunstler: War-Revolution-Weimar, San Diego State Univ Art Gallery, 83; German Expressionist Art: The Robert Gore Rifkind Collection, UCLA, 77; German Expressionist Prints and Drawings: The Robert Gore Rifkind Center for German Expressionist Studies, Los Angeles Co Mus Art & Prestel Verlag, Munich, 89. *Mailing Add:* 10100 Santa Monica Blvd, Suite 250 Los Angeles CA 90067

RIGBY, IDA KATHERINE
CRITIC, HISTORIAN
b Los Angeles, Calif, May 10, 44. *Study:* Stanford Univ, BA, MA; Ecole des Beaux Arts, Tours, France; Univ Calif, Berkeley, MA, PhD(art hist), 74. *Teaching:* Asst prof mod art hist, Univ Montana, Missoula, spring 1972; instr, Newcomb Col, Tulane Univ, New Orleans, 72-74; asst prof, Univ Victoria, BC, 74-76; prof mod & contemp art, San Diego State Univ, 76- *Awards:* Kress Found Grant; Grant, Deutscher Akademischer Austauschdienst, Bonn. *Mem:* Col Art Asn; Art Historians of Southern Calif. *Res:* German Expressionism; German Expressionist artists and politics; politics of opposition and official collaboration in Germany during the 1930's; art criticism. *Publ:* Auth, Karl Hofer, Garland Publ, 76; The Expressionist Artist and Revolution, 1918-1922 & Entartte Kunst, 1933-1938, In: German Expressionist Art: The Robert Gore Rifkind Collection, Univ Calif, Los Angeles Press, 77; Franz Marc's wartime letters from the front, 1880-1916, Univ Calif Berkeley, 79; Wichner Collection, Long Beach Mus Art, 81; An Alle Kunstler! War Revolution Weimar: German Expressionist Prints, Drawings, Posters and Periodicals for the Robert Gore Rifkind Foundation, San Diego State Univ Press, 83. *Mailing Add:* Dept of Art San Diego State Univ San Diego CA 92182

RIGG, MARGARET RUTH
ASSEMBLAGE ARTIST, CALLIGRAPHER
b Pittsburgh, Pa, Dec 14, 29. *Study:* Carnegie-Mellon Univ, 45-50; Fla State Univ, BA, 51; Scarrett Col; Presby Sch, MA, 55; George Peabody Col; Chicago Art Inst, 63; painting with Edmund Lewandowski & Florence Kawa; design & theory with Mathias Goeritz; Chinese calligraphy with Tsutomu Yoshida, Kim Kee-Sung, Kim Hahn & Tennyson Chang; Am calligraphy with Corita Kent & Jan Steward; Brit calligraphy with George L Thompson. *Work:* Tenn Collection, Smithsonian Inst; Yamada Gallery, Kyoto, Japan; Turku Univ Mus, Finland; NH Mus, Manchester; Korea Fulbright House, Seoul. *Comn:* Stained glass windows, Mexico City Nat Cathedral, 61; stained glass window, communion table, lecturn & celtic cross, Univ NC, Chapel Hill, 62; calligraphy mural, Experiment House, Vere, Jamaica; calligraphy letterhead & gates to campus, Eckerd Col, 72. *Exhib:* Ringling Mus Art Arch, Sarasota, Fla; Womanspirit Ann Exhib, 79-; solo shows, calligraphy, Hannover, Ger, 84, calligraphy & paintings, Montreat, NC, 85 & calligraphy, Buenos Aires, Argentiana & Salvador, Bahia, Brasil, 86 & calligraphy, Cultural Olympics, Seoul, Korea, 87; two person exhib, calligraphy, Tokyo, Japan, 88, Garia Pequena, St Petersburg, Fla, 90 & Gararia Pequena, St Petersburg, Fla, 91; group invitational shows, Aura group, Philadelphia, Pa, 92 & St Petersburg visual artists, Univ S Fla, 92; and others. *Pos:* Art dir, Bd Publ, Fla State Univ, 51-53; owner & publ, Possum Press; art ed, Motive Mag, Nashville, Tenn, 54-65. *Teaching:* Artist in residence, Fla Presby Col, 65-67; prof visual art, Eckerd Col, 67-; dir, Elliot Teaching Gallery, Eckerd Col, 81-88. *Awards:* Stone Lectr, Princeton Seminary, Princeton, NJ, 71; Fulbright-Hays Sr Res Grant in Chinese Calligraphy, Korea, 72. *Bibliog:* Meinke (auth), Very Seldom Animals, 69 & 77, Barbara Chaulk (auth), Poems & Why, 75 & Amos N Wilder (auth), Imagining the Real, 78, Possum Press; I Need to Hear You, 69 & Keep in Touch, 70 (films), CBS-TV. *Mem:* Int Soc Women Calligraphers; Soc Italic Handwriting; Nashville Artist Guild (pres, 63-64); Fla Artist Group, Inc; St Petersburg Soc Scribes (founder & 1st pres, 78-); Soc Arts, Religion & Contemp Cult. *Media:* Pen & Ink, Markers, Brush & Chinese Ink, Mixed Media Materials. *Publ:* Pro-Nica, logo & art, Religious Soc Friends (relief to Nicaragua), 89; Front cover design, Human Quest Mag, 90. *Dealer:* Carol Ridge St Petersburg FL 33712. *Mailing Add:* 2960 58th Ave S St Petersburg FL 33712-4616

RILEY, BARBRA BAYNE
PHOTOGRAPHER, EDUCATOR
b Brooklyn, NY, Dec 20, 49. *Study:* Sch Visual Arts, New York, cert(fine arts), 70; Calif State Univ, Sacramento, BA, 72, MA, 74. *Work:* Dallas Mus Art; Mus Fine Art, Houston; Laguna Beach Mus Art; Chase Manhattan Bank, New York; Atlantic Richfield Co. *Comn:* Photographers Portray the Family, Women & Their Work, Nat Endowment Arts, Austin, Tex, 81; 24 photographs, Corpus Christi Nat Bank, 81; Texas Commerce Bank, Corpus Christi. *Exhib:* Solo exhib, Art Mus STex, Corpus Christi, 79; Contemporary Photography as Phantasy, Santa Barbara Mus Art, Calif, 82; Texas Landscape 1900-1986, Mus Fine Arts, Houston, 86; Houston Ctr for Photog, 86; Texas Women, Nat Mus Women in Arts, Washington, DC, 88; 150 Years of Photography, Laguna Gloria Art Mus, Austin, Tex, 89. *Collections Arranged:* Return to Beyond the Valley of Photography, Weil Gallery, Corpus Christi State Univ, 81; Touched by Man--Landscape Photographs from Around the World, Weil Gallery, Corpus Christi State Univ, 90. *Teaching:* From asst prof to prof photog & design, Corpus Christi State Univ, Tex, 82- *Bibliog:* Ellen Wallenstein (auth), Ties that bind, Artweek, 12/81; Suzanne Winkler (auth), Where's the family, Tex Monthly, 1/82. *Mem:* Tex Photog Soc; Houston Ctr for Photog (bd trustees); Art Mus S Tex (bd trustees). *Media:* Silver Prints, Non-Silver Processes. *Dealer:* Lynn Goode Gallery 2719 Colquitt Houston TX 77098. *Mailing Add:* 327 Katherine Dr Corpus Christi TX 78404

RILEY-LAND, SARAH (SARAH AGNES RILEY LAND)
PAINTER, EDUCATOR
b Richmond, Va, July 1, 47. *Study:* Tyler Sch Art, Rome; Va Commonwealth Univ, BFA; Univ Mo, Columbia, MA, 77, MFA, 82. *Work:* William Woods Col Permanent Collection, Fulton, Mo; Springfield Art Mus, Mo; Vivian & Gordon Gilkey Ctr Graphic Arts, Portland, Ore. *Comn:* Painting, Univ Mo Hosp & Clinics, 83. *Exhib:* Va Prints & Drawings, Va Mus Fine Arts, 81; Va Mus Fine Arts Next Juried Show, 83; Watercolor USA, Springfield Art Mus, Mo, 83 & 88; 2nd Nat Small Print & Drawing Exhib, Cobleskill, NY, 84; one-woman shows, Wichita State Univ, 85 & Leedy-Voulkes Gallery, Kansas City, Mo, 90; Mid-Four Ann Juried Exhib, Nelson Atkins Mus, Kansas City, 87; Fourth Clemson Nat Print & Drawing Exhib, SC, 89. *Pos:* Dir, Davis Art Gallery, Stephen's Col, Columbia, Mo, 83- *Teaching:* Prof drawing & painting, Stephens Col, 82-, actg head art dept, 85-86, prog dir art area, 86- *Awards:* First Patroness Award, Mid-Four Ann Juried Exhib, 87; Purchasse Award, Springfield Mus Art, 88; Summer Study Grant, Stephens Col, Columbia, Mo, 89 & 90; and others. *Bibliog:* Donald Hoffman (auth), article, Kansas City Star, 6/20/82; article, New York Art Rev, 88. *Mem:* Col Art Asn; Watercolor USA Hon Soc; assoc mem, Kans Watercolor Soc. *Media:* Drawing, Paint. *Publ:* Charlottesville First Folio, 71. *Dealer:* Reynolds-Minor Gallery 1514 W Main St Richmond VA 23220; Leeder Voulkos Gallery 1919 Wyandotte Kansas City MO 64111. *Mailing Add:* 101 N Glenwood Columbia MO 65201

RINDFLEISCH, JAN
DIRECTOR, CURATOR
Study: Purdue Univ, BS, 62, San Jose State Univ, MFA, 79; Mus Mgt Inst, J Paul Getty Trust, 89. *Collections Arranged:* Art Collectors in and Around Silicon Valley, 4/85; Art of the Refugee Experience, 3/88; Drawing from Experience: Artists over Fifty, 2/90. *Pos:* Dir, Euphrat Gallery, De Anza Col, Cupertino, Calif, 79- *Teaching:* Instr studio art/art hist, De Anza Col, Cuperinto, Calif, 79-85. *Awards:* Asian Heritage Coun Arts Award, 88; Woman Achievement, Santa Clara Co, 89. *Bibliog:* Cordell Koland (auth), Euphrat Gallery fights cultural deprivation in the valley, Bus J, 3/25/85; Theresa Hong Bailar (auth), Focus on Jan Rindfleisch, Silhouette Mag, 4/89; Eric Reyes (auth), A Room of One's Art, Metro, 4/90. *Mem:* Am Asn Mus; Calif Confederation Arts; Western Mus Conf; Comt Arts Policy, Santa Clara Co (comt mem, 85-); Arts Coun Santa Clara Co (bd mem, 88-). *Publ:* Auth, Art, Religion, Spirituality, Euphrat Gallery, 82; Art Collectors in and Around Silicon Valley, Euphrat Gallery, 85; Content: Contemporary Issues, Euphrat Gallery, 86; Art of the Refugee Experience, Euphrat Gallery, 88. *Mailing Add:* De Anza College Euphrat Gallery 21250 Stevens Creek Blvd Cupertino CA 95014

RINDGE, DEBORA ANNE
HISTORIAN, GALLERY DIRECTOR
b Santa Monica, Calif, Dec 5, 56. *Study:* Univ Calif, Santa Barbara, BA (art hist), 78; Ohio State Univ, MA(art hist), 80. *Collections Arranged:* Works by Lowell Nesbitt, 1956-1982 (auth, catalog), 83; 19th Century American Paintings from Washington & Lee University, 84; The Sculptor's View: An Invitational Exhibit, 84; Works on Paper: An Invitational Exhibit, 85; Women at Washington & Lee University: A Historical Exhibit, 86. *Teaching:* Instr art hist & Am & mod art, Univ Ala, Birmingham, 80-82; instr & gallery dir Am art, Washington & Lee Univ, Lexington, Va, 82-86; instr, Smithsonian Inst, Washington DC, 88-91; instr art hist & Am & mod art, Hood Col, Frederick, Md, 92-93. *Awards:* Fel Nat Gallery Art, 88-89; Fel Mid-Atlantic Asn Mus, 90; Fel Huntington Libr & Art Collections, 91-92. *Mem:* Col Art Asn Am; Arch Am Art. *Res:* Cultural meaning of American landscape subjects. *Publ:* Auth, Sara Armstrong, 81, Jim Alexander: Recent Work, 82 & Roger Shimomura, 82, Art Papers; contribr, Catalogue of the American Collection, Columbus Mus Art, Ohio, 89; Frederic Edwin Church, Nat Gallery Art, 90. *Mailing Add:* 7921 Mandan Rd Apt 103 Greenbelt MD 20770-2152

RINEHART, MICHAEL
EDITOR
b Miami, Fla, Dec 27, 34. *Study:* Harvard Univ, BA, 56; Courtauld Inst, Univ London, 57-59. *Pos:* Ed-in-chief, BHA Bibliography of the History of Art. *Mem:* Col Art Asn; ARLIS/NA. *Publ:* Ed, B Berenson, Italian Pictures of the Renaissance, Florentine School, London, 63; auth, A Drawing by Vasari for the Studiolo of Francesco I, Burlington Mag, 64; auth, Practical Support on an International Basis for the Bibliography of Art History, CNRS, Paris, 69; auth, A Document for the Studiolo of Francesco I in Art the Ape of Nature, Abrams, 81; auth, Art databases and art bibliographies: A survey, Art Librs J, 82; and others. *Mailing Add:* 415 Central Park W New York NY 10025

RING, EDWARD A
COLLECTOR
b New York, NY. *Collections Arranged:* Focus on Light, NJ State Mus, Trenton, 67. *Pos:* Owner, Carter Gallery, formerly; mem, NJ State Coun Arts, 67-78, chmn, 71-76; partner, Artnews, formerly. *Mailing Add:* 190 Sayre Dr Princeton NJ 08540

RINGGOLD, FAITH
PAINTER, SCULPTOR
b New York, NY, Oct 8, 30. *Study:* City Col New York, BS, 55, MA, 59; Moore Col Art, Hon PhD, Wooster Col Art, Hon PhD, Brockport State Univ, Hon DSc. *Work:* Chase Manhattan Bank, New York; Studio Mus, Harlem, New York; High Mus Art, Atlanta, Ga; Philip Morris Collection, New York; Newark Mus, NJ; Metrop Mus Art, Solomon R Guggenheim Mus, New York; Boston Mus Fine Art. *Comn:* For the Womens House (mural), Women House Detention, Rikers Island, NY, 71; Williams Col, Williamstown, Mass, 88; Williams Col, Williamstown, Mass, 88; High Mus Art, Atlanta, Ga, 88; Committed to Print, Mus Mod Art, New York, 88; Tradition & Conflict: Images of a Turbulent Decade, 1963-1973, Studio Ms Harlem, New York; Oprah Winfrey, Harpo Prod, 90-91. *Exhib:* Memorial for Martin Luther King, Mus Mod Art, New York, 68; Women Choose Women, New York Cult Ctr, 73; retrospectives, Rutgers Univ Art Gallery, 73, Studio Mus Harlem, New York, 84 & Fine Arts Mus of Long Island, traveling, 90-93; Jubilee, Boston Mus, 75; Second World Black & African Festival Arts & Cult, Lagos, Nigeria, 77; Whitney Biennial, 85; one-person shows, Wooster Col, Columbus, Ohio, 85, Bernice Steinbaum Gallery, New York, 86, Baltimore Mus, Md, 87, Deland Mus Art, Deland, Fla, 87 & Bernice Steinbaum Gallery, New York, 88; The Decade Show, The Studio Mus, Harlem, 90. *Pos:* Founder, Coast to Coast: A Women of Color Nat Artists' book proj, 88; independent cur, Detroit Focus Gallery, 89, African Am Mus Fine Art, 90 & SoHo 20 Gallery, New York, 90. *Teaching:* Prof art, Univ Calif, San Diego, 84- *Awards:* La Napoule Found Award, 90; Coretta Scott King Award, 92; The Caldecott Honor, 92. *Bibliog:* Leslie Sills (auth), Inspirations: Stories about Women Artists, Albert Whitman & Co, Ill, 88; Arlene Raven, Cassandra L Langer & Joanna Frueh (co-eds), Feminist Art Criticism: An Anthology, 88; Faith Ringgold, A 25 Yr Survey, Fine Arts Mus Long Island, 90. *Mem:* Women's Caucus Art; Col Art Asn. *Media:* Mixed. *Publ:* Contribr, Confirmation: An Anthology of African American Women Writers, William Morrow, 83; auth, Tar Beach, Crown Publ, 91; Aunt Harriet's Underground Railroad in the Sky, Crown Publ, 93. *Mailing Add:* 345 W 145th St New York NY 10031

RINGNESS, CHARLES OBERT
EDUCATOR, PRINTMAKER
US citizen. *Study:* St Cloud State Univ, BS, 68; Univ NMex, 70; Tamarind Lithography Workshop, Los Angeles, Master Printer(Ford Fel Grant), 70; Univ Cincinnati, MFA, 83. *Work:* Mus Mod Art, New York; Los Angeles Co Mus Art, Calif; Amon Carter Mus Western Art, Ft Worth, Tex; Canada Coun

Art Bank, Ottawa; Pasadena Art Mus, Calif; Art Gallery, Ont, Toronto. *Exhib:* One-man shows, Univ Cincinnati, Art Gallery, 73, Gallery Moos, Toronto, 79, 81, 83 & 85, Phillis Needlman Gallery, Chicago, 83, Condesso Lawler Gallery, New York, 83 & 84, Art Gallery, Ont, Toronto, 84, Helandenr Rubinstein Gallery, Palm Beach 85 & Malton Art Gallery, Cincinnati, 86 & 90, Lydon Fine Art, Chicago, 90, Peter M David Gallery, Minneapolis, 90; Canadian Biennial, Winnipeg Art Gallery, Man, 81; Condesso/Lawler Gallery, New York, 83 & 84; Van Straaten Gallery, Chicago, 85. *Teaching:* Asst prof, Univ SFla, 70-76, graphicstudio mgr, 71-76; assoc prof, Univ Sask, 76-85, prof, 85- *Awards:* Ford Fel Grant, 68-70; Prizes for prints & drawing, Art Gallery Brant Inc, Brantford, Ont, 80 & 81; Kathleen Fenwick Award, Edmonton Art Gallery, 80; Sask Sr Arts Bd Grant, 82-83. *Bibliog:* Marshall Webb (auth), article, Arts West, 12/79; Carol Phillips (auth), article, Artscanada, 4/80; Charlie Crane (auth), Anti-multiple printmaker, Artmagazine, 6/80; articles in Palm Beach Daily News, Cincinnati Post & NY Times. *Mem:* Col Arts Asn, New York; Print & Drawing Coun Canada; Canada Artists Representation. *Media:* Mixed. *Dealer:* Gallery Moos 136 Yorkville Ave Toronto ON Canada M5R 1C2; Lydon Fine Arts Chicago Ill. *Mailing Add:* Dept Art Univ Sask Saskatoon SK S7N 0W0 Canada

RIOUX (DE MESSIMY), DEENA (COTY) DES
PAINTER, GRAPHIC ARTIST
b Cambridge, Mass, Dec 7, 41; French & US citizen. *Study:* RI Sch Design, 59-62; Brown Univ, 60-62; Ecole de la Grande Chaumiere, Paris, 61; Univ Paris I at Sorbonne, 61 & 63. *Work:* Indiana Univ Art Mus; Int Triennale Graphic Arts, Krakow, Poland; RI Sch Design Mus Art; Laguna Gloria Art Mus, Austin, Tex; Boise State Univ, Idaho. *Exhib:* One-person shows, Ward-Nasse Gallery, New York, 78; Photo-Derived, Nat Competition, Indiana Univ, Bloomington, 89; At the Edge II, Nat Competition, Laguna Gloria Art Mus, Austin, Tex, 90-92; Earth, Nat Competition, La Sierra Univ, Riverside, Calif, 91; Volksgraphic Bumbershoot, Seattle Ctr, Wash, 91; Int Triennale of Graphic Arts, Krakow, Poland/Nuremberg, Ger, 91-92; Maison Francaise/Columbia Univ, New York, 92; Techno-Gods, City Without Walls Gallery, Newark, NJ, 92. *Pos:* Designer package & corp image, free lance illus & design, Boston, 65-69; lectr, Lesley Col, Mass Col Art & Harvard Grad Sch Design, 75-77; founder & dir, 7 at Large, NE Women Artists' Collab, 75-78; exhib consult, Asn Artist-Run Galleries, New York, 81-85; exhib coordr, NY Alumni Chapter, RI Sch Design, 85-86. *Awards:* RI Sch Design Scholar, 59-61; Exhib grant, Art Inst Boston, 75; Boston Mus Sci Grant, 77; named One of New York's Outstanding Artists, Pop Art Collector Ethel Scull, New York, 83; Travel Citation, Midwest Mus Circuit, New York, 90-93; Travel Citation, Mid-Am Arts, Alliance, Tex, 90-92. *Bibliog:* Garry Armstrong (auth), Boston Women Artists, WNAC-TV Channel 7 Spec Feature, Boston, 75; Mary Lou Kelley (auth), Organic visions, Christian Sci Monitor, 78; Joan Shepard (auth), Ethel Scull-Collectors Choice exhibit, Daily News, New York, 83; Robert Atkins (cur/critic),Art Now/New York Gallery Guide, special feature, New York, 85; Mus Mod Arts & Wendy Weitman (catalog Photo & mention), At The Edge II, Tex Fine Arts Asn, Austin; Computer Generations, Providence J Bull, RI, 91; North American Off-Color Exhibition, Idaho Statesman, Boise, 91; Sunday Star-Ledger, Newark, NJ, 92; Robert Hirsch (photo/monogr), Exploring Color Photography, 2nd Ed , Wm C Brown, Dubuque, Iowa, 92. *Mem:* New Mus Contemp Art, New York; Art & Sci Collaborative Inc, Staten Island; Maison Francaise/Columbia Univ, New York. *Media:* Acrylic; Scanner Editions. *Mailing Add:* 251 West 19th St Apt 3B New York NY 10011

RIPPEL, M (MORRIS CONRAD)
PAINTER
b Albuquerque, NMex, Jan 23, 30. *Study:* Univ NMex, BS(Archit Eng), 58. *Work:* NMex Dept Development, Santa Fe; West Texas Mus, Lubbock; Denver Art Mus, Colo; Valley National Bank, Phoenix. *Exhib:* Retrospective, Haley Libr, Tex, 79; Nat Acad Western Art, Nat Cowboy Hall Fame, Okla, 75-81; Artists of Am Exhib, Colo Heritage Ctr, Denver, 81; Western Heritage, Houston, Tex, 81. *Pos:* Design architect, Chambers & Campbell Architects, 64-67. *Awards:* Prix de West, Nat Cowboy Hall Fame, 79; Gold Medal Watercolor, Nat Cowboy Hall Fame, 78 & 79. *Bibliog:* Susan E Meyer (auth), The watercolor page, Am Artist, 72; Mary Carroll Nelson (auth), A serious realist, Southwest Art, 80; Jean Jordan (auth), From blueprints to egg tempera, NMex Mag, 81. *Mem:* Nat Acad Western Art. *Media:* Egg Tempera; Drybrush Watercolor. *Dealer:* Settler's West Galleries 6420 North Campbell Ave Tucson AZ 85718. *Mailing Add:* 1317 Florida St NE Albuquerque NM 87110

RIPPEY, CLAYTON
PAINTER, MURALIST
b La Grande, Ore, Apr 24, 23. *Study:* Northwestern Univ; Stanford Univ, with Daniel Mendelowitz, Ray Faulkner & Anton Refrigier, BA & MA; San Jose State Col, with George Post; Inst Allende, Mex, with James Pinto & Fred Samuelson. *Work:* Cunningham Mus, Bakersfield, Calif; Dance Mag Hq, New York; Wakayama Castle, Japan; Missions of Calif, Mexicali, Bakersfield, Calif; World of Legends, Los Altos, Calif. *Comn:* Pylon design & mural, Bakersfield Col, Calif, 58; two murals, Valley Plaza Mall, Bakersfield, 67; three-dimensional mural, Tenneco Corp Hq, Bakersfield, 69; murals, Bakersfield Californian Publ Hq, 75 & Nat Martinize Corp, 77; and others. *Exhib:* Lucian Labaudt Gallery, San Francisco, 55; Bakersfield Mus Art, Calif, 58, 61 & 66; Circulo de Belles Artes, Palma, Spain, 60; Pioneer & Haggen Mus, Stockton, Calif, 64; Port Townsend Art Ctr, Wash, 65; and over 75 one-man shows. *Pos:* Chmn art dept, Bakersfield Col, 69-72. *Teaching:* Prof art, Bakersfield Col, 49-67 & 69-80; prof art, Maui Comm Col, 68-69. *Awards:* Top 100 Arts for Parks, 90. *Bibliog:* Clayton Rippey, Ora Press, Athens, Greece. *Media:* Acrylics, Watercolor; Mosaics. *Dealer:* Cezanne Gallery Int PO Box 2354 Bakersfield CA 93303; Stary Sheets 14988 Sand Canyon Ave St I-5 Irvine CA 92718. *Mailing Add:* Cederwood Studio PO Box 639 Eastsound WA 98245

RIPPON, RUTH MARGARET
CERAMIST, SCULPTOR
b Sacramento, Calif, Jan 12, 27. *Study:* Calif Col Arts & Crafts, with Antonio Prieto, BA, 47, MFA, 51; San Francisco Sch Fine Arts, with Joan J Pearson, scholar. *Work:* Crocker Art Mus, Sacramento; Vice President's House, Washington, DC; Bemidji State Univ; Calif Expos & Fair, Sacramento; Memorial Gallery Rochester; and many pvt collections. *Comn:* large clay sculpture, comn by Dr & Mrs Malcolm McHenry, 83; two life-sized seated figures, Pavilions, A Robert Powell Develop, Sacramento, 85; life-size clay, Bather, Mr & Mrs Vern Jones, Sacramento, 87; life-size sculpture group, Mother w/children, Pavilious, A Robert Powell Development, Sacramento, 89; Freeport Sq, Sacto Sculpture Lifesize, 91. *Exhib:* One-woman shows, Artists Contemp Gallery, Sacramento, 67, 69, 72, 74, 77, 79, 82 & 86, Univ Pac, Stockton, Calif, 76 & Univ Rochester, NY, 76; Michael Himovitz Gallery, 90; 20-Yr Retrospective, Crocker Art Mus, Sacramento, 71; Oakland Mus, 74; Crocker Kingsley Retrospective, Sacramento, 75; Drawing Show, Sacramento City Col, 78; Col Holy Names, 82; Retrospective Calif State Univ, 87. *Teaching:* Crafts dir, Presidio of San Francisco, 54-56; prof ceramics, Calif State Univ, Sacramento, 56-87 (Prof Emer, 87-). *Awards:* Many Purchase Awards, Calif State Fair & Expos, Sacramento, 48-66; Presidents Wives Series, San Francisco Potters Asn, DeYoung Mus, 69-70, Excellence in craftsmanship, AIA for Lollies, Powell Pavilion, 87. *Bibliog:* Oppi Untracht (auth), Ruth Rippon, Sgraffito Through Glaze, 57 & Fred Ball (auth), Ruth Rippon Retrospective, 71, Ceramics Monthly Mag; Ruth Holland (auth), Rippon Retrospective, Creative Arts League 71 Catalog, 71; Calif State Univ Retrospective catalog, 87. *Mem:* Creative Arts League Sacramento; Asn San Francisco Potters; Crocker Art Gallery Asn. *Media:* Stoneware Clay, Watercolor. *Mailing Add:* 57 Sandburg Dr Sacramento CA 95819

RIPPON, THOMAS MICHEAL
SCULPTOR, COLLECTOR
b Sacramento, Calif, Apr 1, 54. *Study:* Apprenticeship with Robert Arneson, Calif, 70-74; Sch Art Inst Chicago, MFA(Nelson Raymond Fellow), 79. *Work:* San Francisco Mus Mod Art, Calif; Renwick Gallery, Smithsonian Inst, Washington, DC; Contemporary Art Mus, Honolulu, Hawaii; Erie Art Mus, Pa; Crocker Art Mus, Sacramento, Calif. *Exhib:* The Great American Foot, Am Craft Mus, New York, 78; Clay Routes, San Francisco Mus Mod Art, Calif, 79; Wedgewood's Contemporaries, Philadelphia Mus Mod Art, Pa, 80; The Clay Figure, Am Craft Mus, New York, 81; American Porcelain, Renwick Gallery, Smithsonian Inst, Washington, DC, 81; Painting & Sculpture Today, Indianapolis Mus Art, Ind, 82; First Int Crafts Triennial, Art Gallery of Western Australia, Perth, 89; New Masters Exhib (2 person), Huntington Mus Art, WVa, 91. *Pos:* Chmn Dept Art, Univ Montana, 89- *Teaching:* Asst prof fine art, Univ Nev, Reno, 87-89; vis prof fine art, Univ Calif, Davis, 89; assoc prof fine art, Univ Montana, Missoula, Mont, 89- *Awards:* Artist Fel, Nat Endowment Arts, 74, 81. *Bibliog:* Dennis Adrian (auth), Tom Rippon, Arts Mag, 80; Vicki Halper (auth), Clay Revisions, Seattle Art Mus, 87; Ingrid Evans (auth), Cheerful Agglomerations, Artweek, 88. *Mem:* Nat Coun Arts Adminrs; Col Art Asn. *Media:* Porcelain, Ceramic. *Collection:* Contemporary american Folk Art-naive-untrained contemporary painting, drawing & sculpture. *Dealer:* Judith Weintraub Gallery 1723 J St Sacramento CA 95814. *Mailing Add:* University of Montana Dept of Art Missoula MT 59812

RIPPS, RODNEY
PAINTER
b New York, NY. *Study:* York Col, BA, 72; Hunter Col, MA, 72-73. *Work:* Chase Manhattan Bank & Lehman Brothers Collection, New York; Cincinnati Mus, Ohio; Isreal Mus, Jerusalem; Southeast Banking Corp, Miami, Fla; Rothchild Bank, Zurich, Switz. *Exhib:* Critics Choice, Munson-Williams-Proctor Inst, Utica, NY, 77; one-man shows, Nancy Lurie Gallery, Chicago, 77, Brooke Alexander Gallery, New York, 77 & 78 & Galerie Daniel Templon, Paris, 78, Univ Art Mus, Calif State Univ, Long Beach, 84, Carl Solway, Cincinnati, Ohio, 86 & Berkshire Mus, Pittsfied, Mass, 88; Holly Solomon Gallery, New York, 80-81; Univ Kentucky Art Mus, Lexington, 82; Joslyn Art Mus, Omaha, Nebr, 82; Univ Tex, Austin, 83; Jacksonville Art Mus, Fla, 83; Ronald Felman Gallery, New York, 84; Jewish Mus, New York, 86; Berkshire Mus, Pittsfield, Mass, 90; Marisa Del Re Gallery, New York, 91. *Pos:* Vis artist, Art Inst Chicago, 77, Ill State Univ, Bloomington, 78, Marisa Del Re, New York, 85 & Princeton Univ. *Teaching:* Instr painting, Brooklyn Mus Art Sch, 74-76. *Awards:* Nat Endowment Arts, 79 & 90. *Bibliog:* John Russell (auth), Painting 1985, The New York Times, 2/1/85; Anthony Bannon (auth), Anything goes, Buffalo News, 1/18/85; Stephen Westfall (auth), Ripps romantic theatre, Art in Am, 1/86. *Mem:* Abstract Artist Asn. *Mailing Add:* 350 Old Stockbridge Rd Lenox MA 01240

RISBECK, PHILIP EDWARD
GRAPHIC ARTIST, EDUCATOR
b Kansas City, Mo, July 25, 39. *Study:* Univ Kans, BFA, 62, MFA, 65. *Work:* Sheldon Gallery Art, Lincoln, Nebr; Union Soviet Artists Collections, Moscow; Libr Cong; Wilanov Poster Mus, Warsaw; Moravian Mus, Brno, Czechoslovakia. *Exhib:* Int Poster Biennale, Zacheta Mus, Warsaw, 66, 68, 70, 72, 74, 76, 78, 84, 86, 88 & 90; Graphic Design Biennale, Moravian Mus, Brno, Czechoslovakia, 66, 70, 74, 78, 82, 84, 86, 88 & 90; Posters USA, Mead Libr Ideas, New York, 75; American Poster, 45-75, Smithsonian Inst, 76;

Jurors Exhib, Cordegarda Gallery, Warsaw, 80; one-man exhibs, Gallery Union Soviet Artists, Moscow, 83, traveling exhib, 83-84 & Porto Museo de Los Soares, Portugal, 84; and many others. *Pos:* Co-dir, Colo Int Poster Exhib, 79- *Teaching:* Prof art, Colo State Univ, 65- *Awards:* Silver Medal, Int Biennale Graphic Design, Brno, Czechoslovakia, 82; Durrell Award Res, Colo State Univ, 82; Outstanding Prof, Col Arts, Humanities & Soc Sci, Colo State Univ, 83. *Bibliog:* Lanny Sommese (auth), John Sorbie and Phil Risbeck, Colo State Univ & Novum Gebrachsgraphik, Ger, 76; Richard Coyne (auth), Colorado State University Poster Exhibition, Commun Arts Mag, 79; Silas Rhodes (auth), Colorado State University Art Program in Graphics, Graphis, Zurich, 82; Oleg Savostiuk (auth), Philip Risbeck-An artist of the USA, Art Mag, Moscow, 84. *Mem:* Art Dirs Club Denver (pres, 81-82, mem bd, 81-); Univ & Col Designers Asn; Int Typography Alliance; Int Cong Graphic Design. *Publ:* Auth, Eighth International Poster Biennale in Warsaw, Graphis Press, Zurich, 80; Third, Fourth & Fifth Colorado International Poster Exhibition, Graphis, 84, 86 & 88. *Mailing Add:* Colorado State Univ Ft Collins CO 80523

RISE, JOHN ERNEST
PAINTER
b Albuquerque, NMex, Nov 30, 54. *Study:* Tamarind Litho Workshops, with Garo Antresian, 74-75; Ariz State Univ, with Jim Pile, BFA, 76; Univ NMex, with John Wenger, MA(grad asst), 77. *Work:* Mus Albuquerque; Roswell Mus & Arts Ctr, NMex; Prudential Life Insurance Co, Los Angeles; Ariz State Univ, Tempe; Am Oil Co, Denver; and others. *Exhib:* One-man shows, William Sawyer Gallery, San Francisco, 79 & traveling show in Mex, 81-82; Here and Now, Mus Albuquerque, 80; Joslyn Art Mus, Omaha, 80; New Mexico Artists, Sarah Blaffer Mus, Univ Houston, 81; and others. *Pos:* Pres & gen mgr, Best Moulding Frames, 80- *Awards:* Alumni Asn Award, Ariz State Univ, 76; Jurors Award, 8 West Biennial, Grand Junction, Colo, 80. *Bibliog:* Thomas Albright (auth), Decadence, motion, San Francisco Chronicle, 80; William Peterson (auth), New Mexico art, Portfolio Mag, 81; William Peterson (auth), New Mexico art, Art Am, 81. *Mem:* Nat Art Materials Trade Asn. *Media:* Oil, Chalk Pastel. *Dealer:* William Sawyer Gallery 3045 Clay St San Francisco CA. *Mailing Add:* 8712 Canyon Run NE Albuquerque NM 87107

RISELING, ROBERT LOWELL
EDUCATOR, PAINTER
b Sioux City, Iowa, June 5, 41. *Study:* Univ Northern Iowa, BA, 63, MA, 66; State Univ Iowa, 64; Univ Wis-Madison, MFA, 72. *Work:* Memphis Brooks Mus Art, Memphis Col Art, Tenn; Tenn State Mus, Nashville; Hamline Univ, St Paul, Rochester Art Ctr, St Cloud Univ, Anoka-Ramsey St Jr Col, Wilmar & City of St Cloud, Minn; Univ Northern Iowa, Cedar Falls; and many others. *Exhib:* One-man shows, Maka Gallery, Rock Island, Ill, 65 & 71, Univ Northern Iowa, Cedar Falls, 66, Rochester Art Ctr, Minn, 67, Hamline Univ, Minn, 67, 71 & 73, St Cloud State Univ, Minn, 68, 70 & 72, Edythe Bush Theatre, St Paul, Minn, 71 & Univ Wis, Madison, 72; Memphis Col Art, Tenn, 75 & 82, Commerce Sq Gallery, Tenn, 77, Theatre Memphis, Tenn, 78, Galveston Arts Ctr, Tex, 80, Clark Turner Gallery, Tenn, 82, Alice Bingham Gallery, Tenn, 83 & Albers Gallery, Tenn, 86; Jewish Community Ctr, Memphis, Tenn, 87 & Crown Plaza Hotel Gallery, Memphis, Tenn, 88; group shows, Luther Col Fine Arts Festival Exhib, 65 & 67, Luther Col Watercolor, Prints and Drawing, 65-66, 3rd Ann, Waterloo, Iowa, 66, Charles E MacNider Mus Painting and Drawing Exhib, Mason City, Iowa, 66, Minn State Fair, 66, Luther Col Drawing, Water, Print Show, 69 & Minn Printmakers, 70; Midwest Drawing Invitational, N Hennepin State Jr Col, 71, 8th Ann, Waterloo, Iowa, 71, 40th Ann Arrowhead, Tweed Gallery, Duluth, Minn, 73, 17th Ann Delta, Arkansas Arts Ctr, Little Rock, 74, Tenn Bicentennial, Nashville, 76, 11th Ann Prints and Drawings, Ark Art Ctr, Little Rock, 78 & Memphis in May Exhib, 81; Art in the Eighties, Tenn State Mus, Nashville, 81, Tenn State Mus, Nashville, 84, Memphis Ctr Contemp Art, Tenn, 89 & Flora, Goldsmiths Botanic Gardens, Memphis, Tenn, 90. *Teaching:* Instr art, Monticello, Iowa, 63-65; grad asst, Dept Art, Univ Northern Iowa, 65-66; asst dir & resident artist, 66-67, dir art, Rochester Art Ctr, 67; instr dept art, St Cloud State Univ, 67-71; teaching asst, Dept Art, Univ Wis, 71-72; asst prof, Dept Art, St Cloud State Univ, 72-74; asst prof, Memphis Col Arts, Tenn, 74-78, assoc prof, 78-; vis artist, Lake Placid Sch Arts, NY, 81, Univ Northern Iowa, Cedar Falls, 83, Alfred Univ, New York, 83, Pac Northwest Col Art, Portland, Ore, 86 & faculty, Gov Sch Arts Murfreesboro, Tenn, 89 & 90. *Awards:* First Award Painting, 8th Ann, Waterloo, 71; Second Award Painting, 40th Ann Arrowhead, Tweed Gallery, Duluth, Minn, 73; Purchase Award, Tenn Bicentennial, 76. *Media:* Acrylic, Collage. *Mailing Add:* Dept Art Memphis Col Art Overton Park Memphis TN 38112

RISHEL, JOSEPH JOHN, JR
CURATOR
b Clifton Springs, NY, May 15, 40. *Study:* Hobart Col, BA, 62; Univ Chicago, MA, 65. *Collections Arranged:* Painting in Italy in the 18th Century: Rococo to Romanticism (co-ed, catalog), Chicago, Minneaolis & Toledo, 70-71; Art in France Under the Second Empire (auth, catalog), Philadelphia, Detroit, Paris, 78-79; Sir Edwin Landseer (auth, exhib catalog); Cezanne in Philadelphia Collections (auth, exhib catalog); British Painting in the Philadelphia Museum of Art from the Seventeenth through the Nineteenth Century; Claude Monet: Philadelphia, 87; Henry P McIlhenny Collection, 87-88; Masters of 17th-Century Dutch Landscape Painting, 87-88; Masterpieces of Impressionism and Post-Impressionism: The Annenberg Collection, 89. *Pos:* Cur, European painting before 1900 & John G Johnson Collection, Philadelphia Mus Art, 71-; cur, Rodin Mus, Philadelphia. *Teaching:* Instr art hist, Wooster Col, Ohio; lectr spec exhibs, Art Inst Chicago. *Publ:* Co-ed, Museum Studies, Chicago; contribr, Great Museums of the World: The Art Institute of Chicago, Kodnasha, Tokyo, 70; The Hague School: some forgotten pictures in the collection, Philadelphia Mus of Art Bull, 15-27, 7-9/71; auth, Landseer: Queen Victoria's favorite painter copied in America, 19th Century Mag, Vol 7, autumn 81; A Lyonnais flower piece by Antoine Berjon (1754-1843), Philadelphia Mus Art Bull, Vol 78, No 336, 16-24, fall 82. *Mailing Add:* PO Box 7646 Philadelphia PA 19101

RISLEY, JOHN HOLLISTER
SCULPTOR
b Brookline, Mass, Sept 20, 19. *Study:* Amherst Col, BA(cum laude); R I Sch Design, BFA; Cranbrook Acad Art, MFA. *Work:* Wesleyan Univ; Fred Olsen Found, Conn; Hartford Jewish Community Ctr, Conn; Rose Art Gallery, Brandeis Univ. *Comn:* Wood & metal relief, IBM Hq, New York, 65; wrought iron relief, Cleveland Garden Ctr, Ohio, 66; copper relief, Nat Bank, Quarryville, Pa, 71; wood & metal sculptures, Brookside Elementary Sch, Waterville, Maine, 70; bronze sculpture, Univ Maine, Portland, 70. *Teaching:* Prof sculpture, Wesleyan Univ, 54-, chmn dept of art, 68- *Awards:* Drakenfield Prize, 18th Ceramic Ann, 54; New Haven Arts Festival Sculpture Prize, 66; First Prize, Int Festival Humor and Satire, Bulgaria. *Mailing Add:* Dept Art Wesleyan Univ Middletown CT 06457

RISS, MURRAY
PHOTOGRAPHER, EDUCATOR
b Poland, Feb 6, 40; US citizen. *Study:* City Univ New York, BA; Cooper Union Sch Art; RI Sch Design, with Harry Callahan, MFA. *Work:* Mus Mod Art, New York; Bibliot Nat, Paris; Art Inst Chicago; Nat Gallery Art, Can; New Orleans Mus Fine Arts. *Comn:* Photograph Reelfoot Lake, State of Tenn, 72. *Exhib:* Mus Mod Art, New York, 70-71; one-man shows, Minneapolis Mus Fine Art, 71, Visual Studies Workshop (traveling show), New York, 76-78, Projects Inc, Cambridge, 79 & Southern Artist (worldwide traveling exhib), US Info Agency, 76; Fantastic Photography USA, six maj mus in Europe, 78; Photographer's Gallery, London, Eng, 79; Rhodes Col, Memphis, 80; Big Shot, Univ Ala, 83. *Pos:* Vis sr lectr, Univ Haifa, Israel, 75-76; cur, Emerging Southern Photographers, Memphis Col Art, 92. *Teaching:* Prof photog, Memphis Col Art, 68-86, head dept photog, 68-86. *Awards:* Nat Endowment Arts Grant, 79. *Bibliog:* William Parker (auth), Introduction to my portfolio, Ctr Photog Studies, 75. *Publ:* Illusr, Sleep Book, Harper & Row, 74; Good Abode: Architectural History of Shelby County, Towery Press, 83; The Guide to Mud Island, MM Publ, 87. *Mailing Add:* 1306 Harbert Ave Memphis TN 38104

RISSER, JAMES K
DEALER, PAINTER
b Ft Collins, Colo, Nov 8, 47. *Study:* Univ Calif, Santa Barbara, MFA, 72. *Work:* Mus Mod Art, New York; Oakland Mus; Richmond Art Ctr, Calif; NJ State Mus, Clinton; Grunwald Ctr Graphic Arts, Los Angeles. *Exhib:* Photography in Printmaking, Cornell Univ Art Gallery, 77; Aesthetics of Graffiti, San Francisco Mus Mod Art, 78; Santa Barbara Artists Invitational, Santa Barbara Mus Art, 79; Drawing Show Biennale, Newcastle Upon the Tyne, Cleveland, England, 80; solo show, List Gallery, Brown Univ, 80; Love Hate Fear Suicide, Vrije Univ Gallery, Brussels, Belgium, 81; Prints: Acquisitions 1977-1981, Mus Mod Art, New York, 82. *Collections Arranged:* Work of Five Artists, Santa Barbara Mus Art, 79. *Pos:* Owner, Risser Gallery, Pasadena, currently. *Teaching:* Instr drawing & printmaking, Univ Calif, Berkeley, 74-76, Col Creative Studies, Univ Calif, Santa Barbara, 79-82 & Brown Univ, 80-81. *Awards:* Tiffany Found Grant, 77. *Dealer:* Ruth S Schaffner Gallery 128 W Ortega Santa Barbara CA 93101; Kathryn Markel Gallery 50 W 57th New York NY 10019. *Mailing Add:* c/o Hunsaker-Schlesinger Gallery 812 N La Cienega Blvd Los Angeles CA 90069

RITCHIE, (CELIA) ANN
PAINTER
b Providence, RI, Feb 17, 34. *Study:* Univ Wis, Madison, BA, 57; Columbia Univ, MA, 70; Art Students League, New York, with Mario Cooper & Dale Meyers; also with Leo Rabkin, Fay Spahn & Dorothy Gillespie. *Exhib:* Am Watercolor Soc, Nat Acad Galleries, New York, 74-82; Works on Paper, Brooklyn Mus, 75; Nat Arts Club Open, Nat Arts Club, New York, 75-83; Paper, An Invitational Exhib, Michael C Rockefeller Arts Ctr Gallery, State Univ NY Col, Fredonia, 76-77; Nat Arts Club, 82; Salmagundi Club, 83. *Awards:* Award of Merit, Ga Watercolor Soc, 79; Merchandise Award, Inveresk 1979 Artists in Watercolor Competition, 79; House of Heydenryk Award, Nat Arts Club, 83. *Mem:* Am Watercolor Soc (treas, 83-); Allied Artists; Nat Soc Painters in Casein and Acrylic; Audubon Artists; Nat Arts Club. *Media:* Watercolor, Acrylic. *Mailing Add:* 195 W Tenth St New York NY 10014

RITCHIE, WILLIAM (BILL)
PRINTMAKER, VIDEO ARTIST
b Yakima, Wash, Dec 24, 41. *Study:* Cent Wash State Col, BA, 64; San Jose State Col, MA, 66; studied with Rolf Nesch, Norway, 69; intern Nat Ctr for Experiments in Television, 74. *Work:* Philadelphia Mus Art, Pa; US Info Agency, Japan; Seattle Art Mus, Wash; Tacoma Art Mus, Wash; Segovia Biennial, Spain. *Comn:* Print, Henry Gallery Asn, Seattle, Wash, 70; sculpture, City of Seattle, Wash, 77; prints, CDROM Publisher's Club, Seattle, Wash; Videotape, King Co Arts Comn, 80. *Exhib:* Nat Print Exhib, Libr of Cong, Washington, DC, 71; British Int Print Biennale, Bradford Galleries, Eng, 72; NWest Film & Video Exhib, Portland Art Mus, Ore, 73 & 74; Am Printmaking, Brooklyn Mus Art, NY, 76; Boston Printmakers 29th Nat, DeCordova Mus, Lincoln, Mass, 77; Portopia, Kobe, Japan, 81; Perspectives: 100 Yr Washington Art, Tacoma Art Mus, 89; Northwest

Vision, Seattle Art Mus, Wash, 90. *Pos:* Art Prof, Univ Wash, Seattle 66-85; corp exec artist, Ritchie's, Inc, 90. *Teaching:* Prof art, Univ Wash, Seattle, 66-85; vis prof media arts, Evergreen State, Wash, 87. *Awards:* Research Grants, Printmaking, Video & Computer Art, 70-76; First Prize, First NWest Film & Video Festival, Portland Art Mus, Ore, 73; Nat Endowment Arts Fel, 74. *Bibliog:* Korot & Schneider (coauths), Video Art, Harcourt, Brace, Jovanovitch, 76; F Eichenberg (auth), The Art of the Print, Harry N Abrams, 76; V Ancona (auth), Bill Ritchie: Video in the Northwest, Videography Mag, Vol 12, No 6. *Mem:* Washington Software Asn; Print Coun; Nat Fac Exchange; Col Art Asn. *Media:* All print media; Video and Computer Graphics. *Publ:* Auth, Behind Time in the Electronic Age, Ritchie's Video, 82; Print 'N Video News, Ritchie's Video, 85-87; Art of Selling Art, Ritchie's Perfect Press, 89; Reinventing Art Studios: Between Tradition and Technology, 93. *Mailing Add:* 360 Halladay Seattle WA 98109

RITTER, JULIAN
PAINTER, MURALIST
b Hamburg, Ger, Sept 19, 09; US citizen. *Study:* Schnars-Alquist, Hugo, 23; Art Inst Chicago, 26; Art Ctr Sch (scholar), Los Angeles, with Stanley Reckless, 32-34. *Work:* War Dept, Hqs, Second Army, Memphis, Tenn; Last Frontier Hotel, Las Vegas, Nev; Silver Slipper Collection, Las Vegas, Nev; Dept Army, US Army Military Hist Inst, Carlisle Barracks, Pa; US Army Art Activity, Ctr Military Hist, Washington, DC. *Comn:* Paintings, Warner Brothers-First National Studios, Burbank, 28-41; murals, comn by State of Calif, 38; paintings, Metro Goldwyn-Mayer, Culver City, Calif, 35-38; paintings, United Artists Studios, Hollywood, Calif, 35-38; paintings, Paramount, Hollywood, 52. *Exhib:* One-man shows, Vigeveno Galleries, Los Angeles, 47, Assoc Am Artists Galleries, Pasadena, Calif, 48, Maxwell Galleries, San Francisco, 52, Swiss Chalet Galleries, Chicago, 52, Paulsen Galleries, Pasadena, 63 & Howard E Morseburg Galleries, Los Angeles, 75; retrospective, Hui Noeau Visual Arts Ctr, Hawaii, 88. *Bibliog:* Keith Gilcrest (dir), Julian Ritter - Pallete of Passion (video), pvt publ, 90; Phyllis Settecase Barton (auth), Julian Ritter, The Sacred and the Profane, pvt publ, 91; Lloyd Jeffrey Mallan (auth), Chasing Moonlight, 92. *Media:* All. *Mailing Add:* Ritter Project PO Box 518 Kula HI 96790

RITTER, JULIAN STAWSKA FROMM See Ritter, Julian

RITTER, RENEE GAYLINN
PAINTER
Study: Queens Col, NY, BA; Long Island Univ, Greenvale, NY, MFA. *Work:* Islip Art Mus, NY; Hillwood Art Mus, Greenvale, NY; Famli Mus, Hempstead, NY; Danville Mus Art, VA. *Exhib:* Long Beach Mus Art, NY, 79, 82, 86, 87 & 89; Sivermine Guild for Arts, New Canaan, Conn, 81, 83, 86 & 92; Islip Art Mus, NY, 83-87, 89 & 92; Francine Ellman Gallery, Los Angeles, 88-91; one-man shows, Parish Art Mus, Southampton, NY, 84, Exotica, Elaine Benson Gallery, Bridghampton, NY, 88, Women in the Arts, Smithtown Township Arts Coun, NY, 88, Nassau Co Mus Fine Arts, 88 & Joan Hodgell Gallery, Sarasota, Fl, 90-92; Gallery Authentique, Viridian Gallry, Roslyn, NY, 92. *Pos:* Lectr, Nassau Co Mus Art, 79-; exec bd, Nat Drawing Asn, 90- *Teaching:* Asst prof, art, CW Post Ctr, Long Island Univ, NY. *Awards:* Award of Excellence, Nassau Co Mus Fine Arts, 86; First Prize, Islip Art Mus, 87; Don Steward Graphic Award, Heckscher Mus, 90. *Bibliog:* Numerous articles including, NY Times, Newsday, Artspeak & Artists Mag, Christian Sci Monitor. *Media:* Paint, collage. *Dealer:* Reece Gallery 24 W 57 St New York NY. *Mailing Add:* 62 Birchwood Park Dr Jericho NY 11753

RITTS, EDWIN EARL, JR
ADMINISTRATOR, MUSEUM DIRECTOR
b Pittsburgh, Pa, Nov 11, 48. *Study:* Wilmington Col, AB, 70; Univ Cincinnati, grad prog, 71; Univ NC, cert arts mgt, 85. *Collections Arranged:* Andrew Wyeth in Southern Collections, 76; Richard Hunt, Mountain Flight, 77; Pvt collection of Arthur & Holly Magill, 81; New Modern Painting, Harsh Images on Canvas, 84; America's Impressionists, 86. *Pos:* Pres, SC Artist's Guild, 74-75; treas, SC Mus Asn, 74-76; chmn art sect, NC Mus Conf, 89- *Teaching:* Lectr art markets, SC Gov Sch, 82; adj prof mus studies, Univ NC, 84-86. *Mem:* Am Asn Mus; NC Mus Conf. *Mailing Add:* Asheville Art Mus Civic Ctr Asheville NC 28801

RITZ, LORNA J
PAINTER, SCULPTOR
Study: Worcester Art Mus, 63-65; Boston Mus Fine Arts, 65; Art Students League, 66; Skowhegan Sch Painting & Sculpture, Scholar, 68; Pratt Inst, BFA, 69; Cranbrook Acad Art, Bloomfield Hills, Mich, MFA(painting & sculpture), 71. *Work:* Bank of Boston, Int Bank New Eng & High Voltage Eng, Shrafts Ctr, Boston; Mt Holyoke Col Art Mus. *Exhib:* Solo exhibs, Nat Arts Mus, Teguciagalpa, Honduras, 83, Boston Visual Artists Union, 85, Augusta Savage Gallery, New Africa House, Univ Mass, Amherst, 87, Nicole C Gallery, Boston, 90, NACUL Archit Ctr, Amherst, Mass, 90 & Harriet Tubman House, Boston, 91; Art in Embassies Program, Washington, DC, paintings located in Guatemala City, Brazzaville, the Congo, Banjul, The Gambia, Valetta, Malta and Praia & Cape Verde; Lopoukhine Gallery, Boston, 88; Nat Asn Women Artists, Jacob Javits Ctr, New York, 89; Grossman Gallery, Sch Mus Fine Arts, Boston, 89; Lacoste Exhib, Mona Bismarck Found, Paris, 91. *Teaching:* Asst prof painting, Univ Minn, 76-77; vis asst prof, Brown Univ, RI, 78 & Dartmouth Col, NH, 78-79; lectr, univs & insts throughout US and world. *Awards:* US Info Agency Grant Awards, Vt, Partners of Americas, to paint, exhibit, lectr & teach at Univ Honduras, 83, Mass Partners of Americas, to teach, lectr & exhib at Inst de Belles Arted, Medelin, Columbia, 90; Esther & Adolph Gottlieb Found Emergency Grant Award, 88; Pollock-Krasner Found Grant Award, 90. *Mailing Add:* 1245 S East St Amherst MA 01002

RIVERA, ELIAS J
PAINTER
b Bronx, NY, April 18, 37. *Study:* Art Students League, 55-61, with Frank Mason; pvt study with Steve Raffo, 61-64. *Work:* Ga Mus Fine Arts, Athens; Adelphi Univ, Long Island, NY; Vassar Mus, Poughkeepsie, NY. *Comn:* Mural, Banco de Ponce, Rockefeller Plaza, New York, 73; four paintings and one bronze plaque, pvt comn by Fortunoff family, New York, 80. *Exhib:* Community Gallery, Brooklyn Mus, NY, 69; National Acad Design, New York, 71, 73, 74, 77 & 78; Crimes of Passion, Chrysler Mus, Norfolk, Va, 81; Santa Fe Festival Arts, NMex, 83 & 84; Ctr Contemp Arts, Santa Fe, 85. *Awards:* Best Painter, De Puerte Rico Inst, 72; Purchase Prize, Ann Show, Am Acad & Inst Arts & Lett, 78; Creative Artists Pub Serv Award, 81. *Media:* Oil. *Dealer:* Munson Gallery Canyon Rd Santa Fe NM 87501; Georgetown Gallery 3235 P St NW Washington DC 20007. *Mailing Add:* c/o Munson Gallery 225 Canyon Rd Santa Fe NM 87501

RIVERA, FRANK
PAINTER
b Cleveland, Ohio, Aug 28, 39. *Study:* Yale Univ Grad Sch Fine Arts, with Alex Katz & Jack Tworkov, BFA, 62; Univ Pa, with Pi Dorazio, Savelli, Helen Frankenthaler & Ludwig Sander, MFA, 67. *Exhib:* Ann Am Painting & Sculpture, Pa Acad Fine Arts, 68; NJ State Mus Painting & Sculpture Ann, 72; Univ Rochester Gallery Art, 72; Susan Caldwell Gallery, New York, 74; 1975 Biennial Exhib Am Art, Whitney Mus Am Art, 75. *Teaching:* Assoc prof painting & design, Mercer Col, Trenton, NJ, 67- *Awards:* Nat Endowment Humanities Grant for Study & Travel in France, 72-73. *Bibliog:* Elizabeth Stevens (auth), Review Whitney Biennial, This Week Mag, Trenton Times, 3/23/75. *Media:* Mixed. *Mailing Add:* Dept Painting Mercer Co Comm Col PO Box B Trenton NJ 08690

RIVERON, ENRIQUE
PAINTER, SCULPTOR
b Cienfuegos, Las Villas, Cuba, Jan 31, 02; US citizen. *Study:* Acad Villate, Havana, Cuba; Acad San Fernando, Madrid, Spain; La Colarouse & Grand Chaumiere, Paris, France; travel scholar from Cuba, Spain, France, Italy & Belgium. *Work:* Fine Arts Mus, Havana, Cuba; Wichita Art Mus, Kans; Lowe Art Mus, Coral Gables, Fla; Mitchell Wolfson, Jr Collection, Miami-Dade Community Col & Miami Mus Mod Art, Fla. *Exhib:* Retrospective exhibs, Lowe Art Mus, Coral Gables, Fla, 80 & De Armas Gallery, Virginia Gardens, Fla, 80; one-man exhibs, Forma Gallery, Coral Gables, 82-83 & Gallery at Grove Isle, Miami, Fla, 83; Hommage a Joan Miro, Editar Cult Ctr, Geneva, Switz, 83; Moosart Art Gallery, Miami, 84; retrospective, SIBI Art & Cult Ctr, 84-85; Bacardi Art Gallery, Miami, Fla, 87. *Teaching:* Instr cartooning, Wichita Art Asn, Kans, 49-53; instr painting, Wichita Univ, Kans, 58-59. *Awards:* Sculpture Award, Sculptors of Fla, Miami, 70; Sculpture Award, Ft Lauderdale Mus Arts, Fla, 70; Painting Award, Third Ann Pan-Am, Miami, 72; Cintas Found Lifetime Achievement Award, Metro Dade Cult Ctr, Miami, Fla, 88. *Bibliog:* Dore Ashton (auth), Art criticism, NY Times, 4/13/57; Carroll E Hogan (auth), Catalog Preface, Dir Wichita Art Mus, Kans, 5/58; J Gomez-Sicre (auth), Catalog Preface, Dir Visual Arts, Orgn Am States, Washington, DC, 74. *Media:* Steel, Iron; Collage. *Publ:* Illus & cartoons, New Yorker, NY Times, Modern Screen & Cine Mundial, New York, 27-50; contribr, Creating art from anything, 68. *Mailing Add:* 1726 Espanola Dr Miami FL 33133

RIVERS, LARRY
PAINTER
b Bronx, NY, Aug 17, 25. *Study:* Hans Hofmann Sch Fine Arts, 48-49; NY Univ, BA, 51. *Work:* Brooklyn Mus; Corcoran Gallery Art, Nat Gallery Art, Washington, DC; Baltimore Mus Art, Md; Metrop Mus Art, Mus Mod Art, Whitney Mus Am Art, Solomon R Guggenheim Mus, New York; Albright-Knox Art Gallery, Buffalo, NY; Art Inst Chicago, Ill; Dallas Mus Art, Tex; Los Angeles Co Mus Art, Calif; San Francisco Mus Mod Art, Calif; Butler Inst Am Art, Youngstown, Ohio; and many others including pvt collections. *Comn:* Outdoor billboard, First New York Film Festival, 63; cover, Erasing the Past, NY Times Mag, 86. *Exhib:* Pa Acad Fine Arts, 63; retrospective, Art Inst Chicago, 70; Va Mus Fine Art, Richmond, 70; one-man exhibs, Traveling retrospective exhib: Kestner-Gesellschaft, Hannover, 80-82, Marlborough Fine Art Ltd, London, 81, Elaine Horwich Gallery, Phoenix, 83, History of Matzah (The Story of Jews), The Jewish Mus, New York, 84-85, Mus Univ Pa, Philadelphia, 85, Marlborough Gallery, New York, 86 & Simms Fine Art, New Orleans, 87; La Jolla Mus Art, 80; Spoleto Festival USA, Gibbes Art Gallery, 88; restrospective, Larry Rivers: Public and Private, traveling, Butler Inst Am Art & Fedn Arts, 90-92, Larry Rivers: Master Prints, 91-92 & Nassau Co Mus Art, 92; and others. *Teaching:* Artist in residence, Slade Sch Fine Arts, London, 64; Md Inst Col Art; instr, Univ Calif, Santa Barbara, 72. *Awards:* Third Prize, Corcoran Gallery Art, 54. *Bibliog:* Sam Hunter (auth), Larry Rivers (monogr), Abrams, 70; What's Happening in America (television interview), Ital Television, 88; Lana Jokel (film), documentary, 92; and many others. *Media:* All. *Dealer:* Marlborough Gallery Inc 41 E 57th St New York NY 10022. *Mailing Add:* 92 Little Plains Rd Southampton NY 11968

RIVERS, VICTORIA Z
SCULPTOR, PAINTER
b Louisville, Ky, Sept 7, 48. *Study:* Murray State Univ, BFA, MACT, SCT, 70 & 74. *Work:* Evansville Mus Arts & Sci; Liberty Gallery, Louisville Gallery, Louisville, Ky; Crocker Mus Art, Sacramento; Bradley Univ Drawing Collection; Valley Bank, Ariz. *Comn:* Several pvt comns in Ky & Tenn, 77-79; Transcendental Landscape (textile) & Recollections (textile), Opryland Hotel, Nashville, 78; Raley's Corp Offices; Registry Hotel,

Minneapolis. *Exhib:* Solo shows, Am Gallery, Bern, Switz, 82, Mus Neon Art, Los Angeles, 83, Crocker Art Mus, Sacramento, 84, Conduit Gallery, Dallas, Tex, 86 & Light Memory, Self Remembering, Univ Davis, Calif, 88; Crossoners, Gallery Contemp Art, Univ Colo, Colorado Springs, 90; Connected through Fiber, Santa Rosa Jr Col, Calif, 91; Ten Year Anniversary Exhib, Mus Neon Art, Los Angeles, 91; Natural Influence-A National Textile Review, Rochester Inst Technol, NY, 92; & others. *Teaching:* Asst prof art, Volunteer State Col, 74-80; prof design, Univ Calif, Davis, 80-; instr workshops, Summervail, Colo, Fiberworks, Berkeley, Art Inst Chicago, Penland Sch, NC, 89 & 90, Haystack Mountain Sch Crafts, Deer Isle, Maine, 89, Split Rock Arts Prog, Univ Minn, Duluth, 92 & Southwest Craft Ctr, San Antonio, Tex, 92; vis artist, Cranbrook Acad Art, Ga State Univ, Univ Ga, Atlanta Col Art, 86, Kyoto Seika Col, Selan Women's Col, Kyoto Am Ctr, US Info Serv, New Media Arts Group, Osaka & Kyoto, Japan, 87, Old Dominion Univ, Norfolk, Va, 88; vis artist & lectr, Herron SchArt Indianapolis, Ind, 89, Am Ctr, Bombay, India, 90, S Ill Univ Carbondale, 89, Concordia Univ, Montreal, Can, 89, Nat Inst Design, Ahmedabad, India, 90, Lalbhai Dalpatbhai Mus, Ahmedabad, India, 90, Nat Inst Fashion Technl, New Delhi, India, 90, Akron Univ, Ohio, 90 & Univ Nev, Las Vegas, 90. *Awards:* Tenn Arts Comn Fel, 78-79; Nat Endowment Art Visual Artists Fel, 85; Indo-Am Fel, Indo-US Subcomn Educ & Cult, 91-92. *Bibliog:* Ann Corbett (auth), The fine art of making crafts, The Washington Post, 1/27/91; D R Wagner (auth), Transforming the sublime: Victoria Z Rivers, Fiberarts Mag, 3-4/91; The surface designer's art, Altamont Press, 92; & others. *Mem:* Surface Design Asn; Am Crafts Coun. *Media:* Printed Dyed Fabric, Embellished Light-Reflective Surfaces. *Publ:* Auth, Perspectives from the Rim, Am Craft, 91; Allegories of Thread, Surface: Surface Design Asn J, 92; Zardozi of India, Am Craft, 92; Beetle Wings in Indian Art, India Mag (in press), 92; Beetle Wings in Textile and Personal Adornment, Fiberarts (in press). *Mailing Add:* 2131 51st St Sacramento CA 95817

RIVO, SHIRLEY WINTHROPE
PAINTER
b Toronto, Ont, Can, June 28, 25; US citizen. *Study:* Univ Toronto, 46; Kean Col, BA, & teaching certification, 77, MA, 80; studied with Carl Burger, Vito Giacalone, James Howe, Wanda Gromodska, Joseph Loeber, Nicholas Reale. *Work:* Deloitte Haskins & Sells, Morristown, NJ; Morris Mus, Morristown, NJ; Nabisco Gallery, East Hanover, NJ. *Comn:* Crescendo, Morris Mus, Morristown, NJ, 89. *Exhib:* One-woman exhibs, Chemical Bank, New York, 77, St Barnabas Med Ctr, Livingston, NJ, 78, NJ Ctr Visual Arts, Summit, NJ, 79 & 85, Ciba-Geigy Corp, Summit, NJ, 79, Exxon Corp, Linden, NJ, 84, Chubb Corp World Hq, Warren, NJ, 85; two-person show, AT&T, Basking Ridge, NJ, 82; Centennial Brooklyn Bridge, Morris Mus, Morristown, NJ, 83; Merck & Co Visual Arts, Rahway, NJ, 90; Images, NJ Ctr Visual Arts, AT&T, Prudential, Chubb, 88, 90 & 91; Water, Water, Everywhere, Nabisco Brands, East Hanover, NJ, 89; Arts Counc of Morris Area at Schering Ploiugh, Madison, NJ, 92. *Pos:* Window display designer, Display Craft & Belg Stores, 44-53; theatrical design & decor, Actors Co, Toronto, Ont, 51-53; needlepoint design, Creative Yarn Kits Inc, New York, 65-72. *Teaching:* Substitute teacher art, various high schs NJ, 77-90. *Awards:* First Prize Oil Paint, Paper Mill Playhouse, 84; Best in Show, Millburn-Short Hills Art Ctr, 85; Pauline Wick Mem, Am Artist Prof League, 90. *Bibliog:* Eileen Watkins (auth), Art, Sunday Star-Ledger, 1/11/87; Ada Brunner (auth), Artists show their best, Star-Ledger Towns, 4/4/91. *Mem:* NJ Ctr Visual Arts (prog chmn, 79-84); Am Artists Prof League; Millburn-Short Hills Art Ctr (bd trustees, 86-92); NJ Ctr Visual Arts (chmn of classes, 90-92). *Media:* Oil. *Dealer:* A J Lederman Fine Art 309 Court St Hoboken NJ 07030. *Mailing Add:* 32 Summit Rd Murray Hill NJ 07974

RIZZI, JAMES
PAINTER, PRINTMAKER
b Brooklyn, NY, Oct 5, 50. *Study:* Miami Dade Jr Col, AA, 72; Univ Fla, BFA, 74. *Work:* Brooklyn Mus, NY; Isetan Sagamihara, Kanagawa, Japan; Seibu Parco, Chiba, Tokyo, Japan. *Comn:* Eric's, comn by E Nalvin, New York, 74; mural, Sullivan St, Police Athletic League, New York, 76 & 92. *Exhib:* 30 Years of American Printmaking, Brooklyn Mus, NY, 76; one-man shows, Fine Arts Mus Long Island, Hempstead, NY, 88 & Tsukuba City Mus, Japan, 92. *Awards:* Pres Award, Nat Art Show, Nat Arts Club, 78; Best of Show, Printmaking, Wash Sq Outdoor Art Exhib, 78; Ann Exhib, Soc Illusrs, 84. *Bibliog:* Gerrit Henry (intro auth), James Rizzi 3-D, Constructions, 88 & Glenn O'Brien (auth), Rizzi, 92, John Szoke Graphics. *Media:* Acrylic, Oil; Miscellaneous Media. *Mailing Add:* c/o John Szoke Graphics Inc 164 Mercer St 2nd fl New York NY 10012

RIZZIE, DAN
COLLAGE ARTIST, PAINTER
b Poughkeepsie, NY, May 23, 51. *Study:* Hendrix Col, Conway, Ark, BA, 73; Southern Methodist Univ, Dallas, Tex, MFA, 75. *Work:* Dallas Mus Fine Arts & Univ Gallery, Southern Methodist Univ, Tex; Witte Mus, San Antonio, Tex; Brooklyn Mus, NY. *Comn:* Akard Mall banners, City of Dallas, Tex, 79. *Exhib:* Tex Painting & Sculpture, Dallas Mus Fine Arts, 76; one-man shows, Works on Paper, Dallas Mus Fine Arts, 78 & Meadows Mus, Shreveport, La, 79, Focus, Ft Worth Art Mus, 80; On the Right Bank of the Red River, Root Art Ctr, New York, 79; Response, Tyler Mus, Tex, 80; Collage, Brooklyn Mus, 81. *Teaching:* Instr lithography & drawing, Southern Methodist Univ, Dallas, 74-75; instr drawing, Richland Col, Dallas, 75-76; instr painting & drawing, Eastfield Col, Dallas, 76-80. *Awards:* Best of Shows, Tex Painting & Sculpture, 76, Shreveport Ann, 77 & Tarrant Co Ann, 78. *Bibliog:* Janet Kutner (auth), Capricious places, Art News, 12/77; Ned Rifkin (auth), Southwest 1978, Art Week, Vol IX, No 18, 78; M J Smith (auth), Dan Rizzie, Art in Am, 2/80. *Media:* Drawing, Collage. *Mailing Add:* PO Box 1672 Sag Harbor NY 11963

ROATZ See Myers, Dorothy Roatz

ROBB, CHARLES
PAINTER
b Toronto, Ont, Can, June 28, 38. *Study:* Ont Col Art, AOCA, 59, with Jock MacDonald, John Alfson & Carl Schaefer. *Work:* Can Coun Art Bank, Ottawa; Citicorp Ltd, Toronto; Kitchener/Waterloo Art Gallery, Ont; Esso, Calgary, Alta; Art Gallery London, Ont, Can; and others. *Exhib:* One-man shows, Pollock Gallery, Toronto, 77-82; three-man show, Agnes Etherington Art Centre, Queens Univ, Kingston, Ont, 77; Art for Bus Sake, Art Gallery Ont, Toronto, 75; Lefebvre Galleries, Edmonton, Alta, 81; Kitchener/Waterloo Art Gallery, Ont, 81; and others. *Bibliog:* D Adlow (auth), Stripes by Robb, Christian Sci Monitor, 64; Kay Woods (auth), Charles Robb, Arts Canada, 77 & 81; Seeing it Our Way, Portrait of Charles Robb (film), Canadian Broadcasting Corp. *Media:* Acrylic. *Mailing Add:* c/o Gallery One 121 Scollard Toronto ON M5R 1J4 Canada

ROBB, DAVID METHENY, JR
MUSEUM DIRECTOR, HISTORIAN
b Minneapolis, Minn, Apr 12, 37. *Study:* Princeton Univ, BA, 59; Yale Univ, MA, 67; Attingham Summer Sch, 78; Mus Mgt Inst, Univ Calif, Berkeley, 83. *Collections Arranged:* The Book of Hours of Charlotte of Savoy, 73; Star Spangled History--, 75-77; Louis I Kahn: Sketches for the Kimbell Art Museum (auth, catalog), 78; Elisabeth Louise Vigee Le Brun, 82. *Pos:* Res asst, Nat Gallery Art, DC, 63; cur, Collection of Mr & Mrs Paul Mellon, 63-65; curatorial fel, Walker Art Ctr, Minneapolis, 67-69; cur, Kimbell Art Mus, Ft Worth, Tex, 69-74, chief cur, 74-83 & acting dir, 79-80; dir, Telfair Acad Arts & Sci, Savannah, 84-85 & Huntsville Mus Art, Ala, 85- *Awards:* Ford Found Cur Training Fel, 68-69. *Mem:* Col Art Asn; Am Asn of Mus; Soc Archit Historians. *Res:* European and American portrait painting; architecture of museums; architectural and landscape photography. *Publ:* Ed, Kimbell Art Mus Catalogue, 72; Louis Kahn: Sketches for the Kimbell Art Mus, 78; Kimbell Art Mus Handbook, 81. *Mailing Add:* Huntsville Mus Art 700 Monroe St Huntsville AL 35801

ROBB, PEGGY HIGHT
PAINTER
b Gallup, NMex, Sept 14, 24. *Study:* Univ NMex, BFA & MA, with Raymond Jonson & Kenneth Adams; Art Students League, New York, 64. *Work:* Univ NMex, Albuquerque; Guangzhuo Art Inst, China, 84. *Comn:* Stained glass window & portraits, Christian Ctr, Albuquerque, 75; McDonnell-Douglass Aircraft, St Louis, Mo, 79. *Exhib:* Southwestern Fiesta, NMex Art Mus, Santa Fe, 66; Sun Carnival Art Exhib, El Paso, Tex, 71; Centre International D'Art Contemporain, Paris, 83; Inst Art, Guangzhuo, China, 84; NMex State Fair, 86; Biennial exhib, Ariz, Colo, NMex, Tex & Utah, 87; Expressions of Faith, Scottsdale, Ariz, 87; Sacred Arts 200, Civic Ctr Mus, Philadelphia, 89; Graham Ctr Mus, Wheaton, Ill, 87 & 89; Christians in the Visual Arts, Washington, DC, 87. *Pos:* Juror, Statewide Exhib, 81, 87, 89, 91. *Teaching:* Univ NMex, Continuing Educ. *Awards:* First Prize, NMex State Fair, 59 & 63; Exhib Awards, St John's Episcopal Cathedral, Albuquerque, 78 & 79. *Bibliog:* Conceptions Southwest, Southwest Art Mag, Univ NMex, 85. *Mem:* Fel Artists Cult Exchange; Albuquerque Asn United Artists; Christians in the Visual Arts; Albuquerque Arts Alliance. *Media:* Acrylic, Oil. *Mailing Add:* 7200 Rio Grande Blvd NW Albuquerque NM 87107

ROBBIN, ANTHONY STUART
PAINTER
b Washington, DC, Nov 24, 43. *Study:* Columbia Col, BA; Yale Univ Sch Art, BFA & MFA. *Work:* Addison Gallery Am Art, Andover, Mass; Whitney Mus Am Art. *Exhib:* Bykert Gallery, New York, 71; Paley & Lowe Inc, New York, 72; Ann, Whitney Mus Am Art, 72, one-man show, 75. *Media:* Acrylic. *Publ:* Auth, Smithson sites & non sites, Art News, 69; auth, Two ocean projects, 69 & auth, A protein sensibility, 71, Arts Mag; auth, Hutchison ecological art, Art Int, 70; auth, Visual paradox & 4-D geometry, Tracts Mag, 75. *Mailing Add:* 423 Broome St New York NY 10013

ROBBIN, TONY
PAINTER, SCULPTOR
b Washington, DC, Nov 24, 43. *Study:* Columbia Univ, BA, 65; Yale Univ, MFA, 68. *Work:* Whitney Mus Am Art, New York; Neuberger Mus, Purchase, NY; Loch Haven Art Ctr, Orlando; Crysler Mus, Norfolk, Va; Del State Mus, Wilmington. *Comn:* Prudential Insurance, Newark, NJ, 82; Southeast Bank, Miami, Fla, 83; United Bank, Houston, 83. *Exhib:* Le Wouvean Mus, Lyon, France, 80; McNay Art Inst, San Antonio, 83; Loch Haven Art Ctr, Orlando, 83; Concepts in Construct, Neuberger Mus, Purchase, NY, 84; Computers & Art, IBM Gallery, New York, 88; Kaos, Chicago Acad Sci, 89. *Bibliog:* Linda Henderson (auth), Princeton Univ Press, 83; David Curtis (auth), To the Nth Dimension, Inovations/PBS, 87; Cynthia Goodman (auth), Distal Visions, Henry Abrams, 87. *Media:* Acrylic, Oil. *Publ:* Auth, Smithson's non-site sights, Art News, 69; Procelain Sensibility, Arts, 71; Chuangtze, Main Currents, 75; Painting & Physics--4 Dimensions, Leonardo, 84; Quasi crystals for Architecture, Leonardo, 89. *Mailing Add:* 423 Broome St New York NY 10013

ROBBINS, BRUCE
PAINTER, SCULPTOR
b Philadelphia, Pa, July 22, 48. *Study:* Cooper Union Sch Art & Archit, New York, BFA, 73. *Work:* Mus Mod Art, New York; Stedelijk Mus, Amsterdam; St Louis Art Mus; Los Angeles County Art Mus. *Exhib:* Art of the 70's, Venice Biennale, 80; Seven Artists (with catalog), Neuberger Mus, Purchase, NY, 80; Biennial, Whitney Mus Am Art, New York, 81; International Survey Recent Painting & Sculpture, Mus Mod Art, New York, 84. *Bibliog:* Ron Warren (auth), Bruce Robbins, M Knoedler Zurich Gallery, 85; Susan S Harris (auth), Bruce Robbins, Arts Mag, 85. *Media:* Oil & Encaustic on Plaster & Wire Mesh; Canvas & Wood. *Dealer:* Blum Helman 20 West 57th St New York NY 10019. *Mailing Add:* 108 Franklin St New York NY 10013

ROBBINS, DANIEL J
HISTORIAN, MUSEUM DIRECTOR
b New York, NY, Jan 15, 32. *Study:* Univ Chicago, BA, 51; Yale Univ, MA, 56; Univ Paris, Inst Art & Archaeology, 58-59; New York Univ Inst Fine Arts, PhD, 74. *Collections Arranged:* Albert Gleizes Retrosepctive, Guggenheim Mus, 64-65; Jaques Villon, Fogg Mus, Grand Palais, 75-76; 200 Years of American Sculpture, Whitney Mus, 76; Edward Koren, 83; Jean Metlinger, Univ Iowa, 85-86. *Pos:* Cur, Nat Gallery Art, Washington, DC, 59-60; cur, Guggenheim Mus Art, 61-64; dir, Mus Art, RI Sch Design, 64-71; dir, Fogg Art Mus, Harvard Univ, 71-75; bd trustees, Canadian Ctr for Achitecture, Montreal, 89- *Teaching:* Instr, Ind Univ, 55; prof, Brown Univ, 65-71; lectr, Harvard Univ, 71-75; vis prof, Dartmouth Col, 75-80 & Yale Univ, 77; Clark prof, Williams Col, 78-79; Baker prof, Union Col, 80- *Awards:* French Govt Fel, 58 & Fulbright Grant, 59, Paris; Nat Endowment Humanities Sr Fel, 76; Guggenheim Fel, 78-79; Fel, Inst Advan Study, Princeton, 86; Fel, Am Coun Learned Soc, 86. *Mem:* Am Fedn Arts; Collectors Am Art. *Publ:* Auth, Jacques Villon, Fogg Mus, 76; From Statues to Sculpture, 76; Cubist Drawings, 79; co-auth, Henri de Toulouse-Lautrec, 80; contribr, Cataloge Societe Anonyme, Yale, 84. *Mailing Add:* Farcevol Farm Randolph VT 05060

ROBBINS, DAVID A
CONCEPTUAL ARTIST, WRITER
b Whitefish Bay, Wis, Apr 17, 57. *Study:* b Brown Univ, Providence, RI, BA, 79. *Work:* Mus Boymans von Beunigen, Rotterdam, Holland; Univ Chicago. *Exhib:* Presi Per Incantemento, Padiglione d'Arte Contemporanea, Milan, Italy, 88; The Photography of Invention, Nat Mus Am Art, Smithsonian, Washington, DC, 89; Image World, Whitney Mus Am Art, New York, 89; D&S Austellung, Kunstverein, Hamburg, Ger, 89; Das Offentliche Bild, Forum Staatpark, Graz, Austria, 91; numerous solo exhibs. *Bibliog:* Doris Von Dratein (auth), David Robbins, Kunstforum, 88; Joshua Decter (auth), Psychosafari, Artscribe, 91; Olivier Zahm (auth) The Wanderer, Texte Zur Kunst, 91. *Media:* Photographs, Sculpture. *Publ:* Auth, The Camera Believes Everything, Eds Schwarz, Stutgart, 88; Foundation Papers from the Archives of the Institute for Advanced Comedic Behavior, NY, 92; auth of more than 30 essays & articles. *Mailing Add:* c/o Jay Gorney Mod Art 100 Greene St New York NY 10012

ROBBINS, EUGENIA S
WRITER, EDITOR
b New York, NY, Apr 22, 35. *Study:* Smith Col, BA. *Pos:* Art ed, George Braziller Inc, 60-64; bk ed, Art in Am, 64-67; news ed, Art J, Col Art Asn of Am, 67 & Col Art Asn Newsletter, 76-80; ed, Art & Auction, 80; news ed, Art Express, 81-; secy, Iriquois Co, currently. *Res:* Persian art and architecture; modern art and architecture; Art books. *Publ:* Auth & coauth, articles in Studio Int, Art in Am, Art and Auction & NY Post; auth, Art, Collier's Yr Bk; auth, regular column in Art J & rev in Art in Am & Art J; and others. *Mailing Add:* RR 2 Peth Rd Randolph VT 05060

ROBBINS, HULDA D
PAINTER, PRINTMAKER
b Atlanta, Ga, Oct 19, 10. *Study:* Pa Mus Sch Indust Art, Philadelphia; Prussian Acad, Berlin, with Ludwig Bartning; Barnes Found, Merion, Pa. *Work:* Metrop Mus Art, New York; Victoria & Albert Mus, London, Eng; Bibliot Nat, Paris; Art Mus Ont; Smithsonian Inst, Washington, DC. *Exhib:* Portrait of America, New York & Tour, 45-46; Current Am Prints, Carnegie Inst, Pittsburgh, 48; Nat Print Ann, Brooklyn Mus & Tour, 48-49; Nat Exhib Prints, Libr Cong, Washington, DC, 56; US Info Agency Print Exhib Europ Tour, 72- *Teaching:* Instr basic & advan serigraphy, Nat Serigraph Soc Sch, 54-60; instr creative painting, Atlantic Co Jewish Community Ctr, Margate, NJ, 60-67. *Awards:* Purchase Award, Prints For Children, Mus Mod Art, 41; Paintings by Printmakers Award, 47 & Babette S Kornblith Purchase Prize, 49, Nat Serigraph Soc. *Mem:* Print Club; Am Color Print Soc. *Media:* Oil. *Dealer:* Optique Gallery 28 N Union St Lambertville NJ 08530. *Mailing Add:* 16 S Buffalo Ave Atlantic City NJ 08406

ROBBINS, JOAN NASH
PAINTER, COLLAGE ARTIST
b Kalamazoo, Mich, Nov 24, 41. *Study:* Western Mich Univ, BA, 63; Oakland Univ, MA, 69. *Comn:* Jungle Story (series of 4 collages), St Louis Fed Savings & Loan, 84; Growth (series of 4 collages), Gen Am Life, St Louis, 85; Rivers Run (diptych collage), AT&T, St Louis, 85; Dance (diptych collage), AT&T, St Louis, 86. *Exhib:* An Art Affair, Westport, St Louis, 82 & 84-86; San Diego International, 85; Watercolor Missouri, William Woods Col, Fulton, Mo, 85; 10th Oklahoma Annual, Norman Gallery, Lawton, Okla, 85; 10th National Annual, Southern Watercolor Soc, Okla Art Ctr, Oklahoma City, Okla, 86. *Teaching:* Pvt instr, collage & watermedia, in studio & in workshops. *Awards:* Moerschel Award, St Charles 17th Ann Show, 82; Merit Award, An Art Affair, Show, St Louis, 83; Norman Gallom Award, Watercolor, Okla 10th Ann, 85. *Mem:* Southern Watercolor Soc; Midwest Watercolor Soc; St Louis Art Guild; North Coast Collage Soc. *Media:* Watercolor, Collage. *Mailing Add:* 601 North Kings Hwy Sikeston MO 63801

ROBBINS, LEROY (SOUTHWARD)
PHOTOGRAPHER, FILMMAKER
b St Louis, Mo, June 14, 04. *Study:* Apprenticed under artist Oscar Thalinger while working as photographer for St Louis Art Mus, 22-27; Washington Univ Sch Archit, 24-27. *Work:* Mus Mod Art, New York; San Francisco Mus Mod Art; Oakland Mus; Santa Barbara Mus Art; St Louis Art Mus; Nat Mus Art, Washington, DC. *Exhib:* A Pageant of Photog, Golden Gate Int Expos, San Francisco, 40; Image of Freedom, Mus Mod Art, New York, 41; one-man shows, Mexico, San Francisco Mus Mod Art, Calif, 67, Friends of Photog, Carmel, Calif, 72 & Phoenix Art Mus, Ariz, 76; Quartet, Munic Art Gallery, Los Angeles, 73; New Deal Art: Calif, de Saisset Art Gallery & Mus, Univ Santa Clara, 76; retrospective, Sr Cye Gallery, Long Beach, Calif, 80; Offical Images: New Deal Photography, Nat Mus Am Hist, Washington, DC, 87-88; Sandra Berler Gallery, Chevy Chase, Md, 89. *Media:* Black and White Photography. *Publ:* Contribr, A Pageant of Photography, Crocker-Union, San Francisco, 40; auth, Ancient Peru Today (limited ed of photog), privately publ, 75; contribr, New Deal Art, Calif deSaisset Art Gallery, Univ Santa Clara, 76; Official Images: New Deal Photography, 87. *Mailing Add:* 10210 Legend Rock Rd Escondido CA 92026

ROBBINS, TRINA
CARTOONIST, ILLUSTRATOR
b Brooklyn, NY, Aug 17, 38. *Exhib:* Corcoran Gallery, Washington, DC, 69; Global Space Invasions, San Francisco Mus Mod Art, 78; Pork Roasts, Univ BC Fine Arts Gallery, Vancouver, 81. *Awards:* Inkpot Award, San Diego Comic Art, 77. *Bibliog:* Ronald Levitt Lanyi (auth), Trina, Queen of underground comics, Univ Calif, Davis, 78; Sharon R Gunton (ed), Contemporary Literary Criticism, Vol 21, Gale Res, 82. *Publ:* Ed & contribr, It ain't me, Babe, 70 & contribr, Wimmen's Comix No 1-6, 72-76, Last Gasp; ed, contribr, Wet Satin No 1 & 2, Krupp/Last Gasp, 76 & 78; auth & illusr, Flashback Fashions, Price, Stern, Sloan, 83; coauth, Women and the Comics, Eclipse Enterprises, 85; and others. *Mailing Add:* 1982 15th St San Francisco CA 94114

ROBBINS, WARREN M
MUSEUM DIRECTOR
b Worcester, Mass, Sept 4, 23. *Study:* Univ NH, BA, 45; Univ Mich, MA, 49; Lebanon Valley Col, Pa, 75; Int Col, Los Angeles, 79; Univ NH, 79. *Collections Arranged:* African Art--The De Havenon Collection, 71; African Art in Washington Collections, 72; Tribute to Africa--the Photography and the Collection of Elliot Elisofon, 74; African Textiles & Traditional Dress, 75; The Art of Zaire, 76; The Art of Sierra Leone, 76; Religious & Secular Art of Ethiopia, 76-77; The Sculptor's Eye, Chaim Gross Collection, 76; The Traditional Art of the Nigerian People, 77; Art of Zaire: The Bronson Collection, 78; Traditional Sculpture from Upper Volta, 79; The Useful Arts of Kenya, 79; African Puppetry, 80; Permanent Collections, 80-81; Traditional Costumery and Jewelry in Africa, 81; Traditional Costumes and Jewelry of Egypt, 81; Forms and Influence of African Art, 85. *Pos:* Sr scholar & founding dir emer, Nat Mus African Art, Smithsonian Inst, 82; mem, Duke Ellington Sch Arts. *Teaching:* Lectr African art, Mus African Art, Washington, DC, 64-; lectr influence of African sculpture on mod western art, mus & univs in US, 68- *Awards:* Order of Merit, Gov Cameroon, 73; Rothko Chapel Int Human Rights Award, 81; Henry Medal, Smithsonian Inst, 82; Washington DC Mayors Art Award, 85. *Bibliog:* John Coppola (auth), Teaching museum, Topic Mag, 12/76; Barbaralee Diamondstein (auth), Light from the Dark Continent (film), CBS TV, 3/77; article, The Museum of African Art, Sat Rev, 5/77; Peter Vandevanter (auth), Addicted to Art, Washington Home & Garden, 90; Steve Rosoff (auth), The collector, Michigan Almnus, 1/92. *Mem:* Asn Art Mus Dirs; DC Comn Arts & Humanities; Am Asn Mus; Libr Cong. *Res:* Influence of African sculpture on modern western art. *Publ:* Auth, African Art in American Collections, Praeger, Vol 1, 66, Smithsonian, Vol 2, 89; Art of Henry O Tanner, Smithsonian Inst, 69; contribr, Art in Society, Vol 5, No 3; How to Approach Traditonal African Sculpture, Smithsonian, 72; auth, Traditional American values in a World of Hostilities, Adult Educ, 75. *Mailing Add:* 530 Sixth St SE Washington DC 20003

ROBERSON, SAMUEL ARNDT
ARCHITECTURAL HISTORIAN, EDUCATOR
b Honolulu, Hawaii, May 5 39. *Study:* Williams Col, BA, 61, MA, 63; Salzburg-Klessheim Sch, cert, 65; Yale Univ, PhD, 74. *Collections Arranged:* American Paintings from a Private Long Meadow Collection, Amherst Col, 71; Five College Modern Architecture, Amherst Col, 72; Early Chicago Architecture, Herron Sch Art, 80. *Pos:* Consult, Eye of Thomas Jefferson Bicentennial Exhib, Nat Gallery Art, Washington, DC, 74-76; acad coordr, Nat Endowment Humanities Learning Mus Prog, Indianapolis Mus Art, 76-80; dir, Historic Indianapolis Inc, 80-; comnr, Ind Film Comn, 83-; adj assoc prof Am studies, Sch Liberal Arts, Ind Univ, 84- *Teaching:* Instr art hist, Williams Col, 61-63, Yale Univ, 64-66, Princeton Univ, 66-68 & Amherst Col, 69-72; asst prof, Herron Sch Art, 72-76, chmn art hist, 72-80, assoc prof, 76-; vis assoc prof, Ind Univ, Bloomington, 76. *Mem:* Soc Archit Historians; Col Art Asn; and others. *Res:* Eighteenth and nineteenth century American architecture and landscape gardening. *Publ:* Auth, The Technical Creation of the Greek Slave, 65 & coauth, The Greek Slave, 65, Newark Mus; contribr, Praeger Encyclopedia of Art, Praeger Publ, 71; auth, Indiana Historic Sites and Structures Reports, 80-; Historic American Buildings Survey in Indiana Catalog, 83. *Mailing Add:* Herron Sch of Art 1701 N Pennsylvania Indianapolis IN 46202

ROBERSON, WILLIAM
TAPESTRY ARTIST, COLLAGE ARTIST
b Ripley, Miss, Feb 15, 39. *Study:* Memphis State Univ; Memphis Col Art, BFA; Ind Univ. *Work:* Ark Art Ctr, Little Rock; Tenn Craft Collection, Craft Mus, Nashville; 1st Nat Bank, Orlando, Fla; Falls Creek State Park, Tenn; and others. *Comn:* Tapestries, comn by Lausanne Sch, Memphis, 70, Jewish Community Ctr, Memphis, 71, Holiday Inns of Am, Aberdeen, Tex, 73, Opreyland Hotel, Nashville & First Tenn Bank, Memphis. *Exhib:* Young Americans, Mus Contemp Crafts, New York, 69; Piedmont Craft Exhib, Sneed Mus, Charlotte, NC; Miss Arts Festival, Jackson; Southeastern Craftmen Show, San Antonio, Tex. *Pos:* Assoc dean. *Teaching:* Assoc prof fiber design, Memphis Col Art, 69- *Mailing Add:* 694 N Trezevant St Memphis TN 38112

ROBERT, HENRY FLOOD, JR
MUSEUM DIRECTOR
b El Dorado, Ark, Feb 26, 43. *Study:* Palomar Col, AA, 66; Ariz State Univ, BFA, 70, MFA, 73; Harvard Univ, dipl (arts admin), 77. *Work:* Alfred Jocob Miller Collections. *Exhib:* Adolph Gottlieb Exhib, Phoenix Art Mus, Ariz; George Sugarman: The Shape of Space Exhib, Inst Contemp Art, Philadelphia, Pa, Columbus Mus Art, Ohio, Bard Col, Annandale-on-the-Hudson, NY. *Collections Arranged:* Zelda Sayre Fitzgerald Retrospective, 74, Marathon Art by Three Artists, 75, Corporate Collections in Montgomery, 76, George Verdak: Eras the Dance, 76-77 & Art Inc: American Paintings from Corporate Collections, 79, Montgomery Mus Fine Arts, Ala. *Pos:* Dir, Mem Union Gallery, Ariz State Univ, Tempe, 69-70, asst dir, Univ Art Mus, 70-72; asst dir, Loch Haven Art Ctr, Orlando, Fla, 73-74; dir, Montgomery Mus of Fine Arts, 74-79, Joslyn Art Mus, Omaha, 79-88, Knoxville Mus Art, Tenn, 90- *Mem:* Am Asn of Mus; Asn of Art Mus Dirs; Int Conf of Mus. *Publ:* Auth, Paolo Soleri: Arcology and the Future of Man, 75, contribr, Venetian Drawings from the Collection of Janos Scholz, 76, The Throne of the Third Heaven of the Nations Millenium General Assembly, 77 & Anne Goldthwaite: 1869-1944, 77 & auth, Walter Gauknek Retrospective, 78, Montgomery Mus Fine Arts; Auth, Legacy of the West, 82, Karl Bodmer's America, 84, Ancient Greek Pottery, 85, Joslyn Art Mus; contribr, corpus Vasorum Antiquoim, 86, Joslyn Art Mus: Painting and Sculpture from the European and American Collections, 87, Joslyn Art Mus. *Mailing Add:* c/o Knoxville Mus Art 410 Tenth St Knoxville TN 37916

ROBERT, JEAN See Ipousteguy, (Jean Robert)

ROBERTS, BRUCE ELLIOTT
PAINTER
US citizen. *Study:* Art Students League, 37-39; Corcoran Sch Art, 44-45; also design with Paul Rand, New York, 49-51. *Work:* Rosenberg Libr, Galveston; Elliott Mus, Stuart, Fla; La Maritime Mus, New Orleans. *Comn:* Downwind Victory (painting), US Capitol, Washington, DC, 73; History of Florida (painting), Fla Supreme Court, Tallahassee. *Exhib:* Walker Mus Art, Brunswick, Maine, 75; one-man shows, Elliott Mus, Stuart, Fla, 71 & 76 & Mus Arts & Sci, Daytona Beach, Fla, 77; 2nd Ann, Am Soc Marine Art, New York, 79. *Bibliog:* John Alexander (auth), Maritime paintings, USN All Hands Mag, 9/76; Charlotte Moser (auth), Sailing ships, Houston Chronicle, 1/77; Denis McCarthy (auth), Bruce Elliott Roberts, ArtQuest, Vol I, 86. *Mem:* Am Soc Marine Artists; Soc Marine Painters. *Media:* Oil. *Publ:* A Salute to Josh Slocum, Cruising World Publ, 1/77. *Dealer:* Townhouse Galleries 319 Royal St New Orleans LA 70130. *Mailing Add:* 611 Ash St Port St Lucie FL 33452

ROBERTS, CLYDE HARRY
PAINTER, INSTRUCTOR
b Sandusky, Ohio, June 12, 23. *Study:* Cleveland Inst Art, dipl, 46; Columbia Univ, MA, 49; also with John Pike, Robert Brackman, Edgar Whitney & William Schultz. *Work:* Washington Co Mus Fine Arts, Hagerstown, Md; Ford Times Gallery, Dearborn, Mich; State House, Annapolis, Md. *Comn:* Murals, Rocco's Restaurant, 87, Washington Co Tourism Ctr, 89; hist painting, Renfrew Mus, Waynesboro, Pa, 91. *Exhib:* Many exhibs, Baltimore Watercolor Open, Cumberland Valley Exhib, Cleveland Mus May Show; one-man show, Pa State Univ, 79. *Teaching:* instr painting, Hagerstown Jr Col, 57-; supvr art, Washington Co Bd Educ, 68-81; retired; instr watercolor, Mont Alto Campus, Pa State Univ; instr art teacher educ, Shepherd Col, WVa, 89; pvt studio printing, 92. *Awards:* First Prize, Cumberland Valley Artists, 88, 89 & 90; Artists Members Award, Baltimore Watercolor Club, 71 & 74; First Award, Pa Watercolor Soc, 81; and others. *Bibliog:* G Horn (auth), article, Art Today, 68; feature article, Painting--Materials and Techniques, Timmon, 79; article, US News & World Report, 82. *Mem:* Baltimore Watercolor Club; Md Art Asn (secy, 62-64); Nat Art Educ Asn; fel Royal Soc Art; Pa Watercolor Soc. *Media:* Watercolor. *Publ:* Illusr, Ford Times Mag, 58; contribr, Sch Arts, 68; contribr, Artists News Unlimited, 71; contribr, Nat Geog Sch Ed, 73; auth, article, Palette Talk, 80. *Dealer:* Little Gallery Montalto PA 21722; Benjamen's Art Gallery Hagerstown MD 21740. *Mailing Add:* 219 N Colonial Dr Hagerstown MD 21740

ROBERTS, DONALD
EDUCATOR, PRINTMAKER
b Wolfeboro, NH, Nov 24, 23. *Study:* Vesper George Sch of Art, Boston, cert; RI Sch of Design, Providence, BFA; Ohio Univ, Athens, MFA. *Work:* Cleveland Mus of Art; Tate Gallery, London; Rosenwald Collection, Los Angeles; Seattle Mus, Wash; Libr of Cong, Washington, DC. *Exhib:* Dayton Art Inst, Ohio, 60, 65 & 74; 1st-3rd Lithography Ann, Tallahassee, Fla, 64-67; The Print Club, Philadelphia, 68; Contemp Am Prints, Krannert Mus, Champaign-Urbana, Ill, 70; Huntington Galleries, WVa, 71; and others. *Teaching:* Prof printmaking, drawing & painting, Ohio Univ, Athens, 53- *Awards:* Tamarind Lithography Grant, 62; Purchase Award, 9th Ann Paint of the Yr, Mead Corp, 63; Pennypacker Award, 4th Ann Soc Am Graphic Artists, 65. *Bibliog:* William Sargent (auth), American Printmakers, Ashland Oil Corp, 76. *Mailing Add:* 6555 Frum Rd Athens OH 45701

ROBERTS, GILROY
SCULPTOR
US citizen. *Study:* Frankford High Sch Eve Art Class, Philadelphia; Corcoran Gallery Art Sch; also with John R Sinnock & Heinz Warneke. *Work:* US Mint, Philadelphia; Smithsonian Inst, Washington, DC; Franklin Mint, Franklin Center, Pa. *Comn:* Portrait of Anthony Drexel, Drexel Univ, 38; Kennedy half dollar, US Mint, 63; portrait of Albert Einstein, Inst Advan Study, Princeton; portrait of David Sarnoff, RCA Corp; portrait of Ernie Pyle, Scripps Howard News Alliance. *Exhib:* Pa Acad Fine Arts, Philadelphia, 36-37; Corcoran Gallery Art, Washington, DC, 42; Nat Sculpture Soc, New York; Madrid, Spain, 51; Rome, Italy, 61. *Pos:* Picture engraver, Bur Engraving & Painting, Washington, DC, 38-44; chief sculptor & engraver, US Mint, Philadelphia, 48-64; chmn & chief sculptor, Franklin Mint, 64- *Awards:* Honorable Mention, Nat Sculptors Soc, 51; Gold Medal & Citation, Int Exhib Coins & Medals, Madrid, Spain, 51; Gold Medal, Numismatic Asn, 51. *Bibliog:* Willard Garvin (auth), The suburb that has its own mint, Sunday Bull Mag, 1/51; Thomas Baker (auth), The creation of the Kennedy half dollar, Coin Asn Mag, 6/72. *Mem:* Fel Nat Sculpture Soc; Franklin Inst; Philadelphia Sketch Club. *Publ:* Auth, Birth of a dime design, 10/67 & Creating designs in circles, 5/68, Coins Mag. *Mailing Add:* 7 Llangollen Lane Newtown Square PA 19073

ROBERTS, HELENE EMYLOU
LIBRARIAN, EDITOR
b Seattle, Wash, Mar 23, 31. *Study:* Univ Wash, BA, 53, MA, 57, ML, 61. *Pos:* Art librn, Dartmouth Col, Hanover, NH, 63-66 & slide librn, 68-70; cur visual collections, Harvard Univ, 70-; adv ed, Victorian Periodical Newslett, 75-; ed, Visual Resources, currently, Documenting the Image (Bk Series), currently & Encyl Comparative Inconography, currently. *Awards:* Librn Res Fel, Harvard Univ Libr, 80-81; Distinguished Serv Award, Visual Resources Asn, 91. *Mem:* Art Libr Soc NAm; Spec Libr; Res Soc for Victorian Periodicals (treas, 70-75); Am Soc Picture Professionals; Visual Resources Asn. *Res:* Dante Gabriel Rossetti; Victorian Art; Eighteenth and nineteenth century art periodicals; images of women in art; nineteenth century art criticism; history of visual documentation. *Publ:* Auth, The image library, Art Libr J, 3/78; Victorian medievalism: Revival or masquerade, Browning Inst Studies, 8/80; The sentiment of reality, Thackeray's art criticism, In: Studies in the Novel, Vol 13, 81; Exhibition and review: The periodical press and the Victorian art exhibition system, In: Victorian Periodical Press,Leicester Univ Press, 82; Inconographic Index to Old Testament Subjects, Gardand Press, 87. *Mailing Add:* c/o Fogg Art Mus Harvard Univ Cambridge MA 02138

ROBERTS, HOLLY L
PAINTER, PHOTOGRAPHER
b Boulder, Colo, Dec 22, 51. *Study:* Univ NMex, BA, 73; Ariz State Univ, MFA, 81. *Work:* San Francisco Mus Art; Ctr Creative Photog, Tucson, Ariz; Mus Photog Art, San Diego, Calif; Los Angeles Mus Contemp Art; Art Inst Chicago. *Exhib:* Crosscurrents: Recent Additions to the Collection, San Francisco Mus Art, 86; Photography & Art: Interactions Since 1946, Los Angeles Co Mus Art, 87; Explorations: Extending the Boundaries of Contemp Photography, Mus Contemporary Photog, Chicago, 87; Transform (2 person show), Mus Contemp Photog, Chicago, 88; solo exhib, Friends Photog, San Francisco, 89, Lowe Art Gallery, Syracuse Univ, NY, 90, La Photographie en Miettes, Musee Nat d'Art Moderne, Centre Georges Pompidou, Paris, 92 & Presentation House, North Vancouver, BC, Can, 92. *Awards:* Fel Photog, Nat Endowment Arts, 86 & 88. *Bibliog:* Robert Hirsch (auth), Exploring Color Photography, William C Brown Co, 88; David Featherstone (auth), Holly Roberts, Friends of Photography, 90. *Mailing Add:* PO Box 2955 Corrales NM 87048

ROBERTS, LUCILLE D (MALKIA)
PAINTER, EDUCATOR
b Washington, DC. *Study:* Howard Univ; Univ Mich, AM; New York Univ; Acad Grande Chaumiere, Paris; Univ Ghana; also with Jose Gutierriez, Mexico City, Mex. *Work:* Atlanta Univ; WVa State Col; Jefferson Community Col, Water Town, NY. *Exhib:* One-man shows, Porter Gallery, Howard Univ, 71 & Col Mus, Hampton Inst, 72; Nat Exhib Black Artists, Smith-Mason Gallery, Washington, DC, 71; Black Artists Exhib, Afro-Am Cult Ctr, Cleveland State Univ, 72. *Teaching:* Asst prof art, DC Teachers Col, Washington, DC, 65-78, assoc prof, 78-; vis assoc prof African & Afro-Am art, State Univ NY Col Oswego, 70-71; retired. *Awards:* First Prize, Mem Show, 65 & Evening Star Award, 66, Soc Washington Artists; James A Porter Award, Cleveland State Univ, 72. *Bibliog:* Lewis & Wadday (auths), Black Artists on Art, 69; J Edwin Atkinson (auth), Black Dimensions in Contemporary Art, Carnation Co, 70. *Mem:* Nat Conf Artists; Black Acad Arts & Lett; Soc Washington Artists; DC Art Asn. *Media:* Oil, Acrylic. *Mailing Add:* 2445 Lyttonsville Rd No 1116 Silver Spring MD 20910

ROBERTS, PRISCILLA WARREN
PAINTER
b Glen Ridge, NJ, June 13, 16. *Study:* Art Students League; Nat Acad Design. *Work:* Metrop Mus Art, New York; Dallas Mus Fine Arts; Walker Art Ctr, Minneapolis; Butler Inst Am Art, Youngstown, Ohio; IBM Collection, New York; Nat Mus Women Arts, Washington, DC; Shite Mus, Notre Dame, South Bend, Ind. *Exhib:* Carnegie Inst Int, Pittsburgh, 50; Nat Acad Design, New York, 69; Corcoran Gallery Art, Washington, DC; Univ Ill, Urbana; Allied Artists, New York. *Awards:* Hallgarten Prizes & Proctor Portrait Prize, Nat Acad Design, 47; Third Prize, Carnegie Inst Int, 50. *Mem:* Nat Acad Design; hon mem Catharine Lorillard Wolfe Asn. *Media:* Oil. *Dealer:* Grand Central Galleries 24 W 57th St New York NY 10019. *Mailing Add:* Box 716 Georgetown CT 06829

ROBERTS, RICHARD
PAINTER
b Philadelphia, Pa, June 26, 25. *Work:* Nat Acad Design, New York; Butler Inst Am Art, Youngstown, Ohio. *Exhib:* 51st Ann, Pa Acad, Philadelphia, 53; March Exhib, Mus Fine Art, Springfield, Mass, 53; 19th Ann Mid Year, Butler Inst, Youngstown, Ohio, 54; Manhattan Artists, Whitney Mus, New York, 54; 54th Ann Spring Exhib, Delgado Mus, New Orleans, La, 55; The

Seaport, Baltimore Mus, Md, 55; 5th Ann Exhib, Pittsfield Mus, Mass, 56; 153rd Exhib, Nat Acad Design, New York, 78. *Awards:* Louis Comfort Tiffany Found Fel, 54; Purchase Prize, Butler Inst Am Art, 54; Ward Ranger Purchase Award, Nat Acad Art, 78. *Media:* Oil, Acrylic. *Mailing Add:* 175 W 12th St New York NY 10011

ROBERTS, STEVEN K
SCULPTOR, PRINTMAKER
b San Diego, Calif, Dec 2, 54. *Study:* Washington & Lee Univ, Va, BA, 76; also with Ju Ming, Taiwan, 76. *Work:* Nat Mus Am Art & Fed Deposit Insurance Corp, Washington, DC; Nat Mus Hist, Taipei, Taiwan; Gen Motors, Detroit; Am Tel & Tel, Rosalyn, Va. *Comn:* Poster, comn by City Councilman John Wilson, Washington, DC, 80; stained glass window, Rivertown Gen, Occuquan, Va, 80; painting, Am Systs Corp, Annandale, Va, 82; sculptural portrait, pvt comn by Melvin Watson & family, Lynchburg, Va, 84; wall murals, pvt comn by Anita & Burton Reiner, Bethesda, Md, 86. *Exhib:* 36 Hours, Mus Temporary Art, Washington, DC, 78; Sculpture Conference, Lansburg Bldg, Washington, DC, 80; 57th Annual International, Print Club, Philadelphia, 81; American Printmakers in Moscow, US Embassy, Moscow, USSR, 84; North Miami Mus & Art Center, NMiami, Fla, 84; Kathleen Ewing Gallery, Washington, DC, 85. *Bibliog:* Paul Waley (auth), US sculptor deeply influenced, The China News, 9/19/76; Ellen Edwards (auth), Art-Show & Tell, 4/26/80 & Jo Ann Lewis (auth), Art in boxes: surprizes inside, 3/12/83, Washington Post. *Mem:* Washington Proj Arts, DC; Print Club, Philadelphia. *Media:* Wood, Steel; Serigraphy. *Dealer:* Kraskin Gallery 9812 Falls Rd Potomac MD 20854. *Mailing Add:* 1824 B Lamont St NW Washington DC 20010

ROBERTS, TOM (THOMAS KEITH)
PAINTER
b Toronto, Ont, Dec 22, 08. *Study:* Cent Tech Sch, Toronto; Ont Col Art, Toronto. *Work:* Ford Motor Co; Rio-Algom; Seagrams; and other pvt & public collections. *Exhib:* Many ann, Royal Can Acad Arts, Montreal & Toronto; Nat Gallery Can, Ottawa; Montreal Mus Fine Arts; Ont Soc Artists, Toronto, 29-; one-man shows in Montreal, Toronto, Ottawa, Halifax & Vancouver, Can. *Awards:* Ralph Clarke Stone Award, 49. *Bibliog:* Edith G Firth (auth), Toronto in Art. *Mem:* Royal Can Acad; Ont Soc Artists. *Media:* Oil, Watercolor. *Dealer:* Wallack Gallery 203 Bank Ottawa ON Can; Continental Gallery Montreal PQ. *Mailing Add:* 1312 Stavebank Rd Mississauga ON L5G 2V2 Canada

ROBERTS, WILLIAM EDWARD
PAINTER, EDUCATOR
b Cleveland, Ohio, July 1, 41. *Study:* Kent State Univ, BFA, 68, MA, 71; Cornell Univ, lithography with Arnold Singer, 73. *Work:* Everson Mus Art, Syracuse, NY; Kent State Univ, Ohio; IBM Corp, Albany, NY; NY Racing Asn, Elmont; Seagrams Inc, New York. *Exhib:* One-man show, Everson Mus Art, 74; 55 Mercer, New York, 81; Saratoga Performing Art Ctr, NY, 82; Hartell Gallery, Cornell Univ, 82; Dayspring Gallery, Saratoga Springs, NY, 82-86; Handwerker Gallery, Ithaca Col, 83; Schweinforth Art Ctr, Auburn, NY, 85; Shearson Lehman Am Express, Ithaca, NY, 86; Herbert Johnson Mus, Cornell Univ, 91; Tyler Art Gallery, SUNY Oswego, NY, 91. *Pos:* Instr, Cayuga Correctional Facility, 90- *Teaching:* Assoc prof painting, Wells Col, Aurora, NY, 71-86, prof, 86-; instr painting, Auburn Prison, NY, 75-77. *Awards:* Purchase Awards, State Univ NY, Potsdam, 73 & Erie Pa Ann, Marine Midland Bank, 73; Purchase Award, Erie, Pa Ann, Marine Midland Bank, 73; First Place in Painting, Skaneateles Art Assoc, NY, 90. *Bibliog:* Millie Wolff (auth), Artist's racing series has King's excitement, Palm Beach Daily News, 3/14/79; Charlene Johnson (auth), Saratoga on a grand scale, Horsemen's J, 8/83; Lee Scott (auth), Aurora artist paints life on the fast track, Ithaca J, 2/20/84; Message to the Future, Binghamton, NY, 91; and others. *Mem:* Col Art Asn; Am Asn Univ Prof. *Media:* Oil,. *Mailing Add:* Wells Col Aurora NY 13026

ROBERTSON, CHARLES J
ADMINISTRATOR
b Houston, Tex, Sept 12, 34. *Study:* Univ Va, BA, 56; Harvard Univ, MA, 58; Courtauld Inst, Univ London, 60; George Washington Univ, JD, 64. *Pos:* Assoc dir, NC Mus Art, 75-77; asst dir mus resources, 77-86; dep dir, Nat Mus Am Art, 86- *Mem:* Am Asn Mus (treas, 81-83); Soc Archit Historians; Octagon House Mus (adv comt, 89-); Victorian Soc Am (bd dirs, 90-); DC Hist Preserv Rev Bd, 92- *Mailing Add:* Nat Mus Am Art Smithsonian Inst Washington DC 20560

ROBERTSON, E BRUCE
HISTORIAN, CURATOR
b Dunedin, New Zealand, May 14, 55. *Study:* Swarthmore Col, BA(hons), 76; Yale Univ, MA, 78, MPhil, 80, PhD, 87. *Collections Arranged:* The Art of Paul Sandby (auth, catalog), Yale British Art Ctr, 85; Dutch Landscape Prints, Allen Art Mus, 86. *Pos:* Asst cur Am paintings, Cleveland Mus Art, 87- *Teaching:* Instr, Univ Del, Newark, 82 & Oberlin Col, Ohio, 83-87; asst prof, Case Western Reserve Univ, Ohio, 87-90. *Mem:* Col Art Asn, ASECS. *Res:* 18th and 19th century British and American landscape and genre painting. *Publ:* Coauth & ed, The Four Indian Kings, Pub Archives, Can, 85; coauth, Views and visions, Corcoran Gallery Art, 86; auth, Reckoning with Winslow Homer: His Late Paintings and Their Influence, 90. *Mailing Add:* c/o Art Hist Dept Univ Calif Santa Barbara CA 93106

ROBERTSON, JOAN E (JOAN ELIZABETH MITCHELL)
CURATOR, GRAPHIC ARTIST
b Washington, DC, June 11, 42. *Study:* Bucknell Univ, Lewisburg, Pa, BA(art), 64; Univ Iowa, MA(printmaking), 67, studied with Mauricio Lasansky. *Work:* Kemper Group, Long Grove, Ill; Chemical Bank, New York; First Nat Bank, Chicago; Southland Corp, Dallas, Tex; Ill State Mus, Springfield; Blount Inc, Montgomery, Ala. *Exhib:* Works on Paper by Artists of Chicago and Vicinity, Art Inst Chicago, 78; one-person shows, Donnelly Libr Gallery, Lake Forest Col, Ill, 79 & Loyola Univ, Chicago, 81; Nat Prints & Drawing Competition, DeKalb, Ill, 81; Ill State Fair, Prof Art Exhib, 89; Flora 88 & 90, Chicago Botanic Garden, 88 & 90. *Collections Arranged:* Kemper Nat Insurance Companies art collection, purchase, brochure preparation & monthly exhibs, 73-; Couples I and Couples II, Suburban Fine Arts Ctr, Highland Park, Ill, 83 & 84; A Celebration of Women (catalog), David Adler Cult Ctr, Libertyville, Ill, 92. *Pos:* Art cur, Kemper Nat Insurance Companies, Long Grove, Ill, 73-; gallery coordr, Lake Forest Col, Ill, 81-84. *Awards:* Award Merit, Flora, 88; Chicago Botanic Garden, 88; President's Purchase Award, Elgin Community Col, Ill, Works on Paper, 90; and others. *Bibliog:* Lydia Murman (auth), Joan E Robertson, New Art Examiner, 6/81; Sandy Riemer (auth), Color puts life into her pencil drawings, Sunday Herald, 4/81; Garrett Holg (auth), An exhibition for art and nature lovers at Botanic Garden, Waukegan News-Sun, 2/11/88; and others. *Mem:* Asn Corp Art Curators, Chicago (treas); Nat Asn Corp Art Mgt, New York; David Adler Cult Ctr, Libertyville, Ill (bd dirs, 90-93). *Media:* Colored Pencil. *Mailing Add:* c/o Kemper Nat Insurance Co Long Grove IL 60049

ROBERTSON, NANCY ELIZABETH See Dillow, Nancy E (Nancy Elizabeth Robertson)

ROBERTSON, TED WALTER
PAINTER, INSTRUCTOR
b Dunmor, Ky, Nov 21, 42. *Study:* Bergman Art Inst, Denver, 60; Austin PEA State Col, 64; Colo State Univ, 66-67. *Work:* NMex Military Mus, Roswell; Eastern NMex Univ, Portales; Carlsbad Art Mus, NMex; El Paso Art Mus, Tex; Roswell Mus Art Ctr, NMex. *Comn:* Doc Severinson, Ruidoso Chamber Com, NMex, 74; Landscape (mural), Knights Columbus, Danville, Ill, 75; Hondo landscape, 88, Col Godfrey, 89, NMex Military Inst, Roswell. *Exhib:* Ann Show, Carlsbad Mus, NMex, 87; United Coun Artists, Roswell Mus, NMex, 88; Lubbock Invitational, Tex, 89; Invitational Pippins Show, Prescott Regional, Ariz, 90; Charity Fund, Mus Horse, Ruidoso, NMex, 92. *Teaching:* Painting, Carizzo Art Inst, 74-92; art, Roswell Pub Schs, 87-91; art, Seattle Art Inst, 89. *Awards:* Best of Show, United Coun Artists, 88. *Mem:* Pastel Soc Am, New York; Pastel Soc Southwest, Dallas; Portrait Soc Am, La & Calif; Roswell Art League, NMex. *Media:* Pastel, Oil; Watercolor, Etching. *Dealer:* Meyer Gallery 225 Canyon Rd Santa Fe NM; Artistic Gallery Scottsdale AZ. *Mailing Add:* PO Box 74 Lincoln NM 88338

ROBINS, CORINNE
CRITIC, WRITER
b New York, NY, July 31, 34. *Study:* Walden Sch; New York Univ; New Sch Social Res. *Pos:* Asst managing ed, Mademoiselle Mag, 57-59; cur exhib, Soho Ctr Visual Artists, 76; contrib ed, Arts Mag, 76-82, assoc ed, 82-; contribr ed, Am Book Review; curator, AIR Gallery, New York. *Teaching:* Lectr Am art, US Info Serv, Brazil, 72; lectr Drawing Now, Jamaica Art Ctr, 76; lectr art hist, criticism & social change, Pratt Inst, 77, lectr painting seminar, 79-; lectr art hist, Sch Visual Arts, 78-; vis assoc prof, State Univ NY, Binghamton, 84. *Awards:* Critics Fel Award, Nat Endowment Art, 78. *Bibliog:* Grace Glueck (auth), Art people, New York Times, 5/28/76; Essayists Encyclopedia, Art Week, 85; Eric Gibson (auth), Thinking About the Seventies, New Criterion, 5/85. *Mem:* Artist Talk Art; International PEN; Orgn Independent Artists; Art Critics Asn; Poets & Writers; Poetry Soc Am. *Publ:* Auth, Late decorative: Art, artifact and the Ersatz, 4/80 & Ten months of rush hour figuration, 9/82, Arts Mag; Art in the Power (poems), Prat Press, 84; Smart Marxists-Dumb Artists, Am Book Review, 5-6/84; The Pluralist Era, American Art 1968-1981, Harper & Row, 84; East Village Art, East Village Artstore, Artscribe, 9-10/85; and others. *Mailing Add:* 83 Wooster St New York NY 10012

ROBINSON, CHARLOTTE
PAINTER, PRINTMAKER
b San Antonio, Tex, Nov, 24. *Study:* Art Students League, 48; New York Univ, 49; Corcoran Art Sch, 51. *Work:* Mus Espanol de Arts Contemporaneo, Madrid; Philip Morris Inc, New York; McNay Art Mus, San Antonio, Tex; Artery, Washington, DC; Nat Mus Women in Arts, Washington, DC. *Exhib:* Bronx Mus, New York, 76; Mint Mus, Charlotte, NC, 77; Douglass Col, Rutgers Univ, New Brunswick, NJ, 79 & 80; The Artist & The Quilt, Nat Endowment Arts, mus traveling show, 83-86; Solo exhibs, McNay Art Mus, San Antonio, Tex, 86, Lowenstein Libr Gallery, Fordham Univ, New York, 90 & San Antonio Art Inst, Tex, 91; Abstraction Southeastern Ctr Comtemp Art, Winston-Salem, NC, 84; Iowa State Univ, Ames, 92. *Pos:* Trustee, Bronx Mus, New York, 76-77; vis artist, Southwest Craft Ctr, San Antonio, Tex, 85 & 86. *Teaching:* Instr drawing, Smithsonian Assoc Prog, Washington, DC, 76-; instr art world sem, Washington Women's Art Ctr, Washington, DC, 76-80. *Awards:* Scholar, Student Exhib, Corcoran Art Sch, Washington, DC, 51; Grants, Nat Endowment Arts, 77, 78 & 81. *Bibliog:* Mary McKay (auth), Undercurrents, Wash Post, 12/22/90; John B Wilson (prod), Undercurrents, UAV Productions Inc, 90; Lowenstein Libr Gallery (monogr, catalog), Fordham Univ & San Antonio Art Inst, Tex, 90. *Mem:* Nat Women's Caucus Art (bd dirs, 82-84). *Media:* Oil; Lithography. *Publ:* Ed, The Artist & The Quilt, Knopf, 10/83. *Dealer:* de Andino Fine Arts 1609 Conn Ave Washington DC 20009. *Mailing Add:* 6324 Crosswoods Dr Falls Church VA 22044

ROBINSON, CHRIS (CHRISTOPHER THOMAS)
CONCEPTUAL ARTIST, EDUCATOR
b Huntington, NY, Mar 18, 51. *Study:* Fla State Univ, BFA, 73; Univ Mass, MFA, 75. *Work:* Arch Am Art, Washington, DC; Univ South; SC State Art Collection, Columbia; Southern Graphics Coun; Univ Miss. *Comn:* Installations, Ninth Nat-Int Sculpture Conf, New Orleans, 76, Nat Sculpture Conf, Jonesboro, Ark, 77, Arcosanti Festival Art in the Environment, Cordes Junction, Ariz, 78, Col Art Asn, New Orleans, 80 & Eastern Ill Univ, 81, SC State Mus, 89. *Exhib:* Artists Biennial, New Orleans Mus Art, 77; solo exhib, Atlanta Art Workers Coalition Gallery, 80; Installation, Southeastern Ctr Contemp Art, Winston-Salem, NC, 81; Appalachian Nat Drawing Competition, Appalachian State Univ, 81; Netherlands-Am Contemp Exchange Exhib, 82; Printmakers in the South, Southern Arts Traveling Exhib, 83; Southern Satellite Show, 10 on 8, New York, NY; Photostatic Images, Southeastern Ctr Contemp Art, Winston-Salem, 84; Portrait of the South, Rome Exhib, Palazzo Venezia, Rome, Italy, 84; Fact, Fiction and Fantasy: Recent Narrative Art in the Southeast, Traveling Exhib, Ewing Art Gallery, Univ Tenn, Knoxville, 87; Solo exhibs, Univ NC, Col at Charleston, 87, Art in Transit, Arts Festival Atlanta, 89. *Collections Arranged:* Nat Sculpture Exhib, 76, 78 & 79. *Pos:* Dir, Northern Projects, Operation Raleigh, Chile; bd trustees, Lexington Co Sch Dist Five; leader, US Expeditions (sci, serv, adventure), Operation Raleigh, Alaska, Colo & NC, 88; dir grad studies, Univ SC, 90. *Teaching:* Assoc visual arts, Univ Mass, Amherst, 73-75; from instr to assoc prof, Univ SC, Columbia, 75-; guest artist, Univ Ala, Huntsville, 77, Univ South, Greensboro Col, Brevard Col & Univ Cent Ark. *Bibliog:* Elizabeth George (auth), Laser artist beams brush towards space shuttle, Greenville Piedmont, 3/10/78; Ron Jones (auth), Techno-aesthetics in South Carolina, Art Papers, 3-4/81; Linda Shrives (auth), Outline of a dream, Columbia Record, 4/13/84; Michael Farley (auth), USC art instructor lives life full of adventure, The Charlotte Observer, 7/7/85; Beverly E Simmons (auth), University professor leads five month research mission, The State, 1/16/86. *Mem:* Col Art Asn; Southern Asn Sculptors (bd mem, 75-80); Southeastern Col Art Conf. *Res:* Experiential investigation of exploratory processes in science and technology as an impetus to the expansion of the visual arts process. *Publ:* Auth, Astronautics as an impetus to visual art, In: Proceedings of the 33rd International Astronautical Federation Congress, 82; Cultural dichotomy: An artist's role in scientific and space exploration, Art Papers, 5-6/85; Sky Art and Power chap Sky Art Book Ctr for Adv Visual Studies, Mass Inst Technol, in press; Art & Technol, Koger Ctr Prog, 89; The Visual Artist's Role in Scientific & Space Exploration, 41st Int Art Found Congress, Dresden, Ger. *Mailing Add:* 300 Lost Creek Dr Columbia SC 29212

ROBINSON, DUNCAN
DIRECTOR, HISTORIAN
b Kidsgrove Staffs, Eng, June 27, 43. *Study:* Clare Col, Cambridge, Eng, BA, 65, MA, 69; Yale Univ, Mellon Fel, 65-67, MA, 67. *Collections Arranged:* Stanley Spencer (auth, catalog), 75 & William Nicholson, 80, Arts Coun Gt Brit; British Watercolors, Brisbane, Australia, 82; and several exhibs of British Contemp Art. *Pos:* Asst keeper paintings & drawings, Fitzwilliam Mus, Cambridge, Eng, 70-76, keeper, 76-81; dir, Yale Ctr Brit Art, 81- *Teaching:* Lectr art hist, Univ Cambridge, Eng, 70-81; adj prof hist Art, Yale Univ, 81- *Awards:* Fel Royal Soc of the Arts, United Kingdom. *Mem:* Blake Trust (UK); Walpole Soc (UK). *Res:* History of British Art concentrating on later 18th and 19th century contemporary art. *Publ:* Auth, Companion Volume to the Kelmscott Chaucer, Basilisk Press, 75; Stanley Spencer, Phaidon, 79 (rev 90); coauth, Morris & Company in Cambridge, Cambridge Univ Press, 80; auth, Town Country, Shore and Sea: British Drawings and Watercolors from Van Dyck to Nash, Cambridge, 82. *Mailing Add:* Yale Ctr Brit Art Box 2120 Yale Station New Haven CT 06520

ROBINSON, FRANKLIN W
MUSEUM DIRECTOR, HISTORIAN
b Providence, RI, May 21, 39. *Study:* Harvard Univ, BA, 61, MA, 63, PhD, 70. *Pos:* Dir, Williams Col Mus Art, 75-79, Mus Art, RI Sch Design, 79-92 & Herbert F Johnson Mus Art, Cornell Univ, 92- *Teaching:* Asst prof art hist, Dartmouth Col, 69-75; assoc prof & dir grad prog art hist, Williams Col, 75-79. *Mem:* Col Art Asn; Am Asn Mus; Am Asn Mus Dir. *Res:* Baroque art; prints and drawings. *Publ:* Auth, 100 Master Drawings from New England Private Collections, 72; Gabriel Metsu, 75; Dutch Life in the Golden Century, 75; Seventeenth Century Dutch Drawings from American Collections, 77; Dutch and Flemish Paintings from the Ringling Museum, 80. *Mailing Add:* Herbert F Johnsons Mus Art Cornell Univ Ithaca NY 14853

ROBINSON, GAIL E
PAINTER
b San Antonio, Tex, July 16, 49. *Study:* Univ Okla, BFA, 70; Va Ctr Creative Arts, fel, 91-92. *Work:* Painting, Solomon Brothers, New York; painting, Chubb Life Am, Concord, NH; painting, Browning Ferris Industs, Boston; painting, Northern Telecommunications, Manchester, NH; painting, Arthur Anderson & Co, Concord, NH. *Exhib:* Nat Ann Exhib, Pastel Soc Am, New York, 83-90; Statewide Asn Exhib, Currier Mus, Manchester, NH, 83-92; Invitational Nat, Salmagundi Club, New York, 86-87; The Subject is Water, Newport Art Mus, RI, 87; Nat Color Show, Faber Birren Exhib, Stamford, Conn, 88 & 92; and others. *Awards:* Isenberg, Giffuni, Armstrong, Pastel Soc Am Nat, 83, 86 & 88; Grumbacher Gold Medal, Pastel Soc Can, 85; McCarthy, Salmagundi Club, 86. *Mem:* Pastel Soc Am (master status); Copley Soc (full artist status); NH Art Asn; League NH Craftsmen; Womens Caucus, Boston Chap. *Media:* Oil, Pastel. *Publ:* Illusr, Sudden Harbor, Orchises Press, 91. *Mailing Add:* PO Box 255 Mount Vernon NH 03057

ROBINSON, GROVE
PAINTER, PRINTMAKER
b Asheville, NC, May 17, 35. *Study:* Mars Hill Col, 53-55; Univ NC, Chapel Hill, 55-56; Yale Summer Sch Art, Norfolk, Conn, 57; with Bernard Chaet & Gabor Peterdi; Columbia Univ, BFA, 58, MFA, 60, with John Hewker, Edwin Dickinson, Hans Mueller, Meyer Schapiro & Rudolph Wittkower; Fulbright Fel to France, in painting, 58-59; with Marcel Brion, advisor. *Work:* NC Mus Art, Raleigh; Carroll Reece Mus, E Tenn State Univ; Tenn State Mus, Nashville; Tenn All-State Collection, First Am Nat Bank, Nashville; Plough Industs, Memphis, Tenn; High Mus, Atlanta, Ga. *Exhib:* Group shows, Mint Mus, Charlotte, NC, 71, Brooks Art Gallery, Memphis, Tenn, 73, Univ Ga, Athens, 74 & Middle Tenn State Univ, Murphreesboro, 77; one-man show, East Tenn State Univ, 64; Memphis State Univ, 79; Tenn State Mus, 81; and others. *Pos:* Vpres for visual arts, Jackson Art Coun, Tenn, 72-74; crafts adv panel, Tenn Arts Comn, 72-76. *Teaching:* Instr, Meredith Col, Raleigh, 65-71; chmn & prof dept art, Union Univ, Jackson, Tenn, 71-87; lectr grad art hist, Memphis State Univ, 79; independent workshops, 87- *Awards:* Purchase Awards, NC Mus of Art, 56 & Tenn State Mus & Cult Ctr, 81. *Bibliog:* 28th NC Artists Ann Art Review, Veritas Corp Inc, 66; Acquisitions from NC Anns 1946-1966 (catalog), N Mus of Art, 67; Art reviews, Taos News, 7/31/86. *Media:* Water media, Lithography. *Dealer:* The Bell-Ross Gallery Memphis TN; La Paloma de Taos, NM. *Mailing Add:* Dept Art Union Univ Jackson TN 38305

ROBINSON, JAY (THURSTON)
PAINTER
b Detroit, Mich, Aug 1, 15. *Study:* Yale Col, BA; Cranbrook Acad Art, MFA. *Work:* Cranbrook Mus, Bloomfield Hills, Mich; Detroit Inst Art; Houston Mus Fine Arts; J B Speed Mus, Louisville, Ky; Philbrook Art Ctr, Tulsa. *Exhib:* Audubon Artists, New York; Carnegie Inst Int, Pittsburgh; Corcoran Gallery Art Biennial, Washington, DC; Nat Acad Design, New York; Pa Acad Fine Arts, Philadelphia. *Awards:* Louis Comfort Tiffany Found Fel, 49; seven Childe Hassam Fund Purchase Awards, Am Acad Arts & Lett. *Mem:* Artists Equity Asn, New York. *Media:* Miscellaneous. *Mailing Add:* 60 Church St Pleasantville NY 10570

ROBINSON, LIBBY
PAINTER, SCULPTOR
b New York, NY. *Study:* Art Students League(drawing), 49-51; studied painting with John Von Wicht, New York, 49-51. *Exhib:* Discoveries IV, Arsenal Gallery, New York, 88; Women in the Arts at Phoenix, Phoenix Gallery, New York, 88; The Kendall Gallery, New York, 91; Noho Gallery, New York, 91; Noho Invitational, 92. *Awards:* Susan Hirschfeld, Assn Curator, The Solomon Guggenheim Mus, New York, 89. *Bibliog:* Leslie Plummer (auth), article, New York Arts J, 9/79; Renee Phillips (auth), article, News World, East Side Weekly, 12/80; reviews, Artpseak, 9/1/83, 1/15/85, 7/1/86 & 11/16/86. *Mem:* New York Artists Equity; Women in Arts, New York; Women's Caucus Arts. *Publ:* Auth, catalogue, Discoveries V, 89. *Dealer:* Noho Gallery 168 Mercer St New York NY 10012. *Mailing Add:* 240 W 98th St New York NY 10025

ROBINSON, LILIEN FILIPOVITCH
HISTORIAN, EDUCATOR
b Ljubljana, Yugoslavia, Feb 7, 40; US citizen. *Study:* George Washington Univ, BA, 62, MA, 65; Johns Hopkins Univ, PhD, 78. *Pos:* Chmn dept art, George Washington Univ, 76- *Teaching:* Lectr art introd & surveys of Western art, George Washington Univ, 64-65, asst prof 19th century art & surveys of Western art, 65-76, assoc prof 19th century Europ art, 76-79 & prof 19th century Europ art, 80. *Awards:* Outstanding Teacher Award, Columbian Col, George Washington Univ, 88. *Bibliog:* Boris Weintraub (auth), The professor's enthusiasm is contagious, Washington Star, 10/27/79. *Mem:* Col Art Asn. *Res:* 19th-century French painting and academic painting. *Publ:* Auth, Art and Life in Nineteenth Century France in La Vie Moderne, Corcoran Gallery, 83; auth, Collecting as tradition and art, In: The Intimate Scale: Paintings from the Phillips Collection, Dimock Gallery, 83; auth, Jeffrey L Stephanic, Alexandria, Va, 85; Clarice Smith, Wildenstein Galleries, 86; Barye & the Nineteenth Century Sculptural Tradition, Barye and Patronage in Antoine-Louis Barye, Corcoran Gallery Art, Washington, DC, 88. *Mailing Add:* Dept Art Chairperson George Wash Univ 801 22nd St NW Washington DC 20052

ROBINSON, MARGOT (MARGOT STEIGMAN)
PAINTER, SCULPTOR
b New York, NY. *Study:* Art Students League, with Harry Sternberg, 47; Robert Blackburn's Creative Workshop, 49-55; painting with John Von Wicht, 53-55; Gerard Koch Studio, Paris, 68; Donald Mavros Studio, New York, 71-72. *Work:* Am Express Co, New York; Data Processing Co, Boston & Chicago; Continental Grain Co, Columbus, Ohio; Bronze mem, Jervis Pub Libr, Rome, NY. *Comn:* Bronze memorial, Jervis Pub Libr, Rome, NY. *Exhib:* Whitney Mus Am Art, New York; Women's Visions, Themes from Nature, Nabisco Brands Gallery, Hanover, NJ, 89; Womens Caucus Art Painters Puzzle Project, Port Authority, New York, 90; solo exhib, Tom Kendall Gallery, New York, 90 & Noho Gallery, New York, 92; Cincinnati Art Mus, Ohio; Brooklyn Mus, New York; Cie Moderne et Contemporaine, Paris, France, 91; and others. *Pos:* Dir, Creative Graphic Workshop, New York, 52-54; registr, Nat Acad Sch of Fine Arts, New York, 55-57; vpres, Noho Gallery, New York, 76-77, secy, 77-78. *Bibliog:* Sean Simon (auth), Artspeak, 11/89; Claude Le Suer (auth), Artspeak, 1/90; Bruno Palmer Poroner (auth), article, Artspeak, 6/92. *Mem:* New York Artists Equity, (77-); Women in the Arts; Womens Caucus Art, New York & Nat (77-). *Media:* Acrylic, Oil; Miscellaneous Media. *Publ:* Contribr, Modern Sculpture, calendar, Cedco Publ Co, San Rafael, Calif, 90. *Dealer:* Retrospective Gallery 888 La Jolla CA; NoHo Gallery 168 Mercer St New York NY 10012. *Mailing Add:* 141 Joralemon St Brooklyn NY 11201

ROBINSON, MARY ANN
PAINTER, EDUCATOR
b McPherson, Kans, Sept 24, 23. *Study:* Kans State Univ, BS, 45; McCormick Theological Sem, MA, 55; Wichita State Univ, MA, 72; studied under Maude Ellsworth, Jan Lundgren, Robert Kisskaden, Robert Wood & James Pike. *Exhib:* Am Contemp Arts & Crafts, Fla, 73; Birger Sandzen Mem Gallery, 80-92; Kans Watercolor Soc Mem Exhib, Lawrence, Kans, 88; Wichita Art Mus Watercolor Exhib, 89. *Pos:* Supvr art pub sch, McPherson, Kans, 47-49; dir, Friendship Hall Gallery, McPherson Col, Kans, 63-86, Pratt Art Gallery, Pratt, Kans, 92 & Ellsworth Art Gallery, Kans, 91. *Teaching:* Assoc prof art educ & art hist & chmn dept art, McPherson Col, Kans, 63-86, emer prof, 86-*Mem:* Kans Watercolor Soc (bd mem, 77-79); McPherson Mus & Art Found (bd mem, 86-90); Opera House Preserv Co (bd mem, 86-90); McPherson Arts Coun; charter mem Nat Mus Women in the Arts; Aesthetics Ltd (bd mem, 89-92). *Media:* Watercolor, Acrylic. *Publ:* Illustrated Survey of Leading Comtemporaries, 90. *Mailing Add:* 601 S Walnut McPherson KS 67460

ROBINSON, MAURA
PAINTER
b Wilton, Conn, Nov 27, 56. *Study:* State Univ New York, Purchase, BFA, 79. *Work:* Informatics General Corp, New York; Gallery V, Kansas City, Mo; The Boston Co, Boston, Mass; also pvt collections. *Comn:* Wood panel 23k gold & oil, John Kazanjian, New City Theater, Seattle, Wash, 85; oil & copper leaf on paper, Grand Hyatt Hotel, New York, 87; wood panel 22k gold & oil, Capital Hilton Hotel, Washington, DC, 87; oil & copper leaf on paper, Embassy Suites, San Diego, CA, 88. *Exhib:* Gallery V, Kansas City, Mo, 85 & 88; Heatherfield Gallery, New York, 85 & 86; Broadway, Walker & White, New York, 89; L Rostovski Gallery, New York, 86; Genovese Gallery, Boston, Mass, 88, 89, & 90; group exhib, Five Stars, Gallery V, Kansas City, Mo, 88, The Gold Show, 88, Divergent Views, 89, Post Minimalism, 90, Genovese Gallery, Boston, Broadway, Walker & White, New York, 89; solo exhib, Art Space, Los Angeles, 89; Balance Brought Forward, Art Space, Los Angeles, 91. *Bibliog:* Suvan Geer (auth), Los Angeles, 5/89; Mary Sherman (auth), Boston Globe, 8/90; Cate McQuaid (auth), Visions Art Quarterly, Summer 91. *Mem:* Found for Community of Artists. *Media:* Oil, Gilding. *Mailing Add:* 411 E 6th St No 23 New York NY 10009

ROBINSON, SALLY W
PAINTER, PRINTMAKER
b Detroit, Mich, Nov 2, 24. *Study:* Bennington Col, BA; Wayne State Univ, MA & MFA; Cranbrook Acad Art; also with Hans Hofmann, Paul Feeley, Karl Knaths & Leon Kroll. *Work:* Chase Manhattan Bank, New York; Detroit Inst Arts; K-Mart Hq; and pvt collections. *Exhib:* Toledo Mus, Winston Traveling Show; Zella 9 Gallery, London, Eng; Troy Art Gallery, 78; Detroit Inst Arts, 78; Cliche-Verre, nat exhib, Detroit Inst Arts & Houston; and others. *Pos:* Mem, Gov Comn for Art in State Bldgs, Mich, 78-79; bd mem, Mus Art, Univ Mich, formerly. *Teaching:* Instr silk screen, Wayne State Univ, 73-74. *Awards:* Second Prize, Bloomfield Art Asn, 72; Second Prize, Soc Women Painters, 74 & First Prize, 75. *Mem:* Friends Mod Art; Founders Soc; Detroit Artists Market; Soc Women Painters; Bloomfield Art Asn. *Publ:* Contribr, Mich Art J, 76; auth, Cliche-Verre: Hand Drawn, Light Printed, 80. *Dealer:* Klein-Vogel Gallery 4520 N Woodward Royal Oak MI 48053; Rina Gallery E 74th St & Madison New York NY 10021. *Mailing Add:* 840 N Casey Key Rd Osprey FL 34229

ROBINSON, THOMAS V
DEALER, COLLECTOR
b Ft Worth, Tex, Feb 9, 38. *Study:* Tex Christian Univ, 56-57; Carlsbad-Oceanside Col, 57-58; Tex Wesleyan Col, 59-60. *Exhib:* Am Embassy, Mexico City, 81; Edinburgh Int Festival, 83-85; London Int Fair, 85; Am Festival, Glasgow, Scotland, 85; Casa de la Cultura, Quito, Ecuador, 87. *Collections Arranged:* Ben Shahn 1930-1969, 70; Auther G Dove 1920-1940, 71; Am Landscape, 73; Western Am Art 1860-1940 (auth, catalog), 74; Networking, Int Exchange Prog, 82-86 & 87-91. *Pos:* Dir, Robinson Galleries, 69-, pres, 77-90; dir, Ben Shahn Foundation, New York, 71-75; chmn, art travel studies & bd mem, Instituo de Arte Grace, Ecuador, 88. *Awards:* Consulor Corps Comt, 89; Inst Hispanic Cult, 90. *Bibliog:* Thomas V Robinson, SW Art Mag, 71; Donna Tennant (auth), Gallery-Inst Exchange, Houston Chronicle, 81; Internation exchange, Artscene, Houston, 83; Clare Henry (auth), Networking, Glasgow, Scotland, 85; El Commercial, Quito, Ecuador, 87. *Mem:* Cultural Arts Comt Houston Chamber Com; Tex Arts Alliance; Cultural Arts Coun Houston; Houston Art Dealers Asn (treas, 80-81, dir, 83-90). *Specialty:* Nineteenth and twentieth century American art; International contemporary, conceptual, performance, video and all media objects. *Publ:* Coauth, Kachinas-Paone, Encino Press, 76; International Fine Art Collector, 90. *Mailing Add:* Robinson Galleries Inc 3514 Lake St Houston TX 77089

ROBINSON, WALTER
PAINTER, CRITIC
b Wilmington, Del, July 18, 50. *Study:* Columbia Univ, New York, with Brian O'Dougherty & Adja Yunkers, BA, 72. *Work:* Mus Mod Art, New York; Weatherspoon, Univ NC. *Pos:* Co-ed publ, Art Rite Mag, 73-78; contrib ed, Art in Am, 82-; arts ed, East Village Eye, 83-85. *Mem:* Am Section, Int Asn Art Critics. *Media:* Acrylic, Oil. *Res:* Topical art world news reporting. *Dealer:* Metro Pictures 150 Greene St New York NY 10012. *Mailing Add:* 175 Ludlow No 9 New York NY 10012

ROBISON, ANDREW
MUSEUM CURATOR, WRITER
b Memphis, Tenn, May 23, 40. *Study:* Princeton Univ, AB & PhD; Oxford Univ, MA; Fulbright Res Scholar, India. *Collections Arranged:* Giovanni Battista Piranesi & Picasso Prints, 70, Princeton Univ; diverse print & drawing exhib, Nat Gallery of Art, 74-; 18th century Venetian Illus Bks, Grolier Club, 81; Prints From an Alumni Collection, Princeton Univ Art Mus, 82; Uncommon Piranesis, Grolier Club, 88. *Pos:* Cur & head dept prints & drawings, Nat Gallery Art, 74-, sr cur, 83-92, Mellon sr cur 92-; mem ed adv bd, Master Drawings, 81-; pres, Int Adv Comn Keepers Pub Collections Graphic Art, 84-88; bd dirs, Drawing Soc, 84- *Teaching:* Instr & asst prof, Univ Ill, 70-74. *Awards:* Ateneo Veneto, 90. *Mem:* Grolier Club, NY; Master Drawings Asn (int ed adv bd, 81-); Drawing Soc (bd dirs, 84-). *Res:* Eighteenth century Italian graphic art; early German prints and drawings. *Collection:* Prints and 18th century Italian illustrated books. *Publ:* Contemporary American Prints and Drawings, 81; Picasso: The Bull, 82; German Expressionist Prints from the Collection of Ruth & Jacob Kainen, 85; Piranesi: Early Architectural Fantasies: A Catalogue Raisonne of the Etchings, 86; Durer to Diebenkorn, 92; and others. *Mailing Add:* Dept Graphic Arts Nat Gallery Art Washington DC 20565

ROBLES, JULIAN
PAINTER, SCULPTOR
b Bronx, NY, June 24, 33. *Study:* Nat Acad Art & Design, with Robert Phillip; Art Students League, with Sidney Dickinson. *Work:* NMex State Permanent Collection, Albuquerque; Diamond M Mus, Snyder, Tex; 3M Collection, Houston, Tex. *Comn:* Portraits, Adm Edward O McDonnell, Lincoln Family, Oyster Bay, Long Island, 68, Ernestine Evans, Secy State NMex, 69, Margaret Jamison, Santa Fe, NMex, 70, Jean & Merle Rosenbaum, Santa Fe, 71, Bill Acheff, 81; and others. *Exhib:* NMex State Fair Art Exhib, Albuquerque, 71; Gov Galley Show, Santa Fe, 78; one man shows, Diamond M Mus, Snyder, Tex, 73, Pelham, Santa Fe, NMex, 81; Cowboy Hall Fame, 75; and others. *Awards:* Rosenthan Award, Pastel Soc Am, 83; Silver Medal for Oils & Third Place for Pastels, Nat Western Artist Show, 83; 24 national and regional awards; and others. *Bibliog:* Article, SW Art, 8/75; article, Artists of the Rockies, spring 82. *Mem:* Artists Equity; Pastel Soc Am; SW Pastel Soc. *Media:* Mixed; Wood. *Res:* Researching and recording authentic western Indian life and ceremonials. *Dealer:* Grand Central Galleries New York NY; Trailside Galleries Scottsdale AZ. *Mailing Add:* Box 1845 Taos NM 87571

ROCAMORA, JAUME
PAINTER
b Tortosa, Spain, July 6, 46. *Study:* Taller Sch Art, Tortosa, Sapin, 56; studied with Joan Llimona, Cercle Artistic Sant Lluc, Barcelona, 69. *Work:* Mus Popular Contemp Art, Villafamés, Spain; Zabaleta Mus, Quesada; Munic Mus Fine Arts, Cholet, France; Mus Leopod-Huesch, Duren, Alemania; Mus Dibujos, Larres, Spain. *Comn:* Mural collage, Casa Diocesana d'Espiritualitat, Tortosa, Spain, 86; mural collage, Hotel Berenguer IV, Tortosa, Spain, 86; Serigrafía, Ministry of Trabajo, Madrid, 89 & 90. *Exhib:* Elements Primaris, Mus Popular Contemp Art, Villafamés, 84; Oeuvres 1983-1988, Mus Munic Fine Arts, Cholet, 89. *Bibliog:* J Corredor Matheos (auth), El Arte Mental de Jaume Rocamora, catalog, 85; Josep Miquel Garcia (auth), La percepció implica pensament, catalog, 86; Arnau Puig (auth), Intención ensimismada, catalog, 91. *Mem:* Noesis Found, Calaceite, Spain (vpres, currently). *Media:* Collage. *Publ:* Illustr, Textos Bàsic de Edicions de Filosofia, Santa Coloma de Gramenet, 91; Xle, Festival de Música Felip Pedrell, Tortosa, 91; Ediciones del Ministerio de Trabajo, Madrid, 91; L'Organització Territorial en Vegueries, Tortosa, 91. *Mailing Add:* Argentina, 13 Tortosa 43500 Spain

ROCCO, RON (RONALD ANTHONY ROCCO)
SCULPTOR, VIDEO ARTIST
b Fort Hood, Tex, Nov 21, 53. *Study:* Fordham Univ, BS, 71; State Univ NY, Col at Purchase, BFA, (state regents scholar) 76; Ctr Advanced Visual Study/ Mass Inst Technol with Herr Otto Piene, 33. *Work:* Raw Data for the I V, Showing Room, New York, 79; Laser Sculpture/Dance, Herbert F Johnson Mus, Ithaca, NY, 81; Zaroffs Tale, Solomon R Guggenheim Mus, New York, 83; Buddah Meets Einstein at the Great Wall, Asia Soc, New York, 85 & Grammage Theatre, Temple, Ariz, 86. *Comn:* Altair, 77 & Meketra, 78, Festival Ithaca, NY; The Horizon is Nothing More Than the Limit of Our Sight, Brooklyn Mus, NY, 90. *Exhib:* Solo exhibs, New Sculpture, Gallery Danielli, Toronto, Can, 79, Special Projects, PS1, Inst Art & Urban Resources, New York, 87, The Waterline Project, Found Art Garden, Amsterdam, Neth, 89, The Berlin Project, Kunstlerhaus Bethanien & Amerika Haus, Berlin, Gern, Ger, 91; Artist & the Computer, Bronx Mus Art, New York, 85; Technological Muse, Katonah Mus Art, 90, Working in Brooklyn-Installations, Brooklyn Mus Art, New York, 90. *Collections Arranged:* American Video Selections/The Video Image Invitational, Found Georgio Ronchi, Capri, Italy, 85. *Teaching:* Guest lectr, Cornell Univ, Watermargin Ser, Ithaca, NY, 77, Columbia Univ, Sch Art Hist, New York, 82, Harvard, Sch Archit, Cambridge, Mass, 88; guest fac, Banff Ctr Arts, Banff, Can, formerly. *Awards:* NY State Coun Arts Award, In Light of Sound, 85; NY Found Arts Award, The Waterline Project, 89; The Netherland/ America Found Award, The Waterline Project, Dutch Consulate General, 89; Nat Endowment Arts, 77 & 84. *Bibliog:* Jennifer Dunning (auth), Dance--laser sculpture, NY Times, 5/26/81; Jenya Gould (auth), Brooklyn Artists-Open Studios, Greenline Press, 5/90; Jeanne Greenberg (auth), Working in Brooklyn-Installations, Brooklyn Mus, 8/3/90. *Mem:* Resident Video Artist The Experimental TV Center, Owego, NY; United Nations Conference on Communication Technology & Traditional Culture (conf participant, 83); Int

artist-in-residence, Kunst & Complex, Rotterdam, Neth, 92. *Media:* Metal, Video. *Publ:* The Berlin Project, Kunstlerhaus Bethanien, Berlin, Ger, 91. *Dealer:* Kahan Art 123 Bank St New York NY; Gallerie Schoen & Nalepa Pariser Strabe 56 D-1000, Berlin, 15, Ger. *Mailing Add:* 209 President St Brooklyn NY 11231

ROCH, ERNST
DESIGNER
b Osijek, Croatia, Dec 8, 28; Can citizen. *Study:* State Sch Appl Arts, Graz, Austria, MFA, 53; also with Hans Wagula, Graz, Austria; Nova Scotia Col Art & Design, DFA, 88. *Work:* Nat Poster Mus, Warsaw; Nat Archives, Ottawa; Mus Mod Art, New York; Libr Congress, Washington, DC; and others. *Comn:* Visual identitiy prog, comn by Nat Art Ctr, Ottawa, 65; poster, comn by Montreal Olympic Games, 76; postage stamps, Queen Elizabeth II, 63, Canadian Mushrooms, 89. *Exhib:* Nat Libr, Ottawa, Ont, 77; St Mary's Univ, Halifax, 78; NB Mus, St John, 78; Alta Col of Art Gallery, Calgary, 78; York Univ, 79; Montreal Mus Fine Arts, 70; Mus Applied Arts, Belgrade & Zagreb, 73; State Univ Fine Arts, Braunschweig, 74; and others. *Collections Arranged:* The Visual Image of the Munich Games 1972, Montreal Mus Fine Arts, Art Gallery Ont, Toronto, 72; Alliance Graphique Int Posters, Place Ville Marie, Montreal, 82. *Pos:* Founding mem & principal, Design Collaborative, Montreal & Toronto, 65-77; principal, Roch Design, Montreal, 77- *Teaching:* Vis lectr graphic design, Ohio State Univ, Columbus. *Awards:* Fifty Books of the Year, Am Inst Graphic Arts, 72 & 75; Most Beautiful Books of the World, Leipzig, 75; Poster Biennale, Warsaw, 76, 78 & 80; and numerous other awards. *Bibliog:* Hans Kuh (auth), Design Collaborative, Gebrauchsgraphik, Munich, 6/70; T Kirkman (auth), To say the most with the least, Montreal Star, 11/14/70; Allan Harrison & Hans Neuburg (auth), Graphic Designs by Rolf Harder & Ernst Roch, Montreal, 77; Rolf Muller (auth), Ernst Roch, High Quality, Munich 6/86; Ken Cato (ed), Ernst Roch, the Best Choice, Tokyo, 89; and others. *Mem:* Am Inst Graphic Arts; Int Inst Typographic Arts; Soc Graphic Designers Can; Graphic Design Austria; Int Inst Info Design; and others. *Publ:* Ed & designer, Arts of the Eskimo: Prints, 74; Paper Zoo, 74. *Mailing Add:* PO Box 1056 Sta B Montreal PQ H3B 3K5 Canada

ROCHA, RANDOLFO (RANDOLFO SCOTT ROCHA)
PAINTER
b Belo Horizonte, Minas Gerais, Brazil, Mar 31, 50. *Study:* Private study with Yara Tupinamba, Prof Federal Univ Minas Gerais, Brazil, 67-70. *Work:* Rose Art Mus, Brandeis Univ, Watham, Mass; DeCordova Mus, Lincoln, Mass; Babson Col, Wellesley, Mass. *Exhib:* Boston Reacts: Central America, Addison Gallery, Phillips Acad, Andover, Mass, 85; Evils of Power, Southeastern Mass Univ, N Dartmouth, 86; Brockton Triennial, Brockton Art Mus, Mass, 87; Boston Now, Inst Contemp Art, Mass, 88; solo exhib, Real Art Ways, Hartford, Conn, 89. *Bibliog:* Carla McCormick (auth), Exits and Entrances: On Clowns, Artforum, 1/88. *Mem:* Inst Contemp Art, Boston (trustee, 90-); White Columns (trustee 90-). *Dealer:* Stux Gallery 155 Spring St New York NY 10012. *Mailing Add:* 58 Brimmer St Boston MA 02108

ROCHE, ROBERT (RICHARD)
PAINTER
Study: Apprenticeship, studio of Sebastian Cruset, 31-32; Nat Acad Design, New York, 33-36; Art Students League, 36-40. *Work:* NY Racing Asn, Aqueduct, Long Island & Belmont, Elmwood; Nat Mus Racing, Saratoga, NY; Wilmington Race Track, Del; US Air Force, Offutt, Nebr; and others. *Comn:* Saratoga Race Track Series, NY Racing Asn, Long Island, 60, painting of Man O War, 61 & Belmont Race Track Series, 63; plus others. *Exhib:* One-man shows, Frank K M Rehn Galleries, New York, 49 & 52 & Am Watercolor Soc, New York; Silvermine Guild Artists, Norwalk, Conn, 51-54; Salmagundi Club, New York, 54 & 55; Retrospective, USAF, 88; many others. *Pos:* Cur, Mus Fine Arts, Richmond, Va, 47-48; radio art prog, NH Maine, Mass, 68-70; writer, Nat Antiques Rev, Portland, Maine, 69-71; owner, RRR Assoc & RR Prints. *Teaching:* Instr painting & drawing, pvt art sch, 42-64. *Bibliog:* G Leonard Gold (auth), Saratoga Prints, NY Racing Asn, 62. *Mem:* Am Watercolor Soc; Royal Soc Arts. *Media:* All Media. *Publ:* Illusr, Birds and Beasts of Mark Twain, Univ Okla Press, 66; and prints of own work. *Mailing Add:* Windswept Farm York ME 03909

ROCHETTE, ANNE MONIQUE
SCULPTOR
b Oullins, France, Jan 5, 57. *Study:* Ecole Nationale Des Beaux Arts, Paris, dipl fine arts, 79; New York Univ, MA, 82. *Teaching:* Asst prof sculpture, Parsons Sch Design, 87-88; asst prof sculpture, RI Sch Design, Providence, 87-90; instr sculpture, New York Studio Sch, 88-90. *Awards:* Nat Endowment Arts Fel, 90; New York Found Arts Fel, 91. *Bibliog:* Michael Brenson (auth), Emerging sculptors, NY Times, 10/87; Eleanor Heartney (auth), A Hand of Many, Art Am, 4/90; Jennifer Borum (auth), Pains & pleasures, Art Forum, 5/90. *Media:* Sculpture. *Mailing Add:* 315 Berry St No 7N Brooklyn NY 11211

ROCKBURNE, DOROTHEA
PAINTER, SCULPTOR
b Verdun, Quebec; US citizen. *Study:* Black Mountain Col. *Work:* Mus Mod Art, Whitney Mus Am Art & Metrop Mus Art, New York; Philidelphia Mus Art; The Corcoran, Washington, DC; Guggenheim Mus, New York. *Comn:* Hilton Hotel, San Jose, Calif. *Exhib:* One-person exhibs, Margo Leavin Gallery, Los Angeles, Calif, 82, Galleriet, Lund, Sweden, 83, Xavier Fourcade, New York, 86, Arts Club, Chicago, Ill, 87, Andre Emmerich Gallery, 88, 89, 90, 91, 92; The Americans: The Collage, Contemp Arts Mus, Houston, 83; Haags Gemeentemuseum, The Hague, 87; Mus Contemp Art, Chicago, 87;; The Spiritual in Art: Abstract Painting 1890-1985, Los Angeles Art, 87; Drawings from the Eighties, Carnegie Mellon Univ Art Gallery, Pittsburgh, 87; Viewpoints: Postwar Painting & Sculpture, Guggenheim Mus, New York, 89; Making Their Mark Traveling Exhib, 89 & Abstraction, Geometry Painting Travelling Exhib, 90; ten year retrospective, Rose Art Mus, Brandeis Univ, Waltham, Mass, 89. *Pos:* Mem, Artists' Advisory bd, New Mus, NY; Trustee, Independent Curators Inc, New York. *Awards:* Guggenheim Fel, 72-73; Painting Award, Art Inst Chicago, 72; Nat Endowment Arts Fel, 74-75; Brandeis Univ Creative Arts Award, 85. *Bibliog:* Robert Storr (auth), Painterly Operations, Art Am, 2/86 & Rockburne's Wagner (exhib catalog), Andre Emmerich Gallery, 88; Michael Brenson (auth), A new-world painter views the masterpieces of old-world innovators, 4/29/88 & Egyptian art is alive & well in the West, 12/31/89, New York Times; Saul Ostrow (auth), Dorothea Rockburne, Bomb, fall 88; John Yau (auth), Light and Dark (exhib catalog), Andre Emmerich Gallery, 89. *Media:* Miscellaneous Media. *Mailing Add:* 140 Grand St New York NY 10013

ROCKEFELLER, (MR & MRS) DAVID
COLLECTORS
Mr Rockefeller, b New York, NY, June 12, 15. *Study:* Mr Rockefeller, Harvard Univ, BS, 36; Univ Chicago, PhD, 40; LLD, Columbia Univ, 54, Bowdoin Col, 58, Jewish Theol Sem, 58, Williams Col, 66, Wagner Col, 67, Harvard Univ, 69, Pace Col, 70, St John's Univ, 71, Univ Liberia, 79. *Pos:* Trustee & chmn bd trustees, Mus Mod Art, New York. *Collection:* Paintings, modern art. *Mailing Add:* 30 Rockfeller Plaza Rm 5600 New York NY 10112

ROCKEFELLER, (MRS) LAURANCE S
COLLECTOR
b New York, NY, May 26, 10. *Study:* Vassar Col, 27-29; Art Students League, 29-34. *Mem:* Trustee, Whitney Mus Am Art; Metrop Mus Art, New York; Mus Mod Art, New York. *Collection:* Paintings & modern art. *Mailing Add:* c/o George Taylor 30 Rockfeller Plaza Rm 5600 New York NY 10112

ROCKLIN, RAYMOND
SCULPTOR, EDUCATOR
b Moodus, Conn, Aug 18, 22. *Study:* Educ Alliance, New York, with Abbo Ostrovsky; Cooper Union Art Sch, with Milton Hebald & John Havannes, BFA(Skowhegan Scholar). *Work:* Whitney Mus Am Art, New York; Provincetown Mus Art, Mass; Temple Israel, St Louis; Skowhegan Sch Painting & Sculpture. *Comn:* Wall brass, comn by Mrs Beskind, New York, 62; wall brass, comn by Mrs Nina Waller, Baltimore, 63; four religious sculptures, White Plains Hosp, NY, 79; Brass Horse (16'x9'), Mr & Mrs Stahmer, Yorktown Heights, NY, 88. *Exhib:* Young Americans, Whitney Mus Am Art, 56; Oakland Art Mus, 59; Gallerina Tiberina, Rome, 59; Univ Calif, Berkeley, 60; Claude Bernard Gallery, Paris, 60. *Teaching:* Guest artist, Am Univ, 56; asst prof art, Univ Calif, Berkeley, 59-60; guest artist, Ball State Teachers Col, summer 64; prof art, Borough Manhattan Community Col, City Univ New York, currently. *Awards:* Fulbright Grant, Italy, 52-53; Yaddo Found Fel, 56. *Bibliog:* M Seuphor (auth), Raymond Rocklin, The Sculpture of this Century, 61; F Hazan (auth), article, Dictionary Mod Sculpture; and others. *Mem:* Sculptors Guild; Am Abstract Artists; Fedn Mod Painters & Sculptors. *Media:* Mixed. *Dealer:* Sculptors Guild 110 Greene St New York NY 10012. *Mailing Add:* 232B Watch Hill Rd Peekskill NY 10566

RODA (RHODA LILLIAN SABLOW)
PAINTER, TAPESTRY ARTIST
b Port Chester, NY, Nov 26, 26. *Study:* Univ Wis; Rochester Inst Technol; Art Students League; also with Frank Vincent DuMont & Frank Reilly. *Comn:* Cranbrook 50th Anniversary (needlepoint rug), Cranbrook Acad, Bloomfield Hills, Mich, 73; needlepoint designs of main altar area & furniture, Christ Episcopal Church, Detroit, Mich, 75 & main altar rug, 82; needlepoint designs altar seats & kneelers, St James Church, Birmingham, Mich, 83. *Exhib:* Allied Artists Am, Nat Acad, New York, 69; Ahda Artzt Gallery, New York, 70; Needle Arts Gallery, Birmingham, Mich, 71, 74 & 76; Lever House, New York, 77. *Bibliog:* Lesley Umans (auth), Encaustic painting, Reporter Dispatch, AP, 7/70 & Creative stitchery, Women's Wear Daily, 8/71; Lillian Braun (auth), 3-D needlepoint, int, Detroit Free Press, 10/74. *Media:* Oil, Acrylic. *Mailing Add:* Rural Dr Scarsdale NY 10583

RODAN, DON
PHOTOGRAPHER, PAINTER
b Cincinnati, Ohio, June 30, 50. *Study:* Cooper Union Art Sch, BFA, 74. *Work:* Int Mus Photog, George Eastman House, NY; Australian Nat Gallery, Canberra; Williams Col Art Mus, Mass; The Polaroid Collection, Cambridge, Mass; San Francisco Mus Mod Art, Calif; Kunstmuseum, Basel, Switz; Walker Arts Ctr, Minneapolis, Minn; Nat Gallery, Washington, DC. *Exhib:* One-man shows, The Greek Myths, Int Mus Photog, George Eastman House, 77 & Castelli Gallery, New York, 79, Immortal Stories: Recent Color Drawings, Leo Castelli Gallery, New York, 86; One of a Kind Color, Houston Mus Fine Arts & Corcoran Gallery, 79-80; Exploration of a Medium, Rheinisches Landes Mus & Frakfurter Kunst Verein, Germany, 80 & 81; Fabricated to be Photographed, San Francisco Mus Mod Art & Albright-Knox Gallery, 80; New Voices 2, Allen Mem Art Mus, Ohio, 81; La Photographie en Amerique, Galerie Texbraun, Paris, 82; Arranged Images, Boise Gallery Art, Idaho, 83; Three Dimensional Photographs, Herman Wunsche, Bonn, WGer, 83; The Family of Man, PS 1, Long Island City, NY, 84; Extending the Perimeters of Twentieth-Century Photography, San Francisco Mus Mod Art, 85; Fabrications: Staged, Altered and Appropriated Photographs, Int Ctr of Photog, NY 87 & Carpenter Art Ctr, Harvard Univ, Cambridge, Mass, 88. *Awards:* Fel, Nat Endowment Arts, 84-85. *Bibliog:* Richard Whelan (auth), New York Reviews: Don Rodan, Art News, 5/79;

Sally Eauclaire (auth), The New Color, Abbeville Press, 81; Carter Ratcliff (auth), Tableau photography from Mayall to Rodan, Picture Mag #18, fall 81; Andy Grundberg (auth), Exploring the improbable, New York Times, 7/11/82; Ronny H Cohen (auth), Image scavengers, photography, an exhibition, Print Collector's Newletter, 5-6/83; John Russell (auth), Don Rodan, Immortal Stories: Recent Color Drawings, NY Times 3/14/86; Anne Hoy (auth), Fabrications: Staged, Altered and Appropriated Photographs, Abbeville Press, NY 87. *Media:* Color Pencil on Linen, Cibachrome Color. *Mailing Add:* 23 W 12th St New York NY 10011

RODBARD, BETTY
PAINTER
b Boston, Mass. *Study:* Univ Toronto, Can; Univ Buffalo, NY, with Seymour Drumlevich, Walter Prochownik & Sheldon Berlyn. *Work:* Springfield Art Mus, Mo; Univ Utah Art Gallery, Logan; Roswell Park Mem Inst, Buffalo; KFAC Radio Sta, Los Angeles; Cedars-Sinai Med Ctr & City of Hope Med Ctr, Los Angeles. *Comn:* Portraits, Greeting Cards. *Exhib:* Albright-Knox Art Mus, 63; Nat Juried Ann, Butler Inst Am Art, 68, 70 & 73; Pasadena Mus Art; Calif Inst Technol, 80; Tucson Mus Art, 82; Brand XIII, 83; Nat Acad Design, New York; and others. *Teaching:* Pvt instruction in painting. *Awards:* Southwest Mo Mus Award, Mus Assocs, 68; Henry C Pitz Mem Award, Am Watercolor Soc, 77; Nat Watercolor Soc Award, 79; and others. *Mem:* Pasadena Soc Artists (secy treas, 67-71, historian, 76-79); Nat Watercolor Soc (secy, 69-72, treas, 79-80); Women Painters of the West; Los Angeles Art Asn; Watercolor USA Honor Soc. *Media:* Watercolor, Oil. *Dealer:* Los Angeles Art Asn 825 N La Cienega Los Angeles CA 90069. *Mailing Add:* 3422 Calle Azul, No E Laguna Hills CA 92653

RODE, MEREDITH EAGON
PRINTMAKER, EDUCATOR
b Delaware, Ohio, Mar 27, 38. *Study:* Corcoran Sch of Art, 55-58; George Washington Univ, BA, 58; Art Students League, New York, (scholar), study with George Grosz & Harry Sternberg, 59; Univ of Md, MFA, 74. *Work:* Southern Graphics Print Collection, Univ Miss, Oxford; Univ Md Col Permanent Collection; Dundalk College; Univ District Columbia Permanent Collection; Nat Mus of Women In the Arts. *Exhib:* Baltimore Mus of Art, Md, 77; Utah Mus of Fine Arts, Salt Lake City, 77; Contemporary Printmaking in Maryland, (juried) Baltimore, MD, 83; Dundalk Col Gallery Invitational, The Window, 86; US Dept State Art in the Embassies Prog, Nassau, Bahamas, Kinshasa, Zaire, Vienna, Austria, Port-Au-Prince, Haiti, Brazzaville, the Congo, Geneva and Switzerland; and others. *Pos:* Actg chmn, Federal City Col, Washington, DC, 71-72. *Teaching:* Instr studio art, Corcoran Sch Art, 62-68; assoc prof studio art, Univ District Columbia, 68-78, prof, 78- *Awards:* Fac Res Grant, Univ District of Columbia, 85-86, 86-87; Fel, Ctr for Applied Res, 88-89. *Bibliog:* UDC Special Art Collection catalog, 84. *Mem:* Women's Caucus Art (nat vpres, 75-76); Southern Graphics Coun; Asn Am Cultures; and others. *Media:* Multimedia. *Publ:* Auth, articles, Art J, Col Art Asn, 75; Illus, Earth Day, 90, Quicksilver Comm, Inc. *Dealer:* Foundry Gallery 641 Indiana Ave Washington DC. *Mailing Add:* Univ of DC Mt Vernon Campus Washington DC 20001

RODEIRO, JOSÉ MANUEL
PAINTER, MURALIST
b Tampa, Fla, Feb 5, 49. *Study:* Univ Tampa, Fla, BA, 71; Pratt Inst, Brooklyn, MFA, 73; Ohio Univ, Athens, Ohio, PhD, 76. *Work:* Washington Co Mus, Hagerstown, Md; Oscar Cintas Found, New York; The City of Tampa, Fla; Clayton Galleries, Tampa, Fla. *Comn:* Arrival of De Soto in Florida (mural), City Hall, Tampa, Fla, 80; Tampa the Craddle of Cuban Independence (mural), Fla, 90; The Ransoming of Frederick (mural), Walkersville, Md, 92. *Exhib:* Four Allegheny Artists, Md Art Place, Baltimore, 83; one-person shows, Nicholas Roerch Mus, New York, 85 & Washington Co Mus, Md, 88; Inaugural Exhib, Casal de Sarria, Barcelona, Spain, 86; Grace Harkin Gallery, New York, 88; Rosenberg Gallery, Baltimore, Md, 90; Lucia Gallery, New York, 90. *Teaching:* Vis prof, Pratt Inst, Brooklyn, 75-77; adj prof art, Univ SFla, Tampa, 77-79; asst prof, Frostburg State Univ, Md, 79-84, assoc prof, 84-; artist-in-residence, Md State Arts Coun, 92. *Awards:* Visual Artist Fel, Nat Endowment Arts, 85 & 86; Best of Show, Washington Co Mus, 85; Best of Show, Lucia Gallery, 88. *Bibliog:* Henry Scarupa (auth), article, Baltimore Sun, 4/88; Nico Suarez (auth), Amnesis Art, Lascaux Pub, 88; Murals article, St Petersburg Sun Times, 11/11/90. *Mem:* Art South Inc; Md Fedn Art; Md State Arts Coun Visual Arts Panel. *Media:* Oil, Acrylic. *Publ:* Illusr & contribr, The Immanentist Anthology, Smith Horizon Press, 73; contribr, For Neruda for Chile, Beacon Press, 75; From the Hudson to the World, Clearwater, 78; Art of the 60's & 70's, Wash Co Mus Fine Arts, Hagerstown, 90; Contemporary Nicaraguan Art, Frostburg State Univ Press, 91. *Dealer:* Clayton Galleries Tampa FL; Lucia Gallery New York NY. *Mailing Add:* 112 Victoria Lane Frostburg MD 21532

RODGERS, JACK A
ADMINISTRATOR
b Littlefield, Tex, Oct 5, 38. *Study:* Tex Tech Univ, BA(advert & design); Univ Tex Southwestern Med Sch, Dallas, MMA; San Antonio Art Inst, Hon Dr Art. *Pos:* Supvr med illus, Univ Tex Med Br, Galveston, Tex, 64-66; exec dir, San Antonio Art Inst, Tex, 76-80, bd chmn, 81-; spec adv, San Antonio Arts Coun; educ adv, Tex Comn on Arts; bd mem, Tex Arts Alliance. *Teaching:* Asst prof & deputy chmn dept med commun, Univ Tex Med Sch, San Antonio, 67-75. *Awards:* Nat Eaton Award, Nat Student Am Med Asn; First Place, Dept Neurol Exhib, Univ Tex Med Br, Galveston, Tex & Dept Surgery Exhib, Tex Med Asn; Outstanding Young Texan; San Antonio Honor for Leadership & Community Involvement; Deeds Awards for Community Leadership. *Mailing Add:* 431 E Rosewood San Antonio TX 78212

RODMAN, RUTH M
PRINTMAKER, TAPESTRY ARTIST
b Boston, Mass, Apr 13, 28. *Study:* Mass Sch of Art; Boston Mus Sch, with Karl Zerbe; De Cordova Mus, Lincoln, Mass, with Stoltenberg. *Work:* New York Pub Libr; Boston Pub Libr, Mass; Brockton Art Ctr, Mass; Minneapolis Inst of Art, Minn. *Comn:* Annual Appeal Print, DeCordova Mus, 78. *Exhib:* De Cordova Mus, Lincoln, Mass, 73-77; 1st Nat Bank Boston Printmaker Exhib; Silvermine Guild of Artists Nat Print Exhib, Conn, 74; Worcester Mus, Mass, 74-75; Brockton Art Ctr, Mass, 75; Boston Visual Artist Union; Boston Ctr for the Arts. *Teaching:* De Cordova Mus. *Awards:* Purchase Prizes, Boston Printmakers, Rose Art Mus, Brandeis Univ & De Cordova Mus; Nat Print Show, Silvermine Nat Print Exhib. *Bibliog:* J Silverman (auth), feature article, Boston Sunday Globe & Wayland-Weston Town Crier, 75; Carol LeBrun Danikian (auth), review in Christian Sci Monitor, 11/76; Corporations--the new medicis, Newsweek Mag, 11/76. *Mem:* Boston Printmakers; Boston Visual Artists Union; Nat Asn Am Penwomen. *Publ:* Illusr, Collagraph Printmaking, Watson-Guptill, 75; illusr, A Time for Living, Dutton, 75. *Mailing Add:* 16 Linn Lane Wayland MA 01778

RODMAN, SELDEN
WRITER, CRITIC
b New York, NY, Feb 19, 09. *Study:* Yale Univ, 31. *Collection:* Contemporary figurative painting & sculpture, primitive & folk art; collection has been widely shown in the United States & Mexico, and has been catalogued by Vanderbilt University & by San Carlos Academy, Mexico; selections from folk art collection have been donated to Yale University & Ramapo Colege, New Jersey. *Publ:* Auth, The Miracle of Haitian Art, 74; Tongues of Fallen Angels, 74; Genius in the Backlands, 77; Artists in Tune with Their World, Simon & Schuster, 82; Where Art is Joy-Forty Years of Haitian Art, Ruggles De LaTour, 88; and others. *Mailing Add:* 659 Ramapo Valley Rd Oakland NJ 07436

RODRIGUEZ, GENO (EUGENE)
PHOTOGRAPHER, MUSEUM DIRECTOR
b New York, NY, June 2, 40. *Study:* Hammersmith Col Art, London, NDD, 66; Int Peoples Col, Elsinore, Denmark. *Work:* Metrop Mus Art; Everson Mus Art; Int Ctr for Photog, New York; Am Mus Natural Hist, New York; Mus Contemp Art, Caracas, Venezuela. *Exhib:* One & two-person exhibs, Wadsworth Atheneum, Hartford, Conn, 76, Aternative Ctr for Int Arts, New York, Studio Arte 20001, Castressata, Italy & Centro Arte Galeter, Brescia, Italy, 77, Mus Contemp Art, Caracus, Venezuela & II Diaframma Gallery, Milan, Italy, 79, Cayman Gallery, New York & Real Art Ways Gallery, Hartford, Conn, 80, Jayne H Baum Gallery, New York, 86, CEPA Gallery, Buffalo, NY, 87 & Sheldon Memorial Art Gallery, Univ Nebr, Lincoln, 89; Graham Mod, New York, 87; San Diego Mus Art, Calif, 87; Photography on the Edge (catalog), The Patrick & Beatrice Haggerty Mus Art, Marquette Univ, Milwaukee, Wis, 88; The Photography of Invention: American Photographers of the Eighties (catalog), Nat Mus Am Art, Smithsonian Inst, Washington, DC, 89; Fantasies, Fables and Fabrications: Photoworks from the 80's traveling exhib, Univ Mass, Amherst, Herter Art Gallery, also traveling: Delaware Art Mus, Wilmington; Lamont Gallery, Phillips Exeter Acad, Andover, Mass; Univ Mo, Gallery Art, Kansas City; Mus Contemp Art, Ostende, Belgium; Mus Contemp Photog, Antwerp, Belg & Mus Contemp Art, Florence, Italy, 89; and others. *Collections Arranged:* Dia Dos Los Muertos III: Homelessness, 90; Peter Dean: A Retrospective, 90; Keith Morrison: Recent Paintings, 90; Syncretism: Art of the 21st Century, 91; Artists of Conscience: 16 Years of Social & Political Commentary, 92; Made in America: Art of the Great Lakes States, 86. *Pos:* Pres, founder, Inst Contemp Hispanic Art, 72-74, Enfoco: Latin Am Photog Collaborative, 73-74, Alternative Mus, 75- *Teaching:* Instr photog, Rutgers Univ, 77-78; instr photo critique, Sch Visual Arts, New York, 77- *Awards:* Distinguished Am Vis to Africa, Phelps Stokes Fund, 77; Artist Nat Endowment Arts fel, 79; Ludwig Vogelstein Found Fel, 81. *Mem:* Am Asn Mus (cur comt, exec mem, 85-86). *Media:* Photo-assemblage. *Publ:* The Islands: Worlds of the Puerto Ricans, Harper & Row, 74; auth, Mira Mira Mira Puerto Rican New Yorkers, Forum Press, 75. *Mailing Add:* 32 W 82nd St New York NY 10024

RODRIQUEZ, ERNESTO ANGELO
PAINTER, DESIGNER
b New York, NY, Aug 19, 47. *Study:* Parsons Sch Design, 65-68; New Sch Social Res/Parsons, BFA, 79. *Work:* Hudson River Mus, Yonkers, NY. *Comn:* Linen fabric design, comn by Miss Iris Roberts, New York, 89; linen designs, comn by D Calahan, New York, 89; floral fabric designs, comn by H Rodriquez, New York, 90; football fabric, comn by S Brathwait, New York, 90; marine fabric design, comn by S Willard, New York, 90-91. *Exhib:* Hudson River Mus, Yonkers, NY, 81; Hispanic Experience, Long Beach Mus Art, NY, 82; St Francis Assisi, NY, 74. *Teaching:* Coordr, Camp Oakhurst, NJ, 82-86; instr crafts, Jewish Guild for Blind, 86-87; instr art, St Francis Assisi, NY, 84-89, 91-92. *Mem:* Fdn for Community Artist. *Mailing Add:* 55 Overlook Terr 4H New York NY 10033

ROEBLING, MARY G
COLLECTOR, PATRON
b Collingswood, NJ, July 29, 05. *Mem:* Am Art Asn; Arch Am Art; Philadelphia Print Club; NJ Cult Ctr Adv Coun (first chmn). *Collection:* Paintings, sculpture, fine porcelain and glass. *Mailing Add:* Lafayette House 777 W State St Apt No 5B Trenton NJ 08618

ROESCH, ROBERT ARTHUR
SCULPTOR, DESIGNER
b Buffalo, NY, June 25, 46. *Study:* State Univ NY; Pratt Inst, study with David Lee Brown. *Work:* Fidelity Bank, Philadelphia; Marine Midland Bank, New York; State Univ NY, Farmingdale. *Comn:* Sculpture, Cynmark Group, Suffern, NY, 84; sculpture, Boca Raton Redevelopment, Fla, 85. *Exhib:* New Directions in Sculpture, Heckscher Mus, NY, 77; Wistariahurst Mus, Holyoke, Mass, 77; Art Alliance, Philadelphia, 80; Bennison Bldg, Long Island, NY, 81; Beaver Col, Pa, 83. *Teaching:* Adj prof, 3-D design, Southampton Col, NY, 75-84, Parsons Sch Design, New York, 84-85 & Acad Fine Arts, Philadelphia, 86- *Bibliog:* Jessica Darraby (auth), article, in: Designer's West, 86. *Media:* Steel and Similar Metals. *Dealer:* David Segal Gallery 568 Broadway New York NY 10012; Nerlino Gallery 96 Green St New York NY. *Mailing Add:* 1201 S Fifth St Philadelphia PA 19147

ROGALSKI, WALTER
PRINTMAKER, LECTURER
b Glen Cove, NY, Apr 10, 23. *Study:* Brooklyn Mus Sch, with Xavier Gonzalez, Arthur Osver, C Seide & Gabor Peterdi, 47-51. *Work:* Mus Mod Art; Brooklyn Mus; Cleveland Mus Art; Fogg Mus Art; Seattle Art Mus; plus many others. *Exhib:* Six shows, Brooklyn Mus, 51-68; Soc Am Graphic Artists, 66 & 69; Cincinnati Mus Asn, 68; Am Fedn Arts Traveling Exhib, 69; Nat Print Exhib, Potsdam, NY, 69; plus many others. *Teaching:* Prof graphic art, Grad Sch Art & Design, Pratt Inst, currently. *Awards:* Prizes, De Cordova & Dana Mus, 61 & Yale Gallery Fine Arts, 61; Purchase Prize, Assoc Am Artists, 66; plus others. *Mem:* Soc Am Graphic Artists. *Mailing Add:* Dept of Printmaking Pratt Inst Brooklyn NY 11205

ROGERS, ART
PHOTOGRAPHER
b Wilson, NC, Sept 13, 48. *Work:* Joseph Seagrams & Sons Calif Photog Collections, New York; Arch Univ Ariz, Tucson; San Francisco Mus Mod Art, Calif. *Exhib:* SECA, San Francisco Mus Mod Art, Calif, 82; Photographs, CEPA Gallery, Buffalo, NY, 83; 10,000 Eyes, ASMT, Int Ctr Photog, New York, 91. *Awards:* SECA Art Award, San Francisco Mus Mod Art; Guggenheim Fel, 86; Photog Fel, Nat Endowment Arts, 91. *Mem:* Am Soc Mag Photogs; Marin Arts Coun. *Dealer:* Photos/Ruth Silverman Gallery 403 Francisco St San Francisco CA 94133. *Mailing Add:* 11435 Hwy 1 PO Box 777 Pt Reyes Station CA 94956

ROGERS, BARBARA
PAINTER, EDUCATOR
b Newcomerstown, Ohio, Apr 28, 37. *Study:* Ohio State Univ, BSc; Univ Calif, Berkeley, MA. *Work:* San Francisco Mus Mod Art; Oakland Art Mus, Mills Col, Oakland, Kaiser Permanente Hosp, Bank Am, San Francisco, Calif; Evergreen Col, Wash; Univ Calif, Berkeley; Prudential Ins Co, Calif; AT & T, New York; and others. *Exhib:* One-person exhibs, San Francisco Mus Mod Art, 73, Michael Berger Gallery, Pittsburgh, Pa, 78 & 81, Fuller Goldeen Gallery, San Francisco & Univ Pacific Gallery, Stockholm, Calif, 87; plus others; 71st Am Exhib, Art Inst of Chicago, 74; Artist Valentines, San Francisco Art Inst, 85; Sprayed Paint, Ahlone Col, Freemont, 85; Artists Choose Artists, Falkirk Cult Ctr, San Rafael, Calif, 88; Faculty exhib, San Francisco Art Inst, Calif, 89; Primal Forces, Women's Caucus for Art, Nat Exhib, New York, 90; Selections 49, The Drawing Ctr, New York, 90; Bridges: Artists Responses to Disaster, Berkeley Art Ctr, Calif, 90; two-person exhib, Embracing Change, San Jose State Univ, Calif, 89; one-person exhib, Bilder Uber Dem Vasser, Frauen Mus, Erfurt, Ger, 92, Barbara Rogers, Recent Work, Ga State Univ, Atlanta, 93; Human Nature, Allrich Gallery, San Francisco, Calif, 92. *Teaching:* Vis lectr drawing & painting, Univ Calif, Berkeley, 72-73; vis artist painting & grad sem, Univ Wash, Seattle, 75; vis artist painting & drawing, San Francisco Art Inst, 74-76, 83-85, chmn painting, 86-88; instr painting & drawing, San Jose State Univ, 78-82; prof painting, San Francisco Art Inst, Calif, 83-, Univ Ariz, Tucson, 90- *Awards:* Eisner Prize, Univ Calif, Berkeley, 63; Int Travel Grant, Univ Ariz, 91; Prof Develop Grant, Com on the Arts, Ariz, 91. *Bibliog:* William Urban (auth), Barbara Rogers, An Interview, Airbrush Digest, 8/82; Robert Pasckal & Robert Anderson (auths), The Art of the Dot: Advanced Airbrush Techniques, Van Nostrand Reinhold & Co, 85; Thomas Albright (auth), Art in the San Francisco Bay Area, 1945-1980, Univ Calif Press, 85; Angelika Storm-Rushé (auth), Reverence for the Water, General-Anzeiger, 1/92; plus many reviews in magazines & newspapers. *Mem:* Col Art Asn; Women's Caucus for Art. *Media:* Oil, Mixed Media. *Dealer:* Allrich Gallery 251 Post St San Francisco CA 94108. *Mailing Add:* 6161 N Camino Padre Isadoro Tucson AZ 85718

ROGERS, BRYAN LEIGH
CONCEPTUAL ARTIST, EDUCATOR
b Amarillo, Tex, Jan 7, 41. *Study:* Yale Univ, New Haven, Conn, BE, 63; Univ Calif, Berkeley, MS, 66, MA, 69, PhD, 71; Akademie der bildenden Künste, Munich, Germany, 74-75. *Work:* San Francisco Mus Mod Art, Calif. *Exhib:* Umbrella Show, San Francisco Mus Mod Art, Calif, 74 & Laguna Beach Mus Art, Calif, 74; Timepieces, Baxter Art Gallery, Pasadena, Calif, 79; Between Science & Fiction, 18th Int Biennial, Sao Paulo, Brazil, 85; San Francisco/Science Fiction, Clocktower Gallery, New York, 85; Mechanical Contraptions, Objects Gallery, Chicago, 92. *Pos:* ed, Leonardo Journal, San Francisco, Calif, 82-85; dir, Studio for Creative Inquiry, Carnegie Mellon Univ, 89- *Teaching:*, lectr art, Univ Calif, Berkeley, 72-73; prof art, San Francisco State Univ, 75-88; prof art & dept head, Carnegie Mellon Univ, 88- *Awards:* Artist's Fel, Nat Endowment Arts, 81 & 82; Res Fel, Mass Inst Technol, 81; fel, Deutscher Akademischer Austauschdienst, Ger, 74-75. *Bibliog:* Gerhard Lischka (auth), Das Poetische ABC, Benteli Verlag, Bern, 85; Jim Jenkins/Dave Quick (coauth), Motion Motion Kinetic Arts, Gibbs-Smith, 89. *Media:* Electromechanical. *Publ:* The Umbrella Series , Leonardo, Pergamon, 76, Timepieces, 81 & Odyssetron, 84. *Mailing Add:* 5415 Normlee Pl Pittsburgh PA 15217

ROGERS, JOHN H
SCULPTOR, CONSULTANT
b Walton, Ky, Dec 20, 21. *Study:* Eastern Ky Univ; Tyler Sch Art, Temple Univ, BFA & MFA. *Work:* Ala Archives, Montgomery; Marine Corps Art Collection, Marine Corps Mus, Washington, DC; Auburn Univ, Ala; Dept Defense, Pentagon, Washington, DC; NDak Mill, Grand Forks, 81. *Comn:* Bust of Gen H M Smith USMC, Ala Archives, Montgomery, 69; mem plaque of Lt Gen J A Chaisson, USMC, 75; baptistry, St Paul's Episcopal Church, Grand Forks, NDak, 83; Peace Garden Award Medallion, Univ NDak, 85. *Exhib:* Armed Forces of US as Seen by the Contemporary Artist, Smithsonian Inst, Washington, DC, 68; Artists in Vietnam, Smithsonian Traveling Exhib Serv, 68-70; Atlanta Col Art Fac Exhib, High Mus Art, Ga, 72; Inaugural Exhib, USMC Hist Ctr, Washington, DC, 77; solo show, Art Gallery, Univ NDak, 81; and others. *Pos:* Acad dean, Minneapolis Col Art & Design, 64-68; asst head, Marine Corps Combat Art Prog, Washington, 68-69, head, 69-70; dean, Atlanta Col Art, Ga, 70-73; dean col fine arts, Univ NDak, 73-80; sculptor in residence, Syracuse Univ, 80-81. *Teaching:* Sr sem humanities, Atlanta Col Art, 70-71; prof fine arts & sr symp, Univ NDak, 73-80, prof visual arts, 81-85; adj prof basic design, Syracuse Univ, 80-81, emer prof visual arts, 85-; vis lect sculpture, Earlham Coll, 89. *Mem:* Fel & life mem Nat Asn Schs Art & Design; Am Crafts Coun; Int Sculpture Ctr; Tri-State Sculptors Guild. *Media:* Wood; Miscellaneous. *Publ:* Coauth, Aging & creativity, In: Lifelong Learning and the Visual Arts, Nat Art Educ Asn, 80. *Mailing Add:* 5522 Hideaway Dr Chapel Hill NC 27516

ROGERS, JOSEPH SHEPPERD See Nevia, (Joseph Shepperd Rogers)

ROGERS, MILLARD FOSTER, JR
MUSEUM DIRECTOR, HISTORIAN
b Texarkana, Tex, Aug 27, 32. *Study:* Mich State Univ, BA(honors), 54; Univ Mich, MA, 58; Victoria & Albert Mus, London, 59, with John Pope-Hennessy, Xavier Univ, Cincinnati, LHD, 87. *Collections Arranged:* New Eng Glass Co, 1818-1880, Toledo Mus Art, 63; Indian Miniature Painting, 71 & Canadian Landscapes, Univ Wis, 73; Treasure From the Tower of London, 82-83; Masterworks from Munich, Cincinnati Art Mus, 88-89. *Pos:* Asst to dir, Toledo Mus Art, Ohio, 59-63, cur Am art, 64-67; dir, Elvehjem Art Ctr, Univ Wis-Madison, 67-74; Cincinnati Art Mus, 74- *Teaching:* Prof art hist dept, Univ Wis-Madison, 67-74; vis prof, Principia Col, 84; adj prof, Univ Cincinnati, 86- *Awards:* Gosline Fel, Toledo Mus Art, 58-59; Samuel B Sachs Prize, 83. *Mem:* Asn Art Mus Dirs; Am Asn Mus; Mariemont Preservation Found (pres 84-90). *Res:* Junius Brutus Stearns, 1815-1885. *Publ:* Auth, Benjamin West and the caliph: two paintings for Fonthill Abbey, Apollo, 6/66; Nydia, popular Victorian image, Antiques, 3/70; Randolph Rogers, American sculptor in Rome, Univ Mass, 71; Spanish paintings in the Cincinnati Art Museum, 78; Favorite paintings from the Cincinnati Art Museum, Abbeville Press, 80; Sketches & Bozzetti by American Sculptors, 1800-1950, Cincinnati Art Mus, 87. *Mailing Add:* Cincinnati Art Mus Eden Park Cincinnati OH 45202

ROGERS, OTTO DONALD
PAINTER, EDUCATOR
b Kerrobert, Sask, Nov 19, 35. *Study:* Sask Teacher's Col, cert, 53; Univ Wis, BSc(art educ), 58, MA(fine art), 59. *Work:* Nat Gallery Can, Ottawa; Montreal Mus Fine Arts; Nat Mus Iceland, Reykjavik; Fredericton Art Gallery, NB; Windsor Art Gallery, Ont. *Comn:* Sculpture in steel (with George Kerr, architect), Prince Albert Regional Libr, 65. *Exhib:* Biennial, Nat Gallery Can, 66, Royal Can Acad Art Exhib, 70; Directors Choice Exhib, sponsored by Can Coun, Confedn Art Gallery & Mus, Charlottetown, PEI, 68; Art in Saskatchewan, Waddington Fine Arts Gallery, Montreal, 69; Art Bank Can Exhib, Mendel Gallery, Saskatoon, 72. *Teaching:* Prof painting, Univ Sask, 59-, head dept art, 73-88. *Awards:* Sr Award for Study in Europe, 67-68. *Bibliog:* R Harper (auth), History of Canadian Painting, 66; W Townshend (auth), Canadian art today, Studio Int, 70; C McConnell (auth), Otto Rogers, Arts Can, 71. *Mem:* Royal Can Acad Art. *Media:* Acrylic. *Mailing Add:* Box 155 Haifa 31001 Israel

ROGERS, P J
PRINTMAKER, SCULPTOR
b Rochester, NY. *Study:* Wells Col, BA; Univ Buffalo; Acad Fine Arts, Vienna; Art Students League; also with Victor Hammer, Lazlo Szabo & Robert Brackman. *Work:* Dulin Gallery of Art, Knoxville, Tenn; Rockford Col; TRW Corporate Headquarters, Ohio; Cleveland Mus Art; Portland Art Mus, Ore; and others. *Comn:* Murals for Hall of Man, Buffalo Mus Sci, 53-55; portrait of founder, Novatny Elec Co, Akron, 67; poster for opening of new theater, Akron Weathervane Theater, 70; portrait of Dr D J Guzzetta, pres of Univ Akron, 75; spec ed aquatints, Bayvillage, Ohio, 79. *Exhib:* Ann Philadelphia Print Club Int, 82-83 & 90-91; Soc Am Graphic Artists Nat, New York, 83-92; Boston Printmakers Nat, 83, 86, 88 & 91; NDak Nat, 84-86 & 90-92; Hunterdon Nat Print, 84-92; Three persons exhib, Butler Mus Am Art, Youngston, Ohio, 88; and others. *Pos:* Art preparator, Buffalo Mus Sci, 52-55. *Teaching:* Instr painting, Buffalo Mus Sci, 55; instr arts & crafts, Univ Akron Spec Progs, 58. *Awards:* Ohio Arts Coun Fel, 79 & 86; Boston Printmakers Award, 85-86; Purchase Award, Print Club, Philadelphia, 90-91; and others. *Bibliog:* Stevens (auth), Aux Etats-Unis, expositions diverses, P J Rogers, La Rev Mod. *Mem:* New Orgn Visual Arts, Cleveland; Philadelphia Print Club; Boston Printmakers; Soc Am Graphic Artists, New York. *Media:*

Aquatint-etching, Mixed; Wood, Acrylic. *Publ:* Contribr, The Gamut, (six aquatints), Cleveland State Univ, Ohio, 80 & 90. *Dealer:* Collectors Gallery Columbus Mus of Art OH; Toni Brickhead Gallery 342 W Fourth St, Cincinnati Ohio 45202. *Mailing Add:* 954 Hereford Dr Akron OH 44303

ROGERS, PETER WILFRID
PAINTER
b London, Eng, Aug 24, 33. *Study:* St Martins Sch Art, London, Eng. *Work:* Bristol Art Gallery, Eng; Roswell Mus, NMex; Macnider Mus, Mason City, Iowa; Mus Southwest, Midland, Tex. *Comn:* Mural, Tex State Archives & Libr, Austin, 64; 48 paintings & drawings of Alaska, Atlantic Richfield Co, Los Angeles, 70-71; mural, Tex Tech Mus, 74; mural, Anaconda Co, Denver; mural, Arcomex, Mexico City. *Exhib:* One-man shows, Fairmount Gallery, Dallas, 69, Artium Orbis, Santa Fe, 71-72, Grace Cathedral, San Francisco, 73 & Janus Gallery, Santa Fe, 75; Heard Mus, Phoenix, Ariz, 75; plus others. *Media:* Oil, Acrylic. *Publ:* Auth & illusr, A Painter's Quest, Bear & Co. *Mailing Add:* PO Box 214 San Patricio NM 88348

ROGERS, STEVE
SCULPTOR
b Orange, Calif, 1945. *Study:* San Francisco Art Inst, BFA, 74. *Work:* Los Angeles Co Mus Art. *Comn:* Home savings, Sherman Oaks, Calif. *Exhib:* Space Gallery, Los Angeles, 78 & 79; one-man shows, Rosamund Felsen Gallery, Los Angeles, 82-83, 85-86, 88-90 & 92, Installation, San Diego, 84; Olympiad, Koplin Gallery, Los Angeles, 84; Recent Ceramic Sculpture, Univ Art Mus, Univ NMex, Albuquerque, 86. *Teaching:* Instr, Otis Art Inst of Parson Sch of Design, Los Angeles, 86- *Awards:* Nat Endowment Arts, 88. *Bibliog:* Our man in Honduras, Los Angeles Times, 9/17/88. *Media:* Terra Cotta. *Dealer:* Rosamund Felsen Gallery Los Angeles CA. *Mailing Add:* c/o Rosamund Felsen Gallery 8525 Santa Monica Blvd Los Angeles CA 90069

ROGERS-LAFFERTY, SARAH
CURATOR
b Buffalo, NY, Aug 8, 56. *Study:* Wells Col, Aurora, NY, BA, 78; Northwestern Univ, Evanston, Ill, MA, 80. *Collections Arranged:* Art Instruments (auth, video), 84, Body & Soul: Recent Figure Sculpture (auth catalog), 85, Personae: Jenny Holzer - Cindy Sherman (auth, catalog), 86 & On Site Sculpture, Fed Reserve Garden, 86, Standing Ground: Sculpture by Am Women Artists, 86, Ulay & Marina Abramovic, 87, John Alexander Paintings & Drawings, 88 & Jim Dine Drawings 1973- 87, 88, Contemp Arts Ctr, Cincinnati; Arts '86, Cincinnati, Ohio, 86; Doug & Mike Starn, Contemp Arts, Cincinnati, 85-90; Trilogy Anaugral Exhibs, Wexner Ctr, 89-90. *Pos:* Intern, Nat Endowment Arts, Walker Art Ctr, Minneapolis, 80-81; asst dir, New Gallery Contemp Art, Cleveland, 81-82; cur, Contemp Arts Ctr, Cincinnati, 82-; cur exhibs, Wexner Ctr Visual Arts, Columbus. *Awards:* Abby Grey Fel, Nat Endowment Arts, 80. *Mem:* Col Art Asn. *Publ:* Segments I-III, (catalogs), Contemp Arts Ctr, 84-85; Nam Jine Paik, Video Flag X (catalog), Contemp Arts Ctr, 85; interview, Doug & Mike Starn, Abrams, 90. *Mailing Add:* 2793 Bexley Park Columbus OH 43209

ROGNAN, LLOYD NORMAN
ILLUSTRATOR, PAINTER
Study: Am Acad Art, Chicago, 41-42; Acad Grande Chamiere, France, 46-49; Famous Artists Course, Westport, Conn, with Norman Rockwell, 50-52. *Comn:* Italian landscape, Caruso's Restaurant, Chicago, 57; Animal Subjects for 5 Yrs, Goes Litho, Chicago, 92-97. *Exhib:* Lief Erickson, Vesterheim, Norweg Am Mus, Decorah, Iowa, 72; one-man show, Nekoosa Paper Co Mus, Port Edwards, Wis, 82; Mormon Church Hist Mus, Salt Lake City, Utah, 88; Governor Edgar's Art Gallery on Ethnic Art Exhib. *Pos:* Artist & illusr, Meyer Booth Advert, Chicago, Ill, 57-62; artist, Golden Bk Encyl, Chicago, Ill, 62-63; art ed & illusr, United Card Co, Rolling Meadows, Ill, 67-72; illusr, Brown & Bigelow, 74-87 & Renaisance, Auburn, Ind, 87-93. *Awards:* Distinctive Art Award for Most Outstanding of the Year, Meyer Booth Advert, 59; Best of Show, Nekoosa Paper Co Gallery, 82. *Bibliog:* Article, Life Mag, 4/22/46; Western pictures by Rognan, Wis Rapids Tribune, 5/4/83; American Artists, Signatures & Monograms 1800-1989, Scarecrow press, Metuchen, NJ & London, 90. *Media:* Watercolor, Mixed Media. *Publ:* Illus Mt Goat & Kid, limited ed, Rognan Prints, Publ. *Mailing Add:* 3620 Linneman St Glenview IL 60025

ROGOVIN, MARK
MURALIST, MUSEUM DIRECTOR
b Buffalo, NY, July 31, 46. *Study:* Mexico, with Elizabeth Catlett Mora & David Alfaro Siqueiros, 64-68; RI Sch Design, Providence, BFA, 68; Art Inst Chicago, MFA, 70. *Comn:* Outdoor mural (18ft x 89ft), side of Am Nat Bank, comn by Rockford Evening Cosmopolitan Club, Ill, 75; indoor mural, Col of Dupage, Glen Ellyn, Ill, 75; Outdoor mural, comn by several neighborhood orgn on Chicago's West Side, 76. *Exhib:* Murals for the People, Mus of Contemp Art, Chicago, 71; Street Art--Pub Murals in the USA (Bicentennial traveling exhib), Amerika-Haus, W Berlin, 76; Mural Art USA (traveling exhib); porcelain enamel mural, Percent for Art Comn, Chicago. *Pos:* Dir & co-founder, Pub Art Wkshp, 72-81 & Peace Mus, 81-86. *Teaching:* Sch prog artist, Urban Gateways, Chicago, 73-81; artist-in-residence murals, Col DuPage, Glen Ellyn, Ill, spring 75, Univ Nebr, Omaha, 77, Univ Ill, Champaign, 78. *Mem:* Chicago Artists Coalition. *Publ:* Auth, Mural Manual, Beacon Press. *Mailing Add:* 930 Dunlop Ave Forest Park IL 60130

ROGOVIN, MILTON
PHOTOGRAPHER
b New York, NY, Dec 30, 09. *Study:* Columbia Univ, BS, 31; State Univ NY, Buffalo, MA, 72. *Work:* Metrop Mus Art & Mus Mod Art, New York; Libr Cong, Washington, DC; Bibliot Nat, Paris; Albright-Knox Art Gallery, Buffalo, NY. *Comn:* Eight porcelain enamel panel portraits, Niagara Frontier Transit Authority, Buffalo, NY, 83. *Exhib:* One-man exhibs, Int Mus Photog at George Eastman House, Rochester, NY, 71, Fotografi Centrum, Stockholm & Panselinos Gallery, Greece, 78, Capen Gallery, Buffalo, 84; Lower West Side, Int Ctr of Photog, 76 & Canon Photo Gallery, Amsterdam, 82; Working People, Currier Gallery Art, 82, circulated to: Mus Art, Pa State Univ, Charles Burchfield Ctr, State Univ Colo NY, Buffalo, Braithwaite Fine Arts Gallery, Utah; group shows, Hayden Gallery, Mass Inst Technol, 70 & 72, Photog Gallery of London, 78; Nat Mus Am Hist, Smithsonian Inst, 92. *Awards:* W Eugene Smith Mem Fund Award, 83; Arts & Sci Distinguished Achievements Award, State Univ New York, 89. *Bibliog:* James N Wood (auth), Lower West Side, Albright-Knox Gallery Art, 75; Ann Rogovin (auth), Learning by Doing, Westinghouse Learning Corp, 79 & Let Me Do It, Harper & Row, 79; Jack Foran (auth), The workhouse views, Afterimage, Rochester, NY, 4/83; Fred Licht (auth), Photography class acts, Art in Am, New York, 2/84; and many others. *Publ:* Auth, The Forgotten Ones, Univ Wash Press, 88; Portraits in Steel, Cornell Univ Press, 91. *Mailing Add:* 90 Chatham Ave Buffalo NY 14216

ROHLFING, CHRISTIAN
ADMINISTRATOR, CURATOR
b Philadelphia, Pa, Nov 14, 16. *Study:* Univ Chicago. *Pos:* Cur emer, Cooper-Hewitt Mus Design, New York, currently. *Mailing Add:* 343 E 30th St New York NY 10016

ROHM, ROBERT
SCULPTOR
b Cincinnati, Ohio, Feb 6, 34. *Study:* Pratt Inst, BID, 56; Cranbrook Acad Art, Bloomfield Hills, Mich, MFA, 60. *Work:* Mus Mod Art, New York; Kunsthalle, Zurich, Switz; Finch Col Mus, New York; Metrop Mus Art, New York; Whitney Mus Am Art, New York; The Rose Art Mus, Brandeis Univ, Waltham, Mass. *Exhib:* Solo Exhibs, O K Harris Works of Art, New York, 70, 72, 73, 75, 77, 79, 80, 82, 84, 86, 89 & 92, Suzette Schochet Gallery, Newport, RI, Worcester Art Mus, Mass, 78, Nielsen Gallery, Boston, Mass, 85, 86 & 92, Cumberland Gallery, Nashville, Tenn, 86, New Work; Sculpture & Drawing, Fine Arts Ctr, Univ RI, Kingston, 88 & Lenore Gray Gallery, Providence, RI, 90; Totem: Sculpture by Ellen Driscoll, Christopher Hewat, Robert Rohm, Ursula von Rydingsvard, Addison Gallery Am Art, Phillips Acad, Andover, Mass, 89; Common Ground II, Nielsen Gallery, Boston, Mass, 90; Painting/Sculpture/Drawing, Nielsen Gallery, Boston, Mass, 90; 10 Years of Boston Art, Nielsen Gallery, Boston, Mass, 91; Drawing, Lenore Gray Gallery, Providence, RI, 91; and others. *Teaching:* Instr sculpture, Columbus Col Art & Design, 56-59; instr sculpture, Pratt Inst, 60-65; prof sculpture, Univ RI, 65- *Awards:* Guggenheim Found Fel, 64; Fel, RI Coun Arts, 73 & 82; Nat Endowment Arts Award, 74 & 86. *Bibliog:* Kenneth Baker (auth), review, Art Am, 5/84; Ronald J Onorato (auth), Robert Rohm, Arts Mag, 1/85; Robert C Morgan (auth), Review, Arts Mag, Summer, 89. *Publ:* Robert Rohm: Selected Works 1975-1985, Nielsen Gallery, Boston, Mass, 85. *Dealer:* OK Harris Works of Art 383 W Broadway New York NY 10012; Nielsen Gallery 179 Newbury St Boston MA 02116. *Mailing Add:* 103 Shumankanuc Hill Rd Charlestown RI 02813

ROHRER, WARREN
PAINTER
b Lancaster, Pa, Dec 4, 27. *Study:* Eastern Mennonite Col, BA; Madison Col, BS; Pa State Univ; Pa Acad Fine Arts. *Work:* Philadelphia Mus Art; Pa Acad Fine Arts; Metrop Mus Art, New York; Portland Art Mus, Ore; Allentown Art Mus, Pa; Smith Col Mus Art, Northampton, Mass; Del Art Mus, Wilmington. *Comn:* Lithograph, Inst Contemp Art, Philadelphia, 88. *Exhib:* Pittsburgh Int, Carnegie Inst Fine Arts, 55; 154th & 163rd Ann, Pa Acad Fine Arts, Philadelphia, 59 & 68; one-man shows, Makler Gallery, Philadelphia, 63, 65, 67, 69 & 71, Marian Locks Gallery, Philadelphia, 74, 76, 78, 80, 87, 89 & 91, Lamagna Gallery, New York, 76, Morris Gallery, Pa Acad Fine Arts, 82, CDS Gallery, New York, 83 & 86, Millersville Univ, Pa, 90; A Sense of Place: The American Artist & the Land, Joslyn Art Mus, Omaha, 73; Philadelphia: Three Centuries of Am Art, Philadelphia Mus Art, 76; Susan Caldwell Gallery, New York, 77; Philadelphia: Contemporary Drawings, Pa Acad Fine Arts, 78; Philadelphia Collects: Art Since 1940, Philadelphia Mus Art, 86; Contemporary Philadelphia Artists: A Juried Exhibition, Philadelphia Mus Art, 90; Philadelphia Art Now: Artists Choose Artists, Inst Contemp Art, 91. *Pos:* Mem, Pa Coun Arts, 76-79. *Teaching:* Prof painting, Philadelphia Col Art, 67-92. *Awards:* Hon Mention, Pa Acad Fine Arts, 59, Artist Fel Grant, 81; Artist Fel Grant, Nat Endowment Arts, 81-82; and others. *Media:* Oil. *Dealer:* Locks Gallery 600 Washington Sq S Philadelphia PA 19106. *Mailing Add:* 627 St George's Rd Philadelphia PA 19119

ROJEK, CHRISTINE
SCULPTOR
b Chicago, Ill, Jan 15, 49. *Study:* Univ Ill, Champaign-Urbana, BFA, 71; Am Sch Fountainebleau, France, 71. *Work:* Equity Financial & Mgt Co, Chicago; Mus Contemp Art, Chicago; Col DuPage, Glen Ellyn, Ill. *Comn:* Large scale publ sculpture, Sculpture Chicago, 84; sculpture, James Nagle, AIA, Chicago, 88; Capitol Develop Bd State Ill, Percentage for Art Prog, Art & Archit Com Northeastern Ill Univ Physical Ed Bldg, 88-90; Univ Akron, Ohio, 91. *Exhib:* Painting and Sculpture Today, Indianapolis Mus Art, Ind, 76; Art Instruments, Contemp Arts Ctr, Cincinnati, Ohio (and traveling US), 83-86; Small but Hot, Burpee Art Mus, Rockford, Ill, 84; Sculpture Now - Works by Women, Contemp Arts Ctr, Cincinnati, 87; solo exhib, Sonic, Pneumatic, Eccentric Sculpture, Zolla/Lieberman Gallery, Chicago, Col DuPage Performing Arts Ctr Gallery, Glen Ellyn, Ill, 87; Zolla/Lieberman Gallery,

Chicago, 89; Renaissance Soc, Chicago, Ill, 91. *Awards:* Proj Completion Grant, 79, 81 & 82 & Fel Grants, 83, 84, 86, 87 & 89, Ill Arts Coun; Visual Artists Fel Grant, Nat Endowment Arts, 86. *Mailing Add:* c/o Zolla/Lieberman Gallery 325 W Huron St Chicago IL 60610

ROJO, VICENTE
PAINTER
b Barcelona, Spain, Mar 15, 32. *Work:* Mus Mod Art, Mex; Banco Cedulas Hipotecarias SA, Mex; Musée d'art Moderre, Paris; Museo Rufino Tamayo, Mex; Banco Nac de Mex. *Exhib:* Second Biennial De Jovenes, Paris, 61; Mexico: The New Generation Traveling Exhib, US, 66; Expo '67, Montreal, PQ, 67; 1st Triennial India, New Delhi, 68; Contemporary Mexican Painting, Mus Mod Art, Tokyo, 74; and others. *Bibliog:* J J Gurrola (producer), Rojo (film), 66 & J Garcia Ponce (auth), Vicente Rojo, 71, Nat Univ Mex; Octavio Paz (auth), Discos visuales, Ediciones Era, 68. *Media:* Acrylic, Oil. *Dealer:* Galeria Juan Martin Amberes 17 Mexico DF Mexico. *Mailing Add:* Dulce Oliva 57 Coyoacan DF 21 Mexico

ROKEACH, BARRIE
PHOTOGRAPHER, WRITER
b Mansfield, Ohio, Feb 26, 47. *Study:* Univ Calif, Berkeley, BA, 70, MA, 74. *Work:* Oakland Mus Nat Hist; Bank of Am, San Francisco; Hewlett Packard, Consolidated Freightway, Palo Alto; Citicorp, New York. *Exhib:* Images From Above, Ryder Gallery, Chicago, 83; An Intimate Look, Neikrug Gallery, New York, 84; Aerial Photography, Art Ctr, Waco, Tex, 86; Aerial Photography, Tweed Mus, Duluth, Minn, 87; Oakland Mus, Calif, 90; Calif Mus Sci & Indust, Los Angeles, 91; and others. *Teaching:* Instr, Univ Calif Berkeley, 77-78 & 84. *Awards:* Calif Design Award, Art Dirs, 92. *Bibliog:* Paul Raedeke (auth), article, Photo Metro, 83; Lucas Blok (auth), Portfolio, Vantage Point, 84; Brenda Kahn (auth), Aerial photography, Zoom, 86. *Mem:* Am Soc Mag Photogrs (exec bd & ed, 68-). *Publ:* Contribr, 24 Hours in the Life of Los Angeles, Van der Marck, 84; Ireland: A Week in the Life of a Nation, Century Hutchinson, 86; Thailand: Seven Days in the Kingdom, Times Ed, 87; Auth-illusr, Timescapes: California Aerial Images, Westcliffe, 89. *Mailing Add:* 499 Vermont Ave Berkeley CA 94709

ROLLER, MARION BENDER
PAINTER, SCULPTOR
b Boston, Mass. *Study:* Vesper George Sch Art, dipl; Art Students League, with John Hovannes; Greenwich House, with Lu Duble; Queens Col, BA; also watercolors with Edgar Whitney. *Comn:* Head of child, Nassau Ctr Emotionally Disturbed Children, Woodbury, NY, 68; Relief portrait of Ethel Traphagen & commemorative medal, Traphagen Sch, 82-83; portrait of Margaret Sussman, Pen & Brush, 83-84; Women & Youth (7' bronze sculpture), St Mary's Family Services, Syosset, NY, 88; 3 Dancing Figures - in memory of Rosemary Harris (poet), 90; and many private commissions of portraits, figures & animals. *Exhib:* Exhib tour, US Info Serv, Eastern Europe, 78; Catherine Lorillard Wolfe, 79-81; Sculpture Ctr Gallery, 79-85; solo exhib, Hudson Valley Art Asn, 80-81; Allied Artists, 80-89; Nat Sculpture Soc, 80-92; Berkshire Mus; Am Numismatic Soc; US Old Mint, San Francisco, Calif, 84; Nat Acad Design, 86-90; Port of Hist Mus, Philadelphia, Pa, 87; Janus Gallery, Santa Fe, NMex, 88; Helsinki, Finland, 90; Newark Mus, NJ, 90-91; Pen & Brush, 83-92; Transco Energy Gallery, Houston, Tex, 90-91; Can Mus Nature, Ottawa, Ont, 91-92. *Teaching:* Instr art, Fashion Inst Technol, 67-72; instr, Traphagen Sch, 73-, Sculpture Ctr, 77- *Awards:* Pen & Brush Award, 84, 86, 87, 88 & 91; Helen G Oehler Mem, Allied Artists Am, 91; Samuel Cashwan Award, Audubon Artists, 92. *Bibliog:* Gustav Kramer (auth), Profile, Hudson Register Star, 65 & 10/3/75; Ed Reiter (auth), reviews in NY Times, 5/8/83; Helen Barett (ed), article in Pen & Brush Bull, 86; Featured in Film, The Making of a Bronze Monument. *Mem:* Allied Artists Am (asst corresp secy, 66 & 83, corresp secy, 82, dir sculpture, 84-87, vpres, 85-88, pres, 89-91); Pen & Brush (co-chmn, 67, chmn, 82-90, vpres 92-); Fel Nat Sculpture Soc (rec secy, 82-85, sec, 86-89, 91-); Audubon Artists (treas, currently); Fine Arts Fedn (bd dir, 81-, secy, 83-89); Am Medallic Sculpture Asn; Knickerbocker Artists. *Media:* Mixed. *Publ:* Auth, The challenge of space, Nat Sculpture Soc Rev, spring 82; several art book reviews, Nat Sculp Rev, summer 81, 82, 84, 86, 87, 88, 89. *Mailing Add:* 30 W 60th St No 8A New York NY 10023

ROLLER, RUSSELL KENNETH
EDUCATOR, PRINTMAKER
b Chicago, Ill, Oct 6, 38. *Study:* Ill Wesleyan Univ, BFA, 63; Southern Ill Univ, MFA, 65. *Work:* Univ Wisconsin, Eau Claire; Emporia State Col, Kans; Northern State Col, Aberdeen, SDak. *Exhib:* Int Miniature Print Exhib, Pratt Graphics, New York, 79; 34th Ann Exhib Chicago & Vicinity Artists, Art Inst Chicago, 85. *Teaching:* Asst prof printmaking, Emporia State Col, Kans, 65-70; assoc prof printmaking, Northeastern Ill Univ, 70-76, prof & chmn art dept, 76- *Media:* Intaglio, Acrylic. *Mailing Add:* Northeastern Ill Univ Chicago IL 60625

ROLLINS, TIM
PAINTER, INSTRUCTOR
b Pittsfield, Maine, 1955. *Study:* Sch Visual Arts, BFA, 78; New York Univ, MA, 80. *Work:* Philadelphia Mus Art; Mus Mod Art, New York; Mint Mus, Charlotte, NC. *Exhib:* All shows collaborations with KOS; Bi National: Am Art of the Late 80's, Mus Fine Arts, Boston & Kunsthalle, Dusseldorf, 88; Amerika, Dia Art Found, New York, 89-90; Wadsworth Atheneum, Harford, Conn, 90; The Temptation of St Antony, Mus fur Gegenwartskunst, Basel, 90; Amerika, Mus of Contemp Art, Los Angeles, Calif, 90. *Teaching:* Artist & teacher, Learning to Read through the Arts Prog, Bd Educ, New York, 80-82 & Div Spec Educ, New York, 82-; founder, Kids of Survival (KOS) & Art & Knowledge Workshop Inc, 82. *Awards:* Artists-in-Educ Grant, 83 & 84, Expansion Arts Grant, 85 & 86 & Visual Artists Fel, 86, Nat Endowment Arts; Artists-in-Educ Award, 86 & Spec Art Servs Grant, 88, NY State Coun Arts; Joseph Benys Prize, 89. *Bibliog:* Berman (auth), Parkett #20, 89; Amerika, Dia Art Found; Arthur Danto (auth), Tim Rollins & KOS, The Nation, 1/22/90. *Mailing Add:* c/o Mary Boone Gallery 417 W Broadway New York NY 10012

ROLLMAN, CHARLOTTE
PAINTER
b Harrisburg, Ill, Oct 15, 47. *Study:* Murray State Univ, Ky, BFA, 69; Univ Ill, Champaigne, MFA, 71. *Work:* Capitol State Bank, Continental Banking Co, St Louis, Mo; McDonald's Corp, Heart Hanks Radio, Phoenix, Ariz; State of Ill Bldg, Harris Bank, Chicago; Nev State Univ, Reno; Evansville Mus Art & Sciences, Ind; Western Wash State, Bellingham. *Comn:* John Gardener Tennis Resort, Sedona, Ariz; Jan Cicero Gallery, Chicago; Locus Gallery, St Louis, MO; Suzanne Brown, Scottsdale, Ariz. *Exhib:* One person exhibs, Roy Boyd Gallery, Chicago, 84, Suzanne Brown Gallery, 85, Locus Gallery, 88, Univ Wis Ctr/Rock County, Janesville, 91 & Cornucopia, Dorothea Thiel Gallery, S Suburban Col, S Holland, Ill, 91; Farrington-Keith Nat Juried Exhib, Clara Kott von Storch Gallery, Ann Arbor, Mich, 91; 8th Ann Works on Paper Exhib, Elgin Community Col, Ill, 91; 11th Ann Exhib, Fla Pastel Asn, Searle & Kellogg Galleries, Bradenton, 91; Still-Life Gallery Artists, Jan Cicero Gallery, Chicago, 92; Art by Women: Voices & Priorities, Shircliff Gallery Art, Vincennes Univ, Ind, 92; Utopia: Envisioning a Dream, The Forum Gallery at Jamestown Community Col, NY, 92; 16th Harper Nat Print & Drawing Exhib, Harper Col, Palatine, Ill, 92; Owensboro Nat Bank & the Arts: Part IV, Owensboro Mus Fine Arts, Ky, 92; Art on Paper 1992, Md Fedn Art, MFA Gallery on the Circle, Annapolis. *Media:* Watercolor, Drawing. *Publ:* Illusr, New American Dictionary of Music, Penguin Bks, New York, 91. *Mailing Add:* Sch Art Northern Ill Univ De Kalb IL 60115

ROLLY, RONALD JOSEPH
DEALER
b Waterbury, Conn, Dec 31, 37. *Pos:* Dir, Rolly-Michaux Galleries, Boston. *Mem:* Newbury St Merchants League. *Specialty:* 20th century masters and contemporaries; paintings, sculpture and graphics. *Mailing Add:* c/o Rolly-Michaux Galleries 290 Dartmouth St Boston MA 02116

ROLOFF, JOHN SCOTT
SCULPTOR, ENVIRONMENTAL ARTIST
b Portland, Ore, Sept 20, 47. *Study:* Univ Calif, Davis, BA; Calif State Univ, Humboldt, MA. *Work:* Oakland Mus; Univ Art Mus, Berkeley; Lannon Found, Palm Springs; Mus Mod Art, San Francisco; Herbert F Johnson Mus, Cornell Univ, Ithaca, NY; and others. *Exhib:* Clay Images, Calif State Univ, Los Angeles, 74; Clay USA, Fendrick Gallery, Washington, DC, 75; Whitney Mus Am Art, Biennial, New York, 75; Northern California Clay Routes-Sculpture Now, San Francisco Mus Mod Art, 79; solo shows, Fuller-Goldeen Gallery, 79-81, San Francisco, Theo Portnoy Gallery, New York, 81 & San Francisco Art Inst, 82; Six East Bay Artists, Oakland Mus, 82. *Teaching:* Instr ceramics, San Francisco Art Inst, 73-74 & 78-; asst prof ceramics, Univ Ky, 74-78; asst prof, Mills Col, 80- *Awards:* Craftsmens Fel, Nat Endowment Arts, 77; Visual Arts Grant, Nat Endowment Arts, 80; Guggenheim Found Fel, 83. *Bibliog:* Jan Axel & Karen McCready (coauths), Porcelain: Traditions and New Visions, Watson-Guptill, 81; Susan Weschler (auth), Low Fire Ceramics, Watson-Guptill, 81; Joanne Burstein (auth), John Roloff Allegory/Alchemy, Am Ceramics Mag, fall 83. *Publ:* Auth, Kiln projects, Artery Mag, 2-3/83. *Dealer:* Fuller-Goldeen Gallery 228 Grant St San Francisco CA 94108. *Mailing Add:* Dept Art Mills Col MacArthur Blvd & Sem Ave Oakland CA 94613

ROMAN, SHIRLEY
PRINTMAKER, PAINTER
b New York, NY. *Study:* Am Artists Sch; Brooklyn Mus Sch; Queens Col; also with Gregorio Prestopino, Raphael Soyer, Ruth Leaf & Agnes Mills. *Work:* De Cordova Mus, Lincoln, Mass; Readers Digest, Pleasantville, NY; Slater Mus, Norwalk, Conn; Butler Mus Am Art; Libr Cong, Washington, DC; Fed Reserve Bank, Richmond, Va. *Exhib:* Philadelphia Print Club, 69-74; Soc Am Graphic Artists; Pratt Graphics Miniature Show; Boston Printmakers Asn, 73; Audubon Artists, Taipei, Taiwan, 80; Nat Asn Women Artists, 80-92. *Awards:* Purchase Prize, Boston Printmakers 25th Ann, 73; Medals of Hon, Nat Asn Women Artists, 76, 79, 82 & 86; Audubon Artists, 80; and others. *Bibliog:* Ruth Leaf (auth), Intaglio Printmaking Techiques. *Mem:* Nat Asn Women Artists; Soc Am Graphic Artists; Boston Printmakers; Nat Art League. *Media:* Etching; Watercolor. *Dealer:* Printworks 251-27 Gaskell Rd Little Neck NY 11363. *Mailing Add:* 60-41 251 St Little Neck NY 11362

ROMANO, CLARE CAMILLE (MRS JOHN ROSS)
PRINTMAKER, PAINTER
b Palisade, NJ. *Study:* Cooper Union Sch Art, 39-43; Ecole Beaux-Arts, Fontainebleau, France, BFA, 49; Inst Statale Arte, Florence, Italy, Fulbright Grant, 58-59. *Work:* Mus Mod Art, Whitney Mus Am Art & Metrop Mus Art, New York; Libr of Cong & Nat Collection Fine Arts, Washington, DC. *Comn:* Tapestry, Mfrs Hanover Bank, New York, 69. *Exhib:* 2nd Triennial Int Exhib Woodcuts, Ugo Carpi Mus, Italy, 72; American Prints, US Info Agency, Australian Nat Mus, Canberra, 72; Hane Haslem Gallery, Washington, DC, 81; Queensland Col Art, Brisbane, Australia, 82; AAA Gallery, New York, 82; and others. *Teaching:* Asst to Herbert Bayer, 43-46; instr printmaking, New Sch Social Res, 60-73; adj assoc prof printmaking, Pratt Graphic Arts Ctr, 63-87; prof printmaking, Pratt Inst, 64- *Awards:* MacDowell Fel, 74, 76, 78, 82 & 87; Distinguished Teacher Award, Pratt Inst,

79; NJ State Counc Arts Grant, 80; and others. *Bibliog:* Jules Heller (auth), Printmaking Today, Holt, Rinehart & Winston, 72; Fritz Eichenberg (auth), The Art of the Print, Abrams, 77; Eldon Cunninham (auth), Printmaking, A Primary Form of Expression, Univ Press Colo, 92. *Mem:* Soc Am Graphic Artists (pres, 70-72); Print Club Philadelphia; Nat Acad Design (vpres, 87-). *Media:* All. *Publ:* Co-illusr, Leaves of Grass, 64; auth, Artist's Proof, 64 & 66; American Encyclopedia, 71; coauth, The Complete Printmaker, 72 & 89 & The Complete Collagraph, 80, Free Press. *Dealer:* Susan Teller Gallery 568 Broadway New York NY 10012; Jane Haslem Gallery 406 Seventh St NW Washington DC 20004. *Mailing Add:* Dept Visual Arts Pratt Inst Brooklyn NY 11205

ROMANO, SALVATORE MICHAEL
SCULPTOR, KINETIC ARTIST
b Cliffside Park, NJ, Sept 12, 25. *Study:* Art Students League, with Jon Corbino; Acad Grande Chaumiere, Paris, with Edouard Georges & Earl Kerkam. *Work:* Chase Manhattan Bank, New York. *Exhib:* Highlights of the Season, 68-69, Aldrich Mus Contemp Art, Ridgefield, Conn, 69; Monumenta, A Biennial Exhib Outdoor Sculpture, Newport, RI, 74; Wave Hill Sculpture Garden Exhib, New York, 77; Shared Spaces, Bronx Mus Art, 83; Anchorage Brooklyn Bridge Ctr, 83; NJ State Mus, 83; Swimming and Other Pools, Getler, Pall & Sapler Gallery, New York, 84; 5 Sculptors, Arch Grand Army Plaza, Brooklyn, NY, 85; Socrates Sculpture Park, Long Island City, 86; Bali Miller Gallery, New York, 88; Water Installation, Sculpture Ctr, (with catalog), NY, 90. *Teaching:* Adj instr sculpture, Cooper Union Sch Arts & Archit, 68-70; lectr painting & sculpture, Lehman Col, 69-71, prof, 72-; lectr kinetic sculpture, US Info Serv, Brazil, 72 & Rutgers Univ, 79; assoc prof, Lehman Col, 81- *Awards:* Nat Endowment Arts, 79-80; Fac Res Award, City Univ New York, Lehman Col, 80-81; McDowell Coloy Fel, 80 & 81; NY Found Arts Award, 85-86, 89-90. *Bibliog:* Lawrence Alloway (auth), Salvatore Romano's sculpture, 10/77 & Joan Marter (auth), Salvatore Romano's water sculptures, 11/83, Arts Mag; Donald B Kuspit (auth), article, Art Am, 1-2/78; and others. *Mem:* Artist Equity; Int Sculpture Ctr. *Media:* Plastics, Wood; Metal, Water. *Publ:* Auth, article, Lehman Col Art News Lett, 71. *Mailing Add:* 83 Wooster St New York NY 10017

ROMANS, VAN ANTHONY
SCULPTOR, DESIGNER
b Baltimore, Md, Jan 13, 44. *Study:* Univ Calif, Fullerton, BA(art design), studied with Dextra Frankel; Univ Southern Calif, studied 3-D arts & mus design with Lee Chesney, MFA. *Work:* Claremont Grad Sch Gallery, Calif; Univ Southern Calif, Los Angeles; Calif State Univ, Fullerton; Orange Coast Col, Costa Mesa, Calif. *Comn:* Westcliff Shopping Ctr (designed), comn by Richard Marowitz, 76; Courtyard Shopping Ctr (designed), comn by Jerry Stout, 77. *Exhib:* one-man shows, Oakland Mus Art, Calif, 71 & Univ Southern Calif, Los Angeles, 72; Six Promising Young Sculptors, Claremont Cols, Calif, 73; Environments/Spaces, Orange Coast Col, 75; Spaces, Pac Design Ctr, Calif, 76; and others. *Collections Arranged:* Thonet & Thereafter, show of chair hist incl Bauhaus (auth, catalog), Japanese Sword Show, collection from collectors & from Los Angeles Co Art Mus, Western Indian Show--Dan Namingha & Persian Rug Show (designed exhib), 57 rugs from cols & collections, Orange Coast Col Art Gallery. *Pos:* Dir display prog, Orange Coast Col, Costa Mesa, Calif, 73-, dir galleries interior design, 75-; mem, Orange Co Art Alliance, Calif, 77; lectr, Newport Harbor Art Mus, Newport Beach, Calif. *Teaching:* Prof design & exhib design/visual promotion, Orange Coast Col, Costa Mesa, Calif, 73-, prof design & visual promotion, currently; asst prof design, Univ Southern Calif, Los Angeles, 73-82. *Awards:* Most Outstanding Educator, Orange Coast Col, 75. *Bibliog:* Wilson (auth), Sculpture, 74. *Mem:* Am Soc Interior Designers. *Media:* Metal. *Mailing Add:* Dept Art Orange Coast Col 2701 Fairview Rd Costa Mesa CA 92626

ROMBOUT, LUKE
MUSEUM DIRECTOR
b Amsterdam, Neth, May 4, 33; Can citizen. *Study:* Mt Alison Univ, Sackville, NB, BFA, 67. *Pos:* Asst cur, Beaverbrook Art Gallery, Fredericton, NB, 60; actg cur, Owens Art Gallery, Mt Allison Univ, 65-67, cur, 67-68, dir, 68-71; mem arts adv panel, Can Coun, Ottawa, Ont, 69-70, dir art bank, 72-74, head visual arts film sect, 74-75; mem adv comt art, Can Dept Pub Works, 73; mem design adv comt, Can Post, 73; mem fine arts comt, Can Dept External Affairs, 73-75; dir, Vancouver Art Gallery, BC, 75-84. *Teaching:* Lectr Can art hist, Mt Alison Univ, 68-71; lectr art hist, NS Col Art Design, 70-72; asst prof visual arts & chmn prog, Fac Fine Arts, York Univ, Toronto, Ont, 72-74; lectr Can art hist, Univ Ottawa, Ont, 74-75. *Awards:* Fel Royal Soc Arts, 83; Order Can, 87. *Mem:* Can Mus Asn (vpres, 70-71); Can Art Mus Dirs Orgn; Asn Art Mus Dirs; Asn Am Mus Dirs; Can Asn Mus Dirs; and others. *Mailing Add:* Le Cartier 1115 Sherbrooke St W Montreal PQ H4C 1B1 Canada

ROMELING, W B
PAINTER
b Schenectady, NY, Feb 26, 09. *Study:* Pratt Inst, Brooklyn; Syracuse Univ; Sch Fine Arts; also with Ogden Pleissner. *Work:* Schenectady Mus; Cooperstown Art Asn; Canajoharie Libr; Gen Elec Co; Munson Williams, Proctor Inst, Utica, NY. *Exhib:* Central New York, Munson-Williams-Proctor Inst, Utica, NY, 62; one-man shows, Pioneer Gallery, Cooperstown, 83 & Elhoff Gallery, Syracuse, NY, 83; Cooperstown Ann, NY, 70-71; Retrospective, Muggleton Gallery, 77; Southern Vt Art Ctr, 86; Jamaica Gallery, 88; Old Forge Art Ctr, 88. *Teaching:* Instr art, Owen D Young Sch, Van Hornesville, NY, 43-69. *Awards:* Purchase Prize, Schenectady Mus, 63; Trails & Streams Medal, 300 Adirondacks Nat Exhib, 86; The Pulsifer Award, 200 Adirondacks Nat Exhib, 88. *Mem:* Cooperstown Art Asn (pres, 70-72); Southern Vt Artists; Cent NY Watercolor Soc. *Media:* Watercolor. *Publ:* Contribr (watercolor), Am Artist Mag, 12/77. *Mailing Add:* Box 53 Van Hornesville NY 13475

ROMERO, JOSE T
PAINTER
b Tayabas, Quezon, Philippines, US citizen. *Study:* Art Instr Sch, Minneapolis, 72; Paris Am Acad Beaux des Artes, 78; Marquis Giuseppe Scicluna Univ Found, Malta, Dr Art, 86. *Work:* Acad Art Gallery, Val de Grace, Paris, France; Salammbo Gallery, Near Picasso Mus, Paris; Scarab Club, Detroit. *Exhib:* Keatington Art Show, Orion, Mich, 75; Meadow Brook Art Show, Rochester, Mich, 76; one-man shows, Int Art Inst, Detroit, 75, Scarab Club, Detroit, 86, Gallery in the Grove, Sarnia, Can, 87, Watercolor Gallery, Ann Arbor, 87, Acad Art Gallery, Paris, 88 & Beijing Int Convention Ctr, 91. *Awards:* Mich Ann Art Award, Sam Field Studio, 76; Cert Appreciation, Southfield Civic Ctr, 87. *Mem:* Scarab Club; Friends Paris Am Acad; Cranbook Acad Art; Beijing Watercolor Soc. *Media:* Acrylic. *Dealer:* Scarab Club of Detroit, MI; Lawrence Gallery Pontiac, MI. *Mailing Add:* 6414 Wood Pond West Bloomfield MI 48323

ROMERO, MEGAN H
PAINTER, DEALER
b Chicago, Ill, Sept 22, 42. *Study:* Ind Univ, BA, 65; Univ Chicago, with Max Kuhn; Univ NMex, with Charles Mattox, MA, 69. *Work:* Univ NMex Fine Arts Mus, Albuquerque; Mus NMex, Santa Fe. *Exhib:* Intrinsic Art, Friends Contemp Art, 71, Denver; Fall Invitational, Roswell Mus & Art Ctr, NMex, 72; one-man show, Lerner Heller Gallery, New York, 72; Fine Arts Mus NMex, Biennial, 73; Seven Artists, Francis McCray Gallery, Western NMex Univ; and others. *Pos:* Owner, Hill's Gallery, Santa Fe, currently. *Awards:* Southwest Biennial, Mus NMex, 72. *Bibliog:* Donna Meilach (auth), Leather Book, 71; article, Art in Am, 8/72; article, Southwest Art Gallery Mag, 12/72. *Mem:* Mus NMex Found. *Specialty:* Contemporary New Mexico fine arts and crafts. *Publ:* Contribr, Craft Horizons, 12/71; auth, Aiming at the creative environment, Southwest Art Gallery Mag, 11/71 & 1/73. *Mailing Add:* 1469 Canyon Rd Santa Fe NM 87501

ROMERO, RACHAEL L
PAINTER, PRINTMAKER
b Adelaide, S Australia, July 14, 53. *Study:* S Australian Art Inst, 70-72; San Francisco State Univ, 75-78; Antioch Univ, MA, 92. *Work:* Mus Mod Art, New York (artists bks); Cooper Hewitt Mus, New York; Whitney Mus, New York (artists bks); Lahti Mus, Finland; Lib Cong, Washington. *Comn:* Mural, US Post Off, New York; mural, Subway, New York. *Exhib:* Committed to Print, Mus Mod Art, New York & 89, Newport Art Mus, 89; Homeless: The Street and other Venues, DIA Art Found, New York, 89; The Decade Show (with Group Mat), Studio Mus, Harlem, NY, 90; A Different War: Vietnam in Art, DeCordova Mus, Lincoln, Mass, 90, Akron Art Mus, 90 & Whatcom Mus, Bellinham, Wash, 90. *Teaching:* Artist/educ art & printmaking, Third Street Men's Shelter, New Yor, 87-90; artist/educ art educ, Pratt Inst, Brooklyn, 89-90. *Awards:* Award Merit, Hispanic Festival Arts, Mus Sci & Ind, Chicago, 82; Fel, Residency, MacDowell Colony, 89; Fel, Yaddo, Saratoga, NY, 91-92. *Bibliog:* Deborah Wye (auth), Committed to Print, Mus Mod Art, 88; Peter Plagens (auth), A painful war's haunted art, Newsweek, 9/11/89. *Mem:* Col Art Asn. *Media:* All Media. *Mailing Add:* PO Box 281 Prince St Sta New York NY 10012

ROMEU, JOOST A
CONCEPTUAL ARTIST, DESIGNER
b Bremerhaven, Ger, Jan 16, 48; US citizen. *Study:* Drexel Univ, BS. *Work:* Kansas City Art Inst; MTL Gallery, Belg. *Exhib:* Deurle, Belg, 73; Projekt '74, Koln, Ger; Diskussies Omtrent Joost A Romeu, Univ Antwerp, Belg, 75; Idea Warehouse, New York, 75. *Bibliog:* Foote (auth), The apotheosis of the crummy space, Artforum; J L Mackie (auth), The Directon of Causation; Merleau Ponty (auth), Primacy of Perception. *Publ:* Art after philosophy, 73; auth & illusr, ONCE1, ONCE2. *Mailing Add:* 148 Seal Rock Dr San Francisco CA 94121

ROMNEY, HERVIN A R
ARCHITECT
b Havana, Cuba, 1941; US citizen. *Study:* Cooper Union, 62-65; L'Ecole Speciale d'Architecture, Paris, 70; Catholic Univ, Washington, DC, BArchit, 73; Yale Univ Sch Archit, Master's, 75. *Comn:* Il Gattopardo, Ambassador J A Correa, Quito, Equador, 76; Babylon (condominium), Pac Developers, Miami, 77; Atlantis (condominium), Stonecrest Development, Miami, 79; Palace (condominium), Helmsley-Spear, Miami, 79, Helmsley Ctr, 81. *Exhib:* Inst Archit & Urban Studies, Rome, 79; Cooper Hewitt, New York, 79; Yale Art Gallery, New Haven, Conn, 80; Inst Fine Arts, Chicago, 80; Mus Contemp Arts, La Jolla, 81; Contemp Arts Mus, Houston, 82. *Pos:* Designer, Harrison & Abramovitz, New York, 61-65; proj designer, Andrault-Parat, architects, Paris, 69-70; architect & environmental designer, South Am, 75-76; principal & founder, Arquitectonica Int Corp, Miami, 76-; founder & pres, Hervin Romney Architect Inc, Miami, 85- *Awards:* Cintas Fel, UN Inst Int Educ, 74-75; Design Citations, Progressive Archit, 78 & 80; Fla Am Inst Archit, 82; First Prize, Dade County Prototype Sch Competition, Miami, 85. *Bibliog:* Color-architecture, Life Mag, 4/81; articles, Newsweek 11/8/82 & House & Garden, 6/83. *Mem:* Am Inst Architects. *Publ:* Ed, Perspecta 15, Yale Archit Papers, 75. *Mailing Add:* Arquitectonica 1423 Mendavia Ave Coral Gables FL 33146

ROMPPANEN, EINO ANTTI See Eino

RONALD, WILLIAM
PAINTER
b Stratford, Ont, Aug 13, 26; US citizen. *Study:* Ont Col Art, hon grad, 51. *Work:* Mus Mod Art, Guggenheim Mus & Whitney Mus Am Art, New York; Nat Gallery Can, Ottawa, Ont; Carnegie Inst, Pittsburgh, Pa; among others. *Comn:* Acrylic mural, Nat Art Ctr, Ottawa, 70. *Exhib:* Carnegie Int, 58; Brussels World's Fair & traveling exhib, 58; Sao Paulo Biennale, Mus Arte Mod, 59; Can Biennial, Nat Gallery Can, 68; and many others. *Pos:* Host of TV show on arts, Can Broadcasting Corp, Toronto, Ont, 66-67. *Teaching:* York Univ, Toronto, Ont, 66. *Awards:* Watercolor Award, Hallmark Corp Art, 52; Nat Award, Can Sect, Int Guggenheim Awards, 56; Award, Second Biennial Exhib Can Painting, Nat Gallery Can, 57. *Bibliog:* David Ralston & Hugo McPherson (coauth), Ronald Chapel in Toronto Harbour, Can Art, 4/66; William Cameron (auth), Portrait of the artist as a violently honest man, Macleans Mag, 2/71; From crisis to crisis with William Ronald, Sat Night, 7-8/75. *Mailing Add:* 392 Brunswick Ave Toronto ON M5R 2Z4 Canada

ROOD, KAY
PRINTMAKER, DRAFTSMAN
b Omaha, Nebr, May 19, 45. *Study:* Univ Iowa, BA, 68, with Maurico Lasansky, Stuart Edie & James Lechay; Ecole des Beaux Arts, 68. *Work:* Seattle Art Mus; City of Seattle, One Percent For Art, Portable Works Collection; Washington State, One Percent For Art, Art in Public Places; King County Arts Commission Portable Purchase Collection, Portland, Ore, Art Mus. *Exhib:* Washington Women Artists, Eastern Wash State Univ, Cheney, 81; Ten Monotype Artists, 82 & Contemp Seattle Art, 83, Bellevue Art Mus, Wash; Northwest Print Council in China, Cent Fine Arts Acad, Beijing, China, 86; Northwest Now, 86 & Kay Rood: Recent Monotypes, 87, Tacoma Art Mus, Wash; Sixth Ann Northwest Int Art Competition, 86 & Kay Rood, 92, Whatcom Mus, Bellingham, Wash; First Impressions: Northwest Monotypes, Seattle Art Mus, 89. *Pos:* Artist-in-residence, Centrum Found, 84 & Marrowstone Press, Pt Townsend, 86. *Awards:* Juror's Award Painting & Drawing, Sixth Ann Northwest Int Art Competition, 86. *Bibliog:* Matthew Kangas (auth), Kay Rood: The gesture and the void, West Art, 10/22/82; Lynn Smallwood (auth), Studies in monotype, The Seattle Weekly, 10/17/84; Ron Glowen (auth), The fascination of process, Artweek, 5/24/86. *Mem:* Northwest Print Coun, Portland, Ore (bd dirs, 84-). *Media:* Miscellaneous; Monotype, Pastel. *Publ:* Contribr, Perspectives in New Music, Six Images, vol 28, no 2, 90; Five Pears or Peaches (cover art), short stories by Reginald Gibbons, Broken Mold Press, Seattle, 91. *Mailing Add:* 922 E Denny Way Seattle WA 98122

ROOKE, FAY LORRAINE
ENAMELIST, INSTRUCTOR
b Chatham, Ont, Can, Dec 22, 34. *Study:* Ont Col Art, Toronto, AOCA, 56; specialized enamel studies Royal Can Acad Arts, RCA, 83. *Work:* Jean A Chalmers Nat Craft Collection, Ottawa, Ont; Jean A Chalmers Nat Bicentennial Collection, Ont Crafts Coun, Toronto; Claridge Investments, Montreal, Quebec, 89. *Comn:* Cloisonne triptych, Can Int Philatelic Exhib, Toronto, Ont, 78; cloisonne panels (cast bronze gate), 80 & champleve panels, 84 (collab with Endre Fazekas), St Elias Byzantine Cath Church, Homestead, Pa; Infirmary Chapel, Loretto Abbey, Toronto, Ont, 90; Glenn Gould Prize, Toronto, Ont, 90. *Exhib:* 1st Int Shippo Exhib, Tokyo, Japan, 78; 5e & 8e Biennale Int L'Art de L'Email, Chapelle du Lycee Gay-Lussac, Limoges, France, 80 & 86; Enamels: International 1985, Long Beach Mus Art, Calif, 85; Premiere Biennale Int d'Email, La Maison des Arts, Laval, Que, 86; Masterworks-Enamel 87, Taft Mus, Cincinnati, Ohio; L'Art de L'Email (invitational), Limoges, France, 90. *Pos:* Vpres & exec bd mem, South Hills Arts League, Mt Lebanon, Pa, 70-72; found bd dir, Renaissance Ctr Arts, Pittsburgh, Pa, 71-72. *Teaching:* Instr enamel, Dept Technol Studies, Ont Col Art, Toronto, 79-, Novia Scotia Col Art & Design, Halifax, summer 85 & St Lawrence Col, Brockville, Ont, 87-92. *Awards:* Thompson Enamels Award & Alice Wilick Robyns Mem Award, 85. *Bibliog:* Kay Whitcomb (coauth), First international Shippo exhibition, Goldsmith J, 78; Elizabeth Dingman (ed), Fay Rooke enamelist, Craftsman, 78; Margot Fischer Page (coauth), Along feathered lines: Fay Rooke, Ont Crafts Coun, Vol 7, No 3, 9/82; Mary Pat Flaherty (coauth), Wired For Beauty, Pittsburgh Press, 10/3/82; Lois Crawford (coauth), Magnificent project, Weekend Burlington Post, 84; film, Faces in small places: Fay Rooke, CKUR Barrie, Ont-TV Series, 84 & CBC Nat Television, Sunday Arts, 90, 91 & 92. *Mem:* Royal Can Acad Arts (exec bd mem, 86-); Assoc Artists of Pittsburgh; Metal Arts Guild; Ont Col Art Alumni Asn (mem-at-large, 84-85); Enamelist Soc (trustee, 89-). *Mailing Add:* 842 Forest Glen Ave 100 McCaul St Burlington ON L7T 2L2 Canada

ROOSEN, MIA WESTERLUND
SCULPTOR
b New York, NY, 1942. *Study:* Art Students League; New York Univ. *Work:* Montreal Mus Art; Albany Mus Art, Ga; Edward Albee, New York; Metrop Mus Art, New York. *Exhib:* One-woman shows, Shoshana Wayne Gallery, Santa Monica, Calif, 89, Christine Bergin Gallery, New York, 89, Joseloff Gallery, Harry Jack Gray Ctr, West Hartford, Conn, 89, Mia Westerlund Roosen, Univ Hartford, 89 & 91; Forum 76, Montreal Mus Art, 76; Nat Gallery, Ottawa, Can, 80; Varieties of Sculpture Ideas, Max Hutchinson Gallery, New York, 83; Drawing for Sculpture, Thomas Segal Gallery, Boston, 87; Figurative Impulse, Santa Barbara Mus Art, Santa Barbara, Calif, 88; bronze, Atlanta Col Art, Ga, 91; Lennon, Weinberg Inc, New York, 91. *Awards:* Canada Council Art Grant; Nat Endowment Arts, 88-89. *Bibliog:* Ruth Bass, Joan Snyder (authors), Mia Westerlund Roosen, Artnews, 4/83; Alan G Artner, Just four sculptures make for a full show for Roosen, Chicago Tribune, 1/25/91; Micheal Brenson (auth), American Beauties: Images of Softness Rendered in Concrete, NY Times, 3/15/91. *Mailing Add:* c/o Shoshana Wayne Gallery 1454 Fifth St Santa Monica CA 90401-2470

ROOTS, GARRISON
SCULPTOR CONSULTANT
b Abilene, Tex, June 25, 52. *Study:* Mass Col Art, with George Greenmayer, Harris Barron & Jana Longacre, BFA(with hon), 79; Washington Univ, with Howard Jones & James Sterritt, MFA, 81. *Work:* Washington Univ Fine Arts, St Louis; Mountain Bell Telephone, Denver, Colo; Laumeier Sculpture Park, St Louis. *Comn:* Artpark Lewiston, NY, 86; City of Denver, Denver Ctr Performing Arts, 86; Glassell Sch Arts, Houston Mus Fine Arts, Tex, 88; Aspen Art Mus, Colo, 89; City of Denver, New Denver Airport Proj, 90; City of Dallas, 1993 Dallas Conv Ctr Expansion Proj, 91-93. *Exhib:* Boston Area Sculptors: Out of the Woods, Rose Art Mus, Waltham, Mass, 82; Ctr Contemp Art, Sante Fe, NMex, 90; Young American Artist, Mandeville Gallery, Univ Calif at San Diego, La Jolla, 85; Phoenix Biennial, Phoenix Art Mus, 85; Colorado 3-D, Arvada Ctr for the Arts, Colo, 85; Artpark, Lewiston, NY, 86; Univ Colorado, Colorado Springs, 87; solo show, I have so much more to learn, Ft Worth Art Mus, Tex, 83, In hopes of not being seen, Contemp Arts Ctr, New Orleans, La, 84, And so it seems, but who's to say, Alternative Mus, New York, 86, Paper targets; real victims, Cincinnati Artists Group Effort, Ohio, 89 & An installation, Inst Design & Experimental Art, Sacramento, Calif, 92. *Pos:* Med artist/photogr, Mass Eye & Ear Infirmary, Boston, 76-79; asst to dir, Laumeier Sculpture Mus, St Louis, 79-81; artist/consult, Denver Art Ctr, Denver Comn on Cult Affairs, Colo, 86-87. *Teaching:* Teaching/tech asst, Washington Univ, St Louis, 79-80; instr, Swain Sch Design, New Bedford, Mass, 81-82; asst prof, Univ Colo, 82-88, assoc prof, div dir sculpture, 88- *Awards:* Rosenthal Found Award for Sculpture, Silvermine Guild for Artists, 79; Fel Award for Sculpture, Nat Endowment Arts, 81 & 84; Colo Coun Arts & Humanities, 86. *Bibliog:* Beth Chic (auth), Dialouge, 91; Steven Litt (auth), Cleveland Plain Dealer, 91; Randall Davis (auth), Artweek, 92. *Mem:* Nat Endowment Arts; Colo Coun Arts & Humanities; Col Art Asn; FUSE, Boulder, Colo. *Publ:* Donald Locke (auth), Artspace Mag, 86; Tiffany Bell (auth), Artpark still exists, Arts Mag, 86; Irene Rawlings (auth), Denver Post, 88; Owen Marshall (auth), Cincinatti Enquirer, 89; Simone Ellis (auth), Pasatiempo, Santa Fe, NMex, 90. *Dealer:* Robischon Gallery 1122 E 17 Ave Denver CO; William Campbell Gallery Ft Worth TX. *Mailing Add:* Dept Fine Arts Univ Colo Boulder CO 80309

ROPHAR
PAINTER
b Los Angeles, Calif, Dec 19, 35. *Study:* Self taught. *Work:* Bolshoi Theatre, Moscow, Russia; Am Cancer Prevention Ctr, Los Angeles, Calif; Bank Yokohama, Japan. *Comn:* Dancer/Portraits, comn by Ruth St Denis, Los Angeles, Calif, 59; Study of Anna Pavlova, comn by James A Doolittle, Los Angeles, Calif, 72; Total Design Concepts, comn by Liberace, Los Angeles, Calif, 73; 17th Century Fantasy (portrait), comn by Dr Richard Ellenbogen, Los Angeles, 83; White Tigers, comn by Jim Simon, Scottsdale, Ariz, 92. *Exhib:* One-man shows, 21 Turtle Creek Club, Dallas, 71, residence of Baroness von Boehm, Berlin, Ger, 73, Marina City Club, Marina Del Rey, Calif, 76 Regional Conf ASID, Los Angeles, Calif, 81, Pomeroy Gallery Fine Arts, Carmel, Calif, 89 & Ctr Arts Galleries, Hawaii, Honolulu, 90-91. *Awards:* Rotary Club Award, Ann Contest, Rotary Club Int, 51-57; Hon Mem, Regional Conf ASID, Los Angeles Chap, 81. *Media:* Acrylic, All Media. *Mailing Add:* 4242 Beethoven St Los Angeles CA 90066

ROPP, ANN L
PAINTER, GALLERY DIRECTOR
b Lacross, Wis, Nov 14, 46. *Study:* Univ Ill, BFA, 71; Columbia Univ, MFA, 89. *Work:* Evansville Mus Art, Ind; NY Pub Libr, New York. *Pos:* Gallery dir, East Tenn State Univ, Johnson City, Tenn, 89- *Teaching:* Instr printmaking, East Tenn State Univ, 92- *Media:* Oil. *Mailing Add:* 206 W Holston Johnson City TN 37601

ROREX, ROBERT ALBRIGHT
EDUCATOR, HISTORIAN
b Alexandria, La, Sept 9, 35. *Study:* Hendrix Col, BA, 57; Univ Ark, MFA, 60; Princeton Univ, MA, 69, PhD, 75. *Teaching:* Asst prof, Hendrix Col, 60-61; actg asst prof, Univ Kans, Lawrence, 68-70; instr, Univ Iowa, Iowa City, 70-75, asst prof art hist, 75-79, assoc prof, 79- *Mem:* Col Art Asn; Mid-Am Col Art Asn; Midwest Art Hist Soc. *Res:* Chinese art & archeology; Japanese art & archeology; Sung, Ming & Liao painting. *Publ:* Coauth, Eighteen Songs of a Nomad Flute: The Story of Lady Wen-Chi, Metrop Mus Art, 74; auth, Setting out at dawn on an autumn river: A painting by Wang Hui, Artibus Asiae, 79; auth, Eighteen songs of a nomad flute, 8/81 & Chunghi Choo: Works in metal and silk, 10/82, Orientations; auth, Some observations on Harold Osborne's The Aesthetics of Chinese Pictorial Art, J Theory & Criticism Visual Arts, 82. *Mailing Add:* 846 Kirkwood Ave Iowa City IA 52240

ROSAND, DAVID
HISTORIAN, CRITIC
b Brooklyn, NY, Sept 6, 38. *Study:* Columbia Col, AB, 59; Columbia Univ, MA, 62, PhD, 65. *Collections Arranged:* Titian and the Venetian Woodcut (auth, catalog), Nat Gallery Art, Washington, DC, 76; The Pastoral Landscape (coauth catalog), Nat Gallery Art, Washington, DC, Philipps Col, Washington, DC, 88. *Teaching:* Prof art hist, Columbia Univ, New York, 64- *Awards:* Fulbright Fel, 71-72; Nat Endowment Humanities Fel, 71-72, 85-86; Guggenheim Fel, 74-75. *Mem:* Col Art Asn Am; Renaissance Soc Am; Ateneo Veneto; Master Drawings Asn; Drawing Soc. *Res:* Venetian painting; Renaissance tradition; graphic arts; criticism of drawing; Abstract Expressionism. *Publ:* Auth, Titian, Abrams, 78; Painting in Cinquecento Venice: Titian, Veronese, Tintoretto, Yale Univ Press, 82; The Portrait, the Courtier, and Death in Castinglione, Yale Univ Press, 83; The Meaning of the Mark: Leonardo and Titian, Spencer Mus Art, Univ Kansas, 88; coauth, Places of Delight: The Pastoral Landscape, Clarkson N Potter, 88. *Mailing Add:* Dept of Art Hist & Archeol Columbia Univ New York NY 10027

ROSAS, MEL
PAINTER, EDUCATOR
b Des Moines, Iowa, June 1, 50. *Study:* Drake Univ, with Jules Kirschembalm, BFA, 71; Tyler Sch Art, with John Moore & Steven Greene, MFA, 74. *Work:* Mus Am Art, Washington, DC; Cleveland Co Coun, Middlesbrough, Eng; Carnegie-Mellon Inst, Pittsburgh; Chemical Bank, New York; Detroit Inst Art. *Comn:* The Road Show (billboard proj art), First Fed Savings & Loan, Detroit, 80; painting, The Italian Consulate of Detroit, 89; litho, Stewart & Stewart Publ, Birmingham, Mich. *Exhib:* The Road Show, City Detroit, 80; American Drawings in Black and White, Brooklyn Mus, 81; Mich Artists 80-81, Detroit Inst Art, 82; City Walls (solo exhib), Fendrick Gallery, Washington, DC, 82; invitational group exhib, Inst Cult, Zacatecas, Mex, 89 & Alexander Milliken Gallery, New York, 90; Coming Attractions, Maxwell Davidson Gallery, New York, 91; In the Heart of the Country, Dept Cult Affairs, Chicago Pub Libr, 91; and others. *Teaching:* Instr, Univ Calgary, Alberta, 75-76; assoc prof, Wayne State Univ, Detroit, 76- *Awards:* Purchase Award, Third Int Drawing Biennale, Cleveland Co Coun, England, 77; Creative Artists Grant, Mich Coun Arts, 82, 85 & 87. *Media:* Oil, Drawing. *Dealer:* Maxwell Davidson Gallery 415 W Broadway New York NY. *Mailing Add:* 2515 Rochester Rd Royal Oak MI 48073

ROSE, BARBARA
HISTORIAN
b Washington, DC, June 11, 37. *Study:* Columbia Univ, MA, PhD. *Pos:* Contributing ed, Art Int, 63-65, Art in Am & Artforum, 65-72 & Vogue Mag, 64-; ed-in-chief, Journal of Art, 88- *Teaching:* Vis lectr art hist, Yale Univ, 70; vis lectr art hist, Hunter Col, 87. *Awards:* Fulbright Fel, 61-62; Distinguished Art Criticism Award, Col Art Asn, 66 & 69. *Publ:* Auth, American Art since 1900, Holt, Rinehart, 64; Auth, American Painting: Twentieth Century, Skira & Rizzoli, 86; Robert Rauschenberg, Avedon Editions, Vintagew Books, 87; Auto-critique, Weidenfeld & Nicolson, 88; Donald Sultan, Avedon Editions, Vintage Books, 88. *Mailing Add:* c/o Vintage Bks 201 E 50th New York NY 10022

ROSE, DAVID
PAINTER, ILLUSTRATOR
b Malden, Mass, Mar 10, 10. *Study:* Mass Col Art, Boston, dipl drawing-painting, 31, BSc(art educ), 34; Mus Fine Arts, Boston, with Jocovleff, 32; etching with Herman Struck, Haifa, 33; Chouinard Art Inst, Los Angeles, 38-40; Art Ctr Col, 40-42. *Work:* Israel Mus, Jerusalem; Mus Mod Art, Haifa; Bialik Mus, Tel Aviv; Skirball Mus, Los Angeles; US Airforce Art Collection, Washington; Judah L Magnes Mus, Berkeley, Calif, UCLA spec collection; Libr Congress; US Holocaust Mem Mus. *Comn:* Courtroom sketches of famous trials: Pentagon Papers, Patty Hearst, Klaus Barbie in France, Reuters, NBC, 74-75 & ABC, 77-80, New York; film titles, Humanities & The Arts, Coast Community Col Dist, Calif, 78; Los Angeles Subway Doc. *Exhib:* Los Angeles Co Mus Art, 52; Soc Illusr, Calif State Mus, Los Angeles, 70; Skirball Mus, Los Angeles, 78; one-man shows, Univ Calif, Los Angeles, 79 & Univ Ariz, Tucson, 79; Mandeville Gallery, Univ Calif, San Diego, 80; Judah L Magnes Mus, Berkeley, Calif, 87; Klutznick Mus, Washington, DC, 88; City Bridge Gallery, Los Angeles, 90. *Teaching:* Instr artist-reporter, Otis-Parsons Sch Design, Los Angeles, 79-81. *Awards:* US War Dept Commendation, Army Pictorial Serv, Info & Educ, 45; Two Medal Awards, Art Dirs Club Los Angeles, 59; Emmy Nomination for Pentagon Papers trial sketches, TV Acad Arts & Sci, 74; Purchase Award, Los Angeles Union Art, 90; and many others. *Bibliog:* Paul Buscemi (auth), Artists in the courtroom (videotape), Mandeville Gallery, Univ Calif, San Diego, 80; John Gorham (auth), Courtroom art: David Rose draws it as he sees it, Los Angeles Weekly, 3/14-20/80; NBC-TV, CNN interviews. *Mem:* Art Dirs Club Los Angeles; Nat Soc Art Dirs; Soc Illusr Los Angeles; Artists Equity. *Media:* Pen, Felt Markers; Oil, Watercolor. *Publ:* Auth, Western art, (Graphis), Int J Graphic Art, 57; illusr, People's Almanac No 1, Doubleday, 78 & People's Almanac No 2, William Morrow & Co, 79, DeLorean-Zondervan, 85, Quick Draw Artist, Mod Maturity, 85 & Courtroom Artists, Los Angeles Times, 86; Artists Mag, 90; Los Angeles Co Mus Art, 92. *Mailing Add:* 1623 N Curson Ave Los Angeles CA 90046

ROSE, HERMAN
PAINTER, PRINTMAKER
b Brooklyn, NY, Nov 6, 09. *Study:* Nat Acad Design, 27-29. *Work:* Whitney Mus Am Art, Mus Mod Art, New York; Univ Tex; Univ Nebr; Smithsonian Inst Print Collection; and others. *Exhib:* Mus Mod Art, 48 & 52; 15 Americans, Whitney Mus Am Art, 48-58 & 72; Pa Acad Fine Arts, 52; one-man shows, ACA Gallery, 52 & 55-56, Forum Gallery, NY, 62 & Zabriskie Gallery, 67, 69, 72 & 74. *Teaching:* Instr, New Sch Social Res, 54-55 & 63-; instr, Hofstra Col, 59-60; artist in residence, Univ Va, 66; vis prof, Univ NMex, 70-71. *Awards:* Childe Hassam Purchase Award, 71; Benjamin Altman Award, Nat Acad Design, 76; Nat Endowment Arts, 76. *Mailing Add:* c/o Fischbach Gallery 24 W 57th St New York NY 10019

ROSE, JOHN TIMOTHY
PAINTER, PHOTOGRAPHER
b Los Angeles, Calif, Dec 14, 42. *Study:* Otis Parsons Sch, BA 64, MFA, 68. *Work:* Otis-Parsons Sch, Cedar-Sinai Med Ctr & Mitsui Manufacturers Bank, Los Angeles; Dellen Publ, San Francisco; Yergeau Musee Int d'Art, Montreal. *Exhib:* Alexandria Eighth Ann, Alexandria Mus, La, 89; 24th Ann, San Bernardino Mus Art, Calif, 89; Watercolor Invitational, Riverside Mus Art, Calif, 87; New American Talent, Laguna Gloria Mus, Austin, Tex, 91; Landscape Revisited, Bakersfield Mus, Calif, 92; Solo exhibs, Space Gallery, Los Angeles, 87, Allport Gallery, San Francisco, 87 & Tortue Gallery, Santa Monica, 91. *Awards:* Best of Show, 3rd Ann Watercolor, Ojai Art Ctr, 87; Gold Medallion, 24th Ann, Grumbacher Corp, 89; Gold Medals, Discovery Awards, Art in Calif Mag, 91. *Mem:* Col Art Asn. *Media:* Multimedia. *Dealer:* Mallory Freeman/Tortue Gallery 2917 Santa Monica Blvd Santa Monica Calif 90404. *Mailing Add:* 3515 Landa St Los Angeles CA 90039

ROSE, LEATRICE
PAINTER, INSTRUCTOR
b New York, NY. *Study:* Cooper Union, 45; Art Students League, 46; Hans Hofmann Sch, 47. *Exhib:* Artists Ann, Whitney Mus Am Art, 50; one-woman shows, Zabriske Gallery, 65, Landmark Gallery, 74, Tibor de Nagy Gallery, 75, 78 & 81 & Armstrong Gallery, 85, Cyrus Gallery, 89; Women Choose Women, New York Cult Ctr, 73; Nat Acad Design Ann, 74-76; Whitney Mus Am Art, Downtown, 78; Hans Hofmann as Teacher: Drawings by his Students, Metrop Mus Art, 79; Contemp Naturalism, Nassau Co Mus Fine Arts, 80; Contemp Still Life, One Penn Plaza, New York, 85. *Teaching:* Instr painting, State Univ NY, Stony Brook, 74-75, Sch Visual Art, New York 77, Art Students League, currently. *Awards:* Gottlieb Found Award, 80; Esther and Adolph Gottlieb Found Grant, 88; Am Acad Arts and Letts Painting Award, 92. *Bibliog:* John Ashbery (auth), Dash, Dodd & Rose, 3/74 & Lawrence Campbell (auth), article, 10/85, Art in Am; April Kingsley (auth), The Lugano review, Art Int, 3/20/74; Lawrence Alloway (auth), Art, The Nation, 10/25/75; Barbara Guest (auth), article, Arts, summer 85. *Mem:* Artists Equity, NY. *Mailing Add:* 463 West St New York NY 10014

ROSE, MARY ANNE
PAINTER, PRINTMAKER
b San Francisco, Calif, Aug 10, 49. *Study:* Univ Calif, Santa Cruz, AB, 70; Univ Calif, Berkeley, MA, 72, MFA, 73. *Work:* Mills Col, Oakland, Calif; Malmo Mus, Malmohus Lans Landstinget & Skandinaviska Enskilda Banken, Sweden; Art Mus Santa Cruz Co; Chicago Art Inst. *Exhib:* Pasadena Mus Mod Art, 73; San Francisco Mus Mod Art, 73 & 77; Univ Art Mus , Berkeley, 73-77; Los Angeles Ist Contemp Art, 76; two-person show, San Francisco Art Inst, 78; Art Mus Santa Cruz Co, 83; solo show, San Jose Mus Art, 83; Gallerie Oscar, Stockholm, 83 & 86; Lilla Galleriet Helsingborg, Swed, 84 & 86; Artists Space, NY, 85; Landskrona Konsthall, Sweden, 87; Bülowska Gallery, Malmo, Sweden, 89; Bibliot Communale, Milan, Italy, 89. *Pos:* Gallery attendant supervisor, Univ Art Mus, Berkeley, 73-78. *Teaching:* instr artist, Studio-in-a-Sch Asn, New York, 84-88. *Awards:* Studio, Cite Int des Arts, Paris, 78-80; Nat Artist Fel, Sweden, 82; Jerome found Scholar, Printmaking Wkshp, New York, 84-85; and others. *Bibliog:* Thomas Albright (auth), Art in the San Francisco Bay Area 1945, 80. *Media:* Acrylic; Monotype. *Dealer:* Peder Olin Futura Gallery Box 10097 Stockholm Sweden. *Mailing Add:* 222 W 23rd St New York NY 10011

ROSE, MATTHEW ADAM
WRITER, PAINTER
b New York, NY, Mar 15, 59. *Study:* Brown Univ, BA, 81; RI Sch Design. *Work:* Like Most Americans, Boca Raton Mus, Fla. *Exhib:* Under 30, Bryant Libr, Roslyn, NY & Area Gallery, New York, 86; Warsch Art Ctr, Glen Clove, NY, 87; Isabelle Bongard Gallery, Paris, 90; Main St Show, Port Washington, NY, 91; Gallery Stendhal, New York, 92. *Res:* Modern contemporary painting, sculpture and related visual. *Publ:* Auth, Inside Ray Johnson's House, Light Works, 90; Art During Wartime, Journal of Art, 4/91; Meet and Talk Mail Art Value Judgements: Ken Linsren, Art News, 11/91; Fluxus Redux, Connoisseur, 1/92; numerous articles in New York Mag between 87 and 88, Lund Art Press, 91 and 92, Arts & Antiques between 91 and 92. *Dealer:* Gallery Stendhal 622-626 Broadway New York; Isabelle Bangard 4 rue Rivoli 75003 Paris. *Mailing Add:* Atelier 03, 33 rue Raspail Ivry sur Seine 94200 France

ROSE, PETER HENRY
DEALER
b New York, NY, Feb 25, 35. *Study:* Hamilton Col, BA; Univ Pa, MA; Columbia Univ; Ecole Superieure, Univ Paris. *Pos:* Co-owner, Peter Rose Gallery, currently. *Mem:* Arts & Bus Coun New York. *Specialty:* Nineteenth and twentieth century contemporary American art; major French impressionist paintings. *Mailing Add:* c/o Peter Rose Gallery 200 E 58th St New York NY 10022

ROSE, ROBIN CARLISE
PAINTER, SCULPTOR
b Ocala, Fla, Sept 3, 46. *Study:* Fla State Univ, BFA, 68, MFA, 70. *Work:* Corcoran Gallery, Phillips Collection & Nat Mus Am Art, Washington, DC; Jacksonville Mus Fine Art, Fla; Hirshhorn Mus & Sculpture Garden, Washington, DC. *Comn:* IBM, Gaithersburg, Md; Signet Bank, Washington, DC; Shea Beker Gallery, New York; Grand Hyatt, Washington, DC. *Exhib:* M-13 Gallery, New York; WPA, Washington, DC; Corcoran Gallery Art, Washington, DC; White Columns, New York. *Bibliog:* Stephen Westfall (auth), rev, Art in Am, 5/86. *Media:* Encausitic, Silverpoint. *Dealer:* Fendrick Gallery 3059 M St NW Washington DC 20007. *Mailing Add:* c/o Baumgartner Galleries 2016 R St NW Washington DC 20009

ROSE, ROSLYN
COLLAGE ARTIST, PAINTER
b Irvington, NJ, May 28, 29. *Study:* Rutgers Univ; Pratt Graphic Ctr; Skidmore Col, BS. *Work:* NJ State Mus, Trenton; McAllen Int Mus, Tex; AT&T; Newark Mus, NJ; Citibank of New York, Moscow, Russia; Newark Pub Libr, NJ. *Comn:* Etchings, New York Graphic Soc, Ltd, Greenwich, Conn, 70-80 & John Szoke Gallery, New York, 81-85; UNICEF Card, 79-80; etched metal wall-relief, Pub Serv Elec & Gas Co, Newark, NJ, 80. *Exhib:* Wadsworth Atheneum, Hartford, Conn, 65 & 75; Birmingham Mus Arts, Ala,

67; Seattle Art Mus, Wash, 68; Women in the Arts, Florence, Italy, 72; Newark Mus, NJ, 74; The Print Club, Philadelphia, 75; George Frederck Gallery, Rochester, 81; Arnot Art Mus, Elmira, 82; Nathans Gallery, West Patterson, 84, 86 & 89; and others. *Collections Arranged:* Liberated Printmakers (traveling exhib), NJ Coun Arts, 72; Black-White & Color, Printmaking Coun NJ, 82. *Teaching:* Instr printmaking, Newark Mus, 72- *Awards:* Best-in-Show, Tri-State Exhib, Summit Art Ctr, NJ, 69, 71 & 75; Graphic Award, Rochester Int Religious, Coun of Churches & Synagogues, 70; Georgi Memorial Graphic Prize, 77, Innovative Painting Prize, 90, Nat Asn Women Artists. *Bibliog:* J H Newman & L S Newman (auths), Plastics for the Craftsman, Crown, 72; Thelma R Newman (auth), Innovative Printmaking, Crown, 77. *Mem:* Assoc Artists NJ; Nat Asn Women Artists (printmaking jury ch, 86-88); Printmaking Coun NJ (bd dirs, 80-85); Assoc Artists NJ (exec bd, 86); Artist Equity Asn, Inc. *Media:* Acrylic, Oil; Paint, Paper on Canvas. *Publ:* Auth, Outline of Printmaking, NJ Coun Arts, 72. *Dealer:* Nathans Gallery 1205 McBride Ave W Paterson NJ 07424. *Mailing Add:* PO Box 5095 Hoboken NJ 07030

ROSE, SAMUEL
PAINTER, MURALIST
b Cleveland, Ohio, Sept 17, 41. *Study:* Cape Cod Sch Art, Provincetown, with Henry Henche; Cooper Sch & Kent State Univ; Boston Atelier, with R H Ives Gammell; also with Basil Kalashnifoff, Cleveland. *Work:* Maryhill Mus Art & St Ignatius Church, Washington, DC; Nat Fire Protection Asn; Brockton Mus; Pierce Galleries Inc, Hingham, Mass. *Comn:* Many, incl Maharaj Ji, Mrs F Lee Bailey, Patricia Barlow & Patricia Pierce. *Exhib:* Nat Arts Club, New York, 69; Copley Art Soc & Concord Art Asn, 71; Jordan Marsh, Boston, 72-73; one-man shows, Concord Art Asn, 75, Pierce Galleries, Inc, 79, 80, 88 & 90, Hammer Galleries, New York, 85; and others. *Teaching:* Pvt art classes. *Awards:* First Prize, Concord Art Asn, 63, 67 & 69; Greenshields Grant, Montreal, 63-70; Nat Fire Protection Asn; and others. *Bibliog:* The Surreal World of S Rose, Am Antiques, 79; Edmund C Tarbell & The Boston Sch of Painting, 80- *Mem:* Copley Soc; Salmagundi Club; Guild Boston Artists; Concord Art Asn; Am Artists Prof League. *Media:* Oil. *Dealer:* Pierce Galleries Inc Hingham MA. *Mailing Add:* c/o Pierce Galleries Inc 721 Main St Hingham MA 02043

ROSE, STEPHANIE
PAINTER, EDUCATOR
Study: Skidmore Col, BS, BFA, 64; also with David Smith. *Work:* Continental Bank, Chicago; Chase Manhattan Bank, New York; Sydney Lewis Co, Richmond, Va; Prudential Insurance Co Am, Coopers & Lybrand, Boston; Castellani Art Mus, Niagara Univ, NY. *Exhib:* Solo exhibs, Susan Caldwell Inc, New York, 74, Betty Cunningham Gallery, New York, 80, Getler/Pall Gallery, New York, 82 & 84, van Straaten Gallery, Chicago, 83, One Ill Exhib Space, Chicago, 84, Moss/Chumley Gallery, Dallas, 86, fiction/nonfiction, New York, 87, E M Donahue Gallery, New York, 89 & 91 & Bethune Gallery, State Univ NY, Buffalo, 91; Voices for Choice, Soho 20, New York; New Abstractions, HBO Gallery, New York, 90; and many others. *Teaching:* Instr drawing & painting, Pratt Inst Grad Sch Fine Art, 79-80; instr, Parsons Sch Design, 80-; guest critic, Empire State Col, State Univ NY, 82- & State Univ NY Buffalo Grad & Undergrad Schs Fine Art, 91-92. *Awards:* Ludwig Vogelstein Found Grants, 76 & 79; New Sch Soc Res Fac Develop Fund Grant, 91. *Bibliog:* Eleanor Heartney (auth), Stephanie Rose (exhib catalog), E M Donahue Gallery, 89; William Zimmer (auth), Stephanie Rose, Art News, 2/90; A Talk with Stephanie Rose (exhib catalog), E M Donahue Gallery, 91; Eileen Myles (auth), Stephanie Rose, Art Am, 1/92. *Media:* Oil & Acrylic on Canvas. *Dealer:* E M Donahue Gallery 560 Broadway New York NY 10012. *Mailing Add:* 508 Broadway 4th Floor New York NY 10012-4432

ROSE, THOMAS ALBERT
SCULPTOR
b Washington, DC, Oct 15, 42. *Study:* Univ Wis-Madison, 60-62; Univ Ill, Urbana, BFA, 65; Univ Calif, Berkeley, MA, 67, study grant to Univ Lund, 67-68. *Work:* Univ NMex Mus, Albuquerque; Libr Cong, Washington, DC; Minneapolis Inst Art; Walker Art Ctr, Minneapolis; Brooklyn Mus, NY; plus others. *Comn:* Park St Loft One, Springfield, Mass; chapel, St Lukes Episcopal Church, Minneapolis; set design, Fool for Love, Cricket Theater, Minneapolis; set design, Circus, Theater de Veune Lune, Minneapolis. *Exhib:* Walker Art Ctr, Minneapolis, 74; Small Objects, Downtown Whitney, New York; Scale & Environment, Walker Art Ctr; outdoor sculpture exhib, Wave Hill, New York, 81; Sheldon Mus Art, Univ Nebr; Tampa Mus Art, Fla; Minneapolis Inst Art, 92; Thomson Gallery, Minneapolis, 91; and others. *Teaching:* Instr sculpture, Univ Calif, Berkeley, 68-69; instr sculpture & graphics, NMex State Univ, 69-72; instr sculpture, Univ Minn, Minneapolis, 72-81, assoc prof, 81-83, prof, 83- *Awards:* Bush Found Fel, 79-80; McKnight Fel, 82; Minn State Arts Fel, 82; Travel Fel, Jerome Found, 90; Mellon Found, Travel, 92. *Bibliog:* John Ligon (prod), Encounters with Minnesota Artists (film); Eleanor Heartney (auth), Tom Rose: Access to Hidden Worlds (article). *Media:* Miscellaneous Media. *Dealer:* Deson/Saunders Gallery 750 N Orleans Chicago IL; Robert Thomson Gallery 400 Second Ave Minneapolis MN. *Mailing Add:* 5124 Harriet Ave Minneapolis MN 55419

ROSEBERG, CARL ANDERSSON
SCULPTOR, PAINTER
b Vinton, Iowa, Sept 26, 16. *Study:* Univ Iowa, BFA, 39, MFA, 47; Cranbrook Acad Arts, summer 47 & 48; Univ Va, summer 64; Univ Mysore, summer 65; Tyler Sch Art, summer 67. *Work:* Springfield Art Mus, Mo; Chrysler Mus, Norfolk, Va; Va Mus Fine Arts, Richmond; Thalhimers, Richmond; Univ Iowa; Swem Libr, Col William & Mary. *Comn:* Bronze hwy markers, Rockingham Co Citizens Comt, Va, 55; William & Mary Medallion, Marshall-Wythe Sch Law, 67, Medallion, 68, Donald W Davis Commemorative Plaque, Life Sci Bldg, 70 & William G Guy Commemorative Plaque, Rogers Hall, 75, Col William & Mary; Bicentennial Medal, Williamsburg-Jamees City Count, 76; I L Jones Jr Bronze Commemorative Plaque, Bruton Parish House, 85; Carter Lowance Bronze Medallion, Marshall Wythe Sch Law, 88; Lawreng I'anson Bronze Medallion, Marshall Wythe Law Sch, 91. *Exhib:* One-man show, Norfolk Mus Arts & Sci, 63; Am Art Today, New York World's Fair, 64; Va Sculptors Traveling Exhib, 70-72; Tidewater Col Fac Exhib, Chrysler Mus, 72; 1st Int Sculpture Competition & Traveling Show, Mercer Col, 79-80. *Teaching:* Instr, Col William & Mary, 47-52, asst prof fine arts, 52-57, assoc prof, 57-66, prof & Heritage fel, 66-82, emer prof fine arts, 82- *Awards:* Fulbright Fel, India; Award of Honor, Va Chap Am Inst Architects, 68; Thomas Jefferson Award, Robert McConnell Found, 71; and others. *Mem:* Audubon Artists; Twentieth Century Gallery; Middle Plantation Club. *Res:* Art of India. *Publ:* Illusr, Little Red Riding Hood & Big Bad Wolf, 53; illusr roll titles for The Colonial Naturalist (film), 64. *Mailing Add:* 4998 Hickory Signpost Rd Williamsburg VA 23185

ROSEMAN, SUSAN CAROL
PRINTMAKER, PAINTER
b Philadelphia, Pa, June 20, 50. *Study:* Art Inst Pittsburgh, 67; Pa Acad Fine Arts, cert, 68-73. *Work:* Allentown Art Mus, Pa; Deborah Heart & Lung Hosp, NJ 81. *Exhib:* 15th Int Grand Prix Contemp Art, Cong Ctr, Monte Carlo, Monaco, 81; Japan Int Artists Soc, Prefectural Mus, Nara, China, 81-82; NJ State Mus Biennial, 83; Nat Print Exhib, Trenton State Col, NJ, 86; James A Michener Art Mus Bucks Binnial I, Doylestown, Pa, 92; and others. *Pos:* Secy & bd dirs, Open Space, Allentown, Pa, 76; co-chmn exhib, fel, Pa Acad Fine Arts, 91- *Awards:* Warga Award, Princeton Art Asn 10th Ann, 79; Critic's Choice Award, Lehigh Art Alliance Ann, 83; Fel, Pa Acad Fine Arts, Fort History Mus, 88. *Mem:* Philadelphia Print Club; Pa Acad Fine Arts; Woodmere Art Mus. *Media:* All. *Publ:* Auth, rev, Art Matters, 12/84, 10/89. *Mailing Add:* 6588 Groveland Rd Pipersville PA 18947

ROSEN, ANNABETH
CERAMIST, SCULPTOR
b Brooklyn, NY, Jan 15, 57. *Study:* Ny State Col Ceramics-Alfred Univ, BFA, 78; Cranbrook Acad Art, Bloomfield Hills, Mich, 81. *Exhib:* Solo Exhibs, New Gallery, Bemis Found, Omaha, Nebr, 86 & Jane Hartsook Gallery, Greenwich House Pottery, New York, 88; Objects, Jessica Berwind Gallery, Philadelphia, Pa, 91; RI Sch Design Mus, Providence, 91; three person shows, Abington Freinds Sch & Jessica Berwind Gallery, Pa, 92; Ceramic Work, Cheltenham Ctr Arts, Pa, 92. *Teaching:* Instr, Ohio State Univ, Columbus, 87; instr, Cheltenham Ctr Arts, Pa, 88-90; instr, Tyler Sch Art, Temple Univ, Philadelphia, Pa, 89-; instr, RI Sch Design, Providence, 90 & 91; instr, Sch Art Inst Chicago, Ill, 91; instr, Univ Arts, Philadelphia, 91- *Awards:* Craftsman Fel, Nat Endowment Arts, 86 & 79; Craftsman Fel, Pennsylvania Coun Arts, 88; Pen Fel, 92. *Mailing Add:* c/o Greenwich House Pottery/Jane Hartsook Gallery 16 Jones St New York NY 11014

ROSEN, CAROL M
SCULPTOR, PRINTMAKER
b New York, NY. *Study:* Hunter Col, BA, 54, MA, 62; Pratt Graphics Ctr, New York. *Work:* Smithsonian Inst, Washington, DC; Rutgers Univ, Newark, NJ; Scanoil Corp, New York; Silvermine Guild Artists, Conn; Newark Mus, NJ. *Exhib:* 18th Nat Print Exhib, Brooklyn Mus, New York, 73; New Ways with Paper, Smithsonian Inst, Washington, DC, 78; solo exhib, Evocations: Works in Hand Formed Paper, Newark Mus, NJ, 80; Paper, Getler/Pall Gallery, New York, 80; Fiber Structure Nat, Downey Mus Art, Calif, 81; Paperworks, Alberta Col Art, Can, 83; Constructed Image, Constructed Object, Alternative Mus, New York, 84; solo show, NJ State Mus, Trenton, 86. *Teaching:* Teacher Art, Pub Sch, Bronx, NY, 54-59; Printmaking, Painting, Papermaking, Art History, Pub Sch, West Orange, NJ, 59-85. *Awards:* Purchase Award, New Jersey Mus, 69; Fel New Jersey State Coun, 80 & 83. *Bibliog:* Vivien Raynor (auth), Collages from assorted everyday items, New York Times, 80; Pat Malarcher (auth), 16 State fellows at the Noyes, New York Times, 84; Pat Malarcher (auth), An artist's radical shift, New York Times, 86. *Mem:* Printmaking Coun New Jersey (bd dir, 88-90). *Media:* Mixed media. *Publ:* Auth, Donald Judd at Marfa, Arts Mag, 88; 10, 000 Things I know about her: Judy Pfaff's Recent Work, Arts Mag, 89; Sites and installations, Arts Mag, 90. *Mailing Add:* Ten Beavers Rd Califon NJ 07830

ROSEN, DIANE
PAINTER
b New York, NY. *Study:* French Govt Fel Painting, Independent Study, 81; Art Students League, with Robert Beverly Hale & Daniel Greene, 78-80; Nat Acad Design, with Harvey Dinnerstein, 79. *Work:* Pastel Soc Am, National Arts Club, New York. *Comn:* Mural (oil, 5 x 4 1/2 ft), comn by David R Holland, Laconia, NH, 90; screen (oil, 5 x 6 ft), comn by Constance Baumann-Slaughter, London, Eng, 91; mural (oil, 7 x 10 ft), comn by Victoria Hunter-Gohl, New York, 92. *Exhib:* 19th Ann Pastel Soc Am, Nat Arts Club, New York, 91; True Love & Other Stories, Gallery Stendhal, New York, 91; Selections from Pastel Society Members, Mills Pond House Gallery, Smithtown, NY, 92; Ann Combined Media Exhib, Salmagundi Club, New York, 92; Pastels USA, 6th Ann Pastel Soc West Coast Int Open Exhib, Sacramento Fine Arts Mus, Carmichael, Calif, 92; and others. *Pos:* Creative dir, vpres, Wilcox & Assoc, New York, 84-88; creative dir/owner, Diane Rosen Communs, New York, 88-90. *Teaching:* Teacher art, Parsons Sch Design, New York; teacher, Birch Nathen Sch, New York; teacher, Pastel Soc Am Sch, New York. *Awards:* Best Figure Painting, Pastel Soc Am Ann, 80;

William Henry Shelton Award, Salmagundi Club Ann Exhib, 92; President's Award, Ms Marbo Barnard, 6th Ann Pastel Soc West Coast Int Open, 92. *Bibliog:* Palmer Poroner (auth), Maybe it's real, Artspeak, 84; Elizabeth Exler (auth), The classical in the contemporary art of Diane Rosen, Manhattan Arts, 92. *Mem:* Pastel Soc Am (bd dirs & newsletter ed, 90-); Salmagundi Club, New York; Allied Artists Am (bd dirs & awards comt, 91-). *Media:* Oil, Pastel. *Publ:* Auth & ed, Pastelagram, Newsletter Pastel Soc Am, 91, 92. *Dealer:* Gallery Stendhal 622-626 Broadway 3rd fl New York NY 10012. *Mailing Add:* 20 Bond St 2nd fl New York NY 10012

ROSEN, ESTHER YOVITS
PAINTER, MURALIST
b Schenectady, NY, June 3, 16. *Study:* Study with Samuel Brecher, 33-36. *Work:* Bergen Community Mus, Paramus, NJ; Teaneck Pub Libr, NJ. *Comn:* Citrus (triptych), 80, Edibles (mural on ceramic tiles), 91, comn by Mr & Mrs Alan Alda, Los Angeles, 80; Poppies A, B, C (triptych), 80 & Fruit-Flowers (triptych), 81, Judie's Restaurant, Amherst, Mass; New York No 1 (triptych) & New York No 2 (triptych), Nakamoto Design Studio, Tokyo, 84; Musicians (diptych), comn by Shirley & Arnold Schreiber, West Palm Beach, Fla, 92. *Exhib:* Pa Acad Ann, Philadelphia, 38; Am Fedn Arts traveling exhib, 38-39; Impressions of Kostelanetz, Philharmonic Hall, New York, 69; Nat Asn Women Artists traveling exhib, Israel and Egypt, 81; Views by Women Artists, Women's Caucus for Art, New York, 82; solo exhibs: Bodley Gallery, New York, 83, John Harms Ctr Arts, Englewood, NJ, 86, Palm Beach Int Airport, Fla, 91 & Ark Hills, Tokyo, Japan, 92. *Teaching:* Instr art, Teaneck Jewish Community Ctr, NJ, 53-72 & YM-YWHA, Hackensack, NJ, 65-76. *Awards:* Grumbacher Award, 90; Halsey Griffiths Award, 91; Award for Announcement Cover, Artist's Guild Exhib, Norton Gallery Art, 91. *Bibliog:* Article, Palm Beach Arts Mag, Vol IX, No 3, 91; David Volz (auth), interview, Palm Beach Jewish World, 3/92; interview, Artscene, Channel 20, West Palm Beach, 92. *Mem:* Nat Asn Women Artists, Inc; NY Artist's Equity Asn; Artists Guild Norton Gallery Art. *Media:* Oil, Ink. *Publ:* Illusr, Allegro, Assoc Musicians Greater New York publ, 85-86. *Mailing Add:* 13840 Parc Dr Palm Beach Gardens FL 33410

ROSEN, HY (HYMAN JOSEPH)
CARTOONIST, SCULPTOR
b Albany, NY, Feb 10, 23. *Study:* Art Inst Chicago; Art Students League; State Univ NY Albany; Stanford Univ, fel. *Comn:* Seal of City of Albany (over life size bronze sculpture) Tricentennial Park, Albany, NY 86; Christopher Columbus bust (1 1/2 life size), Troy, NY, 92. *Pos:* Ed cartoonist, Albany Times-Union, 45; ed cartoonist, Hearst Newspapers & Heritage Found, Washington, DC. *Teaching:* Instr cartooning, State Univ NY Albany, formerly; instr, Russell Sage Evening Division Col, currently. *Awards:* Top Award, Freedom Found, Valley Forge, Pa, 50, 55 & 60; Top Award, Nat Conf Christians & Jews, 62; Am Legion Fourth Estate Awards, 62nd Nat Conv, 80. *Mem:* Asn Am Ed Cartoonists (pres, 72). *Media:* Ink. *Publ:* Auth, As Hy Rosen Saw It, 70; Do They Tell You What to Draw?, 80. *Mailing Add:* Times-Union Albany-Shaker Rd Albany NY 12201

ROSEN, ISRAEL
COLLECTOR
b Baltimore, Md, Dec 28, 11. *Study:* Johns Hopkins Univ, AB, 31; Univ Md Sch Med, MD, 35. *Pos:* Bd trustees, Baltimore Mus Art, 72-86, hon trustee, 86- *Collection:* Modern art, with special emphasis on abstract expressionism, including works by Pollock, de Kooning, Still, Kline, Rothko, Baziotes, Tobey, Rauschenberg, as well as works by twentieth century European artists such as Picasso, Miro, Schwitters, Klee, Leger & Gris. *Publ:* Auth, Toward a definition of abstract expressionism, Baltimore Mus News, 59; Edward Joseph Gallagher, III memorial collection, Baltimore Mus Art, 64 & Metrop Mus Art, 65; The pleasures and agonies of collecting art, World Fedn Friends Mus, 5/79. *Mailing Add:* One E University Pkwy No 1504 Baltimore MD 21218

ROSEN, JAMES MAHLON
PAINTER, HISTORIAN
b Detroit, Mich, Dec 3, 33. *Study:* Cooper Union, with Franz Klein, Ludwig Sander, Leo Manso & Paul Zucker; Wayne State Univ, with Ernst Scheyer, BA; Cranbrook Acad Art, with Zoltan Sepeshy, MFA; studied with William S Morris, Eminent Scholar Art, Augusta Col. *Work:* Mus Mod Art, New York; Whitney Mus Am Art; Newark Art Mus, NJ; Victoria & Albert Mus, London; San Francisco Mus Mod Art; and others. *Comn:* Entre Nous Restaurant, Fairmont Hotel, Chicago. *Exhib:* Color Field 1890-1970, Albright-Knox Art Gallery, Buffalo, NY, 71; one-man shows, Mus Mod Art Penthouse Show, 73 & Betty Parsons Gallery, New York, 74 & 80; Drawings USA, Minn Mus Art, 73; A Sense of Place, Joslyn Mus, 73; Bluxome Gallery, San Francisco; Galleria Civica d'Arte Mod, & Galleria d'Arte Dosso Dossi, Ferrara, Italy; Mus Contemp Religious Art. *Teaching:* Instr studio, Wayne State Univ, 61-63; asst prof studio & art hist, Univ Hawaii, 65-67; instr art hist, Santa Rosa Jr Col, 67-; vis prof art, Univ Calif, Berkeley, 87-88. *Awards:* Huntington Hartford Found Fel Painting, 63; Yaddo Found Fel Painting, 68 & 72; Nat Endowment Fel, 72-73. *Bibliog:* Alfred Frankenstein (auth), Perception traps, San Francisco Chronicle, 70; John Canaday (auth), art criticism column, New York Times, 74; Thomas Albright (auth), Art in the San Francisco Bay Area, 1945-1980, San Francisco Chronicle, 81; John Dillenberger, Visual Arts and Christianity in America. *Mem:* Fel, Soc Art, Relig & Contemp Cult; Renaissance Soc Am; Soc Southern Artists. *Media:* Oil, Watercolor. *Res:* Perception and structuring in 15th through 17th century Italian art and architecture; the art of William Bartram. *Publ:* Auth, Notes From a Painter's Journal, 60; auth, Qualities of Camouflaging, 70; auth, The Sheer Nonsense of Liking Anything; Objects of Atmosphere-The Sculpture of Michael Brenner, 88; Ambiquity as Continuity in Art, 90. *Dealer:* Gallery Paule Anglim 14 Geary St San Francisco CA 94018. *Mailing Add:* 303 Broad St Augusta GA 30901-1517

ROSEN, JOAN FISCHMAN
PAINTER
b St Louis, Mo. *Study:* Univ Iowa, with Philip Guston & Maurice Lasansky, 43-46; Wash Univ, with Arthur Osver & Fred Becker, BFA, 61, MFA, 65. *Work:* Consolidated Aluminum Corp, St Louis, Mo; Univ Iowa, Iowa City; Taft Hoffman Corp, Fla; Springfield Art Mus, Mo. *Comn:* Poster, St Louis Ice Cream Festival, 79; portrait of Dr Irwin Levy for Barnes Hospital, comn by Maurice Handelsman, St Louis, 80. *Exhib:* William Rockhill Nelson Gallery Art, Kansas City, Mo; Joslyn Mus, Omaha; Watercolor USA (traveled); Va Traveling Exhib; Ten Mo Painters Traveling Exhib, Mo State Coun Arts. *Collections Arranged:* St Louis Artists' Exhib, Bixby Gallery, Washington Univ, 80. *Pos:* Coordr, Visual Catalog, Women's Caucus for Art, 79-80. *Teaching:* Artist-in-residence, Midwest Coun for Aging, 78. *Awards:* Purchase Award, Watercolor USA, Southwestern Mus Asn; Lena Newcastle Watercolor Award, Nat Asn Women Artists. *Bibliog:* Kenneth Shuck (auth), Joan Rosen, Ten Mo Painters, Mo State Arts Coun; R Stevens (auth), article, La Revue Mod, 2/63; Mary King (auth), article, St Louis Post Dispatch, 11/78. *Mem:* Area Coord Coun for Arts; Nat Asn Women Artists; Women's Caucus for Art. *Media:* Watercolor, Oil. *Dealer:* Schweig Galleries 4658 Maryland St Louis MO 63108. *Mailing Add:* 1709 Washington Ave St Louis MO 63102

ROSEN, KAY
PAINTER
Study: Newcomb Col Tulane Univ, BA; Northwestern Univ, MA. *Exhib:* Solo exhibs, Bertha Urdang Gallery, New York, 79, 81, 83; Feature, Chicago, 84, 87, 88, 89, 90 & 92; Broadway Window, New Mus Contemp Art, NY, 84; De Pree Art Gallery, Hope Col, Holland, Mich, 86; Univ Gallery Fine Arts, Ohio St Univ, Columbus, 86; Witte de With (Ctr Contemp Art), Rotterdam, 90; Victoria Miro Gallery, London, 90, Laura Carpenter Fine Art, Santa Fe, NMex, 92, Rhona Hoffman Gallery, Chicago,92 Cleveland Ctr Contemp Art, The Five Core Values, Ohio, 92; Word as Image: American Art 1960-1990 (traveling exhib), Milwaukee Art Mus, 90; The Thing Itself, Feature, NY, 90; In the Beginning -- , Cleveland Ctr Contemp Art, 90; News as Muse, Sch 33 Art Ctr, Baltimore, Md, 91; Awards in the Visual Arts 10 Exhibition (traveling), Hirschhorn Mus, Washington, DC, 91; Painting Culture, Univ Calif, Irvine, 92; Summer '92, Shoshana Wayne Gallery, Santa Monica, Calif, 92; Artists' Books from the Permanent Collection, Mus Contemp Art, Chicago, 92. *Pos:* Cur, Sch Art Inst Chicago, 88; panelist, Sch Art Inst Chicago, 89, Midwest Col Art Asn Conf, Cincinnati, 89, Arts Midwest New Partnership Grants for Visual Artists, 90, Mass Artists Fel Prog Painting Panel, 90 Mountain Lake Symposium XI, Va, 90. *Teaching:* Vis artist, Sch Art Inst Chicago, 88; lectr, Inter-Arts at Columbia, Ser, Columbia Col, Chicago, 89. *Awards:* Nat Endowment Arts Visual Arts Grants, 87, 89; Awards, Visual Arts (AVA) 10 Fel, 90. *Bibliog:* Russell Bowman (auth), Text As Image: American Art 1960-1990 (essay, catalog), Milwaukee Art Mus, 90; Roberta Smith (auth), The Group Show as Crystal Ball, New York Times, 7/6/90, C1 c23; Rhonda Lieberman (auth), Kay Rosen: Feature, Artforum, 95, 4/92. *Mem:* Visual Arts Panel, Ind Arts Comn, 86; Arts Midwest Focus Groups, 88. *Publ:* P-Form, Randolph Street Gallery; White Walls, #21, Chicago, Winter 89; College Art Association Journal, Summer 90; Spunky International, New York, 92; White Walls, Chicago, Summer 92. *Dealer:* Feature 484 Broome St New York NY 10013. *Mailing Add:* 6925 Indian Boundary Gary IN 46403

ROSENBAUM, ALLEN
MUSEUM DIRECTOR
b New York, NY, Jan, 37. *Study:* Queens Col, City New York, BA, 58; Inst Fine Arts, New York Univ, MA, 62. *Pos:* Lectr, Educ Dept, Metrop Mus Art, 64-69, sr lectr, 71-72; asst dir, Shickman Gallery, New York, 72-73; asst dir, The Art Mus, Princeton Univ, 74-, dir, 80- *Teaching:* Instr, Sch Gen Studies, Queens Col, City Univ New York, 61; instr, Sch Fine Arts, Univ Calif, Irvine, 72. *Awards:* Fulbright Fel Hist Art, Rome, 62-63. *Mem:* Asn Art Mus Dirs. *Publ:* Auth, Titian and Giotto in Padua, Marsyas, Studies Hist Art, Vol 8, 66-67; Old Master Paintings from the Collection of Baron Thyssen Bornemisza, Int Exhibs Found, Washington, DC, 79. *Mailing Add:* The Art Mus Princeton Univ Princeton NJ 08544

ROSENBAUM, EVELYN ELLER See Eller, Evelyn (Evelyn Eller Rosenbaum)

ROSENBAUM, JOAN H
MUSEUM DIRECTOR
b Hartford, Conn. *Study:* Hartford Col Women, AA; Boston Univ, BA; Hunter Col(art hist). *Pos:* Cur asst, Mus Modern Art, New York, 66-72; dept head, Mus Prog, NY State Coun Arts, 72-79; trustee, Artist Space, New York, 80-; consult, Michael Washburn & Assocs, Am Asn Mus, Mus Assessment Prog, 79-80; dir, Jewish Mus, New York, 80- *Awards:* European travel grantee, Int Coun Mus, 72; Achievement Award, E Manhattan Chamber Com, 89. *Mem:* Asn Art Mus Dirs (chmn mem comt); Coun Jewish Mus (pres, 86-); Am Asn Mus; Int Coun Mus. *Res:* History of Jewish museums in America and Europe. *Publ:* Introd, Treasures of the Jewish Museum (catalog), Universal, 26; numerous catalog introductions. *Mailing Add:* c/o Jewish Mus 1109 Fifth Ave New York NY 10128

ROSENBERG, ALEX JACOB
CURATOR, CONSULTANT
b New York, NY, May 25 19. *Study:* Philadelphia Mus Art; Albright Col, Hofstra Univ, LHD, 89. *Collections Arranged:* An American Portrait 1776-1976 Traveling Exhib (original print & multiple sculpture portfolio; ed, catalog), 76-77; Marc Tobey Retrospective, 77 & 81; James Coignard Traveling Exhib, 82-83; Henry Moore (Mother & Child, co-cur & assoc ed,

catalog), Mus Traveling Exhib, 87-88; co-cur, The Prints of Romave Bearden, co-ed catalog, Mus Travelling Exhib, 92-94. *Pos:* Publ & ed-in-chief, Transworld Art Corp, New York, 69-88; dir & bd mem, Artist's Rights Today Inc, 76-86; dir, Alex Rosenberg Gallery, New York, 77-88; chmn, Designee, 80; Snug Harbor Cult Ctr, 83 & 88; assoc dir, Ardmore Affiliates Ltd, 85-; trustee, Mus Borough Brooklyn, 86-88; Abbott Group, 87-89; Neikrug-Rosenberg Assoc Inc, 89-; adv comt mem, Hofstra Mus, 89; trustee, Philadelphia Col Textiles & Sci, 91- *Teaching:* Lectr, New Sch Social Res, Parsons Div, 79-88; Appraising Modern Art, NY Univ, 92- *Awards:* Spec Prize Publ, 7th Int Triennial Colored Graphic Prints, Kunstgesellschaft, Grenchen, Switz, 76; and others. *Mem:* Visual Artists & Galleries Asn (trustee, 78-); Asn Artist Run Galleries (bd dirs, 79-); Fine Arts Publ Asn (vpres & dir, currently); Fine Arts Publ Asn (pres, 84-86); sr mem Am Soc Appraisers (bd examiners, 87-); Appraisers Asn Am (vpres, 92-). *Publ:* Ed, The 12 Tribes of Isreal--Dali, 73, The Prophets--R Rubin, 73, Homage to Tobey, 74, Our Unfinished Revolution--Calder, 76 & An American Portrait 1776-1976, 76, Transworld Art; and others. *Mailing Add:* 3 E 69th St New York NY 10021

ROSENBERG, BERNARD
PUBLISHER, BOOK DEALER
b New York, NY, Aug 2, 38. *Study:* City Col of New York, cert advert. *Pos:* Owner, Olana Gallery. *Res:* American art. *Publ:* Auth, Olana's Guide to American Artists, A Contribution Toward a Bibliography, Olana Gallery, 2/78, supplement, vol 2, 80. *Mailing Add:* Drawer 9 Brewster NY 10509

ROSENBERG, CAROLE HALSBAND
ART DEALER, DIRECTOR
b New York, NY, Nov 16, 36. *Study:* Hunter Col, Brooklyn Col, BA; Yeshiva Univ; New York Univ. *Collections Arranged:* An American Portrait 1776-1976; Mark Tobey Retrospective (ed, catalogue), 77 & Yaacov Agam (ed, catalogue), 77. *Pos:* Art ed & exec dir, Transworld Art Corp; exec dir, Alex Rosenberg Gallery; vpres, Ardmore Affiliates Ltd, currently. *Awards:* Spec Prize for Publ, Seventh Int Triennial of Colored Graphic Prints, Grenchen, Switz, 76. *Mem:* Visual Artists & Galleries Asn (bd mem); Nat Arts Club; Women's City Club; Lotos Club (art comt). *Specialty:* Contemporary painting, sculpture, graphics and multiples. *Collection:* Contemporary painting, sculpture, prints and multiples. *Mailing Add:* 3 E 69th St New York NY 10021

ROSENBERG, CHARLES MICHAEL
HISTORIAN, EDUCATOR
b Chicago, Ill, Aug 3, 45. *Study:* Swarthmore Col, Pa, BA, 67; Univ Mich, Ann Arbor, MA, 69, PhD, 74. *Teaching:* Asst prof renaissance art, State Univ NY, Brockport, 74-80; assoc prof renaissance art, Univ Notre Dame, 80- *Awards:* Fel, Harvard Ctr, 85-86. *Mem:* Col Art Asn; Renaissance Soc Am; Centro di Studi Europa delle Corti. *Res:* Renaissance patronage; portraiture. *Publ:* Auth, Courtly decorations and the decorum of interior space, 82, Raphael and the Florentine Istoria, 86 & Borsian imagery in the heavenly zone in the Sala dei Mesi, 89; Fifteenth Century North Italian Painting & Drawing: Bibliography, G K Hall, 86. *Mailing Add:* 410 Manitou Pl South Bend IN 46556

ROSENBERG, HERB
SCULPTOR, DESIGNER
b New York, NY, Feb 4, 42. *Study:* Ecole Des Beaux Arts, Paris, 63; State Univ NY, Binghamton, BA, 64; Pratt Inst, MFA, 67; Hertfordshire Col Art & Design, Eng, PhD, 92. *Work:* Zimerli Mus, New Brunswick, NJ; Robeson Archives, New York; Inst Expressive Arts, Goteborg, Sweden; Seybold Sculputre Garden, Malibu, Calif. *Comn:* Monumental reliefs, Sitmar Cruise Lines, Los Angeles, 82; landscape fountain, Mosbacher Inc, Paris, France, 85; plynth neon, Mobil Oil Corp, New York, 88; Holocaust Memorial, Hollis Hills Temple, New York, 89; interior lobby, JCS Designs, New York, 90. *Exhib:* Light & Illusion, State Mus, Trenton, NJ, 85, The Sculputre Soc, Sydney, Australia, 90, Acad Fine Arts, Beijing, China, 90 & Gallerie des Acts UNESCO, Paris, 91; Salone d'Automne, Paris, 85; New Sweden Invitational, Fine Arts Palace, Stockholm, 88; Art Int Invitational, World Expo '88, Brisbane, Australia; MAC 2000, Paris, 92; and others. *Pos:* Cur, Fine Arts Collection, Jersey City State Col, 85-; exec dir, The Heights Artist Asn, 88. *Teaching:* Instr photog, Baruch Col, New York, 75-78; lectr design, Drexel Inst Design, 69-71; assoc prof sculpture, Jersey City State Col, 71- *Awards:* Design research, Jersey City Col, 86-89; Grant, Canada Coun, 88; Award, Essex Cty Arts Coun, 88. *Bibliog:* Walter Zabinski (auth), Imogene Coca by Herb Rosenberg, Newsweek, 84; Eric Bersh (auth), Light and Illusion, Video Press Packs, 86; CBC Mainstreet, 92. *Mem:* Int Sculpture Ctr; Am Art Therapy Asn; Australian Sculpture Soc; Centre Bras d'Or Cult Ctr. *Media:* Stainless Steel, Bronze Neon. *Publ:* Auth, Drawing within a drawing, Am Art Therapy Asn, 80. *Dealer:* Viridian Gallery 24 W 57th St New York NY 10019. *Mailing Add:* 408 Ogden Ave Jersey City NJ 07307

ROSENBERG, JANE
ILLUSTRATOR, PAINTER
b New York, NY, Dec 7, 49. *Study:* Beaver Col, with Jack Davis, BFA, 71; New York Univ, with Sol Lewitt, MFA, 73. *Work:* Amerada Hess, New York. *Comn:* Scenes of the Operas (notecard ser), Metrop Opera Guild, New York, 86. *Exhib:* Review, Preview, Judith Christian Gallery, New York, 81; Invitational Show, 55 Mercer Gallery, New York, 82; The Original Art: Celebrating the Fine Art of Children's Book Illustration, Master Eagle Gallery, New York, 85-86; The Art of the Fairy Tale, Every Picture Tells A Story Gallery, Los Angeles, 91. *Bibliog:* Faith McNulty (auth), Children's books, New Yorker Mag, 12/2/85; Tessa Rose Chester (auth), Children's Literature, London Times, 4/11/86; San Francisco Chronicle, Bk Rev, 12/3/89. *Mem:* Authors Guild. *Media:* Childrens Books; Watercolor, Encaustic. *Publ:* Auth & illusr, Dance Me a Story: Twelve Tales from the Classic Ballets, Thames & Hudson, 85; Sing Me a Story: The Metropolitan Opera's Book of Opera Stories for Children, 89. *Dealer:* Every Picture Tells A Story: A Gallery of Original Art from Children's Books 836 N LaBrea Los Angeles CA. *Mailing Add:* 2925 Nichols Canyon Rd Los Angeles CA 90046

ROSENBERG, MARILYN R
GRAPHIC ARTIST, PRINTMAKER
b Philadelphia, Pa. *Study:* Empire State Col, State Univ NY, BA(studio art), 78. *Work:* Bibliotheque Nationale, Paris, France; Houghton Libr, Harvard Univ, Fogg Art Mus, Cambridge, Mass; Mus Mod Art, New York; Victoria & Albert Mus, London, Eng; Yale Univ Lib, New Haven. *Exhib:* World Artists' Stamps, Mus Fine Arts, Budapest, Hungary, 87; Artists' Books, Mus Art, Univ Ore, Eugene, 88; Beyond Words, San Francisco Craft Folk Art Mus, 90; Book Arts in the USA, US Info Agency tour Africa, 90-91; International Artistamps, Western Ill Univ Art Gallery/Mus, 91; and others. *Bibliog:* Betty Bright & Karen Wirth (coauths), Copier Books (catalog), Minn Ctr Book Arts, 9/8/90; George Gessert (auth), Green Light: Commentary of Artists' Books, Northwest Rev, 91. *Media:* Miscellaneous. *Publ:* Contribr, Assembling 12 (visual poetry), Charles Doria, 86; contribr (with David Cole), NRG (2 visual poems), Dan Rapheal, 90; auth, ed & illusr, Open House (artists' book with visual poetry), pvt publ, 90; contribr, Kaldron, Karl Kempton, 90; contribr (with David Cole), Rampike (3 visual poems), Karl E Jirgens, 92. *Dealer:* Tony Zwicker 15 Gramercy Park S New York NY 10003. *Mailing Add:* 101 Lakeview Ave W Peekskill NY 10566

ROSENBERG, TERRY
SCULPTOR, PAINTER
b Hartford, Conn, 1954. *Study:* Miami-Dade Community Col, AA, 74; Univ Miami, Coral Gables, BFA, 76; NY State Col Ceramics, Alfred Univ, MFA, 78. *Work:* Albright-Knox Art Gallery, Buffalo; John Michael Kohler Arts Ctr, Sheboygan, Wis; Walker Art Ctr, Minneapolis; Smart Gallery, Univ Chicago. *Exhib:* US Art Now, Nordiska Kompaniet, Stockholm & Goteborgs Konstmuseum, Sweden, 81; Painting & Sculpture Today 1982, Indianapolis Mus Art, Ind, 82; The UFO Show, Queens Mus, Flushing, NY, 82; Raw Edge: Ceramics of the 1980's, Everson Mus, Syracuse, NY, 83; Modern Masks, Whitney Mus Am Art, New York, 84; A Passionate Vision: Contemp Ceramics, DeCordova Mus, Lincoln, Mass, 84; Between Sci & Fiction, Sao Paulo Bienal, Brazil, 85; The Eloquent Object, Traveling Exhib, Philbrook Art Ctr, Tulsa, Mus Fine Arts, Boston & Oakland Mus, Calif, 86- *Bibliog:* Nicholas Moufarrege (auth), Terry Rosenberg, Arts Mag, 9/82; Grace Glueck (auth), Terry Rosenberg, New York Times, 11/9/84; Tim Maul (auth), Terry Rosenberg-Painting & Sculpture, (exhib catalog), Miami-Dade Community Col, 84. *Media:* Mixed. *Dealer:* Sharpe Gallery 152 Wooster St New York NY 10012. *Mailing Add:* 598 Broadway New York NY 10012

ROSENBLATT, ADOLPH
PAINTER, SCULPTOR
b New Haven, Conn, Feb 23, 33. *Study:* Sch Design, Yale Univ, BFA, 56, with Albers, Brooks & Marca-Relli. *Work:* New York Times; Libr Cong, Washington, DC; Ft Wayne Mus Art, Ind; Carlisle Mus Art, Pa; Williamstown Mus, Mass. *Exhib:* Razor Gallery, New York, 78 & 79; one-man shows, Toledo Mus Art, Ohio, 78, Minneapolis Inst Art, 82 & Tibor de Nagy Gallery, New York, 82; Cooperstown Hall of Fame, NY, 83; and others. *Teaching:* From assoc prof to prof, Univ Wis-Milwaukee, 66- *Awards:* Great Lakes Film Festival Award, 76; Res Award, Univ Wis-Milwaukee, 86. *Bibliog:* Robert Berlind (auth), Adolph Rosenblatt, Art in Am, 9-10/78. *Media:* Polychrome, Clay. *Publ:* Auth, Book of Lithographs, Peter Deitsch Gallery, New York, 71; producer, dir & ed, Underpass (film), 74 & Daydream Diner (film), 75. *Mailing Add:* 4211 N Maryland Ave Milwaukee WI 53211

ROSENBLATT, SUZANNE MARIS
PAINTER, WRITER
b Hackensack, NJ, July 2, 37. *Study:* Cent Sch Arts & Crafts, London, 57-58; Oberlin Col, Ohio, BA, 59; Cooper Union, 60; Art Students League, 61-63. *Work:* City Ctr, Libr Performing Art & Guggenheim Mus Artists Books Collection, New York. *Comn:* Courtroom drawings, WISN-TV, Milwaukee, 73-77 & Milwaukee's Pub TV, 74. *Exhib:* One-woman shows, Oshkosh Pub Mus, Wis, 72, New York City Ctr Gallery, 76 & others; Ft Wayne Mus Art, Ind, 76; Performing Arts Ctr, Milwaukee, 76-87; Long Island Univ, Brooklyn, New York, 80. *Awards:* Hon Mention, Media Am, Seattle, Wash, 75; Artreach Teaching Grants, Junior League, 89, Milwaukee Found, 90. *Bibliog:* Dean Jensen (auth), Personal vision of circus magic, Milwaukee Sentinel, 71; Donald Key (auth), Show of painted people shadowed by circus, Milwaukee J, 71. *Mem:* Nat Art Workers Community; and others. *Media:* Acrylic, Ink. *Publ:* Illusr, Jumping rope, 70 & Quiet ethnics, 71, Insight, Milwaukee J; producer, dir & ed, Animated film paintings & drawings of dancers,76; Everyone Is Going Somewhere, Macmillan, NY, 76; auth, Memorandance, Marcel Dekker, 78; Changes in the Lake, 82; Some Poems, 87. *Mailing Add:* 4211 N Maryland Ave Milwaukee WI 53211

ROSENBLUM, ELIZABETH
PAINTER
b Manhattan, NY, 54. *Study:* Barnard Col Columbia Univ, New York, 72-77; Tufts Univ, Medford, Mass, BFA, 80; Boston Mus Fine Arts, dipl, 81, Fifth Yr Cert, 82. *Work:* DeCordova Mus & Sculpture Park, Lincoln, Mass; Fed Reserve Bank Boston, Mass; Fuller Mus Art, Brockton, Mass; Gen Electric, Conn. *Exhib:* Boston Ctr Arts, Mass, 89; Ctr Study & Exhibs Drawings, New York, 89; solo shows, Lillian Immig Gallery, Emmanuel Col, Boston, Mass, 90, Akin Gallery, Boston, Mass, 90, Bunting Inst Radcliffe Col, 92 & Galley

NAGA, Boston, Mass 92; Gallery NAGA, Boston, Mass, 92; and others. *Awards:* Visual Artists Fel, Nat Endowment Arts & Humanities, 87; Fel Painting, Mass Coun Arts & Humanities, 89; Fel, Bunting Inst Radcliffe Col, 91-92. *Bibliog:* Shawn Hill (auth), Impending doom, Bay Windows, 7/4-10/91; Nancy Stapen (auth), Passion fuels nuclear solstice, 7/5/91, Christine Temin (auth), Critic's tip, 5/7/92 & Nancy Stapen (auth), Two Bunting artists' searing explorations of self and society, 5/22/92, Boston Globe; Cate McQuaid (auth), Apocalyptic art, South End News, 7/25-31/91; and others. *Dealer:* Gallery NAGA Fine Art Inc 67 Newbury St Boston MA 02116. *Mailing Add:* 249 A St Boston MA 02210

ROSENBLUM, RICHARD STEPHEN
SCULPTOR
b New Orleans, La, Dec 31, 40. *Study:* Calif Sch Art; Cleveland Inst Art; Cranbrook Acad Art. *Work:* Columbus Mus Art; Addison Gallery Am Art. *Exhib:* Profile of a Gallery, Addison Gallery Am Art, Andover, Mass, 80; one-man shows, Columbus Mus Art, Ohio, 81 & Edwin Ulrich Mus Art, Wichita, Kans, 82, Allanstone Gallery, New York, 89; Narrative Sculpture, Artists Choice Mus, New York, 82; The Re-emergent Figure, Storm King Sculpture Ctr, Mountainville, NY, 87; Revered Earth, traveling exhibition, currently. *Pos:* Guest cur, Artists Choice Mus, New York, 82. *Media:* Bronze, Wood. *Dealer:* Allan Stone Gallery 48 E 86th St New York NY; Howard Yuzerski Gallery Boston MA. *Mailing Add:* 63 Lake Ave Newton Center MA 02159

ROSENBLUM, ROBERT
HISTORIAN
b New York, NY, July 24, 27. *Study:* Queens Col, BA, Hon PhD, 92; Yale Univ, MA; New York Univ, PhD; Oxford Univ, Hon MA, 73. *Teaching:* Instr hist art, Univ Mich, 55-56; assoc prof hist art, Princeton Univ, 56-66; prof hist art, New York Univ, 67- *Awards:* Frank Jewett Mather Award Art Criticism, Col Art Asn Am, 81; Fel Am Acad Arts & Sci. *Res:* Modern art, 1760 to the present. *Publ:* Auth, Cubism and Twentieth Century Art, 60, Transformations in Late Eighteenth Century Art, 67, Ingres, 67, Frank Stella, 70 & Modern Painting and the Northern Romantic Tradition: Friedrich to Rothko, 75; coauth, 19th Century Art, 84; The Dog in Art from Rococo to Post-Modernism, 88; The Romantic Child from Runge to Sendak, 88; Paintings in the Musee d'Orsay, 89; The Jeff Koons Handbook, 92. *Mailing Add:* Dept Fine Arts New York Univ Washington Sq New York NY 10003

ROSENFELD, RICHARD JOEL
DEALER
b Philadelphia, Pa, May 31, 40. *Study:* Pratt Inst, New York, MFA, 64; Univ Pa, Philadelphia & Pa Acad Fine Art (coordinated prog), BFA, 62. *Pos:* Mgr, Artists Galleries, Cheltenham, Pa, 67-72; co-dir, Longman Gallery, Pa, 72-75; dir-owner, Rosenfeld Gallery, Philadelphia, Pa, 76- *Teaching:* Instr painting & art hist, Perkiomen Sch, Pennsburg, Pa, 63-65. *Bibliog:* Susan Perloff (auth), article, Pa Gazette, 6/77. *Mem:* fel Pa Acad Fine Arts. *Specialty:* Contemporary art, all media including crafts. *Mailing Add:* Rosenfeld Gallery 113 Arch St Philadelphia PA 19106

ROSENFELD, SAMUEL L
ART DEALER, COLLECTOR
b New York, NY, July 27, 31. *Study:* Univ Pa, BS, 51; Harvard Univ, MBA, 53. *Pos:* Dir, Artists Unlimited Gallery & Rosenfeld Fine Arts, New York, currently. *Mem:* Appraisers Asn Am (bd dir). *Specialty:* American art in the realist & modernist tradition in all media, mainly from 1910 to World War II emphasizing the WPA period, the Eight & ash can school. *Collection:* Modern American realists, especially WPA period; Trench art; Rogers groups; Doulton Lambeth stoneware pottery; cast iron boot jacks. *Mailing Add:* Rosenfeld Fine Arts 44 E 82nd St New York NY 10028

ROSENFELD, SHARON
PAINTER
b New York, NY, Apr 8, 54. *Study:* Pratt Inst, BFA, 77; New York Univ, MA, 83. *Work:* Mus Nat Arts Found, New York. *Exhib:* Solo exhibs, 80 Washington Sq E Gallery, New York , 83, Mead Data Cent, Pan Am, New York, 90, Mighael Ingbar, New York, 91, Righetti Knie Fine Arts Trading, Muri-Bern, Switz, 92, Century Galleries, Henley on Thames, Eng, 92 & Gallery Galimberti, Vaduz, Liechtenstien, 92; Romantic Paintings, Tracy Garet Asn, New York, 84; American-French Art Exchange (with catalog), Auvers-sur-oise, France, 87; Ibex International, 87 & Mead Data Central, 88, Mus Nat Arts Found, Washington, DC; Primary States, Marymount Col, New York, 88; In Search of the American Experience (with catalog), Mus Nat Arts Found, Fed Plaza, New York, 89 & Deutsch-Amerikanisches Inst, Regensburg, Ger, 89; and others. *Awards:* Ford Found Studio Art Award, 77; Artist in Residence Grant, The Millay Colony for the Arts, 85. *Media:* Acrylic on Linen. *Publ:* Reviews, Arts Mag, 4/84; Contribr, Profile, Manhattan Arts, 6/89. *Dealer:* Claudius Ochsner Bahnhofstr 20 Rapperswil Switz 8640. *Mailing Add:* 201 E 77 St, Apt 12B New York NY 10021

ROSENFIELD, JOHN M
EDUCATOR, CURATOR
b Dallas, Tex, Oct 9, 24. *Study:* Univ Calif, Berkeley, BA, 45; Univ Iowa, Iowa City, MFA, 49; Harvard Univ, PhD, 59. *Collections Arranged:* Japanese Art of Heian Period (auth, catalog), Asia House, New York, 67; Traditions of Japanese Art (auth, catalog), Fogg Mus, Harvard, 70; Courtly Tradition in Japanese Art & Literature (coauth, catalog), Fogg Mus, Harvard, 73; Journey of the Three Jewels (coauth, catalog), Asia House, New York, 79. *Pos:* Cur Asian art, Fogg Art Mus, Cambridge, Mass, 76-91; actg dir, Harvard Univ Art Mus, 82-85. *Teaching:* Asst prof oriental art, Univ Calif, Los Angeles, 57-60; prof japanese art, Harvard Univ, Cambridge, Mass, 65- 91, emer, 91- *Publ:* Auth, Dynastic Arts of the Kushans, Univ Calif, 67; ed, Song of the Brush: Japanese Paintings from the Sanso Collecion, Seattle Art Mus, 79; coauth, The Japanese Courtier: Painting, Calligraphy and Poetry from the Fogg Art Mus, The Philip Hofer Collection, Santa Barbara Mus Art, 80; Masters of Japanese Calligraphy 8th-19th Century, Japan Soc, NY, 84. *Mailing Add:* Dept Fine Arts Harvard Univ Cambridge MA 02138

ROSENHOUSE, IRWIN
PRINTMAKER, PAINTER
b Chicago, Ill, Mar 1, 24. *Study:* Cooper Union, cert, 50, BFA, 78. *Work:* Metrop Mus Art; Cooper Union Mus; New York Pub Libr Graphics Collection; Everhart Mus, Pa; Brooklyn Col. *Exhib:* Am Fedn Arts; Libr Cong; Mus Mod Art, New York; Pa Acad Fine Arts; Boston Printmakers. *Pos:* Resident artist, Huntington Hartford Found, 59 & 61; owner & operator, Rosenhouse Gallery, New York, 63-71; free lance designer & illusr, currently. *Teaching:* Instr drawing, painting & graphics, Mus Mod Art Educ Ctr, 68-70; instr graphics, Brooklyn Col, 72; adj prof art, Nassau Community Col, 73-92, New York Tech Col, 82-83. *Awards:* Award for Graphics, Louis Comfort Tiffany Found; Billboard Ann Award, Huntington Hartford Found Resident. *Mem:* Philadelphia Print Club; New York Artists Equity. *Media:* Graphics, Acrylics. *Publ:* Illusr, What Kind of Feet Does a Bear Have, Bobbs, 63; Have You Seen Trees, Young-Scott, 67; Alternate Celebrations Catalogue, Pilgrim Press, 82; Teenagers Themselves, ADAMA, 83-84. *Mailing Add:* 256 Mott St New York NY 10012

ROSENQUIST, JAMES
PAINTER
b Grand Forks, NDak, Nov 29, 33. *Study:* Univ Minn, Minneapolis, scholar, 48, study with Cameron Booth; Art Students League, 54-55; Aspen Inst of Humanist Studies, Colo, Eastern philo & hist, 65. *Work:* Art Gallery Ont, Toronto; Stedelijk Mus, Amsterdam; Metrop Mus, New York; Mus Mod Art, New York; Musee Nat d'Art Moderne, Paris; and others. *Exhib:* Six Painters & the Object, Solomon R Guggenheim Mus, New York, 63; Mixed Media, 63 & Kid Stuff, 71, Albright Knox Art Gallery, Buffalo, NY; Americans 1963, Around the Automobile, 65, The 1960's, 67 & Works from Change, 74, Mus Mod Art, New York; Sound, Light, Silence, William Rockhill Nelson Gallery Art, Kansas City, Mo, 66; Ann, 67 & Am Pop Art, 74, Whitney Mus Am Art, New York; Documenta IV, Kassel, WGer, 68; New York: The Second Breakthrough, 1959-1964, Univ Calif, Irvine, 69; Prints by Four New York Painters, 69 & New York Painting & Sculpture: 1940-1970, 69-70, Metrop Mus Art, New York; Am Painting, Va Mus Fine Art, Richmond, 70; Art & Technol, Los Angeles Co Mus Art, Los Angeles, 71; American Drawing: 1970-1973, Yale Univ, 73; Am Art-Third Quarter Century, Seattle Art Mus, Wash, 73; one man shows, Nat Gallery Can, Ottawa, 68, Metrop Mus Art, New York, 68, Whitney Mus Am Art, New York, 73, Mus Contemp Art, Chicago, 72 & Portland Art Ctr, Ore, 73; Contemp Art Mus, Houston, 82, Whitney Mus Art, 82 & Mus Fine Arts, Houston, 83; Butler Inst Am Art, Youngstown, Ohio, 88; Mus Fine Arts, Houston, Tex, 88. *Pos:* Commercial display artist, Gen Outdoor Advert Co, 52-54 & Bonwit Teller & Tiffany & Co, New York, 59; coun mem, Nat Endowment Arts, 78- *Teaching:* Vis lectr, Yale Univ, New Haven, Conn, 64. *Awards:* Art Inst Chicago Award, 63; Torcuato di Tella Int Prize, Buenos Aires, 65. *Bibliog:* J Siegel (auth), An Interview with James Rosenquist, Artforum, New York, 6/72; J Loring (auth), Prints: James Rosenquist's Horse Blinders, Artmagazine, New York, 2/73; P Tuchman (auth), Pop: Interview with James Rosenquist, Art News, New York, 5/74. *Media:* Oil. *Mailing Add:* c/o Leo Castelli Gallery 420 W Broadway New York NY 10012

ROSENQUIST, MARC H
SCULPTOR
b Amityville, NY, May 5, 55. *Study:* Syracuse Univ, BFA, 79. *Work:* Newark Pub Libr, NJ; Zimmevli Mus Art, New Brunswick, NJ; NJ State Mus, Trenton; Newark Mus, NJ. *Exhib:* Newark Mus, NJ, 61; NJ Mus, Trenton, 85; Philadelphia Mus Art, Pa, 90. *Awards:* Louise Cramer Found Award, Artnew, Philadelphia Mus Art, 90; Nat Endowment Arts, 90; NJ State Coun Arts, 90. *Bibliog:* Paula Marincola (auth), Contemporary Philadelphia Artists, Philadelphia Mus Art Catalog, 4/90; Anne Levin (auth), Two Trenton residents, Gain Nat Arts Award, Trenton Times, 11/6/90; Vivien Raynor (auth), Creations by Fellowship Winners, NY Times, 7/28/91. *Media:* All. *Mailing Add:* c/o Larry Becker 43 N Second St Philadelphia PA 19106

ROSENTHAL, DEBORAH MALY
CRITIC, PAINTER
b New York, NY, Jan 16, 50. *Study:* Smith Col, with Leonard Baskin, 66-68; Barnard Col, BA, 71; Pratt Inst, with George MacNeil, MFA, 74; Queens Col, with Ilya Bolotowsky, 74. *Exhib:* Purdue Univ, Ind, 73; Metaphor in Painting, Fed Hall Nat Mem, New York, 78; Artists by the Sea, Snug Harbor Cult Ctr, New York, 79 & 80. *Pos:* Critic, Arts, Artforum & New York Arts J, 75-; artist & cur, Cult Coun Fedn, 78-80. *Teaching:* Guest lectr, Queens Col, Univ NH & Parsons Col, 77-; lectr, Sch Visual Arts, New York, 80-82; fac mem, New Sch Social Res, 81- *Awards:* Critic's Award, Nat Endowment Arts, 79-80. *Mem:* Col Art Asn; Int Asn Art Critics. *Media:* Oil. *Publ:* Auth, Metaphor in Painting, 78, auth, The lesson of the master: Paul Klee, 78, auth, Interview with Andre Masson, 80 & coauth, Zone painting, 81, Arts Mag; auth, Ilya Bolotowsky, Harry N Abrams, 82. *Dealer:* Nicholas Rizzo Fine Arts 18 Strong Pl Brooklyn NY. *Mailing Add:* 250 West 85th St No 12G New York NY 10024

ROSENTHAL, DONALD A
MUSEUM DIRECTOR, HISTORIAN
b Jersey City, NJ, Oct 7, 42. *Study:* Yale Univ, BA(magna cum laude); Princeton Univ; Hunter Col, MA; Columbia Univ, MPhil, PhD. *Collections Arranged:* Charlotte Dorrance Wright Collection, Philadelphia Mus Art, 78; George Eastman Collection, Mem Art Gallery, Rochester, 79; Monet in London, High Mus Art, Atlanta, 88; Thomas Cornell: Paintings, Bowdoin Col Mus Art, 90. *Pos:* Res asst, Metrop Mus Art, New York, 74-77; asst cur europ painting, Philadelphia Mus Art, 77-79; cur collections, Mem Art Gallery, Rochester, NY, 79-85; chief cur & cur europ art, High Mus Art, Atlanta, 86-89; assoc dir, Bowdoin Col Mus Art, 89-91; dir, Chapel Art Ctr, St Anselm Col, Manchester, NH. *Teaching:* Lectr fine arts, St Anselm Col, 91- *Mem:* College Art Asn; Int Coun Mus. *Res:* European art of the 18th & 19th centuries; history of photography. *Publ:* Auth, A Mughal Portrait copied by Delacroix, Burlington Mag, 77; Géricault's Expenses for The Raft of the Medusa, Art Bull, 80; Orientalism: The Near East in French Painting, 1800-1880, 82 & La Grande Maniére: Historical and Religious Painting in France, 1700-1800, 87, Rochester. *Mailing Add:* Chapel Art Ctr, St Anselm Col 87 St Anselm Dr Manchester NH 03102

ROSENTHAL, EARL EDGAR
EDUCATOR, HISTORIAN
b Milwaukee, Wis, Aug 26, 21. *Study:* Univ Wis, Milwaukee, BA, 43; New York Univ, PhD, 53. *Pos:* Asst dir, Milwaukee Art Inst & Layton Art Gallery, 52-53. *Teaching:* Prof hist art, Univ Chicago, 54- *Awards:* Order of Merit, King of Spain, 6/89. *Mem:* Col Art Asn Am; Soc Archit Historians (dir, 57-58 & 59-60); Am Soc Hispanic Art Hist Studies; Hispanic Soc Am; corresp mem Acad San Fernando, Madrid. *Res:* Renaissance architecture and sculpture in Italy and Spain. *Publ:* Auth, The Cathedral of Granada, 61 & The Palace of Charles V in Granada, 85 & 88, Princeton Univ Press; Michelangelo's Moses, Art Bulletin, XLVI, 64; Die Reichskrone, In: Jahrbuch der Kunsthistorischen Sammlungen in Wien, 71; Invention of columnar device of Charles V, J Warburg Inst, 73; transl of El Palacio de Carlos V en Granada, Alianza, Madrid, 88 & La Catedral De Granada, Granada, 90. *Mailing Add:* 5529 S University Ave Chicago IL 60637

ROSENTHAL, GLORIA M
COLLAGE ARTIST, PAINTER
b Brooklyn, NY, May 24, 28. *Study:* Com Art Training, Archit Design, Univ Cincinnati; Post Col; Artist in Am Sch; Queen's Col; Provincetown Workshop; Nassau Community Col; Pratt Graphic Ctr; pvt & independent study. *Work:* Bankers Trust, New York; Sperry Gyroscope, Lake Success, NY; Weaver Schs, Milwaukee, Wis; Community Hosp, Glen Cove, NY; Transverse Nat Bank, Pa. *Exhib:* Audubon Artists; Nat Asn Women Artists; Nat Acad Design, 70-75; Silvermine Regional, Silvermine, Conn, 72; one-woman shows, Saratoga Performing Art Ctr, NY, 71 & State Univ NY Farmingdale, 79; Palazzo Vecchio, Florence, Italy, 72; Winners of the Past Ten Years, Brooklyn Mus, 75. *Pos:* Artist-in-residence, Gloria Rosenthal Gallery, Rocky Neck Art Colony, Mass, 71-; artist-in-residence, Col St Benedict, St Joseph, Minn. *Awards:* Medal of Honor, Nat Asn Women Artists, 75 & Grumbacher Award, 79; Am Artist Mag Nat Award, 78. *Mem:* Nat Asn Women Artists; Rocky Neck Art Colony, SFla Art Asn (vpres, 73); Syosset Players (vpres, 66, pres, 67). *Media:* Oil, Collage. *Mailing Add:* 17 Shore Ave Bayville NY 11709

ROSENTHAL, HOWARD
SCULPTOR
b March 4, 48. *Study:* RI Sch Design, Providence, BFA, 69; Pratt Inst, Brooklyn, NY, MFA, 80. *Comn:* Outdoor sculpture, Crosby Gardens, Toledo, Ohio, 89-90; outdoor sculpture, Snug Harbor Cult Ctr, Staten Island, NY, 91. *Exhib:* Solo shows, 22 Wooster Gallery, New York, 86, Intersection Arts, San Francisco, Calif, 86, White Gallery, Tokyo, Japan, 89 & Ihara Ludens Gallery, New York, 90; Pratt Inst, Brooklyn, NY, 91; Cleveland State Univ, Ohio, 91; Int Contemp Art Fair, Yokohama, Japan, 92. *Teaching:* Lects & presentations, var col, mus & univ, 84-91; asst prof art, Conn Col, New London, 84-87 & 88-89; vis instr New Forms, Grad Sch Art & Design, Pratt Inst, Brooklyn, NY, 91-92; vis instr sculpture, Barnard Col, Columbia Univ, New York, 92. *Awards:* Grant, Corp Pub Broadcasting, 85; Nat Endowment Arts Fel, 90. *Bibliog:* Amy Sparks (auth), Unreal vistas, Cleveland Ed, 4/25/91; Gretchen Faust (auth), New York in review, Arts Mag, 11/91; Jennifer Dunning (auth), A collaboration in individuality, NY Times, 1/3/92. *Mailing Add:* 65 Spring St New York NY 10012

ROSENTHAL, JOHN W
PHOTOGRAPHER, PUBLISHER
b Munich, Ger, Mar 25, 28; US citizen. *Study:* Univ of Chicago, BA(liberal arts). *Pos:* Commercial photogr, Koopman-Neumer, Chicago, Ill, 55-65; owner-dir, Rosenthal Art Slides, Chicago, 60- *Teaching:* Helped photograph the collections & taught photogrs at the Art Inst of Chicago & Mus of Contemp Art, 70-77. *Bibliog:* Norine Cashman, Slide Buyer's Guide, Libr Unlimited, 90. *Media:* Slides. *Specialty:* Extensive collection 36,000 of high quality slides pertaining to art and art history. *Publ:* Auth, Rosenthal Art Slides, The 90's Catalog, Part I: Painting and Sculpture, Part II: Architecture & Decorative Arts. *Mailing Add:* 5456 S Ridgewood Court Chicago IL 60615

ROSENTHAL, JUDITH-ANN SAKS See Saks, Judith-Ann (Judith-Ann Saks Rosenthal)

ROSENTHAL, MARK L
CURATOR, HISTORIAN
b Philadelphia, Pa, Aug 9, 45. *Study:* Temple Univ, AB, 63; Univ Iowa, MA, 71, PhD, 79. *Collections Arranged:* Andre, Buren, Irwin, Nordman: Space as Support (auth, catalog), 79; Franz Marc (auth, catalog), 79; Neil Jenney (auth, catalog), 81; Juan Gris (auth, catalog), 83-84; Jonathan Borofsky (auth, catalog), 84-85; Anselm Kiefer (auth, catalog), 87-88; Joseph Johns (auth, catalog), 88-89. *Pos:* Assoc cur, Wadsworth Atheneum, Hartford, Conn, 74-76; cur collections, Univ Art Mus, Berkeley, Calif, 76-83; cur 20th century art, Philadelphia Mus Art, Pa, 83- *Mem:* Col Art Asn. *Res:* Various topics in twentieth century art. *Publ:* Auth, Paul Klee, Phillips Collection, 81; auth, The prototypical triangle of Paul Klee, Art Bulletin, 82; auth, Picasso's night fishing at Antibes, Art Bulletin, 83. *Mailing Add:* 7033 McCallum St Philadelphia PA 19119

ROSENTHAL, RACHEL
PERFORMANCE ARTIST, SCULPTOR
b Paris, France, Nov 9, 26; US citizen. *Study:* New Sch Soc Res, New York; Sorbonne, Paris; also with Hans Hoffmann, Karl Knaths, William S Hayter, John Mason, Merce Cunningham & Erwin Piscator. *Comn:* Los Angeles Festival, 90; Serious Fun, New York, 93. *Exhib:* Rental Gallery, Los Angeles Co Mus, 72; Five-Person Show Performance Art, Contemp Art Ctr, New Orleans, 80; Soldier of Fortune (performance), Art Inst Chicago & others, 81; Was Black, The Kitchen, New York; L O W in Gaia, across US & Europe, 86-90; Rachel's Brain, throughout US & Europe, 87-90; Amazonia, LA County's Bing Theatre & Ojai Music Festival, 90; Pangaean Dreams, Santa Monica Mus, Calif & Lincoln Ctr, New York, 91; and others. *Pos:* Founding mem bd dir, Womanspace, Los Angeles, 72-74, co-chmn, 73-74; dir, Instant Theatre, Los Angeles, 56-66 & 74-76; founding mem, Double X, Los Angeles, 74-76; dir, Espace DBD, Los Angeles, 80-82; exec dir, The Rachel Rosenthal Co, Los Angeles, Calif, 89-90. *Teaching:* Performance, Claremont Grad Sch, Calif, 79, Otis/Parsons Inst Design, Los Angeles, 80-81, Espace DBD, Los Angeles, 81-82 & Univ Calif, Irvine, 82; vis artist, Univ Colo, Boulder, 83 & Calif State Univ, Long Beach, 83, New York Univ & Univ Calif, Los Angeles; workshop residency, Galerie 101, Ottawa, 89; performance lect, San Francisco Art Inst, 90; Art Gaia Art, Univ Calif,Santa Barbara, 91; Who Needs Artists, Carnegie Mellon Univ, Pittsburgh, Pa, 92; Chaos, Movement Res Inc, New York, 92; performance, CSU Summer Arts, Humbolt State Univ, Calif, 91-92. *Awards:* Nat Endowment Fel, 90; Tides Found, Calif, 91; Arts Int Fund for US Artists, New York, 92. *Bibliog:* Ross Weston (auth), Stand Up Shaman, The Village Voice, 8/6/91; Anthony Hayden-Guest (auth), Live Art: Annie Lebovitz Photographs Five Women Who Shock, Vanity Fair Mag, 4/92; Denise Meola (auth), Rachel Rosenthal, OMNI Mag, 8/92. *Mem:* Int Asn Art Critics; New Mus Contemp Art (adv bd); Mus Contemp Art. *Media:* Clay. *Publ:* Futurfax, audio-cassette, 90; My Brazil, Out From Under, Performance Texts by Women, New York, 90; Pangaean Dreams, videotape, 90; In Search of the New Pataphysical Order, audio-cassette, 91; Filename: FUTURFAX, videotape, 92. *Mailing Add:* 2847 S Robertson Blvd Los Angeles CA 90034

ROSENTHAL, SEYMOUR
PAINTER, LITHOGRAPHER
b New York, NY, Aug 14, 21. *Study:* Self Taught. *Work:* Metrop Mus Art, City New York Mus, New York; Technion Bldg, Haifa, Israel; Santa Barbara Mus Art, Calif; Harry S Truman Libr, Independence, Mo; New York Pub Libr; Thirty-nine (39) original Lithos in permanent collection Metro Mus Art, New York; Yale Univ, New Haven, Conn. *Comn:* Drawings of children, New York Bd Educ, 57; painting of Moses, borough pres off, Queens, NY, 62; Pfizer Pharmaceutical; Pfizer, Parke Davis. *Exhib:* Civil Rights Art Show, Brooklyn Mus, 62; one-man shows, Suffolk Mus, 68, ACA Gallery, New York, 69, Daruma Gallery, Cedarhurst, NY, 91 & Educ & Cul Fund Elect Indus, Flushing, NY, 92; Major Drawings of 19th & 20th Century Exhib, Gallery Mod Art, New York, 64-65; Art Dealers Choice Exhib, 67; Indianapolis Mus Art, 72; Creative Journey into an Artist's Mind, Am Jewish Congress House, New York, 90. *Awards:* Saint Gaudens Medal for Fine Draughtsmanship; Citation of Honor from the Benjamin Rosenthal Chapter of the Am Jewish Congress, 92. *Bibliog:* Edwin Newman (commentator), Today Show, NBC TV, 70; Alfred Werner (auth, film), Directions, ABC TV, 71; Life & Works of Seymour Rosenthal, ABC TV, 10/82; Live at Five, NBC TV, 4/1/88. *Mem:* Artists Equity Asn; Comt Arts & Lit in Jewish Life; Jewish Fedn Philanthropies; United Jewish Appeal. *Media:* Watercolor, Oil. *Publ:* Illusr, Parke Davis Med J, & Scope, 56; contribr, Commonwheel, Vol 90, No 15; The World of Seymour Rosenthal, 76. *Dealer:* Frances Rosenthal 161-08 Jewel Ave Flushing NY 11365; Daruma Gallery Inc 554 Central Ave Cedarhurst NY 11516. *Mailing Add:* 161-08 Jewel Ave Flushing NY 11365

ROSENTHAL, STEPHEN
PAINTER
b Richmond, Va, May 28, 35. *Study:* Art Students League, with Edwin Dickinson; Tyler Sch Fine Arts, Philadelphia, with Boris Blai, BFA, 60. *Work:* Arts Club Chicago; Yale Univ Art Gallery, New Haven, Conn; Art Fund, New York; Metrop Mus of Art, New York, NY. *Exhib:* Am Acad Arts & Lett, New York, 63; Amon Carter Mus, Ft Worth, Tex, 64; Int Watercolor Biennial, Brooklyn Mus, NY, 65; Herron Inst, Indianapolis, Ind, 67; Pa Acad Fine Arts Biennial Exhib, Philadelphia, 67; John Gibson Gallery, New York, NY, 87; Steven Rosenberg Gallery, New York, NY, 87; one-man shows, Eric Stark Gallery, New York, 91 & Gallerie Wasserman, Munich, Ger, 92. *Pos:* Bk reviewer, Arts Mag, New York, 71-72. *Teaching:* Instr design, Cooper Union, New York, 66-67; lectr painting, Univ NC, Greensboro, 71-72; vis instr, Parsons Sch of Design, 86- *Awards:* Mason Lord Prize, Baltimore Mus Art, 67. *Bibliog:* Raymond Charmet (auth), Un jeune Americain, Arts Mag, 66; Leach Levy (auth), The drawn line in painting, Parker St 470, 71. *Media:* Tempera. *Dealer:* John Weber Gallery 142 Greene St New York NY 10012. *Mailing Add:* 39 Bond St New York NY 10012

ROSENTHAL, TONY (BERNARD)
SCULPTOR
b Highland Park, Ill, Aug 9, 14. *Study:* Univ Mich, BFA, 36; Cranbrook Acad Art. *Work:* Guggenheim Mus, Mus Mod Art, Whitney Mus Am Art, New York; Israel Mus, Jerusalem; Albright-Knox Art Gallery, Buffalo. *Comn:* Cube, Alamo, New York, 66; large cube, Univ Mich, Ann Arbor, 68; bronze disk, Rondo, New York Pub Libr, 69; Indiana totem, Ind Univ Art Mus, Bloomington, Ind, 71; Police Plaza Sculpture, New York, 74. *Exhib:* Nine Whitney Mus Am Art Ann, 53-72; Recent Sculpture USA, Mus Mod Art, 59; one-man shows, Catherine Viviano, New York, 50-60, Kootz Gallery, New York, 60-66; Knoedler & Co, New York, 66-77; Denise Rene, Paris, 88; Maxwell Davidson, New York, 89. *Awards:* Outstanding Achievement Award, Univ Mich, 67; First Prize, Iron & Steel Inst, 75; Sculpture Award, Am Inst Arts & Letts, 89. *Bibliog:* Gibson Danes (auth), Bernard Rosenthal, Art Int, 68; Sam Hunter (auth), Rosenthal: Sculptures, 68; Edward Albee (auth), Reacting to Rosenthal, Decade, 79. *Dealer:* Andre Emmerich Sculpture Farm Pawling NY. *Mailing Add:* 173 E 73rd St New York NY 10021

ROSENWALD, CAROL
ART DEALER
b New Haven, Conn, Sept 4, 33. *Pos:* Corp art consult, currently. *Specialty:* American, European and Asian 20th century paintings, prints, drawings, sculpture and photographs; framing, installations and corporate exhibitions. *Mailing Add:* 135 E 83rd St New York NY 10028

ROSENZWEIG, DAPHNE LANGE
HISTORIAN, MUSEUM CONSULTANT
b Evanston, Ill, July 7, 41. *Study:* Mt Holyoke Col, AB; Columbia Univ, MA & PhD; Univ Wis; Corcoran Sch Art; Nat Taiwan Univ, spec scholar. *Collections Arranged:* Art of the Orient: Eighth Century to the Present, Univ NMex, 72. *Teaching:* Lectr Oriental art, Univ NMex, Albuquerque, 69-73; asst prof Oriental art, Oberlin Col, 73-77; asst prof, Univ SFla, 78- *Awards:* Fulbright Fel, Repub China, 67-69; Columbia Univ Grant, 69; Mary E Wooley Fel, 70. *Mem:* Japan House; Int House of Japan; Asn Asian Studies; Asia House; China Inst. *Res:* Painting the Ch'ing Dynasty of China, with emphasis on court painting and modern Chinese jades. *Collection:* Chinese paintings, Oriental ceramics; modern Japanese prints. *Publ:* Auth, Landscape Painting by Hsiao Yun-ts'ung, Allen Art Mus Bulletin, 2/74; auth, Court painting and the K'ang-hsi Emperor, Ch'ing Shih Wen t'i, 12/75; auth, Court painting of the K'ang-hsi era: The socioeconomic aspects, Monumenta Serica, 75; auth, Stalking the Persian Dragon: Chinese prototypes for the miniature representations, Kunst des Orients, 80. *Mailing Add:* 5211 Lawnwood Dr Tampa FL 33617

ROSENZWEIG, PHYLLIS D
CURATOR
b Brooklyn, NY, Dec 27, 43. *Study:* Hunter Col, City Univ New York, BA, 64; Inst Fine Arts, New York, 65-69. *Collections Arranged:* The Thomas Eakins Collection (auth, catalog), Hirshhorn Mus & Sculpture Garden, Smithsonian Inst, Washington, DC, 77, Arshile Gorky: The Hirshhorn Museum & Sculpture Garden Collection, 79; The Fifties: Aspects of Painting in New York, 80; Larry Rivers, The Hirshhorn Mus and Sculpture Garden Collection, 81; Directions 1983 & 1986; Content: A Contemporary Focus, 84; Sol Lewitt, 87; Directions: Sherrie Levine, 88; Krzysztof Wodiczko, 88; Daniel Buren Works, 89; Directions, Susana Solano, 89. *Pos:* Curatorial asst, Hirshhorn Mus & Sculpture Garden, 71-78, assoc cur, 78- *Res:* 20th century art. *Mailing Add:* Hirshhorn Mus & Sculpture Garden Smithsonian Inst Washington DC 20560

ROSER, CE (CECILIA)
PAINTER, VIDEO ARTIST
b Philadelphia, Pa. *Study:* Berlin Fine Arts Acad, 52-53. *Work:* Guggenheim Mus, New York; Mus Mod Art, New York; Brooklyn Mus, NY; Nat Mus Art, Washington, DC; The Brit Mus, London, Great Britain; Newark Mus Art, NJ; Bibilotheque Nat, Paris, France; and others. *Exhib:* Int Watercolor Biennial, Brooklyn Mus, 63; Women Choose Women, New York Cult Ctr, 73; Works on Paper/Women Artists, Brooklyn Mus, 75; Art & Poetry, Tweed Mus Art, Duluth, Minn, 77; New Acquisitions, Guggenheim Mus, 82; Am Abstr Artists, Bronx Mus, 86; New Spaces/New Faces, East Hampton Guild Hall Mus, 87; Int traveling show Tikanoja, Rovaniemi & Josensuu Art Museums, Finland, 88; plus many others. *Pos:* Producer & pres, Artists Video Arch, New York, 77- *Bibliog:* Rosemary Daniell (auth), Elegant explosions East and West mingle in Roser act, Atlanta Constitution, Ga, 7/5/67; Lane Dunlop (auth), article, 9/77 & Joan Marter (auth), article, 2/80, Arts Mag; plus others. *Mem:* Founder Women in the Arts (first exec-coordr, 74-76, bd mem at large, 76-78); Women's Caucus for Art; Am Abstr Artists. *Media:* Oil, Watercolor; Collage. *Dealer:* Ingber Gallery 415 West Broadway New York NY 10012. *Mailing Add:* 355 Riverside Dr New York NY 10025

ROSKILL, MARK WENTWORTH
HISTORIAN, CRITIC
b London, Eng, Nov 10, 33. *Study:* Trinity Col, Cambridge (Eng), BA, 56, MA, 61; Harvard Univ, MA, 57; Courtauld Inst, Univ London, 57; Princeton Univ, MFA & PhD, 61. *Teaching:* Instr & asst, Princeton Univ, 59-61; from instr to asst prof, Harvard Univ, 61-68; assoc prof, Univ Mass, Amherst, 68-72, prof, 72- *Awards:* Am Coun Learned Socs Fel, 65-66 & 74-75. *Mem:* Col Art Asn Am. *Res:* Nineteenth & twentieth century art; criticism; history of photography; methodology of art history. *Publ:* Auth, Dolce's Aretino and Venetian Art Theory of the Cinquecento, 68 & Van Gogh, Gauguin and the Impressionist Circle, 70; contribr, Atlantic Brief Lives, 71; auth, What is Art History, 76 & 89; The Interpretation of Cubism, 85; Interpretation of Pictures, 89; Klee, Kandinsky and the Thought of their Time: A Critical Perspective, 92. *Mailing Add:* Dept of Art Univ of Mass Amherst MA 01003

ROSLER, MARTHA (ROSE)
VIDEO ARTIST, CRITIC
b Brooklyn, NY, July 29, 43. *Study:* Brooklyn Mus Art Sch; Brooklyn Col, BA; Univ Calif, San Diego, MFA. *Work:* Canada Coun, Ottawa; Arts Coun Great Britain, London; New England Found Arts; Long Beach Mus Art, Calif; Mus Mod Art, New York. *Exhib:* One-person shows, Long Beach Mus Art, Calif, 77, Whitney Mus Am Art, New York, 77, A-Space, Toronto, 79, Interaction Arts, New York, 80, Dance Theater Workshop, 82 & Installation Gallery, San Diego, 86; Whitney Mus Am Art Biennial, 79 & 83; Issue, Inst Contemp Arts London, 80; 74th Am Exhib, Art Inst Chicago, 82; Documenta 7, Kassel, WGer, 82; Video of the Seventies--The Greatest Hits, Inst Contemp Art, Boston & traveling, 83; New American Video Art: A Historical Survey, Whitney Mus Am Art, New York, 84; Difference: On Representation & Sexuality, 84 & The Art of Memory, the Loss of History, 85, New Mus of Contemp Art, New York. *Teaching:* Instr, San Diego State Univ, 75-76 & Univ Calif San Diego, 75-78; instr photog, Orange Coast Col, Costa Mesa, 77-79; instr film, photog & media, Univ Calif, Irvine, 78-79; vis prof art, Simon Fraser Univ, Vancouver, 80, New York Univ & Cooper Union; asst prof, Rutgers Univ, 80-85, assoc prof, 85-; studio instr, Whitney Independent Study Prog; vis assoc prof, Univ Calif, San Diego, 86. *Awards:* Nat Endowment Arts Fel, 75-77, 80 & 83; Line Artist's Book Grant, 83; NY Found Arts Fel, 85. *Bibliog:* Martha Gever (auth), interview, Afterimage, 10/81; Benjamin Buchloh (auth), Allegorical Procedures: Appropriation & Montange in Contemporary Art, Artforum, 9/82; Moira Roth (auth), Martha Rosler, The Amazing Decade: Women & Performance Art, 83; Craig Owens (auth), The Discourse of Others: Feminism & Postmodernism, The Anti-aesthetic, 83. *Media:* Images & Texts. *Res:* Relationships between representations and power in daily life and in the public sphere. *Publ:* Auth, Service: A triology on colonization, New-Found Career, 78; Martha Rosler: Three Works, NS Col Art & Design Press, 81; Lookers, buyers, dealers, and makers: Thoughts on audience, Art After Modernism, New York, 85; Shedding the Utopian Moment (video), Block, 86. *Mailing Add:* Rutgers Univ New Brunswick NJ 08903

ROSS, CHARLES
ENVIRONMENTAL ARTIST, SCULPTOR
b Philadelphia, Pa, Dec 17, 37. *Study:* Univ Calif, AB, 60, MA, 62. *Work:* Whitney Mus Am Art; Univ Art Gallery, Berkeley, Calif; Indianapolis Mus Art; Walker Art Ctr, Minneapolis; Los Angeles Co Mus Art, Calif; and others. *Comn:* Prism & Spectrum, Fed Bldg, Lincoln, Nebr; Spectrum Bldg, Denver; Cumberland Sta, Chicago; Solar Spectrum, Harvard Bus Sch Chapel; Year of Solar Burns, Chateau D'Oiron, France; and others. *Exhib:* Venice Biennale, Italy; Inst Contemp Art, Philadelphia; Renwick Gallery, Smithsonian, Washington, DC; Stadtizches Mus, W Ger; Centre Georges Pompidou, Paris, 77; Albright Knox, Buffalo; Hirshhorn Mus, Washington, DC; Mus Contemp Art, Chicago; Yale Univ Art Gallery; Stadtisches Mus, WGer; Mus Fine Arts, Boston. *Teaching:* Assoc prof, Cornell Univ, 64; instr, Univ Calif, 65, Sch Visual Arts, New York, 67, 70 & 71 & Herbert Lehman Col, 68. *Awards:* Am Inst Graphic Arts Award, 76; and others. *Bibliog:* Donald Kuspit (auth), Light's measure, Art in Am, 3-4/78; Katharine Chafee & Steve Katz (auths), article, Artspace, fall 81; Eleanor Munro (auth), Art in the desert, New York Times, 12/7/86. *Publ:* Auth, Sunlight Convergence-Solar Burn, Univ Utah Press, 76. *Dealer:* Joyce Schwartz Ltd 17 West 54th St New York NY 10019. *Mailing Add:* 383 W Broadway New York NY 10012

ROSS, CLIFFORD
PAINTER
b New York, NY, Oct 15, 52. *Study:* Skowhegan Sch, 73; Yale Univ, BA(A Conger Goodyear Fine Arts Award), 74; Nat Acad Design, 81. *Work:* Metrop Mus Art, New York; Yale Univ Art Gallery; Corcoran Gallery Art, Washington, DC; Albright-Knox Mus, Buffalo, NY; J P Speed Art Mus, Louisville, Ky. *Exhib:* Award Winners, Am Acad & Inst Art & Lett, New York, 78; Figuratively Sculpting, Inst Art & Urban Resources, New York, 81; Corcoran Gallery Art, Washington, DC, 88; The 1980s: A New Generation, Metrop Mus Art, New York, 88; Big/Little Sculpture, Williams Col Mus, Mass, 88. *Awards:* Rosenthal Award for Young Am Painter of Distinction, Am Acad & Inst Arts & Lett, 78. *Bibliog:* Connie Rogers (auth), article, Arts Mag, 1/79; Paul Goldberger (auth), article, Art in Am, 7/79. *Media:* Oil on Panel. *Publ:* Abstract Expressionism: Creators and Critics, Abrams, 91. *Dealer:* Salander/O'Reilly Galleries 20 E 79th St New York NY 10021. *Mailing Add:* 832 Broadway New York NY 10003

ROSS, CONRAD H
PAINTER, PRINTMAKER
b Chicago, Ill, Apr 26, 31. *Study:* Univ Ill, BFA, 53; Univ Chicago, 54; Univ Iowa, MFA, 59; Masereel Ctr Graphic Arts, Kasterlee, Belgium, 88. *Work:* Libr Cong, Washington, DC; Springfield Art Mus, Mo; Norfolk Mus Arts & Sci, Va; Dallas Mus Fine Arts, Tex; Macon Mus Arts & Sci, Ga. *Exhib:* 1973 Artists Biennial, New Orleans Mus Art, La; one-man show, Augusta Col, Ga, 79; Southeastern Graphics Invitational, 81; Prints, Mint Mus, Charlotte, NC; Washington & Lee Univ, Va, 81; Art Dept Gallery, Jacksonville State Univ, Ala, 85; Exhib US-UK Print Connection, An Int Exchange, Los Angeles Printmakers Soc & Printmakers Coun of Great Brit, 88-89; Artsplosure, Raleigh, NC, 89; Artist Selects, Comer Art Mus, Sylacauga, Ala, 89. *Pos:* Bd dirs, Southeastern Col Art Conf, 79-82; publ, Wycross Press, 89- *Teaching:* Instr drawing, design, lettering & art appreciation, La Polytech Inst, 61-63; asst prof drawing & printmaking, Auburn Univ, 63-81, assoc prof, 81-83, prof, 83-; vis lectr drawing & printmaking, Kans Univ, 68; instr, Arrowmont Sch Arts & Crafts, Gatlinburg, Tenn, 83; artist-in-residence, Univ Ga Summer Abroad Prog, Cortona, Italy, 84. *Awards:* Louis Comfort Tiffany Found Grant printmaking, 60; Auburn Univ Res Grant-in-Aid, 65-68, 70 & 73;

Purchase Award, LaGrange Nat II, Prints and Drawings, Ga, 75. *Mem:* Ala Art League (pres, 78-80); Artist Equity Asn; Col Art Asn Am; Nat Art Workers Community; Southeastern Graphics Coun (vpres, 78-80). *Media:* Watercolor; Etching. *Publ:* Contribr, Artists' proof the annual of prints and printmaking, 70; The monoprint and the monotype: a case of semantics, Art Voices/South, 7-8/79; Approaches to Drawing: Activity in the Southeast, SECAC Rev, 81. *Mailing Add:* Dept Art Auburn Univ Auburn AL 36849

ROSS, DAVID ANTHONY
CURATOR, LECTURER
b New York, NY, Apr 26, 49. *Study:* Syracuse Univ, BS, 71. *Collections Arranged:* Traveling exhib, Circuit: A Video Invitational (survey of video art, 68-72), 72-74; Southland Video Anthology (survey of video art in Southern Calif, 68-75, with catalog), Long Beach Mus Art, 75. *Pos:* Asst dir, Everson Mus Art, Syracuse, 71-72, cur video arts, 71-74; deputy dir TV & film, Long Beach Mus Art, 74-77; chief cur, Univ Art Mus, Univ Calif, Berkeley, 77-; dir, Sam Rayburn House, Bonham, Tex, currently; dir, Boston Inst Contemp Art, currently. *Teaching:* Lectr video performance, San Francisco Art Inst, formerly; lectr video art, Grad Sch, Univ Calif, San Diego, 74-82. *Awards:* John D Rockefeller III Found Res Study Grant, 74. *Mem:* Am Asn Mus; Advocates for Arts. *Res:* Relationship between development of new art and context that supports art in American society and development of new support structures. *Publ:* Coauth, Douglas Davis: Videotapes, Manifestos, Drawings and Objects, 72; coauth, Frank Gillette: Video Process & Metaprocess, 73; coauth, Nam June Paik: Video & Videology, 74; coauth, Peter Campus: Video Works, 74; auth, Southland Video Anthology, 75 & 76-77. *Mailing Add:* Whitney Mus Am Art 945 Madison Ave New York NY 10021

ROSS, DOUGLAS ALLAN
SCULPTOR, INSTRUCTOR
b Los Angeles, Calif, Jan 23, 37. *Study:* Carleton Col, BA, 59; Minneapolis Col Art & Design, 59-61; Univ Minn, MFA, 65. *Work:* Northrup Gallery, Univ Minn, Minneapolis; Ill State Univ, Normal; Sheldon Art Gallery, Lincoln, Nebr; Prudential-Bache Securities, New York; McDonalds Corp, Chicago, Ill. *Exhib:* Okla State Univ, Stillwater, 88; 20th Ann Joslyn Biennial, Joslyn Art Mus, Omaha, Nebr, 88; Central Time Zone Sculpture Exhib, Nebr Weslyan Univ, Lincoln, 89; 6th Ann Exhib, Kansas City Artists Coalition, Mo, 89; 60th Ann Exhib, Art Asn Harrisburg, Pa, 89; 12th Ann Art Exhib, Milford Fine Arts Coun, Conn, 89; Chicago Int New Art Forms, Navy Pier, Chicago, 89; Sculpture Now, Spokane Ctr Gallery, Wash, 89; solo exhibs, Drury Col, Springfield, Mo, 90, Eastern Mont Col, Billings, 90, MC Gallery, Minneapolis, Minn, 90 & Ralston Fine Arts, Johnson City, Tenn, 91. *Collections Arranged:* First Great Plains sculpture Exhib, Sheldon Mem Art Gallery, Lincoln, Nebr, 75; Drawings by Sculptors, SW Mo State Univ, 75 & Syracuse Univ, NY, 76; Second Ann Great Plains Sculpture Exhib, Sheldon Mem Art Gallery, 76; Nebr Alumni, Nebr Mus Fine Arts, 76. *Teaching:* From asst prof to assoc prof sculpture/drawing, Univ Nebr, Lincoln, 66-79, prof, 79-; lectr grade II sculpture, Manchester Polytech, Eng, 69-70. *Awards:* Juror's Award, NJ Ctr Arts, 90; First Prize, Greater Midwest Int III, Warrensburg, Mo, 90; Purchase Award, One-man Show, Muhlenberg Col, 76. *Mem:* Mid-Am Col Art Asn (prog dir & exhib dir, 75-76). *Media:* Mixed. *Dealer:* MC Gallery Minneapolis MN; Anderson-O'Brien Gallery Omaha NE. *Mailing Add:* Dept Art Univ Nebraska Lincoln NE 68583

ROSS, GLORIA F(RANKENTHALER)
TAPESTRY ARTIST
b New York, NY, Sept 5, 23. *Study:* Mt Holyoke Col, Mass, BA, 43; Art Students League, New York, 57-60. *Work:* Denver Art Mus; Int Bank for Reconstruction & Development, Washington, DC; Int Business Machines Corp Hq, Armonk, NY; Kennedy Int Airport, New York; Storm King Art Ctr, Mountainville, NY; Bank of Tokyo, New York; Citibank, NY; Windows on the World; Exec Off, Port Authority of NY & NJ. *Comn:* Tapestry in collaboration with Jack Youngerman, Skidmore Owings Merrill, Upper Ave Nat Bank, Chicago, 70; Robert Motherwell, Westinghhouse Broadcasting Co, Philadelphia, 71; Helen Frankenthaler, Westinghouse Broadcasting Co, Philadelphia, 71 & Winters Bank, Dayton, Ohio, 71. *Exhib:* Tapestries & Rugs by Contemp Painters & Sculptors, Mus Mod Art, New York, 65; Art Market, Kolner Kunstmarkt, Cologne, Ger, 71; Fiber Structures, Denver Art Mus, 72; Beyond the Artists' Hand, Calif State Univ, Long Beach, 76; Tapestries, Jacksonville Art Mus, Fla, 77; Int Biennial, Switz, 77; solo exhibs, Ringling Mus Art, Sarasota, 78 & Mt Holyoke Col Art Mus, Mass, 79; Gallery 10, New York & Scottsdale, Ariz, 84; 50 Years of Contemporary Tapestry, Montreux, Switz, 85; Edinburgh-Dublin Exhib, Scotland, 85. *Collections Arranged:* Gloria F Ross Tapestries, Feigen Galleries, New York & Chicago, 68-69 & 71, Pace Gallery, New York, 73, 75 & 78; Gloria F Ross/Nevelson Tapestries, Pace Gallery, New York, 78. *Pos:* Lectr, Fashion Inst Technol, New Sch Social Research, Pace Edition, Harvard Bus Sch Clubs, NY, Gallery 10, Scottsdale, Ariz, Mt Holyoke Col, South Hadley, Mass, Ringling Mus, Sarasota, Fla & SW Weaving, Santa Fe, NMex. *Bibliog:* Articles in, Archit Digest, 5/78 & Metropolis, 4/85. *Mem:* Am Fedn Arts; Textile Mus; Mt Holyoke Col Art Mus Coun; Am Crafts Coun. *Media:* Flat Tapestry Weave high & low warp, Tufted Weave hooked & handknotted. *Mailing Add:* 21 E 87th St New York NY 10128

ROSS, JAIME
GRAPHIC ARTIST, PAINTER
b New Haven, Conn, Aug 14, 46. *Study:* Princeton Univ; Univ Colo, BA, 69, MFA, 71, studied with Roland Reiss and George Woodman. *Work:* Oslo Fine Arts Mus, Norway; Alvord Mus Fine Art, Portugal; Univ Colo, Boulder; Los Angeles Inst Contemp Art. *Comn:* Billboard, ABC Records, Los Angeles, 76; mural, Fiat, Milan, 78; distributional sculpture, Alvord Inst, Oporto, Portugal, 84; mural, Santa Fe Pub Schs, 85 & NMex Arts Comn, Ojo Caliente, NMex, 86. *Exhib:* Wit and Whimsey, Cambridge Mus Fine Arts, Eng, 77; Small Wonders, Univ BC, Vancouver, 81; Contemporary Cartoons, Lisbon Fine Arts Mus, Portugal, 84; Western States Biennial, Fine Arts Mus NMex, Santa Fe, 82; Color, Oslo Fine Arts Mus, Norway, 83. *Pos:* Artist-in-residence, NMex Arts Comn, 85-86; painter, designer & illusr for various ad agencies, animation studios & mags, Los Angeles, 76-78. *Teaching:* Instr painting & drawing, Univ Ill, 71-72; instr painting, Univ Colo, 75. *Media:* All. *Dealer:* Copeland-Rutherford 403 Canyon Rd Santa Fe NM 87501. *Mailing Add:* Catchwater Farm PO Box 40 Carson NM 87517

ROSS, JANICE KOENIG
PAINTER, INSTRUCTOR
b Harrisburg, Pa, 26. *Study:* Pa State Univ, BA, 47; Univ Ill, MFA, 54; Fulbright-Hays seminar, Pakistan, summer 86. *Work:* Ala Power Co, Auburn Univ; and many corp collections. *Comn:* Numerous pvt portrait comns. *Exhib:* solo exhibs, Ga Inst Technol Student Ctr Gallery, 80 & Chattahoochee Valley Art Asn Gallery, 83; Armory Gallery, Montgomery, Ala, 88; The Human Figure, Arts Festival of Atlanta, 89; Hearthstones I, Space One Eleven, Birmingham, Ala, 91; Patchwork of Many Lives, Huntsville Mus Art, 92; and other regional & nat exhibs. *Pos:* Artist-in-Residence, Art Studios Abroad Prog, Univ Ga, 84. *Teaching:* Prof art, Tuskegee Univ, Ala, 68-91. *Awards:* Nat Endowment Humanities Fel, 81-82; Fulbright-Hays Fel, Pakistan, 86. *Mem:* Col Art Asn; Women's Caucus Art (nat adv bd, 88-91); founder Studio 218; Southeastern Women's Caucus Art (mem secy-treas, 78-80); and others. *Media:* Oil, Pastel. *Publ:* Auth, MFA Survey, Col Art Asn, fall 78; Eight from Auburn, Art Voices South, 1-2/80; Agnes Bradley Taugner profile, Artcraft, 2-3/80. *Dealer:* Portrait Representatives Ltd 6305 Falls Rd Baltimore MD 21209. *Mailing Add:* 447 Wrights's Mill Rd Auburn AL 36830

ROSS, JOAN M
PAINTER, INSTRUCTOR
b Brooklyn, NY, Apr 23, 31. *Study:* St Joseph's Col, Brooklyn, NY, BA, 53; St Elizabeth's Col, Convent Station, NJ(continuing educ), 80-84; studied with Betty Lou Schlemm & Robert Laessig, art Workshops 84-85. *Work:* Highland Lakes Country Club, NJ; Lakeland State Bank, Sparta, NJ, 91. *Comn:* Watercolor-landscapes, Pope John High Sch, Sparta, NJ, 80-84; watercolor-landscapes, J Kane, Hygrade Corp, Philadelphia, Pa, 80; watercolor-landscapes, Midlantic Bank, Newton, NJ, 80; watercolor-landscapes, comn by Mr & Mrs John Reeth II, Highland Lakes, NJ, 89-91; watercolor-landscapes, comn by Senator & Mrs Robert E Littell, Franklin, NJ, 91; and others. *Exhib:* NE Watercolor Soc, Hall of Fame, Goshen, NY, 76-92; Salmagundi Club Ann, New York, 85-92; Am Artists Prof League, Ridgewood Art Asn, NJ, 86-92; Essex Watercolor Club, Bloomfield Civic Ctr, NJ, 86-92; Composers, Authors & Artists Am, Nat Arts Club, New York, 86-92. *Pos:* Treas, vpres & chmn adv bd, Sussex Co Arts Coun, 77-92; pres, Vernon Township Cultural Soc, 80-82; pres, Northeast Watercolor Soc, 86-90. *Teaching:* Chmn & vprincipal dept art & sci, Immaculate Conception Regional Sch, 68-90; instr art & watercolors, Highland Lakes Country Club, NJ, 80-92. *Awards:* First Watercolor Award Composers, Auth, Artists Am, 86, 88; Margaret Pedersen Award, NE Watercolor Soc, 88 & 90; John Pike Mem Award, NE Watercolor Soc, 91. *Bibliog:* Mark Fitzgibbon (auth), Immortalizing Vernon, Vernon News, 3/86; Jim Cordes Beacon (auth), Recording a vanishing scene, NJ Herald, 8/86; Maura Rossi (auth), Beauty around her, The Beacon, Patterson, NJ, 86. *Mem:* Am Artist Prof League; Salmagundi Club; Essex Watercolor Club; Composers, Authors & Artists Am; Northeast Watercolor Soc (vpres, 83-86, pres, 86-88). *Media:* Watercolor. *Dealer:* Cardinal Art Gallery PO Box 1189 Vernon NJ 07462. *Mailing Add:* RR1 Box 94 Highland Lakes NJ 07422

ROSS, JOHN T
PRINTMAKER, EDUCATOR
b New York, NY, Sept 25, 21. *Study:* Cooper Union Art Sch, with Morris Kantor & Will Barnet, BFA; New Sch Social Res, with Antonio Frasconi & Louis Schanker; Columbia Univ, 53. *Work:* Libr Cong, Hirshhorn Mus & Nat Collection Fine Arts, Washington, DC; Metrop Mus Art, New York; Cincinnati Art Mus. *Comn:* Ed prints, Hilton Hotel, 63, Assoc Am Artists, 64, 66 & 72, Philadelphia Print Club, 67, NY State Coun Arts, 67 & Int Poetry Forum, 68. *Exhib:* Second Int Color Print Exhib, Grenchen, Switz, 61; Int Biennale Gravure, Cracow, Poland, 68; Prize-winning Am Prints, Pratt Graphic Art Ctr, New York, 68; Nat Acad Fine Arts, Amsterdam, Neth, 68; Biennial Print Exhib, Calif State Col, Long Beach, 69; and others. *Pos:* Dir, Art Ctr Northern NJ, 66-67; pres, US Comt-Int Asn Art, 67-69. *Teaching:* Instr printmaking, New Sch Social Res, 57-; instr printmaking, Pratt Graphic Ctr, 63-; prof art, Manhattanville Col, 64-; demonstr & lectr, US Info Agency Exhib, Romania & Yugoslavia, 64-66. *Awards:* Louis Comfort Tiffany Found Grant Printmaking, 54; Purchase Prize for 100 Prints of the Year, AAA Gallery, 63; citation for prof achievement, Cooper Union Art Sch, 66. *Bibliog:* Articles, Am Artist, 52-81, Artists Proof, 64 & Art in Am, 65. *Mem:* Soc Am Graphic Artists (pres, 61-65, exec coun, 65-); assoc Nat Acad Design; Boston Printmakers; Philadelphia Print Club; Am Color Print Soc. *Publ:* Illusr, many bks; coauth, The Complete Printmaker, 72 & The Complete Collagraph, 80, Macmillan. *Dealer:* Assoc Am Artists 663 Fifth Ave New York NY 10022. *Mailing Add:* Dept Art New Sch Social Res 66 W 12th St New York NY 10011

ROSS, RHODA HONORE
PAINTER, INSTRUCTOR
b Boston, Mass, Dec 24, 41. *Study:* Carnegie-Mellon Univ, 60-62; RI Sch Design, BFA, 64; Yale Univ, with Jack Tworkov, Al Held, Lester Johnson & Bernard Chaet, MFA, 66; Skowhegan Sch Painting & Sculpture, 86. *Work:* Mus City New York; The White House, Washington, DC; Julliard Sch, Chemical Bank, & Can Imperial Bank of Commerce, New York. *Comn:* Paintings, Russian Tea Room, New York, 82; paintings, Smith Barney, Harris, Upham & Co, New York, 84; Waldorf Astoria Hotel, New York, 84; paintings, First Deposit Corp, San Francisco, Calif, 85; portrait, retiring pres, Lehman Col, New York 90. *Exhib:* Watercolor USA, Springfield Art Mus, Mo, 83; The Subway Show, Lehman Col Art Gallery, New York, 85; Art in the Garden, Cape Mus Fine Arts, Dennis, Mass, 88; Nat Asn Women, Pace Univ Art Gallery, New York 88-89; Artists traveling exhib, Nicolasen Art Mus, Wyo, Lewiston Art Ctr, Mont, Jesse Besser Mus, Mich & S Roper Gallery, Md; Am Univ, Washington, DC, 90; NY Studio Sch, NY, 91. *Pos:* Treas, RI Sch Design Alumni Exec Comt, 86-90; juror, Nat Asn Women Artists, 88-90. *Teaching:* Instr collage, Hebrew Arts School, New York, 87- *Awards:* First Prize, Mademoiselle Mag, 65; Susan B Whedon Prize, Yale Univ, 65-66; Grumbacher Gold Medal, Nat Asn Women Artists, 85. *Mem:* Nat Asn Women Artists; Artists Equity; Womens Caucus Art. *Media:* Oil. *Mailing Add:* 473 W End Ave No 7B New York NY 10024

ROSS, SHELDON
ART DEALER, GALLERY DIRECTOR
b Detroit, Mich, Sep 26, 25. *Pos:* Owner, Sheldon Ross Gallery, Detroit, currently. *Mem:* Detroit Art Dealers Asn (treas, 81-). *Specialty:* German Expressionism including: Max Beckmann, Otto Dix, Lyonel Feininger, George Grosz, Erich Heckel, Ernst Ludwig Kirchner; 20th Century American Realism including: Romare Bearden, Charles Burchfield, Edward Hopper, Reginald Marsh. *Mailing Add:* 250 Martin St Birmingham MI 48009

ROSS, SUEELLEN
PRINTMAKER, PAINTER
b Oakland, Calif, July 12, 41. *Study:* Univ Calif, Berkeley, BA, 65, MA, 69, Sch Visual Arts, New York, NY, 78-79. *Work:* Dyptich of Quail, etchings, Leigh Yawkey Woodson Art Mus. *Comn:* Study of quail, etching, Sequim Pub Libr, Sequim, Wash, 83; heron tryptich, etching, Rainier Bank, Seattle, Wash, 84; tryptich, mixed media, Dean Whitter Reynolds, Wayzata, Minn, 84; tryptich, mixed media, Alaska Pac Bank, Anchorage, Alaska, 85; bittern in reeds, Safeco Insurance Co, Seattle, Wash, 86. *Exhib:* Survival to Sport, Whatcom Mus Hist & Art, Bellingham, Wash, 86; solo exhib, Animal Paintings, Frye Art Mus, Seattle, Wash, 86; Birds in Art, Leigh Yawkey Woodson Art Mus, Wausau, Wis, 87, 89, 91-92; Arts for the Parks, 92; Naturally Drawn, Leigh Yawkey Woodson Art Mus, Wausau, Wis, 92. *Awards:* Region I Winner, poster, Arts for the Parks, 91. *Bibliog:* Les Krentz (auth), American Artists, an illustrated survey, 90; Judy D Hughes (auth), How liberal are the arts, Wildlife Art News, 89; M Stephen Doherty (auth), The American artist collection 1990 selection, Am Artist Mag, 9/90; Artists vignette, Wildlife Art News, 11-12/92. *Media:* Hand Colored Etchings; Mixed Media. *Dealer:* Mill Pond Press Inc 310 Ctr Court Venice Fla 33505; Howard/Mandville Gallery 120 W Dayton Suite D9 Edmonde WA 98020. *Mailing Add:* 1909 SW Myrtle Seattle WA 98106

ROSSE, MARYVONNE
SCULPTOR, MEDALIST
b Palo Alto, Calif, Mar 4, 17. *Study:* Acad Fine Arts, The Hague, Neth, dipl. *Work:* Mus Holland, Mich. *Comn:* Plaques, J Bos, Neth, 38; medals, Koninklyk Begeer, Neth, 38; portraits, D Tutein Noltenius, Neth, 42; garden ornaments, Nederlandshe Olie Fabriek, Delft, Neth, 46; commercial prototypes, D G Williams Inc, Brooklyn, 48-66; Relig images, Our Lady of Grace Church, Howard Beach, NY, 84. *Exhib:* Pulchri Studios, The Hague, 36-47; New York World's Fair, 39; Pen & Brush Club, 67-80; Catharine Lorillard Wolfe Art Club, 67-80; Nat Sculpture Soc, 67-88. *Pos:* Sculpture, D G Williams, Brooklyn, NY, 48-66; ed news lett, Catharine Lorillard Wolfe Art Club, 68-72. *Teaching:* Instr sculpture, Rockland Found, Nyack, NY, 47; instr art, King Coit Theatre Sch Children, New York, 47-48. *Awards:* Pen & Brush Solo Exhib Award, 71; Gold Medal, Catharine Lorillard Wolfe Art Club Ann, 72; Tallix Award, Nat Sculpture Soc, 78. *Mem:* Nat Sculpture Soc; Pen & Brush Club (sculpture chmn, 69-72); Burr Artists (historian, 68-70); Catharine Lorillard Wolfe Art Club (bd mem, 69-73, sculpture chmn, 69-72); Am Medallic Sculpture Asn (secy, 82-88). *Media:* Clay, Plaster; Wood, Bronze. *Mailing Add:* 431 Buena Vista Rd New City NY 10956

ROSSEN, SUSAN F
HISTORIAN, EDITOR
Study: Smith Col, AB(art hist), 63; Univ of Mich, Wayne State Univ, MA(art hist), 71. *Pos:* Asst cur of educ, Detroit Inst of Arts, 64-68, assoc cur European art, 71-72, sr ed & coordr of publ, Detroit Inst of Arts, 72-81; exec dir publs, Art Inst Chicago, 81- *Teaching:* Lectr 19th century art, Univ of Detroit, 71. *Awards:* Am Art Mus Asn; Art Mus Asn, Chicago Book Clinic. *Mem:* Am Asn of Mus; Mus Publ of Am; Women's Caucus for Art, Col Art Asn; Chicago Women in Publ. *Res:* Nineteenth and twentieth century art and women artists, women as patrons of the arts. *Publ:* Ed, Henri Matisse Paper Cut-Outs, 77; The Golden Age of Naples: Art and Civilization Under the Bourbons 1734-1805, 81; The Crest Eastern Temple: Treasures of Japanese Buddhist Art from Todai-gi; ed, The Photography of Coustau Le Cray; auth, Primer for seeing: The Gallery of Art Interpretation of Katharine Kuhs Crusade for Modernism in Chicago, Art Inst Chicago Mus Studios, Vol 16, No 1,90. *Mailing Add:* Art Inst Chicago Michigan Ave & Adams St Chicago IL 60603

ROSSI, BARBARA
PAINTER, PRINTMAKER
b Chicago, Ill. *Study:* Art Inst Chicago, MFA. *Work:* Fogg Mus; Baltimore Mus Art, Md; Nat Collection of Fine Arts, Washington, DC; Mus des 20, Jahrhunderts, Vienna; Art Inst Chicago. *Exhib:* What They're Up To In Chicago, Nat Gallery Can, Ottawa, 72; Directions, Hirshhorn Mus & Sculpture Garden, Washington, DC, 79; one-woman shows, Phyllis Kind Gallery, Chicago, 75, 76 & 80, New York, 78 & Inst Contemp Art, Boston, 80-82; and others. *Teaching:* Vis artist, Art Inst Chicago, 71- *Awards:* Nat Endowment Arts Artist's Fel, 73; Mr & Mrs Frank Armstrong Prize, 74th Artists of Chicago & Vicinity Exhib, Art Inst Chicago, 73; Vielher Award, 78th Artists of Chicago & Vicinity Exhib, Art Inst Chicago, 80. *Mailing Add:* c/o Phyllis Kind Gallery 313 W Superior Chicago IL 60610

ROSSI, JOSEPH O
PAINTER, INSTRUCTOR
b Paterson, NJ. *Study:* Newark Sch Fine & Indust Art; Grand Cent Art Sch; Columbia Univ; private study with John R Grabach, Harvey Dunn & Edgar A Whitney. *Work:* Salmagundi Club Collection; Norfolk Mus, Va; Bergen Mall Collection & Bergen Community Mus, Paramus, NJ; Newark Hospital Collection. *Exhib:* Am Watercolor Soc Ann, Nat Acad Design, New York, 79, Allied Artists Ann, 79 & Audubon Artist Ann, 79; Selected Am Watercolor Soc, Royal Acad, London; Rockport Art Asn, Mass, 79. *Teaching:* Instr watercolor, oil & life drawing, Newark Sch Fine & Indust Art; instr watercolor, Art Students League, New York. *Awards:* Malcolm Tuttle Award, Salmagundi Watercolor Exhib, 74; NJ Watercolor Award, 78; Lena Newcastle Award, Am Watercolor Soc, 79. *Mem:* Am Watercolor Soc; NJ Watercolor Soc; Allied Artists Am; Audubon Artists; Salmagundi Club; Soc Illusrs. *Media:* Watercolor, Oil. *Publ:* Auth, Watercolor Page, Am Artist Mag, 8/72. *Dealer:* Grand Cent Galleries New York NY 10017. *Mailing Add:* Art Students League 215 W 57th St New York NY 10019

ROSSMAN, MICHAEL
PAINTER
b Chambersburg, Pa, Apr 4, 41. *Study:* Pratt Inst, Brooklyn, BID, 63 & MFA(sculpture). *Exhib:* Artists Choose Artists, Inst Contemp Art & More Gallery, Philadelphia, 91. *Teaching:* Prof, Univ Arts, Philadelphia, 66- *Awards:* Nat Endowment Art Fel, 91. *Media:* Graphite Paper. *Dealer:* More Gallery Inc 1630 Walnut St Philadelphia PA 19103. *Mailing Add:* 819 N 21st St Philadelphia PA 19130

ROSSMAN, RUTH SCHARFF
PAINTER, INSTRUCTOR
b Brooklyn, NY. *Study:* Cleveland Inst Art; Case-Western Reserve Univ, BS; Kahn Inst Art; Univ Calif, Los Angeles; also with Sueo Serisawa & Rico Lebrun. *Work:* Pa Acad Fine Arts; Univ Redlands; Nat Watercolor Soc; Brandeis Inst; Ahmanson Collection, Calif; plus others. *Exhib:* Recent Paintings USA: Figure, Mus Mod Art, New York, 61; one-woman shows, Heritage Gallery, Los Angeles, 63, 66 & Univ Judaism, Los Angeles, 79 & 86; Los Angeles Mus Sci & Indust, 78; Crescent Gallery, New Orleans, 77, 78; Rocky Mountain Nat, Colo, 77 & 81; Denver Art Mus; and others. *Teaching:* Teacher art, Pub Sch Syst, Canton; teacher art, Canton Art Inst; instr, Arts & Crafts Ctr, Los Angeles. *Awards:* Purchase Award, Pa Acad Fine Arts, 65; All-City Ann Purchase Awards, Los Angeles, 65 & 69; Rocky Mountain Nat, 77; plus others. *Bibliog:* William Wilson & Henry Seldis (auths), articles, Los Angeles Times, 63 & 6/66; States Item, Times-Picayune World Art, New Orleans, 12/77; Robert Perine (auth), The California Romantics - Harbingers of Watercolorism, Artra Publ Inc, 86. *Mem:* Nat Watercolor Soc (secy, 73-74, 1st vpres, 74-75, pres, 75-76). *Media:* Acrylic, Oil. *Mailing Add:* 401 Cascada Way Los Angeles CA 90049

ROSTER, FRED HOWARD
SCULPTOR, EDUCATOR
b Palo Alto, Calif, June 27, 44. *Study:* Gavilan Col, AA; San Jose State Col, BA & MA; Univ Hawaii, MFA & with Herbert H Sanders. *Work:* Honolulu Acad Art, Hawaii; State Found Cult & Arts, Honolulu; Contemp Arts Ctr Hawaii; Hawaii Loa Col, Kailua; St Francis Hosp, Honolulu. *Comn:* Sand cast mural, Ft Derussy, 75; bronze bust of former Gov John Burns, State Found Cult & The Arts; Kekuanaoa bronze portrait, 79; bronze & stainless steel mural, Physical Educ Facility, Univ Hawaii, Manoa, 82; bronze, stone & stainless steel sculpture, Honolulu Int Airport, 83. *Exhib:* Artists of Hawaii Ann, Honolulu Acad Art, 75-76, 79 & 81; Hawaii Craftsmen's Ann, Honolulu, 69-72 & 75-80; one-man shows, Contemp Arts Ctr Hawaii, 72, Gima's Art Gallery, Honolulu, 75 & 78 & Corpus Christi Univ, Tex, 80. *Teaching:* Instr ceramics, San Jose State Col, 68-69; asst prof sculpture, Univ Hawaii, 69-78, assoc prof, 78- *Awards:* Elizabeth Moses Award, San Francisco Potter's Asn, 68; Sculptural Grant Award, Windward Artists Guild, 71; Hawaii Craftsman Award, 74. *Mem:* Honolulu Acad Art. *Media:* Mixed. *Mailing Add:* Dept Art-123 Univ Hawaii 2500 Campus Rd Honolulu HI 96822

ROTAN, WALTER
SCULPTOR
b Baltimore, Md, Mar 29, 12. *Study:* Md Inst; Pa Acad Fine Arts; also with Albert Laessie. *Work:* Pa Acad Fine Arts; Brookgreen Gardens, SC. *Exhib:* Nat Acad Design; Pa Acad Fine Arts; Art Inst Chicago; Philadelphia Mus Art; Carnegie Inst Art, Pittsburg, Pa; Metropolitan Art Mus, New York, NY. *Teaching:* Head art dept, Taft Sch, Watertown, Conn, 38-53. *Awards:* Cresson Traveling Scholar, 33 & Prize, 46, Pa Acad Fine Arts; four Prizes, Nat Acad Design, 36-45; Prize, Allied Artists Am, 56; Tiffany Found Fel; Penna Acad Fel Prize; and others. *Mem:* Fel Nat Sculpture Soc; Audubon Artists; fel Pa Acad Fine Arts. *Mailing Add:* 45 Christopher St New York NY 10014

ROTENBERG, JUDI
PAINTER, GALLERY DIRECTOR
b Boston, Mass. *Study:* Boston Univ, BFA; studied privately in Paris, Mex & Israel. *Exhib:* Le Salon 80, Soc des Artistes Francais, Paris, 80. *Pos:* Dir, Judi Rotenberg Gallery, Boston & Square Circle Gallery, Rockport, Mass. *Media:* Acrylic, Watercolor. *Specialty:* 20th century American art. *Mailing Add:* Judi Rotenberg Gallery 130 Newberry St Boston MA 02116

ROTH, DAVID
PAINTER
b New York, NY, June 7, 42. *Study:* Ill Inst Technol, study with Harry Callahan & Aaron Siskind. *Work:* Albright-Knox Gallery, Buffalo; Ball State Univ, Ind; Mus Contemp Art, Tehran, Iran; Philadelphia Mus Art; Rockefeller Inst, New York; Brooklyn Mus Art; Newark Mus Art. *Comn:* Johnson & Johnson; Smith-Kline; Chase Manhattan Bank; Swiss Investment Bank; Lehman Brothers; Hess Oil; Amstar Corp. *Exhib:* Thirty-second Ann for Soc Contemp Art, Art Inst Chicago, 72; Painting or Sculpture?, Newark Mus, 72; 8th Nat Print Exhib, Brooklyn Mus, 72; Small Works-Selections from Richard Brown Baker Collection, Mus Art RI Sch Design, 73; Contemp Am Artist, Cleveland Mus Art, 74; Painting & Sculpture Today, Indianapolis Mus Art, 74 & 76; Bradford Col, 88. *Bibliog:* Marcia Hafif (auth), A fusion of real & pictorial space, Arts Mag, 3/72; Tom Hinson (auth), Contemporary American Artists, Cleveland Mus Art, 73; Carter Ratcliff (auth), NY Letter, Art Int, summer 73. *Media:* Liquitex, Acrylic on String, & Canvas. *Dealer:* Elkon Gallery 18 E 81st St New York NY 10028. *Mailing Add:* PO Box 731 Newtown PA 18940

ROTH, FRANK
PAINTER
b Boston, Mass, Feb 22, 36. *Study:* Cooper Union, 54; Hofmann Sch, 55. *Work:* Albright-Knox Art Gallery, Buffalo, NY; Whitney Mus Am Art, Metrop Mus Art, Mus Mod Art, New York, NY; Santa Barbara Mus Art, Calif; Baltimore Mus Art; Walker Art Ctr, Minneapolis; Tate Gallery, London, Eng; David Rockefeller Collection, New York; and others. *Exhib:* Va Mus Fine Arts, Richmond, 70; Indianapolis Mus Art, Ind, 70; Amherst Col, 72; Contemp Am Painting, Lehigh Univ, 72; Finch Col Mus Art, New York, 73; Louise Himmelfarb Gallery, Bridgehampton, NY 77 & 78; one person exhibs, Martha Jackson Gallery, New York, 67, 68, 70 & 71, Gimpel & Weitzenhoffer, New York, 74, O K Harris Works Art, New York, 75, Louis K Meisel Gallery, New York, 81, 82, 84 & 85, Martha White Gallery, Louisville, Ky, 81, Sindin Gallery, New York, 91; David Anderson Gallery, Buffalo, NY, 91; Bologna Lawdi Gallery, East Hampton, NY, 91. *Teaching:* Instr painting, State Univ Iowa, summer 64; instr painting & drawing, Sch Visual Arts, NY, 63-91; Ford Found artist-in-residence, Univ RI, 66; instr, Univ Calif, Berkeley, 68 & Univ Calif, Irvine, 71; vis lectr, Bellville Area Col, Ill, 76, Maryland Inst Art, Baltimore, Md, 77; vis critic, Md Inst Art, Baltimore, 78-80, 82- *Awards:* Guggenheim Fel, 64; Minister Foreign Affairs Award, Int Exhib Young Artists, Tokyo, Japan, 67; Nat Endowment for Arts, 77; Prix de Rome, Nat Endowment Arts. *Bibliog:* William H Gerdts, Jr (auth), Painting & Sculpture in New Jersey, Van Nostrand-Reinhold, 64. *Dealer:* Louis K Meisel Gallery 141 Prince St New York NY 10014. *Mailing Add:* 120 Accabonac Rd East Hampton NY 11973

ROTH, JACK (RODNEY)
PAINTER
b Brockway, Pa, Mar 13, 27. *Study:* Calif Sch Fine Arts, with Mark Rothko & Clifford Still, 49-50; State Univ Iowa, with James Lechay, MFA, 51-53; Duke Univ, PhD, 62. *Work:* Mus Mod Art, New York. *Exhib:* Younger American Painters, Guggenheim Mus, New York, 54; one-man shows, Clocktower, New York, 81, Montclair Art Mus, 82 & NJ State Mus, 83. *Teaching:* Prof math, Ramapo Col, NJ, 71- *Awards:* Guggenheim Fel, 79-80. *Media:* Acrylic, Watercolor. *Dealer:* Snyder Fine Art 588 Broadway New York NY 10021. *Mailing Add:* 32 Clinton Ave Montclair NJ 07042

ROTH, LELAND M(ARTIN)
HISTORIAN, WRITER
b Harbor Beach, Mich, Mar 22, 43. *Study:* Univ Ill, Urbana, BA(archit), 66; Yale, MA, 70, PhD, 73. *Teaching:* Instr, Univ Ill, Urbana, 66-67 & Ohio State Univ, Columbus, 71-73; asst prof, Northwestern Univ, 73-78; assoc prof, Univ Ore, Eugene, 78-90, prof, 90- *Awards:* Founders Award, Soc Archit Historians, 79; Nat Endowment Humanities Fel, 82-83; Kamphoefner Fel, 85. *Mem:* Col Art Asn; Soc Archit Historians (dir, 77-80). *Res:* American architecture, 1850-1950; history of urban America; history of American art, 1850-1930. *Publ:* Ed, Monograph of the Work of McKim, Mead & White, B Blom, 73; auth, The Architecture of McKim, Mead & White, 1870-1920: A Building List, Garland Publ, 78; A Concise History of American Architecture, 79 & rev ed, 93, ed, America Builds: Source Documents in American Architecture, 83, auth, McKim, Mead & White, Architects, 83 & Understanding Architecture, 92, Harper & Row. *Mailing Add:* Art Hist Dept Univ Ore Eugene OR 97403

ROTH, MOIRA
EDUCATOR, HISTORIAN
b London, Eng, July 24, 33. *Study:* New York Univ, BA, 59; Univ Calif, Berkeley, MA, 66, PhD, 74. *Teaching:* Acting asst prof art hist, Univ Calif, Irvine, 70-72; lectr art hist, Univ Calif, Santa Cruz, 73-74; from asst to assoc prof, Univ Calif, San Diego, 74-86, chmn, Visual Arts Dept, 82-83; prof art hist, Mills Col, 86- *Res:* Performance art, Marcel Duchamp, American Multicultural & women's contemporary art. *Publ:* Auth, Marcel Duchamp in America: A self-readymade, 5/77 & auth, Toward a history of California performance, 6/78, Arts; auth, The aesthetic of indifference, 11/77 & auth, Visions and re-visions, 11/80, Artforum; ed & contribr, The Amazing Decade: Women and Performance Art in America, 1970-1980, 83; The Dual Citizenship: Art of Carlos Villa, Visions, fall 89; auth, A Trojan Horse (essay), Faith Ringgold: A Twenty Year Retrospective (catalog), 90. *Mailing Add:* Dept Art Mills Col Oakland CA 94613

ROTH, RICHARD
PAINTER, EDUCATOR
b Brooklyn, NY, June 22, 46. *Study:* Cooper Union, BFA, 69; Tyler Sch Art, Temple Univ, MFA, 77. *Work:* Akron Art Inst, Ohio; Chase Manhattan Bank Collection, New York; New York Univ Art Collection; First Nat City Bank Collection, New York; Wexner Ctr Visual Arts, Columbus. *Comn:* Sculpture, Tipton Assocs, 87; Ohio State Univ Hosp, 89. *Exhib:* 1969 Ann Exhib of Contemp Am Painting, Whitney Mus Am Art, New York, 69-70; Group shows, Contemp Arts Ctr, Cincinnati, 88, Dart Gallery, Chicago, 88, Penine Hart Gallery, New York, 90, Bess Cutler Gallery, New York, 90; One-person shows, Toni Birckhead Gallery, Cincinnati, 90, Feigen Inc, Chicago, 91. *Teaching:* Asst prof & dir, Prog Fundamentals & Spec Classes, Art Inst Chicago, 77-81; assoc prof & dir, Grad Prog, Dept Art, Ohio State Univ, 81- *Awards:* Nat Endowment Arts, Visual Artists Fel, Painting, 91; Ohio Arts Cow Individual Artists Fel, 91. *Mailing Add:* Dept Art Ohio State Univ Columbus OH 43210

ROTHENBERG, BARBARA
PAINTER, COLLAGE ARTIST
b New York, NY, June 21, 33. *Study:* Univ Mich, 52-54; Bennington Col, with Paul Feeley, BA(cum laude), 56; Columbia Univ Teachers Col, MA, 56; New York Univ, with Esteben Vicente & Samuel Adler, 56-58. *Work:* Housatonic Mus Art, Bridgeport, Conn; Westport Town Hall, Conn; Gen Electric Corp, Fairfield, Conn; Marketing Corp Am, Westport, Conn; Chase Manhattan Bank, New York; Pitney-Bowes, Stamford, Conn; Phoenix Mutual, Hartford, Conn; Readers Digest Corp, Pleasantville, NY; CDC Financial, Farmington, Conn. *Comn:* Tapestry, Sofia Assocs, New York, 85. *Exhib:* New Dimensions in Drawing, Aldrich Mus, 81; Northeast USA & Out of Landscape, 83, Silvermine Guild; Conn Art, 88 & Conn Artists, 90, Stamford Mus; Solo-exhib, Paintings and Pastels, Ingber Gallery, New York, 88 & Inside-Outside Series, Conn Gallery, Marborough, 88; The Art of Collage, Hartford, Conn, 89; Newspace Gallery, Manchester Community Col, 91; Modern Times, Katonah Mus, NY, 92. *Pos:* Modevator-organizer, The Gallery & the Artist, Inst Visual Artists; lectr, Picasso and the Musical Image, Paul Klee, An appreciation & a look at the Latest (Whitney Biennial), 87, Georgia O'Keefe, 89; moderator-panelist, On Color, Silvermine Guild Artists, 89. *Teaching:* Instr art, City Col New York, 58-60 & Silvermine Sch Arts, 80-83; adj assoc prof art, Housatonic Community Col, 70-82, Sch Visual Arts, New York, 80-82, Sacred Heart Univ, 80-88 & Fairfield Univ, Conn, 86-; adj prof fine arts, Fairfield Univ. *Awards:* Sacred Heart Univ Grant, 83; Individual Artists Grant for Painting, Conn Comn Arts, 89; Indo-Am Fulbright Grant, 92-93. *Bibliog:* Jacqueline Moss (auth), On Landscape: A new view, Stanford Advocate, 7/3/83; Shirley Gonzales (auth), review, The New Haven Register, 6/85; Nancy Hall-Duncan (auth), First Conn Biennial (catalog), Bruce Mus, Greenwich, 89. *Mem:* Col Art Asn; Womens Caucus Arts; Westport-Weston Arts Coun; Silvermine Guild Ctr Arts (mem bd, 78-80). *Media:* Pastel, Oil. *Publ:* Auth, On painterly painting, Women Artists News, 81; Connecticut women artists, Conn Mag, 81. *Dealer:* Silvermine Guild New Canaan CT. *Mailing Add:* 303 Bayberry Lane Westport CT 06880

ROTHENBERG, SUSAN
PAINTER, PRINTMAKER
b Buffalo, NY, Jan 20, 45. *Study:* Cornell Univ, BFA, 66; George Washington Univ, 67; Corcoran Mus Sch. *Work:* Mus Mod Art, New York; Albright-Knox Art Gallery, Buffalo; Whitney Mus Am Art, New York; Walker Art Ctr, Minneapolis; Museum Fine Arts, Houston. *Exhib:* Extraordinary Women, & New Acquisitions, Mus Mod Art, New York, 77; Susan Rothenberg: Recent Work, Walker Art Ctr, Minneapolis, 78; New Image Painting, 78-79 & Whitney Biennial, 79, 83 & 85, Whitney Mus Am art; Animals in Am Art, Nassau Co Mus Fine Art, 81-82; solo exhibs, Los Angeles Co Mus Art, 83, San Francisco Mus Art, 83, Carnegie Inst, Mus Mod Art, Pittsburgh, 84, Portland Visual Arts Ctr (catalog), Ore, 85-86, Baltimore Mus Art, Md, 88, Greg Kucera Gallery, Seattle, Wash, 91 & Albright-Knox Art Gallery, Buffalo, NY, travelling, 92-94; Prints from Blocks, Gauguin to Now (catalog), Mus Mod Art, New York, 83; Minimalism to Expressionism: Painting and Sculpture since 1965 from the Permanent Collection, Whitney Mus Am Art, New York, 83; 47th Ann Mid-Year Exhib (catalog), Butler Inst Am Art, Youngstown, Ohio, 83; Visions of Childhood: A Contemporary Iconography, Whitney Mus Am Art, New York, 84; An International Survey of Recent Painting and Sculpture (catalog), Mus Mod Art, New York, 84; Images and Impressions: Painters Who Print (catalog), Walker Art Ctr, Minn, 84; Content: A Contemporary Focus, 1979-1984 (catalog), Hirshhorn Mus & Sculpture Garden, Washington, DC, 84-85; States of War: New European & Am Paintings (catalog), Seattle Art Mus, Wash, 85; Four Printmakers, Whitney Mus Am Art, New York, 85; Three Printmakers, Whitney Mus Am Art, New York, 86; 75th Ann of 'The Am Exhib', Art Inst Chicago, Ill, 86; 50th Nat Mid-Year Exhib, Butler Inst Am Art, Youngstown, Ohio, 86; Black and White: Loaned to American Express Company, a Prof Assoc Coun, Art Adv Serv, Mus Mod Art, New York, 86; Boston Collects: Contemporary Painting and Sculpture (catalog), Mus Fine Arts, Boston, 86-87; Devil on the Stairs: Looking Back on the Eighties (catalog), Inst Contemp Art, Philadelphia, traveled to: Newport Harbor Art Mus, Newport Beach, Calif, 91-92; Allegories of Modernism: Contemporary Drawing (catalog), Mus Mod Art, New York, 92. *Collections Arranged:* A Guide to the Collection of the Museum Fine Arts, Houston, Tex; The Image in American Photography &

Sculpture 1950-1980 (auth, catalog), Akron Art Mus. *Awards:* Creative Artists Pub Serv Prog Grant, NY State Coun Arts, 76-77; Guggenheim Fel Painting, 80; Award Painting, Am Acad Arts & Lett, 83. *Bibliog:* Ken Johnson (auth), Susan Rothenberg at Sperone Westwater, Art Am, 9/92; Barbara A MacAdam (auth), Susan Rothenberg, Sperone Westwater, Artnews, 9/92; Souren Melikian (auth), The yearning for figuration, Susan Rothenberg's long, lonely quest for form, Int Herald Tribune, Art Section, 9//5-6/92. *Media:* Acrylic and Flashe or oil on Canvas or Paper, Aquatint; Lithography. *Publ:* Contribr, New Image Painting, Whitney Mus, 78; American Paintings: The Eighties, Barbara Rose/Vista Press, 79. *Mailing Add:* c/o Sperone Westwater Gallery 142 Greene St New York NY 10012

ROTHMAN, SIDNEY
GALLERY DIRECTOR, CRITIC
Study: Brooklyn Col; Columbia Univ, BA(lang & art hist); New York Sch Archit Design. *Collections Arranged:* NJ Artists Show, 68; SAm Collection, 69; Yugoslavian Printmakers, 72; Collection of European Prints, Fordham Univ, 72; NJ Sculptors Asn Show, 86. *Pos:* Art dealer, Philadelphia area, 46-66; gallery dir, Barnegat Light, 58-; assessor of paintings, Long Beach Found Arts & Sci, 71-72; organizer, NJ Artists/Summer 88, Long Beach Island Found. *Teaching:* Lectr art, Women's Club Island, Beach Haven, NJ, 67-68, Deborah Hosp, Browns Mills, NJ, 69 & Long Beach Found, Loveladies, NJ, 71 & 90. *Awards:* Mayors Award, 86; Ocean Co Cult & Heritage Comn Award, 88. *Bibliog:* Miriam Bush (auth), articles, Asbury Park Press, 6/8/75 & 9/8/81; article, Philadelphia Inquirer, 8/3/75 & 6/12/81; article, Summer Times, 6/2/82. *Mem:* Long Beach Found Arts & Sci; Ocean Co Cult & Heritage Comn, US Lighthouse Soc, NJ; Artists Equity Asn; NJ Watercolor Soc. *Res:* Spanish art of time of Velasquez thru Ribera; ukiyo-e Japanese prints and identification. *Specialty:* Showing artists of all mediums. *Publ:* contribr, Arts of Asia, Hong Kong, 71; Sandpaper, Long Beach Island, 5/25/88; US No 1 Princeton, 6/28/88; Toms River Observer, 6/92; Philadelphia Inquirer, 8/14/92; and others. *Mailing Add:* 21st on Central Ave Barnegat Light NJ 08006

ROTHOLZ, RINA
PRINTMAKER
b Israel; US citizen. *Study:* Pratt Graphic Arts Ctr, New York; Brooklyn Mus Art Sch, NY. *Work:* Boston Mus Fine Arts; Rose Art Mus, Brandeis Univ; Mus Mod Art, New York; Israel Mus, Jerusalem; Albright-Knox Art Gallery, Buffalo, NY; and others. *Comn:* Ed of 50 prints, 69 & ed of 200 prints, Commentary Libr Collection of Art Treasure; Blue Disc (greeting card design), UNICEF, 72; 36 ingots (reprod by Franklin Mint), Judaic Heritage Soc, 73-78. *Exhib:* One-man shows, Pucker/Safrai Gallery, Boston, 72, 74, 77 & 81 & Port Washington Libr, New York, 75; Boston Printmakers Ann & Traveling Shows, 67-79; Queens Mus, NY, 74; Potsdam Print Exhib, State Univ NY Col, Purchase, 76; and others. *Teaching:* Lectr & demonstr, Bd Coop Educ Serv, Scholars in Residence Prog, Nassau Co, NY. *Awards:* First Prize for Graphics, Port Washington Ann, 70; Purchase Prize, Nassau Community Graphic Exhib, 72 & 73; Prize in Graphics, Nat Asn Women Artists, 72 & 74. *Mem:* Boston Printmakers; Graphic Arts Coun NY; Nat Asn Women Artists; Prof Artists Guild. *Res:* Discovered process of Tuilegraphy, which is the carving of vinyl asbestos tiles while they are still warm, then printing the tiles as intaglio plates to achieve a variety of textures, shapes, and high reliefs. *Publ:* Auth, Tuilegraphy, Artist's Proof, Vol 7. *Mailing Add:* 42 Shepherd Lane Roslyn Heights NY 11577

ROTHSCHILD, AMALIE (ROSENFELD)
SCULPTOR, PAINTER
b Baltimore, Md, Jan 1, 16. *Study:* Md Inst Col Art, dipl; New York Sch Fine & Appl Art; studied with Herman Maril. *Work:* Corcoran Gallery Art & Phillips Collection, Washington, DC; Baltimore Mus Art, Md; Peale Mus, Baltimore; Honolulu Acad Arts. *Comn:* Design for needlepoint ark curtain, Baltimore Hebrew Congregation, 51; design for Plexiglas & aluminum window, Forest Park High Sch, Baltimore, 81; design for needlepoint wall hanging, Sun Life Ins Co Am, Baltimore, 66; design for aggregate archit panels, Martin Luther King, Jr Elementary Sch, Baltimore, 69; design for needlepoint wall hanging, Walters Art Gallery, Baltimore, 74. *Exhib:* Synagogue Art Today, Jewish Mus, New York, 52; Living Today, Corcoran Gallery Art, 58; Three Artists from Washington & Baltimore, Corcoran Gallery Art, 59; solo exhibs, Baltimore Mus Art, 71, Franz Bader Gallery, Washington DC, 89, 91 & Artist's Pavilion, Tel Aviv, 90-; Celebration for the Artists, Nat Sci Acad, 75; Sculpture/300, Philadelphia Art Alliance, 82. *Teaching:* Instr painting, Metrop Sch Art, Baltimore, 56-59; lectr fine arts, Goucher Col, 60-68. *Awards:* Prize Painting, 50 & Prize Work in Any Medium, 54, Baltimore Mus Art; Award for Painting, Corcoran Gallery Art, 57; Distinguished Alumni Award, Md Inst Col Art, 85. *Bibliog:* Theodore L Low (auth), Man the maker, WMAR-TV & Walters Art Gallery, Baltimore, 60; Lincoln F Johnson, Jr (auth), Amalie Rothschild: Drawings, Goucher Col, 68; Tom Haulk (auth), Amalie Rothschild Retrospective 1933-1983. *Mem:* Artists Equity Asn; Sculptors, Inc; Int Sculpture Ctr. *Media:* Miscellaneous Media Construction, Cast Bronze; Acrylic, Oil. *Dealer:* Franz Bader Gallery 1500 K St NW Washington DC 20005. *Mailing Add:* 2909 Woodvalley Dr Baltimore MD 21208

ROTHSCHILD, CAROLYN ANITA
DEALER
b Baldwin, NY, April 3, 39. *Study:* State Univ NY, Potsdam, BS, 61; Southern Ill Univ, MS(fel), 63; New York Univ, 63-65; Univ Int, Santander, Spain, 65. *Collections Arranged:* Nancy Grossman Exhib, Univ Nev, Reno, 78. *Pos:* Owner, Rothschild Fine Arts, currently. *Specialty:* European and American paintings, drawings and sculptures by the masters, from French Impressionists up through the present. *Mailing Add:* Rothschild Fine Arts Inc 205 West End Ave New York NY 10023

ROTHSCHILD, JOHN D
DEALER
b Chicago, Ill, June 22, 40. *Study:* Mass Inst Technol, BS, 62; Columbia Univ, MBA, 64. *Pos:* Owner, Rothschild Fine Arts Inc, currently. *Specialty:* European and American paintings, drawings and sculptures by the masters, from French impressionists up through the present. *Publ:* Contribr, I Love New York Guide, Macmillan. *Mailing Add:* Rothschild Fine Arts Inc 205 West End Ave New York NY 10023

ROTHSCHILD, JUDITH
PAINTER, COLLAGE ARTIST
b New York, NY. *Study:* Fieldston Sch, Art Students League, with Reginald Marsh; Cranbrook Acad Art; Wellesley Col, BA(art hist); study with Hans Hofmann; Atelier 17, with S W Hayter. *Work:* Metrop Mus Art, Whitney Mus Am Art, Solomon R Guggenheim Mus, New York; Fogg Art Mus, Harvard Univ, Cambridge, Mass; City Art Gallery, Auckland, New Zealand; Baltimore Mus Art, Md; Pa Acad Fine Arts, Philadelphia Mus Art, Pa; Ludwig Mus, Aachen, Ger; Israel Mus, Jerusalem; State Tretyakov Gallery, Moscow; and others. *Exhib:* Solo shows, Annely Juda Fine Art, London, 76, 81 & 87, Williams Col Mus Art, Williamstown, Wellesley Col Art, Mus, Mass, Kenne State Col, NH, Palzaao Grassi, Venice, Italy, Portland Mus Art, Maine, 88, Pa Acad Fine Arts, Philadelphia, 90, State Tretyakov Gallery, Moscow, 91, Univ Mich Mus Art, Ann Arbor, 92; plus over 100 exhibs in the US & abroad. *Pos:* Staff consult, Fine Arts Work Ctr of Provincetown, 71-; corresp ed, Leonardo Mag, Europe, 71-80. *Teaching:* Artist in residence in painting, Univ Syracuse, 70-71; guest artist painting, Pratt Univ, summer 74 & RI Sch Design, summers 75, 76 & 77. *Awards:* Wellesley Achievement Award, 81. *Bibliog:* Richard H Axsom (auth), Judith Rothschild: Relief Paintings, 1972-87, Pa Acad Fine Arts & Portland Mus Art, Maine, 88. *Mem:* Am Fedn Arts (bd mem); MacDowell Colony (mem bd); bd mem, Fine Arts Work Ctr, Provincetown, Mass; Am Abstract Artists (past pres). *Media:* Oil, Relief-Collage. *Dealer:* Galerie Gmurzynska Cologne Ger; Andre Zarre Gallery New York. *Mailing Add:* 1110 Park Ave New York NY 10028

ROTTERDAM, PAUL Z
PAINTER
b Austria, Feb 12, 39; US citizen. *Study:* Acad & Univ Vienna. *Work:* Graphische Sammlung Albertina, Vienna, Austria; Metrop Mus, Mus Mod Art & Guggenheim Mus, New York; Mus Nat d'Art Moderne, Paris; and others. *Exhib:* 4th Biennial, Paris, 65; 8th Biennial, Tokyo, 65; Whitney Biennial Am Art, 75; Acquisitions, Guggenheim Mus, 75; Susan Caldwell Gallery, New York, 75; Mus de l'Abbaye St Croix, Les Sables d'Olonne, France, 76; Mus de Nice, France, 77; Birmingham Mus Art, Ala, 77; and others. *Teaching:* Lectr painting, Harvard Univ, 68-88 & Cooper Union Sch Art, 74-75. *Bibliog:* Alvin Martin (auth), Paul Rotterdam: The 14 Stations of the Cross, Univ Tex, 80; Carter Ratcliff (auth), Paul Rotterdam: Selected Paintings, Storrer, 82. *Dealer:* Denise Cadé 1024 Madison Ave New York NY 10021; Adams Middleton Gallery 3000 Maple Ave Dallas TX 75201. *Mailing Add:* 115 W Broadway New York NY 10013

ROUKES, NICHOLAS M
SCULPTOR, WRITER
b San Jose, Calif, Nov 22, 25. *Study:* San Jose State Col, Calif; Fresno State Col, BA, 49; Stanford Univ, MA, 51. *Work:* Can Coun Art Bank, Ottawa. *Comn:* Kinetic Light, Provincial Judges Court; column, Calgary, Alta, 74. *Teaching:* Prof art educ, design & sculpture, Univ Calgary, Alta, 66-88, prof emer art, currently. *Media:* Mixed Media. *Res:* New media for art creativity. *Publ:* Auth, Masters of Wood Sculpture, 80; Art Synectics, 81; Acrylics Bold and New, 82; Design Synectics, 88; Sculpture in Paper, 92. *Mailing Add:* Dept Art Univ Calgary Calgary AB T2N 1N4 Canada

ROUSSEAU, IRENE VICTORIA
SCULPTOR, WRITER
Study: Hunter Col, with Tony Smith, AB; Claremont Grad Sch, MFA; New York Univ, PhD. *Work:* Metrop Mus Art, Mus Mod Art & Guggenheim Mus Art, New York; Smithsonian Inst, Washington, DC; Philadelphia Mus Art; Brit Mus, London. *Comn:* Mosaic mural, Holocaust Mem, The Brotherhood Synagogue, New York, 86; series of metal wall relief sculptures, Capital Sports Inc, Stamford, Conn, 89-90; mural wall relief, Beacon Hill Club, Summit, NJ, 92; mosaic mural, Overlook Hosp Found, Summit, NJ, 93. *Exhib:* Drawing Exhib, Philadelphia Mus Art, Pa; Invitational Sculptors Exhib, Morris Mus Art & Sci, NJ; On and Off the Wall, Newark Mus, NJ; New Jersey Currents, NJ State Coun Arts & Nat Endowment Arts, traveling, 79; Weatherspoon Art Gallery, Univ NC, Greensboro, 83; Moody Art Gallery, Univ Ala, 83; 50th Anniversary 1936-1986 American Abstract Artists, Bronx Mus Arts, 86; one-person exhib, Gallery Saint Agnes, Denmark, 86; Int Art Competition, Gallery 54, New York, 89-90. *Collections Arranged:* Language of Abstraction & Works on Paper, 79 American Abstract Artists, Betty Parsons Gallery, 79; American Abstract Artists: The Early Years, mus traveling show, 80 & 81; Abstraction in Action, City Gallery, New York, 82. *Teaching:* Former prof, William Paterson Col, Wayne, NJ. *Awards:* Recipient 7 first prize awards for creative work in NJ, ER Squibb and Sons Sculpture Award. *Bibliog:* Roskilde Avis (auth), Drom, fantasi realiteter og Illusioner, 6/28/86; Synagogue to Unveil Mosaic Mural, Town and Village, NY, 5/1/86; Arthur Williams (auth), Sculpture: Technique-Form-Content, Davis Publ, Inc, Worcester, Mass, 88; Ed McCormack (auth), World Class Winners at Art Gallery 54, Artspeak, NY, 1/1/90; Jennifer Lawson (auth), Holocaust mural, The Jewish Week, Inc, New York, 5/9/86. *Mem:* Col Art Asn; ISC; WCA; Fine Arts Federation. *Media:* Metal, Paint. *Res:* Space in light sculpture. *Publ:* Contrib, Perle Fine Arts, 6/82; Hiroshi Murata, Arts, 1/83; Nassos Daphnis: An Artist in the Art World, Arts, 5/83; Offset Technology as a fine arts medium, Arts, 3/84. *Mailing Add:* 41 Sunset Dr Summit NJ 07901

ROUSSEAU-VERMETTE, MARIETTE
TAPESTRY ARTIST, EDUCATOR
Can citizen. *Study:* Ecole des Beaux Arts, dipl, 48; Oakland Col Arts & Crafts, Calif, 48-49. *Work:* Kyoto Mus Mod Art, Japan; Nat Gallery, Ottawa; Mus Contemp Art, Montreal; Winnipeg Art Gallery, Man; Quebec Mus, Quebec City; Metrop Mus Art, New York, NY. *Comn:* Kennedy Ctr theatre curtain, comn by Can Govt, Washington, DC, 70; tapestry mural, Exxon Corp, Rockefeller Ctr, New York, 71; tapestry mural, Royal Bank hq, Toronto, 77; Concert Hall ceiling, Toronto, 77-83; theatre Curtain, Can Embassy, Washington, DC, 88-89. *Exhib:* Mus des Beaux Arts, Montreal, 61; 1st Biennale Tapestry, Mus Cantonal des Beaux Arts, Lausanne, Switz, 62, 65, 67, 71 & 77; Triennale, Milan Mus, 68; Contemporary Tapestries, Mus Mod Art, New York, 68; Retrospective, Quebec City Mus, 72; Fiber Works, Mus Mod Art, Kyoto & Tokyo, Japan, 77-78; New Tapestry, Mus d'Art Contemp, Montreal, 77-78; The Art Fabric-Mainstream, traveling USA, 81-84. *Collections Arranged:* Metiers d'Art 2 & 3, Paris, Brussels, London & traveling; Mikrokosma, Europ & Can cities, 82-85. *Teaching:* Prof art, archit, Banff Sch Fine Arts, 77-80, head fiber arts dept, 80-85. *Awards:* 1st Prize, Concours Artistiques de la Province, Govt Que, 57; 2nd Prize, Can Handicraft Guild, Montreal, 61; Cert Honor, Can Conf Arts, 74. *Bibliog:* André Kuenzi (auth), La Nouvelle Tapisserie, Bibliot des Arts, Paris, 81; Vincent Tovell, interview, Hand & Eye-Fiber, Can Broadcasting Corp, 84; Pasia Schonberg, interview, Life: In a Flash of Lightning, TV Ont, 84-85. *Mem:* Can Soc Decorative Art & Design (vpres, 86); Soc Que de la Tapisserie Contemp (vpres, 81, pres, 86); Royal Can Acad Arts (elected mem, 73); Order Can (officer, 76). *Dealer:* Alice Pauli 9 rue de Port-Franc Lausanne 1003 Switzerland; Mira Godard Gallery 16 Hazelton Toronto ON Can. *Mailing Add:* 373 Rue Morin Ste Adele PQ J0R 1L0 Canada

ROUSSEL, CLAUDE PATRICE
SCULPTOR, EDUCATOR
b Edmundston, NB, Can, July 6, 30. *Study:* Ecole Beaux-Arts, Montreal, PQ, 50-56; Can Coun Sr Traveling Fel, Europe, 61. *Work:* Smithsonian Inst, Washington, DC; NB Mus, St John; Confedn Art Gallery, Charlottetown, PEI; Portland Mus, Maine; Mt Allison Univ, Sackville, NB. *Comn:* Exterior sculpture & interior mural, Univ Moncton Nursing Pavilion, 71; Sailing Olympics, Kingston, Ont, 76; Int Sculpture Garden, Seoul Olympics, 88; Moncton 100 Monument, 90; Clement Cormier Monument, Univ Moncton, 90; and others. *Exhib:* Survey 69, Montreal Mus Fine Arts, 69; Confedn Art Gallery, 70; Air & Space Mus, Smithsonian Inst, 71; Man and His World, Montreal, 71; Owens Art Gallery, 75 & 79; Ctr d'Art du Montreal, Royal, 82; Beaverbrook Art Gallery, 84-88; Univ de Moncton Art Gallery, 84. *Pos:* Asst cur, Beaverbrook Art Gallery, Fredericton, 59-61. *Teaching:* Instr art, Edmundston Pub Schs, 56-59 & Univ Moncton, 63-91 (retired). *Awards:* Allied Arts Medal, Royal Archit Soc Can, 64; St John City Hall Sculpture Competition, City of St John, 72; Winner of Sailing Olympics Sculpture Competition, Kingston, Ont, 76; Order of Can, 84; McCain Exhib, Beaverbrook Art Gallery, Fredericton, NB, 89. *Bibliog:* Painting a province, Nat Film Bd, 60; articles, Arts Atlantic, fall 77 & spring, 83; Claude Roussel, Sculpteur, Sculptor, Edition D'Acadie, 87. *Media:* Wood, Cast Paper. *Publ:* Coauth, The Visual Arts, In: The Acadians of the Maritimes, 82. *Mailing Add:* 905 Amirault Dieppe Moncton NB E1A 1E1 Canada

ROUTON, DAVID F
PAINTER, DRAFTSMAN
b Jackson, Tenn, Dec 6, 31. *Study:* Mexico City Col, BFA, 59; Univ Iowa, MFA, 63. *Work:* Sheldon Mem Art Gallery, Lincoln, Nebr; Univ Nebr, Lincoln; Univ Minn Art Mus, Minneapolis; Sioux City Art Ctr, Iowa; Col Notre Dame Md, Baltimore; & others. *Exhib:* Am Drawing Biennial, 88 & Am Drawing Biennial II, Muscarelle Mus Art, William & Mary Col, Williamsburg, Va, 90; 35th San Diego Art Inst Exhib, San Diego, Calif, 89; Juror's Merit Award, La Grange Nat XV, La Grange Col, Ga, 90; 33rd NDak Ann Print & Drawing Exhib, Univ NDak, 91. *Teaching:* Instr, Mich State Univ, E Lansing, 63-64; Asst prof drawing & painting, State Univ NY, Plattsburg, 64-66 & Univ Minn, Minneapolis, 66-72; prof drawing & painting, Univ Nebr, Lincoln, 76- *Awards:* Purchase Awards, Cent States Expos (2), Pratt Community Col, Kans, 80, 43rd Ann, Sioux City Art Ctr, Iowa, 81, Nat Print & Drawing Show, Univ Wis, Waukesha, 81 & 5th Nat Drawing & Print Competitive Exhib, Col Notre Dame Md, Baltimore, 92; Juror's Merit Award, LaGrange Nat XV, 90; Hon Mention, 49th Ann Juried Competition, Sioux City Art Ctr, Iowa, 90. *Mem:* Col Art Asn. *Media:* Oil; Drawing. *Publ:* Illusr, Ten Years in Nevada, 85, All is But a Beginning, 86, Martha Maxwell, Rocky Mountain in Naturalist, 86, Emily: The Diary of a Hard Worked Woman, 87, Life in Alaska, 88, Univ Nebr Press; Sod House Days, Univ Press, Kans, 83. *Mailing Add:* Dept Univ Nebr at Lincoln Lincoln NE 68583

ROVETTI, PAUL F
MUSEUM DIRECTOR, ADMINISTRATOR
b New Haven, Conn, Jan 29, 39. *Study:* Columbia Univ, BA, 61; Cooperstown Grad Prog, MA, 66. *Collections Arranged:* Watercolors & Prints by Reginald Marsh, 86; Henry C White: Pastels, 86; Harvey Sadow Jr - Toward A Vessel Aesthetic: Ceramic Works 1968-1988, 88; Giorgi Cavallon: A Retrospective View, 90. *Pos:* Dir, Mattatuck Mus, Waterbury, Conn, 66-69; dir, William Benton Mus of Art, Univ Conn, Storrs, 69- *Awards:* Scriven Found Fel, 65-66; Nat Endowment Arts Mus Prof Fel, 73. *Mem:* Am Asn Mus (mem coun, 78-90); New Eng Mus Asn (exec comt, 66-81, Conn rep, 69-78); Int Coun Mus. *Res:* Nineteenth century American painting; nineteenth century American folk art. *Publ:* Auth, Dwight W Tryon: A Retrospective Exhibition (catalog), Univ Conn Mus Art, 71; coauth, The American Earls (catalog), 72 & auth, Nineteenth Century Folk Painting: Our Spirited National Heritage, 73, William Benton Mus Art. *Mailing Add:* William Benton Mus of Art U-140 Univ of Cónn Storrs CT 06268

ROW, DAVID
PAINTER
b Portland, Maine, Aug 31, 49. *Study:* Yale Univ, BA (cum laude), 72, Yale Sch Art, with Al Held, MFA, 75. *Work:* Carnegie Mus Art, Pittsburgh, Pa; Brooklyn Mus Art, NY; Cleveland Mus Art & Progressive Art Collection, Ohio; Thomas Ammann Collection, Zurich, Switzerland; McCrory Corp, New York. *Comn:* Triptych, Richard Lewis Assocs, New York, 87. *Exhib:* New Drawing in America (traveling exhib), Drawing Ctr, New York, 82-83, Maine Biennial, Portland Mus Art, Portland, 85, New Abstraction, J B Speed Mus Art, Louisville, Ky, 89; one-man shows, John Good Gallery, New York, NY, 87, 89 & 91, Galerie Ascan Crone, Hamburg, Ger, 88 & 92, Galerie Thaddaeus Ropac, Salzburg, Aus, 90 & Paris, France, 91, Richard Feigen, Chicago, 91, Fujii Gallery, Tokyo, Japan, 91; Working on Paper, High Mus, Atlanta, 90; Contemp Works on Paper, Sunrise Mus, Charleston, 92. *Teaching:* Instr drawing & photo, Rutgers Univ, NJ, 77-78; instr drawing & color, Sch Visual Arts, New York, 77-91; asst prof, Pratt Inst, Brooklyn, NY, 86-87. *Awards:* Scholar of the House in Painting, Yale Univ, 71-72; Yale-Norfolk Scholar, Norfolk Summer Sch Art & Music, 71; Grant in Painting, Nat Endowment Arts, 87. *Bibliog:* M Brenson (auth), David Row, New York Times, 3/17/89 & 3/15/91; J Gilbert-Rolfe (auth), The Current State of Nonrepresentation, Visions Art Quart, spring 89; P Dagen (auth), On the use of color: two conceptions of painting, David Row and Gerhard Richter, Le Monde, 9/21/91; B Schwabsry (auth), David Row, Arts Mag, 5/91. *Media:* Oil. *Dealer:* John Good Gallery 532 Broadway New York NY 10012; Ascan Crone Isestrasse 121 D-2000 Hamburg W Germany. *Mailing Add:* 476 Broadway New York NY 10013

ROWAN, DENNIS MICHAEL
PRINTMAKER, EDUCATOR
b Milwaukee, Wis, Jan 6, 38. *Study:* Univ Wis, BS, 62; Univ Ill, MFA, 64. *Work:* Art Inst Chicago; Boston Mus Fine Arts; Seattle Art Mus, Wash; Okla Art Ctr, Oklahoma City; Honolulu Acad Arts, Hawaii. *Exhib:* Boston Mus Fine Arts, 61, 64-65, 68-69 & 70; Walker Art Ctr, Minneapolis, 62; Chicago Art Inst, 62 & 66; Pa Acad Fine Arts, 63; Seattle Art Mus, Wash, 63-65, 67, 70 & 71; Okla Art Ctr, 68, 70 & 72; Miami Art Ctr, 73; Brooklyn Mus, NY, 73; Calif Palace Legion Honor, San Francisco, 73; Vienna Graphics Biennale, Austria, 73; US Nat Mus, Washington, DC, 74; Kansas City Art Inst, 75; 3rd Biennale Int de l'Image, Epinal, France, 75; and many others. *Teaching:* Prof art, Univ Ill, Urbana-Champaign, 64-, assoc ctr advan study, 71-, prof sch art & design, currently. *Awards:* Purchase Award, 2nd Biennale Int Gravure, Cracow, Poland, 68; Yorkshire Arts Asn Purchase Prize, Brit Int Print Biennale, 70; Juror's Prize, Graphikbiennale Wien, Europahaus, Vienna, Austria, 72. *Media:* Intaglio. *Publ:* Contribr, Prize-winning graphics, Vol 3, 65 & Vol 4, 66; contribr, John Ross & Clare Romano's Complete Printmaker, Free Press, New York & Collier-Macmillan Ltd, Toronto, 72; contribr, Walter Chamberlin's Etching & Engraving, Thames & Hudson, London, 72 & Viking Press, New York, 73. *Mailing Add:* 143 Art & Design Bldg Univ Ill Champaign IL 61820

ROWAN, FRANCES PHYSIOC
PAINTER, WOODCUT
b Ossining, NY, Dec 17, 08. *Study:* Randolph-Macon Woman's Col, 29-30; Cooper Union, cert, 36; also graphics with Harry Sternberg & woodcuts with Carol Summers, 65-73. *Work:* Randolph-Macon Woman's Col, Lynchburg, Va; Freeport High Sch, NY; Cotton Inc. *Exhib:* Brooklyn Mus 11th Nat Print Show, 58; Audubon Artists, 58 & 59; Am Fedn Arts Traveling Show, 58-59; Knickerbocker Artists, 61; Silvermine Guild Artists 6th & 14th Nat Print Show, 66 & 80; one-man show, Sarasota Art Asn, 81. *Teaching:* Instr drawing & painting, Country Art Gallery, Westbury, NY, 55-66; instr drawing & painting, Five Towns Music & Art Found, 70-72; instr drawing, still life & figure, Longboat Key Art Ctr, 77- *Awards:* First Prizes, Hofstra Univ, 57 & Sarasota Art Asn, 79 & 82; Flax Award, Knickerbocker Artists, 61; and others. *Mem:* Prof Artists Guild; Silvermine Guild Artists. *Media:* Graphics; Oils. *Mailing Add:* 601 Broadway Longboat Key FL 34228

ROWAN, HERMAN
PAINTER, EDUCATOR
b New York, NY, July 20, 23. *Study:* Cooper Union; San Francisco State Col; Kans State Col, BS; State Univ Iowa, MA & MFA. *Work:* Walker Art Ctr, Minneapolis; Brooklyn Mus, NY; Univ Notre Dame, South Bend, Ind; Columbus Mus, Ohio; San Diego Gallery Fine Arts, Calif; Tweed Mus, Duluth, Minn. *Exhib:* Art USA, New York, 60; San Francisco Mus Nat Ann, 63; Southwest Ann, Houston Mus, 63; Walker Art Ctr Exhib, 65; Box-Top Art, Tour NZ Galleries, 71-72; Mitzi Landau Gallery, Los Angeles, 82; Tweed Mus Art, Duluth, Minn, 86. *Teaching:* Prof painting, Univ Minn, Minneapolis, 63- *Awards:* Lyman Award, Albright Gallery, 59; Purchase Prize, San Diego Gallery Fine Arts, 63. *Media:* Oil. *Dealer:* Anderson & Anderson 400 1st Ave N Minneapolis MN. *Mailing Add:* Dept Studio Arts Univ Minn Minneapolis MN 55455

ROWAN, (C) PATRICK
PAINTER, EDUCATOR
b Milwaukee, Wis, Jan 7, 37. *Study:* Univ Wis-Madison, BSArch, 62; Univ Wis-Milwaukee, BFA(painting), 69, MS(painting), 70; Univ Fla, Gainesville, MFA(sculpture), 71. *Work:* Kearney State Col, Nebr; Univ Wis-Milwaukee; Joslyn Art Mus, Omaha, Nebr; Sheldon Art Gallery; Springfield Art Mus, Mo; and others. *Exhib:* One-man exhibs, 25 painting & sculpture, Wis, Fla, Nebr, SDak, Pa, Iowa, Ark, Mo, Colo, 70-90; New Am Talent Nat Exhib, Austin, Tex, 90-91; Nat Juried Exhib, New Orleans, La, 90-91; Dimensions '90 Nat Exhib, Winston-Salem, NC, 90 & 91; one-man exhib, Sticks and Stones, Siva Art Ctr, Joplin, Mo; Northern Nat Art Exhib, Rhinelander, Wis. *Teaching:* Instr, Univ Wis-Milwaukee, 69-70; prof sculpture, painting & drawing, Univ Nebr, Lincoln, 71- *Mailing Add:* 5110 Lenox Lincoln NE 68510

ROWAND, JOSEPH DONN
GALLERY DIRECTOR, ART DEALER
b Champaign-Urbana, Ill, July 11, 42. *Study:* Southern Ill Univ, BFA, 64; Ont Sch Art; Parsons Sch Design, New York. *Collections Arranged:* Vic Huggins, 78, 81, 85, 89 & 93, Dorothy Gillespie, 81, 84, 88 & 92 Maud Gatewood, 83, 87, 89, 91 & 93, Mary Lou Higgins, 84, 87 & 91, Edith London, 82, 84, 86, 89 & 91; Raymond Chorneau, 85, 88 & 91, Andrew Braitman, 92, Will Dexter, 90, Claytopia, 90 & Thomas Sayre, 92; Group Fiber Show 87, Somerhill Gallery, Chapel Hill, NC. *Pos:* Panel mem, How to Buy & Enjoy Contemporary Art, City Gallery Contemp Art, Raleigh, NC, 88; adv bd, City Mag, 91 & NC Home Mag, 92; Town Chapel Hill Public Art Endowment Coun, 91 & 92; owner & dir, Somerhill Gallery, currently; plus numerous juror & adminr positions for arts orgns. *Teaching:* Guest lectr, Sandhills Community Col, Carthage, NC, 85, Arts on the River Festival, Savannah Arts Asn, Ga, 88, Duke Univ Continuing Educ Fac, 89 & 90 & Wake Visual Arts Asn, Raleigh, NC, 92; NC Cent Univ Fine Art of Collecting Symp, 87. *Bibliog:* Kay McClain (auth), Chapel Hill Newspaper, 89; Jo Schwarts (auth), Art Bus News, 90; Katheleen Christianson & Fred Park (auths), article, Bus Properties, 91; and others. *Mem:* NC Mus Art Found; Duke Univ, Mus Art (bd dirs, 92-95); Art Advocates NC; Akland Mus Assocs; Southeastern Ctr Contemp Art; and others. *Specialty:* Contemp American Artists of Southeastern US. *Mailing Add:* Three Eastgate East Franklin St Chapel Hill NC 27514

ROWANTREE, KAREN SMILEY
PHOTOGRAPHER
b Montreal, Que, Jan 6, 47. *Study:* Univ Toronto, BA (fine art), 69, MA (hist art), 70; Mass Inst Technol, with Minor White, 70-71. *Work:* Mus Fine Arts, Boston; St Louis Art Mus, Mo; Addiuson Gallery Am Art, Andover, Mass; Nat Gallery Can, Ottawa; Art Bank of Can Coun, Ottawa. *Exhib:* Photo/works (solo exhib with catalog), Addison Gallery Am Art, Andover, 76; Images of Women, Portland Mus Art, Maine, 77; 14 New England Photographers, Mus Fine Arts, Boston, 78; Maine Biennial, Colby Col Mus Art, Waterville, Maine, 83; Contemporary Canadians, 83 & Environments Here and Now, 85, Nat Gallery Can; Photographic Portraits, St Louis Art Mus, Mo, 83; Photographic Truth (with catalog), Bruce Mus, Greenwich, Conn, 88. *Teaching:* Instr, Nasson Col, Springvale, Maine, 76-77; lectr photog, Univ Mass, Boston, 77-81; vis artist, Univ Southern Maine, Portland, 84. *Awards:* Can Coun Arts Grant Photog, 80, 81 & 82. *Bibliog:* Edgar Allen Beem (auth), article, Maine Art Now, 90; Lorraine Johnson (auth), Public Exposures: One Decade of Contemporary Canadian Photography, Toronto Photos Workshop, 90. *Dealer:* Obelisk Gallery 72 Mt Vernon St Boston MA 02108. *Mailing Add:* PO Box 674 Cape Porpoise ME 04014

ROWE, CHARLES ALFRED
PAINTER, DESIGNER
b Great Falls, Mont, Feb 7, 34. *Study:* Mont State Univ, 52-53; Southern Methodist Univ, 56-57; Univ Chicago, 57-58; Art Inst Chicago, BFA, 60; Tyler Sch Art, Philadelphia, MFA, 68; also with John Rogers Cox, Boris Margo, Max Brill & Leroy Neiman. *Work:* Univ Del; Great Falls Pub Schs. *Comn:* Designed a coord arts coun symbol & related printed materials for Mont Arts Coun, Missoula, 73; designed numerous fabrics for major accounts for Galleon Fabrics, Inc, New York, 74- *Exhib:* One-man shows, C M Russell Mus, Great Falls, Mont, 73 & 81, Pleides Gallery, New York, 77 & Caja de expociones, Almonear, Spain; Butler Inst Art Mid-Year Show, Youngstown, Ohio, 73; Ball State Univ Nat Drawing & Small Sculpture Show, 74; Am Painters in Paris, France, 76-77; World Trade Ctr Exhib, New York, 79; and others. *Pos:* Graphic package designer, Am Can Co, Bellwood, Ill, 60-62; graphic designer, Abrams-Bannister Engraving, Inc, Greenville, SC, 62-64; artist-in-residence, Nat Endowment Arts & Humanities, 72-73. *Teaching:* Prof drawing & painting, Univ Del, 64-; vis artist, Univ Ariz, 83-84. *Awards:* Drawing of Distinction, Mead Painting of the Year Exhib, Atlanta, Ga, 64; Delaware Duck Stamp Winner, 81; Grant, Ctr Advanced Study, Univ Del, 81; and others. *Bibliog:* Artist in residence, Mont Arts, Vol 25, No 1; Artist employs original method and style, Great Falls Tribune, 10/72; Mary Hemple (auth), Charles Rowe, the creator of a new art form, Del Today Mag, 1/73. *Mem:* Soc of Illustr, NY. *Publ:* Illusr, State duck stamps, New York Art Review, Harshman & Houk. *Mailing Add:* 133 Aronimink Dr Chapel Hill Newark DE 19711

ROWE, REGINALD M
PAINTER, SCULPTOR
b New York, NY, Dec 8, 20. *Study:* Princeton Univ, BA, 44; Art Students League, with Louis Bosa, 46-47; Inst Allende, Univ Guanajuato, 58-59, MFA, 59. *Work:* McNay Mus, San Antonio; Arts Coun San Antonio; Univ Tex Health & Sci Ctr; San Antonio Mus Art. *Comn:* Mural & outdoor sculpture, Hemisfair 1968, San Antonio, Tex, 68. *Exhib:* One-man shows, Ruth White Gallery, New York, NY, 70, Marion Koogler McNay Mus, San Antonio, Tex, 77 & Locus Gallery, San Antonio, 87 & 90; San Antonio Art Inst, 80; 12 Texas Painters, Univ Tex, El Paso; Milagros Gallery, San Antonio, Tex, 92; Art Mus S Tex, Corpus Christi, 92; and others. *Pos:* Chmn exhibs, Witte Mus, 65-67. *Teaching:* Instr painting & design, San Antonio Art Inst, 64-84; vis artist, Univ NFla, 75, Southwest Craft Ctr, 84-87 & San Antonio Art Inst, 87- *Awards:* San Miguel Allende, 60. *Bibliog:* Ernest Hemingway (auth), catalog statement for first New York show, 52; reviews in Arts, Art News, Artweek, Pictures on Exhib, Times, Tribune & Art Int, 52-70; rev, San Antonio Express, S A Light, 70-92. *Dealer:* Read Stremmel Gallery San Antonio TX; Wallace Wentworth Gallery Washington DC. *Mailing Add:* 219 W Gramercy San Antonio TX 78212

ROWELL, MARGIT
CURATOR, HISTORIAN
b New Haven, Conn. *Study:* Inst Art Archeologie, Paris, MA; Univ Paris, Nanterre, PhD. *Collections Arranged:* Mondrian Retrospective, 71; Miro, Magnetic Fields (with catalog), 72; Jean Dubuffet, Retrospective (with catalog), 73; Frantisek Kupka, Retrospective (with catalog), 75; The Planar Dimension (with catalog), 79; Art of the Avant-garde in Russia: The George Costakis Collection (with catalog), 81; Julio Gonzalez, Retrospective (with catalog), 83; Torres-Garcia (with catalog), 86; Quest-ce que la Sculpture Moderne (with catalog), 86. *Pos:* Cur, Solomon R Guggenheim Mus, 73-83 & Mus Nat Art Mod, Paris, 83-87; dir exhibs, Fundacio Joan Miro, Barcelona, 86-89; cur, special projects, Centro de Arte Reina Sofia, Madrid, 90, Mus Nat Art Mod, Paris, 91- *Teaching:* Instr art hist, Sch Visual Arts, 69-72; instr contemp art, New Sch Social Res, 74. *Awards:* Frank Jewett Mather Award, Col Art Asn Am, 72; Guggenheim Found Grant, 76; Nat Endowment Arts Grant Mus Prof, 76. *Mem:* Int Asn Art Critics; Am Asn Mus; Int Coun Mus. *Res:* Twentieth century European art and aesthetics. *Publ:* Auth, Joan Miro, Abrams, 71; auth, La Peinture le geste, l'action, Klincksieck, Paris, 72; ed, Joan Miró: Selected Writings and Interviews, G K Hall, Boston, 86. *Mailing Add:* Centre National d'Art Culture Georges Pompidou Musee National d'Art Modern Paris 75191 Cedex 04 France

ROWLAND, ANNE
PHOTOGRAPHER
b Washington, DC. *Study:* Am Univ, 79; Sch Mus Fine Arts, Boston, BFA, 82. *Work:* Bank of Boston; Spencer Mus, Kans; Houston Mus Fine Art, Tex. *Exhib:* Persona, Robert Menschel Gallery, Syracuse, NY, 88; One-person show, Zoe Gallery, Boston, 86, 87 & 91, Tartt Gallery, Washington, DC, 90; Animae Venatories, Tartt Gallery, Washington, DC, 87; The Photography of Invention: American Pictures of the 1980's, Nat Mus Am Art, Smithsonian, Washington, DC; God & Country, Gregg Kucera Gallery, Seattle, Wash, 90; The 80th Ann Exhib; Focus on Photography: 1980-1990, Maier Mus Art, Randolph-Macon Woman's Col, Lynchburg, Va, 91; Family Matters, Tartt Gallery, Washington, DC, 92. *Awards:* Fel, Nat Endowment Arts, 86; Photog Fel, Mass Coun Arts & Humanities, Artists' Found, 85. *Dealer:* Zoe Gallery 207 Newbury St Boston MA 02116; Tartt Gallery 2017 Q St NW Washington DC 20009. *Mailing Add:* 1114 Sixth St No 2 Santa Monica CA 90403

ROYAL, RICHARD P
CRAFTSMAN
Study: Inst de Cultural, Guadalajara, Mex, 73; Cent Wash Univ, 70-74; Pilchuck Glass Sch, Stanwood, Wash, 78-84. *Work:* Washington Trust Bank, Spokane; Wash State Arts Comn, Olympia; Seattle Children's Theater; IBM Collection, New York; High Mus Art, Atlanta. *Comn:* Wash Governor's Award, Wash State Arts Comn. *Exhib:* one-man shows, Foster/White Gallery, 86, 87, 89 & 91, Glass Gallery, Bethesda, Md, 88 & 90, Brendan Walter Gallery, Los Angeles, 89, Vespermann Gallery, Atlanta, 89 & 91, Holt Gallery, Olympia, 90, Grohe Gallery, Boston, Mass, 91 & Christy/Taylor Gallery, Boca Raton, Fla, 91; C Corcoran Gallery, Muskegon, Mo, 88, 89 & 90; Masterworks: Pacific NW Arts and Crafts Now, Bellevue Art Mus, Wash, 91; Clearly Art: Pilchuck's Glass Legacy, Whatcom Mus Hist & Art, Bellingham, Wash, 92; Lewallen Gallery, Santa Fe, NMex, 92; Works in Glass, Elaine Horwitch Gallery, Scottsdale, Ariz, 92. *Pos:* Designer/production artist, Glass Eye Studio, Seattle, Wash, 82-84. *Teaching:* Gaffer, Dale Chihuly Studio, Seattle, Wash, 78- & Benjamin Moore Studio, Seattle, Wash, 85-; instr, Pilchuck Glass Sch, Stanwood, Wash, 81- & gaffer, 83-90; instr, Haystack Mountain Sch Crafts, Deer Isle, Maine, 89; full-time prof artist, currently. *Awards:* Nat Endowment Arts Fel Award, 88; Wash Gov Award, Wash State Arts Comn. *Bibliog:* Regina Hackett (auth), Richard Royal's Glass Art at Foster/White Gallery, Seattle Post-Intelligencer, 4/12/91; Bonnie Miller (auth), rev, GLASS Mag, No 45, fall 91; New Work Mag, No 11, 92; and others. *Mailing Add:* c/o Foster/White Gallery 311 1/2 Occidental Ave S Seattle WA 98104

ROYCE, SUZANNE
CONSULTANT, CURATOR
b Oakland, Calif, Dec 26, 35. *Study:* Univ Calif, Berkeley, BA(hist art), 83. *Collections Arranged:* Parker Edwards, George Scott Miller, Louis Siegriest, 92, Gordon Onslow Ford (auth, catalog), 93, Richard & Martha Shaw, Robert Hudson, Cornelia Schulz-The Stinson Years (auth, catalog), 93, Bolinas Mus, Calif. *Pos:* Spec projs coordr, Phillips Collection, Washington, DC, 83-84, corp progs mgr, 84-86; art communs consult, Suzanne Royce & Assocs, San Francisco, 87- *Mem:* Am Asn Mus; Nat Asn Corp Art Mgt; Coun Univ Art Mus, Berkeley. *Mailing Add:* 1408 Kearny St San Francisco CA 94133

ROYER, MONA LEE
PAINTER
b Dayton, Ohio, June 5, 44. *Study:* Dayton Art Inst, 53; Famous Artists Sch, 66; Wright State Univ, BFA(hons), 78; Georgetown Univ, 85; Alliance Francaise, Paris, 85. *Work:* Joan Rivers, New York; The Embassy of European Economic Community, Washington, DC; Xerox Corp & Ohio Vision Serv, Columbus, Ohio. *Comn:* I Magnin (portrait); Visitors Service Staff, Nat Gallery Art, Washington, DC; D M Graves Jr, Asn Old Crows; Terrance Allen, Allen Antiques; Joan Rivers, New York. *Exhib:* One-man show, Nat Gallery Art, Washington, DC; Toledo Mus Art, Ohio; Columbus Mus Fine Art, Ohio; Iranian Embassy; British Embassy; Capitol Hill; Phillips (mus) Mansion. *Pos:* Commercial artist, Sales Art/Dayton, 67-68; dealer & consult, 69-; exhib aide & art info specialist, Nat Gallery Art, Washington, DC. *Awards:* Second in Painting, Nat Arboretum, Washington, DC, 89. *Bibliog:* Jacqueline Hall (auth), Enjoying paintings, Columbus Dispatch, 78 & 79; Pat Gordon (auth), Personality, Dallas Morning News, 83; Kristen

Hartke (auth), Hill Rag, Art Critic, Washington, DC, 91. *Mem:* Cultural Alliance Washington; Washington Arts Club; Capitol Hill Art League. *Media:* Oil, Watercolor. *Publ:* Delta Queen Cover, CFA program, Cincinnati, 68; Eight art covers, Hill Rag, Washington, DC, 85-91; art covers, Foxhall Gazette, Fagon Publ, Washington, DC, 90-91. *Mailing Add:* 2214 Harbor Terrace Alexandria VA 22308

ROYSHER, HUDSON (BRISBINE)
DESIGNER, ADMINISTRATOR
b Cleveland, Ohio, Nov 21, 11. *Study:* Cleveland Art Inst, grad dipl, 34; Western Reserve Univ, MS, 34; Univ Southern Calif, MFA, 48. *Work:* Univ Buffalo, NY; Univ Southern Calif, Los Angeles; Syracuse Univ, NY; Calif State Univ, Los Angeles; Bethune-Cookman Col, Daytona Beach, Fla. *Exhib:* US State Dept Traveling Exhib, 50-52; Eleven Southern Californians, De Young Mem Mus, San Francisco, Calif, 52; Smithsonian Inst Traveling Exhib, 53-55; Designer Craftsmen of the West Traveling Exhib, 57; Masters of Contemporary American Crafts Exhib, Brooklyn Mus, 61. *Teaching:* Asst prof indust design, Univ Southern Calif, 39-42; head div indust design, Chouinard Art Inst, 45-50; prof art, Calif State Univ, Los Angeles, 50-70, chmn dept art, 70-75, prof emer, 75- *Awards:* Spec Award for Continued Excellence, Cleveland Mus Art, 40 & 46; Outstanding Professor Award, 66 & Outstanding Educator Award, 72, Trustees Calif State Univ & Col. *Bibliog:* A welded steel education, Design Mag, 1/51; H E Winter (auth), Three American silversmiths, Amerika, 5/53; Churches and temples, Progressive Archit, 10/56. *Mem:* Indust Designers Soc Am; Am Asn Univ Prof; Southern Calif Designer Craftsmen; Am Craftsman's Coun; Asn Calif State Univ Prof (chap pres, 63-65 & 71-72). *Mailing Add:* 1784 S Santa Anita Ave Arcadia CA 91006

ROZIER, ROBERT L
PAINTER
Study: St Mary's Seminary Col, Perryville, Mo, BA, 72; Mich State Univ, East Lansing, MFA, 81. *Exhib:* Columbia Art League Ann Exhib, Columbia, Mo, 77; Knollwood Gallery, Western Mich Univ, Kalamazoo, 80; All Area 1985 Exhib, Saginaw Art Mus, Mich, 86; Nat Juried Exhib, Arlington Art Asn, Arlington Mus Art, Tex, 87; Four Views of the Figure, Pontiac Art Ctr, 88; solo exhibs, Flora Kirsch Beck Gallery, Alma Col, 83, Colby-Sawyer Col, New London, NH, 84, Creative Arts Gallery, Mt Pleasant, Mich, 87, Saginaw Valley State Univ, 88. *Teaching:* Instr painting, drawing, watercolor, Art Reach Mid-Mich, Mt Pleasant, 81-82; instr illus, Lansing Community Col, 82; asst prof, Alma Col, Mich, 83- *Media:* Watercolor. *Dealer:* Cade Gallery, Royal Oak, MI. *Mailing Add:* 416 Yale Ave Alma MI 48801

ROZMAN, JOSEPH JOHN
PAINTER, EDUCATOR
b Milwaukee, Wis, Dec 26, 44. *Study:* Univ Wis, Milwaukee, BFA(with honors), 67, MFA, 69. *Work:* Milwaukee Art Mus, Wis; Southwest Tex State Col; Carroll Col; Waukesha, Wis; Charles Wustum Mus Fine Arts, Racine, Wis; De Cordova Mus, Lincoln, Mass. *Comn:* Complete ed of etchings for membership drive, Milwaukee Art Ctr, 69; Award Emblem Design, Lakefront Festival of Arts, Milwaukee Art Ctr, 73 & 77; PBS Great TV Auction (poster), WMVS TV, 78. *Exhib:* 19th, 20th & 21st Boston Printmakers Nat, Boston Mus Fine Arts, 67-69; Nat Print & Drawing Exhib, Okla Art Ctr, Oklahoma City, 67-68 & 72; Int NW Printmakers Exhib, Seattle Art Mus & Portland Art Ctr, 68 & 69; Printmaking: Wisconsin Editions, Milwaukee Art Mus, 72; one-man show, Milwaukee Art Mus, 73 & Joy Horwich Gallery, Chicago, 80 & 83; Artists/Toys Exhib, Milwaukee Art Mus, 77 & 79; Works on Paper, Art Inst Chicago, 78; Wisconsin Directions Two: Here & Now, Milwaukee Art Mus, 78; Watercolor USA, Springfield Art Mus, 81; Prints & Multiples, Art Inst Chicago, 81; Wis Masters Exhib, Wis Acad Arts & Scis, 86; The Aesthetic Excursion: Artists Look at Travel & Transportation, Wustum Mus Fine Arts, Racine, 89; Fourth Int Biennial Print Exhib, Taipei Fine Arts us, Taiwan, Rep of China, 90; Watercolor Wisconsin: Celebrating 25 Years, Charles A Wostum Mus Art, Racine, 91; and others. *Teaching:* Instr design & printmaking, Univ Wis-Milwaukee, 67-69 & 72-73; instr printmaking, Milwaukee Art Mus, 68-76; instr printmaking & painting, Carthage Col, 69-72; vis lectr art, univ Wis-Parkside, 70-71; instr printmaking & design, Layton Sch Art & Design, 73-74; prof printmaking, painting & photography, Mt Mary Col, Wis, 75-; artist-in-residence, Univ Wis-Platteville, 83. *Awards:* Purchase Award, 23rd Nat Boston Printmakers Exhib, De Cordova Mus, 71; Main Award in Painting, Lakefront Festival of Arts, 77, 79 & 81-82; John G Curtis Award, Art Inst Chicago, 81; Edgewood Col Award, Madison Nat Watercolor Exhib, 88; Janey & Carl Moebius Award for Excellence, Alumni Art Show 15, Univ Wis-Milwaukee Art Mus, 89. *Bibliog:* James Auer (auth), They call him the Wizard of Roz, Milwaukee J, 3/11/73; Genene Grimm (auth), Joe Rozman: The busiest boy on the block, Art Scene Mag, 2/69; Dean Jensen (auth), Art in a cold climate, Wisc Acad Rev, 3/83. *Mem:* Am Film Inst, Art Inst Chicago; Racine Art Asn. *Media:* Watercolor; Miscellaneous Media. *Mailing Add:* 5125 Darby Pl Racine WI 53402

ROZZI (JAMES A)
PAINTER, SCULPTOR
b Pittsburgh, Pa, Jan 22, 21. *Work:* State Capitol, Carson City, Nev; Favell Mus, Klamath Falls, Ore; Elks Lodge, Las Vegas; State Bicentennial Comt, Nev. *Comn:* Mural, Valley of Fire State Park Visitors Ctr, Nev, 68. *Exhib:* US Army Nat Art Exhib, Dallas, Tex, 45; Heldorado Western Art Show, Las Vegas, 69-75; Death Valley Western Art Show, Calif, 70-75; Nev Bicentennial Calendar Competition, 75; George Phippen Mem Art Show, Prescott, Ariz, 75. *Pos:* Pres, Arts & Crafts Guild, Las Vegas, 63-65. *Teaching:* Instr, adult educ, San Bernardino Valley Col, Calif, 49-60; teacher drawing, Las Vegas Art League, 67-69. *Awards:* First Place Purchase Awards, Elks Lodge, Las Vegas, 69, 73 & 74; First Place Trophy for Oils, Death Valley 49'ers, 71; Third Place Medal, George Phippen Mem Comt, 75; Grand Champion, Western Art Show, Heldorado Elks Lodge, Las Vegas, 84, Second Prize, Oils, 85. *Bibliog:* Ray Chesson (auth), article, Rev J, 71; Florine Lawlor (auth), article, Las Vegas Sun Newspaper, 71. *Mem:* Nat Cowboy Hall Fame; Nat Soc Lit & Arts. *Media:* Oil, Watercolor; Bronze. *Publ:* Illusr, Loma Linda Med Col Handbook, 51; San Bernardino Valley Col Handbook, 58; auth, Screen Process Mag, 58; illusr, Las Vegas Jazz Festival Mag, 63; True West Mag, 71. *Mailing Add:* 1041 Franklin Ave Las Vegas NV 89104

RUBELLO, DAVID JEROME
PAINTER, PHOTOGRAPHER
b Detroit, Mich, Sept 3, 35. *Study:* La Accademia Di Belli Arti, Rome, with Franco Gentilini, BFA, 61; Det Kongelige Akademi, Copenhagen, with Richard Mortensen, 63-66; Univ Mich, Ann Arbor, with Guy Palazzola, MFA, 72. *Work:* Philip Morris Collection, Washington, DC; Tate Gallery, London; Victoria & Albert Mus, London; Brit Libr; Mus Mod Art, New York; Stanford Univ; Rijksmuseum, The Hague; Book Mus, The Hague; and others. *Comn:* Mural-painting, New Detroit, Inc, Mich, 72; mural-painting, Residential Col, Ann Arbor, Mich, 73. *Exhib:* One-man shows, Slusser Art Gallery, Univ Mich, 78, Shippensburg State Univ, 84 & Gallerie Int, Bloomfield Hills, Mich, 91 & 92; Suprema Invitational, Amsterdam, 91; 3 Dimensions Blank Page 4, London, 90; Kalamazoo Inst Art, 90; Konkretemultiples II, Gallerie L'Idee, Zoetermeer, Netherlands, 90-91; and others. *Pos:* Artist coodr, Italian-Am Archives, Warren, Mich, 87, dir, 88. *Teaching:* Lectr, Univ Mich, Ann Arbor, 73-74; asst prof art, Pa State Univ, University Park, 74-80; assoc prof art, Towson State Univ, Md, 80-81 & Univ Mich, Ann Arbor, 87-90. *Awards:* Ford Found Grants, Pa State Univ, 79 & 80; Fel, Va Ctr Creative Arts, 81; Mich Coun Arts Grant, 87. *Bibliog:* A L Smith (auth), Art & Soul, GMAC Quest, 88; Les Krantz (auth), New York Art Review, Spring 89; Blank page, B-4 Publ, London 90; and others. *Mem:* Mich Photog Soc. *Media:* Acrylic, Wood. *Publ:* Auth, Reflection and form. *Mailing Add:* 22062 27 Mile Rd New Haven MI 48096

RUBEN, ALBERT
PAINTER
b New Orleans, La, Dec 4, 18. *Study:* Univ Calif, Los Angeles, BA(hon; art), 41; Art Students League, with Robert Brackman & F V Dumond, 44-46. *Work:* Elizabeth Greenshields Found, Montreal. *Exhib:* Solo exhib, Regina Gallery, New York, 55, Studio Gallery Workshop, New York, 59 & Doll & Richards, Boston, 61; Butler Mus Am Art, 60; Nat Acad Ann Exhib, New York, 72; Allied Artists Am Ann Exhib, New York, 75-78. *Teaching:* Instr painting, Pels Sch Art, New York, 65-66 & Montserrat Sch Art, Mass, 73-74. *Awards:* Gold Medals, Am Veterans Art Soc, 57 & Rockport Art Asn, 68 & 80. *Mem:* Allied Artists Am; Rockport Art Asn; North Shore Art Asn. *Media:* Oils. *Mailing Add:* Bearskin Neck Rockport MA 01966

RUBEN, RICHARDS
PAINTER, EDUCATOR
b Los Angeles, Calif, Nov 29, 25. *Study:* Chouinard Art Inst. *Work:* Worcester Mus, Mass; Brooklyn Mus, NY; Los Angeles Co Mus Art; Corcoran Gallery Art, Washington, DC; Pasadena Art Mus, Calif. *Exhib:* Sao Paulo, 3rd Biennial, Sao Paulo, Brazil; First Paris Biennial, France, 59; Whitney Mus Am Art, 62-63 & 64; Arte de America y Espana, Madrid, Spain, 63; one-man exib, San Francisco Mus Art, Calif, 71 & Johnson Mus, Cornell Univ; Neuburger Mus, New York, 77; Anita Shapolsky Gallery, New York, 84, 86, 90. *Teaching:* Asst prof drawing & painting, Pomona Col, 58-62; asst prof drawing & painting, New York Univ, 63-82; instr drawing & painting, Pratt Inst, 67-71, 82 & 90; New York Studio Sch, summer 81; Pratt Inst, Venice, Italy, summer 84 & 87-89. *Awards:* Tiffany Grant, 54; Tamarind Fel, 61; Nat Endowment Arts Fel, 80-81. *Bibliog:* Robert Pesurie (auth), Chouinard an Art Vision Betrayed, Antsa, Encintas, Calif; 8 New York Artists, Ex 3 Catalog Text, Kenkeleha Gallery, 87. *Media:* Acrylic, Oil. *Mailing Add:* 85 Mercer St New York NY 10012

RUBENSTEIN, LEWIS W
PAINTER, PRINTMAKER
b Buffalo, NY, Dec 15, 08. *Study:* Harvard Univ, AB, 30; Bacon Traveling Fel, 31-33; painting with Leger & Ozenfant, Paris, fresco with Rico Lebrun, Rome, lithography with Emil Ganso, New York & sumi with Keigetsu, Tokyo. *Work:* Ford Found, New York; Am Univ, Washington, DC; Vassar Col Art Gallery, Poughkeepsie, NY; and others. *Comn:* Frescoes, Fogg Art Mus, 33 & 35; frescoe, Busch-Reisinger Mus, Cambridge, Mass, 37; murals, Post Off, US Sect Fine Arts, Wareham, Mass, 40; mural, Jewish Ctr, Buffalo, 50; and others. *Exhib:* Whitney Mus Am Art, 38; Nat Acad Design, 46, 52, 56 & 63; Libr Cong, Washington, DC, 52-60; Soc Am Graphic Artists, New York, 52-81; Am Watercolor Soc, New York, 55 & 64; retrospective, Vassar Col Art Gallery, 74, Schenectady Mus, NY, 75 & Barrett House, Poughkeepsie, NY, 79, 83 & 90; Fleming Mus, Burlington, Vt, 86; and others. *Pos:* Illusr, Foreign Serv J, 58-66. *Teaching:* Instr fresco painting, Boston Mus Sch Art, 37-38; prof painting, Vassar Col, 39-74. *Awards:* Fulbright Grant, Japan, 57-58; Fairfield Award, Silvermine Guild Artists, 59; Dutchess Exec Co Arts Award, 87; and others. *Bibliog:* The Rubenstein murals, Germanic Mus Bull, Vol 1, No 4, 3/37; Erica Beckh Rubenstein (auth), Lewis Rubenstein's time painting, Vassar Alumnae Mag, 5/57; Masao Ishizawa (auth), Rubenstein and his sumi painting, Hoshun, Japan, 2/25/59; Beatrice Schuller Cohen (auth), Lewis Rubenstein and his time paintings, Am Artist, 11/78. *Mem:* Soc Am Graphic Artists; Dutchess Co Art Asn. *Media:* Watercolor, Sumi; Lithography. *Publ:* Auth, Fresco painting today, Am Scholar, 35; dir, Time Painting by Lewis Rubenstein (film), Vassar Col, 56; Dunes (video), 82; Psalm 104 (video), 87. *Mailing Add:* 153 College Ave Poughkeepsie NY 12603

RUBENSTEIN, MERIDEL
PHOTOGRAPHER
b Detroit, Mich, Mar 26, 48. *Study:* Sarah Lawrence Col, BA, 70; Mass Inst Technol, with Minor White, 72-73; Univ NMex, with Beaumont Newhall, Van Deren Coke & Tom Barrow, MA, 74, MFA, 77. *Work:* Bibliot Nat, Paris; Ctr Creative Photog, Univ Ariz; Mus Fine Arts, Houston; Mus Kunst & Gewerbe, Hamburg, Ger; NMex Mus Fine Arts, Santa Fe. *Exhib:* Solo exhibs, La Gente de la Luz, NMex Mus Fine Arts, Santa Fe, 77 & Mus Kunst & Gewerbe, Hamburg, Ger, 79, The Lowriders, NMex Mus Fine Arts, Santa Fe, 80 & Artists Space, New York, 81, Lifelines, Ctr Creative Photog, Tucson, 83, Calif Mus Photog, 85 & Santa Fe Ctr Contemp Arts, 87; The Portrait Extended, Mus Contemp Art, Chicago, 80; Eleven Photographers from Santa Fe, Int Festival Photog, Arles, France, 81; Unraveling Sound--A Ranch, Paris Biennale, Mus l'Art Mod, Paris, 82; The Essential Landscape, NMex Mus Fine Arts, 85; Contemporary Myth: San Francisco Camerawork, San Francisco, 87. *Pos:* Assoc prof & area head, photog dept, San Francisco State Univ, 85- *Teaching:* Instr photog, Univ NMex, Albuquerque, 76-78 & 85 & Col Santa Fe, 76-80; vis lectr photog & art hist, Univ Colo, Boulder, 80-83. *Awards:* Ferguson Grant, Friends of Photog, 77; Photog Survey Grant, 79 & 82 & Visual Arts Fel, 83, Nat Endowment Arts; Guggenheim Fel Photog, 81-82. *Bibliog:* Dana Ashbury (auth), review, Popular Photog, 2/83; Jonathan Green (auth), American Photography--A Critical History, Abrams, 84; Meridel Rubenstein: Lifelines, NMex Mag, 8/85; David Bell (auth), Report from Santa Fe, Art in Am, 9/85. *Mem:* Soc Photog Educ; Friends Photog; Santa Fe Ctr Photog; San Francisco Camerawork. *Publ:* Auth, La Gente de la Luz, NMex Mus Fine Arts, 77; Photography in New Mexico, 1/77 & Alternative images, 9/79, Afterimage; article, Newslett Friends Photog, 78. *Mailing Add:* Art San Francisco State Univ 1600 Holloway Ave San Francisco CA 94132

RUBEY, TONY (GEORGE ANTON)
PRINTMAKER, EDUCATOR
b Cincinnati, Ohio, May 12, 52. *Study:* Miami Univ, Ohio, BFA, 74; Univ Wis, Madison, MA, 78, MFA, 79. *Work:* Okla Arts Ctr; Alaska State Mus, Juneau; Atlantic-Richfield Co, Anchorge, Alaska; Dulin Gallery Art. *Comn:* Photo-lithographs, Alaska State One Per Cent for Arts Proj, Anchorage, 82. *Exhib:* Collage and Assemblage, Miss Mus Art, Jackson, 81; Lithographs and Constructions, Okla Arts Ctr, 81; Dulin Nat Print Exhib, 82; Colorprint Nat, Tex Tech Univ, 83; solo exhib, Alaska State Mus, Juneau, 83. *Pos:* Studio dir printmaking, Visual Arts Ctr Alaska, Anchorage, 80- *Teaching:* Vis instr printmaking & drawing, Univ Okla, Norman, 79-80; instr printmaking, Univ Alaska, Anchorage, 82- *Awards:* Alaska State Coun Arts Fel, 83. *Mem:* Col Art Asn; Northwest Printmakers Orgn. *Media:* Etching, Lithography. *Dealer:* Miriam Perlman 505 N Lakeshore Dr Suite 5410 Chicago IL 60611. *Mailing Add:* c/o Toni Birckhead Gallery 342 W Fourth St Cincinnati OH 45211

RUBIN, DAVID S
CURATOR, CRITIC
b Los Angeles, Calif, June 18, 49. *Study:* Univ Calif, Los Angeles, AB, 72; Harvard Univ, MA(art hist), 74; Mus Mgt Inst, 89. *Collections Arranged:* Black and White are Colors (auth, catalog), 79, & Contemporary Triptychs (auth, catalog), 82, Galleries Claremont Cols; Jay DeFeo (auth, catalog), 84, Wally Hedrick (auth, catalog), 85 & Concerning the Spiritual (auth, catalog), 85, San Francisco Art Inst; William Baziotes (auth, catalog) 87, Computer Assisted (auth, catalog) 87 & Edward Albee Collection, 88, Freedman Gallery (auth, catalog); Painting from the San Francisco Bay Area (auth, catalog), 88, Paine Art Ctr; Cynthia Carlson (auth, catalog), 89; Contemp Hispanic Shrines (auth, catalog) 90, Freedman Gallery; Art About AIDS, 89, Donald Lipski (auth, catalog) 90, Freedman Gallery; Cruciformed (auth, catalog), Cleveland, Ctr Contemp Art, 91; Petah Coyne (auth, catalog), Cleveland Ctr Contemp Art, 92. *Pos:* Asst dir, Galleries Claremont Cols, 77-; contrib ed, Arts Mag, New York, 79-81; cur, Los Angeles Visual Arts, 82; dir, Santa Monica Col Art Gallery, 82-83; dir exhibs, San Francisco Art Inst, 83-85; adj cur, San Francisco Mus Mod Art, 83-85; guest cur, Paine Art Ctr, Oshkosh, Wis, 86-88; dir, Freedman Gallery, Albright Col, Reading, Pa, 86-90; assoc dir & chief cur, Cleveland Ctr Contemp Art, 90. *Teaching:* Lectr art hist, Sch Visual Arts, New York, 76-77; asst prof art hist, Scripps Col, Claremont, Calif, 77-82. *Awards:* Nat Endowment Arts Mus Fel, Fogg Art Mus, 75-76; summer fel, Guggenheim Mus, 76. *Mem:* Col Art Asn; Int Asn Art Critics; Am Asn Mus. *Res:* Contemporary art, twentieth century art, automatism, abstract expressionism, Californian art. *Publ:* Contribr, Jacques Villon, Fogg Art Mus, 76; auth, critical reviews of exhibitions, 77 & A case for content: Jackson Pollock's subject was the automatic gesture, 79, Arts Mag; Jean St Pierre, Re-Dact, 84. *Mailing Add:* Cleveland Ctr Contemp Art 8501 Carnegie Ave Cleveland OH 44106

RUBIN, DONALD VINCENT
SCULPTOR
b New York, NY, July 10, 37. *Comn:* US Army War Col, Carlisle Barracks, Pa; Am Polled Hereford Asn. *Exhib:* Soc Animal Artists Exhib Conv, NY, 79; one-man shows, Brass Door Galleries, Houston, 77, Hunter Gallery, San Francisco, 77, Indian Paint Brush, Vail, Colo, 77-81 & Huntsville Mus Art, Ala, 78; Nat Sculpture Soc 47th Ann Exhib, New York, 80; and many others. *Pos:* Bd Dirs, Huntsville Mus Art, 81-89. *Awards:* Richman Award for Sculptures, Salmagundi Club, 75, 76, 77 & 80, DeBellis Award, 79; Elliot Liskin Sculpture Award, 81 & 87; and others. *Bibliog:* Ralph Perril (auth), Donald Rubin (Huntsville Alabama), Art Voices South Mag, 7-10/78; Cover Photo Polled Hereford World, 10/88; Francis Robb (auth), Don Rubin American Realistic Sculptor (monogr), Art Press, 11/88. *Mem:* Am Artists Prof League; Soc Animal Artists; Artists Fel; Salmagundi Club. *Media:* Bronze. *Dealer:* J N Bartfield Art Galleries 30 W 57th St New York NY 10019; Indian Paint Brush 183 Gore Creek Dr Vail CO 81657. *Mailing Add:* 712 Forrest Heights Dr Huntsville AL 35802

RUBIN, IDA ELY
CONSULTANT, WRITER
b New York, NY. *Study:* Wells Col, Aurora, NY, BA(with high honors), 44; NY Univ Inst Fine Arts, 44-49; Belg-Am Educ fel, Brussels, 51. *Collections Arranged:* The Guennol Collection (ed, catalog), Metrop Mus Art, New York, 69; Collection of Mr and Mrs John D Rockefeller, III, NY; Collection of Mr and Mrs David Rockefeller, NY; and others. *Pos:* Exec Dir, 20th Int Cong Art Hist, Columbia Univ & New York Univ, 59-61; dir develop, Inst Fine Arts, New York Univ, 62-64; spec consult, Art Gallery, Ctr Inter-Am Rels, New York, 66-69. *Teaching:* Lectr art of Latin Am, Manhattanville Col, Purchase, NY, 70-71. *Mem:* Univ Andes Found; Am Found; Coun Arts Mass Inst Technol; and others. *Res:* Cross-cultural influences of American and European art. *Publ:* Ed, Acts of the 20th International Congress of Art History, 4 vols, Princeton Univ, 63; ed, The Drawings of Morris Graves, New York Graphic Soc, 75; auth, Text on Eduardo Ramirez Villamizar, In: Panorama Artistico Colombiano, Lithografia Arco, Bogota, 77; and others. *Mailing Add:* Indian Head Rd Riverside CT 06878

RUBIN, IRWIN
PAINTER, DESIGNER
b Brooklyn, NY, July 26, 30. *Study:* Brooklyn Mus Sch Art; Cooper Union Art Sch; Yale Univ, BFA & MFA. *Exhib:* Fla State Univ, 60; Baltimore Mus Art, 60; Bertha Schaefer Gallery, New York, 60-63; Stable Gallery, New York, 64; Byron Gallery, 65; and others. *Pos:* Art dir, McGraw-Hill Bk Co, New York, 58-63; art dir, Harcourt Brace Jovanovich, Inc, New York, 71- *Teaching:* Instr drawing & color design, Univ Tex, 55; asst prof, Fla State Univ, 56-58; instr, Pratt Inst, Brooklyn, 64-; assoc prof art Cooper Union Art Sch, 67- *Publ:* Auth, Permanency in collage, Arts Mag, 57. *Mailing Add:* Art Sch Cooper Union Astor Pl New York NY 10003

RUBIN, LAWRENCE
ART DEALER, COLLECTOR
b New York, NY, Feb 22, 33. *Study:* Brown Univ, BA, 55; Univ Paris. *Pos:* Pres, M Knoedler, New York, currently; art adv panel, IRS. *Mem:* Art Dealers Asn (vpres). *Specialty:* Twentieth century contemporary paintings sculpture and drawings; artists Adolph and Esther Gottlieb Found, Inc, Michael David, Richard Diebenkorn, Estate of Herbert Ferber, Glenn Goldberg, Nancy Graves, Howard Hodgkin, Robert Motherwell, Robert Rauschenberg, Estate of David Smith, Frank Stella, Donald Sultan, John Walker. *Collection:* Contemporary painting and sculpture. *Mailing Add:* 19 E 70th St New York NY 10021

RUBIN, SANDRA
PRINTMAKER, LITHOGRAPHER
b Denver, Colo. *Study:* Stanford Univ; Tex Christian Univ, BFA, 67, MFA, 70. *Work:* Ft Worth Art Mus, Tex; Mus NMex, Santa Fe; Univ Ark Gallery, Fayetteville; Univ Colo Gallery, Colorado Springs; Artlink Artspace, Ft Wayne, Ind. *Exhib:* Handmade Paper Objects, Santa Barbara Mus Art, Calif, 76, Oakland Mus, Calif, 77, Inst Contemp Art, Boston, 77, Johnson Mus, Cornell Univ, Ithaca, NY, 77 & Jacksonville Mus Art, Fla, 77; Southwestern Prints & Drawings, Dallas Mus Fine Arts, 78; Fire & Water, Paper as Art, Rockland Ctr for Arts, West Nyack, NY, 80; and others. *Teaching:* Assoc prof printmaking & papermaking, Univ Tex, Arlington, 70-, assoc prof art, currently. *Awards:* Univ Tex, Arlington Organized Res Grant, study handmade paper in Spain, 76 & study handmade paper in Japan, 79; Nat Endowment Arts Ctr for Book Arts Grant, Papermaking Symposium, 77. *Mem:* Col Art Asn Am. *Media:* Intaglio, Embossment. *Dealer:* Adele M Fine Arts Gallery Dallas TX. *Mailing Add:* Dept Art Univ Tex Arlington TX 76019

RUBIN, SANDRA MENDELSOHN
PAINTER
b Santa Monica, Calif, Nov 7, 47. *Study:* Univ Calif, Los Angeles, BA, 76, MFA, 79. *Work:* Los Angeles Co Mus Art; Santa Barbara Mus Art; Univ Calif, Los Angeles; Boise Art Mus, Idaho. *Exhib:* Exhib of Contemp LA Artists, Nagoya City Mus, Nagoya, Japan, 82; A Heritage Renewed, Univ Art Mus, Santa Barbara, 83; solo exhib, Los Angeles Co Mus Art, Calif, 85; American Realism: Twentieth-Century Drawings & Watercolors, San Francisco Art Mus, 86; The Janss Collection, Boise Art Mus, Idaho, 88; California Cityscapes, San Diego Mus Art, 91; and others. *Awards:* Young Talent Purchase Award, Los Angeles Co Mus Art, 80; Nat Endowment Arts, Artist's Fel Grant, 81 & 91. *Bibliog:* Edward Lucie-Smith (auth), American Art Now, William Morrow & Co, 85; Alvin Martin (auth), American Realism, Harry N Abrams, 86; Wendy Beckett (auth), Contemporary Women Artists, Phaidon Press Ltd, 88. *Media:* Oil on Canvas. *Dealer:* LA Louver Gallery 55 N Venice Blvd Venice CA 90291. *Mailing Add:* Box 627 Boonville CA 95415

RUBIN, WILLIAM
CURATOR, HISTORIAN
b New York, NY, Aug 11, 27. *Study:* Columbia Univ, AB, MA & PhD; Univ Paris. *Collections Arranged:* Matta, 57; Dada, Surrealism & Their Heritage (auth, catalog), 68; New Am Painting & Sculpture (auth, catalog), 69; Stella (auth, catalog), 70 & 87, Picasso (auth, catalog), 72 & Miro (auth, catalog), 73, Mus Mod Art; Gerald Murphy (auth, catalog), 74, Anthony Caro (auth, catalog), 75, Andre Masson (auth, catalog), 76 & Cezanne: The Late Work (auth, catalog), 77; Picasso: A Retrospective (auth, catalog), 80; Giorgio DeChirico (auth, catalog), 82; Primitivism in 20th Century Art, 84; Picasso and Brague (auth, catalog), Pioneering Cubism, 89; Ad Reinhardt (auth, catalog), 91; The William S Paley Collection (auth, catalog), 92. *Pos:* Am art ed, Art Int Mag, 58-64; chief cur painting & sculpture, Mus Mod Art, New York, 68-73, dir painting & sculpture, 73-, dir emer, 88-; trustee, Sarah

Lawrence Col, 79-86. *Teaching:* Prof art hist, Sarah Lawrence Col, 52-67; prof, Hunter Col, 54-60; prof, City Univ New York Grad Div, 60-67; adj prof, New York Univ Inst Fine Arts, 69-; dir painting & sculpture, 73-88; dir emer, 88- *Awards:* Knight French Legion of Honor, 79; Award for Distinguished Scholar in Art Hist, Art Dealers Asn Am, 86; Officer French Legion of Honor, 91. *Bibliog:* Calvin Tomkins (auth), Profiles, New Yorker Mag, 11/85; Barbara Rose (auth), The Man From MoMA, Vogue, 8/84. *Mem:* Fel Am Acad Arts & Sci. *Publ:* Auth, Modern sacred art and the Church of Assy, 61, Dada and surrealist art, 69; Jackson Pollock and the Modern Tradition, Parts I-IV, Artforum, 2-5/67; auth, Dada and Surrealist Art, Abrams, 68; Pollock's Jungian Critics, Parts I-II, Art in America, 11-12/79; From Narrative to Iconic in Picasso, Art Bulletin, 83. *Mailing Add:* Mus Mod Art 11 W 53rd St New York NY 10019

RUBINFIEN, LEO H
PHOTOGRAPHER, FILMMAKER
b Chicago, Ill, Aug 16, 53. *Study:* Reed Col; Calif Inst Arts, BFA, 74; Yale Univ Sch Art, MFA, 76. *Work:* Bibliot Nat, Paris; San Francisco Mus Mod Art, Calif; Metrop Mus Art & Mus Mod Art, New York; Corcoran Gallery Art. *Exhib:* Solo exhibs, Castelli Gallery, New York, 81 & Fraenkel Gallery, San Francisco, 82 & 86; The New Color, Int Ctr Photog, New York, 81; New Am Color Photog, Inst Contemp Arts, London, 81; Color & Colored, San Francisco Mus Mod Art, Calif, 81; Color as Form, George Eastman House, Rochester, NY & Corcoran Gallery, Washington, DC, 81; Recent Acquisitions, Mus Mod Art, New York, 84; New Directors, New Films, Mus Mod Art, New York, 89. *Teaching:* Instr photog, Swarthmore Col, 77 & Sch Visual Arts, New York, 78-87; assoc prof art, Fordham Univ, 81-87; vis lectr, Cooper Union, 82. *Awards:* Guggenheim Found Fel, 82-83; Asian Cult Coun Fel, 84. *Bibliog:* Ben Lifson (auth), Cons of collections, Village Voice, 7/22/81; Pete Karmel (auth), The anxious moment, Soho News, 11/4/81; Prudence Carlson (auth), article, Art in Am, 3/82. *Publ:* Auth, Love-Hate Relations, Artforum, 78; auth, The Man in the Crowd, In: Photography in Print, Touchstone Press, 81; 10 Photographs in Camera Mainichi, 5/84; dir & coauth, The Money Juggler (film), 88; dir & coauth, My Bed in the Leaves (film), 90; auth, A Map of the East (in prep). *Dealer:* Fraenkel Gallery 55 Grant Ave San Francisco CA. *Mailing Add:* 230 Riverside Dr No 5L New York NY 10025

RUBINSTEIN, CHARLOTTE STREIFER
WRITER, LECTURER
b New York, NY, Dec 14, 21. *Study:* Brooklyn Col, BA, 41; Teachers Col, Columbia Univ, MA, 46; Otis Art Inst, Los Angeles, MFA, 69. *Collections Arranged:* Women USA Nat Exhib (with catalog), Nat Endowment Arts, 73. *Teaching:* Instr art hist, appreciation & design, Fullerton Col, 71-74; instr art appreciation, women in art, Saddleback Col, 74-84. *Awards:* Best Humanities Bk of 1982, Asn Am Publ, 82; Individual Res Grant, Am Asn Univ Women, 84-85. *Mem:* Col Art Asn; Women's Caucus Art; Art Lib Soc NAm. *Res:* All aspects of history of American women artists. *Publ:* Auth, The early career of Frances Flora Bond Palmer (1812-1876), Am Art J, fall 85; The first American women artists, Women's Art J, spring-summer 82; American Women Artists: From Early Indian Times to the Present, G K Hall/Avon Bks, 82; Chris Peiteys: The Dr Johnson of women artists, Women's Art J, spring-summer, 86. *Mailing Add:* 2680 Victoria Dr Laguna Beach CA 92651

RUBINSTEIN, MEYER RAPHAEL
CRITIC
b Lawrence, Kans, July 22, 55. *Study:* Bennington Col, BA, 79. *Pos:* Managing ed, Flash Art, 89-90. *Publ:* Auth, Europa resurgent: nouveau realisme, 88, Outstations of the post modern, 89 & A hemisphere decentered: Mexican art comes north, 91, Arts Mag; Sight unseen: Derrida at the Louvre, 91 & The painting undone: supports/surfaces, 91, Art Am. *Mailing Add:* 474 Greenwich St New York NY 10013

RUBINSTEIN, SUSAN R See SuZen

RUBY, LAURA
SCULPTOR, PRINTMAKER
b Los Angeles, Calif, Dec 7, 45. *Study:* Univ Southern Calif, BA, 67; San Francisco State Col, MA, 69; Univ Hawaii, MFA(art), 78. *Work:* Contemp Mus, Musicians Asn Hawaii, Honolulu Acad Arts, Hawaii State Fedn Cult & Arts, Honolulu; Erie Mus, Pa. *Comn:* Cromlech (exterior sculpture), Hawaii State Fedn Cult & Arts, Hilo, 80; Richard Street YWCA (serigraph), Hawaii YWCA, 86; Film Crew at Diamond Head (serigraph), Honolulu Printmakers, 88; Stage Set--Mise en Scéne (site specific mixed media sculpture), Hawaii St Fedn Cult & Arts, Honolulu, 91. *Exhib:* Solo exhib, Utah Mus Natural Hist, Salt Lake City, 84; 30th Ann Drawing & Small Sculpture Show, Ball State Art Gallery, Muncie, Ind, 84; 14th Ann Nat Invitational Drawing Exhib, Eppink Art Gallery, Emporia State Univ, Kan, 87; Boston Printmakers 39th NAm Print Exhib, Danforth Mus, Framingham, Mass, 87; Honolulu Acad Arts, 87; Cal-Poly State Univ, Union Gallery, San Luis Obispo, Calif, 88; Bishop Mus, Honolulu, 90; Osaka Trienniale '91, Osaka Mydome, Japan, 91. *Teaching:* Instr, Univ Hawaii, Honolulu, 77-; instr, Chaminade Univ, Honolulu, 80-81. *Awards:* Purchase Award, Erie Clay Nat, Erie Art Mus, Pa, 83; Award in Sculpture, Artquest 86, Los Angeles; Lace Artist Proj Grant New Forms Regional Initiative, Los Angeles, 91-92. *Bibliog:* Marcia Morse (auth), A Tribute to Diamond Head, Honolulu Star Bull, Hawaii, 3/16/86; Ronn Ronck (auth), A printmaker's many visions of Diamond Head, Honolulu Advertiser, 1/21/88; Joan Rose (auth), Installation Sculptures Invite Viewer Participation, Honolulu Star Bull, 4/5/92. *Media:* All; Serigraphy. *Mailing Add:* 509 University Ave 902 Honolulu HI 96826

RUBYLEE, (CHARLES ARMSTRONG LITTLER)
DRAFTSMAN
b Montrose, Colo, Jan 31, 28. *Study:* Univ NMex, BA, 49; Hans Hofmann Sch, New York, 52-54; Alfred Univ, MFA. *Work:* Phoenix Art Mus; Univ NMex Art Mus; Roswell Art Mus, NMex; Univ Ariz Art Mus; Yuma Art Mus, Ariz. *Comn:* Tucson River Park Art Project, Pima County, 90. *Exhib:* One-man shows, Univ Ariz Art Mus, 60 & 78 & Inst Cult, Mex, 64; Ariz Comn Arts, 78; Tucson Art Mus; Phoenix Art Mus, 81. *Pos:* Founder, pres & trustee, Rancho Linda Vista Arts Community. *Teaching:* Prof art, Univ Ariz 58-83; vis artist, Alfred Univ, 60 & Brown Univ, 62. *Awards:* First Purchase Awards, Phoenix Art Mus, 59, Roswell Mus, 61 & Yuma Art Mus. *Bibliog:* Articles in Art in Am & Artspace, fall 81; Ariz Illus, KUAT-TV, 81, 85. *Media:* Charcoal; Mixed Media. *Mailing Add:* Rancho Linda Vista Oracle AZ 85623

RUCKER, HARRISON CAMPBELL
PAINTER, PRINTMAKER
b Louisville, Ky, Apr 7, 30. *Study:* Richmond Prof Inst, cert, 48-52; Cleveland Inst Art, 55-56. *Exhib:* Columbia Mus Art, SC, 69; Seven Major Southern Artists, Mint Mus, Charlotte, NC, 78; Artists of the Rockies Retrospective, Sangre De Cristo Arts Ctr, Pueblo, Colo, 83. *Awards:* First Prize, Exhib Southern Contemp Art, 61; Second Prize, 11th Ann Springs Art Contest, Springs Mills, 69. *Bibliog:* Paula S Jordon (auth), Harrison Rucker, Artists of the Rockies, fall 81. *Mem:* Southeastern Ctr Contemp Art. *Media:* Acrylic, Oil. *Publ:* Auth, article, in: Western Art Digest, Artists of the Rockies & the Golden West, 86. *Dealer:* Hammer Galleries 33 W 57th New York NY 10019. *Mailing Add:* 1407 Lynwood Terrace High Point NC 27260

RUDA, EDWIN
PAINTER
b New York, NY, May 15, 22. *Study:* Columbia Univ, MA, 49; Sch Painting & Sculpture, Mexico City, 49-51; Univ Ill, MFA, 56. *Work:* State of NY Collection, Albany Mall; Indianapolis Mus Art, Ind; Dallas Mus Art, Tex; Nat Gallery of Australia, Canberra; Mass Inst Technol, Cambridge; Corcoran Gallery, Washington; Port Authority of New York. *Exhib:* Smithsonian Traveling Exhib, Latin Am, 66; Systemic Painting, Guggenheim Mus, 66 & Whitney Mus Am Art Painting Ann, 69, New York; Paintings on Paper, Aldrich Mus Contemp Art, Ridgefield, Conn; 73 Biennial, Whitney Mus Am Art, New York; Contemp Am Painting & Sculpture, Krannert Art Mus, Univ Ill, Urbana, 74; 10th Anniversary Exhib 1964-1974, Aldrich Mus Contemp Art, 74; Baltimore Mus, 75, Drawing Show, 76; Benefit Exhib for Udine, Italy, NY Univ, 76; June Kelly Gallery, New York, NY, 87-88; Condeso Lawler Gallery, New York, NY, 87-88. *Pos:* Co-founder, Park Pl Gallery Art Res. *Teaching:* Instr painting, Univ Tex, Austin, 56-59 & 78, Sch Visual Arts, New York, 67-71, Pratt Inst, Syracuse Univ & Ohio State Univ, 78 & Tyler Sch Art, Philadelphia, 79; instr painting, Sch Visual Arts, New York, 67-71. *Awards:* Creative Artists Pub Serv Fel, 78-79. *Bibliog:* Carter Ratcliff (auth), Striped for action, Artnews, 2/72; Dore Ashton (auth), New York commentary, Studio Int, 2/70; Peter Schjeldahl (auth), In and out of step in Soho, New York Times, 10/73. *Publ:* Auth, Park Place 1963-67: some informal notes in retrospect, Art Mag, 67. *Mailing Add:* 44 Walker St New York NY 10013

RUDDLEY, JOHN
PAINTER, CONSULTANT
b New York, NY, Oct 29, 12. *Study:* Cooper Union Sch Art & Archit, with Tully Filmus, Ernest Fiene & Paul Feeley; DaVinci Sch Art; Columbia Univ, BS(hist art) & MA(art educ). *Work:* Corcoran Sch Art & Arts Club Washington, Washington, DC. *Exhib:* Corcoran Gallery Art, Washington, DC, 63; Arts Club Washington, 63; Corcoran Sch Art, 63-64; Avant Gallery, Alexandria, Va, 64; Columbia Univ Gallery, New York, 65. *Pos:* Dean & head, Corcoran Sch Art, 62-65; supvr art, Westchester Co, White Plains, NY, 65-; dir, Westchester Art Workshop, 65-; bd gov, Cooper Union, New York, 69-; bd dirs, Nippon Mus, New York; consult, Mus Mod Art, New York, 84-; researcher, Ringling Mus Art, Sarasota, Fla, 85-; trustee, Hammond Mus, N Salem, NY, 72- *Teaching:* Prof design & painting, Corcoran Sch Art, 62-64; prof hist art, Lab Inst Design, New York, 64-69; prof painting, Pace Col, Pleasantville, NY, 70-71. *Mem:* Am Soc Aesthetics; Arts Club Washington; Inst Study Art; Int Soc Educ Art; Nat Art Educ Asn. *Media:* Acrylic, Oil, Watercolor. *Publ:* Auth, Series of book reviews, Nat Art Educ Asn J, 64-72. *Mailing Add:* 97-40 62nd Drive New York NY 11374

RUDENSTINE, ANGELICA ZANDER
HISTORIAN, CURATOR
b Ger. *Study:* Oxford Univ, Eng, BA, 59, MA, 60; Smith Col, MA, 61. *Collections Arranged:* Art of the Russian Avant-Garde: The George Costakis Collection Traveling Exhib (auth, catalog), 81-84. *Pos:* Cur, Mus Fine Arts, Boston, 60-68 & Guggenheim Mus, New York, 69-82; freelance curator, 82-; ed bd, American Scholar, currently. *Teaching:* Adj prof 19th & 20th century art hist, Inst Fine Arts, NY Univ, 85-86. *Awards:* Guggenheim Fel, 83; Alfred H Barr Award, 87; Mitchell Prize, 88. *Mem:* Col Art Asn Am; Am Acad, Rome (trustee & chmn, fine arts comt, 80-92); Int Coun Mus. *Res:* 20th century European and American art. *Publ:* Auth, Guggenheim Mus Collection: Paintings 1880-1945, 76; Russian Avant Garde Art: The George Costakis Collection, 81; Peggy Guggenheim Collection, Venice, Abrams, 85; Modern Painting-Drawing-Sculpture Collected by Emily & Joseph Pulitzer, Jr, Harvard Univ Press, 88. *Mailing Add:* 33 Elmwood Ave Cambridge MA 02138-4717

RUDMAN, JOAN (COMBS)
PAINTER, INSTRUCTOR
b Owensburg, Ind, Oct 7, 27. *Study:* Mich State Univ, BA(art educ), MA(art); Art Student's League, Woodstock, NY, with Arnold Blanch, Walter Plate & Richard Segalman also with Edgar A Whitney, Walter DuBois Richards, Diana Kan & Charles Reid. *Work:* Combe Inc, Kresgie Mus. *Exhib:* Wadsworth Atheneum; Acad Fine Arts & Watercolor Soc, New Brit Mus Am Art; Nat Arts Club Open Watercolor Show, 69 & 78; Am Watercolor Soc, 74, 77 & 84; Mus Fine Arts, Springfield, Mass, 77; Salmagundi Club, 78; Nat Acad Design, New York, 86; and others. *Pos:* Asst Ed, Newsletter (Am Watercolor Soc). *Teaching:* Instr, King Sch, Stamford, Conn, Round Hill Community House, Greenwich, Conn & Continuing Educ Classes, Stamford, currently; artist-in-residence, Southern Vermont Art Ctr, Manchester, currently. *Awards:* Best in Show & Russell Purchase Award, Old Greenwich Art Soc, 91; Winsor-Newton Plaque & Award, Hudson Art Asn, 91; Hon Mention in Graphics, Catherine Lorillard Wolfe Art Club, 91. *Mem:* Am Watercolor Soc, 84- (bd dir, 87-); Am Artists Prof League; Hudson Valley Art Asn (bd dirs, 71-); Catherine Lorillard Wolfe Art Club (bd dirs, 84-91); Nat Press Club, Washington, DC. *Media:* Watercolor. *Publ:* Artist in Special Tribute, HVAA Catalog Ann, Newspaper Press Releases, Gannett Chain, 72- *Mailing Add:* 274 Quarry Rd Stamford CT 06903

RUDQUIST, JERRY JACOB
PAINTER, EDUCATOR
b Fargo, NDak, June 13, 34. *Study:* Minneapolis Col Art & Design, BFA, 56; Cranbrook Acad Art, MFA, 58. *Work:* Univ Minn Gallery, Minneapolis; St Cloud State Col, Minn; Anoka Ramsey State Jr Col, Minn. *Exhib:* Walker Art Ctr, Minneapolis, 58, 60, 62, 65 & 77; Minn Portfolio (traveling exhib, Middle East & Europe), St Paul Gallery, 60; Denver Art Mus, Colo, 63; Joslyn Mus Art, Omaha, Nebr, 64, 68 & 70; Birmingham Mus Art, Ala, 66; Art in the Embassies Prog, US State Dept, 68-71; Drei Amerikaner aus dem Mittleren Western, Mannheimer Symposion der Kunste, WGer, 72; one-man exhibs, Walker Art Ctr, Minneapolis, 63 & Minneapolis Inst Arts, 64, 71 & 75; Colo 1st Nat Print & Drawing Competition, 74. *Teaching:* Prof art, Macalester Col, 58-; vis lectr & critic art, Boston Univ, summer 69. *Awards:* Spec Donor & Purchase Award, Walker Art Ctr, 62; Purchase Award, Minneapolis Inst Arts, 65; Purchase Award, World Print Competition, San Francisco, 73. *Bibliog:* Dan Paris (auth), Rudquist (film), produced by Minneapolis Inst Arts, Macalester Col & Minn State Arts Coun, 71; Samuel Sachs II (auth), Jerry Rudquist: Recent works, Minneapolis Inst Arts, 71. *Media:* Oil. *Dealer:* Suzanne Kohn Gallery 1690 Grand Ave St Paul MN 55105. *Mailing Add:* c/o Susan Kohn Gallery 1690 Grant Ave St Paul MN 55105

RUELLAN, ANDREE
PAINTER
b New York, NY, Apr 6, 05. *Study:* Art Students League, scholar, 20-22; Maurice Sterne Sch, Rome, scholar, 22-23; Acad Suedoise, Paris, with Per Krogh & Charles Dufresne. *Work:* Fogg Mus, Harvard Univ; Metrop Mus Art, New York; Phillips Mem Gallery, Washington, DC & Columbia Mus Art, SC; Whitney Mus Am Art; Springfield Mus Art, Utah; SC State Mus Art. *Comn:* Murals, Post Off, Emporia, Va, 40 & Lawrenceville, Ga, 41. *Exhib:* 10th Ann, Whitney Mus Am Art; Am Painting Today, Metrop Mus Art, 50; Storm King Art Ctr Retrospective, 66; Artists for Victory, Metrop Mus Art, New York; Pa Acad Fine Arts Ann; Mus City New York; Art Inst Chicago; Corcoran Gallery, Washington, DC; Springfield Mus Art, Mass; Libr Cong, Washington, DC; Va Mus Fine Arts, Richmond; Heckscher Mus, New York; Retrospective, Lehigh Univ; one-person show, Woodstock Artists Asn, 77; Drawing Retrospective, Kraushaar Gallery, 90; and others. *Teaching:* Vis artist, Pa State Univ, summer 57. *Awards:* Pennell Mem Medal, Philadelphia Watercolor Club, 45, Dawson Medal, 50; Guggenheim Found Fel, 50-51; Am Acad Arts & Letts Grant. *Bibliog:* Harry Salpeter (auth), About Andree Ruellan, Coronet, 12/38; Ernest Watson (auth), Andree Ruellan, Am Artist, 10/43; Arthur Zaidenburg (auth), The Art of the Artist, Crown, 51. *Mem:* Woodstock Artists Asn; Art Students League. *Media:* Multi. *Dealer:* Kraushaar Galleries 724 Fifth Ave New York NY 10019. *Mailing Add:* c/o Kraushaan Galleries 724 Fifth Ave New York NY 10019

RUFFING, ANNE ELIZABETH
PAINTER
b Brooklyn, NY. *Study:* Cornell Univ, BS; Drexel Inst Technol; also studied with John Pike. *Work:* Metrop Mus Art, New York; Brooklyn Mus, NY; Nat Gallery Art, Washington, DC; Whitney Mus Am Art, New York; Libr of Nat Collection of Fine Arts, Smithsonian Inst, Washington, DC; and many others. *Comn:* Four Wildlife Drawings, Johnston Hist Mus, North Brunswick, NJ, 76; four hist landmark lithographs, NY State Senate, comn by City of Kingston, NY, 76; porcelain series, Danbury Mint, Norwalk, Conn, 81-82; porcelain series, Oxmoor House, Birmingham, Ala, 83-85; ltd ed print, Nat Wildlife Fedn, Washington, DC, 88. *Exhib:* Rocky Mountain Nat Watermedia Exhib, Golden, Colo, 76; 25th Ann Exhib Painting & Sculpture, Berkshire Mus, 76; one-woman shows, Art in Industry, IBM Corp, New York, 66 & A E Ruffing Exhib, Hall of Fame, Goshen, NY, 71; 4th Ann Exhib, Midwest Watercolor Soc, Manitowoc, Wis, 80; and others. *Awards:* Int Women's Year Award, Int Women's Festival, D Gillespie, 76; Spec Merit Award, Midwest Watercolor Soc, 80. *Bibliog:* Bruce Henry Davis (auth), Introducing the art of A E R, 1/77, Memories of Childhood, 2/77 & Glimpses of yesterday, 7/77, Collector's News, Am Masters Found. *Media:* Watercolor, Ink. *Publ:* Illusr, Ideals Old Fashioned Issue (title page plus two others), Ideals, 75. *Mailing Add:* Box 125 Bloomington NY 12411

RUFFNER, GINNY MARTIN
GLASSBLOWER
b Atlanta, Ga, June 21, 52. *Study:* Univ Ga, BFA(drawing, painting, cum laude), 74, MFA, 75. *Work:* High Mus, Atlanta, Ga; Corning Mus Glass, NY, Cooper-Hewitt Mus, New York; Mus des Arts Decoratif, Lausanne, Switz; Huntington Mus, WVa. *Exhib:* Athens Ann Exhib, Ga, 74; La Grange Ann Exhib, Ga, 75; Nat Art Invitational, Atlanta, Ga, 81; Leigh Yawkey Woodsen Art Mus, Wausau, Wis, 81; Macon Mus Arts & Sci, Ga, 84; Cooper-Hewitt Mus, New York, 85; State Capital Mus, Olympia, Wash, 86; Bellevue Mus, Wash, 86; Louisville Art Gallery, New York, 86; Habatat Gallery, Miami, Fla, 87; Darmstadt Mus, WGer, 87; Mus Modern Art, Hokkaido, Japan, 88; and others. *Teaching:* Adj instr watercolor & art appreciation, DeKalb Col, Clarkston, Ga, 77; vis scholar glassblowing, Penland Sch Crafts, NC, 79; lectr, Nat Sculpture Conf, Cincinnati, 87; lectr, Bellevue Mus, Wash, 88; instr, Pilchuck Sch, 84, 85, 86, 87, 88 & 89; and others. *Awards:* First Place, Art Quest 1985, 85; Cert of Excellence, Int Art Competition, 86; Award of Merit, Post Alley Art Expose, 87. *Mem:* Glass Art Soc; Atlanta Glass Art Guild (charter mem, bd dirs, 84, 85); Am Craft Coun; Am Sci Glassblowers Soc. *Publ:* Auth, NEA Visual Artists Fel 86, Am Craft, 86; New Glass Review II, Corning Mus, 81; Public Domain, Am Craft, 88, Studio Glass Poses Novel Possibilities, Atlanta Journal, 88, Ruffner's Lampworks Will Turn You On, Seattle Times, 88; and others. *Mailing Add:* 84 University No 403 Seattle WA 98101

RUFFO, JOSEPH MARTIN
PRINTMAKER, ADMINISTRATOR
b Norwich, Conn, Dec 6, 41. *Study:* Pratt Inst; Cranbrook Acad Art. *Work:* Ark Art Ctr, Little Rock; Mus Mod Art, Salvador, Brazil; Memphis Col Art, Tenn; Miss Art Asn, Jackson; Sheldon Mem Art Gallery, Lincoln, Nebr; and others. *Comn:* American Tool Co. *Exhib:* Third Biennial Rutgers Nat Drawing Exhib, State Univ NJ, Camden Col Arts & Sci, 79; Potsdam Prints, 16th Nat, 82; 11th Nat Prints & Drawing Exhib, Minot State Col, 82; La Grange Nat, 82; 23rd Nat Print Exhib, Hunterdon Art Ctr, Clinton, NJ, 79; Images Aluminum, Tamarind Prints Traveling Exhib, Macalester Col, 79-80; solo exhib, Sheldon Mem Art Gallery, Lincoln, Nebr, 87. *Pos:* Head dept art, Univ Northern Iowa, Cedar Falls. *Teaching:* Instr art, Memphis Acad Arts, 64-68; instr art, Fla Mem Col, 69-77; asst prof art & chmn dept, Barry Col, 69-74, chmn div fine arts, 74-77; prof art, Univ Northern Iowa, 77-84; chmn dept art hist, Univ Nebr, 84. *Awards:* Fulbright Grant, Brazil, 63; Best in Show, 12th Ann Mid South Exhib, 67; Purchase Prize, 10th Dixie Ann Prints & Drawings, 68. *Mem:* Nat Coun Art Adminrs; Nat Asn Schs Art & Design; Col Art Asn; Am Arbitration Asn. *Media:* All Media. *Mailing Add:* Dept Art & Art Hist Univ Nebr Lincoln 14th & R St Lincoln NE 68588

RUGGIERO, LAURENCE J
MUSEUM DIRECTOR
b Patterson, NJ, Mar 25, 48. *Study:* Univ Pa, BA, 69, MA, 73, PhD, 75; Boston Univ, MBA, 79. *Work:* Ringling Mus Art, Sarasota, Fla; Oakland Mus Asn, Calif; Metrop Mus Art, New York. *Pos:* Consult projs, J Paul Getty Mus Found, Los Angeles & Boston Mus Fine Arts; asst to pres, Metrop Mus Art, New York, 78-81; exec dir, Oakland Mus Asn, Calif, 81-85; dir, John & Mable Ringling Mus Art, Sarasota, 85-92; assoc dir, Charles Hosmer Morse Mus Am Art, Winter Park, Fla, 92- *Teaching:* Asst prof hist art, Univ Ill, Chicago Circle, 73-77. *Mem:* Am Asn Art Mus Dirs; Col Art Asn; Am Asn Mus. *Mailing Add:* c/o Charles Hosmer Morse Mus Am Art 151 E Welbourne Ave Winter Park FL 32789

RUGGLES, JOANNE BEAULE
PAINTER, EDUCATOR
b New York, NY, May 19, 46. *Study:* Akron State Univ; Ohio State Univ, with Sidney Chafetz, BFA(painting) & MFA(painting, printmaking & photography); Univ of Calif, Santa Barbara; Calif Polytechnic State Univ. *Work:* Ohio State Univ, Columbus; Calif Polytech State Univ, San Luis Obispo; Calif State Library, Sacramento; Wesleyan Col, Macon, Ga. *Exhib:* 6th, 7th, 8th & 9th Int Exhib Original Drawings, Mus Mod Art, Rijeka, Yugoslavia, 78, 80, 82 & 84; Ibiza Graphic 80, Mus Art Contemporaneo Ibiza, Spain, 80; Eigth Premio Biella Per L' Incisione, Italy, 80; Second international Exhibition of Prints and Drawings, Mus Arts & Sci, Wesleyan Col, 83-84; Cabo Fio I & II International Print Biennal, Brazil, 83 & 84; Intergraphic '84, Exhibit Ctr, Berlin, 84; Int Print Exhib: 1983 Repub of China, Taipei City Mus Fine Arts, Taiwan, 83-84; Prints USA, Nat Mus, Singapore & Nat Gallery, Bangkok. *Pos:* Reviewer, Applications for Dorland Mountain Arts Colony, 89-; panalist to review art in public places applicants, San Luis Obispo Co, 92- *Teaching:* Lectr drawing & painting, Ohio State Univ, 70-71, Allan Hancock Col, 71-76 & Cuesta Col, 77-79; lectr drawing & printmaking, Calif Polytech State Univ, 73-80, assoc prof, 83-88, prof, dept art & design, 88- *Awards:* First prize graphics, Arts Club of Washington, 81; University Purchase Award, Wesleyan Col, 83; Jurors Award, Cabo Frio Int, Brazil, 83. *Mem:* Los Angeles Printmaking Soc; Calif Soc of Printmakers; Boston Printmakers; World Print Council; Philadelphia Print Club. *Media:* Mixed Media; Oil, Pastels. *Publ:* Co-auth, Darkroom Graphics: Creative Photographic Techniques for Photographers and Artists, Amphoto, 75; contribr, Encyclopedia of Photography, Amphoto/Eastman Kodak, 78. *Mailing Add:* Box 46 San Luis Obispo CA 93406

RUGOLO, LAWRENCE
PRINTMAKER, EDUCATOR
b Milwaukee, Wis, Oct 2, 31. *Study:* Univ Wis, Milwaukee, BA(art & art educ), 54; Univ Iowa, MFA, 59. *Work:* IBM, St Louis, Mo; Hunterdon Art Ctr, Clinton, NJ; State Univ NY Col, Potsdam; Ark Arts Ctr, Little Rock; Arts Coun Collection, Tulsa, Okla; plus others. *Comn:* Mural, First Nat Bank,

Columbia, Mo, 79. *Exhib:* One-man shows, Albrecht Art Mus, 75, Northeast Mo State Univ, 81 & Lindenwood Col, St Louis, Mo, 88; 15th Nat Print & Drawing Exhib, Minot, NDak, 85; Cameron Nat Print Exhib, Lawton, Okla, 85; 15th Ann Works on Paper Exhib, Southwest State Univ, San Marcos, Tex, 87; Nat Print 88, Trenton, NJ, 88; 32nd Nat Print Exhib, Hunterdon Art Ctr, Clinton, NJ, 88. *Teaching:* Prof screenprinting & design, Univ Mo, Columbia, 74-, chmn art dept, 73-76. *Awards:* Purchase Awards, 28th Nat Print Exhib, Hunterdon Art Ctr, Clinton, NJ, 84 & 19th Ann Anderson Winter Show, Ind, 89; Best of Show, No Platte Valley Artist's Guild Nat Juried Art Show, Scottsbluff, Nebr, 90. *Mem:* Print Consortium, St Joseph, Mo; Col Art Asn. *Mailing Add:* Dept Art Univ Missouri Columbia MO 65211

RUHE, BARNABY SIEGER
PAINTER, CRITIC
b New York, NY, Aug 10, 46. *Study:* US Naval Acad, BS, 68; Md Inst, Col Art, with Ed Dugmore, Sal Scarpitta & Babe Shapiro, MFA(painting), 75; New York Univ, PhD, 89. *Work:* Lincoln & Great Neck Schs; Muhlenberg Col, Lincoln & Great Neck; Sidney Lewis Mus; Patterson Mus; Conejo Valley Art Mus. *Comn:* Marathons, City Allentown, 80; Conejo Valley Art Mus, 90. *Exhib:* Pleiades, New York, 76, 77 & 79; 5 solo-shows, Barbara Braathen Gallery, New York, 85-88; Conejo Valley Art Mus, 90. *Collections Arranged:* WC4 Box 83 10,000, New York Mail Concept Exhib. *Pos:* Dir, cur & producer, Whitney Counterweight, New York, 77, 79, 81 & 83; Sr art ed, Art World, 80-90; artist & lectr, Mus Mod Art, New York, 90-91. *Teaching:* Instr, Art hist, US Naval Acad, 72-75; instr Shamanistic painting workshops, Muhlenberg Col & Great Neck Ctr, 81- *Awards:* Nat Endowment Arts Dirs Grant, 77; Prize, Allentown Art Mus, 79; Comn Visual Arts Grant, New York, 83, 86. *Bibliog:* Vic Miles (interviewer), Ruhe marathon painting, CBS TV, New York, 1/79 & NBC TV, 2/80; Myra Goldfarb (auth), Zen in Ruhe Painting, Call Chronicle, 5/79; Brad Swift, Bill Paige & Nina Barbier (dirs), Movies on Ruhe. *Mem:* Founding mem Valley Arts Coun, 76-; bd dirs, Artists Talk on Art, New York, 89-91. *Media:* Oil, House Paint. *Publ:* Auth, Art of Making Boomerangs, American Woodworking, Rodale Press, 91. *Dealer:* Helen Turner 185 E 85th New York NY 10028. *Mailing Add:* RD 2 Box 67 Emmaus PA 18049

RUMFORD, BEATRIX TYSON
ADMINISTRATOR
b Baltimore, Md, June 16, 39. *Study:* Wellesley Col, 58-62; State Univ NY Oneonta & NY State Hist Asn Cooperstown, 64-65; Bath Summer Sch, Courtauld Inst, Univ London travel course, 69; Nat Trust Summer Sch, Attingham Park, Shropshire, Eng & study tour, Oslo, Norway, 70. *Collections Arranged:* The Beardsley Limner, 72-73; Folk Art in America: A Living Tradition, 74-76; and organized five major exhibs on American Folk Art Ann. *Pos:* Art res ed, D C Heath & Co, Boston, 62-64; res assoc, Chicago Hist Soc, Ill, 66-67; from asst cur to assoc cur, Colonial Williamsburg, Va, 67-71, vpres & dir mus, 79-; from assoc dir to dir, Abby Aldrich Rockefeller Folk Art Collection, 71-, vpres mus, 79- *Mem:* NY State Hist Asn; Furnishings Comt, Exec Mansion, Richmond, Va; Bermuda Nat Trust; Antique Collectors Guild, Richmond, Va (exec coun, 74). *Res:* Role of death as reflected in the art and folkways of the Northeast in the eighteenth and nineteenth centuries. *Publ:* Auth, The household accessories at Colonial Williamsburg, 69 & Nonacademic English painting, 74, Antiques; auth, What is American Folk Art?, 74; auth, Folk art, In: World Bk Encycl, 75; ed, American Folk Portraits, 81. *Mailing Add:* 110 Nicholson St Williamsburg VA 23185

RUMSEY, DAVID MACIVER
ENVIRONMENTAL ARTIST, PATRON
b New York, NY, Apr 29, 44. *Study:* Yale Univ, BA, 66, BFA & MFA, 69. *Exhib:* Spaces, Mus Mod Art, New York, 70; Work for New Spaces, Walker Art Mus, Minneapolis, 71; Pulsa & Television Sensoriums, Automation House, 71; Pulsa, Philadelphia Mus Fine Arts, 71; Calif Inst Arts, 72. *Teaching:* Lectr art, Yale Univ, 68-72; vis artist, Calif Inst Arts, 70-73. *Bibliog:* Lucy Lippard (auth), Arts Canada, 12/68; Jim Burns (auth), Arthropods, 72; David Shirey (auth), NY Times, 12/24/70. *Mem:* Pulsa Group; Am Soc for Eastern Arts & Ctr for World Music (assoc dir, 73-75). *Interests:* Life-involved large scale speculative sculpture; patron of Radical Lava Plateau Art Company. *Mailing Add:* 24 Beulah St San Francisco CA 94117

RUPP, SHERON ADELINE
PHOTOGRAPHER, EDUCATOR
b Mansfield, Ohio, Jan 14, 43. *Study:* Denison Univ, BA, 65; Univ Mass, MFA, 82. *Work:* Mus Mod Art, New York; Fogg Art Mus, Harvard Univ; Rose Art Mus, Brandeis Univ; Smith Col Mus Art; Univ Mass, Mead Art Mus, Amherst Col, Mass; Mus Fine Arts, Boston. *Exhib:* Recent Acquisitions, Mus Mod Art, New York, 87; one-man show, Photo Ctr Gallery, New York Univ, Tisch Sch Art, 87, Hart Gallery, Northampton, Mass, 92 & OK Harris Gallery, 92; Rose Art Mus, Waltham, Mass, 88; Portland Sch Art, Maine, 89; Smith Col Mus Art, Northampton, Mass, 89; New Photography-7, Mus Mod Art, 91; Pleasures & Terrors of Domestic Comfort, Mus Mod Art, New York, 91; and others. *Pos:* Mem bd dir, Zone Art Ctr, Springfield, 87- *Teaching:* Instr photog, Northfield Mt Hermon Sch, 82-83 & Holyoke Community Col, 86-88; vis asst prof, Hampshire Col, Amherst, 85-87. *Awards:* Photog Fel, Mass Artists Found, 84 & 87; Visual Arts fel, Nat Endowment Arts, 86; John Simon Guggenheim Mem Award, 90. *Bibliog:* For Kids' Sake - Photographs of Today's Youth, PRC-Boston, 85; Cross Currents, Cross Country, PRC Boston & San Francisco camera work, 88; Northampton Postcards, Smith Col Art Mus, Northampton, Mass, 90; Peter Galassi (auth), Pleasures & Terrors of Domestic Comfort, Mus Mod Art, New York, 91. *Mem:* Photog Resource Ctr; Friends of Photog. *Publ:* Auth, Sheron Rupp Color Photographs, Helicon Nine, J Women's Arts & Lett, 86. *Mailing Add:* 100 Chestnut Florence MA 01060

RUPPERSBERG, ALLEN
CONCEPTUAL ARTIST
b Cleveland, Ohio, Jan 5, 44. *Study:* Chouinard Art Inst, BFA. *Work:* Guggenheim Mus Art, New York; Los Angeles Co Mus, Calif; Mus Mod Art, New York; Whitney Mus Am Art, New York; Mus Contemp Art, Los Angeles, Calif. *Exhib:* Mus Contemp Art, Los Angeles, Calif, 85; New Mus Contemp Art, New York, 85; one-man shows: John Weber Gallery, Projects' Room, New York, 90, Zoetrope from Andre Breton, Ponce de Leon and the Fountain of Youth (installation), Rich Kuhlenschmidt Gallery, Santa Monica, Calif, 90, The Myth of Metaphor, Galerie Gabrielle Maubrie, Paris, Personal Art, Christine Burgin Gallery, new York; Just What is it That Makes Today's Homes So Different, So Appealing, The Hyde Collection, New York, 91; L'Esprit Bibliotheque, Les Editions Belle Haleine, Paris, 91; A Passion for Art, Tony Shafrazi Gallery, New York, 91; One Leading to Another, 303 Gallery, New York, 92; Overlay, Louver Gallery, New York, 92. *Awards:* Grant, Nat Endowment Arts, 76 & 82; Theodoran Award, Guggenheim Mus, 77; Visual Arts Award (AVA), 87. *Bibliog:* Peter Kirby (dir), Allen Ruppersberg (film), 85; Olivier Zahm (auth), Reviews, Paris, Artforum, 112-113, 12/91; Eric Troncy (auth), No Man's Time, Flash Art, 119-122, 11/91. *Publ:* Auth, The Secret of Life and Death, Black Sparrow Press, 85; Artists Paper, Artist's Page, 4-9/88. *Dealer:* 21 Bond St New York NY 10012. *Mailing Add:* 611 Broadway, No 703 New York NY 10012

RUSAK, HALINA R
LIBRARIAN, PAINTER
b Navahradak, Byelorussia; US citizen. *Study:* Douglass Col, New Brunswick, NJ, BA, 54; Rutgers Univ, New Brunswick, MLS, 56, MA, 76. *Exhib:* One-woman shows, NJ State Mus, Trenton, 77, Georgian Court Col, Lakewood, NJ, 77, SOHO 20, New York, 79, 84 & 87, Byelorussion Inst Arts & Sci, New York, 82, Franklin Libr, Somerset, NJ, 82, Ortho Pharmaceutical Corp Art Gallery, Raritan, NJ, 86 & Johnson & Johnson Int Hq Gallery, New Brunswick, NJ, 87; Women Artists, Paul Robeson Gallery, Newark, NJ, 79-80 & Nabisco World Hq, East Hanover, NJ, 80; Women Artists Series, Walters Hall Gallery, New Brunswick, 81 & Douglass Col Libr, 84; Women's Spheres, Middlesex County Mus, Piscataway, NJ, 83-84; Slavic Art Exhib, New York, 88. *Pos:* Art bibliographer & slide librn, Douglass Col, New Brunswick, 56-83; art librn, Rutgers Univ, New Brunswick, 83-; consult ed, Art Reference Services Quarterly, 91- *Teaching:* Bibliog instr, art, Rutgers Univ, New Brunswick, NJ, 83. *Awards:* Preservation Grant for Elephant Folio, State of NJ; Research Coun Grant for publication, Am Abstract Women Painters. *Bibliog:* Portfolio of New Jersey Women Artists, Womens Caucus Art, NJ, 80; Amy Stromsten (auth), Women Artists, Rutgers Univ; Women Artists Series Representative Works, 1971-84, Douglass Col, 84. *Mem:* Art Libr Soc NAm (vchmn, 84-85 & pres, 85-86, NJ chap); Women's Caucus Art; Col Art Asn. *Media:* Acrylic. *Res:* Women's art history; Byelorussian arts history; architectural history and preservation. *Publ:* Auth, Nature interpreted: A Retrospective (exhib catalog), SOHO 20, 89; New and adequate space for the art library, ARLIS/NJ Newsletter, spring, 90; Ann Ryan, In: Past and Promise: lives of New Jersey Women, Scarecrow Press, 90; co-auth, American Women Painters Bosrn After 1900, In: Women Artists in US, G K Hall, 90. *Dealer:* SOHO 20 Gallery 469 Broome St New York NY 10013. *Mailing Add:* Art Libr Voorhees Hall-Rutgers Univ CAC New Brunswick NJ 08903

RUSCHA, EDWARD JOSEPH
PAINTER, FILMMAKER
b Omaha, Nebr, Dec 16, 37. *Study:* Chouinard Art Inst. *Work:* Mus Mod Art & Whitney Mus Am Art, New York; Los Angeles Co Mus Art; Joseph Hirshhorn Collection, Washington, DC; San Francisco Mus Mod Art. *Comn:* Mural, Metrop Dade Co Art in Public Places, 85. *Exhib:* One-man exhib tour, San Francisco Mus Mod Art, 82-83; Whitney Mus Am Art; Los Angeles Co Mus Art; Contemp Arts Mus, Houston; Vancouver Art Gallery; ICA, Nagoya, Japan, 88; and others. *Teaching:* Lectr painting, Univ Calif, Los Angeles, 69-70. *Awards:* Nat Coun Arts Grant, 67; Nat Endowment Arts Grant, 69 & 78; Tamarind Lithography Workshop Fel, 69; Guggenheim Found Fel, 71; Skowhegan Sch Painting & Sculpture Award in Graphics, 74. *Bibliog:* Geoffrey Haydon (dir), Edward Ruscha (film), British Broadcasting Corp, 79; Dave Hickey (auth), Available Light, Hudson Hills Press, 82; Peter Plagens (auth), Ed Ruscha, Seriously, Hudson Hills Press, 82; plus many others. *Publ:* Auth, Twenty six Gasoline Stations, 63, Various Small Fires, 64, Real Estate Opportunities, 70, A Few Palm Trees, 71, Heavy Industry Publs; Guacamole Airlines, Abrams, 80; and others. *Dealer:* Leo Castelli 420 W Broadway New York NY 10012; James Corcoran Gallery 1327 Fifth St Santa Monica CA 90401. *Mailing Add:* 35 S Venice Blvd Venice CA 90291

RUSH, ANDREW
PRINTMAKER, SCULPTOR
b Mich, Sept 24, 31. *Study:* Univ Ill, BFA(hons), 53; Univ Iowa, MFA, 58; Fulbright fel, Florence, Italy, 58-59. *Work:* Uffizi Mus, Florence, Italy; Libr Cong, Washington, DC; Dallas Mus, Tex; Seattle Mus, Wash. *Comn:* Law Prints (portfolio of three offset lithographs), Lawyers Publ Co, 68 & 74; ed etchings, Tucson Art Ctr, 71. *Exhib:* US Info Serv Traveling Exhib to Europe & Latin Am, 60-65; Graphic Art USA, Am prints to Soviet Union, 63; Brooklyn Mus Biennial, 64; 50 American Printmakers, Am Pavilion, New York World's Fair, 64-65; Intag 71, 30 Printmakers, San Fernando State Univ, 71. *Pos:* Founding mem, Rancho Linda Vista Community Arts, 69. *Teaching:* Assoc prof art, Univ Ariz, 59-69; vis artist-in-residence, Ohio State Univ, 70. *Awards:* Seattle Mus Int Printmakers Award, 63; Purchase Award, Brooklyn Mus Biennial, 64. *Bibliog:* Article, Southwest Art Gallery Mag, 3/72. *Mem:* Illusr, A Voice Crying in the Wilderness, St Martins Press, New York, 90. *Media:* All. *Publ:* Illusr, The Rule of Two, Oracle Press, 84; A Voice Crying in the Wilderness, St Martins Press, 90. *Mailing Add:* Rancho Linda Vista Star Rte 2360 Oracle AZ 85623

RUSH, DEBORAH
SCULPTOR, MURALIST
b Buffalo, NY, Oct 29, 52. *Work:* Arabian Horse Trust-Permanent Collection, Westminster, Colo. *Comn:* Town Historical mural, Elma Hist Soc, NY, 76; Pioneer/Indian History, Canuseraga Cent Sch, NY, 86. *Exhib:* Allentown Art Festival, Buffalo, NY, 73; Crabbet Symposium, Denver, Colo, 84; US Nat Arabian Show, Louisville, Ky, 88; World Cup, Tampa, Fla, 89; Egyptian Event, Lexington, Ky, 91. *Teaching:* Creative sculpting ceramic-clay, Iroquair Cent Sch, 72-; drawings & sketching, Adult Educ Prog, Elma, NY, 75- *Bibliog:* D Hamrick (auth), Rush's Passion--, Arabian Horse Express, 9/86; S Leadley (auth), The Easel, Arabian Visions, 2/92. *Mem:* Buffalo Fine Arts League. *Media:* Porcelain; Pencil, Pastel. *Mailing Add:* 10069 Savage Rd Holland NY 14080

RUSH, JEAN C
ADMINISTRATOR, PAINTER
b Bloomington, Ill, Nov 21, 33. *Study:* Ill Wesleyan Univ, BFA, 55; Univ Iowa, MFA, 58; Univ Ariz, PhD, 74. *Exhib:* 13th Nat Exhib Prints, Libr Congress, Washington, DC, 55; 11th Exhib Southwest Prints & Drawings, Dallas Mus Fine Arts, Tex, 61; Ariz Women's Caucus for Art Statewide Show, 79. *Pos:* Coordr art educ prog, Univ Ariz, 78-80 & 81-88; co-ed, Studies in art education, Nat Art Educ Asn, 81-83, sr ed, 83-85; dir, Ariz Inst Elementary Art Educ, 86-87. *Teaching:* Lectr art educ, Univ Ariz, 71-75, asst prof art educ, 75-80, assoc prof, 80-89; prof & admin chmn art dept, Ill State Univ, 89-91, prof, 91- *Awards:* Purchase Prize, Tucson Mus Art, 60; First Prize, Ariz State Fair, 60; Purchase Prize, Dallas Mus Fine Arts, 61. *Mem:* Am Educ Res Asn; Am Psychological Asn; Col Art Asn; Int Soc Educ through Art; Nat Art Educ Asn. *Media:* Oil, Pencil. *Res:* Visual perception, art learning. *Publ:* Research, the river, and art education engineers, Design Arts in Educ, 87; Interlocking images: The conceptual core of a discipline-based art lesson, Studies in Art Educ, 87; The politics of passion: Credibility crisis for academics and practitioners, Art Ed, 89; Coaching by conceptual focus: Problems, solutions and tutored images, Studies Art Educ, 89; Braving the thaw wind: A challenge for academics in basic arts education, Design for Arts Educ, 90. *Mailing Add:* Dept Art Ill State Univ Normal IL 61761

RUSH, JON N
SCULPTOR, EDUCATOR
b Atlanta, Ga, Sept 24, 35. *Study:* Art Inst Chicago, 53-55; Cranbrook Acad Art, with Tex Schiwetz, 55-59, BFA & MFA. *Work:* Columbus Mus Art, Ohio; Univ Mich, Ann Arbor. *Comn:* Sculpture, Briarwood, Ann Arbor, 80, Southwestern Mich Col, Dowagiac, 84, Domino World Hq, Ann Arbor, 88, Univ Mich, 90. *Exhib:* Hong Kong Int Competition, China, 62; Bundy Art Gallery, Waitsfield, Vt, 63; Fifteen Mich Sculptors, City of Lansing, 76; Meadowbrook Outdoor Sculpture, Rochester, Mich, 81; Mich Outdoor Sculpture II, S Field, 89. *Teaching:* Prof sculpture, Univ Mich, 62- *Awards:* Sculpture Award, All Mich Artists, Flint Inst Art, 72; Sculpture Prize, Mich Outdoor Sculpture II, S Field, 89. *Media:* Stainless Steel, Bronze. *Mailing Add:* 7930 Fifth St Dexter MI 48130

RUSH, KENT THOMAS
PHOTOGRAPHER, PRINTMAKER
b Hayward, Calif, Jan 16, 48. *Study:* Calif Col Arts & Crafts, BFA, 70; Univ NMex, Albuquerque, MA, 75; Univ Tex, Austin, MFA, 79. *Work:* Oakland Mus, Calif; McNay Mus, San Antonio; USIA, Washington, DC; City Dallas, Tex; Albuquerque Mus, NMex; Instituto De Obra Gráfica De Oaxaca, Oaxaca, Mex; Humanities Res Ctr, Univ Tex, Austin. *Exhib:* Contemporary Prints, traveling, 73; Madison Art Ctr, Wis, 77; Paperworks: An Exhibit of Texas Artists, traveling, 79-80; Cliche-Verre, Detroit Inst Arts, 80; Aspects of Realism, World Print Coun, Oakland, Calif, 81; Seventh British Int Print Biennial, Bradford Galleries, Eng; Texas Annual, Laguna Gloria Art Mus, Austin, 87; Fotofest 88, Lawndale Art & Performance Ctr, Houston, Tex, 88; Photogr Gallery, London, Eng, 89; Univ Art Mus, Univ NMex, Albuquerque, 90; Instituto Cult Peruano Norte Americano, Lima, Peru, 90; Dowd Fine Arts Ctr, SUNY Cortland, NY, 92. *Teaching:* Instr, San Antonio Art Inst, 76-79; lectr, Calif Col Arts & Crafts, Oakland, 80-81, San Francisco Art Inst, 82; assoc prof, Univ Tex, San Antonio, 82-; instr, Santa Reparata Grafic Arts Ctr, Florence, Italy, 84, Taller Delas Artes Plasticas Rufino Tamayo, Oaxala, Mex, 88 & Universidad Catolica, Lima, Peru, 90. *Awards:* Sr, Fulbright Fel, Taller Rufino Tamayo, Oaxaca, Mex, 88; MidAm Arts Alliance & Nat Endowment Arts Fel in Photog, 90-91. *Bibliog:* Pamela Hammond (auth), Kent Rush at Art Space, Images and Issues, spring 82; Peter Boswell (auth), Urban Imagery, Artweek, 7/31/82; R L Pincus (auth), Los Angeles Times (review), 10/83; Ron Glowen (auth), Kent Rush: Forms & Attitudes (catalog), San Antonio Art League, Tex, 89. *Mem:* Col Art Asn Am; Partners of Am; Sierra Club. *Publ:* Auth, Collotype: An Extension of Lithography, Tamarind Papers, 87. *Mailing Add:* Div Art & Design Univ Tex San Antonio TX 78285

RUSSELL, DR STELLA PANDELL
WRITER, PAINTER
Study: Hunter Col, BFA, 48; Teachers Col, MA, 50; Columbia Univ, PhD, 72; New York Inst Technol, MCA, 87. *Work:* Hunter Col, New York; Fine Art Mus of Long Island, Hempstead, NY; Nassau Community Col, Garden City, NY; Islip Art Mus, NY. *Comn:* Photo/airbrush mural, comn by City of New York for Hunter Col, NY, 50. *Exhib:* Twelfth Ann Competition, Hecksher Mus, Huntington, NY, 83; Yards of Art, Midge Karr Gallery, NY Inst Technol, Green Vale, NY, 84; Focus on the Figure, Islip Art Mus, 85; solo exhibs, To Thine Own Self, Firehouse Gallery, Garden City, NY, 86, Genesis, Fine Arts Mus of Long Island, Hempstead, NY, 87, Fragments & Recollections, Mills Pond House, St James, NY, 88; New York Now, Parsons Inst, 89; Seventh Ann Photog, Mills Pond House, St James, NY, 90. *Pos:* Co-dir, Russell-Pandell Studios, New York, 51-70; consult computer & advert, Marilyn Kass Assocs, Dix Hills, NY, 88- & Pro/Advert, Bellerose, NY, 87- *Teaching:* prof, Hunter Col, 51-70; Prof, Nassau Community Col, 65-; lectr, Huntington Twp Art League, 80-85, Freeport Arts Coun, 88- *Awards:* Prize, Nassau Co Employees, 65; Second Prize, Hecksher Mus, Huntington Twp Art League, 84; Third Prize, Islip Art Mus, 85. *Bibliog:* Phyllis Braff (auth), Computer imagery--paint of the 21st century, NY Times, 1/16/87; Karin Lipson (auth), Brushstrokes for computer graphics, Newsday, 3/27/87; Margaret Mohrman (auth), Multimedia landscapes, Newsday, 8/19/88. *Mem:* Prof Artist Guild (vpres, 80-85); Graphic Eye Gallery Asn (vpres, 87-89); Nat Orgn Women Artists; Hempstead Harbor Artist Asn (2nd vpres, 88-90). *Media:* Computed Graphics, Airbrush. *Publ:* Auth, article, Mona Lisa unmasked by computer, C W Post Col, 87; article, Aesthetics of computer art, Scan (IEEE), 87, 89 & 90; Art in the World, 3 eds, Holt Rinehart Winston, 88 & 4th eds, Harcourt Brace Jovanovich, 93; article, 25 years of masterpiece computer art, Scan Network, 89 & 90; Art in Modern World, 1st ed, Brown Benchmark, 94. *Dealer:* Country Art Gallery Birch Hill Rd Locust Vally NY. *Mailing Add:* 29 Tiffany Rd Oyster Bay NY 11771

RUSSELL, HELEN DIANE
HISTORIAN
b Kansas City, Mo, Apr 8, 36. *Study:* Vassar Col, AB; Radcliffe Grad Sch; Johns Hopkins Univ, PhD; Inst Advan Study, 80-81. *Collections Arranged:* Protest and Social Comment in Prints, 70; Kathe Kollowitz, 71; Rare Etchings by Giovanni Battista & Giovanni Domenico Tiepolo (auth, catalog), 72; Jacques Callot, Prints and Related Drawings (auth, catalog), 75; Europ Countryside: 16th & 17th century prints(auth, catalog); Self-Portraits in Prints (auth, catalog), 79; Claude Lorrain 1600-1682, Washington, DC, 82 & Paris (auth, catalog), 83; Robert Nanteuil, 85; Eva Ave, Woman in Renaissance & Baroque Prints (auth, catalog), 90. *Pos:* Asst to chief, Smithsonian Inst Traveling Exhib Serv, Washington, DC, 60-61; mus cur, Nat Gallery Art, Washington, DC, 64-70, asst cur graphic arts, 70-76, cur French Prints, 76-81, asst head, dept graphic arts, 81-90; dept head, Old Master Prints, 90- *Teaching:* Prof & lect, 15th-17th century Europ painting & graphic arts, Am Univ, Washington, DC, 66-72 & 78, adj prof, 83, 86-; fac mem, Folger Inst, 85; chmn, Folger Colloquium, 87-88. *Awards:* Woodrow Wilson Nat Fel, 58-59; Samuel H Kress Fel, 73; Mus Prof Fel, Nat Endowment Arts, 80-81; Alfred H Barr Award, Art Asn Am, 84. *Mem:* Col Art Asn Am (chmn, Bar Comt, 86); Women's Caucus for Art (adv bd, 77-79); Print Coun Am; Renaissance Soc. *Res:* Prints and drawings of the 16th through 18th centuries. *Publ:* Auth, A museum worker speaks, Washington Print Club Newslett, 72; Francoise Viatte, Dessins de Stefano della Bella, Art Bull, 77; Claude's Psyche Pendants: London and Cologne, Studies Hist Art, vol 14. *Mailing Add:* Nat Gallery Art Washington DC 20565

RUSSELL, JEFFREY See Jeff

RUSSELL, JOHN LAUREL
DEALER, COLLECTOR
b Cochrane, Ont, Aug 14, 16. *Study:* Russell Sch Art, Toronto, 37-38. *Pos:* Owner, Beaver Hall, Gananoque, Ont, currently. *Mem:* Fel Royal Soc Arts; fel Royal Geog Soc; Can Guild Crafts; Order of Can; life gov Montreal Numis & Hist Soc. *Specialty:* General antiques. *Collection:* Early Canadian painting of the eighteenth and nineteenth centuries. *Mailing Add:* Beaver Hall PO Box 490 Gananoque ON K7G 2W7 Canada

RUSSELL, PHILIP C
PAINTER, INSTRUCTOR
b Tulsa, Okla, July 9, 33. *Study:* Colo Springs Fine Arts Ctr, with V Vytlacil; Univ Iowa, with M Lasansky; Univ Calif, Berkeley, with David Park and W Kahn, MA. *Work:* Philbrook Art Ctr, Tulsa; Wichita Mus Art; Dallas Mus Fine Arts; Palace of the Legion of Honor, San Francisco; Butler Inst Am Art, Youngstown, Ohio. *Exhib:* US Info Serv, travelling exhib, SAm, 57-59; Drawings, Dallas Mus Fine Arts, 58-59; Mid Am Ann Exhib, Nelson Gallery, Kansas City, Mo, 58; Philadelphia Mus Art, 58; Calif Soc of Etchers, 44th Ann Nat Exhib, 59; Area Gallery, New York, 61 & 63; New York World's Fair, 63-64. *Collections Arranged:* 10th Street Days--Coops of the 50s, Noho Gallery & Landmark, 77. *Teaching:* Instr drawing, Univ Okla, 57-58; instr composition, Philadelphia Col Art, 62-63; instr art & art hist, Edgemont Sch, Scarsdale, NY, 69-71, chmn arts, 71-88. *Awards:* Purchase Awards, Drawing and Prints, Dallas Mus, 58 & 59, Calif Soc of Etchers, Legion of Honor, San Francisco, 59 & Am Graphic Arts, Wichita Art Assoc, 59. *Bibliog:* John Canaday (auth), Art: Street of strugglers, 12/14/61 & Goodbye forever, a sad farewell to 10th street, 5/9/63, New York Times; Joellen Bard (auth), 10th Street Days, Educ Art & Serv Inc, 12/77. *Media:* Oil, Intaglio. *Mailing Add:* PO Box 14042 Tulsa OK 74159-1042

RUSSELL, RAYMOND See Fink, Ray (Raymond Russell)

RUSSELL, ROBERT PRICE
PAINTER, EDUCATOR
b Rochelle, Ill, June 23, 39. *Study:* Kansas City Art Inst, Mo, BFA, 61; Southern Ill Univ, Carbondale, MFA, 63. *Work:* El Paso Mus Art, Tex; Idaho State Univ, Pocatello; Roswell Mus & Art Ctr, NMex; Springfield Art Mus, Mo. *Comn:* Painting/Drawing, Westin-Crown Ctr Hotel, Kansas City, Mo, 87. *Exhib:* One-person shows, Dubose-Rein Gallery, Houston, 85, Jan Weiner Gallery, Kansas City, Mo, 87, 89 & 92, Kauffman Galleries, Houston, 89 & 91, Buena Vista Col, Storm Lake, Iowa, 89 & Sch Ozarks, Point Lookout, Mo, 90. *Pos:* Artist-in-residence, Area arts prog, Wis, 66-67, Hanover Col, Ind, 73, Roswell Mus & Art Ctr, NMex, 74-75 & Idaho State Univ, Pocatello, 79 & 82. *Teaching:* Instr art, Univ Wis-Stevens Point, 63-66; prof art, Pittsburg

State Univ, Kans, 67- *Awards:* Tech Assistantship Grant in Lithography, Kans Arts Comn & Nat Endowment Arts, 85. *Bibliog:* Greg Field (auth), Readable references rescue abstract art, Forum, 9/87. *Media:* Acrylic, Monotype. *Dealer:* Jan Weiner Gallery 4800 Liberty St Kansas City MO; Kauffman Galleries 2702 W Alabama Houston TX. *Mailing Add:* Pittsburg State Univ Pittsburg KS 66762

RUSSIN, ROBERT I
SCULPTOR, EDUCATOR
b New York, NY, Aug 26, 14. *Study:* City Univ New York, BA & MA; Beaux Arts Inst Design. *Work:* Evanston Post Off, Ill; Duarte Monument, Santo Domingo; Conshohocken Post Office; Pa; Bicentennial Monument, Cheyenne Visitors' Ctr, Wyoming Crystal, State Off Bldg, Cheyenne, Wyo; Chthonodynamis, Granite monument, Dept Energy Bldg, Washington, DC, 92; and others. *Comn:* Spirit of Life, City Hope Nat Med Ctr, Duarte, Calif; Fountainhead (steel), City Hall, Casper, Wyo; marble carving, Univ Wyo; Prometheus (bronze), Casper Pub Libr, Wyo; Helios Dallas (bronze & marble), Lincoln Ctr, Dallas; Joie de Vie, bronze fountain sculpture, Pomona Col, Claremont, Calif; Pan-American Family, Dominican Repub; Einstein, Gershwin, I B Singer medals for Magnes Mus, Berkeley, Calif; Freedom Fighter Monument, Tucson Jewish Community Ctr, Ariz. *Exhib:* Pa Acad Fine Arts Sculpture Biennial, Philadelphia, 66; one-man shows, Colorado Springs Fine Arts Ctr, 67, Palm Springs Desert Mus, 70, Magnes Mus, Berkeley, Calif, 70, Galleria d'Arte Mod, Santo Domingo, 76-77, Fine Arts Mus, Univ Wyo, 77, Tubac Art Mus, Ariz, 88, Riggins Art Gallery, Scottsdale, Ariz, 89 & Univ Wyo Art Mus, 91. *Teaching:* Instr sculpture, Cooper Union Art Inst, 44-47; prof sculpture, Univ Wyo, 47-86, univ artist, 79-86, prof emer, 87. *Awards:* Lincoln Sesquicentennial Medal, US Cong, 59; Charles G B Steele Sculpture Award, Pa Acad Fine Arts, 66; Order of Duarte, Sanchez & Mella, by Pres Joachim Balaguer, Dominican Repub, 77. *Bibliog:* O A Sealy (auth), Russin's metal magic, Empire Mag, 2/56; Tom Francis (auth), Robert Russin, Wyoming sculptor, Am Artist, 1/60; F K Frame (auth), Russin's Lincoln, Empire Mag, 2/26. *Mem:* Sculptors Guild. *Media:* Miscellaneous Media. *Publ:* Contribr, A new sculptural medium, Col Art J, 56; contribr, The Lincoln monument on the Lincoln highway, Lincoln Herald, 61; contribr, A university bronze foundry, Am Artist, 63. *Dealer:* Maxwell Galleries 551 Sutter Ave San Francisco CA; Karen Newby Gallery Tubac AZ. *Mailing Add:* 61 N Fork Rd Centennial WY 82055

RUSSO, ALEXANDER PETER
PAINTER, EDUCATOR
b Atlantic City, NJ, June 11, 22. *Study:* Pratt Inst, 40-42; Swarthmore Col, 47; Bard Col, summer 47; Columbia Univ, BFA(Breevort-Eickenmeyer Fel), 52; Acad Fine Arts, Rome, Fulbright Grant, 52-54; Univ Buffalo, 55. *Work:* Albright-Knox Gallery, Buffalo, NY; Corcoran Gallery Art, Washington, DC; Nat Collection Fine Arts, Washington, DC; Fed Ins Deposit Corp, Washington, DC; Acad Arts & Lett, New York. *Comn:* Encaustic mural, Telesio Interlandi, Capo San Andrea, Sicily, 53; var design comns, Doubleday Publ Co, Dutton Publ, Birge Co & Cohn Hall Marx, 56-60; acrylic painting series, US Navy Dept, 64; acrylic mural, Dr Martin Cherkasky, NY, 70; Vet Mem sculpture, Frederick, Md, 75. *Exhib:* Carnegie Nat, Pittsburgh, 46; Int Exhib, Bordighera, Italy, 53 & 54; Four Am Artists Exhib, Biblioteca, Rome, 54; Albright-Knox Gallery Regional, Buffalo, NY, 56; Corcoran Biennials, Washington, DC; and many one-man shows. *Pos:* Combat artist, US Navy Dept, Washington, DC, 42-46; actg art dir, Sewell, Thompson, Caire Advert, New Orleans, 48-49; freelance artist & designer, var agencies & orgns, New York, 58-60; guest lectr art, Roanoke & Hollins Cols, Univ Southern Ill, Miss Art Asn, and others; art consult, Univ Publications of Am, Frederick, Md, 80-; Guest Art Critic, Southampton Press, summer 88. *Teaching:* Assoc prof painting & drawing, Corcoran Sch Art, 61-70, chmn fac & painting dept, 66-69; prof art & chmn dept, 71-85, prof art, 86-90, prof emer, 90, Hood Col. *Awards:* Guggenheim Fel Painting, 47-50; Purchase Award, Albright-Knox Art Gallery, Buffalo, NY, 56; David Lloyd Kreeger Award, Corcoran Gallery Art, Washington, DC, 63; Hudson Beneficiary Teaching Fel, Hood Col, 83. *Bibliog:* Carl Fortes (auth), Tape on aesthetics and teaching methods of Alexander Russo, Boston Univ, 68; Anne M Jonas (auth), Focus on: Alexander Russo, The Art Scene, 70/71. *Mem:* Col Art Asn; Arts Club Washington (chmn exhibs, 70-71); Artists Equity; Soc Washington Artists; Edward McDowell Colony; Md State Arts Coun. *Media:* Acrylic, Oil. *Publ:* Illusr, To All Hands, an Amphibious Adventure, 44 & Many a Watchful Night, 45, McGraw; auth, The Italian Experience, Inst Int Educ, 53; Profiles on Women Artists, Univ Publ Am, 83; The Challenge of Drawing, Prentice-Hall, 86. *Dealer:* Benton Gallery Benton Plaza 365 County Rd 39 Southampton NY 11968. *Mailing Add:* PO Box 1377 Wainscott NY 11975

RUSSO, MICHELE
PAINTER
b Waterbury, Conn, Apr 30, 09. *Study:* Yale Univ, BFA, 34; Colorado Springs Fine Arts Ctr, studies with Boardman Robinson & George Biddle, fel, 37. *Work:* Portland Art Mus & Collection of Reed Col, Portland; Dayton Art Inst, Ohio; Seattle Art Mus; Univ Ore Art Mus, Eugene. *Exhib:* Santa Barbara Mus, 63; retrospective, Portland Art Mus, 66; Art of the Pacific Northwest, Smithsonian Inst, Washington, DC, 74; Portland Ctr Visual Arts, 77; one-man shows, Portland Ctr Visual Arts, 78, Seattle Art Mus (with monogr), 84, The Laura Russo Gallery, Portland, Ore, 87, 88, 90-92; 38th Corcoran Biennial Exhib Am Painting & Second Western States Traveling Exhib, 82-84, Corcoran Gallery, Washington, DC; retrospective (with catalog), Portland Art Mus, 88. *Teaching:* Instr painting & art hist, Pac Northwest Col Art, Ore Art Inst, Portland, 47-74. *Awards:* State Ore Arts Comn Award, 81; Abrey R Watzek Award, Lewis & Clark Col, 82; City Portland Arts Comn Award, 83. *Bibliog:* Ron Glowen (auth), article, Artweek, 78; Jane Van Cleve (auth), World of Russo, Bigoni Books, 81; 50 Northwest Artists, Chronicle Bks, 83. *Mem:* Metrop Arts Comn, Portland (comnr, 79-81); founder Portland Ctr Visual Arts (pres bd, 71-); founder Artist Equity, Portland; Comt Art Pub Places (chmn, 75). *Media:* Acrylic, Ink. *Dealer:* Laura Russo Gallery 3227 NW 21st Portland OR 97209. *Mailing Add:* 3227 NW Thurman Portland OR 97210

RUSSO, SALLY FULTON HALEY See Haley, Sally (Sally Fulton Haley Russo)

RUST, DAVID E
CURATOR, COLLECTOR
b Bloomington, Ill. *Study:* Harvard Col, BA; NY Univ Inst Fine Arts, MA, 63. *Collections Arranged:* English Drawings & Watercolors, 62; Old Master Drawings from Chatsworth, 69; Nathan Cummings Collection, 70; Francois Boucher: 100 Drawings (asst auth, catalog), 73; French Paintings from the Alisa Mellon Bruce Collection (auth, catalog), 78; Manet and Modern Paris, 82-83. *Pos:* Cur Fr, Brit & Spanish Paintings, Nat Gallery Art, Washington, DC, 61-83; adv panel, Art Pub Places, Dade County, Fla; dir, Tissot Exhib, 84-85. *Collection:* Paintings and drawings, mostly European sixteenth-nineteenth century; American nineteenth century and some contemporary. *Publ:* Auth, Twentieth Century Paintings & Sculpture of the French School in the Chester Dale Collection, 65; Eighteenth & Nineteenth Century Paintings & Sculpture of the French School in the Chester Dale Collection, 65; The drawings of Vincenzo Tamagni da San Gimignano, Report & Studies Hist Art, 68; Small French Paintings from the Bequest of Alisa Mellon Bruce, 78. *Mailing Add:* 2812 P St NW Washington DC 20007

RUST, EDWIN C
SCULPTOR, ADMINISTRATOR
b Hammonton, Calif, Dec 5, 10. *Study:* Cornell Univ; Yale Univ, BFA; also with Archipenko & Milles; Southwestern at Memphis, Hon DFA. *Work:* US Ct House, Washington, DC; Univ Tenn Ctr Health Serv; Univ Miss, Oxford; Univ Tenn, Knoxville; Memphis Acad Arts, Tenn; Ouchita Baptist Univ, Arkadelphia, Ark; Memphis Brooks Mus Art. *Exhib:* Whitney Mus Am Art, New York, 40; Carnegie Inst Int, Pittsburgh, 40; Philadelphia Mus Art, 40 & 49; Mus Mod Art, New York, 42; Brooks Mem Mus, 50 & 52. *Pos:* Dir, Memphis Acad Arts, 49-75, emer dir, 75- *Teaching:* Assoc prof sculpture, Col William & Mary, 36-43, head, Dept Fine Arts, 39-43. *Mem:* Nat Sculpture Soc. *Mailing Add:* 3725 Waynoka Ave Memphis TN 38111

RUSTVOLD, KATHERINE JO
DEALER
b Grand Forks, NDak, Jan 24, 50. *Study:* Univ NDak; Univ Ariz; Univ Neuchatel Switz. *Collections Arranged:* Equestrian Exhib, 10/77; American Impressionists, 5/78; The Impressionist Years, 10/78; Ann Biltmore Celebrity Show, 2/81; Henry Casselli, one-man show, 11/81; San Francisco Equestrian Festival, 87; James Reynolds, one-man show, 89. *Pos:* Owner, Biltmore Galleries, Rancho Santa Fe, Calif, 79- *Mem:* Art Dealers' Asn Calif. *Specialty:* Nineteenth and twentieth century American art; French Impressionists, with emphasis on American Western and Hudson River School, Early California School & selected current artists. *Mailing Add:* 430 Pearl St La Jolla CA 92037

RUTA, PETER PAUL
PAINTER
b Dresden, Ger, Feb 7, 18; US citizen. *Study:* Art Students League, with Morris Kantor & Jean Charlot, 38-42 & 45-46; Acad Fine Arts Venice, 47-49, degree; Acad Venice, with Guido Cadorin, 48. *Work:* Uffizi Gallery, Florence, Italy; Univ Southern Ill; State NMex. *Exhib:* One-man shows, Larcada Gallery, New York, 76, Sunne Savage Gallery, Boston, 80, Sch House Gallery, Truro, Mass, 83, Acad Gallery, New Orleans, 83, 89 & 92 and Munson Gallery, Santa Fe, NMex, 85-88. *Pos:* Ed, Arts Mag, 68-71 & Int Art Exhibs, 69. *Awards:* First Prize, Westchester Art Soc, 65; The Pollack-Krasner Found, 88; Fel, Va Ctr Creative Arts, 89; Santa Fe Poster, 89. *Media:* Oil. *Dealer:* Munson Gallery 225 Canyon Rd Santa Fe NM. *Mailing Add:* 463 West St New York NY 10014

RUTH, SHEILA
PAINTER
b St Louis, Mo, 1951. *Study:* Univ Minn, 69-73; Int Col, MFA, 76. *Work:* Asukenazy Galleries & Hotels, Los Angeles, Calif; Long Beach Mus Art, Calif; Screen Actors Guild, Los Angeles, Calif; New York Pub Libr, NY; Chelsea Sch Art, London, Eng. *Exhib:* Solo Exhibs, New York, Los Angeles City Hall Bridge Gallery, Calif, 82, Recent Painting, Molly Barnes Gallery, Los Angeles, Calif 84 & Styrian Autumn, Palais Attems, Graz, Austria, 88; Flower Imagery in Art, Downey Mus Art, Calif, 84; Galerie Griss, Graz, Austria, 87; Five West Coast Artists, Walter Gallery, Los Angeles, Calif, 88; God of the Fathers, Gallery Kulturzentrum Minoriten, Graz, Austria, 88; Contemp Expressions from Los Angeles, Taiwan Mus Art, Taichung, Taiwan, 89. *Awards:* Calif Arts Coun Grant, 76 & 80; Invited Artist, Meditations 88, Graz, Austria. *Bibliog:* Marlena Donohue (auth), The galleries--La Cienega area, LA Times, 12/14/84; Jack Reilly (auth), A discourse on flowers, Artweek, 1/5/85; Era Platzer (auth), article, Kleine Zwitung, 10/4/88. *Mem:* Artist Equity. *Mailing Add:* 122 Lake Forest Saint Louis MO 63117

RUTHLING, FORD
PAINTER, PRINTMAKER
b Santa Fe, NMex, Apr 23, 33. *Study:* With Randall Davey; largely self taught. *Work:* Mus NMex; Wichita Falls Fine Art Mus; Univ Utah Collection. *Comn:* US Pueblo Pottery Postage Stamp (4 thirteen cent stamps), 77; and

others. *Exhib:* Nelson Atkins Mus; Mus NMex; Oklahoma City Mus Fine Art; Dallas Mus Fine Art; Wichita Falls Mus Fine Art; Roswell Art Mus, 79; and others. *Media:* Oil, Graphics. *Mailing Add:* 313 E Berger St Santa Fe NM 87501

RUTHVEN, JOHN ALDRICH
PAINTER, LECTURER
b Cincinnati, Ohio, Nov 12, 24. *Study:* Cincinnati Art Acad; Cent Acad Com Art; Miami Univ, Ohio, DHL; St Francis Col, Loretto, Pa, DHL. *Work:* Hermitage Mus, Leningrad, Russia; Armstrong Space Mus, Wapakoneta, Ohio; Ruthven Conf Ctr, Middletown, Ohio; Smithsonian Inst, Washington, DC; Cincinnati Natural Hist Mus. *Comn:* Cardinals for Gov Conf, State Ohio, Columbus, 68, Eagle to the Moon, 69; Colonial Williamsburg Ser, Va, 70-75; Cardinal, USSR, 70; Miami Indian, Miami Univ, 74. *Exhib:* Ducks Unlimited, Hilton Head, SC, 72; Ohio State Fair, Columbus, 74; White House Reception, 76; Leigh-Yawkey-Woodson Mus, Wausau, Wis, 76 & 77; Wildlife Festival, Easton, Md, 77. *Pos:* Mem bd dir, Cincinnati Nature Ctr, 69-; trustee, Cincinnati Natural Hist Mus, 75-; trustee, Ducks Unlimited, 75- *Awards:* Sachs Fine Art Award, Cincinnati Art Acad, 69; Printing Industry Am Award, 70-77; Ohioana Career Medal, Martha Kinne Cooper Ohioana Libr, 75. *Bibliog:* Jerry Bowles (auth), John Ruthven, Acquire Mag, 73; Cincinnati Art, Town & Country, 75; Dan Johnston (auth), John Ruthven, Artist, pvt publ, 75. *Mem:* Soc Animal Artists New York. *Media:* Opaque Watercolor. *Publ:* Coauth, Topflight, 69; auth, Carolina Paraquet, Audubon Mag, 72; auth, Regal Series Prints, 68-75, North American Series Prints, 69-75 & Aquatint Series Prints, 71-81, Wildlife Int Publ. *Mailing Add:* 6290 Old State Rte 68 Georgetown OH 45121

RUTLAND, LILLI IDA
PAINTER, ILLUSTRATOR
b Dothan, Ala, Jan 3, 18. *Study:* Univ Ala, 50-52; study with Claude Peacock, 50-52. *Work:* Governors Mansion, Montgomery, Ala; Houston Mem Libr & Rose Hill Elem Sch, Dothan, Ala. *Comn:* Yearbook cover, Young Jr High Sch, Dothan, Ala, 33. *Exhib:* King Alfred Daffodils, Panama City Art Mus, Fla, 60; First Snow and Wild Flowers, Montgomery Mus Fine Arts, Ala, Daytona Mus Arts & Sci, Daytona Beach, Fla, Mobile Art Gallery, Ala & Birmingham Mus Art, Ala, 76; Daybreak, 84 & Southern Magnolias, 84, City Nat Bank Gallery, Dothan, Ala; solo exhib, Southeast Ala Med Ctr Gallery, Dothan, Ala, 85. *Pos:* Illusr, Training Aids, Ft Rucker, Ala, 67-75. *Awards:* First in Watercolor, Houston Co Fair, City of Dothan, 60; First in Watercolor, Dothan Wirgrass Art League, 73; Best of Show in Watercolor, Dothan Bank & Trust Co, 73. *Mem:* Dothan Wirgrass Art League (secy, 62); Portrait Club, Washington, Conn. *Media:* Watercolor. *Mailing Add:* Colony Square Apt No 40 Dothan AL 36301

RUTSCH, ALEXANDER
PAINTER, SCULPTOR
b Austria. *Study:* Acad Fine Art, Belgrade, Yugoslavia; studied in Vienna & Austria; govt study grant, Paris. *Work:* Albertina Graphic Art Collection, Austria; Austrian Gallery, Belvedere, Vienna; Munic Mus, Vienna; Mus Mod Art, Paris; Mus Liege, Belg. *Exhib:* Int Sculptors, Mus Rodin, Paris, 62-63; one-man show, Galerie Vendome, Brussels, Belg, 65; Int Exhib, Grand Palais de Champs Elysees, Paris, 66; Avanti Galleries, 74 & Harkness House Gallery, 75, New York; Bustamante, New York, 89. *Teaching:* Pelham Art Ctr, NY, 82 & Blumka II, New York, 82. *Awards:* Silver Medal Arts, Sci & Lett & Bronze Medal Art, City Paris, 58; First Prize, Salon Artistique Int Sceaux, 54; Int Beaux Arts Artist Year, 76 & 82. *Bibliog:* Carlton Lake (auth), In Quest of Dali, Putnam, 69; Roger Seiler (auth), Inner Eye of Alexander Rutsch (film), IBM, 72; Alexander Rutsch 1991, Ed Lafayette, New York, 91. *Mem:* Burr Artists New York; Accad Ital. *Mailing Add:* 222 Highbrook Ave Pelham NY 10803

RUTTINGER, JACQUELYN
PAINTER, GALLERY DIRECTOR
b Great Falls, Mont, July 21, 40. *Study:* Univ Wash, Seattle, 58-60; Art Inst Chicago, with McKinnon, Fabian, Kauffman & Yoshida, BFA(hon), 63; Northern Ill Univ, with Mahmoud, Beard & Syrek, MA, 76, MFA, 77; Governor's State Univ, 81-83. *Work:* Ill State Mus, Springfield; State Ill Percent Art, Northern Ill Univ, DeKalb & Eastern Ill Univ, Charleston; Millikin Univ, Decatur, Ill; Sheldon Swope Art Mus, Terre Haute, Ind; Western Mich Univ, Kalamazoo, Mich. *Comn:* 2 paintings, Appl Technol Bldg, Grand Rapids Community Col, Mich, 92. *Exhib:* Juried exhibs, 64th Ann West Mich Comp, Muskegon Mus Art, Mich, 91, All Michigan/All Media 2 Show, Krasl Art Ctr, St Joseph, Mich, 91, Michigan Annual XIX, Art Ctr, Mt Clemens, Mich, 91, 12th Mich Artists Comp, Art Ctr Battle Creek, Mich, 91 & Review Comt Selects, Group II, Detroit Focus Gallery, Mich, 92; solo exhibs, Jesse Besser Mus, Alpena, Mich, 87, Saginaw Art Mus, 88 & Kalamazoo Inst Arts, 90; Recent Trends in Painting: The 11th Michigan Biennial, Kresge Art Mus, Mich State Univ, traveling exhib for 89; and others. *Pos:* Dir exhib & vis artist progs, art dept, Western Mich Univ, Kalamazoo, 86- *Teaching:* Instr art, Prairie State Col, 77-81; community prof, Governor's State Univ, 82; chmn art dept, St Mary-of-the-Woods Col, 83-85. *Awards:* First Prize & Purchase Award, 41st Ann Wabash Valley Exhib, Sheldon Swope Art Mus, Terre Haute, Ind, 85; Arts Coun Greater Kalamazoo & The Upjohn Co Mini-Grant, 87-88; Col Fine Arts Fac Res Grant, Western Mich Univ, 90-91. *Bibliog:* Judith Kanin (auth), article, New Art Examiner, 1/79; Adelaide Cooley (auth), Ruttinger & O'Brien, New Art Examiner, 12/81; Nancy Rice (auth), Forecki, Ruttinger & Teczar, New Art Examiner, 12/82. *Mem:* Kalamazoo Inst of Arts; Arts Coun Greater Kalamazoo; Mich Mus Assoc. *Media:* All Media. *Publ:* 33rd Annual Drawing & Small Sculpture Show (exhib catalog), Ball State Univ Art Gallery, 87; Recent Trends in Painting: The 11th Michigan Biennial (exhib catalog), Kresge Art Mus, Mich State Univ, 89; Haworth Col Bus Fine Art Collection (catalog), Western Mich Univ, 91. *Dealer:* Rubiner Gallery West Bloomfield Hills MI; Zaks Gallery Chicago IL. *Mailing Add:* 1110 Dwillard Dr Kalamazoo MI 49001-2259

RUTZKY, IVY SKY
SCULPTOR
b New York, NY, Nov 19, 48. *Study:* Penland Sch, NC, 69; Univ NMex, BFA, 73. *Work:* Glacial, Macomb Community Col, Warren, Mich; New Mus, NY. *Comn:* Silver Phoenix, Detroit, Mich, 79; Hybrid, Ann Arbor, Mich, 80. *Exhib:* One-person shows, Threshold, Kiva, New York, 80, Cranbrook Acad Art, 80 & Berry Col, Ga, 83; Gilbert & Lila Silverman Collection, Cranbrook Acad Art, Bloomfield Hills, Mich, 81; Artists Invite Artists, Limnol, New Mus, New York, 81; Sculpture sites, Amagansett, NY, 81; Spirit-Icon, BACA Downtown, Brooklyn, 85. *Bibliog:* Dennis Nawrocki & Tom Holleman (auth), Art in Detroit Public Places, Wayne State Univ Press, 80; Ruth & Louis Redstone (auth), Public Art/New Directions, McGraw-Hill, 81; Keith Johnson, Threshold, Art Express, 5-6/81. *Media:* Wood, Oil. *Mailing Add:* 317 W 21st St New York NY 10013-3010

RUVOLO, FELIX EMMANUELE
PAINTER, EDUCATOR
b New York, NY, Apr 28, 12. *Study:* In Catania, Sicily. *Work:* Krannert Art Mus, Univ Ill, Urbana; Art Inst Chicago; Walker Art Ctr, Minneapolis; Oakland Mus, Calif; Univ Calif Mus Fine Arts, Berkeley. *Comn:* Colored lithograph, Collectors Press, 67. *Exhib:* Abstract & Surrealist Art in America, Mus Mod Art, New York, 51; 60 Americans--1960, Walker Art Ctr, 60; American Drawing, Moore Col Art Gallery, Philadelphia, 68; Drawings 1969, Ithaca Col Art Gallery, NY, 69; American Drawing & Sculpture, 1948-1969, Krannert Art Mus, 71; Gruenenbaum Gallery, 82. *Teaching:* Prof art, Art Inst Chicago, 44-48, Univ Calif, Berkeley, 50- & Univ Southern Calif, summer 63. *Awards:* San Francisco Mus Art Award, 64; Hall of Justice Compt Award, San Francisco Art Comn, 67; Grants, Univ Calif Inst Creative Arts, 64 & 71. *Bibliog:* K Kuh (auth), Felix Ruvolo, Mag Art, 47 & Painters who teach, Pictorial Living, 59; N Pousette Dart (auth), American Painting Today, Hastings, 57. *Mailing Add:* 13 Oakmont Ave San Rafael CA 94901

RUYLE, LYDIA MILLER
PRINTMAKER, EDUCATOR
Study: Univ Colo, Boulder, BA(magna cum laude), 57; Univ Northern Colo, MA(fine arts), 72; Syracuse Univ, int study, Renaissance Art, Italy; Romanesque Art, France, Spain, 85; Santa Reparata Graphic Arts Ctr Workshops, Florence, Italy, 88-92; Sch Art Inst Chicago, study in Indonesia, 93. *Work:* Nat Mus Women rts, Washington, DC; Citicorp, Denver; McDougal-Littell Publs, Evanston, Ill; Lincoln Ctr, Ft Collins, Colo; Union Colony Civic Ctr, Sr Ctr, Greeley, Colo. *Comn:* Bronze Armilliary Sundial, Rutherford Hill Winery, St Helena, Calif, 72; print ed of lithographs, Am Hist Soc Gers from Russia, Lincoln, Nebr, 80; print eds for United Way, Weld County, Colo, 80-91; environmental sculpture, Artspicnic Festival, Greeley, Colo, 85; cast paper sculptures, Children's Hosp, Denver, 92. *Exhib:* Solo exhib, Paper Press Gallery, Chicago, 91; Art and Healing, Johnson-Humrick Mus, Cochoton, Ohio, 91, Marin County Courthouse, Calif, 91 & Univ Tex Health Scis Ctr, San Antonio, Tex, 92; Better Homes and Goddesses, travelling, 87-92; Nat Asn Women Artists Ann Exhibs, New York, 82-92; Quattro Amici, Santa Reparata Graphic Arts Ctr, Florence, Italy, 92; Exchange Exhib, Travelling Printmaking, Bombay, India, 89-90, throughout US, 92-93; and others. *Pos:* Gov appointed bd mem, Colo Coun Arts Humanities, 77-82; comnr, Colo Comn Higher Educ, 83-85. *Teaching:* Creative Arts Ctr, Greeley, Colo, 68-78; adj fac, Printmaking, Art Hist & Art Appreciation, Univ Northern Colo, 80-; workshop presenter, univs serv clubs, prof asns throughout US & abroad, 85- *Awards:* Juror's Award, Manhattan Nat Print, 84; Printmaking, 86, Works on Paper, 91, Nat Asn Women Artists Ann. *Bibliog:* Judy Chicago (auth), The Birth Project, Doubleday & Co, 85; Linda Anderson (auth), Greeley's Goddesses, Spectrum UNC, 90; Mary Carroll Nelson (auth), Affirming Wholeness, Southwest Art/CBH Publ, 6/92. *Mem:* Nat Asn Women Artists, New York; Los Angeles Printmaking Soc; Women's Caucus Art, Philadelphia; Soc Multi-Media Layerists, Albuquerque, NMex; Colo Art Educs Asn. *Res:* Research and use inherited images of women in collagraph prints; Black Madonnas as icon images of healing. *Publ:* Illusr, Kuche Kochen, Am Hist Soc Gers from Russia, 73-84; contrib, Layering, Soc Layerist in Multimedia, Albuquerque, 91; illusr, The Great Goddess, An Introduction to Her Many Names, Shef, Boulder, 92; Subtle Energies, Int Soc Study Subtle Energies & Energy Med, Golden, Colo, 92; auth & illusr, The Goddess Has A Thousand Faces, Inner Eye Press, Tucson, Ariz, 92. *Dealer:* Madison & Main Gallery. *Mailing Add:* 2101 24th St Greeley CO 80631

RUZU, See Zuckerman, Ruth Victor

RYAN, DAVID MICHAEL
CURATOR
b Lincoln, Nebr, July 10, 39. *Study:* Univ Nebr, BFA & BA, 62; Univ Nebr Law Sch, 62-63; Univ Denver, MA, 65. *Collections Arranged:* Sixth Minn Biennial, 68, Documents as Art, 69, Barry Le Va: Piece One and Two, 69, Richard Avedon, 70, Art Deco, 71 & American Indian Art: Form and Tradition, 72, Minneapolis Inst Art; Aycock, Holste, Singer, 80, Josef Hoffmann, 82, Twentieth Century Drawings, 83, Pop Art Print, 84, Focus Series 79-85; Modernism One and Two, 88-89, Modernist Ceramics, 90-91, Modernist Lighting, 91-92, Norwest Ctr, Minneapolis. *Pos:* Mus intern, Denver Art Mus, 64-65; cur asst, Walker Art Ctr, 65-68; cur exhibs, Minneapolis Inst Arts, 68-72; asst dir, Am Fedn Arts, New York, 73-74; asst

dir mus prog, Nat Endowment Arts, 74-79; dir, Ft Worth Art Mus, 79-85, Des Moines Art Ctr, 86, arts prog, Norwest Corp, Minneapolis, 87- *Mem:* Assoc Prof Art Advs. *Publ:* Auth, Guide to the Painting and Sculpture Collection, 83 & The Pop Art Print, 84, Ft Worth Art Mus; Md Invitational, 88; Baltimore Mus Art, 88; Modernism at Norwest, 89; Modernist Ceramics, Norwest Ctr, Minneapolis, 90. *Mailing Add:* 2001 W 86th St Minneapolis MN 55431

RYAN, ELIZABETH
PAINTER
b New York, NY. *Study:* With Ed Whitney, Ivan Olinsky & Bruce Stevenson. *Work:* Va State Col, Richmond; Frye Mus, Seattle. *Exhib:* Am Watercolor Soc Traveling Exhib, 82-83; Nat Acad Design; Salmagundi Club; and others. *Awards:* Brush Award, 85, Hon Ment, 85-86, Solo Award & Grumbacher Medal, 87 & Watercolor Award, 92, Pen & Brush Inc; Arthur Alexander Mem Award, Knickerbocker Artists; Jordane Art Works Award & Picard Award, 87, Graphic Award, 89 & 90 & Watercolor Award, 90, Salmagundi Club. *Mem:* Am Watercolor Soc (treas, 70-73); Allied Artists Am; Audubon Artists (treas, 84-); Salmagundi Club. *Media:* Watercolor. *Mailing Add:* 14 Sutton Pl S New York NY 10022

RYAN, RICHARD E
PAINTER, PRINTMAKER
b London, Eng, Feb 14, 50, US citizen. *Study:* Stanford Univ, BA, 72; Yale Univ Sch Art, MFA, 79. *Work:* Middlebury Col Gallery, Utah; Calif Mus Legion Hon, San Francisco, Calif. *Exhib:* The Classic Tradition, Aldrich Mus, Ridgefield, Conn, 85; Tradition & Innovation 1500-1989, Calif Palace Legion Hon, San Francisco, 89. *Teaching:* Asst prof, Ind Univ, Bloomington, 79-81; Vassar Col, 81-85; assoc prof, Yale Univ Art, 85- *Awards:* Ingram Merrill Found Grant, 85; Louis Comfort Tiffany Found Grant, 86; Richard & Hinda Rosenthal Award, Am Acad Inst Arts & Letts, 86. *Bibliog:* Charles Jencks (auth), Post Modernism: the New Classicism in Art and Architecture, Rizzoli, NY, 87. *Mailing Add:* Yale Sch Art 180 York St New Haven CT 06520

RYAN, WILLIAM EDWARD
PAINTER
b Oakland, Calif, Oct 26, 36. *Study:* Calif Col Arts Crafts, Oakland, 49-53; Pratt Inst, Brooklyn, NY, BA, 59. *Comn:* Mural in oil, Calif Valley Nat Bank, Delano, Calif, 64; three oil paintings, US Navy Art Collection, Washington, DC, 74; oil painting, Paccar Corp, Bellevue, Wash, 86; mural in oil, Sunset Mem Park, Bellevue, 88. *Exhib:* Puget Sound Area Exhib, Frye Mus, Seattle, 74-78; Nat Exhib Am Soc Marine Artists, Peabody Mus, Salem, Mass, 81 & Mariners Mus, Newport News, Va, 84; Int Exhib Am Soc Marine Artists, Mystic Seaport Mus, Conn, 87-88; Nat Acad Western Art (NAWA), Oklahoma City, 90. *Awards:* Rudolph J Schaefer Award, 87 & Award of Excellence, 88 & 90, Mystic Maritime Gallery Int Exhib. *Mem:* Am Soc Marine Artists; Puget Sound Group NW Painters; US Navy Artists Asn. *Media:* Oil; Watercolor. *Publ:* Auth, The young man and the sea, View Northwest, 74; Northwest marine art exhib 80, 81 & 87, Mystic Int Exhib, Sea Hist, 87-88 & spring 92; An artist looks at USS Fahriou, All Hands US Navy, 82; US Art, 7-8/90. *Mailing Add:* 9855 Vineyard Crest Bellevue WA 98004

RYDEN, KENNETH GLENN
SCULPTOR
b Chicago, Ill, May 16, 45. *Study:* Univ Wis, Superior, BFA; Univ Kans, Lawrence, MFA; study with Bernard Frazer, Eldon Tefft & Victor Timmerman. *Work:* Grover Hermann Fine Arts Ctr, Marietta, Ohio; Swope Art Gallery, Terre Haute, Ind; Southern Ill Univ Art Collection, Edwardsville; Wabash Col Art Collection, Crawfordsville, Ind; Kans State Univ; and others. *Comn:* Delyte Morris Mem, Southern Ill Univ at Edwardsville, 76 & John Rendleman Mem, 76; Greenville City Sq, 80; 10 Yr Mem, Southern Ill Univ, Sch Med, Springfield. *Exhib:* Mainstreams 73, Grover M Hermann Fine Arts Ctr, Marietta, Ohio, 73; one-man exhibs, Univ Wis-Superior, Ark State Univ, Jonesboro, Univ Notre Dame, Kans State Univ, Manhattan & Roberts Wesleyan Col, Rochester; Houghton Col, New York, 80; and many others. *Teaching:* Instr sculpture, Univ Mo, Columbia, 70-73; asst prof sculpture, Southern Ill Univ, Edwardsville, 73-78; assoc prof & chmn art dept, Greenville Col, Ill, 78-; assoc prof, Anderson Col, Ind, 83- *Awards:* Purchase Award, Mainstreams 73, Grover M Hermann Fine Arts Ctr, 73; Top Purchase Award, 33rd Ann Wabash Valley Sheldon Swope Art Gallery, 77; First in Sculpture, Int Platform Asn Artists Exhib, 82. *Mem:* Nat Col Art Asn; Southern Sculptors Asn; Nat Sculpture Ctr; Int Platform Asn; Washington Arts Club, Washington, DC. *Media:* Multimedia, Metals. *Dealer:* Prairie House Gallery 213 S Sixth St Springfield IL 62701; Neville-Sargent Gallery 509 Main St Evanston IL 60202. *Mailing Add:* Dept Art Anderson Univ Anderson IN 46012

RYERSON, MITCH
CRAFTSMAN
Study: Boston Univ, BAA (furniture design), 82. *Work:* Cambridge Publ Libr, Mass; Mus Fine Arts, Boston; ARC Int, New York; Workbench Corp, New York. *Exhib:* New Furniture, Victoria & Albert Mus, London, Eng, 84; Look Before You Sit, Fitchburg Art Mus, Mass, 85; Works in Wood, Dairy Barn Cult Arts Ctr, Ohio, 86; Contemporary Furniture Masterpieces, Gallery Fair, Mendocino, Calif, 87; Contemporary Expressions, Lyman Allyn Art Mus, New London, Conn, 89; Art That Works, Mint Mus Art, Charlotte, NC, 90. *Teaching:* Inst, Penland Sch Crafts, NC, 87 & Swain Sch Design, New Bedford, Mass, 88. *Awards:* Nat Endowment Arts Fel, 88; Cambridge (Mass) Arts Coun Fel, 88. *Bibliog:* Ellen Stasy (auth), Art is a chair, Christian Sci Monitor, 10/3/88; Edward S Cook Jr (auth), New American furniture: the second generation of studio furnituremakers, Mus Fine Arts, Boston, 89; Eric Gibson (auth), Artist crafts imaginative replies to old furniture, Washington Post, 4/24/90. *Mailing Add:* c/o Gallery NAGA 67 Newbury St Boston MA 02116

RYMAN, ROBERT
PAINTER
b Nashville, Tenn, May 30, 30. *Study:* Tenn Polytech Inst, 48-49; George Peabody Col, 49-50. *Work:* Mus Mod Art & Whitney Mus Am Art, New York; Ctr Pompidou, Paris; Carnegie Inst, Pittsburgh; Kunsthaus, Zurich; Albright-Knox Art Gallery; and many others. *Comn:* The Charter Series: A Meditative Room, Gerald S Elliott; Art Inst Chicago. *Exhib:* Solo exhibs, The Charter Series: A Meditative Room for the Collection of Gerald S Elliott, Art Inst Chicago & San Francisco Mus Mod Art, 87-88, Dia Art Found, New York, 88-89, Projects Room, John Weber Gallery, New YOrk, 89, Six Aquatints, Nohra Haime Gallery, New York, 90, New Paintings, Pace Gallery, New York, 90, Renn Espace d'Art Contemporain, Paris, Hallen fur neve Kunst, Schaffhausen, Switz, 91-93 & Versions, Pace Gallery, New York, 92-93; Artifice Artifacts, Galerie de Poche, Paris, 92; Yvon Lambert Collectionne, Musée d'art moderne de la communauté urbaine de Lille, Villeneuve d'Ascq, France & Musée des Beaux-Arts, Tourcoing, France, 92; Abstract Painting Between Analyst and Synthesis, Galerie nachst St Stephan, Vienna, 92; Arte Americana 1930-1970, Lingotto, s r i, Torino, Italy, 92; 15th Anniversary Exhib, Rhona Hoffman Gallery, Chicago, 92; and many other one-man & group exhibs. *Pos:* Mem, Art Comn New York, 82- *Awards:* Medal, Skowhegan Sch Painting, 87. *Bibliog:* Kay Larson (auth), The Wright Stuff, New York, 92; Yve Alain Bois (auth), Robert Ryman, surprise and equanimity, Galeries Mag, 6-7/92; Roberta Smith (auth), Guggenheim reopens on a new chapter, NY Times, 6/92; Decker (auth), What price Guggenheim?, Village Voice, 6/92; Roger Bevan (auth), Guggenheim: bigger and better, Art Newspaper, 6/92; and many others. *Mem:* Mus Mod Art, New York; Comnr, New York City Art Commission; Art Comn, New York. *Dealer:* Pace Gallery New York NY. *Mailing Add:* 17 W 16th St New York NY 10011

S

SAAR, ALISON M
SCULPTOR
b Los Angeles, Calif, Feb 5, 56. *Study:* Otis Art Inst, MFA, 81; Scripps Col, BA, 78. *Work:* Metro Mus Art & Studio Mus Harlem, New York; Trenton Mus Art, NJ; Newark Mus, NJ. *Comn:* Bronze gates, Metro Transit Authority, New York, 90-91. *Exhib:* Recent Acquisitions, Metro Mus Art, New York, 88; Urban Figures, Whitney Mus & Phillip Morris, New York, 89; Frederic Weisman Collection, Wright Mus, Los Angeles, 89; Secrets-Dialogues-Revelations, Chicago Inst Contemp Art, Ill, 90 & Wright Art Mus, Los Angeles, 90. *Awards:* Nat Endowment Arts, 85 & 88; John Solomon Guggenheim Award, 89. *Mailing Add:* 543 Union No L/C Brooklyn NY 11215

SAAR, BETYE
ASSEMBLAGE ARTIST, COLLAGE ARTIST
b Los Angeles, Calif, July 30, 26. *Study:* Univ Calif, Los Angeles, BA; Univ Southern Calif; Long Beach State Col; San Fernando Valley State Col. *Work:* Univ Mass, Amherst; Wellington Evest Collection, Boston; Golden State Mutual Life Ins Collection, Los Angeles; Los Angeles Co Mus Art; Univ Calif Mus, Berkeley. *Comn:* Mural, Los Angeles, 83; mural, Newark Sta, NJ, 84; Metrorail Sta, Miami, Fla, 86. *Exhib:* Sculpture Ann, 70 & Contemporary Black Artists in America, 71, Whitney Mus Am Art, New York; Black Artist Exhib, Los Angeles Co Mus Art, 72; one-woman exhibs, Whitney Mus Am Art, 75, Jan Baum/Iris Silverman Gallery, Los Angeles, 77, 79 & 81, Univ Art Gallery, Univ NDak, 79 & Mandeville Art Gallery, Univ Calif, San Diego, 79; Painting/Sculpture in Calif: Mod Era, San Francisco Mus Mod Art, 76 & Smithsonian Inst, Washington, DC, 77; Monique Knowlton Gallery, New York, 76 & 81; San Francisco Mus Mod Art, 77; Studio Mus Harlem, New York, 80; Connections, Mass Inst Tech, Cambridge, 87; and others. *Teaching:* Vis artist, Calif State Univ, Hayward, fall 71; prof art, Calif State Univ, Northridge, 73-75 & Otis Art Inst, 76-84; instr, Univ Alaska, summer 79 & Univ Calif, Los Angeles, 84- *Awards:* Purchase Award, Calif State Col, Los Angeles, 72; Nat Endowment Arts Award, 74 & 84. *Bibliog:* Spirit Catcher: The Art of Betye Saar, The Originals: Women in Art series, WNET-PBS, New York; Houston Conwill (auth), Interview with Betye Saar, Black Art, 79; Eleanor Munro (auth), Originals: American Women Artists, Simon & Schuster, 79; Lynn Miller & Sally Swenson (auths), Lives & Works: Talks with Women Artists, Scarecrow Press, NJ, 81; Clothier (auth), Betye Saar (catalog), Mus Contemp Art, Los Angeles, 84. *Media:* Multi. *Publ:* Auth, Handbook, 67. *Dealer:* Monique Knowlton New York NY. *Mailing Add:* c/o Ulrike Kantor Gallery 143 Saint Ives Dr Los Angeles CA 90089

SAARI, PETER H
PAINTER, SCULPTOR
b New York, NY, Feb 15, 51. *Study:* Sch Visual Arts, 69-70; C W Post Col, BFA, 74; Tyler Sch Art, Rome, Italy, study with Stephen Greene, 72-73; Yale Sch Art, study with William Bailey & Al Held, MFA(fel), 76. *Work:* Hirshhorn Mus, Washington, DC. *Exhib:* Solo exhibs, Helander Gallery, Palm Beach, FL, 87, OK Haris Works of Art, New York, 87, Robert Schoelkopf Gallery, New York, 88, Tortue Gallery, Santa Monica, Calif, 89

& Fendrick Gallery, Washington, DC, 90; New York-New York, Helander Gallery, Palm Beach, Fla, 86-87; Mainstream America: The Collection of Phil Desind & 51st Ann Nat Mid-Year Exhib, Butler Inst Am Art, Youngstown, Ohio; Classical Myth and Imagery in Contemp Art, The Queens Mus, Flushing, NY, 88. *Teaching:* Asst instr advan painting, Yale Sch Art, New Haven, Conn, 75-76; guest lectr, St Lawrence Univ, 78. *Bibliog:* Ninon Gaulthier (auth), Impressions de New York, Finance, France, 4/87; A Question of Space: Architectural Inquiries (catalog), The Rye Arts Ctr, NY, 87; Richard Martin and Harold Koda (coauthor), The Historical Mode: Fashion and Art in the 1980's, Rizzoli, New York, 80. *Dealer:* Helander Gallery Palm Beach FL 33480. *Mailing Add:* c/o Ivan Karp 383 W Broadway New York NY 10007

SAARINEN, LILIAN
SCULPTOR
b New York, NY, Apr 17, 12. *Study:* Art Students League, with Alexander Archipenko, 28; study with Hans Warneke, 34-36; with Albert Stewart; Cranbrook Acad Art, with Carl Milles, 36-40. *Work:* IBM Collection; Addison Mus Gallery, Andover, Mass; Fogg Art Mus, Harvard Univ. *Comn:* Sculpture for Toffennetti Restaurant, Skidmore, Owings & Merrill, Chicago, 48; eagle for Detroit Fed Reserve Bank, Leineweber Yamasaki & Hellmuth, Detroit, 52; and others. *Exhib:* World's Fair, 39; Los Angeles Co Art Fair, 44; Boston Arts Festival, 54-60; Beverly Farms Regional Art Exhib, Mass, 63; St Gaudens Hist Park, Cornish, NH, 75. *Teaching:* Instr lang of clay, Pratt Inst, Brooklyn, 59-60, Mus Fine Arts, Boston, 63-64 & Mass Inst Technol, 63-67. *Awards:* Jefferson Nat Expansion Mem Competition Award for Sculpture Gateway to the West, 48; Walter B Ford Prize for Eagle, 54; Beverly Farms Regional Art Exhib Award for Portrait Edwin O'Connor, 61. *Bibliog:* Clay sculpture, Arts & Archit, 9/42; Emily Genauer (auth), Super sculpture, This Week Mag, Detroit News, 9/54; Mabel Colgate (auth), Visit with L Saarinen, Boston Globe, 5/7/70. *Mem:* Cambridge Art Asn; St Gaudens Nat Hist Park (trustee, 73-75); Fine Arts Work Ctr Provincetown. *Media:* Terra Cotta, Metal. *Publ:* Auth & illusr, Who Am I?, Reynal & Hitchcock, 46; design for eagle used on book jackets, Americans, 63 & Short Chronology of American History, 63. *Mailing Add:* 224 Brattle St Cambridge MA 02138

SABA, RICHARD
PAINTER
b Minneapolis, Minn, Dec 15, 46. *Study:* Skowhegan Sch Painting & Sculpture, 67; Minneapolis Col Art & Design, BFA, 68; Univ Wash, MFA, 71. *Work:* Mus Art, Ft Lauderdale, Fla; Tomasulo Gallery, Union Col, Cranford, NJ; Prudential Insurance Co of Am, Newark, NJ; IBM Corp, White Plains, NY; E F Hutton Co, New York. *Exhib:* The Irascible Seventeen, Henry Gallery, Seattle, 70; Invitational Shows, Whitney Mus, Art Resources Ctr, New York, 72 & 73; Contemp Am Painters and Sculptors, Nabisco Hq, East Hanover, 78; Invitational Show, Col Mt St Vincent, New York, 81; Invitational Show, Daytona Beach Col, Fla, 82; New Talent-New York, Sioux City Art Ctr, Iowa, 84. *Bibliog:* Eric Gibson (auth), Richard Saba, Art Int, 6/79; Claude Pelieu (auth), Reflections concerning Richard Saba's spaces, Kanal, Paris, 1/85; Robert Berlind (auth), Richard Saba, Art in Am, 5/86. *Media:* Acrylic on Canvas. *Mailing Add:* c/o Jaffe Baker Gallery The Gallery Ctr 608 Banyan Trail Boca Raton FL 33431

SABATELLA, JOSEPH JOHN
ADMINISTRATOR, PAINTER
b Chicago, Ill, May 5, 31. *Study:* Univ Ill, BFA(painting & graphics), 54, MFA(painting & graphics), 58. *Comn:* Acrylic painting on masonite, Campus Cafeteria, Univ Fla, Gainesville, 64. *Exhib:* Hunterdon Print Society, Nat Print Show, 57; Libr Cong, Washington, DC, 57; Society Four Arts, West Palm Beach Fla, 63; Atlantic Artist Show, Clemson Col, SC, 64; one-man shows, Atelier Chapman Kelley, Dallas, Tex, 64 & Visual Arts Comt Jacksonville Coun Arts, Fla, 69; and others. *Pos:* Mgr, Elenhank Designers Inc, Riverside, Ill, 58-59. *Teaching:* Prof drawing & design, Univ Fla, Gainesville, 59-, asst dean, Col Archit & Fine Arts, 66-75, dean, 75- *Awards:* First Award, Arts Festival Six, City of Jacksonville, Fla, 63. *Mem:* Int Coun Fine Arts Deans. *Media:* Oil. *Mailing Add:* 2510 N W 30th Terrace Gainesville FL 32605

SABELIS, HUIBERT
PRINTMAKER, PAINTER
b Wageningen-Gelderland, Neth, Feb 28, 42; Can citizen. *Study:* Tech Sch Art, Neth, with Bloothoofd, 57-60; Art Instr Schs Inc, Minneapolis, 64; lino printmaking with Senggih, 73; Serigraphy with Rol Lampitoc, 81-86. *Work:* Royal Ont Mus, Toronto; Philippine Nat Mus, Manila; UNESCO of Japan, Tokyo; Nat Libr, Paris, France; HRH Prince Bernard of the Neth; Vatican Collection; Librijeciy Art Gallery, Neth; and many others. *Exhib:* One-man shows, Woodstock Public Art Gallery, Can, 80, Laurier Gallery, Toronto, Can, 81 & Galerij 3, The Netherlands, 81, US, Phillipines, Australia, Japan, Israel & Colombia; Saxe Gallery, Toronto, Can, 81. *Awards:* Haiez Award IV, Mostra Mondiale di pittura Cresentino, 79. *Bibliog:* Articles in Arts mag, Arts Queensland, Toronto Calendar Mag. *Media:* Acrylic, Watercolor; Serigraphy. *Mailing Add:* c/o Aaron Gallery 25 Young St E Waterloo ON N2J 2L4 Canada

SABLOW, RHODA LILLIAN See Roda (Rhoda Lillian Sablow)

SABO, BETTY JEAN
PAINTER, SCULPTOR
b Kansas City, Mo, Sept 15, 28. *Study:* Univ NMex; also with Randall Davey, Carl von Hassler, Charles Reynolds & Al Merrill. *Work:* Albuquerque Mus; Mus Sasebo, Japan; Pub Serv Co, NMex; United NMex Bank; Sunwest Bank; Plains Elec Co; Las Vegas, Nev Pub Libr. *Comn:* Baldequino (mural), St Bernadette's Catholic Church, Albuquerque, 61; 15 paintings for children murals, pediatrics ward, St Joseph's Hosp, 66; Leanin' Tree Cards, Artists of the Am West, 77; Christmas Greeting, Phelps-Dodge Collection, 81; 36 Collographs, St Joseph Rehabilitation Hosp, 90. *Exhib:* Albuquerque I, Albuquerque Mus, 68; Catharine Lorillard Wolfe Exhib, Nat Acad, NY, 71 & Nat Arts Club, NY, 72-73; Allied Artists, 78-80; Am Acad Art, New York, 80; Margaret Jamison Prescuts, NMex, 84-86; NMex Tapestries, 84-85; Magnifico, Gov Exhib, Albuquerque; Arte Grande Outdoor Sculpture, Albuquerque, 91; Magnifico 90, Albuquerque; Sedona Sculpture Walk, Ariz, 91; NM Community Found, 91-92. *Pos:* Chmn, Albuquerque Arts Bd, 88-; guest cur, Miniatures/91 & Minatures/92, Albuquerque Mus. *Bibliog:* Flo Wilks (auth), The colorful way of the land, SW Art, 12/77; Women on the Arts, Southwest Art, 4/81; M C Nelson (auth), New Mexico is warm when its Cold, Art Lines, Winter 86-87; S H McGarry (auth), Schooled in the Art of Collecting, Southwest Art, 1/87; J A Baldinger (auth), Colorful Artists Run the Spectrum, NMex Mag, 6/91; Fabulous Fountains, Southwest Art, 8/92. *Mem:* Catharine Lorillard Wolfe Art Club; NMex Art League; Am Artists Prof League. *Media:* Oil, Bronze. *Mailing Add:* 705 Parkland Circle SE Albuquerque NM 87108

SACANGA, ITALO
SCULPTOR, EDUCATOR
b Lago, Italy, June 6, 32; US citizen. *Study:* Mich State Univ, BA, 60, MFA(sculpture), 61. *Work:* Fogg Mus, Cambridge, Mass; Guggenheim Mus, New York; Philadelphia Mus Art; Los Angeles County Mus Art; Mus Mod Art, New York. *Comn:* Figure Holding Fire, Santa Barbara Museo, Mammola, Italy, 84; Figure Holding the Sun, City of San Jose, Calif, 88; wall reliefs, Carlson Companies, Minneapolis, Minn, 89; ceramic heads, pvt comns, La Jolla, Calif, 89 & 90. *Exhib:* Sculpture Ann, 70 & Biennial Exhib, 83, Whitney Mus Am Art; Mus Mod Art, New York, 71; Corcoran Gallery Art, Washington, DC, 71; one-man shows, La Galleria, Lugano, Switz, 85, Simon Neuman Gallery, New York, NY, 87-88, Dorothy Goldeen Gallery, Santa Monica, Calif, 89, Betsy Rosenfield Gallery, Chicago, Ill, 90 & Helander Gallery, New York, 91; The Anxious Edge, Walker Art Ctr, 81; Beyond Modernism, Crysler Mus, Norfolk, Va, 82; The 6th Day: A Survey of Recent Developments in Figurative Sculpture, Univ Chicago, 83; group exhib, Mus Mod Art, New York, 84, Guggenheim Mus Art, New York 85, Cleveland Mus Art, Cleveland, Ohio, 87, Everson Mus Art, Syracuse, NY, 88; Park Wing Gallery, Santa Barbara Mus Art, Calif, 89; Linda Farris Gallery, Seattle, Wash, 90; Joan Pratt Gallery, New York, 91. *Teaching:* Asst prof sculpture, RI Sch Design, 64-66; assoc prof sculpture, Tyler Sch Art, Philadelphia, 67-78; vis assoc prof visual arts, Univ Calif, San Diego, 76-77, prof, 78- *Awards:* Howard Found Grant, Brown Univ, 70; Cassandra Found Grant, 72; Copley Found Grant Chicago, Ill, 72; Nat Endowment Arts, 73 & 80. *Bibliog:* Ron Onorato (auth), article, Art in Am, 78; Christopher Knight (auth), Scanga's object cipher, Art Express, 82; Susan Larsen (auth), cover article, Art News, 11/84; and others. *Mem:* Int Sculpture Ctr. *Media:* Mixed Media. *Mailing Add:* 6717 Vista Del Mar La Jolla CA 92037

SACHS, SAMUEL, II
MUSEUM DIRECTOR, HISTORIAN
b New York, NY, Nov 30, 35. *Study:* Harvard Univ, AB(cum laude); NY Univ Inst Fine Arts, AM. *Collections Arranged:* The Past Rediscovered, XIX Century French Painting 1800-1900, 69; Fakes and Forgeries (with catalog), 73; Grant Wood, 83. *Pos:* Asst prints & drawings, Minneapolis Inst Arts, 58-60, chief cur, 64-73, dir, 73-85; asst dir, Univ Mich Mus Art, 62-64; dir, Detroit Inst Arts, 85- *Teaching:* Lectr art hist, Univ Mich, Ann Arbor, 62-63. *Mem:* Am Fedn Arts; Col Art Asn Am. *Res:* Fakes and forgeries; American 19th and 20th century painting. *Publ:* Auth, Reconstructing the whirlwind of 26th St, Art News, 2/63; Drawings and watercolors of Thomas Moran, In: Thomas Moran (catalog), Univ Calif, Riverside, 63; American Paintings at the Minneapolis Institute of Arts, 71; Art forges ahead, Auction Mag, 1/72; Favorite Paintings from the Minneapolis Institute of Arts, Abbeyville Press, 81. *Mailing Add:* Detroit Inst Arts 5200 Woodward Ave Detroit MI 84202

SACHSE, JANICE R
PAINTER, PRINTMAKER
b New Orleans, La, May 6, 08. *Study:* La State Univ, with Conrad Albrizio; Newcomb Col Art Sch; Corcoran Gallery. *Work:* Two Major Works, New Orleans Mus Art; Anglo Am Mus, La State Univ; Lauren Rogers Mus, Laurel, Miss; Pan American Life Insurance Bldg, New Orleans; Five Major Works, City Nat Bank, Baton Rouge. *Exhib:* New York World's Fair, 65; Volkfest Exhib from New Orleans Galleries, Berlin, Ger, 68; 11th Midwest Biennial, Joslyn Art Mus, Omaha, Nebr, 70; Sally Jackson Gallery, Hong Kong, 70; 50 Year Retrospective, La State Univ, 82; Southern Works on Paper 1900-1950, Southern Arts Fed, Atlanta. *Awards:* Ten juried purchase prizes; Bicentennial Exhib Purchase Prize, 76; First Prize, 65th Anniversary Celebration Exhib, Am Soc Contemp Artists, New York, 83. *Bibliog:* Keith Cooper Marshall (auth), article, Am Artist Mag, 9/80; Richard Cox (auth), Janice Sachse Retrospective, 83. *Mem:* Am Soc Contemp Artists. *Publ:* Auth, article & centerfold, New Orleans Mus Art, Arts Quarterly, 81; article, Am Artist Mag. *Mailing Add:* 3737 Essen Lane No 60 Baton Rouge LA 70809

SACKS, BEVERLY & RAY
CONSULTANTS, COLLECTORS
Study: Beverly: Brooklyn Col, BA; Ray: Pratt Inst. *Exhib:* African American Artists; Woman at Her Easel; The Fine Line; Wonderous Imagery; All the Isms. *Pos:* Beverly: Consult, Phillips & Son & Neale, Am Illusr; owners, Sacks Fine Art; permanent collection, Comt Soc Illusr Mus Am Illus. *Bibliog:* Antique & Arts Weekly, 10/17/80; Maine Antique Digest, 11/80; Buying

American painting, Boston Sunday Globe, 11/23/80. *Mem:* Appraisers Asn Am; Prof Antique Dealers Asn; Soc Illusr. *Specialty:* American paintings; 19th and early 20th century American illustrations and paintings; American works on paper. *Collection:* African American, abstract and surrealists. *Publ:* Rube Goldberg, Early Works, 81; African-American artists of the Harlem Renaissance period and later, 91. *Mailing Add:* 50 W 57th St New York NY 10019

SADE, SHULI
PAINTER, SCULPTOR
b Jerusalem, Israel, Oct 20, 52; Am & Israeli citizen. *Study:* Tel-Hai Sch Painting & Sculpture, 70; Bezalel Acad Art & Design, BFA, 76; Sch Visual Arts (spec student prog), New York, 78. *Work:* Israel Mus, Jerusalem; Haifa Mus, Israel. *Exhib:* Biennale of Young Artists & New Acquisitions, Haifa Mus, Israel, 78; one-woman shows, Bertha Urdang Gallery, New York, 79, Gimmel Gallery, Jerusalem, 80, East-West Performance, Billy Rose Pavillion, Israel Mus, Jerusalem; Tel Hai 80 Biennale, Israel, 80; Borders, Israel Mus, Jerusalem, 80; New Directions, 91, Barrett House, Symbolism in the 90's, Poughkeepsie, 92; Small Works, Parsons Sch Design, New York, 92; Monumental Propaganda, New York & Moscow, 93. *Pos:* Cur, USIS, Jerusalem, Am Embassy, 76-82; art dir, Parade, AZYF, 90-92. *Teaching:* Instr three dimensional design, Parsons Sch Design, 90-91. *Awards:* Painters Fel, Nat Endowmment Arts, 91-92. *Bibliog:* Various interviews & reviews including, Art TV, 6/92 & Art Talk, 8/92. *Media:* Oil; Industrial Materials. *Dealer:* Edmund Yankov 59 Livingston St No 1C Brooklyn NY 11201-4814. *Mailing Add:* 55 W 14th St New York NY 10011

SADEK, GEORGE
EDUCATOR, DESIGNER
b Czech, Oct 12, 28; US citizen. *Study:* Hunter Col; City Univ New York, BA; Ind Univ, MFA. *Work:* Mus Mod Art, New York; Libr Cong; Morgan Libr. *Exhib:* Type Dir Club New York, 69; Am Inst Graphic Arts, 70; Typomondus, Frankfurt, Ger, 71. *Teaching:* From instr to asst prof graphic design, Ind Univ, 60-66; prof graphic design, Cooper Union, 66-, chmn dept art, 66-68, dean, Sch Art, 68- *Bibliog:* Articles, Am Inst Graphic Arts J, 68 & Print, 70. *Mem:* Am Inst Graphic Arts (bd mem, 69-72); Col Art Asn (vpres, 74-76, pres, 76-78). *Mailing Add:* Dept Art Cooper Union Sch Art 41 Cooper Sq New York NY 10003

SADIK, MARVIN SHERWOOD
DEALER
b Springfield, Mass, June 27, 32. *Study:* Harvard Univ, AB, 54, AM, 61; Bowdoin Col, DFA, 78. *Pos:* Curatorial asst, Worcester Art Mus, Mass, 55-57; cur & dir, Bowdoin Col Mus Art, 61-67; dir, Univ Conn Mus Art, 67-69; dir, Nat Portrait Gallery, Smithsonian Inst, 69-81. *Teaching:* Instr fine arts, Harvard Col, 58-60. *Awards:* Knight of Dannebrog, Denmark; Smithsonian Gold Medal For Exceptional Service, 81. *Mem:* Colonial Soc Mass; Am Antiquarian Soc; fel Morgan Libr; Century Asn; Grolier Club. *Publ:* Auth, Colonial & federal portraits at Bowdoin Col, 66. *Mailing Add:* 47 Foreside Common Dr Falmouth Portland ME 04105

SADLE, AMY ANN BRANDON
PAINTER, PRINTMAKER
b Council Bluffs, Iowa, Aug 3, 40. *Study:* State Univ Iowa, 59-61; Ed Whitney Watercolor, 73; State Univ RI, 65- *Work:* Statute of Liberty Mus, New York; Des Moines Art Ctr, Des Moines, Iowa; Indian Comn, Lincoln, Nebr; Mc Cook Col, Nebr; Hilton Hotel, Rapid City, SDak. *Comn:* St Theresa Church, Sta of the Cross, Mitchell, Nebr, 80; Stained Glass Window, Cath Church, Torrington, Wyo, 80; Portrait, Indian Comn, Lincoln, Nebr, 83. *Exhib:* Women our Lives & Experiences, Univ Kansas, Lawrence, Kans, 86; one-man show,Univ NDak, Grand Forks, NDak, 87; Small Works, Brandon Gallery, Fallbrook, Calif, 88; Fla Print Show, Fla Print Club, Winterpark, Fla, 88 & 89; East Meets West, Jacob Javitz Ctr, New York, 89. *Collections Arranged:* Impact the Art of Nebraska Women, 88-90. *Pos:* Art gallery dir, W Nebr Art Ctr, 74-76; corp dir, Columbus, Nebr, Impact, 87. *Teaching:* Instr, Painting, W Nebr Community Col, Scottsbluff, Nebr, 72-81; Dillman Lodge, Lac Flambaue, Wis, 88-89; Red Carpet Travel, 88-89. *Awards:* Top Award, San Diego Print Nat, 84; Nebr Arts Award, A Nac, 88. *Bibliog:* Krantz, Calif Art Review, Country People, 88. *Mem:* N Platte Valley Artists Guild (pres 71-85); Asn Nebr Art Clubs, (comts 75-88); Columbus Area Artists (pres 88-89); Nat Artists Equity; Philadelphia Print Club. *Media:* Woodcut, Watercolor. *Res:* 1987 Daniel Smith Research Grant in Metalics; Encaustic Book; Impact. *Publ:* Auth, ed & illusr, Home of Wooden Men and Iron Ships, private publ, 79; ed, Her Barnyard Brush, Country People, 81; auth, Doing My Thing in Tune, Pallet Talk Mag, 88; ed, Impact, art of Nebr women, private publ, 88. *Dealer:* Myraid Fine Art 800 Miami Cir Suite 200 Atlanta GA 30324. *Mailing Add:* Box H Syracuse NY 68446

SADOWSKI, CAROL (LOUISE) JOHNSON
PAINTER
b Chicago, Ill, Mar 20, 29. *Study:* Art Inst Chicago Scholar, 42-43; Wright Jr Col, AAS, 49. *Work:* Mus Fla Hist, Tallahassee; Elliot Mus, Stuart, Fla; Hollywood Art & Cult Ctr, Fla; Ernest Hemmingway Home & Mus, Key West, Fla; Hemmingway Mus, San Francisco; de Paula, Cuba; The Vatican. *Comn:* Paintings, San Augustin Antiqua Found, St Augustine, Fla, 85; Atlantic Bank, Fort Lauderdale; Bonnet House Fla Trust, Fort Lauderdale. *Exhib:* solo exhibs, Scenes of Fla, Mus Fla Hist, Tallahassee, 84, Hemingway's Haunts, Elliot Mus, Stuart, Hemingway's Home & Mus, Key West, Hist Mus S Fla, Miami, 86, Marjorie Kinnan Rawlings-Cross Creek, Thomas Ctr Arts, Gainesville, Fla, 85 & Mus Fla Hist, Tallahassee 85 & 87; Marjorie Kinnan Rawlins-Cross Creek, Mus Fla Hist, Tallahassee, 85. *Teaching:* Art teacher, adult ed, Malverne High Sch, 68-69. *Awards:* Appreciation Award, City of Hollywood, Fla. *Bibliog:* Gary Schwan (auth), Hemingway's Cuba, Palm Beach Post, 6/23/85; Terri Fox (auth), Hemingway's haunts, Fla Hist Assocs, 9/1/87; Paul Heidelberg (auth), Canvassing Hemingway's life, Ft Lauderdale Sun Sentinal, 5/15/88. *Mem:* Broward Art Guild; Fla Hist Assocs; charter mem Women in the Arts Nat Mus, Washington, DC. *Media:* Oil, Watercolor. *Dealer:* Gingerbread Square Gallery Key West FL 33040; de Ligny Art Galleries 709 E Las Olas Blvd Ft Lauderdale FL 33301. *Mailing Add:* 1930 Scott St Hollywood FL 33020

SAFER, JOHN
SCULPTOR
b Washington, DC, Sept 6, 22. *Work:* Baltimore Mus Art, Md; Corcoran Gallery Art, Washington, DC; Nat Air and Space Mus, (Smithsonian Inst), Washington, DC; Philadelphia Mus Art, Pa; San Francisco Mus Art; and others. *Comn:* Judgement, 15 ft bronze, Harvard Law Sch, 79; Search, 20 ft bronze, Harvard Bus Sch, 84; Web of Space, Nat Air and Space Mus Trophy, 84; Timepiece, (World's largest clock, Guinness Bk of Records), Int Sq Bldg, Washington, DC, 85; Challenge: Christa McAuliffe Mem, Bowie New Town Ctr, Bowie, Md, 88. *Exhib:* One-man shows, US Embassy, London, 72 & 89, Nat Air & Space Mus (Smithsonian Inst), Washington, DC, 84, Norton Gallery Art, Palm Beach, Fla, 85, & Espace Pierre Cardin, Paris, 89. *Bibliog:* Charles Mann (auth), article, An Artistic Bent, Pursuits Mag, 88 (cover); C J Houtchens, (auth), article, Dossier Mag, The Art of John Safer, 89; Walter Boyne (auth), David Finn (photo), book, Art in Flight, 92. *Media:* Metal. *Mailing Add:* 183 Chain Bridge Rd McLean VA 22101

SAFF, DONALD JAY
PRINTMAKER, ADMINISTRATOR
b New York, NY, Dec 12, 37. *Study:* Queens Col, City Univ NY, BA, 59; Columbia Univ, MA, 60; Pratt Inst, MFA, 62; Teachers Col, Columbia Univ, EdD, 64. *Work:* Metrop Mus Art, Mus Mod Art, Brooklyn Mus, & Nelson Rockefeller Collection, New York; William Hayes Fogg Art Mus, Harvard Univ & Mus Fine Arts, Boston, Mass; Lessing Rosenwald Collection, Philadelphia Mus Art & La Salle Col, Pa; Nat Gallery Art, Libr Cong, Washington, DC; Dartmouth Col, NH; Ill State Univ & Southern Ill Univ; Fla Int Univ, Miami; Butler Inst Am Art, Ohio; and many others. *Comn:* Two hundred prints, 67, 200 prints, 68 & 125 prints, 71, Int Graphic Arts Soc. *Exhib:* solo exhibs, Martin Gordon Gallery NY, 65, 66 & 70, Galleria Academia, Rome, 65, La Colomba Gallery, Bologna, Italy, 66, Byron Gallery New York, 68, Toronto Art Gallery, 70, Galleria D'Arte Moderna, Udine, Italy, 81, & Gemini, GEL, Los Angeles, 85; Smithsonian Inst, 61; Soc Washington Printmakers, Washington, DC, 62; Fanesi Gallery, Ancona, Italy, 64; Canadian Int Print Exhib, Vancouver, 67; Loch Haven Art Ctr, Orlando, 70; Edison Community Col, Ft Myers, Fla, 80; Huntsville Mus Art, Ala, 81; Tahir Gallery, New Orleans, La, 81, Dyansen Gallery, New York, 82, Pennell Collection, Libr Cong, 84 and many other one man & group exhibs. *Pos:* Co-dir, Pyramid Arts Ltd, Tampa, Fla, formerly; dir graphic studio, Univ SFla, 68-76 & 85-90; dean Col Fine Arts, Univ SFla, 71-82; dir & cur, Rauschenberg Overseas Cult Interchange, 84-91; consult, Art J, formerly. *Teaching:* Instr printmaking & design, Teachers Col, Columbia Univ, summers 65 & 66; assoc prof printmaking & design, Univ SFla, Tampa, 65-67; chmn visual arts dept, 67-71, distinguished serv prof, currently; dir, SAFF Tech Arts Prog, Md, 90- *Awards:* Fulbright Grant, Italy, 64-65; Patrick Gavin Mem Prize, Boston Printmaking Asn, 66; Grant Proj, Dir, Univ SFla, Nat Endowment Arts, 73-77. *Bibliog:* Article, New York Herald Tribune, 12/65; John Canaday (auth), article, New York Times, 10/68; article, Print Collector's Newslett, 7-8/72, 5/79, 1/81. *Mem:* Nat Coun of Art Adminrs (mem bd dirs, 73-75); Int Coun Fine Arts Deans; Col Art Asn; mem & founder, Nat Coun of Art Adminrs, (bd dir, 73-75). *Publ:* Coauth, Images of Destruction: Monsu Desiderio and Jacques Callot, Queens Col, 64; auth, Modern Masters of Intaglio, Queens Col, 64; coauth, Printmaking History and Technique, Holt, Rinehart & Winston, 77; Fables, 79 & Constellations, 80, Getler/Pall Gallery, New York. *Mailing Add:* Box 408 Royal Oak MD 21662

SAGANIC, LIVIO MICHELE
SCULPTOR
b Vidovici, Yugoslavia, Aug 19, 50, US citizen. *Study:* Pratt Inst, BFA, 74; Yale Univ, MFA, 76. *Work:* Albright-Knox Art Gallery, Buffalo, NY; Montclair Mus, NJ; Newark Mus, NJ; Chase Manhattan Bank, New York; Exxon Corp, New York. *Comn:* Outdoor sculpture for Rio Plaza, Vector Real Estate Corp, New York, 87; outdoor public sculpture for BMW of Am, BMW & City of Oxnard, Calif, 88-89;; outdoor public sculpture, NJ Dept Motor Vehicles, Mays Landing, 90. *Exhib:* Special Proj, PS 1, Inst Art & Urban Resources, Long Island City, NY, 80; solo exhibs, NJ State Mus, Trenton, 82, Univ NC, Chapel Hill, 86, Hal Bromm Gallery, New York, 88 & Montclair Mus, NJ, 88; Landscape into Sculpture, Barbara Krakow Gallery, Boston, 83; Sacred Spaces, Everson Mus, Syracuse, NY, 87; 19th Biennial, Middleheimein Mus, Antwerp, Belg, 87. *Teaching:* Prof fine arts & art dept chmn, Drew Univ, Madison, NJ, 76- *Awards:* Louis Comfort Tiffany Found Award for Sculpture, 79; Sculpture Fel Award, Nat Endowment Arts, 80; Sculpture Fel Award, New York Found Arts, 87. *Bibliog:* William Zimmer (auth), Compelling mundanities in stone & paint, New York Times, 3/10/85; April Kingsley (auth), Obsession is with permanence, Arts Mag, 11/85; Stephen Westfall (auth), review, Art in Am, 9/88. *Media:* Stone, Metal. *Mailing Add:* 245 W 29th St New York NY 10001

SAHLSTRAND, JAMES MICHAEL
PHOTOGRAPHER
b Minneapolis, Minn, May 4, 36. *Study:* Univ Minn, BA, MFA. *Comn:* Photographs SE Wash, Walla Walla Community Col, 76-77 & photographs E Wash, Eastern Wash Univ & Turnbull Game Reserve Res Sta, 77, Wash State Arts Comn. *Exhib:* Young Photographers Traveling Exhib, 68-70; Being without Clothes, Mass Inst Technol, 70; Photo-Media, Mus Contemp Crafts, New York, 71; San Francisco Mus Art, 72; Synthetic Color, Univ Southern Ill, 74. *Pos:* Pres, Roslyn Arts, 72- *Teaching:* Assoc prof photog, Cent Wash Univ, Ellensburg, 65- *Mem:* Soc Photog Educ. *Media:* Color, Multiple Image. *Mailing Add:* Dept Art Central Wash Univ Ellensburg WA 98926

SAHLSTRAND, MARGARET AHRENS
PRINTMAKER, CRAFTSMAN
b St Louis, Mo, Oct 1, 39. *Study:* Lindenwood, Col, St Charles, Mo, 61; Univ of Iowa, Iowa City, printmaking, MFA, 64; also in Japan, 81-83. *Work:* Kobe Mus Fine Arts, Hygo Prefecture Mus Collection, Japan; Okla Art Ctr, Oklahoma City; Wash State Printmakers Collection, Evergreen State Col, Olympia; Nat Collection Art, Washington, DC. *Comn:* Cast paper murals, W Valley Sr High Sch, Yakima, Wash, 80 & Western Paper Co, Kent, Wash, 81. *Exhib:* Solo exhibs, Cast Paperworks, Slocumb Gallery, E Tenn State Univ, Johnson City, 77; 1st Editions Graphics Competition, Ore Arts Comn, Salem, 76; World Print Competition, San Francisco Mus Art, 77; Paper as Medium, SITES, Smithsonian Inst, Washington, DC, 78-; Cast Paper, Pratt Graphics Ctr, New York, 78; Works in Handmade Paper, Jerusalem Theater, Israel, 83; Paper Innovations, Mingei Int Mus, La Jolla, Calif, 85; Arts of the Book, The Akuin Soc, Vancouver, BC, 86. *Pos:* Proprietor, Icosa Studio & Papermill, Ellensburg, currently. *Teaching:* Prof art, Cent Wash Univ, Ellensburg, 65- *Awards:* Cannon Prize, Printmaking, Nat Acad Design, New York, 66; Purchase Award, Statewide Services, Univ Ore, Eugene, 75; Fac Res Grant, Cent Wash Univ, 78; First prize, Paper Fair III Exhib, Vancouver, BC, 85. *Mem:* Northwest Book Arts Guild; Northwest Designer Craftsmen. *Publ:* Auth, Paper clothing, Fiberarts, Vol II, No 2, 84 & Hyakomantoh, No 61, Tokyo, 85; Japanese paper textiles, Paper Innovations, Mingei Int Mus, 85. *Mailing Add:* Art Dept Cent Wash Univ Rte 4 Box 279 Ellensburg WA 98926

SAHRBECK, EVERETT WILLIAM
PAINTER, PHOTOGRAPHER
b East Orange, NJ, Nov 4, 10. *Study:* NY Univ. *Work:* De Cordova Mus, Lincoln, Mass; Montclair Art Mus; Newark Art Mus; Overlook Hosp, Summit, NJ; First Nat Bank Boston. *Exhib:* Am Watercolor Soc Ann, 54-72; Montclair Art Mus Statewide Ann, 55-67; Royal Soc Painters Watercolors, London, 63; Landscape I, De Cordova Mus, 70 & 77; Boston 350th Jubilee, 80. *Pos:* Art dir, Reach, McClinton & Co, 34-68. *Teaching:* Watercolor workshops, Cape Cod Art Asn. *Awards:* Am Watercolor Soc Ann Prize, 61; Silver Medal of Honor, NJ Watercolor Soc, 70; Cape Cod Art Asn Watercolor Prizes, 71-80. *Mem:* Am Watercolor Soc; NJ Watercolor Soc; Cape Cod Art Asn (pres, 71-72). *Media:* Watercolor. *Dealer:* Port Gallery Harwichport MA. *Mailing Add:* Box 401 South Harwich MA 02661

SAIA, JORGE See Zontal, Jorge (Jorge Saia)

SAIDENBERG, DANIEL
DEALER
b Winnipeg, Man, Oct 12, 06. *Study:* Julliard Sch Music. *Pos:* Pres, Saidenberg Gallery. *Specialty:* Twentieth century European and American masters. *Mailing Add:* 1018 Madison Ave New York NY 10021

SAIDENBERG, ELEANORE B
DEALER, COLLECTOR
b Chicago, Ill, Apr 7, 11. *Exhib:* Mus Mod Art & Guggenheim Mus, New York; Art Inst Chicago. *Pos:* Owner & dir, Saidenberg Gallery Inc, New York, currently. *Mem:* Art Dealers Asn Am (bd mem, 65-70). *Specialty:* Picasso, Leger, Klee, Masson, Gris, Braque & others. *Collection:* Picasso and School of Paris; Klee, Kandinsky, Feininger. *Publ:* Auth, Pablo Picasso Paintings, 57, Picasso Exhibition, 67-68, Fernand Leger-Gouaches, Watercolors, Drawings, 68, Paul Klee-A Retrospective Exhibition, 69 & Picasso-Recent Works on Paper-1967-1970, 70, (all catalogs). *Mailing Add:* Saidenberg Gallery Inc 1018 Madison Ave New York NY 10021

ST AMAND, JOSEPH
PAINTER
b New York, NY, Nov 10, 25. *Study:* Univ Calif, Berkeley; Calif Sch Fine Art, San Francisco. *Work:* Cathedral Sch, Kristiansand, Norway. *Exhib:* San Francisco Mus Art 75th Ann, 57; Palace Legion Honor Winter Exhib, Calif, 60-64; Carnegie Inst Int, Pittsburgh, 64; Univ Calif, Santa Cruz, 69; one-man retrospective, Arbes Gallery, San Francisco, 79. *Media:* Oil. *Mailing Add:* 953 Kansas St San Francisco CA 94107

ST CLAIR, MICHAEL
ART DEALER
b Bradford, Pa, May 28, 12. *Study:* Kansas City Art Inst, with Thomas Hart Benton, Vanderslice Scholar; Art Students League, with George Grosz; Colorado Springs Fine Arts Ctr, with Boardman Robinson(scholar). *Exhib:* One-man exhib, Okla Art Ctr, Oklahoma City. *Pos:* Dir, Babcock Galleries, New York, 59- *Teaching:* Instr drawing & painting, Okla Art Ctr Sch. *Mem:* Art Dealers Asn Am; Arch Am Art; Drawing Soc. *Specialty:* Nineteenth and twentieth century American paintings. *Mailing Add:* Babcock Galleries 724 Fifth Ave New York NY 10019

ST DENIS, PAUL ANDRE
PAINTER, INSTRUCTOR
b Chicago, Ill, Nov 16, 38. *Study:* Cleveland Inst Art, BFA; Kent State Univ, MA; additional study with Julian Stanczak. *Work:* Tweed Mus, Duluth, Minn; Massillon Mus, Ohio; Utah State Univ, Logan; Columbia Mus Art, SC. *Comn:* Cleveland Pub Libr. *Exhib:* Butler Inst Am Art, Youngstown, Ohio, 68 & 70; Am Watercolor Soc, Nat Acad Galleries, New York, 71-73, 75 & 77-79; Canton Art Inst, Ohio, 73; Aqueous Open, Pittsburgh Watercolor Soc, 74 & 75; Watercolor West, Utah State Univ, 76-79; Nat Watercolor Soc, Laguna Beach Mus Art, Calif, 76-88; and others. *Pos:* Chmn art dept, Interlochen Ctr Arts, Mich, summers, 69-81. *Teaching:* Prof painting, Kent State Univ, Ohio, 68-70, Cooper Sch of Art, Cleveland, 70-80 & Cleveland Inst of Art, 73- *Awards:* Purchase Prize, Nat Watercolor Soc, Laguna Beach Mus of Art, Calif, 76; Arjomari Award & Purchase Prize, Nat Watercolor Soc, 88; First Prize Gold Medal, Ohio Watercolor Soc, 89. *Bibliog:* The Artist Mag, 9/90; Splash, North Light/F W Publ, 90. *Mem:* Am Watercolor Soc; Nat Watercolor Soc. *Media:* Acrylic, Watercolor. *Dealer:* Belstone Gallery Traverse City MI; Vigland Gallery Benzonia MI. *Mailing Add:* 28007 Sites Rd Bay Village OH 44140

ST FLORIAN, FRIEDRICH GARTLER
EDUCATOR, ARCHITECT
b Graz, Austria, Dec 21, 32; US citizen. *Study:* Tech Univ Graz, dipl(archit), 58; Ecole Nat Superiure d'Archit, Brussels, Belg, 55-56; Atelier, with Victor Bourgeois; Columbia Univ, MArch, 62. *Work:* Mus Mod Art, New York; Mass Inst Technol, Cambridge; Mus Art, Providence. *Exhib:* One-man shows, Mod Museet, Stockholm, 69, Hayden Gallery, Mass Inst Technol, 73, Mus Art, Univ Tex, 76, Drawing Ctr, New York, 79 & Walker Art Ctr, Minneapolis, 80; Inst Contemp Art, London, Eng, 73; Archit Studies & Proj, Mus Mod Art, New York, 75; RI Sch Design Mus Art, 77. *Teaching:* From asst to prof archit design, RI Sch Design, 63-, chmn archit div, 77-78, dean archit, 78-88. *Awards:* Fulbright Fel, 61-62; Fel, Ctr for Advan Visual Studies Fel, Mass Inst Technol, 71-77; Nat Endowment Arts Awards, 73-74 & 76-77; Fel, Am Acad in Rome, 85- *Mem:* Am Inst Architects. *Publ:* Auth, On my imaginary architecture, Leonardo, 77. *Mailing Add:* European Hons Prog RI Sch Design Palazzo Cenci Piazza Cenci 56 Rome 00186 Italy

ST JOHN, ADAM
CRAFTSMAN, FURNITURE ARTIST
b Tampa, Fla, Feb 24, 52. *Study:* Self-taught. *Work:* Mus Fine Arts, Houston, Tex; San Antonio Mus Asn Collection, Texas. *Comn:* Future Perfect One table, Houston, Tex, 86; Paradise: The Chair, West Palm Beach, Fla, 86; Remember the Alamo, Amarillo, Tex, 87; Pueblo Santa Fe chair, Santa Fe, NMex, 89; Texas Virgin Bed, Houston, 90. *Exhib:* The Chair Fair, Int Design Ctr, New York, 86; Materials: Hard & Soft, Denton Arts Coun, Tex, 87; Furniture of the 80's, Hokin-Kaufman Gallery, Chicago, IL, 88; one-man show, Parkerson Gallery, Houston, Tex, 86; two-person show, O'Kane Gallery, Houston, Tex, 90. *Pos:* Int exec dir, Am Soc Furniture Artists, 91- *Teaching:* Painted illusions, Trompe l'Oeil, Art League Houston, 88-; continuing educ Faux finishes, Univ Houston, 90-; art for detained youth, Harris Co Juvenile Detention Ctr, 90- *Awards:* Honor Award, 1986 Furniture Design, Texas Homes Mag, 86; Meadows Found Award, 87; Outstanding Artist Award, IAC New York '88, 88. *Bibliog:* 397 Chairs, Archit League NY, Abrams, NY, 88. *Mem:* Art League Houston (bd dirs, 88-90); Am Craft Coun; Am Soc Interior Designers; Am Soc Furniture Artists (found & Pres, 89-). *Media:* Mixed. *Publ:* Article, Los Angeles Mag, 86, ID, 87, Ambienture, 87, Ultra, 88. *Mailing Add:* PO Box 271001 Houston TX 77277-1001

ST JOHN, TERRY N
PAINTER, CURATOR
b Sacramento, Calif, Dec 24, 34. *Study:* Univ Calif, Berkeley, AB; San Francisco Art Inst, spec study with James Weeks; Calif Col Arts & Crafts, Oakland, MFA. *Work:* Mills Col, San Francisco. *Exhib:* James D Phelan Award Show, Calif Palace Legion Honor, 65; one-man show, Crown Col, Univ Calif, Santa Cruz, 75; 20 Bay Area Painters, Western Asn Art Mus (traveling), 76-79; Univ Miss, 78; Berkeley Art Ctr, 78; Contemp Realist Gallery, San Francisco, 90. *Collections Arranged:* Pilexi Years Revisited, (co-curator, auth, catalog), 83. *Pos:* Asst cur, Oakland Mus, 69-90; head art dept, Col Notre Dame, Belmont, Calif, 90. *Teaching:* Outdoor Painters Proj, Univ Calif, Santa Cruz, 79-88; Col Notre Dame, Belmont, 90. *Bibliog:* Thomas Albright (auth), Art in the San Francisco Bay Area, Univ Calif Press, 85. *Media:* Oil. *Publ:* Auth, Society of Six (catalog), Oakland Mus, 72; Louis Siegriest: A painter's topography, Currant Mag, 75; Impressionism: The California View, Oakland Mus, 81. *Mailing Add:* 2736 Shasta Rd Berkeley CA 93308

ST MAUR, KIRK (KIRK SEYMOUR MCREYNOLDS)
SCULPTOR, PAINTER
Study: Quincy Col; Univ Minn; Carleton Col, BA, 72; Academia di Belle Arti, Florence, Italy, 72-75, studied anat with Harkevitch; asst to R Puccinelli, Univ Int de Belle Arte, 73 & 74; Villa Schifanoia, Florence, MA, studied with E Manfrini; Simi Studio, Florence, 74-78. *Work:* State of Ill Mus, Lindbergh Mus; H M Seymour Libr, Mus Air & Space, France; Pere Marquritta State Park (monument). *Comn:* Heroic bronze of St Michael, Church of Buriano, Italy, 79; Quest (bronze monument), Ore State Univ, 83; The Sentinel (monument), City of Richmond, Calif, 84; Indian monument, City of Duluth, 92. *Exhib:* Knickerbocker Artists, 83, 84, 85, 86, 87, 88 & 89; NAm Sculpture Exhib, 84 & 89; John Pence Gallery, 84; Quincy Art Ctr, 85; Acad Artists Asn, 86, 87, 88, 89 & 91; Int Art Expos, Los Angeles, 88; and others. *Teaching:* Prof sculpture, Gonzaga Univ, 78-79. *Awards:* First Prize for Relig Art, Allied Artists Am, 78; Knickerbocker Artists Award, 84; Acad Artist

Asn Award, 86; Medal of Honor, City of LeBourget, France, 88. *Bibliog:* Mario Bucci (auth), Kirk McReynolds, Sansoni Editrice, Florence, Italy, 77; articles in Rome Daily Am, San Francisco Examiner, 79 & 83 & Oakland Tribune, 84. *Mem:* Fel, Am Artists Prof League; Acad Artists; Knickerbocker. *Media:* Bronze, Oils. *Publ:* Am Arts Quarterly, spring 92. *Mailing Add:* PO Box 177 Payson IL 62360

ST TAMARA
PAINTER, PRINTMAKER
b Navahradak, Repub of Belaruś. *Study:* Western Col, Oxford, Ohio, BA; Columbia Univ, MFA, with John Heliker; Art Students League, with Seong Moy. *Work:* UNICEF, UN, New York Pub Libr, Columbia Univ, New York; Woodbridge Free Pub Libr, NJ; Fine Arts Mus, Asbury Park, NJ; Zimmerli Art Mus, Rutgers Univ. *Comn:* Four Icons, Belarusan Church, Cleveland, Ohio; woodcut portrait of Dr Francisak Skaryna, Dr V Kipel, New York Pub Libr, 68. *Exhib:* Anchorage Audubon Soc Inc, Alaska, 86; Monmouth Mus, Lincroft, NJ, 88; Audubon Artists, Nat Arts Club, New York, 88; Mark of Vision, Traveling Exhib, Md & Washington, DC, 90; Women Artists, Belarusan Cult Tradition, Rutgers Univ, New Brunswick, NJ, 91; and others. *Awards:* Ida Becker Fund for Graphic Award, Catharine Lorillard Wolfe Art Club, 78; Martin T Hannon Mem Award, Salmagundi Club, New York, 80; Merit Award, 61st Nat Exhib, George W V Smith Mus, Springfield, Mass, 80; and others. *Bibliog:* Pat Hipp (auth), Woods enhance her art, Asbury Park Press, 3/13/77; Zina Stankievic (auth), Let's get acquainted with an artist, Byelarus, 77; Americans, TV Prog, Mensk, Repub of Belaruś. *Mem:* Guild of Creative Art; Catherine Lorillard Wolfe Art Club, Inc; Print Club, Albany; and others. *Media:* Oil, Etching. *Publ:* Illusr, Biography of a Polar Bear, G P Putnam's Sons, 72; illusr, Come Visit a Prairie Dog Town, 76, Save That Racoon, 78 & auth & illusr, Chickaree, A Red Squirrel, 80, Harcourt Brace Jovanovich; Animal Games, Holiday House, 76. *Mailing Add:* 235 Hockhockson Rd Tinton Falls NJ 07724

SAITO, SEIJI
SCULPTOR
b Utsunomiya, Japan, 1933. *Study:* Tokyo Univ Art, BFA(sculpture), clay modeling with Tsuruzo Ishii & MFA(stone carving), with Kametaro Akashi, Brooklyn Mus Art Sch, Scholar, 8 yrs; granite carving with Odillo Begg; Ottavino Granite Corp, New York. *Work:* Pepsico Co, Purchase, NY; Methodist Hospital, Brooklyn, NY; Isaac Delgado Mus Art, New Orleans; Non-Ferros Int Corp, New York; The Toyo Trust & Banking Co, Ltd, New York; Wichita Mus; Tochigi Mus, Japan; Taiyo Kobe Bank, New York; Utsukushigahara Open Air Mus, Japan; Kowa Realty, New York; Daiwa Security & Trust Co, NJ. *Comn:* Buddha (stone sculpture), Gyokusendo, Okinawa, Japan, 81. *Exhib:* Azuma Gallery, New York, 75; one-man shows, Samanthe' Gallery, New York, 68 & 70, New Sch, New York, 78, Warner Commun Bldg, 79 & Tokyo Gallery, Tokyo, Japan, 79; Mid-Hudson Art & Sci Ctr, Poughkeepsie, NY 80; Hakone Open Air Mus, Japan; Fed Int Editors Medailles, Florence, 83; and others. *Teaching:* Instr sculpture, Brooklyn Mus Art, summer 74, 76, 84, 85. *Awards:* Outstanding Prize, Ann Art Festival Exhib, Tochigikaikan Gallery, Japan, 58; Cert of Merit, Ann Exhib of Nat Acad Design, New York, 73; Merit Prize, Hakone Open-Air Mus, Japan, 80; Maurice B Hexter Prize, 53 Ann Exhib Nat Sculpture Soc, New York, 86; Silver Prize, 55 Ann Exhib Nat Sculpture Soc, New York, 88. *Mem:* Nat Sculpture Soc. *Media:* Stone, Bronze. *Publ:* Auth, Article, Expressions, McMillan, New York. *Mailing Add:* 925 Union St Apt 1G Brooklyn NY 11215

SAKAOKA, YASUE
SCULPTOR, DESIGNER
b Himaji-City, Hyogo-Prefecture, Japan, Nov 12, 33; Nat US. *Study:* Reed Col, BA, 59; Portland Mus Art Sch, cert; Univ Ore, MFA, 63. *Work:* Portland Mus Art, Ore; Arnot Mus, Elmira, NY; Zanesville Art Ctr, Ohio; Schumacher Gallery, Capital Univ, Columbus. *Comn:* Two outdoor sculptures, Parkside Gardens, Welsh Construct Co, Baltimore, 65; a set of play sculptures, South Hill Park, Va, 71-73; a play sculpture, Columbus Acad, Ohio, 80-81 & Godman Guild, 83; a tapestry, Epiphany Lutheran Church, Pickerington, Ohio, 84-85. *Exhib:* Exhibs in Southern states museums and major galleries, 65-77; American Painter in Paris, Palais des Congress, Paris, France, 76-77; one-man exhib, Arnot Mus, 78; Paper Exhibs, 81 & Best of 1986, 86, Columbus Cult Arts Ctr, Ohio; Public Sculpture in Columbus, Ohio State Univ Art Gallery, 84; Ohio Selection Dayton Art Inst, 89. *Collections Arranged:* Many exhibs at St Paul's Coll in Va including Robert Dilworth's work, 66-77; View of Columbus (with catalog), Artreach Gallery, Columbus, Ohio, 82; A Photographic Exhib: Sculpture on the Grass (with catalog), 83; Franklin Co Sculptors (a catalogue), Columbus, Ohio, 83; Paintings, Art Reader, 87. *Pos:* Adv & dir develop Artreach, Columbus, Ohio, 83-90. *Teaching:* Asst prof art, Saint Paul's Col, Va, 67-77; asst prof sculpture & art hist, Mansfield State Col, Pa, 77-78; lectr, Ohio State Univ Continuing Educ, 80-91; resource fac, Capital Univ Without Walls, Colo, Ohio, 81-86. *Awards:* Development Award, Ohio Arts Coun, 86; Pollock-Krasner Found Award, 87-88; Apprenticeship Award, Ohio Arts Coun, 89-91. *Bibliog:* Fred Kalister (auth), Yasue Sakaoka in Dialogue, Ohio Found Arts, 72; Charles Dietz (auth), Yasue Sakaoka (exhib catalog), Zanesville, Art Ctr, Ohio, 85; John Seto (auth), Sakura in Buckeye, Lima Art Asn, 90-91. *Mem:* Col Art Asn; Int Sculpture Ctr; Ohio Designer Craftsmen. *Media:* All. *Publ:* Auth, article, Sculpture Quart, Vol II, No 1, 74; Fragments: A review of a Whitney exhibtion in sculpture, Southern Asn Sculptors, summer 76. *Dealer:* Ohio Designer Craftsmen Inc 2164 Riverside Dr Columbus OH 43221; Roberta Kuhn's Gallery 641 N High St Columbus OH 43215. *Mailing Add:* PO Box 09428 Columbus OH 43209-0428

SAKS, JUDITH-ANN (JUDITH-ANN SAKS ROSENTHAL)
PAINTER
b Anniston, Ala, Dec 20, 43. *Study:* Tex Acad Art, Houston, 57-58; Houston Mus Fine Arts, 62; Rice Univ, 62; Sophie Newcomb Col, Tulane Univ, BFA(Arthur Q Davis Prize), 66; Univ Houston, 67. *Work:* Marine Transportation Collection, Smithsonian Inst; Royal Libr, Windsor Castle, England; Univ Houston; Harris Co Heritage Soc Mus, Houston; Johnson Manned Space Mus, Clear Lake, Tex. *Comn:* Christmas card design (oil painting), Houston CofC, 70; Drawing of the Straithard, Roberts Steamship Agency, New Orleans, 75; Am Revolution Bicentennial Proj (six oil paintings), Port of Houston Authority, 75-76; four hist paintings, Pin Oak Charity Horse Show Asn, 77; painting, Cruiser Houston Mem Room, Univ Houston. *Exhib:* 59th Ann Exhib, Birmingham Mus Art, Ala, 67; 1st Nat Space Art Show, Brown Palace Hotel, Denver, 69; Images on Paper, Miss Arts Festival & Munic Art Gallery, Jackson, 70; 7th Ann Art Exhib, Mobile Art Gallery, Ala, 72; and others. *Pos:* Cur student art collection, Univ Houston, 68-72. *Awards:* Selected Print, Miss Art Asn, 70-71; Nat First Places, Prints, Am Heritage Comt, NSDAR, 87. *Bibliog:* Ann Absher (auth), Painter on the roof, The Milepost, Columbia Gulf Transmission Co, 6/69; Susanna Friedman (auth), Southern artist, Bull Asn Jewish Libr, 9/79; Judith-Ann Saks, Arch Am Art, Smithsonian Inst, 79. *Mem:* NSDAR; Art League, Houston; Daughter Repub Tex. *Media:* Oil on Linen; Pen and Ink Etchings. *Publ:* Illusr, Southwestern Art Inc, 11/67; illusr, seven covers, Port Houston Mag, 71, 75 & 76; The Catline, Desk & Derrick Club, 72; Maersk Post, A P Moller, Denmark, 8/77; Texas Sesquicentennial drawing for Texas Daughters of the American Revolution, Nat Soc Daughters Am Revolution Nat Mag, 86. *Mailing Add:* PO Box 1793 Bellaire TX 77401

SAKSON, ROBERT (G)
PAINTER
b Trenton, NJ, Feb 13, 38. *Study:* Trenton Jr Col, AA, 58. *Work:* Hunterdon Co Libr, Felmington, NJ; AT&T Longlines, Bedminster, NJ; US Coast Guard, Mich; Ellarslie, Trenton City Mus, NJ; Princeton Univ Art Mus, NJ. *Comn:* Paintings for Caendar, Best Foods Corp, Ridgwood, NJ, 86; paintings of Phillipsburg, NJ, Carteret Savings Bank, 86, 87 & 88; location paintings, Avon Corp, New York, 89 & 90; series paintings, Waterloo Village, Horizon Bank, Morristown, NJ, 88, 89 & 90; painting of Palmer Square, Collins Develop Corp, Princeton, NJ, 90. *Exhib:* Allied Artists Am, Nat Arts Club, New York, 83, 86 & 87; Audubon Artists Ann, Nat Arts Club, New York, 88; Knickerbocker Artists Ann, Salmagundi Club, New York, 89; In Our Circle, James Michener Art Mus, Doylestown, Pa, 91; Historic New Jersey: A Contemporary View, Bristol Myers-Squibb Gallery, Princeton, 91. *Pos:* Instr master classes watercolor, Somerset Art Asn, Far Hills, NJ, 70-; instr watercolor, Morris Co Art Asn, Morristown, NJ, 89- *Awards:* Helen Gapen Ohler Award, 70 & Paul B Remmey Mem Award, 77, Am Watercolor Soc; Gold Medal, Allied Artists Am, 83; Silver Medal of Honor, NJ Watercolor Soc, 76, 83 & 92. *Mem:* Am Watercolor Soc (juror, currently); Allied Artists Am (juror, currently); Audubon Artists Am (juror, currently); Knickerbocker Artists (juror, currently); Pastel Soc Am (juror, currently); NJ Watercolor Soc & Garden State Watercolor Soc. *Media:* Watercolor, Pastel. *Mailing Add:* Ten Stacey Ave Trenton NJ 08618-3421

SAKURAI, JO MARY (JO MARY MCCORMICK-SAKURAI)
PAINTER, PHOTOGRAPHER
b New York, NY, Mar 6, 18. *Study:* Nat Acad Design, 47; Art Students League, scholar, 48; Columbia Univ, 47-55; Empire State Col, BS, 77; Hunter Col, 83; Sch Visual Arts. *Work:* Mus Mod Art Archives. *Comn:* Series of pastel paintings, Grace Manney, 80-; Mus Mod Art; Yale Univ; Columbia Univ. *Exhib:* Burr Gallery, 62; Graphics Show, Nat Arts Club, 63; Barzansky Art Gallery, 65; New York Pub Libr, 72-74; Archives, Mus Mod Art, New York; Urban Wildlife Press Int, 91. *Pos:* Art critic, Pictures on Exhib Mag, 59-75; auth, Wings of Thought and Art Column, New York Column Newspaper, 71-72; writer & photogr, Cats Mag, 83- *Teaching:* Instr journalism, Newspaper Inst Am, 71. *Awards:* Cert Award, NBC-TV, 45; Color Slide of the Yr, 85. *Bibliog:* New Yorker Mag, 64; McNaught Syndicate column, 66; Montgomery, Ala News, 67. *Mem:* Burr Artists; Life mem Art Students League. *Media:* Watercolor, Pen & Ink. *Publ:* Auth, Yasuo Kuniyoshi and Kenzo Okada, 55; illusr, Art: USA Now, 64; auth & illusr, Etti Cat, 64-82; contribr, Am Artist Mag, 71. *Mailing Add:* 444 Second Ave 22A New York NY 10010

SAKUYAMA, SHUNJI
PRINTMAKER, PAINTER
b Harbin, Manchuria, July 29, 40, Japan citizen. *Study:* Tokyo Gakugei Univ, BA, 65; Brooklyn Col, MFA, 72; Pratt Graphics Ctr. *Work:* Brooklyn Mus; Berkshire Mus, Pittsfield, Mass; City Mus, New York; New Sch Art Ctr, New York; New York Hist Soc. *Exhib:* One-man shows, Paintings, 72 & Prints, 79, Berkshire Mus; 21st Nat Print Exhib, 78; New York Album, Brooklyn Mus, 79; New York Collects, City Mus, New York, 81; Gene Baro Collects, Brooklyn Mus, 83. *Teaching:* Instr Japanese brush work, Long Island Univ, Brooklyn Ctr, 77-78. *Awards:* Painting Awards, New England Art Exhib, New Canaan, Conn, 72 & Berkshire Art Asn Exhib, 75. *Mem:* Japanese Artists Asn, NY. *Media:* Lithography; Acrylic, Oil. *Mailing Add:* 915 President St Brooklyn NY 11215

SAL, JACK
PHOTOGRAPHER, PAINTER
b Waterbury, Conn, Mar 28, 54. *Study:* Philadelphia Col Art, BFA, 76; Art Inst Chicago, MFA, 78. *Work:* Detroit Inst Arts, Mich; Ctr for Creative Photog, Tucson, Ariz; Mus Mod Art, New York; Int Mus Photog, Rochester, NY; Yale Univ Art Gallery, New Haven, Conn; and others. *Comn:* Earth

Work, Off Cult Affairs, New Haven, Conn, 79; Grant, Conn Comn for Arts, 80; Fresco mural, Univ Bridgeport, 84; Fresco mural, Padua, Italy, 86. *Exhib:* Prints in the Cliche-Verre, Houston Mus Fine Art, 80; One-man shows, Northlight Gallery, Tempe, Ariz, 80 & Recent Camera Works, Photographics Workshop, New Canaan, Conn, 80; Light Gallery, New York, 81; Int Ctr Photog, New York, 81; Ferns Gallery, Hull, Eng, 82; Mus Mod Art, New York, 83; Hudson Ctr, 85; and others. *Pos:* Cur, Light Gallery, 85- *Teaching:* Assoc prof, Int Ctr Photog-New York Univ, Rutgers Univ, 85; chmn photog dept, Moore Col Art & Design. *Awards:* Mellon Fel, 82; Vis Artist Am Acad in Rome, 86-87. *Bibliog:* S D Peters (auth), Interview/Jack Sal, Int Mus Photog, 79; Roger Baldwin (auth), Jack Sal/camera images, Views, 80; Glassman/Symmes, Prints in the Cliche-Verre, Detroit Inst Arts, 80. *Media:* Pigment, Light-Sensitive Paper. *Publ:* Auth, Cliche-verre: cameraless images, Portfolio Mag, 79; contribr, Prints in the Cliche-Verre, Detroit Inst Arts, 80; contribr, Connecticut Photographers, Art Resources of Conn, 80; contribr, Photographers Hand, Int Mus Photog/George Eastman House, 80; auth, Mark/Making, Combinations Press, 81. *Mailing Add:* 431 E Sixth St New York NY 10009

SALADINO, TONY
PRINTMAKER, PAINTER
b New Orleans, La, June 5, 43. *Study:* La State Univ, BS, 64; self-taught as artist. *Work:* McNeese State Univ, Lake Charles, La; Nassau County Comn Col, Garden City, NY; Univ Wis, Parkside, Kenosha, Wis; The Art Complex Mus, Duxbury, Mass; Parkersburg Art Center, WVa; Nat Mus Fine Arts, Hanoi, N Vietnam; Mus Art & Archaeology, Univ Mo. *Comn:* Mem Hosp, San Antonio, Tex. *Exhib:* Central Texas Biennial, The Art Center, Waco, Tex, 89 & 92; Nat Works on Paper, Univ Miss, 90; Small Impressions 1990, The Printmaking Coun of NJ, Somerville; Pacific States Nat Print Exhib, Univ Hawaii, Hilo, 90; 1990 Am Realism Competition, Parkersburg Art Center, Parkersburg, W VA; The Print Club of Albany, NY, 92; 5th Ann Nat Art Exhib, Cooperstown Art Asn, NY, 92. *Pos:* Instr, 1-wk workshop, Imagination Celebration, Ft Worth Sch District, 90; monotype workshop, Oxbow Summer Sch Art, Saugatuck; instr painting, Mod Art Mus, Ft Worth, Tex, 92- *Awards:* Purchase Award, Am Realism Competition, Parkersburg Art Center (work added to Col Parkersburg Art Ctr), Parkersburg, VA, 90; Purchase Award, McNeese Works on Paper, 88; Purchase Award, 1988 Mid-Am, 88; Purchase Award, Am Realism Competition, Parkersburg Art Ctr, Va, 90. *Bibliog:* article, D&D Disegnare E Dipingere, Milan, Italy, 6/89; article, NY Times, 12/17/89; article, The Art Calendar, 2/92. *Mem:* Tex Fine Arts Asn; Los Angeles Printmaking Soc; Los Angeles Printmaking Soc; Print Club of Albany. *Media:* All Media. *Dealer:* Baker Gallery PO Box 1920 Lubbock Tex 79408; Evelyn Siboel Gallery 3700 W Seventh Ft Worth TX 76107. *Mailing Add:* 756 Norwood Hurst TX 76053

SALEMME, ANTONIO
PAINTER, SCULPTOR
b Gaeta, Italy, Nov 2, 92; US citizen. *Study:* Eric Pape Art Sch, Boston, Mass, studied with George L Noyes; studied sculpture with Angelo Zanelli, Rome. *Work:* Metrop Mus Art, New York; Newark Mus, NJ; Syracuse Mus, NY; Man Centennial Ctr, Winnipeg; Swedish Int Trade Fair Ctr; Rutgers Univ; Harvard Univ; Yale Univ. *Comn:* Gen Dwight D Eisenhower, Columbia Univ Alumni, 65; Dr Josiah Trent, comn by Dr & Mrs James Semans, Duke Univ Med Ctr, 75; bronze portrait of Pres John F Kennedy, Kennedy Mem Library, 77; bronze medallions, Kleinhans Music Hall, Buffalo, NY. *Exhib:* Gen Int Exhib, Salon d'Automne, Paris, France, 33-34; Gen Nat, Pa Acad Fine Arts, 30-50; Art in Am, Metrop Mus Art, 50; Blossom-Kent 3rd Ann Sculpture Exhib, Kent State Univ, 70; one-man shows, Edward-Dean Mus Decorative Arts, Cherry Valley, Calif, 79; Artists Equity Triennial, Philadelphia, Pa; Philadelphia Art Show, 86. *Pos:* Dir, Manhattan Art Proj of WPA for Mural Painting, New York, 34-35. *Teaching:* Instr sculpture, Nat Inst Archit Educ, 20-23; instr sculpture, Roerich Mus Sch Art, New York, 20-23; Spence Sch, New York, 37-38. *Awards:* Guggenheim Fel, 32 & 36; First Prize, Guild Hall, East Hampton, 59; Ingram-Merrill Grant for Sculpture, 74; and others. *Bibliog:* Records (on sculpture & painting), Folkway Records, 78; interview, Tonight Show & Johnny Carson, NBC, 78; eight minute segment on Sunday Today, NBC, 5/26/91. *Mem:* Hon life mem Nat Inst Archit; Artists Equity Asn. *Media:* Oil, Watercolor; Terra Cotta, Bronze. *Dealer:* Neulight Gallery 3479 Hickory Circle Allentown PA 18103; Cavallo Gallery 510 South Delaware Dr Easton PA 18042. *Mailing Add:* 189 Gaffney Hill Rd Easton PA 18042

SALEMME, LUCIA (AUTORINO)
PAINTER, WRITER
b New York, NY, Sept 23, 19. *Study:* Privately with Gustavo Cenci, 30-35; Art Student League, 38. *Work:* Whitney Mus Am Art; Nat Gallery Art, Washington, DC; Vincenzo & Elsa Picone, Rome, Italy; Sam Dorsky, New York; Mrs Randolph Kidder, Washington, DC; Mr Lindsey Gruson, NY Times Washington Bureau, Washington, DC; Ross Contantine Gallery, New York. *Comn:* Mosaic mural, Mayer & Whittlesey, New York, 58; portraits, 59-72; art restoration, Manhattan House murals, 77 & Art Students League collection, 78. *Exhib:* One-woman exhibs, N Y Univ Lubin Ctr, 62, Dorsky Gallery, New York, 65, Grand Central Moderns Gallery, New York, 65 & 86, William Zierler Gallery, New York, 72 & 74, Fair Lawn Libr, NJ, 76, Cape Split Place Gallery, Maine, 77; Pen & Brush Gallery, New York, 88; Susan Teller Gallery, New York, 89; Assoc Am Artists, 90. *Teaching:* Instr, People's Art Ctr, Mus Mod Art, 57-61; adj prof painting & drawing, NY Univ, 59-70; instr painting & drawing, Art Students League, 70- *Awards:* Pen & Brush Graphics Award, 84; Grumbacher Watercolor Award, 85; Oil Awards, 89, 90, 91, 92. *Mem:* Artists' Equity; Pen & Brush, New York. *Media:* Oil, Watercolor. *Publ:* Auth, Color Exercises for the Painter, 70 & Compositional Exercises for the Painter, 73, Watson-Guptill; The Complete Book of Painting Techniques, Macmillan, 82. *Dealer:* Dorsky Gallery 379 W Broadway New York NY 10012; Susan Teller Gallery 568 Broadway New York NY 10019. *Mailing Add:* 55 Bethune St, No B641 New York NY 10014

SALEMME, MARTHA
PAINTER
b Geneva, Ill, Aug 30, 12. *Study:* With Antonio Salemme. *Work:* New York Hosp; Svenska Massan, Swedish Int Trade Fair Ctr, Gothenburg, Sweden. *Exhib:* One-woman exhibs, New York, Paris & Sweden, 48, 63, 74-76, 80, 83 & 87; Hudson River Mus, Yonkers, NY, 58; Jersey City Mus, 59 & 61; Int Platform Asn Exhib, Washington, DC, 69-71, 73, 75, 77 & 81; two-person show, (with Antonio Salemme), Van Diemen-Lilienfeld Gallery, 49; Artists Equity Triennial, Philadelphia, Pa, 84; Int Exhib: Centre Int d'Art Contemporain, Paris, 85; Philadelphia Art Show, 86; and other group exhibs. *Bibliog:* Hugo Johansson (auth), articles, Hyssna, Sweden, 76, 78 & 83; Sonny Mattison (auth), Vastgota-Demokraten, Kinna, Sweden, 83; interview, Twin Co Cable TV, 83, 90. *Mem:* Artists Equity. *Dealer:* Andrea Neulight 3479 Hickory Circle Allentown PA 18103; Cavallo Gallery 510 South Delaware Dr Easton PA 18042. *Mailing Add:* 189 Gaffney Hill Rd Easton PA 18042

SALERNO, CHARLES
SCULPTOR, EDUCATOR
b Brooklyn, NY, Aug 21, 16. *Study:* Art Students League; Acad Grande Chaumiere, Paris; Escuela Pintura Y Escultura, Mexico City; State Univ NY, teaching cert. *Work:* Mus Art RI Sch Design; Ariz State Univ Collection Am Art; Atlanta Art Asn, Ga; Wadsworth Atheneum, Hartford, Conn; Grand Rapids Art Mus, Mich; Nat Acad Design, New York. *Exhib:* Carvers, Modelers, Welders, Mus Mod Art, New York, 50; Am Pavilion, Brussels Fair, Belg, 58; New York World's Fair, 64; one-man shows, Weyhe Gallery, New York; retrospective, Sculpture Ctr, NY, 75; Red Lion Gallery, Vero Beach, Gla, 90. *Teaching:* Asst prof sculpture, City Col New York, 64-74 & Nat Acad Design, 78-80. *Awards:* Louis Comfort Tiffany Found Fel sculpture, 48; Purchase Prize, Staten Island Mus, 59; Margaret Hirsch-Levine Prize in sculpture, Audubon Artists Ann, 71. *Bibliog:* Frances Christoph (auth), Salerno sculpture, Weyhe Gallery, 65; Dona Z Meilach (auth), Contemporary Stone Sculpture, Crown, 70. *Mem:* Audubon Artists; Nat Acad Design; Sculptors Guild; Fel Nat Sculpture Soc. *Media:* Stone. *Mailing Add:* 5828 Lindsay Rd Sebastian FL 32976

SALINAS, BARUJ
PAINTER, PRINTMAKER
b Havana, Cuba, July 6, 35; US citizen. *Study:* Kent State Univ, BArch. *Work:* Art Inst Chicago; Mus de Arte Mod, Mexico City, Mex; San Antonio Mus Art; Museo Arte Siglo XX, Alicante, Spain; McNay Art Inst, San Antonio; and others. *Comn:* Murals, Sephardi Sch, Mex DF; paintings, Edificio la Victoria, Mex DF, 79; paintings, Europ Am Bank, Miami, Fla, 82. *Exhib:* One-man shows, Harmon Gallery, Fla, 75 & 83, EditArt, Geneva, Switz, 75, 77, 79, 83, 85, 88 & 91 Carrillo Gil, Mex, 81, Galeria Joan Prats, New York, 82 & Barbara Gillman Gallery, Miami, 82; Museo De Arte Contemporaneo, Madrid, Spain, 77; Gisele Linder Galerie, Basel, Switz, 85; Mus de Arte Mod, Mexico City, Mex, 88. *Awards:* Cintas Fel, Inst Int Educ, 69 & 70; First Prize, V Bienal, Degrabado Latinoame Ricano de San Juan, PR, 83. *Bibliog:* Wifredo Fernandez (auth), Baruj Salinas su mundo pictorico, Ed Punto Cardinal, 71; Octavio Armand, Carlos Monsivais, Michel Butor, Jose A Valente, (auths), Baruj Salinas, Mus Arte Mod, Mexico City, 88; Gloria Moure, Carlos Franqui, Wifredo Fernandez & Jose A Valente (authors), Baruj Salinas, Ediciones Poligrafa, Espana, 79. *Media:* Acrylic, Miscellaneous Media. *Publ:* Illusr, Calendario del hombre Descalzo, 70; Resumen A I P, 71; Narradores Cubanos de Hoy, 75; Revista Escandalar, NY, 81. *Dealer:* Foster Haarmon Galleries 1415 Main St Sarasota FL 34236. *Mailing Add:* 2740 SW 92nd Ave Miami FL 33165

SALLE, DAVID
PAINTER
b Norman, Okla, Sept 28, 52. *Study:* Calif Inst Arts, Valencia, BFA, 73 & MFA, 75. *Work:* Boymans Mus, Rotterdam, Holland; Basel Kunst Mus, Switz; New York Public Libr; Whitney Mus. *Exhib:* L'Amerique aux Independants, Grand Palais, Paris, 80; Figures Forms and Expressions, Albright-Knox Mus, Buffalo, NY, 81; Figurative Aspects of Recent Art, Hayden Gallery, Mass Inst Technol, 81; solo shows, Mary Boone Gallery, New York, 81-83, 85 & 87-88, Tel Aviv Mus Art, Israel, 89, Mario Diacono Gallery, Boston, Mass, 90, Castelli Graphics, New York, 90, Gagosian Gallery, New York, 91; Larry Gagosian Gallery, Los Angeles, 81; The Anxious Edge, Walker Art Ctr, 82; 74th Am Exhib, Chicago Art Inst, 82; Homo Sapiens, Aldrich Mus, 82; The Americans: Collage 1950-1982, Contemp Art Mus, Houston, 82;; Contemporary American Art, Sara Hilden Art Mus, Finland, 88; Drawing on the East End, 1940-1988, Parish Art Mus, Southampton, NY, 88; The Last Decade: American Artists of the 80's, Tony Shafrazi Gallery, New York, 90; Pintura de los Ochenta en las Americas, Museo de Arte Contemporaneo de Monterrey, Mex, 91. *Awards:* Creative Artists Public Service Program Grant, 79. *Bibliog:* Grace Glueck (auth), Artists who scavenge from the media, New York Times, 1/9/83; Roberta Smith (auth), Appropriation uber allies, Village Voice, 1/11/83; Michael Brenson (auth), New York vs Paris: Views of an art reporter, New York Times, 1/16/83; Eleanor Heartney (auth), David Salle at Mary Boone, ArtNews, 88; Robert Storr (auth), Salle's gender machine, Art Am, 88; Laura Cottingham (auth), David Salle, Flash Art, 88. *Mailing Add:* c/o Gagosian Gallery 980 Madison Ave New York NY 10012

SALLICK, LUCY ELLEN
PAINTER, INSTRUCTOR
b Boston, Mass, Sep 21, 37. *Study:* Univ Mich, 55-58; New York Univ, BA, 59, painting, 60-62; Art Students League, 64-65; Corcoran Sch Art, 66-68. *Work:* Bruce Mus, Greenwich, Conn; Rahr West Mus, Manitowoc, Wis; Housatonic Mus Art, Bridgeport, Conn; Univ Mich Art Mus, Ann Arbor; Town of Westport, Conn. *Comn:* Painting, Brunswick Savings Inst, Maine, 75. *Exhib:* Contemporary Reflections, Aldrich Mus, Ridgefield, Conn, 75; solo exhibs, Rutgers Univ, New Brunswick, NJ, 77, Canton Art Inst, Ohio, 80 & Bowdoin Col Mus Art, Brunswick, Maine, 87; Childe Hassam Purchase Exhib, Am Acad & Inst Arts & Lett, 76-83; Contemporary Naturalism, Nassau Co Mus Fine Arts, NY, 80; Conn Painters, Wadsworth Atheneum, 83; Contemp Landscape Painting, Wesleyan Univ, Conn, 83; Contemporary American Still Life, One Penn Plaza, New York, 85. *Teaching:* Instr painting, Silvermine Guild Sch Arts, 77- & Lyme Acad Fine Arts, 85- *Awards:* Eloise Egan Mem Award, New Eng Ann Silvermine Guild, 75 & Guild Award, 79. *Bibliog:* Lawrence Alloway (auth), Lucy Sallick, Fairleigh Dickinson Univ, 75; John Russell (auth), article, New York Times, 9/23/77; Gerrit Henry (auth), article, Art in Am, 2/83. *Mem:* Women's Caucus Art; Silvermine Guild; Soho 20. *Media:* Oil, Watercolor. *Dealer:* G W Einstein Co Inc 591 Broadway New York NY 10012. *Mailing Add:* 77 Long Lots Rd Westport CT 06880

SALMON, RAYMOND MERLE
CARTOONIST, EDUCATOR
b Akron, Colo, Sept 6, 31. *Study:* Mesa Col; Univ Denver; Chicago Acad Fine Arts; Univ Colo; Calif Col Arts & Crafts; San Francisco State Univ; Colorado Springs Fine Arts Ctr; Univ Northern Colo, BA & MA(fine arts). *Work:* Libr Commun & Graphic Arts, Ohio State Univ. *Exhib:* Univ Denver Art Mus, 55; Colorado Springs Fine Arts Ctr, 61; Tacoma Art Mus, Wash, 64; State Univ Mo, 65; Master Cartoonists Exhib, Parke-Bernet, New York, 71. *Pos:* Free lance graphic artist, Salmon Studios, Calif, 60-; cartoonist; creator cartoon panel, The Little Man. *Teaching:* Art educ, John F Kennedy Univ, 66-74; art educ, commercial dept, Solano Community Col, 71-; Chapman Col, 88. *Mem:* Nat Cartoonists Soc, New York; Soc Prof Journalists. *Media:* Pen and Ink, Watercolor. *Publ:* Cartoons in Saturday Review, FM and the Fine Arts Mag, Writer's Digest & Life. *Mailing Add:* PO Box 712 Vallejo CA 94590

SALOMON, LAWRENCE
SCULPTOR, EDUCATOR
b Chicago, Ill, July 18, 40. *Study:* Art Inst Chicago; Univ Ill, BFA; Univ Chicago. *Exhib:* Chicago Biennial, 68 & Critic Choice, 69, Art Inst Chicago; Lyman Wright Art Ctr, Beloit, Wis, 70; The Five: Public Works, Univ Chicago, 71; Art for Public Places, Dept Housing & Urban Develop Nat Competition, 73; Cool Abstraction, Richard Gray Gallery, Chicago, 76; Romantic Structures: Abstract Art in Chicago Traveling Exhib, Univs Mo & Kans, 78; and others. *Teaching:* Assoc prof fine art, Univ Ill, Chicago Circle, 65- *Awards:* Art in Public Places Award, Nat Competition, Dept Housing & Urban Develop, 73. *Bibliog:* Amy Goldin (auth), Greasy kid stuff, Art Gallery Mag, 73; articles, Art in Am, 77; C L Morrison (auth), Chicago dialectics, Art News, 2/78. *Mem:* The Five; Participating Artists Chicago (secy, 68-70); Art Pub Places (bd dir, 78-). *Media:* Metal. *Dealer:* Jan Cicero Gallery 433 N Clark Chicago IL. *Mailing Add:* 2116 N Bissell Chicago IL 60614

SALT, JOHN
PAINTER
b Birmingham, Eng, 1937. *Study:* Birmingham Col Art, Eng; Slade Sch Fine Arts, London. *Exhib:* Die Metamorphose des Dinges, Palais des Beaux-Arts, Brussels, 71; Relativerend Realisme, Stedelijk van Abbemuseum, Eindhoven, Netherlands, 72; Sharp-Forcus Realism, Sidney Janis Gallery, New York, 72; Verkehrskultur, Westfalische Kunstverein, Munster, W Ger, 72; one-man show, Univ Birmingham, Eng, 66. *Teaching:* Instr, various cols of art, Eng, 60-67 & Md Col Art, Baltimore, 67-68. *Bibliog:* Grace Glueck (auth), New York gallery notes, Art in Am, New York, 11-12/70; J Patrick Marandel (auth), New York Letter, Art Int, Lugano, 1/71; Juergen Weichardt (auth), Neue Landschaft, Mag Kunst, Mainz, 1, 72. *Media:* Oil. *Mailing Add:* c/o O K Harris Works of Art 383 W Broadway New York NY 10012

SALTER, RICHARD MACKINTIRE
PAINTER
b Iowa City, Iowa, May 7, 40. *Study:* Northern Ariz Univ, BA, 64; Univ Guanajuato, Inst Allende, Mex, MFA, 68. *Work:* Arthur Adams Western Collection, Beloit, Wis; US Dept Interior, Washington, DC; Miller Brewing Co, Milwaukee, Wis; Univ Wis, Green Bay; Northern Ariz Univ. *Comn:* Com Design, US Borax Co, Boron, Calif, 65-66; Photography, Orput & Orput, Architects, Rockford, Ill, 71. *Exhib:* Mitchell Mus, Mt Vernon, Ill, 81; Smithsonian Inst, 82; Kennedy Ctr, 82; one-person show, Alverno Col, Milwaukee, 82; Appleton Gallery Fine Arts, Wis, 83; and many other group and one-man exhibs. *Teaching:* Instr painting, Stanislaus State Col, 68; instr creative photog, Univ Wis-Green Bay, 73. *Awards:* First Prizes, Red Cloud Indian Art Show, Pine Ridge, SDak & Heard Indian Art Show, Phoenix. *Bibliog:* Platt Cline (auth), NAU Show, Ariz Daily Sun, 73; Barbara Manger (auth), Salter Exhib, Mid-West Art Mag, 74 & 77. *Mem:* Rockford Art Asn; Wis Painters & Sculptors Asn; Col Art Asn Am. *Media:* Acrylic, Mixed. *Dealer:* Segal Gallery New York NY; Cudahy Gallery Milwaukee Art Ctr Milwaukee WI. *Mailing Add:* Rte 1 Box 902 Lake Geneva WI 53147

SALTMARCHE, KENNETH CHARLES
PAINTER, DIRECTOR
b Cardiff, Wales, Sept 29, 20; Can citizen. *Study:* Ont Col Art, Toronto, assoc, 46; Art Students League, with Julian Levi; Univ Windsor, LLD, 77. *Work:* Art Gallery Hamilton, Ont; London Art Mus, Ont; Govt Ont, Toronto; Confederation Art Gallery, Charlottetown, PEI. *Exhib:* Pollock Gallery, Toronto, 77; Djamkar-Burton Gallery, Hamilton, 77; Prince Arthur Gallery, Toronto, 81; Willistead Manor, Windsor, 87; Art Gallery of Windsor, 89. *Collections Arranged:* Louis Muhlstock: Forty-Five Years, 76; A J Casson Retrospective, 78; Frans Masereel: A Tribute, 81; Glorious Visions: Peter Haworth Designs for Stained Glass, 85. *Pos:* Dir, Art Gallery Windsor, 46-85, emer dir, 85-; art critic, Windsor Star, 47-74. *Awards:* Ont Col Art Fel, Toronto, 83; Order of Canada, 85. *Mem:* Ont Asn Art Galleries (pres, 68-69); Can Art Mus Dirs Orgn (pres, 75-76); Can Mus Asn. *Media:* All Media. *Mailing Add:* 995 Chilver Rd Windsor ON N8Y 2K6 Canada

SALTZ, JERRY
CRITIC, CURATOR
b Chicago, Ill, Feb 19, 51. *Study:* Art Inst Chicago, BFA, 73; Fashion Inst Tech, Grad Studies, 89 & 90. *Collections Arranged:* Recent Tendencies in Black & White, Sydney Janis Gallery, 73; A Drawing Show, Cabel Gallery, New York, 87; and over 75 shows at NAME Gallery, Chicago, 73-78. *Pos:* Founder & dir, NAME Gallery, 73-78; contrib, ed Arts Mag, 87-; contrib ed, Balcon Mag, 89; contribr, Flash Art. *Awards:* Nat Endowment Arts Grant, 80. *Publ:* Coauth, Sketchbook with Voices, Alfred Van der Marck, 86; auth, Beyond Boundaries: New York's New Art, Alfred Van der Marck, 87; numerous exhibition catalog essays. *Mailing Add:* 60 Ave B No 4B New York NY 10009

SALTZMAN, MARVIN
PAINTER, EDUCATOR
b Chicago, Ill, June 16, 31. *Study:* Art Inst Chicago, 54-56; Univ Southern Calif, BFA, 58, MFA, 59. *Work:* Nat Mus Am Art, Washington, DC; Univ Calif, Berkeley Art Mus; Ackland Art Mus, Chapel Hill, NC; Univ Southern Calif, Los Angeles; Portland Mus Art, Ore. *Exhib:* Los Angeles Artists & Vicinity Ann, Los Angeles Co Mus, 57-59; Pasadena Mus Nat Print Festival, Calif, 58; Ball State Ann, 59, 61, 66 & 67; Artists of Ore Painting & Sculpture Ann, 64-65; Northwest Printmakers, Seattle, Wash, 66-67; Solo, Nat Acad Science, Washington, DC, 87; and many others. *Teaching:* Vis lectr printmaking, Univ Southern Calif, 66-67; prof painting, 67-, studio chmn, Univ NC, Chapel Hill, 67-74 & 86-88, chmn fine arts div, 76-79. *Awards:* Poque Fel, 78-79. *Media:* Oil. *Dealer:* Raleigh Contemp Gallery 134 E Hargatt St Raleigh NC 27601. *Mailing Add:* 717 Emory Dr Chapel Hill NC 27514

SALTZMAN, WILLIAM
PAINTER, SCULPTOR
b Minneapolis, Minn, July 9, 16. *Study:* Univ Minn, BS, 40, Art Student's League, 37. *Work:* Mayo Clin, Rochester, Minn; Minneapolis Inst Art & Walker Art Ctr, Minneapolis; Joslyn Mus, Omaha, Nebr; plus many Banks, Hotels, Hospitals & Librs. *Comn:* Stained glass, Univ Minn New Hosp Bldg & Univ Minn New Music Bldg, 86; glass mobile, Wayzata Bank & Trust Co, Wayzata, Minn; St Marks Lutheran Church, North St Paul, Minn; glass mobile, First Bank, Crystal, Minn; tryptic paintings, Lutheran Brotherhood Exec Dining Room, Minn; and many others. *Exhib:* Abstract and Surrealist American Art, 58th Ann Exhib Am Paintings & Sculpture, Art Inst Chicago, 48; 13th Ann Watercolor Exhib, San Francisco Art Asn, San Francisco Mus Art, 49; Ann Exhib Contemp Am Painting, Whitney Mus Am Art, New York, 52; Sculpture, Coast to Coast Stores Hq, Edina, Minn, 78; Sculpture Show, Black Walnut SK Gallery, Minn, 90. *Pos:* Supvr art, Fairmont Pub Schs, Minn, 40-42; camouflage adv, USA Engrs, 42-46; mem gov comt, Minn State Art Soc, 46-50; resident artist & dir, Rochester Art Ctr, 48-64; juror, many exhibs, Iowa, Wis & Minn, 48- *Teaching:* Instr painting & drawing, Exten Div, Univ Minn, asst & actg dir, Univ Minn Gallery, Minneapolis, 46-48; guest instr, St Olaf Col, 51-54; vis prof, Univ Nebr, Lincoln, spring 64; from assoc prof art to prof, Macalester Col, 66-83, emer prof, 84- *Awards:* Best in Painting Award, 48th Ann Minn State Fair, St Paul, 59; Guild for Relig Arch Award, 73; AIA Assoc Art Award, 73; plus others. *Media:* Miscellaneous. *Mailing Add:* 210 N Second St Suite 060 Minneapolis MN 55401

SALVADORI, VIERI R
PHOTOGRAPHER, ADMINISTRATOR
b New York, NY, Dec 1, 43. *Study:* Columbia Univ, AB, 65, MA, 67. *Exhib:* One-man shows at galleries in Rome, Milan & Paris, 75- *Collections Arranged:* Issac Witkin Retrospective, Univ Bridgeport, Conn, 70. *Pos:* Dean, Pratt Inst Art & Design, 84-86. *Teaching:* Prof, Univ Bridgeport, 68-72; prof, Parsons Sch Design, 72-78, dean of students, 75-80, assoc dean, 80-84. *Mailing Add:* 543 Broadway New York NY 10012

SAMARAS, LUCAS
SCULPTOR
b Kastoria, Greece, Sept 14, 36; US citizen. *Study:* Rutgers Univ, with Alan Kaprow, BA, 59; Columbia Univ, with Meyer Schapiro, 59-62. *Work:* Solomon R Guggenheim Mus, Metrop Mus Art, Whitney Mus Am Art, Mus Mod Art, New York; Albright-Knox Art Gallery, Buffalo, NY; Los Angeles Co Mus Art; Fogg Art Mus, Harvard Univ, Cambridge, Mass; Mus Contemp Art, Chicago; Hirshhorn Mus & Sculpture Garden, Smithsonian Inst, Washington, DC; Aldrich Mus Contemp Art, Ridgefield, Conn. *Exhib:* Mixed Media & Pop Art, Albright-Knox Art Gallery, Buffalo, 63; Sculpture Ann, Whitney Mus Am Art, NY, 64; Eleven from the Reuben Gallery, Solomon R Guggenheim Mus, 65; The Richard Brown Baker Collection, Aldrich Mus Contemp Art, Ridgefield, Conn, 65; Young America 1965, Whitney Mus Am Art, NY, 65; Contemp Am Sculpture, Selections, Whitney Mus Am Art, NY, 66; The Object Transformed, Mus Mod Art, NY, 66; Eight Sculptures, The Ambiguous Image, Walker Art Ctr, Minneapolis, 66; Highlight of the '66-'67

Season, Aldrich Mus Contemp Art, Ridgefield, Conn, 67; American Sculpture of the 60's, Los Angeles Co Mus Art, 67; Sculpture: A Generation of Innovation, Art Inst Chicago, 67; Human Concern/Personal Torment, Whitney Mus Am Art, 69; One Man's Choice, Dallas Mus Art, Tex, 69; Sculpture Ann, Whitney Mus Am Art, NY, 70; The Mind's Eye, Philadelphia Mus Art, 70-71; The Twentieth Century: 35 American Artists, Whitney Mus Am Art, NY, 74; 71st Am Exhib, Art Inst Chicago, 74; Two Hundred Years of American Sculpture, Whitney Mus Am Art, NY, 76; American Drawing in Black & White, Brooklyn, NY, 80; Forty Years of Sculpture, Solomon R Guggenheim Mus, NY, 85; 75th Am Exhib, Art Inst Chicago, 85-86; solo exhibs, Jean Bernier Gallery Athens, 86; Mayor Gallery, London, 86; Pace Gallery, NY, 87; Objects & Subjects: 1969-1986 (traveling), Denver Art Mus, Colo, 88-90; Boxes & Mirrored Cell, Pace Gallery, NY, 88; Figures and Still Life, Pace/MacGill Gallery, NY, 88, Waddington Galleries, London, 90; Enigmatic Objects; Sculpture from the Permanent Collection, Whitney Mus Am Art, NY, 88-89; Identity; Representations of the Self, Whitney Mus Downtown Fed Reserve Plaza, NY, 88-89; Vanishing Presence, Walker Art Ctr, Minneapolis, 89; Photographic Treasures from the National Portrait Gallery Collection, Nat Portrait Gallery, Washington, DC, 3/30-8/19/90; Portrait of an American Gallery, Galerie Isy Brachot, Brussels, 4/19-7/23/90; retrospective, Yokohama Mus Art, Hiroshima City Mus Contemp Art, Japan, 91-92; The Endowed Chair, Franklin Parrasch Gallery, New York, 92. *Teaching:* Instr, Brooklyn Col, 71-72. *Bibliog:* Joshua Decter (auth), New York in review, Arts Mag, 1/92; Eleanor Heartney (auth), Through the mind's eye: Samaras's abstractions, Art in Am, 3/92; Marcia E Vetrocq (auth), Report from Turin: Back to basics, Art in Am, 4/92. *Publ:* Auth, Autopolaroid, Art in Am, 11/70, Vol 58, 66-83; The art of portraiture in the words of four New York artists, NY Times, 10/31/76, 29; Clay and bronze, Artforum, 3/82, Vol 20, 57-63. *Mailing Add:* c/o Pace Gallery 32 E 57th St New York NY 10023

SAMBURG, GRACE (BLANCHE)
PAINTER, LITHOGRAPHER
b New York, NY. *Study:* Art Students League, painting with Morris Kantor & Raphael Soyer; New Sch for Social Res, stage design & lighting; Contemp Art Gallery Graphic Workshop, with Michael Ponce de Leon; also with Philip Guston. *Work:* Slide Collection, Mus Fine Arts, Boston. *Exhib:* Silvermine Guild of Artists Ann, New Canaan, Conn, 59; Works on Paper, Brooklyn Mus, NY, 75; Fairleigh Dickinson Univ, NJ, 75; Traveling Exhib, Artist Choice, State Univ NY, Binghamton, 76; Chatham Col, Pittsburgh, Pa, 76; Randolph-Macon Women's Col, Lynchburg, Va, 77; solo exhibs, Kornbluth Gallery, Fairlawn, NJ, 83 & Péne DuBois Gallery, New York, 86; Green Mountain Gallery, New York, 73. *Bibliog:* Lawrence Campbell (auth), article, Art News, 9/73; Gordon Brown (auth), article, Arts Mag, 11/73; Lucy Lippard (auth), From the Center, Feminist Essays on Women's Art, Dutton, 76. *Mem:* Women in the Arts. *Media:* Oil on Canvas. *Publ:* Contribr, Arts Mag, & Art News, 67. *Dealer:* Kornbluth Gallery Fairlawn NJ; Péne DuBois Gallery New York NY. *Mailing Add:* 63 Highwood Terrace Weehawken NJ 07087

SAMERJAN, GEORGE E
DESIGNER, PAINTER
b Boston, Mass, May 12, 15. *Study:* Art Ctr Col, grad, 38; Chouinard Art Inst, 33; Otis Art Inst, 40-41; also with Alexander Brook, Willard Nash & Stanley Reckless. *Work:* San Diego Fine Arts Soc; Fla Southern Col; Abbott Labs; Ford Motor Co Collection; US Airforce Heritage Collection, Pentagon, Washington, DC; plus others. *Comn:* Designed Arctic Commemorative Stamp, 59, Adlai Stevenson Mem Stamp, 65 & Erie Canal Sesquicentennial Stamp, 67, US Post Off Dept; SC Tricentennial, 70. *Exhib:* Nat Acad Design; Pa Acad Fine Arts, Philadelphia; Denver Art Mus; Corcoran Gallery Art, Washington, DC; Liege Belg & Paris, France; plus others. *Pos:* Chmn, Soc Illusrs Sem, 62-63. *Teaching:* Lectr, NY Univ & Pratt Inst, formerly. *Awards:* Art Dirs Clubs New York, Philadelphia, Advert Club Westchester, NY & Calif Watercolor Soc Awards; Am Watercolor Soc Award, Audubon Artists, Oakland Art Gallery; plus others. *Bibliog:* Norman Kent (ed), Seascapes & Landscapes in Watercolor, Watson/Guptill, 56; Norman Kent (auth), 100 Watercolor Techniques, Watson/Guptill, 68; Marlene Park & Gerald E Markowitz (coauths), Democractic Vistas, Post Offices & Public Art in the New Deal, Temple Univ Press, 84. *Mem:* Am Watercolor Soc; Dirs Club; Advert Club, Westchester, NY; Audubon Artists. *Media:* All. *Mailing Add:* Cantitoe St Katonah NY 10536

SAMPSON, FRANK
PAINTER, PRINTMAKER
b Edmore, NDak, Mar 24, 28. *Study:* Concordia Col, BA, 50; Univ Iowa, MFA, 52, printmaking with Mauricio Lasansky, 56-59. *Work:* Libr Cong, DC; Walker Art Ctr, Minneapolis; Nelson-Atkins Mus, Kansas City; Sheldon Mem Art Ctr, Lincoln, Nebr; Joslyn Art Mus, Omaha, Nebr. *Exhib:* One-man shows, Walker Art Ctr, Minneapolis, 54, Sheldon Mem Art Ctr, Lincoln, Nebr, 64 & Denver Art Mus, 75; Mid-Am, Nelson-Atkins Mus, Kansas City, 65; 13th Am Drawing Biennial, Norfolk Mus Arts, Va, 69; 21st Nat Exhib Prints, Libr Cong, Washington DC, 69; Drawings from Nine States, Mus Fine Arts, Houston, Tex, 70; Regionalism: Seven Views, Joslyn Art Mus, Omaha, Nebr, 79; Hanga Annual, Tokyo Metrop Art Gallery, Japan. *Teaching:* Prof painting, drawing & printmaking, Univ Colo, Boulder, 61-90, prof fine arts emer, 90- *Awards:* Best in show, Mid-Am Purchase Fund, 62; Ford Purchase, Walker Biennial, 64; Purchase Prize, Minn Mus Art, St Paul, 71. *Bibliog:* Michele de Ghelderode (auth), D'ou Viens Tu, Beau Nuage?, Le Cahier des Arts, Bruxelles, Belg, 4/61; Walter Simon (auth), The collector, Colo Quart, Univ Colo, summer 77; Merrill Mahaffey (auth), Contemporary western painting, the new western art, Southwestern Art, fall 77. *Media:* Oil, Acrylic. *Dealer:* Sandy Carson Gallery 1734 Wazee Denver CO 80202. *Mailing Add:* 1912 Columbine Ave Boulder CO 80302

SAMUELS, GERALD
PAINTER, SCULPTOR
b Brooklyn, NY, Nov 14, 27. *Study:* Long Island Univ; City Col New York; NY Univ; Pratt Inst; also with Moses Soyer, Phillip Evergood, Hans Hofmann. *Work:* Mass Inst Technol; San Francisco Mus. *Exhib:* One-man shows, Drawing & Sculpture, Molesworth Gallery, New York, 69, Painting, River Run Gallery, Martha's Vineyard, 74 & Painting, Landmark Gallery, New York, 75, 77 & 81; Paintings, Maine Coast Artist, 74. *Pos:* Prog dir, Sundays at JASA, New York. *Teaching:* Instr advan painting, New York, currently; Advan Painting, Northern NJ Arts Ctr. *Awards:* Pollock-Krasner Award for Painting, 90. *Mailing Add:* 799 Greenwich St New York NY 10014

SAMUELS, JOHN STOCKWELL, 3RD
COLLECTOR, PATRON
b Galveston, Tex, Sept 15, 33. *Study:* Tex A&M Univ, BA, 54 & MS, 54; Harvard Univ, BL, 60. *Collection:* American, French, Italian & Pre-Columbian paintings and decorative arts. *Mailing Add:* 1702 Broadway Galveston TX 77550

SAMUELSON, FRED BINDER
PAINTER, EDUCATOR
b Harvey, Ill, Nov 29, 25. *Study:* Sch Art Inst Chicago, BFA, 51 & MFA, 53; Univ Chicago, 46-53. *Work:* Denver Art Mus, Colo; Witte Mus, San Antonio, Tex; Ohio Univ, Athens; Tex Fine Arts Asn, Laguna Gloria Mus, Austin. *Comn:* Acrylic mural, Hemisfair 68, San Antonio. *Exhib:* 60th Ann Exhib Western Art, Denver Art Mus, 54; 20th Ann Tex Painting & Sculpture Exhib, Dallas Mus Fine Art, 58; Southwest Am Art Ann, Okla Art Ctr, 60; Segundo Festival Pictorico Acapulco, 64; 53rd Tex Fine Arts Asn Ann, 64. *Teaching:* Prof painting & drawing, Inst Allende, San Miguel de Allende, Mex, 55-63, head grad studies & painting, 65-; chmn fac, San Antonio Art Inst, 63-64. *Awards:* Purchase Award, Denver Art Mus, 54; Purchase Award, Tex Fine Arts Asn, Laguna Gloria Mus, Austin, 64; Purchase Award, Ohio Univ, Athens, 64. *Bibliog:* Leonard Brooks (auth), Oil Painting Traditional and New, 59 & Wash Drawings, 61, Van Nostrand Reinhold; interview, Time-Life, 65. *Media:* Acrylic. *Dealer:* Hartley Gallery Winter Park FL 32789; Odyssey Gallery San Antonio TX 78209. *Mailing Add:* 133 Valencia Rd Rockledge FL 32955

SANABRIA, ROBERT
SCULPTOR
b El Paso, Tex, Aug 20, 31. *Study:* Univ Md, BA, 65, MFA, 79. *Work:* Snite Mus Art, Univ Notre Dame, Ind; Wichita Art Mus, Kans; SDak Mem Art Ctr, Brookings; Tweed Mus Art, Duluth, Minn; Miss Mus Art, Jackson; Richmond Conv Ctr, Richmond, Va. *Comn:* Abstract steel tree, B F Saul Co, Lexington, Ky, 75; 2 abstract concrete sculptures, City Philadelphia, 80; cast paper relief, Lane & Edson, Washington, DC, 81; concrete sculpture, Md Nat Capitol Park & Plan Comt, Prince Georges Co, 81-82; abstr concrete sculpture, M/G Archit Inc, Milford, Va, 83; bonded bronze abstract relief sculpture, Baltimore Plaza Hotel, Md, 85; bronze relief sculpture, Montgomery Co Pub Sch, Silver Spring, Md, 86; cast paper relief, Charles E Smith Co, Alexandria, Va, 87; bronze/copper abstract tree sculpture, Dr Wm Rutherford, Washington, DC, 91. *Exhib:* Allied Artists Am 68th Ann, Nat Arts Club, New York, 81; Tri-State Sculpture Exhib, Camden, SC, 85; Sculpture 87 at Washington Square, Washington, DC, 87; Columbia Asn Arts, Md, 88; George Mason Univ, Fairfax, Va, 89; Sculpture 89, Washington Square; 819 Gallery, Baltimore, Md, 90; Landmarks, Strathmore Hall, Rockville, 90; Md Col Art & Design, Silver Spring, 90; Fridholm Fine Arts Gallery, Asheville, NC, 91; Invitational Outdoor Sculpture Exhib, Montgomery Col, Rockville, Md, 92. *Teaching:* Instr sculpture, Art League Workshops, Alexandria, Va, 75-78. *Awards:* Artist-in-residence, Fairfax Co Sch, Mobil Oil Co, 92. *Bibliog:* I Winitsky (auth), Private Dream, Public Art, Media Arts Inc, 83; CB Tomlins, (auth) Water Sculpture: USA, 86; Galleries, Washington Post, 90. *Mem:* Artists Equity Asn (pres, Washington, DC chap, 83-85); Loudoun Arts Coun, Leesburg, Va, (vpres, 87-92). *Media:* Miscellaneous Media. *Publ:* Auth, Fees for commissions, Sculptors' Int, Vol 1, No 6, 83. *Mailing Add:* Rte 2 Box 55 A Leesburg VA 22075

SANABRIA, SHERRY ZVARES
PAINTER
b Washington, DC, Oct 18, 37. *Study:* George Washington Univ, BA, 59; Am Univ, MFA, 74. *Work:* Phillips Collection, Columbia Hosp Women, Washington Convention Ctr, Washington Post & Student Loan Marketing Asn, Washington, DC; Phillip Morris Co, Richmond, Va; Frostburg State Col, Md; First Nat Bank Boston, Mass. *Comn:* Crystal City Park IV. *Exhib:* Solo exhib, Phillips Collection, Washington, DC, 80, 22nd Area Exhibition: Works on Paper, Corcoran Gallery, 80, Capitol Art: 12 Artists from Washington, DC, Williams Col Mus Art, Mass, 84, Color as Light, Washington Co Mus Fine Arts, Hagerstown, Md, 86, Baum Gartner Gallery, 88, David Adamson Gallery, 89 & 91, Ellis Island Immigration Mus, 91-92, Marymount Univ, McLean, Va, 92; Washington Light, Art 80, The Armory, Washington, DC, 80; 35th Ann Hassam & Speicher Fund Purchase Exhibition, Am Acad & Inst Arts & Lett, New York, NY, 83; Art for Collectors: A Capital Choice, Fed Reserve Syst, Washington, DC, 85; group exhib, A sense of presence, Vanderbilt Univ, Nashville, Tenn, 89 & Nat Works on Paper, Univ Richmond, Va. *Bibliog:* Alic Thorson (auth), Sherry Zvares Sanabria: Steps to the barrio, City Paper, 5/91; Judith Sloan Deutsch (auth), Views with a room, Washington Jewish Week, 10/91; Peggy McGlone (auth), Ellis Island Pastiche, The Star Ledger, 11/91. *Mem:* Artist Equity; Washington Women's Caucus. *Media:* Acrylic. *Dealer:* David Adamson Gallery 406 Seventh St NW Washington DC 20004. *Mailing Add:* Box 55 A Leesburg VA 22075

SANBORN, JAMES
SCULPTOR
Study: Art & Archeol Prog, Oxford Univ, United Kingdom, 67; Randolph-Macon Col, Ashland, Va, 68; Pratt Inst, MFA(sculpture), 71. *Exhib:* Solo shows, Diane Brown Gallery, Washington, DC, 80, 82 & 86, Artists Space, New York, 81, Nancy Drysdale, Washington, DC, 92 & Corcoran Gallery Art, Washington, DC, 92; Los Angeles Co Mus Art, Calif, 88; Grimaldis Gallery, Baltimore, Md, 91; Phillips Collection, Washington, DC, 92. *Awards:* Visual Arts Grant, 88; Grant, Art Matters Inc, 90; Va Mus Fine Arts, Fel, 91. *Bibliog:* Colin Hughes (auth), Secret messages of the CIA, London Independent, 1/17/90; Joshua Remo (auth), CIA cryptic on artwork, Boston Globe, 7/4/90; Jack Rosenberger (auth), The CIA's top secret sculpture, Art Am, 3/91; and others. *Mailing Add:* c/o Diane Brown Gallery 560 Broadway, 2nd Fl New York NY 10012

SANCHEZ, BEATRICE RIVAS
ADMINISTRATOR, PRINTMAKER
b San Antonio, Tex, June 17, 41. *Study:* Del Art Ctr, 65-69; Montgomery Col, 70-71; Univ Mass, MFA, 75. *Work:* McNay Mus, Trinity Univ, Tex; Univ Tex Health Sci Ctr; Fla State House Rep; St Johns Col, Fla. *Comn:* Two Hundred Years of Graphics (poster), STex Print Soc, San Antonio, 76. *Exhib:* Color Print USA, Tex Tech Univ, 75; Women Artists of San Antonio, Univ Tex, 76; Womens Nat Exhib, Galerie Triangle, Washington, DC, 80; Montgomery Co Regional Juried Exhib, Greater Reston Arts Ctr Ann Juried Exhib, Md, 81; Southern Graphic Couns 190th Ann Conf Exhib, Kansas City, Mo, 91. *Pos:* Mem bd trustees, Native Am & Alaskan Indian Cultural Inst, Santa Fe, NMex; mem Comm on Accredidation, Nat Assoc of Schs of Art & Design; mem Capital Campaign Honorary Comt, Col Art Assn; pres, Kansas City Art Inst, 87-; gov, Am Royal Asn; Adv Bd Mem, Conelo Studios, Chicago. *Teaching:* Artist-in-residence printmaking & drawing, Trinity Univ, Tex, 76; coordr fine arts prog, Fla Sch Art, Palatka, 76-78; acad & assoc dean, Md Col Art & Design, 78-82; dean, Cranbrook Acad Art, 82- *Awards:* Second Prize, Eighth Ann Parkville Art Exhib, Md, 68; Third Place, Dept Commerce Exhib, Washington, DC, 69; First Prize, Creative Painting, Md Sch Art, 69. *Mem:* Nat Coun Art Admin. *Publ:* Contribr, Spectrum Fine Arts, 74 & 75 & Chomo-Uri Mag, summer 75. *Mailing Add:* Kansas City Art Inst 4415 Warwick Blvd Kansas City MO 64111

SANCHEZ, MARY LOWE (ELIZA)
DEALER, COLLECTOR
b Taos, NMex, July 21, 14. *Pos:* Secy & assoc dir, Gallery A (Allied Artists NMex Inc), Taos, 61-70, dir, secy & treas, 70-76, pres & dir, 76-86, 87-88. *Specialty:* Original paintings, etchings and sculpture. *Collection:* Watercolors and etchings by Gene Kloss; aquatints by Doel Reed; pastels and oils by Howard Cook and etchings; watercolors and oils by Barbara Latham; and others. *Mailing Add:* c/o Gallery A 105-107 Kit Carson Rd Taos NM 87571

SANCHEZ, THORVALD
PAINTER
b Havana, Cuba, June 11, 33; US citizen. *Work:* Milwaukee Art Ctr, Wis. *Exhib:* Pintura Cubana, Caracas, Venezuela, 72; 15th Ann Hortt Competition, Ft Lauderdale, Fla, 73; 35th Ann Exhib, Soc Four Arts, Palm Beach, Fla, 73; East Coast Painters, Longboat Key Art Ctr, Sarasota, Fla, 74; Fla Artists, Norton Mus, West Palm Beach, 75. *Awards:* Best of Show Award, Fla Gulf Coast 9th Show, High Mus Art, Atlanta, Ga, 74. *Bibliog:* Georgia Dupuis (auth), Transition theme of Sanchez work, Palm Beach Post, 74. *Mem:* Fla Artist Group. *Media:* Acrylic, Collage. *Dealer:* Center Gallery 327 Acadia Rd West Palm Beach FL 33401. *Mailing Add:* 146 Seminole Ave Palm Beach FL 33480

SANDBACK, FREDERICK LANE
SCULPTOR
b Bronxville, NY, Aug 29, 43. *Study:* Yale Univ, BA, 62-66, Sch Art & Archit, 66-69, BFA & MFA. *Work:* Mus Mod Art & Whitney Mus Am Art, New York; Nat Gallery Can, Ottawa, Ont; Kunsthalle Basel, Switz; Kaiser Wilhelm Mus, Krefeld, Ger; Sprengel Mus, Hannover, Ger; Yale Univ Art Gallery, New Haven, Conn. *Exhib:* Sculpture Ann, Whitney Mus Am Art, 68; Actualite d'un Bilan, Galerie Yuon Lambert, Paris, 72; Solo exhibs, Kunsthalle, Bern, Switz, 73, Mus Mod Art, New York, 78, Marian Goodman, New York, 85, Kestner-Gesellschaft, Hanover, Ger, 87, Westfalian Kunstverein, Münster, Ger, 87, David Nolan, New York, 88, DIA Art Found, New York, 88, Contemp Arts Mus, Houston, Tex, 89, Yale Univ Art Gallery, New Haven, Conn, 89, Magasin 3, Stockholm, Sweden, 91 & Lieu D'Art Contemporain, Hameau du Lac, France, 92; Actualite d'un Bilan, Galerie Yvon Lambert, Paris, 72; Yale Univ Sch Art & Archit, New Haven, Conn, 78; PS 1, Long Island City, NY, 78; Kunsthaus, 85 & Gallerie Anne Marie Verna, 86, Zurich, Switz; Gallerie Fred Jahn, Munich & Kunsthalle Mannheim, Mannheim, WGer, 86. *Awards:* Fel, Guggenheim Found, 75. *Bibliog:* Paul Wember (auth), Frederick Lane Sandback, Mus Hauslange, Krefeld, 69; Hermann Kern (auth), Fred Sandback, Kunstaum München, 75; Robert Creeley (auth), Walking the line, Arts Mag, 4/90. *Media:* Yarn, Pastel. *Publ:* Auth, 16 Variationen von 2 Diagonalen Linien, 72; 16 Variationen von 2 Horizontalen Linien, 73. *Dealer:* Fred Jahn Maximillian Strasse 10 West Germany 0114989-220117; David Nolan 560 Broadway New York NY. *Mailing Add:* E Monomonac Rd Rindge NH 03461

SANDE, RHODA
ART DEALER, SCULPTOR
b New York, NY. *Study:* Pratt Inst & Parsons Sch Design. *Exhib:* Sculpture, 5 Tiffany Windows, 91. *Pos:* Owner, Rhoda Sande Studio, New York, currently; cur, Mus Necca, New Eng Ctr Contemp Art, Brooklyn, Conn, currently. *Specialty:* Twentieth Century American and Mexican paintings, drawings and sculpture; antique American frames & antique prints. *Collection:* Antique Persian calligraphy, antique prints, drawings & sculpture. *Mailing Add:* 220 E 60th St New York NY 10022

SANDEN, JOHN HOWARD
PAINTER, INSTRUCTOR
b Austin, Tex, Aug 6, 35. *Study:* Minneapolis Sch Art, BFA, 56; Art Students League New York. *Work:* US Capitol & NASA Hq, Washington, DC; Fifth Ave Presby Church & New York Univ, New York; Royal Palace, Oyo, Nigeria. *Pos:* Pres & found, Portrait Inst, Washington, Conn, 74-; chmn & found, Nat Portrait Sem, 79- *Teaching:* Instr, Art Students League, 71- *Bibliog:* Doreen Mangan (auth), Portrait of a portraitist, Am Artist Mag, 3/75; Joe Singer (auth), Painting Men's Portraits, Watson-Guptill, 76 & 77; Eunice Agar (auth), John Howard Sanden, Am Artist Mag, 11/83. *Media:* Oil. *Publ:* Auth, Painting The Head in Oil, 76 & Successful Portrait Painting, 81, Watson-Guptill. *Dealer:* Portraits Inc 41 E 57th St New York NY 10022. *Mailing Add:* 881 Seventh Ave No 1010 New York NY 10019

SANDERS, JOOP A
PAINTER
b Amsterdam, Holland, Oct 6, 21; US citizen. *Study:* Art Students League, with George Grosz; also with De Kooning. *Work:* Stedelijke Mus, Amsterdam; Munic Mus, The Hague; Belzalel Mus, Jerusalem; Dillard Univ. *Exhib:* Ninth St Show, 51; Stable Shows, 52-55; one-man retrospective, Stedelijke Mus, 60; Carnegie Inst, 60; Options, Mus Contemp Art, Chicago, 68; one-man show, Alfred Kren Gallery, New York, 86; Gallery Biderman, Munich, Ger, 92. *Teaching:* Vis lectr, Carnegie Inst Technol, spring 65; prof painting, State Univ NY Col, New Paltz, 66-; vis lectr, Univ Calif, Berkeley, spring 68. *Awards:* Longview Found Fel, 60-61; Carnegie Inst Technol Res Found Awards, 71-72. *Media:* Oil, Acrylic. *Mailing Add:* Rte 2 Box 119A Stone Ridge NY 12484

SANDERS, RHEA (RHEA SANDERS RABINOVICH)
PAINTER
b Charleston, SC, Nov 6, 23. *Study:* With Maurice Sterne, 40-44; Pratt Graphics, NY, 83. *Work:* High Mus, Atlanta, Ga; Univ SC, Columbia; British Mus Libr, London; Rare Bks Collection, New York Pub Libr; Gibbes Art Mus, Charleston, SC; and others. *Exhib:* Paintings, Princeton Univ, League Gallery, 86; Theatre of Object, Marymount Manhattan Col, New York, 90; A Salute to Women, Nat Mus Women Arts Libr, Washington, DC, 91; Still Life, First St Gallery, New York, 91; Still Life in Egg Tempera, Moravian Col, Bethlehem, Pa, 91 & Interchurch Ctr, New York, 92; and others. *Awards:* Visual Artists Fel Grant, Nat Endowment Arts, 85. *Media:* Egg Tempera, Watercolor. *Publ:* Auth & illusr, The Fire Gardens of Maylandia, Tradd St Press, 80; Lecture on Egg Tempera, (film), Paragon Cable, New York, 90. *Dealer:* First St Gallery 560 Broadway New York NY 10017; Cortland Jessup Gallery 234 Commercial St Provincetown MA. *Mailing Add:* 617 W End Ave New York NY 10024

SANDERSON, CHARLES HOWARD
PAINTER, EDUCATOR
b Hamilton, Kans, Mar 6, 25. *Study:* Kans State Univ; Emporia State Univ, Kans; Wichita State Univ, BS(art educ); Ft Hays State Univ, Kans, MS(art educ). *Work:* Wichita Art Mus, Kans; Springfield Art Mus, Mo; Hockaday Ctr for the Arts, Kalispell, Mont; Birger Sandzen Mem Gallery, Lindsborg, Kans; Wichita Ctr Arts; and others. *Comn:* Faceted stained glass windows, Ascension Lutheran Church, Wichita, kans, 80; five piece mural, Central State Bank, Junction City, Kans, 86. *Exhib:* One-man show, Wichita Art Mus, Kans, 65-80; Sanderson-Booty Exhib, Galerie Monti-Carlo, Charleroi, Belg, 72; Am Painters in Paris, France, 76; Watermedia Nat, Kalispell, Mont, 85; Rocky Mountain Nat, Golden, Colo, 86; and others. *Collections Arranged:* Group Two--Invitational Kans Exhib, Century II Concert Hall Foyer, Wichita, 72-75; Kans Watercolor Soc Five-State. *Teaching:* Instr art, Kans Pub Schs, 51-85; instr painting, Wichita Art Asn, Kans, 58-71; instr teaching methods, Friends Univ, Wichita, 68-74; lectr & instr, Kans Art Educators Workshop, Wichita, 72-75; instr watercolor, Wichita State Univ Continuing Educ, 75-81, asst prof art, 85- *Awards:* Kans Watercolor Soc Tri-State Exhib Award, 70-73, 75-76 & 80-81; Kans Watercolor Soc Spec Jurer's Award, Wausau Wis Festival of Art, 88; Kans Gov's Art Award, 88. *Bibliog:* Watercolor, Acrylic, Sculpture & Demonstration (four educ videotapes), Wichita Bd of Educ, 77; Eileen O'Hara (auth), The painter and the business manager, Wichitan Mag, 5/81; feature article, Wichita Eagle Beacon, 4/85; Best of Kansas Art & Craft, Kansas Dept of Commerce, 88. *Mem:* Founder Kans Watercolor Soc (pres, 71-72, 79-86 & 89); Wichita Artists Guild; Whiskey Painters Am; Kans Cult Trust, Scholastic Art Awards Comt. *Media:* Watercolor, Acrylic. *Mailing Add:* 902 Waddington Ave Wichita KS 67212

SANDERSON, WARREN
HISTORIAN, CONSULTANT
b Boston, Mass, Feb 9, 31. *Study:* Boston Univ, MA, 56; NY Univ Inst Fine Arts, PhD, 65. *Teaching:* Prof hist art & archit, Univ Ill, Chicago, 66-70; prof art hist & criticism, Concordia Univ, Montreal, 76-; vis prof art hist, Univ Trier, Ger, 77, 78 & 83; vis prof archit hist, Univ Cologne, Ger, 89; vis scholar, Harvard Fine Arts, 90. *Awards:* Fulbright Fel, 66 & 82; Deutsche Forschungsgemeinschaft, 77, 78 & 83; Can Coun Award, 80, 86-89. *Bibliog:* Jeffrey Horrell (auth), article, Art Doc, 10/82; Diane Kay (auth), article, Art Int, 1/3/83; Elaine Cohen (auth), Sharing the joy & discovery of fine works of art, Suburban, 9/28/83. *Mem:* Int Asn Critics Art; Soc Archit Historians; Int Comt Hist Art (pres emer, Can Sect); Univ Arts Asn Can; Avista (pres, 92-). *Res:* Medieval art and architecture; Carolingian Trier; art and

architecture since 1950. *Publ:* Auth, Die Frühmittelalterlichen Krypten von St Maximin in Trier, Trierer Zeitschrift, 68; Monastic reform in Lorraine -- the outer crypt 950-1100, Transactions Am Philos Soc, 71; Archbishop Ratbodus -- Regino of Prüm -- Art & Music circa 900, Jahrbuch Berliner Mus, 82; ed & contribr, International Handbook of Contemporary Developments In Architecture, Greenwood Press, 83; Plan of St Gall Reconsidered, Speculum, 85. *Mailing Add:* PO Box 509 Champlain NY 12919

SANDESON, WILLIAM SEYMOUR
CARTOONIST
b Mound City, Ill, Dec 16, 13. *Study:* Chicago Acad Fine Arts, 31-32. *Pos:* Free-lance cartoonist for nat mags, 32-37; ed cartoonist, New Orleans Item-Tribune, 37-41; cartoonist, picture ed & art dir, St Louis Star-Times, 41-51, daily cartoon feature, Sketching Up with the News, Star-Times; ed cartoonist, Ft Wayne News-Sentinel, Ind, 51-82; retired. *Awards:* Honor Medal, 52, 53 & 56 & Distinguished Serv Award, 71-73, Freedoms Found; George Washington Honor Medal, 54, 55 & 57-60; Ind Sch Bell Award, 67; Pulitzer Prize, 83; and others. *Mem:* Nat Cartoonists Soc; Am Asn Ed Cartoonists; Cong Club; Ft Wayne Press (pres, 65). *Mailing Add:* 119 W Sherwood Terr Ft Wayne IN 46807

SANDGREN, ERNEST NELSON
PAINTER, PRINTMAKER
b Dauphin, Man, Dec 17, 17. *Study:* Univ Ore, BA & MFA; Univ Michoacan, Mex; Chicago Inst Design. *Work:* Portland Art Mus, Ore; Am Embassy Collection; Victoria & Albert Mus, London. *Comn:* Murals, Ore State Univ Libr, Corvallis & Portland. *Exhib:* Denver Art Mus; Santa Barbara Mus Art; Brooklyn Mus; Am Cult Ctr, Paris, Turin & Bordighera, Italy & Johannesburg, SAfrica; 46 USA Printmakers, New Forms Gallery, Athens, Greece, 64. *Pos:* Artist, Am Quintana Roo Mex Exped, 65 & 66 & CEDAM Exped to Durango, Mex, 70. *Teaching:* Instr art, Univ Ore, 47; prof art, Ore State Univ, 48-89; guest instr printmaking, Pa State Univ, 66 & Cent Ore Col, 70-72. *Awards:* M H De Young Mem Mus, 58; Yaddo Fel, 61; K Fisher Award, NW Watercolor Soc, 79; plus others. *Mem:* Ore Artists Alliance; W Coast Watercolor Soc. *Mailing Add:* 421 NW Eleventh Corvallis OR 97330

SANDGROUND, MARK BERNARD, SR
COLLECTOR, PATRON
b Boston, Mass, June 6, 32. *Study:* Univ Mich, BA, 52; Univ Va, LLB, 55 & JD, 71. *Exhib:* Hard on the Cutting Room floor, demonstration of film gestronics, 92. *Teaching:* Prof humanities & cooking, Free Col Belgravia, Lower Sch, 65-66. *Awards:* La Chaine des Les Robsier Chevalier, 71; Klip & Klop Gold Medal, 72; Star of Mex 1992, Order of The Grand Papal Soc for Peace & Friendship, Columbia, 92. *Bibliog:* D Kane (auth), Killer Kane and the White Princess, McGraw, 72; The Gypsie princess (film), Anon, 72. *Mem:* Friends of Corcoran Gallery Art (bd dir, 67-, pres, 68-70); Osuna Gallery. *Res:* Graphic works of Jose Louis Cuevas. *Collection:* Cuevas, Rico Lebrun & Anne Truitt. *Publ:* Auth, Collected letters from unknown artists, 1846-1871, privately publ, 52; Erotica from the Falls Church Collection, 72; Specialties at The Sign of The Whale, 92. *Mailing Add:* 8000 Towers Crescent Dr Suite 660 Vienna VA 22180

SANDLER, BARBARA
PAINTER
b New York, NY, Sept 14, 43. *Study:* Art Students League, George Bridgeman scholar, 63, also with Edwin Dickenson & Robert Beverly Hale. *Work:* Mus Mod Art, New York; Chicago Art Inst; Joseph Hirshhorn Mus, Washington, DC; Chase Manhattan Bank; Manufacturers Hanover Trust; Hearst Corp; Royal Saudi Arabian Naval Base; Dance Collection Lincoln Ctr. *Comn:* Poster & lithograph for Bicentennial, Spec Proj Group, Chicago, 75; posters, Circle in the Square Theatre, New York, 77-78; covers for Harpers & Sat Rev Mag; var record covers for Columbia & Verve Records; poster PBS Mobil Oil Mystery Series. *Exhib:* Danenberg Gallery, 73; Gimpel Weitzenhoffer, 75; Alex Rosenberg Gallery, New York, 79; one-person shows, Segal Gallery, New York, 81 & 83-85, Mary Martin Gallery, Aspen, Colo, 83, Trabia-Macafee Gallery, 89, The Center Show, 89, Art in Embassies-US State Dept, 89 & Dance Collection Lincoln Ctr, 91; Micro '83 Int Exhib, Stockholm, Sweden, 83; Zeus Trabia Gallery, 86. *Awards:* Elizabeth T Greenshields Mem Found Grant, 74. *Bibliog:* Articles, Archit Digest, 2/76, Print Mag, 79, Graphis Mag, 80, Arts Mag, 5/83, 5/84, 4/86 & 5/89, Downtown Mag, 12/86, Village Voice, 89, NY Native, 89 & Dance Mag, 1/89. *Media:* Oil, Graphite. *Publ:* Illusr, The Long View, Knopf, 74; Indian Oratorio, Ballantine Bks, 75; contribr, Super Realism, Dutton, 75. *Mailing Add:* 221 W 20th St New York NY 10011

SANDLER, IRVING HARRY
CRITIC, HISTORIAN
b New York, NY, July 22, 25. *Study:* Temple Univ, BA, 48; Univ Pa, MA, 50; NY Univ, PhD, 76. *Pos:* Art critic, Art News, 56-62 & New York Post, 60-65; contrib ed, Art Am, 72. *Teaching:* Instr art hist, NY Univ, 60-71; prof, State Univ NY Col Purchase, 71- *Awards:* Tona Shepherd Fund Grant Travel in Ger & Austria; Guggenheim Found Fel, 65; Nat Endowment Humanities Fel, 80. *Bibliog:* Jay Jacobs (auth), Of myths and men, Art Am, 3-4/70; Rosalind Constable (auth), The myth of the myth-makers, Washington Post Bk World, 11/29/70; Gesture-makers and colourfieldsmen, Times Lit Suppl, 6/8/71. *Mem:* Int Asn Art Critics (pres, Am Section, 70-75); Col Art Asn Am (bd dirs, 86); Artists Space (co-founder, 73). *Res:* American art since 1930. *Publ:* Auth, The Triumph of American Painting, a History of Abstract Expressionism, 70; The New York School: Painters and Sculptors of the Fifties, Harper & Row, 78; Alex Katz, Abrams, 79; Al Held, Hudson Hills, 84; American Art of the 1960s, 88. *Mailing Add:* 100 Bleecker St New York NY 10012

SANDLIN, DAVID THOMAS
PAINTER, PRINTMAKER
b Belfast, N Ireland, Nov 9, 56. *Study:* Univ Ala, Birmingham, BA, 79. *Work:* Gallery X, Kansas City; Chase Manhattan Bank, New York. *Exhib:* Birmingham Art Asn Show, Birmingham Mus, 79 & 80; Excerpts from East Village, Va Beach Arts Ctr, 84; Innocence and Experience, Greenville County Mus, 85; New Work from New York, Barbara Farber Gallery, Amsterdam, Neth, 85; Painting and Sculpture 1986, Indianapolis Mus, 86; Prints, Public and Private 1986, Brooklyn Mus, 86; Focus New York, Moos Art Gallery, Miami, 86; Investigations, McIntosh-Drysdale Gallery, Washington, DC, 86; solo exhibitions, Kwok Gallery, New York, 83, Gracie Mansion Gallery, New York, 84-86 & Brunswick Gallery, Missoula, Mont, 85. *Pos:* Founding mem, Print Co-op, New York, 80-81. *Teaching:* Mgr, printmaking shop, Sch Visual Arts, 82-, teacher lithography, 85- *Awards:* Jurors Award, Birmingham Art Asn, Birmingham Mus, 79. *Bibliog:* M Brenson (auth), rev, New York Times, 85; M Cone (auth), Prints about prints, Print Collectors Newslett, 85; D Rubey (auth), Sarcastic quotations, Arts Monthly, 85. *Media:* All. *Mailing Add:* 58 E First St Apt 5C New York NY 10003

SANDMAN, ALAN
SCULPTOR, PUBLISHER
b New York, NY, Nov 1, 47. *Study:* Self taught. *Work:* Community Gallery Art, Santa Fe Community Col, Gainesville, Fla. *Comn:* Fountain sculpture, C Beville Landscape Designer, 78; Univ Lutheran Church, 78. *Exhib:* Solo exhibs, Santa Fe Community Col, 75, Springdale Park, Atlanta, 79 & DeKalb Community Col, Clarkson, Ga, 86; Great Garden Sculpture Show (with catalog), Atlanta Botanical Garden, Sculptural Arts Mus, 82; Sculpture Tour (with catalog), Univ Tenn, Knoxville, 85 & 86; Sculpture Tour (with catalog), Walters State Community Col, Morristown, Tenn, 86-87; Sculpture to Touch, Martin Luther King Libr for the Blind (with printed & braille catalogs), Washington, DC, 87. *Pos:* Bd mem, Atlanta Artworks Coalition, 79-82, pres, 80-82; visual arts chmn, Decatur Arts Post, 87. *Awards:* Exhib Grant, Atlanta Bur Cultural Affairs, 79. *Bibliog:* Larry Smith (auth), Sculptor Uses Live Models, Gainesville Sun, 10/12/75; Grant Carrington (auth), Shapes in Stone, Vol 2, No 21, New Look, 10/15/75; Metro Scenes, Atlanta Constitution, 10/18/84. *Mem:* 20th Century Art Soc; DeKalb Coun Arts; Int Sculpture Ctr; Nexus Contemp Art Ctr. *Media:* Cast, Stone. *Dealer:* Art Int 394 Fourth St Atlanta GA 30308. *Mailing Add:* PO Box 5595 Sta E Atlanta GA 30307

SANDMAN, JO
SCULPTOR, CONCEPTUAL ARTIST
b Boston, Mass, Mar 22, 31. *Study:* Brandeis Univ, AB, 52; with Hans Hofmann, Provincetown and NY, 52-53; Hunter Col, with Robert Motherwell, 53; Univ Calif, Berkeley, MA(art), 54; Radcliffe Col, MAT, 56; Harvard Univ, Japanese garden design, with Kinsaku Nakane, 85. *Work:* Aldrich Mus Contemp Art; Addison Gallery Am Art; Dallas Mus Fine Arts; NY Univ; Mass Inst Technol. *Comn:* Video piece for TV, Nat Endowment Arts, Rockefeller Found & Mass Coun Arts, Boston, 75; Removal Drawing, Bicentennial Painting Comn, Boston 200, 75. *Exhib:* Flush with the Walls, Mus Fine Arts, Boston, 71; Drawings from Two New York Galleries, Va Mus Fine Arts, (traveling), 73-75; solo exhib, O K Harris Works Art, New York, 73, 75 & 82, Addison Gallery Am Art, 74, Brockton Art Mus, Mass, 76, Stux Gallery, Boston, 81 & 83, DeCordova Mus, Lincoln, 85 & Thomas Segal Gallery, 89; Prospectus: Art in the Seventies, Aldrich Mus Contemp Art, 79; Boston Now: Abstract Painting, Inst Contemp Art, Boston, 81; Boston Now: Works on Paper, ICA, Boston, 88; MassachusArts: Location and Place, Boston Ctr Arts, Boston, 90. *Teaching:* Vis artist, lectr & critic painting, various art sch & col, 56- *Awards:* Sculpture Fel, Mass Coun on the Arts & Humanities, 84; Mary Ingram Bunting Fel, Radcliffe & Harvard Univ, 86-87. *Bibliog:* Kay Larson (auth), Jo Sandman, Christopher Wilmarth, 5/78 & Pamela Allara (auth), The scope of Boston art is broader than it would appear, 11/81, Art News; Nancy Doll (auth), Added Dimensions (exhib catalog), Tufts Univ, 84; David Bonetti (auth), Drawing, Boston Phoenix, 7/87. *Media:* Miscellaneous. *Dealer:* Thomas Segal Gallery 207 South St Boston MA 02111. *Mailing Add:* One Fitchburg C-507 Somerville MA 02143

SANDOL, MAYNARD
PAINTER
b Newark, NJ, 1930. *Study:* Newark State Col, 52; also with Robert Motherwell. *Work:* Newark Mus Art; Wadsworth Atheneum, Hartford, Conn; Princeton Univ, NJ; Finch Col Mus, New York; Joseph Hirshhorn Collection, Washington, DC; also pvt collections. *Exhib:* Corcoran Gallery of Art, Washington, DC; Mus Mod Art, New York; NJ Pavilion, New York World's Fair; NJ State Mus, Trenton; NJ Masters, 1980; and others. *Bibliog:* William H Gerdts, Jr (auth), Paintings and Sculpture in New Jersey, Van Nostrand, 64. *Media:* Oil, Acrylic. *Mailing Add:* Bunn St Box 364 RR 2 Califon NJ 07830

SANDROW, HOPE
PHOTOGRAPHER
b Philadelphia, Pa, Dec 31, 51. *Study:* Philadelphia Col Art, study with Ray Metzker, 72-75. *Comn:* Portraits, Interview Mag, 80, comn by Regina Trapp/Andrea Grey, New York, 85, Robert & Adrian Mnunchin, New York, 86 & Dakis Joannou, Athens, Greece, 87; Artforum Maga, 90; Vera List 1991, New York. *Exhib:* Neo York, Univ Art Mus, Santa Barbara, Calif, 84; solo exhibs, Philadelphia Col Art, 84, Haggery Mus, Milwaukee, Wis, 86 & Gracie Mansion Gallery, New York, 86, 88, 89 & 91; Painting & Sculpture Today-Biennial, Indianapolis Mus, 86; Directions-Biennial, Hirshhorn Mus, Washington, DC, 86; The New Shape of Content, Whitney Mus Art, 87; Photo on the Edge, Haggerty Mus, Milwaukee, 88; American Photos of the

80s, Nat Mus Am Art, Washington, DC, 89; Sequence (con) Sequence, Blum Art Inst, Bard Col, 89; Fantasies, Fables & Fabrications, Herter Art Gallery, Univ Mass, 89-91; Grey Art Gallery, New York Univ, 91; Dia De Los Muertos, Alternative Mus, 91. *Teaching:* Instr art, photography & creature writing, Katherine Street Shelter, New York, 87-89, Park Ave Shelter, 89- *Awards:* Polaroid Product Grant, 89 & 90; Manhattan Borough Presidents Citation for Excellence in the Arts, 91; Mayor Dinkins Superstar Award, 92. *Bibliog:* Ben Lifson (auth), Hope & Fear (exhib catalog), Gracie Mansion, 86; Phyllis Rosenzweig (auth), Directions 86, (exhib catalog), Gracie Mansion, 86; Julia Ballerini (auth), Sequence con Sequence, Aperture, 89; The New Shape of Content (exhib catalog), Whitney Mus Am Art; Reading in Contemporary Poetry, Dia Found, 88; Am Photo of the Eighties, Nat Mus Art, 89. *Mem:* Artist/Homeless Collaborative (founder & proj dir), NY, 90-92; Visual Aids, 90-; Women's Action Coalition, 92. *Media:* Photography. *Publ:* Art Forum, 80 90 & 91; Art in Am, 84 & 90; Village Voice, 87, 89 & 90; Blast Art, 10/91; Vogue, 91; Art Forum, 80, 90 & 91, Boston Review, 89. *Mailing Add:* 5 E 16th St New York NY 10003

SANDUSKY, BILLY RAY
PAINTER, PRINTMAKER
b Bowling Green, Ky, Oct 23, 45. *Study:* John Herron Sch Art, Ind Univ, BFA, 68, Tulane Univ, New Orleans, La, MFA, 70; Academia di Belle Arte, Florence, Italy, 75. *Work:* Midwest Mus Am Art, Elkhart, Ind; Evansville Mus Arts & Sci, Ind; South Bend Art Ctr, Ind; Santa Raparta Graphic Art Ctr, Florence; Tulane Univ, New Orleans; Wilfrid Laurier Univ, Waterloo, Ont, Can. *Exhib:* One-person shows, Palazzo Strozzi, Florence, 76 & So Bend Art Ctr, 82 & 90, Purdue Univ, Lafayette, Ind, 86; Indiana Artists Show, Indianapolis Mus Art, 83; Realism Today, Mus Arts & Sci, Evansville, 85-86; La Grange National XI, Lamar Dodd Art Ctr, Ga, 86; Art USA, Grand Junction, Colo, 89. *Teaching:* Asst prof painting, St Mary's Col, Notre Dame, Ind, 80- *Awards:* Painting Purchase Award, Fourth Elkhart Regional, 82; Best Painting, South Bend Art Ctr, 83; Airbrush Excellence Competition, 1st Place Fine Arts, Airbrush Action Mag, 90; and others. *Mem:* Col Art Asn; Mid-Am Col Arts Asn (exec bd). *Media:* Acrylic, Oil; Lithography. *Mailing Add:* Art Dept St Mary's Col Notre Dame IN 46556

SANDWEISS, MARTHA ANN
MUSEUM DIRECTOR
b St Louis, Mo, Mar 29, 54. *Study:* Harvard Univ, BA, 75; Nat Endowment for Humanities Fel, Nat Portrait Gallery, Washington, DC, 75-76; Yale Univ, MA, 77, Fel, Ctr Am Art & Mat Cult, 77-79, PhD, 85. *Collections Arranged:* A Knot of Dreamers: The Brook Farm Community, Nat Portrait Gallery, 76; Pictures from an Expedition: Early Views of the American West (auth, catalog), Yale Univ Art Gallery, 78; Carlotta Corpron: Designer with Light (auth, catalog), 80; Masterworks of American Photography (auth, bk), 82; Carleton E Watkins: Photographer of the American West (introd, bk), Amon Carter Mus; 83; Carl Mydans, Amon Carter Mus, 85; Richard Avedon: In the American West, 85; Laura Gilpin: An Enduring Grace (auth, bk), Amon Carter Mus, 86; Eliot Porter (introd, bk), Amon Carter Mus. *Pos:* Cur photographs, Amon Carter Mus, Ft Worth, Tex, 79-86; dir, Mead Art Mus, Amherst Col, 89. *Awards:* George Wittenborn Award, 87; Nat Endowment Humanities Fel for Independent Scholars, 88. *Publ:* Ed, Historic Texas: A Photograhic Portrait, Tex Monthly, 86; Denizens of the Desert, Univ NMex Press, 88; Contemporary Texas: A Photographic Portrait 86; coauth, Eyewitness to War: Prints and Daguerreotypes of the Mexican War, 1846-1848, Smithsonian Press, 89; ed & coauth, Photography in Nineteenth-Century America, Abrams, 91. *Mailing Add:* Mead Art Mus Amherst Col Amherst MA 01002

SANGIAMO, ALBERT
EDUCATOR, PAINTER
b Brooklyn, NY. *Study:* Brooklyn Col, AB; Yale Univ, BFA & MFA. *Work:* Baltimore Mus, Md. *Exhib:* Smithsonian Traveling Exhib Am Drawing, 65; one-man shows, Baltimore Mus, 69, Towson State Col, 71, Decker Art Gallery, Md, 75 & Md Arts Coun Traveling Show, 75. *Teaching:* Instr painting & drawing, Md Inst Col Art, 61-, chmn found dept, 61-73, chmn dept fine arts, 73- *Awards:* Grand Prize, Baltimore Mus, 59; Purchase Prizes, St Paul Arts Ctr, 64. *Media:* Synthetic Charcoal, Acrylic. *Mailing Add:* Md Inst Col Art 1300 Mt Royal Ave Baltimore MD 21217

SANGUINETTI, EUGENE F
ADMINISTRATOR, LECTURER
b Yuma, Ariz, May 12, 17. *Study:* Univ Santa Clara, BA, 39; Univ Ariz, 60-62. *Collections Arranged:* Selected Drawings from the Collection of Edward Jacobson, 70; Drawings by Living Americans, Objects from Buddhist Cultures & Etching Renaissance in France: 1850-1880, 71 (with catalog); Drawings by New York Artists (with catalog), Prehistoric Utah Petroglyphs & Pictographs & Ron Resch and the Computer, 72; Abraham Walkowitz Retrospective (with catalog), 74; plus other retrospectives & one-man exhibs. *Pos:* Dir, Tucson Mus & Art Ctr, Ariz, 64-67; dir, Utah Mus Fine Arts, Univ Utah, Salt Lake City, 67-; judge art shows, Colo, Utah & Idaho, 68-72, Bellevue & Seattle, Wash, 75. *Teaching:* Lectr art hist, Univ Ariz, 62-64; adj prof art, Univ Utah, 67- *Mem:* Asn Am Mus; Western Asn Art Mus; Col Art Asn Am; Asn Archit Historians; Am Fedn Arts. *Res:* American art of the first half of the 20th century. *Specialty:* Paintings, tapestries and furniture from American and European periods; Oriental material; Egyptian and Cyprist antiquities; French and English objects and decoration. *Publ:* Contribr, Alexander H Wyant Retrospective, 68; contribr, John Marin Drawings Retrospective, 69; contribr, Alex Katz Retrospective, 71; contribr, Social Concern and the Worker: French Prints from 1830-1910, 73. *Mailing Add:* 101 Arts & Archit Ctr Univ Utah Salt Lake City UT 84112

SANKOWSKY, ITZHAK
PAINTER, SCULPTOR
b Kishinew, Romania, Mar 9, 08; US citizen. *Study:* Acad Fine Arts & Univ Florence, Italy; Univ Pa, MA; with Arthur B Carles, Jr. *Work:* Philadelphia Mus Art; Jewish Mus Art, New York; Mus Tel Aviv; Harrisburg Mus Art; also in pvt collection of Milton Shapp. *Comn:* Stained glass windows & mem plaques, Har-Zion Temple, Philadelphia, 60-66; candelabra, Philadelphia Psychiat Hosp, 62; stained glass windows, Levine Mem Chapel, Philadelphia, 63-64; sculpture bas-relief, Home for Jewish Aged, Philadelphia, 64-65; illus for book, Jewish Publ Soc, Philadelphia, 67. *Exhib:* Int Watercolor Show, Chicago, 40-69; one-man shows, Arts & Crafts, Pittsburgh, 52, Pa Art Alliance, 56-68, Agra Gallery, Washington, DC, 65 & Franklin & Marshall Col, 67; and others. *Teaching:* Instr painting & sculpture, Philadelphia Mus Art, 48-76, Allens Lane Art Ctr, Philadelphia, 48-51 & Main Line Ctr Art, Philadelphia, 50-53 & 76 (retired). *Awards:* Within the Ghetto Walls, YM-YWHA, Philadelphia, 51; Purchase Prize for Print, Burr Gallery Nat Exhib, 58-59. *Mem:* Philadelphia Print Club; Artists Equity Asn; Am Color Print Soc; Philadelphia Art Alliance. *Media:* All. *Publ:* Auth, Art in Israel, Jewish Frontier, New York, 35; Art in Israel, Bull Har-Zion Temple, Philadelphia, 65; Always time for art, suppl to the Jewish Exponent, Philadelphia, 73. *Mailing Add:* 217 Upland Rd Merion Station PA 19066

SANSONE, JOSEPH F
CRAFTSMAN
b Mount Vernon, NY, Oct 20, 22. *Exhib:* Milton Glazer, Univ Minn, Minneapolis, 88; Frank Stella, Los Angeles; Richard Haas, San Francisco. *Pos:* Pres, Archit Wallcovering Inc, 60-; Painting & Decorating Contractors Am, 70-71. *Teaching:* Instr mural installation, various trade unions (CETA sponsored), 60- *Awards:* First Prize, Painting & Decorating Contractors Am, 87, 88 & 89, Second Prize, 88. *Mem:* Painting & Decorating Contractors Am. *Publ:* Coauth, PWC Mag, Finan Publ, 70-90; coauth, American painter-decorator, Voss Publ, 70-90; coauth, Journal of Prepatory Mgt, NAR, Chicago, 90. *Mailing Add:* 10846 N 34th Pl Phoenix AZ 85028

SAN SOUCIE, PATRICIA MOLM
PAINTER, INSTRUCTOR
b Minneapolis, Minn, Nov 4, 31. *Study:* Univ Wisc, graphics with Warrington Colescott & Alfred Sessler, painting with Dean Meeker, BS(applied art), 53; Drew Univ, NJ, with Lee Hall, 72-73; Summit Art Ctr, NJ, painting with V Fangor, R Reid, William McCartin & Wolf Kahn, 72-81. *Work:* Springfield Art Mus, Mo. *Comn:* Neuberger & Berman Off, New York; Casio Int Off, NJ & New York. *Exhib:* Am Watercolor Soc, 72-76; Solo exhib, Acad Arts, Easton, Md, 83; Butler Inst Am Art, 86; Watercolor USA Hon Soc, 92-93. *Pos:* Jury selection chmn, St Louis Artists Guild, 68-71; gallery exhib comt, Summit Art Ctr, NJ, 73-79; pres, NJ Watercolor Soc, 88-90. *Teaching:* Instr, Princeton Art Asn, NJ, 75-76; fac mem, Summit Art Ctr, NJ, 83- & ARTWORKS, Trenton, NJ, 92- *Awards:* Walser Greathouse Award & Gold Medal, Am Watercolor Soc, 91; Arches Special Papers, Third Award, Aajomari Inc, 91; Ariz Aqueous Award for Excellence, Tubac Ctr Arts, 91. *Bibliog:* Edward Betts (auth), Master Class in Watercolor, Watson-Guptill Publ, 75; Splash I, 90 & Splash II, 92, Northlight Publ; Marilyn H Phillis (auth), Watermedia Techniques for Releasing the Creative Spirit, Watson Guptill Pub, 92. *Mem:* Nat Watercolor Soc; Nat Asn Women Artists; Am Watercolor Soc Assoc; Watercolor USA Honor Soc. *Media:* Watercolor. *Publ:* Auth, article, Artists Mag, 1/91. *Dealer:* Gallery 9 Chatham NJ; Art Forms Redbank NJ. *Mailing Add:* 68 Dortmunder Dr Manalapan NJ 07726

SANTIAGO, RAMON
PAINTER, PRINTMAKER
b Rochester, NY, Sept 4, 43. *Study:* Mt San Antonio Col, Walnut, Calif, AAS, 62; Rochester Inst Technol, NY, ADA, 65. *Work:* New York Univ; Carnegie Mellon Collection, Pittsburgh; Mus Art, Ft Lauderdale, Fla; Hamilton Mus, Hamilton, Ont; Mus Mod Art, Palermo, Italy. *Comn:* Paintings, prints & posters, Camp Good Days & Special Times, Rochester, NY, 80, 84, 85 & 90; paintings & posters, Vietnam Vets Outreach Ctr, Rochester, NY, 84; paintings & prints, Eastman Kodak Co, Rochester, NY, 88; paintings, prints & posters, Sesquicetennial-Irondequoit, NY, 89; prints, Bauch & Lomb, Rochester, NY, 90. *Exhib:* Avanti Galleries, New York, 83, 87 & 90; Galerie Rienzo, New York, 88; Artefino Gallery, Charlotte, NC, 89; Kenan Art Ctr, Lockport, NY, 90; David Barker Gallery, Columbus, Ohio, 90. *Awards:* Silver Award, Rochester Soc Communicating Arts, 87; Alumni Recognition Award, Rochester Inst Technol, 87; Artistic Award, Italian Civic League, 89. *Bibliog:* Frank Barton (auth), Ramon Santiago, his dreams become his art, Delaware Valley Mag, 2/87; Joan Creatura (auth), The business of art: contemporary artist Ramon Santiago, Rochester Business Opportunities Guide, 12/8/89; Lesley Constable (auth), Women celebrated in Santiago's works, Columbus Dispatch, Ohio, 2/25/90. *Mem:* Arts Greater Rochester. *Media:* Oil, Mixed Media. *Dealer:* Frank Communs Inc 17 Fallbrook Circle Rochester NY 14625. *Mailing Add:* c/o Ramon Santiago Gallery 7 Strathallan Park Suite No 4 Rochester NY 14607

SANTIAGO, RICHARD E
SCULPTOR, EDUCATOR
b Mar 29, 48. *Study:* Univ S Fla, Tampa, BA(art educ), 74, MA(art educ) 77; Univ Utah, Salt Lake City, MFA(sculpture), 84; studied with Stephen Antonakos, Sculptor, New York. *Work:* Tampa Mus Art & Berkeley Prep Sch, Tampa, Fla; First Fla Bank, Clearwater, Fla; Univ Utah, Mus Fine Arts, Univ Utah, Art Dept & Salt Lake City Art Ctr, Salt Lake City; Nora Eckles Harrison Mus Fine Art, Logan, Utah; also pvt collections of Stephen Antonakos, Peter Frank & James Whitecotton. *Exhib:* ASA Gallery, Albuquerque, NMex, 83; solo exhibs, Gittins Gallery, Salt Lake City, Utah,

83 & 84, Univ Utah, Mus Fine Arts, Salt Lake City, 83 & 84, U S Garage Gallery, Sarasota, Fla, 86, Fla Ctr Contemp Art, Tampa, 88, Michael Murphy Gallery, Tampa, Fla, 89, Fla Towers Bldg, Tampa, 90, Tampa Mus Art, Fla, 90 & C Company, Chicago, Ill, 91; Utah Arts Coun, Salt Lake City, 84; Bellair Art Ctr, Bellair, Fla, 87; Ridge Art Asn, Winter Haven, Fla, 87; The Arts Ctr, St Petersburg, Fla, 87, 88 & 92; Fla Ctr Contemp Art, Tampa, 87 & 88; PSA Architects Inc, St Petersburg, Fla, 89; N Miami Ctr Contemp Art, Fla, 91; PJC Gallery, Pensacola, Fla, 92. *Teaching:* Instr art, Hillsborough County Pub Schs, Fla, 75-; instr design & sculpture, Univ Utah, Salt Lake City, 80-82 & 91. *Awards:* Emerging Artists Grant, Arts Coun Tampa/Hillsborough, Tampa, Fla, 89; Master Assoc, Atlantic Ctr Arts, New Smyrna Beach, Fla, 89; Individual Artist Fel, Fla Arts Coun, Div Cultural Affairs, Tallahassee, Fla, 90. *Media:* Neon, Site Specific Installation. *Mailing Add:* 7107 N 18th St Tampa FL 33610

SANTLOFER, JONATHAN
PAINTER
b New York, NY, Apr 26, 46. *Study:* Boston Univ, BFA, 67; Pratt Inst, MFA, studied with George McNeil, 69. *Work:* Norton Simon Mus; Inst Contemp Art, Tokyo, Japan; Prudential Corp, Grand Rapids, Mich; Indianapolis Mus Art, Ind; Chase Manhattan Bank, New York; Security Pac Nat Bank, Los Angeles; A T & T, Inc, NJ. *Exhib:* Solo Exhibs, Inst Contemp Art, Tokyo, Japan, 78 & 85, Klein Gallery, Chicago, Ill, 86 & 89, Graham Mod Gallery, New York, 86, 88 & 90, Nina Freudenheim Gallery, Buffalo, NY, 87, Heckscher Mus, Huntington, NY, 87, Galleria Peccolo, Livorno, Italy, 89, Ruth Bachofner Gallery, Los Angeles, Calif, 91; Landscape Constructions, Richard Green Gallery, Los Angeles, Calif, 89; A Good Road, Barbara Toll Gallery, NY, 89; Nina Freudenheim Gallery, Buffalo, NY, 90; Personal/Mechanical, Graham Mod Mus, NY, 90; and others. *Teaching:* Instr art hist/studio, Jersey City State Col, NJ, 74-; instr contemp art, The New Sch, New York, 76- Columbia Univ, currently. *Awards:* Skowhegan Scholar, Summer Painting Grant, Skowhegan Sch of Painting & Sculpture, Maine, 66; Nat Endowment Arts, 81 & 89. *Bibliog:* Peggy Cyphers (auth) rev, Arts, 2/89; Antonella Capitanio (auth), Il Tirreno Estate, 9/8/89; Alan G Artner (auth), rev, Chicago Tribune, 3/30/89. *Media:* Multimedia. *Dealer:* Graham Modern Gallery 1014 Madison Ave New York NY 10021. *Mailing Add:* 151 W 28th St New York NY 10001

SANTOS, ADÈLE NAUDÉ
ARCHITECT, URBAN DESIGNER
Study: Archit Asn, London, dipl, 61; Univ Pa, MArch & MP; Harvard, MArch in UD. *Pos:* Professorships grad prog at Harvard, Rice Univ & Univ Pa, chmn dept archit, 81-87; founding dean, Sch Archit, Univ Calif San Diego, currently. *Awards:* Int design competitions. *Publ:* Published work in journals world-wide. *Mailing Add:* c/o Univ California-San Diego, Sch of Archit 9500 Gilman Dr La Jolla CA 92093-0084

SAPHIRE, LAWRENCE M
WRITER, ART DEALER
b Brooklyn, NY, Jan 12, 31. *Study:* Yale Univ, BA, 52, writing with Robert Penn Warren; Yale Sch Fine Arts, 51-53; Univ Paris I at Sorbonne, two dipl. *Pos:* Dir, Blue Moon Gallery, New York; ed, Blue Moon Press, Yorktown Heights, NY. *Res:* Modern prints, particularly Leger, Andre Masson. *Specialty:* Modern European painting, sculpture, graphics, original print publications in books and albums. *Publ:* Auth & ed, Sea Bird Saga (including Wallace Putnam lithographs), Blue Moon Gallery, 66; Poems (including Andre Masson etchings), Ed de la Lune Bleue, 74; Andre Masson/Second Surrealist Period, 75, The Genius of Andre Masson, 76, Fernand Leger/Complete Graphic Work, 78, Andre Masson/Complete Graphic Work, 90 (catalogs), Blue Moon Press. *Mailing Add:* 808 Broadway New York NY 10003

SAPIEN, DARRYL RUDOLPH
PERFORMANCE ARTIST, GRAPHIC ARTIST
b Los Angeles, Calif, Mar 12, 50. *Study:* Fullerton Col, AA, 71; San Francisco Art Inst, BFA, 72, MFA 76. *Work:* Univ Art Mus, Univ Calif, Berkeley; Oakland Mus, Calif; San Francisco Mus Mod Art; Solomon R Guggenheim Mus, New York. *Comn:* This is Not A Test (participation performance), Soc Encouragement Contemp Art, San Francisco, 76; Pixellage Commissioned Set Design for San Francisco Ballet, 83. *Exhib:* Within the Nucleus (performance), San Francisco Mus Mod Art, 76; Painting & Sculpture in Calif: The Mod Era, San Francisco Mus Mod Art, 76; Gallery of the Nat Collection of Fine Arts, Washington, DC, 77; The Principle of the Arch (performance), PS 1, New York 77; A Bridge Can Also Be a Work of Art (performance), Arte Fiera di Bologna, Italy, 77; Space, Time, Sound, a Decade in the Bay Area, San Francisco Mus Mod Art, 79; Hero (performance), Newport Harbor Art Mus, Calif, 80; 19 Artists--Emergent Americans, Solomon R Guggenheim Mus, New York, 81; Am Roulette, Solomon R Guggenheim Mus, NY, 81; Artspace Painting Grant Award, San Francisco Artspace, 88. *Pos:* Sr computer graphics artists, Amdahl Coop, 84-86. *Teaching:* Lectr, San Francisco State Univ, San Francisco Inst. *Awards:* Nat Endowment Arts Awards, 73 & 79; Louise Riskin Award, Video Pavillion, San Francisco Art Festivel, 75. *Bibliog:* Jack Burnham (auth), Contemporary ritual, Arts Mag, 73; Robert McDonald (auth), The total art of Darryl Sapien, Artweek, 75; William Kleb (auth), Art performance San Francisco, Performing Arts J, 77. *Media:* Live Performance, Paintings. *Publ:* Auth, Splitting the axis & Video art and the ultimate cliche, La Mamelle, 76; contribr, Other Sources (catalog), San Francisco Art Inst, 76; contribr, Oggi in California, Data, 77; auth, Crime in the streets, High Performance, summer 79; auth, What is performance art?, Intersection Newsletter, 81. *Dealer:* Galerie Paule Anglim 710 Montgomery St San Francisco CA 94111. *Mailing Add:* 4333 Balboa St San Francisco CA 94121

SAPP, WILLIAM ROTHWELL
SCULPTOR, EDUCATOR
b Cape Girardeau, Mo, July 4, 43. *Study:* Univ Mo, Columbia, MA, 67; Wash Univ, MFA, 78; Southeast Mo State Univ. *Work:* Univ Ark, Little Rock; Comptroller of the US Currency, Oklahoma City; Harlin Mem Mus, West Plains, Mo. *Comn:* J P Harlin Portrait Sculpture, comn by Harlin family, 73; Timeframe (site sculpture), Ark Arts Coun-Univ Ark, Little Rock, 80. *Exhib:* Energy exhib, New Sch Social Res, New York, 79; Nat Sculpture Traveling Exhib, 79; Last Nat Sculpture Show (with catalog), Univ Ga, Athens, 82; William Sapp New World Exhib, Paris Gibson Ctr Contemp Art, Great Falls, Mont, 84; Mid-Am Winners Exhib, Salina Art Ctr, Kans, 86. *Teaching:* Asst prof sculpture, Adams State Col, 67-73; assoc prof, Univ Ark, Little Rock, 78-86. *Awards:* Nat Endowment Arts Fel, 85; Mid-Am Art Asn Fel, 85; Ark Arts Coun Fel, 86. *Mem:* Int Sculpture Ctr; Mid-Am Col Art Asn. *Media:* Handformed Paper. *Dealer:* Batz-Lawrence Gallery 4116 Pennsylvania Ave Kansas City MO. *Mailing Add:* Visual Arts Building Dept Art Univ Georgia Athens GA 30602

SARET, ALAN DANIEL
SCULPTOR
b New York, NY, Dec 25, 44. *Study:* Cornell Univ, BArch, with Peter Kahn & Alan Atwell; Hunter Col, with Robert Morris. *Work:* Mus Mod Art, Whitney Mus Am Art, New York; Detroit Inst Art; Art Gallery Ont; Ft Worth Art Mus, Tex; Dallas Art Mus & Art Mus S Tex; Allen Art Mus, Oberlin Col. *Exhib:* Whitney Ann, 69 & Whitney Biennial, 77, Whitney Mus Am Art, New York; Recent Acquisitions, Mus Mod Art, New York, 75-76; Recent Developments in Sculpture, Whitney Mus Am Art, 81; Images of the Unknown, PS 1, Long Island City, NY, 86; Natural Form and Forces, MIP Bank Boston, Mass, 86; one-man shows, Charles Cowles Gallery, New York 80 & 82, Rudolph Zwirner Gallery, Cologne, Ger, 81, Nigel Greenwood Gallery, London, 82, Daniel Weinberg Gallery, Los Angeles, 83 & 89, Albright-Knox Gallery Buffalo, NY, 83 Alan Saret: Recent Sculpture & Drawings, Margo Leavin Gallery, Los Angeles, 86 & Lorence Monk Gallery, New York, 89; Eccentric Abstraction, Blum Helman Gallery, New York, 86; Retrospective exhib, Inst Art Urban Resources, PS 1, Long Island City, NY, 90; Home & Away (environmental mosaic on 3 levels), Arrivals Terminal, Pittsburgh Int Airport. *Pos:* Founder & dir, ALAEL, 74-77. *Teaching:* Vis artist sculpture, Univ Calif, Irvine, 78. *Awards:* Guggenheim Fel, 69; Nat Endowment Arts Fel, 75; CAPS Grant, 76. *Bibliog:* Suzanne Muchnic (auth), A show that is wired for brightness, Los Angeles Times, 6/9/86; Cynthia Goodman (auth), Digital Visions, Everson Mus Art, 87; Michael Brenson, rev, NY Times, 5/29/87; Robert Morgan (auth), Eccentric abstraction and postminimalism, Flash Art, 1/2/89; Michael Kimmelman (auth), Exploring the connections in a multi-faceted Career, NY Times, 1/26/90. *Media:* Multimedia. *Publ:* Auth, The Ghosthouse, ALAEL, 76; coauth (with Klaus Kertess) Matter Into Aether, Newport Harbor Art Mus, Newport Beach, Calif, 82. *Dealer:* Margo Leavin Gallery 812 N Robertson Blvd Los Angeles CA 90069. *Mailing Add:* 65 S 11th St Brooklyn NY 11211

SARGENT, J MCNEIL See Braley, Jean

SARGENT, MARGARET HOLLAND
PAINTER, VIDEO ARTIST
b Hollywood, Calif, 27. *Study:* Univ Calif, Los Angeles, 45-47; Tokyo, Japan, 56; with Herbert Abrams, NY, 59-61 & Marcos Blahove, Fairfax, Va, 69; Art Students League, with John Sanden, 74. *Work:* British Piano Mus, Middlesex, Eng; US Military Acad Mus; US Air Force Acad; USA Pentagon; US Naval Acad; US Naval War Col; Hawaii State Found. *Comn:* Portrait, President Gerald Ford, Time, Inc; portrait, Secretary of State Alexander M Haig; portrait, playwright Tennessee Williams; portrait, Jules S Stein; portrait, Prince Turki Saud; portrait, Governor George Ariyoshi, Hawaii; portrait, Army Chief of Staff, General John A Wickham; portrait, Lew R Wasserman; portrait, Dorothy Stimson, Bullitt; and others. *Exhib:* One-man shows, Turkish Am Asn, Ankara, 63, Frye Art Mus, 71 & 84, Woodside Gallery, Seattle, 72 & Excelsior Club, NY, 74-75; plus many others. *Pos:* Owner-dir, Sargent Portraits, Los Angeles, currently. *Teaching:* Instr video, Camelot Productions, currently. *Awards:* H M Salmagundi Award; Naval Award Outstanding Achievement in Oil Painting, 77; First Prize Prof Oils, AFL-CIO's 10th Ann, Los Angeles, 79; and others. *Bibliog:* Three from Hollywood, SW Art, 9/82; Margaret Holland Sargent, Am Artist, 4/83; Margaret Holland Sargent, Palm Springs Life, 12/87. *Mem:* Salmagundi Club; Am Portrait Soc. *Media:* Oil. *Mailing Add:* 2750 Glendower Ave Los Angeles CA 90027

SARGENT, RICHARD
PAINTER, PHOTOGRAPHER
b St Louis, Mo, 1932. *Study:* Univ Southern Calif, BFA, 54 & MFA, 56. *Comn:* Mural, Audio Workshop, New York, 58; painting on environmental electricity, Int Sci & Technol Mag, 63. *Exhib:* One-man shows, New York Times, 58, Nonagon Gallery, New York, 61 & Heads, Berkeley Art Ctr, 68; Drawing & Small Sculpture, Ball State Teachers Col, 57, 58 & 62; West Coast Graphic Design, Am Inst Graphic Arts, 74; Santa Rosa Jr Col, 80; Ammo Gallery, Brooklyn, NY, 85; Festival by the Lake, Oakland, Calif, 87. *Collections Arranged:* David Anderson Sculpture, 72; Karen Breschi, Larry Fuente Sculpture, 73; Berkeley City Limits, 73; Water Works, 75; John Battenberg, Sculpture, 75; Fiber Space, 75; Joseph Rees, Neon-Argon, 75; Three Allegorical Painters: Jimenez, Pratchenko, Ross, 77; Barbara Spring, Wood Sculpture, 77; Berkeley Before 1950: Historical Photographs, 86- *Pos:* Cur, Long Beach Mus Art, 64-65, Berkeley Art Ctr, 69-78 & Berkeley Hist Soc, 85. *Awards:* Hon Mention, 50 paintings, Civic Arts Gallery, Walnut Creek, Calif, 69. *Mem:* Soc Indust Photogr (bd mem). *Media:* Acrylic, India

Ink. *Publ:* Illusr, New York Times, 59, Western J Surgery, Obstet & Gyn, 59, Africa Today, 61 & 62; illusr, Poems Read in the Spirit of Peace & Gladness, 66; San Francisco Earthquake, 68; photos, The Studio Potter, 84, Fine Woodworking, 86, 87 & 88, Am Crafts, 88, Woodwork, 90 & Macrobiotic Times, 90. *Mailing Add:* 2316 McGee Ave Berkeley CA 94703

SARKISIAN, PAUL
PAINTER
b Chicago, Ill, Aug 18, 28. *Study:* Art Inst Chicago; Otis Art Inst, Los Angeles; Mexico City Col. *Work:* Metrop Mus Art, New York; Corcoran Gallery Art, Washington, DC; Santa Barbara Mus, Calif; Chicago Art Inst; Milwaukee Art Ctr, Wis; Sheldon Mem Art Gallery, Lincoln, Nebr. *Exhib:* One-man exhibs, Corcoran Gallery Art, 69, Santa Barbara Mus, 70, Mus Contemp Art, Chicago, 72, Nancy Hoffman Gallery, New York, 78, 80 & 82 & Tomasulu Gallery, Cranfield, NJ, 84; Documenta, Ger, 72; San Francisco Mus, Calif, 76; Kunsthaus Zurich, 77; Nat Mus Fine Arts, Washington, DC, 79; Taft Mus, Cincinnati, Ohio, 83; Nancy Hoffman Gallery, New York, 82, 83 & 84; Columbus Mus Arts & Sci, Ga, 84; Castle Gallerry, Col New Rochelle, NY, 85. *Teaching:* Vis prof painting, Univ Calif, Los Angeles, 70, Univ Ore, Eugene, 71 & Univ S Fla, Tampa, 72. *Media:* Air Brush. *Mailing Add:* Tano Rd Box 252 Sante Fe NM 87501

SARNOFF, ARTHUR SARON
PAINTER, ILLUSTRATOR
b Brooklyn, NY, Dec 30, 12. *Study:* Indust Sch Art; Grand Cent Sch Art; also with Harvey Dunne; Kansas Univ, Hon Dr Art. *Work:* Bass Mus; Springfield Mus; Parrish Mus; Hartford Mus; Nat Art Mus Sport, New York. *Comn:* Fine art prints, Arthur Kaplan Co, Donald Art Co & Cataldi Fine Prints; portraits Pres Kennedy, Bob Hope and others. *Exhib:* Int Art Galleries; Continental Art Galleries; Sports in Action, Grand Cent Art Galleries; Nat Acad Art; De Ligny Gallery; Zantman Gallery; Findley Gallery. *Teaching:* Instr Boca Raton Mus Art, currently. *Awards:* Outdoor advert award, Art Dirs Club; Art League Nassau Award; Allied Artists Award; Allied Artists Awards, 90 & 91. *Mem:* Soc Illusrs; Allied Artists Am; Prof Art Guild. *Media:* Oil, Acrylic. *Publ:* Illusr, Saturday Evening Post, Colliers, Good Housekeeping, Cosmopolitan, Red Book, McCalls, Women's Home Companion, Ladies Home J and others. *Mailing Add:* 6462 Woodbury Rd Boca Raton FL 33433

SARNOFF, LOLO
SCULPTOR, COLLECTOR
b Frankfurt am Main, Ger, Jan 9, 16; US citizen. *Study:* Reimann Art Sch, Berlin, Ger, grad, 36. *Work:* Nat Acad Sci, Washington, DC; Nat Air & Space Mus, Washington, DC; Kennedy Ctr, Washington, DC; Corning Glass Ctr, Corning, NY; Federal Nat Mortgage Asn, Washington, DC. *Comn:* Flame, Kennedy Ctr, 71; spiral galaxy, Nat Air & Space Mus, Washington, DC, 78; Nat Inst for Music Theatre, 86. *Exhib:* One-person shows, Agra Gallery, Washington, DC, 68, Corning Mus Glass, NY, 70 & Franz Bader Gallery, Washington, DC, 76, Galerie Les Hirondelles, Geneva, Switz, 88 & Watergate South, Washington, DC, 90; Franz Bader Gallery, 76; Gallery von Bartha, Basel, 78 & 82; Gallery K, Washington, DC, 82; Pfalzgalerie, Kaiserslautern, WGer, 85; Int Sculpture Cong, Washington, DC, 90; and others. *Awards:* Gold Medal, Accademia Italia Arti Lavoro. *Mem:* Artists Equity Asn; Am Artists. *Media:* Acrylic, Fiberoptics. *Collection:* Nineteenth and twentieth century drawings, paintings and sculptures; 18th century Fayence; Chinese porcelain and snuff bottles. *Dealer:* Gallery K 2010 R St NW Washington DC 20036. *Mailing Add:* 7507 Hampden Lane Bethesda MD 20814

SARSONY, ROBERT
PAINTER, PRINTMAKER
b Easton, Pa, Jan 1, 38. *Work:* Butler Inst Am Art, Youngstown, Ohio; NJ State Mus, Trenton; Joslyn Art Mus, Omaha, Nebr; Nat Mus Am Art, Smithsonian Inst, Washington, DC; Univ Kans Mus Art, Lawrence; and others. *Exhib:* Allied Artist Show, New York, 63-65; one-man shows, Capricorn Galleries, Bethesda, Md, 67-78; Christopher Gallery, New York, 78-80; Meinhard Galleries, Houston, Tex, 82-83; Harris Gallery, Dallas, Tex, 85-87; and others. *Bibliog:* John S Le Maire (auth), Robert Sarsony, NJ Bus Mag, 69; Philip Desind (auth), article, Southwest Art, 4/80; Dennis Wepman (auth), article, Sunstorm Arts Mag, fall 91. *Media:* Oil, Watercolor; Serigraph, Lithography. *Dealer:* Wally Findlay Galleries New York NY Chicago IL Palm Beach FL. *Mailing Add:* 60 Gristmill Rd Randolph NJ 07869

SARU, GEORGE
PAINTER, MURALIST
b Checea-Timis, Romania, Mar 1, 20. *Study:* Acad Fine Arts, Jassy, Romania, BA, 44; Acad Fine Arts, Bucharest, Romania, MFA, 48; Academia Di Belle Arti Pietro Vannucci, Perugia, Italy, 63; Order Cult Merit, Bucharest, Romania, Laureate, 68. *Work:* Hermitage Mus, Leningrad, USSR; Mus Fine Arts, Bucharest, Romania; Mus Mod Art, Galati, Romania; Art Mus, Jassy, Romania; Arts Mus, Timisoara, Romania. *Comn:* Monumenta public square, comn Ministry Cult, Jassy Romania, 64; monumental public square, comn Ministry Cult, Suceava, Romania, 66; monumental mosaic, comn Ministry Culture, Tecuci, Romania, 70; mural mosaic, comn Ministry Cult, Bucharest, Romania, 76; monumental tapestry, comn Ministry Cult, Bucharest, Romania, 76. *Exhib:* Biennale di Venezia, Italy, 54 & 56; Exposition D'Art au Mus Nat d'Art Moderne, Paris, France, 61; Exposition Int, Mus Mod Art, Sczecin, Poland, 65 & 75; Triennial Exhib of Realistic Painting, Mus Art, Sofia, Bulgaria, 76; Mus Fine Arts, Bucharest, Romania, 77. *Teaching:* Prof, painting, Acad Fine Arts, Bucharest, Romania, 48-83. *Awards:* Laureate of the State Prize, Ministry Culture, Romania, 51; Inter Award, World Youth Festival, 53; Gold Medal, Triennial Exhib Realist Painting, 76. *Bibliog:* Rene Huyghe (auth), L'Art et l'Homme, Paris, 61; Bernard Dorival (auth), Peintres Contemporains, Mazenod, Paris, 64; Dan Grigorescu (auth), George Saru (monogr), Editura Meridiane, 83. *Mem:* Fine Arts Guild, Romania; Nat Asn Fine Arts, Unesco; Int Asn Fine Arts. *Media:* Acrylic, Oil; All Media. *Publ:* Auth, articles in Arta (Bucharest), Art News, Art in Am & Artspeak. *Dealer:* Carmen Morin Miller Galleries 119 W 57th Street 805 New York NY 10019. *Mailing Add:* 43-39 39 Place Apt 36 Sunnyside NY 11104

SASAKI, TOSHIO
SCULPTOR, ENVIRONMENTAL ARTIST
b Kyoto, Japan, Nov 24, 46. *Study:* Aichi Prefectual Univ Fine Art, BFA, 72; Brooklyn Mus Art Sch, 74. *Work:* Manhattan Psychiatric Ctr Sculpture Garden, Ward's Island, NY; NY Aquarium, Brooklyn, NY. *Comn:* Wall sculpture, comn by New York City. *Exhib:* Japanese Artist in Brooklyn, Brooklyn Mus, 75; Drawing in Lead, Storefront for Art Archit, New York, 82; Modern Mythology, Fordham Univ, 85; South Beach III, S Beach Psychiatric Ctr, Staten Island, NY, 86; Transculture Transmedia, Exit Art Mus, New York, 86; In the Making, Sculpture Ctr, New York, 88; Crossed Cultures, Rotunda Gallery, Brooklyn, NY, 89; Metaphysical Vistas, Cleveland State Univ, Ohio, 91; solo exhibs, 112 Workshop Inc, New York, 78, Storefront Art & Architecture, New York, 82. *Awards:* CAPS grant, NY State Coun Arts, 79; Visual Artist fel, Nat Endowment Arts, 86. *Bibliog:* Japan art at War Memorial, Daily News, 11/8/89; Asian influence on the Brooklyn art scene, Phoenix, 11/30/89; Metaphysical vistas, a real challenge at CSU, Plain Dealer, 4/13/91. *Mem:* Int Sculpture Ctr. *Mailing Add:* 788A Union St Brooklyn NY 11215

SASSONE, MARCO
PAINTER, PRINTMAKER
b Florence, Italy, July 27, 42. *Study:* Ist Galileo Galilei, Florence; Acad Fine Arts, with Silvio Loffredo, Florence. *Work:* Los Angeles Co Mus Art; Nat Art Gallery, Wellington, NZ; Galleria d'Arte Int, Florence; Hunt-Wesson; Laguna Art Mus, Calif. *Comn:* Nat Acad Design, New York, 77; Laguna Art Mus, Calif, 79; Munic Art Gallery, Los Angeles, Calif, 88; Los Angeles Contemp Exhib (LACE), Calif, 92. *Exhib:* One-man shows, Wally Findlay Galleries, Beverly Hills & New York, 77-79, Wally Findlay Galleries, Beverly Hills, Calif, 82, Bernheim-Jeune, Paris, France, 88, Diane Nelson Gallery, Laguna Beach, Calif, 87, Buschlen-Mowatt Gallery, Vancouver, Can, 90 & Ital Cul Inst, San Francisco, Calif, 89 & 91. *Pos:* Lectr-guest artist, Bowers Mus, Santa Ana, Calif, 70, San Bernardino Mus Art, Calif, 78, Laguna Beach Mus Art, 78, Orange Coast Col, Costa Mesa, Calif, 78, Leonardo da Vinci Soc, Univ Calif, San Francisco, 87 & Kern Co Art Educ Asn, Bakersfield, Calif, 79. *Awards:* Gold Medal, Ital Acad Arts, Lit & Sci, 78; Off Knight, Ital Repub, 82. *Bibliog:* Phyllis Barton (auth), monogr, 10/73 & Donelson F Hoopes (auth), monogr, 79, Arti Grafiche Il Torchio, Florence, Italy; John Wilson (producer), Sassone (film), Fine Arts Films Inc, 76. *Media:* Oil; Watercolors. *Publ:* Auth, William Wilson, Los Angeles Times, 11/14/75; Sassone's personal renaissance, Southwest Art, Houston, Tex, 11/75; Sassone Serigraphs, Arti Grafiche, Florence, Italy, 9/84; Janet Dominik (auth), Sassone (catalog), Bernheim-Jeune, Paris, France, 88; Peter Clothier (auth), Sassone (catalog), Ital Cult Inst, San Francisco, Calif, 91. *Mailing Add:* 2140 Bush St San Francisco CA 94115

SATO, MASAAKI
PAINTER
b Kofu, Japan, Feb 28, 41. *Study:* Kofu Saito Fine Arts Inst, Japan; Heatherley Sch Fine Arts, London, Eng; Brooklyn Mus Art Sch, NY; Pratt Inst. *Work:* Aldrich Mus Contemp Art, Ridgefield, Conn; Mus Honolulu Acad Art; Minn Mus Art, Minneapolis; ETenn State Univ; Mus Mod Art, La Tertulia, Cali, Columbia; and others. *Exhib:* One-man shows, Brooklyn Mus Little Gallery, 73, Soho Ctr Visual Artists, New York, 76 & Edward Williams Col, NJ, 77; Yamanashi Prefectural Mus, Japan, 79; OK Harris West Gallery, Scottsdale, Ariz, 82; OK Harris Works of Art, New York, 85; and many others. *Bibliog:* Richard Walker (auth), Gallery reviews, Art Rev, 8/31/68; Arthur Bloomfield (auth), An artist of many styles, San Francisco Examiner, 9/24/73; Malcolm Preston (auth), Westbeth connection, Newsday, 7/31/75; John Canaday (auth), It's spring in Connecticut and new talent blooms, 5/9/76; Michael Brenson (auth), Off the beaten paths at city treasure houses, 1/13/84 & Michael Brenson (auth), Weekend reviews, 6/21/85, New York Times. *Mem:* Contemp Artists Orgn; Am Soc Contemp Artists. *Media:* Acrylic, Oil. *Dealer:* Wenger Galleries 5721 La Jolla Blvd La Jolla CA 92037; OK Harris 383 W Broadway New York NY 10012. *Mailing Add:* Studio A-931 463 West St New York NY 10014

SATO, NORIE
VIDEO ARTIST
b Sendai, Japan, July 19, 49. *Study:* Univ Mich, BFA, 71; Univ Wash, MFA, 74. *Work:* Brooklyn Mus; Philadelphia Mus Art; Seattle Art Mus; Guggenheim Mus. *Comn:* King County Courthouse, Wash, 85; IBM, Gaithersburg, MD, 87; Clark Col, Vancouver, Wash, 88; Phase 1, Denver Int Airport, 90. *Exhib:* Thirty Yrs Am Printmaking, 76 & Eight West Coast Printmakers, Brooklyn Mus, 78; 5th Int Brit Print Biennale, Bradford, Eng, 76; Northwest '77, Seattle Art Mus, 77; Proj Video XXIV, Mus Mod Art, New York, 79; Lande, Ritchie & Sato, Vancouver Art Gallery, BC, 79; Videoviewpoints, Mus Mod Art, New York, 80; 19 Artists-Emergent Americans, Guggenheim Mus, 81; solo shows, Linda Farris Gallery, 81, 82, 83, 86, 87 & 90; 13th & 15th Northwest Film-Video Festival, Portland Art Mus, 85; Seattle Art Mus, 84; Reed Col, 87; 15th Ave Studio II, Henry Art Gallery, Seattle, 87; Home Show, Santa Barbara Contemp Arts Forum, 88. *Teaching:* Cornish Col, Seattle, 84-87; Western Wash Univ, Bellingham, fall 89. *Awards:* Nat Endowment Arts Fel, 78 & 81; Wash State Arts Comt, 90. *Mem:* COCA, Seattle; 9-H, Seattle; WESTAF, Santa Fe, (bd mem). *Media:* Electronic, Mixed. *Dealer:* Linda Farris Gallery 322 Second Ave S Seattle WA 98104. *Mailing Add:* 619 Western Ave Box 14 Seattle WA 98104

SATO, TADASHI
PAINTER, DESIGNER
b Maui, Hawaii, Feb 6, 23. *Study:* Honolulu Sch Art; Brooklyn Mus Art Sch; New Sch Social Res, New York; also with Ralston Crawford, Stuart Davis, John Ferren & Wilson Stamper. *Work:* Albright-Knox Art Gallery, Buffalo, NY; Guggenheim Mus & Whitney Mus Am Art, New York; Honolulu Acad Arts, Hawaii; Univ Art Gallery, Tucson, Ariz. *Comn:* Concrete relief wall & oil mural , State Libr, Kahului, Maui, 63; mosaic floor design, Hawaii State Capitol Bldg, Honolulu, 69; mosaic mural, West Maui Mem Gym, Maui, 72; ceramic floor mural, Tsunami Mem, Hilo; oil mural, Kapalua Bay Club, Maui, 80 & Halekulani Hotel, Waikiki, 85. *Exhib:* 52 Young Painters of America, Guggenheim Mus, 54; Pacific Heritage Exhibit, Los Angeles, Calif, 63; Four Contemporary Painters, McRoberts & Tunnard Ltd, London, 64; White House Festival of Arts, White House, Washington, DC, 65; American Paintings in Berlin Art Festival, Ger, 67; one-man shows, Seattle, Wash, New York & Honolulu. *Awards:* John Hay Whitney Found Opportunity Fel, 53; McInerny Found Honolulu Community Fel, 55; Best Painting in Show, Honolulu Acad Arts, 57. *Mem:* Hawaii Painters & Sculptors League. *Media:* Oil. *Mailing Add:* 1600 Kuuipo St PO Box 476 Lahaina HI 96761

SATORSKY, CYRIL
PRINTMAKER, ILLUSTRATOR
b London, Eng. *Study:* Leeds Col Art, nat dipl design; Royal Col Art, Royal scholar, traveling scholar, res scholar, ARCA & first class hon degree. *Work:* Cincinnati Art Mus; Wooster Col; Essex Community Col. *Exhib:* Philadelphia Print Club Ann; Rental Gallery, Baltimore Mus, 70; Sixth Dulin Nat Print Show, Knoxville, Tenn, 70; one-man show, Gallery Four, Alexandria, Va, 74 & Grimaldo Gallery, Baltimore, 78. *Pos:* Adv to univ publ, Univ Tex, Austin, 62-65. *Teaching:* Prof illus & printmaking, Md Inst Col Art, 65- *Publ:* Auth & illusr, A pride of Rabbis, Aquarius, 70; illusr, Frenchman & the Seven Deadly Sins, Scribners, 71; illusr, Sir Gawain & the Green Knight, Limited Ed Club, 72; Illusr, Country J. *Dealer:* Gallery K 2032 P St NW Washington DC 20036. *Mailing Add:* 5707 Berkeley Ave Baltimore MD 21215

SATTERFIELD, JOHN EDWARD
GOLDSMITH, EDUCATOR
b Clearwater, Fla, Sept 14, 31. *Study:* Univ Fla, BDesign; Univ Kans, MFA; study with Hekki Seppa, Earl Krentzin, Fred Feuster & Eleanor Moty. *Work:* Renwick Gallery; Mint Mus, Charlotte, NC; Gilchrist Mills, NC; E Carolina Univ, NC; and others. *Exhib:* Goldsmith 1974, Renwick Gallery, Washington, DC, 74; Southeastern Crafts Invitational, Greenville Co, SC, 75; Southeastern Ctr for Contemp Art, 78, 79 & 81-85; SNAG Europ exhib, 79-80; Southern Fedn Art traveling exhib, 79-82; Jewelry USA, Am Crafts Coun, NY, and traveling, 84-86. *Pos:* Art dir, Advertising Design Studio, Clearwater, Fla, 57-63; Peace Corps Vol arts & crafts develop, Peru, 63-65. *Teaching:* Prof design & metal, E Carolina Univ, 67-, assoc prof art, Univ Abroad Prog, Univ Nac Heredia, Costa Rica, 75- *Awards:* Mus Purchase, Mint Mus Art, 78; Kans Designer Craftsmen Exhib Award, Wichita, 83; NC Mus Hist Award, 83. *Bibliog:* American Craftsmen, John Satterfield (film), Cinemasonics Inc, 74; article, Goldsmith J, Vol 3, 12/77. *Mem:* Am Crafts Coun; Soc NAm Goldsmiths; Piedmont Craftsmen; Southeastern Ctr Contemp Art; and others. *Media:* Precious Metal. *Mailing Add:* Box 34 Rte 1 Greenville NC 27834

SATTLER, JILL
JEWELER, PAINTER
b New York, NY, Jan 3, 47. *Study:* Chouinard Art Inst, Los Angeles, 68 (with scholarship & honors), Univ Calif, Santa Barbara; pvt study as well as manuscript painting with student of Royal Scribe to Queen of Eng. *Work:* Pvt collections of Cher (worn during acceptance of Acad Award for Moonstruck), Diane English (writer, exec producer of Murphy Brown & featured in ELLE Mag). *Comn:* Many public & pvt comns. *Exhib:* Southern Calif assemblage, Past & Present, Contemp Arts Forum, Santa Barbara & Art Mus Santa Cruz Co; Peregrine Gallery, Montecito, Calif, 90-91; Spectrum Multi Cult Art Exhib, Antioch Univ, Santa Barbara, 90; Instore, Santa Barbara Contemp Arts Forum, 90-91; one-woman show, La Luz Blanca, Taos Art Festival, NMex, 90; C L Clark Galleries, Bakersfield, Calif, 91. *Bibliog:* Chouinard: An Art Vision Betrayed, Astra Publ Inc, 86; A Survey of the States Museums, Galleries and Artists, Calif Art Rev, 90 & A Survey of Leading American Contemporaries, 90, Am References Publ Co. *Publ:* Jewelry photos only in Elle Mag, Ladies Home J Memories Mag (front cover), Artspace Mag Scene, Los Angeles Times. *Mailing Add:* 924 C Garden St Santa Barbara CA 93101

SATUREN, BEN
PAINTER, PRINTMAKER
b Somerset, Pa, Dec 10, 48. *Study:* Iowa State Univ, BS, 70; NAUI Cert for Scuba diving, 81; Calif Col Art & Crafts, 84. *Work:* Chinese Med Acad Sci, Beijing, China & Shanghai Second Med Univ; Leigh Yawkey Woodson Art Mus, Wausau, Wis; Bell Mus Natural Hist, Minneapolis, Minn. *Comn:* Silkscreen seriagraph, comn by Dr William Bigler, San Francisco State Univ, Calif, 85; World Wildlife Fund/SAO Tome Cachets & Stamps, Comn by Intercontinental Philatelics, Inc, Southampton, NJ, 92; Marine Wildlife Poster, Comn by Nature Discovery Press, Hull, Mass, 90. *Exhib:* Pac Rim Wildlife Art, Snake Lake Nature Ctr, Tacoma, Wash, 88, 89, 90, 91 & 92; 9th Ann Wildlife Art, Vt Inst Sci, Woodstock, 88, 89, 90, 91 & 92; Mus Sci, Boston, Mass, 89-90; Birds in Art, Leigh Yawkey Woodson Art Mus, Wausau, Wis, 89; Art and the Animal, Roger Tory Peterson Inst, Jamestown, NY, 92; and others. *Awards:* Hon Mention, Calif Works 82, Calif State Fair, 82; Cash Award Winner, Artist's Liaison, 88; Third Place, Seascape, and Merit Awards, Wildlife Art Show, Los Angeles Audubon, 87. *Bibliog:* Colleen Francis (auth), Diving for Art, Calif Diving News, 88; Colleen Francis (auth), Below the Surface, Artist's Mag, 4/89; Colleen Francis (auth), Artist Vignette: Ben Saturen, Wildlife Art News, 3-4/90. *Mem:* Soc Animal Artists; Artists Guild San Francisco. *Media:* Oil; Silkscreen Serigraphy. *Publ:* Bay Area Naturalist, Marjorie Ruegg, 82; 1987 Artists' Profile, Wildlife Art News, 87, 89, 90; Profile of Wildlife Artists, Southwest Art, 88. *Dealer:* Saturen Studio PO Box 2151 Petaluma CA 94953. *Mailing Add:* PO Box 2151 Petaluma CA 94953

SATZ, JANET M
PAINTER, EDUCATOR
b Chicago, Ill, Apr 20, 33. *Study:* Pratt Inst, BFA, 74; NY Univ, MA, 77, Doctor of Arts fel, 77-79. *Work:* Smithsonian Inst; Gen Electric Corp & Fairfield Univ, Fairfield, Conn; Housatonic Col Mus Art, Bridgeport, Conn; Town Westport Collection Art, Conn. *Comn:* Wall mural, comn by Town of Norwalk, Conn, 78. *Exhib:* Chicago & Vicinity Ann, Art Inst Chicago, 69; one-person exhibs, Caravan Gallery, New York 73, Silvermine Guild Ctr Arts, New Canaan, Conn, 80, Henry Chauncey Conf Ctr, Princeton, NJ, 81, Stamford Mus, ART/EX Gallery, Conn, 87, Conn Gallery, Marlborough, 88; New Reflections, Aldrich Mus Contemp Art, Ridgefield, Conn, 77; 40th Art of Northeast USA, Silvermine Guild Ctr Arts, New Canaan, Conn, 89; Kansas Nine, 90 & Kansas Ten, 91, Mulvane Art Mus, Washburn Univ, Topeka; Greater Midwest International VI, Cent Mo State Univ, Warrensberg, 91. *Pos:* Branch Mgr, dir educ, Whitney Mus Am Art, Fairfield Co, Stamford, Conn, 81-89, educ consult, 89-90; Kans Arts Comn appointment, major grants panelist, prof develop panelist, 90-93. *Teaching:* Lectr & dir mus docent training, Whitney Mus Am Art, Stamford, Conn, 81-90. *Awards:* Winsor-Newton, Hudson River Ann, Yonkers, NY, 72; Bowater Inc Award for mixed media, 38th Art of Northeast USA, Silvermine Guild Ctr Arts, New Canaan, Conn, 87; Lithography Proj Grant, Kans Arts Comn, 91. *Bibliog:* J Burnham (auth), monograph, Arts Mag, 2/73; Jacqueline Moss (auth), Stamford Museum celebrates, The Advocate, 4/13/82; Vivien Raynor (auth), Contemporary Solo Shows in Hartford and Marlborough, NY Times, 1/24/88. *Mem:* Westport/Weston Arts Coun, Conn; Visual Artists & Galleries Asn, NY; Artist Equity, New York; Kans City Artists Coalition; Nat Art Educ Asn. *Media:* Acrylic, Mixed. *Mailing Add:* 3713 Quail Creek Ct Lawrence KS 66047

SAUER, JANE GOTTLIEB
CRAFTSMAN, SCULPTOR
b St Louis, Mo, Sept 16, 37. *Study:* Wash Univ, BFA, 59. *Work:* Wash Univ Steinberg Mus, St Louis, Mo; Erie Art Mus, Pa; Nordenfjeldske Kunstinndustrimuseum, Tronndheim, Norway; Wadsworth Atheneum, Hartford, Conn; Mus Suwa, Japan. *Exhib:* Solo exhib, Jane Sauer Currents, St Louis Art Mus, Mo, 88; Knots & Nets, Johnson Mus Art & tour, Ithaca, NY, 88-90; The Tactile Vessel, Am Craft Mus & thru US, New York, 88-91; Crafts Today USA, Mus Eastern & Western Europe & Russia, 89- 91; Meeting Ground: Basket Traditions & Sculptural Forms, First Street Forum & Ariz State Univ Art Mus, St Louis, Mo, 90. *Pos:* Lectr, various univs & orgns, US, 77- *Awards:* Visual Artists Grant, Nat Endowment Arts, 84 & 90; Biennial Visual Artist Grant, Mo Arts Coun, 88. *Bibliog:* Crissa Falconer (auth), Knots in her life, Fiberarts, 5-6/86; Patricia Degener (auth), Emotive basketry, Am Craft, 8-9/88; M J Van Deventer (auth), Jane Sauer, Art Gallery Int, 6/89. *Mem:* Craft Alliance; Am Craft Coun (bd trustees, 92-); St Louis Artist Coalition (bd trustees, 84-86); Forum Contemp Art, St Louis, Mo (bd dir, 90-). *Media:* Structured fiber. *Dealer:* Okun Gallery 301 N Guadalupe Santa Fe NM 87501; Elliot Smith Contemp Art 4727 McPherson St Louis MO 63108. *Mailing Add:* 6332 Wydown Blvd St Louis MO 63105

SAUL, PETER
PAINTER
b San Francisco, Calif, Aug 16, 34. *Study:* Stanford Univ; Calif Sch Fine Arts, 50-52; Wash Univ, with Fred Conway, BFA, 56. *Work:* Art Inst Chicago; Whitney Mus Am Art, New York; Mus Mod Art, New York; Univ Mass. *Exhib:* One-man exhibs, Frumkin & Struve, Chicago, 84, Rena Bransten Gallery, San Francisco, 86, Allan Frumkin Gallery, New York & Chicago, 87, Tex Gallery, 87 & 90, Frumkin/Adams Gallery, New York, 89-90, Galerie Thomas R Monahan, Chicago 90 & Galerie Du Ctr, Paris, 91; Pop Apocalypse, Gracie Mansion Gallery, New York, 88; Unknown Secrets: Art and the Rosenberg Era (with catalog), Hillwood Art Gallery, Long Island Univ-C W Post, 88; Reagan: American Icon, traveling exhib (with catalog), Bucknell Univ, Lewisburg, Pa, 89; Art on Paper, Weatherspoon Art Gallery, Univ NC, Greensboro, 89; Retrospective exhib, Aspen Art Mus, Colo, Mus Contemp Art, Chicago, Laguna Gloria Art Mus, Austin, Tex, Contemp Arts Ctr, New Orleans, 89-90; Calif A to Z and Return, Butler Inst, Youngstown Ohio, 90; American Art Today: The City, Fla Int Art Mus, Miami, 90; Word as Image: American Art 1960-1990, traveling exhib (with catalog), Okla City Mus, Contemp Arts Mus, Houston, 90; Drawings, Tex Gallery, Houston, 90; and many others. *Awards:* New Talent Award, Art in Am Mag, 62; William & Norma Copley Found Grant, 62; Nat Endowment Arts Grant, 80. *Mailing Add:* c/o Frumkin/Adams Gallery 50 W 57th St New York NY 10019

SAULS, FREDERICK INABINETTE
SCULPTOR, PAINTER
b Seattle, Wash, Mar 22, 34. *Study:* Stanford Univ, BA; Calif Col Arts & Crafts, MFA Prog; Univ Calif, MA. *Work:* Mus Mod Art, Skopje, Yugoslavia; Ithaca Mus Art, Cornell Univ, NY; Univ Calif Mus; Picker Art Gallery, Colgate Univ, Hamilton, NY; Univ Minn Mus Art. *Exhib:* San Francisco Mus Mod Art Ann, Calif, 60-63; Paris Biennale, Paris Mus Mod Art, 64; Sauls Sculpture, Univ Ky Mus, 66; Sauls Graphics, Univ Minn Mus, 67; UNESCO Int traveling exhib mod art, 68. *Teaching:* Assoc sculpture, Univ Calif, Berkeley, 63-64; vis artist sculpture, Univ Ky, 65-67; asst prof sculpture, Univ

Minn, 68. *Awards:* Grand Prize, Am Sculptors, Paris Mus Mod Art, France, 63; Harry Lord Ford Grad Prize, Univ Calif, 65. *Media:* Bronze, Aluminum. *Mailing Add:* c/o R Mutt Gallery 6161 Santa Monica Blvd Suite 100 Los Angeles CA 90038

SAULSON, HAROLD
PAINTER
b New York, NY, Dec 10, 53. *Study:* Bard Col, BFA, 76. *Exhib:* Ann Plumb Gallery, New York. *Awards:* Nat Endowment Arts Grant, 87. *Mailing Add:* 73 Leonard St New York NY 10013

SAUNDERS, EDITH DARIEL CHASE
PAINTER, INSTRUCTOR
b Waterville, Maine, Mar 19, 22. *Study:* Univ NC, Greensboro, with Robert Partin, Boris Margo, Gilbert Carpenter & Madam Sun To-Ze Hsu; John Brady Sch Art, Blowing Rock, NC; studied with Maria D'Annuzio in Florence, Italy & Leroy Neiman. *Work:* Wachovia Bank; Reynolds Tobacco; Southport Libr, NC; Hunt Mfg Co Collection; Westminster Presbyterian Church, Knoxville, Tenn. *Exhib:* Island Gallery, Manteo, NC; Contemp Graphic Artists (traveling exhib); Weatherspoon Art Gallery, Greensboro; Regional Gallery, Boone, NC; Assoc Artists of NC; Mint Mus Art, Charlotte, NC; and others. *Collections Arranged:* Arts Coun Gallery, Winston-Salem, 57, 62, 64, 65, 77 & 81; Southeastern Art Festival, Winston-Salem; Arts & Sci Mus, Statesville, NC; Herman Art Gallery, Statesville, NC; Contemp Graphic Artists (nat traveling exhib); Regional Gallery, Boone, NC; Hickory Mus of Art, NC; Greenville Art Gallery, NC; Caldwell Arts Coun, Lenoir, NC. *Pos:* Art chmn-coordr, Winston-Salem Women's Club, 60-61; columnist, Edy and Art (weekly), The Suburbanite, 74-76 & 77-78. *Teaching:* Inst privately in home, painting. *Awards:* Purchase Prizes, Northwest Art Exhib, Lowe's Collection, Lowe's Co, 62 & Southport Art Festival, City of Southport, NC, 63; Hunt Mfg Purchase Award, Watercolor Soc of NC, 75. *Mem:* Assoc Artists Winston-Salem; Watercolor Soc NC. *Media:* Acrylic, Watercolor. *Publ:* Artists of Florida vol II, Mountain Productions Tex, Inc; Artists of North Carolina vol I, Mountain Productions Tex, Inc. *Dealer:* Erl Originals 124 Fayette St Winston-Salem NC 27101. *Mailing Add:* 2250 Hilltop Dr Winston-Salem NC 27106

SAUNDERS, J BOYD
PRINTMAKER, EDUCATOR
b Memphis, Tenn, June 12, 37. *Study:* Memphis State Univ, BS; Univ Miss, MFA; Bottega Arte Grafica, Florence, Italy. *Work:* Denison Univ; SC State Collection, Mus Art, Columbia; Bottega Arte Grafica; Cent Art Acad, Beijing, China. *Comn:* Mixed media altar panel, Guess Chapel, Univ Church, Oxford, Miss, 62; mem portrait comn, Tipoff Club, Columbia, SC, 69; oil mural, Univ House, Univ SC, 72. *Exhib:* Soc Washington Printmakers 24th Nat, Smithsonian Inst, 62; First Int Printmaker's Exhib, Gallerie Bottega & Arte Grafica, Florence, 67; 34th Graphic Arts & Drawing Nat, Wichita, Kans, 69; Fifth Dulin Print & Drawing Competition Nat, Knoxville, Tenn, 70; 15th NDak Print & Drawing Ann, Grand Forks, 72. *Pos:* Staff artist, Dan Kilgo & Assocs, Tuscaloosa, Ala, 59-60; designer & illusr, Chaparral Press, Kyle, Tex, 63-65. *Teaching:* Instr art, Univ Miss, 61-62; instr art, Southwest Tex State Col, 62-65; prof art, Univ SC, 65- *Awards:* Third Prize, Sixth Ann Mid-South Exhib Paintings, Prints & Drawings, Memphis, Tenn, 61; Grand Prize, Guild Columbia Artists, 71; Purchase Prize, 15th NDak Ann Print & Drawing Competition, 72. *Bibliog:* Jack Morris (auth), Boyd Saunders, printmaker, Contemp Artists SC, 69; Beryl Dakers (producer), Boyd Saunders (video tape), WSCE-TV, 79; Gita Maritzer Smith (auth), The Storyteller's Art of Boyd Saunders, WLC Press, 84. *Mem:* Print Coun Am; Guild SC Artists; Columbia Art Asn; Southeastern Graphics Coun; Am Asn Univ Prof. *Publ:* Illusr, Bosque Territory: A History of an Agrarian Community, 64; illusr, Lyndon Baines Johnson: The Formative Years, 65; auth, A summer's printmaking in Florence, Art Educ J, 68. *Dealer:* Trans Designs Inc 1000 Transart Pkwy Woodstock GA 30188. *Mailing Add:* 533 Mallard Dr Chapin SC 29036

SAUNDERS, RAYMOND JENNINGS
PAINTER
b Pittsburgh, Pa, Oct 28, 34. *Study:* Pa Acad Fine Arts, nat scholastic scholar, 53-57; Univ Pa, nat scholastic scholar, 54-57; Carnegie Inst Technol, BFA, 60; Calif Col Arts & Crafts, MFA, 61. *Work:* Mus Mod Art, Whitney Mus Am Art, Andover Collection Am Art, Nat Inst Art & Lett, Metrop Mus Art, New York; Pa Acad Fine Arts; Seattle Art Mus, Wash; Addison Gallery Am Art, Andover, Mass; San Francisco Mus Mod Art; and others. *Comn:* Los Angeles Bicentennial Anniversary Poster Comn, 80; exhib poster, Hunsaker/Schlesinger Gallery, Los Angeles, 87; US Olympic poster, 84. *Exhib:* Mus Mod Art, New York, 68, 70, 72-73 & 74; Philadelphia Art Mus, Pa, 68, 72-73, 74 & 78; Afro-American Artists 1800-1969, Philadelphia Art Mus, Pa, 69; Thirty Contemporary Black Artists, San Francisco Mus Art, Calif, 69; Boston Mus Fine Art, Mass, 70; Metrop Mus, New York, 70; Card Design, Mus Mod Art, New York, 70; Whitney Mus Am Art, New York, 70, 74; Recent Acquisitions, Mus Mod Art, New York, 71; Contemporary Black Artists in America, Whitney Mus Am Art, New York, 71; one-man shows, San Francisco Mus Mod Art, Calif, 71, Seattle Art Mus, Wash, 81, Addison Gallery Am Art, Andover, Mass, 87 & 89, Pa Acad Fine Arts, Philadelphia, 90, Tampa Mus Art, Fla, 92, Stephen Wirtz Gallery, San Francisco, Calif, 93 & Galerie Resche, Paris, France, 93; Pa Acad Fine Arts, Philadelphia, 72-73, 74 & 78; San Francisco Mus Mod Art, Calif, 72-73 & 74; Whitney Biennale, Whitney Mus Am Art, New York, 72-73; Corcoran Gallery Art, Washington, DC, 74; Tweed Mus Art, Duluth, Minn, 74; Va Mus Fine Arts, Richmond, 74; Graffitti, San Francisco Mus Mod Art, Calif, 78; Paper on Paper, San Francisco Mus Mod Art, Calif, 79; Masterpieces from the Permanent Collection, San Francisco Mus Mod Art, Calif, 80; Resource/Reservoir: Collage and Assemblage, San Francisco Mus Mod Art, Calif, 82; Second Western State Exhib/The 38th Corcoran Biennial Exhib of Am Painting, Corcoran Gallery Art, Washington, DC, 83, Brooklyn Mus, New York, 84, Long Beach Mus, Calif, 84 & San Francisco Mus Mod Art, Calif, 84; Resource/Reservoir: CCAC 75 Years, San Francisco Mus Mod Art, Calif, 83; The Human Condition: SFMMA Biennial III, San Francisco Mus Mod Art, Calif, 84; Made in USA, Univ Art Mus, Berkeley, Calif, Traveling: Nelson-Atkins Mus Art, Kans, Mo & Va Mus Fine Art, Richmond, 87; The Appropriate Object, Albright-Knox Art Gallery, Buffalo, New York, 89; Present Tense, Univ Wis at Milwaukee, 92; Spirit Made Visible, John Natsoulas Gallery, Davis, Calif, 92; Drawings as Poems, Armory Ctr Arts, Pasadena, Calif, 92; and others. *Pos:* Nat consult urban affairs, Vol Teaching Serv, New York, 68; art consult, Dept Black Studies, Univ Calif, Berkeley, 69. *Teaching:* Prof painting, Calif State Univ, Hayward, 68-; Ais critic, RI Sch Design, 68, vis artist, 72; vis artist, Yale Univ, 72. *Awards:* Nat Inst Arts & Lett Award, 63; Guggenheim Award, 76; Nat Endowment Arts Award, 77 & 84; Visual Arts, Southeastern Ctr Contemp Art, 89. *Bibliog:* Rene Duer (auth), Raymond Saunders at Stephen Wirtz Gallery, Artweek, 6/6/91; Stephen Litt (auth), Using or abusing a powerful symbol?, Plain Dealer, 9/8/91; Bruce Nixon (auth), Expatriates: Paris connections at Bomani Gallery, Artweek, 2/13/92; and others. *Mem:* Fel Am Acad Rome. *Media:* All. *Publ:* Auth, Black is a color, pvt publ, 68. *Mailing Add:* c/o Stephen Wirtz Gallery 49 Geary 3rd Floor San Francisco CA 94108

SAUNDERS, RICHARD HENRY
MUSEUM DIRECTOR, HISTORIAN
b Rochester, NY, Aug 13, 49. *Study:* Bowdoin Col, BA, 70; Univ Del (Winterthur Prog), MA, 73; Yale Univ, MA, 76, PhD, 79. *Collections Arranged:* Daniel Wadsworth: Patron of Arts, Wadsworth Atheneum, 81; Celebrating Vermont: Myths and Realities, Middlebury Col, 92. *Pos:* Cur, Am paintings, Wadsworth Atheneum, Hartford, Conn, 78-81; dir, Christian A Johnson Mem Gallery, Middlebury Col, Vt, 85-91; Middlebury Col Mus Art, 92- *Teaching:* Lectr, art hist, Yale Univ, 77-88; asst prof art hist, Univ Tex, Austin, 81-85 & Middlebury Col, Vt, 85- *Awards:* Samuel H Kress Found Fel, Courtalld Inst, London, 76-77; Andrew Wyeth Fel, Yale Univ, 75-76. *Mem:* Col Art Asn; Nat Trust Hist Preservation. *Publ:* Coauth, American Colonial Portraits: 1700-1776, Smithsonian Inst, Ore, 87; auth, Collecting th West: The C R Smith Collection of Western American Art, Univ Tex Press, 88. *Mailing Add:* Middlebury College Christian A Johnson Memorial Gallery Middlebury VT 05753

SAUNDERS, WADE
SCULPTOR, CRITIC
b Berkeley, Calif, Sept 13, 49. *Study:* Wesleyan Univ, Conn, BA, 71; Univ Calif, San Diego, MFA, 74. *Work:* Corcoran Gallery Art; Baltimore Mus Art; Milwaukee Mus Art; Seattle Art Mus; Metrop Mus Art. *Exhib:* Solo exhibs, Newspace Gallery, Los Angeles, 77, 79, 81, 83 & 85, Charles Cowles Gallery, New York, 81 & 82, C Grimaldis Gallery, Baltimore, 83, 84 & 88, Lawrence Oliver, Philadelphia, 84 & 86, Diane Brown Gallery, 84, 85, 86 & 88; Charles Cowles Gallery, New York, 81 & 82; Lawrence Oliver Gallery, Philadelphia, Pa, 84 & 86; Betsy Rosenfield Gallery, Chicago, Ill, 90. *Teaching:* Asst prof, Tyler Sch Art, 78-82, Pa State Univ, 82-84; Assoc prof, RI Sch Design, 84-90. *Awards:* Penny McCall Foun, 87; Art Matters Inc, 87; Nat Endowment Arts, 88; Indo-Am Fel, 88; John Simon Guggenheim Fel, 89. *Bibliog:* David Tannous (auth), article, Art in Am, 10/80; Reagan Upshaw (auth), article, Art in Am, 6/82; Phyllis Derfner (auth), Art in Am, 11/85; Michael Brenson (auth), article, NY Times, 4/27/85; Nancy Princenthal (auth), Art in Am, 11/88. *Publ:* Auth, Art Inc, 79, Hot Metal, 80, Touch and Eye "50's" Sculpture, 82, Risk & Balance; Mark di Suvero, 83, Talking Objects, 85, At Critical Mass, 86, Art in Am. *Dealer:* Diane Brown Gallery 560 Broadway New York NY 10012. *Mailing Add:* 315 Berry St Seven North Brooklyn NY 11211-5112

SAVAGE, JERRY
PAINTER
b Chicago, Ill, Sept 2, 36. *Study:* Art Inst Chicago, BFA, 59; Univ Southern Calif, MFA, 62. *Work:* Kemper Collection, Longrove, Ill; Krannert Art Mus, Urbana, Ill; pvt collection, George Irwin, Quincy, Ill. *Exhib:* Solo exhibs, Allen Frumkin Gallery, 69, Zaks Gallery, 78, 81, 86 & 88, Chicago, Ball State Univ, Muncie, Ind, 87 & Gallery K, Washington, DC; Human Concern-Personal Torment, Whitney Mus Am Art, New York, 69; Extraordinary Realities, Whitney Mus Am Art, New York, 69; Illinois Artist '76 Traveling Exhib, Ill, 76; Contemporary Currents in American Art, Fung Ping Shun Mus, Hong Kong, 82; Illinois Artists, Nat Gallery Art, Kuala Lumpur, Malaysia, 83; Am Art, Bejing, China, 87; Kunstwerke Aus Papier, Hamburg, Ger, 87; Hamburg Media Serv, Hamburg, Ger, 88. *Teaching:* Prof painting, Univ Ill, Champaign, 62- *Awards:* Drawing Award, Los Angeles Co Mus, 61; Guggenheim Fel, 64-65; Ctr Advanced Study Assoc, Univ Ill, 74-75; Ford Found Grant, 75-76. *Bibliog:* Franz Schultz (auth), rev, Chicago Sun Times, 69; Dennis Adrian (auth), profile, Art Now-USA, 5/86; Daniel Reich (auth), rev, New Art Examiner, summer 86. *Media:* All Media. *Dealer:* Zaks Gallery 620 N Michigan Ave Chicago IL. *Mailing Add:* 209 W California Ave Urbana IL 61801

SAVAGE, NAOMI
PHOTOGRAPHER
b NJ, June 25, 27. *Study:* Bennington Col; and with Man Ray. *Work:* Mus Mod Art, New York; Fogg Mus, Boston; NJ State Mus; Univ Kans, Ill & Princeton. *Comn:* 8 x 50 ft wall of photo engravings, LBJ Presidential Libr, Austin, Tex, 72; 60 tennis photographs, Youth Tennis Found, Princeton, NJ,

73-74. *Exhib:* Always the Young Stranger, Mus Mod Art, New York, 53; Photography as Printmaking, Mus Mod Art, 68; Two Generations of Photographs-Man Ray & Naomi Savage, NJ State Mus, 68; Light & Lens-Methods of Photography, Hudson River Mus, Yonkers, NY, 73; Women of Photography, San Francisco Mus Art, 75; Photographic Disclosures, Squibb Gallery, Princeton, NJ, 82; one-man exhibs, Photographs, Noyes Mus, Oceanville, NJ, 83. *Awards:* Photography, Cassandra Found, 70; Nat Endowment Arts Grant, 71. *Bibliog:* Julia Scully (auth), Everchanging faces of Naomi Savage, NJ State Mus, 68; Contemporary Photographers, St Martins Press, NY, 82; N Rosenblum (auth), A World History of Photography, Abbeville Press, NY, 84. *Media:* Miscellaneous Media. *Dealer:* Witkin Gallery 415 W Broadway New York NY 10012. *Mailing Add:* 41 Drakes Corner Rd Princeton NJ 08540

SAVAGE, ROGER
PAINTER, PRINTMAKER
b Windsor, Ont, Sept 25, 41. *Study:* Mt Allison Univ, Sackville, NB, Can, BFA, 63; study with Alex Colville, Lawren Harris, Jr & E B Pulford. *Work:* Confederation Ctr Art Gallery & Mus, PEI; Art Gallery of Nova Scotia, Halifax; Can Coun Art Bank, Ottawa, Ont; Glenbow Mus, Calgary; Gotlands Kommun, Visby, Sweden; and others. *Comn:* Can $100 Gold Commemorative Coins, Royal Can Mint, Ottawa, 78 & 81; watercolors, Bowater Mersey Paper Co, 81; serigraphs, Halifax Sheraton Hotel, 85; etchings, Royal Bank of Canada, 89; drawings, Liverpool Int Theatre Festival, 92. *Exhib:* Art Gallery NS, Halifax, 79; FGK Galleri, Visby, Sweden, 81; Aschaffenburg, WGer, 81; Inst Cultura, Tunja, Colombia, 86; Watercolors from Crete, Soho Gallery, Halifax, 89; Aquarelles, Centre de Congres, Montreux, 90; Arctic in Palmengarten, Palmengarten, Frankfurt, 91; Gotlands Konst Mus, Visby, 92; Can Printmakers, Gallery 206, St Joseph, Man, 92. *Pos:* Vis artist, Art Gallery, Corner Brook, Nfld, 77, Summerside, PEI, 78 & Univ Moncton, 79, Arctic Awareness Prog, 91, Camp Otto Fiord, 92; Printworkshop BBK, Berlin, 88, 89, 90 & 91. *Teaching:* Instr, Annapolis Royal Community Arts Coun, NS, 86 & other self-conducted painting workshops. *Awards:* Can Coun Grants, 70 & 80; Brucebo Found Scholar, 80; Award, Province NS, 80; NS Skills Dev for Prof Artist, 89. *Bibliog:* Pat Laurette (auth), Roger Savage: A Survey, Art Gallery NS, 79; Elizabeth Jones (auth), Roger Savage: An intractable essence, Arts Atlantic, 3/81; Marilyn Vance (auth), Roger Savage: Artist, Visual Arts News, Vol 7, No 4, 85. *Mem:* Can Artists Representation; Visual Arts NS; Royal Can Acad Arts; The Pring Consortium; Vis-Art Copyright Inc. *Media:* Watercolor; Serigraphy. *Dealer:* Roger Savage 611 Mersey Point Rd Liverpool NS B0T 1K0. *Mailing Add:* 611 Mersey Point Rd, RR1 Liverpool NS B0T 1K0 Canada

SAVAS, JO-ANN
PAINTER, INSTRUCTOR
b Opelika, Ala, Jan 30, 34. *Study:* Auburn Univ, BS(art educ; Alpha Delta Pi Scholar). *Exhib:* New York World's Fair; Chateau de la Napole, Cannes, France; Southern Contemporaries Collection of Sears-Roebuck; Int Women's Show; Nat Women's Watercolor Exhib; and others. *Pos:* Tech illusr, Army Ballistic Missile Agency, Redstone Arsenal, Ala, 57-58; brochure designer, Huntsville Symphony Orchestra, 72-; dir art dept, Madison Acad, Huntsville, Ala, 74-77; chmn dept art, Stone Middle Sch. *Teaching:* Pvt art instr, Huntsville. *Mem:* Huntsville Art League & Mus Asn; Huntsville Art Educ Asn; Nat Asn Women Artists. *Media:* Multimedia. *Mailing Add:* 3506 May Dr SE Huntsville AL 35801

SAVENOR, BETTY CARMELL
PAINTER, PRINTMAKER
b Boston, Mass, Sept 2, 27. *Study:* Jackson von Ladau Sch Fashion; Mass Col Art; Brandeis Col, with Mitchel Siporin. *Work:* De Cordova Mus Corp Rental Gallery, Lincoln, Mass; Fairfield Med Asn, Vackerville, Calif; Bank Boston; First Capital Bank Concord, NH; New Eng Life Insurance Co; and others. *Comn:* Needlepoint design, Temple Sinai, Springfield, Mass, 88. *Exhib:* Boston Printmakers, Rose Art Mus, Waltham, Mass, 80; New Eng Watercolor, Fitchburg Art Mus, Mass, 86; RI Watercolor Soc Nat Exch, Tokyo, Japan, 87-88; Nat Asn Women Artists USA Centennial (traveling), New York, 88-89; Nat Asn Women Artist 100 Works (traveling), India, 89-90. *Teaching:* Instr in home studio. *Awards:* First Prize, Graphics & Best in Show, Cambridge Art Asn, 82; Best Contemp Painting, New Eng Watercolor Soc Open Exhib, 90; Cape Cod Art Asn Juror's Merit Award, 92. *Bibliog:* Mary Ann Wenninger (auth), Collograph Printing, Watson Guptil, 80. *Mem:* Nat Asn Am Penwomen; New Eng Watercolor Soc (secy, 85-); Depot Sq Artists (past pres); Copley Soc Boston; Monotype Guild New Eng. *Media:* Watercolor; Miscellaneous Media. *Dealer:* Art Three Manchester NH; Diane Levine Gallery MA. *Mailing Add:* PO Box 414 West Falmouth MA 02574-0414

SAVILLE, KEN
SCULPTOR, CRAFTSMAN
b Hanging Rock, WVa, Jan 9, 49. *Study:* Austin Peay State Univ, BS, 71. *Work:* Albuquerque Mus; Mus NMex, Santa Fe; Libr Cong; New Mus, New York; Univ Idaho. *Comn:* Sculpture, City of Albuquerque, one percent for the Arts Prog, 86. *Exhib:* Drawings USA, Minn Mus Art, 77; Artwords and Bookworks, Los Angeles Inst Contemp Art, 78; New Epiphanies, Gallery Contemp Art, Univ Colo, 82; Arteder, Muestra Int Arte Grafico, Bilboa, Spain, 82; Arts New Mexico, Gallery Contemp Art Latin Am, Washington, DC, 84; Mus NMex, 91; Roswell Mus, 91. *Pos:* NMex Arts Div Grants Awards Juror, 84. *Teaching:* Artist in residence, NMex Arts Div, 78-83, 88-91; Tex Comm Arts, 90. *Awards:* Jurors Award, Southwest Fine Arts Biennial, 76; Award Merit, Craftworks V, 83. *Bibliog:* Susan Zwinger (auth), Walking the edge of precipitous sacrilege: Ken Saville, Craftrange, summer 83; Michael Reed (auth), article, Artspace, summer 83; Sandy Ballatore (auth), New Mexico Sculptors, El Palacio, spring/summer 90. *Media:* Polychromed Wood; Colored Pencil. *Dealer:* Janus Gallery 225 Canyon Rd Santa Fe NM 87501. *Mailing Add:* Box 4662 Albuquerque NM 87196

SAVINAR, TAD
VIDEO ARTIST
b Portland, Ore, 1950. *Study:* Colo Col, BA. *Work:* Portland Art Mus, Ore; Mus Mod Art, New York; Nat Archives, Smithsonian Inst, Washington, DC; Chase Manhattan Bank, New York; J Berggruen, San Francisco, Calif. *Comn:* State Lands Bldg, Boise Cascade, Ore, 90; US Customs Off, Nat Endowments Arts, 90; Mentor Graphics Hdq, Ore, 90; Harborview Hosp, Seattle, Wash, 91-96; Westside Light Rail, Design Team, Portland, Ore, 92-97. *Exhib:* Solo exhibs, Los Angeles Inst Contemp Art, 83, Ctr Contemp Art, Seattle, Wash & Reed Col, Portland, Ore, 84, New Mus Contemp Art, New York, 85, Elizabeth Leach Gallery, Portland, Ore, 88, 89, 91 & 92; Artists Space, New York, 84; Greg Kuccra Gallery, Seattle, Wash, 85; CEPA, Buffalo, NY, 86; Baskerville-Watson Gallery, New York, 87; Portland Art Mus, Ore, 91. *Teaching:* Instr, Marylhurst Col, Ore, 79-86. *Awards:* Fel, Ore Arts Comn, 83; Fel & Grant, Nat Endowment Arts, 84; Grant, Metrop Arts Comn, 84, 86 & 87. *Publ:* Auth, The 4 Mickies, Artists Repertory Theatre, 88; Brushfires, Portland Civic Theater. *Dealer:* Elizabeth Leach Gallery 207 SW Pine St Portland OR 97204. *Mailing Add:* 2246 NW Pettygrove St Portland OR 97210

SAVITT, SAM
PAINTER, ILLUSTRATOR
b Wilkes-Barre, Pa. *Study:* Pratt Inst; Art Students League; drawing with Paul Brown, painting with Howard Trafton & John Vickery & sculpture with Seymour Lipton. *Work:* St Lawrence Univ, Canton, NY; Grumbacher Collection, New York; and pvt collections including William Randolph Hearst, Jr, Raymond Firestone, August Busch, Dr Jere Lord, Jr, George C Haas, Howard H Newman & Meriwether Hudson. *Comn:* Posters, Nat Horse Show, New York, 80, 89 & Lipizzaner Stallions, 82; polo poster, BMW, 86; Ky Derby, 91. *Exhib:* Int Sports Core, Oak Brook, Ill, 75; one-man shows, Piccolo Mondo, Palm Beach, Fla, 74, Gallery at Noroton, Darien, Conn, 81 & Northridge Gallery, Ridgefield, Conn; Am Acad Equine Artists, Morven Park, Leesburg, Va, 81; Soc Animal Artists, Acad Natural Sci, Philadelphia, 81; Bancroft Libr, Berkeley, Calif, 86; and others. *Pos:* Official artist, US Equestrian Team, 60- *Teaching:* Guest lectr horses in art, 55-; yearly workshop, drawing & painting, Scottsdale Artists' Sch, Scottsdale, Ariz; Am Acad Equine Art, Lexington, Ky. *Awards:* Jr Bk Award, Boys Clubs Am, 58; Literary Guild Award, 73. *Bibliog:* Anthony Amaral (auth), About cowboys and broncos, Ariz Hwy, 5/70; Nancy Boyce (auth), Sam Savitt speaks, Horse Play, 4/74; Annette Cummings (auth), Profile, Lead Line, 3/78; Felice Buckvar (auth), Animals fascinate artist, NY Times, 11/11/84; Nancy T Marr (auth), Savitt is a true aficionado, Chronicle of the House, 2/86; Equus Mag, 11/87. *Mem:* Soc Animal Artists; Soc Illusr; Graphic Artists Guild; Authors Guild; Am Acad Equine Art (dir, painting). *Media:* Mixed. *Publ:* Auth & illusr, Vicki and the Brown Mare, 76, Dingle Ridge Fox and Other Stories, 78 & One Horse, One Hundred Miles, One Day, 81, Dodd Mead Co; auth & illusr, Draw Horses with Sam Savitt, Viking Press, 81; auth, A Horse to Remember, Viking Press, 84. *Dealer:* Northridge Gallery 418 Main St Ridgefield CT 06877. *Mailing Add:* PO Box 302 North Salem NY 10560

SAVOY, CHYRL LENORE
SCULPTOR, EDUCATOR
b New Orleans, La, May 23, 44. *Study:* La State Univ, BA(art); Acad Fine Arts, Florence, with Gallo & Berti; diploma di Profitto, Universita degli Studi di Firenze, Florence; Wayne State Univ, MFA(sculpture); T H Harris Vocation Tech Sch, diploma (welding), 72. *Work:* Alexandria Mus Art, La; Couvent St Dominique de la Gloire de Dieu, Maison Mere des Dominicaines, Flavigny, France; Our Lady Star of the Sea, Cameron, La; Sixtus Vezie, Cath Mission, Willowvale, Transkie, SAfrica; Savoy Med Ctr, Mamou, La. *Comn:* St John the Baptist (sculpture design), Our Lady Star of the Sea, Cameron, La, 73; portrait, comn by F C Barksdale Assocs, Savoy Med Ctr, Mamou, La; Digi Hactus (sculpture), comn by Alexandria Mus Art, 91. *Exhib:* 14th Ann Delta Art Exhib, Arkansas Art Ctr, Little Rock, Ark; Sculpture Invitational, Closson 78 Gallery, Cincinnati, Ohio, 87; Galeria de Academia de Artes Plasticas, Monterrey, Mex, 87; New Orleans Contemp Art Ctr, 89; Alexandria Mus Art, 90; and others. *Teaching:* Asst prof fine arts, La State Univ, Shreveport, 73-77; asst prof sculpture & drawing, Univ Southwestern La, Lafayette, 78- *Awards:* Artists Biennial Exhib Artists Southeast & Texas, New Orleans Mus, 71; hon mentions, 13th Ann Piedmont Painting & Sculpture Exhib, Mint Mus Art, 73; Samuel Wiener Sculpture Award, 51st Regional Exhib, R S Barnwell Mem Garden & Art Ctr, 73. *Bibliog:* Les Krant (ed), American Artists: an illustrated survey of leading contemporary Americans, Krantz Co, 85; Virginia Watson-Jones (auth), Contemporary American Women Sculptors, Oryx Press, 86; Arthur Williams (auth), Sculpture: Technique-Form-Content, Davis Publ Inc. *Mem:* Artist's Alliance. *Media:* Wood, Metal. *Mailing Add:* PO Box 573 Youngsville LA 70592

SAWADA, IKUNE
PAINTER
b Japan, Aug 30, 36. *Study:* Kyoto Art Univ, BFA. *Work:* Seattle Art Mus; Art Gallery Gtr Victoria, BC; Brooklyn Col; Art Univ Kyoto. *Comn:* Mural, Puget Sound Mutual Savings Bank, Seattle, 75; King Co Bldg, Seattle, Wash, 76; Safeco Insurance Co, Seattle, 80. *Exhib:* Ann Exhib Northwest Artists, Seattle Art Mus, 71-75; Wash State Artmobile Exhib, 72; Ann Puget Sound Area Exhib, Charles & Emma Frye Art Mus, Seattle, 72 & 75; Nat Art Competition, Springfield Art Mus, Utah, 75; Asian Artist Exhib, Western

Wash State Col Mus, 75. *Teaching:* Teacher art & art hist, Pub High Sch, Japan, 60-65. *Awards:* Lulu Fairbanks Award, Found Int Understanding Through Students, 70; Second Place Award, Fed Way Arts Festival, Washington, 72; Honorable Mention Award, Ann Exhib Northwest Artists, Seattle Art Mus, 74. *Bibliog:* Natsuhiko Tsutsumi (auth), People in Seattle, Katei-Zenka, 75. *Media:* Oil, Watercolor. *Mailing Add:* Francine Seders Gallery 6701 Greenwood Ave N Seattle WA 98103

SAWAI, NOBORU
PRINTMAKER, EDUCATOR
b Takamatsu, Japan, Feb 18, 31; US citizen. *Study:* Augsburg Col, Minneapolis, BA, 66; Univ Minn, MFA, 69; Yoshida Hanga Acad, Tokyo, woodcut printmaking with Toshi Yoshida, 70. *Work:* Nat Gallery Can, Ottawa; Glenbow Mus, Calgary, Alta; Edmonton Art Gallery, Alta; Winnipeg Art Gallery, Man. *Comn:* Sculpture, Trinity Lutheran Congregation, Minneapolis, 67. *Exhib:* 38th Ann Exhib, Japan Printmakers Asn, Tokyo, 70; Can Nat Exhib, Toronto, 73; 1st Ann Nat Print Exhib, Los Angeles, 73; 2nd NH Int Graphics Ann, 74; 11th Int Biennial Graphic Art, Ljubljana, Yugoslavia, 75. *Teaching:* Instr printmaking, drawing & art hist, Berea Col, Ky, 70-71; asst prof printmaking, Univ Calgary, 71- *Awards:* Manisphere Award, Manisphere 10th Ann Show, 73; Purchase Award, London Mus, Ont, 74; Edition Award, Art Gallery Brant, Brantford, Ont, 75. *Bibliog:* Dennis Elliot (auth), 12th Annual Calgary Graphic Show, Arts Can Mag, 72; Ruth Weisberg (auth), Prints of wit and humor, W Coast Art Works, 5/4/74; Rino Boccaccini (auth), Noboru Sawai, Voce di Ferrara, 9/21/74. *Media:* Woodcuts, Etching. *Dealer:* Thomas Gallery 460 River Ave Winnipeg Man Can. *Mailing Add:* Dept Art Univ Calgary 2500 Univ Dr NW Calgary AB T2N 1N4 Canada

SAWKA, JAN A
PAINTER, PRINTMAKER
b Zabrze, Poland, Dec 10, 46. *Study:* Polytech Inst, MA, 72 & Art Acad, MA, 72, Wroclaw, Poland. *Work:* Mus Mod Art, New York; Centre Georges Pompidou, Paris, France; Stedelijk Mus, Amsterdam, Holland; Libr Cong, Washington, DC; Nat Mus, Warsaw, Poland. *Comn:* Grateful Deat-Stadium Sets, 89 & 93. *Exhib:* Solo shows, Wilanow Mus, 76 & Poster Mus, Warsaw, Poland, 80; Musee d'Art Moderne, Paris, 78; Smithsonian Tour Show, 79-80; Toyoma Mus, Japan, 85; Musee D'Affiche, Paris, 86. *Pos:* Resident artist, Pratt Manhattan Ctr, 82-86. *Awards:* Oscar De La Peinture Award, 7th Int Painting Festival, Cagnos-sur-Mar, France, 75; Gold Medal, 7th Int Poster Biennale, Warsaw, Poland, 78; Silver Medal, 14th Int Graphic Art Biennale, Brno, Czechoslovakia; Artist Laureate, 7th Int Poster Exhib, Ft Collins, Colo. *Bibliog:* Syzmon Bojko (auth), Jan Sawka, Graphics Mag, Zurich, Switz, 81; James Beck (auth), The conversation, Arts Mag, 83. *Media:* Acrylic, Mixed Media. *Publ:* A Book of Fiction, Clarkson N Potter, New York, 86. *Mailing Add:* c/o State Univ Col Col Art Gallery New Platz NY 12561

SAWYER, ALAN R
CONSULTANT
b Wakefield, Mass, June 18, 19. *Study:* Bates Col, BS, 41; Boston Mus Fine Arts Sch; Boston Univ, 47-48; Harvard Univ, MA(art hist), 49; Bates Col, Hon DFA, 69. *Collections Arranged:* Designer-Craftsmen USA, 54, Design in Scandinavia, 56, coordr of Midwest Designer-Craftsmen Exhib, 57 & installation of all primtive art exhibs, 52-59, Art Inst Chicago; installation of rug & textile exhibs, Textile Mus, 59-71. *Pos:* Cur primitive art, Tex Woman's Univ, 49-52; asst to cur decorative arts, Art Inst Chicago, 52-54, asst cur decorative arts in charge Early Americana & pre-Columbian art, 54-56, assoc cur in charge primitive art, 56-58, cur primitive art, 58-59; dir, Textile Mus, 59-71. *Teaching:* Instr art dept, Tex Women's Univ, 49-52; group discussion leader, Looking at Modern Art, Ford Found, Art Inst Chicago, 55-57; lectr, Pub Lect Prog, Univ Chicago-Art Inst Chicago, 59; adj prof art & archaeol, Columbia Univ, 68-69; lectr, Smithsonian Assocs, 71-73; prof art, Univ BC, 75- *Mem:* Archaeol Inst Am; Soc Am Archaeol; Inst Andean Studies. *Publ:* Auth, Handbook of the Nathan Cummings Collection of Ancient Peruvian Art, 54 & Animal Sculpture in Pre-Columbian Art, 57, Art Inst Chicago; auth, A group of early Nasca sculptures in the Whyte Collection, Archaeol Mag, 62; auth, Ancient Peruvian Ceramics, Metrop Mus Art, 66; auth, Ancient Peruvian Art, 68; plus numerous other articles & catalogs on Peruvian art. *Mailing Add:* 1799 W King Edward Vancouver BC V6J 2W1 Canada

SAWYER, CHARLES HENRY
MUSEUM DIRECTOR
b Andover, Mass, Oct 20, 06. *Study:* Yale Univ, AB; Harvard Law Sch & Harvard Grad Sch; Amherst Col, LHD; Univ NH, DFA; Clark Univ, LHD. *Pos:* Dir, Addison Gallery Am Art, Andover, Mass, 30-40, mem art comt, 40-55; dir, Worcester Mus Art, Mass, 40-47; mem Mass Art Comn, 43-45; trustee, Corning Mus Glass, 50-76; mem, Smithsonian Art Comn, 54-80; dir, Univ Mich Mus Art, 57-72; mem art gallery coun, Univ Notre Dame, 72-84. *Teaching:* Prof hist art, Sch Archit & Design, Yale Univ, 47-56; prof mus practice & hist art, Univ Mich, Ann Arbor, 57-75, prof emer, 76. *Mem:* Am Asn Mus; Asn Art Mus Dirs; Col Art Asn Am; Am Antiquarian Soc; Am Acad Arts & Sci. *Publ:* Auth, Art Education in English Public Schools, 37; auth, Report of Committee on Visual Arts at Harvard, 54-55; auth, Integration in the arts, 57 & The college art department and the work of art, 65, Col Art J; contribr, var art mags. *Mailing Add:* 2 Highland Lane Ann Arbor MI 48104

SAWYER, HELEN
PAINTER, WRITER
b Washington, DC. *Study:* Masters Sch, Dobbs Ferry; Nat Acad Design Sch, with Charles Hawthorne. *Work:* Whitney Mus Am Art; Pa Acad Fine Arts; Toledo Mus; Atlanta Mus; Indianapolis Mus. *Comn:* Paintings, Blue Ridge Spring, Chesapeake & Ohio RR, New York, First Nat City Bank & Circus Parade, G Lister Carlyle. *Exhib:* Carnegie Nat & Int, Pittsburgh; Am Painting Today, Metrop Mus Art; Century of Progress, Chicago; San Francisco World's Fair; New York World's Fair; and many others. *Teaching:* Instr, Art Students League, New York Farnsworth Sch Art, Cape Cod & Fla. *Awards:* Award for The Bareback Rider, Ringling Mus; First Hon Mention for Trees by the Turn, Art Inst Chicago; First Prize for landscape & still life, Atlanta Mus. *Bibliog:* Ernest Watson (auth), Helen Sawyer, Am Artist. *Mem:* Nat Acad Design; Fla Artists Group; Audubon Artists; Nat Asn Women Painters & Sculptors; Fel, Royal Acad. *Media:* Oil, Watercolor. *Res:* Material on life and work in Syracuse University Archives and Archives of American Art. *Publ:* Auth, Paintings in oils on paper, Am Artists; Living Among the Modern Primitives, Scribner; Peter Sawyer (auth), Master Mariner, Cape Cod Compass. *Dealer:* Corbino Gallery. *Mailing Add:* 3482 Flamingo Ave Sarasota FL 34242

SAWYER, JOHN R
CURATOR, LECTURER
b Chicago, Ill, Jan 6, 53. *Study:* State Univ NY, Purchase, BA(with honors), 80, Brown Univ, Providence, RI, MA, 83. *Collections Arranged:* Highway as Habitat: A Roy Stryker Documentation, 1943-1955, 87, Influence of Paul Klee on American Art, 88, Masters of Contemporary Art in Poland, 88, Photo League: 1936-1951, 88, 51st Annual Exhibition: Artists of Central New York, 89, Munson- Williams-Proctor Inst, NY. *Pos:* assist cur, St Louis Art Mus, 85-87; cur 20th century art, Munson-Williams-Proctor Inst, Utica, NY, 87-89; cur, Contemp Arts Center, Cincinnati, Ohio, 89-92. *Teaching:* Asst instr, RI Sch Design, 82-85; lectr, Wright State Univ, Dayton, Ohio, 92. *Awards:* Grant, Nat Endowment Humanities, 72. *Publ:* Contribr, All the Banners Wave: Art and War in the Romantic Era, 1792-1851, Brown Univ, Providence, RI, 82; auth, Currents 34: Mel Kendrick, St Louis Art Mus, 87; 50th Annual Exhibition: Artists of Central New York, Munson- Williams-Proctor Inst, 88; co-auth intro & contribr, One Hundred Masterpieces at the Munsun-Williams-Proctor Institute, Abrams, 89. *Mailing Add:* 1007 Kinmont Ave Cincinnati OH 45208

SAWYER, MARGO
SCULPTOR, PAINTER
b Washington, DC, May 6, 58. *Study:* Brighton Polytechnic Fac Art, Gt Britain, 76-77; Chelsea Sch Art, London, Hon BA, 77-80; Skowhegan Sch Painting & Sculpture, 80; Yale Univ, MFA, 80-82. *Work:* Leon Hess; Prudential Insurance; Chemical Bank; Samuel P Harn Mus Art, Univ Fla; Progressive Corp. *Comn:* Birdhouse Proj, Hong Ning Apts, New York, 86; set & costume design, Sharir Dancer Co, Austin, Tex, 92. *Exhib:* Sculptors Drawing, Yale A & A Gallery, New Haven, Conn, 81; solo exhibs, British Coun, Bombay, India, 83, Special projects, PS1, Long Island, NY, 89, Barbara Toll Fine Arts, New York, 89 & 91, Women & Their Work, Austin, Tex, 92; Borsisti Americani, Am Acad in Rome, Italy, 87; Sculptors Working, Socrates Sculpture Park, Long Island, 88-89; Fresh Ideas-Idiosyncratic Perspectives, Meyers-Bloom Gallery, Santa Monica, Calif, 89; 52nd, 90 & 53rd, 92, Art Fac Exhib, Archer M Huntington Art Gallery, Austin, Tex; Visions of Beauty, Baure House, Austin, Tex, 92; The Box, Silent Auction Women & Their Work, Austin, Tex, 92. *Awards:* Nat Endowment for Visual Arts, 86; Fel, A Acad in Rome, 86-87; Grant, New York State Coun for Arts, 87. *Bibliog:* John Robertson (auth), Artistic Faculties, Austin Chronicle, Vol X, No 14, 11/3/90; Lee Kelly (auth), Austin American Statesman, 5/14/92 & 6/20/92; Rebecca Levy (auth), The Artists' Eye, Austin Chronicle, Vol XI, No 41, 6/12/92. *Mailing Add:* Dept Art & Art Hist, Tex 23rd & San Jacinto Austin TX 78712

SAWYER, MARIA ARTEMIS PAPAGEORGE See Artemis, Maria (Maria Artemis Papageorge Sawyer)

SAWYER, WILLIAM
DEALER, COLLECTOR
b Lindsay, Okla, Feb 16, 20. *Pos:* Dir, William Sawyer Gallery, San Francisco, Calif. *Specialty:* Contemporary American painting, sculpture and graphics. *Collection:* Contemporary American and Mexican paintings, sculpture and graphics. *Mailing Add:* 3045 Clay St San Francisco CA 94115

SAXE, ADRIAN A
CERAMIST
b Glendale, Calif, 1943. *Study:* Chouinard Art Sch, 65-69; Calif Inst Arts, BFA, 74. *Work:* Everson Mus Art, Syracuse, NY; Los Angeles Co Mus Art, Calif; Mus Art, Carneige Inst, Pittsburg, Pa; Nelson-Atkins Mus Art, Kansas City, Mo; Renwick Gallery, Nat Collection Am Art, Smithsonian Inst, Washington, DC; plus many more. *Exhib:* Solo exhibs, Garth Clark Gallery, New York, 85, 87, 88 & 90 & Los Angeles, 85, The Am Hand, Washington, DC & Univ Mo Art Gallery Kansas City, 87 & 89; Contemp Ceramics, Muscarelle Mus Art, Col William & Mary, Williamsburg, Va, 86; Craft Today: Poetry of the physical, Am Craft Mus, New York, 86; Am Potters Today, Victoria & Albert Mus, London, 86; New Clay, Univ Art Gallery, Calif State Univ, San Bernardino, Calif, 86; Am Ceramics Now, Everson Mus, 87; Chinese Influence on Am W Coast Contemp Art, 88; Kansas City Collects, Nelson Atkins Mus, Mo, 89; American Clay Artists, Port Hist Mus, Philadelphia, 89, Vessels From Use to Symbol, Am Craft Mus, New York, 90. *Teaching:* Instr, Calif State Univ, Long Beach, 71-72; assoc prof art, Univ Calif, Los Angeles, 73- *Awards:* Fac Grant, Art Coun, Univ Calif, Los Angeles, 84; Artist Fel, Nat Endowment Arts, 86; US/France Exchange Fel, US Info Agency & Govt France, 87. *Bibliog:* Garth Clark (auth), Adrian Saxe: an interview, Am ceramics, Fall 82; Jan Axel & Karen McCready (auths), porcelain: Traditions and New Visions, Watson-Guptill, 81; Judith

Bettleheim, Pacific Connections, Am Crafts, 4/86; Barbara Mayer (auth), Contemporary American Craft Art: A Collector's Guide, Peregrine Smith Books, 88. *Mailing Add:* c/o Garth Clark Gallery 170 S La Brea Ave Los Angeles CA 90036

SAXE, HENRY, OC
SCULPTOR
b Montreal, Que, Sept 24, 37. *Study:* Ecole Des Beaux Arts, Montreal, 56-62; post grad studies with Albert Dumouchel, 61-62; studied in London, 68. *Work:* Nat Gallery Can; Montreal Mus Fine Arts; Musee Art Contemporain, Montreal; Musee de Quebec; Queens Univ, Ont; and others. *Exhib:* Agnes Etherington Art Ctr, Kingston, 74 & 83; Les Cents Jours, Montreal, 85; Aurora Borealis, Ctr Int d'Art Contemp, Montreal, 85; Olga Korper Gallery, Toronto, 85, 87, 89 & 92; 49th Parallel Gallery, New York, 89; and many others. *Awards:* Grants, 67-69 & Sr Awards, 73, 77, 81, 84, 87 & 91, Can Coun Arts; Order Can, 88. *Bibliog:* Jennifer Lynton (auth), Abstract Beauty in Sculpture, Queen's J, Kingston, 10/83; Elio Grazioll (auth), Aurora Borealis, Flash Art, No 124, Milan, 10/11/85. *Dealer:* Olga Korper Gallery Toronto; Gallery Esperanza Montreal. *Mailing Add:* PO Box 143 Tamworth ON K0K 3G0 Canada

SAYLES, EVA
PAINTER
b, June 10, 28. *Study:* Brooklyn Col, BA, 49; Art Students League, with Will Barnet, Burban & Palumbo, 60-62 & 84-86; Sch Visual Arts. *Exhib:* Greenwich Village Art Show, 61; Vera Lazuk Gallery, New York, 66; Marcolio Ltd, New York, 69; Pen & Brush Club, New York, 70; solo exhibs, St Bartholemew's Church, New York, 70, Pen & Brush Club, 71 & Amos Eno, New York, 92; Knickerbocker Artists; Queens Mus, 83. *Awards:* First Prize, Pen & Brush Club; Scholarships, Art Students League, 84 & 85. *Mem:* Nat Asn Women Artists (chairperson pub relations comt, 86-88). *Media:* Oil. *Dealer:* Amos Eno Art Gallery Soho New York NY. *Mailing Add:* Box 510 Port Chester NY 10573

SAYLORS, JO AN
SCULPTOR, PAINTER
b Lewisberg, Tenn, Apr 23, 32. *Study:* Scottsdale Artists Sch, studied with Edward Fraughton, 86. *Work:* Will Rogers Mus, Claremore, Okla; Collection of Pres Suharto, Jakarta, Indonesia; Territorial Mus, Guthrie, Okla; Am Petroleum Mus, Ponca City, Okla. *Comn:* World Trophy, Pewte Corp, Stillwater, 78; Stations of the Cross, Episcopal Church, Ponca City, 80; seal fountain, comn by Margo Kay Shorney, Oklahoma City, 82; life-sized bronze, Ponca City Libr, 88; Lady of Justice, Okla Found, 91. *Exhib:* Sculpture Today, Okla Mus Art, 78; Nat Sculpture Soc Ann Show, New York, 78; Am Royal Art Show, Am Royal Bldg, Kansas City, Mo, 81; Art Annual III & IV, Oklahoma City & Tulsa, 82-83; Nat Audubon Soc Invational, Tulsa, 83; N Am Sculpture Show, Golden, Colo, 84. *Awards:* Gallery Owners Award, Art Ann III, Oklahoma City, 82; First Prize for Sculpture, Nat Audubon Soc, 83; Merit Award, Int Western Wildlife Show, Okla Gallery Owners Asn, 85. *Bibliog:* Article, Southwest Art, 4/89, Vail Mag, winter 90; cover, Santa Faen, 12/89. *Media:* Bronze. *Dealer:* Driscol Galleries Denver Vail Beaver Creek. *Mailing Add:* c/o The Knox Galleries 555 17th St Denver CO 80202

SAYRE, ELEANOR AXSON
CURATOR
b Philadelphia, Pa, Mar 26, 16. *Study:* Bryn Mawr Col, AB, 38; Harvard Univ, 38-40. *Collections Arranged:* Rembrandt: Experimental Etcher, in collaboration with Morgan Library; Albrecht Duerer: Master Printmaker; Goya. *Pos:* Asst in exhibs, Yale Univ Art Gallery, 40-41; gallery asst, Lyman Allyn Mus, New London, Conn, 42; asst dept educ, RI Sch Design Mus, 42-45; asst cur prints & drawings, Mus Fine Arts, Boston, 45-67, cur, 67-. *Teaching:* Lectr, Harvard Univ & Radcliffe Col. *Awards:* Lazo de Dama of the Order of Isabel la Catolica, 75. *Mem:* Real Academia de Bellas Artes de San Fernando; Print Coun of Am; Hispanic Soc Am. *Publ:* Auth, A Christmas Book, 66; coauth, Rembrandt: Experimental Etcher, 69; auth, Late Caprichos of Goya, 71; coauth, Duerer: Master Printmaker, 71; auth, Goyas Spanian, Tiden och Historien, Nationalmuseum, Stockholm, Sweden, 80. *Mailing Add:* 23 Sibley Ct Cambridge MA 02138

SAZEGAR, MORTEZA
PAINTER
b Teheran, Iran, Nov 11, 33; US citizen. *Study:* Univ Tex, El Paso, BA, 55, BS, 56; Baylor Univ Col Med, 56-57; Cornell Univ, 58-59. *Work:* Whitney Mus Am Art, New York; San Francisco Mus Art; Corcoran Gallery Art, Washington, DC; Prudential Ins Co, Newark, NJ; Tehran Mus Contemp Art. *Exhib:* One-man shows, Poindexter Gallery, New York, 64-77; Art Inst Chicago, 65; Whitney Mus Am Art Ann, 69-70; Cleveland Mus Art, 72; Corcoran Gallery Art, 73. *Bibliog:* Donald B Goodall (auth), Color Forum, Univ Tex Art Mus, 72; Gene Baro (auth), The Way of Color, Corcoran Gallery Art, 73; Lucy R Lippard (auth), Intricate Structural Repeated Image, Tyler Sch Art, Temple Univ, Philadelphia, Pa, 79. *Media:* Acrylic, Watercolor. *Dealer:* Poindexter Gallery 1160 Fifth Ave New York NY 10029. *Mailing Add:* RR 1 Cochranville PA 19330

SCALA, JOSEPH (A)
PAINTER, EDUCATOR
b Queens, NY, Feb 20, 40. *Study:* C W Post Col, BS, 62; Cornell Univ, MFA(sculpture), 71. *Work:* Metrop Mus Art, New York; Herbert Johnson Mus, Ithaca, NY; Battelle Mem Inst, Acad Contemp Problems, Columbus, Ohio. *Comn:* Laser sculpture, Andrew Dickson White Mus, Ithaca, NY, 70; Sound/Light Sculpture, Rochester Jr League, 70; Cybernetic Fountain, Cornell Univ Physics Dept, 72. *Exhib:* Some More Beginnings, Brooklyn Mus, 68; Mirrors, Motors, Motion, Albright-Knox Gallery, Buffalo, NY, 70; one-person one-piece show, Everson Mus, Syracuse, NY, 72; Can Comput Show Art Exhib, Toronto, Ont, 75; one-man show, Westbroadway Gallery, New York, 76; Computers & Art, IBM Gallery, New York, NY & traveling, 87-88. *Collections Arranged:* Current-New York (auth, catalog), Syracuse Univ Lowe Art Gallery, 80; Tibor de Nagy Collection, Syracuse Univ Lubin House Gallery, 80; A Contemporary Art Collection: Clement Greenberg, Syracuse Univ. *Pos:* Pres & founder, Collaborations in Art, Sci & Technol Inc, 69-79; dir, Lowe Art Gallery, Syracuse Univ, 78-85, dir, Lubin House Gallery, 79-82. *Teaching:* Instr multi-media, Cornell Univ, 70 & 71; assoc prof art & technol, Syracuse Univ, 71-85, chairperson museology prog, 78-85, prof computer graphics & museolosy, 85-86, prof computer graphics art. *Awards:* Winner Young Sculptors Competition, Sculptors Guild, New York, 69; New York State Coun Arts Grants, 70-85; Inst Mus Serv, Nat Endowment Arts, 85-86. *Bibliog:* Milford Kime (auth), Laser art, Laser Focus, 73. *Mem:* Am Asn Univ Profs; Col Art Asn Am; Nat Comput Graphics Asn. *Media:* Acrylic; Computer. *Mailing Add:* 266 W Seneca Tpke Syracuse NY 13207

SCALISE, NICHOLAS PETER
PAINTER, SCULPTOR
b Meriden, Conn, June 4, 32. *Study:* Horace C Wilcox Tech Sch, Meriden; Paier Sch Art, New Haven, Conn. *Work:* Meriden World War II Mem Hosp, Meriden; Town Hall, Meriden, Conn. *Exhib:* Nat Art League, New York, 69; Butler Inst Am Art, Youngstown, Ohio, 69 & 87-88; Nat Soc Painters in Casein, New York, 70 & 91; Wadsworth Atheneum, Hartford, Conn, 72; Silvermine Exhib, Conn, 77 & 81; New England in Winter Watercolor Exhib, De Cordova Mus, Lincoln, Mass, 77 & 78; Addison Gallery Am Art, Phillips Acad, Andover, Mass, 81; Holyoke Mus, Mass; New Brit Mus, Conn. *Teaching:* Instr drawing & painting, Famous Artists Sch, Westport, Conn, 59-69. *Awards:* Meriden Hall of Fame, 87; Second Prize Watercolor, Susquehanna Art Soc, Pa, 92; Cert Merit Watercolor, Nat Acad Design, New York, 92; and many others. *Bibliog:* Articles, North Light Mag, 7-8/77 & Am Artist Mus, 7/78, Am Artist Diary, 11/80; article & cover, Palette Talk, 80. *Mem:* Springfield Acad Artist; Meriden Arts & Crafts, Conn; Conn Acad Fine Arts, Hartford; Conn Watercolor Soc, Hartford; Knickerbocker Artists, New York. *Media:* Oil, Watercolor. *Dealer:* Capricorn Gallery 4849 Rugby Ave Bethesda MD; Munson Gallery 653 Canyon Rd Santa Fe NM & Main St Chatham MA. *Mailing Add:* 59 Susan Lane Meriden CT 06450

SCARBROUGH, CLEVE KNOX, JR
MUSEUM DIRECTOR, HISTORIAN
b Florence, Ala, July 17, 39. *Study:* Univ NAla, BS, 62; Univ Iowa, MA, 67. *Collections Arranged:* Pre-Columbian Art of the Americas, 70, Graphics by Four Modern Swiss Sculptors, circulated by Smithsonian Traveling Serv, 72- & Completed Charlotte Museum of History, 76, Mint Mus Art, Charlotte, NC. *Pos:* Dir, Mint Mus Art, 69-76, Hunter Mus Art, Chattanooga, Tenn, 76-; mem visual arts adv panel, Tenn Arts Comn, 76, chmn comt, 77-81, rev comt, Art in Pub Places, 78. *Teaching:* Grad asst, Univ Iowa, 64-67; asst prof art hist, Univ Tenn, Knoxville, 67-69. *Mem:* NC Mus Coun (bd mem, 70-75); Southeastern Mus Assoc (bd mem & adv comt, 78-81 & 86-89); Chattanooga Cent City Coun (adv, 81-); Coun Am Asn Mus, 86-89; and others. *Publ:* Ed, North Carolinians Collect, 71; Graphics by Four Modern Swiss Sculptors, 72; British Painting from NC Museum of Art, 73; Mountain Landscapes by Swiss Artists, 75. *Mailing Add:* Hunter Mus Art 10 Bluff View Chattanooga TN 37403

SCARPA, DOROTHEA
PAINTER, EDUCATOR
b Brooklyn, NY, July 24, 26. *Study:* Art Students League, wood sculpture with Chaim Gross, 47-50. *Work:* East Stroudsburg Univ Collection. *Exhib:* East Stroudsburg Univ Exhibs, 79-86; Celebration of the Arts-Outdoors, Delaware Water Gap, Pa, 81-85; Lehigh Art Alliance Spring Shows, Muhlenburg Col, Allentown, 84; Spring Show, Hunterdon Art Ctr, Clinton, NJ, 88-89; and many others. *Pos:* Bd mem, Community Art Asn, East Stroudsburg Univ, 80-84, pres, 85 & vpres, 86- *Teaching:* Artist-in-residence, Dept Early Childhood & Elem Educ, E Stroudsburg Univ, 83-88, Pocono Mt, Elem Ctr, 87 & Family of Artist Prog, Stroudsburg, Pa, 88-91; Special Arts Festival, E Stroudsburg Univ, 88-90; Asst prog dir & Artist-in-Residence Penna Ctr of the Arts, Delaware, WaterGap, Pa, 91-92. *Awards:* Purchse Prize, 79 & Hon Mention, 82 & 84, Fall Show, East Stroudsburg Univ; First Prize Theme, Celebration of the Arts, Delaware Water Gap, 85. *Bibliog:* Karen Fisher (ed), Dorothea Scarpa, an artist after a challenge, Pocono Rec, Stroudsburg, Pa, 11/24/81. *Mem:* Hunterdon Art Ctr, Clinton, NJ. *Media:* Painting, Collage. *Publ:* Illusr, Museums & Other Resources in Education(MORE), East Stroudsburg Univ, 11/83. *Mailing Add:* Coolbaugh Road Box 4767 East Stroudsburg PA 18301

SCARPITTA, SALVATORE
SCULPTOR, PAINTER
b New York, NY, 1919. *Study:* Study in Italy, 36-40, Royal Acad, Rome, Italy. *Work:* Stedelijk Mus, Amsterdam, Holland; Albright-Knox Art Gallery, Buffalo, Mus Mod Art, New York; Los Angeles Co Mus Art; Nat Mus, Milan Italy; Tel-Aviv Mus, Israel; Mus Mod Art, New York. *Exhib:* 28th Corcoran Biennial, Corcoran Gallery Art, Washington, DC, 63; 67th Ann Exhib: Painting & Sculpture, Art Inst Chicago, 64; one-man shows, Studio Bonifacio, Genova, Italy, 86, Not Vital, Studio Guenzani, Milan, Italy, 88, Salvatore Scarpitta: Matrix (in cooperation with Leo Castelli), Univ Art Mus, Berkeley, Calif, 89, Sal Scarpitta (in cooperation with Leo Castelli), Scott Hanson Gallery, New York, 90, Sal Scarpitta: Race Car on Idaho Potato Track, Greenburg Wilson Gallery, New York, 90, Studio Guenzani, Milan, Italy, 90

& Galleria d'Arte Niccoli, Parma, Italy, 90-91; Pre/Pop Post-Appropriation, Stux Gallery, New York, 89; The Road Show, John Michael Kohler Arts Ctr, Sheboygan, Wis, 89; Buena Vista, John Gibson Gallery, New York, 89; All Quiet on the Western Front?, Espace Dieu, Paris, France, 90; and others. *Teaching:* Artist-in-residence, Md Inst, Col Art, 66- *Bibliog:* Harriet Janis & Rudi Blesh (auth), Collage, Personalities-Concepts-Techniques, Chilton, 62; Allen S Weller (auth), The Joys & Sorrows of Recent American Art, Univ Ill, 68; B H Friedman (auth), The ivory tower, Art News, 4/69. *Media:* All. *Mailing Add:* 307 E 84th St New York NY 21217

SCHAB, MARGO POLLINS
ART DEALER
b Cincinnati, Ohio, Aug 4, 45. *Pos:* Pres, Margo Pollins Schab, New York. *Specialty:* Important prints, drawings, paintings and sculpture of the 19th and 20th century. *Mailing Add:* 1000 Park Ave New York NY 10028

SCHABACKER, BETTY BARCHET
PAINTER
b Baltimore, Md, Aug 14, 25. *Study:* Conn Col Women; Marian Carey Art Asn, Newport, RI; Coronado Sch Art, Calif, with Monty Lewis; also with Gerd & Irene Koch, Ojai, Calif. *Work:* B K Smith Gallery, Lake Erie Col, Painesville, Ohio; First Nat Bank Pa, Erie; Western Union, New York; McGraw Edison, Columbia, Mo; Erie Zoo, Pa; and others. *Exhib:* Butler Inst Am Art Ann, 64-77; Audubon Artists, 67-79; Nat Watercolor Soc Ann, 79; 17 solo shows, Nat Acad Design; Acad Natural Sci, Philadelphia, 81-82; St John's Col, Santa Fe, NMex, 90; Soc Animal Artists Traveling Show, 91-92; and others. *Pos:* Artist-in-residence, Lake Erie Col, 71. *Awards:* Nancy Hubbard Lance Award, Lake Erie Col, 71; First Toastmaster, Ann Fine Art Series, 73; Second Award, Nature Interpreted, Cincinnati Mus Natural Hist, 80; and others. *Mem:* Nat Watercolor Soc; Audubon Artists; Soc Animal Artists. *Media:* Watercolor, Cloth Collage. *Dealer:* Lightside Gallery 225 Canyon Rd Santa Fe NM 87501. *Mailing Add:* 738 Camino Mirada Santa Fe NM 87501

SCHACHTER, JUSTINE RANSON
GRAPHIC ARTIST, ILLUSTRATOR
b Brooklyn, NY, Dec 18, 27. *Study:* Tyler Sch Fine Arts, Temple Univ, scholar; Brooklyn Mus Art Sch, with John Bindrum, Milton Hebald & John Ferren; Art Students League, with Will Barnett. *Work:* Bellmore Pub Libr, NY; Island Trees Pub Libr, Levittown, NY; Wantagh High Sch, NY. *Comn:* Poster, NY State Parent-Teacher Asn, 70-73. *Exhib:* One-woman show, Ruth White Gallery, 61; Nat Asn Women Artists Traveling Graphics Show, US & Europe, 69-70; Am Soc Contemp Artists, New York, 69-91; and others. *Pos:* Dir graphic arts, Audio-Visual Educ TV, Mineola Pub Sch, 64-65; exec dir, Art Forms Creative Ctr, 71-73; owner, The Artist's Studio Gallery, 74-; designer & partner, Justine & Ruth Cards, 85-; art dir, The Pink Pages, 85- *Teaching:* Artist in residence, Community Arts Prog, Wantagh High Sch, 72 & Syosset High Sch, 74. *Awards:* Award for graphics, Brooklyn Soc Artists Ann, 49; awards for mixed media, Nassau Co Off Cult Develop, 70 & Am Soc Contemp Artists, 71 & 75. *Bibliog:* Elyse Sommer (auth), Rock and Stone Craft, Crown, 72. *Mem:* Am Soc Contemp Artists (chmn admis, 68-71); Nat Asn Women Artists; Artists Equity Asn; Int Asn Arts. *Media:* Pen, Ink; Paper, Stone. *Publ:* Illusr, Long Island Free Press, 70-71; illusr, Make a Glad Sound, Consort Music, Inc, 74; illusr, You Can Play a Recorder, Music Minus One, illusr, Treasury of Stories, Waldman, 78. *Mailing Add:* 14 Trumpet Lane Levittown NY 11756

SCHACTMAN, BARRY ROBERT
PAINTER, EDUCATOR
b Newark, NJ, May 10, 30. *Study:* Univ of Miami; Art Students League; Rutgers Univ; Tyler Sch of Art of Temple Univ; Yale Univ Sch of Art, BFA, 58, MFA, 60, study with Josef Albers & Rico Lebrun. *Work:* Yale Univ Art Mus, New Haven, Conn; St Louis Univ, Mo; Mus of Israel, Jerusalem; Minn Mus Art, St Paul; Weatherspoon Art Gallery, Univ NC, Greensboro. *Exhib:* Drawing Soc National Traveling Exhib, Am Fedn Arts, 70-72; Drawing USA (nat traveling exhib), Minn Mus Art, St Paul, 71-73; Nat Invitational Drawing Exhib, Mitchell Gallery, Southern Ill Univ, Carbondale, 75; Drawing Mo 1976, Bicentennial Invitational Exhib (traveling exhib), Albrecht Art Mus, St Joseph, Mo, 76; 30th Ann Hassam Purchase Fund Exhib, Am Acad & Inst Arts & Lett, New York, 78. *Pos:* Assoc dean, Sch Fine Arts, Washington Univ, St Louis, Mo, 77-79. *Teaching:* Instr drawing & design, Univ Tex, Austin, 59-61; prof drawing & painting, Washington Univ, St Louis, Mo, 61- *Awards:* Purchase Prize, Drawing USA, Minn Mus Art, St Paul, 71; plus others. *Bibliog:* Gerald M Monroe (auth), Teaching drawing: The personal approach of Barry Schactman, Drawing Soc, 81 & Am Artist, 82; Bernard Chaet (auth), The Art of Drawing, Holt, Rinehart and Winston Inc, 83. *Media:* Pen and Ink, Charcoal; Oil. *Mailing Add:* 437 E Glendale Rd St Louis MO 63119

SCHAECHTER, JUDITH
STAINED GLASS ARTIST, PAINTER
b Gainsville, Fla, Feb 14, 61. *Study:* RI Sch Design, BFA(sculpture), 83. *Work:* Julie & Neil Courtney, Robert Ingersoll & John Wineman, Philadelphia, Pa; Corning Mus Glass, NY; Renwick Gallery, Nat Mus Am Art, Washington, DC. *Exhib:* Size Isn't Everything, Nexus Gallery, 87; solo exhibs, Beckoning Graves, Nexus Gallery, 88 & Challenge Show, Samuel S Fleisher Art Mem, Philadelphia, Pa, 90; Light, Momenta Gallery, Philadelphia, 88; Art Around the Edges, Port Hist Mus; Contemp Philadelphia Artists, Philadelphia Mus Art, Pa, 90; Renwick Gallery, Smithsonian Inst, 90; and others. *Teaching:* Artist-in-Residence, glass prog, RI Sch Design, 85 & guest lectr, glass prog, 88; guest lectr glass prog, Tyler Sch Art, Temple Univ, 88, RI Sch Design, 88-90 & Glass Art Soc Conf, Kent State, Ohio, 88; guest lectr painting dept, Univ Arts, 89 & sculpture dept, Moore Col Art, 89; panelist, New Art Forms Expos, Chicago, Ill, 91. *Awards:* Fels in Visual Arts, Nat Endowment Arts, 86 & 88; Louis Comfort Tiffany Found Award, 89; Pa Coun Arts Fel Grant, 91; and others. *Bibliog:* Jeanne Nugent (auth), Through the glass darkly, Scan Mag, 5/89; Maralyn Lois Polak (auth), Interview, Judith Schaechter: is her art a crime, Philadelphia Inquirer Sunday Mag, 1/20/90; Susanne K Frantz (auth), Conversation, Glass, spring/summer 90; and others. *Mem:* Found Today's Art, Nexus, 83- *Media:* Acrylic, Oil. *Dealer:* Snyderman Gallery. *Mailing Add:* 1532 Rodman St Philadelphia PA 19146

SCHAEFER, CARL FELLMAN
PAINTER
b Hanover, Ont, Apr 30, 03. *Study:* Ont Col Art, Toronto, with J E H MacDonald & Arthur Lismer; Cent Sch Arts & Crafts, London; Ont Col Art, Fel, 76; Univ Waterloo, Ont, Hon DLett, 76. *Work:* Nat Gallery Can; Art Gallery Ont; Art Gallery Hamilton; Art Gallery London; Va Mus Fine Arts, Richmond. *Comn:* Ser of paintings on prod, Can Packers, Ltd, Toronto, 42. *Exhib:* Century of Can Art, Tate Gallery, London, 38; 18th Int Art Inst Chicago, 39; 11th Int, Brooklyn Mus, 41; 1st Biennial, Sao Paulo Mus Arte Mod, 51; Retrospective 1926-1969, Sir George Williams Univ, Montreal, 69-70; Aviation Paintings, Can War Mus, Ottawa, 72; Can Paintings to People's Repub of China, 75; Can Paintings in the Thirties, Nat Gallery Can, 75; Ont Community Collects, Art Gallery Ont, Toronto, 75; Retrospective 1932-1967, Robert McLauglin Gallery, Oshawa, 76; Can Paintings in Univ Toronto, Art Gallery Ont, 77-78; Hanover Edmonton Art Gallery, 80; and many others. *Pos:* Off war artist, Europ Theatre Opers & Iceland, RCAF, 43-46. *Teaching:* Instr painting, Cent Tech Sch, Toronto, 30-40; dir art, Hart House, Univ Toronto, 34-40; instr & dir painting, Ont Col Art, 48-55, emer chmn dept drawing & painting, 68- *Awards:* Queen's Coronation Medal, Elizabeth II, 53 & Can Silver Jubilee Medal, 52-77 & 78; Mem, Order of Can, 78. *Bibliog:* Donald W Buchanan (auth), The Growth of Canadian Painting, Collins, 50; J Russell Harper (auth), Painting in Canada, a History, Univ Toronto Press, 66; Can Artists Series, Carl Schaefer, Gage Publ, 77. *Mem:* Can Soc Graphic Art; Can Soc Painters Watercolour; fel Royal Soc Arts; Royal Can Acad Arts; life fel Int Inst Arts & Lett. *Media:* Watercolor, Egg Tempera. *Publ:* Auth, Iceland, Atlantis on the Arctic Circle, Can Art Mag, 46. *Dealer:* Roberts Gallery 641 Yonge St Toronto ON Can; Downstairs Gallery Edmonton Can. *Mailing Add:* 157 St Clements Ave Toronto ON M4R 1H1 Canada

SCHAEFER, GAIL
SCULPTOR
b NJ, June 11, 38. *Study:* Art Students League, with Kaz-Simon, 77-80, Scolar, 85-86; Ramapo Col, NJ, BA, 79; Nat Acad Design, Lucchesi scholar, 80-83. *Comn:* North Jersey Automobile MEM Plaque; BEC Manufacturing Corp; Trautwein Farms Inc. *Exhib:* Catherine Lorrilard Wolfe Nat Arts Club, New York, 78, 82 & 83; Allied Artists Am, Nat Acad Galleries, New York, 78, Am Acad & Inst Arts & Lett, 80 & Nat Arts Club, 81, 83, 87, 89, 90 & 91; Salmagundi Club, New York, 80; Nat Acad Design 157th Ann, New York, 82. *Teaching:* Instr studio classes, 77-; instr sculpture, Old Church Cult Ctr, Demarest, NJ. *Awards:* William Averbach-Levy Award, Nat Acad Design, 81; Medal Hon, Printers & Sculptors Soc NJ, 82; Anna Hyatt Huntington Award, Catherine Lorrilard Wolfe Art Club, 83. *Bibliog:* David Spengler (auth), Women of the arts, Record, 10/28/76; Diana Drew (auth), Sculptress has a way with children, Town News, 6/21/78; Terry Meyer (auth), Gail Schaefer's talent, Sunday Post, 7/16/78. *Mem:* Allied Artists Am; Painters & Sculptors Soc NJ; Catherine Lorrilard Wolfe Art Club; Nat Sculpture Soc. *Media:* Clay, Bronze. *Dealer:* Whychoff Galery Whychoff NJ; Saddle River Gallery Saddle River NJ. *Mailing Add:* 103 Commander Black Oradell NJ 07649

SCHAEFER, RONALD H
PRINTMAKER, EDUCATOR
b Milwaukee, Wis, June 2, 39. *Study:* Univ Wis-Milwaukee, BS(art), 62; Univ Wis-Madison, MS(art), 63, MFA, 64. *Work:* Joslyn Mus, Omaha, Nebr; Tampa Pub Libr; First Nat Bank Minneapolis; and others. *Exhib:* Five Okla Printmakers Ann, 64-72; three Boston Printmakers Ann, 65-67; 12th & 19th Ball State Univ Drawing & Small Sculpture Ann, 66 & 73; Miami Biennial Print, 73; NH Int Ann, 73; and others. *Teaching:* Prof printmaking & chmn dept, Univ NDak, 65- *Awards:* Twenty-five Printmakers Nat Invitational Purchase Award, Minot State Col, 71; Graphic Chem & Ink Co Award, First NH Print Int, 73; Purchase Award, Los Angeles, Print Exhib, 73. *Mem:* Print Club. *Media:* Etching, Intaglio. *Mailing Add:* 119 Conklin Ave Grand Forks ND 58203

SCHAEFER, SCOTT JAY
CURATOR, HISTORIAN
b Chicago, Ill, Mar 30, 48. *Study:* Univ Ariz, BA, 70; Bryn Mawr Col, MA, PhD, 75. *Pos:* Asst cur paintings, Philadelphia Mus Art, 74; asst cur prints, Fogg Art Mus, Cambridge, Mass, 76-78; asst cur paintings, Mus Fine Arts, Boston, 78-80; cur Europ paintings and sculpture, Los Angeles Co Mus Art, 80-87; dir mus serv, Sotheby's, NY, 88-91, vpres, Old Master Drawings & Paintings, 91. *Teaching:* Lectr, Philadelphia Col Art, 71-72; lectr, Harvard Univ, Cambridge, Mass, 76-79. *Mem:* Southern Calif Art Hist; Am Mus Asn. *Res:* Late 16th & 17th century Italian painting, 19th century French paintings. *Publ:* Auth, Drawings of the Studiolo of Francesco; a catalogue, Master Drawings, XX, 83; Drawings by Martin Freminet, Gazette Des Beaux-Arts, 1371, 83; Europe and beyond: Some paintings for the studiolo, Coun Europe, 3/84; A day in the country, Impression and the French Landscape, 84; Guido Reni, 88. *Mailing Add:* c/o Sotheby's 1334 York Ave New York NY 10021

SCHAEFFER, KATE
DEALER, COLLECTOR
b Berlin, Ger; US citizen. *Collections Arranged:* Carl Hofer (auth, catalog), 35. *Pos:* Owner, Schaeffer Galleries, New York, currently. *Specialty:* Fine Old Master paintings and drawings early 19th century. *Mailing Add:* Schaeffer Galleries Inc 983 Park Ave New York NY 10028

SCHAEFFER, MARTHA J
DEALER
b Springfield, Mass, Jan 14, 48. *Study:* St Bonaventure Univ; Herbert Lehman Col, BA, 74. *Collections Arranged:* Joan Miro, Works on Paper, 82; Sandra Chia, Sculpture & Prints, 84; Paintings by Cassatt, Renoir, Monet and Pissarro, 85; Works on Paper by Gonzalez, Helion, Leger, Matisse, Toulouse-Lautrec and Vuillard, 85; Sculpture by Arp, Calder, DeKooning, Gargallo, Lipschitz and Renoir, 86; Recent Painting by Jackie Battenfield at The First Women's Bank, 87; Paintings by Botero, LAM, Matta, Tamayo, Torres-Garcia, 88; James Harrison, Works on Paper (55-84), 89. *Pos:* Owner, Schaeffer Fine Art, currently. *Bibliog:* Sandra Salmas (auth), Personal finance, 1/25/81 & Good buys in fine arts, 1/25/81, New York Times. *Mem:* Private Art Dealers Asn, Inc. *Specialty:* Twentieth Century Masters: Paintings, drawings, prints & sculpture; also emerging artists. *Mailing Add:* 500 E 77th St Suite 512 New York NY 10162

SCHAEFFER, S(TANLEY) ALLYN
PAINTER, INSTRUCTOR
b Franklin, NJ, Nov 3, 35. *Study:* W Lester Stevens Studio, 50-60; Nat Acad Design, with Ivan Olinsky, 54-55; Art Students League (Schanackenberg Merit Scholarship), with Robert Brackman, 54-56, New York. *Work:* Shering Plough, Madison, NJ; Pastel Soc Am, New York; NJ Sports & Exposition Authority, East Rutherford, NJ; Monmouth Park, Oceanport, NJ; NJ Bell Telephone Co, Newark. *Comn:* Raceing Paintings, Monmouth Park, Oceanport, NJ, 80-92; Revolutionary War Mural, (6x12), State Bank NJ, Springfield, 79; Mural School Life, (8x12), Long Branch Pub Sch, NJ, 83; Historic Drawing, Muhlenberg Hosp, Plainfield, NJ, 84; History of the Hambletonian, NJ Sports Authority, East Rutherford, 92. *Exhib:* Hudson Valley Art Asn Ann, White Plains Co Ctr, NY, 75-92; Pastel Soc Am Ann, Nat Arts Club, New York, 80-92; Hudson Valley group show, Hammond Mus, NY, 80; Pastel Soc Am Traveling Show, Eastern States, Fla & New England, 86. *Pos:* Art ed, NJ Life Mag, Maplewood, 70-76; art ed, NJ Music & Arts Mag, Chatham, 81. *Teaching:* Instr anatomy figure drawing, Du Sch Arts, Plainfield, NJ, 70-76; instr anatomy figure drawing, Spectrum Inst, Hillsboro, NJ, 75-80; instr painting, NJ Ctr Visual Arts, Summit, 82- *Awards:* Pearl Paint Award, Pastel Soc Am 19th Ann, Pearl, 91. *Bibliog:* Wendon Blake (auth), Painting in Alkyd, Am Artists Mag, Billboard Publ, 80; George Maganan (auth), Interview S Allyn Schaeffer, Todays Art & Graphics, Sindicate Mag Inc, 81. *Mem:* Pastel Soc Am (bd mem, 91-); Hudson Valley Art. *Media:* Oil, Pastel. *Publ:* Auth, The Oil Painters Guide to Painting Trees, The Oil Painters Guide to Painting Skies, 85, The Oil Painters Guide to Painting Water, 86, Color Composition & Light in the Landscape, 87 & Big Book of Painting Nature in Pastel, 93, Watson/Guptill. *Dealer:* The Sporting Gallery Inc 11 W Washington St Middleburg VA 22117. *Mailing Add:* PO Box 254 Middleburg VA 22117

SCHAFFER, CLAUDIA POST
PAINTER, INSTRUCTOR
b Bridgeport, Conn, Jan 11, 45. *Study:* NY-Phoenix Sch Design, New York (summer scholar), 61-62; Art Ctr Col Art, Los Angeles, 63-64; studied with Frank Covino, 78 & Daniel Greene, 79-80; studied with Albert Handell (master pastellist), NMex, 79, Richard Clive, Rockport, Mass 89 & Herman Margolis (master pastellist), Conn. *Work:* Portrait, Donna Diers, Dean Sch Nursing, Yale Univ, 87; Waterbury Court House, Conn Bar Asn. *Comn:* Portrait, Judge McGrath & Judge Tellalian, Conn Bar Asn, 89; two 3' x 5' murals, Town Cheshire Conn Lawyers Group, Comn by A H Fred Hitt, 89; many individual & family portraits spanning 25 yrs by pvt clients & through gallery representation. *Exhib:* Knickerbocker Artists Ann Exhib, Salmagundi Club, New York, 88, 89 & 90; Academic Artists Nat Ann, Springfield, Mass 89, 90, 91 & 92; Am Artists Prof League Nat Ann, Salamagundi CLub, New York, 89, 90 & 92; Pastel Soc Am Ann Exhib, Nat Arts Club, New York, 90, 91 & 92; Catherine Lorillard Wolfe Art Club Nat Ann, New York, 90, 91 & 92; North Shore Art Asn Ann Exhib, Gloucester, Mass, 90, 91 & 92; Am Realism '92, Parkersbury Art Ctr, WVa, 92; Pastel Soc NFla, Pensacola Mus Art, 92. *Pos:* Dir & Founder, Post Acad Fine Arts Ctr, 75-81; dir art instr prog, Cheshire, 76-79; dir art workshops, Rockport, 79-80. *Teaching:* teaching art grant, Conn Commission Arts, 76-77; fine arts portraiture, Quinnipiac Col, Hamden, Conn, 80-81; artist-in-residence, Milford Fine Arts Pub Schs, 82-83; artist-in-residence, S Maarten, 90. *Awards:* Top Honor Award for pastel, Acad Artists Asn, 90, 91 & 92; Second Prize, Founders Award, Pastel Soc NFla, 92; Bd Dirs Award, Pastel Soc West Coast, 92. *Mem:* Signature mem, Pastel Soc Am, New York; Salmagundi CLub, New York; Catherine Lorillard Wolfe Art Club, New York; Conn Pastel Soc; Am Artists Prof League, New York. *Media:* Pastel. *Mailing Add:* 176 Captains' Dr Westbrook CT 06498

SCHAFFER, DEBRA S
SCULPTOR, INSTRUCTOR
b New York, NY, Nov 22, 36. *Study:* Montclair State Col, BA, 58; Univ Md, with Kenneth Campbell, 79; Westchester County Ctr, with Anthony Padovano, 82; Art Life Studio with Sebastiano Mineo; Pietra Santa Italy; Jane B Armstrong, VT. *Work:* Blue Heron Gallery, Wellfleet, Mass; Images Gallery, Briarcliff, NY; Le Boeuf Lamb Lieby & Mac Rae, New York; Temple B'nai Yisrael, Armonk, NY. *Comn:* Three fish, comn by Renee San Marco, Briarcliff, NY; owls, comn by Dr & Mrs Bruce Brofman, Armonk, NY; harp seal, comn by Dr & Mrs David Schaffer, Philadelphia, Pa. *Exhib:* Visual Individualists United, E Stuhr Mus of Great Plains, Nebr, 89; Allied Artists Am, NY, 89; two-person show, Westchester Community Col, NY, 90; Bergen Co Mus Arts & Sci, NJ, 90; Salmagundi, Club, New York, 91; Am Acad Sci, New York, 91. *Pos:* Pres, bd mem, juror, Mamaroneck Artists Guild, 77-88; Juror, Nat Asn Women Artists. *Teaching:* Instr sculpture, Northern Westchester Ctr for Arts, Outreach Prog, 82-85; Heritage Hills, Somers, NY, 82-; Home Studio, 77- *Awards:* Merit Award, Mamaroneck Artist Guild, V Sonynas, 82; Jeffrey Childs Willis Mem Award, Nat Asn Women Artists, David Burt, 87; Gretchen Richardson Freelander Mem Award for Carving, Chaim Gross, 89. *Mem:* Nat Asn Women Artists; Stone Sculpture Soc, NY; Hudson Valley Art Asn; Art Life Guild (mem chmn, 88-89). *Media:* Wood, Stone. *Dealer:* Images Gallery Briarcliff Manor NY 10510; Rose Gallery Kent Ct. *Mailing Add:* Ten Windmill Pl Armonk NY 10504

SCHAFFNER, INGRID L
CRITIC, CURATOR
US citizen. *Study:* Mount Holyoke Col, AB, 83; Whitney Mus Am Art, ISP Prog, fel, 83-84; New York Univ, IFA, MA, 89. *Collections Arranged:* Christopher Wilmarth Estate (auth, catalog); The Feminine Gaze, Whitney Mus, 84; Constructing Images: Synapse of Sculpture and Photography, (travelling), Saul Lieberman, New York, Ctr Creative Photog, Tuscon & San Jose Mus Art, Calif, 91-92; The Return of the Cadavre Exquis, The Drawing Ctr, NY, 92-93. *Pos:* Cur, Richard Artschwager Studio, 91- *Publ:* Auth, feature, Marlene Dumas, Arts, 91; rev, Rebecca Horn, Sculpture, 91; feature, Genevieve Cadieux, Artscribe, 91; feature, Marlene Dumas, Kunst & Mus J, 92. *Mailing Add:* 24 Taaffe Place Brooklyn NY 11205

SCHAFFNER, J LURAY See Luray, J

SCHAPIRO, MEYER
EDUCATOR, HISTORIAN
b Shavly, Russia, Sept 23, 04; US citizen. *Study:* Columbia Univ, AB, MA & PhD. *Teaching:* Prof hist art, Columbia Univ, 28-75, prof emer, 75- *Awards:* Comdr l'Ordre Arts & Lett, France; Aby Warburg Award, Homberg, Ger, 84; British Fel, Brit Acad, 91. *Mem:* Fel Am Acad Arts & Scis; Am Philos Soc; Nat Inst Arts & Lett; Medieval Acad Am. *Res:* Early Christian, medieval and modern art. *Publ:* Auth, Words and Pictures: On the Literal and the Symbolic in the Illustrations of a Text, Mouton, 73; Romanesque Art, 77, Late Antique, Early Christian & Medieval Art: Selected Papers, 79 & Modern Art, 82, Braziller; and others. *Mailing Add:* 279 W Fourth St New York NY 10014

SCHAPIRO, MIRIAM
PAINTER, SCULPTOR
b Toronto, Ont, Nov 15, 23; US citizen. *Study:* Univ Iowa, BA, 45, MA, 46, MFA, 49; Col Wooster Ohio, Hon DFA, 83; Calif Col Arts & Crafts, Hon Dr Fine Arts, 89. *Work:* Whitney Mus Am Art, Mus Mod Art, New York; Stanford Univ, Palo Alto, Calif; Oberlin Hirshhorn Mus; Boston Mus Fine Arts, Mass; Mass Mus Contemp Art. *Comn:* Temple Shalom, Chicago, Ill; Kaemper Co, Rosslyn, Va; Orlando Airport, Fla; Pasquerilla Performing Arts Ctr, Johnstown, Pa. *Exhib:* Solo exhibs, Bernice Steinbaum Gallery, New York, 86, 88, 90 & 91, Gibbes Art Gallery, Charleston, SC, 87, Simms Fine Art Gallery, New Orleans, La, 87, Phyllis Rothman Gallery, Fairleigh Dickinson Univ, Madison, NS, 90, New Allen/Butler Fine Art, Santa Fe, NMex, 90, The Nature of Miriam Schapiro, Colo State Univ, Ft Collins, Colo, 92 & The Politics of the Decorative, Guild Hall Mus, East Hampton, NY, 92; Prints of the Eighties, Guild Hall Mus, East Hampton, NY, 90; In Bloom, Phizer Corp, New York, 90; The Art of Fashion, Bernice Steinbaum Gallery, New York, 90; The Complete Printmaker, Sylvan Cole Gallery, New York, 90; Floored Art, Bernice Steinbaum Gallery, New York. *Pos:* Co-originator feminist art prog, Calif Inst Arts, 72-75; co-found, Feminist Art Inst, New York, 79. *Awards:* Guggenheim Fel Award, 87; Women's Caucus Art Award, 88; and others. *Bibliog:* Skira Annual--Actual Art, 80; Jensen & Conway (auths), Ornamentalism, Clarkson N Potter, 82. *Mem:* Women's Caucus Art (nat adv bd, currently). *Media:* Acrylic, Oil. *Publ:* Coauth, Womanhouse (catalog), 72; ed, Anonymous Was a Woman, 74 & Art: A Woman's Sensibility, 75, Feminist Art Prog, Cal Inst Arts; auth, Women and the Creative Process, Univ Man, 74; Rondo: An Artist's Book, Bedford Press, 88; Gardner, Art Through the Ages, 9th Ed, Harcourt Brace Jovanovich Inc, 90. *Mailing Add:* 393 W Broadway New York NY 10012

SCHAR, STUART
ADMINISTRATOR, EDUCATOR
b Chicago, Ill, Aug 27, 41. *Study:* Univ Chicago, BFA, 63, MFA, 64, PhD(arts admin), 67. *Comn:* Painting for Frank Lloyd Wright house, Brookfield, Ill, 73; lithograph for Lyons Twp High Sch, City of LaGrange, Ill, 74; painting for Aurora Pub Libr, City of Aurora, Ill, 75. *Exhib:* Art Inst Chicago, 60-64, 70 & 74; Lexington Studios, Chicago, 64-65, 75-76; Printmaking 1969, Northern Ariz Univ, Flagstaff, 69; John Hancock Ctr, Chicago, 73; Columbus Gallery Fine Arts, Ohio, 76; Oberlin Col, Ohio, 77; Western Art League Asn, 77; and others. *Pos:* Res assoc higher educ, NCent Asn Cols & Sec Schs, 65, asst to exec secy, 66; admin asst to chmn art dept, Univ Ill, Chicago Circle, 66-69, actg chmn art dept, 69; artist-in-residence, Joliet Art League, Ill, 70-72; dir, Sch of Art, Kent State Univ, 75-83; co-dir, Blossom Kent Art, Music & Theatre summer progs, 75-83; dir, James A Michener Mus, Univ Galleries, Eells Outdoor Gallery & Jack Lord Purchase Collections, 75-83; coordr, Div Res & Serv, La State Univ, 84-86; dean, Hartford Art Sch, 86-; assoc vpres, Arts, 89-; actg dean, Hartt Sch Music, 89-90. *Teaching:* Asst prof rendering & drafting, Chicago Tech Col, 64, asst prof design & graphics, 65; asst prof art, Univ Ill, Chicago Circle, 66-70, assoc prof urban sci, 70-75; prof art, Kent State Univ, 75-83; Distinguished Prof, La State Univ, 83; prof art, Hartford

Art Sch, 86- *Awards:* Best of Show, Midway Studios, 72; Gen Motors Purchase Award, Art Inst, Chicago, 74; Best of Show, Western Art League Asn, 77; Lady Bing Fel Award, 86. *Mem:* Col Art Asn; Am Asn Univ Prof; Am Inst Planners. *Publ:* Coauth, Guide for the Evaluation of Institutions of Higher Education, NCent Asn Cols & Sec Schs, 66; auth, The education of an art student, Tallyrand, Vol 3, 70; coauth, A Self Study Report: The University of Illinois at Chicago Circle, Univ Ill, 71; Central Themes of Louisiana Architecture, Art & Humanities Coun, Baton Rouge, 84; Pathways to Art through Numbers, Apple Educ Found, 86; A Video Pilot: Significant Interiors Survey, Am Soc Interior Designers. *Mailing Add:* Art Sch Univ Hartford West Hartford CT 06117

SCHARF, KENNY
PAINTER
b Los Angeles, Calif, 58. *Study:* Sch Visual Arts, New York, BFA, 80. *Comn:* Installation, The Palladium, New York, 85. *Exhib:* Solo exhibs, Tony Shafrazi Gallery, New York, 83-88, 91-92, Akira Ikeda Gallery, Tokyo, 86, 88 & 90, Michael Kohn Gallery, Los Angeles, 89, Hans Mayer Gallery, Dusseldorf & Galerie Beaubourg, Paris, 90, AC&T Corp, Tokyo & Studio Trisorio, Naples, 91, Edward Totah Gallery, Milan & London, 92; Object trouvés d'artistes, Galerie du Jour, 91 & 92; American Art of the 80's, Palazzo delle Albere, Trento, Italy, 91; Variations Gitanes, a La Grande-Villette, Paris, 92; 1492, Museo de Art Contemporaneo de Monterrey, Mex, 92; and others. *Bibliog:* Rosemary Grillo (auth), Changing Channels, Son of Pop Keeps Up, Cover Arts, 4/90; John Howell (auth), Don't Bungle the Jungle, Elle Mag, 8/90; Olivier Zahm (auth), Kenny Scharf--Beaubourg, Flash Art, 11-12/90; Glen O'Brien (auth), rev, Artforum, 3/85. *Media:* All. *Mailing Add:* c/o Tony Shafrazi Gallery 130 Prince St New York NY 10012

SCHARF, WILLIAM
PAINTER
b Media, Pa, Feb 22, 27. *Study:* Samuel Fleisher Mem Art Sch, Philadelphia, Pa; Pa Acad of the Fine Arts, Philadelphia; The Barnes Found, Merion, Pa. *Work:* Nat Mus Am Art, Smithsonian Inst, Washington, DC; Newark Mus, NJ; Boston Inst Contemp Art, Mass; Guggenheim Mus & Brooklyn Mus, New York; and others. *Exhib:* Pa Acad Anns, Philadelphia, 47-; Inst Contemp Art, Boston, 51; Aldrich Mus, Ridgefield, Conn, 63; Brandeis Univ, Waltham, Mass, 63; San Francisco Art Inst, 70; The Neuberger Mus, Purchase, NY, 76; High Mus, Atlanta, Ga, 78; Guggenheim Mus, New York, 84; Smith Col Mus, Northampton, Mass, 85; Am Acad & Inst Arts & Lett, New York, 91; Univ Mich Mus, 92. *Teaching:* Instr painting, San Francisco Sch Fine Arts, 63, 66, 69 & 74, Sch Visual Arts, New York, 65-69; Lectr, Art Students League, 87-92. *Mem:* Artists Equity Asn. *Media:* All. *Mailing Add:* 75 Central Park W New York NY 10023

SCHARFF, CONSTANCE KRAMER
PRINTMAKER, PAINTER
b New York, NY. *Study:* Brooklyn Mus Art Sch, grad; also with Adja Jounkers & Abraham Rattner. *Work:* Brooklyn Mus; Philadelphia Mus Art; Columbia Univ; Smithsonian Inst Archives; Butler Inst Am Art, Youngstown, Ohio; Greenville Mus, SC; Libr Cong, Washington, DC. *Comn:* Ed prints, Contemp Arts Asn, NY, 56 & 60 & Am Asn Contemp Arts, 68. *Exhib:* Potsdam Nat Print Show, 66; Soc Am Graphic Artists, 72-81; Award Winners Show, Community Church, NY, 74; Traveling Juried Show, Israel & Egypt, 81 & 82; Invitation Show, Pelham Art Ctr, 85. *Teaching:* Private lessons at home studio, 84-85. *Awards:* Grumbacher Award, Nat Asn Women Artists, 73; Edna Stauffer Award, Audubon Artists, 73; Elsie-Jet-Key Mem Award, ASPCA, 88. *Mem:* Soc Am Graphic Artists; Nat Soc Painters Casein & Acrylic (rec secy, 67-90); Nat Asn Women Artists; Am Soc Contemp Artists (rec secy 75-81, exec bd, 82-); Audubon Artists (dir, 85). *Media:* Woodcut; All. *Mailing Add:* 115 Jaffrey St Brooklyn NY 11235

SCHARY, EMANUEL
PAINTER, PRINTMAKER
b Feb 27, 24; US citizen. *Study:* Carnegie Inst Technol Sch Fine Arts; Art Students League; Pratt Graphics Ctr; and with Edwin Dickenson, Howard Trafton, Frank Reilly, Ivan Olinsky, Robert Hale & Jurgen Fischer. *Work:* Nat Fine Art Collection, Smithsonian Inst, Washington, DC; Metrop Mus Fine Art, New York; Israel Mus, Jerusalem; Vatican Mus, Rome, Italy; Brooklyn Mus, New York; and others. *Comn:* New York World's Fair Pavilion, Weizmann Inst Sci, 64-65; large painting, West Hempstead Community Ctr, NY; numerous litho ed for var group collectors; designed & stained glass windows from old works art, Crescent Hill Synojogue, NY, 92. *Exhib:* One-man shows, Tel-Aviv, Israel, 68 & Kean Col, NJ, 73; Brooklyn Mus, 70; New York, Assoc Am Artists, 74; Kansas City Country Club Plaza, 74; Guild Gallery, New York, 78, 79 & 81. *Bibliog:* Ann Shapiro (auth), New York artist comes to Kansas City, Kansas City Chronicle, 9/74; Rusty Hoffland (auth), Art show '75, NSide News, Atlanta, Ga, 2/6/75. *Mem:* Life mem Art Students League; Univ Mich Artists & Craftsmen's Guild; Artists Equity Asn, Inc. *Media:* Acrylic, Graphics. *Mailing Add:* 8 Nottingham Gate Rock Hill NY 12775

SCHAUMBURG, DONALD ROLAND
EDUCATOR, CERAMIST
b Oakland, Calif, Aug 23, 19. *Study:* Calif Col Arts & Crafts, Oakland, BA(art educ), 41; Claremont Col, MFA, 51; graduate studies with Marguerite Wildenhain, 57-59. *Work:* Folk Art Mus, Santa Fe, NMex; Univ Art Collections, Ariz State Univ, Tempe; Int Minerals Corp Collection, Skokie, Ill. *Comn:* Ceramic wall panel, Valley National Bank, Tempe, Ariz, 81. *Exhib:* One-man shows, Phoenix Art Mus, 62 & 68, Univ Art Collections, Tempe, Ariz, 74, Hand and the Spirit Gallery, Scottsdale, Ariz, 75 & 82 & Grossmont Col, El Cajon, Calif, 88; Southwestern Craftsmen, Mus Int Folk Art, NMex, 65. *Pos:* Chmn, Palomar Col, 46-49. *Teaching:* Instr ceramics, San Diego State Univ, 53; prof ceramics, Ariz State Univ, 53-88, prof emer, 88. *Awards:* Merit Awards, Tucson Mus, 60-62; First Prize, Heard Mus, 75; Mary Soule Mem, Ariz Designer Craftsman, 76. *Bibliog:* Krevanic (auth), Keramos, Kendall-Hunt, 70; Glenn Nelson (auth), Ceramics Handbook, Holt Reinhart Winston, 78; John H Conrad (auth), Contemporary Ceramic Techniques, Prentic-Hall, 79. *Mem:* Nat Council Educ of Ceramic Arts. *Media:* Porcelain Clay, Raku Clay. *Dealer:* The Hand and the Spirit Crafts Gallery Scottsdale AZ. *Mailing Add:* 5410 E Vernon Phoenix AZ 85008

SCHEER, LISA N
SCULPTOR
Study: Bennington Col, Vt, BA, 74-79; Yale Sch Art, New Haven, MFA, 79-81. *Comn:* Clarence DuBurns Arena, City of Baltimore, Coplans, Hort & Macht Architects, Md. *Exhib:* Solo exhibs, Rice Fine Arts, Philadelphia, Pa, 85, McIntosh/Drysdale Gallery, Washington, DC, 87, Md Invitational, Baltimore Mus Art, 88, Am Inst Architects, Wash, 89, Tartt Gallery, 90, Nancy Drysdale Gallery, 92, The Phillips Collection, Washington, DC, 92; The Later Years, Bennington Artists, 1960-1980, Usdan Gallery, Bennington, Vt, 85; Recollections, Wash Proj Arts, 87 & 88, Wall Sculpture & Freize, Addison/Ripley Gallery, Washington, DC, 90; Washington Artists, PS 122, New York, 87; Wash Co Mus Fine Arts, Hagerstown, Md, 88; Strathmore Hall Arts Ctr, Rockville, Md, 88. *Awards:* Fac Develop Grant, St Mary's Col Md, Baltimore, 83 & 85; Md Arts Coun Fel, Baltimore, 87; Nat Endowment Arts, 90. *Bibliog:* JoAnn Lewis (auth), Lisa Scheer at McIntosh/Drysdale, Wash Post, 12/5/87; Dan Cameron (auth), Is there any hope of art in Washington, New Art Examiner, 3/88; J W Mahoney (auth), Washington, DC critic's poll, New Art Examiner, 11/88. *Mailing Add:* PO Box 73452 T St Sta Washington DC 20009

SCHEER, SHERIE (HOOD)
PHOTOGRAPHER, PAINTER
b Estherville, Iowa, Feb 15, 40. *Study:* Univ Iowa, 58-60; Univ Calif, Los Angeles, BA, 69, MA, 71. *Work:* Metrop Mus Art, New York; Fogg Art Mus, Harvard Univ; Israel Mus, Jerusalem; Minneapolis Inst Art, Minn; San Francisco Mus Mod Art. *Exhib:* Contemporary Hand-Colored Photography, DeSaisset Mus, Santa Clara, Calif, 81; Summer Show V, Los Angeles Co Mus Art, 81; Five Photographers, Los Angeles Inst Contemp Art, 82; Artists' Tribute to Bertha Urdang, Israel Mus, Jerusalem, 82; Invitational: Bertha Urdang, London Regional Gallery, Ont, 83. *Teaching:* Instr photog, Univ Calif, Los Angeles Exten, 82-84. *Bibliog:* Barbara Noah (auth), J Golden & S Scheer at the Womens Building, Art in Am, 3-4/78; Colin Westerbeck (auth), Reviews: New York, Artforum, 3/81; Anne Wagner (auth), Selections from An Interview with Sherie Scheer together with some suggestions for their use, J Womens Studies, winter 92. *Media:* Painted Photographs, Mixed Media. *Dealer:* Sherie Scheer Studio 31 Park Ave Venice CA 90291. *Mailing Add:* 31 Park Ave Venice CA 90291

SCHEIN, EUGENIE
PAINTER, PRINTMAKER
US citizen. *Study:* Hunter Col, BA; Columbia Univ, MA; Art Students League, with De Muth & Bridgeman; studies in art & aesthetics at New York Univ & Univ NMex; Martha Graham Sch Dance. *Work:* Carvell Mus, La; Ga Mus Art, Athens; Lowe Art Mus, Coral Gables, Fla; Miami Mus Mod Art, Fla. *Exhib:* Int Watercolors, Brooklyn Mus; Cincinnati Mus; Riverside Mus, New York; Soc Four Arts, Palm Beach; Lowe Mus, Univ Miami, Coral Gables, Fla; Hollywood Art & Cult Ctr, Fla; Butler Inst, Youngstown, Ohio; one-person shows, Midtown Gallery, Uptown Gallery & Salpeter Gallery, New York, Mexico City, Havana, PR, Barzasky Gallery, NY. *Teaching:* Instr, Hunter Col, 26-55 & Univ Miami, 56-60. *Mem:* Artists Equity Asn (vpres, 72-); Fla Artists Group; Nat Asn Women Artists. *Media:* Acrylic, Oil; Graphics. *Mailing Add:* 1070 Stillwater Dr Miami Beach FL 33141

SCHENCK, WILLIAM CLINTON
PAINTER, PRINTMAKER
b Aug 19, 47; US citizen. *Study:* Columbus Col Art & Design, 65-67; Kansas City Art Inst, BFA, 69. *Work:* Va Art Mus, Richmond; Rose Art Mus, Boston; Security Pac Bank, Brussels, Belg; Nat Bank Switz, Geneva; Scottsdale Ctr Arts, Ariz; Wells Fargo, Los Angeles; First Interstate Bank, Salt Lake City. *Comn:* Paintings, Sky Harbor Int Airport, Phoenix, 79; paintings, IBM Corp, Tucson, Ariz, 81. *Exhib:* Wadsworth Atheneum, Hartford, Conn, 74; Rose Art Mus, Boston, 75; Grand Hornu Gallery, Belg, 76; Edwin Ulrich Mus, Wichita, Kans, 76; Navy Pier, Chicago, 81; 15-Year Retrospective, Scottsdale Ctr for the Arts, Ariz, 83; and others. *Bibliog:* Gregory Battcock (auth), Super-Realism: A Critical Anthology, E F Dutton, New York, 75; John Perrault (auth), Impressions of Arizona, Art Am, 81; Barbara Perlman (auth), Schenck's brand, Ariz Arts & Lifestyle, 81. *Media:* Oil; Serigraph. *Dealer:* Jo Anne Lyon Gallery 525 E Cooper Ave Aspen CO 81611; Trailside Gallery 105 N Center St Jackson WY 83001. *Mailing Add:* c/o Elaine Horwitch Galleries 4211 N Marshall Way Scottsdale AZ 85251

SCHENK, JOSEPH BERNARD
DIRECTOR
b Glendale, Ariz, March 28, 53. *Study:* Huntingdon Col, Montgomery, Ala, BA, 75; Ball State Univ, Muncie, Ind, MA, 79; Univ Calif, Berkeley, Mus Mgt Inst, 86. *Collections Arranged:* Indiana Collects, 78; 20th Century Am Art, 79; Collections in Anderson, pvt collection survey, 79; The Cochran Collection, 20th Century Graphics, 86; Art: On the Move, Nat Juried Invitational, 87; Mobile Collect, pvt collection survey, 92; FAMOS Collection Highlights 1991; Out of the Woods: Turned Wood by American

Craftsmen, 92. *Pos:* Dir, Anderson Fine Arts Ctr, Ind, 76-79, Chattahoochee Valley Art Mus, 83-88 & Fine Arts Mus South, Mobile, Ala, 88- *Teaching:* Instr art appreciation, W Ga Col, Carrollton, 86-87. *Mem:* Am Asn Mus; Southeastern Mus Conf; Ga Citizens for Arts (treas, 87-88); Ala Mus Asn. *Res:* 19th & 20th century American art. *Mailing Add:* Fine Arts Mus South PO Box 8426 Museum Dr Mobile AL 36689

SCHEPIS, ANTHONY JOSEPH
INSTRUCTOR, PAINTER
b Cleveland, Ohio, Mar 6, 27. *Study:* Cooper Sch Art, dipl; Cleveland Inst Art, cert; Kent State Univ, MA. *Work:* Akron Art Mus, Ohio; Albion Col, Mich; Massillon Mus Art, Ohio; Butler Inst Am Art, Youngstown, Ohio; Washington & Jefferson Col, Pa. *Exhib:* Nat Mid-Year Show, Butler Inst Am Art, 55-74; Avanti Gallery, New York, 71; May Show, Cleveland Mus Art, 73-89; Univ Mus, Ind Univ, Pa, 83; Cleveland/Toronto Exhib, Harbourfront Gallery, Toronto, 78; one-person shows, B K Smith Gallery, 80 & Univ Columbia Fine Arts Gallery, 80, Mo; New Realism, Robert L Kidd Assoc Gallery, Mich, 85; Albion Col, Mich, 85; and others. *Teaching:* Prof drawing & painting, Cleveland Inst Art, Ohio, 79- *Awards:* Edwin C Shaw Purchase Award, 47th All-Ohio Exhib, Akron Art Inst, 70; Purchase Award, Nat Mid-Year Show, Butler Inst Am Art, 74; Individual Artists fel, Ohio Arts Coun; and others. *Bibliog:* Article, Ft Wayne J, 3/26/80; article, Cleveland Mag, 6/78; Cleveland Mus Art Bulletin, 5/88. *Mem:* New Orgn Visual Arts, Cleveland. *Media:* Oil, Silkscreen. *Dealer:* Robert L Kidd Asn Inc Birmingham MI. *Mailing Add:* 34720 Sherwood Dr Solon OH 44139

SCHERER, HERBERT GROVER
LIBRARIAN, LECTURER
b Brooklyn, NY, May 16, 30. *Study:* Western Reserve Univ, BA(art), 53, MA(art hist), 60, MLS, 63. *Collections Arranged:* Marquee on Main Street: Jack Liebenberg's Movie Theaters, 1928-1941 (auth, catalog), Univ Minn Art Gallery, 82. *Pos:* Art librn, Syracuse Univ, 63-66 & Univ Minn, Minneapolis, 66- *Teaching:* Instr art hist & methodology, Univ Minn, Minneapolis, 66- *Awards:* Res Grant, Am Philos Soc, 67, Univ Minn, 67, 86 & 87, Nat Endowment Humanities, 79 & 86 & MacMillan Fund Grant, 87. *Mem:* Art Libr NAm (charter mem & founder, 72). *Publ:* Auth, Program of the thirty-nine ceiling paintings of the Jesuit Church of St Ignatius in Antwerp, painted by P P Rubens in 1620, Am Philos Soc Yearbk, 68; auth, Minneapolis art deco extravaganza, Arts Mag, summer 71; dir, Streamlined Dreams (TV doc), KTCA, 80; auth, Marquee on Main Street: Jack Liebenberg's Movie & Theatres, J Decorative Arts, spring 86; Tickets to Fantasy, Hennepin Co Hist, fall 87; A tarnished Art Deco Gem, Minneapolis-St Paul, 3/88; Merging Subject Collections or Love's Labor Lost, The Architecture Library of the Future: Complexity and Contradiction, Ann Arbor Univ, Mich Press, 89, 105-111; Modernism at Norwest: An Interview with David Ryan, Journal of Decorative and Propaganda Arts, 14, Fall 89, 112-127. *Mailing Add:* 5 Wilson Libr Univ Minn 309 19th Ave S Minneapolis MN 55455

SCHERPEREEL, RICHARD CHARLES
EDUCATOR, PAINTER
b Mishawaka, Ind, Dec 1, 31. *Study:* Univ Notre Dame, BFA & MFA; McMurry Col, MEd; George Peabody Col for Teachers, EdD. *Comn:* STex totems, Tex A&I Univ, Kingsville, 75. *Exhib:* Mid States Artist Exhib, 66-68; Found Exhib, Art Mus S Tex, 70-78; Del Mar Nat Drawing & Small Sculpture Exhib, 71; Tex Fine Arts Asn, 72-74. *Teaching:* Instr art, Irving Pub Schs, Tex, 59-60 & Elkhart, Ind, 60-63; prof & chmn dept art, Bloomsburg State Col, Pa, 64-68 & Tex A&I Univ, 68- *Mem:* Nat Coun Art Adminr (bd dirs, 72-78, secy-treas, 72-78); Art Mus STex (bd mem, 74-); Tex Fine Arts Asn (bd dirs, 71-74); S Tex Art League (pres, 72-73); Coastal Bend Art Educ Asn (pres, 73-74). *Mailing Add:* 1631 Santa Cecilla Dr Kingsville TX 78363

SCHEU, LEONARD
PAINTER, LECTURER
b San Francisco, Calif, Feb 19, 04. *Study:* Calif Sch Fine Arts, San Francisco; Art Students League, drawing with George Bridgeman. *Work:* Ford Motor Co Collection, Dearborn Mus, Mich. *Exhib:* Butler Inst Am Art, Youngstown, Ohio, 68; Holyoke Mus, Mass, 69; Erie Pub Mus, Pa, 70; Anchorage Fine Arts Mus, 71; Nat Drawing Exhib, Del Mar Col, Corpus Christi, Tex; Drawing & Small Sculpture Exhib, Ball State Univ; Purdue Univ, Ind. *Pos:* Juror, local & nat exhibs, 53- *Teaching:* Instr painting & drawing, Whittier Sch Syst, Calif, 61-70; prof art, Banff Sch Fine Arts, Univ Alta, 62-65; instr painting, drawing & art hist, Orange Coast Col, 62-67. *Awards:* Honorable Mention, Laguna Beach Art Asn. *Bibliog:* M Jackson (auth), article in Laguna Beach Post, 55; Margaret Paige (auth), article in SCoast News, 64; article in St Vincent, Latrobe, Pa, 66. *Mem:* Laguna Beach Art Asn (mem bd, 56-, pres, 56-57, exhib chmn, 56-58); Calif Nat Watercolor Soc; Nat Soc Painters Casein (bd mem, 56-59). *Media:* Watercolor, Oil. *Publ:* Illusr, Good ghost towns never die, Lincoln Mercury Times, 54; Saga of Cinnabar, New Almaden, 54 & Gold rush town that took its time, 61, Ford Times. *Dealer:* Stary-Sheets 14988 Sand Canyon Ave Suite 1-5 Irvine CA 92718. *Mailing Add:* 309 Agate St Laguna Beach CA 92651

SCHEUER, RUTH
PAINTER, TAPESTRY ARTIST
b Wilson, NC, Aug 20, 52. *Study:* Univ NC, BFA(cum laude), 70; Les Manufactures Nationales Des Gobelins, Paris, France, invitational studies, 79-80; Univ Calif, San Francisco, MA(fine art), 81. *Work:* Am Embassy, Warsaw, Poland; Univ NC, Weatherspoon Gallery, Greensboro. *Comn:* Tapestry, IBM, White Plains, NY, 87; tapestry, Nabisco-RJR, Altanta, Ga, 87; tapestry, Touche-Ross, Houston, Tex, 88; tapestry, Wilmington Trust Bank, Del, 89; tapestry, Bell Atlantic Hq, Philadelphia, Pa, 91. *Exhib:* Solo exhib, NJ State Mus, Trenton, 85, Weatherspoon Gallery, Univ NC, Greensboro, 91 & Va Ctr Arts, Richmond, 92; International Textile Exhib, Kyoto Cult Mus, Japan, 87 & 92; The Narrative Voice (touring), Musée D'Aubusson, France, 89; International Tapestry, Anchorage Mus, Alaska, 90 & Textile Mus; World Tapestry Today (touring), West Pac Gallery, Melbourne, Australia, 88. *Pos:* Founder & dir, Scheuer Tapestry Studio, 82-89; founder & pres, Ctr Tapestry Arts, New York, 89-92, InterArt Ctr, New York, 92- *Awards:* Visual Arts Fel, Midatlantic/Nat Endowment Arts, 89; Fel Grant, NY Found Arts, 90. *Bibliog:* Manson Kennedy (dir), Narrative Voice (film), 89; Pamela Scheinman (auth), cover article, Urban Tapestry, Am Craft, 89; Beatrijs Sterk (auth), Stromungen Der Zeit Tap, Deutsches Textilforum, 90. *Mem:* Distant Lives/Shared Voices, Lodz, Poland (int steering comt, 92); Am Tapestry Alliance (vpres & bd dirs, 82-89); San Francisco Tapestry Workshop (co-founder, 76-79). *Media:* Miscellaneous. *Mailing Add:* 167 Spring St New York NY 10012

SCHIAVINA, LAURA M
PAINTER
b Springfield, Mass, Nov 27, 17. *Study:* Traphagen Sch Fashion, NY, cert, 44-46; Art Students League, with Will Barnet, 73; studied with Paul Puzinas, Carl Molno & Don Stacy. *Work:* Metrop Club, New York. *Exhib:* Ann Exhib Nat Assoc Women Artists, New York, 90-92; Stuhr Mus Prairie Pioneer, Grand Isle, Nebr, 90; Bergen Mus Art & Sci, Paramus, NJ, 91; Sumner Sch Mus, Washington, DC, 92; Trotting Horse Mus, Goshen, NY, 92; and many others. *Awards:* Gold Medal oil/acrylic, 60th Mems Show, Nat Art League, 90; Cert Excellence, Manhattan Arts Mag, 92; Hon Mention for oil, NY & Conn& Conn Chap, Am Artist Prof League, 92; and others. *Bibliog:* rev, France-Amerique, Le Courrier des Estats Unis, 69; Dorothy Hall (auth), rev, Park East, New York, 69; article, Mixing pensions and painting, Marsh & McLennan News, 90; Artist in the 1990's, Manhattan Arts Mag, 9-10/92. *Mem:* Salmagundi Club; Nat League Am Pen Women; Burr Artists; Nat Asn Women Artists; Audubon Artists; and others. *Media:* Acrylic on Canvas, Watercolor; Pencil. *Mailing Add:* 35-25 78th St Jackson Heights NY 11372

SCHIEBOLD, HANS
PAINTER
b Freiberg, Ger, Feb 12, 38; US citizen. *Study:* Brigham Young Univ, Utah, BA, 68; Hartford Art Sch of Univ Hartford, Conn, MFA, 70. *Work:* Aldrich Mus Contemp Art, Conn; New Britain Mus Am Art, Conn; Brownsville Art Mus, Tex; Wichita Art Mus, Kans; Southern Conn State Col, New Haven. *Comn:* Mural, Sedgewick Co Courthouse-Co Comnr, Kans, 81; 12 public murals, Kans Arts Commission & Wichita Arts Board, Kans, 80; 3 outdoor murals, Wesleyan Univ, Conn, 76. *Exhib:* Invitation Acad Exhib, Wadsworth Atheneum, Conn, 71-73; Contemporary Reflections, Aldrich Mus, Conn, 74; one-man shows, Ctr Arts, Wesleyan Univ, Conn, 74, Razor Gallery, New York, 77, Mus Art, Okla, 80 & Wichita Art Mus, Kans, 81. *Teaching:* Asst prof painting & drawing, Wesleyan Univ, Conn, 70-78 & Wichita State Univ, Kans, 78-82. *Awards:* Best in Show, Greater Hartford Arts Festival, 72; First Prize, Conn Acad, 74 & Springfield Art League, Mass, 75. *Media:* Acrylic, Graphite. *Dealer:* Runnings Gallery Seattle WA. *Mailing Add:* 13705 SW 118th Ct Portland OR 97223

SCHIEFERDECKER, IVAN E
PRINTMAKER, PAINTER
b Keokuk, Iowa, Apr 14, 35. *Study:* Univ Ill, BFA; Univ Iowa, MFA. *Work:* Colorado Springs Art Ctr; Ohio Univ; Dulin Art Gallery, Knoxville, Tenn; Springfield Art Mus, Mo; Montgomery Art Mus, Ala. *Exhib:* Pa Acad Fine Arts Ann Prints & Drawings, 65; Nat Print Show, Cent Wash State Col, 75; J B Speed Art Mus, Louisville, Ky, 77; Nat Print & Drawing Competition, Minot, NDak, 79; Prints, Drawings, Watercolor Show, Eastern Ky Univ, 79; 1st Mid-Am Exhib, Owensboro Art Mus, Ky, 79; and others. *Teaching:* Assoc prof printmaking, Western Ky Univ, 64-81. *Mem:* Col Art Asn. *Mailing Add:* 1024 High St Bowling Green KY 42101

SCHIETINGER, JAMES FREDERICK
SCULPTOR, EDUCATOR
b Baltimore, Md, Sept 27, 46. *Study:* Fla Presby Col, 64-66; Fla Atlantic Univ, 67; Univ SFla, BA, 68, MFA, 71. *Work:* Univ SFla; Norton Gallery Art, West Palm Beach. *Exhib:* Twenty-fifth Ceramic Nat, Everson Mus, Syracuse, 69; New Photographics, Cent Wash State Col, 71; Photo-Media Show, Mus Contemp Crafts, New York, 71; Light and Lens: Methods of Photography, Hudson River Mus, NY, 73; Images-Dimensional, Moveable, Transferable, Akron Art Inst, 73. *Teaching:* Instr art hist, Fla Atlantic Univ, 71; instr ceramics, Univ SFla, 71-72; instr art, Miami-Dade Community Col, Miami, 72-73; asst prof art, Univ Vt, Burlington, 77-78 & Millikin Univ, 78- *Awards:* First Prize in Sculpture, Winter Park Art Show, 70; Technol & Artist-Craftsman Symposium Award, Octagon Art Ctr, 73; Best in Show, Los Olas Art Festival, Ft Lauderdale, 75. *Mem:* Am Crafts Coun. *Media:* Clay. *Mailing Add:* Art Dept-Millikin Univ 1184 W Main St Decatur IL 62522

SCHIFF, (ADELE M)
ASSEMBLAGE & ARTISTS, COLLEGE ARTIST, SCULPTURE
b Calif, Jan 1, 15. *Study:* Studied at Long Island Univ Art Students League, 6 yrs. *Work:* Nassau Mus Fine Arts, Roslyn, NY; Huntington Mus, NY; Marvin Horowitz, NY Sch Technol, Long Island, NY; House of Representatives, Washington, DC. *Comn:* Numerous comns in Israel, France & Italy. *Exhib:* Nassau Mus, NY; Nat Asn Women Artists, NY; Huntington Mus, NY; Northwest Univ; 2 yr travelling exhib for Mus. *Teaching:* Painting, Studio 6, 52-72. *Awards:* La Review Moderne, France. *Mem:* Nat Asn Women Artists; Great Neck Libr Art Comt. *Publ:* Painting, front page, Metrop Revue; La Revue Mod; Frontpiece, Asn Madison Inst. *Mailing Add:* Five Lake Rd Great Neck NY 11020

SCHIFF, JEAN
ILLUSTRATOR
b Keokuk, Iowa, Oct 20, 29. *Study:* Chicago Art Inst, 49-52; Washburn Univ, 57-60; Univ Kans, 61-63; Col San Mateo, 63-64; Univ Denver, BFA, 66; Univ Colo, Boulder, MFA, 70; Art Students League, NY, 82, Michael Howard Studio, NY, 88-89; Ruth Franklin, Audio, NY, 89. *Work:* St Paul Fine Art Ctr, Minn; Wichita Art Asn; Bucknell Univ; Francis McCray Gallery, Western NMex Univ; Mulvane Art Ctr, Washburn Univ; and others. *Comn:* Illustration, Scott Printing Co, Denver, 75; illustration, Rocky Mountain Mag, 80 & 81; Frederick Ross Co, 82. *Exhib:* Del Mar Col, Corpus Christi, Tex, 79; Minot State Col, NDak, 79; Memphis State Univ, Tenn, 81; Colo Women's Col, Technology Exhib, 81; Objects, Objects, Emanuel Gallery, Denver, 86; Gensler Design Asn, 90, Kyle Benlding Gallery, 92, One Over One Gallery, 92, Spark Gallery, Denver, 92; Univ Delaware, 90; One West Contemp Art Ctr, Ft Collins, Colo, 91. *Teaching:* Instr drawing, Univ Colo, Denver, summer 70; instr drawing, Metrop State Col, 70-71, prof, 71-; vis prof drawing & video workshops, Univ Colo, Colorado Springs, 75, Colo State Univ, Ft Collins, 77, 78 & 82 & Red Deer Col, Alta, Can, 77, Chicago Art Inst, 82, Inst de Arte Federico Brandt, Caracas, Venezuela, 89. *Awards:* Grad Fel, Univ Colo, Boulder, 70; Purchase Award, Stanislaus State Col, 72; Video Workshop fel, Chicago Art Inst, 82; and others. *Mem:* Alliance for Contemp Art; Denver Art Mus, Women's. *Media:* Drawing, Installation. *Mailing Add:* 1276 Corone B-3 Denver CO 80218

SCHIFF, LONNY
PRINTMAKER, CONSERVATOR
b Columbus, Ohio. *Study:* Univ Ill, BA(hons), 53; Worcester Art Mus Sch, fine arts cert, 64; Impressions Workshop, etching study, 65; papermaking study, Rugg Road Handmade Papers, 84-87. *Work:* Fogg Art Mus; Brooklyn Mus; Am Express Co, New York; Publishers Clearing House, Long Island; Nat Mus Am Art, Washington, DC. *Comn:* Complete restoration of oils by Enneking, A C Goodwin, Largelliere, 80-84; wall graphics designer, Framingham Union Hosp, 82; Restoration Folk Paintings of Framingham Hist Soc, 86-89; First Street Cafe, East Cambridge, Mass, 88; NASA Space Ctr Mus, Cape Canaveral, Fla, 88-90. *Exhib:* Mus Mod Art, Gannett Corp, 87; solo shows, Randall Beck Gallery, 86 & 88; Franz Bader Gallery, Washington, DC, 88; First Impressions Gallery, Toronto, Ont, 90; Space Explorer's Asn Show, Riyadh, Saudi Arabia, 90. *Teaching:* Instr oil painting, Adult Classes, Worcester Art Mus, 63-67; instr art appreciation & techniques, Sudbury Art Asn, 68-69; instr printmaking workshop, Charles River Art Ctr, 68, lectr & demonstr of conservation Am folk art, 70- *Awards:* Patron's Prize, Philadelphia Print Club, 86; Morse Graphics Prize, N Coast Collage Soc, Hiram, Ohio, 87; Top Prize, Berkshire Mus, Pitts Field, Mass, 82; plus others. *Mem:* Int Inst Conservators Art, London, Eng; Philadelphia Print Club; NASA Art Team, 88- *Media:* All Media. *Publ:* New York Review of Art, 3rd ed, 88. *Dealer:* Randall-Beck Gallery 123 Newbury St Boston MA 02116. *Mailing Add:* Box 2156 Framingham Center MA 01701

SCHILDKNECHT, DOROTHY E
PAINTER
b Chicago, Ill, Sept 30, 43. *Study:* Am Acad Art. *Work:* St Patrick High Sch, Chicago. *Exhib:* Women Artists on the West, Calif, 90-91; Nat Asn Women Artists, New York, 91; NMex Nat Small Painting Exhib, 91; Okla Art Ann Nat Exhib, Tulsa, 92; Oil Painters Am, Chicago, 92. *Teaching:* Oil painting, Mt Prospect Park Dist & Glenview Park Dist, 88-92, Studio Long Grove, Ill, 91-92. *Awards:* Purchase Award, St Patrick High Sch, 77; Third Place, Nat Exhib NMex Small Picture, 91. *Mem:* Nat Asn Women Artists, New York; Oil Painters Am, Chicago; Palette & Chisel Acad Fine Art, Chicago; Kans Acad Oil Painters, Wichita. *Media:* Oil. *Dealer:* Rosequist Tucson AR. *Mailing Add:* 1356 Whitcomb Des Plaines IL 60018

SCHILLER, BEATRICE
PAINTER, GRAPHIC ARTIST
b Chicago, Ill. *Study:* Inst Design; Ill Inst Technol; Art Inst Chicago; also with Richard Florsheim, Jack Kearney, Herbert Davidson, Kwak Wai Lau & Stanley Mitruk. *Work:* Standard Oil Bldg, Chicago; Excel Packing Co, Wichita, Kans; Univ Ill Med Ctr, Chicago. *Exhib:* Nat Exhib Small Paintings, Purdue Univ, West Lafayette, 64; 17th Ann Nat Exhib Realistic Art, Mus Fine Arts, Springfield, Mass, 66; Butler Inst Am Art, Youngstown, Ohio, 67; New Horizons in Sculpture & Painting, Chicago, 70; Draw 82, Boulder, Colo, 82; one-man exhibs, Later Impressions, 89, State Ill Ctr, 89 & Old Town Triangle Asn Gallery, Chicago, 90; and others. *Awards:* Reinhard Jahn Purchase Award, Union League Club Exhib; Second Prize, Chicago Soc Artists, 90. *Bibliog:* Louise D Yochim (auth), Role and Impact: The Chicago Society of Artists; Louise D Yochim (auth), Harvest of Freedom, a survey of Jewish artists in Am. *Mem:* Chicago Soc Artists (bd mem); Ill Inst Technol (alumni); Arts Club Chicago (prof mxem); Munic Art League Chicago; plus others. *Media:* Watercolor, Graphic. *Mailing Add:* 3150 N Lake Shore Dr Chicago IL 60657

SCHIMANSKY, DONYA DOBRILA
LIBRARIAN, HISTORIAN
b Yugoslavia; US citizen. *Study:* Univ Belgrade, Yugoslavia, BA & MA(art hist); Univ Cologna, WGer, study with Prof Hans Kaufmann; Univ Hamburg, medieval art with Prof Wolfgang Schone; City Univ New York, MLS. *Pos:* Asst to chmn, The Cloisters, New York, 69-73; asst chief librn, Metrop Mus Art Libr, 73-76, mus librn, 76- *Mem:* Int Ctr Medieval Art (secy, 69-74); Spec Libr Asn, New York (secy/treas, 78); Yugoslav Am Art Asn (bd dir, 79-); Art Libr Soc NAm. *Res:* Wall painting in Byzantine art; classification of art books. *Publ:* Auth, The study of medieval ecclesiastical costume, 71 & On stained glass, 72, Metrop Mus Art Bulletin; auth, The Metropolitan Museum of Art Library Classification System: how it works, Art Libr Soc Newsletter, 76; auth, Museum art libraries collection development policy in the United States, Art Librs J, 81. *Mailing Add:* 2025 Broadway No 14C New York NY 10023

SCHINSKY, WILLIAM CHARLES
ADMINISTRATOR, CONSULTANT
b Santa Monica, Calif, Oct 11, 46. *Study:* Calif State Univ, Fullerton, BA, 74, MA, 77. *Pos:* Dir visual arts prog, Southern Arts Fedn, Atlanta, 82-86; independent consult. *Mem:* Am Asn Mus; Southeastern Mus Conf. *Interests:* Administer a regional program for the enhancement and cultivation of art from the Southeast, also administration of regional fellowship program with the National Endowment Arts. *Mailing Add:* 999 Eden Ave SE Atlanta GA 30316

SCHIPPER, MERLE SOLWAY
HISTORIAN, CRITIC
b Toronto, Ont; US citizen. *Study:* Univ Toronto, BA, 43; Univ Calif, Los Angeles, MA(art), 71, PhD(art hist), 74. *Exhib:* Young Italian Art, Otis Art Inst of Parsons Sch Design, Los Angeles, 91. *Collections Arranged:* Americans in Paris: The 50s (auth, catalog), Art Gallery, Calif State Univ, Northridge, 79; 1931 America: The Artists View (auth, catalog), Sierra Nev Mus Art, Reno, 82; Visions of Inner Space, Univ Col Los Angeles & Gallery Mod Art, New Delhi (auth, catalog), 88, 89; Marmo: The New Italian Stone Age, Los Angeles Mus Sci & Ind (auth, catalog), 89. *Pos:* Interviewer Los Angeles art community, Oral Hist Prog, Univ Calif, Los Angeles, 76-77; contribr ed, Artweek, 85-89, corresp Los Angeles, Artnews, 85-87; project dir, Santa Monica Arts Com, 87; researcher, Santa Monica Art Found, Calif, 88-; critic, Los Angeles Daily News, Calif, currently; columnist, Artscene, Los Angeles. *Teaching:* Lectr 20th century art, Calif State Univ, Northridge, 76-78 & Univ Calif, Los Angeles, 77-79; lectr, Univ Southern Calif, 85. *Awards:* Res Fel, Indo-US Subcom Educ & Cult, 88; Travel Grant, Partners Amers, 89. *Bibliog:* Photographic memories: local art historian paints a bright future, Santa Monica Evening Outlook, 7/21/88. *Mem:* Col Art Asn Am; Int Asn Art Critics. *Res:* California women artists, 1900-1920; Southern California art of 1950s & 60s. *Publ:* Auth, Redact, 1984, Willis, Locker & Owens, 84; The Interpretive Link: Surrealism into Abstraction, Newport Harbor Art Mus, 86 & 87; auth, Contemporary Artists, St James Press, London, 89; On the beach: Santa Monica & Venice 1955-1975, Antiques & Fine Art, 9-10/90; Dialogue: Prague/Los Angeles, Visions, 12/90. *Mailing Add:* 835 Grant St No 3 Santa Monica CA 90402

SCHIRA, CYNTHIA
WEAVER, TAPESTRY ARTIST
b Pittsfield, Mass, June 1, 34. *Study:* RI Sch Design, BFA, hon DFA, 56 & 89; L'Ecole D'Art Decoratif, Aubusson, France, 56-57; Univ Kans, MFA, 67. *Work:* Mus Bellerive, Zurich, Switz; Chicago Art Inst, Ill; Renwick Gallery, Nat Mus Am Art, Smithsonian, Washington, DC; Metrop Mus Art, New York; Philadelphia Mus Art, Pa. *Exhib:* Third Triennale Textiles, Lodz, Poland, 78; solo exhibs, Mus Bellerive, Zurich, 79, Spencer Mus Art, Univ Kans, Lawrence, 87, Renwick Gallery, Nat Mus Am Art, Smithsonian, Washington, DC; Textiles 81, Linz, Austria; The Art Fabric: Mainstream, San Francisco Mus Mod Art, 81; Sixth, Eighth & 14th Int Biennale Tapestry, Lausanne, Switz; Fiber R/Evolution, Milwaukee Mus Art, 86; Eloquent Object, Philbrook Art Mus, Tulsa, Okla, 87; Craft Today, Am Crafts Mus, 87; Int Textile Competition '89, Kyoto, Japan; Jacquard Project, Mus Industriel Kultur, Nurnberg, Ger. *Pos:* Chairperson Bd trustees, Haystack Mountain Sch Crafts, Maine, 89-92. *Teaching:* Prof textile design, Univ Kans, 76- *Awards:* Louis Comfort Tiffany Award, 66-67; Nat Endowment Arts Craftsman's Fel, 74- & 83; Kansas Art Commission Fel, 90. *Bibliog:* Betty Park (auth), Poetic Evocations-The Woven Cloth of Cynthia Schira, Vol 45, No 5, Am Craft Mag, 11/85; Nancy Corwin (auth), Cynthia Schira-New Work, Spencer Mus of Art Univ Kans, 87; Charles Talley (auth), Evocative Landscape Weaving, Artweek, vol 19, no 15, 4/16/88. *Mem:* Am Crafts Coun. *Dealer:* Franklin Parrasch Gallery 588 Broadway Suite 403 New York NY 10012. *Mailing Add:* 1700 New Hampshire St Lawrence KS 66044

SCHJELDAHL, PETER
CRITIC, EDITOR
b Fargo, NDak, 42. *Study:* Carlton Col; New Sch, 60-65. *Pos:* Art critic, New York Sunday Times, 70-75, Village Voice, 81-82, Vanity Fair, 83-84 & 7 Days, currently; contrib ed, Art Am, currently. *Awards:* Frank Jewett Mather Award, Col Art Asn, 80. *Publ:* Auth, Cindy Sherman, Pantheon Books, 84; Eric Fischl, Art Am/Stewart, Tabori & Chang, 88; and articles in Artforum, Art News, Art Int, Art & Antiques, Camera Arts, Am Craft and others. *Mailing Add:* 53 St Marks Pl New York NY 10003

SCHLAGETER, ROBERT WILLIAM
ADMINISTRATOR
b Streator, Ill, May 10, 25. *Study:* Univ Ill, BA & MFA; Univ Heidelberg, cert; Univ Chicago; Harvard Univ. *Collections Arranged:* Fifty Years of American Art (1900-1950), 68; Winslow Homer's Florida (1886-1909), 77; George Inness, Florida & the South, 80; Martin Johnson Heade: St Augustine Years (with catalog), 81; Robert Henri & George Bellows (with catalog), 81. *Pos:* Dir, Mint Mus Art, Charlotte, NC, 58-66; assoc dir, Downtown Gallery, New York, 67; assoc dir, Ackland Art Ctr, Univ NC, Chapel Hill, 67-; dir, Cummer Gallery Art, Jacksonville, Fla, 76- *Teaching:* Asst prof art hist, Univ Tenn, Knoxville, 52-58. *Publ:* Auth, Winslow Homer: Florida Years, 77; George Inness in Florida, 80; Martin Johnson Heade in Florida, 81. *Mailing Add:* c/o Cummer Gallery Art 829 Riverside Ave Jacksonville FL 32204

SCHLAM, MURRAY J
SCULPTOR
b Tyczyn, Austria, May 7, 11; US citizen. *Study:* Langfuhr Univ, Free City Danzig; Arthipenko Art Sch; New York Univ, with Prof Ross; Art Students League, with Robert Brackman; Nat Acad. *Work:* Fordham Univ, Lincoln

Ctr, New York; Einstein Med Col, Bronx, NY; Mus Bat-Yam, Israel; Univ Miami, Fla; St Francis Hosp, Miami. *Comn:* Dr Bela Schick, Einstein Med Col, 59; Herman Muehlstein, Muehlstein Plastic Co, New York, 60; Dr Leo Michel, Grossinger Country Club, NY, 62; Rocky Marciano, pvt collection, 64; Leo Lowenstein, Fordham Univ, Lincoln Ctr, 68; and others. *Exhib:* Madison Ave Gallery, New York, NY, 75; one-man show, Nat Mus Fine Arts, Santiago, Chile, 77; Metrop Mus Art, New York, 79; Mus Fine Arts, Rio Quatro, Arg, 79; Centro Lincoln, Buenos Aires, Arg, 79; Int Art Expo, New York, NY, 86. *Pos:* Art dir, Grossinger Hotel, 53-67 & Second Masonic Dist, 62-64. *Teaching:* Asst dir sculpture, Art Life Sch, New York, 53-57; instr drawing, City Col New York, 61-63; instr sculpture, Albert Pels Art Sch, New York, 64-66. *Awards:* Gold Medal, Second Masonic Dist, New York, 62. *Mem:* Fel Royal Soc Art, London; Nat Soc Arts & Lett. *Media:* Bronze. *Mailing Add:* 25 Chateau Dr Melville NY 11747

SCHLANGER, JEFF
SCULPTOR
b New York, NY, 37. *Study:* Swarthmore Col, BA; Cranbrook Acad Art, with Maija Grotell. *Work:* Sheldon Mem Art Gallery, Univ Nebr, Lincoln; Am Craft Mus, New York; Cranbrook Art Mus, Bloomfield Hills, Mich. *Comn:* Tile mural, Performing Arts Ctr, 82. *Exhib:* Total Cup, Kanazawa City, Tokyo, Kyoto, Japan, 73; Contemp Crafts of the Americas: 75, Ft Collins, Colo, 75; The Object as Poet, Renwick Gallery, Smithsonian Inst, Washington, DC & Mus of Contemp Crafts, New York, 77; one-man shows, State Col Ceramics, Alfred, NY, 78 & City Univ New York Grad Ctr Mall Gallery, 80; and others. *Teaching:* Instr ceramics, Hunter Col, 75 & Pratt Inst Grad Sch, 77; instr sculpture, State Univ NY, Purchase, 82; ceramics, Cranbrook Acad Art, 84. *Awards:* Tiffany Found Scholar, 67; Craftsmen's fel Nat Endowment Arts, 73; fel NY State Creative Artists Pub Serv, 81. *Mem:* Am Craft Coun; Int Sculpture Ctr. *Media:* Clay, Wood. *Publ:* Auth, Maija Grotell, Craft Horizons, 11/69. *Mailing Add:* 556 Stratton Rd New Rochelle NY 10804

SCHLEEH, HANS MARTIN
SCULPTOR
b Königsfeld Schwarzwald, Ger, Oct 9, 28; Can citizen. *Work:* Montreal Mus Fine Arts; Tel Aviv Mus, Israel; Art Gallery Winnipeg; Vancouver Art Gallery; Univ Sherbrooke, Can; Musée Contemporain. *Comn:* Limestone sculpture, Ciba Ltd, Montreal, 56; Swan (carrara marble), Pl Arts, Montreal, 65; copper sculptures, Arthur Maron Enterprises, Montreal, 67; limestone sculpture, Freiman Stores, Ottawa, 73. *Exhib:* Solo exhibs, Dominion Gallery, Montreal, 60-70, Que Sculptors Asn, Montreal, 65-70, Salon Jeune Sculpture, Paris, 66-67 & Expo 67, Montreal, 67; Exposition Int, Rodin Mus, Paris, 71; and others. *Bibliog:* Guy Robert (auth), L'Art au Quebec Depuis 1940, 40 & Ecole de Montreal, 64, La Presse. *Mem:* Royal Can Acad Arts. *Media:* Stone, Metal. *Mailing Add:* 20 Edgecliffe Golfway Apt 604 Don Mills ON M3C 3A4 Canada

SCHLEMM, BETTY LOU
PAINTER, INSTRUCTOR
b Jersey City, NJ, Jan 13, 34. *Study:* Phoenix Sch Design, New York, scholar; Nat Acad Design, New York, scholar. *Work:* US Navy; 1st Nat Bank Boston; Andrew Mellon Collection; American Telephone & Telegraph; also in many other pvt & public collections. *Exhib:* Am Watercolor Soc; Butler Inst Am Art; Nat Acad Design; Allied Artists Am; Audubon Artists. *Pos:* Vpres, Boston Watercolor Soc; regional vpres, Am Watercolor Soc, 89-90 & dir, 90-. *Awards:* Gold Medal, Rockport Art Asn, 81; Frederick B Robinson Award, Academic Artists, 81; Dolfin Fel, Am Watercolor Soc, 81 & Silver Medal, 64; and others. *Bibliog:* 100 Watercolor Techniques, Watson-Guptill, 69; Stephen Doherty (auth), Being An Artist, 92; Lewis Lehrman (auth), North Light, 92; and others. *Mem:* Am Watercolor Soc; Allied Artists Am (secy, 64-65); Rockport Art Asn (mem bd, 70-); Boston Watercolor Soc (vpres, 76-); and others. *Media:* All. *Publ:* Auth, Watercolor page, Am Artist, 64 & 76; auth, Painting with Light, Watson-Guptill, 78, 2nd ed, 79 & 3rd ed, 92. *Dealer:* Guild of Boston Artists 162 Newbury St Boston MA 02116; Rockport Art Asn 10 Main St Rockport MA 01966. *Mailing Add:* Caleb's Lane Rockport MA 01966

SCHLEMOWITZ, ABRAM
SCULPTOR
b New York, NY, July 19, 11. *Study:* Beaux-Arts Inst Design, 28-33; Art Students League, 34; Nat Acad Design, 35-39. *Work:* Chrysler Mus, Provincetown, Mass; Univ Calif, Berkeley; City Univ New York, Kingsborough Col; Univ NC, Greensboro. *Exhib:* One-man shows, Howard Wise Gallery, 61 & 62; Collaboration: Artist & Architect, Mus Contemp Crafts, 62; 12 New York Sculptors, Riverside Mus, 62; Humanists of the 60s, New Sch Social Res, 63; Art in Embassies Traveling Exhib, Mus Mod Art, circulated internationally, 63-64; Retrospective 1960-1977, Kingsborough Col, City Univ New York, 77; and others. *Pos:* Organizing chmn, New Sculpture Group, 57-58. *Teaching:* Instr, Pratt Inst, 62-63; lectr, Univ Calif, Berkeley, 63-64; lectr, Univ Ky, 65; prof, Univ Wis, 65-67; Distinguished lectr, Kingsborough Col, City Univ New York, 70-76; lectr, NY Univ, 78-79, Sculpture Ctr, 80, New Sch Soc Res, 83. *Awards:* Longview Found, 60; Guggenheim Fel, 63; Gottlieb Found Award, 82. *Media:* Bronze, Steel. *Mailing Add:* 139 W 22nd St New York NY 10011

SCHLITTER, HELGA
PAINTER, SCULPTOR
b Mexico City, Mex; Can citizen. *Study:* Studied with Marcel Jean, 68-75. *Work:* Musee du Quebec; Ministry Multicultural Communities, Quebec Govt. *Exhib:* Prêt d'oeuvres d'art, Musee du Quebec, 83, 85 & 86; Femmes-Forces Musee du Quebec, 87; Noel Reinvente, Musee du Civilisation, Quebec, 88; Quetzalpapalotl, le temple de l'oiseau-papillon, 84 & Recent Work, 86, La Chambre Blanche; Tout l'art du monde, itinerary exhib to Montreal, Sherbrooke, Quebec & other cities, 85 & 86; Recent Work, Powerhouse, Montreal, 86; Des jaguar-des serpents-et des temples, Axe-Neo 7, Hull, Que, 86; Encore des animaux, Espace Virtuel, Chicoutimi, Que, 86. *Pos:* Mem exec coun, La Chambre Blanche, Quebec, 80-83, pres, 82-83; pres, Atelier le 88, Quebec, 80-88; mem exec coun, L'Oeil du Poisson, Quebec, 88. *Awards:* Artist-in-residence, Can Art Coun, 84; Quebec Cult Ministry Scholar, 88. *Bibliog:* Marie Delagrave (auth), Architec & paysages imaginaires, 1/28/84 & Helga Schlitter et le temple des papillons, 4/14/84, Le Soleil; Chantal Boulanger (auth), Atelier de l'artiste, Vanguard, 84. *Media:* Multimedia. *Mailing Add:* 635 St-Cyrille Ouest Quebec PQ G1S 1S7 Canada

SCHLOSBERG, CARL MARTIN
ART DEALER
b Los Angeles, Calif, Feb 5, 36. *Study:* Univ Calif, Los Angeles, BS, 58. *Pos:* Dir, Carl Schlosberg Fine Arts, 72- *Mem:* Graphic Arts Coun, Los Angeles Co Mus; Univ Calif, Los Angeles Art Coun; Los Angeles Inst Contemp Art; Nat Soc Lit & Arts; Artists Equity Asn. *Specialty:* Contemporary paintings, graphics, tapestry, sculpture; publisher of Lee Waisler editions; twentieth century master prints; twentieth century American sculpture: Aldo Casanova, George Rickey, Oliver Andrews. *Mailing Add:* 15447 Valley Vista Blvd Sherman Oaks CA 91403

SCHLOSS, ARLEEN P
PAINTER
b Brooklyn, NY, Dec 12, 43. *Study:* Parsons Sch Design, cert; New York Univ, BA; Art Students League. *Work:* Aldrich Mus Contemp Art, Ridgefield, Conn; Am Tel & Tel Longlines, NJ; Mus Mod Art Libr, New York; Lenbachhaus Mus, Munich, Ger. *Exhib:* Tenth Anniv Exhib, Aldrich Mus, Conn, 74; Contemporary Reflections, 1971-74 Traveling Show, Am Fedn Arts, 75-77; Artists Books USA, Allen Mem Art Mus, Oberlin Col, 79; one-woman show, Diagrams, Rush Rhees Gallery, Rochester Univ, 75. *Teaching:* Artist-in-residence art & music, New York Pub Schs, 67-75; guest lectr art, Rochester Univ, 75. *Bibliog:* Jill Dunbar (auth), Avant-Garde--The other end, The Villager, 12/8/77; Enrico Baj (auth), Panorama Mag, 6/86; Frances DeVuono (auth), New York Art Examiner, 89; and others. *Media:* Audio & Visual Materials. *Publ:* Contribr, Weaving: A Handbook of The Fibre Arts, Holt, Rinehart & Winston, 78. *Mailing Add:* 330 Broome St New York NY 10002

SCHMALTZ, ROY EDGAR
PAINTER, EDUCATOR
b Belfield, NDak, Feb 23, 37. *Study:* Otis Art Inst, Los Angeles, 59-60; Univ Wash, Seattle, 60-61; Akademie Der Bildenden Kunste, Munich, Ger, 65-66; San Francisco Art Inst, BFA, 63, MFA, 65. *Work:* Frye Art Mus, Seattle; San Francisco Art Inst & M H De Young Mem Art Mus, San Francisco; Mills Col, Oakland; Amerika-Haus, Munich, Ger; Univ Hawaii, Hilo; and others. *Exhib:* M H De Young Mem Art Mus, San Francisco, 69; San Francisco Mus Mod Art, 71; Oakland Art Mus, 79; Springfield Art Mus, Mo, 81; Butler Inst Am Art, Youngstown, Ohio, 81; Crocker Art Mus, Sacramento, 82; Appalachian State Univ, NC, 82; Univ Hawaii, Manoa, 83; and others. *Pos:* Artists bd, San Francisco Art Inst, 89-92. *Teaching:* Lectr, Col Notre Dame, Belmont, Calif, 68-70; lectr, M H De Young Art Mus, San Francisco, 69-70; prof, St Mary's Col, Moraga, Calif, 69- *Awards:* Fel, Fulbright, Munich, Ger, 65; Walnut Creek Civic Art Ctr Award, 82; San Francisco Art Comn Award, 85. *Bibliog:* Thomas Albright (auth), Art of the San Francisco Bay Area 1945-1980, Univ Calif Press, Berkeley; Bay Area Artists Calendar-1984, KQED TV; Les Krantz (auth), The Calif Art Review, Second ed, Am References, Chicago. *Media:* Oil, Watercolor. *Dealer:* Collectors Gallery Oakland Art Mus 1000 Oak St Oakland CA 94607. *Mailing Add:* 1020 Whistler Dr Suisun City CA 94585

SCHMALZ, CARL (NELSON), JR
PAINTER, EDUCATOR
b Ann Arbor, Mich, Dec 26, 26. *Study:* Eliot O'Hara Watercolor Sch, summers 43 & 44; Harvard Univ, AB, 48, MA, 49, PhD, 58; Amherst Col, Hon MA, 69. *Work:* Walker Art Mus, Brunswick, Maine; Jones & Laughlin Steel Corp, Cleveland, Ohio; Diners Club Am; Blue Cross-Blue Shield; Hampshire Col; Kalamazoo Art Ctr; plus others. *Exhib:* Am Watercolor Soc, 66, 68 & 70; Watercolor USA, Springfield, Mo, 70 & 84; Wichita Centennial Nat Art Exhib, Kans, 70; Wall of Fame Bicentennial Exhib, Baltimore Watercolor Soc, 76 & 85; Boston Atheneum, 79; Govt House Gallery, Hamilton, Bermuda, 79 & Invitation, 86; plus others. *Pos:* Vpres & mem bd dirs, Portland Mus Art, 57-62; art consult, O'Hara Picture Trust, 69- *Teaching:* Asst prof art hist & assoc dir, Bowdoin Col, 53-62; prof art hist, Amherst Col, 62-; dir pvt watercolor workshops, Kennebunkport, Maine, 70-89; private workshops nationally, currently. *Awards:* First Prize for Watercolor, Cambridge Art Asn Ann, 47; First Prize for Traditional Watercolor, Virginia Beach Boardwalk Show, 65; Southern Mo Trust Purchase Award, Watercolor USA, 70; Watercolor USA Honor Soc, 85. *Mem:* Col Art Asn. *Media:* Watercolor, Serigraph. *Publ:* Contribr, A staining and transparent palette, In: Watercolor Portraiture, Putnam, 49; auth, Watercolor Lessons from Eliot O'Hara, 74, Watercolor Your Way, 78 & Finding and Improving Your Painting Style, 86, Watson-Guptill; plus others. *Dealer:* Harmon-Meek Gallery 1258 Third St S Naples FL 33940; Mast Cove Gallery Kennebunkport ME. *Mailing Add:* c/o Harmon Meek Gallery 4262 Gulfshore Blvd N Naples FL 33940

SCHMANDT-BESSERAT, DENISE
HISTORIAN, ARCHAEOLOGIST
b Ay-Champagne, France, Aug 10, 33. *Study:* Ecole du Louvre, Paris, 65. *Collections Arranged:* Permanent exhib, Near Eastern Collections (with catalog), Peabody Mus, Harvard Univ, 68; The Legacy of Sumer, the First Civilization (with catalog & children's catalog), 75 & Ancient Persia--The Art of an Empire, 78, Univ Tex Art Mus. *Pos:* Adv ed, Technology & Cult, 78-92; adv bd, Visible Language, 85- *Teaching:* Prof Paleolithic art & ancient Near East, Univ Tex, Austin, 72-; vis assoc prof, Dept Near Eastern Studies, Univ Calif, Berkeley, 87; guest scholar, Ger Archaeological Inst, Berlin, WGer, 87; guest scholar, Tsukuba Univ, Hiroshima Univ, Japan, 90. *Awards:* Radcliffe Fel, Radcliffe Inst, Cambridge, Mass, 69-71; Nat Endowment Arts Grant, 74-75 & 77-78; Nat Endowment Humanities, 79-80 & 91; Am Coun of Learned Soc Grant, 84; Inst Research in the Humanities Fel, Univ Wis, Madison, 84-85; German Acad Exchange Serv Grant, 86. *Mem:* Archaeol Inst Am (pres, Cent Tex Chap, 74-76, gov bd, 85-); Am Oriental Studies; fel Am Anthropological Asn; Am Sch Oriental Res. *Publ:* Auth, Tablet and tokens: Reexaminaton of the so-called numerical tablets, Vol 15, No 3, 81; The emergence of recording, Am Anthropologists, Vol 84, No 4, 82; Tokens and Counting, Biblical Archaeologist, Vol 46, No 2, 83; Ton Marken and Bilder Schrift, Das Altertum, Vol 31, No 2, 85; The origins of writing, Written Communication, Vol 13, No 1, 86; Before Writing, Univ Tex Press, 92. *Mailing Add:* 11 Hull Circle Austin TX 78746

SCHMID, RICHARD ALAN
PAINTER
b Chicago, Ill, Oct 5, 34. *Study:* Am Acad Art, Chicago, 52-55, with William Mosby. *Exhib:* Invitational Drawing Exhib, Otis Art Inst, Los Angeles, 66; 33rd Ann, Butler Inst Am Art, Youngstown, Ohio, 68; 23rd Ann Drawing Biennial, Norfolk Mus Arts & Sci, 69; 164th Ann, Pa Acad Fine Arts, Philadelphia, 69; Am Watercolor Soc Ann, Nat Acad Design Galleries, New York, 70-71; and many one-man shows throughout US, 58-72. *Awards:* Jane Peterson Prize, Allied Artists Am, 67; Gold Medal of Honor, Am Watercolor Soc, 71, Gold Medal of Honor for Marianne, Am Artist, 72; and others. *Media:* Oil, Watercolor. *Publ:* Auth, Richard Schmid Paints the Figure, 73 & auth, Richard Schmid Paints Landscapes, 75, Watson-Guptill. *Dealer:* Talisman Gallery 115 SE 12th Bartlesville OK 74003. *Mailing Add:* c/o Tailsman Gallery 115 SE 12th Bartlesville OK 74003

SCHMIDT, ARNOLD ALFRED
PAINTER, SCULPTOR
b Plainfield, NJ, Jan 9, 30. *Study:* Art Students League, 49-50; Cooper Union, cert, 56; Hunter Col, BA & MA, 65; also with Hannes Beckmann, Neil Welliver & Tony Smith. *Work:* Mus Mod Art; Rose Art Inst, Brandeis Univ; Newark Mus; Fairleigh Dickinson Univ; Stedelijk Mus, Schiedam, Netherlands. *Exhib:* The Responsive Eye, 65, Optical Art, 66 & Recent Acquisitions, 66, Mus Mod Art, New York; Op Art and Others, Newark Mus, 67; Form and Color, Stedelijk Mus, 67; American Paintings of the Nineteen Sixties, Currier Mus Art, 72; plus others. *Bibliog:* Alfred Barr (auth), What is Modern Art, 67 & Painting and Sculpture in the Museum of Modern Art 1929-1967, Mus Mod Art; Ray Faulkner & Edwin Ilegfeld (auth), Art Today, Holt, Reinhart & Winston, 69. *Media:* Acrylic. *Mailing Add:* 505 La Guardia Pl New York NY 10012

SCHMIDT, CHARLES
PAINTER
b Pittsburgh, Pa, Mar 4, 39. *Study:* Carnegie-Mellon Univ, Pittsburgh, BFA(painting), 60; Cranbrook Acad Art, Bloomfield Hills, Mich, MFA(painting), 67. *Work:* Nat Air & Space Mus, Nat Gallery Art Rosenwald Collection, DC; San Francisco Mus Art; Philadelphia Mus Art; Butler Mus, Youngstown, Ohio; Europ Space Agency, Paris, France. *Comn:* Painting, Nat Aeronautics & Space Admin, 80, 82, 83, 86 & 87; Mem mural of Challenger astronauts, US Senate for US Capitol, dedicated 87. *Exhib:* 164th Ann Exhib, Pa Acad Fine Arts, Philadelphia, 69; Nat Drawing Exhib, San Francisco Mus Art, 70; one-man shows, Lowe Art Mus, Syracuse Univ, NY, 73 & Rosenfeld Gallery, Philadelphia, 76, 80 & 83; Small Works, Newcastle upon Tyne Polytech Mus Art, Eng, 79; Artist and the Space Shuttle int tour, 82-87; Visions of Flight, int tour, 88-91; The Art of Silverpoint, nat tour, 89. *Pos:* Calligrapher, White House Social Staff, DC, 61-62. *Teaching:* Instr, Atlanta Col Art, Ga, 63-65; asst prof, Tyler Sch Art, Temple Univ, Philadelphia, 67-72, assoc prof, 72-81, prof, 81-; asst prof, Temple Abroad Tyler Sch Art Rome, Italy, 70-72. *Awards:* Dana Watercolor Medal, Pa Acad Fine Arts, 69; Purchase Award, Southern Ill Univ, Carbondale, 75; Purchase Award, West Collection, West Publ Co, St Paul, 84. *Bibliog:* Art for armor, Life Mag, 9/21/53; Life on the new frontier, Look Mag, 1/2/62; The watercolor page, Am Artist Mag, 10/77. *Mem:* The Drawing Soc. *Media:* Oil. *Publ:* Illusr, Bioscience, by Platt & Reid, Reinhold Publ, 67. *Dealer:* J Rosenthal Fine Arts Ltd Chicago IL; Capricorn Gallery Bethesda MD. *Mailing Add:* 347 Harrison Ave Elkins Park PA 19117

SCHMIDT, EDWARD WILLIAM
PAINTER
b Ann Arbor, Mich, April 19, 46. *Study:* Art Students League, with R Beverly Hale, 66-69; Skowhegan Sch Painting & Sculpture, 67; Pratt Inst, BFA, 71; Ecole Beaux Arts, Paris, with R Chaplain-midi, 67-68; Brooklyn Col, MFA, 74. *Work:* Bayly Mus Art, Univ Va, Charlottesville; Am Acad Rome; Nat Acad of Design, New York. *Comn:* Mural, Alwyn Court, New York, 77; eight statues, Cincinnati Orchestra Pavilion, comn by M Graves, 85; four murals, Hotel Giorgio, Denver, 87. *Exhib:* Salon Nat Beaux Arts, Grand Palais, Paris, 68; solo exhibs, Bayly Mus Art, Univ Va, Charlottesville, 80, Robert Schoelkopf Gallery, NY, 82, Stiebel Mod, New York, 92, New York Acad Art, New York, 92 & Contemp Realist Gallery, San Francisco, 93; Art & Architecture & Landscape, San Francisco Mus Mod Art, 85. *Teaching:* Assoc prof, New York Acad Art, 82-92. *Awards:* Prix de Rome, Am Acad Rome, 82-83; Ingram Merrill Found Grant, 84-85; Nat Endowment Arts, 85-86. *Bibliog:* Jed Perl (auth), Life of the object, 12/77 & George M Tapley (auth), Arcadian ethos, 2/83, Arts Mag; Lawrence Campbell (auth), article, Art in Am, 2/83; Charles Jencks (auth), Post-Modernism, 87. *Mem:* Soc Fel Am Acad in Rome (vpres). *Media:* Oil. *Dealer:* Stiebel Modern 32 E 57 St New York NY 10022; Contemporary Realist Gallery 23 Grant Ave San Francisco CA 94108. *Mailing Add:* 79 Circuit Rd Tuxedo Park NY 10987

SCHMIDT, FREDERICK LEE
PAINTER, EDUCATOR
b Hays, Kans, Dec 11, 37. *Study:* Univ Northern Colo, BA; Univ Iowa, with Eugene Ludins & Stuart Edie, MFA; also with Joe Patrick & Howard Rogovin. *Work:* Joint Educ Consortium, Arkadelphia, Ark; Worthen Bank, Ark Arts Ctr, Historic Capitol Hotel, Ark State Capitol, Little Rock; Kimberly-Clark, Conway, Ark; Systematics-Little Rock, Ark; La Gas Co, Little Rock; St Vincents Hosp, Little Rock; KPMG Peat, Marwick, Cleveland, Ohio. *Comn:* Stuck, Frier, Lane, Scott Archit, 82; Allison, Moses & Redden Archit, 86; J B Hunt Trucking Co & Cromwell Archit, 90. *Exhib:* Little Rock Arts & Design Fair, 77; 12th Ann Ark Artists Exhib, 78 & 79; 23rd & 24th Ann Delta Exhibs, Little Rock, Ark, 80 & 81; Arkansas Art on Exhibit, Arkadelphia, 82; one-man shows, Heights Gallery, 86 & Terretorial Restoration, Little Rock, Ark, 87; Terretorial Restoration, 89; Ark Art Ctr, Vineyard, Little Rock, 92. *Teaching:* Asst prof art, Northwestern Col, 68-70, Western Carolina Univ, 70-72 & Va Polytech Inst & State Univ, 72-76; instr, Ark State Univ & Ark Arts Ctr, 76-77, Univ Ark, Pine Bluff, 77-78, Ark Arts Ctr, 78- & Mann Arts Magnet, Little Rock. *Awards:* Purchase Awards, 12th Ann Ark Artists Exhib, 79 & 24th Ann Delta Exhib, 81; Governor's Award, Little Rock Arts & Design Fair, 80; Painting Invitational, Hendrix Col, Ark. *Mem:* Nat Col Art Asn. *Media:* Acrylic, Oil. *Dealer:* Cromwell Interior Design & Architects Inc; Boody Fine Arts Inc St Louis MO. *Mailing Add:* 11 Forest Maple Ct Little Rock AR 72212

SCHMIDT, FREDERICK LOUIS
PAINTER, ILLUSTRATOR
b New York, NY, Mar 21, 22. *Study:* Am Sch Design, scholar, 39-41; Phoenix Sch Art, New York, 45-46. *Work:* Federal Home Loan Bank, Executive Offices, Brooklyn Union Gas Co, Hofstra Univ & Calvary Hospital, NY; Nat Bank NC. *Exhib:* Painters & Sculptors Soc NJ, Jersey City Mus, 70; Bergen Co Artists Guild, Bergen Co Mus, NJ, 75; one-man show, Hofstra Univ Club, Long Island, NY, 78; Knickerbocker Artists, Nat Arts Club, New York, 79-80; Am Artists Prof League, Equitable Life US Gallery, New York, 81. *Pos:* Asst art dir, Fairchild Publ Co, New York, 65-77; art dir, Marshall/Altman Adv, New York, 77-82, Newmark, Posner & Mitchell Adv, 82- *Awards:* Second Prize, Salmagundi Spring Auction, 80; Gold Medal, Nat Art League, 80; Lee Loeb Mem Award, Knickerbocker Artists, 81. *Mem:* Nat Art League; Knickerbocker Artists; Artists Fel; Am Artists Prof League; Salmagundi Club. *Media:* Acrylic, Oil. *Mailing Add:* c/o L'Idee Corporate Art Concepts 945 Hatch St Cincinnati OH 45202

SCHMIDT, JULIUS
SCULPTOR
b Stamford, Conn, June 2, 23. *Study:* Okla Agr & Mech Col; Cranbrook Acad Art, BFA & MFA; with Ossip Zadkine, Paris, France, 53; Acad Belle Arti, Florence, Italy, 54. *Work:* Mus Mod Art, New York; Art Inst Chicago; Albright-Knox Art Gallery, Buffalo; Hirshhorn Mus; Whitney Mus Am Art, New York; 38 pub collections. *Exhib:* Sixteen Americans, Mus Mod Art, New York, 59; The Hirshhorn Collection, Guggenheim Mus, New York, 62; Seventh Biennial, Sao Paulo, Brazil, 63; Sculpture in the Open Air, Battersea Park, London, Eng, 63; Biennial, Middleheim, Belg, 71; and 35 one-man shows. *Teaching:* Chmn dept sculpture, Kansas City Art Inst, 54-59; vis artist sculpture, RI Sch Design, 59-60 & Univ Calif, Berkeley, 61-62; chmn dept sculpture, Cranbrook Acad Art, 62-70; head dept sculpture, Univ Iowa, 70- *Awards:* Guggenheim Fel, 64. *Bibliog:* H Read (auth), Concise History of Modern Sculpture, Praeger, 64; Redstone (auth), Art in Architecture, McGraw, 68; Feldman (auth), Varieties of Visual Experience, Prentice-Hall. *Media:* Cast Bronze & Cast Iron. *Mailing Add:* Sch Art Univ Iowa Iowa City IA 52242

SCHMIDT, MARY MORRIS
LIBRARIAN
b Minneapolis, Minn, June 28, 26. *Study:* Univ Minn, BA, 47, MS(libr sci), 54 & MA(art hist), 55; Univ Paris, Fulbright fel, 56-57; New York Univ, 62-65. *Pos:* Art librn, Univ Minn, Minneapolis, 53-55; cataloger-reference librn, Metrop Mus Art, New York, 57-58; indexer, Art Index, H W Wilson Co, Bronx, 58-65, ed, 65-69; fine arts librn, Columbia Univ, New York, 69-77; librn, Marquand Libr, Princeton Univ, NJ, 77-89; spec projs librn, Princeton Univ, NJ. *Mem:* Art Libr Soc NAm; Col Art Asn Am. *Interests:* Romantic book illustration; 19th century American art journals. *Mailing Add:* Marquand Libr Princeton Univ Princeton NJ 08544

SCHMIDT, RANDALL BERNARD
SCULPTOR, EDUCATOR
b Ft Dodge, Iowa, Oct 2, 42. *Study:* Hamline Univ, BA; Univ NMex, MA. *Work:* Univ NMex Art Mus, Albuquerque; Univ Art Collections, Ariz State Univ, Tempe; Col Art Collection, Ariz Western Col, Yuma; Univ Art Collections, Pac Lutheran Univ, Tacoma, Wash; Yuma Fine Arts Asn. *Exhib:* Nat Crafts Exhib, Univ NMex Art Mus, 68; 25th Ceramics Nat, Everson Mus Art, Syracuse, NY, 68-70; Media 68 & Media 72, Civic Arts Gallery, Walnut

Creek, Calif, 68-72; Southwest Crafts '70, Am Crafts Coun, Los Angeles, 70; Crafts 72, Richmond Art Ctr, Calif, 72. *Teaching:* Asst prof ceramics, Ariz State Univ, 68-75, assoc prof, 75-; guest artist, Pac Lutheran Univ, summer 71. *Awards:* Best of Show, 1st Ann Art Exhib, Phoenix Jewish Community Ctr, 68; Award, Media 68, Civic Arts Gallery, 68; Award, Four Corner Painting & Sculpture Biennial, Phoenix Art Mus, Ariz, 71; and others. *Mem:* Ariz Designer-Craftsmen; Nat Coun Educ Ceramic Arts. *Media:* Ceramics, Vinyl. *Res:* Exploration of expanded vinyl as a sculptural material. *Publ:* Contribr, Teaching Secondary School Art, W Brown Co, 71. *Mailing Add:* 834 W 12th St Tempe AZ 85281

SCHMITT, MARILYN LOW
HISTORIAN, ADMINISTRATOR
b Chicago, Ill, May 24, 39. *Study:* Lawrence Univ, Wis, BA, 60; Univ Calif, Berkeley, MA, 62; Seminar, Bibliotheque Royale, Brussels, 62; Yale Univ, PhD, 72. *Pos:* Dir, Int Ctr Medieval Art; dir, Abraham A Low Inst. *Teaching:* Vis lectureships, Univ of Nebr, 63, Univ of Colo, 75 & Southern Methodist Univ, 77; instr, Dickinson Col, Carlisle, Pa, 64-66; actg instr, Yale Univ, 69-70; asst prof art hist, Southern Conn State Col, New Haven, 70-75; asst prof, Univ Miami, 75-78, assoc prof, 79-82; prog officer, J Paul Getty Trust, 83-84; prog mgr, Getty Art Hist Info Prog, 85. *Awards:* Woodrow Wilson Fel, 60-61; Am Asn Univ Women Fel, 68-69; Individual Res Fel, Nat Endowment Humanities, 81-82; Earthwatch Research Expedition, 82. *Mem:* Col Art Asn Am; Int Ctr Medieval Art. *Res:* Romanesque sculpture in France; computerization of art-historical info. *Publ:* Auth, The carved gable of Beaulieu-les-Loches, Gesta, 75; auth, Alice Neel, Arts Mag, 78; auth, Random reliefs and primitive friezes: Re-used sources of Romanesque sculpture?, Viator, 80; auth, Traveling carvers in the Romanesque: The case history of St Benoit-sur-Loire, Selles-sur-Cher, Meobecq, Art Bulletin, 81; coauth, Object, Image, Inquiry: The Art Historian at Work, 88. *Mailing Add:* c/o Getty Art Hist & Info Prog 401 Wilshire Blvd Suite 1100 Santa Monica CA 90401

SCHMUTZHART, BERTHOLD JOSEF
SCULPTOR, EDUCATOR
b Salzburg, Austria, Aug 17, 28; US citizen. *Study:* Acad Appl Art, Vienna, Austria; masterclass for ceramics & sculpture. *Work:* Mr & Mrs Hirshhorn Collection; Fredericksburg Gallery Mod Art, Va. *Comn:* Christ (wood), St James Church, Washington, DC, 62, Christ (bronze), 64; bacchus fountain, Fredericksburg Gallery, 67; Christ (steel), St Clements Church, Inkster, Mich, 68, processional cross (bronze), 71; cross (guilded wood), Church of Reformation, Washington, DC, 74. *Exhib:* Washington Artists, Massilon Mus, Ohio, 69; Twenty Washington Artists, Nat Collection Fine Arts, Washington, DC, 70; Art Barn, US Dept Interior, Washington, DC, 71; Franz Bader Gallery, Washington DC, 78-81; Nat Gallery Mod Art, New Delhi, India, 90; and others. *Teaching:* Assoc prof sculpture & chmn sculpture dept, Corcoran Sch Art, Washington, DC, 63-81, prof, 81- *Awards:* First Prizes, Wash Relig Arts Soc, 60 & Southern Sculpture, 66; First Prize Silver Medal, Audubon Soc, 71. *Bibliog:* Off Econ Opportunity (auth), A Face for the Future (film), Booker Assocs, Reston, Va, 65; Tools for Learning (film), Kingsbury Ctr, Washington, DC, 71. *Mem:* Am Asn Univ Prof; Guild Religious Archit; Artist's Equity Asn (pres, Washington, DC Chap, 73). *Media:* Multimedia. *Publ:* Auth, The Handmade Furniture Book, Prentice-Hall, 81. *Dealer:* Franz Bader Gallery 1701 Pennsylvania Ave NW Washington DC 20006. *Mailing Add:* 18 Ninth St NE Washington DC 20002

SCHMUTZHART, SLAITHONG CHENGTRAKUL
INSTRUCTOR, SCULPTOR
b Bangkok, Thailand, Jan 1, 34; US citizen. *Study:* Corcoran Sch Art, Washington, DC, dipl sculpture, 68, dipl ceramics, 70; Univ DC, BA(fine arts), 77; George Washington Univ, MFA(sculpture), 83. *Comn:* Polychromed wood altar relief, Sr Citizens Home, Inkster, Mich; polychromed wood relief, comn by Dr Morton Ehudin for dental off, Oxon Hill, Md, 77; Corten steel standing figure, comn by Mr & Mrs Leon Baer, Alexandria, Va, 77; polychromed wood relief, comn by James Ellison, Capitol Hill, Washington, DC, 77; corten steel figure, comn by Dr & Mrs W Proctor Harvey, McLean, Va. *Exhib:* Nat Collection Fine Arts, Washington, DC, 68; Textile Mus, Washington, DC, 73-74; Columbus Mus, Ga; Corcoran Gallery, 75 & Phillips Gallery, 76, Washington, DC; one man shows, Franz Bader Gallery, Washington, DC, 77, Univ DC, 77, Mt Vernon Col, 78, 79, 86 & 92 & Antioch Univ, Md, 79. *Teaching:* Asst instr sculpture, Off Economic Opportunity, Job Corps, 65-66; instr art, Lab Sch, Kingsbury Ctr, Washington, DC, 68-71 & Northern Va Community Col, 78-; lectr studio art, Mt Vernon Col, 78- & Am Univ, Washington DC, 79-; asst prof sculpture, Corcoran Sch Art, Washington DC, 80. *Awards:* Ford Found Scholar in Sculpture, 66. *Bibliog:* Sarah B Conroy (auth), Living in style, Washington Post, 2/71; Benjamin Forgey (auth), Washington's Artists, Sunday Star, 12/71; Anne Ogden (auth), New Ways with Stained glass, House Beautiful, 8/73. *Mem:* Artists Equity Asn. *Media:* Welded Steel, Woodcarving. *Dealer:* Franz Bader Gallery 1701 Pennsylvania Ave NW Washington DC 20006. *Mailing Add:* 1011 E Capitol St Washington DC 20003

SCHNABEL, JULIAN
PAINTER
b New York, NY, 51. *Study:* Univ Houston, Tex, BFA, 73; Whitney Independent Study Prog, New York, 73-74. *Work:* Tate Gallery, London; Centre Georges Pompidou, Paris; Whitney Mus Am Art, Mus Mod Art & Metrop Mus Art, New York; Fogg Art Mus, Harvard Univ, Boston; Lannan Found, Lake Worth, Fla; Mus Contemp Art, Los Angeles; and many others. *Exhib:* Graphische Arbeiten 1983-1991, Galerie Daniel Blau, Munich, 91 & 92, Gallerie Bruno Bischofberger, Zurich, 92, Pace Eds, New York, 92, Olatz, Pace Gallery, New York, 92, The End of the Summer, Pace Gallery, New York, 92 & Hurricane Bob, Pace Gallery, New York, 92; Yvon Lambert Collectionne, Musée d'art Moderne de la Communauté Urbaine de Lille, Villeneuve d'Ascq, France & Musée des Beaux-Arts, Tourcoing, France, 92; Contemporary Masters, Margaret Lipworth Fine Art, Boca Raton, Fla, 92; 15th Anniversary Exhibs, Rhona Hoffman Gallery, Chicago, 92; Max Hetzler/Thomas Borgmann, Cologne, 92; sculpture, Waddington Galleries, London, Eng, 92; and many other one-man & group exhibs. *Bibliog:* Guy Davenport (auth), Artists' Sketchbooks, Matthew Marks, New York, 91; Julian Schnabel: Graphische Arbeiten 1983-1991, Galerie Daniel Blau, Munich, 91; Sculpture, Waddington Galleries, London, 92; Gabriella De Ferrari (auth), Olatz/The End of the Summer/Hurricane Bob, Pace Gallery, New York, 92; Jean-Christophe Ammann & Jerry Salz (auths), Robert Gober, On Kawara, Mike Kelly, Martin Kippenberger, Jeff Koons, Albert Oehten, Julian Schnabel, Cindy Sherman, Thomas Struth, Philip Taaffe, Christopher Wool, Max Hetzter/Thomas Borgmann, Cologne, 92; and many others. *Dealer:* Pace Gallery 32 E 57th St New York NY 10022. *Mailing Add:* 24 E 20th St New York NY 10003

SCHNACKENBERG, ROY
PAINTER, SCULPTOR
b Chicago, Ill, Jan 14, 34. *Work:* Whitney Mus Am Art, New York; Art Inst Chicago. *Exhib:* Whitney Recent Acquisitions Show, 67 & Whitney Ann, 67-69; New American Realists, Goteberg, Sweden, 70; Beyond Illustration, The Art of Playboy World Tour, 71-; Recent Acquisitions Show, Art Inst Chicago, 71; Dept Interior Bicentennial Exhib, Corcoran Gallery, Washington, DC; and numerous one-man & group shows. *Awards:* Copley Found Award, 67. *Mailing Add:* 1919 N Orchard Chicago IL 60614

SCHNEEBAUM, TOBIAS
PAINTER
b New York, NY, Mar 25, 21. *Study:* Work Prog Admin, 35-36; City Col New York, BA, 42; Brooklyn Mus Art Sch, with R Tamayo, 46 & A Osver, 47; Goddard Col, Vt, MA;(cultural anthrop). *Work:* Mus Estado, Guadalajara, Mex; Mus Nat, Cuzco, Peru. *Exhib:* Smithsonian Inst, Washington, DC, 55; Peridot Gallery, 55-70; Univ Nebr, 63; Art Inst Chicago, 64; Univ Colo, 65; Goldwater Libr, Metrop Mus Art, 85. *Teaching:* Instr painting, Ajijic Sch Art, Mex, 47-49; instr primitive art, New Sch for Social Research, NY. *Awards:* Fulbright Fel, 55 & 56; Creative Artists' Pub Serv Prog, 74; Firefly Fund Award, 75; John D Rockefeller III Found, 75 & 83; Ingram Merril, 82. *Media:* Oil, Pen & Ink. *Publ:* Illusr, The Girl in the Abstract Bed, 54; auth, Keep the River on Your Right, Grove Press, 69; Wild Man, Viking Press, 79; Asmat: Life with the ancestors, 81 & Asmat Images, 85. *Mailing Add:* 463 West St New York NY 10014

SCHNEEMANN, CAROLEE
PAINTER, FILMMAKER
b Fox Chase, Pa, Oct 12, 39. *Study:* Univ Ill, Urbana, MFA; Bard Col, MA; Columbia Univ Sch Painting & Sculpture, New York; New Sch Social Res, New York; Univ de Puebla, Mexico. *Work:* Mus Contemp Art, Chicago; Erotica Archives Mus, Yugoslavia; Philadelphia Mus Art; Inst Contemp Art, London; Cincinnati Mus Art. *Exhib:* Fluxfestival, Forum Theatre, Berlin, 71; Up to and Including Her Limits, Univ Art Mus, Berkeley, Calif; Anthology Film Archives, New York, 74; Palazzo Reale, Milan, 81; Max Hutchinson Gallery, New York, 82-83; Contemp Arts Ctr, Cincinnati, 90; Venice Bienbnale, Italy, 90; Mus Mod Art, San Francisco, 91; and others. *Pos:* Founder-dir, Kinetic Theatre, New York; vis artist, San Francisco Art Inst, Calif, 92. *Teaching:* Instr art, Art Inst Chicago, Ill, Rutgers Univ, NJ, Univ Colo, Univ Ohio & Univ Calif, Los Angeles. *Awards:* Nat Endowment Arts Grants, 74 & 77; Creative Artists Pub Serv Grant, NY, 78; Visual Artist Fel, Nat Endowment Arts, 83 & 85. *Mem:* Women's Caucus Art; Col Art Assoc. *Publ:* Auth, Kenneth Anger's Scorpio Rising, Film Culture No 32, New York, 64; Love Paint Ritual Technicians of the Sacred, New York, 69; Banana Hands, Plays for Children to Direct, London, 70; More Than Meat Joy (complete performance works & selected writings), 78 & Carolee Schneeman: Early & Recent Work (monography of painting--constructions 1963-1983), 83, Documentext. *Dealer:* Emily Harvey New York NY. *Mailing Add:* 114 W 29th St New York NY 10001

SCHNEIDER, IRA
VIDEO ARTIST, PHOTOGRAPHER
b New York, NY, Mar 2, 39. *Study:* Brown Univ, AB, 60; Univ Wis, MA, 64. *Work:* Mus Mod Art Film Arch, New York; Donnell Film Libr, New York; Anthology Film Arch, New York; Long Beach Mus Art, Calif. *Comn:* Wipe Cycle (video installation, with Frank Gillette), Howard Wise Gallery, New York, 69; Manhattan is an Island (video installation), 74 & Video 75 (video installation), 75, The Kitchen, New York. *Exhib:* Videotape (circuit), Los Angeles Co Mus, Los Angeles, 73; Manhattan is an Island (video installation), Whitney Mus Am Art, New York, 77; Proj XIII (videotape), Mus Mod Art, New York, 77; Palais de Beaux Art, Brussels, 84; Kunst Halle Mannheim, 85; Musee Mod Art, Lyon, 85; Mus Moderne Kunst, Vienna, 86; Barbican, London, 86; Wipe Cycle (installation), Kunstverein, Köln, 89; Kongresshalle, Berlin, 89; and others. *Pos:* Ed, Radical Software, Raindance Mag, 70-74; pres, Raindance Found, New York, 72- *Teaching:* Vis lectr video art, Univ Calif, San Diego, 76-77, 78-79; adj assoc prof art, Cooper Union, New York, 79-92. *Awards:* Film Contest Award, Philharmonic Hall, Lincoln Ctr, New York, Nat Student Asn, 67; Nat Endowment Arts Individual Artist Fels, 76 & 79; Guggenheim Found Fel, 77. *Bibliog:* David Antin (auth), Aspects of the video medium?, Artforum, 76; Russell Conor (auth), Panorama--video gallery, WNET Pub Broadcasting System, 77; Grace Glueck (auth), Critics choice, New York Times, 5/3/81. *Publ:* Contribr, Guerillo Television, Holt Rinehart

& Winston, 71; co-ed (with Beryl Korot), Video Art, Harcourt Brace Jovanovich, 76; and others. *Dealer:* Electronic Art Intermix 636 Broadway New York NY 10012. *Mailing Add:* 51 Fifth Ave No 11-D New York NY 10003

SCHNEIDER, JANET M
MUSEUM DIRECTOR, PAINTER
b New York, NY, June 6, 50. *Study:* Queens Col, City Univ New York, BA(fine arts, summa cum laude), 72; Boston Univ Tanglewood Inst, special study, fine arts, 71. *Exhib:* Long Island Invitational, CW Post Art Gallery, 81; The First Eight Years, The Artists Choice Mus, 84. *Collections Arranged:* Sons and others: Women Artists See Men (auth, catalog), 75; Urban Aesthetics (auth, catalog), 76; Masters of the Brush: Chinese Painting and Calligraphy from the Sixteenth to the Nineteenth Century (auth, catalog), 77; Symcho Moszkowicz: Portrait of the Artist in Postwar Europe (auth, catalog), 78; Shipwrecked 1622: The Lost Treasure of Philip IV (auth, catalog), 81; Michelangelo: A Sculptor's World (auth, catalog), 83; Joseph Cornell, Revisited, (auth, catalog), 92. *Pos:* Cur, Queens Mus, 73-75, prog dir, 75-77 & exec dir, 77-89. *Teaching:* Instr mus cert prog, Hofstra Univ, 85-86. *Mem:* Gallery Asn NY State (bd dirs, 79-81); Artists Choice Inc (bd trustees, 79-82); Cult Inst Group (chmn, 86-87); Mayor's Adv Comn Cult & Arts, New York (pres, 91). *Media:* Oil. *Dealer:* Prince St Gallery 121 Wooster New York NY 10012. *Mailing Add:* 35-39 159th St Flushing NY 11419

SCHNEIDER, JO ANNE
PAINTER
b Lima, Ohio, Dec 4, 19. *Study:* Sch Fine Arts, Syracuse Univ. *Work:* Butler Inst Am Art, Youngstown, Ohio; Syracuse Univ; Allentown Mus, Pa; St Lawrence Univ; Metrop Mus Art, New York; and others. *Exhib:* Corcoran Gallery Art, Washington, DC; Whitney Mus Am Art Ann, New York; 50 Years of Am Art, Am Fedn Art, 64; Childe Hassam Fund Exhib, Am Acad Arts & Lett, 71; plus one-man exhibs, 54-85. *Awards:* First Prize, Guild Hall, 67; Marion K Haldenstein Mem Prize, Nat Asn Women Artists, 70; Stanley Grumbacher Mem Award, Audubon Artists, 72. *Media:* Oil. *Mailing Add:* 35 E 75th St New York NY 10021

SCHNEIDER, JULIE (SAECKER)
PAINTER, DRAFTSMAN
b Seattle, Wash, Mar 7, 44. *Study:* Univ Wis, Madison, BS(art); Univ Wis, MFA(two-dimensional painting), 76. *Work:* Minn Mus Art, St Paul; Algur Meadows Mus, Shreveport, La; Rutgers Univ, Camden, NJ; State Univ NY Col, Potsdam; Indianapolis Mus Art; Lakeview Mus, Peoria, Ill; Birke Art Gallery, Marshall Univ; Glenn C Janss Collection, Boise Art Mus; Shepherd Col Art Mus. *Exhib:* Drawings USA Nat Exhibs (traveling show), Minn Mus Art, Saint Paul, 75 & 77; Am Drawings, Tidewater Art Coun & Portsmouth Community Art Ctr, Va, 76 & 78; Davidson Nat Print & Drawing Competition, Appalachian Nat Drawing Competition, Boone, 76, NC; Smithsonian Travel Exhibs, 76 & 78; Bradley Print & Drawing Competition, Bradley Univ, Peoria, Ill, 77, 79 & 85; Drawing Invitational, Goucher Col, Towson, Md, 85; Washington Community Artists, Jane Haslem Gallery, Washington, DC, 85; solo exhibs, Am Int Col, 80, Arlington Arts Ctr, Va, 85, Recent Work, Arlington Arts Ctr, Va & Drawings, Fairweather-Hardin Gallery, 86, Jane Haslem Gallery, Washington, DC, 89 & Tretyakov Gallery, Moscow USSR, 90-91; Am realists (with catalog), San Francisco Mus Mod Art, Calif, 85-86; Realism/Idealism (with catalog), Jane Haslem Gallery, Washington, DC; Am Drawing, Boca Raton Mus Art; 12th Ann Int Drawing Invitational, Emporia, Kans; and others. *Teaching:* Adj prof, Williams Col, 82-84; lectr, Northern Va Community Col, Alexandria; instr, Interlochen Ctr Arts; asst prof, No Va Community Col, currently; vis lectr, Va Mus Artists-in-residence series, Md Inst Col Art, Interlochen Ctr Arts, Towson State Univ. *Awards:* Purchase Awards, Rutgers Nat Drawing 77, Drawings USA-77, Minn Mus of Art, St Paul, 77 & Bradley Print & Drawing, 79; Finalist, Mass Artist Found Grants, 80; Fel, Mid Atlantic Found, 88. *Bibliog:* Sandra Conn (auth), Julie Schneider-Jerry Torn at the Fairweather-Hardin Gallery, Reader, 4/2/82; Susan Blake (auth), Julie Schneider-Jerry Torn, Fairweather-Hardin, New Art Examiner, 5/82; Susan Heller (auth), Figurative artists - Washington DC, Arts Mag, 1/83; Michael Welzenbach (auth), article in Washington Times, 5/15/85; Nichols Coleman (auth), Shifting images, Washington Post, 5/16/85; American Realism, San Francisco Mus Mod Art & Abrams Press, 85; Pamela Kessler (auth), Galleries, Washington Post, 5/20/87. *Mem:* Col Art Asn; FATE. *Media:* Graphite, mixed media. *Dealer:* Fairweather-Hardin Galleries 101 E Ontario Chicago IL 60611; Quadrum Gallery Chestnut Hill MA 02167. *Mailing Add:* 3550 Wilson Boulevard Arlington VA 22201

SCHNEIDER, LISA DAWN
DEALER, CRITIC
b Brookline, Mass, Nov 16, 54. *Study:* Boston Mus of Fine Arts Sch, Mass; DeCordova Mus; Syracuse Univ, Visual & Performing Arts Sch; Finch Col; Arts Sch League; Marymount Col, BA(fine arts). *Pos:* Asst dir, Galerie Denise/Rene, 76-77; art critic & art ed, Women's Week, 77-79; dir, Robert Freidus Gallery, New York, 78; assoc dir, Bertha Urdang Gallery, New York, 79-; exec dir, Cur Consul & Galleries, NY & Boston, 80-; cur, Fisher Brothers Collection, 82- *Awards:* Third Annual Interiors Award, Ramco Co Art Collection. *Specialty:* Nineteenth & twentieth century Europe & American paintings, drawings, photography & sculpture. *Mailing Add:* 135 E 54th St New York NY 10022

SCHNEIDER, NOEL
SCULPTOR, PAINTER
b New York, NY, July 31, 20. *Study:* Art Students League, with William Zorach; City Univ NY, AS(fine arts, hons), 85. *Work:* Permanent collection Kingsborough Community Col, City Univ New York. *Comn:* Willner Mem Bas Relief, Bergen Co YMHA, 64. *Exhib:* Two-man show, Meet Sculptor Ser, Sculpture Ctr, New York, 69; 28th Ann Nat Exhib Painters & Sculptors, Jersey City Mus, 69; Salmagundi Club, 70; Nat Arts Club, 74; Brooklyn Mus, NY, 76, 77 & 79; US Customhouse Mus, 79 & 81. *Awards:* Gold Medal Sculpture, Salmagundi Club, 70; First Prize Sculpture, Nat Arts Club, 74; First Prize Sculpture, US Customhouse Mus, 82. *Bibliog:* Feature, New York Sunday News, 4/22/56; interview, New York World Telegram & Sun, 2/21/62; article, New Writers, 9/74. *Mem:* Artists Equity Asn. *Media:* Welded Metal, Wood. *Mailing Add:* 124 Oxford St Manhattan Beach Brooklyn NY 11235

SCHNEIDER, RICHARD DURBIN
CERAMIST, CRAFTSMAN
b Toledo, Ohio, April 5, 37. *Study:* Univ Toledo, BA, 63; Bowling Green State Univ, MA, 68. *Work:* Utah Mus Fine Arts, Salt Lake City; Cleveland Mus Art; Ohio Wesleyan Univ; Libbey-Owens, Ford Collection, Toledo. *Exhib:* Eighteenth Nat Las Vegas Art Exhib, Las Vegas Art Mus, 75; Materials & Techniques of 20th Century Artists, Cleveland Mus Art, 76; Lake Superior 4th Biennial Int Exhib, Tweed Mus Art, Duluth, Minn, 77; Beaux Art Designer, Columbus Mus Art, Ohio, 79; Eighth State Ann Craft Exhibition, JB Speed Art Mus, Louisville, Ky, 80; 28th Annual National Drawing & Sculpture, Ball State Univ, Muncie, Ind, 82; First Annual American Ceramic National, Downey Mus Art, Calif, 83. *Teaching:* Asst prof ceramics, Monroe Co Community Col, Mich, 69-71; assoc prof, Cleveland State Univ, Ohio, 71- *Awards:* Special Award Sculpture, Cleveland Mus Art, 72; Purchase Award Ceramics, Butler Mus Am Art; Juror's Award for Drawing, Kansas 6th National Exhib, Ft Hays State Univ, 81. *Bibliog:* Lynette Rhodes (auth), Nine artisans, Craft Horizons, 74; Elizabeth McClelland (auth), Ceramic sculpture, Nat Orgn Visual Artists News, 80; Roger Welchans (auth), Dialogue, Ohio Arts J, 83. *Publ:* Auth, Large thrown forms, 76 & Surface decoration on ceramic functional ware, 82, Ceramics Monthly. *Dealer:* Sylvia Ullman Gallery of American Crafts Larchmere Woodland Shaker Heights OH 44121. *Mailing Add:* 2610 Exeter Rd Cleveland Heights OH 44118

SCHNEIDER, SHELLIE
COLLAGE ARTIST, PRINTMAKER
b Brooklyn, NY, Oct 12, 32. *Study:* Cooper Union Art Sch, with Nick Marsicano & Leo Manso, 54; Hunter Col, with Tony Panzera, BA(cum laude, printmaking), 74; Queens Col, with Walter Kendra, MS(art educ), 77. *Work:* Voluntary Hosps Asn, Tampa, Fla; Chalgrin Co Ltd, Osaka, Japan; Am Stock Exchange, New York. *Comn:* Triptych (collage), comn by Mr & Mrs Kurtz, Long Island, NY, 90. *Exhib:* Ann Nat Asn Women Artists, Fed Plaza, New York, 80-92; Plandome Gallery, New York, 83; Nat Works on Paper '88, Firehouse Gallery, Nassau Community Col, Garden City, NY, 88; one-person show, From There to Here--In a Decade, Graphic Eye Gallery, Port Washington, NY, 91; Multi-Media Art Forum & Exhib, Hempstead House, Sands Point, New York, 91. *Pos:* Co-pres, Graphic Eye Coop Gallery, Port Washington, New York, 86-87. *Teaching:* Art instr K-12 & adult educ, Port Washington, New York, 74-92; adj instr printmaking, C W Post Univ, New York, 80. *Awards:* First Place, Sheffield Art League, 86; Award Excellence, Nassau Co Mus Fine Art, 86; Medal Honor, Nat Asn Women Artists, Leila Sawyer Mem, 88. *Mem:* Nat Asn Women Artists (jury selection, printmaking, 88); Sheffield Art League; Port Washington Libr Art Adv Counc (rec secy, 92); Graphic Eye Gallery (coop gallery) 80-92. *Media:* Paint; Serigraphy. *Mailing Add:* 43 Driftwood Dr Port Washington NY 11050

SCHNEIDERMAN, DOROTHY
DEALER
b New York, NY, Apr 11, 19. *Pos:* Dir, Harbor Gallery, 65- *Mem:* Int Fine Print Dealers Asn (bd mem). *Specialty:* Nineteenth & twentieth century fine prints. *Mailing Add:* 24 W 57th St New York NY 10019

SCHNEIDERMAN, RICHARD S
MUSEUM DIRECTOR
b NJ, June 27, 48. *Study:* Hartwick Col, BA, 70; Univ Cincinnati, MA, 73; State Univ NY Binghamton, PhD, 76. *Collections Arranged:* West Meets East, Impressionism in Nineteenth Century Prints, 78-80; J M W Turner Watercolors from the British Museum (auth introd, catalog), 82; Guardians of the Spire: The Gargoyle Image in Prints, 84; Drawings as Drawings: Works from the Ackland and the Weatherspoon, 87-88; Robes of Elegance: Japanese Kimono from the Sixteenth-Twentieth Centuries, 88; Nature into Art: English Landscape Watercolors from the British Museum, 91. *Pos:* Cur prints & drawings, Ga Mus Art, Univ Ga, Athens, 76-86, dir, 81-86; dir, NC Mus Art, Raleigh, 86- *Teaching:* Adj prof hist art, Tompkins-Cortland Community Col, Cortland, NY, winter 76; lectr mod art, State Univ NY Binghamton, summer 76; adj assoc prof, dept art, Univ Ga, 83-86. *Mem:* Am Asn Mus; Am Soc Aesthet; Col Art Asn; Asn Art Mus Dirs; Print Coun Am. *Res:* History of prints, primarily English and northern European. *Publ:* Contribr, A Catalogue Raisonne of the Prints of Sir Francis Seymour Haden, Robin Garton Fine Art Publ, 83; Masterpieces of European Printmaking: 15th-19th Centuries, Ga Mus Art, 84; A Catalogue Raisonne of the Prints of Charles Meryon (with Frank W Raysor II), Garton & Co, Scolar Press, 90. *Mailing Add:* NC Mus Art 2110 Blue Ridge Rd Raleigh NC 27607

SCHNEIER, DONNA FRANCES
DEALER
b St Louis, Mo, Mar 30, 38. *Study:* Brandeis Univ, BA; NY Univ, MFA; Inst Fine Art, NY Univ, PhD(art history). *Pos:* Pres, Gallery 6M, New York, 66-73; pres, Donna Schneier Fine Arts, 73- *Mem:* Am Craft Coun (bd trustees); Am Craft Mus (chairman & collections comt); First NY Bank For Business (bd advisors); Sch of For Serv, Georgetown Univ (bd govs). *Specialty:* Post World War II Ceramics, Glass, Fiber, Metal & Wood. *Mailing Add:* 910 Fifth Ave New York NY 10021

SCHNITZER, ARLENE
PATRON
b Salem, Ore, Jan 10, 29. *Study:* Univ Wash, Seattle, 47-48; Portland Art Mus Sch, 59-61; studied with Michele Russo. *Pos:* Dir, Fountain Gallery of Art, Portland, Ore, currently; emer dir, ArtQuake, City of Portland; trustee, Reed Col, currently; vpres, Harsh Investment Corp; dir US Dist Court Historical Soc; Nat trustee, Nat Symphony Orch, Washington, DC. *Awards:* Portland Art Asn Award, 79; Aubrey Watzek Award, Lewis & Clark Col, 81; Pioneer Award, Univ Ore, 85; Portland Arts Award, 85. *Mem:* Portland Ctr Visual Arts; Oregon Art Inst; Ore Symphony Asn (bd dirs & vpres exec comt, currently. *Collection:* Primarily most noted artists of the Northwest; largest collection outside a museum of works by C S Price, including carvings. *Mailing Add:* Fountain & Assoc PO Box 2708 Portland OR 97208

SCHNITZER, KLAUS A
PHOTOGRAPHER
Study: State Univ NY, Albany, BA, 67; Ohio Univ, Athens, MFA, 71. *Work:* Mus Mod Art, New York; Witkin Gallery, New York; Brookdale Community Col, Lincroft, NJ. *Exhib:* Invitational, Bertha Urdang Gallery, New York, 77; one-man shows, Newark Mus, NJ, 77, Mem Fine Arts Ctr, Univ Colo, Boulder, 81 & Art Inst Chicago, Ill, 81; Hunterdon Art Ctr, Linton, NJ, 78; NY Univ East Galleries, 78; and many others. *Awards:* Nat Endowment Arts Photog Fel, 80; Montclair State Col Alumni Asn Grants, 78 & 80; Montclair State Col Research Grant & Release Time, 81-82. *Publ:* Ed & contribr, Sans Silver, Camera 25 Mag, 10-12/74; illusr, Ancient Glass at the Newark Mus, Newark Mus, 77; auth, New Jersey: Unexpected pleasures, United Jersey Banks & NJ Monthly, 80; auth, Capitol Story, New York State Publ, 82. *Mailing Add:* 555 Upper Mountain Ave Art Dept Montclair State Upper Montclair NJ 07043

SCHNORRENBERG, JOHN MARTIN
HISTORIAN, ADMINISTRATOR
b New York, NY, Dec 1, 31. *Study:* Univ NC, Chapel Hill, AB(Phi Beta Kappa), MA, 53; Princeton Univ, MFA, 57, PhD, 64. *Teaching:* Instr art hist, Columbia Univ, 58-59; from asst prof to prof art hist, Univ NC, Chapel Hill, 59-76; chmn & prof art, Univ Ala, Birmingham, 76- *Awards:* Tanner Award for Excellence in Teaching, Univ NC, Chapel Hill, 66; Nat Endowment for Humanities, Jr Fel, 67-68. *Mem:* Col Art Asn; Medieval Acad Am; Soc Archit Historians; Archeol Inst Am; Southeastern Col Art Conf (ed, Review, 66-70, pres, 75-76 & 79-80). *Res:* Late gothic architecture, gothic survival, modern architecture. *Publ:* Ed & contribr, A Medieval Treasury From Southeastern Collections, Ackland Art Ctr, 71; ed & contribr, Comedy in Western Art, Visual Arts Gallery, 78. *Mailing Add:* 3824 11th Ave S Birmingham AL 35222

SCHNURR, ELINORE
PAINTER
b Sandusky, Ohio. *Study:* Cleveland Inst Art, BFA. *Work:* Cleveland Mus Art, Ohio; Mus Fine Art, St Petersburg, Fla; Nat Mus Am Art, Washington, DC; US State Dept, Washington, DC; Manufacturer's Hanover Trust, New York; NCR Corp, Columbus, Ohio; and others. *Exhib:* ROKO Gallery, New York, 77, Tirca Karlis Gallery, Provincetown, Mass, 79, Cleveland Inst Art, Ohio, 79, Capricorn Galleries, Bethesda, Md, 84 & 87, Chautauqua Art Asn Galleries, Chautauqua, NY, 86, Studio K Gallery, Long Island City, NY, 87; New Acquisitions, Cleveland Mus Art, Ohio, 83; The Landscape, Park Ave Atrium, New York, 85; New Acquisitions, Nat Mus Am Art, Washington, DC, 85; 161st, 163rd & 165th Juried Exhibition, Nat Acad Design, New York, 86, 88 & 90; Paper in Particular, Columbia Col, Mo, 86 & 88; and others. *Awards:* Childe Hassam Purchase Award, Am Acad Arts & Letters, New York, 76; CAPS Fel, NY State Coun Arts, 79; Patron Purchase Award, Watercolor USA, Springfield Art Mus, Mo, 80; Thomas B Clarke Award, 161st Juried Exhib, Nat Acad Design, 86. *Media:* Oil, Watercolor. *Mailing Add:* 10-09 50th Ave Long Island City NY 11101

SCHOEN, (MR & MRS) ARTHUR BOYER
COLLECTORS
Mr Schoen, b Pittsburgh, Pa, Apr 17, 23; Mrs Schoen, b New York, NY, Sept 27, 15. *Study:* Mr Schoen, Princeton Univ, BA; Mrs Schoen, Columbia Univ; Grand Cent Sch Art, New York. *Pos:* Mr Schoen, bd adv, Ocean Learning Inst, West Palm Beach, Fla; dir & secy, Aqua Sol Inc; dir, Solar Micro Inc. *Mem:* Parrish Art Mus (Mrs Schoen, pres, 70-76, trustee); Meadow Club, Southampton. *Collection:* Paintings: 18th century English and American furniture; archaeological artifacts; Chinese porcelains; 10th & 12th century Persian pottery. *Mailing Add:* 17 E 89th St New York NY 10028

SCHOENER, ALLON
DESIGNER, CONSULTANT
b Cleveland, Ohio, Jan 1, 26. *Study:* Yale Univ, BA, 46, MA, 49; Courtauld Inst Art, Univ London, 47-48. *Collections Arranged:* Lower East Side: Portal to American Life, Jewish Mus; Erie Canal: 1817-1967, NY State Coun Arts, 67; Harlem on My Mind, Metrop Mus Art, 69; Word From Jerusalem, Jewish Mus, 72; Life Aboard the Tall Ships for South Street, Seaport Mus, 76; The Family of Nations for the United Nations, Vienna, Austria, 79; Jewish Life in America, New York Pub Libr, 83; The Italian Americans--per terre assai lontane, Archivi Alinri, Florence, Italy, 89; Ellis Island, New York, 92. *Pos:* Asst dir, Jewish Mus, 66-67; visual arts prog dir, NY State Coun Arts, 67-72; consult traveling exhib, Smithsonian Inst, Washington, DC & Jewish Mus, New York; consult multiple exhib prog, Libr of Cong, Washington, DC. *Awards:* Nat Endowment Arts Proj Fel, 82. *Publ:* Ed, Portal to America, Holt, Rinehart & Winston, 67; Harlem on My Mind, Random House, 69 & Dell, 79; The American Jewish Album, Rizzoli Int Publ 83; The Italian American, Macmillan, 87; Gli Italo-Americani, RCS Rizzoli Libri, Italy, 88. *Mailing Add:* Grafton VT 05146

SCHOENER, JASON
PAINTER, EDUCATOR
b Cleveland, Ohio, May 17, 19. *Study:* Cleveland Inst Art, dipl; Western Reserve Univ, BS; Art Students League; Columbia Univ, MA. *Work:* Cleveland Mus Art; Whitney Mus Am Art, New York; Calif Palace Legion of Honor, San Francisco; Columbus Gallery Fine Art; Rochester Mem Art Gallery, DeCordova Mus, Lincoln, Mass; and others. *Exhib:* San Francisco Mus Art Painting Ann, 53-65; Brooklyn Mus Int Watercolor Exhibs, 59 & 61; Pa Acad Fine Arts Watercolor Ann, 59-69; Calif Palace Legion of Honor Winter Invitationals, 68 & 70; Landscape I & II, DeCordova Mus, Lincoln, Mass, 70 & 71; Wichita Art Asn, Kans, 75; Kalamazoo Art Inst, Mich, 75; Expressions From Maine, Hobe Sound Galleries, Fla, 76; 76 Maine Artists, Maine State Mus, 76; 41st & 43rd Ann Butler Art Inst Am Art, Youngstown, Ohio; one-man shows, Guangzhou Art Gallery, Canton, China, 88, St Mary's Col, Md, 93. *Teaching:* Instr, Munson-Williams-Proctor Inst, 49-53; assoc prof, Calif Col Arts & Crafts, Oakland, 53-61, dir pub rels & spec serv, 53-55, chmn dept fine arts, 55-70, dir, Eve Col, 55-69, prof, 61-87, dir, Div Fine Arts, 70-78, dean advanced studies, 78-87; prof, Calif Col Arts & Crafts, 61-87; vis lectr, Mills Col, 62-63; vis prof, Athens Technol Inst, Greece, 64-65. *Awards:* Calif State Award, 58; Award, Maine Art Gallery, 61; Childe Hassam Award, Am Acad Arts & Lett, 78. *Mem:* Art Students League. *Media:* Multimedia. *Publ:* Contribr, Art patronage in Greece, Art J, winter 66-67. *Dealer:* Midtown Payson Galleries 745 Fifth Ave New York NY 10151; Gumps Gallery 250 Post St San Francisco CA 94118. *Mailing Add:* 74 Ross Circle Oakland CA 94618

SCHOENHERR, JOHN (CARL)
PAINTER, ILLUSTRATOR
b New York, NY, July 5, 35. *Study:* Art Students League; Pratt Inst, BFA, study with Will Barnet & William A Smith. *Work:* Nat Park Serv, DC; Kerlan Col, Univ Minn, Maples, Minn; Zimmerli Art Mus, Rutgers Univ, NJ; Genesee County Mus, Mumford, NY. *Exhib:* Artists of America, Denver, Colo Hist Soc, 84, 85, 86, 87; Soc Illusr, New York, 64-68, 71 & 75; Contemp Am Illusr of Children's Bks, Rutgers Univ, NJ, 74; Royal Ont Mus, Toronto, Can, 75; Kent State Univ, 83. *Awards:* Soc Animal Artists Medal, 79 & 85; Silver Medal, Philadelphia Acad Natural Sci, 84; Caldecott Medal, 88. *Bibliog:* Kingman, Foster & Lontoft (auths), Illustrators of Childrens Books 1957-1966, Horn Bk Inc, 68; Diana Klemin (auth), The Illustrated Book, Clarkson N Potter Publ, 70; C Hume (ed), From The Wild, Summerhill Press, 86. *Mem:* Soc Illusr; Soc Animal Artists. *Media:* Polymer Tempera, Oil. *Publ:* Illusr, Rascal, E P Dutton, 63; auth & illusr, The Barn, Atlantic Mo Press, 68; illusr, Julie of the Wolves, Harper & Row, 72; illusr, Dune, Berkeley, 78; Illusr, Owl Moon, Philomel, 87. *Dealer:* Carson Gallery Denver CO; King Gallery New York NY. *Mailing Add:* 135 Upper Creek Rd Stockton NJ 08559

SCHOFIELD, ROBERTA
PAINTER
b Ronceverte, WVa, July 9, 45. *Study:* Univ S Fla, BA, 73, MFA, 79. *Work:* Federal Reserve Bank, Richmond, Va & Miami, Fla; Valencia Community Col, Orlando; Jamestown Community Col, Olean, NY; Strathmore Hall Found, Rockville, Md; Deland Mus Art, Fla; and others. *Exhib:* Contemporary American Paintings, Soc Four Arts, Palm Beach, Fla, 86; solo shows: Capricorn Gallery, Bethesda, Md, 85; Union St Gallery, Olean, NY, 86; Moon Gallery, Berry Col, Rome, Ga, 87; Stein Gallery, Tampa, Fla, 90; Jacksonville Coalition Visual Arts, Fla, 91; and others. *Pos:* Artistic dir, Fla Ctr Contemp Art, 87-88; exhib coordr, Tampa City Coun, 87-89 & 92. *Teaching:* Instr, S Fla Jr Col, Avon Park Fla, 79-82, Univ Wis, Eau Claire, Wis, 83-84 & St Petersburg Jr Col, Clearwater, Fla, 89. *Awards:* First Prize, Arts West 5, Eau Claire Arts Coun, 84; Fla Arts Coun Fel, 87-88; Hillsborough County Artists Grant, 90; and others. *Bibliog:* Janet Heller (auth), Art Uncovers Drama in Cloth, Fla Flambeau, Tallahassee, Fla, 9/89; Mary Ann Marger (auth), Fabric of her life, St Petersburg Times, 9/90; Maggie Hall (auth), Schofield's art, Tampa Tribune, 9/90; and others. *Mem:* Col Art Asn; Women Caucus Art (chap secy, 87, treas, 88, publicity, 90); Fla Ctr Contemp Art (bd secy, 88-89, Treas, 89-90). *Media:* Oil, Color Pencil. *Publ:* Auth-illusr, Gallerie Women's Art, Gallerie Pubs, 88. *Dealer:* Clayton Galleries 4105 S MacDill Ave Tampa FL 33611. *Mailing Add:* PO Box 10561 Tampa FL 33679

SCHOLDER, FRITZ
PAINTER, SCULPTOR
b Breckenridge, Minn, Oct 6, 37. *Study:* Univ Kans; Wis State Univ; Sacramento City Col, with Wayne Thiebaud; Sacramento State Univ, BA; Univ Ariz, MFA; Hon DFA, Rippon Col, 84, Univ Ariz, 85, Concordia Col, Minn, 86 & Col Santa Fe, NMex, 90. *Work:* Tucson Mus Art; Boston Mus Fine Arts; Bibliotheque Nat, Paris, France; Milwaukee Art Ctr, Wis; Philadelphia Mus Art; Mus Mod Art, New York; Nat Mus Am Art, Washington, DC. *Exhib:* Winter Invitational, Calif Palace Legion Hon, San

Francisco, 61; Two American Painters, Nat Collection Fine Arts, Smithsonian Inst, 72 & traveling, Madrid, Berlin, Bucharest, Belgrade, Ankara, Athens, London & San Francisco Mus Art, 76-77; one-man shows, Oakland Mus, Calif, 77, Scottsdale Ctr Arts, 81, Fresno Art Ctr, Calif, 81 & El Paso Mus Art, 82 & 83; retrospectives, Tucson Mus Art, 81, Arco Plaza, Southwest Mus, Los Angeles, 85; Anshutz Collection, The Hermitage, Leiningrad, Russia, 90. *Pos:* Artist-in-residence, Dartmouth Col, 73. *Teaching:* Guest artist, Okla Summer Arts Inst, Quartz Mt. *Awards:* Am Acad Arts & Lett Painting Award, 77; Int Prize, Lithography, Aintergrafiks, Berlin, 80; Gov's Award, NDak, 81 & NMex, 83; Distinguished Achievement Award in the Arts, Ariz State Univ, Tempe, 83. *Bibliog:* Fritz Scholder/An American Portrait (film), Pub Broadcasting Serv, 83; Fritz Scholder/Paintings and Monotypes, Twelve Tree Press, 88; Afternoon Nap, Nazraeli Press, 91. *Publ:* New York Times Mag, 1/70; Chicago Tribune Mag, 2/73; People Mag, 7/77; School Arts, 5/87; Art & Antiques, 12/89; Zone, 90. *Dealer:* Louis Newman Galleries 322 N Beverly Dr Beverly Hills CA 90210; Riva Yares Gallery 3625 Bishop Lane Scottsdale AR 85251. *Mailing Add:* 118 Cattle Track Rd Scottsdale AZ 85253

SCHOLDER, LAURENCE
PRINTMAKER, EDUCATOR
b Brooklyn, NY, Nov 23, 42. *Study:* Carnegie Inst Technol, BFA; Univ Iowa, MA. *Work:* Ft Worth Art Ctr, Tex; Houston Mus Fine Arts; Brooklyn Mus, NY; Dallas Mus Fine Arts, Tex. *Exhib:* American Graphic Workshops '68, Cincinnati Art Mus, 68; Multiples USA, Western Mich Univ, Kalamazoo, 70; Midwest Biennial, Joslyn Art Mus, Omaha, Nebr, 70 & 72; Seattle Print Int, Seattle Art Mus, 71; Libr of Cong 22nd Print Nat, Washington, DC, 71. *Teaching:* Asst prof printmaking, Southern Methodist Univ, 68-73, assoc prof, 73-81, prof, 81- *Awards:* Purchase Awards, Young Printmakers, Herron Art Inst, 67 & Print & Drawing Nat, Okla Art Ctr, 68; Merit Award, Southwest Graphics, San Antonio, 72; Nat Endowment Arts Printmaker's Fel, 75. *Media:* Intaglio. *Dealer:* Delahunty Gallery 2611 Cedar Springs Dallas TX 75201. *Mailing Add:* 5239 Goodwin Ave Dallas TX 75206

SCHON, NANCY QUINT
SCULPTOR
b Boston, Mass, Sept 24, 28. *Study:* Tufts Univ, BA; Boston Mus Sch (with honors, sculpture, teaching fel). *Work:* Easter Seal Collection, NJ; Children's Patio Newton Free Libr, Mass; Plotkin Mus, Phoenix, Ariz; M Maloney Properties, Boston, Mass; Beth Shalom, Needham, Mass. *Comn:* Brandeis Univ, Waltham, Mass; Nat Acad Sci, Washington, DC; Sweet Briar Col, Va; Jewish Home for the Elderly, Fairfield, Conn; Make Way for Ducklings, Boston Pub Garden, Mass & Novodevichy Park, Moscow, Russ, 91; and others. *Exhib:* One-person shows, Bristol Art Mus, RI, 78, Jerusalem Theatre Gallery, Israel, 79, Mass Inst Technol, Cambridge, Pierce Galleries, Hingham, Mass & Schönhaus Preview, Newton, Mass, 85; Concourse Art Gallery, Boston, 78; Richards Galleries, Hyannis, Mass, 80-81; Riji Gallery, New York, 81; Small Works, Rochester, NY, 84; Aetha Inst, Hartford, Conn, 84-85; Catherine Lorrilard Wolfe Ann, New York, NY 84-85; New England Sculptors' Asn Invitational, Boston, Mass, 85; Worcester Craft Mus, 86; Boston Mus, Mass, 86. *Pos:* Gov's task force, Accessibility of the Arts (gov's comm), Boston, Mass, 72-74; Gov's Coun on Arts & Humanities, Boston, Mass, 72-75. *Awards:* Carroll Ctr for the Blind Mem Award, Mass, 71; Good Samaritan Award, Easter Seal/Sculpture Competition, 73; Fel, Va Ctr Creative Arts, 85; Boston Preserv Award, Pub Art, 88. *Media:* Bronze. *Mailing Add:* 291 Otis St West Newton MA 02165

SCHONWALTER, JEAN FRANCES
PAINTER, SCULPTOR
b Philadelphia, Pa. *Study:* Moore Col Art, scholar, BFA; Pa Acad Fine Arts, grad fel. *Work:* Philadelphia Mus Art; Brooklyn Mus, NY; Slater Mus, Norwich, Conn; New York Pub Libr; NJ State Mus; Notre Dame Univ; Am Numismatic Mus. *Comn:* Two paintings of Temple B'nai Jeshurun, NJ, 59. *Exhib:* Libr Cong, Washington, DC; Boston Mus Exhibs; Butler Inst Am Art, Youngstown, Ohio; Nat Acad Design, New York; Int Print Exhib, Taipai, Taiwan; Prints Around the World, Asia; Brit Mus; Helsinki Mus. *Teaching:* Instr life painting, Newark Sch Fine & Indust Art, NJ, 69- *Awards:* Pennypacker Prize for Graphics, Soc Am Graphic Artists, 66; Purchase Prize, NJ State Mus, 67; First Prize & Medal of Honor for Graphics, Nat Asn Women Artists, 71. *Bibliog:* Dona Meilach (auth), Direct Metal Sculpture, Crown, 58; E F Singer (auth), Meet the artist--Jean Schonwalter, Suburban Life, 70. *Mem:* Artists Equity Asn NJ; Soc Am Graphic Artists; Assoc Artists NJ; Nat Asn Women Artists. *Media:* Oil; Bronze. *Dealer:* Bobker Gallery 74 Church St Montclair NJ 07042. *Mailing Add:* 67 Cummings Circle West Orange NJ 07052

SCHONZEIT, BENJAMIN
PAINTER
b Brooklyn, NY, May 9, 42. *Study:* Cooper Union, BFA, 64. *Work:* Brooklyn Mus Art; Del Art Mus, Wilmington; Denver Art Mus; Eindhoven Mus, Holland; Palace Legion of Honor, San Francisco; Guggenheim Mus, New York; Kunsthalle, Basel, Switz; Metrop Mus Art, New York; Miss Mus Art, Jackson; Mus Contemp Art, Chicago; Worcester Art Mus, Mass. *Exhib:* Lowe Art Mus, Univ Miami, Fla, 72; Storm King Art Ctr, Mountainville, NY, 73; Art Inst Chicago, 74; Wadsworth Atheneum, Hartford, Conn, 74; Albright-Knox Art Gallery, Buffalo, NY, 75; Whitney Mus Downtown, New York, 75; Baltimore Mus Art, 75-76; Butler Inst Am Art, Youngstown, Ohio, 76; solo exhibs, Michael Berger Gallery, Pittsburgh, 79, Tomasulo Gallery, Union Col, Crawford, NJ, 79, Gibbes Art Gallery, Charleston, SC, 80, Nancy Hoffman Gallery, New York, 81 & DeGestlo Gallery, Cologne, Ger, 81, Del Art Mus, Wilmington, 84, Galerie 99, Bay Harbor Island, Fla, 88; Brooklyn Mus, 80; Guggenheim Mus, New York, 85; American Icons, Fairleigh-Dickinson Univ, New Brunswick, NJ, 89. *Awards:* Butler Prize, Butler Inst Arts. *Bibliog:* Edward Lucie-Smith (auth), Superralism, Phaidon Press Ltd, 79; Louis K Meisel (auth), Photorealism, Abrams, Inc, New York, 80; Art Business News, 7/89. *Dealer:* Ann Jolle Gallery Miami FL 33154. *Mailing Add:* 109 Mercer St New York NY 10012

SCHOOLEY, ELMER WAYNE
PAINTER, EDUCATOR
b Lawrence, Kans, Feb 20, 16. *Study:* Univ Colo, BFA, 38; State Univ Iowa, MA, 41. *Work:* Mus Mod Art & Metrop Mus Art, New York; Hallmark Collection, Kansas City; Mus NMex, Santa Fe; Roswell Mus, NMex; Albuquerque Mus; Tucson Mus. *Comn:* Fresco (with Gussie Du Jardin), Las Vegas, NMex Hosp, 50. *Exhib:* Houston Southwestern Exhib, 62; Kansas City Mid-Am Exhib, 64; Tucson Festival Art Exhib, 64; Eight State Exhib, Oklahoma City, 68; Biennial Southwestern Exhib, Santa Fe, 72; One-man shows, Tucson Mus Art Mus, New York & Roswell Mus, NMex, 92. *Pos:* artist-in-residence, Roswell Mus, NMex, 77-78. *Teaching:* Asst prof, NMex Western Univ, 46-47; prof arts & crafts, NMex Highlands Univ, 47-77. *Awards:* Purchase Prize, Ford Found, 62; Honorable Mention, Kansas City Hallmark Purchase, 64; Prizes, Southwest Biennial, Santa Fe, 70, 72 & 74; NMex Governor's Award for Excellence in Visual Art, 86. *Media:* Oil. *Dealer:* Munson Gallery 225 Canyon Rd Santa Fe NM 87501. *Mailing Add:* Rt 1 1403 W Berrendo Roswell NM 88201

SCHORR, JUSTIN
PAINTER, EDUCATOR
b New York, NY, June 10, 28. *Study:* City Col New York, BSS, 50; Columbia Univ Teachers Col, EdD, 62. *Work:* Butler Inst Am Art, Youngstown, Ohio; Waldemar Res Found; Lock Haven State Col; Columbia Univ; NY Hosp. *Exhib:* Brooklyn Mus, 58; Nat Acad Design, New York, 59; Pa Acad Fine Arts, Philadelphia, 63; Butler Inst Am Art, 64; Union Theological Seminary, 83; Columbia Univ, 87, 90; Rutgers Univ, Ohio, 89. *Teaching:* Prof painting, Columbia Univ Teachers Col, 62- *Media:* Oil, Acrylic. *Publ:* Auth, Aspects of Art, Barnes, 67; Toward the Transformation of Art, Fairleigh Dickinson Univ, 74; Way of the Painter, Barlewmir House, NY, 86. *Mailing Add:* Dept Art-Educ Columbia Univ-Teachers Col 525 W 121st St New York NY 10027

SCHORRE, CHARLES
PAINTER, PRINTMAKER
b Cuero, Tex, Mar 9, 25. *Study:* Univ Tex, BFA, 48. *Work:* Mus Fine Arts, Houston, Tex; Sheldon Mem Art Gallery Collection, Univ Nebr, Lincoln. *Comn:* Transworld Airways, Kans City, Mo, 70; Borlenghi Towers, Houston; Westlake Hilton, Houston; Shell Oil Corp, Houston; Transco Tower, Houston; Mobil Corp, New York. *Exhib:* One-man show, Laguna Gloria Art Mus, Austin, Tex, 74; 20th Exhib Prints & Drawings, 75 & Works on Paper-Southwest, 78, Dallas Mus Fine Arts, Tex; New Orleans Triennial, New Orleans Mus Art, La, 80; Houston Area Exhib, Blaffer Gallery-Univ House, Houston, 80 & 88; Pages from Books Unpublished, Contemp Arts Mus, Houston, 81; The Americans: The collage (with catalog), Contemp Arts Mus, Houston, 82; Fresh Paint (with catalog), 85, Texas Landscape (with catalog), 86, Mus Fine Arts, Houston. *Awards:* Pages for Books Unpublished, Nat Endowment Arts, 79; Artist-in-residence, Saudi Arabia, Mobil Oil Corp, 80. *Publ:* Auth, Drawings & Notes I & II; Life Class. *Dealer:* Merideth Long & Co 2323 San Felipe Houston TX 77019. *Mailing Add:* c/o Meredith Long & Co 2323 San Felipe Houston TX 77019

SCHOTTLAND, M
ILLUSTRATOR, PAINTER
b Brooklyn, NY, Nov 18, 35. *Study:* Pratt Inst, BFA, 57; New Sch, printmaking with Antonio Frasconi, painting with Gregorio Prestodino, 58-60. *Work:* Soc of Illustrators Permanent Collection, New York; US Army Military Hist, US Air Force Art Prog, Pentagon & Nat Parks Serv, DC. *Comn:* Postage stamp, US Postal Serv, DC, 76; painting, US Air Force, DC, 77; paintings for nat advert, Ingersoll Rand Corp, NJ, 78; painting for bk illus, Franklin Libr, New York/Philadelphia, 79; NASA, 83; and others. *Exhib:* Indust Arts Methods Ann Show, New York, 76; 200 Yrs Am Illus, New York Hist Soc, 77; Soc Publ Designers Ann Show, New York, 78-79; Soc Illustrators Ann Show, New York, 78 & 79 & 50 Yrs of Award Winners, 79; Art in Sci, Cincinnati Mus Art, 79; Smithsonian Inst, 83. *Pos:* Chmn Air Force Art Prog, US Air Force/Soc Illustrators, 76-79. *Teaching:* Guest lectr illus, Soc Illustrators, New York, 77, Sch Visual Arts, New York, 78, Fashion Inst Technol, New York, 79 & Philadelphia Col Art, 79. *Awards:* Hamilton King Award, Soc Illustrators Ann Show, 71; Best of Show, Indust Arts Methods Ann Show, 76; Awards of Distinctive Merit, Soc Publ Designers Ann Show, 77 & 79. *Mem:* Soc Illusrs; Comt to Save New York Libr Picture Collection (vpres, 78-80); Graphic Artists Guild, New York. *Media:* Tempera. *Mailing Add:* 2201 Massachusetts Ave NW Washington DC 20008

SCHRAG, KARL
PAINTER, PRINTMAKER
b Karslruhe, Ger, Dec 7, 12; US citizen. *Study:* Ecole Beaux Arts, Geneva & Paris; Acad Ranson, Paris; Art Students League, with Lucien Simon, Roger Bissiere, Harry Sternberg & S W Hayter. *Work:* Nat Gallery Art, DC; Metrop Mus Art; Mus Mod Art; Whitney Mus Am Art; Guggenheim Mus, NY; Uffizi Gallery. *Exhib:* Several one-man shows, Kraushaar Galleries, New York, 47-; Mod Art in US, Tate Gallery, London & other Europ mus, 56; Am Fedn Arts one-man exhib, Brooklyn Mus & Tour, 62; Whitney Mus Am Art Painting Ann, NY, 65; Assoc Am Artists, 71, 80, 86, 90 & 92; Retrospective Exhib Prints, Nat Collection Fine Arts, Washington, DC, 72 & Farnsworth Mus, Rockland, Maine, 92; Mus Mod Art & Metrop Mus Art, 86. *Teaching:* Dir

etching, Atelier 17, New York, 50-51; instr printmaking, Brooklyn Col, 53-54; instr drawing & printmaking, Cooper Union, 54-68. *Awards:* Purchase Awards, Brooklyn Mus Print Ann, 47 & 50; Cert of Merit for Best Exhib US, Fourth Int Exhib Contemp Art, New Delhi, India, 62; Am Acad Arts & Lett Grant, 66. *Bibliog:* US Info Agency Staff (auths), Printmakers USA (film), Sidney Stiber Prod, 61; 80 page catalog, Retrospective Exhib, Farnsworth Mus. *Mem:* Soc Am Graphic Artists; Artists Equity Asn; Art Students League; Nat Acad Design. *Media:* All. *Publ:* Auth, Some Thoughts on Art, Cable, 58; Happiness and torment of printmaking, Artist's Proof, 66; The artist alone versus the artist in the workshop, New Univ Thought, autumn 67; Light & darkness in contemporary printmaking, Print Rev, 7/77. *Dealer:* Kraushaar Galleries 724 Fifth Ave New York NY 10019; Assoc Am Artists 20 W 57th St New York NY 10022. *Mailing Add:* 127 E 95th St New York NY 10028

SCHRECK, MICHAEL H
PAINTER, SCULPTOR
b Austria; US citizen. *Work:* Ft Lauderdale Mus of Art; Heckscher Mus, New York; Metrop Mus, Miami; Mus Fine Arts, Lausanne, Switz; Tel Aviv Mus & Mus Mod Art, Haifa, Israel; Jacksonville Art Mus, Fla; Norton Gallery Arts; Currier Gallery Art, Manchester, NH; and others. *Comn:* Masada Monument, Hollywood, Fla. *Exhib:* Mus Mod Art, Paris, 64; Palm Beach Gallery, Fla; Rauchbach Gallery, Bay Harbor, Fla, 82; Dyansen Gallery, New York; Patricia Judith Gallery, Boca Raton, Fla; Boca Raton Mus, Fla; and others. *Awards:* Grand Prix Int, Deauville, France; City of Hollywood Appreciation Award, Fla, 75; Academic Gold Medal, Accademia, Italia, 80; Diploma-Maestro Di Pittura, 82; Prix Int, Vichy, France. *Bibliog:* Alfred Werner (auth), Michael Schreck Sculpture, Univ Miami, 75; Richard A Madigan (auth), Michael Schreck Sculpture, Mus Palm Beach, 79. *Mem:* Life fel Royal Soc Arts, London; Am Fedn Arts; Artists Equity Asn; Accademia Italia, Italy. *Media:* Acrylic, Oil; Miscellaneous Media. *Mailing Add:* 3111 N Ocean Dr Hollywood FL 33019

SCHRECKENGOST, VIKTOR
DESIGNER, SCULPTOR
b Sebring, Ohio, June 26, 06. *Study:* Cleveland Sch Art, 25-29; Univ Vienna, Austria, 29-30. *Work:* Cleveland Mus Am Art; Metrop Mus Art; Whitney Mus Am Art, New York; Memphis Mus Art; also in pvt collections. *Comn:* Designer K K Culver Air Trophy, Oberlin Mem Tablet; sculpture for bird bldg, Cleveland Zoo, Pachyderm Bldg, 50; Cleveland Hopkins Airport, 56. *Exhib:* Major mus in US; also Century Progress, Chicago, San Francisco & New York World's Fair, Paris Expos. *Pos:* Head designer, Murray Ohio Mfg Co, Nashville; consult designer, Harris-Intertype Corp & divs; designer, Am Artists Group, Inc, New York; mem fine arts adv comt, Cleveland Planning Comn, 61- *Teaching:* Instr, Cleveland Sch Art, 30-, head dept indust design, 36- *Awards:* Spec & First Award, Cleveland Mus Art, 55; Gold Medal Fine Arts, Am Inst Architect, 58; Visual Arts Award, Women's City Club Cleveland, 73. *Mem:* Fel Int Inst Arts & Lett; Cleveland Soc Artists; NY Archit League; Indust Designers Soc Am (past nat vpres & dir); Am Watercolor Soc; plus others. *Mailing Add:* Dept Indust Design Cleveland Inst Art 11141 E Blvd Cleveland OH 44106

SCHREIBER, EILEEN SHER
PAINTER, PRINTMAKER
b Denver, Colo. *Study:* Univ Utah, 42-45; NY Univ Exten, 66-68; Montclair State Col, 75-79. *Work:* Citibank; AT&T Co; Johnson & Johnson; Georgia Pacific; Champion Int Paper; New York Univ; Public Serv NJ, Morris Mus. *Comn:* NJ Beach Area, Broad Nat Bank, Newark, 70; Mitzubushi, Barclay Bank of England. *Exhib:* NJ Mus, Trenton, 69 & 73; Am Watercolor Soc Nat, Nat Acad Galleries, New York; Audubon Artists, New York; Pallazzo Vecchio, Florence, Italy; Va State Mus, 75; Art Expo, New York, 86 & 87. *Awards:* Best in Show Cash Award, Short Hills State Show, 76; Purchase Award, Tri-State Exhib, Somerset Co Col, 77; Best in Show, Tri State Exhib, Somerset Col, 80; and others. *Bibliog:* M Lenson (auth), article, Newark Eve News, 4/70; article, Newark Star Ledger, 6/74; Addison Parks (auth), article, Arts Mag, 12/79. *Mem:* Nat Asn Women Artists (chmn, 73-75); Artists Equity Asn, NY; Printmakers Coun; NJ Visual Arts. *Media:* Acrylic, Watercolor; Collage, Monoprints. *Dealer:* Robin Hutchins Gallery 176 Maplewood Ave Maplewood NJ 02040; Matter of Taste Broad St Red Bank NJ. *Mailing Add:* 22 Powell Dr West Orange NJ 07052

SCHREIBER, MARTIN
SCULPTOR, PAINTER
b Berlin, Ger, Nov 8, 23; US citizen. *Study:* Art Students League; Brooklyn Mus Art Sch; also with Ruben Tam. *Work:* Nassau Community Col, NY; Contemp Arts Ctr, Cincinnati, Ohio; Mary Washington Col, Univ Va; Corcoran Mus, Washington, DC. *Exhib:* Silvermine Ann; Gallery MacKay, Montreal, 68; Razor Gallery, New York, 78; Documenta Gallery, Sao Paulo, Brazil, 79; one-man show, Spectrum Gallery, New York, 71; and others. *Awards:* First Prize in Acrylic, Silvermine, Conn, 65. *Media:* Chrome Plated Steel; Acrylic. *Dealer:* Pleiades Gallery 164 Mercer St New York NY 10029. *Mailing Add:* 1578 Pea Pond Rd North Bellmore NY 11710

SCHRERO, RUTH LIEBERMAN
SCULPTOR, DRAFTSMAN
b New York, NY. *Study:* Columbia Univ, with Oronzio Maldarelli; Art Students League, with George Grosz; Tyler Sch Art of Temple Univ; Pratt Graphics Workshop & Manhattan Graphics Workshop. *Work:* Maywood Pub Libr, NJ; Harsen & Johns, Architects, Rochelle Park, NJ; Nabisco Brands Corp, Parsipanny, NJ; NY Univ Sch Law. *Comn:* Bronze portrait Hon Edward Weinfeld, comn by New York Univ Sch Law, 77. *Exhib:* Newark Mus, 79; American Drawings, Morris Mus, 84; Monmouth Mus, 88; Libr Port Washington, NY, 88; Trenton City Mus, 89; and others. *Teaching:* Community Schools, Fairlawn & Glen Rock, NJ. *Awards:* Estelle Goodman Prize, Nat Painters & Sculptors Soc, 75; Exhib Am Drawings, Morris Mus, 84; Anna Hyatt Huntington Bronze Medal for Sculpture, Catharine Lorillard Wolfe Art Club, 84 & 89, and others. *Bibliog:* New York Times, 79 & 84. *Mem:* Artists Equity Asn New York; New York Soc Women Artists; Sculptors Asn NJ; Catharine Lorillard Wolfe Art Club; life mem Art Students League. *Media:* Clay, Miscellaneous Media; Ink, Mixed Media. *Mailing Add:* 377 Rutland Ave Teaneck NJ 07666

SCHREYER, GRETA L
PAINTER, PRINTMAKER
b Vienna, Austria, July 28, 23; US citizen. *Study:* Columbia Univ, with Seong Moy; Art Students League; Pratt Inst; also with Moses Soyer & Fred Taubes. *Work:* Oesterreichische Gallerie Belvedere, Vienna, Austria; Museen der Stadt Wien, Vienna, Austria; Jewish Mus, New York; Univ Windsor, Can; Loyola Marymount Univ, Los Angeles; Vassar Col, Poughkeepsie, NY; Albertina, Vienna, Austria. *Exhib:* Four shows, New Sch Art Ctr, New York, 60-68; Knickerbocker Artists, New York; one-man shows, St Olaf Col, 66 & Fairleigh Dickinson, Univ NJ, 79 & 83; Roko Gallery, New York, 72-78; Inbger Gallery, 85, 87, 88 & 89; Oesterreicische Gallerie, Vienna, Austria, 87. *Awards:* Grumbacher Awards, 56 & 69. *Mem:* Arch Am Art; Artists Equity Asn New York; Art Students League. *Media:* Oil, Watercolor; Lithography. *Mailing Add:* 170 West End Ave Apt 6N New York NY 10023

SCHROECK, R D
PAINTER, CONCEPTUAL ARTIST
b Buffalo, NY, June 28, 49. *Study:* Rosary Hill Col, BFA, 76. *Work:* Dartmoth Col Mus & galleries, Hanover, NH; Georgia State Univ, Atlanta; Cleveland Col Art & Design, Middlesbrough, Eng; Gold Dome Bank, Buffalo, NY; Cleveland Co Coun, Middlesbrough, Eng. *Exhib:* Western New York Exhib, Albright Knox Art Gallery, Buffalo, NY, 76, 80 & 86; 16th Biennal De Sao Paulo, 81; New Art of 1980-1990, Atelier Galeria, Dijon, France, 81; The Charles Rand Penney Collection of 20th Century Art, Rochester Art Gallery, NY, 83-84. *Media:* Acrylic, oil. *Mailing Add:* Lily Art Studio PO Box 150 Holland NY 14080

SCHRUT, SHERRY
PAINTER, PRINTMAKER
b Detroit, Mich, Apr 27, 28. *Study:* Wayne State Univ, Detroit, BA(art), 50; Long Beach State Col, Calif & Univ Calif, Los Angeles. *Work:* Security Pac Nat Bank, Palm Desert, Calif; Cedars-Sinai Med Ctr, Thalians Bldg, Los Angeles; Int Cult Ctr for Youth, Jerusalem, Israel; Hebrew Union Col Skirball Mus, Los Angeles; Atlantic Richfield Co, Los Angeles; Wayne State Univ, Mich; IBM, Atlanta, Ga; Xerox Corp. *Comn:* Southern Calif Psychoanalytic Inst, Beverly Hills, 71 & 74; Sheraton Grande Hotel, Tokyo, Japan; MGM Grand Air, Lax Terminal Airport, Los Angeles; and others. *Exhib:* Los Angeles Inst Contemp Art, Century City, 75; Laguna Beach Mus Art, 76; Works on Paper, Newport Harbor Art Mus, Calif, 77; one-woman shows, Brand Libr & Art Ctr, Glendale, 72 & 79 & Galeria Del Sol, Santa Barbara, 76; Calif Mus Sci & Indust, 81; Hank Baum Gallery, San Francisco, 82; Eva Cohon Gallery, Chicago, Ill, 86. *Teaching:* Instr, Craft & Folk Art Mus, Los Angeles, 73-74. *Awards:* Second Prizes, Wayne State Univ, Detroit, 51 & Long Beach Mus Art, 53; First Prize, Westwood Ctr Arts, 68 & Riverside Mus Art, 80, Calif; Lucille Simon Purchase Award, Skirball Mus, Los Angeles. *Bibliog:* Barbara Probstein (auth), The fiery art, Home Mag, Los Angeles Times, 73 & Cloisonne enameling, Sch Arts Mag, Davis Publ, 1/75; W F Alexander (auth), Cloisonne Extraordinaire, California Contemporary Artists, In: Cloisonne & Related Arts, Wallace-Homestead Bk Co, 77; Designers West, Calif, 86. *Mem:* Southern Calif Designer-Crafts, Inc (treas, 75-78); Enamel Guild-West (mem bd, 77); Am Crafts Coun; World Crafts Coun. *Publ:* Contribr, Creative Stitchery, Crown Publ, 70; Porcelain Enamel, Historical, Contemporary, Industrial and Artistic, San Diego Univ Press, 76; Enameling for Secondary Schools, Lawrence Univ Press, RI, 76; Crafts 1976, Southern Calif Designer-Crafts, Inc, 76; The Center Mag, Ctr Democratic Insts, Santa Barbara, Calif, 78 & 79. *Dealer:* Ruth Bachofner Gallery Beverly Hills CA. *Mailing Add:* c/o Artrageous 5350-A Eastgate Mall San Diego CA 92121

SCHUCKER, CHARLES
PAINTER
b Gap, Pa, Jan 19, 08. *Study:* Md Inst Fine & Mech Arts, grad, 33; traveling scholar, Europe, 34. *Work:* Whitney Mus Am Art, NY; Brooklyn Mus; Archit Digest; Paul L Ferber pvt collection; Roy Newberger; John I H Baur; Pratt Inst; and others. *Comn:* Painting, Woodhull Hosp, 76. *Exhib:* Solo exhibs, Whitney Mus Am Art, 71, Max Hutchinson Gallery, Soho, 72-80, Camino Real, Boca Raton, Fla, 80, 81, 84, & 86, Katonah Mus Art, NY, 81, 90 & 91, Brooklyn Borough Hall Rotunda, 81, Great East River Bridge Show, Brooklyn Mus, 83; Nat Watercolor Ann, Baltimore Mus Art, 49; Am Painting Today, Metrop Mus Art, New York, 50; Am Painting, Walker Art Ctr, Minneapolis, 50; Whitney Mus Am Art, 52-57, 59, 63 & 73; Art in 20th Century, San Francisco Mus Art, Calif, 55; Brooklyn Mus Biannual, NY, 56; Pratt Inst Gallery, 82, 90 & 91. *Pos:* Mem Fed Art Proj, Works Prog Admin, 38-42. *Teaching:* Art instr, New York Univ, 47-54; prof art, Pratt Inst, New York, 56-75, emer prof, 75-85. *Awards:* Oil painting, Brooklyn & Long Island Biennial, Brooklyn Mus, 48, 60; Audubon Prize for oil painting, 49; Hassam Prize, AAAL, 52; Guggenheim Found Fel, 53. *Bibliog:* Robert Goldwater (auth), article, Mag Art, 53; Carter Ratcliff (auth), article, Art Int, 78, catalog essay, 90; Anne Sharp (auth), article, Arts Mag, 78; Charles Schucker, Portrait in Color, Pratt Video Dept, Archiv Am Art. *Mem:* Yaddo Found (bd dirs). *Media:* Oil. *Dealer:* Camino Real Banyon Trail Boca Raton FL; Studio 33 Middagh St Brooklyn NY 11201. *Mailing Add:* Studio 33 Middagh St Brooklyn NY 11201

SCHULE, CLIFFORD HAMILTON
PAINTER, SCULPTOR
b Brooklyn, NY, Aug 2, 18. *Study:* Art Students League; Pa Acad Fine Arts. *Work:* Hershey Mus, Pa; Lankenau Hosp Mus, Philadelphia; Pa Hosp Portrait Gallery, Philadelphia; Cornell Univ, Ithaca, NY; Princeton Univ, NJ. *Comn:* Henry Kissinger, State Dept, Washington, Dc; Bob Hope, Valley Forge Military Acad, Pa; Nizar Hamdoon, Ambassador Iraq, Washington, DC; Austin Kipplinger, Cornell Univ, Ithaca, NY; Eric Ritter, India House, New York. *Exhib:* Allied Artists Am Ann, New York; Salmagundi Club Ann & Others, New York; Art Dirs Ann, Philadelphia; Hudson Valley Asn, White Plains, NY. *Pos:* Portrait painter & illusr, free lance, 47-72; Art dir & supervisor, Franklin Mint, 72-82, portraity painter & sculptor, 82-92. *Awards:* Gold Medal Honor & Ada D Rosario Award, Allied Artists Am; Best in Show, First Prize Oil, Franklin Mint. *Bibliog:* Articles, Newsweek, Wash Post, Evening Bull; and others. *Mem:* Salmagundi Club; Allied Artists Am; Hudson Valley Art Asn; Coast Guard Art Prog. *Media:* Oil, Pastel. *Publ:* Illusr, Saturday Evening Post; Alfred Knopf; Western Publishing; Lippincott, Winston; and others. *Dealer:* Newman Galleries 1625 Walnut St Philadelphia PA 19103; Portraits Inc 985 Park Ave New York NY 10028. *Mailing Add:* 1350 Old Plain Rd Pennsburg PA 18073

SCHULE, DONALD KENNETH
SCULPTOR, INSTRUCTOR
b Madison, Minn, June 17, 38. *Study:* Univ Minn, sculpture with Richard Randall, Robert Mallory & James Wines, BFA, 64, MFA, 67. *Work:* Walker Art Ctr, Minneapolis; Sheldon Art Mus, Lincoln, Nebr; Univ Notre Dame, South Bend, Ind; Wichita Art Mus, Kans; Minn Mus Art, St Paul. *Exhib:* Walker Art Ctr, Minneapolis, 62 & 64; solo shows, Minneapolis Inst Arts, 70, Contemp Arts Mus, Houston, 75, Sheldon Art Mus, Lincoln, Nebr, 78 & Phyllis Kind Gallery, Chicago, 78; Allan Stone Gallery, New York, 73 & 77; Whitney Mus Am Art, New York, 77; Indianapolis Mus Art, 78; Nelson Mus, Kansas City, 83; Karen Lennox Gallery, Chicago, 83; Janet Fleisher Gallery, Philadelphia, 83; and others. *Teaching:* Assoc prof, Wichita State Univ, 67-78; lectr, Southwest Tex State Univ, San Marcos, 81-88 & Pa State Univ, 89-90. *Awards:* Purchase Prizes, Ford Found, 64 & Nat Endowment Arts, 70; 1st Prize, Wichita Art Asn, 72. *Bibliog:* Dona Z Meilach (auth), Woodworking: The New Wave, Crown Publ Inc, 81. *Media:* Wood, Stone. *Mailing Add:* 1721 Linden Hall Rd Boalsburg PA 16827

SCHULER, MELVIN ALBERT
SCULPTOR, PAINTER
b San Francisco, Calif, Apr 29, 24. *Study:* Calif Col Arts & Crafts, BA, 46, MFA, 47; Danish Royal Acad Fine Arts, Copenhagen, 55-56. *Work:* Hirshhorn Mus & Sculpture Garden, Nat Collection Fine Arts, Smithsonian Inst, Washington, DC; Storm King Art Ctr, Mountainville, NY; Portland Mus Art, Ore; La Jolla Mus Contemp Art, Calif; Fresno Art Mus. *Comn:* Sculpture (copper over redwood), Tri-Met Mall, Portland, 77; sculpture (copper over redwood), Deschutes Co Justice Bldg, Bend, Ore, 79; sculpture (copper over redwood), Greenwood Park Mall, Indianapolis, 79; sculpture (copper over redwood), Alderwood Ctr, Lynwood, Wash, 79; Pacific Lumber Co, San Francisco (copper over redwood); Spanish Bay Resort, Pacific Grove. *Exhib:* Portland Mus Art, Ore, 73 & 76; Henry Gallery, Univ Wash, Seattle, 75; Univ Ore Mus Art, Eugene, 76; Palm Springs Desert Mus, Calif, 78; Fresno Art Mus, 88. *Teaching:* Prof art, Humboldt State Univ, Arcata, 47-77. *Media:* Watercolor, Wood, Copper over redwood. *Dealer:* Louis Newman Galleries 322 N Beverly Dr Beverly Hills CA 90210; Gumps Gallery 250 Post St San Francisco CA 94108. *Mailing Add:* c/o Ankrum Gallery Box 612 Arcata CA 95521

SCHULLER, NANCY SHELBY
LIBRARIAN, HISTORIAN
b Austin, Tex, Aug 20, 42. *Study:* Univ Tex, Austin, BFA, 63, MA, 69. *Pos:* Prof librn dept art, Univ Tex, Austin, 67-77, cur visual arts, 77- *Teaching:* Sr lectr, Univ Tex, Austin, 78- *Awards:* President's Award, Visual Resources Asn, 87. *Mem:* Art Libr Soc NAm (pres Tex chap, 80-83); Col Art Asn; Mid-Am Col Art Asn (chair, visual resources group, 77-79); Spec Libr Asn; Visual Resources Asn (vpres, 82, treas, 83-87). *Res:* Automated process for slide and photograph collections in the visual arts; subject indexing of slides and photographs of works of art; the image bank in visual arts. *Publ:* Auth, Slide collections, Tex Libr J, Vol 47, No 4; Strake College Book of Hours, Gothic & Renaissance Illuminated Manuscripts, Univ Tex, 71; compiler, Standard Abbreviations for Image Descriptions for Use in Fine Arts Visual Resources Collections, VRA Special Bull, No 2, 87; auth, Management for Visual Resources Collections, Librs Unlimited, 89; The Curator's Job Description: Development & Evaluation, Visual Resources, Vol 1, No 4, 90. *Mailing Add:* Art Dept Univ Texas at Austin Austin TX 78712

SCHULMAN, ROBERT
PAINTER, DIRECTOR
b Springfield, Mass, June 17, 24. *Study:* Whitney Sch Art, New Haven, Conn, 46-47; Corcoran Sch Art, Washington, DC, figure painting with Edmond Archer, 47-49. *Work:* NASA Art Prog Collection, Smithsonian Inst, Washington, DC. *Comn:* Painting (oil on canvas), commemorating the first landing of the Space Shuttle Columbia, NASA, Washington, DC, 82. *Exhib:* The Artist & the Space Shuttle, Nat Air & Space Mus, Smithsonian Inst, Washington, DC, 82; Space Paintings, Danforth Mus Art, Framingham, Mass, 84; 48th Ann Nat Mid-Year Exhib, Butler Inst Am Art, Youngstown, Ohio, 84; Artist's View of Space, Cornell Fine Arts Ctr, Rollins Col, Winter Park, Fla, 85; Artists and Space, El Paso Mus Art, Tex, 86; 28th & 29th Ann of American Illustration, Mus Am Illus, Soc Illusr, New York, 86. *Pos:* Art dir, Dept Com-Census, Washington, DC, 68-75; dir, NASA Fine Art Prog, Washington, DC, 75-; pres, Fed Design Coun, Washington, DC, 78-79. *Awards:* First Presidential Award for Design Excellence, Fed Art & Design, The White House, Nat Endowments Arts, 85; NASA Hon Award, Fine Arts Prog, Washington, DC, 85; Gold Medal Award, 27th Ann Am Illus, Soc Illusr, New York, 85. *Bibliog:* Dennis Overbye (auth), The artist & the space shuttle, Discover Mag, 12/82; Pam Hait (auth), Space: The final frontier, Western Art Dig, 10/85; Phoebe Hoban (auth), The artronauts, Omni Mag, 11/85. *Mem:* Soc Illusr, New York; Nat Endowment Arts (graphics evaluation panel). *Media:* Oil. *Publ:* Contribr, Space art, Brit Aerospace Quart, 11/84; Illustrators 27-The Society of Illustrators, Madison Sq Press, 86; Challenger crew memorial: The future belongs to the brave, Omni Mag, 5/86. *Mailing Add:* 1877 Cherry Rd Annapolis MD 21401

SCHULSON, SUSAN
PAINTER
b Racine, Wis, Nov 21, 41. *Study:* Lawrence Univ, BA, 63; Univ Ill, MFA(teaching asst), 78. *Work:* Mus Contemp Art, Chicago. *Exhib:* With Paper, About Paper, Albright-Knox Art Gallery, Buffalo, NY, 80; Basel, Switz, 80 & 81; Navy Pier, Chicago, 81; Heresies, Grey Art Gallery, New York, NY, 81; Swen Parson Gallery, 83; Ornaments as Sculpture, Sculpture Ctr, New York, 83; and others. *Pos:* Ed, Le Corbusier Sketchbooks vols II-IV, Archit History Found, New York, 81-82. *Teaching:* Instr printmaking, Evanston Art Ctr, Ill, 75-76, Univ Ill, 76-78, Searing Sch, New York, 80-81; lectr, Univ Chicago, 75-76. *Bibliog:* Joanna Frueh (auth), Susan Schulson at Zolla/Lieberman, Art Am, 79. *Mem:* Col Art Asn; Artist Equity. *Media:* Oil, Acrylic. *Dealer:* Galerie Farideh Cadot 77 rue des Archives Paris France. *Mailing Add:* 121 Wooster St New York NY 10012

SCHULTE, (MR & MRS) ARTHUR D
COLLECTORS
Mr Schulte, b New York, NY, 06. *Study:* Mr Schulte, Yale Univ; Mrs Schulte, Hunter Col, Columbia Univ, NY Univ. *Collection:* French, American, Italian and Greek paintings and sculpture. *Mailing Add:* 810 Fifth Ave New York NY 10021

SCHULTZ, CAROLINE REEL
PAINTER, LECTURER
b Evansville, Ind. *Study:* Art Ctr Col Design, Los Angeles, 58; Univ Ill-Urbana, 60-62; Wellfleet Sch, with W Kennedy, 60; Art Mart Sch, Martha's Vineyard; European Sch, Mallorca, Spain, 61; also with Nichola Ziroli & Billy M Jackson. *Work:* Mt Kenya Safari Club, EAfrica; Pavillon, Scottsdale, Ariz; New Masters, Carmel, Calif; Bruners Fine Art, Santa Rosa, Calif. *Comn:* Wildlife (screen), comn by John Batten, III, Twin Disc Corp, Racine, Wis, 75. *Exhib:* Game Coin, San Antonio, 75; Shikar Safari Club 75, San Diego Zoo, 75; Safari Int, Las Vegas, 76; Abercrombie & Fitch, San Francisco, 76; and other group and one-woman shows. *Pos:* US art dir, EAfrican Wild Life Soc, 75. *Teaching:* Lectr animal anat & Africa through the eyes of an artist, currently. *Awards:* Purchase Award, Comedians Classic, 72; Lenten Art Festival, San Diego, 72; Spec Award, Mt Kenya Safari Club, E African Wildlife Soc, 91; and others. *Mem:* San Diego Art Inst; La Jolla Art Asn; Desert Art Ctr, Palm Springs, Calif; Spanish Village Art Ctr. *Mailing Add:* 10405 Viacha Dr San Diego CA 92124

SCHULTZ, DOUGLAS GEORGE
DIRECTOR
b Oakland, Calif, Oct 3, 47. *Study:* Univ Calif, Berkeley, BA(art hist), 69, MA(art hist), 72; Inst Arts Admin, Harvard Univ, 71. *Collections Arranged:* Antoni Tapies: Thirty-Three Years of His Work, 77, In Western New York (coauth, catalog), 77, Piero Dorazio: A Retrospective, 79, Kenneth Nelson, 81, Chryssa: Urban Icons, 82, Robert Motherwell, 83, Beverly Pepper, 86, Albright-Knox Art Gallery. *Pos:* Curatorial intern, Albright-Knox Art Gallery, 72-73, asst cur, 73-75, assoc cur, 75-76, cur, 77-79, chief cur, 80-83, acting dir, 83, dir, 83-; mem professional adv comt, Arts Develop Servs, Buffalo, NY. *Teaching:* Adj prof art hist, State Univ NY, Buffalo, 75-79. *Mem:* NY State Coun Arts; Arts Develop Serv. *Mailing Add:* 1285 Elmwood Ave Buffalo NY 14222

SCHULTZ, HAROLD A
PAINTER, EDUCATOR
b Grafton, Wis, Jan 6, 07. *Study:* Layton Sch Art; Northwestern Univ, BS & MA. *Exhib:* Art Inst Chicago; Chicago Soc Artists; Brooklyn Mus; Ferargil Gallery. *Teaching:* Lectr, American Art Today; head dept art, Francis W Parker Sch, Chicago, 32-40; prof art & design, Univ Ill, Urbana-Champaign, 40-75, emer prof, 75- *Media:* Miscellaneous. *Publ:* Coauth, Art in the Elementary School, 48. *Mailing Add:* 101 Windsor Rd Apt 4102 Urbana IL 61801

SCHULTZ, JOHN BERNARD
EDUCATOR, HISTORIAN
b Pittsburgh, Pa, Nov 26, 48. *Study:* John Carroll Univ, BA, 70; Univ Pittsburgh, MA, 73, PhD, 82. *Pos:* Bd dirs, Monongalia Arts Ctr, Morgantown, WVa, 82-84; chmn, div art, WVa Univ, Morgantown, 89- *Teaching:* Instr art hist, John Carroll Univ, Cleveland, Ohio, 74-75; from instr art hist to prof, WVa Univ, Morgantown, 77-90. *Awards:* Outstanding Teacher, 81, Innovation-Excellence Award, 85, Art Div, WVa Univ; Distinguished Prof Art, WVa Art Alumni Assoc, 88. *Mem:* Col Art Asn Am; Am Asn Hist Med; Soc Ancient Med; Nat Coun Art (Adminr). *Res:* Historical interrelationships between medicine and art. *Publ:* Auth, Art and Anatomy in Renaissance Italy, UMI Res Press, 85; A Fifteenth Century Papal Brief on Human Dissection, Medical Heritage, 86; coauth, Art Past/Art Present, Abrams, 90; Study Guide for Janson's History of Art, 4th ed, Prentice- Hall, 91; With Gratitude to Eva Hubbard: A Celebration of Women Artists at WVa Univ (exhib catalog), 91. *Mailing Add:* Dept Art WVa Univ Morgantown WV 26506

SCHULTZ, SAUNDERS
SCULPTOR
b July 16, 27. *Study:* Wash Univ, St Louis, Mo, BFA, 50; Univ Ill, Urbana, MFA, 52; special study with Max Beckman, Paul Burlin & Fred Conway. *Work:* Morris Arboretum/Sculptural Park, Philadelphia; Broward Co--Art in Public Places Collection, Pompano Beach, Fla; Univ Ark Art Collection, Little Rock; Sculpture Fountain, Kansas City; St Louis Univ Hosp, Mo. *Comn:* Cosmos, Juffall Hq, Jedda, Saudi Arabia, 83; Light Rays, Maridian Hotel, Singapore, 83; Nurturing, Cath Cemeterics, St Louis, Mo, 89; Battle Bows, Tri-State Vet Mem, Dubuque, Iowa, 89; Flamma, One Pacific Place, Omaha, Nebr, 90-91. *Exhib:* Sculpture in Architectural Context, Fordham Univ, New York, 79; Centennial Alumni Exhib, Bixby Hall Gallery, Wash Univ, St Louis, Mo, 79; Sculpture Outdoors, Temple Univ, Philadelphia, Pa, 80; Int Sculpture Competition, Mercer Col, Trenton, NJ, 80; Interfaith Forum Exhibition on Religion, Art & Architecture, Washington, DC, 84; Sch Environ Design, Calif State Polytechnic, 88; Miss State Univ, 89. *Teaching:* Guest lectr, numerous cols & univs incl Harvard Univ Sch Grad Sch Design, Columbia Univ Archit, Planning & Preserv, 77- *Awards:* First Prize, Univ Wis, Green Bay, 75, Broward Co Housing Authority, 80, Washington, DC Hebrew Cong, 83, Nat Competition to create sculpture for Washington Hebrew Congregation, DC, 84, Tri-State Vets Mem, 87; Preservation by Design Award, Swain Sch Design, 89. *Bibliog:* George McCue (auth), Sculpture City: St Louis, Hudson Mills Press, 88; Lineatus, Hotel & Motel Mgt, Harcourt Brace & Jovanovich, cover photo, 88; plus others. *Media:* All. *Publ:* contribr, Nat Community Arts Program, US Dept Housing Urban Development, 73; auth, Washington Univ Mag, Washington Univ, St Louis, Mo, 79; auth, Religion and Theatre, Bethel Col, St Paul, Minn, 8/80; contribr, A Christian Response to the Holocaust, Stonehenge Books, 81; coauth, Art Guidelines, Salt River Project, Phoenix, 89. *Mailing Add:* 27 Covington Rd Olivette MO 63132

SCHULTZ, STEPHEN WARREN
PAINTER, EDUCATOR
b Chicago, Ill, Aug 28, 46. *Study:* RI Sch Design, 65-67; San Francisco Art Inst, BFA, 71; Stanford Univ, MFA, 74. *Work:* Equitable Life Assurance Corp, New York; Univ Iowa Mus, Iowa City; Stanford Univ; Regis Corp, Minneapolis; Syntex Corp, Saratoga, Calif; McNay Art Mus, San Antonio, Tex; Hallmark, St Louis, Mo. *Exhib:* Elvehjem Mus Art, Madison, Wis, 77; Walker Art Ctr, 77; Awards in Visual Arts, Nat Mus Am Art, Washington, DC, 82, Denver Art Mus, 83 & Des Moines Art Ctr, 83; Iowa Artists, Des Moines Art Ctr, 82; Sid Deutsch Gallery, New York, 84 & 86; Minneapolis Mus Art, 86; Artists Who Teach, Fed Res Gallery, Wasnington, DC, 87- *Pos:* Rockefeller Found artist-in-residence, Bellagio Ctr, Lake Como, Italy, 84; artist-in-residence, George Rickey Workshop, East Chatham, NY & Camargo Found, Cassis, France, 85; Juror, Ill Art Coun Fellowships, 90. *Teaching:* Prof, Univ Iowa, 75-; vis artist, Univ Tex, Arlington, 80 & Belgrade Acad Fine Arts, Yugoslavia, 86-87. *Awards:* Tiffany Found Fel, 79; Awards in Visual Arts, Southeastern Ctr Contemp Arts, 81; Fulbright Fel, Int Exchange Scholars, 86; fels painting, Nat Endowment Arts, 90. *Bibliog:* Southeastern Ctr Contemp Art, Awards in Visual Arts (film), PBS TV, 83; R S Coburn (auth), Raising veil of emerging artist, Smithsonian Mag, 5/82; All art considered (interview), Nat Pub Radio, 5/19/82. *Dealer:* Sid Deutsch Gallery 20 W 57th St New York NY. *Mailing Add:* c/o Ovsey Gallery 170 S La Brea Ave Los Angeles CA 90036

SCHULZ, ANNE MARKHAM
HISTORIAN, EDUCATOR
b New York, NY, Mar 3, 38. *Study:* Radcliffe Col, BA, 59; New York Univ, Inst Fine Arts, MA, 62, PhD, 68. *Teaching:* Asst prof Renaissance art, Univ Ill, Chicago Circle, 67-68; vis lectr to vis asst prof & res assoc, Brown Univ, 68- *Awards:* Basic Res Grant, Nat Endowment Humanities, 82-86; Am Coun Learned Socs Sr Fel, 87-88; Assoc I Tatti Grant, Italy, 83-84. *Mem:* Col Art Asn; Renaissance Soc. *Res:* Venetian Renaissance sculpture; early Renaissance art. *Publ:* Auth, The Columbia altarpiece & Roger van der Weyden's stylistic development, Münchner Jahrbuch, 71; The Sculpture of Bernardo Rossellino and his Workshop, 77 & Antonio Rizzo, Sculptor & Architect, 83, Princeton Univ Press; The sculpture of Giovanni & Bartolmeo Bon, Transactions Am Philos Soc, 78; Niccolo di Giovanni Fiorentino and Venetian Sculpture of the Early Renaissance, CAA Monographs, 78; Giambattista and Lorenzo Bregno, Cambridge Univ Press, 91. *Mailing Add:* 192 Bowen St Providence RI 02906

SCHULZ, CHARLES MONROE
CARTOONIST
b Minneapolis, Minn, Nov 25, 22. *Study:* Anderson Col, Hon LHD, 63. *Exhib:* Louvre Musee des Arts Decoratifs, Paris; Mus Fine Arts, Montreal; Pavilion Flaminio, Rome; Smithsonian Inst, Washington, DC; Los Angeles Mus Natural Hist; Oakland Mus; Palm Springs Desert Mus; Brooklyn Children's Mus; Univ Minn Art Mus. *Pos:* Cartoonist, St Paul Pioneer Press & Sat Eve Post, 48-49; created syndicated comic strip Peanuts, 50- *Teaching:* Instr, Art Instr Sch, Minn, 46-50. *Awards:* Six Emmy awards for animated television specials 65-80; Cartoonists Hall of Fame, 87; Commandeuer des Artes et Lettres, French Ministry of Cult, 90. *Bibliog:* Joan Roebuck (auth), The Graphic Art of Charles Schultz; Umberto Eco (auth), The World of Charlie Brown; John Culhane (auth), A Boy for all Seasons, Mus Broadcasting. *Publ:* Auth & illusr, Boy Named Charlie Brown, 81 & Look Out Behind You Snoopy, 82, Fawcett; auth & illusr, Classroom Peanuts, 82 & You're Weird, Sir, 82, Holt, Rinehardt & Winston; auth & illusr, Some Day You'll Find Her, Charlie Brown, Random House, 82; and more than 200 others. *Mailing Add:* c/o Nancy Nicolelis United Feature Syndicate 200 Park Ave New York NY 10166

SCHULZ, JUERGEN
EDUCATOR, HISTORIAN
b Kiel, Ger, Aug 18, 27; US citizen. *Study:* Univ Calif, Berkeley, BA, 50; Courtauld Inst Art, Univ London, PhD, 58. *Collections Arranged:* Master Drawings from California Collections (coauth, catalog), 68; Caricature and Its Role in Graphic Satire (coauth, catalog), 70; The Origins of the Italian Vedanta (coauth, catalog), 78. *Teaching:* From instr to prof hist art, Univ Calif, Berkeley, 58-68; assoc cur Renaissance art, Art Mus, 64-68; prof, Brown Univ, 68-, A V Rosenthal prof hist art, 90- *Awards:* Grande Ufficiale, Stella Solidarieta Repub Italiana, 68. *Mem:* Col Art Asn Am; Renaissance Soc Am (mem exec bd, 72-74); Soc Archit Historians. *Res:* History of Italian medieval architecture and urbanism; history of Italian 16th century art and architecture. *Publ:* Auth, Venetian Painted Ceilings of the Renaissance, Univ Calif Press, 68; Printed Plans and Panoramic Views of Venice, Fondazione G Cini, 72; Michelangelo's unfinished works, 74 & Jacopo de Barbari's View of Venice, 78, Art Bulletin; The houses of Titian, Aretino and Sansovino, Titian, 82. *Mailing Add:* Program Hist Art, Box 1855 Brown Univ Providence RI 02906

SCHULZ, KEN
PAINTER, LECTURER
b Racine, Wis, Jan 19, 20. *Study:* Layton Sch Art, Milwaukee; also with Gerhard C F Miller. *Comn:* Many pvt & corp comns. *Exhib:* Ann Allied Artists Am, NY; Ann Knickerbocker Artists, NY; Ann Audubon Artists, Inc, NY; Ann Nat Acad Design, NY; Academic Artists, Springfield, Mass. *Pos:* Artist-owner, Ken Schulz Gallery, Gatlinburg, Tenn, 66- *Teaching:* Pvt art classes & watercolor workshops, Arrowmont Sch, Gatlinburg, 66- *Awards:* Best of Show, Circa 1964, Wustom Mus Fine Arts, Wis; Kathrine M Howe Mem Prize, Knickerbocker Artists, 72; Tenn Waterfowl Stamp Print, 82-83. *Bibliog:* Karen Tansel (auth), article, Racine J Times, 72; Flo Gullockson (auth), Knoxville News-Sentinel, 75; Deborah Walther (auth), article, Decor Mag, 12/77. *Mem:* Am Watercolor Soc; Salmagundi Club; Allied Artists Am; Audubon Artists; Knickerbocker Artists. *Media:* Watercolor, Oil. *Mailing Add:* PO Box 396 Gatlinburg TN 37738

SCHULZE, FRANZ
EDUCATOR, CRITIC
b Uniontown, Pa, Jan 30, 27. *Study:* Northwestern Univ, 43; Univ Chicago, PhD, 45; Art Inst Chicago, BFA, 49, MFA, 50; Acad Fine Arts, Munich. *Pos:* Art critic, Chicago Daily News, 62-78; corresp ed, Art in Am, 65-; contrib ed, Art News, 75-; contrib ed, Inland Architect, 75-, Chicago Sun-Times, 78-85. *Teaching:* Instr, Purdue Univ, 50-52; prof, Lake Forest Col, 52-74, Hollender prof art, 75- *Awards:* Ford Found Critics Fel, 64; Harbison Award, Danford Found, 71; Graham Found Advan Fine Arts Fel, 71 & 80; and others. *Mem:* Col Art Asn Am (bd dirs, 81-82); Arch Am Art; Am Asn Univ Prof; Ragdale Found; Koffler Found. *Res:* Art and architecture in the Midwest, especially Chicago. *Publ:* Auth, Art, Architecture and Civilization, 68; Fantastic Images: Chicago Art Since 1945, 72; 100 Years of Architecture in Chicago, 76; Mies van der Rohe: A Critical Biography, 85; A Heritage: The University Club of Chicago, 87; ed, Mies van der Rohe, Critical Essays, 89. *Mailing Add:* Dept Art Lake Forest Col Lake Forest IL 60045

SCHULZE, JOHN
PHOTOGRAPHER, COLLAGE ARTIST
b Scottsbluff, Nebr, June 7, 15. *Study:* Emporia State Univ, Kans, BS; Univ Iowa, MFA. *Work:* Nihon Univ, Tokyo; Hayden Gallery, Mass Inst Technol; Univ Ala; Oakland Mus; Smithsonian Inst; Union League Club Archives, Chicago. *Comn:* Photog mural, Sci Bldg, Univ Northern Iowa, 71. *Exhib:* American Photography: The Sixties, Sheldon Mem Art Gallery, Nebr, 66; Photography in Fine Arts V, Metrop Mus Art, New York, 67; Photography USA, De Cordova Mus, 68; Focus Gallery, San Francisco, 68; Exposure Gallery, New York, 73; travelling retrospective, 85. *Teaching:* Prof photog, Sch Art, Univ Iowa, 48-85; artist-in-residence, Washburn Univ, 72 & Northwest Mo State Col, 72; instr, Sun Valley Ctr Arts, 77. *Awards:* Hon Educ, Soc Photo Educ, 85. *Bibliog:* Elusive Shadow (film), Univ Iowa Camera, 65. *Mem:* Soc Photog Educ (chmn, 70); Col Art Asn Am; Mid Am Col Art Asn. *Publ:* Camera Int, 65, Contemp Photogr, 67, Aperture, 69, Photog Ann, 69 & Fotografie, Int Fotokunst, 79; article, John Schulze in search of the elusive shadow, Photog Forum, 85. *Mailing Add:* 5 Forest Glen Iowa City IA 52240

SCHULZE, PAUL
DESIGNER
b New York, NY, Feb 7, 34. *Study:* Parsons Sch Design, cert; NY Univ, BS(indust design), 60. *Comn:* Crystal cross, Steuben Glass, St Clement's Episcopal Church, New York. *Exhib:* Studies in Crystal 1966, Steuben Glass, NY, 65; Islands in Crystal, Steuben Glass, NY, 66; New Glass, Corning Mus Glass, 79. *Pos:* Off interior design, Bus Equip Sales Co, New York, 60-61; designer, Steuben Glass, 61-69, asst dir design, 69-70, dir design, 70-87. *Teaching:* Instr eng drawing & three dimensional design, Parsons Sch Design, 62-70. *Awards:* Student Competition Award, Am Soc Indust Designers, 59. *Mem:* Guild for Organic Environment; Nat Alumni Coun Parsons Sch Design; NY State Craftsmen. *Media:* Glass, Mixed. *Publ:* Illusr, Organics, Steendrukkerij & Co, Holland, 61. *Mailing Add:* PO Box 134 New Suffolk NY 11956-0134

SCHURR, JERRY M
PAINTER, PRINTMAKER
b Philadelphia, Pa, May 4, 40. *Study:* Univ Pa, 58-59; Pa Acad Fine Arts, 58-60 & 65-69; Temple Univ, 61-63. *Work:* Philadelphia Mus Art, Pa; Delaware Art Mus, Wilmington, Del; Portland Mus Art, Ore; Minneapolis Mus Art,

Minn; US Dept State (Vienna Embassy), Vienna. *Exhib:* Ann Fel Show, Pa Acad Fine Arts, Philadelphia, 68, 69, 70, 74 & 86; Philadelphia Print Club, 74, 77, 78 & 86; The Philadelphia Civic Ctr Mus Exchange Exhib, Tel Aviv, Israel, 80; 65th Ann Multiple Impressions Traveling Show, Philadelphia Print Club, 80; Fel Show PAFA, Noyes Mus, NJ, 86; Nat Acad Art for the Parks, Smithsonian Inst, Washington, DC, 87. *Teaching:* Instr serigraphy, Tyler Sch Art, Elkins Park, Pa, 77-78. *Awards:* Thouron Prize, Pa Acad Fine Arts, 66; Eugene Feldman Mem Prize, Philadelphia Print Club, Philadelphia Mus Art, 77; Nat Arts Club Purchase Prize, 79. *Bibliog:* Victoria Donahoe (auth), The panorama of the west, Philadelphia Inquirer, 4/11/86; Talking Posters, Art Business News, 11/85; Article, Print Collectors Newsletter, 4/83. *Mem:* Artist Equity; Philadelphia Print Club; Pa Acad Fine Arts (alumni). *Media:* Acrylic; Serigraphy, Silkscreen. *Mailing Add:* 1105 Melrose Ave Melrose Park PA 19126

SCHUSELKA, ELFI
PAINTER, SCULPTOR
b Vienna, Austria, Feb 13, 40. *Study:* Art hist & theatre, Univ Vienna; Acad Arts, Vienna; photog, Graphic & Experimental Inst, Vienna; studied with Oskar Kokoschka, Sch of Vision, Salzburg, Austria; Art Students League, New York; Pratt Graphics Ctr, New York. *Work:* Albertina, Vienna, Austria; Amon Carter Mus Western Art, Ft Worth, Tex; Bibliot Nat, Paris, France; Nat Mus Hist, Taipei, Taiwan; Mus Mod Art, New York; Mus Contemporary Art, Ibiza, Spain; Mus Int Contemp Graphic Art, Fredrikstad, Norway; Mus d'Art Contemporian, Skoplje, Yugoslavia. *Exhib:* Int Print Biennale, Cracow, Poland, 70, 76, 78 & 80; Brooklyn Mus Print Exhib, NY, 70 & 76; Int Exhib Graphic Art, Ljubljana, Yugoslavia, 75, 79, 81, 83 & 85; Int Print Biennale, Fredrikstad, Norway, 76-86; solo exhibs, 55 Mercer Gallery, New York, 77, 79, 82 & 84, Condeso/Lawler, 80, 83, 85 & 87, Joan Hodgell Gallery, Sarasota, Fla, 85, Broadway Windows, New York Univ, 88 & Neue Galerie, Vienna, 88, Henry Chauncey Conf Ctr, Princeton, NJ, 90; Monumental Drawing, Brooklyn Mus, 86; Int Biennial Graphic Art Ljubljana, Tokyo, Japan, 88-89; Exhib Graphic Art, Frechen, Ger, 76, 78, 83 & 90; Int Biennale Varna, Bulgaria, 89; Plaster in Contemp Art, Queens Mus, NY, 90. *Teaching:* Instr printmaking, Sch Visual Arts, New York, 70-73; instr art, Pratt/Phoenix Sch of Design, New York, 74 & Pratt Graphics Ctr, 78-80, Baruch Col, City Univ New York, 89. *Awards:* Int Exhib Graphic Art Medal, Frechen, Germany, 78; Award, Ibizagraphic 82, Spain; New York Found Arts Grant, 86. *Bibliog:* Tiffany Bell (auth), article, Arts Mag, 1/78; Vivien Raynor (auth), New York Times, 8/6/78 & 12/26/82; Nancy Unger (auth), Gannett Newspaper, 1/21/83; Grace Glueck (auth), article, New York Times, 3/29/85. *Dealer:* Condeso/Lawler Gallery 76 Greene St New York NY 10012; Galerie Al Lōwenstr 43B 7000 Stuttgart 70 Germany. *Mailing Add:* 133 Eldridge St New York NY 10002

SCHUSTER, CITA FLETCHER (SARAH E)
PAINTER, CONSULTANT
b El Paso, Tex, Sept 12, 29. *Study:* Vassar Col, AB, 50; Univ Tex, El Paso, with David Deming & Sally Bishop; Univ Calif, Los Angeles, Am Soc Appraisers sem fine arts; conservation & restoration with Nikoli Poloskov, 81; Cornucopia V, Am Soc Appraisers sem fine arts, London, 85. *Exhib:* One-man exhibs, Univ Tex, El Paso, 75 & 78; Int Woman's Art Slide Festival, 76; 19th Ann Sun Carnival Nat, El Paso Mus Art, Tex, 76-77; El Paso Designer Craftsmen Invitational, Univ Tex, El Paso, 78; Toys Designed by Artists, Ark Art Ctr, 79-80. *Pos:* Owner-dir, Two-Twenty-Two Gallery, El Paso, 63-; fine art appraiser, 63- *Bibliog:* Betty Chamberlain (auth), Professional page, Am Artist, 11/74; guest appearance, Spectrum - appraising fine arts, KCOS-TV, 86. *Mem:* Charter mem Visual Artists & Galleries Asn Inc; Appraisers Asn Am; founder Valuors Consortium, Houston; La Watercolor Soc; co-founder, UT El Paso, Friends Art, 87; sr mem Am Soc Appraisers, recertified, 88-93. *Media:* Watercolor, Acrylic. *Specialty:* Nineteenth and twentieth century painting, print and sculpture. *Publ:* Co-auth, The Status Game, Avalon Hill, 82. *Mailing Add:* 6109 Pinehurst El Paso TX 79912

SCHUSTER, EUGENE IVAN
DEALER, HISTORIAN
b St Louis, Mo, Dec 8, 36. *Study:* Wayne State Univ, BA & MA; Univ Mich, Ann Arbor, 59-62; Univ London, Warburg Inst, Fulbright scholar with E H Gombrich & Courtauld Inst, 62-65; London Sch Econ, 62-65. *Pos:* Dir, London Arts Gallery. *Teaching:* Lectr art hist, Wayne State Univ, 59-62, Eastern Mich Univ, 60, Rackham Exten, Univ Mich, 61 & Nat Gallery, London, 62-65. *Mem:* Founders Soc, Detroit Inst Arts; Detroit Art Dealers Asn; Appraisers Asn Am. *Res:* Quattrocento in Florence, especially formative changes caused by humanistic studies and leading to the Renaissance. *Specialty:* Old and modern master graphics; American and European painting and sculpture from the 15th to the 20th centuries. *Publ:* Auth, Les Peintres Maudits: A Study of the Cultural Relationship of the Jewish Artists of Paris, 60; Sir Charles Locke Eastlake, Plymouth Art Mus, Eng. *Mailing Add:* 321 Fisher Bldg Detroit MI 48202

SCHUSTERMAN, GERRIE MARVA
ART DEALER, GALLERY DIRECTOR
b Chicago, Ill, July 6, 28. *Study:* Univ Mich; Soc Arts & Crafts, Detroit; Univ Southern Calif, Irvine. *Pos:* Gallery director, Art Angles Gallery, Orange, Calif, 71- *Teaching:* Teacher & coordr, Rancho Santiago Community Col, 80- *Mem:* Prof Picture Framers Asn; Art Dealers Asn, (bd mem). *Specialty:* Established regionalist artists. *Mailing Add:* Art Angles 3411 E Chapman Orange CA 92669

SCHUTTE, THOMAS FREDERICK
ADMINISTRATOR
b Rochester, NY, Dec 19, 35. *Study:* Valparaiso Univ, Ind, AB, 57; Ind Univ, Bloomington, MBA, 58; Univ Colo, Boulder, DBA, 63. *Pos:* Asst dean, Wharton Sch, Univ Pa, Philadelphia, 73-75; pres, Philadelphia Col Art, 75-83; dir, Union Independent Cols Art, 75-; pres, RI Sch Design, 83- *Interests:* American 18th and 19th century decorative arts. *Publ:* Auth, Is the antiques dealer aware of his economic position in the market place?, 1-5/63 & A salesmanship model for the antiques dealer, 4/64, Antiques Dealer; ed, An Uneasy Coalition: Design & Corporate America, Univ Pa, 75. *Mailing Add:* 132 Bowen St Providence RI 02906

SCHUTZ, ESTELLE
PAINTER, PRINTMAKER
b New York, NY, Oct 10, 07. *Study:* Cooper Union, cert; Pratt Graphic Ctr. *Work:* Philadelphia Mus of Art; Brooklyn Mus, NY; McAllen Int Mus, Tex; Portland Art Mus, Ore; Seattle Art Mus, Wash. *Exhib:* Brooklyn Mus, NY; Pa Acad Fine Arts, Philadelphia; Philadelphia Mus of Art; Boston Printmakers Exhib, Mass; one-woman shows, Kans State Univ, Manhattan, Western Mich Univ, Kalamazoo, Fla State Univ, Tallahassee & Hofstra Univ, Hempstead, NY; Essex Col, Baltimore, Md; and others. *Pos:* Juror, art exhib, & exhib comt. *Teaching:* Pvt teacher for graphics in Frederick, Md for students with art degrees. *Awards:* John Taylor Arms Award/Printmaking, Audubon Ann, New York; Bankers Trust, Long Island, NY; Audobon Soc Award & purchase for Print, NAWA; Frederick County Annuals, Md; over 30 awards for prints & paintings. *Bibliog:* Articles in Newsday, 70-82, Diversions, 5/89, Frederick News-Post, 87-90, The New Paper, 89-90. *Mem:* Soc Am Graphic Artists; Nat Asn Women Artists; Delaplaine Visual Arts Ctr; Frederick Art Coun, Frederick, Md. *Media:* Acrylics; Etching. *Mailing Add:* 7076 Catalpa Rd Frederick MD 21701

SCHWABSKY, BARRY
EDITOR, CRITIC
b Paterson, NJ, Oct 26, 57. *Study:* Haverford Col, BA, 79; Yale Univ, MA, 81. *Pos:* Managing ed, Flash Art, Milan, Italy, 87-88; ed, Arts Mag, New York, 88- *Publ:* Auth, Awards in the Visual Arts 6, Southeastern Ctr Contemp Art, 87; coauth, Rotella Sovrapitture, Studio Marconi, Milan, 88; coauth, Alain Kirili, Musée d'Art Moderne, Saint-Etienne, 92. *Mailing Add:* C/O Arts Magazine 561 Broadway New York NY 10012

SCHWALB, SUSAN
PAINTER, INSTRUCTOR
b New York, NY, Feb 26, 44. *Study:* Carnegie-Mellon Univ, BFA, 65; Fel, Va Ctr Creative Arts, 73 & 92; MacDowell Colony, 74, 75 & 89; Yaddo, Saratoga Springs, NY, 81. *Work:* Mus Mod Art, Belgrade, Yugoslavia; Ark Arts Ctr, Little Rock; Chase Manhattan Bank, New York; Fogg Art Mus, Harvard Univ; Norton Gallery of Art, West Palm Beach, Fla; Boston Public Libr. *Exhib:* One-woman shows, Creation Ser, Hudson Gallery, 87, Silverpoint Drawings, SOHO 20 Gallery, NY, 89 & Brad Cooper Gallery, Tampa, Fla, 89, Creation Ser: 15 Years of Silverpoint, Yeshiva Univ Mus, New York, 90, Chase/Freedman Gallery, Greater Hartford JCC, West Hartford, Conn, 92, May Mus Judaica, Lawrence, NY, 93 & B'nai B'rith Klutznick Mus, Washington, DC, 93; Uncommon Ground, Brad Cooper Gallery, Tampa, Fla, 91; Selections from the National Drawing Association, Thesis Gallery, Md Inst, Col Art, Baltimore, 92; Europa-America: 360 E-VENTI (catalog), Pino Molica Gallery (travelling), 92; Silverpoint Etcetera: Contemporary American Metalpoint Drawings (catalog), travelling, 93; Sacred Artifacts, Objects of Devotion, Alternative Mus, 82-83; solo exhibs, Am Ctr, Belgrade, Yugoslavia, 83, Silverpoint Drawing, SOHO 20 Gallery, New York, 85 & 89, Simmons Col, Boston, Mass, 85, Brad Cooper Gallery, Tampa, Fla, 89 & "The Creation Series: 15 Years of Silverpoint", Yeshiva Univ Mus, New York, 90; The Fine Line: Drawing with Silver in America, Norton Gallery Art, West Palm Beach, Fla, 85-86; Mus Fine Arts, Springfield, Mass, 85-86; Saints & Sinners: Contemporary Responses to Religion, DeCordova & Dana Mus & Park, Lincoln, MA, 86; Jewish Community Mus, San Francisco, Calif, 87; group exhib, Abstract American Drawings, Arkansas Art Ctr, 88-90, Drawing: Line or Image, Newport Art Mus, 89. *Pos:* Art dir, Aphra, Literary Mag, 74-75 & Women Artist News, 75-77. *Teaching:* Instr, Kean Col of NJ, 78-79, City Univ New York, 79-82 & Parsons Sch Art, 82; assoc prof, Mass Col Art, 82-; spec instr, Simmons Col, 88; vis assoc prof, Mass Col Art, Boston, 82-91. *Awards:* Comt for the Visual Arts Grant, New York, 77 & 85; Int Commun Agency Travel Grant, 81. *Bibliog:* Elin A Bard (auth), Drawing at Benson, Dan's Papers, 6/14/91; Elaine Adler (auth), Contemporary Jewish Artist: Susan Schwalb, fall 91; and others. *Mem:* Coalition of Women's Art Orgn (exec comt, 77-78, vpres, 85-86); Col Art Asn; Women's Caucus for Art (bd mem, 78-79, coord, Boston Chap, 82-83). *Media:* Silverpoint Drawing, Acrylic. *Publ:* Illusr, Issue of Aphra, 73; contribr, Crafting with Plastics, Chilton Bk Co, 75; contribr, Women Artist News, Mid-March Assoc, 75-77; auth, Notes From Houston, Womanart, 78. *Mailing Add:* 10 Winsor Ave Watertown MA 02172

SCHWARCZ, JUNE THERESA
CRAFTSMAN, ENAMELIST
b Denver, Colo, June 10, 18. *Study:* Univ Colo, 36-38; Univ Chicago, 38-39; Pratt Inst, 39-41; Inst Design, Chicago, with Moholy Nagy. *Work:* Lannan Found, Palm Beach, Fla; Johnson Wax Collection; Kunstgewerbemuseums, Zurich, Switz; Nat Collection Fine Arts, Smithsonian Inst, Washington, DC; Mus Contemp Craft, New York; and others. *Comn:* Enameled bowl with technique demonstration bowls, Mus Contemp Crafts, 58. *Exhib:* New Talent USA, Art in Am, 60; Objects USA, Johnson Wax Collection & Exhib, 69; one-man shows, Mus Bellerive (Kunstgewerbermuseum), Zurich, Switz, 71,

Schmuckmuseum, Pforzheim, Ger, 72 & Mus Contemp Crafts, New York; two-man show, de Young Mus, San Francisco; Living Treasures of California, Crocker Mus, Sacramento, Calif, 85; Craft Today, Am Craft Mus NY, 86; Eloquent Object, Philbrook Mus Tulsa, Okla, 87. *Awards:* Ceramic Nat Purchase Award, Everson Mus, Syracuse, 60; First Calif Craftsmen's Biennial, Oakland Mus, 61; Goldsmith 70, Minn Mus Art, 70; Fel, Am Craft Coun. *Bibliog:* Ventura (auth), June Schwarcz: Electroforming, Crafts Horizons, 11/65; Hammel (auth), June Schwarcz: Enamelist, Am Craft Mag, 10/81; Bennett (auth), article, Metalsmith, 83. *Mem:* Am Crafts Coun. *Media:* Enamel, Copper. *Publ:* Contribr, Craftmen's World, 59 & Research in Crafts, 61, Am Crafts Coun; auth, The arts turn to plating, J Electroplaters Soc, 11/67. *Mailing Add:* c/o The Sylvania Gallery 301 W Fourth St Royal Oak MI 48087

SCHWARTZ, ADRIENNE CLAIRE See Mim, Adrienne C (Adrienne Claire Schwartz)

SCHWARTZ, ALAN E
COLLECTOR
Study: Univ Mich, BA, 47; Havard Law Sch, LLB, 50; Wayne State Univ, LLD, 83; Univ Detroit, LLD, 85. *Exhib:* Master Prints of Five Centuries, Detroit Inst Arts, Mich, 91. *Mailing Add:* 4120 Echo Rd Bloomfield Hills MI 48302

SCHWARTZ, AUBREY E
PRINTMAKER, SCULPTOR
b New York, NY, Jan 13, 28. *Study:* Art Students League; Brooklyn Mus Art Sch. *Work:* Nat Gallery Art, Washington, DC; Brooklyn Mus Art; Philadelphia Mus Art; Libr Cong, Washington, DC; Art Inst Chicago. *Comn:* Ed lithographs, Predatory Birds, Gehenna Press, 58, Midget & Dwarf, Tamarind Workshop, 60 & Bestiary, Kanthos Press, 61. *Exhib:* Young Am, Whitney Mus Am Art, 57; Print Coun Am Show, 57; one-man show, Grippi Gallery, New York, 58; Art USA, New York Coliseum, 59; Contemp Graphic Art, US State Dept, 59. *Teaching:* Prof art, State Univ NY, Binghamton, currently. *Awards:* Guggenheim Found Fel Creative Printmaking, 58-60; Tamarind Fel Creative Lithography, 60; First Prize Graphic Art, Boston Arts Festival, 60. *Mailing Add:* Dept Art & Art History PO Box 6000 Binghamton Univ Binghamton NY 13901-6000

SCHWARTZ, BARBARA ANN
PAINTER, SCULPTOR
b Philadelphia, Pa, Aug 23, 48. *Study:* Carnegie-Mellon Univ, BFA, 70. *Work:* Guggenheim Mus, New York; Albright Knox Mus, Buffalo; Mus Fine Arts, Mus Contemp Art, Chicago; Neuberger Mus, Purchase, NY; Pa Acad Fine Arts, Philadelphia; and others. *Exhib:* Brooklyn Mus, 74; Whitney Biennial Exhib Contemp Am Art, 75 & 79; Artpark, Lewiston, NY, 76; Willard Gallery, New York, 76, 78 & 79; Art in Pub Spaces, New York, 77; Contemp Arts Ctr, Cincinnati, 78; Dart Gallery, Chicago, 79, 80 & 84; Three Dimensional Painting, Mus Contemp Art, Chicago, 80; David Heath Gallery, Atlanta, Ga; Morris Gallery, Pa Acad Fine Arts, Philadelphia, 88; Hirshl & Adler Mod Gallery, NY, 83, 87; Koplin Gallery, Los Angeles, 88; Barbara Green Gallery, Miami, Fla, 90; Unique Prints, Pace Prints, New York, 91; 15 Years Dieu Donne', Ctr Bk Arts, New York, 91; New Editions, Pace Ed, New York, 91; Presswork: The Art of Woman Printmakers, Nat Mus Woman Arts, Washington, DC, 91; one-persons exhibs, Solo Press, New York, 91, Hirschl & Adler Modern, New York, 91 & 92. *Teaching:* Instr drawing, Brooklyn Mus Art Sch, 74-75; instr drawing & sculpture, Sch Visual Arts, New York, 77-90. *Awards:* Creative Artists Pub Serv Prog, 82-83. *Bibliog:* Jeanne Siege (auth), articles, Art Am, 75, 77, 81 & 84; Rose C S Slivka (auth), From the Studio, 2/28/91; Richard Kalina (auth), Review Art in Am, 6/91. *Publ:* Ed, Art News, 71-72; auth, Young New York artists, 72 & auth, New York sculpture (column), 72-75, Craft Horizons; auth, SoHo, an interview with a neighborhood, Bolaffi Arte, 74. *Dealer:* Hirschl & Adler Modern New York NY. *Mailing Add:* 416 Cedar Hill Rd Tivoli NY 12583

SCHWARTZ, BELLA
PAINTER, COLLAGE ARTIST
b New York, NY. *Study:* George Washington Univ, Washington, DC, BA, MA; Am Univ, Washington, DC. *Exhib:* Corcoran Gallery Art, Washington, DC, 56-57; Philadelphia Mus Art, 70; Washington Artists Equity, traveling, 72-73; Works on Paper Traveling Exhib, Kuumba Learning Ctr, 80. *Mem:* Washington Water Color Asn (pres, 72-74); Artists Equity Asn (pres, Washington area chap, 77-79); Women's Caucus Art. *Media:* Mixed. *Publ:* Ed, Paper: A Group Exhibition of Changing Uses and Concepts (exhib catalog), 12/79 & Clay: As Art and As Function, 11/81, Gallery 10 LTD, Washington, DC. *Dealer:* Studio Gallery 2108 R St NW Washington DC 20008. *Mailing Add:* 2122 Massachusetts Ave NW Washington DC 20008

SCHWARTZ, BUKY
PAINTER
b Jerusalem, Israel, 1932. *Study:* Avni Sch Art, Tel Aviv, Israel, 57-59, St Martin's Sch Art, London, Eng, 59-62. *Work:* Am Jewish Mus, Philadelphia; Rutgers Univ, New Brunswick, NJ; Jewish Mus, Bank Leumi Trust, Maritime Div Discount Banking, Ardin Co, Whitney Mus Am Art, New York; Israel Mus, Jerusalem; Tel Aviv Univ, Israel. *Exhib:* Solo exhibs, Eric Stark Gallery, New York, 89, Speces, Cleveland, Ohio, 89, Delta Gallery, Dusseldorf, Germany, 89, Spokane Ctr Gallery, Eastern Washington Univ, 90; Videosculpture Retrospective and Actual 1963-1989, Koln, Berlin, Zurich, 89; House 1990, Artists' Studios, Tel Aviv, Israel, 90; Frieze 1990, Paule Anglim Gallery, San Francisco, 90; Bookish Work, Reinpire Gallery, New York, 91; Video Sunflowers, Mucca Mus, Belg, 91; Video Sculpture, Middlebury Col, Vt, 92. *Awards:* Artpark, NYSCA Video Art Production Award, 83; Guggenheim Fel, USA, 87; Sculpture Grant, Nat Endowment Arts, 88; Guggenheim Grant for Publication, 90. *Mailing Add:* 519 Broadway New York NY 10012

SCHWARTZ, CARL E
PAINTER, PRINTMAKER
b Detroit, Mich, Sept 20, 35. *Study:* Art Inst Chicago, BFA; Univ Chicago, BFA. *Work:* Art Inst Chicago; Libr Cong & Smithsonian Inst, Washington, DC; Brit Mus; Brooklyn Mus Art; and many others. *Exhib:* Am Painting Exhib, Smithsonian Inst, Washington, DC & traveling, 72; 18th Nat Print Exhib, Brooklyn Mus, 72-73; Calif Palace Legion of Honor, San Francisco, 73; Eight State Painting Exhib, J B Speed Mus Art, 75; one-man exhibs, Ill State Mus, 77, Ill Inst Technol, 77, Gallery 4, Alexandria, VA, 78, Harmon Gallery, Naples, Fla, 81 & Art Inst Chicago, Jan Cicero Gallery, Chicago, 90; and many others. *Teaching:* Instr figure painting & drawing, NShore Art League, 58-85, Surburban Fine Arts Ctr, 60-85 & Deerpath Art League, Lake Forest, Ill. *Awards:* Purchase Awards, J B Speed Mus Art, 73, Ill State Mus, 74 & Dickinson State Univ, 76; Artist Grumbacher Award, Logan Medal Art Inst Chicago, Ill, 88. *Bibliog:* Allan Davidson (auth), article, Art League News, 67; Thomas Carbol (auth), The Printmaker in Illinois, Ill Art Educ Asn, 72; Les Krantz (pub), American Artists, 85-90. *Mem:* NShore Art League; Fla Artist Group. *Media:* Acrylic; All. *Dealer:* Jan Cicero Gallery 221 W Erie St Chicago Ill 60610; Harmon Gallery 1415 Main St Sarasota FL 33577. *Mailing Add:* 13872 Pine Villa Lane SE Ft Myers FL 33912

SCHWARTZ, ELLIOTT S
PHOTOGRAPHER
Study: Univ Cincinnati, 71; Calif Inst Arts, BFA, 72; Yale Univ, MFA, 74. *Work:* Metrop Mus Art, New York; Int Ctr Photog, New York; Australian Nat Gallery, Canberra, Australia. *Exhib:* Photography as Fine Arts, Univ Fla, Gainesville, 74; Sequential Imagery in Photography, Broxton Gallery, Los Angeles, 76; Certain Landscapes, Castelli Photog, New York, 78; one-man shows, Galerie T Venster, Rotterdam, Neth, 80, Sonnabend Gallery, New York, 81, Palazzo Dei Diamanti, Ferrara, Italy, 83, ICA, Boston, 85, Int Ctr Photog, NY, 87 & Jayne H Baum Gallery, New York, 90. *Awards:* Nat Endowment Arts Fel, 78 & 88. *Bibliog:* Stephen Westfall (auth), Art in America, 3/88. *Mailing Add:* c/o Jayne H Baum Gallery 588 Broadway New York NY 10012

SCHWARTZ, EUGENE M
COLLECTOR, PATRON
b Butte, Mont, Mar 18, 27. *Study:* New Sch Social Res; NY Univ; Columbia Univ; Univ Wash. *Pos:* Acquisitions comt, Whitney Mus Am Art, NY, 67-79, 91-; mem, 20th Century Comt, Metrop Mus Art, NY, 75-; Photogr Acquisitions Comt, Metrop Mus Art, 89. *Collection:* Contemporary American art since World War II, chiefly of the sixties: parts of the collection shown as a group at Jewish Museum, Everson Museum of Art and the Albany Institute; also individual pieces exhibited at Metropolitan Museum of Art, Museum of Modern Art, Whitney Museum Am Art, New York, Los Angeles County Museum and Tate Gallery. *Mailing Add:* 1160 Park Ave New York NY 10028

SCHWARTZ, HENRY
PAINTER, INSTRUCTOR
b Winthrop, Mass, Oct 27, 27. *Study:* Sch Mus Fine Arts, Boston, dipl(traveling fel), 53; Akad Bildendekunst, Salzburg, Austria, with Oskar Kokoschka, dipl. *Work:* Mus Fine Arts, Boston; Wheaton Col, Mass; DeCordova Mus; Boston Pub Libr. *Exhib:* Five one-man shows, Boris Mirski Gallery, 56-68; Carnegie Inst Int, 61; Harvard Univ, 75; Boston Atheneum, 80; four one-man shows, Gallery Maga, 80-; Boston Expressionism, retrospective, De Cordova Mus, 86; 40 Year Retrospective, Fuller Mus, Brockton, Mass, 90. *Teaching:* Instr painting, Sch Mus Fine Arts, 56- *Awards:* Mus Sch Fel, 53; Ford Found Grant, 80. *Bibliog:* Christine Temin (auth), Boston Globe Profile, 90. *Media:* Oil. *Publ:* Illusr, filmstrip, United Churches of Christ, 61; illusr, Boston Mag, 64-65; Retrospective Catalog, Fuller Mus, Brockton, Mass, 90. *Dealer:* Gallery Naga 67 Newbury St Boston MA 02116. *Mailing Add:* 8 Garrison St Boston MA 02116

SCHWARTZ, LILLIAN (FELDMAN)
FILM, VIDEO, AUTHOR
b Cincinnati, Ohio, July 13, 27. *Study:* Univ Cincinnati; Kean Col, NJ, LHD, 88. *Work:* Mus Mod Art, New York; Moderna Museet, Stockholm, Sweden; Stedlijk Mus Art, Amsterdam, Holland; Los Angeles Co Mus Art; Newark Mus Art, NJ. *Comn:* Painting/collage, Columbia Univ, New York, 67; murals, Int Bus Machines, Zurich, Switz, 72, sculpture, Miami, Fla, 77; New York Philharmonic, 76; mural, Am Telephone & Telegraph, Basking Ridge, NJ, 76; Hitachi, 88. *Exhib:* Mus Mod Art, New York, 68-69; Metrop Mus, New York, 72 & 73; Whitney Mus Am Art, New York, 73; 25th Int Film Festival, Cannes, France, 74; Hirshhorn Mus, Washington, DC, 75; Albright-Knox Art Gallery, Buffalo, NY, 76; Huntsville Mus, Ala, 78; Venice Biennial, 80; Grand Palais, Paris, 80; ELECTRA, La Musee d'Art Moderne de la Ville de Paris, France, 83; Lavillette, 88; IBM Gallery Sci & Art, 88. *Pos:* Consult, AT&T Bell Labs, Bellcore Commun Research, IBM, currently. *Teaching:* Prof, Univ Md, 77-; adj prof, Kean Univ, Union, NJ, 81-, Rutgers Univ & Sch Visual Arts Master Prog, New York. *Awards:* Video Expos, Victor Co, Japan, 80; Artist of the Month, Hitachi, Japan, 88; Fel, World Acad Art & Sci; and others. *Bibliog:* McCauley (auth), Computers and Creativity, Praeger, 75; Keating Productions, The Artist and the Computer (film), Am Telephone & Telegraph, 76; Jankel (auth), Creative Computer Graphics, Cambridge Press, 84. *Mem:* Artists Equity Asn (NY & NJ); Artists League Cent NJ; Nat Acad

Television Arts & Sci; Soc Motion Pictures & Television Engineers; Independent Cinema Artists & Producers; and others. *Media:* Computer, Video Books. *Publ:* Appropriation Art, Calculation & Creativity-Pixim 88, L'image Numerique a Paris, 10/88; The Identities of the Mona Lisa, Computer Vision (in press); The Computer Artist's Handbook (with Laurens R Schwarts), Norton Publ, 92; The Mask of Shakespeare, Pixel, 92; Electronic Restoration, Piero de lle Francesca, Visual Computer, 92; and others. *Mailing Add:* 524 Ridge Rd Watchung NJ 07060

SCHWARTZ, MARJORIE WATSON
PAINTER
b Trenton, Tenn, Jan 4, 05. *Study:* Newcomb Col Art Sch, Tulane Univ, BFA(design), 27. *Work:* Opryland Hotel, Nashville, Tenn; Memphis Pub Libr, Baptist Mem Hosp, NBC Bank & Mid-South Fair, Memphis, Tenn. *Comn:* 7 Landscapes, Mem Park Funeral Home, Memphis, Tenn, 69; painting, Crippled Children's Hosp, Memphis, Tenn, 80. *Exhib:* One-woman shows, Memphis Brooks Mus & Gallery, 53 & Memphis Athletic Club, 75, Tenn; Watercolor USA, Springfield Art Mus, Mo, 72; Art Collection, Eastwood Hosp, Memphis, 80; Central South, Parthenon Gallery, Nashville, 81; Tennessee Art, Pickwick Dam Visitor's Ctr, Tenn, 84; two-woman show, Memphis Publ Co, Tenn, 85; Mid-South Art Exhib, Brooks Mem Gallery, 5 times. *Teaching:* Instr, watercolor by eight workshops, Memphis State Univ, 79-81 & Germantown Art League, 80, Memphis, Tenn. *Awards:* First Prize Watercolor, Mid-South Fair's Permanent Collection, 72; Purchase Prize, Watercolor USA, 74. *Mem:* Tenn Watercolor Soc (charter mem); Memphis Watercolor Soc; Ky Watercolor Soc; Southern Watercolor Soc; and others. *Media:* Watercolor. *Mailing Add:* 1117 Whiting Memphis TN 38117

SCHWARTZ, MARVIN D
HISTORIAN
b New York, NY, Feb 15, 26. *Study:* City Col New York, BS, 46; Inst Fine Arts, NY Univ, 47-51; Univ Del, MA, 54. *Pos:* Jr cur, Detroit Inst Arts, 51-52; cur decorative arts & indust design lab, Brooklyn Mus, 54-68, ed publ, 59-60; adv dept design, Sears, Roebuck & Co, 64-72; auth, weekly antiques column, New York Times, 66-72; lectr & consult, Metrop Mus Art, 68-; NY ed, Antique Monthly, 74- *Teaching:* Lectr, City Col New York, 48-51 & 56-64; lectr, State Univ NY Col Purchase, 69-82. *Awards:* Stipend, Belg-Am Educ Found. *Mem:* Soc Archit Historians; Col Art Asn Am; fel H F DuPont Winterthur Mus. *Publ:* Auth, Collectors Guide to American Clocks, 75; auth, Collectors Guide to American Silver, 75; plus many others. *Mailing Add:* Off Community Educ Metrop Mus of Art 5th Ave & 82nd St New York NY 10028

SCHWARTZ, ROSALYN
PAINTER
b St Louis, Mo, Aug 6, 52. *Study:* Washington Univ, St Louis, Mo, BFA(summa cum laude), 75; Fontbonne Col, St Louis, Mo, MFA, 79. *Work:* Arthur Anderson Cos, Minneapolis, Minn; Beckman Inst Advanced Sci & Technol, Univ Ill, Urbana; Gen Mills Corp, World Hq, Minneapolis, Minn; Prudential Ins Co, Newark, NJ; Squibb Pharmaceutical Cos Inc, Trenton, NJ. *Exhib:* Solo Exhibs, Parkland Col Gallery, Champaign, IL, 89, Recent Paintings, Gallery Nine, Univ Ill, Champaign, 89 & Kiehle Gallery, St Cloud State Univ, Minn, 89, Landscape Paintings, Fontbonne Col Gallery, St Louis, 90, Paintings, Gwenda Jay, Chicago, 90, Merwyn Gallery, Ill Wesleyen Univ, Bloomington, 92 & Betsy Rosenfield Gallery, Chicago, 93; Group Exhib, Gwenda Jay Gallery, Chicago, 92; May 1992, Betsy Rosenfield Gallery, Chicago Int Art Expo, 92; six-person show, Betsy Rosenfield Gallery, Chicago, 92; Nature Fabrilis, Steibel Modern, New York, 92; and others. *Teaching:* Instr painting, Univ Minn, Minneapolis, 84-87 & Minneapolis Col Art & Design, 86-88; asst prof painting, Univ Ill, Champaign, 88-92. *Awards:* Fel Visual Arts, McKnight Found, Minneapolis, Minn, 86; Fel Visual Artists, Bush Found, Minneapolis, Minn, 87; Grant, Finalist, Awards in the Visual Arts, Winston-Salem, NC, 88. *Bibliog:* James Yood (auth), Rosalyn Schwartz, ArtForum, 1/91; John Brunetti (auth), Rosalyn Schwartz, New Art Examiner, 11/91; Holland Cotter (auth), Nature Fabrilis, NY Times, 7/3/92. *Media:* Oil on Canvas. *Mailing Add:* c/o Betsy Rosenfield Gallery 212 W Superior St Chicago IL 60610

SCHWARTZ, RUTH
PAINTER, INSTRUCTOR
Study: NY Univ, with Leo Manso; Empire State Col, 84. *Work:* John T Mather Mem Hosp, Port Jefferson, NY; Atlantic County Publ Libr, Atlantic City, NJ. *Exhib:* Hudson River Annual, Hudson River Mus, Yonkers, NY, 84; Long Island Artists, Nassau County Mus Fine Arts, Roslyn Harbor, NY, 85; 43rd Western New York Exhib, Albright-Knox Gallery, Buffalo, NY, 90; Chautauqa Inst, NY; Burchfield Ctr, State Univ NY, Buffalo; State Col, Buffalo; and others. *Teaching:* Instr, Ctr Performing & Creative Arts, Wheatley Heights, Long Island, NY, 81-88; Albright-Knox Art Gallery, Buffalo, NY, 89- *Awards:* Audobon Artists Citation of Merit, Am Acad & Inst Arts & Letters, 80; C Whinston Memorial Works on Canvas Award, Nat Asn Women Artists, 88. *Bibliog:* Park East (auth), article, Artspeak, 82; Malcolm Preston (auth), An invitational show, Newsday, 84. *Mem:* Nat Asn Women Artists (oil jury chmn, 80-81); Audobon Artists; Artist's Equity of NY; Buffalo Soc Artists (steering comt, 90). *Media:* All. *Dealer:* Members Gallery Albright-Knox Art Gallery Elmwood Ave Buffalo NY 14222. *Mailing Add:* 214 N Autumn Williamsville NY 14221

SCHWARTZ, SING-SI
PHOTOGRAPHER
b New York, NY, Oct 20, 54. *Study:* New Sch for Social Res, advan photo printing with George Tice; psychol portraiture with Phillippe Halsman, 73; Rochester Inst Technol, AAS, 75, BS, 77. *Comn:* Photograph, Burma Airline & posters, Burma Govt, 71; photograph, Vt Bi-Centennial Comn, 75; photographic mural, Wool Bur, Chicago Hq, 81; Eastern Spirit Western World, Transparencies in the film on artist, Diana Kan, 88. *Exhib:* One-man shows, Pen & Brush Club, New York, 77 & 85, Rochester Inst Tecnol, NY, 77, Dawson Gristmill Gallery, Vt, 77, Portchester Libr, NY, 78, Photographers Place, 86, Backer and Spielvogel, 86 & Nat Arts Club, NY, 88. *Pos:* Mem staff, Villager Newspaper, New York, 68-74; photogr/correspondent, Cosmorama Pictorial, Hong Kong, 70-; photogr ed, New York Air, 83-85, & The New York Scene, 83-87. *Teaching:* Instr, Int Ctr Photog, New York, 81-88; adj prof, New York Univ, 83-84; Instr, New Brunswick Craft Sch, British Columbia, Can, 85. *Awards:* Elected as one of 100 outstanding Chinese abroad for accomplishments in photography, Chinese Govt, Taiwan, 71-77. *Bibliog:* Beautiful girls of Hong Kong seen through the eyes of photographer Sing-Si Schwartz, Ming-Pao Weekly, Hong Kong, 8/15/71; article, Interior Design, 10/81. *Mem:* Nat Arts Club; Am Soc Mag Photogr; assoc Allied Artists Am; Overseas Press Club. *Publ:* Photogr, Creating with Card Weaving, Crown Publ Inc, 73; photogr, The How and Why of Chinese Painting, Van Nostrand, 74; contribr, 40 American Watercolorists & How They Work, Watson-Guptill, 77; photogr, Joan Whitney Payson Gallery of Art, Westbrook Col, Maine, 77; photogr, A guide to flowers and flower painting, North Light, 80; Scientific Experiments for Kids, Harper & Row, 88; From the Desk of, Harcourt Brace Jovanovich, 89. *Mailing Add:* 15 Gramercy Park S New York NY 10003

SCHWARTZ, THERESE
PAINTER, WRITER
b New York, NY, Dec 7, 28. *Study:* Corcoran Sch Art, Washington, DC; Am Univ; Brooklyn Mus Art Sch. *Work:* Corcoran Gallery Art, Smithsonian Inst & Howard Univ, Washington, DC; Nelson/Atkins Mus, Kansas City, Mo; Pepsico Collection, Purchase, NY; Ciba-Geigy Corp; Brooklyn Mus & New Sch Social Res, New York; Huntington Mus, San Francisco. *Exhib:* Humphrey Gallery, New York, 87-89; Ctr Performing Arts, Bucknell Univ, Lewisburg, Pa, 88; ARCO Int Art Fair, Madrid, Spain, 88; Humphrey Fine Art, New York, 89 & 92; Andrea Ross Gallery, Santa Monica, Calif, 90; and others. *Pos:* Ed, New York Element, 68-72; contrib ed, Feminist Art J; mem bd dirs, Princeton Arts J. *Awards:* Second Prize for Oils, Corcoran Gallery Art Regional Show, 52; New Talent USA Award, Art Am, 62; Women Artists Year Three, Mabel Smith Douglass Libr, Rutgers Univ, 73. *Bibliog:* Eleanor Heartney (auth), Art in America, 10/87; Eleanor Heartney (auth), Art News, 9/88; Gerrit Henry (auth), Art in America, 6/92. *Mem:* Artists Equity. *Media:* All Media. *Publ:* Auth, Plastic Sculpture and Collage, Hearthside, 69; The politicalization of the avant-garde (ser), Art in Am, 11/71, 3/72, 3/73 & 1/74. *Mailing Add:* Apt 9A 161 W 75th St New York NY 10023

SCHWARZ, JUDITH
SCULPTOR, DRAFTSMAN
b Can, Nov 26, 44. *Study:* Univ BC, BA, 66; York Univ, MFA, 78. *Work:* Nat Gallery Can & Can Coun Art Bank, Ottawa, Ont; Windsor Art Gallery, Windsor, Ont; City of Vancouver, BC; Univ Ore, Portland, Ore. *Comn:* Bronze sculpture, Skydome Corp, 90. *Exhib:* Cella, PS 1, Long Island, NY, 82; New City of Sculpture, Toronto, Ont, 84; Exposicion Canadiense, Inst Cultura Yucatan, Merida, Mex, 85; Canada Collects, Washington, DC, 85; York Faculty, Zheijiang Acad, Hangzhou, China, 86; Continuum, Southern Alta Art Gallery, Lethbridge, 86; Artscape, Burlington Cult Ctr, Ont, 87; Plato's Cave, Windsor Art Gallery, Ont, 89. *Pos:* Mem bd, Mercer Union Gallery, 80-, Toronto Sculpture Garden, 84-88; pres, Mercer Union Gallery, 83-88; bd mem, Art Gallery York Univ, Toronto, 89- *Teaching:* Asst prof sculpture & drawing, York Univ, Toronto, Can, 78- 89, assoc dir MFA Prog, 87-89. *Bibliog:* Jamelie Hassan (auth), Judith Schwarz, C Mag, 85; Christopher Dewdney (auth), Continuum (exhib catalog), Southern Alta Art Gallery, 86; Gary-Michael Dault (auth), Judith Schwarz, Can Art, 88. *Mem:* Adv mem Ont Arts Coun. *Publ:* Judith Schwarz (catalog), Art Gallery Windsor. *Dealer:* S L Simpson Gallery 515 Queen St W Toronto Ont M5V 2B4. *Mailing Add:* 26 Noble St Unit 17 Toronto ON M6K 2C7 Canada

SCHWARZ, MYRTLE COOPER
DESIGNER, MOSAIC ARTIST
b Breckenridge Co, Ky, Dec 10, 1900. *Study:* Western Ky State Univ, AB; Col William & Mary, MA; Columbia Univ, MA, PhD. *Exhib:* One-man shows, Col William & Mary, Okla State Univ & Univ Wis; Art Club & Art Ctr, St Petersburg, Fla; Gulf Coast Art Ctr, Clearwater, Fla; Beaux Arts Gallery, Pinellas Park, Fla; and numerous nat & regional shows. *Pos:* Chmn math & pres art sect, Va Educ Asn; mem comt, Seven Coop Univs Teacher Training; chmn Lang Arts Develop, Va State Curriculum; mem comt, Prof Standards & Develop, Nat Educ Asn; dir, Community Art Ctr, Enid, Okla. *Teaching:* Instr, Exten Serv, Univ Ky; prof educ, Col William & Mary; prin high sch & supt schs, Va & Ky; prof art educ & dir, Community Ctr, Phillips Univ; prof educ & dir art educ, Okla State Univ; vis prof, Monticello Col; prof Eng, Wis State Univ; instr creative crafts, Continuing Educ, Inst for Lifetime Learning. *Awards:* Many prizes at Nat Exhib. *Mem:* Enid Artists League; Univ Women's Serv Club; Nat Art Educ Asn (chmn Div Higher Educ & Teacher Training); Acad Senior Prof Eckerd Col. *Media:* Mixed. *Publ:* Auth, articles in Va J Educ, Ky & Okla J Educ. *Mailing Add:* 705 Chestnut Grove Rd Elizabethtown KY 42701-9725

SCHWEBEL, RENATA MANASSE
SCULPTOR
b Zwickau, Ger, Mar 6, 30; US citizen. *Study:* Antioch Col, BA, 53; Columbia Univ, MFA, 61; Art Students League, 68. *Work:* Columbia Univ, New York; Antioch Col, Ohio; Colt Industries, New York; Southwest Bell, Houston;

Heinrich Gruber House, Berlin, Ger; Mus Foreign Art, Sofia, Bulgaria; Comcraft Indust, Nairobi, Kenya; Am Airlines, Irvine, Calif. *Exhib:* Silvermine Guild New England Ann, Conn; Hudson River Mus Competitions, NY; Wadsworth Atheneum; New Britain Mus; one-woman show, Sculpture Ctr, New York; Katonal Gallery, Pelham Art Ctr, Berman/Daferner Gallery, New York. *Pos:* Dir, Fine Arts Fedn NY, 84; trustee, Sculpture Ctr, New York, 82, cmn exhib comt, 84-86. *Awards:* Chaim Gross Found Award, 80; Medal of Honor, Nat Asn Women Artists, 81; Medal of Honor, Audubon Artists, 82. *Bibliog:* Padavano (auth), The Process of Sculpture, Doubleday, 81; Watson-Jones (auth), Contemporary American Women Sculptors, Oryx Press. *Mem:* Sculptors Guild (pres, 80-83); Audubon Artists; Nat Asn Women Artists; Artist-mem Katonah Gallery; Silvermine Guild. *Media:* Welded Metal, Wood. *Dealer:* Berman/Daferner Gallery 568 Broadway #103A New York NY 10012. *Mailing Add:* Donbrook Rd RR No 3 Box 165 Pound Ridge NY 10570

SCHWEISS, RUTH KELLER
SCULPTOR, DESIGNER
US citizen. *Study:* Washington Univ, St Louis, fine arts cert; Cranbrook Art Acad, Bloomfield Hills, Mich, three yr int fel, sculpture with Carl Milles. *Work:* Many private collections. *Comn:* Bear for pool garden, comn by J A Baer, II, St Louis, 70; Blachette (bronze), Founder Monument, St Charles, Mo, 72; Children in the Rain, Ger Coun, Hamm, Ger, 73; Still Point (12 ft bronze fountain), Ritz-Carlton, Hotel, St Louis, Mo; bronze mem, Leif Sverdrup, St Louis, 79; Plaza Fronter: In Paradise, St Louis, Mo, 87. *Exhib:* Nat Acad Design, New York, 43; Detroit Art Mus Regional Show, Mich, 43; Pacific Show, Hawaiian Art Mus, Honolulu, 44; Int Art Show, Rotunda Gallery, London, 73; Ars Longa Gallery, Houston, 74. *Awards:* Mus Purchase Prize, Cranbrook Art Mus, 42; Ruth Renfrow Sculpture Prize, St Louis Art Mus, 45; Thalinger Sculpture Prize, St Louis Artists Guild, 50. *Bibliog:* Ruth Keller Schweiss, Gonterman Assoc, 65; The World of Ruth Keller Schweiss (film), Rick Noel, 74; picture story, St Louis Home/Garden, 79. *Mem:* Acad Prof Artists (exec dir, 68-83); Nat Soc Arts & Lett (corresp secy, 69-71, treas, 75-); Media Nine; St Louis Artists Guild (secy & mem bd, 65-67). *Media:* Bronze Castings of Limited Editions from Any Carved or Modeled Medium. *Mailing Add:* 4 Daniel Rd St Louis MO 63124

SCHWEITZER, M R
DEALER, GALLERY DIRECTOR
b Sept 7, 11. *Collections Arranged:* Waters, Salt & Sweet (with catalog), 59; Americans at Home & Abroad from 1850's (with catalog), 67; 40th Anniversary Exhib (with catalog), 70. *Pos:* Owner, Schweitzer Gallery, NC. *Mem:* Charter mem, Am Soc Appraisers. *Res:* American painting. *Specialty:* American painting, 1830-1930; European painting, 16th to 19th centuries. *Collection:* American and English 19th century; Catalan, Spanish and Italian 17th century; French, Scandinavian, Russian. *Mailing Add:* 18 E 84th St New York NY 10028

SCHWEIZER, PAUL DOUGLAS
ART HISTORIAN, MUSEUM DIRECTOR
b Brooklyn, NY, Nov 26, 46. *Study:* Marietta Col, Ohio, BA, 68; Univ Del, MA, 74, PhD, 79. *Collections Arranged:* Avant-Garde Painting & Sculpture in America: 1910-25 (collab effort, co-auth, catalog), Del Art Mus, spring 75; Edward Moran, Del Art Mus, 79; North Country Folk Art, 82, Cole's Course of Empire, 83 & The Voyage of Life: Paintings, Drawings, & Prints, 85, Munson-Williams-Proctor Inst, Utica, NY; 200 Yrs of Am Art, 86-87, The Art of Trenton Falls, 89, Munson-Williams-Proctor Inst, Utica, NY, 86-87; Alex Katz: A Drawing Retrospective, 91. *Pos:* Res consult, Choptank Collection, Middletown, Del, 76-77; cur collections, St Lawrence Univ, Canton, NY, 77-78, dir, Richard F Brush Art Gallery, 78-80; dir, Mus Art, Munson-Williams-Proctor Inst, Utica, NY, 80-; pres, bd of trustees, Williamstown Regional Art Conservation Lab, 87-91. *Teaching:* Instr art hist, Univ Del, Wilmington, 76; instr art hist, St Lawrence Univ, 77-78, asst prof fine arts, 78-80. *Awards:* Unidel Fel, Univ Del, 72-76. *Mem:* Col Art Asn; Asn Art Mus Dirs. *Res:* John Constable and the Rainbow; American Painting and Sculpture of the 19th & 20th centuries. *Publ:* Auth, John Constable, Rainbow Science and English Color Theory, Art Bulletin, 82; Literary source for Cole's Voyage of Life, 83 & Washington Irving's Friendship with William E West and the Impact of his History of New York on John Quider, spring 85, Am Art J; Who Was the Utica Artist, Clarion, 83; A note on the sources for W H Rinehart's Sleeping Children, MWPI Bulletin, 2/85; gen ed, Masterworks of Am Art at the Munson-Williams-Proctor Inst, Abrams, 88. *Mailing Add:* Munson-Williams-Proctor Inst 310 Genesee St Utica NY 13502

SCHWENINGER, ANN ROZZELLE
ILLUSTRATOR
b Boulder, Colo, Aug 1, 51. *Study:* Univ Colo, 69-72; Calif Inst Arts, BFA, 73-75; also with Uri Shulevitz and Peter Hopkins, 75- *Awards:* Notable Bk Award, Am Libr Asn, 82. *Media:* Watercolor, Pencil. *Publ:* Illusr, ABC Cat, Harper & Row, 83; illusr, Tales of Amanda Pig, Dial Press, 83; illusr, The Musicians of Bremen, 83 & illusr, Silent Night, 83, Western Publ; auth & illusr, Christmas Secrets, Viking Press, 84; and many others. *Mailing Add:* 319 E 24th St No 15D New York NY 10010

SCHWIDDER, ERNST
SCULPTOR, DESIGNER
b St Louis, Mo, Nov 9, 31. *Study:* Univ Wash, BA, 53 & MFA, 55. *Comn:* Our Saviour Lutheran Church, Richmond, BC, Can, 88; Lutheran Church of the Resurrection, Huntington Beach, Calif, 89; Ascension Lutheran Church, Thousand Oaks, Calif, 89; St Columban Cath Church, Yelm, Wash, 90; Advent Lutheran Church, Charlotte, NC, 90; and many others. *Exhib:* Eight Washington Artists, Portland Art Mus, 55; Mus Mod Art Int Biennial, Sao Paulo, Brazil, 55; Pacific Coast Art, San Francisco Mus Art, 56; Artists West of the Mississippi, Colorado Springs Art Ctr, 57; Cult Exchange Expos, Moscow, USSR, 59. *Pos:* Owner, Ernst Schwidder Assoc. *Teaching:* Chmn sculpture & design, Valparaiso Univ, Ind, 58-61 & Seattle Pac Univ, 63-67; chmn sculpture & design, Pac Lutheran Univ, Tacoma, 67-, prof, 75- *Media:* Wood. *Mailing Add:* 1660 S Wilton Rd #4 Tacoma WA 98465

SCHWIEGER, C ROBERT
EDUCATOR, PRINTMAKER
b Scottsbluff, Nebr, Dec 5, 36. *Study:* Nebr Western Col, AA; Chadron State Col, BFA(educ); Univ Northern Colo, MA; Univ Denver, MFA. *Work:* Ohio State Univ; Miss Art Asn; Ga Inst Technol; Olivet Col, Mich; Oklahoma Art Ctr, Oklahoma City; and others. *Comn:* Gilded gold & mixed media on glass mural, Univ Northern Colo, 66. *Exhib:* Recent Trends & New Directions in Printmaking, Northern Ill Univ; Am Printmakers Invitational, Univ SDak; St Cloud State Univ; Univ Dallas; Prints of the 80's, Pratt Manhattan Gallery & Schafler Gallery, New York, 90; and others. *Teaching:* Assoc prof, Minot State Univ, 67-81, coordr art & prof, 81- 90, prof & chmn, dept art; prof & chmn, art dept, Mo Southern State Col, 90-91, prof art, 91- *Awards:* Purchase Award, Univ Tex, Austin; Northwest Printmakers Int Jury Commendation, Seattle Art Mus, 71; 16th Nat Print & Drawing Exhib Jury Commendation, Okla Art Ctr, 74. *Bibliog:* The Complete Printmaker, Ross-Romano-Ross, rev ed, 89. *Mailing Add:* 1424 Tyson Dr Joplin MO 64801

SCOTT, ARDEN
SCULPTOR
b Port Chester, NY, Oct 21, 38. *Comn:* Nassau Co Mus Fine Arts, NY, 77; pub sculpture, Riverhead, NY, 81; Atlanta Arts Festival, 83; Greenport Maritime Monument, 86. *Exhib:* Whitney Mus Biennial, 73; one-person show, 112 Greene Gallery, NY, 74; O K Harris Gallery, New York, 75 & 80; Forms in Focus, Coop City Gallery, 77; Elvehjem Mus Art, Madison, Wis, 80; 55 Mercer Gallery, 82; Ga State Univ, 83; Aberdeen Arts Mus, Scotland, 83; Ways of Wood, Queens Col, NY, 84; Sculpture Ctr, New York, 84; Guild Hall Mus, EHampton, NY, 85; Live Steam Voices (performance), New York Harbor, 87 & Erie Canal, 88; Nat Print Exhib, Brooklyn Mus Art, 89. *Teaching:* Prof sculpture, Bard Col, 75- & Parsons Sch Design, 78. *Awards:* NY State Coun Arts Award, 77; Guggenheim Fel, 81; Fel, NY State Found Arts, 88. *Bibliog:* Marcia Tucker (auth), Making it big, Ms Mag, 4/74; Brentano & Savitt, 112 Workshop/112 Greene, NY Univ Press, 81; Poppy Johnson (auth), Sculpture and fiction, Bomb Mag, No 6, 83; Michael Brenson (auth), article, New York Times, 12/2/84; Jack Somer (auth), A modern monument, Yachting Mag, 1/86. *Media:* Miscellaneous. *Mailing Add:* 73 Leonard St New York NY 10013

SCOTT, B NIBBELINK (BARBARA GAE SCOTT)
PAINTER, SCULPTOR
b Columbia, Mo, July 23, 44. *Study:* With Daniel Greene, 82-83, Albert Handell, 84 & Herman Margulies, 85. *Work:* Wichita Art Asn & Fourth Financial Ctr, Wichita, Kans; Am Ambassador's Collection, London. *Exhib:* Kans Pastel Soc First Nat, Wichita Art Asn Gallery, 86-87; Pastel Soc Am, Nat Arts Club, New York, 86-90; Third Salon des Pastellistes France, Centre Culturel de la Ville, Lille, France, 87; Am Aid Soc, Mall Gallerie's, London, 88; Fourth Salon des Pastellistes France, Centre Culturel de la Ville de Compiegne, France, 88; Cassalt Pastel Soc, Berkley Gallery, Scottsdale, Ariz, 89. *Pos:* Prog chmn 83-84, pres, 84-85, Community Art Guild, Wichita, Kans. *Awards:* Honorary Award, Kans Small Oil Painting Exhib, 82; Prix de International Honneur, Third Salon des Pastellistes de France, 87; First Place US, Fifth Salon des Pastellistes de France, 89. *Mem:* Kans Pastel Soc (founder, pres, 84-90); Pastel Soc Am; Salmagundi Club; Societe des Pastellistes de France (hon pres US, 87-90); Kans Acad Oil Painters. *Media:* Pastel, Oil; Clay. *Publ:* Auth, Discovering my potential with pastel, Am Artists, 7/87. *Mailing Add:* 301 N Crestway Wichita KS 67208

SCOTT, C(HARLES) A(RTHUR)
SCULPTOR
b San Diego, Calif, Dec 2, 40. *Study:* San Diego State Univ, BA, 68; Univ Calif, Santa Barbara, MFA, 70. *Work:* San Diego State Univ, Calif; Univ Calif, Santa Barbara; Western Wash Univ & Whatcom Mus Hist & Art, Bellingham, Wash; Favell Mus Western Art & Artifacts, Klamath Falls, Ore. *Exhib:* 58th Ann NW Artists, Seattle Art Mus, 72; Gov's Ann, State Capitol Mus, Olympia, Wash, 72 & 73; Western Gallery, Bellingham, Wash, 72-74; Santa Barbara Mus Art, Calif, 74; Whatcom Mus Hist & Art, Bellingham, Wash, 80; 8th Ann Western Art Asn Exhib, Ellensburg, Wash, 80; and others. *Pos:* Vis artist, Fonderiaversillia, Pietrasanta, Italy, 77; asst to Mark di Suvero for Handel (sculpture), Bellingham, Wash, 73-74. *Teaching:* Instr, Western Wash Univ, Bellingham, 70-77. *Awards:* Purchase Prizes, 9th & 10th Ann Small Sculpture, Western Gallery, Bellingham, Wash, 72 & 73; First Prize, Design Competition, Seattle Water Dept, 74. *Bibliog:* Barry Kahn (auth), Things are seldom what they seem, Bellingham Herald, 11/28/80. *Mem:* Southwest Parks & Monuments Asn. *Media:* Clay. *Interests:* Pre-historic Southwest art, architecture and cultures and their replication. *Collection:* Extensive: Archaic to Contemporary. *Mailing Add:* 2629 Humboldt Bellingham WA 98225

SCOTT, CAMPBELL
PRINTMAKER, SCULPTOR
b Milngavie, Scotland, Oct 5, 30; Can citizen. *Study:* Studied with S W Hayter, Paris; Glasgow Sch Art, Scotland. *Work:* British Mus, London; Bibliot Nat, Paris; Scottish Nat Gallery Mod Art; Montreal Mus Art Can; Victoria & Albert Mus; Art Gallery Ont Can. *Comn:* Bronze sculpture, Pub Libr, Niagara Falls, Can; wood sculpture, Pub Libr, St Catharines, Can. *Exhib:*

FAAP Gravura, Sao Paulo, Brazil, 68; 1st British Int Print Biennale, Gt Brit, 69; Traveling Exhib, Nat Gallery Can, Ottawa, 69; 4th Am Biennial Engraving, Santiago, Chile, 70; Exhib Can Graphics, Can Embassy, Washington, DC, 71 & Pratt Inst, New York, 71. *Mem:* Can Graphic Arts Soc. *Publ:* (Auth), article, City and Country Home, Maclean Hunter Publ, 9/85; article, House and Garden (Brit ed), Conde Publ, 11/87. *Mailing Add:* 89 Byron Niagara on the Lake ON L0S 1J0 Canada

SCOTT, DAVID WINFIELD
ADMINISTRATOR
b Fall River, Mass, July 10, 16. *Study:* Art Students League; Harvard Col, AB; Claremont Grad Sch, MA & MFA; Univ Calif, Berkeley, PhD. *Pos:* From lectr art to prof, Scripps Col, 46-63; dir, Nat Collection Fine Arts, Washington, DC, 64-69; consult, Nat Gallery Art, Washington, DC, 69-84; mus consult, 84-; dir, Corcoran Gallery Art, Washington, DC, 90. *Mailing Add:* 3016 Cortland Pl NW Washington DC 20008

SCOTT, DEBORAH EMONT
CURATOR
b Passaic, NJ. *Study:* Rutgers Univ, BA; Oberlin Col, MA. *Collections Arranged:* Veda Reed, 79; Alan Shields (auth, catalog), Memphis Brooks Mus Art, Memphis, Tenn, 83-84. *Pos:* Asst cur, Allen Mem Art Mus, Oberlin, Ohio, 77-79; cur, Memphis Brooks Mus Art, Memphis, Tenn, 79-83; cur, 20th century art, Nelson-Atkins Mus Art, Kansas City, 83- *Mem:* Col Art Asn. *Res:* 20th century art. *Publ:* Auth, Neil Welliver: The fact of the painting, Univ Mo, 86. *Mailing Add:* c/o Nelson-Atkins Mus Art 4525 Oak St Kansas City MO 64111

SCOTT, JOHN
ILLUSTRATOR, PAINTER
b Camden, NJ, Dec 1, 07. *Study:* La France Art Inst, Philadelphia, illus with Joseph Clement, 28. *Work:* Mus Am Illus, New Britain, Conn; Hist Arch US Army, Washington, DC. *Comn:* Biblical subjects, Mormon Church, Salt Lake City, 68 & 78, Independence, Mo, 71 & Washington, DC, 73; painting, Permian Oil Mus, Midland, Tex, 70. *Pos:* Illusr, Sports Afield Mag, Hearst Publ, 48-75. *Bibliog:* Zack Taylor (auth), article, Sports Afield, 8/79; Jack Hines (auth), article, Art West, 7/81. *Mem:* Soc Illusr, New York. *Media:* Oil, Gouache. *Dealer:* Settlers West Gallery 6420 N Campbell Tucson AZ 85718. *Mailing Add:* c/o Victor Fischer Gallery 350 Stuart St San Francisco CA 94119

SCOTT, JOHN
PAINTER
b Windsor, Ont, 50. *Study:* Ont Col Art, Toronto, AOCA, 76; Univ Toronto; Centennial Col, Toronto. *Work:* Nat Gallery Can, Can Coun Art Bank, Ottawa; Art Gallery Ont, Toronto; London Regional Art Gallery, Ont; Art Gallery Stratford, Ont. *Exhib:* Solo exhibs, Carmen Lamanna Gallery, Toronto, 81, 83-84 & 86; Fragments, Content, Scale, 49th Parallel Gallery, New York, 83; Modern Times: The Artist as Social Critic, The Gallery, Stratford, Ont, 83; Attitude, Can Nat Exhib, Toronto, 83; Chromaliving, ChromoZone Gallery, Toronto, 83; Toronto Painting, Art Gallery Ont, 84; XIIeme Biennale de Paris, Musee de la Moderne de la Ville de Paris, France; New Forms of Figuration, Ctr Inter-Am Relations, New York, 84-85. *Awards:* Can Coun Grants, 77-81; Floyd S Chalmers Fund Award, Ont Arts Coun, 82; Ont Arts Coun, 83. *Bibliog:* John Bentley Mays (auth), Scott's obsession still compelling, Globe and Mail, 11/28/81; Charlotte Townsend-Gualt & Terrence Heath (auths), Visions: Contemporary Art in Canada, Douglas & McIntyre, Vancouver, 83. *Mailing Add:* Dept Newmedia Ont Col Art 100 McCaul St Toronto ON M5T 1W1 Canada

SCOTT, JOHN BELDON
HISTORIAN, EDUCATOR
b Scottsburg, Ind, Aug 3, 46. *Study:* Ind Univ, BA, 68; Rutgers Univ, MA, 75, PhD, 82. *Pos:* Ed, Rutgers Art Rev, 78-79. *Teaching:* Instr, Rutgers Univ, 77-79; lectr, Univ Pa, 81-82; assoc prof, Univ Iowa, 82- *Awards:* Am Acad Rome Fel, 79-81; Delmas Found Fel, 82; Am Coun Learned Soc Fel, 84; Am Philos Soc Grant, 84; Andrew W Mellon Fel, Univ Pa, 85. *Mem:* Col Art Asn; Soc Archit Historians; Renaissance Soc Am. *Res:* Italian Renaissance and Baroque; northern Baroque. *Publ:* S Ivo Alla Sapienza and Borromini's symbolic language, J Soc Archit Historians, 82; Urban VIII, Bernini and the Contess Matilda, L'Âge D'or Du Mécénat (1598-1661), Paris, 85; The Meaning of Perseus and Andromedia in the Farnese Gallery and on the Rubens House, J of the Warburg and Courtauld Inst, 88; Pietro da Cortona's Painted Ceilings of Palazzo Barberini, Princeton Univ Press, 90; Images of Nepotism: The Painted Ceilings of Palazzo Barberini, Princeton Univ Press, 90. *Mailing Add:* c/o Victor Fischer Galleries 3560 Stewart St San Francisco CA 94119

SCOTT, JOHN FREDRIK
HISTORIAN, EDUCATOR
b Westfield, NJ, May 14, 36. *Study:* Princeton Univ, AB, 58; Johns Hopkins Univ, MAT, 62; Columbia Univ, PhD, 71. *Collections Arranged:* Before Cortes (auth, catalog), Metrop Mus Art, 70; Ecuadorian Art (auth, catalog), Johnson Mus Art, 82; Taino Art from Dominican Republic (auth, catalog), Univ Fla Gallery, 85; Ancient Mesoamerica, Univ Fla Gallery, 87; Lowe Art Mus, Univ Miami, 90. *Pos:* Research assoc, Metrop Mus Art, New York, 68-71; adj cur, Mus Fine Arts, Houston, 78-80. *Teaching:* Asst prof primitive art, Cornell Univ, Ithaca, NY, 71-77; Rice Univ, Houston, 77-81; assoc prof Latin Am art, Univ Fla, Gainesville, 81- *Awards:* Nat Endowment Humanities Grant, 74-75; Foreign Area Fel, 66-68; Fel, US-Spanish Joint Comm, 88. *Mem:* Col Art Asn Am; Archaeology Inst Am (vpres Houston soc, 80-81, pres Gainesville Soc, 83-); Asn Latin Am Art (vpres Precolumbian, 83-86, pres, 87-88). *Res:* Pre-Columbian art, especially sculpture. *Publ:* Auth, Danzantes of Monte Alban, Dumbarton Oaks, 78; Post-Olmec Art in Veracruz, Antrop Americanista, 80; Monuments of Los Idolos, Veracruz, J New World Archeol, 82; Latin America: Perspectives on a region, Latin Am Art & Arc; Role Mesoamerican Funerary Figurines, Arte Funerario, II, 87; Potbellies & Fat gods, J New World Archeol, 88. *Mailing Add:* Art Dept Univ Fla Gainesville FL 32611

SCOTT, JOHN TARRELL
PRINTMAKER, SCULPTOR
b New Orleans, La, June 30, 40. *Study:* Xavier Univ La, BA, 62; Mich State Univ, MFA, 65. *Work:* Johnson Publ Co, Chicago, Ill; Golden State Mutual Life Insurance Co, Los Angeles, Calif; Pan American Life, New Orleans, La; One Canal Place, New Orleans, La. *Comn:* Relief wall sculpture, Civic Ctr, Naples Co, Fla, 60-61; bronze pieta, Edgewood United Church, Lansing, Mich, 64; Madonna & St Joseph, St Angela Marici Church, Metaire, La, 68; steel figure, Mt Carmel High Sch, New Orleans, 76; Ruggles Station, Boston, 86. *Exhib:* Black Am Artists Nat, Ill Bell Tel Co, Chicago, 70; Fiske Univ, Nashville, Tenn, 73; The Classic Revival, Ill Bell Tel Co, 75; Migrations, Colombia, SAm, 76; Mitchell Mus, Mt Vernon, Ill, 76; Simonne Stern Gallery, La, 84 & 86; Harris Brown Gallery, Boston, Mass, 85. *Pos:* Mem visual arts comt, Contemp Arts Ctr, currently. *Teaching:* Prof printmaking & sculpture, Xavier Univ of La, New Orleans, 65- *Awards:* Hand Hollow Found, 83; United Negro Col Fund Grant, 83, Distinguish Scholar Award, 86. *Mem:* New Orleans Arts Coun (bd dirs, currently); Congo Square Arts Collective (asst dir, currently). *Media:* Mixed. *Mailing Add:* c/o Alexandria Museum of Art 933 Main St Alexandria LA 71309-1028

SCOTT, JONATHAN
PAINTER
b Bath, Eng, Oct 30, 14. *Study:* Heatherly Sch, London; Mauritz Heymann Sch, Munich; The Accad, Florence. *Work:* Laguna Mus Art & Pasadena Art Mus, Calif; Col Santa Fe, NMex; Lindsay Art Asn, Calif; Harwood Mus, Taos, NMex; G G de Silva Collection, Los Angeles. *Comn:* Paintings, USN Art Prog, 63-64; also portrait comns. *Exhib:* One-man shows, Pasadena Mus Art, Santa Barbara Mus Art, Calif & McNay Art Inst, San Antonio, Tex; Los Angeles Mus; Mus NMex; Occidental Col, Los Angeles; Ringling Mus, Sarasota, Fla; Stables Gallery, Taos, NMex; Past Pres Exhib, Nat Watercolor Soc, Glendale, Calif, 87; Seven Contemp Painters, Carlsbad Mus, NMex, 87. *Teaching:* Instr drawing & painting, Univ Southern Calif, 46, Pasadena Art Mus, 47-48, Riverside Art Asn, 62-63; instr watercolor, workshops, Taos, 82-83. *Awards:* Calif Watercolor Soc, 55, Laguna Beach Art Asn, 61 & NMex Watercolor Soc, 74. *Mem:* Nat Watercolor Soc; Taos Art Asn. *Media:* Oil, Watercolor. *Dealer:* Lumina Gallery Taos NM 87571. *Mailing Add:* PO Box 1047 Ranchos De Taos NM 87557

SCOTT, JOYCE
WEAVER
b Baltimore, Md, Nov 15, 48. *Study:* Md Inst Col Art, BFA, 66-70; Instituto Allende, San Miguel de Allende, Guanajuato, Mex, MFA(crafts); Haystack Mountain Sch Crafts, weaving, beadworking, dyeing, 73 & 76. *Work:* Bannecker-Douglas Mus, Annapolis, Md; Baltimore Mus Art, Md; Westfield State Col, Mass; Morgan Univ, Baltimore, Md; Towson Univ, Md; and many other pub & pvt collections. *Exhib:* One-person exhibs, Drew Univ Art Gallery, Madison, NJ, Brooklyn Col Art Gallery, NY & Esther Saks Fine Art Ltd, Chicago, Ill, 92; Diggs Gallery, Winston-Salem State Univ, NC, 92; Visual Arts Ctr, NC State Univ, Raleigh, 92; Eubie Blake Cult Ctr, Baltimore, Md, 92; and others. *Pos:* Guest cur, Walter's Art Gallery, Baltimore, Md, 88-89 & Artscape, Baltimore, Md, 89; lectr, var cols, mus & univs, 75-92; guest artist, Md Inst Col Art, Baltimore, Pratt Art Ctr, Seattle, Wash, Split Rock Art Prog, Duluth, Minn, The Shepardess, San Diego, Calif & Haystack Mountain Sch Crafts, Deer Isle, Maine, 92; artist-in-residence, Univ Del, Newark, 90, Contemp Arts Ctr, Cincinnati, Ohio, 92 & Pilchuck Glass Sch, Seattle, Wash, 92; bd trustees, Mus Contemp Arts, Baltimore, Md, currently; adv bd, Pub Art Fund, New York & Baltimore Film Forum, currently; hon bd, James Renwick Alliance, Smithsonian Inst, Washington, DC, currently. *Awards:* Nat Endowment Arts Fel, 88-89; Nat Printmaking Fel, Rutgers Ctr Innovative Printmaking, New Brunswick, NJ, 90; Art Matters Inc, NY, 92. *Bibliog:* Stefany Tomalin (auth), Beads, David & Charles Publs, Devon, Eng; The Art of Politics, Contemporanea/Int Art Mag, Vol 1, No 4, 11-12/88; Arlene Raven (auth), Mojotech, Village Voice, 3/28/89. *Mailing Add:* 2417 Woodbrook Ave Baltimore MD 21217

SCOTT, MARIAN (DALE)
PAINTER
b Montreal, Que, June 26, 06. *Study:* Montreal Art Asn, scholar, 17-20; Monument Nat, with Dionnet, 18-20; Ecole Beaux Arts, Montreal, 23-25; Slade Sch, London. *Work:* Nat Gallery Can, Ottawa; McGill Univ Art Collection, Montreal; Montreal Mus Fine Arts; Edmonton Art Gallery; Dept External Affairs, Ottawa, Mus Art Contemporain, Montreal; and others. *Comn:* Oils & murals, McGill Univ, 43 & Montreal Gen Hosp Chapel, 58. *Exhib:* New York World's Fair, 39; Panorama, Peinture du Quebec, Mus Art Contemporain, 40-66; Biennale, Sao Paulo, Brazil, 51-53; 50 Years of Canadian Painting, Nat Gallery Can; Expos Createurs Quebec, 71; La Collection Inaugural, Mus Contemp Art, 92. *Teaching:* Instr painting, St George's Sch, Montreal, 37-39; instr painting, Montreal Mus Fine Arts, 42-45. *Awards:* First Prize for Painting, Can Group Painters, 66; Purchase Award, Thomas More Inst, Montreal, 67; Baxter Purchase Award, Ont Soc Artists. *Mem:* Les Artistes pour la Paix; Can Acad Arts. *Media:* Acrylic. *Mailing Add:* 451 Clarke Ave Montreal PQ H3Y 3C5 Canada

SCOTT, MARTHA F
PRINTMAKER, SCULPTOR
b Washington, DC, Nov 11, 16. *Study:* Md Inst Col Art, cert, 36; Johns Hopkins Univ-Teacher's Col, 37; Cleveland Inst Art, studied printmaking with H C Cassill, 60-64. *Exhib:* Solo exhibs, Baltimore Mus Art, 69, Original Intaglio Prints, Univ de Picardie, Amiens, France, 76, Space Telescope Sci Inst, Johns Hopkins Univ, Md, 85; Oklahoma Art Ctr, Oklahoma City, Okla, 69-74; Miami Mus Art, Fla, 75; North American Print Conference, City Hall Galleries, Baltimore, Md, 83; Women on Paper, Running Gallery-Luther Col, Decorah, Iowa, 84; and 90 others. *Pos:* Designer, Norcross Co, New York, 37-41; illusr, Children's books, Wilcox & Follett, 42-44; arts dir & pub relations dir, Cross Keys Community Ctr, Baltimore, Md, 67-86. *Teaching:* Instr stone sculpture, Cross Keys Community Ctr, Baltimore, Md, 70-86; Private classes, Baltimore Md Medfield Comm Ctr, 86-90. *Awards:* Purchase Prizes, Jewish Community Ctr, Cleveland, Ohio, 62-64 & Cooperstown Art Assoc, Muggleton Gallery, 67. *Bibliog:* Feature article, Today's Woman Mag, 46; feature article, Sunday Sun Mag, Baltimore, 48 & 77. *Mem:* League of NH Craftsmen Found. *Media:* Etching, Stone. *Publ:* Auth, numerous articles about exhibitions, in: Cleveland Plain Dealer and Baltimore Sun Papers. *Mailing Add:* RR 13 No 123 Concord NH 03301

SCOTT, ROBERT MONTGOMERY
ADMINISTRATOR, PATRON
b May 22, 29; US citizen. *Study:* Harvard Col, AB, 51; Univ Pa Law Sch, LLB, 54. *Pos:* Trustee, Pa Mus Art, 65-, pres, 80-, chief exec officer, 82- *Awards:* Superior Hon Award, US State Dept, 73. *Mem:* Greater Philadelphia Cult Alliance; Am Asn Mus. *Mailing Add:* Philadelphia Mus Art Box 7646 Philadelphia PA 19101

SCOTT, SAM
PAINTER
b Chicago, Ill, Apr 7, 40. *Study:* Univ Mich, BFA, 65; Md Inst Col Art, MFA, 69; also with Grace Hartigan, David Hare, Joseph Goto, Zubel Kachadoorian. *Work:* Mus NMex, Santa Fe; Roswell Mus Fine Art, NMex; AT&T Corp Building, New York; Univ Iowa Fine Arts Mus, Iowa City; Phoenix Fine Arts Mus, Ariz; Midlands Bank, Denver; Albuquerque Mus Contemp Art, NMex; and others. *Comn:* Mural painting, Westinghouse Elec Corp Bldg, Norman, Okla, 72; mural, Jelco Corp Bldg, Minneapolis, Minn, 72. *Exhib:* Keats Gallery, Santa Fe, 85; Conlon Grenfelly Gallery, San Diego, 86; Robischon Gallery, Denver, 87; Sena West Gallery, Santa Fe, 87; Tucson Fine Art Mus, Tucson, 87; 10 Take 10 (retrospective), Colorado Springs Fine Arts Mus, 77; Phoenix Art Mus, 79-80. *Pos:* Artist-in-residence, Sun Valley Ctr Arts & Humanities, Idaho, 75 & 76 & Tucson Fine Art Mus Sch, Ariz, 87, E Caroline Univ, Greenville, 88; panel coord mem, Tucson Vis Artists Consortium, 78-80. *Teaching:* Instr painting, Md Inst Col Art, 67-69; instr painting, St Johns Col, Santa Fe, 71; asst prof art, Univ Ariz, 78- *Awards:* Res & Mat Grant, Univ Ariz, Tucson, 80; Panel mem, Art in NMex, Int Contemp Art Fair, Los Angeles, 86; NMex Arts Comn Prize, 73. *Bibliog:* Linda Durham (auth), Artists of New Mexico, 88; Ernesto Mayans (auth), Men of the River, 88. *Media:* Oil on Canvas. *Publ:* Auth, Sam Scott, Southwest Profiles Mag, 87; and others. *Dealer:* Watson de Nagy Gallery 1106 Berthea Houston TX 77006; Sebastian Moore Gallery Denver CO. *Mailing Add:* 2930 Revere No 200 Houston TX 77098-5607

SCOTT, SANDY (SANDRA LYNN)
SCULPTOR
b Dubuque, Iowa, July 24, 43. *Study:* Kansas City Art Inst. *Work:* Wildlife World Mus, Monument, Colo; El Paso Zoo, Tex; Gilcrease Mus, Tulsa, Okla. *Comn:* Rodeo Events (etchings), Nat Cowboy Hall Fame, Oklahoma City, 78; Grand Slam, 79 & Bears of North America, 80, Nat Sporting Fraternity Ltd, New York; Kodiak Bears, WesTex Oil Co, El Paso, 80; Wood Ducks, Albuquerque, NMex, 81. *Exhib:* Am Artists Prof League, New York, 82 & 83; Catharine Lorillard Wolfe Art Club, New York, 82 & 83; Salmagundi Open Sculpture Exhib, New York, 83; New York Pen & Brush, 83; Ann Soc Am Impressionists Show, 84; more than fifty one-woman shows at galleries throughout the country. *Pos:* Background artist, Calvin Motion Pictures, Kansas City, Mo, 62-65. *Awards:* New York Pen & Brush Award, Ann Sculpture Exhib, 83; Medal Hon Sculpture, Catharine Lorillard Wolfe Art Club, 83; Barett-Colea Award & Salmagundi Club Cert Merit, Salmagundi Club Open Sculpture Exhib, 83; Sculpture Award, Pen & Brush, 83; Graphics Award, Am Artists Prof League, 84, Medal of Honor, sculpture, 85; Harriett W Frishmuth Mem Award, Catharine Lorillard Wolfe Art Club, 85. *Bibliog:* Sandy Scott: Etchings, Prints Mag, 7-8/81; Carrol Nelson (auth), Sandy Scott, In: Masters of Western Art, Watson-Guptill, 82; article, Artists of the Rockies, spring 83. *Mem:* Soc Animal Artists; Am Artists Prof League; New York Pen & Brush; Soc Am Impressionists. *Media:* Cast Bronze, Bronze. *Publ:* Illusr, The Ultimate Fishing Book, Houghton-Mifflin, 81. *Mailing Add:* Knox Gallery 1632 Market St Denver CO 80202-1514

SCOTT, WALTER
PAINTER, ARCHITECT
b Pittsburgh, Pa, May 24, 19. *Study:* Carnegie Inst Technol, with Sam Rosenberg, Kindred McCleary & Camille Grapin, BA, 41. *Exhib:* One-man shows, Mamaronek Artists Guild, NY, 72 & Briarcliff Col, 75; Nat Soc of Painters in Casein & Acrylic Ann, New York, 72-86; Hudson River Open, Hudson River Mus, Yonkers, NY, 76-79, 83; NJ Painter & Sculptors Soc Ann, Nat Arts Club, New York, 86; Catskill Art Soc Ann, 90; and others. *Pos:* Architect, Harrison & Abramovitz, Architects, New York, 48-83; pvt architectural practice, 83- *Awards:* Silvermine Guild Award, 72 & Koenig Art, 74, New Eng Exhib; Hyplar Award, Nat Soc Painters Casein & Acrylic Ann, Grumbacher, 72; and others. *Mem:* Silvermine Guild Artists; Nat Soc Painters Casein & Acrylic (bd dir, 77-78); Hudson River Contemp Artists; Artists Equity Asn; Am Inst of Architects; Catskill Art Soc, 89. *Media:* Multimedia. *Dealer:* Silvermine Guild of Artists New Canaan CT 06840. *Mailing Add:* Box 196 Ferndale NY 12734

SCOVILLE, JONATHAN ARMSTRONG
PAINTER, PRINTMAKER
b New York, NY, Nov 13, 37. *Study:* Art Students League, 56-57 & 64-65; NY Univ, 60-62. *Work:* Metrop Mus Art, New York; Boston Pub Libr Wiggin Collection; Butler Inst Am Art; Nat Collection Fine Art; Chemical Bank, NY; Lloyds Bank Int, NY; Dow Jones & Co, Inc, NY; and others. *Comn:* Landscape, Berkshire Life Insurance Co, Pittsfield, Ma; landscape, Sohio Petroleum Co, Houston; landscape, Mobil Oil Co. *Exhib:* One-man shows, Slater Mem Mus, Norwich, Conn, 79, Mattatuck Mus, Waterbury, Conn, 80, four exhibs, Condeso/Lawter Gallery, NY, 81-88, Old State House, Hartford, 83 & New Brit Mus Am Art, Conn, 85; Berkshire Mus Ann Exhib, Pittsfield, Mass, 70's & 80's; Nat Acad Design, Ann Exhibs, NY, 60's, 70's & 80's; Landscape, Seascape & Cityscape, Contemp Arts Ctr, New Orleans, La, 86 & New York Acad Art, 86; Art Awards & Exhib, Am Acad & Inst Arts & Lett, 87-91. *Awards:* Residence fels, Yaddo, 67, MacDowell Colony, 69-71 & 75-80 & Millay Colony, 77; Conn Comn Arts Grants, 76, 79 & 91. *Bibliog:* Michael Brenson (auth), article, NY Times, 4/84 & 12/85; Stephen Westfall (auth), article, Arts Mag, 9/84; Ronny Cohen (auth), article, Art Forum, 3/86. *Media:* Oil, Pastel; Watercolor Etching. *Dealer:* Condeso/Lawler Gallery 76 Greene St New York NY 10012. *Mailing Add:* Old Town Rd West Cornwall CT 06796

SCRIBNER, CHARLES, III
HISTORIAN, LECTURER
b Washington, DC, May 24, 51. *Study:* Princeton Univ, AB, 73, MFA, 75, PhD, 77. *Pos:* Vpres, MacMillan Publ Co, 84- *Teaching:* Instr Baroque art, Princeton Univ, 76-77, mem adv coun, Dept Art & Archaeol, 83-91. *Awards:* Thesis Prize, Princeton Univ, 73. *Mem:* Asn Princeton Univ Press. *Res:* Baroque art, especially religious art of Rubens, Bernini and Caravaggio--cultural world of the Counter-Reformation. *Publ:* Auth, Sacred architecture: Rubens' Eucharist tapestries, Art Bulletin, 75; Daniel Hopfer's Venus and Amor, Princeton Univ Art Mus Rec, 76; In Alia Effigie: Caravaggio's London Supper at Emmaus, Art Bulletin, 77; The Triumph of the Eucharist: Tapestries by Rubens, UMI Res Press, 82; Rubens and Bernini, Ringling Mus J, 83; Rubens: Baroque Artist, Renaissance Man, Abrams, 89; Gianlorenzo Bernini, Abrams, 91. *Mailing Add:* 655 Park Ave No 4B New York NY 10021-5937

SCRIVER, (BOB) ROBERT MACFIE
SCULPTOR, CURATOR
b Browning, Mont, Aug 15, 14. *Study:* Dickinson State Univ, NDak, BM; Vandercook Col, Chicago, MM; postgrad study, Northwestern Univ, Evanston & Univ Wash, Seattle; Carroll Col, Helena, Mont, Hon PhD(art), 76. *Work:* Glenbow Mus, Calgary, Alta; Whitney Gallery Western Art, Cody, Wyo; Mont Hist Soc, Helena; Panhandle Plains Mus, Canyon, Tex; Cowboy Hall Fame, Oklahoma City. *Comn:* Bill Linderman (statue), Rodeo Cowboy Asn, Cowboy Hall Fame, Oklahoma City, 68; Lewis & Clarke & Sacajawea (statue), Fort Benton, Mont; An Honest Try (cowboy & bull statue), Board of Trade Bldg, Kansas City, Mo; Symbol of the Pros (cowboy on bucking bronco statue), Pro Rodeo Hall of Champions, Colorado Springs, Colo; Int Peace Mem (statue), Cut Bank Peace Comt, Cut Bank, Mont; Lewis, Clark, York & dog Seaman, Overlook Park, Great Falls, Mont; National Guardsman, Nat Guard Armory, Helena, Mont. *Exhib:* Acad Western Art, Cowboy Hall Fame, Oklahoma City, 73; Allied Art Ctr, Calgary, Alta, 73; solo exhib, Stremmel Galleries, Security Nat Bank, Reno, 75; Rodeo in Bronze Ser, Wells Fargo Bank, San Francisco, 76; Grand Cent Art Gallery, New York, 76; Traveling Sculpture Exhib, Blackfeet Indians; Mont Hist Soc, Helena. *Pos:* Cur, Scriver Mus Mont Wildlife, 56 & Hall of Bronze, 84- *Awards:* Gold Medals, 69-71 & Silver Medal, 72, Cowboy Hall Fame; Silver Medal, Nat Acad Western Art, 73; Governor's Citation, 76 & 89. *Bibliog:* Articles, Am Artist, 63, Rev Mod, 64 & SW Artist Mag, 84. *Mem:* Salmagundi Club; Nat Sculpture Soc; Cowboy Artists Am; Nat Acad Western Art; Soc Animal Artists. *Media:* Bronze; Oil. *Publ:* Auth, An Honest Try, 75; No More Buffalo, 82 &; The Blackfeet-Artists of the Northern Plains, Lowell Press. *Mailing Add:* Scriver Mus of Mont Wildlife Box 172 Browning MT 59417

SCUCCHI, ROBIE (PETER), JR
EDUCATOR, PAINTER
b Lake Village, Ark, Apr 10, 44. *Study:* Ark State Univ, with Dan F Howard, BS(painting), 67; Southern Ill Univ, Edwardsville, painting with John Richardson, 70-71; Inst Allende, Univ Guanajuato, Mex, with James Pinto & Fred Samuelson, MFA(painting), 71. *Work:* Claypool-Young Art Gallery, Morehead State Univ, Ky; Matrix Art Gallery, Ind Univ, Bloomington; Grinstead Art Gallery, Cent Mo State Univ, Warrensburg; Jackson Hall Art Gallery, Ky State Univ, Frankfort; Gallery Fine Arts, Univ Ark, Little Rock. *Exhib:* Washington & Jefferson Col Gallery, Washington, Pa, 73 & 79; Birmingham Mus Art, Ala, 74; one-man shows, Jackson Hall Art Gallery, Ky State Univ, Frankfort, 81, Claypool-Young Art Gallery, Morehead State Univ, Ky, 81 & Matrix Art Gallery, Ind Univ, Bloomington, 82; and others. *Teaching:* Instr & head painting, drawing & design, NW High Sch, House Springs, Mo, 67-71; assoc prof art, Miss State Univ, Starkville, 71- *Awards:* Best Show Awards, St Charles Art Guild 4th Ann, Mo, 69 & Ark Bicentennial, 76; 2nd Place Purchase, Am Inst Architects, 72. *Mem:* Nat Soc Painters Casein & Acrylic; Col Art Asn Am; SE Col Arts Conf; Miss Mus Art Asn; Nat & Miss Art Educ Asn (state assemblyman, 78-79, state vpres, 78-80). *Media:* Charcoal, Acrylic. *Mailing Add:* Art Dept Miss State Univ Mississippi State MS 39762

SEABERG, STEVE (STEVENS)
ASSEMBLAGE ARTIST, PERFORMANCE ARTIST
b Evanston, Ill, Sept 30, 30. *Study:* Northwestern Univ, BS, 52, MA, 61; Academie Grande Chaumiere, Paris, 56. *Work:* Art Bus Collection, State Ga, Atlanta; Albany Mus Art, Albany, Ga. *Comn:* Mural, comn by Ted Berrigan, New York, 66; mural, comn by Melvin Wildberger, Brooklyn, NY, 67; Lex et Domus (mural), The Law Office, Atlanta, 76; The Black Arts (mural), Nat Endowment Arts, Atlanta, 78; Hulsey Yard (murals), Seaboard Railway, Atlanta, Ga, 86. *Exhib:* Chicago and Vicinity, 60, Biennial Print & Drawing Exhib, 62, Art Inst Chicago; solo exhibs, Here Come de Judge-ment!, Clocktower Gallery, New York, 79 & Ancestors, Malmö Konsthall, Sweden, 81; Artists in Georgia, High Mus Art, Atlanta, 80; Collage & Assemblage, Miss Mus Art, Jackson, 82; Leisure America, Tampa Mus Art, Fla, 83; Birmingham Biennial, Birmingham Mus Art, Ala, 83. *Pos:* Artist & artist preparator, Field Mus Natural Hist, Chicago, 67-65; painter in residence, Neighborhood Art Ctr, Atlanta, 76-79; program dir, Arts Interface, Atlanta, 80-83, Atlanta Urban Design Comn, 85- *Teaching:* Vis lectr art hist, Northwestern Univ, 61-64; lectr & asst prof studio & art hist, Rutgers Univ, 67-70; instr humanities, Clark Col, Ga, 70-73. *Awards:* Nat Endowment Arts Visual Artist Fel, 78; Site Work Grants, Arts Festival Atlanta, 79-81; Third Prize, Birmingham Biennial, Birmingham Art Asn, 83. *Bibliog:* Öyvind Fahlström (dir, film), Sweden's TV, 68; Ann Livet (auth), Steve Seaberg's skeletons, Art Papers, 6/79; Tom Patterson (auth), Who is Steve Seaberg?, Brown's Guide to Ga, 8/82. *Publ:* Contribr, Chapters in the prehistory of eastern Ariz, Field Mus Natural Hist, 64; auth, Sunlight in Jungleland, private publ, 65; coauth, Guds Ansikte, Raben & Sjögran, 65; illusr, Om Baddräkter, Författerförlaget, 77; Song of Atlanta, Ali Baba, 81. *Mailing Add:* 683 Queen St SW Atlanta GA 30310

SEABOURN, BERT DAIL
PAINTER, PRINTMAKER
b Iraan, Tex, July 9, 31. *Study:* Oklahoma City Univ, cert(art); Famous Artists Schs, Westport, Conn, cert(art); Okla Cent State Univ; Okla Univ. *Work:* Okla Art Ctr, Okla City; Five Civilized Tribes Mus, Muskogee, Okla; Heard Mus, Phoenix; Vatican Mus Mod Religious Art, Italy; Nat Palace Mus, Taipei, Taiwan. *Comn:* Bronze sculptur, Southwestern Bell Telephone, Oklahoma City, Okla, 86. *Exhib:* Kennedy Ctr Performing Arts, 76 & 83; New Britain Mus Am Art, Conn, 79; Pintura Amerinda Contemp/EUA, 80; Kimball Art Ctr, Park City, Utah, 80; Denver Mus Natural Hist, Colo, 80; Native Am Ctr Living Arts, Niagara Falls, NY, 81; Mus Natural Hist, Smithsonian Inst, Washington, DC, 83; and others. *Pos:* Artist & journalist, USN, 51-55; art dir & artist, Okla Gas & Elec Co, Oklahoma City, 55-77. *Awards:* Grand Award, Red Cloud Indian Ann, 74; Gov Art Award, Okla, 81; Grand Award, Master Artists, Five Civilized Tribes Mus, 88. *Bibliog:* Dick Frontain (auth), Cherokee artist Bert D Seabourn, Prairie Hawk, 79; Gary L Roberts (auth), The spiritual paintings of Bert Seabourn, Art Voices South, 80; Tricia Hurst (auth), Bert Seabourn common ties, Southwest Art, 81. *Mem:* Okla Art Guild (pres, 70); Okla Watercolor Asn; Indian Artist Craftsman Asn; Master Artists Five Civilized Tribes. *Media:* Watercolor, Oil; Etching, Monotype. *Publ:* Auth & illusr, Indian Gallery, 72; auth & illusr, Master Artists of the Five Civilized Tribes, 76. *Mailing Add:* 6105 Covington Lane Oklahoma City OK 73132

SEABOURN, CONNIE
PAINTER, PRINTMAKER
b Purcell, Okla, Sept 20, 51. *Study:* Univ Okla, BFA, 81. *Work:* Gilcrease Mus, Tulsa; Talley Indust, Phoenix; Southwestern Bell Tel Co, Washington, DC; Heritage Ctr, Red Cloud Indian Sch, Pine Ridge, SDak; Tyson Foods Corp, Fayetteville, Ark. *Exhib:* Nat Printmaking & Drawing Show, Okla Art Ctr, 81; Night of the First Americans, John F Kennedy Ctr, Washington, DC, 82; Selected Works from Night of the First Americans, Smithsonian Mus, 82; Traditions & Transformations, Somerstown Gallery, Somers, NY, 83; Native American Art--Three Artists, Twenty Six Horses, New York, 83; two-person exhib, New Trends Gallery, Santa Fe, 83; Eye of My Mind, San Diego Mus Man, 85; Southern Plains Indian Mus, Anadarko, Okla, 86; Kimball Art Ctr, Park City, Utah, 89. *Awards:* Powers Award, Red Cloud Art Show, 83. *Bibliog:* Jimmie Marshall (auth), The emerging of an artist, Art Gallery Mag, winter 80; Jimmie Marshall (auth), The best of both worlds: Connie Seabourn Ragan, Okla 81, 11/81; Dick Frontain (auth), The rising star of Connie Seabourn Ragan, Indian Trader, 10/82. *Mem:* Soc Layerists Multi Media. *Media:* Watercolor, Serigraphy. *Publ:* Auth, The Artist as Printmaker, 8/86. *Mailing Add:* c/o El Taller Gallery 1221 W Sixth St Austin TX 78703

SEAMAN, DRAKE F
PAINTER
US citizen. *Study:* Kachina Art Sch, with Jay Datus, 59-63; also murals with Ray Strong, 70. *Work:* Whitney Gallery of Western Art, Cody, Wyo. *Comn:* Landscape mural, Seventh Day Adventist Church, Santa Barbara, Calif; Prodigal Son (mural), St Joseph's Catholic Church, Williams, Ariz, 83. *Exhib:* Troys Cowboy Art Gallery, Scottsdale, 71-72; El Prado Gallery, Sedona, Ariz, 74-78; Am Painters in Paris, France, 75; Phippen Mus Western Art, 92; McAdoo Gallery, Santa Fe, New Mexico, 92; plus others. *Teaching:* Instr landscape, Brooks Fine Arts Ctr, Santa Barbara, 69-70. *Bibliog:* Bob Austin (auth), Reflections on Oil, Austin Gallery, 70; article in SW Art, 4/76. *Media:* Oil. *Publ:* Auth (autobiog), Modern Veterinary Practice, 74; Animal Cavalcade, 74. *Mailing Add:* PO Box 23 Williams AZ 86046

SEAMANS, BEVERLY BENSON
SCULPTOR
b Boston, Mass, Oct 31, 28. *Study:* Mus Sch Fine Arts, Boston, 48-50; with George Demetrios & Peter Abate, 46-48. *Work:* Essex Inst & Peabody Mus, House of Seven Gables, Salem, Mass; Salem Hosp, Mass; Am Cathedral, Paris, France. *Comn:* Bronze, First Nat Bank Boston, Mass, 69; bronze, Salem Hospital, Mass, 76; bronze, Mass Inst Technol, 80; bronze, Camp Kieve, Nobleboro, Maine, 81; and other pvt collections. *Exhib:* Nat Sculpture Soc, New York, 73, 76-80; one-person shows, Essex Inst, Salem, 74, Mus Sci, Boston, 76, Pingree Sch, Hamilton, 75 & 77, Peabody Mus, Salem, 79-80, House of Seven Gables, Salem, Mass, 86, North Haven Gallery, Maine, 87 & Mem Art Gallery, Rochester, NY, 88, plus others; Abbot Pub Libr, Marblehead, Mass, 85. *Awards:* First Prize, Marblehead Arts Asn, 76, 78 & 87; Silver Medal, Nat Sculpture Soc, 78. *Bibliog:* Sharron King (auth), Woman 75, Channel 4, Boston, 75. *Mem:* Nat Sculpture Soc; New Eng Sculptors Asn; Copley Soc; Cambridge Arts; Marblehead Arts; Rockport Art Asn, Mass. *Media:* Bronze, Marble. *Mailing Add:* Five Harbor View Lanen Marblehead MA 01945

SEARLES, CHARLES
PAINTER, SCULPTOR
b Philadelphia, Pa. *Study:* Pa Acad Fine Arts, four-year cert, 73. *Work:* First Pa Bank, Philadelphia; Harlem State Bldg, New York; Smithsonian Inst; Howard Univ; Philip Morris Corp; Arco Chemical Co; First Dist Self-Help Inc, Philadelphia, Pa, 90. *Comn:* Celebration (mural), Gen Serv Admin, Philadelphia, 76; Playtime (mural), City Philadelphia, 78. *Exhib:* Black Artist in America, Whitney Mus Am Art, 71; Invisible Artist, Philadelphia Mus Art, 73; Jubilee, Boston Mus Fine Arts, 75; Afro-American Abstract, PS1 Gallery, New York, 81; one-person shows, Landmark Gallery, New York, 81, Peale Gallery, Pa Acad Fine Arts, 82 & Sande Webster, Philadelphia, 83, 85, 87, 90 & 92; Black Art: Ancestral Legacy, Dallas Mus Art, Tex, High Mus, Atlanta, Ga. *Teaching:* Lectr drawing, Philadelphia Col Art, 73- *Awards:* Cresson Award, Sr Show, Pa Acad Fine Arts, 71; Nat Endowment Fel Arts, 78; Creative Artists Pub Serv Fel, 80 & 81. *Media:* Acrylic; Painted Wood Sculpture. *Mailing Add:* c/o Sande Webster Gallery 2018 Locust St Philadelphia PA 19103

SEARLES, STEPHEN
SCULPTOR, PAINTER
b Leonia, NJ. *Study:* Art Students League, with George Bridgman, Charles Chapman, Frank V DuMond & Reginald Marsh; Grand Cent Sch Art, New York, with Georg Lober & Harvey Dunn; Gloucester with Emile Gruppe; also with Dennis Gelin, Fontainebleau, France. *Work:* Gloucester Fishermen's Mus; Leonia Pub Libr, NJ; Dwight-Englewood Sch, Englewood, NJ; John F Kennedy Sch, Somerville, Mass. *Comn:* Our Lady of Good Voyage Statue, Church of Our Lady of Good Voyage, Gloucester, Mass; portrait busts, Norman Rockwell, Howard C Crristy, James Montgomery Flagg, Gordon Grant & Arthur Fielder; also bronzes of athletes & fishermen. *Exhib:* Sculpture, Grassy Gallery, Biarritz, France, 46, Salmagundi Club, New York, 52, Guild of Boston Artists, 72 & Rockport Art Asn, 72. *Teaching:* Instr drawing & sculpture, Biarritz Am Univ, 45-46; instr life drawing & sculpture, Newark Sch Fine & Indust Art, 50-53; instr life drawing, Vesper George Sch Art, Boston, 62- *Awards:* Sculpture Awards, Salmagundi Club, 52, Am Artists Prof League, 76 & 77 & Rockport Art Asn, 77, 78, 81, 83, 85 & 89. *Bibliog:* Article, Artists by artists, winter 82 & Artists are his subjects, winter 83, Sculpture Review. *Mem:* Nat Sculpture Soc; Am Artists Prof League; Rockport Art Asn; Nat Arts Club; Hudson Valley Art Asn, New York. *Media:* Bronze, Stone. *Publ:* Auth, Farewell to John (poem with sculpture), Veterna's Voices, spring, 82. *Mailing Add:* Guild of Boston Artists 162 Newbury St Boston MA 02116

SEARS, STANTON GRAY
PAINTER, SCULPTOR
b Bethlehem, Pa, Oct 22, 50. *Study:* RI Sch Design, BFA, 73; Pa State Univ, MFA, 76. *Comn:* Sculptures, NH Art Asn, Manchester, 79 & 80; sculptures, Phillips Exeter Acad, NH, 81. *Exhib:* Stedman Art Gallery, Rutgers Univ, Camden, NJ, 79; Lee Hall Gallery, Northern Mich Univ, Marquette, 79; Allentown Art Mus, Pa, 79; De Cordova Mus, Lincoln, Mass, 79; Currier Gallery Art, Manchester, NH, 81; solo show, Plymouth State Col Art Gallery, Plymouth, NH, 81; Silvermine Guild Artists, New Canaan, Conn, 81; and others. *Teaching:* Instr, Pa State Univ, State Col, 75-78; instr, Univ NH, Durham, 80-81; instr, Manchester Inst Arts & Sci, NH, 81-83. *Awards:* Drawing Award, Educ Ctr Arts, New Haven, Conn, 78; Currier Award, NH Art Asn 34th Ann, Currier Gallery, 80; Award for Advanc Am Art, Arts Coun Holyoke, Mass, 81. *Bibliog:* David Elliot (auth), What are those stripes in the ravine, Univ NH Newspaper, 81; Laura Holland (auth), Sears' high overhead, Valley Advocate, 81; John Wharton (auth), David Fullam, Stanton Sears, Art New Eng, 81. *Mem:* Col Art Asn Am; NH Art Asn. *Media:* Graphite, Pastel; Welded Aluminum. *Dealer:* Boston Art Work 2345 Washington St Newton Lower Falls MA 02162. *Mailing Add:* 1477 Ashland Ave St Paul MN 55104

SEAWELL, THOMAS ROBERT
PRINTMAKER, PHOTOGRAPHER
b Baltimore, Md, Mar 17, 36. *Study:* Washington Univ, BFA, 58; Tex Christian Univ, MFA, 60. *Work:* Pushkin Mus, Moscow; Brit Mus, London; Libr Cong, Washington, DC; Mem Art Gallery, Rochester, NY; Brooklyn Mus, NY; DeCordova Mus, Lincoln, Mass. *Comn:* Rochester Print Club; Geldermann Print Comn, 85-92; Merchants Nat Bank & Trust, 90. *Exhib:* 2nd Miami Graphics Biennial, Metrop Mus & Art Ctr, 75; 30 Yrs of Am Printmaking Including 20th Nat Print Exhib, Brooklyn Mus, 76; Int Biennial, Philadelphia Print Club, 79; Contemporary American Prints, US Consul Gen, Leningrad, USSR, 84-85; A Sense of Place, Southern Arts Fedn, 86-87 & traveling; Collagraph Invitational, Univ Mont, Missoula, 87-90; retrospective exhib, The Oswego Years, Tyler Art Gallery, State Univ NY, 91; and others.

Pos: Vis artist, numerous sch art, 77-89, E Tex State Univ, spring, 83 & Print Symposium, Ox Bow, summer, 85, Univ Dallas, 89. *Teaching:* Prof drawing & printmaking, State Univ NY, Oswego, 63-91; Retired. *Awards:* State Univ NY Res Found Printmaking Fels, 67, 70 & 74. *Bibliog:* 30 Years of American Printmaking including the 20th National Exhibition, Brooklyn Mus, 76; The Complete Collagraph, Romano & Ross, The Free Press, Macmillan, NY, 80; Eldon Cunningham (auth), Printmaking: A Primary Form of Expression, Univ Colo Press, 92. *Mem:* Boston Printmakers; Soc Am Graphic Artists; Philadelphia Watercolor Club. *Media:* All. *Dealer:* Miriam Perlman Inc 505 N Lakeshore Dr Suite 5410 Chicago IL 60611; Joyce Paulson Fine Arts Box 277 Cambridge MA 02238. *Mailing Add:* 1513 Park Commerce TX 75428

SEAWRIGHT, JAMES L, JR
SCULPTOR, EDUCATOR
b Jackson, Miss, May 22, 36. *Study:* Univ Miss, BA, 57; Art Students League, NY, 61-62. *Work:* Mus Mod Art, Whitney Mus Am Art & Solomon R Guggenheim Mus, New York; Larry Aldrich Mus, Ridgefield, Conn; Wadsworth Atheneum, Hartford, Conn. *Comn:* Electronic Environ, Seattle-Tacoma Int Airport, 73; outdoor sculpture, NJ State Mus, Trenton, 76; outdoor sculpture, Mobile Tech Ctr, Pennington, NJ; Sculpture Terminal, C Logan International Airport, Boston. *Exhib:* Whitney Ann, Whitney Mus Am Art, 67; The Sixties, Mus Mod Art, 67; Focus on Light, NJ State Mus, Trenton, 68; Magic Theater, Nelson Gallery Performing Arts Found, Kansas City, Mo, 68; Cybernetic Serendipity, Inst Contemp Art, London, 69; Theodoron Awards Show, Solomon R Guggenheim Mus, New York, 69; Works for New Spaces, Walker Art Ctr, Minneapolis, 71; Art of the Space Age, Huntsville Mus Art, Ala, 78; American Rennaissance Mus of Art, Fort Lauderdale, Fla; one-man show, David Bermant Found, New York. *Pos:* Dir visual arts prog, Princeton Univ, 74- *Teaching:* Teacher sculpture, Sch Visual Arts, New York, 67-69; lectr sculpture, Princeton Univ, NJ, 69-, prof visual arts, 92- *Awards:* Theodoron Found Award, Guggenheim Mus, 69; fel Graham Found Walker Art Ctr, 70-71; Nat Endowment Arts Comn, NJ State Mus, 76; Award of Merit, Miss Inst of Arts & Letters, 83. *Bibliog:* Article, Life Mag, 4/67; Douglas Davis (auth), interview, Art Am, 1-2/68; Ralph T Coe (auth), The Magic Theater, Circle Press, 70. *Mem:* Am Abstract Artists. *Media:* Miscellaneous. *Publ:* Contribr, On the Future of Art, Viking, NY, 70. *Mailing Add:* 155 Wooster St New York NY 10012

SEBASTIAN
SCULPTOR
b Chihuahua, Mex, Nov 16, 47. *Study:* Nat Sch Plastic Arts, Univ Mex, 69; Res Fel, Nat Univ Mex, 79- *Work:* Mus Mod Art, Mexico City, Jerusalem, Rio de Janeiro & Caracas; Schubladen Mus, Bern, Switzerland. *Comn:* Construccion (mural), Col Civil Engineers, Mexico City, 74; Trono de Netzahaulcoyotl, gift from Govt Mex to Vancouver, Can, 78; Glorieta (sculpture), Gucadigose, Villahermosa, Mexico, 76; Tlaloc (sculpture) & Ctr Sculptural Space, Nat Univ Mex, Mexico City, 79. *Exhib:* One-man shows, Palace Fine Arts, Mexico, 74, Mus Mod Art, Mexico, 76, Loeb Gallery, Bern, Switzerland, 80; Graphic Arts Biennial, Florence, Italy, 74; Mus Mod Art, Paris, 77, Rio de Janeiro, 78 & Caracas, Venezuela, 78; Alpha Gallery, Denver, 79. *Collections Arranged:* Arte Correro (auth, catalog), Carrillo Gil Mus, 79; Mex Sculptors in Can, Capilano Col Art Gallery, Vancouver, Can, 80. *Teaching:* Instr urban sculpture, Escuela Nac de Arte Plastico, Mexico City, 70-78; instr painting, La Esmeralda, Mexico City, 75-77; prof res, Univ Nac Autonoma Metrop, Mexico City, 78-81. *Awards:* First Prize, I Biennial Art, Mexico, 74. *Bibliog:* Roberto Pontual (auth), Geometric sensivel, Edicones J Brasil, 78; Frank J Malina (auth), Visual Art, Mathematics & Computers, Pergamon Press, 79; Louis G Redstone (auth), Public Art-New Directions, McGraw-Hill, 81. *Mem:* Mex Asn Visual Artists (pres, 81-). *Media:* Steel, Aluminum. *Publ:* Auth, My Transformable Structures Based on the Mobius Strip, Leonardo, Vol 8, Pergamon Press, 75; co-auth, Extructura y Biografia de un Objeto, Nat Univ Mex, 79. *Dealer:* Rutherford Barnes Collection 1415 Larimer Sq Denver CO 80202. *Mailing Add:* c/o Alpha Gallery 959 Broadway Denver CO 80203

SEBASTIAN, JILL C
ENVIRONMENTAL ARTIST, SCULPTOR
b Libertyville, Ill, Mar 24, 50. *Study:* Univ Wis-Milwaukee, MFA, 79. *Work:* Burpee Art Mus, Rockford, Ill; Marquette Univ, Milwaukee, Wis. *Comn:* Installation, performance, Madison Art Ctr, Wis, 83; sculpture, 1st Bank Milwaukee, Wis, 83. *Exhib:* Solo exhibs, Purdue Univ, WLafayette, Ind, 83, Kit Basquin Gallery, Milwaukee, 83, Charles Wustum Mus, Racine, Wis, 84, Bertha Urdang Gallery, New York, 85 & Loho Gallery, Louisville, Ky, 86; Wisconsin Directions III & IV, Milwaukee Art Mus, 81 & 85; Wisconsin Drawing & Painting, Kohler Arts Ctr, Sheboygan, Wis, 82; Colorado 3-D, Arvada Ctr Arts, Denver, 85. *Teaching:* Lectr film, design & drawing, Univ Wis-Milwaukee, 79-84; asst prof sculpture, Univ Denver, Color, 84-85. *Awards:* Grants, Wis Arts Bd, 81 & 82, Milwaukee Artists Found, 82; Nat Endowment Arts Fel, 85. *Bibliog:* Christine Buth-Furness (auth), Jill Sebastian, New Art Examiner, 4/83; John Mominee (auth), Jill Sebastian, Wis Acad Rev, 3/85. *Mem:* Col Art Asn; Chicago Artists Coalition. *Publ:* Auth & illusr, Cream City Rev, 81; Aviva Rahmani, rev, & Jim Brozak, rev, New Art Examiner, 84. *Dealer:* Bertha Urdang Gallery 23 E 74 St New York NY 10021. *Mailing Add:* c/o Alpha Gallery 959 Broadway Denver CO 80203

SEBELIUS, HELEN
PAINTER
b Assiniboia, Sask, 1953. *Study:* Univ Regina, Sask, 71-72; Alberta Col Art, Calgary, Dipl, 74-78; Banff Ctr, Alta, 80; Nova Scotia Col Art & Design, Halifax, MFA, 87. *Work:* Alberta Art Found; Can Coun Art Bank & Dept External Affairs, Ottawa; Grant MacEwan Col, Edmonton; Nickle Arts Mus, Calgary; Red Deer Col. *Exhib:* Solo exhibs, Drawings and Constructions, Gallery O, Toronto, Ont, 81, Source/History, Anna Leonowens Gallery, Halifax, NS, 87 & Drawings--Rotation Series, New Gallery, Calgary, Alta, 87; Paper Variations, Beaver House Gallery, Edmonton, Alta, 86; Papiers Transforms 11 (with catalog), Langage Plus, Alma, PQ, 87; Contemporary '88 Calgary (with catalog), Virginia Christopher Galleries, 88, Visions of Alberta, Muttart Art Gallery, 88 & Drawings/Motivations, Glenbow Mus, 88, Calgary, Alta. *Pos:* Guest speaker, Calif Col Arts & Crafts, Oakland, 81; asst dir, Snyder Hedlin Fine Art Consult, Calgary, Alta, 81-83; bd dirs, Off Centre, Calgary, Alta, 84-85; adv bd, New Gallery, Calgary, Alta, 88- *Teaching:* Instr textile & foundations, Alta Col Art Calgary, 81-85; vis artist & instr textiles, 87-88, instr drawing, 88-; instr foundations, Univ Calgary, Alta, 84, instr drawing 88-; instr papermaking, David Thompson Univ, Nelson, BC, 84, Red Deer Col, Alta, 85; teaching assitantships, Nova Scotia Col Art & Design, Halifax, 85-87, instr drawing, 87. *Awards:* Alberta Cult Assistance Award, 79; Project Grant, 82-83, Short Term Grant, 84, Travel Grant, 85, Can Coun; Project Grant, Alta Cult Project, 82-83. *Bibliog:* Nancy Tousley (auth), 5 plus 5, 9/27/85 & Drawings/Motivations, 10/5/88, Calgary Herald; Christiane Laforge (auth), Papiers Transformes 11, Le Quotidien, 5/16/87. *Media:* All media. *Mailing Add:* Olga Korper Gallery 17 Morrow Ave Toronto ON M6R 2H9 Canada

SEBOROVSKI, CAROLE
PAINTER
b San Diego, Calif, 1960. *Study:* Calif Col Arts & Crafts, BFA, 82; Hunter Col, MFA, 87. *Work:* Metrop Mus Art, Mus Mod Art, New York; Brooklyn Mus, NY; Carnegie Mus Art, Pittsburgh; Cleveland Ctr Contemp Art, Ohio; San Francisco Mus Mod Art, Calif. *Exhib:* Geometric Perspectives, Pfiser Inc, arranged by Mus Mod Art, NY, 91; Amerikanische Druckgraphik, Galerie Cora Höisl, Dusseldorf, 91; Modern Drawings, Anthony Ralph Gallery, New York, 91; Small Works on Paper, John Berggruen Gallery, San Francisco, 91; one-person shows, Hunter Col Art Gallery, New York, Damon Brandt Gallery, New York, 86, Lorence-Monk Gallery, New York, 88 & 89, Galerie Karsston Grove, Paris, 91, Angles Gallery, Santa Monica, Calif, 91 & 92, Galerie Karsten Grove, Ger. *Awards:* Grant, Pollock-Krasner Found, 86; Agnes Bourne Fel Visual Arts, 90; Grant, Nat Endowment Arts, 91. *Bibliog:* Peter Frank (auth), Constructive Concepts, Jerald Brainin, Carole Seborovski, LA Weekly, 6/28-7/4/91; Ann Cremin (auth), Mixed Media-Artists Tend Towards Textural Testimonies, Paris Boulevard, p 30-31, 2/91; Sean Wainbird (auth), Drawn in the Nineties (exhib catalog), 92. *Mailing Add:* c/o Betsy Senior Contemporary Prints 375 Broadway New York NY 10012

SECKEL, PAUL BERNHARD
PAINTER, PRINTMAKER
b Osnabrueck, Ger, July 18, 18; US citizen. *Study:* London Cent Sch Arts & Crafts; Univ Buffalo, BFA; Yale Univ, MFA. *Exhib:* Recent Drawings, USA, Mus Mod Art, New York, 56; Drawings by Invitation, Flint Inst Art, 57; Exhib of Paintings Eligible for Purchase, Am Acad Arts & Lett, 63; Audubon Artists Ann. *Awards:* Emily Lowe Award, 63. *Mem:* New York Artists Equity Asn. *Media:* Acrylic, Oil. *Publ:* Auth, How to Make Original Color Lithographs--A Manual for Professional Artists, 70. *Mailing Add:* 12 Van Etten Blvd New Rochelle NY 10804

SECKLER, DOROTHY GEES
CRITIC, PAINTER
b Baltimore, Md, July 9, 10. *Study:* Teachers Col, Columbia Univ, BS(art educ); Md Inst Art, dipl traveling scholar, 31; NY Univ; also in Europe. *Comn:* Everson Mus, Syracuse, NY. *Exhib:* One-woman show, Leonore Ross Gallery, Provincetown, Mass, 80; Provincetown Mus, 80-81; two-woman show, Outermost Gallery, Provincetown, Mass, 82. *Pos:* Assoc ed, Art News & Art News Ann, 50-55; gallery ed, Art in Am, 55-61, contrib ed, 61-68; spec contribr fine arts, MD (Med News Mag), 57-73. *Teaching:* Lectr art hist, Mus Mod Art, 45-49; adj instr, NY Univ, 47-52; lectr & instr, City Col New York, 57-60 & Pratt Inst, 60-61. *Awards:* Am Fedn Arts Award Art Criticism, 54; Adolph & Esther Gottlieb Found Artists Grant, 85; Pollock-Krasner Found Artists Grant, 90. *Bibliog:* Archives Am Art, Smithsonian Inst, Washington, DC; Robert Taylor (auth), 80 Years at Provincetown, Boston Sun Globe, 9/11/77. *Mem:* Provincetown Art Asn & Mus. *Media:* Acrylic, Collage. *Publ:* Coauth, The questioning public, Mus Mod Art Bulletin, 49; Figure Drawing Comes to Life, 57; contribr, Encycl World Art, 59; auth, Provincetown Painters, Everson Mus, Syracuse, NY, 77; contribr numerous articles, Arts, Art Am & Art News, also rev on exhibs & monogr. *Mailing Add:* 64 Sagamore Rd Bronxville NY 10708

SECUNDA, (HOLLAND) ARTHUR
PAINTER, COLLAGE ARTIST
b Jersey City, NJ, Nov 12, 27. *Study:* NY Univ; Art Students League; Acad Grande Chaumiere; Acad Julian; with Zadkine & L'hote, Paris, 48-50; Inst Meschini, Rome; also study in Mex. *Work:* Smithsonian Inst, Libr Cong & Nat Collection Find Arts, Washington, DC; Mus Mod Art, New York; Art Inst Chicago; Brooklyn Mus; plus many others in US, Sweden, Belgium, Switz, France, Israel & Canada. *Exhib:* One-man shows, La Jolla Art Mus, Calif, 66, Galerie Richard Foncke, Gent, Belg, 68, Konstsalongen Kavaletten, Uppsala, Sweden, 71, Galerie Leger, Malmo, Sweden & Arras Gallery, New York, 75; plus many other including over 80 one-man shows. *Teaching:* Sierra-Nevada Col, Incline Village, Nev. *Awards:* Tamarind Fel, Calif, 70 & NMex, 72. *Media:* Acrylic, Oil. *Dealer:* Galerie P Cramer 11 Grand Rue Geneva Switz; Owl Gallery 1074 Broadway Woodmere NY 11598. *Mailing Add:* PO Box 6363 Beverly Hills CA 90212

SEDERS, FRANCINE LAVINAL
DEALER
b Paris, France, Dec 12, 32; US citizen. *Study:* Univ Paris Law Sch, MLaws; Univ Wash, MLS. *Pos:* Mgr, Otto Seligman Gallery, Seattle, Wash, 65-66; pres & dir, Francine Seders Gallery Ltd, Seattle, 66- *Mem:* North Seattle Community Col Adv Coun Humanities, 83-90. *Specialty:* Contemporary paintings, sculpture and graphics. *Mailing Add:* 6701 Greenwood Ave N Seattle WA 98103

SEED, SUZANNE LIDDELL
PHOTOGRAPHER, WRITER
b Gary, Ind, Mar 8, 40. *Study:* Yale Univ Summer Sch Music Art, 61; Ind Univ, with Henry Holmes Smith, BA, 63; Art Inst Chicago, MFA, 82. *Work:* Chrysler Mus; Chase Manhatten Bank, NY; Exchange Nat Bank, Chicago. *Exhib:* Los Angeles Inst Contemp Art's Photog, Downey Mus Art, 80; Chicago Contemp Photog, Los Angeles Ctr Photographic Studies, Calif, 81; Women/Image/Nature, Tyler Sch Art, Philadelphia, Pa & Rochester Inst Technol, NY, 81; and others. *Mem:* Soc Photogrs Communications; Soc Photogrs Educ; Writers' Guild. *Publ:* Auth & illusr, Saturday's Child, J Philip O'Hara, 73; contribr, Women See Men, McGraw Hill, 77; contribr, Women Photograph Men, Morrow, 77; auth & illusr, Fine Trades, Follett, 79. *Dealer:* Marjorie Neikrug 224 East 68th St New York NY 10021. *Mailing Add:* 175 E Delaware Chicago IL 60611

SEEMAN, HELENE ZUCKER
WRITER, CURATOR
b New York, NY, Apr 20, 50. *Study:* Boston Univ, BA; Queens Col, NY, MLS. *Collections Arranged:* Photorealism Traveling Exhibition, NZ mus, 75-76; Audrey Flack, Univ Bridgeport, Conn, 75; Look Again, Taft Mus, Cincinnati, Ohio, 76; Rothmans of Pall Mall Traveling Exhibition, 77-78; New Realism, Jacksonville Mus, Fla, 77; Off the Beaten Path, Brainerd Gallery, State Univ NY Col, Potsdam, 77. *Pos:* Cur, Prudential Ins Co, NJ, 80- *Teaching:* Lectr, New Sch, NY, 80 & 83, Avila Col, 81, Scripps Col, 82, Walker Art Ctr, 83 & Fairleigh Dickinson Univ, NJ, 86. *Bibliog:* Randy Rosen (auth), Corporate collecting at a crossroads, Nat Arts Guide, 11-12/80; Connoisseur's corner, Wall St Transcript, 6/28/82; Keepers of corporate art, Fortune, 3/21/83; The corporate collector, Village Voice, 10/23/84. *Mem:* Asn Corporate Art Curators. *Interests:* Organization, research and published documentation of artists and special exhibitions. *Publ:* Coauth, SoHo, Neal Schuman, 79; The PhotoRealists, Abrams, 79; contrib, Alternative Careers for Librarians, Neal Schuman, 79. *Mailing Add:* Art Prog, Prudential Insurance Co 745 Broad St Newark NJ 07101

SEEREY-LESTER, JOHN VERNON
PAINTER
b Manchester, Eng, Dec 6, 45. *Study:* Salford Col Art, Lancashire, Eng, dipl art, 62. *Work:* Salford Art Gallery, Lancashire, Eng; Manchester Art Gallery, Eng; Leigh Yawkey Woodson Art Mus, Wausau, Wis. *Comn:* Drawing, Royal Lytham & St Ann's Golf Club, Cancer Soc fund raiser, British Open, 74; portrait of Lord Chalfont, Brit Indust Develop Corp, Eng, 75; painting of Giant Panda, World Wildlife Fund, 81. *Exhib:* Solo exhib, World Wildlife Fund, Ann Conf, Manchester, Eng, 82; Birds in Art, Leigh Yawkey Woodson Art Mus, Wausau, Wis, 83-86; World Wildlife Fund, Washington, DC, 84; Soc Wildlife Art for the Nation, Inaugural Exhibition, Guildhall Art Gallery, London, 85; Birds in Art, 87-92; Seerey-Lester Wildlife Art Seminars, Can, Fla & Alaska Masters, Watson-Guptill Publ, 85. *Teaching:* Seerey-Lester Wildlife Art Seminars, Can, Fla & Alaska. *Awards:* Artist of the Year, Miniatures 85 & Northwoods Wildlife Rehab Ctr Ann Show, 85; Artist of the Year, Pacific Rim, 91. *Bibliog:* Chuck Wechsler (auth), The arrival of John Seerey-Lester, Wildlife Art News, 85; Face to Face with Nature: The Art of John Seerey-Lester; other articles in Midwest Art News, Southwest Art News & Prints. *Mem:* World Wildlife Fund; Soc Wildlife Art for the Nation (SWAN); Wilderness Soc; Audubon Soc. *Media:* Oil on Canvas. *Mailing Add:* c/o Lindart Inc 439 S Tamiami Trail Suite 207 Venice FL 34285

SEGAL, BARBARA JEAN
SCULPTOR, CRAFTSMAN
b Bronxville, NY, Jan 27, 53. *Study:* Pratt Inst Technol, NY, 70-72; L'Ecole Nationale Superieuve Des Beaux-Arts Paris, 72-74; New Sch Soc Res, 80-83. *Work:* Malcomb Forbes Collection, New York. *Comn:* Marble jacket, comn by Morey Chaplick, Toronto, Can, 90; marble tuxedo (with Greek figures), comn by Sheila Lampert, New York, 90. *Exhib:* New Talent, Alan Stone Gallery, New York, 84-85; Art of Northeast America, Silvermine Gallery, Conn, 86, 87 & 88. *Teaching:* Instr, private, formerly; instr stone carving, Sch Visual Arts, New York, 90. *Awards:* Claudia & Maurice Stone Memorial Award, Silvermine Gallery, 88; Sculpture Award, Int Art Competition, 88. *Bibliog:* Nancy Helle (auth), Stone age artist, Profiles, 8/86; John Sailer (auth), How to create marble art with lamination, Stone World, 2/89. *Media:* Stone. *Publ:* Co-auth, Barbara Segal Sculptor, EGG, 90. *Mailing Add:* c/o Gallery Henoch 80 Wooster St New York NY 10012

SEGAL, GEORGE
SCULPTOR
b New York, NY, Nov 26, 24. *Study:* NY Univ, BS(art educ), 49; Rutgers Univ, MFA, 63. *Work:* Mus Mod Art, New York; Mus Mod Art, Stockholm, Sweden; Art Gallery Ont, Toronto; Nat Gallery Can, Ottawa, Ont; Art Inst Chicago; Mus Mod Art, Seibu Takanawa, Karuizawa, Japan; Tamayo Mus, Mexico City, Mex; Hirshhorn Mus & Sculpture Garden, Smithsonian Inst, Washington, DC. *Comn:* The Holocaust, Lincoln Park, San Francisco, 83. *Exhib:* Galerie Speyer, Paris, 69; Expo '70, Japan; Munson-Williams-Proctor Inst, Utica, NY, 72; one-man shows, Onnash Galerie, Basel Art Fair, Switz, 74, Santa Barbara Mus Art, Calif, 76, Serge DeBloe, Brussels, Belg, 79, Akron Art Inst, Ohio, 80, Israel Mus, Jerusalem, 83, Sidney Janis Gallery, New York, 84, Galerie Maeght-Lelong, Paris, 85, Galerie Brusberg, Berlin, 86 & Yares Gallery, Scottsdale, Ariz, 88; Whitney Mus Am Art, 78; retrospective, Walker Art Ctr, 78-79; Galerie Kornfeld, Zurich, 80; New Reliefs, Sch Visual Arts, New York, 82; The Innovative Still Life, Holly Solomon Gallery, NY, 84; American Sculpture, Margo Leavin Gallery, Los Angeles, 84. *Awards:* Walter K Gutman Found Award, 62; First Prize, Art Inst Chicago, 66; Governor's Walt Whitman Arts Award, 89. *Bibliog:* George Segal, Artsmag, 12/74; Ellen Zeiffer (auth), George Segal: sculptural environments, Am Artist, 1/75; Robert Pincus Witten (auth), Reviews: George Segal, Artforum, 1/75; Phyllis Tuchman (auth), George Segal, Abbeville Press, 83; Sam Hunter & Don Hawthorne (coauth), George Segal, Ediciones Poligrafa, Barcelona, 84. *Dealer:* Sidney Janis Gallery 6 W 57th St New York NY 10019. *Mailing Add:* Davidsons Mill Rd New Brunswick NJ 08901

SEGAL, TAMA & DAVID
DEALER, DIRECTOR
Tama, b Brooklyn, NY, Feb 13, 49, David, b Bronx, NY, Aug 31, 40. *Study:* Tama, Brooklyn Mus; Pratt Inst; New Sch; David, City Col, New Sch Social Res, BFA, 64. *Pos:* Owners, Segal Gallery, 77- *Teaching:* Guest lectr contemp Native Am painting & sculpture, New Sch Soc Res. *Mem:* Munic Art Soc New York; Santa Fe Festival Arts; Mus Am Indian. *Mailing Add:* 12032 Parks Farm Lane Charlotte NC 28277

SEGALOVE, ILENE JUDY
VIDEO ARTIST, PHOTOGRAPHER
b Los Angeles, Calif, Nov 24, 50. *Study:* Univ Calif, Santa Barbara, BFA; Loyola Univ, MA(commun arts). *Exhib:* Artists Choice, Los Angeles Co Mus Art, 75; Southland Video, Long Beach Mus Mod Art, 75; Documentary Tapes, Mus Mod Art, New York, 75; Whitney Biennial, New York, 75 & 77; Los Angeles Inst Contemp Art, Calif, 76; Long Beach Mus Art, Calif, 77; one-person show, Univ Calif, Irvine, 78; Mus Contemp Art, Chicago, 80; Paris Biennele, 81; Contemp Mus Art, Houston, 82; Media Art Ctr, NY, 82; Inst Contmep Art, Boston, 83; and others. *Awards:* Nat Endowment Arts Grant, 76, 79 & 83; Am Film Inst, 80; James D Phelan Award in Video, Rocky Mountain Film, 83. *Bibliog:* Interview, KCET Public TV, 83. *Mailing Add:* c/o Los Angeles Munic Art Gallery 4804 Hollywood Blvd Los Angeles CA 90027

SEGAN, KEN AKIVA
DRAFTSMAN, PAINTER
b New York, NY, Feb 19, 50. *Study:* Southern Ill Univ, BA, 77; Univ Mo, MFA, 80, Acad Fine Arts, Cracow, 84, Jagiellonian Univ, Cracow, 85. *Work:* Musee d'Art Juif de Paris; Musee Des Beaux-Arts, Budapest; Albertina Graphic Arts, Vienna; Mus Mod Art, Haifa; Ore Art Inst, Portland. *Exhib:* La Peur de L'autre/Fears of Others, Vancouver, BC, 89 & Int tour, US & Can, 90-91; Bumbershoot, Seattle, 90; Prints & Artists Books, Recent Acquisitions 78-88, Bibliotheque Nationale, Paris, 90; Under the Wings of G-D: Ten Drawings from the Fifty Drawing Suite in Commemoration of the Warsaw Ghetto Uprising, 1943-93, Hillel Found, Seattle, 92 & 93; and others. *Pos:* Int artist-in-residence, Aberdeen Art Gallery, Scotland, 87. *Awards:* Purchase Prize, West 80-Art & the Law, West Publ Co, 80. *Bibliog:* Susan Auerbach (auth), A Jewish Printmaker at Work, Jewish Transcript, Seattle, 3/9/85; Anne Flann (auth), Aberdeen Gallery Hosts Ideological Battler ar AIR, London, 7/10/87; Ramona Gault (auth), Martyrs Take Wing Under Artists Hand, Warsaw Ghetto Uprising Anniversary, Northwest Ethnic News, Seattle, 4/92. *Media:* Ink, Mixed Media Drawing. *Publ:* The late Mayor in bra, panties-Times editorial insensitive to blacks, Seattle Times, 5/19/88; The old De Hirsch synagogue a priceless treasure, Jewish Transcript, Seattle, 11/24/88; Fear of Others (exhib catalog), Arts Action Soc, Vancouver, BC, 89; Citys Loss of Historic Buildings a Disgrace, Seattle-Post-Intelligencer, 1/9/91. *Dealer:* Yvonne Banks Art Consult 316 Occidental S Seattle WA 98104; Mahler Fine Arts Consulting 85 S Wash Seattle WA 98104. *Mailing Add:* Tsigana Art Studio 1514 Western Art Palaces Seattle WA 98101

SEGGER, MARTIN JOSEPH
HISTORIAN, MUSEUM DIRECTOR
b Felixtowe, Eng, Nov 22, 46; Can citizen. *Study:* Univ Victoria, BA, 69, with Alan Gowans, dipl, 70; Warburg Inst, Univ London, with E H Gombrich, MPhil, 73. *Collections Arranged:* Arts of the Forgotten Pioneers (with catalog), Maltwood Mus, 71; Samuel Maclure-Architect, 74 & House Beautiful, An Exhibit of Decorative Arts 1860-1920 (with catalog), 75, BC Prov Mus; Colonial Painters of British Columbia, 79; The Victoria Portrait, 81; To Sir Yehudi Menuhin, 85; John Wright, Architect, 90. *Pos:* Dir, Maltwood Mus, Victoria, 71-, BC Heritage Trust, Provincial Heritage Adv Bd, Heritage Can & Int Coun Monuments & Sites Can; consult mus training, Egypt/UNESCO, 83; consult, Heritas Inc, 83; Consult, Icom, Costa Rica, 89. *Teaching:* Lectr art hist & mus studies, Univ Victoria, BC, 71- *Awards:* Am Asn State & Local Hist & Commun Award, Heritage Can Found; Lieut Gov Medal, BC Heritage, 89. *Mem:* Soc Archit Historians; Can Mus Asn (nat exec mem, 75-77); Soc Study Archit Can (dir, currently); Royal Soc Arts Fel; and others. *Publ:* Auth, the British Columbia Parliament Buildings, 79; Heritage of Canada, 81; Museum Operations Manual, 83; Samuel Madure: An Architectural Biography, 86; The Development of the Gordon Head Campus, 88. *Mailing Add:* 1035 Sutlej St Victoria BC V8V 2V9 Canada

SEGUIN, JEAN-PIERRE
PAINTER, PHOTOGRAPHER
b Montreal, Que, Feb 12, 51. *Study:* Cegep du Vieux-Montreal, DEC, 72; Universite de Que, Montreal, BA, 75, MA, 79. *Work:* Musée du Que; Conseil

des Arts du Can, Ottawa; Universite du Que a Montreal. *Comn:* Stained-glass window, Govt du Que, Ville de la Baie, 86. *Exhib:* Gravure du Quebec, Musée d'Art Contemporain, Montreal, 74; SCAN, Vancouver Art Gallery, BC, 74; Forum 1976, Musée des-Beaux-Arts, Montreal, 76; Works on Paper, Sir George Williams Univ, Montreal, 76; Galerie Nationale, Ottawa, Ont, 77; Biennale II du Quebec, Musée du Centre Saidye Bronfman, Montreal, 79; Jeune Contemporain 80, London Art Gallery, Ont, 80; ACTFART, Musée du Saguenay-Lac-St-Jean, Chicoutimi, Oue, 85; Nommage à A Wharol, Galerie 13, Montreal, 87; Histoire De Collections, Musée Dart Contemporain, Montreal, 88; Passages, Musée Du Saguenay, Que, 89; Le Blanc of MFS Nuits, éoifice Belgo, Montreal, 91. *Teaching:* Charge de cours activite de synthese, Univ Que, Montreal, 76-78 & prof painting & drawing, Univ Que, Chicoutimi, 79-717. *Awards:* Greenshield Fel, 75; ler Prix, Concours de Dessin & Biennale du Que, Govt du Que, 79; ler Prix Biennale Du, Que, 89. *Bibliog:* René Payant (auth), Dépeindre le photographique, Galerie Graff, 83; Giles Daigneault (auth), Jean-Pierre Seguin: Peindre ou feindre, Le Devoir, 83; Pierre Ouellet (auth), Le Savoir peint, Revue Protée, 85. *Media:* All. *Publ:* Coauth, Du neuf a cinq, Articule, 80; Entre le corps et la matiére, Intervention, 81; Ou, Langage Plus, 83; illusr, Langage et savoir, Protée, 85; Un Printemps Costaud, Vie Des Arts, 91. *Mailing Add:* Univ Quebec a Chicoutimi, Art Dept Chicoutimi PQ G7H 2B1 Canada

SEGUR, ELEANOR CORINNE
PAINTER, INSTRUCTOR
b Toledo, Ohio, Aug 2, 23. *Study:* Buffalo Univ; Pratt Inst, illus, Sch Visual Arts, New York, advert; Art Students League; also with Edgar Whitney, Rex Brandt, George Post & Carl Molno. *Work:* Smithsonian Inst & Pentagon Bldg, DC; Craft Students League, New York. *Exhib:* Artist of the Month, Brunswick, NJ, 70; Nat Arts Club, 15 Gramercy Pk, New York, 70-80; solo exhib, Art Asn Padukah, Ky, 75; Brooklyn Watercolor Soc, Brooklyn Mus, NY, 76 & Metrop Mus Art, New York, 77; NJ Watercolor Soc, Morristown, NJ Mus, 77-79; Princeton Art Asn, McCarter Theatre, NJ, 80. *Pos:* Draftsman & sr artist, Ford Instrument Co, New York, 60-63; demonstr & lectr, Nat Arts Club, 72, 74 & 78, Metrop Mus Art, New York, 72-80 & Catharine Lorillard Wolfe Art Club Inc, 74. *Teaching:* Lectr landscapes & portraits, Craft Students League, New York, 69-80; demonstr design, figures & flowers, Nat Art League New York, 71-80; instr watercolors, New York Botanica Gardens, 72-77. *Awards:* Seven Scholarships, Washington Sq Outdoor Art Show, 65-69; Four First Prizes, Jackson Heights Art Club, New York, 68-71. *Mem:* Catharine Lorillard Wolfe Art Club (co-chmn, 66-70); Nat Art League NY; Artists Equity; Brooklyn Watercolor Soc; Island Art Guild; and others. *Media:* Watercolor, Pen & Ink. *Publ:* Auth & illusr, Watercolor Workbook (manual), Va Graphics, 74 & 76. *Mailing Add:* 42-42 80 St Apt 7P Elmhurst NY 11373

SEHRING, ADOLF
PAINTER, SCULPTOR
b Urupino, Russia, June 8, 30; US citizen. *Study:* Berlin Acad Art, 46-49. *Work:* Chrysler Mus, Norfolk; Bayly Mus, Va; St Mary's Inst, Mich; US Dept State Embassy, Rome & London; Mellon Collection, Pa. *Comn:* Portrait of Pope John Paul II, St Mary's Inst Eastern Art (Now in the Vatican Collection, Rome), 78. *Exhib:* Youth Paints, Victoria & Albert Mus, London, Eng, 47; Qualite dela Vie, Grandpalais Salon, Paris, 75; Virginia Scene, Bayly Mus, Charlottesville, 78; Adolf Sehring, St Mary's Collection Mus, Mich, 78; Biannual Exhib, Va Mus Art, Richmond, 81; Chrysler Mus, 83. *Pos:* Lectr, Lehigh Valley Art Groups, 75; lectr, Varied Civic Groups, 72-81. *Awards:* First Prize of Germany, Rias, Berlin, 46. *Bibliog:* Levin Houston (auth), Adolf Sehring and Realism, Kembel Publ, 77; S Bullard (auth), Sehring Paints, Daily Progress, 78; Rome Accepts Papal Portrait by Sehring, Associated Press, 78; The Real World of A Sehring, English/Japanese. *Mem:* NY Artist's Equity Asn. *Media:* Oil, Watercolor; Bronze, Lithographs. *Mailing Add:* Tetley Plantation Somerset VA 22972

SEIDE, PAUL A
SCULPTOR
b New York, NY, Feb 15, 49. *Study:* Egani Neon Glassblowing Sch, cert, 71; Univ Wis, BS(art), 74. *Work:* Nat Mus Mod Art, Kyoto, Japan; Corning Mus Glass, Corning, NY; Chrysler Mus Art, Norfolk, WVa; Mus des Arts Decoratifs, Lausanne, Switz; Lannan Found Mus, Palm Beach, Fla; and others. *Exhib:* One-man exhib, Heller Gallery, New York, 82, 84 & 88, Kurland Summers Gallery, Los Angeles, Calif, 84 & 86 & Habatat Galleries, Bay Harbour Islands, Fla, 85 & 87; Corning Mus Glass, NY, 78-79; Leigh Yawkey Woodson Art Mus, Wausau, Wis, 79, 81 & 88; Hokkaido Mus Mod Art, Sapporo, Japan, 82; Illumination: The Quality of Light, Pittsburgh Ctr for the Arts, Pa, 85; Luminosity, The Alternative Mus, New York, 86; The Saxe Collection, Mus Am Craft, New York, 87; Light and Transparency, Mus Bellerive, 88 & Illuminated Sculpture, Sanske Gallerie, 88, Zurich, Switz; Expressions en Verre II, Musee des Artes Decoratifs, Lausanne, Switz; Building a Permanent Collection, Mus Am Craft, New York, 90. *Pos:* Design dir & vpres, Milropa Studios, New York, 75- *Teaching:* Instr, Milropa Studios, New York, 75-76 & New Sch Social Res, New York, 76-77. *Awards:* Res Grant, Union Molycorp, Los Angeles, 82. *Bibliog:* Judy Spurgin (auth), article, Art Craft Mag, 10-11/80; Sylvia Netzer (auth), Rays of Glass-Paul Siede, Neus Glas Mag, 3/88. *Mem:* Glass Art Soc. *Dealer:* Leo Kaplan Mod Art 969 Madison Ave New York NY 10021; Kurland Summers Gallery 8742A Melrose Ave Los Angeles CA 90069. *Mailing Add:* 29 W 17th St New York NY 10011

SEIDEN, ARTHUR
PAINTER, ILLUSTRATOR
b Brooklyn, NY. *Study:* Queens Col, BA(cum laude), 74; Art Students League, 8 yrs study with Will Barnet, S Dickinson, Charles Alston & Mario Cooper; New Sch, with Stuart Davis. *Work:* Kerlan Collection, Univ Minn; Philip Morris Corp & Kennedy Gallery, New York; Rutgers Univ, New Brunswick, NJ. *Exhib:* Am Watercolor Soc, Nat Acad Design, New York, 64, 67 & 68; one-man show, Lotos Club, New York, 74; Union Carbide Bldg Gallery; Lotos Club, 75. *Teaching:* Guest instr, New York City Community Col. *Awards:* Bk Awards, Am Inst Graphic Arts, 54, 57 & 61. *Mem:* Am Watercolor Soc; life mem Lotos Club; life mem Art Students League; Artist's Equity NY Inc; Soc Illusr. *Media:* Transparent Watercolor. *Publ:* Illusr, Train to Timbuctoo, Golden Bks, 51; Greek Gods and Heroes, 61, Big Treasure Book of Fairy Tales, 64 & Big Book of Kittens, 68, Grosset & Dunlap; Doc stops a war, Reader's Digest. *Mailing Add:* 380 Howard Ave Woodmere NY 11598

SEIDEN, KATIE
SCULPTOR, ASSEMBLAGE ARTIST
b New York, NY. *Study:* Sarah Lawrence Col, Bronxville, NY, BA, 58; New York Univ, New York, NY, MA, 60. *Work:* House of Humor & Satire, Gabrova, Bulgaria; Grand Manan Mus, New Brunswick, Can; Wash Co Mus Fine Arts, Hagerstown, Md; Helen S Keller Nat Ctr, Kingspoint, NY; Saint Mary Abbey, Mechanicsville, Md; Islip Art Mus, E Islip, Mid-Houston Arts & Sci Ctr, Poughkeepsie, NY. *Comn:* Sculpture (3 feet), comn by Mr & Mrs David Wood, Berkeley, Calig, 84; sculpture (7 feet), comn by Stephen Style, New York, 85. *Exhib:* Solo exhibs, Edward Williams Gallery, Hackensack, NJ, 84, Cent Hall Gallery, Soho, New York, 79, 82, 84, Five & Dime, East Village, NY, 87, Wash Co Mus Fine Arts, Hagerstown, Md, 88 & Sensory Evolution Gallery, NY, 87 & 88, San Francisco Int Airport, Calif, 88 & Myth & Reality, Gallery 10, Washington, DC, 90; Lines of Vision I: Drawings by Contemporary Women Traveling Exhib, Islip Art Mus, E Islip, NY, 92, ARC Gallery, Chicago, 92; Lines of Vision II: Drawings by Contemporary Women, US Info Agency Traveling Exhib, 89-90; Centennial Exhib Nat Asn Women Artists Traveling Exhib, 89- 90; The Expressionist Surface & Contemporary Art in Plaster, Queens Mus, Flushing, NY, 90; Original Sin, Hillwood Art, Brookville, NY, 91. *Pos:* Arts ed & critic, Boulevard Mag, 87, 88 & 89; Exec ed & critic, Country Plaza Mag, 89, 90 & 91; arts ed & reviewer, The Gold Coast Gazette, Glen Cove, NY, 91- *Awards:* Artists Grant, Artist Space, New York, 88-91; Puffin Found, 92; NY Found for the Arts & E End Arts Coun, 92. *Bibliog:* Michael Brenson (auth), Sculpture that springs from surrealism, The Sunday New York Times, 3/8/87; Karin Lipson (auth), Katie Seiden - The Outpost Artist, Newsday, 6/1/87; Diane Ketchum (auth), Katie Seiden - About Long Island, 12/4/88; Barbara Matilsky (auth), The Expressionist Surface: Contemporary Art in Plaster-Katie Seiden (exhib catalog), 90; Michael Brenson (auth), Plaster as a medium, not just an interim step, New York Times, 7/13/90. *Mem:* Nat Asn Women Artists; Hempstead Harbor Artists (bd mem, 84-85); Women's Caucus Arts. *Media:* Plaster, Miscellaneous Media. *Publ:* Auth, article, Central Hall Artists Newsletter, 76; Women Artists News, Midmarch Asn, 77; illusr, Sinister Wisdom, 84; feature art exhib (monthly), Boulevard Mag, 87, 88 & 89; illustr, Spiral Though, Front Cover, 89. *Dealer:* Country Art Gallery Locust Valey NY; Sensory Evolution Gallery 420 E 13th St East Village NY. *Mailing Add:* 52 Cromwell Pl Sea Cliff NY 11579

SEIDL, CLAIRE
PAINTER, PRINTMAKER
b Greenwich, Conn, May 17, 51. *Study:* London Polytech, Sir John Cass Col Art, 72; Syracuse Univ, Col Visual & Performing Arts, BFA(cum laude), 73; City Univ New York, Hunter Col, MFA, 82. *Work:* Albright Col, Pa; Aldrich Mus, Conn; Gen Instrument Corp & Mobil Oil Corp, New York; Richardson-Vicks Corp, Conn; and others. *Exhib:* Solo exhibs, Contemp Arts Gallery, Loeb Ctr, New York Univ, 75, Freedman Gallery, Albright Col, Reading, Pa, 79, 22 Wooster Gallery, New York, 81, Hunter Gallery, New York, 82 & John Davis Gallery, Akron, Ohio, 83 & 85; A Look Forward-A Look Back, 82, The Art of the 70's and 80's, 85 & Recent Acquisitions, 86, Aldrich Mus, Ridgefield, Conn; Avida Dollars Gallery, Milan, Italy, 84; Collector's Gallery, McNay Art Mus, San Antonio, Tex, 86; Space, Scale, Structure, Ben Shahn Galleries, William Paterson Col, Wayne, NJ, 89; Hunter Col Faculty Exhib, Hunter Col, New York, 89. *Teaching:* Vis artist, Ill State Univ, 84 & Syracuse Univ, NY, 85 & 86; instr, Hunter Col, City Univ, NY, 85-90. *Awards:* Nancy Ashton Mem Fund Prize, 82; William Graf Fel, 82; Fel, Cummington Community of the Arts, 83. *Bibliog:* Valentin Tatransky (auth), Ten downtown, Arts Mag, 9/78; Jacqueline Moss (auth), The symphonic interplay of looking at the '60's and '70's, 3/21/82; Marina Vaizey in Berlin: New work--New York, London Sunday Times, 10/30/83; John Yau (auth), article, 12/84 & Stephen Westfall (auth), article, 2/85, Arts Mag; Benjamin Forgey (auth), article, Washington Post, 7/20/85. *Mem:* 22 Wooster (treas, 79-80). *Media:* Oils; Lithography. *Dealer:* John Davis Gallery 61 S Main St Akron OH 44308; Stephen Rosenberg Gallery 115 Wooster St New York NY 10012. *Mailing Add:* c/o Stephen Rosenberg Gallery 115 Wooster St New York NY 10012

SEIDLER, DORIS
PAINTER, PRINTMAKER
b London, Eng. *Study:* Atelier 17, New York, with Stanley William Hayter. *Work:* Smithsonian Inst, Washington, DC; Philadelphia Mus Art; Brooklyn Mus; Seattle Mus Art; Whitney Mus Am Art, New York; British Mus, London, Eng; Pallant House Col, Chichester, Eng. *Exhib:* Vancouver Int Print Exhib; First & Second Hawaii Nat Print Exhib, Honolulu Acad Arts; Pa Acad Fine Arts, Philadelphia; Soc Am Graphic Artists, Kennedy Gallery, 71;

Jewish Mus, New York; Atelier 17, Brooklyn Mus, 78; Whitney Mus Am Art; Libr Cong, Washington, DC; Nassau Co Mus Fine Art, NY; Pallant House, Chichester, Eng, 91. *Awards:* MacDowell Artists Colony Fel, 66 & 75; Purchase Award, Brooklyn Mus, 68; Medal for Creative Graphics, Audubon Artists, 72; awards, Soc Am Graphic Artists, 82, 83 & 85. *Mem:* Soc Am Graphic Artists (rec secy, 64-71, vpres, 81). *Media:* Acrylic, oil; All Media. *Publ:* Auth, articles in Artist Proof. *Dealer:* Anita Shapolsky Gallery 99 Spring St New York NY 10012. *Mailing Add:* 14 Stoner Ave Great Neck NY 11021

SEKIGUCHI, RISA
PAINTER
b Yokosuka, Japan, Feb 28, 62; US citizen. *Study:* Art Inst Chicago, BFA, 84. *Work:* City of Chicago, Harold Washington Libr; First Nat Bank Chicago; Mus Contemp Art, Chicago. *Exhib:* Solo Exhibs, Amano Gallery, Osaka, Japan, 86, CompassRose Gallery, Chicago, 89, Chicago Cult Ctr, 92 & Betsy Rosenfield Gallery, Chicago, 93; Towards the Future: Contemporary Art in Context, Mus Contemp Art, Chicago, 90; Silent Dramas: Paintings by L J Douglas, David Hodges & Risa Sekinguchi, Rockford Art Mus, Ill, 91; From America's Studio: Drawing New Conclusions, Betty Rymer Gallery, Sch Art Inst Chicago, 92; May 1992, Betsy Rosenfield Gallery, Chicago Int Art Expo, 92; six person show, Betsy Rosenfield Gallery, Chicago, 92; Small, Really Small, Tiny, Steibel Mod, New York, 92; and others. *Awards:* Individual Artist Fel, Ill Arts Coun, 86 & 88; Visual Arts Fel Award, Arts Midwest/Nat Endowment Arts Regional, 88-89. *Bibliog:* Sue Taylor (auth), Risa Sekiguchi at CompassRose Gallery, Art Am, 11-12/89; Joe Scanlan (auth), Risa Sekiguchi, Artscribe, 11-12/89; Garrett Holg (auth), Risa Sekiguchi at the Chicago Cultural Center, Art News, summer 92. *Media:* Oil on Board. *Mailing Add:* c/o Betsy Rosenfield Gallery 212 W Superior St Chicago IL 60610

SELBY, PATRICIA LOUISE
PAINTER, INSTRUCTOR
b Ronceverte, WVa, Nov 14, 44. *Study:* Spec educ classes, Univ of Akron, 78; Workshop, Al Brouilette, 84, Carole Barns, 92; Irving Shipero, 83; Maxsine Masterfield, 82. *Work:* Akron General Med Ctr, Ohio; Brecksville Schools System, Ohio. *Exhib:* 52nd Area Artist Ann, Butler Inst Am Art, Youngstown, Ohio; Midwest Watercolor Soc, 80; Nat Miniature, Gallery La Luz, NMex, 81, 83, 91; Mont Nat Miniature, Billings, 83, 84, 85; Ohio Regional, Cuyahoga Valley Art Ctr, Cuyahoga Falls, 89; Festival of Flowers, Cuyahoga Valley Art Ctr, Cuyahoga Falls, 91. *Pos:* Pres, Cuyahoga Valley Art Ctr, Cuyahoga Falls, Ohio, 77-87; secy, Front St Merchants Asn, Cuyahoga Falls, Ohio, 85-87. *Teaching:* Drawing & painting, Cuyahoga Valley Art Ctr, Cuyahoga Falls, Ohio, 87-; drawing & painting, Akron, Ohio, 88- *Awards:* Third Place, Nat Miniature, Gallery La Luz, 81 & 83; Second Place, Ohio Regional Exhib Cuyahoga Valley Art Ctr, 86; First Award, 52nd Area Artist Ann, Mahoning Co Watercolor Soc, 90. *Bibliog:* Directory Regional Artists, Am Art, 91. *Mem:* Life mem, Cuyahoga Valley Art Ctr (pres, 77-87); life mem, Whiskey America; Women's Art League Akron; assoc mem, Am Watercolor Soc. *Media:* Mixed. *Dealer:* Lock Loft Gallery Box 21 Elkton OH 44415. *Mailing Add:* 3191 Elmo St Akron OH 44319

SELBY, ROGER LOWELL
ADMINISTRATOR, MUSEUM DIRECTOR
b Philadelphia, Pa, July 4, 33. *Study:* Univ Md, AB, 60; Claremont Grad Sch, 61; Ind Univ, 65; Univ NMex, with Beaumont Newhall, 84. *Pos:* Cur educ, Nat Gallery Art, 61-62, Corcoran Gallery Art, Washington, DC, 65-68, Wadsworth Atheneum, Hartford, Conn, 68-74; dir, Winnipeg Art Gallery, Man, 74-83 & Boca Raton Mus Art, Fla, 84- *Teaching:* Instr art hist, Grad Sch US Dept Agr, 61-63, Corcoran Sch Art, Washington, DC, 65-68 & Hartford Art Sch, Conn, 69-71. *Awards:* Queens Silver Jubilee Medal, Can Govt, 78; Hon Prof, Univ Winnipeg, Man, 79-83. *Bibliog:* Sally Calhoun (auth), On the edge of vision, Mus News, 4/74; Newsom & Silver (editors), The Art Museum as Educator, Univ Calif Press, 78. *Mem:* Am Mus Asn. *Publ:* Auth, Contemporary Posters in America, USIA, 69; coauth, Professional Practice & Ethics in Art Museums, Can Art Mus Dir Orgn, 76; auth, By-laws for volunteer groups, Mus News, 77; Director's Report, Winnepeg Art Gallery, 77-83. *Mailing Add:* 801 W Palmetto Park Rd Boca Raton FL 33432

SELCHOW, ROGER HOFFMAN
PAINTER, SCULPTOR
b Greenwich, Conn, Feb 13, 11. *Study:* Grand Cent Sch Art, New York; Columbia Univ; also with Dong Kingman; Acad Grande Chaumiere, Paris; also with Andre Lhote & Fernand Leger, Paris; Inst Statale d'Arte, Florence, Italy. *Work:* Mus Beaux-Arts, Liege, Belg; Wadsworth Atheneum; NY Univ; Brooklyn Mus; Metrop Mus Art, New York; plus others. *Exhib:* Groupe Espace Paris, Vaison-la-Romaine, France, 59; Vingt-Ans d'APIAW, Mus Beaux Arts, Liege, Belg, 65; retrospective, Bruce Mus, Greenwich, Conn, 69; Images Gallery, New York, 83; Isoa Gallery Group, Grennwich, Conn, 83. *Pos:* Dir, Atelier Vieux Vaison, Vaison-la-Romaine, France, 53-60. *Awards:* Two First Place Medals, Grand Cent Sch Art, 33; First Prize, Greenwich Soc Artists, 54. *Bibliog:* Robert Vrinat (auth), Portrait d'Artiste--Selchow, Actualite Artistique Paris, 4/53; Gilbert Chaboud (auth), Un Americain Vaisonnais: Selchow, Le Meridionale-La France Orange, 3/55. *Media:* Oil, Watercolor; Electro-Wire. *Dealer:* Raydon Gallery 1091 Madison Ave New York NY 10028; Isoa Gallery 151 Clapboard Ridge Rd Greenwich CT 06830. *Mailing Add:* 5 E 22nd St Apt 7C New York NY 10010

SELIG, (MR & MRS) MANFRED
COLLECTORS, PATRONS
b Ger, Feb, 09. *Exhib:* Henry Art Gallerie; Seattle Fry Mus. *Bibliog:* Michael Brenson (auth), New York Times, 12/16/88. *Collection:* Old and modern paintings; graphic art. *Mailing Add:* 803 32nd Ave S Seattle WA 98144

SELIGER, CHARLES
PAINTER
b New York, NY, June 3, 26. *Work:* Metrop Mus Art, Mus Mod Art, Solomon R Guggenheim Mus & Whitney Mus Am Art, New York; Hirshhorn Mus, Washington, DC. *Exhib:* One-man shows, Andrew Crispo Gallery, New York, 74-81; Intimate Abstractions, Jacksonville Art Mus, Jacksonville, Fla, 81; The Soloman R Guggenheim Mus, NY, 86; Gallery Schlesinger-Boisante, New York, 85, 86, 87 & Galerie Lopes, Beethovenstrasse 7, Zurich, Switz, 86, 89, 90; Nature into Art, Munson-Williams-Proctor Inst, Utica, NY, 87; Peggy Guggenheim's Other Legacy, The Soloman R Guggenheim Mus, NY, 87; Visions of Inner Space, Univ Calif, Los Angeles, Wight Art Gallery, Los Angeles and Nat Gallery of Mod Art, New Delhi, India, 87-88; Abstract Expressionism: Other Dimensions, Jane Voorhees Zimmerli Art Mus, Rutgers Univ, NJ, and the Whitney Mus Am Art at Philip Morris, New York, 90. *Pos:* Distinguished vis prof, Robert H & Clarice Smith, George Washington Univ, 41-90; lectr, Katonah Art Mus, Katonah, NY, 4/90; panelist, Terra Mus Am Art, Chicago, 2/90; Whitney Mus Am Art, Philip Morris, New York, 11/90. *Bibliog:* Addison Parks (auth), Through the keyhole: some meaning and method to Charles Seliger, Arts Mag, 6/80. *Media:* Oil, Acrylic. *Dealer:* Galerie Lopes Agency Beethovenstrasse 7 Zurich Switzerland; Michael Rosenfeld Gallery New York NY. *Mailing Add:* 10 Lenox Ave Mt Vernon NY 10552

SELIGMAN, THOMAS KNOWLES
DIRECTOR
b Santa Barbara, Calif, Jan 1, 44. *Study:* Stanford Univ, BA, 65; Acad of Art Col, San Francisco, BFA, 67; Sch of Visual Arts, New York, MFA, 68. *Collections Arranged:* Eskimo Art from the Toronto-Dominion Bank, 72, Man and Animals in Pre-Columbian Mesoamerica, 73, Australian Aboriginal Art from the Louis Allen Collection, 74, African & Ancient Mexican Art-The Loran Collection (coauth, catalog), 74-75, Fire, Earth & Water-Sculpture from the Land Collection of Mesoamerican Art (ed, catalog), Honolulu Acad of Arts & Seattle Art Mus, 75 & Masterpieces of Primitive Art from the Museum of Primitive Art in New York, 77, San Francisco Mus Fine Arts; Form & Freedom, Rice Inst Arts; The Art of Being Huichol, Field Mus, Chicago & Am Mus Natural Hist, New York; Treasures of Ancient Nigeria, co-organized with Detroit Inst Arts & Metrop Mus Art, 78-80; Bay Area Collects (coauth, catalog); Spirits, Gods and Kings; Forms and Forces: Dynamics of African Figurative Sculpture (coauth, catalogue), 88. *Pos:* Dir, Africana Mus, Liberia, Africa, 69-71; deputy dir educ & exhibs, Fine Arts Mus of San Francisco, 72-89; deputy dir operations and planning, Fine Arts Mus of San Francisco, 89-; dir, Stanford Univ Mus Art, 91- *Teaching:* Asst prof African art hist, Cuttington Col, Liberia, Africa, 69-71. *Awards:* Aid to Mus Prof Award, Nat Endowment for the Arts, 75, 87. *Mem:* Am Asn Mus; Friends of Ethnic Arts (dir, 74-); Am Fedn Arts (trustee & vpres); Cult Property Adv Comt to Pres of US, 88-92. *Res:* African aesthetics; art in context in Liberia, Sierra Leone and Ivory Coast, Tuareg art of Niger and Algeria. *Publ:* Auth, African art at the M H de Young Memorial Museum, African Arts, Univ Calif, Los Angeles, Vol 7 (4); Educational use of an anthropology collection in an art museum, Curator, fall 74; An indigenous concept of fakes--authentic African art?, African Arts, Univ Calif, Los Angeles, Vol 9 (3); An Unexpected Bequest and an Ethical Dilemma featuring serpents and flowering trees, Fine Arts Mus of San Francisco, 88. *Mailing Add:* Stanford Univ Mus Art Stanford CA 94305-5060

SELLA, ALVIN CONRAD
PAINTER, EDUCATOR
b Union City, NJ, Aug 30, 24. *Study:* Yale Univ Sch Art; Art Students League, with Brackman & Bridgman; Columbia Univ, with Machau; Col Fine Arts, Syracuse Univ; Univ NMex; also in Mex. *Work:* Bristol Iron & Steel Co; Collectors of Am Art; Sullins Col. *Exhib:* Am Fedn Arts Traveling Exhib, 61-62; one-man exhibs, Centenary Col, Lauren Rogers Mus Art, Laurel, Miss, Munic Art Gallery, Jackson, Miss & Birmingham Mus Art, Ala, 69 & Dick Jemison Gallery, Birmingham, 76; Birmingham Mus Art, 76; Watercolor Soc Ala, 76; Frank Fedele Fine Art, 84-86; Univ Ark, 85; and others. *Teaching:* Head, Dept Art, Sullins Col, 48-61; prof art, Univ Ala, 61-; vis prof, Spring Workshops, Miss Art Colony, 62-64 & Shreveport Art Colony, 64-68; artist in residence, Summer Sch Arts, Univ SC, 68. *Awards:* First Award, 54th Ann Miss Exhib; Third Prize, 7th Mobile Art Exhib, 72; 32nd Ann Watercolor Exhib First & Second Prize, Birmingham Mus Art, 72. *Mem:* Art Students League; Am Asn Univ Prof; Col Art Asn Am; fel Int Inst Arts & Lett. *Media:* Miscellaneous. *Mailing Add:* Dept of Art Univ of Ala University AL 35486

SELLERS, JOHN LEWIS
EDUCATOR, DESIGNER
b Alexander City, Ala, Aug 28, 34. *Study:* Auburn Univ, BAA; Peabody Col, MA; also with Maltby Sykes for printmaking & Harry Lowe for painting. *Pos:* Art dir, Motive Mag, Nashville, Tenn, 65-67; assoc creative designer, McDonald & Saussy Agency, Inc, Nashville, 65-68; partner & creative dir, Les Hart Agency, Inc, Nashville, 68-70; art dir, Syracuse Scholar, 79-85, ed, 85-; co-dir, Drawing Nat, Everson Mus, 85-86. *Teaching:* Prof, Col Visual & Performing Arts, Syracuse Univ, 73-, chmn dept visual commun, 78-, chmn, Independent Study MFA progs, 73- *Awards:* Magazine of the Year Award Runner Up, Mag Publ Asn, Mag Ed Asn & Columbia Univ Sch Journalism, 67; Best US Travel Brochure, Int Asn Travel Agents, 68; Merit Awards, NY Art Dir Club, 80, 82, 84 & 86. *Bibliog:* Don Barron (auth), Syracuse U: Preparation for the big world, Art Direction, 10/76; Jo Yanow (auth), John Sellers: The professional as educator, Graphics Today, Spring, 77; Paul Palange (auth), A teacher first, Syracuse Alumni Mag, Fall 77. *Mem:* Art Dirs Club New York; Am Inst Graphic Arts. *Res:* Creativity; Strategy. *Mailing Add:* Syracuse Univ Visual Commun 102 Shaffer Syracuse NY 13244-1210

SELLERS, WILLIAM FREEMAN
SCULPTOR
b Bay City, Mich, June 1, 29. *Study:* Univ Mich, BA, 54, MFA, 62. *Work:* Suspension, Six Cubes & Converging Cubes, Mem Art Gallery, Rochester, NY. *Comn:* Four Squares (painted steel), Student Asn, State Univ New York, Cortland, 69; reprogression, Pyramid Art Ctr, Rochester, NY. *Exhib:* Sculpture & Prints Ann, Whitney Mus Am Art, New York, 66, Contemp Am Sculpture Ann, 68; Plus by Minus: Today's Half-Century, Albright-Knox Art Gallery, Buffalo, 68; American Sculpture of the Sixties, Grand Rapids Art Mus, Mich, 69; Painting and Sculpture Today, Indianapolis Mus Art, 70; Carleton Col, 81; Contemporary Sculpture, State Univ NY, 83; sculpture installation, Pyramid Arts Ctr, Rochester, NY, 87; working drawing & studies, Monroe Community Col, Rochester, NY, 87. *Teaching:* Instr design, Rochester Inst Technol, 62-65; asst prof sculpture, Univ Rochester, 66-70; asst prof art, Lehman Col, 70-, chmn dept art, 75-77; vis artist-teacher, Carleton Col, 81-; instr sculpture, Nazareth Col, 87. *Awards:* Jurors' Show Award, Mem Art Gallery, 66. *Media:* Metal, Wood. *Mailing Add:* 192 Abedeeb Rochester NY 14619

SELLIN, DAVID
LECTURER, CURATOR
b Philadelphia, Pa, Apr 13, 30. *Study:* Skolds Atelier, Stockholm, Sweden, 46-47; Univ Pa, BA, 52; Royal Acad Art, Stockholm, painting, 52-53; Univ Pa, MA, 56, PhD, 68; Univ Rome, Italy, 56-57; Univ Cologne, 67-68. *Collections Arranged:* American Art in the Making (auth catalog), Smithsonian Inst & circulated to nine mus, 76; Eakins, MacDowell and Kenton (consult & auth catalog), Northcross, Roanoke, Va, 77; Art and Architecture of the US Capitol, installed in Capitol, Washington, DC, 80-90; American Artists in Brittany and Normandy (auth, catalog), traveling to Pa Acad, Amon-Carter Mus, Ft Worth, Tex, Phoenix Art Mus, Ariz & Nat Mus Am Art, Washington, DC, 82-83. *Pos:* Asst cur, Philadelphia Mus Art, 58-60; dir schs, Pa Acad Fine Arts, 60-62; gallery dir, Colgate Univ, 63-67 & Wesleyan Univ, 70-72; spec cur, Smithsonian Inst, Washington, DC, 74-76; cur, Off Archit, US Capitol, Washington, DC, 76-80; guest cur, Phoenix Art Mus, 80-83; vis scholar, NPG/NMAA, Smithsonian Inst, 88-89; consult, Nat Hist Ladmarks, US Dept of Interior, 92. *Teaching:* Instr art hist, Univ Pa, 53-56; prof art hist, Pa Acad Fine Arts, 60-62; asst prof art hist, Colgate Univ, Hamilton, NY, 63-67; assoc prof, Wesleyan Univ, Middletown, Conn, 68-72; vis prof art hist, Newcomb Col, Tulane Univ, New Orleans, 67-68; distinguished vis prof, Univ Tex, Austin, 79; adj prof, Am Univ, DC, 79; vis prof, Univ Mass, Amherst, 83. *Awards:* King Gustav V Fel, 52; Fulbright-Hays Fel, Rome, 56; Smithsonian Inst Fel, 72. *Bibliog:* D Delouche (auth), Paintres Americans en Bretagne, Arts de L'Ouest, 83. *Mem:* Victorian Soc Am; Hist Soc Washington, DC (bd mem); Soc Arch Historians; Potomac Soc of Stereo Photographers; Cult Heritage Preserv Group. *Res:* Nineteenth century American art and its sources; French artist colonies. *Publ:* The First Pose: Eakins Roberts and the Nude in Philadelphia, Norton, 75; Americans in Brittany and Normandy, 1860-1910, Phoenix, 82; Robert Wylie et Pont-Aven, Pont-Aven, Arts de L'Ouest, 86; Childe Hassam a Pont-Aven, Arts de L'Ouest, 89; Innkeepers as Art Patrons: Pont-Aven, 19th Century, VSA, 92. *Mailing Add:* 1834 16th St NW Washington DC 20009

SELSER, CHRISTOPHER
DEALER, COLLECTOR
b Omaha, Nebr, Sept 15, 50. *Study:* Univ Ariz, BA, 77. *Collections Arranged:* 1000 Years Southwest Ceramic Art (auth, catalog), ACA Gallery, 81. *Pos:* Owner, Selser Gallery, Tucson; owner & dir, ACA Am Ind Arts, New York, formerly; Zaplin Lampert Gallery, Santa Fe, NMex. *Teaching:* Lect, New Sch, New York, 85. *Specialty:* American Indian Art. *Publ:* Auth, Navajo Weaving Tradition, E P Dutton, New York, 85. *Mailing Add:* PO Box 9328 Santa Fe NM 87504-9328

SELSOR, MARCIA LORRAINE
SCULPTOR, CERAMIST
b Philadelphia, Pa, Feb 1, 49. *Study:* Philadephia Univ Arts, BFA, 70; Southern Ill Univ, MFA, 74. *Work:* Northern Ariz Univ Galleries, Flagstaff; Yellowstone Art Ctr, Billings, Mont; Ill State Mus, Springfield; Mus Plastic Arts, Tumen, Russia; Mus Fine Art, Riga, Latvia. *Comn:* Raku plaques, Deaconess Med Ctr, Billings, Mont, 89. *Exhib:* Electrum , Holter Mus Art, Helena, Mont, 91; Western Ceramic Artists, N Ariz Univ Gallery, Flagstaff, 91; Dzintari Creative Arts, Ceramic Symp: Exhib Dzintari Creative Arts Ctr, Jurmala, Latvia, 91; solo exhibs, Marking the Millennium, Yellowstone Art Ctr, Billings, Mont, 91 & Recent Raku, Minot Art Gallery, NDak, 92; and others. *Pos:* Chairperson, Art Dept Eastern Mont Col, Billings, 87-92; vis artist, Dzintari Creative Arts Ctr Soviet Artists Union, 91 & Uzbekisani Artists Union, 92. *Teaching:* Prof ceramics, Eastern Mont Col, Billings, 75-92. *Awards:* Fulbright Scholar, US-Spaing Joint Comt Educ & Cult Exchange, 85-86; Merit Award, 12th Ann NDak Nat Juried, Minot Art Gallery, 89; Member of Doboshu, Northern Ariz Univ, 91. *Bibliog:* David Barnes (auth), Marcia Selsor, Ceramics Monthly, 2/92. *Mem:* Col Art Asn; Nat Coun Educ Ceramic Arts (dir-at-large, 90-91); Fulbright Asn; Am Anthropological Asn; Medieval Hispanists Soc. *Media:* Clay. *Dealer:* Toucan Gallery 2505 Montana Ave Billings MT 59101. *Mailing Add:* 703 Burlington Billings MT 59101-0298

SELTZER, JOANNE LYNN
PAINTER, PRINTMAKER
b Philadelphia, Pa, June 21, 46. *Study:* Northwestern Univ, cert, 63; Univ Mich, BFA(painting & ceramics), 69; New Sch Social Res, 73; Pratt Inst, 74; Pratt Graphics Ctr, 74; NY Univ, MA(photog), Parsons Sch Design, 86-88 (perspective & drawing). *Work:* Brookly Mus; Worcester Art Mus, Mass; Interlochen Ctr Arts, Mich; Sunrise Mus, Charleston, WVa; WVa State Mus, Charleston; Belgian Flemish Ministry Cul, Brussels; and others. *Exhib:* Travaux Sur Papier, Ctr Cult-Jacques Prevert, Paris, 81; Mapped Art, Charts, Roots, Regions traveling exhib, 81-83; Hundreds of Drawings, Artists Space, New York, 83; Independent Cur Benefit, 85; Works in the Space, permanent collection, Sunrise Mus, Charleston, WVa, 93; and others. *Pos:* Inst, Nat Soc Col Dames State New York-Art Archit & Decorative Arts Col Am, 86-88. *Teaching:* Guest lectr, Univ Iowa, 79, Univ Va, 79, Koninklijke Akad Bosch, Holland, 80 & 82, NY Univ, 81 & Drew Univ, 81. *Bibliog:* Peter Frank (auth), article, Art News, 9/76; Lucy Lippard (auth), From the Center, E P Dutton, 77; Jos Knaepen (auth), article, Bulletin, Belg, 1/22/82. *Mem:* New York Junior League. *Media:* Oil; Silkscreen-Serigraphy. *Publ:* Contribr, Mus J, Amsterdam, 76, Kunstlerinnen Int, 77 & Flash Art, 77. *Dealer:* Gallerie Yaki Kornblit Willemsparkweg 69 Amsterdam 1071 GS Holland. *Mailing Add:* 210 Centre St New York NY 10013

SELTZER, PHYLLIS
PAINTER, PRINTMAKER
b Detroit, Mich, May 17, 28. *Study:* Univ Iowa, BFA & MFA; Lasansky's Workshop, sr study hist of technol, with M Kranzberg; Case Western Reserve Univ. *Work:* Brooklyn Art Mus; Cleveland Mus Art; Minn Mus Art, Minneapolis; Nat Gallery Art, Ottawa, Ont; Butler Mus, Youngstown, Ohio; Cleveland Clinic, Ohio; Citibank, New York, NY; B P America, Cleveland, Ohio. *Comn:* Bicentennial print, Cleveland Area Arts Coun, 75; ed of 25, Exodus print, Cleveland Health Dept; elevators & etched mirrors, Stouffer's Inn on the Square, Cleveland, Ohio; Murals, Bistro des Artistes, Cleveland, Ohio. *Exhib:* May Show, Cleveland Mus Art, Ohio, 87 & 90 & Year in Review, 90; Fla Printmakers Soc Ann, Tampa, 89; Art Expo, New York, 90; New York, New York traveling, WGer, 90; NY Print Fair, 92; and others. *Pos:* Coordr fine arts, Cleveland Col, Case Western Reserve Univ, 66-70; interior designer, Dalton, Van Dijk, Johnson, Cleveland, 72-74; interior designer, 75-87. *Teaching:* Lectr art hist & printmaking, Lake Erie Col, Painesville, Ohio, 70-72; lectr art fund, Cleveland State Univ, 69-71. *Awards:* Purchase Award, Brooklyn Mus 19th Nat, 75; Tiffany Fel, Nat Congress Art & Design, 88; Artlink, 90. *Bibliog:* William Bierman (auth), Artist Improves on Technology, Akron Beacon J, 3/23/75; Helen Cullinan (auth), Venice is Source of Inspiration, Cleveland Plain Dealer, 8/7/88; Helen Cullinan (auth), A New Pespective on Spring Tradition, Cleveland Plain Dealer, 4/6/90. *Mem:* New Orgn Visual Arts (secy, 73, vpres, 74); Print Club Cleveland (pres, 83 & 84). *Media:* Oil; Heat Transfer Printing, Miscellaneous Media. *Publ:* Printworld, 83-87 & 90; Art Examiner, 90; An Illustrated Survey of Leading Contemporaries, Am Artists, 89 & 90; NY Gallery Guide, 90. *Dealer:* The Bonfoey Gallery Cleveland OH; John Szoke Gallery New York NY. *Mailing Add:* 1220 W Sixth St Cleveland OH 44113

SELVIG, FORREST HALL
HISTORIAN, WRITER
b Tacoma, Wash, Jan 3, 24. *Study:* Harvard Col, AB, 49; Univ Calif, Berkeley, 53-56. *Collections Arranged:* Selections From Richard Brown Baker Collection, 60; The Nabis, 61; Pavel Tchelitchew, 64; Jean Helion, 65; Charles Demuth (with catalog), 68; and others. *Pos:* Asst dir, Minneapolis Art Inst, Minn, 61-63; asst dir, Gallery Mod Art, New York, 63-65; dir, Akron Art Inst, 66-68; ed, New York Graphic Soc, Greenwich, Conn, 68-71. *Bibliog:* Ben Shahn Talks with Forrest Selvig, Arch Am Art J, Vol 17, 77. *Mem:* Am Asn Mus. *Res:* Late 19th century French painting, especially the Nabis and the Symbolists. *Publ:* Auth, The Nabis and Their Circle, 62; American Collections, 63; ed, 19th Century Landscape Painting, 71; Mosaic Deterioration and Preservation, 80; ed & trans, Views of Florence in 120 Paintings by Fabio Borbottoni, Firenze Perduta, 82. *Mailing Add:* 1580 Massachusetts Ave Apt 7-A Cambridge MA 02138

SELVIN, NANCY
CERAMIST, SCULPTOR
b Los Angeles, Calif, 1943. *Study:* Univ Calif, Berkeley, BA, 69, with Voulkos & Ron Nagle, MA, 70. *Work:* Kohler Art Gallery, Sheboygan, Wis; Oakland Mus, Calif; Hokkoku Shimbun, Tokyo; Ariz State Univ Art Gallery, Tempe; Calif Crafts Mus, Palo Alto; Los Angeles Mus Mod Art; Nora Eccles Mus, Utah. *Exhib:* Mus Contemp Crafts, New York, 76; San Francisco Mus, 77; Reality and Illusion, traveling, 79-80; Calif Crafts Mus, Palo Alto, 82; Scripps Col Gallery, Claremont, Calif, 82; Oxford Gallery, Eng, 83; Leverett Ctr, 88; Acad Art, Honolulu, 89; Grossmont Col, El Cajon, Calif, 90; Syboris Gallery, Detroit, 92; and others. *Teaching:* Instr ceramics, State Univ NY, Albany, 70-72; dir, After Sch Art, 86-, San Francisco State Univ, 92. *Awards:* Craftsman Fel, 80 & Artist Fel, 88, Nat Endowment Arts; Skaggs Found Prog Develop Grant, 86; Business Arts Award, Oakland, 90. *Bibliog:* Suanne Muchnic (auth), article, Los Angeles Times, 12/18/81; Elaine Levin (auth), Ceramic metaphors, Artweek, 12/23/81 & History American Ceramics; Melinda Levine (auth), Parallel views, Am Craft, 4/82. *Mem:* Nat Coun Educ Ceramics Arts; Pro-Arts (pres & bd dirs); Pub Art Adv Comt, Oakland. *Media:* Mixed. *Publ:* Auth, Bulmer brick & tile, Am Craft, 6-7/83; How I Got Here, Ceramics, 11/89. *Mailing Add:* 745 Page St Berkeley CA 94710

SELZ, PETER H
HISTORIAN, CURATOR
b Munich, Ger, Mar 27, 19. *Study:* Univ Chicago, fel, 46-54, MA & PhD; Univ Paris, Fulbright Award, 49-50; Calif Col Arts & Crafts, hon DFA, 67. *Collections Arranged:* Directions In Kinetic Sculpture (catalog), 65; Funk (catalog), 67; Richard Lindner, 69; Pol Bury, 70; Excellence, 70; Harold Paris (catalog), 72; Ferdinand Hodler (catalog), 72; The American Presidency in Political Cartoons (coauth, catalog), 76; German and Austrian Expressionism (catalog), 78; Two Decades of American Painting: 1920-1940 (catalog),

Dusseldorf, Zurich & Brussels, 79; and many others. *Pos:* Head art educ prog, Inst Design, Ill Inst Technol, 53-55; chmn dept art & dir art gallery, Pomona Col, 55-58; chief cur painting & sculpture exhibs, Mus Mod Art, 58-65; dir, Univ Art Mus, Univ Calif, Berkeley, 65-73; ed, Art Am; mem consult comt, Art Quart; proj dir, Christo's Running Fence Project, Calif, 74-76. *Teaching:* Asst prof art hist, Inst Design, Univ Chicago, 53-54; chmn, Art Dept, Pomona Col, 55-58; prof art hist, Univ Calif, Berkeley, 65-88. *Awards:* Belg-Am Educ Found Fel, 53; Order of Merit, Fed Ger Repub, 63; Sr Fel, Nat Endowment Humanities, 72; and others. *Mem:* Col Art Asn Am (dir, 59-68). *Publ:* Auth, Max Beckmann, 64; Art in a Turbulent Era, 65; Art in Our Times, 81; Sam Francis, second ed, 82; Chilida, 86; and others. *Mailing Add:* Dept Art Hist Univ Calif Berkeley CA 94720

SEMAK, MICHAEL
PHOTOGRAPHER, EDUCATOR
b Welland, Ont, Jan 9, 34. *Study:* Ryerson Polytech Inst, Toronto, cert archit technol, 59. *Work:* Nat Gallery Can, Pub Arch, Ottawa; George Eastman House, Rochester, NY; Mus Mod Art, New York. *Comn:* Photographing Canada, Nat Film Bd, Ottawa, 64, 66, 67, 72 & 74; Photographing Tunisia, Nat Geog Soc, Washington, DC, 67; Photographing WVa, Time-Life Bks, New York, 68; Photographing Italy, Can Coun, Ottawa, 71; Photographing USSR, York Univ, Toronto, 75. *Exhib:* Ghana Image 4, Nat Film Bd, Ottawa, 69; Ghetto, New Sch Social Res, New York, 70; Mixed Subjects, Image Gallery, New York, 71; Italy 1971, Il Diaframma Gallery, Milan, 73; Mixed Subjects, Deja Vue Gallery, Toronto, 75. *Pos:* Toronto chmn interarts, Canada-USSR Asn, 73- *Teaching:* Lectr photog, Visual Arts Dept, Fac Fine Arts, York Univ, Toronto, 71-73, asst prof, 73-76, assoc prof, 77- *Awards:* Gold Medal for Photog Excellence for Ghana Show, Nat Film Bd, 69; Award of Excellence in Photo-Jour, Pravda Newspaper, Moscow, 70 & 72; Excellence Int Fedn Photog Arts Dipl, Switz, 72. *Bibliog:* Don Long (auth), Tell a story, Can Photo Ann, 75. *Mem:* Royal Can Acad Art. *Publ:* Ed, Concerned photographer, Popular Photog, 70; Semak portfolio, Creative Camera, 70 & 73, Camera Can, 71 & Nuova Fotografia, 73; co-auth, Michael Semak monograph, Impressions Mag, 74; and others. *Mailing Add:* 1796 Spruce Hill Rd Pickering ON L1V 1S4 Canada

SEMANS, JAMES HUSTEAD
PATRON
b Uniontown, Pa, May 30, 10. *Study:* Princeton Univ, AB; Johns Hopkins Univ, MD. *Pos:* Chmn bd trustees, NC Sch Arts, 64-81; bd mem, Mary Duke Biddle Found. *Publ:* Auth, Siena-Six Summers of Music, 74. *Mailing Add:* 1415 Bivins St Durham NC 27707

SEMCHISHEN, OREST M
PHOTOGRAPHER
b Mundare, Alta, Jan 9, 32. *Work:* Nat Film Bd, Can Coun Art Bank, Pub Archives, Ottawa; Edmonton Art Gallery, Alta; Nickle Art Mus, Calgary; Winnipeg Art Gallery, Can Ctr Archit, Montreal. *Comn:* Photog proj, Alta 75th Anniversary Comn, 80. *Exhib:* Byzantine Churches of Alta, Edmonton Art Gallery, 76, Confedn Art Gallery, Charlottetown, PEI, 77, Prov Mus, Edmonton, 81, and others; Banff Purchase, Glenbow Mus, Calgary, 79; Points of View: Photos of Architecture, Vancouver Art Gallery, BC, 81 & Mus de Beaux Arts, Montreal, 81. *Bibliog:* James Adams (auth), World through a radiologist's camera, Edmonton J, 81; Terry Fenton (auth), 4 Photographers, Update, Edmonton Art Gallery, 82. *Mem:* Friends Photog. *Publ:* Contribr, Byzantine Churches of Alberta, Edmonton Art Gallery, 76; contribr, The Banff Purchase, Banff Ctr, 79; contribr, Keepsake, Western Emerging Arts, 81. *Mailing Add:* 4208 - 109A St Edmonton AB T6J 2R8 Canada

SEMMEL, JOAN
PAINTER
b New York, NY, Oct 19, 32. *Study:* Cooper Union, dipl, 52; Art Students League, with Morris Kantor, 58-59; Pratt Inst, BFA, 63, MFA, 72. *Work:* Mus Contemp Art, Houston; Aldrich Mus, Ridgefield, Conn; Michener Collection, Mus Univ Tex, Austin; Newport Beach Mus; Chysler Mus, Norfolf, Va; and others. *Comn:* Portraits of: Rosemary MacNamara, Chris Connell, Evelyn Wexler, Robin Oz, Frank Oz, Taylor Reznick, Eric Nord & Pres of Vassar Col. *Exhib:* Solo exhibs, Maurice M Pine Pub Libr, Fairlawn, NJ, 85, Tomasulo Gallery, Union Col, Cranford, NJ, 85, Manhattanville Col, Purchase, NY, 85, Univ Missouri, St Louis, 86, Benton Gallery, Southhampton, NY, 87, Gruenebaum Gallery, New York, 87, East Hampton Ctr Contemp Art, NY, 89; Through the Looking Glass, Bernice Steinbaum Gallery, New York, 89; At the Waters Edge, Tampa Mus Art, Fla, 90; Nathan Contemp, New York, 90; Sex and Subtext, Ceres Gallery, 90; Gender & Representation, Zoller Gallery, Pa State, Univ Park, 90; Designing Women, Douglas Col, New Brunswick, NJ, 91; Greenville County Mus, SC, 91; State Univ NY, Albany, 92; Skidmore Col, Saratoga Springs, NY, 92. *Teaching:* Prof painting, Mason Gross Sch Art, Rutgers Univ. *Awards:* Off Educ EPDA Fel, 70-72; Creative Artists Pub Serv Prog Award, NY State Coun on Arts, 75-76; Nat Endowment Arts Grant, 80 & 85. *Bibliog:* Calvin Alberts (auth), Figure Drawing Comes to Life, Prentice-Hall, 2nd ed, NY, 1/87; Kenna Love (auth), Exposure (text, Arlene Raven & Betty Ann Brown), Newsage Press, 89; Judy Collishan VanWagoner, Lines of Vision (color reproduction), Hills Press, 89. *Mem:* Women in the Arts; Womens Ad Hoc Comt. *Media:* Oil. *Mailing Add:* 109 Spring St New York NY 10012

SEMOWICH, CHARLES JOHN
HISTORIAN, PAINTER
Study: State Univ NY, Binghamton, BA, 71; Cath Univ Am, MFA, 72; Int Col, PhD, 81; Woodstock Sch Art, NY, 89. *Work:* Roberson Ctr, Binghamton, NY; Woodstock Sch Art, NY; Print Club Albany, NY. *Exhib:* 36th Nat, Village Libr, Cooperstown, NY, 73; 23rd Cent Adirondack, Old Forge Ctr, NY, 76; Hudson River Watercolor, Woodstock, NY, 91; Schweinfurth Art Ctr, Auburn, NY, 92. *Collections Arranged:* Please Be Seated, Roberson Ctr, NY, 80; 16th Nat Print Show, Print Club Albany, NY, 89; D Lathrop Retrospective (with catalog), State Univ NY, Albany, 91; 17th Nat Print Exhib, Print Club Albany & Schenectady Mus, 92. *Pos:* Cur, Susquehanna Co Hist Soc, 76; pres, Print Club Albany, 88-; chmn, Mus Print Club Albany, 89-; mem, Mayor's Task Force Arts, Albany, 90-; book reviewer, Antiquer's Guide. *Teaching:* Adj, Empire State Col, 78- & Chautauqua Inst, NY, summers 88-90. *Awards:* NY State Fair Awards Art, 72. *Bibliog:* Article, Capital District Bus Rev, 1/18/92. *Mem:* Aerosciences Mus, Schenectady, NY, 90-; Empire State (chairperson, art comt); Capital Area Archivists (secy, 92); and others. *Media:* All Media. *Res:* American art, both fine and decorative; Joseph Antione Hekking; New York state furniture. *Publ:* Coauth, Technical Leaflet 116, Am Asn State Local Hist, 80; auth, Historical ceramics-Englebert, Bulletin NY State Archeol Soc, 80; American Furniture Craftsmen Working Prior to 1920, Greenwood, 84; co auth, Dorothy Lathrop-A Centenary Celebration State Univ, New York, 92. *Mailing Add:* 242 Broadway St Rensselaer NY 12144

SENDAK, MAURICE BERNARD
WRITER, ILLUSTRATOR
b Brooklyn, NY, June 10, 28. *Study:* Art Students League, 49-51. *Work:* Rosenbach Found, Philadelphia, Pa. *Exhib:* One-man show, Gallery Sch, Visual Arts, New York, 64; Ashmolean Mus, Oxford, Eng, 75; Morgan Libr, 88. *Pos:* Writer & illusr children's bks, 51-; Stage designer (costumes & sets), 80- *Awards:* Caldecott Award for Where the Wild Things Are, 63, In the Night Kitchen, 70 & Outside Over There, 81; Hans Christian Andersen Illusr Award, 70; Laura Ingalls Wilder Award, 83. *Publ:* Auth & illusr, Where the Wild Things Are, 63, In the Night Kitchen, 70 & Maurice Sendak's Really rosie: Starring the Nutshell Kids, Harper & Row, 75; illusr, Some Swell Pup, Farrar, Straus & Giroux, 76; ed, The Disney Poster Book, Crown, 77; auth & illusr, Seven Little Monsters, 77 & Outside Over There, 81, Harper & Row; auth, Caldecott & Co (a book of essays); illus, Dear Mili, 88. *Mailing Add:* 200 Chestnut Hill Rd Ridgefield CT 06877

SENIE, HARRIET
HISTORIAN, CRITIC
b New York, NY, Sept 23, 43. *Study:* Brandeis Univ, BA, 64; Hunter Col, New York, MA, 71; Inst Fine Arts, New York, PhD(art hist), 81. *Collections Arranged:* Fabric into Art Traveling Exhib (auth, catalog), 80, William King Traveling Exhib (auth, catalog), 80, South Africa-South Bronx (auth, catalog), 81 & Landscape-Sculpture (auth, catalog), Amelie A Wallace Gallery, State Univ NY, Old Westbury; Sculpture for Public Spaces (auth, catalog), Marisa del Re Gallery, 86; George Rickey: Projects for Public Sculpture (auth, catalog), Neuberger Mus, 87. *Pos:* Dir, Amelie A Wallace Gallery, State Univ NY, Old Westbury, 79-82; assoc dir, The Art Mus, Princeton Univ, 82-86; dir, Mus Studies Prog, City Col NY, 86- *Teaching:* Adj prof art hist, Hunter Col, 74-78; asst prof, State Univ NY, Old Westbury, 79-82; assoc prof, City Col NY, 86- *Awards:* Eisner Scholars Award, City Col, 89; Nat Endowment Asn Mus studies grant, 87; PSC-City Univ UNY Res Grant, 88 & 92. *Mem:* Col Art Asn; Am Asn Mus; Soc Am Art Historians; Am Studies Asn. *Res:* Public art and contemporary culture. *Publ:* The Tomb of Leo XI by Alessandro Algardi: Art Bull, 78; Urban Sculpture: Origins and New Approaches, 79, The Right Stuff, 84 & King's Kingdom, 86, Art News; co-ed & contribr, Critical Issues in Public Art, Art J, 89; Contemporary Public Sculpture: Tradition, Transformation and Controversy, Oxford Univ Press, 92; co-ed & contribr, Critical Issues in Public Art: Content, Context and Controversy, Harper Collins, 92. *Mailing Add:* 215 Sackett St Brooklyn NY 11231-3604

SENSEMANN, SUSAN
PAINTER, EDUCATOR
b Glen Cove, NY, Oct 6, 49. *Study:* Tyler Sch Art, Rome Italy, 70; Syracuse Univ, NY, BFA, 71; Tyler Sch Art, Philadelphia, MFA, 73. *Work:* Ill State Mus, Springfield; Southern Ill Univ Mus, Edwardsville; Lakeview Mus, Peoria, Ill; Univ Rochester, NY; Appalachian Col, Boone, NC. *Comn:* Five oil paintings, Ill Agricultural Asn, Bloomington, Ill, 79; two acrylic paintings, Hyatt Regency Hotel, Flint, Mich, 81; two watercolors, Western Hotels, Houston, Tex, 84; five paper pieces, Paper Press, Chicago, Ill, 84; two oils, IBM Tower, Atlanta, Ga, 88. *Exhib:* Women in Art, Col St Catherine, St Paul Minn, 90; Ill Painters, Western Ill Univ, Macomb, 92; Open Surface: Nardi, Sensemann, Tinsley, State Ill Gallery, Chicago, 92; Roy Boyd Gallery, Chicago, Ill, 92; Artemesia, Chicago, Ill, 92; and others. *Teaching:* Assoc prof, Univ Ill, Urbana, 73-81, Chicago, 81- *Awards:* Rice Award, Vicinity Show, Art Inst Chicago, 79; Capital Develop Bd, State Ill, 91. *Bibliog:* Giselle Atterberry (auth), Abstract Art in Chicago, New Art Examiner, 4/85; Alan Artner (auth), Sensemann puts the unseen of canvas, Chicago Tribune, 8/85; Kristen Schleifer (auth), Susan Sensemann Review, New Art Examiner, 6/92. *Media:* Oil. *Publ:* Patty Carroll, James Yood, Spirited Visions, Univ Ill Press, 91. *Mailing Add:* University of Illinois at Chicago PO Box 4348 Chicago IL 60680

SEPLOWIN, CHARLES JOSEPH
SCULPTOR
b New York, NY, July 19, 45. *Study:* Univ NH, BA(art); RI Sch Design, MFA(sculpture). *Work:* Municipal Fire House Ctr, New York; Titan Steel Corp, New York; Montclair State Col; Univ NH; Sherson-Hutton, NY. *Comn:* Gates, Caleia Fine Arts, Upper Montclair, NJ; One percent Prog for Art. *Exhib:* Aldrich Mus, 75; one-man show, Elizabeth Weiner Gallery, New York, 80; Sculpture Ctr, New York, 83; Cheltenham Art Ctr, Philadelphia, 83; Mus Mod Art Latin Am, Washington, DC, 83; Leslie Cecil Gallery, 86-;

Recent Acquisitions, Art Mus Ams, Washington, DC, 92; and others. *Teaching:* Assoc prof, Montclair State Col, 74- *Bibliog:* Articles in Craft Horizons, 8/74 & Arts Mag, 9/74. *Mailing Add:* 463 West St New York NY 10014

SEPPA, HEIKKI MARKUS
GOLDSMITH, EDUCATOR
b Sakkijarvi, Finland, Mar 8, 27; US citizen. *Study:* Georg Jensen Silversmiths, Copenhagen, 48-49; Cranbrook Acad Art, 60-61; Goldsmith Sch Helsinki, Cent Sch Indust Arts, Finland, Master Silversmith, 63. *Work:* Evansville Mus Sci & Art, Ind; Steinberg Gallery Art, Washington Univ, St Louis, Mo; Tex Tech Univ, Lubbock; Cranbrook Acad Art, Bloomfield Hills, Mich; St Louis City Art Mus. *Comn:* Over 200 pvt collections, St Louis area patrons, 65-78; The Search, W G Elliot Soc of Washington Univ, 69; Menorah Shaare Emeth Temple, St Louis, Mo, 80; Church St Michael & St George, 90. *Exhib:* The Metalsmith, Phoenix Art Mus, Ariz, 77; 3-Exhib, Burnaby Art Gallery, BC, 77; Goldsmiths Hall, London, Eng, 78; Schmuck Mus Pforzhaim, Ger, 79; solo shows, Ten Arrow, Cambridge, Mass, 82 & Wichita Arts Asn, 86. *Pos:* Head metal-arts studies, Art Ctr Sch, Louisville, Ky, 61-65; head metalsmithing, Sch Fine Arts, Washington Univ, 65-92. *Teaching:* Prof art metalsmithing, Washington Univ, St Louis, 65-92; prof emer, frequent workshop leader in prominent summer progs,penland, Haystack, Craft orgns & univs. *Awards:* Craftsman Fel, Nat Endowment for the Arts, 75; dipl for lifetime work in profession, Precious Metal Indust League of Finland; Col of Fellows, Am Crafts Coun, 87. *Bibliog:* Excellence, Am Craft Mag, 8/79; article, Form Mag, Seoul, Korea, 80; Washington Univ Mag, spring 81; and others. *Mem:* Soc NAm Goldsmiths; Am Crafts Coun; Soc NAm Silversmiths. *Media:* Gold, Silver. *Publ:* Article on roll printing, Artisan/Craftsman, Can Craft Asn, 70; Auth, Form Emphasis for Metalsmiths, Kent State Univ Press, 78; Chapter on Reticulation, In: Metals Technic, Brynmorgan Press, 92. *Mailing Add:* 8 Price Court St Louisc MO 63132

SERENYI, PETER
HISTORIAN, ADMINISTRATOR
b Budapest, Hungary, Jan 13, 31. *Study:* Dartmouth Col, AB, 57; Yale Univ, MA, 58; Washington Univ, PhD, 68. *Collections Arranged:* Contemporary Architecture in India, 76 & Le Corbusier in India, 80, Northeastern Univ Art Gallery & traveling; Hungarian Art: 1920-1970, Northeastern Univ Art Gallery, 81; Additions to Buildings: 1972-1982, 83 & Boston Architectural Competitions: 1960-1983, 84, Northeastern Univ Art Gallery & Boston Archit Ctr. *Teaching:* Chmn dept art & archit, Northeastern Univ, 81- *Awards:* Northeastern Univ Faculty Development Grant, 84-85; Smithsonian Inst Award, India, 84-85; Northeastern Univ Fac Develop Grant, 91; and others. *Mem:* Soc Archit Historians (vpres, New Eng chap, 77-78, pres, 78-79, dir, 79-82); Mass Comt Preserv Archit Records (dir, 79-81); Citizen Ambassador Prog Art Educ Deleg to People's Repub China, 91. *Res:* Le Corbusier; modern architecture in India. *Publ:* Auth, Le Corbusier, Fourier and the Monastery of Ema, Art Bull, 67; ed, Le Corbusier in Perspective, Prentice-Hall, 75; auth, Mies' New National Gallery, Harvard Archit Rev, 80; Le Corbusier's Architecture in India, Le Corbusier Archive, 83; Sixty years of housing in Delhi, Techniques et Architecture, 85. *Mailing Add:* Dept Art & Archit Northeastern Univ 360 Huntington Ave Boston MA 02115

SERISAWA, SUEO
PAINTER
b Yokohama, Japan, Apr 10, 10; US citizen. *Study:* Study with Yoichi Serisawa (father) & George Barker; Otis Art Inst. *Work:* Metrop Mus Art, New York; Los Angeles Co Mus Art; Santa Barbara Mus Art; Smithsonian Inst, Washington, DC; San Diego Fine Arts Gallery; and others. *Exhib:* Carnegie Inst Int, Pittsburgh, 52; Tokyo Int, Japan, 52; Sao Paulo Biennale, Brazil, 55; Whitney Mus Am Art, New York, 60; Pacific Heritage, US State Dept, Berlin, Ger, 65; plus others. *Teaching:* Instr painting, Kann Inst Art, 48-51; instr painting, Scripps Col, 49-50 & Univ Southern Calif, Idyllwild Campus, 75- *Awards:* Carol H Beck Gold Medal, Pa Acad Fine Arts, 47; Purchase Award, Metrop Mus Art, 50; Purchase Award, Los Angeles Co Mus, 50, 56 & 57. *Bibliog:* Arthur Millier (auth), Inner development of artist, Am Artist, 50; Ed Biberman (auth), 20 Artists (film), Los Angeles Mus & Univ Calif, Los Angeles, 70; Joe Mugnaini (auth), Oil Painting Techniques and Materials, 69 & Logics of Drawing, 73, Reinholt; plus others. *Media:* Sumi Ink, Woodcut. *Dealer:* I Serisawa Gallery 8320 Melrose Ave Los Angeles CA 90069. *Mailing Add:* PO Box 511 Idyllwild CA 92549

SERRA, RICHARD
SCULPTOR
b San Francisco, Calif, Nov 2, 39. *Study:* Univ Calif, Berkeley; Univ Calif, Santa Barbara, BA; Yale Univ, BA & MFA. *Work:* Whitney Mus Am Art & Guggenheim Mus, Met Mus Art, New York; Stedelijk Mus, Amsterdam; Moderna Museet, Stockholm; Tate Gallery, London; Yale Univ Art Gallery, New Haven, Conn; Larry Aldrich Mus, Ridgefield, Conn; Allen Mem Art Mus, Oberlin, Ohio; and numerous pvt collections. *Comn:* Outdoor sculpture, London Stock Exchange, 87; Sculpture, Pijksmuseum Kroller-Muller park, Otterlo, Neth, 88; Fin (sculpture), 11th floor, Sky Lobby, Swiss Bank Corp - US Hq, 90; Stacks, Yale Univ, New Haven, 90. *Exhib:* Whitney Mus Am Art, 75-77 & Matrix Gallery, Univ Art Mus, Univ Calif, Berkeley, 79; solo exhib, Mus Mod Art, New York, 78, Richard Hines Gallery, Seattle, 79, Univ Calif, Berkeley, 79, KOH Gallery, Tokyo, 79, Galerie Schmela, Dusseldorf, 79, Synagoge Stommelin, Pulheim, Ger, 92, Blancpain/Stepczynski, Geneva, Switz, 92, Pace Gallery, New York, 92; Venice Biennale, Venice, Italy, 81; Akira Ikeda Gallery, Nagoya, Japan, 82; Connections-Bridges, Ladders, Ramps, Staircases, Tunnels, Inst Contemp Art, Univ Pa, 83; American Sculpture, Margo Leavin Gallery, Los Angeles, 84; The Sculptor as Draftsman, Visual Arts Mus, NY, 85; Tony Shafrazi Gallery, New York, 91-92; Pace Gallery, New York, 92; Lingotto, Srl, Torino, Italy, 92. *Awards:* Skohegan Sch Medal, 75; Kaiserring Award for Sculpure,Goslar, WGer, 81; Hon Fel, Bezalel Acad Arts & Design, Jerusalem, 83. *Bibliog:* John Russell (auth), Art: Startling Sculpture from Richard Serra, NY Times, 2/28/86; A M Hammacher (auth), Modern Sculpture: Tradition and Innovation, New York, 88; Klaus Honnef (auth), Kunst der Gegenwart, Taschen, 88; Dennis Adrian (auth), Elliott exhibit proves instructive, Chicago Sun-Times, 5/90; Amy Jinker-Lloyd (auth), Musing on Museology, Art Am, 6/92. *Publ:* Coauth (with Clara Weyergraf) Richard Serra, Hudson River Mus, Yonkers, NY; auth, Richard Serra: Sculpture 1985-1987, (exhib catalog) Pace Publn, NY, 87; Richard Serra: Sculpture 1987-1989 (exhib catalog), Pace Gallery, NY, 89. *Dealer:* The Pace Gallery 32 E 57th St New York, NY 10022. *Mailing Add:* 173 Duane St New York NY 10013

SERRA, RUDY
SCULPTOR
b San Francisco, Calif, Apr 9, 48. *Study:* City Col San Francisco, AA; San Francisco State Col, BA; Univ Calif, Berkeley, MA & MFA. *Exhib:* San Francisco Art Inst, 73 & 76; 1975 Whitney Biennial, New York, 75; San Francisco Mus Mod Art, 77; Faculty Exhib, Univ Conn, 80-82; one-person shows, Univ Houston, 80, Baruch Col, 82 & Marianne Deson Gallery, 83; Oakland Mus, 82; Nassau Mus, NY, 85; Tomoko Liguori Gallery, NY, 88. *Teaching:* Vis asst prof sculpture, Calif State Univ, Chico, 75; asst prof, Am River Col, Sacramento, 76-77; vis asst prof sculpture, Univ Calif, Davis, fall 78; asst prof sculpture & drawing, Univ Conn, Storrs, 79-; State Univ NY, Purchase, 84, Sarah Lawrence Col, NY, 86-87, Bennington Col, Vt, 88. *Awards:* Nat Endowment Arts Grant, 76, 78 & 85. *Bibliog:* Roberta Smith (auth), Biennial review, Artforum, 5/75; Amy Goldin (auth), The New Whitney Biennial, Art Am, 5-6/75; Judith Dunham (auth), Introduction 75, Artweek, 7/75; Michael Brenson (auth), article, New York Times, 88. *Media:* Concrete, Hydracol. *Mailing Add:* 108 Franklin St New York NY 10013

SERRA-BADUE, DANIEL F
PAINTER, EDUCATOR
b Santiago de Cuba, Sept 8, 14. *Study:* Escuela Munic Bellas Artes, Santiago de Cuba, 24-26; Borrell-Nicolau & Luis Muntane, Escuela Bellas Artes, Barcelona, 32-36; Art Students League, Nat Acad Design & Columbia Univ, 38-40; Escuela Nac Bellas Artes, Havana, 43; Pratt Inst Graphic Art Ctr, 64; Art Critics Workshop, Am Fedn Arts, 67. *Work:* Mus Mod Art, New York; Museo Nac, La Habana; Inst Cult Hispanica, Madrid; Mus Contemp Latin Am Art, Washington, DC; Metrop Mus Art, New York. *Comn:* Print ed, Columbus Quircentenary, Print Club Albany, NY, 92. *Exhib:* Whitney Mus Am Art, New York, 40; Museo de Arte Moderno, Barcelona, 55; Six Cuban Painters Working in New York, Ctr Inter-Am Relations, New York, 75; 149th Ann Exhib, Royal Scottish Acad, Edinburgh, 75; Ibizagrafica 80, Mus Art, Ibiza, 80, 82 & 84; International Biennial Print Exhibit, Fine Arts Mus, Topie, Taiwan, 83, 87 & 89; Ann Exhib, Nat Acad Design, New York, 84 & 90; Outside Cuba/Fuera de Cuba, Rutgers Univ Mus, NJ, 87; The Latin American Spirit: Art and Artists in the United States, 1920-1970, Bronx Mus Arts, New York, 88. *Pos:* Asst dir, Cult Dept, Ministry Ed, Havana, 59-60. *Teaching:* Prof, Sch Plastic Arts, Santiago de Cuba, 45-60; instr art, Univ Oriente, Cuba, summers 48 & 50; prof design, Sch Journalism, Santiago de Cuba, 54-59; prof, Nat Sch Fine Arts, Havana, 60-62; lectr painting, Columbia Univ, 62-63; instr drawing & painting, Brooklyn Mus Art Sch, 62-85; asst prof art hist, St Peter's Col, NJ, 67-70, chmn dept, 67-77, assoc prof, 70-77, prof, 77-85, emer prof, 85- *Awards:* Guggenheim Fel, 38-39; Oscar B Cintas Found Fel, 63 & 64; Cert Merit in Graphics, Nat Acad Design, 84; plus others. *Bibliog:* Al Brunelle (auth), Daniel Serra-Badue, Art News, 2/73; Rafael Santos Torroella (auth), Serra-Badue, El Noticiero Universal, Barcelona, 6/5/73; Alberto del Castillo (auth), Daniel Serra-Badue, Goya, Madrid, 7-8/73. *Mem:* Am Soc Contemp Artists; Col Art Asn Am; Soc Am Graphic Artists; Artists Equity New York; Circulo de Cultura Bramericano. *Media:* Oil, Lithography. *Publ:* Auth, weekly articles in Diario de la Marina, Havana, 46-47; weekly articles in Diario de Cuba, Santiago de Cuba, 57-58. *Mailing Add:* 15 W 72nd St No 10T New York NY 10023

SERRANO, ANDRES
PHOTOGRAPHER, CONCEPTUAL ARTIST
b New York, NY, Aug 15, 50. *Study:* Brooklyn Mus Art Sch, 67-69. *Work:* New Mus Contemp Art, New York; Brooklyn Mus, NY; First Bank Systems, Minneapolis, Minn. *Exhib:* Solo exhibs, Galerie Hufkens-Noirhomme, Brussels, Belg, 87, Greenberg Wilson Gallery, New York, 88 & Stux Gallery, 88, 89 & 90, BlumHelman Gallery, Santa Monica, Calif, 90, Denver Mus Art, Colo, 91 & Inst Contemp Art, Amsterdam, Holland, 92; Past, Present, Future, 86 & FAKE, 87, New Mus Contemp Art, New York; Awards in the Visual Arts, Los Angeles Co Mus, 88; Abstraction in Question, John & Mable Ringling Mus, Sarasota, Fla, 89; Photog Invention, Smithsonian Inst, Washington, DC, 89; Quotations, Aldrich Mus Contemp Art, Ridgefield, Conn, 92; Dirt and Domesticity: Constructions of the Feminine, Whitney Mus Am Art, 92; Political/Advocacy Art, Aldrich Mus Contemp Art, Ridgefield, Conn, 92. *Awards:* Fel, NY Found Arts, 87; Fel, Louis Comfort Tiffany Found, 89; NY State Coun Arts Sponsored Proj, 90. *Bibliog:* Marvin Heiferman (auth), Scared to Breath (exhib catalog), Perspektief, Neth, 87; Michael Brenson (auth), Andres Serrano: Provocation & Spirituality, New York Time, 12/8/89; Lucy Lippard (auth), Andres Serrano: The Spirit & Letter, Art in Am, 4/90. *Dealer:* Stux Gallery 155 Spring St New York NY 10012. *Mailing Add:* 171 Johnson St Brooklyn NY 11201

SERRANO, LUIS
PAINTER
b Guayaquil, Ecuador, 1955. *Study:* Otis Art Inst, Los Angeles, Calif, BA, 78, MFA, 81. *Exhib:* Miles Above, Otis/Parsons Art Gallery, Los Angeles, 83; Sunshine & Shadow, Fisher Gallery, Univ S Calif, 84; The Right Foot Show, San Francisco Int Airport, 87; Expresiones Hispanas 88/89, Mexican Cult Inst, San Antonio, Tex, & travelling, 88; Solo shows, Southwest Col, Los Angeles, 82, Diurnal/Nocturnal, Saxon-Lee Gallery, 86 & 88, I, The Spectator, Saxon-Lee Gallery, Los Angeles, 88, Still Lifes, Da Vinci Hall Art Gallery, Los Angeles City Col, 89, Introductions 1990, K Kimpton Gallery, San Francisco, 90 & A Sense of the Familiar, Daniel Saxon Gallery, Los Angeles, 91; Parallel Realities, Transamerica Ctr Galleries, Los Angeles, 90; Of Nature & the Human Spirit, Daniel Saxon Gallery, Los Angeles, 91; Chicano & Latino: Parallels & Divergence, Daniel Saxon Gallery, Los Angeles (traveling to the Kimberly Gallery, Washington, DC & the El Paso Mus Art, Tex), 91. *Bibliog:* Zan Dubin (auth), Southwest exhibit goes in all directions, Los Angeles Times, 7/3/88; Kenneth Baker (auth), Luis Serrano's Space at K Kimpton, San Francisco Chronicle, 8/1/90; Suvan Geer (auth), Art Reviews, Los Angeles Times 4/18/91. *Media:* Acrylic. *Mailing Add:* Daniel Saxon Gallery 7525 Beverly Blvd Los Angeles CA 90036

SETLOW, NEVA C
SCULPTOR, PAINTER
b New Haven, Conn, Dec 29, 40. *Study:* Univ Conn; Southern Conn State Col; Empire State Col, BA. *Work:* Assoc Univs, Brookhaven Nat Lab, Upton, NY; Pittsfield City Bank, Mass. *Exhib:* Aldrich Mus, Ridgefield, Conn, 76; Guild Hall, 86-92; Giordano Gallery, 89; Sculpture '90, Islip Mus, Long Island, NY; Goodman Gallery, Southampton, NY, 92; Ward Nasse, New York, 92; and others. *Awards:* Silvermine Guild Artists 50th Ann Award, 72; Sculpture House Award, West Chester Art Soc, 73; Award of Excellence, Huntington Art League, 74. *Mem:* Artists Equity Asn; E End Arts Coun; Smithtown Coun; Southampton Artists; Int Sculpture Ctr. *Media:* Plastic, Wood. *Dealer:* Goodman Gallery Southampton NY. *Mailing Add:* Four Beachland Ave East Quogue NY 11942

SEVERSON, WILLIAM CONRAD
SCULPTOR
b Madison, Wis, Nov 22, 24. *Study:* Univ Wis, Madison, BS, AA, 47; Syracuse Univ, with Ivan Mestrovic, MFA(sculpture), 49; Susquahanna Univ, Hon PhD, 85. *Work:* Nat Cathedral Washington DC; Concordia Seminary, St Louis, Mo; St Louis Sculptors' Gallery, Mo; Cheltenham Art Asn, Philadelphia, Pa; Morris Arboretum, Philadelphia, Pa. *Comn:* Ciborium, Shrine Our Lady of Snows, Belleville, Ill, 64; Connectors, Blue Cross/Blue Shield, Chapel Hill, NC, 74; Solaris (bronze, solar), Tampa Electric Co, Fla, 80; Protein Cube, Ralston Purina, St Louis, Mo, 72; Primogenesis, Friends Mus Sci Nat Hist, St Louis, Mo, 81; Tri-State Vets Mem, Dubuque, Iowa, 89. *Exhib:* NY World's Fair, Mo Pavilion, New York, 65; Chillicothe, Mo State Council Arts, 65; Casa D'Artes, Taos, NMex, 70; Sculpture in Archit Concept, Fordham/Lincoln Ctr, New York, 76; 7th Ann, Shidonaa, Santa Fe, NMex, 81. *Pos:* Pres, St Louis Sculptors' Gallery, 64-68. *Awards:* First Place, Univ Wis, Green Bay, 77; Purchase Prize, Philip & Muriel Berman, 79. *Bibliog:* Thelma R Newman (auth), Plastics as Art Form, Chilton, 64; Theodore F Wolff (auth) Something for all to share, Christian Sci Monitor, 80; Louis G Redstone (auth), Public Art--New Directions, McGraw-Hill, 81. *Mem:* Int Sculpture Conf; Ecumenical Coun Drama & Art. *Media:* Steel, Bronze. *Mailing Add:* Two St Mary's Knoll St Louis MO 63124-1809

SEVIGNY, MAURICE JOSEPH, II
EDUCATOR, ADMINISTRATOR
b Amesbury, Mass, July 24, 43. *Study:* Mass Col Art, BSEd, 65; Ohio State Univ, MA, 69, PhD, 77. *Teaching:* Asst prof art educ, Western Ky Univ, 69-76; teaching assoc, Ohio State Univ, 76-78; assoc prof art, chair, Div Art Educ, Bowling Green State Univ, Ohio, 78-81, dir, Sch Art, 79, prof, 81-; chmn dept art & Marguerite Fairchild centennial prof, Univ Tex, Austin, 86. *Awards:* Award Excellence Dissertation Res, Rev Res Visual Arts Educ, 79; Ann Hollis Moore Award Distinguished Serv, Bowling Green State Univ Student Union, 82. *Mem:* Nat Coun Policy Studies Art Educ; Ohio Art Educ Asn (adv coun rep, 78, chmn Higher Educ, 79); Nat Art Educ Asn Higher Educ Div (chmn elect); Nat Coun Art Adminr; Nat Soc Schs Art & Design. *Res:* Discipline based art education, studio learning and performance; assessment at the university level from the triangulated perspective of teacher, student, classroom ethnographer; lanquage and gender differences in non-verbal communication. *Publ:* Auth, Triangulation and descriptive research, Rev Res Visual Arts, 5/78; auth, Utilizing recorded materials for the clinical component of teacher training, In: Human Relations and the Clinical Component, Ohio Dept Educ, 80; auth, Triangulate inquiry: A methodology for the analysis of classroom interaction, In: Analysis of Discourse: Ethnographic Approaches, Ablex Publ, 81; Discipline Based Art Education and Teacher Education, J P Getty Ctr Educ, 86. *Mailing Add:* Univ Arizona Deans Office Faculty Fine Arts, Music Bldg 111 Tucson AZ 85721

SEVY, BARBARA SNETSINGER
LIBRARIAN
b Montpelier, Vt, June 4, 26. *Study:* Univ Vt, BS; Drexel Univ, MSLS. *Pos:* Librn, Philadelphia Mus Art, 68- *Mem:* Art Libr Soc NAm (secy, 81-83); Am Libr Asn (chmn art sect, 74); Spec Libr Asn (secy mus div, 68-69). *Mailing Add:* 242 Mather Rd Jenkintown PA 19046

SEWELL, DARREL L
CURATOR, HISTORIAN
b Cushing, Okla, Dec 21, 39. *Study:* Univ Chicago, BA, 62, MA, 62. *Collections Arranged:* Modern Jewelry, 64-86; Philadelphia: Three Centuries of American Art (auth, catalog), 76; Installation of American Collections, 77; American Presidential China, 77; The University of Pennsylvania: Collector and Patron of Art, 1779-1979, 79; Copley from Boston (auth, catalog), 80; Thomas Eakins: Artist of Philadelphia (auth, catalog), 81-82; One Hundred Years of Acquisitions, 83; Benjamin West in Pennsylvania Collections, 86; Diego Rivera, 86; The Helen Drutt Collection, 86-87; The Fairmount Waterworks, 88; Henry O Tanner (auth, catalog), 91. *Pos:* Intern, Conservation Dept, Art Inst Chicago, 65; cur educ, Nat Collection Fine Arts, 70-73; cur, Am Art, Philadelphia Mus Art, 73- *Teaching:* Instr art hist, Ohio State Univ, Columbus, 66-67 & Univ Ill, Chicago Circle, 68-70. *Publ:* Auth, What you see is what you get: An approach to the use of museums for education, Art Educ, 12/71. *Mailing Add:* Philadelphia Mus Art PO Box 7646 Philadelphia PA 19101

SEWELL, JACK VINCENT
MUSEUM CURATOR
b Dearborn, Mo, June 11, 23. *Study:* St Joseph Jr Col, Mo, 41-43; City Col New York, 43-44; Univ Chicago, MFA, 50; Harvard Univ, 51-53. *Collections Arranged:* Complete reinstallation of Oriental Collections, Art Inst Chicago, 58. *Pos:* Mem staff, Oriental dept, Art Inst Chicago, 50-56, assoc cur Oriental art, 56-58, cur, 58- *Mem:* Far Eastern Ceramic Group; Japan-Am Soc Chicago; The Cliff Dwellers; Arts Club Chicago. *Res:* Indian and Far Eastern art; arts of China; strength in delicacy--archaic Chinese bronzes and sculptures of Gandhara. *Publ:* Contribr, Archaeol & Chicago Art Inst Quart. *Mailing Add:* 618 S Prospect St Galena IL 61036

SEWELL, LEO
SCULPTOR, ASSEMBLAGE ARTIST
b Anapolis, Md, Sept 7, 45. *Study:* Univ Del, MA, 70. *Work:* Please Touch Mus, Philadelphia, Pa; Express-Ways Children's Mus, Chicago; Ripley's Believe It Or Not Mus, St Augustine, Fla; Sci Mus, Palm Beach, Fla; Lehigh Univ Galleries, Bethlehem, Pa. *Comn:* NBC Corp Hq, Comn by Brandon Tartikoff, New York, 80; The Family, comn by Philip & Muriel Berman, Allentown, Pa, 83; Rocky, comn by Sylvester Stallone, Los Angeles, Calif, 85. *Exhib:* Earth Art, Mus Philadelphia Civic Ctr, Pa, 73; Artist's Toys, Please Touch Mus, Philadelphia, Pa, 82; Inaugural Exhib, Unsinus Col, Collegeville, Pa, 86; Two-man show (with Jim Henson), Albany Mus Art, Ga, 87; Bits & Pieces, Brockton Art Mus, Mass, 88; solo exhib, Children's Mus RI, Pawtucket, 89 & Danville Mus Fine Art & Hist, Va, 90; Trash Menagerie, Express-Ways Children's Mus, Chicago, Ill, 90. *Bibliog:* Domerque (auth), Artists Design Furniture, Abrams, 84; Brommert & Horn (coauths), Arts in Your Visual Environment, 88. *Media:* Found Objects. *Publ:* Featured on many TV productions including You Asked For It, 81, Ripley's Believe It or Not, 82, Captain Noah, 85 & Earth Week Celebration on Mr Roger's Neighborhood, 90. *Dealer:* Rena Branstein Gallery 77 Geary St San Francisco CA 94108. *Mailing Add:* 3614 Pearl St Philadelphia PA 19104

SEWELL, RICHARD GEORGE
PRINTMAKER, PAINTER
b St Louis, Mo, Aug 22, 42; Can citizen. *Study:* Univ Nac Autonoma de Mexico, 65; Kansas City Art Inst, Mo, 66; Univ Mo, Kansas City, BA, 67. *Work:* Can Coun, Ottawa; The Gallery, Stratford, Ont; Nova Scotia Art Gallery, Halifax; Owens Art Gallery, Mt Allison, NB; Winnipeg Art Gallery, Man. *Exhib:* Beyond the Repeatable Image, Heywood, Tamasauskas, Sewell, England, Spain, Belgium, Scotland, France, 84-85; New Work, May, Besant, Parker, Sewell, Alberta Col Art, Calgary, 88; Agnes Etherington Art Ctr, Kingston, Ont, 85; Univ Toronto, Erindale Campus, 90; solo exhib, Mem Univ St John's Newfoundland, 90. *Pos:* Co-founder & dir, Open Studio, Print Workshop, Toronto, Ont, 70-82; chmn, Print and Drawing Coun Canada, Toronto, Ont, Can, 89-91. *Teaching:* Univ Saskatchewan, Saskatoon, 81; Alberta Col Art, Calgary, 84-86; Sheridan Col, Oakville, Ont, 86-; Ontario Col Art, Toronto, 88- *Bibliog:* Linda Beattie (auth), Beyond the Repeatable Image, Heywood, Tamasauskas, & Sewell, Visual Arts, Ont, Toronto, 84; Louise Dompierre (auth), Paratactic Images Agnes Etherington Art Ctr, Kingston, Ont, 85; Deidre Hanna (auth), Chaos/Relief, NOW Mag, Toronto, Ont, 1/90. *Media:* All; Acrylic, Oil. *Publ:* Contribr, Open Studio-Ten Years (catalog), Open Studio, Toronto, Ont, 80; auth, StoneGrain Cycle, The Prints of Mark Critoph, The Gallery/Stratford, Ont, 84. *Mailing Add:* 49 Appleton Ave Toronto ON M6E 3A4 Canada

SEXAUER, DONALD RICHARD
INSTRUCTOR, PRINTMAKER
b Erie, Pa. *Study:* Col William & Mary; Edinboro State Col, BS; Kent State Univ, MA. *Work:* Butler Inst Am Art, Youngstown, Ohio; New York Pub Libr; Mint Mus Art, Charlotte, NC; Nat Mus Art, Smithsonian, Washington, DC; Libr of Cong, Washington, DC; and others. *Comn:* Print eds, Make Believe Print Club of Albany, Int Graphic Art Soc, 66, To Fly, To Fly, 66; Vietnam Fragments (folio), Off, Chief Mil Hist, Washington, DC, 71; Mecklenburg Bicentennial Comn (folio). *Exhib:* Soc Am Graphic Artists, 64-; New Talent In Printmaking, New York, 66; 140th Ann, Nat Acad Design, 66; San Diego Print Exhib, 71; 16th Hunterdon Nat, Clinton, NJ, 72. *Teaching:* Prof printmaking, Sch Art, E Carolina Univ, 60- *Awards:* Print Prize, Nat Acad Design 140th Ann, 66; Purchase Awards, Piedmont Print Ann, Mint Mus, 69-74; Purchase Awards, Bradley Print Show, Peoria, Ill, Soc Am Graphic Artists, 79 & 80 & Hunterdon Art Ctr, Clinton, NJ, 83 & 86. *Mem:* Soc Am Graphic Artists; Boston Printmakers; Audubon Artists. *Media:* Intaglio. *Publ:* Illusr, Red clay reader number 5, Southern Lit Rev, 68. *Mailing Add:* 109 Greenbriar Dr Greenville NC 27834

SEXTON, JOHN (WILLIAM)
PHOTOGRAPHER
b Maywood, Calif, May 22, 53. *Study:* Photog workshops with Ansel Adams, Wynn Bullock, Paul Caponigro & Brett Weston, 73-74. *Work:* Univ Ariz Ctr Creative Photog, Tucson; Polaroid Corp Collection, Clarence Kennedy Gallery, Cambridge, Mass; Newport Harbor Art Mus, Newport Beach, Calif; Monterey Peninsula Mus Art, Calif; China Photogrs Asn, Bening, Chica. *Exhib:* One-man exhib, Chapman Col, Orange, Calif, 76; Bell Gallery, Brown Univ, Providence, RI, 80; New Landscapes, Friends Photog Gallery, Carmel, Calif, 80; Message From The West Coast, Photo Gallery Int, Tokyo, 81; Focus Gallery, San Francisco, 81; and others. *Pos:* Co-dir & instr, Owens Valley Photog Workshops, Agoura, Calif, 76-; tech consult to Ansel Adams, Carmel, Calif, 79-82. *Teaching:* Instr, Cypress Col, Calif, 77-79; instr, Univ Calif, Santa Cruz, 80-81; instr, Ansel Adams Yosemite Workshops, 80- *Awards:* Imogen Cunningham Award, Focus Gallery, San Francisco, 81. *Bibliog:* Ron Eggers (auth), Working with the masters, Rangefinder, 80. *Mem:* Friends Photog; Soc Photog Educ. *Publ:* Contribr, Photo-Image Mag, Lodestar Press, 76; Darkroom Photog Mag, Sheptow Publ, 79; The negative, New York Graphic Soc, 81; Zoom Mag, Joel Laroche-France, 81; coauth, Quiet Light, essays, 51 black & white reproductions, Bulfinch Press/Little, Brown & Co, 4/90, 2nd printing, 5/90. *Dealer:* Weston Gallery PO Box 655 Carmel CA 93921. *Mailing Add:* 291 Los Agrinemsors Carmel Valley CA 93924

SEYFFERT, J ROBERT
PAINTER
b Bryn Mawr, Pa, Dec 9, 52. *Study:* Yale Sch Music & Art, Norfolk, 74; Md Inst, Col Art, BFA, 75; Parsons Sch Design, with Paul Resika, MFA, 81. *Work:* Acad Arts, Easton, Md; Holtzman Gallery, Towson State Univ; Signet Bank, Baltimore; Manekin Corp, Baltimore; Center Club, Baltimore; Chateau Mus, Rocheforten Terre, France. *Comn:* Oil portrait, James Michener, 79; and other private portrait comm. *Exhib:* Baltimore Mus Biennial, 76; solo exhib, Gregg Galleries, Nat Arts Club, New York, 81, 83, 86 & 88, Houston-North Gallery, Lunenberg, NS, 85 & 87, Gallery 819 (pastels), Baltimore, 88; Landscapes, Md Hist Soc, Baltimore, 83; Maryland Landscapes, Kawasaki Cult Hall, Japan, 83; Critical Perspectives in Contemporary Landscapes, State House, Annapolis, 83; Md Art Place, Baltimore, 84 & 86; solo exhib, Houston-North Gallery, Lunenburg, NS, 85 & 87. *Teaching:* Adj instr drawing, Johns Hopkins Univ, 86 & 87; instr painting, Baltimore Sch Arts, 88-89. *Awards:* Greenshields Fel, 77. *Bibliog:* Chris Lamb (auth), Robert Seyffert, Am Artist, 10/83; Recent landscapes by Robert Seyffert, Daily Record, Baltimore, 2/24/86; Elizabeth Stevens (auth), Color distinguishes paintings, Baltimore Sun, 2/28/86; John Dorsey (auth), Landscape Seyffert's Metier, Baltimore Sun, 2/19/88. *Mem:* Nat Arts Club. *Media:* Oil, Pastels. *Mailing Add:* c/o 819 Gallery 817 S Broadway Fells Pt Baltimore MD 21231

SEYLE, ROBERT HARLEY
SCULPTOR, DESIGNER
b National City, Calif, Oct 9, 37. *Study:* La Sierra Col, Riverside, Calif; Otis Art Inst, Los Angeles, BFA, MFA. *Work:* Storm King Art Mus, Corning, NY; Palm Springs Desert Mus, Calif; Beneficial Ins Group, Los Angeles; Metro Media Studios, Hollywood, Calif. *Comn:* Nail sculpture 11, Henry J Ittleson, Jr, Palm Springs, 67; nail sculpture 89, Julian Brody, Des Moines, Iowa, 72; nail sculpture 110, Dr Alonzo Proctor, Lodi, Calif, 74; nail sculpture 125, Arthur Elrod Interiors, Palm Springs, 75; nail sculpture 154, Steve Chase, Palm Springs, Calif, 81. *Exhib:* One-man show, Palm Springs Desert Mus, 74; group show, Calif State Capitol Bldg, Sacramento, 75; Ankrum Gallery, Los Angeles, 78; Riverside Art Ctr, Calif, 78; San Bernardino Co Mus, 78; and others. *Bibliog:* Ray Faulkner & Edwin Ziegfeld (auths), Art Today, Holt, Rinehart & Winston Inc; Bernard Morris (auth), California people, Eyewitness News, ABC-TV, 74; Noonday WVa, Channel 12, Clarksburg, WVa, 80. *Mailing Add:* 545 Howell Mountain Rd Angwin CA 94508-9757

SHACKELFORD, BUD (LYNE T)
PAINTER, INSTRUCTOR
b Washington DC, Nov 15, 18. *Study:* Univ Ala; Chouinard Sch Art, Los Angeles, Calif; Art Students League. *Exhib:* Am Watercolor Soc, 68-78, Ann, 78 & Audubon Artists, 73, Nat Acad, New York; Watercolor USA, Springfield Art Mus, Mo, 68-72; Butler Art Inst Ann, Youngstown, Ohio, 71-72; Watercolor West, Riverside Art Mus, Calif, 75-77. *Pos:* Animator, Walt Disney Studios, 39-40; art dir, Phillips Ramsey Advert Co, 51-61; pres, Art Assocs Inc, San Diego, Calif, 61-66. *Teaching:* Instr watercolor, San Diego Art Inst, 70-72, Hewitt Painting Workshops, 70-77 & Painting Holidays, 78-79. *Awards:* Over 200 awards. *Bibliog:* Watercolor Page, Shackelford advocates strong design, Am Artist Mag, 3/67; Marlene Schiller (auth), Artists as demonstrators, Am Artist Mag, 2/79; Linda Lewis (auth), Life and excitement--Bud Shackelford, Southwest Art Mag, 5/73. *Mem:* Am Watercolor Soc; Nat Watercolor Soc; Nat Soc Art Directors; San Diego Watercolor Soc (pres 68-69); San Diego Art Guild (dir 71-72). *Media:* Watercolor, Acrylic. *Publ:* Auth, As I See It, Alfred Knopf, 45; Fun with Watercolor, pvt publ, 73; Experimental Watercolor Techniques, Watson-Guptill, 80; Draw Animals, pvt publ, 92. *Mailing Add:* Rolling Hills Dr El Cajon CA 92020

SHADBOLT, JACK LEONARD
PAINTER
b Shoeburyness, Eng, Feb 4, 09. *Study:* Euston Rd Group, London, Eng; with Andre L'Hote, Paris; Art Students League; hon degrees from Univ BC, Victoria Univ, Simon Fraser Univ & Bishop's Univ. *Work:* Art Gallery Toronto, Ont; Nat Gallery Can; Montreal Mus Fine Arts; Seattle Art Mus, Wash; Vancouver Art Gallery; and others. *Comn:* Murals, Edmonton Int Airport & Charlottetown Mem Ctr; Metrop Life Bldg, Ottawa; CBC Bldg, Vancouver; other comn in pvt collections. *Exhib:* Sao Paulo, Brazil; Caracas, Venezuela; Carnegie Int, 56; Seattle World's Fair, 62; Retrospectives, Nat Gallery Can & touring, 69 & Vancouver Art Gallery, 78; Glenbow Mus, Calgary & travelling, 92- *Teaching:* Head drawing & painting sect, lectr, juror, Vancouver Sch Art, formerly. *Awards:* Molson Award, Can Section Guggenheim Int, 78; Freedom of the City of Vancouver, 89; Order of BC, 90; and others. *Bibliog:* Joan Lowndes (auth), Jack Shadbolt Retrospective Catalog, Nat Gallery Can, 69; Jack Shadbolt, Seven Years, Vancouver Art Gallery, 74; Retrospective catalog, Vanguard, 81 & 83; Scott Watson (auth), Jack Shadbolt, 50 Years, 90; Correspondences, restrospective catalogue, Glenbow Mus, 92. *Publ:* Auth, In Search of Form, 69, Mind's I, 73 & Act of Art, 81, McClelland & Stewart. *Dealer:* Bau-Xi Gallery 3045 Granville Vancouver BC V6H 3J9 Canada. *Mailing Add:* 5121 Harborview Rd N Burnaby BC V5B 1C9 Canada

SHADDLE, ALICE
SCULPTOR, COLLAGE ARTIST
b Hinsdale, Ill, Dec 21, 28. *Study:* Oberlin Col; Univ Chicago; Sch Art Inst Chicago, BFA & MFA. *Work:* Smithsonian Inst, Washington, DC; Muskegon Mus, Mich; State Ill Ctr Mus. *Exhib:* Made With Paper, 67, Chicago Needs Famous Artists, 69, & Alternative Spaces, 84, Mus Contemp Art; Soc for Contemp Art, 69, Exhib by Artist in Chicago & Vicinity, 75 & 85 & Prizewinners, 79, Art Inst, Chicago; Indianapolis Mus Art, Ind, 76; 26th Ill Invitational, Ill State Mus, Springfield, 76; Nat Drawing Show, Kohler Arts Ctr, Sheboygan, Wis, 76; Ill Traveling Sculpture Exhib II, 78-79. *Teaching:* Instr printmaking & drawing, Roosevelt Univ, Chicago, 65-67; children's painting teacher, Hyde Park Art Ctr, 55-92 & Triangle Art Ctr, 78-88, Chicago. *Awards:* Logan Medal, 75th Exhib by Artist of Chicago & Vicinity, Art Inst Chicago, 75; Ill Arts Coun Grant, 78; Nat Endowment Arts Grant, 79. *Bibliog:* Meilach & Ten Hoor (auth), Collage & Assemblage, Crown, 73; C L Morrison (auth, rev), Artforum, 76 & 78; Holly Day (auth), revs, Art in Am, 78 & 79. *Mem:* Artemisia Gallery & Fund (treas, 77-79); Hyde Park Art Ctr, Chicago. *Media:* Paper, Oil on Canvas. *Publ:* Contribr, Art: Choosing & Expressing, Benefic Press, 77, Leonardo, Vol II, Pergamon Press, 78, London, Eng. *Mailing Add:* 4858 S Kenwood Chicago IL 60615

SHADRACH, JEAN H
PAINTER
b La Junta, Colo. *Study:* Univ NMex; Sumie, Okinawa; Constantine & Roman Chatov Studio, Atlanta, Ga; Alaska Methodist Univ. *Work:* Anchorage Fine Arts Mus & Aleyeska Pipeline Co, Anchorage; Frye Mus, Seattle; Standard Oil Co Calif; Murray, Bradley & Rockney; Price Waterhouse; Senator & Mrs Ted Stevens. *Comn:* Anchorage Beautification, 70; Executive suites, ARCO & Aleyska Pipeline, 75; SOHIO painting, 80. *Exhib:* All Alaska Art Exhib, Anchorage, 68-72; Northwestern Watercolor Soc Ann, Seattle, 70; Design I, Anchorage, 71; Artists of Alaska, traveling, 71-75; Frye Mus, Seattle, 85; Sumie Soc Am, 87, 88 & 91. *Pos:* Found, Artique, Ltd, Fine Art Gallery, Anchorage, 71-87. *Teaching:* Workshops, Foothills Art Ctr, Golden, Colo, 89-90; artist-lectr aboard Cunard Lines cruise ships, 89-90 & 91-92. *Awards:* Drawing Award, All Alaska Art Exhib, 70; Gov Award, Alaska, 70; Best Show, Alaska Watercolor, 88. *Bibliog:* Leo Krantz (auth), Contemporary Am Artists, 85 & 89; Article in Am Artist, 4/85 & Midwest Art, 9-10/87; Elizabeth Leonard (auth), Floral Painting, 86. *Mem:* Alaska Artist Guild (pres, 70-71); Artists Equity Asn; Sumie Soc Am; Alaska Watercolor Soc. *Media:* Acrylic, sumi-e. *Publ:* Auth, Okinawa Sketchbook, 62. *Mailing Add:* 3530 Fordham Dr Anchorage AK 99508

SHAFFER, FERN
PAINTER
b Chicago, Ill, Mar 29, 44. *Study:* Univ Ill, BFA, 81, Columbia Univ, MA, 91. *Exhib:* Detroit Focus, Mich 87; Wichita Art Asn, Kans, 89; Tropical Rain Forrest, Sundered Ground, New York, 89; For the Birds, Wustum Mus, Racine, Wis, 90. *Pos:* Pres, Artemisia Gallery, 83-92. *Teaching:* Instr, Humanities Inst, 89-90. *Awards:* Ill Arts Coun Award, Chicago, 86; Community Arts Award, Chicago, 87; Columbia Col Fel, 90. *Bibliog:* Suzi Gablik (auth), Psychological Prospectives & Reenchantment of Art the World & I, 88; Gloria Oreinstein (auth), Reflowering of the Godess, MacMillen, 90. *Mem:* Womens Caucus Art (chmn, 90-91); Chicago Artists Coalition. *Media:* Acrylic, Oil. *Mailing Add:* Artemisia Gallery 700 N Carpenter Chicago IL 60622

SHAFFER, RICHARD
PAINTER, PRINTMAKER
b Fresno, Calif, Mar 17, 47. *Study:* Univ Calif, Santa Cruz, BA(philos), 69; New Sch Social Res, New York, grad study philos; San Francisco Art Inst, BFA(painting), 73; Stanford Univ, Palo Alto, Calif, MFA(painting), 75. *Work:* Santa Barbara Mus Art, Calif; Roswell Mus & Art Ctr, NMex; La Jolla Mus Contemp Art, San Diego; Dallas Mus of Art, Tex; Nova Corp, Canada. *Exhib:* Roswell Mus 20th Anniversary Exhib, Roswell, NMex, 87; Am Acad & Inst Arts & Lett, New York, 86; La Jolla Mus Contemp Art, La Jolla Calif, 88; Nat Mus Am Art, Washington, DC, 82; John Berggruen Gallery, San Francisco, Calif, 88; and others. *Pos:* Artist-in-residence, Roswell Mus, 75-76, MacDowell Colony, Peterborough, NH, fall 77, Yaddo, Saratoga Springs, NY, spring 78, Ossabaw Found, Savannah, Ga, spring 79; vis artist, Univ Iowa, Iowa City, fall, 81; artist in residence, Bellagio Study & Conference Ctr, Lake Como, Italy, 83. *Teaching:* Instr printmaking, Univ Calif, Santa Cruz, summer 75; assoc prof painting & drawing, Univ Tex, Arlington, 78-83. *Awards:* Fulbright fel, Fulbright-Hays Exchange Act, 76-77; Nat Endowment Arts, painting, 81; Visual Arts Award for Painting, 82. *Bibliog:* Harry Rand (auth), Awards in the Visual Arts I, Southeastern Ctr Contemp Art, 82; Richard Shaffer (LA Lower, Susan Freudenheim) (coauth), article, Venice,

Calif, 84; Annette Carlozzi (auth), 50 Texas Artists, Chronicle Books, San Francisco, Calif, 86. *Mem:* MacDowell Colony Fellows. *Publ:* Auth, Andenken, L A Louver Publications Inc, 82. *Mailing Add:* c/o L A Louver Inc 55 N Venice Blvd Venice CA 90291

SHAFFER, ROSALIND
SCULPTOR, PAINTER
b Brooklyn, NY, Apr 7, 49. *Study:* Syracuse Univ, BFA, 70; Brooklyn Col, 73. *Exhib:* Year of the Woman: Reprise, Bronx Mus, 76; Norton Mus Art, West Palm Beach, Fla, 77; Working, San Francisco De Young Mus, 78; Between Sculpture and Painting, Evanston Art Ctr, 85; Current Trends in Art, Columbus Mus, 85. *Pos:* Chairperson new artists studio, Soho 20 Gallery, New York, 79-82. *Bibliog:* Ellen Lubell (auth), Women artists, Arts Mag, 4/75 & 4/77; San Francisco-working (article), San Francisco Examiner, 10/78; Jo Ann Wein (auth), Politics in art, Queens Col, 2/84. *Media:* Oil, Wood. *Publ:* Illusr, What's new in art, Oui Mag, 75; 6 women artists, Viva Mag, 77; Read On, Speak Out, Newberry House-Harcourt Brace, 78; Marriage and the Family, Random House, 82; Physicians & Surgeons Mag, 84. *Mailing Add:* 57 Strawberry Hill Norwalk CT 04351

SHAHEEN, GARY EDWARD
ADMINISTRATOR, COLLAGE ARTIST
b Binghamton, NY, Oct 21, 52. *Study:* Royal Univ Malta, with Charles Eldred, 75; State Univ New York, Binghamton, with Angelo Ippolito & Aubrey Schwartz, BA(art), 75; Syracuse Univ Maxwell Sch, with Joseph Scala, 86. *Work:* Security Mutual Life Corp, Binghamton, NY. *Exhib:* State Univ New York-Binghamton Alumni Invitational, Univ Art Gallery, 83; Central Regional Exhib, Robinson Mem, Binghamton, NY, 86; Artists of Achievement, Lever House, New York, 88 & Stuhr Mus, Grand Island, Nebr, 90. *Pos:* Dir, Studio Sch & Art Gallery, Binghamton, NY, 80-87; bd mem, Broome Co Arts Coun, 85-87, Schnectady Co Arts Coun, 87-90; exhibs comt mem, Schenectady Mus, NY, 89-90. *Teaching:* Instr drawing, Robinson Mem, Binghamton, NY, 82-86; instr printmaking, Studio Sch/Art Gallery, Binghamton, NY, 84-86. *Awards:* Purchase Prize, Security Mutual Life, 82; Hon Mention, Visual Individualists, 89. *Mem:* Schenectady County & Coun (bd dirs, 87-90, visual arts comt, 90); Schenectady Mus & Planetarium (exhib comt, 89-90); A Place for Jazz Inc (bd mem, 90). *Mailing Add:* 1002 Bill Rd Schenectady NY 12303

SHAHLY, JEHAN
PAINTER
b Detroit, Mich, Dec 12, 28. *Study:* Mich State Univ, BA; Art Students League; New Sch Social Res; Hunter Col, MA. *Work:* San Francisco Mus Art; Univ Southern Ill; Univ Mass; Geigy Collection; Bradford Jr Col. *Exhib:* Grand Central Mod Gallery, New York, 62 & 63; Six Painters, Kansas City Mus, 63; one-woman shows, Green Mountain Gallery, New York, 73, Ulster Co Community Col, 76 & Landmark Gallery, New York, 78; Caldbeck Gallery, Rockland, Maine, 86 & 88; and others. *Pos:* Lectr, Guggenheim Mus, formerly; Gallery & mus tour guide, Great Neck Adult Prog, NY, presently. *Awards:* Purchase Prizes, San Francisco Mus Art, 56 & Wichita Mus, Kans, 57; Creative Artists Pub Serv Grant, 76. *Bibliog:* Lawrence Campbell (auth), article, Art News Mag, 11/73; April Kinsley (auth), article, Art Int, 1/74; Robbie Ehrlich (auth), article, Arts Mag, 12/78. *Media:* Oil. *Mailing Add:* 799 Greenwich St New York NY 10014

SHAHN, ABBY
PAINTER
b Long Branch, NJ, July 31, 40. *Study:* Skowhegan Sch Painting & Sculpture, 59-61; Calif Sch Fine Arts, San Francisco, 60; Art Students League, 60-61. *Work:* Hirshhorn Mus & Sculpture Garden, Washington, DC; Portland Mus, Maine; Colby Col, Waterville, Maine; Union Carbide; Walker Mus, Bowdoin Col, Brunswick, Maine. *Comn:* Door panels, Railroad Square Cinema, Waterville, Maine, 81; three paintings, Solon Elem Sch, Maine, 83; four paintings, Dept Disability, Old Max Bldg, Augusta, Maine, 85; mural, Univ Southern Miane, 90. *Exhib:* All Maine Biennial, Bowdoin Col, 79 & Portland Mus, 85; Ghost Dance, Univ Maine, Farmington, 83; Abstraction, Maine Coast Artists, Rockport, 85; Here and Now in Maine, Westbrook, 85; solo exhibs, Midtown, New York, 87-89. *Pos:* Mem, Maine Biennial Comt, Portland Mus Art, 81-83 & Visual Arts Panel, Maine State Comn, 79-83. *Teaching:* Instr mural proj, Skowhegan High Sch, 85 & Univ Southern Maine, 86; instr gifted class art, Madison High Sch, 86. *Bibliog:* Edgar Allen Beam (auth), 2 stars of the 3rd magnitude, Maine Times, 85; Susan Elizabeth Ryan (auth), Roy Slamm and Abby Shahn making art up country, Artists in Maine, summer 86; Ken Greenleaf (auth), One of the best artists, Maine Times. *Mem:* Union of Maine Visual Artists. *Media:* Egg Tempera. *Publ:* Illusr, Visions Mag, 70. *Dealer:* Midtown Payson Galleries 745 Fifth Ave New York NY 10151. *Mailing Add:* Box 95 Solon ME 04979

SHAHN, BERNARDA BRYSON
PAINTER, WRITER
b Athens, Mar 7, 03. *Study:* Ohio Univ, 21-26; Cleveland Sch Art; John Huntington Evening Sch; New Sch for Soc Res. *Work:* Ammon-Carter Mus, Wichita, Kans. *Comn:* Murals, Bronx Post Off, Bronx, NY,; Roosevelt Community Bldg, Roosevelt, NJ. *Exhib:* Annual Exhib, Whitney Mus Am Art, New York, 30; Brooklyn Mus; Springfield Mus Art, Utah, 84; Politics in Art: The Art of Politics, Mus of the Borough of Brooklyn, 84; Trenton City Mus, NJ, 85; Realism Between the Wars, Transco Bldg, Houston, Tex, 85; Prints by American Women, Asn Am Artists, New York, 86; Modern Mythology, travelling show, 87-88. *Pos:* Mem, bd gov, Skowhegan Sch Painting & Sculpture, currently. *Teaching:* Instr etching & lithography, Columbus Mus Sch, formerly. *Awards:* Rembrandt Graphics Award, NJ Print Club; First Place, Springfield Nat Figurative Show. *Bibliog:* Russell Lynes (auth), Bernarda Bryson Shahn: Illustrator, Print, Vol 10 No 7, 55; Edward Rubin (auth), Bernarda Bryson Shahn, Art News, 1/84; Raymond J Steiner (auth), Bernarda Bryson Shahn, Art Times, 6/86. *Mem:* Artists Union, 34- *Publ:* Auth & illusr, The Twenty Miracles of Saint Nicholas, Little Brown, 60; The Zoo of Zeus, Grossman Publ, 64; Gilgamesh: Man's First, Holt, Rinehart & Winston, 67; Lettering in the Work of Ben Shahn, Graphics, Vol 208, 81; Ben Shahn, Harry N Abrams, 72; Garrity US History, Harcourt, 82. *Dealer:* Midtown Payson Galleries 745 Fifth Ave New York NY 10151. *Mailing Add:* c/o Midtown-Payson Galleries 745 Fifth Ave New York NY 10151

SHAINMAN, JACK S
ART DEALER, GALLERY DIRECTOR
b Pittsfield, Mass, July 21, 57. *Study:* Am Univ, BA, 82. *Pos:* Owner, Jack Shainman Gallery, New York, NY. *Specialty:* Contemporary American, Canadian and European art of all media. *Publ:* Numerous reviews of the Jack Shainman Gallery in newspapers and mags. *Mailing Add:* Jack Shainman Gallery 560 Broadway 2nd Fl New York NY 10012

SHALKOP, ROBERT LEROY
CONSULTANT
b Milford, Conn, July 30, 22. *Study:* Maryville Col, Tenn, 40-42; Univ Chicago, 46-50, MA, 49; Sorbonne, Univ Paris, 51-52. *Collections Arranged:* Arroyo Hondo, the Folk Art of a New Mexican Village (with catalog); Reflections of Spain: a Comparative View of Spanish Colonial Sculpture (with catalog), 68; Reflections of Spain II: Spanish Colonial Painting (with catalog), 69; 100 Years of Painting in the Pike's Peak Region (with catalog); Russian Orthodox Art in Alaska (with catalog), 73; Sydney Laurence, an Alaskan Impressionist (with catalog), 75; Eustace Ziegler (with catalog), 77; Contemporary Native Art of Alaska (with catalog), 79; Henry Wood Elliot (with catalog), 82. *Pos:* Dir, Rahr Civic Ctr, Manitowac, Wis, 53-56, Everhart Mus, Scranton, Pa, 56-62, Brooks Mem Art Gallery, Memphis, Tenn, 62-64; assoc dir, Colorado Springs Fine Arts Ctr & cur, Taylor Mus, 64-71; Dir, Anchorage Mus Hist, 72-87; Freelance Mus Consult, 88- *Mem:* Asn Art Mus Dirs; Am Asn Mus; Art Mus Asn. *Publ:* Auth, Wooden Saints, the Santos of New Mexico, 67; Sydney Laurence, His Life and Work, 82. *Mailing Add:* 309 W Marsh St Salisbury NC 99501

SHAMAN, SANFORD SIVITZ
MUSEUM DIRECTOR, CURATOR
b Pittsburgh, Pa, July 11, 46. *Study:* Ohio Univ, Athens, BFA, 68; State Univ NY Binghamton, 70-71; Villa Schifanoia Grad Sch Fine Arts, Florence, Italy, MFA, 74. *Collections Arranged:* Contemporary Chicago Painters (auth, catalog), Ohio State Univ, Fla State Univ, Univ SFla & Univ Northern Iowa Gallery Art, 77-78; De Kooning 1969-1978 (auth, catalog), Univ Northern Iowa Gallery Art, St Louis Art Mus, Contemp Arts Ctr, Cincinnati & Akron Art Inst, 78-79; Standards by Allan Kaprow (auth, catalog), Univ Northern Iowa Gallery Art; The Contemporary Amercan Potter (ed & contribr, catalog), 80-82 & Noritake Art Deco Porcelains: Collection of Howard Kottler (auth, catalog), 82-84, Smithsonian Inst Traveling Exhibs; Philip Pearlstein: Painting to Watercolors (auth, catalog), Wash State Univ & Univ Northern Iowa, 83-84; Rodney Alan Greenblat's Reality & Imagination, Two Taste Treats in One (auth, catalog), Penn State Univ; Inst of Contemp Art, 86-87; Robert Yarber Paintings: 1980-88 (auth, catalog), Penn State Univ; Mus of Fine Arts. *Pos:* Cur, Huntington Galleries, WVa, 74-75; asst cur, Mem Art Gallery, Rochester, NY, 75-77; Dir, Gallery of Art, Univ Northern Iowa, Cedar Falls, 77-80; dir, Museum Art, Wash State Univ, Pullman, 80-84, Pa State Univ, 80-89; Evaluator, Am Asn Mus, Mus Assessment Prog, 85-88; dir Fine Arts, Univ of Haifa, Israel, currently. *Teaching:* Vis lectr, WVa State Col, 75; adj faculty, Univ Northern Iowa, 78. *Awards:* Villa Schifanoia Grad Sch Fine Arts Scholar, Florence, 72; Univ Northern Iowa Fac Res Award, 79-80; Nat Endowment Arts Fel, 83; B'nai B'rith Hillel Found Leadership Fel, Jewish Acad. *Bibliog:* Donald Miller (auth), A new art museum is his dream at Pennsylvania State, Pittsburgh Post Gazette, 2/24/87; Ethics and professionalism, Museum News, 12/88. *Mem:* Am Asn Mus; Pa Coun Arts, vchmn mus adv panel; Eastern Wash State Hist Soc (trustee, 82-84); Asn Col & Univ Mus & Galleries (vpres, 81-82, pres, 82-83); and others. *Publ:* Philip Pearlstein: Painting to Watercolors, Arts Mag, 10/84; Auth, Rodney Alan Greenblat's Reality and Imagination: two tastes in one, Arts Mag, 5/87; In step with the new vulgarity, New Art Examiner, 12/87; An interview with Philip Pearlstein, Art in Am, 9/81; contribr, Arts Voice, Atlanta Art Papers & New Art Examiner, 83; and others. *Mailing Add:* Art Dept Univ of Haifa Mt Carmel Haifa 31999 Israel

SHANER, (GEORGE) DAVID
CERAMIST, CRAFTSMAN
b Pottstown, Pa, Nov 11, 34. *Study:* State Col, Kutztown, Penn, BS(art ed), 56; NY State Col Ceramics, Alfred Univ, MA(ceramic design), 59. *Work:* Royal Ont Mus, Toronto; Mus Contemp Crafts, New York; Everson Mus Art, Syracuse, NY; Nat Arts Collection, Smithsonian Inst, Washington, DC; Kansas City Art Inst, Mo. *Exhib:* Everson Mus Art, New York, 66 & 79; Craftsman USA, Mus Contemp Crafts, New York, 66; US Info Agency Exhib, Far East, Middle East, South Am & Africa, 74; Smithsonian Inst, Washington, DC, 79; Potters Dozen-NCECA, Univ Mich, Ann Arbor, 80; 8th Chunichi Int Exhib Ceramic Arts, Nagoya, Tokyo & Kanazawa, Japan, 80. *Pos:* Asst prof art, Univ Ill, Urbana, 59-63; res potter & dir, Archie Bray Found, Helena, Mont, 63-70; self-employed studio potter, Bigfork, Mont, 70- *Awards:* Louis Comfort Tiffany Scholar Award, 63; Nat Endowment Arts craftsman fel, 73 & 78. *Bibliog:* Garth Clark (auth), A Century of American Ceramics: 1878-1978, 79; Peter Sabin (auth), David Shaner: Montana Conversation, Studio Potter Vol 8, No 1, Daniel Clark Found, 79; Harrington (auth), Northwest Ceramics, Univ Wash Press, 79. *Mem:* Archie Bray Found (trustee, 70-, chmn 76-); Mont Arts Coun (vchmn, 77-). *Mailing Add:* c/o Hookaday Center for the Arts Second Ave E & Third St Kalispell MT 59901

SHANGRAW, CLARENCE FRANK
HISTORIAN, CURATOR
b Burlington, Vt, Aug 9, 35. *Study:* Inst Far Eastern Lang, Yale Univ, cert; Univ Calif, Berkeley, AB(with high honors), MA(Oriental lang & lit). *Collections Arranged:* Avery Brundage Collection of Asian Art Permanent Collection, 65-; Chinese Gold, Silver & White Porcelain from the Carl Kempe Collection, 71; Ancient Indonesian Art of the Central & Eastern Japanese Periods, 71; Rarities of the Musee Guimet: Asian Art from a French Museum, winter 75; Exhibition of Archeological Finds of the People's Republic of China, summer 75; 5,000 Years of Korean Art (contribr, catalog), 79; Chinese Blue-and-White Porcelain from Drake's Bay, 79; Treasures from the Shanghai Museum--6,000 Years of Chinese Art (contribr & translr, catalog), Asian Art Mus, 83; Masterworks of Ming: 15th century blue and white porcelains, 85; Marvels of Medieval China: Song and Yuan Lacquers, 86; Looking at Patronage: Recent Acquisitions of Asian Art (contrib, catalog), 89. *Pos:* Res asst, De Young Mus, San Francisco, 65-66, asst cur, 66-67; cur, Asian Art Mus, San Francisco, 69-71, sr cur, 72-84, actg dir, 85, chief cur, 85-, dep dir, 90- *Teaching:* Adj prof, John F Kennedy Univ, Sch Museum Studies, 79- *Mem:* Oriental Ceramics Soc, London; Am Asn Mus; Archeol Inst Am. *Res:* Early Chinese ceramics, prehistoric to the Han; Chinese Buddhist sculpture; archaeology in China; Asiatic canine breeds; chinese glass. *Publ:* Auth, A Cross-section of Chinese Blue and White Porcelains in the Asian Art Museum, 7/80 & Chinese Cloissone and Painted Enamels in the 18th Century, 7/80, Apollo; Korean art in western collections: The Asian Art Museum of San Francisco, Korean Cult, 1/82; coauth, The Drake and Cermeno Expeditions' Chinese Porcelains at Drakes Bay, California, 82; auth, Archaeological treasures from Shanghai, Archaeol, 5/83; Fifteenth century blue and white porcelains in the Asian Art Mus of San Francisco, 5/85 & Chinese Lacquers in the Asian Art Mus of San Francisco, 4/86, Orientations. *Mailing Add:* Asian Art Mus Golden Gate Park San Francisco CA 94118

SHANKMAN, GARY CHARLES
PAINTER
b Washington, DC, Sept 30, 50. *Study:* Sch Fine & Applied Arts, Boston Univ, BFA, 68-73; Sch Arts & Sci, Am Univ, MFA, 73-75; Koninklijke Academie voor Schone Kunsten, Belg, 75-76; Skowhegan Sch, 78. *Work:* Mabee-Gerrer Mus Shawnee, Okla; Superior Ct Art Trust, Washington, DC; Nat Home Furnishings Asn, Chicago, Ill. *Comn:* Cover design ITT Int Fel Yearbook. *Exhib:* solo exhibs, Still Life & Landscapes, Seta House, Antwerp, Belg, 76, H C Dickens, London, Eng, 82, Patterns of Light, Mickelson Gallery, Washington, DC, 85, Reflections, 88 & Confections, 92, Painters Light, Shelnutt Gallery & Rensselger Polytechnic Inst, Troy, NY, 89; 48th Ann Midyear Exhib, Butler Inst Am Art, 84; New Work for the Nineties, George Sherman Union Gallery, Boston Univ, Mass, 90; 14th Ann Landscape Competition, Rensselaer Co Coun Arts, Troy, NY, 90; Sage Studios, Fac Exhib, Russell Sage Col, Troy, NY, 91; Six Realist Painters, Miller Gallery, Cincinnati, 92; Home and Family Matters, Warren St Gallery, Hudson, NY, 92; and others. *Pos:* Artist-in-residence, State of Okla, 80. *Teaching:* Instr drawing & painting, Smithsonian Inst, Washington, DC, 78- & Md Col Art & Design, 81-86; assoc prof drawing & design, Sage Jr Col Albany, NY, 86- *Awards:* First Place, Nat Home Furnishing Asn, 85; First Place, Nat Landscape Competition, Tolley Galleries, Washington, DC, 83. *Bibliog:* John Greenya (auth), Painter's progress, Washington Post Mag, 80; Merrie Aiken (auth), An American artist paints English scene, 82 & Lucia Anderson (auth), Time to do something for themselves, 84, Potomac News. *Media:* Oil. *Dealer:* Mickelson Gallery 707 G St Washington DC 20001; Miller Gallery 2715 Erie Ave Hyde Park Sq Cincinatti, OH 45208. *Mailing Add:* 157 S Lake Ave Albany NY 12208

SHANNON, CHARLES
PAINTER
b Montgomery, Ala, June 22, 14. *Study:* Emory Univ, 30-32; Cleveland Sch Art, dipl(cum laude), 36. *Work:* War Dept Collection Combat Paintings, Washington, DC; Montgomery Mus of Fine Arts. *Exhib:* Nat Gallery, 44; Metrop Mus Art, New York, 50; retrospective, Southeastern Ctr Contemp Art, Winston-Salem, NC, Hunter Mus Art & others, 81-82; Southern Works on Paper, 1900-1940, 81-82 & Southern Drawings and Prints, 83-84, Southern Arts Fedn; Painting in the South, 1546-1980, Va Mus, 83-84; West 83--Art and the Law Traveling Exhib, 83-84. *Pos:* Picture ed & illusr, Army Info & Educ Div, New York, 44-46. *Teaching:* Artist in residence, WGa Col, 40-42; instr, Univ Ala Exten Ctr, Montgomery, 58-68; prof art & dept head, Auburn Univ, Montgomery, 69-79. *Awards:* First Award Figure Composition, Cleveland Mus Art Ann May Show, 36; Third Prize Int Div, Golden Gate Exposition, San Francisco, 39; Purchase Award, West 83--Art and the Law, West Publ Co, 83. *Mailing Add:* 1470 Midlane Ct Montgomery AL 36101

SHANNONHOUSE, SANDRA
SCULPTOR
b Petaluma, Calif, May 19, 47. *Study:* Univ Calif, Davis, BS, 69, MFA(dramatic art), 73. *Work:* Utah Mus Fine Arts, Salt Lake City. *Exhib:* One-man shows, Quay Gallery, San Francisco, 75, 78 & 80, Stephen Wirtz Gallery, 82, 84, 86; A Decade of Ceramic Art 1962-1972, San Francisco Mus Mod Art, Calif, 73; R Joseph Monson Collection, Seattle Mus Art Washington, DC, 74; Birthday Show, Mus Contemp Crafts, New York, 76; Calif Clay I & II, Braunstein/Quay Gallery, New York, 76 & 77; An Exhibiton of Bay Area Ceramics, Fine Arts Mus, San Francisco, 77; Nothern California Clay Routes: Sculpture Now, San Francisco Mus Mod Art, 79; Clay Attitudes, Queens Mus, New York, 79; One plus One Equals Two, exhib organized by Bernice Steinbaum Gallery, New York, 84-86; Works in Bronze: A Modern Survey, Sonoma State Univ Travelling Show, 85-86. *Teaching:* Lectr form in theatre, Univ Calif, Davis, 74; instr ceramics & drawings, Am River Col, Sacramento, Calif, 75-76; guest artist, Otis Art Inst, Los Angeles, Calif, 76-78; artist-in-residence ceramics, Oxbow Summer Sch Art, Saugatuck, Mich, 76. *Bibliog:* Suzanne Foley (auth), A Decade of Ceramic Art, San Francisco Mus Art, 72; Sandy Ballatore (auth), The California Clay Rush, Art in Am, 76; Mac McCloud (auth), Dealer's choice, Images & Issues, 9-10/83; Beth Coffelt (auth), Recent Bronzees, Stephen Writz Gallery. *Media:* Bronze, Clay. *Dealer:* Stephen Wirtz Gallery 345 Sutter St San Francisco CA 94108. *Mailing Add:* c/o John Natsoulas Gallery 140 F St Davis CA 95616

SHAP, SYLVIA
PAINTER
b Toledo, Ohio, Mar 29, 48. *Study:* Otis Art Inst, 65; Univ Judaism, 68-71. *Work:* Art Mus South Texas, Corpus Christi; Atlantic Richfield Co, Anchorage, Alaska; Downey Mus Art, Calif; South Calif Gas Co; Los Angeles Music Ctr, Calif. *Comn:* Portrait, comn by Audrey & Billy Wilder, Los Angeles, Calif, 82; portrait, comn by Henry Mancini, Los Angeles, 84; portrait, comn by Eileen & Peter Norton, Los Angeles, 87; portrait, comn by Victoria Principal, Beverly Hills, 92. *Exhib:* Contemp Southern Calif Art, Mus Fine Arts, Taipei, Taiwan & Los Angeles Municipal Gallery, 87; Hollywood: Portraits of Stars, Otis/Parsons, Los Angeles, 88; Some Members of My Family, Los Angeles Municipal Gallery, 88 & Art Mus S Tex, Corpus Christi, 89; solo exhib, Art Mus S Tex, 89; portraits, Jose Drudis-Biada Gallery, Los Angeles, 90. *Pos:* Instr, Calif State, Fullerton, 83, Yeshiva Univ, Los Angeles, 86. *Teaching:* Gifted Children's Prog, Otis-Parsons, Los Angeles, 92; lectr, mus & univs; TV appearances. *Bibliog:* Art in America, 86; Gregory Firlotte (auth), The image makers, Designers West, 87; Joanna Krotz (auth), How to Commission a Portrait, Money Mag, 90. *Mem:* Los Angeles Mus Art. *Media:* Oil, Miscellaneous Media. *Mailing Add:* 648 N Laurel Rd Los Angeles CA 90048

SHAPERO, ESTHER GELLER See Geller, Esther (Esther Geller Shapero)

SHAPIRO, ADRIAN MICHAEL
LECTURER, WRITER
b Galveston, Tex, April 13, 50. *Study:* Univ Tex, Austin, BA(cum laude), 72, MA, 73; Ind Univ, Bloomington, PhD, 77. *Collections Arranged:* Slavko Kopac--Recent Work (coauth, catalog), 82; Claude Bellegarde--Homage to Color, 82. *Pos:* Contrib ed, Art Happenings mag, 80-86; Managing partner, FAME Gallery, Houston, 80-86; dir, Post Oak Fine Art Distribr, Houston, 81-88; sec, Texas Mod Art Foun, 82-87; mem, Mus Fine Arts, Houston & B'nai B'rith Int, currently. *Teaching:* Lectr, Univ Houston, 77-79; Our Lady of the Lake Univ, 87-, Texas Mod Art Foun, 87- *Specialty:* Contemporary prints and art appreciation lectures. *Publ:* The origin of print collecting, Art Happenings Mag, 81; The search for original prints, Southwest Art Mag, 82; Corporate art collections, Art Happenings Mag, 83. *Mailing Add:* 5230 Arboles St No C-1 Houston TX 77035

SHAPIRO, BABE
PAINTER, ADMINISTRATOR
b Irvington, NJ, May 4, 37. *Study:* NJ State Teachers Col, Newark, BS; Hunter Col, with Robert Motherwell, MA. *Work:* Newark Mus; Andrew Dickson White Mus, Cornell Univ; Albright-Knox Art Gallery, Buffalo; Corcoran Gallery Art, Washington, DC; Scottish Nat Gallery of Mod Art, Edinburgh. *Exhib:* Biennial Exhib Contemp Am Painting, Univ Ill, 63; New York World's Fair, 65; Cincinnati Art Mus, 66; Indianapolis Mus Art, 70; New Museum Acquisitions, Colorado Springs Fine Arts Mus, 72; plus others. *Pos:* Dir, Mount Royal Grad Sch Painting, Md Inst Col Art, Baltimore, currently. *Teaching:* Artist in residence, Quincy Art Club, 66. *Awards:* Newark Mus Triennial Purchase Prize Award, 58 & 61; First Prize in Painting, Monmouth Col, NJ, 63. *Media:* Acrylic. *Dealer:* Paula Allen Gallery 110 Greene St New York NY 10012; Dalsheimer Gallery 336 North Charles St Baltimore MD 21201. *Mailing Add:* 31 Walker St New York NY 10013

SHAPIRO, DAVID
PAINTER, PRINTMAKER
b Brooklyn, NY, June 26, 44. *Study:* Skowhegan Sch Art, Maine, 65; Pratt Inst, BFA, 66; Ind Univ, Bloomington, MFA, 68. *Work:* Brooklyn Mus, Guggenheim Mus & Mus Mod Art, New York; San Francisco Mus Mod Art; Ft Lauderdale Mus Art, Fla. *Exhib:* Poindexter Gallery, New York, 71, 73, 74 & 77; Gloria Luria Gallery, Fla, 79, 81, 83, 85 & 88; Getler/Pall/Saper Gallery, New York, 81, 83 & 85; Jan Turner Gallery, Los Angeles, 87; Dolan/Maxwell Gallery, Philadelphia, 87 & 88; Fay Gold Gallery, Atlanta, 88. *Teaching:* Instr, Pratt Inst, 69-71; vis artist, Barnard Col, 72; guest artist, Kansas City Art Inst, 73; instr, Parsons Sch Design, 74-80. *Bibliog:* M L Thompson (auth), Cosmos and chaos, Arts Mag, 10/80; Jon R Friedman (auth), Elucidation in the art of David Shapiro, Arts Mag, 11/85. *Media:* Acrylic. *Dealer:* Dolan/Maxwell Gallery 154 Wooster St New York NY 10012. *Mailing Add:* 315 Riverside Dr New York NY 10025

SHAPIRO, DAVID
PAINTER, LECTURER
b New York, NY, Aug 28, 16. *Study:* Educ Alliance Art Sch, 33-35; Am Artists Sch, 36-39. *Work:* Metrop Mus Art, New York; Brooklyn Mus, NY; Philadelphia Mus Art; Nat Mus Am Art; Libr Cong, Washington, DC; and others. *Comn:* Black & white intaglios, Assoc Am Artists Gallery, New York, 70-75; color lithographs, Litografie Int, Milan, Italy, 70; stained glass windows, Garden Jewish Ctr, Flushing, NY, 70; black & white intaglio,

Ferdinand Roten Galleries, 77; original print, Collectors Group, 76, 77 & 82. *Exhib:* Pa Acad Ann, Philadelphia, 47; Whitney Ann, New York, 52; Brooklyn Mus Print Ann, 53; Libr Cong Print Ann, 53; Corcoran Biennial, Washington, DC, 59. *Pos:* Art ed, Hofstra Rev, Hofstra Univ, 65-70. *Teaching:* Instr studio art, Smith Col, 46-47; asst prof studio art & art hist, Univ BC, 47-49; prof studio art & art hist, Hofstra Univ, Hempstead, NY, 61-81, prof emer, 81-; artist in residence & prof Am art, Univ Belgrade, 81. *Awards:* Fulbright Fel, 51-53 & 81; Purchase Awards, Brooklyn Mus Print Ann, 46, Libr Cong Print Ann, 50 & Mus Fine Arts, Springfield, Mass, 57. *Mem:* Soc Am Graphic Artists (pres, 68-70, exec coun, 70-); Col Art Asn Am. *Media:* Acrylic, Oil. *Res:* American art with emphasis on art of the 30's. *Publ:* Auth, Stanley William Hayter, expression of the unconscious (catalog essay), 4/70; Social Realism: Art as a Weapon, Frederick Ungar Publ Co, 73; contribr, Search for an American image, Am Art Rev, 5-6/74; Abstract expressionism: the politics of apolitical painting, Prospects, 77; auth, Abstract Expressionism: A Critical Record, Cambridge Univ Press, 89. *Dealer:* Woodstock Gallery of Art Gallery Pl Woodstock VT 05091; Chaffee Art Ctr 16 S Main St Rutland VT 05701. *Mailing Add:* RFD 77 Cavendish VT 05142

SHAPIRO, DAVID (DAVID JOEL SHAPIRO)
CRITIC, EDUCATOR
b Newark, NJ, Jan 2, 47. *Study:* Columbia Col, BA, 68; Clare Col Cambridge, Eng, BA, MA, 70- 74; Columbia Univ, PhD, 73. *Pos:* Ed Assoc, Art News, 69-70, Architectures Mag, 89-; ed bd, RES, Harvard. *Teaching:* Assoc prof, William Paterson, Wayne, NY, 80-; vis prof, architecture, Cooper Union, NY, 80-; asst prof, Columbia Univ, 73-79, Brooklyn Col, Princeton Univ. *Awards:* Zabel Prize, Nat Acad Inst Arts & Letters,77; Nat Endowment Humanities, for research in poetry & painting, 78; Nat Endowment Art, for poetry, 79. *Bibliog:* Stephen Paul Miller (auth), David Shapiro, Jasper Johns: An Analogy (Master's Thesis, City Col); Michael Simon, Padgett Shapiro Master's Thesis, Brown Univ. *Mem:* ed bd, RES Mag, Harvard/Peabody Mus; advisor, Poet's House. *Res:* Interdisciplinary modern Semiotics and aesthetics. *Publ:* Auth, John Ashbery's Poetry, Columbia Univ Press, 77; Jim Dine: Painting What One Is, Abrams, 80; Jasper Johns' Drawings, Abrams, 84; Mondrian Flowers, Abrams, 91; coauth, Artistic Collaboration in the 20th-Century Art, Smithsonian Inst Press, 84. *Mailing Add:* 3001 Henry Hudson Pkwy Linden House 3B Bronx NY 10463

SHAPIRO, DEE
PAINTER, LECTURER
b Brooklyn, NY, Nov 30, 36. *Study:* Univ Mex, 56; Queens Col, BA, 58, MS, 60. *Work:* Newark Mus; Oklahoma Art Mus, Oklahoma City; Guggenheim Mus; NY Univ; Dayton Art Inst, Ohio; Everson Mus, Syracuse, NY. *Exhib:* Solo exhibs, Nassau Co Mus Fine Arts, Roslyn, NY, 74 & 83, Andre Zarre Gallery, NY, 76-78, 80, 81, 83, 85-87 & 91, Everson Mus, Syracuse, NY, 81, Dubins Gallery, La, 82 & Ana Sklar Gallery, Fla, 83; Brooklyn Mus, 75; Albright-Knox Mus, Buffalo, NY, 80; Suzanne Brown Gallery, Scottsdale, Ariz, 81. *Pos:* Gallery dir & cur, North Shore Community Arts Ctr, 79-81; cur, Wunsch Art Ctr, Glen Cove, NY; contrib ed, Stylist-Rebus Inc, New York. *Teaching:* Instr, Adelphi Univ, 81-, Empire State Col, 83-86. *Awards:* Nat Asn Women Artists Award, 73; Award Excellence, Heckscher Mus, 74; Video Tex Grant, Nat Endowment Arts, 86. *Bibliog:* Judith Tannenbaum (auth), Dee Shapiro, Arts Mag, 78; Barbara Flug Colin (auth), The pattern of a painter, New York Arts J, 81. *Mem:* Col Art Asn. *Publ:* Bordering on the Decorative, Central Hall Newsletter, 80. *Dealer:* Andre Zarre 194 Wooster St New York NY 10012. *Mailing Add:* 28 Clover Dr Great Neck NY 11021

SHAPIRO, IRVING
PAINTER, INSTRUCTOR
b Chicago, Ill, Mar 28, 27. *Study:* Art Inst Chicago; Chicago Acad Fine Art; Am Acad Art, Chicago. *Work:* Univ Vt; Columbus Mus Art, Ga; Lakeview Mus Art, Peoria, Ill; Ill State Mus, Springfield; Macon Mus Art, Ga. *Exhib:* Am Watercolor Soc Ann, Nat Acad Design Gallery, 58-72; Union League Club Chicago, 55, 57 & 59; Butler Inst Am Art, Youngstown, Ohio, 62; Art Inst Chicago Sales & Rental Galleries, 66-68. *Teaching:* Instr watercolors, Am Acad Art, 45-, dir, 71- *Awards:* Am Watercolor Soc Award, 81; Grumbacher Silver Medal, 81; Winsor & Newton Bronze Medal, 82. *Mem:* Am Watercolor Soc; Midwest Watercolor Soc. *Media:* Watercolor. *Publ:* Auth & illusr, article, Am Artist, 59 & 79; auth & illusr, Watercolor Techniques, 70; auth & illusr, Acrylic Watercolor, 71; auth & illusr, Palette Talks, 72 & 79. *Dealer:* Gallery of the Ravens Estes Park CO 80517; R H Love Galleries, Chicago IL. *Mailing Add:* 650 Onwetsia Highland Park IL 60035

SHAPIRO, JOEL (ELIAS)
SCULPTOR
b New York, NY, Sept 27, 41. *Study:* NY Univ, BA & MA. *Work:* Fogg Art Mus; Metrop Mus Mod Art & Whitney Mus Am Art, New York; Albright-Knox Art Gallery, Buffalo; Stedelijk Mus, Amsterdam; Israel Mus, Jerusalem; Philadelphia Mus Art, Pa; Moderna Museet, Stockholm, Switz; Cleveland Mus Art; NC Mus Art, Raleigh; Des Moines Art Ctr. *Comn:* Sculpture, One Logan Sq Assoc, Philadelphia; sculpture, Kawamura Mem Mus, Tokyo; Creative Artists Agency, Los Angeles; US Federal Building and Curthouse, Los Angeles; Hood Mus Art, Dartmouth, NH; Fukuoka Sogo Bank, Fukuoka, Japan. *Exhib:* One-man shows, Kunstmus Dusseldorf, 86, Hans Strelow, Dusseldorg, 88; Galerie Daniel Templon, Paris, 88; Waddington Gallery, London, 89; Museet I Varberg (with catalog), Varberg, Sweden, 90; IVAM Ctre Julio Gonzalez (with catalog), Valencia, Spain, 90; Ctr for Fine Arts, Miami (with catalog), 91; Drawings-Sculptures, Inst Contemp Art, Boston, 80; Am Drawing in Black and White, Brooklyn Mus, NY, 80; Whitney Biennial, Whitney Mus Am Art, NY, 81; New Dimensions in Drawing, Aldrich Mus Contemp Art, Conn, 81; Drawings from Georgia Collections, 19th & 20th Centuries, High Mus Art, Atlanta, 81; New Acquisitions, Whitney Mus Am Art, NY, 81; Akron Art Mus, Ohio, 81; Documenta 7, Kassel WGer, 82; An American Renaissance: Painting & Sculpture since 1940, Mus Art, Ft Lauderdale, 86; group exhib, The Saatchi Collection, London, 88; and others. *Awards:* Brandeis Award, 84; Skowhegan Medal for Sculpture, 86; Merit Medal for Sculpture, Am Acam & Inst Arts & Letts, 90. *Bibliog:* Jeremy Gilbert-Rolfe (auth), Joel Shapiro: works in progress, 12/73 & Marc Field (auth), On Joel Shapiro's sculptures and drawings, summer 78, Artforum; Carter Ratcliff (auth), Joel Shapiro's drawings, Print Collector's Newlett, 3-4/78; Joel Shapiro: Sculpture and Drawing, Whitechapel Gallery, London, 80. *Mailing Add:* c/o Paula Cooper 155 Wooster St New York NY 10012

SHAPIRO, MICHAEL EDWARD
MUSEUM DIRECTOR
b New York, NY, Nov 15, 49. *Study:* Hamilton Col, BA, 72; Williams Col, MA(Kress Fel), 76; Harvard Univ, MA(Teaching Fel), 78, PhD, 80. *Collections Arranged:* Frederic Remington: the Masterworks, St Louis Art Mus, 88, Buffalo Bill Hist Ctr, Cody, Wyo, 88, Mus Fine Arts, Houston, Tex, 89 & Metrop Mus Art, New York, 89; Modern Art from the Pulitzer Collection: Fifty Years of Connoisseurship (auth, brochure), Fogg Art Mus, Harvard Col, 88 & St Louis Art Mus, 88; New Sculpture/Six Artists, 88 & Currents 41: Judy Pfaff, 90, St Louis Art Mus; George Caleb Bingham, St Louis Art Mus & Nat Gallery of Art, Washington, DC, 90. *Pos:* Guest cur, Nat Mus Am Art, 80-81; cur 19th & 20th Century art, St Louis Art Mus, 84-92, chief cur, 87-92, secr bd comnrs, 89-91; dir, Los Angeles Co Mus Art, 92-. *Teaching:* Asst prof, dept art, Duke Univ, Durham, NC, 80-84. *Publ:* Auth, Nature into sculpture: Nancy Graves and the tradition of direct casting, Arts, 11/84; Twentieth-Century American sculpture, Bull St Louis Art Mus, winter 86; George Caleb Bingham, Antiques, 7/90; Gerhard Richter: Paintings, Photographs and Prints in the Collection of the St Louis Art Mus, Bull St Louis Art Mus, summer 92. *Mailing Add:* 5291 Westminster Pl St Louis MO 63108

SHARITS, PAUL JEFFREY
FILM ARTIST, PAINTER
b Denver, Colo, Feb 7, 43. *Study:* Univ Denver, BFA(painting), 64; Ind Univ, MFA(visual design), 66. *Work:* Mus Mod Art, New York & Paris; Albright-Knox Art Gallery, Buffalo, NY; Ga Mus Art, Athens; Arco Ctr Visual Arts, Los Angeles; Art Inst Chicago; and others. *Comn:* Four-screen film environment, Contemp Arts Mus, Houston, 71; four-screen film environment, Artpark, State of NY, Lewiston, 75; three-screen film environment, Walker Art Ctr, 74. *Exhib:* Projected Images, Walker Art Ctr, Minneapolis, 74; one-man shows, Albright-Knox Gallery (film), Buffalo, 76, Art Gallery Ont (film), Toronto, 78, Whitney Mus (film), New York, 84, Amsterdam Art Fair (ed of prints), Galerie A, 90, Big Orbit Gallery, Buffalo, 91 & ICON, Buffalo, 91; A History of the American Avant-Garde Cinema, Mus Mod Art, New York, 76; film retrospective, Centre Nat d'Art et de Cult Georges-Pompidou, Paris, 77 & 3 complete progs on film, Berlin, 91; Film Installation, Whitney Biennial, 81; 3 screen film installation, Whitney Mus, 86; Begin Fluxus Fashion Designs, The Gallery, 91; Musi for Eyes & Ears, Emily Harvey Gallery, New York, 91; New Fluxus Work, Emily Harvey Gallery, New York, 92; Fluxattitudes, New Mus, New York, 92; Fluxus, Wieshaden, Ger, 92; var exhibs at major mus incl Mus Mod Art, Hayden Gallery, Whitney Mus Am Art & Albright-Know Art Gallery; and others. *Pos:* Artist in Residence, Calif Inst Arts, Valencia, 3/90; guest panelist, Stadtwerkstaff--TV, Buffalo Pub Access Cable TV Channel 32, 7/90; mem Acad Coun, Nautilus Found, 91; panelist & lectr var asns. *Teaching:* Instr film, Md Art Inst, Baltimore, 67-70; asst prof film, Antioch Col, Yellow Springs, Ohio, 70-73 & State Univ NY, Buffalo, 70-73; prof film, Dept Media Study, State Univ NY, Buffalo, 73-. *Awards:* Nat Endowment Arts Grant for film, 79 & 82; State Univ NY Creative Proj Grant, 83; DAAD Fel, Berlin, 87 & 89; and others. *Bibliog:* Susanne Deicher, Farbe-Vision: The Unpublished Diaries of Paul Sharitz, Berlin, 10/89; Annette Michelson (auth), Situations Americaine: les annees 60-70, Peinture Cinema-Peinture, 10/89; Jean Claude Lebensztein, Mournings Brilliance, Franco Maria Ricci, 2/90. *Mem:* Col Art Asn Am. *Media:* Film. *Publ:* Auth, Prepared Box for John Cage (catalog), Chicago Int Art Exposition, 5/87; Words per Page, Esthetics Contemp (rev ed), Prometheus Books, Buffalo, NY, 89; After Effect Special: The Cinematic Object, Geneva: Editions Fabriart, 90. *Dealer:* Galerie Ricke Friesenplatz 23 Cologne Ger. *Mailing Add:* 537 Lafayette Ave Buffalo NY 14222

SHARON, RUSSELL
PAINTER, SCULPTOR
b Minn, 1948. *Study:* Univ Ams, Sch of Liberal Arts, Mexico City, Mex, 68-72; MIT, Student Art Asn, Cambridge, Mass, MA, 74-75. *Comn:* Outdoor sculptures, comn by Mr & Mrs Orton, Calif, 88. *Exhib:* Solo exhibs, Ctr for Fine Arts, Miami, Fla, 87, The Gallery, New York, 89, Barbara Greene Gallery, Miami, Fla, 90, Minneapolis Inst Art, Minn, 90. *Bibliog:* John Herzfeld (auth), article, Art News, 4/87; Helen H Kohen (auth), article, Miami Herald, 2/16/88; Leslie Judd Ahlander (auth), On Site Sculpting at Art Center, Miami News, 3/11/88. *Mailing Add:* c/o Hal Bromm 90 W Broadway New York NY 10007

SHARP, ANNE
PAINTER, PRINTMAKER
b Red Bank, NJ, Nov 1, 43. *Study:* Pratt Inst, Brooklyn, NY, BFA, 65, with Richard Lindner; Brooklyn Col, MFA, with Lee Bontecou. *Work:* Smithsonian Inst, Nat Air & Space Mus, Washington, DC; Albright-Knox Art Gallery, Buffalo, NY; St Vincent's Hosp, New York; New York Pub Libr; New York Life Insurance Co Am. *Exhib:* One-man shows, Pace Editions,

New York, 74, Ten Downtown, 74 & NY Pub Libr, Epiphany Branch, 88, Books & Co, New York, 89, Kendall Gallery, New York, 90; Arteder 82, Bibao, Spain, 82; Cabo Frio Biennale 85-86, Int Print Show, 85-86, Cabo Frio, Brazil; Hempstead Harbor Art Assoc, Glen Cove, NY; Paper Art Exhib, Int Mus Contemp Art, Bahia, Brazil, 86; New York Pub Libr, Epiphany Br, 88; Kendall Gallery, New York, 88; Parsons Sch Design Gallery, Exhib Ctr, 89; FMK Gallery, Budapest, Hungary, 89; Q sen do Gallery, Kobe, Japan, 89; Anchorage Mus Hist & Art, Alaska, 90-91; Coos Art Mus, Ore, 90; Univ Alaska, Anchorage, 90, 91; Nat Mus Women Arts, Washington, DC, 91; Mus Ostdentsche Krungbou, South Bohemia, Czech. *Teaching:* Instr, NY Univ, 78, Sch Visual Arts, 78-89, Pratt Manhattan Ctr, 82-, State Univ NY, Purchase, 83, Parsons Sch Design, New York, 84-90. *Awards:* Teaching fel, Artist's Show, Brooklyn, NY, 72; Artist sponsor, Great Lakes Col Asn Apprenticeship Prog, 73-76; Artist in Residence, Va Ctr Creative Art, 75, Artpark, 80; Pippin Award, OurTown, 84. *Bibliog:* Helen Harrison (auth), The Budapest Gallery, Hungary; Art of Today II (catalog), 87; Galleries Fur Moderne Kunst, Schaurzenberg, Ger; The Wall (catalog), 90; NY Post, 12/7/91; Jerry Tallmer (auth), A Sharp View of the World. *Mem:* Nat Mus Women Arts; The Planetary Soc; Nat Space Inst; Alaska Natural Hist Asn; Pratt Alumni Asn; Col Art Asn Am. *Media:* Oil, Acrylic; Collage. *Publ:* Auth, Women Artists and the Business of Art, 78; Charles Schucker at Max Hutchinson Gallery, Arts Mag, 78; Swimming in the mainstream with her, fall 86, Thoughtlines, fall 86, Univ Va Mag. *Dealer:* Novo Arts 57 E 11th St New York NY 10003. *Mailing Add:* PO Box 100480 Anchorage AK 99510-0480

SHARP, LEWIS INMAN
DIRECTOR
b New York, NY, Dec 22, 41. *Study:* Lewis & Clark, Col, Portland, Ore, BA, 65; Univ Del, MA, 68 & PhD, 80. *Pos:* Asst cur Am paintings & sculpture, Metrop Mus Art, New York, 72-75, assoc cur Am paintings & sculpture, 75-82, adminr Am wing & curator, 82-86; dir, Denver Art Mus, 89- *Mem:* Asn Art Mus Dirs, 89- *Publ:* Auth, John Quincy Adams Ward: History & contemporary influences, The Am Art J, Vol IV, 11/72; The Smith Memorial, Sculptures of a City: Philadelphia's Treasures in Bronze & Stone, Walker Publ Co, 74; New York Public Sculpture by 19th Century American Artists, Metrop Mus Art, 74; contribr, The Architecture of Richard Morris Hunt, Univ Chicago Press, 86. *Mailing Add:* 661 Franklin St Denver CO 80216-3625

SHARP, SUSAN S
PAINTER
b North Bergen, NJ, Jan 4, 42. *Study:* Syracuse Univ, 60-62; Univ Hartford, BS, 64. *Work:* Chase Manhattan Bank, Kidder/Peabody, New York; Town of Fairfield, General Electric, Conn; Huntington Bank, Columbus, Ohio. *Exhib:* Conn Watercolor Soc, Wadsworth Atheneum, Hartford, 81; Conn Women Artists, John Slade Sly House, New Haven, 82; Winners Conn-Painters & Sculptors, Stamford Mus, 82; Art of Northeast, Silvermine Guild, New Canaan, Conn, 83, 85 & 89; Solo show, Water & Memory, Soho 20, 92; Abstract Connections, Silvermine Guild, 92. *Bibliog:* Roger Baldwin (auth), Art on the Town, Art New Eng, 85; Jude Schwendenwien (auth), A survey of Connecticut art, Art New Eng, 9/90; James Fox (auth), Gallery reviews, Art & Antiques, summer 92. *Mem:* Silvermine Guild (bd 85-86); Inst Visual Artists (pres 90-91). *Media:* Acrylic, Oil. *Dealer:* Soho 20 469 Broome St New York NY 10013. *Mailing Add:* 53 Wyldewood Rd Easton CT 06612

SHARP, WILLOUGHBY
VIDEO ARTIST, CONSULTANT
b New York, NY, Jan 23, 36. *Study:* Brown Univ, BA; Univ Paris; Univ Lausanne; Columbia Univ, MA. *Work:* Guggenheim Mus & Mus Mod Art, New York; Boston Mus Fine Arts; Nat Gallery Art, Calif; plus others. *Exhib:* Information, Mus Mod Art, New York, 70; Earth, Air, Fire, Water: Elements of Art, Boston Mus Fine Art, 71; Circuit: A Video Invitational, Everson Mus Art, Syracuse, NY, Henry Gallery, Univ Wash, Cranbrook Acad, Bloomfield & Los Angeles Co Mus, plus others, 73-74; Kunst Bleibt Kunst: Project, 74, Cologne, Ger, 74. *Pos:* Dir, Kineticism Press, 68-; pres, Avalanche Video, 70-; vpres, Ctr New Art Activities, Inc, (Sharpcom), 74-; dir, Franklin Street Arts Ctr, New York, 76-82; dir, Worldpool, Toronto, 79; cur videos, Guggenheim Mus, New York, 79-80. *Teaching:* Prof humanities & sci, Sch Visual Art, 83- *Awards:* Rockefeller Found Grant, 71; Kaplan Fund Grant, 71; Nat Endowment Arts Grant, 72 & 80; and others. *Bibliog:* Robert E Dallos (auth), Sculpture, NY Times, 8/30/67; Anthony Bannon (auth), Sharp puts himself into his art literally, Buffalo Eve News, 3/17/75; Douglas David (auth), Art, Newsweek, 7/21/75. *Dealer:* Electronic Arts Intermix Inc 84 Fifth Ave New York NY 10011. *Mailing Add:* 120 E 86th St No 5A New York NY 10028

SHARPE, (NORMAN) BLAIR
PAINTER
b Montreal, Que, July 25, 54. *Study:* Kent Sch, West Germany, A level, 72; Ottawa Sch Art, 73-74. *Work:* Can Coun Art Bank, Ottawa, Ont; Esso Resources Can--Petro Plaza Collection, Calgary, Alta; City of Ottawa Collection; Arts Court Gallery & Regional Municipality of Ottawa-Carleton, Ottawa, Ont. *Comn:* Painting, Mr & Mrs R McNally, Toronto, Ont, 88; mural, Jack Purcell Pool, comn by City of Ottawa, Art in Pub Pls Prog, 89; floor work, Smyth Transitway Station, Regional Municipality Ottawa-Carleton, Transart Prog, 90-91. *Exhib:* Regional Exhib, Agnes Etherington Art Ctr, Kingston, Ont, 81; Paint: The Expressive Touch, Gallery 111, Univ Manitoba, Winnipeg & Gairloch Gallrey, Oakvill, 81, SAW Gallery, Ottawa, Ont & Cedar Ridge Gallery, Scarborough, Ont, 82; A Selection of Canadian Paintings, Art Gallery at Harbourfront, Toronto, 81; Ottawa in The Hague, Artoteek The Hague, Netherlands, 86; Studios: Work in Progress, Arts Court Gallery, 89; Blair Sharpe: 15 Years of Work, Arts Court Gallary, Ottawa, 89 & Library and Gallery, Cambridge, Ont, 90. *Teaching:* Instr, drawing & painting, Ottawa Sch Art, 74-79, 88-, instr, Painting, Drawing & Studio Seminar II, 88-; instr, Workshops Ottawa Sch Art, 88- *Awards:* Post A Award, British Forces Educ, 73; Project Grant, Ont Arts Coun, 76, 77 & 80; Can Coun Arts Grant, 82. *Bibliog:* David Burnett (auth), article, Artscanada, 5-6/77; Anna Babinska (auth), article, Artmag, Can, 2-3/80; Mayo Graham (auth), Blair Sharpe: 15 Years of Work (exhib catalog & monogr), Arts Court Gallery, Ottawa, 90. *Mem:* Canadian Artists' Representation, Ont, (spokesperson, 83-86); SAW Gallery Inc, Ottawa, Ont (trustee, 81-87); Arts Court (gallery adv comt, 89-91) Ottawa, Ont; Coun Art in Ottawa; Gallery 101 Artist's Ctr, Ottawa, Ont (bd mem, 90-). *Media:* Acrylic, Watercolor. *Publ:* Auth, Juried exhibitions, In: Information for Artists, Canadian Artists Representation, Toronto, Ont, 88; Kenneth Lochhead: A Garden of Delights, Coun Arts in Ottawa, 88; review, John Sadler, 9-10/89 & La premier recit: Carla Whiteside at Gallery 101, 1-2/90, ARTicles, Coun Arts in Ottawa. *Dealer:* Lake Galleries 624 Richmond St W Toronto ON M5V 1Y9; Wallack Galleries 203 Bank St Ottawa ON Canada. *Mailing Add:* 32 Lewis St Ottawa ON K2P 0S3 Canada

SHARROW, SHEBA
PAINTER, EDUCATOR
b Brooklyn, NY, Apr 28, 26. *Study:* Art Inst Chicago, BFA, 48; Pa Acad Fine Art, 52; Tyler Sch Art, Temple Univ, MFA, 68. *Work:* Millersville State Col, Lancaster, Pa; Citibank, New York; Va Ctr Creative Arts, Sweet Briar, Va. *Exhib:* Art Inst Chicago, 48-51; State Mus Ill, Springfield, 49; Pa Acad Fine Art, Philadelphia, 52 & 64; Butler Inst Am Art, Youngstown, Ohio, 68; Nat Acad Design, New York, 69 & 79; Philadelphia Art Alliance, 63, 65, 69 & 70; William Penn Mem Mus, Harrisburg, Pa, 71, 75 & 78-80. *Teaching:* Assoc prof, Millersville State Col, Pa, 68-; retired. *Awards:* Resident Fels, Va Ctr Creative Arts, 78 & 79. *Mem:* Artists Equity Asn; Col Art Asn; Women's Caucus Art. *Media:* Acrylic. *Publ:* Contribr, chap, Women's Studies and the Arts, Hacker Art Books, 79. *Dealer:* Rosenfield Gallery Philadelphia PA. *Mailing Add:* 910 Abington Rd Cherry Hill NJ 08034-3902

SHASHATY, YOLANDA VICTORIA
PAINTER
b Chicago, Ind, Aug 13, 50. *Study:* Oberlin Col, BA, 72; Univ Wis-Madison, MA, 74. *Work:* Sunrise Mus, Charleston, WVa. *Exhib:* Directions 1986, Hirshhorn Mus, Washington, DC, 86; A View to Nature, Aldrich Mus Contemp Art, Ridgefield, Conn, 86. *Bibliog:* Michael Brenson (auth), New York Times, 86; Everett Potter (auth), Arts Mag, 88; Nancy Grimes (auth), Art News, 88. *Media:* Oil on Canvas. *Mailing Add:* 425 Riverside Dr Apt 4D New York NY 10025

SHATALOW, VLADIMIR MIHAILOVICH
PAINTER
b Belgorod, Russia, July 20, 17; US citizen. *Study:* Inst Art, Kharkov, 34-36 & Inst Art, Kiev, USSR, 38-41. *Work:* Nat Acad of Design, New York; Mint Mus of Art, Charlotte, NC; Woodmere Art Mus, Philadelphia, Pa; San Diego Fine Arts Gallery; Sun Co Collection, Radnor, Pa. *Exhib:* Butler Inst Am Art, Youngstown, Ohio, 68; Watercolor Show, Pa Acad Fine Arts, Philadelphia, 69; Am Watercolor Soc Ann, New York, 70; Wichita Centennial Watercolor Competition, Kans, 71; Watercolor USA Nat, Springfield, Mo, 72; Marietta Col, Ohio; Nat Acad Design, NY. *Awards:* Adolph and Clara Obrig Prize, 86 & 89, Paul and Margaret Bertelsen Prize, 88, Nat Acad Design, New York; Murray Kupferman Award, Audubon Artists, New York, 86; Philadelphia Watercolor Club Prize, Noyes Mus, Oceanville, NJ, 92. *Mem:* Nat Academician Nat Acad Design; Allied Artists Am; Philadelphia Watercolor Club; Am Watercolor Soc. *Media:* Oil, Tempera. *Mailing Add:* 2104 Poplar St Philadelphia PA 19130

SHATTER, SUSAN LOUISE
PAINTER
b New York, NY, Jan 17, 43. *Study:* Pratt Inst, BFA, 65; Skowhegan Sch Painting & Sculpture, summer 65; Boston Univ, MFA, 72. *Work:* Boston Mus Fine Arts; Univ Utah Mus, Salt Lake City; Art Inst Chicago; Philadelphia Mus Art; Dartmouth Col Art Mus. *Comn:* Colorado River in Utah (4ft x 8ft painting), America 1976, US Dept Interior, 75; Panorama of Manhattan Island (3 1/2ft x 12 1/2ft), Am Tel & Tel Co, New York, 77; seascape (5ft x 12ft), Bank New Eng, 88. *Exhib:* New Talent Knoedler Gallery, New York, 71; solo exhibs, Fischbach Gallery, New York, 73, 75, 78, 80, 82, 84, 87 & 88, Harcus Gallery, Boston, 84 & 87, John Berggruen Gallery, San Francisco, 86 & Heath Gallery, Atlanta, 87; Boston Watercolor Today, Mus Fine Arts, Boston, 76; America 1976 (traveling exhib), Corcoran Gallery Art, Washington, DC, 77; New York Now, Phoenix Mus, Ariz, 79; Am Realism since 1960, Pa Acad, 81-83; Gund Collection, Mus Fine Arts, Boston, 82; Realist Watercolors, Fla Int Univ, 83; American Realism: Twentieth-Century Drawings and Watercolors (traveling exhib), San Francisco Mus Mod Art, 85-86; A Contemporary View of Nature, Aldrich Mus Contemp Art, Ridgefield, Conn, 86-87; The Subject is Water, Newport Art Mus, RI, 87; The World is Round: Contemporary Panoramas, Hudson River Mus, Yonkers, NY, 87-89. *Pos:* Bd govt, Skowhegan Sch Photog, chmn 88-; instr, Sch Visual Arts, 83. *Teaching:* Vis artist, Univ Pa, Philadelphia, 74-75 & 79, act chmn, 83-84; mem fac painting, Skowhegan Sch Painting, Maine, summers 77 & 79 & Benninton Col, 79; vis artist, Tyler Sch Art, 85, San Francisco Art Inst, 89 & Brooklyn Col, NY, 91-92. *Awards:* Radcliffe Inst Fel, Boston, 75; Ingram-Merrill Found Grant, New York, 76; Nat Endowment Arts Grants, 80 & 87; NY State Found Arts Grant, 85. *Bibliog:* M Stephen Doherty (auth), Watercolor today: Ten contemporary painters, Am Artist, 2/83; Michael Brenson (auth), article & reviews, New York Times, 2/5/84, 10/19/84 & 1/9/87; Sebby Wilson Jacobson (auth), THESE are landscapes?, Times-

Union Rochester, 3/3/88; John Ashbery (auth), Review of Fischbach show, New York Mag, 3/80; Ken Baker (auth), American watercolor today, Portfolio, 9-10/82; Donald Kuspit (auth), Review of Fischbach show, Art Am, 10/82. *Media:* Watercolor, Oil. *Publ:* Illusr, Am Watercolors & Drawings (auth, John Arthur), Graphics Soc, NY, 80; Am Realism, Alvin Martin Abrams, NY, 85; Graphic Muse Prints by Contemp Am Women, Mt Holyuke Press, 87; Twentieth Century Watercolor, Christopher Finch, Mabeville Press, NY, 88. *Dealer:* Fischbach Gallery 29 W 57th St New York NY 10019; Harcus Gallery Seven Newbury St Boston MA 02116. *Mailing Add:* 26 W 20th St New York NY 10011

SHAW, COURTNEY ANN
LIBRARIAN, HISTORIAN
b Hagerstown, Md, Feb 10, 46. *Study:* Univ Wis-Madison, BA; Case Western Res Univ, MSLS; Ariz State Univ; also weaving, Atelier, France; Univ Md, PhD. *Exhib:* Am Tapestry Weaving Since the 1930s and its European Roots, Art Gallery, Univ Md. *Pos:* Asst librn, Yavapai Jr Col, Prescott, Ariz; art librn, Ariz State Univ; head fine arts libr, Lake Placid Sch Art; head art libr & expert Medieval, Renaissance & modern tapestries studies, Univ Md. *Teaching:* Instr art hist, Lake Placid, NY; lectures on history of textiles, Univ of Md. *Awards:* Md Humanities Coun Grant, Art Gallery for Am Tapestry Weaving Exhib. *Mem:* Art Libr Soc; Art Libr Soc NAm; Washington Art Libr Resource Comt. *Publ:* Auth, Regional Cooperation-Collection Development, Art Documentation, winter 85; American Tapestry Weaving since the 1930s and its European Roots; auth, Historical Overview of Tapestry, Int Tapestry Network #1, 90; auth, (4 articles), Dictionary of Art, (in prep); Books by & about Jean Tureat, Int Tapestry Network Newsletter. *Mailing Add:* Art-Sociology Bldg Univ Md College Park MD 20742

SHAW, DONALD EDWARD
SCULPTOR, PAINTER
b Boston, Mass, Aug 24, 34. *Study:* Boston Mus Sch Fine Arts. *Work:* Ark Arts Ctr, Little Rock; Atlantic Richfield Co, Los Angeles; Chast Manhattan Bank, New York; Mus Fine Arts, Houston, Tex; Smithsonian Inst, Washington, DC. *Comn:* Ark Arts Ctr, Little Rock, 88; Ark Col, Bateville, 92; Am Capitol, Houston. *Exhib:* Tex 30, Nave Mus, Victoria, Tex, 77; Kornblatt Gallery, Baltimore, Md, 77; one-man show, Moody Gallery, Houston, Tex, 78 & 79; Mus Fine Arts, Houston, Tex, 89; Mid Am Mus, Hot Springs, Ark, 92; and others. *Awards:* Travel Grant to Arg, Casa De'Arg, 77. *Bibliog:* Ann Holmes (auth), Fantastic artists, Southwest Art Gallery Mag, 2/72; N Laliberte & A Mogelon (auths), Art in Boxes, Van Nostrand, Reinhold Co, 74; Susie Kaul (auth, essay cat), Don Shaw, Ark Arts Ctr, Little Rock, 89. *Media:* Mixed. *Publ:* Contribr, Agencia Noticias Mex, 69 & cover illus, Southwest Art Gallery Mag, 72; Poverty Point, Sky Drawings Video, 91. *Mailing Add:* 210 W Barraque PO Box 8751 Pine Bluff AR 71601

SHAW, ERNEST CARL
SCULPTOR, WOOD
b New York, NY, Apr 17, 42. *Work:* Aldrich Mus Contemp Art, Ridgefield, Conn; Indianapolis Mus; Nelson Rockefeller; Wichita Art Mus, Kans; and others. *Comn:* Orlando Int Airport, Reading, Pa. *Exhib:* Storm King Art Ctr, Mountainville, NY, 77; Contemp Reflections, Aldrich Mus Contemp Art, 77; one-man shows, Storm King Art Ctr, 78, Hamilton Gallery Contemp Art, 78, Sculpture Now, New York, 78, Allentown Art Mus, 81, Wichita Art Mus, 81, Huntington Galleries, WVa, 81, Althea Viafora, New York, 86, Maxwell Davidson, New York, 88 & Williams Col Art Mus, Williamstown, Mass, 88; three-man show, Hamilton Gallery Contemp Art, 78; A M Sachs Gallery, 80; and other group and one-man shows. *Media:* Steel, Wood. *Mailing Add:* 2 Wawarsing Rd New Paltz NY 12561

SHAW, ISABEL
SCULPTOR, GRAPHIC ARTIST
b New York, NY. *Study:* Bard Col, BFA, 52; Sch Visual Arts, Cooper Union. *Exhib:* Harrison Coun Arts, Visual Arts Gallery, Purchase, NY, 83; Dimensions, Legler Barn Mus, Lenexa, Kans, 87; NAm Sculpture Exhib, Foothills Art Ctr, Golden, Colo, 87; Roslyn Sailor Fine Arts, Margate, NJ, 88, 89, 90, 91 & 92; Tutwiler Asn, Miami, Fla, 88, 89, 90; and others. *Awards:* Merrit Award, New Rochelle Artists, NY, 74; First Place Sculpture, Beaux Arts Finale, Westchester Co, NY, 74; Sculpture Award, Mamaroneck Artists Guild, Lyla J Weiss Mem, 84. *Mem:* NY Soc Woman Artists; NY Artists Equity; Contemp Artists Guild New York; Hudson River Contemp Artists; Sculpture League, New York. *Media:* Bronze, Wood. *Publ:* Contemp Women Artists (calendar), 88. *Dealer:* Sandra Neustadter Gallery Delray Beach FL; Bruton St Gallery Ltd London Eng. *Mailing Add:* 19 Black Birch Lane Scarsdale NY 10583

SHAW, JIM
PAINTER
b Midland, Mich, Aug 8, 52. *Study:* Univ Mich, BFA, 74; Calif Inst Arts, MFA, 78. *Exhib:* TV Generation, Los Angeles Contemp Exhibs, Los Angeles, 86; Los Angeles Hot & Cool, Ctr Visual Arts, Los Angeles, 87; solo exhibs, Gartn Clark Gallery, Los Angeles, 90 & Feature Art, New York, 90, New Works from 'My Mirage', Linda Cathcart Gallery, Santa Monica, Calif, 91, Tex Gallery, Houston, 92, Massimo de Carlo, Milan, Italy, 92, Metro Pictures, New York, 92, Horror A Vacui, Linda Cathcart Gallery, Santa Monica, Calif, 92; True Stories, Inst Contemp Arts, London, Eng, 92; Re: Framing Cartoons, Wexner Ctr Arts, Ohio State Univ, Columbus, 92; Songs of Innocence/Songs of Experience, Whitney Mus Am Art, Stamford, Conn, 92. *Awards:* Nat Endowment Arts Grant, 87. *Bibliog:* Christopher Knight (auth), An Art of Darkness at MOCA, Los Angeles Times, 1/28/92; Janet Kutner (auth), An artist with a thirst for Pop, 6/12/92; Colin Gardner (auth), Jim Shaw/Benjamin Weissman, vol XXXI, no 1, 9/92 & Helter Skelter at the Temporary Contemporary, Artforu, 4/92. *Dealer:* Linda Cathcart Gallery 924 Colorado Ave Santa Monica CA 90401. *Mailing Add:* 1522 Micheltorena No 4 Los Angeles CA 90026

SHAW, JOHN PALMER
PAINTER, PRINTMAKER
b San Mateo Calif, Apr 23, 48. *Study:* Art Students League; Pratt Inst; Md Inst Col Art, BFA, 72. *Work:* Mus Mod Art, New York; Brooklyn Mus, NY; Bank Am, San Francisco. *Exhib:* Five Baltimore Artists, Baltimore Mus Art, 73; Manifesto Show, Collaborative Projs, New York, 79; The Ritz Show, The Ritz, Washington, DC, 83; Terminal Show, Brooklyn Terminal, 83; The Great East River Bridge Show, 83 & New Aquisitions, 86, Brooklyn Mus; New Talent, Leo Castelli Uptown, New York, 84. *Bibliog:* Barbara Gold (auth), A show with a subtle message, Baltimore Sun, 3/11/73; Jed Stevenson (auth), A room with a view, NY Times, 1/12/78; Beverly Mitchell (auth), Home again, Montreal Gazzette, 7/12/92. *Media:* Encaustic, Oil. *Publ:* Ed, New Observations No 8, Lucio Pozzi, 83. *Dealer:* Patrick Gusway Galerie Stornaway 1069 Rue BLevry Montréal Québec Canada. *Mailing Add:* 2202 Rue Panet Prince St Sta Montreal PQ 10012 H2L 3H6 Canada

SHAW, JOSEPH WINTERBOTHAM
HISTORIAN, EDUCATOR
b Chicago, Ill, July 6, 35. *Study:* Brown Univ, BA, 57; Wesleyan Univ, MA, 59; Univ Pa, PhD, 70; Brown Univ, LHD, 87. *Teaching:* Asst prof, Univ Toronto, 70-73, assoc prof, 73-77, prof, 77- *Awards:* Various research grants for Aegean Bronze Age architecture and archaeology. *Mem:* Can Mediterranean Inst; Am Sch Classical Studies; Archaeological Inst Am (pres, Toronto chap, 79-82, vpres). *Res:* Bronze Age Aegean archaeology and art. *Publ:* Auth, Minoan Architecture: Materials and Techniques, Inst Poligraphico, Rome, 73; coauth, Kenchreai, Vol 1, Brill, 78; auth, Consideration of the Site of Akrotiri as a Minoan Settlement, Thera & Aegean World, 78; Evidence for the Tripartite Shrine, Am J Archeol, 78; Excavation at Kommos, Crete, Hesperia, 76-86; The Early Helladic II Corridor House, Am J Archeol, 87; Phoenician Shrine at Kommos, Am J Archeol, 89. *Mailing Add:* Fine Art/Grad Dept Hist Art Univ Toronto Toronto ON M5S 1A1 Canada

SHAW, KAREN
PAINTER
b Bronx, NY, Oct 25, 41. *Study:* Hunter Col, City Univ New York, BFA, 65; grad work Hunter Col & C W Post, 70-71. *Work:* The Herbert F Johnson Mus Art, Ithaca, NY; The Israel Mus, Jerusalem; City Univ Grand Ctr, New York; Erasmus Haus, Basel, Switzerland; Mus Mod Art, New York. *Comn:* 11 large paintings, Mall, City Univ Grad Ctr, New York, 80; Installation: Effects of Acid Rain on the Great Lakes, LI Univ, Southampton Campus, 88; Installation, Het Apollohus, Eindhoven, Netherlands, 90; Pandora's Box, The Effects of Burning Fossel Fuels on the Environment, 90; Plato's Box in Pandora's Cave, Dowling Col, 91. *Exhib:* Book Works, Albright Knox Art Gallery, Buffalo, NY, 77; one woman shows, Bertha Urdang Gallery, New York, 76 & 83, Dany Keller Galerie, Munich, WGer, 78 & 81, City Univ Grad Ctr, New York, 80 & 86, Corinne Hummel Galerie, Basel, Switz, 83, C Kermit Ewing Gallery Art & Archit, Univ Tenn, Knoxville, 86 & 91, Southampton Col, Long Island Univ, New York, 88, Het Apollohuis, Eindhoven, Netherlands, 90; Artists Books, Walker Art Ctr, Minneapolis, Minn, 81; Albright Knox Art Gallery, Buffalo, NY, 82; Dowling Col, Oakdale, New York; Women's Art Caucus, The Environment Show, Bronx, NY, 90; Anchorage Mus Hist & Art, Alaska, 90; Vital Signs, Artists Address the Environment, Henry St Settlement, New York, 90. *Pos:* Cur, Islip Art Mus, 81- *Teaching:* Asst prof art, Univ Tenn, 89-90; instr, Silvermine Art Sch, New canaan, Conn, 89- *Awards:* Nat Endowment Arts, US Govt, 78-79; Foundation Karolyi, Vence, France, 88 & 89; New York Found Arts Grant, 92-93. *Bibliog:* Lenore Malen (auth), Karen Shaw: the reckoner, Arts Mag, 4/79; Helen Harrison (auth), New York Times, 9/22/91. *Media:* Acrylic, Oil. *Publ:* Contribr, A Big Jewish Book, Anchor Press Doubleday, 78; auth, Market Research, Univ Akron, Ohio, 78. *Dealer:* Tony Zwicker 15 Gramercy Park NY 10003. *Mailing Add:* c/o Islip Art Mus 50 Irish Lane East Islip NY 11730

SHAW, (GEORGE) KENDALL
PAINTER
b New Orleans, La, Mar 30, 24. *Study:* Ga Inst Technol, 44-46; Tulane Univ, BS, 49, MFA, 59; La State Univ, 50; New Sch Social Res, 50-52; Brooklyn Mus Art Sch, 53; also with Edward Corbett, Ralston Crawford, Stuart Davis, O Louis Guglielmi, George Rickey & Mark Rothko. *Work:* Albright-Knox Art Gallery, Buffalo, NY; Mus Contemp Art, Nagaoka, Japan; NY Univ; Chase Manhattan Bank, NY; Everson Mus, Syracuse, NY; Neue Galerie Sammlung Ludwig, Aachen. *Exhib:* One-man exhibs, Tibor de Nagy Gallery, New York, 64, 65, 67 & 68, John Bernard Myers Gallery, New York, 72, Alessandra Gallery, New York, 77 & Lerner-Heller Gallery, 79, 81 & 82, Nature Morte Gallery, New York, 83, Bernice Steinbaum Gallery, New York, 91, Artists Space, New York, 92; Contemp Painting, Mus Contemp Art, Nagaoka, Japan, 65; Modular Painting, Albright-Knox Art Gallery, 70; Sets for The First Reader by Gertrude Stein, Mus Mod Art & Metrop Mus Art, New York, 70-71; Pattern Painting, PS 1, New York, 77; and others. *Teaching:* Columbia Univ, New York, 61-66; Hunter Col, New York, 66-68; Parsons Sch Design, New York, 66-86; Lehman Col, New York, 68-70; Brooklyn Mus Art Sch, Brooklyn, NY, 70-76. *Bibliog:* Articles, Arts Mag, 1/77 & Art News, summer 82; Art & Artists, 8-9/86. *Mem:* Col Art Asn Am; Art Workers Coalition. *Media:* Miscellaneous. *Mailing Add:* 458 Broome St New York NY 10013

SHAW, LOUISE
DIRECTOR
Study: Clark Univ, Worchester, Mass, BA, 73; Syracuse Univ, MFA, 81. *Pos:* Exec dir, Nexus Contemp Art Ctr, 83-; freelance cur & consult, 80- *Awards:* Nat Endowment Arts Mus Fel, 88. *Mem:* Cult Olympiad; Mayor's Adv Arts Comt; Ga Asn Mus & Galleries; Art & Cult Comt, Atlanta. *Publ:* Vital signs, Nexus Contemp Art Ctr, 91. *Mailing Add:* Nexus Contemporary Art Center 535 Means St Atlanta GA 30318

SHAW, MARY TODD
SCULPTOR, PAINTER
b Gadsden, Ala. *Study:* Atlanta Col Art, cert, 41; Univ NC, Charlotte, BCA, 74. *Work:* Columbia Mus, SC; Mint Mus Art; Gibbs Gallery Art, Charleston, NC; Hickory Mus Art, NC. *Comn:* Monotypes, Art Coalition Charlotte, NC, 82. *Exhib:* Nat Asn Women Artists Exhib, Nat Acad, New York & Royal Scottish Acad, Edinburgh; Piedmont Exhib, Mint Mus Art; State Dept Show, Mus Bella Artes, Buenos Aires; Hunter Mus Art Ann; Allied Artists Exhib, Nat Arts Club, New York; Exhib Va Artists, Va Mus Fine Arts; Southeastern, High Mus Art. *Teaching:* Instr drawing & painting, Mint Mus Art, 64-74; instr painting, Spirit Sq, 76- & Cent Piedmont Col, 79-80. *Awards:* Best in Show, Arts & Sci Exhib, Charlotte, NC; Best of Show, Roanoke Va Ann Outdoor Exhib; Henri Bendel Award, Nat Asn Women Artists Exhib; Yaddo Fel, 80 & 81; Tyrone Power Guthrie Found Fel, New Bliss, Ireland; Va Ctr Fel, Sweet Briar, Va, 84 & 85; Banff Ctr Fel, Alta, Canada; Best in Show, Springfest, Charlotte, NC, 86. *Bibliog:* Charlene Whisnant (auth), Red Clay Reader, Vol 1, 67, Vol 4, 68 & Vol 7, 70; Donaz Meilach & Evie Ten Hoor (auths), Collage & Assemblages, Crown Publ, 73; Virginia Watson Jones (auth), Contemporary American Woman Sculptors, Oryx Press, 86. *Mem:* Southern Graphics Asn; Tri-State Sculptors; Int Sculptors; Nat Asn Women Artists; NC Print & Drawing Soc. *Media:* Boxes. *Publ:* Auth, Tri State Sculptors Catalog, 85, 86, 87. *Mailing Add:* 6611 Burlwood Rd Charlotte NC 28211

SHAW, NANCY (RIVARD)
CURATOR, HISTORIAN
b Saginaw, Mich. *Study:* Oakland Univ, Mich, BA(studio art), 69; Wayne State Univ, Mich, MA(art hist), 73; Attingham Summer Inst, England, 77. *Collections Arranged:* Heritage & Horizon: American Painting 1776-1976 (with catalog), 76; Daniel Chester French: An American Sculptor, 77; John Singer Sargent and the Edwardian Age, 79; American Masters: The Thyssen-Bornemisza Collection, 84; Sharing Traditions: Five Black Artists in Nineteenth Century America, 86; The Art That is Life: The Arts and Crafts Movement in America 1875-1920, 87; Thomas Hart Benton: An American Original, 89; American Paintings from the Manoogian Collection,90; Gari Melchers: A Retrospective Exhibition, 90; Henry Ossawa Tanner, 91. *Pos:* Asst cur Am art, Detroit Inst Arts, 72-75, actg cur, 75-77, cur, 77- *Bibliog:* Cotopaxi, Detroit Inst Arts Bull, 78. *Mem:* Decorative Art Chap, Soc Archit Hist. *Res:* Late Nineteenth and early twentieth century painting and sculpture. *Publ:* Contribr, American paintings acquired during the last decade, Detroit Inst Arts Bull, 77; auth, Curatorial notes on the collection: Cotopaxi, Detroit Inst Arts Bull, 78; American paintings at The Detroit Institute of Arts, Antiques Mag, 11/78; contribr, The Quest for Unity: American Art Between World's Fairs, 1876-1893 (exhib catalog), 83; auth, Rebellion, Defiance and Beauty: Two Centuries of American Painting, Apollo Mag, 12/86; contribr, American Paintings from the Manoogian Collection, (exhib, catalog), 89; auth introd to, American Paintings in the Detroit Institute of Arts: Works by Artists Born Before 1916, (1st of 3 vol on the collections), 91. *Mailing Add:* The Detroit Inst of Arts 5200 Woodward Ave Detroit MI 48202

SHAW, PAUL JEFFERSON
CALLIGRAPHER, DESIGNER
b Ann Arbor, Mich, Sept 28, 54. *Study:* Reed Col, BA, 76; Columbia Univ, MA, 78, MPh, 80. *Comn:* Corp typeface for origins, 91-92. *Exhib:* Writing, Illuminating & Lettering, Calligraphy Space 2001, New York, 78; Words & Images, Folger Libr, Washington, DC, 82; Brooklyn Art Mus, 83; Chicago Calligraphy Collective in Paris, France, 86; Words & Images, Donnell Libr, New York, 85; Rhythm-a-ning, Newark, 87. *Collections Arranged:* Calligraphy in the Graphic Arts, 81-89. *Pos:* Corresp, Calligraphy Rev, currently. *Teaching:* Prof calligraphy, Sch Visual Arts, 79-85, Long Island Univ, 81-89 & Parsons Sch Design, 85-; prof lettering design, New York Inst Technol, 81- *Awards:* Fels, Newberry Libr, 80 & Smithsonian Inst, 80. *Mem:* Soc Scribes Ltd (bd gov, 78-85); Type Director's Club; Soc Typographic Artists; Am Inst Graphic Artists; Asn Typografique Int. *Media:* Ink, Gouache and Paper; Collage. *Publ:* Auth, Constant surprises: The Calligraphy of George Salter, Scripsit, 81; WAD as Lettering Artist: Pattern and Motion, private publ, 83; The Letter G, Visible Language, 83; W A Dwiggins, Design Issues, 84; Letterforms, pvt publ, 87. *Mailing Add:* 785 West End Ave New York NY 10025

SHAW, PEGGY
PAINTER, PHOTOGRAPHER
b Oak Park, Ill, Apr 23, 58. *Study:* Univ Ill, Champaign, BFA, 82; Art Inst Chicago, MFA, 86. *Work:* Readers Digest, Pleasantville, NY. *Exhib:* Solo exhibs, Photo Collages, Ind Univ Northwest, Gary, 90, Betsy Rosenfield Gallery, Chicago Int Art Expo, 90, Living Systems, Hal Katzen Gallery, New York, 91, Betsy Rosenfield Gallery, Chicago, 91 & 93, Milliken Univ, Decatur, Ill, 91 & Pa Sch Art & Design, Lancaster, 92; New Work, Betsy Rosenfield Gallery, Chicago Int Art Expo, 91; Artfair/Seattle, Betsy Rosenfield Gallery, 92; May 1992, Betsy Rosenfield Gallery, Chicago Int Art Expo, 92; Reoganized Realities, Reicher Gallery, Barat Col, Lake Forest, Ill, 92; and others. *Pos:* Producer, videographer, ed, Parkland Col, Champaign, Ill, 86-; videographer ed, DeYoung Productions, Champaign, 86- *Teaching:* Photog teaching asst beginning photog, Art Inst Chicago, 85 & photog teaching asst large format photog, 86; instr basic television production, Parkland Col, Champaign, Ill, 86- *Awards:* Artist Fel Award, Ill Arts Coun, 88; Visual Arts Fel Award, Arts Midwest/Nat Endowment Arts Regional, 88; Visual Arts Finalist Award, Ill Arts Coun, 91 & 92. *Bibliog:* Susan Snodgrass (auth), Resurgence, New Art Examiner, 9/89; John Brunetti (auth), Peggy Shaw, New City, 3/91; Elisabeth Condon (auth), Peggy Shaw, Lillian Heard, New Art Examiner, 5/91. *Media:* Pigment, Transparencies. *Mailing Add:* c/o Betsy Rosenfield Gallery 212 W Superior St Chicago IL 60610

SHAW, REESEY
PAINTER, SCULPTOR
b Jacksonville, Fla, Jan 11, 43. *Study:* Sch Fine & Appl Art, Boston Univ, 60-62; Md Inst Col Art, BFA, 64, MFA, 66. *Work:* Kaufman & Broad Collections, Los Angeles, Calif; AT&T, Los Angeles, Calif; Arco Corp Collection, Los Angeles, Calif. *Exhib:* La Jolla Mus Contemp Art, Calif, 74, 78 & 86; solo exhibs, San Diego Mus Art, 75 & Los Angeles Inst Contemp Art, 80, Calif; Personal Myth, Queens Mus, NY, 78; Private Icons, Bronx Mus, NY, 79; Painted Sculpture, Munic Art Gallery, Los Angeles, Calif, 82; Sunshine & Shadow, Univ Southern Calif, Los Angeles, 85; Retrospective, Selected Works 1980-1990 (auth, catalog), Mesa Col Art Gallery, San Diego. *Pos:* Dir Galleries, Ctr for the Arts, Escondido, Calif. *Awards:* Art Guild Award, San Diego Mus Art, 75. *Bibliog:* John Russell (auth), When Art Imitates Anthropology, NY Times, 4/78; David Rubin (auth), Contemporary Tryptichs, Calif Technol-Pamona Col, 82; Ballatore (auth), The Psychological Tightrope, Images & Issues, 1/82. *Media:* Encaustic Paint; Wood. *Publ:* Illusr, cover photogr, John Hopkins Mag, 66; auth, Double Exposure, Images & Issues, 81. *Mailing Add:* 7793 Senn Way La Jolla CA 92037

SHAW, RENATA VITZTHUM
ADMINISTRATOR
b Mänttä, Finland, July 21, 26; US citizen. *Study:* Univ Chicago, MA(art hist), 49; Univ Helsinki, Finland, MPhilos(art hist), 51; Ecole de Louvre, Paris, dipl(museology), 52; Catholic Univ Am, MS(libr sci), 62. *Pos:* Reference librn art, Prints & Photog Div, Libr Congress, Washington, DC, 62-67, supervisory librn art, 67-71, bibliog specialist art, 71-81, asst chief prints & photog div, 82, actg chief prints & photog div, 83-84, asst chief prints & photog, 84-90. *Teaching:* Lectures in the Library of Congress on visual resources. *Mem:* Art Librn North Am; Spec Libr Asn; Am Libr Asn. *Res:* Art bibliography; collection development; visual librarianship; organization of visual collections; automation of library holdings, visual resources, production of videodisk of visual resources and retrieval of visual information. *Interests:* Development of a research collection in the field of art history. *Publ:* Auth, Handbook of Latin American Studies: Book Annotations, Univ Fla, 74; Quarterly Journal of the Library of Congress: Essays, Libr Cong, 75; Encyclopedia of Library & Information Science, Marcel Dekker, 77; Graphic Sampler: A Century of Photographs, 1846-1946, Libr Cong Collection, 80. *Mailing Add:* 79 King St Charleston SC 29401

SHAW, RICHARD BLAKE
SCULPTOR
b Hollywood, Calif, Sept 12, 41. *Study:* Orange Coast Col, 61-63; San Francisco Art Inst, BFA(Agnus Brandenstein Fel), 65; Alfred Univ, 65; Univ Calif, Davis, MA, 68. *Work:* Oakland Mus, Calif; San Francisco Mus; Nat Mus Art, Tokyo; Stedelijk Mus, Amsterdam, Holland; Whitney Mus Am Art, New York. *Exhib:* One-man shows, San Francisco Mus Art, 73 & Braunstein Gallery, 81-90; Whitney Mus Am Art, New York, 70 & 81; International Ceramics, 1972, Victoria & Albert Mus, London, 72; The Chosen Object: Europ & Am Still Life, Joslyn Art Mus, Omaha, Nebr, 77; Newport Harbor Art Mus, Calif, 81; San Jose Mus Art, Calif, 81; Boise Gallery Art, Idaho, 81; Palm Springs Desert Mus, 87. *Teaching:* Chmn, ceramics dept, San Francisco Art Inst, 65-; mem fac, Univ Wis-Madison, summer 71; prof ceramics, Univ Calif, Berkeley, 87- *Awards:* Nat Endowment Arts Grant, 70; Nat Endowment Arts Crafts Grant, 74. *Bibliog:* Articles in Viking Press, 69 & Arts Can, summer 71; Catalog, Ceramic Sculpture, 78 & 81-83. *Mem:* Order Golden Brush; Int Soc Ceramists. *Media:* Ceramics, Mixed Media. *Mailing Add:* Ceramics Dept Univ Calif Berkeley Berkeley CA 94720

SHAY, ED
PAINTER
b Boston, Mass, Nov 12, 47. *Study:* Murray State Univ, Ky, BFA, 69; Univ Ill, Champaign, MFA, 71. *Work:* Minn Mus Art, St Paul; Univ NDak, Grand Forks; Dulin Gallery Art, Knoxville, Tenn; Bradley Univ, Peoria, Ill; Calif Col Arts & Crafts, San Francisco. *Comn:* Oil Planetarium, Ponderosa Collection, Dayton, Ohio, 74; wall graphic, Skate Away, Muncie, Ind, 77; billboard, Indianapolis Art League, Ind, 78. *Exhib:* 74th Chicago Artists & Vicinity Show, Chicago Art Inst, 73; World Print Competition, Calif Col Arts & Crafts, San Francisco, 73; Works On Twinrocker Handmade Paper, Ind Mus Art, Indianapolis, 75; Crimes of Passion, Univ Ky, Lexington, 77; Rutgers Nat Drawing 77, Camden Col of Arts & Sci, NJ, 77; My Backyard: A Mid Career Retrospective of Paintings, Mt Vernon, Ill, 90 & State of Ill Art Gallery, Springfield, 91; Contemp Ill Watercolor Art Asn, 91; 8th Biennial Exhib, Tarble Arts Ctr, Charleston, Ill, 91. *Collections Arranged:* Rollman-Shay, Not In New York Gallery, Cincinnati, Ohio, 74 & 76; Krannert Gallery, Univ Evansville, Ind, 74; Nancy Lurie Gallery, Chicago, Ill, 76; Roy Boyd Gallery, Chicago,. *Teaching:* Prof art & design, Southern Ill Univ, Carbondale, 78- *Awards:* Purchase Awards, 55th Soc Am Graphic Artists Nat Print Exhib, New York, 77 & Drawings & Prints 77, Miami Univ, Oxford, Ohio, 77; Bronstein Purchase Award, Mid-States Exhib, Evansville Mus Art, Ind, 77. *Bibliog:* Ellen Brown (auth), Ed & Charlotte Rollman-Shay, Art in Am, 3-4/76; Lynn Karn (auth), Ed & Charlotte Rollman-Shay, New Art Examiner, 1/77; Franz Schulze (auth), Illinois Artists, Chicago Daily News, 1/23/77. *Media:* Oil, Watercolor. *Mailing Add:* Sch Art & Design Southern Ill Univ Carbondale IL 62901

SHEA, JUDITH
SCULPTOR
b Philadelphia, Pa, Nov 13, 48. *Study:* Parsons Sch Design, 69; Parsons/New Sch, BFA, 75. *Work:* Neuberger Mus, State Univ New York Col, Purchase; Hirschhorn Mus & Sculpture Garden, Washington, DC; Dallas Mus Fine Art; Walker Art Ctr, Minneapolis; La Jolla Mus Contemp Art, Calif; Minneapolis Sculpture Garden; Brooklyn Mus. *Comn:* Minn Sculpture Garden; Laumeier Sculpture Park, St Louis, Mo. *Exhib:* Biennial, Whitney Mus Am Art, New York, 81; Milwaukee Arts Ctr, 83; Directions 83, Hirshhorn Mus, 83; Sculpture Now, Va Mus Contemp Art, 83; two-person show (with Nick Vaughn), Walker Art Ctr, Minneapolis, 84 & (with Robert Moskowitz), Hayden Gallery (with catalog), List Visual Arts Ctr, Mass Inst Technol, Cambridge, Mass, 85; one-person show, Pa Acad Fine Arts, Philadelphia, 86; Sculpture Inside/Outside, Walker Art Ctr, Minn & Mus Fine Arts, Houston, Tex; La Jolla Mus Contemp Art, Calif, 88; Nelson Atkins Mus Art, Kansas City, Mo, 89; Nat Mus of Women Arts, Washington, DC, 90; Monuments & Statues, Whitney Mus Am Art, Phillip Morris, NY, 92. *Teaching:* Instr, Parsons Sch Design, New York, 79-86, New York Univ, 80-86; vis prof, Univ Calif Davis, 91; vis fac grad sculpture, Yale Univ, fall 92. *Awards:* Nat Endowment Arts Grant, 84 & 86; Solomon R Guggenheim Sculptor-in-Residence at Chesterwood, Mass, 89. *Bibliog:* Peter Schjeldahl (auth), Metaphysics of Skin, The Village Voice, Art, 99, 4/16/91; Robert Taplin (auth), Judith Shea at Max Protetch Gallery, Art Am, 151-152, 10/91; Robert Mahoney (auth), Judith Shea: Monument Statuary, Arts Mag, 9/91. *Media:* Bronze, Wood. *Publ:* Auth, Beyond Fashion: Mariano Fortuny, Art Am, 11/82; Valentino, Artforum, 12/82. *Dealer:* Max Protetch Gallery, New York, NY; John Berggruen Gallery, San Francisco, CA. *Mailing Add:* 124 Chambers St New York NY 10007

SHEAD, S RAY
PAINTER, PRINTMAKER
b Cartersville, Ga, Nov 27, 38. *Study:* Atlanta Art Inst, BFA, 60; Art Ctr Col Design, BPA, 63; Ga State Univ, MVA; Inst Allende, Mex; also with John Rodgers & Loser Fiedelson, Los Angeles. *Work:* Columbus Mus, Ga; Montgomery Mus, Ala; Opelika Art League, Ala; Atlanta High Mus, Ga; Southwest Ga Art Mus, Albany. *Comn:* Painting, Chrysler Corp, Atlanta, 60; sculpture, Dibco-Wayne Corp, Atlanta, 68; painting, Callaway Gardens, Ga, 70. *Exhib:* Dixie Ann, Montgomery, Ala, 60; 6th Ann Callaway Gardens Exhib, Ga, 69; 49th Shreveport Art Exhib, La, 70; Ga Artists Exhib I & II, Atlanta, 71-72; SC Artists, 74. *Pos:* Art dir, Compton Advert, New York, 63-67; art dir, Marschalk Co, Atlanta, 67. *Teaching:* Assoc prof art & head dept, LaGrange Col, 68-74; head dept art, Presby Col, 74-76; chmn commercial art, Dekalb Col, 77-86. *Awards:* Second Dixie Ann Award, 60; Southern Contemp Award, 69; 6th Ann Columbus Exhib Award, 70. *Mem:* Col Art Asn Am. *Media:* Acrylic, Epoxy. *Dealer:* Beverly Singlee Atlanta GA 30034. *Mailing Add:* 2320 Cape Courage Way Suwanee GA 30174-2763

SHEAKS, BARCLAY
PAINTER, WRITER
b East Chicago, Ind. *Study:* Va Commonwealth Univ, BFA; Col William & Mary, teaching cert. *Work:* Va Mus Fine Arts, Richmond; Butler Inst Am Art, Youngstown, Ohio; Columbia Mus Fine Arts, SC; Mobile Mus, Ala; Chrysler Mus, Norfolk, Va. *Comn:* Portrait of USS Enterprise, comn by off of ship, 65; portrait of USS John F Kennedy, City of Newport News, 69; painting series, Exec Suite, Tenneco Corp, Newport News Shipyard, 72; space paintings, NASA, Langley Res Ctr, Hampton, Va; painting depicting surface of Mars, US Bicentennial Expo on Sci & Technol, Kennedy Space Ctr, 76; and others. *Exhib:* Nat Drawing Biennial (drawing selected for Smithsonian Inst Nat Traveling Exhib), Norfolk Mus, Va, 65; Butler Inst Am Art Mid-Year Show Am Painting, 65, 66 & 67; 99 Exhibition, Am Watercolor Soc, Nat Acad Design, New York, 66; Juried Art Exhib, Corcoran Gallery Art, Washington, DC, 67; Ten Top Realists SE, Gallery Contemp Art, Winston-Salem, NC, 69-70. *Pos:* Art consult, Hunt Mfg Co, Philadelphia, 65; lectr, Va Mus, Richmond, 70; artist in residence, Richmond Humanities Ctr, 71 & Va Mus, Richmond, 78; art consult & TV host, Painting with Acrylic with Barclay Sheake, PBS-TV, 85. *Teaching:* Head art dept, Newport News Pub Schs, 49-69; assoc prof art & distinguished res artist, Va Wesleyan Col, 69- *Awards:* Va Comn Arts & Humanities Top Award, 79. *Bibliog:* Russel Woody (auth), chap, In: Painting in Synthetic Media & Complete Guide to Polymer Paintings, Van Nostrand Reinhold. *Mem:* Tidewater Artists Asn. *Media:* Acrylic, Polymer. *Publ:* Auth, Painting with Acrylics from Start to Finish, 72, Drawing and Painting the Natural Environment, 74, Painting with Oils, Davis & Drawing Figures and Faces, 87. *Dealer:* Chester Smith Seaside Art Gallery P O Box 1 Nags Head NC 27959. *Mailing Add:* Dept Art Va Wesleyan Col Wesleyan Dr Newport News VA 23502

SHEARD, WENDY STEDMAN
HISTORIAN, EDUCATOR
b New Haven, Conn, July 24, 35. *Study:* Vassar Col, BA, 57; Yale Univ, with Charles Seymour Jr, MA, 65, PhD, 71. *Exhib:* Antiquity in the Renaissance (auth, catalog), Smith Col Mus Art, 78. *Teaching:* Asst prof art hist, Mt Holyoke Col, 78-79; vis asst prof, Univ Hartford, 79-80 & Boston Univ, 83-84; vis assoc prof, Boston Univ, spring 88; vis scholar in art, Wesleyan Univ, spring 90. *Mem:* Col Art Asn; Asn Independent Art Historians. *Res:* Relationships between sculpture and painting in Renaissance Venice. *Publ:* Ed, Collaboration in Italian Renaissance Art, Yale Univ Press, 78; auth, Asa Adorna: The Prehistory of the Vendramin Tomb, Jahrbuch Berliner Mus, Vol 20, 78; auth, Giorgione and Tullio Lombardo in Giorgione, Convegno Int Studi, Castelfranco, Italy, 79. *Mailing Add:* 693 Leetes Island Rd Stony Creek CT 06405

SHEARER, LINDA
DIRECTOR
b Long Island, NY, Feb 13, 46. *Study:* Sarah Lawrence Col, Bronxville, NY, BA, 68. *Pos:* Solomon R Guggenheim Mus, New York, 69-80; exec dir, Artists Space, New York, 80-85; cur, Dept Painting & Sculpture, Mus Mod Art, New York, 85-89; dir, Williams Col Mus Art, 89- *Teaching:* Instr, Sch Visual Arts, New York, 73-79 & Williams Col Mass, 91- *Mem:* Am Asn Mus Dirs. *Mailing Add:* Williams Col Mus Art Williamstown MA 01267

SHEARER, RHONDA ROLAND
SCULPTOR, WRITER
b Aurora, Ill, June 12, 54. *Study:* Central Col, Chicago, Ill; Boston Univ, 70-74. *Work:* Hallmark Corp, Kansas City, Mo; Hartz Mountain Corp, New York, NY. *Comn:* Lifesize bronze horse, Goffs Bloodstock Sales Co, Kildare, Ireland, 84. *Exhib:* Solo show, Elements of Chaos, Am Asn Advan Sci, Washington, DC, 90; Ambiguous Figures, Feingarten Gallery, Los Angeles, Calif, 90. *Bibliog:* Lawrence Gowing (auth), Still Lifes in Bronze (exhib catalog), Wildenstein Gallery, 87. *Media:* Bronze. *Res:* New science of chaos; fractal geometry's potential influence in art & ecology. *Publ:* Auth, National Symposium: The Role of Horticulture in Human Well-Being and Social Development, Timber, 91 & 92; Beyond Romanticism: The Significance of Plants as Form in the History of Art, Chap 40; Chaos Theory and Fractal Geometry: Their Potential Impact on the Future of Art, Leonardo, Vol 25, Issue 2, 3/92. *Dealer:* Wildenstein Gallery 19 E 64th Street New York NY 10021. *Mailing Add:* 285 Spring St New York NY 10013

SHECHTER, BEN-ZION
PAINTER, ILLUSTRATOR
b Tel Aviv, Israel, Aug 7, 40; US & Israel citizen. *Study:* Bezalel Sch Art, Jerusalem, BFA, 66; Sch Visual Arts, New York, 67-69. *Work:* Whitney Mus Am Art & New York Pub Libr, New York; Mus Fine Art, Boston; Brooklyn Mus; Houghton Libr, Harvard Univ, Cambridge, Mass; Univ Iowa Mus. *Exhib:* Interiors-Exteriors: Figurative Artist, Brooklyn Mus, 80; solo exhibs, Wustum Mus, Racine, Wis, 82, Capricorn Gallery Bethseda, Md, 89; Univ Iowa Mus, 83; Ark Art Ctr, Little Rock, 86; Carnegie Inst, Pittsburg, Pa, 88; Hunt Inst, Pittsburg, Pa, 88; Buther Inst; and others. *Awards:* Purchase Award, West Publ, 80. *Bibliog:* Lawrence Alloway (auth), Park Slope: The Urban Subject, Brooklyn Mus, 80; Susan Paul (auth), Interiors/Exteriors, Phoenix, Brooklyn, 80; N Scott Marraday (auth), Recent Press Book, Fine Print, 81. *Media:* Gauache; Pen & Ink, Watercolor. *Publ:* Illusr, Common Ground, Bieler Press, 80. *Dealer:* Martin Sumers Graphics 50 W 57th St New York NY. *Mailing Add:* 429 4th St Brooklyn NY 11215

SHECHTER, LAURA J
PAINTER, DRAFTSMAN
b Brooklyn, NY, Aug 26, 44. *Study:* Brooklyn Col, BA, 65. *Work:* Boston Mus Fine Arts, Mass; Brooklyn Mus, NY; Indianapolis Mus Art, Ind; Albright-Knox Art Gallery; Art Inst, Chicago, Ill. *Exhib:* One-man shows, Suffolk Mus, Stony Brook, NY, 71, Wuster Mus, Wis, 82, Greenville Co Mus Art, SC, 82, Univ Richmond, Va, 91 & Raton Guest Mus, Wis, 91; The New American Still Life, Westmoreland Co Mus Art, Greenburg, Pa, 79; Am Drawing in Black & White, Brooklyn Mus, NY, 80 & 81; Still Life, Albright-Knox Art Gallery, Buffalo, NY, 81; West 81/Art & the Law, Minn Mus Art, St Paul, 81; Contemporary Art-Gund Collection, Boston Mus, 82; Perspectives on Contemporary Realism, Pa Acad Fine Art, 82 & Art Inst Chicago, 83; American Realism, San Francisco Mus, 85; Intimate Views, Spive Art Mus, Joplin, Mo, 91. *Teaching:* Instr, Parson Col, 84 & Nat Acad Fine Art Sch, New York, 85- 88. *Awards:* Creative Artists Pub Serv Prog Grant, 81-82. *Bibliog:* Ralph Poweroy (auth), Laura Shechter, Arts Mag, 81; Eric Widing (auth), Laura Shechter, Am Artist, 83; Romen Cohen (auth), Laura Shechter (mus catalog, Wis & Va), 91. *Mem:* Artists Equity. *Media:* Oil, Watercolor; Pencil, Silverpoint. *Dealer:* Katharine Rich Perlow Gallery 560 Broadway New York NY 10012. *Mailing Add:* 429 4th St Brooklyn NY 11215

SHECHTMAN, GEORGE HENOCH
DEALER
b Paterson, NJ, Dec 8, 41. *Study:* Rutgers Univ, BA(art hist), 64. *Pos:* Dir, Gallery Henoch, New York, currently. *Specialty:* Contemporary American paintings. *Mailing Add:* c/o Gallery Henoch 80 Wooster St New York NY 10012

SHECTER, PEARL S
PAINTER, CONSULTANT
b New York, NY, Dec 17, 10. *Study:* Hunter Col, BFA; Columbia Univ, MFA; Hans Hofmann Sch Painting; Archipenko Sch Art, New York; New Bauhaus Sch Design, with Moholy-Nagy; Acad Grande Chaumiere, Paris. *Work:* NY Univ; John F Kennedy Libr; Miami Univ, Ohio; Int Rels Found, New York; also in many pvt collections. *Exhib:* Walker Art Ctr, Minn, 63; Mfs Hanover Trust Bank, 70 & 71; Union Carbide Gallery, New York, 72, 75 & 78; Bankers Trust Gallery, 80-81; Warner Communications Gallery, New York, 82; Bankers Trust Gallery, 83; Lever House Gallery, 85-87; Cork Gallery, 90; Lincoln Ctr, New York. *Pos:* Art dir, Elisabeth Irwin High Sch, 75. *Teaching:* Lectr studio courses, NY Univ, 58-69; instr studio courses, Newton-Harvard Creative Art Ctr, 63. *Awards:* Carnegie Found Grant, 50; Gold Medal, Patronato Scholastico Arti, Italy, 63; Gold Medal, Academia Italia, 81; World Victory Cult Prize, Italy Ctr Study & Research, 85; Elected Hon Mem Int Child Art Ctr, Fort Dei MarMi, Italy, 87. *Bibliog:* Artists New York (tape), Voice of Am, 72. *Mem:* Artists New York (pres, 72-76); NY Soc Women Artists (secy). *Media:* Acrylic, Gold Leaf. *Publ:* Contribr, Art News, Art Digest, Art Now, 63-70, Park East, 80 & Art Speaks, 85. *Mailing Add:* 60 E Ninth St New York NY 10003

SHEDD, GEORGE J
PAINTER, ILLUSTRATOR
b Yonkers, NY, Sept 19, 22. *Study:* Cambridge Jr Col, 40-41; Mass Col Art, 41-43 & 47-48; Sch Mus Fine Arts, Boston, 49-50. *Work:* Barn Restaurant, Kennebunkport, Maine; First Nat Bank Gallery, Boston, Mass. *Exhib:* Opening Shows, Salmagundi Club Galleries, New York, 82-85; New Eng Watercolor Soc Show, Nashua Arts & Sci Ctr, NH, 83-85; one-man show, Guild of Boston Artists, Nov, 88; Simagundi Club, 89-90; Allied Artists Am, 90; and others. *Pos:* Instr watercolor, Lexington Arts & Crafts Soc, Mass, 70-; art dir, Rust Craft Greeting Cards, Inc, 75-81; instr watercolor workshops, Falmouth, 85, Orleans & Concord, 86, Mass. *Teaching:* Watercolor Workshops in Bermuda, 82, Fort Myers, Fla, 88, Barnstable, Cape Cod, Mass, 89-90. *Awards:* Salmagundi Club Award for Watercolor, spring 88, 91 & 92; Allied Artists Am, 91; Guild Boston Artist, 91. *Mem:* Am Watercolor Soc; Allied Artists Am; Guild Bostons Artists; Lexington Arts & Crafts Soc; New Eng Watercolor Soc (secy-treas, 78-80). *Media:* Watercolor. *Publ:* Contribr, Scenic Impressions, calendar paintings, Rust Craft Publ, 78; Seascapes, 83 & The Way We Were, 84, calendar paintings, Gibson Greetings Cards; 4th of July in Rockport, cover, Yankee Mag, 7/83; Watercolor Page, Am Artist Mag, Dec, 88; Cover, Yankee Mag, May 90. *Dealer:* Laura Erlich 19 Fox Run Rd Bedford MA 01730. *Mailing Add:* 46 Paulson Dr Burlington MA 01803

SHEDOSKY, SUZANNE
PAINTER
b Joliet, Ill, Sept 11, 55. *Study:* Brookwood Gallery/Merfeld Atelier with Gerald Merfeld, 76-92. *Exhib:* Allied Artists Am, New York, 84, 87, 88 & 91; Am Artists Prof League, New York, 86; Midwest Pastel Soc, Chicago, Ill, 86 & 87; Catharine Lorillard Wolfe Art Club, New York, 86; Nat Small Oil Painting Exhib, Wichita Art Asn, 88; Oil Painters Am Premier Nat Exhib, 92; Akron Soc Artist-Grand Exhib, 92. *Pos:* Studio asst, Brookwood Gallery/ Merfeld Atelier, 83-92. *Teaching:* Brookwood Gallery, 89-91. *Awards:* Ann & Richard Sauter Award for Pastel, Allied Artists Am, 84; Special Excellence Award, Harness Tracks Am, Lexington, Ky, 87; Ella Shaw Mem Best of Show Award & Lucille Warner Award, Phidian Art Club, Dixon, Ill, 88 & 91. *Media:* All Media. *Dealer:* Thum'prints Art Gallery Hilton Head Island SC. *Mailing Add:* 1120 Hahnaman Rd Rock Falls IL 61071

SHEEHAN, DIANE
CRAFTSMAN
Elizabeth, NJ, Dec 22, 45. *Study:* Montclair State Col, BA, 68; Indiana Univ, MFA, 72. *Work:* Ind Univ Art Mus; Ctr Visual Arts, Ill State Univ. *Exhib:* Mano Galleries, Chicago, Ill, 76; Vatican Mus, Rome, Italy, 78; Univ Hawaii, Manoa, Hawaii, 81; Brainerd Art Gallery, State Univ Col Arts & Science, Potsdam, NY, 84; Indianapolis Mus Art, Ind, 85; Univ Art Mus, Univ Wis-Milwaukee, Wis, 86. *Teaching:* From asst prof to assoc prof, Purdue Univ, 72-85. *Awards:* Lilly Endowment Fel, 80; Mayflower Corp Award, 83; Nat Endowment Arts, 87. *Dealer:* Katie Gingrass Gallery 241 N Broadway Milwaukee WI 53202. *Mailing Add:* 3452 Crestwood Dr Madison WI 53705

SHEEHAN, EVELYN
PAINTER
b Hymera, Ind, Dec 27, 19. *Study:* Scripps Col, with Jean Ames; also study with Phil Dike & Rex Brandt. *Work:* Lytton Collection, Los Angeles; Calif Bank, San Francisco; Mus Art, Univ Ore, Eugene; Tacoma Bank, Wash. *Exhib:* Spokane Ann Art Exhib, Cheney-Cowles Mus Art, Wash, 69; Watercolor USA, Springfield Art Mus, Mo, 70; 32nd Ann Northwest Exhib, Seattle Art Mus, Wash, 71; Dimensional Construction Exhib, Portland Contemp Craft Gallery, 77; Exhib of Paintings, Governor's Ceremonial Chambers, Salem, 77; one-man show, Mus Art, Univ Ore, Eugene, 71. *Awards:* Lytton Purchase Award, Watercolor USA, 67; Mo Award, 32nd Ann Nat Watercolor Soc, 71; Cash Award, 62nd Ann Nat Watercolor Soc, 82. *Mem:* Nat Soc Painters in Casein; Nat Watercolor Soc; Portland Art Asn. *Media:* Water Media, Collage. *Mailing Add:* 3935 SW Corbett Ave Portland OR 97201

SHEEHAN, MAURA A
SCULPTOR, PAINTER
b New York, NY, Dec 2, 54. *Study:* Art Students League, 68-72; Carnegie-Mellon Univ, Pittsburgh, Pa, 72-74; San Francisco Art Inst, Calif, BFA, 74-76. *Work:* Art in Public Spaces, Hamden, Conn; The Weatherspoon, Univ NC, Greensboro. *Comn:* De Appel Foundation, Amsterdam, Hollan, 84; Urban Sited Sculpture, Comn The Seattle Arts Comn, 84. *Exhib:* solo exhibs, Simon Watson, New York, 89, Beaver Col Art Gallery, Philadelphia, PA, 89, Facchetti Gallery, New York, 89 & 90, Anderson Gallery, VA Commonwealth Univ, Richmond, 90; Orchard Gallery, Derry, Northern Ireland, 89; Parcours-Prives, Paris, France, 10/90; Casino Fantasimo, Venice, Italy, 6/90; The New Metaphysical Art, Amy Lipton Gallery, New York, 9/90. *Teaching:* Assoc prof art, Sch Visual Arts, New York, 88- *Awards:* Painting Award, Nat Endowment Arts, 87; Sculptor Award, New York State Arts Grant, 91. *Bibliog:* Philadelphia Inquirer, 10/15/89; Roger Denson (auth), rev, Artscribe, 1/90; Ken Johnson (auth), rev, Art in America, 1/90. *Media:* Installation, Multimedia. *Dealer:* Bruno Facchetti 476 Broadway New York NY 10012; Barbara Flynn 113 Crosby St New York NY 10012. *Mailing Add:* PO Box 20752 New York NY 10009

SHEEHE, LILLIAN CAROLYN
PAINTER, ENAMELIST
b Conemaugh, Pa, Oct 16, 15. *Study:* Indiana Univ Pa, BS(art); ceramics & sculpture with Sheldone Grumbling, majolica with Hugh Geise & painting & sculpture with George Ream. *Comn:* Golf mural, comn by J Cover, Johnstown, Pa, 44; designed & printed Christmas cards, Pa Rehab Ctr & Bur Voc Rehab, 59-71; emblem design, Lee Hosp Rehab Med Dept, 66; fired glass picture, Pepsi Cola Co, Washington, DC, 78 & Johnstown, Pa, 79. *Exhib:* All Allied Artists Shows, 36-; Allied Artists Graphic Arts Show, 70; Sheraton '75; Field Glass, Johnstown Chamber of Com, 76; First three-generation show, Community Art Ctr, 82; one-man show, Indiana Univ Mus Galleries, Pa, 87. *Teaching:* Art supvr, East Conemaugh Schs, 36-42; instr art & world hist, Westmont High Sch, 44-45 & 53-54; instr art & art supvr, Ferndale-Dale Grade & High Schs, 55-59; instr arts & crafts, Pa Voc Rehab Ctr, 59-75. *Awards:* Phoebe Jerema Award, Pittsylvania Ceramic Guild, 71; David Glosser Libr Craft Award, 73; Chrysanthemum Soc Sweepstakes Award, 78; A B Crichton Award,83, Allied Artists Ann Show & Gold Award, 84; Gold Award, Allied Artists Am Show, 88; Prof Artists League Ann Award for Best Enamelling, 90. *Bibliog:* George Mengelson (producer), Art Exhibit (two TV shows on glass work), 69; article, Johnstown Tribune-Democrat, 7/76; Catholic Register, Altoona, Pa, 5/76. *Mem:* Allied Artists (pres, 70-72); Area Arts Coun (pres, 75-77); Arts Assocs; Cult Affairs Comt; Am Artists Prof League; Chrysanthemum Soc (pres, 78-80). *Media:* Mixed. *Res:* Experimented twenty-years on uses of fired glass and its combinations for pictorial work. *Publ:* Auth & illusr, Allied Artists Fall Show Catalog (also cover design), 58; Useless to useful, Leather Craftsman Mag, 61; auth & illusr, Antiquity in a day, Ceramics Arts & Crafts, 64 & Textbook on Photo--Tinting--Color--Oils, Bur Voc Rehab, 65; auth, I Dreamed in Glass, Antique Trader, 7/77; and others. *Mailing Add:* 1333 Christopher St Johnstown PA 15905

SHEFFIELD, MARGARET
CRITIC, CURATOR
b New York, NY. *Study:* New York Univ Grad Sch Arts & Sci, MA, 66, MSW, 93. *Collections Arranged:* The Hudson River, Broadway Mall Ctr, 89; Barbara Kulicke, Arsenal Gallery, New York, 91. *Pos:* NY corresp, Studio Int, London, Eng, 76-77; art critic, Int Daily News, Rome, Italy, 78-79. *Teaching:* Instr, Eng, Forum Sch, Rome, Italy, 76-78; instr, eng lit, The New Sch, 86-87; instr, eng lit, Marymount Manhattan Col, NY, 87-91. *Publ:* Auth, Cy Twombly: Major Changes in Space, Ideas, Time, 5/79 & Perfecting the Imperfect: Noguchi's Personal Style, Artforum Mag, 4/80; Frame Ups and Downs, Connoisseur Mag, 3/88; Roll Over Rembrandt: Franz Hals gets his First Great Show Anywhere, Connoisseur Mag, Dec/89; Tyrone Mitchell: The Mythic & the Minimal, Art News, 12/90 & 8/92; Elise Asher: Nightfall (catalog), June Kelly Gallery, 11/91. *Mailing Add:* 45 Christopher St New York NY 10014

SHEIRR, OLGA (KROLIK)
PAINTER
b New York, NY, June 7, 31. *Study:* Art Students League, with Reginald Marsh, 48-50; Brooklyn Col, with Rothko, Reinhardt & Still, BA, 53; New York Inst Fine Arts, 54; Pratt Graphics Ctr, with Michael Ponce de Leon, 65-70. *Work:* Mus City New York; St Vincents Hosp, New York; Greenville Co Mus, SC; Nat Mus Women Arts, Washington, DC. *Comn:* Serigraph eds, Art Resources and Treasures, New York, 79 & Summit Fine Arts, New York, 79. *Exhib:* one-person shows, Noho Gallery, 75-92, New Sch Social Res, New York, 84, Barbizon Gallery, Greenwich, Conn, 84, Farleigh Dickinson Univ, 85 & 90- 91, Kendall Gallery, New York, 86, Passaic Co Community Col, Patterson, NJ, 90; Guild Hall, East Hampton, New York, 89-92; Compagnie Moderne Et Contemporaine, Paris, France, 91; 165th Ann Exhib, Nat Acad Design, New York, 90; HTAL 35th Ann Long Island Exhib, Heckscher Mus, Huntington, NY, 90; Ninth Ann Small Works, 80 Washington Sq E Galleries, New York, 85; The Newark Mus, Newark, NJ, 92. *Collections Arranged:* Noho Gallery Invitational Exhib, 76 & Madness on Mercer, 86, New York; Twenty Three Artists at Ten Studios (auth, catalog), New York, 77; Six at the Arsenal (auth, catalog), New York, 78. *Pos:* Instr, art workshop, Fla Gulf Coast Art Ctr, Belleair, 87; watercolor workshop, Barkly Art Ctr, Custer, SDak, 90; The Education Alliance, New York, 89; Lectr, Rutgers Univ, New Brunswick, NJ, 90. *Awards:* Adolf & Clara Obrig Prize, Nat Acad Design, 90; Nora Mirmont Hambuechen Award, Heckscher Mus, 90; New York Artist Equity Annual Award, 91. *Bibliog:* James T McCartin (auth), article, Arts Mag, 5/82; Stephen DiLauro (auth), article, Am Artists Mag, 86; Ed McCormack (auth), article, Artspeak, 11/89. *Mem:* Women in Arts; New York Soc Women Artists; New York Artists Equity; Womens Caucus Art; Artist for Mental Health. *Media:* Watercolor, Oil. *Dealer:* Noho Gallery 168 Mercer St New York NY 10012. *Mailing Add:* 360 First Ave Apt 11G New York NY 10010

SHELBY, LILA (LILA NORMA WALLACE)
PAINTER
b Simsboro, La, Jan 30, 1900. *Study:* Columbia Univ, 40-41; The Arts Students League, New York; Studied with George Bridgeman, Frank Reilly, Harry Carnahan, Carl Blenner, MA Rasko & Wayman Adams, 40-43. *Comn:* Portrait, 1951 Crusade; portrait, US Supreme Court Justice, Tom Clark; portrait, Dr Reverend Billy Graham. *Exhib:* New York Worlds Fair, Colorama Gallery, 50; Art In Religion, Birmingham Mus, Ala, 66. *Awards:* Hon Mention, Acad Allied Artists, 40; Hon Mention, Nat Art Digest, 41. *Mem:* Nat Asn Women Artists Inc; Life mem, Arts Students League. *Mailing Add:* 718 Green Acres Rd Metairie LA 70003

SHELTON, PETER T
SCULPTOR
b Troy, Ohio, Jan 18, 51. *Study:* Pomona Col, BA(fine arts), 73; Hobart Sch Welding Technol, cert, 74; Univ Calif, Los Angeles, MFA, 79. *Work:* State Wash; Artpark, Lewiston, NY. *Comn:* Artpark, Lewistown, NY; Exposition Park, Los Angeles. *Exhib:* Solo exhibs, Chapman Col, Orange, Calif, 80 & Malinda Wyatt Gallery, Los Angeles, 81; Los Angeles Co Mus Art, 81; Open Space Gallery, Victoria, Can, 82; Artists Space, New York, 82; Mus D'Art Mod, Paris, 82; Ctr Contemp Art, Seattle, 83; Portland Ctr Visual Arts, 84; and others. *Teaching:* Lectr sculpture, Otis/Parsons Sch Art & Design, 80-; lectr sculpture, Claremont Grad Sch, 81- *Awards:* Purchase Award, State Wash, 77; Fel, Nat Endowment Arts, 80. *Bibliog:* Christopher Knight (auth), Your Place or Shelton's, Los Angeles Herald Examiner, 81; Merle Schipper (auth), Peter Shelton's Places and Spaces, Images & Issues, 81; Melinda Wortz (auth), Peter Shelton at the Santa Barbara Contemporary Arts Forum, Artnews, 83. *Media:* Multi-Media. *Publ:* Contribr, Neckwall, Footscreen, Sleeper, Dreamworks, Human Sci Press, 82. *Dealer:* Malinda Wyatt Gallery 76 Market St Venice CA 90291. *Mailing Add:* c/o LA Louver Gallery 55 N Venice Blvd Venice CA 90291

SHELTON, ROBERT LEE
DESIGNER, EDUCATOR
b Memphis, Tenn, Apr 8, 39. *Study:* Memphis State Univ, BFA; Univ Ala, MA. *Work:* South Central Bell, Regional Off, Birmingham, Ala; First Nat Bank, Montgomery, Ala; Ambassadors Off, Fed Repub Ger. *Exhib:* Nat Small Painting Biennial, Purdue Univ, 66; Nat Black & White Prints, Kans State Univ, 66; Mid-South Ann, Memphis, Tenn, 69; Hunter Gallery Ann, Chattanooga, Tenn, 69; Graphics USA, Dubuque, Iowa, 70. *Teaching:* Asst prof drawing & design, Auburn Univ, Ala, 64-68; prof printmaking & design, Birmingham-Southern Col, Ala, 68- *Awards:* First Prize, Macon Mus, 68; First Purchase Award, Columbus Mus Art, 69 & 72; First Purchase Award, Montgomery Mus Art, 70. *Bibliog:* Martin Hames (auth), Robert Shelton, 1975 Birmingham Festival of Arts Bull, 3/75. *Mem:* Birmingham Art Asn (bd mem, 74-75, pres, 81-); Tenn Valley Art Asn. *Media:* Crayon, Oil. *Publ:* Auth, Contemporary printmaking in the US, Birmingham Festival Bulletin, 73. *Dealer:* Courtyard Gallery 2800 Sixth Ave S Birmingham AL 35208. *Mailing Add:* 10 Fifth St Birmingham AL 35217

SHEMESH, LORRAINE R
PAINTER
b Jersey City, NJ, Mar 27, 49. *Study:* Boston Univ, BFA(magna cum laude), 71; Tyler Sch Art, Rome, 71-72; Tyler Sch Art, MFA(painting fel), 73. *Work:* DeCordova Mus, Lincoln, Mass; Mus RI Sch Design, Providence; Am Tel & Tel, Chicago; Mus City of New York; Boise Art Mus, Idaho. *Exhib:* solo shows, Alpha Gallery, Boston, 78, Allan Stone Gallery, New York, 83, 85, 88 & 91; Painting New York, Mus City of New York, 83-84; American Realism: 20th Century Drawings, San Francisco Mus Mod Art, 85-86; Duke Univ, Mus Art, Durham, NC, 87; Akron Art Mus, Ohio, 87; Am Broadcasting Corp, New York, 90; and others. *Teaching:* Asst prof painting & drawing, RI Sch Design, 73-80 & Amherst Col, 80-81. *Awards:* RI State Coun Arts Grant, 79; Yaddo Fel, 81. *Bibliog:* Review, Art in America, 9/88; review, Artspeak, 3/88 & 12/89; Daniel Mendelowitz, Wane A Wakeham, A Guide to Drawing, Holt, Rinehart & Winston, 88. *Media:* Oil, Graphite. *Dealer:* Allan Stone Gallery 48 East 86th St New York NY 10028. *Mailing Add:* 548 East 82nd St Apt 2A New York NY 10028

SHEON, AARON
HISTORIAN, ADMINISTRATOR
b Toledo, Ohio, Oct 7, 37. *Study:* Univ Mich, AB, MA, 60; Inst d'Art et d'Archeolgie, Paris, 62; Princeton Univ, MFA, PhD, 66. *Teaching:* Assoc prof, Univ Pittsburgh, Pa, 66-78, prof, 78-; vis mem, Inst Advan Study, Princeton, 84-85. *Awards:* Bowman Fac Award, Univ Pittsburgh, 76; Hon Award, Pa Soc Architects, 82; Gould Found Fel, 86. *Mem:* Col Art Asn; Soc Fr Art Hist. *Res:* French 19th and 20th century art history; art and scientific thought; educational role of the museum. *Publ:* Auth, Monticelli, His Contemporaries, His Influence, 79; Organic Vision: The Architecture of Peter Berndston, 80; Octave Tassaert's Le Suicide, Arts, 81; Courbet, French realism and discovery of unconscious, Arts, 81; 1913: Forgotten cubist exhibitions in America, Arts, 83; Monticelli Centennial Exhib, Marseille, 86; Paul Guigou, 87. *Mailing Add:* Dept of Fine Arts Univ Pittsburgh Pittsburgh PA 15260

SHEPARD, LEWIS ALBERT
DEALER, HISTORIAN
b East Orange, NJ, May 24, 45. *Study:* Rutgers Univ, New Brunswick, BA, 67; Ind Univ, Bloomington, MA, 70. *Collections Arranged:* Cowboys, Indians, Trappers & Traders (with catalog), Mead Art Gallery, Amherst Col, 73 & Am Painters of the Arctic (with catalog), 75. *Pos:* Trainee catalog & dept head, Sotheby Parke Bernet, New York, 70-72; cur, Mead Art Gallery, Amherst Col, 72-77; proprietor, dealer & appraiser, pvt pract, Worcester, Mass, 77- *Teaching:* Asst instr mod art, Ind Univ, Bloomington, 69-70; instr Am art, Amherst Col, 73-76 & Clark Univ, 80 & 84. *Mem:* Col Art Asn; Worcester Heritage Preserv Soc (bd dirs, 79-84); Appraisers Registry. *Res:* American 19th and 20th century painting; Western Americana; Arctic exploration; arts and crafts movement. *Specialty:* American and European 19th and 20th century art. *Collection:* American drawings 1830-1930. *Publ:* Auth, Willard Metcalf Exhibition--a Review, Am Art Rev, 77; American Art at Amherst Collage--a Summary Catalogue, Amherst Col, 78. *Mailing Add:* 2 Congress St Worcester MA 01609

SHEPHERD, HELEN PARSONS
PAINTER
b St John's, Nfld, Jan 16, 23. *Study:* Mem Univ Nfld, LLD, 41-42; Ontario Col Art, hons grad, 48. *Work:* Mem Univ Gallery, St John's Nfld, Can; Beaverbrook Gallery, Fredericton, New Brunswick, Can; Gov General Shreyer's Portrait, Readeau Hall, Ottawa, Ont, Can; Reader's Digest Coll, Can; Coll Northern Telecom, Can Ltd. *Comn:* Portraits, mayors, St John's, 73; portrait, Lord Taylor of Harlow, Mem Univ, 73; portrait, Prince Philip, Government House, St John's, Royal Canadian Legion, 76. *Exhib:* Maritime Art exhib, Beaverbrook Gallery, 64; Expo 67, Montreal; Montreal Mus Fine Arts Exhib, 68; Solo exhib, Mem Univ, Nfld, 75, Erindale Col, Toronto, 75, The Gallery-Mauskoph, St John's, Nfld, 85; Mem Univ Gallery 25th Ann Exhib, St John's, 86; Helen Parsons Shepherd & Reginald Shepherd - Four Decades, Mem Univ Gallery, 89. *Pos:* Co-founder & teacher, Nfld Acad Art, 49-61. *Teaching:* Instr drawing & painting, Nfld Acad Art, 49-61. *Awards:* Royal Can Acad Arts; Mem Univ, Nfld, LLD. *Bibliog:* Rex Murphy (dir), Here & Now (film), Can Broadcasting Corp TV, 76; Neil Murray (auth), Profile, Nfld Herald, 79; Helen Parsons Shepherd & Reginald Shepherd, Four Decades, Peter Gard (art critic). *Mem:* Royal Can Acad Arts; St Michael's Print Shop. *Media:* Oil, Graphic Drawing. *Mailing Add:* 26 Oxen Pond Rd St John's NF A1B 3J3 Canada

SHEPHERD, REGINALD
PAINTER, PRINTMAKER
b Portugal Cove, Nfld, Can, Mar 28, 24. *Study:* Ont Col Art, Toronto, AOCA, 49. *Work:* Mem Univ Gallery, St John's, Nfld, Can; Univ Ore, Corvallis; Art Gallery London, Ont; Dalhousie Art Gallery, Halifax, NS; Mt Allison Univ Gallery, Sackville, NB. *Comn:* Reredos, St Patricks Roman Cath Church, St John's, Nfld, 62; 12 watercolors, City of St John's, Nfld, 73; oil mural in Atlantic Pl, Crosbie & Co, St John's, Nfld, 75; Canada Postage Stamp Commemorating Canada's 125th Year of Confederation. *Exhib:* First Biennial Exhib, Nat Gallery Can, Ottawa, 55; Survey 64, Montreal Mus; solo exhibs, Mem Univ Gallery, St John's, Nfld, 72, Canada House Gallery, London, Eng, 83, Univ Leeds Gallery, Eng, 83 & Piazza Cardelli, Rome, Italy, 83-84; Traveling Print Exhib, Univ Ore, Corvallis, 76; Exhib Helen Parsons Shepherd & Reginald Shepherd, Four Decades, Memorial Univ, 89c. *Teaching:* dir & instr drawing & painting, Nfld Acad Art, 49-61; vis lectr art educ, Mem Univ, St John's, 51-61; specialist fine arts, Prince Wales Col, 62-80. *Awards:* Can Govt Fel for study in Holland, Royal Soc Can, 56-57; LLD Honoris Causa, Mem Univ, Nfld, 88. *Bibliog:* Rex Murphy (dir), Here & Now (film), Can Broadcasting Corp TV, 76; Neil Murray (auth), Profile, Nfld Herald, 79; Colleen Lynch (auth), Watercolours Reflect Human Values, Nfld Daily News, 1/84; Peter Gard (art critic), Helen Parsons Shepherd-Reginald Shepherd, Four Decades; James Wade (art critic), Evening Telegram, St John's, Nfld. *Mem:* Royal Can Acad Arts (provincial vpres, 78-83); fel Int Inst Arts & Lett. *Media:* Watercolor, Serigraphy. *Dealer:* The Gallery 284 Duckworth St St John's Nfld Can A1C 5M9; Contemporary Fine Art Services 411 Richmond St E Suite 103 Toronto ON M5A 355 Canada. *Mailing Add:* 26 Oxen Pond Rd St John's NF A1B 3J3 Canada

SHEPHERD, WILLIAM FRITZ
PAINTER
b Casper, Wyo, April 1, 43. *Study:* Univ Wyo, BA, MFA, 72. *Work:* Amoco Oil Co, Houston; Univ Wyo Art Mus, Laramie; IT&T, Basking Ridge, NJ; NMex Fine Arts Mus, Santa Fe; pvt collection of Mrs Joseph Hirshhorn, Washington, DC. *Exhib:* New Works New Mexico, Blaffer Gallery, Univ Houston, 81; Rosalind Constable Selects, Sweeney Ctr, Santa Fe, 81; Best of Decade, Hills Gallery, Santa Fe, 81; one-person show, Amarillo Art Ctr, Tex, 86; Boundless Realism, Rockwell Mus, Corning, NY, 87; The Face of the Land, Southern Alleghenies Mus Art, Loretto, Pa, 88; The Art Collection of Abassador and Mrs Keith Campham Brown, Am Embassy Residence, Copenhagen, Denmark, 90-92; Events About a Rectangle, Cedar Rapids Mus Art, Iowa, 91; Events About a Rectangle, Eiteljorg Mus, Indianapolis, Ind, 91. *Awards:* Spec Jurors Prize, Washington & Jefferson Col, 74. *Bibliog:* Harold Olejarz (auth), article, Arts Mag, 1/79; William Peterson (auth), Smoke Rings, Shinto Shrines, Doktor Thrill and the Snake Lady, Art News, 12/80; Carol Everingham (auth), Bi-lateral--bi-literal rocks, spring 83, Town & Country, 7/84 & Art & Antiques, 4/86, Artspace. *Media:* Oil on Canvas. *Mailing Add:* PO Box 9816 Santa Fe NM 87501

SHEPP, ALAN
SCULPTOR
b Cleveland, Ohio, Nov 11, 35. *Study:* Bowling Green State Univ, BA, 57; Cleveland Inst Art, BFA, 58; Univ Wash, Seattle, MFA, 63. *Work:* London Co Coun, Eng; Seattle Art Mus; Walker Art Ctr; Univ Wis, Menomie; Cleveland Mus Art. *Comn:* Marble relief, Mill Valley City Hall, Calif, 82; slate relief, Bank Am, San Francisco, 83; Pan Pac Singapore Hotel, Singapore, 86; IBM, Alameda, Calif, 86; Hewlett Packard, Mountain View, Calif, 86. *Exhib:* Toledo Mus Art, 57; May Show, Cleveland Mus Art, 58; Seattle Art Mus, 63; Fulbright Artists Group Exhib, Palazzo Venezia, Rome, Italy, 64; Contemp

Mus Art, Chicago, 70; Art and Technology, Mus Mod Art, Tel Aviv, Israel, 71; Aesthetics of Graffiti, San Francisco Mus Mod Art, 78. *Teaching:* Instr, Goldsmiths Col, Univ London, 64-66; Minneapolis Col Art, 66-70; Univ Victoria, 70; Calif State Univ, Hayward, 71- *Awards:* Fulbright Fel to Italy, 63-64; Calif State Univ Res Grant, 74; Nat Endowment Arts Fel, 79. *Bibliog:* Robert McDonald (auth), Manifestations of Graffiti, Artweek, 78; Robert Yaskowitz (auth), article, Arts Mag, 79; Joanne Burstein (auth), Sculpture 82, Artweek, 82; Robert Atkins (auth), Alan Shepp, Recent Sculpture (catalog), Stephen Wirtz Gallery, 83. *Media:* Slate. *Publ:* Auth, 1968 Biennial of Painting and Sculpture, Walker Art Ctr, 68; RE-DACT, Willis, Locker & Owens, 84. *Mailing Add:* c/o Stephen Wirtz Gallery 49 Geary San Francisco CA 94108

SHEPPARD, CARL DUNKLE
HISTORIAN
b Washington, DC, Jan 11, 16. *Study:* Amherst Col, BA; Harvard Univ, MA, 42, PhD, 47. *Teaching:* Instr, Univ Mich, Ann Arbor, 46-49; from asst prof to prof, Univ Calif, Los Angeles, 50-64; prof art hist & chmn dept, Univ Minn, Minneapolis, 64-83, prof emer, 83-86. *Awards:* Fulbright Grants, Italy, 53-54 & Turkey, 67-68; Del Amo Found Grant, Spain, 57; McMillan Travel Grant, Italy, 68; Kress Found Grant, 83 & 84; Gaspar Perez Villagra Award, Hist Soc NMex, 88. *Mem:* Soc Archit Historians; Int Ctr Medieval Art; Medieval Acad. *Publ:* Auth, Carbon 14 dating & Santa Sophia, Dumbarton Oaks Papers, Istanbul, 65; Byzantine carved marble slabs, Art Bulletin, 3/69; Classicism in Tuscan Romanesque sculpture, 77, A note on the date of Taq-i-bustan, 81, Pre-romanesque sculpture: Evidence for the cultural evolution of the people of Dalmation Coast, 84 & Excavations, Frankish Cathedral Androvida, 86, Gesta; Creator of Santa Fe Style: Isaac Hamilton Rapp, Archit Univ of NMex Press, 88. *Mailing Add:* 1234 Camino De Cruz Blanca PO Box 5773 Santa Fe NM 87501

SHEPPARD, JOSEPH SHERLY
PAINTER, SCULPTOR
b Owings Mills, Md, Dec 20, 30. *Study:* Md Inst Col Art, cert (fine art); also with Jacques Maroger. *Work:* Butler Inst Am Art; Fine Arts Mus, Mobile, Ala; Baltimore Mus Art, Md; Carnegie Inst; Westmoreland Art Mus, Greenburg, Pa; and others. *Comn:* Murals, Police Dept Hq Bldg, Baltimore; mural, Equitable Trust Co, Baltimore; bronze bas-relief, Baltimore Fire Dept; bronze, Holocaust Mem, Baltimore; mural, Palmer House Hotel, Chicago, Ill; Peabody Court Hotel, Baltimore, Md, 85. *Exhib:* One-man shows, Butler Inst Am Art, 64 & 72, Westmoreland Co Mus, 66, 72 & 82 & Davenport Munic Art Gallery, Iowa, 67 & 83; consecutive shows, Florence, Italy, 77-; and others. *Pos:* Owner studio, Pietrasanta, Italy. *Teaching:* Instr painting & artist-in-residence, Dickinson Col, 56-57; instr drawing, painting & anat, Md Inst Col Art, 60-75. *Awards:* Prize for Figure Painting, 63 & Paul Puzinas Award, 84, Allied Artists; John J McDonough Prize, Butler Inst Am Art, 67; Gov Prize, Md Artists Exhib, Baltimore Mus, 71; Tallix Foundry Prize, 83 & Agop Agopoff Mem Prize, 86, Nat Sculpture Soc; Award of Merit, Soc Animal Artists, 83. *Mem:* Allied Artists Am; Nat Sculpture Soc; Soc Animal Artists; Knickerbocker Artists. *Publ:* Auth, Anatomy, 75, Drawing the Female Figure, 75, Drawing the Male Figure, 76, Learning From the Masters, 79 & Drawing the Living Figure, 84, Watson-Guptill; auth, Keeping Christmas, Stemmer House, 81. *Dealer:* Carolyn Hill Gallery 109 Spring St New York NY 10012. *Mailing Add:* 3908 N Charles St Baltimore MD 21218

SHEPPARD, NINA AKAMU See Akamu, Nina

SHER, ELIZABETH
VIDEO ARTIST, PRINTMAKER
b Washington, DC, Feb 13, 43. *Study:* Smith Col, Mass, 60-62; Univ Calif, Berkeley, BA, 64, MA, 67; San Francisco Art Inst, 65-66. *Work:* US Info Agency, Washington, DC; Oakland Mus; Calif Palace Legion Hon; Sierra Mus Art; Carnegie Mellon Univ. *Exhib:* Fifty-seven Calif Printmakers, Calif Palace Legion Hon; Edinburgh Int Film Fest, 82; First Int Video Fest, Montbeliard, France, 82; San Francisco Int Film Fest, 82 & 83; Athens Int Film & Video Fest, Mich, 83; AFI Women in Film III, John F Kennedy Ctr, Washington, DC, 83; Ann Arbor Film Fest, Mich, 83; Milan Fest Am Independent Cinema, 83; Video on the Rock, La Rochelle, France, 84; Calif Collection, Fortuny Mus, Venice, Italy, 84; New Music USA, Musee d'Art Moderne de la Ville de Paris, 85. *Collections Arranged:* Guest cur, Mixed Media on Paper, Berkeley Art Ctr, 78. *Pos:* Dir, IV Studios, Berkeley, Calif, 82- *Teaching:* Assoc prof, Calif Col Arts & Crafts, 77- *Awards:* Purchase Award, Seventh Nevada Ann, 80; Union of Independent Art Col Fac Grant, 82 & 83; Most Humorous Video, Hollywood Erotic Film & Video Fest, 84; Western Regional Media Arts Fel, 84. *Bibliog:* Articles, San Diego Mag, 81 & Artweek Mag, 82; Video, Ego Mag, 82; Showing a head for video, Chicago Tribune, 4/85; review, St Louis Post-Dispatch, 9/12/85; Totally tubular artists, Calif Living Mag, 9/15/85. *Mem:* Film Arts Found; Calif Soc Printmakers; Bay Area Video Coalition; Women's Caucus Art; Canyon Cinemateque Film Soc. *Media:* Mixed Media. *Publ:* Illusr, A Child's Library of Dreams, Celestial Arts, 78. *Mailing Add:* IV Studios 985 Regal Rd Berkeley CA 94708

SHERBELL, RHODA
SCULPTOR, CONSULTANT
b Brooklyn, NY. *Study:* Art Students League, with William Zorach & Reginald Marsh; Brooklyn Mus Art Sch, with Hugo Robies; study in Italy, France, Eng & Switz, with Mervin Honig. *Work:* William Benton Mus Art, Conn; Colby Col Art Mus, Waterville, Maine; New York Pub Libr, Queens Mus & Brooklyn Mus, New York; Smithsonian Inst; Nat Portrait Gallery; Mus Mod Art, New York; Jewish Mus, New York. *Comn:* Marguerite & William Zorach Bronze, Nat Arts Collection, Smithsonian Inst, Washington, DC, 64; bronzes of Aaron Copland, Eleanore Roosevelt, & Yogi Berra, Montclair Art Mus; Casey Stengel, Country Art Gallery Long Island, Baseball Hall of Fame, Cooperstown, NY; Yogi Berra, comn by Percy Uris. *Exhib:* Pa Acad Fine Arts, 60; Brooklyn Mus Art Award Winners Exhib, 65; Nat Acad Design, 67, 72, 80 & 82; Jewish Mus, NY; Nat Arts Club, Allied Artists Am, William Benton Mus; solo exhibs, Brooklyn Mus, New York Cult Ctr & Bronx Mus Art, New York; and over 20 solo exhibs. *Pos:* Pres bd, Friends Emily Lowe Gallery; dir sculpture, Allied Artists; dir pub rels, Audubon Artists, currently. *Teaching:* Instr, Mus Mod Art, Art Students League, Nat Acad Design; prof art, Hofstra Univ, New York. *Awards:* Am Acad Arts & Lett Awards; Louis Comfort, Tiffany Found Award; Ford Found Award; Gold Medals, Audubon Artists Am, Allied Artists & Nat Asn Woman; and many others. *Bibliog:* Articles, Mus Mag, 4/82 & McCall's Mag, 8/82; Woman in Bronze (film), PBS TV; and many others. *Mem:* Allied Artists Am; Audubon Artists; life mem Art Students League; Am Inst Arts & Letters; assoc mem Am Watercolor Soc; Nat Acad Design; and many others. *Media:* Bronze. *Collection:* Contemporary American realistic work, including M & R Soyer, W Zorach, Marguerite Zorach, Mervin Honig, Harry Sternberg, John Koch, Agostine, H Jackson, Margit Beck and others. *Mailing Add:* 64 Jane Ct Westbury NY 11590

SHERIDAN, HELEN ADLER
CURATOR
b Kansas City, Mo. *Study:* Ohio State Univ; Univ Kans, BA; Univ Calif Los Angeles, MA; Western Mich Univ, MLS. *Collections Arranged:* Super Realism from the Morton G Neuman Family Collection (ed, catalog), 81; New Image-Pattern & Decoration from the Morton G Neumann Family Collection (ed, catalog), 83; Kirk Newman Retrospective (ed, catalog), 84; A Century of Caring: American Realism , 1880's-1980's (ed, catalog), 86, Kalamazoo Inst Arts, Mich; The Cutting Edge, New Directions in Handmade Papers (ed, catalog), 88; Meetings in The Garden: The Art of John Himmelfarb (catalog), 89; Richard Hunt: Sculpture Past, Present, & Future (catalog), 90. *Pos:* Head librn & cur collections, Kalamazoo Inst Arts, Mich, 75-82, asst to dir collections & exhibs, 83-88; dir collections & exhib, 89- *Teaching:* Instr arts of the 20th century, Western Mich Univ, 66-75. *Mem:* Col Art Asn; Midwest Mus Asn; Am Asn Mus; Mich Mus Asn. *Res:* Contemporary American art and artists; documentation of Mich artists and art collections. *Interests:* American arts of the twentieth century; regionalist art; photography. *Publ:* Co-ed, The Vagaries of Invention, 81. *Mailing Add:* c/o Kalamazoo Inst Arts 314 S Park St Kalamazoo MI 49006

SHERIDAN, SONIA LANDY
MEDIA ARTIST
b Newark, Ohio, Apr 10, 25. *Study:* Hunter Col, AB, 45; Columbia Univ, 46-48; Taiwan She Da Univ, 58; Yoshida Studio, Tokyo, 59; with Nathan Oliveira, 60; Calif Col Arts & Crafts, MFA, 60. *Work:* Art Inst Chicago; Mus Sci & Indust, Chicago; San Francisco Mus Art; George Eastman House, Rochester, NY; Nat Gallery, Ottawa, Can; Tokyo Metrop Mus Photog. *Exhib:* two-person show, Projects, Mus Mod Art, New York, 74; Women of Photography, San Francisco Mus Art, 75; retrospective, Univ Iowa Mus Art, 76; Mus Mod Art, Paris, 83; Photog & Art, Los Angeles Co Mus, 87; Am Women Artists: 20th Century, Knoxville Mus Art & Queensboro Community Art Col, NY, 89-90; Infinite Illusion, Smithsonian, 90; Tokyo Metrop Mus, 91; Vasarely Museum, Budapest, 92; Trivial Machines, Osthaus Mus, Hagen, Ger, 92; Circulo des Belles Artes, 92. *Collections Arranged:* Traveling exhib, The Inner Landscape & the Machine (assembled, catalogued), Visual Studies Workshop, Rochester, 72- *Pos:* Co-ed, Leonardo, Int J Art, Sci, Tech, currently; hon dir, Mus fur Fotocopie, Mulheim an der Ruhr. *Teaching:* Instr art educ & design, Calif Col Arts & Crafts, 60-61; founder, prof & area head generative systems, Sch Art Inst Chicago, 61-80, prof emer, 80- *Awards:* Guggenheim Fel, 73; NEA Workshop Grant, 74, Union Independent Cols Art Grant, 75; Pub Media Grant, 76 & Artist Grant, 81-82. *Bibliog:* Raymond Synard (ed), Color Theory and Imaging Systems, Soc Photog Scientists & Engrs, 73; Diane Kirkpatrick (auth), Chicago the City and Its Artists, Univ Mich, 78; Richard Wickstrom (auth), NMex State Univ, Art Science, 78; The Computer Revolution in Art, Univ Fla Press, 3/88; Gardner's Art Through the Ages (auth, 9th ed), De la Croix, Tansey, Kirkpatrick. *Mem:* Founding mem, Int Soc Interdisciplinary Study Symmetry, Budapest, Hungary. *Media:* Still Imaging. *Publ:* Symmetry/Asymmetry: An Artist's View, Symmetry in a Kaleidoscope, Int Soc Interdisciplinary Study of Symmetry, Budapest, Hungary, 89; Guest ed & auth, New Foundations: Lessons in Art/Science/Technology, Leonardo: Int J Art, Sci, Tech, Vol 23, No 2/3 Pergammon Press, Berkeley, Calif, 90; Timescope: Patterns in Flow Symmetrically, Symmetry: Culture & Science, Budapest, Hungary, 92. *Dealer:* Visual Studies Workshop 31 Prince St Rochester NY 14607; Photo Researchers Inc New York NY 10022. *Mailing Add:* 718 Noyes Evanston IL 60201

SHERMAN, CINDY
PHOTOGRAPHER
b Glen Ridge, NJ, 1954. *Study:* State Univ NY, Buffalo, 76. *Work:* Mus Mod Art, Metrop Mus Art, & Brooklyn Mus, New York; Tate Gallery, London; Walker Art Ctr, Minneapolis, Minn; San Francisco Mus Art, Calif; Corcoran Gallery Art, Washington, DC. *Exhib:* Eight Artists: The Anxious Edge, Walker Art Ctr, Minneapolis, 82; Recent Color, San Franciso Mus Mod Art, 82; New Figuration in America, Milwaukee Art Mus, 82; Biennial, Whitney Mus, New York, 83, 85 & 91; Big Pictures by Contemporary Photographers, Mus Mod Art, New York, 83; Facets of the Collection: Recent Acquisitions, San Francisco Mus Contemp Art, 83; Alibis, Centre Pompidou, Musee d'Art Moderne, Paris, 84; Color Photographs: Recent Acquisitions, Mus Mod Art, Paris, 84; Self-Portrait, Mus Mod Art, New York, 85; Stills: Cinema and

Video Transformed, Seattle Art Mus, 86; The American Exhib, Art Inst Chicago, 86; Avante-Garde in the Eighties, Los Angeles Co Mus Art, 87; Photography and Art: Interaction Since 1946, Los Angeles Co Mus Art, traveling exhib, 87; 1988: The World of Art Today, Milwaukee Art Mus, 88; The Photographer's Eye: A Selection by Chris Kellep, Victoria & Albert Mus, London, 88; Surrogate Selves, Corcoran Art Gallery, Washington, DC, 89; The Art of Photography: 1839-1989, Mus Fine Arts, Houston, 89; Making Their Mark: Women Artists Move into the Mainstream, 1970-85, Cincinnati Art Mus, travelled to Pa Acad Fine Arts, New Orleans Mus Art & Denver Art Mus, 89; The Photography of Invention: American Pictures of the 1980's, Nat Mus Art, Smithsonian Inst, Washington, DC, 89; Photography Now, Victoria & Albert Mus, London, 89; A Forest of Signs: Art in the Crisis of Representation, Mus Contemp Art, Los Angeles, 89; Invention and Continuity in Contemporary Photography, Metrop Mus Art, New York, 89; Image World: Art and Media Culture, Whitney Mus Am Art, New York, 89; Photography Until Now, Mus Mod Art, New York, 90; solo shows, Univ Art Mus, Univ Calif, Berkeley, 90, Saatchi Collection, London, Milwaukee Art Mus (travelled to Ctr Fine Arts, Miami & Walker Art Ctr, Milwaukee), Basel Kunsthalle, Switz (travelled to Staatsgaleri Moderner Kunst, Munich & Whitechapel Gallery, London), 91, Metro Pictures, New York, Linda Cathcart Gallery, Santa Monica & Museo de Monterrey, Mex, 92; Affinities and Intuitions: The Gerald S Elliot Collection of Contemporary Art, Art Inst Chicago, 90; Figuring the Body, Mus Fine Arts, Boston, 90; Quotations--The Second History of Art, Aldrich Mus Contemp Art, Ridgefield, Conn, 92; Pleasures and Terrors of Domestic Comfort, Mus Mod Art, New York, 92; More than Photograhy, Mus Mod Art, New York 92; and others. *Bibliog:* Amei Wallach (auth), Tough images to face, Los Angeles Times, 6/7/92; Barry Schwabsky (auth), Shamelessness, Sculpture, p 44-45, 7-8/92; John M Cavalho (auth), Repetitions--appropriation representation in contemporary art, Philos Today, p 307-323, winter 92; and others. *Mailing Add:* c/o Metro Pictures 150 Greene St New York NY 10012

SHERMAN, CLAIRE RICHTER
HISTORIAN, EDUCATOR
b Boston, Mass, Feb 11, 30. *Study:* Radcliffe Col, BA(Fulbright Scholar), 51; Univ Mich, with Marvin J Eisenberg, MA(Am Univ Women Fel), 58; Johns Hopkins Univ, with Adolf Katzenellenbogen, PhD, 64. *Pos:* Sr fel, Ctr Advan Study Visual Arts, Nat Gallery Art, 81-82; consult, J Paul Getty Trust, 83; sr res assoc, Ctr Advan Study Visual Arts, Nat Gallery Art, 86- *Teaching:* Instr art hist, Univ Mich, 58-59; lectr art hist, Am Univ, 66-72; vis assoc prof of art, McIntire Dept of Art, Univ of Va, 76. *Awards:* Grant in Aid, Am Coun Learned Socs, 75 & 82; Grants, Am Philos Soc & Nat Endowment Humanities, 86. *Mem:* Col Art Asn Am; Women's Caucus Art. *Res:* Illustrations of Aristotle's Ethics & Politics in fourteenth and fifteenth century manuscripts; women scholars in the arts. *Publ:* Auth, The Portraits of Charles V of France (1338-80), 69; Representations of Charles V of France as a Wise Ruler, 71; The Queen in Charles V's Coronation Book, Viator, Medieval & Renaissance Studies, Vol 8, 77; Some visual definitions of the illustrations of Aristotle's Nichomachean Ethics and Politics in the French translation of Nicole Oresme, Art Bull, Vol 59, 77; ed & contribr, Women as Interpreters of the Visual Arts, 1820-1979, 81; and many others. *Mailing Add:* 4516 Que Lane NW Washington DC 20007

SHERMAN, LENORE (WALTON)
PAINTER, WRITER
b New York, NY, May 11, 20. *Study:* With Leon Franks, Hayward Veal, Orrin A White & Sergei Bongart, watercolor with James Couper Wright & portrait with Eignar Hansen. *Work:* San Diego Law Libr; var banks. *Exhib:* Southern Calif Expos, Del Mar, 70-72; Calif Fedn Women's Club Fine Arts Festival, 71; Southern NMex State Fair, 81 & 82; and others. *Teaching:* Instr oil painting, San Diego Art Inst, 60-67, Foothills Art Asn, La Mesa, Calif, summer 72 & Las Cruces Arts & Crafts Asn, NMex, 80-81 & 88. *Awards:* First Award Oils, 82 & Best in Show, 82, NMex State Fair; and others. *Bibliog:* Ed Ainsworth (auth), The Cowboy in Art, World Publ, 68; articles in San Diego Union, 60-72; articles, Las Cruces Sun News, NMex, 80-81. *Mem:* Salmagundi Club, New York. *Media:* Oil. *Publ:* Auth, Impressionistic Flowers, Impressionistic Landscapes, Walter Foster Art Bks, 75 & 80. *Dealer:* Linda Gallery 618 S Alameda Blvd Las Cruces NM. *Mailing Add:* 1425 Country Club Circle Las Cruces NM 88001

SHERMAN, SARAI
PAINTER, SCULPTOR
b Philadelphia, Pa, 1922. *Study:* Tyler Sch Art, Temple Univ, BFA, BS(educ); Barnes Found; Univ Iowa, MFA. *Work:* Whitney Mus Am Art & Mus Mod Art, New York; Hirshhorn Collection, Smithsonian Inst, Washington, DC; Uffizi Gallery Print Collection, Florence, Italy; Collection Mod Art, Southwestern Methodist Univ, Dallas; Univ Nebr, Lincoln; Wichita Mus, Kans; Okla Art Ctr. *Comn:* 18th Century Chapel, 10 murals, ceramic altar wall, sculpture, Villa Guiliemi, Cortona, Italy, 88-92. *Exhib:* Recent Painting USA: The Figure, Traveling Show, Mus Mod Art, New York, 62-63; Venice Biennial, Int Graphics: USA, Italy, 72; Childe Hassam Acquisition Fund, 75; 30 Years--Painting, Sculpture, Drawing, Palazzo Acad, Tod, Italy, 83; Forum Gallery, New York, 86; Idiomi Della Scuttura Contemp, Verona, 89; and others. *Pos:* Juror for Artists' Awards, Fulbright Comn, 89-91. *Awards:* Award for Painting, Nat Inst Arts & Lett, 64; Europ Community Prize, Premio Marzotto, 67; Ann Painting Award, Repub San Marino, 75; Proctor Prize, Nat Acad Design, 76. *Bibliog:* Bryant (auth) & Venturoli (auth), Painting of Sarai Sherman (monogr), Galleria Penelope, Rome, 63; Sarai Sherman, Edizioni Enrico Vallecchi, Florence, 83; Geske (auth), American Painting Collection, Sheldon Mem Gallery, Univ Nebr, 83. *Media:* All; Ceramic Sculpture. *Dealer:* Forum Gallery 1018 Madison Ave New York NY 10021; Galleria Giula Via Givlia 148 Rome Italy. *Mailing Add:* 17 W Ninth St New York NY 10011

SHERMAN, Z CHARLOTTE
PAINTER
b Los Angeles, Calif. *Study:* Univ Calif, Los Angeles; Kann Art Inst; Otis Art Inst, scholar. *Work:* Munic Art Gallery, Los Angeles; Palm Springs Mus, Calif; Glass Container Corp Am; Winthrop Rockefeller Found, Ark; Laguna Art Mus; Vincent Price Gallery. *Exhib:* Los Angeles Co Mus Art, 56 & 58; Heritage Gallery, Los Angeles, 63-89; Grand Prix Int de Deauville, Paris, 72; Prix de Rome Palais des Beaux Artes, Rome, 73; Palm Springs Mus, 76, 77, 80 & 81; Laguna Art Mus, 80; and others. *Awards:* Phelan Found Award, 61; Pasadena Mus Ann Award, 61; All City Exhib Award, Barnsdale, Los Angeles, 63 & 65; and others. *Bibliog:* Joseph Mugnaini (auth), Oil Painting Techniques, Van Nostrand, 63; Bertrand Sorlot (auth), article, La Rev Mod, Paris, 74; Don Rothenberg (producer), Z Charlotte Sherman, Portrait of a Woman Artist (film), 77, 79. *Mem:* Nat Watercolor Soc. *Media:* Oil, Watercolor. *Dealer:* Heritage Gallery 718 N La Cienega Blvd Los Angeles CA 90069. *Mailing Add:* 1300 Chautauqua Blvd Pacific Palisades CA 90272

SHERR, RONALD NORMAN
PAINTER
b Plainfield, NJ, July 17, 52. *Study:* DuCret Sch Art, Plainfield, NJ; Nat Acad Design Sch Fine Art; also with Burton Silverman. *Work:* Phoenix Mus Art, Ariz; Nat Portrait Gallery, Washington, DC. *Exhib:* Ann Exhib, Nat Acad Design, New York, 78; Hassam Fund Exhib, Inst Arts & Letters, New York, 78; Painting & Sculpture Today, Indianapolis Art Mus, Ind, 78; Drawing Exhib, Univ NH, 79; A Heritage Renewed: Representational Drawing Today Traveling Exhib, 83. *Pos:* Instr painting seminar, Galeria San Juan, PR. *Teaching:* Instr painting, Nat Acad Sch Fine Art, & Art Students League, New York, currently. *Awards:* Benjamin Altman Figure Prize, Nat Acad Design, New York, 78; Award for Excellence, Int Ed Design Competition, 83; Allied Artists Am Gold Medal of Honor, New York, 86; Hubbard Art Award for Excellence, Ruidoso, NMex, 91. *Bibliog:* Smithsonian Mag, 7/88; Am Artist, 9/91; Southwest Art, 8/91. *Media:* Oil, Drawing. *Publ:* Illusr, Illusr 25, 29. *Mailing Add:* 584 Cafferty Rd Upper Black Eddy PA 18972

SHERRILL, MILTON LEWIS
SCULPTOR, PAINTER
b New York, NY, May 30, 49. *Study:* Cooper Union, New York, 72; City Univ New York, BA, 74; Pratt Inst, New York, MFA, 76. *Work:* Studio Mus in Harlem, New York; Schomburg Collection, New York. *Comn:* Momenta I (steel sculpture), City of Mt Vernon, NY, 78; bronze abstraction, Selchow & Righter Co, New York, 83; lifesize bronze figures, City of New York, 83 & Apollo Theater, New York, 87. *Exhib:* Solo exhib, Studio Mus in Harlem, 76; Emerging Artists, Neuberger Mus, Purchase, NY, 80; 35 Under 35, Lever House, New York, 80; Ideas in Bronze, Los Angeles Co Mus, Calif, 83; two-man exhib (with Robert P Dilworth), Isobel Neal Gallery, Chicago, Ill, 88. *Teaching:* Teacher sculpture, State Univ NY, Mt Vernon Co-Op Col, 70-72; dir, Artists in Schs Prog, Mt Vernon, 73-74; teacher, Studio Mus Co-Op Sch Prog, 74-75. *Bibliog:* C Gerald Fraser (auth), Guide going out, New York Times, 83; Terrie S Rouse (auth), From painter to sculptor, Rev African Am Art, 84. *Mem:* Artists' Equity Asn; Orgn Independent Artists. *Media:* Bronze, Steel; Oil, Acrylic. *Mailing Add:* PO Box 2421 Mt Vernon NY 10550

SHERROD, PHILIP LAWRENCE
PAINTER, WRITER
b Pauls Valley, Okla, Oct 12, 35. *Study:* Okla State Univ, BS, 57, BA(etching, pottery & drawing), 59; Art Students League, Am Fed Arts & Lett Scholar, 63. *Work:* Rose Art Mus, Brandeis Univ, Waltham, Mass; Herbert Johnson Gallery, Cornell Univ, Ithaca, NY; Smithsonian Inst, Hirshhorn Mus & Sculpture Garden, Washington, DC; Worcester Fine Arts Mus, Mass; Mus City New York. *Exhib:* Street Painters, Arbitrage Gallery & Art Student's League, New York, 80, 83 & 90; Inside Out, Joslyn Art Mus, 81; Painting New York, Mus City New York, 83; Bodies & Souls, Artist's Choice Mus, 83; one person show, Il Ferro di Cavallo, Rome, Italy, 85 & Prix de Rome, Fellow-Painting, Amer Acad, Rome, 85-86. *Pos:* Pres & founder, Street Painters, New York. *Teaching:* Instr color & design, Okla State Univ, 59; asst painting, Art Students League, 60 & instr, 84-90; instr, Morristown Art Asn, NJ, 73-74 & NJ Ctr Visual Arts, 77-90. *Awards:* Nat Endowment Arts Grant, 82; Prix de Rome Grant, Am Acad in Rome, 85-86; The Pollock-Krasner Found Grant, 89. *Bibliog:* Barry Schwartz (auth), Arts in Society (Humanist Alternative), Univ Wis, 4/73; Barry Schwartz (auth) New Humanism: Art in a Time of Change, Praeger, 74. *Media:* Oil, Etching. *Publ:* Auth, 30 Mentaltalia (poems & paintings), Merging Media Publ, 80; Black Truck (poems), Mirronic Pub, 81; Mr Wigley Cums (poems), Mirronic Pub, 83; Images Below the Belt (poems & paintings), Carrousel Pub, 84; Sex (I) Con! (poem), Carrousel Pub, 85. *Dealer:* Allan Stone Gallery 48 E 86th St New York NY 10028. *Mailing Add:* 41 W 24th St New York NY 10010

SHERRY, WILLIAM GRANT
PAINTER
b Amagansett, NY, Dec 7, 14. *Study:* Acad Julian, Paris, cert, with Pierre Jerome; Heatherly Sch Art, London, with Ian McNab. *Work:* Farnsworth Mus, Rockland, Maine; Zellerbach Collection, San Francisco; Wintersteen Collection, Philadelphia; Mod Mus Art, Ft Lauderdale, Fla; Springfield Mus Fine Art, Mass; Am Embassy, Pakistan; Mary Johnston, Philadelphia, Lee Ault, New York, Erwin Panofsky (art historian), Princeton Univ. *Exhib:* De Young Mus, San Francisco; Colby Col, Maine; Ringling Mus, Sarasota, Fla, 49; Grand Palais des Champs-Elysees, Paris, 52; Boston Arts Festival, 56; Allied Artists Am, New York, 60; Art USA, Madison Square Garden, New York, 58; Soc Four Arts, Palm Beach, Fla; Farnsworth Mus, Rockland, Maine. *Teaching:* Chief instr painting & art dir, Fla Gulf Coast Art Ctr, Belleair, Fla, 57-64; art instr, Hamilton AFB, Ignacio, Calif, 65-67. *Awards:*

Laguna Beach Festival Arts, Nat Painting Contest, 51; Mr & Mrs Chauncey A Steiger Purchase Prize, Springfield Mus, 57, Theodor Ogden Mus, Mountainville, NY. *Media:* Oil. *Mailing Add:* 51 Park Terr Mill Valley CA 94941

SHERSHER, ZINOVY
PAINTER, MURALIST
b Birobidian, Russia, Apr 12, 47; US citizen. *Study:* Sch Fine Arts & Design, Kursk, Russia, 62-65; Univ Fine & Applied Arts, Kursk, Russia, MA, 65-70; Sch Visual Arts, New York, 81-82. *Work:* Mus Fine Art, Kursk, Russia; Funds Russian Mod Art-Ministry Cult, Moskow, Russia; Rental Gallery Los Angeles Co Mus Art, Calif; Platt Art Gallery, Univ Judaism, Los Angeles, Calif; Finegood Art Gallery/Art Coun Jewish Fedn, West Hills, Calif. *Comn:* We have a Future (2000 ft mural), Int Inst Los Angeles, Calif, 91; Jewish Soul (8 stained glass windows, 300 ft), Russian Chabad Synagogue, West Hollywood, Calif, 92. *Exhib:* Solo Exhibs, Art Expo New York, Jawits Ctr, 90, The Sound of Color, Window Gallery, Beverly Hills, Calif, 91 & Art Expo Calif, Convention Ctr, Los Angeles, Calif, 92; Multi-cultural LA, Platt Gallery Univ Judaism, Los Angeles, Calif, 90; Int Small Painting Show, Oil Pastel Asn, Nyack, NY, 91; Artist as Emigre, Finegood Art Gallery/Jewish Fedn Coun, West Hills, Calif, 91; 15th Non-member juried Exhib, Salmagundi Club, New York, 92; Rental Gallery Los Angeles Co Mus Art, 92. *Pos:* Artistic Dir, Sherberg Gallery, Los Angeles, Calif, 89-90; dir, Art Sch Children, Chabad Synagogue, West Hollywood, Calif, 92- *Teaching:* Instr, painting & composition, Art Sch Children, Chabad Synagogue, West Hollywood, 92-; guest speaker, mural, Clif State Univ, Northrige, Calif, 92- *Awards:* Award, Int Small Painting, Oil Pastel Asn, 91; Grant, We Have a Future Mural, Clif Community Found, 91; Cert Appreciation, City of Los Angeles, Los Angeles City Hall, 92. *Bibliog:* Encyclopedia of Living Artists in America, Dir Guild Publishers, 90; Miles Corwin (auth), The Big Picture, Los Angeles Times, 91; Documentary, The Sound of Color, RCN Tv Production Century Cable, 92. *Mem:* Oil Pastel Asn; United Pastelists Am; LAART. *Media:* Oil, Pastel. *Publ:* Illustr, New Paper, 84; coauth, Group Helps USSR Artists Find Supplies, Art Business News, 90; auth, The Wall of Future, Panorama, Almanach, 92; Art World of Vl Atanian, Art Catalog, Artists Union, Moscow, Russia, 92. *Mailing Add:* 6260 Morse Ave North Hollywood CA 91606

SHERWOOD, KATHERINE
PAINTER
b New Orleans, La, 1952. *Study:* Univ Calif at Davis, BA, 75; San Francisco Art Inst, MFA, 79. *Exhib:* One-person shows, Anna Gardner Gallery, Stinson Beach, Calif, 77, Nelson Gallery, Davis, Calif, 81, ARC Gallery, Sacramento, 82, M O David Gallery, New York, 84, 8 BC, New York, 85 & Gallery Paule Anglim, San Francisco, 88 & 92; This Side of Paradise, Concord Gallery, New York, 81; Sex, Sharpe Gallery, New York, 83; Bruno Facchetti Gallery, New York, 88; Pac Rum Art Now, 91. *Pos:* Asst prof painting. *Teaching:* Instr, San Francisco Art Inst, 79, New York Univ, 83-88 & Univ Calif, Berkeley, 88- *Awards:* McDowell Colony Fel, 84; Nat Endowment Arts, 89. *Bibliog:* Kenneth Baker (auth), Katherine Sherwood at Paule Anglim, San Francisco Chronicle, 8/13/92. *Mailing Add:* 10950 E 14th St #210 Oakland CA 94603

SHERWOOD, LEONA
PAINTER, INSTRUCTOR
b New York, NY. *Study:* Studied with John Chetcuti, New York, 46-48; workshop critiques with Philip Hicken, Mass, 58, Robert Gelinas, Fla, 65, Leon Berkowitz, New Coll, 80. *Work:* Hickory Mus Art, NC; Edison Col, Fort Myers, Fla; Collegiate Sch Boys, New York; Diamond Shamrock Co, Cleveland, Ohio; Barnett Bank, Bradenton, Fla. *Comn:* 42 paintings for Strathmore Co, Sarasota, Fla, 67-; painting, Lido Ambassador, Sarasota, 71; paintings, Thru Hang-up Gallery, Sarasota, 81; and others. *Exhib:* One-person show, Hickory Mus Art, NC, 79; Metrop Art Mus, Miami, Fla, 77; Boca Raton Art Mus, Fla, 83; Color of Greece, Sarasota, Fla, 86; Cornell Fine Arts, Rollins Col, 89; Polk Co Col, Winter Park, FL, 90; Sumner Mus, Washington, DC, 92; and others. *Teaching:* Instr contemp painting & drawing, Longboat Key Art Ctr, Fla, 69- & Art League Manatee, Bradenton, Fla, 74-89; instr workshops, NC & Fla Art Ctrs, 79-, Chateau de Lanapoule Art Found, France, 86-87 & 89-91, Corfu, 89, O'Neill Art Ctr, Ireland, Madeira, Port, 90, Wilson Art Ctr, Wales, 91 & Malta, 92. *Awards:* First in Painting, Nat League Pen Women State Biennial, 71- 72 & 76-78 & First Award, 79 & 91; Am Artist Award Watercolor, Fla Suncoast Ann, 90; Best of Show & Merit Award, Nat Biennial Nat League Am Penwomen, Washington, DC, 92. *Bibliog:* Sheila Scotter (auth), An artist, cook & gardener, Australian Women's Weekly & Tatler, London, Eng, 79; Jane Roehr (auth) Art for the Artists Sake, Sarasota Times, 89; Penwoman, biennial issue, 92. *Mem:* Fla Artist Group; Nat League Am Pen Women; Fla Watercolor Soc; Fla Suncoast Watercolor Soc; Artists Fel, New York. *Media:* Multimedia, Watercolor. *Publ:* Auth, Learn to really see, not just look, Islander, 81. *Dealer:* The Hang-Up Gallery, Palm Ave Sarasota, FL. *Mailing Add:* 615 Buttonwood Dr Longboat Key FL 33548

SHESTACK, ALAN
MUSEUM DIRECTOR, HISTORIAN
b New York, NY, June 23, 38. *Study:* Wesleyan Univ, Middletown, Conn, BA, 60; Harvard Univ, Cambridge, Mass, MA, 62; Zentralinstitut Fur Kunstgeschichte, Munich, 63-64; Wesleyan Univ, DFA, 78. *Collections Arranged:* Master E S (auth catalog), Philadelphia Mus Art, 67; Fifteenth-century Engravings (auth catalog), Nat Gallery Art, Washington, DC, 67-68; Graphic Art of the Danube School (with catalog), Yale Art Gallery, St Louis Art Mus, Philadelphia Mus Art, 68-69; Hans Baldung Grien (auth, catalog), Nat Gallery Art, Washington, DC, 81. *Pos:* Mus cur graphic art, Nat Gallery, 65-67; cur prints & drawings, Yale Univ Art Gallery, New Haven, Conn, 68-71, dir, 71-85; bd dir, Am Fedn Art, 81-88; indemnification panel, Nat Endowment Arts, 80-84; pres, Asn Art Mus Dir, 83-84; dir, Minneapolis Inst Art, 85-87, Boston Mus Fine Arts, 87- *Teaching:* Adj prof hist art, Yale Univ, 71- *Awards:* Woodrow Wilson Fel, 61-62; David E Finley Fel, Nat Gallery, 63-65; Ctr Advan Studies Visual Arts Sr Fel, 84. *Mem:* Visiting comt, Mus Mod Art; Internal Revenue Serv (art adv panel 84-88); Smithsonian Coun; Visiting comt, Harvard Univ Art Mus. *Res:* Fifteenth and sixteenth century printmaking in Europe; German art of 15th and 16th centuries. *Publ:* Auth, The Complete Engravings of Martin Schongauer, 68; Master LCz & Master WB, 71; co-auth, Hans Baldung Grien: Prints and Drawings, Univ Chicago Press, 81. *Mailing Add:* c/o Museum of Fine Arts 465 Huntington Ave Boston MA 02115

SHEYA
PAINTER, INSTRUCTOR
b Brooklyn, NY. *Study:* Hunter Col, BA(fine arts), 42; Grand Cent Art Sch, with Harvey Dunn, 44-45; Wayne State Univ, 59-62. *Work:* Educ Exhibitors Traveling Show in Schs, Long Island, NY. *Exhib:* Birmingham Artists Ann, Cranbrook Mus, Mich, 60; Landscape Artists, Smithsonian Inst, Washington, DC, 64; Fifty New York Artists, Harkness House Gallery, New York, 78; Reflections of Winter, Town Hall, Manhasset, NY, 78-79; one-person show, US Customs House Exhib Hall, New York, 79 & Nassau Co Mus, Roslyn, 86;; NY State Prebiennial, Lever House, 83 & 87;; Long Beach Mus, 83; Americana Mus, Va, 86; Mallet Gallery, Garden City; Cork Gallery, Lincoln, Conn, 89; Hutchins Gallery, C W Post. *Pos:* Dir art, Rose-Martin, New York, 44-46, Hayes-Endler, New York, 46-80, Luckoff & Wayburn, Detroit, 53-56 & Hecht Co, Washington, DC, 63-64. *Teaching:* Instr, Detroit Continuing Educ, 55-59, Port Washington Adult Educ, Long Island, NY, 65-81; pvt art classes, 66- *Awards:* Cult Rep State of NY, Brazilian Acad Arts, Rio de Janeiro, Brazil. *Mem:* Nat League Am Pen Women (NY art chmn, 82-84 & pres, Queens branch, 84-86); Artists Equity Asn; Metro Portrait Soc. *Media:* Oil, Watercolor. *Mailing Add:* 44 Jayson Ave Great Neck NY 11021

SHIBLEY, GERTRUDE
PAINTER
b Brooklyn, NY. *Study:* Brooklyn Col, BA; with Francis Criss, 42; Hans Hofmann Sch Fine Arts, 52-53. *Work:* Wichita State Univ Mus Collection, Kans; Guild Hall Mus, Easthampton, NY; Univ Ala, Birmingham; Provincetown Art Asn & Mus, Mass; St Vincent's Med Ctr, New York. *Exhib:* Nat Asn Women Painters, Nat Acad Design Gallery, 51; Prizewinners Village Art Ctr, Whitney Mus Am Art, New York, 54; New York WPA Art, Then & Now (with catalog), Parsons Sch Design, 77; Tenth St Days: The Co-ops of the 50s (with catalog), New York, 77; Abraham Rattner Ctr Arts, Sag Harbor, NY, 79-80; Provincetown Art Asn & Mus, Mass, 80-81; The Gathering of the Avante-Garde: 1948-70, Ken Keleba Gallery, New York, 85. *Pos:* Ceramist, Design Technics, 44-48. *Teaching:* Instr painting, Halloran Hosp, Staten Island, 42-44 & Ruth Ettinger Sch, New York, 55-56. *Awards:* Prize for One-man Show, Village Art Ctr, 49; Hon Mention, Terry Art Award, Miami, Fla, 52. *Mem:* Guild Hall; Provincetown Art Asn; Am Soc Contemp Artists. *Media:* Acrylic, Oil. *Dealer:* Atlantic Gallery 164 Mercer St New York NY 10012; Ross-Constantine Gallery 65 Prince St New York NY 10012. *Mailing Add:* 351 W 24th St New York NY 10011

SHIELDS, ALAN J
PAINTER
b Lost Springs, Kans, Feb 4, 44. *Study:* Kans State Univ; Univ Maine. *Work:* Mus Mod Art, Whitney Mus Am Art, Guggenheim Mus, New York; Akron Art Inst, Ohio; Hirshhorn Mus, Washington, DC. *Exhib:* One-man shows, Williams Col, Mass, 79, Bowdoin Col Mus Art, Brunswick, Maine, 81, Neuberger Mus, State Univ NY, Purchase, 82, Gallery Veda, Tokyo, Japan, 83, Cleveland Ctr Contemp Art 86, NJ Ctr Visual Arts, Summitt, 87, Contemp Art Gallery, Ahmedabad, India, 89, Works on Canvas & Paper, Paula Cooper Gallery, New York, 91; American Painting in the 70's, Albright-Knox Art Gallery, 78; Dorry Gates Gallery, Kansas City, Mo, 81; Alan Shields Retrospective, Memphis Brooks Mus Art, 84; Lowe Art Mus, Coral Gables, Fla, 84; Nelson Atkins Mus Art, 84; Papers from Tyler Graphics, Walker Art Ctr, Minneapolis, Minn, 85; Made in India, Mus Mod Art, New York, 86; The Cutting Edge: New Directions in Handmade Paper, Kalamazoo Inst Arts, 88; First Impressions: Early Prints by Forty-six Contemp Artists, Walker Art Ctr, Minneapolis, 89; Aspects of Collage, Guild Hall Mus, East Hampton, 91. *Awards:* Guggenheim Fel, 73. *Bibliog:* Deborah Emont-Scott (auth), Alan Shields, 84; Nancy Cohen & Pat Kettering (coauths), Alan Shields: Color and Form, 87; Charlotta Kotik (auth), The Cutting Edge: New Directions in Handmade Paper, Kalamazoo Inst Arts, 88; article in Print Col Newsletter, 220-21, 90. *Media:* Mixed Media. *Dealer:* Paula Cooper 155 Wooster St New York NY 10012. *Mailing Add:* PO Box 1554 Shelter Island NY 11964

SHIELDS, ANNE KESLER
PAINTER, ASSEMBLAGE ARTIST
b Winston-Salem, NC, Jan 27, 32. *Study:* Hollins Col, Roanoke, Va, BA, 54; studied with Hans Hoffman, Provincetown, Mass, 57; Univ NC, Greensboro, MFA, 59. *Work:* NC Mus Fine Art, Raleigh; Mint Mus, Charlotte, NC; Weatherspoon Gallery, Univ NC, Greensboro; Mus Fine Arts, Montgomery, Ala; Cornell Univ, Ithaca, NY. *Comn:* Portrait of James English, Conn Bank & Trust, Hartford, 70; urban wall mural, Arts Coun, Winston-Salem, NC, 75; portraits (4), Wake Forest Univ, Winston-Salem, NC, 80, 82, 83 & 88; portraits (3), Trinity Col, Hartford, Conn, 88 & 89. *Exhib:* Xylon IV, Int Exhib Woodcuts, Musee d'art et d'historie, Geneva, Switz, 65; 20th Nat Exhib Prints, Libr Cong, Washington, DC, 66; Printmakers, US Pavillion, Japan

Expo, 70; solo exhibs, Silvermine Guild, New Canaan, Conn, 70 & Southeastern Ctr Contemp Art, Winston-Salem, NC, 77; 200 Years of Art in NC, NC Mus Art, Raleigh, 76; Five Winston-Salem Printmakers, Southeastern Ctr Contemp Art, NC, 83; After Her Own Image, Woman's Work, Salem Fine Arts Ctr, NC, 85. *Awards:* Atwater Kent Award, Soc Four Arts, Palm Beach, Fla, 64; E J Arden Prize, Boston Printmakers, Mass, 70; Va Ctr Creative Arts fels, 87, 88 & 90. *Bibliog:* Joanna L Krotz (auth), New traditions, Money Mag, 6/90; Genie Carr (auth), Face to face, portrait-group, Winston-Salem J, 8/25/91; Jean S Rodgers (auth), Women of letters, a group portrait of North Carolina writers, Winston-Salem, 3/18/92. *Mem:* Artworks Gallery (Artists Cooperative, Winston-Salem). *Media:* Oil on Canvas. *Publ:* Illustr, Whedbee--Legends of the Outer Banks & Tarheel Tidewater, Blair Publ Co, 66. *Dealer:* Portraits Inc 985 Park Ave New York NY 10028; Portraits South 4008 Barrett Dr Suite 106 Raleigh NC 27609. *Mailing Add:* 1134 Burke St Winston-Salem NC 27101

SHIH, JOAN FAI
PAINTER, INSTRUCTOR
b Shantou, China. *Study:* Studied Chinese painting & calligraphy in Hong Kong, 49-52; Art Students League New York, 53; Kansas City Art Inst, BFA, 56, MFA, 61; Pa Acad Fine Arts, 57-59, 61-63. *Work:* ARCO Chemical Co, Newtown Square, PA, 91; Methodist Hosp, Philadelphia, PA. *Exhib:* Pa Acad Fine Arts Mus Galleries, Philadelphia, 62, 63, 69 & 72; Philadelphia Art Alliance, 66, 68, 79 & 83; Mus Philadelphia Civic Ctr, 70, 74, 79, 80 & 82; Nat Asn Women Artists Traveling Exhib, 78-80, 80-82, 83-85, 85-87; Nat Asn Women Artists Ann, Fed Bldg, New York, 79-83, 85; Woodmere Art Mus, Philadelphia, 79, 81 & 87; Peele Hoe Galleries, Pa Acad Fine Arts, 82; Bergen Mus, Paramus, NJ, 83; Plastic Club Annual Art Exhib, Philadelphia, 85, 88-91; solo exhib, Danville Mus Fine Arts, Danville, Va, 86, Penn Wynne Library, Wynnewood, Pa, 91; Art Inst Philadelphia, 87, 90 & 91; John Geiszel All Transparent Watercolor Annual Exhib, Philadelphia, 88-91; group show, Chester Co Art Asn, West Chester, Pa, 91. *Teaching:* Instr, Kansas City Art Inst, Mo, 59-61; instr, Converse Col, Spartanburg, SC, 66-67; lectr, Rosemont Col, Pa, 69-88. *Awards:* Elizabeth Erlanger Mem Prize, Nat Asn Women Artists 91st Ann, New York, 80; Marion Cohee Mem Award (First Prize), Plastic Club Open Juried Ann Art Exhib, Philadelphia, 89; First Prize, Plastic Club All Media Atr Exhib, Philadelphia, Pa, 90. *Mem:* Nat Asn Women Artists; Philadelphia Watercolor Club; Hong Kong Art Club; fel Pa Acad Fine Arts. *Media:* Watercolor, Oil. *Dealer:* Plum Gallery 1800 E Lancaster Ave Paoli PA 19301. *Mailing Add:* 2013 Locust St Philadelphia PA 19103

SHIKLER, AARON
PAINTER
b Brooklyn, NY, Mar 18, 22. *Study:* Tyler Sch Fine Arts, Temple Univ, BFA, BSEd & MFA; Barnes Found; Hans Hofmann Sch. *Work:* Metrop Mus Art, New York; Mint Mus Art, Charlotte, NC; Sheldon Mus Art, Lincoln, Nebr; New Britain Mus Am Art, Conn; Charleston Art Gallery of Sunrise, WVa. *Comn:* Portraits of President & Mrs John F Kennedy for White House. *Exhib:* New Britain Mus Art, Conn, 64; Gallery Mod Art, New York, 65; Nat Acad Design, 65; Brooklyn Mus, 71; Calif Palace Legion Honor, San Francisco, 71; and others. *Awards:* Thomas B Clarke Prize, 61; US Dept State Traveling Grant, 76; Benjamin Figure Prize, Nat Acad Design, 76; and others. *Bibliog:* articles, Am Artist, 9/71 & Current Biog, 12/71. *Mem:* Nat Acad Design; Century Asn. *Publ:* Contribr two chaps, In: Pastel Painting, 68. *Dealer:* Davis & Long Co 746 Madison Ave New York NY 10021. *Mailing Add:* c/o Doule & Langdale Co 231 E 60th St New York NY 10022

SHILLEA, THOMAS JOHN
PHOTOGRAPHER
b Peckville, Pa, May 7, 47. *Study:* Kutztown State Univ, BS(art educ), 69; Rochester Inst Technol, MFA(photog), 79. *Work:* Rochester Inst Technol; Johnson Matthey Corp; Philadelphia Col Art; Philadelphia Mus Art; Baltimore Mus Art; Ariz State Univ. *Exhib:* Solo exhibs, Tyler Sch Art, Philadelphia, 81, Photog Place Gallery, Philadelphia, 82 & Lehigh Univ, Bethlehem, Pa, 85; Daniel Wolf Gallery, New York, 80-81; Pennsylvania Photographers, Harrisburg, 80 & Allentown, Pa, 82; Lowe Fine Arts Gallery, Syracuse Univ, 83; Platinum Prints, New Orleans Mus Art, 83; The Print Club, Philadelphia, 84-85; A Breath of Light, NJ State Mus, Trenton, 86. *Pos:* Photog consult, Eastman Kodak Co, 84 & Johnson Matthey Corp, 84-. *Teaching:* Vis lectr photog, Rochester Inst Technol, 83-84. *Mem:* Am Soc Mag Photogr; Friends Photog; Visual Studies Workshop; Soc Photog Educ. *Publ:* Coauth, The Platinum Print, Graphic Arts Res Ctr, Rochester, 79; contribr, Time Life Photog Series, 82; article, Art Direction Mag, 5/85; The history of Platinum Printing, Photog Conserv Newslett, 2/85; The Return of Platinum Photography, The Rangefinder Mag, Vol 34, 2, 2/85; Platinum Printing Instruction Manual, Johnson Matthey Inc, 86. *Dealer:* Harold Simon 20 Church St Montclair NJ 07042. *Mailing Add:* 3915 Terrace St Philadelphia PA 19128

SHILSON, WAYNE STUART
PAINTER, ILLUSTRATOR
b Minneapolis, Minn, July 14, 43. *Study:* Univ Minn, BS(art educ), 71, MFA, 72; study with Katherine Nash, 68-70; with J P Weisberg, 87-89. *Work:* Parks Fine Art Gallery, Sycamore, Ill; Arthur's Int Gallery, Las Vegas, Nev; Meadowcreek Gallery, Edina, Minn; Framstyles Gallery, Kenwood, Minneapolis, Minn; Southdale/Hennipen Publ Libr, Edina, Minn. *Comn:* Paintings, Bernard Picture Co, Stamford, Conn, 86; paintings, comn by Willima George, Minneapolis, Minn, 88; paintings, Arthur's Int, Honolulu, Hawaii, 88-90; paintings, Scafa-Tornabene, Nyack, NY, 90. *Exhib:* One-man shows, Sky Gallery, St Paul, Minn, 76 & 79, Minn Inst Arts, Minneapolis, 79 & 80, Horizon Gallery, Bloomingdale, Ill, 86, Authurs Int, Honolulu, Hawaii & Las Vegas, Nev, 87-90 & Minn State Fair, St Paul, 90; five-year retrospective, Normandale Central Gallery, Bloomington, Minn, 87-89; ten-year retrospective, Lutheran Brotherhood, Minneapolis, Minn, 89; Eagan Auction, Eagan Rotary, Minn, 90. *Pos:* Artist & illusr, Honeywell, Minneapolis, Minn, 74-; pres, Household Landscapes, 87- *Awards:* Award, Sky Gallery, St Paul, 76 & Art Ctr Minn, 80; Second prize, Eagan Rotary Club, 90. *Bibliog:* David Peifer (auth), The independent, Farmington newspaper, 8/87; Christy Dejoy (auth), Nestine Biography, Eagan Newspaper, 3/85; Diana Martin-Hoffman (ed), The artists market, Writers Digest Bks, 91. *Media:* Acrylic on Canvas. *Publ:* Article, Go Gallery News, Art Views, 85; article, Art Paper, 4/85; article, Streamlines: Minn J Creative Writing, spring, 87; Park Rapids Enterprise, 11/91; illusr, Keyboard Classic, Sept-Oct, 92. *Dealer:* Marvin C Arthur 2508 Ocean Front Dr Las Vegas NV 89129. *Mailing Add:* RR 1, Box 149 Park Rapids MN 56470

SHIMIZU, YOSHIAKI
HISTORIAN, CURATOR
b Tokyo, Japan, Feb 27, 36. *Study:* Harvard Col, BA, 63; Univ Kans, MA, 68; Princeton Univ, MFA, 71, PhD, 74. *Pos:* Cur Japanese art, Freer Gallery Art, Smithsonian Inst, Washington, DC, 79-84; bd adv, Japan Soc NY, 81- & Arthur Sackler Gallery, Ctr Asian Art, Smithsonian Inst, Washington, DC, 84; ed bd, Arch Asian Art, 82-; consult cur, Nat Gallery Art, Washington, DC, 84-89; bd dir, Col Art Asn Am, 87-91; adv comt, Asia Soc Galleries, 92. *Teaching:* Asst prof art & archeol, Princeton Univ, 73-75, vis lectr, 81-84, prof, 84-, Marquand prof, 92-; asst prof Oriental art, Univ Calif, Berkeley, 75-78, assoc prof art hist, 78-79. *Mem:* Japan Art Hist Soc; Col Art Asn Am. *Res:* Primarily Japanese art of the medieval period with reference to Chinese art. *Publ:* Coauth, Masters of Japanese Calligraphy: 8th-19th Centuries, Asia Soc-Japan Soc, New York, 84; auth, A Chinese album leaf from the former Ashikaga Collection in the Freer Gallery of Art, Arch Asian Art, Vol 38; Zen Art? Zen in China, Japan and East Asian Art, Swiss Asian Studies, Vol III, Peter Lang, Berne-New York, 85; ed & coauth, Japan: The Shaping of Daimyō Culture 1185-1868, Nat Gallery Art, 88; The Vegetable Nehan of Itō Jakuchū, in Sanford, LaFleur and Nagatouri, Flowing Traces: Buddhism in the Literary and Visual Arts of Japan, Princeton Univ Press, 92; and others. *Mailing Add:* Dept Art & Archeol McCormack Hall Princeton Univ Princeton NJ 08544

SHIMODA, OSAMU
SCULPTOR
b Manchuria, June 4, 24. *Study:* St Paul Univ, Tokyo; Acad Grande Chaumiere, Paris. *Work:* St Paul Univ, Tokyo; Syracuse Mus; Nat Mus Mod Art, Tokyo; Mus Mod Art, Saitama, Japan, 88; Contemp Art Mus Toyama, Japan, 89. *Comn:* Kuala Lumpur, Malaysia, 83; Kushiro Pub Univ, Hokkaido, Japan, 88; Toyota Seiki Corp, Yamanashi, Japan, 88; Kings, Borough Community Col, Brooklyn, 85; Riverhead Shopping Ctr, Long Island, NY, 77. *Exhib:* Solo exhibs, Andrew Crispo Gallery, New York, 84 & Contemp Sculpture Ctr, Tokyo, 87; Sculptors Guild Group Show, 72-83; Windows on the East, World Trade Ctr, New York, 79; Sculpture Ctr, New York, 76, 79 & 83; Bronx Botanical Garden Outdoor Show, 81; Imprimatra Gallery, Minneapolis, Minn, 84; Schulman Sculpture Garden Outdoor Show, 84; Music Mountain Sculpture Show, Conn, 84. *Bibliog:* Articles in J Art, 12/89 & New York Art Rev, 89. *Mem:* Sculptors Guild (bd mem, currently). *Media:* Iron. *Dealer:* Contemp Sculpture Ctr Tokyo. *Mailing Add:* 300 Seventh St Brooklyn NY 11215

SHIMOMURA, ROGER YUTAKA
PAINTER, PERFORMANCE ARTIST
b Seattle, Wash, June 26, 39. *Study:* Univ Wash, BA(graphic design), 61; Syracuse Univ, MFA(painting), 69. *Work:* Seattle Art Mus; Nat Mus Amer Art; Nelson Atkins Mus, Kansas City, Mo; Denver Art Mus; Birmingham Art Mus, Ala. *Comn:* Mural (120" x 420"), Westlake Station, Metro, Seattle, 90. *Exhib:* Pyramid Galleries Ltd, Washington, DC, 76; Morgan Gallery, Kansas City, Kans, 77, 79; Dobrick Gallery, Chicago, 77, 80; Elaine Horwitch Gallery; Bernice Steinbaum Gallery, NY, 89 & 92; and many others. *Teaching:* prof art, Univ Kans, Lawrence, 69- *Awards:* Japan Found Grant, 75; Nat Endowment for the Arts Grant, 77, 89 & 91; fourteen gen res grants, Univ Kans; and numerous others. *Bibliog:* Harold Haydon (auth), An unexpected sensation, Chicago Sun-Times, 5/17/74; JoAnn Lewis (auth), The American ethic, Washington Post, 6/3/76; David L Shirley (auth), Twitting the Samurai style, NY Times, 11/23/76. *Media:* Acrylic on Canvas. *Dealer:* Greg Kucera Gallery Seattle Wash; Bernice Steinbaum Gallery New York NY. *Mailing Add:* 1019 Delaware Lawrence KS 66044

SHINE, VINCENT
SCULPTOR
b Kingsport, Tenn, 62. *Study:* Columbus Col Art & Design, Ohio, BFA, 85; Univ Chicago, Midway Studios, Chicago, MFA, 87. *Exhib:* One-person exhibs, Jeffrey Neal Gallery, New York, 88, Robbin Lockett Gallery, Chicago, 88 & 91, Galerie Grita Insam, Vienna, Austria, 89, Laure Genillard Gallery, London, Eng, 90, Michael Kohn Gallery, Los Angeles, 90 & 92, Postmasters Gallery, New York, 91, Galleria Toselli, Milan, Italy, 92; Up the Garden Path, Wolff Gallery, 90, 3-man show, Postmasters Gallery, 90, How it is, Tony Shafrazi Gallery, New York, 92; Vonder Natur in der Kunst (with catalog), Wiener Festwochen, Vienna, Austria, 90; The (Un)making of Nature (with catalog), Whitney Mus Am Art, Stamford, Conn, 91; Gullivers Reisen-Gulliver's Travels, Galerie Sophia Ungers, Cologne, Ger, 91; Through the View Finder, De Appel Found, Amsterdam, 92; Twist, Laure Genillard Gallery, London, Eng, 92; Abigail Lane, Cathy de Monchaux, Vincent Shine, Verein Kunsthalle Luzern, Switz, 92. *Bibliog:* Maureen Sherlock (auth), Screened Memories, Arts Mag, Vol 66, No 2, 44-47, 10/91; Kathryn Hixson (auth), Vincent Shine, Arts Mag, 5/91; Susan Kandel (auth), Vincent Shine (rev), LA Times Calendar, 7/23/92. *Mailing Add:* 312 N Laslan St Chicago IL 60607

SHIPLEY, ROGER DOUGLAS
SCULPTOR, EDUCATOR
b Cleveland Heights, Ohio, Dec 27, 41. *Study:* Am Sch Fontainebleau, France, with Monsieur Goetz, cert (painting), 62; Otterbein Col, Ohio, BA, 64; Cleveland Inst Art, painting & sculpture, 64-65; Cranbrook Acad Art, Mich, MFA, 67. *Work:* Nat City Bank, Cleveland, Ohio; Kalamazoo Inst Arts, Mich; Cranbrook Acad Art; Lock Haven State Col, Pa; Northern Cent Bank, Williamsport, Pa. *Comn:* Achievement award, comn by Williamsport/Lycoming Found, 91; recognition award, comn by N Cent Pa Conservancy, 91. *Exhib:* 31st Ann Mid-Year Show, Butler Inst Am Art, Youngstown, Ohio, 66; A Plastic Presence, Jewish Mus Art, New York, Milwaukee Art Ctr, Wis & San Francisco Mus Art, 69-70; Transparent & Translucent Art, St Petersburg & Jackson, Fla, 71; Soft and Light Exhib, Taft Mus, Cincinnati, Ohio, 73; 49th to 64th May Shows, Cleveland Mus Art, Ohio, 67-83; Henri Gallery, Washington, DC, 86; Penn's Landing, Port Hist Mus, Philadelphia, 83; AAV/108 Nat Competition Metal Sculpture, Millerville Univ, Pa, 84; Group Exhibs, B & S Galleries, Williamsport, Pa, 85-90; Two-person sculpture Exhib, Extension Gallery, Johnson Atelier, Mercerville, NJ, 88; and many others. *Teaching:* Prof painting, drawing, printmaking, two-dimensional design & color theory, Lycoming Col, coord Commercial Design Major, 67- *Awards:* Second Place Sculpture Award & Charlie Gohn Sculpture Award, William Penn Mus, Harrisburg, Pa, 83; May show, Cleveland Mus Art, 83. *Bibliog:* Bringing the art of plastics into focus, Chicago Tribune, 2/70; The brightness of lesser lights, Cincinnati Enquirer, 10/73; Penns landing sculpture show, in doors and out, Philadelphia Inquirer, 8/83; and others. *Mem:* Int Sculpture Ctr; Greater Williamsport Community Arts Coun (bd mem); Doshi Ctr Contemp Art; Community Arts Ctr, Williamsport, Pa (bd mem). *Media:* Cast Bronze, Plexiglass. *Publ:* Severin Roesen, Greater Williamsport Community Arts Coun, Bucknell Univ Press, 92. *Dealer:* Island Art Gallery Box 265 Manteo NC 27954; Tangerine Fine Arts 310 N 2nd St Harrisburg Pa 17101. *Mailing Add:* 264 Lehman Drive Cogan Station PA 17728-9228

SHIRAI, AKIKO
PAINTER, PRINTMAKER
b Darier, Manchuria. *Study:* Tokyo Nat Univ Fine Arts, BA(oil, painting), 59, MA(printmaking), 64. *Work:* Mus Mod Art, NY; Philadelphia Mus Art, Pa; Libr Cong, Washington, DC; Nat Mus Mod Art, Tokyo, Japan; British Mus, London, Eng. *Comn:* Mural, comn by Dr I Okazaki, Urawa, Japan, 66; mural, comn by Dr T Hinose, Bronx, NY, 74; mural, Shimano Am Corp, Passippany, NJ, 79; mural, Int Plant Ctr, Chiba, Japan, 87-88; The Picture of Dorian Gray, Louisville Ballet Co, Louisville, Ky, 88; Madame Butterfly, Louisville Ballet Co, Ky, 89. *Exhib:* Mainichi Contemp Japan Art Exhib, Tokyo Metrop Art Mus, 62, 64 & 66, 5th Tokyo Int Biennial Exhib Print, 66 & Artists in the Americas, Nat Mus Mod Art, Tokyo, Japan, 73-74; 9th San Paulo Int Biennial Exhib, San Paulo, Brazil, 67; 4th Int Trieminal of Original Colored Graphic, Grenchen, Switz, 67; Contemp Japanese Arts, Ville De Paris Mus, Paris, France, 70; Contemp Japanese Prints, Mex Nat Mus Art, Mex, 75. *Teaching:* Instr drawing & painting, Shibaura Inst Technol, 62-66. *Awards:* Excellent Work Prize, Shell Oil Co, 63; Study Fel, Rockefeller Found, 66; Alice Standish Buell Mem Award, Soc Am Graphic Artists, 67. *Bibliog:* T Okada (auth), The Artist in Her Studio, Abe Publ, 78; Paul Watabe (auth), Behind the Scenes With the New York Art World, Sun Art, 81; Shozou Yoshida (auth), Japanese Printmakers for the Collector Trendo Shupan, 88. *Mem:* Japan Print Asn, 62-; Japan Artist Asn, 63-; Soc Am Graphic Artist, 83- *Publ:* Illusr, Expo 70 Osaka, Time/Life, 69; contrib, About Akiko Shirai, Gallery Shirota, 77; ed, Philosophy & Originality, pvt publ, 83; Monotypes-Spontaneous Painting, pvt publ, 83; Artists in America, Cent Mus, 85. *Dealer:* AAA Gallery 20 W 57 St New York NY 10019; Susan Teller Gallery 568 Broadway No 405A New York NY 10012. *Mailing Add:* 905 Madison Ave No 2R New York NY 10021

SHIRE, PETER
SCULPTOR
b Los Angeles, Calif, Dec 27, 47. *Study:* Chouinard Art Inst, BFA, 70. *Work:* Mus Mod Art, Lodz, Poland; Art Inst Chicago; Los Angeles Co Mus, Mod Art; Brooklyn Mus, New York; Oakland Mus Art, Calif; Victoria & Albert Mus, London. *Comn:* Olympic Villages USC, UCLA, 84; Santa Ana Venture, 86; Tropicana Hotel, 88; Encanto Park, Phoenix Arts Comn, Ariz, 91. *Exhib:* Janus Gallery, Los Angeles, Calif, 75-83; Modernism, San Francisco, Calif, 80-85; Am Hand, 81; MOCA, Los Angeles, 85; Saxon-Lee, 86-87; Dixon Art Gallery, 87; Davis-McClain, Austin, Tex; Los Angeles Munic Gallery, 88; Nev Inst Contemp Art, 88; solo exhibs, Roger Van Den Doel Gallery, Grarenhage, Holland, 89, Moderism, San Francisco, 89, Saxon-Lee Gallery, Los Angeles, 89, William Traver Gallery, Seattle, Wash, 90, Hokin Kaufman Gallery, Chicago, Ill, 90, Teapots of Steel, Daniel Saxon Gallery, Los Angeles, Modernism, San Francisco & William Traver Gallery, Seattle, Wash, 91 & Recent Furniture & Paintings, Daniel Saxon Gallery, Los Angeles, 91; Greninger Mus, Holland, 90; Stedelijk Mus, Amsterdam, Holland, 90. *Teaching:* Guest instr ceramics, Calif State Univ, Los Angeles, spring 81, Univ Calif, Los Angeles, spring 82, Hochschule Angewandte Kunst, Vienna, spring 83, Otis Parsons Sch Design, Los Angeles, fall 83, San Diego State Univ, 85, spring & Polytech Univ, Pomona, 86; workshop, Palo Alto Cult Ctr, Calif, 88; So Calif Inst Archit, Santa Monica, 89-91. *Awards:* Design Team of XXIII Olympiad, Inst Architects, 84; Esquire Register, 85. *Bibliog:* Marie W Payzant (auth), Bucolic splendor moves up market, Designers West, 3/91; Jeffrey Book (auth), Shades of shire, Angeles, 12/90; Keiko Nelson (auth), Expanding the Rich Local Color of Echo Park, Design J, Korea, 1/90. *Media:* Metal, Wood. *Publ:* Auth, Teatypes, Tea Garden Press, 80. *Dealer:* Saxon-Lee Gallery 7525 Beverly Blvd Los Angeles CA 90036. *Mailing Add:* Daniel Saxon Gallery 7525 Beverly Blvd Los Angeles CA 90036

SHIRK, HELEN Z
CRAFTSMAN
Study: Skidmore Col, BS, 63; Kunsthaandvaerkerskolen, Copenhagen, Denmark, 63-64; Indiana Univ, Bloomington, Ind, MFA, 69. *Work:* Carnegie Mus Art, Pittsburgh; Nat Mus Mod Art, Kyoto, Japan; Minnesota Mus Art, St Paul, Minn; Schmuckmuseum, Pforzheim, Ger; Univ Tex, El Paso. *Exhib:* Young Americans '62, Mus Contemp Crafts, New York, 62; Objects & Crafts, Indianapolis Mus Art, 73; Am Craft Mus, New York, 82; Galveston Arts Ctr, Galveston, Tex, 86; Wita Gardiner Gallery, San Diego, Calif, 87; Los Angeles Co Mus, 88; The Oriental Expression, Joan Robey Gallery, Denver, 90; Five in One Metals, Zoller Gallery, Penn State Univ, Pa, 90. *Teaching:* Asst prof art, Ind Univ, 71-73; instr jewelry & metalsmithing, Des Moines Art Mus, 73-75; lectr, Silversmithing Dept, Camberwell Sch Arts & Crafts, London, Eng, 83; prof art, San Diego State Univ, 75- *Awards:* Fulbright Grant to Denmark, 63; Nat Endowment Arts, 78 & 88. *Bibliog:* Peter Dormer & Ralph Turner (auths), The New Jewelry: Trends & Traditions, Thames & Hudson, 85; Weidenfeld & Nicholson (auths), Craft Today: Poetry of the Physical, Am Craft Mus, 86; Barbara Mayer (auth), Contemporary American Craft Art: A Collector's Guide, Peregrine Smith Bks, 88. *Mem:* Soc N Am Goldsmiths; Am Crafts Coun. *Dealer:* Joan Robey Gallery 939 Broadway Denver CO 80203. *Mailing Add:* San Diego State Univ San Diego CA 92182-0214

SHISHIM, FRANCIS See Bob & Bob

SHIVES, ARNOLD EDWARD
PAINTER, PRINTMAKER
b Vancouver, BC, Dec 27, 43. *Study:* Univ BC, 62-64; San Francisco Art Inst, BFA, 66; Stanford Univ, MA, 69. *Work:* Achenbach Found Graphic Arts; Nat Gallery Ottawa; New York Pub Libr. *Exhib:* One-man shows, The Pollock Gallery, Toronto, 75 & 76, Art Gallery of Greater Victoria, BC, 83-84; World Print Competition, San Francisco Mus Mod Art, 77-79; New Acquisitions, 1940-1984, Achenbach Found, Calif Palace of Legion of Honor, San Francisco; Paul Kuhn Fine Arts, Calgary, 84-92; Heffel Gallery, Vancouver, 89 & 90. *Awards:* Carnegie Corp New York Fel, 66 & 68; Can Coun Arts Grant, 76 & 77; Distinguished Citizen Award, North Vancouver Centennial, 91. *Bibliog:* Paddy Moore (auth), Octogon Artists Exped, Can Broadcasting Corp, Vancouver, 88; John K Grande (auth), Arnold Shives, Vie des Arts, Montreal, summer 92; Anne Rosenberg (auth), The Vancouver Sun, 7/4/92. *Mem:* North Shore Arts Comn, 91-93. *Publ:* Arnold Shives Prints (auth, catalog), Art Gallery Greater Victoria, 83. *Dealer:* Paul Kuhn Fine Arts 722 11th Ave SW Calgary T2R 0E4. *Mailing Add:* 4217 Prospect Rd North Vancouver BC V7N 3L6 Canada

SHLIEN, HELEN S
CURATOR
b Kansas City, Mo. *Study:* Sarah Lawrence Col, BA, 41; Univ Chicago, MA, 64. *Pos:* Owner, Contemp Prints & Drawings Gallery, Chicago, 65-67; cur, Inst Contemp Art, Boston, Mass, 69-72; gallery dir, Boston Visual Artists Union, 74-75; owner, Helen Shlien Gallery, Boston, 78-85; independent cur, 85- *Awards:* Nat Endowment Arts Grant, 77. *Mem:* Bd mem, The Space, Boston, Mass. *Specialty:* Contemporary painting and sculpture. *Publ:* Auth, Artists' Associations in the USA, A Descriptive Directory, pvt publ, 77. *Mailing Add:* 14 Reservoir Rd Wayland MA 01778

SHOEMAKER, INNIS HOWE
CURATOR
b Reading, Pa, Feb 7, 42. *Study:* Vassar Col, Poughkeepsie, NY, AB, 64; Columbia Univ, New York, MA, 68, PhD, 75. *Collections Arranged:* Promised Gifts '77, Vassar Col Art Gallery, Poughkeepsie, NY, 77; Drawings About Drawing Today (auth, catalog), Ackland Art Mus, 78; The Engravings of Marcantonio Raimondi, Ackland Art Mus & traveling to: Spencer Mus Art, Univ Kans, Lawrence & Wellesley Col Mus, 81-82; Paul Cézanne: Two Sketchbooks, Philadelphia Mus of Art, 89 (exhib & cat co-auth). *Pos:* Cur, Vassar Col Art Gallery, Poughkeepsie, NY, 73-76; asst dir, Ackland Art Mus, Univ NC, Chapel Hill, 76-78, acting dir, 78, dir, 83-86; sr cur prints, drawings & photogr, Philadelphia Mus Art, 86- *Teaching:* Vis lectr, dept art, Wesleyan Univ, Middletown, Conn, 75; adj prof, dept art, Univ NC, Chapel Hill. *Awards:* Travel Grant, Samuel H Kress, 70; Rome Prize Fel, Hist Art, Am Acad Rome, 71-73. *Mem:* Am Asn Mus; Print Coun of Am; Col Art Asn Am; Conservation Ctr for Art and Historic Artifacts (bd dir). *Publ:* Auth, Drawings after the antique by Filipino Lippi, Master Drawings, 78; Marcantonio Raimondi, Art News, 80; ed, The Ackland Art Museum: A Handbook, 83; auth, A University collects: Drawings at the Ackland Art Museum, University of North Carolina, Drawing, 5-6/84. *Mailing Add:* Philadelphia Museum of Art Philadelphia PA 19130

SHOEMAKER, PETER
PAINTER
b Newport, RI, Jan 9, 20. *Study:* Calif Sch Fine Arts, San Francisco, with Clyfford Still, Clay Spohn, Elmer Bischoff & David Park, cert, 50; Univ Calif, Berkeley, BA, 51. *Work:* Calif Palace of Legion of Honor, San Francisco; Richmond Art Ctr, Calif; Oakland Mus, Calif. *Exhib:* Corcoran Biennial, Washington, DC, 57; Pacemakers, Contemp Arts Mus, Houston, 57; Carnegie Int, Pittsburgh, 58; Bay Area: Painting Invitational, 79, Three Calif Artists, 80 & 30th Painting Ann, 83, Richmond Art Ctr, Calif; Breakfast Group, Col Notre Dame, Belmont, Calif, 87; one-man show, Kennedy Art Ctr, Holy Names Col, Oakland Calif, 88, Carlson Gallery, San Francisco, 90; group Six Gallery show, Natsoulos/Noveloso Gallery, Davis, Calif, 90. *Teaching:* Prof painting, Calif Col Arts & Crafts, Oakland, 60-84, prof emer, 84. *Awards:* 27th Ann Painting Prize, Richmond Art Ctr, 80. *Bibliog:* Mary Fuller (auth), Was there a San Francisco school?, Artforum, 1/71; Thomas Albright (auth), Art in the San Francisco Bay Area: 1945-1980, Univ Calif Press, 85. *Mem:* San Francisco Art Inst. *Mailing Add:* 622 Panoramic Way Berkeley CA 94704

SHOEMAKER, VAUGHN
EDITORIAL CARTOONIST, PAINTER
b Chicago, Ill, Aug 11, 02. *Study:* Chicago Art Inst; Chicago Acad Fine Arts, Ill. *Work:* Huntington Libr, San Marino, Calif; Syracuse Univ, NY; Wheaton Col, Ill. *Exhib:* Obrien Galleries, Chicago, 35 & 36; Marshall Field Galleries, Chicago, 38; El Prado Galleries Inc, Sedona, Ariz. *Pos:* Cartoonist, Chicago Daily News, 22-25, chief ed cartoonist, 25-52; ed cartoonist, New York Herald Tribune, 56-61; chief ed cartoonist, Chicago Am-Chicago Today, 61-72. *Teaching:* Instr ed cartooning, Chicago Acad Fine Arts, 27-42; instr ed cartooning, Studio Sch Art, Chicago, 43-45. *Awards:* Pulitzer Prizes, Columbia Univ, 38 & 47; Headliners Award, Atlantic City, 43. *Bibliog:* Gerald W Johnson (auth), The Lines are Drawn, Lippincott, 58. *Mem:* Hon mem Palette & Chisel Acad Fine Arts, Chicago; Sigma Delta Chi; Soc Western Artists, San Francisco; hon mem Ridge Art Asn, Chicago. *Media:* Acrylic, Oil. *Publ:* Auth, '38 A D, '39 A D, '40 A D, '41-42 A D, '43-44 A D & '45; plus others. *Mailing Add:* c/o El Prado Galleries By the Creek Tlaquepaque Arts & Crafts Village PO Box 1849 Sedona AZ 86336

SHOOK, GEORG
PAINTER
b Miss, May 24, 34. *Study:* Univ Fla; Ringling Inst Art, Sarasota, Fla; with Bernard Robinson, Orlando, Fla. *Work:* Ellen J Martin & T H B Dunnegan Collections, Springfield, Mo; City of Springfield & Watercolor USA Collections, Springfield Art Mus; Lloyd O Angell Collection, Golden, Colo; Nat Bank of Com; Artists Registry, Memphis Brooks Mus Art, Tenn. *Exhib:* 9th-29th Tenn All-State Artists Ann, Nashville, 69-89; 14th-18th Mid-South Ann, Brooks Art Gallery, Memphis, 69-73; Watercolor USA, Springfield Art Mus, 70-92; Cent South Ann, Parthenon Galleries, Nashville, 70-92; 105th, 106th, 109th & 110th Ann Am Watercolor Soc, New York, 72, 73, 76 & 77; plus others. *Pos:* Creative dir, Memphis Publ Co, 61- *Teaching:* Demonstrations and workshops. *Awards:* Four consecutive Purchase Awards, Watercolor USA, Springfield, Mo; ten consecutive Awards, Tenn Watercolor Soc; CFS Award, Am Watercolor Soc, New York; over 100 nat & int awards. *Bibliog:* Feature article, Am Artist Mag, 4/73, 3/80, 12/84; cover & feature article, North Light Mag, 9/77; cover & feature article, Art Voices S Mag, 8/77, 3/78; Sharp Focus Watercolor Painting, 81, Painting Creative Watercolors from Photographs, 83, 40 Watercolorists and How They Work, Watercolor Painting Techniques & Still Life Painting Techniques, Watson-Guptill. *Mem:* Memphis watercolor Soc (co-founder & dir, 69-); Am Watercolor Soc; Art Dirs Club Memphis (pres, 70-72); Tenn Watercolor Soc (pres, 71-72); Southern Watercolor Soc (pres, 77-78); Watercolor USA Hon Soc (co-founder, 86-, pres, 91-92). *Media:* Watercolor, Mixed Media. *Mailing Add:* 41 Union Ave #3 Memphis TN 38103

SHOOP, WALLY (WILLIAM WALTER)
SCULPTOR
b Sioux City, Iowa, Feb 17, 41. *Study:* Self edocated. *Work:* Nat Mus Australia; Nat Mus Ger; Nat Mus Japan; Wolves Minn Zoo. *Comn:* Star Eagle, Isuzu; Catch the Spirit, 3M; Eagles, Cenex Land O Lakes; Wolverine, Univ Mich; Hawk, Univ Iowa. *Pos:* Pres, Soc Minn Sculptors & Ann Bronze Castng. *Media:* Bronze. *Mailing Add:* 728 Prospect Ave Osceola WI 54020

SHOOTER, TOM
PAINTER
b Williamsport, Pa, Aug 18, 41. *Study:* Lycoming Col, 59-61; Sch Mus Fine Arts, Boston, cert, 65 & grad cert, 66; with Jan Cox, Boston, 66; Tufts Univ, MFA, 71. *Work:* Tufts Univ Collection; Sch Mus Fine Arts Collection, Boston; Spaulding & Sly Corp Collection, Boston; Tufts New Eng Med Ctr Collection, Boston; Commercial Assurance Union Collection, Boston. *Comn:* The Boston Bicentennial Art Collection, 78. *Exhib:* Works on Paper, Fogg Mus, Harvard Univ, 74; Corporations Collect, De Cordova Mus, Lincoln, Mass, 74; Painting Invitational, Brockton Art Ctr, Mass, 75; Painted in Boston, Inst Contemp Art, 75; Art of the State, Rose Mus, Brandeis Univ, 79; New Paintings, Sunne Savage Gallery, Boston, 79; Recent Work, George DePaul Gallery, New York, 87-88; J Johnson Gallery, New York, 90; Wetherholt Gallery, Washington, DC, 91. *Teaching:* Instr painting, Sch Mus Fine Arts, Boston, 65-66; instr painting, Tufts Univ, Naples, Italy, 68-69; instr painting & drawing, Cambridge Ctr Adult Educ, 70-78; instr painting, Sch Mus Fine Arts, Boston, 76-78; instr painting & drawing, Educ Alliance Art Sch, New York, 92-93. *Awards:* 34th James William Paige Fel, Boston Mus Fine Arts, 66; Nat Endowment Arts & Humanities Grant, 66; Mass Found Arts & Humanities Grant, 79; Adolph & Esther Gottlieb Found, 85. *Bibliog:* Kay Larson (auth), Boston, identity crisis, Art News & The flowering of Boston art, 2/75; Jane Holtz-Kay (auth), On view in Boston, summer 76, Art News; Les Krantz (ed), NY Art Rev, 3rd ed, 88. *Mem:* Found Community Artists, New York. *Media:* Oil, Watercolor. *Dealer:* Sunne Savage 135 Cambridge St Winchester MA 01890. *Mailing Add:* 463 West St #107H New York NY 10014

SHORE, MARY (MCGARRITY)
PAINTER
b Philadelphia, Pa, Mar 19, 12. *Study:* Cooper Union Art Sch, scholar; Art Inst Chicago. *Work:* Addison Gallery Am Art, Andover, Mass; Fitchburg Art Mus, Mass; Baltimore Art Mus. *Exhib:* Solo exhibs, Mus Mod Art, New York, Boris Mirsky Gallery, Boston, 64, Town Wharf Gallery, Blue Hill, Maine, 64, Philadelphia Art Alliance, 65, Fitchburg Art Mus, Mass, 65 & 66, Jeffrey Gallery, Boston, Mass, 69 & Hilliard Gallery, Martha's Vineyard, 71; Paintings & Sculpture, Fitchburg Art Mus, Mass, 71; Horizon Gallery, Newton & Rockport, Mass, 73-82; Rockport Art Asn group show, 85; Point Hill Gallery, 85-86; Judy Rotenberg Gallery, Boston, 87; and many others. *Awards:* Blanche E Coleman Art Found Award, 66. *Mem:* Artists Equity Asn (past pres New Eng Chap & nat dir); Nat Mus Women Arts, Washington, DC. *Media:* Oil, Watercolor. *Mailing Add:* Studio on Way Rd Gloucester MA 01930

SHORE, STEPHEN
PHOTOGRAPHER
b New York, NY, Oct 8, 47. *Work:* Metrop Mus Art, Mus Mod Art, New York; Int Mus Photog, Rochester, NY; Mus Fine Arts, Boston; Art Inst Chicago. *Exhib:* Solo exhib, Metrop Mus Art, New York, 71, Mus Mod Art, New York, 76, Kunsthalle, Dusseldorf, Ger, 76 & Ringling Mus, Sarasota, Fla, Art Inst, Chicago, 83; New Topographics, Int Mus Photog, Rochester, NY, 75; Counterparts, Metrop Mus Art, New York. *Teaching:* Prof photog, Bard Col, 82- *Bibliog:* Tony Hiss (auth), The framing of Stephen Shore, Am Photog, 2/79. *Publ:* Auth, Uncommon places, 82 & The gardens at Giverny, 83, Aperture. *Dealer:* Pace-MacGill E 57th St New York NY. *Mailing Add:* c/o Bard Col Annandale-on-Hudson NY 12504

SHORES, (JAMES) FRANKLIN
PAINTER
b Hampton, Va, Nov 9, 42. *Study:* Pa Acad Fine Arts, Cresson Europe Traveling Scholar, Eakins Figure Painting Prize. *Work:* Pa Acad Fine Arts, Philadelphia; Camden Pub Libr, Maine. *Exhib:* Pa Acad Fine Arts Ann, 67 & 69; Philadelphia Watercolor Club Exhibs, 68-; Cabrini Col, 86. *Teaching:* Instr art, Pa Acad Fine Arts, 65-86. *Awards:* Harry Deitch Mem Prize, Philadelphia Watercolor Club, 78. *Mem:* Philadelphia Watercolor Club (hon pres, currently). *Media:* Watercolor, Oil. *Mailing Add:* 612 S Ninth St Philadelphia PA 19147

SHORNEY, MARGO KAY (MCIVER)
ART DEALER, SCULPTOR
b Great Falls, Mont, July 5, 30. *Study:* Col Educ, Great Falls, Mont, with Sister Mary Trinitas, 49-51; Univ Denver, with Clarence Van Duzer & Mrion Buckan, 51-53. *Work:* Great Falls Pub Lib, Mont; Cooper West Insurance Agency, Elk City, Okla; John Thompson Movie Service, Oklahoma City; Dr R G Williams Medical Offices, Tulsa, Okla; Country Club Pub, Oklahoma City. *Comn:* Christmas mural, Lake View Country Club, Oklahoma City, 69; Oil Depicting Old & New, Delta Gamma Society, Norman, Okla, 79. *Exhib:* Eleventh Mem Ann, 77 & 17th Ann Artists Salon, 78, Okla Mus Art; Okla Spring Gala, N Park Mall, Oklahoma City, 81; Okla Sculpture Soc, Kirpatrick Ctr, Oklahoma City, 81; First Ann Women's Invitational, Quail Springs Mall, Oklahoma City, 81; Am Art Bronze Invitational, Tulsa, 84; Okla Sculpture Soc Show, Kirkpatrick Ctr, 85. *Collections Arranged:* Okla Art Guild Spring Regional, 78; 25th Anniversary, Okla Art Guild, 79. *Pos:* Owner & dir, Shorney Gallery, 76- *Teaching:* Lectr, Okla Art Guild, 82-83 & 91, S Oklahoma City Asn, 82-83 & Edmond Art League, Okla, 92; judge, Ponca City 12th Ann Fine Arts, 86; lectr & critic, Norman Art League, 87 & 90. *Mem:* Charter mem Okla Sculpture Soc; Okla Art Gallery Owners Asn (pres, 81-82); Okla Art Guild (bd dirs, 79-82); Great Falls Mont Inst Arts (pres, 52-54). *Media:* All. *Specialty:* Originals only, National, regional and emerging artists, featuring a variety of media including graphics, sculpture, oils, watercolors, acrylics, pastels, pottery, weaving & jewelry. *Mailing Add:* 6616 N Olie Oklahoma City OK 73116

SHORR, HARRIET
PAINTER
b New York, NY, May 14, 39. *Study:* Swarthmore Col, BA, 60; Yale Sch Art & Archit, BFA, 62. *Work:* Utah Mus Fine Arts, Salt Lake City; Lehman Brothers, Main Hurdman & Citibank, New York. *Exhib:* Eight Women-Still Life, New Britain Mus, Conn, 82; Painterly Realism, 82 & Contemporary Women Painters, 83, Rahr West Mus, Manitowac, Wis; American Realism, William Sawyer Gallery, San Francisco, 85 & San Francisco Mus Fine Art, 85-86; Artists Choosing Artists, Artists Choice Mus, New York, 85; The Object Revitalized, Paine Arts Ctr, Oshkosh, Wis, 85-86; Contemporary American Still Life, One Penn Plaza, New York, 85-86. *Teaching:* Assoc prof painting, State Univ NY, Purchase, 79- *Awards:* Nat Endowment Arts Grant, 80. *Bibliog:* Tak Inagaki (dir), Harriet Shorr, Nippon Television, Japan, 81; Robert Berlind (auth), Harriet Shorr at Fischbach, Art Am, 5/81; Janice Oresman (auth), Still life today, Arts, 12/83. *Media:* Oil. *Publ:* Auth, A painter's reflections on real painting, Arts, 79. *Dealer:* Peter Tatistcheff 50 W 57th St New York NY 10019. *Mailing Add:* 117 Mercer St No 5 New York NY 10012

SHORT, PATRICIA ANN REILLY
PAINTER
b Oakland, Calif, Aug 6, 41. *Study:* Univ Calif, Irvine, BFA, 72; study with John Paul Jones, S Serisawa, Rex Brandt & Tony DeLap. *Work:* Imperial Savings & Loan Hq, San Diego, Calif; Hemet Bank, Hemet, Calif; Hyatt Hotel, Fisherman's Wharf, San Francisco, Calif; Hilton Hotel, Pasadena, Calif. *Exhib:* Artist Members Exhib, 78-80 & Bagged Art & Boxed Art, 82-83, Laguna Beach Mus Art; Watercolor West, Riverside Art Mus, Riverside, Calif, 80, 84 & 88; Traditional Artists Exposition, San Bernardino Mus, San Bernardino, 80 & 83; Brand XII, Brand Mus, Glendale, Calif, 82; solo exhib, Robertson Gallery, Riverside, Calif, 85; Five Women in Watercolor, Art Angles Gallery, 87; Audubon Soc, New York, 88; Kathrine Lorillard Wolfe Club, New York. *Pos:* Mem, artists steering comt, Laguna Beach Mus Art, currently, studio tour coordr, 84. *Teaching:* Private watercolor workshops, 76-; art instr, Saddleback Col, Mission Viejo, Calif, 78-90. *Awards:* Richter-Moore Award, 79 & Cert Merit, Ann Membership Show, Laguna Beach Mus Art; Cert Merit, Catharine Lorillard Wolf Art Club, 84. *Bibliog:* Earl Beecher (auth), Meet the artist, Pat Short, Dawn Mag, 5/81; Sarah Ahearn (auth), Patricia Short, emerging artist, Am Artist, 8/86; Patricia Short-Business Supplement, Am Artist, 6/89. *Mem:* Nat Asn Women Artists; assoc mem Nat Watercolor Soc; assoc mem Watercolor West. *Media:* Watercolor, Oil. *Dealer:* Laguna Fine Arts Gallery 1045 Newport Ctrs Dr Newport Beach CA 92660. *Mailing Add:* c/o Laguna Fine Arts Gallery 1045 Newport Centers Dr Newport Beach CA 92660

SHOSTAK, ED (EDWIN BENNETT)
SCULPTOR
b New York, NY, Aug 23, 41. *Study:* Ohio Univ, 59-60; Cooper Union, 60-61. *Work:* Many pvt collections including: Phillip Johnson, New Canaan, Conn, Sydney Lewis, Richmond, Va & Mrs Horace Solomon, New York. *Exhib:* Am Exhib of Am Sculpture, 70 & Biennial, 73, Whitney Mus Am Art, New York; 76 Jefferson St, Mus Mod Art, New York, 75; Selections for New & Old Collections, Art Mus STex, Corpus Christi, 76; Non-Collectible Art from the Collection of Holly Solomon, Sarah Lawrence Col, Bronxville, NY, 77; A Collection, A Collector, Norman Fisher Collection, Jacksonville Art Mus, 79. *Awards:* Creative Artists Pub Serv Award, 73; Guggenheim Fel, 74. *Bibliog:* Robert Hughes (auth), In search of the new; Pursuit of the old, Time Mag, 1/71; Le Salon des Artists Independents, Grand Palais, Paris, France, 80; Decorative Sculpture, Sculpture Ctr, New York, 81; plus numerous others. *Media:* Wood, Metals. *Mailing Add:* 303 E Houston St New York NY 10002

SHOULBERG, HARRY
PAINTER, GRAPHIC ARTIST
b Philadelphia, Pa, Oct 25, 03. *Study:* Am Artists Sch; also with Carl Holty & Sol Wilson. *Work:* Metrop Mus Art, New York; Carnegie Inst, Pittsburgh; Norfolk Mus Arts & Sci, Va; Denver Mus, Colo; Butler Inst Am Art; Rutgers Univ, NJ. *Exhib:* American Oil Painting, Corcoran Gallery Art, Washington, DC, 41; Print & Watercolor Exhib, Pa Acad Fine Arts, Philadelphia, 46; Libr Cong Print Exhib, Washington, DC, 47; Audubon Artists 28th Ann, New York, 70; Nat Acad Design 146th Ann, New York, 71 Channel 13, WNET, 1/89; Nat Soc of Painters in Casein & Acrylic at the Nat Acad of Design, New York, 76 & 77; one-man show, Harbor Gallery, Cold Spring Harbor, NY, 80, Park Avenue South Gallery, 82. *Awards:* Elanie & James Hewett Award, Am Soc Contemp Artists, 77; Pearl Award, Painters & Sculptors Soc NJ, 79; and others. *Bibliog:* H Shokler (auth), Artists manual for silk screen printmaking, 46, A Reese (auth), American prize prints of the 20th century, 49 & The New York Art Review, 88. *Mem:* Audubon Artists; Am Soc Contemp Artists; NJ Soc Painters & Sculptors; Artists Equity Asn; Nat Soc Painters Casein & Acrylic. *Media:* Oil. *Mailing Add:* 223 W 21st St New York NY 10011

SHOWELL, KENNETH L
PAINTER
b Huron, SDak, Oct 22, 39. *Study:* Kansas City Art Inst, BFA, 63; Ind Univ, MFA, 65. *Work:* Art Inst Chicago; Whitney Mus Am Art, New York; Michener Collection, Univ Tex, Austin; Akron Mus, Ohio. *Exhib:* Whitney Mus Am Art Ann, 67-69; Highlights of the 1969-1970 Art Season, Aldrich Mus, Ridgefield, Conn; Lyrical Abstraction, Whitney Mus Am Art, New York, 71; Spray, Santa Barbara Mus Art, 71; Painting & Sculpture Today 1972, Indianapolis Mus Art, Ind, 72; one-man shows, Parr Gallery, 86. *Bibliog:* R Pincus-Witten (auth), New York, Artforum, 1/70; C Ratcliff (auth), The new informalists, 2/70 & J Weissman (auth), Showdown in Soho, 11/74, Art News. *Media:* Acrylic, Oil. *Mailing Add:* 82 Forsyth New York NY 10002

SHUBIN, MORRIS JACK
PAINTER, LECTURER
b Mansfield, Wash, Feb 25, 20. *Work:* Utah State Univ, Logan; Las Vegas Art Mus, Nev; Home Savings & Loan, Calif; City La Mirada, Calif; Philip H Greene Collection; and others. *Comn:* Painting (brochure), Robert Mondavi Winery, Calif, 90. *Exhib:* Nat Watercolor Soc Ann, Palm Springs Art Mus, Calif, 81; Art and the Law, Atlanta, 83; Utah State Univ, Logan, 83; 161st Ann Exhib, Nat Acad Design, 86, 88 & 92; Am Watercolor Soc Invitational, Museo de la Acurela Mexicana, Mexico City. *Teaching:* Instr watercolor workshops, Fla, Tex, NMex, Ore, Colo, Mo & Mex, 74-84, Spain, 85, Canada, 90. *Awards:* Addeso Franklin Page Award, Owensboro Mus, Ky, 83; Samuel J Bloomingdal Mem Award, Am Watercolor Soc, 118th Ann Exhib, Canton Art Inst, 85; Crandall Norton Award, Downey Art Mus, 90. *Bibliog:* Gerald Brommer (auth), Transparent Watercolor, Davis, 73; Susan Meyer (auth), 40 Watercolorists and How They Work, Watson-Guptill; McClelland & Last (coauths, publ), The California Style, 85. *Mem:* Am Watercolor Soc (vpres, 87-89); Nat Watercolor Soc (treas, 70-72, 89-90, vpres, 72-73); WCoast Watercolor Soc; Pasadena Soc Artists; Watercolor USA Hon Soc. *Media:* Multimedia. *Publ:* Auth, Watercolor page, Am Artists, 8/74; producer, Nat Watercolor Soc Ann Catalog, 89-90. *Dealer:* Eileen Kremen's Gallery 619 N Harbor Blvd Fullerton CA; Sandra Zahn Oreck Gallery 529 Wilkinson Row New Orleans LA 70130. *Mailing Add:* 313 N 12th St Montebello CA 90640

SHUEBROOK, RON (RONALD LEE)
PAINTER, EDUCATOR
b Ft Munroe, Va, July 29, 43. *Study:* Haystack Mountain Sch, Maine, 65 & 67; Kutztown State Col, Pa, BS, 65, MEd, 69; Kent State Univ, Ohio, MFA, 72. *Work:* Art Gallery Onc, Toronto; Nat Gallery Can, Ottawa; Art Gallery Hamilton, Ont; Art Gallery, Windsor, Ont; Confederation Ctr PEI; and others. *Exhib:* Solo exhib, Recent work, Concordia Univ Art Gallery, Montreal, 86, Paintings, Drawings & Construction (catalog), Art Gallery Hamilton, traveled to Beaverbrook Art Gallery, Fredericton, NB, Kitchener-Waterloo Art Gallery, Ont, Mendel Art Gallery, Saskatoon, Saskatchewan, 87-88, Galerie Maghi Bettini, Amsterdam, 88 & 91, Forest City Gallery, London, Ont, 89; Select Acquisitions 1975-1988, Art Gallery Nova Scotia, Halifax, 88; 49th Parallel, New York, 89; Secession Mus, Vienna, 81. *Pos:* Assoc prof, Nova Scotia Col Art & Design, 79 & 86-87, chmn studio div, 80-83, coordr painting & drawing, 83-84 & coordr drawing & fdn art, 84-85; exec dir, Ottawa Sch Art, Ont, 87-88; chmn art dept, Univ Guelp, Ont, 88. *Awards:* Grants, NS Col Art & Design, 80, 81, 83 & 86 & Can Coun, 85 & 90; Fel, McDowell Colony, Peterborough, NH, 81. *Bibliog:* Gloria Hickey (auth), Ron Shuebrook, Artsatlantic 30, winter 88; Kit Lort (auth), Interview with Ron Shuebrook, Artsatlantic, summer 88; Ingrid Jenkner (auth), Ron Shuebrook in Guelph, MacDonald Stewart Art Ctr, Guelph, Ont, 90. *Publ:* Thinking and Making: Notes for the Duration, Ron Shuebrook: Recent Work, Concordia Art Gallery, 3-4/86; Richard Gorman, Canadian Art, winter 87; John Greer, Vanguard, Vancouver, 9/87; Rockwell Kent at Dalhousie, Canadian Art, summer 87; Context and Paradigm, Ron Shuebrook in Guelph, MacDonald Stewart Art Ctr, Guelph, Ont, 90. *Dealer:* Olga Korper 17 Morrow Ave Toronto Ont M6R 2H9 Canada. *Mailing Add:* Dept Fine Art Univ Guelph Guelph ON N1G 2W1 Canada

SHUFF, LILY (LILLIAN SHIR)
PAINTER, PRINTMAKER
b New York, NY. *Study:* Hunter Col, BA & MA; Columbia Univ; Brooklyn Acad Fine Art; Art Students League, with Morris Kantor; also with Adja Junkers & Jerry Farnsworth. *Work:* Metrop Mus Art, New York; Libr of Cong, Washington, DC; Yale Univ Art Gallery, New Haven, Conn; Butler Inst Am Art, Youngstown, Ohio; Ga Mus Am Art; Archives Am Art, Smithsonian Inst, Washington, DC; plus 33 other nat mus collections. *Exhib:* Ten Years of American Prints 1947-1956, Brooklyn Mus, NY, 56; Munic Mus Art, Uneo Park, Tokyo, 60; Mus Nac Bellas Artes, Buenos Aires, 63; Royal Scottish Acad, Edinburgh, Scotland, 63; Int Cult Ctr, New Delhi, India, 66; slides of paintings circulated in universities & colleges in US by Ga Mus Fine Art, Athens; one-woman shows, East Side Gallery, New York, 66, Univ Maine, 68, Rosenberg Libr, Galveston, Tex, 70, Pack Mem Gallery, Asheville, NC, 71, Studio Angelico, Adrian, Mich, 72, Holy Cross Seminary, La Cross, Wis, 72 & State Univ, Morrisville, NY, 74; and others. *Awards:* Allied Artist Am, Nat Casein Soc, 63, 65, 69, 73, 76, 77, 81 & 83-85; Shiva Prize, 84; Soloway Mem Prize for Casein Reverie, Casein Soc, 90; and others. *Bibliog:* Article in Think, 59; Alfred Khouri Collection, Norfolk Mus, 63; Archives of American Art, Smithsonian Inst, Washington, DC. *Mem:* Nat Asn Women Artists (chmn mem jury, 56-58 & 64-66, bd dirs, 58-67); Nat Soc Painters Casein (rec secy, 57-64 & corr secy, 68-83); New York Soc Women Artists (bd gov, 56-71); Audubon Artists (graphics dir, 70-72); NJ Painters & Sculptors (admis jury, 71). *Media:* Oil, Watercolor. *Publ:* Contribr, Art Collector's Almanac, 65; Today's Art, 70, 74 & 77; How to Paint a Prize Winner, 70. *Mailing Add:* 155 W 68th St New York NY 10023

SHUKMAN, SOLOMON
PAINTER, PRINTMAKER
b Bobr Prov, USSR, July 5, 27; US citizen. *Study:* Col Fine Arts & Theater Design, Moscow, BA, 49; Stroganoff Inst Art, Moscow, BA, 52. *Work:* Mankind and Work (monumental composition), Moscow; Energy/Metal (monumental composition), Paris; Summer, Spring, Autumn (monumental composition), Ehrfurt, EGer; Majakovski (collage), New York; Transport (3 decorative compositions), Prague. *Comn:* Mankind & Oil (mural), Art Found USSR, Moscow, 68; Morning, Union Soviet Artist, Moscow, 69; Cosmos, Union Soviet Artist, Moscow, 69; Country and Army (mural), Art Found USSR, Moscow, 71; Men and Cloth, Art Found USSR, Moscow, 72. *Exhib:* Solo exhibs, Loeb Rhode Market Gallery, 75, Panteon Gallery, 77 & Nathan Gallery, 78, San Francisco & Magnes Mus (with catalog), Berkeley, Calif, 78-79; Int Art Expo, NY Coliseum, New York & Los Angeles Convention Ctr, 85. *Awards:* First Praise, Int Expo, Moscow, 69 & 72, 2nd Praise, 73. *Bibliog:* Article, Best show of the year, Art in the USSR Mag, 72. *Mem:* Int Soc Artists; Graphic Arts Coun; Ctr Visual Arts; World Print Coun. *Media:* Murals, Graphics. *Dealer:* Solo Art Studio PO Box 1337 Menlo Park CA 94026. *Mailing Add:* 554 Beresford Ave Redwood City CA 94061

SHULER, THOMAS H, JR
PHOTOGRAPHER, EDUCATOR
b Detroit, Mich, Apr 15, 49. *Study:* Princeton Univ, BA, 71; Univ Del, MA, 78. *Work:* Corcoran Gallery Art; Mus Francais Photog, Bievres, France; Bibliot Nat, Paris; Libr Cong, Washington, DC. *Exhib:* Recent Acquisitions, 77 & Still Life, 78, Corcoran Gallery Art; Focus Gallery, San Francisco, 79; MFA Gallery-The Platinotype, Rochester Inst Technol, 79; Photographer's Gallery, London, England, 79; Nuages, Bibliot Nat, Paris, 80; Invisible Light, Harvard Univ, 81; and others. *Teaching:* Instr photog, Smithsonian Inst, 75-76; chmn, asst prof & prog head photog, Northern Va Community Col, 76-. *Awards:* Medaille Verrieres Buisson, Mus Francais Photog, 78. *Bibliog:* Ben Forgey (auth), A sense of the moment when everything's right, Washington Star, 5/5/78; Time-Life Photo Annual, 79; Hafey & Shillea (auth), The Platinum Print, Graphic Arts Res Ctr, Rochester Inst Technol, 80; and others. *Mem:* Soc Photog Educ. *Publ:* Ed, Places, Infrared Photographs 1976-1978, pvt publ, 78. *Mailing Add:* 3715 Cardiff Rd Chevy Chase MD 20815

SHULL, CARL EDWIN
PAINTER, EDUCATOR
b Greenup, Ill, Dec 8, 12. *Study:* Eastern Ill Univ, BA(educ), 39; Peabody Col, MA, 40; Chicago Art Inst, advan work, 40-42; Ohio State Univ, PhD, 54. *Work:* Canton Art Inst, Ohio; Lakeview Ctr Arts & Sci, Ill; Eastern Ill Univ Collection. *Comn:* Murals, US Navy, South Pac Area, 44-45; Space Flight, pvt comn, Terre Haute, Ind, 71; Sports in Art (35 paintings on sports), Field House, Lakeland Col, Mattoon, Ill, 74. *Exhib:* One-man shows, Univ Ill, 62, Evansville Mus Arts & Sci, 71 & Univ Wis, Platteville, 74; Mid Year Am Painting Exhib, Butler Inst Am Art, Youngstown, Ohio, 53 & 63; Nat Painting Show, Sheldon Swope Art Gallery, Terre Haute, Ind, 67; Tarble Art Ctr, Eastern Ill Univ, Charleston, 82 & 83. *Pos:* Comm artist, Graham & Nugent Studios, Chicago, Ill, 41-42. *Teaching:* Instr arts & crafts, Univ Mo, 46-47; prof painting & drawing, Eastern Ill Univ, Charleston, 47-80; retired. *Awards:* Purchase Awards, Wabash Valley Exhib, Sheldon Swope Art Gallery, Terre Haute, Ind, 68 & 71, Tri-State Exhib, Evansville Mus Art & Sci, Ind, 71 & Wabash Col Brubeck Gallery, 83;; Award, Ill Watercolor Show, Tarble Art

Ctr, Eastern Ill Univ, 89. *Bibliog:* Shull & Wiseman (coauth), Approaches in Life Drawing (film), 70 & Willis Waltman (auth), Shull's Life Class Relates Work to Other Art Areas, 77, Eastern Ill Univ. *Media:* Oil, Watercolor. *Publ:* Auth-illusr, Techniques in Life Drawing, 74, Elements in Landscape Painting, 74, Heads, Heads, Heads, 75, Lore and Design of Nature's Harvest, 76 & Lore and Legend of Birds in Design, 77, Eastern Ill Univ. *Mailing Add:* RR4 Charleston IL 61920

SHULZKE, MARGOT SEYMOUR
PAINTER, WRITER
b San Francisco, Calif. *Study:* Brigham Young Univ, BA, 59, additional study with Albert Handell, Constance Flavell Pratt, William Schultz, Richard Yip, Richard Pionk & Frank Zuccarelli. *Comn:* Shirley Canyon (pastel painting), Squaw Valley Auburn Diagnostic Ctr, Calif; Provo River Canyon II (pastel), Auburn Faith Hosp, Calif; Larry Remmel (portrait), comn by Mr & Mrs Richard Remmel, Auburn, Calif; Megan (portrait), comn by Mr & Mrs Steven Martini, Bellingham, Wash; Jordan Walker (portrait), comn by Mr & Mrs Neil Walker, Stockton, Calif. *Exhib:* Pastel Soc Am Nat Open Exhibs, Nat Arts Club, New York, 86-92; Pastel Soc West Coast Nat Open Exhibs, Ctr Galleries, Sacramento Fine Arts Ctr, Calif, 86-92; Degos Pastel Soc Nat Biennial, Open Exhib, New Orleans, La, 88; Contemp Pastels, Pastel Soc Am, Quincy Art Mus, Ill, 89; 3rd Ann Orig Art Showcase, Prestige Gallery Ltd, Toronto, Can, 91. *Pos:* Pres (founding), Pastel Soc West Coast, 85-88 & advisory bd mem 88- *Teaching:* Week Tours, Lectr, creativity oil painting, Brigham Young Univ, Educ, 66-67; instr pastel & oil, Roseville Arts Ctr, 85-; instr pastel, Ultima Nat Art Symp, Yellowstone, 91. *Awards:* First Place, Eclectic Three Exhib, Roseville, Calif, 88; Distinguished Pastelist, Pastel Soc West Coast (5 awarded nationally to date), 89; First Place, Sacramento Fine Arts Ctr, 3rd Nat Open, 90. *Mem:* Full mem Knickerbocker Artists, New York; Pastel Soc Am, New York; Degas Pastel Soc, New Orleans; Pastel Soc West Coast, Sacramento; Soc Western Artists, San Francisco. *Media:* Pastel, Oil. *Res:* The arts. *Publ:* Auth, Art on Anita Wolff, Am Artist Mag, 87; On the Wing, Gloria Burt Publ, 90-91; contribr, Pastel Interpretations by Madlyn Ann C Woolwich, Northlight, fall 93; auth & illustr, Another Angle on Perspective, 1/92 & Pastel Corrections Made Easy, 6/92, Artist's Mag. *Dealer:* Art Works Gallery 10239 Fair Oaks Blvd Fair Oaks CA 95628. *Mailing Add:* 1840 Little Creek Rd Auburn CA 95602

SHUMACKER, ELIZABETH WIGHT
PAINTER
b Chattanooga, Tenn, Sept 25, 12. *Study:* Univ Chattanooga, BA, postgrad work in painting & graphics; spec drawing & printmaking classes, Hunter Mus, Chattanooga, Tenn. *Work:* High Mus Art, Atlanta, Ga; Brooks Mem Gallery, Memphis, Tenn; Inst Cult Mexicano-Norteamericano, Guadalajara, Mex; Hunter Mus, Chattanooga; Tenn Arts Comn; First Nat Bank, Nashville, Tenn; Chattanooga Corp, Tenn; and many others. *Comn:* New York Times; Chattanooga Times. *Exhib:* High Mus, Atlanta, 53-58 & 61; Butler Inst Am Art, Youngstown, Ohio, 55 & 62; Brooks Mem Art Gallery, Memphis, Tenn, 56-69; Smithsonian Inst, Washington, DC, 60 & 81; Springfield Art Mus, Mo, 62; Heal's Art Gallery, London, 78-79; 33 one-man shows including six Mex cities; Salon des Nations Invitational, Ctr Int d'Art Contemporain, Paris, France, 83; and others. *Teaching:* Instr beginning, intermediate & advan painting, Hunter Gallery Art, Chattanooga, Tenn, 55-75; vis instr advan painting, Univ Chattanooga, spring 69 & Univ Tenn, Chattanooga, spring 73. *Awards:* First Prize Water Color, Southeastern Ann, Atlanta, 57 & Mid-South Exhib, Brooks Mem Gallery, Memphis, Tenn, 57; First Prize & Best in Show, 2nd Nat Small Painting Exhib, Gallery North, Mt Clemens, Mich, 74; First Prize Painting, Firehouse Arts & Crafts Festival, Dalton, Ga, 75; Honorable Mention, St Andrews Arts Festival, Sewanee, Tenn, 76; Cash Award Painting, Atlanta Arts Festival, 76 & Tenn Watercolor Soc, 77. *Bibliog:* Numerous reviews from around the nation. *Mem:* Tenn Water Color Soc. *Media:* Acrylic, Collage. *Mailing Add:* 1400 Riverview Rd Chattanooga TN 37405

SHUTE, ROBERTA E
SCULPTOR, PRINTMAKER
b Saskatoon, Sask. *Study:* Corcoran Mus Art Sch, 49-52; Am Univ, 52-53; study with Hans Hofmann, 53. *Work:* Alice Denny Collection; Henri Goetz Collection, Paris; Tremaine Collection, New York. *Comn:* Environ sculpture (with Maxine Cable), Noche Crist, engrs & technicians, Allied Chem, New York, 70; maj installation, Wolf Trap, summer 71. *Exhib:* Baltimore Mus, 53; Corcoran Mus, 53, 54, 56, 59, 65 & 67; Pa Acad, 54; Art: USA Nat, New York, 58; Nat Acad Sci, 72; Happening for Summers in the Park Prog, Nat Park Serv, Washington, DC, 72; Installations, Textile Mus, Washington, DC, 74; Sculpture on Grounds, Rockville City, 90. *Teaching:* Painting, Corcoran Mus Sch, 51-52; guest lectr plastic sculpture, Am Univ, 72; sculpture, Glen Echo Creative Adult Educ Prog, 73; pvt classes. *Awards:* Nathan Goodman Estate Award, 51; Second Prize, Washington Soc Artists, 62; First Prize, Art & Religion, 63. *Mem:* Washington Sculptor's Group; Int Sculpture Ctr. *Media:* Poly-Adam Concrete System; Fabric. *Mailing Add:* 3536 Edmunds St NW Washington DC 20007

SIAMIS, JANET NEAL
PAINTER
b Cleveland, Ohio, July 31, 38. *Study:* Rollins Col, Winter Park, Fla, 56-57; Antelope Valley Col, Lancaster, Calif, 78-81; study with Ralph Love, Temecula, Calif. *Work:* Home Savings Am; Fluor Corp, Irvine, Calif; Kaiser Permanente; Security Pacific Bank; Embassy Suites Hotel; Marriott Hotel, Presidential Suites, New Orleans, La; Marriott Lincolnshire, Exec Suites, Chicago, Ill; Marriott Hotel, Ballrooms & Hospitality Suites, Anaheim, Calif. *Exhib:* All Media Exhib, Lancaster Mus, Calif, 85; Tallahassee City Hall Art Show, 88 & 89; Fla Watercolor Ann, St Petersburg, 91. *Awards:* Judge's Choice Award, Fla Watercolor Soc, 91. *Bibliog:* J S Ayres (auth), Brushes, Am Artist Mag, 86, Making Watercolor Monotypes, 88, Mediums & Methods Monotype, Watson-Guptill, 91; Dorothy Hoyal (auth), Taking oneself seriously as an artist, Am Artist Mag, 6/86. *Mem:* Fla Watercolor Soc. *Media:* Watercolor. *Publ:* Illusr, A Christmas to Remember, Antelope Valley Press, 80. *Dealer:* Riggs Galleries 875 Prospect La Jolla CA 92037; The Nice Picture Co Havana FL 32333. *Mailing Add:* P O Box 1383 Hwy 98 Crawfordville FL 32327

SIBERELL, ANNE HICKS
PAINTER, SCULPTOR
b Los Angeles, Calif. *Study:* Univ Calif, 2 yrs; Chouinard Art Inst, BFA; Silvermine Col Art, New Canaan, Conn, painting with John Wheat & Richard Lytle; Rowayton Art Ctr, Conn, printmaking with Antonio Frasconi; Col San Mateo, Calif, etching. *Work:* Kerlan Collection, Walter Libr, Univ Minn, Minneapolis; Univ Alta, Edmonton, Can; DeGrummond Collection, Univ Southern Miss; Cleveland Art Inst; Victoria & Albert Mus, London; Nat Mus Women Arts. *Comn:* Ed 100 woodcuts, Silvermine Guild Art, Silvermine Col Art, 66. *Exhib:* International Artists Book Show, Art Inst Chicago, Ill, 81; The Book Thought Through, Metrop Mus Art, New York, 85; Forwarding the Book in California, Victoria & Albert Mus, London, Eng, 88; Bound in the USA, Evanston Art Ctr, Ill, 88; Book Exhibition, Fuller Gross Gallery, San Francisco, Calif, 88; Books and Bookends, Strathmore Hall Arts Ctr, N Bethesda, Md, 89; A Book in Hand, Arvada Ctr Arts and Humanities, Colo, 89; one man exhibs, College of Notre Dame, Calif, 70, Montalvo Ctr Arts, Calif, 81, San Francisco Cons Music Gallery, 82, Rolando Castellon Contemp Art, San Francisco, 87, 88. *Pos:* Asst art ed, Walt Disney Prods, Inc, 56-59; ed filmstrip prep from children's lit, Weston Woods Studios, Conn, 60; artist-in-residence, Women's Graphics Ctr, Los Angeles & Nat Endowment Arts, 83 & Ragdale Found, Lake Forest, Ill, 90. *Teaching:* Art for Children, Silvermine Col Art, 66-68 & Martin Luther King, Jr Ctr, San Mateo, 68-70; woodblock printmaking, San Mateo Adult Educ, 70, illus children's lit, 74-75 & teaching, 76-78; guest lectr, Bakersfield Col, Calif, 77,Univ Ky, 80 & Mills Col, Oakland, Calif, 86; guest lectr, Univ Ky, 80, Mills Col, Oakland, Calif, 86 & Sonoma State Univ, 92. *Awards:* Award for Color Woodcut, Conn Mus Show, Hartford, 68; Rounce & Coffin Award for Bk Design & Illus, 73; San Francisco Art Festival Award, Palo Alto Cult Ctr, 77; Peninsula Community Found Grant, Burlingame, Calif, 87. *Bibliog:* Design without Clients, Fortune Mag, 75; TV interview, Festival of the Arts, San Carlos, Calif, 75. *Mem:* Los Angeles Printmaking Soc; Calif Soc Printmakers; Appeltree Etchers, Inc (bd dirs, 72-74); Ctr Bk Arts, New York; Pac Ctr Bk Arts. *Media:* Oil Based Paint and Ink; Collage and Metals. *Publ:* Illusr, Emanuel Thayer's, Climbing Sun - The Story of a Hopi Indian Boy, Dodd, Mead, 80; auth & illusr, Whale in the Sky, E P Dutton, 82; coauth & illusr, Who Found America, 83 & Feast of Thanksgiving, 84, Children's Press; auth & illusr, A Journey to Paradise, Henry Holt, 90. *Mailing Add:* 1041 La Cuesta Rd Hillsborough CA 94010

SIBLEY, CHARLES KENNETH
PAINTER, EDUCATOR
b Huntington, WVa, Dec 20, 21. *Study:* Ohio State Univ, BS; Art Inst Chicago; Columbia Univ, MA; State Univ Iowa, MFA. *Work:* Metrop Mus Art, New York; NC Mus, Raleigh; Va Mus, Richmond; Rochester Mem Mus, NY; Chrysler Mus, Norfolk, Va; and others. *Comn:* Panels, USS Kennedy, 71; Virginia Landscape (oil), Gov Mansion, Richmond, 72; mural, Old Dominion Univ Libr, Norfolk, Va, 77; mural, AT&T Study Ctr, 86. *Exhib:* Carnegie Inst, Pittsburgh, 57; Whitney Mus Am Art Bi-Ann, New York, 57-59; Nat Soc Arts & Lett, 59; Nat Acad Design, 61; 50 Artists--50 States, Am Fedn Arts, 68. *Pos:* Mem bd dirs, Norfolk Va Children's Art Ctr. *Teaching:* Instr painting & design, Duke Univ, 50-51 & Tex State Univ, 52-54; prof painting & design, Old Dom Univ, 55-82, chmn dept, 55-70, Louis I Jaffe chair, 75-82, prof emer, 82- *Awards:* Louis Comfort Tiffany Grant, 55; Stern Medal, Nat Acad Design, 61; Irene Leache Mem First Prize, Norfolk Mus, 71. *Mem:* Nat Soc Mural Painters. *Media:* Mixed. *Mailing Add:* 5212 Vick St Portsmouth VA 23701

SICA
PRINTMAKER, SCULPTOR
b New York, NY, May 21, 32. *Study:* Art Students League, 49-50; Pratt Graphic Ctr, 69-70. *Work:* Mus Mod Art, Paris, France; Victoria & Albert Mus, London, Eng; Montreal Mus Fine Arts, Can; Brooklyn Mus, NY; Los Angeles Mus, Calif. *Comn:* Edition 30 Prints, Yugoslav Consal, Montenegro, 80. *Exhib:* British Biennial, Bradford Mus, Eng, 72-79; Shiedam Mus, Rotterdam, 73; 1st Miami Graphic Biennial, Miami Mus, Fla, 73; New Graphics, New Berger Mus, Purchase, NY, 76; US Graphics, Tokyo Central Mus, Japan, 79. *Awards:* NJ State Mus Graphics, 76. *Media:* Collage, Clay. *Dealer:* Langman Editions 218 Old York Rd Jenkintown PA 19046. *Mailing Add:* c/o Raydon Gallery 1091 Madison Ave New York NY 10028

SICKLER, MICHAEL ALLAN
PAINTER, EDUCATOR
b Milwaukee, Wis, Aug 11, 45. *Study:* Layton Sch Art, Milwaukee, Wis, BFA, 70; Univ Wis-Milwaukee, MFA, 73. *Work:* Univ Potsdam, NY; Layton Sch Art, Milwaukee, Wis; Keith Corp, Salmon Brook, Conn. *Comn:* Painting-mural, Keith Corp, Glastonbury, Conn, 84; 2 paintings, Birnbaum & Assoc, Syracuse, NY, 85; painting, comn by Sheraton Hotel, Liverpool, NY, 86. *Exhib:* Regional, 76 & New Paintings, 77, Everson Mus, Syracuse, NY; 42nd Ann, Munson-Williams-Proctor, Utica, NY, 79; Recent Paintings, Univ London, Ctr Related Arts, Eng, 83; Six Syracuse Painters, Skidmore Col, Saratoga, NY, 85. *Pos:* Art dir & sole auctioneer, WCNY, WCFE, WNPE & WNPI, NY State PBS, 83- *Teaching:* Assoc prof studio art & art hist, Syracuse

Univ, NY, 73- *Awards:* Ford Found Grants, 79-83; First Prize, WCNY Invitational, PBS Sta, NY, 83; Golden Poet Award, World Poetry Press, 85 & 86. *Bibliog:* James Auer (auth), He draws plein-air, Milwaukee J, 74; article, Art enters the workplace, Glastonbury News, 4/84; George Zaiser (auth), Six from Syracuse, Skidmore News, 10/85. *Media:* Acrylic on Canvas, Watercolor. *Dealer:* Arlene McDaniel Gallery 10 Phelps Lane Simsbury CT 06070. *Mailing Add:* Art Dept Syracuse Univ Syracuse NY 13210

SICKMAN, JESSALEE BANE
PAINTER, INSTRUCTOR
b Denver, Colo, Aug 17, 05. *Study:* Univ Colo; Goucher Col; Corcoran Sch Art, Washington, DC; also with Richard Lahey & Eugen Weisz. *Work:* Corcoran Gallery Art. *Comn:* Portrait, comn by Mr Pach, Cleveland, Ohio, 51; Pigeons, comn by Mrs Bruton, Alexandria, Va, 55; Figure Study, comn by Mrs Woods, San Diego, Calif, 71; figure study & still life, comn by Mr & Mrs Ira Glackens, Shepherdstown, WVa. *Exhib:* One-man Watercolor Show, Pub Libr, Washington, DC, 42; Corcoran Gallery Art Biennial Exhibs, 42-50; Colony Club, Washington, DC, 58 & 62; Soc Washington Artists, Smithsonian Inst, 68 & Arts Club. *Teaching:* Instr still life, Warrentown Country Sch, Va, 40; instr life portrait, Corcoran Sch Art, 40-63; instr portrait & still life, Sickman Studios, Washington, DC, 64- *Awards:* Landscape Award, Corcoran Sch Art, 37; Alice Barney Mem Portrait Award, 38. *Mem:* Artists Equity Asn; Soc Washington Artists. *Media:* Oil. *Mailing Add:* 1115 Massachusetts Ave NW Washington DC 20005

SIDEN, FRANKLIN
DEALER, LECTURER
b Highland Park, Mich, Nov 16, 22. *Study:* Soc Arts & Crafts, 32-36; Meinzinger Art Sch, 40; Univ Ill, BS, 47; Wayne State Univ, MA(art hist), 77. *Pos:* Owner, Franklin Siden Gallery, Detroit, Mich, 64-72 & West Bloomfield, Mich, 72-82 & Bloomfield Hills, 82- *Teaching:* Lectr art, Bloomfield Birmingham Art Asn, 74 & 76-77; lectr art & collecting prints, Univ Courses in Adult Educ, 78-80 & Jewish Community Ctr, 81-82. *Bibliog:* Six Detroit dealers who are serving a growing art market, The Art Gallery, 66; Kick out the jams: Detroit's cass corridor 1963-1977, Detroit Inst Arts, 80. *Mem:* Fel Founders Soc, Detroit Inst Arts; Friends of Mod Art, Detroit Inst Arts; Mus Mod Art, New York; Cranbrook Acad Arts, Bloomfield Hills. *Specialty:* Contemporary paintings, drawings, sculptures and prints. *Mailing Add:* 3649 Quail Hollow Bloomfield Hills MI 48302

SIEBER, ROY
EDUCATOR, HISTORIAN
b Shawano, Wis, Apr 28, 23. *Study:* New Sch Social Res, BA, 49; Univ Iowa, MA, 51, PhD, 57. *Pos:* Mem foreign area fel prog, Africa Screening Comt, 59-63; cur primitive art, Ind Univ Fine Arts Mus, 62-; mem primitive art adv comt, Metrop Mus Art; mem joint comt Africa, Am Coun Learned Socs-Social Sci Res Coun, 62-70; trustee, Mus African Art. *Teaching:* From instr to asst prof art hist, Univ Iowa, 50-62; mem fac, Ind Univ, 62-64, prof art hist, 64-74, chmn fine arts dept, 67-70, Rudy Prof Fine Arts, 74-; vis prof, Univ Ghana, 64 & 67; vis prof, Univ Ife, Nigeria, 71; Benedict Distinguished Vis Prof, Carleton Col, 76-77. *Awards:* African-Am Univ Grant, 64; Ind Univ Int Studies Grant, 64 & 67; Nat Endowment for Humanities Sr Fel, 70-71 & 80-81; plus others. *Mem:* African Studies Asn; Col Art Asn Am; Am Asn Univ Prof; Midwest Art Asn (secy, 63). *Res:* African art. *Publ:* Auth, Sculpture of Northern Nigeria, Mus Primitive Art, NY, 61; co-auth, Sculpture of Black Africa, Los Angeles Co Mus Art, 68; auth, African Textiles & Decorative Arts, Mus Mod Art, NY, 72; auth, African Furniture and Household Objects, Am Fedn of Arts, 80. *Mailing Add:* Nat Mus African Art Smithsonian Inst Washington DC 20560

SIEBNER, HERBERT
MURALIST, PAINTER
b Stettin, Ger, Apr 16, 25; Can citizen. *Study:* Atelier Max Richter, Stettin, 41-43; Berlin Acad, under Carl Hofer, with Kaus & Schumacher, 46-49. *Work:* Seattle Art Mus; Confedn Art Mus, PEI; Nat Gallery Ottawa; City of West Berlin; Victoria Art Gallery. *Comn:* Sgraffito, Crown House, Victoria, BC, 60; sgraffito-encaustic, Univ Victoria, 65; planetary hist, Mus Victoria, 68; life-frieze, Govt BC, 75; opening the Weisenstein Foundation, Victoria, 92. *Exhib:* Int Graphic Expos, Lugano, Switz, 58, Lubljana, Yugoslavia, 59; Can Biennial, Ottawa, 58 & 62; Int Triennial of Xylographia, Carpy, Italy, 69; Int Graphic Exhib, Spain, 71, Italy, 72; retrospective show, Univ Victoria, 79, Victoria Art Gallery, 84 & City of Berlin, 86; Int Graphic Biennial, Lubljana, 89, 4 decades retrospective, Calgary, 91. *Teaching:* Vis prof painting, Univ Wash, 63 & Univ BC, 64, Univ Alta, 65; lectr painting, Univ Victoria, 67 & 69. *Awards:* Reid Award for Graphic, 56; Can Coun Sr Grant, 62; Guest of Hon, Berlin Acad, 63; Hon Citizen, City of Victoria, BC, 73; Can Coun Grant, 86. *Bibliog:* Anthony Emery (auth), Art of Herbert Siebner, Can Art Mag, 58; Robin Skelton (auth), The man & the vision, Malahat Rev, Univ BC, 71; Creative Canada, Univ Toronto, 72. *Mem:* Union Prof Artists, Ger; Can Group Painters; Soc BC Artists; Royal Can Acad; The Limners. *Media:* Sgraffito, Acrylic. *Publ:* Illusr, Inscriptions, 67 & Muse Book, 72; auth, Colour, Line & Form, 70; H Siebner, 25 years: Monograph, Univ Victoria, 79; 30 Years of BC Art, Victoria Art Gallery, 84; Human Landscape, Berlin, 86; Siebner Before Canada Retroex, Winchester Jal, Victoria, BC, 89 & Large Book: The Art of H Siebner, 92. *Mailing Add:* 270 Meadow Brook Rd Victoria BC V8X 3X3 Canada

SIEG, ROBERT LAWRENCE
SCULPTOR, EDUCATOR
b Cement, Okla, Aug 10, 38. *Study:* Cent State Univ, Okla, BA, 63; Inst Allende, Univ de Guanajuato, MFA, 68. *Work:* Ark Arts Ctr, Little Rock; Okla Art Ctr, Oklahoma City; Mus Art, Univ Okla, Norman; Okla Arts & Humanities Coun Collection, Oklahoma City. *Exhib:* Past Jurors Invitational, Okla Art Ctr, 69; Eight-State Exhib Painting & Sculpture, Okla Art Ctr, 73; Goddard Arts Ctr, Okla, 78; Inter-D Exhib, McAllen Int Mus, Tex; Midwest Biennial Joslyn Art Mus, Omaha, Nebr; Monroe Ann, Masur Mus Art, La; Delta Art Exhib, Ark Art Ctr; Werkstatt Menschen, Okla State Univ, 84. *Teaching:* Asst prof art, ECent Okla State Univ, 66-86, chmn art dept, 90- *Awards:* Sculpture Award, 15th Mid-Am, Nelson Gallery Art, Kansas City, 65; Inter-Am Craft Alliance Award, McAllen Int Mus, Tex, 70; Purchase Awards, Toys Designed by Artists, Ark Art Ctr, 74. *Bibliog:* B J Smith (auth), Features artist, Cimarron Rev, 4/73. *Media:* Wood, Metal. *Mailing Add:* 1017 E Central Blvd Ada OK 74820

SIEGEL, (LEO) DINK
ILLUSTRATOR, CARTOONIST
b Birmingham, Ala. *Study:* Nat Acad Design; Art Students League; Am Sch Art; also with Robert Brackman. *Mem:* Soc Illusr. *Media:* Watercolor, Ink. *Publ:* Illusr, Redbook, Cosmopolitan, Saturday Evening Post, Field & Stream Mag, Good Housekeeping, New Yorker & Playboy. *Mailing Add:* 100 W 57th St New York NY 10019

SIEGEL, FRAN
PAINTER
b Mar 10, 60. *Study:* Tyler Sch Art, Temple Univ, BFA(magna cum laude), 82; Yale Univ Sch Art, MFA, 87. *Exhib:* Solo shows, New Gallery, Houston, Tex, 84, 86, 87, 89 & 91, James Turcotte Gallery, Los Angeles, 84, Attack Gallery, 85 & Genovese Gallery, Boston, Mass, 92; Works on Paper, Yale Art & Architecture, New Haven, Conn, 85; Rex Wignall Mus, Alta Loona, Calif, 85; Emerging Artists, Westport Arts Coun, Conn, 86; Wright Gallery, Dallas, Tex, 86; The Drawing Show, Koslow Rayl Fine Art, Los Angeles, 88; Drawings by Ten, Univ Calif, San Diego, 88. *Teaching:* Instr, two-dimensional drawing, Yale Univ Sch Art, 87; adj lectr-drawing, Dowling Col, 88; two-dimensional design & color, Cooper Union; color theory, Parsons Sch Design, 90. *Awards:* First Prize, Bay Arts, 83; Harriet Wooley Scholarship, Found des Etats Unis, 87. *Bibliog:* Articles in Los Angeles Weekly, 11/83, Artlines, 10/84, Reader, 11/84, Artweek, 5/85 & Arts Mag, 3/85. *Mem:* Womens Action Coalition. *Media:* Oil on Aluminum. *Dealer:* Genovese Gallery Boston MA; New Gallery Houston TX. *Mailing Add:* 65 W Broadway New York NY 10007

SIEGESMUND, RICHARD
MUSEUM DIRECTOR
Study: Trinity Col, Hartford, Conn, BA, 73; Univ Hawaii, Manoa, Honolulu, Hawaii, grad study, 73-75; Fel Arts Mgt, Visual Arts Prog, Nat Endowment Arts, Washington, DC, 81. *Pos:* Dir, The Fabric Workshop, Philadelphia, Pa, 89-90, San Francisco Mus Mod Art, currently; consult, guest cur, guest lectr, & panelist for numerous programs. *Mem:* The Photo Rev (bd mem); Pyramid Atlantic (bd mem). *Mailing Add:* San Francisco Museum of Modern Art 401 Van Ness Ave San Francisco CA 94102

SIGALA, STEPHANIE CHILDS
LIBRARIAN, EDUCATOR
b Berkeley, Calif, Nov 1, 47. *Study:* Univ Calif, Los Angeles, BA, 68, MA, 70; Univ Ill, MLS, 84. *Pos:* Slide cur, Univ Wisc, Milwaukee, 73-74; Archit librn, Auburn Univ, 84-85; Head Librn, St Louis Art Mus, 85- *Teaching:* Instr art hist, Univ Wis, Whitewater, 71-73; asst prof, art hist, Ill State Univ, 78-83; adj prof libr sci, Univ Mo, 88- *Awards:* Kress Found Grant, 69; Fel, Univ Ill, 74-75. *Mem:* Art Libraries Soc of N Am (chapter pres, 88-90); Special Libraries Asn (chapter dir, 89-90); Am Library Asn. *Res:* Greek and Roman art; mus librarianship; history of the St Louis Art Mus. *Publ:* Auth, A Decade of Professional Literature for Slide Curators, VRA Bulletin, 85; auth, Exhibition Catalogs on Exchange, Art Documentation, 88; auth, Art of the Ancient World, St Louis Art Mus, 89; auth, The Museum Building: Inside and Out, St Louis Art Mus, 90; contribr, History of American Mass Market Magazines, Greenwood Press, 90. *Mailing Add:* St Louis Art Mus St Louis MO 63110

SIGISMUND, VIOLET M
PAINTER, PRINTMAKER
b New York, NY. *Study:* Art Students League; also with Sidney Laufman & George Grosz. *Comn:* Many portrait comns. *Exhib:* Butler Inst Am Art, Youngstown, Ohio, 62; print show, Albany Inst Arts, 71; print show, Washington Co Mus, Md, 71-73; print show, Cayuga Mus, 73; one-woman show, Paul Kessler, Provincetown, Mass, 73; Nat Asn Women Artists Traveling Group Oil Show, US, 75-77, Israel & Egypt, 81-82 & Traveling Group Print Show, 79-81; NY Nat Acad, Audubon; and others. *Awards:* Sargent Prize, Nat Asn Women Artists, 63; Provincetown Art Asn, 83; Pen & Brush, 91; and others. *Mem:* Knickerbocker Artists; Nat Asn Women Artists; Provincetown Art Asn; NY Artists' Equity Asn (chmn mem, 60-73, mem bd dirs, 81-82); Pen & Brush, NY. *Media:* Oil, Watercolor; Woodblock, Lithography. *Mailing Add:* One Sheridan Sq New York NY 10014

SIGLER, HOLLIS
PAINTER
b Gary, Ind, Mar 2, 48. *Study:* Moore Col Art, BFA, 70; Sch Art Inst Chicago, MFA, 73. *Work:* Mus Contemp Art, Chicago; Indianapolis Mus Art; Seattle Art Mus; Madison Art Ctr, Wis; Univ S Fla, Tampa. *Exhib:* 1981 Whitney Biennial, Whitney Mus Am Art, New York, 81; The Anxious Edge (with catalog) Walker Art Mus, Minneapolis, 82; Back to the USA Traveling Show, Bonn & Stuttgart, Ger, 83; Selection-Art Since 1945, Mus Mod Art, New York, 84; 39th Biennial, Corcoran Gallery Art, Washington, DC, 85; one-

woman shows, Akron Art Mus, 86, SW Craft Ctr, San Antonio, Tex, 89 & Nat Mus Women Arts, Washington, DC, 91, Printworks Gallery, Chicago, 91, Priebe Art Gallery, Univ Wisc, Oshkosh, 92, Susan Cummins Gallery, Mill Valley, Calif, 92, Interiors, Steven Scott Gallery, Baltimore, Md, 92; The Edge of Childhood, Hechsher Mus, Huntington, NY, 92; In Celebration of Women: An Exhibit of Outstanding Women Artists in Ill, 92; Face to Face: Self Portraits by Chicago Artists, David Adler Cult Ctr, Libertyville, Ill, 92. *Teaching:* Instr painting & drawing, Columbia Col, Chicago, 84-; faculty, Columbia Col, Chicago, Ill, 78- *Awards:* Anne Louis Raymond Traveling Fel, Sch Avt Inst of Chicago, 73; First Prize for Watercolor, Union League Club of Chicago, Ill, 76; Golden Heritage Award, Rocky Mountain Nat Watermedia Exhib, Foothills Art Ctr, Golden, Colo, 77; Emilie L Wild Prize for Painting, The Art Inst of Chicago, Ill, 80; Individual Artist Grant & Chmn's Grant, Ill Arts Coun, 86; Cash award, Southeastern Ctr for Contemp Art, Winston-Salem, NC, 87; Visual Fel Grant, Nat Endowment for Arts, 87. *Bibliog:* Joanne Freuh (auth), Hollis Sigler, Arts Mag, 80; Lynn Blummenthal & Kate Horsefield (coauths), Profile: Hollis Sigler, Sch Art Inst, 83; Joanna French (auth), exposures: Women and their Art, Raven Brown, New Sage Press, 89; article, Art Am Mag, 90. *Media:* Oil on Canvas. *Publ:* Illusr, Room with a view-and no people, New York Times, 85; Corners of the mouth, Ridescience, 85; Mothermania, 86; A Cloud On Sand (cover), Roman Borgen, 91. *Dealer:* Dart Gallery 750 N Orleans Chicago IL 60610; Printworks Gallery 311 W Superior Chicago IL 60610. *Mailing Add:* 22663 N Prairie Rd Prairie View IL 60069

SILBER, MAURICE
PAINTER, ILLUSTRATOR
b Brooklyn, NY, Apr 12, 22. *Study:* Cooper Union; Art Students League; Empire State Col, Saratoga Springs, NY, 80; Pratt Inst, indust design with Donald Dohner; study with Ed Whitney, Robert E Wood, Tom Hill & John Pike; New York Univ, MA, 83. *Work:* USAF Art Collection & USN Combat Art Collection, Washington, DC; Nat Park Serv, Washington, DC; Marine Mus, Amagansett, NY; Allianca Francaise, Costa Rica; Teatro Nacional, Costa Rica. *Comn:* Philadelphia Naval Shipyard, NACAL Assignment, 72-74 & 80; Eglin AFB, USAF, Fla, 72; San Antonio, Tex, USAF, 73; US Dept Interior, Nat Park Serv, 75; USAF NORAD & USAF Acad, Colorado Springs, 76. *Exhib:* Salmagundi Club, New York, 71-83; Guild Hall East Hampton, New York, 87; Teatro Nacional, San Jose, Costa Rica, 77-83; Knickerbocker Artists Ann, 78-83 & 88; Gallery 80, New York Univ, 83; St Johns Univ, 83; Society of Illustrators, 90; American Merchant Marine Mus, 90. *Teaching:* Watercolor, Queensborough, Community Col; Univ Costa Rica, San Jose. *Awards:* First Prize & Spec Award, Am Inst, Westinghouse, New York World's Fair, 39; Anco Award, Knickerbocker Artists, 79; and others; Watercolor Award, Knickerbocker Artists Ann, 88; Graphic Watercolor & Watercolor Awards, Salamagundi Club, New York, 88. *Bibliog:* Air Force Art, Bolling Beam, Morkap Pub Co, 10/73; Air Force Art, Seacoast Flyer, Star Press, Maine, 9/74; AFSA, US Air Force, Impressions at Eglin, 12/74. *Mem:* Salmagundi Club (chmn admis, 72-74); Soc Illusrs; Artists Equity of New York; Knickerbocker Artists of NY; Art League Nassau County; Am Soc Marine Artists. *Media:* All Media. *Publ:* Auth & illusr, The Water Color Page, Am Artist, 6/72. *Mailing Add:* 183-07 69th Ave Fresh Meadows NY 11365

SILBERMAN, ARTHUR
LIBRARY DIRECTOR, WRITER
b Antwerp, Belg, Jan 8, 29; US citizen. *Collections Arranged:* From Pictographs to Jerome Tiger Traveling Educ Exhib, 68-72; American Indian Painting Traveling Educ Exhib, 72-75; 100 Years Native American Painting (auth, catalog), 78, Okla Mus Art, Oklahoma City; The Legacy, Governor's Gallery, Okla State Capitol, 87; Charles W Hogan Mem Exhib, Goddart Ctr, Ardmore, Okla, 91; Beyond the Prison Gates, travelling exhib, 92-93. *Pos:* Dir, Native Am Painting Ref Libr, Oklahoma City, 75-; hon cur, Native Am Painting, Okla Hist Soc Mus, Oklahoma City, 76-78; guest cur, Okla Mus Art, Oklahoma City, 78; consult, Okla TV Authority, 78, WABC-TV, New York, 79, Am Indian Inst, Univ Okla, Norman, 80, Mus Am Indian, New York, 81, Ctr of Am Indian, Oklahoma City & Philbrook Art Ctr, Tulsa, 85- *Teaching:* Adj fac Native Am art hist, Oklahoma City Univ, 88- *Awards:* Oklahoma City Univ Distinguished Native Am Arts Award, 81; Govs Spec Recognition Award, 88. *Res:* All phases of history and development of Native American painting. *Interests:* To increase the appreciation of Native American painting by making reference material available to educators, writers, publishers and museums; to increase public awareness through lectures, media presentations, publications and exhibits. *Publ:* Auth, Tiger, 71 & Early Kiowa Art, 73, Okla Today Mag; 100 Years of Native American Painting, Okla Mus Art, Oklahoma City, 78; Making Medicine, Ledger Drawing Art from Fort Marion, Ct of the Am Indian, Oklahoma City, 84; Animals in Indian Art (sound slides), Native Am Painting Ref Libr, 86; A Selection of Native American Art, Tamaqua, 91. *Mailing Add:* 8912 Sheringham Dr Oklahoma City OK 73132

SILBERSTEIN-STORFER, MURIEL ROSOFF
ART EDUCATOR, INSTRUCTOR
b Brooklyn, NY. *Study:* Carnegie Inst Technol, BFA; Philadelphia Mus Art, with Hobson Pitman; Inst Mod Art, with Victor D'Amico, Donald Stacy & Jane Bland. *Comn:* Prog drawings, Philadelphia Symphony Orch Children's Concerts, 49; murals & other projs, Mt Sinai Hosp & Philadelphia Psychiat Hosp. *Exhib:* Jewish Community Ctr Group Show, 71-72; one-woman shows, Panoras Gallery, New York, 72, Pacem in Terris Gallery, New York, 75 & Gallery 84, 78 & 83; Pacem in Terris Gallery, New York, 76-77. *Pos:* Assoc tech dir & scene designer, Pittsburgh Playhouse, 44-46; interior display designer, var Pittsburgh Dept Stores, 46-47; art educ consult, Staten Island Ment Health Schs, Head Start, Staten Island Community Col Mus Mod Art, The Met Mus Art & others; founder & creative dir, Doing Art Together, Inc, 82; art ed adv bd, Art Table & Binney Smith Inc. *Teaching:* Instr, Inst Mod Art, Mus Mod Art, New York, 63-70, Int Playgroups Art Workshops, New York, 70-71, Staten Island Community Col, 70-71, Metrop Mus Art, 72-; guest lectr art educ, var cols & community education groups, New York, 67- *Awards:* Woman of Achievement, Staten Island Advan, 67; Art Commission Service Award, Mayor of New York, 85; Arts Partnership Award, SI Counc Arts, 89. *Bibliog:* The Museologist, Vol 47, No 169, winter 85; New York Mag, 1/88; Art News, Vol 88, No 6, summer 89. *Mem:* New York Art Comn (comnr, 70-85); Metrop Mus Art (trustee, 71-77 & emer trustee, 77-); Assoc Art Comn City New York (vpres, currently); Snug Harbor Cult Ctr (trustee 76-87). *Media:* Assemblage, Collage. *Res:* Art education; community arts projects. *Publ:* Auth, pamphlet for parent-child workshops, Metrop Mus Art, New York; Doing Art Together, Simon & Schuster, 82. *Mailing Add:* 1200 Broadway New York NY 10001

SILER, PATRICK W
PAINTER, CERAMIST
b Spokane, Wash, 1939. *Study:* Wash State Univ, Pullman, BA, 61; Univ Calif, Berkeley, MA(painting), 63. *Work:* Johnson's Wax, Racine, Wis; Utah Mus Fine Arts, Salt Lake City; Cranbrook Inst, Bloomfield Hills, Mich. *Exhib:* Solo exhibs, Leedy Voulkos Gallery, Kansas City, Mo, 90, Southwest Craft Ctr, San Antonio, Tex, 90, Spokane Falls Community Col, Wash, 90, Whatcom Mus, Bellingham, Wash, 91, Univ Puget Sound, Tacoma, Wash, 91, Bemis Found Alternative Worksite, Omaha, Nebr, 92; Wash State Univ Mus Art, 91; Sybaris Gallery, Royal Oak, Mich, 91; Moira-James Gallery, Las Vegas, 91; Ceramic Show cur by Dean Moniz, Jennifer Pauls Gallery, 92. *Teaching:* Artist-in-residence & instr, Univ SDak, Vermillion, 68; instr ceramics, Univ Calif, Berkeley, 71; assoc prof found drawing & ceramics, Wash State Univ, Pullman, 73- *Awards:* Fel, Wash State Arts Comn, 86; Residency Award, Alternative Workspace, Omaha, Nebr, 86-87; Ceramic Sculpture Fel, Nat Endowment Arts, 90. *Bibliog:* Feature article, Ceramics Monthly Mag, 90; article, Craft Arts Int Mag, Sydney, Australia, 91; Kippy Stroud (auth), An Industrious Art, 92. *Mailing Add:* 325 NW Dillon St Pullman WA 99163

SILER, TODD (LAEL)
PAINTER, SCULPTOR
b Long Island, NY, Aug 21, 53. *Study:* Smith Col, with Leonard Baskin, 73-74; Bowdoin Col, BA(cum laude), 75; Mass Inst Technol, MS(visual studies), 81, PhD(intedisciplinary studies in psychol & art), 86. *Work:* The Solomon R Guggenheim Mus; Denver Art Mus; Whitehead Inst Biomed Res; and pvt collections of Otto Plene, Keitero Takagi, Drs Herbert & Gabrielle Kayden, Jack Nash, Lynn Epsteen, Robert & Maryse Boxer, Jean Charles Lignel, Stewart & Judy Colton, Ronald & Frayda Feldman & Jack Ronick; Metrop Mus Art, Mus Mod Art, Pushkin Mus Moscow. *Comn:* Sculpture, Alvin I Schragis, New York City, 88. *Exhib:* Reality of Illusion, Denver Art Mus & traveling, 79-81; Schemes: A Decade of Installation Drawings, Mus D'Art Contemp, Montreal & traveling, 81; Revolutions Per Minute (The Art Record), Ronald Feldman Fine Arts, Tate Gallery, Documenta, Germany & Biennale De Paris, 82; Alea(s), Mus D'Art Mod, Paris, 82; The New Culture, Ctr Peace Through Cult, Toronto, 83; The Year One: 1984-2001, Chrysler Mus, Norfolk Mus, Va, 84; Brainworks, Munic Art Gallery, Los Angeles, 85; Sao Paulo Bienal, Sao Paulo, Brazil, 85; Light: Perception-Projection, Ctr Int D'Art Contemp de Montreal, 86; solo exhib Inquiries Into the Biomirror, 81 & Thoughts/Thought Assemblies, 83, Ronald Feldman Fine Arts, New York, Cerebral Forms, Grey Art Gallery, New York Uni, 85, Psi- Phi: The Hidden Territory, Ronald Feldman Fine Arts, 87, The Art of Thought, Saidye Bronfman Ctr, Montreal, 87, & Metaphorms: Forms of Metaphor, The New York Academy of Sci, New York, 88. *Pos:* Res fel, Ctr Adv Visual Studies, 81-; co-pres & consult, United Sciences & Arts, 83-; Res Affil, Computer-Aided Design Lab, Dept Mech Eng, Mass Inst Technol, 86-91. *Teaching:* Instr visual design, Mass Inst Technol, 82-83. *Awards:* IBM Thomas J Watson Fel to Paris, IBM, 75-76; Fulbright Fel to India, 85-86; Mass Artists Found Fel in Painting, 87; Meitec Fel, Nagoya, Japan, 89. *Bibliog:* Martha Fleming (auth), Todd Siler, Galerie France Morin, Vanguard Mag, 12/81-1/82; Michael Schrage (auth), Cerebreactors, Omni Mag, 10/82; Ellen Handy (auth), article, Arts Mag, 11/83; Marguerite Feilowitz (auth), Where art and medicine meet, MD Publ, 2/85; Patricia Phillips (auth), Todd Siler at Ronald Feldman Gallery, Artforum, 5/87; Phillip Evans-Clark (auth), Todd Siler, Ronald Feldman Gallery, Tema Celeste, 5/87. *Media:* All. *Publ:* Cerebreactors, 81, The Biomirror, 83, Ronald Feldman Fine Arts, NY; Neurocosmology, In Leonardo Journal, Vol 18, No 1, 85; The Art of Thought Centre Saidye Bronfman, Montreal, 87; Metaphorms: Forms of Metaphor The New York Academy Sci, 88; Breaking the Mind Barrier, New York, Simon & Schuster, 90. *Dealer:* Ronald Feldman Fine Arts Inc 31 Mercer St New York NY 10013. *Mailing Add:* c/o Ronald Feldman Fine Arts 31 Mercer St New York NY 10013

SILKOTCH, MARY ELLEN
PAINTER
b New York, NY, Sept 12, 11. *Study:* Van Emburgh Sch Art; also with Jonas Lie, Sigismund Ivanowski & Dudley Lloyne Summers. *Work:* In pvt collections. *Exhib:* Nat Asn Women Artists; Montclair Art Mus, NJ; Am Artists Prof League; Atlantic City Art Ctr; Irvington Mus & Art Asn; and others. *Pos:* Vpres, Trailside Mus Arts Ctr, NJ, 66-67; vpres, Academic Artists, 67-69. *Teaching:* Instr art, Van Emburgh Sch, Plainfield, 44-64; instr art, Adult Educ, Dunellen, NJ, 48-57; instr art, Bound Brook Adult Educ, 50-57; instr art, North Plainfield, 51-54. *Awards:* Prizes, Am Artists Prof League, Plainfield Art Asn & East Orange, NJ; and others. *Mem:* Nat Asn

Women Artists; Am Artist Prof League (pres, NJ chap, 69-71); Artists Equity Asn. *Media:* Acrylic, Oil. *Dealer:* Jaro Art Gallery 955 Madison Ave New York NY 10021. *Mailing Add:* 60780 Coyote Canyon Box 237C Star Rte 1 Anza CA 92539

SILL, GERTRUDE GRACE
EDUCATOR, CURATOR
b New York, NY. *Study:* Smith Col, with Oliver Larkin, BA, 48; Wesleyan Univ, with Samuel Greene & Richard Field, MA, 78. *Collections Arranged:* George Cope 1863-1933 (auth, catalog), Brandywine River Mus, 78; George Brainerd Burr-Old Lyme Impressionist (with catalog), 84; John Haberle, Master of Illusion (auth, catalog), Mus Fine Arts, Springfield, Mass, 85-86; Realism and Romanticism in 19th Century New England Seascapes, Whitney Mus Am Art, Stamford, Conn, 89. *Pos:* Writer & art critic, Connoisseur, Antiques, Portfolio and others, 68-; art critic, Bridgeport Post Telegram, 86- *Teaching:* Lectr & consult, Metrop Mus Art, New York, 75-78; lectr, Southern Conn State Univ, New Haven, 80-81, Whitney Mus Am Art, 89, New Brit Mus Am Art, 89, Yale Univ, 89, Mus Fine Art, Houston, Tex, 90, Smith Col Sem, 91, Mus Fine Arts, Boston, Mass, 91, Portland Mus Art, Maine, 92 & Col Art Asn, 93; lectr, introd, American art, impressionism, Fairfield Univ, Conn, 76- *Awards:* Nat Endowment Humanities Grant, 78; Nat Endowment Arts Grant, 85 & 86. *Mem:* Col Art Asn; Archives Am Art; Asn Am Art Historians; PEN. *Res:* John Haberle (1853-1933) for book in progress. *Collection:* 19th century american still-life and landscape paintings. *Publ:* Auth, Handbook of Symbols in Christian Art, Macmillan, 75; George Cope, West Chester's Home Painter, Brandywine River Mus, 78; essay on Francis, Haberle, Hanet etc, Dictionary of Art, 89; John Haberle: Master of Illusion, Mus Fine Arts, Springfield, Mass; Realism and Romanticism in 19th Century New England Seascapes, (exhib catalog), Whitney Mus Am Art, 89. *Mailing Add:* 46 Willow St Southport CT 06490

SILLS, THOMAS ALBERT
PAINTER
b Castalia, NC, Aug 20, 14. *Work:* Whitney Mus Am Art, Metrop Mus Art, Mus Mod Art & Chase Manhattan Collection, New York; Sheldon Mem Gallery, Lincoln, Nebr; and many others. *Exhib:* Wilson Col, Chambersberg, Pa, 68; Student Ctr Art Gallery, Brooklyn Col, NY, 69; New American Painting & Sculpture, The First Generation, Mus Mod Art, New York, 69; Afro-Am Artists Exhib, Mus Philadelphia Civic Ctr, Pa, 69; Mt Holyoke Col, South Hadley, Mass, 69; and other group & one-man exhibs. *Awards:* William & Norma Copley Found Award, 57. *Media:* All. *Mailing Add:* 240 W 11th St New York NY 10014

SILVA, ERNEST
PAINTER, SCULPTOR
b Providence, RI, Dec 11, 48. *Study:* Univ RI, BFA, 71; Tyler Sch Art, Temple Univ, MFA, 74. *Work:* Fogg Art Mus, Cambridge, Mass; San Diego Mus Contemp Art, La Jolla, Calif; Laguna Mus Art, Calif; Grand Rapids Art Mus, Mich; de Saisset Mus, Santa Clara, Calif; Newport Harbor Art Mus, Newport Beach, Calif. *Exhib:* Solo exhibs, Inst Contemp Art, Boston, Mass, 72, Artist's Space, New York, 75, Roy Boyd Gallery, Chicago, 82-84 & 87, Vanderwoude Tananbaum Gallery, NY, 86, Dietrich Jenny Gallery, San Diego, 89, Jan Baum Gallery, Los Angeles, 89 & 91 & Lenore Gray Gallery, Providence, RI, 92; Corcoran Art Gallery, Washington, DC, 75,; La Jolla Mus Contemp Art, Calif, 86; Nancy Lurie Gallery, Chicago, 88; De Saisset Mus, Santa Clara, Calif, 88; Laguna Beach Mus Art, Calif, 90; Mia Gallery, Seattle, 90; and many others. *Teaching:* Instr painting, Univ RI, Kingston, 77-79; assoc prof, painting & sculpture, Univ Calif, San Diego, 79- *Awards:* Nat Endowment for the Arts, Visual Artists Fel, 89-90. *Bibliog:* Susan Larsen (auth), Los Angeles-Ernest Silva, Artnews, 2/83; Ellen Lee Klein (auth), New York-Ernest Silva, Arts Mag, 4/84; Suvan Geer (auth), Ernest Silva, Los Angeles Times, 2/5/89; Leah Ollman (auth), Los Angeles Times, 9/22/89. *Dealer:* Jan Baum Gallery Los Angeles CA. *Mailing Add:* Visual Arts Dept Univ Calif San Diego La Jolla CA 92093

SILVER, LARRY ARNOLD
CURATOR, HISTORIAN
b Los Angeles, Calif, Oct 14, 47. *Study:* Univ Chicago, BA, 69; Harvard Univ, MA, 71, PhD, 74. *Pos:* Vis cur, St Louis Art Mus, 81-82; vis res cur, Art Inst Chicago, 81-84; vis cur, Block Gallery, Northwestern Univ, 89- *Teaching:* Asst prof Medieval & Renaissance art, Univ Calif, Berkeley, 74-79; prof Medieval, Renaissance & Baroque art & chmn dept, Northwestern Univ, 79- *Awards:* Porter Prize, Col Art Asn, 75; Col Art Asn. *Mem:* Renaissance Soc Am; Soc Values in Higher Educ; Col Art Asn (vpres, 90-92, pres, 92-). *Res:* Painting and graphics in northern Europe, 15th and 16th century. *Publ:* Coauth, Flemish Dutch Paintings (catalog), Ringling Mus, 80; auth, Early Northern European Paintings (catalog), St Louis Art Mus, 82; Forest primeval: Albrecht Altdorfer and --- landscape, Simiolus, 83; The Paintings of Quinten Massys, 84; Rembrandt, 92; and others. *Mailing Add:* Dept Art Hist 254 Kresge Hall Northwestern Univ Evanston IL 60208

SILVER, RAWLEY A
EDUCATOR, PAINTER
b New York, NY. *Study:* Cornell Univ, BA, 39; Art Students League, with George Grosz, 48, 50; Columbia Univ, MA(fine arts educ), 64, EdD(fine arts educ), 66. *Exhib:* Mamaroneck Artists Guild Ann, NY, 55-; Hudson River Mus Invitational, Yonkers, NY, 76; solo invitational, Women's Resource Ctr, Sarasota, Fla, 92. *Collections Arranged:* Shout in Silence (auth, catalog), 69-77 & Art as Language (auth, catalog), 79-82, Smithsonian Inst Traveling Exhib. *Teaching:* Instr art, 61-73; adj assoc res prof art therapy, Col New Rochelle Grad Sch, 74-81. *Awards:* Biennial Award Res, Am Art Therapy Asn, 76 & 80; Res Grants, US Off Educ, Nat Inst Educ & NY State Dept Educ. *Bibliog:* Kristen Vilstrup (auth), rev, Am J Art Therapy, Vol 22, No 2, 83; Ellen G Horovitz (auth), rev, Art Therapy, Vol 2, No 1, 85; Marcia L Rosal (auth), rev, Art Therapy, fall 90. *Mem:* Hon life mem Am Art Therapy Asn; Nat Asn Women Artists; Mamaroneck Artists Guild; Hon life mem Art Therapy Asn Fla. *Media:* Watercolor, Oils. *Res:* Developing and assessing cognitive skills and adjustment nonverbally through drawing; assessing gender & age differences. *Publ:* Auth, Developing Cognitive and Creative Skills Through Art, Univ Park Press, 78, rev ed, 86, Albin Press, 89; Stimulus Drawings and Techniques in Therapy, Development, and Assessment, Albin Press, 82, rev ed 89; Silver Drawing Test of Cognitive and Creative Skills, Spec Child Publ, 83, rev ed Albin Press, 90; Draw-A-Story: Screening for Depression & Emotional Needs, Albin Press, 88; coauth (with Felix Carrion), Using the silver drawing test in schools and hospitals, Am J Art Therapy, vol 30, 11/91; Gender differences in drawings: a study of self-images, autonomous subjects & relationships, Art Therapy, 9/92; and others. *Mailing Add:* 3332 Hadfield Greene Sarasota FL 34235

SILVER, SHELLY ANDREA
VIDEO ARTIST, FILMMAKER
b Manhattan, NY, July 16, 57. *Study:* Cornell Univ, Col Arts & Sci, BA, 79, Col Art & Archit, BFA, 79; Whitney Mus Am Art Independent Studio Prog, 80-81. *Work:* Mus d'Arte Moderne Centre Georges Pompidou, Paris, France; Long Beach Mus Art, Los Angeles, Calif. *Exhib:* Fake, The New Mus, New York, 87; Television for Real, Halle Sud, Geneva, Switz, 88; D & S, Kunstverein in Hamburg, Ger, 89; Images of American Pop Culture, Laforet Art Mus, Tokyo, Japan, 89; Talking Heads, Int Ctr Photog, New York, 89; It's Evening in America, Gulbenkian Found, Lisbon, Port, 89; Video Poetics, Long Beach Mus Art, Los Angeles, Calif, 90; Tendance Multiples, Centre Georges Pompidou, Paris, France, 90. *Awards:* NY State Coun on the Arts Grant, 87 & 89; Nat Endowment Arts Fel, 89; Checkerboard Found Grant, 90. *Mem:* Media Alliance; Asn of Independent Video and Filmmakers. *Dealer:* EAI 536 Broadway New York NY; Video Data Bank 37 S Wabash 10th Floor Chicago IL 60603. *Mailing Add:* 22 Catherine St #6 New York NY 10038

SILVERBERG, ELLEN RUTH
PAINTER, ART DEALER
b New York, NY, Mar 7, 47. *Study:* Art Students League; Cooper Union, BFA, 67. *Pos:* Dir, Art Gallery Studio 53 Ltd, New York, 73- *Specialty:* Contemporary limited edition graphics and oils, specializing in Miro, Delacroix, Rockwell, Chagall, Gorman, Wyeth, Matisse, Tobiasse, Alvar & Haring. *Mailing Add:* c/o Studio 53 424 Park Ave New York NY 10022

SILVERBERG, JUNE ROSELYN
PAINTER
b Brooklyn, NY. *Study:* Brooklyn Col, BA, 56; Yale Univ, with Joseph Albers, 56-57; Art Students League, Pratt Inst, MS, 69. *Work:* Arthur Andersen Corp Collection, Minneapolis, Minn; Bryn Mawr Col Libr Collection, Pa; Art Students League, New York. *Exhib:* Mimes & Minatures, BACA's Downtown Cult Ctr, Brooklyn, NY, 84; Ninth Ann Small Works, 80 Wash Sq E Galleries, 85, Audubon Artists Nat Exhib, Nat Arts Club, New York, 91 & 92; Am Drawing Biennial II, Muscarelle Mus Art, Williamsburg, Va, 90; Works on Paper, QCC Art Gallery City Univ New York, Bayside, 90; Int Exhib Miniature & Small Format Art, Metro Toronto Conv Ctr & Del Bello Gallery, Can, 90 & 91. *Awards:* Premier Prix, Salon du Portrait de Montreal, 91. *Mem:* Audubon Artists; life mem, Art Students League NY. *Media:* Oil, Oil Pastels. *Dealer:* Bowery Gallery 121 Wooster St New York NY 10012. *Mailing Add:* Rm 1205, 32 Union Sq New York NY 10003

SILVERMAN, BURTON PHILIP
PAINTER, ILLUSTRATOR
b Brooklyn, NY, June 11, 28. *Study:* Pratt Inst; Art Students League, 46-49; Columbia Univ, BA, 49. *Work:* Brooklyn Mus, NY; Philadelphia Mus Art; Butler Inst Am Art, Youngstown, Ohio; Nat Mus Am Art, Nat Portrait Gallery, Washington, DC; Parrish Mus Art, Southampton, NY. *Comn:* Portrait, Paul Moore, Jr, Episcopal Bishop of New York; portrait, Joseph Flom, Sr Partner of Skadden, ARPS, Meagher & Flom. *Exhib:* Pa Acad Art Ann, Philadelphia, 49; Butler Inst Am Art Ann, Ohio, 54-70, 71, 74, 76, 79, 82, 86, 90 & 92; Nat Acad Design Ann, New York, 59-92; Pa State State Mus of Art, 76; Portsmouth Mus of Art, WVa, 76, 78, 80 & 82; Am Watercolor Soc Ann, New York, 78-91; Artists of America, Colo Hist Soc, Denver, 81, 82, 86, 87, 90 & 92. *Teaching:* Instr drawing & painting, Sch Visual Arts, New York, 64-67; lectr & workshops, Nat Acad Design, New York, 90- *Awards:* Henry W Ranger Purchase Prize, 65 & 83, Benjamin Altman Figure Prize, 69 & Isidor Gold Medal, 92, Nat Acad Design, New York; Purchase Prize, Am Drawings II & IV, Portsmouth, WVa, 79 & 83; Gold Medal, 79 & Silver Medal, 84, Am Watercolor Soc; Hall of Fame, Soc Illusrs, New York. *Bibliog:* Fredrick Whitaker (auth), Four realists, 10/64, Elizabeth Case (auth), Burton Silverman captures the moment, 6/71 & Pat Van Gelder (auth), Drawing the human figure, an interview with Burt Silverman, 7/81, Am Artist Mag; and others. *Mem:* Am Watercolor Soc; academician, Nat Acad Design. *Media:* Oils, Watercolors. *Publ:* Auth, Homage to Thomas Eakins, 67 & Art for Pablo Picasso's Sake, 68, Book World; A Portfolio of Drawings, 68; Painting People, 77 & Breaking the Rules of Watercolor, 83, Watson-Guptill; Realism rediscovered, Artist's Mag, 90; and others. *Dealer:* Joseph Keifer Gallery 28 E 72 St New York NY 10021; Capricorn Galleries 4849 Rugby Ave Bethesda MD 20014. *Mailing Add:* 324 W 71st St New York NY 10023

SILVERMAN, JOY
ADMINISTRATOR
Study: George Wash Univ, BA, 75; Mus Mgt Inst, summer, 83. *Exhib:* Nat Arts Emergency (co-prodr & ed); State of the Art-Art of the State? (asst prodr). *Pos:* Learning ctr coordr, Smithsonian Inst, Div Performing Arts, Nat Am Prog, 75-76; asst dir, Wash proj Arts, 80-83; exec dir, Los Angeles Contemp Exhibs, 83; co-founder & dir, Nat Campaign for Freedom of Expression, 90-91; contrib ed, Artforum, 90- *Awards:* Outstanding Young Woman Year, 84; Fel Art Matters Inc, 90. *Mem:* Fel, Nat Endowment Arts, 78; Elizabeth Straub Ringside Inc & Nat Campaign; mem steering comt, New Music Am Festival, 83-85, Nat Asn Artists Orgn, 83-85 & New Music LA Festival, 86-87, Visual AIDS; adv comt, J Paul Getty Fund Visual Arts, 87-88 & Los Angeles Cultural Master Plan; bd mem, Nat Campaign Freedom of Expression. *Mailing Add:* 450 W 24th No 12E New York NY 10011

SILVERMAN, LANNY HARRIS
DIRECTOR, CURATOR
b Philadelphia, Pa, Oct 16, 47. *Study:* Case Western Reserve Univ, BA, 69. *Collections Arranged:* Magic: Artist as Alchemist (auth, catalog), 86; Didier Nolet: Dreams of a Man Awake, 90; Sowers of Myth (catalog), 91; Michiiko Itatani: Paintings Since 1984 (interview, catalog), 92. *Pos:* Educ asst, Akron Art Mus, 80-81; cur educ & pub prog, Madison Art Ctr, Wis, 81-84; dir, NAME Gallery, Chicago, 85-87; asst dir, Evanston Art Ctr, 87-89; cur, Chicago Cult Ctr, 89- *Teaching:* Instr art, poetry & performance, Cleveland Mus Art, 74-78. *Bibliog:* Barbara Newsom & Adele Silver (ed), The Museum as Educator, Univ Calif Press, 78. *Specialty:* Experimental art; mixed media; installations; performance art; new music. *Mailing Add:* Dept Cult Affairs Visual Arts Dept 78 E Washington 4th Floor Chicago IL 60602

SILVERMAN, RONALD H
EDUCATOR, WRITER
b Cleveland, Ohio, Aug 2, 26. *Study:* Univ Calif, Los Angeles, BA, 52; Los Angeles State Col, MA, 55; Stanford Univ, EdD, 62. *Pos:* Consult, Nat Assessment Educ Progress Art; assoc dir, Getty Inst Educators Visual Arts. *Teaching:* Prof emer art, Calif State Univ, Los Angeles, 55-88. *Awards:* Outstanding Prof Award, Calif State Univ, Los Angeles, 78; Award, Nat Art Educ Asn, 81; Distingued Fel, Nat Art Educ Asn, 91. *Mem:* Life mem, Nat Art Educ Asn; Calif Art Educ Asn. *Publ:* Auth, Spectrum of Music, Macmillan, 74; Goals and roles in art education of children, In: The Arts, Human Development and Education, McCutchan, 76; A comprehensive model for teaching art, In: Report of the NAEA Commission on Art Education, Nat Art Educ Asn, 77; ed, Art, Education and the World of Work, Nat Art Educ Asn, 80; The egalitarianism of discipline-based art education, Art Educ, 3/88. *Mailing Add:* Art Dept Calif State Univ Los Angeles CA 90032

SILVERMAN, SHERLEY C
PAINTER, SCULPTOR
b Maywood, Ill, Jan 20, 09. *Study:* Univ Ill; Chicago Acad Fine Arts; Frederick Grant; worked in Pietrasanta, Italy, 63-65; also with John Kearney & Ralph Bormacher. *Work:* B'nai B'rith Exhib Hall, Washington, DC; also in many nat & int collections, as well as in numerous pvt collections, notably that of Mr & Mrs Harold Green, Palm Springs, Calif. *Comn:* Welded steel sculpture, comn by Hon Philip Klutznick; Ode to Eleanor (painting), comn by Mrs Nelson Hartstone, Palm Beach; Mother & Child, comn by Mr & Mrs Richard Tucker. *Exhib:* Patronat Premi Int, DiBuix Joan Miro, Barcelona, Spain; UNESCO; Int Biennale Della Regioni, Italy; Tournoi Int Des Beaux Arts, France; Int Contemp Exhib, Rome, Italy; among many others. *Pos:* Hon past pres, Mid-Am Art Asn, Chicago, 68-70. *Teaching:* Pvt art classes, 60- *Awards:* Gold Medal of Recognition & Bronze Plaque, La Scala Gallery, Florence, Italy; Int Medal of Honor, Int Centro Studi E Scambi; Honoris Causa Silver Medal, Acad Int, Tommaso, Campanella. *Mem:* US Commite Int Centro Studi E Scambi; Int Arts Guild (comdr); Acad Int Leonardo Da Vinci; Acad Int, Tommaso, Campanella. *Media:* Acrylic, Oil; Welded Metal. *Mailing Add:* 9929 SW 16th St Quincy Park Pembroke Pines FL 33024

SILVERSTEIN, IDA
PAINTER
b New York, NY. *Study:* New Sch Social Res, 61; Art Student League, 62-65, Scholar, 67; Contemp Sch Painting, 81. *Exhib:* Allied Artists, New York, 64-67; Audubon Artists, New York, 66-67 & 71; Am Acad Arts & Letters, New York, 69; Painters & Sculptors Soc, NJ, 69-70; Butler Inst Am Art, Ohio, 73. *Awards:* Nat Asn Women Artist Award, 74; Nat Soc Contemp Artist Award, 75. *Mem:* Nat Asn Women Artists; Am Soc Contemp Artists. *Media:* Acrylic. *Dealer:* Jain Gallery 979 Third Ave New York NY 10022. *Mailing Add:* 2 Fifth Ave New York NY 10011

SILVERTOOTH, DENNIS CARL
SCULPTOR
b Killeen, Tex, Aug 20, 57. *Study:* Corpus Christi Community Art Ctr, with Maurice Schmidt & Ann Armstrong, 74. *Exhib:* American Cowboy: Fact & Fiction, Eastman Kodak, New York, 75; Tex Art Classic, Tarrant Co Convention Ctr, Ft Worth, 76-79; Shidoni Summer Sculpture Show, Shidoni Foundry & Gallery, Santa Fe, NMex, 77-81; Philbrook Presents Sculpture, Philbrook Mus, Tulsa, Okla, 78; Midland Col Sculpture Show, Tex, 78-81; and others. *Awards:* Best Sculpture, Art About Town, Dallas Crippled Childrens Soc, 77; Best Sculpture, 34th Ann American Indian Artist Exhib, Philbrook Mus, Okla, 79; Artist of the Year, Santa Fean Mag, 80. *Bibliog:* Donn Puca (auth), A young artist working magic, Southwest Art Collector, 12/79; Marion Love (auth), article, Santa Fean Mag, 8/80; Joseph Cain (auth), article, Art Voices/South, 9-10/80. *Media:* Bronze, Plaster. *Mailing Add:* 3014 Pimlico Corpus Christi TX 78418

SIMEL, ELAINE
PRINTMAKER, PAINTER
b New York, NY. *Study:* High Sch Music & Art, New York; Black Mountain Col, NC; Syracuse Univ, NY, BFA; studied with Josef Albers, Robert Motherwell, Harry Sternberg & Ruth Leaf. *Work:* De Cordova & Dana Mus, Lincoln, Mass; Publ Clearing House, Port Washington, NY; Hunt Inst Botanical Doc, Pittsburgh; Reader's Digest, New York; Comptroller of US Currency. *Exhib:* Huntington Twp Art League, Heckscher Mus, NY, 77; Soc Am Graphic Artists, Am Art Asn Gallery, New York, 77; Boston Printmakers 29th Nat Exhib, De Cordova & Dana Mus, 77; Audubon Artists 35th Ann Exhib, Nat Acad Galleries, New York, 77; Philadelphia Art Show, Philadelphia Civic Ctr, 89; Long Island Art Experience, Westfair Office Park, 90. *Awards:* John Carl Georgi Mem Prize, Nat Asn Women Artists, 76; Hortense Ferne Mem Prize, Nat Asn Women Artists, 79. *Bibliog:* Malcolm Preston (auth), Newsday, 4/75; David Shirey (auth), Artistic Cooperation, NY Times, 3/76; Malcolm Preston (auth), article, Newsday, 7/77. *Mem:* Nat Asn Women Artists; Graphic Arts Coun NY; Soc of Am Graphic Artists. *Media:* Etching; Oil. *Publ:* Contribr, Ruth Leaf's Printmaking Techniques, Watson-Guptill, 76. *Dealer:* Assoc Am Artists 663 Fifth Ave New York NY 10022. *Mailing Add:* 40-47 235 St Douglaston NY 11363

SIMIONOV, ALEXANDRU
SCULPTOR, GRAPHIC ARTIST
b Bucharest, Romania, Mar 19, 50. *Study:* Art Inst Bucharest, MA(sculpture), 69-73. *Work:* Romanian Nat Mus, Bucharest; Art Mus, Tulcea, Romania. *Comn:* Vertical Horizon (monument), 75, Ana (stone monument), 78, Romanian Arts Coalition, Buzău; Rainbow (stone monument), 79, Cariatide (stone monument), 84, Trap (wood), 85, Romanian Arts Coalition. *Exhib:* Biann, Dales Mus, 74 & 75, Bucharest, Romainia; one man shows, Simeza Mus, 76, Romanian TV, 70, Bucharest & Romanian Cult Ctr, Chicago, Ill, 90. *Pos:* Set Designer, Romanian TV, 79-80; sculptor, Anima Film Studios, Bucharest, 80-87; pres, Romanian Cultural Ctr, Chicago, Ill, 91-92. *Bibliog:* Marin Nicolau Golfin (auth), Alexandru Simionov, Art Mag, 76; Ruxandra Handoreanu Nesbit (auth), Alexandru Simionov, Democratic Romanian, 90. *Mem:* Art Inst Chicago; Chicago Artists Coalition. *Media:* Stone, Marble. *Mailing Add:* 6132 N Paulina Chicago IL 60660

SIMKIN, PHILLIPS M
SCULPTOR
b Philadelphia, Pa, Jan 19, 44. *Study:* Tyler Art Sch, Temple Univ, BFA; Cornell Univ, MFA; Univ Pa, post grad fel. *Comn:* Sculpture, Pub Ctr for Collection & Dissemination of Secrets, Inst Contemp Art, Univ Pa, 73; Displacement Proj I (with Doris Olafson), Inst Contemp Art, Boston, 74; Displacement Proj II (with Doris Olafson), Philadelphia Mus Art, 74; Artpark (with Thom Farmer), Lewiston State Arts Park, New York, 75. *Exhib:* Displacement Proj II-a Public Event, Philadelphia, 74; Commodity Exchange, Human Puzzle, Lewiston, NY, 75; Choices Maze, Inst Art & Urban Resources, PS1, New York, 76; Project Looking Glass, Three Centuries of Am Art exhib, Philadelphia Mus of Art, 76; Proj--Is There Anything Else You Want to Tell Me?, Brooklyn Mus, 77; solo proj, Pa Acad of Fine Arts, Philadelphia, 78; Sculpture Performance Comn, Nat Fine Arts Comt, XIII Winter Olympics, Lake Placid, NY, 80; and others. *Pos:* Art dir, Earthweek Inc, Philadelphia, 71-73; co-dir (with John Formicola), The Luncheonette Inc Artist Ctr, Philadelphia, 75; adv bd mem, Dept Community Programs, Philadelphia Art Mus, 77-82. *Teaching:* Assoc prof studio fine arts, York Col, City Univ New York, 73-; adj asst prof studio fine arts, Moore Col Art, Philadelphia, 73-; artist-in-residence, Brooklyn Mus, 77. *Awards:* Nat Endowment Arts Artist Fel, 75-76; Creative Artists Pub Serv Sculpture Grant, New York, 76; Artist Fel Grant, Pa State Coun Arts, 80. *Mailing Add:* 1434 S Broad St Philadelphia PA 19146

SIMMONS, CLEDA MARIE
PAINTER, GRAPHIC ARTIST
b Douglas, Wyo, June 24, 27. *Study:* Univ NMex, Albuquerque, with Ralph Douglas & Raymond Jonson; studied seven yrs in Madrid, Spain. *Work:* Pan Am Gallery, San Antonio, Tex; Ateneo de Belles Artes, Madrid. *Exhib:* US Info Serv Traveling Show, Mus Mod Art, Paris & Madrid, 53; two-woman show, Jonson Gallery, Univ NMex, 56; Detroit Art Inst, 64; Denver Art Mus, 70; EQUUS, Denver, Colo, 77; RI Sch Design, Providence, 81; and others. *Pos:* Graphic artist, ESA Women Int, Loveland, Colo, 69-70, art ed, 70-73, art dir, 73-77; assoc ed & art dir, Jonquil Mag, 77-78. *Teaching:* workshops, Boston, Ma & Southern Calif. *Awards:* Purchase Award, Ateneo de Belles Artes, Madrid, Spain, 54. *Bibliog:* Mary Hagen (auth), The challenge of art, Southwest Art Mag, 1/77; article in Int Soc Artists Communicator, 7-8/78. *Mem:* Boston Visual Arts Union; Copley Soc Boston; Vistas Inst for Visual Arts. *Media:* Mixed; Collage. *Publ:* Illusr, Our Government, 69; coauth, Art of Editorship, ESA Women Int, 72; illusr, Beneath the Peaks, ESA Women Int, 73; illusr, This is Loveland, League of Women Voters, 76. *Dealer:* East Park Galleries 13310 Ralston Ave Sylmar CA 91342; DeVorzon Gallery Inc Pacific Design Ctr 8687 Melrose Ave Los Angeles CA 90069. *Mailing Add:* 724 Osborne St Vista CA 92084

SIMMONS, GARY PAUL
GRAPHIC ARTIST, EDUCATOR
b Vergennes, Ill, Feb 10, 41. *Study:* Southern Ill Univ-Carbondale, with Buckminster Fuller, BA, 63, MA, 65; Ind Univ-Bloomington, with Henry Smith, EdD(photog), 72. *Work:* Koh-I-Noor, Rapidograph Permanent Collection, Touring, Bloomsbury, NJ. *Comn:* Hall Fame Trainer Jack Van Berg (portrait), Van Berg Farms, Goshen, Ky, 84; Jane Ross (portrait), Ross Found, Arkadelphia, Ark, 90; Governor Bill Clinton, Little Rock, Ak, 92. *Exhib:* One-man shows, Neil Rizk Gallery, Houston, 77, Univ Ozarks,

Clarksville, Ark, 91 & Univ WVa, Morgantown, 92; Artistry Int Portrait, Fed Reserve Bank, Philadelphia, 90; Ark Art 80 & 92, Henderson State Univ, Arkadelphia, 92; Knickerbocker Artists, New York, 92. *Pos:* Bd dirs, Hot Springs Art Ctr, Ark, 83-86. *Teaching:* Instr drawing, Garland Co Community Col, Hot Springs, Ark, 76-78; lectr pen & ink, Nat Workshops Koh-I-Noor Rapidograph, 89-92; asst prof graphics, Henderson State Univ,Arkadelphia, Ark, 91-92. *Awards:* Visual Arts Achievement Award, Hot Springs Arts Ctr, 91; John J Karpick Award for Drawing, Knickerbocker Artists, 92; Merit Award, Ark Art '92, Joint Educ Consortium, 92. *Bibliog:* The art of Gary Simmons, Arkansan Mag, 80. *Mem:* Hot Springs Art Ctr (bd dirs). *Media:* Pen & Ink. *Publ:* Ed, Since Feeling is First, Scott Foresman, 71; auth, Headlines in Visual Design, Audio Visual Instruction, 73; Message Design: The Prodigal Son, Med & Biological Illus, 75; Fundamentals of Pen & Ink, Decorative Arts Digest, 90; The Technical Pen: Techniques for Artists, Watson-Guptill, 92; Instruction in Pen and Ink, Paint Works, issue 6, 2/93. *Mailing Add:* 800 Central Ave Hot Springs National Park AR 71901

SIMMONS, JOHN HERBERT
EDUCATOR, HISTORIAN
b Springfield, Mo, Mar 23, 38. *Study:* Drury Col, BA, 60; Univ Ark, MA, 73; Univ Rome, DA, 78. *Collections Arranged:* All cataloged, Ernest Trova, Work by Contemp Sculptor, 71, Classical Greek Ceramics, Early Movement Through Gallo Rome, 75, Sung Dynasty Ceramics, Chinese Ceramics, 75, Egyptian Art, Works from the Duncan Collection, 78, Chinese Art, Neolithic Through Ching Dynasty, 79 & Alice Neel, 80. *Pos:* Chmn bd trustees, Springfield Art Mus, Mo, 79-80; art critic, Springfield News Leader, 87-. *Teaching:* Prof & chmn art dept, Drury Col, 69-83. *Mem:* Col Art Asn; Am Inst Archaeol; assoc Am Inst Archit. *Res:* Chinese art with papers published and read on Ku kai chih; also early printing in Europe. *Interests:* Chinese art, especially ceramics, and early European printed books. *Publ:* Auth, Ku kai chih, an Early Chinese Painter, 73, Ching-te-Chan, 74 & The Loud Brothers of Philadelphia, 75, Gallery. *Mailing Add:* 2059 S Mayfair Springfield MO 65804

SIMMONS, JULIE LUTZ
PAINTER, COLLAGE ARTIST
b San Diego, Calif. *Study:* Murray State Univ, BS, 64, with Miles Batt, Ed Betts, Virginia Cobb, Maxine Masterfield, Barbara Nechis, Charles Reid, Frank Webb & Daniel Green; Southeast Mo State Univ. *Work:* Southwestern Bell, St Louis, Mo; Coca Cola Inc, Atlanta, Ga; Marriot Hotels, Atlanta, Ga; First Bank Fla; First Bank Tenn. *Comn:* Watercolor collage, comn by Dr Edwin Noffel, Cape Girardeau, Mo, 83, John Virant, Chesterfield, Mo, 83; Directions in Design, St Louis, Mo, 85, 86, 87, 88 & 89; portraits, Dr Charles Moore, Tallahassee, Fla; collage, Embassy Suites, La Jolla, Calif, 84; mural, PGA W Resort Golf Club, Landmark Landco Calif Inc, 90; Congregation Shalom, Milwaukee, Wis. *Exhib:* two person exhib, Latzer Gallery, St Louis, 85 & 86; Six Artists-Six States, Univ Wis, Aaron Bohrod Fine Arts Gallery, 86; La Watercolor Int, New Orleans, 86; North Coast Collage Soc Ann Exhib, 86 & 87; Shawnee Col, Ill, 87; Abstein Gallery, Atlanta, Ga, 86-90; Soc Layerists Multi Media, 88 & 90; Barucci's Gallery, St Louis, Mo, 90; Sun Cities Mus, Sun City, Ariz, 92; Durfee Gallery, Scottsdale, Ariz, 92. *Teaching:* Instr studio workshops watercolor, Charleston, Mo, 70-; instr, studio workshops, Medford, Ore, Monroe, La, 86 & 89, Sikeston, Mo, 86, Lighthouse Art Ctr, Crescent City, Calif, 88, 89 & 91, Geneseo Art League, Ill, 88 & 89, E Cent Col, Union, Mo, 88, Ill Art League, Peoria, 89, Sun Cities, Ariz, 90-, Friends of the Arts & Sciences, Sarasota, Fla, 91 & Left Bank Art League, Moline, Ill, 91. *Awards:* First Prize, Midwest Watercolor Soc Seventh Ann Exhib, 83; Ky Watercolor Soc Exhib Award, 84; An Art Affair Award, St Louis, 85; Ga Watercolor Soc Award, 86; La Watercolor Int Award, 86; Ariz Watercolor Soc Award, 91. *Bibliog:* Article, The watercolor page, Am Artist, 1/86; rev, St Louis Globe-Democrat, 5/17-18/86. *Mem:* Soc Layerists Multi-Media; N Coast Collage Soc; Nat Watercolor Soc; Am Watercolor Soc; Soc Layerists Multi Media; Ariz Watercolor Asn; Ariz Artists Guild. *Media:* Watercolor; Mixed. *Publ:* Auth, article, The watercolor page, Am Artist, 1/86; Interior design, Southern Accents, 9/89; Architectural Design Collaborators 2, 91; Am Artists, 91. *Mailing Add:* 10250 E Mountain View #229 Scottsdale AZ 85258

SIMMONS, LAURIE
PHOTOGRAPHER
b Long Island, NY, Oct 3, 49. *Study:* Tyler Sch Art, Temple Univ, BFA, 71. *Work:* High Mus, Atlanta, Ga; Mus Art Contemp, Montreal, Can; Birmingham Mus Art, Ala; Philadelphia Mus; Walker Art Ctr, Minneapolis; St Louis Mus, Mo; Fogg Mus Art, Boston; Albright-Knox Gallery, Buffalo, NY; Mus Mod Art, New York; and many others. *Exhib:* One-woman shows, Daniel Weinberg Gallery, Los Angeles, 89 & 92, Galerie Jablonka, Cologne, 89 & 90, Metro Pictures, New York, 81, 83, 88, 89 & 91, San Jose Mus Art, Calif, 90, Galerie Carola Mosch, Berlin, Orangerie München, Munich; Biennial Exhib, Whitney Mus Am Art, New York, 91; Pleasures & Terrors of Domestic Comfort, Mus Mod Art, New York, 91; American Art of the 80s, Palazzo delle Albere, Trent, Italy, 91; The Surrogate Future: Intercepted Identities in Contemporary Photography, Ctr Photog, Woodstock, NY, Cooley Mem Art Gallery, Reed Col, Portland, Ore, Rosa Esman Gallery, New York, 91; More Than One Photog (with catalog), Mus Mod Art, New York, 92; Devil on the Stairs: Looking Back on the Eighties, ICA, Philadelphia, Newport Harbor Art Mus, Newport Beach, Calif, 92. *Awards:* Nat Endowment Arts, 84. *Bibliog:* Richard Kaline (auth), Laurie Simmons at Metro Pictures, Art Am, 2/90; Peggy Cyphers (auth), Laurie Simmons, Arts Mag, 2/90; Kathryn Hixsin (auth), Chicago in Review,Arts, summer 90; Charles Hagen (auth), Two Goals in One Show: Diversity and Unity, NY Times, C28, 5/29/92. *Dealer:* Metro Pictures 150 Greene New York NY 10012. *Mailing Add:* 547 Broadway New York NY 10012

SIMMONS, PERCY SLOTSKY
COLLECTOR
b London, Eng, Dec 27, 06; US citizen. *Study:* City of London Col, 27-29. *Exhib:* Piranesi, Ind Univ Art Mus, Bloomington, Ind Exhib, New York & The Drawing Society. *Collections Arranged:* Prints and Master Drawings, Indianapolis Collectors, Indianapolis Mus Art, 79. *Pos:* Mem exec bd, Eureka Col Art Coun, Ill, currently; co-founder, Print & Drawing Soc, Indianapolis Mus Art, Ind. *Awards:* Nat Order of Merit, Pres Fr Repub, 74. *Mem:* Col Art Asn Am; Master Drawings Asn. *Collection:* Old master drawings and prints, etchings of seventeenth and eighteenth centuries and Chiascuro prints of sixteenth, seventeenth and eighteenth centuries. *Mailing Add:* 5602 Central Ave Indianapolis IN 46220-3012

SIMON, DAVID L
HISTORIAN, EDUCATOR
b Lawrence, Mass, June 14, 46. *Study:* Boston Univ, BA, 69, MA, 71; Courtauld Inst Art, Univ London, PhD, 77. *Teaching:* Chmn & assoc prof, State Univ NY Col, Cortland, 74-81; chmn & Ellerton M Jette prof art, Colby Col, 81- *Awards:* Am Coun Learned Soc Travel Grant, 78; US-Spanish Comt Educ & Cult Affairs Res Fel, 78-79; Mellon Found Fel, Metrop Mus Art, 80-81. *Mem:* Col Art Asn; Int Ctr Medieval Art. *Res:* Romanesque sculpture. *Publ:* Auth, Daniel and Habakkuk in Aragon, J Brit Archaeol Asn, 75; Roland, the Moor and the Pilgrim and Spanish Romanesque sculpture, Acta, 75; Still more by the Cabestany master, Burlington Mag, 79; Le Sarcophage de Dona Sanch a Jaca, 79 & L'Art Roman, Source de L'Art Roman, 80, Cahiers St-Michel Cuxa; Romanesque Sculpture in North American Collections, The Metrop Museum of Art, Gesta, XXIII, XXV, XXVI, 84, 86 & 87; San Adrian de Sasave and Sculpture in Altoaragon, Romanesque & Gothic: Essays for George Zarnecki, 87. *Mailing Add:* Art Dept Colby Col Waterville ME 04901

SIMON, HELENE
SCULPTOR
b Bagdad, Iraq; US citizen. *Study:* Bedford Col, London; Am Univ, Beirut, Lebanon; Islamic Art with Mary Devonshire, Cairo, Egypt; painting with Anthony Toney & Jacob Lawrence; New Sch, sculpture with Lorrie Goulet. *Work:* Phoenix Art Mus, Ariz; Jewish Mus, New York; Hirshhorn Mus, Washington, DC; NY Univ Art Collection, New York; Fordham Univ Art Collection, Bronx; Pepsico, Purchase, NY. *Comn:* Merck & Co; Banca Nazional del Lavoro, NY. *Exhib:* One-man shows, Bodley Gallery, New York, 71 & 73, Fordham Univ, 75 & Haber Theodore Gallery, 80; Sculptors 9, Caravan House, New York, 71; Stable Gallery, Scottsdale, Ariz, 73; Habib Anavian Gallery, 81-83; Carolyn Hill, Soho, 86-90. *Bibliog:* Andrea Mikotajuk (auth), In the galleries, 12/71 & 1/72 & Gordon Brown (auth), In the galleries, 12/73, Arts Mag; article in Artworld, 2/80; articles in Artspeak, 2/80, 86, 87 & 4/88. *Mem:* Artists Equity Asn, New York. *Media:* Marble, Bronze. *Mailing Add:* 200 E 74th St New York NY 10021

SIMON, HERBERT BERNHEIMER
SCULPTOR
b Nashville, Tenn, Sept 20, 27. *Study:* Brooklyn Mus Art Sch; Hans Hofmann Studio, NY; Colorado Springs Fine Art Ctr; Hunter Col, study with Robert Motherwell; NY Univ, BA & MA, study with Philip Guston. *Work:* Everhart Mus, Scranton, Pa; Lehigh Univ, Bethlehem, Pa; Roberson Ctr Arts & Sci, Binghamton, NY; State Mus Pa, Harrisburg; Asheville Art Mus, NC. *Comn:* Two Modules (sculpture), Coal St Park, Wilkes-Barre, Pa, 77; Facets (aluminum relief), Wilkes Col, Wilkes-Barre, Pa, 77; Aluminum Relief, Schaeffer Residence, Mountaintop, Pa, 78. *Exhib:* Drawings USA, Mus Mod Art, New York, 55; one-man shows, Phoenix Gallery, NY, 64 & 66 & Sordoni Art Gallery, Wilkes-Barre, Pa, 74-80; William Penn Mus, Harrisburg, Pa, 72 & 80; Regional Exhib, Everhart Mus, Scranton, Pa, 76; Fed Hall, New York, 82; 84 Sculptors for 1984, Rodger LaPelle Gallery, 84, 85, 86 & 90; Five Sides & Some Tops, Southern Ohio Mus & Cult Ctr, Portsmouth, Ohio, 85; Sordoni Art Gallery, Wilkes Col, Wilkes-Barre, Pa, 86; Susquehanna Regional Art Exhib, Roberson Mus, Binghamton, NY, 88 & 92; Mayfair Juried Art Exhib, Allentown Art Mus, Allentown, Pa, 89, 90 & 91; Katharina Rich Perlow Gallery, New York, NY, 89; Penn State Univ, 90, State Mus Pa, 91 & 92; Contemp Gallery, Marywood Col, Scranton, Pa, 90, 91 & 92; Bixler Gallery, Stroudsburg, Pa, 91; Riverwalk Juried Exhib, York, Pa, 92; Col Miseriocordia Dallas, Pa, 92. *Teaching:* Instr painting & drawing, Sch Design, NC State Col, Raleigh, 56-58; prof sculpture & 3-D design, Wilkes Univ, Wilkes-Barre, Pa, 69-92. *Awards:* Award, William Penn Mus, Harrisburg, Pa, 71; Purchase Prize Regional Art Exhib, Everhart Mus, Scranton, Pa, 76; Artist-in-Residence, Johnson Atelier, Mercerville, NJ, 86. *Bibliog:* William Sterling (auth), Herbert Simon: Metal Sculpture 1976-1980, Wilkes Col, Wilkes-Barre, Pa, 80. *Media:* Welded Steel, Aluminum. *Mailing Add:* 25 E Center St Shavertown PA 18708

SIMON, JEWEL WOODARD
PAINTER, SCULPTOR
b Houston, Tex, July 28, 11. *Study:* Atlanta Univ, AB(summa cum laude), 31, painting with Hale Woodruff, 46; pvt study with B L Hellman, 34; sculpture with Alice Dunbar, 47; Atlanta Col Art, BFA, 67; Art Instr Inc, cert grad, 62; Tamarind Inst, lithography, 81; Univ NMex. *Work:* Educ Dept, Ringling Mus, Sarasota, Fla; Atlanta Univ Gallery; Du Sable Mus, Chicago; Carver Mus, Tuskegee, Ala; Kiah Mus, Savannah, Ga; Atlanta Life Insurance Co, Ga; and others. *Comn:* Portrait of Frankie Adams, Atlanta Sch Social Work, 70; portrait of A F Herndon, founder, Atlanta Life Insurance Co, 70; oil landscapes, cover design, The Vision, Atlanta Life Ins Co, Atlanta, Memphis & Dallas, 73; plus others. *Exhib:* One-woman shows, Clark Col, 73 & Carver Mus, Tuskegee, Ala, 74; Huntsville Mus, 79; Int Soc Artists, New York, 79;

Chicago Mus Sci & Indust; Ariel Gallery, Soho, New York; three-women show, Variety in Works on Paper, 90 & 91; and many other group & one-woman shows. *Collections Arranged:* South Eastern, 50, End of Year Show, 64-67, Show of Georgia Artists, 71 & Highlights of Atlanta University Collection Touring Show, 73, High Mus Art, Atlanta. *Pos:* Slide lectures and exhibs, various cols & univs; career consult, High Schs & Elem Schs. *Awards:* Arts Serv Award, Phoenix Arts & Theater Co, 78; Golden Dove Heritage Award, Kappa Omega Chap, A K A Sorority, 79; Bronze Jubilee Award, 81; and others. *Bibliog:* Samella S Lewis & Ruth C Waddy (auths), Black Artists on Art, 69; Marion Brown (auth), The Negro in the Fine Arts, Negro Heritage Libr, Vol 2, 70; Women Artists in America, II, Art Dept, Univ Tenn, Chattanooga. *Mem:* Nat Conf Artists (co-founder & nat treas, 58-73, bd dir, 59-); Graphic Soc; Black Artists Atlanta (treas, 73-87); Ga Arts Coun; High Mus Collectors. *Media:* Oil, Watercolor; Multimedia. *Publ:* Contribr, Prints by American Negro Artists, Cult Exckange Ctr, 64, Black Dimensions in Art, Carnation Co, 70 & American Printmakers, Graphic Group, Arcadia, Calif, 74; Two Thousand Notable American Women, First Illusr Ed, 89. *Mailing Add:* 67 Ashby St SW Atlanta GA 30314

SIMON, LEONARD RONALD
ADMINISTRATOR, WRITER
b Norristown, Pa, Dec 9, 36. *Study:* Ohio State Univ. *Collections Arranged:* Two Centuries of Black American Art (coauth, catalog), 75. *Pos:* Registr, Stanford Mus, 65-69; deputy dir, Calif Arts Coun, 77-80. *Teaching:* Instr Black Am art, Univ Calif, Riverside, 76-77 & 80- *Mem:* Col Art Asn. *Res:* Black American artists. *Publ:* Auth, The American presence of the Black artist, Am Art Rev, 76; The sound of people, Arts in Soc, Vol 12, No 1. *Mailing Add:* 360 S Mills Ave Claremont CA 91711

SIMON, MICHAEL A
PHOTOGRAPHER
b Budapest, Hungary, June 20, 36; US citizen. *Study:* Budapest Tech Univ, 54-56; Pa State Univ, 57-58; Wis Arts Bd photog fel, 80, Rochester Inst Technol, MFA. *Work:* Mus Mod Art, George Eastman House, Rochester, New York; Univ Kans, Lawrence; Minneapolis Inst Arts, Minn; Sheldon Mem Art Gallery, Lincoln, Nebr; Theodore Lyman Art Ctr, Beloit Col; Wis State Hist Soc, Madison. *Exhib:* Contemp Photog VII, George Eastman House, Rochester, NY, 72; Midwest Invitational, Walker Art Ctr, Minneapolis, 73; one-man shows, Wright Art Ctr, 77, 78 & 80, Minneapolis Inst Arts, Minn, 79, Write Art Ctr, Beloit Col, 80, TUBE Gallery, Write Art Ctr, Beloit Col, 83, Write Art Mus, Beloit Col, Univ Rochester, 85, Malone Gallery, Rochester, NY, 86; Recent Acquisitions, Minneapolis Inst Arts, Minn, 76; Madison Art Ctr, Wis, 83; Aspen Ctr Visual Arts, Colo, 83; Wright Art Mus, Beloit Col, 85; Univ Rochester, NY, 85; Malone Gallery, Rochester, NY, 86. *Pos:* Cur photog, Wright Art Ctr, Beloit Col, currently; consult, Andre Kertes Retrospective exhib, Art Inst Chicago, 83-85; guest cur, exhib, Hungarian Photog from 1839 to Present, Fratelli Aliari, Florence, Italy, 87-89. *Teaching:* Assoc prof photog, Beloit Col, Wis, 69-; artist-in-residence photog, Univ Del, 74; vis artist photog, Art Inst Chicago, 78; artist-in-residence, Avila Col, Kansas City, Mo, 81; instr workshop, Chilmark Photog Workshop, Martha's Vineyard, Mass, 86; prof art & chmn dept art & art hist, Beloit Col, currently. *Awards:* Nat Endowment Arts Photog Survey Grant, 80; Nat Endowment Arts Exhib Grant, 81; grant, Wis Humanities Comt, 81; Purchase Awards, Mus Mod Art, NY, George Eastman House, Rochester, NY, Univ Kans, Lawrence, Minneapolis Inst Arts, Minn & Sheldon Mem Art Gallery, Lincoln, Nebr. *Bibliog:* Diaframma Italiana, Milan, Italy, 1-2/75. *Mem:* Soc Photog Educ (nat bd mem, 76-84, chmn nat bd dirs, 79-81, chmn reg affairs comt, 81-83, chmn educ comt & mem steering comt, 83-84); Szechenyi Soc Hungary. *Res:* Mellon Foundation grant for the research of the history of photography in Hungary (76-80). *Publ:* Auth, Massachusetts Review of Photography, Vol II, No 3, 81; co-ed, Center of the Eye, Aspen Ctr Visual Arts, 83; auth, article, Newslett Photog teachers, Polaroid Corp, summer 85; auth, three Hungarian Photographers (exhib catalogue), Wright Mus Art, Beloit Col, Beloit, Wis; auth, article, Newslett Photog teachers, Polaroid Corp, summer 85; auth, essay in exhib catalogue for Contemp Hungarian Photogr, Allen Mus, Oberlin Col, Ohio, 89; auth, three Hungarian Photographers (exhib catalogue), Wright Mus Art, Beloit Col, Beloit, Wis. *Mailing Add:* 925 Church St Beloit WI 53511-5433

SIMON, MICHAEL J
CERAMIST
b Springfield, Minn, Dec 27, 47. *Study:* Univ Minn, BA, 70; Univ Ga, MFA, 80. *Exhib:* Solo exhibs, Baltimore Clayworks, Md, 89, Arvada Ctr Arts & Humanities, Denver, Colo, 89, Fla Gulf Coast Art Ctr, Belleair, Fla, 90; group shows, Pro Art Gallery, St Louis, Mo, 90; Expressive Teapot, Swidler Gallery, Royal Oak, Mich, 90; McKenzie Legacy, Manchester Craftsmen Guild, Pittsburgh, 91; and many others. *Pos:* Many workshops & lectr including, Stetson Univ, Deland, Fla, 88, Fla Gulf Coast Art Ctr, Belleair, 90, Arrowmont Sch, Gatlinburg, Tenn, 91, Pa State Univ State Col, 91. *Awards:* Fel, Ford Found, 81; Craft Fel, Nat Endowment Arts, 90. *Bibliog:* Michael Simon (auth), Old & New Pots: A Ceramics Monthly Portfolio, Ceramics Monthly, p 53-62, 6/83; Andy Nasisse (auth), A Coffee Bowl, Ceramics Monthly, p 63, 6/83; and others. *Mailing Add:* 2111 Watson Springs Rd Watkinsville GA 30677

SIMON, NETTY D
PAINTER
Study: Escuela de la Bellas Artes, Lima, Peru; Utica Col; Art Students League; C W Post Col. *Work:* NY Tel Co; W C Grace Co, New York; Bethlehem Steel Co, New York; East Meadow Publ Libr, NY; Tower Mus, Philadelphia, Pa. *Exhib:* Solo shows, Steinhardt Gallery, Long Island, NY, 78, Sonnenberg Gallery, Rapperswil, Switz, 80 & 81, Halsten Gallery, Stockbridge, Mass, 81, Loring Gallery, Long Island, NY, 84 & Joy Berman Gallery, Philadelphia, 87; Audubon Artists, New York; Nat Acad Galleries, New York. *Awards:* First prize-oil, Locust Valley Art Show, 76 & 77 & St John's Univ, 80; Grumbacher Award, 78. *Bibliog:* articles in Interior Design, 8/78, Art Speaks, 8/81 & Uptown News, 1/90. *Mailing Add:* 487 Richmond Rd East Meadow NY 11554

SIMON, NORTON
COLLECTOR
b Portland, Ore, Feb 5, 07. *Pos:* Pres, Norton Simon Mus, Pasadena, Calif; pres, Norton Simon Found & Norton Simon Inc Found. *Collection:* Old Master European paintings from the Renaissance through the mid-20th century, including paintings by Renoir, Cezanne, van Gogh and others; complete bronze modeles by Degas; sculpture by Maillol, Moore, Rodin, Giacometti and others; graphic works by Rembrandt, Goya and Picasso; Indian and Southeast Asian bronze and stone sculpture. *Mailing Add:* PO Box 2248 Beverly Hills CA 90213

SIMON, ROBERT BARRY
CONSULTANT, HISTORIAN
b New York, NY, Nov 27, 52. *Study:* Columbia Col, BA, 73; Columbia Univ, MA, 75, MPhil, 76, PhD, 82. *Collections Arranged:* Sixteenth Century Portraits (auth, catalog), Soprintendenza, Florence, Italy, 80-82; US Info Agency Permanent Collection (auth, catalog), 82; Haggerty Mus, Marquette Univ (auth, catalog), 84; Discoveries in una nuova luce (auth catalog), 88 & Devotion and Delight (auth catalog), 89, Piero Corsini Gallery, New York. *Pos:* Chester Dale Fel, Metrop Mus Art, New York, 76-78; dir, Fine Arts Group Crosson Dannis, 82-85 & Robert B Simon Fine Arts Consultant and Appraisers, 85-92. *Teaching:* Lectr Ital renaissance art, Juilliard Sch, 82-; lectr appraisal old master paintings, Marymount Col, 91. *Mem:* Col Art Asn; Am Soc Appraisers; Am Asn Mus; Appraisers Asn Am (bd dirs, 90, treas, 92); Unione Amici Cane & Gatto, Italy. *Res:* Bronzino, Crivelli, Opie & Smetham; problems of portraiture, Mannerism. *Publ:* Auth, Bronzino's portrait of Cosimo I De'Medici, Burlington Mag, 83, Giulio Clovio's Eleonora Di Toledo, 89; Sofonisba Anguisciola, 86 & Dore in the Highlands, 89, Walters Art Gallery J; Yo Pontormo, J Art, 89. *Mailing Add:* Satis House Tower Hill Rd Tuxedo Park NY 10987

SIMON, SIDNEY
SCULPTOR, PAINTER
b Pittsburgh, Pa, May 21, 17. *Study:* Carnegie Inst Technol; Pa Acad Fine Arts, Emlen Cresson fel, 40 & Edwin Austin Abbey fel, 40-41, BFA, Univ Pa, BA; Barnes Found. *Work:* Metrop Mus Art, New York; Corcoran Gallery; Am Embassy, Paris; Cornell Univ Med Ctr, Kramer Col, Ithaca, NY; Colby Col, Waterville, Maine; and others. *Comn:* Entrance sculpture, 747 Bldg, New York, 72; West Point Jewish Chapel, 85; Graham Bldg, Philadelphia, 86; fountain, World Wide Plaza, 88; Hakone Open Air Mus, Japan, 91; and others. *Exhib:* Pa Acad Fine Arts Ann, 48-52 & 62-72; Am Painting, Metrop Mus Art, 50; 20 one-man shows, Whitney Mus Am Art Ann, 50-; Mus Mod Art Assemblage Exhib, 62; L'Aquarelle Contemporaine aux Etats Units, State Dept, 63; Sculpture Retrospective, Sculpture Ctr, New York, 78; Long Point Gallery, Provinceton, Mass, 77, 81, 83, 85, 87, 89 & 91. *Pos:* Mem, New York City Art Comn, 75-78. *Teaching:* Instr & founding dir, Skowhegan Sch Painting & Sculpture, Maine, 45-58 & 75-76, acad dir, 81-84; Artist in residence, Am Acad Rome, 69-70; vis sculptor, Sarah Lawrence Col, 71-72; vis prof, Salzburg Sem Am Studies, 71; instr, Art Students League, 73-; vis artist, Univ Pa, 77 & 80, Columbia Univ, 85-86. *Awards:* Gold Medal, 81 & Greer Prize, 83, Nat Acad Design; Award, Acad Arts & Letters, 81; Silver Medal, Nat Arts Club, 82; Prize, Nat Sculpture Soc, 89. *Bibliog:* Richard McLanathan (auth), Sidney Simon, Grippi Gallery, 75; J Place (auth), article in Am Artist, 11/79; April Kingsley (auth), Provinceton Mag, 90. *Mem:* Artists Equity Asn; Sculpture's Guild; Sculpture Ctr, New York (vpres); Nat Sculpture Soc; Nat Acad Design. *Media:* Wood, Bronze; All. *Mailing Add:* 95 Bedford St New York NY 10014

SIMONDS, CHARLES FREDERICK
SCULPTOR, ARCHITECT
b New York, NY, Nov 14, 45. *Study:* Univ Calif, Berkeley, BA, 67; Rutgers Univ, Douglass Col, New Brunswick, NJ, MFA, 67. *Work:* Mus Mod Art, Guggenheim Mus & Whitney Mus Am Art, New York; Walker Art Ctr, Minneapolis; Mus Contemp Art, Chicago; Centre Georges Pompidon, Paris. *Comn:* Dwellings, over 300 works constructed in the streets of New York for an imaginary civilization of little people migrating through the city, 70-; Project Uphill-La Placita (park playlot sculpture), Lower East Side Coalition for Human Housing, 74; full scale Dwellings, 74 & Growth House, 75, Art Park; Refuge (full scale work), 1988 Seoul Olympics; Olympiades des Arts, Seoul, Korea, 88. *Exhib:* Biennial of Paris, 73 & 75; Whitney Biennial, 75 & 77; Made by Sculptors, Stedelijk Mus, Amsterdam, Neth, 78; Contemp Sculpture, Selections from the Collection of the Mus Mod Art, New York, 79; one-person shows, Projects: Picaresque Landscape, Mus Mod Art, New York, 76 & 77, Temenos, Albright-Knox Art Gallery, Buffalo, NY, 77, Floating Cities & Other Archit, Westfalischer Kunstverein, Munster, 78, Mus Sables D'Olonne, France, 79, Architekturmuseum, Basel, 85, Galerie Maeghtlelong, Paris, 86, Galerie Baudoin Lebon, Paris, 87, Corcoran Gallery, Washington, DC, 88 & Leo Castelli Gallery, New York, 89 & 92; Circles & Towers Growing, traveling exhib, Mus Contemp Art, Chicago, Los Angeles Co Mus Art, Ft Worth Art Mus & Contemp Arts Mus, Houston, Tex; Solomon R Guggenheim Mus, New York; House Plants and Rocks, Leo Castelli Gallery, New York, 84. *Awards:* Artist in Residence Grant, 74 & Young Artists Grant, Nat Endowment Arts, 74-75; Nat Endowment Arts, 80; Mem, Soc Fels Am

Acad Rome. *Bibliog:* John Beardsley (auth), Charles Simonds: Extending the metaphor, Art Int, Vol 22, No 9, 2/79; Mark Stevens (auth), The dizzy decade, Newsweek, 3/26/79; Kate Linker (auth), Charles Simonds' emblematic architecture, Artforum, 3/79; and many others. *Publ:* Auth, Microcosm to macrocosm, 2/74 & Three peoples, 75, Art Forum. *Mailing Add:* 26 E 22nd St New York NY 10010

SIMONE (MILDRED SIMONSON)
SCULPTOR, PAINTER
b New York, NY. *Study:* Art Students League, with Yasuo Kuniyoshi & Louis Bosa, 45-47; Rockport Art Sch, Provincetown, with Hans Hoffman, 46; New Sch Social Res, with Louis Bosa, 50; Brooklyn Mus, with Xavier Gonzales & Vincent Glinsky, 50; Hunter Col, Hon BA, 28. *Work:* Brooklyn Mus. *Exhib:* Mother's Day Bouquet, Brooklyn Mus, 47; San Miguel de Allende, Whitney Mus, 50; Mother and Child, Nat Acad, New York, 53; Chiquita, Smithsonian Inst, 58; To Market, Riverside Mus, New York, 59; various works, Assoc Am Artists, New York, 59-62; David & Saul, Calif Legion Honor, San Francisco, 60; Motherhood, Miami Beach Publ Libr, 77. *Awards:* Second Prize, Whither Thou Goest, Brooklyn Mus, 52; Second Place, Milk Weed Pods, Oil Riverdale Mus, 92. *Bibliog:* Article, New York Times, 4/27/52; America discovers art, New York Post, 10/58. *Mem:* Charter mem Artists Equity; Brooklyn Soc Artists. *Media:* Bronze, Marble; Oil. *Publ:* Illusr & compiler, In the Beginning Cookbook, Progressive Synagogue, 69. *Dealer:* Lincoln Mall Gallery Miami Beach FL; Cambi Gallery Bay Harbor Island FL. *Mailing Add:* 2550 Webb Ave, Apt 12E Bronx NY 10468

SIMONI, JOHN PETER
PAINTER, EDUCATOR
b Denver, Colo, Apr 12, 11. *Study:* Colo State Col Educ, BA & MA; Nat Univ Mex; Kansas City Art Inst, with Thomas Hart Benton; Univ Colo, with Max Beckmann; Ohio State Univ, PhD; Mass Inst Technol; also in Trentino, Italy; Int Univ Art, Florence, Italy, cert specialization (museology, conserv & restoration), 79. *Work:* Colo Friends Art Collection. *Comn:* Mural paintings, The Kerr McGee Ctr, Oklahoma City, Okla, 75, The Mid-Kans Savings & Loan Bank of Wichita, 76, Reading & Bates Petroleum Ctr of Tulsa, Okla, 76 & Sheplers of Wichita, Kans, 76; Wall Painting, BPOE Lodge 2617, Estes Park, Colo, 88-; and others. *Exhib:* Mulvane Mus Art; Wichita Art Mus; Colo State Univ; Birger Sandzen Mem Gallery, Lindsborg, Kans; Univ Wichita. *Pos:* Gallery dir, Baker Univ, 37-55; dir Univ Galleries, Univ Wichita, 57-63; designer, John Coultis Interiors, 57-76; color consult, Western Lithograph Co, Wichita, Kans & Houston, Tex, 61-63; co-dir Univ Gallery, Wichita State Univ, 64-67. *Teaching:* Head dept art, Baker Univ, 37-55; prof art, Univ Wichita, 55-57, chmn dept art, 57-63; prof art, Wichita State Univ, 64-78; retired. *Awards:* Decorated Knight Order of Crown, Italy, 47; Knight Officer, Order of Merit, Repub Italy, 66; Academician of Italy with Gold Medal, Accademia Italia Arti Lavoro, 80. *Mem:* Am Soc Aesthet; Col Art Asn Am; Kans Fedn Art; Southwestern Col Art Conf (pres, 62-64); fel Int Inst Arts & Lett; and others. *Publ:* Columnist, Wichita Eagle; columnist, Baldwin Ledger, 65-68; columnist, Estes Park Trail Gazette, 60-; columnist, Art in the Bluestream, El Dorado Times, 76-; Writings on Art Criticism in 19th Century America, 51; Art Critics & Criticism in 19th Century America, 52; The Structure of Form in Painting & Design, 73. *Mailing Add:* PO Box 1154 Estes Park CO 80517

SIMONIAN, JUDITH
PAINTER
b Los Angeles, Calif, 45. *Study:* Calif State Univ, Northridge, BA, 67; MA, 74. *Work:* Chemical Bank, New York; Security Pac Bank, New York & Los Angeles; Prudential Savings Insurance Co, NJ, Kaufman & Broad, Los Angeles & Paris, France; Newport Harbor Mus, Calif. *Comn:* Alteration, Downtown Los Angeles in Santa Barbara, Santa Barbara Mus Art, 80; sculpture, MacArthur Park Pub Art Prog, Los Angeles, Calif, 85; sculpture, Barbara Sinatra Children's Ctr, Palm Springs, Calif, 86; street installation, Washington Proj Arts, Washington, DC, 87; site sculpture, Art on the Beach, NY, 88. *Exhib:* Seibu Mus, Tokyo, Japan, 79; Fresh Paint, San Francisco Mus Mod Art, 82; one-person exhib, Ovsey Gallery, Los Angeles, Calif, 82, 83, 84, 86, 88, 90 & 91, Leila Taghinia-Milani, New York, 84, Newport Harbor Art Mus, Calif, 84 & Jane H Baum Gallery, New York, 89, Peter Miller Gallery, Chicago, Ill, 84 & 91; Viewing Recent Contemporary Landscape Painting, Calif State Univ, Los Angeles, 84; Fresno Art & Mus, Calif, 88; Mus Bochum, WGer, 88; Altos de Chavon, La Romana, Dom Repub, 90; American Art Today, Fla Int Univ, Miami, 90; Selections from the permanent collection, Newport Harbor Mus Art, Calif, 92; Hells Kitchen, Salon de Guerre, New York, 92. *Teaching:* Instr drawing, Moorpark Community Col, 74-78; East Los Angeles Community Col, 78-82; instr color theory & graphic art, Calif State Univ, Long Beach, 80-81; instr drawings & painting, Otis Parson Sch of Design, Los Angeles, Calif, 81-85; vis artist, Clairmont Grad Sch, Calif, 83 & 88. *Awards:* Fel, Calif confederation of the Arts, 78; Fel, Nat Endowment Arts, 87; Artist in Residency Prog Altos de Chavon, Dominican Repub, 90. *Bibliog:* Kathy Norklon (auth), First Newport Biennial-Los Angeles, Newport Harbor Art Mus, 84; Robert L Pincus (auth), Art as Artifact, Flash Art, summer 85; Terry Bissell (auth), Art: Judith Simonian, Southern Calif Home & Garden, 11/88. *Media:* Acrylic, Miscellaneous Media. *Mailing Add:* 361 W 36th St, #12 New York NY 10018

SIMOR, SUZANNA B
LIBRARIAN, GALLERY DIRECTOR
b Prague, Czech; US citizen. *Study:* Inst Fine Arts, NY Univ, MA, 74; Grad Sch Libr & Info Sci, Pratt Inst, MLS, 76. *Collections Arranged:* Italian Art--15th to 18th Century (auth catalog), Godwin-Ternbach Mus, Queens Col, 86. *Pos:* Head Art Libr, dir Art Ctr, Queens Col, City Univ NY, 80- *Teaching:* Asst prof art librarianship, Queens Col, City Univ NY, 77- *Awards:* Nat Endowment Arts Grant, 85; PSC/City Univ NY Grant, 86-87. *Mem:* Art Librs Soc NAM (chmn, 77, NY chapter chmn, 90-); Col Art Asn; Special Librs Asn-Mus-Arts and Humanities Div; Am Libr Asn; Libr Asn City Univ NY (chmn, 77-). *Res:* Art librarianship; art bibliography and research methods; late medieval and Renaissance art; 20th century art. *Interests:* Medieval and Renaissance art; art of the 20th century contemporary art and artists. *Publ:* Auth, articles, Basic Materials for Reference & Research in Art History, Queens Col, 81-86; auth & ed, Art of E Africa Slide Collection, IFLA, Art Librs Sect, 84; ed, NY Membership Directory, ARLIS/NY, 85; coauth, Italian Art--15th to 18th Century, Queens Col, 86; auth, Necessary luxury: art exhibitions in academic libraries, 90; The Credo in Context: Endorsing Other Themes, Pensee - image et communication en Europe medievale, 91. *Mailing Add:* Queens Col Art Libr City Univ New York Flushing NY 11367

SIMPER, FREDERICK
PAINTER
b Mishawaka, Ind, July 31, 14. *Study:* Self-taught. *Work:* Detroit Inst Arts; South Bend Art Mus, Ind; US Embassies Collection. *Exhib:* Detroit Inst Arts, 38-68; Art Inst Chicago, 48; Watercolor USA, Springfield, Mo, 65; Butler Inst Art, Youngstown, Ohio; Pa Acad Fine Arts, Philadelphia; one-man shows, Arwin Gallery, Detroit, 78 & The Herman Frankel Orgn, W Bloomfield, 86. *Pos:* Art dir, D'Arcy, Macmanus Int, 49-80. *Teaching:* Instr watercolor, Soc Arts & Crafts, Detroit, 48-51; instr watercolor, Bloomfield Art Asn, Birmingham, Mich, 68-70. *Awards:* Detroit Inst Arts Founders Soc Award, 42; Baltimore Sun Award for Black & White Drawing, 45; Mich Watercolor Soc Award, 72. *Mem:* Mich Watercolor Soc. *Media:* Watercolor. *Mailing Add:* PO Box 562 Leland MI 49654

SIMPSON, BUSTER
SCULPTOR
b May 29, 42. *Study:* Univ Mich, BA, MFA, 63-69. *Work:* City Seattle, Portland, Ore, Cleveland, Ohio, Anaheim, Calif, State of Wash, Denver Int Airport, Metrop Boston Transit Authority. *Exhib:* Keating/Simpson, Seattle Art Mus, 79; one-man show, Western Front, Vancouver, BC, Can, 80; Images & Latitude, Paris, 88; Face Plate, Installation, Hirshhorn Mus & Sculpture Garden, Washington, DC, 89; Alexandria Marsh Gardens, Va, 90-92; Material in the Service of Meaning, Tacoma Art Mus, Wash, 91. *Pos:* Comnr, Pike Pl Market Hist Dist Comn, Seattle, Wash, 83; artist consult, Schmidt Copeland Assoc, Oakland County, Mo, 87-88, Redondo Seawall, Federal Way, Wash, 88-89, New Denver Airport, Colo, 90-91, Central Artery/Tunnel, Boston, Mass, 91-92. *Teaching:* Instr drawing & mixed media, Flint Jr Col, Mich, 69; artist in residence, Artpark, Lewiston, NY, 78; vis lectr, Univ NC, Chapel Hill, 92. *Mailing Add:* 901 Yakima Ave Seattle WA 98114

SIMPSON, DAVID
PAINTER, EDUCATOR
b Pasadena, Calif, Jan 20, 28. *Study:* Calif Sch Fine Arts, with Clifford Still & others, BFA, 56; San Francisco State Col, MA, 58. *Work:* San Francisco Mus Art; Oakland Art Mus, Calif; Mus Mod Art, New York; Philadelphia Mus Art; Baltimore Mus Art; Panza Collection, Milan, Italy; Univ Art Mus, Berkeley, Calif; Laguna Art Mus, Laguna Beach, Calif. *Exhib:* Americans 1963, Mus Mod Art, New York, 63; Retrospective, Oakland Mus, Calif, 78; Mincher/Wilcox Gallery, San Francisco, 90-92; Angles Gallery, Santa Monica, Calif, 91-92; Anthony Ralph Gallery, NY, 92; John Good Gallery, NY, 92; Bemis Found, Omaha, Nebr, 92; and others. *Teaching:* Prof art emer, Univ Calif, Berkeley, 65- *Awards:* Nat Endowment Arts Grant, 90. *Media:* Acrylic. *Dealer:* Mincher/Wilcox Gallery 228 Grant St San Francisco CA 94108. *Mailing Add:* 565 Vistamont Berkeley CA 94708

SIMPSON, GAIL A
SCULPTOR
b Baltimore, Md. *Study:* Wash Univ, St Louis, Mo, BFA; Art Inst Chicago, MFA. *Work:* Chicago Title & Trust, Ill. *Exhib:* Par Excellence, Ill State Mus & Sch Chicago Art Inst, 88; About Devices, White Columns Gallery, New York, 89; two-person exhib, Cage Gallery, Cincinnati, Ohio, 90; Omnibus, Herron Gallery, Indianapolis, Ind, 91; three-person exhibit, Abel Joseph Gallery, 92. *Teaching:* Asst Prof sculpture, Ill State Univ, 89- *Awards:* Nat Endowment Arts, 88- *Mem:* Col Art Asn; Int Sculpture Soc. *Mailing Add:* 103 S Clinton Bloomington IL 61701

SIMPSON, LEE
PAINTER
b Cisco, Tex, Oct 9, 23. *Study:* Columbia Univ, with Arnold Leondar; also with Louise Nevelson & Elaine De Kooning, New York. *Work:* Empire Savings & Loan, Denver; Midland Fed Savings & Loan, Denver; Am Express, Denver; Int Bus Machines, Dallas; Beech Aircraft, Wichita; and others. *Comn:* Mural, Perryton Nat Bank, Tex, 69; lithograph, PBS TV, Denver, 78. *Exhib:* Spec Group Show, Panhandle-Plains Hist Mus, Canyon, Tex, 69; 9th & 10th Ann Awards Show, Taos Art Asn, 71 & 72; Southwest Fine Arts Biennial, Mus NMex, Santa Fe, 72; one-man show, WTex State Univ, Canyon, 68. *Pos:* Owner & instr oil painting, Simpson Gallery & Studio, Amarillo, 62-70. *Teaching:* Guest lectr oil painting, WTex State Univ, 69; guest instr oil painting, Amarillo Jr Col, 69-70. *Awards:* Juror's Citation Award, State Citation Show, Tex Fine Arts Asn, 68 & 69; First Award, 9th Ann Awards Show, Taos Art Asn, 72. *Bibliog:* Whitney Meeckum (auth), The man is the medium, Southwest Art Mag, 4/70. *Media:* Oil, Pastel. *Dealer:* Ledoux Gallery PO Box 2418 Taos NM 87571; Adelle M Fine Art 3317 McKinney Ave Dallas TX 75204. *Mailing Add:* c/o El Prado Galleries-Patio Azul Tlaquepaque Arts & Crafts Village PO Box 1849 Sedona AZ 86336

SIMPSON, MARIANNA SHREVE
HISTORIAN, EDUCATOR
b Washington, DC, Nov 17, 49. *Study:* Univ Pa, BA, 70; Johns Hopkins Univ, 71-72; Harvard Univ, PhD, 78. *Pos:* From asst to actg registr, Baltimore Mus Art, 71-72; res assoc, Freer Gallery Art, Smithsonian Inst, 79-80; asst dean, Ctr Advan Study Visual Arts, Nat Gallery Art, Washington, DC, 80- *Teaching:* Lectr, Harvard Univ, Cambridge, Mass, 78 & Georgetown Univ, Washington, DC, 80-; vis asst prof, Univ Calif, Los Angeles, 80. *Awards:* Mus Intern Fel, Nat Endowment Arts & Fogg Art Mus, Harvard Univ, 76-77; Pre-Doctoral Fel, Smithsonian Inst, 77-78; Grant-in-aid, Am Coun Learned Soc, 79. *Mem:* Middle East Studies Asn; Col Art Asn. *Res:* Medieval Islamic art, with focus on problems in illustrated manuscript studies of fourteenth through sixteenth centuries. *Publ:* Auth, Arab and Persian Painting in the Fogg Art Mus, Fogg Art Mus, 80; auth, The Illustration of an Epic: The Earliest Shahnama Manuscripts, Garland, 79; auth, The narrative structure of a medieval Iranian beaker, 81 & The production and patronage of the Haft Aurang by Jami in the Freer Gallery of Art, 82, Art Orientalis; auth, The role of Baghdad in the formation of Persian painting, In: Art et Societe Dans le Monde Iranien, Paris, 82. *Mailing Add:* Georgetown Univ Dept of Fine Arts 37th & O St NW Washington DC 20001

SIMPSON, MARILYN JEAN
PAINTER, INSTRUCTOR
b Birmingham, Ala. *Study:* Univ Ala; Art Students League; Inst Allende, San Miguel Allende, Mex; Madison Art Sch, Conn; with Robert Brackman; Am Univ Avignon, France; Rome & Florence, Italy. *Exhib:* Am Arts Prof League; Kottler Gallery; Smithsonian Inst, Washington, DC; Pastel Soc Am, NY; Pastel Soc NMex; and others. *Pos:* Founder, Pastel Soc North Fla; dir, Sch Pastel Painting, Ft Walton Beach, Fla. *Teaching:* Dir & instr, Acad Fine Arts, Ft Walton Beach, Fla. *Awards:* Gold Medal, Acad Rome; Am Artists Prof League Cash Award, Grand Nat Exchange, NY; Dick Blick Award; Golden Egg Gallery Award, Dallas, Tex; Golden Centaur Award, Rome, Italy; Pastel Soc Am Plaque, Pastel Soc, NMex Nat; Am Artist Award, Pastel Soc NFla, Nat, Pensacola. *Mem:* Signature mem Pastel Soc Am, NY; Pastel Soc Southwest, Dallas, Tex; Pastel Soc N Fla, Ft Walton Beach, Fla; Allied Artist Am, NY. *Media:* Pastel, Oil. *Dealer:* Gallery Fine Arts Hwy 98 East Destin Fl. *Mailing Add:* Rte 1 Box 43-C Mary Esther FL 32569

SIMPSON, MERTON D
PAINTER, DEALER
b Charleston, SC, Sept 20, 28. *Study:* NY Univ; Cooper Union Art Sch, with Robert Motherwell & Baziotes; also with William Halsey. *Work:* James J Sweeney Collection, Guggenheim Mus; Howard Univ, Washington, DC; Scott Field Mus, Chicago; Atlanta Univ; Gibbs Art Gallery. *Exhib:* Guggenheim Mus & Metrop Mus Art, New York; Brooklyn Mus, NY; Nat Gallery, Paris; Nat Mus Japan. *Pos:* Owner, Merton D Simpson Gallery, New York. *Awards:* Red Cross Exchange Exhib Award, Tokyo & Paris, 50; Atlanta Univ Awards, 50, 51 & 56; Oakland Art Mus Award, 52. *Specialty:* Primitive art, especially African. *Mailing Add:* 1063 Madison Ave New York NY 10028

SIMPSON, WILLIAM KELLY
HISTORIAN, EDUCATOR
b New York, NY, Jan 3, 28. *Study:* Yale Univ, BA, 47, MA, 48, PhD, 54; Ecole Practique Hautes Etudes, Paris. *Collections Arranged:* The Pennsylvania-Yale Expedition to Nubia, Peabody Mus, Yale Univ, New Haven, Conn, 63; Recent Accessions in Egyptian & Ancient Near Eastern Art & The Horace L Mayer Collection, 72, Mus Fine Arts, Boston; Metrop Mus, New York; Univ Pa Mus, Philadelphia. *Pos:* Cur Egyptian art, Mus Fine Arts, Boston, 70-87. *Teaching:* Prof Egyptol, Yale Univ, 56-; vis prof Egyptol, Univ Pa. *Awards:* Guggenheim Found Fel, 65. *Mem:* Archaeol Inst Am; Am Oriental Soc; Am Res Ctr in Egypt; Int Coun Mus Mod Art, New York; and others. *Res:* Art, history, and literature of ancient Egypt. *Publ:* Auth, Papyrus Reisner I-Records of a Building Project, 63; auth, Papyrus Reisner II-Accounts of the Dockyard Workshop, 65; auth, Papyrus Reisner III-Records of a Building Project in the Early Twelfth Dynasty, 69; coauth, The Ancient Near East: A History, 71; coauth, The Literature of Ancient Egypt, 72; auth, The Mastaba of Queen Mersyankh III, 74. *Mailing Add:* Katonah's Wood Rd Katonah NY 10536

SIMS, LOWERY STOKES
HISTORIAN, CURATOR
b Washington, DC, Feb 13, 49. *Study:* Queens Col, City Univ New York, BA, 70, MPhil, 90; Johns Hopkins Univ, MA, 72; Md Inst, Baltimore, LHD, 88. *Collections Arranged:* John Marin: Selection Works from Mus, Metrop Mus, New York, 81; Charles Burchfield, Metrop Mus, New York, 83; Romare Bearen: And Artists' Odyssey, (catalog essay & organizer), 86; Race and Representation, (catalog essay), Hunter Col Gallery, New York, 87; New York; New Venues, The Work of Herb Aach, Joan Semmel and Al Loving, (auth, catalog essay), Mint Mus, Charlotte, NC 87; Art as a Verb, The Evolving Continuum, (co-curator & essay), Maryland Inst Col of Art, Baltimore, Md, 88-89; Next Generation, Southern Black Aesthetic, (catalog essay), Southern Center Contemp Art, Winston-Salem, NC, 90. *Pos:* Asst mus educ, Metrop Mus Art, New York, 72-75, assoc cur 20th century art, 75- *Teaching:* Adj lectr survey art, Queens Col, City Univ New York, 73-76, adj lectr African art, 75; lectr found art hist & curatorship, Sch Visual Arts, 75-76 & 81-86; vis critic, Md Inst, 87, Penn Academy Arts, 88. *Awards:* Frank Jewett Award, Col Art Asn, 91. *Mem:* Col Art Asn; Int Asn Art Critics; NY State Coun Arts. *Res:* 20th century painting, sculpture and architecture especially of the last 30 years, with special interest in Afro-American, Latin American, Asian and Native American artists. *Publ:* In Search of Wilfredo Lam, Arts Mag, Vol 63, No 4, 50-55, 12/88; 'Heat' and Other Climatic Manifestations: Urban Bush Women, Thought Music and Craig Harris with the Dirty Tones Band, Vol 12, No 1, 22-27, Spring 88; Words Into Vision: The Art of Hachivi Edgar Heap of Birds, (essay for the catalog), Hachivi Edgar Heap of Birds: Claim Your Color, Exit Art, New York, 89; The Mirror, the Other: The Politics of Esthetics, Art Forum, Vol XXVIII, No 7, 111-115, 3/90; Race Riots - Cocktail Parties - Black Panthers - Moon Shoots and Feminists: Faith Ringgold's Observations on the 1960's in America, (essay), Faith Ringgold: A 25 Year Survey, Fine Arts Mus Long Island, Hempstead, New York, 90; Beulahland (for Marilyn Monroe), An Icon for America, (essay), IDA Applebroog: Happy Families, A Fifteen-Year Survey, Comtemp Arts Mus, Houston, 90; Cultural Diversity or the Americanist Canon: The Aesthetic Dialog of the 1990's, (catalog essay), The Decade Show, New Mus Comtemp Art, Studio Mus Harlem & Mus Comtemp Hispanic Art, New York, 90. *Mailing Add:* Metrop Mus Art Fifth Ave at 82nd St New York NY 10028

SIMS, PATTERSON
CURATOR
b Philadelphia, Pa, Nov 17, 47. *Study:* Chestnut Hill Acad, Philadelphia, Pa; Darrow Sch, New Lebanon, NY; Trinity Col, Hartford, Conn; New Sch Social Res, New York, BA, 72. *Collections Arranged:* Seven Decades of MacDowell Colony Artists, James Yu Gallery, 76; On Canvas, 76, 30 Years of American Art, Whitney Biennial Exhibition, American Art 1900-1950 & Selections from the Promised Gift of Mrs Percy Uris, 77 & American Art 1920- 1945, 77-78, Whitney Mus Am Art, New York; School of Visual Arts 1977 End of the Year Show, 77; American Art 1900-1950, 77, Jasper Johns: A Selected View, 89 & Made in New York: The New York School: 1945-1965, 89, Seattle Art Mus; Mark Tansey: Art and Source, 90, Documents Northwest Series: Buster Simpson, 91 & Dale Chihuly: Installations 1964-1992 (auth, catalog), 92, Seattle Art Mus; Jacob Lawrence: The Early Decades 1935-1950, Katona Mus, New York, 92. *Pos:* Asst dir, O K Harris Works of Art, New York, 69-76; assoc cur permanent collection, Whitney Mus Am Art, 76-87; assoc dir art & exhibs & cur mod art, Seattle Art Mus, Wash, 87- *Teaching:* Part-time instr, Sch Continuing Educ, New York Univ, 75-77 & 84-86. *Publ:* Auth, Alan Shields, Moore Col Art, Pa, 77; Jan Matulka: A Life in Art, Smithsonian Press, 79; Whitney Museum of American Art: Selected Works from the Permanent Collection, 86; Documents Northwest Series: CT Chew, 88, Figures of Translucence, 89 & Crossed Cultures, 89 (exhib brochures), Seattle Art Mus. *Mailing Add:* c/o Seattle Art Museum Volunteer Park Seattle WA 98112

SIMS, PETER ANDREW
GALLERY DIRECTOR, HISTORIAN
b Pottsville, Pa, April 19, 59. *Study:* Paul Mellon Ctr Brit Art, London, cert, 80; Yale Univ, BA, 81. *Pos:* Art ed, Yale Literary Mag, New Haven, Conn, 81-86; asst to the dir, Weintraub Gallery, New York, 86- *Awards:* Am Literary Soc Fel, 83 & 84. *Res:* Work on: Igor Galanin, George Stubbs, Marc Chagall and others. *Specialty:* 20th century masters, Picasso, Chagall, Moore, Calder, Leger, Arp and others. *Mailing Add:* c/o Weintraub Gallery 968 Madison Ave New York NY 10021

SIMSON, BEVLYN A
PAINTER, PRINTMAKER
b Columbus, Ohio, Sept 9, 17. *Study:* Ohio State Univ, BFA & MFA; mus in Europe & Japan. *Work:* Chase Manhattan Bank, New York; Kresge Collection, Detroit; Columbus Mus Art; J B Speed Mus, Louisville, Ky; Tyler Mus, Tex; and others. *Comn:* Nine paintings, Lobby, Ohio State Nisonger Ctr; three-panel paintings, First Investment Co, 69 & First Community Bank, 81. *Exhib:* One-person shows, J B Speed Mus, Louisville, Ky, 70, City Hall, Columbus, Ohio, 73, Capital Univ, 77, Springfield Art Mus, 80, Franklin Univ, 81 & Collectors Gallery, Columbus Mus Art, 83; 37th Nat Painting Show, Butler Inst Am Art, Youngstown, Ohio, 73; Contemp Prints for Collectors, Columbus Mus Art, 74 & 75; Represented US at 2nd Int Art Exhib, Parimaribo, Suriname, 74; Ohio Women Artists: Past & Present, Butler Inst Am Art, 76; Legacy of Hoyt Sherman, Denver Mus Art & Ohio State Univ Gallery, 82; Centre Int d'Art Contemp, Paris, 83; and others. *Awards:* Dipl di Merito, Univ della Arte, Acad Ital, 82; Best of Show, State of Ohio Competition, Nat League Am PEN Women, 85; Shared Best of Show Award, 29th Ann Fall Exhib, Bexley Art Guild, Trinity Lutheran Sem, 90; and others. *Bibliog:* Jacqueline Hall (auth), Bevlyn Simson displays works internationally, Columbus Dispatch, 4/9/75; Mary Bridgman (auth), Bevlyn Simson rhymes colors & shapes, Columbus Dispatch, 12/11/77; Tricia & Mat Herban (auths), Bevlyn Simson neo-geometrics show a technique of modern art, Columbus Citizen-J, 5/16/83. *Mem:* Nat Mus Women in the Arts, Columbus Mus Art; Am Fedn Arts; Nat League Am Pen Women; Bexley Area Art Guild; Columbus Art League (past pres). *Media:* Acrylic; Lithograph, Silkscreen. *Publ:* Auth, Prints & Poetry, 69. *Mailing Add:* Bevlyn Simson Gallery 289 S Roosevelt Ave Columbus OH 43209

SINA, ALEJANDRO
KINETIC ARTIST, SCULPTOR
b Santiago, Chile, May 10, 45. *Study:* Univ Chile, MBA, 73; Ctr Advan Visual Studies, Mass Inst Technol, with Gyorgy Kepes & Otto Piene, fel, 73-79. *Work:* Mus Sci & Indust, Chicago; Nat Mus Fine Arts, Santiago; Nat Sci Mus, Veno Park, Tokyo; Saitama Childrens Mus, Higashi-Matsuyama, Japan; Bruce Mus, Greenwich, Conn. *Comn:* Neon Rainbow, Creative Times, New York, 76; neon mobile, comn by Graham Gund, Hyatt Regency, Cambridge, Mass, 77; participatory kinetic lightworks, Art Pub Space, Rye, NY, 78-80, 82 & 83; kinetic light sculpture, Cambridge Arts Coun, Mass, 82-84; Neon Veils, Cambridge Side, NEng Development, Cambridge, Mass, 90. *Exhib:*

Gaslight Phenomena, Inst Contemp Art, Boston, 77; Five Artists, Five Technologies, Grand Rapids Art Mus, Mich, 79; 16th Biennial Arte, Sao Paulo, Brazil, 81; Art in Light and Illusion, Isetan Mus Art, Tokyo, 82; Light: Recent Issues in Illumination, Morris Mus, Morristown, NJ, 82; Color-Light-Motion, Wadsworth Atheneum, Hartford, Conn, 84; PULSE, New York, 87; Images des Futur, Montreal, Can, 88; ARTEC 89, Nagoya, Japan; PULSE 2, Univ Calif, Santa Barbara, 90. *Teaching:* Instr, Ctr Advan Visual Studies, Mass Inst Technol, 73-77. *Awards:* Fulbright Fel, 73-75; Nat Endowment Arts Grant, 76-77. *Bibliog:* Milan Ivelic & Gaspar Galaz (auths), La Pintura en Chile, Univ Catolica, Valparaiso, 82; Sixto Escobar (producer), The Art of Alejandro Sina, La Plaza Prog, TV Channel 7, Boston, 83; Michael Webb (auth), The Magic of Neon, Gibbs M Smith Inc, 83; Michael Webb (auth), Liquid Fire, Gibbs Smith, 90; Rudi Stern (auth), Contemporary Neon, Larry Fuersich Retail Reporting, 91. *Media:* Neon, Electronics; Glass. *Mailing Add:* 21 Andem Pl No 1 Brookline MA 02146

SINCLAIR, ROBERT (W)
PAINTER, SCULPTOR
b Saltcoats, Sask, Can, Feb 9, 39. *Study:* Univ Manitoba Sch Art, BFA, 61; Univ Iowa, MA, 65, MFA, 67. *Work:* Art Gallery, Windsor, Ont; Agnes Etherington Art Gallery, Queens Univ, Kingston, Ont; Confederation Art Gallery, Charlottetown, PEI; Glenbow Mus, Calgary, Alta; Edmonton Art Gallery, Alta; Royal Collection, Windsor Castle Libr, Eng. *Comn:* Foyer painting (acrylic stain), Oxford Develop Group, Royal Trust Tower, Edmonton, Alta, 79; Slumped Glass Landscape (sculpture), Brit Petroleum, Calgary, Alta, 89. *Exhib:* A Response to the Environment, Rutgers Univ Gallery, NJ, 75; Changing Visions, Art Gallery Ont, Toronto, 76-77; one-man shows, Gallery-Stratford, Ont, 76 & Edmonton Art Gallery, Alta, 82-83; Pertaining to Space, Art Gallery Ont, Toronto, 76-77; Diamond Jubilee Collection, Royal Libr, Windsor Castle, Eng, 86; Spaces & Places, Alta Art Found, traveling China & Japan, 86-90; Heaven-and-Earth, Whyte Mus Can Rockies, Banff, Alta, 91; Artists in Wilderness: Images of a Vanishing Alberta, Provincial Mus, Edmonton, 92. *Teaching:* Prof art painting & drawing, Dept Art & Design, Univ Alta, 65-; vis artist, Univ Iowa, 73 & Banff Sch Fine Art, 76. *Bibliog:* Four Praire Artists (film), Can Broadcasting Corp, 85. *Mem:* Royal Canadian Acad Arts; Can Soc Painters Watercolour. *Media:* Watercolor, Acrylic Stain. *Dealer:* Kathleen Laverty Gallery 10411 124 St Edmonton Alta T5N 3Z5; Ingram Fine Arts 697 Mt Pleasant Rd Toronto Ont M4S 2N4. *Mailing Add:* 10819 52 Ave Edmonton AB T6H 0P2 Canada

SINDELIR, ROBERT JOHN
GALLERY DIRECTOR, ADMINISTRATOR
b Olivia, Minn, June 12, 32. *Study:* Univ Miami, Coral Gables, Fla, with Virgil Barker, AB, 57. *Collections Arranged:* Christo, Wrapped Coastline, 72; Lee Krasner, Selected Paintings, 73; Duane Michals, Photographs, 77; Philip Pearlstein, Selected Paintings, 78; Komar and Melamid, Monotype Prints, 90. *Pos:* Dir, Art Pub Places Prog, Miami, Fla, 74-76, Mitchell Wolfson Gallery, 83-90, Kendall Campus Art Gallery, 90- *Teaching:* Instr humanities, Miami-Dade Community Col, 70-74. *Publ:* Auth, African Tribal Art (exhib catalog), Miami-Dade Community Col, 83; contribr, Journal of Decorative and Propaganda Arts, Wolfsonian Found, 86; auth, Susana Sori (exhib catalog), Thomas Ctr, 88; Julio Antonio (exhib catalog), Elite Fine Art, 89; Lynn Davison (exhib catalog), Miami-Dade Community Col, 91. *Mailing Add:* 11011 SW 104th St Miami FL 33176-3393

SINGER, CLIFFORD
PAINTER, PRINTMAKER
b Great Neck, NY, May 19, 55. *Study:* Alfred Univ, BFA, 77; Empire State, 77; Hunter Col, 77-79, City Col New York, MFA, 90; Staten Island Col, City Univ New York, 92. *Work:* Mus Mod Art, New York Pub Libr, Chelsea Sch Art & Lincoln Ctr, New York; Gemeente Mus & Riyksmuseum, Meermano, Den Haag; Victoria & Albert Mus and Victoria Mira, London; Found Pro, Neth; and many others in US and abroad. *Comn:* Lemma III (three paintings), Mobil Oil Corp Hq, New York, 83; Didecameter Suite, paintings, AT&T, Atlanta, Ga, 85; Poster, Lincoln Ctr, New York, 91. *Exhib:* Acquisitions Since 1980, Aldrich Mus Contemp Art, 86; solo exhibs, Art Investors Int, Trump Plaza, West Palm Beach, Fla, 86 & Vasarley Ctr, New York, 88; Bayley Gallery, New York, 87; Art Res Ctr, Kansas City, Mo, 88; Ann Jacob Gallery, Atlanta, Ga, 89; Gemini Gallery, Palm Beach, Fla, 89; Art Res Ctr, Kansas City, Mo, 91; Lincoln Ctr/Tokyu Bunkamura, New York & Tokyo; and many others. *Awards:* Change Found Grant, Rober Rauchenberg, 89. *Bibliog:* Articles in Arts Mag & Art Investors Int, 86; BH Friedman (auth), Clifford Singer, Vasarely Ctr, Whitney Mus Art, 88; Les Krantz (auth), New York Art Review, 88. *Mem:* Visual Artists & Galleries Asn, Inc; Orgn Independent Artists, Inc. *Media:* Acrylic; Silkscreen. *Publ:* Chris Hunter (auth), Paintings blaze of color, Palm Beach Daily News, 4/22/86; Les Krantz (auth), NY Art Rev, 88; B H Friedman (auth, trustee), Vasarely Ctr, Whitney Mus Am Art, 88. *Mailing Add:* 510 Broome St New York NY 10012

SINGER, CLYDE J
PAINTER
b Malvern, Ohio, Oct 20, 08. *Study:* Columbus Art Sch, Ohio; Art Students League, with Kenneth Hayes Miller, John Steuart Curry & Thomas Hart Benton. *Work:* Pa Acad Fine Arts, Philadelphia; Wadsworth Atheneum, Hartford, Conn; Thomas Gilcrease Inst Hist & Art, Tulsa, Okla; Butler Inst Am Art, Youngstown, Ohio; Canton Art Inst, Ohio. *Comn:* Skaters (mural), Post Off, New Concord, Ohio, 40. *Exhib:* Over 40 exhibs in maj mus, 35-58, incl Carnegie Mus Int, Pittsburgh, Pa, 36-39; Corcoran Gallery Art Biennial, Washington, DC, 37; Golden Gate Int Expos, San Francisco, 39; Whitney Mus Am Art Painting & Sculpture Biennial, 41; Artists for Victory, Rockefeller Ctr, New York, 45; The Neglected Generation of American Realist Painters, 1930-1948, Wichita Art Mus, Kans, 81. *Pos:* Art critic, Vindicator, Youngstown, 40-; asst dir, Butler Inst Am Art, 40- *Awards:* Norman Wait Harris Silver Medal, Art Inst Chicago, 35; First Hallgarten Prize, Nat Acad Design, 38; Pagasus Award, Ohioana Libr Asn, 72; Alumni Award, Columbus Col Fine Arts, Ohio, 89. *Bibliog:* Roger Bonham (auth), Clyde Singer; Ohio painter, Am Artist, 2/69; Clyde Singer's New York, Butler Inst, 2/87; M J Albacete (auth), Clyde Singer's New York, Canton Art Inst, 11/89; Eliz McClelland (auth), The Art of Clyde Singer, Regional Artists Inc Ser, 92. *Media:* Oil. *Mailing Add:* 210 Forest Park Dr Youngstown OH 44512

SINGER, ESTHER FORMAN
PAINTER, CRITIC
b New York, NY, Oct 14, 28. *Study:* Art Students League, 39-41; Temple Univ, 41-44; NY Univ, 47-49; New Sch Social Res, 68-70; Fairleigh Dickinson Univ, pvt study with Hans Hoffman, Brackman, George Gross & Tosun Bayrak; Hon degree, Universita d'ell Arte Contemporania, Parma, Italy, 82. *Work:* NJ State Mus, Trenton; Finch Mus Contemp Art, Whitney Mus Permanent Collection, New York; Yonkers Mus, New York; Morris Mus Arts & Sciences, Morristown, NJ; Newark Mus, NJ; Libr Congress; Sen Nelson Stamler Collection. *Comn:* Many works in pvt & pub collections. *Exhib:* Chubb Art Gallery, Warren, NJ, 86; Shering-Plough, Madison, NJ, 88; Johnson & Johnson Corp Hq, 90; Governors Club, Palm Beach, Fla, 90; Aids Project, Hyacinth Found, 91; and others. *Pos:* Guest panelist, Art Forms, WOR-TV, 67-68; ed, Newark News, 70-74; art critic, Am Artist Mag, 72- & Worrall Press, 74- *Teaching:* Instr elementary art, Baird Community Ctr, South Orange, NJ, 69-; pvt instr at own studio, South Orange, NJ, 68-70. *Awards:* Gov Purchase Award, Art from NJ 10; Painting Prize, Mus Mod Art, Paris, 73. *Bibliog:* Carlotte Winslow (auth), article in NJ Suburban Life Mag, 3/70; article, New York Art Rev Mag, 87; Art Views (film), Ch 36, 10/91; and others. *Mem:* Artists Equity Asn, NJ & NY; Old Bergen Art Guild; Painters & Sculptors Soc, NJ; Am Veterans Soc Artists. *Media:* Acrylic. *Dealer:* Helander Gallery Palm Beach FL; Key Gallery Soho NY. *Mailing Add:* 15 Lawrence Way Cedar Grove NJ 07009

SINGER, MICHAEL
SCULPTOR
b 1945. *Study:* Cornell Univ, BFA, 63-67; Rutgers Univ, New Brunswick, grad study, 68; Yale Univ, Klorfolk Prog, 68. *Exhib:* Solo exhibs, Galerie Zabriskie, Paris, 81, J Walter Thompson Art Gallery, New York, 83, Solomon R Guggenheim, New York, 84, Sperone Westwater, New York, 86, Michael Singer Ritual Series, Retelling, Fine Arts Ctr, Art Gallery, State Univ NY-Stonybrook & Michael Singer-Ritual Series, Santa Barbara Contemp Arts Forum, 87, Artworks: Michael Singer, Williams Col Mus Art, Williamstown, Mass, 90; Sculpture Inside Outside, Walker Art Ctr, Minneapolis, 88; Collage, Robinson Orange Gallery, Boston, 89; Arts on Paper, Weatherspoon Art Gallery, Univ NC, Greensboro, 90-91; The Transparent Thread: Asian Philosophy in Recent American Art (travel), Hofstra Mus, Hofstra Univ, Hempstead, NY, 90 & many other mus, 90-92; Art for the Land, Five Points Gallery, E Chatham, NY, 91. *Bibliog:* Patricia C Phillips (auth), Michael Singer: Williams College, Artforum, 131-132, 1/91; Michele Cone (auth), Baroque Nature, Arts Mag, 3/91; Ann Wilson Lloyd (auth), Michael Singer at Williams College Museum of Art, Art in Am, 4/91. *Mailing Add:* Shearer Hi Rd Wilmington VT 05363

SINGER, NANCY BARKHOUSE
DEALER
b St Louis, Mo, Oct 5, 12. *Study:* Univ Wis, BA, 33; Wash Univ, St Louis. *Collections Arranged:* Laumeier Int Sculpture Park, St Louis, Mo; Univ Mo, St Louis; First St Forum, St Louis; Wichita Col Art Gallery. *Pos:* Dir, Nancy Singer Gallery, currently. *Mem:* First St Forum; Contemp Art Soc; Print & Drawing Soc; Friends of St Louis Art Mus; lifetime mem, Laumeier Sculpture Park Bd. *Specialty:* Contemporary master prints. *Mailing Add:* 31 Crestwood Dr St Louis MO 63105

SING HOO
SCULPTOR, PAINTER
b Canton, China, May 15, 08; Can citizen. *Study:* Toronto Col Art; Ont Col Art, with A Barnes & Emmannual Hahn, AA; Slade Sch, Univ London, with Turner. *Work:* London Mus, Eng; Nat Gallery Ottawa; Royal Ont Mus, Toronto. *Comn:* Sun Dial & bronze figures of daughter & gardener, Parks, Toronto. *Exhib:* Ont Soc Artists, 32-68; Can Nat Exhib, 32-68; Royal Can Acad Art, 36-72; Sculptor's Soc Can, 40-67. *Pos:* Asst, Paleont Dept, Royal Ont Mus, 34-40. *Teaching:* Lectr Oriental & Western art, Chinese Sch, 36-40. *Mem:* Royal Can Acad Arts. *Media:* Bronze, Marble. *Mailing Add:* 139 Livingstone Ave Toronto ON M6E 2L9 Canada

SINGLETARY, MICHAEL JAMES
PAINTER
b New York, NY, Jan 23, 50. *Study:* Art Student League; Vt Acad, 68; Univ Ghana, W Africa, 69; Guadalajara Univ, Mex, 70; Ecole De Beaux Art, Fountainbleau, France, 71; Syracuse Univ, BFA, 72; RI Sch Design, 73; Lehman Col, New york, 74; State Univ New York, 88; Bob Blackburn Printmaking Workshop, 88. *Comn:* Eight painting ser, Am Contract Designers, New York, NY; 12 painting ser for Grand Paradise Island Hotel, Creative Concepts, New York; 7 painting ser for hotel chain, Sheraton Inn, Roanoke, Va; Tribute to Woodie Shaw, New York Jazz Committee; Martin Luther King, painting, Ariel Mgt Corp, Chicago, Ill; 23 portraits, New York City Basketball Hall of Fame. *Exhib:* solo exhibs, US Fed Court House, NY, 82-84, 112 Greene St Gallery, Soho, NY, 90 Jazz Series, Dalcour Fine Art, 90, Mercy Col, Dobbs Ferry, NY, 90, Iona Col, New Rochelle, NY, 90,

Heritage Show, New York Univ, 90; Printmakers Show, Kent State Univ, 90; Edwin A Ulrich Mus Art, Wichita, Kans, 90; The Humanist Icon, New York Acad Art, New York & Univ Va, 90; Bayly Art Mus, 90; and others. *Pos:* Assoc dir, CBS Inc, 75-86. *Teaching:* Artist-in-residence, Bronx Mus Art, 72-73; master teacher mosaic, Cloister Mus, Metrop Mus Art, New York, 73; teacher art, New York City Bd Educ, 74; artist in residence, Studio Mus, 74; Sarah Lawrence Col Gallery Sch, Bronxville, NY, 89-90. *Awards:* First Prize Portrait, Bridgeport Art League Exhib, Bridgeport Mus, 85. *Bibliog:* Television appearances, Best Talk in Town, WPIX, New York, 88, Phil Donahue Show, WNBC, New York, 89 & State of the Art Show, WDMC, 90; Fine arts and collectibles, Emerge Mag, 10/89; numerous other mag & newspaper articles. *Mem:* Dir Guild Am; Writers Guild Am; Harrison Art League; Found Community Artists; New York Artist Equity ASN. *Media:* Acrylic, Oil. *Publ:* The artist life - A Master of Improvisation, Artist Mag, 3/91; The art of Basketball, Daily News, New York, 9/24/91; Inside Track Michael Singletary: Guilding Light Gets Jazzy, Soap Opera Digest; Own Way, Art Sect, Kenichi Ishizuka, Tokyo, Japan, winter 91. *Mailing Add:* 375 Hawthorne Terr Mt Vernon NY 10552

SINNARD, ELAINE (JANICE)
PAINTER, SCULPTOR
b Ft Collins, Colo, Feb 14, 26. *Study:* Art Students League, 48-49, with Reginald Marsh; NY Univ, 51, with Samuel Adler; also with Robert D Kaufmann, 51; Sculpture Ctr, 55, with Dorothea Denslow; Acad Grande Chaumiere, Paris, 56. *Comn:* Five wall hangings (with Mrs Cris Darlington, Marlin Studios), Scandinavian Airline, New York, 61; three oil paintings, Basker Bldg Corp 5660, Miami Beach, 70. *Exhib:* One-woman shows, Ward Eggleston Galleries, New York, 59, Fairleigh Dickinson Univ, NJ, 60 & Lord & Taylor Art Gallery, 63-78; Sinnard Art Studio, New York; Chevy Chase Gallery, Kensington, Md; Bergdorf Goodman, Nina's Choice Gallery, New York. *Bibliog:* Article in Art News, 54; James E Duffy (auth), article in World Telegram, 59; Fran Hepperle (auth), article in Times Herald Rec, 73, 83 & 86; Art in Am, 75. *Mem:* Nat Arts Club, NY. *Media:* Oil; All. *Dealer:* Bergdorf Goodman c/o Nena's Choice Gallery Fifth Ave at 57th St New York NY 10019. *Mailing Add:* Box 304 New Hampton NY 10958

SINTON, NELL (WALTER)
PAINTER, EDUCATOR
b San Francisco, Calif. *Study:* San Francisco Art Inst, with Maurice Sterne; Inst Creative & Artistic Develop, Oakland, Calif. *Work:* San Francisco Mus Art; Oakland Mus Art, Calif; Chase Manhattan Bank, New York; Am Tel & Tel Co, NJ; Mills Col, Oakland; Nat Mus Women Arts, Washington, DC; and others. *Exhib:* San Francisco Mus Art, 57, 63 & 70; Staempfli Gallery, New York, 60; Am Acad Arts & Lett, New York, 67; Triennial Exhibs, Braunstein Gallery, San Francisco, 68-90; Univ Calif, Berkeley, 72; The Modern Era, Smithsonian Inst, DC, 77; 30 yr retrospective, Mills Col, 81; Arch Am Art Symp, Calif Palace Legion Hon, San Francisco, 88; Oakland Mus, 90; Lines of Force, Nat Poetry Asn, Ft Mason Ctr, San Francisco, Calif, 90; For Better or Worse, Artists' View on Romance, Monterey Peninsula Mus Art, 91-92; Krannert Mus, Univ Ill, Urbana, 92. *Pos:* Artist mem, San Francisco Art Comn, City & Co, 58-63. *Teaching:* Instr drawing, San Francisco Art Inst, 70-71; lectr symp, Mt Holyoke Col, Mass, 76; artist-in-residence, La State Univ, 77 & Univ of Ill, Urbana, 78; instr drawing & painting, Col Marin, 80-89. *Awards:* San Francisco Art Inst Award, De Young Mus, 56; Oakland Mus Art Awards, 58 & 61; Award of Hon for Painting, San Francisco Art Commission. *Bibliog:* M Tapie (auth), Morphologie autre, 60; F Martin (auth), Review San Francisco, Art Int, 63 & Artforum, 63 & 67; Kenneth Baker (auth), Review San Francisco Chronicle, 89, ArtForum, 89. *Media:* Watercolor, Oil. *Collection:* Pre-Columbian pottery, contemporary American and European paintings and sculptures. *Publ:* Auth, Oral History, Bancroft Libr, Univ Calif, Berkely, 92. *Dealer:* Braunstein Gallery 254 Sutter St San Francisco CA 94108. *Mailing Add:* 1020 Francisco St San Francisco CA 94109

SIPIORA, LEONARD PAUL
MUSEUM DIRECTOR, MUSEOLOGIST
b Lawrence, Mass, Sept 1, 34. *Study:* Vanderbilt Univ; Univ Mich, Ann Arbor, AB(cum laude), 55, MA, 56. *Collections Arranged:* Ann Nat Sun Carnival Exhib; Biennial, Int Designer Craftsmen; W S Horton Retrospective, 70; Tom Lea Retrospective, 71; Walter Griffin Retrospective, 71. *Pos:* Co-founder & pres, El Paso Arts Coun, 69-70, dir, 71-; dir, El Paso Mus Art, 67-; retired. *Awards:* Knight Grand Cross of Malta. *Mem:* Tex Asn Mus (pres, 77-79); Am Asn Mus; Am Fedn Arts; Am Platform Asn; Asn Art Mus Dir. *Res:* Nineteenth and twentieth century American painting. *Collection:* American paintings and graphics. *Publ:* Auth, The Universality of Tom Lea (catalog), 71; A community oriented art museum, Southwest Gallery Art Mag, 71; auth foreword, Biography of John Enneking, 72. *Mailing Add:* 1012 Blanchard El Paso TX 79902

SIRENA (CONTESSA ANTONIA MASTROCRISTINO FANARA)
PAINTER, LECTURER
b White Plains, NY. *Study:* Self taught. *Work:* Mus Campidoglio, Mus Mod Art, Rome, Italy; Mus Castello Sforzesco, Milano, Italy; Mus Eureka, Ill; Regione Fruili Venezia Giulia, Regione Siciliana; Regione Sarda; Voorhees Zimmerli Art Mus, NJ; New England Ctr Mus; Mus Art & Sci, Daytona, Fla. *Comn:* Paintings for Federico Fellini, Frankie Laine, Gina Lollobrigida, Vittorio de Sica, The Vatican, Pope Paul XI & Pope John Paul II, Vatican Mus; 3 paintings, Family Bible Encycl, Vol 19-20, Curtis Bks & Copylab, 72. *Exhib:* One-woman shows, Gallerie Andre Weil, Paris, 68, Mike Douglas TV Show Exhib, 68, Palazzo delle Esposizioni, Comune di Roma, Rome, 69 & State Gallery in Teatro Massimo, Palermo, Sicily, 70; C W Post Univ Gallery, 77; Lowenstein Gallery, NY, 83; Wapner Gallery, NY, 86; Wash Mus Fine Art, 66; Hostra Mus, 87; Pouce Univ, 89. *Pos:* Dir, Sirena Art Studios, New York, formerly. *Teaching:* Lectr, Fordham Univ, NY, 85- *Awards:* Gold Cup, Quadrennale, Rome, 68; Gold Medal of Pres of Senate, Italy & Mayor of Rome, 72; Gold Medal Award, Accad of Paestum; Medal of Vatican, Pope John Paul II, Vatican Mus, 84; Artist of Love Trophy, 86. *Bibliog:* Guilio Bolaffi (auth), Bolaffi on modern art, Torino, Italy, 70 & 72. *Mem:* Accad of Paestum; Accad dei 500; Accad Tiberina; Int Comt Cult, Rome; Metrop Mus Art; Accademia Burgkart, Rome (deleg for USA, 90). *Media:* Acrylic, Oil. *Publ:* Illusr & auth, autobiography, MPH Publ, 76; The Roses and the Thorns, prt publ, 89; Visions of Women Artist, prt pubi, 89. *Mailing Add:* 1035 Fifth Ave New York NY 10028

SIRES, JONATHAN
SCULPTOR
b Savannah, Ga, 1955. *Study:* Kent State Univ, BFA, 79; Cranbrook Acad Art, MFA, 82. *Work:* Ga State Univ, Atlanta; Butler Inst Am Art, Youngstown, Ohio; Weber State Col, Ogden, Utah. *Comn:* NC Mus Natural Hist, NC Arts Coun, 88; Governor's Bus Awards, Governors Bus Coun on the Arts & Humanities. *Exhib:* Beaux Arts Designer-Craftsman, Columbus Mus Art, Columbus, Ohio, 79; one-man shows, Canton Art Inst, Canton, Ohio, 79 & Barry Merrit Gallery, Rochester, NY, 83; Salon D'Hiver, Invitational, Spaces Gallery, Cleveland, 84; NC Invitational, Hickory Mus Art, Hickory, NC, 89; Two Views, Wilson Arts Ctr, Wilson, NC, 90; New Generation Group Exhib, Ctr Earth Gallery, 91; RSVP Six Artists Respond Tides of Knowledge, Hans & Walter Bechtler Gallery, Carillon, Charlotte, NC, 92. *Pos:* Dir/artist in res Clay Works, Spirit Sq Ctr Arts, Charlotte, NC, 83-89; dir studio prog Visual Arts Dept, Spirit Sq Ctr Arts, 89-92; co-owner, Ctr Earth Gallery, 90- *Awards:* Individual Artist Fel Grant, Ohio Arts Coun, 83; NC Visual Artist Fel Grant, NC Arts Coun, 88; Nat Endowment Arts, 88. *Bibliog:* Terra Firma, Charlotte Observer, 3/2/87. *Publ:* Auth, Artist Profile, Charlotte Mag, 2/86; Terra Firma, Charlotte Observer, 3/2/87; Nat Endowment Fel, Ceramics Monthly, 2/89; J Paul Sires, Studio Potter, 6/89; CITI Mag, summer 90. *Mailing Add:* c/o Center of The Earth 3204 N Davidson St Charlotte NC 28205

SIRKIS, NANCY
PHOTOGRAPHER, EDUCATOR
b New York, NY, Aug 22, 36. *Study:* RI Sch Design, BFA, 58; Hunter Col, New York, MA, 82. *Work:* Skidmore Col Art Gallery, Saratoga, NY; First Bank of Boston. *Exhib:* Solo shows, Witkin Gallery, 70, New York; Addison Gallery, Andover, Mass, 72; Douglass Col, New Brunswick, NJ, 74; and others. *Teaching:* Staff instr, Int Ctr Photog, 76-; instr photog, Marymount Manhattan Col, 78-79. *Mem:* Col Art Asn. *Publ:* Auth, Newport: Pleasures and Palaces, 63, Boston, 65, Reflections of 1776: The Colonies Revisited, 74 & Massachusetts: From the Berkshires to the Cape, 77, Viking Press; One Family, Little Brown & Co, 70. *Mailing Add:* 310 Riverside Dr Apt 1707 New York NY 10025

SIRUGO, SAL (SALVATORE)
PAINTER
b Pozzallo, Italy; US citizen. *Study:* Art Students League, 48-49; Brooklyn Mus Art Sch, NY, 50-51. *Work:* NY Univ; Pace Univ, New York; Vassar Col, Poughkeepsie, NY; Lannan Mus, Los Angeles, Calif; Ciba-Geigy Corp, Ardsley, NY; Zimmerli Art Mus, New Brunswick, NJ; and others. *Exhib:* Whitney Mus Am Art Ann, New York, 52; Pa Acad Fine Arts Ann, Philadelphia, 53; one-man exhibs, Tanager Gallery, 61, Great Jones Gallery, 66, Landmark Gallery, 76, 78 & 81; group exhibs, Gallery Asn New York, traveling exhib, 78-80, First Int Exhib Watercolor Painting, Korea, 91; Whitney Mus Am Art Philip Morris, 90; Sixth Asia Int Watercolor Painting, Nagoya, Japan, 91; and others. *Awards:* Longview Found Award, 62; Creative Artists Pub Serv Prog Fel, 79-80; Adolph & Esther Gottlieb Found, 82 & 84. *Bibliog:* Joellen Bard (auth), Sal Sirugo, Arts, 12/78; Tram Combs (auth), Sirugo's miniature sublime, Woodstock Times, 2/19/81; Jeffrey Wechsler (auth), Abstract Expressionism: Other Dimensions 1940-1965 (catalog), Zimmerli Art Mus, Rutgers Univ, 89. *Mem:* Life mem Art Students League; Artists' Club. *Media:* Acrylic, Inks. *Mailing Add:* 321 W 24th St New York NY 10011

SISCHY, INGRID B
EDITOR, CURATOR
b Johannesburg, SAfrica, Mar 2, 52; Brit citizen. *Study:* Sarah Lawrence Col, BA, 73. *Exhib:* In the Twenties: Portraits from Photog Collection, Mus Mod Art, New York, 79 & 80. *Pos:* Asst ed, Print Collector's Newslett, 75-76 & assoc ed, 76-77; curatorial intern, Dept Photog, Mus Mod Art, New York, 78-79; dir, Printed Matter Inc, 78-80; ed, Artforum, 80-88; consult ed & staff writer, New Yorker, 89-; ed-in-chief, Interview Mag, 89- *Awards:* Hon Phd, Moore Col Art. *Mailing Add:* c/o Interview Magazine 575 Broadway, 5th Fl New York NY 10012

SISCO, ELIZABETH
EDUCATOR, PHOTOGRAPHER
b Cheverly, Md, Aug 21, 54. *Study:* Univ Calif, San Diego, BFA(cum laude), 78; MFA, 81, teacher educ prog, 87; Southwestern Col, 92; Photoshop, digital imaging Macintosh, Univ Calif Exten, 92. *Work:* La Jolla Mus Contemp Art; Kans City Art Inst, Mo; Lynne Schutte, San Diego; Univ Wis, Milwaukee; Univ Calif, San Diego, La Jolla. *Exhib:* Solo shows, Ctr US-Mex Studies, La Jolla, Calif, 85 & SUSHI, San Diego, Calif, 85; John Michael Kohler Arts Ctr, Sheboygan, Wis, 92; Cameraworks, San Francisco, 92; Univ Art Gallery, Calif State Polytechnic Univ, Pamona, Calif, 92. *Pos:* Div Arts & Humanities, Southwestern Col, Chula Vista, Calif, currently. *Teaching:* Instr, Univ Calif, San Diego Exten, 80-88, lectr dept visual art, summer 82, 83, 84, 85, 87 & 88

& spring 85-88; instr, Southwestern Col, Chula Vista, Calif, currently. *Awards:* Artist-in-residence, Banff Ctr, 6-7/91; Art Matters Inc, 92; Artist Fel, Calif Arts Coun Arts, 92. *Bibliog:* Mark Alice Durant (auth), Activist art in the shadow of rebellion, Art Am, 7/92; Susan Otto (auth), NHI project, Art Papers, 7-8/92; Susanne Skubik (auth), Artswatch, Vol III, No 2, Ms Mag, 9-10/92. *Publ:* Coauth (with D Small, C Kirkwood, S Kessler & L Hock), NHI (catalog), 92; The NEA is dead, La Jolla Light, 3/26/92; NHI (bk), 92; coauth (with D Small, L Hock & D Avalos), High School Art and Criticism Learning Guide, New Mus New York, in prep; auth, The Cultural Battlefield, Artist, Citizen, Taxpayer, Avocus Press, Washington, DC, in prep. *Mailing Add:* 903 26th St San Diego CA 92102

SISSOM, EVELYN JANELLE See Lee-Sissom, E

SISSON, LAURENCE P
PAINTER
b Boston, Mass, Apr 27, 28. *Study:* Worcester Mus Sch, grad, 49; Yale Univ, summer sch, scholar, 48-49; Portland Sch Arts, Hon DFA, 92. *Work:* Mus Fine Arts, Boston; Portland Mus, Maine; Dartmouth Col; DeCordova Mus, Mass; Worcester Mus, Mass. *Comn:* Four murals, Boston Five Cent Saving Bank Br Offs, 55-67; mural, Worcester Polytech Inst, 66; mural, Carrick Agency, Whitinsville, Mass, 72. *Exhib:* Hallmark Int Exhib, 49; Ill Art Festival, 51; Am Watercolor Soc, 55-60; one-man shows, Gallery Mod Art, New York, 69 & Brockton Art Ctr, Mass, 72. *Pos:* Corporator, Worcester Art Mus, 72- *Teaching:* Teacher & dir, Portland Art Mus Sch, Maine, 54-58. *Awards:* Fourth Am Prize, Hallmark Int Show, 49; First Prize, Boston Arts Festival, 56 & 64 & Boston Watercolor Soc, 57. *Bibliog:* Maine Harvesters of the Sea (film), Film Group, 69; W Caldwell (auth), The man and the artist, Down E Mag, 68. *Media:* Oil, Watercolor. *Publ:* Auth, Along Time River, 75. *Dealer:* Wadle Galleries 128 W Palace Santa Fe NM 87501; Midtown-Payson Galleries 745 Fifth Ave New York NY 10021. *Mailing Add:* 2204 Calle Cacique Santa Fe NM 87505

SISTO, ELENA
PAINTER
b Boston, Mass, Jan 11, 52. *Study:* Brown Univ, BA(art/art hist), 72-75; RI Sch Design, BA(art/art hist); New York Studio Sch of Drawing, Painting & Sculpture, with Nicholas Carone, 75-77. *Work:* Newark Mus, NJ; First City Capital Corp, New York, NY; Prudential Bache Securities, Newark. *Comn:* Eight page design for actors' charter, Screen Actors' Guild, Los Angeles, 79. *Exhib:* One-man shows, Vanderwoude Tananbaum Gallery, New York, 84 & 86 & Damon Brandt Gallery, New York, 90; Is This a Small Picture?, Henry Feiwel Gallery, New York, 89; Immanent Space, Ruggiero Henis Gallery, New York, 89; Field and Frame: Meyer Schapiro's Semiotics of Painting, New York Studio Sch, NY, 89; Damon Brandt Gallery, New York, 89; Personal Icons, City Gallery, New York Dept Cult Affairs, 89; Drawings, Fawbush Gallery, 89; Re: Framing Cartoons, Loughelton Gallery, New York, 90; Eros/Thanatos, Death & Desire, Tom Cugliani Gallery, New York, 90. *Teaching:* Guest lectr & sr painting critiques, Bates Col, 86; instr drawing, State Univ NY, 88; instr drawing, RI Sch Design, 87-90; instr painting & drawing, NY Studio Sch, 87-90; vis artist, Bard Col, 90. *Awards:* Skowhegan School Fel, 76; Nat Endowment Arts Visual Arts Fel, 83-84 & 89-90; Artists' Residency, Millay Colony Arts, 87. *Bibliog:* Stephen Westfall (auth), review of one-person show, 2/87 & Ken Johnson (auth), review of one-person show, 6/90, Art in Am; Charles Hagen (auth), review of one-person show, Artforum, summer 90; Robert Mahoney (auth), review of one-person show, Arts, summer 90, Arts Mag. *Media:* Oil on Canvas. *Dealer:* Vanderwoude Tananbaum 24 E 81 St New York NY 10028. *Mailing Add:* 138 W 10th St New York NY 10014

SITTON, JOHN M
PAINTER, LECTURER
b Forsyth, Ga, Jan 9, 07. *Study:* Yale Univ, BFA, 29; Am Acad Rome, fel painting, 29-32; with Eugene Savage & Barry Faulkner. *Work:* Addison Gallery Am Art, Andover, Mass; Mint Mus, Charlotte, NC; Lubbock Art Mus, Tex. *Comn:* Mural painting, Bd Room, Fed Res Bldg, Atlanta, Ga, 37; mural, Riverside Mem Chapel, New York, 38. *Exhib:* One-man exhib, Grand Cent Art Galleries, New York, 33, High Art Mus, Atlanta, 39, Light House Gallery, Tequesta, Fla, 71 & Parker Playhouse, Ft Lauderdale, Fla, 71; American Painters in Paris, 76; plus others. *Pos:* Dir, Finch Summer Sch Painting, 38; dir life drawing, NY Sch Appl Design Women, 38-41. *Teaching:* Instr art anat, NY Univ, 32; instr watercolor, Columbia Univ, 36-37; asst prof painting & art hist, Cornell Univ, 40-44. *Awards:* Prix di Rome, Am Acad Rome, 29; Nat Mural Competition, Riverside Mem Chapel, 38; First Award Portraiture (oil), Broward Art Guild, Ft Lauderdale, 75; Water Color Prize, Fla Tri-Co Award Ann Exhib, 78. *Mem:* Life mem Century Asn; life mem Allied Artists Am; Alumni Asn Am Acad Rome; Boca Raton Art Ctr; Artist Equity Asn. *Media:* Oil, Watercolor. *Publ:* Auth, An adventure in painting, 38 & Painting of my silk decorations, 38, Art Instr Mag. *Mailing Add:* 4745 NW 9th Ave Pompano Beach FL 33064

SKALAGARD, HANS
MARINE PAINTER, LECTURER
b Skuo, Faroe Islands, Europe, Feb 7, 24; nat US. *Study:* Royal Acad Art, Copenhagen; with marine artist Anton Otto Fisher, New York. *Work:* Constitution, Dudley Knox Libr & War of 1812 Constitution & Guerriere, Hermann Hall, Naval Post Grad Sch, Monterey, Calif; Casco, Reid Hall, Robert Louis Stevenson Sch, Pebble Beach, Calif; Frigate Ship United States, Salvation Army Hq & Savannah US Frigate, Allen Knight Maritime Mus, Monterey; and others. *Comn:* Olivebank Deck View, comn by Dr Wm Rustad, Sea Cliff, San Francisco, 68; USN BB Maine, comn by Hal Whitten, Dean Witter & Assoc, San Mateo, Calif, 73; Anna Maerske, comn by Capt Olsen, Port Capt Maersk Line, San Francisco, 75; and other pvt collections. *Exhib:* Calif Palace of the Legion of Honor, 60; Lucein Labaudt Art Gallery, San Francisco, 60; Robert Louis Stevenson Sch, 67, 68 & 69; Galerie De Tours, San Francisco, 72; Gallerie Vallombreuse, Biarritz, France, 75; New Los Angeles Maritime Mus, 80; Skaalegaard's Square-Rigger Art Gallery, Carmel, Calif, 81; and others. *Pos:* Dir, Skaalegaard's Square-Rigger Art Gallery, Carmel, 66-; Calif hist librn, Mayo Hayes O'Donnel Libr, Monterey Hist & Art Asn, 72 & 73; dir bd, Allen Knight Maritime Mus, 72-76; cult dir, Sons of Norway, Monterey, 74-76. *Awards:* Silver Medal & Hon Dipl, 70; Gold Medal & Title Master Painter, Tommaso Campanella Acad Arts, Lett & Sci, Rome, 72; Gold Medal, Academia Italia Delle Arti e Del Honoro, Parma, 80. *Bibliog:* Judith A Eisner (auth), Carmel closeup, Pine Cone, Carmel, 9/14/72; and others. *Mem:* Life hon Academia Italia Delle Arti e Del Honoro. *Media:* Multimedia. *Mailing Add:* Los Cortes Bldg PO Box 6611 Carmel CA 93921

SKELLEY, ROBERT CHARLES
EDUCATOR, PRINTMAKER
b Bellevue, Ohio, Jan 15, 34. *Study:* Ind Univ, AB & MFA. *Work:* Libr of Cong, Washington, DC; Mint Mus, Charlotte, NC; Montgomery Mus Art, Ala; Springfield Col, Mass; Southern Ill Univ, Carbondale. *Exhib:* Dixie Ann Graphic Exhib, Montgomery Mus Art; Boston Printmakers, Mass; Mint Mus Ann Graphics; Libr Cong Print Ann; American Graphics, Col of Pac, Stockton, Calif. *Teaching:* Prof graphic design, Univ Fla, Gainesville, 61-81. *Awards:* Dixie Ann Best in Show Purchase, Montgomery Mus Art; Boston Printmakers Hon Mention, Boston Mus Art; Libr of Cong Purchase Award; Humanities Coun Res Grant. *Bibliog:* Graphic rev in La Rev Mod, 1/65 & Art Rev Mag, 4/66; Norman Kent (auth), Robert Skelley wood cuts, Am Artist Mag, 1/71; Lanny Sommesse (auth), Robert Skelley Woodcuts, Novum Gebrauchs Graphik, 10/76. *Mem:* Soc Am Graphic Artists; Southern Graphic Artist Circle. *Publ:* Auth, articles in Am Artist Mag, Novum Gebrauchs Graphic Mag & 30 Years of Am Printmaking. *Mailing Add:* Dept Art Univ Fla Gainesville FL 32611

SKINNER, ORIN ENSIGN
DESIGNER
b Sweden Valley, Pa, Nov 5, 1892. *Study:* Rochester Atheneum Art Sch, NY, with Herman J Butler, dipl, 15; also res in France & Eng, 23-25. *Comn:* Stained glass windows, Princeton Univ Chapel, 30, St John the Divine Cathedral, New York, 32, Heinz Mem Chapel, Univ Pittsburgh, 38, St Patrick's Cathedral, New York, 56 & Grace Cathedral, San Francisco, 66. *Exhib:* Boston Art Club. *Pos:* Designer, Charles A Baker, Rochester, 12-16; designer, R Toland Wright, Cleveland, 17-19; mgr, treas & pres, Charles J Connick Assocs, 20-; ed, Stained Glass, 30-48; pres, Charles J Connick Stain Glass Found, 85- *Teaching:* Crafts related to Architecture, stained glass, sculpture in stone, wood carving, YMCA & Franklin Inst, Boston. *Awards:* Master Craftsman, Boston Soc Arts & Crafts, 40. *Bibliog:* History & Practice of Stained Glass, Documentary film of O E Skinner, 4/90. *Mem:* Fel Int Inst Arts & Lett; fel Stained Glass Asn Am (pres, 48-49). *Media:* Stained Glass. *Res:* Restoration of Great Western Rose Window of Rheims Cathedral. *Publ:* Contribr, Am Architect, 27, Stained Glass Quart, 33-47, Liturgical Arts, 37, Am Fabricks, 50 & Holy Cross Mag, 67. *Mailing Add:* 37 Walden St Newtonville MA 02160

SKLAR, DOROTHY
PAINTER
b New York, NY. *Study:* Univ Calif, Los Angeles, BE; Chouinard Art Ctr Sch, Los Angeles; also with S Macdonald Wright & Millard Sheets. *Work:* Los Angeles Munic Art Comn, Los Angeles City Hall; Baptist Univ, Shawnee, Okla; Westside Jewish Community Ctr, Los Angeles; private collections. *Exhib:* Oakland Art Mus, 44 & 50; Denver Mus, 45, 46, 51 & 53; Calif State Fair, Sacramento, 49, 52, 54, 55, 57, 59, 60-66; Pa Acad Fine Arts, 53, 54 & 57; Los Angeles Co Mus Art, 54 & 55; Butler Inst Am Art, Youngstown, Ohio, 55, 58, 60, 62, 63 & 68; Nat Soc Painters in Casein & Acrylic, 56-63 & 77; Riverside Mus, New York, 57; Am Watercolor Soc, 58; Long Beach Mus; Pasadena Art Mus; Montgomery Mus Art, Ala; Frye Mus, Seattle, Wash, 58-63, 66. *Teaching:* Instr art, Santa Monica City Schs, 43. *Awards:* Award in Oil & Watercolor, Laguna Mus Art, 45-48, 52-54, 59, 60 & 66. *Mem:* Nat Watercolor Soc; Nat Artists Equity; Nat Soc Painters in Casein & Acrylic; Women Painters of the West; Nat Asn Women Artists. *Media:* Watercolor, Acrylic. *Mailing Add:* 6612 Colgate Los Angeles CA 90048

SKLARSKI, BONNIE J
PAINTER, EDUCATOR
b Elma, NY, July 16, 43. *Study:* Pratt Inst, BFA, 65; Brooklyn Col, MFA, 70. *Work:* Ind Univ, Bloomington. *Exhib:* Sense of Place, Wichita Art Mus, Kans, 73 & Sheldon Mem Art Gallery, Nebr, 73; one-man exhib, Paul Creative Arts Ctr, NH, 77; Artists Choice, Fischbach Gallery, New York, 80; Contemp Landscape Painters, Md Inst Gallery, 89; Tradition in Contemp Am Landscape, Gibbs Mus, Charleston, SC, 90 & Bayly Mus, WVa, 90. *Pos:* Graphic artist, Dell Publ, 70. *Teaching:* Asst prof anatomy & painting, Ind Univ, 70-76, assoc prof, 76-93, prof, 83- *Bibliog:* John Arthur (auth), Landscape Painting and the American Tradition, Bullfinch, 89. *Media:* Oil. *Publ:* Auth, Wilderness and Garden, Artist Choice Newsletter, 79; illusr, The sciences, NY Acad Sci, 88. *Dealer:* Robert Schoelkopf Gallery 50 W 57th St New York NY 10019. *Mailing Add:* 522 N Washington Bloomington IN 47408

SKLAR-WEINSTEIN, ARLENE (JOYCE)
PAINTER, PRINTMAKER
b Detroit, Mich, Oct 25, 31. *Study:* Parsons Sch Design; Mus Mod Art, New York, scholar & study with Bernard Pfreim; Albright Art Sch; New York Univ, with Hale Woodruff, BA, 52, MS(art educ), 55; Pratt Graphics Ctr, with Andrew Stasik; Ctr for Understanding Media, 74; Col New Rochelle, 75 & 81; Columbia Univ, 85-86. *Work:* Mus Mod Art, New York; New York Pub Libr Permanent Print Collection; Grace Gallery, New York City Community Col, Brooklyn; Hudson River Mus Permanent Collection, Yonkers, NY; Metrop Mus Art, Slide Libr; Manufacturers Hanover Trust Co; Pepsico Art Collection. *Exhib:* Regional graphics, Albright-Knox Gallery, Buffalo, NY, 52; Yonkers Art Asn Regional, Hudson River Mus, 70 & 71; one-person shows, Evolutions, Hudson River Mus, 71 & West Broadway Gallery, 72-73, 75-76, 78 & 80; Nat Asn Women Artists Nat, Lever House, New York, 72; Pelham Art Ctr, 86. *Pos:* Visual arts coordr, Coun Arts Westchester, White Plains, NY, 69-70. *Teaching:* Art specialist, Hillside Sch, Hastings-on-Hudson, NY, 73-81; lower sch art specialist, Marymount Sch of NY, 81- *Awards:* Geigy Award for Painting, Ciba-Geigy Corp, 69; First Prize, Hudson River Mus Regional, Yonkers Art Asn, 71; Print Competition Award, Gestetner Corp, 71. *Bibliog:* Masters & Houston (auths), Psychedelic Art, Grove, 68; H H Arnason (auth), History of Modern Art, Abrams, 69. *Mem:* Yonkers Art Asn, Hudson River Mus (pres, 70-72); Women in Art (rotating leadership, 72); The Abraxas Group, Westchester; Mamaroneck Artist Guild; Hastings Creative Arts Coun (bd mem, 73-). *Media:* Acrylic; Fiber, Relief Prints. *Mailing Add:* 18 Harvard Lane Hastings-on-Hudson NY 10706

SKOFF, GAIL LYNN
PHOTOGRAPHER
b Los Angeles, Calif. *Study:* Univ Calif, Berkeley, 67-69; San Francisco Art Inst, BFA, 72, MFA, 79. *Work:* Nat Mus Am Art, Smithsonian Inst; Bibliot Nat, Paris; Oakland Mus, Calif; Ctr Creative Photog, Tucson, Ariz; Smith Col Art Gallery. *Exhib:* Exchange, Ft Worth Mus Art & San Francisco Mus Mod Art, 75-76; Attitudes: Photography in the '70's, Santa Barbara Mus Art; Soc Encouragement Contemp Art Photog Invitational, San Francisco Mus Mod Art, 80; Contemporary Hand-Colored Photographs, DeSaisset Mus, Univ Santa Clara, 81; American Photographers and the National Parks, traveling to New York Pub Libr, Los Angeles Co Mus, Amon Carter Mus, Corcoran Gallery, and others; In Color: Ten California Photographers, Oakland Mus, 83; Exposed and Developed, Nat Mus Am Art, Smithsonian Inst, Washington, DC, 84; The Colored Image: Hand Applied Color in Photography, Friend of Photog, Carmel, Calif, 85. *Teaching:* Instr photog and hand-colored photog, Univ Calif Extension, San Francisco, 76-; instr photog, Univ Calif, Berkeley, summer 80. *Awards:* Nat Endowment Arts Photogr Fel, 76. *Bibliog:* Hal Fisher (auth), article, Artforum, 80; Contemporary hand-colored photography, Picture Mag, 81; Dana Asbury (auth), Gail Skoff/Judy Dater, Popular Photog, 83; Kermit Lynch (auth), Adventures on the Wine Route, Farran Straus, 88. *Mem:* Friends of Photog, Carmel, Calif. *Publ:* Contribr, The young romantics, Newsweek, 79; New Landscapes & Untitled 24, Friends Photog, 81; Photography Year, Trends, Time-Life Books, 82; Cliches, Brussels, 84; Chez Panisse Cooking, Random House, 88. *Dealer:* Jones Troyer Gallery 1614 20th St NW Washington DC 20009; Terry Etherton Gallery 424 E 6th St Tucson Ariz 85705. *Mailing Add:* 1718 Jaynes St Berkeley CA 94703

SKOGLUND, SANDY
PHOTOGRAPHER, SCULPTOR
b Boston, Mass, Sept 11, 46. *Study:* Smith Col, BA, 68; Univ Iowa, MFA, 72. *Work:* Metrop Mus Art, Chase Manhattan Bank, New York; St Louis Mus Art, Mo; Art Inst Chicago; The Brooklyn Mus, NY; Centre Georges Pompidou, Paris, France; Eastman House Int Mus Photog, Rochester, NY; Tampa Mus Art, Fla; Univ Mass Mus Art, Amherst, Mass; Walker Art Ctr, Minneapolis, Minn. *Exhib:* Solo exhibs, New Work & Food Still Lifes, Janet Borden Inc, New York, 92, In the Last Hour (with catalog), Fred Jones Jr Mus Art, Univ Okla, Norman, Okla, 92, The Green House, Aspen Art Mus, 92, Radioactive Cats (with catalog), L'Espace Photog de la Ville de Paris, France, 92, Fundacio la Caixa, Sala Catalunya, Barcelona, Spain, 92, Lowe Art Mus, Coral Gables, Fla, 92, Tampa Mus Art, Fla, 92; Whitney Mus Am Art, New York; Fox Games (with catalog), L'Invention d'un Art, Centre Georges Pompidou, Paris, France, 89; Los Angeles Munic Art Gallery, Calif, 89; Biennale de Marseille, Musee de Marseille, France, 90; Lo Specchio/In/Fedele: Padiglione d'Arte Contemp di Milano, Milan, Italy, 91; Fotografia Am del Segle XX: Centre Cult de la Fundacio, Barcelona, Spain, 91; The Intuitive Eye: Photog from the David C I Sarajean Ruttenberg Collection, Art Inst Chicago, Ill, 91 & 92. *Teaching:* Prof art, Univ Hartford, Conn, 73-76, vis prof, 92; prof, Rutgers Univ, Newark, NJ, currently. *Awards:* New York Found Arts, 88; The Bd of Trustees Award for Excellence in Res, Rutgers Univ, New Brunswick, NJ, 91; Richard Koopman Distinguished Chair in the Visual Arts, Hartford Art Sch, Univ Hartford, Conn, 92. *Bibliog:* Andy Grundberg (auth), Weekend Reviews: Sandy Skoglund; The Green House at Janet Borden Inc, New York Times, 9/14/90; Nan Richardson (auth), Sandy Skoglund: Wild at Heart, Art News, 4/91; Gloria Picazo (auth), Paradoxes of Photography - On the work of Sandy Skoglund (catalog), Barcelona, Spain, 92, reprinted Paris, France, 92. *Publ:* Auth, Spirituality in the Flesh, Artforum Int, 2/92. *Dealer:* Janet Borden Inc 560 Broadway New York NY 10012; PPOW Gallery 532 Broadway New York NY 10012. *Mailing Add:* 476 Broome St 2B New York NY 10013

SKURKIS, BARRY A
PAINTER, SCULPTOR
b Chicago, Ill, Nov 21, 51. *Study:* Col Du Page, with Karl Owen; AA, 71; Sch Art Inst Chicago,With T Karpalis, R Yoshida & C Wirsum, BFA, 75; Univ Notre Dame, with Don Vogl, MA, 78. *Comn:* Bronze casting, Archbishop N Popp, Detroit, Mich, 81; oil painting, Dr Wallace Schwass, Richmond, Ill, 82; watercolor, Robert Malorny, DDS, Westmont, Ill, 82; oil painting, Edward Mazurowski, Westmont, 82; watercolor, Dean Bunting, Downers Grove, Ill, 82. *Exhib:* Solo exhibs, Aurora Univ, Ill, 88 & N Cent Col, Naperville, 88; Seventh Ann Maine/Maritime Int Flatwork Exhib, Marguerite Pullen Galley, Presque Isle, Maine, 89; Northern Nat Exhib, Rhinelander, Wis, 89; Sixth Ann Miniature Art Exhib, Fells Point Art Gallery, Baltimore, Md, 89; Fourth Ann Int Exhib Miniatures, Del Bello Gallery, Toronto, Can, 89-90; Baer Competition, Beverly Art Ctr, Chicago, Ill, 89-90; Ill State Fair Prof Art Exhib, Springfield, Ill, 89-90; Fred Wells 14, On Paper of Paper, Elder Gallery, Lincoln, Nebr, 90; Faxart, Gallery 400, Chicago, 90; Nat Small Works Exhib, Schohaire Co Arts Coun Gallery, Cobleskill, NY, 90; Fifth Clemson Nat Print and Drawing Exhib, SC, 91; Shades of Pastels, Baltimore, Md, 91; Midwest Small Sculpture Exhib, Cape Girardeau, Mo, 91; 41st Spiva Ann Competition, Joplin, Mo, 91; San Diego Art Inst, The Prints and the Paper, Calif, 91; Nat Small Works Exhib, Cobleskill, NY, 91; Newport Art Musuem: Lost Landscape, RI, 91; Mountain Valley Fine Art Exhib, Guntersville, Ala, 91; Louisville Ann Art Exhib, Colo, 91; Wiseman Gallery, Grants Pass, Ore, 91; Soc Movement Gallery, Nashville, Tenn, 91; Historical Crosscuts: Private Response to World Events Flint, Mich, 92; 42nd Spiva Ann Competition, Joplin Mo, 92; and many others. *Collections Arranged:* The Holocaust: 1933-1945, 89. *Pos:* Gallery cur, N Cent Col, Naperville, Ill, 83-90; mem bd dirs & vpres, Sch Art Inst Chicago Alumni Asn, 88; bd dirs, Riverwalk Sculpture Garden, 88-89 & chmn, 89-90; pres, Chicago Soc Artists, 89, 90, 91 & 92. *Teaching:* Instr, Col DuPage, Glen Ellyn, Ill, 75-83; vis lectr painting, drawing & design, N Cent Col, 80-83, chmn, dept art, 83-91, assoc prof, 91. *Awards:* Third Place, Linoleum Print Competition, Chicago Soc Artists, 90; 11th Ann Juried Exhib of the Soc of Watercolor Artists, Ft Worth, Tex, 92; Daniel Smith Award, Nat Small Works Exhib, Schohaire Co Arts Coun, Cobleskill, NY, 90. *Bibliog:* Mementy's, Featured Artist, Linoleum Prints, 88; Chicago Soc Artists Block Print Calendar, 86- *Mem:* Chicago Soc Artists; Art Inst Chicago; Wedge Pub Cult Ctr Arts (bd mem, 78-84); Chicago Soc Artists (mem bd dirs, 87-); Chicago Artists Coalition, 88. *Media:* Acrylics, Watercolor; Bronze, Wood. *Mailing Add:* N Cent Col 30 N Brainard St Naperville IL 60566

SKY, ALISON
ENVIRONMENTAL ARTIST
b New York, NY, Aug 1, 46. *Study:* Columbia Univ, 62; Adelphi Univ, with Peter Lipman-Wulf, BA(fine arts), 67; Art Students League, with Jose de Creeft & John Hovannes, scholar, 67-69. *Work:* Smithsonian Inst, Washington, DC; Mus Mod Art, New York; and others. *Comn:* Best Products Co Inc, Richmond, Va, 78; Nat Shopping Ctrs Inc, 77-78; WilliWear Ltd, 82; McDonald Corp, 83; Formica Corp, 83; and others. *Exhib:* Louvre, Paris, 75; Cooper-Hewitt Mus, New York, 78; America Now, traveling, Hudson River Mus, New York & Wadsworth Atheneum, Hartford, Conn, 79; Mus Mod Art, New York, 79; and others. *Pos:* Vpres & co-founder principal, SITE Projects Inc, 78- *Awards:* Int Design, Am Soc Interior Designers, 79; Award, Progressive Archit, 80; Ward for Showroom Design, Interiors Mag, 83 & 85; Nat Endowment Arts Design Fel, 84. *Mem:* Fel Am Acad Rome. *Media:* Multi-Media. *Publ:* Auth, Sky Book, Profile Press, 72; ed, On SITE On Energy, SITE/Scribners, 74; co-auth, Unbuilt America, McGraw-Hill, 76; coauth, SITE: Projects and Theories 1969-78, Dedalo Libri, 78; coauth, SITE: Architecture as Art, Acad Ed & St Martin's Press, 81. *Mailing Add:* c/o SITE 60 Greene St New York NY 10012

SKY, CAROL VETH
PAINTER, EDUCATOR
b Cleveland, Ohio, Aug 30, 34. *Study:* Univ Houston, BFA, 79; Univ Iowa, MA, 82; Univ Iowa, MFA, 83. *Work:* Nat Mus Women Arts, Washington, DC; Univ Iowa, Iowa City; Univ St Thomas, Houston; Col Mainland, Texas City. *Exhib:* Nat Drawing & Sculpture, Del Mar Col, Corpus Christ, Tex, 75; National on Paper Show, Terrance Gallery, Palenville, NY, 83; Focus International: American Women in Art, United Nations World Conf, Nairobi, Kenya, 85; Visions, Westbeth Gallery, New York, 90; Salute To Women, Nat Mus Women Arts, Washington, DC, 91; WPA at the Hemicycle, Corcoran Gallery Art, Washington, DC, 92. *Pos:* Dir, art gallery, Col Mainland, Texas City, 73-79; dean acad affairs, Md Col Art & Design, Silver Spring, 88-, actg pres, 89. *Teaching:* Instr drawing, Col Mainland, Texas City, 75-79; instr drawing painting, Md Col Art & Design, Silver Spring, 87-88; instr drawing, Georgetown Univ, Washington, DC, 88. *Awards:* Judges Cash Award, James Boynton, Graphic Arts, 75. *Bibliog:* Janet Wilson (auth), Today's collages, pieces of the past, Wash Post, 6/20/92; Michael Welzenbach (auth), Landscapes of light & shadow, Wash Post, 7/11/92. *Mem:* Nat Artists Equity (East Coast reg vpres, 88-92); Wash Artists Equity (bd dirs & vpres, 84-); Women's Caucus Art (nat exhib comt, 84 & nat prog comt, 91); Arts Action Coalition (bd dir, 92); Nat Arts Med Ctr (artistic adv bd, 92). *Media:* All. *Publ:* Auth, Brazilian Art & History; Focus on Modernism, Univ Iowa, 83; William Christenberry, Photographer, Painter, Sculptor, Wash Artist News, 85; Ethical & Political Considerations of Being An Artist, Nat Artist Equity, 87; Art, Funding, Choice, Accountability & Censorship: Orienting Students to Issues & Realities, Nat Asn Schs Art & Design, 90; The Role of Art Colleges for the Artist, ACA/Inst Asn Art Critics, Pub Policy Forum, 88-92. *Dealer:* Mahler Gallery 406 Seventh St NW Washington DC 20004. *Mailing Add:* 522 First St SE Washington DC 20003

SLADE, ROY
PAINTER, MUSEUM DIRECTOR
b Cardiff, Wales, July 14, 33. *Study:* Cardiff Col Art, NDD, 54; Univ Wales, ATD, 54. *Work:* Arts Coun Gt Brit; Contemp Art Soc; Nuffield Found;

Westinghouse Corp; Brit Overseas Airways Corp. *Exhib:* Nat Print Club, Nat Col Fine Art, Washington, DC, 72; Pyramid Gallery, Washington DC, 76 & 77; Robert Kidd Gallery, Birmingham, Mich, 81; The Cranbook Vision, touring exhib, 86; Cranbook Contemp, touring exhib in Latin Am, 86; & others. *Pos:* Chmn, Comt Art in Pub Places, State of Mich, 83-85; comnr, Comn on Inst Higher Educ, NCentral Asn Col & Sch, 83-; chmn, Design Mich Adv Coun, 78-; mem, Mus Prog Overview Panel, Nat Endowment Arts, 90-93. *Teaching:* Sr lectr post-grad studies, Leeds Col Art, Eng, 64-69; prof painting, Corcoran Sch Art, Washington, DC, 67-68, dean, 70-77, dir, Gallery, 72-; pres, Cranbrook Acad Art, Bloomfield Hills, Mich, 77- *Awards:* Fulbright-Hays Scholar, 67; Welsh Soc of Philadelphia Award; Knight, First Class, Order of the White Rose, Finland, 85. *Mem:* Nat Soc of Lit & Arts; Nat Coun Art Admin (chmn, 81-); Asn Art Mus Dir; Nat Asn Schs Art & Design; Soc Bolivariana de Arguitectors, hon mem; Am Inst Architects (hon mem, Detroit chap). *Publ:* Auth, Report from Washington, Studio Int, 1/72; Studio Int; A new cultural center, Yorkshire Post, 2/69; Artist in America, Contemp Rev, 5/69; The Temple Flourishes, Nat Council of Art Administrators Publ, 80; Toward understanding and collaboration, Nat Asn Sch Art & Design Publ & Asn Art Mus Dir Publ, 82. *Dealer:* Osung Gallery 1919 Q St NW Washington DC 20003; Robert Kidd Gallery 107 Townsend Birmingham MI 48011. *Mailing Add:* c/o Cranbrook Acad Art 500 Lone Pine Rd PO Box 801 Bloomfield Hills MI 48013

SLATE, JOSEPH FRANK
PAINTER, WRITER
b Holliday's Cove, WVa, Jan 19, 28. *Study:* Univ Wash, BA, 51; printmaking, Tokyo, Japan, 57; Yale Univ Sch Art & Archit, Alumni fel & BFA, 60; study of sumi-e painting, Kyoto, Japan, 75. *Work:* Drawings, Yale Univ; Poems & Prints (bk), Newberry Collection of Rare Bks, Univ Chicago; Painting, Kenyon Col. *Exhib:* 12th Nat Print Show, Brooklyn Mus, 60; Whitney Mus, New York, 74; Cent Ohio Watercolor Soc, Schumacher Gallery, Columbus, 75; Hopkins Hall Gallery, Columbus, Ohio, 76; Mus Art, Port Huron, Mich, 78; Retrospective, 1956-1988, Olin Gallery, 88. *Pos:* Consult, studies on aesthet & perception, Yale Univ Dept Psychol, 60-65; mem exec comt, Kress Found Consortium Art Hist, 65-69; consult, Nat Endowment for the Arts, 77-78; Juror, Soc Children Book Writers, 86. *Teaching:* Prof Art, Kenyon Col, 62-88, chmn dept, 64-72 & 81-82, chmn fine arts div, 67-69, emer prof, 88- *Awards:* Yale Alumni Fel, 60; Painting Award, Ohio Expo, 62; Outstanding Educator of Am, 73; Placed on Ohio Reader's Circle List, 82, 83 & 85; Ohioana Libr Asn Award for Distinguished Contribution to Children's Lit, 88. *Bibliog:* Janice Prindle (auth), Before we sleep, Village Voice, 10/82; Wash Alumnus, fall 82; reviews, Publishers Weekly, 5/21/82, 7/2/82, 9/16/83, 10/28/88; Something about the author, vol 38, Contemporary Authors, vol 110; Kenyon Alumni Bull, Fall 88. *Mem:* Soc Children's Book Writers; Authors Guild; and others. *Publ:* Auth, Those Old Italians, 62 & Respect, 64, New Yorker; The Star Rocker, Harper & Row, 82; The Mean, Clean, Giant Canoe Machine, Crowell, 83; Lonely Lulu Cat, Harper & Row, 85; Who is Coming to Our House? Putnam, 88. *Mailing Add:* 15107 Interlachen Dr Apt 701 Silver Spring MD 20906

SLATER, GARY LEE
SCULPTOR
b Montevideo, Minn, Oct 27, 47. *Study:* Univ Minn, BFA, 70; Ariz State Univ, MFA, 73. *Work:* Sky Harbor Int Airport, Phoenix, Ariz; Mus Fine Arts, NMex; City Monterey Park, Calif; City Palo Alto, Calif; Tucson Mus Art, Ariz. *Comn:* Ambassador Row Ctr, Lafayette, La, 86; Gwinett Com Ctr, Atlanta, Ga, 87; Ctr Park II, Calverton, Md, 88; Univ Ariz, Cancer Ctr, Tucson, 89; Chase Manhattan Bank, Tempe, Ariz, 92; and others. *Exhib:* Corten Steel: Contemporary Sculpture, Bowers Mus, Santa Ana, Calif, 74; SW Fine Arts Biennial, Santa Fe, NMex, 76; Summer Outdoor Sculpture Exhib, Palo Alto, Calif, 77; Ariz Biennial, Tucson Mus Art, 80; NAm Sculpture Exhib, Golden, Colo, 83; and others. *Awards:* Nat Endowment Arts Grant, 73-74; Purchase Awards, 9th Ann Drawing & Sculpture Show, Del Mar Col, Corpus Christi, Tex, 75 & Ariz Outlook 76, Tucson Mus of Art, 76. *Media:* Metal. *Dealer:* Elaine Horwitch Gallery 4200 N Marshall Way Scottsdale AZ 85251. *Mailing Add:* 638 W Contessa Circle Mesa AZ 85201

SLATKES, LEONARD J
HISTORIAN
b Hartford, Conn, Jan 11, 30. *Study:* Syracuse Univ, BFA, 52; Oberlin Col, MA, 54; Inst Fine Arts, NY Univ, 56-58; Columbia Univ, 58-60; Univ Utrecht, Fulbright Fels, US Educ Found, PhD, 62, Sr Fulbright Scholar, 79-80. *Teaching:* Asst prof art hist, Univ Chicago, 62-64 & Univ Pittsburgh, 64-66; assoc prof art hist, Queens Col, City Univ New York, 66-81, prof, 81- *Awards:* Research Grants, City Univ New York, 69, 78, 81, 82 & 85; Nat Endowment Humanities, 83-84; Senior Fulbright Fel, 86-87; and others. *Mem:* Col Art Asn; Historians of Northern Europ Art. *Res:* Northern Renaissance art; Northern mannerism; Italian and Northern Baroque art; history of graphic arts. *Publ:* Auth, The Netherlandish Artists, Vol I, 79; Rembrandt, 80; Vermeer and His Contemporaries, 81; Rembrandt and Persia, 83; Rembrandt, complete paintings, 92; and others. *Mailing Add:* Attn: Mrs Gershoff Dept Art Hist Klapper Hall Queens Col Flushing NY 11367

SLATKIN, WENDY
HISTORIAN
b New York, NY, June 20, 50. *Study:* Barnard Col, Columbia Univ, with Barbara Novak, BA, 70; Villa Schifanoia Grad Sch Fine Arts, Florence, Italy, MA, 71; Univ Pa, with John McCoubrey, PhD, 76. *Teaching:* Asst prof art hist, survey & post-renaissance, Camden Col Arts & Sci, Rutgers Univ, 76-83; vis lectr, Univ Calif, Riverside, 83-85, Univ Redlands, 85- 90; prof, Calif Polytech, Pomona, Calif, currently. *Publ:* Auth, The genesis of Maillol's la Mediterranee, Art J, spring, 79; The early sculpture of Maillol, Gazette des Beaux Arts, 10/80; Reminiscences of Maillol: A conversation with Dina Vierny, Arts Mag, 2/80; Maternity and sexuality in the 1890's, Woman's Art J, spring 80; Women Artists in History, Prentice-Hall, 84, 2nd rev ed, 90. *Mailing Add:* 1343 Lakewood Ave Upland CA 91786

SLATTON, RALPH DAVID
PRINTMAKER, GRAPHIC ARTIST
b Trumann, Ark, March 19, 52. *Study:* Ark State Univ, BFA, 81, MA, 86; Univ Iowa, MFA, 90. *Work:* Taiwan Mus Art, Taichung; Print Consortium, Kansas City, Mo; Proj Home, Baltimore, Md; Found Arts, Little Rock, Ark; Ark Artists Registry, Little Rock. *Exhib:* Univ Wis, Madison, 91; Choice, AIR Gallery, New York, 91; 5th Int Print, Taipei Art Mus, Taiwan, 91; 15th Harper Nat, William Harper Raney, Palatine, Ill, 91; 35th Anne Steele Marsh, Hunterdon Art Ctr, Clinton, NJ, 91. *Teaching:* Asst prof printmaking, E Tenn State Univ, Johnson City, 90- *Awards:* Purchase Award, 17th La Ann, Sulzer Escher Wyss Serv Ctr, 90; Purchase Award, Henley Southeastern Spectrum, 91; Purchase Award, 21st Prints & Drawings, Ark Arts Found, 91. *Mem:* Print Consortium; Philadelphia Print Club; Asociacion Difusora Obra Grafica Int. *Media:* Etching. *Mailing Add:* Dept Art, Box 23740A E Tenn State Univ Johnson City TN 37614-0002

SLAVICK, SUSANNE MECHTILD
PAINTER, EDUCATOR
b South Bend, Ind, Apr 1, 56. *Study:* Yale Univ, with B Chaet, Samia Halaby, R Reed, G Peterdi, BA, 78; Tyler Sch Art, with David Pease, Margo Margolis & John Moore, Philadelphia, MFA, 80. *Work:* Madison Art Ctr, Wis; Prairie State Col, Chicago Heights, Ill; Wabash Col, Crawfordsville, Ind. *Exhib:* Anderson, Lane, Slavick, Minn Mus Art, St Paul, 83; 80th Chicago Vicinity Exhib, Art Inst Chicago, 84; Wisconsin Directions 4, Milwaukee Art Mus, 84; solo exhibs, Slusser Gallery, Univ Mich, Ann Arbor, 86, Hewlett Gallery, Carnegie-Mellon Univ, Pittsburgh, Pa, 86, Struve Gallery, Chicago, 87, Brody's Gallery, Washington, DC, 88, Pittsburgh Ctr Arts, Pa, 88, CAGE Gallery, Cincinnati, 89 & Foster Art Gallery, Univ Wis, Eau Claire, 89; Perspectives from Pa, Carnegie-Mellon Art Gallery, 89; Coming of Age, Madison Art Ctr, Wis, 89; Regarding Art, Kohler Art Ctr, Sheboygen, Wis, 90-; Nature, Normalcy & Nonsense, Pittsburgh Ctr Arts, 91; Anxious Nature, Univ Nebr, Lincoln, 91; and others. *Teaching:* Instr art, Kutztown State Col, Pa, 80-81; asst prof, Univ Wis, Madison, 81-84; assoc prof, Carnegie-Mellon, Pittsburgh, Pa, 84- *Awards:* Broadus James Clarke Mem Prize, 80th Chicago & Vicinity Exhib, 84; Pa Coun Arts Fel in Painting, 84; Nat Endowment Arts Grant, 87. *Bibliog:* Michael Bonesteel (auth), rev, Art Am, 10/87; Carol Weiss (auth), article, Arts Indiana, 88; Paulette Roberts (auth), article, Art Papers, 88; Mary Jean Kenton (auth), Perspectives from Pa, New Art Examiner, 89. *Media:* Oil, Acrylic. *Dealer:* Tom & Judy Brody 1706 21st St Washington DC 20009. *Mailing Add:* 14 Swan Dr Pittsburgh PA 15237-2375

SLAVIN, ARLENE
PAINTER, SCULPTOR
b New York, NY, Oct 26, 42. *Study:* Cooper Union, BFA, 64; Pratt Inst, MFA, 67. *Work:* Brooklyn Mus, Metrop Mus Art, Chase Manhattan & Hudson River Mus, Yonkers, NY; Fogg Art Mus, Cambridge, Mass; Allen Mem Art Mus, Oberlin, Ohio; Berkely Univ Art Gallery, Calif; Norton Mus Art, Palm Beach, Fla; Prudential Life Insurance, NJ. *Comn:* Greeting card, Mus Mod Art, New York, 80; mural, Univ Colo, Colorado Springs, 81; Albert Einstein Hosp, Public Art Fund, New York Aquarium, Brooklyn, New York; mural & ceramic fountain, Bellevue Hosp Ctr, NY, 86; design of iron gates, Cathedral of St John the Divine, 89; design of iron fence & gate (55 ft), Henry St Settlement, NY, 92; metal work main stairway, Desoto Sch, NY, 93. *Exhib:* Whitney Biennial Contemp Art, 73 & Am Drawings 1967-1973, Whitney Mus; solo exhibs, Alexander F Milliken Gallery, New York, 79-83, Am Embassy, Belgrade, Yugoslavia, 84, Painterly Panels, Heckscher Mus, NY, 87 & Simultaneous Landscapes, Rich Perlow Gallery, 88, Chauncey Gallery, Princeton, NJ, 90, The Gallery: Benjamin N Cardozo Sch Law, Screen Retrospect, New York, 91; Useable Art, Queens Mus, Flushing, NY, 81; Ornamentalism, Hudson River Mus, Yonkers, NY; Large Drawings, Santa Barbara Mus Art, Calif, 86; group exhib, Noahs Art, NY Parks & Recreation, Central Park, 89. *Teaching:* Instr painting, Hofstra Univ, Long Island, NY, 71-72, Pratt Inst, 74 & Skowhegen Art Sch, Maine, 75 & 76; vis critic, Grad Sch, Univ Pa, 77; vis artist, Syracuse Univ, NY, 79. *Awards:* Printmaking grant, Nat Endowment for the Arts, 77. *Bibliog:* Art Work at Chase Manhattan Bank, E P Dutton Inc, 84; Nancy Love (auth), The Screen as Art, Town & Country, 10/85; Christopher Crossman (auth), Painterly Panels, Heckscher Mus, 7/87; Helen Harrison (auth), Painterly Panels: Hybrid Art, NY Times, 8/23/87; Pat Van Gelder (auth), Animals as subjects in contemporary art, Am Artists Mag, 89. *Media:* Acrylic, Oil; Metal. *Dealer:* Denise Levy 135 Central Park West New York NY 10023. *Mailing Add:* 119 E 18th St New York NY 10003

SLAVIN, NEAL
PHOTOGRAPHER
b New York, NY, Aug 19, 41. *Study:* Scholar, Lincoln Col, Oxford Univ, Eng, 61; Cooper Union, BFA, 63. *Work:* Metrop Mus Art, Mus Mod Art, Photog Arch, Int Ctr Photog, New York; Int Mus Photog, George Eastman House, Rochester, NY; Akron Art Inst, Ohio. *Comn:* The official cabinet portraits, Carter Administration, Nat Portrait Gallery, Washington, 80. *Exhib:* One person exhibs, Allen St Gallery, Dallas, Tex, 86, Kennedy Gallery, Cambridge, Mass, 87, Photogr Gallery, London, Eng, 87, Foto Forum, Frankfurt, Ger, 87, Festival at Arles, Arles, France, 87, Chase Manhattan Corp Hq, New York, 87 & Centre National De La Photographie, Palais De Tokyo, Paris, 90; solo exhibs, Underground Gallery, New York, 65 & 71,

Royal Ont Mus, Toronto, 71, Wadsworth Atheneum, Hartford, Conn, 76, Ctr Creative Photog, Tucson, Ariz, 76, Oakland Mus, Calif, 76, Light Gallery, New York, 76, Akron Art Inst, Ohio, 80, Nat Mus Photog, Film & TV, Eng, 86, Int Ctr Photog, New York, 86, Foto Forum, Frankfurt, Ger, 87 & Festival at Arles, France, 87; Rooms, Mus Mod Art, New York, 76; Venezia, The History of Polaroid, Venice, Italy, 79; Aspects of Am Photog, Galerie Spectrum, Hannover, West Germany, 81; The New Color, 81, Review, 86 & Legacy of Light, 87, Int Ctr Photog, New York; Color as Form: A History of Color Photog, Int Mus Photog & George Eastman House, Rochester, NY, 81; Va Mus Fine Arts, Richmond, 87; Zilkha Gallery Wesleyan Univ, Middletown, Conn, 92; Multiple Exposure: The Group Portrait in Photography, Zabriskie Gallery, New York, 92; plus many others. *Pos:* Lectr, Cooper Union Forum, New York, 75, Int Mus Photog, Rochester, NY, 75, Int Ctr Photog, New York, 77, Univ Calif, Los Angeles, 77, Milan workshops, Italy, 78, Ansel Adams Workshop, Yosemite, Calif, 77 & 80 & Smithsonian Inst, Washington, DC, 81. *Awards:* Nat Endowment Arts Grant, 72 & 76; Augustus Saint Gaudens medal for Art, Cooper Union Sch Art & Archit, 88; Recipient of Press & Poster Gold Lion, Cannes Festival, 92; Communications Arts Award, Water Country Usa, 92. *Bibliog:* New frontiers in color, Newsweek, 4/76; Fox Style News, Fox Network, 91; Photo Dist News, 6/92. *Mem:* Am Soc Mag Photogrs. *Publ:* Auth, Britons, Andre Deutsch Ltd, London & Aperture, New York; Athletes: Photographs 1860, 1986 Knopf, New York, 87; American Photography, Edward Booth-Clibborn, Rizzoli Int Publ Inc, 89; A Photographer's Source, 1989 by Henry Horenstein, Simon & Schuster; The Meaning of Life, Time Life Bks, 92. *Mailing Add:* 62 Greene St New York NY 10012

SLAYMAKER, MARTHA
PAINTER, SCULPTOR
b Saratoga, Ind, 1935. *Study:* Edinboro Col, Pa; Ohio State Univ, Columbus; John Herron Sch Art, Ind Univ. *Work:* Indianapolis Mus Art, Ind; Albuquerque Mus Art, Hist & Sci, NMex; NMex Mus Fine Arts, Santa Fe; Univ Northern Ariz, Flagstaff; Univ Western Ont, London; Eiteljorg Mus Am Indian & Western Art, Indianapolis, Ind. *Comn:* Relief sculptures, comn by Harrison Eiteljorg, Indianapolis, Ind, 78; art awards, Ind Arts Comn, Indianapolis, 79; IBM Corp, 85; Mayo Clinic, Scottsdale, Ariz, 88; Hannock-Weisman PC, New Jersey, 90. *Exhib:* One-woman shows, Univ NMex, 75 & 77, Galerie Motte, Geneva, Switz, 80, La Commanderie, Poet La Val, France, 83, Dubins Gallery, Los Angeles, 89; Dartmouth St Gallery, Albuquerque NMex, 90; Editions Ltd, Indianapolis, Ind, 91; Governor's Invitational Magnifico! Art Exhib, Convention Ctr, Albuquerque, NMex, 92; Med Artist World Exhib, Lincoln Ctr, New York, 92; and others. *Pos:* Cur, Viva la Vida, Viva el Arte: Confronting Cancer Through Art, Albuquerque, NMex, 88, 90, 91, 92. *Teaching:* Symposium Art & Healing, Univ Fla, 90; presenter, MedArt World Cong, New York, 91; presenter, Soc Layerists Multi-media, Agonquit, Maine, 92 & San Antonio, Tex, 92. *Awards:* Med Art World Cong Exhib Award, Lincoln Ctr, New York, 92. *Bibliog:* Mary Carroll Nelson (auth), Mixed media mixes with archeology, Today's Art & Graphics, 12/81, Martha Slaymaker: Collograph printing techniques, Am Artist, 9/85 & Layering, Leonardo J, Int Soc Arts, fall 86; Daniel Gibson (auth), Time and the shard, Artlines, 9/83; Fourth Dimension, Southwest Art, 8/87. *Mem:* NMex Artists Peace (chairperson); Soc Layerists in Multimedia (bd dirs, 83-89); Living through Cancer 1983-1992, Albuquerque, NMex. *Media:* Mixed; Relief. *Publ:* Auth, Art and healing, Southern Med J, 2/91. *Mailing Add:* 451 Gavilan Pl NW Albuquerque NM 87107

SLEIGH, SYLVIA
PAINTER, INSTRUCTOR
b Llandudno, Wales. *Study:* Brighton Sch Art, Eng. *Work:* Everson Mus Art, Syracuse, NY; Smart Mus, Univ Chicago; Milwaukee Art Mus. *Exhib:* One-artist shows, Bennington Col, Vt, 63, Soho 20 Gallery, 73, Fine Arts Ctr, Univ RI, Kingston, 74 & AIR Gallery, 74, 76 & 78, Milwaukee Art Mus, 90, Ball State Univ, Muncie, Ind, & Butler Inst, Youngstown, Ohio; Tokyo Int Biennial: New Image in Painting, 74; G W Einstein Co, Inc, 80 & 83; Zaks Gallery, Chicago, 85. *Pos:* Selection Comt, Women Choose Women, New York Cult Ctr, 73; ann grants adv, Adolph & Ester Gottlieb Found, 88. *Teaching:* Instr life painting, New Sch Social Res, 74-80; Kreeger Wolf Distinguished Prof, Northwestern Univ, 77; vis artist, Baldwyn Seminar, Oberlin Col, Ohio, 82; Cornell Univ, Nancy C Dickinson, 87. *Awards:* Nat Endowment Arts Visual Artists Fel Grant, 82; Pollock-Krasner Found Grant, 85. *Bibliog:* John Russell (auth), Sylvia Sleigh, Lerner-Heller Gallery, New York, 72; Linda Nochlin (auth), Some women realists, Arts, 74; John Perreault (auth), Male nudes, Village Voice, New York, 10/18/73; Joanna Frueh (auth), Sylivia Sleigh at Zaks Gallery, Art in Am, 86; Grace Glueck (auth), Artists & Model, New York Times, 6/86. *Mem:* Women's Caucus For Art; Col Art Asn. *Media:* Acrylic, Oil. *Publ:* Contribr, Anonymous was a Woman, 74 & Art: A Woman's Sensibility, 75, Feminist Art Prog, Calif Inst of the Arts. *Dealer:* Zaks Gallery 620 N Michigan Ave Chicago IL 60611. *Mailing Add:* 330 W 20th St New York NY 10011

SLETTEHAUGH, THOMAS CHESTER
ASSEMBLAGE ARTIST, EDUCATOR
b Minneapolis, Minn, May 8, 25. *Study:* Univ Minn, BS, 49, MEd, 50, with Walter Quint, Peter Lupori, Malcolm Myers & John Rood; Pa State Univ, DEd, 56, with Viktor Lowenfeld; spec study, Williams Col, Univ SC, Univ Ga & Syracuse Univ. *Work:* Bucharest Univ, Romania; Cult Ctr, Budapest, Hungary; Univ Belgrade, Yugoslavia. *Comn:* Symbol of Excellence, Miss Univ Women, 70; Miss Univ Women Crest for Apollo 14, Alumni Asn, 71; Architectural Graphics, Newman Ctr, 86. *Exhib:* Carnegie Mus Regional, Pittsburgh, 70; Heidelberg Univ Gallery, 75; Serigraphs, Cambridge Univ, Eng & Centro de Altos Estudios, Madrid, Spain, 76; Serigraph Techniques, Nat Gallery, Budapest, Hungary, 77; Klienen Gallery, Vienna, Austria, 78; Univ Ctr, Dubrovnik, Yugoslavia, 80; Taller Gallery, Barcelonia, Spain, 83-90; Centro Para Las Artes, Montevideo, Uruguay, 90. *Collections Arranged:* Max Klager--Printmaker, Heidelberg Univ, WGer; John Jackson--Drawings, Cambridge Univ, Eng; Charlotte Strobele Graphics, Univ Vienna, Austria; Zheng Sheng Tian Paintings, Hangzhou, PRC; Juan Carlos Ferreyra Santos-Acrylics, Punta del Este, Uruguay. *Teaching:* Prof fine arts, Miss Univ Women, 68-70; assoc prof grad studies art educ, Univ Minn, 70-; vis prof, Kenyatta Univ, Kenya, 86-88; Centro Paralas Artes, Montevideo, Uruguay, 90; Kossuth Univ, Debrecen, Hungary, 90. *Awards:* Psychoaesthetics Develop Award, Col Educ, Univ Minn, 71; Minneapolis Arts Comn, 86-89; Minnesota Fine Arts, Color Photog, 88. *Bibliog:* Hans Stumbauer (auth), Art education in Austria, Art Sch Linz, 71; Paul Cornel Chitic (auth), articles in Tribune & Art Rev, Bucharest, Romania, 72. *Mem:* Int Soc Educ in Art; Int Soc Aesthet; Int Soc Art Hist; Int Soc Empirical Aesthet; Int Union Architects. *Publ:* Auth, The analysis & synthesis of psychoaestheics, Cambridge Univ, 75; Southern Hemisphere Research, Aboriginals in Australia and Maori in New Zealand, 78 & Oriental Seminar in People's Republic of China, Hong Kong, Japan and Philippines, Int Soc for Educ through Art, United Nations Educ, Sci & Cult Orgn, 79 & 81; Taller de la Flor, Centro Artistico Antesanal, Buenos Aires, Argentina, 84. *Mailing Add:* 49 Williams Ave SE Minneapolis MN 55414

SLIDER, DORLA DEAN
PAINTER
b Tampa, Fla, Sept 9, 29. *Study:* Study with Dr Walter Emerson Baum, 40-48. *Work:* Allentown Art Mus, Pa; Plymouth Meeting Mall Asn, Pa; Brandywine River Mus, Chadds Ford, Pa; DuPont Corp, Del; Cedar Crest Col, Pa; and others. *Exhib:* Am Watercolor Soc, New York; Allied Artists of Am, Nat Acad Design, 67-77; Pa Acad Fine Arts, Philadelphia, 69; William Penn Mus, Harrisburg, Pa, 75; Watercolor USA, Springfield, Ohio; Butler Inst of Am Art, Ohio. *Awards:* Gold Medal, Knickerbocker Artists New York, 77; Doris Kennedy Mem Award, Audubon Artists, New York, 79; Arjomari/Arches/Rives Award, Nat Soc Painters Casein & Acrylic, New York, 91; plus others. *Bibliog:* Henry C Pitz (auth), Brandywine Tradition, Houghton Mifflin Co, Boston, 69; articles in Brandywine Bugle, Trade Mag, Pa, 71-74. *Mem:* Am Watercolor Soc; Nat Soc Painters in Casein & Acrylic; Knickerbocker Artists; Artists Equity Asn; Audubon Artists; plus others. *Media:* Watercolor, Acrylic. *Publ:* Artists Fla, 89-90. *Dealer:* Lippincott Gallery Second and Buttonwood Sts Phoenixville Pa 19460; H C Mann Gallery West Reading PA 19611. *Mailing Add:* 268 Estate Rd Boyertown PA 19512

SLIGH, CLARISSA T
PHOTOGRAPHER, PAINTER
b Wash, DC, Aug 30, 39. *Study:* Hampton Inst, BS; Howard Univ, BFA; Univ Pa, MBA. *Work:* Mus Mod Art, New York; Women's Mus, Wash, DC; Schomburg Ctr for Res in Black Cult, New York Pub Libr; Australian Nat Gallery, Canberra. *Comn:* Washington State Arts Commission, Walker Art Ctr. *Exhib:* One-woman shows, Modernage Discovery Gallery, 82, Rockland Community Col, Suffern, NY, 85, CEPA Satellite Space, Buffalo, 87, White Columns, New York, 90, Wash Proj for the Arts, 91, Menschel Gallery, Syracuse Univ, 91, Art in General, New York, 92, Ctr Photog, Woodstock, 92; Crossing Over/Changing Places: Collaborative Print Projects & Paperworks, Print Club, Philadelphia, 91; Convergence, Photog Resource Ctr, Boston Univ & traveling, 91; Recent Acquisitions: Prints & Drawings, Mus Mod Art, New York, 91; Bridges & Boundaries: African Americans & American Jews, Jewish Mus, NY Hist Soc & traveling, 92; The Presence of the Past, Newhouse Ctr Contemp Art, Snug Harbor, Cultural Ctr, Stten Island, NY, 92. *Teaching:* Instr, City Col NY, 86-87; vis artist faculty, Minn Col Art & Design, Minneapolis, Minn, spring term, 88-89; instr, Lower Eastside Printship, New York, winter 88-90; distinguished vis artist/teacher, Carlton Col, Northfield, Minn, spring term, 92. *Awards:* Nat Endowment Arts, 88; New York Found Arts, 88; NY State Coun Arts, 90; Artiste En France Award, Greater NY Links, French Govt, Moet & Chandon, 92. *Bibliog:* Laura U Marks (auth), Reinscribing the Self: An Interview with Clarissa Sligh, Afterimage, 17:5, 12/89; Linda S Klinger (auth), Where's the Artist? Feminist Practice & Poststructural Theories of Authorship, Art J, 50:2, 39-47, summer 91; Laura U Marks (auth), Healing the Cultural Body: Clarissa Sligh's Unfinished Business, Center Quarterly, No 50, 18-22, 92. *Mem:* Coast to Coast Nat Women Artists Color; Women's Caucus Art Col Art Asn. *Publ:* Contribr, What's Happening with Momma & Reading Dick and Jane With Me, 89, Artist Bookwork; On Being An American Black Student, Heresies, Vol 7, No 1, issue 25, 90; Women of Color? (catalog essay), Coast to Coast Nat Women Artists Color, 91; Witness to Dissent: It Wasn't Little Rock, IKON, No 12/13, 92. *Mailing Add:* 465 W Broadway New York NY 10012

SLIVE, SEYMOUR
HISTORIAN, MUSEUM DIRECTOR
b Chicago, Ill, Sept 15, 20. *Study:* Univ Chicago, AB, 43, PhD, 52. *Pos:* Dir, Fogg Art Mus, Harvard Univ, 75-82; Elizabeth & John Moors Cabot dir, Harvard Art Mus, emer. *Teaching:* Instr fine arts, Oberlin Col, Ohio, 50-51; asst prof art & chmn dept, Pomona Col, Calif, 52-54; from asst prof to prof fine arts, Harvard Univ, 54-73, Gleason prof fine arts emer, 73-91. *Awards:* Officer of Order of House of Orange-Nassau, 62; Charles Rufus Morey Prize, Col Art Asn Am, 70; Award for Achievement in Art Hist, Art Dealers' Asn Am, 79. *Mem:* Fel Am Acad Arts & Sci; hon mem Karel van Mander Soc; Col Art Asn (dir, 58-62 & 65-69); Renaissance Soc; foreign mem Dutch Soc Sci. *Res:* Baroque art. *Publ:* Auth, Drawings of Rembrandt, 2 vols, Dover Publ, New York, 65; coauth, Dutch Art and Architecture: 1600-1800, Penguin Bks, Baltimore, 66; auth, Frans Hals, 3 vols, Phaidon Press, London, 70-74; Jacob van Ruisdael, Abbeville Press, New York, 81; Frans Hals, Prestel Press, Munich, 89; and others. *Mailing Add:* Fogg Art Mus Harvard Univ Cambridge MA 02138

SLIVKA, DAVID
SCULPTOR
b Chicago, Ill. *Study:* Calif Sch Fine Arts. *Work:* Univ Pa, Philadelphia; Baltimore Mus; Rutgers Univ, Camden, NJ; Everson Mus, Syracuse, NY; Brooklyn Mus, NY. *Exhib:* Mus Mod Art, 62; Hirshhorn Collection Mod Sculpture, Guggenheim Mus, 62-63; Mus Fine Arts, Boston, 68; Selections from Chase Manhattan Bank Collection, 71; Albright-Knox Art Gallery, Buffalo, NY, 74; one-man shows, Southern Ill Univ, Carbondale, 68, Everson Mus, Syracuse, NY, 74 & Univ Pa, Philadelphia, 75. *Teaching:* Prof sculpture, Univ Mass, Amherst, 64-67; artist in residence, Southern Ill Univ, Carbondale, 67-68; instr, Queens Col, NY, 71-73; prof, Pa Acad Fine Arts, Philadelphia, 72-88. *Awards:* Brandeis Univ Creative Arts Award for Am Sculpture, 62; Louis Comfort Tiffany Award-Sculpture, 77; Pollock-Krasner Found Award, 85-86. *Bibliog:* Harvey Arnason (auth), Modern Sculpture from the Joseph Hirshhorn Collection, Guggenheim Mus, 62; Georgine Oeri (auth), The sculpture of David Slivka, Quadrum, 63; Harold Rosenberg (auth), The anxious object, Illus, 65. *Media:* Miscellaneous. *Mailing Add:* 549 W 52nd New York NY 10019

SLOAN, JEANETTE PASIN
PAINTER, PRINTMAKER
b Chicago, Ill, Mar 18, 46. *Study:* Marymount Col, Tarrytown, NY, BFA, 67; Art Inst of Chicago; Univ Chicago, MFA, 69. *Work:* Nat Mus Am Art, Smithsonian Inst, Washington, DC; Cleveland Mus Fine Arts; Art Inst Chicago; Minneapolis Inst Art; Yale Univ Art Gallery; Metrop Mus Art, New York; and others. *Exhib:* G W Einstein Co, New York, 77, 79, 80, 83 & 85; one-person shows, Frumkin & Struve Gallery, Chicago, 81 & Ill State Mus, Springfield, 81; Roger Ramsay Gallery, Chicago, 87 & 92; Adams-Middleton Gallery, Dallas, 87; David Adamson Gallery, Washington, DC, 87; Leedy-Voulkos Gallery, Kansas City, Mo, 87; Thimmish Gallery, Minneapolis, Minn, 92. *Awards:* Ill Arts Coun Fel, 86. *Bibliog:* Gerrit Henry (auth), rev, Art News, 1/78 & rev, Art in Am, 6/85; Anne I Lockhart (auth), Jeanette Pasin Sloan, Arts, New York, 4/79; Michele Vishney (auth), Still-Life and the Art of Jeanette Pasin Sloan, Arts, 3/83. *Media:* Oils, Colored Pencils; Lithography, Watercolor. *Dealer:* Roger Ramsey Gallery Chicago Ill; Landfall Press Chicago Ill. *Mailing Add:* 535 Keystone River Forest IL 60305

SLOAN, MARK
MUSEUM DIRECTOR
b Durham, NC, Nov 16, 57. *Study:* Univ Richmond, BA, 80; Va Commonwealth Univ, MFA, 84. *Exhib:* Photographs: Rimma and Varleriy Gerlovin, 91; Intimate Technologies/Fictional Personas, 92; Dear Mr Ripley, 93. *Pos:* Asst dir, San Francisco Camerawork, 86-89; dir, Roland Gibson Gallery, Potsdam, NY, currently. *Mem:* Am Asn Mus; Col Art Asn; Soc Photog Educ. *Publ:* Spirit in the Land: Photographs from the Bible Belt, Southern Accents; Spectacular Photographs: Unforgettable Faces, Facts and Feats, 89; Hoaxes, Humbugs and Spectacles, Villard/Random House, 90; Dear Mr Ripley, Bulfinch/Little, Brown & Co, 93. *Mailing Add:* Roland Gibson Gallery State Univ NY Potsdam NY 13676

SLOAN, RICHARD
PAINTER, ILLUSTRATOR
b Chicago, Ill, Dec 11, 35. *Study:* Am Acad of Art, Chicago, Ill. *Work:* Denver Mus Natural Hist; Ill State Mus, Springfield; Leigh Yawkey Woodson Art Mus, Wausau, Wis. *Comn:* The Raptors of Arizona (paintings), Ariz Wildlife Found, Ariz Game & Fish Dept, & Univ Ariz Press, in progress. *Exhib:* Birds in Art Exhib, Leigh Yawkey Woodson Art Mus, 79-81, 83-89 & 91-92, Field Mus Natural Hist, Chicago, 88; Woodson Art Mus Int Exhib, Bejing Mus Natural Hist, Bejing, People's Repub China, 86-87; Wildlife in Art, 87; Cummings Nature Ctr, Rochester Mus Sci Ctr, Rochester, 88; Animals in Art, Soc Animal Artists, Jamestown, NY, 92. *Pos:* Staff artist, Lincoln Park Zoo, Chicago, 62-65. *Awards:* Award of Excellence, Cincinnati Mus Natural Hist, Cincinnati, 84; Award of Merit, Nat Art Exhib Alaskan Wildlife, Anchorage Audubon Soc, Anchorage, 85; Award of Excellence, Soc Animal Artists, 90. *Mem:* Soc Animal Artists, New York. *Media:* Acrylic. *Publ:* Roger Tory & Virginia Marie Peterson (auths), Audubon's Birds of America, 81; Artist of the Ancient Forest, Int Wildlife, 7-8/86; illusr, In the Rainy Season, Field Mus Natural Hist Bull, 88; cover, The sunlit ruins, US Art Mag, 3/89; From Hawks to Hornbills and Back Again: The Art of Richard Sloan, Wildlife Art News, 11-12/91. *Dealer:* Thomas Nygard Inc 127 E Main Bozeman MT 59715; Gregory & Falk 540 First St San Francisco CA 94107. *Mailing Add:* Rte 2 Box 2138 Soldiers Grove WI 54655-9610

SLOAN, ROBERT SMULLYAN
PAINTER
b New York, NY, Dec 5, 15. *Study:* City Col New York, AB, 36; Inst Fine Arts, NY Univ, 37-39. *Work:* IBM Collection; Bradford Jr Col, Haverhill, Mass; Herbert F Johnson Mus, Ithaca, NY; Nat Portrait Gallery, Washington, DC. *Comn:* Many covers & spec features, Time, Coronet & Colliers, 41-50; posters, Russian War Relief, 43 & Doing All You Can, Brother, US Treas, 43. *Exhib:* Corcoran Biennial, 49; Portraits of Year, Portraits, Inc, 49; Am Watercolor Soc Exhib, Nat Acad Design Gallery, 56; one-man shows, Leger Galleries, White Plains, NY, 55, Herbert F Johnson Mus, Cornell Univ, 74 & Capricorn Galleries, Bethesda, Md, 75; Time Salutes Pennsylvania, Hist Soc Pa, 82; Traveling exhib, The Seasoned Eye III, 90-91; Ending, Kennedy Ctr, Washington, DC. *Awards:* Citation for Distinguished Serv, US Treas, 43; Watercolor Div Award, Nat Soldier Art Show, USA, 45; Distinguished Achievement Award, The Seasoned Eye III, Mod Maturity Mag, 90. *Bibliog:* George Wiswell (auth), Discovery of a Copley portrait, Am Heritage Mag, 60. *Mem:* Appraisers Asn Am; Mamaroneck Artists Guild (pres, 54). *Media:* Oil. *Publ:* Illusr, Army Educ Prog & other mags. *Mailing Add:* 1412 Arlington St Mamaroneck NY 10543

SLOAN, RONALD J
PAINTER
b Brooklyn, NY, Jan 8, 32. *Study:* Central State Univ, Edmond, Okla, MA(art educ), 65; Univ Albany, NY, MA, 75; Univ Ky, Lexington, MFA(painting), 79. *Work:* Univ Potsdam Gallery, New York; Provincetown Mus, Cape Cod, Mass; Chase Manhattan Bank, New York; Gen Elec Corp, Conn; Northwestern Community Col, Winsted, Conn. *Exhib:* Dreamscapes-Surreality in Conn, Mattatuck Mus, Waterbury, 88; Art New Eng Exhib, Silvermine Guild, New Canaan, 88; Berkshire Invitational Exhib, Pittsfield Mus, Mass, 88; Conn Watercolor Show, Saltbox Gallery, West Hartford, 88; solo exhib, Bushnell Gallery, Hartford, Conn, 89; Works on Paper, Berkshire Mus, Pittsfield, Mass, 90; Bruce Mus, Greenwich, Conn, 91. *Awards:* Provincetown Fine Arts Work Ctr Fel, 84-85; Nat Endowment Arts, 87-88. *Mem:* Conn Acad Fine Arts; New Haven Paint & Clay; Springfield Art League. *Media:* Acrylic. *Mailing Add:* 52 Lovely St Winsted CT 06098

SLOANE, JOSEPH CURTIS
HISTORIAN
b Pottstown, Pa, Aug 8, 09. *Study:* Princeton Univ, AB, 31, MFA, 34, PhD(Hodder fel), 49. *Teaching:* Instr art hist, Princeton Univ, 35-37; asst prof art hist & chmn dept art, Rutgers Univ, 37-38; from assoc prof art hist to prof & chmn dept art, Bryn Mawr Col, 38-58; prof art hist & chmn dept art, Univ NC, Chapel Hill, 58-78, emer dir, William Hayes Ackland Art Ctr, currently. *Awards:* Fulbright Sr Res Grant, 52; NC Award (Arts), 76; Morrison Award, Roanoke Island Hist Asn, 82. *Mem:* Col Art Asn Am (past pres); NC Art Soc (past pres); hon life mem Asn Art Mus Dirs. *Res:* Nineteenth and twentieth century art, especially painting. *Publ:* Auth, French Painting Between the Past & the Present, Princeton Univ, 51; Paul Marc Joseph Chenavard, Univ NC, 62; The American Situation, Univ NC Publ, 76; articles in Art Bulletin, Art Quart, Gazette Beaux-Arts, Art J & others. *Mailing Add:* 3117 Carol Woods Weaver Dairy Rd Chapel Hill NC 27514

SLOANE, PHYLLIS LESTER
PAINTER, PRINTMAKER
b Worcester, Mass. *Study:* Carnegie-Mellon Univ, BFA. *Work:* Cleveland Mus of Art, Ohio; Philadelphia Mus of Art, Pa; Canton Art Ctr, Ohio; Rutgers Univ Archives, NJ; Mus Fine Art, Santa Fe, NMex. *Comn:* Mural (on bldg side), Cleveland Area Arts Coun, Am Inst of Architects & NOVA, 74; ed of print La Nue, Univ Print Club, Cleveland, 77; 4 print eds, Transworld Art Corp, 79; presentation print, Cleveland Print Club, 83; portfolio, Image Resource Ctr, NOVA, Cleveland, 83. *Exhib:* Ohio Women Artists: Past & Present, Butler Inst of Am Art, Youngstown, 76; Hunterdon Nat Print Exhib, 78, 79 & 81; Boston Printmakers Exhib, 79-81, 84 & 85; Cleveland Play House Gallery, 83 & 85; The Printed Image, Hudson River Mus, Yonkers, NY, 87; and others. *Awards:* Graphics Awards, Cleveland Mus Art May Show, 78; Cleveland Visual Arts Award, 82; First Prize, Miami Int Print Biennial, 84; Purchase Awards, NC Print & Drawing Ann & Anderson Ind Print Show, 85. *Bibliog:* Printworld, 82, 83, 85 & 86; Print World, winter 91; Color in Contemporary Painting, Charles Le Clair; Screenprinting Mag, 2/92. *Mem:* New Orgn Visual Arts (bd trustees, 73-79). *Media:* Watercolor; Miscellaneous Media. *Dealer:* Bonfoey & Co 1710 Euclid Ave Cleveland OH 44115; Cleveland Ctr Contemp Art 8500 Carnegie Ave Cleveland OH 44106. *Mailing Add:* 13800 Shaker Blvd No 1204 Cleveland OH 44120

SLOAT, RICHARD JOEL
PAINTER, PRINTMAKER
b Easton, Pa, Sept 18, 45. *Study:* Univ Pa, BA, 69; Art Students League, 72. *Work:* British Mus, London; Israel Mus, Jerusalem; Fogg Mus, Cambridbe, Mass; Mus of City of New York; Taipei Mus, Taiwan. *Comn:* 5 Print Editions, New York Graphic Soc, Greenwich, 72-80. *Exhib:* Silvermine Biennial, Silvermine Guild, New Cannan, 72, 88 & 92; Juried exhib, Nat Acad, New York, 74, 86 & 88; 15 Years of Figurative Alliance, The Studio Sch, New York, 84; 38th NAm Print Exhib, DeCordova Mus, Boston, 86; Solo exhib, Martin Sumers Gallery, NY, 87 & Wood and Stone Gallery, Taipei, 90; two person show, FalkenStern Fine Art, New York, 90. *Awards:* Hon Mention, Audubon Artists, 74; First Presby Church Award, Wash Sq, New York, 76; Leo Messner Prize, Nat Acad, 86. *Bibliog:* Michael Brenson (auth), Art Sect Rev, New York Times, 4/21/86; Vivien Raynor (auth), Sunday New York Times, 3/6/88; Wu Jin Fa (auth), Min Chung Dailey News, Taiwan, 9/1/89. *Mem:* Alliance of Figurative Artists (prog dir, 82-85); Sky Wheel Configurist Group (co-founder); Print Consortium; Boston Printmakers. *Media:* Oil; Woodcut. *Publ:* Illusr, Good Times, San Francisco Newspaper, 69-70; Floating Weeds, Bk by Hung Su-Li, 82; Configurism, Artist Manifesto, 86; United Daily News Taipei, 89; Mythic City & Friends, Book by Artist, 91. *Mailing Add:* 148 Henry St New York NY 10002

SLOBODKINA, ESPHYR (MRS URQUHART)
PAINTER, WRITER
b Siberia, Russia, Sept 22, 08; US citizen. *Study:* Pvt art tutors, Russian High Sch, Manchuria, attended Nat Acad Design. *Work:* Met Mus of Art Whitney Mus Art, New York; Corcoran Nat Mus Am Art, Washington, DC; Philadelphia Art Mus. *Exhib:* Many national and international exhibitions. *Pos:* Designer, experimental textile printing plant, 35-44. *Teaching:* Pvt art class, Great Neck, NY, 50-62. *Awards:* McDowell & Yaddo fels. *Mem:* Am Abstract Artists (pres, secy & tres, 36-84); founding mem Fed of Modern Painters & Sculptors. *Media:* Oil on Gesso Board. *Publ:* Auth & illusr, Caps For Sale, Harper & Row, in print continuously since 1940; auth, Notes For a Biographer 3 vol set, Urquhart-Slobodkina, Inc, 82-85; auth & illusr of over 20 children's books. *Dealer:* Snyder Fine Arts Gallery 588 Broadway New York NY 10012. *Mailing Add:* 309 SW Eighth St Hallandale FL 33009

SLONE, SANDI
PAINTER, INSTRUCTOR
b Boston, Mass, Oct 1, 39. *Study:* Wheaton Col, 57-59; Mus Fine Arts Sch, Boston, 70-73; Wellesley Col, BA, 74. *Work:* Mus Fine Arts, Boston; Mus Mod Art, NY; Hirshhorn Mus & Sculpture Garden, Washington, DC; Rose Art Mus, Brandeis Univ; New Mus Contemp Art, Barcelona, Spain; De Cordova Mus, Lincoln, Mass; Hood Mus, Dartmouth Col, Hanover, NH; Federated Union Black Artists Gallery, Johannesburg, S Africa. *Exhib:* Drawing Made Material, Hayden Gallery, Mass Inst Tech, Cambridge, 78; The New Generation (with catalog), Andre Emmerich Gallery, NY; Azure Cooperative, Portugal, 80-81; Carpenter Ctr, Harvard Univ, Cambridge, 83; Casa de la Caritat, Barcelona, Spain, 87; Stephen Rosenberg Gallery, New York, 88; Levinson Kane Gallery, Boston, 89; Smith Jariwala Gallery, London, 90; one-person exhibs, Galleria Uno Granollers, Barcelona, Spain, 90, Smith Jariwala Gallery, London, 90, Miyoko Gallery, Tokyo, 91; Reams of Pleasure, Jan Weiss Gallery, 90, Gesture and Light, Ulysses Gallery, New York, 91; Big Talent, Levison Kane Gallery, Boston, 90; Sensuous Geometry, Bernard Jordan Gallery, Paris, 90; Mostra Int D'Art Contemp, Acad de Belles Artes, Sabadell, Spain, 91; Olympia Int Art Fair, 91, The New Abstraction, Smith Jariwala Gallery, London, 91; Cologne Art Fair, Koln, Ger, 91. *Teaching:* asst prof painting, Brandeis Univ, 76-77; MFA Prog, Sch Visual Arts, New York, 89-90; painting fac, Sch of Mus Fine Arts, Boston, 71- *Awards:* Mus Fine Arts Traveling Fel, 77 & 81; Artist-in-Residence, City Hall, Barcelona, Spain, 87 & 89; Mus Fine Arts Sabbatical, China, 85-87. *Bibliog:* Miles Unger (auth), Sandi Slone, Levinson Kane Gallery, Art New Eng, 12/89; Karen Wilkin (auth), In the Galleries, Partisan Rev, spring 90; Tim Hilton (auth), Critic's Choice, The Guardian, 10/28/90. *Mem:* ART/OMI Int Artists' Forum (found dir). *Media:* Paint. *Dealer:* Acquavella Contemp Art 18 E 79th St New York NY 10021; Levinson Kane Gallery 14 Newbury St Boston MA 02116. *Mailing Add:* 13 Worth St New York NY 10013

SLONEM, HUNT
PAINTER, MURALIST
b Kittery, Maine, July 18, 51. *Study:* Skowhegan Sch Painting & Sculpture, 72; Tulane Univ, BA, 73. *Work:* Metrop Mus Art, New York; Birmingham Mus Art, Ala; Hunter Mus Art, Chattanooga, Tenn; Va Mus Fine Arts, Richmond; Mint Mus, Charlotte, NC; Newark Mus. *Comn:* Fan Dance (mural), World Trade Port Authority Ctr, New York, 80. *Exhib:* Figurative Drawings, Va Mus Art (with catalog), Richmond, 85; Narrative Painting Since 1980, Phoenix Art Mus, Ariz, 86; Realism & Abstraction, Newark Mus, NJ, 87; Stamford Mus, Conn, 88; Contemporary Mus, Honolulu, Hiawaii, 89; Feathers, Fur & Fin, Laguna Gloria Mus, Austin, Tex, 90; Menagerie, Mus Mod Art, 90; solo exhibs, Galerie Witteveen, Amsterdam, Holland, 89, Ben Shahn Galleries, William Paterson Col, Wayne, NJ, 90, Helander Gallery, New York & Palm Beach, 90, Gallerie Eewal, Leewarden, Holland, Bergen Mus Art & Sci (with catalog), Paramus, NJ, 90, Tilden-Foley Gallery, New Orleans, La, 91, Harcourts Contemp Art, San Francisco, Calif, 91; Contemp Mus, Honolulu, Hawaii; Bergen Mus, NJ. *Awards:* Greenshields Found Grant for Painting, 76; Millay Colony Arts, 82; Colony Fel, 83, 84 & 86. *Bibliog:* Elizabeth Hess (auth), Review: Slonem at Paul Allen Gallery, Village Voice, 5/23/89; Jami Bernard (auth), Hunt Slonem, Hamptons, 90; Brooks Adams (auth), Vogue, 7/90; Roberta Smith (auth), article, NY Times, 88; Brooks Adams (auth), article, Vogue, 90; Jay Murphy (auth), article, Contemporanea, 90. *Media:* Oil on Canvas. *Dealer:* Harcourts Contemporary & Modern 460 Bush St San Francisco CA 94108. *Mailing Add:* 87 E Houston New York NY 10012

SLOSBURG-ACKERMAN, JILL
SCULPTOR, JEWELER
b Omaha, Nebr, Aug 28, 48. *Study:* Tufts Univ, BFA, 71, MFA, 83. *Work:* Mass Col Art, Boston. *Exhib:* Solo exhibs, Body Sculpture at The Harcus-Krakow Gallery, Boston, Mass, 78, 80 & 85, Helen Shlien Gallery, Boston, Mass, 80 & 82, Cohen Arts Ctr, Tufts Univ, Medford, Mass, 82 & Van Buren/Brazelton/Cutting Gallery, Cambridge, Mass, 85; Amerricky Sperk, Mus Decorative Arts, Prague, 91; Other Voices, Nancy Margolis Gallery, New York, 91; Of Power, Myth, and Memory, Bellevue Art Mus, Wash, 92; Crossroads, ARTWEAR, New York, 92; Material Boundaries Between the Sexes, Genovese Gallery Albany, Boston, 92. *Teaching:* Prof arts, Mass Col Art, 72-; artist in residence, Cranbrook Acad Art, 93. *Awards:* Mary Ingraham Bunting Inst Fel, 85-86; 20 x 24 Photog Grant, Polaroid Corp, 88; Finalist, Artist Found, 91. *Bibliog:* Norman Keyes Jr (auth), Danforth Installation Explores Beach Culture, Boston Globe, 3/21/86; Alicia Faxon (auth), Nature Observed, Art New Eng, 4/86; Michael Dunas (auth), Form Beyond Function, Metalsmith, spring 86. *Media:* Wood; Precious Metal. *Publ:* Auth, Angela Fisher's Africa Adorned, Art New Eng, 11/86; A Show of Vessels: Duncan Miller, Claire Sanford, Metalsmith, winter 87; Marilyn Pappas (exhib catalog), winter 87; Art Jewelry, Art New Eng, 12-13, 5/87; Lisa Gralnick, Metalsmith, fall 89. *Mailing Add:* 12 Coolidge Hill Rd Cambridge MA 02138

SLOSHBERG, LEAH PHYFER
MUSEUM DIRECTOR
b New Albany, Miss, Feb 21, 37. *Study:* Miss State Col Women, BFA, 59; Tulane Univ, La, MA, 61. *Pos:* Cur arts, NJ State Mus, Trenton, asst dir, 69-71, dir, 71- *Mem:* Am Asn Mus; Conserv Ctr Art & Artifacts (bd mem, 79-); Mid-Atlantic Asn Mus. *Res:* American art; museum management. *Mailing Add:* New Jersey State Mus 205 W State St Trenton NJ 08625

SLOTNICK, MORTIMER H
PAINTER, EDUCATOR
b New York, NY, Nov 7, 20. *Study:* City Col New York; Columbia Univ. *Work:* In pvt collections of Mrs Harry S Truman, Mrs Cordell Hull and others; New Brit Mus Am Art, Conn; Nat Mus Am Art, Smithsonian Inst; Johnson Art Mus, Cornell Univ; Nat Archives; and others. *Exhib:* Whitney Mus Am Art, Riverside Mus, Hudson River Mus, New Rochelle Pub Libr, Nat Acad Design, New York; and others. *Teaching:* Adj prof art & art educ, City Col New York; supvr arts & humanities, City Sch Dist, New Rochelle, NY; adj prof art educ, Col New Rochelle; adj prof educ, Pace Univ; principal, Davis Elem Sch, New Rochelle, NY. *Mem:* Allied Artists Am; Am Artists Prof League; Artists Equity, NY; Am Vet Soc Artists; Knickerbocker Artists, NY. *Media:* Oil. *Publ:* Works publ by Am Artists Group, Donald Art Co, Bernard Picture Co, Scafa-Tornabene Art Publ & McCleery-Cummings Co. *Mailing Add:* 43 Amherst Drive New Rochelle NY 10804

SLUSKY, JOSEPH
SCULPTOR, EDUCATOR
b Philadelphia, Pa, June 7, 42. *Study:* Univ Calif, Berkeley, BA(arch), MA(art), studied with James Prestini, Ibram Lassaw, James Melchert, Wilfred Zogbaum, Sidney Gordin, Harold Paris, Richard O'Hanlon, William King & Robert Hudson. *Work:* Hayward Area Festival of the Arts, Calif; City San Francisco; San Francisco Dept Water. *Comn:* Outdoor sculpture, City Berkeley, 81; interior lobby sculpture, San Francisco Dept Water, 84; interior lobby sculpture, Peerless Lighting Corp, Berkeley, Calif, 89. *Exhib:* Sculpture, Dorothy Weiss Gallery, San Francisco, Calif, 88; sculpture & drawings, Holy Names Col, Oakland, Calif, 90; Tex Sculpture Assoc, Fifth Ann Nat Jurried Exhib, Excellence, 90, Plaza of the Am, Dallas, Tex, 90; A Selection of Bay Area Drawings, Richmond Art Ctr, Richmond, Calif, 92; sculpture & drawings, Smith Andersen Gallery, Palo Alto, Calif, 92; and many others. *Teaching:* Lectr sculpture & visual studies, Univ Calif, Berkeley, 69-70 & 78-; instr sculpture & drawing, Ohlone Col, Fremont, Calif, 72-85; lectr sculpture, Calif State Univ, San Francisco, 78, and others. *Awards:* Purchase Award, Hayward Festival of the Arts, 75 & 79; First Place Award, Bay Arts, Belmont, Calif, 87 & 90; Sculpture Award, Calif State Fair, 85, 88, 91 & 92; and others. *Bibliog:* Johanna Drucker (auth), Construction & revery: the work of Joe Slusky, J of CED, UCB, Vol 17 No 6, 84; Chiori Santiago (auth), Art and the evolution of things, The Daily Californian, 3/19/86; Victoria Powers (auth), Contrasts of concepts and form, Artweek, 3/29/86. *Media:* Metal, Acrylic. *Dealer:* Barclay Simpson Fine Arts Gallery 3669 Mt Diablo Blvd Lafayette CA 94549; Smith Andersen Gallery 200 Homer Ave Palo Alto CA 94301. *Mailing Add:* 2612-A Regent St Berkeley CA 94704

SMALL, DEBORAH
PAINTER
b Mariemont, Ohio, Oct 38, 48. *Study:* Univ Calif, San Diego, MFA, 83. *Exhib:* MiscegeNATION, Istanbul Biennale, 92. *Teaching:* Asst prof visual arts, Calif State Univ, San Marcos, 92- *Awards:* Painting Fel, 87 & 89 & Interarts Grant, 90 & 91, Nat Endowment Arts. *Mailing Add:* 4437 Via DeLos Cepillos Bonsall CA 92003

SMALL, NEAL
DESIGNER, SATIRIST
b New York, NY, Aug 4, 37. *Study:* Tex A & M Sch Archit, 54-55; WVa Wesleyan, 56-57. *Work:* Mus Mod Art, New York; Brooklyn Mus; Philadelphia Mus Art; Albright-Knox Art Gallery, Buffalo, NY; Dallas Mus Fine Arts; Mus of Museums, Waregem, Belg. *Exhib:* Excellence in Design, 67, 68 & 69, Brooklyn Mus, 67, Smithsonian Inst, DC, 68 & Mus Sci & Indust, Chicago, 69; Flint Invitational, Flint Inst Art, De Waters Art Ctr, Flint, Mich, 71; one-man show, Mus Univ SFla, 71; AIR Gallery, 81. *Collections Arranged:* Environment, St Louis Mus, 70; US Info Agency Show, Zagreb, Yugoslavia, 71, Bucharest, Romania, 72. *Pos:* Pres, Neal Small Designs, New York, 66-73 & Squire & Small, 74-79. *Awards:* Awards for excellence of design, An Design Revs, Indust Design, 68-70. *Mem:* St Simian Soc. *Media:* Acrylic, Bronze and Collage. *Publ:* Articles, NY Times; articles, Industrial Design Mag; articles, Home Furnishings Daily; articles, Life Mag; Plastic as Design Form, Chilton. *Dealer:* George Beylerian 16 E 77 New York NY 10021. *Mailing Add:* 178 Fifth Ave New York NY 10010

SMALLEY, DAVID ALLAN
SCULPTOR, EDUCATOR
b New London, Conn, Dec 17, 40. *Study:* RI Sch Design, 58-60; Univ Conn, with Antony Padovano, BFA, 63; Ind Univ, MFA, 65. *Work:* Lyman Allyn Mus & Conn Col, New London; State of Conn Superior Ct. *Comn:* Warlock III (cor-ten steel), Conn Commission Arts, New London, 73; State of Conn Ocean Clouds 35 ft suspended kinetic, Conn Comn on the Arts; Ad-Astra, stainless steel (10 ft), Conn Col. *Exhib:* Conn Painting, Drawing & Sculpture, Univ Bridgeport, New Britain Mus & Conn Col, 79; Penwith Gallery, Cornwall, Eng, 79; Krausaar Galleries, New York, 80-81; one-man show, Lyman Allyn Mus, New London, Conn, 81 & Kraushaar Galleries, New York, 84, 87 & 90; Vangarde Gallery, New London, Conn, 87 & 90. *Pos:* Bd dirs, Art Resources Conn, 75-80; pres, Vangarde Co-op Gallery, 86; co-dir, Ctr Arts Technol, Conn Col. *Teaching:* Prof sculpture, Conn Col, 65- *Awards:* Ingram Merrill Found Grant, 69; Research Grant, Dana Found, 80. *Bibliog:* Barbara Zabel (auth), Profile, Art Voices, 7-8/81 & review, Arts Mag, 4/84, review Sculpture Mag, 9/87. *Mem:* Mystic Art Asn; Vangarde Co-op Gallery. *Media:* Stainless Steel, Brass. *Dealer:* Kraushaar Galleries 724 5th Ave New York NY. *Mailing Add:* 190 Old Norwich Rd Quaker Hill CT 06375

SMALLEY, STEPHEN FRANCIS
EDUCATOR, PAINTER
b Rockville, Conn, Apr 14, 41. *Study:* Mass Col Art, BS, 63; State Col, Boston, MEd, 65; Pa State Univ, DEd, 70. *Work:* Bridgewater State Col, Mass; Mansfield State Col, Pa; RI Col. *Exhib:* Boston 78, Brockton Art Mus, Mass, 78; one-man shows, Norman, Boston Gallery, Mass, 78, Crewe & Alsager, Cheshire, Eng, 89, Gallery 800, Monmouth Coll, NJ, 91; The New Figure Again, Currier Gallery, Manchester, NH, 84; Bridgewater State Col Fac Exhib, Shanxi Teachers Univ, Linfen, China. *Teaching:* Fac art, Rindge Technical High Sch, Cambridge, Mass, 63-65; teaching asst design & printmaking, Pa State Univ, 65-67; assoc prof & chmn, Dept Art Educ, Tyler Sch Art, 67-72; chmn dept art, Bridgewater State Col, Mass, 72-84, prof, 72- *Awards:* Summer Res Award, Tyler Sch Art, 71; Prof Develop Award, 81 & 88 & Distinguished Serv Award, 86, Bridgewater State Col, Mass; Outstanding Art Teacher Award, Mass Art Educ Asn, 85. *Mem:* Nat Art Educ Asn; Mass Art Educ Asn (coun mem, 79-81 & 85-87); Mass Dirs Art Educ; Int Soc Educ through Art; US Soc Educ through Art. *Media:* Acrylics, Pen & Ink. *Mailing Add:* Bridgewater State Col Bridgewater MA 02324

SMART, MARY-LEIGH
CONSULTANT, PATRON
b Springfield, Ill, Feb 27, 17. *Study:* Oxford Univ, dipl Extra Mural Delegacy, 35; Wellesley Col, BA, 37; Columbia Univ, MA, 39; also with Bernard Karfiol, 38-39. *Collections Arranged:* Art: Ogunquit, A National Exhibition of Artists Who Have Worked in Ogunquit (auth, catalog), 67, Peggy Bacon, A Celebration (auth, catalog), 79 & three exhibitions each season, 80-86, Barn Gallery, Ogunquit, Maine. *Pos:* Founding secy & prog dir, Barn Gallery Assocs, Ogunquit, Maine, 58-78, cur, Hamilton Easter Field Art Found Collection, 66-79, pres, 69-70 & 82-87, hon dir, 71-78, cur exhibs, 79-86; founding mem bd adv, Univ Art Galleries, Univ NH, 73-89, vpres, 75-81, pres, 81-89; mem coun adv, Farnsworth Libr & Art Mus; mem mus panel, Maine Arts Comn, 83-86; mem collections comt, Payson Gallery, Westbrook Col, Portland, Maine, 87-90; founder, Surf Point Found, a non-profit art found, York, Maine, 88. *Awards:* Deborah Morton Award, Westbrook Col, Portland, Me, 88. *Bibliog:* Edgar Allen Beem (auth), An artists best friend, Maine Times, 6/24/88; Rose Safran (auth), Meet Mary-Leigh Smart--art patron, The York Weekly, 6/15/88; Louise Balch Hatfield (auth), Art Foundation, Wellesley, summer 92; and others. *Mem:* Fel Portland Mus Art, Maine; Nat Comt Friends Art, Wellesley Col. *Interests:* Contemporary art. *Collection:* Twentieth century New England painting and sculpture; American, European and Asian contemporary graphics; photography. *Publ:* Auth, Hamilton Easter Field Art Foundation Collection (catalog), 66; A Century of Color, Ogunquit Maine's Art Colony, 1886-1986, 87. *Mailing Add:* 30 Surf Point Rd York ME 03909

SMEDLEY, GEOFFREY
EDUCATOR, SCULPTOR
b London, Eng, Feb 24, 27. *Study:* Camberwell Sch Art, London; Slade Sch Fine Arts, London, 54. *Work:* Victoria & Albert Mus & Arts Coun Gt Brit, London. *Comn:* Sculpture Garden, Commune Pirano, Istria, Yugoslavia, 72; Southern Arts Asn Eng, Portsmouth, 74; set design, Freddy Wood Theatre; Rowingbridge, a 50 foot high kinetic sculpture, Expo 86. *Exhib:* Whitechapel Art Gallery, 72; Arts Coun, traveling, 73 & 76; Agnes Etherington Art Ctr, Queen's Univ, Kingston, Ont, 78; Nature as Material, traveling, Eng, 80-81; solo exhib, Vancouver Art Gallery, BC, 82; Vancouver Art & Artists, Vancouver Art Gallery (with catalog), 83; Canada Collects, Art Bank & traveling USA; Making History, Vancouver Art Gallery, 86. *Teaching:* Prof fine arts, Univ BC, 78- *Awards:* Proj Art Award, Arts Coun Great Brit, 72; Sculpture award, West Gate Plaza Expo 86; Materials Grant, 85 & Sr Grant, 87, Can Coun. *Bibliog:* Scott Watson (auth), article, Vanguard, 2/82; J J McColl, review, Can Broadcasting Co, 1/27/82; John Bentley Mays (auth), several articles, The Globe & Mail, Vancouver, 83 & 84; Max Hymans (auth), articles, The Province, 84 & 85; Keith Alldritt (auth) The ambassadors, Parachute, spring 84. *Publ:* Auth, My sculptural array at Forma Viva, Leonardo, vol 8, Pergamon, 75; contribr, The Arts Council Collection, 1942-78, Arts Coun Gt Brit, London, 78; Visions, Douglas & McIntyre, Vancouver, 83; Open Air Sculpture in Britain, Zwemmer/The Tate Gallery, London, 84; The Arts Council Collection, 1979-83, Arts Coun Gt Brit, London, 84. *Mailing Add:* 113 RR3 Gambier Island Gibson BC V0N 1V0 Canada

SMIGOCKI, STEPHEN VINCENT
PAINTER, PRINTMAKER
b Washington, DC, Nov 20, 42. *Study:* Univ Md, BA(fine arts), 64, MA(drawing), 68; Univ SFla, Tampa; Fla State Univ, painting with Karl Zerbe, PhD(art educ). *Work:* Ringling Mus, Sarasota, Fla; Huntington Gallery, WVa; WVa Sci & Cult Complex, Sunrise Gallery, Charleston. *Exhib:* Dallas Summer Arts Festival Nat Competition, Tex, 71; Biennial I Six-State Painting Competition, Va Commonwealth Univ, 73; Drawings '74 Nat Exhib, Wheaton Col, Norton, Mass; Thirteen State Regional Exhib, Appalachian Corridors, Charleston, WVa, 75; All WVa Exhib, Charleston, 79, 81, 83, 85 & 89; Huntington Galleries, 79, 83 & 88. *Pos:* Graphic artist, Univ Md Ctr Adult Educ, 64-66. *Teaching:* Prof art, Fairmont State Col, WVa, 72- *Awards:* Purchase Awards, Huntington Galleries Exhib 280, WVa, 72 & Appalachian Corridors, 75; merit award, All WVa Exhib, Charleston, 79. *Bibliog:* Art Pedagogy of Paul Klee and Wassily Kandinsky (dissertation). *Mem:* Los Angeles Printmaking Soc. *Media:* Etching; woodcut. *Publ:* Contribr, Echo Without Sound, Northwoods Press, 80; illus, Perspectives Mag Fairmont State Col, Fall, 91. *Dealer:* Bill Tomlinson Garo Gallery Morgantown WV. *Mailing Add:* Dept Art Fairmont State Col Locust Ave Fairmont WV 26554

SMITH, ALBERT E
PAINTER
b San Francisco, Calif, 1929. *Study:* Univ Calif, Berkeley; self taught. *Work:* Achenbach Found, Mus of Legion of Honor, San Francisco; Crocker Mus, Sacramento, Calif; Univ Calif, Davis. *Exhib:* Roger Ramsay Gallery, Chicago, 89; 871 Fine Arts, San Francisco, 91-93; DeSaisset Mus, Santa Clara Univ; Calif State Univ, Hayward; Calif State, Modesto; and others. *Dealer:* Anthony Ralph Gallery New York NY; Anne Berthoud Gallery London England. *Mailing Add:* 1616 El Camino Real Menlo Park CA 94025

SMITH, ALEXIS (PATRICIA ANNE)
COLLAGE ARTIST, CONCEPTUAL ARTIST
b Los Angeles, Calif, Aug 24, 49. *Study:* Univ Calif, Irvine, 66-70, BA(art), 70; study with Robert Irwin & Ed Moses. *Work:* Whitney Mus Am Art; Mus Contemp Art, Los Angeles; Walker Art Ctr, Minneapolis. *Comn:* The Grand, Keeler Grand Foyer, DeVos Hall, Grand Rapids, Mich, 83; Monuments, MacArthur Park Pub Art Prog, Los Angeles, 86; Snake Path, Stuart Collection, Univ Calif, San Diego, La Jolla; South & West Lobby Terrazzo floors, Los Angeles Conv Ctr Expansion. *Exhib:* Lowe, Munger, Smith, Wilson, Los Angeles Co Mus Art, 72; Four Los Angeles Artists, Corcoran Gallery Am Art, Washington, DC, 75; Whitney Biennial, Whitney Mus Am Art, New York, 75, 79 & 81; solo exhibs, Whitney Mus Am Art, 75, Rosamund Felsen Gallery, 78, 80 & 82, De Appel, Amsterdam, 79, Walker Art Ctr, 86 & Inst Contemp Art, Boston, 86; Margo Leavin Gallery 82, 85, 88 & 90; Aspen Art Mus, 87; Brooklyn Mus, 87-88; Am Narrative/Story Art, Contemp Art Mus, Houston, Tex, 77; Narration, Inst Contemp Art, Boston, 78; Holly Solomon Gallery, 77, 78, 79, 81 & 83; Museum as Site, Los Angeles Co Mus Art, 81; New Directions, Hirshhorn Mus & Sculpture Garden, 83; Verbally Charged Images, Independent Curators, 84-86; Mus Mod Art, New York, 84; Individuals, Mus Contemp Art, Los Angeles, 86-88; Josh Baer Gallery, 90; Retrospective exhib, Whitney Mus Am Art, Mus Cont Art, Los Angeles, 91-92. *Teaching:* Instr, Univ Calif, Los Angeles, 79-88, Skowhegan, 90. *Awards:* New Talent Award, Contemp Arts Coun, Los Angeles Co Mus Art, 74; Nat Endowment Arts Fel Grant, 76-77, 87-88. *Bibliog:* Nancy Marmer (auth), Alexis Smith: The narrative act, Artforum, 12/76; Leo Rubinfien, Through western eyes, Art in Am, 9-10/78; Hunter Drohojowska (auth), Alexis Smith: The Public Works, Artspace, Summer 91; Richard Armstrong (auth), Alexis Smith (catalog Bk), publ Rizzoli, 91. *Media:* Multimedia, Public Art. *Publ:* Contribr centerfold, Avalanche, fall 75; auth, Alone, 77; contribr, Italics, Paris Rev, spring 79; Shanghai Express, Los Angeles Herald-Examiner, 11/81. *Dealer:* Margo Leavin Gallery 812 N Robertson Blvd Los Angeles CA 90069; Josh Baer Gallery 476 Broome St New York NY 10013. *Mailing Add:* 1907 Lincoln Blvd Venice CA 90291

SMITH, ANN Y
MUSEUM DIRECTOR, CURATOR
b Alma, Mich, Oct 7, 50. *Study:* Univ Mich, BA, 72; State Univ NY, MA, 73; Univ Conn Law Sch, JD, 91. *Collections Arranged:* Fiddlebacks and Crooked-backs, 82; Connecticut Masters, 86; Brass Valley, 86. *Pos:* Asst cur, Hist Soc York Co, Pa, 73-74; dir, Lyme Hist Soc, Conn, 74-76; Mattatuck Mus, Waterbury, Conn, 76- *Teaching:* Adj fac, Univ Conn, Archit Hist. *Mem:* Conn Comn Arts: Art Selection Panel; New Eng Mus Asn; Am Asn Mus; Conn Mus Asn (steering comt, 89-). *Publ:* Ed, Minds and Machines: Waterbury at Work, Mattatuck Hist Soc, 80. *Mailing Add:* Mattatuck Mus 144 W Main St Waterbury CT 06702

SMITH, ANNE L
SCULPTOR
b Orange, NJ, 1958. *Study:* Boston Univ, BFA, 80; Alfred Univ, State Col Ceramics, MFA, 90. *Work:* Mus Fine Arts, Boston, Mass; Purdue Univ Art Gallery, Lafayette, Ind; General Electric Co, Fairfield, Conn; Wash Sch Dist, Auburn. *Exhib:* Combinations, Danforth Mus, Framingham, Mass, 80; Art for Your Collection, RI Sch Design Mus, Providence, 83; American Ceramics Now, 87 & Young Americans, 88, Am Craft Mus; MFA Selections, Soc Arts & Crafts, Boston, 88; Surface & Form, Nat Mus Ceramic Art, Baltimore, 89; solo exhibs, Garth Clark Gallery, New York, 86, McIntosh Drysdale Gallery, Washington, DC, 87, Thomas Segal Gallery, Boston, Mass, 88 & 91 & Alfred Univ, NY, 90. *Pos:* Vis Artist, Sch Mus Fine Arts, Boston, 85-86 & Philadelphia Col Art, 86-87; Instr ceramic, State Univ NY Col, New Paltz, 87-88 & Bennington Col, Vt, 88; workshop instr, Art New England Summer Prog, Bennington Col, Vt, 88 & Castle Hill Ctr Arts, Truro, Mass, 88. *Awards:* Artist's Found Fel, Mass Coun Arts & Humanities, 82 & 88; Visual Arts Fel, Nat Endowment Arts, 88; Artist's Found Fel, Finalist in Ceramics, 88. *Bibliog:* Christine Temin (auth), Smith makes a breakthrough, Boston Globe, 9/27/85; Angelea Fina (auth), Articles, Ceramics Monthly, 9/87. *Media:* Ceramics. *Dealer:* Thomas Segal Gallery 207 South St Boston MA 02111. *Mailing Add:* 51 Warren St Somerville MA 02143

SMITH, ARTHUR HALL
PAINTER, EDUCATOR
b Norfolk, Va, Mar 23, 29. *Study:* Ill Wesleyan Univ, BFA, 51; Ecole Beaux-Arts, Paris, Fulbright fel, 51; Atelier 17, Paris, with S W Hayter, 52; grad study, Univ Wash, 55; also with Mark Tobey, Seattle, Wash, 55-57. *Work:* Chrysler Mus, Norfolk; Corcoran Gallery Art, Washington, DC; Phillips Collection, Washington, DC; Baltimore Mus Art, Md; Seattle Art Mus. *Comn:* Centennial murals, Mem Ctr, Ill Wesleyan Univ, Bloomington, 50; Mammals in World Art, Mammal Hall, US Mus Natural Hist, Smithsonian Inst, Washington, DC, 58; Truckee Storage Triptych, Bur Water Reclamation, US Dept Interior, Washington, DC, 72. *Exhib:* Va Artists Ann, Va Mus Fine Arts, Richmond, 51; The American Artist and Water Reclamation, Nat Gallery Art, Washington, DC, 72; 25 Yr Retrospective, Exhib Hall, Cathedral

St John the Divine, New York, NY & Dimock Gallery, Washington, DC, 76; Grafik aus den USA, Bawag Found, Vienna, Austria, 76; one-man shows, Washington Artists Series, Corcoran Gallery Art, 61 & Editions of One, Fine Arts Pavilion, Montgomery Jr Col, Takoma Park, Md, 77; and others. *Teaching:* Asst prof painting, George Washington Univ, 74-81, assoc prof, 81-85, prof, 86- *Awards:* Merwin Medal for Painting, Bloomington Art Asn, 48; Painting Prize, 15th Area Exhib, Corcoran Gallery Art, 62; Hereward Lester Cooke Found Grant, 83-84. *Bibliog:* Benjamin Forgey (auth), article, Art News, 4/76; Lilien Robinson (auth), Paris and other rooftops, (catalog essay), Dimock Gallery, 85; M A Turner (auth), Arthur Hall Smith, Art Gallery Int, Vol VIII, ed 5, July-Aug, 87. *Media:* Mixed. *Publ:* Auth introductory essay, Mark Tobey Exhib, St Alban's Sch, Washington, DC, 59; auth intro, Drawings of Kevin MacDonald Exhib, Phillips Collection, Washington, DC, 77; auth catalog essay, James McLaughlin, A Retrospective: In Memoriam, Phillips Collection, Washington, DC, 82; auth, catalog essay, Michel Green, An Appreciation, Dimock Gallery, 88. *Dealer:* Franz Bader Gallery 2124 Pennsylvania Ave NW Washington DC 20037. *Mailing Add:* Academic Ctr A-101A George Washington Univ Washington DC 20052

SMITH, B J
MUSEUM DIRECTOR, INSTRUCTOR
b Beaver, Okla, Aug 22, 31. *Study:* Okla State Univ, Stillwater, BFA, 55; Univ Okla, Norman, MFA, 59. *Work:* Joslyn Art Mus, Omaha, Nebr; Mus Art, Univ Okla, Norman; State Collection of Okla Artists & Craftsmen, Oklahoma City; Okla Art Ctr, Oklahoma City. *Exhib:* Ann Eight State Exhib, 63, 64, 68, 70 & 74, 13 Artists You Should Collect, 65, Okla Art Ctr, Oklahoma City; solo exhib, WNebr Arts Ctr, Scottsbluff, 83, Tex Wesleyan Col, Fort Worth, Tex, 86, W Nebr Arts Ctr, Scottsbluff, 87 & Western Okla Images, Pioneer Mus, Woodward, 87; Pioneer Mus & Arts Ctr, Woodward, Okla, 83; Small Wonders, Kirkpatrick Ctr, Oklahoma City, 90; Okla Small Works 2, E Cent, Ada, 92; Tom Preston Mem Exhib, Alexandra, La, 92; 25th Ann, W Nebr Arts Ctr, Scottsbluff, 92; and others. *Pos:* Asst to dir, Okla Art Ctr, Oklahoma City, 61-65; dir, Gardiner Art Gallery, Okla State Univ, 65- *Teaching:* Assoc prof color & design, Okla State Univ, 65-81, assoc prof, 81- *Awards:* Purchase Awards, Ninth Midwest Biennial, Joslyn Art Mus, Omaha, 66, Okla Biennial, Okla Art Ctr, Oklahoma City, 67 & Okla Artists Ann, Philbrook Art Ctr, Tulsa, 68. *Media:* Acrylic, Masonite. *Mailing Add:* 2132 W Sunset Dr Stillwater OK 74074

SMITH, BARBARA LEE
COLLAGE ARTIST
b Camden, NJ, Apr 1, 38. *Study:* Douglas Col, BS, 59; Governors State Univ; George Williams Col; Col Dupage; Northern Ill Univ, MFA, 78. *Work:* Mohawk Col, Hamilton, Ont, Can; Springfield Art Asn, Ill; Moraine Valley Col, Palos Hills, Ill. *Comn:* Mural, Off Controller Currency, Chicago, 87; mural, Am Nat Bank, Chicago, 87; three murals, Am Med Asn, Chicago, 88; two murals, Exec House, Chicago, 88; Madeira Threads, Thirsk, Eng, 91. *Exhib:* Needle Expressions, travelling exhib, 81, 83, 85, 88, 90 & 92; Gayle Willson Gallery, Southampton, NY, 86; Embroidery Invitational, Dunedin Art Ctr, New Zealand, 87; Moving, Textile Arts Ctr, Chicago, 87; Expressions Gallery, Seattle, 93; and others. *Pos:* Asst ed, Coun Am Embroiderers, 72-74. *Teaching:* Tutor, Arrowmont Sch Crafts, Gatlinburg, Tenn, 77 & 83; tutor design & embroidery, Brescia Col, London, Ont, 79 & 85; vis lectr & tutor design & creativity (touring), Asn New Zealand Embroiderers, 87 & 90; vis lectr & tutor, Australia, Embroiderers' Guilds; vis lect & tutor, London Embroiderers' Guild, Eng. *Awards:* Purchase Awards, Stitchery '79, Pittsburgh Nat Bank & Needle Expressions, pvt donor, 88; First Prize, Oakbrook Invitational, Oakbrook Ctr, 83; Purchase Award, Needle Expressions, 88 & 92. *Mem:* Am Crafts Coun (Ill rep, 74-80); Surface Design Asn; Coun Am Embroiderers; Textile Arts Ctr, Chicago (bd dirs, 86-87). *Publ:* Auth, Creativity, Threads, New Zealand, 87 & Flying Needle, 87; Celebrating the Stitch: Contemporary Embroidery of North America, Taunton Press, 91. *Mailing Add:* 7349 Maidson PO Box 365 Forest Park IL 60130-0365

SMITH, BARBARA TURNER
INSTRUCTOR, VIDEO & PERFORMANCE ARTIST
b Pasadena, Calif, July 6, 31. *Study:* Pomona Col, BA, 53; Chouinard Art Inst, with Emerson Woelfer, 65; workshops with Alex Hay, 68 & Steve Paxton, 69; Univ Calif, Irvine, with Bob Irwin & Larry Bell, MFA, 71. *Work:* Newport Harbor Art Mus, Newport Beach, Calif. *Comn:* Capp Street Proj, 84; SPARC, 89. *Exhib:* People Who Should Be Seen, Los Angeles Co Art Mus, Los Angeles, 65; All Night Sculptures, Mus Conceptual Art, San Francisco, 73; Performance Conf, Womanspace & Woman's Bldg, 73, 75 & 77; Retrospective (auth, catalog), Univ Calif, San Diego, 74; Irvine Milieu, La Jolla Mus Contemp Art, Calif, 75; Tortue Gallery, Los Angeles, Calif, 81. *Pos:* Co-founder, F-Space Gallery, Santa Ana, Calif, 70-72; founding mem, Grandview I & II Gallery, Los Angeles, 73-75; organizer, New Dimensions in Sci series, Los Angeles Inst Contemp Art, 75. *Teaching:* Fac fel art, Univ Redlands, Calif, 75-; vis performance artist, Univ Calif, San Diego, 77; vis artist, San Francisco Art Inst, 78; lectr, Univ Calif, Los Angeles, 79-82. *Awards:* Nat Endowment Arts Grants, 74 & 79. *Bibliog:* G S Lischka,(ed), die Lowin, Switz, 12/75; Nancy Buchanan (auth), Barbara Smith: Communication/communion, Portrait Rev, Vol V, 76; Emily Hicks (auth), Performing sex as ritual, Artweek, 9/81. *Media:* Body and Video. *Publ:* Auth, Rope, pvt publ, 71; auth, Burden case tried, dismissed, Artweek, 73; auth, Women in industry, Los Angeles Inst of Contemp Art J, 74; contribr, Buddha mind performance, In: Vision, Crown, 75; auth, Rachel Rosenthal performs Charm, Artweek, 2/77. *Mailing Add:* 801 Coeur d'Alene Venice CA 90291

SMITH, BERYL K
LIBRARIAN, CURATOR
b Milwaukee, Wis. *Study:* Douglass Col/Rutgers Univ, BA, 82, MLS, 83, MA, 86. *Collections Arranged:* Rep works 1974-1984, Women Artists Series, 84. *Pos:* Cur, Douglas Col, New Brunswick, 83-; asst art libr, Rutgers Univ, New Brunswick, 86- *Mem:* Art Libr Soc NAm; College Art Asn; Am Libr Asn. *Interests:* Contemp art of women, northern and southern renaissance painting, am crafts. *Publ:* Coauth, Faculty Status: A Realistic Survey, NJ Libr, Fall 83; auth, Mary H Dana Women Artists Series (catalog), Rutgers Univ, 86-90; ed, Art Documentation J, Art Libr Soc NAm. *Mailing Add:* 11 Whitehall Road East Brunswick NJ 08816

SMITH, CARY
PAINTER
b Puerto Rico, 1955; US citizen. *Study:* Sir John Cass Art Sch, London, Eng, 76; Syracuse Abroad, Florence, Italy, 76; Syracuse Univ Art Sch, NY, BFA, 77. *Work:* Whitney Mus Am Art, New York; Brooklyn Mus, NY; Osaka Art Mus, Japan; Wadsworth Atheneum, Hartford, Conn. *Exhib:* Solo exhibs, Koury Wingate Gallery, New York, 90, Linda Cathcart Gallery, Santa Monica, 91, Stephen Wirtz Gallery, San Francisco, Calif, 91, Rubin Spangle Gallery, New York, 92; Grids, Vrej Baghoomian Gallery, 90, Small Works, Koury Wintgate Gallery, 90, Selections from the Collection; Art of the 80's, Whitney Mus Am Art, 91, Rubin Spangle Gallery, New York, 92; Outside America; Going into the 90's, Fay Gold Gallery, Atlanta, Ga, 91. *Awards:* Conn Comn Arts, Grant, 83 & 86, Art in Pub Spaces Award, 85. *Bibliog:* Dena Shottenkirk (auth), Artforum, 9/90; Saundra Goldman (auth), Tema Celeste, Nov/Dec, 90; Openings, Art & Antiques, 3/92. *Mailing Add:* PO Box 924 Farmington CT 06034

SMITH, CLYDE
PAINTER
b Pa, June 20, 32. *Study:* Dartmouth Col, BA, 54; Art Ctr Col Design, BFA, 58. *Work:* Mus City of New York; Chrysler Mus, Norfolk; Harvard Col. *Teaching:* Instr painting, & drawing, Sch Visual Art, formerly. *Media:* Oil. *Publ:* Contribr, Painting Men's Portraits & Painting Women's Portraits, Watson-Guptill, 77. *Dealer:* Portraits Inc New York NY; Portraits Brokers Am Montgomery AL. *Mailing Add:* 189 Valley Rd Cos Cob CT 06807

SMITH, DAVID LOEFFLER
PAINTER, EDUCATOR
b New York, NY, May 1, 28. *Study:* Bard Col, BA; Cranbrook Acad Art, MFA; also with Hans Hofmann & Raphael Soyer. *Exhib:* Seligman Gallery, New York; one-man shows, First St Gallery, New York, 72-73, 76-77,79, 82 & 85; M13 Gallery, New York, 86, 87 & 90; Water Street Gallery, Mass, 88; Nemasket Gallery, Fairhaven, Mass, 90; The News as Muse, Baltimore, 91; and others. *Teaching:* Actg chmn dept art, Chatham Col; vis critic, New York Studio Sch, Md Art Inst, Queens Col, State Univ New York, Grad Sch Painting, Parson's Sch Design; prof painting, Southeastern Mass Univ, North Dartmouth, Mass, formerly. *Awards:* Henry Posner Prize, Carnegie Inst, 61. *Media:* Oil. *Publ:* Auth, articles, Am Artist, 59-62, Antiques Mag, 11/67, Arts Mag, 3/68 & Art & Artists, 1/70 & 5/71. *Dealer:* M13 Gallery 72 Greene St New York NY 10012-4373. *Mailing Add:* 122 Hawthorn St New Bedford MA 02740

SMITH, DINAH MAXWELL
PAINTER, PHOTOGRAPHER
b New York, NY. *Study:* L'Academie Julian; RI Sch Design, BFA(painting), 63; Masters Prog, Santa Fe Inst Fine Arts, Wayne Thiebaud Workshop, 88. *Work:* Bridgeport Mus, Conn; Coast Grill Restaurant; Frozen Moments Inc; Chemical Bank; The Rolling Stones; Ferragamo, Inc; O'Neal Enterprises, Inc; and pvt coll. *Comn:* Art in the Garden (poster), Bridgehampton, NY, 92. *Exhib:* Solo exhibs, Nat Arts Club, 75, City Ctr & Kulicke Gallery, New York, 76, Sarah Rentschler Gallery, Bridgehampton, New York, 82, Townhouse Gallery, New York, 84, Read Gallery, Palm Beach, Fla, 86, Union Legue Club, New York, 88 & 92 & Gallery Wessel, Hamburg Ger, 91; Guild Hall Members Show, East Hampton, 82-92; East End Arts Coun Photog Show, Riverhead, NY, 85-90; Guild Hall Members Show, East Hampton, NY, 80-92; Members', EEAC, 85-92; Gallery Wessel, Hamburg, Ger, 90-92; two person show, Clayton-Liberatore Gallery, Bridgehampton, NY, 91; Elaine Benson Gallery, 92. *Teaching:* Instr, Watercolor, Parrish Art Mus, Southampton, NY, 79. *Awards:* Nat Arts Club Graphics Prize, 72 & Special Award, 74; Fourth Prize, Five Towns M & A Found, 85; Third Prize, Photog Show, 89, First Prize, Painting Show, 89, East End Arts Coun. *Bibliog:* New York Reviews, Artnews, 5/82; James R Genovese (auth), Light at the end of the island, 5/28/83 & Phyllis Braff (auth), From the studio, 9/22/83, Hamptons Newspaper Mag; Helen Harrison (auth), New York Times. *Mem:* Nat Arts Club; East End Arts Coun; Southampton Artists; Nat Arts Clubs; Jimmy Ernst Artist Alliance. *Media:* Oils; Black & White Photography. *Mailing Add:* 300 E 51st St, Suite 8B New York NY 10022

SMITH, DOLPH
PAINTER, EDUCATOR
b Memphis, Tenn, July 26, 33. *Study:* Memphis State Univ; Memphis Acad Arts, BFA, 60. *Work:* Ark State Univ, Jonesboro; Brooks Mem Art Gallery, Memphis, Tenn; Southwestern at Memphis; Tenn Arts Comn, State of Tenn, Nashville; NC Nat Bank, Charlotte. *Comn:* Paintings for various locations nationwide, Holiday Inns Am, 65-72; painting for Tenn Exec Mansion Christmas Card, comn by Gov & Mrs Winfield Dunn, 71; painting for Sen Albert Gore, Democratic Party, Shelby Co, Tenn, 71. *Exhib:* One-man shows, Brooks Mem Art Gallery, 65, Charles Bowers Mem Mus, Santa Ana, Calif, 67 & Cheekwood, Nashville, Tenn, 73; Brooks Mem Art Gallery, 69;

Vanderbilt Univ Fac Club, Nashville, Tenn, 70; Memphis Acad Arts, Tenn, 72 & 77; and others. *Pos:* Art dir, Ward Archer Assoc, Memphis, 64-67. *Teaching:* Asst prof painting & drawing, Memphis Acad Arts, 64-81, prof, 81-; vis instr painting, Southwestern Col, 66-68. *Awards:* First Prize for Watercolor, Mid-South Exhib, 64 & Grand Award 76, Brooks Mem Art Gallery; Purchase Prize, Tenn Bicentennial Art Competition, 76. *Bibliog:* Jo Potter (auth), The Real World of Dolph Smith, WKNO TV, 65; William Thomas (auth), Dolph Smith's Mid-South, Mid-South Mag, 2/9/69. *Media:* Watercolor. *Publ:* Iliusr, Delta Rev Mag, 10/67, 11-12/69 & fall 70; illusr, Mid-South Mag, 12/71. *Dealer:* Memphis Academy Arts Overton Park Memphis TN 38104. *Mailing Add:* c/o Albers Fine Art Gallery 1102 Brookfield Rd Memphis TN 38119

SMITH, DONALD C
PAINTER, PRINTMAKER
b Dexter, Mo, July 10, 35. *Study:* Univ Mo, BA & MA; Santa Reparata Graphic Art Ctr, Florence, Italy; also painting with Fred Conway & printmaking with Maricio Lasansky. *Work:* ABC Broadcasting Corp; Spiva Art Ctr, Joplin, Mo; Santa Reparata Stamperia d'Arte Grafica, Florence. *Exhib:* One-man shows, NW Mo State Univ, Maryville, 63, RI Col, 69 & 82, Wheelock Col, 71, Lowell State Univ, 83, Wheeler Gallery, Providence, RI, 92; Boston Printmakers Ann, 75 & 76; Davidson Printmaking, 76; RI Painters Ann, RI Sch Design Mus, 82; Invitational Group, Duxbury Art Complex, Duxbury, Mass, 88. *Pos:* Dir, Spiva Art Ctr, Joplin, Mo, 60-64. *Teaching:* Prof painting, drawing & printmaking, RI Col, 64- *Awards:* Univ Fel, Univ Mo, 58; Faculty Res Grant, RI Col, 83-84 & 86-87; Emerson Award, Wheeler Ann, Providence, RI, 87. *Media:* Etching. *Publ:* Auth, Edwin Dickinson, draftsman/painter, Arts New England, 7-8/82. *Mailing Add:* 132 Pine Hill Ave Johnston RI 02919

SMITH, ELIZABETH
GRAPHIC ARTIST
b New Britian, Conn, Aug 13, 43. *Study:* Univ Vermont, Cent Conn State Univ, BS, 69; Univ Hartford, Cent Conn State Univ, MS, 74. *Exhib:* Knickerbocker Artists New York, Salmagundi Club, 86-87, 89-91; Audubon Artists, Nat Arts Club, New York, 87-88, 90-92; Allied Artists Am, Nat Arts Club, New York, 88-89 & 91; Nat Acad Design, New York, 88; Pastel Soc Am, Nat Arts Club, New York, 90-92. *Pos:* Bd dirs, New Eng Chap Artists Equity 80-81, Gallery on the Green Canton 81-86; Coun mem 91-92, pres, 92-, Conn Acad Fine Arts. *Awards:* Catharine Lorillard Wolfe Medal of Honor, 86, IBM Award, 87, Ida Becker Mem Award, 89, Catharine Lorillard Wolfe Art Club; Silver Medal of Honor, Knickerbocker Artists, New York, 86 & 91; Nydia Preede Award, 87, C L Mason & A V Mason Mem Award, 89, Nat Asn Women Artists; Coun Am Artists Soc Award, Am Artists Prof League, 88; Artist's Mag Painting Competition Finalist, 91 & 92. *Bibliog:* Article, Farmington Valley Herald, 7/81; Bernard Hanson (auth), article, Hartford Courant 6/86; Karin Leite (auth), Interview, Avon News, 5/89. *Mem:* Audubon Artists; Knickerbocker Artists, New York; Catharine Lorillard Wolfe Art Club; Pastel Soc Am; Am Artists Prof League. *Media:* Pastel, Graphite. *Mailing Add:* Ten Ardsley Way Avon CT 06001

SMITH, ELLIOT STEVEN
DEALER, HISTORIAN
b St Louis, Mo, Sept 22, 42. *Study:* Washington Univ, St Louis, AB, 66; Univ Mo, MEd, 68. *Pos:* Founder & vpres, 87-88, St Louis Gallery Contemp Art; dir, Elliot Smith Gallery, St Louis, Mo & New York, NY, currently. *Teaching:* Assoc prof, English & speech, Washington Univ, St Louis, 68-73; assoc prof Am studies, St Louis Univ, 81-84. *Mem:* St Louis Gallery Asn (treas, 85-86 & vpres, 87); Friends Pub Art (founder & pres, 86-). *Res:* Early 20th century American architecture. *Specialty:* Paintings and sculpture of bold imagery and strong intellectual content. *Publ:* Auth, Louis Sullivan, The Last Romantic, St Louis Univ Press, 84. *Mailing Add:* Elliot Smith Contemporary Art 4727 McPherson Ave St Louis MO 63108

SMITH, ERNEST JOHN
ARCHITECT, DESIGNER
b Winnipeg, Man, Dec 17, 19. *Study:* Univ Man, BArch(hons), 44; Mass Inst Technol, MArch(fel), 47; Banff Sch Advan Mgt, 68. *Work:* Nat Gallery Ottawa Royal Can Acad Collection; Sch Archit, Univ Man. *Comn:* Centennial Centre, Centennial Bd, Winnipeg, Man, 65; Lombard Place Complex, Winnipeg, 68; Winnipeg Sq Develop, Trizec Corp, Winnipeg, 74; Great West Life Centre, Winnipeg, 78; Simons, Texada Development, Vancouver, BC, 81; and others. *Exhib:* Residence, East Kildonan, Man, 61; Sch Archit, Univ Man, 61; Man Asn Archit, Winnipeg & Montreal, 68; Kiwanis Ctr Deaf, Winnipeg, 75. *Teaching:* Sr design critic, Univ Man, formerly. *Awards:* Can Gold Medal, Royal Archit Inst Can, 44. *Bibliog:* George Derksen (auth), Smith Carter Parkin prepares for the future, Man Bus J, 6/70; Deanna Waters (auth), Interview with the professionals, Opportunity, 74; and others. *Mem:* Man Asn Archit (pres, 53-54, 58-61, mem exec comt, 49-54); Nat Joint Comt Co Construction Materials (chmn, 63-65); Fel Royal Archit Inst Can (dean, 72-75, chancellor, 79-82); academician Royal Can Acad Arts (mem coun, 74); Ont Asn Archit; and others. *Publ:* Contribr, Can Archit. *Mailing Add:* Lot 19 Berchwood Dr Hillside Beach MB R0E 2A0 Canada

SMITH, FRANCES KATHLEEN
CURATOR, HISTORIAN
b Bolton, Eng, Nov 19, 13; Can citizen. *Study:* London Univ, Eng; Queen's Univ, Kingston, Ont, BA, 56; Oxford Univ, Eng, with Pope Hennessey, Italian sculpture, 56-57. *Collections Arranged:* Andre Bieler: 50 Years (auth, catalog), Retrospective, traveled, Can, 70-71; Heritage Kingston (contribr, catalog), 73; Painting Now 1976/77 (auth, catalog); Henry Moore, Sculpture, Prints, Drawings, 78; Daniel Fowler of Amherst Island, (auth, catalog), traveled, Can, 79; The Brave New World of Fritz Brandtner Traveling Show (coauth, catalog), 81-82; Kathleen Moir Morris (auth, catalog), 83; John Herbert Caddy (auth, catalog), 85; Andre Bielerin Rural Quebec (auth, catalog), 88-89. *Pos:* Cur, Agnes Etherington Art Ctr, Kingston, Ont, Can, 57-79, cur emer, 79- *Awards:* Merit Award, Ont Asn Art Galleries, 80; Merit Award, Can Mus Asn, 81; Distinguished Serv Award, Queen's Univ, 87; Celebration 88, Cert Merit, Olympic Comt, 88. *Mem:* Can Mus Asn (nominating comt, 78); Ont Asn Art Galleries (secy, 68-69). *Res:* Canadian artists: Daniel Fowler, Andre Bieler, Fritz Brandtner, John Herbert Caddy and others. *Publ:* Coauth, A Permanent Collection of the Agnes Etherington Art Centre, 68; auth, George Harlow White 1817-1887, 75 & Daniel Fowler of Amherst Island, 79, Art Ctr, Queens Univ, Kingston, Ont; Andre Bieler: An Artist's Life and Times, Merritt Publ Co, Toronto, 80. *Mailing Add:* RR#1 Bateau Channel Kingston ON K7L 4V1 Canada

SMITH, FRANK ANTHONY
PAINTER
b Salt Lake City, Utah, Aug 4, 39. *Study:* Univ Utah, BFA, 62, MFA, 64. *Work:* Univ Utah Mus Fine Art; Utah State Univ; Salt Lake Art Ctr; Nat Gallery, Washington, DC. *Comn:* design (dance pieces), Repertory Dance Theatre, 66, 71 & 73; stimuli sensory environ for children, Salt Lake Art Ctr, 70; mural, Univ Utah Biol Bldg, 72. *Exhib:* Look Again, Illusionist Painting, Taft Mus, Cincinnati, 76; Reality of Illustion, Univ Southern Calif, 79; Four Corners Biennial, Phoenix, Ariz, 81; Illusions, Faire Int D'art Contemp, Grand Palais, Paris, 82; solo exhib, Suellen Haber Gallery, New York, 82; and others. *Pos:* Illusr, Star Trek: The Movie, 77. *Teaching:* Prof painting & drawing, Univ Utah, 68- *Awards:* San Francisco Art Dirs Gold Medal, 64; Purchase Award, 3rd Intermountain Biennial, 68. *Media:* Acrylic. *Dealer:* Osuna Gallery Washington DC; Phillips Gallery Salt Lake City UT. *Mailing Add:* c/o Osuna Gallery 1919 Q St NW Washington DC 20009

SMITH, GARY
SCULPTOR, GALLERY DIRECTOR
b Portland, Ore, Nov 25, 49. *Study:* Lewis & Clark Col, Portland, Ore, BA, 71; Univ Calif, Santa Barbara, MFA, 75. *Work:* Art Mus Santa Cruz County, Calif; St Mary's Col, Moraga, Calif; Calif Polytechnic Inst, San Luis Obispo. *Exhib:* Large Scale Sculpture, Univ Calif, Davis, 79; Recent Sculpture, Quay Gallery, San Francisco, 80; Departure Gallery, New York, 83-86; Summer Int, Keramik Studio, Vienna, Austria, 84; Recent Sculpture, Cuesta Col, San Luis Obispo, Calif, 85. *Collections Arranged:* Hartnell Col Farm Security Administration Photograph Collection (auth, catalog), 82; Leslie Fenton Netsuke Collection (auth, catalog), 85; Virginia Baker Huichol Artifact Collection (auth, catalog), 86; Daniel Rhodes: The California Years (auth, catalog), 86. *Teaching:* Instr ceramics-art, Hartnell Col, Salinas, 76-, dir gallery, 76- *Mem:* Col Art Asn. *Media:* Clay. *Mailing Add:* 19518 Creekside Ct Salinas CA 93908

SMITH, GARY DOUGLAS
DRAFTSMAN, PAINTER
b San Francisco, Calif, July 29, 48. *Study:* Calif Col Arts & Crafts, BFA(scholoarship), 71; extensive study in Mexico; Atelier 17, Paris; etching with S W Hayter, also engraving with George Ball, also Mezzotint with Yozo Hamaguchi. *Work:* Palm Springs Mus Art, Calif; Achenbach Found Graphic Arts, San Franicisco; De Saisset Mus, Santa Clara, Calif; Calif Acad Sciences, San Francisco; Calif Col Arts & Crafts, Oakland. *Exhib:* San Francisco Mus Mod Art, 70 & 77; Anchorage Hist & Fine Arts Mus, Alaska, 77; El Paso Mus Art, Tex, 77; World Print Competition & Traveling Show, 79; Krannert Art Mus, Ill, 79; Toledo Mus Art, Ohio, 79; Achenbach Found Graphic Arts, San Francisco, 83; solo exhibs, Historic Olema Inn, Calif, 83, Vorpal Galleries, Soho, NY, 85, Laguna Beach, Calif, 85 & San Francisco, 86, Inverness Studio, Calif, 87-90, Robert Mondavi Winery, Oakmille, Calif, 90; Inverness Ridge Assoc, Calif, 87; San Francisco Arts Comn, Calif, 88; Concordia-Argonaut Club, San Francisco, 88 & 89. *Teaching:* Lectr/demonstration, Fine Art Mus San Francisco, 85; lectr, Calif Col Arts & Crafts, Oakland, 87 & 88. *Awards:* Silver Prize, Calif Col Arts & Crafts, 69. *Bibliog:* Thomas Albright (auth), Landscapes in translation, San Francisco Chronicle, 7/7/71; John Marlowe (auth), interview, Currant Art Mag, 76; Carol A Hayes (auth), Profile of an artist, Bay View Mag, 9/81; Al Morch (auth), Too much of a good thing, San Francisco Chronicle, 11/9/81; Diana Freedman (auth), The catalyst in creation, Arts/Speak NY, 83. *Mem:* Graphic Arts Coun; World Print Coun. *Media:* Prismacolor Pencil, Silverpoint. *Publ:* Cover, Floating Island I, 76. *Dealer:* Claudia Chapline Gallery Stinson Beach CA; Waterworks Gallery Harbor Bay WA. *Mailing Add:* PO Box 244 Inverness CA 94937

SMITH, GORDON
PAINTER
b Brighton, Eng, June 18, 19. *Study:* Winnipeg Sch Art; Vancouver Sch Art; Calif Sch Fine Arts; Harvard Univ Summer Sch; Simon Fraser Univ, LLD, 74. *Work:* Collaboration with architect Arthur Erickson, Osaka Worlds Fair; Mus Mod Art, New York; Victoria & Albert Mus, London; Albright-Knox Art Mus, Buffalo, NY; Art Gallery Ont; and others. *Comn:* Osaka World's Fair (collab with Arthur Erickson, Architect); mural, New Canadian Chancery, Washington, DC. *Exhib:* one-man shows, Toronto, Montreal, New York & Vancouver; Can Biennial, 63; Seattle World's Fair, 63; New Design Gallery, Vancouver, BC, 64; Graphic Biennials, Yugoslavia, Ger, Norway & New York; exhib current paintings, Vancouver Art Mus, 87. *Teaching:* Emer prof art, Univ BC. *Awards:* Can Biennial, 56; Can Coun Sr Fel for Study Abroad, 60-61; Allied Arts Medal, Can Archit Inst, 78. *Mem:* BC Soc Art; Can Soc Painter-Etchers & Engravers; assoc Royal Can Acad Arts; Can Group Painters. *Media:* Acrylic on Canvas, Graphic Media. *Mailing Add:* 5030 The Byway West Vancouver BC V7W 1L7 Canada

SMITH, GRAHAM
HISTORIAN, EDUCATOR
b Banff, Scotland, May 30, 42. *Study:* St Andrews Univ, Scotland, MA(with hon), 64; Edinburgh Univ, Scotland, dipl(hist art), 65; Princeton Univ, MFA, 68, PhD, 71. *Teaching:* Asst prof hist art, Univ BC, 69-72; assoc prof, Univ Mich, 75-83, prof, 83- *Awards:* Vis mem, Inst Adv Study, Princeton, 83; guest scholar, J Paul Getty Mus, Malibu, 85; Fel, Royal Soc Arts, London, 88. *Mem:* Scottish Soc Hist Photog; Midwest Art Hist Soc. *Res:* Sixteenth century Florentine painting; 19th century British photography. *Publ:* Auth, The Casino of Pius IV, Princeton Univ Press, 77; Sixteenth Century Tuscan Drawings from the Uffizi, Oxford Univ Press, 88; Sun Pictures in Scotland, Univ Mich Mus Art, 89; Disciples of Light: Photographs in the Brewster Album, 90. *Mailing Add:* Dept Hist Art Univ Mich Ann Arbor MI 48109

SMITH, GREGG SHERWOOD
PAINTER, GRAPHIC ARTIST
b Easton, Pa, June 13, 51. *Study:* Duke Univ, BFA, 73; Pa Acad Fine Arts, 73. *Work:* Chemical Bank Corp Collection, New York. *Comn:* Portrait, comn by Ashton Hawkins, New York, 81; triple portrait, comn by Alan Power, Nevada City, 82; portrait, comn by Yasuo Yamamori, Boulder, 84; double portrait, comn by Veronica Veiss, New York, 84; double portrait, comn by Erling & Carey Madsen, New York, 85. *Exhib:* The Tunnel Wall Mural Series, The Tunnel Discotheque, New York, 87; Prodigy Videotex Art Gallery, Viewed across USA, 88-90; Reagan: American Icon, Bucknell Univ, Lewisburg, Pa, 89; Scenic Views, Willoughby Sharp Gallery, New York, 90; New Landscape Paintings, Willoughby Sharp Gallery, New York, 91; Wiesner Gallery, New York, 92; and others. *Pos:* Sr artist, Prodigy Videotex Servs, 87-90. *Teaching:* Instr desktop publ, MacIntosh Sch Visual Arts, 87. *Bibliog:* Richard Johnson (auth), Page six, NY Post, 4/90; Patty Harris (auth), 4 summer art shows, Downtown, 9/90; Gary Azon (auth), Art Around Town, Downtown, 4/91; and others. *Mem:* Spec Interest Group Computer Graphics & Interactive Techniques, Asn Computer Machinery. *Media:* Oil, Acrylics; Computers. *Publ:* Illusr, East Village Eye, 84, New York Talk, 84, Paper, 85, High Times, 86 & Videotex World, 86. *Dealer:* Elston Fine Arts 560 Broadway New York NY. *Mailing Add:* 106 W 13th St New York NY 10011

SMITH, HARRY WILLIAM
MINIATURIST, ILLUSTRATOR
b Chicago, Ill, July 12, 37. *Study:* Washington Univ, St Louis; Command Mgt Art Sch, Ft Belvoir, Va; Chicago Acad Fine Arts. *Work:* Yorktown Mus, NY; Gibbes Art Gallery, Charleston, SC; Miniature Mus, Kansas City, Mo. *Comn:* Federal Parlor of Maine (miniature), Colby Col Art Mus, 76. *Exhib:* Mid-States Exhib, Evansville Mus Art, 70; Int Exhib Paintings, Marshall Fields Gallery, Chicago, 70 & 71; solo exhib, Brown Co Art Gallery, Nashville, Ind, 71; Maine Forms of American Architecture, Colby Mus Art, Maine, 76; Copley Soc Boston, 77-78; Maine State Mus, Augusta, 83; Mystic Seaport, Mystic, Conn, 84; Neiman Marcus, 87; Farnsworth Mus, 90. *Pos:* Chmn, Maine Libr Comn, 79-83. *Teaching:* Instr advan art, Camden Sch, Maine, 77-84. *Bibliog:* Let it be wee, New York Mag, 83; article, Nutshell News, 90; article, Miniature Collector, 90. *Mem:* Copley Soc; Brown Co Art Gallery Asn (bd dirs, 70-71); Am Soc Marine Artists; Int Miniature Artists. *Publ:* Auth & illusr, Michael and the Mary Day, 79, ABC's of Maine, 80, Windjammers of the Maine Coast, 82, ABC's of New Hampshire, 84, Down East Books; The Art of Making Furniture in Miniature, Greenberg Publ Co, 92. *Dealer:* Coe Kerr Gallery 49 E 82nd New York NY. *Mailing Add:* 50 Harden Ave Camden ME 04843

SMITH, HASSEL W, JR
PAINTER
b Sturgis, Mich. *Study:* Northwestern Univ, BS(cum laude), 36; Calif Sch Fine Arts; San Francisco Art Inst, Hon Dr Art, 91. *Work:* Whitney Mus; Tate Gallery, London; San Francisco Mus Mod Art; Dallas Mus Contemp Art; Los Angeles Co Mus Art; Houston Mus Art; Stanford Univ; Oakland Mus; Hirshhorn Collection, Washington, DC; Univ Calif, Berkely Mus; Crocker Art Mus, Sacramento, Calif; Harrison Mus, Logan, Utah. *Exhib:* Solo exhibs, Calif Palace Legion Hon, 48 & 53, Galleria del Ariete, Milan, Italy, 62, Bristol Art Gallery, England, 72, Gallery Paule Anglim, San Francisco, 77, 81 & 82, Oakland Mus, 81, San Jose Mus Art, Calif, 83 & John Berggruen Gallery, San Francisco, 85; retrospectives, Pasadena Art Mus, Calif, 61 & San Francisco Mus Mod Art, 75; Natsoulas Novelozo Gallery, Davis, Calif, 88. *Teaching:* Lectr painting, Univ Calif, Berkeley & San Francisco Art Inst, 78-79, vis artist, 81; principal lectr painting, Fac Art & Design, Bristol Polytechnic, Eng, 66-77, vis lectr, 78-81. *Awards:* Nat Endowment Arts Award, 68; San Francisco Art Comn Award, 81; Distinguished Career Award, Peter & Madeleine Martin Found, 90. *Media:* Acrylic on Canvas. *Mailing Add:* The Old Rectory 6 Bradford Rd Rode Bath Avon BA3 6PR England United Kingdom

SMITH, J WELDON
MUSEUM DIRECTOR, HISTORIAN
b Richmond, Va. *Study:* Yale Univ, BA, 55; Cambridge Univ, 59 & 69; Northwestern Univ, PhD, 62. *Collections Arranged:* African Pragmatism (catalog), Boise Art Mus, Sonoma State Univ, 85; The Painter as Sculptor and Collector: John Haley, 90. *Pos:* Dir, Fiberworks-Ctr Textile Arts, 81-86, San Francisco Craft & Folk Art Mus, 86- *Teaching:* Prof aesthetics, Mac Murray Col, 65-80; vis prof African art, Inst Allende, Mex, 76 & 80, San Francisco Art Inst, 85. *Mem:* Am Asn Mus. *Res:* Investigation of the socio-religious aspects of African traditional art. *Publ:* Various articles in African Arts; A Report: Journal of San Francisco Craft & Folk Art Mus, African Traditional Art: Haley Collection. *Mailing Add:* San Francisco Craft & Folk Art Mus Ft Mason Ctr Bldg A San Francisco CA 94123

SMITH, JAMES MICHAEL
PAINTER, ASSEMBLAGE ARTIST
Study: Univ Kans, Lawrence, BFA, 71, Univ Ill, Champaign-Urbana, MFA, 73. *Work:* Chase Manhattan Bank, New York; The Byers Mus, Evanston, Ill; Univ Tex Collection, El Paso; Saks Fifth Avenue, New York; Barnes Hospital, St Louis, MO. *Exhib:* Solo exhibs, Festival Gallery, Krannert Ctr Performing Arts, Univ Ill, Urbana, 77, Joy Horwich Gallery, Chicago, Ill, 80, 81, 82, 83, 84 & 89, Louis D Beaumont Gallery, Maryville Col, St Louis MO, 80, Fontbonne Col Gallery, St Louis, MO, 81, Locus Gallery, St Louis, MO, 85, 87, Sch of Ozarks, Lookout Point, MO, 87; The New York Connection, Florissant Valley Community Col, St Louis, MO, 89; Locus Gallery, St Louis, MO, 90; Flora '90, Chicago Botanical Gardens, Ill, 90; Painted Constructions, St Louis Community Col, Forest Park, 90. *Pos:* Juror, Ill Small Painting Competition, Western Ill Univ, Macomb, 87; panelist, Careers in the Arts Seminar, St Louis Community Col, Florissant, 88. *Teaching:* Vis artist lectr, Nat Philosophical Soc, Joy Horwich Gallery, 83; vis artist, Sch of Ozarks, Lookout Point, MO, 88. *Awards:* Award of Merit, 30th Ann Art Exhib, Elizabeth M Sinnock Gallery, Quincy, Ill, 80; Award of Merit, 22nd Ann Art Exhib, Oklahoma Art Ctr, 80; Cash Award, Louis E Seiden Mem Award, Chautauqua 27th Ann Nat Exhib, NY, 84. *Mailing Add:* c/o Locus 710 N Tucker No 315 Saint Louis MO 63101

SMITH, JAMES MORTON
HISTORIAN
b Bernie, Mo, May 28, 19. *Study:* Southern Ill Univ, BEd, 41; Univ Okla, MA, 46; Cornell Univ, PhD, 51. *Pos:* Ed, Inst Early Am Hist & Cult, 55-66; dir, State Hist Soc Wis, 70-76; dir & dir emer, Winterthur Mus, 76-84. *Teaching:* Prof hist, Cornell Univ, 66-70; prof hist, Univ Wis, 70-76; prof hist, Univ Del, 76-89. *Mem:* Asn Art Mus Dirs; Am Hist Asn; Orgn Historians; Am Asn Mus. *Res:* Early American history and culture. *Mailing Add:* 120 Sharpless Dr Elkton MD 21921

SMITH, JAUNE QUICK-TO-SEE
PAINTER
Study: Framingham State Col, Mass, BA; Univ NMex, MA. *Work:* Birmingham Mus Art, Ala; Am Med Asn, Continental Bank, Chicago, Ill; Steinberg Mus, St Louis, Mo; Denver Art Mus, Colo; Nat Mus Am Art, Washington, DC. *Comn:* Sculpture Garden, Yerba Buena Park, Moscone Ctr, San Francisco, Calif. *Exhib:* Myth and Magic on the Americas, Museo de Arte Contemporaneo de Monterrey, Mex, 91; Encuentro-Invasion of the Americas and the Making of the Mestizo, Artes de Mex, Venice, Calif, 91; The Edge of Childhood, Heckscher Mus, Huntington, NY, 92; Columbus Drowning, Rochdale Art Gallery, Eng, 92; In Plural America: Contemporary Journeys, Voices and Identities, Hudson River Mus, Yonkers, NY, 92; solo exhibs, LewAllen Gallery, Santa Fe, NMex, 92, Bernice Steinbaum Gallery, New York, 92, Chrysler Mus, Norfolk, Va, 93. *Collections Arranged:* Our Land/Ourselves, Am Indian Contemp Artists, State Univ NY at Albany, 91. *Teaching:* Speaker, Minneapolis Col Art & Design, Women's Caucus Art, Chicago, Ill. *Awards:* Purchase Award, Acad Arts & Letts, NY, 87; Asn Am Cult Arts Serv Award, 90; Hon Doctorate, Minneapolis Col Art & Design, Minn, 92. *Bibliog:* Ann R Langdon (auth), Women Visual Artists You Might Like to Know, Women in the Arts, New Haven, 90; Mito y Magia en America: Los Ochenta (catalog), Museo de Arte Contemporaneo de Monterrey, 91; Jackson Rushing (auth), Critical Issues in Recent Native Am Art, Art J, fall 92. *Mem:* Col Art Asn; ATLATL, Indian Orgn for the Arts, Phoenix, Ariz. *Dealer:* Steinbaum Krauss Gallery 132 Greene St New York NY 10012. *Mailing Add:* Drawer F Corrales NM 87048

SMITH, JO-AN
DESIGNER, CRAFTSMAN
b Eugene, Ore, Apr 8, 33. *Study:* Ind Univ, 65; pvt studies in Buenos Aires, Arg, 66, San Salvador, El Salvador, 67, Panama, 68-70; Univ Tex, El Paso, BA, 71, NMex State Univ, MA, 75. *Work:* Smithsonian Inst, Washington, DC; plus others. *Comn:* Award Medallions, NMex State Univ, 85-92. *Exhib:* Update: Body Ornament, Am Craft Coun, Winston-Salem, NC, 77; Marietta Col Craft Nat, Ohio, 77; Am Goldsmith Now, St Louis, Mo, Santa Fe Festival Arts, 78; Gold, Las Cruces, NMex, 79; Renaissance Craft Fair Treasure Trio, 85-90; Arts a Poppin, Dona Ana Arts Coun, 85-88. *Pos:* Proprietor & designer, Jos Studio, 71-92. *Teaching:* Instr, NMex State Univ, 75-81. *Awards:* Second Place Purchase Prize in Crafts, Llano Estacado Art Asn, 74; First Place in Show, Las Cruces Chap, NMex Designer Craftsmen, 74; Hon Mention, The Metalsmith, Phoenix & Seattle, 76-77. *Bibliog:* Soc N Am Goldsmiths Film Libr. *Mem:* Soc NAm Goldsmiths; Dona Ana Arts Coun. *Media:* Metals. *Publ:* Contribr, Bead J, Craftsman's Gallery, Design, Golddust, Goldsmith's J & Working Craftsman. *Dealer:* Glenn Cutter Jewelers 1374 Mesilla Valley Mall Las Cruces NM 88001. *Mailing Add:* Box 426 Dona Ana NM 88032

SMITH, JOHN IVOR
SCULPTOR, EDUCATOR
b London, Eng, Jan 28, 27; Can citizen. *Study:* McGill Univ, BSc, 48; Montreal Mus Fine Arts; study with Arthur Lismer, Jacques de Tonnancour & Eldon Grier. *Work:* Art Gallery Ont, Toronto; Provincial Mus Que, Quebec City; Winnipeg Art Gallery, Manitoba; London Pub Art Mus, Ont; Edmonton Art Gallery, Alta. *Comn:* 20' Fiberglass chimeric figure, Expo '67, Montreal, 67; 9' Fiberglass female figure, Can Govt Exhib Comn, Ottawa, 67; 13' Fiberglas sculpture, Nat Capital Comn, Ottawa, 86. *Exhib:* Nat Outdoor Sculpture Show, Ottawa, Ont, 60; Can Sculpture, Dorothy Cameron Gallery, Toronto, Ont, 64; Sculpture '67, City Hall, Nat Gallery Can, Toronto, 67; Expo '67, Montreal; Can Sculpture, Rodin Gallery, Paris, France, 70; La Sculpture Au Quebec, Musee Du Quebec, Quebec, Canada, 92. *Teaching:*

Assoc prof sculpture, Concordia Univ, Montreal, 66-84. *Awards:* First Prizes, Winnipeg Art Gallery, 59-61; Grand Centennial Award, Montreal Mus Fine Arts, 60; Senior Art Awards, Can Coun, 67, 69 & 73. *Mem:* Royal Can Acad. *Media:* Fiberglas reinforced epoxy. *Dealer:* Galerie Dresdnere 12 Hazelton Ave Toronto ON M5R 2E2 Can. *Mailing Add:* RR2 Belvedere Cr Duncan BC V9L 1N9 Canada

SMITH, JOS(EPH) A(NTHONY)
PAINTER, ILLUSTRATOR
b Bellefonte, Pa, Sept 5, 36. *Study:* Pa State Univ, with Hobson Pittman, 55-57 & 60; Pratt Inst, BFA. *Work:* Lauren Rogers Mus, Miss; Univ Miss, Oxford; Kassel Documenta Arch, Ger; Coeln Ludwig Mus, Ger; Stuttgart Staatsgalerie Grafische Sammlung, Ger; and others. *Exhib:* Pa Acad Fine Arts, 61, 67 & 69; solo exhib paintings, drawings & sculpture, Staten Island Inst Arts & Sci, 66; Bethel Gallery, Conn, 78; Newhouse Gallery, Staten Island Cult Ctr, NY, 82; Adirondak Community Col, NY, 87; Artists Select Artists, Trenton City Mus, NJ, 92; The Art of Drawing VII, Staemfli Gallery, NY, 92; and others. *Pos:* Design consult, Brooks Bros, 70-75; exhib designer & consult, Staten Island Inst Arts & Sci, 70-75; mem bd dirs, Staten Island Coun Arts, 71-76. *Teaching:* Prof fine art, Pratt Inst, 61-; asst prof fine art, Pa State Univ, University Park, summers 69-73. *Awards:* Mary S Litt Award for Watercolor, 100th Ann Am Watercolor Soc, 67; Merit Award, NY Soc Illusr, 73, 74, 79 & 82; Merit Award, Nat Works on Paper, Univ Miss, Oxford; and others. *Bibliog:* Jane Cottingham (auth), The imaginary drawings of Joseph A Smith, Am Artist, 7/81; Albert, Seckler & Albert (auth), Figure Drawing Comes to Life, 2nd ed, Prentice Hall, 86; Suzi Galik (auth), The Reenchantment of Art, Thames & Hudson, 91; and others. *Mem:* New York Visionary Artists. *Media:* Oil, Pencil. *Publ:* Illusr, Mackinlay kantor (auth), Andersonville, Franklin Libr, 76; Eric Jong (auth), Witches, Abrams, 80; Susan Cooper (auth), Matthew's Dragon, McElderry Bks, 91; auth, Pen & Ink Book, Watson-Guptill Publ, 92; illusr, D Wolkenstein (auth), Step By Step, Morrow Jr Bks, 93; and others. *Mailing Add:* Dept Painting & Drawing Pratt Inst 200 Willoughby Ave Brooklyn NY 11205

SMITH, KEITH A
PHOTOGRAPHER, PRINTMAKER
b Tipton, Ind, May 20, 38. *Study:* Art Inst of Chicago, BAE, with Aatis Lillstrom, Ken Josephson, Vera Berdich & Sonia Sheridan; Inst Design, Ill Inst Technol, MS(photog), with Aaron Siskind, Arthur Siegel & Misch Kohn; Guggenheim Fel in Photog, 72 & 80. *Work:* Mus Mod Art, New York; Art Inst of Chicago; Int Mus Photog, George Eastman House, Rochester, NY; Nat Gallery of Can, Ottawa, Ont; Houghton Rare Books Libr, Harvard Univ. *Exhib:* Solo exhibs, Light Gallery, New York, 76, Chicago Ctr Contemp Photog, 78 & Stuart Wilber Inc, Chicago, 78, 79 & 80; Mirrors and Windows: American Photography Since 1960, Mus Mod Art, 78 & traveling, 78-80; American Photography of the Seventies, Art Inst Chicago, 79; Cliche Verre: 1939 to the Present, Detroit Inst Arts, 80; Hand-Colored Photographs, Philadelphia Col Art, 80; and others. *Teaching:* Instr photog, Univ Calif, Los Angeles, 70; instr photog generative systems, Sch of Art Inst Chicago, 71-74; coordr of printmaking, Visula Studies Workshop, Rochester, 74- *Awards:* Guggenheim Fel, 72 & 80; Nat Endowment Arts Grant, 78. *Media:* Photography; Etching with Photoetching. *Publ:* Auth, When I Was Two, Visual Studies Workshop, 77; auth, Book 91, 82 & Book 89 Patterned Apart, 83, Space Heater Multiples; coauth (with Jonathan Williams), Lexinton Nocturne, A Poem by Jonathan Williams as Interpreted by Keith Smith, private publ, 83; auth, Book 95 Structure of the Visual Book, Visual Studies Workshop Press, 83. *Mailing Add:* 22 Cayuga St Rochester NY 14620

SMITH, KENT ALVIN
SCULPTOR
b White Earth Indian Reservation, Minn, Dec 23, 43. *Study:* Univ Minn, Minneapolis, with Katherine Nash, BA(sculpture), 71, MFA(sculpture), 75. *Work:* General Mills Inc, Univ Minn Galleries, Fed Reserve Bank, Minneapolis; Bemidji State Univ, Minn. *Comn:* Outdoor sculpture, Portfolio Management Corp, Minneapolis, 75. *Exhib:* Bois Fort Gallery, Ely, Minn, 74 & 75; Ojibwe Exhib, Bemidji State Univ & Minn State Hist Soc, St Paul, 74 & 75; Flatland Sculpture, Drake Univ, Des Moines, Iowa, 75; Drawing Show, Univ Minn, 75. *Pos:* Res asst, Ceramic Shell, Univ Minn, 68-69; sculpture asst to Katherine Nash, Minneapolis, 68-69; gallery technician, Univ Minn Galleries, 69-73. *Teaching:* Artist in residence, Bemidji State Univ, 74-75, instr contemp Am Indian sculpture & painting, 74-82. *Bibliog:* Gerald Vizenor (auth), The Everlasting Sky, Collier-Macmillan, 70; Brian Anderson (auth), The present: Is there Indian art, Minneapolis Tribune, 10/22/72; Don Morrison (auth), Ojibwe art 1974, Minneapolis Star, 6/74. *Mem:* Col Art Asn; Ojibwe Art Asn. *Media:* Cast Metal, Wood. *Dealer:* Art Lending Gallery 2500 Groveland Terrace Minneapolis MN 55403. *Mailing Add:* 1001 Bemidji Ave Bemidji MN 56601

SMITH, LAWRENCE BEALL
PAINTER, SCULPTOR
b Washington, DC, Oct 2, 09. *Study:* Art Inst Chicago, Univ Chicago, PhB, 31; with Ernest Thurn, Gloucester, Mass; also with Charles Hopkinson & Harold Zimmerman, Boston. *Work:* William Hayes Fogg Art Mus, Cambridge, Mass; Libr Cong, Washington, DC; Metrop Mus Art, New York; Addison Gallery, Andover, Mass; Wichita Art Mus, Kans; Worcester Found, Shrewsbury, Conn; and others. *Comn:* Normandy Invasion, Abbott Labs, Washington, DC, 44; Paintings of Missouri, Scruggs-Vandervort-Barney, Univ Mo, 46; portraits of Robert Hutchins, Univ Chicago, 52, Harold Swift, 60, Charles Merrill, Jr, Boston, 65, Hudson Hoagland, 79 & Thomas Ragle, 80; and others. *Exhib:* Whitney Mus Am Art, New York, 60; Nat Acad Design Ann, New York, 74 & 75; Katonah Gallery, NY; Maine Coast Artists-Rockport, Maine; Wichita Mus, Kans; and others. *Pos:* Mem adv bd, Katonah Mus, AR, 54-90. *Awards:* Cert of Excellence, Am Inst Graphic Arts, 53; Purchase Prize, Norfolk Mus, 67; Ellen C Speyer Prize, Nat Acad Design, 76. *Bibliog:* Harry Salperer (auth), The shorthand caricaturist, Esquire Mag, 42. *Media:* Oil; Wood, Bronze. *Publ:* Illusr, Robin Hood, Grossett, 54; Girls are Silly, Ogden Nash (auth), Watts, 62; Henry Fielding's Tom Jones, Bk Month Club, 64; Henry James's Washington Square, 71 & Edith Wharton's Age of Innocence, 73, Ltd Ed Club. *Mailing Add:* Rte 121 Cross River NY 10518

SMITH, LAWRY
DIRECTOR, CURATOR
b Cleveland, Ohio, Aug 29, 52. *Study:* Baldwin Wallace Col, BA, 74; Cleveland State Univ, MFA, 77. *Collections Arranged:* Artist's Adopt, St Vincent Charity Hosp, 89; Ken Burgess (retrospective), La Mama La Galleria, 89, Danforth Mus, 90, Art Students League, 91. *Pos:* Dir, cur, Lamama Lagalleria, New York 85-, Citicorp Ctr, New York, 86-87, Cleveland Public Theatre Ohio, 90; Nat Pub Radio, WBOE, 77-80. *Awards:* Recepient Twyia M Conway Radio-TV Award; Hastings Grant. *Mem:* Screen Actors Guild; Am Fedn TV & Radio Artists. *Specialty:* Emerging artists. *Mailing Add:* La Mama-La Galleria 6 E First St New York NY 10003

SMITH, LAWSON WENTWORTH
SCULPTOR, EDUCATOR
b Havana, Cuba, Apr 20, 47; US citizen. *Study:* Okla State Univ, BFA, 70; Univ Nebr, MFA, 74. *Work:* Ctr Visual Arts Gallery, Ill State Univ, Bloomington & Normal; Sioux City Art Ctr, Sioux City, Iowa; and others. *Exhib:* One man shows, Contemp Arts Found, Oklahoma City, 71, Henri Gallery, Washington, DC, 75, 77, 79 & 82, Foreman Gallery, Hartwick Col, Oneonta, NY, 85, Penelec Gallery, Allegheny Col, Meadville, Pa 86 & Schweinfurth Art Mus, Auburn, NY, 88; Rutgers Nat Drawing Exhib, 79 & 81; OK Harris Gallery, New York, 82; Nat Works on Paper, Great Falls, NDak, 87. *Teaching:* Instr sculpture, Wichita State Univ, Kans, 74-75; assoc prof & head sculpture dept, Syracuse Univ, NY, 76-92. *Awards:* Purchase Award, Ball State Univ, 76; Purchase Award, 35th Ann Exhib, Sioux City Art Ctr, Iowa, 73; Sculpture Award, Fingerlakes Regional, Mem Art Gallery, Rochester, NY, 80; and others. *Media:* All. *Dealer:* Henri Gallery 21st & P St NW Washington DC 20036. *Mailing Add:* Syracuse Univ Syracuse NY 13244

SMITH, LEON POLK
PAINTER, COLLAGE ARTIST
b Chickasha, Okla, May 20, 06. *Study:* E Cent Univ Okla, BA, 34; Columbia Univ, MA, 38. *Work:* Guggenheim Mus; Metrop Mus Art; Mus Mod Art; Hirshhorn Mus, Washington, DC; Whitney Mus Art; Nat Gallery, Berlin; Nernberg Mus. *Exhib:* Museo de Bellas Artes, Venesulia, 63; retrospective, San Francisco Mus, Ft Worth Mus Mod Art & Rose Mus, 68; Paris-New York, Musee Nat d'Art Mod, Georges Pompidou (Beaubourg), Paris, France; Nat Mus, Berlin, 84; Nat Gallery, Washington, DC, 84; retrospective (with catalog), William Hack Mus, Ludwigshaffen, WGer, 89; retrospective (with catalog), Grenoble Mus, France, 89; Brooklyn Mus, NY, 92. *Teaching:* Lectr, Brandeis Univ, 68; resident artist, Univ Calif, Davis, 72; lectr, State Univ NY, Old Westbury, 78, Ace Gallery, Vancouver, Can & Venice, Calif, 79. *Awards:* Grants, Nat Coun Arts, 67 & Tamarind, 68; Hassam/Speicher Fund Purchase Exhib, Am Acad & Inst Arts & Lett, NY, 79; and others. *Media:* Acrylic, Oil. *Mailing Add:* 31 Union Sq W Studio 14E New York NY 10003

SMITH, LOWELL ELLSWORTH
PAINTER
b Canton, Ohio, Nov 20, 24. *Study:* Miami Univ, Ohio, BFA, 48; Famous Artists Schs, dipl, 55. *Work:* Canton Art Mus, Ohio; Akron Art Mus; Frye Mus, Seattle; Cowboy Hall Fame, Oklahoma City. *Exhib:* Nat Acad Western Art, Cowboy Hall Fame, Oklahoma City, 78 & 81-83; The Oaxaca Experience, Frye Mus, Seattle, 80; Western Heritage Show, Houston, 81-85; Artists of American, Colo Hist Soc, Denver, 82-85; Am Watercolor Soc Exhib, Nat Acad, New York. *Teaching:* Instr landscape & figure painting, privately, 60- *Awards:* Gold Medal Watercolor, Nat Acad Western Art, 82 & 83; Prix West, Nat Acad Western Art Show, Cowboy Hall Fame, 83; Silver Medal, Watercolor, 85, Gold Medal, 88 & Silver Medal, Nat Acad Western Art, 90; Silver Medal, Nat Acad Western Art, 90. *Bibliog:* Don Blanchard (producer), The Mood, the Moment (TV film), Metrop Libr, Oklahoma City, 82; Mary Bowman (auth), article, Artists of Rockies, 82; Susan Dodd Whelan (auth), Light washed shadows, Southwest Art Mag, 83; article, Art West Mag, 89. *Mem:* Ohio Watercolor Soc; Am Watercolor Soc; Nat Acad Western Art; Northwest Renderus Group. *Media:* Watercolor. *Dealer:* Linda McAdoo Santa Fe NM; Shriver Gallery Taos NM. *Mailing Add:* 152 Elm St Hudson OH 44236

SMITH, LUTHER A
PHOTOGRAPHER
b Tishomingo, Miss, Mar 16, 50. *Study:* Univ Ill, Urbana, with Art Singabaugh & Bart Parker, BA, 72; RI Sch Design, with Harry Callahan & Aaron Siskind, MFA(photog), 74. *Work:* Portland Mus Art, Maine; Mass Inst Technol; Ark Arts Ctr, Little Rock; Monmouth Col, Ill; La Grange Col, Ga; Chicago Art Inst, Ill; Houston Mus Fine Arts, Tex. *Exhib:* Photography, Kansas City Art Inst, Mo, 78; Black & White & Color, Mass Inst Technol, 79; Contacts, Western Heritage Mus, Omaha, Nebr, 80; Invisible Light, Smithsonian Inst Traveling Exhib, 80-83; Second Sight, Carpenter Ctr, Harvard Univ, 81; Road & Roadside, Chicago Art Inst, 87; one person exhib, Waco Art Ctr, Tex, 87 & Springfield Art Mus, Mo, 91. *Teaching:* Vis lectr, Univ Ill, Urbana, 74-75, instr art, 75-78, asst prof, 78-81, assoc prof, 81-; assoc prof art dept, Tex Christian Univ, 83; prof art, Tex Christian Univ, 92- *Awards:* Purchase Prizes,

Allied Arts Asn, 79, Chattahoochi Art Asn, 80 & Ark Art Ctr, 80; Sesquicentennial Award, Tarrant County Works on Paper, Fort Worth, Tex. *Mem:* Soc Photographic Educ. *Publ:* Illusr, Camera, 75; illusr, Chicago Mag, 78; illusr, Darkroom Dynamics, 78, Electronic Flash Photography, 80 & Photographing Indoors With Your Automatic Camera, 81, Curtin-London. *Mailing Add:* Art Dept Tex Christian Univ PO Box 30793 Ft Worth TX 76129

SMITH, MICHAEL A
PHOTOGRAPHER
b Philadelphia, Pa, Feb 16, 42. *Study:* Self-taught. *Work:* Mus Mod Art, Metrop Mus Art, New York; Art Inst Chicago; Mus Fine Arts, Boston; Philadelphia Mus Art. *Comn:* To Photograph Toledo, Toledo Mus Art, 80; Study of Princeton NJ, Princeton Gallery Fine Art, 84; To Photograph New Orleans, Historic New Orleans Collection, 85; Art in Public Places, Broward County, Fla, 89. *Exhib:* Solo exhibs, Sheldon Mem Art Gallery, 76, Del Art Mus, 78 & Ringling Mus Art, 80; Landscapes 75-79, Stanford Univ Mus Art, 81, Toledo Mus Art, 81 & Norton Gallery Fine Art, West Palm Beach, Fla, 82; Foto Biennal Enschede, The Netherlands, 84; Lowe Art Gallery, Syracuse Univ, 86; Loyola Col, Baltimore, 87; Michael A Smith: A Visual Journey, Inter Mus Photo at George Eastman House, 92. *Teaching:* Vis prof, Philadelphia Col Art, 70-72, Bucks Co Community Col, 71-73. *Awards:* Photogr Fel, Nat Endowment Arts, 77; Best Photog Bk of Yr, Le Grand Prix DuLivre, Recontres Int dela Photog, Arles, France, 81. *Bibliog:* Estelle Jussim (auth), A dead straight picture: The landscapes of Michael A Smith, Boston Rev, 2/77; James Enyeart (auth), Intro to Landscapes 1975-1979, Lodima Press, 81; Richard Trenner (auth), A portrait of the artist, Ont Rev, fall-winter 82-83; John Bratnober (auth), A Visual Journey, Lodima Press, 92. *Media:* Photography. *Publ:* Auth & illusr, Twelve Photographs 67-69, pvt publ, 70; auth, On teaching photography, Exposure, J Soc Photog Educ, 76; auth & illusr, Landscapes 1975-1979 (exhib catalog), Lehigh Univ, 81; Landscapes 1975-1979 (monogr), Lodima Press, 81; Eight Landscape Photographs, Regnis Press, 83; illusr, Michael A Smith: A Visual Journey (monogr), Lodima Press, 92. *Mailing Add:* PO Box 400 Bunker Hill Rd Ottsville PA 18942

SMITH, MOISHE
PRINTMAKER
b Chicago, Ill, Jan 10, 29. *Study:* New Sch Social Res, BA, 50; Univ Iowa, with Lasansky, MFA, 53; Skowhegan Sch Painting & Sculpture; Acad Florence; also with Giorgio Morandi. *Work:* Mus Mod Art & Metrop Mus Art, New York; Kestner Mus, Hannover; Galleria Degli Uffizi, Florence; Nat Gallery Art, Washington, DC; and others. *Comn:* Powwow (etching, 100 proofs), Utah Olympic Bid Comt, 91; Absolut Utah, Absolut Statehood, 92. *Exhib:* Print Coun Am Traveling Exhib, 59 & 62; Int Prints, Cincinnati Mus, Ohio, 62; Salon de Mai, Paris, 65; Libr Cong, 69, 71 & 73; Cracow Int, 78, 80, 84, 86 & 88; Ljubljana Int, 81; Frechen Inst, 80; Grenchen Int, 82; World Print Four, 83; Taiwan Int, 88. *Teaching:* Vis artist printmaking, Univ Wis, 66-67, Ohio State Univ, spring, 71, Univ Iowa, fall, 71; assoc prof, Univ Wis-Parkside, 72-77; prof, Utah State Univ, Logan, 77- *Awards:* Four Seasons Res Grant, Southern Ill Univ, 57; Fulbright Fel, 59-61; Guggenheim Fel, 67-68; Eastern Europe Res Grant, Univ Wis-Parkside, 76; Mountain Landscape & Nat Monuments Res Grants, Utah State Univ, 83; Utah Artist of the Year, 88; others. *Mem:* Nat Acad Design; Soc Am Graphic Artists. *Media:* All. *Mailing Add:* Dept Art Utah State Univ Logan UT 84322-4000

SMITH, NAN S(HELLEY)
SCULPTOR, CERAMIST
b Philadelphia, Pa, Nov 10, 52. *Study:* Tyler Sch Art, Temple Univ, Philadelphia, BFA, 74; Ohio State Univ, Columbus, MFA, 77; Univ Ill, Japan House, with Shozo Sato, 79. *Exhib:* Solo exhibs, Inner Dimensions, McQuade Gallery, Merrimack Col, N Andover, Mass, 84, Portrayals of Faith, East Campus Gallery, Valencia Community Col, 85, Inner Views, Patrons Gallery, Voc's Ctr for Crafts, 90; Ann Juried Mem Exhibs, Orlando Mus Art, 87; Fla Craftsmen Juried Exhib, Polk Mus Art, 89; 38th Ann All Fla Juried Exhib, Boca Mus Art, 89. *Teaching:* Vis instr design & ceramics, Univ Ill, Champaign-Urbana, 77-79; assoc prof ceramics, Univ Fla, Gainesville, 79- *Awards:* Individual Artists fel, Div Cult Affairs, Dept State, Fine Arts Coun Fla & Nat Endowment Arts, 80-81; Grad Fac Res Grant, Univ Fla, 80, 83-84 & 90-91; Res Develop Award, Univ Fla, 86; Honor to Artists Contributing to Arts in Alachua County, Alachua County Arts Coun, 87. *Bibliog:* Alan Saperstein (dir), You Gotta Have A Dream (film), WUFT Public TV, 81; Gene Kleinsmith (dir), Twenty Americans in Clay (multimedia prog), Pompidou Ctr Arts, Paris, 84; Gene Kleinsmith (dir), Clay Artists, America's Best (multimedia prog), Int Identite Ceramique Conf, Auxerre, Yonne, France, 85; Gene Kleinsmith (auth), Clays the Way, Victor Valley Pr, 88; Les Krantz (ed), American Artists, an Illustrated Survey of Leading Contemporaries, 2nd Ed, Am Ref Publ Corp, 89. *Mem:* Col Art Asn; Nat Coun Educ Ceramic Arts; Fla Craftsmen Inc; Int Sculpture Ctr. *Media:* Clay, Wood; Plaster. *Publ:* Auth, A blend of institution and logic, Ceramics Monthly Mag, fall 90. *Mailing Add:* 2310 NW 142nd Ave Gainesville FL 32609-4022

SMITH, PAUL J
MUSEUM DIRECTOR
b Sept 8, 31. *Study:* Art Inst Buffalo; Sch Am Craftsman; Parsons Sch Design; New Sch Social Res, Hon Dr Fine Arts, 87. *Pos:* Bd dirs, Louis Comfort Tiffany Found, currently; adv trustee, Haystack Mountain Sch Crafts, Deer Isle, Maine, currently; adv bd, Atlantic Ctr Arts; Int Coun Pilchuck Glass Sch; dir emer, Am Craft Mus, currently. *Awards:* Hon Degree, Fine Arts, Parsons Sch Design New Sch for Soc Res, 87; Hon Fel, Am Craft Coun, 89. *Mem:* Hon Fel Am Craft Coun. *Publ:* Craft Today: Poetry of the Physical Am Craft Mus, Weidemfeld & Nicholson, 86. *Mailing Add:* 1349 Lexington Ave New York NY 10028

SMITH, RALPH ALEXANDER
WRITER, EDUCATOR
b Ellwood City, Pa, June 12, 29. *Study:* Columbia Univ, AB, Teachers Col, MA & EdD. *Pos:* Exec secy, Coun for Policy Studies Art Educ, 78-82. *Teaching:* Instr art hist & art educ, Kent State Univ, 59-61; asst prof art hist & art educ & chmn dept art, Wis State Univ-Oshkosh, 61-63; asst prof art hist & art educ, State Univ NY Col New Paltz, 63-64; asst prof aesthet educ, Univ Ill, Urbana, 64-67, assoc prof, 67-71, prof cultural and educ policy, 71- *Awards:* First Barkan Mem Award; Distinguished Fel, Nat Art Educ Asn; Distinguished Univ visiting Prof, Ohio State Univ. *Mem:* Am Soc Aesthet; Philos Educ Soc; Nat Art Educ Asn. *Res:* Theoretical foundations of aesthetic and humanities education; cultural and educational policy analysis. *Publ:* Co-ed, Aesthetic and Arts Education, Univ Ill Press, 91; ed, Cultural Literacy and Art Education, Univ Ill Press, 91; coauth, Art Education: A Cultural Necessity, Univ Ill Press, 91; co-ed, The Arts, Education and Aesthetic Framings, Univ Chicago Press, 92; Public Policy and the Aesthetic Interest, Univ Press, 92. *Mailing Add:* 1310 S Sixth St Univ Ill Champaign IL 61820

SMITH, RAYMOND WALTER
CURATOR, PHOTOGRAPHER
b Newark, NJ, Oct 26, 42. *Study:* Stetson Univ, BA, 64; Yale Univ, MA, 66 & MPhil, 68. *Work:* Yale Univ Art Gallery, New Haven; Univ Tex, Gernsheim Collection, Austin. *Exhib:* Connecticut Photography, Greater Hariford Arts Festival, Hartford, 74 & 75; America As Found Photos by Ray Smith, Yale Univ Libr, New Haven, 75; Photographs by Ray Smith, Stetson Univ Art Gallery, Deland, Fla, 76; Beyond Documentary Four Photographers, John Slade Ely House, New Haven, 77. *Pos:* Cur, John Slade Ely House, New Haven, 85- *Mem:* Art Libr Soc-N Am. *Publ:* Contribr, Photos Published in Chicago Review, New Am, 75; Articles in American Art Review, 75, Photographic Rev, 79-80; ed, 15 Painters & Sculptors (exhib catalog), John Slade Ely House, 85; auth, Artists From People's Republic of China (exhib catalog), 91, Architecture and Process (exhib catalog), 92, John Slade Ely House. *Mailing Add:* John Slade Ely House 51 Trumbull St New Haven CT 06510

SMITH, ROBERT CHARLES
DESIGNER, EDUCATOR
b Buffalo, NY, Jan 21, 26. *Study:* Albright Art Sch, Univ Buffalo, BFA, 50; Univ Cincinnati. *Work:* Morton D May Collection, St Louis, Mo; Washington Univ Gallery Art, St Louis, Mo; Butler Inst Am Art. *Comn:* Fountain, Pub Libr Hamilton Co, Cincinnati, Ohio, 60; fountain, Temple Ark & Eternal Light, Glen Manor Temple, Cincinnati, 64; fountain, Munic Opera Asn Forest Park, St Louis, Mo, 74; fountain, Boone Co Nat Bank, Columbia, Mo, 75 & 86; Corporate Identity, City Town & Country, Mo, 92. *Exhib:* Print Ann, Brooklyn Mus, NY, 50-52; Fountains 69, Taft Mus, Cincinnati, 69; Multiples '80, Contemp Arts Ctr, New Orleans, La, 80; one-man shows, Univ City Pub Libr, & Martin Schweig Gallery, St Louis, 81, Cent Mo State Univ, Warrensburg, 86. *Pos:* Art dir, Writer's Dig, Cincinnati, Ohio, 54-69 & Environ Mag, St Louis, Mo, 65-70; graphics consult, City of University City, Mo, 77-80 & City of Bridgeton, Mo, 80-86. *Teaching:* Instr design, Albright Art Sch, 50-52; instr design & drawing, Art Acad Cincinnati, 52-65; prof design, Sch Fine Arts, Wash Univ, 65- *Awards:* Community Arts Award, Community Arts Prog, US Dept of Housing & Urban Develop, 73; Purchase Award, Ann Drawing Show, Ball State Univ Art Gallery, 74. *Bibliog:* K Hanna (auth), Fountains '69, Taft Mus, 69; S Pollack (auth), R C Smith--Waterworks, New Art Examiner, 81; E Dempsey (auth), Create Studio, Wash Univ Mag, 91; and others. *Mem:* Am Ctr Design; Col Art Asn. *Media:* Graphics; Artists Books. *Publ:* Auth, Basic Graphic Design, Prentice-Hall, 86, 2nd ed, 92; Main By Line, 91, Sunrise-Sunset, 91 & Master's Pieces, 92, Eclectic Press. *Mailing Add:* 6316 Washington Ave St Louis MO 63130

SMITH, ROBERT LEWIS
DESIGNER, EDUCATOR
b Salem, Ohio, Aug 5, 40. *Study:* Univ Southern Calif; Univ Calif, Los Angeles, BA, 63, MFA, 66. *Collections Arranged:* Three Photographers--Bullock, Sommer, Teske, 68; Jud Fine, 72; Narrative Themes: Audio Works, 78; Sound, 79; Leroy Neiman-Andy Warhol, 81; Changing Trends: Content and Style, 82. *Pos:* Gallery dir, Calif State Univ, Northridge, 66-70 & Brand Lib Art Ctr, Glendale, Calif, 70-73; dir & founder, Los Angeles Inst Contemp Art, 74-86. *Teaching:* Prof & design, Calif State Univ, Nortridge, 66- *Awards:* DAAD Fel, 85. *Bibliog:* Michael Auping (auth), Interview with Bob Smith, La Mamelle, Berkeley, Calif, 75. *Publ:* Auth & designer numerous exhib catalogs. *Mailing Add:* Dept Art Calif State Univ 18111 Nordoff St Northridge CA 91330

SMITH, ROWENA MARCUS
PAINTER, COLLAGE ARTIST
b Bethel, Vt, June 6, 23. *Study:* Syracuse Univ, BFA, 43; Hofstra Univ, MS, 66; studied with Rex Brandt, Joan Irving, Miles G Batt, Frank Webb, Charles Reid, Barbara Neghis, Don Andrews, 77-90. *Work:* Broward Community Col, Bailey Concert Hall, Davie, Ft Lauderdale; Floyd L Wray Found, Flamingo Botanical Gardens, Davie; Broward Co Libr Found, Ft Lauderdale; Oakland Park Libr, Oakland Park, Fla; Coral Springs Libr, Fla; Nat Asn Women Artists Collection, Zimerilli Mus Douglas Col, Rutgers Univ. *Comn:* Ltd ed print 4-color lithography, Floyd L Wray Found, Davie, 88. *Exhib:* Showcase 88, Nat Asn Women Artists, India Traveling Exhib to Bombay, Baroda & Ahmedebad; Rocky Mountain Nat Watermedia Exhib, 89-90; Nat Asn Women Artists, 100 Years-100 Works, Women Artists of Today Salute their Centennial, USA traveling exhib; Way of Women Artists, Hollywood Art Cult Ctr, 90; Men by Women, Ganymede Gallery, New York, 92; Governors Gallery, Capital Mus, Spokane, Wash, 92; Midwest Watercolor Soc, 16th

Ann, 92. *Pos:* Coordr, Masters Degree Prog in Creative Arts Therapy, Hofstra Univ, 75; exec secry, Gold Coast Watercolor Soc; mem, co-chmn, 2 plus 3 Artists Orgn. *Teaching:* Watercolor & collage, Broward Art Guild, 80-90, Floyd L Wray Found Flamingo Gardens, 87-; workshop leader painting & drawing, Art Adventures Inc, Ft Lauderdale, 84-89; Holiday Park Community Ctr, Ft Lauderdale, 91-93. *Awards:* Savior Faire Lana Award, Midwest Watercolor Soc, 92; Merit Award, North Coast Collage Soc, 92. *Bibliog:* Daily Oklahoman, 2/1/90; Yergean-Musé Int D'Art, Montreal, Can; Joan Davenport (auth), Art Notes, Village Press, 3/92. *Mem:* Miami Watercolor Soc; Am Watercolor Soc; Nat Asn Women Artists; 2 + 3 Artists Asn, (co-chmn); signature mem, Midwest Watercolor Soc; and others. *Media:* Watercolor, Acrylic. *Publ:* Cultural Arts Newsletter, Vol 6, No 9, Broward Art Coun, 87; Complete Guide to Creative Watercolor, Creative Art Pubs, 88; Artists of Fla, vol I and vol II. *Dealer:* Ganymede Gallery New York NY; Dover Gallery Boca Raton FL. *Mailing Add:* 5313 Bayberry Lane Tamarac FL 33319

SMITH, RUTH REININGHAUS See Reininghaus, Ruth (Ruth Reininghaus Smith)

SMITH, SAM
PAINTER, EDUCATOR
b Thorndale, Tex, Feb 11, 18. *Study:* With Randall Davey, Jack Levine, Ben Turner & Carl von Hassler. *Work:* War Dept Hist Properties Sect; Santa Fe Mus; Univ NMex; NMex State Fair Collection; Panhandle Mus Fine Art. *Comn:* Mural, Camp Barkley, Tex, War Dept, 42; paintings, Infantry Weapons, Camp Barkley, 42. *Exhib:* One-man show, Corcoran Gallery Art, Washington, DC, 48; Santa Fe Mus Fine Art, NMex, 49; Botts Mus Art, Albuquerque, NMex, 64; Panhandle-Plains Hist Mus, Canyon, Tex, 64; Roswell Mus Art, NMex, 65. *Teaching:* Prof art, Univ NMex, 56-84, prof emeritus, 84- *Awards:* Questa, NMex Purchase Prize, 62 & First Prize for Watercolor, 62, NMex State Fair; First Prize for Watercolor, Ouray Alpine Show, Colo, 64. *Bibliog:* Robert Ruark (auth), Sam Smith, artist, Assoc Press, 48. *Mem:* Life mem NMex Art League; Artists Equity Asn. *Media:* Watercolor, Oil. *Mailing Add:* PO Box 2006 Telluride CO 81435-2006

SMITH, SHERRI
WEAVER, EDUCATOR
b Chicago, Ill, Mar 21, 43. *Study:* Stanford Univ, Calif, BA, 65; Cranbrook Acad Art, Bloomfield Hills, Mich, MFA, 67. *Work:* Art Inst Chicago; Hackley Art Mus, Muskegon, Mich, Am Tel & Tel Co; Borg Warner Corp; Colorado Springs Fine Arts Ctr, Colo. *Comn:* Wall hangings, Detroit Plaza Hotel, 77; Fed Bldg, Ann Arbor, 78; Du Page Co Hosp, Ill, 78; Int Business Machines, Atlanta. *Exhib:* Mus Mod Art, New York, 69; Biennale of Tapestry, Lausanne, Switz, 71-77; Three-Dimensional Fibers, Govett-Brewster Art Gallery, New Plymouth, NZ, 74; Am Crafts 76, Mus Contemp Art, Chicago, 76; Fiberworks, Cleveland Mus Art, Ohio, 77; one-person show, Hadler Gallery, New York, 78; Mainstream, the Art Fabric Traveling Exhib; and others. *Teaching:* Instr weaving & textile design, Colo State Univ, Ft Collins, 71-75; prof weaving & textile design, Sch Art, Univ Mich, Ann Arbor, 75- *Bibliog:* Larson & Constantine, Beyond Crafts, The Art Fabric, Van Nostrand, 75; Kuenzi (auth), La nouvelle tapisserie, Bonvent, 75; Waller (auth), Textile sculptures, Studio Vista, 77. *Dealer:* Jacques Baruch Gallery 900 N Michigan Ave Chicago IL 60611; Modern Masters Tapestries 11 E 57th New York NY 10022. *Mailing Add:* c/o Alice Simsar Gallery 301 N Main St Ann Arbor MI 48104

SMITH, SHIRLEY
PAINTER
b Wichita, Kans. *Study:* Kans State Univ, BFA; Provincetown Workshop Art Sch, Mass; Art Students League. *Work:* Whitney Mus Am Art, New York; Univ Calif Art Mus, Berkeley; Aldrich Mus Contemp Art, Ridgefield, Conn; Phoenix Art Mus, Ariz; Prudential Insurance Co Am, Newark, NJ; and others. *Exhib:* Am Painting 1970, Va Mus, Richmond; Lyrical Abstraction, Aldrich Mus Contemp Art, 70; Recent Acquisitions & Lyrical Abstraction, Whitney Mus Am Art, New York, 71; From the Mus Collection Art by Women, Univ Calif Art Mus, Berkeley, 73; Auditorium Installation Exhib, Everson Mus, Syracuse, NY, 76-79; Views by Women Artists, Women's Caucus Art, New York, 82; 161st Ann Exhib, Nat Acad Design, New York, 86; Animal Life, 87 & Nature in Art, 88, One Penn Plaza, New York; solo show, Art/EX Gallery, Stamford Mus & Nature Ctr, Conn, 87; Am Acad Inst Arts & Lett Invitational, New York, 90 & 91. *Teaching:* Instr, painting, Teamsters Local 237, New York, 88-92. *Awards:* Grumbacher Artists Mat Co Award Mixed Media, New Eng Exhib, Silvermine, 67; Acad Inst Award, Am Acad Inst Arts & Lett, New York. *Bibliog:* Rosemary Mayer (auth), article, Arts, 2/73; Dorothy Beldon (auth), The Wichita Eagle Beacon, 3/78; Susan Rife (auth), Wichita Eagle, 7/91; Matt Bartel (auth), The Newton Kansan, 7/89 & 7/91. *Mem:* Artists Equity. *Mailing Add:* 141 Wooster St New York NY 10012

SMITH, SUSAN
PAINTER, COLLAGE ARTIST
b Greensburg, Pa. *Study:* Art Students League, 55-57, with Edwin Dickinson; Briarcliff Col, BS, 71; Hunter Col, New York, NY, MA, 76. *Work:* Weatherspoon Art Gallery, Univ NC, Greensboro; Copenhagen Handelsbank, Denmark. *Exhib:* Solo exhib, Westmoreland Mus, Greensburg, Pa, 86; Intericon 1986, Charlottenborg, Copenhagen, Denmark, 86; After Matisse, Travelling Exhib, Worcester Art Mus, Mass, Portland Mus Art, Maine, Queens Mus, Flushing, NY, Chrysler Mus, Norfolk, Va, Dayton Art Inst, Ohio & Phillips Collection, Washington, DC, 86-87. *Teaching:* Lectr art & painting, Sch Visual Arts, New York, 69-70; adj asst prof color, Pratt Inst, Brooklyn, NY, 74; asst prof art, Wagner Col, Staten Island, NY, 82-92. *Awards:* MacDowell Colony Fel, Peterboro, NH, 69; New York Creative Artists Pub Serv Prog Fel, 75-76; Artist Fel Grant, Nat Endowment Arts, Washington, DC, 81. *Bibliog:* Peggy Cyphers (auth), Susan Smith, Arts Mag, 9/91; Stephen Bann & William Allen (coauths), Interpreting Contemporary Art, 91; Yve-Alain Bois (auth), Susan Smith's Archeology, Edinburgh: Reakton Books & New York: Harper Collins Inc, 91; and others. *Media:* Oil. *Dealer:* Margarete Roeder Gallery 545 Broadway New York NY 10012. *Mailing Add:* 39 Bond St New York NY 10012

SMITH, SUSAN CARLTON
PAINTER, SCULPTOR
b Athens, Ga, June 30, 23. *Study:* Univ Ga, Athens, BS & MFA. *Work:* Ga Mus Art & Univ Ga, Athens; Duke Univ Mus Art; Trent Collection, Duke Univ Med Ctr Libr, Durham; Health Affairs Libr, Univ NC; State Botanical Garden, Univ Ga, Athens; Hunt Inst Botanical Doc, Carnegie-Mellon Univ, Pittsburgh, Pa. *Comn:* Portrait, Venus Flytrap (watercolor), Hunt Botanical Libr, Carnegie-Mellon Univ, Pittsburgh, Pa; Nature Sculpture, Am Dance Festival; postcard, Garden Club Am; watercolors, State Botanical Garden, Ga. *Exhib:* NC Wildlife Artists Show, State Mus Natural Hist, Raleigh, 69; Nature Interpretations: Watercolors & Sculptures, Duke Univ Mus Art, 71-; Int Exhib of Botanical Art, Johannesburg, S Africa, 73; Boston Mus Sci, Mass, 74; NC Botanical Garden, 76; Int Mycological Cong, Fla, 77; Traveling Exhib of NC Artists, 78; Second Int Exhib of Botanical Art and Illus, Inst Botanical Doc, Carnegie-Mellon Univ, Pittsburgh, Pa; and many others. *Pos:* Asst cur, Trent Collection, Med Ctr Libr, Duke Univ, retired; conservator, Duke Med Ctr Libr, 77-89. *Teaching:* Instr nature sculpture workshops, Duke Univ & State Botanical Garden Ga, Univ Ga, retired. *Awards:* Best Children's Bk Illus for Ladybug, Ladybug, Am Inst Graphic Arts, 69; Printing Indust Am Award for Illus for Hey Bug & Other Poems About Little Things, 72. *Bibliog:* Watercolors & nature sculptures, Athens Banner Herald, 77; Ann Commire (auth), Something About the Author, Vol XII. *Media:* Watercolor; Natural Materials. *Publ:* Illusr, Wildflowers of North Carolina, Univ NC Press, 68; illusr & contribr, Ladybug, Ladybug, 69 & illusr, Hey Bug! & Other Poems About Little Things, 72, Am Heritage Press, New York; illusr, A Child's Book of Flowers, Doubleday Publ Co, 76; A Book of Flowers, Sacrum Press, 86. *Dealer:* John Hawkins Assoc 71 West 23rd St Suite 1600 New York NY 10010. *Mailing Add:* 145 Woodhaven Ridge Athens GA 30606

SMITH, V JOACHIM
PAINTER, WRITER
b Grand Island, Nebr, Apr 3, 29. *Study:* Chouinard Art Inst, Los Angeles; Calif State Univ, Long Beach, BA, MA. *Work:* San Francisco Mus Art, Calif; Long Beach Mus Art; Newport Harbor Art Mus, Newport Beach, Calif; Laguna Art Mus, Calif; La Jolla Mus Contemp Art, Calif; plus others in Europe and America. *Exhib:* Mus Mod Art, Turin, Italy, 62; Mus-Manifeste (traveling exhib), Austria, WGer & Italy, 64-65; one-man shows, Long Beach Mus Art, 60, Santa Barbara Mus Art, Calif, 62, Pasadena Art Mus, Calif, 63, Los Angeles Munic Art Gallery, 68, Los Angeles Co Mus Art, Los Angeles, 72, Newport Harbor Art Mus, 75 & Calif State Univ, 85; plus others. *Teaching:* Prof drawing & painting, Calif State Univ, Fullerton, 62-80, chmn art dept, 76-77, vchmn art dept, 77-80, prof emer, 81. *Awards:* Over seventy-five awards for painting in Calif. *Bibliog:* Michele Tapie (auth), Morphologie Autre, Int Inst Aesthetic Res, Turin, 60; article in Artforum, Vol 1 (1962); Allan S Weller (auth), Contemporary American painting & sculpture, Univ Ill Press, 67; T Holst (auth), Vic Joachim Smith Retrospective, Calif State Univ, Fullerton, 85. *Media:* Mixed. *Publ:* Auth, Morris Graves, 63 & The Pacific Coast Invitational, 63, Artforum; numerous other gallery/museum publications, art and literary journals, since 1962. *Mailing Add:* Dept Art Calif State Univ Fullerton CA 92634

SMITH, VERNELL EDWARD
CARTOONIST, ILLUSTRATOR
b Ipswitch, Mass, Oct 8, 38. *Study:* Famous Artists Sch, Westport, Conn, 59; Mus Fine Arts, Boston, Mass, 62. *Work:* Equestrian Collection, Palm Beach, Fla. *Comn:* Be-But, comn by Abigail Fuller, Rye Beach, NH, 91; Unsung Heros, comn by Clint Nangle, Highland Beach, Fla, 91; Nuggett, comn by Tim Clark, Hamilton, Mass, 92; Near Side Fore Shot, comn by Peter Bundy, Hamilton, Mass, 92; The Prince of Wales, comn by HRH Prince Charles, Buckingham Palace, Eng, 92. *Publ:* Illustr, New Zealand, Polo Auceland, NZ, 90; Polo Sidelines, Palm Beach, Fla, 90 &91; Austrailian Polo, Melborne, 89; Hurlingham Polo, Buenos Aries, Arg, 91. *Mailing Add:* c/o Gulfstream Equity Management 21301 Powerline Rd No 206 Boca Raton FL 33433

SMITH, VINCENT D
PAINTER, PRINTMAKER
b Brooklyn, NY, Dec 12, 29. *Study:* Art Students League New York with Reginald Marsh, 53; Brooklyn Mus, NY, 54-56; Skowhegan Sch Painting & Sculpture, Maine, studied with Sidney Simon & Ben Shann, 55; Bub Blackburn Printmaking Workshop, New York, with Krisna Reddy & Bob Cale, 71. *Work:* Mus Mod Art, New York; Columbus Gallery Fine Art, Ohio; Newark Mus Asn, NJ; Brooklyn Mus, NY; Ackland Art Mus. *Comn:* One mural on canvas, Boys & Girls High Sch, Brooklyn Bd Educ, New York, 76; mural, Crotona Social Serv Ctr Human Resources Admin, New York, 80; mural, Oberia P Dempsey Multi-Serv Ctr, 88; two mosaic murals, 116th St subway sta, Metrop Transit Authority, New York. *Exhib:* Contemp Black Am Artist, Whitney Mus Am Art, New York; People & Places, Whitney Mus Downtown, New York, 74; one-man shows, Kibo Art Gallery, Mt Kilimanjaro, Tanzonia, 73, Reading Pub Mus, Pa, 74, Portland Art Mus Maine, 74, Erie Art Ctr, Pa, 77 & Larcada Gallery, New York, 67, 68, 70, 73, 75 & 77; Passages East/West - A Retrospective 1964-1989, Schenectady

Mus, NY; solo traveling show, Riding on a Blue Note, Louis Abrons Art Ctr, New York, 90. *Teaching:* Instr painting & printmaking, Whitney Mus Am Art, New York, 67-76; artist-in-residence, Cite des Arts' Int, Paris, France, summer 78. *Awards:* Nat Endowment Arts Travel Grant, 73; Childe Hassam Fund Purchase Award, Am Acad Arts & Letters, 73-74; Thomas B Clarke Award, 149th Ann Exhib, Nat Acad Design, 74. *Bibliog:* The Pulse of Afro-American Culture, 30 minute film on Vincent Smith, his work and influence, WTVG; Peter Mark (auth), African influences in contemporary Black American painting, Art Voices, 1-2/81; Judith Wilson (auth), Afro-American artists in the 20th century, Art Am, 80. *Media:* Acrylic, oil; Etching. *Publ:* Contribr, Atticia Book, Custom Commun Systs, 73; illusr, Folklore Stories from Africa, Garrard Publ, 75. *Mailing Add:* 264 E Broadway New York NY 10002

SMITHER, EDWARD MURRAY
DEALER, CONSULTANT
b Huntsville, Tex, July 23, 37. *Study:* Sam Houston State Univ, BS, 58; Dallas Mus Fine Arts Sch, 59. *Pos:* Dir, Cranfill Gallery, Dallas, 70-72; owner & dir, Smither Gallery, Dallas, 72-74; co-owner, Delahunty Gallery, Dallas, 74-82; pvt dealer & consult, 83-; adv, AH Belo Corp, Estates of Otis Dozier, Jerry Bywaters, Charles Taylor Bowling, Dallas. *Mem:* Dallas Mus Art. *Mailing Add:* 1934 Kessler Pkwy Dallas TX 75208

SMITH-THEOBALD, SHARON A
MUSEUM DIRECTOR
b New Jersey, Feb 12, 42. *Study:* State Col NJ, BA; Hofstra Univ, MA. *Pos:* Dir, Bridgton Art Gallery, 69-75; exec dir, Greater Lafayette Mus Art, 78-89; bd mem, Ind State Coun, 82-92. *Teaching:* Lectr commun, Wilfrid Laurier Univ Can, 75-77; instr art appreciation, Greater Lafayette Mus Art, 78-89. *Awards:* Estabrook Award, Hofstra Univ, 87. *Mem:* Am Asn Mus (chair, Small Mus Adminrs Comt, 87-89); Am Soc Appraisers, Ind Chap (pres, 92; state dir, 93). *Res:* Women artists, specifically Laura Anne Fry and Alice Baber. *Publ:* Auth, Media, metaphor, manipulation, New Art Examiner, 81; Sculpture in the Space Age, 85 & Laura Anne Frye: Rookwood and Beyond, 86, Greater Lafayette Mus Art; Latin American Visions I, Am Express Found, 88; Arts Indiana, 88. *Mailing Add:* Greater Lafayette Art Museum 101 South 9th St Lafayette IN 47901

SMITH-WARREN, KATHARINE
CURATOR, CONSULTANT
b Huntington, NY, June 5, 45. *Study:* Marymount Col, Tarrytown, NY, BFA, 67; Hunter Col, City Univ New York, MA, 71. *Collections Arranged:* The Fine Art of Health Care-Art from the Kaiser Permanente Collection, Boulder Ctr Visual Arts, 87. *Pos:* Colo ed, Artspace: Southwestern Contemp Arts Quart, 77-82; pres, Art Mgt Planning Serv, 79- *Teaching:* Adj fac, Univ Col, Univ Denver. *Bibliog:* The War Between the Collectors, Forbes, 8/19/91; Working with Art, US Air Mag, 5/91. *Mem:* Asn Prof Art Adv (pres, 90-92). *Res:* Contemporary art, photography and crafts with emphasis on the American West; nineteenth century art; art & politics. *Publ:* Auth, Visions of the West, Rocky Mountain, 81; Contemporary Indian painting, Portfolio, 82; A Western Vision of Art, History and Work (catalog), 82; contribr, Contemporary Artists, St Martins Press, 83; Land Escapes (catalog), 91. *Mailing Add:* Art Mgt Planning Services Inc 1660 Wynkoop St, Suite 1060 Denver CO 80202

SMOKLER, STANLEY B
SCULPTOR
b Bronx, New York, Nov 27, 44. *Study:* Univ Pittsburgh, studio art with Virgil Cantini, BFA, 67; Pratt Inst, with George McNeil & Calvin Albert, MFA, 75; also, study with Anthony Caro, 85. *Work:* Fifth Ave Raquet Club; Morgan Trust, New York; Minskoff Realty, 88. *Comn:* Steel sculpture (abstract), comn by Nitkin Alkalay-Robbins, New York, 82; steel sculpture abstractions, Penn & Schoen Assoc, 84, Edelman Pub Relations, 84; wall-relief sculpture (steel), Tanenbaum-Haber Co, New York, 85. *Exhib:* Sculpture Exhib, Salmagundi Club, New York, 81; Terminal Art Show, Brooklyn, NY, 83; In the Courtyard, PS 1, Long Island, NY, 83; Objects, Paulo Salvador, New York, 85; New Art in New York, Parsons Sch Design, New York, 85; Biennial, Everson Mus, Syracuse, NY, 85; Abstractions, Hudson Highland Mus, Cornwall, NY, 86; Heads, Mokotoff Gallery, New York, 86; Case de Picos, Segovia, Spain, 86; one-person shows, Allegheny Col, 88 & Ledis Flam, NY, 89; Three Rivers Arts Festival, Pittsburgh, Pa; Delaware Art Mus, Wilmington, 90; Bill Bace Gallery, New York, 91. *Pos:* Artist-in-residence, Art Park, Nat Heritage Trust, Lewiston, NY, 85; guest lectr contemp art, IBM, New York, 85; fel, Triangle Artists, Pinc Plains, NY, 86. *Teaching:* Guest lectr mod art, NY Univ, 84. *Awards:* NY Heritage Trust Grant, 85; City of New York Grant, 86. *Bibliog:* Palmer Paroner (auth), New Sculpture, Artspeak, 6/81; Susan Drew (auth), Art in public places (radio interview), WBAI, 8/83; The ladies mile, NY Times, 6/86. *Mem:* Found Community Artists; Col Art Asn Am; Int Sculpture Ctr; Lincoln Neighborhood Ctr Arts (adv comt). *Media:* Cast Steel. *Mailing Add:* 873 Broadway No 401 New York NY 10003

SMOLAREK, WALDEMAR
PAINTER, PRINTMAKER
b Warsaw, Poland, Sept 5, 37; Can citizen. *Study:* Warsaw Sch Art, 52; Warsaw Acad Fine Arts, 57, with Zygmunt Tom-Kiewicz & Wincenty Sliwinski. *Work:* Miami Mus Mod Art; Mus Mod Art, Stockholm; Mus Nat, Warsaw, Poland; Artist Coop, San Francisco; Selected Artist Gallery, New York. *Exhib:* One-man shows, Toporow Gallery, Los Angeles, 60 & Santa Barbara, Calif, 61; Gallery, Miami, 62; Schramm Galleries, Ft Lauderdale, 63; Espozione Int Pittura Scultura, Padova, Italy, 63; Langton Gallery, London, 77; Harrison Galleries, Vancouver, BC, 86. *Teaching:* Instr form & color composition, Warsaw Sch Art, 57-60. *Media:* Oil, Watercolor; Serigraphy, Woodcut. *Publ:* North Star News, (article), 8/18/76. *Dealer:* Art Emporium 2928 granville St Vancouver BC V6H 3H7 Can; Osborne Marquis Ltd 32 Lafayette Pl 2nd fl Greenwich CT 06830. *Mailing Add:* 807-1424 Nelson St Vancouver BC V6G 1L9 Canada

SMONGESKI, JOSEPH LEON
PAINTER, DESIGNER
b Two Rivers, Wis, Feb 6, 14. *Study:* Art Inst Chicago; Univ Chicago; Univ Wis-Madison. *Work:* Boston Mus Fine Arts; Thomas Mann Publ Libr, Two Rivers; Copley Soc, Boston; Chicago Art Inst; Rahr West Art Mus, Manitowoc, Wis; Milton Art Mus, Mass; and others. *Comn:* Mural, Arnold Nickerson Castle; portraits, Mr & Mrs Nickerson, Dr Slomkoski, Joanna Ganger, Betty Lape, James T Lape, Jane Jordan. *Exhib:* Art Inst Chicago, 39; Copley Soc Boston, Boston Mus Fine Arts, 58 & 71-75; One-man shows, Oshkosh Pub Mus, Wis, 82 & Art Complex Mus, Duxbury, Mass, 84; Sandwich Mass Pub Lib, 87-; Rahr-Wesst Art Mus, Manitowoc, Wis, 89; Milton Art Mus, Mass, 90; Wellesley Community Col, Mass, 92; Bentley Col, Waltham, Mass, 93. *Pos:* Color consult, Western Publ Co, New York, 41-46; designer, D C Heath & Co, Boston, 46-65; art dir, D C Heath & Raytheon, Lexington, Mass, 65-77. *Teaching:* Instr painting, S Shore Art Ctr; Milton Adult Educ Ctr, Mass. *Awards:* New Eng Book Show Award, Bookbuilders of Boston, 73; Drawing Award, Salmagundi Club. *Bibliog:* Articles, Quincy Patriot Ledger, 74; Articles, Boston Globe, 74-75, 84 & 90. *Mem:* Copley Soc Boston; Milton Art Asn; Salmagundi Club New York; S Shore Art Ctr, Cohasset, Mass; and others. *Media:* Watercolor, Oil; Lithographs. *Publ:* Retrospective color brochure, Rahr West Art Mus & Milton Art Mus, 89-90. *Dealer:* Chapellier Gallery 815 Park Ave New York NY 10021; Crane Collection 121 Newbury St Boston MA 02116. *Mailing Add:* 42 Brook Wollaston MA 02170

SMUSKIEWICZ, TED
PAINTER, EDUCATOR
b Chicago, Ill, Sept 22, 32. *Study:* Am Acad Art, AA, 56-60. *Work:* Northern Indiana Public Service Co, Hammond, Ind. *Exhib:* Union League Club Exhib, Chicago, 78 & 81; one-man show, Freeport Art Mus, Ill, 79; Realist Exhib, Mongerson Gallery, Chicago, 80; Impressionist Exhib, El Pardo Gallery, Scottsdale, Ariz, 83; Denver Rotary Club's Artists of Am, Denver, Colo, 88 & 90; Butler Inst of Am Art, 88 & 89; Salmagundi 11th Ann Exhib, New York, NY, 88; 4th Ann Arts for the Parks Nat Competition, 90; Oil Painters Am, 1st Nat Exhibit, Chicago, Ill, 92. *Teaching:* Instr oil & pastel painting & life drawing, Am Acad Art, Chicago, 79- *Awards:* Diamond Medal, Palette & Chisel Acad, 70; Finalist, Am Artist Mag Competition, 78; 1st Place Award, Municipal Art League Chicago, 90. *Bibliog:* Article, Back of the yards artist, Chicago Back Yards J, 70; article, Midwest Art Mag, 5/87. *Mem:* Palette & Chisel Acad Fine Arts, Chicago, Ill; Oil Painters Am, Park Ridge, Ill. *Media:* Oil, Pastel. *Publ:* Auth, Expressive painting, Am Artist Mag, 84; Creative Painting of Everyday Subjects, Watson-Guptill, 86; Oil Painting Step By Step, North Light, 92. *Dealer:* De Lind Gallery Milwaukee WI; Prince Galleries Chicago IL. *Mailing Add:* 1356 Whitcomb Des Plaines IL 60018

SMYTH, CRAIG HUGH
ADMINISTRATOR, HISTORIAN
b New York, NY, July 28, 15. *Study:* Princeton Univ, AB, 38, MFA, 41, PhD, 56; Harvard Univ, Hon MA, 75. *Pos:* Res asst & sr mus aide, Nat Gallery Art, Washington, DC, 41-42; dir, Harvard Univ Ctr for Ital Renaissance Studies, Florence, 73-85; adv comt & consult chmn, Getty Ctr Hist Art & Humanities, 82-; trustee, The Burlington Mag, 87- *Teaching:* Lectr, Frick Collection, New York, 46-50; from asst prof to prof, Inst Fine Arts, NY Univ, 50-73, actg dir & actg head dept fine arts, 51-53, dir & head grad dept fine arts, 53-73; prof fine arts, Harvard Univ, 73-85, prof emeritus, 85-; Samuel Kress prof, Ctr Advan Study Visual Arts, Nat Gallery Art, Washington, DC, 87-88. *Awards:* Acad Arts & Sci Fel, 78- *Bibliog:* Renaissance Studies in Honor of Craig Hugh Smyth, 2 vols, edited by A Morrogh, F Superbi Giofredi, P Morselli, E Borsook, Florence, Giunti Barbera, 85. *Mem:* US Nat Comt Hist Art (55-85); Metrop Mus Art (hon trustee, 68-); Am Philos Soc (mem, 79-); Comt Ctr Advan Study Visual Art, Nat Gallery Art, Washington, DC (Samuel Kress prof, 87-88); Inst Advan Study (mem, 78, vis, 71, 83, 85-86); and others. *Res:* 16th century Italian painting and drawing; 16th century Italian architecture. *Publ:* Auth, Bronzino as draughtsman, 71; coauth, Michelangelo & St Peter's--II: Observations on the interior of the Apses, a model of the Apse vault, and related drawings, Romisches Jahrbuch fur Kunstgeschichte, 75; Michelangelo Architect, the Facade of San Lorenzo and the Drum and Dome of St Peters, Olivetti, Milan, 88; Repatriation of Art from the Central Collecting Point in Munich after World War II, 88; Mannerism & Maniera, rev ed, 92; ed, Michelangelo Drawings, Nat Gallery Art, Washington, DC, 92; and others. *Mailing Add:* PO Box 39 Cresskill NJ 07626

SMYTH, ED
ILLUSTRATOR, PAINTER
b New York, NY, May 21, 16. *Study:* Pratt Inst; Columbia Univ with Mario Cooper; Wash Univ with Gustav Goetsch & Fred Carpenter. *Exhib:* Wyo State Art Mus, Cheyenne, 75; Royal Watercolor Soc, Nat Cowboy Hall of Fame, Oklahoma City, 76; Wyo Image, State Capitol, Cheyenne, 77. *Bibliog:* Archie L Nash (auth), Ed Smyth, Artist with brush & camera, Western Horseman Mag, 9/67; Jack Rice (auth), Artist with camera is drawn to horses, St Louis Post-Dispatch Mag, 10/67; Diane Simmons (auth), article, Art West, 8-9/82; Harold & Peggy Samuels (coauth), Contemporary Western Artists, 78. *Mem:* Wyo Artists' Asn; Sheridan Artist's Guild. *Media:* Watercolor; Pen & Ink, Conte. *Publ:* Auth & illusr, Born to buck, Western Horseman, 10/67;

Hooked by the Wily Trout, Saturday Evening Post, 9/72; illusr, Murchison's moose, Saturday Evening Post, fall 74; auth & illusr, Big Horn art bonanza-Bradford Brinton Mem, Art West, Fall 1977; calendar illusr, Purina Mills/Cattle Horse chows, 89; illusr, Story Artist Ed Smyth Shares Special Vision Through His Paintings, Jim Newsom, Wyo Rural Elec News, Nov 88. *Mailing Add:* The Line Camp Gallery 18 Rosebud Ln Story WY 82842

SNEED, PATRICIA M
COLLECTOR, CONSULTANT
b Spencer, Iowa, Oct 24, 22. *Study:* Drake Univ, 40-42; Univ Cincinnati, 45-46. *Collections Arranged:* Fifty Artists for Fifty States (nat art exhib), 65-; Art in Other Media, 70. *Pos:* Founder & mem women's bd, Rockford Art Mus, currently. *Mem:* Am Fedn Arts. *Collection:* Contemporary American art. *Mailing Add:* 1311 Parkview Ave No 206A Rockford IL 61107

SNELL, ERIC
SCULPTOR
b Guernsey, Channel Islands, 1953. *Study:* Birmingham Polytechnic, London, Eng, 72-73; Hornsey Col Art, London, 73-76, DAAD Artist-in-Berlin Prog, 85-86. *Work:* Univ E Anglia, Norwich, Eng; Mus Mod Art, Linz, Austria; Art Gallery of Hamilton, Ont; La Jolla Mus Contemp Art. *Exhib:* Solo exhibs, Galerie Work, Kaiserslauterm, WGer, 88, Galerie Bernard Jordan, Paris, France, 88, CREDAC, Centre d'Art Contemporain, Ivry, France, 88, Galerie Corla Feuhr, Munich, Ger, 89, Galerie Schoeller, Dusseldorf, Ger, 89, Galerie Fortlaan 17, Ghent, Belgium, 90; Distances, 86, Ephemerite, 87, Chapelle St Louis de la Salpetriere, Paris, France; Konstruktion, Kontemplation, Expression, Galerie im Trudelhaus, Baden, Switz, 87; Mathematik in der Kunst der letzen Dreizig Jahre, Wilhelm- Hack-Mus, Ludwigshafen, Ger, 87; Die Ecke, Kantonales Kunstmuseum, Sion, Switz & Austellungsraume, Ger, 88; 49th Parallel, New York, 89. *Bibliog:* John Bentley Mays (auth), Drawing's physical qualities focus of artist's work, Globe & Mail, Toronto, 12/16/88; Liliana Albertazzi (auth), Paris, Contemporanea, 1-2/89; Susan Freudenheim (auth), La Jolla: Eric Snell, Artforum Int, 1/89. *Mailing Add:* c/o Olga Korper Gallery 17 Morrow Ave Toronto ON M6R 2H9 Canada

SNELSON, KENNETH D
SCULPTOR, COMPUTER
b Pendleton, Ore, June 29, 27. *Study:* Black Mountain Col, NC, 48-49; with Fernand Leger, Paris, 50. *Work:* Whitney Mus Am Art & Mus Mod Art, New York; Staedelijk Mus, Amsterdam, Holland; City Buffalo, NY; Storm King Art Ctr; Albright-Knox Art Gallery, Buffalo, NY; Hirshhorn Mus & Sculpture Garden, Washington, DC; Japan Iron & Steel Fedn, Osaka. *Comn:* Baltimore Inner Harbor, Md, 80; Albright-Knox Art Gallery, 82; Stanford Univ, Calif, 82; Mus Mod Art, Shiga, Japan. *Exhib:* Int Sculpture Symp, Osaka, Japan, 69; one-man shows, Ger, 71, Wilhelm Lehmbruck Mus, Ger & Berlin Nationalgalerie, 77, Hirshhorn Mus, 81 & Albright-Knox Art Gallery, 81; Portrait of an Atom Traveling Exhib, 79-83; Addison Gallery Am Art, Phillips Acd, Andover, Mass, 84; Toledo Mus, Ohio, 84; Aldrich Mus Contemp Art, Ridgefield, Conn, 85; Cleveland Ctr Contemp Art, Ohio, 85; solo exhib, The Nature of Structure, Nat Acad of Sci, Washington, DC, 90. *Awards:* Deutscher Akad Austauschdienst for Berlin Kunstlerprogram, 76; Am Inst Archit Medal, 81; Amer Acad & Inst Arts and Letters, Artist Award, 87. *Bibliog:* Articles, Artforum, 5/77 & Art News, 2/81; Martica Sawin (auth), Kenneth Snelson: unbounded space, Arts Mag, 9/81; article, Print Collector's Newsletter, 84. *Media:* Mixed. *Publ:* Auth, A design for the atom, Indust Design, 2/63; auth, Continuous Tension, Discontinuous Compression Structures, 65 & A Model for Atomic Forms, 66 & 78, US Patent Off; Portrait of An Atom, 81. *Mailing Add:* 140 Sullivan St New York NY 10012

SNIDOW, GORDON E
PAINTER, SCULPTOR
b Paris, Mo, Sept 30, 36. *Study:* Art Ctr Col Design, BA. *Work:* Nat Cowboy Hall Fame, Oklahoma City; Phoenix Mus, Ariz; Gilcrease Mus, Tulsa, Okla; Mont Hist Soc, Helena; Cowboy Artists Am Mus, Kerrville, Tex. *Exhib:* Cowboy Artist Am Ann Exhib, Nat Cowboy Hall Fame & Phoenix Art Mus, 65-75 & 78; two-man show, Nat Cowboy Hall Fame, 70; one-man show, C M Russell Gallery, Mont Hist Soc, 73; Cowboy Art Exhib, Grande Palais, Paris France, 80; Am Western Art Exhib, Beijing, China, 81; retrospective, Gilcrease Mus, Tulsa, Okla, 81; The American Cowboy, Libr Cong, 83. *Teaching:* Instr workshop, Cowboy Artists Am Mus, Kerrville, Tex, currently. *Awards:* Silver Medal for Watercolor, Cowboy Artist of Am, 74, Mem Award, 78; Gold Medal, 75, 77-79 & 81, Best of Show, 77, 78 & 82, Colt Award, 79, Silver, 84, Western Assoc, Phoenix Art Mus; and numerous other awards. *Bibliog:* Meigs (auth), The Cowboy in American Prints, Sage Swallow, 72; Broder (auth), Bronzes of the American West, Abrams, 74; Hassrick (auth), American Painting Today, Watson-Guptill, 75. *Mem:* Cowboy Artist Am (secy-treas, 67-68, vpres, 68-69, pres, 78-79 & 84-85). *Media:* Gouache. *Publ:* Contribr, Persimmon Hill, 70; auth, Gordon Snidow, Chronicler of the Contemporary West, 73; Hanging On: Gordon Snidow Portrays the Cowboy Heritage, Northland Press. *Mailing Add:* 41 Hobb Rd Los Lunas NM 87031

SNODGRASS-KING, JEANNE OWENS (MRS M EUGENE KING)
CONSULTANT, WRITER
b Muskogee, Okla, Sept 12, 27. *Study:* Art Instr, Inc; Northeastern State Col; Okla Univ. *Collections Arranged:* 214 exhibs of Indian art & artifacts, Philbrook Art Ctr, 55-68; Am Indian Artists Nat Competition Ann, Philbrook Art Ctr, 55-68; Beaver-McCombs Mem Exhib; Oscar Howe Retrospective, 1979-1982. *Pos:* Asst to dir & cur Am Indian Art, Philbrook Art Ctr, 55-68; admin asst to pres, Educ Dimensions, Inc, 69-71; registr, Gilcrease Mus, 73-90; assoc, Am Indian Affairs & mem Arts & Crafts Adv Comt; juror, many nat & regional Indian Art Exhibs. *Teaching:* Lectr, American Indian painting. *Awards:* Outstanding Contrib to Indian Art Award, US Dept Interior, 67. *Mem:* Okla Mus Asn (charter secy); Tulsa Hist Soc; Am Asn Mus. *Publ:* Ed, American Indian Basketry, 64; auth, American Indian Painters: A Biographical Directory, Heye Found, 68; American Indian Painting, Amarillo Art Ctr, Tex, 81; contribr, Oscar Howe, A Retrospective Exhibition, 82; auth, articles, Gilcrease Mag, 73-82, Southwestern Art Mag, 82-85 & Am Indian Art Mag, 85. *Mailing Add:* 3931 S Madison Ave Tulsa OK 74105

SNOW, CYNTHIA REEVES
PAINTER
b Laurel Springs, NC, Oct 2, 07. *Study:* Univ NC, Greensboro, AB; Peabody Col, Nashville, Tenn, MA; NY Univ; Univ Minn; Walter Art Ctr. *Work:* Thaw (oil), New Britain Mus Am Art, Conn; watercolors, SDak Mem Art Ctr, Benton Mus Art, Storrs, Conn & Eastern Conn Col, Willimantic; Southern Conn Univ, New Haven; Weatherspoon Art Gallery, Greensboro, NC. *Exhib:* Eastern Connecticut Artists, Slater Mem Mus, 73; San Diego Mus Art; Quint Gallery Invitational, Landscape Theme, 87; exhib & rev, TV Channel 38, Del Mar, Calif; Adobe Gallery, Vista, Calif; and others. *Teaching:* Instr, Fla State Univ, Tallahassee, 40-47; prof, Univ Conn, Storrs, 48-78, emer prof, 78-*Awards:* Watercolor Prize for Landscape Theme-9b, New Eng Ann, Mystic, Conn, 73; John Slade Ely Award, Nat Soc Women Artists, 74; First Prize, Conn Watercolor Soc, 77; First Prize, Del Mar Centennial, Calif, 85. *Mem:* San Diego Art Guild; Nat Soc Women Artists; Conn Acad Fine Arts. *Media:* Watercolor, Oil. *Mailing Add:* 13663 Mar Scenic Dr Del Mar CA 92014

SNOW, JOHN
PRINTMAKER, PAINTER
b Vancouver, BC, Dec 12, 11. *Study:* Univ Calgary, LLD, 84. *Work:* Victoria & Albert Mus, London, Eng; Nat Gallery Can; Univ Toronto; Can Coun. *Exhib:* Premiere Expos Bienale Int Gravure, Tokyo & Osaka, Japan, 57; 5th Int Biennial Color Lithography, Cincinnati, 58; Royal Acad Arts, London, 63; Cardiff Commonwealth Arts Festival, Cardiff & Brit Isles, 65; Salon Beaux Arts, Paris, 69; one-man retrospective, Edmonton Art Gallery, 89. *Awards:* C W Jeffrey's Award, Can Soc Graphic Art, 61; Jessie Dow Award, Montreal Mus Fine Arts, 62. *Bibliog:* Ken Jones (dir), The Sad Phoenician and Friends (film), Clopton Films. *Mem:* Can Soc Graphic Art; Royal Can Acad Arts. *Media:* All. *Mailing Add:* 915 18th Ave SW Calgary AB T2T 0H2 Canada

SNOW, LEE ERLIN
PAINTER, INSTRUCTOR
b Buffalo, NY, Jan 2, 24. *Study:* Univ Buffalo, BA, 47; Otis Art Inst, with Joseph Young, scholar; Univ Calif, Los Angeles, with Neda Al-Hilali. *Work:* Skirball Mus, Los Angeles; Halls Crown Ctr, Kansas City; Craft & Folk Art Mus, Los Angeles. *Comn:* Mosaic portrait Bess Hawes, Folk Music Classes Univ Calif, Los Angeles; Mosaic portrait Rebecca Berman, Teaneck, NJ. *Exhib:* Solo shows, Southwest Craft Ctr Gallery, San Antonio, 75, Front Rm, Dallas, Tex, 76 & Galeria de Sol, Santa Barbara, Calif, 76; Art Rental Gallery, Los Angeles Co Mus Art, 76-80; Jewish Fedn Craft Show, Los Angeles, 83; Los Angeles Art Asn Exhib, Craft & Folk Art Mus; Santa Barbara Art Asn, 84-92; Juried Weavers Guild, 84 & 85; Adult Educ Fac Shows 85-92; Gallery 113, Santa Barbara, Calif. *Pos:* Interviewer, Starship Earth, KHJ Radio, Los Angeles. *Teaching:* Instr multimedia fibre, Barnsdall Arts & Crafts Ctr, Los Angeles, 72-76 & Los Angeles Co Mus Art, 75; workshop leader non-loom weaving, World Crafts Conf, Toronto, Ont, 74; instr, Necklace Design-Adult Educ, Santa Barbara, 85-92; Beads, Santa Barbara Art Mus, 87. *Awards:* Third Prize Painting & Award Study, Westwood Art Asn, 63. *Bibliog:* Lois McAfee (auth), Oh, what a tangled web, Sun-Tel, San Bernardino, 1/75; article, Los Angeles Times Home Mag, 12/17/78; Santa Barbara News Press, 92. *Mem:* Los Angeles Art Asn; Am Crafts Coun; Southern Calif Weavers Guild; Santa Barbara Art Asn; Goleta Valley Art Asn. *Media:* Oil, Watercolor. *Publ:* Coauth (with Dona Mellach), Weaving Off-Loom, 73 & contribr, Creating Art From Fibers and Fabrics, 74, Regnery; contribr, How to Create Your Own Designs, Doubleday, 75; Exotic Needlework, 78 & Ethnic Jewelry, 81, Crown; coauth, Creative Stitchery with Dona Meilach, Regnery. *Mailing Add:* 333 Old Mill Rd No 284 Santa Barbara CA 93110

SNOW, MARY R
PAINTER
b Logan, Utah, Mar 06, 08. *Study:* Univ Utah, BA, 29; studied with Nicolai Cikoysky, Corcoran Gallery, 34-39, Karl Knaths, Philips Gallery, 41, Max Pechstein & Karl Hofer, Berlin, 47-48. *Work:* Massillon Mus, Ohio; Lighthouse Gallery, Tequest, Fla; Children to Children Mus, Washington, DC. *Exhib:* Nat Asn Women Ann, Nat Acad Design, New York, 66-89; Soc Wash Ann, Smithsonian Inst, Washington, DC, 53-68; Metrop Mus New Talent, Va Mus Fine Arts, Richmond, 51; Fla Ann Exhib, Norton Gallery, W Palm Beach, Fla, 75-80; Major Fla Artists, Harmon Gallery, Naples & Sarasota, Fla, 78; Sarasota Ann, Sarasota Art Asn Gallery, Fla, 89; one-man show, Gov's Club Christmas Show, West Palm Beach, Fla, 91-92; Fla Artists Group Gallery, Long Boat Key, Fla, 92; and others. *Pos:* Pres, Soc Washington Artists, DC, 51-53, (1st woman pres); pres, Artists Guild, Washington, DC, 58-59; bd dirs & exhib chmn, Lighthouse Gallery Found, Tequesta, Fla, 69-89; state of Fla chmn, Florida Artist Group, 90- *Teaching:* Box Elder High, Brigham, Utah, 29-30; Art, Granite High, Salt Lake City, Utah, 31-34. *Awards:* Gold Medal, 1st Award, Soc Wash Artists, Smithsonian, 52; Watercolor Award, Nat Asn W A Grumbacher, 66 & 78; Ann Watercolor Award, Norton Gallery, Norton, 79; President's Award, Cornell Fine Arts Mus, Rollins Col, 87,; Honorable Mention, Harmon Gallery, Naples & Sarasota, Fla, 89. *Bibliog:* Washington Artists Today, Artists Equity, 67; Profile An Artist, Courier News, Lighthouse Gallery, 78; Artists of Florida, Mountain Productions, NMex, 88. *Mem:* Nat Asn Women Artists; Lighthouse Gallery (bd dirs, 69-89); Artists Guild, Norton Gallery (bd dirs, 74-74); Fla Artist Group (chap chmn, 88-90); Women Art Mus, Washington, DC (chap chmn, 88-90). *Media:* Acrylic, watercolor. *Mailing Add:* 291 River Dr Tequesta FL 33458

SNOW, MICHAEL
PAINTER, FILMMAKER
b Toronto, Ont, Dec 10, 29. *Study:* Ont Col Art, Toronto. *Work:* Mus Mod Art & Albright-Knox Art Gallery, New York; Art Gallery of Ont, Toronto; Montreal Mus Fine Arts; Nat Gallery Can, Ottawa; Univ Waterloo, Ont. *Comn:* Photo-sculpture works, Gov't Can Bldg, North York, 78; Flightstop, Cadillac Fairview Comn, Toronto Eaton's Ctr, 79; Hologram Gallery, Round House, Expo '86, Vancouver, BC, 86; Audience, Skydome, Toronto, Ont, 88-89; photo mural, Reflections, Can Embassy, Wash, 89. *Exhib:* Solo exhibs, Isaacs Gallery, 79, 82, 84, 86, 87, 88, 89 & 91, Forest City Gallery, London, Ontario, 87, Mississauga Civic Centre Art Gallery, Ontario, 87, Hara Mus Contemp Art, Tokyo, Japan, 88 & Ruine der Kunste Berlin, Germany, 88; Festival des Arts Electroniques de Rennes, France, 88; Images du Eutur 88, Art et Nouvelles Technologies, Montreal, 88; Vanishing Presence, Traveling, 88-90; The Isaacs Gallery, 90; Passages de l'image, Centre Georges Pompidou, Paris, Barcelona, Toronto, Columbus, San Francisco, 90-92; Robert Fones, Robert McNealy, Michael Snow, SL Simpson Gallery, Toronto, Ont, 92. *Teaching:* Prof advan film, Yale Univ, 70; vis artist, Nova Scotia Col Art & Design, Halifax, 70 & 74 & Ont Col Art, Toronto, 73, 74 & 76; vis prof, Princeton Univ, 88. *Awards:* Guggenheim Fel, 72; Best Independent Experimental Film, Los Angeles Film Critics' Asn , 83; Visual Arts Award, Toronto, 86. *Bibliog:* Regina Cornwell (auth), Snow Seen, Peter Martin Assoc, 80; Gerald Needham (auth), Michael Snow at the Isaacs Gallery, Arts Canada, Dec/Jan, 80; Regina Cornwell (auth), Michael Snow: The Decisive Moment Revised, Arts Canada, Apr/May, 80. *Mem:* Royal Can Acad Arts. *Publ:* Illusr, cover to cover, NS ser, NS Col Art & Design, Halifax, 75; High School, Impulse Ed, The Isaacs Gallery, 79; Diacritics: A review of contemporary criticism, Fall, 84. *Dealer:* SL Simpson Gallery 515 Queen St W Toronto Ont Can MSV 1B4. *Mailing Add:* c/o Isaacs Gallery 179 John St Ctr Toronto ON M5T 1X4 Canada

SNOWDEN, GILDA
PAINTER, WRITER
b Detroit, Mich, July 29, 54. *Study:* Wayne St Univ, BFA, 77, MA, 78, MFA, 79. *Work:* Art Ctr of Battle Creek, Mich; Dayton Hudson Corp, Post/Newsweek Corp, Mich Bell Tel & Edward F Duffy Co, Detroit; Detroit Inst Arts. *Comn:* Painting/construction, Post/Newsweek, Detroit, 83. *Exhib:* View Point-Out of Square, 84 & Detroit Artist Update, 86, Cranbrook Acad Art Mus, West Bloomfield, Mich; Transformations, 88 & Signature Images, 90, Detroit Inst Art; Black Creativity, Mus Sci & Indust, Chicago, Ill, 88; Coast to Coast, Univ Mich Mus Art, Ann Arbor, 89. *Pos:* Dir, Detroit Repertory Theater; contribr, Detroit Focus Quarterly, Focus Gallery & New Art Examiner, currently. *Teaching:* Instr fine arts, Wayne State Univ, Detroit, 79-85; asst prof fine arts, Ctr Creative Studies, Detroit, 81- *Awards:* Artists Grant, Mich Coun Arts, 82, 85, 88 & 90; Arts Midwest Award, Nat Endowment Arts, 90. *Bibliog:* Edsel Reid (dir) 15 Black Artists (video), 88; Jan Vander Marck (auth), Signature Images (exhib catalog), Detroit Inst Arts, 90. *Mem:* Nat Conf Artists; founders soc Detroit Inst Arts. *Media:* Painting, Drawing. *Publ:* Contribr, City Mag, Sutton Publ, 87; Detroit Artist Market J, 90; Chicago New Art Examiner, 92. *Dealer:* Paul Holoweski 430 N Washington Royal Oak MI 48067; Sherry Washington Gallery 1274 Library Detroit MI 48226. *Mailing Add:* 427 E Edsel Ford Detroit MI 48226

SNYDER, DAN
SCULPTOR
b Philadelphia, Pa, July 23, 48. *Study:* Pa State Univ, BFA, 70; Univ Calif, Davis, MFA, 72. *Work:* Oakland Mus, Calif; E B Crocker Art Mus, Sacramento; Am Acad, Rome, Italy; Univ Calif, Davis. *Comn:* Welcome Wall (sculpture), Art Comm San Francisco, 83. *Exhib:* Oakland Mus, Calif, 73; Am Acad, Rome, 75; Allrich Gallery, San Francisco, 77, 79, 81 & 82; San Francisco Mus Mod Art, 79; Monterey Peninsula Mus Art, 83; and others. *Teaching:* Instr sculpture, Pa State Univ, 75-76. *Awards:* Spec proj grant, Nat Endowment Arts, 73; Fel, Prix de Rome, 73-75. *Media:* Ceramics, Mixed. *Mailing Add:* c/o The Allrich Gallery 251 Post St San Francisco CA 94108

SNYDER, HILLS
SCULPTOR
b Lubbock, Tex, Dec 1, 50. *Study:* Univ Kans, Lawrence, 69-70; Tex Tech Univ, Lubbock, 70, 72-73. *Work:* Univ Tex, El Paso; Ucross Found, Ucross, Wyo. *Exhib:* Sculpture on the Wall, San Antonio Art Inst, Tex, 83; Touch with the Eyes, Feel with the Mind, Laguna Gloria Art Mus, Austin, Tex, 83; Visual Short Stories: Five from Austin, The Art Ctr, Waco, Tex, 83; Texture, Line, Form and Color, Dallas Mus Art, 84; Constructed Image-Constructed Object, Alternative Mus, New York, NY, 84; New Works by Austin Artists, Laguna Gloria Art Mus, 84; Hills Snyder: Constructions and Drawings (with catalog), Tyler Mus Art, Tyler, Tex, 85; Transpositions-Collaborations, San Antonio Art Inst, Tex, 86; Hills Snyder: Dimensional Works, Words and Drawings, Brown-Lupon Gallery, Tex Christian Univ, Ft Worth, 86; Third Coast Review: A Look at Art in Texas, Aspen Art Mus, Aspen, Colo, 87; June Rise Ramble (with catalog), Custer County Art Ctr, Miles City, Mont, 87; Garage Optimism, Patrick Gallery, Austin, Tex, 87; West Texas Homecoming, Lubbock Fine Arts Ctr, 88; Subjecting the Shed to a Little Light, Cult Activities Ctr, Temple Tex, 89. *Teaching:* Artist-in-educ drawing & sculpture, Custer County Art Ctr, Miles City, Mont, 86-87; Mont Arts Coun Artist in the Schools/Communities, 86-88. *Awards:* Best of Show, Spar Nat Exhib, City of Shreveport, La, 83. *Bibliog:* Bernice Torregrossa (auth), Spellbinding Spaces (review), Austin American-Statesman, 8/85; Janet Kutner (auth), Hills Snyder (review), Artnews, 11/85. *Media:* Mixed-media. *Dealer:* Patrick Gallery Austin TX; Natsoulas-Novelozo Gallery Davis CA. *Mailing Add:* 3205 Dancy Austin TX 78722

SNYDER, JOAN
PAINTER
b Highland Park, NJ, Apr 16, 40. *Study:* Douglas Col, BA, 62; Rutgers Univ, MFA, 66. *Work:* Metrop Mus Art, Mus Mod Art & Whitney Mus Am Art, New York; Dallas Mus Fine Arts, Tex; Neuberger Mus, Purchase, NY; and others. *Exhib:* Biennial exhib, Whitney Mus Am Art, New York, 81; American Abstraction Now, Inst Contemp Art, Virginia Mus, Richmond, 82; Nielsen Gallery, Boston, Mass, 86; Joan Snyder, Hirschl & Adler Mod, New York, 88; Travel exhib, David Winton Bell Gallery, Brown Univ, Providence, Rhode Island, Fine Arts Ctr, Stony Brook, New York, Contemp Arts Forum, Santa Barbara, Calif; New Paintings, Compass Rose, Chicago, 89; Hirschl & Adler Modern, New York, 90; Monotype Project 88-89 Victoria, Munroe, NY, 90; Ann Jaffe Gallery, Bay Harbor Islands, Fla, 91; Nielsen Gallery, Boston, Mass, 91; Hirschl & Adler Mod, New York, 10/92. *Teaching:* State Univ New York, Stony Brook, 66-; Yale Univ, New Haven, Conn; Atlanta Col Art, Ga; Parsons Sch Design, New York, 90-; Vt Studio Sch, 90, 92; Princeton Univ, NJ. *Awards:* Nat Endowment for Arts Grant, 74; Guggenheim Grant, 83. *Bibliog:* Jed Perl (auth), article, The New Criterion, 2/86, Joan Snyder, Vogue, 3/88; Susan Gill (auth), Painting from the Heart, Artnews, 4/87; Gerrit Henry (auth), article, Art in Am, 2/86, Arts, summer 90; Patrick Pacheco (auth), The New Faith in Painting, Art & Antiques, 4/91; Bill Jones (auth), Joan Snyder, Arts, summer 90; Nancy Grove (auth), Art & Antiques, 4/90; Helen Harrison (auth), New York Times, 12/9/90. *Media:* Oil, Acrylic. *Dealer:* Nielson Gallery Boston MA. *Mailing Add:* c/o Hirschl & Adler Modern Mus Art 851 Madison Ave New York NY 10021

SNYDER, KIT-YIN
SCULPTOR, ENVIRONMENTAL ARTIST
b Canton, China; US citizen. *Study:* City Col, New York, BSEE; Univ Mich, Ann Arbor; Claremont Grad Sch, Calif, MFA. *Work:* Margaret Mitchell Square, Atlanta, Ga; White St Detention Ctr, New York. *Exhib:* Rome, Italy, 89; State Univ NY, Stonybrook, 90; Snug Harbor, Staten Island, NY, 90; Kunstraum, Ger, 91; Reed Col, Portland, Ore, 91; State Univ, NY, Brockport, 92. *Awards:* Nat Endowment Arts Grant, 80, 82 & 86; NY Found Arts Fel Sculpture, 86 & 91; Award Excellence in Design, White St Detention Ctr, New York, 89. *Mailing Add:* 80 Warren St Apt 13 750 N Oleans St, Suite 303 New York NY 10007

SNYDER, RUTH (COZEN)
PAINTER, SCULPTOR
b Montreal, Can; US citizen. *Study:* Univ Calif, Los Angeles; Otis Art Inst. *Work:* Frederick S Wight Gallery, Univ Calif, Los Angeles; Laguna Beach Art Mus, Calif; US Embassy, Lisbon, Portugal; Clorox Corp, San Francisco; Smithsonian Inst, Washington, DC; Coos Art Mus, Coos Bay, Ore. *Comn:* Smithsonian Inst, Washington, DC; The Wall, bronze, Capital Grounds, Sacramento, Calif; Completing the Circle, bronze column, Reseda Home Aged; US State Dept, US Embassy, Riyadh, Saudi Arabia; US State Dept, US Embassy, Lisbon, Portugal. *Exhib:* Galerie Arcadia, Paris; Palm Springs Desert Mus, Calif; Laguna Beach Mus Art, Calif; Butler Inst Am Art, Youngstown, Ohio; Tokyo Metrop Mus, Osaka, Japan; Dept Health & Human Serv Invitational, Washington, DC; and others. *Collections Arranged:* Light, Illusion and Reality & Three from Los Angeles, Riverside Art Ctr & Mus, Calif. *Pos:* Exec bd mem, Watercolor West, Riverside, Calif, 77-80; guest cur, Riverside Art Ctr, Calif, 85; juror, San Diego Int Water Color Soc, currently. *Teaching:* Lectr, Brigham Young Univ, Provo, Utah, 83. *Awards:* Annenberg Award, Nat Watercolor Soc, 78; Scottsdale Ctr Arts Juror's Award; Sculpture & Watercolor Award, San Bernandino Mus Art; and others. *Bibliog:* Neil Menzes (auth), article, 11/80 & Souvan Geer (auth), articles, 85, Artweek; Peggy Loar (auth), article, Ocular, 81; David S Rubin (auth), article, 4/84 & Ann Japenga (auth), article, 84, Los Angeles Times; Art in America, 9/84. *Mem:* Nat Watercolor Soc; Artists Equity; Watercolor West; Womens Caucus Arts; Int Sculptor Soc. *Media:* Mixed Media; Bronze. *Publ:* Contribr, Creative Seascape Painting, by Edward Betts, Watson-Guptill; and others. *Mailing Add:* 2200 Main St Santa Monica CA 90405

SNYDER, WILLIAM B
PAINTER, EDUCATOR
b San Francisco, Calif, Sept 26, 28. *Study:* Chouinard's Art Inst, 43; San Francisco State Col; Stanford Univ, fel, 61-62. *Work:* Oakland Art Mus, Calif; City Chico, Calif; Haggin Mus, Stockton, Calif; Richmond Art Ctr, Richmond, Calif; and others. *Comn:* Portrait, USS Posco Steel Mills, Korea/USA; portrait, John F Kennedy Univ, Calif; mural, Cretaceous period, Calif Acad Sci, San Francisco, 90. *Exhib:* Phelan Award Biennial De Young Mus, 65; Christmas Show, San Francisco Mus Mod Art, 70; one-man shows, Wooster Col, Ohio, 74, Sacramento State Univ, Calif, 77 & San Francisco Art Comn, 78; Jos Chowning Gallery San Francisco (Dealer), 80-; Comic Iconoclasm Show, ICA Gallery, London, Eng, 87-88; Les Misquetes Show, Courbevoie Cult Ctr, Courbevoie, France, 90; Columbus 500th Anniversary Show, Triton Mus, Santa Clara, Calif, 92; and others. *Pos:* Art teacher, Laney Col, Oak, Calif, 65-, Stamford Univ, 61-62 & Sonoma State Col, 80-81; illusr, Bay Area Illusr Tech, 84- *Teaching:* Instr drawing, Stanford Univ, 61-62; instr art, Foothills Jr Col, 62-63; instr drawing & painting, Laney Col, Oakland, Calif, 64- *Awards:* First Prize, San Joaquin Valley Regional Fall Arts Festival, Stockton Art League, Calif, 58; Teaching Fel, Stanford Univ, Chico, Calif, 61-62; Purchase Award, Chico Savings & Loan, 66 & Fairfield Art Comn, 74. *Bibliog:* Tom Albright (auth), $5,000: Study for nightwatch, Art Gallery Mag, 3/73 & Interview: William Snyder, Currant Art Mag, 8/75; Ralph Pomeroy (auth), Triumph of Disneyanity, Art & Artists, London, 8/74; Alfred Jan (auth), article, Flash Art, Italy, summer 84. *Media:* Oil, Watercolor. *Publ:* Illusr, Monterey Advocate, Panadero, 66-68. *Dealer:* Joseph Chowning Gallery 1717 17th St San Francisco CA 94103. *Mailing Add:* PO Box 563 Woodacre CA 94973

SOBOL, JUDITH ELLEN
MUSEUM DIRECTOR, CURATOR
b Washington, DC, June 1, 46. *Study:* Univ Calif, Los Angeles, BA, 68; George Washington Univ, MA, 70. *Collections Arranged:* Intaglio: An Appreciation, 82; New Architecture-Maine Traditions (with catalog), Payson Gallery, 83; Len Jenshel: Photographs, 10/83; Guy Bourdin: Sighs & Whispers, 84; Mainers Away, 85; Sue Coe, Porkopolis, 90. *Pos:* Asst cur Univ Collection, Georgetown Univ, 70-72; supvr interpretive serv, Minneapolis Inst Arts, 73-77; chair, div educ, Baltimore Mus Art, 77-78; exec dir, Don't Tear It Down, Washington, DC, 78-81; dir, Joan Whitney Payson Gallery Art, Westbrook Col, 81-91 & Grand Rapids Art Mus, 91- *Teaching:* Lectr fine arts, Georgetown Univ, 70-72; instr Am art, Westbrook Col, 82-83, Elderhostel, Westbrook Col, 83- *Mem:* New Eng Mus Asn; Am Asn Mus. *Res:* Contemporary art, impressionism and post-impressionism; American art and architecture, especially 1880-1920, art nouveau. *Publ:* Auth, Gilbert Stuart Portrait, Bull, Minneapolis Inst Arts, 77; Neighborhood coalitions, Univ New Orleans, 82; Polly Brown: Drawings, Payson Gallery, 10/83. *Mailing Add:* Grand Rapids AA Mus 155 Division N Grand Rapids MI 49503

SOFFER, SASSON
ENVIRONMENTAL ARTIST, CONCEPTUAL ARTIST
b Baghdad, Iraq, June 1, 25; US citizen. *Study:* Brooklyn Col, with Mark Rothko & others, 50-54. *Work:* Indianapolis Mus Fine Art; Albright-Knox Gallery, Buffalo; Rockefeller Inst, New York; Butler Inst Am Art, Youngstown, Ohio; Whitney Mus Am Art, New York. *Exhib:* Whitney Mus Am Art, New York; one-man shows, Betty Parsons Gallery, New York, 61-63, Corpus Christi Mus, Tex, 64, Portland Mus, Maine, 66, Montclair State Col, NJ, 74 & Battery Park, New York, 75 & 76; and others. *Pos:* Ford Found artist in residence, Portland Mus, 66. *Awards:* Ford Found Purchase Award, Whitney Mus Am Art, 62 & Portland Mus, Maine, 64; North Jersey Cult Coun, 74 & Nat Endowment Arts. *Bibliog:* Sasson Soffer in the City of New York, 85; Sasson Soffer, Metal Sculpture, 85. *Media:* Stainless Steel, Glass. *Mailing Add:* 78 Grand St New York NY 10013

SOKOL, DAVID MARTIN
HISTORIAN, MUSCOLOGIST
b New York, NY, Nov 3, 42. *Study:* Hunter Col, AB, 63; Inst for Fine Arts, NY Univ, MA, 66, PhD, 70. *Pos:* Cur, Terra Mus Am Art, 81-85; interim dir, Spertus Mus, 85-86; adj cur, Maver Mus Art, 88-90. *Teaching:* Instr art hist, Kingsborough Community Col, Brooklyn, NY, 66-68; asst prof art hist, Western Ill Univ, Macomb, 68-71; assoc prof art & archit hist, Univ Ill, Chicago, 71-82, chmn dept, 77-84, prof, 82-, dir, grad studies, 90-; vis asst prof, New York Univ, 70; vis prof, Randolph-Macon Women's Col, 88-89. *Awards:* Univ Scholar, New York Univ, 70; First Award for scholarship in contributions in the Arts in Ill, Ill Acad Fine Arts, 92. *Mem:* Col Art Asn (placement comt, 77 & prof practices comt, 91-); Am Studies Asn (nat coun, 76-78); Am Asn Univ Prof (comt T, 75-78); Asn Historians Am Art (treas, 79-89); Am Cult Asn; Art & Archit(area chmn); Fel, Inst Humanities (exec comt). *Res:* American painting and decorative arts; relations between American and European art; history of art patronage in the US, F L Wright. *Publ:* Auth, John Quider: Painter of American Legend, Wichita Art Mus, 73; auth, American Architecture & Art, 76 & American Decorative Arts & Old World Influences, 79, Gale; coauth, History of American Art, Abrams, 79; auth, Otto Neumann, 82 & Heidelberger Kunstverein, Solitude, 82, Terra Mus Am Art; ed, Cambridge Monographs on America Artists, 84- *Mailing Add:* 330 S Taylor Ave Oak Park IL 60302

SOKOLOW, ISOBEL FOLB
SCULPTOR
b Brooklyn, NY. *Study:* Silvermine Col Art, 65-68; Art Students League; Nat Acad Design; Educ Alliance Art Sch; Independent Study in Italy. *Work:* Westchester Community Col, NY. *Comn:* Private collections in US & Italy. *Exhib:* Audubon Artists, Nat Acad Design, NY, 78; Yonkers Art Asn, Hudson River Mus, Yonkers, NY, 80; Art on Loan Installation, Schulman Realty, White Plains, NY, 85-88; Sculptors Alliance, Lever House, NY 87; Am Soc Contemp Artists, Westbeth Gallery, NY, 88; Nat Asn Women Artists, Monmouth Mus, Red Bank, NJ, 88; solo exhibs, N Shore Sculpture Ctr, 80, Harkness House, 81, Musaui Gallery, 84, Atlanta Gallery, 88, 90, 92. *Pos:* Co-dir fine arts, Pratt Sch Design, 85-; dir, Westchester Art & Cult Asn, 80-92. *Teaching:* Instr art, Jewish Guild for the Blind, Home for the Aged Blind, Yonkers, NY, 74-76 & Clay & Marble Workshops, Pietrasanta, Italy, 84-86. *Awards:* Silver Medal, Audubon Artists; Best in Show, Am Soc Contemp Artists, 88 & 90; Tre Jolie des Arts, Nat Asn Women Artists. *Bibliog:* Enrico Moreti (critic), Il Progresso-An American Artist in Florence, 80; Malcom Preston (auth), Review, Newsday, 82; Angela Pegani (dir), Isobel Folb Sokolow (TV doc), Swiss/Italian TV, 87; State of the Art (TV series), 89. *Mem:* Am Soc Contemp Artists (dir, 79-80); NY Artists Equity (dir, 75-80, vpres, 80-84); Nat Asn Women Artists; Art Students League. *Media:* Steel, Bronze. *Dealer:* Atlantic Gallery 164 Mercer St New York NY 10012. *Mailing Add:* Winding Rd Ardsley NY 10502

SOKOLOWSKI, LINDA ROBINSON
PRINTMAKER, PAINTER
b Utica, NY, May 20, 43. *Study:* RI Sch Design, BFA(painting), 65; Univ Iowa, with Mauricio Lasansky & James Lechay, MA, 70 & MFA, 71. *Work:* State Univ NY, Potsdam; Libr Congress, Washington, DC; Ball State Univ; Pepsico, IBM. *Exhib:* One-man shows, Kraushaar Galleries, New York, 76, 79, 82, 86, 89 & 91; More than Land or Sky: Art from Appalachia, Nat Mus Am Art, Smithsonian Inst, 81; Realist Tradition in Central New York, Munson-Williams Proctor Inst; 43rd, 44th & 56th Ann Painting Exhib, Butler Inst Am Art; 154th, 161st & 165th Ann Exhib, Nat Acad Design; Artists who teach, Fed Reserve Bd, Washington, DC, 87; Summer Pleasures, Kornbluth Gallery, Fairlawn, NJ, 89; The Art Show, Art Dealers Asn, New York, 89 & 90. *Teaching:* Assoc prof art, State Univ NY, Binghamton, 71- *Awards:* Childe Hassam Purchase Award, Am Acad & Inst of Art & Lett, 78; Research grants, State Univ New York, Binghamton, 90. *Bibliog:* G Henry (auth), Art News (review), 86; Wendy Beckett (auth), Contemporary Women Artists, Universe Books, 88; Vivien Raynor (auth), A show meant to give Pleasure, New York Times, 7/16/89. *Publ:* Auth, The Original Prints and Restrikes from the Plates of Kaethe Kollwitz, Univ Iowa Press, 70. *Dealer:* Carole Pesner Kraushaar Galleries 724 Fifth Ave New York NY 10028. *Mailing Add:* Art Dept Binghamton Univ Binghamton NY 13902-6000

SOLBERG, MORTEN EDWARD
PAINTER
b Cleveland, Ohio, Nov 8, 35. *Study:* Cleveland Inst Art. *Work:* Nat Gallery Art, Washington, DC; Cleveland Mus Art; Am Bicentennial Gallery, Huntington Beach, Calif; Nat Acad Design, New York. *Comn:* Painting of hist fountain, Marriott Hotels, Newport Beach, Calif, 75; painting of hist settings, Irvine Co, Newport Beach, 75. *Exhib:* Nat Acad Design, New York, 66 & 76; Watercolor USA, Springfield, Mo, 67; Soc Painters in Casein & Acrylic, New York, 67; Am Watercolor Soc, New York, 68 & 74-76; Nat Watercolor Soc, Los Angeles, 70-75. *Pos:* Art dir, Am Greeting Corp, Cleveland, 58-68; art dir, Buzza Cardoza Corp, Anaheim, Calif, 68-71; pres, Calif Graphics, Design Studio, Orange, 71-73. *Awards:* Paul B Remey Mem Award, Am Watercolor Soc, 68; Soc Animal Artists Medal; San Bernardino Co Mus Award; and others. *Bibliog:* Angie McCance (auth), Morten Solberg, Artist, Register, 74; Janell Gregg (auth), Contributing artist, Orange Co Illus, 75; Ray Merchant (auth), article in Am Artist Mag, 10/76; articles in Sports Afield, 11/85 & Am Artist, 11/86. *Mem:* Soc Animal Artists, NY; Nat Watercolor Soc (ad hoc bd mem, 74, first vpres, 75); Am Watercolor Soc. *Media:* Mixed. *Dealer:* Mill Pond Press Venice FL. *Mailing Add:* 6260 Vine Hill Rd Sebastopol CA 95472

SOLDNER, PAUL EDMUND
SCULPTOR, CERAMIST
b Summerfield, Ill, Apr 24, 21. *Study:* Bluffton Col, BA; Univ Colo, MA; County Art Inst, Los Angeles, MFA; Wesminster Col, Hon DFA, 92. *Work:* Victoria & Albert Mus, London; San Francisco Mus Art; Oakland Art Mus, Calif; Emerson Mus, Syracuse, NY; Smithsonian Mus, Washington, DC; and others. *Comn:* Ceramic mural, Home Savings & Loan Asn, Los Angeles, 56. *Exhib:* Am Potters Today, Victoria & Albert Mus, London, 86; Poetry of the Physical, Am Craft Mus, NY, 86; Esther Saks Gallery, Chicago, Ill, 86 & 88; Cal Prifysgol Cymru, Aberyothwyth, Wales, 87; Eloquent Object, Oakland Mus, Calif, 88; Traveling retrospective exhib, 91-94; and others. *Teaching:* Prof ceramics, Scripps Col & Claremont Grad Sch, Calif, 55-66 & 70-92; vis prof ceramics, Univ Colo, Boulder, 66-67; prof ceramics, Univ Iowa, 67-68. *Awards:* Louis Comfort Tiffany Found Grant, 66 & 72; Purchase Award, Victoria & Albert Mus, 72; Craftsmen's Fel Grant, Nat Endowment Arts, 76. *Bibliog:* John W Conrad (auth), Contemporary Ceramics, Prentice-Hall, 77; Donald Campbell (auth), Using the Potter's Wheel, Van Nostrand Reinhold, 77; Paul Soldner, A Retrospective, Univ Washington Press, 91; & others. *Mem:* Am Craft Coun; Nat Coun Educ Ceramic Arts; Acad Int de Céramique. *Media:* Clay, Metal. *Mailing Add:* PO Box 90 Aspen CO 81612

SOLEM, (ELMO) JOHN
CERAMIST, EDUCATOR
b St Paul, Minn, Aug 10, 33. *Study:* Minn Sch Art, 51-53; Wartburg Col, Waverly, Iowa, BA, 59; Univ Calif, Los Angeles, MA, 62. *Work:* Santa Barbara Mus Art, Calif; Atlantic Richfield Corp Art Collection, Los Angeles; US Embassy, Oslo, Norway; Los Angeles Printmaking Soc; Tex Tech Univ, Lubbock. *Exhib:* Ann Exhib, Artists of Los Angeles, Los Angeles Co Mus Art, 61; Northwest Printmakers' 34th Int Exhib, Seattle Art Mus, 63; 19th Nat Exhib Prints, Libr Congress, DC, 63; 14th Nat Print Exhib, Brooklyn Mus, 64; Arts of Southern Calif XVI: Prints, Long Beach Mus Art, Calif, 65; Prints Calif, Oakland Mus, Calif, 75; Artists-Teachers in Southern Calif, Santa Barbara Mus Art, Calif, 75; Early Sixties, Frederick Wight Gallery, Univ Calif, Los Angeles, 78; Los Angeles Bicentennial Exhib, Mus Sci & Industry, 81. *Teaching:* Extension instr art, Univ Calif, Los Angeles, 63-76; prof art, printmaking, drawing & painting, Calif Lutheran Univ, Thousand Oaks, 67- *Awards:* Tiffany Found Grant, Graphics, 63; Purchase Awards, 5th Ann Colorprint, USA, Tex Tech Univ, 74 & Los Angeles Printmaking Soc 2nd Nat Exhib, 74. *Bibliog:* Louis Newman (auth), Recent works on paper, Monograph, 78; Betts Kimball (auth), John Solem: a portrait of the artist, Westlake Mag, 79. *Media:* Sculptor, Clay. *Mailing Add:* PO Box 296 Topanga CA 90290

SOLERI, PAOLO
ARCHITECT, SCULPTOR
b Torino, Italy, 1919. *Study:* Polytech Torino, Frank Lloyd Wright fel. *Work:* Mus Mod Art, New York. *Comn:* Dome House, Cave Creek, Ariz, 49; Ceramica Artistica Solimene, Ceramics Factory, Vietri Sul Mare, Italy, 50; Native American Theater (amphitheater), Santa Fe, NMex, 68; Il Donnone (sculpture), Phoenix, Ariz, 72. *Exhib:* Corcoran Gallery Art, Washington, DC, 70; Whitney Mus Am Art, New York, 70; Mus Contemp Art, Chicago, 70; Nat Conf Ctr, Ottawa, Can, 71; Univ Art Mus, Berkeley, Calif, 71; Two Suns Arcology Exhib, Xerox Corp-sponsored, 76; New York Acad Sci, 89. *Teaching:* Distinguished vis lectr, Ariz State Univ, Sch Archit, currently. *Awards:* Graham Found, 62; Guggenheim Found, 64 & 67; Gold Medal, World Biennale Archit, Sofia, Bulgaria, 81. *Publ:* Auth, Arcology: The City in the Image of Man, 69 & The Sketchbooks of Paolo Soleri, 71, Mass Inst

Technol; The Bridge Between Matter & Spirit is Matter Becoming Spirit, Doubleday, 73; Fragments, Harper & Row; Paolo Soleri's Earth Casting, Peregrine-Smith, 84; Technology and Cosmogenesis, Paragon House, 86. *Mailing Add:* Cosanti Found 6433 Doubletree Ranch Rd Paradise Valley AZ 85253

SOLINGER, DAVID M
COLLECTOR, PATRON
Study: Art Students League New York; Hans Hofmann Sch. *Pos:* Mem bd trustees, Am Fedn Arts, 53-90; mem bd trustees, Whitney Mus Am Art, 61-, pres, 66-74, chmn, 74-77, hon pres, 77-; chmn mus coun, Cornell Univ, 73-88 & chmn com collections, 88- *Mem:* Art Students League New York. *Collection:* 20th century paintings and sculpture. *Mailing Add:* 33 East 70th St New York NY 10021

SOLMAN, JOSEPH
PAINTER
b Vitebsk, Russia, Jan 25, 09; US citizen. *Study:* Nat Acad Design, New York, 26-29; Art Students League, 29-30. *Work:* Whitney Mus Am Art, New York; Phillips Collection, Washington, DC; Fogg Mus, Cambridge, Mass; Butler Inst Am Art, Youngstown, Ohio; Los Angeles Co Mus; British Mus; Wichita Mus, Kans. *Exhib:* Retrospective oils, Phillips Collection, Washington, DC, 49; ACA Galleries, New York, NY, 50-; Whitney Mus Am Art Ann, 52, 53 & 55; retrospective, Wichita Mus, Kans, 84. *Pos:* Treas, Nat Acad Design, 79-84. *Teaching:* Instr oil painting, Mus Mod Art, 52-54, New Sch Social Res, 64-66 & City Col New York, 67-75. *Awards:* Nat Inst Arts & Lett Award for Painting, 61; Isaac N Maynard Prize for Portrait, 69 & Saltus Gold Medal for Merit, 71, Nat Acad Design. *Bibliog:* D Seckler (auth), Solman paints a picture, Art News, summer 51; S Burrey (auth), Joseph Solman: the growth of conviction, Arts, 10/55; Una E Johnson (auth introd), The Monotypes of Joseph Solman, Da Capo Press, 77. *Mem:* Fedn Mod Painters & Sculptors (pres, 65-67, vpres, 67-). *Media:* Monotype; Oil, Gouache. *Publ:* Auth, Joseph Solman, Crown, 66. *Dealer:* Salander-O'Reilly Galleries 20 E 79 St New York NY 10021. *Mailing Add:* 156 Second Ave New York NY 10003

SOLMSSEN, PETER
ADMINISTRATOR
b Berlin, Ger, Nov 1, 31; US citizen. *Study:* Harvard Col, AB, 52; Univ Pa Law Sch, JD, 59. *Exhib:* One-man photog exhib, Mus Art, Sao Paulo, Brazil, 70. *Pos:* US cult attache, Sao Paulo, 67-70; adv on the Arts, US Dept State, 74-80; pres, Arts Int, 81-83; pres, The Univ Arts, 83- *Publ:* Auth & illusr, Sao Paulo, 70. *Mailing Add:* The Univ Arts Broad & Pine Sts Philadelphia PA 19102

SOLOCHEK, SYLVIA See Walters, Sylvia Solochek

SOLODKIN, JUDITH
LITHOGRAPHER, PUBLISHER
b New York, NY, Apr 7, 45. *Study:* Brooklyn Col, BA, 65; Fulbright Hays Scholar alternate, France & Prix de Rome, Italy, 66-67; Columbia Univ, MFA(cum laude), 67; Tamarind Inst, Ford Found Grant, Tamarind Master Printer, 74. *Work:* Art Mus, Univ NMex; Tamarind Inst Collection, NMex; Pratt Graphics Ctr, Printmaking Workshop, New York. *Exhib:* Dallas Mus Fine Arts, 72; one-person shows, Douglass Col, Rutgers Univ & Elizabeth Pub Libr, NJ, 76, Razor Gallery, 77, Grey Gallery, ECarolina Univ 78 & Walters Art Gallery, Rutgers Univ, 79; and others. *Pos:* Master printer, Petersburg Press & SOLO Press, 74-78; partic artist apprenticeship prog, Great Lakes Col Asn, 76 & 78 & Parsons-New Sch, 77; proprietor & master printer, SOLO Press, 78. *Teaching:* Instr lithography, Univ Ind, Bloomington, 74; instr lithography, Pratt Graphics Ctr, 74-, Sch Visual Arts, 75- & Douglass Col, Rutgers Univ, 77-79. *Awards:* Louis Comfort Tiffany grant to SOLO Press Apprenticeship Prog, 77. *Bibliog:* Lisa Weinberg (auth), Judith Solodkin on SOLO Press, Woman Artists Newsletter, 77; Amy Goldin (auth), Pattern and print, Print Collectors Newslett, 3-4/78. *Mem:* Nat Print Asn; Graphics Art Coun NY; Artists Equity Asn. *Dealer:* Kathryn Markel Fine Arts 50 W 57th St New York NY 10019. *Mailing Add:* 520 Broadway 8th Floor New York NY 10012-3227

SOLOMON, BERNARD ALAN
PRINTMAKER, EDUCATOR
b Chicago, Ill, June 21, 46. *Study:* Art Inst Chicago, with Raymond Martin & Adrian Troy, BFA, 68; Inst Design, Ill Inst Technol, with Misch Kohn, MSVD, 70. *Work:* McDonald Corp, Pittsburgh, Pa; Nat Collection Fine Arts, Washington, DC; Skirball Mus Judaica, Los Angeles; High Mus, Atlanta, Ga; Huntsville Mus Art, Ala; Book Mus, Leipzig, Ger; State of Ga. *Exhib:* Over 50 int, nat & regional juried exhibs, 60 group exhibs & invitationals; over 70 major & one-man exhibs incl Sparbankasse: Tubingen, Ger & Pedagogsche Hochschule, Ludwigsborg, Ger; Univ Ala/Huntsville, Scheduled, Yeshiva Univ Mus, 94. *Pos:* First Nat Color Blend Print Exhib, 78-80, Comparisons & Contrasts, 80-82, & Prints Today: Holland/USA, 82-84; co-cur, Ga Artists' Bks Exhib, Ger, 92-93. *Teaching:* prof, Ga Southern Univ. *Awards:* Mus Purchase, Greenville Co Mus, 76; Edinboro Print Competition Award, 79; Bronze Medal Illus, Int Bk Design Exhib, Leipzig, 82; GSC Award for Excellence Res/Creative Endeavor, 88. *Mem:* Southern Graphics Coun (secy, 78-80, co-found & mem, 71-); Southeastern Col Arts Conf, 71- *Media:* Relief, Intaglio. *Publ:* Producer, Babi Yar, 67, The Zaddick Christ, 74, Small Town America, 74, Words & Fonts, 75, Song of Songs, 83, The Legend of St Julian, 84, Lilith, 85, Johannas Faustus, 87 & Icelandic Sagas, 88, An Artists' Hagaddah, 91, Someday Songs (illus), 92, all pvt publ. *Dealer:* The Print Barn Meredith NH; Tony Zwicker New York NY. *Mailing Add:* c/o Boxwood Press PO Box 2362 Statesboro GA 30458

SOLOMON, GERALD
DEALER
Pos: Pres-dir, Solomon & Co Fine Art, New York, currently. *Specialty:* 20th century American and European paintings, graphics, drawing and sculpture. *Mailing Add:* Solomon & Co Fine Art 959 Madison Ave New York NY 10021

SOLOMON, HOLLY
DEALER, COLLECTOR
b Fairfield, Conn. *Study:* Vassar Col; Sarah Lawrence Col, BA. *Pos:* Dir, Holly Solomon Gallery Inc, New York. *Teaching:* Instr art hist, Fashion Inst Am, 73-75. *Awards:* Award for Film, Edinborough Film Festival, 73. *Bibliog:* Andy Worhol (auth), 50 Best Friends, 65. *Specialty:* Avant-garde American. *Collection:* Pop art, conceptual art, narrative art, performing art & decorative art. *Mailing Add:* 724 Fifth Ave New York NY 10019

SOLOMON, RICHARD H
PUBLISHER, ART DEALER
b Boston, Mass, May 12, 34. *Study:* Harvard Col, AB, 56; Harvard Bus Sch, MBA, 58. *Pos:* Pres, Pace Editions Inc/Pace/Masterprints, Pace Primitive & Ancient Art, New York, currently; chmn, Pace/MacGill Inc 20th Century Photog Gallery, formerly; chmn, Overseers Vis Comt, Visual & Environ Studies Dept, Harvard Col, formerly. *Mem:* Art Dealers Asn Am; Primitive Art Dealers Asn Am; Int Fine Print Dealers Asn. *Specialty:* Contemporary and modern old master prints and drawings, contemporary modern photography, African, Oceanic and Nepalese. *Collection:* Contemporary art and primitive art. *Mailing Add:* c/o Pace Editions Inc 32 E 57th St New York NY 10022

SOLOMON, ROSALIND
PHOTOGRAPHER
Study: Goucher Col, Towson, Md, BA, 51; study with Lisette Model, 74-76. *Work:* Metrop Mus Art, New York; Nat Portrait Gallery, Washington, DC; Eastman House, Rochester, NY; Mus Mod Art, New York; Musee de la Ville de Paris; Victoria & Albert Mus. *Exhib:* One-person show, Mus Mod Art, 86. *Awards:* John Simon Guggenheim Mem Fel, 80; Nat Endowment Arts, 88; Am Inst Indian Studies, 81-83; Art Matters Inc, 88. *Mailing Add:* 712 Broadway New York NY 10013

SOLOMON, (MRS) SIDNEY L
COLLECTOR
b Boston, Mass, May 15, 09. *Study:* Radcliffe Col, AB; Simmons Col, BS. *Exhib:* Sargent, Whitney Mus, New York. *Collection:* Sculpture of the twentieth century to contemporary, including Giacometti, Lipschitz, Marini, Nevelson, Dubuffet, Arp, Chadwick, Calder, Schmidt, Doris Cassar & Trova; painting collection includes Sargent, Vuillard, Tomayo, Leger, Giacometti, Monet and Matta; drawings of Maillol, Archipenko, Degas, Lachaise & many others; watercolors of Nolde & Marini; also a collection of pop art; Picasso Print 1907 Master Drawings. *Mailing Add:* 834 Fifth Ave New York NY 10021

SOLOMON, SYD
PAINTER
b Uniontown, Pa, July 12, 17. *Study:* Art Inst Chicago, 35; Acad Beaux Arts, Paris, 45. *Work:* Whitney Mus Am Art & Solomon R Guggenheim Mus, New York; Philadelphia Mus Art; Wadsworth Atheneum, Hartford, Conn; Joseph H Hirshhorn Mus, Washington, DC; and many others. *Exhib:* National & international exhibs incl, Univ Ill, Corcoran, Biennial, Whitney Mus, Corcoran Gallery Art, Washington, DC; Guggenheim Mus; Art Inst Chicago, Nat Acad, New York; retrospective, Ringling Mus, Sarasota, Fla & New York Cultural Ctr, 74; Ft Lauderdale Mus, 75; St Petersburg Mus, 79; Syd Solomon- a dialogue with nature, (auth, catalog), Ringling Mus, 90-91; Polk mus, Butler Inst Am Art, 92. *Pos:* Camouflage designer, Engrs Bd, Washington, DC, 42; dir fac, Famous Artists Sch, 53-73. *Teaching:* Instr, Art Inst Pittsburgh, 47, Ringling Mus Art, 48-50, Sarasota Sch Art, 50 & 55 & Famous Artist Sch Inc, 54-67; prof art, New Col, Sarasota, Fla, 64-65 & 67-69; instr painting, Univ Ill, 68, Robertson Ctr Arts & Sci, Binghamton, NY, 69 Tampa Bay Art Ctr, 72, Univ Calif, 76 & Boca Raton Ctr Art, 77. *Awards:* The Florida Prize, New York Times, 87. *Mem:* Nat Soc Lit & Arts. *Dealer:* Art Sources Jacksonville FL; Harmon-Meek Gallery Naples FL. *Mailing Add:* 9210 Blind Pass Rd Sarasota FL 34242

SOLOMON, VITA PETROSKY
PAINTER, PRINTMAKER
Study: Moore Col Art, dipl, 37; Tyler Sch Fine Arts, Temple Univ, BFA, BS(educ), 58, MFA, 60. *Work:* Philadelphia Mus Art; City Hall, Philadelphia; Nat Portrait Gallery, Smithsonian Inst, DC; US Court House, Philadelphia, Pa; Univ Pa, Philadelphia. *Comn:* Portraits, Pearl S Buck, Pearl S Buck Found, Smithsonian Inst, Washington, DC, 67, Judge Raymond Pace Alexander, Philadelphia Bar Asn, Law Libr, 70, Alfred Williams, Governor, Fed Reserve Bank, Philadelphia, 75, Keith Doms, dir, Free Libr Philadelphia, 79 & Chief Judge Joseph S Lord III, US District Court, 81. *Exhib:* Am Watercolor Soc, Metrop Mus, New York; Royal Acad Arts, London, Eng; Paris Salon, Paris, France; Pa Acad Fine Art, Philadelphia; Philadelphia Mus Art; Nat Acad, New York; Ann Juried Exhib, Detroit Inst Art; Ann Juried Exhib, Royal Inst, London, Eng. *Teaching:* Instr art hist & coordr art dept, Cheltenham High Sch, 67-82. *Awards:* Silver Medal, Paris Salon, Paris, France, 66; Jane Peterson Medal, Audubon Artists, New York, 75; Eugenia Atwood Prize, Philadelphia Print Club, Philadelphia Mus Art, 75. *Bibliog:* Leon Witconis (auth), Portrait Pros, Focus, Business Weekly, 74; Ralph Fabri (auth), Vita P Solomon paints a portrait, Today's Art, 75. *Mem:* Am Watercolor Soc; Allied

Artists Am; Artists' Equity Asn; Cheltenham Art Ctr Print Guild; Philadelphia Watercolor Soc. *Media:* Watercolor, Oil; Lithography, Pastel. *Mailing Add:* c/o Primarily Portraits The Studio 3 Lehman Lane Philadelphia PA 19144

SOLOWAY, RETA BURNS
PAINTER
b Washington, DC. *Study:* Corcoran Sch Art; Parsons Sch; Philadelphia Mus Sch Art, 31- 35; Philadelphia Graphic Sketch; Nat Acad Sch, 69; New Sch Social Res, 71; Sarah Lawrence Col, 756-77; Hofstra Univ, 76-79; and with Umberto Romano, Thornton Oakley, Henry Pitz, Joseph Stefanelli, EricIsenburger & Susan Schell. *Work:* Gregory Mus, Hicksville, NY; Bank of New York; Univ Pa; Nat Arts Club. *Comn:* Portraits, Maj Gen Arthur Gaines, Denver, Colo, 70 & Dean Emer Charles Smythe, Pennington Prep Sch, 71, Gardiner Gregory, Hicksville, 75, Daniel Moore, Dr Henry Heimlich, Isaac Asinov. *Exhib:* Malverne Artists Long Island, 65-80; Allied Artists Am, 69-90; Catharine Lorillard Wolfe Art Club, 75-90; Islip Mus Art & Nat Soc of Painters Casein & Acrylic; Audubon artists. *Pos:* Pres, Allied Artists Am, 80-84; treas, Nat Soc Painters Casein & Acrylic. *Teaching:* Demonstr, Nat Acad, 66-75 & 77, Nat Arts Club, 73-77, Malverne Libr, 70-80 & IPA Nat Conv, Washington, DC, 72- 74 & 90, Pen & Brush, 79. *Awards:* Pen & Brush Club Award & Watercolor, 80 & 87; Grumbacher Watercolor Award, 81; Michael Eugel Award, Nat Soc Painters Casein & Acrylic, 88- 90; Paul Puzmas Award, Allied Artists Am , 89. *Mem:* Allied Artists Am (corresp secy, 79-81, pres, 81-84, dir watercolor, 86, hon life pres 78-90); Nat Arts Club Exhibiting mem; Nat Soc Painters Casein & Acrylic (treas); Catharine Lorillard Wolfe Art Club; Am Artists Prof League; Audubon Artists. *Media:* Oil, Watercolor. *Publ:* Contribr, Portrait in Occupational Therapy, 46 & Portrait of the World, 65; The Little Brown Spot, 78; NY Art Rev, 89. *Mailing Add:* 145 Lexington Ave Franklin Square NY 11010

SOLWAY, CARL E
DEALER
b Chicago, Ill, Jan 12, 35. *Pos:* Dir, Carl Solway Gallery, Cincinnati. *Mem:* Art Dealers Asn Am. *Specialty:* 20th century American and European painting, sculpture and graphics; video installations; publisher of graphic works by John Cage, Buckminster Fuller, Richard Hamilton, Nancy Graves, Nam June Paik, Matt Mullican, Peter Nagy, Julia Wachtel & Vito Acconci. *Mailing Add:* 314 W Fourth St Cincinnati OH 45202

SOMBERG, EMILIJA O K
PAINTER
b Utena, Lithuania, Feb 20, 24; US citizen. *Study:* Univ Hamburg, BA, 49; Southern Conn State Col, MS, 62; NY Univ, 64. *Work:* Tweed Mus; Lithuanian Embassy & Libr Cong, Washington, DC; Southern Conn State Col; Univ Minn, Minneapolis; Maison Baltique De Paris. *Exhib:* Green Ross Gallery, New York, 65; retrospectives, Normandale Community Col, 78, Nobles Co Art Ctr, Worthington, Mich, 78, Custer Co Arts Ctr, Miles City, Mont, 81 & Tweed Mus, 81 & Alternative Mus, Minneapolis, 85 & Murphy Art Gallery, St Paul, Minn, 87; Minneapolis Inst Art, 79; Minn Mus Art, 80; Invitational, Univ Minn, 86; Moon Art Gallery, Minneapolis, Minn, 91. *Teaching:* Instr art, pub schs, New York, Conn & NJ, 64-74. *Awards:* Distinguished Serv Award, Mayor A Hofstede, Minneapolis, Minn, 79 & Mayor, Fraser, 91. *Bibliog:* Martin Keller (auth), Somberg achieves liberation through art, Insight, 9/78; Elizabeth Miller (auth), Somberg's retrospective, Univ Minn Rev, 3/79; Mary Scarvalone (auth), Somberg's art, Minn Daily, 5/79. *Mem:* Artists' Guild, West Palm Beach, Fla. *Media:* Oil. *Mailing Add:* 1131 Monroe St NE Minneapolis MN 55413

SOMERS, FREDERICK D(UANE)
PAINTER
b Omaha, Neb, Feb 26, 42. *Study:* Univ Omaha, BFA, 65; Univ Iowa, MA(drawing), MFA(painting). *Work:* Univ Minn Hosp, Minneapolis; Nebr Mus Art, Kearny. *Comn:* Northland Insurance, St Paul, Minn, 91-92; Wausau Insurance, Wis; Radison Hotels, Scottsdale, Ariz; Mayo Clinic, Rochester, Minn; Lutheran Brotherhood, Minneapolis. *Exhib:* Charles H MacNider Mus, 10th Ann Area Competition, Mason City, Iowa, 75; Solo shows, Light in Tangent, Smaland Mus, Vaxjo, Sweden, 84, Am Swed Inst, Minneapolis, 84 & Homeland, Am Swed Inst, 88; Contemporary Realism, Nat Exhib, Yuma Art Ctr & Leslie Levy Gallery, Scottsdale, 85-86; Nebraska Artists Retrospective, Nebr Mus Art, Kearny, 90; Nat Wetlands Exhib, Yonkers, NY, 92. *Teaching:* Instr drawing, painting & printmaking, Carleton Col, Northfield, Minn, 70 & 73 & St Olaf Col, 71, 72, 74, 75 & 80; Watercolor painting, Musssjo Folkhogskola, Sweden, 89. *Awards:* Various Peoples & Jurors Choice Awards. *Bibliog:* Article, US Art Mag, 3/89. *Mem:* Full mem, Pastel Soc Am. *Media:* Pastels, Oils. *Mailing Add:* 9775 Dennison Blvd S Northfield MN 55057

SOMERS, H(ARRY W)
PAINTER, PRINTMAKER
b Zweibruecken, Ger, May 28, 22; US citizen. *Study:* Dookie Col, Australia; City Col New York, cert; Art Students League; Brisbane Art Ctr, Australia; also with Joseph Schwartz & S Greene. *Work:* Dookie Col, Victoria, Australia; Stadtmuseum Zweibruecken, Ger; Lowe Art Mus, Coral Gables, Fla; Metrop Mus & Art Ctr, Miami, Fla; Nat Art Gallery, Wellington, NZ; and others. *Exhib:* Mayer Gallery, Ft Lauderdale, 76-79; Klein Gallery, Beverly Hills, 78-79; Artworld Gallery, San Diego, 80-82; Frances Aronson Gallery, Atlanta, 83-89; Park Shore Gallery, Naples, 88; one man shows, Tokyo, London, Paris, Brussels, Dallas, Houston, San Francisco, Laguna Beach, Los Angeles, Caracas, San Diego, Phoenix, Washington & Palm Springs; and others. *Bibliog:* Charles Z Offin (auth), articles, 70, 71 & 72 & Beatrice Dain (auth), article, 3/74, Pictures on Exhibit; Lawrence Dame (auth), Somers the impressionist, Palm Beach Post, 1/78. *Mem:* Am Artists Prof League; Artists Equity Asn. *Media:* Acrylic, Oil; Serigraphy, Silkscreen. *Publ:* Auth, The Art of Collecting, 63. *Dealer:* D Treff Box 26624 Tamarac FL 33320. *Mailing Add:* 7362 La Reserve Circle Tamarac FL 33321

SOMERSON, ROSANNE
CRAFTSMAN, EDUCATOR
b Philadelphia, Pa, June 21, 54. *Study:* RI Sch Design, BFA, 76. *Work:* Mus Fine Arts, Boston, Mass; Brockton Art Mus, Mass; Yale Gallery Fine Arts, New Haven, Conn; RI Sch Design Mus; Kohn Pedersen Fox & Conway, New York. *Exhib:* Craft Today USA, Mus Decorative Arts, Louve Mus, Paris, France & traveling Europe, 89-90; New American Furniture, Mus Fine Arts, Renwick Gallery, Smithsonian Inst, Washington, DC, 90 & Oakland Mus, Calif, 90. *Teaching:* Grad furniture design faculty, RI Sch Design, 84- *Awards:* Grand Prize Winner, Am Crafts Guild, 87; Nat Endowment Arts Visual Arts Fel, 84 & 88; Mass Artists Fel, 88. *Bibliog:* Barb Meyer (auth), Contemporary American Craft Art, Smith Books, 88; Edward S Cooke Jr (auth), New American Furniture: The Second Generation, Mus Fine Arts, Boston, Mass, 89; Kulturweltspiegel: Furniture as Art, Ger Television Ard 1, 90. *Mem:* Am Craft Coun; WARP. *Media:* Furniture Design. *Publ:* Auth, Looking Back & Forth & Furniture of the 90's (catalogue), Essay Conn Vis & Performing Arts, Tex Med Ctr; Perfect Sweep, Am Craft, June/July. *Dealer:* Peter Joseph Gallery 745 Fifth Ave New York NY 10151; Pritam & Eames Gallery 29 Race Lane East Hampton NY 11937. *Mailing Add:* 771 Division Westport MA 02790

SOMERVILLE, ROMAINE STEC
ADMINISTRATOR
b Scranton, Pa, May 24, 30. *Study:* Marymount Col, BA, 51; Columbia Univ, MA, 53; Yale Univ, 58-60. *Collections Arranged:* The Peale Collection of the Maryland Historical Society, 75 (coauth, catalog) & Life in Maryland in the 18th Century, Bicentennial Exhib, 76, Md Hist Soc. *Pos:* Cur art, Everhart Mus, Scranton, Pa, 54-58; cur decorative art, Baltimore Mus Art, 60-63; exec dir, Baltimore City Comn Hist & Archit Preservation, 66-72; asst dir & chief cur, Md Hist Soc, 72-78, dir, 78-84; field consult, Nat Endowment Arts, 84-86; consult cur, Bicentennial Exhib, Roman Cath Archdiocese of Baltimore, 86-90. *Teaching:* Lectr art hist, Marywood Col, Scranton, Pa, 54-58; lectr Am decorative arts, Johns Hopkins Univ evening sch, 78-82. *Mem:* Preserv Md; Baltimore Heritage; Am Asn Museums; Victorian Soc Am; Art Students League. *Res:* Nineteenth century American architecture, decorative arts and painting. *Publ:* Contribr, Maryland Heritage, Five Baltimore Institutions Celebrate the American Bicentennial, Md Hist Soc, 76. *Mailing Add:* 118 W Lafayette Ave Baltimore MD 21217

SOMMER, FRANK H, III
HISTORIAN, ARCHEOLOGIST
b Newark, NJ, July 30, 22. *Study:* Yale Col; Yale Grad Sch; Corpus Christi Col, Cambridge Univ, Henry Fel, 47-48; Art Students League. *Work:* Yale Univ Art Gallery; Peabody Mus, Yale Univ; Brooklyn Mus, NY; Mus Mod Art, New York; Wintherthur Mus, Del. *Collections Arranged:* Pennsylvanian German Folk Art, 62; Recent Accessions, Winterthur Libr, 63-78 & Winterthur Mus. *Pos:* Keeper folk art, Winterthur Mus, 58-63, head of libr, 63-87. *Teaching:* Teaching asst, Yale Univ, 46-48; from instr to prof anthrop & art hist, Univ Del, 48-87 Pos, Coordr, Winterthur Prog, Univ Del, 52-55. *Res:* Design books, trade catalogues, architectural books; Anglo-American classicism and United States folk art. *Publ:* Auth, NW Argentine Archeology, 42, Excavations, 49 & Metamorphoses of Britannia, 76, Yale Univ; Triumph of Neptune, Warburg, 61; Thomas Jefferson's First Plan, Friends Independence Hall Nat Park, 76; Arts of the Pennsylvania Germans, Winterthur Mus, 83. *Mailing Add:* 1203 N Clayton St Wilmington DE 19806

SOMMER, FREDERICK
PHOTOGRAPHER, LANDSCAPE ARTIST
b Angri, Italy, Sept 7, 05; US citizen. *Study:* Cornell Univ, Ithaca, NY, MA(landscape archit), 27; Univ Ariz, Hon DFA, 79. *Work:* Ctr Creative Photog, Univ Ariz, Tucson. *Exhib:* one-man shows, Photogs, Paintings & Drawings, Inst Design, Ill Inst Technol, Chicago, 57, Art Inst Chicago, 63, Drawings & Objects, Washington Gallery Mod Art, Washington, DC, Pasadena Art Mus, 65, Philadelphia Col Art, Pa, 68 & Light Gallery, New York, 72; and others. *Pos:* Coordr, Fine Arts Studies, Prescott Col, Ariz, 66-71. *Awards:* Distinguished Career in Photography, Friends Photog, 82. *Bibliog:* Cynthia Jaffee McCabe (auth), The Golden Door, Artist-Immigrants of America, 1876-1976, Hirshhorn Mus & Sculpture Garden, Smithsonian Inst, Washington, DC, 76. *Publ:* Auth, The Poetic Logic of Art & Aesthetics, 72. *Mailing Add:* c/o Turner Krull Gallery 9006 Melrose Ave Los Angeles CA 90069

SOMMESE, LANNY BEAL
EDUCATOR, DESIGNER
b East Moline, Ill, May 14, 43. *Study:* Univ Fla, Gainesville, BD(graphics), 65, BFA(painting), 66; Univ Ill, Urbana, MFA(graphic design), 70. *Work:* Libr Cong; Zachata Art Gallery, Warsaw, Poland; Lahti Art Mus, Finland; Colo State Collection, Ft Collins; Moravian Gallery, Brno, Czech. *Exhib:* Warsaw Poster Biennale, Poland, 74, 76, 78, 80, 84, 86 & 88; New York Art Dirs Club, 76, 82 & 86; Colo State Biennale, Ft Collins, 79, 81, 83, 85 & 87; Lahti Poster Biennale, Finland, 79, 81, 83, 85 & 87; Brno Graphic Design Biennale, Czech, 80, 82, 84, 86 & 88; Toyama Triennial of Poster, Japan, 85. *Teaching:* Instr, Univ Ill, Urbana, 70; from instr to prof & head graphic design, Pa State Univ, 70- *Awards:* Merit Award, New York Art Dirs Club, 76, 79 & 82; Gold Medal, Univ & Col Design Asn, 79. *Bibliog:* Gibbons & Kinser

(auths), article, Graphis 202, 78; Fukuda (auth), article, Idea 176, 83; Neumeier (auth), article, Communication Arts, 5-6/83; Von Conta (auth) article, Novum Gebrauchsgraphik, 7/88; article, Design J, 4/88. *Mem:* Am Inst Graphic Arts. *Publ:* Auth, James McMullan, Graphis 213, 82; Tom Carnase, Ligature, 82; McRay Magleby, Print, 82; Design and technology, 7/83 & coauth, Design training USA, 9/83, Novum Gebrauchsgraphik; auth, On Campus: Personal Motives and Publis Interest, Am Inst Graphic Arts J, Vol VII, 88; Design Resource 7/88, Mobium Corp for Design & Commun, 10/88, Novum Gebrauchsgraphic. *Mailing Add:* Dept Visual Arts Penn State Univ University Park PA 16802

SONDAY, MILTON FRANKLIN, JR
CURATOR
b Hamburg, Pa, Dec 18, 39. *Study:* Wyomissing Inst Fine Arts, Pa, 55-61; Carnegie-Mellon Univ, Pittsburgh, Pa, 57-61, BFA(painting & design), 61; Penland Sch Crafts, NC, summer 66; ETenn State Univ (Penland Sch), summer 67; US Dept Agr Grad Sch, Washington, DC, fall 67; The Textile Mus (seminar), 67; The New Sch, New York, 68; Ctr Int d'Etude des Textiles Anciens, Lyon, France, 69. *Exhib:* Student Exhib, Carnegie Inst of Technol, 57-61; Reading Pub Mus & Art Gallery, Pa, 63; Gallery Mod Art, Fredricksburg, Va, 63. *Pos:* Mus assst & staff artist, Textile Mus, Washington, DC, 62-65, keeper of rugs, 65-67; asst cur textiles, Cooper Union Mus, New York, 67-68; cur textiles, Cooper-Hewitt Mus Design, Smithsonian Mus, New York, 68- *Awards:* New York Home Fashion League Art Award, 72. *Mem:* Ctr Int d'Etudes des Textiles Anciens, Lyon, France. *Publ:* Illusr, Tiahnuaco Tapestry Design, 63 & Principles of Tixtile Conservation Science, 63-64, The Textile Mus; auth, Counterchange & New Color, Handweaver and Craftsman, summer, 69; coauth, with N Kajitani, A Type of Mughal Sash, 70 & A Second Type of Mughal Sash, 71, The Textile Mus J. *Mailing Add:* c/o Cooper-Hewitt Mus 2 East 91st St New York NY 10128

SONENBERG, JACK
PAINTER, SCULPTOR
b Toronto, Ont, Dec 28, 25; US citizen. *Study:* Ont Col Art, Toronto; NY Univ; Washington Univ, BFA. *Work:* Guggenheim Mus, Whitney Mus Am Art & Metrop Mus Art, New York; Nat Gallery Can, Ottawa. *Exhib:* Whitney Mus Am Art, 67 & Biennial, 73; Cut, Folded & Torn, Mus Mod Art, New York, 74; Small Scale in Contemp Art, Chicago Art Inst, 75; Sitesights 1980, Pratt Inst; Contemporary American Prints and Drawings 1940-80, Nat Gallery, Washington, DC, 81; Drawing by Sculptors--Two Decades, Seagram Col, 84; Large Drawings, Independent Curators, 84-85; Painting Beyond the Death of Painting, Artists Union, Moscow, 89; Painting Self-Evident, Piccolo Spoleto, Charleston, 92. *Pos:* Ford Found & Am Fedn Arts Artist in resident grant, Hampton Inst, 66. *Teaching:* Instr painting & sculpture, Pratt Inst, 68- *Awards:* First Prize for Painting, 13th New Eng Ann, 62; NY State Coun Creative Artist Serv Prog Grant, 73 & 76; Guggenheim Found Grant, 73; Sculpture Award, Nat Endowment Arts, 84-85; Painting Award, New York Found for Arts, 89. *Media:* Miscellaneous Media. *Mailing Add:* 217 E 23rd St New York NY 10010

SONFIST, ALAN
ENVIRONMENTAL ARTIST
b New York, NY, Mar 26, 46. *Work:* Mus Mod Art, Albright-Knox Mus, Mus Mod Art, New York; Boston Mus Fine Art; Oberlin Art Mus, Ohio; Wallarf-Richartz Mux, Koln, Ger; Power Inst, Sydney, Australia; Mus Contemp Art, Chicago; High Mus, Atlanta, Ga; J B Speed Mus, Louisville, Ky. *Comn:* Four Seasons (sculpture), Temple Univ, Pa; 5 Time Enclosures with Forrest Seeds, Grove Isle, Fla; Time Landscape: Dual History Forrest, St Louis, Mo; Time Landscape, Greenwich Village, NY; Time Landscape, Redhook, NY; Hemlock Forrest, Bronx, NY; Towers of Growth, Louisville, Ky; Sun Monument, Kingston, RI; Earth Wall, Buffalo, NY; Rock Monument of Buffalo, NY; 100 Foot Column of Earth, Morgan City, La. *Exhib:* One-man shows, Smithsonian Inst, 78, High Mus Art, Atlanta, 79, Albright-Knox Mus, Buffalo, NY, 80, J B Speed Art Mus, Louisville, Ky, 81, Corcoran Mus, Washington, DC, 84, World's Fair, Osaka, Japan, 88 & Max Protetch Gallery, New York, 90; Boston Mus Fine Arts, 71 & 77; Stedelijk Mus, Holland, 71; Nature of Things, Harcus Karkow, Boston, 71; Interaction with the Environment, Whitney Mus Am Art, 78; Hudson River Artists, Vassar Col Art Mus, 79; Artist Parks and Gardens, Mus Contemp Art, Chicago, 81; Metamanhattan, Whitney Mus Am Art, Downtown, New York, 84; The Artist As Social Designer, Los Angeles Co Mus, 85; World's Fair in Osaka, Japan, 88; Public Sculpture Show, Whitney Mus Am Art, Downtown, New York, 90; Green, Max Protetch Gallery, New York, 91; and others. *Awards:* Creative Artists Pub Serv Grant, 77; Nat Endowment Arts Grant, 78 & 79. *Bibliog:* Robert Hobbs (auth), Review, Sculpture Mag, 12/90; Regina Hackett (auth), Heavyweight artists discuss public works, stress collaboration, Seattle Times, 5/20/91; Giuliano Gori (auth), Living with art: Skeletons, stairways, and thunderbolts, ARTNews, 1/91. *Mailing Add:* 205 Mulberry St New York NY 10012

SONNABEND, JOAN
ART DEALER, COLLECTOR
b Boston, Mass, July 9, 28. *Study:* Sarah Lawrence Col, BA, 50. *Specialty:* Contemporary American and European, drawings, painting, sculpture and prints. *Mailing Add:* 72 Mt Vernon St Boston MA 02108

SONNEMAN, EVE
PHOTOGRAPHER, FILMMAKER
b Chicago, Ill, Jan 14, 46. *Study:* Univ Ill, Urbana-Champaign, BFA, 67; Univ NMex, Albuquerque, MA, 69. *Work:* Mus Mod Art, New York; Mus Fine Arts, Houston; Art Inst Chicago; Minneapolis Inst Art; Menil Found, Houston; Metrop Mus Art, New York. *Exhib:* One-man shows, Art Resources Ctr, Whitney Mus, New York, 73, Galerie Farideh Cadot, Paris, France, 77, 80 & 83, Castelli Gallery, New York, 77, 78, 80, 82, 84, 86 & 89, Cirrus Gallery, Los Angeles, 81 & 83 & Tucson Mus Art, Ariz, 81; Mus Mod Art, New York, 78-80; Ctr Beabourg, Paris, 80 & 84; Venice Biennale, 79 & 81; Charles Cowles Gallery, New York, 92; and others. *Teaching:* Vis artist photog, Rice Univ, 71-72; vis instr photog, Sch Visual Arts, New York, 75-89; vis instr art, Cooper Union Col Art & Architecture, 75-85. *Awards:* Photography grants, Nat Endowment Arts, 71-72 & 78; Cartier Fel, France, 89. *Bibliog:* Group Portrait: 3 New York Photographers (film), Cable Arts, NY State Coun Arts, 75; Real Time, Printed Matter Press, New York, NY; Carter Ratcliff (auth), article, Art Am, Vol 65, No 6; Naomi Rosenblum (auth), A World History of Photography, Abbeville Press, 85; America's Cottage Gardens, Random House, 90. *Publ:* Auth, Realtime, Printed Matter, 76; Roses Are Read, Editions Generations, Paris, 82. *Dealer:* Leo Castelli Gallery 420 W Broadway New York NY 10012. *Mailing Add:* 503 W 43 St New York NY 10036

SONNENBERG, FRANCES
SCULPTOR
b Brooklyn, NY. *Study:* With Prof Alfred Van Loen. *Work:* Hall of Fame. *Comn:* Five ft carved acrylic sculpture, Aquarius, Fla, 75. *Exhib:* One-woman shows, Stephan Gallery, New York, Buyways Gallery, Fla, Shelter Rock Gallery, NY, Cedar Crest Col, Pa & Adelphi Univ, NY; and others. *Teaching:* Sculpture classes in own studio, 72- *Mem:* Nat Asn Women Artists; NY Soc Women Artists (secy, 73-74, rec secy, 74-); Metrop Painters & Sculptors (rec secy, 73-, secy, 74-); Am Soc Contemp Artists; Artist Craftsman. *Media:* Acrylic. *Mailing Add:* Rockhill Rd Roslyn Heights NY 11577

SONNIER, KEITH
SCULPTOR
b Mamou, La, July 31, 41. *Study:* Rutgers Univ, NJ, MFA, 66. *Work:* Hara Mus Contemp Art, Tokyo; Mus Mod Art & Whitney Mus, New York; Australian Nat Gallery, Canberra; Von Abbe Mus, Eindhoven, Holland; Moderna Museet, Stockholm, Sweden; Dr Peter Ludwig Collection, Aachen, WGer; Mus Contemp Art, LA Calif; Mus Haus Lange, Krefeld, WGer. *Comn:* Neon work & bamboo sculptures, Ahmedabad, India, 81; neon installations, Segrams Co, 82 & Palladium, 85, New York. *Exhib:* Leo Castelli Gallery, New York, 70's & 82, 84 & 85, 89 & 90; Kunsthalle Basel, Switz, 81; Postminimalism, Aldrich Mus, Ridgefield, Conn, 82; PS 1 (with catalog), Long Island City, NY, 83; Madi in India, Mus Mod Art, New York, 86; Galerie Montemy, Paris, 86 & 89; Blum-Helman Gallery, New York, 86 & 90; Tony Shafrazi Gallery, New York,86 & 89; Domaine de Kerguehennec, Rennes, France, 87; Keith Sonnier/Lynda Benglis, Alexandria Mus, Alexandria, La, 87; solo exhibs Neon Sculpture, Chrysler Mus, Norfolk, Va, 88 & Expanded file series: 1969-1989, Stadtisches Mus, Abteiber; Hirshhorn Mus, Nat Gallery, Wash, DC; The New Sculpture 1965-1975; Between Geometry and Gesture, Whitney Mus Am Art, NY, 90. *Teaching:* Instr art & art hist, Rutgers Univ, NJ, 69-72, Sch Visual Arts, New York, 72-84 & Bard Col, Rhinebeck, NY, 84-86. *Awards:* Guggenheim Fel, 74; First Prize, Tokyo Prints Biennale, 74; Nat Endowment Arts, 86. *Bibliog:* Donald Kuspit (auth), Interim Shrines: The Sculptures of Keith Sonnier (catalog), 89; Richard Armstrong and Richard Marshall (auth), The New Sculpture 1965-75: Between Geometry and Gesture (catalog); Linda McGreevy, The Janus Strategy: Keith Sonnier Looks East and West, Arts, 10/89. *Dealer:* Leo Castelli Gallery 420 W Broadway New York NY 10012. *Mailing Add:* 145 Chambers St New York NY 10007

SOORIKIAN, DIANA TASHJIAN
PAINTER
b Philadelphia, Pa, Sept 16, 28. *Study:* Philadelphia Col Art, BFA, 50; Columbia Univ, with Jack Tworkov, MFA, 73. *Work:* NJ State Mus, Trenton; Columbia Univ; Becton Dickinson Co, Paramus, NJ. *Exhib:* Pa Acad Fine Arts Ann Exhib, 57 & 67; Silvermine Guild Artists Exhib, 72, 73 & 74; Trenton State Mus Ann Exhib Painting & Sculpture, 73 & 74; NJ Artists Third Biennial, Newark Mus, 81-82; Bergen Co Artists, Bergen Community Mus, Paramus, NJ, 82-83. *Pos:* Asst art dir, Johnstone Inc, New York, 58-62; graphics designer, fashion illus, Market Signs, New York, 81- *Teaching:* Prof fine arts, Fairleigh Dickinson Univ, Hackensack, NJ; drawing instr, Art Ctr, NJ. *Awards:* Eloise Egan Mem Award, 23rd New England Exhib, 72; Purchase Prize, Trenton State Mus Ann Exhib Painting & Sculpture, 74; Fel, NJ State Coun Arts, 87-88. *Bibliog:* David Spengler (auth), The self got lost, Bergen Rec, 7/4/74; Piri Halasz (auth), Jersey artists saluted, 6/9/75 & Helen Harrison (auth), Self portraits, 12/1/85, New York Times. *Mem:* Assoc Artists NJ. *Media:* Oil, Graphite. *Mailing Add:* 430 W 14th St No 309 New York NY 10014

SOPPELSA, GEORGE
PAINTER, COLLAGE ARTIST
b Youngstown, Ohio, July 16, 39. *Study:* Ohio State Univ, BFA, 61. *Work:* Mulvane Art Ctr, Topeka, Kans. *Exhib:* One-man shows, Int Art Galerie Reich, Köln, 77, 81, 84, 87, 90, Mulvane Art Ctr, Topeka, 85, John Szoke Gallery, New York, 89, Univ Conn, 90; Ann Midyear Exhib, Butler Inst Am Art, Youngstown, 85, 90, 92; Works on Paper, Berkshire Mus, Pittsfield, 86; Dreamscapes-Aspects of Surreality in Connecticut, Mattatuck Mus, Waterbury, 88; ARCHA Soc Touring Mus Exhib, Ger, 93. *Awards:* Nat Endowment Arts Fel, 87; Vt Studio Colony Fel, 88; Conn Comn on the Arts, Individual Artist Grant, 91. *Bibliog:* Christine Smith (auth), Classical balance within the new realist idiom, Int Art Galerie, Köln, 81; C Charles Rump (auth), Tanzer aus Goldeiner Zeit, Kölnische Rundschau,3/22/84; Vivian Raynor (auth), A miscellany of figures in American art, New York Times, 7/10/88; Leo Forte (auth), Bridges Between Two Worlds of Light, Int Art Galerie Reich, Köln, 89. *Media:* Acrylic. *Mailing Add:* 135 Central Ave East Hartford CT 06108

SORBY, J RICHARD
PAINTER, DESIGNER
b Duluth, Minn, Dec 21, 11. *Study:* Univ Minn; Univ Northern Colo, AB, 37, MA, 51; Art Inst Chicago; Univ of the Am, Mexico City; Univ Calif, Los Angeles, with John Ferren; Univ Colo, with Jimmy Ernst. *Work:* William Rockhill Nelson Gallery, Kansas City, Mo; Denver Art Mus; Joslyn Mem Mus Art, Omaha; San Jose Mus Art; Brigham Young Univ; and many others. *Comn:* Spaulding Mem, Univ Northern Colo, Greeley, 58; Little Theatre of the Rockies; Ford Motor Co. *Exhib:* Denver Art Mus Ann Western Artists, 40-59; Nat Watercolor Competition, Nat Gallery Art, Washington, DC, 41; Mid-Am Ann Exhibs, Nelson Gallery Art, Kansas City, Mo; Nat Rocky Mountain Watermedia Exhib, Golden, Colo, 79; Calif State Fair Exhib; Whitney Mus Am Art, New York; Pa Acad Fine Arts, Philadelphia; Oakland Art Mus, Calif; Crocker Art Gallery, Sacramento; San Diego Art Mus; solo exhibs, Denver Art Mus, San Jose State Univ, Casa Guleria, Casa de las Campanas San Diego, Calif, 91; and others. *Teaching:* Instr art, Univ Nebr, Lincoln, 40-42; assoc prof painting, Sch Art, Univ Denver, 47-59; prof painting & design, Calif State Univ, San Jose, 59-72, emer prof, 72- *Awards:* Purchase Award, 4th Biennial 10 State Exhib, Joslyn Mem Mus, 56 & Ann Metro Exhib, Denver Art Mus, 64; First Prize for Non-objective Painting, Univ Santa Clara, 66; Purchase Awards, Mid-Am Ann, Kansas City & Nat Watercolor Competition, Washington, DC; First Prize & Purchase Award, Southern Utah State Univ. *Bibliog:* Arneil (auth), Work of Richard Sorby, Empire Mag, Denver Post, 11/58; M L Stribling (auth), Painting in Found Materials, 71. *Media:* Acrylic, Watercolor; Mixed. *Publ:* Illusr, Lincoln-Mercury Times, 54, Ford Times, 56 & Empire Mag, Denver Post, 58. *Mailing Add:* 18655 W Bernardo Dr San Diego CA 92127

SORCE, ANTHONY JOHN
PAINTER
b Chicago, Ill, Apr 30, 37. *Study:* Am Acad Art, dipl, 57; Univ Notre Dame, BFA, 61, MFA, 62. *Work:* Kalamazoo Inst Art, Mich; Wichita Art Mus, Kans; J B Speed Mus, Louisville, Ky; Chase Manhattan & IBM, New York, NY. *Comn:* Sculpture, Wichita Art Mus, Kans, 70; painting, TRW, Linhurst, Ohio, 84-85; painting, Arby's Inc, Atlanta, Ga, 90. *Exhib:* Solo exhibs, Kalamazoo Inst Art, Mich, 66, Jewish Mus, New York, 70, Wichita Art Mus, Kans, 70, O K Harris Works of Art, New York, 77, 79, 80, 82, 84 & 86; Midyear Exhibition, Butler Inst Art, Youngstown, Ohio, 62; Watercolor USA, Springfield Art Mus, Mo, 63; 2nd Flint International, Flint Inst Art, Mich, 70; New York Gallery Showcase, Okla Art Ctr, Oklahoma City, 81. *Teaching:* Instr art, Nazareth Col of Kalamazoo, Mich, 62-67; assoc prof art, Nazareth Col of Rochester, Mich, 67-68; prof art, Manhattan Community Col, City Univ New York, 71- *Awards:* Guggenheim Fel, 68; Fac Res Award for Painting, City Univ, New York, 73-74, State Univ, NY, 74-75. *Media:* Rhoplex, Acrylic. *Dealer:* O K Harris Works of Art 383 West Broadway New York NY 10012. *Mailing Add:* 155 Bank St Apt 939B New York NY 10014

SOREFF, HELEN
PAINTER
b New York, NY. *Study:* Atlanta Art Inst, BFA(High Mus Art Scholar, Beaux Arts Scholar), 52; Art Students League, Grand Concours, 53; NY Univ; C W Post Col, Long Island Univ, MA, 76. *Exhib:* Solo exhibs, Lamagna Gallery, 75, 55 Mercer Gallery, 77, Bertha Urdang Gallery, 77 & 78, Condesco-Lawler Gallery, 83, Guild Hall Mus, East Hampton, NY, 88 & Islip Mus, New York, 90; Clocktower, New York, 86; Graham Mod Gallery, 86; Guild Hall Mus, East Hampton, New York, 87; East Hampton Gallery, New York, 89; Am Abstract Artists, Gallery 55, Mercer, New York, 89; Lines of Vision, Blum Helman Gallery, New York, 89; and many others. *Teaching:* Instr, Parsons Sch of Design, Liberal Studies, New York, 88- 90. *Awards:* Adolph Gottlieb Found Grant, 86; Fel painting, New York Found Arts, 87. *Bibliog:* Peggy Cyphers (auth), Arts Mag, 10/89; Walter Thompson (auth), Art Am, 11/89; Peter Frank (auth), Kunst forum, Ger, 1-2/90. *Mem:* Am Abstract Artists Asn. *Media:* Acrylic. *Dealer:* M-13 Gallery 72 Greene St New York NY 10012. *Mailing Add:* 79 Mercer St New York NY 10012

SOREFF, S See Soreff, Stephen

SOREFF, STEPHEN
CONCEPTUAL ARTIST, PAINTER
b New York, NY, Feb 2, 31. *Study:* Brooklyn Col, BA, 54; Pratt Inst, BA, 60. *Work:* Mus Mod Art Libr & Whitney Mus Libr, New York; Hirshhorn Mus Libr, Washington, DC; Nat Mus, Stockholm Sweden. *Exhib:* Solo exhibs, Betty Parsons Gallery, New York, 75, Artworks Gallery, New York, 81, Lucus Gallery, Los Angeles, Calif, 83 & Hillwood Gallery, Long Island Univ, Brookville, NY, 86; Cologne Mus, Ger, 81; Hasselt Mus, Belg, 83; Sotheby's, New York, 86; Graham Gallery, New York, 86; Mus Hudson Highlands, Cornwall, NY, 87; Guild Hall Mus, East Hampton, NY, 88; Benton Gallery, Southampton, NY, 88; Chauncy Gallery, Princeton, NJ, 90. *Pos:* Staff reviewer, Artworld, 74, 57th Street Rev, 74-75, Art Economist, 80-81; sr ed, Art & Artists, 81-83; ed & publ, Avant Garde Art Rev, 80-90. *Teaching:* Prof art & design, Long Island Univ, Brookville, NY, 70- *Awards:* Res grants, Long Island Univ Res Comt, 80, 83 & 90; Residency, MacDowell Colony, Peterborough, NH, 83; Residency, Va Colony Arts, Sweet Briar, Va. *Bibliog:* Michael Buono (auth), Stephen Soreff, Art News, 64; In the art galleries, New York Post, 64; The big thing show?, Seattle Times, 69. *Mailing Add:* 79 Mercer St New York NY 10012

SOREL, EDWARD
ILLUSTRATOR, WRITER
b New York, NY, Mar 26, 29. *Study:* Cooper Union, dipl, 51. *Work:* 966-3949. *Exhib:* One-man shows, Graham Gallery, New York, 73, New Sch Social Res, 74 & Galerie Bartsch & Chariau, Munich, 86; Push Pin Style, Mus des Arts Decoratifs, Paris, 70; Susan Conway Galleries, Washington, DC, 92. *Pos:* Co-founder, Push-Pin Studios, New York, 53-56; art dir, CBS Promotion Art, New York, 56-57; syndicated cartoonist, King Features, 69-71; contribr, Atlantic Mag, 69-; contrib ed, New York Mag, 72-78 & GQ Mag, 84-; cartoonist, Village Voice, 74-78; cartoonist, The Nation, 85, New Yorker, 90- *Awards:* St Gauden's Medal, Cooper Union, 73; George Polk Award for Satiric Drawing, 81; Page One Award, Newspaper Guild, 88. *Bibliog:* Carlos C Drake (auth), Edward Sorel, Graphis, No 105, 63; Jerome Snyder (auth), Edward Sorel, Graphis, No 154, 71-72. *Mem:* Soc Illusrs; The Century Asn. *Media:* Pen & Ink, Watercolor. *Publ:* Illusr, Word People, 70; Magical Storybook, 72; auth & illusr, Moon Missing, 72; Making the World Safe for Hypocrisy, 72; Superpen, 78. *Mailing Add:* 156 Franklin St New York NY 10013

SORELL, VICTOR ALEXANDER
HISTORIAN, ADMINISTRATOR
b Mexico City, Mex, Oct 31, 44. *Study:* Shimer Col, BA; Univ Chicago, with Joshua C Taylor and John Rewald, MA; Univ Chicago. *Collections Arranged:* Mexposicion I (with catalog in Eng & Span), 75 & Mexposicion II: Photographic Images of the Mex Revolution by Agustin Victor Casasola, 76, A Montgomery Ward Gallery, Univ Ill, Chicago Circle; Hispanic American Art in Chicago & Chilean Arpilleras, Univ Galleries, Chicago State Univ, 80. *Pos:* Co-ed, Abrazo (Embrace) J, 76-; prog adminr, Park Forest Art Ctr, 78 & 79; coordr, Hispanic Am Cult Enrichment Progs, Chicago State Univ, 79-80 & 83; fac fel art hist & sr prog officer, Nat Endowment Humanities, 80-83. *Teaching:* Chmn art dept, Chicago State Univ, 75-80 & 83. *Awards:* Fac Scholar, Inst Bilingual Educ, Educ Prof Develop Act, 75; Grant, Ill Humanities Coun, 76; Grants, Ill Arts & Humanities Coun, 80. *Mem:* Col Art Asn Am; el Movimiento Artistico Chicano (chmn, 79). *Res:* Documentary investigation of modern (1900-present) Canadian, Mexican & US mural art; Chilean arpilleras and subject of human rights as reflected in visual arts. *Publ:* Auth, Barrio murals in Chicago: Painting the Hispanic-American experience on our community walls, In: Revista Chicano--Riquena, Ind Univ-Northwest, 75; co-reviewer articles in American studies sect, Am Quart, 69-73; transl, Jose David Alfaro Siqueiros (auth), Como se Pinta un Mural (How to Paint a Mural), 78; ed, Guide to Chicago Murals: Yesterday and Today, 1st ed, 78, 2nd ed, 79; auth, Hispanic American Art in Chicago (catalog), 80. *Mailing Add:* 10420 S Wood St Chicago IL 60643

SORENSEN, JEAN
PAINTER
b San Diego, Calif. *Study:* San Jose State Univ; study with Eliot O'Hara, Erick Oback, Rex Brandt, Robert Moesle, Robert E Wood & Tom Hill; Univ Calif, Santa Cruz. *Work:* Permanent city collections in Okayama, Japan and Syktyvkar, Russia. *Comn:* Watercolor, City of Los Altos, Calif, 90. *Exhib:* Nat Asn Women Artists 83rd Ann Exhib, Nat Acad Design, New York, 72; Mostra in Italy, Palazzo Vecchio, Florence, 72. *Teaching:* Instr watercolor, De Anza Col, Cupertino, Calif, 84. *Awards:* Gene Alden Walker Award, Nat Asn Women Artists, 72. *Bibliog:* A study of contemporary art in America, Le Revue Moderne, Paris, 71 & 74; Robert & Phyllis Boverie (coauths), Artists of Central and Northern California, Vol 1, Mountain Publ Tex Inc, 89. *Mem:* Nat Asn Women Artists; Soc Western Artists. *Media:* Watercolor. *Mailing Add:* 8422 Chenin Blanc Ln San Jose CA 94135

SORGE, WALTER
PAINTER, PRINTMAKER
b Forestberg, Alta, Oct 25, 31. *Study:* Univ Calif, Los Angeles, BA, 54, MA, 55; Columbia Univ, EDD, 64; also with Stanley William Hayter, Paris, 61-62 & 68. *Work:* Victoria & Albert Mus, London, Eng; J B Speed Mus, Louisville, Ky; Sheldon Swope Art Gallery, Terre Haute, Ind. *Exhib:* One-man show, Inst Mex NAm Relationes Cult, Mexico City, 71; Sheldon Swope Art Gallery, Terre Haute, Ind, 71, Am Embassies, Ankara, Izmir & Istanbul, Turkey, 74-75; Second Can Biennial, 57 & Canadian Watercolors, Drawings & Prints, 66, Nat Gallery Can; Smithsonian Inst Traveling Exhib, Washington, DC, 67; and others. *Pos:* Chmn dept painting, drawing & printmaking, Ky Southern Col, 64-69 & Hardin-Simmons Univ, Tex, 69-70; chmn dept, Eastern Ill Univ, Charleston, 70-75, prof art, 75-; exchange prof, Portsmouth Polytech Inst, England, 77. *Awards:* C W Jefferys Award, 26th Ann Exhib, Can Soc Graphic Art, 59; Jr League Purchase Award, Mid-States Art Exhib, Evansville Mus Arts & Sci, Ind, 67; Helen Van Aken Purchase Award, Fifth Ann Gulf Coast Exhib, Mobile Art Gallery, 70. *Media:* Watercolor, Mixed Media; Intaglio. *Mailing Add:* c/o The Chicago Street Gallery 204 S Chicago St Lincoln IL 62656

SORKIN, EMILY
ART DEALER, GALLERY DIRECTOR
b New York, NY. *Study:* New York Univ, BS(art): Hunter Col, NY, MA(fine arts). *Collections Arranged:* New York to Bennington: Paintings (auth, catalog), 83 & Matter & Spirit, 85, Bennington Col, Vt; Seven Painters, State Univ NY, Purchase, 83; Ontogeny: Sculpture and Painting by 20th Century American Sculptors, New York Studio Sch, 85; Portraits and Self-Portraits, Sorkin Gallery, New York, 86. *Pos:* Dir, Robert Freidus Gallery, 76-77, John Gibson Gallery, 79-81 & Sorkin Gallery, 85-90, New York. *Bibliog:* Peter Gallo (auth), rev, Rutland Herald, Vt, 10/85; Barry Schwabsky (auth), rev, Arts Mag, 6/86; Vivien Raynor (auth), rev, New York Times, 4/86. *Specialty:* 20th century art. *Publ:* Auth, Intro to Bill Jensen Etching Portfolio, Universal Ed, 85; Matter & spirit, Bennington Col, Vt, 85; contribr, Bill Jensen Etchings (exhib catalog), Mus Mod Art, New York, 86; auth, The sculpture of Ronald Bladen, Arts Mag, 86; Introd to Margrit Lewczuk (exhib catalog), Heland Thorden Wetterling Galleries, Stockholm, Sweden, 87. *Mailing Add:* 150 Franklin St New York NY 10013

SORMAN, STEVEN
PAINTER, PRINTMAKER
b Minneapolis, Minn, June 14, 48. *Study:* Univ Minn, BFA, 71. *Work:* Mus Mod Art, New York; Whitney Mus Am Art, New York; Art Inst Chicago; Stedlijk Mus, Amsterdam; Walker Art Ctr, Minn. *Comn:* Springhill Found, Minn; Prudential Insurance; IBM; Honeywell; Hyatt Regency. *Exhib:* Printmakers Midwest Invitational, Walker Art Ctr, Minn, 73; Corcoran Biennial, Corcoran Gallery Art, Washington, DC, 75; Paper as Medium, Smithsonian Inst, Washington, DC, 78; Painting and Sculpture Today, Indianapolis Mus Art, Ind, 78; 21st Nat Print Exhib, Brooklyn Mus, New York, 78; 13th Int Biennial Graphic Art, Ljubljana, Yugoslavia, 79; Artist and Printer, Walker Art Ctr, Minn, 80; Bienal Americana de Artes Graficas, Museo de Arte Moderno La Tertulia, Colombia, 81; 24th Nat Print Exhib, Brooklyn Mus, 86; First Impressions, Walker Art Ctr, 89; The 1980's: Prints from the Collection of Joshua P Smith, Nat Gallery, 89; Contemp Illus Books, Words & Image, 67-88, Independent Curators Inc, 90. *Awards:* Bush Found Artist's Fel, 79; Merit Award, San Francisco Mus Mod Art, 80; Rockefeller Found, Am Ctr Artist in Residence, Paris, 82. *Bibliog:* Madeleine Deschamps (auth), La Peinture Americaine, Paris, 81; Richard Field (auth), Prints: History of an Art, Contemporary Trends, Geneva, 81; Tyler Graphics Catalogue Raisonne, New York, 87; Pat Gilmour (ed), Lasting Impressions: Lithography as Art, Canberra, 88. *Mailing Add:* 400 Maple Marine On St Croix MN 55047

SOROGAS, SOTIRIS
PAINTER
b Greece. *Work:* Nat Art Gallery, Athens, Greece; Collection Ion Vorres, Athens, Greece; Collection Pierides, Athens, Greece. *Exhib:* Bienale Sao Paolo, Brazil, 81; Bienale of Engravings Baden-Baden, Ger, 82; Palacho Venecia Rome, 84; China - Greece, Karkazis Gallery, Chicago, 84; Nat Gallery, Athens, Greece, 85. *Pos:* Asst prof, Nat Fine Art Sch Athens, Greece, currently. *Mailing Add:* c/o Rodi Karkazis Gallery 168 N Michigan Ave No 300 Chicago IL 60601

SOROKIN, JANET
GRAPHIC ARTIST, PAINTER
b Hartford, Conn, April 2, 32. *Study:* Simmons Col, 50-52, Univ Hartford Art Sch, with Paul Zimmerman; Trinity Col; Wesleyan Univ. *Work:* Mass Mutual Insurance Co, Springfield; Metrop Fed Bank, Nashville; Dewey Ballantine, New York; Allied Corp, Trumbull, Conn. *Comn:* 3 acrylic-collage paintings, Aetna Life & Casualty, Hartford, 84; 8 serigraphs chosen by Cesar Pelli & Assocs for the Cleveland Clinic, Ohio. *Exhib:* Boston Printmakers, De Cordova Mus, Lincoln, Mass, 79; Nat Acad Design, New York, 81, 84 & 90; NAWA Exhib, Bergen Community Mus, Paramus, NJ, 83; Conn Acad Fine Arts Exhib, William Benton Mus, Univ Conn, Storrs, 85 & 88; two-person exhib, Univ Minn at Morris, Humanities Fine Arts Gallery, 92; and others. *Awards:* First Prize, The Slater Mem Mus Ann Exhib, 81 & 88; Binney & Smith Award, 83; Janet Turner Award, Nat Asn Women Artists Ann Exhib, 85; and over 58 other awards. *Mem:* Nat Soc Painters Casein & Acrylic; Nat Asn Women Artists; Conn Watercolor Soc (bd mem); Conn Women Artists (bd mem); Conn Acad Fine Arts (coun, 82-90). *Media:* Acrylic on Canvas. *Publ:* Illusr, The Other Side II (poster), Modern Art Ed, 85; poster, In: Room Design, House Beautiful, 6/85; Contemporary Graphic Artists, Gale Res Co, New York, 88. *Dealer:* Signature Art Gallery West Hartford CT; Atrium Gallery St Louis MO. *Mailing Add:* 101 Mohawk Dr West Hartford CT 06117

SOROKIN, MAXINE ANN
PAINTER, EDUCATOR
b Brooklyn, NY, Dec 15, 48. *Study:* Kingsborough Community Col, AA, 67; Brooklyn Col, with Philip Pearlstein, Jimmy Ernst, Robert Wolff & Samuel Gelber, BA(cum laude), 70, MFA, 72. *Comn:* Window & portal paintings, Congregation of Kehillath Jacobs Synagogue, Newton, Mass, 73; paintings, Solomon Schechter Day Sch, Newton, Mass. *Exhib:* Invitational, Newton City Hall, Mass, 73-76; Meetinghouse Gallery, Boston, 73; Boston Visual Artists Union, 74 & 75; two-person exhibs, Goethe Inst, Boston, 80, Jewish Community Ctr Southern NJ, Cherry Hill, 80, Young Adult Ctr, Boston, 84 & Warner House Gallery, Univ Cincinnati, 86, and more. *Teaching:* Fel & grad asst painting, Brooklyn Col, 71-72; lectr art, Univ Mass, Boston, 72-73; assoc prof, Art Inst of Boston, 87-; visual arts coordr, Jewish Community Ctr, Stoughton-Newton, Mass, 87-; art specialist, Schecter Day Sch, 90, Harvard Hillel Children's Sch, 90 & The Rashi Sch, 91. *Awards:* Eisler Award Painting Excellence, City Univ New York, 70. *Bibliog:* Lisa Taylor (producer), Woman 76, WBZ Television, 76. *Mem:* Boston Visual Artists Union; West Roxbury Artists Asn (vpres, 77-78); West Roxbury Hist Soc; Victorian Soc. *Media:* Oil, Pen & Ink. *Publ:* Auth, Harvard Hillel Children's Sch Curric, Cambridge, Mass, 90-91. *Dealer:* Boston Fine Arts 420 Boylston St Boston MA; Crieger Art Assocs 35 Newbury St Boston MA 02116. *Mailing Add:* 61 Perham St West Roxbury MA 02132

SORRENTINO, RICHARD MICHAEL
MOSAIC ARTIST, MURALIST
b Brooklyn, NY, Nov 9, 49. *Study:* MEBA Sch Eng, Baltimore, AA(marine eng), 69; Byam Show Sch Painting, 73-74; Royal Acad London, 73-74; Pratt Inst, BFA, 75; MAAT Sch Art Inst Chicago, 93. *Work:* US Post Office, Tampa, Fla, 90. *Comn:* Tile flooring restoration, Tampa Theatre Bldg, Fla, 85; mural re-creation (painted tile), Mayfair in the Grove, Mayfair Hotel, Miami, 86; 22 ceramic panels, Fla Endowment, Tampa, 88. *Exhib:* Speed of Light, Fla Ctr Contemp Art, Tampa, 88. *Pos:* Pres, El Sama Non-Profit Arts Group, Tampa, 81-82 & Ceramica Europa Inc, Tampa, 82-91; bd mem, Fla Ctr Contemp Art, 82-85; quincentenial consult, Christopher Columbus; consult, Southeastern Pa Transporation Authority, Philadelphia, 90. *Teaching:* TA heavy metal, sculpture dept, Sch Art Inst Chicago, 92. *Bibliog:* Gayla Jameson (dir), 100 Years of Ybor City (film), Fla Endowment Humanties, 90. *Media:* Handpainted Ceramic Tile, Venetian Glass Mosaics. *Publ:* Coauth with L Peterson, Mural Making and its Role in the Art Therapy Process, Focusing on Prevention, Intervention and Restoration, Am Art Therapy Asn with Cata Conf Can Art Therapy Asn Conf, Toronto, 92. *Mailing Add:* 4728 N Dover St Chicago IL 60640

SOSNOWITZ, HENRY ABRAM
COLLECTOR, PATRON
b Warsaw, Poland, July 13, 40; US citizen. *Study:* Lublin Univs, Warsaw, BA; also with Henryk Sienkiewicz. *Work:* Sosnowitz collection of artist Kenneth Hari in Vatican, Rome, Trenton State Mus, NJ, Lincoln Ctr Libr & Mus Collection, Sport Mus & Metrop Mus Art, New York. *Interests:* American art to create a renaissance in the US. *Collection:* Picasso, Kenneth Hari, G'Miglio, J A Whistler, Mary Cassett, F Leyendecker & Larry Rivers. *Mailing Add:* Box 243 Keasbey NJ 08832

SOTTUNG, GEORGE (K)
PAINTER, ILLUSTRATOR
b Chicago, Ill. *Study:* Art Inst Chicago, grad; DePaul Univ; Brooklyn Mus Art, apprentice to Haddon H Sundblom. *Work:* Bethesda Naval Hosp Rotunda, Washington, DC; Princeton Univ, NJ; US Naval War Col, Newport, RI; US Military Acad, West Point; US Air Force Acad, Colorado Springs, 90. *Comn:* First Atlantic Crossing, 75, Capt Healy, 78 & Invasion of Normandy, 79-80, US Govt; US Military History oil paintings series, United Technologies, 84-85; Hist Portrait, Lt Elmer Stone, 89; many portrait comns for pvt individuals and corps. *Exhib:* Grumbacher Exhib, Scott-Fanton Mus, Danbury, Conn, 66; Allied Artists Am Exhib, Nat Acad Galleries, New York, 75 & Am Watercolor Soc Exhib, annually; Am Painters in Paris Exhib, Palais des Cong, France, 75 & 76; Art Inst Chicago; Smithsonian Inst; Fogg Mus; Nat Acad Design, 167th Ann Exhib, 92. *Pos:* Illusr, Chicago Tribune Co, 54-62, Charles E Cooper Studios, New York, 62-64; freelance artist & painter (style & technique, realism and abstraction), 64- *Awards:* President's Show Silver Medal, 80; Art Students League Award, New York, 83; Conn Watercolor Soc Award, 90. *Bibliog:* US Navy Artists (film), US Govt, 74; Ellen Anderson (auth), Meet George Sottung, North Light/Fletcher Art Serv, 76. *Mem:* Salmagundi Club; Am Watercolor Soc; Soc Illusr; Berkshire Art Asn; Chicago Press Club. *Media:* Oil, Acrylic; Watercolor. *Mailing Add:* 111 Tower Rd Brookfield Center CT 06804

SOUGSTAD, MIKE
GRAPHIC ARTIST, EDUCATOR
b Madison, SDak, June 18, 39. *Study:* Dakota Wesleyan Univ, Mitchell, SDak, BA, 61; Univ Wyo, MFA, 85. *Work:* Pioneer Mus, Wyo State Fairgrounds, Douglas, Wyo; Univ Wyo Art Mus, Laramie; Friends of the Middle Border Mus & Dakota Wesleyan Univ Collection, Mitchell, SDak. *Comn:* Naval Special Operations (ser of paintings), US Navy, San Diego, Calif, 65; Leader from the West (Reagan painting), Republican Party, Pierre, SDak, 81; Three Trains at Lead, Black Hill Civitan Club, Rapid City, SDak, 85. *Exhib:* Hot Springs National Show, Sandstone Gallery, Hot Springs, SDak, 82, 84 & 85; Wyoming 83, Nichoylisen Gallery, Casper, Wyo, 83; Mini-Show Artist, 83 & Featured Artist, 84, Dahl Fine Art Ctr; Wyoming State Fair, Pioneer Mus, Douglas, Wyo, 84 & 85; Coors Corporation Show, Corp Hq, Golden, Colo, 85; Faculty Art & MFA Show, Univ Wyo Art Mus, Larmie, 85-86. *Pos:* Freelance artist & illusr, 57-; ed, Dakota West (mag), SDak Cowboy & Western Heritage Hall of Fame, 75; mgr, Dakota Western Art Gallery, Lead, SDak, 86- *Teaching:* Vis lectr art, Univ Wyo, Laramie, 84- *Awards:* Best of Show, Hot Springs National, Hot Springs Art Guild, 83; Juried Award, Coors Corp Show, Adolf Coors Corp, 85; Purchase Award, Wyo State Fair, State of Wyo, 84. *Bibliog:* Tony Brown (auth), Republicans mix art, politics, Sioux Falls Argus Leader, 5/81; Ruth Brennan (auth), Trains are important element in Sougstad's landscape, 9/17/82 & Jan Nauman, Saugstad's art mixes railroads with paint, 1/27/84, Rapid City J. *Mem:* Foothills Art Ctr, Golden, Colo. *Media:* Acrylics, Pencil. *Publ:* Illusr, Dakota Panorama, SDak Territorial Comn, 61; Navy UDT Handbook, US Navy, 66; Buffalo!, 73-74; Old West Trail Vacation Guide, Old West Trail Found, 81-86. *Mailing Add:* Arapahoe Community Col Commercial Art Dept 2500 W College Dr Littleton CO 80160-9002

SOUTHARD, JAMES BRUCE
LECTURER, PAINTER
b Brooklyn, NY, Mar 31, 21. *Study:* Nat Acad Design, 39-41; Beaux Arts Inst Design, 41; Arts Students League, 46-49; Escuela de Pintura y Escultura, Mex; also studied with Robert Brackman, Reginald Marsh, Kenneth Hayes Miller & Jon Corbino. *Work:* Palace Legion Honor, San Francisco; Stockton Mus Art (San Joaquin), Calif; Health Ctr No 3, Dept Health, San Francisco; San Francisco Gen Hosp. *Comn:* Painting, 68, etching edition, 72, City & Co San Francisco; Home Savings S in L, Los Angeles, 69; Health Ctr-Nurses Lounge, San Francisco, 74; Bancroft Libr, Univ Calif, Berkeley, 86. *Exhib:* One-man shows, Galleria Arte Moderno, Mexico City, 51, Galleria Caracalla, Guadalajara, Mex, 51, Three Arts, Poughkeepsie, NY, 53, Lucian Labault Gallery, San Francisco, 54, St Mary's Col, Moraga, Calif, 64, San Joaquin Pioneer Mus, Stockton, Calif, 65 & San Francisco Art Comn (watercolor show), 77; Oakland Mus, AEA Ann, 62-63; John Bolles Gallery, San Francisco, 76; Calif State Fair, 77-78; Kensington Gallery, Calif, 81; Eleonore Austerer Gallery, San Francisco, 90; and others. *Teaching:* Pvt painting classes. *Awards:* Home Savings Purchase Award; Awards of Merit, San Francisco Arts Festival; Purchase Award, San Francisco Arts Comn. *Mem:* Artists Equity Asn; Int Soc Artists; Soc Western Artists; East Bay Watercolor Soc; Duchess Co Art Asn. *Dealer:* Maxwell Galleries 551 Sutter St San Francisco CA 94102; Ebert Gallery San Francisco CA. *Mailing Add:* 555 Buena Vista W San Francisco CA 94117

SOUTHEY, TREVOR J T
PAINTER, SCULPTOR
b Zimbiabwe, Rhodesia, Jan 12, 40; US citizen. *Study:* Brighton Col Art, Eng, 59; Natal Technical Col, Durban, S Africa, 60; Brigham Young Univ, Provo, Utah, BFA, 67, MA, 69. *Work:* Utah State Mus, Salt Lake City & Springville Mus Art, Utah; Rhodes Nat, Zimbabwe; Brigham Young Univ; Mormon Mus, Salt Lake City. *Comn:* Painting, Decision Making Information, Santa Ana, Calif, 71; painting, Brigham Young Univ, Provo, Utah, 75; mural, Salt Lake Int Airport, 81; life size sculpture, Univ Utah Medical Ctr, Salt Lake City, 81; Painter Freeze, Univ Scranton, Pa; Monumental Bronze, Trammell Crow Corp, Atlanta, Ga & Phoenix, Ariz. *Exhib:* Utah State Mus, Salt Lake City, 79 & Ill Ctr, Chicago, 79; Twenty Utah Printmakers, traveling show, Utah Arts Coun, 82; and others. *Teaching:* Asst prof drawing & painting, Brigham Young Univ, Provo, 69-76. *Bibliog:* Trevor Southey/Stephen Doherty, Images and Ideas, Am Artist, 80; Steven P Sondrup (auth), Trevor Southey - the art and the man, Artists of the Rockies and the Golden West, summer 82. *Mem:* North Mountain Artists Cooperative; Alpine Community Arts (chmn, 78-); Calif Print Makers Asn. *Media:* Oil, Etchings; Bronzes. *Publ:* Illusr, The Search, 69, Doubleday; illusr, The Growing Season, Bookcraft, 75; illusr, Marriage and Divorce, Deseret Book, 76; illusr, The Sex Book, Pelton, 78; illusr, A Widening View, Bookcraft, 83; and others. *Dealer:* Lowe Galleries Atlanta GA & Santa Monica CA; Vorpal Gally San Francisco CA. *Mailing Add:* c/o OTG Fine Art Box 2521 444 Main St Park City UT 84060

SOUTHWELL, WILLIAM JOSEPH
PAINTER, WRITER
b Philadelphia, Pa, Jan 14, 14. *Study:* Pa Acad Fine Arts, Philadelphia, 33-37; Univ Pa, Philadelphia, BFA, 40, MFA, 41; Univ London, England. *Comn:* Murals, Stockton Inn, NJ, 84-85. *Exhib:* Pa Col Fac, Lehigh Univ, Bethlehem, Pa, 72; Sketch Club Exhib, Philadelphia, 86; Galeria Savant, 87; Matrix Gallery, 88. *Pos:* Contribr, New Art Examiner, Chicago, Photo Rev, Langhorne, Rotkin Rev, New York, Len's on Campus, Garden City, Art Matters & Perspective, Philadelphia, 86-; Academy Review, Philadelphia Fellowship (PAFA) Newsletter. *Teaching:* Studio arts & hist, Studio Sch, Philadelphia, 63-83; prof studio arts & hist, Northampton Co Col, 69-73 & Art Inst Philadelphia, 73-83; instr of private classes in drawing, painting and sculpture. *Awards:* First Award Figurative Art, City of Philadelphia, Pa, 32; Henry Rankin Poore Composition Award, Pa Acad Fine Arts, 36. *Bibliog:* Globe-Times, Bethlehem, Pa, 70; Writers That Matter: Bill Southwell, Art Matters, Philadelphia, Pa, 89. *Mem:* Authors League, New York; Fel Pa Acad Fine Arts (bd dirs & rec secy, 90); Am Asn Univ Prof. *Media:* Acrylic, Watercolor. *Res:* Delaware River-New Hope School; history of Pennsylvania Academy of Fine Arts, Thomas Eakins. *Publ:* Auth, Diaghilev, 81 & Fall & rise of decadence; Functional photography of Thomas Fakins, Philadelphia Photo Rev, 82; A survey of women in photography, On Campus Mag, 82; The Frudakis Academy of Fine Arts, Art Matters, 86. *Mailing Add:* 1855 Edgehill Rd Abington PA 19001

SOWERS, MIRIAM R
PAINTER, ART DEALER
b Bluffton, Ohio, Oct 4, 22. *Study:* Miami Univ, BFA; Art Inst Chicago; Univ NMex. *Work:* Tex A&I Univ; Mus of NMex Art Gallery; Lovelace Clin, Albuquerque; Sheldon Swope Gallery, Terre Haute, Ind; Nat Arch, Washington, DC. *Comn:* Over 500 portraits. *Exhib:* Butler Inst Am Art; one-person show, Am Bible Soc Gallery, New York & Tex A&I Univ; Springfield Art Ctr, Ohio, 88; Saint Johns Col, Santa Fe, NMex, 89; Provenance Gallery, Lahaina, Hawaii, 89; Holiday Gallery, King Kameamea Hotel, Kailua-Kona, Hawaii, 90; Wakefield Gardens, Honaunau, Hawaii, 91; and others. *Pos:* Owner, Symbol Gallery Art, 61-79; owner, Sowers Symbolic art Studios, currently. *Awards:* Prizes, Toledo Mus Art, Ouray Colo Nat & NMex State Fair; plus others. *Bibliog:* Mary Carroll Nelson (auth), article in, Southwest Art Mag; articles in Albuquerque J & Tribune & The Santa Fe New Mexican; Mary Carroll Nelson (auth), Miriam Sowers, Art Voices, 9-10/81; article in Encore Poetry Mag, 86. *Mem:* Soc of Layerists in Multi-Media. *Media:* Oil. *Specialty:* Oils on gold leaf; silver and copper; symbolism of man and nature. *Publ:* Auth, Parables from Paradise, Branden Press; The Suns of Man, Symbol, 81. *Dealer:* Wakefield Gardens Gallery Honaunau, HI; Weems Gallery Albuquerque NM. *Mailing Add:* c/o Symbolic Art Studio 3020 Glenwood Dr NW Albuquerque NM 87107

SOWINSKI, STANISLAUS JOSEPH
PAINTER, ICONOGRAPHER
b Milwaukee, Wis, May 7, 27. *Study:* San Diego Sch Arts, 48-49; San Diego State Univ, BA, 52. *Work:* Dept Defense, Pentagon; Univ Calif, Sacramento and La Jolla; San Diego State Univ; City Escondido, Calif. *Comn:* 21 Major icons, Sts Constantine & Helen Church, Solana Beach, Calif, 82-90; 3 large paintings, City Escondido, Calif, 88; full length portraits, City Escondido, Calif, 88; numerous large paintings, San Diego State Univ, Calif, 89-91; 3 large paintings, Poway, Calif, 90. *Exhib:* Royal Watercolur Soc, London, 65 & 66; solo exhibs, US Embassy, London, 67 & Escondido Hist Mus, Calif, 83; Royal Soc Brit Artists, London, 67; Royal Acad, London, 67; solo exhib, A Huney Gallery, San Diego, Calif, 89. *Pos:* Demonr watercolor, Grumbacher Inc, New York, 76-79 & Inveresk Paper Co, Bath, UK, 79-86. *Teaching:* Instr watercolor workshops, Calif, Ore & SDak, 71-76; watercolor painting, San Diego Art Inst, 76-77. *Media:* Watercolor, Oil; Acrylic, Pen & Ink. *Dealer:* Galerie du Bois 407 E Hyman Aspen CO. *Mailing Add:* 13040 Cedilla Pl San Diego CA 92128

SPAETH, ELOISE O'MARA
COLLECTOR, WRITER
b Decatur, Ill, June 19, 04. *Study:* Millikin Univ. *Pos:* Trustee, Dayton Art Inst, 38-44, dir, Mod Gallery, 40-44; trustee, Am Fedn Arts, 45-, chmn exten serv, 47-59; trustee, Guild Hall Mus, 50-, chmn acquisitions comt, 62-; trustee, Arch Am Art, 59, chmn, currently; mem, Smithsonian Inst Fine Art Comn. *Awards:* Smithson Medal, Smithsonian Inst, 79. *Mem:* Am Asn Mus; Col Art Asn Am; Art Collectors Club. *Collection:* Contemporary religious art; antiquities; contemporary American and European art. *Publ:* Auth, American Art Museums and Galleries, 60, 66 & 69; auth, Collecting Art, 68; contribr to art & relig publ. *Mailing Add:* 65 E 76th St New York NY 10021

SPAFFORD, MICHAEL CHARLES
EDUCATOR, PAINTER
b Palm Springs, Calif, Nov 6, 35. *Study:* Pomona Co, BA, 59; Harvard Univ, MA(art hist), 60. *Work:* Seattle Art Mus, Wash; Galeria de Inst Mexicano-Norte Americano, Mexico City; Undergrad Libr, Univ Wash; Pac NW Bell, Seattle. *Comn:* Mural, Kingdome, Seattle, Wash, 79; murals, House Chambers State Capitol Bldg, Olympia, Wash, 81; mural, Seattle Opera House, 85. *Exhib:* Art Across America Traveling Exhib, Knoedler Gallery, New York, 65-67; Drawing Society 1970 Traveling Exhib, Am Fedn Arts, New York, 70-71; 73rd Western Ann Invitational, Denver Art Mus, 71; Art of the Pacific Northwest from 1930s to the Present, Smithsonian Inst, 75; one-man shows, Labors of Hercules & Other Works, Utah Mus Fine Arts, 75, Am Acad & Inst Arts & Letters Awards Selection Show, New York, 80 & 83 & Seattle Art Mus, 82 & 86. *Teaching:* Instr painting, Mexico City Col, 61-62; assoc prof painting-drawing, Univ Wash, 63-78, prof, 78- *Awards:* Louis Comfort Tiffany Found Grant Painting, 66; Prix de Rome, Am Acad Rome, 67-69; Award in Painting, Am Acad & Inst Arts & Lett, 83. *Media:* Oil on Canvas. *Dealer:* Francine Seders Gallery 6701 Greenwood Ave N Seattle WA 98103. *Mailing Add:* c/o Francine Seders Gallery 6701 Greenwood Ave N Seattle WA 98103

SPAGNOLO, KATHLEEN MARY
PRINTMAKER, ILLUSTRATOR
b London, Eng, Sept 12, 19. *Study:* Bromley Art Sch; Royal Col Art, London, Royal scholar & Princess of Wales scholar, 39-42; Sch Design, with E W Tristram; Am Univ, with Robert Gates & Krishna Reddy. *Work:* Dept of Interior, Washington, DC; Univ Va, Charlottesville; George Washington Univ; Libr Cong, Washington, DC. *Comn:* Rendering (bench), Index Am Design, Nat Gallery Art, Washington, DC, 69. *Exhib:* Corcoran Gallery Art, Washington, DC, 62; Silvermine Guild Artists, 63; Soc Washington Printmakers, 69-75; one-man exhib, Va Mus Fine Arts, 78; All Hallows by the Tower, London, 82. *Mem:* Soc Washington Printmakers; Washington Watercolor Asn; Washington Print Club; Artist's Equity Asn. *Media:* Graphics. *Dealer:* Gallery 4 115 S Columbus Alexandria VA 22314. *Mailing Add:* 7401 Recard Lane Alexandria VA 22307

SPAMPINATO, CLEMENTE
SCULPTOR
b Italy, Jan 10, 12; US citizen. *Study:* Acad Fine Arts, Rome, Italy; Fr Acad Nude, Rome; Sch Governatorate, Rome; Royal Sch Medal, Rome. *Work:* Nat Mus Sport, New Madison Square Garden, New York; Rockwell Gallery Western Art, Corning, NY; Isaac Delgado Mus Art, New Orleans, La; Notre Dame Univ, Ind; Okla Art Ctr, Oklahoma City. *Comn:* The Navy Goat (bronze statue), Naval Acad Annapolis, Md, 57; Archit reliefs, Bd Educ & Dept Pub Works, New York, 57-75; two limestone bas reliefs, Brooklyn Heights Br Libr, NY, 60; three different bronze statues of Columbus, Huntington, NY, 64, Mineola, NY, 65 & Bridgeport, Conn, 71; Fox Chase (bronze statue), St Charles, Chicago, 73; Bobby Jones (sculpture), World Golf Hall Fame, Pinehurst, NC, 74; The Trail Hunter (bronze statue), Falls Church Va, 87. *Exhib:* Sport Sculpture Nat, Rome, 40-48; Allied Artists Am, New York, 46-51; Am Artists Prof Art League, New York, 51; Nat Sculpture Soc, New York, 52-78; Nat Acad Design, New York, 64-76. *Awards:* First Prize, Nat Competition Sport Figure, Rome, 39; First Prize, Nat Competition Ski Trophy Olympic Games, Rome, 40; Gold Medal, Grand Award Munic Art League, Chicago, 70. *Mem:* Fel Nat Sculpture Soc; Circolo Artistico Int; Int Fine Arts Coun; Int Am Inst. *Media:* Bronze, Marble. *Dealer:* Regency Gallery Inc 1050 Second Ave New York NY 10022. *Mailing Add:* 36 Littleworth Lane Sea Cliff NY 11579

SPANDORF, LILY GABRIELLA
PAINTER, MURALIST
Study: Acad Arts, Vienna, dipl. *Work:* Smithsonian Inst, Libr Cong, White House, Washington, DC; Washington Co Mus Fine Arts, Hagerstown, Md; Munic Mus, Rome, Italy; Kiplinger Collection, Calvert Collection, Washington DC; National Mus Women Arts and others. *Comn:* Paintings, comn by President Lyndon B Johnson, presented to Princess Margaret, Chung Hee Park & Asgeir Asgeirsson; 13 drawings, comn by Folger Shakespeare Libr, presented to Archbishop of Canterbury & others; 23 drawings of embassies, comn by Meridian House Int, presented to Ambassadors; paintings, comn by Am Red Cross, presented to vmayors & chmn Red Cross in Nanking, Peking & Tientsin, China; designed Christmas postage stamp, 63. *Exhib:* Solo exhib, Agra Gallery; Folger Shakespeare Libr's Anne Hathaway Gallery, 81; American University Paintings of Yugoslavia, Yugoslavian Embassy, 85; Nat Mus Women Arts, Washington DC, 88; Nat Press Club, 88, 89 & 90; 5 paintings, Bicentennial, DC Mayor's Off Gallery, 91; At Home & Abroad, Arts Club Washington, 92; and others. *Pos:* Contrib artist, Washington, DC newspapers, NASA & many other publications. *Awards:* Lily Spandorf Day, Mayor of Washington, DC, 3/8/81; numerous awards in Italy, England & US; Decoration of Hon for Serv to the

State & City of Vienna, Austria, 86. *Mem:* Nat Press Club; Artist's Equity Asn; hon mem Washington Watercolor Asn; Am News Women's Club; hon mem Arts Club Washington; and others. *Media:* Gouache, Watercolor; Mixed. *Publ:* Auth, editorial, Washington Star, 3/11/81; Book-full colour reproductions: Lily Spandorf's Washington Never More, summer 88; A view from the street, the Art of Lily Spardorf (doc film), PBS & Am Film Inst, Kennedy Ctr; Mus & Arts article, Mag, Wash Post, Wash Times. *Mailing Add:* 1603 19th St NW Washington DC 20009

SPANDORFER, MERLE SUE
PAINTER, PRINTMAKER
b Baltimore, Md, Sept 4, 34. *Study:* Syracuse Univ, 52-54; Univ Md, BS, 56. *Work:* Metrop Mus Art, Mus Mod Art & Whitney Mus Am Art, New York; Libr Cong, DC; Philadelphia Mus Art; Baltimore Mus; Israel Mus. *Comn:* Fifty-four graphics, Inland Steel Corp, Alexandria, Va, 75; graphics, Thiokol Corp, Newtown, Pa, 76; Mellon Bank, 83; Temple Univ, 84; Univ Pa, Inst Contemp Art, 91. *Exhib:* Md Regional, Baltimore Mus Art, 74; 21 one-woman shows including RI Sch Design, Providence, 79, Governor's Residence & Yoseido Gallery, Tokyo, Japan, 81; Tyler Sch Art, Philadelphia, Pa, 85; Univ City Sci Ctr, 86; Gov's Residence, Harrisburg, Pa, 87; Wennizer Graphics Gallery, Provincetown, Mass, 89; Phila Mus Art, 90; Mangel Gallery, 92; and others. *Teaching:* Instr painting, Cheltenham Sch Fine Arts, 65-; instr printmaking, Tyler Sch Art, Philadelphia, 79-84 & Pratt Inst, New York, 85-86. *Awards:* Outstanding Art Educators Award, Philadelphia Art Educ Asn, 82;; Harry Rockower Mem Award, Cheltenham Ctr Arts, 88; Grant Award, Philadelphia Coun Arts, 89; and others. *Bibliog:* Rob Joymon (auth), Environment, Press, 6/89; Victoria Donohoe (auth), Philadelphia Inquirer, 5/10/92; Edward Sozanski (auth), Philadelphia Inquirer, 5/14/92. *Mem:* Artists Equity; Am Color Print Soc. *Media:* Acrylics, Water-based Printing Inks. *Publ:* Auth, Making Art Safely, Van Nostrand Reinhold, 92. *Dealer:* Mangel Gallery 1714 Rittenhouse Sq Philadelphia PA 19103. *Mailing Add:* 8012 Ellen Lane Cheltenham PA 19012

SPANGENBERG, KRISTIN L
CURATOR, HISTORIAN
b Palo Alto, Calif, June 3, 44. *Study:* Univ Calif, Davis, AB, 68; Univ Mich, MA, 71. *Collections Arranged:* Cincinnati Collects Photographs (auth, catalog) & German Expressionist Prints (auth, catalog), Cincinnati Art Mus, 85. *Pos:* Asst cur prints, drawings & photographs, Cincinnati Art Mus, 71-73, cur, 74- *Mem:* Print Coun Am. *Publ:* Auth, Eastern European Printmakers, 75, French Drawings, Watercolors & Pastels 1800-1950, 78, ed, Nineteenth Century Drawings from the Grand Duchy of Baden, 83 & auth, Photographic Treasures from the Cincinnati Art Mus, 89, Cincinnati Art Mus; Innovation & Tradition, Twentieth Century Japanese prints from The Howard & Caroline Porter Collection, 90; ed & contribr, Six centuries of master prints: Treasures from the Herbert Greer French collection, Cincinnati Art Mus, 1/93. *Mailing Add:* c/o Cincinnati Art Mus Eden Park Cincinnati OH 45202-1596

SPARKMAN, GENE (CARL), JR
PAINTER, ILLUSTRATOR
b Kansas City, Kans, Feb 19, 41. *Study:* Emporia State Teachers Col, Kans, 59-60; San Diego City Col, 67-71; Art Ctr Col Design, Los Angeles, BFA, 75. *Work:* Franklin Libr, Franklin Center, Pa; Pastel Soc Am. *Comn:* Portrait of author Morris West, First Ed Soc, Franklin Libr, Franklin Center, Pa, 78; portrait of Meshulim Ricklus, Rapid Am Corp, New York, NY, 81; portrait of Howard Cosell, ABC-TV/New York Times Inc, 83; portrait of Amanda Fusscas, State Rep Peter Fusscas, Marlborough, Conn, 85. *Exhib:* Image Makers, Mus Art, Sci & Indust, Bridgeport, Conn, 80-85; Curator's Selected Works, Hermitage Mus, Norfolk, Va, 83, 84 & 85; American Annual Works on Paper, Zaner Gallery, Rochester, NY, 84; Soc Am Impressionists, Mo Athletic Club Gallery, St Louis, 85; Pastel Soc Am: Members' Show, Monmouth Mus, NJ, 85; Artists Night at the Museum, Bergen Mus Art & Sci, Ridgewood, NJ, 86. *Pos:* Dir, Pastel Soc Am, 83-, adv bd, 85-, Master Pastelist, 84- *Teaching:* Instr illus, Pratt Inst, Brooklyn, NY, 77-79; asst prof art, Sacred Heart Univ, Bridgeport, Conn, 80-82; instr fine arts illus, Art Students League of New York, 84- *Awards:* Purchase Award, Los Angeles County Documentary Art Exhib, Los Angeles County Sheriff's Dept, 75; Kenneth B Spaulding Award, Hudson Valley Art Asn 55th Ann Open Exhib, K B Spaulding Mem, 83; Most Innovative Use of Pastel Award, Pastel Soc Am 13th Ann Open Exhib, Carson-Arches-Rives Paper Co, 85. *Bibliog:* James Muse (dir), Gene Sparkman (film), 75; Thom Romeo (auth), Gene Sparkman-Master Pastelist, Art-Talk Mag, 12/84. *Mem:* Pastel Soc West Coast (adv bd, 85-); Artists Fel New York; Art Students League New York; Knickerbocker Artists New York. *Media:* Pastel. *Publ:* Illusr, Pride and Prejudice (1815, by Jane Austen), 83 & Tess of the d'Urbervilles (1891, by Thomas Hardy), 85, Readers Digest Bks; And Ladies of the Club (by Helen Hooven Santmyer), Book-of-the-Month Club, 84; Conversations with Eudora Welty, Simon & Schuster Pocket Bks, 85. *Dealer:* GWS Galleries 2600 Post Rd Southport CT 06490; The Connecticut Gallery 4 Austin Dr Marlborough, CT 06447. *Mailing Add:* Art Students League 215 W 57th St New York NY 10019

SPARKS, JOHN EDWIN
PRINTMAKER, INSTRUCTOR
b Washington, DC, Sept 14, 42. *Study:* Richmond Prof Inst; Yale-Norfolk Summer Sch Art & Music; Md Inst Col Art, BFA; Univ Ill, Urbana, MFA. *Work:* Libr of Cong, Washington, DC. *Exhib:* 36th Int Exhib, Northwest Printmakers, Seattle, 65; Libr of Cong Print Exhib, Washington, DC, 66; 47th Exhib, Soc Am Graphic Artists, New York, 66; 3rd Print Show, Eastern Mich Univ, Ypsilanti, 70; 10th Nat Print Exhib, Silvermine Guild Artists, Conn, 74. *Pos:* Cataloger, George A Lucas Print Collection, Union of Independent Cols Art, 69; dir first restrike ed, Rodolphe Bresdin's etching Flight into Egypt, 70; art adv, Md Arts Coun, 70-71. *Teaching:* Instr lithography & intaglio, Md Inst Col Art, 66-, chmn, Printmaking Dept; instr intaglio & lithography, Lake Placid Summer Workshop, 71-75; instr intaglio, NS Col of Art & Design, 77. *Awards:* Printmaking Grant, Louis Comfort Tiffany Found, 67. *Media:* Intaglio, Lithography. *Mailing Add:* Maryland Inst Col Art 1300 Mt Royal Ave Baltimore MD 21217

SPEAR, LAURINDA HOPE
ARCHITECT
b Rochester, Minn, Aug 23, 50. *Study:* Brown Univ, BA, 72; Columbia Univ, MArch, 75; Mass Inst Technol, currently. *Comn:* Babylon, Pacific Developers, Miami, Fla, 77; The Atlantis, Stonecrest Development, Miami, Fla, 78; The Palace, Helmsley Enterprises, Miami, Fla, 78; Imperial at Brickell, Harlon Group, Miami, Fla, 79; Overseas Tower, Overseas Finance Corp, Miami, Fla, 80. *Exhib:* New Americans, Inst Archit & Urban Studies, 79 & Pa State Univ, 80; Work of Arquitectonica, Fla AIA, Orlando, 79; Young Architects, Yale Univ, New Haven, Conn, 80; Work of Arquitectonica, Univ Va, 81. *Pos:* Principal, Arquitectonica, Coral Gables, Fla, 77- *Awards:* Design Award, NY Soc Architects, 75; Rome Prize in Architecture, Am Acad, Rome, 78; Citation--75,78 & 80, Progressive Archit, 80. *Mem:* Archit Club Miami; Dade Co Historic Preservation Bd. *Mailing Add:* Arquitectonica 2151 LeJuene Rd, Ste 300 Coral Gables FL 33134

SPEAR, RICHARD EDMUND
EDUCATOR
b Michigan City, Ind, Feb 3, 40. *Study:* Univ Chicago, BA(art hist); Princeton Univ, MFA(art hist) & PhD(art hist). *Pos:* Dir, Allen Mem Art Mus, Oberlin Col, 72-83; pres, Intermuseum Conserv Asn, 75-77; ed-in-chief, Art Bulletin, 85-88. *Teaching:* Mildred C Jay prof art hist, Oberlin Col, 64-; distinguished vis prof, George Washington Univ, 83-84. *Awards:* Premio Daria Borghese Gold Medal, Rome, 72. *Mem:* Col Art Asn. *Res:* Seventeenth century painting. *Publ:* Auth, Caravaggio and His Followers, Cleveland Mus Art, 71 & Harper & Row, rev ed 75; Renaissance and Baroque Paintings from the Sciarra and Fiano Collections, Pa State Univ Press & Ugo Bozzi, Rome, 72; Domenichino, Yale Univ Press, 82. *Mailing Add:* Dept Art Oberlin Col Oberlin OH 44074

SPECTOR, BUZZ (FRANKLIN MAC SPECTOR)
CONCEPTUAL ARTIST, CRITIC
Chicago, Ill, Mar 13, 48. *Study:* Southern Ill Univ, Carbondale, BA(studio art), 72; Univ Chicago, MFA, 78. *Work:* Mus Contemp Art, Chicago; Getty Mus, Malibu, Calif; Ill State Mus, Springfield; Univ Alberta Art Mus, Edmonton; Art Inst, Chicago; Lannan Found, Los Angeles. *Comn:* Los Angeles Pub Libr. *Exhib:* EarthArt, Mus Contemp Art, Chicago, 83-84; Found Language, Franklin Furnace, NY, 84; Book Made Art, Univ Chicago Libr, 86, Systems, Los Angeles Munic Art Gallery, 90, Transgression, Corcoran Gallery Art, Washington, DC, 90; Solo exhibs, Art Inst Chicago (with catalog), 88 & Spertus Mus of Judaica, Chicago, 88; Newport Harbor Art Mus (with catalog) 90. *Pos:* Ed, WhiteWalls, 78-87. *Teaching:* vis lectr art hist & criticism, Art Inst Chicago, 83-88; vis artist, Univ Calif, Santa Barbara, 88; vis lectr, Art Ctr Col Design, Pasadena, Calif, 89- *Awards:* Fel for Drawing, 82-83, Fel for Artists Books, 85-86, Nat Endowment Arts; Ill Arts coun Fel, 88. *Bibliog:* Neal Benezra (auth), Buzz Spector: The Library of Babel, exh cat, Art Inst Chicago, 88; David Pagel (auth), article, Arts, 9/89; Maria Porges (auth), Buzz Spector (exhib catalog), Newport Harbor Art Mus, 90; Michael Anderson (auth), rev, Art Am, 5/90; Colin Gardner (auth), rev, Artforum, summer, 90. *Publ:* Auth, Objects and Logotypes: Relationships Between Minimalist Art and Corporate Design (exhib catalog), Renaissance Soc, 80; coauth, Words as Images (exhib catalog), WhiteWalls, 81; ed, The Flue, Quart J Franklin Furnace, New York, Vol 3, No 1; Expos, Quart J Soc Photog Educ, Vol 21, No 3; auth, Michiko Itatani: Recent Works (exhib catalog), Alternative Mus, New York, 85; auth, Jo Ann Callis: Objects of Reverie (exhib catalog), Des Moines, Art Ctr, 90. *Mailing Add:* c/o Roy Boyd Gallery 1547 Tenth St Santa Monica CA 90401

SPECTOR, JACK J
HISTORIAN, EDUCATOR
b Bayonne, NJ, Oct 2, 25. *Study:* City Col New York, BS, 56; Columbia Univ, MA, 59, PhD, 64; Fulbright Fel, Paris, 60-61. *Pos:* Ed Bd Amer Imag, 89- *Teaching:* Prof art hist, Rutgers Univ, 62-79 & distinguished prof, 88; vis prof Romanticism, City Univ New York Grad Ctr, 79; vis distinguished prof, Columbian Col, George Washington Univ, Washington, DC, 85; vis scholar, Univ Queensland, Brisbane, Australia, 89. *Awards:* Am Coun Learned Socs Grant, 70; Sr Fel, Ctr Advanced Study Visual Arts, Nat Gallery Art, 85; Fel Rutgers Ctr Hist Analysis, 90-91. *Mem:* Col Art Asn; Am Soc for Aesthetics. *Res:* Nineteenth century French Romanticism, chiefly Eugene Delacroix; psychoanalytic approaches to 19th and 20th century art. *Publ:* Auth, The Murals of Eugene Delacroix at Saint-Sulpice, Col Art Asn, 67; contribr, The method of Morelli and its relation to Freudian psychoanalysis, Diogenes, Paris, 69; auth, The Aesthetics of Freud, Penguin, 72, Praeger, 73, Kindler, 74, Mursia, 77 & Monte Avila, Venezuela, 79; auth, Delacroix's Death of Sardanapalus, Penguin, 75; contribr, The Vierge du Sacre-Coeur: Religious politics & personal expression in an early Delacroix, Burlington Mag, 4/81; auth, Form & Fetish: The Avant-garde Object, RES, autumn 86; The State of Psychoanalytic Research in Art History, Art Bull, 3/88; The Politics of Dream, Am Imago, spring, 89. *Mailing Add:* 28 Spring St Somerset NJ 08873

SPECTOR, NAOMI
WRITER
b Lynn, Mass, Mar 6, 39. *Study:* Brandeis Univ, BA, 60; NY Univ, MA, 66. *Pos:* Asst dir, Byron Gallery, New York, 63-64; mgr, Fischbach Gallery, New York, 67-70; dir, John Weber Gallery, New York, 73-75. *Res:* Contemporary art. *Specialty:* Minimal-conceptual. *Publ:* Auth, Dorothea Rockburne (catalog essay), Contemp Art Ctr, Cincinnati, 75; Dorothea Rockburne: New Color Work (catalog essay), John Weber Gallery, New York, 76; Robert Ryman: Six Aquatints, The Print Collector's Newsletter, 3-4/77; Robert Ryman (catalog), Whitechapel Art Gallery, London, Eng, 77; and others. *Mailing Add:* 435 W Broadway New York NY 10012

SPEED, (ULYSSES) GRANT
SCULPTOR
b San Angelo, Tex, Jan 6, 30. *Study:* Brigham Young Univ, BS; also with Soloman Aranda. *Work:* Whitney Mus, Cody, Wyo; Diamond M Mus, Snyder, Tex; Devonian Found, Calgary, Alta; Repub Nat Bank, Dallas. *Comn:* Sculpture, Brigham Young Univ Animal Sci Dept, 75-76, 76-77 & 77-78; monuments, Charlie Goodnight, Mesa Petrolium, Amarillo, Tex, 79, Buddy Holly, city of Lubbock, Tex, 79 & John Wayne, comn by Ron Chamnis, Dallas, 80. *Exhib:* Ann Preview Exhib, Tex Art Gallery, 71-78; Phoenix Art Mus, 73-75; two-man show, Tex Art Gallery, Dallas, 75; Spec Exhib, Whitney Mus, Cody, 75; Montrail Galleries, Scottsdale, Ariz, 77. *Awards:* Achievement Award Art, Brigham Young Univ Animal Sci Dept, 72; Purchase Award, Men's Art Coun Phoenix, 73; Gold Medal Award/ Sculpture, Cowboy Artists of Am Ann, 76. *Bibliog:* Ed Ainsworth (auth), Cowboy in Art, World, 68; Pat Broder (auth), Bronzes of the American West, Abrams, 74; Don Hedgpeth (auth), From Broncs to Bronzes, 79. *Mem:* Cowboy Artists Am (pres, 72-73, bd dirs, 73-74 & 76-78). *Media:* Bronze. *Publ:* Auth, Hooked on cowboyin', Western Horseman, 70. *Dealer:* Tex Art Gallery 1408 Main St Dallas TX 75202; Main Trail Galleries Jackson WY 83001. *Mailing Add:* 139 S 400 East Lindon UT 84042

SPEIGHT, JERRY BROOKS
EDUCATOR, WRITER
b Murray, Ky, Nov 27, 42. *Study:* Murray State Univ, Ky, BS, 64, MA, 68; Memphis State Univ. *Comn:* YMCA Supergraphic, City of Somerset, Ky, 75. *Exhib:* Mid-States Art Exhib, Evansville Mus Arts & Sci, Ind, 70 & Mid-States Craft Exhib, 70 & 73; All Ky Drawing Competition, Univ Ky, Lexington, 78; one-man show, Owensboro Mus Arts & Sci, Ky, 79. *Pos:* Regional corresp for Art Voices South Mag, Art Voices Publ Co, West Palm Beach, Fla, 78- *Teaching:* Art dept chmn, Brescia Col, Owensboro, Ky, 70-74; instr art educ, Univ Ky, Lexington, 74-75 & Murray State Univ, Ky, 75- *Awards:* Merit Award, All Ky Drawing Competition, 78; Ky Art Educator Year, 80. *Mem:* Ky Art Educ Asn (vpres, 77-78); Nat Art Educ Asn. *Media:* Watercolor, Graphite. *Res:* Artists' work from a technical and conceptual standpoint. *Publ:* Auth, John Thomas Bensing, Sch Arts, 11/80; auth, Wear an original painting, Fiberarts, 1/81; auth, Richard Abrams, Art Voices, 4-5/81; auth, Basic photography experiences, Sch Arts, 5/81; auth, A shoe recall, Sch Arts, 10/81; and many others. *Mailing Add:* Dept Art Murray State Univ Murray KY 42071

SPEIGHT, SARAH BLAKESLEE See Blakeslee, Sarah

SPEISER, STUART M
COLLECTOR, PATRON
b New York, NY, June 4, 23. *Exhib:* Stuart M Speiser Collection of Photorealism, shown at 20 museums, including, Addison Gallery Am Art, Andover, Mass, 74, Allentown Art Mus, Pa, 74, Witte Mem Mus, San Antonio, Tex, 74, Brooks Mem Mus, Memphis, Tenn, 75 & Krannert Mus, Champaign, Ill, 75; donated to Smithsonian Inst, 78. *Awards:* James Smithson Medal, Smithsonian Art Inst, 79. *Bibliog:* Judy Beardsall (auth), Stuart M Speiser Photo-Realist Collection, Art Gallery Mag, 10/73; Phyllis Derfner (auth), New York letter, Art Int Lugano Rev, 11/73; Gregory Battcock (auth), New York, Art & Artists, London, 3/74. *Interests:* Promoting new art movements and pioneering in law as it pertains to artists, in capacity as an attorney. *Collection:* Photorealism. *Mailing Add:* 140 E 45th St New York NY 10017

SPELMAN, JILL SULLIVAN
PAINTER
b Chicago, Ill, Feb 17, 37. *Study:* Hilton Leech Art Sch, Sarasota, Fla, 55-57; and with Paul Ninas, New Orleans, 56-58. *Work:* Univ Mass, Amherst. *Exhib:* Watercolor USA, Springfield Art Mus, Mo, 67; Mainstreams '70, Marietta Col, Ohio, 70; Salon 72, Ward Nasse Gallery, New York, 72; one-man shows, Phoenix Gallery, New York, 73, 75 & 77 & Ward-Nasse Gallery, New York, 77; and others. *Pos:* Pres, Phoenix Coop Gallery, 72-74; assoc ed, Artists Rev Art, 77-78. *Teaching:* Lectr, Ringling Mus Art, Sarasota, 58-60. *Awards:* Sarasota Art Asn First Prize, Art Student Exhib, 57; Hamel Prize, Sarasota Art Asn Ann, 58; Grumbacher Oil Prize, Knickerbocker Artists Ann, 70. *Mem:* Asn Artist-Run Galleries. *Media:* Acrylic. *Dealer:* Rhodd Sande Gallery 61 E 57th St New York NY. *Mailing Add:* 22 W 96th St New York NY 10025

SPENCE, ANDREW
PAINTER
b Bryn Mawr, Pa, Oct 4, 47. *Study:* Tyler Sch Art, Temple Univ, Philadelphia, BFA, 69; Univ Calif, Santa Barbara, MFA, 71. *Exhib:* One-man shows, Barbara Toll Fine Arts, New York, 90, Compass Rose Gallery, Chicago, 90, James Corcoran Gallery, Los Angeles, 90, Insights: Ann Messner & Andrew Spence, Wooster Art Mus, Mass, 91 & Max Protetch Gallery, New York, 92. *Awards:* Painting, Nat Endowment Arts, 87. *Media:* Acrylic, Oil. *Mailing Add:* Six Varick St New York NY 10013

SPENCER, DEIRDRE DIANE
LIBRARIAN, EDUCATOR
b Indianapolis, Ind, Sep 28, 55. *Study:* Ind Univ, Bloomington, AB, 77, MLS, 85; Univ Chicago, MA, 84; Univ Mich, Ann Arbor, PhD study presently. *Pos:* Asst art & archit librn, Univ Fla, Gainesville, 86-88; head fine arts libr, Univ Mich, Ann Arbor, 88- *Teaching:* Instr hist art, Martin Ctr Col, Indianapolis, Ind, 1/83-8/83; adj instr hist art, Herron Sch Art, Ind Univ-Purdue Univ, Indianapolis, currently. *Awards:* Univ Mich Rackham Merit Fel for doctoral study; Univ Mich Fel, Ctr for Educ of Women. *Bibliog:* Martha Keller (auth), Technology may radically alter the way art history is taught, Ann Arbor News, 2/12/89. *Mem:* Art Libr Soc NAm (chmn, Muehsam Award Comt, 90); Art Libr Soc Mich (pres, 90). *Res:* Ancient art; 18th & 19th century art; 19th century African-American art; computer usage in art library reference. *Interests:* Ancient art; 18th & 19th century Western art; issues of race & gender in the history of art; art theory. *Publ:* Auth, Lockefield gardens, Ind Preservationist, 81. *Mailing Add:* Univ Mich Fine Arts Library 260 Tappan Hall Ann Arbor MI 48109

SPENCER, HAROLD EDWIN
HISTORIAN, PAINTER
b Corning, NY, Oct 1, 20. *Study:* Art Students League, 41-42; Univ of Calif, BA(highest honors in art), 48 & James Phelan scholar, MA, 49; Harvard Univ (summer scholar), 58, Fac of Arts & Sci Fel, 60-61 & Frank Knox Fel, 64, PhD, 68. *Work:* William Benton Mus Art. *Exhib:* Mo Exhib, St Louis Art Mus, 52, 55, 59 & 61; Ann Drawing and Print Exhib, San Francisco Art Mus, 55-56; Washington Printmakers Soc, Smithsonian Inst, Washington, DC, 57 & 62; Conn Acad of Art Ann, Wadsworth Atheneum, Hartford, Conn, 76; Monotypes Today I-IX, 77-90; solo exhib, Slater Mus, Norwich, Conn, 87 & Benton Mus, Storrs, Conn, 90. *Pos:* Chmn art dept, Blackburn Col, Carlinville, Ill, 49-62; assoc prof, Occidental Col, Los Angeles, Calif, 62-68, chmn art dept, 63-68; assoc prof, Univ Conn, Storrs, 68-69, prof, 69-, assoc dept head, 77-79, prof emeritus, 88- *Awards:* Merit Award, 65th Ann Springfield Art League, 84; Paier Prize, New Haven PCC, 87; First Prize, Conn Artists Ann, Slater Mus, 87; and others. *Bibliog:* Roberta Capers (auth), Reviews of Readings in Art Hist, Art Bull, 71; Henri Dorra (auth), article in Art J, summer 78. *Mem:* Col Art Asn; Conn Acad of Arts & Sci. *Media:* Oil. *Res:* Nineteenth Century European Painting and American Art. *Publ:* Ed, readings in Art History, Scribner's 82 & 83; auth, On some works by Maurice Prendergast, William Benton Mus Art Bull, 85; Thoughts in Retrospect (exhib catalog), William Benton Mus Art, 90; Some Notes on teh Phelan Collection, Florence Griswold Mus, 92; coauth (with Elizabeth Kornhauser), Pride of Place: The Artistic Heritage of Connecticut, 1790-1920 (exhib catalog), Wadsworth Atheneum, 89; and others. *Mailing Add:* 294 Mansfield Rd Ashford CT 06278

SPENCER, HOWARD DALEE
CURATOR, PRINTMAKER
b Dayton, Ohio, Mar 23, 50. *Study:* Ind State Univ, BS(art educ), 72, MFA, 76. *Collections Arranged:* Through the Looking Glass: Works by Grandma Layton, 80; Legendary Wichita Bill: A Retrospective Exhibition of Paintings by John Noble (auth, catalog), 82,; Colleen Browning: Recent Paintings (auth, catalog), 82; Robert Grilley: A Retrospective (auth, catalog), 87; Angelo Savelli: White on White Paintings (auth, catalog), 88; John Batternberg: Recent Sculptures, Prints and Paintings (author, catalog), 92. *Pos:* Interim dir, Sheldon Swope Art Gallery, Terre Haute, Ind, 78; cur collections & exhibs, Wichita Art Mus, Kans, 79-89; cur collections & exhibs, Nev Mus Art, Reno, 92- *Media:* Etching. *Res:* American art & architecture. *Mailing Add:* Nevada Mus Art 160 W Liberty St Reno NV 89501

SPENCER, JEFFREY PAUL
PAINTER
b Omaha Nebr, Oct 31, 62. *Study:* Univ Nebr, Omaha, BFA, 87; Univ Tenn, Knoxville, MFA, 90. *Work:* Ewing Gallery Art, Univ Tenn, Knoxville. *Exhib:* Water Tower Ann, Water Tower Gallery, Louisville, Ky, 90; solo exhib, Krantz Gallery, Louisville, Ky, 90; Book Art, Garden Zodiac Gallery, Omaha, Nebr, 91; Recent Work, Univ Nebr Art Gallery, Omaha, Nebr, 92; Salina Art Ctr Ann, Kans. *Pos:* Preparator, Ewing Gallery Art, 88-89; head gallery preparator, Knoxville Mus Art, 89-90. *Teaching:* Art, Metrop Community Col, Omaha, Nebr, 90-92. *Awards:* Visual Arts Fel, Nat Endowment Arts, 91; Best of Show, Salina Arts Ctr Ann, 92. *Bibliog:* Kyle MacMillan (auth), Grant winning artist does user friendly abstracts, Omaha World Herald, 6/10/92. *Mem:* Col Art Asn. *Media:* Oil on Canvas. *Dealer:* Anderson O'Brien Gallery. *Mailing Add:* 13334 N 66th St Omaha NE 68152

SPENCER, JOHN R
HISTORIAN, ADMINISTRATOR
b Moline, Ill, Sept 20, 23. *Study:* Grinnell Col, BA, 47; Yale Univ, MA, 51, PhD, 53; also with Charles Seymour, Jr; Grinnell Col, Hon DFA, 72. *Pos:* Dir mus, Oberlin Col, 62-72; dir mus prog, Nat Endowment Arts, 72-78. *Teaching:* Instr & asst prof art, Yale Univ, 52-58; assoc prof art & actg chmn dept, Univ Fla, 58-62; prof hist art, Oberlin Col, 62-72; prof & chmn art dept, Duke Univ, 78- *Mem:* Col Art Asn Am (secy, 67, vpres, 71); Am Asn Mus; Asn Art Mus Dir; Instituto per la Storia dell'arte lombarda; Am Fedn Arts. *Res:* 15th century Italian art, with emphasis on painting and theoretical writings. *Publ:* Auth, L B Alberti, on painting, 55 & 67; Filarete's treatise on architecture, 65. *Mailing Add:* Dept Art Duke Univ Durham NC 27708

SPENCER, SUSAN ELIZABETH
PAINTER, INSTRUCTOR
b Buffalo, NY, Oct 31, 54. *Study:* Sullivan Co Community Col, AA(graphic art), 74, Onondaga Community Col, 79-83. *Work:* Kidder-Peabody Inc, New

York; Trustmark Nat Bank, Jackson, Miss; Neville Public Mus, Green Bay, Wis. *Comn:* Historical sites of Clay, NY, Marine Midland Bank, Syracuse, 85; painting of Crouse Col, King & King Architects, Syracuse, 86. *Exhib:* Pa Watercolor Soc, Port Hist Mus, Philadelphia, 87; 17th Int Exhib La Watercolor Soc, World Trade Ctr, New Orleans, 87; Audubon Artists Exhib, Nat Arts Club, New York, 88; Midwest Watercolor Soc, Neville Pub Mus, Green Bay, Wis, 88 & 89; Watercolor West, Brea Civic Ctr Gallery, Calif; and others. *Teaching:* Pvt classes in watercolor, Syracuse, NY, 84-; instr, workshops for var organizations & institutes throughout central New York. *Awards:* Trustmark Purchase Award, Miss Watercolor Show, 86; Mary Garrison Award, Cooperstown Nat Exhib, 87; Outstanding Adirondack Painting, Central Adirondack Show, Enchanted Forest, 88. *Bibliog:* Sherry Chayat (auth), rev, Syracuse Herald-Am, 85; Stephen Doherty, article, Am Artist, Watercolor, 90. *Mem:* Pa Watercolor Soc; Nat League Am Penwomen; Cent NY Watercolor Soc (secy, 87-89); Camillus Art Asn. *Media:* Watercolor, pencil. *Publ:* Illustr, Conservationist Mag, NY State Dept Environ Conserv, 86; Security Mag, Security Mutual Insurance, 86; Nat Catalogue Arts, Assoc Arts Orgn, 87. *Dealer:* Ed Fynmore Gallery II Manilius NY 13104. *Mailing Add:* 306 Gordon Pkwy Syracuse NY 13219

SPERAKIS, NICHOLAS GEORGE
PAINTER, PRINTMAKER
b New York, NY, June 8, 43. *Study:* Pratt Inst, 60; Nat Acad Design Sch Fine Art, New York; Art Students League, 63; Pratt Graphic Art Ctr. *Work:* Kunst Mus, Fine Arts Mus Bern, Switz, Permanent Print Collection; The Ulmer Mus, ULM, WGer, Permanent Print Collection; The Australian Nat Gallery, Canberra, Australia, Permanent Print Collection; The Israel Mus, Jerusalem, Permanent Print Collection; Yale Univ Art Gallery, New Haven, Conn, Permanent Print Collection; Pratt Inst, The Schafler Gallery, Brooklyn, NY, Permanent Print Collection; The Stedman Art Gallery, Fine Arts Ctr State Univ NJ Rutgers, Camden, Permanent Print Collection; and many others; and others. *Exhib:* Brooklyn Mus Biennials, 64, 66 & 70; Ann Print Exhib, Honolulu Acad Fine Arts, Hawaii, 71; Reading & Bucks Co Collect, Reading Mus Art, Pa, 77; Friends of Corcoran, Corcoran Gallery Art, 81; Ann Acquisition Exhib, Midwest Mus Am Art, Elkart, Ind, 81; one-man exhibs, Washington Irving Gallery, New York, 82, Galerie Taub, Philadelphia, 82-83, Arbitrage Gallery, New York, 83 & Retrospective of Woodcuts, Museo Universitario Del Chopo, Mexico City, 84, Univ Mass, Herter Art Gallery, 87, Leonardo Di Mauro Gallery, 88, Galerie Leopold, Hamburg, WGer, 88; Forum Gallery, New York, 84; and others. *Teaching:* Instr painting, New Sch Social Res, New York, 72-; teacher, Fashion Inst Technol, New York, 72-; adj asst prof, Long Island Univ, Brooklyn Campus, 85-86; adj asst lectr, Sch Painting & Sculpture of Columbia Univ, New York, 86-; and others. *Awards:* Lawrence & Hinda Rosenthal Fel, Am Acad Arts & Lett & Nat Inst Arts & Lett, 69; J S Guggenheim Mem Found Fel Graphics, 70; MacDowell Colony Summer Residency, Peterborough, NH, 76. *Bibliog:* Robert Henkes (auth), The crucifixion as depicted by contemporary artists, Nazarine Col, 72; Barry Shwartz (auth), 20th Century Humanist Art, Praeger, 73; articles, Arts Mag, 75-78 & 80. *Mem:* Am Fedn Modern Painters & Sculptors; Rhino Horn Orgn Humanist Art; Am Fedn Art; Soc Am Graphic Artists. *Dealer:* Paul Kessler Gallery 108 Commercial St Provincetown MA 02657. *Mailing Add:* 245 W 29th St 12A New York NY 10001

SPERANTZAS, VASSILIS
PRINTMAKER
b Athens, Greece, 38. *Exhib:* Univ D'Aix-En-Provence, 70; Origraphica, Malmo, Sweden, 77; Maison Des Beaux Arts, Paris, France, 83; Biblioteque Nat, Paris, France, 83; Musee D'Art Moderne, Paris, France, 83; and others. *Pos:* Assoc prof lithography, Ecole Des Beaux Arts, Paris, France. *Media:* Lithography. *Mailing Add:* c/o Rodi Karkazis Gallery 168 N Michigan Ave No 300 Chicago IL 60601

SPERO, NANCY
PAINTER, COLLAGE ARTIST
b Cleveland, Ohio, Aug, 24, 26. *Study:* Art Inst Chicago, BFA, 49; Atelier Andre L'Hote; Ecole des Beaux Arts, 49-50; Art Inst Chicago, Hon Dr Art, 91. *Work:* Mus des Beaux Arts, Montreal; Ulmer Mus, Ulm, Ger; Mus Mod Art, New York; Australian Nat Gallery; Philadelphia Mus Art; Centro Cultural, Mexico City. *Comn:* Mus Contemp Art, Los Angeles, 88; Rebirth of Venus (wallprinting Installation), Cupola Schirn Kunsthalle, Frankfurt, Ger, 89; To Soar II & Notes in Time on Women (wallprinting installations), Smith Col, Northampton, Mass, 90; To Soar III, Harold Washington Libr Ctr, Chicago, 91; El Sueno Imperativo, Circulo de Bellas Artes, Madrid, Spain, 91. *Exhib:* Issue Social Strategies by Women Artists, Inst Contemp Art, London, 80; Barbara Gross Galerie, Munich, 88; solo exhibs, Works Since 1950's (traveling), Everson Mus Art, Syracuse, NY, 88 & Bilder 1958 bis 1990 (traveling), Haus am Walsee, Berlin, Ger; Committed to Print, Mus Mod Art, New York, 88; Making Their Mark--Women Artists More Into the Mainstream 1970-1985, Cincinnati Art Mus, 89; The Decade Show, Mus Contemp Hispanic Art, New York, 90; Goya to Beijing Centre Int d'Art Contemporain, Montreal, PQ, 90; Gallery Hibell, Tokyo, Japan, 90; Works on Paper 1981-1991, Salzburger Kunstverein, Künstlerhaus Salzburg, Austria, 91; Ulmer Mus (retrospective exhib), Ulm, Ger, 92; Allegories of Modernism: Contemporary Drawing, Mus Mod Art, New York, 92. *Awards:* NY State Coun for the Arts Creative Artists Pub Serv Prog fel, 76-77; Nat Endowment for Arts grant, 77-78. *Bibliog:* Nancy Spero: Rebirth of Venus, Art Random, Kyoto Shoin, Japan, 89; Jon Bird (auth), Nancy Spero--Zwischen den Zeiel--Die Frau (catalog essay), Haus am Waldsee, Berlin, Ger, 90; Nancy Spero: Woman Breathing, Ulmer Mus (exhib catalog), Ed Cantz, Ostfildern, Ger, 92. *Mem:* Women's Caucus Art. *Media:* Collage on Paper. *Publ:* Co-ed, Rip-off file, Ad Hoc Comt Women Artists, 73; auth, Ende, Woman's Studies, England, 78; auth, Sky goddess - Egyptian acrobat, Artforum, No 7, 3/88; contribr, The Discovered Uncovered, M/E/A/N/I/N/G, No 2, 11/87; auth, Tracing Ana Mendieta, Art Forum, 4/92. *Dealer:* Josh Baer Gallery 476 Broome St New York NY 10013; Rhona Hoffman Gallery Chicago IL. *Mailing Add:* 530 La Guardia Pl New York NY 10012

SPERRY, ROBERT
CERAMIST
b Bushnell, Ill, Mar 12, 27. *Study:* Univ Sask, BA, 50; Art Inst Chicago, BFA, 54; Univ Wash, MFA, 55. *Work:* Smithsonian Inst; Everson Art Mus, Syracuse; Lannon Found, Palm Springs, Fla; Johnson Wax Collection; Craft Mus, New York. *Comn:* Chubb Insurance Co, NJ, 81; Sheraton Hotel, Seattle, 82; IBM-FE Educ Ctr, Atlanta, 83; Seattle Art Comn, 85; Safeco Insurance Co, Seattle, 88. *Exhib:* Ceramic Nat, Syracuse, 54-64; Young Americans, New York, 55-56; Int Ceramic Exhib, Ostend, Belg, 59; Third Int Exhib Contemp Ceramics, Prague, 62; Am Studio Potter, Victoria & Albert Mus, Eng, 66. *Teaching:* Prof ceramics, Univ Wash, 55- *Awards:* Tiffany Grant, 57; Ctr Asian Arts Award, 63; Japan Soc Award, 66; NEA Grant, 84. *Bibliog:* Painterly ceramic exploration, Artweek, 10/31/81; Planetary Clay, American Craft, 12/81; Mathew Kangus (auth), Robert Sperry a Retrospective, 86. *Media:* Clay. *Publ:* Producer, The Village Potters of Onda (film), 66; producer, Profiles Cast Long Shadows (film), 68. *Mailing Add:* 120 E Edgar St Seattle WA 98102

SPEYER, NORA
PAINTER
b Pittsburgh, Pa, Nov 24, 22. *Study:* Tyler Col Fine Art, Philadelphia, Pa. *Work:* Carnegie Inst, Philadelphia Mus Art, Pa; Corcoran Gallery, Washington, DC; Nelson Rockefeller Pvt Collection. *Exhib:* Darethea Speyer Gallery Paris, France, 70, 74 & 89; Landmark Gallery, New York, 78, 80 & 82; Emotional Impact, Art Mus Asn (traveling exhib), 84-86; Ingber Gallery, New York, 87. *Bibliog:* Dore Ashton (auth), Nora Speyer, New York Times, 4/57; Judith Applegale (auth), Nora Speyer, Art Int, 10/70; William P Scott (auth), The Sensousness of Point-Nora Speyer, Am Artist, 5/84. *Media:* Oil on Canvas. *Publ:* Auth, Painting the Landscape, Watson-Guptill, 86. *Mailing Add:* 178 Prince St New York NY 10012

SPICER, JEAN (DORIS) UHL
PAINTER, INSTRUCTOR
b Philadelphia, Pa, Nov 5, 35. *Study:* Philadelphia Col Art, dipl, 57; also with Domenic DiStefano, Charles Reid, Frank Webb, Judi Betts, Claude Crooney, 71 & Nita Engle. *Work:* Price Waterhouse, Pa; Haverford Sch Dist, Pa; Superior Models, Del; Stroemann Bread Co, Pa; John Sabatino Architects, Pa. *Comn:* Exhibitor/Flower Show, Philadelphia, 80; paintings, Havertown Sch Dist, Pa, 83. *Exhib:* Philadelphia Mus Art, 73; Bicentennial Cult Exchange Show, Wales, Gt Brit, 76; Salmagundi Club, New York, 79; Artists Equity Asn, traveling, Philadelphia, 80; Knickerbocker Ann, New York, 85; Philadelphia Watercolor Club Ann, Pa, 89. *Teaching:* Instr, Watercolor Workshop, Sydney, Australia, 86, Wayne Art Ctr, 86 & 87, Naples & Ft Myers, Fla, 88 & 89, Bermuda & Cornwall, England, 90; instr, Wallingford Community Art Ctr, 85- & Wayne Art Ctr, 87. *Awards:* Silver Medal, Art Dirs Club, 76; Gold Medal, Rittenhouse Sq, 83; Cash Awards, Philadelphia Water Club, 85 & Pittsburgh Aqueous, 86; Gold Medal, Philadelphia Sketch Club, 88; Gold Medal, Pa Watercolor Soc, 87. *Bibliog:* Sally Kistler (auth), Local artist joins Rittenhouse Show, News Delaware Co, 76; Gen Tully (auth), Art news, Suburban & Wayne Times, 77; Joseph Dempsey (auth), Dynamic duo, Living Mag, 78. *Mem:* Pa Soc Watercolor Painters; Philadelphia Watercolor Club; Artists Equity Asn; Assoc Am Watercolor Soc; Salmagundi Club, New York; Catharine Lorillard Wolfe Art Club, New York. *Media:* Watercolor, Charcoal. *Mailing Add:* No 11 Tenby Rd Havertown PA 19083

SPIEGEL, LAURIE
COMPUTER ARTIST, AUDIO-VISUAL ARTIST
b Chicago, Ill, Sept 20, 45. *Study:* Oxford Univ, 66-67; Shimer Col, BA, 67; Julliard Sch, 69-72; City Univ New York, MA, 75. *Exhib:* 2nd, 3rd & 4th International Computer Arts Festival, New York, 74, 75 & 76; Fur Augen und Ohren, Akademie der Kunst, Berlin, Ger, 79; Crossovers, Just Above Midtown Gallery, New York, NY, 81; Space Probes, Nexus, Atlanta, Ga, 81; Art by Computer and Video, Mus of the Surreal & Fantastique, New York, 82. *Teaching:* Instr & dir computer music studio, Cooper Union, 80-82 & New York Univ, 82-83. *Awards:* Creative Artists Pub Serv Fel, NY State Coun Arts, 75-76 & 79-80; Artist-in-Residence Production Support Grant, Experimental TV Lab WNET-New York, 76; New York Found Arts Fel Award, 91-92. *Bibliog:* Larry Oppenheimer (auth), Laurie Spiegel: Computer Music Pioneer, Mix Mag, 2/86; Bakers Biographical Dict Music & Musicians; New Grove Dict Am Music. *Media:* Electronic & Computer Media, Interactive Computer Media; Video, Graphics. *Publ:* Auth, numerous articles on technol in the arts, Ear Mag, 78-86, Keyboard, Electronic Musician, Computer Music J & others. *Mailing Add:* 173 Duane St New York NY 10013

SPIEGELMAN, LON HOWARD
PAINTER, PUBLISHER
b Los Angeles, Calif, Nov 25, 41. *Study:* San Jose State Univ, BA, 65. *Work:* Univ Md, Catorsville; Gallery Laraviney, Paris, France; Galleria D'Arte Nuova 13, Alessandra, Italy; Univ Sidney, Australia; Syracuse Univ, NY. *Comn:* Stamp sheet, Vancouver Museo Internacionaleda Neu Art, 89; illus written article, Art Unidentified Japan, 90; drawing, Belgium Mus of Museums, 91; painting, Pasadena Armory Ctr Arts, 91. *Exhib:* Omaha Flow Systems, Joslyn Art Mus, Omaha, Nebr, 73; 16th Ann Art Unlimited,

Downey Mus Art, Calif, 74; Mail Art Archive Wein, Univ Wein, Austria, 78; First Int New Dada, Univ Lund, Sweden, 79; Poste-Restant Show, Liverpool Acad Arts, Eng, 79; Nuove Cartoline, Mus del Folklore, Rome, Italy, 80. *Collections Arranged:* The Postman Always Rings Twice, Santa Monica Col, 81; Help Teach Mailart, Otis Art Inst Los Angeles, 83; Target Earth, Los Angeles Alliance Survival, 85. *Pos:* Cur, Santa Monica Col, Otis Art Inst Los Angeles & Los Angeles Alliance Survival. *Teaching:* Instr phototype, Santa Monica Col, Calif, 78-81; instr mail art, Otis Art Inst, Los Angeles, 80-81 & Los Angeles Co Art Mus, Calif, 81; instr, self publ, Calif State Univ, Los Angeles, 88-90. *Awards:* First Place, Westwood Art Asn, 73, Los Angeles Art Asn, 76 & Civic Fine Arts Asn, 80. *Bibliog:* Nancy Howell-Kochler (auth), Photo Art Processes, Davis Publ, 80; Randy Hardson (auth), SWAK, Workman Publ, 81; Linda Burnham (auth), High performance, Astro Arts, 81. *Media:* Mixed. *Publ:* Auth, The Fence is Always Browner on the Other Side of the Grass, 70, The Sayings of Poor Lon, 75, Lee's Alphabet, 78 & Penelope, 78, pvt publ; contribr, Umbrella, Astro Arts, 80-81; ed & publ, Spiegelman's Mailart Rag, 84-90; A HALO, Hettorney KFT Budapest, 91; Mailart, An Annotated Bibliography, Scarecros Press Inc, 91. *Mailing Add:* 1556 Elevado St Los Angeles CA 90026

SPIER, PETER EDWARD
ILLUSTRATOR, WRITER
b Amsterdam, Neth, June 6, 27; nat US. *Study:* Ryks Acad Voor Beeldende Kunsten, Amsterdam, 45-47. *Pos:* Jr ed, Elsevier's Weekly, Amsterdam, 50-51 & Elsevier Publ Co, Houston, 52; free-lance auth & illusr, New York, 52-; speaker & lectr, schs & libr. *Awards:* Caldecott Medal, 78; Christopher Award, 70 & 78; NY Times Award, 77. *Publ:* Auth & illusr, Noah's Ark, 77, Oh, Were They Ever Happy!, 78, Bored, Nothing to Do, 78, The Legend of New Amsterdam, 79 & People, 80; illusr, over 150 bks; contribr illus, many nat mags. *Mailing Add:* 55 Wardencliff Rd PO Box 210 Shoreham NY 11786-9998

SPIESS-FERRIS, ELEANOR
PAINTER
b Las Vegas, NMex, July 3, 41. *Study:* Under Kenneth Adams, 59-60 & 64-67; Univ NMex, BFA, 60-62; Art Inst Chicago. *Work:* State of Ill Bldg, Chicago; Portland Art Mus, Ore; Ill State Mus, Springfield, Ill; Col of Du Page, Ill; Kemper Group Art Collection, Long Grove, Ill; and others. *Comn:* Prints, Plucked Chicken Press, Evanston, Ill, 85. *Exhib:* New Horizons, Chicago Cultural Ctr, 73-74, 80-82 & 85-86; Still and Not-So-Still Lives, Marianne Deson Gallery, Chicago, 77; Chicago Drawing, Columbia Univ, 79; American Drawing IV, Portsmouth Mus, Va, 82; one-person show, Van Straaten Gallery, Chicago, 84; 80th and 81st Exhibition by Artists of Chicago and Vicinity, Art Inst Chicago, 84 & 85; Fetish Art, Rockford Art Mus, Ill, 86; one-person show, Univ Wis at Green Bay, Wustum Mus, Racine, Zaks Gallery; Chicago Show, Chicago Cultural Ctr; Sansker Kendra Mus, Ahmedebad, India; Watercolor '88, Springfield Arts Mus, Mo; American Drawing IV, Portsmouth Mus, Va. *Collections Arranged:* Shelters, 83, Chicago 1984 Contemporary Furniture, 84, Alter Egos-Masks, 85, Indoor-Outdoor Sculpture: An Overview, 85 & Vernal Woods, 86, Evanston Art Ctr, Ill. *Teaching:* Instr figure painting & art fundamentals, Evanston Art Ctr, Ill, 86. *Awards:* Viehler Award, 80th Exhib by Artists of Chicago & Vicinity, 84; Ill Arts Coun Artists Fel Grant, 89; Arts Midwest Fel Grant, 91. *Bibliog:* James Bone (auth), Erotic dreams, The Reader, 84; Harry Boris, Art review, WTTW-FM Radio, 84; Estell Lauter (auth), Women as Mythmakers, Ind Univ Press; Stanely Marcus (auth), Exploring Imaginary Subjects, Am Artist Publ, 88; James Wood (auth), Eleanor Spiess-Ferris, Artforum, 91; and others. *Mem:* Arts Club Chicago; Art Inst Chicago (artists adv bd, 84-86). *Media:* Oil, Gouache. *Dealer:* Zaks Gallery 620 N Michigan Ave Chicago IL 60611; Payton/Wrigt Gallery 128 E Marcy St Santa Fe NM 87501. *Mailing Add:* c/o Evanston Art Ctr 26003 Sheridan Rd Evanston IL 60201

SPINK, FRANK HENRY
PAINTER
Ill, Sept 23, 35. *Study:* Univ Ill, Urbana, BArch, 58; Univ Wash, MUP, 64. *Work:* Chung Cheng Art Gallery, St John's Univ, Jamaica, NY. *Exhib:* Soc Western Artists, DeYoung Mus, San Francisco, 67; Palace Fine Arts Dedication Festival, San Francisco, 67; 12th-27th Ann Sumie Soc Shows, New York, 75-86, Washington, DC, 87-91, Mobile, Ala, 92; Va Watercolor Soc Annuals, 80-85, 91-92. *Pos:* Dir publ, Urban Land Inst, 72-88; dir, Non Residential Res, 83-88, vpres publ, 88- *Awards:* Summer Sketch Prize, Univ Ill, 55. *Mem:* Sumie Soc Am; Va Watercolor Soc; Potomac Valley Watercolorists; Art Club Washington. *Media:* Watercolor, Sumie. *Res:* Adaptive reuse of existing buildings, Shopping Centers, Suburban Activity Centers. *Publ:* Ed, Community Builders Handbook Series, 75-86; contribr, Shopping Center Development Handbook, 1st ed, 77, 2nd ed, 85; Residential Develop Handbook, 78; Downtown Develop Handbook, 80; Shopping Centers USA, 81; Dollars and Cents of Off Price Shopping Centers, 86. *Mailing Add:* 5158 Piedmont Pl Annandale VA 22003

SPINK, WALTER M
EDUCATOR, ADMINISTRATOR
b Worcester, Mass, Feb 16, 28. *Study:* Amherst Col, BA(summa cum laude), 49; Harvard Univ, MA(art hist), 50, PhD, 54; Fulbright grant, Dept Anthrop, Indian Mus, Calcutta 52-53. *Pos:* Cur, Brandeis Univ Art Collection, 56-61, acting chmn, Dept Fine Art, 59-60; dir, Asian Art Arch, Univ Mich, Ann Arbor, 62; dir, Photog Exped to India, 64-68. *Teaching:* Instr, Dept Fine Arts, Brandeis Univ, 56-61, assoc prof, 61-68; vis lectr, Dept Art, Brown Univ, 60; from assoc prof to prof art hist, Univ Mich, Ann Arbor, formerly; vis lectr, Dept S Asian Studies, Univ Chicago, summer 72. *Awards:* Fulbright Grant, 90-91; Guggenheim Grant, 91-92. *Mem:* Am Inst Indian Studies (trustee, 62-65 & 72-73); Asn Asian Studies, Indian Asn Art Historians, Col Art Asn, Am Comt S Asian Art (pres,72-76, dir color slide proj, 74-). *Publ:* Auth, Ajanta to Ellora, 67, Krishnamandala, 71, Ctr & Southeast Asian Studies, Univ Mich; The Axis of Eros, Schocken, 73 & Penguin, 75; Jogeswari, J Indian Soc of Oriental Art, 77; The Great Cave at Elephanta, with a study of sources, In: The Gupta Period, 77. *Mailing Add:* Dept Art Hist Univ Mich Main Campus Ann Arbor MI 48109

SPINOSA, GARY PAUL
SCULPTOR
b Memphis, Tenn, Dec, 26, 47. *Study:* Yale Univ Summer Sch Art & Music, 70; Cleveland Inst Art, BFA(Agnes Gund Mem Traveling Scholar), 72, Edinboro Univ, Pa, MFA, 88. *Work:* Southern Alleghenies Mus Art, Pa; Cleveland Art Asn, Ohio; Butler Inst Am Art; Lockhaven Univ, Pa. *Comn:* Public sculpture, Ohio Arts Coun, 78. *Exhib:* May Show, Cleveland Mus Art, 71-82; Eight State Ann, Speed Mus Art, Louisville, 74; Butler Inst Am Art, 74-75; European Triannual Sculpture Exhib, Paris, 78; one-man shows, Kent State Univ, 80, Ashland Col, 81 & Sandusky Cult Ctr, 82; Canton Art Inst, 89. *Awards:* Fel Grant, Ohio Arts Coun, 79; First Place for Sculpture, May Show, Cleveland Mus Art, 81; Pa Coun Arts Fel, 88. *Mem:* Int Sculpture Ctr, Washington, DC. *Media:* Clay, Mixed Media. *Dealer:* Lucky Street Gallery 919 Duval St Key West FL 33040; Folkarte Gallery 2026 Murray Hill Rd Cleveland OH 44106. *Mailing Add:* RD 1 Box 156 Venango PA 16440

SPINSKI, VICTOR
SCULPTOR, EDUCATOR
b Newton, Kans, Oct 10, 40. *Study:* Kans State Teachers Col, BSE, 63; Ind Univ, Bloomington, MFA, 67. *Work:* State Univ NY Potsdam; Haystack Mountain Sch Crafts, Deer Isle, Maine; Elmira Col, NY; Del Art Mus, Wilmington. *Exhib:* Coffee, Tea & Other Cups, Mus Contemp Crafts, New York, 71; Int Exhib Ceramics, Victoria & Albert Mus, London, Eng, 72; Soup Tureens, Campbell Mus, Camden, NJ, 76; Century of Ceramics in US, Everson Mus Art, Syracuse, NY, 79; Clay Attitudes, Queens Mus, New York; 11th Regional Sculpture Exhib, Mus Philadelphia Civic Ctr, Pa; Ten East Coast Potters, Brooklyn Mus Art Sch, NY; Ind Crafts, Herron Mus Art, Indianapolis. *Teaching:* Grad teaching asst, Ind Univ, 67; prof ceramics, Univ Del, 67-; summer fac, Haystack Mountain Sch Crafts, 68 & 70, Brooklyn Mus Art Sch, 70 & Council Grove Craft Sch, Missoula, Mont, 74-76. *Bibliog:* Judith Schwartz (auth), Victor Spinski, Current, 76; Lisa Hammel (auth), She wants her gallery to shake people up--and it does, New York Times, 76; Clark & Hughto (auth), Century of Ceramics in the United States, E P Dutton, 79. *Mem:* Nat Coun Ceramic Arts; Am Crafts Coun; Int Acad Ceramics. *Media:* Ceramics; Photography. *Publ:* Auth, Ceramic Photosilkscreening, Nat Coun Educ Ceramic Arts, 70. *Dealer:* Theo Portnoy Gallery 56 W 57th St New York NY 10019. *Mailing Add:* Art Dept Univ Del Newark DE 19716

SPIRA, BILL
SCULPTOR
b Antwerp, Belg, Oct 24, 35; US citizen. *Study:* Ill Inst Technol, with L Mies Van der Rohe, L Hillberseimer & Walter Peterhans, BS, 58. *Work:* Am Broadcasting Co, New York; Phillips Petroleum Co; also pvt collections of Richard Brown Baker, New York, Graham Gund, Boston & William King. *Exhib:* Penthouse Group, Mus Mod Art, New York, 65; Play Ball (with catalog), Queens Mus, NY, 78; On-Off the Wall, Va Beach Arts Ctr, 86. *Teaching:* Chmn Wood Arts Fieldston Sch. *Bibliog:* Ellen Lee Klein (auth), Bill Sprira, Arts, 1/84 & 4/87;; Edmund Leites (auth), rev, Art in Am, 4/84. *Media:* Clay, Wood. *Dealer:* Vanderwoude Tananbaum 24 E 81st St New York NY 10028. *Mailing Add:* 30 Waterside Plaza Apt 28F New York NY 10010

SPITLER, CLARE BLACKFORD
ART DEALER
b Findlay, Ohio, Feb 2, 23. *Study:* DePauw Univ; Univ Mich, AB, 44. *Pos:* Owner & dir, Gallery One, Findlay, Ohio, 65-76, Gallery One, Ann Arbor, Mich, 77-81 & Clare Spitler Works of Art, Ann Arbor, Mich, 81-; art writer, bi-weekly column, Art Dealings, Ann Arbor News, Mich, 82-83. *Specialty:* Contemporary American paintings, sculpture, graphics and selected crafts, often featuring Midwestern artists; additional European artists. *Mailing Add:* Clare Spitler Works of Art 2007 Pauline Ct Ann Arbor MI 48103

SPITZ, BARBARA S
PRINTMAKER
b Chicago, Ill, Jan 8, 26. *Study:* Art Inst Chicago; RI Sch Design; Brown Univ, AB. *Work:* Art Inst Chicago; Philadelphia Mus Art; Smart Gallery, Univ Chicago; DeCordova Mus, Lincoln, Mass; Los Angeles Co Mus, Calif. *Comn:* First Ill Print Comn Prog, 73. *Exhib:* Art Inst Chicago 71st Ann, 68; Soc Am Graphic Artists Ann, Kennedy Galleries, New York, 71 & 79; Smithsonian Traveling Exhibs, 73 & 74; Libr Cong & Nat Collection Fine Arts, 73 & 74; Tokyo Cent Mus, 77; Nat Acad Design, New York, 77; Pratt Graphic Ctr, New York, 77; Nat Aperture, 86; Loyola Univ, Chicago, 88. *Awards:* Childe Hassam Purchase Award, Am Acad of Arts & Lett, 73; First Prize, 77 & Purchase Award, 78, Ill Regional Print Show; Stuart M Egnal Prize, Int Biennial Print Exhib, Print Club, Philadelphia, 77. *Bibliog:* Article, Printmaker in Illinois, Ill Educ Asn, 72, Illinois Printmakers I Proj, Ill Arts Coun, 74 & others. *Mem:* Artist Equity Asn; Arts Club Chicago; Los Angeles Printmaking Soc; Boston Printmakers; Soc Am Graphic Artists. *Media:* Intaglio; Photography. *Mailing Add:* 1106 Somerset Lane Newport Beach CA 92660

SPIVY-ANDERSON, C ALEXANDRA
CRITIC, WRITER
b Boston, Mass, May 14, 42. *Study:* Sarah Lawrence Col, BA, 61; Sorbonne, France, 63. *Pos:* Art ed, Paris Rev, 73-78; art ed, Village Voice, 74-77; sr ed, Portfolio Mag, 79-83; ed in chief, Art & Antiques, 83-84; exec ed, Am Photogr, 85-87; arts ed & exec ed, Smart Mag, 88; contrib art ed, Esquire Mag, 90- *Awards:* Nat Endowment Arts Critic Grant, 78. *Mem:* Int Asn Art Critics; Am Soc Mag Ed; Art Table; Colby Col Art Mus Adv Comt (chmn); Contemp Arts Coun, Mus Mod Art. *Res:* Contemporary art and artist's publications; 20th century art. *Publ:* Co-auth, Anderson and Archer's Soho: The Essential Guide to Art and Life in Lower Manhattan, Simon & Schuster, 79; Living with Art, Ruzzoli, 88; auth, Passions & Tenderness: Portraits of Olga by the Baron de Meyer, Graystone Books, 92. *Mailing Add:* 125 W 12th St New York NY 10011

SPOFFORD, SALLY(SARAH H SPOFFORD)
PAINTER
b New York, NY, Aug 20, 29. *Study:* Swarthmore Col, BFA, 52; Art Students League, studied with Bernard Klonis & George Grosz, 53-54; The China Inst, New York, studied with Ya-Hung Wang, 53. *Work:* NJ State Mus, Trenton; Newark Mus, Newark, NJ; Owens Corning Fiber Glass, Corning, NY; AT&T Corp Hq, Basking Ridge, NJ; Murray Invesments, Dallas, Tex. *Exhib:* Transformations: A Show of Contemporary Masks, Hunterdon Art Ctr, Clinton, NJ, 88; solo exhib, Morris Mus, Morristown, NJ, 89, Schering-Plough Gallery, Madison, NY, 89 & Phoenix Gallery, New York, 90; Archit in the Arts, Nabisco Brands Gallery, East Hanover, NJ, 89. *Teaching:* Hunterdon Art Ctr, 83-85, 88 & 90. *Mem:* Allied Artists Am; Assoc Artists NJ (pres, 85-87). *Media:* Watercolor, Oil. *Mailing Add:* 210 Mt Harmony Rd Box 443 Bernardsville NJ 07924

SPOHN, FRANZ FREDERICK
PRINTMAKER, ILLUSTRATOR
b Columbus, Ohio, June 6, 50. *Study:* Ohio State Univ, BFA, 73, MFA, 75. *Work:* Glenbow Mus, Calgary, Alta; Ohio State Univ. *Comn:* Print, Philadelphia Art Alliance, 88. *Exhib:* The Confectioner's Art, Am Craft Mus, NYC, (3 yr traveling exhib); Collaboration: Printmaking in Philadelphia, Glen Vivian Mus, Swansea, Wales & Strozzi Palace, Florance, Italy; one-man show, Glenbow Mus, Calgary, Alta, 81; Collage & Assemblage Traveling Exhib, Miss Mus Art, Jackson, 81-83; Feast Your Eyes, Philadelphia Mus Art, 82; Material Illusions, Unlikely Materials, Taft Mus, Cincinnati, 83; and others. *Collections Arranged:* Eighteen Buys Twenty, Portico Gallery, Philadelphia, 83. *Awards:* Commissioned print by Philadelphia Art Alliance, Philadelphia, 88. *Bibliog:* Nancy Tousley (auth), Artist sweetens his biting satire, Calgary Herald, 2/12/81; Keith Morrison (auth), Realistic self portraits, New Art Examiner, 4/81; Jo Ann Lewis (auth), Artistic couples, Wash Post, 5/31/81. *Mem:* Col Art Asn; Print Club Philadelphia. *Media:* Serigraphy, Silkscreen. *Mailing Add:* PO Box 53402 Philadelphia PA 17105-3402

SPONENBURGH, MARK
HISTORIAN, SCULPTOR
b Cadillac, Mich, June 15, 16. *Study:* Cranbrook Acad Art, scholar, 40; Wayne Univ; Ecole Beaux-Arts, Paris, France; Univ London; Univ Cairo; Hon DFA, 70. *Work:* Detroit Inst Art; Portland Art Mus; Univ Ore; Willamette Univ; Oregon State Univ. *Comn:* Architectural sculpture, McGruder Veterinary Hosp, 80; Fisherman's Mem, Newport, Ore, 88; Town & Gown, bronze group, Willamette Univ. *Exhib:* North Am Sculpture, Paris Salon, France; Mus Mod Art, Cairo; and 35 one-man exhibs, sculpture. *Pos:* Consult, curator & museologist. *Teaching:* Assoc prof, Univ Ore, 46-56; vis prof, Royal Col Arts, 56-57; prof & dean, Nat Col Arts, Pakistan, 58-61; prof, Ore State Univ, 61-, chmn art dept, 82-, emer prof, 84- *Awards:* Distinguished Lecturer, Phi Kappa Phi, 82; Distinguished Prof, Ore State Univ, 82. *Mem:* Int Asn Egyptologists; Royal Soc Arts; Royal Soc Antiquaries; Int Asn Art Historians; Am Res Ctr in Egypt; Oxford Soc. *Media:* Wood, Stone. *Res:* Stylistic analogies in Coptic & Celtic; sculpture of Moukhtar; modular systems in Egyptian sculpture. *Publ:* Contribr, Arts Quart, J Inst Egypte, Rev Caire, Near E Bull & J Near E Studies; Royal Soc Antiquaries; and others. *Mailing Add:* 5562 NW Pacific Hwy Seal Rock OR 97376

SPRAGUE, MARK ANDERSON
PAINTER, EDUCATOR
b Champaign, Ill, Jan 5, 20. *Study:* Univ Ill, BFA, 46, MFA, 49. *Work:* Ill State Univ Mus, Bloomington. *Comn:* Painting for Great Ideas of Western Man, Container Corp Am, Chicago, Ill. *Exhib:* Am Fedn Arts Circulating Exhib, Washington, DC, 49; Art Inst Chicago 60th Am Ann, 51; Western Art Ann, Denver, Colo, 51-52; Corcoran Gallery Art Biennial, Washington, DC, 51-53; Nat Acad Design Ann, New York, 58-62. *Teaching:* Prof art, Univ Ill, Champaign, 46-80. *Media:* Oil, Polymer. *Mailing Add:* 912 Devonshire Dr Champaign IL 61821

SPRAGUE, PAUL EDWARD
HISTORIAN, CONSULTANT
b Cumberland, Md, Feb 28, 33. *Study:* Rutgers Univ, BA, 54; Oberlin Col; Princeton Univ, MA, 63, PhD, 69. *Pos:* Consult, Hist Preserv Serv, 74- *Teaching:* Asst prof archit hist, Univ Notre Dame, 64-68; asst prof art hist, Univ Chicago, 68-74; assoc prof archit hist, Univ Wis, Milwaukee, 78-84, prof, 84- *Awards:* Sr Fel Nat Endowment Humanities, 86-87. *Mem:* Soc Archit Hist (mem bd dirs, 73-75 & 82-85, 1st vpres, 90-92); Victorian Soc Am (mem bd dirs, 75-81); Int Coun Monuments & Sites (mem bd dirs, 75-78); Asn Col Schs Archit; Midwest Art Hist Soc. *Res:* Louis Sullivan, Frank Lloyd Wright and their students and colleagues. *Publ:* Coauth, The Hasbrouck-Sprague Survey of Historic Architecture in Oak Park, Ill, 74; auth, Frank Lloyd Wright and the Prairie School in Oak Park, 76, Village Oak Park; Drawings of Louis Sullivan, Princeton Univ Press, 79; Origin of balloon framing, Soc Archit Historians J, 82; Louis Sullivan, In: Macmillian Encyclopedia of Architecture, Free Press, 82; ed & contribr, Frank Lloyd Wright in Madison, Elvehjem Mus, 90. *Mailing Add:* 39609 Golden Cedar Oconomowoc WI 53066

SPRANG, ELIZABETH
PAINTER, SCULPTOR
b Capitol View, Md. *Study:* Univ Calif, Los Angeles, 3 yrs; studied painting with F Tolles Chamberlain, lithography with Lynton Kistler & Richard Haines, Calif; Naropa Inst, Colo, studied American & Meso-American art & symbolism with Jose Arguelles & Tibetan thangka painting with Glen Eddy. *Exhib:* Los Angeles Co Mus Art, Los Angeles, 50; Libr Cong Ann Print Show, 52-55; Oakland Art Mus, Calif, 53; Pa Acad of Fine Arts, 55; solo shows, Heard Mus, Phoenix, Ariz, 66, Sun Spirits Gallery, Santa Fe, NMex, 75 & Los Llanos Gallery, 77, 79 & 81. *Mem:* Int Sculpture Ctr. *Media:* Acrylic, Oil; Celluclay. *Publ:* Illusr, Conspicuous California Plants, San Pasqual Press, 38; auth & illusr, Art, Beauty and Country life in Utah, Dialogue Mag, 70; auth & illusr, Good-bye River, Mojave Books, 79, reprint by Kiva Press, 93. *Dealer:* Lightside Gallery Santa Fe NMex. *Mailing Add:* Rte 4 Box 16-B Santa Fe NM 87501

SPRATT, FREDERICK R
GALLERY DIRECTOR, PAINTER
b Cedar Rapids, Iowa, June 15, 27. *Study:* Dallas Mus Fine Art, studied painting, 58; Iowa Wesleyan Col, BA, 51; Univ Iowa, MA, 56. *Work:* Iowa Wesleyan Col, Mt Pleasant; State Univ Iowa, Iowa City; De Saisset Mus, Univ Santa Clara, Calif; San Jose Mus Art; Coldwell-Banker Corp, Washington, DC. *Exhib:* Four Contemporary California Artists, Calif Arts Comn, Humboldt, 68; California Landscape, Lytton Ctr Visual Arts, Los Angeles, 68; Biennial of American Painting and Sculpture, Univ Ill, Urbana, 68; O K Harris Gallery, New York, 76; Janus Gallery, Los Angeles, 78; The Clocktower, Inst Art & Urban Res, New York, 79; Northern California Art of the Sixties, De Saisset Mus, Santa Clara Univ, San Jose, 82; Ten California Colorists, traveling exhib, Redding, San Jose & Palm Springs, Calif, 85-86. *Pos:* Partner/Dir, d p Fong & Spratt Galleries, San Jose. *Teaching:* Prof art, San Jose State Univ, 56-; retired. *Bibliog:* Dorothy Burkhart (auth), Fred Spratt, Arts Mag, 78; Peter Frank (auth), Los Angeles Art, Art in Am, 78. *Specialty:* Contemporary American & Asian Artists with focus on West Coast & Pacific Rim. *Publ:* Auth, Art Production in Discipline Based Art Education, J Paul Getty Educ Prog, 86. *Mailing Add:* 920 S First St San Jose CA 95110

SPROAT, CHRISTOPHER TOWNSEND
SCULPTOR
b Boston, Mass, Sept 23, 45. *Study:* Skowhegan Sch Painting & Sculpture, 69; Boston Univ; Boston Mus Sch Fine Arts; also with George Aarons. *Exhib:* One-man show, Inst Contemp Art, Boston, 70; Elements of Art, Mus Fine Arts, Boston, 71-72 & Rohm/Sproat, 74; Whitney Mus Am Art Biennial, New York, 73; Hayden Gallery, Mass Inst of Technol, Cambridge, Mass; Marian Goodman Gallery, New York, 80; Bette Stoler Gallery, New York, 83 & 85; The Silent Studio, Boston Athenaeum, Mass, 84; Barbara Krakow Gallery, Boston, Mass, 85. *Awards:* Mass Arts & Humanities Found Fel, 75 & 78; Nat Endowment for Arts Grant, 75-76 & 80-81; Grant, Nat Endowment Arts, 84-85; Grant, NY Found Arts, 85. *Bibliog:* Kenneth Baker (auth), Sproat & Samaras, Boston Rev Arts, 4/72; Carl Belz (auth), Deliberating with color, drawing with light, Art in Am, 5-6/72; and others. *Mem:* NY Artists Equity. *Dealer:* Barbara Krakow Gallery 10 Newbury St Boston MA 02116. *Mailing Add:* Box 2086 New York NY 10013

SPROUL, ANN STEPHENSON
PAINTER, INSTRUCTOR
b DeWitt, Mo, Aug 9, 07. *Study:* Cent Mo State Univ; also with William B Schimmel, Ariz, John Pike & Edgar Whitney, New York & John Pellew, Conn. *Work:* Pvt galleries in Chile, Switzerland, Czechoslovakia, England & Canada. *Comn:* Mural of Frontier Town, Silver Spur Saloon & Restaurant, Cave Creek, Ariz; Christmas card designs, Mr & Mrs Dow Patterson, Phoenix, 73-74 & Cave Creek Community Schs, 74; illus Christmas letter, Armstrong Congoleum, Cecil Armstrong, Carefree, Ariz, 74. *Exhib:* Plaza Art Fair, Kansas City, Mo, 63-69; Greater Kansas City Art Asn, Kansas City Mus, 64; Ararat Temple Beaux Arts, Ararat Temple Auditorium, Kansas City, 64; one-man show, Am Asn Univ Women, Sophian Plaza, Kansas City, 65; Discovery of Art Mag Exhib, Kansas City, 68. *Pos:* Owner & demonstr watercolor & brush tech, Ann Sproul Watercolor Gallery, Cave Creek, 83- *Teaching:* High Sch teacher art & art supvr, Carrollton Pub Schs, Mo, 59-69; instr watercolor, broadline pencil sketching & charcoal, Cave Creek, 86. *Awards:* First in Watercolor, Greater Kansas City Art Asn, 64 & Mo Div, Nat League Am Pen Women, 65; Publisher's Award, Discovery of Arts Mag, 68. *Bibliog:* Article in Ariz Desert Foothills, Mesa, Ariz, 75; Watercolor Techniques by Ann Sproul (film of tech demonstrations for schs), Outdoor Pictures, Anacortes, Wash, 75. *Mem:* Nat League Am Pen Women. *Media:* Watercolor, Pencil. *Publ:* Auth, The Art of Poster Making, Kappa Delta Pi Scroll, 28; illusr, Of Time & Space (poems), 74. *Dealer:* Grapevine Gallery Box 132 Oklahoma City OK 73101; Beach Front Gallery Box 1028 Cambria CA 93428. *Mailing Add:* 5924 E Carriage Dr PO Box 93 Cave Creek AZ 85331

SPRUCE, EVERETT FRANKLIN
PAINTER, PRINTMAKER
b Faulkner Co, Ark, Dec 25, 08. *Study:* Dallas Art Inst, 25-29; pvt study with Olin H Travis & Thomas M Stell. *Work:* Whitney Mus Am Art, Metrop Mus, New York; Dallas Mus Fine Arts, Tex; Walker Art Ctr, Minneapolis, Minn;

and many others. *Exhib:* Carnegie Inst, Pittsburgh; Corcoran Gallery Art, Washington, DC; Brussels, Belg & Bordighera, Italy; Ford Found Retrospective, circulated nationally by Am Fedn Arts; Pan-Am Union, Washington, DC; Dallas Mus Fine Arts; one-man show, Paintings & Drawings, 1950-1979, Huntington Gallery, Univ Tex, Austin, 79; and others. *Pos:* Gallery asst, Dallas Mus Fine Arts, 31-34, registrar, 35, asst dir, 35-40; chmn dept art, Univ Tex, Austin, 48-50. *Teaching:* Instr, Dallas Mus Sch, 36-40; instr art, Univ Tex, Austin, 40-44, asst prof, 44-47, prof art & mem grad fac, 54-74, emer prof, 75- *Awards:* Bordighera, Italy, 54; D D Feldman Award, Tex State Fair, 55; Dallas Mus Fine Arts Prize, 55; and others. *Bibliog:* Portfolio of Paintings, Vol I, In: Blaffer Series, Univ Tex. *Media:* Acrylic, Oil; All. *Mailing Add:* 15 Peak Rd Austin TX 78746

SPURGIN, JOHN EDWIN
ADMINISTRATOR, PAINTER
b Indianapolis, Ind, Dec 17, 32. *Study:* Ind State Univ, BS & MA; Mich State Univ, with Angelo Ippolito; Univ Cincinnati, with Robert Knipschild, MFA. *Work:* Mich Educ Asn, East Lansing; Hubbard Milling Co, Mankato, Minn; Gustavus Adolphus Col, St Peter, Minn; Southwest State Univ, Marshall, Minn; Univ Cincinnati, Ohio. *Exhib:* Biennial of Painting & Sculpture, Walker Art Ctr, Minneapolis, 66; Okla Art Ctr, Oklahoma City, 67; Minn Mus, St Paul, 70; Miami Univ, Oxford, Ohio, 72; Northeast La Univ, Monroe, 74; one-man shows, Univ Wis, Marshfield, 75, Southwest State Univ, Marshall, 77 & Art Ctr, Minn, 83; Pillsbury Competitive Exhib, Minneapolis, 81; and others. *Collections Arranged:* American National Bank Collection Exhibition, St Paul, Minn, 74; Mankato Clinic, Ltd, Minn, 81. *Pos:* Gallery dir, Gallery Five Hundred, Fine Arts, Inc, Mankato, 69-72 & Nichols Gallery, Mankato State Univ, 73-75. *Teaching:* Instr art educ, Flint Inst Art, Mich, 60-64; prof design, painting, Mankato State Univ, 65-, chmn art dept, 75-89; vpres acad affairs, Milwaukee Inst Art & Design, 89- *Awards:* First Prize Painting, Rochester Area Artists, Rochester Art Ctr, Minn, 66; Best-in-Show, Southern Minn Art Exhib, Mankato Free Press, 67 & 72; Minn State Individual Artists Grant, 77-78. *Media:* Mixed Media. *Mailing Add:* 7840 W Canterbury Ct Franklin WI 53132

SPURLING, NORINE M
GRAPHIC ARTIST, EDUCATOR
b Bermuda Islands, Jan 16, 30. *Study:* Moore Col Art, Philadelphia; Pa Acad Fine Art, Philadelphia; State Univ NY, Buffalo, MFA, 75. *Work:* West Publ Co, St Paul, Minn; Charles Rand Penney Upstate NY Collection, Lockport; Corporate Art Collection, The Kemper Group, Long Grove, Ill; Members Gallery, Albright-Knox Art Gallery, Buffalo, NY; Burchfield Art Center, Buffalo, NY. *Exhib:* West '80 Art & the Law, Minn Mus Art, St Paul, 80; solo exhibs, Deland Mus, Fla, 77, Shelia Nussbaum Gallery, Millburn, NJ, 83 & Access to the Arts, Dunkirk, NY, 84; Printed by Women, Port History Mus, Philadelphia, 83; Nat Drawing, Trenton, NJ, 83; Col Mainland Nat Exhib, Texas City, 83; 27th Nat Print Exhib, Clinton, NJ, 83; plus many others. *Pos:* Exhib coordr, AAO Gallery, Buffalo, 76; gallery dir, AC Gallery, Buffalo, 77-79. *Teaching:* Art dept, State Univ of NY, Buffalo. *Bibliog:* Bryce Kanbara (auth), Norine Spurling: Drawings, the Blue Hush, Hamilton Artists Inc, 82. *Mem:* Buffalo Soc Artists (pres, 75-76); Col Art Asn; Womens Caucus Art; Nat Mus for Women in the Arts, Upstate NY Com. *Media:* Pastel, Charcoal. *Publ:* Illusr, Lightworks: A Handbook of Photographic Alternatives by J Arnow, Van Nostrand Reinhold, 80; Western NY Women Artists Calendar, 83; ed, Western NY Artists (catalog), AAO Gallery, 83. *Dealer:* Barbara Schueller Art Associates 345 Franklin Ave Buffalo NY 14202. *Mailing Add:* c/o Oxford Gallery 267 Oxford St Rochester NY 14607

SPURLOCK, WILLIAM
HISTORIAN, CRITIC
b Chicago, Ill, Oct 23, 45. *Study:* Trinity Univ, San Antonio, Tex, BA; Univ NMex, Albuquerque, MA; Union Grad Sch, PhD. *Collections Arranged:* Vito Acconci (auth, catalog), Wright State Univ Art Gallery, 76; Barry Le Va (auth, catalog), Stephen Antonakos, Dennis Oppenheim, 77; Larry Bell (auth, catalog), Laurie Anderson, William Wegman, Alice Aycock & Pat Steir, 76; Photo-Realist Painting in Calif (auth, catalog), Santa Barbara Mus Art, 80; Herbert Bayer: Sited Sculpture and the Environment (auth, catalog), Roland Reiss, Sam Richardson, 81; and others. *Pos:* Fine art consult, Atlantic Richfield Co, Los Angeles, 79-84; cur exhibs & contemp art, Santa Barbara Mus Art, 78-81. *Teaching:* Asst dir educ in art hist & admin, Des Moines Art Ctr, Iowa, 72-74; asst prof art hist & dir, Fine Arts Galleries, Wright State Univ, Dayton, 74-78; assoc prof art hist, 82-, chair dept art, Univ Tex at Arlington, 82-86. *Mem:* Int Asn Art Critics; Col Art Asn; Am Asn Mus; Int Coun Mus; Am Fedn Arts; Nat Coun Art Adminr; Nat Asn Sch Art & Design. *Res:* Modern and contemporary art forms; environmental arts; criticism & theory; museology. *Publ:* Auth, Social & Ecological Issues in Contemporary Art, National Arts Guide, 3-4/80; Cecile Abish, 78; Richard Fisher, Current Charts: Chosen Lands, 78; Federal Art Patronage in the State of New Mexico: 1933-1943 (catalog), Mus NMex, 78; Dialogue-Discourse-Research: Eleanor Antin, Helen and Newton Harrison, Fred Lonidier, Barbara Strasen, Santa Barbara Mus Art, 79; numerous articles & essays on contemp art & artists. *Mailing Add:* Dept Art & Art History Univ Tex Arlington TX 76019

SPYROPOULOS, GEORGE YORGO See Yorgo (George Yorgo Spyropoulos)

SQUADRA, JOHN
PAINTER
b New York, NY, June 25, 32. *Study:* RI Sch Design, BFA, 53. *Work:* San Francisco Mus Mod Art. *Exhib:* Artist's Showcase, Mus Art, Bridgeport, Conn, 78; one-man shows, Nonson Gallery, Soho, NY, 79, Gallery Lory, Norwalk, Conn, 88 & Gallery-Musee des Duncan, Paris, 80; Vered Int Art Gallery, East Hampton, NY, 80; People 81, Hudson River Mus, Yonkers, NY. *Teaching:* Teacher oils, acrylics, watercolor, Rowayton Arts Ctr, Conn, 74-87. *Awards:* Top Ten, Irene Leache Mem, Norfolk Mus, Va, 55; Second Prize, Darien Art Show, 82; First Prize, Rowayton Arts Ctr, 85. *Bibliog:* Article, Le Nouveau J, Paris, 11/80; article, Playboy Mag, 2/81; Hudson River Mus Show, New York Times, 10/81; rev, Playboy Mag, 2/81; rev, Hudson River Mus Show, 10/81; and others. *Media:* Oil, Acrylic. *Publ:* Illusr, Songs from Silences, 76; auth & illusr, Dr Miraculous, 81. *Dealer:* John Ames Gallery 68 68 Main St Belfast ME 04915. *Mailing Add:* RFD No 2 PO Box 1440 Brooks ME 04921

SQUIER, JACK LESLIE
SCULPTOR, EDUCATOR
b Feb 27, 27; US citizen. *Study:* Ind Univ, BS, 50; Cornell Univ, MFA, 52. *Work:* Mus Mod Art & Whitney Mus Am Art, New York; Hirshhorn Mus, Washington, DC; Everson Mus, Syracuse, NY; Johnson Mus, Cornell Univ; Stanford Univ Mus; Houston Mus, Tex; St Lawrence Univ Mus, NY; Lipman Found, New York. *Comn:* Disc (fiber glass & aluminum leaf sculpture), Ithaca Col, 68. *Exhib:* Carnegie Int, Pittsburgh; Brussels World's Fair; Recent Sculpture USA, Mus Mod Art; 30 Americans Under 35, Whitney Mus Am Art, 57; Hirshhorn Mus, Washington, DC; Mus Fine Arts, Boston; Art Inst Chicago; Denver Art Mus; Albright-Knox Art Gallery, Buffalo, NY; Los Angeles County Mus Art; Rochester Mem Art Gallery. *Teaching:* Prof sculpture, Cornell Univ, 58- *Bibliog:* William Lipke (auth), Disc, by Jack Squier, Cornell Univ, 68. *Mem:* Int Asn Art; Sculptors Guild. *Media:* Bronze, Fiberglass. *Mailing Add:* 221 Berkshire Rd Ithaca NY 14850

SQUIERS, CAROL
WRITER, CURATOR
b Oak Park, Ill, Dec, 25, 48. *Study:* Univ Ill, Chicago, BA(art hist), 71; Hunter Col, New York. *Pos:* Cur photog, PS 1, Inst Art & Urban Resources, New York, 80-84; photog critic, Village Voice, New York, 82-83 & Vanity Fair, 83-84; assoc ed, Am Photogr Mag, 86-89, sr ed, 89- *Awards:* Nat Endowment Arts Fel, 81. *Bibliog:* Andy Grundberg (auth), Mixing art & commerce, NY Times, 5/81; Sharon Gill (auth), Curator as critic: Carol Squiers, New York Photo District News, 9/82; Brian Wallis (ed), Silvia Kolbowski, Discordant Voices, Blasted Allegories: An Anthology of Writings by Contemporary Artists, New Mus Contemp Art, New York & Mass Inst Technol Press, Cambridge, Mass, 87. *Res:* The politics of photographic representation. *Publ:* Auth, Color photography: The Walker Evans legacy & the commercial tradition, 78 & Looking at "Life," 81, Artforum; Photography: Tradition and decline, Aperture, 83; Diversionary (Syn)tactics: Barbara Kruger Has Her Way With Words, Art News, 87; Picturing Scandal: Iranscam, the Reagan White House, and the Photo Opportunity, The Critical Image: Essays on Contemporary Photography, Bay Press, Seattle, 90. *Mailing Add:* 218 Thompson St No 15 New York NY 10012

SQUIRES, GERALD LEOPOLD
PAINTER, GRAPHIC ARTIST
b Nfld, Nov 17, 37. *Study:* Danforth Tech, Toronto; Ont Col Art, Toronto; mainly self-taught. *Work:* Mary Queen of the World Church, Mount Pearl, Nfld; Can Coun Art Bank, Ottawa; Mem Univ Nfld; Dept Mines & Energy, Can Govt; Saidye & Samuel Bronfman Collection, Montreal. *Comn:* Many paintings & drawings for bks, Breakwater Bks, St John's, Nfld, 71-88; Portrait of Lt Governor James McGrath, Government House, St John's, Nfld; painting, comn by Can Cath Conf Asn for New Can Sunday Mass Bk, Ottawa, 76; painting for Hibernia poster, Dept Mines & Energy, Govt Can, 88. *Exhib:* The Legacy of Surrealism in Canadian Art, Queen's Univ, Kingston, Ont, 78-79; An International Exhibition of Fine Art, Le Salondes Vendages de Cognac, Cercle des Beaux-Arts Pouton-Charentes, Govt House, Paris, 85; The Political Landscape 1, Tom Thomson Mem Art Gallery, Owen Sound, Ont, 89; one man shows, Portraits, 78, Ferryland Downs, 79-81, Cassandra Series, 83 (traveling exhib), Crucifixion-Resurrection, The Last Supper & St John's, Nfld, 87, Mem Univ, Nfld, Gerald Squires: A Retrospective, Atlantic Arts Gallery, St John's, Nfld, 81; plus others. *Pos:* Artistic dir, Breakwater Books Publishing Co, St John's; bd dirs, Artist's Coalition Nfld & Labrador. *Teaching:* Instr art, Mem Univ Nfld, 70-88; workshops and lectrs in pub schs & art asns throughout Nfld & Labrador. *Awards:* Community Artist-in-Residence, Mem Univ Exten, Nfld, 73-75; Ted Drover Award for Achievement in the Visual Arts, Nfld & Labrador Arts Coun, 84; Can Coun Arts B Award, 87. *Bibliog:* Gov Nfld, Making Pictures (video), 86; James Wade (auth), A medieval saint in a secular world, The Nfld Herald, 10/1/88; Joan Marie Sullivan (auth), Nfld roots nurture Squires work, Globe & Mail, Toronto, 88. *Mem:* Great Northern AUK Workshop; founding mem Oshawa Art Gallery. *Media:* Acrylic; Pen & Ink, Pencil. *Dealer:* Emma Butler Gallery 111 George St St John's Nfld; Christine Parker Contemporary Graphics 127 Queen's Rd St John's Nfld. *Mailing Add:* General Delivery Bennett's Rd Holyrood NF A0A 2R0 Canada

SQUIRES, NORMA JEAN
PAINTER, SCULPTOR
b Toronto, Ont; US citizen. *Study:* Art Students League; Cooper Univ, BFA, 61; also spec studies with James Rosati; Calif State Univ, Northridge, MA, 83. *Work:* Sterling Forest Gardens, Long Island, NY; Galeria Vandres, Madrid, Spain; Warner Brothers, Burbank, Calif; V-Tek Corp, Santa Monica, Calif; Siemens Pacesetter Systems, Los Angeles; Redwood City Pub Libr, Calif. *Exhib:* 4x4 plud 4x8, Newport Harbor Mus, 75; Dimensions II, Los Angeles Co Mus Art, 87; solo exhibs, Mendenahall Gallery, Whittier Col, Calif, 90, Walker & Walker Gallery, Santa Monica, 90, Contemp Images, Sherman Oaks, 90, Kosmont Assoc, N Hollywood, 91, Maturango Mus,

Ridgecrest, 91, LA Artcore, Los Angeles, Calif, 91; Mt St Mary's Col Gallery, 90, Lancaster Art Mus Invitational, 90, Art Fair at Los Angeles Conv Ctr, 90, Boritzer/Gray Gallery, Los Angeles, 90; Elements of Creation, Finegood Art Gallery, West Hills, Calif, 91; Poetic Directions, Platt Gallery, Univ Judaism, Los Angeles, 91; Introductory Exhibit, Ouvre Multi-Talents, R Mutt Gallery, Hollywood, Calif, 92; Haunted Visions/Celestial Ecstacy, N Brand Gallery Glendale, Calif, 92; The Frame multiplied & Extended, Security Pac Gallery, Costa Mesa, Calif, 92; and many others. *Pos:* Agent & partner, Contemp Fine Artists Reps, 85-; grant writer & publicist LA Art Core, 90- *Teaching:* Instr sculpture, Lucinda Art Sch, Tenafly, NJ, 67-69. *Awards:* Sarah Cooper Hewitt Award Advan Sci & Art, Cooper Union, 61. *Bibliog:* Nancy Ann Jones (auth), Toward a Personal Universe, Artweek, 11/8/90; Gerald Hopman (auth), Visions Art Quart, fall 91; Review in Artscene, 12/91. *Mem:* Women's Caucus Art; Artists Equity; Los Angeles Contemp Exhibs; Seeing It Through Exhibs; Pub Corp Arts. *Media:* Mixed. *Publ:* Illusr, three children's bks, Addie Ripple Co, 78. *Dealer:* Valerie Miller Fine Arts 72-785 Hwy 111 Palm Desert CA 92260; R Mutt 1917 Gallery 6161 Santa Monica Blvd Suite 100 Hollywood CA 90038. *Mailing Add:* 2764 Woodwardia Dr Los Angeles CA 90077

SRAGOW, ELLEN
GALLERY DIRECTOR
b New York, NY. *Study:* Hofstra Univ, BA, 64; New York Univ, MA, 66. *Pos:* Registr & asst cur, New York Univ Art Collection, 67-71; dir, Prints on Prince St Gallery, 74-76 & Sragow Gallery, 76- *Mem:* Int Fine Print Dealers Asn; Art Table Inc. *Specialty:* Contemporary prints, drawings, works on paper and paintings; American prints, drawings, paintings from the 1930's-early 1940's, including the WPA period. *Mailing Add:* 73 Spring St New York NY 10012

STACK, FRANK HUNTINGTON
PAINTER, PRINTMAKER
b Houston, Tex, Oct 31, 37. *Study:* Univ Tex, Austin, BFA; Art Inst Chicago; Univ Wyo, Laramie, MFA; Acad Grande Chaumiere, Paris. *Work:* Minneapolis Inst of Art, Minn; Sheldon Mem Gallery, Univ of Nebr; Madison Art Ctr, Wis; Mo Hist Soc, Columbia; Kalamazoo Art Inst, Mich. *Comn:* Outdoor mural, First Nat Bank, Columbia, Mo. *Exhib:* Ten Missouri Painters, 69; one-man shows, Etchings, US Info Serv, US Embassy, Turkey, Prints, Kalamazoo Art Inst, Mich, 76 & Watercolors, Va Tech Univ, 86 & Harwell Mus, Poplar Bluff, Mo, 87; From Zap to Zippy, San Francisco, 89; Misfit Lit Show, Seattle, 91; and others. *Pos:* contrib ed, The Comics J, 88. *Teaching:* Prof art, Univ Mo-Columbia, 63- *Awards:* Summer Res Fel, 68, 74 & 76 & Foreign Study Grant, 70, Univ Mo Res Coun; Mo Arts Coun Awards, 86. *Bibliog:* Sidney Larson (auth), Etchings and Lithographs by Frank Stack, Singing Wind Publ, 76; exhib catalog, Watercolors by Frank Stack, Mo Arts Coun, 77. *Mem:* Kansas Watercolor Soc; Columbia Art League; and others. *Media:* Oil, Watercolor; Etching, Lithography. *Publ:* Contribr, Nat Lampoon, 81, Ripoff Comix, 86-88, Am Splendor, 87-92, Wierdo, 88, Village Voice, 88-89 & Drawn and Quarterly, 90-92; co-auth, A selection of etchings by John Sloan, Univ Mo, 68; auth, A metal plate sketchbook, Am Artist, 10/75; auth, New Adventures of Jesus, 69-73, Feelgood Funnies, 71, 84, Dorman's Doggie, Kitchen Sink Press, 90, Amazon, Fantagraphics, 90; ed, Alley Oop 46-48, by V T Hamlin reprint of comic strip, 90-92. *Dealer:* The Lakeside Studio 150 S Lakeshore Rd Lakeside MI 49116; Harco Gallery Rte 2 Box 34A Columbia MO 65201. *Mailing Add:* 409 Thilly Ave Columbia MO 65201

STACK, GAEL Z
PAINTER, EDUCATOR
b Chicago, Ill, Apr 28, 41. *Study:* Univ Ill, Champaign, BFA; Southern Ill Univ, MFA. *Work:* Mus Fine Art, Houston; Solomon R Guggenheim Mus, New York; Dallas Mus Art, Tex; Menil Collection, Houston Tex. *Exhib:* 19 Artists-Emergent Americans: 1981 (catalog), Solomon R Guggenheim Mus, New York, 81; solo exhibs, Hadler-Rodriguez Galleries, New York, 85, Brown-Lupton Gallery, Fort Worth, Tex, 85, Janie C Lee Gallery, Houston, Tex, 83, 85, 87 & 89, Beitzel Fine Arts, New York, 88, Sarah Campbell Blaffer Gallery, Univ Houston, Tex, 89, Univ Ark, Little Rock, 89, Moody Gallery, Houston, Tex, 90; Emerging Artists 1978-1986: Selections from the Exxon Series (catalog), Guggenheim Mus, New York, 87; The Artist's Eye: Fourteen Collections Diverse Works, Houston, Tex, 89; Women View Women, RGK Found Gallery, Austin, Tex, 90; Tradition and Innovation: A Museum Celebration of Texas Art, Mus Fine Arts, Houston, Tex, 90; Northwest X Southwest: Painted Fictions (catalog), Palm Springs Desert Mus, Calif, 90; Art from Houston in Norway, Stavanger Mus, 82; New Art from a New City, Frankfurter Kunstverein, Ger, 82; New Orleans Trienniale, New Orleans Mus Art, 83; Fresh Paint, The Houston Sch, Mus Fine Arts, 85; Texas Currents, San Antonio Art Inst, 85; and others. *Teaching:* Instr, Univ Wis, La Crosse, 72-73; from asst prof to assoc prof, Univ Houston, 74-85, prof, 85- *Awards:* Nat Endowment Arts Artists Grant, 82, 89; Cult Arts Coun Houston Award Visual Arts, 85; Tiffany Found Award, 86. *Bibliog:* Michael Ennis (auth), Gael's Force, Domain, 5-6/89, 12, 14, 16; Elizabeth McBride (auth), Gael Stock, Artspace, 9-10/89, 65-65; Ann Holmes (auth), What artists collect, Houston Chronicle, 11/14/89, Sect D, 1, 4. *Dealer:* Janie C Lee Gallery 1209 Berthea Houston TX 77006. *Mailing Add:* c/o Moody Gallery 2815 Colquitt Houston TX 77098

STACK, MICHAEL
PAINTER, SCULPTOR
b Chicago, Ill, Oct 30, 41. *Study:* Univ Ill, BFA, 64; Univ Fla, MFA, 66. *Work:* Okla Art Ctr; Olivet Univ; Nelson-Atkins Mus Art; Yellow Freight Corp, NCAA Headquarters, Overland Park, Kans; Hallmark Collection, Twentieth Century Investments, Dean Witter Reynolds, Kansas City, Mo; and others. *Comn:* Garden of Earthly Delights (painting), KCRF Inc, Hayworth, Ill, 69; painting, MLLJN Inc, Bloomington, Ill, 73; Tensegrity structure, Metrop Life Insurance, Overland Park, Kans, 83; Dancin' (serigraph), Kansas City Arts Coun & Crown Ctr Redevelopment Corp, Kansas City, Mo, 83; mural, Sharon & John Hoffman, Kansas City, 86; bronze sculpture, Pauline & Patrick Dolan, Kansas City, Mo. *Exhib:* Ultimate Concerns, Ohio Univ, Athens, 65; Art Across American, Knoedler Gallery, New York & traveling, 65-66; Fla State Fair Fine Art Exhib, Tampa, 65 & 66; 72nd Chicago & Vicinity Exhib, Art Inst Chicago, 69; Nat Print & Drawing Exhib, Western Ill Univ, 70; Mid-Four Painting Exhib, Nelson-Atkins Mus Art, 80; Three Painters, Mulvane Art Ctr, Topeka, Kans, 83. *Teaching:* Instr painting, Ill State Univ, 67-70; vis artist, NS Col Fine Arts, 69 & Kansas City Art Inst, 76, 87. *Awards:* Third Prize, Chicago Fine Arts Exhib, 63; Merit Award, Fla State Fair, 65; Third Prize, Mid-Four Painting Exhib, 80; Award of Merit, Kansas City Artists Coalition Exhib, 88. *Bibliog:* Mary King (auth), Fishbowl taxicab, Stack-ed deck, St Louis Post Dispatch, 4/11/80; Mary Sprague (auth), article, New Art Examiner, 7/80; Donald Hoffmann (auth), 4 articles in Kansas City Star, 10/9/83 & 11/23/86; Ellen Goheen (auth), Parton Prompts painter, Forum, Vol 15, No 4, 90; Janet Majure (auth), Whirling dancers cast in bronze, Kansas City Star, 4/22/90. *Mem:* Col Art Asn; Kansas City Artists Coalition. *Media:* Acrylic, Oil; Bronze. *Mailing Add:* 400 Admiral Blvd Kansas City MO 64106-1508

STACKHOUSE, ROBERT
SCULPTOR
b Bronxville, NY, 42. *Study:* Univ S Fla, Tampa, BA, 65; Univ Md, College Park, Mass, 67. *Work:* Mus Mod Art, New York; Mus Contemp Art, Chicago; Walker Art Ctr, Minneapolis; Baltimore Mus Art, Md; Corcoran Gallery Art, Washington, DC. *Comn:* Sculpture, Prudential Life Insurance Co Am, Minneapolis; bronze, On the Beach Again, Australia Nat Gallery, Canberra; painted wood, St Louie Bones, Laumeier Sculpture Park, St Louis; Oliver Ranch Project/Russian River Bones, Geyserville, Calif, 89; extruded red brass, Delaware Passage, Del Art Mus, Wilmington. *Exhib:* Solo exhibs, Va Mus Fine Arts, Richmond, 90, Contemp Art Mus, Univ S Fla, Tampa, 91, Dolan/Maxwell Gallery, Philadelphia, Pa, 91, Delaware Art Mus, Wilmington, 91, Posner Gallery, Milwaukee, Wis, 92, Pace Prints, New York, 92; Voyages of the Modern Imagination, William A Farnsworth Libr & Art Mus, Rockland, Maine, 90; New Editions, Pace Prints, 90, 91, 43 Annual Purchase Exhib, Am Acad & Inst Arts & Lett, New York, 91; 5th Int Biennial Print Exhibit, Taipei, Taiwan, 91. *Teaching:* Vis artist & lectr, Univ Hawaii, Manoa, 90, Univ S Fla, Tampa, 91, Univ Denver, Colo, 92. *Bibliog:* Sidney Lawrence (auth), Sculpting the Land at Oliver Ranch, Garden Design Mag, 12/91; Stackhouse Commission Dedicated at University, Hawaii Artreach, Nov/Dec, Vol 7, No 5, 91; Ina Pasch (auth), Artist's Passage: Printmaker Enjoys Journey's to Tandem, Wis State Jour, 2/6/92. *Mailing Add:* 110 Mercer St New York NY 10012

STACY, DONALD L
PAINTER, EDUCATOR
b West Paterson, NJ, Sept 3, 25. *Study:* Newark Sch Fine Art; Art Students League; Univ Paris Sch Art & Archeol; Univ Aix-Marseille; Pratt Graphic Art Ctr; New Sch Social Res. *Work:* Print Dept, Mus Mod Art; Birla Acad Art, Calcutta; Casa de Xilogravra, São Paulo, Brazil. *Comn:* Three decorative wall panels, US Plywood. *Exhib:* Documenta II, Kassel, Ger; Kyoto Gallery, Japan; Grenchen, Switz; Philadelphia Print Club; Knoedlers, York. *Pos:* Dir, Stacy Studio Workshop, 69- *Teaching:* Mem fac, Dept Art, Inst Mod Art, Mus Mod Art, 57-69, Dept Art, Sch Visual Arts, New York, 69-70 & Dept Art, New Sch Social Res, 67- *Awards:* Fulbright Grant, 53-55. *Bibliog:* Michael Lastnite (dir), Don Stacy--Art & the Autonomy of the Psyche (video), On the Otherhand Productions, 90. *Mem:* Am Inst Conserv Hist & Artistic Works; Engadiner Kollegium, Zurich. *Media:* Acrylic, Oil. *Publ:* Auth, The Runaway Dot: A Concept Book for Children, Bobbs, 69; contribr, articles in: Main Currents in Mod Thought, 69-74; Emergent Man, Gordon & Breach, 73; auth, Experiments in Art, Scholastic, 75; Drawing and Painting from Imagination, Stravon Press, 80. *Mailing Add:* 17 E 16th St New York NY 10003

STACY, JOHN RUSSELL
ILLUSTRATOR, JEWELER
b Denver, Colo, Mar 18, 19. *Study:* Denver Art Inst, dipl, 39; Univ Wash, 47. *Work:* Boy Scouts Am Hq, Cimarron, NMex; Yellowstone & Grand Teton Nat Parks, Wyo; Libr Cong, Washington, DC. *Comn:* Painting, Izaac Walton League Am, Denver, Colo, 39; illus, Colo Sch Mines, Golden, 60-70; illus, Geological Soc Am, Boulder, Colo, 60-70. *Pos:* Illusr, US Geological Survey, Denver, Colo, 50-74; dir & illusr, Rocky Mountain Nature Asn, Estes Park, Colo, 74. *Awards:* Meritorious Serv Award, Stewart Udall, Secy Interior, 68; O'Brien Faceting Trophy, Calif Fedn Mineralogical Soc, 84; Best Single Piece of Jewelry, Int Faceters Fair, 86. *Mem:* Life Santa Cruz Art League (bd dirs, 81-82). *Media:* Oil. *Publ:* Auth & illusr, Terrain Diagrams in Isometric Projection--Simplified, Annals Asn Am Geographers, 58; illusr, Philmont Country, Professional Paper 505, 64, Geologic Story of Yellowstone National Park, 73, Geologic Story of Canyonlands National Park, 74 & Geologic Story of Arches National Park, 75, US Geological Survey. *Mailing Add:* 12681 SW Peachbale Tigard OR 97224

STADLER, ALBERT
PAINTER
b New York, NY, Aug 12, 23. *Study:* Univ Pa; Univ Fla. *Exhib:* Corcoran Gallery Art, Washington, DC; Dayton Art Inst, Ohio; Los Angeles Co Mus Art, Calif; Walker Art Ctr, Minneapolis, Minn; Art Gallery Toronto, Ont; 20th Nat Print Exhib, Brooklyn Mus, NY, 77; and many others. *Media:* Acrylic. *Interests:* Color, in all its changing hues, chromas and lights. *Mailing Add:* 54 Beach St New York NY 10013

STAEMPFLI, GEORGE W
DEALER, PAINTER
b Bern, Switz, Dec 6, 10; US citizen. *Study:* Univ Erlangen, PhD, 35. *Exhib:* One-man shows, M Knoedler & Co, New York, 41 & 47, Forum Gallery, New York, 78, Aberbach Gallery, London, Eng, 78, Levy Gallery, Hamburg, Germany, 79, Capricorn Gallery, Washington, DC, 80, 83, 85, & 87, Stobler Gallery, Hofheim, Ger, 85 & Leighton Gallery, Blue Hill, Maine, 89 & 90. *Pos:* Cur, Mus Fine Arts, Houston, Tex, 55-57; coordr fine arts, Am Pavilion, Brussels Expo, 57-58; pres, Staempfli Gallery, 59-92. *Specialty:* Contemporary European, Asian and American painting and sculpture. *Mailing Add:* 47 E 77th St New York NY 10021

STAFFEL, DORIS
PAINTER, EDUCATOR
b New York, NY, 1921. *Study:* Tyler Sch Art, 39-44; Iowa Univ, MA, 45; Hans Hoffman Sch, 45-47. *Work:* Iowa Univ; Tylor Woodruff, London, Eng; Wills Eye Hosp; Cigna Mus. *Exhib:* One-woman shows, Chatham Col, Pittsburgh, Pa, 65, Tyler Abroad, Rome Gallery, Italy, 68 & Gross McCleaf Gallery, Philadelphia, Pa, 79 & 82; Broad Spectrum, Allentown Art Mus, Pa, 81; Ann Drawing Exhib, Beaver Col, Glenside, Pa, 81. *Teaching:* Assoc prof painting, Philadelphia Col Art, 61- *Awards:* Purchase Prize, Beaver Col, 78. *Media:* Oil, Watercolor. *Mailing Add:* 2128 Wallace St Philadelphia PA 19130

STAFFEL, RUDOLF HARRY
CERAMIST, INSTRUCTOR
b San Antonio, Tex, June 15, 11. *Study:* Chicago Art Inst, Ill; Escuela Para Maestros, San Juan Teotihuacan, Mex; pvt study with Jose Arpa & Xavier Gonzalez, San Antonio. *Work:* Mus of Contemp Crafts, New York; Philadelphia Mus Art; Smithsonian Inst, Washington, DC; Dartmouth Col Galleries & Collections, Hopkins Ctr, Hanover, NH; Everson Mus, Syracuse, NY. *Exhib:* Twenty-Five Years of Art in Clay USA, Lang Art Gallery, Scripps Col, 69; Objects USA, Johnson Collection Exhib, Smithsonian Inst, Washington, DC, 69; Ceramics 70 Plus Woven Forms, Everson Mus Art, Syracuse, NY, 70; Thirty Ceramists USA, Victoria & Albert Mus, London, Eng, 72; Contemp Clay--Ten Approaches, Dartmouth Col Galleries, Hanover, NH, 76; 300 Years of American Art, Philadelphia Mus Art, 76; Tureens 1976, Campbell Mus, Camden, NJ, 76; one-man show, Helen Drutt Gallery, Philadelphia, 76. *Teaching:* Prof ceramics, Tyler Sch Art, Temple Univ, 40-82; retired. *Awards:* Lindbach Award, Excellence in Teaching, Temple Univ, 66; Merit Award, Ceramic Arts--USA--1966, Int Mineral and Chemicals Corp, 66; Craftsman Fel, Nat Endowment Arts, Washington, DC, 77. *Bibliog:* Richard B Petterson (auth), Ceramic Art in America, Prof Publ Inc, 69; Roger D Bonham (auth), Full Cover, Ceramic Monthly, 2/75; Robert & Paula Winokur (auth), The Light of Rudolf Staffel, Craft Horizons, 4/77. *Mem:* Nat Coun for Educ Ceramic Arts; Am Asn Col Prof. *Media:* Ceramic Clay. *Dealer:* Helen Drutt Gallery 1625 Spruce St Philadelphia PA 19103. *Mailing Add:* c/o Temple Univ Tyler Sch Art Temple Gallery 3835 Cresson St Philadelphia PA 19127

STAHL, ALAN M
CURATOR, HISTORIAN
b Providence, RI, Aug 7, 47. *Study:* Univ Calif, Berkeley, BA, 68; Univ Pa, MA, Phd, 77. *Collections Arranged:* The Beaux-Arts Medal in America, loan exhib, Am Numismatic Soc, NY, 87-88; USA Exhib, Int Fedn Medal, Helsinki, Finland, 90 & British Mus, 92. *Pos:* Cur medals, Am Numismatic Soc, 80- *Mem:* Am Medallic Sculpture Asn (pres, 83-87); Fedn Int de la Medaille, (USA delgate, 85-); Nat Sculpture Soc (coun, 91-). *Res:* History of the medal in USA & abroad; art of medieval coinage of Europe. *Publ:* Auth, The American Industrial Medal, The Numismatist, 84; Lauffer's Medal Cabinet, Medallic Sculpture, 85; coauth, The Beaux Art Medal in America, Am Numismatic Soc, 87; ed, The Medal in America, New York, 88; American Indian Peace Medals of the Colonial Period in Money of Pre-Federal America, New York, 92. *Mailing Add:* Am Numismatic Soc 155th St & Broadway New York NY 10032

STALEY, CHRISTOPHER P
CERAMIST
b Boston, Mass, July 8, 54. *Study:* Wittenberg Univ, BFA, 77; Kans City Art Inst, Special Student, 77-78; Alfred Univ, MFA, 80. *Work:* Victoria & Albert Mus, London, Eng; Wichita Art Mus, Wichita Art Asn, Kans; Daniel Jacobs, New York; Lannon Found, Fla; Ariz State Univ, Art Mus, Tempe, Ariz. *Exhib:* One-man shows, George Ciscle Gallery, Baltimore, Md, 88, Garth Clark Gallery, New York, 85, 87, 88 & 91, Pro Art Gallery, St Louis, Mo, 87 & 89, Fla Gulf Coast Art Ctr, Belleair, Fla, 91, NHCC Fine Art Gallery, Houston, Tex, 91, Manchester Craftsmens Guild, Pittsburgh, Pa, 92; Craftsman's Gallery, Rhode Island Sch Design, 83; Clay USA 1984, Radford Univ, Va, 84; Works Gallery, Group Invitational, Philadelphia, 85; Archie Bray Found Show, Maveety Gallery, Portland, Ore, 90; The Expressive Teapot, Swidler Gallery, Royal Oak, Mich, 91; Clay Coast to Coast, Trisolini Gallery Ohio Univ, Athens, Ohio, 91; A Decade of Crafts, Auction, Am Craft Mus, New York, 91; Nat Ceramic Invitational Exhib, W Chester Univ, Pa, 92. *Pos:* Lectures and workshops at many colleges, universities, and institutions, 80-92. *Teaching:* Summer School fac, Rhode Island Sch Design, 82, 84, 85, ceramic technician, 80-82, adj prof, 82-85; asst prof, Wichita State Univ, 85-89, Penn State Univ, currently; artist-in-residence, Archie Bray Found, Mont, 85-89. *Awards:* Award for Excellence, Clay USA 1984, 84; Nat Endowment Arts Fel Grant, 86 & 88; Governor's Arts Award, Kans, 89. *Bibliog:* Richard Zakin (auth), Ceramics, Mastering the Craft, Chilton Bk Co, 90; American Ceramics (rev), 9/91; Janet Mansfield (auth), Salt Glazed Ceramics, An Int Perspective, Chilton Bk Co, 91. *Mem:* Nat Coun Educ for the Ceramic Arts (mem bd dirs), 88; Col Art Asn Am. *Mailing Add:* 120 W Lytle Ave State College PA 16801

STALLER, ERIC P
PHOTOGRAPHER, SCULPTOR
b Mineola, NY, Sept 14, 47. *Study:* Univ of Mich, BArch, 71. *Work:* Mus Mod Art, New York; Everson Mus, Syracuse; Int Mus Photog, Rochester; Nat Acad Sci; State Univ New York, Stony Brook. *Comn:* Lighting installations, Int Ctr of Photog, New York, 79, City Univ New York, 79 & Md Inst Col Art, Baltimore, 79; light sculptures, Port Authority NY & NJ, 83; Three Rivers Art Festival, Pittsburgh, 85; Anchorage Performing Arts Ctr, Alaska, 86. *Exhib:* Biennials, Indianapolis Mus, 76 & Taft Mus, Cincinnati, 76; Samual Wagstaff Collection, Corcoran Gallery, Washington, DC, 79; Nat Acad Sci, Washington DC, 81; Lightmobile, City Univ Graduate Ctr, New York, 85; City Lights, Int Ctr Photog, New York, 86. *Awards:* Creative Arts Pub Serv Prog Grant, 77; Nat Endowment Arts Grant, 78. *Bibliog:* Owen Edwards (auth), Tripping the light fantastic, Am Photog Mag, 4/78; article, The New York Times, 4/22/84; article, Wall St Jour, 8/8/85; article, Darkroom Mag, 11/85. *Media:* Light. *Mailing Add:* 201 S Kemp St Topton PA 19562

STALLWITZ, CAROLYN
PAINTER, PHOTOGRAPHER
b Abilene, Tex, Apr 27, 36. *Study:* W Tex State Univ, with Clarence Kincaid, Jr, BS(art); also with Emilio Caballero, Stefan Kramer & Lee Simpson. *Work:* Pioneer Natural Gas Co, First Nat Bank, Amarillo, Tex; Sunray State Bank, Dumas, Tex; Kracke-Gober Corp, Houston; Cliff Dwellers, Los Alamos, NMex. *Exhib:* Tex Watercolor Soc Exhib, 70; Wichita Centennial Nat Art Exhib, 70; Best of Southwest, 71; Amarillo Fine Art Asn Citation Show, 73; Denver Audubon Wildlife Art Show, 77. *Teaching:* Instr drawing, Amarillo Art Ctr, 73-74, instr watercolor, 74-75; Crab Art Ctr, 80-92. *Mem:* Moore Co Arts Asn (pres, 69-70); Tex Arts Alliance; Amarillo Fine Art Asn; Tex Fine Art Asn; Tex Watercolor Soc. *Media:* Watercolor, Pencil. *Publ:* Window on the Prairie, Feather Press, 81. *Dealer:* Colony Art & Frame Shop 2604 Wolflin Ave Amarillo TX 79109; The Cliff Dwellers Los Alamos NM 87544. *Mailing Add:* Box 1225 Dumas TX 79029

STAMATS, PETER OWEN
COLLECTOR, PATRON
b Cedar Rapids, Iowa, July 20, 29. *Study:* Dartmouth Col, BA, 51. *Pos:* Mem, Iowa State Arts Coun, 66-70. *Interests:* Support of Cedar Rapids Museum of Art. *Collection:* Fifteenth century to 20th century prints; vintage American photography; 19th century Aymara weavings; 19th & 20th century Mexican dance masks; Luristan Bronzes; Chancay ceramics & painted textiles. *Mailing Add:* 427 Sixth Ave SE Cedar Rapids IA 52406

STAMELOS, ELECTRA GEORGIA MOUSMOULES
PAINTER, GRAPHIC ARTIST
b Jersey City, NJ. *Study:* Corcoran Mus Sch, study with Aurelius Battaglia & Heinz Warneke, 43-45; Nat Art Sch, 45-48; Magda Sch Design, Am Univ, Washington, DC, 46; work with Margaret Cramer, 61-63; Univ Mich, study with Guy Palazola, 64; Ctr Creative Studies, 65-68 & 79; Wayne State Univ, BA(painting), 70; Eastern Mich Univ, MFA(watercolor), 76. *Work:* Nat Watercolor Soc, Calif; Northwest Br, YWCA, Detroit; State Farm Ins Co, Dearborn, Mich; Brown,& Lund, Washington, DC; Eastern Ill Univ; Jessie Bessard Mus, Alpena. *Comn:* Hardedge acrylic, Northwest Br, YWCA, Detroit, 70; Lithograph, Ctr for Creative Studies. *Exhib:* Source Detroit, Cranbrook Art Mus, Birmingham, Mich, 76; Butler Inst Am Art, Youngstown, Ohio, 76-77 & 79-80; Watercolor USA, 77, 79 & 86, Springfield Art Mus, 77 &80; Nat Watercolor Soc, Fine Arts Gallery, Calif State Univ, Northridge, 77-81; Watercolor USA, 77, 79 & 86; Detroit Realist, Oakland Univ, 79; Slusser Gallery, Univ Mich, 85; Springfield Art Asn, Ill, 86; Rocky Mountain Nat Watermedia Exhib, Foothills Art Ctr, Golden, Colo. *Pos:* Dir art exhibs, Acquisitions, Univ Mich. *Teaching:* Instr drawing & painting, Nat Art Sch, Washington, DC, 45-48; instr drawing & painting, Northwest Br, YWCA, Detroit, 68-72; instr watercolor, Ann Arbor Asn, Mich, 77-78; instr, Birmingham Bloomfield Art Asn, 79-, lectr, Applied Arts, Univ Mich, Dearborn, 80- *Awards:* Purchase Award, Mich Nat Watercolor Soc, 76, 90, 91 & 92; Purchase Award, 7 for 76, Eastern Ill Univ, 76; Purchase Award, Battle Creek Art Ctr. *Mem:* Nat Watercolor Soc, Calif; Mich Watercolor Soc; Birmingham-Bloomfield Art Asn; Ann Arbor Art Asn; Watercolor USA, Honor Soc. *Media:* Watercolor, Acrylic; Pencil, Pastel. *Publ:* Auth, Bibliography of Georgia O'Keefe, J Nat Art Educ Asn, 76; illusr, The Tree House (24 drawings), 76; illusr, SE Michigan Calendar, 82; Splash, Northlight Books, 90. *Dealer:* Lemberg Gallery 538 N Woodward Ave Birmingham MI 48011; Phillipps Gallery Salt Lake City UT. *Mailing Add:* 5118 Royal Vale Ln Dearborn MI 48126-2617

STAMM, GEOFFREY EATON
ADMINISTRATOR, HISTORIAN
b Washington, DC, July 30, 43. *Study:* Univ Paris, CPLF cert, 64; Hamilton Col, AB, 65; Am Univ, Washington, DC; Corcoran Sch Art, Washington, DC; Inst Art Admin, Harvard Univ, cert, 74. *Pos:* Coordr spec proj, Indian Arts & Crafts Bd, Washington, DC, 69-74, asst to gen mgr, 74-78, asst gen mgr, 78-, dir mus, exhib & publ, 89-; mem, Fed Interagency Crafts Comt, Washington DC, 76- *Mem:* Am Crafts Coun; World Crafts Coun; Native Am Art Studies Asn; Am Asn Mus. *Res:* Twentieth century American Indian, Eskimo and Aleut fine arts and handcrafts. *Publ:* Contribr & illusr, Institute of American Indian Arts, 68, illusr, Future Directions in Native American Art, 73 & ed, Protection for Native American Artists and Craftsmen, 74, US Dept Interior; contribr, Authentic Indian Jewelry, Gro-Pub, 75; auth, The Federal Agency as Mentor: Developing Native American Arts, US Dept Interior, 80; and others. *Mailing Add:* 4920 Weaver Terr NW Washington DC 20016

STAMOS, THEODOROS (S)
PAINTER
b New York, NY, Dec 31, 22. *Study:* Am Artists Sch. *Work:* Addison Gallery Am Art, Phillips Acad, Andover, Mass; Albright-Knox Art Gallery, Buffalo, NY; Aldrich Mus Contemp Art, Ridgefield, Conn; Art Gallery Ont, Toronto, Can; Art Inst Chicago, Ill; Baltimore Mus Art, Md; Brooklyn Mus, NY; Corcoran Gallery Art, Washington, DC; Fogg Art Mus, Harvard Univ, Cambridge, Mass; Metrop Mus Art, Mus Mod Art, Solomon Guggenheim Mus, Whitney Mus Art, New York; Milwaukee Art Ctr, Wis; and others. *Comn:* Oil mural, SS Arg, Moore McCormack Lines, 46, tapestry, New York, 71; two murals, Buro Klaus Hoebeck, Cologne, 83. *Exhib:* Abstr Expressionists & Imagists, Guggenheim Mus, New York; Dada, Surrealism & Their Inheritors, Mus Mod Art; Corcoran Gallery Art, Washington, DC; Whitney Mus Am Art, New York; Metrop Mus Art, New York; Joslyn Art Mus, Omaha, Nebr, 73; Mus Knoedler, Zurich, 83, 84 & 85; solo exhibs, M Knoedler, Zurich, Switz, 84, Galerie Wurthle, Vienna, Austria, 85, Grimaldis Gallery, Baltimore, Md, 86, Pierides Gallery Mod Art, Athens, Greece, 87, Mus Morsbroich, Leverkusen, Ger, 88, Ileana Tounta Contemp Art Ctr, Athens, Greece & ACA Galleries, New York, 91-92; Ericson Gallery, 85; Kouros Gallery, 85 & 86; and others. *Teaching:* Instr art, Art Students League, 55; lectr art, Columbia Univ; prof art, Brandeis Univ. *Awards:* Brandeis Univ Creative Arts Award, Tiffany Found Fel; Nat Arts Grant, 67; Mainichi Newspaper Award, Tokyo, Japan, 61. *Bibliog:* K Sawyer (auth), Stamos, Mus Poche Paris, 60; R Pomeroy (auth), Theodoros Stamos, Abrams, 73. *Mem:* Life fel Metrop Mus Art. *Media:* All. *Publ:* Illusr, Sorrows of Cold Stone, Dodd, 51; The Hidden Airdome and Uncollected Poems, 56. *Mailing Add:* 37 W 83rd St New York NY 10024

STAMPFLE, FELICE
CURATOR, WRITER
b Kansas City, Mo, July 25, 12. *Study:* Washington Univ, AB & AM; Radcliffe Col. *Pos:* Cur drawings & prints, Pierpont Morgan Libr, 45-83, cur emer, 84; ed, Master Drawings, 63-83. *Res:* Drawings, especially 17th century Dutch and Flemish & 18th century Italian. *Publ:* Auth, var articles, reviews & exhib catalogs; drawings, Netherlandish Drawings, in the Morgan Library, Vol I, 91. *Mailing Add:* 450 E 63rd St New York NY 10021

STAMSTA, JEAN
PAPER ARTIST
b Sheboygan, Wis, Nov 2, 36. *Study:* Univ Wis, Milwaukee, BS, 58; Haystack Mountain Sch Crafts, 66; Fiberworks Ctr Textile Research, 81. *Work:* Cleveland Mus Art, Ohio; Am Craft Mus, New York; Milwaukee Art Mus, Wis; Mus Fine Arts, Columbus; US Vice President's House, Washington, DC; Wustum Mus, Racine, Wis. *Comn:* wall hanging, First Nat Bank, Amarillo, Tex, 77; woven panels, Bank of Commerce, Milwaukee, 78; wall hanging, Sentry Insurance, Wis, 78; wall hangings, Miller Brewing Co, Milwaukee, 79; fiber sculpture, Ohio Bell, Cleveland, 84. *Exhib:* 5th Biennial Tapestry, Lausanne, Switz, 71; one-man shows, Am Craft Mus, New York, 71, Mem Union Gallery, Univ Wis, Madison, 82, David Barnette Gallery, Milwaukee, 86 & Lawrence Univ, Appleton, Wis, 90; 2nd Int Exhib Miniature Textiles, British Crafts Ctr, London, 76; Fiberworks (with catalog), Cleveland Mus Art, Ohio, 77; Fiber R/Evolution(with catalog), Milwaukee Art Mus, 86; Wis Tri-Ann, Madison Art Ctr, Wis, 87 & 90; Wis Triannual, Madison Art Ctr, (with catalogs) 87 & 90; Paper, Fine Arts Mus, Budapest, Hungary, 92 (with catalog); USA-Today, Textile Mus, Tilburg, Neth, 93 (with catalog); and others. *Pos:* Guest cur, Fiber R/Evolution exhib, 86. *Teaching:* Instr weaving, Mt Mary Col, Milwaukee, Wis, 70-73; instr weaving, Univ Northern Mich, summer 77; instr weaving, Rochester Inst Technol, New York, summer, 80 & Univ Wis, Milwaukee, 84. *Awards:* Purchase Award, Columbus Mus Fine Arts, 72; First Prize, Marietta Col Crafts Nat, 74; Nat Endowment Arts Craftsman Fel, 74; Honorable Mention, Wis Arts Bd Fel, 86. *Bibliog:* Mildred/Larsen Constantine & Jack Lenor (coauth), The Art Fabric: Mainstream, Van Nostrand Reinhold Co, New York, 81; Elizabeth A Bard (auth), Great Lake series, Fiberarts, 4/83. *Mem:* Int Asn Handpaper Makers & Artists; Friends of Dard Hunter Paper Mus. *Media:* Paper, Fabric. *Publ:* Coauth, Fiber R/Evolution (exhib catalog), 86. *Dealer:* Katie Gingrass Gallery 241 N Broadway Milwaukee WI 53202. *Mailing Add:* W 299 N 9313 Center Oak Rd Hartland WI 53029

STANBRIDGE, HARRY ANDREW
PAINTER, PRINTMAKER
b Quesnel, BC, July 23, 43. *Study:* Vancouver Sch Art, dipl(hons), 68; Univ BC, BA(art educ), 74, MA, 82. *Work:* City of Vancouver, BC; Seattle Art Mus; Nat Gallery Can Libr, Ottawa; Provincial Collection, Victoria, BC; Univ Alta Libr, Edmonton; Art Gallery of Greater Victoria; Can Coun Art Bank, Ottawa; Can Embassy, Australia. *Exhib:* Woman, Burnaby Art Gallery, BC, 72; Kinesis, Art Gallery Victoria, BC, 76; Victoria Artist, Art Gallery Victoria, BC, 86; Come Zion, Art Gallery of Greater Victoria, BC, 87; two-person show (with P Coupey), Surrey Arts Ctr, BC, 88; and others. *Teaching:* Instr drawing & painting, Spectrum Community Sch, Victoria, BC, 74-. *Awards:* Grant, Can Coun, 69; Purchase Award, Northwest Printmakers 40th Ann, Seattle Art Mus, 69. *Bibliog:* Charles Shere (auth), Four days from a diary, Arts Canada, 75; Frank Nowasad (auth), Moments of cocksure bravado, Monday Mag, 86; N Tuele (auth), Come Zion, Recent Paintings by H Stanbridge (exhib catalog), Art Gallery of Greater Victoria. *Media:* Acrylic, Oil. *Publ:* Auth & illusr, Mirrored Barriers, Takao Tanabe, 68. *Dealer:* Bau-Xi Gallery 3045 Granville Vancouver BC V6H 3J9 Canada. *Mailing Add:* 4526 Hughes Rd Victoria BC V8X 3X1 Canada

STANCZAK, JULIAN
PAINTER, EDUCATOR
b Borownica, Poland, Nov 5, 28; US citizen. *Study:* Uganda, Africa & London, Eng; Cleveland Inst Art, BFA, 54; Yale Univ, with Albers & Marca-Relli, MFA, 56. *Work:* Carnegie Inst, Pittsburgh; Albright-Knox Art Gallery, Buffalo; Larry Aldrich Mus, Ridgefield, Conn; Corcoran Art Mus, Washington, DC; Nat Gallery, Washington, DC; the Tulsa Mus, Okla; Hirshhorn Mus, Washington, DC; and others. *Comn:* Altar piece, St John's Unitarian Church, Cincinnati, 68; mural, Cleveland City Canvasses, 74; flag, City of Rottweil, Ger, 74; atrium layout, Dracket Co, Cincinnati, 84. *Exhib:* One-man exhibs: Corcoran Art Gallery, Washington, DC, 72, Ohio State Univ, Columbus, 76, Butler Inst Am Art, 80, Nat Mus, Warsaw, Poland, 81 & Standard Oil Co World Hq, Cleveland, Ohio, 87. *Teaching:* Instr, Art Acad Cincinnati, 57-64; prof painting, Cleveland Inst Art, 64-; artist-in-residence, Dartmouth Col, 68. *Awards:* Cleveland Fine Arts Award, 70; Outstanding Educ Am, 70; Ohio Arts Coun Award, 72. *Bibliog:* Art/Search & Self Discovery, 68; Jean Lipman (auth), Provocation Parallels: Naive Early American/International Sophisticates, Dutton Inc, New York, 75; Decades of Light, 40 years of works by Julian Stanczak, State Univ New York at Buffalo, 90; and others. *Mem:* Am Abstract Artists; Am Int Platform Asn. *Media:* Acrylic. *Res:* Pioneer in optical art. *Dealer:* David Anderson Gallery Martha Jackson Place Buffalo NY 14214; Cleveland Ctr Contemp Art 8499 Carnegie Ave Cleveland OH 44106. *Mailing Add:* 6229 Cabrini Lane Seven Hills OH 44131

STANDEN, EDITH APPLETON
HISTORIAN
b Halifax, NS, Feb 21, 05; US citizen. *Study:* Oxford Univ, BA (hon fel). *Pos:* Art secy, Joseph Widener Collection, Elkins Park, Pa, 29-42; assoc cur, Metrop Mus Art, New York, 49-70, consult, 70- *Mem:* Col Art Asn Am. *Res:* European post-medieval tapestries. *Publ:* Auth, var articles in Metrop Mus Bulletin, Metrop Mus J, Art Bulletin & others, 51-77; coauth, Art Treasures of the Metropolitan, 52; Decorative Art from the Samuel H Kress Collection, 64; European Post-Medieval Tapestries & Related Hangings in the Metropolitan Museum of Art, 85. *Mailing Add:* Metrop Mus of Art Fifth Ave & 82nd St New York NY 10028

STANFORD, GINNY C
PAINTER, ILLUSTRATOR
b Lamar, Mo, Sept 3, 50. *Study:* St Olaf Col, Northfield, Minn, 67; Southwest Mo State Col, 68. *Work:* Mills Col, Oakland, Calif; Ft Smith Art Ctr, Ark. *Comn:* Two paintings, Kaiser Hosp, Santa Rosa, Calif, 89 & 90; three paintings, Kaiser Permanente Med Group, Santa Rosa, Calif, 89-91; painting, Bronson, Bronson & McKinnon, Santa Rosa, Calif, 91. *Exhib:* Hassam Speicher Fund Purchase Exhib, Am Acad Arts & Letters, New York, 79; American Realism, William Sawyer Gallery, San Francisco, 85; Fire and Ice, Downey Mus Art, Calif, 88; Mind Over Matter, Angels Gate Cult Ctr, San Pedro, Calif, 89; Figurative Forms, Eastern Wash Univ, Cheney, 90. *Awards:* Western States Art Fedn Corp Collectors Project Award, Nat Endowment Arts, 90; Sonoma County Found, Ind Artists Fel, Nat Endowment Arts, 90; Sonoma Found Grant, Individual Artist Fel, Sonoma Co Found & Nat Endowment Arts, 91. *Bibliog:* Lowell Downey (auth), Introductions 90 Artists: A compelling mix, San Francisco Arts Wkly, 7/90; Laurie Cohn (auth), An American painter, KFTY Television, Santa Rosa, Calif, 4/91; James Carroll (auth), The Paper, Study of an Assassination: Ginny Stanford's Poem Mourning John F Kennedy, 5/91. *Media:* Acrylic on Canvas. *Publ:* Illusr, Victory Over Japan, Little Brown & Co, 86; Mr Bridge/Mrs Bridge, N Point Press, 88; Remember Me, Mercury House, 91; The Light the Dead See, Univ Ark Press, 91. *Dealer:* Michael S Bell 2325 20th St San Francisco CA 94110; Somerhill Callery 3 Eastgate E Franklin St Chapel Hill NC 27514-5816. *Mailing Add:* PO Box 2014 Sebastopol CA 95473

STANFORD, LINDA OLIPHANT
ADMINISTRATOR, HISTORIAN
b Hollis, NY, Feb 11, 46. *Study:* Hunter Col, AB, 67; Indiana Univ, MS, 68; Univ NC, Chapel Hill, PhD, 76. *Pos:* Mem, State of Mich Hist Preserv Rev Bd, 79-; assoc chairperson, Mich State Univ, 85-89; Assoc Dean, Col Arts & Letters, Mich State Univ, 90- *Teaching:* Asst prof art hist, design, Campbell Univ, Buie's Creek, NC, 68-75; from instr to prof, Mich State Univ East Lansing, 75- *Awards:* Fel, Am Coun on Educ, 89-90. *Mem:* Col Art Asn; Soc Archit Historians; Nat Trust Hist Preserv. *Publ:* Auth, W K Kellogg and His Gull Lake Home, Mich State Univ, 83; Railway designs by Fellheimer and Wagner, Queen City Heritage, 85; The Powerless and the Powerful: A Look at Rape by Kathe Kollwitz, Kresge Art Mus Bull, 85; Art and the Elem Sch Experience, Inst for Research on Teaching, Mich State Univ. *Mailing Add:* 200 Linton Hall Michigan State Univ East Lansing MI 48824-1119

STANFORTH, MELVIN SIDNEY
EDUCATOR, PAINTER
b Tuscaloosa, Ala, Sept 22, 37. *Study:* Univ Ala, BFA; Wayne State Univ, MFA. *Work:* Duke Univ Med Ctr; R J Reynolds; Kaiser Permanente, Raleigh, NC; East Carolina Univ, Greenville, NC; Burroughs-Wellcome Corp; and others. *Exhib:* Regional Painting Exhib, 73-76 & Regional Drawing & Prints Exhib, 73-77, Southeastern Ctr Contemp Arts, Winston-Salem, NC; Ball State Univ Nat Drawing Exhib, Muncie, Ind, 74; Potsdam Nat Drawing Exhib, NY, 75; Piedmont Graphics, Greenville Co Mus, Greenville, SC, 77-78; Award Winners Exhib, NC Mus of Art, Raleigh, 79; NC Artists Exhibit, Rutgers Gallery, 80; Works on Paper, National-Weatherspoon Gallery, 87; Drawing/Photography, WVa Juried Show, 87; Outerbanks to Infinity (Nat Photography Show), 87-88; three man show, East Carolina Univ, 88, Boykin Gallery, Wilson, NC, 89; solo exhibs, Art Ctr, Goldsboro,

91, Greenville Mus Art, Spirit Sq Ctr, Charlotte, NC, 92. *Teaching:* Prof drawing & painting, E Carolina Univ, Greenville, NC, 69- *Awards:* Second Purchase Award, NC Artists Exhib, NC Arts Coun, 71; Purchase Awards, Regional Painting Exhib, 73 & Regional Drawing & Prints Exhib, 73, Southeastern Ctr Contemp Arts, Winston-Salem, NC. *Mem:* Durham Art Guild. *Media:* All Media. *Publ:* Contribr, Art Papers, 5-6/88, 8-9/90. *Mailing Add:* 2205 E Fifth St Greenville NC 27858

STANLEY, BOB
PAINTER
b Yonkers, NY, Jan 3, 32. *Study:* Ogelthorpe Univ, BA; High Mus Art, Atlanta, 52; Columbia Univ; Art Students League; Brooklyn Mus Art Sch, Max Beckman painting scholar, 54-56. *Work:* Whitney Mus Am Art, New York; Milwaukee Art Ctr; Fogg Art Mus, Cambridge, Mass; Corcoran Gallery Art; Metrop Mus Art, New York; and others. *Comn:* Painting, Milwaukee Art Ctr, 69. *Exhib:* Whitney Mus Am Art Painting Ann, 67, 69 & 72 & 73 Biennial; two-man show (with Bart Wasserman), PS1, Long Island City, NY, 77; one-man shows, Stockholm Art Fair, Galleri Johnny Ericsson, 88 & Basel Art Fair, Galerie G Lavrov, Basel, Switzerland, 88, Gallery Bebert, Rotterdam, Netherlands, 89, The Painted Bride, Art Ctr, Philadelphia, Pa, 90, Greenville County Art Mus, Greenville, SC, 91, Barbierto Arte Contemporanea, Asiago, Italy & Moderne Kunst Dietmarwerle, Köln, Ger, 92; Group Shows: Worcester Art Mus, Mass, 81; Am Acad & Inst Arts & Letters, 82; Art Mus, Princeton Univ, 85; High Mus, Atlanta, Ga, 88. *Teaching:* Instr, Sch Visual Arts, New York, 70-72 & 84-; vis artist, La State Univ, Baton Rouge, 76, Syracuse Univ, 78, Princeton Univ, 79-80 & St Lawrence Univ, Canton, NY, 78. *Awards:* Cassandra Found Award, 69; Igor Found Award, 87. *Bibliog:* Carter Ratcliff (auth), Bob Stanley & Bart Wasserman at PS1, Art in Am, 1-2/78; Mario Amaya & Naomi Spector (auth), Monograph: Bob Stanley's Louisiana Sweet, publ by artist & Siena Studios, New York, 78; Michael Floresco (auth), article, Arts Mag, 11/80; Richard Artschwager (auth), Robert Stanley, Parade in the Face of Death, Galeries Mag, Paris, France, 8-9/87; Robert Pincus-Witten (auth), Robert Stanley, 25 Years Later, (catalog), Gallery Bebert Exhib, Rotterdam, Netherlands, 11- 12/89; Wim van Sinderen (auth), Robert Stanley, Opererecenti (catalog), Barbierato Arte Contemporanea Exhib, Asiago, Italy, 1-2/92. *Media:* Oil. *Publ:* Auth & illusr, Tracks: A Poem with 8 Etchings, X-Press, New York, 86. *Mailing Add:* 3 Crosby St New York NY 10013

STANLEY, JOHN JACOB
PAINTER
b Alliance, Ohio, 1929. *Study:* Yale Summer Art Prog, studied under Joseph Albers; Cincinnati Art Acad, 55. *Exhib:* Solo exhibs, Chaim Fleichman Gallery, 55, Upstairs Gallery, 70, Last Picture Show Gallery, 75 & Michael Lowe Gallery, 83; Art USA, Madison Square Garden, 62; Cincinnati Zoo Exhibit, 68 & 69; Benedictine Liquor Exhibit, New York, 73; 60th Biennale Int, Ville de Merignar, France, 84; The Imaginative Works of John Jacob Stanley, Madison Road Gallery, Cincinnati, Ohio, 88. *Mailing Add:* Madison Road Gallery 1991 Madison Rd Cincinnati OH 45208

STANLEY, M LOUISE
PAINTER
b Charleston, WVa, Aug 28, 42. *Study:* La Verne Col, BA, 64; Calif Col Arts & Crafts, BFA, 67, MFA, 69. *Exhib:* Solo shows, Univ Art Mus, Univ Calif, Berkeley, 78, PS1, Queens, NY, 78, Quay Gallery, San Francisco, 83 & Rena Bransten Gallery, 86; The Work Show, Downtown Ctr Fine Arts Mus, San Francisco, Calif, 78; Events, The New Mus, New York, 80; Humor, Los Angeles Inst Contemp Art, Calif, 81; Drawings by Painters, Long Beach Mus Art, Calif, 82; Second Sight: Biennail IV, San Francisco Mus Mod Art, 86. *Teaching:* Instr painting & drawing, San Francisco State Univ, Calif, 77-78; asst prof painting, drawing & watercolor, La State Univ, Baton Rouge, 78-79; instr painting, San Francisco Art Inst, Calif, 82-; vis artist, Univ NC, Chapel Hill, 84; instr painting, Univ Calif, Berkeley, 85-86. *Awards:* Nat Endowment Arts Grant, 83. *Bibliog:* David Winter (auth),Artists the critics are watching, 11/84 & M Louise Stanley, 3/86, Art News; Richard Martin (auth), Dr Spock's generation: a crystal palace of childhood, Art J, 80; David Winter (auth), Louise Stanleys' work merits three stars, Peninsula Times Tribune, 10/28/81. *Mem:* Charter mem Calif Fedn Art Teachers Local 1. *Media:* Oil & Gonache. *Publ:* Auth, portfolio, Paris Review, Winter 84. *Mailing Add:* c/o Rena Bransten Gallery 254 Sutter St San Francisco CA 94108

STANTON, HARRIET L
PAINTER
b New York, NY, Mar 27, 24. *Study:* Cornell Univ, 41; Richmond Prof Inst, Col William & Mary, Cert, 44; Art Student's League, 46-47. *Work:* Milwaukee Art Ctr, Wis; Yale Univ Art Gallery, New Haven, Conn; C W Post Col Mus, Brookville, NY; US Embassy, Paris, France; Univ NC, Chapel Hill. *Exhib:* San Francisco Mus Art, Calif, 63; Artists Use of Paper, Suffolk Mus, Stony Brook, NY, 74; New Talent, Gimpel & Weitzenhuffer, New York, 74; Graphics, Albright-Knox Mus, Buffalo, NY, 78; Art in Bloom, Mem Art Mus, Univ Rochester, NY, 78; American Printmakers, Tokyo Central Mus, Japan, 78; Elaine Benson Gallery, Bridgehampton, NY, 90 & 91. *Teaching:* Instr drawing & painting, Nassau County Mus, Roslyn, NY; NY Univ, New York, 67-71 & Hofstra Univ, Homestead, NY, 68-75. *Awards:* Art Honor Award, Richmond Prof Inst; Emily Lowe Found Award; Premier Prix Int, Cannes, France. *Mem:* Nat Drawing Asn; Asn Women Artists. *Media:* Oil. *Dealer:* Szoke Koo 164 Mercer St New York NY 10012. *Mailing Add:* 119 Malverne Ave Malverne NY 11565

STANTON, PHIL
CONCEPTUAL ARTIST, KINETIC ARTIST
b Tex, Nov 16, 59. *Study:* Evangel, theatre, 83. *Work:* New Mus Contemp Art (performance), New York; Milwaukee Art Mus (performance), Wis; Contemp Art Ctr New Orleans (performance), Fla. *Awards:* Obie, Tubes, Village Voice, 91; Drama Desk, Tubes, 92; Lucille Lortel Found Award, Tubes, 92. *Bibliog:* Alisa Soloman (auth), Pissing on propriety, Village Voice, 1/15/91; Vicki Goldberg (auth), Hi tech meets God with Blue Man Group, NY Times, 1/17/91; Thomas M Disch (auth), Blue Man Group: Tubes, Nation, 1/20/92. *Media:* Performance. *Mailing Add:* 575 West End Ave New York NY 10024

STANTON, TOM-ERIC
PAINTER
b Hollywood, Calif, Feb 2, 47. *Study:* Univ Calif, Irvine, with Bas Jan Ader, Tony Delap, Craig Kauffman & John Paul Jones, BA, 75, with David Askevold & Lawrence Weiner, MFA, 78; Claremont Grad Sch, with Michael Brewster, 76. *Work:* Art Space, Prudential Insurance Co & Space Gallery, Los Angeles, Calif; Chemical Bank, New York. *Exhib:* Irvine Mileux, La Jolla Mus Contemp Art, Calif, 75; Masks, Newport Harbor Mus Art, Newport Beach, Calif, 84. *Pos:* Vchmn, Artists Comt, San Francisco Art Inst, 83-86, mem, Exhib Comt, 83-85, trustee, Bd Trustees, 84-86. *Teaching:* Instr design, Brooks Col Design, Long Beach, Calif, 81-83; prof painting, Laguna Beach Col Art & Design, 81-83, lectr art-performance, 82-83. *Awards:* Brython P Davis Fel, 78. *Bibliog:* Price Amerson (dir), Palace Rudel (video), Univ Calif, Davis; Marie DeAlquaz (auth), Ceci N'est Pas Le Surrealisme (catalog), Univ Southern Calif-Art in Calif Bks. *Mem:* San Francisco Art Writers Guild, 84-86. *Media:* Performance, Installation-Video. *Publ:* Artweek, 3/85 & 6/85. *Dealer:* Space Gallery 6015 Santa Monica Blvd Los Angeles CA 90038; Bruce Vellick Gallery 371 Eleventh St San Francisco CA 94103. *Mailing Add:* 229 Harrison St No 205A Oakland CA 94607-4127

STAPEN, NANCY
CRITIC, WRITER
b New York, NY, Dec, 3, 50. *Study:* Brandeis Univ, BA(fine art, magna cum laude), 72. *Collections Arranged:* Robert Henry Logan Retrospective, 84. *Pos:* Asst dir, Clark Gallery, Lincoln, Mass, 81-; coordr, Museum Goers Month, var Boston mus, 83; sr art critic, Boston Herald, 84-90; exclusive Boston rep, Artforum, 85-88; feature writer, Christian Sci Monitor, Artnews & ELLE, 87-; Boston corresp, Artnews, 88-; art critic, Boston Globe, 90- *Teaching:* Chmn fine arts, Belvoir Terrace Fine Arts, Lenox, Mass, summers 76-78; instr sculpture, Concord-Carlisle High Sch, Mass, 79-80; instr learning through art, De Cordova Mus, 81-83; dir Docent Prog, DeCordova Mus, 83-84. *Awards:* Manufacturers Honorer Arts World Award for distinguished newspaper art criticism, 87 & 90; Hon Men, Best Visual Arts Critic, Boston Mag, 86; Chemical Bank Award, Distinguished Newspaper Art Critics, 92. *Mem:* Am Asn Art Critics; Women's Caucus Art; PEN, New Eng; Nat Writers Union; Art Table. *Res:* Visual arts; specializing in contemporary art. *Publ:* Auth, John Imber, Paintings, 78-89, (catalog essay) Fitchburg Art Mus, 9-11/90; Annette Lemieux, New Work, Paris Exhib, 9/91. *Mailing Add:* 25 Euston St Brookline MA 02146

STAPLETON, JOSEPH F
LECTURER, PAINTER
b Brooklyn, NY, Mar 20, 21. *Study:* St John's Univ, Brooklyn, NY, BS(summa cum laude); Brooklyn Col; Columbia Univ; Art Students League, with Vytlacil, Dumond, Kantor, Olitsky, Holty & Barnet. *Work:* Birla Inst, Calcutta, India; Art Students League; Pratt Inst, New York. *Exhib:* Am Painting Today, Metrop Mus Art, New York, 50; Ann Invitational, Pa Acad Art, Philadelphia, 52; one-man show, Hofstra Col, Long Island, 56; Ten-Yr Retrospective, Avant Garde Gallery, New York, 57; Charles Egan Gallery, New York, 63-64. *Teaching:* Instr painting, Metrop Mus Art, New York, 57-59; instr painting & drawing, Pratt Inst, 70-, adj asst prof, currently; instr painting & drawing, Art Students League, New York, 73- *Bibliog:* Russell Arnold (auth), Portfolio of drawings--Joseph Stapleton, Crucible, Atlantic Christian Col, fall 68. *Media:* Oil, Ink. *Publ:* Auth & illusr, Leaflets in Japanese for psychological warfare, US Govt, 44-45; illusr, Who Wrote the Classics?, John Day Co, 68. *Mailing Add:* 427 Washington St No 2W New York NY 10013

STAPP, RAY VERYL
PAINTER, PRINTMAKER
b Norton, Kans, July 10, 13. *Study:* Bethany Col, Kans, with Birger Sandzen, BFA; Kansas City Art Inst, with Thomas Hart Benton; Art Students League, with Dumond, Reilly & Trafton; Teachers Col, Columbia Univ, with Ziegfield, MA; Pa State Univ, with Lowenfeld, EdD. *Work:* Painting, Lowenfeld Mem Collection, Pa State Univ. *Comn:* Portraits, 5 Augustana Lutheran pastors, 90. *Exhib:* Ninth Colorprint USA 1980, Lubbock, Tex; Rocky Mountain Regional Print Show, 81. *Pos:* Engraver & lithographer, Hallmark Card Co, 37-39; advert artist, Armstrong Cork Co, 48-49; prod illusr, Boeing Airplane Co, 56-57. *Teaching:* From instr to asst prof design & art educ, Bethany Col, 49-56; from asst prof to assoc prof art, Edinboro State Col, 57-64; from assoc prof to prof design & art educ, Eastern Ill Univ, 79; retired. *Media:* Oil; Serigraph, Ceramics. *Res:* Relationships of measures of creativity, general intelligence and memory; extension of research used as criteria for evaluating children in grades 4-8. *Dealer:* Miriam Perlman Inc 505 N Lake Shore Dr Lake Point Tower Ste 5410 Chicago IL 60611. *Mailing Add:* 1200 S Monaco Pkwy No 16 Denver CO 80224

STAPP, WILLIAM F
CURATOR
b McKinney, Tex, Mar 2, 45. *Study:* Tulane Univ, BA, 67; Univ Pa, MA, 70; Goddard Col, MA, 76; Princeton Univ, with Peter Bunnell. *Collections Arranged:* Survey of the Photographic Collection, Princeton Univ, 74-76; Artists on Paper--Prints, Photographs, and Drawings from the National Portrait Gallery Collection, 85; Brady Imperials--A Selection from the Collection of Imperial Prints by Mathew Brady at the Fogg Museum, Harvard, 86; Stage Portraits--Photographs by Mathew Brady from the Frederick Hill Meserve Collection, 87; Studies from Life--Portrait Photographs by Julia Margaret Cameron from the Collection of the J Paul Gerry Museum, 87; The Instant Likeness--Polaroid Portraits, 88; Photographic Treasures from the National Portrait Gallery Collection, 90; Irving Penn Master Images, 90. *Pos:* Res asst, Princeton Univ Art Mus, 75-76; cur of photog, Nat Portrait Gallery, 76- *Teaching:* Instr mus collections, Philadelphia Mus Art, 71-76; instr hist photog, Moore Col Art, Philadelphia, 75-76 & Philadelphia Col Art, 75-76. *Awards:* Guest Scholar, J Paul Getty Mus, 89. *Mem:* Oracle Con; Daguerrian Soc; Smithsonian Forum on Mat Cult; Scottish Soc Hist of Photography; Archeol Inst Am. *Res:* History of photography; nineteenth century and portrait photography; Civil War photography; photography and archeology in Egypt: 1839-1860. *Publ:* Auth, Early attempts to improve the daguerreotype, Image, 76; contribr, Philadelphia: Three Centuries of American Art, Philadelphia Mus Art, 76; auth, Robert Cornelius: Portraits from the Dawn of Photography, Smithsonian Inst Press, 83; contribr, Daguerreotypes onto Stone: The Life and Work of Francis D'Avignon, In: American Portrait Prints--Proceedings of the Tenth Annual American Print Conference, Press Va, 84, 194-231; Subjects of strange and of Fearful Interest: Photojournalism from Its Beginnings in 1839, In: Eyes of Time--Photojournalism in America, NY Graphics, Soc, 88 1-33; The Nineteenth Century Portrait, In: The Art of Photography 1839-1989, Yale Press, 89, 44-46; coauth, Irving Penn Master Images: The Collections of the National Museum of American Art and the National Portrait Gallery, Smithsonian Inst Press, 90. *Mailing Add:* Nat Portrait Gallery Washington DC 20560

STAPRANS, RAIMONDS
PAINTER, SCULPTOR
b Riga, Latvia, Oct 13, 26; US citizen. *Study:* Sch Art, Esslingen, Stuttgart, 46; Univ Wash, BA, 52; Univ Calif, MA, 55; also with Archipenko. *Work:* Calif Palace Legion Hon, San Francisco; Oakland Mus, Calif; Santa Barbara Mus, Calif; Los Angeles Co Mus; Phoenix Art Mus. *Exhib:* Portland Art Mus, Ore, 56 & 57; Oakland Art Mus, 57; Calif Palace Legion Hon Winter Invitational, 57, 59 & 60; Litton Industs, 62; Am Acad Arts & Lett, New York, 70; and many one-man shows, in US, Can & Europe. *Teaching:* Instr, Univ Alaska, 78 & 81. *Awards:* San Francisco Art Festival. *Bibliog:* California Canvas (film), KRON, San Francisco, 66; Artists Eye (film), Motion Media, 67. *Media:* Oil; Plastic. *Dealer:* Maxwell Galleries 551 Sutter San Francisco CA 94102. *Mailing Add:* 2052 20th St San Francisco CA 94107

STARK, BRUCE GUNSTEN
CARTOONIST, ILLUSTRATOR
b Queens, NY, Feb 17, 33. *Study:* Sch Visual Arts, New York, 55-58. *Work:* Everett Dirksen Libr; L B Johnson Libr; Baseball Hall of Fame, Cooperstown, NY; Basketball Hall of Fame, Mass. *Exhib:* One-man shows, Art Inst Pittsburgh, 68, Univ Kutztown, Pa, 70 & NY Bank for Savings, New York, 71; Nat Art Mus Sport, New York, 71. *Pos:* Artist, cartoonist, NY Daily News, 61- *Awards:* Nat Cartoonist Soc Reuben Awards, 66, 68 & 75; Page One Award for Best Sports Cartoon, 70 & 73; Most Outstanding Achievement Award, Sch Visual Arts, 82. *Mailing Add:* 212 Elm Ave Melbourne Beach FL 32951

STARK, GEORGE KING
EDUCATOR, SCULPTOR
b Schenectady, NY, June 14, 23. *Study:* State Univ NY Col Buffalo, BS(art educ); Teachers Col, Columbia Univ, MA; State Univ NY Buffalo, EdD; and with Dorothy Denslow. *Work:* IBM Collection; Lowe Art Mus, Univ Miami, Fla; Am Art Clay Co; State Univ NY Col Buffalo; State Univ NY Col Oswego; also in pvt collections. *Comn:* Sculptured light fixtures, Savoy Hilton Hotel, New York, 59; space modulator, Sheraton-Palace Hotel, San Francisco, 60; divider screen, Park-Sheraton Hotel, New York, 60; wall relief sculpture, Prudential Steamship Lines, New York, 61; sculptured fountain, comn by Robert E Maytag, Newton, Iowa, 71. *Exhib:* 17th & 19th Ceramic Nat, 52 & 56 & Ceramic Int Exhib, 58, Syracuse Mus Fine Arts; Western NY Ann, Albright-Knox Gallery, Buffalo, 57 & 60; one-man show, Lowe Art Mus, 67. *Teaching:* Prof art, State Univ NY, New Paltz, Buffalo & Oswego, 53-85; retired. *Awards:* Shared First Prize for Ceramic Sculpture, 19th Ceramic Nat, 56; Am Inst Architects Sculpture Award, Albright-Knox Gallery, 57 & 60. *Media:* Welded Brass & Cast Bronze. *Res:* Analysis of artist-teacher's statements on their creativity. *Publ:* Auth, Silent images, 11/63 & Mass communication and faculty/student dialogue, 4/69, Art Educ J; auth, On sculpture, Sch Arts, 3/64; auth, Games theory in education, Sch & Soc, fall 67; auth, Think stream, S & W, fall & winter 69-70. *Mailing Add:* 149 Bermuda Way North Port FL 34287

STARK, ROBERT
PAINTER, PHOTOGRAPHER
b Sidney, NY, Mar 27, 39. *Study:* Studied photog with Minor White, 61-64; also painting restoration with Robert Scott Wiles, Corcoran Gallery of Art, 71-74. *Work:* Mus Modern Art, New York; Phillips Collection, Corcoran Gallery Art. *Comn:* Sullivan & Cromwell, Washington, DC, 89. *Exhib:* One-person shows, Corcoran Gallery, 69, Phillips Collection, Washington, DC, 79 & Cheekwood Fine Arts Ctr, Nashville, 82. *Pos:* Visual Arts Adv Panel, Pa Coun on the Arts, 89-91. *Awards:* Belin Arts Scholar, 88. *Media:* Acrylic, Oil. *Mailing Add:* Susquehanna Studio Union Dale PA 18470

STARKWEATHER-NELSON, CYNTHIA LOUISE
PAINTER
b Moline, Ill, July 29, 50. *Study:* Northern Ill Univ, BFA, 72; Univ Minn, Minneapolis, MFA, 76. *Work:* Gen Mills, New York; Bank Am, San Francisco; Prudential Insurance Co, Northwestern Life Insurance, Faegre & Benson Law Firm, Minneapolis; Champion Paper Co, Washington, DC. *Comn:* WCCO-TV, Minneapolis. *Exhib:* One-woman show, Am Gallery, Bern, Switz, 81; Drawing, Minneapolis Inst Arts, 81; Works on Paper, Davis-McClain Gallery, St Louis, 82; Of, On, Or About Paper, USA Today, Arlington, Va, 82; New American Paperworks, US & Far East, 82-84; and others. *Pos:* Printer, Vermillion Ed Ltd, Minneapolis, 76-79. *Awards:* Minn State Arts Bd Grants, 78 & 80. *Bibliog:* Mary A Martin (auth), Landscape portraiture, Twin Cities Mag, 80. *Dealer:* Peter M David Gallery 430 Oak Grove Minneapolis MN. *Mailing Add:* 3351 Saint Louis Ave Minneapolis MN 55416-4394

STARN, DOUGLAS See Starn Twins

STARN, MIKE P See Starn Twins

STARN TWINS
PAINTERS, PHOTOGRAPHERS
b Absecon, NJ, May 18, 61. *Study:* Sch Mus Fine Arts, Boston, 5 yr cert, 80-85. *Work:* Mus Fine Arts, Boston, Mass; Metrop Mus Art, New York; Art Inst Chicago, Ill; Ringling Mus Art, Sarasota, Fla; Los Angeles Co Mus; Israel Mus, Jerusalem; Everson Mus Art, Syracuse, NY. *Exhib:* Boston Now: Photography, Inst Contemp Art, Boston, Mass, 85; Whitney Biennial, Whitney Mus Am Art, New York, 87; The New Romantic Landscape, Whitney Mus Am Art at Fairfield Co, Stamford, Conn, 87; Post Abstract Abstraction, Aldrich Mus Contemp Art, Ridgefield, Conn, 87; Binational: American Art of the Late 80's, travelling, Mus Fine Arts & Inst Contemp Art, Boston, Mass, 88; solo exhibs, The Christ Series, Mus Mod Art, San Francisco, Calif, 88, travelling, Contemp Arts Ctr, Cincinnati, Ohio, 90, Fred Hoffman Gallery, Santa Monica, Calif, 90, Mario Diacono Gallery, Tokyo, Japan, 90, travelling, Baltimore Mus Art, Md, 91, Pace/MacGill Gallery, New York, 91 & Leo Costelli Gallery, New York, 92; Invention and Continuity in Contemporary Photography, Metrop Mus Art, New York, 89; Baltimore Mus Art, Md, 89; Wadsworth Atheneum, Hartford, Conn; Selections from the Collection of Marc and Livia Staus, Aldrich Mus Contemp Art, Ridgefield, Conn, 89; Photography Now, Victoria & Albert Mus, London, Eng, 89; With the Grain: Contemporary Panel Painting, Whitney Mus Am Art at Fairfield Co, Stamford, Conn, 90; Boston Now: 10th Anniversary Exhibition, Inst Contemp Art, Boston, Mass, 91; Open Mind: The LeWitt Collection, Wadsworth Atheneum, Hartford, Conn, 91-92; ARCO 92, Parque Ferial Juan Carlos, Madrid, Spain, 92; Amnesty International Benefit, Hotel des arts, Paris, France, 92; Picture in Space/Space in Picture, Lumo '92, Alvar Aalto Mus, Jyvaskyla, Finland, 92; Quotations, The Second History of Art, travelling, Aldrich Mus Contemp Art, 92; Regeneration: Hannah Collins and Mike and Doug Starn, Power Plant, Toronto, Ont, Can, 92; Freedom of Expression '92, Metro Pictures Gallery, New York, 92; Allegories of Modernism, Mus Mod Art, New York, 92; and others. *Awards:* Nat Endowment Arts Grant. *Bibliog:* Joe Jacobs (auth), Doug & Mike Starn: Christ Series (exhib catalog), Ringling Mus, 87; Richard Woodward (auth), It's Art but is it Photography?, New York Times Mag, 88; Andy Grundburg (auth), A pair of shows, NY Times, 88 and Mike & Doug Starn, introduc, Robert Rosenblum. *Media:* Miscellaneous. *Publ:* Contrib, The Art of Robert Bateman, 81 & The World of Robert Bateman, Ramsay Derry, 84; A Day in the Life of Robert Bateman, Charles Kuralt, Can Broadcasting Corp, 85; Twentieth Century Wildlife Artists, Nicholas Hammond, 86; Painting Birds, Susan Rayfield, 88; Robert Bateman: An Artist in Nature, Rick Archbold, 90. *Mailing Add:* c/o Castelli Gallery 420 W Broadway New York NY 10012

STARPATTERN, RITA
SCULPTOR, ADMINISTRATOR
Study: Univ Tex Austin, BSA(cum laude, studio art), 67, NDEA Portuguese Fel, 67, HEW Art Educ Grad Study Fel, 69-70, Sems, 72, 80 & 82. *Exhib:* Solo shows, Moody Hall Atrium, St Edwards Univ, 81 & Art Gallery, Univ Tex Permian Basin, Odessa, 90; Patrick Gallery, Austin, Tex, 86; Laguna Gloria Art Mus, 89; Galeria Sin Fronteras, 90; and others. *Pos:* Adv panel, Tex Comn Arts, 84-85, prog admins, 86-; panelist, var orgns, 85-90; Austin cable comnr, 85-86, Art Pub Places subcomt, 86; exec dir, Women & Their Work, 76-86. *Awards:* Cover story, Ms Mag, 1/80; Amicus Award, Friends Dougherty Cult Arts Ctr, 83; Phoenix Award Women & Minorities Arts, Black Arts Alliance. *Bibliog:* Michael Ennis (auth), Public gestures, Tex Monthly, 5/85; Mel McCombie (auth), Art administrators show talents in Patrick exhibition, 1/23/86 & Austin Annual energetic and strong, 9/5/86, Austin Am-Statesman; photo, Sculpture, winter 87; and others. *Mailing Add:* 6408 Haney Austin TX 78723

STASACK, EDWARD ARMEN
PAINTER, PRINTMAKER
b Chicago, Ill, Oct 1, 29. *Study:* Univ Ill, BFA & MFA. *Work:* Libr Cong, Washington, DC; Honolulu Acad Arts; Mus Mod Art, New York; Metrop Mus Art, New York; Art Inst Chicago. *Comn:* Precast concrete murals, City Honolulu, Fort St Mall, 68 & Honolulu Community Col, 72; Captain Cook Series (print portfolio), Hawaii State Found Cult & Arts; outdoor sculpture & wall sculpture, Hawaii State Intake Serv Ctr, Honolulu. *Exhib:* One-man show, Honolulu Acad Arts, Hawaii, 76-78; Cleveland Inst Art, 76; Amfac Exhib Rm, Honolulu, 77; Ryan Gallery, Kailua, Hawaii, 81; Honolulu Acad Arts, 88. *Teaching:* Prof art, Univ Hawaii, 69-88, chmn dept, 69-72; emer

prof, 88. *Awards:* Tiffany Found Fel, 58 & 62; McDowell Colony Found Fel, 71 & 75; Award of Last Days of Capt Cook, Hawaii State and US Bicentennial Comm Grant, 76. *Bibliog:* George Tahara (dir), Drawing-Painting-Stasack (film), 67; Neogy & Haar (auth), Artists of Hawaii, 74. *Mem:* Soc Am Graphic Artists; Honolulu Printmakers (pres, 59-61); Am Rock Art Research Asn. *Media:* Acrylic, Oil; Collagraph. *Publ:* Auth, Hawaiian petroglyphs, Malamalama Mag, 67; reviews, Honolulu Star-Bull, 68 & 74; coauth, Hawaiian petroglyphs, Bishop Mus, 70. *Mailing Add:* HC-30, Box 895 Univ Hawaii Prescott AZ 86301

STASIK, ANDREW J
PRINTMAKER, CURATOR
b New Brunswick, NJ, Mar 16, 32. *Study:* NY Univ; Columbia Univ, BFA, 54; Univ Iowa; Ohio Univ, MFA, 56. *Work:* Mus Fine Arts, Budapest, Hungary; Nat Mus, Krakow, Poland; Metrop Mus Art, New York; Libr Cong, Nat Collection Fine Arts, Washington, DC; and many others. *Exhib:* Int Biennale Graphics, Krakow, Poland, 66, 68, 70 & 72; 4th Am Biennale Santiago, Chile, 70; one-man exhibs, Molloy Col, 71 & Jacques Baruch Gallery, 73; two-man exhib, Montclair State Col, 74; and others. *Pos:* Dir, Int Graphic Arts Found, currently; Independent cur, Arts adminr. *Awards:* Purchase Award, Okla Art Ctr, 70; Purchase Prize, Multiples Exhib, Western Mich Univ, 70; President's Award in Graphics, Audubon Artists Ann, 70; and many others. *Publ:* Auth & illusr, Prints & poems (folio), 63; ed, Honore Daumier: A Centenary Tribute, 80; founder & ed, Print Review Mag. *Mailing Add:* 18 E Bay Way Lavallette NJ 08735

STATMAN, JAN B
PAINTER, INSTRUCTOR
b New York, NY. *Study:* Hunter Col, with William Baziotes, Bernard Klonis & Richard Lippold, AB. *Work:* Mus Mod Art Alto Aragon, Huesca, Spain; Civic Mus Contemp Art, Sasso Ferrato, Italy; Longview Mus & Arts Ctr, Tex. *Exhib:* Solo exhibs, Longview Mus & Arts Ctr, Tex, 84, McAllen Int Mus, Tex, 85, Wichita Falls Art Asn, Tex, 90 & Milam Gallery, Dallas, Tex, 92; and others. *Pos:* Auth, Art Notes (weekly column), Longview News, 65-70, Artists World (weekly column), Gtr Longview Post, 70-77 & Final Word (weekly column), Dallas Morning News, 81-82. *Teaching:* Instr painting, Longview Mus & Arts Ctr, Tex, 72- & Kilgore Col, 82-84; artist-in-residence, Tex Comn Arts, State of Tex, 85- *Awards:* First Prize Painting, 33rd Ann Cedar City Nat Art Exhib, Utah, 73; Jr League Purchase Award, 25th Ann Exhib, Longview Mus & Arts Ctr, 83; Second Prize Painting, 19th Ann Juried Competition, Masur Mus Art, Monroe, La, 92; and others. *Bibliog:* Ruth Winegarten (auth), A New York Yankee in Longview Texas, Equal Times, Dallas, Tex, 76; Donna Berliner (auth), Jan B Statman, Art Voices-South, 12/78. *Mem:* Tex Press Women; Nat Fedn Press Women; Nat Women's Caucus Art; Dallas Women's Caucus Art. *Media:* Acrylic, Watercolor. *Publ:* The Battered Woman's Survival Guide, Taylor Publ Co, Dallas, Tex, 90. *Mailing Add:* 27 Country Pl Longview TX 75601

STAUFFER, RICHARD L
SCULPTOR, EDUCATOR
b New Cambria, Kans, Apr 1, 32. *Study:* Kans State Teachers Col, with Norma Eppink, BSE, 55; Kans Univ, with Rueschoff & Timmerman, MS, 63; Wichita State Univ, MA, 69. *Work:* Jewish Community Ctr, Kansas City, Kans; Joslyn Art Mus, Omaha, Nebr; Hays Art Coun, Kans; Hutchinson Art Asn, Kans; Birger Sandzen Gallery, Lindsborg, Kans. *Comn:* Concretes, Friends of Art, Emporia, Kans, 72; welded steel, Rock Springs Camp, Junction City, Kans, 78; stone sculpture, St Mary's, 84; concretes, Libr Group Carve Emporia, 86. *Exhib:* Western Arts, Walker Art Ctr, Minneapolis, Minn, 64; 7th Nat Crafts, Jackson, Miss, 71; Objects Mid-Am, Sheldon Mem Art Gallery, Lincoln, Nebr, 73; Glass Now, Joslyn Art Mus, Omaha, Nebr, 78; Business & Arts, Wichita Art Mus, Kans, 79; Hot & Cold Glass, Nebr Arts, Omaha, 79; Chalice, Seattle, Wash, 88 & 89. *Pos:* Treas & mem, Western Arts & Kans Artist Crafts, 71-77; area ed, Kans Art Educ Asn, 78-; dir, Kans High Sch Art Festival, 78-; ed newsletter, Kans Art Educ Asn, 80-85. *Teaching:* Asst prof art educ, Kans State Teachers Col, Emporia, 59-63; assoc prof sculpture, glassblowing & art educ, Emporia Kans State Univ, 63- *Awards:* Governor's Artist, 84; Outstanding Art Educator, Kansas, 85; Best of Show, NAEA Elect Gallery, Washington, DC, 89. *Bibliog:* Hoffaman (auth), Kansas designer crafts, Kansas City Star, 74; Kwolek-Holland (auth), article, Manhattan Mercury, 82; four articles in Kans Art Ed Journal, 84-88. *Mem:* Kans Artist Craftsman Asn (treas, 77); Kans Art Educ Asn; Western Arts Asn; Community Arts Inc (pres, 72); Kans Sculptor Asn (vpres, 90). *Media:* Found Object. *Mailing Add:* 2001 Lincoln St Emporia KS 66801

STAUM, SONJA
LIBRARIAN
b St Joe, Mich, May 9, 59. *Study:* Ind Univ, Bloomington, BA, 84, MLS, 89; Univ Ga, Athens, MFA, 86. *Pos:* Mus librn, Mus Contemp Art, Chicago, Ill, 89- *Mem:* Art Libr Soc of NAm (co-moderator, space planners round table, 90); Special Libr Asn; Am Libr Asn; Soc Am Archivist. *Mailing Add:* Mus Contemp Art Libr 237 E Ontario Chicago IL 60611

STAVANS, ISAAC
PAINTER
b Tampico, Mex, Aug 25, 31. *Study:* Mexico City Col, BA, 52; Brooklyn Col, MA, 53; apprentice to Arnold Belkin, 56-60. *Work:* Pedagogical Mus, Mex Inst Cult Relations, Mexico City; Centro Asturiano de Mexico. *Exhib:* Solo exhibs, Int Week of the Plastic Arts, Mus City, Mex, 77, Artists House, Jerusalem, 77, Recent Works, Misrachi Gallery, Mex City, 79, Univ Ariz, 81, Mus Art & Hist, Ciudad Juarez, Mex, 83, Lourdes Chumacero Gallery, Estocolmo, Mex, 86, Centro Asturiano, 2/90 & Fragments, Gallery Torre del Reloj, 91. *Teaching:* Instr painting, CDI Art Sch, 65-74, Hispanic-Mex Univ, 65-74 & privately, 74- *Bibliog:* Alfonso de Neuvillate (auth), Stavans: Reminiscences and evolations, Novedades Newspaper, 2/5/76; Berta Taracena (auth), Art: Recent shows, Tiempo Mag, 7/19/76; Bryan Johnstone (auth), Stavans inner landscapes, Ariz Daily Wildcat Newspaper, 1/23/81; Alfonso de Neuvillate (auth), Stavans: An opalescent beauty, Novedades Newspaper, 4/4/86. *Mem:* Mex Soc Visual Artists. *Media:* Oil, Mixed Techniques. *Dealer:* Misrachi Gallery Genova No 20 Mexico 6 DF Mex 06600; Lourdes Chumacero Gallery Estocolmo 34 Mexico 6 DF 06600. *Mailing Add:* Bosque Minas 55B Apt 1104 Bosques Herradura Estado Mexico 53920 Mexico

STAVARIDIS, PAT(RICIA ANN)
ART DEALER
b New York, NY, Nov 27, 42. *Study:* Trapnagen Sch Fashion & Design, dipl, 63; Mus Sch Fine Arts, Boston, 74-78; Univ Mass, BA(cum laude), 80. *Pos:* Artist & dir, Loweth National, New York, 64-68; consult, 78-79; dir, Stavaridis Gallery, Boston, 80- *Bibliog:* Robert Taylor (auth), Art moves to the warehouse district, Boston Globe, 78; Linda Stone (auth), Opening gallery doors, Boston Monthly, 79; Faces to watch in 1981, Boston Mag, 81. *Mem:* Friends Boston Art. *Specialty:* Contemporary art; emerging Boston and New York artists. *Mailing Add:* 111 Marlborough Boston MA 02116

STAVEN, LELAND CARROLL
PRINTMAKER, PAINTER
b Milwaukee, Wis, Dec 17, 33. *Study:* Univ Wis-Milwaukee, BFA, 56; Layton Sch Art, 57; Calif Col Arts & Crafts, MFA, 60; Ill Inst Technol, 63. *Work:* Univ Ga Art Mus; Ga Tech Univ Art Gallery; South DeKalb Col; LaGrange Col. *Exhib:* 18th Southeastern Ann Exhib, Atlanta, Ga, 63; Contemp Southern Art Exhib, 64; 1st S Cent Exhib, Nashville, Tenn, 66; 1st Ann Greater Birmingham Arts Alliance Exhib, Ala, 75; 2nd Ann Nat Dogwood Festival Art Show, Atlanta, 75; Georgia Artists Show, 86; Carrollton Regional Exhibition, III, 86. *Pos:* Vchmn, Ga Comn Arts, Atlanta, 67-72. *Teaching:* Chmn dept painting, drawing & printmaking, Berry Col, 60-68 & Mercer Univ Atlanta, 68-69; assoc prof painting, drawing & printmaking & cur, Dalton Galleries, Agnes Scott Col, 70- *Awards:* Purchase Awards, Asn Ga Artists, 61 & Fourth Ann Callaway Gardens Art Exhib, 67; Achievement Award, Appalachian Corridors: Exhib I, 68. *Mem:* Southeastern Col Art Conf; Southern Graphics Coun; Georgia Poetry Soc. *Media:* Acrylic, Oil. *Publ:* Auth, poetry in: Motive, Discourse & Odessa Poetry Rev. *Mailing Add:* 31 View Dr Rome GA 30161-8911

STAVRINOS, GEORGE PHILIP
ILLUSTRATOR
b Boston, Mass, Mar 13, 48. *Study:* RI Sch Design, BA(graphics), 70. *Work:* Metrop Mus Art, New York; Fashion Inst Technol, New York. *Exhib:* Cover '75-Catch the Eye, 75, Commun Graphics, 75-76 & The Mental Picture III, 77, Am Inst Graphic Arts, New York; 26th Soc Illus Am Nat Exhib, New York, 84; 64th Ann Exhib, Art Dirs Club, New York, 85. *Awards:* Cert of Excellence, Cover '75 & Mental Picture III, 77, Am Inst Graphic Arts; Honorable Advisor, Tokyo Designer's Gakuin Col, 84; Merit Award, 64th Ann Exhib, Art Dirs Club, 85. *Bibliog:* Philip Smith (auth), Stavrinos: Fashion & Art, Arts Mag, 10/81; Lori Simmons Zelenko (auth), George Stavrinos, Am Artist, 9/83; Camille Duhe (auth), Attention to detail, HOW-Graphic Design Mag, 5-6/86. *Media:* Graphite Pencil. *Publ:* Contribr, Cheap Chic, 78 & Fame, 80, Harmony Books; Graphic Illustration, Prentice-Hall, 82; The Blue Book, Indigo Books, 83; Fashion Illustration in New York, Graphic-Sha, Japan, 85. *Mailing Add:* c/o Eleanor Ettinger Inc 155 Sixth Ave New York NY 10013

STAYTON, JANET
PAINTER
b Natchez, Miss, Sept 2, 39. *Study:* Tex Christian Univ, BFA, 61; Tulane Univ, MFA, 63. *Work:* MacArthur Arts Ctr, Little Rock, Ark; Brooklyn Mus Fine Arts; Chase Manhattan Bank Collection, New York; Prudential Insurance Co, Newark, NJ; Chicago Art Inst; and others. *Exhib:* One-woman exhibs, Hamilton Gallery, New York, 77, 79 & 80, Van Straaten Gallery, Chicago, 81, Galerie Nord, Randers, Denmark, 82 & Il Ponte, Rome, 86; Patricia Heesy Gallery, New York, 84-85, 87; Raymond J Hage Inc, Huntington, WVa, 88; Out of the House, Whitney Downtown Mus Art, 78; Expressions of Self, Douglass Art Gallery, Rutgers Univ, 79; 100 New Acquisitions, Brooklyn Mus, 81; Ancient Currents, Fisher Gallery, USC, Los Angeles, 86; Washington Arts Club 89; Ray Hage Gallery, Huntington WV 88. *Bibliog:* Hilton kramer (auth), One-person show, Hamilton Gallery, New York Times, 11/77; Hilton Kramer (auth), One-person show, Hamilton Gallery, New York Times, 11/77; Essay Janet Stayton "Paintings", Patricia Heesy Gallery, 85; Donna Stein (auth), "Ancient Currents" catalog essay, USC, 86. *Media:* Oil. *Dealer:* Patricia Heesy Gallery New York NY 10019; Raymond J Hage Inc 401 11th St Huntington WV 25701. *Mailing Add:* 216 Lafayette St New York NY 10012

STEADMAN, DAVID WILTON
MUSEUM DIRECTOR
b Honolulu, Hawaii, Oct 24, 36. *Study:* Harvard Col, BA(magna cum laude), 60; Harvard Univ, MAT, 61; Univ Calif, Berkeley, MA(art hist), 66; Princeton Univ, PhD, 74. *Collections Arranged:* P P Rubens before 1620 (with catalog), Princeton Art Mus, 71; Selections from the Norton Simon, Inc Mus Art (with catalog), 73; Graphic Art of Francisco Goya (with catalog), Galleries of Claremont Cols, 75, 18th Century Drawing from California Collections (with catalog), 76 & Works on Paper 1900-1960 from Southern Calif Collections (with catalog), 77. *Pos:* Lectr, Frick Collection, New York,

70-71; asst dir, Art Mus, Princeton Univ, 71-72, actg dir, 72-73, assoc dir, 73; dir, Galleries of Claremont Cols, 74-80; res cur, Norton Simon Mus, Pasadena, Calif, 77-80; dir, Chrysler Mus, Norfolk, Va, 80-89; dir, Toledo Mus Art, 89- *Teaching:* Asst prof 17th & 18th centuries art, Pomona Col, 74-78, assoc prof, 78-80. *Awards:* Nat Defense Educ Act fel, 66-69; Chester Dale Fel, Nat Gallery Art, 69-70. *Mem:* Am Asn Mus Dirs; Col Art Asn; Art Mus Assoc (trustee). *Res:* 17th and 18th century drawings. *Publ:* Auth, Abraham van Dipenbeeck, UMI Res Press, 82; coauth, A Tricentennial Celebration: Norfolk 1682-1982, 82. *Mailing Add:* Toledo Mus Art PO Box 1013 Toledo OH 43697

STEARNS, ROBERT
CURATOR, ADMINISTRATOR
b Los Angeles, Calif, Aug 28, 47. *Study:* Calif State Univ, San Luis Obispo, 68; Univ Calif, San Diego, BFA, 70. *Collections Arranged:* Dimensions of Black (auth, catalog), La Jolla Mus, 70; Kes Zapkus: Paintings 1968-78 (auth, catalog), 78, Robert Wilson: From A Theater of Images (auth, catalog), 80, Alex Katz: Paintings and Drawings 1959-79, 81 & Dynamix and The New Art of Energy (auth, catalog), 82, Contemp Arts Ctr, Cincinnati; Tableaux, 82, Scott Burton Chairs, 83 & Word Works (auth, catalog), 84, Walker Art Ctr, Minneapolis; Robert Wilson: Knee Plays for the Civil Wars, 85 & Trisha Brown & Nancy Graves: Lateral Pass, 86, Tokyo Arts Festival; Art in Europe and America: The 1950s and 1960s, Art in Europe and America: The 1960s and 1970s, 90, New Works for New Spaces: Into the 90s, Wexner Ctr for the Arts, 91. *Pos:* Asst dir, Paula Cooper Gallery, New York, 70-72; dir, The Kitchen Ctr for Video & Music, New York, 72-78; founding dir & pres, Artists Television Network, New York, 76-77; dir, Contemp Arts Ctr, Cincinnati, 78-82, Wexner Ctr for the Arts, Ohio State Univ, Columbus, 88-92; dir performing arts, Walker Art Ctr, Minneapolis, 82-88. *Teaching:* Lectr performance art & alternative media, var US cols & univs; assoc dean & adj asst prof, Dept Art, Col Arts, Ohio State Univ, 88-92. *Awards:* Rank of Chevalier, Order of Arts and Letters, the French Cult Ministry, 88. *Mem:* Haleakala Inc for the Kitchen Ctr for Video & Music (bd dir, 73-); Minn Independent Choreographers Alliance (bd dir, 83-88); Wexner Ctr Found (bd trustees, 90-92); Trisha Brown Dance Co (bd dir, 90-); Asn Art Mus Dir. *Publ:* Ed, The Kitchen Center Annual, Haleakala Inc, 75 & 76; contribr, Video Art: An Anthology, Harcourt Brace, 76; auth, The Wexner Center for the Visual Arts: The Ohio State University (essay), Rizzoli Int, 89; exec ed & forward, Breakthroughs: Arant Garde Artists in Europe and America: 1950-1990, Rizzoli Int, 91. *Mailing Add:* Wexner Ctr Visual Arts Ohio State Univ 30 W 15th St Columbus OH 43210

STEARNS, THOMAS ROBERT
SCULPTOR, EDUCATOR
b Oklahoma City, Okla, Sept 4, 36. *Study:* Memphis Acad Art, Tenn, 55-57; Cranbrook Acad Art, 57-60; Acad Belli Arti, Venice, Italy, 60-61. *Work:* Minn Mus Art, St Paul; Venini Mus, Venice, Italy; Mus Art, Iowa City, Iowa; Ringling Mus, Sarasota, Fla; Victoria & Albert Mus, London. *Comn:* Sculpture, J Huston Collection, Gaughwell, Ireland, 61-62. *Exhib:* Seattle World's Fair, Wash, 61; Brussels Int, Belgium, 61; Venice Biennale, Venice, Italy, 62; Glass: Czechoslovakia & Italy, Mus Contemp Crafts, New York, 64; Am Oil Painting & Sculpture, Pa Acad Fine Arts Mus, 66; Johnson Collection, Objects, Smithsonian Inst, Washington, DC, 69; Drawing USA, Minn Mus, St Paul, 71; Pacemakers and Trendsetters, Detroit Inst Art, Mich, 73; Venini Retrospective Renwick, Nat Mus Am Art, Washington, DC, 81. *Pos:* Guest research designer, Venini Glass, Venice, Italy, 60-62. *Teaching:* Assoc prof sculpture, Philadelphia Col Art, 70- *Awards:* Fulbright Travel Grant, 60; Italian Govt Award Fel, 60-61; John Simon Guggenheim Fel, 65-66; Nat Inst Arts & Letters Grant, 65-66. *Bibliog:* Domas (auth), Thomas Stearns per Venini, Domasmagazine, Italy, 62; New York Commentary, Thomas Stearns, Willard Gallery, Studio Int, 64. *Media:* Mixed, Charcoal. *Mailing Add:* Univ of Arts 320 S Broad St Philadelphia PA 19102

STEBBINS, THEODORE ELLIS, JR
HISTORIAN, ADMINISTRATOR
b New York, NY, Aug 11, 38. *Study:* Yale Univ, BA, 60; Harvard Univ Law Sch, JD, 64, Harvard Univ, PhD, 71. *Collections Arranged:* Luminous Landscape, Fogg Art Mus, 66; Martin Johnson Heade, Whitney Mus Am Art, 69; New Haven Scene, New Haven Colony Hist Soc, 70; Richard Brown Baker Collects, Yale Univ, 75; Am Landscapes at the Wadsworth Atheneum, Hudson River Sch, 76; Am Master Drawings, Whitney Mus, 76. *Pos:* Assoc cur, Garvan Collections, Yale Univ Art Gallery, 68-77, cur Am painting & sculpture, 71-77; cur Am painting, Mus of Fine Arts, Boston, Mass, 77- *Teaching:* Instr hist art, Smith Col, 67; asst prof hist art, Yale Univ, 69-75, Morse fel, 72, assoc prof, 75-77; vis prof, Boston Univ, 78, prof art hist, 82- *Awards:* Chester Dale Fel, Nat Gallery Art, Washington, DC, 66; Morse Fel, Yale Univ, 70; Joseph Coolidge Shaw Soc Medal, Boston Univ, 85. *Mem:* Col Art Asn Am; Am Fedn Arts. *Res:* American landscape painting of the nineteenth century; history of American drawings and watercolors. *Collection:* Nineteenth and twentieth century American art. *Publ:* coauth, The Lane Collection: 20th Century Paintings in the American Tradition, 83 & A New World: Masterpieces of American Painting, 1760-1910, 83, Mus Fine Arts, Boston; auth, Life and Works of Martin Johnson Heade, Yale Univ Press, 75; coauth, Boston Collects: Contemporary Painting and Sculpture, 86 & Charles Sheeler: The Photographs, Mus Fine Arts, Boston, 88; Introductory Essay in a Book by Anselm Kiefer, George Braziller Inc & Mus Fine Arts, Boston, 88; auth, Weston's Westons: Portraits and Nudes, 89; The Lyre of Italy: American Artists and the Halian Experience, 1760-1914, 92. *Mailing Add:* Mus of Fine Arts Boston MA 02115

STECKEL, ANITA
COLLAGE ARTIST, PAINTER
b New York, NY. *Study:* Cooper Union; Art Students League, with Edwin Dickenson. *Work:* Patrick Lannan Mus Found, Calif. *Exhib:* Whitney Mus, 70, Portland Mus, 74, Bronx Mus, 76; Am Fedn Art, 77; Brooklyn Mus, 77; Krannert Mus, Ill, 77; Biennial, Columbia, SAm, 81; Documenta Seven, Kassel, Ger, 82; Patrick Lannan Mus, Palm Beach, Fla, 82; Rutgers Col, 85; Security Pacific Women's Show, 85; Kingsboro Col, NY, 89; PS1, New York, 90. *Teaching:* Lectr, Sarah Lawrence Col, NY Univ, Rutgers, New Rochelle Col, Univ RI & Queens Col; instr, Parson Sch Design, 79- & Art Students League, 85. *Awards:* Nat Endowment Arts Grant Painting, 83. *Bibliog:* Phyliss Rosser (auth), New directions for women; Arlene Raven (auth), Ms Mag, 20th anniversary issue; plus many other articles in NY Mag, Art News, Woman Art, NY Times & Chrysallis. *Media:* Collage, Oil. *Publ:* Auth, The Art of New York, Abrams, 83; auth, The Male Nude, Paddington Press; contribr, Feminist Art Criticism, an Anthology, Arlene Raven (ed), Univ Microfilms Inc Press. *Mailing Add:* 463 West St New York NY 10014

STECKLER, STUART JAY
ART DEALER, COLLECTOR
b New York, NY, Sept 29, 31. *Pos:* Owner, Ex Libris Art Books, Scottsdale, Ariz, currently. *Collection:* Contemporary American art; New York school; abstract illusionism; photorealism; contemporary American Indian sculpture. *Mailing Add:* 6711 E Camelback Rd No 32 Scottsdale AZ 85251

STECZYNSKI, JOHN MYRON
DRAFTSMAN, EDUCATOR
b Chicago, Ill, June 22, 36. *Study:* Art Inst Chicago; Craft Ctr, Worcester, Mass; Univ Notre Dame, BFA(magna cum laude), 58; Yale Univ, MFA, 61; Acad Fine Arts, Warsaw; and with Umberto Romano. *Comn:* Wood relief panels, Ursuline Provincialate, Kirkwood, Mo, 57-58; dossals for Easter, 71, Christmas, 71, Lent, 73 & Pentecost, 75, Univ Lutheran Church, Cambridge, Mass; drawing, Boston Col, 83; Hilton Hotel, West Palm Beach, Fla, 84; Advent Hangings, Blessed Sacrament Church, Jamaica Plain, Mass, 85; and others. *Exhib:* Dom Akademicki, Warsaw, Poland, 61; Helen Shlien Gallery, Boston, 80; Boston Col Gallery, 81 & 84; Tichnor Lounge, Harvard Univ, 84; Mills Gallery, Boston Ctr for the Arts, 84; and others. *Teaching:* Instr studio art, Worcester Art Mus Sch, 61-64; instr art hist, Boston Mus Fine Arts Sch, 64-67 & Tufts in Italy, Naples, 67-68; asst prof & chmn dept studio art & art history, Newton Col Sacred Heart, 68-75; asst prof studio art, Boston Col, 75-79, asst chmn dept fine arts, 77-81, assoc prof, 79-88, acting chmn, 81-82, assoc chmn, 85-88, prof, 88- *Awards:* Woodrow Wilson Found Fal, 58; Mellon Found Grant, 82; and others. *Bibliog:* Christine Temin (auth), John Steczynski: a figure outside the gallery scene, Boston Globe, 10/24/85; S Avery Brown (auth), The triumph of order, BC Mag, 86; and others. *Mem:* Drawing Soc, New York; The Copley Soc Boston. *Media:* Pen & Ink, Acrylic. *Publ:* Auth, Visual thinking in education, In: Inscape: Studies Presented to Charles F Donovan, SJ, 77; A meditation on nudity as mask in Western art, ACM, spring 89. *Dealer:* Ginsburg Hallowell & Assoc Fine Art 125 Newbury St Boston MA 02116. *Mailing Add:* Dept Art Boston Col 885 Center St Newton MA 02159

STEEL, VIRGINIA OBERLIN
GALLERY DIRECTOR, CURATOR
b Pa, Sept 27, 50. *Study:* Carnegie-Mellon Univ; Univ Hartford, BA, 73; Univ Mass-Amherst, MA, 75. *Collections Arranged:* Rutgers National Works on Paper Competition, 77, 79, 81, 83, 85 & 87; Contemp Artists Exhibs, 77, 78, 82, 84-88. *Pos:* Dir, Stedman Art Gallery, Rutgers Univ, Camden, NJ, 76- *Teaching:* Mus Studies Prog, Rutgers Univ, Camden, NJ, 79- *Mem:* Am Asn Mus. *Mailing Add:* c/o Stedman Art Gallery Rutgers Univ The State Univ of NJ Camden NJ 08102

STEELE, BENJAMIN CHARLES
PAINTER, EDUCATOR
b Roundup, Mont, Nov 17, 17. *Study:* Cleveland Inst Art, dipl; Kent State Univ, BS; Denver Univ, MA; Univ Ore; Ill State Univ; Mont State Univ. *Work:* Eastern Mont Col; Univ Mont; Mont Inst Arts, Permanent Collection. *Comn:* Arts of the West (mural), Denver Univ; Indoor and Outdoor Sports (mural), Eastern Mont Col; and pvt collections. *Exhib:* Mont Arts & Crafts Exhib, Senate Caucus Room, Washington, DC; Mont Inst Arts Little Festival, 75-; one-man shows, Ga Tech, Mont Hist Soc, Yellowstone Art Ctr, Scottsdale Ctr Arts, C M Russell Mus & Minneapolis VA Med Ctr; WWII POW Collection, Eastern Mont Col, Miles Community Col & Univ Mont, 86-87; Spirit of Modernism, Paris Gibson Ctr, Great Falls, Holter Mus, Helene, 87-88; and others. *Teaching:* Art teacher, New London, Ohio High Sch, 51-52; crafts dir, Fort Riley, Kans, 53-54; staff crafts dir, Mil District Wash, 54-56 & Fort MacPherson, Ga, 54-59; prof art & head dept, Eastern Mont Col, Billings, 59-82, prof emer, 82- *Awards:* Teaching Merit Award, Eastern Mont Col, 77; Distinguished Prof Award, Eastern Mont Col, 80; Mont Arts Coun Governors Award, Outstanding Achievement Arts, 92. *Bibliog:* Dorothy Larsen (auth), Man of gentle fiber & Nancy Olson (auth), Briefly biographical, Mont Arts Mag; also feature art in Washington Post, Altanta Const, Kansas City Star & many others. *Mem:* Mont Inst Arts Found Bd; Billings Art Asn; Mont Inst Arts (pres); Yellowstone Art Ctr; and others. *Media:* Oil, Watercolor. *Publ:* Auth, Craft Directors Handbook, 55; illusr, Code of the US fighting man, Army Digest, 66; cover design, Mont Arts, 73; illusr, cover designs & illustrations, Horizons O'er the Musselshell, 74, Along the Zimmerman Trail, 74, Tracking Billings' Past, 78, Of Two Minds, 81, Bataan Diary, 84, Some Survived, 84 & Cabanatvan: Japanese Death Camp, 85, Soochow & the 4th Marines, 87, Correqidor, from Paradise to Hell, 88, Gates Left Open, 89, Prisoner of Hope, 89 & We Remember Bataan & Correqidor, 90. *Mailing Add:* 2425 Cascade Ave Billings MT 59102

STEEN, CAROL J
SCULPTOR, PAINTER
Highland Park, Mich, Nov 6, 43. *Study:* Mich State Univ, BA, 65; Cranbrook Acad Art, MFA, 71. *Work:* Printmaking Workshop, New York; Smithsonian Archives Am Art; Am Craft Mus, New York; Detroit Inst Arts. *Exhib:* 12 Years, 55 Mercer Street Gallery, New York, 83, 85, 87, 89 & 91; Cade Gallery, Royal Oak, Mich, 88; Brody's Gallery, Washington, DC, 88 & Philadelphia Mus Art, 89 & 90; B4A Gallery, New York, 91; C A Wustum Mus, Racine, Wis, 92; and others. *Teaching:* Ford Found vis lectr studio art, Univ Mich, 75; asst prof studio art, William Paterson Col, 77-82 & Touro Col, 83- *Awards:* Grant, Printmaking Workshop, New York, 82; NY Found Arts Fel, 86-87; Materials for the Arts, New York, 87; and others. *Bibliog:* Vered Lieb (auth), Artists on art, Re-View Mag, 79; Jon Friedman (auth), article, Arts Mag, 12/82; Marsha Miro (auth), article, Detroit Free Press, 11/88; Joy Hakanson Colby (auth), Detroit News, 3/90. *Mem:* Col Art Asn, New York; 55 Mercer St Gallery, New York (pres, 82-, bd dirs, 83-). *Media:* Metal; Acrylic, Oil. *Dealer:* Steven Rosenberg Gallery 115 Wooster NY 10012. *Mailing Add:* 163 Bowery New York NY 10002

STEFAN, ROSS
PAINTER
b Milwaukee, Wis, June 13, 34. *Study:* Primarily self-taught; collab with Dan Muller, Milwaukee, Dale Nichols, Antigua, Guatemala & Frederic Whitaker, La Jolla, Calif. *Work:* Ford Motor Co; Milwaukee Jour; Harmsen's Western Americana, Denver; Gilcrease Inst Am Hist & Art, Tulsa; Amerind Found, Dragoon, Ariz. *Exhib:* One-man shows, Rosequist Galleries, Tucson, 70-82 & 83-86; Our Western Heritage, Univ Ariz, 62; Grand Central Art Galleries, New York, 72; 42nd Ann Ariz Exhib, Rosequist Galleries, 90; Stefan's Southern England, Rosequist Galleries, Tucson, Ariz, 93; and others. *Awards:* Artist of the Yr, Tucson Festival Soc Award, 78; Artist Am, Denver, Colo. *Bibliog:* Sen Barry Goldwater (auth), Ross Stefan 1975, Wollheims' Rosequist Galleries; John K Goodman (auth), Ross Stefan: An Impressionistic Painter of the Contemporary Southwest, Northland Press, 77; Jon Stefan (auth), article, Artists of the Rockies, fall 79. *Media:* Oil on Canvas. *Res:* Painters of the Southwest as it is today; since 1948, Southern Arizona, Navajo and Hopi country, the Rio Grande North to Santa Fe and Taos, New Mexico. *Publ:* Articles in Ariz Highways, Reader's Digest, Ford Times, Am Artist, Southwest Art. *Mailing Add:* c/o Rosequist Galleries 1615 E Fort Lowell Rd Tucson AZ 85719

STEFANELLI, JOE
PAINTER
b Philadelphia, Pa, Mar 20, 21. *Study:* Philadelphia Mus Col Art, 38-40; Pa Acad Fine Arts, 40-41; New Sch Social Res, New York, 49-50; Art Students League, 50-51; Hans Hofmann Sch Painting, New York, 51-52. *Work:* Whitney Mus Am Art; Walker Art Ctr; Norfolk Art Mus; Baltimore Mus; NY Univ; and others. *Comn:* Mural, Brooklyn Bd Educ, 77. *Exhib:* Whitney Mus Am Art; Mus Mod Art, New York; Pa Acad Fine Arts; Walker Art Ctr, Minneapolis; Corcoran Gallery Art; Carnegie Inst Int; Art Inst Chicago; one-man shows, Westbeth Galleries, 71, New Sch Social Res, 72, Ingber Gallery, 84, Armstrong Gallery, 88 & Cyrus Gallery, 89; and others. *Teaching:* Instr, Univ Calif, Berkeley, summers 60 & 63; vis critic, Cornell Univ; artist in residence, Princeton Univ, 63-66; vis critic, Univ Ark; instr, Columbia Univ, 66-74; instr, New Sch Social Res, 66-, Wash Univ, St Louis, 89. *Awards:* Fulbright Award for Rome, 58-59; Am Res Ctr Egypt Fel, 66-67; NY State Coun Arts Award, 71; and others. *Mem:* Fel Am Research Ctr Egypt. *Dealer:* M13 Gallery. *Mailing Add:* 463 West St D1006 New York NY 10014

STEFFLER, ALVA W
EDUCATOR, CURATOR
b Philadelphia, Pa, June 22, 34. *Study:* Pa Art Acad; Ind Univ, MAT; Northern Ill Univ, MFA. *Pos:* Cur & dir Am art collection, Wheaton Col, Ill, 71- *Teaching:* Asst prof art hist, painting & sculpture, Grace Col, Winona Lake, Ind, 67-69; prof studio, Wheaton Col, Ill, 70- *Res:* American art history and museology. *Mailing Add:* Dept Art Wheaton Col 501 East Wheaton IL 60187

STEG, JAMES LOUIS
PRINTMAKER, PAINTER
b Alexandria, Va. *Study:* Rochester Inst Technol, cert; State Univ Iowa, BFA & MFA. *Work:* Libr Cong, Washington, DC; Smithsonian Nat Collection, Washington, DC; Brooklyn Mus, NY; Mus Mod Art, New York; Fogg Mus, Cambridge, Mass. *Exhib:* One-man shows, Weyhe Gallery, 45 & Assoc Am Artists, 64, New York; Big Prints USA, State Univ NY Col New Paltz, 68; USIS Cult Ctr, Ankara, Turkey, 75; 30 Year Retrospective Traveling Exhib, New Orleans Mus Art, 78; and others. *Teaching:* Instr drawing & painting, Cornell Univ, 49-51; prof drawing & printing, Tulane Univ La, 51-92. *Awards:* Purchase Prize, Eighth Int Print & Drawing Exhib, Lugano, 64; Purchase Prizes, State Univ NY Col Potsdam Print Exhib, 64-68; Printmaker emeritus, Southern Graphics Art Coun, 90. *Bibliog:* Barry Schwartz (auth), Humanism in Art. *Mem:* Am Color Print Soc. *Publ:* Auth, article, Artists Proof, 66. *Mailing Add:* Dept Art 215 Newcomb Ave Tulane Univ 6823 St Charles Ave New Orleans LA 70118

STEGEMAN, CHARLES
PAINTER, EDUCATOR
b Ede, Netherlands, June 5, 24; US citizen. *Study:* Acad Beeldende Kunst, The Hague; Acad Royale Beaux Arts, Brussels; Inst Nat Superieur Beaux-Arts, Antwerp. *Work:* Nat Gallery Can; Ont Art Gallery; Vancouver Art Gallery; Art Gallery Gtr Victoria; Univ BC. *Exhib:* Toronto Art Gallery, 61; Winnipeg Biannual, 61; Montreal Mus Fine Arts, 62; Chicago Centennial Exhib, Ill, 63; Stratford Art Festival Exhib, Ont, 70; Vancouver Art & Artists 1931-1983, 83; First Int Invitational, Anniversary Israel, Baltimore, 88. *Pos:* Founding pres, Asn Villard de Honnecourt, Medieval Technol, Sci Art, 84-90. *Teaching:* Prof painting, Art Inst Chicago, 62-69; prof painting & chmn dept fine arts, Haverford Col, 69- *Awards:* Humanities Fel, Medical Col Pa, 81-83; Purchase Award, 76 & Merit Grant, 78, Belg Govt; Fedn Field Res Grant, Calif & Chartres, France, 90. *Mem:* Int Ctr Medieval Art, New York, 85- *Media:* Oil, Acrylic. *Mailing Add:* Art Dept Haverford Col Haverford PA 19041

STEGMAN, PATRICIA
PAINTER, PRINTMAKER
b San Antonio, Tex, Nov 27, 29. *Study:* Kansas City Univ, Mo, 48-49; Kansas City Art Inst, Mo, BFA, 52; Art Students League, study with Reginald Marsh, Will Barnet, Vaclav Vytlacil & Morris Kantor, 54-57. *Exhib:* Drawings, Atlantic Gallery, New York, 77, 84 & 86; Landmark Gallery, New York, NY, 77; Tenth St Days--Retrospective of Art of the 50s, Fourteen Sculptors Gallery, New York, 77; one-artist shows, Brata Gallery, New York, 61 & 63 & Gallery 91, Brooklyn, 75 & 76. *Pos:* Scenic artist/designer, Circle Repertory Co, New York, 74 & Big Apple Theatre Co, Brooklyn, 74 & 75; staff writer, Artists Review Art, New York & Phoenix (newspaper), Brooklyn, 76- *Teaching:* Instr painting & drawing, Kansas City Art Inst, 52. *Mem:* Art Students League. *Media:* Oil, Watercolor; Etching, Lithography. *Dealer:* Atlantic Gallery 458 W Broadway New York NY 10012. *Mailing Add:* 245 Dean St No 1 Brooklyn NY 11217

STEIDER, DORIS (MRS C B MCCAMPBELL)
PAINTER, SCULPTOR
b Decatur, Ill, Apr 10, 24. *Study:* Purdue Univ, BS(appl design), 45; Kirksville Col Osteopathy, Cert Lab Technician, 49; Univ NMex, with Kenneth Adams, MA(fine art), 65. *Work:* WTex Mus, Lubbock; NMex Governor's Collection, Santa Fe; Holt, Rinehart & Winston; NMex State Fair Collection; Loewen Group, Burnaby, BC, Can. *Comn:* Sixteen wall panels, St Joseph's Hosp, Albuquerque, 66. *Exhib:* Nat League Am Pen Women, Smithsonian Inst, Washington, DC, 63; Army Traveling Print Shows, US Army, 63-64; Ann Competition by Invitation, Witte Mus Western Art, San Antonio, Tex & Mont State Hist Soc Mus, Helena, 65; solo exhibs, Triton Mus, San Jose, Calif, 68 & Purdue Univ, 92; Ft Sill Int Show, Okla, 74; Spring Panorama Art, Baker Gallery Fine Art, Lubbock, Tex, 81; Magnifico & Art of Albuquerque Invitationals, 92; plus many others. *Awards:* First Sculpture, 13th Ann Nat Art Show, La Junta, Colo, 81; Doris Steider Street Alburquerque NMex, 88; First Painting, SW Arts Festival, Indio, Calif, 89. *Bibliog:* Mary Carroll Nelson (auth), Doris Steider chose egg tempera, Am Artist Mag, 78; Mary Carroll Nelson (auth), Masters of Western Art, Watson-Guptill, 82; Female Artists in the USA 1900-1985, Rutgers Univ, 86. *Media:* Egg Tempera; Bronze. *Dealer:* Weems Gallery Albuquerque NM. *Mailing Add:* Rte 5 30 Silverhills Lane Albuquerque NM 87123

STEIGMAN, MARGOT See Robinson, Margot (Margot Steigman)

STEIN, CLAIRE A
ADMINISTRATOR
b New York, NY, Sept 19, 23. *Study:* Art Students League; Adelphi Col, BA; sculpture with Robert Cronbach. *Collections Arranged:* Nat Sculpture Soc Ann, 68-86; North Shore Community Art Ctr Exhib, 60s. *Pos:* Bd dir, North Shore Community Art Ctr, 57-62; exec dir, Nat Sculpture Soc, retired. *Mem:* Art Table. *Publ:* Contribr, Nat Sculpture Rev, fall 73, winter 74 & 75 & spring 75; contribr sculpture suppl, Grolier Encyclopedia, 70-73. *Mailing Add:* 6 Dorchester Dr Manhasset NY 10030

STEIN, DONNA MICHELE
CURATOR, CRITIC
b Los Angeles, Calif, Oct 2, 42. *Study:* Univ Calif, Los Angeles, BA, 63; NY Univ Inst Fine Arts, MA, 65. *Collections Arranged:* Selected Prints from the Private Collection of Farah Pahlavi, Her Imperial Majesty, the Shahbanou of Iran (with catalog), Negarestan Mus, Tehran, 76; Drawings by 14 Young American Artists (with catalog), Galerie Litho, Tehran, 76; Nature: 12 Americans (with catalog), Iran-Am Soc, Tehran, 78; Cubist Prints-Cubist Books (with catalog), Franklin Furnace, New York, 83; Illuminating Color, Pratt Manhattan Ctr (with catalog), New York, 85; Products and Promotion (with catalog), San Francisco Camerawork, 86; Sam Francis Works on Paper: 1953-1986, The Ranchito Collection, The Branstater Gallery Loma Linda Univ, Riverside, 87; LIBRI CUBISTI (with catalog), Museo CIVICO, SIENA, 88; The Private Work of Public Artists, Plaza Gallery, Security Pac Bank, Los Angeles, 89; Cotemporary Illustrated Books: Words and Image 67-88 (with catalog), Independent Cur Inc, New York, 90; The Berlin Wall, Raleigh Interprises, Los Angeles, 90; 10 Sculptors of the New York Sch (with catalog), Manny Silverman Gallery, Los Angeles, 91-92; Judy Dater Cycles (with catalog), Matsuya Dept Store, Ginza, Pac Press Serv, Tokyo, 92. *Pos:* Registr, Pasadena Art Mus, 64; asst cur dept prints & illus bks, Mus Mod Art, 66-72; cur, RCA Corp Collection, 73-75; consult mod art & mus, Spec Bureau of Her Imperial Majesty, the Shahbanou of Iran, 75-77; consult/archivist, 1 Universal Ltd Art Ed, West Ilsip, NY, 78-81. *Teaching:* Adj fac hist of prints, New Sch Social Res, New York, 73-75; fac contemp art, NY Univ, 74-75. *Awards:* Nat Endowment Fel, 72-73; French Govt Grant, summer 80; Nat Endowment Arts Design Arts, 83. *Mem:* Col Art Asn; Art Table. *Res:* Late 19th and 20th century art, architecture, prints and photography. *Publ:* Auth, Women Artist in the Avant Garde: 1919-1935, 84, Jean Helion: Abstraction into Figuration 1934-1948, 85 & Towards the Restructuring of the Universe: One View of the 1920's, NY 86, Rachel Adler Gallery; Joan Mitchell, Spanning Thirty years, Manny Silverman Gallery, 88; Recent Large Scale

Sculpture, Bret Price, Santa Ana Mod Mus Art, 89; Arthur Secunda, Galerie Int, Bloomfield Hills, Mich, 92; Lyrik Kabinet, Vincent Fitgerald & Co: A Catalogue Raisonne of the First Ten Years, Munich & Franklin Furnace, NY 92; and others; Auth, Women Artist in the Avant Garde: 1919-1935, 84, Jean Helion: Abstraction into Figuration 1934-1948, 85 & Towards the Restructuring of the Universe: One View of the 1920's, NY, 86, Rachel Adler Gallery; Joan Mitchell, Spanning Thirty years, Manny Silverman Gallery, 88; Recent Large Scale Sculpture, Bret Price, Santa Ana Mod Mus Art, 89; Arthur Secunda, Galerie Int, Bloomfield Hills, Mich, 92. *Mailing Add:* 926 S Highland Ave Los Angeles CA 90036

STEIN, FRITZ HENRY
DEALER
b New York, NY, July 25, 32. *Study:* Univ RI, BA; New York Sch Interior Design; also with Harve Stein & Murray Kupferman. *Pos:* Art dir, G Fox Co, Hartford, Conn, 55-60; co-owner, Constitution Galleries, West Hartford, Conn & Gloucester, Mass, 60-63; interior designer, Silberman's of Norwich, Conn, 63-71; owner, Stone Ledge Studio Art Galleries, Noank, Conn, 71- *Mem:* Noank Hist Soc, Conn (dir); Mystic Art Asn, Conn (dir & pres, 83-86). *Specialty:* Eighteenth and nineteenth century collectors gallery; contemporary American artists. *Mailing Add:* 59 High St Mystic CT 06355

STEIN, HARVE
PAINTER, ILLUSTRATOR
b Chicago, Ill, Apr 23, 04. *Study:* Art Inst Chicago, 22-26; Julian Acad, Paris, France, 27; Art Students League, 30-33; and with Harvey Dunn & Jacques Maroger. *Work:* US State Dept; Univ Minn; Soc Illusrs Mus; Pub Arch, Toronto; Norwich Art Mus, Conn; and others. *Exhib:* Nat Watercolor Exhibs throughout US. *Pos:* Restorer, Stone Ledge Studio Art Galleries, Noank, Conn, 63- *Teaching:* Prof fine art, RI Sch Design, 44-69, emer prof, 69-; instr painting, Conn Col, 46, 47 & 51; instr, New London Art Students League, 48-59; Mitchell Col, summer sessions, 55-56. *Awards:* Providence Watercolor Club Award, 56; New Haven Paint & Clay Club, 57; Providence Art Club, 63; plus others. *Mem:* Hon life mem Soc Illustrators; life mem Am Watercolor Soc; life mem Art Asn Mystic, Conn; Appraisers Asn Am; and others. *Media:* Watercolor. *Publ:* Illusr, many bks; contribr, nat mags; auth, Illustrator explains, Am Artist Mag, 58. *Mailing Add:* PO Box 9237 59 High St Noank CT 06340

STEIN, JUDITH ELLEN
HISTORIAN, CURATOR
b New York, NY, June 27, 43. *Study:* Barnard Col, Columbia Univ, BA(art hist), 65; Univ Pa, MA(art hist), 67, PhD(art hist), 81. *Collections Arranged:* Red Grooms: A Retrospective, 1956-1984, (auth, catalog), 85; Betye Saar: Sentimental Sojourn, 87; The Figurative Fifties: New York Figurative Expressionism, (auth catalog), 87. *Pos:* Staff lectr, Philadelphia Mus Art, 66-71; arts reviewer, Art in Am, 74-86 & Nat Pub Radio, Philadelphia, 79-83; coordr, Morris Gallery, Pa Acad Fine Arts, 81-; asst cur, Pa Acad Fine Arts, 83-85, assoc cur, 85- *Teaching:* Instr, Tyler Sch Art, Philadelphia, 71-78; Univ PA, 80. *Mem:* Col Art Asn; Int Art Critics Asn; Women's Caucus Art (nat adv bd, 79-81). *Publ:* Auth, Lester Johnson: The Likeness of Things Unlike, New York Gallery Press Ltd, 87; Collecting the art of the times, In: Searching Out the Best, Penn Acad Fine Arts, 88; Making Their Mark: Women Artists Move Into the Mainstream 1970-1985, Abbeville, 89. *Mailing Add:* 2400 Waverly St Philadelphia PA 19146

STEIN, LEWIS
PHOTOGRAPHER, CONCEPTUAL ARTIST
b New York, NY. *Study:* Mass Inst Technol, 64-66; Univ Calif, Berkeley, 66-68. *Work:* Mus de Stadt, Aachen, Ger; Greenville Mus Art, SC; Ludwig Mus, Cologne, Ger; Yale Univ Art Mus, New Haven, Conn; Univ Art Mus, Berkeley, Calif. *Exhib:* Whitney Biennial, Whitney Mus Am Art, New York, NY, 69. *Bibliog:* Pratt J Archit, 88. *Media:* Photography, Sculpture. *Mailing Add:* 450 Broome St New York NY 10013

STEIN, LUDWIG
PAINTER, EDUCATOR
b Wyoming, Del, Mar 20, 38. *Study:* Kutztown State Col, BFA, 64; Tyler Sch Art, with Steve Green, David Pease & Charles Schmitt, MFA, 69. *Work:* Sheldon Mem Gallery Art, Univ Nebr, Lincoln; Everson Mus Art, Syracuse, NY; Philadelphia Mus Art; Univ Belfast, Ireland; Long Beach Art Found, NJ. *Exhib:* One-man shows, Barbara Gillman, Miami, Fla, 86, Adele M Gallery, Dallas, Tex, 86, John Christian Gallery, New York, 86, Basel Art Fair, Switz, 87, Schoeneck Gallery, Basel, Switz, 90; and many others. *Teaching:* Instr, Wis State Univ, Eau Claire, 69-71; Univ Calif, Northridge, 71-72; prof, Syracuse Univ, NY, 72- *Awards:* Best Show, Waterloo Regional, Iowa, 71; Jurors Award, Tyler Alumni, 76; Grant, Northern British Arts Coun, 77. *Mem:* Col Art Asn. *Media:* Oil. *Mailing Add:* c/o Barbara Gilman Gallery 3898 Biscayne Blvd Miami FL 33137

STEIN, ROGER BREED
HISTORIAN, EDUCATOR
b Orange, NJ, Mar 29, 32. *Study:* Harvard Univ, AB, 54, AM, 58, PhD, 60. *Collections Arranged:* Susquehanna: Images of the Settled Landscape (with catalog), Roberson Ctr, Binghampton, NY; Seascape & American Imagination (with catalog), Whitney Mus of Am Art; Susquehanna: Images of the Settled Landscape (with catalog), Roberson Ctr, Binghamton, NY. *Teaching:* Assoc prof & prof, State Univ NY, Binghamton, 70-86; Sr Fulbright lectr, Gt Brit, 76-77; prof art hist, Univ Va, 86- *Awards:* Prize in Humanities, Am Acad Arts & Sci, 60; Guggenheim Fel, 68-69; Smithsonian Fel, Nat Collection Fine Arts, 77-78; Dan Walker Prize, Western Lit Asn, 85. *Mem:* Am Studies Asn; Mod Lang Asn; Col Art Asn. *Res:* 17-19th Century American painting and art in its cultural context; Winslow Homer; interpretive strategies in museum exhibitions; regional approaches to American art, literature and culture. *Publ:* Auth, John Ruskin & American Aesthetic Thought, 1840-1900, 67; Copley's Watson and the Shark and Aesthetics in the 1770's, Discoveries and Considerations, State Univ NY Press, 76; Charles Willson Peale's expressive design, Prospects, No 6, 81; Thomas Smith's self-portrait: image/text as artifact, Art J, No 44, 84; Packaging the Great Plains: the role of the visual arts, Great Plains Quart, No 5, winter 85. *Mailing Add:* Fayerweather Hall, McIntire Dept Art Univ Va Charlottesville VA 22903

STEIN, RONALD JAY
PAINTER, SCULPTOR
b New York, NY, Sept 15, 30. *Study:* Cooper Union, cert fine art, with Will Barnet; Yale Univ, with Joseph Albers, BFA; Rutgers Univ, MFA. *Work:* Carnegie Inst, Pittsburgh, Pa; Guggenheim Mus, New York; Joseph H Hirshhorn Collection, Washington, DC; Wadsworth Atheneum, Hartford, Conn; Finch Col Mus, New York. *Comn:* Mosaic murals (with Lee Krasner Pollock), Uris Bros, New York, 58; sculpture, Playboy Mag; sculpture, Debeers Ltd, 70; Am Cyanamid; Ford Corp; and others. *Exhib:* Art Inst Chicago Int, 60; one-man shows, Marlborough Gallery, London, Eng, 67, Irving Gallery, Milwaukee, 71 & Hokin Gallery, Palm Beach, Fla, 73; Art in the Mirror, Mus Mod Art, New York, 70; Finch Col Mus Art, 73; Hokin Gallery, Palm Beach, Fla, 74; Bologna & Landi Gallery, East Hampton, NY, 83; Bensen Gallery, Bridgehampton, NY, 88; Benton Gallery, Southampton, NY, 88 & 89; and others. *Bibliog:* Interview, Long Island Originals (TV prog, channel 21), NY, 88; article, New York Newsday, Long Island, NY, 88; article & cover, Dans, Long Island, NY, 88. *Media:* All. *Dealer:* Marlborough Gallery 40 W 57th St New York NY 10019; Benton Gallery Southampton NY. *Mailing Add:* 836 Fireplace Rd East Hampton NY 11937

STEINBACH, HAIM
SCULPTOR, CONCEPTUAL ARTIST
b Israel, Feb 25, 44; US citizen. *Study:* Pratt Inst, BA, 68; Yale Univ, MFA, 73. *Work:* Mus Contemp Art, Chicago, Ill; Los Angeles Co Mus Art, Calif; Israel Mus, Jerusalem; Centre Georges Pompidou, Paris, France; Milwaukee Art Mus, Wis. *Comn:* Coat of Arms, mixed media construct, Gruppo GFT, Torino, Italy, 88. *Exhib:* Brokerage of Desire, Otis Art Inst, Los Angeles, 86; Les Courtiers du Desir, Centre Georges Pompidou, Paris, 87; Documenta 8, Kassel, W Ger, 87; one-man show, Cape Mus D'Art Contemporain, Bordeaux, 88; Binational, Mus Fine Arts, Boston & Kunsthalle, Dusseldorf, W Ger, 88. *Teaching:* Instr, Middlebury Col, 73-77 & Cornell Univ, 77-80. *Awards:* CAPS Award, NY State Coun on the Arts, 83. *Bibliog:* Germano Celant (auth), Haim Steinbach's Wild Wild Wild West, Artforum, 87; John Miller (auth), The Consumption of everyday life, Artscribe, 88; Holland Cotter (auth), Haim Steinbach shelf life, Art in Am, 88. *Media:* Mixed. *Dealer:* Sonnabend Gallery 420 W Broadway New York NY 11222; Jay Gorney Modern Art 100 Greene St New York NY 10012. *Mailing Add:* 85 Quay St No 3A Brooklyn NY 11222

STEINBAUM, BERNICE
DEALER
b Flushing, NY, Jan 3, 41. *Study:* Queens Col, BA, 61; Hofstra Univ, MA, 69. *Pos:* Pres, BFM Gallery, New York, 77-81; pres, P M & Stein Gallery, New York, 81- *Teaching:* Instr fine arts, Hofstra Univ, 69-71 & Farmingdale Univ, 71-77. *Awards:* Entreprenurial Woman of the Year, Nat Orgn Women, 88. *Specialty:* American contemporary painters and sculptures. *Mailing Add:* Bernice Steinbaum Gallery 132 Greene New York NY 10012

STEINBERG, LEO
EDUCATOR, HISTORIAN
b Moscow, USSR, July 9, 20; US citizen. *Study:* Slade Sch Art, Univ London, dipl(fine arts), 40; Inst Fine Arts, NY Univ, PhD, 60; Philadelphia Col Art, Hon Dr, 81; Parsons Sch Design, Hon Dr, 86; Mass Col Art, Hon Dr, 87. *Teaching:* Prof art hist, Hunter Col & Grad Ctr City Univ New York, 61-75, Univ Pa, 75-91, prof emer, 91- *Awards:* Am Acad Arts & Sci fel, 78; Univ Col fel, London, 79; Award in Literature, Am Acad & Inst Arts & Letters, 83; Mather Award for Art Criticism, 84; MacArthur Found Fel, 86. *Publ:* Auth, Other Criteria, 72; Michelangelo's last judgment as merciful heresy, Art in Am, 11-12/75; Resisting Cezanne: Picasso's three women, Art in Am, 11-12/78; The Line of Fate in Michelangelo's Painting, Critical Inquiry 6, spring 80; A Corner of the Last Judgment, Daedalus, spring 80; The sexuality of Christ in Renaissance Art & in Mod Oblivion, 83. *Mailing Add:* Dept Art Hist Univ Pa Philadelphia PA 19174

STEINBERG, RUBIN
COLLAGE ARTIST
b Chicago, Ill, May 31, 34; US citizen. *Study:* Chicago Teachers Col, BE, 52-57; Art Inst Chicago, MFA, 52- 68; Roosevelt Univ, ME, 60-61; IIT, Inst Design, 59-60. *Work:* Southern Ohio Mus, Portsmouth; Ill State Mus, Springfield; Spertus Mus Judaica, Chicago, Ill; McDonalds Corp, Oakbrook, Ill; Borg Warner, Chicago, Ill. *Comn:* Sudler & Co, Chicago, Ill, 65; Malow Cordage Corp, Irving Malow, Mt Prospect, Ill, 68; Madison Steel Co, L A Morgan, Skokie, Ill, 70-75. *Exhib:* Old Orchard Art Festival, North Shore Art League, 71, 91 & 92; Art Inst Chicago, Chicago & Vicinity Show, 68-73; Midwest Craft Festival, North Shore Art League, 74, 78, 86; Oak Brook Crafts Exhib, 79, 80, 91 & 92; Mask, Southern Ohio Mus, Portsmouth, 83; Chicago Soc Artists Reprospective, Mus Science & Industry, 83; one-man shows, Bernard Horwich Jewish Community Ctr, Chicago, 4 Arts Assoc, Evanston, One Ill Ctr, Chicago, Monroe Gallery, Chicago, Oak Park Libr,

Park Forest Art Ctr, Northbrook Racquet Club No 2, and many more; ARC Gallery, Chicago, Ill, and many more. *Awards:* First Prize, Am Jewish Art Club, 79. *Bibliog:* Diana Liu (auth), Rubin Steinberg, New Art Examiner, 79; Michael Karzen (auth), Rubin Steinberg One of Chicago Finest, Sch Art Mag, 87; Laura Nilges-Matias (auth), Artist Uses Bits, Pieces in a Big Way, Pulitzer-Lerner Newspaper, 4/6/88. *Mem:* Chicago Soc Artists (bd dir, 78-88); Am Jewish Art Club (bd dir, 78-90); Chicago Artists Coalition. *Media:* Collage, Acrylic Painted Sculptural Weaving. *Publ:* Auth, The art of mosaic masks, 87, Repousse - metal embossing, 88, Janus Masks - a metal sandwich, 89, Applique Owls - and a few other birds, 89, Dreaming Transformed, 90, Arts & Activities. *Mailing Add:* 3127 W Jerome Ave Chicago IL 60645

STEINBERG, SAUL
CARTOONIST
b Ramnicul-Sarat, Bucharest, Rumania, June 15, 14, US citizen. *Study:* Univ Bucharest, 32; Polytechnic Sch Milan, 40. *Work:* Metrop Mus Art, Mus Mod Art, New York; Baltimore Mus Art; Albright-Knox Art Gallery, Buffalo, NY; Fogg Mus, Harvard Univ, Cambridge, Mass; Victoria & Albert Mus, London; and many others. *Comn:* Mural, Terrace Plaza Hotel, Cincinnati, Ohio, 48. *Exhib:* Solo exhibs, Columbus Mus Art, Ohio, 86, Pace Gallery, New York, 87 & 91, Stadt Nurnberg Kunsthalle,, Ger, 88, Galerie Adrien Maeght, Paris, 88, Galleria Seno, Milan, 90, Tables and Works on Paper, John Berggruen Gallery, San Francisco, 90 & Western Drawings, Blum Helman, Santa Monica, 91; 20th century collage, Margo Leavin Gallery, Los Angeles, 91; The Art Show, Seventh Regiment Armory, New York, 91; Le Cabinet des dessins, Fondation Maeght, St Paul de Vence, 91; Aspects of Collage, Guild Hall Mus, East Hampton, New York, 91; Selected Works on Paper, O'Hara Gallery, New York, 91; and many other one-man & group exhibs. *Pos:* Cartoons, Bertoldo, Milan, 36-39; staff, New Yorker, formerly. *Teaching:* Artist-in-residence, Smithsonian Inst, Washington, DC, 67. *Bibliog:* John Gruen (auth), The Party's Over Now, Viking Press, New York, 77; Samuel Green (auth), American Art: an Historical Survey, Ronald Press, New York, 77; Karin Lipson (auth), A show inspired by 100th birthday, Newsday, 12/20/85; John Updike (auth), The Complete Book of Covers from the New Yorker: 1925-1989, Alfred A Knopf, New York, 89; Ian Frazier & Saul Steinberg (auths), Canal Street, Libr Fels, Whitney Mus Am Art, New York, 90; and many others. *Mem:* Am Acad & Inst Arts & Letts. *Publ:* Illusr, Cartoons published in Sombra, Brazil, Cascabel, Argentina & Settebello, Italy; auth, All in Line, The Art of Living & The Passport, New York, 45; auth, Steinberg Dessins, Paris, 55; coauth, Anti-Photographer Masks, In: Creative Camera, London, 2/69; Auth, The Inspector, Viking Press, 73. *Dealer:* Sidney Janis Gallery 6 W 57 St New York NY 10019; Pace Gallery 32 E 57th St New York NY 10022. *Mailing Add:* c/o The New Yorker 25 W 43rd St New York NY 10036

STEINER, MICHAEL
SCULPTOR, PAINTER
b New York, NY, 1945. *Work:* Storm King Art Ctr; Boston Mus Fine Arts; Mus Mod Art; Solomon R Guggenheim Mus; Denver Art Mus; Mass Inst Technol Mus; Edmonton Art Gallery; Walker Art Ctr; Musee d'Art Moderne et d'Art Contemp. *Exhib:* Whitney Mus Am Art, 70 & 72; Edmonton Art Gallery, Alta, 72; solo exhib, Andre Emmerich Galleries, 75-87, Martha White Gallery, Louisville, Ky, 83, Meredith Long & Co, Houston, Tex, 85, Galerie Elca London, Montreal, Que, 83, Douglas Drake Gallery, Kansas City, 85, Salander-O'Reilly Galleries, New York, 90 & Helander Gallery, Palm Beach, Fla, 90; Mus Contemp Art, Chicago, Ill, 85; Sierra Nevada Mus Art, Reno, 86; Meredith Long & Co, Houston, Tex, 89; Bruce Mus, Greenwich, Conn, 89; Security Pacific Gallery, Costa Mesa, Calif, 89; Steven Scott Gallery, Baltimore, Md, 90; Univ Mich Art Mus, 90; and many others. *Teaching:* Instr, Emma Lake Workshop, Univ Sask, Regina, 69; vis artist, Cranbrook Art Inst, Bloomfield Heights, Mich, 69. *Awards:* Guggenheim Award, 71. *Bibliog:* Anthony Haden-Guest (auth), Alternate States: City & Country Addresses of Michael & Phyllis Steinen, Architectural Digest, 7/86; Susan Gill (auth), Michael Steiner at Andre Emmerich, Artnews, 11/87; Ann E Berman (auth), Sculptors - in Progress, Town & Country, 9/87. *Media:* Steel, Aluminum. *Dealer:* Salander-O'Reilly 20 E 79th St New York NY 10021. *Mailing Add:* 704 Broadway New York NY 10003

STEINER, PAUL
WRITER, CRITIC
b Ger; US citizen. *Study:* NY Univ, BS. *Work:* Calif Mus Photogr. *Exhib:* Reinhold & Brown, New York; Karl Junghans & Galerie Michael Schultz, Berlin; multiples show, Frankfort, Berlin, Switzerland, Japan, Canada, 90. *Pos:* Assoc ed, Esquire, Inc, 47-52; feature writer & columnist, NAm Newspaper Alliance, Women's News Serv, 60-80; writer, Pop Scene Serv (syndicated rev of New York mus exhibs), 67-72; contrib ed, Nat Jeweller, 76, 77 & 78; columnist, Murray Hill News, 77-79, New York Entertainer, 79-82, Stagebill, 81-, Artspeak, 81-, TV Today, 82-83, Jewish J, 83-86, Reuters, 83-, New York Sunday News, 84-, USA Today, 84-, Cable TV World, 84-, Theater Week, 87-, Cover Arts & Jewish Herald, Greenwich Village News, 92-; corresp, New York Post, 77-82, New York Mag, Star Mag, US Mag, 78-, People Mag, New York Daily News, 81-, Omni, 81-, Broadway Mag, 85-86 & Metrop Home, 91; contrib ed, Metro Jewish Life, Show Illus, 81-83; NY Business News, 89-. *Awards:* Columnist Award, 69 & Press Award, 70, Book Author Award, 91, Beaux Arts Soc NY; Int Press Award, New York, 81; World Culture Prize, Italy Centro Studi Recherche dell Nazione, 85. *Publ:* Auth of 17 books; interviews with Chagall, Warhol, LeRoy Neiman & O'Keefe, Artspeak, 81. *Mailing Add:* 161 West 54th St New York NY 10019

STEINFELS, MELVILLE P
PAINTER, DESIGNER
b Salt Lake City, Utah, Nov 3, 10. *Study:* Art Inst Chicago; Chicago Sch Design. *Work:* Murals (buon fresco, fresco secco, mosaic, ceramic tile), Church of the Epiphany, Chicago, Loyola Univ, Chicago, Our Lady of Sorrows Church, Farmington, Mich, Newman Club, Ann Arbor, Mich, St Mary Magdalen Church, Melvindale, Mich & many others. *Comn:* Mosaic murals, All Saints Mausoleum, Des Plaines, Ill, Resurrection Mausoleum, Justice, Ill & Queen of Heaven Mausoleum, Hillside, Ill; ceramic tile, Crucifixion Mausoleum, Hillside, Ill, 81. *Pos:* Retired. *Teaching:* Resident artist, Siena Heights Col, 45-50; instr drawing, painting & design. *Publ:* Illusr, Monthly Missalette (covers), J S Paluch Co Inc, 81-85. *Mailing Add:* 332 Talcott Pl Park Ridge IL 60068

STEINHARDT, ALICE
PAINTER, PHOTOGRAPHER
b New York, NY, Feb 9, 50. *Study:* Univ Miami, Coral Gables, BA, 72; Int Ctr Photog, New York, 75. *Work:* Ctr Creative Photog, Tucson; Corcoran Gallery Art; Los Angeles Co Mus Art. *Exhib:* Recent Acquisitions, Corcoran Gallery Art, 80; solo exhib, G Ray Hawkins Gallery, Los Angeles, 80 & 84, Photog Gallery, La Jolla, 82 & Light Gallery, New York, 84; California Colour, Photogr Gallery, London, 81; Color Photography, Brown Univ Mus, 84. *Awards:* Purchase Prize, LaGrange III, 77. *Bibliog:* Article, Photo Bulletin, 80. *Mem:* Friends Photog; Los Angeles Ctr Photog Studies. *Media:* Oil on Silver Print. *Mailing Add:* 69 McKeen St Brunswick ME 04011

STEINHOFF, MONIKA
PAINTER, PRINTMAKER
b Swinemuende, Ger, Oct 19, 41. *Study:* Univ Calif, Los Angeles, BA, 64, MA, 66; Univ Calif, Berkeley, 69. *Work:* Smithsonian Inst, Washington, DC; IBM, New York, NY. *Comn:* Portrait, David Wynne Family, NMex, 83; poster paintings, Plaza Hotel, Las Vegas, NMex, 85, Strater Hotel, Durango, Colo, 85 & Cloudcroft Lodge, NMex, 86; interior painting, comn by Julian Heldman, 86; Denillos Garden, comn by Don Meredith; family portrait, comn by Eugene Talbert, Tyler, Tex. *Exhib:* Mus Cincinnati, Ohio, 61; Mus Albuquerque, NMex, 78; Fine Arts Mus, Santa Fe, NMex, 84; Governors Gallery, Santa Fe, NMex, 86; one-person shows, Dewey Gallery, 87, Zaplin-Lampert Gallery, Santa Fe, 88, Edith Lambert, 90, Peyton-Wright, 91 & Gallerie Jakob Kohnert, Berlin, Ger, 92; Fine Arts Mus Southwest, 90. *Teaching:* Instr, Col Santa Fe & Univ Calif, Berkeley, formerly. *Media:* Egg Tempera; Aquatint. *Dealer:* Brandywine Galleries Inc Morningside Albuquerque NM; Robertson Gallery Beverly Hills CA. *Mailing Add:* 1298 Lejano Lane Santa Fe NM 87501

STEINHOUSE, TOBIE (THELMA)
PAINTER, PRINTMAKER
b Montreal, Que. *Study:* Sir George Williams Univ; Art Students League, with Morris Kantor & Harry Sternberg, 46-47; Ecole Beaux-Arts, Paris; Atelier 17, Paris, France, with W S Hayter, 61-62. *Work:* Nat Gallery Can, Ottawa; Montreal Mus Fine Arts, PQ; Confederation Art Gallery, Charlottetown, PEI; Ministry of External Affairs of Can, Moscow Embassy, USSR; McMichael Conserv Collection, Kleinburg, Ont. *Comn:* Ed 250 prints, Carousel, Heuga Co, 81; ed 110 prints, Paysage de Rue, Sheraton Hotel, 82; ed 75 prints, Pastorale Québecoise, Int Conf Opthamology-Sherbrooke, Que. *Exhib:* Solo exhibs, Galerie Lara Vincy, France, 57, Montreal Mus Fine Arts, 59, 63 & 78, Galerie du Parc, Trois-Rivières, 83, 92, L'Éuivoue Gallery, Ottawa, 80, 86, 90 & Gallery Arts Sutton, Que, 91; Montreal Mus Fine Arts, 59 & 63; 2nd Int Biennial Engraving, Santiago, Chile, 65; 1st & 3rd Brit Int Print Biennial, Bradford, Eng, 68 & 72; 9th Int Biennial Art, Menton, France, 72; 50 Year Retrospective of Atelier 17, Elvehem Art Centre, Wis, 77; Biennial de Grabado de America, Venezuela, 82; Museo de la Estampa, Mex, 92; and others. *Awards:* Sterling Trust Award, Soc Can Painter-Etchers & Engravers, 63; Jessie Dow First Prize Award, Montreal Mus Fine Arts, 63; Govt Can Centennial Medal of Honor, 67; and others. *Bibliog:* Guy Viau (auth), La Peinture Moderne au Canada Francais, Ministere Affaires Cult, PQ, 64; Guy Robert (auth), Ecole de Montreal, Collection Artistes Can, 65; V Nixon (auth), Tobie Steinhouse-artist, Vie des Arts Mag, summer 72; L'Estampe Originale au Québec - 1980-1990, Bibliotheque National du Québec, 91; and others. *Mem:* Royal Can Acad Arts; Can Group Painters (pres, 66-68); L'Atelier Libre Recherches Graphique; Soc Can Painter-Etchers & Engravers; life mem Art Students' League; and others. *Media:* Oils & Watercolours; Etching & Engraving. *Publ:* Songes et Limiére, portfolio of eight prints, La Guilde Graphique, Montreal, Que, 72; Into my Green World, portfolio of six prints, La Guilde Graphique, 75; and many other editions of prints, 70-92. *Dealer:* La Guilde Graphique 9 St Paul St W Montreal PQ H2Y 1Y6 Can; Galerie L'autre Equivoque 333 Cumberland Ottawa Can K1N 7J3. *Mailing Add:* 208 Cote St Antoine Rd Montreal PQ H3Y 2J3 Canada

STEINKE, BETTINA
PAINTER
b Biddeford, Maine, June 25, 13. *Study:* Fawcett Art Inst, Newark, NJ; Cooper Union, New York; Phoenix Art Inst, New York. *Work:* Nat Cowboy Hall of Fame & Western Heritage, Oklahoma City; Ft Worth Mus, Tex; Gilcrease Mus, Tulsa, Okla; Philbrook Mus, Tulsa; also in pvt collections in US & abroad. *Comn:* 54 yrs of Portraits of Wellknown People. *Exhib:* One-man shows, Well Known Personalities, Eskimo, Winnipeg, 56, Portraits Around US, Oklahoma City, 68 & Palm Springs Desert Mus, 78; Watercolor Show, Curacao, Neth, 47; two-man show, O'Brien's Art Emporium, Scottsdale, Ariz, 75; one-man retrospective & sales, Gilcrease Mus, Tulsa, Okla, 87. *Teaching:* Workshops at Scottsdale Artists Sch, Portraits & Heads. *Awards:* Silver Medals for Drawing, 74 & 76 & Prix de West, 78, Nat Acad

Western Art; Artist of Year Award, Tucson Festival Soc, Ariz, 80; Gold Medal Draw, 84. *Bibliog:* Fred Whitaker (auth), Painter of people, Am Artist, 1/71; Don Hedgpeth (auth), Bettina, Portraying Life in Art, Northland Press, 78; and many others. *Mem:* Pastel Soc Am; Soc Illusr; Nat Acad Western Art. *Media:* Oil, Pastel. *Publ:* Illusr, NBC Symphony Orch, 37; illusr, articles, Lamp, 50-53; also illusr for var mags & bks. *Mailing Add:* 653 Canyon Rd Santa Fe NM 87501

STEINMETZ, GRACE ERNST TITUS
PAINTER
b Lancaster, Pa. *Study:* Pa Acad Fine Arts; Barnes Found; Millersville State Col, BS; Univ Pa, MS. *Work:* Univ Southern Fla, Lakeland; Franklin & Marshall Col; Elizabethtown Col, Pa; Millersville State Col, Pa; Lancaster Co Art Asn, Pa. *Exhib:* Knickerbocker Soc, 70; Nat Soc Painters Casein & Acrylis, 81 & 86; Audubon Artists, 81; Allied Artists Am, 81; Catherine Lorillard Wolfe, 85. *Teaching:* Assoc prof art hist, Elizabethtown Col, 64-65; adj prof oil painting, 69 & 73-74; instr, Lancaster Co Art Asn, 86-88. *Awards:* Best of Show, Lancaster Co Art Asn, 67 & 75; Award for Non-traditional Watercolor, Painters & Sculptors Soc NJ, 68; Grumbacher First Prize, Nat Soc Painters Casein & Acrylic, 69; Cash Award, Berks Art Alliance for Gilbert Commonwealth Engineers & Consultants, 83. *Mem:* Nat Soc Painters Casein & Acrylic; Echo Valley Art Group; fel Royal Soc Arts; fel Pa Acad Fine Arts; Lancaster Co Art Asn. *Media:* Casein, Oil. *Mailing Add:* 2115 James Buchanon Dr Elizabethtown PA 17022-3101

STEINWORTH, SKIP (WILLIAM EUGENE JR)
GRAPHIC ARTIST, PRINTMAKER
b St Paul, Minn, May 2, 50. *Study:* St Cloud State Univ, Minn, BA, 74, MA, 79. *Work:* Springfield Civic Collection, Ill; Plains Mus, Moorhead, Minn; Univ NDak, Grand Forks; Kemper Insurance Corp Collection, Chicago; City of Winter Park, Fla. *Exhib:* Red River Nat, Plains Mus, Moorhead, Minn, 80; 62nd Nat Exhib, George Walter Vincent Smith Mus, Springfield, Mass, 81; Chautaugua Nat Exhib Art, NY, 82; Works on Paper, Univ Wis, Superior, 82. *Awards:* Best of Show, Northern Lights, Lakewood Col, St Paul, Minn, 82; Best of Show, Plaza Art Festival, Kansas City, 88; Best of Show, Winter Park Arts Festival, Fla, 89. *Bibliog:* Betsy Goldman-Schein (auth), Skip Steinworth, Am Artist, 6/89. *Media:* Pencil. *Dealer:* Louis Newman Galleries 322 N Beverly Dr Beverly Hills CA 90210. *Mailing Add:* 1745 Dellwood Ave St Paul MN 55113

STEIR, PAT
PAINTER
b Newark, NJ, 1940. *Study:* Boston Univ, 60; Pratt Inst, 62. *Work:* Mus Mod Art, New York; Metrop Mus Art, New York; Walker Art Ctr, Minneapolis, Minn; Brooklyn Mus, NY; Tate Gallery, London. *Exhib:* Solo exhibs, Brooklyn Mus, NY, 84 & 92, Harcus Gallery, Boston, Mass, 86, Baltimore Mus Art, Md, 87, New Mus Contemp Art, NY, 87, Tate Gallery, London, 88, Musee d'Art Contemporain, Lyon, 90 & Nat Gallery Art, Washington, DC, 90; First Impressions (traveling exhib), Walker Art Ctr, Minneapolis, Minn, 89-90; Inconsolable, Louver Gallery, NY, 90; Some Seventies Works, Robert Miller Gallery, NY, 90; Contemp Prints & Multiples, Norah Haime Gallery, NY, 90; Twenty Years of Landfall Press, Landfall Press, Chicago, Ill, 90; 3 person installation shows, Le Magazine, Grenoble, Switz, 90; Installations, Ecole Des Beaux Arts, Tourcoing, France, 90; Le Diaphane, Musee des Beaux-Arts, Tourcoing, France, 90-91. *Awards:* Nat Endowment Arts, 74; Fel Guggenheim, 82. *Bibliog:* John Howell (auth), A Bloom of One's Own, Elle Mag, 2/88; Pat McCoy (auth), Pat Steir: Knoedler, Artscribe, 2/88; Michael Kimmelman (auth), This American in Paris kept True to New York, New York Times, 4/17/88. *Mailing Add:* 81 Wooster St New York NY 10012

STELLA, FRANK
PAINTER
b Malden, Mass, May 12, 36. *Study:* Phillips Acad, with Patrick Morgan; Princeton Univ, with William Seitz & Stephen Greene; Princeton Univ, Hon DA, 84; Dartmouth Col, Hanover, NH, hon degree, 85. *Work:* Mus Mod Art; Whitney Mus Am Art; San Francisco Mus Art; Albright-Knox Art Gallery, Buffalo, NY; Walker Art Ctr, Minneapolis, Minn; Hirshhorn Mus & Sculpture, Washington, DC; Moderna Museet, Stockholm, Sweden; Kitakyushu Munic Mus, Japan; and many others. *Exhib:* 30th Biennial of Contemporary American Painting, Corcoran Gallery Art, Washington, DC, 66; American Abstract Painting: Selections from the Whitney Mus Collection, Whitney Mus Am Art, New York, 75; Second American Exhibition, Art Inst Chicago, Ill, 76; Acquisition Priorities: Aspects of Postwar Painting in America, Solomon R Guggenheim Mus, New York, 76; American Painting of the 1970's, Albright-Knox Art Gallery, Buffalo, 78; Selections from the Meyerhoff Collection, Baltimore Mus Art, MD, 78; Stella Since 1970, Ft Worth Art Mus, Tex, 78; 73rd American Exhibition, Art Inst Chicago, IL, 79; Emergence and Progression, Milwaukee Art Ctr, 79; Biennial Exhibition, Whitney Mus Am Art, New York, 79; Morton G Newmann Family Collection, Nat Gallery Art, Washington, DC, 80; 37th Annual Exhibition of Contemporary Art American Painting (catalog), Corcoran Gallery Art, Washington, DC, 81; The New York School: Four Decades Guggenheim Museum Collection, Major Loans, Solomon R Guggenheim Mus, New York, 82; Changes, Aldrich Mus Contemp Art, Ridgefield, Conn, 83; Selections from the Twentieth Century Art Collection, Los Angeles County Mus Art, Calif, 83; solo exhibs, Frank Stella "The Waves' 1985-88, Akira Ikeda Gallery, Nagoya, Japan, 89, Frank Stella: Les annees 80, Galerie Beaubourg, Paris, 90, Frank Stella, Galerie Jamileh Weber, Zurich, 90, Frank Stella, 65 Thompson St, New York, 90-91, Frank Stella, Casino Knokke, Belg, 91, Frank Stella, Galerie Daniel Tempon, Paris, 91, Frank Stella 1958-1990, Kawamura Mem Mus Art, Japan, 91; Seven Master Printmakers: Innovations in the Eighties, Mus Mod Art, New York, 91; Selection, Musee d'Art Contemporain Fondation Asher Edelman, Lausanne, Switz, 91; La Sculpture Contemporaine apres 1970, Fondation Daniel Templon Musee Temporaire, Frejus, France, 91; Selections from the Lannan Foundation Collection - Abstraction, Lannan Found, Los Angeles, 91. *Awards:* Charles Eliot Norton Professorship of Poetry, Harvard Univ, Cambridge, Mass, 83-84; NY Univ Resident Fel, Soc Fels; Award Am Art, Pa Acad Fine Arts, Philadelphia, 10/25/85. *Bibliog:* Philip Leider (auth), Shakespearean Fish, Art Am, 10/90; Jillen Lowe (auth), Modern Master, Dutchess, 11-12/91; Michael Kimmelman (auth), Frank Stella Crosses the Sculpture Threshold, NY Times, 10/16/92. *Mem:* Coun US and Italy. *Publ:* Auth, On Caravaggio, NY Times Mag, 2/3/85; Working Space, Harvard Univ Press, 86. *Dealer:* Knoedler & Co 19 E 70th St New York NY 10021; Leo Castelli Gallery 420 W Broadway New York NY 10012. *Mailing Add:* M Knoedler & Co Inc 19 E 70th St New York NY 10021

STELZER, MICHAEL NORMAN
SCULPTOR, INSTRUCTOR
b Brooklyn, NY, Jan 6, 38. *Study:* Pratt Inst, 56; Art Students League, 60-62; Nat Acad Sch Fine Arts, Edward Mooney traveling scholar, 66 & Nat Sculpture Soc Joseph Nicolosi grant, 67; and with Nathaniel Choate, 64, Michael Lantz, 64-67 & Donald DeLue, 68 & 69. *Comn:* 12 ft relief, Worchester Polytech Inst, 64. *Exhib:* Am Artists Prof League Grand Nat, 63, 76 & 77; Nat Arts Club, 63-64; Nat Acad Design, 64-67, 70-71 & 74-77; Allied Artists Am, 67 & 71-81; Nat Sculpture Soc Ann Exhib, 68-81. *Teaching:* Instr sculpture, Fashion Inst Technol, New York, 79. *Awards:* Helen Foster Barnett Prize, Nat Acad Design, 66; Gold Medal, Hudson Valley Art Asn, 76; Gold Medal, Grand Nat Exhib, Am Artists Pro Prof League, 76; Allied Artists Am Award, 81; Hudson Valley Art Asn Award, 85. *Bibliog:* Article in, Pen & Brush, 66; Opportunities offered the young sculptor, 67 & Interpreting the human figure, 68, Nat Sculpture Rev. *Mem:* Nat Sculpture Soc; Hudson Valley Art Asn; Allied Artists Am; Am Artists Prof League. *Mailing Add:* 8 Everit St Brooklyn NY 11201

STEPHANSON, LORAINE ANN
PAINTER
b Edmonton, Alta, Apr 19, 50. *Study:* Univ Alta, BED & MVA, 78; Univ Sask, Emma Lake Wkshps with Friedl Dzubas, John Elderfield & Kenworth Moffett, 79-80; Triangle Wkshp, New York, wtih Larry Poons & Michael Fried, 86. *Work:* Univ Alta, Edmonton; Prov of BC Collection; Air Canada, Montreal; Royal Trust, Vancouver; Triangle Trust, New York. *Exhib:* Solo exhib, University Art Gallery & Mus, Edmonton, 78; Nat Travelling Show, Young Contemporaries, London Regional Art Gallery, Ont, 78 & 80; Emma Lake '79, 79-80, Alberta Now, 80 & Canadian Contemporary Art, 83, Edmonton Art Gallery; The Joy of Form, Burnaby Art Gallery, Vancouver, 86; Celebrations, Univ Art Gallery, Edmonton, 87; Grand Forks Art Gallery, 92. *Pos:* Illusr, Brit Inst Archeol-Univ Alta Classics Dept, Gravina, Italy, 70-71. *Teaching:* Lectr painting, Univ Alta, Edmonton, 78-80, asst prof, 85. *Awards:* Univ Alta Prize Art & Design, 76; Heinz Jordan Mem Scholar, Heinz Jordan Co, Toronto, 77; Can Coun Grant, 80. *Bibliog:* R Lawrence (auth), Review, Vanguard Mag, 85. *Media:* Oil on Wood, Watercolor. *Dealer:* Wade Gallery 750 N La Cienega Blvd Los Angeles CA 90069. *Mailing Add:* 608 Oliver St Victoria BC V8S 4W3 Canada

STEPHANY, JAROMIR
PHOTOGRAPHER, EDUCATOR
b Rochester, NY, Mar 23, 30. *Study:* Rochester Inst Technol, AAS, 56, with Ralph Hattersley, Miner White & B Newhall, BFA, 58; Ind Univ, with Henry Holmes Smith, MFA, 60. *Work:* George Eastman House; Univ Md, Baltimore Co; Detroit Inst Arts; Mus Fine Arts St Petersburg, Fla; Baltimore Mus Fine Arts. *Exhib:* Mus Mod Art, New York, 60; Smithsonian Inst, Washington, DC, 69; Baltimore Mus Art, 70; Addison Gallery Am Art, 75; one-man shows, Dundalk Community Col, Md, 77, Mus Without Walls, Md, 75-76, Catskills Ctr Photog, 79, Int Ctr Photog, 80 & Dalsheimer Gallery, 81; and others. *Pos:* Series writer, Developing Image, Extended Learning Inst, Channel 53-TV, Va. *Teaching:* Lectr hist photog, Md Inst Col Art, 66-77; assoc prof, Dept Visual Arts, Univ Md, Baltimore Co, 72- *Awards:* Univ Md Baltimore Co Summer Fel, 83. *Mem:* Soc Photog Educ (chmn & ed newsletter, Mid-Atlantic Region, 74-80). *Dealer:* G H Dalsheimer Gallery 519 N Charles St Baltimore MD 21201. *Mailing Add:* Art Dept Univ MD Baltimore Col Campus 5401 Wilkins Ave Catonsville MD 21228

STEPHEN, FRANCIS B
JEWELER, SCULPTOR
b Dublin, Tex, Mar 7, 16. *Study:* Fine Art Ctr, Colorado Springs, Colo; Univ Okla, study with Jean Charlot & Robert von Neumann, MFA. *Work:* Witte Mem Mus, San Antonio, Tex; Okla Art Ctr; Hallmark Collection, Mo. *Exhib:* The Patron Church, Mus Contemp Crafts, New York, 61; 11th Mid-Am Exhib, Nelson Gallery, Kansas City, Mo, 61; Craft Exhib, Dallas Mus Fine Arts, 71-74 & 78; South Central States Crafts Exhib, Denver Art Mus, Colo, 73; Contemporary Crafts of The Americas, Denver Art Mus, 74; Lake Superior Int Crafts Exhib, Tweed Mus Art, Univ Minn, Duluth, 74-75; The Metalsmith, Phoenix Art Mus, Ariz, 77; one-man show, Mus of Art, Okla Univ, 79; and others. *Teaching:* Asst prof jewelry & sculpture, North Tex State Univ, Denton, 64-67; prof jewelry, Tex Tech Univ, Lubbock, 67- *Awards:* Swarovski Award, Great Designs in Jewelry, Swarovski & Co, 67; Grand Award, 15th Tex Crafts Exhib, 71; Purchase Award, Miniature Works, Tex Tech Mus Art, 75. *Mem:* Soc of NAm Goldsmiths. *Media:* Miscellaneous Media. *Dealer:* Schneider-Bluhm-Loeb Gallery Inc 230 W Superior St Chicago IL 60610. *Mailing Add:* 4610 29th Lubbock TX 79410

STEPHENS, CURTIS
DESIGNER, PHOTOGRAPHER
b Athens, Ga, Dec 13, 32. *Study:* Univ Ga, MFA. *Work:* Objects USA, Johnson's Wax Collection; Ill State Mus, Springfield. *Exhib:* Designed for Production, Mus Contemp Crafts, 64; Objects USA, Johnson's Wax Collection, Smithsonian Inst, 69; 24th & 25th Ill Exhib, Ill State Mus, 71 & 72. *Pos:* Designer, Callaway Mills, LaGrange, Ga, 63-66; photogr, 1960 Pandora (Popular Photog Award-Winning Yearbk, Univ Ga). *Teaching:* Asst prof art, LaGrange Col, 61-63; asst prof art, Univ Northern Mich, 66-68; assoc prof art & design, Univ Ill, Champaign-Urbana, 68-, assoc dir sch, 75-90. *Bibliog:* Lee Nordness (auth), Objects: USA, Viking Press, 70; Jay Hartley Newman & Lee Scott Newman (auth), Plastics for the Craftsman, Crown, 72. *Media:* Papers, Plastics. *Mailing Add:* Sch of Art & Design Univ of Ill 138 Fine Arts Bldg Champaign IL 61820

STEPHENS, THOMAS MICHAEL
KINETIC ARTIST, DESIGNER
b Elkins, Ark, Feb 21, 41. *Study:* Univ Kans, 59-63; pvt study & travel. *Exhib:* New Tendencies 4 & 5, Galeria Grada Zagreba, Zagreb, Yugoslavia, 69 & 73; 20th Century Am Photog, Nelson-Atkins Mus, Kansas City, Mo, 74; Cybernetic Symbiosis, Lawrence Hall Sci, Berkeley, Calif, 79; Critica I, Mus Graphics, Terme, Italy, 81; Univ Ctr Gallery, Lawrence, Kans, 81; one-man shows, Lawrence Gallery, 81, Rockhurst Gallery, 82 & Batz Gallery, 83. *Pos:* Principal, T M Stephens Design Assoc, currently. *Teaching:* Instr sculpture, Kansas City Art Inst, 86-87. *Awards:* Proclamation of Commendation by Mayor of Kansas City, 85. *Bibliog:* Peter Von Ziegesar (auth), article, Kansas City Mag, 7/86; Virginia Hillix (auth), article, New Art Examiner, 10/86. *Mem:* Comput Art Soc; assoc Hypergraphics Int Alliance; Kansas City Art Gallery Asn (bd dirs). *Mailing Add:* 7676 High Dr Shawnee Mission KS 66208

STEPHENS, WILLIAM BLAKELY
EDUCATOR, PAINTER
b Corpus Christi, Tex, June 8, 30. *Study:* Univ Tex, BFA, 56, with Hiram Williams, MEd, 57, MFA, 66; Univ Fla, EdD, 72. *Work:* Mus E Tex, Lufkin. *Exhib:* 23rd Ann Tex Painting & Sculpture, Dallas Mus Fine Arts, 61; Art on Paper, Weatherspoon Gallery, Greensboro, NC, 67; Super Graphics, Brooks Mem Art Mus, Memphis, Tenn, 74; one-man show, Emerging Figures, Univ Tex at Tyler, 82; Contemp Art of the USA, Hamburg, WGer, 89 & Bonn, WGer, 90; USAid Mission, Tegucigalpa, Honduras, 91; and others. *Pos:* art ed, New Voices in Educ, 71-72. *Teaching:* Asst occup ther, Univ Fla, 70-71; assoc prof art educ, Memphis State Univ, 72-76; prof art, Univ Tex, Tyler, 76- & chmn dept, 76-84. *Awards:* Univ Tex at Tyler Fac Res Grants, 78, 80 & 90. *Mem:* Life mem Tex Fine Arts Asn. *Media:* Acrylic, Gouache. *Res:* Artists' personality types; monuments and myths. *Publ:* Auth, Blue Ridge Studies, Fac Publ, Appalachian State Univ, 5/69; On creativity and teaching: talk with Hiram Williams, Art J, summer 71; Relationship between selected personality characteristics, Studies in Art Educ, spring 73; University art departments and academies of art: The artists' psychological types to their specialities and interests, Bull of Res in Psychological Type, summer 77; Hiram Williams, Memphis State Univ, 78. *Mailing Add:* Dept Art Univ Tex Tyler TX 75701

STEPHENSON, JOHN H
SCULPTOR, EDUCATOR
b Waterloo, Iowa, Oct 27, 29. *Study:* Univ Northern Iowa, BA; Cranbrook Acad Art, MFA. *Work:* Int Mus Ceramics Faenza, Italy; Everson Mus, Syracuse, NY; Portland Art Mus; Detroit Inst Arts; St Paul Art Ctr. *Comn:* Champion No 3 (sculpture), Mich Mall, Battle Creek, Mich, 76. *Exhib:* 1977 Ceramic Conjunction, Long Beach Mus of Art, Calif, 77; Contemp Ceramic Sculpture, Univ of NC, Chapel Hill, 77; one-man show, Gallery 7, Fisher Bldg, Detroit, 78; Century of Ceramics in the United States, Everson Mus, Syracuse, 79-80, Swipler Gallery, Royal Oak, Mich, 91; Clay Attitudes, Queens Mus, Flushing, 80; retrospective, Sustained Visions, Detroit, 88. *Teaching:* Instr ceramics, Cleveland Inst Art, 58-59; prof ceramics & interim dean, Univ Mich, Ann Arbor, 59- *Awards:* Rackham Res Grants, Japan, Univ Mich, 62; Medagla Oro Della Citta Faenza, 65; Mixed Media Prize, Univ Mich, 69. *Bibliog:* Century of Ceramics in the USA, Objects USA. *Media:* Ceramic, Mixed. *Publ:* Auth, Form & Color, Studio Potter, 83; Perception/ Inner & Outer Vision, Studio Potter, 88. *Mailing Add:* Art Dept Main Campus Univ Mich Ann Arbor MI 48109

STEPHENSON, SUSANNE G
CERAMIST, EDUCATOR
b Canton, Ohio, Nov 5, 35. *Study:* Carnegie-Mellon Univ, BFA; Cranbrook Acad of Fine Art, Bloomfield Hills, Mich, MFA. *Work:* Mus of Contemp Crafts, New York; Butler Inst of Am Art, Youngstown, Ohio; Univ Mich Mus of Art, Ann Arbor; Columbus Gallery of Fine Arts, Ohio; El Paso Mus Art. *Comn:* Ceramic Planters, Burroughs Corp, Detroit, Mich, 70, Grosse Pointe Br, Nat Bank of Detroit, 72 & Harper Hosp, Detroit, 72; Liturgical Vessels, Lutheran Chapel, Eastern Mich Univ, Ypsilanti, 72. *Exhib:* Works in Fiber, Metal, Clay by Women, Bronx Mus, NY, 78; Century of Ceramics, USA, 1878-1979, Everson Mus Art, Syracuse, NY, 79; Contemporary American Potter, Univ N Iowa, Smithsonian Traveling Exhib, 80-81; Garth Clark Gallery, New York, 86; Sustained Vision, two-person retrospective, Focus Gallery, Detroit, 88; solo exhib, Carnegie Inst Mus Art, Pittsburgh, Pa, 85; and many others. *Teaching:* Instr ceramics, Univ Mich, Ann Arbor, 60-61; prof ceramics, Eastern Mich Univ, 63- *Awards:* Mich Ceramics Award, 78, 81, 85 & 88; Best in Ceramics, Beaux Arts Designer Craftsmen Exhib, Columbus, Ohio; Regional Visual Arts Fel, 87; Mich Coun Arts Grant, 87. *Bibliog:* Garth Clark & Margie Hughto (coauths), Century of Ceramics, E P Dutton, 79; Garth Clark (auth), American Potters, Watson Guptill, 81; Janet Koplos (auth), Alternations--the ceramics of Susanne Stephenson, Am Crafts, 1/83. *Mem:* Am Craftsmen's Coun; Mich Potters Asn; Nat Coun Educ for Ceramic Arts; Am Asn Univ Prof. *Media:* Porcelain, Stoneware. *Dealer:* Detroit Gallery of Contemp Crafts 301 Fisher Bldg Detroit MI 48202; Garth Clark Gallery 170 S La Brea Blvd Los Angeles CA 90036. *Mailing Add:* 4380 Waters Rd Ann Arbor MI 48103

STERMER, DUGALD ROBERT
ILLUSTRATOR, DESIGNER
b Los Angeles, Calif, Dec 17, 36. *Study:* Univ Calif, Los Angeles, BA, 60; printmaking with John Paul Jones. *Comn:* Designer, Olympic Games Official Medals, 84. *Exhib:* One-man show, Andre's, San Francisco, 69; group show, Greengrass Gallery, 78; Mus Exhib, Calif Acad Sci, 86. *Pos:* Consult ed, Communication Arts, Palo Alto, Calif, 74-; art dir & designer, Oceans, San Francisco, 77-81; design consult, Sierra, San Francisco, 82- *Teaching:* Lectr advan design, Acad Art, San Francisco, 78; instr illus, Artists in Print, San Francisco, 78-79, inst advanced illus, Calif Col Arts Crafts, San Francisco. *Awards:* Excellence Award, Ann Exhibs, Soc Illustrators; Illustr Ann, Communication Arts, 76-90; Am Illusr Awards; plus others. *Bibliog:* Martin Fox (auth), The graphics of dissent, Print, 66; Richard Coyne (auth), Dugald Stermer, Communication Arts, 72; 50 Important US Designers, Idea, 78; Steven Heller (auth), Call of nature, Print, 89. *Mem:* Am Inst Graphic Design; Am Inst Graphic Arts (bd dirs, 89-91); San Francisco Soc Communicating Arts. *Media:* Watercolor, Graphite. *Publ:* Auth, The Art of Revolution, McGraw-Hill, 71; ed, The enviroment, Richard Coyne, 72 & ed & illusr, Vanishing creatures, 80, Communication Arts; auth & illusr, Vanishing Creatures, Lancaster-Miller, 80. *Mailing Add:* 600 Embarcadero San Francisco CA 94107

STERN, ARTHUR I
STAINED GLASS ARTIST, ARCHITECT
b June 18, 50; US citizen. *Study:* Dept Archit, Univ Ill, 68-72; Calif Col Arts & Crafts, BFA (environ design), 73. *Comn:* Leaded glass, Ital Cemetary Mausoleum, Calif, 86; City Ctr, Bramalea Pacific, Oakland, Calif, 87; mural, Imperial Bancorp, Oakland, Calif, 88; St Marys Cath Church, Lakeport, Calif, 88; Las Vegas Temple, LDS Church, Las Vegas, Nev, 88. *Exhib:* One-man shows, Bank Am Gallery, San Francisco, 83 & Calif Col Arts Crafts Gallery, 83; Nat AIA Col, Phoenix, 84, San Francisco, 85 & New York, 88; Image, Light & Structure, Pontiac, Mich, 84; Nat Glass, Downy Art Mus, Los Angeles, 86; Design 1987, Galleria Design Ctr, San Francisco, 87. *Collections Arranged:* CCAIA, Arch Glass, 81; AIA Nat Conv, Arch Craft, 85. *Teaching:* Instr sculpture, Calif Col Arts & Crafts, Oakland, Calif, 87 & instr glass, 88. *Awards:* Glass Mag Awards in Archit Glass, 81; AIA Excellence in Design & Craftsmanship, 83; IFRAA, Art in Archit Award, 87 & 90. *Media:* Architectural Glass. *Mailing Add:* 1221 8th Ave Oakland CA 94606

STERN, H PETER
COLLECTOR
Study: Harvard Univ, AB(magna cum laude), 50; Columbia Univ, MA, 52; Yale Univ Law Sch, LLB, 54. *Pos:* Pres, Storm King Art Ctr, Mountainville, NY; vchmn World Monuments Fund, New York; pres, Ralph Ogden Found, Mountainville, NY; hon dir, Friends of Vassar Art Gallery, Poughkeepsie, NY; chmn bd, Star Expansion Co, Mountainville, NY; pres, Star Expansion Indust Corp, Mountainville. *Collection:* Contemporary paintings, graphics and sculpture; Indian & Turkish art. *Mailing Add:* Otterkill Rd Mountainville NY 10953

STERN, IRENE MONAT
PAINTER
b Nov 20, 32; US citizen. *Study:* New Sch Social Res; classes at Mus Mod Art & Whitney Mus; mainly self-taught. *Work:* Nat Collection of Fine Arts, Smithsonian Inst, Gen Elec World Hq, Joseph H Hirshhorn Mus, First Nat City Bank, Int Off, Washington, DC; and others. *Comn:* Am Broadcasting Co Western Hq; Atlantic Richfield Collection; Pac Mutual Life Ins Co Exec Hq. *Exhib:* Esther Robles Gallery, Los Angeles, 73; Color-73, Brand Mus & Libr; Am Acad Arts & Lett, 74; Downtown Gallery, Honolulu, 74; Source Gallery, San Francisco, 75; Expose IV, Los Angeles Co Mus, 83; and others. *Bibliog:* Articles in Life Mag, 4/24/72, Interiors, 74 & Artweek, 5/31/75. *Media:* Acrylic. *Mailing Add:* PO Box 1817 Santa Monica CA 90406

STERN, JAN PETER
SCULPTOR
b Nov 14, 26; US citizen. *Study:* Col Fine Arts, Syracuse Univ, BID; New Sch Social Res. *Work:* Hirshhorn Mus, Nat Collection Smithsonian Inst, Capitol Mall, Washington, DC; Pasadena Art Mus; Univ Mich Inst Sci & Technol; and others. *Comn:* Monumental sculptures, Prudential Ctr, Boston, 66, Maritime Plaza, Golden Gateway Ctr, San Francisco, 67, Alcoa Hq, Chicago, 68, Cardinal Spellman Retreat House, New York, 69 & Los Angeles City Hall Mall, 72. *Exhib:* Phoenix Art Mus, 67; Mus Contemp Art, 68; St Louis Art Mus, 68; San Francisco Mus Art, 70; Marlborough Gallery, New York, 70; and other group & one-man shows. *Bibliog:* Monumental sculpture show, Artforum, 2/68; Louis Redstone (auth), Art in Architecture, 68 & Garrett Eckbo (auth), Landscape We See, 69, McGraw, documented by Nat Educ TV; and others. *Media:* Stainless Steel, Metals. *Mailing Add:* PO Box 1817 Santa Monica CA 90406

STERN, LOUIS
DEALER, CONSULTANT
b Jan 7, 45; US citizen. *Study:* Calif State Univ, Northridge, BA. *Pos:* Pres, Wally Findlay Galleries, Beverly Hills, Calif, 80-82; pres, Louis Stern Galleries, Beverly Hills, Calif, currently. *Mem:* Los Angeles County Mus Art;

Los Angeles Art Coun; Int Found Art Res, New York; Friends of French Art; Am Friends of Blerancourt; Art Dealers Asn Calif. *Specialty:* Impressionist, post-impressionist, Pont-Aven and 20th century American and European painting. *Mailing Add:* 9528 Brighton Way Beverly Hills CA 90210

STERN, LOUISE
PRINTMAKER, PAINTER
B New Haven, Conn, April 24, 21. *Study:* Syracuse Univ, 39-42; Boston Univ, BA, 43; Mus Mod Art, 60-62; Art Students League & Roberto DeLamonica & Edgar A Whitney (watercolor); study with Don Stacy. *Work:* Morani Art Gallery, Med Col Pa, Philadelphia; Gen Foods Corp, Tarrytown, NY; Cabrini Med Ctr, Dobbs Ferry, NY; Brown Chemical Corp, New York; Simpson, Thacher & Bartlett, New York. *Exhib:* Grassroots, Gallery Hastings, NY, 80 & 82; Fukuoka Mail Art Exhib, Fukuoka Art Ctr, Japan, 81; Of Light and Land, Hudson River Mus, Yonkers, NY, 82; Bridge Gallery, Co Off Bldg, White Plains, NY, 83; Silvermine Collection, Pitney Bowes, Stamford, Conn, 87, 88 & 89; Prints International 1990 & 1992, Silvermine Guild Artists, New Canaan, Conn; Audubon Artists, Nat Acad Galleries, New York; Heaton Gallery, Rockland Ctr Arts, West Nyack, NY; Adelphi Univ, Manhattan Ctr, 91; Grass Roots Alumni, Gallery Hastings, 91; Union Am Hebrew Congregations, New York, 92; The Printed Image, Gallery Hastings, 92. *Teaching:* Children's class, Mamaronk Artists Guild, 90. *Awards:* Stelly Sterling Mem Award, 87; First Prize, graphics, New Rochelle Asn, NY, 89; Dr & Mrs I C Gayner Award, 90. *Mem:* Artist Equity NY; Nat Asn Women Artists, New York (chmn, print jury, 88-90 & chmn, nominating committee, 90-92); Silvermine Guild Artists, New Canaan, Conn; Mamoroneck Artists Guild, Larchmont, NY (exhib chmn); New Rochelle Art Asn, NY (exhib co-chmn); Am Asn Univ Women. *Media:* Watercolor, Graphics. *Mailing Add:* 120 Lakeshore Dr Eastchester NY 10707

STERNBERG, HARRY
GRAPHIC ARTIST, PAINTER
b New York, NY, July 9, 04. *Study:* Art Students League; graphics with Harry Wickey. *Work:* Mus Mod Art & Metrop Mus Art, New York; Walker Art Ctr, Minneapolis; Whitney Mus; Victoria & Albert Mus, London; Brooklyn Mus; Fogg Mus, Boston; Libr Cong, Washington, DC; Bibliothique Nat, Paris; Hirshhorn Mus, New York; Cleveland Mus. *Comn:* Murals, US Treas Dept, Sellersville, Pa, 36 & Chicago, Ill, 38. *Exhib:* Whitney Mus Am Art Ann, New York, 48-50; Timber Gallery, Idyllwild, Calif, 81; one-man shows, Galeria Palomas, PR, 81 & 82, San Diego Print Club, 82, 91 & 92 & Deicas Gallery, La Jolla, 82; Idyllwild Sch Music & Art, 82 & 91; Mary Ryan Gallery, New York, 84, 91 & 92; San Diego Print Club, SDak, 86; Civilians, La Jolla Mus Art, San Diego, 88; Am Masters, Prints & Drawings, Catherine Burns Gallery, Seattle, 88; Serigraph, Nat Acad Design, New York, 88; Assoc Am Artists, 90; The Athenium Libr, La Jolla, Calif, 92; and others. *Teaching:* Instr painting & graphics, Art Students League, 34-68; instr graphics, New Sch Social Res, 42-45; head dept art, Idyllwild Sch Music & Art, Univ Southern Calif, 59-69, instr, 80-84; instr, Palm Springs Desert Mus, 80-83. *Awards:* J S Guggenheim Mem Found Fel, 63; Purchase Award, Am Acad Arts & Lett, 72; Draw 82 Award, Nat Exhib, Denver, 82. *Media:* Woodcut; Mixed. *Publ:* Auth, Silk Screen Color Printing & Modern Methods and Materials of Etching, McGraw Hill; Composition, Abstract-realist Drawing & Woodcut, Pitman Publ; dir & producer, The Many Worlds of Art (film); auth, Catalogue de raissone Sternberg Graphics, Wichita State Univ, 76; auth, My Life, a book of woodcuts, Brighton Press Calif, 91. *Dealer:* Susan Teller Gallery New York NY; Brighton Press San Diego CA. *Mailing Add:* 2234 Hiltonhead Glen Rd Escondido CA 92026

STERNBERG, PAUL EDWARD, SR
CURATOR, CONSULTANT
b Holland, Mich, May 10, 34. *Study:* Univ Md, 61. *Collections Arranged:* Master American Impressionists (auth, catalog), Marietta-Cobb Fine Arts Ctr, 83; Cobb-Marietta Collects (auth, catalog), Marietta-Cobb Fine Arts Ctr, 86; American Sampler-Collection of Fred Bentley (auth, catalog), mus tour, 86-; Paintings by American Women (auth, catalog), mus tour, 88-; American art, Selections from the Collection of Louise and Alan Sellars (auth, catalog), Ga Govs Off, 89; Centennial Exhib, Nat Asn Women Artists (auth, catalog), Brenau Col, 90; Art by American Women, Brenau Col, 91, Knoxsville Mus, 92 & St Petersberg Mus Art, 93. *Pos:* Art appraiser, 69-; cur, Knoke Galleries, Marietta, Ga, 82-87 & Art by Am Women, Louise & Alan Sellars Collection, Marietta, Ga, 87- *Mem:* Int Soc Appraisers; Art Libr Soc NAm. *Res:* American women artists prior to 1950. *Mailing Add:* 2120 Cornerstone Lane Marietta GA 30064

STERNE, HEDDA
PAINTER
b Bucharest, Romania, Aug 4, 16; US citizen. *Study:* Pvt study in Paris, Bucharest & Vienna. *Work:* Univ Ill; Metrop Mus Art, Mus Mod Art, Whitney Mus Am Art, New York; Albright-Knox Art Gallery, Buffalo, NY; Univ Nebr; Art Inst Chicago; and others. *Exhib:* Solo exhibs, Mortimer Brandt, NY, 46, Betty Parson Gallery, NY, 47-78, Lee Ault & Co, NY, 75, Fairweather Hardin Gallery, Chicago, 75, Montclair Art Mus, NJ, 77, CDS Gallery, NY, 82, 84, 87 & 90, The Queens Mus, 85; 58th Exhib Am Painting & Sculpture, Art Inst Chicago, 47; 143ed-145th Ann Exhib of Painting & Sculpture, Pa Acad Fine Arts, Philadelphia, 48, 49 & 50; 21st Biennial Exhib 1949, Corcoran Gallery Art, Washington, DC, 49 & 50; Ann Exhib Contemp Am Painting, Whitney Mus Am Art, NY, 49; Contemp Painting in the US, Los Angeles Co Mus Art, 51; 61st Am Exhib: Paintings & Sculpture, Art Inst Chicago, 54; 50 Ans d'Art aux Etats-Unis: Collections fu Museum of Modern Art de New York, Musee National d'Art Moderne, Paris, 55; Am Artists Paint the City, Art Inst Chicago, 56; 62nd Exhib Am Painting & Sculpture, Art Inst Chicago, 57; Ann Exhib: Sculpture, Paintings, Watercolors, Whitney Mus Am Art, 57; 26th Biennial Exhib, Corcoran Gallery Art, 59; Ann Exhib--Contemp Am Painting, Whitney Mus Am Art, 59; 155th Ann Exhib Am Painting & Sculpture, Pa Acad Fine Arts, 60; 64th Am Exhib: Painting, Sculpture, Art Inst Chicago, 61; 65th Am Exhib: Some Directions in Contemp Painting & Sculpture, Art Inst Chicago, 62; 28th Biennial Exhib, Corcoran Gallery Art, 63; 159th Ann Exhib Am Painting & Sculpture, Pa Acad Fine Arts, 64; Ann Exhib Contemp Am Painting, Whitney Mus Am Art, 67; Vintage Artists, Penn Plaza, NY, 83; CDS Gallery, NY, 82, 84, 86, 88, 90 & 92. *Teaching:* Instr art hist, Carbondale Col, 64; conducted workshop for art teachers, NY State Coun Arts, 68. *Awards:* Fulbright Fel, painting, Venicer, 63; Childe Hassam Purchase Award, Am Acad Arts & Lett, NY, 71; Hassam & Speicher Purchase Fund Award, Am Acad Arts & Lett, 84. *Bibliog:* Robert Motherwell & Reinhardt (ed), Modern Artists in America, Wittenborn, 51; Nathaniel Pousette-Dart (ed), American Painting Today, Hastings, 56; Herbert Read (auth), The Quest and the Quarry, Rome-New York Art Found Inc, 61; and others. *Mailing Add:* c/o CDS 13 E 75th St New York NY 10021

STERRITT, COLEEN
SCULPTOR
b Morris, Ill, Jan 8, 53. *Study:* Univ Ill, BFA, 76; Otis Art Inst, MFA, 79. *Work:* Mus Contemp Art, Los Angeles. *Exhib:* Solo exhibs, Karl Bornstein Gallery, 84 & 86, Seaver Col Art Gallery, Pepperdine Univ, Malibu, Calif, 87 & Santa Monica City Col, Santa Monica, Calif, 88, Cal State Univ, Los Angeles, 90; On the Horizon: Emerging in California, Fresno Art Ctr Mus, Fresno, Calif, 87; Raw Grace, Otis Art Inst, Parsons Sch Design, Los Angeles, Calif, 88; Natural Forces in Los Angeles Sculpture, Munic Art Gallery, Los Angeles, 90; Selections from the Permanent Colect: 75-91, MOCA, Los Angeles, 91. *Pos:* Treas & bd dirs, Los Angeles Contemp Exhibs, 86-92, chmn, 91-92. *Teaching:* Vis artist, Claremont Grad Sch, 85, 88, 89, 90, 91 & 92, Calif State Univ, Fullerton, 86-87, Pepperdine Univ, 87-88; instr drawing, Univ Southern Calif, 85-86, instr sculpture, 89-; instr sculpture, Otis Art inst, Parsons Sch Design, 87- *Awards:* Fel, Nat Endowment Arts, 86. *Bibliog:* Colin Gardner (auth), The galleries, Los Angeles Times, 1/24/86; Beyond gender in: Raw Grace, Los Angeles Times, 8/13/88. *Mem:* Int Sculpture Ctr; Los Angeles Contemp Exhib. *Media:* Mixed. *Mailing Add:* 450 Seaton St Los Angeles CA 90013

STETSON, DANIEL EVERETT
MUSEUM DIRECTOR, CURATOR
b Oneida, NY, Jan 3, 56. *Study:* State Univ NY Col Potsdam, BA, 78; Syracuse Univ, NY, MFA(grad asst), 81. *Collections Arranged:* Focus 1 Michael Boyd (auth, catalog), Focus 3 The Art of Haiti: A Sense of Wonder (auth, catalog), 89, Focus 6 Contemp Developments in Glass (auth, catalog), 90, Stieglitz and 40 other Photographers: The Development of a Collection (auth, catalog), 91-92, New Works: Featuring Austin and Central Texas Artists (auth, catalog), 92. *Pos:* Actg dir, Picker Art Gallery, Colgate Univ, Hamilton, NY, 80-81; dir, Gallery Art & cataloger, Permanent Collection, Univ Northern Iowa, Cedar Falls, 81-87, Davenport Mus Art, Iowa, 87-91; exec dir, Laguna Gloria Art Mus, Austin, Tex, 91- *Teaching:* Museology, Colgate Univ, 80-81; Univ Northern Iowa, 81-87; Mem adv comt MBA Course of Study Styles & Strategies Non-Prof Orgn, St Ambrose Univ, 89-91. *Awards:* Fel, Northeast Mus Conf, 79; Scholar ALI-ABA, 84. *Mem:* Am Asn Mus; Tex Asn Mus; and others. *Mailing Add:* Lagune Gloria Art Museum 3809 W 35 St, Box 5568 Austin TX 78763

STETTNER, LOUIS
PHOTOGRAPHER
b New York, NY, Nov 7, 22. *Study:* Princeton Univ, 42-44; Inst Hautes Etudes Cinematographiques, BA, 49. *Work:* Victoria & Albert Mus, London; Bibliotheque Nat, Paris; Mus Mod Art, Int Ctr Photog & Metrop Mus Art, New York; Nat Mus Am Art; Mus de Elysee, Switzerland; Chicago Art Inst; San Francisco Mus Art; Smithsonian Inst, Washington, DC; Carnaualet Mus, Paris. *Exhib:* Bibliotheque Nat, Paris, 49; Photography in the Fine Arts, Chicago Inst Art, 61 & traveling exhib; Photo League, Int Ctr Photography, New York, 81; Critics Choice, Victoria & Albert Mus, London, 83; Subjective Photography, San Francisco Mus Mod Art, 84; Neikrug Gallery, NY, 85; Daniel Wolf Gallery, NY, 86; Ctr Photog, Geneva, 86; Retrospective Early Work Photofind Gallery, New York, 88; New York Trilogy, Union Sq Gallery, 88; Comptoir de la Photographie, Paris, 89; Kate Heller Gallery, London, 90; Vision Gallery, San Fransisco, 90; Gallery Spectrum, Zaragoza, Spain, 90; Recent Work Howard Greenberg Gallery, 92. *Awards:* Photog Fel, Yaddo, 56; Creative Photog Grant, NY State Coun Arts, 73 & Nat Endowment Arts, 74. *Bibliog:* Norman Hall (auth), The Indestructable Image, Brit Photog, 67; Alan Porter (auth), monograph, Swiss Camera, 72; Ken Poli (auth), Delights of the Quiet Eye, Popular Photog, 83. *Media:* Black and White. *Publ:* Auth, Paris Street Scenes, Two Cities Publ, 49; Weegee the Famous, Knopf Publ, 78; Sur Le Tas, Cercle D'Art, 79; Streetwork, Symbax Inc, 81; photgr, Poster Series by Flammarion, Flammarion Publ, 86; Early Joys Photographs from 1947-72, J Iffland, Pub, 86; Wisdom Cries Out in the Streets Photographs from 1972-89, Editions Marval, Paris, 90. *Dealer:* Howard Greenberg Gallery New York NY 10012. *Mailing Add:* 172 W 79th St New York NY 10024

STEVANOV, ZORAN
PAINTER, SCULPTOR
b Novi Sad, Yugoslavia, June 25, 45; US citizen. *Study:* Fla Atlantic Univ, Boca Raton, BA, 68; Wichita State Univ, Kans, MFA, 70. *Work:* Wichita State Univ; Emporia State Univ, Kans; Ft Hays State Univ, Kans. *Comn:* Sculpture fountain, State Kans, Emporia State Univ Libr, 71-73. *Exhib:* Nat Exhib Drawing & Sculpture, Muncie, Ind, 67; Nat Ann Exhib, Monroe, La,

71; Kans Biennial Art Exhib, Lindsborg, 72; Eight State Ann Exhib, Oklahoma City, 74; three-man show, Lynn Kottler Gallery, New York, 75. *Teaching:* Instr sculpture & design, Emporia State Univ, 70-73; assoc prof design, Ft Hays State Univ, 73-, assoc prof art, currently. *Awards:* Second Prize Ann State Exhib, Fort Lauderdale, Fla, 67; First Prize Ann State Exhib, Hollywood, Fla, 68; Third Prize Nat Art Exhib, Winter Park, Fla, 68; and others. *Mem:* Col Art Asn. *Mailing Add:* Dept Art 600 Park St Fort Hays State Univ Hays KS 67601

STEVEN, JAMES MICHAEL
PAINTER, EDUCATOR
b Chicago, Ill, Jan 11, 38. *Study:* Sch Art Inst Chicago, BFA, 63, MFA(George Brown Fel), 65. *Work:* Columbia Mus Art, SC State Collection & Univ SC, Columbia; Dayton Art Inst, Ohio; Calif State Univ, Stanislaus, Turlock. *Exhib:* Solo exhib, Columbia Mus Art, SC, 79; Cincinnati Biannual, Cincinnati Mus Art, Ohio, 67; Dayton Art Inst, Ohio, 69; Arana National Open, Binghamton, NY, 78; Mint Mus Biannual, Charlotte, NC, 79; Society Four Arts Annual, Miami, 82; Portrait of the South, Palazzo Venezia, Rome, 84; Southeastern Center Contemporary Art, Winston-Salem, NC, 84. *Pos:* Dir, Middletown, Fine Arts Ctr , Ohio, 66-68, McKissick Mus Art Gallery, Columbia, SC, 70-71. *Teaching:* Instr painting & drawing, Dayton Art Inst, Ohio, 68-70; assoc prof painting & drawing, Calif State Univ, Stanislaus, Turlock, 70-73, Univ SC, Columbia, 76- *Awards:* All Ohio Painting & Sculpture Exhib Award, Ohio Arts Coun, 69; First Award, Painting, Arana Nat Open, Binghamton, NY, 78. *Dealer:* Great American Gallery 1925 Peachtree Rd NE Atlanta GA 30309. *Mailing Add:* Dept Art Univ SC Columbia SC 29208

STEVENS, ANDREW RICH
CURATOR, HISTORIAN
b Dubuque, Iowa, Feb 1, 56. *Study:* Iowa State Univ, BA, 78, MA, 80; Univ Kans, MA(art hist), 88. *Collections Arranged:* Prints by Richard Bosman 1978-1988 (auth, catalog), 89; Chushingura Japanese Prints, 91; Chiaroscuros From the Horlbeck Collection, 91; American Color Woodcuts (with James Watrous; auth, catalog), 93. *Mem:* Print Coun Am; Am Asn Mus; Col Art Asn; Midwest Art Hist Soc. *Res:* History and aesthetic of printed art. *Publ:* Contrib, The World in Miniature: Engravings By the German Little Masters (exhib catalog), Spencer, 88; Visions and Revisions: Works on Paper by Robert Cumming (exhib catalog), Elvehjem Mus, 91. *Mailing Add:* c/o Elvehjem Mus Art Univ Wis Madison WI 53706

STEVENS, ELISABETH GOSS
WRITER, CRITIC
b Rome, NY, Aug 11, 29. *Study:* Wellesley Col, BA, 51; Columbia Univ, MA(high hons), 56. *Pos:* Ed assoc, Art News, 64-65; art critic, Washington Post, 65; free lance art critic & writer, 65-78; columnist, The Gallery, Wall St J, 69-71; Sunday art columnist, Trenton Times, 74-77; art & archit critic, Baltimore Sun, 78-86. *Teaching:* Journalistic Criticism, Writers' Ctr, Washington, DC. *Awards:* Citation for Critical Writing, & A D Emmart Award, Baltimore-Washington Newspaper Guild, 80; MacDowell Colony, 81; Fel, Va Ctr Creative Arts, 82, 84, 85, 88, 89, 90 & 91; Ragdale Found, 83, 89 & Yaddo, 91; Works-in-progress Grant, Md State Arts Coun, 86; Mayor's Comt on Art & Culture Creative Develop Grant, 86. *Mem:* Soc Archit Hist; Col Art Asn; Am Studies Asn; Mod Lang Asn; Popular Culture Asn. *Publ:* Auth, The urban museums crisis (sr), Washington Post, 6-7/72; contribr, Black Arts Ctr Mus News, 3/75; Auth, Howard Russell Butler (exhib catalog), E R Squibb & Sons, 77; Elisabeth Stevens' Guide to Baltimore Inner Harbor, Stemmer House, 81; Fire & Water: Six Stories, Perivale Press, 83; Children of dust; Portraits & preludes, New Poet Series, 85; Horse and Cart: Stories from the Country, Wineberry Press, 90. *Mailing Add:* 6604 Walnutwood Circle Baltimore MD 21212

STEVENS, JACQUIE (JAQUELINE LAUREN)
CERAMIST, INSTRUCTOR
b Omaha, Nebr, April 3, 49. *Study:* Univ Colo; Inst Am Indian Arts, Santa Fe, AFA, 78; Col Santa Fe, BA, 81. *Work:* Inst Am Indian Arts Mus, Santa Fe. *Exhib:* Fifteenth Ann NAm Arts Show, Heard Mus, Phoenix, 82; One With the Earth, Smithsonian Inst, 83; The Clay Sings, Wheelwright Mus, Santa Fe, 83; Ceramics, Gallery Mack, New York, 83; Exhibit of New Work, Magic Mountain Gallery, Taos, NMex, 83; Recent Works, Robert Dean Gallery, Scottsdale, Ariz, 84. *Teaching:* Instr pottery & ceramics, Armand Hammer United World Col Am West, Montezuma, NMex, 83-84. *Awards:* Blue Ribbon Contemp Pottery, Heard Mus, Phoenix, 82; Southwest Am Indian Artists Fel, 83; Blue Ribbon, 62nd Indian Market, Santa Fe, 83. *Bibliog:* American Indian Art, Am Indian Art Mag, 83; Carolyn Meyer (auth), Art Scene, Channel 6, Santa Fe, 83. *Media:* Ceramics. *Dealer:* Wheelwright Mus Box 5153 Santa Fe NM 87502. *Mailing Add:* c/o Gallery Ten 225 Canyon Rd Santa Fe NM 87501

STEVENS, JANE ALDEN
PHOTOGRAPHER
b Rochester, NY, March 8, 52. *Study:* St Lawrence Univ, BA, 74; Rochester Inst Technol, MFA, 82; Univ Vienna, Austria, 72-73. *Work:* Int Mus Photog, Rochester, NY; Mus da Imagem e do Som, Mus de Arte Contemporanea, Sao Paulo, Brazil; Camera Club, New York; Cincinnati Art Mus. *Exhib:* One-man show, Galerie Greisinghaus, WGer, 83, Fourth St Gallery, Cincinnati, 86 & Ctr for Photog Woodstock, NY, 90; Rochester: An American Center of Photography, Int Mus Photog, Rochester, NY, 84; Contemporary American Photographers, Galerie Triangle, Washington, 86; Photovisions, Contemp Arts Ctr, Cincinnati, 87; Extended Image, Photo Central Gallery, Hayward, Calif, 89; Pan Horama, Tampere, Finland, 91. *Teaching:* Asst prof photog, Univ Cincinnati, 83-88, assoc prof, 88- *Awards:* Individual Artist Grant, Ohio Arts Coun, 90; Juror's Award of Excellence, Illuminance 86, Lubbock Fine Arts Ctr, 86; Purchase Award, Bicentennial Photog Exhib, Images Gallery, 87. *Mem:* Col Art Asn; Soc Photog Educ; Int Asn Panoramic Photog. *Media:* Photography. *Publ:* Contribr, A Moment of Vision, Dark Sun Press, 81; Solos do Imagem: Visao American-Janelos Brasilei (exhib catalog), 82; Governor's Residence Art Collection (exhib catalog), 86; Photovisions (exhib catalog), 87; Camerawork of Jane Alden Stevens, Adirondac Mag, 88. *Mailing Add:* 515 Terrace Ave Cincinnati OH 45220-1916

STEVENS, JANE M
PHOTOGRAPHER, ADMINISTRATOR
b Chicago, Ill, Oct 1, 47. *Study:* Univ Ill Chicago, BA(anthopology), 72; Sch Art Inst Chicago; State Univ New York, Buffalo, MA(experimental video), 81. *Work:* Visual Arts Collection Pensacola Col, Fla; Ill State Mus, Springfeild; McCartney Award Portfolio, Women in Photography, London, Eng. *Exhib:* Women in Photography Int, Portland Mus Art, Maine, 90; Women in Photography, Royal Photog Soc, Bath, Eng, 90; Heat Wave, Ariz State Univ, Union Gallery, Tempe, Ariz, 90; Positive/Negative, Coos Art Mus, Coos Bay, Ore, 89; 7th Nat Exhib, Alexandria Mus Art, La, 88; and others. *Pos:* Asst cur, Chicago Hist Soc, 78-85; asst admin, State Ill Art Gallery, Chicago, 85- *Teaching:* Instr photogr, Morton Col, Cicero, Ill, 87-90. *Awards:* Project Completion, Solitude, Ill Arts Coun, 81; Purchase Award, Pensacola Portrait Exhib, Pensacola Col, 84; Award Portfolio, McCartney Award, Women in Photography, 88. *Bibliog:* Garrett Holg (auth), Jane Stevens, portraits, New Art Examiner, summer 83; Catharine Reeves (auth), Jane Stevens, transformations, Chicago Tribune, 3/31/89; Abigail Foerstner (auth), Artists Residents Chicago Gallery, Burke/Stevens, Chicago, Tribune, 4/12/91. *Mem:* Artists Residents Chicago (pres, 92-93, grants 91-92); Chicago Artists Coalition; Soc Photg Educ; Col Art Asn; Am Asn Mus. *Publ:* Contribr, Computer Art: Pushing the Boundaries, Ill State Mus, 92. *Dealer:* Artists Residents Chicago Gallery 1040 W Huron Chicago IL 60622. *Mailing Add:* 1631 N Nagle Ave Chicago IL 60635

STEVENS, LINDA LEE
PAINTER, EDUCATOR
b Niles, Mich, Feb 11, 42. *Study:* Occidental Col, Calif, 59-61; Univ Calif, Los Angeles, BA, 64; Calif State Univ, Long Beach, MA, 77, MFA, 80. *Work:* 24 paintings, Home Savings of America, Los Angeles; Greensburg Deposit Bank, Ashland, Ky; Univ Calif, Irvine. *Comn:* 6 paintings, Nat Bank of La Jolla, Calif, 85. *Exhib:* Solo exhibs, California Contemporary Artists IV, Laguna Beach Mus Art, Calif, 82, Louis Newman Galleries, 86, 88 & 90, Cerritos Col, Norwalk, Calif, 86 & Westmont Col, Santa Barbara, Calif, 92; Chatauqua National Exhibition American Art, NY, 82; American Watercolor Society, Nat Acad Galleries, New York, 82; Contemporary Realism, Leslie Levy Gallery, Scottsdale, Ariz, 83; The Church of Jesus Christ of Latterday Saints Mus Art & Hist, Salt Lake City, Utah, 88 & 91; Watercolor: Contemporary Currents, Riverside Art Mus, Riverside Calif, 89. *Teaching:* Part-time instr painting & drawing, Calif State Univ, Long Beach, 81-86; part-time instr painting, Saddleback Col, Mission Viego, Calif, 86-88, Goldenwest Col, Huntington Beach, Calif, 90 & Fullerton Col, Calif, 90. *Awards:* Gold Medal, 82, Walter S Greathouse Medal, 88 Am Watercolor Soc; Gold Medal for Watercolor, Allied Artists Am, 82. *Bibliog:* Suvan Geer (auth), Reading the land, rev, Artweek, 1/25/86; Gerald F Brommer & Nancy Kinne (auths), Exploring Painting, Davis Publ Inc, 88; Diane Casella Hines (auth), Working with Fresh Transparent Glazes, American Artist, Watercolor, 89, 2/89; Ross C Anderson (auth, exhib catalog), Riverside Art Mus, 89; Watercolor: Contemporary Currents, Splash 1, North Light Bk Co, 91. *Mem:* Women Painters West; Nat Watercolor Soc; Watercolor West; West Coast Watercolor Soc. *Media:* Transparent Watercolor. *Publ:* Auth, Building vibrant color--layer by layer, Artist's Mag, 5/85; contribr (with Valerie Shesko), Finding your center of interest, Artist's Mag, 4/86. *Mailing Add:* 9622 Zetland Dr Huntington Beach CA 92646

STEVENS, MAY
PAINTER
b Boston, Mass, June 9, 24. *Study:* Mass Col Art, BFA, 46; Art Students League, 48; Acad Julian, Paris, 48. *Work:* Whitney Mus Am Art; Brooklyn Mus; Herbert F Johnson Mus, Cornell Univ; San Francisco Mus Art; Ohio State Univ; New Mus Contemp Art, New York; Boston Mus Fine Arts. *Exhib:* Recent Acquisitions & Women Artists From Permanent Collection, Whitney Mus Am Art, 70; Johnson Mus, Cornell Univ, 73; Everson Mus, Syracuse, NY, 76; Int Feminist Exhib, Gemeente Mus, Neth, 79-80; Int Exhib of Women's Polit Art, Inst Contemp Art, London, 80; Art of Conscience: The Last Decade, Wright State Univ, Dayton, Ohio; Rosa Luxemburg, Pentonville, London, Eng, 86; New Mus Contemp Art, New York, 88; Orchard Gallery, Derry, Northern Ireland; A Different War: Vietnam in Art, De Cordova Mus, Lincoln, Mass, 90; Concrete Utopia, Dusseldorf, Germany, 90; Herter Gallery, Univ Mass, Amherst, 91; Exit Art Gallery, New York, 93. *Teaching:* Instr painting, Sch Visual Arts, 62-; vis artist, Cornell Univ, 73, Rhode Island Sch Design, 77, Cal State Univ, Long Beach, 90; Skowhegan Sch Printing & Sculpture, 92. *Awards:* Nat Endowment Arts Grant for Painting, 83; Yaddo Artists Colony Award, 85; Fel Painting, Guggenheim Found, 86. *Bibliog:* Moira Roth (auth), Visions and re-visions, Artforum, 11/80; Peter Selz (auth), Art In Our Times, Abrams, 81; Lisa Tickner (auth), May Stevens, Block 5, 81; Donald Kuspit (auth), Crowding the picture, Artforum, 5/88; Carol Jacobsen (auth), Two Lives: Ordinary Extraordinary, Art Am, 2/89; Whitney Chadwick (auth), Women, Art and Society, Thames & Hudson, 90. *Mem:* Col Art Asn. *Media:* Oil, Acrylic. *Publ:* Auth, Working It Out, Pantheon, 77; Between Women, Beacon Press, 84; Fire Over Water, Tanam Press, 86; Visibly Female, Camden Press, 87. *Mailing Add:* 97 Wooster St New York NY 10012

STEVENS, MICHAEL KEITH
SCULPTOR
b Gilroy, Calif, July 14, 45. *Study:* Am River Col, 63-65; Calif State Univ, Sacramento, BA, 67, MA, 69; Univ Guadalajara, Mex, 66. *Work:* Univ NMex, Albuquerque; Israel Mus, Jerusalem; Lexecon Inc, Chicago, Ill; Squadron Press, Kansas City, Mo; Persis Corp, Honolulu, Hawaii. *Exhib:* The Animal Image: Contemporary Objects & the Beast, Renwick Gallery, 81; Sculpture Invitational, Alaska Arts Coun, Anchorage, Fairbanks & Juneau, 81; Humor in Art, Los Angeles Inst Contemp Art, 81; Works in Wood, Morgan Gallery, Shawnee Mission, Kans, 81; Bay Area Figurative Sculpture, Transamerica Pyramid Gallery, San Francisco, 82; Northern California: Focus on the Figure, Brentwood Gallery, St Louis, 82; The Slant Step Revisited, Richard L Nelson Gallery, Univ Calif, Davis, 83; Contemporary American Wood Sculpture, Crocker Art Mus, Sacramento, 84; Works in Wood, Monterey Peninsula Mus Art, 85; Fetishes, Burpee Art Mus, Rockford, Ill, 86; solo exhibs, Braunstein-Quay Gallery, NY, 78, Braunstein Gallery, San Francisco, 77, 79, 82, 84, 86 & 89 & Betsy Rosenfield Gallery, Chicago, 81, 83, 85 & 88; and many others. *Awards:* Phelan Award, Sculpture, San Francisco Found, 82. *Bibliog:* Dona Z Meilach (auth), Woodworking: The New Wave, Crown Publ, 81; Peggy Bagley (auth), Artist's profile, Art Voices, 1-2/82. *Mem:* Col Art Asn. *Dealer:* Betsy Rosenfield Gallery 212 W Superior St Chicago IL 60610. *Mailing Add:* c/o Braunstein-Quay Gallery 250 Sutter St San Francisco CA 94108

STEVENS, NELSON L
PAINTER, EDUCATOR
b Brooklyn, NY, Apr 26, 38. *Study:* Ohio Univ, BFA, 62; Kent State Univ, 69. *Comn:* Work to Unify African People, United Community Construct Worker, Roxbury, Mass, 73; I am a Black Woman, Univ Year for Action, Springfield, Mass, 74; Tuskegee Univ, Centennial Mural, 79. *Exhib:* Afri-Cobra I, II & III & Afri-Cobra 77, Philadelphia, Pa; one-man show, Studio Mus in Harlem, NY; Levels & Degrees, Fisk Univ, Nashville, Tenn; FESTAC 77, Lagos, Nigeria & Janet Carter Gallery, New York, 77. *Pos:* Publisher, Spirit Wood Productions Inc. *Teaching:* Instr, Cleveland Pub Sch Syst, 62-66 & Cleveland Mus Art, 66-68; asst prof art, Northern Ill Univ, DeKalb, 69-72; assoc prof art, Dept Afro-Am Studies, Univ Mass, Amherst, 72- *Mem:* Col Art Asn Am; Nat Conf Artists; Afri-Cobra. *Media:* Acrylic, Acrylic Spray. *Publ:* Illusr, The Cry of My People, Archie Shepp Album, ABC Dunhill, 72; illusr, There is a Trumpet in My Soul, Archie Shepp Album, Artista, 75; Art in the Service of the Lord Calendar, 93. *Mailing Add:* 81 Florida St Springfield MA 01109

STEVENS, THELMA K
EDUCATOR, DEALER
b New York, NY, Dec 4, 32. *Study:* Pratt Inst, Brooklyn, NY, BS, 54; Queens Col, Flushing, NY, MS, 59; Fordham Univ, NY, PhD, 80. *Pos:* Owner & pres, Isis Gallery, 82- *Teaching:* Art instructor, painting & sculpture, various NY State schs, grades K-12, 54-; instr reading & art, Fordham Univ Grad Sch, 79. *Awards:* Art Educator of the Year, NY State, 83; Award, Innovative curriculum design, Cromacyl Paint Co, 83. *Mem:* Nat Art Educ Asn (dir secondary educ, Eastern Region USA & Canada, 86-88); Int Soc Educ through Art (NY State Rep, 88-); US Soc Educ Art; NY State Art Teachers Asn; Long Island Art Teachers Asn. *Res:* Cognition and art. *Specialty:* Contemporary paintings and sculpture. *Publ:* Coauth, Super sculpture, Using Science and Technology, Van Nostrand Reinhold, 74; contribr, Art theory, In: Tapestry, Collegium Book Publ, Inc, 79; auth, articles in Clearing House, Sch Arts. *Mailing Add:* 29 Georgian Lane Great Neck NY 11024

STEVENS, WILLIAM ANSEL, SR
PAINTER, CARTOONIST
b Akron, Ohio, Sept 6, 19. *Study:* Kent State Univ; NMex State Univ; also with E Ladislaw Novotny, Fredric Taubes, Gerry Pierce, Kenneth Barrack & Ramon Froman. *Work:* US Naval Air Station Corpus Christi, Tex Hist Collection; White Sands Missile Range, NMex; US Forest Serv; White Sands Nat Monument; CofC, Alamogordo. *Comn:* Various oil portraits & landscapes throughout the US, Ger, Japan and Australia. *Exhib:* NMex State Fair, Albuquerque, 65; Llano Estacado Art Exhib, Hobbs, NMex, 67-68; Sun Carnival Art Exhib, El Paso, Tex, 68-69; Nat Wild Turkey Fedn Show, 78; Law West Exhib, 78, Ballut Abyad Shrine Temple, Albuquerque, NMex, 83 (permanent). *Pos:* Owner, Art Enterprises, Alamogordo, 60-; ed cartoons for three newspapers, 67-69; ed & illusr, Mgt Digest, 74-75. *Awards:* Grand Champion Art Award, Otero Co Fair, Alamagordo CofC, 62; Grand Champion Art Award, US Forest Serv, White Sands, NMex, 64 & 71; First Place Art Award, CofC Banquet, Alamogordo, 71. *Bibliog:* B Schwartz (auth), Sun dial, El Paso Times Sunday Mag, 5/75; J Baldwin (auth), articles in art sect, Alamogordo Daily News; E White (auth), article in Missile Ranger, White Sands Missile Range, Dept Defense Publ. *Mem:* Black Range Artists Inc; NMex Desert Arts League (pres, 69-70). *Media:* Oil, Watercolor, Pen & Ink. *Publ:* Illusr, Capabilities of the White Sands Complex, 75 & 77; auth, Dear Smudge (weekly art column), 79-80. *Mailing Add:* 1416 Taft Ave Alamogordo NM 88310

STEVENSON, A BROCKIE
PAINTER, EDUCATOR
b Montgomery Co, Pa, Sept 24, 19. *Study:* Pa Acad Fine Arts, Philadelphia; Barnes Found, Merion, Pa; Skowhegan Sch Painting & Sculpture, Maine. *Work:* Corcoran Gallery Art & Nat Mus Am Art; State Univ NY, Potsdam; Woodward Found, Washington, DC; Phillips Collection, Washington, DC. *Exhib:* Eight Washington Artists, Columbia Mus Art, SC, 71; Pyramid Galleries, Washington, DC, 73; Our Land, Our Sky, Our Water, Spokane World's Fair, 74; retrospective, Northern Va Community Col, Annandale, 74; Images of the '70s: Nine Washington Artists, Corcoran Gallery Art, DC, 80; one-man shows, Fendrick Gallery, Washington, DC, 78, 84 & 88. *Pos:* War artist corresp, European Theater Operations, 43-45. *Teaching:* Instr compos, Sch Fine Arts, Washington Univ, 60-62; prof design, drawing & painting, Corcoran Sch Art, Washington, DC, 65- *Bibliog:* Paul Richard (auth), article, Washington Post, 4/29/78 & 5/28/88; Benjamin Forgey (auth), articles, Washington Star-News, 5/7/78 & Washington Post, 5/12/84; David Tannous (auth), article, Art Am, 9-10/78; among others. *Media:* Acrylic, Silkscreen Prints. *Dealer:* Fendrick Gallery 3059 M St Washington DC 20007. *Mailing Add:* 6106 Yale Ave Glen Echo MD 20812

STEVENSON, HAROLD
PAINTER
b Idabel, Okla, Mar 11, 29. *Study:* Univ Okla, Norman; Univ Mex, Mexico City; Art Students League, New York. *Work:* Whitney Mus, New York; Ctr George Pompidou, Paris. *Exhib:* Ann Exhib, Whitney Mus Am Art, New York, 62; Galleria La Medusa, Rome, 73; Americans in Paris, Mus Nat Art Mod, 79; La Famille des Portraits, Louvre Mus Portrait of Francois de Menil, 79-80; and many others. *Teaching:* Artist-in-residence, Austin Col, Sherman, Tex, formerly. *Bibliog:* Andy Warhol (dir), Harold (film), New York, 64; Lucy Lippard (auth), Pop Art, New York, 66; Iris Clert (auth), Iris-Time l'artventure; Andre Morain (auth), Le Milieu de L'Art. *Dealer:* Gallery Medusa Athens Greece; Keith Green Gallery 500 Park Ave New York NY 10022. *Mailing Add:* 21-14 45th Ave Long Island City NY 11101

STEVENSON, RUTH CARTER
COLLECTOR, PATRON
b Ft Worth, Tex, Oct 19, 23. *Study:* Sarah Lawrence Col, BA, 45. *Pos:* Chmn bd, Amon Carter Mus; emer trustee, Ft Worth Art Mus; founder, Ft Worth Art Coun; vpres, Int Coun Mus Mod Art, 67-72; nat chmn collector's comt, Nat Gallery of Art, 74-; mem vis comt, Fogg Mus, Cambridge, Mass, 77-83; trustee, Nat Gallery Art, 79-; pres, Amon G Carter Found, 82-; chmn, Ft Worth Cult Dist Comt, 86-89; trustee, Nat Trust Hist Preservation, 89-93. *Mem:* Nat Endowment of the Arts; Ft Worth City Art Comn (chmn, George Rickey Sculpture Comt, 74-75). *Collection:* French 19th century; European and American sculpture and graphics. *Mailing Add:* 1200 Broad Ave Ft Worth TX 76107

STEVENSON, RUTH ROLSTON
PAINTER, INSTRUCTOR
b Brooklyn, NY, May 27, 1897. *Study:* Pratt Inst, dipl-BFA, 20; Art Students League, with John Sloan, 37. *Work:* Huntington Mus, WVa; Norfolk Mus Arts & Sci, Va. *Comn:* Two murals, Pratt Inst, Brooklyn, 20; Celebrated Musicians Collection, Nat Art Club, New York, 67 & 72. *Exhib:* Nat Asn Women Artists Travel Exhib, Europe, 54-59, Witte Mus, San Antonio, Tex, 59, Ill State Mus, Springfield, 60 & Nat Acad, New York, 64 & 73; Invitational, Southern Vt Art Asn & Hudson Valley Art Asn, 60; Catherine Lorillard Wolfe, Nat Acad, New York, 59; Am Watercolor Soc Travel Exhib, Europe, 67; retrospective exhib, Grand Central Gallery, New York, 81. *Teaching:* Instr drawing & painting, Pratt Inst, Brooklyn, NY, 20-24 & Newark Pub Sch Fine & Indust Arts, NJ, 27-36. *Awards:* Gold Medal, Nat Arts Club, 57; First Prize Watercolor, Nat Asn Women Artists, 60; Am Watercolor Soc Award, 67. *Mem:* Am Watercolor Soc; Nat Arts Club; Pen & Brush Club; Nat Asn Women Artists; Am Artists Prof League. *Media:* Watercolor, Oil. *Mailing Add:* 26 W Ninth St New York NY 10011

STEVOVICH, ANDREW VLASTIMIR
PAINTER, PRINTMAKER
b Salzburg, Austria, July 2, 48; US citizen. *Study:* RI Sch Design, BFA(painting; Sydney Richmond Burley Award; Presidential Fel Travel in Europe), 70; Mass Col Art, MFA(painting), 80. *Work:* Fuller Art Mus, Mass; Danforth Mus, Framingham, Mass; Portland Mus Art, Maine; Mus Fine Arts, Boston, Mass; New Britain Mus Am Art, Conn. *Exhib:* Triennial, Brockton Art Mus, 78 & 81; one-man show, Clark Univ Art Gallery, 80, Coe Kerr Gallery, New York, 83, 85, 87 & 90, Tatistcheff Gallery, Santa Monica, Calif, 89 & Adelson Gallery, New York, 92; 20th Anniversary Exhib, Corcoran Gallery Art, 81; Boston Artists Work on Paper, Boston Univ Art Gallery, 81; Realistic Directions, Pa State Univ, University Park, 83; New England Impression, The Fitchburg Art Mus, Mass. *Bibliog:* Ronny Cohen (auth), review, Artforum, 4/90. *Media:* Oil, Pastel; Etchings. *Dealer:* Adelson Gallery 25 E 77th New York NY 10021. *Mailing Add:* 120 Sewall Ave Brookline MA 02146

STEWART, ARTHUR
PAINTER
b Marion, Ala, July 29, 15. *Study:* Auburn Univ; Art Inst Chicago; and with Kelly Fitzpatrick. *Work:* Birmingham Mus Art, Ala; Montgomery Mus Art, Ala; Atlanta Art Asn, Ga; also in collection of Queen Elizabeth II, Eng. *Comn:* Four murals (with Kelly Fitzpatrick), Bank of Tallassee, Ala. *Exhib:* Art in War Traveling Exhib, Life Mag, 41-42; four Southeastern Ann, 49-59; Norfolk Mus Arts & Sci Traveling Exhib, 64; Ala Watercolor Soc, 69-70; Palm Beach Gallery, 79; Wensten Gallery, Vero Beach, Fla, 84; Country Gallery, Locust Valley, NY, 84; Naples Art Gallery, Fla, 85; B'haru Mus Art, 86. *Teaching:* Instr drawing, Birmingham Mus Art, formerly; pvt instr. *Awards:* Purchase Award for Spanish Bouquet, Norfolk Mus Arts & Sci, 64; Award for Early Light, Meade Co, 64; Harriete Murray Award for Rosalie, Birmingham Centennial Exhib, 72; Purchase Award, Blount Compt, Montgomery, Ala, 86. *Bibliog:* Alfred Frankfurter (auth), Parisian scenes, San Francisco Chronicle, 49; Richard Howard (auth), Arthur Stewart florals, Crescenzi Gallery, 67. *Mem:* Birmingham Art Asn (vpres, 65-66); Ala Watercolor Soc (pres, 65-67); Ala Art League; Ala Art Asn. *Media:* Watercolor, Oil; Acrylic. *Dealer:* Art South Inc 4862 McArthur Blvd Washington DC 20007; Naples Art Gallery 275 Broad S Naples FL 33940. *Mailing Add:* 2969 Pump House Rd Birmingham AL 35243

STEWART, BILL
SCULPTOR, CERAMIST
b Plattsburgh, NY, June 21, 41. *Study:* State Univ NY Col, Buffalo, BS(art educ), 63; Ohio Univ, MFA, 66. *Work:* Burchfield Ctr, Buffalo; Mus Contemp Crafts, New York; Campbell Mus, Camden, NJ; Mem Art Gallery, Rochester; Univ Iowa Mus Art. *Comn:* Environmental sculpture, Greater Rochester Int Airport, NY, 91. *Exhib:* Clayworks--20 Americans, Mus Contemp Crafts, New York, 71; Figure and Fantasy, Renwick Gallery, 74; Clay, Whitney Mus, 74; Clay USA, Fendrick Gallery, Washington, DC, 75; Sculptureens USA, Campbell Mus, Camden, NJ, 76; Contemporary Ceramic Sculpture, Achland Mem Art Ctr, Univ NC, Chapel Hill, 77; Tribute to Josiah Wedgewood, Philadelphia Mus Art, 80; Ancient Inspirations--Contemporary Interpretations, Roberson Ctr, Binghamton, NY, 82; solo exhibs, Dawson Gallery, Rochester, NY, 87 & Munsom Williams Proctor Mus Art, Utica, NY, 89; Expressions in Color: Ceramics, NJ Ctr Visual Arts, Summit, NJ, 88. *Teaching:* Prof art, State Univ NY, Brockport, 66- *Awards:* Nat Endowment Arts Res Grant, 76; Lillian Fairchild Award, Univ Rochester, 79; Chancellor's Award Excellence in Teaching, State Univ NY, 82. *Mem:* Nat Coun Educ Ceramic Arts. *Media:* Ceramics. *Dealer:* Theo Portnoy Gallery New York, NY; Dawson Gallery Rochester NY. *Mailing Add:* 2489 Roosevelt Hwy Hamlin NY 14464

STEWART, DOROTHY S
PAINTER, PRINTMAKER
b Brooklyn, NY. *Study:* Art Students League; Nat Acad Sch Fine Art, New York; NY Univ. *Comn:* In pvt collections. *Exhib:* Catharine Lorillard Wolfe Art Club 68-93rd Ann, 65-91; Allied Artists Am 56-72nd Ann, 69-91; Academic Artists, 88; Hudson Valley Art Asn, 89, 90, 91. *Teaching:* Instr art, Malverne Sr High Sch, NY, 65-66. *Awards:* Catharine Lorillard Wolfe Club Award, 74, 79, 83, 85, 87 & 89; Kent Art Assoc Awards, 74, 78, 80, 84, 89, & 91; Conn Classic Arts - Oil Painting Award, 89 & 91; and others. *Mem:* Catharine Lorillard Wolfe Art Club (dir, 70, 2nd vpres, 71-74); Allied Artists Am (asst corresp secy, 78-79); Knickerbocker Artists; Kent Art Asn (pres, 77-78); life mem Art Students League; among others. *Media:* Oil, Watercolor. *Publ:* Contribr, Prize-winning art book 7, Allied Publ, Inc, Ft Lauderdale, Fla, 67. *Mailing Add:* 14 Club Dr Candlewood Trails New Milford CT 06776

STEWART, DUNCAN E
COLLAGE ARTIST
b St Paul, Minn, Sept 30, 40. *Study:* Calif State Univ, San Diego, BA, 67, MA, 69; Fla State Univ, 74. *Work:* Pensacola Mus Art, Fla. *Exhib:* Solo exhibs, Fla State Univ-Florence Study Ctr, Italy, 82, LeMoyne Art Found, Fla, 84 & Univ New Orleans, 86; The Glove Invitational, Valencia Jr Col, Orlando, Fla, 87; The Box, SE Ctr Contemp Artists, Raleigh, 85; Pensacola Mus Art, Fla, 88; Fla A & M Univ, 89. *Pos:* Dir, Univ West Fla Art Gallery, Pensacola, currently. *Awards:* Fla Arts Coun Individual Artists Fel, 82. *Mem:* Col Art Asn; Southeastern Col Art Asn. *Dealer:* Mario Villa Gallery 3908 Magazine St New Orleans LA 70115. *Mailing Add:* Dept Humanities & Fine Arts Univ W Fla Pensacola FL 32514

STEWART, F CLARK
DRAFTSMAN, PAINTER
b Evansville, Ind, July 18, 42. *Study:* Univ Redlands, Calif, BA(art), 64; Claremont Grad Sch & Univ Ctr, Calif, MFA(painting), 66. *Work:* Mint Mus Art, Charlotte, NC; Tenn State Mus, Nashville; Dulin Gallery Art, Knoxville; Austin Peay State Univ, Clarksville, Tenn; Clemson Univ, SC. *Exhib:* Solo exhibs, Hunter Mus, Chattanooga, 82 , WVa Univ, Morgantown, 87 & Cheekwood Fine Arts Ctr, Nashville, 88; More Than Earth & Sky, Nat Mus Am Art, Washington, DC, 81; Art Quest 86, Video Exhib, Los Angeles; Fact, Fiction, Fantasy-Recent Art in the Southeast, Touring Exhib, Univ Tenn, 87; Clemson Print & Drawing Show, Lee Hall Gallery, Clemson Univ, SC, 87; Festival Int de Louisiane, Lafayette Art Gallery, 91; and others. *Teaching:* Prof drawing, Univ Tenn, Knoxville, 66- *Awards:* Purchase Prizes, Tenn Asn Mus, 76, Marietta Nat Print & Drawing Show, 81 & Clemson Nat Print & Drawing Exhib, 85; AAVW Prize, Northern Nat Art Exhib, Rhinelander, Wis, 90. *Bibliog:* Dale Cleaver (auth), illus rev, Art Express, Vols 1 & 2, 82; Fred Moffat (auth), illus rev, Art Papers, Vols 4 & 6; Susan Knowles (auth), rev, New Art Examiner, Vol 16, No 10, 6/89. *Mem:* Col Art Asn. *Media:* Graphite on Paper; Mixed Media. *Publ:* Illusr, The Marriage of Heaven and Hell, Darkpool Press, Tenn, 72. *Mailing Add:* Dept Art Univ Tenn 1715 Volunteer Blvd Knoxville TN 37996

STEWART, J(OHN) DOUGLAS
HISTORIAN
b Kingston, Ont, Jan 28, 34. *Study:* Queen's Univ, Kingston, Ont, BA(hons), 55; McGill Univ, BLS, 56; Courtauld Inst, Univ London, PhD, 68. *Teaching:* Lectr art hist, Univ Toronto, 64-65; asst prof art hist, Queen's Univ, Kingston, Ont, 65-70, assoc prof, 70-80, prof, 80- *Awards:* Best Local Hist Award, Can Hist Asn, 74; Leave Fels, Can Coun, 74-75 & 81-82. *Res:* 17th century English painting, sculpture and architecture; 19th century Canadian architecture. *Publ:* Auth, Sir Godfrey Kneller, Nat Portrait Gallery, 71; coauth, Heritage Kingston, Agnes Etherington Art Ctr, 73; coauth, English Portraits of the Seventeenth and Eighteenth Centuries, W A Clark Mem Libr, 74; auth, Sir Godfrey Kneller and the English Baroque Portrait, Oxford Univ Press, 83. *Mailing Add:* Dept Art Queen's Univ Kingston ON K7L 3N6 Canada

STEWART, JACK
PAINTER, EDUCATOR
b Atlanta, Ga, Jan 27, 26. *Study:* With Steffen Thomas, Atlanta; Yale Univ Sch Fine Arts, under Albers & deKooning, BFA; Columbia Univ Sch Archit; NY Univ, MA, PhD. *Work:* Yale Univ Art Gallery; Columbia, SC, Mus Fine Arts; Greenville Mus, SC. *Comn:* Six mosaic murals on SS Santa Paula, Grace Lines, 57; mosaic mural on facade of Hotel Aruba Caribbean, Netherlands Antilles, 58; two mosaic murals in Pub Sch 28, Manhattan, NY, 58; stained glass, Cinerama, Inc, New York, 60; cloth mosaic mural, Cluett Peabody, Inc, New York, 88. *Exhib:* Pa Acad Fine Arts, Philadelphia, 53; Collegeo Raffaello, Urbino, Italy, 73; NY Univ, 75; one-man shows, Washington Sq East Galleries, NY, 75 & Woods Gerry Gallery, Providence, RI, 76, Blue Hill Cultural Ctr, Pearl River, NY, 89 & The Broome St Gallery, NY, 91-92. *Pos:* Pres, Stewart Studio, New York, 51- & New York Artists' Equity Asn, 87-89. *Teaching:* Lectr art & archit, New Sch Social Res, 53-58; instr design, Pratt Inst, 55-61; lectr drawing & painting, Columbia Univ, 67-76; instr drawing & painting, Cooper Union Sch Art & Archit, 60-71, assoc prof & chmn dept, 71-74; instr graphics & drawing, Queens Col, New York, 74-76; instr painting & drawing, New York Univ, 74-76; provost & vpres acad affairs, RI Sch Design, 76-77; prof art & chmn dept, Ind State Univ, Terre Haute, 78-80. *Media:* Acrylic, Watercolor. *Publ:* Contribr, Mosaic Art Today, 59; ed, Modern Mosaic Techniques, Watson Guptill, 67; auth, short articles on drawing & mosaic, In: Jefferson Encycl, World, 69; contribr, Art of Mosaic, 69; article on Richard Meier's New Harmony Atheneum, In: USA Today, 1/84. *Mailing Add:* 31 E Seventh St New York NY 10003

STEWART, JOHN (JOHN STEWART HOUSTON)
DEALER
b Orange, NJ, Dec 24, 45. *Study:* Miami Univ, BA, 68. *Collections Arranged:* Works by Van Selm, Barnwell Art Ctr, Shreveport, La, 78; Sculpture of Russell Jacques, Abilene Fine Arts Mus, 79; Watercolors by Jo Taylor, El Dorado Art Ctr, Ark, 80; Figurative Works by Charles Campbell, Univ Tex, Dallas, 81; Mardi Gras by Arie Van Selm, Dallas City Hall, 81, Int House, New Orleans, 81 & touring in Europe; Nathan Jones Touring Exhib, Randall Gallery, New York, 81, Fed Reserve Bank, Cleveland, 81, Fed Reserve Bank, Cincinnati, 81, Univ Tex, Arlington, 81, Univ Calif, Los Angeles, 82 & Fisk Univ, 82; Landscapes by Jeff Tabor, Tex Womens Univ, 82; Artists from the Stewart Gallery, Abilene Christian Univ, 83; Black Heritage Today, Longview Mus, Tex, 83; Landscapes by Four American Artists, Coninck Gallery, Holland. *Pos:* Designer & planner, Galleria des Bellas Artes, Phoenix, 71 & White Gallery, Westlake Village, Calif, 80; founder & dir, Stewart Gallery, Dallas, 72-; dir & mgr, Artists Courtyard, 76-; partner, Jones-Houston Graphics, currently. *Specialty:* Art by young, contemporary artists. *Mailing Add:* 7139 Azalea Dallas TX 75230

STEWART, JOHN LINCOLN
EDUCATOR, WRITER
b Alton, Ill, Jan 24, 17. *Study:* Denison Univ, AB, 38; Ohio State Univ, MA, 39, PhD, 47; Denison Univ, hon DA, 64. *Pos:* Assoc dir, Hopkins Art Ctr, Dartmouth Col, 62-64; dir, Mandeville Ctr for Arts, Univ Calif, San Diego, 75-76. *Teaching:* From asst prof to prof, Dartmouth Col, 49-54; prof Am lit & provost, John Muir Col, Univ Calif, San Diego, 64- *Awards:* Howard Found Fel, 53-54; Dartmouth Fac Fel, 62-63. *Res:* Contemporary American and British literature. *Publ:* Auth, John Crowe Ransom, Univ Minn, 62; auth, Burden of Time, the Fugitives and Agrarians, Princeton Univ, 65; co-auth, Horizons Circled, Univ Calif, 74; plus others. *Mailing Add:* 9473 La Jolla Farms Rd La Jolla CA 92037

STEWART, JOHN P
PAINTER, PRINTMAKER
b Ft Leavenworth, Kans, Mar 11, 45. *Study:* Univ Colo, with Roland Reiss & Wendel Black, BFA, 67; Univ Calif, Santa Barbara, MFA, 69. *Work:* Corcoran Gallery Art, Washington, DC; Whitney Mus Am Art, New York; Ponce Mus, PR; New Orleans Mus of Art, La; Mint Mus, NC; Cincinnati Art Mus. *Comn:* Painting, Rubloff Inc, Bicentennial, Cincinnati, 88. *Exhib:* Recent Acquisitions, Whitney Mus, New York, 72; Osuna Gallery, Washington, DC, 81, 82, 86; Foire Internationale D'Art Contemporain, Grand Palais, Paris, 82; Carl Solway Gallery, Cincinnati, Ohio, 85; Works of the Figure, Allegheny Col, Pa, 86; Landscapes, Southern Ohio Art Mus, 91; and others. *Teaching:* Prof, Univ Cincinnati, 73- *Awards:* Individual Artist Grant, Ohio Arts Coun, 78 & 82. *Dealer:* Osuna Gallery 1919 Q St NW Washington DC 20001; Carl Solway Gallery 314 W Fourth St Cincinnati OH 45202. *Mailing Add:* 2510 Moorman Ave Cincinnati OH 45206

STEWART, NORMAN
PRINTMAKER, PUBLISHER
b Detroit, Mich, Mar 31, 47. *Study:* Univ Mich, BFA, 69, MA, 72; Cranbrook Acad Art, studied with Irwin Hollander & Sewell Sillman, MFA, 77. *Work:* Brooklyn Mus, NY; Cleveland Mus Art, Ohio; Detroit Inst Art, Mich; Univ Ariz Mus Art, Tucson; Toledo Mus Art, Ohio; Kalamazoo Inst Arts, Mich. *Comn:* Print Comn, PBS, WTVS, Detroit, Mich, 75; Creative Artist Grant, Mich Coun Arts, Detroit, 81; print commission, Detroit Inst Arts, Founders Soc, Detroit, Mich, 82; Collaborative Print Comns, Univ Mich Sch Art, Ann Arbor, 84 & Mt Holyoke Col, South Hadley, Mass, 87. *Exhib:* 25th Nat Print Travelling Exhib, Smithsonian Inst & Nat Col Fine Arts, Wash, DC, 77-79; 21st & 22nd Nat Invitational Print Exhib, Brooklyn Mus, NY, 78-79 & 81-82; 7th British International Invitational, Print Biennale, Bradford, Eng, 81; 20th Century Prints & Drawings, Detroit Inst Arts, Mich, 81-82; New Am Graphics Two Invitational, Madison Arts Ctr, Wis, 82; Cabo Frio Int Print Biennial-82, Brazil, 82-83; Gene Baro Collects, Brooklyn Mus, 83; On the Leading Edge, Gen Elec Hq, Fairfield, Conn, 85; A Graphic Muse, Mt Holyoke Col Art Mus, Mass, Yale Univ Art Gallery, Conn, Santa Barbara Mus Art, Calif, Va Mus Fine Arts, Nelson-Atkins Mus Art, Mo, 87-88; Collaboration in Print, Stewart & Stewart Prints, 1980-1990 (with catalog), touring 91-93. *Pos:* Partner & master printer, Stewart & Stewart, Bloomfield

Hills, Mich, 80- *Teaching:* Guest artist screenprinting, Wayne State Univ, Detroit, Mich, 79-80; adj asst prof screenprinting , Sch Art, Univ Mich, Ann Arbor, 79-85; guest artist & lectr screenprinting, numerous art schools & museums across USA, 79- *Bibliog:* Simon Zalkind (auth), 21st Nat Print Exhib, Arts Mag, 2/79; Marsha Miro (auth), His art leaves a lasting impression, Detroit Free Press, 1/83; Joy Hakanson Colby (auth), Flying the colors for a Renaissance in screenprint, Detroit News, 8/85; Lynn Baxter (auth), Norm Stewart: Printmaker and Publisher, Screenprinting, 10/86; M Stephen Doherty (auth), Expanding your market with multiples, Am Artist, 5/87. *Publ:* Contribr, Screenprint in the making: Sondra Freckleton collaborates with Norman Stewart (video), Stewart & Stewart Printer/ Publisher of Fine Prints, 85. *Mailing Add:* c/o Stewart & Stewart 5571 Wing Lake Rd Bloomfield Hills MI 48301

STEWART, PAUL LEROY
PRINTMAKER, EDUCATOR
b Cleveland, Ohio, June 28, 28. *Study:* Cleveland Inst Art, 46-48; Albion Col, BA, 53; Univ Mich, Ann Arbor, MA, 59. *Work:* Detroit Inst Art; Libr Cong; Metrop Mus Art, New York; Minneapolis Inst Art; Cleveland Mus Art, Ohio. *Comn:* Bicentennial print, Mich Workshop Fine Prints, Detroit, 75. *Exhib:* Solo exhibs, DeWaters Art Ctr, Flint, Mich, 79, Lill Street Gallery, Chicago, Ill, 87, Deutsch-Amerikanisches Inst, Tubingen, Ger, 87 & Gallery Nishiazabu, Tokyo, Japan, 91; 11th 12th Int Print Exhib, Krakow, Poland, 86, 88 & 91; Second & Third Biennial Exhib of Prints in Wakayama, Japan, 87; 63rd Ann Int Competition, Print Club, Philadelphia, 87; Third & Fourth Int Print Exhibs, Taipei Fine Arts Mus, China, 87 & 90; 40th N Am Print Exhib, Brockton Art Mus, Mass, 88; The Electronic Print, Britol Polytech Inst, Bristol, Eng, 88; First Kochi Int Triennial Exhib of Prints, Kochi, Japan, 90; Osaka Triennale 91, Japan. *Teaching:* Assoc prof art, Albion Col, 59-72; prof, Univ Mich, Ann Arbor, 73-; guest instr lithography, Univ NMex, Albuquerque, summer 79. *Awards:* Malina Purchase Award & Medalist, 12th Int Print Biennal, Krakow, Poland, 88; First prize, First Kochi Int Triennial Exhib Prints, Kochi, Japan, 90; First Prize, 10th Norwegian Int Graphic Triennial, Fredrikstad, Norway, 92. *Bibliog:* C Overvoorte (auth), article, For the Time Being Fine Arts Mag, Vol II, No 2, 73; Artists in Michigan of the 20th Century, Smithsonian Inst Arch Am Art; Artists in Michigan, 1900-1976, Wayne State Univ Press. *Mem:* Mich Asn Printmakers. *Media:* All Media. *Publ:* AXIS World Design J, No 44, Tokyo, Japan, summer 92. *Dealer:* Gallery G 211 Ninth St Pittsburgh PA 15222; Art Search 111 N First Ann Arbor MI 48105. *Mailing Add:* 2281 Ayrshire Rd Ann Arbor MI 48105

STEWART, ROBERT GORDON
CURATOR, HISTORIAN
b Baltimore, Md, Mar 5, 31. *Study:* Univ Pa, BFA, 54. *Collections Arranged:* Nucleus for a National Collection, 1st Exhib Nat Portrait Gallery, Smithsonian Inst, 65, Recent Acquisitions, 66; National Gallery of 19th Century Distinguished Americans (with catalog), 69; Henry Benbridge (with catalog), 71; Robert Edge Pine (with catalog), 79. *Pos:* Architect & cur, Jefferson Barracks Hist Park, St Louis, Mo, 58-61; dir properties, Nat Trust Hist Preservation, 61-64; sr cur, Nat Portrait Gallery, Smithsonian Inst, 64-, consult ed, The Papers of George Washington, 91- *Teaching:* Vis lectr museology, George Washington Univ, 67-70. *Mem:* The Walpole Soc, Asn Historians Am Art. *Res:* American portraiture from 18th century to present; James Earl (1761-1796). *Publ:* Contribr, In the Minds and the Hearts of the People, 74; The Dye is Now Cast, 75; Abroad in America, 76. *Mailing Add:* 4104 46th St NW Washington DC 20016

STEWART, SHEILA L
DIRECTOR, CURATOR
Study: Ga Southern Col, BA, 76; Southern Ill Univ, MFA, 81. *Work:* Univ Mus, Carbondale, Ill; Alexandria Art Mus, La; Art Mus Southeast Tex, Beaumont. *Collections Arranged:* Laughing to Keep from Crying, Alexandria Mus, 85; Southeast Tex Collects Am Art (auth, catalog), 87; 500 Main: Installations (auth, catalog), Art Mus Southeast Tex, 85; Curator's Choice (auth, catalog), 88; James Surls, Art Mus Southeast Tex, 88. *Pos:* Cur, Alexandria Art Mus, 81-83, exec dir, 83-86; exec dir, Art Mus Southeast Tex, 86- *Awards:* Alexandria Mus Art, 84; Special Exhib Award, Nat Endowment Arts, 85 & 87; Art Mus Southeast Tex, 89. *Publ:* Laughing to Keep from Crying (catalog), 85; Annual Report (catalog), 87-92; John Alexander (catalog), 90; Paths to Grace (catalog), 91; Paul Maness (catalog), 92. *Mailing Add:* Art Mus of Southeast Tex 500 Main St Beaumont TX 77701

STEWART, WILLIAM
PAINTER
b Waco, Tex, Aug 18, 38. *Study:* Univ Tex, BFA, 60, MFA, 62, int artists seminars, Fairleigh Dickinson Univ, Madison, NJ, summers 61 & 62. *Work:* Fordham Univ, Bronx, NY; Fairleigh Dickinson Univ, Madison, NJ; Mus Mod Art, Vienna, Austria. *Exhib:* One-man shows, O K Harris Gallery, New York, 69, Rudolf Zwirner Gallery, Cologne, Ger, 70, Pergola Gallery, San Miguel de Allende, 78, Regional Mus, Oaxaca, Mex, 79, Bonnafont Gallery, San Francisco, Calif, 79, Regional Mus, Oaxaca, Mex, 79 & Old Jail Art Mus, Albany, Tex, 85; group exhibs, Biennale de Paris, France, 71, Newark Mus, NJ, 71, Thomas Moore Chapel, Fordham Univ, Bronx, NY, 76 & Charles Furr Gallery, Sante Fe, Mex, 85. *Teaching:* Asst dir educ dept & instr, San Francisco Mus Art, Calif, 63-64; art instr, Baleares Int Sch, Palma de Mallorca, Spain, 66-67; instr, dept art, Fairleigh Dickinson Univ, Madison, NJ, 68- 70, City Col NY, 71, Ed Dept, Newark Mus, NJ, 73-74; instr drawing & painting, Instituto Allende, San Miguel de Allende, Guanajuato, Mex, 77-78; vis artist, dept art & art hist, Univ Iowa, Iowa City, 81; art instr, Taos Valley School, NMex, 85; instr, dept art, Northern NMex Community Col, NMex, 90- *Bibliog:* Cindy Nimser (auth), Sculpture and the new realism, Arts Mag, 4/70; Emily Wasserman (auth), New York, Art Forum, 3/70; Rosalind Constable (auth), New sites for new sights, NY Mag, 12/70; William Stewart at Zwirner Gallery, Kölner Kulturspiegel, 9/70; Colin Naylor (ed), Contemporary Artist, St James Press Ltd, London, 77. *Media:* Oil, Watercolor. *Mailing Add:* 4161 NDCBU Taos NM 87571-6007

STEYNOVITZ, ZAMY
PAINTER
b Liegnitz, Poland, Jan 15, 51; US citizen. *Study:* Avni Inst, Tel-Aviv, 70-72; Royal Acad, London, 72-75; Art League, New York, 76-80. *Work:* Museo Simon Bolivar, Caracas, Venezuela; Ana Frank Mus, Amsterdam, Holland; Nat Mus Art, San-Jose, Costa-Rica. *Comn:* medal, Judaic Heritage Soc, New York, 79; mural, Mus Simon Bolivar, Caracas, Venezuela, 83. *Exhib:* One man shows, Ramat-Gan, Israel, 70, Jewish Mus, Cleveland, Ohio, 80, Nat Mus Art, San-Jose, Costa-Rica, 83; Tribute to John Lennon, Abraham-Goodman House, New York, 81; Homage to Bolivar, Simon Bolivar Mus, Caracas, Venezuela, 83. *Bibliog:* Saul Mayzlish (auth), Zamy Steynovitz, Revivim Publ, 80; Alex Meilichson (auth), Zamy Steynovitz, Kshatot Arts, 92. *Media:* Oils, Litographe. *Publ:* Auth, Peace Litographe between Israel & Egypt, NY Times & Harold Tribion Int, 79; Art Book of Steynovitz in Colors, Revivim Israel, 80 & Kshatot Israel, 92; Medal Ana Frank, NY Times, sunday 80. *Dealer:* Baruch Kutany 6721 North Corie lane Westhills CA 91307. *Mailing Add:* 67-12 Yellowstone Blvd Forest Hills NY 11375

STICKER, ROBERT EDWARD
PAINTER
b Jersey City, NJ, Dec 26, 22. *Study:* Art Students League, with Frank Reilly. *Work:* IBM Corp, AT&T & Nat Distillers, New York. *Exhib:* Mystic Maritime Gallery Group Shows. *Pos:* Mem bd control, Art Students League, 59- *Awards:* Gold Medal, Franklin Mint Nat Marine Competition, 74; Award of Excellence, Mystic Int, 89. *Mem:* Fel Am Soc Marine Artists. *Media:* Oil, Watercolor. *Publ:* Illusr, Famous small boat voyages, 69-72 & Classical work boats of America, 73- (ser of paintings), Yachting Mag; Steam on the Rivers (prints), Janus Lithograph. *Dealer:* Mystic Maritime Gallery. *Mailing Add:* RD 1 Pleasant Mt PA 18453

STIEBEL, ERIC
DEALER
b Frankfurt, Ger, July 22, 11; US citizen. *Study:* Univ Frankfurt, 29-30; Univ Munich, 30-31; Univ Berlin, 31-32. *Pos:* Chmn, Rosenberg & Stiebel, currently. *Mem:* Nat Antique & Art Dealers Asn Am; Art & Antique Dealers League Am; Art Dealers Asn Am; Int Confedn Dealer in Works Art; Syndicat Nat des Antiquaires. *Specialty:* Old master paintings and drawings; important French 18th century furniture; Renaissance bronzes. *Mailing Add:* 912 Fifth Ave New York NY 10021

STIEBEL, GERALD GUSTAVE
DEALER
b New York, NY, Sept 28, 44. *Study:* C W Post Col, BA, 65; Courtauld Inst, London, 65-66; Study Centre Fine & Decorative Arts, London, dipl, 66; Columbia Univ, MA(art hist), 67. *Collections Arranged:* Grand Gallery Exhib, Metrop Mus Art, New York, 74-75; Experts Choice, Va Mus Art, 83; Chez Elle Chez Lui: At Home in 18th Century France, 87; Collecting at the top, 88; Of Knights & Spires: Gothic Renewal in France & Germany, 89; Louis XV and Madame de Pompadour: A Love Affair with Style, 90. *Pos:* Treas, Rosenberg & Stiebel Inc, 68-71, vpres, 71-85, pres, 85- *Teaching:* Lectr, numerous universities & museums incl Guggenheim Mus & Metrop Mus Art, New York. *Mem:* Nat Antique & Art Dealers Asn Am (secy, 71-73, vpres, 73-77, pres, 77-79, bd dirs, 79-84); La Confederation Int Negociants Oeuvres d'Art (permanent deleg, 72-, pres, 81-84, counr, 84-85, life councillor, 90-); Art Dealers Asn Am (bd dirs, 80-89). *Specialty:* Old master paintings and drawings; important French 18th century furniture; renaissance bronzes. *Publ:* Auth, The Passionate Collector, Designer Mag, 72; Collector's Handbook, Cincinnati Art Mus, 78. *Mailing Add:* 32 E 57th St New York NY 10022

STIEBEL, PENELOPE HUNTER See Hunter-Stiebel, Penelope

STILLMAN, DAMIE
HISTORIAN, EDUCATOR
b Dallas, Tex, July 27, 33. *Study:* Northwestern Univ, BS, 54; Univ Del, MA, 56; Columbia Univ, PhD, 61. *Collections Arranged:* Architecture & Ornament in Late 19th Century America (ed, catalog), 81. *Teaching:* Asst prof art hist, Oakland Univ, 61-65; assoc prof, Univ Wis, Milwaukee, 65-67, prof, 67-77; prof, Univ Del, 77-89, chmn dept, 81-86, prof, 89-; John W Shirley, Prof Univ Del, 89- *Awards:* Nat Endowment Humanities Fel, 70-71 & 86-87; Founders Award, Soc Archit Historians, 75; Gottscalk Prize, Am Soc for 18th Century Study, 88. *Mem:* Col Art Asn Am; Soc Archit Historians (mem bd dirs, 75-78 & 84-87, second vpres, 78-80, first vpres, 80-82, pres, 82-84); Am Soc for 18th Century Study; Victorian Soc. *Res:* American and British architecture and decorative arts with special emphasis on neo-classicism. *Publ:* Co-ed, American Colonial Painting, Harvard Univ Press, 59; auth, New York City Hall: Competition and execution, J Soc Archit Historians, 64; auth, The Decorative Work of Robert Adam, Tiranti, 67; ed, Architecture & Ornament in Late 19th Century America, Univ Del, 81; auth, English Neo-classical Architecture, Zwemmer, 88. *Mailing Add:* Dept Art Hist Univ Del Newark DE 19716

STILLMAN, E CLARK
COLLECTOR
b Eureka, Utah, Oct 24, 07. *Study:* Univ Mich, AB & AM. *Res:* African sculpture; medieval and modern book illumination and illustration. *Collection:* Traditional Congolese sculpture; manuscript and printed Books of Hours. *Mailing Add:* 24 Gramercy Park South New York NY 10003

STILLMAN, GEORGE
PAINTER
b Laramie, Wyo, Feb 25, 21. *Study:* Calif Sch Fine Arts, cert, 49; Ariz State Univ, BFA, MFA, 70. *Work:* Oakland Mus Art, Calif; High Mus Art, Atlanta, Ga; Laguna Art Mus, Calif; Metro Mus Art, New York; Nat Mus Am Arts, Smithsonian, Washington, DC. *Comn:* Murals, comn by Wash Art Comn, Olympia, La Cross, 78, Medical Lake, 78, Omak, 80, Naches, 80, Burbank, 80; and others. *Exhib:* 2nd Ann Int Drawing & Painting Show, Calif Palace of the Legion of Honor, San Francisco, 47; San Francisco Mus Art 69th Ann, 49; two-man show, Lucien Labaudt Gallery, San Francisco, 49; one-man shows, Galeria Arte Mod, Mexico City, 51 & Columbus Mus, Ga, 72; Gallery Inago, San Francisco, Calif, 89; 100 Years of Washington Art, Tagona Mus, Washington, 90; and others. *Teaching:* Prof & chmn, Dept Art, Columbus Col, Ga, 70-72; prof & chmn, Dept Art, Cent Wash Univ, 72-84, prof, 85- *Awards:* Bender Award, San Francisco Art Asn, 49; Ann Bremer Award San Francisco Mus Art, 49; Fel in painting, Nat Endowment Asn, 90. *Bibliog:* articles in Diebenkorn Catalog: Published Lithographs, Mill Valley, Calif, 49; David Park (catalog), Whitney Mus Am Art, New York; Caroline Jones (auth), Bay Area Figurative Art 1950-1965, Univ Calif, Berkeley. *Mem:* Col Art Asn; Nat Watercolor Asn. *Media:* All. *Dealer:* Foster-White Gallery Seattle WA. *Mailing Add:* 1127 Franklin Ave Ellensburg WA 98926

STILLMAN, LUCILLE T
PAINTER
b Chicago, Ill. *Study:* Art Inst Chicago; Acad Fine Arts, Chicago, BA; Col Arts and Crafts, Calif, MFA. *Work:* UNICEF, New York; Smithsonian Mus Galleries, Washington; Martin County Found Arts, Va; IBM Corp, New York; Clifford House, Bridgeport, Conn. *Comn:* US Coast Guard Rescue, Governor's Island, 85; Mrs Correa-Founder of the Fleming Sch, comn by Dr & Mrs Edwin Fondo, New York, 90. *Exhib:* Solo show, Fairfield Univ, Conn, 83, Seaport Mus, Norwalk, Conn, 85, Univ Conn, Stamford, 89; Int Women Artist, Nat Mus, Belgrade, Yugloslavia, 87; Nat Arts Club, New York, 88, Pen and Brush Club, New York, 89. *Awards:* Best in Show, Nat League of Am Penwomen, 89; Best in Show, Kent Art Asn, 89; Gold Medal, Pen and Brush Club, 89. *Bibliog:* Kathleen Paradiso (auth), Feistily Flouting Trends, Women Artists News, 1/86; Ron Lister (auth), Drawing With Pastels, Prentice Hall, 86; People In Action, Spotlight Connecticut Mag, 1/87. *Mem:* Art Students League (life mem); Pastel Soc Am; Salmagundi Club; Catherine Lorillard Wolfe Art Club. *Media:* Oil. *Publ:* Contribr, Connecticut Mag, 8/86; Art News, 6/86; Drawing with Pastels, Prentice-Hall, 86. *Dealer:* Soho 20 Gallery 469 Broome St New York NY 10013. *Mailing Add:* 8 Drum Hill Ln Stamford CT 06902

STINNETT, HESTER A
PRINTMAKER
b Baltimore, Md, June 29, 56. *Study:* Hartford Art Sch, Univ Hartford, Conn, BFA, 78; Tyler Sch Art, Temple Univ, Philadelphia, MFA, 82. *Work:* Walker Art Ctr, Minneapolis; West Chester Univ, Pa; Philadelphia Mus Art, Pa. *Exhib:* Fleisher Art Mem, Philadelphia, 82; 16th National, Potsdam State Univ, NY, 82; Rutgers National, Stedman Art Gallery, Camden, NJ, 84; Solo exhibs, Denison Univ, Ohio, 85 & Haverford Col, Pa, 86; Prints from Blocks: 1900-1985, Assoc Am Artists, New York, 85; Cassa di Risparmio di Biella, Biella, Italy, 87; Pertainting to Philadelphia, Philadelphia Mus Art, 92. *Pos:* Dir, Philadelphia Col Art printmaking workshop, 84-86. *Teaching:* Adj lectr printmaking, Philadelphia Col Art, 82-86; lectr printmaking, Bryn Mawr, Col Pa, 85-86; asst prof printmaking, Tyler Sch Art, Temple Univ, Philadelphia, 86-92, assoc prof & assoc dean, 92. *Mem:* Col Art Asn; Philadelphia Print Club. *Media:* Woodcut. *Publ:* Water-based Inks: A Screenprinting Manual for Studio and Classroom, Univ Arts, Philadelphia, Pa, 87. *Dealer:* Dolan/Maxwell Gallery 1701 Walnut Street Philadelphia PA 19103. *Mailing Add:* 1110 S Franklin St Philadelphia PA 19147

STINSMUEHLEN-AMEND, SUSAN
COLLAGE ARTIST, PAINTER
b Baltimore, Md, Nov 5, 48. *Study:* Hood Col, Indiana Univ & Univ Tex, 66-72. *Work:* Leigh Yawkey Woodson Mus, Wausau, Wis; Wagga Wagga City Art Gallery, New South Wales, Australia; Pilchuck Glass Ctr, Stanwood, Wash; Corning Mus Glass, New York; Detroit Inst Arts, Mich; Marshall Fields Corp Collection, Chicago; Radisson Hotel, Austin, TX; Jewish Mus & Am Craft Mus, New York. *Comn:* Glass entrance, comn by Youens, Houston, 82; glass wall mural, Veteran's Admin Med Ctr, Dallas, 83; leaded glass entrance, comn by Charles Travis, Austin, TX; leaded glass walls, Reunion Bank, Dallas, 87; leaded glass facade, comn by Jerry & Simona Chazen, Nyack, NY, 88; leaded glass mural, Christ Church Cathedral, Houston, TX, 91; and others. *Exhib:* Texas Crafts, Dallas Mus Fine Arts, 81; Americans in Glass, Leigh Yawkey Woodson Mus, Wis, Cooper Hewitt Mus, New York & Krannert Mus, Ill, 81; solo exhibs, Mattingly Baker Gallery, Dallas, 84, Kurland Summers Gallery, Los Angeles, 85, 88, 90 & 92, Traver Sutton Gallery, Seattle, 86 & Habitat Galleries, Detroit, 91; Pilchuck Exhib, Traver Gallery & Pilchuck Glass Exhib, Sea-Tac Airport, Seattle, 91; Nineteenth Int Glass Invitational, Habatat Galleries, Detroit, Mich, 91; Selections from the Chordokoff Collection, Detroit Inst Arts, Mich, 91; New Glass, Joanne Rapp Gallery, Scottsdale, Ariz, 92; Twentieth Int Glass Invitational, Habatat Galleries, Detroit, Mich, 92; Second Australian Int Crafts Triennial, Design Visions, Art Gallery of Western Australia, 92; Glass from Ancient Craft to Contemp Art: 1962-1992 and Beyond, Morris Mus, NJ, Fine Arts Mus South, Ala, Art Mus STex, Scottsdale Ctr Arts, Ariz, Philbrook Mus Art, Okla, 92; Clearly Art: Pilchuck's Glass Legacy, Whatcom Mus, Bellingham, Wash, 92; A Decade of Craft, Recent Acquisitions, Am Craft Mus, New York, 92; Extended Boundaries, Bath House, Atlanta Arts Festival, Ga, 92; Venice Art Walk, Calif, 92. *Pos:* Owner & designer, Renaissance Glass Co, Austin, Tex, 73-87; lead artist, Hollywood Blvd Streetscape Team, Design for Public Art in Hollywood, Calif, 91-92. *Teaching:* Guest artist & lectr Pilchurch Glass Sch, 80-92, Glass Art Soc Conference, 81, 87 & 90, Calif Col Arts & Crafts, 85, 89 & 92, Santa Monica City Col, 88 & 92, Calif State Univ, Fullerton, 91, Cleveland Art Inst, 91, San Francisco Art Inst, 92; and many others. *Awards:* Nat Endowment Arts Fel, 82 & 88; Tex Home Design Competition Honor Award, 86. *Bibliog:* Galleries, Los Angeles Times, 2/2/90; Patricia Conway (auth), Art for Everyday: The New Craft Moveme; Lloyd E Herman (auth), Art That Works: Decorative Arts of the Eighties Crafted in America, Univ of Was Press, Seattle, 90; Rick Mashburn (auth), The new gleam in stained glass, Diversion, 90, p145-47 & 228-29; Ben Marks (auth), Short reviews, Artweek, 2/1/90; Showcase: Screens and dividers, Professional Stained Glass, The Edge Publishing Co, Brewster, NY, 8/91; Shawn Waggoner (auth), Southern California's glass artists: Diversity defined, Glass Art, Jan/Feb 92; Ben Marks (auth), Susan Stinsmuehlen-Amend and the aesthetics of anarchy, Glass, summer 92, No 48. *Mem:* Hon life mem, Glass Art Soc (bd dirs, 82-84, pres, 84-86); Am Craft Coun (bd trustee, 88-92). *Media:* Glass, Mixed Media. *Dealer:* Kurland Summers Gallery Los Angeles CA. *Mailing Add:* c/o Impresa Inc 1112 N Tamarind Ave Hollywood CA 90038

STINSMUEHLEN-AMEND, SUSAN See Stinsmuehlen-Amend, Susan

STIRNWEIS, SHANNON
PAINTER, ILLUSTRATOR
b Portland, Ore, Feb 26, 31. *Study:* Univ Ore, 49-50; Art Ctr Col Design with John Lagatta, BFA, 50-54; Study with Joseph Henniger & Reynold Brown, 56. *Work:* Parks Dept, US Dept Interior, US Air Force Hist & Mus Collection, US Army Hist Mus Collection, Washington, DC; Univ Wyo, Laramie; Calif Fed Savings Collection. *Comn:* Reindeer Being Loaded on Coast Guard Ship, US Coast Guard, 88; Jennings-All American (portrait), US Air Force Acad, Colo. *Exhib:* Soc Illustrators Ann Exhib, Mus Am Illus, New York, 68-75; 200 Years of American Illustration, Mus City New York, 76; Governors Show, Cheyenne, Wyo, 85. *Awards:* Best Dog Book of Year, Dog Writers Asn, 65; Award of Merit, Soc Illus Ann Exhib, 68-75 & 86. *Bibliog:* R Bolivar (auth), An artist who has returned to the West, Southwest Art, 10/77; Samuels (auth), Contemporary Western artists, Southwest Art; Walt Reed (auth), Illustrator in America 1880-1980, Madison Square Press. *Mem:* Soc Illus, New York; Graphic Artists Guild, New York. *Media:* Oil. *Publ:* Illusr, Dogs of the World, Whitman, 65; Ah, Wilderness, Ltd Editions Club, 72; Auth, Art of Painting the Dog, 77, Art of Painting the Cat, 77 & Art of Painting the Wild West, 78, Grumbacher. *Dealer:* Connally Alterman & Morris 3461 W Alabama Houston TX 77027; Troy's Western Heritage Gallery 7190 Main St Scottsdale AZ 85251. *Mailing Add:* 31 Fawn Place Wilton CT 06897

STIRRATT, BETSY (ELIZABETH ANNE)
PAINTER, GALLERY DIRECTOR
b New Orleans, La, Sept 22, 58. *Study:* Louisiana State Univ, BFA, 80; Ind Univ, MFA, 83. *Exhib:* Dark Ages, Indianapolis Mus Art, 91; Language & Symbol in Contemporary Art, Greater Lafayette Mus Art, Ind, 92; Salon Show, Art in General, New York, 92; Primarily Paint, Laguna Gloria Art Mus, Houston, Tex, 92; recent paintings, South Bend Regional Mus Art, South Bend, Ind, 93; and others. *Awards:* Master's Fel, Ind Arts Comn, 89; Fel, Arts Midwest, 89; Visual Arts Fel, Nat Endowment Arts, 90. *Mailing Add:* 2504 Poplar Ct Bloomington IN 47401

STITT, SUSAN (MARGARET)
MUSEUM DIRECTOR
b East Liverpool, Ohio, Jan 24, 42. *Study:* Col William & Mary, AB; Univ Pa, MA. *Pos:* Asst to dir, Hist Soc Pa; dir, Mus Albemarle; adminr, Mus Early Southern Decorative Arts; asst to dir, Brooklyn Mus; proj dir surv placement & training, Old Sturbridge Village, Mass; dir, Mus at Stony Brook, 74-88; consult, Mus Historical Gallery, 88; Hist Soc of Pa, currently. *Teaching:* Adj assoc prof, State Univ NY, Stonybrook, 75-78. *Awards:* Women of the Year in Art, Village Times, 87; Kathleen Coffey Award, Mid-Atlantic Asn Mus, 87; Ward Melville Community Award, Three Village Historical Soc, 88. *Mem:* Am Asn Mus; Long Island Mus Asn; NE Mus Conf; New York State Asn Mus (coun mem); and others. *Publ:* Auth, The will of Stephen Charlton & Hungars Parish, Va Mag Hist & Biog, 7/69; auth, Museum of Early Southern Decorative Arts, 70; auth, Today's labor practices, the search for equality, Mus News, 9-10/75; auth, Trustee orientation: A sound investment, Mus News, 5-6/81; Bryant F Tolles, Jr (ed), The Diamond Link: The Director as Internal Communicator and Human Resources Manager, in Leadership for the Future: Changing Directoral Roles in American History Museums and Historical Socities, 89. *Mailing Add:* c/o Historical Soc of PA 1300 Locust St Philadelphia PA 19107

STOCKDALE, JOHN A D
PAINTER, PHOTOGRAPHER
b Ipswich, Queensland, Australia, Mar 15, 36; US citizen. *Study:* Univ Sydney, Australia, BSc(Hons II), 58, MSc, 60; Univ Tenn, PhD, 69. *Work:* Nat Gallery Victoria, Melbourne; Art Gallery New South Wales, Sydney; San Francisco Mus Mod Art; Corcoran Gallery Art, Washington, DC; Univ Calif Art Mus, Berkeley. *Exhib:* Sao Paolo Biennial, Brazil, 61; Portals, Marlborough Gallery, New York, 76; Warm Truths, Cool Deceits, traveling, 77 & 78; Solo exhibs, Univ Calif Art Mus, Berkeley, 77, Australian Ctr Photog, Sydney, 78, Southeastern Ctr Contemp Art, Winston-Salem, NC, 80; The American Experience, Bass Mus, Miami, Balch Inst, Philadelphia & traveling, 85-86. *Awards:* Clint Prize, Contemp Art Soc Australia, 56; Guggenheim Found Fel, Painting, 70; Sproul Assoc, Univ Calif, 78. *Bibliog:* Joan Murray (auth), John Stockdale photographs, Art Week, Oakland, Calif, 2/77; Alfred Frankenstein (auth), John Stockdale photographs, San Francisco

Chronicle, 2/77; Max Kozloff (auth), Photography and Fascination, Addison House, 79. *Media:* Oils, Color Photography. *Dealer:* Bertha Urdang Gallery 23 E 74th St New York NY 10021. *Mailing Add:* 1325 E Juana Ave San Leandro CA 94577

STOEVEKEN, ANTHONY CHARLES
PRINTMAKER, EDUCATOR
b Milwaukee, Wis, Oct 28, 38. *Study:* Univ Wis-Milwaukee, BS(art educ), 60, MS(art), 66; Tamarind Lithography Workshop, Los Angeles, Master Printer(Ford Found Fel), 68. *Work:* Mus Mod Art, New York; Gruenwald Graphic Arts Found, Univ Calif, Los Angeles; Los Angeles Co Mus Art; Nat Gallery Art, Wash, DC; Crocker Nat Bank, San Francisco, Calif. *Comn:* Ed of prints, Edgewood Orchard Galleries, Fish Creek, Wis, 74; exterior mural, John Michael Kohler Art Ctr, Sheboygan, Wis, 77; mural, Wis Art Bd's Percent for Art, 85. *Exhib:* Northwest Printmakers 41st Int Exhib, Seattle Art Mus & Portland Art Mus, Ore, 70; 42nd Ann Seattle Print Int, Seattle Art Mus, 71; IX Salon de Grabado, Inst Cult Peruano--Norte Americano, Lima, Peru, 73; 74th Exhib by Artists of Chicago & 77th Exhib, Works on Paper, Chicago Art Inst, 73 & 78; Wis Directions Two, Milwaukee Art Ctr, 78; 50 Artists-50 Printers, Univ NMex Art Mus, 85; Contemporary Realism, K Gingross Gallery, 89. *Pos:* Asst studio mgr, Tamarind Lithography Workshop, Los Angeles, 68; tech dir, Graphicstudio, Univ Fla Tampa, 68-70. *Teaching:* Asst prof art, lithography, Univ SFla, Tampa, 68-70; prof art, lithography, Univ Wis-Milwaukee, 70- *Awards:* Univ Wis-Milwaukee grad sch grant, aluminum plate & lithography, 75 & 86; Wis Arts Bd res grant, Chine-Colle, 79. *Bibliog:* Donald Key (auth), Graphic by University of Wisconsin-Milwaukee teacher, Milwaukee J, 72; Barbara Manger (auth), Tucholke and Stoeveken at the Kohler Art Center, Mid-West Art, Gary Pizarick, 76; James Auer (auth), Fantasy in the family, Milwaukee J, 80. *Mem:* Col Art Asn; Mid-America Col Art Asn (pres, 81). *Media:* Lithography, Drawing. *Dealer:* Edgewood Orchard Gallery, Fish Creek, Wis 54212. *Mailing Add:* 5074 N Hollywood Ave Milwaukee WI 53217

STOEVEKEN, CHRISTEL E See Tucholke, Christel-Anthony (Christel E Stoeveken)

STOFFA, MICHAEL
INSTRUCTOR, PAINTER
b Hlinne, Czech; nat US. *Study:* Newark Sch Fine & Indust Arts, NJ, 48; Pa Acad Fine Arts, Philadelphia, 50-51. *Work:* Canojoharie Mus, New York; Art Students League, New York; New England Telephone. *Comn:* Pvt portraits for personal collections, 58-; and others. *Exhib:* Summer Juried Exhib, Rockport Art Asn, Mass, 73-88 & North Shore Art Asn, Gloucester, Mass, 65-92; Annual Exhib, Salmagundi Club, 77- *Pos:* Owner & art teacher, Michael Stoffa Gallery Studio, Westfield, NJ, 58-68; co-owner, Michael Stoffa Gallery, Rockport, Mass, 63- *Teaching:* Instr art painting, various art asns, NJ, 58-68, workshops, Cape Cod Art Asn, 81-91. *Awards:* Distinguished Serv Award, North Shore Arts Asn, 90; Top Ten North Shore Volunteer, 90; Rockports Small Bus Person of the Year, 92. *Mem:* North Shore Art Asn, Gloucester (bd mem, 80-); Salmagundi Club; Art Fel Inc; Burr Artist. *Media:* Oil. *Publ:* Contribr, Newsweek, New York Times, Boston Globe, ArtistMag, Art & Antique, 88. *Mailing Add:* 49A Main St Rockport MA 01966

STOFFLET, MARY
CURATOR, CRITIC
b Long Branch, NJ, Dec 23, 42. *Study:* Skidmore Col, BA, 64; NY Univ, MA, 69; M H de Young Mem Mus, San Francisco, Rockefeller-Nat Endowment Arts Fel Mus Educ, 75-76. *Collections Arranged:* International Rubber Stamp Art Exhibition, La Mamelle Arts Ctr, San Francisco, 76; Cityscapes, 77 & Yosemite, 79, Fine Arts Mus San Francisco, Downtown Ctr; Construction, San Francisco Int Airport, 82; Dr Seuss from Then to Now, 86, More Then Meets the Eye, 87, Cultural Currents, 88, San Diego Mus Art, 88; Faberge: The Imperial Eggs, 89, Li Huai: An Artist in Two Cultures, 89, Latin American Drawings Today, 91, San Diego Mus Art; Calif Cityscapes, 91 & The Frederick R Weisman Collection of Contemporary California Art, 91, San Diego Mus Art. *Pos:* Newsletter ed, Western Asn of Art Mus, Oakland, 74-77; contrib ed, Artweek, 74-81; assoc ed, La Mamelle, 75-77; ed, Front, 76-; coordr intern prog, M H de Young Mem Mus, 77-80; contrib ed, Images & Issues, 80-; asst cur, San Francisco Int Airport, 82-84; cur educ, San Diego Mus Art, 85-88; cur, Mod Art, San Diego Mus Art, currently. *Teaching:* Instr art hist, Oakland Mus, Calif, 77-; lectr art hist, San Francisco State Univ, 77 & 81, Univ Calif San Diego Extension, 87. *Awards:* Critic's Fel, Nat Endowment Arts, 81. *Mem:* Col Art Asn; Am Asn Mus; Int Asn Art Critics; San Diego Independent Scholars Publications; Art Table Inc. *Publ:* Auth, American Women Artists: 20th Century, Slides & Notes, 78 & Women Artists: Sculptors-Photographers, Slides & Notes, 79, Harper & Row; ed, Correspondence Art: Sourcebook for the Network of International Postal Art Activity, Contemp Arts Press, 84; auth, Dr Seuss From Then to Now, San Diego Mus Art, 86 & Random House, 87; essayist & coordr ed, Latin American Drawings Today, San Diego Mus Art & Univ Wash Press, 91; auth & coordr ed, California Cityscapes, San Diego Mus Art & Universe, 91. *Mailing Add:* 3560 1/2 Fifth Ave San Diego CA 92103

STOIANOVICH, MARCELLE
PAINTER, PRINTMAKER
Study: Col d'Art Applique a l'Industrie, Paris, France. *Work:* Work in pvt collections. *Comn:* Window display, Guerlain, Paris; book jacket designs for Doubleday & Co. *Exhib:* Salon des Artistes Francais, Paris, France; Galerie Pierre Hautot, Paris; Assoc Am Artists, New York; Mitsukoshi Galerie, Paris, France; FAR Galleries & Weyhe Gallery, New York; Venable Gallery, Washington, DC; France Garo, Tokyo; Zimmerli Art Mus, New Brunswick, NJ; and others. *Awards:* Hon Mention for Watercolor, Beaux-Arts, Paris, 50; Selected Film Credits, Festival Am Films, Deauville, France, 75. *Bibliog:* New York Art Review, 89; Chicago Art Review, 89. *Mem:* Metrop Mus Art, New York City. *Media:* Miscellaneous Media, Lithography. *Publ:* The Art of Heflin Video 88. *Dealer:* Mitsukoshi Paris France; Heflin Gallery Rockford Ill. *Mailing Add:* 60 Rector St Metuchen NJ 08840

STOKES, LOUIS (WALTER)
SCULPTOR, EDUCATOR
New York, NY, June 23, 41. *Study:* Duquesne Univ, BA, 63; Hollins Col, MA, 65; Univ Calif, Berkeley, PhD, 68. *Work:* Can Coun Art Bank, Ottawa; Robert McLaughlin Gallery, Oshawa, Ont. *Comn:* Fiberglass water fountain sculpture, McMaster Univ, Hamilton, Ont, 72; outdoor wood wall relief, Metrop Toronto Zoo, 74; laminated wood wall sculpture, Ont Govt, Newmarket, 80; environmental steel sculpture, Nat Capital Comn, Ottawa, 80; ann award sculpture (bronze), Acad Can Cinema, Toronto, 81. *Exhib:* Solo exhibs, Alchemy Spirals, Dalhousie Art Gallery, Halifax, NS, 80, Wood Sculptures 1976-1982, Art Gallery Windsor, Ont, 82, Sacred Trees, Toronto City Sculpture Garden, 82-83, Trees of Life, Recent Sculpture 1982-1984, Agnes Etherington Art Ctr, Queens Univ, & Kingston & Not Really Trees, Art Gallery of York Univ, Toronto, Ont, 86, Sculpture In the Park, Can Nat Exhib, Toronto, 82; Contemp Outdoor Sculpture at the Guild, Toronto, 82; Windsor Exhib: New Canadian Sculpture, Art Gallery of Windsor & Community Sculpture '85, Cambridge Art Gallery, Cambridge, 85, Ont; and others. *Bibliog:* Peter Such (auth), Contemporary outdoor sculpture at the Guild, Artmag, 9-10/82; Dale McConathy (auth), Architecture as imagination of the future: Sculpture as speculation on the past, Artscanada, 11/82; Ted Fraser (auth), Louis Stokes: Sculpture 1976-1982, Artmag, spring 83; Louise Dompierre (auth), Louis Stokes: Trees of life, decoding form and reconstructing meaning, Art Post, Vol 2, No 3, 11-12/84. *Mem:* bd dir Royal Can Acad Arts. *Media:* All. *Mailing Add:* 5735 Knights Dr Manotick ON K4M 1B2 Canada

STOKSTAD, MARILYN
HISTORIAN, EDUCATOR
b Lansing, Mich, Feb 16, 29. *Study:* Carleton Col, BA, 50; Mich State Univ, MA, 53; Univ Mich, PhD, 57. *Pos:* Cur, Spencer Mus Art, 67-; res cur medieval art, Nelson-Atkins Mus Art, Kansas City, 69- *Teaching:* Prof hist art, Univ Kans, 58-79, chmn dept, 61-72, dir, Mus Art, 61-67, assoc dean, Col Arts & Sci, 72-76, Univ Distinguished Prof, 79- *Awards:* Humanities Inst Fel, 76-77; Dumbarton Oaks Fel, 81-82; Smithsonian Fel, 86, 90. *Mem:* Midwest Col Art Conf (pres, 64-65); Col Art Asn Am (pres, 78-80); Am Asn Univ Prof; Soc Archit Historians; Int Ctr Medieval Art (vpres, 90-). *Res:* Medieval art; Spanish art; art of the British Isles. *Publ:* Auth, Renaissance art outside Italy, Art Horizons, 68; ed & auth, Hortus Imaginum: Studies in Western Art, Humanistic Series 45, Univ Kans, 74; auth, Santiago de Compostela in the Age of the Pilgrimages, Okla Univ, 79; Scottish Culture, Abrams, 81; ed & auth, Museums, Humanities and the Educated Eye, Univ Kans, 82; Medieval Art, Harper & Row, 86. *Mailing Add:* 4703 Balmoral Dr Lawrence KS 66046

STOLL, (MRS) BERRY VINCENT
COLLECTOR
b Louisville, Ky, Feb 2, 06. *Study:* Bryn Mawr Col; Louisville Art Sch. *Pos:* Vpres emer, J B Speed Art Mus, Louisville, currently. *Collection:* Paintings and antiques. *Mailing Add:* 3905 Lime Kiln Ln Louisville KY 40222

STOLL, TONI
PAINTER
b New York, NY, Nov 5, 22. *Study:* Syracuse Univ, BFA, 41; Rutgers Univ, Grad Sch, 54; workshops with Dong Kingman, Miles Batt, Charles Reid, Frank Webb & Edward Betts, 80-90. *Work:* New Brunswick Pub Libr, NJ; Pub Serv Gas & Elec Co, Newark, NJ; Terra Bank Bldg, Miami, Fla; Ryder Systems Bldg, Miami, Fla; Art & Cult Ctr, Hollywood, Fla. *Comn:* Numerous portraits in watercolor, 55-90. *Exhib:* Am Artist's Prof League, Smithsonian Inst, Washington, DC, 61 & 63; Am Artist's Prof League, Nat Arts Club, New York, 61 & 62; Painters & Sculptors Soc, Jersey City Mus, NJ, 61-66; NJ Tercentenary, Douglass Col Gallery, New Brunswick, 64; Watercolors West XVI, Riverside Art Ctr, Calif, 84; Thomas Ctr & Capital Bldg, Gainsville & Tallahassee, Fla, 88; Miami Watercolor Soc, Metrop Mus Art, Coral Gables, Fla, 86- 88; Of the Figure II, Vero Beach Ctr Arts, Fla, 90; Aqueous '91, Ky Watercolor Soc, Wrather W Mus, Murray, 91. *Pos:* Instr painting, New Brunswick Art Ctr, NJ, 54-72; bd mem, art in public places, Broward County, Fort Lauderdale, Fla, 89-90; mem art task force, Comt of Broward Cult Affairs Coun, Ft Lauderdale, Fla, 90- *Teaching:* Art, Lafayette Sch, Highland Park, NJ, 54-58; instr painting, New Brunswick Art Ctr, NJ, 54-72; private classes, Home Studio, Highland Park, NJ, 54-72. *Awards:* Award for Excellence, Miami Watercolor Soc, 86; Best in Show, Gold Coast Watercolor Soc, 88; Best in Show, Am Artists Prof League, Miami Chap, 90. *Bibliog:* Don Webb & Wendy Blazier (auths), Expressions, W-LRN-TV, 89; Paula H Asslocker (auth), Outstanding Women of New Jersey, Women in the Arts, Univ Women Mag. *Mem:* Life signature mem, Florida Watercolor Soc; life signature mem, Gold Coast Watercolor Soc; life mem, Am Artist's Prof League; Women's Caucus for Art; Broward Art Guild. *Media:* Watercolor. *Publ:* La Revue Moderne, Publication Mensuelle, Paris, France, 61. *Mailing Add:* 1703 St Andrews Rd Hollywood FL 33021

STOLLER, JOHN CHAPMAN
DEALER
b Minneapolis, Minn, Feb 7, 40. *Study:* Univ Minn, BA(art hist). *Pos:* Owner, John C Stoller & Co, presently. *Mem:* Art Dealers Asn Am; CINOA (Confederation International des Negociants en Oeuvres D'Art). *Specialty:* Contemporary American and European paintings, drawings, sculpture and graphics. *Mailing Add:* 81 Ninth St S 380 Minneapolis MN 55402

STOLOFF, CAROLYN
PAINTER, COLLAGE
b New York, NY. *Study:* Univ Ill; Columbia Univ, BS; Art Students League; Atelier 17; with Xavier Gonzalez, Eric Isenburger & Hans Hofmann. *Work:* Norfolk Mus Arts & Scis; Canadian Imperial Bank Commerce. *Exhib:* Whitney Mus Am Art; Pa Acad Fine Arts; Audubon Artists; Oakland Art Mus; one-person shows, Dubin Gallery, Pa & Manhattanville Col, New York, NY; Pine Pub Libr Gallery, Fairlawn, NJ, 89; Kendall Gallery, New York, 90. *Pos:* Chmn dept art, Mahattanville Col, 60-65. *Teaching:* Asst prof painting & drawing, Manhattanville Col, 57-74, lectr, Art & Eng, 69-74; vis writer, Stephens Col, 75 & Hamilton Col, 85. *Awards:* Silver Anniversary Medal, Audubon Artists, 67; Award, Nat Coun Arts, 68; MacDowell Grants, 61, 62, 70 & 76; Michael M Engel Sr Mem Award, 72; Robert Phillips Mem Award, 90; and others. *Bibliog:* Jean Gould (auth), Modern American Women Poets, Dodd Mead & Co, 85, 349. *Mem:* NY Artists Equity Asn; Authors Guild; Poetry Soc Am; Audubon Artists. *Media:* Oil. *Publ:* Auth, Stepping Out, Unicorn Press, 71; Dying to Survive, Doubleday & Co, 73; Swiftly Now, Ohio Univ Press, 82; A Spool of Blue: New and Selected Poems, Scarecrow Press, 83; and others. *Mailing Add:* 24 W Eighth St New York NY 10011

STOLPE, DANIEL OWEN
PAINTER, PRINTMAKER
b Los Angeles, Calif, Nov 14, 39. *Study:* Pasadena City Col, AA, 60; Los Angeles Co Art Inst, 59-60; apprentice with Don La Viere Turner, 61-62 & Joe Funk, 65-66. *Work:* Portland Art Mus; Fogg Art Mus; Boston Pub Libr; Univ Tex Humanities Res Ctr, Austin; Grunwald Ctr Graphic Arts, Univ Calif, Los Angeles. *Comn:* Endangered Wildlife Drawings, World Mint Asn, San Clemente, Calif, 71; Sculpture installation, Santa Cruz City Mus, 86. *Exhib:* Ore Art Inst, Portland, 88; San Jose Art League, 89; Grand Prix D'Aquitaine, Bordeaux, France, 89; Coyote Gallery, Idyllwild, Calif, 89-90; Huntington Mus, Univ Tex, Austin; NMex Mus Fine Arts, Santa Fe. *Teaching:* Artist-in-residence mythology, Univ Calif, Santa Cruz, 78; master printer, Native Images Inc, 81- *Awards:* Spec Proj Grant, Calif Arts Coun, 78; Santa Cruz City Arts Commission, Sculpture project, 86; 1st Place, Affaire in the Gardens, Beverly Hills, Calif, 89 & 90. *Bibliog:* Vickie Ware (auth), Trickster, Art Business News, 81; Marilyn Hanson & Daniel Stolpe (auths), Myths and Images, Coyote Suites I & II, Aptos Press, 82; Eric Mathes (producer & dir), Mythic Imagery of Daniel O Stolpe, Ampersand Video Arts, 83. *Publ:* Illusr, Atlantic Monthly, 72 & Smithsonian Mag, 72; On the Way Home, Houghton-Mifflin, 73; Native American Series, Univ Calif, Los Angeles, 78; Southwest Art Mag, 2/90. *Dealer:* Trojanowska Gallery 2157 Union St San Francisco CA; Gallery Piazza 819 Bridgeway Sausalito CA 94965. *Mailing Add:* 2539 Mission St Santa Cruz CA 95060

STOLTENBERG, DONALD HUGO
PAINTER, PRINTMAKER
b Milwaukee, Wis, Oct 15, 27. *Study:* Inst Design, Ill Inst Technol, BS(visual design). *Work:* Boston Mus Fine Art; Addison Gallery Am Art, Andover, Mass; DeCordova Mus, Lincoln, Mass; Portland Mus Art. *Exhib:* Venice Observed, Fogg Mus, Cambridge, Mass, 56; Boston Arts Festival, 56-61; Corcoran Gallery Art Exhib, Washington, DC, 63; Landscape, DeCordova Mus, 71; Am Art Exhib, Art Inst Chicago; Mass Open, Worcester Art Mus, 77. *Teaching:* Instr painting & printmaking, DeCordova Mus Sch; vis critic, RI Sch Design. *Awards:* Grand Prize, Boston Arts Festival, 57, First Prize in Painting, 59; First Purchase Prize, Portland Mus Arts Festival. *Mem:* Boston Printmakers; Am Watercolor Soc; fel, Am Soc Marine Artists; New Eng Watercolor Soc. *Media:* Oil, Watercolor. *Publ:* Auth, Collagraph Printmaking, 75 & The Artist and the Built Environment, 80, Davis. *Mailing Add:* 947 Satucket Rd Brewster MA 02631

STOMPS, WALTER E, JR
EDUCATOR, PAINTER
b Hamilton, Ohio, July 13, 29. *Study:* Miami Univ, BFA; Art Inst Chicago, with Boris Anisfeld, Paul Weighardt, Isabelle MacKinnon & Edgar Pillet, MFA; Syracuse Univ. *Work:* Cleveland Mus Art; Miami Univ. *Comn:* Ctr City Murals Proj, Nat Endowment Arts, Dayton, 72; Gen Motors (Frigidaire), Dayton; Bicentennial Poster Proj, Dayton. *Exhib:* Mid-States Exhib, Evansville, Ind, 77, 79 & 80; Cent S Exhib, Nashville, Tenn, 77; 1st Ann Mid-Am Exhib Art, Owensboro Mus Art, Ky, 79; Eight States Exhib, Speed Mus Art, Louisville; Print Invitational, Univ Kans, Lawrence, 80; and others. *Teaching:* Prof painting & drawing, Western Ky Univ, 75- *Awards:* James Nelson Raymond Award, Art Inst Chicago, 59; Purchase Awards, Dayton Art Inst, 66 & 68, Owensboro Mus Art, Ky, 79 & Evansville Mus Art & Sci, Ind, 86; and others. *Media:* Acrylic, Watercolor. *Publ:* Illusr, Dayton USA, 72. *Mailing Add:* Art Dept Western Kentucky Univ Bowling Green KY 42101

STONE, DON
PAINTER
b Council Bluffs, Iowa, Mar 27, 29. *Study:* Vesper George Sch Art, Boston, 51. *Work:* Marietta Col, Ohio; Mobile Art Mus, Ala; Charles Greenshield Collection, Montreal; Peabody Maritime Mus, Salem, Mass. *Comn:* Large egg tempera, Univ NH, Durham, 79. *Exhib:* Nat Acad Design & Am Watercolor Soc, New York; Boston Soc Watercolor Painters, Boston Mus Fine Art, 71; Winter, 77 & New England Painters, 78, DeCordova Mus, Lincoln, Mass. *Teaching:* Instr art, Vesper George Sch Art, Boston, 60-65; instr, New Eng Sch Art, Boston, 60-65; Monhegan Island Workshop, Maine. *Awards:* Gold Medals, Franklin Mint, 74 & 75 & Hudson Valley Art Asn, 80. *Mem:* Assoc Nat Acad Design; Am Watercolor Soc; Guild Boston Artists; New Eng Watercolor Soc; Hudson Valley Art Asn. *Media:* Egg Tempera, Watercolor. *Publ:* Auth, Watercolor page, Am Artist, 62. *Dealer:* Whistlers Daughter Art Gallery 88 S Finley Ave Basking Ridge NJ 07920. *Mailing Add:* PO Box 305 Monhegan Island ME 04852

STONE, FRED J
ART DEALER, CONSULTANT
b Vienna, Austria, Oct 2, 19; US citizen. *Collections Arranged:* Work About Women (assembled, arranged, cataloged), Bergen Mus Art & Sci. *Pos:* Assoc cur art, Bergen Mus Art & Sci, 86-; art consult, Saint Peters Col, Jersey City, 87- *Mem:* Appraisers Asn Am (pres, 81-82, mem bd dirs, 78-). *Specialty:* Nineteenth century European paintings: emphasis on the Barbizon School of France; New Jersey XIX Century Paintings. *Mailing Add:* 245 Prospect Ave, Suite 2-C Hackensack NJ 07601

STONE, GWEN
PAINTER, COLLAGE ARTIST
b New York, NY, Feb 1, 13. *Study:* Col Marin, Kentfield, Calif; San Francisco Art Inst, Calif; Univ Calif, Berkeley, teaching cert; also with Walt Kuhlman. *Work:* Monterey Peninsula Mus Art, Calif; Clorox Corp, Oakland, Calif; San Francisco Art Comn, Calif; Univ Calif, Berkeley, Libr; Standard Oil; Univ Tex at Austin. *Comn:* Siskiyou Arts Coun Grant, Res & 5 lectrs with slides, Yreka Community Theatre, 87; Yreka City Partial Grant (video), The Eye, the Paint and the Brush, 88-89. *Exhib:* San Francisco Mus Mod Art Ann, 59-67; one person shows, Calif Palace Legion Honor, San Francisco, 66 & 67, The Pillowbook Series (collage), Redding Mus, 83 & Rogue Gallery, Medford, Ore, 90; Four Views (collage), Shasta Col Art Gallery, Calif, 83; Col Marin Invitational, 84; Mixing It Up (collage), Coos Art Mus, Coos Bay, Ore, 88; 30th Retrospective, Shasta Col Art Gallery, Calif, 91; and others. *Pos:* Guest cur, More Blue is Bluer, Shasta COl, Redding, Calif, 89; guest inst, collage workshop, Sitka Art Ctr, Otis, Ore, 90, 91 & 92. *Teaching:* Instr life drawing, Col Marin, Kentfield, 67-79, instr design, 67-70, instr collage & assemblage, 75-79; instr collage, Art Sch, Belvedere, 77-79. *Awards:* Kingsley Ann, Crocker Art Gallery, 79; Painting Ann Award, Redding Mus, 85; 5,000 Grant Award, Pollock-Krasner Found, NY, 90. *Bibliog:* E M Polley (auth), East Bay, 65 & Marilyn Hagberg (auth), San Diego, 65, Artforum; Lynn Grant (auth), article, Visual Dialog, Vol 2 (1976); Maggie Hazell-Rosen (auth), Artweek, 73. *Mem:* Rogue Gallery, Medford, Ore. *Media:* All. *Publ:* Auth, Conversation with Robert Arneson, 76, Eleanor Bender talks with Gwen Stone, 76, Women Artists: Realities, 77 & Conversation with Wayne Thiebaud, 77, Visual Dialog. *Mailing Add:* 17530 Pilar Rd Montague CA 96064

STONE, JEFFREY INGRAM
PAINTER, INSTRUCTOR
b Richmond, Va, Mar 14, 45. *Study:* Univ Calif, Northridge, BA, 67; Pratt Inst, MFA, 69. *Work:* Mus Mod Art, New York. *Exhib:* Eighteenth Nat Print Exhib, Brooklyn Mus, 73; Fourth Ann Nat Print Exhib, Atlanta Art Mus, 73; Second Ann Int Norwegian Biannale, Norway Nat Arts Mus, 74; Premio Int Biella Per l'Incisione, Biella's Art Mus, Italy, 80; NMex Univ, 83; Gallery of the Royal Melbourne Inst, 87. *Teaching:* Adj assoc prof printmaking, Pratt Inst, Brooklyn, NY, 70-; guest instr, Yale Univ, 74-75; Head Art & Film Dept, Loyola Sch, 87- *Awards:* Purchase Award, Fourth Ann Nat Print Exhib, Ga, 73. *Bibliog:* Fletcher Kastner (auth), Jeffrey Ingram Stone Graphics, Galaxy Press, 79. *Mem:* Artist Equity NY. *Media:* Oil, Watercolor. *Publ:* Illusr, The psychiatric holocaust, Penthouse Mag, 79; Sweet songs of spring, New York Mag, 78. *Mailing Add:* Printmaking Dept Pratt Inst 200 Willoughby Ave Brooklyn NY 11205

STONE, JEREMY
DEALER
b Boston, Mass, Nov 15, 57. *Study:* Cooper Union, 74-75; NY Univ, 76. *Pos:* Spec activities coordr, Commonwealth Cult Preservation Trust, Boston, 79; art consult, Boston, 78-80; proj & res manager, Anne Kohsr Asn, San Francisco, 80-82; owner & dir, Jeremy Stone Gallery, San Francisco, 82-91; exec dir, Learning Through Educ in the Arts Proj, 92-; consult, 92- *Teaching:* Vis lectr, Univ of Washington, Pullman, 84, Calif Col Arts & Crafts, Oakland, 84-86, Univ Calif, Berkeley, 84 & 86, Stanford Univ Sch Law, 85, This Business of Art, Calif Lawyers for Arts, Hastings Col Law, 9/89. *Bibliog:* Dwight Chapin (auth), Color her artfully, San Francisco Examiner, 4/19/83; Sandy Nelson (auth), Gallery history, Images & Issues, 11-12/83; Lloyd Watson (auth), Profile of a Gallery on the Move, San Francisco Chronicle, People in Business, 6/5/87; Dorothy Burkhardt (auth), The Power Dealers, San Jose Mercury News, 1/10/88; Linda Franklin (auth), article in California Executive, 11/88. *Mem:* San Francisco Art Dealers Asn; San Francisco Art Inst (bd of trustees). *Specialty:* Twentieth century American drawings and paintings. *Publ:* Thirty Years of Box Construction, Sunne Savage Gallery, Boston, MA, 79; Bay area's younger collectors select work that expresses their own tastes, San Francisco Business Journal, 2/22/88. *Mailing Add:* 949 Filbert St San Francisco CA 94133

STONE, JIM (JAMES J)
PHOTOGRAPHER, AUTHOR
b Los Angeles, Calif, Dec 2, 47. *Study:* Mass Inst Technol, with Minor White, SB, 70; RI Sch Design, with Harry Callahan & Aaron Siskind, MFA, 75. *Work:* Corcoran Gallery Art, DC; Fogg Art Mus, Harvard Univ, Cambridge, Mass; Int Mus Photog, Rochester, NY; Los Angeles Co Mus Art; Polaroid Collection, Offenbach, Ger & Cambridge, Mass; Mus Mod Art, New York; Nat Mus Am Art, Washington, DC; and others. *Exhib:* Photovision, Boston Ctr Arts, 72; New Eng Experience, De Cordova Mus, Lincoln, Mass, 72; Photog Unlimited, Fogg Art Mus, Harvard Univ, 74 & Contemp Photog, 76; Still Life, Corcoran Gallery Art, Wash, DC, 79; Venezia '79, Venice, Italy, 79; Boston Now: Photog, ICA, 85; Photographs Beget Photographs, Minn Inst Arts, 87; Twelve Photogs Look at US, Philadelphia Mus Art, 87; Future of Photog, Corcoran Gallery Art, Wash, DC, 87; Between Home and Heaven, Nat Mus Am Art, 92. *Pos:* Artist-in-residence, Lightwork, Syracuse, NY, 84,

Visual Studies Workshop, Rochester, NY, 85, Nat Col Arts, Lahore, Pakistan, 86 & Ariz Western Col, Yuma, Ariz, 88; ed, PhotoEducation: A Polaroid Newsletter for Teachers of Photography, 88- *Teaching:* Instr, Boston Col, 73-88; instr, RI Sch Design, 75-78. *Awards:* Mass Arts & Humanities Found photog fel, 76 & 88. *Bibliog:* Channing (ed), Art of the State/State of the Art, Addison House, 78; Shamlian (auth), article in Philadelphia Photo Rev, 78; Hughes (ed), Photography Annuals, Popular Photog, 80 & 86. *Mem:* Boston Photog Resource Ctr (bd dirs, currently); Soc Photog Educ. *Media:* Black and White Gelatin-Silver Prints. *Publ:* Ed, Darkroom Dynamics: A Guide to Creative Darkroom Techniques, Focal Press, 79; auth, A User's Guide to the View Camera, Harper Collins, 87. *Dealer:* Robert Klein Gallery 207 South St Boston MA 02111. *Mailing Add:* 124 Ashmont St Dorchester MA 02124

STONE, M LEE
ART DEALER
b Chicago, Ill, Apr 11, 37. *Study:* Univ Ill, BS, 58; Univ Ill Col Med, MD, 62. *Pos:* Pvt dealer, M Lee Stone Fine Prints, 78- *Mem:* Int Fine Print Dealers Asn. *Specialty:* American artists, 1900-1960. *Mailing Add:* 2101 Forest Ave Suite 130 San Jose CA 95128

STONE, SYLVIA
SCULPTOR
b Toronto, Ont, June 18, 28; US citizen. *Study:* Pvt study in Can; Art Students League, New York. *Work:* Walker Art Ctr, Minneapolis; Whitney Mus Am Art, New York; Hartford Atheneum, Conn; Xerox Corp, New York; Larry Aldrich Mus, Ridgefield, Conn. *Comn:* Xerox Corp, New York, 69; Sunrise Mall, Massapequa, NY, 72; Gen Serv Agency, Fed Court House, Ft Lauderdale, Fla, 79. *Exhib:* One-woman shows, Andre Emmerich Gallery, 72, 75, 77 & 79 & Bennington Col, 77; 14 Sculptors--Industrial Edge, Walker Art Ctr, Minneapolis, 69; Whitney Mus Am Art Sculpture Ann, New York, 69, 71 & 73; Plastic Presence, Jewish Mus, Milwaukee Art Ctr & San Francisco, 70; 200 Yrs Am Sculpture, Whitney Mus Am Art, New York, 75; Hayward Gallery, London, Eng, 75; 3rd Biennalle Small Sculpture, Budapest, Hungary, 75; Perspective 1976, Albright Col, 76; and others. *Teaching:* Prof emer art, Brooklyn Col, 68-89. *Awards:* Creative Artist Pub Serv Award, NY State, 71; Nat Endowment for the Arts, 76. *Bibliog:* Irv Sandler (auth), Sylvia Stone at Emmerich, Art in Am, 72 & Sylvia Stone's Egyptian gardens, Arts Mag, 4/77; Corrinne Robbins (auth), The edges of illusion, Art Spectrum, 75. *Mem:* Col Art Asn. *Media:* Aluminum; Plexiglas. *Mailing Add:* Andre Emmerich Gallery 41 E 57th St New York NY 10022

STONEBARGER, VIRGINIA
PAINTER, EDUCATOR
b Ann Arbor, Mich, Mar 9, 26. *Study:* Antioch Col, BA, 50; Colorado Springs Fine Arts Ctr, 50-51; Art Students League, 51-52; Hans Hofmann Sch, 54; NY Univ, 54 & 56; Univ Wis-Milwaukee, MS, 72. *Work:* Mrs Harry Lynde Bradley, Milwaukee, Wis. *Comn:* Painting & reproduction of bldg, Nat Bank of Tucson; two paintings, Arlington Race Course, Arlington Heights, Ill. *Exhib:* Univ Wis, 59; Milwaukee Art Ctr, 59-61; one-woman shows, Lakeland Col, 69, Univ Wis, 71, Jewish Community Ctr, Milwaukee, 78 & Galleria Simon, 79; plus many others. *Teaching:* Instr art, Univ Lake Sch, Hartland, Wis, 59-62, Waukesha Co Tech Inst, 70-72 & Milwaukee Area Tech Col, 73-77; instr painting, Univ Wis, Milwaukee Exten, 82-; lectr art, Univ Ariz, 83-92. *Awards:* Danforth Found Fel, 69; Merit Award, Nat League of Am Pen Women, Tucson; Awards, Southern Ariz Watercolor Guild, 86 & 90. *Mem:* Southern Ariz Watercolor Guild; Nat League Am Pen Women. *Media:* Watercolor, Oil. *Dealer:* El Persidio Gallery 120 N Main Tucson AZ 85701. *Mailing Add:* 855 E River 8A Tucson AZ 85718

STONEHAM, JOHN
LIBRARIAN
b Eng, Oct 1, 29; US citizen. *Pos:* Co-ed, The Lively Arts, Baltimore, 59-61; head librn, Md Inst, 65- *Teaching:* Teacher lit, Md Inst. *Mem:* Founding mem Worst Verse Conspiracy Baltimore; Art Libr Soc NAm. *Res:* Bad verse; military costume; curiosa; Chaucer; Malory. *Mailing Add:* Deker Libr Md Inst Col of Art 1400 Cathedral St Baltimore MD 21201

STONER, JOYCE HILL
CONSERVATOR, EDUCATOR
b Washington, DC, Oct 9, 46. *Study:* Col William & Mary, BA(fine arts; summa cum laude); NY Univ, Inst Fine Arts, Conserv Ctr, MA(fine arts) & dipl conserv, spec grad study with Bernard Rabin & John Brealey. *Work:* Freer Gallery Art; Winterthur Mus, Del; Va Mus Fine Arts, Richmond; Del Art Mus; and others. *Comn:* Edward Laning murals, New York Pub Libr. *Collections Arranged:* Know What You See, a traveling exhib organized by Louis Pomerantz, Found Am Inst Conserv & Smithsonian Inst Traveling Exhib Serv, 76; Flaking, Foxing and Fine Works, conserv exhib, Del Art Mus, 77. *Pos:* Managing ed, Art & Archeol Tech Abstracts, 69-86; consult conserv paintings, Freer Gallery Art, 75-76; exec dir, Found Am Inst Conserv, 75-79; paintings conservator, Winterthur Mus, Del, 76-82, supv conserv section, 81-82; vis scholar painting conserv, Metrop Mus Art, 80; guest scholar, Getty Mus Painting Conserv, 85; trustee, Williamstown Regional Art conserv lab, 89- *Teaching:* Assoc prof intro art conserv, Va Commonwealth Univ, 75-76; asst prof paintings conserv, Univ Del, 76-79, assoc prof, 79-, assoc dir, Art Conserv Prog, 80-82, dir, Art Conserv Prog, 82-, chair, Art Conserv Dept, 90- *Awards:* Kress Grant, 80; Getty Guest Scholar Grant, 85; Del State Arts Coun Grant, 91 & 92. *Mem:* Fel Int Inst Conserv Historic & Artistic Works; Fel Am Inst Conserv Historic & Artistic Works; Am Asn Mus; Fac Energy Conserv Workshops, Am Asn Mus; Int Coun Mus; Nat Mus Act Advisory Coun, 81-84; Nat Inst for Conserv Proj Dir (vpres, 84); Col Art Asn; Am Asn Mus. *Res:* History of art conservation in America; the technique of contemporary artists Whistler, J McNeill. *Publ:* Auth, Art Conservation in the United States: One View of its history, Cultural Resources Management, 88; Washington Allston: Poems, Veils and Titian's Dirt, J Am Inst Conserv, spring 90; Art Historical and Technical Evaluation of Works by Three Nineteenth Century Artists: Allston, Whistler and Ryder, United Kingdom Inst Conserv Preprints, London, 6/90; Approaching the Cleaning of Whistler's Peacock Room: Retrieving Surface Interrelationships in Harmony in Blue and Gold, Int Inst Conserv Preprints, Brussels, 9/90; and others. *Mailing Add:* 303 Old College Univ Del Newark DE 19716

STONES, MARGARET ALISON
EDUCATOR, HISTORIAN
b Eng, Mar 11, 42. *Study:* Univ London, BA, 64, PhD(hist art), 70. *Teaching:* Assoc prof Medieval art, Univ Minn, 69-81, prof, 81-83; vis prof, Univ Reading, 75; prof, Univ Pittsburgh, 84- *Awards:* APS Grant, 71 & 79; Am Coun Learned Soc Grant, 73; Nat Endowment Humanities Grant, 73, 77, 78, 82, 85 & 92-93. *Mem:* Medieval Acad Am; Brit Archaeol Asn; Int Arthurian Soc; Int Ctr Medieval Art; Soc Nat des antiquaires de France. *Res:* Manuscript illumination. *Publ:* auth, Notes on three illuminated Alexander manuscripts, In: The Medieval Alexander Legend and Romance Epic, Essays in Honour of David J A Ross, Millwood/London/Nendeln, 82; auth, Wace, La Vie de Sainte Marguerite, Tübingen, 90; contrib, Arthurian Art Since Loomis, Medievalia, Lovanensia, 90; auth, Prolegomena to a Corpus of Illuiminated Lea Vincent of Beauvais Manuscripts, Vincent de Beauvais, Paris & Montreal, 90; Le Maitre de La Viede Sainte Benoite O'Origuy: Noureous Considerations, Buu de la Soc Nat des Antiquaires de France, 90. *Mailing Add:* Dept of Fine Arts Univ of Pittsburgh 104 Frick Fine Arts Bldg Pittsburgh PA 15260

STOOKER, HENDRIK CORNELIS
CURATOR, GALLERY DIRECTOR
Neth. *Study:* Kunstoefening Acad Fine & Indust Arts, Arnhem, Neth, teaching degree(art educ); Univ Calif, Los Angeles, MA(art hist). *Collections Arranged:* Intermittent Compositions, Mineko Grimmer, 88; The State of Being, Emerson Woelffer, 89; Exhibition of Graphic Work, Masami Teraoka, 89; Atlas Worked/Central Meridian, Michael C McMillen, 90; Tribute to Figurative African-American Art, Charles White & Richmond Barthe, 90. *Pos:* Sr cur/gallery dir, Occidental Col, 87- *Mailing Add:* Occidental College Weingart and Coons Galleries 1600 Campus Rd Los Angeles CA 90041

STOPPERT, MARY KAY
SCULPTOR, EDUCATOR
b Flint, Mich, Aug 19, 41. *Study:* Western Mich Univ, Kalamazoo, BS, 64; Sch Art Inst Chicago, MFA, 68. *Work:* Mus Contemp Art & Northeastern Ill Univ, Chicago; Michael Rockefeller Art Ctr, State Univ NY, Fredonia; Northern Ill Univ, DeKalb; Kemper Insurance Co, Long Grove, Ill. *Exhib:* Solo exhib (with catalog), New Mus Contemp Art, New York, 82; Painting and Sculpture Today, Indianapolis Mus Art, Ind, 76; Works on Paper, Art Inst Chicago, 78; Detroit and Chicago Art of the 70s, Detroit Inst Arts, 78; Art Inst Chicago, 74, 77 & 79; Museo de Arte Contemporanea, Sao Paolo, Brazil, 80; Chicago: Some Other Traditions, San Francisco Mus Art, 83; The Figure in Chicago Art, Mus Contemp Art, Chicago, 85. *Teaching:* Prof art, Northeastern Ill Univ, Chicago, 70- *Awards:* Frank G Logan Award, 75th Chicago and Vicinity Show, 74, John G Curtis Jr Award, 77th Chicago and Vicinity Show, 78, Art Inst Chicago; President Merit Award, Northeastern Ill Univ, Chicago, 79; Nat Endowment of Arts Visual Artist Fel, 86. *Bibliog:* Grace Glueck (auth), rev, in: New York Times, 6/18/82; Christopher Lyon (auth), rev, in: Chicago Sun Times, 3/11/84. *Mem:* Col Art Asn; Women's Caucus Art (bd adv 76-79, 81-85); Chicago Women's Caucus Art (pres, 79-83); Int Sculpture Ctr. *Media:* Mixed. *Dealer:* Phyllis Kind Gallery 136 Greene Street New York NY & 313 W Superior Chicago Il 60610. *Mailing Add:* Northeastern Ill Univ Chicago IL 60625

STORER, FRANCES NELL
PAINTER, INSTRUCTOR
b Central City, Ky, June 17, 17. *Study:* Ward-Belmont Conserv, Nashville, Tenn, 34-37 & 39-41, Cincinnati Conserv Music, Ohio, 37-39; Rex Brandt Summer Sch, Corona del Mar, Calif, 56-75, with Joan Irving Brandt, George Post, Jae Carmickell & Elliot O'Hara, also studied with James Hu, Hawaii. *Work:* Citizens Fidelity Bank & Trust; Liberty Bank; First Nat Bank, Louisville, Ky; Hilliard & Lyons Corp Collection; and others. *Exhib:* Am Watercolor Soc, New York, 63-64, 65-68, traveling exhib, 65 & 100th Ann Show, 67; Brooks Mus, Memphis, Tenn, 64; Corp Collection Exhib, J B Speed Mus, Louisville, 77; one-person show, Owensboro Mus, Ky, 79 & Ky Watercolor Soc, United Ky Bank Inc, 80, Harpeth Hall Sch, Nashville, Tenn, 81, Arts Club, 84 & Merida Gallery, Louisville, Ky, 85; Paducah Art Asn, Ky, 82; Ky Traditions in Am Landscape Painting, Owensboro Mus Fine Arts, Ky, 83 & 85; Jr League Louisville, Creative Progressiors, Washington, DC, 87-88; and others. *Pos:* Operator, Storer Gallery, 60-65; painter, Ill Cent Mag, 64- *Teaching:* Taught classes in own studio & Storer Gallery, Central City, Ky, 58-65; pvt classes, Louisville, Ky. *Awards:* Woman of the Yr, Times Argus, Central City, Ky, 62. *Mem:* Am Watercolor Soc; Art Ctr Asn & Arts Club, Louisville; Ky Watercolor Soc; MacDowell Music Club. *Media:* Watercolor. *Publ:* La Revue Moderne, Paris, 65. *Mailing Add:* c/o Storer Gallery 8405 Nottingham Pkwy Louisville KY 40222

STORER, INEZ MARY
PAINTER
b Santa Monica, Calif, Oct 11, 33. *Study:* Univ Calif, Berkeley, 54-55; San Francisco Art Inst, with Nathan Oliviera, 55; Los Angeles Art Ctr, with Lorser Feitleson, 56; Dominican Col, BA, 70; San Francisco State Univ, MA,

71. *Work:* Oakland Art Mus, Calif; Univ Calif, Davis; Fairmont Hotel, Chicago, Ill; Libr Tower, IM Pei, Los Angeles, Calif; Univ Calif Davis; Mulvane Art Ctr, Topeka, Kans. *Comn:* Mural in Libr Tower Bldg, I M Pei, archit, Los Angeles, Calif; mural, Lobby First Interstate World Ctr, Maguire Thomas, IM Pel, Archit of Los Angeles; In the Shadow of the Star, Light/Saraf Films; Feature Length Documentary; Oscar 92; Bill Cosby Productions, New York, 92; Savoy Brasserie, San Francisco, Calif, 91. *Exhib:* Univ Calif, Davis, 80; San Francisco Art Inst, 87; Rena Branstein Gallery, 87; San Francisco Int Airport, 88; Triton Mus Art; Chicago Art Fair, 88; San Francisco Mus Art, 80; Richard Demarco Gallery, Edinburgh, Scotland, 80; one-man shows, Jeremy Stone Gallery, San Francisco, CAlif, 90, Aki Ex Gallery, Tokyo, Japan, 92, Nina Frost Gallery, Santa Monica, Calif, 92 & Olga Dollar Gallery, San Francisco, Calif, 92. *Pos:* Dir, Lester Gallery of Contemp Art, 73-80; invited artist, Int Inst Experimental Printmaking, San Francisco, 76. *Teaching:* prof painting, Col Marin, Kentfield, 69-78, Calif State Col, Sonoma, 76-82, Univ Calif, Santa Cruz, 76; lectr, San Francisco State Univ, 70-72; vis artist, Univ Calif, Davis, 80, San Francisco Art Inst, 83-; San Francisco Art Inst, 81- *Awards:* Faculty Grant, San Francisco Art Inst, 92. *Bibliog:* Dorothy Burkhart (auth), Critic's Choice, San Jose Mercury, 87; Kenneth Baker (auth), article, San Francisco Chronicle, 7/87; Donna Brookman (auth), A Bay area diversity, Artweek, Oakland, Calif, 10/88; Dorothy Burkhart (auth), Feminine Statements, San Jose Mercury, San Jose, Calif, 88; William Berkson (auth), Art Forum, New York 4/90; Mary Hull (auth), Between Thee and Me, Artweek, 6/92. *Mem:* San Francisco Art Dealers Asn (mem bd dirs, 75-). *Media:* Mixed Media. *Publ:* Illusr, Laura N Baker's O Children of the Wind and Pines, Lippincott, 67; illusr, Floating Island: Collection of Poetry, Michael Sikes, 77; illusr, Floating Island: Up My Coast, Joanne Kyger (auth). *Dealer:* Smith Anderson 200 Homer St Palo Alto CA 94301; Olga Dollar San Francisco CA. *Mailing Add:* PO Box 117 Inverness CA 94937

STOREY, DAVID
ILLUSTRATOR
b Madison, Wis, 1948. *Study:* Univ Calif-Berkeley, 66-68; Univ Calif-Davis, BA, 70 & MFA, 72. *Exhib:* Solo exhibs, Concord Contemp Art, 81, 83 & 84, Jay Gorney Mod Art, 85, Hirschl & Adler Mod, New York, 87, 91 & 92, Lino Silverstein Gallery, Barcelona, Spain, 89, Jorge Albero Arte Contemporaneo, Madrid, Spain & Davis-McClain Gallery, Houston, Tex, 90, Betsy Senior Contemp Prints, New York, 91; Surface Printing in the 80's, Zimmorli Art Mus, Rutgers Univ, NJ, 90; 42nd Ann Purchase Exhib, Am Acad & Inst Arts & Letts, New York, 90; The Unique Print 70s into 90s, Mus Fine Arts, Boston, 90; A Bestiary, Paula Cooper Gallery, New York, 91. *Awards:* NY State Found Arts Grant, 89; Nat Endowment Arts Fel, 91. *Bibliog:* Susan Tallman (auth), Many Monotypes, Arts Mag, 1/91; Peggy Cyphers (auth), review, Arts, 9/91; Lisa Liebmann (auth), review, Artforum, 10/91. *Publ:* Contribr, Bestiary, Brad Morrow (auth), 90. *Dealer:* Hirschl & Adler Modern 851 Madison Ave New York NY 10012. *Mailing Add:* 134 W Broadway New York NY 10013

STORM, HOWARD
PAINTER, SCULPTOR
b Newton, Mass, Oct 26, 46. *Study:* Denison Univ; J Ferguson Stained Glass Studio, Weston, Mass, apprenticeship; San Francisco Art Inst, BFA, 69; Univ Calif, Berkeley, MA, 70, MFA, 72. *Work:* Roswell Mus, NMex; Denison Univ; Mt St Joseph Col, Ohio; Ky Arts Comn, Frankfort; Baylor Univ. *Comn:* Pioneer Award, Northern KY Chamber Commerce. *Exhib:* One-man shows, Berkeley Mus, 72 & Baylor Univ, 73; Huntington Galleries, 72-74; Univ Cincinnati, 74; Cincinnati Art Mus, 75; plus others. *Pos:* Artist-in-residence, Roswell Mus, 71-72. *Teaching:* Prof art, Northern Ky Univ, 72-, chmn art dept, currently. *Awards:* Eisner Prize, Univ Calif, Berkeley, 72; Purchase Award, Preview '73; Purchase Award, Huntington Galleries. *Media:* Acrylic, Oil; Wood. *Publ:* Left Alone, Logan Elm Press, Ohio State Univ, 85. *Mailing Add:* Dept Arts Rm 224, Fine Arts Bldg Northern Ky Univ Highland Heights KY 41076

STORM, LARUE
PAINTER
b Pittsburgh, Pa. *Study:* Univ Miami, AB & MA; Art Students League, Woodstock; also printmaking with Calvaert Brun, Paris & study in Los Angeles & Mich. *Work:* Lowe Mus, Coral Gables, Fla; Columbia Mus Art, Ga; Norton Gallery Art, West Palm Beach, Fla; Peabody Col, Nashville, Tenn. *Exhib:* Corcoran Gallery Art Biennial, Washington, DC, 57; Butler Inst Am Art, Youngstown, Ohio, 58-60; Miami Six, El Paso Mus, 65; Fla Creates, var mus Fla, 71-; one-man show, Lowe Mus Art, Norton Gallery Art & Columbia Mus Art; and others. *Teaching:* Adj asst prof drawing & design, Univ Miami, 67-84. *Awards:* Purchase Award, Columbia Mus Art, SC. *Media:* Collage, Assemblage. *Publ:* Auth, Jose Guadalupe Posada: Guerrilla Fighter of the Throwaways, Carrell, 70. *Mailing Add:* 3737 Justison Rd Coconut Grove Miami FL 33133

STORM, MARK (KENNEDY)
PAINTER, SCULPTOR
b Valdez, Alaska, Sept 4, 11. *Study:* Univ Tex, 30-34. *Work:* Mus Natural Sci, Houston; Corpus Christi Mus; Houston Livestock Show & Rodeo. *Comn:* Oil painting, Int Ropes Ltd, Eng, 69; oil paintings, Houston Livestock Show & Rodeo, 73; oil paintings, Melacres Ranch, Chapel Hill, Tex, 74 & Pearce Indust Inc, Houston, 77. *Exhib:* Ann Tex Cowboy Artists Asn Shows, Tex, 73-; When You Say Cowboy, Amarillo Art Ctr, Tex, 74; Tex Cowboy Artists, Phippen-O'Brien Gallery, Scottsdale, Ariz, 74; Tex Cowboy Artists, Stamford Art Found, Tex, 74; Mus Art Am West, Houston, 86; Transco Tower, Houston, 87. *Awards:* Best of Show, Tex Cowboy Artists Show, 76. *Bibliog:* Jim Scarbrough (auth), Mark Storm, Quarter Horse J, 71; article in Gulf Coast Cattleman, 83. *Mem:* Tex Cowboy Artists Asn (pres, 75-76). *Media:* Oil, Pen and Ink. *Publ:* Illusr, Picture Tales from Mexico, 41; Marsmen in Burma, 49; Texas Brags, 50; auth & illusr, Gruyo of the Flying H, 56; contribr, XIT--The American Cowboy, Oxmoor; The Texas Cowboy, TCU Press, 86. *Dealer:* Southwest Galleries 2433 Bissonnet Houaton TX 77005. *Mailing Add:* 2322 University Blvd Houston TX 77005

STORY, WILLIAM EASTON
PAINTER, MUSEUM DIRECTOR
b Valley City, NDak, Feb 13, 25. *Study:* Art Inst Chicago, BFA; Ball State Teachers Col, MA; also with Stanley William Hayter. *Work:* Butler Inst Am Art, Youngstown, Ohio; Ball State Univ Art Gallery. *Exhib:* Whitney Mus Am Art Ann, 57; Corcoran Gallery 25th Biennial, Washington, DC, 57; Cincinnati Art Mus 2nd Interior Valley Competition, 58; Artistas Brasileiros E Am, Mus Art Mos, Sao Paulo, Brazil, 60; Collages by American Artists, Ball State Univ Art Gallery, 72. *Pos:* Asst dir, Am Mus in Brit, Bath, Eng, 66-68; dir, Parrish Art Mus, Southampton, 68-69; Ella Sharp Mus, Jackson, Mich, 69-72; Ball State Univ Art Gallery, 72-81; Saginaw Art Mus, formerly. *Teaching:* Asst prof art & supvr art gallery, Ball State Univ, 56-66. *Mem:* Am Asn Mus; Midwest Mus Asn; Mich Mus Asn. *Publ:* Contribr, America in Britain, 67 & 68. *Mailing Add:* PO Box 1594 Fairhope AL 36532

STORY WILSON, MARTHA REDY
CONCEPTUAL ARTIST, MUSEUM DIRECTOR
b Philadelphia, Pa, Dec 18, 47. *Study:* Wilmington Col, Ohio, BA; Dalhousie Univ, Halifax, NS, Can, MA & studies for PhD. *Exhib:* Circa 7500 (traveling exhib of women conceptual artists), 73-74; Autogeography, Downtown Whitney Mus Am Art, New York, 75; Four Evenings, Four Days, Whitney Mus Am Art, New York, 76. *Pos:* Found & dir, Franklin Furnace Archives Inc, 76- *Teaching:* Lectr lit, NS Col Art & Design, 72-74; lectr 20th century art, Brooklyn Col, NY, 75. *Awards:* Grants, Nat Endowment Arts Fel, Performance Art, 78 & 83. *Bibliog:* Moira Roth (auth), The Amazing Decade: Women's Performance Art in America 1970-1980, Astro Artz, Los Angeles, 83; Heresies: Acting Up: Women in Theatre and Performance, Heresies Collective, NY, 84, vol 5 No 1 issue 17; Randy Rosen & Catherine C Brower (auths), Making Their Mark: Women Artists Move into the Mainstream 1970-1985, Abbeville Press, NY, 89. *Mem:* Col Art Asn; Gallery Asn NY State. *Media:* Mixed. *Publ:* Auth, The Arnotated Alice, pvt publ, 76. *Mailing Add:* Franklin Furnace 112 Franklin St New York NY 10013

STOTT, DEBORAH
HISTORIAN
b Minneapolis, Minn, June 11, 42. *Study:* Wellesley Col, BA, 64; Columbia Univ, MA, 66, PhD, 75. *Teaching:* Instr art hist, Wheaton Col, Mass, 70-75; asst prof, Intercollegiate Ctr Classical Studies, Rome, 75-76; assoc prof, Univ Tex, Dallas, 76- *Awards:* Am Acad Rome Fel, 80-81; Delmas Found Grant, 80 & 82; Bunting Inst Fel, Radcliffe Col, 82-83. *Mem:* Col Art Asn Am; Midwest Art Hist Asn; Soc Fels Am Acad (regional rep). *Res:* Style and theory in Italian Renaissance reliefs. *Publ:* Auth, Jacques Lipchitz and Cubism, Garland Publ, 78; auth, Jacopo Sansovino's Bronze Reliefs and Venetian Colorism, Hofstra Univ, 82; auth, Fatte a sembianza di pittura: Jacopo Sansovino's bronze reliefs in San Marco, Art Bulletin, spring 82. *Mailing Add:* Sch Arts & Humanities Univ Tex PO Box 830688 Richardson TX 75083-0688

STOUFFER, DANIEL HENRY, JR
PAINTER
b Paulding, Ohio, Sept 26, 37. *Study:* Ohio State Univ, BFA, 59. *Work:* Ohio State Univ, Columbus; Amoco Oil Co, Houston; Pub Serv Co, NMex; Sandia Fed Savings & Loan Bank, Albuquerque. *Comn:* Ann commemorative painting, Pub Serv Co NMex, Albuquerque, 76; ann commemorative poster, Weems Artfest, 90; painting, Sandia Fed Savings, Albuquerque, 86; Ann commemorative poster, NMex Arts & Crafts Fair, 88. *Exhib:* Albuquerque Mus, 82 & 83; Two Watercolorists, Carlsbad Mus, NMex, 84; Watercolor USA, 87; Rocky Mountain Nat Watermedia Exhib, 87 & 88; Nature Conservancy Show, Gingrass Gallery, Milwaukee, 90; Arts for the Parks, Jackson Hole, Wyoming, 92; Governor's Show, Albuquerque, 92. *Pos:* Artist & dir design, Charles Merrill Publ, Columbus, Ohio, 60-72; art dir, Univ NMex Press, Albuquerque, 72-79. *Awards:* First Prize, Brush & Palette Exhib, Grand Junction, Colo, 82; First Prize, Nat Small Painting Show, 83; First Prize Weems Artfest, 87; Award of Merit, NMex Arts & Crafts Fair, 88; First Prize, Nat Small Painting Show, 89. *Media:* Watercolor. *Publ:* Acoma: Pueblo in the Sky, 76, This Shining Land, 82, The Galaz Ruins: Mimbres Pottery, 83, Univ NMex Press; illusr & collabr, In Celebration of The Book, NMex Book League, 82; Who's Who In The West, Marquis (23rd ed), 92. *Dealer:* Weems Gallery 2801 M Eubank NE Albuquerque NM 87112. *Mailing Add:* 3817 Chelwood Drive NE Albuquerque NM 87111

STOUT, FRANK J
PAINTER, SCULPTOR
b Lynn, Mass, Feb 17, 26. *Study:* Boston Mus Sch, 49-50; San Gimignano, Siena, Italy, painting & sculpture, 82-84; Marlboro Col sch yr abroad, Italy, 85. *Work:* Springfield Mus, Mass; Wichita Art Mus, Kans; Sheldon Swope Art Gallery, Terre Haute, Ind; Vermont State House, Montpelier; Univ Vt, Burlington; Am Embassies in Peru & Brazil. *Comn:* Members portrait, Nat Acad Design, New York, 79; portrait, Ex-Gov Emerson, Montpelier, Vt, 80; monumental sculpture, Burlington, Vt, 81; plaza fountain, Burlington, Vt. *Exhib:* Solo exhibs, Landmark Gallery, New York, 79-81 & Mercer Price Gallery, Putney, Vt, 83; By the Sea, Queens Mus, New York, 79; Vermont Landscape, Fleming Mus, Burlington, Vt; Nat Acad Design, New York, 83;

Vermont Skies, Brattleboro Mus, Vt, 86. *Pos:* Mem, Vt Coun Arts, 75-80, New Eng Found Arts, 79-81. *Teaching:* Chmn dept arts, drawing, painting & sculpture, Marlboro Col, Vt, 66-86. *Awards:* H W Ranger Award, Nat Acad Design, New York, 82. *Bibliog:* Rev, Arts Mag, 2/65; rev, Art News, 2/65; Wolf Kahn (auth), The subject matter in new realism, Am Artist, 11/79. *Media:* All. *Dealer:* William Price 1205 Bolton St Baltimore MD 21217. *Mailing Add:* Butterfield Rd PO Box 75 Marlboro VT 05344

STOUT, RICHARD GORDON
PAINTER
b Beaumont, Tex, Aug 21, 34. *Study:* Cincinnati Art Acad, 52-53; Sch Art Inst Chicago, BFA, 57; Univ Tex, MFA, 69. *Work:* Mus Fine Arts, Houston; Dallas Mus Fine Arts; Marion Koogler McNay Art Mus, San Antonio; Rice Univ; Univ Houston. *Exhib:* Momentium Mid Continental Exhib, Chicago, 56-57; One Hundred Contemporary American Draftsmen, Univ Mich, 63; Marion Koogler McNay Art Inst, 64 & 71; Contemporary Arts Mus, Houston, 75; Jurgen Schweinebroden, Berlin, 80. *Pos:* Mem adv bd, Mus Fine Arts, Houston, 73- *Teaching:* Instr painting, Mus Fine Arts, Houston, 58-67; assoc prof drawing & painting, Univ Houston, 69- *Awards:* Longview Purchase Prize, Jr Serv League, 65 & 72; Tex Fine Arts Asn Awards, 66 & 71; Houston Area Exhib First Prize, Blaffer Gallery, Univ Houston, 75; and others. *Media:* Acrylic. *Dealer:* Graham Gallery 1431 W Alabama Houston TX 77006. *Mailing Add:* 1213 Bonnie Brae Houston TX 77006

STOVALL, LUTHER MCKINLEY (LOU)
PRINTMAKER
b Athens, Ga, Jan 1, 37. *Study:* RI Sch Design; Howard Univ, BFA. *Work:* Washington Post Co, Corcoran Gallery Art, Nat Collection Fine Arts, Smithsonian Inst, Washington, DC; Ringling Mus. *Comn:* Poster, Houston Mus Fine Arts, 70; posters, Corcoran Gallery Art, Washington, DC, 70 & 71; Bikes Have Equal Rights (poster), DC Dept Motor Vehicles, Washington Ecol Ctr, 70-72; print, Equal Employment Opportunity Comn Portfolio, Washington, DC, 73; A Sense of Amity, AFL-CIO, 76. *Exhib:* Prints & Posters, Corcoran Gallery Art, Du Pont Ctr, Washington, DC, 69-71; Johns Hopkins Ctr Advan Inst Study, Washington, DC, 70-71; Atlantic Christian Col, NC, 72; Traveling Exhib Prints & Posters, Baltimore Mus Art, Md, 72-73; two-man show, Fendrick Gallery, Washington, DC, 74; 'Tis Mindful of Sweetness, Fendrick Gallery, Washington, DC, 77. *Pos:* Dir, Workshop, Inc, 68- *Teaching:* Master printmaking & silkscreen, Workshop, Corcoran Gallery Art, 69-72. *Awards:* Stern Grant, 68-72; Individual Artist Grant, 72 & Workshop Grant, 72-76, Nat Endowment Arts. *Bibliog:* Jay Jacobs (auth), We have to like the way you look, Art Gallery, 3/70; Paul Richard (auth), The community art spirit, 3/73 & Art & energy, 11/13/74, Washington Post. *Mailing Add:* Workshop Inc 3145 Newark St NW Washington DC 20008

STOVER, DONALD LEWIS
CURATOR
b Staunton, Va, Jan 8, 43. *Study:* Va Polytechnic Inst Col Archit, 61-65; St Marys Univ, BA, 72; Univ Del Winterthur Prog, 75-77. *Collections Arranged:* Early Texas Furniture and Decorative Arts (auth, catalog), 72 & Tischlermeister Jahn (auth, catalog), 75, San Antonio Mus Asn; Art of Louis C Tiffany (auth, catalog), 81, American Sculpture (auth, catalog), 82 & Pennsylvania German, 83, Fine Arts Mus San Francisco. *Pos:* Cur furniture, San Antonio Mus Asn, 72-75; cur-in-charge, Decorative Arts & Sculpture, Fine Arts Mus San Francisco, 81-83, cur-in-charge, Am Decorative Arts & Sculpture, 83- *Mem:* Soc Winterthur Grads; Decorative Arts Trust; Am Decorative Arts Forum Northern Calif; Western Region Arch Am Art (chmn, currently). *Res:* Nineteenth century Texas cabinetmakers; mid-19th century emmigrant cabinetmakers, New York; Louis Comfort Tiffany; American sculpture. *Publ:* Coauth, Early Texas Furniture, Trinity Press, 74; auth, American decorative arts: Recent acquisitions, Apollo Mag, 80. *Mailing Add:* Fine Arts Mus San Francisco Palace of Legion of Honor San Francisco CA 94121

STRAIGHT, ELSIE H
LIBRARIAN, SCULPTOR
b Cumberland, Eng. *Study:* Art Inst Pittsburgh, dipl(illus), 39; New York Sch of Applied Design for Women, with Kimon Nicholaides, dipl(des), 41; Roger Williams Col, BA, 66; Univ RI, MLS, 72. *Pos:* Librn, Ringling Sch Art Libr, 74-, retired; rare books & libr res, Univ So Fla. *Mem:* Art Libr Soc NAm, Southeastern Region (chmn, 80); Sch Libr Asn (secy, 70); Nat Sculpture Soc. *Media:* Stone, Clay. *Res:* John Simmons Collection of French Revolutionary Statesmen and military leaders; 17th century prints. *Interests:* Portrait artists, painters and sculptors; Pre-Columbian art. *Mailing Add:* 435 Edward Sarasota FL 33580

STRAND, SALLY (SALLY STRAND ELLIS)
PAINTER
b Denver, Colo, Oct 11, 54. *Study:* Am Acad Art, Chicago, 75-75; Denver Univ, BFA, 78; Art Students League, New York, 81-82. *Work:* IDAK, Am Express, Minneapolis; Goldman-Sachs, New York. *Exhib:* Pastel Soc Am, Nat Arts Club Gallery, New York, 83, 85, 89- 92; Am Watercolor Soc, Salmagundi Club, New York, 83; All Media '83 Exhib, Laguna Beach Mus Art, Calif, 83; Pastel Soc Am, Special Invitation, Monmouth Mus, Monmouth, NJ, 85; Pastel Soc Am, Special Invitation, Hermitage Mus, Norfolk, Va, 85; and others. *Teaching:* Fac color theory, Colo Inst Art, Denver, 78-79; fac pastel/mixed media, Scottsdale Artist's Sch, Ariz, 90- *Awards:* Purchase Award, Sixth Ann Open Exhib Watercolor, Okla, 91; Anna Hyatt Huntington Bronze Medal Watercolor, Catharine Lorilland Wolfe 85th Ann Open Exhib, Anna Hyatt Huntington, 81; Thomas & Margery Leighton Mem Award, Pastel Soc West Coast, 92. *Bibliog:* Carole Katchen (auth), Ordinary people, great paintings, Artist's Mag, 9/87; Jacqueline M Pontello (auth), Sally Strand, Southwest Art Mag, 6/89; Martin Parsons (auth), The singular glory of pastel, Artspeak, 9/90. *Mem:* Pastel Soc Am. *Media:* Pastel. *Publ:* Contribr, Light, How to See It, How to Paint It, 88, Drawing with Colour, 89 & Creative Painting with Pastel, 90, North Light Books; The Encyclopedia of Pastel Painting, 92 & Hands, Faces and Figures, 92, Quarto. *Dealer:* J Cacciola Galleries 125 Wooster St New York NY 10012. *Mailing Add:* 33402 Dosinia Dr Monarch Beach CA 92677

STRASEN, BARBARA ELAINE
PAINTER, CONCEPTUAL ARTIST
b Brooklyn, NY, Aug 12, 42. *Study:* Yale Univ Sch Art, summer 62; Carnegie-Mellon Univ, BFA, 63; Univ Calif, Berkeley, MA, 64. *Work:* Allen Mem Art Mus, Oberlin, Ohio; Best Products Collection, Richmond, Va; Callas, Powell, Rosenthal & Bloch Advert, Lafayette, Calif; Dorothy & Herman Vogel pvt collection, New York, NY. *Exhib:* Biennial Contemp Art, Whitney Mus Am Art, 75, AIR Gallery, 83, New York; Artists Investigate the Environment, Munic Art Gallery, Los Angeles, Calif, 78; Santa Barbara Mus Art, 79; PS1, New York, 79 & 80; San Diego State Univ, 82, San Diego Natural Hist Mus, 82; one-woman shows, La Chambre Blanche, Quebec, Can, 84 & Fisher Gallery, Univ Southern Calif, Los Angeles, 85; Animal Art, Steirischer Herbst, Graz, Austria, 87; Grey Art Gallery, New York Univ, NY, 90; Appollohuis, Eindhoven, Netherlands, 90. *Teaching:* Instr visual arts, Southwestern Col, Calif, 71-73; asst prof visual arts, Univ Calif, San Diego, 73-78. *Awards:* Individual Artists Fel, Nat Endowment Arts, 75-76; Creative Arts Grant, Regents of Univ of Calif, 76; res proj grants, Univ Calif, San Diego, 76 & 77. *Bibliog:* Sanda Agalidi (auth), Oblique portraits, Artweek, 6/28/86; Giorgio Fernando Borges, Intervista a Barbara Strasen, Modo Mag, Italy, 11/86; Judith Margolis (auth), A Shared Excellence, Artweek, 8/22/87. *Media:* Acrylic, Mixed; Photography. *Publ:* Auth, Immigrants, J Los Angeles Inst Contemp Arts, 2/75; auth, Desert Notes, Santa Barbara Mus Art, 79. *Dealer:* Lynn Crandall Art Serv 2002 Greenfield Ave Los Angeles CA. *Mailing Add:* 1724 S Pacific Ave San Pedro CA 90731

STRASSBERG, ROY I
CERAMIST, SCULPTOR
b Brooklyn, NY, Sept 18, 50. *Study:* State Univ NY Col, Oswego, BA, 72; Univ Mich, MFA, 74. *Work:* Tenn State Mus, Nashville; SDak Mem Art Ctr, Brookings; Mint Mus Art, Charlotte, NC; Sourwood Regional Art Ctr, Jonesboro, Tenn. *Exhib:* J B Speed Mus, Louisville, Ky, 76; Mint Mus Art, Charlotte, NC, 76; Mus Contemp Crafts, New York, 78; Ft Wayne Mus Art, Ind, 80; Wichita Mus Art, Kans, 81; Plains Art Mus, Moorehead, Minn, 81; and others. *Teaching:* Fel ceramics, Univ Mich, 73-74; instr, Memphis State Univ, 74-76; asst prof, Mankato State Univ, 76- *Awards:* Grand Prize, Miss River Crafts, Brooks Mem Art Gallery, 75; Second Prize, Midwest Craft Exhib, Rochester Art Ctr, Minn, 77; Purchase Award, Plains Art Mus, 79. *Mem:* Nat Coun Educ Ceramic Arts. *Media:* Clay. *Publ:* Contribr, Ceramics Monthly, 5/76-5/80 & Am Craft Mag, 8/76-12/81. *Dealer:* Cooper/Lynn Gallery 54 Seventh Ave S New York NY 10014; Robert L Kidd & Assocs 107 Townsend St Birmingham MI 48011. *Mailing Add:* c/o Tweed Mus of Art 10 University Dr Univ Minn at Duluth Duluth MN 55812

STRATAKOS, STEVE JOHN
CRAFTSMAN, TAPESTRY ARTIST
b Chicago, Ill, Nov 26, 54. *Study:* Italian Univ, Perugia, Italy, 74-75; Sch Art Inst Chicago, BFA, 77. *Work:* DuSable Mus African/American Art, Chicago, Ill; Chicago Public Libr, Chicago, Ill. *Comn:* Five banners, DeVry Tech Inst, Chicago, Ill, 85; 2 appliques, Brookfield Zoo, Brookfield, Ill, 87; bedspread, rug, wallpaper design, Univ Chicago, 87; 7 applique banners, Ruby Mem Hosp, Morgantown, WVa, 88. *Exhib:* New Horizons in Art, Chicago Pub Libr Cult Ctr, Chicago, Ill, 84; Artist as Quiltmaker, 84 & 86 and Fantasies in Fabric, 87, F A V A Gallery, Oberlin, Ohio; At the Table, Soc Arts & Crafts, Boston, Mass, 88; Manmade Quilts, Geneva Courthouse, Ill, 90. *Pos:* Banner designer & fabricator, Advert Flag & Banner, Chicago, Ill, 79-82; sr artist/designer, Brookfield Zoo, Ill, 83-90. *Bibliog:* Dimeta Karis (auth), First Prize Quilts, Simon & Schuster, 84; Roberick Kiracofe, The Quilt Digest 5, Quilt Digest Press, 87; The Guild, Sourcebook, Kraus Sikes, 87 & 88. *Media:* Fabric. *Dealer:* Sandy Friedman 107 Edinburgh South Cary NC 27511. *Mailing Add:* 40 N Tower Rd Oak Brook IL 60521

STRATTON, DOROTHY (MRS WILLIAM A KING)
PAINTER, PRINTMAKER
b Worcester, Mass, Dec 21, 08. *Study:* Pratt Inst, cert, 42; Brooklyn Mus Sch, 42-43; Academie Grande Chaumiere, with Andre Lhote, Paris, 47-48; Univ Calif, with Rico Lebrun, 56-57; Univ Calif, Los Angeles, 61; Univ Calif, San Diego, 66-67. *Work:* Long Beach Mus Art; Tunisian Ministry Cult Affairs, Tunis; Los Angeles Munic Art Collection, City Hall; Art in Embassies, Dept of State, Washington, DC; Southwestern Col, Calif. *Exhib:* Solo shows, Pasadena Art Mus, 59, La Jolla Mus Contemp Art, 62, Univ San Diego, 73 & 80, San Diego State Univ, 79, 30 yr Retrospective, Washington Printmakers Gallery, DC, 85 & 88, Barry Gallery, Marymount Univ N Va, 90; Art in Embassies Prog, 65-90; Calif Soc Printmakers Nat Traveling Shows, 72-74 & 82-90; Pratt Graphics Ctr, New York, 80-83; Int Exchange Printmakers Coun Great Britain, Los Angeles Print Soc, 88-90. *Pos:* Special effects decorator, Paramount Studios, George Pal Productions, Hollywood, 45-47; gallery receptionist & ed publicity, Munic Art Dept, Los Angeles, 52-61; registr & mem secy, La Jolla Mus Art, 64-65, vol art ref libr, 66-74; mem, Contemp Art Comt, San Diego Mus Art, 72-82. *Teaching:* Instr seminars printmaking, Univ Calif, 67, 73-75, 76. *Awards:* 36 Awards through 1988. *Bibliog:* Martin Peterson (auth), Applause, San Diego Mag & The Urban Eye, 10/80; Terry Parmelee (auth), Abstract Print Retros, Wash Print Club Newsletter, Vol 24

No 3 Summer, 88; St Michaels Printshop, An Exciting Future, A Romantic Past J Print World, Vol 12, #4, 89; San Diego Res Mus Art, taped interview, 90. *Mem:* Calif Soc Printmakers; Artists Equity Asn; Nat Mus Women Arts; Washington Printmakers Found; San Diego Mus Art & Art Guild, Calif. *Mailing Add:* c/o San Diego Mus Art Membership Dept PO Box 2107 San Diego CA 92112-2107

STRATTON, MARGARET MARY
PHOTOGRAPHER, EDUCATOR
b Seattle, Wash, Nov 12, 53. *Study:* Evergreen State Col, BA, 77; Univ NMex, MA, 83, MFA, 85. *Work:* Univ NMex Mus, Albuquerque; First Bank Minneapolis; Seattle Arts Comn; Ctr Photog Northwest, Seattle; Univ Iowa Mus Art, Iowa City. *Comn:* Light box installation, Seattle Art Comn, 91. *Exhib:* Nuclear Matters, Camerawork, San Francisco, 90; Critical Reactions, Rena Branstan Gallery, San Francisco, 91; 3 Decades of Midwestern Photo, Davenport Mus Art, Iowa, 92; New Northwest Artist Series, Henry Gallery, Seattle, 92; Moving Light: Seeing Is Believing, Kohler Art Ctr, Wis, 92. *Pos:* Nat Bd Mem, Soc Photo Educ, Dallas, 90-; New Forms Grant Adv, Regional NEA, Arts, Midwest, 90-; Chmn, Nat Conf, Soc Photog Ed, 92-93. *Teaching:* Assoc prof, photog, Univ Iowa, Iowa City, 86-; vis prof photog, Sch Art Inst, 92-93. *Awards:* Nat Endowment Arts Fel, 87 & Rockfeller/NEA Interdisciplinary Award, Intermedia Arts, 88; Nat Endowment Arts Fel, Wash, DC, 90; Artists 1990 Public Works Award, Seattle Art Comn, 91. *Bibliog:* David McCraken (auth), Exhib has fun/serious side, Chicago Tribune, 89; Helen Slade (auth), Courting the Mammoth, Reflex, 91; Regina Hackett (auth), 9 Artists Link Vision, Seattle Times, 92. *Mem:* Coll Art Asn; Soc Photog Educ (bd mem). *Publ:* Auth, Taking it to the Streets, 90 & Images In Action, 91, Afterimage; Nuclear Matters-Camerawork Quarterly, Camerawork, San Francisco, 91; Robbie Steinback's Women-XS Gallery, Western Nev Col, 91; New Feminist Photography, Temple Univ Press, 93. *Mailing Add:* 2032 N Winchester Chicago IL 60614

STRATTON, SUZANNE L
MUSEUM DIRECTOR
b Baton Rouge, La, Nov 23, 43. *Study:* La State Univ, BA, 64; Univ NC, Chapel Hill, MA, 66; Hunter Col, MA, 77; Inst Fine Arts, New York Univ, PhD, 83. *Collections Arranged:* Barcelona Plazas, 87; Drawings of Federico Garcia Lorca, 87; Spanish Golden Age in Miniature, 88; Paintings of Ribalta, 88; Ignacio Zuloaga in America 1909-1925, 89. *Pos:* Cur exhibs, Span Inst, New York 85-90 & dir, fine arts & cult progs, 90- *Teaching:* Asst prof art hist, Rutgers Univ, Newark, NJ, 79-87. *Awards:* Grant-in-Aid, Am Learned Soc, 84-85; Travel Grant, Am Philos Soc, 86. *Mem:* Col Art Asn; Am Soc Hispanic Art Hist Studies (officer in charge ann meetings, 86-88 & gen secy, 88-90); Historians Early Mod Europe; Renaissance Soc Am. *Res:* Spanish art & architecture, 16th-17th centuries. *Publ:* Auth, La Inmaculada Concepcion en el arte espanol, Fundacion Universitaria, Madrid, 89; and many other exhib catalogs. *Mailing Add:* c/o Spanish Inst Gallery 684 Park Ave New York NY 10021

STRATTON, Z' RUSSELL See Z'

STRAUS, SANDY
PAINTER
b Omaha, Nebr, Mar 15, 38. *Study:* Art Inst Chicago, BFA, 76. *Comn:* Jessica Hahn (mural), The Tunnel, New York, 88; Billy Boggs (billboards), Mars Steel Corp, New York, 88; Clarence Darrow (billboard), D Fiedler, 89; Salmon Rushdie (poster), C Carson, New York, 90; Prejudice, Beat It Billboards, W Giles, New York, 93. *Exhib:* Concept: A Million Marks, Smart Gallery, Univ Chicago, Ill, 76; American Women Artists, Mus Arte Contemporange, Sao Paulo, Brazil, 78; Special Project, PS 1, New York, 84; solo exhibs, Fashion Moda, Bronx, NY, 86, Germans Van Eck Gallery, Sensory Evolution Gallery, New York; Women in the Arts, Empire State Mus, 89; Summer Studios, Lake George Art Ctr, 91. *Bibliog:* Newsweek Mag, 11/24/86; Sharon Churcher (auth), Art imitates death, Reuters Ltd, 1/14/88; Art & Artists Cover, Vol 17, 1/89. *Media:* Oil, Charcoal. *Dealer:* Steven Style 439 E Sixth St New York NY; Suzan Cooper Woodstock NY. *Mailing Add:* 124 Thompson St Apt C New York NY 10012-3131

STRAUSER, STERLING BOYD
PAINTER
b Bloomsburg, Pa, Aug 15, 07. *Study:* Bloomsburg State Col, with George Keller, BA. *Work:* Cheekwood Mus, Nashville, Tenn; Everhart Mus, Scranton, Pa; Lehigh Univ; Vanderbilt Univ; Am Mus Brit, Bath, Eng; Allentown Mus, Allentown, Pa; Maier Mus Art, Lynchburg, Va. *Exhib:* Art: USA, 58, New York, 58; Sports & Recreation Panorama, Munic Art Gallery, Davenport, Iowa, 59; one-man show, Lehigh Univ, 61, Lyzon Gallery, Nashville, 65- & William Penn Mus, Harrisburg, Pa, 73, Barry White Gallery, Malibu, Calif, 90; retrospective, Haas Gallery Art, Bloomsburg Univ, 82; Worthington Ave Gallery, Shawnee-on-Delaware, Pa, 92. *Awards:* Top Award Regional Art Exhib, Everhart Mus, 58; Celebration Arts Award, Del Water Gap, 89. *Bibliog:* Lee Nordness (auth), The great momentalist, 6/58 & David Burliuk (auth), American momentalist, 6/61, Color & Rhyme. *Media:* Oil. *Publ:* Illusr, Mademoiselle, 6/56. *Dealer:* Lyzon Gallery 411 Thompson Lane Nashville TN 37211. *Mailing Add:* 150 Analomink St East Stroudsburg PA 18301

STRAWN, BERNICE I
SCULPTOR
b Vallejo, Calif. *Study:* Univ Calif, Berkeley, BA, MA, 52. *Work:* Adrian Col, Mich; Western Michigan Univ, Kalamazoo; McDonald's Corp, Chicago, Ill. *Comn:* Bas relief, Christ on the Mountain Church, Denver, Colo, 81; crucifix, St Michael's Church, Aurora, Colo, 82; crucifix, holy family cast bronze, life size, St Francis & Mother Cabrini relief, St Joseph's Church, Golden, Colo, 85. *Exhib:* Nat Religious Art Exhib, Nat Cathedral, Washington, DC, 83; Colorado 3D Invitational, Arvada Ctr, Denver, 85; Kalamazoo Inst Art, Mich, 87; one-person shows, Mesa Col Gallery, Grand Junction, Colo, 90 & Western State Col, Gunmson, Colo, 92; two-person show, Sangre de Cristo Art Ctr, Pueblo, Colo, 91 & Herr-Chambliss Gallery, Hot Springs, Ark, 92; and others. *Teaching:* Art video instr, Adams Cty Sch Dist #12, Northglenn, Co lo, 80- 87. *Mem:* Int Sculpture Conf. *Media:* Wood, bronze. *Publ:* New Lines, Portfolio of Drawings with Mel Strawn, Kalamazoo Press, 57. *Mailing Add:* 8905 Hwy 285 Salida CO 81201

STRAWN, JARRETT W (JASON)
SCULPTOR, EDUCATOR
b Decatur, Ala, June 28, 43. *Study:* Middle Tenn State Univ, Murfreesboro, BS(art), 67; Univ SFla, Tampa, MFA(sculpture & multi-media), 73; New York Studio Sch; Teachers Col, Columbia Univ; New Sch; Univ Tenn, Arrowmont. *Work:* Tenn Arts & Crafts Comn, Nashville; Rudy Farms Collection, Nashville, Tenn; Atlanta Festival Arts; Wright Art Ctr, Beloit, Wis; Wustum Mus, Racine, Wis; and others. *Comn:* Jermy, Jeremy, Jeremey Set, comn by Larry Manness, Rome, Italy, 69; Mem for Kent State, St Leo Col, Fla, 70; Tower-Steps, Manuel Alum Dance Co, New York, 73-74; Flyer, Lar Lubovitch, New York, 74; Garden and Cruciform, First United Methodist Church, Beliot, Wis, 82. *Exhib:* One-man show, Sculpture, Wright Art Ctr, Beliot, Wis, 77; Nat Sculpture Traveling Show, 77; Wis Biennial Exhib, Madison Art Ctr, Wis, 78; Wis Sculpture 1979, Wustum Mus, Racine, Wis, 79; Rockford Ann, Burpee Mus, Rockford Ill, 79; and others. *Pos:* Nat liaison & mem design comt, Off City Planning, Beloit, Wis, 78-; proj co-dir, Nat Endowment for Arts residency, 80, dir, 80-; owner-mgr, Southouse, Inc, New York, Tenn & Wis. *Teaching:* Vis instr, St Leo Col, Fla, 69-70; instr ceramics, Ridgewood Sch Art, NJ, 73-74; instr design, Parsons Sch Design, New York, 76-77; mem fac sculpture & design, art dept, Beloit Col, 77-82, chmn dept, 77-80. *Awards:* Merit & Purchase Award, Atlanta Festival Arts, 71; Second Award, Nat Sculpture, '76, 76. *Bibliog:* Martin (auth), Beds and cars, Tampa Mag-Tribune, 69; Auer (auth), Thinking big in Beloit, 78 & Salsini (auth), Wisconsin in the 80's, 80, Milwaukee J. *Mem:* Col Art Asn; Nat Asn Schs Art; Tenn Artist-Craftsmen Asn; Art Squad; Mid-Am Col Art Asn. *Media:* Wood, Steel. *Publ:* Ed, The child, In: An Anthology of Poetry, Middle Tenn State Univ, 66-67; coauth, Refinishing, Popular Mechanics, 76; auth, Fine arts in college: A proposal for redesigning the curriculum, 77 & Designing a sculpture studio, 2/81, Am Artist. *Mailing Add:* 723 Church St Beloit WI 53511

STRAWN, MELVIN NICHOLAS
PAINTER, SCULPTOR
b Boise, Idaho, Aug 5, 29. *Study:* Chouinard Art Inst; Los Angeles Co Art Inst; Jepson Art Inst; Calif Col Arts & Crafts, BFA & MFA. *Work:* Oakland Art Mus; Antioch Col; Colo State Univ; Colo Springs Fine Arts Ctr; Western Mich Univ; Ohio State Univ; Ottowa Univ. *Comn:* Environ design (sculpture), Ottawa Col, Kans, 72. *Exhib:* Colo State Univ Centennial Exhib, 70; Cedar City Nat, Utah, 72; I-25 Artists Alliance, Colorado Springs Fine Arts Ctr, 72; Colorado Springs Biennial, Colorado Springs Fine Arts Ctr, 81; and others. *Teaching:* Instr art, Midwestern Univ, Mich State Univ, Antioch Col & Univ Denver, 56-72; chmn dept art, Antioch Col, 66-69 & Western Mich Univ, 85-88; prof & dir, Sch Art, Univ Denver, 69-85. *Awards:* First Purchase Award, Centennial Exhibs Colo State Univ, 70. *Media:* Oil; All. *Mailing Add:* 8905 Hwy 285 Salida CO 81201

STREETER, TAL
SCULPTOR, EDUCATOR
b Oklahoma City, Okla, Aug 1, 34. *Study:* Univ Kans, BFA & MFA; Colorado Springs Fine Arts Ctr, with Robert Motherwell; Colo Col; with Seymour Lipton, 3 yrs. *Work:* Mus Mod Art, New York; San Francisco Mus Art; Corcoran Gallery Art, Washington, DC; Storm King Art Ctr, Mountainville, NY; and others. *Comn:* Large-scale sculpture, Ark Art Ctr, Little Rock; High Mus Art, Mem Arts Ctr, Atlanta, Ga; Sculpture in Environment, New York City Parks Dept, 70; Libr for the Blind, Trenton, NJ, 81-83; Nat Mus Contemp Art, Seoul, Korea, 88. *Exhib:* Whitney Ann, 65, New York World's Fair, 65; Cool Art & Highlights of the Season, Aldrich Mus, 68 & 70; Drawings by Sculptors, Corcoran Gallery, 78; Sky Art, Mass Inst Technol, 80 & 81; Bruckner Festival, Linz, Austria, 82; solo exhib, Univ Ky Mus Art, 82; Kunst and Technik, Munich, Ger, 83; Minimal Line, Milton Avery Mus, Bard Col, NY, 85; Dayton Art Inst, Ohio, 90. *Pos:* Cur, Feather on the Wind, EPCOT Ctr, Orlando, Fla, 85; Ice & Air Show, Lake George, NY, 90. *Teaching:* Vis artist, Fairleigh Dickinson Univ, 62; vis artist in residence, Dartmouth Col, Hanover, NH, 63 & Sun Valley Ctr for Arts, Idaho, 86; vis artist, Univ NC, Greensboro, 70 & 72-73 & Penland Sch Crafts, NC, 74-76; Fulbright prof, Seoul, Korea, 71; vis lectr, US Info Serv, Japan, 72; adj prof, Queen's Col, 73; founder III-D/media area, prof, State Univ NY Col Purchase, 73-; assoc fel & prof, Ctr Advan Visual Studies, Mass Inst Technol, 84-; Sun Valley Ctr Arts, Idaho, 86. *Awards:* State Univ NY Int Studies Grant, Japan, 69; Collaborations in Art, Sci, & Technol, New State Coun Arts Grant, 78; Artpark Artist, Lewisboro, NY, 78; and others. *Bibliog:* G A Ruda (auth), Kitesmanship: Tal Streeter, Craft Horizons, 74; Donald Ritchie (auth), Kite crazy, Natural Hist, 75; Carter Ratcliff (auth), Tal Streeter: Beyond absolutes, Arts Mag, 77; article, Sky painting, Newsweek, 8/80; and others. *Media:* Multimedia, Welded Metal. *Publ:* Auth, The Art of the Japanese Kite, Weatherhill, 74 & 82; Heavenly humors: The modern kite, Am Craft, 79; Art That Flys: Jacquie Matisse Mannier, Dayton Art Inst Press, 90; Dragon Artist, Ahn Bk Publrs, Seoul, Korea, 91; and others. *Dealer:* Saem Art Gallery 8-14 Nonhyum-Dong Kangnam-ku Seoul Korea; Lippincott Large-Scale Sculpture 400 Sackett Point Rd North Haven CT 06473. *Mailing Add:* RR2-38 Romig House Verbank NY 12585

STREETMAN, JOHN WILLIAM, III
ADMINISTRATOR
b Marion, NC, Jan 19, 41. *Study:* Western Carolina Univ, AB; Lincoln Col, Oxford Univ, cert. *Collections Arranged:* The Eye and The Heart: Watercolors of John Stuart Ingle, 87-88; Two American Realists: William Bailey and DeWitt Hardy, 73 & 74; Simplicity, A Grace: Jacob Maentel in Indiana, 89; Beverly Hallam: The Flower Paintings, 90. *Pos:* Founding dir, Jewett Creative Arts Ctr, South Berwick, Maine, 66-70; exec dir, Polk Pub Mus, Lakeland, Fla, 70-75; dir, Mus Arts & Sci, Evansville, Ind, 75- *Awards:* Mayor's Arts Award, Evansville, Ind, 90. *Mem:* Am Asn Mus; Midwestern Mus Conf. *Mailing Add:* 411 SE Riverside Dr Evansville IN 47713

STREETT, TYLDEN WESTCOTT
SCULPTOR, EDUCATOR
b Baltimore, Md, Nov 28, 22. *Study:* Johns Hopkins Univ; St John's Col; Md Inst Col Art, with Sidney Waugh & Cecil Howard, BFA & MFA; also asst to Lee Lawrie. *Comn:* Eight foot bronze figure, Baltimore Firefighter's Mem, Baltimore, 88; medallion, Mayor Clarence Du Burns, 89; portrait, Walter Sondheim Jr, 90; John O'Donnell (bronze portrait statue), O'Donnell Sq, Baltimore, 79; archit sculpture (relief on facade), Waverly Sch, Baltimore, 82; Former Presidents of Seafarers International Union (heroic bronze portraits), Washington, DC & Piney Point, Md, 83; life-sized garden figure, Greater Baltimore Med Ctr, 84. *Exhib:* Corcoran Gallery Art, Washington, DC, 60; Baltimore Mus Art, 69. *Teaching:* Prof sculpture, Md Inst Col Art, Baltimore, 59-, dir, Grad Studies, 66-72; instr sculpture, Jewish Community Ctr, Baltimore, 63-65. *Awards:* John Gregory Award, 62; Union Independent Col Art Grant, 71; Ford Found Grant, 80; and others. *Mem:* Nat Sculpture Soc; Artists Equity Asn; Sculptors Inc. *Media:* Miscellaneous Media. *Publ:* Auth, Plaster Casting Using a Waste Mold (film), 70. *Mailing Add:* 4622 Keswick Rd Baltimore MD 21210

STRICKLAND
PAINTER, INSTRUCTOR
b Waycross, Ga. *Study:* Studied with Eliot O'Hara, 53-68; Lee Atkyns, 61. *Work:* Represented in collection of Fairfax, Va; Chevy Chase Ctr, Bethesda, Md; Rockville Civic Ctr, Md. *Comn:* Drawings & paintings, Fairfax City Govt, Va, 89; fifteen watercolors, Fairfax Bank & Trust, Va, 91; majority of work comn by pvt collectors here & abroad; also comn by law offices & social orgns. *Exhib:* 11th Ann Area Exhib, Corcoran Gallery, Washington, DC, 56; 12th Ann Area Exhib, Corcoran Gallery, 57; 13th Int Dogwood Festival Art Show, Ga Tech Student Ctr Gallery, Atlanta, 86; Spotlight on the Arts, Fairfax City Govt, Va, 87 & 92; group show, Side Porch Gallery, Fairfax, Va, 90. *Pos:* Vpres, Side Porch Gallery, Fairfax, Va, 89-91. *Teaching:* Basic watercolor, Fairfax Co Adult Educ, Va, 80-88; basic watercolor, Side Porch Gallery, Fairfax, Va, 89-90. *Mem:* Fairfax Art League. *Media:* Transparent Watercolor. *Publ:* Dir & producer, Watercolors by Strickland (18 part television series on how to paint watercolors), 7-9/92. *Mailing Add:* c/o Ten Penny Studio PO Box 54 Fairfax Station VA 22039

STRICKLAND, THOMAS J
PAINTER
b Keyport, NJ, Dec 28, 32. *Study:* Newark Sch Fine & Indust Arts, NJ; Am Art Sch & Nat Acad Fine Arts, New York, with Robert Philipp & Gordon Samstag. *Work:* Elliott Mus, Stuart, Fla; Hollywood Art Mus, Fla; St Hugh Catholic Church; Salem Col; St Vincent Col; and others. *Exhib:* Butler Inst Am Art Fine Arts Festival, Youngstown, Ohio, 63; 7th Grand Prix Int Peinture Cote d'Azur, Cannes, France, 71; Hollywood Art Mus, 72, 75 & 76; Cape Coral Nat Art Show, Fla, 73; Martin Co Hist Soc, Elliott Mus, Fla, 74; Am Painters in Paris, 75; and others. *Awards:* First Prize, Hollywood Arts & Crafts Guild Ann Mems Art Exhib, 72 & Hollywood Art Mus Ann Regional Show, 73, Fla; Charles Hawthorne Mem Award, Nat Arts Club, 77; plus others. *Bibliog:* Ann D Browne (auth), Personality of the month, Directions, 12/73; Lawrence T Mahoney (auth), The 2703 faces of Tom Strickland, Tropic, 8/15/76. *Mem:* Blue Dome Art Fel; Miami Palette Club; Pastel Soc of Am; Fla Pastel Asn; and others. *Media:* Oil, Pastel. *Publ:* Auth, A painting demonstration by Thomas J Strickland, Directions, 5 & 7/74; The impressionistic pastels of Thomas J Strickland, 5/76, Painting self-portraits, 7/76 & How Thomas Strickland paints a still life, 3/77, Today's Art. *Mailing Add:* 2595 Taluga Dr Miami FL 33133

STRICKLER, SUSAN ELIZABETH
CURATOR, HISTORIAN
b Baltimore, Md, Jan 23, 52. *Study:* Ecole du Louvre, Paris, 1st yr cert, 72; Mt Holyoke Col, BA, 73; Univ Del, MA, 77. *Collections Arranged:* John Ritto Penniman 1782-1841: An Ingenious New England Artist, 82; John Frederick Kensett: An American Master, 85. *Pos:* Res assoc, Toledo Mus Art, Ohio, 78-79; spec proj dir, Va Mus, Richmond, 79-80; cur Am art, Worcester Art Mus, Mass, 81-, dir curatorial affairs, 87- *Mem:* Col Art Asn; Am Asn Mus; New Eng Mus Asn; Decorative Arts Chap, Soc Archit Historians. *Res:* American painting, especially eighteenth & nineteenth centuries. *Publ:* Auth, American paintings (catalog), Toledo Mus Art, 79; ed, John Frederick Kensett; An American Master, Worcester Art Mus & W W Norton, 85; ed & contribr, American Traditions in Watercolor: The Worcester Art Museum Collection, Worcester Art Mus & Abbeville, 87; auth, American Portrait Minatures: The Worcester Art Mus Collection, 89; co-auth, The Second Wave: American Abstraction of the 1930's & 1940's, Selection from the Penny & Elton Yasuna Collection, 91. *Mailing Add:* Worcester Art Museum Worcester MA 01609-3196

STRIDER, MARJORIE VIRGINIA
SCULPTOR, PAINTER
b Okla. *Study:* Kansas City Art Inst, Mo; Okla Univ, BFA. *Work:* Guggenheim Mus, New York; Storm King Art Ctr, NY; Wadsworth Atheneum, Hartford, Conn; Larry Aldrich Contemp Art Mus, Conn; Hirshhorn Mus, Washington, DC; and others. *Comn:* Carnegie Ctr, Princeton, New Jersey. *Exhib:* Whitney Sculpture Ann, Whitney Mus Am Art, 70; one-woman shows, Hoffman Gallery, New York, 73 & 74, The Clocktower, New York, 77, Grad Ctr, City Univ New York, 77 & Bernice Steinbaum Gallery, New York, 83 & 84; 10 Years Work Traveling Exhib, C W Post Ctr, Long Island Univ, Sculpture Ctr, New York, Joslyn Art Mus, Omaha, McNay Art Inst, San Antonio & elsewhere, 82-85; Broadway Windows, New York, 86; Andre Zarre Gallery, New York, 93; and others. *Teaching:* Prof sculpture, Sch Visual Arts, New York, 68-; prof sculpture, Univ Iowa, summer 70 & Univ Ga, summer 72; also lectr var univ & col throughout US. *Awards:* Nat Endowment Arts Grant, 74 & 80-81; Pollack-Krasner Grant, 90; Florsheim Fund, 92. *Bibliog:* Lucy Lippard (auth), Six Years, Praeger, 73; Lawrence Alloway (auth), Great Drawings of the Western World, Shorewood Publ, 80; Robert Pincus-Witten (auth), Post Minimalism, Out of London Press, London, 80; plus others. *Media:* Bronze; Acrylic. *Publ:* Auth, Moving out-moving up, Art News, 1/71; Radical scale, Art & Artists, 1/72; illusr & contribr, Modern American Painting & Sculpture, Abrams, 72. *Mailing Add:* 7 Worth St New York NY 10013

STRIKER, CECIL L
HISTORIAN, EDUCATOR
b July 15, 32. *Study:* Oberlin Col, AB, 56; Inst Fine Arts, NY Univ, MA, 60, PhD, 68; Univ Pa, Hon MA, 73. *Pos:* Field archeologist, Dumbarton Oaks Ctr Byzantine Studies, 66- *Teaching:* From instr to asst prof medieval art, Vassar Col, 62-68; from assoc prof to prof Byzantine & Medieval art & arch, Univ Pa, 68-, chmn dept art hist, 79-86. *Mem:* Col Art Asn Am; Archeol Inst Am; Asn Field Archeol; Am Res Inst Turkey (pres, 78-84); Coun Am Overseas Res Ctrs (chmn, 81-84); corresp mem German Archaeol Inst; Koldewey Gesellschaft. *Res:* Byzantine architecture and archeology; medieval architecture. *Publ:* Coauth, Work at Kalenderhane Camii in Istanbul: Preliminary reports, Dumbarton Oaks Papers, 67-74; auth, The Myrelaion (Bodrum Camii) in Istanbul, Princeton Univ Press, 82; coauth, Tree ring dating in the Aegean & neighboring regions, J Field Archeol, 84 & 88; and others. *Mailing Add:* Dept Art Hist Univ Pa Philadelphia PA 19104-6311

STRINGER, MARY EVELYN
EDUCATOR, ART HISTORIAN
b Huntsville, Mo, July 31, 21. *Study:* Univ Mo, AB; Univ NC, AM; Harvard Univ, univ traveling fel, 66-67, with Ernst Kitzinger, PhD, 73. *Teaching:* Prof art, Miss Univ Women, 47- *Awards:* Fulbright Scholar, 55-56; Danforth Found Grant, 59-60 & 64-65. *Mem:* Col Art Asn Am; Medieval Acad; Int Ctr Medieval Art; Southeastern Col Art Conf; and others. *Res:* Stained glass windows in America. *Publ:* Auth, Review of Andrew Martindale, Gothic Art, 69; auth, Composite nativity-adoration of English medieval alabasters, NC Mus Art Bulletin, 70; auth, Three Faces of A-T-AH: Artist-Teacher-Art Historian, Southeastern Col Art Conf Rev, 80; auth, Review of Avril Henry, Biblia Pauperum, Facsimile and Edition, SE Col Art Conf Rev, 89. *Mailing Add:* 416 South 10th Columbus MS 39701

STRISIK, PAUL
PAINTER
b Brooklyn, NY, Apr 21, 18. *Study:* Art Students League, with Frank Vincent Dumond. *Work:* Parrish Mus Art, Southampton, NY; Percy H Whitney Mus, Fairhope, Ala; Mattatuck Mus, Conn; Utah State Univ; Peabody Mus, Salem, Mass; and many prominent corp collections. *Exhib:* Allied Artists Am Ann; one-man shows, Grand Cent Art Gallery, New York, 60-70, Rockport Art Asn, 69-75, Gordan Col, Mass, 72, Johnson-Welch Gallery, Kansas City, Mo, 78 & Francesca Anderson Gallery, Boston, Mass, 86; Dodson Gallery, Oklahoma City, Okla, 90; and others. *Awards:* Best in Show, Am Artists Prof League Grant Nat, 72; Gold Medal, Nat Acad Western Art, Okla, 81 & 84; Artist Yr, Santa Fe Rotary, 86; over 160 awards, incl 16 gold medals. *Mem:* Knickerbocker Artists; Int Soc Marine Painters; Santa Fe Watercolor Soc; Rockport Art Asn (pres, 68-71); Am Artists Prof League, New York; and others. *Media:* Multimedia. *Publ:* Auth, Watercolor page, Am Artists, 4/70; auth, article, Am Artists, 79; auth, article, SW Art Mag, 3/81; auth, Art W Mag, 1/83; auth, The Art of Landscape Painting, Watson-Gutpil Publ, 83. *Mailing Add:* 123 Marmion Way Rockport MA 01966

STROH, CHARLES
PRINTMAKER, PAINTER
b Aberdeen, SDak, Feb 20, 43. *Study:* Minneapolis Sch Art, with Eugene Larkin, BFA, 65; Univ Wis, Milwaukee, with T Stoeveken, MS, MFA, 72; US Peace Corps, Kabul, Afghanistan; Northern State Col. *Work:* Milwaukee Art Mus, Wis; Washington Co Mus Fine Arts, Md; Roanoke Mus Fine Arts, Va; Weinstein Collection, Va; Coe Col Collection, Cedar Rapids, Iowa. *Exhib:* Southeastern Ctr Contemp Arts, Winston-Salem, NC, 74; Va Mus, Richmond, 76; Spiva Art Ctr, Joplin, Mo, 77; Des Moines Art Ctr, Iowa, 77; Davenport Munic Gallery, 78; Blanden Mus, Ft Dodge, Iowa, 78; Bharat Bhavan Int Biennial Prints, 89; exhibs in various locations in India, 89, 90; and others. *Collections Arranged:* The Hand-Printed Lithograph (auth, catalog), traveling, Iowa Arts Coun, 80-81; Prints from Kans State Univ Permanent Collection, 81 & Gordon Parks: Photographer (auth, catalog), Kans State Univ, 81; Gordon Parks: Photographer, Miami-Dade Community Col, 82 & traveling exhib US, 84-85; Contemp Printmaking in India, Mt Kailash Meets Mt St Victoire, travelling exhib (auth, catalog), 87-89. *Pos:* Art writer, Cedar Rapids Gazette, Iowa, 78-80; Bd dirs, Manhattan Arts Coun, 80-84; dir, Kans

State Univ Friends of Art, 80-89. *Teaching:* Instr, Northern Mich Univ, Marquette, 72-73; asst prof, Roanoke Col, Salem, Va, 73-76; assoc prof & chmn dept, Coe Col, Cedar Rapids, Iowa, 76-80; prof & head dept, Kans State Univ, Manhattan, 80-89, prof, 89-; lectr at various art schs in India, 85, 89, 90. *Awards:* various awards in juried exhibits, 72-90; Lectr & Res Fel, Am Inst Indian Studies, India, 85; Sr Fulbright Lectureship, India, 89-90; Reston Prize, Design for Arts in Educ, 89. *Mem:* Found Art: Theory & Educ; Nat Coun Art Adminrs. *Media:* Lithography, Acrylic. *Publ:* Auth, articles, Art Educ, 74, 81 & 83, New Art Examiner, 80, Midwest Quarterly, 82, Print Collectors Newsletter, 86, The Tamarind Papers, 87, Print News, 87 & 89, Arts of Asia, 88, Design for Arts in Education, 89 & Span Mag, 90. *Mailing Add:* 331 North 14th St Manhattan KS 66502

STROMSDORFER, DEBORAH ANN
PAINTER, GRAPIC ARTIST
b Aurora, Ill, Dec 18, 61. *Study:* Northern Illinois Univ, BFA(painting), 84, MFA(drawing), 89. *Work:* Arlington Heights Mem Libr, IL; Schaumburg Township Libr, IL; Kelley-Williamson Corp, Rockford, IL; Swed Am Hosp, Rockford, IL; Sycamore Munic Hosp, IL. *Comn:* Triptych (44"h x 60"w) Lasalle Consult Ltd, 89; Growth (3 panels), Rockford Clinic, IL, 91. *Exhib:* 25th Ann Exhib, San Bernardino Co Mus, Redlands, Calif, 90; Women Artists of Am, Chautauqua Art Asn Galleries, NY, 90; Inter Art Exhib, Helio Galleries, New York, 91; 6th Inter Small Works Exhib, Del Bello Gallery, Toronto, Can, 91; Nat Art Competition Winners, UND, Witmer Art Ctr, Grand Forks, NDak, 92; NAm Invitational, Mus Without Walls Inter, Bemus Point, NY, 92; Gray Gallery, Quincy Col, Ill, 92; one woman exhib, Clack Art Ctr, Alma, Mich, 92. *Pos:* Graphic Designer, Northern Ill Univ, DeKalb, Ill 83-87; graphic designer, Univ Ill Col Med, Rockford, Ill, 87-90. *Teaching:* Art instr design/drawing, Rock Valley Col, Rockford, Ill, 90- *Awards:* Best of Show, Rockford Vicinity Exhib, Gallery Ten, 88; Special Award, Nat Contemp, Chim Gregg Gallery, Calif, 90; Best of Show, Art Ctr '91, Elk Grove Village, IL, Talman Home Fed, 91. *Bibliog:* Bebe Raupe (auth), 1986 Floral Competition Winners (2nd place), Artist's Mag, 12/86. *Mem:* Col Art Asn; Chicago Artists' Coalition; Nat Asn Women Artists. *Media:* Colored Pencil, Pastel. *Dealer:* Robert Galitz Fine Art 166 Hilltop Dundee IL 60118. *Mailing Add:* 3602 Grenoble Ct Rockford IL 61114

STRONG, BEVERLY JEAN See Jean, Beverly (Beverly Jean Strong)

STRONG, BRETT-LIVINGSTONE
PAINTER, SCULPTOR
b Junee, New South Wales, Oct 31, 53. *Study:* Self taught. *Work:* Art Gallery New South Wales, Sydney, Australia, 72; Angule Art Ctr, The Rocks Sydney Cove, Australia, 72; Sydney Opera House, Australia, 73; Mus Contemp Art, Tokyo, Japan, 73; Armand Hammer Mus, Los Angeles, Calif, 77. *Comn:* Oil painting & invitation for Royal Opening of the Royal Sydney Opera House, 72-73; US Constitution Bicentennial, Philadelphia, Pa, 87; Official Bicentennial Lithograph (ltd ed commemorative), Sydney Bicentennial Authority, 88; Presidency Monument, Washington, DC, 89; World Friendship Monument, World Fellowship Foundation, Moscow, Russia, 91. *Exhib:* First exhib (charcoal drawing), age 8; one-man show, Sebert Art Gallery (age 16), Sydney. *Media:* Oil, Watercolor; Bronze, Marble. *Mailing Add:* c/o Gallery Rodeo 421 N Rodeo Dr Beverly Hills CA 90210

STRONG, CHARLES RALPH
PAINTER, EDUCATOR
b Greeley, Colo, Dec 25, 38. *Study:* Coronado Sch Fine Art, 57; San Francisco Art Inst, BFA, 62, MFA, 63; also with Elmer Bischoff, Jack Jefferson, Frank Lobdell & James Weeks. *Work:* De Saisset Art Gallery, Univ Santa Clara; Oakland Mus, Calif; San Francisco Art Inst. *Exhib:* Three-artist show, Painted Images, Oakland Mus, 71; Linda Farris Gallery, Seattle, 74; Eastern Wash Hist Soc Traveling Exhib, Western US & Can, 74-76; Works on/of Paper, Zara Gallery, San Francisco, 77; Smith-Andersen Gallery, Palo Alto, 78; and others. *Teaching:* Instr painting & drawing, San Francisco State Col, 65-68; lectr painting & drawing, Stanford Univ, summers 70, 71 & 74; from assoc prof art to prof, Col Notre Dame, Calif, 70-, gallery dir, 76- *Awards:* Fulbright Fel to Eng, 64. *Bibliog:* Work in The Paper Revolution, Am Artist, 8/77; Jules Heller (auth), Paper--the white art, 78; article, Visual Dialogue Mag, 78. *Dealer:* Smith-Andersen Gallery 200 Homer Ave Palo Alto CA 94301. *Mailing Add:* Dept Art Col Notre Dame 1500 Ralston Ave Belmont CA 94002

STRONG, LESLIE (LESLIE STRONG SUTTER)
SCULPTOR, CERAMIST
b Newport News, Va, Dec 1, 53. *Study:* Skidmore Col, Saratoga Springs, NY, BS(art), 76; Syracuse Univ, NY (Univ Fel), MFA, 85. *Work:* President's Collection, Skidmore Col, NY; Roland Gibson Collection, State Univ NY, Potsdam; Richard Brush Art Gallery, St Lawrence Univ, Canton, NY; North Ga Col Art; Key Corp Tower (Swawite), Albany, NY. *Comn:* Exterior wall sculptures, State Univ NY, Cobleskill, 82. *Exhib:* Solo exhib, Work in Transition, St Lawrence Univ, NY, 85; Mindscapes, Wilson Art Gallery, LeMoyne Col, Syracuse, NY, 84; Of the Earth, Schoharie Gallery, Cobleskill, NY, 85; Clay Nat, Upton Hall Gallery, State Univ NY, Buffalo, 85; Artist's Central New York, 1991, 89. *Pos:* Consult & in-house conservator, Brush Gallery, St Lawrence Univ, Canton, NY, 85-88. *Teaching:* Art teacher, Burnt Hill Jr High Sch, NY, 81-83; instr, Skidmore Col, 84-88, Potsdam High Sch, 87- *Awards:* Honorable Mention, AEIOU Exhib, Massena, NY, 86; Roland Gibson Award, N County Regional Exhib, Gibson Gallery, Potsdam, NY, 88; First Prize, Small Sculpture Exhib, N Georgia Col, Delongena, Ga, 90. *Media:* Clay, Bronze. *Dealer:* Upstairs Gallery Main St Canton NY 13617. *Mailing Add:* 11 New St Norwood NY 13668

STRONGHILOS, CAROL
PAINTER
b New York, NY. *Study:* Hunter Col, MA; Art Students League; Brooklyn Mus Art Sch, study with Reuben Tam. *Exhib:* NJ State Mus, 72; Monmouth Col, 72; Brooklyn Mus, 74; Larry Aldrich Mus, 75; Women in the Arts, 76 & 77; Newark Mus, 77; Art in Pub Bldg, NY Orgn of Independent Artists, World Trade Ctr, 77; Women 78, Women's Caucus for the Arts, City Univ New York, 78; one-woman shows, Brooklyn Mus, 71 & Whitney Mus, 75. *Pos:* Founder, NY Feminist Art Inst, New York; consult, Am the Beautiful Fund, 76-77; dir, Art Sch-Mid Westchester, 83. *Teaching:* Instr painting, Brooklyn Mus Art Sch, 71-77 & Brooklyn House of Detention, 74-77; instr painting & drawing, Five Towns Music & Art Ctr, 74-76, Feminist Art Inst, 79-80. *Awards:* Fac & Alumni First Prize, Brooklyn Mus, 70; Grant, Adolph Gottlieb, 86. *Mem:* Women in the Arts; Woman's Caucus for Art, Col Art Asn. *Media:* Acrylic, Oil. *Mailing Add:* 15 Laight St New York NY 10013

STROPPEL, BETTY MACNAIR
PAINTER, INSTRUCTOR
b Woodbridge, NJ, Feb 26, 27. *Study:* Miami Univ, Oxford, Ohio, BFA, 48. *Exhib:* Am Watercolor Soc, Nat Acad Art & Salmagundi Club, New York, 77 & 84; Grand Nat, Salmagundi Club, New York, 90 & 92; The Tree-An Artists Gift, Bergen Mus, Paramus, NJ, 91; Philadelphia Watercolor Club, Noyes Mus, Oceanville, NJ, 92; Audubon Artists, Nat Arts Club, New York, 92; and others. *Teaching:* Instr watercolor, studios & classrooms, NJ, 71-93; Union Co Col, Cranford, NJ, 74-86; Du Cret Sch Arts, Plainfield, NJ, 79-80. *Awards:* Medal of Honor, NJ Watercolor Soc, 79; Mrs John C Newington Watercolor Award, Hudson Valley Art Assn, 90; Gehner Watercolor Award, Nat Asn Women Artists, 91. *Mem:* Nat Asn Women Artists; Audubon Artists; Catharine L Wolfe Club; Hudson Valley Art Asn; NJ Watercolor Soc. *Media:* Watercolor. *Mailing Add:* 115 Sweetbriar Lane North Plainfield NJ 07060

STROSAHL, WILLIAM
PAINTER
b Brooklyn, NY, June 11, 10. *Study:* Self-taught; Dolphin Fel. *Exhib:* Royal Watercolor Soc, London, Eng, 62; 200 Yrs Watercolor, Metrop Mus Art, New York, 64; Am Watercolor Soc (traveling show), Mus Fine Arts, St Petersburg, Fla, 76 & Fry Mus, Seattle, Wash, 77; six one-man shows. *Pos:* Art dir, J Walter Thompson, New York, 30-41; exec art dir, William Esty Co, New York, 42-55, creative dir, 55-69. *Awards:* Gold Medal, Allied Artists Am, 58; Gold & Silver Metals, Audubon Artists, 80; Walter Biggs Award, Nat Acad Design, 80 & 85; and 54 others. *Bibliog:* Wendon Blake (auth), Acrylic Painting, 72 & Norman Kent (auth), 25 Watercolorists, 75, Watson-Guptill; Sue Myers (auth), Fairfield group, Am Artist Mag, 74. *Mem:* Am Watercolor Soc (hon pres); Nat Soc Painters in Casein & Acrylic (dir); Nat Acad Design; Audubon Artists; Allied Artists of Am; Art Dirs Soc, 89. *Media:* Watercolor; Acrylic. *Mailing Add:* 301 Haviland Rd Stamford CT 06903

STROTHER, JOSEPH WILLIS
ADMINISTRATOR, PAINTER
b New Orleans, La, Dec 14, 33. *Study:* La Col, BA; Univ Ga, MA & EdD. *Work:* Rapides Nat Bank Collection; NC Nat Bank Collection; Wachovia Bank State Collection; Ga Mus; Dillard Collection, Weatherspoon Gallery, Univ NC, Greensboro. *Exhib:* Mead Painting of Year, Atlanta, 61; four shows, Nat Art on Paper, Greensboro, 64-69; NC Artist Ann, 71-74; Ga Artist Ann, 72-74; Tex Ann, 74. *Teaching:* Art supvr, Marietta City Schs, Ga, 57-61; instr art, Montgomery Co, Md, 61-64; instr art, Univ NC, Greensboro, 64-66; assoc prof art, Univ Ga, 66-76; prof art & dir, Sch of Art/Archit, La Tech Univ, 76- *Awards:* Award, Ocala Jr Col, 69; Purchase Award, NC Sch Ment Health Exten, Chapel Hill, 71; Purchase Awards, Alexandria, La, 77 & 80. *Mem:* Nat Asn Schs Art & Design; Col Art Asn Am. *Media:* Acrylic, Encaustic Monoprints. *Mailing Add:* Sch of Art/Archit La Tech Univ Ruston LA 71272

STROTHER, VIRGINIA VAUGHN
PAINTER
b Ft Worth, Tex, July 19, 20. *Study:* Tex Christian Univ, BFA(with hons), Spec Div Courses printmaking; watercolor with Barse Miller. *Work:* Tex Fine Arts Asn Permanent Collection, Austin; Univ Tex, Arlington; Sci Dept, Tex Christian Univ; Woman's Club Ft Worth Permanent Collection; and many others. *Exhib:* El Paso Mus Nat Exhibs, 72 & 76; Eight State Exhib Painting & Sculpture, Okla Art Ctr, Oklahoma City, 74; Monroe Nat Ann, Masur Mus Art, La, 73; Southwestern Watercolor, 82; Soc Watercolor Artists, 82, 83, 85 & 86; and fourteen one-person exhibs. *Teaching:* Dir, preparatory workshop art, Tex Christian Univ, 50-54. *Awards:* Citations & Travel Awards, Tex Fine Arts Asn, 69, 70, 72, 75 & 78; Award of Merit, NMex Art League, Albuquerque, 71; Award, Ft Worth Art Mus, 73; Award Works on Paper, Tarrant Co Jr Col NW, 83. *Mem:* Southwestern & Tex Watercolor Socs; Tex Fine Arts Asn (state adv bd, 68-75); Nat League Am Pen Women (pres, Ft Worth Br, 70-72); Soc Watercolor Artists. *Media:* Oil, Watercolor. *Mailing Add:* 4109 Shannon Dr Ft Worth TX 76116

STROUD, PETER ANTHONY
PAINTER, EDUCATOR
b London, Eng, May 23, 21. *Study:* Teacher Training Col, London Univ, Central Hammersmith Schs Art, 48-53. *Work:* Tate Gallery, London; Guggenheim Mus, New York; Los Angeles Co Mus; Detroit Inst Fine Arts; Pasadena Art Mus. *Comn:* Mural, Int Union Archit Congress Bldg, London, 61; mural, State Sch Leverkusen, Ger, 63; mural, Mfrs Hanover Trust Co, New York, 69. *Exhib:* Carnegie Inst Int, Pittsburgh, 61 & 64; Guggenheim Mus Int, 64; The Responsive Eye, Mus Mod Art, New York, 65; Mus Mod Art, Oxford, Eng, 69; Nat Gallery Victoria, Melbourne, Australia, 70; Univ

Calif, Santa Barbara, 70; Ulster Mus, Belfast, Northern Ireland, 71; Finch Col, New York, 72; Retrospective New Jersey, State Mus, Trenton, NJ. *Teaching:* Prof visual studies, Bennington Col, 63-68; prof painting, Grad Sch, Rutgers Univ, New Brunswick, 68- *Awards:* Pasadena Mus Fel, 64. *Bibliog:* Dore Ashton (auth), Peter Stroud's relief-paintings, Studio Int, 66; John Coplans (auth), Interview with Peter Stroud, Artforum, 66. *Media:* Acrylic. *Mailing Add:* 171 Nichol Ave New Brunswick NJ 08901

STRUCK, NORMA JOHANSEN
PAINTER
b West Englewood, NJ. *Study:* New York Phoenix Sch Design, 47-50; study with Paul Burns, 69; Art Students League, New York, 76-77; master class, John Sanden, 78. *Work:* Pentagon, Navy Historical Mus, US Navy Combat Mus, Coast Guard Art Collection, Washington, DC; Governor's Island, New York. *Comn:* First Woman in White House Ceremonial Guard, 79, Rosalyn Carter, Christening of Nuclear Sub "Georgia", Groton, Conn, 79 & First Woman Line Admiral, Washington, DC, 82, US Navy; Admiral Wayne Caldwell, 84 & Vice Admiral Paul Yost, Commandant, 86, US Coast Guard, Governor's Island, NY; Vice Admiral Donald C Thompson, US Coast Guard, 88; Vice Admiral James Irwin. *Exhib:* US Navy Presents: Tall Ships, Navy Hist Ctr, Washington, DC, 77; Navy Combat Art, Navy Combat Art Gallery, Washington, DC, 77-86 & Salmagundi Club, New York, NY, 77-82; Catherine Lorillard Wolfe, Nat Arts Club, New York, 78; Am Artist Prof League, World Trade Ctr, New York, 79; Coast Guard Traveling Art Show, 80-86. *Pos:* Comt mem, Navy Art Coop & Liaison, 80-84. *Awards:* Second Coast Guard Award, Governors Island, 90; Louis E Seley Award, US Navy Art Prog, 79; George Gray Award, US Coast Guard, 83. *Bibliog:* John Pangburn (auth), People, the Record, 82; Linda Bruhn (auth), Guard duty, Profile Mag, 83. *Mem:* Salmagundi Club; Hudson Valley Art Asn (bd dir, 85-88); Am Artists Prof League; life mem Art Students League; Coast Guard Art Prog (comt mem, 80-86). *Media:* Oil, Acrylic. *Publ:* Illusr, World Trade Ctr News, 79; Sea Power, Navy League USA, 82, 84; contribr, Profile: Art for Your Country, Am Portrait Soc, 83; illusr, Retiree News, US Coast Guard, 86. *Mailing Add:* 910 Midland Rd Oradell NJ 07649

STRUPPECK, JULES
SCULPTOR, EDUCATOR
b Grangeville, La, May 29, 15. *Study:* Univ Okla, BFA; La State Univ, MA. *Work:* Univ Okla; Tulane Univ; Ball State Univ; Waite Phillips Col. *Comn:* Courthouse, Iberia Parish, La, 39. *Exhib:* Am Fedn Arts Traveling Exhib, 41; Bertha Schaefer Gallery, 53; Whitney Mus Am Art, 54; Archit League, 54; San Francisco Mus Art, 66. *Pos:* Adv Bd, Internat Sculpture Conf. *Teaching:* Prof sculpture, Newcomb Col, Tulane Univ La, 46-80. *Awards:* Prizes, Gallery Art, Miami, Bertha Schaefer Gallery & Marine Hosp, New Orleans, La; plus others. *Media:* Bronze, Plastics. *Publ:* Auth, The Creation of Sculpture, Holt, Reinhart & Winston, 52; contribr, Design Mag. *Mailing Add:* 1438 Pleasant New Orleans LA 70115

STRUVE, WILLIAM WALTER
DEALER
b Wilkes-Barre, Pa, Dec 16, 36. *Study:* Mich State Univ; Northwestern Univ, BA, 60. *Pos:* Dir, Allan Frumkin Gallery, Chicago, Ill, 60-70; pvt dealer, East Haddam, Conn, 70-79; partner, Frumkin & Struve Gallery, Chicago, Ill, 79-83; owner, Struve Gallery, Chicago, 83- *Mem:* Chicago Art Dealers Asn (past pres). *Specialty:* 20th Century American painting, sculpture, drawings and prints. *Mailing Add:* Struve Gallery 309 W Superior St Chicago IL 60610

STUART, DONALD ALEXANDER
DESIGNER, CRAFTSMAN
b Toronto, Ont, Aug 25, 44. *Study:* Ont Col Art; Sch Am Craftsmen, Rochester Inst Technol, MFA. *Work:* Massey Found, Nat Mus Can; Jean A Chalmers Nat Craft Collection, Can Crafts Coun; Chalmers Collection, Ont Crafts Coun. *Comn:* Elmwood Club, Toronto, 82; sterling chalice, Reverend Ron Raab, South Bend, Ind, 83; altar cross, Rosedale Presbyterian Church, Toronto, 84; silver medal, Victoria Col, Univ Toronto, 84; sterling presentation bowl, Glenn Gould Mem Found, 86; Benton St Baptist Church, Kitchoner, 89; Imperial Oil Ltd, 90; and others. *Exhib:* solo exhib, Brampton Art Gallery, 81 & Craft Gallery, Toronto, 82; Hamilton Art Gallery, Ont, 84; Richmond Art Gallery, BC, 85; Tom Thomson Mem Art Gallery, Owen Sound, Ont, 85; Shelton Gallery, Barrie, Ont, 86; Electrum Gallery, London, Eng, 88; Cambridge Gallery, 89; Koffler Gallery, Toronto, 90. *Pos:* Mgr, Weaving indust in Pangnirtung, Baffin Island, for Eskimo women, 69-72. *Teaching:* instr master weaving, jewelry & design, Georgian Col, Barrie, Ont, 72-; instr in various workshops in USA & Can. *Awards:* Visual Artist Award, 81, Craftsman Grant, 85 & 88, Ont Arts Coun; Gold Award, 82 & Silver Award, 83, Can Jewellery Design; Royal Can Acad Arts. *Bibliog:* The Craftsman's Way, Univ Toronto Press, 81; Donald Stuart, Metalsmith, Vol 2, No 4, fall 82; Works of Craft, Nat Mus Man, 84; article, City & Country Home, 11/89. *Mem:* Ont Crafts Coun (bd dir 74-78 & 82-85); Can Crafts Coun (bd dir, 83-85, 88-90); Visual Arts Ont (bd dir, 84-85); Soc NAm Goldsmiths (conf chmn, 84-85); hon life mem Metal Arts Guild; Royal Can Acad (bd dir, 87-90). *Media:* Jewelry, Holloware. *Publ:* Contribr, The wonderful world of crafts, Toronto Star, 76; auth, Teaching contracts, Craftsnews, 77; The technique of inlaying, Craftsman, Ont Crafts Coun, 81; Pangnirtung weavers, Shuttle, Spindle & Dyepot, fall 85. *Dealer:* Ontario Crafts Coun 35 McCaul St Toronto ON M5T 1N7. *Mailing Add:* 4 Maple Crescent RR3 Barrie ON L4M 4S5 Canada

STUART, JACQUELINE (MRS DAVID)
DEALER
b Kansas City, Mo. *Study:* Kansas City, Col William & Mary, Va. *Pos:* Dir, David Stuart Galleries. *Mem:* Art Dealers Asn Am; Ethnic Arts Coun Los Angeles; Bd Art Dealers Calif. *Specialty:* Contemporary painting and sculpture; pre-Columbian and African arts. *Mailing Add:* c/o David Stuart Galleries 748 N LaCienega Blvd Los Angeles CA 90069

STUART, JOSEPH MARTIN
PAINTER, MUSEUM DIRECTOR
b Seminole, Okla, Nov 9, 32. *Study:* Univ NMex, BFA, 59, MA, 62. *Work:* Art Mus, Univ NMex, Albuquerque; Salt Lake Art Ctr, Salt Lake City; Col of Idaho, Caldwell; Sioux City Art Ctr, Iowa. *Exhib:* Northwest Artists 50th & 52nd Ann, Seattle Art Mus, 64 & 66; Midwest Biennial, Joslyn Art Mus, Omaha 74 & 76; Drawings USA, Minn Mus of Art, St Paul, 77; Nat Drawings, Rutgers Univ, Camden, NJ, 77; solo exhib, The Canyon Suite, WTex State Univ, Canyon, 82. *Collections Arranged:* Jannis Spyropoulos: Paintings, Roswell Mus & Art Ctr, NMex, 62; Edward Kienholz: Sculpture, Boise Gallery Art, Idaho, 67; Art of South Dakota, 74, The Calligraphic Statement, 77, Berry Collection of Asian Arts & Crafts, 79, Sioux Art Collections, 86, Art for a New Century, 89 & Seiferle Collection of American Art, 92, SDak Art Mus, Brookings. *Pos:* Cur, Mus Art, Univ Ore, 62-63; dir, Boise Gallery Art, 64-68, Salt Lake Art Ctr, 68-71 & SDak Art Mus, 71- *Teaching:* Lectr art, Univ Utah, 69; prof art hist, SDak State Univ, 71- *Awards:* First Prize in Painting, Cheney Cowles Mem Mus, Spokane, 65; Salt Lake Art Ctr Purchase Award, 67; Purchase Award, Sioux City Art Ctr, 73. *Mem:* Col Art Asn; Am Asn Mus; Artists Equity Asn. *Media:* Acrylic. *Res:* Art history of South Dakota; Native American Tribal Art. *Publ:* Auth, Stimuli, Utah Archit, fall 69; Art of South Dakota, SDak State Univ, 74; Architecture of Harold Spitznagel, Brookings, 75; South Dakota Collection, 88; The Legacy of South Dakota Art, Pierre: Robinson Mus, 90. *Dealer:* Gallery 306 310 South Phillips Sioux Falls SD 57102. *Mailing Add:* SDak Art Mus Medary Ave at Harvey Dunn St Brookings SD 57007

STUART, KENNETH JAMES
DIRECTOR, ILLUSTRATOR
b Milwaukee, Wis, Sept 21, 05. *Study:* Pa Acad Fine Arts, with Arthur B Carles; also in Paris, France with Constantin Brancusi & Jules Pascin. *Work:* Hitler, Libr Cong, Washington, DC; Cover of Saturday Evening Post. *Exhib:* Drawings, Whitney Mus. *Pos:* Mag & bk illusr & painter, 44; art ed, Sat Eve Post, Philadelphia, 44-62; art dir, Reader's Digest, New York, 62-77, develop lit & graphic work, 77-79; graphics dir, Am Hist & Cult Soc, Washington, DC, 75- *Teaching:* Head dept illus, Moore Col Art, Philadelphia, 39-44, bd mgr, 44-56. *Awards:* Salmagundi Gold Medal, 60; Typographic Excellence Award, Type Dir Club New York, 62; Show Award for Outstanding Work in Mag Illus, Soc Illustrators, 66; and many others. *Bibliog:* Ernest W Watson (auth), American Artist-Interview with Kenneth Stuart; S Neil Fujita (auth), Aim High, Richards Rosen Press; Norman Rockwell & The Saturday Evening Post: The Intimate Story with Ken Stuart (film), Video Arts, 86. *Mem:* Salmagundi Club; Coffee House; Dutch Treat Club; Players Club. *Media:* Watercolor, Drawing. *Publ:* Reader's Digest, article on Norman Rockwell plus prefaces to many bks on illus. *Mailing Add:* 454 Danbury Rd Wilton CT 06897

STUART, MICHELLE
PAINTER, SCULPTOR
b Borrego Springs, Calif, Feb 10, 40. *Study:* Chouinard Art Inst, Los Angeles; apprenticed to Diego Rivera, Mex; New Sch Social Res. *Work:* Mus Mod Art, Brooklyn Mus, New York; Walker Art Ctr, Minneapolis, Minn; Nat Collection Australia, Canberra; Mod Museet, Stockholm, Sweden; Kaiser-Wilhelm Mus, Krefeld, Ger. *Comn:* Painting, Union Cent Life Insurance, Forest Park, Ohio, 87; painting, Security Pac Nat Bank, 87; bronze sculpture & corresponding painting, Col Wooster, Ohio, 87-88; anchorage, painting diptych, Nuritional Ctr, 88; Battery Park City, New York, 92; and others. *Exhib:* One person shows, Haags Gemeentemuseum, Hague, Netherlands, 83, Walker Art Ctr, Minneapolis, Minn, 83, Neuberger Mus, Purchase, NY, 84, Brooklyn Mus, NY, 86, Rose Art Mus, Waltham, Mass, 88 & Wadsworth Atheneum, Hartford, Conn, 88; Mus Mod Art, 76 & 84; Nat Mus Mod Art, Kyoto, Japan, 83; Mus Contemp Art, Chicago, Ill, 84; Moderna Museet, Stockholm, Sweden, 85; San Francisco Mus Mod Art, Calif, 86; Cleveland Mus Art, Ohio, 86; and many other group & one person shows. *Awards:* Nat Endowment Arts, Fel Individual Artists, 74, 77, 80, & 89; For the Arts Fel, New York State Found, 86; Award for Excellence in Design, Arts Comn, New York, 90; and others. *Bibliog:* Stephen Westfall (auth), Melancholy mapping, Art in Am, 2/87; Carey Lovelace (auth), Michelle Stuart's silent gardens, Arts Mag, 9/88; Susan L Stoops (auth), Michelle Stuart: Silent Gardens: The American Landscape (catalog), Rose Art Mus, Brandeis Univ, 88. *Media:* Encaustic; Bronze, Marble. *Publ:* Auth, The Fall, Printed Matter Inc, New York, 76; A Complete Folk History of the United States at the End of the Century, Wright State Univ, Ohio, 78; From the Silent Garden, Williams Col, Mass, 79; I-80 Series: Michelle Stuart, Joslyn Art Mus, Omaha, Nebr, 81; Sacred Precincts: From Dreamtime to the South China Sea, Neuberger Mus, State Univ, New York, 84. *Dealer:* Fawbush Gallery 76 Grand St New York NY 10013. *Mailing Add:* 152 Wooster St New York NY 10012

STUART, SIGNE NELSON See Nelson, Signe (Signe Nelson Stuart)

STUBBS, LU
SCULPTOR
b New York, NY, Aug 16, 25. *Study:* Sch Boston Mus Fine Arts, MA, 64, studied with Harold Tovish & Nathaniel Neujean; L'Accademia di Belle Arti, Perugia, Italy, 71. *Comn:* Three Women (bronze monument), Combined Insurance Co Am, Brookline, Mass, 75; Torso (life-sized bronze), Women's Div Greater Springfield Chamber Com, Mass, 77; life-sized bronze, Sharon Hist Soc, Mass, 89; life-sized children (bronze), Browne Fund/City of Boston, Charlestown, Mass, 90-91; Mr Frog, bronze fountain, Children's Hosp, Boston, Mass, 90. *Exhib:* One-person shows, Attleboro Mus, Mass, 73, Brockton Art Mus, 73-74 & DeCordova Mus (with catalog), Lincoln, 77; Art in Transition-A Century of the Museum School, Mus Fine Arts, Boston, 77; Sculpture Outdoors, Schulman Sculpture Forum, White Plains, NY, 80-82; National Sculpture Society Celebrates the Figure, Port Hist Mus, Philadelphia, 87. *Teaching:* Instr sculpture, Boston Ctr Adult Educ, 63-77, Milton Acad, 67-68 & Boston Univ, 76-77. *Awards:* Exhib grant, Nat Endowment Arts & Humanities, 77; First Prize, New Eng Artist Showcase, Univ Mass, 81; Best of Show, New Eng Sculptors Asn, 86. *Bibliog:* Deborah Minsky Jackson (auth), Celebration of life-the sculptor's view, Nat Sculpture Review, fall 83; Liz Kowalczyk (auth), This woman's place was in the revolution, Patriot Ledger, 10/24/88. *Mem:* Fel, Nat Sculp Soc, 92; New Eng Sculptors Asn; Boston Visual Artists Union. *Media:* Bronze, Wood. *Mailing Add:* 4 Wayside Lane Sharon MA 02067

STUDSTILL, PAMELA
CRAFTSMAN
b San Antonio, Tex, Sept 27, 57. *Study:* Univ Tex, San Antonio, BFA, 78. *Work:* Bank South, IBM Corp & High Must Art, Atlanta, Ga; Fidelity Financial Services, Boston, Mass; Jack Lenor Larsen, New York; Bank San Antonio, San Antonio Arts Coun; Helen Allen Collection, Univ Wis, Madison; and many others. *Exhib:* Solo exhibs, Contemporary Quilts and Sewn Paper, 86, Art Quilts and Sewn Paper Pieces, 87 & Mastworks, Connell Gallery, 90, Great Am Gallery, Atlanta, Ga; Quilts: Tradition and Innovation, Soc Art in Crafts, Pittsburgh, 87; New Art Forms Exposition, Great Am Gallery, Chicago, 88-89; Nat Objects Invitational, Ark Arts Ctr, Decorative Arts Mus, Little Rock, 89; Belles Artes Gallery, Santa Fe, 89; Studio Art Quilts: Seven Innovative Artists, Chelsea Gallery, Western Carolina Univ, Cullowhee, NC, 91; and many others. *Awards:* Nat Endowment Arts Visual Arts Fel, 83 & 88; Nat Endowment of the Arts, Visual Arts Fel, 83 & 89. *Bibliog:* Penny McMorris (auth), A new generation of quilts, Creative Ideas for Living, Birmingham, 1/87; Betsa Marsh (auth), with brush and needle, Creative Ideas for Living, Birmingham, 7-8/88; Annual Report, 1988-1989, High Mus Art, Atlanta, 89; Penny McMorris (auth), Quilts at the end of the 80's, Fiberarts Mag, Asheville, NC, 11-12/89; Nat Objects Invitational (exhib catalog), Ark Arts Ctr Decorative Arts Mus, 89; and many others. *Dealer:* Connel Gallery Great American Ballery 333 Buckhead Ave Atlanta GA 30305. *Mailing Add:* PO Box 63276 Pipe Creek TX 78063

STUHL, MICHELLE
SCULPTOR, ENVIRONMENTAL ARTIST
b Toledo, Ohio, 57. *Study:* Univ Wis-Madison, BS, 78; RI Sch Design, MFA, 82. *Work:* Corning Mus Glass, NY. *Comn:* Phoenix Art Comn, Large Pub Gateway Comn, 89. *Exhib:* New Glass Traveling Exhib, Corning Glass Ctr, Metrop Mus Art, New York, Smithsonian Inst, De Young Mem Mus, Victoria & Albert Mus, and others, 79; Mass Col Art, Boston, 80; List Art Ctr, Brown Univ, 81; Mus Fine Art, Providence, 82; Sculpture Invitational, Barrington Col, RI, 82; Ctr for the Arts, State Univ NY at Purchase, 84; Mid Hudson Art Ctr, 89. *Bibliog:* Suzanne K Frantz (auth), Contemporary Glass, 89. *Mailing Add:* Old Route 28 Mt Tremper NY 12457

STUKEY, VIRGINIA
PAINTER, ASSEMBLAGE ARTIST
b New York, NY. *Study:* Scudder-Colver Col, Guatemala City, Guatemala, AA, 47; Sch Fine Arts, Columbia Univ; Art Students League; studied under Pietro Mangravite, Pierre Lamotte, Pierre Loos, Howard Trafton, Dora DeVries, Dagmar Freuchen & Roberto Delamonica. *Work:* Hinton Rural Life Ctr, Hinton, NC; Riverside Church, New York. *Comn:* Noah's Ark (mural), Church of the Good Shepherd, Bergenfield, NJ, 84. *Exhib:* Solo exhibs, Fantasy, 81, Painting, Collage & Constructions, 83, Windows & Posts, 84, Keane Mason Gallery, New York; Interfaith Ctr, New York, 87; One Hundred Years, One Hundred Artists (5 US Mus); Small Works, Marbella Gallery, New York, 90; First NJ Small Works, 90. *Pos:* Art asst, Barbara Schwinn Mag Illus, 48; commercial illusr, C Hulling Studio, New York, 53-55; artist, Keane Mason Gallery, 81-85; gallery artist, Salon Des Artistes, Mercer St, New York, 88-90. *Teaching:* Instr painting, arts & crafts prog, Riverside Church, New York, 65-75. *Bibliog:* Renee Phillips (auth), Allegorical images, Artspeak, 81; Muriel Jacobs (auth), What can a small museum offer?, NY Times, 85. *Mem:* Nat Asn Women Artists (nominating chmn, 88-90, publ relations chmn, 90-91, 1st VPres 91-92); New York Artists Equity; Am Soc Contemp Artists; Painters Affils, NJ. *Media:* All. *Dealer:* Hugo de Pagano Salon des Artistes 79 Mercer St New York NY 10012. *Mailing Add:* 87 Bennett Rd Teaneck NJ 07666

STULER, JACK
PHOTOGRAPHER, EDUCATOR
b Homestead, Pa, Aug 30, 32. *Study:* Phoenix Col, 57; Ariz State Univ, BA, 60, with Van Deren Coke, MFA, 63; workshop with Ansel Adams, 66. *Work:* George Eastman House, Rochester, NY; Gen Aniline Films, New York; Univ Collections, Ariz State Univ, Tempe; Yuma Art Ctr, Ariz; Phoenix Col; Bibliotheque Nationale, Paris; San Francisco Mus Mod Art. *Exhib:* George Eastman House, 63; Photog In Twentieth Century, Nat Gallery Can, 67; Am Photog: The Sixties, Sheldon Mem Art Gallery, Univ Nebr, Lincoln, 66; Photog USA, DeCordova Mus, Lincoln, Mass, 68; Celebrations, Hayden Gallery, Mass Inst Technol, 74; Ariz Arts Showcase, John F Kennedy Ctr for the Performing Arts, Washington, DC, 74; First Light, Focus Gallery, San Francisco, Calif, 75; one-man show, Univ of Ore, Eugene, 76. *Teaching:* Asst prof photog art, Ariz State Univ, 66-72, assoc prof, 73-75, prof, 75-, currently. *Awards:* First Award Biennial Photog, Phoenix Art Mus, 67; Southwestern Art Best of Show, Yuma Fine Arts Asn, 68; Summer Fel, Ariz State Univ, 68. *Bibliog:* Nathan Lyons (auth), The younger generation, Art Am, 12/63; Helmut Gernsheim (auth), A Consise History of Photography, Dover Publ Inc, New York, 86; Jack Stuler in the Nature of Things (monogr), Nazraeli Press, Munich, Ger, 90. *Mem:* Soc Photog Educ; Inst Cult Exchange Through Photog (mem adv bd, 66-). *Publ:* Contribr, Photography in the Twentieth Century, Horizon, 67; Being without clothes, Aperture, 15:3, 70; Camera, Lucerne, Switz, 11/71; Concise History of Photography, Dover Publ. *Mailing Add:* Dept Art Arizona State Univ Tempe AZ 85287

STULL, JEAN HIMROD
PAINTER
b Waterford, Pa, Jan 30, 29. *Study:* Edinboro State Col, BS(art educ); Pa State Univ. *Work:* Mus Fine Arts, Springfield, Mass; Frye Mus, Seattle; First Nat Bank of Pa, Erie; Time Equities, New York; Erie Insurance Exchange, Pa; and others. *Comn:* Pa Wild Plants of Concern Poster, Wild Resource CF. *Exhib:* Watercolor USA, Springfield, Mo, 66-68 & 75; Pa Soc of Watercolor Painters Annual, 80 & 81; Pa Artists, Capitol Bldg, Harrisburg, 81-82; Invitational for Pa Govs Mansion, Harrisburg, 81-82; Erie Art Mus, 88; plus many others. *Teaching:* Teacher art, Bessemer Sch Dist, Pa, 49-51 & Ft LeBoeuf Sch Dist, Waterford, Pa, 56-84; retired. *Awards:* Rocky Mountain Nat Watermedia Award, 75 & 81; Best of Show, Cincinnati Mus Nat Hist, 82; Distinguished Alumni, Arts & Humanities, 90 & Art Achievement Award, 91, Edinboro Univ, Pa; and others. *Bibliog:* Meyer (auth), Forty Watercolorists and How They Work, Watson-Guptill, 76. *Mem:* Am Watercolor Soc; Northwestern Pa Artists Asn. *Media:* Watercolor. *Publ:* Contribr & illusr, The Sandpiper, 56-64; auth & illusr, untitled weekly column in Erie Times-News, 57-58; Finding Birds on Presque isle, 65; auth, The Watercolor Page, Am Artist, 1/75; coauth & illusr, Birds of Erie County, Pa, 85. *Mailing Add:* 661 Benson Rd Waterford PA 16441

STULL, ROBERT J
SCULPTOR, ADMINISTRATOR
b Springfield, Ohio, Nov 4, 35. *Study:* Ohio State Univ, BS, 62, MA, 63; NY Univ Japanese Language Sch, 64-65; Fulbright Res Scholar Ceramics, Japan, 65-67. *Work:* Smithsonian Inst; Cent State Univ, Ohio; Kyoto Col Fine Arts, Japan. *Comn:* Ceramic sculpture, First Nat Bank, Chicago, 69, Martin Luther King Libr, Columbus, Ohio, 72, SAI Archit & Assoc, Boston, 73 & Gallery Seven, Detroit, Mich, 77; mural painting, St John's Parrish Ctr, Columbus, Ohio, 75. *Exhib:* Brooklyn Mus, 66; Everson Mus, Syracuse, NY, 68; Mus Contemp Crafts, New York, 70; Detroit Inst Art, 71; Mus Art Mod, Paris, 72; Eastern Mich Univ, Ypsilanti, 72-80; L'Domo et L'Arte, Milan, Italy, 73. *Pos:* Founder & gen partner, JDS Assoc, Columbus, 74- *Teaching:* Assoc prof ceramics, Univ Mich, 68-72; prof ceramics & visual commun, Ohio State Univ, 72-, chmn art dept, 75-79, assoc dean, Col Arts, 79-86. *Awards:* Outstanding Achievement Award, African Studies Ctr, Univ Mich, 75; Elizabeth Catlett Moro Award & Virginia Kiah Award, Nat Conf Artists, 78. *Bibliog:* Cover, Ceramics Mo Mag, 65; Four Artists, Ind Univ Press, 69; Lee Nordness (auth), Objects USA, Viking Press, 70. *Mem:* Col Art Asn; Nat Conf Artists (bd dirs, 76-, chmn, 78); Kuumba Theatre, Chicago. *Media:* Ceramic, Acrylic. *Collection:* African art; Japanese, Chinese and Korean ceramics. *Publ:* Producer & dir, TV tapes, Nat Guard Bur, Washington, DC, 77. *Dealer:* Gallery Seven/Charles McGee Gallery Fisher Bldg Detroit MI. *Mailing Add:* 2287 Brookwood Rd Columbus OH 43209

STUMP, M PAMELA (PAMELA STUMP)
SCULPTOR
b Detroit, Mich, July, 8, 28. *Study:* study with Carl Milles, 46, Marshall Fredericks & Thomas McClure, 49-51; Cranbrook Acad Art, 47; Univ Mich BA, 50, MA, 51; Oakland Univ & Univ Mich, 69. *Work:* Rochester Hills Libr, Children's Reading Room, Mich; Saginaw Civic Ctr, Mich; Theodore Roosevelt High Sch, Wyandotte, Mich; Univ Mich Alumni Ctr, Ann Arbor. *Comn:* bronze sculpture, Providence Hosp, Southfield, Mich, 89; six bronze sculptures, Cranbrook Educational Community, Bloomfield Hills, Mich, 90; bronze fountain, Grosse Ile Presbyterian Church, 92; four sculptures, St Stephens Episcopal Church, Troy, Mich. *Exhib:* Mo Artists Show, City Art Mus, St Louis, 51; Mich/Pa Artist Show, Pa Acad Fine Arts, Philadelphia, 59; Oakland Univ, 91-92; New York Acad Scis, 91; Urban Park Gallery, Detroit, 92; Arc Gallery, Chicago, 92; Jr League Travelling Show, 92; and others. *Teaching:* Instr ceramic sculpture, Saginaw Mus Art, 59-64; Instr design, Washtenaw Community Col, 66; Instr sculpture, Cranbrook Kingswood, 69-90. *Awards:* 3rd Prize, First Int Cult & Artistic Exhib, 59; Jurors Award, Mich Fine Arts Competition, 87; Distinguished Alumna Medal, Cranbrook Kingswood, 88. *Bibliog:* Virginia Watson-Jones (auth), Contemporary American Women Sculptors, Oryx Press, 86; C Stokes (auth), Odyssey, Artspeak, New York, 91. *Mem:* Founders Soc Detroit Inst Arts; Int Sculptors; Nat Asn Women Artists; Nat Mus of Women in Arts. *Media:* Cast Metal, Welded Metal. *Publ:* Auth, Michigan Voices (poems), Mich Voices, 50; Mich Alumnus Quarterly Rev, Univ Mich, 56-60; The Moment in Time, pvt publ, 70; auth & illusr, Cranbrook Rev, Cranbrook Sch, 85-92. *Mailing Add:* 19629 Park Ln Grosse Ile MI 48138

STURGEN, WINSTON
PHOTOGRAPHER, PRINTMAKER
b Harrisburg, Pa, Aug 27, 38. *Study:* Pa State Univ, BS, 60, MF, 64; studied with Gerhard Bakker, 80-83. *Work:* Helene Wurlitzer Found, Taos, NMex; Carlsbad Mus, NMex. *Comn:* Photo mural, Sta Rite Industries, Delavan, Wis, 84; photo mural, Phelps Dodge Corp, Phoenix, Ariz, 92. *Exhib:* Int Exposition Prof Photog, Prof Photogrs Am, 83-84 & 86-87; solo exhib, Metamorphosis: 1946-1988, Univ NMex, Albuquerque, 88; Nat Catalogue, Artists' Liaison, Venice, Calif, 88; Beyond Photography, Tex Fine Arts Asn, touring, 91-93; Nat Art Show, Epilepsy Soc, New York, 92. *Pos:* Certified prof photogr, Prof Photogrs Asn Am, Des Plains, Ill, 83-88; various bd offs, Prof Photogrs Asn, NMex, 85-88. *Teaching:* The art photog, Western NMex Univ, 88-91; The image photog, Silver City, 89-91; The color photog, NMex, 90-91. *Awards:* Award Merit, Int Exposition Photog, Prof Photogrs Asn Am, 83-84 & 86-87; Residency Grants, Wurlitzer Found, 87-89; Third Place, Sister Kenny Int, 92. *Bibliog:* Francis de Buda (auth), Art Photography Show, 89 & Metamorphosis Reviewed, 89, Wilderness Outlook; Pete Szilagyi (auth), Photgraphy's Fuzzy Edges Explored, Austin Am Statesman, 91. *Mem:* Resources Artists Disabilites; Enabled Artists United; Disabled Artists Network; Fuller Lodge Mus Art Ctr. *Media:* Assemblage. *Publ:* Auth, Park Cafe, est 1932 (poem), Single Life, 84; Art, artists and photography, 86, Is photography an art from?, 87 & What if?, 87, Prof Photogrs Asn NMex; Death is Not the Parting Way (poem), Singing Wings, 89. *Mailing Add:* 212 W Broadway PO Box 370 Silver City NM 88062

STURGEON, JOHN FLOYD
VIDEO ARTIST, SCULPTOR
b Springfield, Ill, Jan 6, 46. *Study:* Yale Univ, Yale-Norfolk fel, 67; Univ Ill, BFA, 68; Cornell Univ, MFA, 70. *Work:* Mus Mod Art, New York; Los Angeles Co Mus Art; Long Beach Mus Art; Kunstmuseum, Bonn, WGer; Biennale Venice, Italy; and others. *Comn:* Satellite, interactive Video performance, Conf Univ Iowa, 82; No Earth-No Earth Station (video performance), Los Angeles Mus Art, 83; I Will Take You (video installation), Long Beach Mus Art, 84. *Exhib:* Whitney Mus Am Art, 75; Long Beach Mus, 75-76 & 84; San Francisco Mod Art, 76; one-man shows, Mus Mod Art, New York, 78, Los Angeles Inst Contemp Art, 78 & Inst Contemp Art, Boston, 83 & 86; Mus Mod Art, New York, 79-80 & 82-90; Los Angeles Co Mus Art, 83; Night Flight, USA Cable, 83; Cablecast & VPRO Dutch Cable, 85; TV-Broadcast, PBS, New TV Series, 88-90; and others. *Pos:* Video artist, Los Angeles Inst Contemp Art, 78-79; vis artist, Sch Art Inst Chicago, 80 & 83; Univ Iowa, 82. *Teaching:* Instr, Univ Calif, Los Angeles, 79-80; vis artist fac, Claremont Grad Sch, Calif, 80, Art Inst Chicago, 80, 82 & 83; assoc prof, Rensselaer Polytechnic Inst, 83-; mem art fac, State Univ New York, at Purchase, 85- *Awards:* Individual Artists Fels, 75, 77 & 80, Video Production Grant, 84, Nat Endowment Arts; Guggenheim Found Fel, 81; Individual Artists, NY Found for the Arts, 86; and others. *Bibliog:* Louise Lewis (auth), Art as alchemy, Artweek, 7/28/79; Barbara London (auth), Independent Video: The first fifteen years, Artforum, 9/80; Michael Nash (auth), Present tense rights of passage, Art-Com, fall 83; Kathy Huffman (auth), The Second Link (exhib catalog) & Video Art Personal Medium; Margot Lovejoy (auth), Postmodern Currents, Art & Artists in the Age of Electronic Media, UMI Press, 89. *Publ:* Contribr, Video Art, Harcourt Brace Jovanovich, 76; Two Video Installations, Long Beach Mus Art, 78; auth, Spinning dream, Dreamworks, fall 80; US Film & Video Festival (catalog), 83; Polulism--Report from the Field, Art-Com, spring 83; and others. *Dealer:* L A Louver Gallery 55 North Venice Blvd Venice CA 90291; Data Bank Sch of the Art Inst of Chicago Columbus at Jackson Blvd Chicago IL 60603. *Mailing Add:* Art Dept/The Col of Fine Arts 5000 Forbes Ave Pittsburgh PA 15213-3890

STURGEON, MARY C
HISTORIAN
b Los Angeles, Calif, Dec 6, 43. *Study:* Univ Minn, BA(summa cum laude), 65; Bryn Mawr Col, MA, 68, PhD(classical archaeol & Greek), 71; Am Sch Class Studies in Athens, 68-70 & 70-71. *Teaching:* Asst prof Greek & Roman Art, Oberlin Col, 72-77; assoc prof Greek art, Univ NC, Chapel Hill, 77-85, prof, 85- *Mem:* Archaeol Inst Am; Col Art Asn; Am Sch Classical Studies in Athens; Am Philological Asn. *Res:* Greek sculpture. *Publ:* Auth, A new group of sculptures from ancient Corinth, Hesperia, 75; auth, A Hellenistic lion-bull group in Oberlin, 75 & A bronze statuette of Hercules, 76, Allen Mem Art Mus Bulletin; auth, The reliefs of the Theatre of Dionysus in Athens, Am J Archaeol, 77; auth, Corinth IX 2: Sculpture, The reliefs from the theater, Princeton-Am Sch, 77 & Isthmia IV; Sculpture I, 1952-1967, 87. *Mailing Add:* Dept Art Univ of NC Chapel Hill NC 27514

STURGES, HOLLISTER
CURATOR, HISTORIAN
b Kingston, NY. *Study:* Cornell Univ, BA, 62; Univ Calif, Berkeley, MA, 69. *Pos:* Dir, Univ Mo Art Gallery, Kansas City, 76-78; cur European art, Joslyn Art Mus, 80- *Teaching:* Instr, Univ Mo, Kansas City, 72-80; lectr, Univ Nebr, Lincoln, 83. *Mem:* Col Art Asn. *Res:* 18th and 19th century French printing with emphasis on social themes; contemporary American. *Publ:* Auth, Christo's aesthetics of manipulation; Kansas City's wrapped walkways, New Art Examiner, 78; auth, Chicago abstractionists: Romanticized structures, Univ Mo, Kansas City, 78; auth, Angels and urchins: Images of children at the Joslyn, 80, I-80 series: Mario Merz, 81 & Jules Breton and the French Rural Tradition, 82, Joslyn Art Mus; coauth, Art of the Fantastic: Latin America, 1920-1987, 87; coauth, Collection Handbook, Indianapolis Mus Art, 88. *Mailing Add:* 10 Chestnut St Springfield MA 01103

STURMAN, EUGENE
PAINTER, SCULPTOR
b New York, NY, Jan 28, 45. *Study:* Alfred Univ, BFA, 67; Univ NMex, MFA, 69; Tamarind Lithograph Workshop, 70. *Work:* Metro Media Studios, Hollywood, Calif; Warner Bros Records, Universal City, Calif; Los Angeles Co Mus; Newport Harbor Mus. *Comn:* Pub sculpture, City of Los Angeles, 85. *Exhib:* LA Six 74, Los Angeles Co Mus, 74; 24 from Los Angeles, Barnsdall Munic Gallery, Los Angeles, 74; Basel Art Fair, Switz, 74 & 75; Whitney Mus Am Art Biennial, 75; Chicago Art Fair, 82; Los Angeles Co Mus, 83. *Teaching:* Instr printmaking, Long Beach State Univ, 72-74; lectr printmaking, painting & drawing, Univ Calif, Los Angeles, 73-78; instr, Otis-Parsons Sch Design, Los Angeles, 84-91; lectr, Pepperdine Univ, 92. *Awards:* Michael Levins Award, Alfred Univ, 66; New Talent Award, Los Angeles Co Mus, 74; Nat Endowment Arts Grant, 75. *Media:* Copper, Lead,. *Mailing Add:* 190 Loma Metisse St Malibu CA 90265

STURTEVANT, E
PAINTER, SCULPTOR
b Lakewood, Ohio, Aug 23, 30. *Study:* Univ Iowa, BA, 47; Columbia Univ, MA, 74; Chicago Art Inst; Art Students League; Univ Zurich. *Work:* Mus Mod Art, Paris, France; Mus Contemp Art, Los Angeles, Calif; Everson Mus, Syracuse, NY; Stedelijk Mus, Amsterdam, Holland; Staats Galerie, Stuttgart, Ger. *Exhib:* Art in the Mirror, Mus Mod Art, New York, 67; solo exhibs, Everson Mus, Syracuse, NY, 73, Kunstverein, Stuttgart, Ger, 92, Diechtorhallen, Hamburg, Ger, 92 & Villa Arson, Nice, France, 93; Prospect 89, Kunstverein, Frankfort, Ger, 89; Dos Ausstellung, Kunstverein, Hamburg, Ger, 89; Aspect de l'Art XXeme, Siecle Abbaye St Andre, Meyuac, France, 91. *Bibliog:* E Swartz & P Davis (coauth), A Double Take on Sturtevant, File Mag, 86; Norbert Messler (auth), Sturtevant, Noema, 89; F Derrin & W Arning (coauths), Sturtevant, Uwe Krauss GmbH, 92. *Publ:* Auth, Sturtevant, J Contemp Art, 89, Artforum, 91 & Der Spiegel, 92; Sampling Art, Bijutsu Techo, 90; Les Mirror Reflechis, Galerie Ropal, 91. *Mailing Add:* 23 rue des Lombards Paris 75004 10012 France

STUSSY, MAXINE KIM
SCULPTOR
b Los Angeles, Calif, Nov 11, 23. *Study:* Univ Southern Calif, art scholar, 43; Univ Calif, Los Angeles, AB, 47; also res & pvt study in Rome, France, Eng, Ger, 59 & 63. *Comn:* Bob Hope Award Trophy, Bob Hope Athletic Award Comn, 60; Bob Hope New Talent Award, Universal Studios, 61; Wall Sculptures in Wood, Neuropsychiatric Hosp Lobby, Univ Calif, Los Angeles, 68; Wood Sculpture, St Martin of Tours Church, Brentwood, 72; Bronze Horse, Westport, Conn, 92. *Exhib:* Los Angeles Co Mus, 54, 58, 59, 61; Galleria Schneider, Rome, Italy, 59; Denver Art Mus, 60; 25 Calif Women of Art, Lytton Ctr of Visual Arts, Los Angeles, 68; Bednarz Gallery, Los Angeles, 76; Zara Gallery, San Francisco, 77; Sindin Gallery, 86; Coslow Gallery, Los Angeles, 89. *Awards:* First Prize, Sculpture, Bronze, Los Angeles Co Art Mus, 61. *Bibliog:* Bea Miller (auth), The anatomy of an artist, Home Mag, Los Angeles Times, 70; Beverly Edna Johnson (auth), Sculptures evolved from wood, Home Mag, Los Angeles Times, 75; Kathleen Reinoehl (auth), The many faces of Maxine Kim Stussy, Am Artist Mag, 7/75. *Media:* Multimedia. *Mailing Add:* 2280 The Terrace West Los Angeles CA 90049

STUX, STEFAN VICTOR
ART DEALER, DIRECTOR
b Timisoara, Romania, Oct 28, 42; US citizen. *Study:* New York Univ, PhD, 75. *Pos:* Pres & dir, Stux Gallery, Boston, 80- & Stux Gallery, New York, 86- *Specialty:* Contemporary American painting, sculpture and photography; Boston artists. *Mailing Add:* Stux Gallery 163 Mercer St New York NY 10012

SUBA, SUSANNE (MRS BERTAM BLOCH)
PAINTER, ILLUSTRATOR
b Budapest, Hungary; US citizen. *Study:* Pratt Inst, grad. *Work:* Metrop Mus Art, New York; Brooklyn Mus, NY; Art Inst Chicago; Mus City of New York; Kalamazoo Inst Art, Mich. *Exhib:* Ansdell Gallery, London, Eng; Hammer Gallery, New York; Kalamazoo Inst Art; Art Inst Chicago; Mus Mod Art, New York; Works on Paper, Weatherspoon Gallery, Chapel Hill, NC. *Pos:* Teacher, Nelson Univ, Nelson, BC & Community Col, NY. *Awards:* Awards, Am Inst Graphic Art, Art Dirs Club New York & Art Dirs Club Chicago. *Media:* Watercolor, Black Ink. *Publ:* A Rocket in My Pocket; The Monkeys and the Pedlar; The Man with the Bushy Beard. *Mailing Add:* 200 E 66th St New York NY 10021

SUBLETT, CARL C
PAINTER
b Johnson Co, Ky, Feb 4, 19. *Study:* Western Ky Univ; Univ Study Ctr, Florence, Italy; Univ Tenn. *Work:* Nat Acad Design, New York; Hunter Gallery Art, Chattanooga, Tenn; Mint Mus, Charlotte, NC; Springfield Art Mus, Mo; Tenn Arts Comn, Nashville; Knoxville Mus Art, Tenn. *Exhib:* Southeastern Art Ann, Atlanta, Ga; Paintings of Yr, Atlanta; New Painters of South, Birmingham, Ala; Watercolor USA, Springfield, Mo, 64-72; Am Watercolor Soc, New York, 72; one-man retrospective, Tenn State Mus, Nashville, 83 & Knoxville Mus Art, Tenn, 91. *Teaching:* Prof art, Univ Tenn, emer, 82- *Awards:* Rudolph Lesch Award, Am Watercolor Soc, 72; Purchase Awards, Am Collection, Hunter Gallery Art, 72 & Collection Tenn Art League & Parthenon, Nashville, 72; Art in Embassies Prog State Dept, 68-83, 87-90. *Bibliog:* Prize Winning Watercolors, Allied Publ, Inc, 65; Invitational Carl Sublett Exhibition Catalog, Tenn State Mus, 83. *Mem:* Nat Acad Design; Knoxville Watercolor Soc; Tenn Watercolor Soc; Port Clyde Arts & Crafts Soc, Maine; Watercolor USA Hon Soc. *Media:* Watercolor, Oil. *Publ:* Illusr, (exhib catalog), Tenn State Mus, 83. *Dealer:* Collector's Gallery Nashville TN; Bennett Galleries Knoxville TN. *Mailing Add:* 2104 Lake Ave Knoxville TN 37916

SUDLOW, ROBERT N
PAINTER, PRINTMAKER
b Holton, Kans, Feb 25, 20. *Study:* Univ Kans, BFA; Univ Calif, Berkeley; Calif Col Arts & Crafts, Oakland, MFA; Acad Grande Chaumiere, Paris; Acad Andre L'Hote, Paris. *Work:* City Art Mus, St Louis, Mo; Yellow Freight Collection, Kansas City, Mo; Joslyn Art Mus, Omaha; Sheldon Art Mus, Lincoln, Nebr; Menninger Found, Topeka, Kans. *Exhib:* One man show, Am Legacy Gallery, Kansas City, Mo, 90, Beauchamp Gallery, Topeka, 84-90; Kansas Landscapes, traveling show, 85 & 87. *Teaching:* Prof art, Univ Kans, 47-87; retired. *Awards:* Gov Artist, 76; Baker Univ Citation, 90. *Media:* Oil, Watercolor; Lithography. *Publ:* Landscapes in Kansas, Kans Univ Press, 87. *Dealer:* Am Legacy Gallery 5911 Main Kansas City MO 66103. *Mailing Add:* Rt 5 Box 225B Lawrence KS 66046

SUEÑOS, CARLOS
PRINTMAKER, PAINTER
b San Juan, PR, May 25, 52; US citizen. *Study:* Art Student League PR, 73; Univ PR, BA(art), 77, study with Bonilla Norat, Balossi; with Bob Blackburn, Admando Rubbo & Lloyd Reiss in New York. *Work:* Nat Libr, Paris; Nat Libr, Madrid; Omar Rayo Mus, Colombia; Fine Arts Mus, Caracas, Venezuela; Inst Fine Arts, Mexico City. *Comn:* Limited edition etching, comn by Cartón y Papel, Colombia, Venezuela & Mex, 81. *Exhib:* Mus Art & Anthrop, San Juan, PR, 75; Ponce Mus Fine Arts, San Juan, 77; Fine Arts Mus, San Juan, 77; Inst Puerto Rican Cult, San Juan, 78; Mus Mod Art, Mexico City, 81; Am Mus Natural Hist, New York, 83; Latin American Print Biennials, 84 & 88; Urbino Univ, Italy, 84; 10th Drawing Exhibition, Rijeka, Yugoslavia, 86. *Pos:* Cur, exhibs & collections, Printmaking Workshop, 79-83, Ollantay Ctr for the Arts, New York, 90-; registrar, Mus del Barrio, New York, 88-90; cur exhibs, Ollantay Gallery, Queens, NY, 90- *Teaching:* Vis artist anthrop studies in art, Hamilton Col, Clinton, NY, 82; vis artist printmaking, Memphis Acad Arts, 83. *Awards:* Honorable mention, 4th UNESCO Painting Salon, PR, 78; 3rd Prize, 2nd Am Print Biennial, Maracaibo, Venezuela, 82; 1st Prize Graphics, 34th Show, Urbino Univ, Italy, 84; Nat Endowment Asn Fel, Printmaking, 90. *Bibliog:* Suenos, not just a dreamer, San Juan Star, 82. *Mem:* Printmaking Workshop, New York. *Media:* All. *Dealer:* Maximillion Gallery New York NY; Printmaking Workshop 114 W 17th St New York NY 10011. *Mailing Add:* 41-18 29th St No 5D Long Island City NY 11101

SUGARMAN, GEORGE
SCULPTOR, PAINTER
b New York, NY, May 11, 12. *Study:* City Col New York, BA; Atelier Zadkine, Paris, 51. *Work:* Walker Art Ctr, Minneapolis; Kunstmuseum, Zurich, Switz; Metrop Mus, Mus Mod Art & Whitney Mus Am Art, New York; Chicago Art Inst. *Comn:* Allegheny Landing, Pittsburgh, PA, Columbia Plaza, Cincinnati, OH, 85; NCNB Plaza, Tampa, Fla, 88; Violl Ctr, Irvins, Calif, 89; Pavillions at Backland Hills, Manchester, Conn, 90; GTE Bldg, Irving, Tex, 91; and others. *Exhib:* Whitney Mus Am Art Sculpture Ann, 60-; Carnegie Inst Int, Pittsburgh, 61; Sao Paulo Biennal, Brazil, 63; Sculpture of the Sixties, Los Angeles Co Mus Art, 67; Int Pavilion, Venice Biennal, 69; Retrospective, Stedelijk Mus, Amsterdam, Holland, 69-70; 200 Yrs Am Sculpture, Whitney Mus Am Art, New York, 76; retrospective, Joslyn Art Mus, Omaha, Nebr, 81; and others. *Teaching:* Assoc prof sculpture, Hunter Col, 60-70; vis prof sculpture, Grad Sch Art & Archit, Yale Univ, 67-68. *Awards:* Second Prize for Sculpture, Pittsburgh Int, 61-62; Longview Found Grants, 61-63; Nat Art Coun Award, 66. *Bibliog:* I Sandler (auth), Sugarman-Sculptural Complex, First Nat Bank, St Paul, 71; Sam Hunter (auth), American Art of the 20th Century, 72; Holliday T Day (auth), The Shape of Space: The Sculpture of George Sugarman, 81; and others. *Media:* All; Acrylic. *Mailing Add:* 21 Bond St New York NY 10012

SUGGS, DON
PAINTER, PHOTOGRAPHER
b Ft Worth, Tex, Mar 16, 45. *Study:* Univ Calif Los Angeles, MA, 71, MSA, 72. *Work:* San Diego Mus Contemp Art, Calif; Univ Calif, Los Angeles. *Exhib:* Clearing, Los Angeles Co Mus, Calif, 89. *Teaching:* Lectr painting drawing, UCLA, 83- *Awards:* Artist Fel, Nat Endowment Arts, 91. *Mailing Add:* 423 Molino St Los Angeles CA 90013

SUGGS, PAT(RICIA) ANN
PAINTER, CONCEPTUAL ARTIST
b Reedley, Calif, Mar 17, 36. *Study:* The Leighton Art Acad, San Francisco, 74-81; student of the late Thomas Leighton & Margery Lester Leighton; Old World Acad Training. *Comn:* Roses floral painting, comn by Joe & Inez Wilson, San Jose, Calif, 82; Floral painting, comn by Drace & Pat Kutnewsky, San Jose, Calif, 85; Pastel portrait painting, comn by Melody Grey, Santa Rosa Calif, 86; Pastel floral painting, comn by Elaine Clarke, Grants Pass, Ore, 91; Pastel landscape painting, comn by James & Helen Riley, Saratoga, Calif, 92. *Exhib:* Pastel Society of America, Nat Arts Club, Nat Open Show, New York, 80; Pastel Society of the West Coast, Sacramento Fine Arts Ctr, Nat Open Show, Carmichael, Calif, 89-92; Pastel Society of the West Coast, Runnings Gallery, Seattle, 90; Pastel Society of America, Ashland Gallery, Ashland, Ky, 90; Society of Western Artists 41-42nd Annual, San Francisco, 91-92. *Pos:* Judge fine arts, Arts Clubs, The Peninsula, Northern Calif & San Joaquin Valley, 84-92 & Sonoma Co, Alameda Co & Santa Clara Co Fairs, 89-91. *Awards:* Lee & Vincent Award for Best Floral, 80, Pastel Soc Am, NY; Award of Merit, Pastel Soc WCoast, Seattle, Wash, 90. *Bibliog:* George A Magnan (auth), Painting Flowers in Pastels, Today's Art, 11/79; Margaret Kock (auth), San Jose Show, Santa Cruz Sentinel, 2/22/82; John Lehman (auth), Three Native Daughters' Show, The New Outlook, 6/6/83. *Mem:* Pastel Soc Am, New York; Pastel Soc WCoast, Carmichael, Calif (adv bd, 86-92); Soc Western Artists (trustee, 86-92); Allied Artists West (dir, exhibs, 91-92); The Nat League Am Pen Women, Las Artes Br. *Dealer:* Carol A Dabb 41 Sunkist Lane Los Altos CA 94022. *Mailing Add:* 4127 Beebe Circle San Jose CA 95135-1010

SUJO, CLARA DIAMENT
GALLERY DIRECTOR, DEALER
b Argentina. *Pos:* Mem bd dirs, Mus Bellas Artes Caracas, 58-63; dir, Estudio Actual, Caracas, 68- & CDS Gallery, New York, 81- *Teaching:* Prof art hist & fine Arts, Cristobal Rojas Sch Fine Arts, Caracas, 58-65; teacher, Neumann Found Inst Design, 67-70. *Mem:* Int Asn Art Critics; Art Table Inc. *Specialty:* International contemporary art. *Publ:* Auth, Art in Latin America Today, Panamerican Union, 62; coauth, Joseph Albers, Kellar Velag, 67; contribr, The Emergent Decade, Cornell Univ, 65. *Mailing Add:* 76 E 79 St New York NY 10021

SULLIVAN, ANNE DOROTHY HEVNER
PAINTER, PRINTMAKER
b Boston, Mass, Mar 17, 29. *Study:* Northeastern Univ, Boston, Mass, 72-74; Univ Lowell, Mass, BA, 77; DeCordova Mus, with King Coffin, Carlton Plummer, Glen Bradshaw & K Chang Liu. *Work:* The New England Permanent Collection, Boston, Mass; Shawmut Bank, Boston, Mass; Bay Banks of New Eng, Boston, Mass; Sheraton Corp, Boston, Mass; Amoskeag Banks, Manchester, NH. *Exhib:* Okla Watercolor Exhibit, Okla Univ, 85; Nat Asn Women Artists, traveling graphics, USA, 87-89; Nat Asn Women Artists, traveling painting, USA, 88-90; NAmOpen Show, Fed Reserve Gallery, Boston, Mass, 90 & 92; Emerging Boston Painters, Brush With Hist Gallery, Lowell, Mass, 90; Midwest Mus Am Art, Elkhardt, Ind, 91; Summer Mus, NLAPW Biennial, Washington, DC, 92; Catharine Lorillard Wolfe Art Club Inc, 96th Ann at Nat Arts Club, New York, 92. *Pos:* Vpres, Whistler Mus, 77-79; chmn, Lowell Arts Lottery Coun, 79-81; bd mem, Mass Arts & Humanities Adv Comt, 81-82. *Teaching:* Dir & instr art program, Whistler Mus, Lowell, Mass, 75-76; dir & instr art workshop, AID Prog, Univ Lowell, Mass, 74-82. *Awards:* Martha Reed Memorial Award, Nat Asn Women Artists, 88; Award of Excellence, Nat League Pen Women, Kansas City, 90; 2nd Prize, watercolor, Cahoon Mus Open Competition, Cotuit, Mass, 91. *Bibliog:* Ann Schecter (auth), Sun Art critics review, Lowell Sun, Mass, 4/8/79 & 4/6/84; Marie Geary (auth), Art is, Chelmsford Weekly, Mass, 4/3/80. *Mem:* New Eng Watercolor Soc (dir, 83-92); Nat Asn Women Artists, New York; Nat League Penwomen, Musicians & Artists, Washington, DC; Copley Soc of Boston, Mass; Monotype Guild of New Eng (pres, 92-93). *Media:* Mixed Media. *Mailing Add:* 28 Rindo Pk Dr Lowell MA 01851

SULLIVAN, BILL
PAINTER, PRINTMAKER
b New Haven, Conn, Sept 10, 42. *Study:* Silvermine Col Art, 60-65; Univ Pa Grad Sch Fine Arts, MFA, 68. *Work:* Cleveland Mus Art, Ohio; Mus de Arte Mod, Bogota, Colombia; Reading Mus, Pa; Metrop Mus Art, New York; Hudson River Mus, NY. *Exhib:* solo exhibs, Siegal Contemp Art, 81, David Findlay Jr Gallery, 84, G W Einstein, 86 & 89 & Schreiber Cutler, 86, New York; Susan Schreiber Gallery, New York, 90; Am Acad & Inst Arts & Letters, New York, 90; Painting Calif: Five NY Artists Look at Los Angeles & Plein Air Painting: Capturing the Moment, Tatistcheff Gallery, Santa Monica, Calif, 90; Land/Sea/Air, Steven Scott Gallery, Baltimore, Md, 90; Pa Prints: 30 Years of Printmaking at the univ Pa, Arthur Ross Gallery, Philadelphia, Pa, 90. *Awards:* Premio Quirama, Inst de Integracion Cult, Medelin, Colombia, 79; Ingram Merrill Found Fel, 81; Nat Endowment Arts Fel, 90. *Bibliog:* Gerrit Henry (auth), Painterly realism and the mod landscape, Art in Am, 9/81; John Arthur (auth), The Spirit of Place: Am Landscape Painting, 90; Lori Simmons Zelinko (auth), Bill Sullivan's Reality, Am Artist, 10/90. *Mem:* Artists Equity Asn. *Media:* Oil on Canvas, Pastel. *Dealer:* Susan Schreiber Gallery 171 Spring St New York NY 10012; Tatistcheff Gallery 1547 10th St Santa Monica CA 90401. *Mailing Add:* 687 Eighth Ave New York NY 10036

SULLIVAN, DAVID FRANCIS
PAINTER, PRINTMAKER
b Stoughton, Mass, Apr 13, 41. *Study:* Univ NH, 57-61; Chouinard Sch Fine Arts, Los Angeles, Calif; Boston Mus Fine Arts Sch. *Work:* Addison Gallery Am Art, Andover, Mass; Montreal Mus Art; Philadelphia Mus Art, Pa; Cleveland Mus, Ohio; Minn Mus Art, St Paul. *Exhib:* Twenty-Fifth Nat Exhib Prints, Smithsonian Inst, 77; Art in Transition, Mus Fine Arts, Boston, 77; Nat Print Exhib, Trenton State Col, NJ, 78; Art of the State, Hayden Gallery, Mass Inst Technol, Cambridge, 78; Printmaking Biennial, Brooklyn Mus, NY, 78; Recent Trends in Am Printmaking, Mitchell Mus, 79; New Am Still Life, Westmoreland Co Mus Art, Greensburg, Pa, 79. *Awards:* Purchase Awards, De Cordova Mus, 76 & Trenton State Col, 78; Stuart M Egnal Prize, Philadelphia Mus Art, 77; Blanche E Coleman Found Grants, 80, 81 & 82. *Bibliog:* Pamela Allara (auth), New Editions, Artnews, 9/82. *Media:* Oils; Silkscreens, Drawings. *Mailing Add:* 94 N Main St Andover MA 01810

SULLIVAN, FRANCOISE
PAINTER
b Montreal, Que, June 10, 25. *Study:* Ecole des Beaux Arts de Montreal. *Work:* Nat Gallery, Ottawa; Le Musée d'Art Contemporain, Montreal; La Banque d'Art du Canada; Univ Sask. *Comn:* Sculpture, Toronto City Hall, comn by City of Toronto, Ont, 67; sculpture, Expo '67, & Les Jeux Oly Piques (artwork), 76, comn by City of Montreal. *Exhib:* Art and Engineering, Art Gallery Ont, Toronto, 65; New Directions in Canadian Sculpture, Dorothy Cameron Gallery, Toronto, 65; 11th Biennial, Middleheim, Anvers, Belg, 71; Su Proust, Arte Studio, Brescia, Italy, 74; Chi E Pandora, Galleria Unimedia,

Genova, Italy, 81; retrospective (with catalog), Musée d'Art Contemporain, Montreal, 81; Montreal Painting, Second Look, Memorial Univ Art Gallery, St Johns, Nfld, 85; Le Musée Imaginaire, Saidye Bronfman Ctr, Montreal, 86; Station, Centre Int d'Art Contemp, 87, Consenses et Contestation, 92, L'Amarchie resplendissaute de la peinture, Galerie de l'UQAM, Montreal, 92; Kunst aus Canada, Galerie Clara Maria Sels, Dusseldorf, Ger, 92; Présence québecoise, Chateau de Biron, Dordogne, 92, La Ferune du Buisson, Marne la Vallee, France, 92; Naissauce et persistance de la sculpture, Musée de Que, 92. *Teaching:* Instr drawing & painting, Concordia Univ, Montreal, 77- *Awards:* Martin Lynch Staunten Award, Can Coun, 84; Prix Borduas, 87-; Royal Acad Arts, 92. *Bibliog:* Manon Lapointe (auth), Francoise Sullivan: Renouer avec la presence du passe, ETC, printemps, 88; Claire Gravel (auth), Francoise Sullivan: La parole retrouvee, Vie des Arts, mar, 88; Gilles Daigneault (auth), L'Art au Quebec depuis Pellan-Une histoire des prix Borduas, Mus du Que, mai, 88. *Mem:* Vehicule Art Inc. *Publ:* Poème, Da Vinci, Montréal, No 2, p 64, 74; sans titre, tiré (catalog), Péiriphéries, Musée d'artcontemp-Véhicule Art Inc, Montréal, 74; Sans titre, texte d'une conférence sur l'art conceptuel donnée à l'Université du Qué à Montréal, 75; Francoise Sullivan, David Moore, textes de F Sullivan et de D Moore, et texte commun des deux artistes, Galerie Véhicule Art, Montréal (catalog d'exposition), 77; contribr, Three Holes in the Ground, de David Moore, édition de 50, Maker Press, 81. *Dealer:* Dominion Gallery Montreal PQ. *Mailing Add:* 375 St Madeline St Montreal PQ H3K 2K8 Canada

SULLIVAN, JIM
PAINTER
b Providence, RI, Apr 1, 39. *Study:* RI Sch Design, Providence, Fulbright scholar, 61; Stanford Univ, 62-63. *Work:* Whitney Mus Am Art, New York; Worcester Art Mus, Mass; Albany State Mus; Wadsworth Atheneum, Hartford, Conn; Metrop Mus, New York. *Exhib:* Whitney Mus Am Art Ann, 72; Small Works Group Show, Mus Mod Art, New York, 71; Ind Mus Art, Indianapolis, 72; Nancy Hoffman Gallery, New York, 80, 82, 84, 86 & 88; McNay Mus, San Antonio, Tex, 81; American Still Life 1945-1983, Contemp Arts Mus, Houston, 83; New York Painting Today, Three Rivers Festival, Pittsburgh, 83; Folker Skulima Gallery, Berlin, 83; Dart Gallery, Chicago, 84. *Teaching:* Prof painting, Bard Col, 65- *Awards:* Guggenheim Found Grant, 72; Nat Endowment Arts Grant, 83. *Bibliog:* Kay Larson (auth), article, New York Mag, 1/19/81; Vivian Raynor (auth), article, New York Times, 1/9/81; Gerrit Henry (auth), Rev, Art in America, 10/86; and others. *Publ:* Empire State Collection, Art for the Public, Tiffany Bell, 87; American Still Life, Linda Cathcart, 83; New York Painting Today, Donald Kuspit, 83; Diamonds are Forever, Peter Gordon, 87. *Dealer:* Nancy Hoffman 429 W Broadway New York NY 10012. *Mailing Add:* 59 Wooster St New York NY 10013

SULLIVAN, LINDA SUSAN
MUSEUM DIRECTOR
b Bethesda, Md, Mar 8, 52. *Study:* Univ Md, Col Park, BS(craft design), 75; Columbia Univ, New York, MFA(arts admin), 91. *Pos:* Dir, Univ Md Art Ctr, 76-81; dir development, Washington Proj Arts, 84-86; exec dir, Acad Arts, Easton, Md, 86-92; exec dir, Miss Mus Art, Jackson. *Mem:* Am Asn Mus; Md 1992 Comn; Md Air & Space Mus Comn. *Mailing Add:* c/o Mississippi Mus Art 201 E Pascagoula St Jackson MS 39201

SULLIVAN, R(ONALD DEE)
SCULPTOR, EDUCATOR
b Norman, Okla, Feb 6, 39. *Study:* Univ Okla, BFA, 63; Calif State Univ, Sacramento, MA, 69; ETex State Univ, postgrad. *Comn:* sculpture garden, Incarnate Word Acad, Corpus Christi, Tex, 89. *Exhib:* Art Mus STex, Corpus Christi, 76; one-man shows, Temple Univ, Philadelphia, 72 & Joseph A Cain Gallery, Del Mar Col, Corpus Christi, Tex, 92. *Pos:* Conservator, var pub & pvt collections, 89- *Teaching:* Prof sculpture, drawing, Del Mar Col, Corpus Christi, 70- *Awards:* Fac Develop Grant, Del Mar Col, 89-92. *Bibliog:* The Mystery and Magic of Glass, Channel 16, Corpus Christi, Tex, 78. *Mem:* Tex Assoc Sch Art. *Media:* All Media. *Publ:* Auth, Hillabee to Weogufkee, Del Mar Col, 89; Ron George (auth), Red Earth Images, Caller-Times, 92. *Mailing Add:* 2845 Topeka Corpus Christi TX 78404

SULLIVAN, RUTH WILKINS
CURATOR, AUTHOR
b Boston, Mass, Nov 20, 26. *Study:* Wellesley Col, AB. *Collections Arranged:* Chinese Export Porcelain, 65; American Painting from 1830 (with catalog), 65; Chinese Art from the Cloud Wampler Collection (with catalog), 68; Wealth of the Ancient World: The Nelson Bunker Hunter & William Herbert Hunt Collections (with catalog), 83. *Pos:* Admin asst, Everson Mus Art, 58-60, registr, 60-62, cur & ed publ, 63-70, cur collections, 66-70; consult, Mus Am China Trade, 71; cur educ, Kimbell Art Mus, 71-82, res cur, 83- *Awards:* Woman Achievement Arts, Post Stand, 68. *Mem:* Col Art Asn Am. *Res:* Early Italian painting. *Collection:* Early American silver. *Publ:* Auth, Some Old Testament Themes on the Front Predella of Duccio's Maesta, Art Bulletin, 86; contribr, In Pursuit of Quality: The Kimbell Art Museum, Abrams, NY, 87; auth, Duccio's Raising of Lazarus Reexamined, Art Bulletin, 88; Mary Magdalen Annointing Christ: A New Devotional Subject, Arte Christiana, 90; International Dictionary of Art and Artists, St James Press, London, 90; and others. *Mailing Add:* 4500 Westridge Ave Unit 1 Ft Worth TX 76116

SULLIVAN, SCOTT A
HISTORIAN, EDUCATOR
b Cleveland, Ohio, May 22, 47. *Study:* John Carroll Univ, BA, 69; Case Western Reserve Univ, MA, 72, PhD, 78. *Teaching:* Asst prof art hist, Univ N Tex, 75-81, assoc prof, 81-87, prof, 87-, chmn dept, 87-92, actg dean, 92- *Mem:* Historians of Netherlandish Art; Col Art Asn Am; Midwest Art Hist Soc (secy-treas, 85-87, pres, 87-89); Am Asn Netherlandic Studies; Nat Coun Art, admin. *Res:* 17th century Flemish and Dutch painting, especially still life. *Publ:* Auth, Rembrandt's self portrait with a dead bittern, Art Bull, 80; F Snyders: Still Life with Fruit, Vegetables and Game, Detroit Art Inst Bull, 81; The Duth Gamepiece, Allanheld & Schram, 84; In the Shadow of Caravaggio: Pietro Paolini's Bacchic Concert, Dallas Mus Art Bull, 85; Abraham van Beyeren's Visserij-bord at the Groote Kerk, Maassluis Oud Holland, 87. *Mailing Add:* Dept Art Univ N Tex PO Box 5098 Denton TX 76203

SULLO, JOSEPH ANTHONY
PAINTER, DESIGNER
b New York, NY, June 13, 21. *Study:* Pratt Inst, cert(indust design), 42. *Exhib:* One-man show, Ormond Beach Mem Mus & Art Gallery, Fla, 79, Bardavon Opera House, Poughkeepsie, 86 & Main Street Gallery, Pine Bush, NY, 88; Festival of the Masters, Lake Buena Vista, Disneyworld, Fla, 83; Hudson Valley Art Asn 56th Ann Exhib, Westchester Co Ctr, White Plains, 84; Halifax Art Festival, The Casements, Ormond Beach, 87; Pres Show, Kent Art Asn, Conn, 89; Eighth Regional Open Jury Show, Ridgewood Art Inst, NJ, 90. *Awards:* First Place, Pine Bush Area Arts Coun Show, 88; Best in Show, Eighth Ann Art Exhib, Newburgh Free Libr, 89. *Bibliog:* R Lane Herron (auth), Doll artistry-the sullos, Antiques J, 4/80; LaClaire T Wood (auth), This is no ordinary dollhouse, Poughkeepsie J, 7/20/80; Drew Murphy (auth), Together, Morning J, 7/2/83. *Mem:* Kent Art Asn; Dutches Co Art Asn; Garrison Art Ctr; Ridgefield Guild of Artists. *Media:* Oil. *Mailing Add:* 16 Briar Hill Rd Rt 52 Hopewell Junction NY 12533

SULTAN, ALTOON
PAINTER
b Brooklyn, NY, Sept 29, 48. *Study:* Brooklyn Col, BA, 69, MFA, 71, study with Phillip Pearlstein; Boston Univ at Tanglewood, 69; Skowhegan Sch Painting & Sculpture, study with Gabriel Laderman, 70. *Work:* Princeton Univ Libr; Hunter Mus, Chattanooga, Tenn; Yale Univ Art Gallery; Metrop Mus Art, New York; Walker Art Ctr, Minneapolis, Minn. *Exhib:* One-woman shows, Marlborough Gallery, 77, 79, 81, 84, 85, 88 & 90, Middendorf Gallery, Washington, DC, 87 & Hokin- Kaufman Gallery, Chicago, 90; New York Showcase, Okla Art Ctr, 81; Collectors Gallery, Columbus Mus Art, 81; A Private Vision: Contemporary Art from the Graham Gund Collection, Boston Mus Fine Arts, Mass, 82; Lower Manhattan from Street to Sky, Whitney Mus Am Art, 82; Small Pictures, New Britain Mus Am Art, 82; Painted Light, Reading Pub Mus, Butler Inst Am Art, 83; American Realism: 20th Century Drawings & Watercolors, San Francisco Mus Mod Art, 85; The Landscape in 20th Century American Art: Selections from the Metropolitan Mus Art, Philbrook Mus Art, Tulsa, Okla; and others. *Teaching:* Vis critic, Univ Pa, Philadelphia, 85-88; Resident fac, Skowhegan Sch Painting & Sculpture, 88; asst prof, San Jose State Univ, Calif, 91- *Awards:* MacDowell Colony Fel, 72 & 74; Yaddo Fel, 75 & 76; Nat Endowment Arts Fel Grant, 83 & 89. *Bibliog:* June Cutler (auth), article, Am Artist, 5/83; John Arthur (auth), The remembrance of tranquility: Altoon Sultan's new paintings, Arts Mag, 3/84; John Russell (auth), review, 1/15/85 & Micheal Brenson (auth), review, 12/13/85, New York Times; Gerrit Henry (auth), review, Art News, 3/86. *Media:* Oil, Govache. *Dealer:* Marlborough Gallery 40 W 57th St New York NY 10019. *Mailing Add:* 131 Allen St New York NY 10002

SULTAN, DONALD K
PAINTER, PRINTMAKER
b Asheville, NC, May 5, 51. *Study:* Univ NC, Chapel Hill, BFA, 73; Art Inst Chicago, MFA, 75. *Work:* High Mus Art; Dallas Mus Fine Arts; Albright-Knox Art Gallery; Mus Mod Art, New York; La Jolla Mus, Calif; Guggenheim Mus, New York; Art Inst Chicago; Kitakyushu Munic Mus Art, Tobataku Kitakyushu, Japan. *Exhib:* Solo exhib, Mus Mod Art, 88, Richard Green Gallery, New York, 89, The Greenberg Gallery, St Louis, 89, Galeria Trauma, Barcelona, Spain, 92, Meredith Long & Co, Houston, Tex, 92, Knoedler & Co, New York, 92, Hill Gallery, Birmingham, Mich, 92; Prints from Blocks--Gaugin to Now, Mus Mod Art, New York, 83; Boston Mus Fine Arts, 83; Boston Collects: Contemp Painting & Sculpture, Mus Fine Arts, Mass, 86; New Romantic Landscape, Whitney Mus Am Art, Stanford, Conn, 87; Projects and Portfolios: 25th Nat Print exhib, Brooklyn Mus, New York, 89; Pharmakon 90, Nippon Convention Ctr, Makuhari Meese, Japan; Inaugural exhib, One Hundred years of American & European Art, Adelson Galleries, New York, 90; Art Inst Chicago (with catalog), 92; Nassau Co Mus (with catalog), Roslyn Harbor, NY, 92; Tucson Mus Art, Ariz, 92; Bibliotheque Nationale (with catalog), Paris, France, 92. *Teaching:* Lectr, Greenberg Gallery, St Louis, Mo, 89; lectr, Meadows Sch Arts, 89; lectr, Hirshhorn Mus & Sculpture Garden, Washington, DC, 89. *Awards:* Creative Artists Pub Serv Grant, 78-79; Nat Endowment Arts Grant, 80-81. *Bibliog:* Helen A Harrison (auth), Another First: Sultan Survey, review, NY Times, p 1, 8/16/92; Roberta Smith (auth), Art LI Shows, NY Times, 8/21/92; Adrienne Lesser (auth), The Arts, East End Stars: Art World's Big Guns on Target in New Show, Southampton Press, p B1, B6, 8/13/92. *Dealer:* M Knoedler & Co Inc 19 E 70th St New York NY 10021. *Mailing Add:* 54 N Moore St New York NY 10013

SULTAN, LARRY A
PHOTOGRAPHER
b July 13, 46. *Study:* Univ Calif, BA, 68; San Francisco Art Inst, MFA, 73. *Work:* Mus Mod Art, New York; Ctr Creative Photog, Univ Ariz; Fogg Art Mus; Univ Alaska, Fairbanks; Bibliot Nat, Paris; San Francisco Mus Mod Art. *Comn:* Plexiglas map, Atlantic Richfield Co, Los Angeles, 79. *Exhib:* Contemporary Photographs, Fogg Art Mus, 76; Evidence, San Francisco Mus Mod Art, 77 & Chicago Mus Contemp Art, 79; Beyond Color, San Francisco

Mus Mod Art, 80; Attitudes: Photography in 1970s, Santa Barbara Mus Art, 80; Photographs From the Museum of Modern Art, Seibu Art Mus, Tokyo, 82; Color as Form, Corcoran Gallery, 82; Newsroom, Univ Art Mus, Berkeley, 83. *Teaching:* Instr photog, Univ Calif, Berkeley, 73-78 & San Francisco Art Inst, 78-; asst prof art, Lone Mountain Col, 74-78. *Awards:* Grant, 76 & fel, 80, Nat Endowment Arts; Guggenheim Found Fel, 83. *Bibliog:* Ben Lifson (auth), Modern dreams, Village Voice, 9/77; Douglas Davis (auth), Harvards challenging evidence, Newsweek, 6/8/78; Kathryn Livingston (auth), article, Am Photogr, 8/80. *Dealer:* Stephan Wirtz Gallery 345 Sutter St San Francisco CA 94108. *Mailing Add:* c/o Stephen Wirtz Gallery 49 Geary St San Francisco CA 94108

SUMM, HELMUT
PAINTER, EDUCATOR
b Hamburg, Ger, Mar 10, 08; US citizen. *Study:* Univ Wis, grad, 30; Marquette Univ, MEd, 46; also with Umberto Romano, Carl Peters & Robert Von Neumann. *Work:* Milwaukee Art Ctr, Milwaukee J Gallery, Milwaukee; Milwaukee J Gallery Wis Art; Univ Wis-Green Bay Contemp Art Collection; Lakeland Col Collection Wis Art. *Comn:* Mural, St John's Lutheran Sch, Glendale, Wis, 56; mural, Home for Aged Lutherans, Milwaukee, 57. *Exhib:* Milwaukee Art Mus Friends of Art, 64-; Wis Watercolor Soc, 74; Retrospective Exhib, Fine Arts Galleries, Univ Wis, Milwaukee, 78; Artist in Full Maturity, Charles Allis Art Libr; Bergstrom Art Ctr, Neenah, Wis, 79. *Teaching:* Instr art, Milwaukee Pub Schs, 31-48; dir dept art, Univ Wis-Milwaukee Exten, 48-56, prof art & art educ, Univ Wis-Milwaukee & Exten, 56-78, emer prof, 78- *Awards:* Purchase Award for Oil, Beloit & Vicinity Exhib, 64; Watercolor Award, Wis Salon, 65; Purchase Award, Milwaukee Art Commission, Ozaukee Co Exhib, Wis Watercolor Soc. *Bibliog:* Don Key (auth), Review of Theodore's Gallery, 65 & Violet Dewey (auth), What's new in art, 67, Milwaukee J. *Mem:* Wis Watercolor Soc; Wis Painters & Sculptors (pres, 63); Delta Phi Delta. *Media:* Oil, Watercolor. *Publ:* Auth, University of Wisconsin Extension Art Programs, WTMJ. *Dealer:* Friends of Art Milwaukee Art Mus 750 N Lincoln Memorial Dr Milwaukee WI 53202. *Mailing Add:* 6183 N Lake Dr Milwaukee WI 53217

SUMMER, (EMILY) EUGENIA
PAINTER
b Newton, Miss, June 13, 23. *Study:* Miss Univ for Women, BS; Columbia Univ, MA; Art Inst Chicago; Calif Col Arts & Crafts; Penland Sch Crafts, NC; Seattle Univ. *Work:* Miss Mus Art & First Nat Bank, Jackson; Nat Bank Commerce Collection, Columbus, Miss; First Nat Bank, Laurel, Miss; First Miss Nat Bank, Hattiesburg. *Exhib:* Delta Ann Exhib, Ark Art Ctr, Little Rock, 60, 62-63, 74 & 82; Art in Embassies Prog, US State Dept, Rio de Janeiro, Brazil, 66-67; Eighth Decade: Painters Choice, Ga Col Milledgeville, 71; 5th Greater New Orleans Int Art Exhib, 75; Nat Asn Painters Acrylic & Casein, Nat Arts Club, New York, 80. *Pos:* Bd dir, Southeastern Col Art Conf, 81-83. *Teaching:* Prof art, Miss Univ Women, 50-, head div fine & performing arts, 82-86, emeritus prof, 86- *Awards:* Dumas Milner Purchase Award, Nat Watercolor Exhib, Jackson, 62, Jurors Award, 68; Purchase Prizes, Lauren Rogers Mus Exhib & Miss Southern Univ Exhib; Award of Merit, Miss Mus Art, 83. *Mem:* Col Art Asn Am; Miss Art Asn; Southeastern Col Art Asn; Kappa Pi; Nat Asn Schs Design. *Media:* Acrylic, Watercolor. *Mailing Add:* Mississippi Univ For Women Columbus MS 39701

SUMMERS, CAROL
PRINTMAKER
b Kingston, NY, Dec 26, 25. *Study:* Bard Col, BA, 51, PhD, 75. *Work:* Corcoran Gallery Art, Libr Cong, Nat Gallery, Washington, DC; Metrop Mus Art & Mus Mod Art, New York; Kunstmuseum, Malmö, Sweden; and many others. *Comn:* Posters NY Film Festival, US Park Serv, Ojai Festival, Venice Biennial and many others. *Exhib:* One-person shows, Mus Mod Art, New York, 64-66, AAA Gallery, New York, 67 & Bard Col, 68; Retrospective, San Francisco Mus Art, Calif, 67; 20th Nat Print Exhib, Brooklyn Mus, 77; ADI Gallery, 77; plus others. *Teaching:* Instr, Brooklyn Mus Sch Art, 54, Pratt Graphic Art Ctr, 62, Hunter Col, 63, Sch Visual Arts, New York, 65, Pa State Univ, 68, Columbia Univ, New York, 69 & San Francisco Art Inst, 73; US Info Serv tour of India, 74 & 79. *Awards:* Ital Govt Grant, Italy, 55; Louis Comfort Tiffany Found Fels, 55 & 60; Guggenheim Found Fel, 59. *Mem:* Print Coun Am (artist adv bd); Print Club Philadelphia. *Media:* Wood. *Mailing Add:* 2817 Smith Grade Santa Cruz CA 95060

SUMNER, GEORGE
ENVIRONMENTAL ARTIST, PAINTER
b San Francisco, Calif, Apr 29, 40. *Study:* City Col, San Francisco, 61; San Francisco Art Inst, 62-63; Skyline Col, San Mateo, Calif, 66; self-taught. *Work:* Univ Hawaii, Honolulu; Stanford Univ, Calif; Whale Mus, Friday Harbor, Wash; Univ Dunedin, NZ; Statue of Liberty Mus, New York, NY. *Comn:* Whales (oil painting), Univ Hawaii, Oahu, 81; abstract oil paintings, Unicure Corp, Atlanta, Ga, 83-86; Whales (oil painting), Greenpeace USA, San Francisco, 85; abstract oil painting, Make A Wish Found, San Francisco, 86; Lighthous (oil painting), Nat Park Serv, Pt Reyes, Calif, 86. *Exhib:* Los Angeles Design Ctr, 84; The Houstonian, Houston, Tex; Maui Marine Art Expo, Intercontinental Hotel, Wailea, Hawaii, 85-86; New York Int Art Expo, Jacob Javitts Ctr, New York, 86; Statue of Liberty, NY. *Pos:* Painting instr, pvt studio, 65-69; publisher, Sumner Studios, Inc, 81-, lectr, 84- *Teaching:* Art instr for special programs on broadcast media. *Awards:* First Place, Sausolito Art Festival; First Place, Felton Art Exhib; First Place, Reno Art Festival. *Bibliog:* In Studio, KCOP TV Channel 13, Los Angeles, 83; Artist Residence, Cable 6, San Francisco, 84; Evening Mag, KCRA Channel 3, Sacramento, 86. *Mem:* Artists for Social Responsibility; Artist Guild of San Francisco (pub relations dir, 80-82); Marin Arts Coun. *Media:* Oil on Canvas. *Publ:* Contribr, Hawaii-In Flight Mag, Ocean Sports Mag, This Week (Maui info mag) & Passages (med journal). *Mailing Add:* 480 Gate 5 Rd Studio 325 Sausalito CA 94965

SUNDBERG, CARL GUSTAVE
ENAMELIST, DIRECTOR
b Erie, Pa, June 23, 28. *Study:* Albright Art Sch, Univ Buffalo, grad; study with Joseph Plaucan, Virginia Cuthbert, Albert Blaustien, Letterio Calipia & Robert Bruce. *Work:* Butler Inst Am Art, Youngstown, Ohio; Tyler Mus Art, Tex; Erie Pub Mus; Erie Art Mus; Albright-Knox Rental Art Gallery. *Comn:* Six porcelain panels (mod motif with coins), Union Bank, Erie, 69; three porcelain enamel panels, Gannon Resource Ctr, Erie, 73; three enclosure set (Plexiglas-enamel), St Vincent Hosp, Erie, 74. *Exhib:* Midyear Shows, Butler Inst Am Art, Youngstown, 68 & 70-82; Washington & Jefferson Col Nat Exhib, 69, 72 & 74; Miss Nat Arts Festival, 70; Audubon Artists, New York, 71; two-persons show, Thiel Col, Greenville, Pa, 77; Pa Woodwinds, traveling exhib, 81; Erie Art Mus Exhib, 84; Int Enamelist Soc Exhib, 89; The Cutting Edge, Frye Mus, Seattle, Wash, 92. *Pos:* Art dir, Erie Ceramic Arts Co, 53-; dir, Galerie 8, Erie, 67-74. *Teaching:* Instr painting, Erie Art Ctr, 64-78; enamel screen print workshop, Kent State Univ, 90. *Awards:* Purchase Prize & Hon Mention, Butler Inst Am Art Mid Year Show, 70 & 81; Purchase Prize, Tyler Mus Art 7th Nat Exhib, 70 & Int Enamelist Exhib, Newport, KY, 80; Prize for Non-Traditional, Chautauqua Exhib, 72 & 76; Jurors' Choice Award, Pittsburgh North Hills Exhib, 87; Purchase Award, Int Enamelist Exhib, Newport, Ky, 89. *Bibliog:* Clyde Singer (auth), article, Youngstown Vindicator, 6/28/70; Ada C Turner (auth), article, Chautauqua Daily, 8/17/70; Peggy Krider (auth), Art Demonstration (film), Villa Maria Col, 70. *Mem:* Erie Art Ctr (pres, 67-69); Erie Arts Coun (vpres, 70-71); Pittsburgh Soc of Artists; Northwestern Pa Artist Asn (co-dir); Enamelist Soc, 88. *Media:* Porcelain Enamel, Graphic. *Mailing Add:* 5518 Bondy Dr Erie PA 16509

SUNDBERG, WILDA (REGELMAN)
PAINTER, INSTRUCTOR
b Erie, Pa, Oct 5, 30. *Study:* Albright Art Sch, Univ Buffalo, 49-51; Gannon col, 64-66; Mercyhurst Col, Pa, 78-79; with Al Broulette, Harrisburg, 82; Edinboro Univ, 85 & 86; Tony Couch, Union Deposit, Pa, 86. *Work:* Thiel Col, Greenville, Pa; Erie Pub Libr; Erie Art Mus; Regional Cancer Res Ctr, Erie, Pa; Eat n Park Restaurant Chain, Pa; and others. *Exhib:* Albright-Knox Mem Gallery, Buffalo, 71-90; one-women show, Waterford Community Ctr, Pa, Thiel Col, Pa, 77, Gannon Univ, Eric, Pa, 76,79,81, & Erie Art Mus, 84; Butler Inst Am Art, Ohio; Counterpoint II, Pittsburgh, Pa, 81; Pa Gov Mansion, Harrisburg, 81-82; McClelland Gallery, Melbourne, Australia, 83; La Roche Col, Pittsburgh, Pa, 85; Access to the Arts, Dunkirk, NY, 85; North Hills, 86-88; Jamestown Community Col, NY, 87; St Vincent Col, Latrobe, Pa 88; Blair County Arts Festival, Altoona, Pa, 88; Aqueous 89 & 91 Nat Watercolor; Lahaina Arts Soc, Maui, Hawaii, 90; one person exhibs, Erie Art Mus, 84 & 92, Gannon Univ, Erie, Pa, 76, 79, 81, Thiel Col, Greenvilla, Pa, 77. *Teaching:* Instr art, Erie Art Mus, 64-90; instr drawing & painting, Mercyhurst Col, 79-90; Behrend, Pa State Instr Watercolor; Harbor Creek Pub Sch, Enrichment Prog, 90. *Awards:* Chautauqua Nat Watercolor Award, Chautauqua Art Asn, 70; Nat Scholastic Scholar; Award Purchase, North Hills Pittsburgh, Pa. *Mem:* Pittsburgh Watercolor Soc; NW Pa Artist Asn; Watercolor Soc, Pa. *Media:* Transparent Watercolor. *Dealer:* Glass Growers 701 Holland St Erie PA 16503. *Mailing Add:* 5518 Bondy Dr Erie PA 16509

SUNDERLAND, NITA KATHLEEN
EDUCATOR, SCULPTOR
b Olney, Ill, Nov 9, 27. *Study:* Duke Univ; Bradley Univ, BFA & MA. *Work:* Fed Plaza, Chicago; Civic Ctr, Peoria, Ill. *Comn:* Archit sculpture, Bradley Univ Bookstore, 64, monumental sculpture, Williams Hall Mall, 67; archit sculpture, St John's Cath Church, Woodhull, Ill, 69; stone and bronze sculpture, Ill State Univ, State Ill capital develop bd, 90. *Exhib:* Chicago Mus Without Walls, 78; 31st Ill Invitational, 79; Selections from the Collection of George M Irwin, 80; 30 Years of Pub Sculpture in Ill, 81; Eighteen Ill Sculptors, 83. *Teaching:* Prof emer art, Bradley Univ, 56-88. *Bibliog:* Three Illinois Artists (film), Ill Arts Coun, WCBV-TV, Peoria, 79. *Mem:* Am Soc Testing & Materials. *Media:* Bronze, Stone. *Publ:* Contribr, Contemporary American Women Sculptors, Watson-Jones, Oryx Press, 86. *Mailing Add:* Bradley Univ Peoria IL 61625

SUNDIN, ADELAIDE TOOMBS
CERAMIST, SCULPTOR
b Boston, Mass, May 8, 15. *Study:* Mass Col Art, with Cyrus Dallin & Raymond Porter, BS(educ), 38; Mass Inst Technol, 42-47. *Work:* Mass Inst Technol. *Comn:* Bronze bas-relief, comn by family of Dr Otis, Otis Airfield, Mass, 36. *Exhib:* Pa Acad Fine Arts Ann, 41 & 42; Corcoran Gallery Art Ann Exhib, 42; solo exhib, Centerville Gallery, Wilmington, 77 & Hudiksvall Mus, Sweden, 80; Women at MIT, Boston Athenaeum, 77 & Mass Inst Technol, 81; Am Medallic Sculpture Asn, Am Numismatic Soc, New York, 83; Pen & Brush, New York, 92; Portraits Inc & Portraits South, New York, 92; Somerville-Manning Gallery, Wilmington, Del, 92. *Bibliog:* Jane Guernsey (auth), An ancient art revived, Philadelphia Inquirer, 79. *Mem:* Portraits Inc New York; Am Medallic Sculpture Asn. *Media:* Parian Porcelain. *Mailing Add:* 132 Hedge Apple Lane Wilmington DE 19807

SUNKEL, ROBERT C
HISTORIAN, ADMINISTRATOR
b Clarksville, Tex, Jan 19, 33. *Study:* Kilgore Col, Tex, AA; Tex Christian Univ, BFA & MFA; Herron Sch Art, Ind Univ; Temple Univ; Northern Ill Univ. *Pos:* Cur, Percival DeLuce Mem Collection, Northwest Mo State Univ, 74-78. *Teaching:* Instr art, Henderson State Col, 58-60; from instr to asst prof art, Northwest Mo State Univ, 60-74, actg chmn dept, 63-71, assoc prof, 74-, chmn dept, 76-78, head div fine arts, 78-81, dean col arts-humanities, 81- *Mem:* Soc Archit Historians; Am Asn Univ Prof; Col Art Asn Am; Mid-Am Col Art Conf; Midwest Art Hist Soc. *Res:* English Baroque and Palladian architecture, particularly the work of Wren, Gibbs and Hawksmoor. *Mailing Add:* Northwest MO State Univ Maryville MO 64468

SUPERIOR, MARA R
CERAMIST
b New York, NY, Dec 1, 51. *Study:* Hartford Art Sch, Univ Conn, 70-71; Univ Conn, Storrs, BFA(painting), 75; Univ Mass, Amherst, MA, MAT, 80. *Work:* Charles A Wustrum Mus Fine Arts, Racine, Wis. *Exhib:* Solo shows, DeCordova Mus, Lincoln, Mass, 91 & Ferrin Gallery, Pinch Pottery, Northampton, Mass, 91; Creative Arts Workshop, New Haven, Conn, 91; Am Craft Mus, New York, 91; John MichaelKobler Art Ctr, Sheboygan, Wis, 91; and others. *Pos:* Co-owner, Contemp Craft Shop/Gallery, Pinch Pottery, Northampton, Mass, 79-; founder, East St Clay Studios, Hadley, Mass. *Teaching:* Grad teaching assoc design, Univ Mass, Amherst, 79, 80; instr ceramics, Pinch Pottery, Northampton, Mass, 81. *Awards:* Guild Am Craft Award, 88, 89 & 90; Fel, Mass Artists Fel, 88, 91; Fel, Nat Endowment Arts, 90. *Bibliog:* Angela Finn (auth), rev, Am Ceramics, 4/90; Philadelphia Craft Show Portfolio, Ceramics Monthly, 5/90; Randi Danforth (auth), Pride of the Yankees, Bon Appetit, 11/91; and others. *Mem:* Am Crafts Coun; Asparagus Valley Potters Guild. *Mailing Add:* Eight Williams St Williamsburg MA 01096

SURES, JACK
CERAMIST, EDUCATOR
b Brandon, Man, Nov 20, 34. *Study:* Univ Man, BFA, 57; Mich State Univ, MA, 59. *Work:* Montreal Mus Fine Arts; Can Coun Art Bank, Ottawa; Sask Art Bd, Regina; Burlington Cult Ctr, Ont; Can Guild Potters, Toronto; Pecs Mus, Hungary; Norman Mackenzie Art Gallery; Tajimi Mus, Japan. *Comn:* Clay mural, Sch Archit, Winnipeg, Man, 64; clay mural, Col Veterinary Med, Saskatoon, Sask, 69; 2900 square foot mural, Province of Sask, Saskatoon, 79; clay wall, Waterloo Potters Workshop, Ont, 86; mural, Mus Civilization, Holl, Que, 89. *Exhib:* Nat Gallery, Ottawa, Ont, 67; Kunstnerforbundet, Oslo, Norway, 83; Rosemont Art Gallery, Regina, 85; Moose Jaw Art Mus, 87; Franklin Silverstone Gallery, Montreal, 87-89; Ashton's, Toronto, ll/91; and others. *Pos:* Chmn, Can Craftsman's Asn, 68-70; bd mem, Can Coun Arts, 69-71. *Teaching:* Prof ceramics, Univ Regina, 65- *Awards:* Best in Show, Ceramics, 67, Can Potters Guild, 67; Medal d'Honneur, Geneva Int Ceramics, 67; Senior Award, Can Coun Arts, 72; Grand Prix Mino, Tajimi, Japan, 89. *Mem:* Hon mem Waterloo Potters Guild; Nat Coun Educ Ceramic Arts; Ceramics Can. *Media:* Clay. *Publ:* Coauth, Down to Earth, Nelson, 80. *Mailing Add:* 2237 Rae St Regina SK S4T 2G1 Canada

SURGALSKI, PATRICK J
PAINTER, PRINTMAKER
b Detroit, Mich, Mar 17, 53. *Study:* San Jose State Univ, BFA, 79; Cranbrook Acad Art, MFA, 81. *Work:* Brooklyn Mus, New York; Cranbrook Mus, Bloomfield Hills, Mich. *Exhib:* Bay Area Printmakers, Santa Rosa Col, Calif, 79; Mich Asn Printmakers, Kalamazoo Art Inst, 80; Summer Invitational, Cranbrook Mus, Bloomfield Hills, Mich, 81. *Pos:* Dir, Mantissa Press, Northville, Mich, 79-82; artist-in-residence, Cranbrook Acad Art, 81. *Media:* Oil; Monotype, Lithography. *Mailing Add:* Sch Art & Design, San Jose State Univ 1 Washington Sq San Jose CA 95192-0089

SURLS, JAMES
SCULPTOR, EDUCATOR
b Terrell, Tex, 1943. *Study:* Sam Houston State Col, BS, 65; Cranbrook Acad Art, MFA, 69. *Work:* Whitney Mus Am Art, New York; Solomon R Guggenheim Mus; Mus Mod Art, New York; Dallas Mus Art, Tex; Mus Fine Arts, Houston; Liquid Paper Corp, Dallas; Albright Knox Gallery, Buffalo, NY; Ft Worth Art Mus, Tex; Seattle Art Mus; Los Angeles County Mus, Calif; Nelson-Atkins Mus, Kansas City, Mo; Stedejlik Mus, Amsterdam; Bennington Mus, Vt; and others. *Comn:* Pine Flower (treated pine & steel), Buford TV Inc, Tyler, Tex, 79; The Brazos Flower (painted steel & oak), Brazos Ctr & Arena/Pavilion Complex, Bryan, Tex, 86; There Used to be a Lake (with Robert Creeley), Poets Walk, Citicorp Plaza, Los Angeles, Calif, 88; Points of View (painted steel & pine), Market Sq Park Proj, Houston, Tex, 91; To the Point (painted steel & redwood), GTE Telephone Opers World Hq, Hidden Ridge, Irving, Tex, 91. *Exhib:* Exchange DFW/SFO, San Francisco Mus Mod Art, 75; Nine Artists: Theodoron Awards, Solomon R Guggenheim Mus, New York, 77; Whitney Biennial Exhib, Whitney Mus Am Art, 79 & 85; Fine Art for Federal Buildings, 1972-79, Nat Collection Fine Arts, Smithsonian Inst, Washington, DC, 80; 20 American Artists: Sculpture 1982, San Francisco Mus Mod Art, 82; Minimalism to Expressionism: Painting and Sculpture since 1965 from the Permanent Collection, Whitney Mus Am Art, 83; A Century of Modern Sculpture: 1882-1982, Mus Fine Arts Houston, Tex, 83; Am Art Since 1970: Painting, Sculpture and Drawings from the Collection of the Whitney Mus Am Art, New York, 84; 75th Ann Exhib, Art Inst Chicago, 86; Structure to Resemblance, Albright-Knox Art Gallery, Buffalo, NY, 87; one-man exhibs, Cranbrook Acad Art Mus, Bloomfield, Mich, 87, LA Louver Gallery, Venice, Calif, 88, Arthur Roger Gallery, New Orleans, La, 89, Barry Whistler Gallery, Dallas, Tex, 89, Hiram Butler Gallery, Houston, Tex, 89, Jan Weiner Gallery, Kansas City, Mo, 90 & Contemp Mus, Honolulu, Hawaii, 91; One Plus One: Collaborations by Artists and Writers, Glassell Sch, Mus Fine Arts Houston, Tex, 88; Direction & Diversity, Mus Fine Arts, Houston, 88; The Boat Show: Fantastic Vessels, Fictional Voyages, Renwick Gallery, Smithsonian Inst, Washington, DC, 89; Word As Image American Art 1960-1990, Milwaukee Art Mus, Wis & Contemp Art Mus, Houston, Tex, 90; Image & Likeness, Whitney Mus Am Art, 91; Texas, The State I'm In, Dallas Art Mus, 91; Braustein/Quay Gallery, San Francisco, 92; Art and Nature, Hiram Butler Gallery, Houston, Tex, 92; Thirty Prints, Barry Whistler Gallery, Dallas, Tex, 92; Summer Invitational, Jan Weiner Gallery, Kansas City, Mo, 92; Some of Houston's Known and Underknown, Allen Ctr Gallery, Tex, 92. *Teaching:* Instr sculpture, Southern Methodist Univ, Dallas, 70-75; assoc prof, Univ Houston, 75-83. *Awards:* Nat Endowment Arts Fel, 79; Tex Artist Yr, Houston Area Art League, 91. *Bibliog:* Wendy Paris (auth), James Surls, Siren 9/90; Gary McKay (auth), On the town, 11/90 & Sandy Sheehy (auth), Arts power, 3/92, Houston Metrop Mag; Janet O'Grady (auth), The making (and unmaking) of art, Aspen Mag, holiday 90-91; and others. *Media:* Wood. *Publ:* Contibr, Tom Klobe (auth), The 3rd International Shoebox Sculpture Exhibition, 16, 17, 88 & Tom Klobe (dir), the 4th International Shoebox Sclpture Exhibition, 140, 91, Univ Hawaii Art Gallery, Honolulu; Patterson Sims (auth), Figure as Subject: The Revival of Figuration Since 1975, Whitney Mus Art, New York, 7, 21, 88; Joan Simon (auth), Sculpture Inside Outside, Walker Art Ctr, Minneapolis, Rizzoli, New York, 25, 88; Sarah Maline (auth), Guest Artists in Printmaking, Archer M Huntington Gallery, Col Fine Arts, Univ Tex, 46, 47, 89; James L Fisher (auth), Forty Texas Printmakers, Mod Mus Ft Worth, 78, 79 & 90. *Dealer:* Marlborough Gallery New York NY 10019. *Mailing Add:* Rt 7 Box 569 G Midline Rd Cleveland TX 77327

SURREY, MILT
PAINTER
b New York, NY, Mar 18, 22. *Work:* Cincinnati Art Mus; Columbia Mus Art, SC; Detroit Inst Arts; Evansville Mus Art, Ind; Miami Mus Mod Art; and many others. *Exhib:* Soc Four Arts, Palm Beach, 69; Nat Arts Club, New York, 69; Cape Coral Nat Art Show, 70; George Walter Vincent Smith Art Mus, Springfield, Mass, 70; Parrish Art Mus, Southampton, NY, 70. *Awards:* John Knecht Mem Award, Berwick Arts Festival, 69. *Media:* Oil. *Mailing Add:* 425 E 58th St New York NY 10022

SUSSMAN, ARTHUR
PAINTER
b Brooklyn, NY, Mar 30, 27. *Study:* Syracuse Univ, BFA; Brooklyn Mus Sch Art. *Work:* NMex Mus Fine Art, Santa Fe; Okla Art Ctr; Skirball Mus; Univ NMex; Albuquerque Mus Fine Art; Jewish Mus New York; Am Mus Jewish History, Philadelphia; Okla Art Ctr. *Comn:* Ethicon; Joe G Maloof Corp; Pub Serv NMex; Monte Vista Christian Church, Albert, NMex; Congregation Albert, Albert, NMex; and others. *Exhib:* One-man shows, Miami Mus Mod Art, 64, Chagall House, Haifa, Israel, 64, Univ NMex, 67 & 77, Nat Acad Design, New York, 69, NMex Mus Fine Arts Biennials, 72 & 74, Plant Gallery Univ Judaism, Los Angeles, 88; Gallery 16, New York, 86. *Pos:* Art & film ed, KOAT TV, Albuquerque, formerly; pub TV film critic, indust art consult & courtroom sketch artist, currently; owner, A Sussman Gallery, Albert, NMex, currently; rep, Preusser Galleries, Taos, NMex. *Teaching:* Artist in residence, Univ Albuquerque, formerly. *Awards:* Oriental Studies Found Grant, 62; Prize Award, NMex So West Invitational Arts & Craft Show, 78. *Bibliog:* Am Jewish Arch, 70; Southwest Arts, 73; Contemp Western Artists-Samuels, 82; Nat Catholic Report, 4/87. *Mem:* Nat Mural Painters Soc. *Media:* Oil, Mixed. *Mailing Add:* c/o Arthur Sussman Gallery PO Box 13493 Albuquerque NM 87192

SUSSMAN, BARBARA J
PAINTER
b Hackensack, NJ, Apr 14, 55. *Study:* RI Sch Design, 72-73; Art Students League, study with Richard L Seyffert, 72-77. *Work:* Susan Blanchard Gallery, New York; Union Mutual, Portland, Maine; Hoglund & Pearce, Portland, Maine. *Comn:* Tryptych, B S R Ltd, New York, 80. *Exhib:* Nat Arts Competitional Oils Open, Nat Arts Club, New York, 82 & 83; Skowhegan Artists, Colby Mus, Waterville, Maine, 82 & 83; Four Generations: An American Art Family, Ridgewood Art Inst, NJ, 83; solo exhib, Hobe Sound Gallery, Hobe Sound, Fla, 85; Hobe Sound Galleries, N Portland, Maine, 85; Of Land & Sea, Midtown Gallery, New York, 86; St Gaudens Nat Hist Park, Cornish, NH, 87; Southern Vt Art Ctr, Manchester, Vt, 88; Albany Biennial, 92. *Pos:* Dir, Fine Arts Studio, New York, 78- *Teaching:* Dean, Skowhegan Sch Painting & Sculpture, Maine, 83 & 84. *Awards:* Best in Oils, State Show, Somerset, NJ, 78. *Bibliog:* Rev, Art Critic, Maine Times, 12/16/83; Schenectady Gazzette, 90; Manchester News, 7/22/92. *Mem:* Kent Art Asn; Life mem Art Students League. *Media:* Oil. *Dealer:* Midtown Payson Galleries 745 Fifth Ave New York NY 10151; Hobe Sound Galleries One Milk St Portland ME. *Mailing Add:* Fog Hill Rd Hoosick Falls NY 12090

SUSSMAN, BONNIE K
DEALER, GALLERY DIRECTOR
b Minneapolis, Minn. *Study:* Univ Minn, BS. *Pos:* Dir-owner, Peter M David Gallery, Minneapolis, 70- *Mem:* Metrop Art Dealers Asn, Twin Cities of Minnesota. *Specialty:* Contemporary American and English paintings, sculpture, prints, drawings, watercolor, photography, handmade paper. *Mailing Add:* 3351 St Louis Ave Minneapolis MN 55416-4394

SUSSMAN, ELISABETH SACKS
DIRECTOR
b Baltimore, Md, July 16, 39. *Study:* Simmons Col, BS, 60; Boston Univ, MA(art hist), 64. *Pos:* Spec asst, Mus Fine Arts, Boston, 72-75; cur, Inst Contemp Art, Boston, 76-, dept dir, currently. *Teaching:* Museology, Tufts Univ, 75- *Mem:* New Eng Coun, Am Asn Mus. *Publ:* Coauth, Building with nature: Roots of the San Francisco Bay Tradition, Peregrin-Smith, 74; Florine Steltheimer: Still Lifes, Portraits, Panoramas, Inst Contemp Art, 80; contribr & co-ed, Dissent: The Issue of Modern Art in Boston, ICA, 85; Endgame: Reference & Simulation in Recent Painting & Sculpture, MIT & ICA, 86; Utopia Post Utopia: configurations if Nature & Culture in Recent sculpture & photography, MIT & ICA Press, 88; In the Passage of of a Few People through a Rather Brief Period of Time: The Situation is International, ICA-MFA, 90. *Mailing Add:* c/o Whitney Mus 945 Madison Ave New York NY 10021

SUSSMAN, GARY LAWRENCE
SCULPTOR, DIRECTOR
b New York, NY, Feb 15, 52. *Study:* Art Students League, apprentice to Jose de Creeft, 71-75; Ecole des Beaux Arts, Paris, France, 74; Academy, Florence, Italy, 74. *Work:* Sunnyside State Park, Tarrytown, NY; Storm King Sch, Mountainville, NY; Mt Carmel Sch, Ridgewood, NJ; Art Students League, New York; Mus Art & Sci, Los Angeles, Calif. *Comn:* Bronze busts, Washington Irving, Irving Trust Bank, New York, 83, Walter Read, comn by Dolly Borgia, New York, 84; large relief sculpture, Rockefeller Ctr, 88; bronze cloisonre, Radio City Music Hall, New York, 88; temple doors, Bethel Synagogue, Bennington, Vt, 89; marble bust of Giomatti, Yale Univ, 91. *Exhib:* Solo exhibs, Art Students League, New York, 74, Bergen Co Mus, Paramus, NJ, 77 & St Gaudens Nat Hist Park, Cornish, NH, 87; Newark Mus Invitational, NJ, 78; Discovery, Rediscovery, 82, Toys by Artists, 84 & Drawings by Artists, 84, Sculpture Ctr, New York; Skowhegan Artists, Colby Mus, Waterville, Maine, 83 & 84; Portraits by Artists, Bethune Gallery, State Univ NY, Buffalo, 84. *Pos:* Pres, Fine Arts Studio, Hoosick Falls, NY, 76; dir, Sculpture Ctr Studio, Sculpture Ctr, Inc, New York, 79-88. *Teaching:* Sculpture technician, Skowhegan Sch Painting & Sculpture, Maine, 76 & 77, dean, 83-84; prof sculpture, Sculpture Ctr, 79-89; adj lectr, City Col New York, 83-84. *Awards:* McDowell Fel, Art Students League, New York, 73; William Zorach Mem Scholar, New York, Bd Control Scholar, ASC, New York; Am Artist in Residence 90, Musie Roche, Fort en Terre, Brittany, France, 90. *Mem:* Life mem Art Students League, New York; Artists Equity; Nat Sculpture Soc; Audubon Artists; Artist Fel Inc. *Media:* All Media. *Mailing Add:* Fine Arts Studio Fog Hill Rd Hoosick Falls NY 12090

SUSSMAN, JILL
GALLERY DIRECTOR
b New York, NY, June 29, 54. *Study:* RI Sch Design, 75; State Univ Alfred, NY, BA, 76. *Pos:* Cur asst, Whitney Mus Am Art, New York, 77-81; dir, Marian Goodman Gallery, New York, 81- & Multiples Inc, New York, currently. *Specialty:* Contemporary American and European painting, sculpture, photos & prints. *Mailing Add:* c/o Marian Goodman Gallery Multiples Inc 24 W 57th St New York NY 10019

SUSSMAN, WENDY
PAINTER
b Brooklyn, NY, June 3, 49. *Study:* Empire State Col, State Univ NY, BA, 77; Brooklyn Col, MFA, 79. *Exhib:* An Appreciation of Realism, Munson-Williams-Proctor Inst, Utica, NY, 82; Painted Light, traveled to Queens Mus, Butler Art Inst, Redding Mus, 83; Am Acad & Inst Arts & Letters, New York, 84; Am Acad in Rome-Ann Exhib, Italy, 87; John Berggruen Gallery, San Francisco, 92; San Francisco Arts Comn Gallery, 92. *Teaching:* Asst prof, Univ Calif, Berkley, 89- *Awards:* Rome Prize, Am Acad Rome, 86-87; Grant, Pollock-Krasner Found, 88; Grant, Nat Endowment Arts, 89. *Media:* Oil. *Mailing Add:* 4934 Telegraph Avenue Oakland CA 94609

SUSSMANN, M HAL See McGarry, Susan Hallsten

SUTER, SHERWOOD EUGENE
EDUCATOR, PAINTER
b Bluffton, Ohio, Sept 22, 28. *Study:* Western Mich Univ, BS(art), 50; Columbia Univ, MFA & Fine Arts Educ, 56. *Work:* Abilene Savings Asn, Tex; Bank One, Abilene, Tex. *Exhib:* State-wide Show of Paintings, Abilene Fine Arts Mus, Kendall Art Mus, San Angelo, Tex, Women's Art Forum, Wichita Falls & Howard Payne Col, Brownwood, 70-71; one-man show, Abilene Chamber of Commerce, 76. *Collections Arranged:* American Watercolor Society Annual Show, McMurry Col, Abilene. *Pos:* Instr painting, Abilene Fine Arts Mus, 74- *Teaching:* Prof art, McMurry Col, 57- *Awards:* Top Award-Watercolor, 70 & Top Award-Oil, 71, Abilene Fine Arts Mus, Abilene Savings Asn. *Mem:* Nat Coun Art Administrators. *Media:* Watercolor; Oil. *Mailing Add:* c/o Art Dept Box 8 McMurry University Abilene TX 79697

SUTTENFIELD, DIANA
GRAPHIC ARTIST, PAINTER
b Washington, DC, Nov 20, 44. *Study:* Md Inst Col Art, Baltimore, BFA(painting), 72. *Work:* Sunrise Mus, Charleston, WVa; Washington Co Mus Fine Arts, Hagerstown, Md. *Comn:* McDonalds Restaurants, Md and WVa, 85-89; Univ Md Hosp, Physicians Complex, Baltimore, 86; Peat Marwick Main & Co, Baltimore, 87; Jackson & Kelly, Charleston, WVa, 88-92; AT&T, Martinsburg, WVa 89. *Exhib:* Midyear Show, Butler Inst Am Art, Youngstown, Ohio, 81; West Virginia Juried Exhibition, Cult Ctr, Charleston, WVa, 83, 85, 87, 89 & 91; Mid-Atlantic Regional Watercolor Exhibition, Johns Hopkins Univ, Baltimore, Md, 85; Images of the Land, Sunrise Mus, Charleston, WVa, 86; Cumberland Valley Artists, Washington Co Mus Fine Arts, Hagerstown, Md, 81, 83-85, 88-90 & 92; Md Pastel Soc, Johns Hopkins Univ, 91 & 92; Pastel Soc Am, New York, 91; Allied Artists of WVa, 87 & 92. *Awards:* Woman of the Year in Art, WVa Woman's Comn, 85; Best of Show, Washington County Mus Fine Arts, Hagerstown, MD, 90; Merit Award, Allied Artists of WVa, Charleston, 92. *Mem:* Baltimore Watercolor Soc; Maryland Pastel Soc; WVa Allied Artists. *Media:* Pastel, Color Pencil; Watercolor. *Publ:* Auth, Shepherdstown Sketchbook, 76; Martinsburg Sketchbook, 79; Pen & Ink Drawings of Harpers Ferry, 80; C and O Canal: An Illustrated History, 81. *Dealer:* Mary Bell Galleries 415 W Superior St Chicago IL; TAF (The Artists Fund) Rt 1 Box 351 Alderson WV. *Mailing Add:* PO Box 832 Shepherdstown WV 25443

SUTTER, JAMES STEWART
SCULPTOR, EDUCATOR
b Milwaukee, Wis, Feb 12, 40. *Study:* Univ Wis, BA(art educ), 64; Univ Iowa, MA(sculpture), 65; Univ Mass, univ fels, 65-67, MFA(sculpture), 67. *Work:* St Lawrence Univ, Canton, NY; Roland Gibson Art Found Inc, Concord, NH; Mus Fine Arts, Springfield, Mass; Lutheran Brotherhood Ins Co, Minneapolis; Millersville Univ, Pa; and others. *Exhib:* one-man shows, Hansen Galleries, 75 & 80, Fredric Remington Mus, 81, New York, Art Ctr Gallery, State Col, Oneonta, 86; R K Parker Gallery, New York, 82 & 83; Int Sculpture Ctr, Washington, DC, 83; Peter Drew Gallery, Palm Beach, Boca Raton, Fla, 83-89; Tenth Anniversary Drawing Invitational, Artist Space Gallery, New York, 84; La Petite Gallery, Burlington, Vt, 92; and others. *Teaching:* Drawing asst, Univ Mass, 66-67; assoc prof sculpture, State Univ NY Col Potsdam, NY, 67-79, prof art, 79-; guest prof sculpture & drawing, Skidmore Col, Saratoga Springs, 79-88. *Awards:* First Prize, 5th Ann Arena Nat, Binghamton, NY, 78; Sculpture Prize, Cooperstown Nat, NY, 84; Prize, Nat Metal Sculpture Compt, Millersville Univ, Pa, 84; Prize for Sculpture, Nat Small Works Exhib, Schoharie Arts Coun, Cobleskill, NY, 85; Artist Fel, NY State Found Arts, 87. *Mem:* Col Art Asn. *Media:* Bronze, Aluminum. *Publ:* Coauth, with Dr Frank Seiberling, The Role of Sculpture in Modern Architecture, Univ Iowa, 65. *Dealer:* Peter Drew Gallery Worth Crocke Ctr Boca Raton FL; Judith Posner Associates Milwaukee WI. *Mailing Add:* 11 New St Norwood NY 13668

SUTTER, LESLIE STRONG See Strong, Leslie (Leslie Strong Sutter)

SUTTMAN, PAUL
SCULPTOR
b Okla, July 16, 33. *Study:* Univ NMex, BFA, 56; Cranbrook Acad Art, MFA, 58. *Work:* Joseph H Hirshhorn Mus, Washington, DC; Mus Mod Art, New York; Art Mus, Macomb Col, Mich; Kalamazoo Art Ctr; Roswell Art Ctr. *Comn:* Two figures, Eastland Shopping Ctr, Detroit, 65; figure, Martha Cooke Bldg, Univ Mich, 68. *Exhib:* Sculpture From Hirshhorn Collection, Guggenheim Mus, 62; Biennale Sculpture Contemp, Rodin Mus, Paris, 68 & 70; US Info Serv Traveling Exhib, Istanbul & Ankara, Turkey, 72; After Surrrealism, Metaphors & Similes, Ringling Art Mus, Sarasota, Fla, 72; Los Angeles Mus, 77; Jodi Scurry Gallery, 77; Mus of Albuquerque, 78; Terry Riutenfess Gallery, New York, 66, 68, 70 & 73-80; Robinson Galleries, Houston, 70-72, 74, 82 & 87. *Teaching:* Instr sculpture, Univ Mich, Ann Arbor, 58-62; artist in residence, Dartmouth Col, spring 73; vis prof art, Univ NMex, 76- *Awards:* Rackham Found Res Grant, Italy, 60; Fulbright Fel Paris, Inst Int Educ, 63; Prix de Rome Fel, Am Acad Rome, 65-68. *Bibliog:* The Bronze Man, Nat Educ TV, 60. *Media:* Bronze, Marble. *Mailing Add:* c/o Robinson Galleries 3514 Lake St Houston TX 77098

SUTTON, CAROL (LORRAINE)
PAINTER
Norfolk, Va, Sept 3, 45. *Study:* Richmond Prof Inst, BFA, 67; Univ NC, MFA. *Work:* Mus Fine Arts, Boston; Nat Collection Fine Art, Smithsonian Inst; Weatherspoon Art Gallery, Greensboro, NC; Edmonton Art Gallery, Alta; Agnes Etherington Gallery, Kingston, Ont. *Exhib:* Certain Traditions: Recent British & Canadian Art, Edmonton Art Gallery, Alta & traveling through Canada, England & Wales, 78; The New Generation: A Critic's Choice, Andre Emmerich Gallery, New York & traveling to Berlin, Ger & Am Cult Ctr, Paris, 80; Edmonton Art Gallery, Alta, 81; Viewpoint 29 x 9, Art Gallery Hamilton, Ont, 81; Heritage of Jack Bush, Robert McLaughlin Gallery & traveling in Canada, 81. *Bibliog:* James Clark (auth), The Problem of Fundamental Ontology Book, Limits Bk Co, 81; Karen Wilkin (auth), Toronto: Fans, flickers & penny arcades, Art News, 2/82. *Media:* Acrylic on Canvas. *Dealer:* Salander O'Reilly New York NY. *Mailing Add:* 27 Davies St Toronto ON M4M 2A9 Canada

SUTTON, PAT (LIPSKY)
PAINTER
b New York, NY, Sept 21, 41. *Study:* Cornell Univ, BFA, 63; Hunter Col, with Tony Smith, MA, 68. *Work:* Hirshhorn Mus & Sculpture Garden; Whitney Mus Am Art, New York; San Francisco Mus Fine Arts; Walker Art Ctr; Brooklyn Mus; Wadsworth Atheneum. *Exhib:* Lyrical Abstraction, Aldrich Mus Contemp Art, 70 & Whitney Mus Am Art, 71; Highlights 1969-1970, 70 & Ten Years, 74, Aldrich Mus Contemp Art; solo exhibs, Everson Mus, 70, Andre Emmerich Gallery, New York, 71, 72, 74 & 75, Deitcher O'Reilly Gallery, New York, 76, Promenade Gallery, 87, Gloria Luria Gallery, Bar Harbor Island, Fla, 88, Slater-Price Gallery, 89 & Andre Zarre Gallery, 91; Vistas, G W Einstein Gallery, New York, 87; Still Life Painting, Univ Mass, Amherst, 87; Interior Visions, Herbert Johnson Mus, Ithaca, NY, 88; group shows, Andre Zarre Gallery, 90, Celebrative Formalism, Schulte Gallery, S Orange, NJ, 92; and others. *Pos:* Mem adv coun, Col Art & Archit, Cornell Univ, 88- *Teaching:* Instr, Fairleigh Dickinson Univ, 68 & Hunter Col, 72; vis artist, San Francisco Art Inst, 74; instr, State Univ NY, Purchase, 79-80; asst prof, Hartford Art Sch, Univ Hartford, 83- *Awards:* Va Ctr Creative Arts Fel, 86; NY Found Arts Fel, 92; Grant, Winsor & Newton Paint Co, 92; and others. *Bibliog:* Karen Wilkin (essay), Announcement Brochure, 89; Karen Wilkin (auth), Fast track, New York Mag, 89; Pat Rosoff (auth), Pat Sutton, Arts Mag, 91; and others. *Media:* Oil on Linen. *Mailing Add:* 11 Riverside Dr New York NY 10023

SUTTON, PETER C
CURATOR, HISTORIAN
b Mar 30, 49. *Study:* The Gunnery, Washington, Conn, 68; Harvard Col, AB, 72 (Fel 72); Yale Univ, (Fel 73-76) MA, 75, PhD, 78. *Collections Arranged:* Masters of Seventeenth-Century Dutch Genre Painting (auth, catalog),

Philadelphia Mus Art & tour to West Berlin & London, 84; Renoir, 85-86 & Manet to Matisse, 86, Mus Fine Arts, Boston; Masters of Seventeenth-Century Dutch Landscape Painting (auth, catalog), Rijksmus Amsterdam & tour to Boston & Philadelphia, 87-88; Prized Possessions: European Paintings from Private Collections, Mus Fine Arts, Boston, 92. *Pos:* Asst cur Europ paintings before 1900, Philadelphia Mus Art, 79-83, assoc cur, 83-85; Mrs Russell Baker cur Europ paintings, Mus Fine Arts, Boston, 85- *Awards:* Kress Travel Grant Summer, 75; David E Finley Fel, Nat Gallery Art, 76-79; Alfred Barr Award Most Distinguished Mus Pub of 1984, Col Art Asn, 86. *Publ:* Auth, Pieter de Hooch (1629-1684): Complete Edition, Phaidon Press 80; European Paintings, Mus Fine Arts, Boston, 85; Masterpiece Paintings from the Museum of Fine Arts, Boston, Abrams Press, 86; Dutch Art in America, Eerdmans Publ Co, 86; Dutch & Flemish Seventeenth-Century Paintings, The Harold Samuel Collection, Cambridge Univ Press, 92. *Mailing Add:* Mus Fine Arts 465 Huntington Ave Boston MA 02115

SUZEN
PHOTOGRAPHER, DESIGNER
b New York, NY, May 17, 46. *Study:* Brooklyn Mus Art Sch; Am Univ, BA(fine arts & graphic design); Art Ctr Col Design, Los Angeles, with Todd Walker. *Work:* Denver Mus Art; Yale Univ Art Gallery; Exchange Nat Bank Chicago; Mus Art & Hist, Fribourg, Switz; Het Sterckhof Mus, Antwerp, Belg; Libr of Cong, Washington, DC; Santa Barbara Mus; Bibliotheque Nat, Paris. *Exhib:* Solo exhibs, Herbert F Johnson Mus, Ithaca, NY, 77, Bertha Urdang Gallery, New York, 80, Canon Photo Gallery, Geneva, Switz, 81, Galerie Karin Steins, Frankfurt, WGer, 82, Howard Univ, Washington, DC, 82 & Mus Ludwig, Cologne, WGer, 84; Fac Exhib, Int Ctr Photog, New York, 80; Independent Am Photog, Warsaw, 80; Live from New York, Lowe Gallery, Syracuse, NY, 82; Works in Progress, Heller Gallery, New York, 83; Spirit of Spring Festival of the Arts, Performance, at Port Authority, New York, 84. *Pos:* Founder/dir, Art for the People. *Teaching:* Instr photog, Hunter Col, 78-79, Marymount Manahattan Col, 78-, Int Ctr Photog, 79-82 & Asphalt Green/Murphy Ctr, 85-90, New York; artist-in-residence, Apeiron Workshops, Millerton, NY, 79, NY Found Art/Guggenheim Mus, 85. *Awards:* NY State Coun Arts grant, 84; Nat Endowment Arts/Inter Arts grant, 85. *Bibliog:* John Hunter (auth), Ironic reality, Art Week, 1/75; Jacques J Halber (auth), Brief vit Belge, Foto, 3/77; Arthur Secunda (auth), article, Visual Dialogue, winter 77-78; article, Kolner Stadt-Anseiger, WGer, 84; article, New York Daily News, 11-12/84. *Mem:* Soc Photog Educators. *Media:* Light. *Publ:* Illusr, The Love Story of Sushi & Sashimi: A Cat Tale, Capra Press, 90. *Dealer:* Leslie Cecil Gallery 16 E 72nd St New York NY 10021. *Mailing Add:* 55 Bethune St #D816 New York NY 10014

SUZUKI, JAMES HIROSHI
PAINTER
b Yokohama, Japan, Sept 19, 33. *Study:* Sch of Fine & Appl Art, Portland, Maine, 52; Corcoran Sch Art, 53-54; privately with Yoshio Markino. *Work:* Corcoran Gallery of Art, Washington, DC; Wadsworth Atheneum, Hartford, Conn; Rockefeller Inst, New York; Nat Mus Mod Art, Tokyo, Japan; Toledo Mus Art, Ohio. *Exhib:* Corcoran Gallery Art, 56, 58 & 60; Whitney Mus Am Art; Baltimore Mus Art, Md; Contemp Painters of Japanese Origin in Am, Inst Contemp Art, Boston; Everson Mus Art, Syracuse, NY, 58; Wadsworth Atheneum, 59; Waning Moon and Rising Sun, Mus Fine Arts of Houston, 59; San Francisco Mus Art, 63 & 64; solo exhibs, Quay Gallery, 73, Braustein Quay Gallery, 76 & 78 & Sacramento State Univ, 78; Aesthetics of Graffiti, San Francisco Mus Mod Art, 78. *Teaching:* Instr, Univ Calif, Berkeley, 62-63 & Univ Ky, 66-68; assoc prof art, Sacramento State Univ, currently. *Awards:* Eugene Weiss Scholar, Corcoran Gallery Art, 54; John Hay Whitney Fel, 58; Larry Aldrich Prize, Silvermine Guild, 59. *Dealer:* Braunstein Quay Gallery 254 Sutter St San Francisco CA 94108. *Mailing Add:* Art Dept Calif State Univ Sacramento CA 95819-6061

SUZUKI, KATSKO (KATSKO SUZUKI KANNEGIETER)
ART DEALER
b Nagoya, Japan. *Study:* Kinjyo Female Col, Nagoya; Bunka Gakuin, Tokyo, Japan. *Work:* Mus Mod Art, New York; Kyoto Mus, Japan; Mus Mod Art, Paris, France; Pub Libr, New York; Brooklyn Mus, New York. *Exhib:* Chrysler Mus, Norfolk, Va. *Pos:* Dir & pres, Suzuki Graphics Inc, New York, 70- *Bibliog:* E Stern (auth), article, in: New York Mag, 6/13/77; N Sano (auth), article, in: The Mainichi Graph, 4/9/78; S Sawyer & B Fasciani (auths), article, in: The Executive Female, 3-4/81. *Media:* Works on Paper. *Specialty:* Mainly specialized in graphics; many gallery artists are international; extended for small paintings, sculptures and other media at Suzuki Gallery (subsidiary). *Publ:* Auth, articles in Hanga Geijyutsu (Arts in Graphics), 74-75. *Mailing Add:* 24 W 57th St Suite 603 New York NY 10019-3918

SUZUKI, SAKARI
PAINTER
b Iwateken, Japan; US citizen. *Study:* Calif Sch Fine Arts, San Francisco; Art Students League, NY Metrop Scholar, 34. *Work:* High Mus Art, Atlanta, Ga; Dept Labor, Washington, DC. *Comn:* Mural, Willard Parker Hosp, New York, 37. *Exhib:* Corcoran Gallery Art, Washington, DC, 34; one-man shows, ACA Gallery, New York, 36, Artists Gallery, New York, 48 & 51 & Mandel Bros Art Gallery, Chicago, 55; Pa Acad Fine Arts, Philadelphia, 52. *Pos:* Scenic artist, Munic Opera, St Louis, Mo, 53-55, Starlight Theatre, Kansas City, Mo, 56-69, Gen Motors Futurama, 62-64 & Lyric Opera, Chicago, 65-70. *Teaching:* Instr painting, Am Artists Sch, New York, 38-40. *Awards:* Am Artists Cong Prize, 36. *Mem:* United Scenic Artists Am. *Media:* Oil. *Mailing Add:* 5040 Marine Dr Apt B8 Chicago IL 60640

SUZUKI, TARO
SCULPTOR, PAINTER
b New York, NY, Nov 17, 53. *Study:* Syracuse Univ, 71-72; Sch Visual Arts, 72-73; Cooper Union, BFA, 76. *Comn:* Installation, comn by Shorr, Aspen, Colo, 80; installation, comn by J Shore, Cincinnati, 82; installation, comn by M Sklar, New York, 82; installation, comn by C Cameron, New York, 83. *Exhib:* L'Amerique Aux Independents, Grand Palais, Paris, France, 80; Energie NY, ELAC, Lyons, France, 82; C31, Walker Arts Ctr, Minneapolis, 85; Science Meets Fiction, Sao Paulo Biennale, Brazil, 85; Galeria Fucares, Madrid, 87; Daniel Newberg Gallery, New York, 88-89; Scott Hanson Gallery, New York, 90; Marta Cerveras Gallery, New York, 90; White Columns, New York, 90; Fay Gold Gallery, Atlanta, 91; Rempire Gallery, New York, 91. *Pos:* Dir, Space Force, New York, 80-84 & 92-; mem bd dirs, Ocean Earth Construct & Develop, New York, 80-84. *Teaching:* Teacher sculpture, RI Sch Design, 85. *Awards:* Nat Endowment Arts, Grant, 82; Pollock Krasner Grant, 89. *Bibliog:* Grace Glueck (auth), review, The New York Times, 3/12/83; Marc Balet & Robert Becker (coauths), Assemblages, Interview Mag, 11/84; Roberta Smith (auth), article, 87; Michael Kimmelman (auth), article, NY Times, 88; Alan Jones (auth), article, Arts Mag, 89. *Media:* All. *Mailing Add:* 201 E 10th St New York NY 10003

SVENDSEN, LOUISE AVERILL
CURATOR
b Old Town, Maine, Nov 22, 15. *Study:* Wellesley Col, BA; Yale Univ, MA & PhD. *Pos:* Assoc cur, The Solomon R Guggenheim Mus, 62-66, cur, 66-78, sr cur, 78- *Teaching:* Instr hist of art, Duke Univ, Durham, NC, 43-45; asst prof, Goucher Col, Baltimore, Md, 45-50 & Am Univ, Washington, DC, 51-52; lectr, The Solomon R Guggenheim Mus, New York, 54-62. *Publ:* Auth, Rousseau, Redon and Fantasy, 68, Ilya Bolotowsky, 74 & Frank Lloyd Wright, Architect, 75, Guggenheim Mus; Alberto Giacometti, Sculptor and Draftsman, Am Fedn Arts, 77. *Mailing Add:* 16 Park Ave New York NY 10016

SVENSON, JOHN EDWARD
SCULPTOR
b Los Angeles, Calif, May 10, 23. *Study:* Claremont Grad Sch, Calif. *Work:* Ahmandson Ctr, Los Angeles; San Bernardino County Mus; Skagway, Alaska Sch Dist; Civic Ctr, Garden Grove, Calif; Smithsonian Air Mus; Foothill Ranch, Laguna Hills, Calif; and others. *Comn:* Gold portrait medallions of King Hussein, Jordan & Ibn Saud Saudi Arabia; bronze porpoise fountain, Ritz Carlton, Laguna Niguel, Calif; hist panels, San Gabriel Mission Chapel, Calif; bldg facade & sculpture, Purex Corp, Lakewood, Calif; Alaska Tlingit Medal, Soc Medallists An Issue; and others. *Exhib:* Los Angeles Co Mus Art, 62; Newman Galleries, Philadelphia, 71; Kennedy Galleries, New York, 72; Alaska State Mus; Green Galleries, Anchorage; Stary-Sheets Gallery, Irvine, Calif; and others. *Pos:* Trustee, Alaska Indian Arts, Inc, Port Chilkoot, 67- *Awards:* Awards for Excellence in Sculpture, Am Inst Archit, 57 & 61; First Prize, Laguna Art Festival, 61; and others. *Bibliog:* Nat Sculpture Rev, 77; Inland Empire Mag, 8/82; Elan Mag, 3/90. *Mem:* Fel Nat Sculpture Soc; Soc Medalists, New York. *Media:* Wood, Bronze. *Dealer:* Svenson Arts Gallery 2480 Vista Dr Upland CA 91786. *Mailing Add:* 2480 Vista Dr Upland CA 91786

SVERDLOVE, ZOLITA
PAINTER, PRINTMAKER
b New York, NY, Feb 21, 36. *Study:* Art Students League, 49-52; Cooper Union Art Sch, cert, 56, BFA, 77; San Francisco State Univ, 59-60; Calif Sch Fine Arts, 60; Pratt Graphic Arts Ctr, 67; Southern Methodist Univ, 70-74. *Work:* Owens-Corning Collection, Toledo Mus, Ohio; Dallas Mus Fine Arts, Tex; Purdue Univ, Ind; Marymount Col, New York; plus many others. *Comn:* Grand Hotel, Houston, 79; Fluor Corp, Los Angeles 67. *Exhib:* Tex Painting & Sculpture Ann, Dallas Mus Fine Arts, 71, 1st Tex Invitational, 72 & 75, Yrs at Dallas Mus Fine Arts, 78; one-person shows, Hooks-Epstein Gallery, Houston, 78 & Longview Mus, Tex, 79, Peabody Clouds, 91; Pasadena Art Alliance Gallery, 91; Satellite Galleries, Los Angeles, 91; Structure & Movement, Art Store, Pasadena, 91; Arroyo Landscape, Occidental Col, 92; and others. *Awards:* Purchase Prize, Purdue Univ, 70; Top Prize, Dallas Mus Fine Arts, 72; Nat Endowment Arts Grant, 73-74; and others. *Bibliog:* article, Dallas Morning News, 11/77; review & photograph, by Glenna Parks, Art Wk, 11/4/78; Women in Art (TV-video), Women's Caucus for Art, 89. *Mem:* Los Angeles Printmakers Soc; Women's Coalition for Arts; Los Angeles County Mus Graphic Arts Coun; Philadelphia Print Club. *Media:* Monotype. *Publ:* Designed & publ five booklets for Nat Endowment for Arts grant, 73-74; contribr, Mundus Artium, Univ Tex, Dallas, 76. *Dealer:* Allan Stone 48 East 86th New York NY; Valley House Gallery 6616 Spring Valley Rd Dallas TX. *Mailing Add:* 1445 Indiana Ave South Pasadena CA 91030

SWAIN, ROBERT
PAINTER
b Austin, Tex, Dec 7, 40. *Study:* Am Univ, Washington, DC, BA. *Work:* Corcoran Gallery of Art, Washington, DC; Walker Art Ctr, Minneapolis; Denver Art Mus, Colo; Albright-Knox Mus, Buffalo, NY; Everson Art Mus, Syracuse, NY. *Comn:* Painting (8 1/2ft x 20ft), Schering Labs, Bloomfield, NJ, comn by Skidmore, Owings & Merrill, New York, 70; painting (5ft x 10ft), Phillip Mallis of Kahn & Mallis Assocs, New York, 72; painting (4ft x 27ft), IBM, Charlotte, NC, 81; painting (5ft x 9ft), Tupperware World Headquarters, Kissimmee, Fla, 81. *Exhib:* The Art of the Real, Mus of Mod Art, New York, 68; one-man shows, Susan Caldwell Gallery, 74, 76, 78 & 81, Everson Art Mus, Syracuse, 74 & Columbus Gallery of Fine Arts, Ohio, 76; 31st Biennial, Corcoran Gallery of Art, 69; The Structure of Color, Whitney Mus of Am Art, 71; Painting & Sculpture Today, Indianapolis Mus of Art,

Ind, 74; Color as Language (traveling exhib, Latin Am), Mus of Mod Art, New York, 74-75; Nina Freudenheim Galley, Buffalo, NY, 78; Toni Birckhead Gallery, Cincinnati, Ohio, 80. *Teaching:* Prof fine arts, Hunter Col, New York. *Awards:* Guggenheim Fel, 69; Nat Endowment for Arts Grant, 76. *Bibliog:* Scott Burton (auth), Light from Aten to Laser, MacMillan Co, 69; B Wasserman (auth), Modern Painting, Davis Publ, 70; Roberta Smith (auth), Artforum, 76. *Media:* Acrylic. *Mailing Add:* 57 Leonard St New York NY 10013

SWAIN, ROBERT FRANCIS
GALLERY DIRECTOR
b Halifax, NS, Oct 25, 42. *Study:* Carleton Univ, BA. *Collections Arranged:* Joan Frick, 74; Robert Sinclair, 76; Made Glorious: 25 Years of Stratford Design, 76; A History of Children's Book Illustrations, 77; Fantastic Shakespeare; Coasts: The Sea and Canadian Art. *Pos:* Dir, Agnes Etherington Art Ctr, Kingston, Ont. *Mem:* Int Comt Mus; Ont Asn Art Galleries (dir); and others. *Publ:* Auth, many exhib catalogs. *Mailing Add:* 43 Jorene Dr Kingston ON K7M 3X5 Canada

SWAN, BARBARA
PAINTER
b Newton, Mass, June 23, 22. *Study:* Wellesley Col, BA; Boston Mus Sch. *Work:* Philadelphia Mus Art; Boston Mus Art & Boston Pub Libr, Boston; Worcester Mus; Fogg Art Mus. *Exhib:* Carnegie Ann, 49; Contemp Am Painting, Univ Ill, 50; View 1960, Inst Contemp Arts, Boston, 60; Brooklyn Mus Biennial Print Exhib, 65; New Eng Women, De Cordova Mus, 75; Eight New Eng Artists, Works on Paper, Boston Mus Fine Arts, 77; New England Realists, Danforth Mus, 80. *Teaching:* Instr painting, Wellesley Col, 46-49; instr art, Milton Acad, 51-54; instr painting & drawing, Boston Univ, 60-65. *Awards:* Albert Whitin Traveling Fel, Boston Mus Art, 48; Assoc Scholar, Inst Independent Study, Radcliffe Col, 61-63; George Roth Prize, Philadelphia Print Club, 65. *Media:* Oil. *Dealer:* Alpha Gallery 122 Newbury St Boston MA 02116. *Mailing Add:* 808 Washington St Brookline MA 02146

SWANSON, J N
PAINTER, SCULPTOR
b Duluth, Minn, Feb 4, 27. *Study:* Col Arts & Crafts, Oakland, Calif; Carmel Art Inst; also with Donald Teague & Armin Hansen. *Work:* Read Mullin Collection, Phoenix; Sunset Mag Collection Art; Leaning Tree Mus, Boulder, Colo; Diamond M Mus, Tex; Cowboy Artist Am Mus, Kerrville, Tex; and others. *Comn:* Pvt comn only. *Exhib:* Monterey Co Fair Prof Div, Calif, 67; Springville Regional Show, Utah; Cowboy Artists Ann Show, Hall Fame, Okla, 70-75; Soc Western Artists, De Young Mus, San Francisco, 71. *Teaching:* Horse anat, Cowboy Artist Mus, Kerrville, Tex. *Awards:* San Francisco Best of Show Award, Monterey Co Fair, 67; Soc Western Artists Atelier Award, De Young Mus, 71. *Bibliog:* Ainsworth (auth), Cowboy in Art, World, 68; Paul Weaver (ed), Cowboy Artists Ann Exhib Bks, Northland, 69-75; Broder (auth), Bronzes of the American West, Abrams, 74. *Mem:* Cowboy Artists Am (vpres, 70). *Media:* Oil; Plastilene Clay. *Res:* Complete Western library for research into historical Western painting; first hand knowledge of the cowboy subject of present day. *Dealer:* Kyle Gallery Los Olivus CA. *Mailing Add:* 18865 Cachagua Rd Carmel Valley CA 93924

SWANSON, RAY V
PAINTER
b Alcester, SDak, Oct 4, 37. *Study:* Northrop Inst, BS, 60. *Work:* Indianapolis Mus Art; Riverside Art Collection Mus, Calif. *Exhib:* Wichita Nat Art Exhib, Kans, 70; Franklin Mint Gallery Am Art, 73-74; Capitol Bldg, Phoenix, Ariz, 75; Nat Acad Western Art, Cowboy Hall of Fame, 76. *Awards:* Gold Medal, Nat Acad Western Art, Cowboy Hall of Fame, 75; Silver Medal, Royal Western Watercolor, Cowboy Hall of Fame, 75; Gold Medal, Franklin Mint Gallery, 75-76. *Bibliog:* J & J Ward (auth), Renaissance of Western Art, Franklin Mint Gallery, 74; Tom Cooper (auth), The Best of Arizona Highways, Ariz Hwys, 75; Royal B Hassrick (auth), Western Painting Today, Watson-Guptill Publ, 75. *Mem:* Prescott Fine Arts Asn. *Media:* Oil; Watercolor. *Publ:* Contribr, Artist of the Rockies, Colo Publ, 75; contribr, Illuminator, Grand Cent Publ, 75. *Dealer:* Husberg Fine Arts Gallery 330 Hwy 179 Sedona AZ 86336. *Mailing Add:* 6542 E Old Paint Tr PO Box 937 Carefree AZ 85377

SWANSON, VERN GROSVENOR
MUSEUM DIRECTOR, HISTORIAN
b Central Point, Ore, Feb 4, 45. *Study:* Brigham Young Univ, Provo, Utah, BA, 69; Univ Utah, Salt Lake City, MA(art hist), 75; Univ London, Courtauld Inst Art, PhD(art hist), 89. *Collections Arranged:* The Work of Eugene Higgins (auth, catalog), 75 & An Exhibition of British and American Paintings (auth, catalog), 76, Auburn Univ; The Unknown Alma-Tadema (auth, catalog), Brigham Young Univ, Utah, 79; Permanent Collection (auth, catalog), 81 & National April Salon (auth, catalog), 81-89, Springville Mus Art; over 25 other temporary exhibs at the Springville Mus. *Pos:* Mus aide supervisor, National Gallery Art, Washington DC, 69-70; gallery dir, House Fine Arts, Provo, Utah, 70-71; art consult British classical art, major auction houses, 73-; mus dir, Springville Mus Art, Utah, 80-; art hist, Brigham Young Univ, 87-88. *Teaching:* Asst prof art hist, Auburn Univ, Ala, 73-76. *Awards:* Prof of the Year, Auburn Univ, 73-74; Research grant, Paul Mellon Inst Studies Brit Art, 88 & Am Acad Art, 88; George S & Delores Dore' Eccles Found, 89. *Mem:* Am Asn Mus; Victorian Soc Am; Art Mus Asn; Utah Mus Asn (vpres, 86-87); Grand Cent Art Galleries Educ Asn (bd dirs, 88-). *Res:* The fine arts among the Mormons in Utah; Catalogues Raisonnies on John William Godward & John Hapen; Preparation fo book on LDS theology entitled "Sticking with the Mysteries and Leaving the Basics Alone"; Editing and writing book on Utah art from the Springville collection. *Publ:* Coauth, The Apodyterium and the Voice of Spring, The Other Nineteenth Century, 78; auth, Alma Tadema: The Painter of The Victorian of The Ancient World, C Scribner's, 77; Ed Fraugaton: Quest for Perfection, 10/82, Bruce Hixson Smith: Beyond Splendor, 10/82 & Gary E Smith: Rooted Substance and Surface, 8/84, Southwest Art; Utah Grandeur (exhib catalog) Springfield Mus Art, 10/89; The Life and Works of Sir Lawrence Alma-Tadema, Garton & Co, 90; The Biography & Catalogue Raisonne of the Paintings of Sir Lawrence Alma-Tadema, Garton & Co, 90; Utah Art, Peregrine-Smith, 91; Mormon art & beliefs movement, Southwest Art Mag, 12/91. *Mailing Add:* 1440 E Hobble Creek Dr Springville UT 84663

SWARD, ROBERT S
EDITOR, WRITER
b Chicago, Ill, June 23, 33. *Study:* Univ Ill, BA(hons), 56; Univ Iowa, MA, 58; Univ Bristol, Eng, 60-61 & Middlebury Col, 56-60 (post grad). *Work:* Archive Collection, City Hall, Toronto, Ont; Provincial Mus Collection, BC Provincial Govt. *Exhib:* Travelling Exhib, The Toronto Islands (auth, catalog), Toronto City Archive, Can, 80-83. *Pos:* Ed, Soft Press Publ, Victoria, BC, 70-79 & Business to Business Network, Santa Cruz, 86-88; ed-in-chief, Hancock House Publ, Vancouver, BC, 75-79; vis artist poetry & bk-making, Ont Arts Coun, Toronto, 81-85; vis artist poetry, bk-making & illus, Cult Coun Santa Cruz, 86-; freelance writer, ed & consult, currently. *Teaching:* Instr creative writing, Univ Calif Ext, currently; instr creative writing, Foothill Col; Eng prof, Monterey Peninsula Col, Calif, 85-87; instr, Univ Calif, Santa Cruz Extension, 86-87; prof eng, Cabrillo Col, 87- *Awards:* Guggenheim Fel Poetry, 65; D H Lawrence Fel Poetry, Univ NMex, 66; Grants, Can Coun, Ontario Arts Coun & Ontario Heritage Found, 81-84; Villa Montalvo Literary Arts Award, 90. *Bibliog:* William Meredith (introd), Kissing the Dancer, Cornell Univ Press, 64; John Malcolm Brinnin (auth), NY Times Book Review; Tina Barr (auth), Harvard Rev, 6/92. *Mem:* Nat Writer's Union; fel Yaddo, MacDowell Colony & Djerassi Found, 60-90. *Media:* Book-making, Mixed Media; Printed Word Illustrations. *Res:* Small Press Publications in the USA and Canada (bks & mags). *Publ:* Ed, Victorian Architecture of Port Townsend, Wash, Emily Carr: The Untold Story, 78 & The Art of the Haida, Argillite, 80, Hancock House; auth, Half a Life's History: New & Selected, Aya Pressm 83; Poet Santa Cruz, Jazz Press, 85; auth, Four Incarnations, New & Selected Poems, 1957-1991, Coffee House Press, 91; Contemp Authors Autobiography Series, Gale Research, vol 13, 90. *Mailing Add:* PO Box 7062 Santa Cruz CA 95061-7062

SWARTZ, BETH AMES
PAINTER
b New York, NY, Feb 5, 36. *Study:* Art Students League; Cornell Univ, BS, 57; NY Univ, MA, 60. *Work:* Jewish Mus, New York; Nat Mus Am Art, Washington, DC; Phoenix Art Mus; San Francisco Mus Art; Mus Fine Art, Santa Fe, NMex. *Exhib:* solo exhibs, Elaine Horwitch Galleries, Scottsdale, Ariz, 79, 80, 82, 84, 86 & 88, A Moving Point of Balance, traveling show, 85-92, Plaka Art Gallery, Athens, Greece, Nafplion Art Gallery, Greece, 89, Galeria Yolanda Rios, Sitges, Barcelona, Spain, 89, New Gallery, Houston, Tex, 89 & Elaine Horwitch Galleries, Palm Springs, 89; Paper: Surface and Image, Rutgers Univ, touring, 81-82; Artists in the American Desert Touring Show, 81-82; Artist as Shaman, Women's Bldg, Los Angeles, 86; Artists of the Western States Biennial, Elaine Horwitch Galleries, Palm Springs, 87; New Sacred Art: Prayers for Peace, White Light Gallery, New York, 87; Newhouse Ctr Contemp Arts, Staten Island, NY, 88; The Transformative Vision, Phyllis Weil & Co, New York, 89; and many others. *Teaching:* Assoc, Exten Dept, Ariz State Univ, 63-74. *Awards:* Nat Endowment Arts Grant, 75; Ariz Comn Arts & Humanities Educ Grant, 77. *Bibliog:* Margaret Carde (auth), Beth Ames Swartz: Celestial visitations, Artspace, summer 88; Lynn Pyne (auth), Artist approaches life from a different angle, Phoenix Gazette, 4/20/88; Victoria Beaudin (auth), Artist's work depicts heavenly inspiration, Scottsdale Progress Weekend Mag, 5/6/88. *Mem:* Nat & Ariz Art Educ Asns. *Media:* Fire on Paper; Mixed-Media. *Publ:* Are we stifling our children's creativity?, Point West Mag, 63; Help your child create, Art Handbook for Parents, 65; auth, Inquiry into fire, Ariz Artist, fall 77. *Mailing Add:* 5346 E Sapphire Lane Paradise Valley AZ 85253

SWARTZ, LINDA
PHOTOGRAPHER
b New Bedford, Mass, Mar 29, 50. *Study:* Wheaton Col, 68-71; Boston Univ, 71; Art Inst Boston, 80-81. *Work:* Rose Art Mus, Brandeis Univ, Waltham, Mass Inst Technol Photog Archives, Cambridge, Boston Pub Libr, Mass. *Exhib:* The Artist's Lens: Work in Progress, local traveling exhib, Boston Pub Libr, Roxbury, Mass, 86; solo exhib, Columbia Point Photographs, Hampshire Col, Amherst, Mass, 86; Collected Visions: Twelve Contemporary Photographers, Rose Art Mus, Brandeis Univ, Waltham, Mass, 86; Along the El, traveling exhib, State Transportation Bldg & Boston Pub Libr, Mass, 87; Fellowship III, Artists Found Gallery, Boston, Mass, 88; Columbia Point, Photog Resource Ctr, Boston, Mass, 89; Mass, Boston Ctr Arts, 90; Documentary 4, Mus Contemp Photog, Chicago, Ill, 90; Seven Photographers on Transportation, Artists Found, Boston, Mass, 90; Film in the Cities, Minneapolis, Minn, 91. *Pos:* Owner & mgr, photog studio & darkroom, Boston, Mass, 81- *Teaching:* Instr photog, Univ Mass, Boston, 88- *Awards:* Purchase Award, Rockport Photog Soc, 81; Visual Artist Fel, Artists Found, Mass Coun Arts & Humanities, 84 & 87; Visual Artist Fel Photog, Nat Endowment Arts, 86; Mass Productions Grant, Coun Arts Humanities, 87. *Bibliog:* Images of youth (review), Daily Free Press, Boston, 12/4/85; A long look at life "along the el" (review), Boston Globe, 7/22/87; Along the el (review), Views, Potog Resource Ctr, fall, 87. *Mem:* Photog Resource Ctr, Boston, Mass; Intermedia Arts, St Paul, Minn. *Publ:* Contribr, New American Nudes, Morgan & Morgan, 81; For Kids' Sake (exhib catalog), Photog Resource Ctr & WBZ-TV, Boston, 85; auth, article & photographs, Views, Vol 7, No 4, 86. *Mailing Add:* 1707 Cambridge St Cambridge MA 02138

SWARTZMAN, ROSLYN
PRINTMAKER, SCULPTOR
b Montreal, Que, Aug 17, 31. *Study:* Montreal Artists Sch; Montreal Mus Fine Arts; Ecole des Beaux Arts, with Albert Dumouchez. *Work:* Nat Gallery Can, Ottawa, Ont; Montreal Mus Fine Arts, Que; DeCordova Mus, Boston; Brooklyn Mus, NY; New York Pub Libr; and many others. *Comn:* Aluminium bas-relief sculpture, Arctic Forms, Montreal, 83-84; aluminium wall sculpture, Oiseau de Feu, Place Bonaventure Entrance Lobby, St Antoine & Univ, Montreal, 90-91. *Exhib:* 2nd Int Graphics Biennial, Miami, 75; Jewish Experience in the 20th Century, Mt St Vincent Univ, Halifax, NS; Can Landscape through Drawings & Prints, Mus Fine Arts, Montreal; Boston Printmakers, 78; one-man show, Burnaby Art Gallery, BC, 80 & Saidye Bronfman Ctr, 81; and others. *Teaching:* Teacher & dir graphics dept, Sayde Bronfman Ctr, Montreal, 71-; printmaking instr, Univ Haifa, Israel, 88; art instr, Israel Painting Workshop Tour, 89; founder & coordr comprehensive art prog, Saidye Bronfman Centre, Montreal, Que, 90- *Awards:* two patron selection awards, Boston Printmakers 30th Exhib; Thomas Moore Purchase Award, Montreal, 80; Travel Grant to Israel, Can-Israel Cult Found, 88; and others. *Bibliog:* Nicole Malenfant (auth), L'Estampe - La Documentation Québécoise, 79; Gilles Daigneault & Ginette Deslauriers (auths), La Gravure Au Québec - 1940-1980; Elyse (auth), Musée du Québec, 81; Marcel Broquet (auth), Musée du Québec, 86; Idea of North, Royal Can Acad Arts, 83. *Mem:* Royal Can Acad; Graphic Arts Coun Can; Print & Drawing Coun Can; Graphics Soc NH. *Media:* Intaglio; Bas-Relief. *Dealer:* La Guild Graphique 9 St Paul Ouest Montreal Can. *Mailing Add:* 4174 Oxford St Montreal PQ H4A 2Y4 Canada

SWAY, ALBERT
PAINTER, ETCHER
b Cincinnati, Ohio, Aug 6, 13. *Study:* Cincinnati Art Acad; Art Students League. *Work:* Metrop Mus Art, New York; New York Pub Libr; Carnegie Inst; Cincinnati Art Mus; Libr Cong, Washington, DC. *Exhib:* Libr Cong, Washington, DC, 43-45; Albright-Knox Art Gallery, 51; Soc Am Graphic Artists, 51-; Royal Soc Painters, Etchers & Engravers, London, Eng, 54; Am-Japan Contemp Print Exhib, Tokyo, 67; Garden State Watercolor Soc Ann Exhib, NJ, 83-85; and many one-man shows. *Teaching:* Instr drawing & painting, New York Hosp League, 63-64. *Awards:* First Prize in Graphics, Cincinnati Mus Asn, 39; Winsor-Newton Award, 22nd Ann Juried Show Garden State Watercolor Soc, 91. *Mem:* Soc Am Graphic Artists; Garden State Watercolor Soc. *Publ:* Illusr filmstrips on New York State history, produced by Our York State, NY, 50-; med illusr, A Syllabus for Health Visitors, Navajo Tribal Coun, Ariz, 60; Respiratory diseases, Nat Tuberculosis Asn, 61; Hepatic Excretory Function (ser filmstrips); Am Gastroenterol Asn, 72; med illusr, Congenital Malformations of the Heart, Grune & Stratton, 75; plus med illus in sci jour; Cosmetic Surgery, Alfred E Greenwald, MD, 88. *Mailing Add:* PO Box 43 Kendall Park NJ 08824

SWEENEY, J GRAY
HISTORIAN, CURATOR
b Jacksonville, Fla, Nov 20, 43. *Study:* Univ NMex, BA, 66; Ind Univ, MA, 69, PhD, 75. *Collections Arranged:* Themes in American Painting (auth, catalog), Grand Rapids Art Mus, 77; Artists of Grand Rapids: 1840-1980 (auth, catalog), 81; Great Lakes Marine Painting of the 19th Century (auth, catalog), Muskegon Mus Art, 83, Artists of Michigan from the 19th Century (auth, catalog), Muskegan Mus Art, 87. *Pos:* Cur, Themes in Am Painting, Grand Rapids Art Mus, 75-77, Tweed Mus, 80, Grand Rapids Art Mus, Mich, 81 & Muskegon Mus Art, 83 & 86. *Teaching:* Asst prof 19th & 20th century Am painting, Grand Valley State Univ, 71-78, assoc prof, 78-85; assoc prof, Ariz State Univ, 86-88, prof, 89- *Awards:* Fels, Carnegie Found, 67 & 70 & Samuel H Kress Found, 70-71; Senior fel, Smithsonian Inst, Nat Mus Am Art, 84-85. *Mem:* Col Art Asn; Asn Hist Am Art. *Res:* Nineteenth century American landscape painting; influence of Thomas Cole; Regional and Western Am Art. *Publ:* Auth, Endued with Rare Genius, In: To the Memory of Cole (auth, Frederic E Church), Smithsonian Studies in American Art, winter, 88; The Nude of Landscape Painting: Emblematic Personification in the Art of the Hudson River School, Smithsonian Studies in Am Art, fall 89; A very peculiar picture: Martin J Meades Thunderstorm over Narragansett Bay, Archs Am Art J, #4, 88; Masterpieces of Western American Painting, 91; The Columbus of the Woods: Daniel Boone & Manifest Destiny (catalog), 92. *Mailing Add:* 6908 E Latham St Scottsdale AZ 85257

SWEET, MARY (FRENCH)
PAINTER
b Cincinnati, Ohio, Oct 10, 37. *Study:* Stanford Univ, with Daniel Mendelowitz, AB(art), 59, MA(art), 60. *Work:* Carlsbad Art Mus, NMex; La Posada Hotel & Menninger Clinic, Albuquerque NMex; First Nat Bank, Albuquerque, NMex; NMex Educ Credit Union. *Comn:* Painting, USS Barb Submarine, 63; NMex Educ Credit Union, Albuquerque, 88. *Exhib:* Oakland Art Asn Ann, Oakland Art Mus, 68; Watercolor New Mexico, Mus NMex, Santa Fe, 74; El Paso Sun Carnival, El Paso Mus Art, 74; Introductions, 76 & Watercolor New Mexico, 81, Albuquerque Mus; Am Watercolor Soc Ann, New York, 86 & 88; Am Artist Mag Golden Ann Travelling Exhib, San Francisco, New York & St Louis, 87; Western Fedn Watercolor Soc 16 Exhib, Corpus Cristi Mus, 91; Western Fedn Watercolor Soc 17 traveling exhib, Albuquerque Mus, NMex, 92. *Awards:* Jurors Award Excellence, Santa Fe Festival Arts, 79; Lena Newcastle Award, Am Watercolor Soc, 88; Merit Award, Tubac Ctr Arts, 90. *Bibliog:* Mary Carroll Nelson (auth), Wilderness landscapes by Mary Sweet, Am Artist, 9/82; Joseph Traugott (auth), Abstract form, vivid colors typify works, Albuquerque J, 10/30/83; Elizabeth Leonard (auth), Mary Sweet: Flattening Out Three Dimensional Subjects, In: Painting The Landscape, Watson-Guptill, 84; SPLASH, America's Best Contemporary Watercolors, North Light Books, 91. *Mem:* NMex Watercolor Soc; Albuquerque United Artists. *Media:* Acrylics, Mixed Media. *Dealer:* Weyrich Gallery 2935D Louisiana NE Albuquerque NM 87059; Hummingbird Originals 4319 Camp Bowie Blvd Ft Worth TX 76107. *Mailing Add:* PO Box 280 Tijeras NM 87059

SWEET, ROGER
SCULPTOR, CERAMIST
b Huntington Park, Calif, Jan 22, 46. *Study:* Orange Coast Col, Costa Mesa, Calif, AA, 70; Whitney Mus Independent Study Prog, New York, 73; Univ Calif, BFA, 72, MFA, 75. *Work:* Univ NMex, Albuquerque. *Exhib:* Solo exhibs, Bowers Mus, Santa Ana, Calif, 75, Fine Arts Gallery, Tex Tech Univ, Lubbock, Tex, 87 & Jonson Gallery, Univ NMex, Alburquerque, NMex, 88; Everson Mus Art, Syracuse, NY, 79, catalogue; Allentown Art Mus, Allentown, Pa, 81; Mus Fine Arts, Santa Fe, NMex, 86; Playing with Fire, Ctr Contemp Arts, Sante Fe, NMex, 90; Overlay, Graham Gallery, Albuquerque, NMex, 90; Cafe Gallery, Albuquerque, NMex, 92. *Teaching:* Instr, Univ NMex, ceramics & sculpture, 75-80, art hist, ceramics & sculpture, 83- *Bibliog:* Artists of 20th Century NMex, Mus NMex Press, 92. *Mailing Add:* PO Box 562 Jemez Springs NM 87025

SWEET, STEVE (STEVEN MARK)
COLLAGE ARTIST, KINETIC
b Boston, Mass, Mar 13, 52. *Study:* Antioch Col, with Paul Sharits, Allan Jones & Tony Conrad, BA(visual arts), 74. *Work:* Pan-Am Life Insurance Corp, New Orleans; United Media Enterprises, New York; New Orleans Mus Art; Contemp Arts Ctr. *Comn:* The Appliance Giant Mural, comn by Tony Campo, New Orleans, 83; City of New Orleans, 89; New Orleans Int Airport, 90. *Exhib:* Louisiana Major Works, Contemp Arts Ctr, New Orleans, 79; New Orleans Triennial, New Orleans Mus Art, 80 & 86; Focus, Ft Worth Art Mus, 81; Art of New Orleans, Southeast Ctr Contemp Arts, Winston-Salem, NC, 84; New Music America 83, Hirshhorn Mus & Sculpture Garden, 83; Birmingham Biennial, Birmingham Mus Art, 85; Corcoran Biennial, Corcoran Gallery, Washington, DC, 89. *Pos:* Artist-in-residence, La Superdome, 86. *Awards:* Services to the Field, Contemp Arts Ctr & Nat Endowment Arts, 80; Nat Endowment Arts Fel, 81 & Interarts grant, 85; Rockefeller Grant, Southeastern Interdisciplinary Fund, 89. *Bibliog:* Roger Green (auth), Flattened people: Portraits in depth, Times Picyunne-States Item, 1/83; Jeff Zeldman (auth), Picture perfect, City Papers, Washington, DC, 10/14/83; David Rive (auth), SteveSweet, Art Papers, 5/87. *Mem:* Contemp Arts Ctr. *Dealer:* Arthur Roger Gallery 314 Julia St New Orleans La 70130. *Mailing Add:* 827 Louque Pl New Orleans LA 70124

SWEITZER, CHARLES LEROY
MURALIST, PAINTER
b Brownsville, Pa, Mar 23, 39. *Study:* Univ NC, BA, 76; NC Cent Univ, MA, 88; NC Cent Univ, MA(clin psychology), 91. *Comn:* History of North Carolina, comn by Dwight Phillips, Charlotte, NC, 68; Man's Relationship to God, Douglas MacArthur Acad, Tex Baptist, Brownwood, 72; Nashville Civil War Cyclorama, comn by Sam Fleming, Franklin, Tenn, 79; Place in Time, Othal Brand, Loma Linda, Calif, 85. *Teaching:* Instr visual art, Sweitzer Sch Art, 85-87; instr painting, Cent Piedmont Col, 80-82. *Bibliog:* Judith Sands (dir), Making a Mural (film), Media Consultants, 72; Carrol DeWhit (auth), The cyclorama at Franklin, Southern Living Mag, 79. *Mem:* Nat Soc Mural Painters, New York; NC Coun Arts; Wake Co Visual Artists. *Media:* Oil on Canvas. *Mailing Add:* 1302 Timber Dr Garner NC 27529-4730

SWENSEN, J(EAN) MARY JEANETTE HAMILTON
GRAPHIC ARTIST, CALLIGRAPHER
b Laurens, SC, June 25, 10. *Study:* Columbia Univ, with Hans Mueller, BS, 56, with Arthur Young, MA(graphic arts), 60; Fine Arts Sch for Am, Fountainbleau, France, with Lucien Fontanerosa; Ariz State Univ, with Arthur Hahn, 5 summers. *Work:* Metrop Mus Art, New York; Nat Graphic Arts Collection, Smithsonian Inst, Washington, DC; Graphic Arts Collection, New York Pub Libr; Laurens Pub Libr, SC. *Exhib:* Soc Western Artists, M H de Young Mus, San Francisco, 64; Nat Art Roundup, Las Vegas, Nev, 65; Fine Arts Bldg, Colo State Fair, Pueblo, 65; Duncan Gallery, Paris, 74; Co Fed Savings & Loan Asn, Denver, Colo, 78. *Awards:* Honorable Mention for Drawing, Soc Western Artists, 64; Duncan Gallery Prix de Paris, 74. *Mem:* Delta Phi Delta. *Mailing Add:* 684 W 99th Ave Denver CO 80221

SWENSON, ANNE (BEATRICE)
PAINTER, INSTRUCTOR
b Stafford Springs, Conn. *Study:* Art Students League; studied with W Fisher & V Drennan; City Univ New York, BA(art hist, summa cum laude), 80, MS, 85; NY State Teachers Licence(art), 81. *Work:* Pvt collections in USA, Italy & England. *Exhib:* Metrop Mus Art, 75 & 77; Snug Harbor Cult Ctr, NY, 76-83; Artists Equity Asn Exhib, 77; Goldsboro Art Ctr, NC, 77; Salmagundi Club, New York, 81; Nat Americana Mus, Yorktown, Va, 86. *Teaching:* Instr, St Peters Elem Sch, 60-63, S B Wagner High Sch, 74 & Our Lady Good Counsel & Immaculate Conception Elem Schs, 80- *Awards:* Anna B Morse Gold Medal, Gotham Painters, 66; Art Achievement Award, Centennial Comt 7th Regiment, Armory, NY, 80. *Bibliog:* With photos of work, Staten Island Advan, 59, 60 & 69. *Mem:* Burr Artists (dir, 67-81); Gotham Painters (treas, 74-88); New York Artists Equity Asn; gold medal mem Accad delle Arti del Lavoro, Parma, Italy. *Media:* Oil, Pen and Ink. *Publ:* Auth, Rugs Through the Ages, New Bull Staten Island Mus, Vol 9, No 3; articles, Perceptual and Motor Skills: Modeling and Verbal Instruction, 2/85; Relationships: Art Education, Art Therapy and Special Education, 2/91. *Mailing Add:* 10 Phelps Pl Staten Island NY 10301

SWERGOLD, MARCELLE M
SCULPTOR
b Antwerp, Belg, Sept 6, 27; US citizen. *Study:* NY Univ, painting with Aaron Berkman & Henry Kallem; Art Students League, with John Hovanes & Jose deCreft; wax with Harold Caster. *Work:* New Britain Mus Am Art, Conn; Yad Vashem-Sculpture Garden, Jerusalem, Israel. *Comn:* Mudge, Rose, Guthrie, Alexander & Feldon, 82; Yad Vashem, Jerusalem, 90. *Exhib:* Fairleigh Dickinson Univ, Teaneck, NJ, 72; Cork Gallery, Philharmonic Hall, Lincoln Ctr, New York; Allied Artists, Nat Acad Gallerie, New York; Audubon Artist Ann, New York, 78; New Britain Mus Am Art, Conn, 80; and others. *Awards:* First Prize, Womanart Gallery, New York, 77 & Stanley Richter Asn Arts, Danbury, Conn, 85; Vincent Glinsky Mem Award, Audubon Artists, 86; Union Carbide, First Prize. *Bibliog:* Article, Museum collection grows again, The Herald New Britain, Conn, 12/80; article, Jerusalem Post, 10/90; Mizrachi Magazine (Amit), 82. *Mem:* New York Soc Women Artists (corresp secy, 77-79, pres, 79-81, exec vpres, 81-); Artists Equity Asn, New York; Contemp Artist Guild. *Media:* Bronze, Stone. *Mailing Add:* 2231 Broadway New York NY 10024

SWETCHARNIK, SARA MORRIS
PAINTER, SCULPTOR
b Shelby, NC, May 21, 55. *Study:* Schuler Sch Fine Art, 73-79; Art Students League, 80-82. *Work:* Haussners Restaurant & Mus, Baltimore, Md. *Comn:* Portrait sculpture, comn by Walter Finch Esq, 78. *Exhib:* Pastel Soc Am Annual Exhib, Nat Arts Club, New York, 79 & 81; solo exhibs, Weinberg Ctr for Arts, Frederick, Md, 80 & Landon Sch Gallery, Bethesda, Md, 90; Mount St Mary's Col, Emmitsburg, Md, 81; Allegheny Int Art Exhib, Bluefield, WVa, 89; Frederick Community Col Gallery, Frederick, Md, 92. *Awards:* First Place Award, Allegheny Int Art Exhib, 89; Residency, Va Ctr for Creative Arts, 90. *Bibliog:* Cassle Hagan (auth), Art Eden, News & Daily Advance, 7/8/90. *Media:* Oil, Terracotta. *Mailing Add:* 7044 Woodville Rd Mt Airy MD 21771

SWETCHARNIK, WILLIAM NORTON
PAINTER, SCULPTOR
b Philadelphia, Pa, Oct 18, 51. *Study:* RI Sch Design, 69-71; Univ Calif, San Diego, with Manny Farber, 73-76; Towson State Univ, Md, BS, 77. *Work:* Art Mus, Fla Int Univ, Miami, Fla; Cintas Found, New York; Comm Cult Exchange between United States & Madrid, Spain; Psychiatric Inst Greater Washington, Silver Spring, Md; Salisbury St Hosp, Salisbury, Md. *Exhib:* Solo exhibs, Weinberg Ctr Arts, Frederick, Md, 80, Mt St Mary's Col, Emmitsburg, Md, 81, Harbor Gallery, New York, Cold Spring Harbor, Foxhall Gallery, Washington, DC, John Pence Gallery, San Francisco, Calif, Md Col Art & Design, Silver Spring, Md, 86, Washington Cty Mus Art, Hagerstown, Md, forthcoming, 91; Ann Nat Salon, Springfield Mus Art, Utah, 85 & 86; Washington County Mus Art, Hagerstown, Md, 81, 86-89; Md Art Place, Baltimore, 90; Nat Acad Design, New York, 90. *Awards:* Cintas Found Fel, Inst Int Educ, 85-86; Yaddo Residency, 87; Fulbright Int Fel, 87-89. *Bibliog:* Robin Longman (auth), Emerging artists, Am Artist, 84. *Mem:* Artists Equity; Pastel Soc Am. *Media:* Oils. *Mailing Add:* 7044 Woodville Rd Mt Airy MD 21771

SWICK, LINDA ANN
SCULPTOR
b Bedford, Ohio, Sept 9, 48. *Study:* Kent State Univ, BA, 70; Fla State Univ, MFA, 77. *Exhib:* Solo show, Washington Proj Arts, Washington, DC, 79; Rutgers Univ, Camden, NJ, 79; Laguna Gloria Art Mus, Austin, 80; Middendorf Lane, Washington, DC, 80; Corcoran Gallery, Washington, DC, 81; Lawndale, Univ Houston, 82. *Pos:* Set designer for animated films, Broadcast Arts, Washington, DC, 80- *Awards:* Fel, City Washington, DC, 82. *Bibliog:* Sylvia Shauck (auth), interview, Art & Craft Mag, 6/80; Charlotte Moser (auth), Washington art, Art News, 10/81. *Media:* Wood. *Dealer:* Gallery K 2032 P St Washington DC. *Mailing Add:* 1728 S St NW Washington DC 20009

SWIGART, LYNN S
PHOTOGRAPHER
b Kansas City, Mo, Aug 22, 30. *Study:* Bradley Univ, Peoria, Ill, BS(psychol, philos); also photog with Minor White & George Tice. *Work:* Carpenter Ctr for the Visual Arts, Harvard Univ, Cambridge, Mass; Stanford Univ; Ill State Mus; Lakeview Mus. *Exhib:* One-man shows, Univ Conn, 77, Stanford Univ, 78, Univ Iowa, 78, Ill State Mus, 78, Lakeview Mus, Peoria, Ill, 80, Cape Ann Hist Mus, Glouchester, Mass, 81; Radius 76, Burpee Art Mus, Rockford, Ill, 76; Twelfth Biennial Michiana Regional, 82; Arts Works Nat Photog Exhib, Brattleboro, Vt, 82; Camera Movements, Moore Col Art, Philadelphia, Pa, 82; Ill Photogr, 85; Ill State Mus, 85. *Teaching:* Instr photog, Multi-Media Arts Inst, Bradley Univ, summer 73 & 74. *Mem:* Lakeview Ctr for Arts; Peoria Art Guild. *Publ:* Contribr, Olson's Gloucester, LSU Press, 80, The Best of Photog Ann, 82 & NDak Quart, 85. *Mailing Add:* 3 Weston Rd Weston CT 06883

SYKES, (WILLIAM) MALTBY
PAINTER, PRINTMAKER
b Aberdeen, Miss, Dec 13, 11. *Study:* With Wayman Adams, John Sloan, Diego Rivera, Andre Lhote, Fernand Leger & Stanley William Hayter. *Work:* Mus Mod Art & Metrop Mus Art, New York; Stedlijk Mus, Amsterdam; Boston Mus Fine Arts, Mass; Philadelphia Mus Art, Pa. *Comn:* Color engravings ed (210 prints), Trellis, Int Graphic Arts Soc, 55, Cathedral Interior, 58 & Floating Still Life, 62. *Exhib:* Salon d'Automne, Paris, 51; Int Biennial Contemp Color Lithography, Cincinnati Art Mus, 52; Am Watercolors, Drawings & Prints, Metrop Mus Art, New York, 52; Curator's Choice Exhib, Philadelphia Print Club, 56; Contemp Am Graphic Art, US Info Agency & Tour Abroad, 61. *Teaching:* Prof art, Auburn Univ, 42-77, artist-in-residence, 68-77, emer prof, 77- *Awards:* Albany Inst Hist & Art Purchase Award, Print Club, Albany, 63; Philip & Esther Klein Award, Am Color Print Soc, 65; Sabbatical Award, Nat Endowment Arts, 67-68. *Mem:* Soc Am Graphic Artists. *Media:* Acrylic, Oil; Etching, Lithograph. *Publ:* Auth, The Multimetal lithography process, Artists Proof, 68; contribr, Printmaking Today, Holt, Rinehart & Winston, rev ed, 72; The Print, Abrams, 75; auth, Recollections of a lithographile, Tamarind Papers, Vol 6, No 3, summer 83; Diego Rivera and the hotel reforma murals, Arch Am J, Vol 26, No 1-2, 85. *Mailing Add:* 712 Brenda Ave Auburn AL 36830

SYLVAN, RITA M
PHOTOGRAPHER, PAINTER
b Minneapolis, Minn, Mar 21, 28. *Study:* Minneapolis Sch Art, Univ Minn with Ralston Crawford & Paul Burlin, BA, 48; Columbia Univ, MA, 67; Fine Arts Inst; Penland Sch; Bennington Col. *Work:* Rose Mus, Brandeis Univ, Waltham, Mass; Columbia Univ, New York; Boca Raton Mus Art. *Exhib:* Regional Exhib, Minneapolis Inst Art, 48; 50 NJ Artists, Newark Mus, 65; US State Dept, Nat Asn Women Artists Traveling Exhib, India & Pakistan, 65-66; Philharmonic Hall Invitational, New York, 69; NJ State, Biennial, NJ State Mus, Trenton, 69; Ann Artists Guild Exhib, Norton Gallery Art, Palm Beach, Fla, 84-89; All Fla Exhib, Boca Raton Mus Art, Fla, 86, 87, 88 & 89; 32nd Ann Hortt Exhib, Ft Lauderdale Mus Art, Fla, 90; one-man show, Art in Public Places, Boca Raton Nat Endowment for the Arts, Bergen Mus. *Pos:* Asst cur photog, Brooklyn Mus, NY, 50-51; asst dir photog, Mus Mod Art, New York, 52-53. *Teaching:* St Andrews Sch, Boca Raton, Fla; instr & dir art, Art Ctr of Northern NJ, Tenafly, 68-73, Boca Raton Mus. *Awards:* Ann Award, Nat Asn Women Artists, 66; Best 2-D, Prof Artists Guild Ann Exhib, 89; First Prize, Norton Gallery, 92. *Bibliog:* Bruce Weber (auth), Artcetera (auction catalog), Broward Art Guild, 90. *Mem:* Prof Artists Guild (admin chmn, 86-90); Women's Caucus Art; 2 plus 3--Artists Orgn, Ft Lauderdale, Fla; Broward Art Guild. *Media:* Color photography; Mixed Media, Watercolor. *Publ:* Contribr, Edward Steichen: A memoir, Connoisseur, 2/88. *Mailing Add:* PO Box 145 Boca Raton FL 33429

SYLVESTRE, GUY
CRITIC, WRITER
b Sorel, Que, May 17, 18. *Study:* Col Ste Marie, Montreal; Univ Ottawa, MA. *Pos:* Ed, Gants du Ciel, 43-46; nat librn, Nat Libr, Ottawa, 68-83. *Mem:* Can Libr Asn; Soc Ecrivains Can; Royal Soc Can Acad Can Francaise. *Publ:* Auth, Anthologie de la Poesie Canadienne-Francaise, Beauchemin, 64 & 74; Panorama des Lettres Canadiennes Francaises, 64 & Literature in French Canada, 67, EOQ; Ecrivains Canadiens, HMH, 64 & McGraw, 67; Structures Sociales du Canada Francais, Laval, 66; and many others. *Mailing Add:* 2286 Bowman Rd Ottawa ON K1H 6V6 Canada

SYROP, MITCHELL
CONCEPTUAL ARTIST
b Yonkers, NY, Dec 21, 53. *Study:* Pratt Inst, Brooklyn, NY, BFA, 75; Calif Inst Arts, Valencia, MFA, 78. *Work:* Mus Contemp Arts, Los Angeles; Newport Art Mus, Newport Beach, Calif; La Jolla Mus Contemp Art, Calif; Lannan Found, Los Angeles, Calif; Tampa Mus Art, Fla. *Comn:* Seattle Arts Comn, Washington, 89; Los Angeles Central Libr, Calif, 89; Progressive Corp, 89. *Exhib:* Solo exhibs, Matri Gallery, Univ Art Mus, Univ Calif, Berkeley, 87, Univ Art Mus, Univ Calif, Santa Barbara, 89; Avante-Garde in the Eighties, Los Angeles Co Mus Art, 87; The Photography of Invention: American Pictures of the Eighties, Nat Mus Am Art, Washington, DC, Mus Contemp Art, Chicago, Walker Art Ctr, Minneapolis, 89; A Forest of Signs: Art in the Crisis of Representation, Mus Contemp Art, Los Angeles, 89; Hacia el Paisaje (Toward Landscape), Centro Atlantico de Arte Moderno, Las Palmas, Spain, 90; Individual Realities, Sezon Mus, Tokyo, Japan & Tsukashin Hall, Osaka, Japan, 91; Body/Language, Lannan Found, Los Angeles, 91; and others. *Teaching:* Instr, Calif Inst Arts, Valencia, 90-91. *Awards:* Nat Endowment Arts Grant, 87. *Bibliog:* Lane Relyea (auth), rev, Art Am, 3/87; Christopher Knight (auth), Constellations: Yearbook of Adolescent Yearning, rev, Los Angeles Times, 4/23/92. *Dealer:* Rosamund Felsen Gallery 8525 Santa Monica Blvd Los Angeles CA 90069. *Mailing Add:* 1640 Point View Los Angeles CA 90035

SZABO, JOSEPH GEORGE
CARTOONIST, EDITOR
b Budapest, Hungary, Feb 4, 50; US citizen. *Study:* Sch Masters Typography, cert, 69; Hungarian Acad Journalism, BA(summa cum laude), 74; Sch Com, cert, 78. *Work:* Cult Ctr Scharpoord, Knokke-Heist, Belg; Yomiuri Shimbun, Tokyo; Cartoon Art Mus, San Francisco. *Exhib:* Humorfoto '82-'86, Cult Ctr Scharpoord, Kuokke Heist, Belg, 82-86; Man and His World, Int Salon Cartoons, Montreal, 84-86; Yomiuri Int Cartoon Contest, Tokyo, 85-86; Everything is Cabaret, World Cartoon Gallery, Skopje, Yugoslavia, 86; South Africa, Montevideo, Uruguay, 86; Int Simavi Cartoon Competition, Istanbul, Turkey, 86. *Pos:* Assoc art dir, Nōk Lapja (weekly), Budapest, Hungary, 75-78; managing graphics ed & ed cartoonist, Magyar Nemzet (daily), Budapest, Hungary, 78-80; art dir & cartoonist, Sting (satirical mag), Ctr Sq, Philadelphia, 84-85. *Awards:* Press Prize, Humorfoto '84, Belg, 84; Bronze Medals, Yomiuri Int Cartoon Contest, Tokyo, 85 & 86. *Bibliog:* Istvan Molnar (auth), article, Magyar Grafika, 2/80; Gloria Sipes Paleveda (auth), Hungarian political cartoonist, Philadelphia Inquirer, 6/23/85; Ann Whiteside (auth), Cartoonist's sketches span the globe, Montgomeryville Spirit, 4/30/86. *Mem:* Nat Cartoonists Soc; Asn Am Ed Cartoonists. *Media:* Coated Cardboard, Marker. *Publ:* Auth, Photo-Cartoon Calendar, self-publ, 83; Illus, Animal Farm, by George Orwell, Rainbow Publ, 84; auth, Never pointing a different way, Target, 85; ed, WittyWorld, Int Cartoon Mag, 87; Finest International Political Cartoons of our Time, 92, Witty World Books, 92. *Mailing Add:* PO Box 1458 North Wales PA 19454

SZABO, STEPHEN LEE
PHOTOGRAPHER
b Berwick, Pa, July 17, 40. *Study:* Art Ctr Col Design, Los Angeles, Calif; Pa State Univ. *Work:* Int Ctr Photog, Mus Mod Art, New York; Corcoran Gallery Art, Libr Cong, Washington, DC; Int Mus Photog, George Eastman House, Rochester, NY. *Exhib:* Old Techniques by Young Photographers, Eastern Shore, Phillips Collection, Washington, DC, 73, Springfield Art Mus, Mo, 77, Hunter Mus Art, Chattanooga, Tenn, 77, Int Ctr Photog, NY, 77, Fine Arts Mus of the South, Mobile, Ala, 77 & Baltimore Mus Art, Md, 77. *Teaching:* Inst, Corcoran Sch Art, Washington, DC. *Awards:* Nat Endowment Arts, 86. *Bibliog:* Paul Richard (auth), Of time and the photograph, Washington Post, 72; A dialogue with the present to document the past, Camera, 76; Mark Power (auth), Washington photographs and the contact print, Washington Rev Arts, 77. *Publ:* Illusr, Where We Live, Fed Home Loan Mortgage Corp, 73; auth-illusr, The Eastern Shore, Addison House, 76. *Mailing Add:* c/o Kathleen Ewing Gallery 1609 Connecticut Ave Washington DC 20009

SZASZ, FRANK V
PAINTER, PRINTMAKER
b Budapest, Hungary, Aug 1, 25; US citizen. *Study:* Sch Graphic Arts, studied graphic design with Gustav Vegh & Sandor Bortnyik, 41-42, grad, 43. *Work:* Kansas City Mus & City Hall of Kansas City, Mo; Fed Bur Investigation, Washington, DC; Harry S Truman Pres Libr, Independence, Mo; Missouri Supreme Court, Jefferson City. *Comn:* President Truman (portrait), comn by Margaret Truman, Independence, Mo, 73; President Ford (portrait), Repub Nat Election Comn, Kansas City, Mo, 76; George Clay (portrait), Fed Reserve Bank, Kansas City, Mo, 76; Anwar Sadat (portrait), Govt Egypt, Cairo, 81; Mrs Marvin Davis (portrait), Children's Diabetes Fund, Denver, 83. *Exhib:* Heritage Exhibits, Kansas City Mus, Mo, 60-70. *Pos:* Art dir, Juvenile Publ House, Budapest, 53-56; dept head, Hallmark Cards, Inc, Kansas City, Mo, 63-65; art dir, Global Int Airways, Kansas City, Mo, 80-85. *Teaching:* instr painting, Kansas City Art Inst, 63-65, Kansas City Art Guild, 65-75; instr art survey, Rockhurst Col, Kansas City, Mo, 68-69. *Bibliog:* Frank Spurlock (auth), article, Kansas City Star, 71; Marina's Portrait, television program, Kansas City Pub Television, 72; Kent Politsch (auth), Artist in great style, Kansas City Monthly Mag, 5/80. *Publ:* Illusr, Henri Barbusse: A Tuz, Új Magyar Kõnyvkiadó, Budapest, 56; Animal Stories, Simon & Schuster, 57; John F Kennedy: Words to Remember, Hallmark Cards, Inc, 67. *Mailing Add:* 8104 Lee Blvd Leawood KS 66206

SZESKO, JUDITH CLARANN See Jaidinger, Judith C

SZESKO, LENORE RUNDLE
PAINTER, PRINTMAKER
b Galesburg, Ill, Mar 13, 33. *Study:* Art Inst Chicago, BFA(drawing, painting, illus), 61, MFA(painting), 66; wood engraving with Adrian Troy. *Work:* Standard Oil Co, Chicago; NJ State Mus; Jayell Publ House, Miami, Fla; Springfield Col; Kemper Ins Co Collection, Long Grove, Ill. *Exhib:* Conn Acad Fine Arts 62nd Ann, Wadsworth Atheneum, Hartford, Conn, 72; Cedar City Ann Fine Art Exhib, Utah, 72-75; Contemp Am Graphics, Old Bergen Art Guild, Bayonne, NJ (traveling exhib), 72-80; Soc Am Graphic Artists 52nd Nat Print Exhib, New York & Chicago, 73; NH Print Club 1st & 2nd Int, Nashua, 73-74. *Awards:* James R Marsh Mem Purchase Prize, Hunterdon Art Ctr 16th Print, Clinton, NJ, 72; Muth Award, Miniature Painters, Sculptors & Gravers Soc of Washington, DC, 73; Award Highest Merit-Drawing, Miniature Art Soc of Fla Nat Exhib, 76; and others. *Mem:* Audubon Artists, Inc, New York; Painters & Sculptors Soc NJ; Boston Printmakers, Mass; Miniature Art Soc NJ; La Watercolor Soc. *Media:* Multimedia. *Collection:* American Indian and Pre-Columbian, some African art; antique furniture and dolls. *Mailing Add:* 5728 N Austin Ave Chicago IL 60646-6231

SZILVASY, LINDA MARKULY
PAINTER, WRITER
b Granite City, Ill, Oct, 7, 40. *Study:* Lindenwood Col Women, St Charles, Mo, BA, 61; George Peabody Col, Nashville, Tenn, MA, 62. *Work:* Eden Theol Sem, Webster Groves, Mo; US Army Chaplain Mus, Ft Hamilton, NY; Lindenwood Col Women; George Peabody Col. *Comn:* Paintings used for official Christmas cards, First Cavalry Div, Ft Hood, Tex, 72, III Corps, Ft Hood, 73 & 75 & Officer Wives Club, Ft Leonard Wood, Mo, 75; jeweled ostrich shells painted symbols of longevity, comn by Charlene Franz for Premier Sun Yun-hsuan & Pres Chiang Ching-kuo, Taiwan, 78; jeweled egg by Am Egg Board for First Lady Nancy Reagan, 80. *Exhib:* One-woman show, Petite Pigalle Gallery, St Louis, Mo, 62; Invitational, Lindenwood Col Women Gallery, St Charles, Mo, 67 & Jeweled Eggs, 77; Ann Show, Women's Club Gallery, Houston, 72; 10th Ann Arts & Crafts Festival, Killeen, Tex, 73; jeweled eggs, Galeria de las Artes, Las Cruces, NMex, 80; Centennial Mus, Univ Tex El Paso, 86; Glorietta's Gallery, El Paso, Tex, 86-*Pos:* Co-chmn Arts Comt, Metamora Woman's Club, 91-92. *Teaching:* Art instr, Omaha Pub Sch System, Nebr, 63-66, Killeen Independent Sch Dist, Tex, 72-73 & var eggs-ibits, Dallas, Mich & Md, 75- *Awards:* Sweepstakes Winner, 10th Ann Arts & Crafts Festival, Killeen, Tex, 73; Best in Show Eggs-ibits: Dallas, 75, New Carrollton, Md, 75 & 76 & Oklahoma City, Okla, 76; Best Depicting Texas History, Tex Guild Egg Shell Artists, 86. *Bibliog:* Barbara Brabec (auth), The jeweled egg, Artisan Crafts, 4/75; ed staff, The egg and leather, Make It With Leather Mag, 1/77; ed staff, Eggs, $250 a dozen and up, El Paso Today Mag, 4/80. *Mem:* Am Crafts Coun; Artists' Equity Asn; Tex Guild Egg Shell Artists (1st vpres, 85-86); Nat Egg Art Guild. *Media:* Jeweled Egg Shells, Paintings and Sculptures Inside; Paintings on Canvas. *Publ:* Illusr, Dottie Miller's Around the World in 99 Beds, Eden Publ House, 73; contribr, A bit of the woods, Creative Craft Mag, 6/75; auth, The Jeweled Egg: A Handbook for Beginning and Advanced Craftsmen, Asn Press, 76; contribr, Barbara Brabec's, Creative Cash: How to Sell Your Crafts, Countryside Bks, 79; Aline Becker's Almost Everything About Heirloom Eggs, pub, 80. *Mailing Add:* 101 S Hanover St PO Box 684 Metamora IL 61548

SZNAJDERMAN, MARIUS S
PRINTMAKER, PAINTER
b Paris, France, July 18, 26; US citizen. *Study:* Sch Plastic Arts, Caracas, Venezuela, with Rafael Monasterios, Ramon Martin Durban & Ventrillon-Horber, 47-48; Columbia Univ, BS, with printmaker Hans Mueller, BS, 53; T C Colombia, MFA, 58. *Work:* Mus Mod Art, Jewish Heritage Mus, Mus Contemp Hispanic Art, New York Pub Libr, Yeshiva Univ Mus, Yivo Inst, New York; Rayo Mus, Roldanillo, Colombia; Yad Washem Mus, Jerusalem, Israel; Nat Gallery, Mus Contemp Art, Caracas, Venezuela; B'nai B'rith Klutznick Mus, Washington, DC; Fine Arts Mus, Caracas, Venezuela; Lib Cong, Washington. *Comn:* Prints, Agrupacion Grafica Pan Americana, 78-86; Carton de Venezuela, 86; Holocaust, brass monument, Temple Bethel, Hackensack, NJ. *Exhib:* one-man shows, Estevez Vilas Gallery, Cincinnati, 82-84, Rayo Mus, Colombia, 82 & Galeria Borkas, Lima, 82, Mus Contemp Hispanic Arts, New York, 89 & Corinne Timsit Int Gallery, San Juan, PR, 90; Galeria Venezuela, New York, 89 & 90; Corinne Timsit Int Galleries, San Juan, PR, 89; Jewish Community Ctr Palisades, Tenafly, NJ, 90; Mus Contemp Art, Caracas, Venezuela; and others. *Pos:* Dir, Galeria Venezuela, New York, 74-83. *Teaching:* Instr art hist & painting, Sch Visual Arts, New York, 65-71; lectr, Fairleigh Dickinson Univ, Madison, NJ, 69-73; artist-in-residence, AIM Prog, NJ Pub Sch, 74-77. *Bibliog:* Hispanic Culture in New Jersey (film), NJ Pub TV, 78; Carlos Silva (auth), Historia De La Pintura en Venezuela, Tomo III, Caracas, 89. *Media:* All. *Publ:* Illusr, Magicismos, Colleccion Rasgos Comunes, Caracas, 89. *Dealer:* Kerygma Gallery 38 Oak St Ridgewood NJ 07450. *Mailing Add:* 242 Summit Ave Hackensack NJ 07601

SZOKE, JOHN
DEALER, PUBLISHER
US citizen. *Study:* NY Univ, BS, 72; Grad Sch Bus Admin, MBA, 73. *Pos:* Owner, John Szoke Graphics, New York. *Teaching:* Asst prof, Baruch Col, City Univ New York, 75-79. *Mem:* Fine Art Publ Asn (pres, formerly, treas, currently). *Media:* Prints, Works on Paper. *Mailing Add:* 164 Mercer St New York NY 10012

T

TABACHNICK, ANNE
PAINTER
b Derby, Conn, July 28, 37. *Study:* Hans Hofmann Sch (scholar), three yrs; Hunter Col, BA; Univ Calif, Berkeley; NY Univ. *Work:* Hyde Collection, Glens Falls, NY; Mus of Univ Calif, Berkeley; Mus Of Univ Mass, Amherst; Metrop Mus Art; Dayton Art Inst, Ohio; Nueberger Mus; Montclair Mus. *Exhib:* Many one-woman shows in New York & other cities, 51-86; Mus Mod Art Traveling Show-Hofmann & His Students, 62; one-woman shows, Dayton Art Inst, 65, La State Univ Gallery, 75 & Hyde Collection, 76. *Pos:* Reviewer, Art News, 66-67. *Teaching:* Instr art, Dayton Art Inst, 65-67 & Harvard Univ, 68-69; instr art, Harvard Univ, 68-69; prof painting, Md Inst Col Art, 70-; vis artist, La State Univ, Baton Rouge, 75, 78 & 81. *Awards:* Creative Artists Pub Serv Fel, NY State Coun on Arts, 74 & 78; Adolph & Esther Gottlieb Grant, 82 & 89; Guggenheim Grant, 83; Nat Endowment of Arts, 90. *Bibliog:* D Cochrane (auth), Hans Hofmann's students, 3/74 & Tabachnick-lyrical expressionist, 6/74, Am Artist; George Nelson Preston (auth), Against the grain: The paintings of Anne Tabachnick, Arts, 1/79. *Media:* Acrylic, Watercolor. *Dealer:* Erika Meyerovich Gallery 231 Grant Ave San Francisco CA 94108. *Mailing Add:* 463 West St New York NY 10014

TABACK, SIMMS
ILLUSTRATOR, DESIGNER
b New York, NY, Feb 13, 32. *Study:* Cooper Union, BFA; Sch Visual Arts. *Exhib:* Soc Illusr Ann Exhib, 63-86; Art Dir Club Show; Am Inst Graphic Arts; Soc Publ Designers; Type Dir Club. *Teaching:* Instr illus & design, Sch Visual Arts, New York, 67-82. *Awards:* Cert of Merit, Soc Illusr Show & Ten Best Illus Children's Books, New York Times, 67. *Mem:* Soc Illusr; Illusr Guild (pres, 75-76); Graphic Artists Guild (pres, 79-80). *Media:* Pen & Ink; Watercolor. *Publ:* Auth-illusr, Joseph Had a Little Overcoat, Random House, 77; illusr, Fishy Riddles, Dial, 83; Hide & Peek Books, Grosset & Dunlap, 84; On Our Way Books, Harper & Row, 85; Baby Bookstore, Simon & Schuster, 86; Ruggy Riddles, Dial, 86. *Dealer:* Milton Newborn 135 E 54th St New York NY 10022. *Mailing Add:* PO Box 325 Shokan NY 12481

TABAK, CHAIM
PAINTER, SCULPTOR
b Bamberg, Ger, Nov 13, 46, US citizen. *Study:* Brooklyn Col, 70-71; Art Students League New York, cert, 75. *Work:* Brooklyn Mus; Wichita Art Mus, Kans; Weatherspoon Art Gallery, Univ NC. *Exhib:* On Radioactive Waste, Harvard Univ, 77 & Yale Univ, 78; International Printmakers, Snug Harbor Cult Ctr, Staten Island, NY, 82; Artists Protest, Pratt Graphics Ctr, New York, 82; Art and the Law, Landmark Ctr, Minneapolis, 82; HRCA 67th Ann, Hudson River Mus, Yonkers, NY, 82; War & Peace & Art, Rotunda Gallery, Brooklyn, NY, 84; Book Arts, Hand in Hand Gallery Invitational, New York,

85; The Radwaste and Stonehenge Series (with catalog), Wichita Art Mus, Kans, 85, nat tour, 86- *Bibliog:* Anthony S Maulucci (auth), Radioactive waste as a subject of art, New Haven Register, 2/5/78; Nancy Pate (auth), Books are art with a message, Wichita Eagle Beacon, 4/7/85. *Mem:* Ctr Book Arts. *Dealer:* Dorsky Galleries Ltd 58 W 58th St New York NY 10019. *Mailing Add:* 65 Prospect St New Paltz NY 12561

TABASCO, EVANGELINE (SAM WIENER) See Wiener, Sam (Evangeline Tabasco)

TABOR, VIRGINIA S
PAINTER, PRINTMAKER
b Putnam, Conn, Mar 28, 26. *Study:* Bethany Col, BA, 47; Cornell Univ, MA, 50; Pa Acad Fine Arts, 66-70; also critiques with Myron Barnstone, 88-92. *Exhib:* Allentown Art Mus, Pa, 76-84; Newark Mus, NJ, 83; Audubon Artists, New York, 83-86; Kemerer Mus, Bethlehem, Pa, 84 & 87; 49th American Color Prints Soc, 84-87; National Print Exhibition-Hunterton Art Ctr, Clinton, NJ, 84; Boston Printmakers, 87; Provident Nat Bank, Philadelphia, Pa, 87; Philadelphia Art Show, Philadelphia, Pa, 90 & 91. *Teaching:* Vis instr painting & design, Lehigh Univ, fall, 72 & 73; instr painting & drawing, Lehigh County Community Col, 75-84. *Awards:* Pen & Brush Award, Salmagundi Club, New York, 83; Purchase Awards, Printmaking Coun NJ, Red Devil Corp. 83 & 85-87; 1st Place Pastels, Rittenhouse Sq Fine Arts Ann, 92. *Bibliog:* Jill Stewart Narrow (auth), Virginia Tabor-Artist & Printmaker, Theatrical Faces Mag. *Mem:* Lehigh Art Alliance (pres, 78-80); fel Pa Acad Fine Arts; Artists Equity; Philadelphia Watercolor Club. *Media:* Pastel; Silkscreen. *Dealer:* Tabor Studio 46 Covington Pl Catasauqua Pa 18032. *Mailing Add:* 46 Covington Pl Catasauqua PA 18032

TACHA, ATHENA
SCULPTOR, EDUCATOR
b Larissa, Greece, Apr 23, 36; nat US. *Study:* Nat Acad Fine Arts, Athens, MA(sculpture), 59; Oberlin Col, Ohio, MA(art hist), 61; Univ Paris, PhD(aesthetics), 63; Col Wooster, OH, , Hon FA, 90. *Work:* Mus Fine Arts, Houston; Nat Col Fine Arts, Washington, DC; Cleveland Mus Art, Ohio; Allen Art Mus, Oberlin, Ohio; Univ Utah Art Gallery, Salt Lake City. *Comn:* Blair Fountain, Arkansas River, Tulsa, 83; Marianthe, Univ SFla, Ft Myers, 86; Merging, Case Western Reserve Univ, Cleveland, 86; Green Acres, Dept Environ Protection, Trenton, NJ, 87; Connections, Franklin Town Park, Philadelphia, 92. *Exhib:* One-woman shows, Zabriskie Gallery, New York, 79 & 81; Max Hutchinson Gallery, New York, 84; retrospective, High Mus Art, Atlanta, 89; many other exhibs throughout the world, 66- *Pos:* Cur mod art, Allen Art Mus, Oberlin, Ohio, 63-73. *Teaching:* Prof art, Oberlin Col, Ohio, 73- *Awards:* Fel, Ctr Advan Visual Studies, Mass Inst Technol, 74; Artist's Grant, Nat Endowment Arts, 75; Artist's Grant, Ohio Arts Coun, 91. *Bibliog:* Articles, Landscape Architecture, 5/78, Artforum, 1/81, Arts Mag, 10/88. *Mem:* Int Sculpture Asn; Col Art Asn Am (dir, 73-76); Artists' Equity. *Publ:* Auth, Rodin Sculpture, Cleveland Mus Art, 67; Brancusi's Birds, 69; ed, Art in the Mind, 70; auth, Athena Tacha: Public Sculpture, 82; Forms of Chaos: Drawings by Athena Tacha, 88. *Mailing Add:* 291 Forest St Oberlin OH 44074

TACLA, JORGE
PAINTER, MURALIST
b Santiago, Chile, 58. *Study:* Univ de Chile, Santiago, BFA, 79. *Work:* Archer M Huntington Art Gallery, Univ Tex, Austin; High Mus Art, Atlanta; Walker Hill Art Ctr, Seoul, South Korea; ECO Art, Rio de Janeiro, Brazil. *Comn:* Mural, Bronx Housing Ct, Percent Arts, New York, 91-92. *Exhib:* Myth & Magic in the Americas, Museo de Monterrey, Mex, 91; Cruciformed, Ctr Contemp Art & Travel, Cleveland, 91-92; solo exhibs, High Mus, Atlanta, 91 & Lehman Col, Bronx, 92; Migrations, RI Sch Design, Providence, 92; and others. *Awards:* Grant, NY Found Arts, 87 & 91; Grant, J S Guggenheim Found, 88. *Bibliog:* Donald Kuspit (auth), Jorge Tacla: Hemispheric Problem, 91 & Bruce Guenther (auth), Jorge Tacla-Borders, 92, Nohra Haime Gallery; Carrie Pryzbilla (auth), Art on the Edge: Tacla, High Mus Art, 91. *Media:* Oil on Canvas. *Mailing Add:* c/o Nohra Haime Gallery 41 E 57th St Sixth Floor New York NY 10022

TAFT, FRANCES PRINDLE
HISTORIAN, LECTURER
b New Haven, Conn, Dec 12, 21. *Study:* Vassar Col, AB 42; Yale Univ, grad sch, MA 48; with George Heard Hamilton, George Kubler & Sumner McKnight Crosby. *Pos:* Prof art hist 50-, actg dean, Cleveland Inst Art, 73-74. *Teaching:* Chmn liberal arts & instr art survey, 19th & 20th century art, pre-Columbian art, Cleveland Inst Art, 52-; instr, Cleveland Col, Case Western Reserve Univ; freelance lect, 20th century art, archit hist, Primitivism, Pre-Columbian art & European Megaliths. *Mem:* Col Art Asn Am; Western Reserve Archit Historians (pres, 71-72); Art Asn Cleveland; Cleveland Mus Art (prog chmn, 72, trustee, 72-); Womens Coun, Cleveland Mus Art. *Res:* Pre-Columbian art in Mesoamerica & Peru; study of Megaliths of W Europe. *Collection:* Small pre-Columbian collection and collection of painting, sculpture & prints with a focus on Cleveland artists. *Mailing Add:* 6 Pepper Ridge Rd Cleveland OH 44124

TAGGART, WILLIAM JOHN
PAINTER, SCULPTOR
b Buffalo, NY, Aug 8, 40. *Study:* Art Inst Chicago, BFA; Univ NMex, MFA. *Work:* Int Arrivals Bldg, JFK Airport, New York; Installation, Pub Sch 3, New York; Univ NMex, Albuquerque; Art in the Embassies Prog, Bonn, Ger & New Delhi, India; Mus Contemp Art, Chicago. *Comn:* Sculpture, Port Authority, New York, 73. *Exhib:* Whitney Mus Am Art, New York, 74; Off the Wall, Pace Univ, New York, 74; Hokin Gallery, Chicago, 80; Nina Freudenheim Gallery, Buffalo, NY, 81; Betty Parsons Gallery, New York, 81; Appalachian State Univ, Boone, NC, 82; and others. *Pos:* Vis artist, Sch Art Inst Chicago, 78- *Teaching:* Instr printmaking, Cooper Union, New York, 68-71; instr visual fundamentals, York Community Col, 75; instr, Montclair State Col, NJ, 77- *Mailing Add:* 429 Broome 5th Floor New York NY 10013

TAHEDL, ERNESTINE
STAINED GLASS ARTIST, PAINTER
b Vienna, Austria, Oct 10, 40; Can citizen. *Study:* Acad for Appl Arts, Vienna, Austria, with Franz Herbert, MA in Graphic Arts, 61; with Prof Heinrich Tahedl, collab in design & execution of stained glass works, 61-63. *Work:* Paintings represented in public galleries in Vienna, Japan, Montpellier, France, London, Ont & Mus de Que, Can. *Comn:* Stained glass murals, Fed Revenue Bldg, Quebec, Que, 71, Bibliotheque Varennes, Quebec, 81, Greenfield Park Libr, Quebec, 82 & Ctr D'Accueil, St Bruno, Quebec, 82, Annunciation Church, Ottawa, 87, St Peters Church, Toronto, 90; Restoration, Christkoenigs Church, Klagenfurt, Austria, 89-90. *Exhib:* Solo exhibs, J Arends Gallery, Edmonton, Alta, 77-78 & 80-88, Gallery Quan, Toronto, 83-90 & Tudor Collection, Montreal, 83; Third & Fourth Int Print Biennale, Korea, 81 & 83; 15th Int Biennial Graphic Art, Ljubljana, Yugoslavia, 83; Hanga Int Print Exhib, Metrop Mus, Tokyo, Japan, 85-87; 3rd Int Biennal Print Exhib, Taipei, Taiwan. *Pos:* Vpres, Royal Can Acad Arts. *Awards:* Allied Arts Medal, Royal Archit Inst Can, 66; Can Coun Arts Award, 67. *Bibliog:* Guy Robert (auth), Art Actuel au Quebec, Iconia, Quebec, 83; Joel Russ & Lou Lynn (auth), Contemporary Stained Glass, Doubleday, Toronto, 85; Guy Simard (auth), Verriers du Quebec, Ed Broquet, Ottawa, 89. *Mem:* Royal Can Acad Arts; Ont Soc Artists. *Publ:* Ltd ed portfolio etchings, Circle of Energy, Art World Int, 81. *Dealer:* Shayne Gallery 5471 Royalmount Montreal PQ Can; Schieder Assocs Gallery 33 Hazeton Lane Toronto ON. *Mailing Add:* 79 Collard Dr RR One King City ON L0G 1K0 Canada

TAHIR, ABE M, JR
DEALER, CONSULTANT
b Greenwood, Miss, Feb 18, 31. *Study:* Univ Miss, BBA; George Washington Univ, MBA. *Exhib:* With Nothing On: Prints and Drawings of the Nude by American Artists, New Orleans Mus Art, 2-3/90; Gerald L Brockhurst: A Retrospective of Prints and Drawings, New Orleans Mus Art, 9-10/91. *Pos:* Dir, Tahir Fine Arts currently. *Specialty:* Original prints. *Publ:* Auth, Jacques Hnizdovsky, Woodcuts and Etchings, 87. *Mailing Add:* Tahir Fine Arts PO Box 56577 New Orleans LA 70156

TAI, JANE S
ADMINISTRATOR
b Poughkeepsie, NY, May 14, 44. *Study:* Syracuse Univ, BA, 67. *Pos:* Exhib coordr, Everson Mus Art, Syracuse, NY, 67-69; exhib coordr, Am Fedn Arts, New York, 70-75, asst dir, exhib dir, 75-78, assoc dir prog, 78-83, assoc dir & exhib prog dir, 83-87; owner, Tai Assoc, Int Inc, NY, Exhib Serv, currently. *Mailing Add:* 529 E 87th St No 1W New York NY 10128

TAIRA, MASA MORIOKA
DIRECTOR, CURATOR
b Kagoshima City, Japan, Nov 25, 23; US citizen. *Study:* Studio Prog, Honolulu Acad Arts, with Joseph Feher & Ron Kowalke, studied gallery mgt with David Asherman & Tom M Klobe; materials tech, Univ Hawaii Art Dept with Don Dugal; painting with Helen Gilbert & intermediate & adv drawing with Ron Kowalke, Univ Hawaii; Life Drawing with Sara Frankel; Sculpture with Rick Mills & David Landry. *Exhib:* Honolulu Printmakers, Amfac Plaza, Honolulu, Hawaii, 75; Paintings/Drawings, Univ Hawaii-Manoa, Commons Gallery, 89 & 90; Undergrad Show, Univ Hawaii, Manoa Gallery, 89, 90 & 92. *Collections Arranged:* Human Form: From Egypt to the Renaissance, Queen Emma Gallery, 84 & traveling, 84-86; Monouri: Street Vendors of Old Japan, Queen Emma Gallery, 85 & traveling, 86; Kumulipo: Hawaiian Chart of Creation, Visual Perspectives traveling, 88. *Pos:* Founder & chmn, Queen Emma Gallery, Honolulu, 76-85, dir, 85- *Publ:* Auth, Human Form: From Egypt to the Renaissance, Humanities News, 84. *Mailing Add:* Queen Emma Gallery PO Box 861 Honolulu HI 96808

TAIT, WILL(IAM) H
PRINTMAKER, PAINTER
b Edinburgh, Scotland, Apr 1, 42; nat US. *Study:* Art Students League NY, 69-71; San Francisco Art Inst, 74. *Work:* Achenbach Found, Calif Palace Legion Honor, San Francisco. *Exhib:* Northwest Regional, Grants Pass, 76; Berkeley Nat Show, Berkeley Art Ctr, 84; Contemp Prints, Western NMex Univ, Silver City, 84. *Pos:* Coordr, Berkeley Art Ctr, Calif, 83-85. *Teaching:* Instr life drawing, painting, Rogue Community Col, Oreg, 76-77 & Monterey Peninsula Col, Calif, 81-82. *Bibliog:* Feature article, Printing J, Mar/89. *Mem:* Int Soc Art, Sci & Tech. *Media:* All Media. *Dealer:* San Francisco Mus Mod Art Rental Gallery San Francisco CA; Mission Gallery Mission Plaza Carmel CA. *Mailing Add:* c/o San Francisco Mus Mod Art Rental Gallery Bldg A Ft Mason San Francisco CA 94123

TAJIRI, SHINKICHI
SCULPTOR, EDUCATOR
b Los Angeles, Calif, Dec 7, 23. *Study:* Art Inst Chicago, with Ossip Zadkine; with F Leger, Paris; Acad Grande Chaumiere, Paris. *Work:* Stedelijk Mus, Amsterdam; Mus Mod Art, New York; Louisiana, Copenhagen; Boysman Mus, Rotterdam; CNAC, Paris. *Comn:* AKU fountain, 60; Overhand Knot, Schiphol Airport, Amsterdam, 74; Friendship Knot, Los Angeles, 81; Connections, Shell Int, Der Haag, 86- *Exhib:* Stedelijk Mus, 60-67; Venice

Biennial, 62; Andre Emmerich Gallery, New York, 65; Kunsthalle, Basel, Switz, 69; Kunsthalle Lund, Sweden, 71. *Teaching:* Guest prof sculpture, Minneapolis Col Art & Design, 64-65; prof sculpture, Hochschule der Kunste, West Berrlin, Ger, 69- *Awards:* Golden Lion, 8th Int Festival Amateur Films, Cannes, France, 55; Mainichi Shibum Prize for Sculpture, Mainchi Newspapers, Tokyo, 63; Grand Prix, The Wet Dream Film Festival, Amsterdam, 70. *Bibliog:* L Freed (auth), Seltsame Spiele, Barmieyer & Nikel, 69; Tajiri, SDU, 91; Tajiri, ABP, 91. *Publ:* Auth, The Wall, 70; ed, Ferdi, 70; ed, Portrait, Self-portrait & Measurements, 72; and others. *Mailing Add:* Castle Scheres Baarlo Netherlands

TAKACH, MARY H
MUSEUM DIRECTOR, HISTORIAN
b New York, NY. *Study:* State Univ NY Binghamton, BA(art hist & humanities), MA(art hist), 73. *Pos:* Cur, asst prof, asst dir, Joe & Emily Lowe Art Gallery, Syracuse Univ, NY, 74-77; dir special exhib, House on Admin Comt, US House of Representatives, 78; consult humanities adminr, Nat Endowment for Humanities, DC, 78; dir, Pensacola Mus Art, Fla, 80-88. *Teaching:* Asst prof art hist survey & grad mus studies prog, Syracuse Univ, NY, 74-78; adj prof, Univ West Fla, 82-; instr art, Greene, NY, currently. *Awards:* Jennie F Snapp scholar, 70; Ruth Fraizer res scholar, Eng Delta-Kappa Gama Hon Teaching Soc, 74. *Mem:* Col Art Asn; Am Asn Mus; Fla Art Mus Dir Asn. *Res:* Transcribe, annotate and index letters of Benjamin West (1738-1820); catalog raisonne of works by Thomas Doughty. *Publ:* Contribr, Strictly Academic, a Study of Life Drawing in the 19th Century, 74 & Binghamton Collects (exhib catalog), 75, Univ Art Gallery, State Univ Binghamton, NY; The Mural Art of Ben Shahn (exhib catalog), 78, Lowe Art Gallery, Syracuse Univ. *Mailing Add:* 215 Taylor Ave Endicott NY 13760

TAKAL, PETER
PAINTER, PRINTMAKER
b Bucharest, Romania, Dec 8, 05; US citizen. *Study:* Paris, France, largely self-taught. *Work:* Mus Mod Art, Metrop Mus Art & Whitney Mus Am Art, New York; Art Inst, Chicago; Brooklyn Mus; Cleveland Mus Art; Los Angeles Co Mus Art; and in over 100 museums collections in US & abroad. *Comn:* City Roofs (print), 56, Trees & Fields (print), 57, Print Club Cleveland; four prints, Int Graphic Arts Soc, New York, 56-65; Meditation (print), Assoc Am Artists, New York, 58; Of Nature Of Man (suite of 20 lithographs), Tamarind Lithography Workshop, Los Angeles, 64; two prints, Hollander Workshop, New York, 69; and others. *Exhib:* Pa Acad Fine Arts, 53-69; Whitney Mus Am Art Ann, 55-69; Recent Drawings USA, Mus Mod Art, New York, 56; one-man shows, Cleveland Mus Art, 59 & Smithsonian Inst, 59-60; American Prints Today Traveling Exhib, Print Coun Am, 59, 62 & 63; Kestner Mus Hanover Travel Exhib Germ, 61-62; The White House, Washington, DC, 66 & 70; and more than 50 one-man shows in US & abroad, 32-77 & Fiac, Paris (Grand Palais), 86. *Teaching:* Lectr art, Cleveland Mus Art, 58 & Cent Col, 68; artist-in-residence, Beloit Col Mus, 65. *Awards:* Fel, Yaddo Found, 61; Purchase Award, 3rd Nat Print Exhib, Pasadena Art Mus, 62; Ford Fel, Tamarind Lithography Workshop, 63-64; and others. *Bibliog:* Pierre Mornand (auth), Takal portraitiste lineaire evocateur de l'insaisissable, Le Courrier Graphique, 37; Leona E Prasse & Louise Richards (auth), Recent Works of Peter Takal, Cleveland Mus Art, 58; Catalog raisonne, Kresge Art Mus, Mich State Univ, 86; Takal Drawings 1930-1990, Editart, Geneva. *Mem:* Artists Equity Asn New York; Soc Am Graphic Artists; Asn Ind Arts Plastiques; Soc des Peintres, Sculpteub, Architectes Suisses. *Media:* Intaglio, Lithography; Drawing, Painting. *Publ:* Auth, Selected Works of Peter Takal, Drawings & Poems, Int Univ, 45; auth & illusr, Drawings by Peter Takal, New Am Libr, 58; auth, Artist's Proof, Vol 1, No 2; auth, About the Invisible in Art, Wright Art Ctr, Beloit Col, 65; Danses (portfolio 32 drawings), Weber, 92; and others. *Dealer:* Galerie Alain Blondel 4 Ave Aubry Le Boucher 75004 Paris France; Gallery Weber 13 rue de Monthoux CH1201 Geneva Switzerland. *Mailing Add:* 40 Rue du Mole CH1201 Geneva Switzerland

TAKAMORI, AKIO
CERAMIST
b Nobeoka, Miyazaki, Japan, 50. *Study:* Musashino Art Col, Tokyo, Japan, 69-71, Koishiwara-ware, Fukuoka, Japan, 72-74, Kansas City, Art Inst, Mo, BFA, 76; NY State Col Ceramics, Alfred Univ, MFA, 78. *Work:* Carnegie Inst Art Mus, Pittsburgh, Pa; Los Angeles Co Mus, Calif; Victoria & Albert Mus, London; Kansas City Art Inst; Rhode Island Sch Design Mus. *Exhib:* One-person exhibs, Himawari Gallery, Miyazaki, Japan, 80, Garth Clark Gallery, Los Angeles, 83, 85, 88, 90, Garth Clark Gallery, NY, 84, 86, 87, 89, Everson Mus, Syracuse, NY, 89; American Potters Today, Victoria and Albert Mus, London, 86; Smits Collection, Los Angeles County Mus Art, Calif, 87; The Vessel: Studies in Form and Media, Craft & Folk Art Mus, Los Angeles, Calif, 89; American Ceramic Art, The Vessel: 1940 to the Present, Pine Street Lobby Gallery, San Francisco, Calif, 89; Surface and Form, Nat Mus Ceramic Art, Baltimore, Md, 89; Archie Bray Foundation Show, Maveety Gallery, Portland, Ore, 90. *Teaching:* Instr, Sheridan Col Appl Art & Technol, Mississauga, Ont, Can, 81, Emily Carr Col Art, Vancouver, Can, 82, Kansas City Art Inst, Mo, 86, Rhode Island Sch Design, Providence, 86, Univ Wash, Seattle, 88-89; Montana State Univ, Bozeman, 83-84; resident artist, Archie Bray Found, Helena, Mont, 85-87. *Awards:* Fel, Nat Endowment Arts, 86 & 88. *Bibliog:* Andy Nasisse (auth), The battleground of Eros: Akio Takamori, Am Ceramics, 5/1/86; Garth Clark (auth), American Ceramics 1876 to the Present, Abbeville Press, 88; The Book of Cups, Abbeville Press, NY, 90. *Publ:* Auth, Artists at Work, Alaska Northwest Books, 90; Art Random, Ceramic Art: 7 Individuals, Kyoto Shoin, 90; Clay Today, Los Angeles Co Mus Art, 90. *Mailing Add:* 14018 SW 220th St Vashon WA 98070

TAKASHIMA, SHIZUYE VIOLET
ILLUSTRATOR, PAINTER
b Vancouver, BC, June 12, 28. *Study:* Ont Col Art, BA, 53; Fine Arts Inst, San Miguel, Mex (weaving), 65; Pratt Art Ctr Graphic Arts, New York, 66. *Work:* Nat Gallery, Ottawa, Can; Imperial Oil; Can Titanium Pigments Ltd, Montreal; Montreal Standard Publ Co, Montreal; Midland Computer Bldg, Syracuse, NY. *Comn:* Four Posters, Midwestern Regional Libr, Kitchener, Ont, 78. *Exhib:* Hamilton Art Gallery, Ont, 61; Hart House, Univ Toronto, 61; VI Biennial Exhib, Nat Gallery Ottawa, 65; Mystic Circle Traveling Show, Burnaby Art Gallery, 74; five-man show, Montreal Mus Fine Arts, 65; four-man show, Art Gallery Ont, Toronto, 60; one-man shows, Burnaby Art Gallery, BC, 65 & 78 & Japanese Can Cult Ctr, Toronto, 74. *Pos:* Assoc ed, Rika Mag, 76-79, Inner City Angels, Toronto, 79-84. *Teaching:* Instr drawing & painting, Forest Hill Learning Resources, 71 & Ont Col Art, Toronto, 76- *Awards:* Can Coun Grant, 71 & 73; Bronze Award, Can Asn Children's Libr Asn, 72; Sankai Shinbun Ann Literary Award, Tokyo, 74; VI Premio Europeo di Litteratura Gioranite Award, Padua, Italy, 76. *Bibliog:* Robin Mathews (auth), Young Artists, Can Forum, 61; David P Silcox (auth), Young Artists, Can Art Mag, 62. *Media:* Oils, Watercolor. *Publ:* A Child in Prison Camp, Tundra Books, Montreal, 71; Illusr, Watercolors: Kenji and the Cricket, Adele Wiseman Porcupine & Quill Inc, 88. *Dealer:* Gallery House Sol Georgetown ON Can. *Mailing Add:* 21 Raglan Ave Toronto ON M6C 2K7 Canada

TAKEMOTO, HENRY TADAAKI
CRAFTSMAN, SCULPTOR
b Honolulu, Hawaii, July 23, 30. *Study:* Univ Hawaii, BFA; Los Angeles Co Art Inst, MFA. *Work:* Smithsonian Inst. *Exhib:* Int Exhib Contemp Ceramics, Ostend, Belg, 59; 3rd Int Exhib Contemp Ceramics, Prague, Czech, 62; Studio Potter Exhib, Victoria & Albert Mus, London, Eng, 66-70; Objects: USA, Johnson Wax Collection Contemp Crafts, Smithsonian Inst, Washington, DC, 70-73; Contemp Ceramic Art, US, Can, Mex, Japan, 71-72. *Pos:* Designer & glaze chemist, Wedgewood of Eng, 69- *Teaching:* Instr ceramics, Calif Sch Fine Arts, San Francisco, formerly; instr ceramics, Scripps Col, 65-69; instr ceramics, Otis Art Inst, formerly. *Awards:* Double Purchase Prize, Wichita Art Asn, 59; Silver Medal for Sculpture, Ostend, Belg, 59; Bronze Medal, Mus Contemp Crafts, NY, 60; and others. *Media:* Ceramics. *Mailing Add:* 3209 Landa St Los Angeles CA 90039

TALABA, L (LINDA TALABA CUMMENS)
SCULPTOR, PRINTMAKER
b Detroit, Mich, July 15, 43. *Study:* Detroit Inst Technol, with Maxwell Wright; pvt instr with Lois Pety; Ill Wesleyan Univ, with Fred Brian, BFA; Southern Ill Univ, with David Folkman & Lewis Brent Kinston, MFA. *Work:* Henry Ford Found Print Collection, Detroit; Can Arts Coun; Albion Univ Print Collection; Leopold Schepp Found Collection, New York; Detroit Art Inst Rental Collection; St John's Univ Prints; and others. *Comn:* Painting, Waterford Twp Bd Educ, 61; Isaac E Crary Jr High Sch, 63; Burton Title & Abstract Co, Detroit, 67; bronze door ornaments, Little Grassy Mus, Southern Ill Univ, 70; bronze sculpture, Dir & Bur Budget, State of Ill, Springfield, 75; and other comn by individuals. *Exhib:* Libr of Cong Print Show, 65; Ball State Nat Drawing & Small Sculpture Exhib, 65; one-woman shows, Renee Gallery, Detroit, 68, Lewis Towers Gallery, Loyola Univ, 75 & Deerfield Courts Gallery, 84-85; Western Ill Univ, Macomb, 79; NShore Art, 80; Rotunda City Hall, Highland Park, 85; Cook Mem Libr Gallery, 88; Kraft Co Gallery, 89. *Pos:* Dir, sch art, Suburban Fine Art Ctr, 84-85. *Teaching:* Guest artist, sculpture, Springfield Art Asn, 74-78, Sangamon State Univ, 75-78, Col Lake Co, 80-85, Suburban Fine Art Ctr, Highland Park, Ill, 83-86, Dist #113 Continuing Educ, 83-; art fac, Park Dist Highland Park, 86- *Awards:* The Intimate Eye, Artemesia Gallery, 88; Beacon St Gallery, Chicago Women's Caucus Award, 90, Northern Ill Art Mus, 90-91; Recent Works Award, Col Lake Co, 91. *Mem:* NShore Art League; and others; Am Asn Univ Women (co-vpres, 86-); Art Inst Chicago; Chicago Artists Coalition; and others. *Media:* Bronze; Graphics, Handmade Paper. *Publ:* Illusr, Lakeland's Paradise, Bd Educ Oakland Co, Pontiac, Mich, 61; art ed, The Argus Newspaper, 62 & illusr, The Black Book (literary mag), 63-65, Ill Wesleyan Univ; illusr, Experimental Math Books, Cent Mid-Western Regional Educ Labs, 70; illusr & co-auth, Helping Your Doctor - A Children's self- Healing Guide, 84. *Mailing Add:* 1316 Oxford Rd Deerfield IL 60015

TALBERT, RICHARD HARRISON
PAINTER, ENVIRONMENTAL ARTIST
b Rockville Centre, NY, Apr 23, 57. *Study:* RI Sch Design, 75-77; Sarah Lawrence Col, BA(philos), 80; Inst for Archit & Urban Studies, 82-83; Univ Cambridge, cert, 86; Univ Miami, BA(archit), 92, MA(archit), 93. *Work:* Dana Roth Collection, Ft Lauderdale, Fla; Susie & Robert Lafer Collection, New York; Hyundai Motor Co, Seoul, Korea; Robert Scull Collection, New York; Michael & Katherine Karolyi Mus Collection, Vence, France. *Comn:* Papering the Walls (acrylic painting), City Without Walls Mus, Newark, NJ, 84; City Scapes Mural, Hoboken Arts Coun, NJ, 84; Water Tower Mural, 85, Banners, 85, Karolyi Found, Vence, France; mixed media/oil on canvas/neon, Mrs Dana Roth, Ft Lauderdale, Fla, 90. *Exhib:* Solo exhibs, Michael Karolyi Found, Vence, France, 85, Esta Robinson Gallery, New York, 86, Gallery des Artiste, West Palm Beach, Fla, 90, Bonwit Teller's Atrium Gallery, Bal Harbor, Fla, 90 & La Gallerie Presidence, Bordeaux, France, 91; Summer Exhibition, Royal Acad Arts Mus, London, Eng, 86; Image Gallery, Stockbridge, Mass, 89; Berkshire Artisans, Pittsfield, Mass, 91. *Teaching:* Asst to Vincent Scully, hist of archit, Univ Miami, 92. *Awards:* Jane B W Whitney Award, Whitney Found, NY, 78; Michael Karolyi Fel, Karolyi Found, Vence, France, 85; Hon Travel Fel, Kettle's Yard Art Gallery, Univ Cambridge, Eng, 85. *Mem:* NY Artist Equity. *Publ:* Auth, Art on Madison Avenue, Art Speak, 83; article in Views, RI Sch Design, 90. *Mailing Add:* 410 W End Ave New York NY 10024

TALBOT, JAROLD DEAN
PAINTER, DIRECTOR
b Solano, NMex, Aug 28, 07. *Study:* Tiffany Found, 37; Cumming Sch of Art, Des Moines, Iowa; Grand Cent Sch of Art, New York; studied with Edmund Greacen, Ivan Olinsky, Keith Shaw Williams; Millikin Univ, AB, 51. *Work:* Iowa State Hist Bldg-36; Works Progress Admin Art Proj, 36-42. *Exhib:* Nat Acad Design, 38; Audubon Artists, New York, 48; Ohio Valley Oil & Water Color Show, Cincinnati, 54; Interior Valley Show, Cincinnati Art Mus, 58; Ann Exhib, Ill State Mus, Springfield, 59; 14th Ann Exhib, N Miss Valley Artists, 60. *Collections Arranged:* Ann Exhib Cent Ill Artists, 48-60; Tri-State Exhib of Painting & Sculpture, 60-63 & Nat WVa Centennial Exhib of Painting & Sculpture, 63, Huntington Galleries; Ann Exhib New Mexico Artists, Mus of Fine Arts, Santa Fe, 63; Photo Show, Orange Co, New York Hist Churches, 66-67. *Pos:* Dir, Decatur Art Ctr, Ill, 47-60, Huntington Galleries, WVa, 60-63, assoc dir, Fine Arts Gallery, Mus Fine Art, Santa Fe, NMex, 63, dir, Smith Clove Mus Folk-life, Monroe, NY, 64-71; cur, Hill-Stead Mus, Farmington, Conn, 72-82, retired. *Teaching:* Instr art, Bradley Univ, Peoria, Ill, 46; asst prof art, ceramics, Millikin Univ, Decatur, Ill, 46-60. *Awards:* Fourth Award, Iowa State Fair, 36; First Award, All Iowa Exhib, 37. *Mem:* Am Asn Mus; Nat Trust Hist Preserv. *Media:* Oil. *Mailing Add:* 24 Main St PO Box 123 Monson MA 01057

TALBOT, JONATHAN
PAINTER, COLLAGE ARTIST
b New York, NY, Nov 14, 39. *Study:* Brandeis Univ; New Sch Social Res; San Francisco Acad Art. *Work:* Smith Col Mus, Northampton, Mass; Byer Mus Arts, Evanston, Ill; Everhart Mus, Scranton, Pa; Toronto Cent Libr, Ont; Newark Mus, NJ; and others. *Exhib:* Museum Managerie, Mus Mod Art, New York, 76; Nat Acad Ann, New York, 81 & 82; The World of Jonathan Talbot, Byer Mus Arts, Evanston, Ill, 84; Surrealism After Surrealism, Ark Arts Ctr, Little Rock, Ark, 86; Recent American Works on Paper, Smithsonian Inst Traveling Exhib Serv, 85-87; The Humanist Icon, Bayly Art Mus, Univ Va, Charlottesville, NY Academy Art, New York & Ulrich Mus Art, Wichita, Kans, 90; solo exhib, Res & Devel, Gallery Contemp Art, Sacred Heart Univ, Fairfield, Conn, 90; and others. *Awards:* Ranger Fund Purchase Award, Nat Acad, 82; Audubon Artists Award, 41st Ann Exhib, Nat Arts Club, 83; C R Gibson Award, Art of Northeast USA, 83; and others. *Bibliog:* Amy Goldberger (auth) Collage of conscience, Orange Mag, 89. *Dealer:* Gimpel/Weitzenhoffer Gallery 415 W Broadway New York NY 10012. *Mailing Add:* 7 Amity Rd Warwick NY 10990

TALLEY, DAN R
CURATOR, WRITER
b Hogansville, Ga, Jan 6, 51. *Study:* Atlanta Col Art, BFA, 73; Univ Hartford, MFA(art), 76. *Pos:* Asst ed, Contemp Art-Southeast, Atlanta, 76-77; ed, Art Papers, 79-82; gallery dir, Contemp Art Ctr, Atlanta, 87-89; visual arts initiative, Forum Gallery, Jamestown, NY, 89-91, dir, 91- *Teaching:* Issues in contemp art, Jamestown Community Col, 92- *Bibliog:* Catherine Fox (auth), Nexus gallery's director, Dan Talley, hopes to define its role in art world, 5/24/87 & Talley trades Nexus job for NY arts spot, 4/29/87, Atlanta J & Consitution. *Publ:* Auth, Kimberly Burleigh: Recent Works, 3/90 & Aging: The Process, the Perception, Forum Gallery Publ, 8/90; Elegy: An Intuitive Chronicle of War, Review, Art Papers, Atlanta, Ga; and others. *Mailing Add:* 9 Falconer St Jamestown NY 14701

TAMBURINE, JEAN HELEN
PAINTER, SCULPTOR
b Meriden, Conn, Feb 20, 30. *Study:* Traphagen Sch, New York, 48-49; Art Students League, New York, with Jon Corbino & John Groth, 48-50; also with Elizabeth Gordon Chandler. *Work:* Middletown Pub Libr & State Libr, Middletown, Conn; Nashville Pub Libr, Tenn; Strong Sch, Hartford, Conn; and others. *Comn:* Heritage (bronze sculpture), Wallingford Pub Libr, 86. *Exhib:* Town & Country Club Exhib, West Hartford, Conn, 69; George Walter Vincent Smith Art Mus, Springfield, Mass; one-woman show, L'Heure Joyeux, Paris, France, 69; Pearl S Buck Found Exhib, Meriden Pub Libr, 72; Ellsworth Gallery, Simsbury, Conn, 76; and others. *Pos:* Comnr, Conn Comn on Arts, State Conn, 63-65; chmn & organizer, Cult Comn for Art Appointments to Pub Bldg, 66-70. *Awards:* Founders Prize, Pen & Brush, New York, 81; Asn Members Prize, Academic Artists Asn, Inc, Springfield, Mass, 81; Martha Moore Mem Award for Excellence in Portrait, Rockport Art Asn, 83. *Mem:* Acad Artists Asn; Rockport Art Asn, Mass; Am Artists Prof League; Salmagundi Club; Guild Boston Artists; Am Medallic Sculpture Asn. *Publ:* Auth & illusr, How Now, Brown Cow, Abington Press, 67; illusr, It's Nice To Be Little, Rand-McNally, 65; The Complete Peddlers Pack, Univ Tenn Press, 67; Something Was Missing, Follett, 69; Five Busy Bears, Rand-McNally, 69; and others. *Mailing Add:* c/o The Bertolli Studio 73 Reynolds Dr Meriden CT 06450

TANCOCK, JOHN LEON
ADMINISTRATOR, HISTORIAN
b London, Eng, June 11, 42. *Study:* Downing Col, Cambridge Univ, Eng, MA, 63; Courtauld Inst Art, Univ London, PhD, 77. *Collections Arranged:* Multiples the First Decade (auth, catalog), Philadelphia Mus Art, 71. *Pos:* Assoc cur, Philadelphia Mus Art, 67-73; head dept contemp art, Sotheby Parke Bernet, 73-76, dir dept impressionist & mod painting, 78-, worldwide dir scholar & res, 91- *Publ:* Auth, The influence of Marcel Duchamp, In: Marcel Duchamp, Philadelphia Mus Art & Mus Mod Art, New York, 73-74; The Sculpture of Auguste Rodin, Philadelphia Mus Art & David Godine, 76. *Mailing Add:* c/o Sotheby's 1334 York Ave New York NY 10021

TANGER, SUSANNA
PAINTER, WRITER
b Boston, Mass, June 9, 42. *Study:* Boston Mus Sch; Univ Colo; Univ Calif, Berkeley. *Exhib:* Post Washington NY Cent Hall Gallery, 75; City of Paris Mus Mod Art, 75; PS 1, New York, 76; Hal Bromm Gallery, New York, 76; Galerie Rencontres, Paris, France, 76; Moore Col of Art Gallery, Philadelphia, 77; and others. *Mailing Add:* 141 Wooster St No 8C New York NY 10012

TANGREDI, VINCENT
SCULPTOR
b Compobasso, Italy, May 15, 50. *Study:* Ont Col Art, Toronto, AOCA, 73. *Work:* Can Coun Art Bank, Ottawa; Art Gallery Ont; Nat Gallery Can; York Univ, Downsview, Ont. *Exhib:* Information and Perception, Art Gallery Ont, 72; solo shows, Carmen Lamanna Gallery, Toronto, 75-80, 82-83 & 86; Transparent Things, Vancouver Art Gallery, 76; Nine Canadian Artists, Kunsthalle, Basel, Switz, 78; 49th Parallel, NY, 84; Project Studios One, New York, 84; Fifth Biennale of Syndey, Art Gallery New South Wales, Australia, 84; Toronto Painting, Travelling Exhib, 84; MacDonald Stewart Art Ctr, Guelph, Ont, 85; Thomas Barry Fine Arts, Minneapolis, Minn, 85. *Awards:* Grants, Ont Art Coun, 74-78 & Can Coun, 76, 78, 79 & 83. *Bibliog:* Walter Klepac (auth), article, Artscanada, 75. *Publ:* Contrib ed, Impulse Mag, Vol V, No 3, 77. *Mailing Add:* 3 MacDonell Toronto ON M6R 2A3 Canada

TANKSLEY, ANN
PAINTER, PRINTMAKER
b Pittsburgh, Pa, Jan 25, 34. *Study:* Carnegie Inst Technol, with Samuel Rosenberg & Balcomb Green, BFA; Art Students League, with Norman Lewis; New Sch Social Res, with Robert Conover; Bob Blackburn Printmaking Workshop. *Work:* Johnson Publ Co, Chicago; Studio Mus In Harlem, New York; Sewickley Acad, Pa; Duquesne Light Co of Pittsburgh; Medgar Evers Col, New York; Nat Mus of Women in the Arts, Washington, DC. *Comn:* Book cover, The Stretch of a Satisfied Soul by Gavin Moses, Zeitgeist Press, Calif, 90; poster image, Visions Gallery, Pa, 90. *Exhib:* Solo exhibs, Black Hist Mus, 72, Acts of Art, New York, 73-74, Dorsey Gallery, 86, Campbell Gallery, Sewickley, Pa, 87, Jamaica Arts Ctr, New York, 87, Spiral Gallery, New York, 88 & Isobel Neal Gallery, Chicago, Ill, 90; Carnegie Inst, Pa; Queens Mus, NY; Hudson River Mus, Yonkers, NY; Salmagundi Club, New York; Am Women in Art, Nairobi, Kenya; Indianapolis Mus Art; Langston Hughes Libr, Queens, NY; Christie's, New York; Savacou Galleries, New York. *Pos:* Consult, NY State Coun Arts. *Teaching:* Adj art instr, Suffolk Co Community Col, 73-75. *Awards:* Harlem Cult Coun Grant, 81. *Bibliog:* Elton C Fax (auth), Black Artists of the New Generation, Dodd, Mead & Co, 77; Grace Glueck (auth), Women artists 80, Art News, 10/80; Palmer & Poroner (auths), Art to illustrate man's kinship to nature, Art Speak, 5/27/82; Jean Bryant (auth), Standing out, Pittsburgh Press, 2/87; Clara Heron (auth), In Celebration of Black History, Pittsburgh Post Gazette, 2/5/87; Arna Alexander Bontemps Stephenson (auth), Forever Free: Art by African-American Women, 1862-1980. *Mem:* Artists Equity Asn. *Media:* Oil, Charcoal. *Dealer:* Cinque Gallery 560 Broadway 5th Floor New York NY 10012; Isobel Neal Gallery 200 West Superior Chicago IL 60610. *Mailing Add:* c/o California College of Arts & Crafts 5212 Broadway Oakland CA 94618

TANNENBAUM, BARBARA LEE
CURATOR, HISTORIAN
b Chicago, Ill, Aug 15, 52. *Study:* Reed Col, Portland, Ore, BA, 75; Univ Mich, Ann Arbor, MA, 77. *Collections Arranged:* The Art of Seymour Rosofsky, KrannertArt Mus, Champaign-Urbana, Ill, 84 & Cultural Ctr, Chicago, Ill, 85; Hollis Sigler, Akron Art Mus & Cult Ctr, Chicago, 87; SeeTV: An Exhibition of Video Art, Akron Art Mus, 87; Aminah Robinson: Painting and Sculpture, 87, Susan Shie: Diary Quilts, 87, Ohio Perspectives: New Work in Clay, Glass, Textiles and Metals (auth, catalog), 88 & The Cuyahoga Valley: Photographs by Robert Glenn Ketchem (travelling exhib), 89, Akron Art Mus catalog), Akron Art Mus, 88-89; Ralph Eugene Meatyard: An American Visionary (co-cur), Akron Art Mus, San Francisco Mus Mod Art & traveling, 91. *Pos:* Cur, Seymour Rosofsky Mem Found, 81-85 & Akron Art Mus, 85- *Teaching:* Vis instr art hist, Univ Ill, Chicago, 82; vis prof art hist, Univ Wyo, Laramie, 83; inst art hist, Oberlin Col, Ohio, 83-85; NE Ohio Univ Col Med, 88- *Awards:* Danforth Postbaccalaureate Fel, 79; Marion Talbot Endowed Fel, Am Asn Univ Women, 80; Henry Luce Found Grant, Univ Mich, 88. *Mem:* Am Asn Mus; Col Art Asn; Women's Caucus Art. *Res:* Contemporary art, photography. *Publ:* Auth, Politics, economics and personality as media: the art of the Christos, Nat Arts Guide, 80; ed, The Edwin C Shaw Collection of American Impressionist and Tonalist Painting, Akron Art Mus, 86; The soul cannot exist without the body: contemporary artists' books, In: Artists' books-Illinois: A Travelling Exhibition, 87; Balancing opposites: the imagism of Seymour Rosofsky, In: Seymour Rosofsky and the Chicago Imagist Tradition, Mus Art, Univ Wis, Milwaukee, 88; ed & contribr, Ralph Eugene Meatyard: An American Visionary. *Mailing Add:* c/o Akron Art Mus 70 E Market Akron OH 44308

TANNENBAUM, JUDITH E
CURATOR, CRITIC
b Bronx, NY, Oct 26, 44. *Study:* Douglass Col, Rutgers Univ, New Brunswick, NJ, BA(Eng), 66; Hunter Col, City Univ New York, MA(art hist), 73. *Collections Arranged:* Concept, Narrative, Document: Recent Photographic Works from the Morton Neumann Family Collection & Three Dimensional Painting, Mus Contemp Art, Chicago; Landscape in Sculpture, Day In/Day Out: Ordinary Life as a Source for Art, Art in Public Places & The Ceramics of Betty Woodman (auth, catalog), 81, Freedman Gallery, Albright Col; Peter

Campus: Selected Works 1973-1987, Investigations, 86-89, Innst Contemp Art, Philadelphia. *Pos:* Ed-in-chief, Noyes Art Books, New York, 75-77; acting cur, Mus Contemp Art, Chicago, 78-79; contrib ed, Arts Mag, New York, 73-81; dir, Freedman Gallery, Albright Col, Reading, Pa, 81-86; asst dir, Inst of Contemp Art, Univ of Pa, 86- *Mem:* Col Art Asn Am. *Res:* European and American modern and contemporary art. *Publ:* Auth, Ilya Bolotowsky, 74, Arts Mag; auth, Blythe Bohnen: The kinesthetic of form, 77, Arts Mag; ed, New York Art Yearbook, Noyes Art Books, 76; contribr, Handbook of the Guggenheim Museum Collection, S R Guggenheim Mus, New York, 80. *Mailing Add:* Inst Contemp Art, Univ Pa 36th & Samson Sts Philadelphia PA 19104

TANNER, JAMES L
CRAFTSMAN
b Jacksonville, Fla, July 22, 41. *Study:* Fla A&M Univ, BA, 64; Aspen Sch Contemp Art, summer 64; Univ Wis-Madison, MS, 66, MFA, 67; also studied with Harvey Littleton, Donald Reitz, Hal Lotterman & Amos White. *Work:* Del Mus Art, Wilmington; St Paul Companies, Minn; Ray & Lee Grover Antiques, Inc, Cleveland, Ohio; North Hennepin State Jr Col, Minneapolis; Mus Contemp Crafts, New York; Everson Mus, Syracuse, NY; Moukinha Mus Leningrad, USSR. *Exhib:* Objects USA, circulated by Smithsonian Inst, 69-70; Glass 2000 BC-1971 AD, John Michael Kohler Art Ctr, Sheboygan, Wis, 71; Reflections on Glass, Long Beach Mus Art, 71-72; Brooks Mem Art Gallery, Memphis, Tenn, 79; East West, Calif Afro-Am Mus, Los Angeles, 86; 10th Anniversary Exhib, Minneapolis Inst Art, 86; Maurine Littleton Gallery Ceramic Invitational, Washington, DC, 86; Eloquent Object, Philbrook Mus Art, Tulsa, Okla, 87; 44th Ceramics Ann, Galleries Claremont Col, Claremont, Calif, 88; Craft Today/USA, Am Craft Mus, NY, traveling Europe, 89; The Clay Studio, Philadelphia, PA, 89; 28th Ceramic Nat Exhib, Everson Mus, NY, 90; Figures in Ceramics, La State Univ, Baton Rouge, 90; SDak Art Mus, Brookings, 90. *Teaching:* Prof art ceramics, Mankato State Univ, Minn, 68- *Awards:* Visual Artist Fel Grant, NEA, 84; Sculpture Award, Int Festival Des Saint Germain Des Pres, New York, 80; Minn State Arts Bd Individual Artist Grant, 80. *Bibliog:* Lee Nordness (auth), Objects USA, 70; Ray Grover & Lee Grover (coauth), Contemporary Art Glass, Crown Publ Co Inc, 75; Paul Donhauser (auth), The History of American Ceramics--Studio Potter, W C Brown, Kendall/Hunt Publ, 78. *Mem:* Nat Coun Educ Ceramic Arts; Am Craftsman Coun; Minn Craftsman Coun (bd dirs, 72-77). *Media:* Ceramics. *Dealer:* Maurine Littleton Gallery 3222 N St NW Georgetown Ct Wash DC 20007. *Mailing Add:* Rte 3 Box 189 Janesville MN 56048

TAPER, GERI
PAINTER, ENVIRONMENTAL ARTIST
b Pittsburgh, Pa, Dec 5, 29. *Study:* Carnegie Mus Sch, 37-47; Univ Pittsburgh, BS, (summa cum laude), 51; Carnegie-Mellon Grad Studies, 70-72. *Work:* Allentown Mus Art, Pa; Carnegie Mus Art, Pittsburgh; Pittsburgh Nat Bank; Chase Manhattan Bank & Citibank NAm, New York. *Comn:* The Seasons, Pittsburgh Nat Bank, 73; Dancers (triptych), Carnegie Libr, Pittsburgh, 74; Lobby, 401 N Broad Bldg, Philadelphia, 81; Public Spaces, Ctr Bldg, New York, 85; interior & exterior art work, Redstone Bldg, New York, 86; The Falchi Bldg, NY, 87-90; creator of banner sculpture, Colorfield, MTA Transit Prog, NY, 89; Celebrating the Boroughs Van Project, Bronx Community Col, NY, 90; Seniors Early Childhood Mural, Sunnyside Communicty Childhood Ctr, NY, 91. *Exhib:* Westmoreland Mus, Greensburg, Pa, 73-75; William Penn Mem Mus, Harrisburg, Pa, 75; Springfield Art Mus, Mo, 75; solo exhibs, Carnegie Mus Art, Pittsburgh, 76, Movement in Space and Time, 5-year retrospective, New York, 82, Sculpted Paintings Accessible to the Blind and Visually Impaired, New York, 84, Space, Time and Infinity, 20-year retrospective, 1971-1991, New York, 91; Bicentennial Invitational, Madden Galleries, London, 76; Nancy Poole Internatinal Exchange, Toronto, 79; Grey Art Gallery Invitational, New York, 81; and others. *Pos:* Artist in residence, Indust Complexes, Long Island City, NY, 80-90. *Teaching:* Instr adult educ, Univ Pittsburgh, 69-70; instr, Duquesne Univ, 71-72 & Laroche Col, 72-73; community educator handicapped audiences, Metrop Mus Art, NY, 84; environ art teacher in community, NY, 86-90. *Awards:* Carnegie Mus Friends of Art Award, 72; Juror's Award, Carnegie Mus Art, 76; Alcoa Corp Award, 76. *Bibliog:* Harry Schwalb (auth), Taking it to New York, 8/77 & New York, New York, 6/82, Pittsburgher Mag; Rachel Chodorov (auth), Geri Taper, Arts Mag, 2/82. *Mem:* Found Community Artists New York; Artists Equity, New York; charter mem Nat Mus Women in the Arts, Washington, DC. *Media:* Acrylic, All. *Dealer:* Harold Hart 156 W 86th St New York NY 10024. *Mailing Add:* 458 Broome St New York NY 10013

TARADASH, MERYL
ENVIRONMENTAL ARTIST, KINETIC ARTIST
b Passaic, NJ, Jan 25, 53. *Study:* Conn Col, New London, 70-71; Pratt Inst, New York, BFA, 74, MFA, 78. *Work:* Newark Mus, NJ; Colgate-Palmolive Co, New York; AT&T Longlines, Bedminister, NJ; Bellevue Hosp Ctr, New York; NY State Legislature, Albany. *Comn:* Light Dance, suspended installation, State NJ, Rutgers Med Sch, 84; Frozen Rain Series, suspended installation, David Bermant Hamden Plaza, Conn, 88; Waves, suspended installation, ARA Servs Inc, Philadelphia, 89; Wind Dancing, (wind-driven Outdoor Sculpture), David Bermant Found, Santa Barbara, Calif, 92. *Exhib:* Group Fac Exhib, Montclair Art Mus, NJ, 78; solo exhib, Sounds of the Environment, Newark Mus, NJ, 79; NJ Arts Inclusion Program 1978-84, Rutgers Univ, New Brunswick, NJ, 85; Ornaments, New Mus Contemp Art, New York, 86; Stalking the Light, Noyes Mus, Oceanville, NJ, 87; Personal Patterns, Elaine Benson Gallery, Bridgehampton, NY, 89; Kinetic Sculpture Show, Hastings Gallery, Hastings-on- Hudson, NY, 90-91. *Teaching:* Vis specialist contemp art, Montclair State Col, NJ, 88 & life drawing I-IV, 89 & art & civilization I, 90. *Awards:* Ford Found Grant, 78; Post-Production Video Funds for Documentary Light Dance, NJ State Coun Arts, 85; Fel Panelist Sculpture, NJ State Coun Arts, 92. *Bibliog:* Vivien Raynor (auth), Art from state buildings, New York Times, 85; Kent Kiser (auth), Commissions, Int Sculpture, 86; Jessica Althoz (auth), Commissions, Sculpture Mag, 88. *Mem:* Int Sculpture Ctr; Col Art Asn. *Media:* Acrylic & Aluminum Prisms, Reflected Light. *Dealer:* Gallery Henoch 80 Wooster St New York NY 10012. *Mailing Add:* 503-511 Broadway New York NY 10012

TARBELL, ROBERTA KUPFRIAN
HISTORIAN, CURATOR
b Mineola, NY, Jan 6, 44. *Study:* Cornell Univ, Ithaca, NY, BS, 65; Univ Del, Newark, MA, 68, PhD, 76. *Collections Arranged:* Early Paintings by Marguerite Zorach (auth, catalog), Smithsonian Inst, 73; Peggy Bacon: Personalities and Places (co-auth, catalog), Smithsonian Inst, 75; Chaim Gross (auth, catalog), 77; Vanguard American Sculpture (coauth, catalog), Rutgers Univ Art Gallery, 79; Figurative Tradition (coauth, catalog), Whitney Mus Am Art, 80; Hugo Robus (auth, catalog), Smithsonian Inst, 80; Ezekiel's Vision (coauth, catalog), 85. *Pos:* Research assoc, Nat Mus Am Art, Smithsonian Inst, 74-80; guest cur, Jewish Mus, 76-77, NY & Philadelphia, 85; guest cur, Whitney Mus Am Art, Rutgers Univ Art Gallery & Farnsworth Art Gallery, 79-80; adj prof art hist, Winterhur Mus, 86- *Teaching:* Asst prof Am art, Univ Del, 76, vis assoc prof Am & modern art, 79-84; asst prof art hist, Rutgers Univ, 84-90, assoc prof art hist, 90- & actg chair art dept, 90-92. *Awards:* John Sloan Mem Res Grant, 83 & 90; Res Grant, Rutgers Univ, 85-; Smithsonian Inst Post-Doctoral Fel, 89; and others. *Mem:* Col Art Asn; Soc Archit Historians. *Res:* Twentieth century American art; modern sculpture. *Publ:* Ed & coauth, Walt Whitman and the Visual Arts, Rutgers Univ Press, 92. *Mailing Add:* 628 Montgomery Woods Dr Hockessin DE 19707

TARBET, URANIA CHRISTY
PAINTER, INSTRUCTOR
b Dec 19, 31. *Study:* Pasadena Col, 78; Otis Art Inst, 79-81; Sergei Bongart Sch Art, 81-83. *Work:* Loomis, Sayles Co Inc, Pasadena, Calif; South Gate Art Asn Collection, Calif. *Comn:* Watercolor & ink painting (floral), comn by Florance Knerr, Whamo Corp, Arcadia, Calif, 85; pastel painting/landscape, comn by Mr & Mrs Brent Howell, Grants Pass, Ore, 89; pastel portraits, comn by Mr Lyn Nofziger, communication dir to Pres Reagan, Washington, DC, 90; pastel floral painting, comn by Ms M Burton, Casablanca Fan Corp, Newport Beach, Calif, 92. *Exhib:* Society of Western Artists, Rosecrusian Mus, San Jose, Calif, 87; Pastel Society of America, Ashland Art Mus, Ky, 90; Pastel Society of America, Quincey Art Mus, Ill, 90; Degas Pastel Society, Lauren-Rogers Mus Art, Laurel, Miss, 90; Women Artists of the West, Chinese Cultural Mus, Visallia, Calif, 92; and others. *Pos:* Co-founder & vpres, Pastel Soc West Coast, 84-85; pres & founder, Cassatt Pastel Soc/A Nat Soc Prof Artists, 88-90. *Teaching:* Instr oil, pastel, art marketing, art workshops throughout US, Mex & Europe, 83-92; instr oil, pastel, St Mary's Art Ctr, 91-92. *Awards:* Neva Rall Mem, Soc Western Artists, 87; Award Excellence, Degas Pastel Soc, 90; Pastel Award Excellence, Women Artists West, Ben Konis, 91. *Bibliog:* Dan Lombard (auth), Artist profile, Designer's Illus, 5-6/92; Carole Katchen (auth), Deepen the power of pastel, Artist Mag, 6/92. *Mem:* Otis Art Inst Alumni; Pastel Soc Am; Cassatt Pastel Soc Prof Artist (pres, 88-90); Pastel Soc Can; Nat League Am Pen Women (vpres, 92). *Media:* Pastel, Oil. *Publ:* Auth, One artist's experience, Am Artist Mag, 7/89. *Mailing Add:* Lazy UB Ranch Box 1032 Diamond Springs CA 95619

TARBOX, GURDON LUCIUS, JR
MUSEUM DIRECTOR, ADMINISTRATOR
b Plainfield, NJ, Dec 25, 27. *Study:* Mich State Col, BS, 52; Purdue Univ, MS, 54. *Pos:* Trustee, Brookgreen Gardens, Murrells Inlet, SC, 59-, dir, 63 & pres, 90. *Publ:* Contribr, A Century of American Sculpture - Treasures of Brookgreen Gardens, Abbeville Press, 81. *Mailing Add:* Brookgreen Gardens US Hwy 17 S Murrells Inlet SC 29576

TARDO, (MANUEL) RODULFO
SCULPTOR
b Matanzas, Cuba, Feb 18, 19; US citizen. *Study:* Nat Fine Arts Sch, Havana, Cuba, prof(sculpture & drawing); Clay Club & Art Students League, scholar. *Work:* Nat Mus Cuba; Sch Archit, Havana; Sch Pedagogy, Havana Univ; Art Gallery Matanzas; Cathedral of St John the Divine, New York. *Comn:* Eagles, Califano Mansion, Glen Cove, NY, 70; bust, Mother Cabrini Park, Newark, NJ, 75; image, Nat Shrine of Immaculate Conception, Washington, DC, 75-76; outdoor bronze sculpture, Church Immaculad Corazon de Maria, Elizabeth, NJ; indoor sculptures, Church Immaculad Corazon de Maria, Newark, NJ, 83. *Exhib:* Philadelphia Mus Art, 49; Mus Nat D'Art Mod, Paris, France, 51; Bienal Hispanoamericana de Arte, Madrid, Spain, 52; Brooklyn Mus, NY, 73; Metrop Mus Art, New York, NY, 76; one-man shows, Galerie Int, New York, 71, Cisnero Gallery, New York, 73 & Horizon Galleries, New York, 82. *Pos:* Dir, Art Mag, Matanzas, 50-52. *Teaching:* Prof drawing, Sch Plastic Arts, Matanzas, 41-51, dir, 44-49, prof sculpture, 51-61. *Awards:* Gold Medals, Tampa Univ, 52 & Accad Italia Delle, 80. *Bibliog:* Articles, Art News, 2/70 & Arts Mag, 11/70; Jeanne Paris (auth), Rodulfo Tardo, Long Island Press, 71. *Mem:* Artisti Contemp Accad Italia. *Publ:* Auth, Tendenze e Testimonianze dell Arte Contemporanea, Nicole Panepinto & Calogero Panepinto, 83. *Mailing Add:* c/o Raydon Gallery 1091 Madison Ave New York NY 10028

TARGAN, JUDY
PRINTMAKER, PAINTER
b New York, NY, Oct 12, 31. *Study:* Smith Col, BA(magna cum laude), 53; Rutgers Univ, 55; Fairleigh Dickinson Univ, 56-59. *Work:* State Mus,

Trenton, NJ; Newark Mus, NJ; Libr Cong, Washington, DC; Univ Pa, Philadelphia; and many others. *Comn:* Women's Div, Jewish Community Fedn, Metropolitan, NJ, 80; Nat Women's Div, Albert Einstein Col Medicine, NJ, 81; UNICEF greeting cards. *Exhib:* Nat Print, Hunterdon Art Ctr, NJ, 78; State Mus, Trenton, NJ, 78; Boston Mus Fine Arts, Mass, 78; Newark Mus, NJ, 79; Outstanding Women Artists of NJ, YMHA & YWHA, 79; Art for the Table, Philadelphia Art Alliance, Pa, 80. *Awards:* Roth Award, Nat Asn Women Artists, 77; Purchase Award, Irvington Art Asn, NJ, 78; First Prize, Summit Art Ctr Regional Show, 79. *Mem:* Artists Equity; Printmaking Coun NJ; Nat Asn Women Artists. *Media:* Mixed media. *Publ:* UNICEF notecards, New York Botanical Garden, 78. *Mailing Add:* 40 Glenside Rd South Orange NJ 07079

TARIN, GILBERTO A
PAINTER, PRINTMAKER
b San Antonio, Tex, Feb 19, 43. *Study:* Univ of Americas, Puebla, Mex, with Victor Cuevas & Fernando Belain; Our Lady of Lake Univ, San Antonio, Tex. *Work:* San Antonio Art League; SW Craft Ctr, San Antonio. *Exhib:* One-man shows, Galeria Rewi, Mexico City, 71 & Galeria Agustin Arrieta, Puebla, 72; Okla Art Mus, Oklahoma City, 74; Walker & Guthrie Art Ctr, Minneapolis, Minn, 74; McNay Art Inst, San Antonio, 77; and others. *Awards:* Purchase Prize, Tex Watercolor Soc, 74; Cash Award, 26th Ann Tex Watercolor Soc, James K Naylor Mem, 75; First Prize, 47th Ann San Antonio Artists Exhib, Julian Onderdonk Mem, 77. *Mem:* Tex Watercolor Soc. *Media:* Pen & Ink, Gouache; Lithography. *Dealer:* Maggie L Reed 2222 Nacogdoches St San Antonio TX 78209. *Mailing Add:* 927 SW 38th St San Antonio TX 78237

TARSHIS, JEROME
WRITER
b New York, NY, June 27, 36. *Study:* Columbia Col, AB, 57. *Awards:* Nat Endowment Arts Art Critic's Fel, 79. *Publ:* Contribr, Smithsonian, American Heritage, Atlantic Monthly, Art in Am, Christian Sci Monitor & Vogue. *Mailing Add:* 1315 Polk St San Francisco CA 94109

TASCONA, ANTONIO TONY
PAINTER, PRINTMAKER
b St Boniface, Man, Mar 16, 26. *Study:* Winnipeg Sch Art, dipl, 50; Univ Man Sch Fine Arts, 50-53. *Work:* Winnipeg Art Gallery, Man; Confederation Art Gallery & Mus Charlottetown, PEI; Art Gallery Ont, Toronto; Nat Gallery Can, Ottawa; Can Coun Art Bank; S J Drake Collection, Univ Man Law Sch; Vancouver Art Gallery. *Comn:* Aluminum bas relief, Man Centennial Art Ctr, 67-68; epoxy resin disks, in steel rings, Fed Dept Pub Works for Freshwater Inst, Univ Man, 72; hanging stabiles, Law Courts Bldg, Winnipeg, 84 & St Boniface Hosp Med Res Bldg, Winnipeg, 86; mural, lounge of Assinaboine Dome Car for Via Rail, Park Cars Proj, Montreal, 88. *Exhib:* One-man shows, Carman Lamana Gallery, Toronto, 68, La Gallerie Int, Ribe, Denmark, 76 & The Dynamics of Tony Tascona (traveling exhib), 84-85; Manitoba Mainstream, Nat Gallery Can (traveling exhib), 72; Manitoba Artists Overseas, Winnipeg Art Gallery (traveling to London, Paris & Brussels), 84; and others. *Awards:* Arts Medal, Royal Archit Inst Can, Ottawa, 70; Can Coun Arts Award Fel, 72; Can Silver Jubilee Medal, Govt Can, 77; Gold Medal, Accademia Italia, 80; and others. *Bibliog:* Virgil Hammock (auth), Tony Tascona: Le succes interieur, Vie Des Arts Mag, winter 75; Visions: A Definition of Space-Prairie Visual Artists, TV Ontario, 83; Arthur Kroker & Kenneth J Hughes (auths), Technology and emancipatory art: The Manitoba vision, Can J Political & Social Theory, 2/86. *Mem:* Royal Can Acad Art (vpres, Prairie Region, 79-81); Can Conf Arts; Can Artists' Representation. *Mailing Add:* 208 Provencher Blvd Winnipeg MB R2H 0G4 Canada

TASENDE, JOSE MARIA
GALLERY DIRECTOR, DEALER
b Bilbao, Spain, 1932; US citizen. *Study:* Inst Bilbao, Basque Country, BA, 48. *Collections Arranged:* Francisco Zuniga: Exhibit of Drawings & Sculpture, Fine Arts Gallery San Diego, 71 & Everson Mus, 77; Jose Luis Cuevas: An Exhibition of Recent Works, Phoenix Art Mus, 75 & Calif Palace Legion Hon, 75; Jose Luis Cuevas Drawings, Brigham Young Univ, 77; Giacomo Manzu: Exhibition of Sculptures & Drawings, Springfield Mus Art, Mo, 78; Roberto Matta: Paintings & Drawings, Metrop Mus, Coral Gables, Fla, 81; Henry Moore Sculptures & Drawings, Blanden Mem Art Gallery, Ft Dodge, Iowa, 82; An Irreverent Approach (exhib), The Meadows Mus, Southern Methodist Univ, Dallas, 90; Pasadena City Col, Calif, 92; Univ Iowa Mus Art, Iowa City, 93. *Mem:* Art Mus Asn Am. *Publ:* Image and Specter (exhib catalog), Jose Luis Cuevas Letters, Tasende Gallery, 81; Personal Approach (exhib catalog), Figure, Space, Image, Tasende Gallery, 85; The American Factor (exhib catalog), Andres Nagel, Tasende Gallery, 90. *Mailing Add:* Tasende Gallery 820 Prospect St La Jolla CA 92037

TASH, JOY ALENE
ART DEALER, COLLECTOR
b Des Moines, Iowa, Nov 11, 43. *Study:* Private study in art marketing with Calvin Goodman, 83. *Collections Arranged:* A Retrospective-Pena, Scottsdale Ctr Arts, 87. *Pos:* Owner, Joy Tash Gallery, Scottsdale, Ariz, 76-. *Mem:* Phoenix Art Mus; Scottsdale Ctr Arts. *Specialty:* Contemporary American, European, Western & Mexican art. *Publ:* A Retrospective-Pena, Scottsdale Ctr Arts, 87. *Mailing Add:* 4234 N Craftsman Court Scottsdale AZ 85251

TASSE, M JEANNE
EDUCATOR, CALLIGRAPHER
b Worcester, Mass. *Study:* Anna Maria Col, AB, 55; Univ Notre Dame, MA, 62; Boston Univ, PhD, 72. *Comn:* Calligraphy, comn by The Mountain State Co, Easter Seals and pvt comns. *Exhib:* By Women's Hands, ECC Faculty Art Show. *Teaching:* Prof art & music, Anna Maria Col, 55-75; prof art, Marietta Col, 75-90. *Bibliog:* Calligraphy, The Marietta Times. *Mem:* Col Art Asn; Int Ctr Medieval Art; Nat Soc Arts & Lett (pres Ohio Valley chap formerly); founding mem Marietta Calligraphy Soc (pres formerly); Nat Resolutions (chmn). *Media:* Pen and Ink. *Res:* Iconcographic source study of the circular illustrations in the Beatus manuscripts; medieval sculpture. *Collection:* Medieval manuscript folios; miniature prints and paintings. *Mailing Add:* 100 Becker Lane Marietta OH 45750

TATA, SAM BEJAN
PHOTOGRAPHER
b Shanghai, China, Sept 30, 11; Can citizen. *Study:* Self-taught; Concordia Univ, LLD, 82. *Work:* Nat Gallery Can, Pub Arch Can & Nat Film Bd Can, Ottawa; Mus Mod Art, New York. *Exhib:* Phoenix Art Ctr, Ariz, 57; George Eastman House, Rochester, NY, 58; Nat Film Bd, Ottawa, 71; Nat Gallery Can, Ottawa, 81; Saidye Bronfiman Ctr, Montreal, Can Mus Contemp Photo, 88. *Awards:* Life Achievement Award, 90; Kodak Chair Lectr Ser, 90-91; Can Ctr Archit, 92; and others. *Bibliog:* Norman Hall (auth), Sam Tata's rebellion, Photog, London, 56; John Linder (auth), review, Photoage, Montreal, 62; Hugh Hood (auth), article, Can Fiction Mag, 79. *Mem:* Royal Photog Soc, London; Royal Can Acad Arts. *Publ:* Illusr, Expos 67 Sculpture, Tundra Bks, 67; Marcel Braitstein, Sculpteur, 70; A Certain Identity, 50 Portraits, Deneau Publ, 83; auth, Shanghai 1949, End of an Era, Batsford London, New Amsterdam Bks, New York & Deneau, Toronto, 89; Portraits of Canadian Writers, 40 Portraits, 91. *Mailing Add:* 4361 Beaconsfield Ave Montreal PQ H4A 2A5 Canada

TATE, BLAIR
TAPESTRY ARTIST, EDUCATOR
b New York, NY, Aug 28, 52. *Study:* RI Sch Design, BFA, 74; Haystack Mountain Sch Crafts, studied with Jack Larsen, 78. *Work:* Mass Inst Technol, Cambridge; Boston Trade Bank. *Comn:* Inset (tapestry), Rocky Mountain Energy Co, Broomfield, Colo, 81; Crossover (tapestry in two parts), Conn Comn for Arts Stamford, Conn, 83-85; Revisions (tapestry), Southeastern Mass Univ, N Dartmouth, 89; Seton Hall Sch Law, Newark, 92. *Exhib:* Contemporary Crafts Americas, Colo State Univ, Ft Collins & traveling, 75; American Academy, Rome, 77; Three Dimensional Possibilities, Rose Art Mus, Brandeis Univ, Waltham, Mass, 79; National Miniature Textile Exhib, Textile Mus, Washington, DC & traveling, 79-81; Crafts of the Commonwealth, Berkshire Mus, Pittsfield, Mass & traveling, 80-81; Skidmore Col Invitational, Saratoga Springs, NY, 84; Fiber R/Evolution, Univ Art Mus, Milwaukee & traveling, 86-87; one-person show, La Jolla Mus Contemp Art, 87, Am Craft Mus, New York, 91. *Pos:* Studio artist, 75-. *Teaching:* Lectr textiles & weaving, Mass Col Art, Boston, 83 & RI Sch Design, 83-87; instr weaving, Sch Art Inst Chicago, 87. *Awards:* Fel, Mass Artists Found, Crafts, 80 & Project Completion Award, 82; Bunting Fel, Bunting Inst, Radcliffe Col, 83-84. *Bibliog:* Jack Larsen & Mildred Constantine (auths), The Art Fabric: Mainstream, Van Nostrand Reinhold, 81 & 85; Barbara Mayer (auth), Contemporary American Craft - A collectors guide, Peregrine Smith Bks, 88. *Mem:* Am Craft Coun. *Media:* Fiber. *Publ:* Auth, The Warp: A Weaving Reference, Van Nostrand Reinhold, 84. *Mailing Add:* 209 Clinton St No 2R Brooklyn NY 11201

TATE, GAYLE BLAIR
PAINTER
b Abilene, Tex, Apr 3, 44. *Study:* Univ Wyo, Laramie, 62-64; Fla State Univ, Tallahassee, BS, 67; Loch Haven Art Ctr, Orlando, Fla, 71-72. *Comn:* Trompe l'oeil paintings, comn by Robert Smith, Tampa, Fla, 87 & 88 & Ken Allen, Hendersonville, NC, 88, 89 & 90; Ron Hall, Dallas, 90; Robert Griffin, Charlotte, NC, 1-92. *Exhib:* ERL Originals, Winston-Salem; Ann Jacob Gallery, Highlands, NC; S & S Dillon, Clayton, Ga; The Picture House, Charlotte, NC; Scottie's, Hendersonville, NC; and others. *Pos:* Pres, Tate Gallery, Tallahassee, 72-; pres, Interarts Inc/Tate Galleries, Tampa, 73-83; pres, Southeast Prof Art Dealers Asn, 80-83. *Teaching:* Lectr art & Christianity, 77-; guest lectr, Univ Tampa, 82; Biblical Principles, 85- *Awards:* First, Second & Third in Painting, Best of Show, Charlotte Spring Show, 90; First & Third in Painting, Charlotte Spring Show, 91; Exhibitor's Award, Merrimon Galleries, Asheville, NC, 92. *Bibliog:* American Artists, Illustrated Survey 1986, New York Art Review, 89; Men of Achievement 1986, Internationale Biographie, 85. *Mem:* Founding mem, Seven Artists' Alliance, Asheville, NC, 92. *Media:* Oil, Watercolor. *Publ:* Auth, Miro, The Early Works, Interarts Inc, 78; auth, Chapter One, Verse One, Living Waters Press, 89. *Dealer:* Ken Allen 225 N Main St Hendersonville NC 28792; Gesner Fine Art Largo FL. *Mailing Add:* PO Box 333 Black Mountain NC 28711

TATHAM, DAVID FREDERIC
HISTORIAN
b Wellesley, Mass, Nov 29, 32. *Study:* Univ Mass, AB; Syracuse Univ, MA & PhD. *Teaching:* Prof hist art, Syracuse Univ, 68- *Awards:* Am Art J Award, 84; H A Moe Prize, NY State Hist Asn, 91. *Mem:* Col Art Asn; Am Antiq Soc. *Res:* American painting and graphic arts of the nineteenth and twentieth centuries. *Publ:* Auth, The Lure of the Striped Pig, Imprint Soc, 74; Winslow Homer's Drawings, Lowe Art Gallery, 79; Winslow Homer in the 1880's, Everson Mus, 83; ed, Prints and Printmakers of New York State 1825-1940, Syracuse Univ Press, 86; Winslow Homer and the Illustrated Book, Syracuse Univ Press, 91. *Mailing Add:* Dept of Fine Arts Syracuse Univ Syracuse NY 13210

TATISTCHEFF, PETER ALEXIS
DEALER, GALLERY DIRECTOR
b New York, NY, Dec 12, 38. *Study:* Yale Univ, New Haven, Conn. *Collections Arranged:* New Images, Figuration in American Painting, Queens Mus, NY, 74, New Figurative Painting Tour, 77, First Charleston Ann Tour, 77. *Pos:* Pres & dir, Tatistcheff & Co Inc, New York & Tatistcheff Gallery, Inc, Los Angeles. *Specialty:* Contemporary American painting, drawing. *Mailing Add:* 50 W 57 St New York NY 10019

TATOSSIAN, ARMAND
PAINTER
b Alexandria, Egypt, Sept 26, 48; Can citizen. *Study:* Painting with Adam Sherrif Scott, 66-69; McGill Univ, 67-69; Cararra Acad, Bergamo, Italy, mural techniques with Langarette, 70; also painting & lithography with Carzou, Paris, 71. *Work:* Nat Gallery Can, Ottawa; Nat Gallery Athens, Greece; Mus Fine Arts Soviet Armenia; Quebec Mus; Joliette Art Mus. *Comn:* Fight for Liberation (painting), Ecole Polytechnique, Athens, Greece, 74; paintings, Bank Can Nat, Montreal, 74. *Exhib:* Solo exhibs, Kaspar Gallery, Toronto, 79, Pub Arch Can, Ottawa, 80, Linchrist Gallery, Ontario, 80 & Galerie Bernard Desroches, Montreal, 81 & 83; Fed Reserve Bank Gallery, Boston, 81. *Teaching:* Prof, Art Educ, Concordia Univ, 71-74. *Bibliog:* Jean Trepanier (auth), Cent peintres du Quebec, 80; Guy Robert (auth), Art au Quebec, 83 & Art au Quebec depuis trois siecles, 83. *Mem:* Assoc Royal Can Acad Art; res mem Arts Club Montreal; Arts & Lett Club Toronto; Conseil peinture Quebec. *Media:* Oil, Acrylic. *Dealer:* Galerie Bernard Desroches 1444 Sherbrooke St W Montreal PQ Can. *Mailing Add:* 2121 Tupper St Apt 416 Montreal PQ H3H 1D1 Canada

TATRO, RONALD EDWARD
SCULPTOR, INSTRUCTOR
b Kankakee, Ill, Jan 12, 43. *Study:* Southern Ill Univ, BA & MFA. *Work:* San Jose Mus Art, Calif; Southwestern Col. *Comn:* Flour Corp, Irvine, Calif; San Diego Co, Ruffin Rd Annex Bldg, Calif; Pargon Group, Redwood City, Calif; San Diego Co Health Ctr, Calif; Saddleback Col, Mission Viejo, Calif. *Exhib:* Fourteenth Ann Purchase Prize Competition, Riverside Art Ctr & Mus, Calif, 76; Calif Hawaii Biennial, San Diego Mus Art, 76; San Jose Mus Art, Permanent Collection Exhib, Calif, 85; New Art Forms-Chicago Int Expos, Nave Pier, Ill, 88; Art 17, 86, Art 19, 88, Art 20, 89, Art 21, 90, Basel Art Fair, Switz; and others. *Teaching:* Instr basic art, Southern Ill Univ, Carbondale, 66-67; asst prof art, Va State Col, 67-68; instr sculpture, Grossmont Col, 68- *Awards:* Third Prize in Sculpture, San Diego Art Inst, 75; Juror's Award, Crafts-Sculpture-Painting-Graphics, Orange Co Art Asn, 76; Muckenthaler Cult Ctr, Fullerton, Calif, 79. *Media:* Steel. *Dealer:* Erika Meyerovich Gallery San Francisco CA; Valerie Miller Fine Art Palm Desert CA. *Mailing Add:* Dept Art Grossmont Col 8800 Grossmont Col El Cajon CA 92020

TATTI, BENEDICT MICHAEL
SCULPTOR, PAINTER
b New York, NY, May 1, 17. *Study:* Masters Inst Roerich Mus, with L Slobodkin; Da Vinci Art Sch, with A Piccirilli; State Univ NY; Art Students League, with William Zorach & O Zadkine; Hans Hofmann Sch Art. *Work:* In pvt collections of Mr & Mrs Cass Canfield, New York, Mr & Mrs Zero Mostel, New York & Mr & Mrs Sam Golden, NJ. *Comn:* Sundial, comn by R W Bliss for Dumbarton Oaks, Washington, DC, 52; Bison, comn by E Taylor for Tokyo Park, Japan, 60; D'Aragon Mem, comn by A D'Aragon, Hartsdale, NY, 69; medallions of D Sarnoff, D Eisenhower & Mark Twain, Newell & Lennon, New York. *Exhib:* Artists for Victory, Metrop Mus Art, New York, 42; Pa Acad Fine Arts, Philadelphia, 50-54; Mus Mod Art, New York, 60; Claude Bernard Gallery, Paris, France, 60; Roko Gallery, New York, 67. *Pos:* Consult restoration, Alexanders Sculpture Studio, 46-72; sculptor-designer, Loewy-Smith Assocs, 52-65; artist in residence, Nat Ctr Experiments TV, San Francisco, 69. *Teaching:* Instr sculpture & head dept, H S Art & Design, formerly; instr sculpture, Craft Students League, 66-67. *Awards:* Creative Arts Prog Grant, NY State Coun Arts, 72; Medal of Honor for Sculpture, Painters & Sculptors Soc NJ, 72; Rennick Award for Sculpture, Audubon Artists, 88. *Mem:* Am Soc Contemp Artists; Sculptors League, New York; Painters & Sculptors Soc NJ; life mem Art Students League; Am Medallic Sculpture Asn; Audubon Artists (dir sculpture, currently). *Dealer:* Alexander Gallery 117 E 39th St New York NY 10016. *Mailing Add:* 214 E 39th St New York NY 10016

TAUBES, TIMOTHY EVAN
CRITIC, CURATOR
b New York, NY, June 6, 55. *Study:* Ohio Univ, BA, 77; Hunter Col, art history with Rosalind Krauss & E C Goosens, MBA, 79. *Work:* Artists' Choice Mus, New York. *Exhib:* Abstractscapes, Longboat Key, Fl, 88. *Collections Arranged:* Frederic Taubes Memorial Retrospective, Butler Inst Am Art, Youngstown, Ohio, Canton Art Inst, Ohio & Westmoreland Mus, Greensberg, Pa, 83; Frederic Taubes-Paintings & Drawings, Marymount Manhattan Col Art Gallery, New York, 84; Realist Antecedents, Artists' Choice Mus, New York, 85. *Pos:* Exec dir, Artists' Choice Mus, New York, 83-86; dir, Gallery Educ Ctr, Longboat Key, Fl, 87. *Teaching:* The Educ Ctr, Longboat Key, Fl, 87. *Bibliog:* Article in Art World Mag, 10/84, 3/85. *Res:* 20th century American painting. *Publ:* Contribr, J Artists' Choice Mus, Vols 5-8, 84-86. *Mailing Add:* 1156 Ctr Pl Sarasota FL 34236

TAVENNER, PATRICIA
PAINTER, PRINTMAKER
b Doster, Mich. *Study:* Mich State Univ, BA; Calif Col Arts & Crafts, Oakland, MFA. *Work:* San Francisco Mus Art; Oakland Mus Art, Calif; Royal Mus Fine Arts, Antwerp, Belgium; Cornell Univ, Inica, NY; Mus Mod Art, New York. *Comn:* Facade, Mus Contemp Crafts, New York, 71; sect of wall, Can Nat Res Libr, Ottawa, 73. *Exhib:* Inst Environ, Paris, France, 74; solo exhibs, Mills Col, Oakland, 74, OHS Parsens, Los Angeles, Calif, 82, Atkins Mus Fine Arts, Kansas City, Mo, 85, Mus Mod Kunst, Weddel, Ger, 87, Univ Calif, Berkeley Exten, 85, 89 & 92; Mus Fine Arts, Budapest, Hungary, 87; Am Hist, Atlanta Col of Art, 88; Davidson Gallery, Seattle, Wash, 89. *Pos:* Univ Calif Davis, 87. *Teaching:* Instr, Univ Calif, Berkeley Exten, 67-92; asst prof art, Calif State Univ, San Jose & Calif State Univ, San Francisco. *Awards:* Acquisitions, San Francisco Mus Mod Art; Residency, Centrum Frans, Belgium. *Bibliog:* Thomas Albright (AUTH), Bay Area Art, Univ Calif Press. *Mem:* Womens Caucus for Art; Pro Arts, (bd dirs). *Media:* Collage; Monoprint. *Publ:* Contribr, Art et Communication Marginale, 74; contribr, Women See Women, 75; contribr, Art: A Womans Sensibility, 75; contribr, Rubber Stamp Art, 78. *Mailing Add:* PO Box 11102 Oakland CA 94611

TAWNEY, LENORE
WEAVER, ASSEMBLAGE ARTIST
b Lorain, Ohio. *Study:* Univ Ill, 43-45; Inst Design, Ill, with Archipenko, 46-47; also with Martta Taipale, Finland, 54. *Work:* Mus Contemp Crafts, New York; Mus Mod Art, New York; Kunstegwerbe Mus, Zurich; Art Inst Chicago; Brooklyn Mus; and others. *Exhib:* Art Inst Chicago, 79; one-person show, Tacoma Art Mus, Wash, 81; Fiber 82, Hunterdon Art Ctr, Clinton, NJ, 82; Katonah Gallery, NY, 82; Port Hist Mus, Philadelphia, 83; 75th Int Bienniale Tapestry Exhib, Lausanne, Switzerland, 84; Am Craft Mus, Ny, 86-89; Milwaukee Art Mus, Wis, 86-88; Monmouth Mus Art, Lincroft, NJ, 86-88; and others. *Awards:* Fel Am Crafts Coun, 75; Women's Caucus for Arts Honor Award for Outstanding Achievement in Visual Arts, Port of Hist Mus, Philadelphia, 83; Gold Medal, Am Crafts Coun, 87. *Bibliog:* Gloria Overstein (auth), Lenore Tawney: The Craft of the Spirit, Feminist Art Journal, winter, 73-74; Aclavio Paz (auth), In Praise of Hands, NY Graphic Soc, 74; Charlotte Streifer Rubenstein (auth), American Women Artists, Avon Books, 82. *Media:* Linen, Collages. *Mailing Add:* 32 N 20th St 5th Fl New York NY 10011

TAYLOR, AL C
SCULPTOR, PRINTMAKER
b Springfield, Mo, 1948. *Study:* Yale-Norfolk Summer Session, 69; Whitney Mus Art Resources Ctr, New York, 69; Kansas City Art Inst, 70. *Work:* Mus Fine Arts, Boston, Mass; Mus Mod Art, New York; NY Public Libr, New York; Walker Art Ctr, Minneapolis, Minn. *Exhib:* Solo exhibs, Galerie Alfred Kren, Cologne, Ger, 89 & 91, Galerie 86, Europäische Adademie für Bildende Kunst, Trier, Ger, 90, David NolanGallery, New York & Galerie Jahn und Pusban, Munich, 92; Projects & Portfolios, Brooklyn Mus, NY, 89; Diverse Representations, Morris Mus, Morristown, NJ, 90; The Unique Print, Mus Fine Arts, Boston, Mass, 90; Drawings, Lorence Monk Gallery, New York, 91; Sean Scully, Al Taylor, David Row, Martin Beck, NY, Galerie 86, Trier, Ger, 92; Drawn in the Nineties, Katonah Mus Art, New York, 92. *Awards:* Fel, Nat Endowment Arts, 88. *Bibliog:* Robert Mahoney (auth), Al Taylor, Arts Mag, 2/89; Shoichiro Higuchi (auth), Artist in New York: Al Taylor, Anthropos, 9/90; Brooks Adams (auth), Al Taylor at Lorence Monk, Art in Am, vol 79, no 4, pg 160-161, 91. *Media:* All Media. *Publ:* BOMB, spring, 88. *Mailing Add:* 72 Franklin Street New York NY 10013

TAYLOR, ANN
PAINTER
b Rochester, NY, Mar 23, 41. *Study:* Vassar Col; New Sch Soc Res, BA, 62; self-taught painter. *Work:* Bank Am, Houston; Bausch & Lomb Inc & Xerox, Rochester; Palm Springs Desert Mus, Calif; Honeywell Inc, Minneapolis; and others. *Comn:* Paintings, Central Trust Co, Cincinnati, Ohio, 75; Third Nat Bank, Dayton, Ohio, 79; A C Neilson Corp, Northbrook, Ill, 85. *Exhib:* Butler Inst Am Art, Youngstown, Ohio, 66; Gallery Mod Art, New York, 67; Saginaw Art Mus, 68 & 84; Mem Art Gallery, Univ Rochester, 70; Scottsdale Ctr Arts, Ariz, 82 & 84; Rochester Mus & Sci Ctr, 84; Palm Springs Desert Mus, 84; Yuma Fine Arts Ctr, 84; Reed Whipple Cultural Ctr, 84; Beaumont Art Mus, 85. *Awards:* Commemorative Lithograph Competition, Scottsdale Ctr for the Arts, 85. *Bibliog:* Donna Marxer (auth), Painting the very air, Southwest Art, 2/78; Carol Kotrozo (auth), Ann Taylor, Artspace, 4/81; Donald Locke (auth), Ann Taylor, Arts Mag, 2/83 & 3/84; Barbara Cortright (auth), The Reach of Solitude: The Paintings of Ann Taylor, Paul S Eriksson Publ, 83. *Media:* Oil, Lithographs. *Dealer:* Marilyn Butler Fine Art 4160 N Craftsmans Ct Scottsdale AZ 85251; Gallery Henoch 80 Wooster St New York NY 10012. *Mailing Add:* c/o Oxford Gallery 267 Oxford St Rochester NY 14607

TAYLOR, BILL (WILLIAM BRADLEY)
SCULPTOR, INSTRUCTOR
b Atlantic City, NJ, Jan 1, 26. *Study:* Inst Contemp Arts, DC, with Alexander Giampietro, cert, 51. *Work:* Talladega Col Mus, Ala; Miami Dade Co Pub Libr Exhib, Miami, Fla. *Exhib:* 200 Yrs of Black Am Art, Los Angeles Co Mus Art; High Mus Art, Atlanta, Ga, 77; Mus Fine Arts, Dallas, 77; Brooklyn Mus Art, 77; 18th Ann Art Fac Exhib, Howard Univ, Washington DC, 88. *Teaching:* Instr sculpture, Corcoran Sch Art, DC, 65-68; asst prof sculpture, Univ DC, 68-83. *Awards:* Sargent Johnson Award, Nat Exhib Black Artists, Smith Mason Gallery, DC, 71. *Bibliog:* Carol L Myers (auth), Black Power in the Arts, Flint, Mich, 70. *Media:* Granite Field Stones; Welded Steel. *Mailing Add:* Nat Gallery of Art Washington DC 20565

TAYLOR, BRIE (BENJAMIN DE BRIE)
EDUCATOR, PAINTER
b Paris, France, Mar 5, 23; US citizen. *Study:* Harvard Univ, BS, 47; Art Students League New York, dipl, 55. *Work:* Johnson Mus, Cornell Univ; Mus Mod Art Miami, Fla. *Exhib:* Butler Inst Biennial, 57; American Artists, Dallas Mus Fine Arts, 57; Brooklyn and Long Island Artists, Brooklyn Mus, 58 & 60-62; solo exhib, Mus Mod Art Miami, Fla, 59; Contemporary American Painting, Whitney Mus, 60; Corcoran Gallery Biennial, 61; West Side Artists, Riverside Mus, New York, 66; Indiana Artists, Indianapolis Mus Art, 71. *Pos:* Dean, Parsons Sch Design, 68-70 & Herron Sch Art, Ind Univ, 70-73; dir, Inst Design, Ill Inst Technol, 73-75. *Teaching:* Instr painting & drawing, Pratt Inst, 60-68; instr drawing & visual communications, Parsons Sch Design, 67-70; prof drawing & art hist, Inst Design, Ill Inst Technol, 73-87, prof emer, 87- *Awards:* Fels, MacDowell Colony, 62 & Yaddo, 62. *Bibliog:* James R Mellow (auth), In the galleries, Arts Mag, 10/58; Dore Ashton (auth), Art, New York Times, 10/3/58; Henry Butler (auth), New Herron dean, Indianapolis News, 10/30/70. *Mem:* Col Art Asn; Art Students League New York. *Media:* Oil, Watercolors. *Res:* Art and natural history. *Publ:* Auth, Towards a plastic revolution, Art News, 64; auth, A problem in painting, Sch Arts, 67; auth, John Heliker, Arts Mag, 68; auth, articles, In: Art, Crowell-Collier, 70; auth, Design Lessons From Nature, Watson-Guptill, 74. *Mailing Add:* 26 Wild Goose Rd Wakefield RI 02879-6702

TAYLOR, GRACE MARTIN
PAINTER, PRINTMAKER
b Morgantown, WVa. *Study:* Pa Acad Fine Arts; WVa Univ, AB & MA; Ohio Univ; Art Inst Chicago; Art Students League; Bisttram Sch Art; Hans Hofmann Sch Fine Arts. *Work:* Am Color Print Soc; Hallmark Co; Charleston Art Gallery, WVa; WVa Culture Ctr, Charleston; WVa Univ Creative Art Ctr, Morgantown. *Exhib:* Metrop Mus Art, 43 & Nat Acad Design, 44 & 48, New York; Am Watercolor Soc, New York, 58 & 59; Am Drawing Biennial, Norfolk Mus, 65; Contemp Gallery, Palm Beach, 67; one-man shows, Artist of the Yr, WVa Univ, 58 & 67 & WVa Univ Creative Arts Ctr, 74; Smithsonian Inst, Washington, DC, 85. *Pos:* Dean, Mason Col Music & Fine Arts, 50-55, pres, 55-56. *Teaching:* Assoc prof art & head dept, Mason Col Music & Fine Arts, 34-56; assoc prof art, Morris Harvey Col, 56-68; lectr, WVa Univ Div Exten Credit, 67-71. *Awards:* First Prize for Prints, Seven State Exhib, Va Intermont Col, 48; Three State Ann First Prize & Jurors Award, Huntington Galleries, 54 & 64; Citizen of the Yr in Art in WVa, WVa Rhododendron Arts Festival, 71 & First Prize Drawing, 74; Purchase Award Drawing, Allied Artists of WVa, WVa Arts Coun, 73; Distinguished WVa Award, Gov John D Rockfeller, 82. *Bibliog:* Haas & Packer (auth), Instruction in Audio-Visual Aids, 50 & Morris Davidson (auth), Painting with Purpose, 64, Prentice-Hall. *Mem:* Provincetown Art Asn; Allied Artists WVa (pres, 35-36); Am Asn Univ Prof. *Media:* Oil, Casein. *Mailing Add:* c/o Michael Lowe Gallery 338 W Fourth St Cincinnati OH 45202

TAYLOR, HARRY GEORGE
PRINTMAKER, PHOTOGRAPHER
b Detroit, Mich, Aug 17, 18. *Study:* Sch, Art Inst, Chicago, MFA, 49, studied with Boris Anisfeld, S W Hayter & Moise Smith. *Work:* Utah State Fine Arts, Capitol, Salt Lake Art Ctr & MS Soc NY, Salt Lake City, Utah; Ogden Bd Educ Sch Mus, Utah; Co Sch Mus, Pleasant View, Utah; Union Pac; Nora Eccles Harrison Mus, Logan, Utah. *Comn:* Eight ft wooden cross, 67 & 12ft wooden sculpture, 68, St James Church, Ogden, Utah; Mini-Show of Graphics, Ogden City Rd Educ, 70; etching for 100th anniversary, Eccles Community Art Ctr, 85; etching for 25th anniversary, YWCA, 86; Presentation Edition Prints, Ogden Arts Coun. *Exhib:* Ft Wayne Print Show, Ind, 86; Odense, Denmark 88, 89; Rembrandt, New York, Cleveland & Pasadena, 88; San Francisco Franklin Gallery, 90; Moss Rehab, Philadelphia, Penn, 92; and others. *Pos:* Art dir, Meridian Publ Co, Ogden, Utah, 60-84. *Teaching:* Instr painting & drawing, St Bonaventure-Olean, NY, summer, 47; instr oil & watercolor, Weber State Col, Ogden, Utah, 59, 75 & 80. *Awards:* Purchase Awards, Chicago Veterans, US Army, 49, Capital Show, State of Utah, 52 & Utah State Collection, 84; First Place Graphics, 18th Ann Exhib, Ogden Palette Club, 77. *Bibliog:* Bob Halliday (auth), article, 70 & Charlotte, 72, Salt Lake Tribune; Article, Deseret News, 91 & 92; Article, Standard Examiner, 91 & 92. *Mem:* Calif Soc Printmakers; Sch of the Art Inst Alumni Asn; Ogden Palette Club (vpres, 67); Venice Int. *Media:* Etching. *Publ:* Illusr, Improvement Era, Norman Press, 60; Hill Air Force Guide, US Air Force, 74; Exhibit for the Blind, Weber Col, 76; A Book of Korean Recipes, Twink Lee-Miller, 77; Petrglyph, vol 2, Spring 90. *Mailing Add:* 905 Rancho Blvd Ogden UT 84404

TAYLOR, HUGH HOLLOWAY
HISTORIAN, EDUCATOR
b Charlottesville, Va, July 18, 41. *Study:* Col of William & Mary, Williamsburg, Va, AB(art hist), 63; George Washington Univ, MA(art hist & theory), 65, with Lawrence Leite. *Collections Arranged:* Dir cataloging of collection of Washington Co Hist Soc, Pa, 76-77. *Teaching:* Prof art hist, Washington & Jefferson Col, Washington, Pa, 65-, Edith M Kelso Chair Art Hist, currently. *Mem:* Soc Archit Historians; Nat Trust Hist Preserv; Washington Co (Pa) Hist & Landmarks. *Res:* Nineteenth century architecture of western Pennsylvania. *Mailing Add:* Dept Art History Washington & Jefferson Col Washington PA 15301

TAYLOR, IRA MOONEY
PRINTMAKER, SCULPTOR
b Hot Springs, Ark, Feb 5, 35. *Study:* Ark Tech Univ, BS, 68; La State Univ, MA, 70, MFA, 73. *Work:* La State Univ Gallery, Baton Rouge; Centro de Arte Moderno, Guadalajara, Mexico; First State Bank Gallery, Abilene, Tex. *Comn:* Print, Lion's Club Governor, Abilene, Tex, 75; stained glass window (collabr, Bob Howell), First Baptist Church, Guthrie, 79, pvt comn, Abilene 80 & Aldersgate Methodist Church, Abilene, Tex, 82. *Exhib:* Univ Ga Invitational, 89. *Teaching:* Prof printmaking & sculpture, Hardin-Simmons Univ, Abilene, Tex, 70- *Awards:* First Place Prints, La State Exhib, 70; First Place Sculpture, Soggetto Religioso, Diocese of Cortona, Italy, 78. *Mem:* Tex Asn Schs Art; Artists League Tex. *Media:* All; Stone, Bronze. *Mailing Add:* 1641 Sandefer St Abilene TX 79601

TAYLOR, JANET R
TAPESTRY ARTIST, WEAVER
b Lima, Ohio, Jan 19, 41. *Study:* Cleveland Inst Art, dipl, 63; Syracuse Univ Sch Art, MFA, 65. *Comn:* Tapestries, Morris Knudson hq, Boise, Idaho, 81; tapestries, Corpus Christi Bank, Tex, 82; tapestry, Neshaminy Complex, Trevose, Pa, 85; tapestries, The Boulders Resort, Carefree, Ariz, 86; tapestries, Westcourt in the Buttes, Tempe, Ariz, 86. *Exhib:* Solo exhibs, Swan Gallery, Philadelphia, 83 & Willingheart Gallery, Austin, Tex, 85; The Creative Spirit, Maier Mus Art, Lynchburg, Va, 85; Woven Works, Univ Wis, Green Bay & traveling, 85; Fiber and Clay, Augustana Col, Rock Island, Ill, 85; The Hand and the Spirit Gallery, Scottsdale, Ariz. *Teaching:* Asst prof fiber art, Kent State Univ, Ohio, 69-76; prof fiber art, Sch Art, Ariz State Univ, Tempe, 77- *Bibliog:* Tapestries by Janet Taylor, Fiberarts Mag, 9-10/82; Contemporary tapestry, Interior Design, 11/85; Commissions, Am Craft Mag, 4-5/86. *Mem:* Am Craft Coun. *Media:* Tapestry. *Mailing Add:* 1012 E Palmcroft Dr Tempe AZ 85282

TAYLOR, JOSEPH RICHARD
SCULPTOR
b Wilbur, Wash, Feb 1, 07. *Study:* Univ Wash, BFA, 31, MFA(cum laude), 32; Univ Okla; Columbia Univ, 40. *Work:* Western Hemisphere Collection, IBM; De Golyer Collection, Univ Okla Libr; Philbrook Mus, Tulsa. *Comn:* W B Bizzell Mem Statue, Univ Okla, 50. *Exhib:* Kansas City Art Inst Ann Midwest Exhib, 33-40; New York World's Fair, 38-39; San Francisco World's Fair, 40; Mus Mod Art, New York, 40; Univ Okla Art Mus; plus others. *Pos:* Lectr & art judge, art clubs & festivals, 69-; actg dir, Art Sch, Univ Okla. *Teaching:* Prof art & head dept sculpture, Fine Arts Col, Univ Okla, 32-63, David Ross Boyd prof, 63-71, emer prof, 71- *Awards:* Okla Hall of Fame, 60; Distinquished Serv Citation, Okla Univ, 77; Distinguished Lifetime Serv in Arts Governor's Award, 78; Best of Show, Okla Sculpture Soc, 81; and others. *Bibliog:* Article, Fortune Mag, 4/61 & fall 69; article, Nat Sculpture Rev Mag, fall 70 & summer 71. *Mem:* Okla Sculpture Soc; Okla Artists Asn. *Media:* All Media. *Mailing Add:* 701 W Brooks St Norman OK 73069

TAYLOR, KENDALL FRANCES
ADMINISTRATOR, HISTORIAN
b New York, NY. *Study:* Univ Oslo, Norway, cert achievement, 60; Fairleigh Dickinson Univ, Rutherford, NJ, BA(lit), 62; Vanderbilt Univ, Nashville, Tenn, MA(lit), 63, MAT(lit), 64; Syracuse Univ, MA(art hist, Grad Fel), 75, PhD(interdisciplinary humanities), 79. *Collections Arranged:* Philip Evergood in the Hirshhorn Mus Collection (auth, catalog), Smithsonian Inst, Washington, DC, 78; Political Comment in Contemporary Art (auth, catalog), Brainerd Gallery, 79 & Black and White: Two Views of New York City During the Depression (auth, catalog), 79; The Benefactors: 20th Century Patronage of the Arts (auth, catalog), 80; Arnold Genthei The Celebrity Portraits (auth, catalog), Libr of Congress, Washington, DC; Philip Evergood Retrospective Traveling Exhib (auth, Ctr Gallery, catalog), 87; Food/Art/USA, (contrib cur, catalog) Bard Col, 89. *Pos:* Chairperson coun, State Univ NY Gallery & Exhib Dirs, 79-80; dir, Brainerd Art Gallery, State Univ NY Col Potsdam, 79-80; dir traveling exhibs, Libr Cong, Washington, DC, 81-84; dir, Arts Management Assoc, Washington, DC, 84-, Artbank, 90-; Acad Dir Wash Sem Prog Art & Archit, Am Univ, 88- *Teaching:* Lectr Brit & Am lit, Univ Md, Europ Div, 65-69; instr mus studies, State Univ NY Col Potsdam, 79-80; instr mus studies, George Washington Univ, Washington, DC, 81-; vis prof, St Lawrence Univ, 85; prof art & archit, Am Univ, Washington, DC, 88. *Awards:* Fels, Ford, 63, Florence Fine Arts, 76-77, & Smithsonian, 77-79. *Mem:* Am Asn Mus; Col Art Asn; Univs Art Asn Can; Writers Guild Am; Fla Asn Mus. *Res:* Twentieth century American art and cultural history. *Publ:* Auth, The Philip Evergood Papers & Ryder Remembered, Arch Am Art J, 79; Never Separate from the Heart: The Life and Work of Philip Evergood, Bucknell Univ Press, 87; The Auction Trade Boom, Mus & Arts Mag, 88; Woman and Museum Work, An Hist Perspective Smithsonian Inst, 92; Ideologism and Am Art, The Courier, 92. *Mailing Add:* 2707 Adams Mill Rd NW Washington DC 20009

TAYLOR, MARY CAZORT
CURATOR, HISTORIAN
b Little Rock, Ark. *Study:* Washington Univ, St Louis, Mo, BFA, 53; Univ Mich, Ann Arbor, MA, 61, PhD, 70. *Pos:* Cur prints & drawings, Nat Gallery Can, Ottawa, 70- *Teaching:* Adj prof art hist, Carleton Univ, Ottawa, 77- *Mem:* Keepers of Pub Graphic Collections; Print Coun Am. *Res:* European drawings, concentration in North Italian, particularly Bolognese, late eighteenth century. *Publ:* Coauth & ed, European Drawings from the National Gallery of Canada, Toronto, 69; auth, The pen and wash drawings of the Brothers Gandolfi, Master Drawings, Vol 14 (1976), 159-65; coauth (with Catherine Johnston), Bolognese Drawings in North American Collections, Ottawa, 80. *Mailing Add:* 380 Sussex Dr PO Box 427 Sta A Ottawa ON K1N 9N4 Canada

TAYLOR, MICHAEL (ESTES)
INSTRUCTOR, SCULPTOR
b Lewisburg, Tenn, May 10, 44. *Study:* Middle Tenn State Univ, BS, 67; ETenn State Univ, MA, 68, MFA, 77; Penland Sch Arts & Crafts; Univ Wis; Univ Utah. *Work:* Corning Mus of Glass, NY; Lannon Found, Palm Beach, Fla; Mus fur Kunsthandiwerk, Frankfurt, WGer; Vanderbilt Univ, Tenn State Mus & Metrop Govt, Nashville; Fur Kunst Und Gewerbe, Hamburg, Ger; Del Mus Art, Wilmington; Feder's Glass, Mexico City; Hunter Art Mus, Chattanooga, Tenn. *Comn:* Sculptural glass panel, Vanderbilt Univ, Nashville, 73; two clear glass sculptures, Standard Oil Corp, Chicago, 75; New York State Gov Arts Awards, 87. *Exhib:* One-man shows, Univ SC, Columbia, 73, Glass Art Gallery, Toronto, Ont, 83 & Heller Gallery, New York, 84; Glass: American, Europe and Japan, Mus fur Kunsthandiwerk, Frankfurt, 74, Contemporary World Glass, Kunst Haus Am Mus, Koln, 75, WGer; Elaine Potter Gallery, San Francisco, Calif, 79 & 81-83; Boise Gallery of Art, Rosenthal Gallery Art, Caldwell, 80, Idaho; Habatat Galleries, Dearborn, 80, Lathrup Village, 83-85, Bay Harbor Islands, Fla, 85; Contemp Art Glass Gallery, Toronto, Ont, 82; Fabrications in Glass, New York Experimental Glass Workshop, NY, 84; Elaine Potter Gallery, San Francisco, Calif, 84-85; Glass Now 85, Yamaha Nippon Gakki, Hamamatsu, World Glass Now '85, Hokkaido Mus Mod Art, Sapporo, Shimonoseki City Art Mus, 85, Japan; Sculptural Glass Invitational, Erie Art Mus, Pa, 85; Int Glass Craft Exhib, Kanazawa, Japan, 88. *Pos:* Chmn arts fac, George Peabody Col, 76-79; chmn art dept, Col Idaho, Caldwell, 80-81; bd gov's NY State Found for Arts, NY. *Teaching:* Assoc prof, Vanderbilt Univ, Nashville, 71-79, chairperson, 75-79; vis artist, glass, Konfax Skolen, Stockholm, Sweden, 74 & Gerrit Rietuield Akad, Amsterdam, Holland, 74; chmn art dept, Col Idaho, 79-81; prof, head of glass prog, Rochester Inst Technol, 81- *Awards:* Lewis Comfort Tiffany grant, Tiffany Found, 69; Thord Gray Fel, Am-Scand Found, 74; Fulbright-Hayes Scholar, 74; Hans Christinsen Mem Award for Excellence in Craftsmenship & Design in a Sculptural Material, Rochester Mus Art, 83; Visual Artist Fel, 84-85, Visual Artists Forums Grant, 85-86, Nat Endowment Arts; Visual Artist Exhib Grant, NY State Coun Arts, 85-86; Grand prize, Int Glass Exhib, Kanazawa, Japan, 89. *Bibliog:* Richard Skull (dir), Michael Taylor: Glass (film), Micki Colman, 68; Rusty Chapman (dir), Glass Craft (film); Glass Art Soc Jour, 88 & 90. *Mem:* Tenn Artists-Craftsmen Asn (pres, 70-71); Am Crafts Coun; Glass Art Soc (bd dirs, 78-82); Am Asn Univ Prof. *Media:* Clay, Metal. *Mailing Add:* Glass Dept Rochester Inst Technol Rochester NY 14623

TAYLOR, MICHELE F
PAINTER
b Nov 1, 46; US citizen. *Study:* Ore State Univ, BA(fine arts), 68; Chouinard Art Inst, BS, 70. *Work:* Portland Art Mus, Ore; Univ Ore Mus; Ga Pac, Atlanta; Payne-Webber, Portland, Ore; Marriott Corp, Washington, DC; and others. *Exhib:* Northwest Watercolor, Bellevue Art Mus, Wash, 82; Ore Printmakers Invitational, Gresham, 83; Art About Agriculture, Ore State Univ, Corvallis, 84; Summer Images, Seattle Art Mus, 84; solo exhibs, Fountain Gallery, Portland, Ore, 84, Foster-White Gallery, Seattle, 85, Ft Hunter Mus, Harrisburg, 90 & Galerie Lareuse, Washington, DC, 91; Susan Blanchard Gallery, New York, 86; Conacher Gallery, New Stars, San Francisco, 90; Galerie Ranut, Munchen, Ger, 91. *Teaching:* Guest lectr, Corcoran Sch Art, Washington, DC, 89. *Awards:* First Award, Garden Invitational, Salem Art Mus, 79; Cash Award, Art in Agriculture, Ore State Univ, 83. *Bibliog:* Article, Art Gallery Mag, 5/85; Mus & Arts Mag, 89; article, Alaskan Airlines Mag, 90; Apprise Mag, Harrisburg, 90; Archit Dig, 92; and others. *Media:* Oil. *Mailing Add:* 465 Country Club Rd Camp Hill PA 17011

TAYLOR, RENE CLAUDE
MUSEUM DIRECTOR, HISTORIAN
b London, Eng, Dec 9, 16. *Study:* London Univ, PhD, 73. *Pos:* Dir, Museo de Arte de Ponce, PR, 62- *Mailing Add:* Museo de Arte de Ponce Las Americas PO Box 1492 Ponce PR 00731

TAYLOR, ROBERT
CRITIC, WRITER
b Newton, Mass, Jan 19, 25. *Study:* Colgate Univ, AB, 47; Brown Univ Grad Sch, 48. *Pos:* Art critic, Boston Herald, 52-67; Boston corresp, Pictures on Exhibit, 54-59; mem staff, Boston Globe Mag, 68-72, art critic, 72-, arts ed, 73-76, columnist, 76-82, chief bk & art critic, 82- *Teaching:* Prof Eng, Wheaton Col, 60-; lectr art hist, Boston Univ, 72-74. *Mem:* St Botolph Club, Boston; Mass Hist Soc. *Publ:* Auth, In Red Weather, 61; ed, publs, Inst Contemp Art, Boston, 67; auth, Treasures of Massachusetts, 72; Saranac, 86; Fred Allen, 89. *Mailing Add:* 1 Thomas Circle Marblehead MA 01945

TAYLOR, ROSEMARY
CERAMIST, SCULPTOR
b Joseph, Ore. *Study:* Cleveland Inst Art; NY Univ; Greenwich House; Arrowmount Col. *Work:* Westchester Col. *Exhib:* Taylor Gallery, Baltimore, 81; Hudson River Gallery, New York, 81; Am Crafts, Cleveland, Ohio, 85-92; Guild Gallery, Princeton, NJ, 85-90; Sign of the Clef, Savannah, Ga, 91-92; & others. *Pos:* Juror, Fulbright Award & Grants, 81-82; pottery consult, McCall's Mag, 62-72; standards chmn, NJ Designer-Craftsman, 92. *Teaching:* Instr, Rahway Art Ctr, 50-60. *Bibliog:* Arthur Williams (auth), Sculpture, Craft Report Mag. *Mem:* NJ Designer-Craftsman; Am Craft Coun; Nat Pen Women. *Media:* Stoneware. *Publ:* Contribr, McCall's Needlework, Craft Mag & Craft Report; and others. *Mailing Add:* Box 282 Stockton NJ 18559

TAYLOR, SANDRA ORTIZ
PAINTER, PRINTMAKER
b Los Angeles, Calif, Apr 27, 36. *Study:* Univ Calif, with William Brice & Sam Amato, BA; Iowa State Univ, with Byron Burford, MA. *Work:* Univ Iowa; Macy's Corp, New York; Univ Calif Res Libr, Los Angeles; Oakland Mus. *Exhib:* Calif Small Works 1991, Calif Mus Art, Luther Burbank Ctr, Santa Rosa, Calif, 91; Old & New Glory, Calif Crafts Mus, Ghirardelli Sq, San Francisco, 92; Many Mansions: The Art of Shelter, San Francisco Craft & Folk Art Mus, 92; Cross Currents: Book Works from the Edge of the Pacific, Selby Gallery, Ringling Sch Art, Sarasota, Fla, 92; The Shrine, Falkirk Cult Ctr 16th Exhib, San Rafael, Calif, 92; and others. *Pos:* Gallery asst, John Bolles Gallery, 70-71. *Teaching:* Instr, San Francisco Community Col, 66- & Indian Valley Col, Marin, Calif, 74. *Bibliog:* Dwight Johnson (auth), article, Palo Alto Times, 74; Lois Fishman (auth), article, Artweek, 74; Alfred Frankenstein (auth), article in San Francisco Chronicle, 74; and others. *Mem:* Col Art Asn Am; Women's Caucus Art; Artists Equity; and others. *Media:* Multimedia. *Mailing Add:* Ephemera Studio 2854 Harrison St San Francisco CA 94110

TAYSOM, WAYNE PENDELTON
SCULPTOR, EDUCATOR
b Afton, Wyo, Oct 10, 25. *Study:* Univ Wyo; Columbia Univ; Univ Utah, BFA, 48; Ecole Beaux-Arts, Paris; Teachers Col, Columbia Univ, MA, 50; Cranbrook Acad Art. *Work:* Ore State Univ Mem Union; Corvallis Clin, Ore; Univ Ore Erb Mem Union; US Nat Bank Ore, Portland. *Comn:* Archit sculpture, Lane Co Courthouse, Eugene; Corvallis Br, US Nat Bank Ore; fountain & doors, Ore State Univ Libr; coun chamber doors, Salem Civic Ctr, Ore; St Mary's Cath Church, Corvallis; and others. *Exhib:* One-man show, Portland Art Mus, 54, Paper Works, 72; Seattle World's Fair, 62; Am Crafts Coun, Western Craftsmen, 64; Hunnicutt Art Gallery, Hawaii, 67; and others. *Teaching:* Instr sculpture, Univ Ore, 51-52; prof sculpture, Ore State Univ, 53-88, prof emer, currently. *Awards:* Purchase Prize, Portland Art Mus, 56. *Mem:* Portland Art Asn; Corvallis Art Asn. *Mailing Add:* 1765 NW Alta Vista Dr Corvallis OR 97330

TCHAKALIAN, SAM
PAINTER
b Shanghai, China, 1929. *Study:* San Francisco City Col, AA, 50; San Francisco State Col, BA, 52, MFA, 58. *Work:* San Francisco Mus Mod Art; Oakland Mus; Milwaukee Art Ctr; Albright-Knox Art Gallery, Buffalo, NY; Brooklyn Mus, NY; Milwaukee Art Ctr, Wis. *Exhib:* Ann exhibs, San Francisco Mus Mod Art, 58-65; Pointdexter Gallery, Los Angeles, 61; one-man shows, Dilexi Gallery, San Francisco, 60, John Bolles Gallery, San Francisco, 66, Molly Barnes Gallery, Los Angeles, 68, Portland Ctr for Visual Arts, Portland, Ore, 79, Modernism, San Francisco, 86, 87 & 91, Nat Mus Contemp Art, Seoul, Korea, 89; Levi Strauss Collection, San Francisco Mus Mod Art, 74; A City Collects, Transamerica Corp, San Francisco, 85; Security Pac Gallery, San Francisco, 91. *Teaching:* Guest lectr, Calif Col Arts & Crafts, Oakland, 62-63; painting instr, Col San Mateo, Calif, 64-65; painting fac, San Francisco Mus Mod Art, 61. *Awards:* 80th Ann Painting Award, San Francisco Mus Mod Art, 61; Adaline Kent Award, San Francisco Art Inst, 81; Nat Endowment Arts, 75, 81 & 89. *Mailing Add:* c/o Modernism 685 Market St Suite 290 San Francisco CA 94105

TCHETCHET, TATIANA
PAINTER
b Moscow; US citizen. *Study:* Moscow Art Sch. *Work:* Human Resources Ctr, Great Neck; Art Gallery Am Merchant Marine Acad. *Exhib:* Am Artist Prof Art League, US Custom House Mus, New York, 80; Hechscher's Mus, Huntington, NY, 80; one-person show, Am Merchant Marine Mus, Kings Point, NY, 82; Nat Art League, Douglaston, New York, 88; 58th Ann Members Exhib, Nat Art League Inc, Douglaston, NY, 88. *Teaching:* Pvt lessons at studio in Kings Point, NY, 57-62; instr drawing & painting, Great Neck Cult Art Ctr, 63-67. *Awards:* First Prize Art Exhib, Murray Hill News, 57; Third Prize, Nat Art Show, 80; Second Prize, Am Artist Prof League, 80; Bronze Medal, 58th Ann Mem Exhib, Nat Art League, 88. *Mem:* Am Artists Prof League; Nat Art League. *Media:* Oil, Pastel. *Publ:* Illusr, Picture Play, Street & Smith, 33; Breezy Stories & Romantic Love, Youngs Mag, 35. *Mailing Add:* 80 Knightsbridge Rd Great Neck NY 11021

TEAGUE, EDWARD H
LIBRARIAN, EDUCATOR
Study: Univ NC, Chapel Hill, BFA, 73, MSLS, 78; Univ Ga, MA(art hist), 76. *Pos:* Reference librn, Valdosta State Col, Ga, 78-80; head reference dept, Univ NC, Charlotte, 82-84; archit & fine arts librn, Univ Fla, Gainesville, 84-; ed, Art References Services Quarterly, Haworth Press, 90- *Mem:* Art Libr Soc NAm (exec bd, 88-91); Asn Archit Librns; Asn Archit Sch Librns. *Res:* Reference and research services for design disciplines. *Interests:* Architecture, modern art, ancient art, landscape architecture, interior design, building construction. *Publ:* Auth, Henry Moore: Bibliography & Reproductions Index, McFarland, 81; World Architecture Index, Greenwood Press, 91; Index to Italian Archit, Greenwood Press, 92. *Mailing Add:* PO Box 12872 Gainesville FL 32604

TECZAR, STEVEN W
PAINTER, EDUCATOR
b St Joseph, Mo, Aug 8, 48. *Study:* Univ Mo, Columbia, BA, 70, MA, 72; Washington Univ, St Louis, MFA, 86. *Work:* Greenville Co Mus Art, SC; Southeastern Ctr Contemp Art, Winston-Salem, NC; Va Mus Fine Arts, Richmond; Charleston Art Gallery Sunrise, WVa; Suwa Munic Art Mus, Suwa, Japan; Nanjing Sch Fine Arts, Nanjing, China. *Exhib:* 1940-80

Fellowship Recipients, Va Mus, Richmond, 80; The Next Juried Show, Va Mus, Richmond, 83; Currents 29: Drawing in St Louis, St Louis Art Mus, 85; St Louis Contemp Works, Nanjing Sch Fine Arts, Nanching, China, 88; Suwa Munic Art Mus, Suwa, Japan, 88; Four Square Feet, Sazama/Brauer Gallery, Chicago, Ill, 88; New Work on paper & Constructions, B S Wagman Gallery, St Louis, 89; New Constructions and Drawings, Atrium Gallery, St Louis, 91; & others. *Pos:* Prin, Design Collaborative Richmond, Va, 74-78. *Teaching:* Asst prof drawing & design, Va Commonwealth Univ, Richmond, 72-79; prof & art div chmn, Maryville Univ St Louis, 79- *Awards:* WVa Arts & Humanities Coun Purchase Award, Charleston Art Gallery Sunrise, 74; Va Mus Purchase Award, 75; Purchase Award, 46th Southeastern Competition, Southern Ctr Contemp Art, 78; Va Mus Prof Artist Fel Painting & Drawing, 78-79; Nat Endowment Arts to Print Workshop, Richmond, Va, 79-80; Fac Prof Travel Grant, Maryville Col, St Louis, 87. *Bibliog:* Alexandra Bellos (auth), Contrasting Approaches at Galleria Exhibition, St Louis Post-Dispatch, 2/16/89; Alexandra Bellos (auth), Sea Views, Riverfront Times, St Louis, 1/91; Karen Schmitendorf (auth), Teczar's Trailing Lines, St Louis Post-Dispatch, 2/2/91. *Mem:* Col Art Asn Am; Nat Asn Schs Art & Design; Art St Louis. *Media:* Oil Pastel, Acrylic. *Publ:* Drawing in St Louis, 85, Art St Louis, 86-89 & St Louis Contemp Works: An Invitational Exchange, 87; Currents 29: Drawing in St Louis, 85; American Drawings, 76. *Dealer:* Carolyn Miles Atrium Gallery 815 Olive St St Louis MO 63101. *Mailing Add:* 518 Cornelia Ave St Louis MO 63119-1807

TEFFT, ELDEN CECIL
SCULPTOR, EDUCATOR
b Hartford, Kans, Dec 22, 19. *Study:* Univ Kans, BFA, 49, MFA, 50; Cranbrook Acad Art, 51-52; with Bernard Frazier, William McVey. *Comn:* Franklin D Murphy (bronze), Sculpture Garden, Univ Calif, Los Angeles, 69; Moses (bronze), Kans Sch Religion, Lawrence, Kans, 82; Ida B Wells (bronze bust), Wells Journalistic Ann Award, 83; Buddy Award, a bronze sculpture presented ann by the Kans Univ Dept Theatre & Media Arts & the Univ Theatre, 87-; Keepers of the Universe (limestone triptych), City of Lawrence, Kans, 88. *Exhib:* One-man show, Philbrook Art Ctr, Tulsa, Okla, 48; San Francisco Mus Art, Calif, 50; Carnegie Mus, Philadelphia, Pa, 50; The Midwest Show, Joslyn Art Mus, Nebr, 52; 58th Ann Exhib for Western Artists, Denver Art Mus, Colo, 53; Mid-Am Invitational, William Rockhill Nelson Gallery Art, Kans City, Mo, 55; Missouri Show, City Art Mus, St Louis Art Mus, 59; Kans Sculptors Asn Outdoor Ann Exhib, Lawrence, Kans, 88-89 & 91-92; two-man show with Kim T Tefft, Baker Univ, Baldwin, Kans, 92. *Pos:* Chmn, Nat-Int Sculpture Conf, 60-78; dir, Nat Sculpture Ctr, Lawrence, Kans, 67-77, Int Sculpture Ctr, Lawrence, Kans, 77-80, Sculpture Research Ctr, Univ Kansas, Lawrence, 80-90; dir emer, Int Sculptor Ctr, Washington, DC, 80-; prof emer, Univ Kans, 90- *Teaching:* Prof sculpture, Univ Kans, 50-90; vis prof, Univ Philippines, Quezon City, 64, Univ Ore, Eugene, 64, Univ Costa Rica, San Jose, 71, Cent Inst Fine Art Beijing, Shanghai Jiao Tong Univ, China, 86 & Ateno Paraquayo, Asuncion, Paraguay, 88; workshop, Baker Univ, Baldwin, Kans, 92. *Awards:* 17th Mo Show, City Art Mus St Louis, 59; First Award Arch Sculpture Competition, Fidelity State Bank, Topeka, Kans, 67; Nat Sculpture Conf, Jonesboro, Ark, 77. *Bibliog:* Dennis Kowal & D Meilach (auths), Sculpture Casting, Crown Publ, Inc, NY, 72; Robert Rose (cinematographer), Moses, The Creation of a Heroic Sculpture, Sculpture Research Ctr, Lawrence, Kansas, 85. *Media:* Bronze, Stone. *Res:* World sculpture founding techniques and their effect on the creative process. *Publ:* Auth, Bronze Casting of Sculpture (film), Int Film Bureau, Chicago, 60; Lost Wax Sculpture Foundry Equipment & Design: Ceramic Shell Supplement, Sculpture Res Ctr, 83; Lost Wax Sculpture Founding, An Exploration, Sculpture Res Ctr, Univ Kans, 92. *Mailing Add:* Sculpture Res Ctr Univ Kans Lawrence KS 66045

TEICHMAN, MARY MELINDA
PRINTMAKER, CHILDRENS BOOK ILLUSTRATOR
b Newark, NJ, Sept 8, 54. *Study:* Cooper Union, New York, BFA, 76. *Work:* Corcoran Gallery, Washington, DC; Brooklyn Mus, New York; Mus Art, Carnegie Inst, Pittsburgh; Columbus Mus Arts & Sci, SC; Mus Art & Archaeol, Columbia, Mo; Duxbury Art Complex Mus; Art Inst, Portland. *Exhib:* Solo exhibs, A Clean Well Lighted Place, New York, 82 & 91 & Univ Minn, Morris, 87, Nat Inst Health, Bethesda, Md, 88 & 90, Univ New Brunswick, NJ, 89; Soc Am Graphics Artists Competition, New York, 79, 86, 88, 91 & 92; Print Club, Philadelphia, 80-81; Brooklyn Mus, New York, 81; Hunterdon Art Ctr, NJ, 81, 83 & 85; Assoc Am Artists, New York, 82, 84, 85, 87, 89 & 92; Contemporary Images, Mus City New York, 82-92; Boston Printmakers International, De Cordova Mus, Lincoln, Mass, 82-84 & 86; Nat Acad Design, New York, 81, 86 & 88; Mid-Hudson Art & Sci Ctr, Poughkeepsie, NY, 88. *Awards:* Boston Printmakers Award, 88; Chancellor's Purchase Award, 62nd Nat Print Exhib, Univ Wis, 89; Merit Award, Purdue Univ, Ind, 90; and others. *Mem:* Boston Printmakers; Soc Am Graphic Artists; Western Mass Illusr Guild. *Media:* Color Etching. *Dealer:* Assoc Am Artists 20 W 57th St New York NY. *Mailing Add:* 7 Liberty St No 1 East Hampton MA 01027-1403

TEILHET-FISK, JEHANNE HILDEGARDE
HISTORIAN, EDUCATOR
b Palo Alto, Calif, May 16, 39. *Study:* Univ Calif, Los Angeles, BA, 62, MA, 67 & PhD(art hist), 75. *Collections Arranged:* Arts of East Africa, Los Angeles Mus Sci & Indust, 67; Dimensions of Black (auth, catalog), La Jolla Mus Art, 70; Dimensions of Polynesia (auth, catalog), San Diego Fine Arts Gallery, 73; Gauguin: Polynesian Sources, Mus A Gauguin, Tahiti, 81. *Pos:* Asst cur, Jos Mus, Nigeria, 67-68; consult ed, Tofua Press, San Diego, Calif, 75-77; filmmaker, Tapa Production in Tonga, 76- *Teaching:* Prof non-Western art hist, Dept Visual Arts, Univ Calif, San Diego, 68- *Awards:* Kress Found & Nat Endowment Arts Awards, Dimensions of Polynesia, 73; Univ Research Grants, 87 & 88; Distinguished Teaching Award, Univ Calif, 90. *Res:* Focus on non-Western arts of Oceania, Native American & Afro-Am with special interests in woman's art forms & folk art. *Publ:* Auth, The Role of Women Artists in Polynesia and Melanesia, Dunmore Press, 83; Paradise Review: An Interpretation of Gauguin's Polynesian Symbolism, UMI Press, 83; Tongan Grave Art: Indicators of Social Change, Univ Hawaii, 90; To Beat or Not to Beat; A Study on Acculturation and change in an Art Making Process, Pacific Studies, 91; Clothes in Tradition: The Ta'ovala and Kiekie as Social Text and Aesthetic Markers of Custom and Identity in contemporary Tongan Society, Part I & II, Pacific Arts, 92. *Mailing Add:* Dept Visual Arts B-027 Univ Calif San Diego La Jolla CA 92093

TELBERG, VAL
PHOTOGRAPHER, PAINTER
b Moscow, Russia, Feb 14, 10; US citizen. *Study:* Wittenberg Col, BA, 32; Art Students League, 42-56. *Work:* Mus Mod Art, New York; San Francisco Mus Mod Art; Minn Inst Art; Getty Mus, Malibu, Calif; Smithsonian Inst. *Exhib:* Solo exhib, Brooklyn Mus Art, 48, Smithsonian Inst, 51, Parrish Mus Art, Southampton, NY, 65, Hudson River Mus, Yonkers, NY, 66, Guild Hall Mus, East Hampton, NY, 82, New Orleans Mus Art, 82 & San Francisco Mus Mod Art, 83, Elaine Benson Gallery, Bridgehampton, NY, 91; Gallery Huit, Paris, France, 51; Impact of Surrealism on American Art, Whitney Mus, New York, 88; Boca Raton Mus Art, Fla, 89; Univ Md, College Park, 90. *Teaching:* Instr photog, Southampton Col, 66 & 85; co-dir, Youth Theatre Workshop, Guild Hall, East Hampton, NY, 71-76. *Awards:* Yaddo Fel, 53 & 54; Huntington Hartford Fel, 54. *Bibliog:* Coke (auth), Photography: A Facet of Modernism, Hudson Hill Press, 86; Belinda Rathbone (auth), Photography and Surrealism in America, Centro Atlantico De Arte Moderno, Canary Islands, 90; Steven Carothers & Gail Roberts (auths), Photographer's Dialogue, Boca Raton Mus Art, Fla, 89; Cynthia Wayne (auth), Dreams, Lies and Exaggerations-Photomontage in America, Univ Md, Collage Park, 91. *Mem:* Art Students League; Jimmy Ernst Artists Alliance, Amagansett, NY. *Media:* Photomontage. *Publ:* Illusr, House of Incest, Swallow Press, 58. *Dealer:* Laurence Miller 138 Spring St New York NY 10012. *Mailing Add:* PO Box 920 Bay St Sag Harbor NY 11963

TELLER, DOUGLAS H
PAINTER, EDUCATOR
b Battle Creek, Mich, June 1, 33. *Study:* Western Mich Univ, BA, 56; Mich State Univ, George Washington Univ, MFA, 62. *Work:* Corcoran Gallery Art, State Dept, George Washington Univ, Smithsonian Inst & Libr of Cong, Washington, DC. *Exhib:* Corcoran Gallery Touring Show, 59 & 60; Relig Arts Show, Smithsonian Inst, DC, 61; Provincetown Art Asn, Chrysler Mus, Mass, 63; Soc Washington Printmakers Int Show, Nat Collection Fine Arts, DC, 64; one-man show, Corcoran Gallery Art, 65; Massillon Mus Invitational, Ohio, 69; two-man show, Dimock Gallery, George Washington Univ, DC, 79; George Washington Univ, annually; Cosmos Club, 87; and others. *Teaching:* Prof serigraphy & watercolor, George Washington Univ, DC, 63- *Awards:* Third Graphics Award, Arts Club Washington, 61; Third Relig Art Show Award, Smithsonian Inst, 61; First & Purchase Award, Corcoran Gallery Art, 65. *Mem:* Va Watercolor Soc. *Media:* Watercolor. *Publ:* Auth, Art and Design, George Washington Univ, 60. *Mailing Add:* c/o Mariposa Gallery Inc 2116 18th St NW Washington DC 20009

TEMES, MORT (MORTIMER ROBERT TEMES)
CARTOONIST, DESIGNER
b Jersey City, NJ, Apr 15, 28. *Study:* Art Students League, with William McNulty, Jon Corbino, Frank Reilly & Robert B Hale, 47-49; NY Univ, BA, 53. *Pos:* Prof free lance cartoonist, 50-; dir spec serv, NJ Inst Technol, 58-88; dir off serv, 88-91. *Teaching:* Newark Col Eng, 60-65. *Mem:* Nat Cartoonists Soc; Life mem, Art Students League. *Media:* Pen, Ink; Pencil, Watercolor. *Publ:* Illusr, Engineers & Engineering--Some Definitions, 68; Making Tomorrow Happen, 70; cartoons have appeared in many nat mags & cartoon anthologies. *Mailing Add:* 10 Sycamore Dr Hazlet NJ 07730

TEMPEST, GERARD FRANCIS
PAINTER, SCULPTOR
b San Donato, Italy, Feb 23, 18; US citizen. *Study:* Mass Sch Art, studio art, 39; Tufts Univ, Mus Sch, Boston, Mass, 45; pvt study with Giorgio de Chirico, Rome, 48, Univ NC, BA, 49. *Work:* Vatican Mus Art, Vatican City, Italy; Akiraniasaki Collection, Tokyo, Japan; NC Mus, Raleigh; La Fondation Michelange, Venaco, Corsica; Monte Cassino Mus, Cassino, Italy. *Comn:* Empress Farah Diba (HIM), comn by Shah of Iran, Teheran, 74. *Exhib:* Salon D'Automne de Lyon, France, 67; Mus Fine Arts, Boston, 68; solo exhibs, Duke Mus Art, Durham, NC, 78 & Bergen Co, NJ, 91. *Awards:* Purchase Award, NC Mus Art, Raleigh, 49; Gold Medal, II Biennale Azureen, Cannes, France, 67. *Bibliog:* Sarah Margaret Cameron (auth), Tempest: Abstract Spiritualism, De Luca, Rome, Italy, 73. *Media:* Oil on Canvas; Cast Metal. *Mailing Add:* 106 Central Park S New York NY 10019

TEMPLE, BYRON
CERAMIST
b Ind, 33. *Study:* Ball State Univ, 51-52. *Work:* State Mus NJ; Harrison Mus Art; Ball State Univ Mus; Am Craft Mus; Peat Marwick Montvale Art Collection. *Exhib:* One-man shows, Concept Design, Lambertville, NJ, 85, Univ Calif, San Diego, 86, Caja Rural, Granada, Spain, 87, Sargadelos, Madrid, Spain, 87, Sordoni Art Gallery, Wilkes-Barre, Pa, 89, Swearingen Gallery, Louisville, Ky, 89, Amaury St Gilles, Tokyo, 89; Contemporary Crafts: An Expaning View, Monmouth Mus & Squibb Gallery, NJ; Craft Today-Poetry of the Physical, Am Craft Mus, New York, 86; Art in Craft II,

Bellas Artes, Santa Fe, NMex, 87. *Pos:* Independent studio potter. *Bibliog:* Dawna Richard-Hyde (auth), Byron Temple's Quest for Beauty and Utility, Ceramics Art & Perception, No 6, 91. *Mailing Add:* 1259 Ray Ave Louisville KY 40204

TEN BROEKE, JAN
PAINTER
b Marienberg, Netherlands, June 8, 30. *Exhib:* Newark Mus, 61; one-man shows, Flemington Studio Arts, NJ, 71, Upstairs Gallery, Somerville, NJ, 72 & Papermill Playhouse, Milburn, NJ, 72; Plainfield Regional Art Mus, NJ, 79; Ctr Int D'Art Contemporain, Paris, France, 84; Mandragore Int Galerie D'Art, Paris, France, 86; and others. *Awards:* Wally's Award, Plainfield Art Asn, 66, First Prize in Oils, 69; Tracy Long Mem Award, Summit Art Ctr, 66. *Bibliog:* Doris Brown (auth), Surrealist's exhibit opens, 5/3/70, Franklin artist, 8/8/71 & Dutch-born artist, 6/25/72, Sunday Home News. *Mem:* Hunterdon Co Art Ctr; NJ Print Coun; Artists Equity. *Media:* Oil. *Mailing Add:* Box 498 RD 1 Somerset NJ 08873

TEN EYCK, CATRYNA (CATRYNA TEN EYCK SEYMOUR)
PAINTER, PRINTMAKER
b New York, NY, June 30, 31. *Study:* Smith Col; Art Students League. *Work:* Nat Collection Fine Arts, Smithsonian Inst, Washington, DC; Calif Palace Legion Hon, San Francisco; Denver Art Mus; Honolulu Acad Arts; Munson-Williams-Proctor Inst, Utica, NY. *Media:* Graphic, Acrylic. *Publ:* Auth, Enjoying the Southwest, Lippincott, 73. *Mailing Add:* Box 363 Salisbury CT 06068

TENGROTH, MIRRA See Mirra, (Mirra Tengroth)

TENNANT, DONNA KAY
WRITER, EDITOR
b Waynesburg, Pa, Nov 28, 49. *Study:* Univ Rochester, NY, BA(art hist), 71; Univ NMex, Albuquerque, MA(art hist), 79; also with Beaumont Newhall. *Pos:* Art critic, Houston Chronicle, Tex, 79-81; asst dir, Jeremy Stone Gallery, San Francisco, 82-84 & 89-91, Sherry French Gallery, New York, 84-85; assoc ed, Mus Fine Arts, Houston, 85-86; adminr, Houston Art Dealers Asn, 87-89 & 91-; ed, Orange press, 91- *Res:* Second-generation abstract expressionism; 19th & 20th century art, history of photography. *Publ:* Ibsen Espada (catalog), McMurtrey Gallery, 89; Ferne Koch (catalog), FotoFest, 90; Nine in Fiber, Artspace, 90; Art Car--Icon of Our Time, Orange Press, 92; Jacob Lawrence, Painter, Mus & Arts Mag, 92. *Mailing Add:* 2603 Parana Houston TX 77080

TENZER, (DR & MRS) JONATHAN A
COLLECTORS
Dr Tenzer, b New York, NY, May 21, 40. *Study:* Dr Tenzer, Univ Vt, BA, 62; Univ Pa, DMD, 66. *Collection:* A Wyeth, Moses (Anna Robertson), Rockwell; Michele Delacroix. *Mailing Add:* 2332 River Bend Rd RD 2 Allentown PA 18103

TERAOKA, MASAMI
PAINTER, SCULPTOR
b Onomichi, Japan, Jan 13, 36. *Study:* Kwansei Gakuin Univ, Kobe, Japan, BA(esthetics), 59; Otis Art Inst, BA, MFA, 68. *Work:* Oakland Mus; Achenbach Found Graphic Arts, Fine Arts Mus San Francisco; Los Angeles Co Mus Art; Nat Mus Am Art, Washington, DC; Minneapolis Inst Arts. *Comn:* Cover illus, Time Mag, 3/30/81. *Exhib:* Solo exhibs, Masami Teraoka: AIDS Ser, Grey Art Gallery, NY Univ, 90, Henry Art Gallery, Seattle, Wash, 91, Schmidt/Dean Gallery, Philadelphia, Pa, 91, Macquarie Galleries, Rushcutters Bay, Australia, 92, Rebecca Hossack Gallery, London, Eng, 92 & Pamela Auchincloss Gallary, New York, 90 & 92; All for Love, Tyler Galleries, Temple Univ, Pa, 91; In the Looking Glass, Mint Mus, Charlotte, NC, 91; Parallel Visions: Modern Artists & Outsider Art, Los Angeles Co Mus Art, 92; From Media to Metaphor: Art About AIDS, organized by Independent Cur Inc (travelling), 92; and others. *Pos:* Lectr, Art Gallery New South Wales, Victorian Col Arts, Melbourne, Australia, 89 & San Francisco Art Inst, Calif, 89. *Teaching:* Artist in res, Victorian Col Arts, Melbourne, Australia. *Awards:* Artists Fel, Nat Endowment Arts, 80 & 89; Kay Nielsen Mem Purchase Award, Los Angeles Co Mus Art, 78. *Bibliog:* Howard Link (auth), Masami Teraoka, Whitney Mus Am Art, 79; Gerald Haggerty (auth), Masami Teraoka, Oakland Mus, 83; Howard Link (auth), Waves & Plaques: The Art of Masami Teraoka, Contemp Mus, Honolulu, 88. *Media:* Watercolor. *Mailing Add:* c/o Pamela Auchinclose Gallery 558 Broadway New York NY 10012

TERKEN, JOHN
SCULPTOR
b Rochester, NY, Jan 11, 12. *Study:* Beaux Arts Inst Design, with Chester Beach, Lee Lawrie & Paul Manship; NY Sch Fine & Indust Arts; Columbia Sch Fine Arts; also Europ art ctrs. *Work:* Roswell Mus, NMex; Gregory Mus, Hicksville, NY. *Comn:* Eagle Fountain, Salisbury Park, East Meadow, NY, 61; New Horizons, Hempstead Town Plaza, 69; Richard Henry Dana Monument, San Juan Capistrano Hist Soc, Calif, 72; Colonial Lad (bicentennial figure), East Meadow, Pub Libr, NY, 77; Three Metaphysical Pioneers, comn by Phineas Parkhurst Quimby, Emma Curtis Hopkins & Ernest Holmes, 79; and others. *Exhib:* Nat Acad Design, New York, 68; Nat Arts Club, New York, 70; Hudson Valley Art Asn, Westchester, NY, 71; Acad Artists Asn, Springfield, Mass, 71; Nat Sculpture Soc, New York, 72. *Pos:* Advert mgr, Nat Sculpture Rev, 49-65, mem ed bd, 70-72, mem, Bd Coop Educ Serv, Long Island Dist, 69-74, deleg to Fine Arts Fedn New York, 70-72. *Teaching:* Lectr sculpture, East Meadow High Sch. *Awards:* Louis Comfort Tiffany Found Award, 49; Lindsey Morris Mem Prize, Nat Sculpture Soc, 65; Coun Am Artists Award, Am Artists Prof League, 72. *Mem:* Fel Nat Sculpture Soc (mem coun, 62-, secy, 68-70, first vpres, 77-78 & 78-79); fel Hudson Valley Art Asn; assoc Int Inst Conservators; Acad Artists Asn; Art League Nassau Co; and others. *Media:* Bronze. *Mailing Add:* 386 Chambers Ave East Meadow NY 11554

TERMES, (DICK A)
PAINTER, PHOTOGRAPHER
b San Diego, Calif, Nov 7, 41. *Study:* Black Hills State Col, BS, 64; Univ Wyo, Laramie, MA(art), 69; Otis Art Inst, Los Angeles, MFA, 71. *Work:* Denver Art Mus; Otis Art Inst, Los Angeles; Coca Cola Corp, Atlanta, Ga; SDak Art Mus, Brookings. *Comn:* 5 1/2 ft centennial sphere for State of SDak; Pull to the North (sphere), North Pole, Alaska; Order/Disorder (sphere), Law Enforcement Acad, Wyo. *Exhib:* Pillsbury Am Art Exhib, Tenn, 81; Spherical Thinking and Total Photos, Col Archit Gallery, Ariz State Univ, 82 & Univ Ky, Lexington, 83; Mus of Fun (15 cities), Japan, 84; Air & Space Mus, Smithsonian Inst, 87; Montana Moon Gallery, Chicago, Ill, 88; Gallery on the Green, Lexington, Mass, 89; San Francisco State Univ, 90. *Teaching:* Instr art, Henley High Sch, Klamath Falls, Ore, 64-66, Sheridan High Sch, 66-68 & Black Hills State Univ, 71-72. *Awards:* SDak Arts Coun Fel, 76 & 80; Artistic Achievment Citation, SDak Mus Art, 86. *Bibliog:* Susan O'Neill (auth), Six point perspective--the total view, Denver Post, 77; David Miller (auth), Total photographer has whole world in his hands, 80, Mod Photog, 80; Daralice Boles (auth), Termes total photo, Progressive Archit, 83; Shaping Space, 88; Curvilinear Perspective, 87. *Media:* Lexan Plastic Globe Canvas, Acrylic. *Publ:* Contribr, Vantage Paint, Am Coun Arts, 10/88; Art Gallery Int Mag, 8/89. *Mailing Add:* Rte 2 Box 435B Spearfish SD 57783

TERMINI, CHRISTINE
PAINTER, SCULPTOR
b Brooklyn, NY, Sept 30, 47. *Study:* Pratt Inst, BFA; Hunter Col, study with Tony Smith & Robert Walker, MFA. *Exhib:* Long Beach Mus, NY, 80 & 81; Nat Soc Painters Casein & Acrylic, 81; one-woman show, Univ Pa, 82; Art Views, East Hampton, 83; Sound Shore Gallery Inc, Portchester, 83; Laguna Beach Mus Art, Calif, 84; Newport Harbor Art Mus, Calif, 84; EAC Gallery, New York, 85-90; Beaux Arts Gallery, Southbury, Conn, 88; Phoenix Gallery, New York, 88. *Pos:* Art dir, Circle Galleries, New York, 76-77, Jack Gallerie, New York, 76-77, Gallerie La Grande Illusion, New York, 77, Neill Gallery, New York, 78-79, Atelier Royce Ltd, 81, Hanover Fine Arts, Mass, 83. *Teaching:* Lectr galleries, New Sch, Sch Visual Arts, New York, 77-78; adj prof, La Guardia Community Col, 89-90. *Bibliog:* Chris Jones (auth), The 24 Hour Room, Am Home Mag, 5/77; New York Art Rev, 88. *Media:* Acrylic, Oil; Clay. *Mailing Add:* 250 Gorge Rd Apt 12F Cliffside Park NJ 07010

TERRA, DANIEL J
COLLECTOR, PATRON
b Philadelphia, Pa, June 8, 11. *Study:* Pa State Univ, BS, 31; Lehigh Univ, Columbia Univ & Northwestern Univ, 31-36; MacMurray Col, JD, 73; Nat Col Educ, hon DFA, 80. *Pos:* Founder, sponsor & pres, Terra Mus Am Art, Evanston, Ill, currently; US ambassador at large for cult affairs, 81- *Mem:* Nat Arts Club, New York. *Collection:* Early John Singleton Copley portrait; Samuel F B Morse's Gallery of the Louvre and George Caleb Bingham's The Jolly Flatboatmen; a growing number of important Luminist and other nineteenth century paintings; strong representation of American Impressionist works; Maurice Predergast oils, watercolors and monotypes; and many other select works up to and including paintings by Andrew Wyeth and Kenneth Noland. *Mailing Add:* 664 N Michigan Ave Chicago IL 60611

TERRIS, ALBERT
SCULPTOR
b New York, NY, Nov 10, 16. *Study:* With Aaron J Goodelman, 33; Works Progress Admin Art Sch, New York; Beaux Arts Inst Design, New York 33-34; City Col New York, with George W Eggers, BSS, 39; Inst Fine Arts, New York Univ, with Walter Friedlander, Richard Krautheimer & A Phillip McMahon, 39-42. *Comn:* Signature piece (with Jimmy Ernst), for Pontiac Hour, Television, Playwrights 56, comn by Nat Broadcasting Co, 56; Sun (for Wide, Wide World), comn by Abe Liss of Electra Films, 58; Words: Strong, Weak, Argonne Nat Lab, Downers Grove, Ill, comn by Dr Ted Novy, 62; In the Beginning Was the Word, Dr Bill Gerhard, 63; 50 Years, Brooklyn Col Anniversary, 80. *Exhib:* One-man shows, Artist Space, 75 & Gloria Cortella Gallery, New York, 77; Carnegie Int; Brooklyn-Long Island Artists Biennale, Brooklyn Mus, NY, 60; Sculpture Show, Mus Mod Art, New York, 62; Bundy Int Sculpture Exhib, Waitsfield, Vt, 63; Treasures of 20th Century Art, Maremont Collection, Washington Gallery Mod Art, Washington, DC, 64; Critics Choice, Sculpture Ctr New York, 72; Artist in the Civil Service, Brooklyn Col Gallery, 85; and others. *Pos:* Deputy chmn in charge of Dept Art, Sch Gen Studies, Brooklyn Col, NY, 58-70, emer prof, 86. *Teaching:* Prof sculpture & theory of art, Dept Art, Brooklyn Col, NY, 47-86. *Awards:* First Prize, Long Island Artists Biennale, Brooklyn Mus, 60. *Bibliog:* Sidney Geist (auth), Month in review, Arts Mag, 1/58; Irving Sandler (auth), Am construction sculpture, Evergreen Review, Vol 2, No 2, spring 59; James A Schinneller (auth), Search & Self Discovery, Int Textbook Co, 68. *Media:* Steel Welded. *Publ:* Contrib, Artists on the Current Scene, Arts Yearbook 4, 60; The Private Myth, Tanager Gallery, 60; auth, Retrospective 1950-1975, Metal Sculpture, Freeport Mem Libr, 77. *Mailing Add:* 280 S Ocean Ave Freeport NY 11520

TERRY, HILDA
CARTOONIST
b Newburyport, Mass, June 25, 14. *Study:* Art Students League; Nat Acad Design; NY Univ. *Comn:* Fulton Fish Market (acrylics), comn by Sam Marg, New York, 71. *Pos:* Dir, Hilda Terry Gallery, New York; computer animator for electronic score boards; pres & dir, Computered Scoreboard Graphics Exchange Inc; dir archs, Reeder & Terry Ltd. *Teaching:* Instr cartooning, New Sch Social Res, 68 & New York Phoenix Sch Art & Design, 69-71, & Art Students League, 90. *Awards:* Wohelo Award, Camp Fire Girls; Best Waste-Not Cartoon, New York Times, 42; NCS Best Animations Cartoonist, 79. *Mem:* Nat Cartoonists Soc; NYMUG; lat Women's Writing Guild; Writers Union. *Specialty:* Computer art and science. *Publ:* Auth, Teena, comic strip, 41-64, comic bks, 46-49; Originality in Art, 54; assoc ed, Art Collectors Almanac, 65; Baseball Lights Up, 86; Does God Eat Us?, 90; Strange Bod Fellows. *Mailing Add:* 8 Henderson Pl New York NY 10028

TESFAGIORGIS, FREIDA
PRINTMAKER, EDUCATOR
b Starkville, Miss, Oct 21, 46. *Study:* Graceland Col, Lamoni, Iowa, AA, 66; Northern Ill Univ, De Kalb, BS, 68; Univ Wis, Madison, with Ray Gloeckler & Robert Grilley, MA, 70, MFA, 71. *Work:* Grad Sch, Univ Wis, Madison; Du Sable Mus of African & Afro-Am Art, Chicago; S Side Community Art Ctr, Chicago; Afro-Am Ctr, Univ Wis. *Comn:* Mixed-media drawing, Afro-Am Arts Inst, Univ Ind, Bloomington, 76; prints & drawings, Wis Arts Bd, 78. *Exhib:* Sixth Concours Int de la Palme d'Or des Beaux Arts, Palmares, Monte Carlo, France, 74; Prints & Drawings, MAMA Gallery, Madison, Wis, 76; Beloit Vicinity Ann Exhib, Wright Art Ctr, Wis, 76; 15th Nat Print Exhib, Art Gallery, Bradley Univ, Peoria, Ill, 76; Midwestern Black Artist, Performing Arts Ctr, Milwaukee, Wis, 76. *Pos:* Artist-in-residence, Univ Wis, Madison, 71-72. *Teaching:* Asst prof African/Afro-Am art, Univ Wis, Madison, 72-77, assoc prof African/Afro-Am art, 77- *Awards:* Wis Arts Bd Art Grant, 77; City Arts Grant, Prints & Drawings, Off of the Mayor, Madison, 77. *Bibliog:* Interest in African art is on the increase in US, Capital Times, 7/75; James Auer (auth), PAC surveys midwestern Black art, Milwaukee J, 2/76; Shirley Carley (auth), Starkville native making name in field of art, Starkville Daily News 3/76. *Mem:* Wis Women in the Arts; Nat Conf of Artists (regional coordr, 74); Nat Coun for Black Studies. *Media:* Woodcut. *Publ:* Illusr (cover), Ba Shiru, Univ Wis, 71 & 76-77; contribr, Center debut: A Black artist's view, Milwaukee J, 11/75. *Dealer:* Assoc Am Artist 663 Fifth Ave New York NY 10022. *Mailing Add:* Dept Afro-Am Studies Univ Wis 4231A Humanities 455 N Park St Madison WI 53706

TESKE, EDMUND RUDOLPH
PHOTOGRAPHER
b Chicago, Ill, Mar 7, 11. *Study:* Huettle Art Sch, Chicago; Art Inst Chicago; Univ Chicago. *Work:* Mus Mod Art, New York; Chicago Art Inst; San Francisco Mus Mod Art; George Eastman House, Rochester, NY; Frederick Wight Gallery, Univ Calif Los Angeles. *Exhib:* Photog 1974, Los Angeles Co Mus Art, 74; one-man shows, San Francisco Mus Art, 63, Art Inst Chicago, 70, Friends of Photog, Carmel, Calif, 75, Revision Gallery, Santa Monica, 75, Susan Spiritus Gallery, Newport Beach, Calif, 76 & Visual Studies Workshop, Rochester, NY, 77; Witkin Gallery, New York, 79. *Pos:* Fel, Taliesin Fel, Frank Lloyd Wright, Spring Green, Wis, 36-37. *Teaching:* Instr, New Bauhaus Inst Design, Chicago, 37-38 & Fed Arts Proj, Chicago, 39-40; asst prof art, Chouinard Art Inst, Los Angeles, 62-64; vis prof photog, Col Fine Arts, Univ Calif Los Angeles, 65-70 & 79 & Immaculate Heart Col, Los Angeles, 74. *Awards:* Grants, Frank Lloyd Wright, 36 & Nat Endowment Arts, 75. *Bibliog:* Wright & Brownell (auth), Architecture & Modern Life, Harper & Bros, 37; Hitchcock (auth), In the Nature of Materials, Duell, Sloan & Pearce, 42; Life-the Art of Photography, Time-Life Books, 71. *Publ:* Auth, Edmund Teske, pvt pub, 74. *Dealer:* Lee Witkin Witkin Gallery 41 E 57th St New York NY 10022. *Mailing Add:* 1652 N Harvard Blvd Los Angeles CA 90027

TETERS, J CHARLENE
PAINTER, ILLUSTRATOR
b Spokane, Wash, Apr 25, 52. *Study:* Special study with Sergai Bongart; Inst Am Indian Arts, Santa Fe, Nmex, 86; apprenticeship with Sylvia Sleigh, New York, 86. *Work:* Heritage Ctr Inc, Red Cloud Sch, Pine Ridge, SDak; Sioux Indian Mus, Rapid City, SDak; Spokane City Hall, Wash; Spokane Tribal Mus, Wellpinit, Wash. *Comn:* Emblem-Logo, Nat Tekewitha Orgn, Great Falls, Mont, 82. *Exhib:* American Indian Art Show, Heard Mus, Phoenix, Ariz, 80 & 86; Seattle American Indian Art Show, Nat Exhibit, Seattle, Wash, 80-82; Art in Public Places Show, Spokane, Wash, 82; Red Cloud Art Show, Pine Ridge, SDak, 82-86; Inter Tribal Exhib, Pembroke, NC, 85; Tribute to Native American Women, Inst Am Indian Arts, Santa Fe, NMex, 85. *Awards:* Thunderbird Found Scholar, Red Cloud Art Show, Heritage Ctr, 85-86; Helen Hardin Mem Award, Inst Am Indian Arts, Capistrano Galeria, 86; Second Award, 65th Indian Market, Southwestern Asn Indian Affairs, 86. *Mem:* Southwestern Asn Indian Affairs; Canyonlands Field Inst; Canyonlands Arts Coun. *Media:* Oil. *Publ:* Illusr, Finding A Way Home, Coulee Dam, 83. *Mailing Add:* c/o Inst Am Indian Arts PO Box 20007 Santa Fe NM 87504

TETHEROW, MICHAEL
PAINTER
b Tacoma, Wash, 1942. *Study:* San Francisco Art Inst, BFA, 68. *Work:* Dallas Mus Art, Dallas, Tex; Seattle Mus Contemp Art, Seattle, Wash; Syracuse Univ Art Collection, NY; Neuberger Mus Art, Southampton, NY; Whitney Mus Am Art, New York; Brooklyn Mus, NY; New York Pub Libr. *Exhib:* Bykert Gallery, New York, NY, 72; solo exhibs, Daniel Weinberg Gallery, San Francisco, Calif, 74, Bonlow Gallery, New York, NY, 82, Contemp Art Mus, Houston, Tex, 83, Fabian Carlson Gallery, Goteborg, Sweden, 83, Forum Int Art Fair, Hamburg, Ger, 88 & Seven Years on Paper, Jason McCoy Inc, New York, 92; US Art Now, Nordiska Kompaniet, NK-Teatern, Stockholm Swed, 81; Konstallen Gotaplatsen, Goteborg, Swed, 82; Parrish Art Mus, Southampton, NY, 83; Baskerville & Watson, New York, NY, 86; Nina Freudenheim Gallery, Buffalo, NY, 89-90; Vital Forces: Nature in Contemporary Abstraction, Heckscher Mus, Huntington, NY, 91; New York Collection 1991-92, Albright-Knox Art Gallery, Buffalo, NY, 91. *Awards:* Fel, Nat Endowment Arts, 79 & 87; Engelhard Found Award, 85. *Bibliog:* Ken Johnson (auth), Michael Tetherow, Art in Am, 10/91; Charles Hagen (auth), Inspiration from Dreams, Spirits and the Center of the Earth, NY Times, 11/8/91; Gary Schwan (auth), NY Exhibition Intentive, Cheeky, Palm Beach Post, 1/31/92. *Mailing Add:* Jason McCoy Inc 41 E 57th St New York NY 10022

TETTLETON, ROBERT LYNN
PAINTER, EDUCATOR
b Ruston, La, Dec 23, 29. *Study:* La Polytech Inst, BA, 50; La State Univ, Baton Rouge, MEd, 53; studied painting with Louis Guglielmi, 53 & Hale Woodruff, 63; New York Univ, 63-64. *Exhib:* Mid-South Art Show, Brooks Mem Art Gallery, Memphis, Tenn, 69; one-man shows, Little Theater, Monroe, La, 54, Mary Buie Mus, Oxford, Miss, 70, Sardis Pub Libr, Miss, 79, Univ Gallerie, Univ Miss, 81; Teacher's Touch, Miss Mus Art, Jackson, 83; plus others. *Pos:* Interior designer, Sears Roebuck & Co, Shreveport, La, 59-61; local site coordr, Very Special Arts, 78-88. *Teaching:* Instr art, Port Arthur Independent Sch Dist, 50-51 & Northeast La State Col, 55-56; asst prof art, Univ Fla, 61-65; prof art, Univ Miss, 65-, chmn art dept, 65-76. *Awards:* Hon mention, La Art Comn Exhib, 54; Governors Award, Volunteers, 87. *Mem:* Nat Art Educ Asn; Southeastern Col Art Asn; Col Art Asn; Miss Art Educ Asn (pres, 79-82); Am Soc Interior Designers; and others. *Media:* Oil, Acrylic. *Mailing Add:* 137 Leighton Rd Oxford MS 38677

TEWES, ROBIN J
PAINTER, PRINTMAKER
b Queens, NY, Sept 16, 50. *Study:* Hunter Col, BA(fine arts), 78. *Work:* Prudential Life Insurance; Cabrini Nursing Home. *Exhib:* Critical Perspectives, 81 & The New Portrait, 84, PS 1 Inst, New York; Ann Exhib Art on Paper, Weatherspoon Mus, Greensboro, NC, 82; The Human Figure in Contemporary Art (with catalog), Contemp Arts Ctr, New Orleana, La, 82; Ann Competition, Provincetown Mus, Mass, 83; Portrait on a Human Scale (with catalog), Whitney Mus, New York, 83; And---the Living is Easy, Visual Arts Mus, New York, 84; Situations, Mus Modern Art, New York, 85. *Awards:* NY Found Arts, 89. *Bibliog:* Vivien Raynor (auth), Downtown art comes uptown, 6/26/81 & William Zimmer (auth), Styles designed to capture likeness & personalities, 6/24/84, New York Times; Ronny Cohen (auth), review, Art Forum Mag, 9/83. *Media:* Acrylic, Oil; All. *Publ:* Auth, Art for the Eighties (catalog), Scott Cook, 80 & Episodes (catalog), Carter Ratcliff, 81, Borgenicht Gallery; 26 paintings-Robin Tewes, Hanging Loose Press, 82. *Mailing Add:* 532 LaGuardia Pl, Apt 2 New York NY 10012

TEWI, THEA
SCULPTOR
US citizen. *Study:* Nat Acad Fine Arts, Berlin; Art Students League; Greenwich House; New Sch Social Res. *Work:* Nat Collection Fine Arts, Smithsonian Inst, Washington, DC; Cincinnati Art Mus; Chrysler Mus, Norfolk, Va; Univ Notre Dame; Am Ins Co Corp Collection, Galveston, Tex; Citicorp, New York; City of New York, Dept of Parks; Brooklyn Botanic Garden, New York; plus many others. *Exhib:* 18th-20th Ann New Eng Exhib, Silvermine Guild Artists, 65 & 67-69; Nat Arts Club Exhib Relig Art, 66; one-person shows, La Boetie Gallery, New York, 66, 68 & 70, Hallway Gallery, Washington, DC, 76 & 80, Randall Gallery, New York, 77, 79, 81 & 83, Vorpal Gallery, New York, 85 & NY Acad Sci, 92; Erie Summer Festival Arts, Pa State Univ, 68; 6th Bienniale of Sculpture, Carrara, Italy, 69; and many others. *Awards:* First Prize for Sculpture, Am Soc Contemp Artists, 71, 75, 76 & 79; Nat Arts Club Medal of Merit, 74 & 75; Sculpture Prize, Nat Asn Women Artists, 75 & 76; and others. *Bibliog:* D Meilach (auth), Contemporary Stone Sculpture, Crown, 70; Prize Winning Art, Harold Publ, 67; Art in Public Places, Bowling Green Press, 68. *Mem:* Am Soc Contemp Artists; Sculptors League (pres, 71-); Nat Asn Women Artist; Am Soc Contemp Artists. *Media:* Stone. *Mailing Add:* 100-30 67th Dr Forest Hills NY 11375

TEYRAL, JOHN
PAINTER, INSTRUCTOR
b Yaroslav, Russia, June 10, 12. *Study:* Cleveland Inst Art; Boston Mus Fine Arts Sch; Grande Chaumiere, Paris; Accad Belli Arti, Florence, Italy. *Work:* Cleveland Mus Art; City of Cleveland, Ohio; Butler Inst Am Art; Pepsi Cola Collection; Montclair Mus Art, NJ. *Comn:* Mural, President Garfield Mem, Cleveland; many portraits of prominent persons. *Exhib:* Carnegie Inst Int; Metrop Mus Art; Va Mus Fine Arts; Corcoran Gallery Art; Univ Nebr; and others. *Teaching:* Instr drawing, Boston Mus Sch Fine Arts, 36-37; instr painting & drawing, Cleveland Inst Art, 39-77; retired. *Awards:* Prizes, Cleveland Mus Art, 41-61 & Butler Inst Am Art, 44; Fulbright Grant to Italy, 49-50; and others. *Publ:* Auth, Encaustic--the hot wax medium, In: Portraits in the Making, Phoebe Flory Walker, G P Putnam's Sons, 48. *Dealer:* Harmon Gallery Naples FL 33940. *Mailing Add:* Rte 2 Box 176 Whiteside Cove Rd Highlands NC 28741

THACHER, ANITA
INSTALLATION ARTIST, FILMMAKER
b New York, NY, April 4, 36. *Study:* Antioch Col; New Sch Social Res, BA, 64; New York Studio Sch Drawing, Painting & Sculpture, 65-66; Millennium Film Sch, 67. *Work:* Metrop Mus Art, New York; Chicago Art Inst; Neuberger Mus, State Univ NY, Purchase; SC Art Inst, Columbia; Inst Arts, Rice Univ Mus; Mus Mod Art. *Exhib:* New Directors--New Films, Mus Mod Art, New York, 75; New American Filmmakers, Whitney Mus, 75; Int Festival Jeune Cinema Hyeres, France, 79; Film as Installation, Clocktower, New York, 80 & 83; Schemes: A Decade of Installation Drawings Traveling Show, 81; 19th New York Film Festival, Lincoln Ctr, 81; Film Installation, PS1 Inst Art & Urban Res, New York, 81; Directions 83, Hirshhorn Mus & Sculpture Garden, 83; Film, Fabric & Construction Installation, Fabric Workshop, New York, 85; Mus Mod Art, 91; Anthology Film Arch New York, 91. *Awards:* NY State Coun Arts, 72, 75, 78 & 82; Nat Endowment Arts, 77, 78, 80 & 87; Martin E Segal Award, Lincoln Ctr, 88; and others. *Bibliog:* Joanne Silver (auth), Boston Sunday Herald, 7/21/91; Nancy Stapen (auth), Boston Globe, 7/20/91; Marion Boulton Stroud (auth), An Industrious Art, Innovation in Pattern and Print at the Fabric Workshop, W W Norton & Co, 91. *Mem:* New York Women in Film; Filmmakers Co-op (bd dirs, 85-86); MacDowell Colony (mem bd dirs, 80-85). *Media:* Film, Video. *Publ:* Contribr, Frames, 78, Cover Mag, summer 80, Idiolects J, 83 & Film as Installation Catalog, 83. *Mailing Add:* PO Box 1625 New York NY 10276

THACKSTON, R KING
PAINTER, MURALIST
b Greenville, SC, Dec 21, 48. *Study:* Atlanta Col Art, BFA, 74. *Work:* Albany Mus Art, Ga; State Ga, Atlanta; SC Nat Bank, Greenville. *Comn:* Illusionary graphic mural, Bur Cult Affairs, Atlanta, Ga, 84; 200' Street of Shops, Dewar's Fine Foods, Atlanta, Ga, 89. *Exhib:* Ga Artists, High Mus Art, Atlanta, 73; Piedmont Graphics Exhib, Greenville Mus Art, SC, 75; Murders & Miracles, Albany Mus Art, Ga, 93. *Collections Arranged:* Johnny Detroit's Brunch (40 placesettings by males), 89-90; The Cross Show (70 interpretations of the cross), 90; Taboo's Angry Love, Arts Festival Atlanta, 92. *Pos:* Mem, TABOO Curatorial Group, 88- *Awards:* First Award Drawing, Arts Festival Atlanta, 76; Artist Initiated Grant, Bur Cult Affairs, 83; Art Acquisition Prog, Ga Coun Arts, 86-88. *Media:* Drawing; Mural Painting. *Dealer:* Gallery MSL 75 Bennett St Atlanta GA 30309. *Mailing Add:* 370 Loomis Ave Atlanta GA 30312-2217

THAMES, EMMITT EUGENE
PAINTER
b Brookhaven, Miss, Oct 28, 33. *Study:* Self taught. *Work:* Lauren Rogers Mus Art, Laurel, Miss; Deposit Guaranty Nat Bank, Jackson, Miss; Miss Power Co, Gulfport, Miss; Ivey's Inc, Kosclusko, Miss; Hancock Bank, Gulfport, Miss. *Exhib:* Solo exhibs, Miss Art Asn, Jackson, Miss, 76, Lauren Rodgers Mus Art, Laurel, Miss, 78 & R W Norton Art Gallery, Shreveport, La, 84; The Return to Realism, 77 & America the Beautiful, 17 Points of View, 79, Merrill Chase Galleries, Chicago; Meridian Mus Art, Miss, 87. *Awards:* First Place Watercolor, Edgewater Tri-State, Edgewater Merchants Asn, 66 & Tri-State Exhib, Biloxi Art Asn, 70; Purchase Award, Watercolor USA, Mellers Photo Lab, 71. *Bibliog:* A conversation with Emmitt Thames (film), Miss Educ TV, 75; Marda Kaiser Burton (auth), Emmitt Thames, more feeling than formula, Southwest Art, 1/81; Carter Hillyer (auth), An interview with Emmitt Thames, Miss Mag, 11-12/83; Barbara Salloum (hostess), The Art of Emmitt Thames, (interview), WLOX-TV, 3/13/86 & 3/14/86. *Mem:* Miss Art Asn; Gulf Coast Arts Coun; Mobile Art Asn. *Media:* All Media. *Dealer:* James L Brown 3011 N State St Jackson MS 39216. *Mailing Add:* 100 45th St Gulfport MS 39507

THAW, EUGENE VICTOR
DEALER, COLLECTOR
b New York, NY, Oct 27, 27. *Study:* St John's Col, BA, 47; Columbia Univ (art hist), 47-49; Hartwick Col, Oneonta, NY, Hon Dr Art, 90. *Exhib:* Pvt collection, Pierpont Morgan Libr, Cleveland Mus, Art Inst Chicago & Nat Gallery Can, 75-76; Part II, Thaw Collection, Pierpont Morgan Libr, 85 & Mus Fine Arts, Richmond, Va, 86. *Pos:* Art dealer & pres, E V Thaw & Co, Inc, 50-; writer, Spectator, London, 76-77 & Times, London, 77-78; vchmn, Artemis, S A, 76-; contrib ed, New Republic, 83-; trustee, St John's Col, Annapolis & Santa Fe, 75-83, Glimmerglass Opera Theater, Cooperstown, NY, 83, Hartwick Col, Oneonta, NY, 86-89, Pierpont Morgan Libr, New York, 88 & World Monuments Fund, 90; pres, Pollock-Krasner Found Inc, New York. *Teaching:* Vis lectr fine arts, St John's Col, 73, Asn Art Mus Dirs, 83, Nat Gallery, Washington, DC, 83, Mus Fine Arts, Boston, 83, Pierpont Morgan Libr, 84-85 & Ft Worth Art Mus, 86. *Mem:* Art Dealers' Asn Am (bd dir, 64-, secy & treas, 66-68, vpres, 68-70 & pres, 70-72); IRS Art Adv Panel, 68-71; fel perpetuity, Pierpont Morgan Libr, New York; Grolier Club, New York; Century Asn, New York. *Collection:* Master drawings. *Publ:* Coauth, Jackson Pollock: A Catalogue Raisonne, Yale Univ Press, 78; auth, articles, New York Review of Books, 80, New Criterion, 83 & New Republic, 83; Am Scholar, 83-84 & New York Times Bk Rev, 84; The Abstract Expressionists, Metrop Mus Art, Bulletin, winter 86/87. *Mailing Add:* 726 Park Ave New York NY 10021

THEA, CAROLEE B
SCULPTOR, ENVIRONMENTAL ARTIST
b Brooklyn, NY, Dec 13, 42. *Study:* Skidmore Col, Saratoga Springs; Columbia Univ, BS, 64; Hunter Col, City Univ NY, MA, 76. *Work:* Hofstra Univ Mus, LI, NY; Fla Int Univ Mus, Miami; AMOCO, Denver, Colo; Best Products, Va. *Comn:* Gullivers Blocks, environ sculpture, Md Inst Art, Baltimore, 80; Hellgate Maze, earth work, AREA, Ward Island, NY, 81. *Exhib:* Hudson River Mus, Yonkers, NY 81; Private Icon, Bronx Mus, 81; Landmarks, Bard Col, Blum Art Ctr, Annandale, NY, 84; Out of Square, Cranbrook Acad Mus, Bloomfield, Mich, 84 & 85; Intermedia, Aldrich Mus, Ridgefield, Conn, 84; Still Life, East Hampton Ctr Contemp Art, NY, 89; Journal, Queens Mus, NY, 89; Hofstra Mus, Hempstead, NY, 91. *Pos:* Educ rep to UN Women's Year, 75; contribr revs, Arts Mag & Woman Art Mag, 77-78. *Teaching:* Instr & coordr art dept, Sch of New Resources, Col New Rochelle, NY, 73-78; instr art, Parsons/New Sch, New York 79-; distinguished vis artist, Bard Col, 85, Syracuse Univ, 87-88 & Skidmore Col, 87. *Awards:* Nat Endowment Arts Award, 90; CAPS Finalist, 77, 78 & 79; Athena Found Award, 88. *Mem:* Nat Orgn Women Artists & Writers (co-founder & chmn, Westchester Co, NY, branch, 74-76). *Media:* All Media. *Publ:* Contribr, Eve's idle hand, Art J, 75; Masks power & sisterhood in African Society, Heresies, 78; auth, Self Portraits (catalog essay), Skidmore Col, 88. *Dealer:* Ann Jaffe Gallery 1088 Kane Concourse Bay Harbor Islands FL 33154. *Mailing Add:* 534 La Guardia Place New York NY 10012

THELIN, VALFRED P
PAINTER, LECTURER
b Waterbury, Conn, Jan 8, 34. *Study:* Layton Sch Art; Art Inst Chicago; Int Design Conf Ctr, Insel Mainau, WGer; art seminars in six European countries & Mex. *Work:* Reading Mus, Pa; Ft Wayne Mus, Ind; Butler Inst Am Art, Youngstown, Ohio; Corcoran Gallery Art; Inst Cult Rels, Mexico City. *Exhib:* Watercolor USA, Springfield Mus, Mo, 63-72; Am Watercolor Soc, Nat Acad Galleries, New York, 63-72; Art in the Embassies, sponsored by Smithsonian Inst, Washington, DC, 68-73; Landscape 1 & Art Expo '72, De Cordova Mus, Lincoln, Mass, 70 & 72; Six by Eight, Philbrook Art Mus, Tulsa, Okla, 71; Smithsonian Inst, 78 & 79; Metropolitan Mus Art, 79; Nat Arts Club, New York, 88. *Teaching:* Artist-in-residence, Univ Wis. *Awards:* Second Prize, Golden Gate Expos, IBM Fine Arts Collection, 39; Third Prize for Oil, Soc Four Arts, 47; First Prize for Drawing, Norton Gallery Art, 60; Golden Centaur Award, Venice, Italy, 84; Gardner Nat Acad, 84. *Bibliog:* Joshua Kind (auth), Chicago, Art News, 2/66; Safer (auth), New York reviews, Arts Mag, 4/68; B Sheaks (auth), Painting with acrylics, Davis, 6/72. *Mem:* Ogunquit Art Asn; life mem Rockport Art Asn; Pa Acad Fine Arts; Sarasota Art Asn; Am Watercolor Soc; Salmagundi Club, New York; Soc Four Arts. *Media:* Watercolor, Acrylic. *Publ:* Contribr, Art in Am, 3/67, 68 & 72 & The Art Gallery, 71 & 72; auth, Watercolor page, Am Artist, 12/74; Watercolor, Let the Media Do It, Watson-Guptill, 88. *Mailing Add:* Box 473 Shore Rd Ogunquit ME 03907

THENHAUS, PAULETTE ANN
PAINTER, WRITER
b St Louis, Mo, Nov 8, 48. *Study:* Webster Univ, St Louis, Mo, BA, 71; San Francisco Art Inst, with Perkle Jones, Calif; Southern Ill Univ, Carbondale, Ill, MFA(Phi Kappa Phi), 87. *Work:* Evansville Mus Art & Sci, Ind; Tarble Art Ctr, Eastern Univ, Charleston, Ill; Woodstock Sch Art, NY; Granite City Steel Collection, Ill; Giant City State Park Ctr, Makanda, Ill. *Comn:* Trailing the American Dream (painting), pvt collector, San Francisco, Calif, 84; Percent for Art (2 paintings), Ill State, Carbondale, 87. *Exhib:* One-woman shows, In the Field, Seghi Gallery St Louis, Mo, 86, The Land with Additions, Northeast Mo State, Kirksville, 90; 38th Ann Mid-States, 86 & Winter Dreams, 87, Evansville Mus, Ind; Watercolor: Illinois '89, Tarble Art Ctr, Charleston, 87; Horizontal Traditions, New Harmony Contemp Gallery, Ind, 87; 44th Ann Washington Valley Exhib, Sheldon Swope Gallery, Terra Haute, Ind, 88; 20th Joslyn Biennial, Joslyn Mus, Omaha, Nebr, 88. *Collections Arranged:* Pressworks Ill Printmakers (catalog), 91; Collage/Assemblage (catalog), 92. *Pos:* Asst dir, Peoria Art Guild, Ill, 87-88; mus ed, Blanden Mem Mus, Iowa, 89-90; dir, Galesburg Civic Art Ctr, Ill, 90- *Teaching:* Art educator studio art, Branson Sch, Marin, Calif, 78-84; artist-in-residence, Dorland Colony, Temecula, Calif, 85 & Woodstock Studio Space, NY, 87. *Awards:* Best of Show (mus purchase), 38th Mid-States Exhib, 86; Award, 20th Joslyn Biennial, 88; Best of Show (purchase), Tarble Art Ctr, 89. *Mem:* Am Asn Museums; Cent Ill Artists Coalition; Galesburg Civic Art Ctr, Ill (dir, currently). *Media:* Acrylic, Oil. *Publ:* Auth, Tapping the power of ritual, Artweek, Vol XV, No 5, 2/84; Form beyond function, New Art Examiner, Vol XIII, No 13, 6/86; Paul Flexner, 88 & James Fritz/Lisa Sheets, 89, New Art Examiner. *Dealer:* Locus Gallery St Louis MO. *Mailing Add:* 1492 E Knox Galesburg IL 61401

THEOBALD, GILLIAN LEE
PAINTER, LITHOGRAPHER
b La Jolla, Calif, Nov 17, 44. *Study:* Studied with Byam Shaw, London, 64-65; San Diego State Univ, BA, 67, MA, 71. *Exhib:* Solo exhib, Cirrus Gallery, Los Angeles, 83, 86, 88, 89, 90 & 93, Patty Aande Gallery, San Diego 85-87, Palomar Col, San Marcos, 88; Watercolors: A Contemp Survey, San Diego State Univ Gallery, 84; To the Astonishing Horizon, Los Angeles Design Ctr, 85; A San Diego Exhib (with catalog), La Jolla Mus Contemp Art, 85; Spectrum Los Angeles (with catalog), Gallery Akmak, Berlin, Ger, 85; Scapes (with catalog), Univ Art Mus, Univ Calif, Santa Barbara, 85; Reaching the Summit: Mountain Landscape, Laguna Beach & Saddleback Col, 86; On the Horizon: Emerging Art in California, Fresno Mus, 87; Lines of Vision; Drawings by Contemporary Women (with catalog), Long Island Univ, NY, 89; Waterfall as Image, Occidental Col, Los Angeles, 90; The Contemporary Drawing: Existence, Passage & the Dream (with catalog), Rose Art Mus, Brandeis Univ Mass, 91; The Spirtual Landscape, Biota Gallery, Los Angeles, 91; Soul Survivors; The Courage to go Beyond (with catalog), Beacon St Gallery, Chicago, Ill, 90; Eye of the Creator; Artist's Self Portraits, Bush Art Ctr, Salem, Ore, 92; Summer, 92 Cirrus Gallery, Los Angeles, Calif, 92. *Bibliog:* Theobald's new paintings are on the "must see" list, Los Angeles

Times, 2/14/87; Leah Olman (auth), San Diege-Gillian Theobald, Artnews, 5/87; Mac McCloud, Metaphors in earth and water, Artweek, 3/26/88; Nancy Stapen (auth), Drawings at Brandeis Ask Profound Questions, The Boston Globe, 3/91; Dr Judy Collischan Van Wagner (auth), Lines of Vision: Drawings by Contemporary Women, Hudson Hills Press, NY, 89; Jan Butterfield (auth), The Art Collection of Pacific Enterprises, Pacific Enterprises, Los Angeles, Calif, 91. *Media:* Oil; Ink, Charcoal. *Dealer:* Cirrus Gallery 542 S Alameda St Los Angeles CA 90013; David Lewinson Gallery 1555 Camino Del Mar Del Mar CA 92014. *Mailing Add:* 9610 7th Ave NE Seattle WA 98115

THEOFILES, GEORGE
HISTORIAN, DEALER
b Reading, Pa, July 28, 47. *Study:* Md Inst Col Art, BFA(graphics), 69. *Pos:* Owner, catalog publ & seller, Miscellaneous Man, Vintage Graphics, New Freedom, Pa, 70- *Awards:* Gold Medal Poster Design, Baltimore Md Art Dir Club, 70- *Mem:* Co Military Historians; Int & New England Antique Appraiser's Asn; Poster Soc (bd); Ephemera Soc. *Specialty:* American and European poster art and communication graphics, 1850-1950. *Publ:* Publ, Catalog of Original Poster Art and Graphics (tri-ann), 71-; auth, American Posters of World War I, Dafran House, 72. *Mailing Add:* Miscellaneous Man-Vintage Graphics Box 1776 New Freedom PA 17349

THEROUX, CAROL
PAINTER
b Cardwell, Mo, Aug 10, 30. *Study:* Cerritos Col Calif, with Reynold Brown, Donald Putman, Gerome Grimmer, life teaching credential, 76; Scottsdale Art Sch, 90; Scholar Art Ctr Design, La, 48. *Work:* Northwestern Bell Corp, Omaha, Nebr. *Comn:* Drawing of Borglum Statue, Prescott C of C, Ariz, 86; Buffalo Child (painting to celebrate NE Indian Arts Show), State of Nebr, Omaha, 88. *Exhib:* Ten one-woman shows, Mammen Gallery, Scottsdale, Ariz, 81-91; Classic-Am Art Show, Invitational, Beverly Hills, Calif, 89-91; C M Russel Art Show & Auction, Great Falls, Mont, 90-92; Pastel Soc Am, New York, 91; The Albuquerque Miniatures, Albuquerque Mus, NMex, 91-92. *Teaching:* Artist, drawing & painting, S Calif Studios, 63-78; artist, demonstrations, All S Calif Art Asns, 70-80; artist, Bellflower High Sch, 75-77. *Bibliog:* Susan Vreeland (auth), Dancing the ancient steps, Southwest Art Mag, 4/83; Vicki Stavic (auth), One on One, 87 & Artists to watch, 89, Art West Mag. *Mem:* Charter mem, Pastel Soc Am; Pastel Soc W Coast; Pastel Soc Southern Calif; Nat Mus Women Arts. *Media:* Pastel. *Mailing Add:* 17825 Canehill Ave Bellflower CA 90076

THIBERT, PATRICK A
SCULPTOR
b Windsor, Ont, Feb 25, 43. *Study:* Univ Windsor, Ont, BFA, 72; Fla State Univ, Tallahassee, MFA, 74. *Work:* McIntosh Art Gallery, Univ Western Ont, London; Can Coun Art Bank, Ottawa; Laurentian Univ Mus & Art Ctr, Sudbury, Ont; Art Gallery of Ont, Toronto; Kitchener-Waterloo Art Gallery, Ont. *Exhib:* Solo shows, Factory 77, Toronto, 81, Trajectory Gallery, London, Ont, 83, At Cite, windsor, Ont, 85, Art Gallery Hamilton, Ont, 86, Kitchener-Waterloo Art Gallery, 86, Forest City Gallery, London, Ont, 87, London Regional Art & Hist Mus, London, Ont, 92; Sculpture Tour, Univ Tenn, Knoxville, 83-85, 87-88; Outdoor sculpture exhib, Burlington Cult Ctr, Ont, 87; Experiencing Drawing: Its Discipline, Technique & Purpose, McIntosh Gallery, Univ Western Ont, 87; Group Alumni Exhib-25th Anniversary, Sch Visual Art, Univ Windsor, Ont, 88. *Pos:* Cur, Forest City Gallery. *Teaching:* Grad teaching asst, Fla State Univ, Tallahassee, 73-74; instr, St Clair Col Applied Art & Technol, Windsor, Ont, 74-75; prof, Fanshawe Col Applied Art & Technol, London, Ont, 75- *Awards:* Ont Arts Coun Mat Grants, 75-83 & 92. *Bibliog:* David Burnett & Marilyn Schiff (auths), Contemporary Canadian Art, Hurtig Publ Ltd, 83; Dennis Peacock (auth), Sculpture Tour 84/85, Univ Tenn, 84; Judith Maclean Rodger & Patrick Thibert (auth), Transitions 1979-1987, London Regional Art & Hist Mus, 92. *Mem:* Forest City Gallery, London, Ont. *Media:* Metal, Wood. *Dealer:* Olga Korper Gallery 157 Morrow Ave Toronto ON Canada M6R 2H9. *Mailing Add:* RR 1 Mt Bridges ON N0L 1W0 Canada

THIEBAUD, (MORTON) WAYNE
PAINTER, EDUCATOR
b Mesa, Ariz, Nov 15, 20. *Study:* Sacramento State Col, BA, 51 & MA, 52; Calif Sch Arts & Crafts, Hon Dr, 73; Dickenson Col, Hon DFA, 83, San Francisco Art Inst, Hon DFA, 87. *Work:* Mus Mod Art; Whitney Mus Am Art; Libr Cong; Albright-Knox Art Gallery; Washington Gallery Mod Art; plus many others. *Comn:* Fountain mobile structure, Calif State Fair, 52; mosaic mural, Munic Utility Dist Bldg, Sacramento, 59; producer 11 educ motion pictures, Bailey Films, Hollywood, Calif; Time, Inc. *Exhib:* One-man shows, De Young Mem Mus, 62, Whitney Mus Am Art, 71, Wayne Thiebaud: Survey 1947-76, Phoenix Art Mus, 76, Works on Paper, from the Collection of the Artist, Arts Club of Chicago, 87 & Works on Paper, 1947-1987, Richard L Nelson Gallery and travelling, 88-90; Environments USA 1957-1967, Sao Paulo Bienal, Brazil, 67; Int Contemp Art, Houston, Tex; San Francisco Mus Art; Kompas 4-West Coast USA, Stedlijk Abbemuseum, Eindhoven, Neth, 69; Documenta 5: Inquiry into Reality--Today's Image, Kassel, Ger, 72; Los Angeles Munic Mus, Calif, 73; Delphian Gallery, Sheridan, Ore, 77; Contemporary Realism, Palo Alto Cult Ctr, 87; plus many other group and one-man shows. *Teaching:* Chmn art dept, Sacramento City Col, 51; guest instr, San Francisco Art Inst, 58; prof art, Univ Calif, Davis, 60-; prof art & artist in residence, Cornell Univ, 66; artist in residence, Yale Univ, 74 & Rice Univ, 75. *Awards:* Creative Res Found Grant, 61; DFA(hon), Calif Col Arts & Crafts, 74; Citation Most Distinguished Art Studio Teacher of Year, Col Art Asn Am, 81. *Bibliog:* Sam Hunter (ed), New Art Around the World: Painting and Sculpture, Abrams, 66; Lucy R Lippard (auth), Pop Art, Praeger, 66; Allen S Weller (auth), The Joys and Sorrows of Recent American Art, Univ Ill Press, 68. *Publ:* Auth, American Rediscovered, 63 & Delights, 65; Wayne Thiebaud: Private Drawings-The Artist's Sketchbook, Harry F Abrams Publ, 87. *Mailing Add:* Dept Art Univ Calif Davis CA 95616

THIELEN, GREG GLEN
CURATOR
b St Peter, Minn, Sept 21, 40. *Study:* Southwest Mo State Univ, BA(cum laude), 70, MA, 80. *Collections Arranged:* Fish, Fowl and Other Fauna, 81; Guileless Visions: Paintings by Robert E Smith (auth, catalog), 84; James L Richardson: Tribute to a Printmaker (auth, catalog), 87; Frederick Kieforndorf: Journeys Near & Far (auth, catalog), 88; View From the Mountain: Watercolors by William McNamara (auth, catalog), 89; Atavistic Images: Sculpture & Drawings by Jerry Hatch (auth, catalog), 89; Intimate Light: Paintings by Robert Natkin (auth, catalog), 90; Amerindian Beadwork from the Deaderick Collection (auth, catalog), 90; The Drawings, Prints and Antics of Robert A Nelson (auth, catalogue), 91; Brocade, Tupperware and Other Stuff: Soft Sculptures by Holly Hughes (auth, catalogue), 91; Penumbral Images: Paintings & Prints by James G Davis (auth, catalogue), 91; Of Tinmen and Swans: Watercolors & Engravings by Brian Paulsen (auth, catalogue), 91; Fragments from Nature: Drawings by Dale Leys (auth, catalogue), 92. *Pos:* Art reference librn & registr, Springfield Art Mus, Mo, 71-76, actg dir, 1-6/76 & 9/87-6/88, cur of collections, 77- *Publ:* Auth, Japanese painted porcelain, Glaze, 2/81; Fruit crate art, Art Voices, 1-2/82; coauth, Harry Truman in Caricature and Cartoon, Iowa State Univ Press, 84; auth, Through Rose Colored Glasses: The Drawings and Illustrations of Rose Cecil O'Neill, Springfield Art Mus, 85; Watercolor Now, Fed Reserve Bank Fine Arts Gallery, Kansas City, 88. *Mailing Add:* 1111 E Brookside Dr Springfield MO 65807

THIES, CHARLES HERMAN
PAINTER, PRINTMAKER
b Poplar Bluff, Mo, Aug 22, 40. *Study:* SE Mo State Univ, BS(fine arts educ), 63; Kans State Univ, MA(drawing & painting), 70. *Work:* Minn Mus Art, St Paul; Utah Mus Fine Arts, Salt Lake City; Margaret Harwell Art Mus, Poplar Bluff, Mo; Univ Mus, Cape Girardeau, Mo; Kans State Univ; and others. *Comn:* Exterior mural, Ford Found Sponsored Prog at Kans State Univ, 69; six canvases, Marriott Hotel, Ft Collins, Colo, 85. *Exhib:* Thirty Miles of Art, Nelson Gallery-Atkins Mus, Kansas City, Mo, 76; Western Ann Nat Drawing Exhib, Western Ill Univ, 76; Drawings/USA, Minn Art Mus, St Paul, 77; Joslyn Biennial, Joslyn Art Mus, Omaha, Nebr, 78; one-man exhibs, Margaret Harwell Art Mus, Popular Bluff, Mo, 82 & 88 & Univ Art Mus, Cape Girardeau, Mo, 87; All Colo Art Exhib, 86, 88, 91 & 92; and others. *Pos:* Asst dir of admis, Kansas City Art Inst, Mo, 76-77. *Teaching:* Instr drawing, design & figure drawing, Florissant Valley College, St Louis, Mo, 69-76; instr 3-D design, Johnson Co Community Col, Overland Parks, Kans, 76. *Awards:* Painting Award, Exhib 70, St Louis, N Co Art Asn, 70; Drawing Award, Quincy Ill Fine Arts Asn, 71; Purchase, Drawings/USA 1977, Minn Mus of Art. *Bibliog:* Int Personalities, Parma, Italy, 81. *Mem:* Nat Art Educ Asn. *Media:* Oil; Etching, Lithography. *Mailing Add:* 8518 Thunderbird Rd Parker CO 80134

THIEWES, RACHELLE R
JEWELER
b Owatonna, Minn, Jan 11, 52. *Study:* Southern Ill Univ, BA, 74; Kent State Univ, MFA, 76. *Work:* Evansville Art Mus, Ind; Univ Tex, El Paso; Art Inst Chicago; Ark Art Ctr, Little Rock. *Exhib:* Craft Today USA, touring several Europ Mus, 89-; Silver: New Forms & Expressions II, Atlanta Mus Art & Design, 91; Capirotada, El Paso Mus Art, 91; Rachelle Thiewes, Dartmouth Col, 91; Design Visions, American Jewellery & Metalwork, Art Gallery Western Australia (Perth & Traveling), 92; and others. *Teaching:* Prof art, Univ Tex, El Paso, 76- *Awards:* Visual Artist Fel, Nat Endowment Arts, 88. *Bibliog:* Vanessa S Lynn (auth), Provocative performers, Metalsmith, summer 87. *Mem:* Bridge Ctr Contemp Art, El Paso (bd dirs, 87-90 & vice pres, 88-89); Soc N Am Goldsmiths (bd dirs, 88-90). *Dealer:* Adair Margo Gallery 415 E Yandell El Paso TX. *Mailing Add:* 5160 Cielo Del Rio El Paso TX 79932

THIRY, PAUL (ALBERT)
ARCHITECT, COLLECTOR
b Nome, Alaska, Sept 11, 04. *Study:* Ecole des Beaux Arts, Fontainebleau, dipl, 27; Univ Wash, BArchit, 28; St Martins Col, DFA, 70; Lewis & Clark Col, Arts D(hon), 79. *Comn:* State Libr, Capitol Comt, State Wash, Olympia, 58; Embassy, US Dept State, Santiago, Chile, 60; Seattle Ctr Coliseum, City Seattle, 64; Contemp Arts Pavilion, Seattle Art Mus, 64; World War II Monument, US 4th Inf Div, permanently located at Utah Beach, France, 68. *Exhib:* Salon d'Art Sacre, Mus Mod Art, Paris, 54; Nat Gold Medal Exhib, Archit League, New York, 56; Architectura Actual de Am, Madrid, 65; Ann Exhib, Nat Acad Design, New York, 68; New Am Archit, US Info Agency, New Delhi, India, 73. *Pos:* Mem & vchmn, Hist Am Bldg Surv, 56-61; prin architect, Century 21 Expos, Seattle, 57-62; mem, President's Coun for Pennsylvania Ave, 62-65; prof adv, Int Sculpture Competition Treaty Tower, Libby Dam, Mont, 74-75. *Awards:* Officier d'Acad, Repub France, 50; Distinguished Citizen in the Arts, City Seattle, 62; Herbert Adams Mem Medal, Nat Sculpture Soc, 74 & Henry Hering Medal, 76. *Bibliog:* Monogr, Nuestra Arquitectura, Arg, 7/49; Robert Koehler (auth), monogr, Pac Architect & Builder, Seattle, 2/61; Esther McCoy (auth), monogr, Arts & Archit, Los Angeles, 1/65. *Mem:* Hon mem Am Inst Interior Design; fel Am Inst Architects (chancellor, 62-64); hon mem Nat Sculpture Soc; academician Nat Acad Design; life mem Soc Archit Historians (dir, 67-70). *Collection:*

Primitive arts of the Alaskan Eskimo and the Indians of the Northwest Coastal Areas. *Publ:* Coauth, Churches & Temples, Reinhold, 53; ed, Washington in transition, 1/63 & auth, Planning of Washington as a Capital, 4/74, Am Inst Architects J; auth, Architectural treatment of dams, Arts & Archit, 8/67; coauth (with Mary Thiry), Eskimo Artifacts, Designed for Use, Super Publ Co, Seattle, Wash, 78. *Mailing Add:* 18330 SE May Valley Rd Issaquah WA 98027

THISTLETHWAITE, MARK EDWARD
EDUCATOR, HISTORIAN
b Baton Rouge, La, Jan 26, 48. *Study:* Univ Calif, Santa Barbara, BA, 70, MA, 72; Univ Pa, Kress Found Fel, PhD, 77. *Collections Arranged:* Guest cur, The Artist as Interpreter of American History (auth, catalog), Pa Acad Fine Arts, Philadelphia, 76; co-cur, Ed Blackburn, Tex Christian Univ, Ft Worth, 82 & co-cur, Dan Rizzie, Kimbell Art Mus, 90. *Pos:* Trustee, Mod Art Mus Ft Worth. *Teaching:* Lectr mod art, Univ Pa, Philadelphia, 74-75; lectr Am & mod art, Philadelphia Col Art, 74-76; from asst prof to prof, Am & mod art & archit, Tex Christian Univ, Ft Worth, 77- *Awards:* Tex Christian Univ Grants, 79, 81, 84-85, 88-89 & 90-91; Honors Fac Recognition Award, 88; Chancellor's Award Distinguished Teaching, 90. *Mem:* Col Art Asn; Midwest Art Hist Soc (mem bd dirs); Southeastern Col Art Conf. *Res:* American art and architecture, especially 19th century history painting and contemporary art. *Publ:* Auth, The Image of George Washington: Studies in Mid-Nineteenth Century American History Paintings, Garland, 79; coauth (with W Gerdts), Grand Illusions: History of Painting in America, 88; William Ranney: East of the Mississippi, Brandywine River Mus, 91; plus numerous articles, exhibition reviews and criticism. *Mailing Add:* Dept Art & Art Hist Tex Christian Univ Ft Worth TX 76129

THOLLANDER, EARL
ILLUSTRATOR, GRAPHIC ARTIST
b Kingsburg, Calif, Apr 13, 22. *Study:* Univ Calif, BA. *Exhib:* Fifty-three one-man shows. *Bibliog:* Earl Thollander Discusses Painting, 4/54 & Artist reporter on tour, Am Artist Mag, 3/60; Adrian Wilson (auth), The Design of Books, Reinhold Studio Vista, 67; Diana Klemin (auth), The Illustrated Book, Clarkson N Potter, 70. *Media:* Drawing; Acrylic, Watercolor. *Publ:* Auth & illusr, Backroads of California, Sunset Books, 71; Barns of California, Calif Hist Soc, 74; Back Roads of Arizona 78, Back Roads of Texas, 90, Northland Press; Back Roads of Oregon, 79, Earl Thollander's Back Roads of California, 82, Back Roads of the Carolinas, 85 & Earl Thollander's San Francisco, 87, Potter; Back Roads of Washington, Sasquatch Bks, rev ed, 92. *Mailing Add:* 19210 Hwy 128 Calistoga CA 94515

THOMAS, C DAVID
PRINTMAKER
b July 15, 46. *Study:* Portland Sch Art, Maine, dipl, 68; Tufts Univ, BFA, 72; RI Sch Design, MFA, 74. *Work:* Brooklyn Mus; Mus Fine Art, Boston; DeCordova Mus, Lincoln, Mass; Philadelphia Mus Art; Portland Mus, Maine. *Exhib:* Thirty Years of American Printmaking, Brooklyn Mus, 78; Recent Prints, Gallery Nat Asn Graphic Artists, Boston, 83. *Teaching:* Asst prof art, Emmanuel Col, 78- *Awards:* Bort Award, Boston Mus Sch, 72; Emmanuel Col Fac Develop Grant, 83. *Mem:* Boston Printmakers (exec bd, 79-); Philadelphia Print Club; Los Angeles Print Soc; Nat Asn Graphic Artists (chair, 80-). *Media:* Lithography. *Dealer:* Gallery Nat Asn Graphic Artists 67 Newbury St Boston MA 02116. *Mailing Add:* Dept Art Emanuel Col 400 Fenway Boston MA 02115

THOMAS, ELAINE FREEMAN
EDUCATOR, ADMINISTRATOR
b Cleveland, Ohio, July 21, 23. *Study:* Northwestern Univ, Evanston, 44; Tuskegee Inst, BS(magna cum laude), 45; Black Mountain Col, 45, with Josef Albers & Robert Motherwell; NY Univ, Bodden fel, MA, 49, with Hale Woodruff; Mexico City Col, 56; Berea Col, 61; Univ Paris, 66; Southern Univ Workshop, 68; Columbia Univ, 70. *Collections Arranged:* One-man exhib, Winston-Salem State Univ, 70; Discovery 70, Univ Cincinnati; George Washington Carver Exhib, White House, 71; Ala Black Artists Exhib, Birmingham Festival Art, 72; plus others. *Teaching:* Ast prof art & chmn dept, Tuskegee Inst, 45- *Awards:* Distinguished Participation, Am Artists Prof League, 68; Beaux Arts Festival Award. *Mem:* Am Asn Mus; Col Art Asn Am; Nat Art Educ Asn; Nat Conf Artists; Ala Art League. *Mailing Add:* Art Dept Tuskegee Univ Tuskegee AL 36088

THOMAS, HELEN (DOANE)
WRITER, PAINTER
b Portland, Ore. *Study:* Philadelphia Col Art; Art Students League, New York. *Work:* Chase Manhattan Bank, New York; Mus Univ Wichita, Kans; Finch Mus, New York; Univ Ala, Birmingham; New Eng Ctr Contemp Art, Brooklyn, Conn. *Exhib:* Albright-Knox Art Gallery, Buffalo, NY, 70-72; Philadelphia Mus Gallery, Pa, 72-75; Phoenix Gallery, New York, 73, 75, 77 & 80; Maison de la Cult, Cluses & Annemasse, France, 76; Ga Inst Technol, Atlanta, 76; Univ Ala, Birmingham, 76. *Pos:* Treas, Phoenix Gallery, New York, 72-74, pres, 74-79; art critic, Arts Mag, 77-79. *Bibliog:* Article, Arts Mag, 10/77. *Mem:* Nat Asn Women Artists. *Media:* Oil on Canvas. *Publ:* Auth, The application of the Ostwald System in my painting, Leonardo Mag, winter 79; Simulation of colored illumination in painting using the Ostwald System, Color-Research & Application, Vol 9, No 3, fall 84. *Mailing Add:* 241 University Dr Coral Gables FL 33134

THOMAS, JOHN
PAINTER, PRINTMAKER
b Bessemer, Ala, Feb 4, 27. *Study:* Univ Ga, 46-48; New Sch Social Res, New York, BA, 51; NY Univ, with William Baziotes, MA, 54; Univ Stranieri, Perugia, Italy, 54. *Work:* Hirshhorn Collection, Smithsonian Inst; Hawaii State Found Cult & Arts Collection, Capitol Bldg, Honolulu; Contemp Art Ctr of Hawaii, Honolulu; Detroit Inst Art; Univ Iowa. *Comn:* Mural, Hawaii State Found Cult & Arts, 78; paintings, Hemmeter Corp, 82 & Delta Airlines, 86. *Exhib:* Second Pac Coast Biennial, Seattle Art Mus, Portland Art Mus, Santa Barbara Mus & San Francisco Legion of Honor, 57-58; Whitney Ann Am Art, New York, 59; Contemp Am Painting & Sculpture Biennial, Univ Ill, Champaign-Urbana, 61-65; Artists of Hawaii Ann Exhib, Honolulu Acad Arts, 65-; American Painting, 1966, Va Mus Fine Arts, Richmond, 66; Contemp Art Ctr of Hawaii, Honolulu, 76-79; Biblioteca Americana, Bucharest, Romania, 77; Fifth Hawaii Nat Print Exhib, 80; Visions of the Volcano, traveling exhib, 89-90. *Teaching:* Vis prof life drawing, State Univ Iowa, 62-63; prof art, Univ Hawaii, Manoa & Hilo, 65-67 & 70-74; vis artist painting, Univ Wash, 68-69. *Awards:* Nat Endowment Arts Grant, 77; Hawaii State Senate Congratulations (for Boy with Goldfish), 77; Hawaii Artists League Juror's Award, Ann Exhib, Honolulu, 78. *Bibliog:* Betje Howell (auth), article, Am Artist, 2/78; Tanner Thomas & Elliott Siu (coauths), Boy with Goldfish, multi-arts concept, Prem Honolulu Symphony Orchestra, 76 & London Symphony Orchestra, 79; Harvey Hess (auth), article, Aloha Mag, 1/80; Pat Pitzer (auth), article, Hawaii Mag, 8/82; cover, Western World, 8/84 & Am Artist Mag, 3/85. *Mem:* Hawaii Artists League; Honolulu Acad Art; East Hawaii Cult Coun; The Contemp Mus; West Hawaii Arts Guild. *Media:* Oil, Watercolor. *Publ:* Auth, Orchid Art and the Orchid Isle, Malama Arts Inc, 82; Hawaii Island Artists, premiere ed, Malama Arts Inc, 89 & vol II, 91. *Dealer:* Malama Arts Inc PO Box 1761 Honolulu HI 96806. *Mailing Add:* PO Box 1478 Kailua Kona HI 96740

THOMAS, KATHLEEN K
SCULPTOR, ASSEMBLAGE ARTIST
b Jan 1, 40; US citizen. *Study:* Wichita State Univ, BA (art educ), 75, BA (art hist, cum laude), 76; Ind Univ Masters Prog, 77; Helena Rubenstein Fel, Whitney Mus Am Art, 77. *Work:* Chase Manhattan Bank, New York; Deste Found Contemp Art, Athens; pvt collections, Ms Anne Dayton, Mr & Mrs Saul Skolar & others. *Exhib:* Solo exhibs, Barbara Gladstone Gallery, New York, 81 & 84, Fashion Moda Gallery, Bronx, NY, 81 & Civilian Warfare Gallery, New York, 86; Beelden/Sculpture 83 (with catalog), Rotterdam Arts Coun, Netherlands, 83; Materialisms (with catalog), Visual Arts Gallery, State Univ NY, Purchase, 84; Preview: 1984 (with catalog), Ronald Feldman Gallery, New York, 84; Precious (with catalog), Grey Art Gallery & Study Ctr, New York Univ, 85; International High Tech Art Festival (with catalog), Seibu Mus, Tokyo, 85; Solo exhib, Studio Bergemeinde, Frankfurt, WGer, 88, Max Fish, New York, 90. *Collections Arranged:* Co-cur, Outside New York (contribr, catalog), 78, Sustained Visions (contribr, catalog), 79, In a Pictorial Framework (contribr, catalog), 79, Ree Morton Retrospective: 1971-1977 (coauth, catalog), 77 & traveling, 80-81, New Mus Contemp Art. *Pos:* Assoc cur, New Mus Contemp Art, New York, 77-79. *Awards:* Helena Rubenstein Fel, Whitney Mus Am Art, 77; Deste Found Contemp Art Fel, 86. *Bibliog:* Ronnie H Cohen (auth), rev, Artforum Mag, 9/80; Jamie Gambrell (auth), Kathleen Thomas, East Village Eye, 10/84; Annelle Pohlen (auth), Skulptur '85, Kunstforum, 5-6/85; Jamie Gambrell (auth), rev, Art in Am Mag, 5/86. *Media:* Contemporary electronic, industrial, military, automotive and often unidentified machine-made components. *Publ:* Coauth, The 1970's: New American Painting, US Info Agency, 80. *Mailing Add:* 114 E First St Apt 19 New York NY 10009

THOMAS, LARRY W
PAINTER, PRINTMAKER
b Memphis, Tenn, Oct 29, 43. *Study:* Memphis Acad Arts, BFA, 66; San Francisco Art Inst, MFA, 79. *Work:* Oakland Mus, Calif; Memphis Col Art, Tenn; Bank Am Corp, San Francisco, Calif; San Francisco Mus Mod Art, Calif; Achenbach Found Graphic Arts, Palace Legion Hon, San Francisco, Calif; Nat Mus Am Art, Washington, DC. *Comn:* Series of monotypes, Achenbach Found Graphic Arts, San Francisco, Calif, 86; edition of lithographs, Fairmont Hotels, Chicago, Ill, 87; large scale drawing, No 44 Montgomery St, San Francisco, 87. *Exhib:* Solo exhib, San Francisco Mus Mod Art, 84, Recent work, Fuller Goldeen Gallery, San Francisco, 87, Ruminations, Susan Cummins, Gallery Mill Valley, Calif, 92, Drawing II, Marti Koplin Gallery, Santa Monica, Calif, 92; Contemp Art from Calif, Ore & Wash, Alternative Mus, New York, 84; Visual Dialogues of the '80's, Univ Metrop, Mexico City & San Jose Inst Contemp Art, Calif, 84-85; Recent 20th Century Acquisitions, Oakland Mus, 85; Public and Private: American Prints Today, Brooklyn Mus (and traveling), 86-87; Graphica Creativa, Alvar Aalto Mus, Jyvaskyla, Finland, 87; A Drawing Show, San Francisco Art Inst, Calif, 87; Recent Acquisitions, Works on Paper, Nat Mus Am Art, Washington, DC, 91; Macau Printmaking 92 (catalog), Cult Inst Macau, Macau, 92. *Teaching:* Instr drawing, Santa Rosa Jr Col, 81-84; instr drawing & printmaking, San Francisco Art Inst, 83- & Stanford Univ, Palo Alto, Calif, 89-, chair, dept print, 92- *Awards:* Individual fel, Nat Endowment Arts, 80-81 & 87-88 & Djerassi Found, 86; SECA Art Award, San Francisco Mus Mod Art, 84. *Bibliog:* Thomas Albright (auth), An etcher stands out, San Francisco Chronicle, 7/9/80; Judith Dunham (auth), Larry Thomas, Vanguard Mag, 4/84; Donna Graves (auth), Larry Thomas, San Francisco Mus Mod Art, 84. *Dealer:* Susan Cummins Gallery 12 Miller Ave Mill Valley CA 94941; Experimental Workshop PO Box 77504 San Francisco CA 94107. *Mailing Add:* 601 Chenery St San Francisco CA 94131

THOMAS, TAMARA B
CONSULTANT
b Calif. *Study:* Univ Calif, Berkeley, BA(art hist); Univ Geneva. *Collections Arranged:* Security Pacific Nat Bank, 70; United Bank Denver; Pacific Bell; Investment Mortgage Int, San Francisco; plus many others. *Pos:* Pres, Fine Arts Services Inc, Los Angeles, 70-; dean's coun, Univ Calif, Los Angeles Grad Sch Archit & Urban Planning, formerly; bd mem, Asn Professional Art Advisors, New York; trustee, Inst Art & Urban Resources, New York, formerly; Consultation to major private collectors, corporations, and real estate developers, architects and interior design firms on art acquisitions, display and integration. *Mem:* Friends of Whitney Mus, New York; Mod & Contemp Art Coun, Los Angeles Mus Art. *Res:* Explanatory material on works acquired, bridging gap between public and contemporary art. *Mailing Add:* Fine Arts Serv Inc 107 S Irving Blvd Los Angeles CA 90004

THOMAS, THALIA ANN MARIE
PAINTER, EDUCATOR
b Wilkes Barre, Pa, Apr 22, 35. *Study:* Col Misericordia, BA, 56; Columbia Univ, MA, 62; Plus XII Inst, 63; Univ Guanasuato, Mus Fine Art, 76; Marywood Col, MA, 87. *Work:* Gallery, Col Misericordia, Dallas, Pa; Contemp Gallery, Marywood Col, Scranton, Pa; Galerie Internationale, New York. *Comn:* Paianting, Col Misericordia, Dallas, Pa, 87. *Exhib:* Retrospective, Windsor Studio, Scranton, Pa, 82; one-woman shows, United Penn Bank, Forty Fort, Pa, 83 & Wyoming Seminary, Kingston, Pa, 84; Retrospective, Penn State Univ, Scranton, 86; Retrospective, Col Misericordia, Dallas, Pa, 87; Art as Therapy, John Heinz Ctr, Wilkes Barre, Pa, 88; Kappa Pi & Alumni Show, Marywood Col, Scranton, Pa, 88; Pennsylvania Educators, William Penn Mus, Harrisburg, Pa. *Pos:* Regist Art Therapist, Am Asn Artists Therapist Inc, 87- *Teaching:* Asst prof art, Marywood Col, 62-85; asst chmn art, Scranton, Pa, 77-85. *Awards:* Cor Mariae Pro Fide et Cultura, Marywood Col, 82; Melvin Medal, Marywood Col, 85. *Bibliog:* Artists,USA, 76; Women Artists of America-18th Century to the Present, 80; International Directory of the Arts, 86. *Mem:* Northeastern Pennsylvania Creative Arts Therapy Asn (pres, 87-88); Am Asn Univ Profs; Wyoming Valley Art League; Am Asn Artists Therapists; Kappa Pi, Zeta Omicron Chap. *Media:* Acrylic. *Publ:* ed, Contemporary Art, Degree Studies, ICS, 85. *Mailing Add:* 18 Welles St Forty Fort PA 18704

THOMAS, YVONNE
PAINTER
b Nice, France. *Study:* Cooper Union; Art Students League; studied with Hans Hoffman, Amedee Ozenfant, B Neurman & Robert Motherwell. *Work:* Guggenheim Mus; Corcoran Gallery; Atlantic Richfield, Los Angeles; Brandeis Univ; Loeb Ctr, NY Univ; Nat Gallery Art, Washington, DC; Ciba-Geigy, Greensboro, NC. *Exhib:* American Abstract Artists, 48; Eleven Americans, Riverside Mus, New York, 55; Women in the Arts, New York Cult Ctr, 73; Brooklyn Mus, 75; The Magic Circle, Bronx Mus, 77; Acad & Inst Arts & Lett, New York, 82; Fond Nat D'Art Contemp, Paris, France, 88. *Teaching:* Instr painting & drawing, Colo Mountain Col, summers 67-72 & La State Univ, 73. *Bibliog:* Lawrence Campbell (auth), article, Art News, Vol 72, 3/73; Grace Glueck (auth), article, NY Times, 5/12/78; Kim Levin (critic), article, Art News, Vol 64, 5/65; Gerrit Henry (critic), article, Art Am, Vol 74, 12/86. *Media:* Oil, Acrylic. *Mailing Add:* c/o Phillippe Briet Gallery 558 Broadway New York NY 10012

THOMASON, MICHAEL VINCENT
PHOTOGRAPHER, CURATOR
b West Palm Beach, Fla, June 20, 42. *Study:* Univ South, Sewanee, Tenn, BA, 64; Duke Univ, MA, 66, PhD, 68. *Exhib:* Work & Leisure in Turn Century Mobile, Fine Arts Mus South, Mobile, 80; Allied Arts Competition, 77, Mobile, 77; The Image of Progress: Alabama Photographs 1877-1917, Birmingham Mus Art, Ala, 81; Buildings Reborn: Adaptive Re-use Proposals, traveling exhib, Ala, 80. *Collections Arranged:* Work & Leisure Turn Century Mobile (auth, catalog), 80; The Image of Progress (auth, catalog), Birmingham, Ala, 81; Mobile's Black Heritage in Photographs, 83; Mardi Gras from the Gay Nineties to the Great Depression, 83; Trying Times: Alabama Photographs, 1917-1945 (auth, catalog), 85. *Pos:* Dir, Photo Archives, Univ South Ala, Mobile, 78- *Teaching:* Prof, Univ S Ala, 78- *Awards:* First Prize, Allied Arts Competition, 77. *Media:* Black & White. *Res:* Uses of photography in history; the photography as a historical source. *Publ:* Coauth, Mobile: American River City, Easter, Mobile, 75; coauth, Mobile: The Life and Times of a Great Southern Seaport, Windsor, Calif, 81. *Mailing Add:* Dept History Univ S Ala 307 University Blvd Mobile AL 36688

THOMASON, TOM WILLIAM
JEWELER, PAINTER
b Shawnee, Okla, Oct 28, 34. *Study:* Univ NMex, BFA, 62. *Work:* Am Inst Architects, Albuquerque, NMex. *Comn:* Bronze Sculpture, Arlene Vanderbilt Webb, New York, 67; Cross & Collection Plates, St Mark's Episcopal Church, Albuquerque, 68; Archit Awards, Am Inst Architects, Albuquerque, 69; Archit Medals, Univ NMex, 70; Desk Award Plaques, NMex Coun Exceptional Children, 77-79. *Exhib:* Young Americans, Mus Contemp Crafts, New York, 62; 1st Survey Contemp Am Crafts, Univ Tex Art Mus, Austin, 67; one-man shows, Art Ministry, Tananarive, Madagascar, 67 & Wichita Art Asn Mus, Kans, 80; Southwestern Craftsmen, Dallas Mus of Fine Arts, Tex, 68; Silver & Gold, Corcoran Gallery Art, Washington, DC, 72; Contemp Crafts Biennial 1st, Folk Art Mus, Santa Fe, NMex, 76. *Collections Arranged:* Contemporary Crafts Exhibition, New Mexico Pavilion, World's Fair, New York, 64; Santeros of New Mexico, Studio Gallery, Albuquerque, 68. *Pos:* Owner & mgr, Studio Gallery, Albuquerque, 63-; design & sales adv, Zuni Arts & Crafts Coop, NMex, 68. *Teaching:* Guest artist design, Univ Madagascar, Tananarive, 67. *Awards:* Purchase Award, NMex Contemp Crafts, Am Inst Architects, Albuquerque, 70; First Prize, Metal, NMex Contemp Crafts, NMex State Fair, 73; First, Third & Fourth Prizes, Metal, Tulsa Gallery of Fine Arts, Okla, 73. *Bibliog:* Lois E Franke (auth), Handwrought Jewelry, McKnight & McKnight, 67. *Mem:* NMex Designer Craftsmen (vpres 62-65, pres, 65-66); Albuquerque Designer Craftsmen (pres, 62-65); Corrales Art Asn (vpres, 64 & 66); Albuquerque Gallery Asn (pres, 78); World Crafts Coun. *Media:* Watercolor. *Specialty:* Contemporary art in painting, sculpture and art crafts. *Publ:* Contribr, Marcilla Chamberlain, auth, Making Metal Jewelry, Watson-Guptill, US & Pitman Ltd, Eng, 77. *Mailing Add:* 615 16th St NW Albuquerque NM 87104

THOMPSON, BRADBURY
DESIGNER, ART DIRECTOR
b Topeka, Kans, Mar 25, 11. *Study:* Washburn Univ, AB, 34 & DFA, 65; RI Sch Design, DFA, 83, Parsons Sch Design, DFA, 89. *Work:* Yale Univ; Harvard Univ; Brit Libr. *Comn:* Book design for ann of advert art, 43 & 54, graphic arts prod yearbk, 48 & 50, Westvaco Inspirations & Am Classics, 38-83, Homage to the book, 68, Designer, 105 US Stamps, 58-92, The Art of Graphic Design, Yale, 88; plus many others. *Exhib:* Int Exhib Graphic Art, Paris, 55, London, 56, Milan, Italy, 61, Amsterdam, 62 & Hamburg, 64; traveling one-man exhibs, Am Inst Graphic Art, 58 & 75, Bradbury Thompson by Westvaco, 88-92. *Pos:* Art dir, Capper Publ, 34-38, Rogers-Kellogg-Stillson, 38-41, Off War Info, 42-45 & Mademoiselle, 45-59; design dir, Art News & Art News Ann, 45-72; consult, Westvaco Corp, 38-92, McGraw Hill Publ, 60-78, Time-Life Bks, 64-70, Harvard Bus Rev, 64-67, Field Enterprises, 64-78, Cornell Univ, 65-75, Menninger, 77-92 & Oxford Univ Press, 79-80; designer, Smithsonian Mag, 69, Washburn Col Bible, 69-80; bd trustees, Washburn Univ, 70-; mem Citizens Stamp Adv Comt, 69-92. *Teaching:* Vis prof, Sch Art, Yale Univ, 56- *Awards:* New York Printers Wall of Fame, 83; Soc Publ Designers Award, 86; Medal, Type Director's Club, 86; and others. *Bibliog:* Article, Smithsonian, 6/79; article, Town & Country, 12/79; article, Communication Arts, 1-2/80; article, Gutenberg & Family, 1/85. *Mem:* Art Dirs Club (first vpres, exec comt); Soc Illusr; Am Inst Graphic Arts (bd dirs); Alliance Graphique Int; Nat Soc Art Dirs; plus others. *Publ:* Auth, The Monalphabet, 45 & Alphabet 26, 50; The Art of Graphic Design, Yale Univ Press, 88. *Mailing Add:* 25 Jones Park Drive Riverside CT 06878

THOMPSON, CAPPY (CATHERINE)
PAINTER
Study: Fairhaven Col, Bellingham, Wash, 70-71; Factory Visual Arts, Seattle, Wash, 71-72; Evergreen State Col, Olympia, Wash, BA, 76. *Work:* Corning Mus Glass; Mountlake Terrace Pub Libr, Wash; Safeco Insurance Co, Seattle, Wash; Pac First Centre, Seattle, Wash; Microsoft Corp, Bellevue, Wash; and others. *Exhib:* Watcom Co Mus Art, Bellingham, Wash, 92; Art Gallery Western Australia, Perth, 92; William Traver Gallery, Seattle, Wash, 92; Betsy Rosenfield Gallery, Chicago, Ill, 92; and others. *Pos:* Studio coordr, Pilchuck Sch, Stanwood, Wash, 87, printmaker, 90. *Teaching:* Artist-in-residence, Pilchuck Sch, Stanwood, Wash, 84, fac, 88, 89 & fac, Seattle, Wash, 90; fac, Pratt Fine Arts Ctr, Seattle, Wash, 90 & 91; Int Conf Workshop, Glass Art Soc, Monterey, Mex, 92. *Awards:* Nat Endowment Arts Fel Visual Arts, 90. *Bibliog:* Bonnie Miller (auth), Out of the Fire: Contemporary Glass Artists and their Work, Chronicle Bks, 91; New Glass Review, Corning Mus Glass, 92; Cappy Thompson's fabled world, GLASS, spring 92; and others. *Mem:* Glass Art Soc (bd dirs, 89-92, secy, 90-92); Pilchuck Glass Sch (artistic adv comt, 92). *Mailing Add:* 707 S Snoqualmie No 4A Seattle WA 98108

THOMPSON, DAVID ELBRIDGE See Hompson, Davi Det (David Elbridge Thompson)

THOMPSON, DONALD ROY
PAINTER, ASSEMBLAGE ARTIST
b Fowler, Calif, Mar 2, 36. *Study:* Calif State Univ, Sacramento, BA, 60, MA, 62. *Work:* Oakland Mus, Calif; Seattle First Nat Bank; Crocker Art Mus, Sacramento, Calif; IBM Santa Teresa Lab, San Jose, Calif; Art Mus Santa Cruz Co, Calif. *Exhib:* One-man shows, Cabrillo Col, Aptos, Calif, 70, 80 & 90, Foster Goldstrom Fine Arts, San Francisco, 82, Santa Cruz Arts Resource Ctr, Calif, 85 & 86 & Santa Clara Univ, Calif, 90; West '81/Art and the Law, Minn Mus Art, St Paul; Art Mus Ann-Works on Paper/Clay, Art Mus Santa Cruz, Calif, 85; Smith Andersen Gallery, Palo Alto, Calif, 86; d p Fong & Spratt Galleries, San Jose, Calif, 92; Composer's Choice: Selections from the Collection of Lou Harrison, Octagon Mus, Santa Cruz, Calif, 92; and others. *Teaching:* Instr art, Cabrillo Col, 71- *Awards:* Purchase Award, West '81/Art & the Law, West Publ Co, 81. *Bibliog:* Charles Johnson (auth), Color is form and subject, Sacramento Bee, 1/26/75; Mark Levy (auth), Vital fabrications, Artweek, 12/18/82; Claude Lesuer (auth), Rare summer pleasures, Artspeak, 6/23/83. *Media:* Acrylic. *Dealer:* D P Fong & Spratt Galleries San Jose CA. *Mailing Add:* 2395 Delaware Ave Unit 70 Santa Cruz CA 95060

THOMPSON, DOROTHY BURR
EDUCATOR, LECTURER
b Delhi, NY, Aug 19, 1900. *Study:* Bryn Mawr Col, AB, 23, European fel, 23, AM, PhD, 31; Wooster Col, Hon DFA, 72. *Collections Arranged:* Comment in Clay, Royal Ont Mus, 47. *Pos:* Actg dir, Royal Ont Mus, 46-47. *Teaching:* Lectr archaeol for circuit, Archaeol Inst Am, retired; lectr class archaeol, Univ Toronto, 43-47; prof class archaeol, Univ Pa, 54 & 68; vis lectr archaeol, Oberlin Col, 68; prof class archaeol, Princeton Univ, 69-70; vis lectr, Univ Sydney, 72. *Awards:* Order of Phoenix, Govt Greece, 56. *Mem:* Archaeol Inst Am (exec comt, 48-52); Deutsches Arch-ologisches Inst. *Res:* Classical Greek

subjects such as figurines, garden art and private life. *Publ:* Auth, Terracottas from Myrina in Museum of Fine Arts, Boston, privately publ, 34; auth, Swans and Amber (transl of Greek lyrics), Univ Toronto Press, 49; auth, Troy, the Terracotta Figurines of the Hellenistic Period, Princeton Univ Press, 63; auth, Ptolemaic Oinochoai and Portraits in Faience, Oxford Press, 73; contribr var jour. *Mailing Add:* Inst for Advan Study Princeton NJ 08540

THOMPSON, ERNEST THORNE, JR
SILVERSMITH, PAINTER
b South Bend, Ind, Nov 9, 28. *Study:* Huguenot Sch Art, with Courtney Allen, Charles R Kingnan, Ernest T Thompson, Sr, dipl; Sch Mus Fine Arts, Boston, with Joseph L Sharrock, Sr & Hazel Olsen Brown, dipl, independent study in Japan. *Work:* Mus Sci, Boston, Mass; USAF Chapel, Bien Hoe, Vietnam; Corp Plate, Boston, Gt Brit. *Comn:* Industrial comns & pvt collections; chapel & altar pieces, Miles Mem Hosp Chapel. *Pos:* Trustee, Soc Arts & Crafts, 61-64; juror, Sterling Silver Design Competition, 75; owner & partner, Thompsons Studio Inc. *Teaching:* Dept head jewelry & silversmith, Boston Mus Sch, 61-70 & Portland Sch Art, 69-80. *Bibliog:* Bill Cauldwell (auth), Stop, silversmith at work, Ford Times Mag, 10/69; Richard Stilwell (auth), Ernest Thompson unselfish in silver, Maine Guide Dir, 74; article in House Beautiful Mag, 2/80; Damon Ripley & Lawrence Willard (auths), Thompson's silversmith studio, Yankee Mag, 12/81. *Mem:* Pemaquid Group of Artists. *Media:* Gold, Silver; Oils, Watercolor. *Mailing Add:* Back Meadow Rd Box 340 RR 1 Damariscotta ME 04543

THOMPSON, JACK
SCULPTOR, EDUCATOR
b Los Angeles, Calif, May 25, 46. *Study:* Calif State Univ, Northridge, BA, 70; San Francisco Art Inst, 71; Tyler Sch Art, Temple Univ, MFA,73. *Work:* Int Acad Ceramics, Calgary; John Michael Kohler Arts Ctr Mus, Sheboygan, Wis. *Comn:* Ltd ed teapot, Helen Drutt Gallery, Philadelphia, 81. *Exhib:* New Photographics, Central Wash State Univ, Ellensburg, 76 & 77; Long Beach Mus Art, 77; 36th Ceramics Ann, Scripps Col, Pomona, Calif, 80; Homage to Josiah Wedgwood, Mus Philadelphia Civic Ctr, 80; John M Kohler Arts Ctr Mus, Sheboygan, Wis, 81; The Animal Image, Renwick Gallery, Smithsonian Inst, Washington, DC, 81; and others. *Teaching:* Asst prof, Moore Col Art, Philadelphia, 74-82. *Awards:* Cash Award & Medal, Int Acad Ceramics, 73; fel, Pa State Coun Arts, 81. *Bibliog:* Kent E Wade (auth), Alternative photographic processes, Morgan & Morgan Inc, Dobbs Ferry, NY, 78; Surreal genetics, Philadelphia Evening Bull, 4/27/80; Michael Monroe (auth), The Animal Image, Smithsonian Inst Press, 81. *Mem:* Bucks Co Coun Arts. *Media:* Acrylic. *Mailing Add:* 705 Almshouse Rd Chalfont PA 18914

THOMPSON, JEAN DANFORTH
TAPESTRY ARTIST, PAINTER
b Baltimore, Md, May 3, 33. *Study:* Md Inst Art, 50; Univ Md, BA, 54; Wright State Univ, MA, 72. *Work:* Univ Md; Am Embassy, Bonn, WGer; US Cent Intelligence Agency, McLean, Va; US Dept of State; Marriott Corp, Washington, DC; Sheraton Hotel, Baton Rouge, La. *Comn:* Xerox, Arlington, Va, 80, Nat Rural Electric Coop Asn, Washington DC, 80, McDonalds Corp, Fairfax, Va, 81, Am Apparel Asn, Rosslyn, Va, 83 & Paffrather Raiffeisen Bank, Cologne, WGer. *Exhib:* Am Craft Coun Exhib, Textile Mus, Washington, DC, 79; Am Textile Exhib, Folger Mus Gallery, Washington, DC, 80; Art USA, Textural Art Gallery, London, 80; solo exhib, Geilsdorfer Gallerie, Cologne, W Germany, 82-84 & 86; Gayle Wilson Gallery, Southampton, NY, 83; Arverne Art Int, Ltd, New York, NY, 83; Leighton-Richey Gallery, Columbia, 92. *Collections Arranged:* Art USA, London, 80. *Mem:* Torpedo Factory Artists Asn (pres, 79-80, bd mem, 76-86); Fiber Workshop; Artists Equity. *Media:* Fiber, Collage. *Mailing Add:* Studio 16 Torpedo Factory Art Ctr 105 N Union St Alexandria VA 22314

THOMPSON, JUDITH KAY
PAINTER
b Kansas City, Kansas, May 28, 40. *Study:* William Jewell Col, Liberty, Mo, 60; Kans City Art Inst, Wilbur Neiwald, BFA, 65; Univ Cincinnati & Art Acad, MFA, 67. *Exhib:* Works on Paper, Fairleigh Dickinson Univ, Hackensack, NJ, 75 & Brooklyn Mus, NY, 75; 96th Ann Nat Exhib Asn, Jacob K Javits Fed Bldg, New York, 85. *Teaching:* Instr drawing, Cincinnati Art Mus, 66; instr draw, 2-D & 3-D design, St Cloud State Univ, Minn, 69; instr painting & draw, St Benedict's Col, Minn, 69. *Awards:* Goldie Paley Award, Celebration Bicentennial, Nat Asn Women Arts, 76. *Bibliog:* Notable Women of Tex, 84; New York Art Review, 87. *Mem:* Nat Asn Women Artists. *Mailing Add:* 9337 Westwood Village Dr Houston TX 77036

THOMPSON, KENNETH WEBSTER
ILLUSTRATOR, PAINTER
b New York, NY, Apr 26, 07. *Study:* Grand Cent Sch Art; also with George Pierce Ennis. *Work:* Wartime illus, Libr Cong, Washington, DC. *Exhib:* Am Watercolor Soc Ann; Soc Illusr; Nantucket Artists Asn; Nat Arts Club; Cerberus Gallery. *Awards:* Thirteen awards, Chicago Art Dir Club; three awards, Am Inst Graphic Arts; seven awards, incl three medals, NY Art Dir Club; and others. *Mem:* Life mem Soc Illusr; life mem Am Watercolor Soc; Nantucket Artists Asn; Artists Guild. *Media:* Gouache, Watercolor. *Publ:* Illusr, The continent we live on (series), 62-68; The sea, 66. *Mailing Add:* 20 W 11th St New York NY 10011

THOMPSON, LOCKWOOD
COLLECTOR
b Cleveland, Ohio, 01. *Study:* Williams Col, AB, 23; Harvard Law Sch, LLB, 26. *Pos:* Mem adv coun, Cleveland Mus Art, 49-, chmn 81-83; co-organizer & first pres, Cleveland Soc for Contemp Art, 61; mem, Int Coun Mus Mod Art, New York, 63-; legal coun & pub mem comn accreditation, Nat Asn Schs Art; mem adv bd, Cleveland Inst Art & Friends of the Tate Gallery, London; mem, Akron Ohio Mus. *Mem:* Cleveland Pub Libr bd, 90-97; Fel & life mem Nat Asn Art & Design, 87. *Collection:* Contemporary art, primarily Henry Moore. *Mailing Add:* 1010 Euclid Ave Apt 401 Cleveland OH 44115

THOMPSON, LYNN P
PAINTER, PHOTOGRAPHER
b Plainfield, NJ, July 22, 22. *Study:* Bennett Jr Col, 39-40; Douglas Col, BA, 43; Cornell Med Col, MD, 46; Nat Acad Design; Art Students League. *Work:* New York Hosp; Khanbegian Gallery, Sonogee, Bar Harbor, Maine; Inglemoor, Englewood, NJ; Kodak Artcart Collection, 86- *Comn:* El Molino (oil), comn by George Moore, Sotogrande, Spain, 80; seascape, comn by Dr Eibl, Vienna, 80; Maine seascape, Drawing Room, Pennsula, Ohio, 81; painting (oil), New York Hosp, 83; Series Watercolors, David Elliott; plus many others. *Exhib:* Solo exhib, Bergen Mus, Paramus, NJ, 74 & El Molino, Spain, 79; Federated Art Asn, NJ State Mus, Trenton, 75; New York Physicians Art Asn Ann, Union Carbide, 76; New York Physicians Art Exhib, New York Acad Med, 76-79. *Pos:* Dir, New York Hosp Art Comn, 66-74 & 77-80 & Child Life Ctr, New York, 82-; dir & adv, Circulating Art Cart Prog, 78; coordr, Hosp Audiences, New York, 82-; 300 progs underway in 31 states, Quebec, Can, Am Hosp, Paris; exec comm assoc, Healthcare Art Admin, 89- *Teaching:* Instr watercolor, Sonogee, Bar Harbor, Maine, 79-, Mainescape Gallery, Bar Harbor, Maine. *Awards:* Prix Etats-Unis, Duncan Gallery, New York & Paris, 75; First & Second Awards, New York Physicians Art Asn Ann, 76-79; Bocour Award, Orange Art Asn, 78; Volunteer of Year Award for Art in Nursing Homes, Am Health Asn, 88. *Bibliog:* Marguerite Logan (auth), Circulating art program brings new vistas to facility life, Am Health Care Asn J, 85; Judy Haberek (auth), Nursing home volunteers circulate art & heart in Bergen county, Voluntary Action Leadership, winter 86; Marian (auth), Doctor Finds Art the Best Medicine, Lancet, Art in Health care facilities, 12/88. *Mem:* Salmagundi Club; Catharine Lorillard Wolfe Club; Allied Artists Am; New York Physicians Art Asn (dir, 78-); Bergen Co Artists Guild. *Media:* Watercolor, Oil. *Publ:* Contribr, Cornell Med Col Alumni News, 81 & 84. *Dealer:* Upper Gallery 34B-435 E 70th St New York NY 10021; Mainescape Gallery 54 West St Bar Harbor ME 04609. *Mailing Add:* 11 Creston Ave Tenafly NJ 07670

THOMPSON, MALCOLM BARTON
PAINTER
b Coraopolis, Pa, Dec 25, 16. *Study:* Pratt Inst, grad; Art Students League; also illus with Nicholas Riley. *Comn:* US Army in Action Ser, Pentagon, 49. *Exhib:* Soc Casein Artists, New York, 70; Slater Mem Mus, Norwich, Conn, 71; Conn Watercolor Soc, Hartford, Conn, 71; Mainstreams '71, Marietta, Ohio, 71; Am Watercolor Soc Traveling Exhibs, 72 & 73. *Teaching:* Instr watercolor & anat, McLane Art Inst, New York, 38-40. *Awards:* Marjorie Salembier Award, Conn Classic Arts, 68; First Prize, New Canaan Art Show, 70; Grumbacher Acrylic Award, Am Artists Prof League, 71 & 75. *Mem:* Am & Conn Watercolor Soc; Silvermine Guild Artists. *Media:* Acrylic, Watercolor. *Dealer:* Newman Galleries 1625 Walnut St Philadelphia PA 19103; Settlers West Galleries 6420 N Campbell Ave Tucson AZ 85718. *Mailing Add:* 40 Honey Hill Rd Wilton CT 06897

THOMPSON, MARK L
SCULPTOR
Study: Univ Calif, Berkeley, BA, 72, MA, 73. *Exhib:* San Francisco Civic Ctr Plaza Exhib, 74; Headlands Ctr Arts, Fort Barry, Calif, 86 & 87; Springhouse, Artpark, Lewiston, NY, 89; Invocations, Whitechapel Art Gallery, London, 90; Dance of the Honeybees: An Exploration of San Francisco's Mission District, Exploratorium, San Francisco, Calif, 92. *Pos:* Panel mem, Going Public: Western Regional Pub Art Forum, San Francisco, 88, Earth Day: Artists Respond to the Environmental Crisis, Palo Alto Cult Ctr, Calif, 90 & Installation Art, Discussion with Chris Burden and Mark Thompson, Whitechapel Art Gallery, London, Eng, 90. *Teaching:* Var lect-film presentations, 77-92; lectr art-conceptual design, San Francisco State Univ, 88 & 89, lectr sculpture, 91, grad workshop, 92; vis lectr sculpture, Univ Col London, Slade Sch Fine Art, 90. *Awards:* Nat Endowment Arts, 80, 89 & 90; Artist Fel Grant, Awards In The Visual Arts, 91-92; New Genre Artists Fel, Calif Arts Coun, 92; and others. *Bibliog:* Beate Eickhoff (auth), Seven obsessions, Kunstforum Int, Vol 111, 1-2/92; Makiyo Matsushima (auth), Art News Review, Ryusei Ikebana, Tokyo, Japan, No 384, 92; Raul Alas (auth), Interview: Mark Thompson, KDTV, Channel 14, San Francisco, Calif, 92; and others. *Publ:* Auth, A House Divided, White Walls: A Journal of Language and Art, No 25, White Walls Inc, Chicago, Ill, 90; Edge 90, Art & Life in the Nineties, Mediamatic, Vol 4, No 4, The Edge Biennale Trust, London, Eng & Mediamatic Mag, Amsterdam, Neth, 90; Animalia: Stellvertreter (catalog), Haus am Waldsee, Berlin, Ger, 90; Seven Obsessions (catalog), Whitechapel Art Gallery & Performanc Mag, No 63, London, Eng, 11/90; and others. *Mailing Add:* 4701 San Leandro St No 24 Oakland CA 94601

THOMPSON, NANCY KUNKLE
JEWELER, EDUCATOR
b Marion, Ind, Dec 30, 41. *Study:* Ball State Teachers Col, BS(art), 63; Ind Univ, MFA(jewelry design & metalsmithing), 68. *Work:* Ind Univ Mus Art, Bloomington; Greenville Co Mus Art, SC. *Exhib:* Extraordinary Vehicles, J M Kohler Arts Ctr, Sheboygan, Wis, 74; Southeastern Crafts, Greenville Co Mus Art, SC, 74; Bicentennial Craft Invitational, Ind Univ Art Mus, 76; Wearables, Renwick Gallery, DC, 79; The Next Juried Show, Va Mus Fine Arts, 83; New Art Forms: Virginia, Hand Workshop, 88. *Teaching:* Prof jewelry & metalwork, Va Commonwealth Univ, 73- *Awards:* Exp Metalwork,

Carnegie Found, 68; Slide Doc of Hist Jewelry-Ornamental Devices, Va Commonwealth Univ, 71, Fac Grant-in-Aid, 76. *Bibliog:* Geff Reed (auth), Thompson/Kerrigan, Craft Horizons, 72. *Mem:* Am Crafts Coun; Col Art Asn; Soc NAm Goldsmiths. *Media:* Precious Metals, Nonmetallic Materials. *Mailing Add:* Dept Crafts Va Commonwealth Univ 910 W Franklin St Richmond VA 23284

THOMPSON, RENA
WEAVER, PAINTER
b New York, NY, Jan 22, 50. *Study:* Moore Col Art, BFA, 78; Tyler Sch Art, Temple Univ, MFA, 80. *Work:* Provident Mutual Life Insurance Co, Philadelphia, Pa; Chase Manhattan Bank, New York; First Am Bank Va, Richmond; Central Trust Bank Jefferson City, Mont; Bristol-Myers, NJ. *Exhib:* Solo exhibs, Marian Locks Gallery, Philadelphia, Pa, 87, Leedy-Voulkos Gallery, Kansas City, Mo, 87 & Del Ctr Contemp Art, Wilmington, 92; Pa Coun Arts Fel Exhib (with catalog), Soc Arts Craft, Pittsburgh, 88; Fiber Chronicals (with catalog), Moore Col Art, Philadelphia, Pa, 88; Out of the Woods, Fairmount Park, Philadelphia, 90; Bucks Biennial I, James Michener Art Mus, Doylestown, Pa, 92; Threads in Common, Philadelphia Art Alliance, PA, 92; and others. *Teaching:* Artist in residence, State of Pa, 88- *Awards:* Visual Arts Fel, Nat Endowment Arts, 80 & 87; Pa Coun Arts Fel, 83, 88 & 91. *Media:* Acrylic, Oil. *Mailing Add:* 705 Almshouse Rd Chalfont PA 18914

THOMPSON, RICHARD CRAIG
PAINTER
b McMinnville, Ore, June 27, 45. *Study:* Ore State Univ, 63-65; Univ NMex, BFA, 67, MA, 72; painting with John Kacere; also lithography with Garo Antresian. *Work:* San Antonio Mus Art, Tex; Roswell Mus, NMex. *Comn:* Twenty Sculpture Pieces, Univ Md, 69; Impermanent Sculpture, Mich Arts Coun, Detroit, 74; Cowboy Nights, Warehouse Living Arts Ctr, Corsicana, Tex. *Exhib:* Solo exhibs, Roswell Mus, NMex, 81, Monique Knowlton Gallery, New York, 81, 82 & 84, Art Mus STex, Corpus Christi, 84, Harris Gallery, Houston, 85; Biennial of Contemp Am Art, Whitney Mus, New York, 75; Space Gallery, Los Angeles, 80 & 84; Fresh Paint, Mus Fine Arts, Houston; Hill's Gallery, Santa Fe, NMex, 75-78; Scottish Arts Festival, Edinburgh, Scotland, 80; and others. *Teaching:* Lectr painting & drawing, Univ Albuquerque, 72-75; vis lectr color, Wayne State Univ, spring 74; instr design-color, Univ NMex, 75-78; vis prof, Univ Tex, San Antonio, 84; asst prof, Univ Tex, Austin, 84- *Awards:* Nat Endowment Arts Fel, 78; Artist-in-residence, Australia Arts Coun, 82; Mid-Am Art Alliance Award, 86; artist-in-residence grant, Roswell Mus, NMex. *Bibliog:* Charlotte Moser, New Mexico, open land and psychic elbow room, ARTnews, 12/77; article in New America, Univ NMex, 79; Portfolio, Paris Review, Summer 79. *Mem:* Col Art Asn; Nat Watercolor Honor Soc. *Media:* Acrylic, Oil. *Dealer:* Harris Gallery 1100 Bissonnet Houston TX 77005; Space Gallery 6015 Santa Monica Blvd Los Angeles CA 90038. *Mailing Add:* c/o Roischon Gallery 1740 Wazee St Denver CO 80202

THOMPSON, RICHARD E, JR
DEALER, COLLECTOR
b Oak Park, Ill, Dec 30, 39. *Study:* Univ Wis; Wayland Acad. *Collections Arranged:* Richard Thompson, Sr, 77. *Pos:* Dir, Richard Thompson Gallery, San Francisco, 77- *Specialty:* Twentieth century American impressionists. *Collection:* American impressionists. *Mailing Add:* 80 Maiden Lane San Francisco CA 94108

THOMPSON, ROBERT CHARLES
PAINTER, EDUCATOR
b Conroe, Tex, Nov 5, 36. *Study:* Univ Tex, BFA; Stephen F Austin State Univ, MA & MFA. *Work:* Southeast Ark Arts & Sci Ctr, Pine Bluff; First Nat Bank, Conway; Witte Mus, San Antonio, Tex; Pulaski Fed Savings & Loan Asn, Little Rock. *Exhib:* Young Artists Am, Xavier Univ, 60; Miniature Painter, Sculptors & Gravers Nat, Washington, DC, 68; Small Painting Nat Exhib, Univ Pac, 70; 4th Ann Nat Print & Drawing, Northern Ill Univ, 71; Ann Mid-South Exhib, Brooks Gallery, Memphis, Tenn, 71; Visual Arts Ctr, Texarkana, Tex, 87; Miniature Art, Cantrell Gallery, Little Rock, Ark, 87. *Teaching:* Asst prof art, Univ Cent Ark, 68-78, assoc prof, 78-88, prof, 88- *Awards:* Tex Watercolor Soc Purchase Award, 65; Invitational Exhib Award, 70 & First Place Oils & Acrylics, 73, Ann Ark Festival Arts; Four State Ann, Purchase Award, Texarkana, 88. *Media:* Oil, Watercolor. *Mailing Add:* Rte 7 Box 299 Conway AR 72032

THOMPSON, TAMARA
ASSEMBLAGE ARTIST, PAINTER
b Anderson, Ind, Apr 8, 35. *Study:* Univ Ky, BA(art); Ind Univ, MFA; study with Leon Golub & Creighton Gilbert. *Work:* Ind Univ, Bloomington; Colgate Univ; Univ Ky; Syracuse Univ. *Comn:* Mural, Children & Sports, Albuquerque Pub Schs, 85. *Exhib:* 17 Connecticut Artists, Wadsworth Atheneum, Hartford, 60; Arts of Cent New York 36th & 38th Ann, Munson-Williams-Proctor Inst, Utica, 73 & 75; solo exhibs, Picker Art Gallery, Colgate Univ, 78, Photogenesis, Albuquerque, 81 & Hoshour Gallery, Albuquerque, 83; Electroworks, Int Mus of Photog, George Eastman House, Rochester, 79-80; Mutiples 80, Contemp Arts Ctr, New Orleans; Spring Arts Festival, Taos, 85; On the Wall-Off the Wall, Ctr for Contemp Arts, Santa Fe, 85; Statements 88 Invitational, Albuquerque, 88; Magnifico, Albuquerque, 91. *Pos:* Dir art classes, Wadsworth Atheneum, 59-61; vis artist in residence, Univ Ky, 65, Everson Mus, Syracuse, 79 & Int Mus Photog, George Eastman House, Rochester, 80. *Teaching:* Instr art, Univ Ky, 65-66; instr fine arts, Colgate Univ, 72-80, asst prof, 80; art specialist, The Montessori Sch, Albuquerque, 86- *Awards:* First Prize, Hartford Soc Women Painters, 60 & 61; Colgate Univ Fac Develop Fund Grant, 77-78, Res Coun Grant, 79-81. *Bibliog:* Catherine Lord (auth), Women and photography, Afterimage, 1/80 & Modern photography, 9/80; Ellen Land-Weber (auth), Processes: Copying Machines, Afterimage. *Mem:* Col Art Asn Am; Albuquerque United Artists. *Media:* Multi. *Publ:* Contribr, Drawings of the Italian Renaissance, Ind Univ Press, 58. *Mailing Add:* 1400 Marron Circle NE Albuquerque NM 87112

THOMPSON, WADE S
PAINTER, EDUCATOR
b Moorhead, Minn, July 30, 46. *Study:* Macalester Col, BA, 68; Bowling Green State Univ, MA, MFA, 72; Pratt Inst, 85. *Work:* IBM Corp, Kansas City, Mo; M-Bank Corp, Houston, Tex; Freeport-MacMahon Corp, New Orleans, La; Provincetown Art Asn, Mass; Shell Oil Co, Houston, Tex; Hoyt Institute of Fine Arts, New Castle, Pa; Jena Int, Wash, DC. *Exhib:* 63rd Nat Exhib, Laguna Gloria Art Mus, Tex Fine Art Asn, Austin, 74; American Drawing 1976, Smithsonian Inst Traveling Exhib, Portsmouth Arts Ctr, Va, 76; one-man shows, Hansen Galleries, New York, 77, Jack Meir Gallery, Houston, Tex, 85, 87, 88, 91 & 93, Mary Bell Gallery, Chicago, 84, 85, 87, 88 & 89, Martin Schweig Gallery, St Louis, 86 & Still-Zinzel New Orleans, 90; 2nd Ann Art Competition for Spoleto, Marble Arch Gallery, Charleston, SC, 83; Greater Midwest/Int Invitational, West Surrey Col Art & Design, Farnham, Surrey, Gt Brit, 84; 11th Nat Art Exhib, New Orleans Art Asn, Int Trade Mart, La, 84-86; 67th Nat Exhib, George Walter Vincent Smith Art Mus & Mus Fine Arts, Springfield, Mass, 84 & 86; Peter Drew Gallery, Boca Raton, Fla, 88; Nat Juried Exhib, Arlington Art Mus, Arlington, Tex, 89; Aaron Gallery, Washington, DC, 90. *Pos:* Designer, Assoc Design, St Paul, Minn, 70-71; co-chmn, Art, Design & Psychology Interest Group, Inter-Soc, Color Coun , 88- *Teaching:* Asst prof art, Tyler Sch Art, Temple Univ, 75-79; prof art and design, Southwest Mo State Univ, 79-91, Distinguished Scholar, 92- *Awards:* Purchase Award, Nat Graphics Competition, Provincetown Art Asn, Mass, 76; Award for Acrylic, 27th Ann Chautauqua Nat Exhib Am Art, 84; Arlington Art Asn Award, Nat Juried Exhib, Arlington Mus, Tex, 89. *Bibliog:* Howard Derrickson (auth), Exhibit at Schweig Gallery, West End World, 86; Betsy Goldman (auth), Wade Thompson, New Art Examiner, Chicago, 86; Stephen Bachman (auth), Three at Still-Zinsel, The New Orleans Art Rev, 6/90. *Mem:* Inter-Society Color Coun (co-chmn, art, design, & psych); and others. *Media:* Acrylic on Canvas. *Dealer:* Jack Meier Gallery Houston TX. *Mailing Add:* Southwest Missouri State Univ Springfield MO 65804

THOMPSON, WILLIAM JOSEPH
EDUCATOR, SCULPTOR
b Denver, Colo, Apr 19, 26. *Study:* RI Sch Design, with Valdimir Raemaesch; Cranbrook Acad Art, with William McVey; Art Students League, Woodstock, NY, with Kuniyoshi. *Work:* Columbus Mus Fine Arts, Ohio; Ga Art Comn, Atlanta; Ga Mus, Atlanta; Pembroke State Col; Ga Power Co. *Comn:* Bronze portrait figure (14 ft) of R B Russell, State of Ga, 73-75; bronze group, Gov Comt for Ga Prisoner of War Mem, Americus, Ga, 73-76; bronze sculpture, St John of the Cross, Western Springs, Ill, 80; bronze portrait sculpture of Robert W Woodruff, Woodruff Art Ctr, Atlanta, Ga, 83; wood carving, Madonna and Child, 6 1/2 ft, Saint Mary's Cathedral, Saint Cloud, Minn, 83. *Exhib:* Southeastern Ann Exhibs, High Mus, Atlanta, 65, 66 & 67; one-man exhibs, Grand Cent Mod, New York, 66 & US Embassy Cult Ctr, Brussels, Belg, 88; Southern Sculpture 67; Smithsonian Inst Traveling Exhib, 69-70; Ga Artists Exhib, High Mus, Atlanta, 72 & 74. *Teaching:* From instr to asst prof sculpture, Ohio State Univ, 54-64; from assoc prof to prof sculpture & drawing, Univ Ga, 64-, prof emer, 90. *Awards:* First Prize in Sculpture, Columbus Mus Fine Arts, 56; Columbus Chap, Am Inst Architects Award for Comn: St Andrew, 60; First Prize, Southern Sculpture 67. *Bibliog:* Articles, La Rev Mod, Paris, 68 & Atlanta Mag, Inc, 74. *Mem:* Nat Acad Design. *Media:* Bronze. *Mailing Add:* 168 Red Fox Run Athens GA 30605

THOMSON, CARL L
PAINTER, ART APPRAISER
b Brooklyn, NY, Mar 6, 13. *Study:* Pratt Inst. *Work:* Salmagundi Club; Burr Artists Group. *Exhib:* Salmagundi Club Ann Watercolor & Oil Shows, 59-72. *Pos:* Advert designer, C Thomson Assoc, 47-59; art dir, Am Home Prod Corp, 59-70; owner, Thomson Gallery; pres, Equitable Appraisal Co, Inc, New York, 70- *Teaching:* Instr drawing, Salmagundi Club, 61-63. *Awards:* Graphic Arts Award, Printing Industs Am, 69; Cert Spec Merit, Printing Industs Metrop New York, 70. *Mem:* Salmagundi Club (pres, 81-83). *Media:* Watercolor, Oil. *Mailing Add:* 19 E 75th St New York NY 10021

THOMSON, COLIN (H)
PAINTER
b London, Eng, 49. *Study:* Lake Forest Col, Ill, BA, 71; Skowhegan Sch Painting & Sculpture, Maine, 74; New York Studio Sch, 72-75; Yale Univ, New Haven, Conn, MFA, 77. *Work:* Albright-Knox Mus; Centro Cult, Arte Contemporaneo, Mexico City; Chase Manhattan Bank; Chemical Bank; Equitable Life Assurance Soc; M & T Bank; and others. *Exhib:* Solo shows, Nine Freudenheim Gallery, Buffalo, NY, 87, 88 & 92 & Lieberman & Saul Gallery, New York, 89 & 91; Int Sculpture Ctr, Washington, DC, 88; Nina Freudenheim Gallery, Buffalo, NY, 88 & 91; Lieberman & Saul Gallery, New York, 92; David Beitzel Gallery, New York, 92; and others. *Awards:* Nat Endowment Arts Fel, 91-92. *Bibliog:* William Wilson (auth), Review, LA Times, 6/9/87; Richard Huntington (auth), Review, 6/9/87 & 5/6/88 & Elizabeth Licata (auth), The other side of summer, 7/5/91, Buffalo News; Justin Spring (auth), Review, Artforum, 113, summer 91; and others. *Mailing Add:* 142 Henry St 1FW New York NY 10022

THON, WILLIAM
PAINTER
b New York, NY, Aug 8, 06. *Study:* Art Students League, 24-25; Bates Col, Hon DFA, 57. *Work:* Metrop Mus Art; Butler Inst Am Art; Brooklyn Mus; Calif Palace Legion Honor, San Francisco; Whitney Mus; and over 45 maj US mus. *Exhib:* Corcoran Gallery Art, Washington, DC; Pa Acad Fine Arts, Philadelphia; Va Mus Fine Arts, Richmond; Art Inst Chicago; Whitney Mus Am Art, New York; and many others. *Pos:* Trustee, Am Acad in Rome. *Awards:* Prix Di Rome, 47; Dawson Medal, Philadelphia Watercolor Club, 68; Altman Prize, Nat Acad Design, 69; Gold Medal of Honor, Am Watercolor Soc, 70. *Bibliog:* Alan Gruskin (auth), William Thon--The Artist and His Technique, Viking Press, 64. *Mem:* Am Watercolor Soc; Dolphin Soc; Am Inst Arts & Lett; Nat Acad Arts & Lett. *Media:* Oil, Watercolor. *Dealer:* Midtown Payson Galleries 745 Fifth Ave New York NY 10151. *Mailing Add:* c/o Midtown-Payson Galleries 745 Fifth Ave New York NY 10151

THORNE-THOMSEN, RUTH T
PHOTOGRAPHER, EDUCATOR
b New York, NY, May 13, 43. *Study:* Southern Ill Univ, Carbondale, BFA(painting), 70; Columbia Col, Chicago, BA(photog), 73; Art Inst Chicago, MFA(photog, John Quincy Adams fel), 76. *Work:* Art Inst Chicago; San Francisco Mus Mod Art; Santa Barbara Mus Art, Calif; Walker Art Ctr, Minneapolis; Hallmark Photog Collection, St Louis; Mus Fine Arts, Houston. *Exhib:* Solo exhibs, Allan Frumkin Gallery, Chicago, 80, Art Inst Chicago, 81, Marcuse Pfeifer Gallery, New York, 83 & Jones Troyer Gallery, Washington, DC, 84; The Photographer and the City, Mus Contemp Art, Chicago, 77; Landscape Images, La Jolla Mus Contemp Art, Calif, 80; Midwest Photography (with catalog), Walker Art Ctr, Minneapolis, 81; Timed and Spaced, Alchemic Gallery, Boston, 83; Extending the Perimeters of Twentieth Century Photography & Sign of the Times, San Francisco Mus Mod Art, 85; Photographs from the Getty Museum & City Light, Int Ctr Photog, New York, 85; Photographic Fiction (with catalog), Whitney Mus Fairfield County, Stamford, Conn, 86. *Teaching:* Instr photog, Columbia Col, Chicago, 74-83; asst prof, Univ Colo, Denver, 83- *Awards:* Nat Endowment Humanities Fel, Paris, 79; Nat Endowment Arts Fel, 82. *Bibliog:* Discoveries, In: Photography Year 1980, Time-Life Bks, 80; Jon Cook, The marvelous journey: Photographs of Ruth Thorne-Thomsen, Nits & Wits Mag, 3-4/82; Owen Edwards (auth), Tripping the light fantastic, Am Photographr, 3/84; Lisbeth Morano (auth), Ruth Thorne-Thomsen at Marcuse Pfeifer, Art in Am, 4/84; Lauren Smith (auth), The Visionary Pinhole, Peregrine Smith Bks, Salt Lake City, 85. *Mem:* Soc Photog Educ. *Mailing Add:* c/o Robischon Gallery 1740 Wazee St Denver CO 80202

THORNLEY, WENDY ANN
SCULPTOR, CRAFTSMAN
b Bolton, Lancashire, Eng, Feb 28, 48; US citizen. *Study:* Southern Conn State Univ, BS, 70, MS 78; Wesleyan Univ, MA(lib studies), 92. *Work:* Reichold Chemical, White Plains, NY; Aetna Insurance, Hartford, Conn. *Comn:* Wall relief (paper), Bank Boston, Hartford, Conn, 88; wall relief (paper), Halloran, Sage Law Off, Hartford, Conn, 90. *Exhib:* Fiber Structure Nat, Calif State Univ, Los Angeles, 82; Grand Renwick Souvenir Show, Renwick Gallery, Washington, DC, 82; Art Northeast USA, 83, 86 & 89 & Paperworks, 88, Silvermine Galleries, New Canaan, Conn; Twenty-fifth Contemp Crafts Exhib, Del Art Mus, Wilmington, 85; New Artists, Currier Gallery, Manchester, NH, 89; Containers, Lyman Allyn Art Mus, New London, Conn, 92; and others. *Teaching:* Art instr, Bristol Eastern High Sch, 72- *Awards:* Best in Show, Ann Exhib, Soc Conn Craftsmen, 82, 84 & 91; Binney & Smith Award, Ann Exhib, Conn Women Artists, 85; Best in Fiber, Ann Exhib, Soc Conn Craftsmen, 90. *Bibliog:* Waterbury Republican-American, 2/22/87; Art New England, Rev, 12/89; Who's Who in the East, 92. *Mem:* Nat Asn Women Artists; Conn Women Artists; Soc Conn Craftsmen (bd dirs, 81-88); Artworks Gallery (bd dirs, 87-91); New Eng Sculptors Asn. *Media:* Handmade paper. *Mailing Add:* 97 Summit PO Box 7094 Prospect CT 06712

THORNS, JOHN CYRIL, JR
DESIGNER, PAINTER
b Denver, Colo, Apr 14, 26. *Study:* Ft Hays State Univ, BA; Ind Univ, with Henry Hope & George Rickey, MA(art hist); Univ Iowa, with John Schulze & Lester Longman, MFA(archit design). *Work:* Hastings Col, Nebr; Friends of Art Collection, Kans State Univ; Marian Col, Wis; Hansen Mus, Logan, Kans; Ft Hays State Univ, Hays, Kans. *Comn:* Bldg design, First Presby Church, Hays, Kans, 74; campanile design, Campus, Ft Hays State Univ, 75. *Exhib:* Nat Decoration Arts Show, Wichita Art Asn Gallery, 58 & Kans Watercolor Soc, 72-88; Am Craftsman Coun Exhib, Mus Contemp Crafts, New York, 62 & 63; Watercolor USA, Springfield Art Mus, Mo, 63 & 64; Smoky Hill, 80, 83, 85-92; Kans Nat Small Paintings, Drawings, Prints, 91-92; numerous one-man exhibs. *Pos:* Pres, Hays Arts Coun, Kans, 72-74. *Teaching:* Mem fac, Ft Hays State Univ, 54-72, prof art hist & design & chmn dept art, 72-90. *Awards:* Governor's Artist, Kans, 85-86; Moss Thorn Gallery Art, 87; Best Kans, Ft Hays State Names Art Gallery, 88; and others. *Mem:* Col Art Asn Am; Delta Phi Delta (pres, 70-73); Kans Watercolor Soc; Kans Art Educ Asn; Nat Coun Art Adminr; and others. *Media:* Collage; Acrylic, Watercolor. *Publ:* Illusr, Frontier Mag, 57-62; contribr, Ft Hays Studies, Ser 1 & 2, Ft Hays State Univ, 60 & 66; ed, Palette, spring 66-70 & 73. *Mailing Add:* 500 W 36th St Hays KS 67601

THORNTON, RICHARD SAMUEL
EDUCATOR, WRITER
b Columbia, Mo, Aug 5, 34. *Study:* Univ Mo, BA, 56; Cranbrook Acad Art, MFA, 57. *Teaching:* Prof graphic design, Wash State Univ, 60-77, chmn art dept, 72-76; head art dept, 77-87 & prof graphic design, 77-, interim dean, Sch Fine Arts, 89-90, Univ Conn, Storrs. *Awards:* Teacher of the Yr, Wash State Univ, 77-78; Fulbright Scholars Award, Japan, 90-91. *Mem:* Fulbright Assocs; Grapahic Design Educ Asn; Conn Art Dirs Club. *Res:* Japanese graphic design history. *Publ:* Auth, Education of the Japanese designer, Graphis, 69; New generation Japanese graphic designers, Print Mag, 84; SEVEN, seven graphic designers, Grapha-Sha, 85; Japanese Posters: The First 100 Years, Design Issues J, 89; Essay, Best 100 Japanese Posters 1945-1989, Tokyo, Kodansha 90; Graphic Spirit of Japan, Van Nostrand Reinhold, 91. *Mailing Add:* Dept of Art Univ Conn Storrs CT 06268

THORNYCROFT, ANN
PAINTER
b Petersfield, Hampshire, Eng, Feb 29, 44. *Study:* Central Sch Art, London, BA, 66; Chelsea Sch Art, London, Dipl(art), 68. *Work:* Los Angeles County Mus Art, Calif; Pepsico, NY; Transamerica, Los Angeles, Calif. *Exhib:* Drawings by Painters, Long Beach Mus Art, Calif, 82; Michael & Dorothy Blankfort Collection, Los Angeles County Mus Art, Calif, 82. *Awards:* Individual Artist Grant, Nat Endowment Arts, 82. *Media:* Oil, Watercolor. *Dealer:* Mark Moore Works Gallery 106 W Third St Long Beach Calif. *Mailing Add:* c/o Irene Drori 13 N Orange Dr Los Angeles CA 90036

THORPE, HILDA (SHAPIRO)
PAINTER, SCULPTOR
b Baltimore, Md, Dec 1, 19. *Study:* Am Univ. *Work:* Nat Mus Am Art; Phillips Collection; Corcoran Gallery Art; US Info Agency, Smithsonian Inst, Pakistan; Dept Health, Educ & Welfare, Washington, DC. *Comn:* Atrium installation (sculpture), Manikee Bldg, Rockville, Md, 86; sculpture, Int Telecommun Satellite Orgn, Washington, DC, 86; Marriott Suites Hotel, Washington, DC, 90. *Exhib:* Small Sculpture Int Prog, Smithsonian Inst, Pakistan, 70; solo exhib, 75 & American Art, 76, Phillips Collection; New Ways With Paper, Nat Collection Fine Arts, 77; The Collage Medium, Pensacola Mus Art, Fla, 81; Retrospective Exhib, 63-88; Athenaeum, Alex, Va, 88. *Teaching:* Adj prof, Am Univ, 71-81. *Awards:* Best in Sculpture, Friends 20th Anniv Exhib, Corcoran Gallery Art Washington, DC, 81. *Bibliog:* Ben Forgey (auth), Art, Washington Star, 9/30/79; David Tannous (auth), Sculpture shows in Washington, Aura, winter 80; Jo Ann Lewis (auth), The N tion, Washington, DC, Art News, 12/80; Ben Forgey (auth), Galleries, Washington Post, 12/3/88; Elvira de Galvez (auth), Cultural, Cronicas, El Comerrio, Lima, Peru; Elizabeth Tebow (auth), Hilda Thorpe, Sculpture, Paperwork, Paintings, 63-88, Athenaeum, Northern Va Fine Arts Asn, Alexandria, 88. *Mem:* Artists Equity; Washington Sculptors Group. *Media:* Handmade Paper and Painted Canvas. *Dealer:* Mahler Gallery Washington DC 20007. *Mailing Add:* 200 King St Alexandria VA 22314

THORPE, JAMES GEORGE
DESIGNER, ILLUSTRATOR
b Fort Dix, NJ, May 4, 51. *Study:* Univ Md, College Park, BA, 73, MFA, 75; studied painting with Frank Bunts, sculpture & design with Claudia Demonte. *Work:* Poster Collection, Libr Cong, Washington, DC; Lahti Poster Mus, Finland; Warsaw Poster Mus, Poland; Musee de la Publicite, Paris, France; Hiroshima Mus Art, Japan. *Comn:* Hiroshima Appeals '85 (poster), Shoshin Soc Am, Washington, DC, 85. *Exhib:* 22nd Ann Irene Leache Exhib, Chrysler Mus, Norfolk, Va, 74; Maryland Biennial, Baltimore Mus Art, 76; 1st Triennial Toyama Poster Exhib, Toyama Mus Art, Japan, 85; Lahti Poster Biennale Int, Lahti Poster Mus, Finland, 85; Hiroshima Appeals '85 Invitational, Hiroshima Mus Art, Japan, 85; Colo Int Poster Biennial, Univ Colo Mus, Ft Collins, 85; 10 year retrospective, Univ & Col Designers Assoc, Chicago, Ill, 85; Warsaw Poster Biennale, Warsaw Poster Mus, Poland, 86; Lahti Poster Bienale, Lahti, Finalnd, 87; Moscow Int Peace Poster Exhib, USSR, 87; one-man exhib, posters, Am Cult Ctr, Brussels, Belgium, 88. *Pos:* Designer-illusr, US Army European Command, 77-78 & Md Nat Capital Park & Planning Comt, 78; freelance designer-illusr, James Thorpe Graphic Design, 77. *Teaching:* Lectr graphic design-illus, Univ Md, College Park, 80-85, asst prof graphic design, 85- *Awards:* Design Excellence Award, Nekoosa Paper Corp, 81. *Bibliog:* Walter Herdeg (auth), Graphis Posters, 84 & Glenn Beal (auth), Images for Survival, 12/85, Graphis Press; Ann & Ha Hanna (auths), the art of peace, ID Mag, 12/85. *Mem:* Univ & Col Designers Assoc. *Media:* Montage, Posters. *Publ:* Contribr, Print Mag-Reg Design Ann, R C Publ, NY 83 & 84; American Illustration Ann, Abrams, NY, 84; Graphis Poster Ann, Graphis Press, Zurich, 84; ID Mag, 85. *Mailing Add:* Housing & Design Dept, Rm 1401 Marie Mount Hall Univ Md College Park MD 20742

THORSON, ALICE R
EDITOR, CRITIC
b Hinsdale, Ill, Sept 22, 53. *Study:* Western Ill Univ, BA, 75; Northern Ill Univ, MA, 81; Univ Chicago, PhD prog, 80-82. *Pos:* Managing ed, New Art Examiner, Chicago & Washington, DC, 82-; Art Critic, Washington Times, Washington, DC, 87-90, Kansas City Star, Mo, 91- *Teaching:* Adj Prof, Corcoran Sch Art, Washington, DC, 89-91. *Res:* Contemporary visual art. *Publ:* Contribr, The Earthly Chimera & The Femme Fatale (exhib catalog), Univ Chicago, 81; auth, Hirshhorn's content swamps issues, 85 & 49th Carnegie International sets the record straight, 86, New Art Examiner; Morris Yarowsky: Paintings 1971-1991 (exhib catalog), McLean Project for the Arts, 91. *Mailing Add:* 1406 P St NW Washington DC 20005

THRALL, ARTHUR
PRINTMAKER
b Milwaukee, Wis, Mar 18, 26. *Study:* Univ Wis, Milwaukee, BS & MS; Univ Wis, Madison; Univ Ill, Urbana; Ohio State Univ. *Work:* Brit Mus, London, Eng; Libr Cong, Washington, DC; Art Inst Chicago; Brooklyn Mus, NY; Tate

Gallery, London, Eng. *Comn:* 50 print ed, Wis Arts Found, 84. *Exhib:* Carnegie Inst Int Print Exhib, Pittsburgh, 51; Young American Printmakers, Mus Mod Art, New York, 53; one-man show, Smithsonian Inst, 60; 160th Ann, Pa Acad Art, Philadelphia, 64; 143rd Ann, Nat Acad Design, New York, 67; 43rd Ann, Audubon Artists, NY, 85. *Teaching:* Assoc prof art, Milwaukee-Downer Col, 56-64; prof art, Lawrence Univ, 64-, chairperson, Art Dept, 81-86; vis prof art, Univ Wis-Madison, 66-67 (retired 90). *Awards:* Louis Comfort Tiffany Found Fel Graphics, 63; Purchase Award, Brooklyn Mus 14th Ann, 63; Cannon Prize, Nat Acad Design 143rd Ann, 67. *Bibliog:* M Fish (auth), Arthur Thrall, Wis Architect, 65; D Anderson (auth), The Art of Written Forms, Holt Rinehart & Winston, 69; J Watrous (auth), A Century of American Printmaking, Univ Wis Press, 84. *Mem:* Soc Am Graphic Artists; Boston Printmakers; Audubon Artists. *Media:* All Media. *Dealer:* Bradley Galleries Milwaukee WI; Benjamin--Beattie Gallery Chicago IL. *Mailing Add:* 4225 N Worthburn Shorewood WI 53211

THRELKELD, DALE
PAINTER
b Mo, Apr 11, 44. *Study:* Northeast Mo State Col, BS, 66; Ball State Univ, MA, 70; Southern Ill Univ, Edwardsville, MFA, 75. *Work:* Brooklyn Mus Art, NY; Arco Collection Los Angeles; Ill State Mus. *Exhib:* New Talent Exhib, Gimpel & Weitzenhoffer Gallery, New York, 74; Los Angeles Print Soc Nat Print Exhib, 74; 28th Ann Ill Invitational, Ill State Mus, 75; Unique Works on Paper, Frank Marino Gallery, New York, 75-79; Arco Collection, Los Angeles; and others. *Teaching:* Art instr drawing, Belleville Area Col, Ill, 71- *Awards:* Purchase Awards, Dulin Gallery Art, 70, Ark Arts Ctr, 71 & Ill State Mus, 75. *Media:* Mixed, oil on canvas. *Mailing Add:* Dept Humanities & Soc Scis Belleville Area Col 2500 Carlyle Belleville IL 62221

THURMAN, CHRISTA CHARLOTTE MAYER
CURATOR
b Darmstadt, Ger, Dec 12, 34; US citizen. *Study:* Finch Col, NY, BA, 58; NY Univ Inst Fine Arts, MA, 66. *Collections Arranged:* Masterpieces of Western Textiles: A Handbook on the Art Institute of Chicago's Western Textile Collection (auth, catalog), Art Inst Chicago, 69; Coverlets: a Handbook on the Collection of Woven Coverlets in the Art Institute of Chicago (coauth, catalog), 73, Raiment for the Lord's Service: a Thousand Years of Western Vestments (auth, catalog), 76 & Claire Zeisler: a Retrospective (auth, catalog), 79; Ancient Textiles from Nubia (coauth, catalog), Art Inst Chicago & Univ Chicago, 79. *Pos:* Conserv apprentice, New York, 59-61; asst cur dept textiles, Cooper Union Mus, New York, 61-67; assoc cur dept textiles, Art Inst Chicago, 67-68 & cur, 68-82. *Teaching:* Vis asst prof hist archit & art, Univ Ill, Chicago Circle, 74. *Bibliog:* Alan G Artner (auth), The department of textiles, 1/16/78 & Peter Gorner (auth), Nubian textiles, 5/24/79, Chicago Tribune. *Mem:* Fel Am Inst Conserv Hist & Artistic Works; Centre Int d'Etude Textiles Anciens; Am Asn Mus; Int Comt Mus & Collections Costumes & Textiles; Costume Soc Am. *Mailing Add:* 464 Greenbay Rd PO Box 458 Winnetka IL 60093-0458

THURMER, ROBERT
SCULPTOR, GALLERY DIRECTOR
b Vienna, Austria, Oct 8, 53; US citizen. *Study:* Syracuse Univ, Col Visual & Performing Arts, BFA, 77; Univ Nebr, Lincoln, RI Sch Design, MFA, 81. *Work:* Cleveland Mus Art, Ohio; Everson Mus Art, Syracuse, NY; RI Sch Design Mus, Providence; Annmary Brown Mem, Providence, RI; B K Smith Gallery, Lake Erie Col, Painesville, Ohio. *Comn:* Indoor monumental installations, numerous pvt individuals, Cleveland, New York, San Diego & Chicago, 86-92; indoor monumental installation, Jacobs/Visconci/Jacobs, Cleveland, 90. *Exhib:* May Show, Cleveland Mus Art, 86-88; Int Selected Group Show, Lucia Gallery, New York, 89; Int Art Horizons, Art 54 Gallery, New York, 89-90; Sculpture Survey, Metro Gallery (Tri-C), Cleveland, 92; Body and Soul, Beck Ctr Mus, Lakewood, Ohio, 93; and others. *Collections Arranged:* Nature in Art, Cleveland Mus Art, 85; North Coast-New Imagery, Beck Ctr Mus, 86; Sculpture Exposed essay, Everson Mus Art, 89; Metaphysical Vistas, Cleveland State Art Gallery, 91; Vision Quest, Cleveland State Art Gallery, 92. *Pos:* Exhib specialist, Cleveland Mus Art, 83-83, gallery dir, 90-; cur educ, Everson Mus Art, Syracuse, 88-90; gallery dir, Cleveland State Univ Art Gallery, 90-; mem, visual arts & craft review panel, Ohio Arts Coun, 92. *Teaching:* Lectr 3-d design, State Univ NY, Oswego, 82-83; instr 3-d design, Cazenovia Col, NY, 88-90; acad appointment 3-d design & sculpture, Cleveland State Univ, 90- *Mem:* Col Art Asn; SPACES; New Organization Visual Arts; Charter mem, d'Art Bd, 89-90. *Media:* Miscellaneous. *Mailing Add:* Cleveland State University Art Gallery 2307 Chester Ave Cleveland OH 44114

THURSTON, JACQUELINE BEVERLY
EDUCATOR, PAINTER
b Cincinnati, Ohio, Jan 27, 39. *Study:* Carnegie-Mellon Univ, BFA(painting), 61; Stanford Univ, MA(painting), 62. *Work:* Libr Cong; San Francisco Mus Mod Art; Oakland Mus, Calif; St Louis Mus Art; Henry Gallery, Univ Washington, Seattle; and other pub & pvt collections. *Exhib:* Observations/Translations--Four Photogr, Oakland Mus, Calif, 72; Two Photogr, Oakland Mus, 75; Photography 2 (exhib catalog), Jack Glenn Gallery, Newport Beach, Calif, 75; Am Photogr: Past into Present (exhib catalog), Seattle Mus Art, Wash, 76; Graham Nash Collection (exhib catalog), Univ Santa Clara, Calif, 79, San Francisco Mus Mod Art, 80; one-person show, Susan Spiritus Gallery, Newport Beach, 77, 80 & 93; La Photographie Creative (exhib catalog), Pavillon des Arts, Paris, France, 84. *Teaching:* Prof art, San Jose State Univ, Calif, 65-; lectr, Stanford Univ, Calif, Calif Inst Technol, Pasadena, 78, St Joseph's Hosp, Costa Mesa, Calif, Sacred Heart Schs, Atherton, Calif, 80, Summer Arts Inst, Kirkwood, Calif, 88, C G Jung Inst, San Francisco, Calif, 89 & San Francisco Psychoanalytic Inst, Calif, 92. *Awards:* Fac Artist Residence, Arts Fac Inst, 88; Meritorius Performance & Prof Promise Award, San Jose State Univ, 89; CSU Summer Arts Exchange, 92; and others. *Bibliog:* Thomas Albright (auth), Observations/translations - four photographers, 9/11/72 & Two photographers, 8/6/75, San Francisco Chronicle; Joan Murray (auth), Observations/translations - four photographers, 9/23/72, Dorothy Burkhardt (auth), rev, 76 & Rebecca Palmer (auth), Dioramas, 86, Artweek. *Mem:* Soc Photog Educators. *Media:* All. *Publ:* Coauth (with Ronald Carraherr), Optical Illusions and the Visual Arts, Van Nostrand Reinhold, 66; auth, Geoff Winningham & Jacqueline Thurston (exhib catalog), Calif Inst Technol, Pasadena, 78; Individual Visions (exhib catalog), 82 & A Show of Hands (exhib catalog), 82, San Francisco Mus Mod Art; contribr, The Voice of the Image, Cameraworks, 89. *Mailing Add:* Dept Art San Jose State Univ San Jose CA 95192

THWAITES, CHARLES WINSTANLEY
PAINTER, MURALIST
b Milwaukee, Wis, Mar 12, 04. *Study:* Univ Wis; Layton Sch Art. *Work:* Univ Wis; Gimbel Collection; Edgar Kaufman Collection; Cottonwood Hist Soc Mus, Windom, Minn; Milwaukee Art Ctr. *Comn:* Murals, US Post Off, Greenville, Mich, Plymouth & Chilton, Wis & Windom, Minn; portraits, pres of St John's Col, Annapolis, Md & Santa Fe, NMex; mural designs for fed bldgs, Pub Bldgs Admin. *Exhib:* Chicago Art Inst; Corcoran Biennials, Washington, DC; Pa Acad Fine Arts; Metrop Mus Art, New York; Whitney Mus Am Art, New York; Nat Acad Design, New York; Walker Art Ctr, Minneapolis; Calif Palace Legion Honor, San Francisco; Nelson-Atkins Gallery, Kansas City; Colorado Springs Fine Arts Ctr, Colo; Mus NMex, Santa Fe; Univ Minn Traveling Exhib of Govt Art 1930-1940, 77-78; and others. *Pos:* Artist in residence, St John's Col, Santa Fe, NMex, 73-74. *Awards:* Forty-eight State Mural Competition Prize, 39; Prizes & Medal, Calif Palace Legion Honor, 46. *Bibliog:* Article, The Studio, London, Eng, Vol 131, No 634; Dr Francis V O'Connor (auth), Federal art patronage, Univ Md, 66; Forbes Watson (auth), American painting today, Am Fedn Arts. *Mailing Add:* 1860 Sun Mountain Dr Santa Fe NM 87505

TIBBS, THOMAS S
EDUCATOR, MUSEUM DIRECTOR
b Indianapolis, Ind, Aug 30, 17. *Study:* Univ Rochester, AB & MFA; Columbia Univ. *Exhib:* Craftsmanship in a Changing World, 56; Louis Comfort Tiffany Retrospective, 58; Six Decades of American Painting, 61; Affect & Effect, 68; Jose de Rivera Forty Year Retrospective, 72. *Pos:* Assoc dir educ, Rochester Mem Art Gallery, 47-52; dir, Huntington Galleries, WVa, 52-56; Mus Contemp Crafts, New York, 56-60; Des Moines Art Ctr, Iowa, 60-68; La Jolla Mus Contemp Art, 68-73; retired, currently. *Teaching:* Lectr art hist, Calif State Univ, San Diego, 69-90, retired. *Mem:* Am Asn Mus; Asn Art Mus Dir; fel Royal Soc Art, London. *Mailing Add:* 8639 Circle R Course Lane Escondido CA 92026

TICE, GEORGE ANDREW
PHOTOGRAPHER, AUTHOR
b Newark, NJ, Oct 13, 38. *Study:* Newark Vocational & Tech High Sch, NJ, 55. *Work:* Metrop Mus of Art, New York; Mus of Mod Art, New York; Art Inst of Chicago; Bibliot Nat, Paris, France; Victoria & Albert Mus, London, Eng. *Comn:* Two 55ft photog murals, Field Mus of Natural Hist, Chicago, 75; photog, Liberty Park, Mus Mod Art, NY, 79; photog, Bank Archit, Mus Fine Arts, Houston, 90. *Exhib:* One-man shows, Metrop Mus Art, New York, 72, NJ State Mus, 76, Mus Mod Art, New York, 79, Witkin Gallery, New York, 81 & Photo Gallery Int, Tokyo, 82; Photpgraphy in America, Whitney Mus, 74; Mirrors & Windows, Mus ModArt, 79; and others. *Teaching:* Instr master class photog, The New Sch, New York, 70- *Awards:* Grand Prix, Festival d'Arles, France, 73; Nat Endowment for Arts Fel, 73; Guggenheim fel, 73-74; Fel, Nat Mus Photog & Bradford & Ilkley COl, Bradford, England, 90-91. *Bibliog:* Gerry Badger (auth), Recent books, British J Photog, 3/77; Barbara Lobron, Romantic notions, Camera Arts, 6/83; Peggy Sealfon (auth), Meet the masters, Peterson's Photographic, 10/83. *Publ:* Auth, Paterson, 72, Urban Landscapes, 75 & Lincoln, 84, Rutgers; Artie Van Blarcum, Addison House, 77; Urban Romantic, The Photographs of George Tice, Godine, 82; Hometowns, Graphic Soc, 88; Stone Walls, Grey Skies, Nat Mus Photog Film & Television, Eng, 91. *Dealer:* The Witkin Gallery 415 West Broadway New York NY 10012. *Mailing Add:* 323 Gill Lane 9B Iselin NJ 08830

TIEGREEN, ALAN F
PAINTER, ILLUSTRATOR
b Boise, Idaho, July 6, 35. *Study:* Univ Southern Miss, AB, 57; Art Ctr Col Design, 61. *Work:* High Mus Art, Atlanta, Ga. *Comn:* Painting, Atlanta Bur Cult Affairs, Ga, 75; mural, Simmons Corp, Atlanta, 76; paintings, Hilton Hotels, Knoxville, Tenn, 81. *Exhib:* Nat Drawing Exhib, High Mus, Atlanta, 65; Prof Art Am, Smithsonian Inst, Washington, DC, 66; SEastern Ann Exhib, 67 & Ga Artists Exhib, 68, High Mus, Atlanta; SEastern Regional, Columbus, Ga, 70. *Teaching:* Prof, Ga State Univ, 65- *Awards:* First Award, Nat Drawing Soc, 65; Purchase Prize, Atlanta Arts Festival, Ga, 68; 1st Award, Decatur Sesquicentennial, Ga, 72. *Bibliog:* Clyde Burnette (auth), Charcoal drawings, Atlanta Newspapers, 2/80; article, Art Voices, 7/81; article, American Illustrators, Dell, 81. *Media:* Acrylic; Ink, Charcoal. *Publ:* Illusr, Doodle & the Go-Cart, Viking, 72; illusr, Ramona the Brave, Morrow, 75; illusr, Silver Woven in my Hair, Atheneum, 77; illusr, Kelly's Creek, Crowell, 77; illusr, Ramona Age 8, Morrow, 81. *Dealer:* Artists Assocs Gallery 3261 Roswell Rd Atlanta GA 30305. *Mailing Add:* 4279 Wieuca Rd NE GA State Univ, University Plaza Atlanta GA 30342

TIEMANN, ROBERT E
PAINTER, SCULPTOR
b Austin, Tex, Jan 12, 36. *Study:* Univ Tex, Austin, BFA, 58; Univ Southern Calif, MFA, 60. *Work:* Los Angeles City Collection; San Antonio Mus Art, Tex; Am Tel & Tel Collection, New York; Univ Tex & Laguna Gloria Mus, Austin. *Comn:* Voyage to Cythera (mural), Charles Butt Found Hemisfair, San Antonio, Tex, 68; mural, Citizens Nat Bank, Austin, Tex, 74; Joffrey Ballet Program Cover, Soc Performing Arts, San Antonio, Tex, 80. *Exhib:* Solo exhibs, Witte Mem Mus, San Antonio, Tex, 66, Roswell Mus & Art Ctr, NMex, 71 & McNay Art Inst, San Antonio, Tex, 75; Invitational Texas Artists Show, Dallas Mus Fine Arts, 72; Laguna Gloria Art Mus, Austin, Tex, 74; San Antonio Mus Art, Tex, 82. *Pos:* Art therapist, Audie Murphy Veterans Hosp, San Antonio, 75-77; design consult, Chumney-Urrutia Archit Firm, San Antonio, 85- *Teaching:* Prof art, Trinity Univ, San Antonio, 65-, chmn dept, 82-; prof art, Harvard Univ, summers, 82-84. *Awards:* Nat Endowment Arts Grant, 68; Fac Res & Develop Grant, Trinity Univ, San Antonio, 78. *Bibliog:* Martha Utterback (auth), Robert Tiemann (exhib catalog), Univ Tex, Austin, 4/67; Henry Hopkins (auth), Contemporary art in Texas, Art News, 5/73; Susan Platt (auth), rev, Artforum, 4/80. *Mem:* Col Art Asn; The Blue Star-Contemp Art for San Antonio (bd mem, 86). *Publ:* Auth, art criticism column, San Antonio Express-News, Tex, 78. *Mailing Add:* Dept Art Trinity Univ 715 Stadium Dr San Antonio TX 78212

TIERNEY, PATRICK LENNOX
HISTORIAN, EDUCATOR
b Weston, WVa, Jan 28, 14. *Study:* Univ Calif, Los Angeles, EdB(cum laude), 36; Columbia Univ, New York, MA, 44; Sogetsu-Ryu, Tokyo, Japan, Seizan I, 52. *Pos:* Cur, Asian Art, San Diego Mus Art, 74-82; mem & trustee, Mingei Mus, San Diego, 77- *Teaching:* Chmn arts fac, Pasadena City Col, Calif, 46-71; lectr, Univ Calif, Los Angeles & San Diego, 52-71; assoc dean col fine arts & prof hist Oriental art, Univ Utah, 71-; prof, Univ Pittsburgh, 89-90, 90-91. *Awards:* Emmy, Acad Television Arts & Sci, 67; Honors Citation, Resolution of Bd of Trustees, Pasadena City Col, Calif, 71. *Mem:* Royal Asiatic Soc, Seoul, Korea; Pacificulture Found, Pasadena, Calif (dir, mus div, 61-70, mem bd dir, Asian Mus, 61-); Acad Television Arts & Sci; Salt Lake Art Ctr (mem bd dir, 71-); Japan-Am Soc, Southern Calif (dir, 72-); and others. *Res:* Folk art of Japan. *Publ:* Coauth, Japan, Int Publ, 58; coauth, Chanoyu, as a form of non literary art criticism, Chanoyu J, Kyoto, 76; coauth, Cambodia, Khmer Remains, 79. *Mailing Add:* Dept Art Univ Utah Salt Lake City UT 84112

TIFT, MARY LOUISE
PRINTMAKER, EDUCATOR
b Seattle, Wash, Jan 2, 13. *Study:* Univ Wash, BFA(cum laude); Art Ctr Col Design; San Francisco State Univ. *Work:* Philadelphia Mus Art, Pa; US Art in the Embassies; Achenbach Print Collection, San Francisco; Brooklyn Mus; Libr Cong, Washington, DC; Seattle Art Mus. *Exhib:* First Int Print Biennale, Segovia, Spain, 74; US Mission to UN, Geneva, Switz, 74; World Print II, San Francisco Mus Mod Art, 77; one-man show, Gumps' Gallery, San Francisco, Calif, 77, 86, 89 & Brooklyn Mus, NY, 78; retrospective, Ore State Univ, 81; Utah State Univ, 83; UN-UK Impressions, Eng, 88. *Pos:* Coordr design, San Francisco Art Inst, 57-60. *Teaching:* Asst prof design, Calif Col Arts & Crafts, Oakland, 49-57. *Awards:* Purchase Awards, Northwest Printmakers Int, 69, Nat Exhib Prints, Nat Gallery, Washington, DC, 73 & Hawaii Nat Print Exhib, 78. *Bibliog:* Leonard Edmonson (auth), Etching, Reinhold; article, Am Artist Mag, 12/80 & 2/87; Mary Tift, Prints, Gumps Gallery, 85. *Mem:* Int Graphic Arts Found; Print Club Philadelphia. *Media:* Etching, Silkscreen. *Dealer:* Gump's Gallery San Francisco CA. *Mailing Add:* 112 Industrial Ctr Bldg 480 Gate 5 Road Sausalito CA 94965

TIGERMAN, STANLEY
PAINTER, ARCHITECT
b Chicago, Ill, Sept, 20, 30. *Study:* Mass Inst Technol, 48-49; Inst Design, 49-50; Yale Univ, BArch, 60 & MArch, 61. *Work:* Art Inst Chicago; Metrop Mus Art, New York; Mus Mod Art; Deutshes Arch Museum. *Comn:* Modular structure, Metrop Structures, Chicago, 71. *Exhib:* Eight Chicago Artists, Walker Art Ctr, Minneapolis, Minn, 65; one-man shows, Evanston Art Ctr, Ill, 69, Art Res Ctr, Kansas City, Mo, 69 & Springfield Arts Asn, Ill, 70; IBA, Deutches Architekus Mus, Frankfurt, WGerm, 86; Chicago Arch 1872-1922, Art Inst, Chicago, 89; Gulbenkian Found, Lisbon, Portugal, 89. *Pos:* Prin, Stanley Tigerman & Assocs, Chicago, 62- *Teaching:* Prof archit & art, Univ Ill, Chicago Circle, 65-71, dir, Sch Arch, 80-; archit-in-residence, Am Acad in Rome, 80. *Awards:* AIA-DBA Suburban Village, 91; AIA Interior Archit Award Excellence, Am Standard, 92; AIA Int Archit Award, The Ernest Graham Study Ctr Art Inst Chicago, 92; AIA INT Archit Award, The Arts Club Chicago, Ill Acad Fine Arts, 92. *Bibliog:* R A M Stern (auth), New Directions in American Architecture, Braziller, 69; Faulkner & Ziegfield (auth), Art Today, Holt, Rinehart & Winston, 69; Dahinden (auth), Urban Structures of the Future, Praeger, 72. *Mem:* Am Inst Architects; Yale Art Asn; Ill Arts Coun; Yale Club NY; Arts Club Chicago. *Media:* Acrylic. *Publ:* VERSUS: An American Architect's Alternatives, 82; Chicago's Architectural Heritage: A Romantic Classical Image--Work of the Current Generation of Chicago Architects, Arquitectura, 79; Stanley Tigerman Architoons, 88; The Architecture of Exile, 88; Stanley Tigerman: Buildings & Projects 1966-1989. *Mailing Add:* Arch Dept Univ Ill at Chicago Chicago IL 60680

TILLENIUS, CLARENCE (INGWALL)
PAINTER, WRITER
b Sandridge, Man, Aug 31, 13. *Study:* Teulon Col, with A J Musgrove; Univ Winnipeg, hon LLD, 70. *Comn:* Collection of wildlife painting, North American Life Assurance Co, Winnipeg, 54-80; dioramas, habitat groups, Nat Mus Can, Ottawa, Ont, 60-72, BC Mus, Victoria, 65-70 & Mus Alta, Edmonton, 72-74; dioramas, paintings, Man Mus Man & Nature, Winnipeg, 69-79. *Exhib:* Two one-man shows, London Art Gallery, London Shute Inst, 54; one-man exhibs, Monarch Life Bldg, 62, Whitney Gallery Western Art, Cody, Wyo, 64, Man Mus Man & Nature, 74 & Glenbow-Alta Inst, 75; Soc Wildlife Art Nations Opening Exhib, Eng, 88. *Pos:* Diorama dir, Nat Mus Can, Ottawa, 62-72. *Teaching:* Lectr art appreciation, Man, 50-52; lectr wildlife painters, Glenbow Inst, 70; dir wildlife drawings, Okanagan Summer Sch Arts, Penticton, BC, 73-82. *Awards:* Man Centennial Medal Honor, Gov Gen, Prov Man, 72; Seton Medal, 85. *Bibliog:* Peter Kelly & Paul Guyot (coauth), Tillenius on the Prairies (film), Can Broadcasting Corp, 63; Eric Mitchell (auth), Clarence Tillenius, Nature Can Mag, 73; Richard Savage (auth), Tokens of Myself--Tillenius, the Man and the Art (film), Wilderness Trail Motion Picture Co, 78, rev and copyrighted by artist, 84. *Mem:* Explorers Club, New York; Soc Animal Artists; life mem Man Naturalist Soc; Royal Geographical Soc, London, Eng; Soc Wildlife Art Nations, Eng. *Media:* Oil, Watercolor. *Res:* Lifetime study of wild animals, wilderness travels across North America into Yukon and the arctic. *Publ:* Illusr, Little Giant, 51; illusr & auth, Fur Bearers of Canada, 51; Monarchs of the Canadian Wilds, 54-75; auth, Sketchpad Out of Doors, 56 & 62; illusr, Orphan of the North, 58. *Dealer:* Trails of the Interlake Studio 441 Dominion St Winnipeg Man R3G 2M8 Can. *Mailing Add:* 441 Dominion St Winnipeg MB R3G 2M8 Canada

TILLEY, LEWIS LEE
PAINTER, VIDEO ARTIST
b Parrott, Ga, May 17, 21. *Study:* High Mus Sch Art, 37-39; Emory Univ, 37-39; Univ Ga, BFA, 42; Colorado Springs Fine Arts Ctr, with Boardman Robinson, Adolph Dehn & John Held, 42-45; Inst Allende, Mex, MFA, 68; British Film Inst, 72-75, Univ Ga, Cortona, Italy, 85. *Work:* Post Card No 2, Colorado Springs Fine Arts Ctr, Colo; Ga Art Asn; Southern States Art League; Canñon City Art Ctr, Colo. *Comn:* Mural, Broadmoor Cheyenne Mountain Zoo, Colorado Springs, 58; dragon wall mural, Victor Hornbein House, Denver, 59; mural, First Nat Bank, Colorado Springs, 59; four polyester resin sculptures, Colorado Springs Eye Clin, 60; exterior wall mural, Horace Mann Jr High Sch, Colorado Springs, 62. *Exhib:* Am Fedn Arts; Graphic Arts Chicago; Denver Ann & Biennial; Artists West of Mississippi; Washington Cathedral Relig Exhib; Southern State Art League; Dallas Print & Drawing Show. *Pos:* Producer & dir, Alexander Film Co, 58-62; artist-in-residence, Univ Ga, Cotona, Italy, 85; columnist, Your Amiga, London. *Teaching:* Instr painting, life drawing & design, Colorado Springs Fine Arts Ctr, 45-51; prof art, Univ Southern Colo, 65-86, prof emer, currently. *Awards:* First Purchase Award for oil, Canon City Blossom Festival, 69; First Purchase Award for oil, Colo State Fair, 70. *Bibliog:* Discovery No 49, Mod Photog, 58; Info 64, 9/85. *Media:* All Media, Computer Graphics. *Publ:* Auth, History of writing and painting, 63; illusr, English with the twins, 63; History of medicine, 63; ed, The story of Nok culture, 63. *Mailing Add:* Box 115 Parrott GA 31777

TILLIM, SIDNEY
PAINTER, INSTRUCTOR
b Brooklyn, NY, June 16, 25. *Study:* Syracuse Univ, BFA, 50. *Work:* Joseph H Hirshhorn Mus & Sculpture Garden; Univ Tex, Austin; Equitable Life Assurance Co, New York; Mod Art Mus, Ludwig Col, Vienna; Michener Col, Austin; and others. *Exhib:* Aspects of New Realism, Milwaukee Art Ctr, 69; 22 Realists, 70 & Ann, 72, Whitney Mus Am Art; 30th Ann, Chicago Art Inst, 70; one-man shows, Robert Schoelkopf Gallery, New York, 65 & 67, Noah Goldowsky Gallery, New York, 69 & 74, Edmonton Art Gallery, Alta, 73 & 76, Tibor de Nagy Gallery, New York, 77, Meredith Long Contemp, New York, 79, Bennington Col, Vt, 86, Perimeter Gallery, Chicago, 90 & Galerie Burgis Geismann, Cologne, 90; Realism in American Art Since 1960, Pa Acad Fine Arts, Philadelphia, 81; Diamonds are Forever; Baseball & Am Art, NY State Mus, Albany & tour, 87-89; Galerie Löl, Möchengladbachefour, 91; Slow Art, Painting in NY; PS1 Mus, Long Island City, NY, 92. *Pos:* Contrib ed, Arts, 59-65; contrib ed, Artforum, 65-69. *Teaching:* Instr art hist & drawing, Pratt Inst, 64-68; instr painting, Bennington Col, 66- *Awards:* Painting Grants, Nat Endowment Arts, 74 & Ingram-Merrill Found, 76; Pollock-Krasner Found, 90. *Bibliog:* Interview with Sidney Tillim by R Rubenstein & D Wiener, Arts, 12/87. *Media:* Acrylic. *Publ:* Auth, The new avant garde, Arts, 2/64; Walker Evans: Photography as representation, 3/67, Earthworks and the new Picturesque, 12/68 & The View from Past Fifty, 4/84, Artforum; Criticism and Culture: Greenberg's Doubt, Art in Am, 5/87; Ideology and difference: Reflections on Olitski and Koons, Arts Mag, 3/89; Helen Levitt: Photography as Remembrance, Artforum, 12/91. *Mailing Add:* 17 Bleecker St New York NY 10012

TILLMAN, PATRICIA ANN
SCULPTOR
Study: Univ Tex, Austin BFA(painting, drawing), 76; Univ Okla, Norman, MFA(painting, mixed media constructions), 78. *Exhib:* Solo shows, Koehler Cult Ctr, San Antonio Col, Tex, 80, Brown-Lupton Gallery, Tex Christian Univ, Ft Worth, Tex, 84 & Ft Worth Gallery, Tex, 85, 87 & 90; Texas Exhibit (auth catalog), Nat Mus Arts, Washington, DC, 88; A Century of Sculpture in Texas, 1889-1989 (auth, catalog), Archer M Huntington Gallery, Univ Tex Austin, 89; Austin Visual Arts Asn, Tex, 90; and others. *Teaching:* Adj lectr art dept, Baylor Univ, Waco, Tex, 82, part-time adj lectr, 83-89; part-time instr art dept, McLennan Community Col, Waco, Tex, 83-, adj instr, 85 & 90; lectr, var univ & col, Tex. *Awards:* Nominee, Awards Visual Arts, 86, 87; Nat Endowment Arts Fel Grant, 86. *Bibliog:* Annette Carlozzi (auth), 50 Texas Artists, A Critical Selection of Painters and Sculptors, Chronicle Bks, San

Francisco, 98, 99, 86; Mark Smith (auth), Laguna Gloria exhibit embodies substance of women's souls, Austin Am-Statesman, F4, 3/23/89; Janet Kutner (auth), Figurative art: Patricia Tillman's sculpture evolves, Dallas Morning News, 5C-6C, 5/5/90; and others. *Mailing Add:* c/o Fort Worth Gallery 901 Boland St Fort Worth TX 76107

TIMMAS, OSVALD
PAINTER, LECTURER
b Estonia, Sept 17, 19; Can citizen. *Study:* Tartu State Univ; Atelier Sch Tartu & Tallinn, Estonia, with Nicholas Kummits & Gunther Reindorff. *Work:* London Art Mus, Ont; Art Gallery Hamilton; Art Gallery Windsor; Rodman Hall Art Ctr, St Catharines, Ont; Art Gallery Ont, Toronto. *Exhib:* Can Watercolors, Drawings & Prints, Nat Gallery Can, Ottawa, 66; Audubon Artists, 66-69, Am Watercolor Soc, 66, 67 & 69 & Nat Acad Design, 67, 68 & 71, New York; Royal Can Acad Arts, Nat Gallery Can, 70; OSA Image (circulating show), Ont Pub Galleries, 75-77 & 79; Watercolour Painting in Canada, A Survey, Univ Waterloo, 79; and one-man shows. *Awards:* Medal & Award for creative aquarelle, Audubon Artists, 67 & 68; Major Award for watercolor painting, Coutts-Hallmark Co Can, 69 & 70; Lacana Grant, 79. *Bibliog:* Anthony Ferry (auth), A floating world, 2/20/65 & It's now time for Timmas, 11/11/65, Toronto Star; Stevens (auth), Osvald Timmas, La Rev Mod, 11/66. *Mem:* Royal Can Acad Arts; Am Watercolor Soc; Can Soc Painters Watercolor; Ont Soc Artists (vpres, 71-75). *Media:* Watercolor, Acrylic. *Dealer:* Karney Daniels Gallery 11 Yorkville Ave Toronto ON M4W 1L2. *Mailing Add:* 776 Marlee Ave Toronto ON M6B 3J9 Canada

TIMMS, PETER ROWLAND
MUSEUM DIRECTOR
b Philadelphia, Pa, Aug 26, 42. *Study:* Brown Univ, Providence, RI, BA, 64; Harvard Univ, MA, 69 & PhD(anthrop), 76. *Pos:* Dir, Fitchburg Art Mus, Mass, 73- *Teaching:* Instr, Int Col, Beirut, Lebanon, 68; teaching fel, Harvard Univ & Mass Inst Technol, 69-73; vis lectr, Fitchburg State Col, 78; instr, Applewild Sch, 78-79. *Mem:* Am Asn Mus (chmn, State Comt Energy, 78); Applewild Sch (trustee, 82-); Nashua Arts & Sci Ctr (trustee, 83-). *Publ:* Auth, Flint Implements of the Old Stone Age, Shire Publ, United Kingdom, 74, 2nd ed, 79; Consult ed & illusr, Human Biology & Ecology, Albert Damon, W W Norton & Co, New York, 77; auth, Accreditation and the small museum, Mus News, 7-8/80. *Mailing Add:* c/o Fitchburg Art Mus 185 Elm St Fitchburg MA 01420

TIMOTHY, GROVER See Whiten, Tim

TIMPANO, ANNE
MUSEUM DIRECTOR, HISTORIAN
b Osaka, Japan; US citizen. *Study:* Col William & Mary, Williamsburg, Va, BA, 72; George Washington Univ, Washington, DC, MA, 83. *Collections Arranged:* William Christenberry: A Southern Perspective, 87; A Select View: American Paintings from Columbus Museum, 87; Paintings and Sculpture from the Permanent Collection, 91; Starstruck: Images from Hollywood's Golden Age, 92. *Pos:* Docent prog coord, Nat Mus Am Art, Washington, DC, 77-80, res asst, 80-83 & prog mgt asst, 83-86; dir, Columbus Mus, Ga, 86- *Awards:* David Lloyd Kreeger Prize in the History of Art. *Mem:* Asn Art Mus Dirs; Am Asn Mus; Col Art Asn; Southeast Mus Conf. *Res:* American art & architecture. *Publ:* A Select View: American Paintings from the Columbus Museum, 87; Starstruck: Images from Hollywood's Golden Age, 92. *Mailing Add:* Columbus Museum 1251 Wynnton Rd Columbus GA 31906

TIMS, MICHAEL WAYNE See Bronson, A A (Michael Wayne Tims)

TING, WALASSE
PAINTER
b Shanghai, China, Oct 13, 29. *Work:* Mus Mod Art, New York; Guggenheim Mus, New York; Carnegie Inst, Pittsburgh; Stedelijk Mus, Amsterdam, Holland; Israel Nat Mus, Jerusalem. *Exhib:* Paul Facchetti, Paris, France, 54; Martha Jackson Gallery, 60; Carnegie Inst Int, 61, 64, 67 & 70; Galerie Birch, 63; Galerie France, 68; Lefebre Gallery, 71. *Awards:* Guggenheim Fel, 70. *Dealer:* Lefebre Gallery 47 E 77th St New York NY 10028. *Mailing Add:* 463 W St New York NY 10014

TING SHAO KUANG
PAINTER
b Beijing, Oct 7, 39, US citizen. *Study:* Cent Acad Arts & Crafts, BA, 62. *Work:* Ginza Art Mus, Tokyo, Japan; Tainan Fine Art Mus, Repub of China; Nat Mus China, Beijing; Shanghai Fine Art Mus, China; Great Hall of the People, Beijing, China. *Exhib:* Solo exhibs, Ginza Art Mus, Tokyo, Japan, 88, Tainan Fine Art Mus, China, 91, Historic Mus Art, Beijing, China, 92 & Shanghai Mus Art, China, 92. *Pos:* Chmn, Chinese Overseas Artist Asn, 91- *Teaching:* Prof painting, Cent Acad Arts & Crafts, Beijing, China, 62-80. *Bibliog:* Anna Macdonnell (auth), Segal Fine Art, 89; Tetsuro Murobushi (auth), Kodansha Ltd, 89; Ann Wicks (auth), People's Publ House, 91. *Media:* Chinese Stone Painting, Acrylic. *Publ:* Contribr, The Art of Ting Shao Kuang, Kodansha, 89; Ting Shao Kuang Serigraphs, Segal Fine Art, 91; Painting Paradise-The Art of Ting Shao Kuang, People's Fine Art Publ House, 92. *Dealer:* Segal Fine Art 21220 Erwin St Woodland Hills CA 91367. *Mailing Add:* 707 N Alpine Dr Beverly Hills CA 90210

TINKLER, BARRIE KEITH
PAINTER
b Tyler, Tex, 1935. *Study:* Univ Houston, BFA, 62; pvt study with Guido Fulignot; Mus Fine Arts, Houston (scholor); study with Emil Bisttram. *Work:* Canvas murals, Historic Garcia Opera House, Socorro, NMex; Hotel Plaza, Liberty Bank & Banker's title Bldg, Houston, Tex; H E Stratagraph Inc, Lafayette, La. *Comn:* Portrait, comn by R C Gorman, 83. *Exhib:* Art Ctr for Southwestern La & La Landmarks Soc Exhib of La Artists, Lafayette; Taos Festival of Arts, NMex, 80; Art Expo, New York, 84; Daffodil Arabian Horse Asn, Washington, DC, 84. *Awards:* Purchase Prize, Brazosport Art League, Tex; First Prize, J K Ralston Mus & Art Ctr, Sidney, Mont, 82; Second Place, 11th Ann Nat Small Painting Exhib, 83, NMex Art League. *Publ:* John Gaines (auth), article, Astrology J, 5/70; Houston Scene Mag, 8/76; Prime Times, Albuquerque, NMex, 82. *Mailing Add:* 10607 Benavides St SW Albuquerque NM 87121

TINNING, GEORGE CAMPBELL
PAINTER
b Saskatoon, Sask, Feb 25, 10. *Study:* Elliot O'Hara Sch, Maine; Art Students League. *Work:* Nat Gallery Art, Ottawa, Ont; Nat War Mus, Ottawa, Ont; Montreal Mus Fine Arts, McGill Univ, Montreal; Charlottetown Art Mus, PEI; George Campbell Tinning Collection, Can Nat Archives, Ottawa, Ont; and others. *Comn:* Mural, Jenkins Valve Co, Lachine, Que, 60; mural, Bank Montreal, 61; Legends of Quebec (drawing), Baie Comeau Hotel, Que. *Pos:* War artist, Hist Sect, Can Army, 43-46. *Teaching:* Pvt classes. *Awards:* Dow Awards for watercolor, 42 & 48, Montreal Mus Fine Arts. *Mem:* Academician Royal Can Acad Art; Can Soc Painters Watercolour. *Media:* Watercolor, Acrylic. *Publ:* Auth, Can Art, spring, 49; auth & illusr, Lincoln Mercury Times, 50-59. *Dealer:* Galerie Dominion 438 Sherbrooke St W Montreal PQ H3G 1K4. *Mailing Add:* Apt 52 1509 Sherbrooke St W Montreal PQ H3G 1M1 Canada

TINSLEY, BARRY
SCULPTOR
b Roanoke, Va, Feb 19, 42. *Study:* Col William & Mary, Williamsburg, Va, BA, 64; Sch Art & Hist, Univ Iowa, Iowa City, MA, 67, MFA, 68. *Work:* S W & B M Koffler Found Collection, Nat Mus Am Art, Washington, DC; Lakeview Mus, Peoria, Ill; Ctr Visual Arts Gallery, Normal, Ill. *Comn:* Jetty (corten steel), comn by City of Chicago, Ill, 80; Silver Oak, (stainless steel & painted aluminum), Green Co, Miami, Fla, 85; Silver Blade (stainless steel relief), Borg Warner Corp, Chicago, Ill, 84; Urban Moraine, comn by State of Ill, Chicago, 84. *Exhib:* Solo exhibs, Ill State Mus, Springfield, 79, Piedmont Arts Asn, Martinsville, Va, 84 & Ordean Ct, Tweed Mus, Duluth, Minn, 86; Mayor Byrne's Mile of Sculpture, Int Art Expo, Navy Pier, Chicago, Ill, 82; Festival of the Arts, Arts Coun Oklahoma City, 85; Chicago Sculpture, Rockford Col, Ill, 85; Sculpture Campus Tour, Univ Tenn, Knoxville, 85-86; Traveling Exhib, New Traditions in Sculpture, Ill Grant, 86. *Pos:* Treas, Chicago Sculpture Soc, 82-; vis artist, Visual Arts Ctr Alaska, 83; bd mem, Sculpture Chicago, Burham Park Planning Asn, 84- *Teaching:* Instr art & sculpture, Eastern Ky Univ, Richmond, 68-70; assoc prof art & sculpture, Ill State Univ, Normal, 70-78. *Awards:* Dick Blick Mem Award, Galex X, Galesburg, Ill, 76; Chicago Sculpture Syposium Award, 83. *Mem:* Ill Arts Coun (visual artist panel); Chicago Artists Coalition (adv bd, 86). *Mailing Add:* c/o Conlon Gallery 125 N Guadalupe Sante Fe NM 87501

TOBEY, ALTON S
PAINTER, MURALIST
b Middletown, Conn, Nov 5, 14. *Study:* Yale Univ Sch Fine Arts, BFA, 37, MFA, 47. *Work:* Smithsonian Inst; MacArthur Mem, Norfolk, Va; Am Bur Shipping, Paramus, NJ; Metrop Opera Gallery Mus, Jewish Mus, Sea, Air Space Mus & Mus City of New York; Sea, Air Space Mus, New York; Mus City New York; Westport Mus, Westport, NY. *Comn:* Mural, East Hartford Post Off, 38; Life of Gen MacArthur (six murals), Edwin Abbey Mural Fund for MacArthur Mem, 65; two murals on anthrop, Smithsonian Mus Natural Hist, 67; mural, Am Bur Shipping, Paramus, NJ; Sea, Air Space Mus, New York; and others. *Exhib:* solo shows, Hudson River Mus, Yonkers, NY, Gallerie Alliance, Copenhagen, Denmark, 74, Am Ctr, Stockholm, Sweden, 75, Silvermine Galleries, New Canaan, Conn, 83; Univ Pa Art Mus, Philadelphia; Albany Mus, NY; Casa Acquarela, Mexico City. *Teaching:* Instr & lectr styles, techniques & hist art, Yale Sch Fine Arts, 45-49; lectr hist art, City Col New York, 50-51; lectr mural painting, Westchester Art Teachers, 86-90. *Awards:* Grumbacher Award, 82; Artist of Yr, Westchester Council Arts, NY. *Bibliog:* New York Times, 65 & 89; Am Artists Mag, 76; Plate Collectors, 81; Spotlight, 85. *Mem:* Abraxas; Silvermine Artists Guild; Artists Equity New York (dir, 70-79, pres emer, 79-); Nat Soc Mural Painters (pres, 72-); Mamaroneck Art Guild. *Media:* Oil, Acrylic. *Publ:* Contribr, Man & Power, Golden Bks; Epic of Man, Life Bks. *Mailing Add:* 296 Murray Ave Larchmont NY 10538

TOBIA, BLAISE JOSEPH
PHOTOGRAPHER, EDUCATOR
b Brooklyn, NY, Jan 20, 53. *Study:* Brooklyn Col, with Walter Rosenblum, George Krause, Bob D'Allesandro & Philip Pearlstein, BA, 74; Univ Calif, San Diego, with David Antin, Allan Kaprow & Newton Harrison, MFA, 77. *Work:* Mus City New York; Delaware Mus Art. *Comn:* Many commissioned photographic catalogs as well as documentations of artist-performances. *Exhib:* Image-Text (with catalog), Franklin Furnace, New York, 84; Encampments, Randolph St Gallery, Chicago, 89; Philadelphia Photographers in Transit, Art Now, Philadelphia, 89; Biennial '91, Delaware Art Mus, 91; Surveillance: 6 Days, CEPA Gallery, Buffalo, 91; American Pie: Myth Representation, Abington Arts Ctr, Philadelphia, 92. *Teaching:* Vis photogr, Univ Calif, San Diego, 79, Wayne State Univ, Detroit, 81; assoc prof photog, prog head, Drexel Univ, 85- *Awards:* Ford Found Grant, 77; Fac Res Award, Drexel Univ, Philadelphia, 86; Nat Endowment Humanities Res Fel, 88. *Bibliog:* Victoria Donohue (auth), Focusing on emotions in pictures of city life, Philadelphia Inquirer, 90; Miles Orvell (auth), Democracy, Disorder, and

the New Political Art, American Pie (exhib catalog), Abington/CEPA, 92. *Mem:* Col Art Asn; Soc Photog Educ. *Publ:* ed, Works for Freedom, Ikon, 85; auth, Wrestling with questions, In: Upfront, 85; Making the Invisible Visible, Art & Artists, 88 & Atlanta Art Papers, 88; Demolished by neglect, Artpapers, 88; Connie Coleman, coauth (with Alan Powell), New Art Examiner, 88; Undermining Documentary, Afterimage, 90; auth, From Resistance to Embrace: Text/Image Relationships in 20th-Century Fine-Art Photographic Practice, Word & Image, fall 92. *Dealer:* TandM Arts 3410 Baring St Philadelphia Pa 19104. *Mailing Add:* 3410 Baring St Philadelphia PA 19104

TOBIAS, ABRAHAM JOEL
PAINTER, SCULPTOR
b Rochester, NY, Nov 21, 13. *Study:* Cooper Union Art Sch, 30-31; Art Students League, 31-33; Fed Art Proj, New York, 38-40. *Work:* Brooklyn Mus, NY; Los Angeles Co Mus Art; New York Pub Libr; Rochester Pub Libr, NY; Nat Mus Am Art, Smithsonian, Washington, DC. *Comn:* Two Plexiglas panels for entrance, Polytech Inst Brooklyn, 58; mosaic & terrazzo mural, Henrietta Szold Sch, New York Bd Educ, 60; Freedom Movement, Brooklyn Bicentennial Comn, New York, 76; History of Science (mural, 60' x 9'), entrance, Polytech Univ, New York, 92. *Exhib:* Mus Mod Art, New York; San Francisco Mus; Brooklyn Mus; Adelphia Col; Archit League New York; Art for the People, Hofstra Univ, New York, 78; one-man retrospective, Zimmerli Mus, Rutgers Univ, New Brunswick, NJ, 87-88, travelled to Queens Mus, New York, 88 & Ga Mus Art, Univ Ga, Athens, 89; The Technological Muse, Katonah Mus Art, New York, 90-91; and others. *Pos:* Art dir, Intelligence Div, USAF, Washington, DC, 43-44; graphic designer, Off Strategic Serv, Washington, DC, 44-45. *Teaching:* Lectr mural painting, Howard Univ, 45; artist in residence, Adelphi Univ, 47-57; lectr mural painting, Asn Am Cols Prog, 52 & 55; inst artist, Polytech Inst Brooklyn, 70- *Awards:* Award for Mural Painting, Archit League New York, 52. *Bibliog:* Joseph L Young (auth), Mosaics: Principles & Practice, Reinhold, 64; Lawrence N Jensen (auth), Synthetic Painting Media, Prentice Hall, 64; Louis Botto (auth), In the know, Look Mag, 69. *Mem:* Fine Arts Fedn New York (exec bd); Nat Soc Mural Painters; Artists Equity NY. *Media:* Multimedia. *Publ:* Auth, Mural painting, 2/57 & auth, A mural painting for science & technology, 3/69, Am Artist Mag. *Mailing Add:* 98-51 65th Ave Rego Park Flushing NY 11374

TOBIAS, JULIUS
SCULPTOR, INSTRUCTOR
b New York, NY, Aug 27, 15. *Study:* Atelier Fernand Leger, Paris, 49-52. *Exhib:* Pa Acad Fine Arts, Philadelphia, 58; Mus Mod Art Traveling Exhib, Tokyo, 59; New Eng Exhib, Silvermine, Conn, 60; Whitney Mus Am Art Sculpture Ann, 68; Indianapolis Mus Art, Ind, 70; BYA Gallery, New York, 91; Staller Ctr Arts, Stony Brook, NY, 92; Artemisia Gallery, Chicago, Ill, 92. *Teaching:* Instr painting, New York Inst Technol, 66-71; instr sculpture, Queens Col (NY), 71-74; vis artist, Ind Univ, Bloomington, 74-75, Univ Minn, Minneapolis, 77, Univ NC, Chapel Hill, 78, Univ Calif, Los Angeles, 83. *Awards:* Guggenheim Mem Found Fels, 72 & 78; Nat Endowment Arts Grant, 75 & 81; Adolf & Esther Gottlieb Found Grant, 80 & 91; Pollock-Krasner Foun Grant, 86 & 91. *Bibliog:* James R Mellow (auth), Two sculptors worlds apart, 1/31/71 & Pater Schjeldahl (auth), A journey well worth making, 1/20/74, NY Times; Corinne Robins (auth), Julius Tobias: a decade of spatial dialogue, Arts Mag, 3/77; Judith Lopes Cardozo (auth), article, Artforum Mag, 12/77; April Kingsley (auth), catalogue essay, A Boulder in the Mainstream, 92. *Mailing Add:* 9 Great Jones St New York NY 10012

TOBIAS, RICHARD
PAINTER
b New York, NY, 52. *Study:* Philadelphia Col Art, Pa, 72-74; Independent Study Prog, Whitney Mus Am Art, 73-75; Pratt Inst, BFA, 75. *Exhib:* Solo exhibs, Brooke Alexander, 84, 86 & 87; Selections from the Independent Study Prog, Whitney Mus Am Art, NY, 74; Black & White, Art Advisory Serv, Mus Mod Art, NY, 86 Abstract Painting, Asher Faure Gallery, Los Angeles, 87; Generations of Geometry, Whitney Mus Am Art, NY, 87; Art Against AIDS, Brook Alexander, 87; Logical Foundations, Art Advisory Serv, Mus Mod Art, NY, 88; Visiting Artists, Ewing Gallery, Univ Tenn, Knoxville,88; Columnar, Hudson River Mus, Yonkers, NY, 88. *Awards:* Edward F Albee Found, Montauk, NY, 83; Pollock-Krasner Found, New York, 86; Nat Endowment Arts, 87. *Bibliog:* Jed Perl (auth), Versions of pastoral, New Criterion, 6/86; Margaret R Lazzri (auth), Evasion of abstraction, Artweek, 5/9/87. *Mailing Add:* c/o Brooke Alexander Gallery 59 Wooster St New York NY 10012

TOBIAS, ROBERT PAUL
PAINTER, SCULPTOR
b Reading, Pa, Dec 14, 33. *Study:* Ariz State Univ, BS(appl arts, ceramics), 64, MFA(sculpture), 69. *Work:* Matthews Ctr, Ariz State Univ, Tempe; Univ Ariz Mus Art, Tucson; Ariz Western Col, Yuma; Phoenix Art Mus, Ariz. *Comn:* Monumental sculpture, La Placita, City of Tucson, 74. *Exhib:* Painting, 1973 Four Corners Exhib, Phoenix & 1974 Mainstreams, Marietta Col, Ohio; sculpture, Nelson Art Mus, Kansas City, Mo, 70, Yuma Invitational, 73 & Arizona's Outlook '74, Tucson Art Ctr. *Teaching:* Instr design, Univ Kans, Lawrence, 69-71; assoc prof sculpture & design, Univ Ariz, Tucson, 71- *Awards:* Sculpture Purchase Award, Wis State Univ, Platteville, 67; Painting Award, 1972 Yuma Invitational, Ariz Western Col; Sculpture Exhib Award, Tucson Art Mus, 74. *Bibliog:* Tobias show in Lawrence, Kansas City Star, 3/22/70; Darrell Dobraus (auth), Artists review, Desert Silhouette, Tucson, 10/75. *Dealer:* Gekas/Nicholas Gallery 6538 East Tangue Verde Rd Tucson AZ 85715. *Mailing Add:* Dept of Art Bldg 2 Univ Arizona Tucson AZ 85721

TOBIN, NANCY
DESIGNER, EDITOR
b New York, NY, Aug 31, 43. *Study:* Syracuse Univ Sch Art, BFA, 65. *Pos:* Art dir, Buffalo Mag, 65-75, asst ed, 65-69; art critic, Courier Express, Buffalo, 71-77, ed, Sunday Mag, 78-81; news art dir, Buffalo Courier Express, formerly; freelance writer, Art News, New York Times & Progressive Archit; asst prof, S I Newhouse Sch Pub Commun, Syracuse Univ, 85-87; design dir, Asbury Park Press, 87-89; dir publ, Univ at Buffalo, 89- *Awards:* Awards for Ed Content & Visual Content for Buffalo Mag, Am Asn Com Publ, 66-71; Merit Award for Criticism, Am Newspaper Guild, 75; 1st & 2nd Place Awards, newspaper design & headline writing, Am Newspaper Guild; Award of Excellence, Soc Newspaper Design, 84. *Mem:* Soc Newspaper Design (bd mem, pres, 93); Albright-Knox Art Gallery Coun for the Support & Advan Educ. *Publ:* Auth, Understanding changes in the growth and shape of newspaper art departments, Soc Newspaper Design, 10/85. *Mailing Add:* 140 Linwood Ave #B-12 Buffalo NY 14209

TODD, MICHAEL CULLEN
SCULPTOR, PAINTER
b Omaha, Nebr, June 20, 35. *Study:* Univ Notre Dame, BFA, 57; Univ Calif, Los Angeles, MA, 59; Woodrow Wilson Fel, 59; Fulbright Fel, France, 61. *Work:* Whitney Mus Am Art, New York; Los Angeles Co Mus Art; Oakland Mus; Hirshhorn Mus & Sculpture Garden, Washington, DC. *Exhib:* Whitney Mus Am Art Sculpture Ann, 64-70; Sculpture of 60's, Los Angeles Co Mus Art, 65 & Philadelphia Mus, 66; Living Am Art, Maeght Found, France, 71; Exhibs Large Scale Sculpture, Lippincott Corp; Charles Cowles Gallery, New York, 81; and others. *Teaching:* Instr sculpture, Bennington Col, 66-68; asst prof sculpture, Univ Calif, San Diego, 68-76. *Awards:* NEA. *Bibliog:* Catalog: 25 Year Survey, Palm Springs Desert Mus. *Media:* Steel, Aluminum. *Dealer:* Tortue Gallery 2817 Santa Monica Blvd Santa Monica CA 90404; Klein Gallery 400 N Morgan Chicago IL 60622. *Mailing Add:* 2817 Clearwater Los Angeles CA 90039

TOKER, FRANKLIN
HISTORIAN, EDUCATOR
b Montreal, Que, Apr 29, 44; US citizen. *Study:* McGill Univ, BA, 64; Oberlin Col, AM, 66; Harvard Univ, PhD, 73. *Exhib:* Poussin en detail, fogg Art Mus, Harvard Univ, 67. *Pos:* Archeol dir excavations, Cathedral of Florence, Italy, 69-74 & 80. *Teaching:* A W Mellon vis prof fine arts, Carnegie-Mellon Univ, Pittsburgh, 74-76, assoc prof, 76-80; assoc prof, Dept Fine Arts, Univ Pittsburgh, 80-87, prof, 87; vis prof hist art, Univ Florence, Italy, 89; vis prof hist archit, Univ Rome, Italy, 91. *Awards:* A K Porter Prize, Col Art Asn Am, 80; Sr Fel Nat Endowment Humanities, 85; Interpretive Res Grant, Nat Endowment Humanities, 92-94. *Bibliog:* Ada Louise Huxtable (auth), The current age of rediscovery, New York Times, 11/27/77 & Henry Tanner (auth), Florence cathedral credited to sculptor, 5/7/80; Brendan Gill (auth), Skyline, New Yorker, 1/9/89. *Mem:* Life mem Medieval Acad Am; Inst Advan Study, Princeton; life mem Col Art Asn; life mem Soc Archit Historian (dir, 85-88, vpres, 90-); Archaeological Inst Am. *Res:* Medieval art; American and 19th century architecture and urban design; Early Christian archaeology. *Publ:* Coauth, Florence cathedral: The design stage, 78, & Gothic architecture by remote control, 85; Arnolfo's S Maria del Fiore, J Soc Archit Hist, 83; Alberti's ideal architect, Renaissance Studies honoring Craig Hugh Smyth, Florence, 85; Pittsburgh: An Urban Portrait, Univ Pittsburgh Press, 86; Building on Paper: The Role of Architectural Drawings in Late-Medieval Italy, Actes du XVIIe congres International de l'Histoire de l'Art, Strasbourg, 92. *Mailing Add:* Dept Fine Arts Univ Pittsburgh Pittsburgh PA 15260

TOLEDO, ANGELES
ART DEALER, MUSEOLOGIST
b Mexico City, Mex, Mar 13, 58. *Study:* Nat Autonomous Univ, Mex, BA, 80; Nat Inst Fine Arts, Mex, cert, 81. *Pos:* Asst to dir, Mus Mod Art, Mexico City, 82-84; co-dir, Artmart Gallery, New York, 84-86; partner, Gallery Casas Toledo Oosterom, New York, formerly; art consult, Zona Gallery, New York; dir, El Galeon Art Consultants, Mexico City. *Mem:* Int Coun Mus. *Specialty:* Contemporary art. *Mailing Add:* PO Box 965 New York NY 10009

TOLEDO, FRANCISCO
PAINTER, PRINTMAKER
b Minatitlan, Oaxaca, Mex, July 17, 40. *Study:* Nat Inst fine Arts, grad, 59; study with Stanley William Hayter in Paris, 60. *Exhib:* Solo exhibs, Martha Jackson Gallery, New York, 75 & Everson Mus, Syracuse, NY, 80; retrospective, Mus Art, Mexico City, 80; Nat Mus Mod Art, Tokyo, 74; Mus Mod Art, Mexico City, 76; Mus Contemp Art, Bogota, Colombia, 77; Mus Biblioteca Pape, Monslova, Mex, 79; and many others in US, Canada, South America, Europe and Asia. *Bibliog:* Josh Teplow (auth), Phantasmagoric art, Artspeak, 85; Dag Buxell & Carlos Stoll (auths), article, in: El Buho, Excelsior, 85. *Publ:* Illusr, Coyote va a la fiesta de Chihuitan, Ayuntamiento Popular de Juchitan, Oaxaca; Los signos de vida, Found de Cultura Economica, 79; article, in: Novaro Editions, 81. *Mailing Add:* c/o TwoSixtyOne Art 261 Broadway Suite 8A New York NY 10007

TOLL, BARBARA ELIZABETH
DEALER, CURATOR
b Philadelphia, Pa, June 8, 45. *Study:* Goucher Col, Towson, Md, AB, 67; Radcliffe Col, 67; Pratt Inst, New York, MFA, 69. *Pos:* Dir, Hundred Acres Gallery, New York, 70-77; freelance cur & dealer, 77-81; dir, Barbara Toll Fine Arts, New York, 81- *Specialty:* Contemporary works of art in all media. *Mailing Add:* c/o Barbara Toll Fine Arts 146 Greene St New York NY 10012

TOLLES, BRYANT FRANKLIN, JR
EDUCATOR, CONSULTANT
b Hartford, Conn, Mar 14, 39. *Study:* Yale Univ, BA, 61, MAT, 62; Boston Univ, PhD, 70. *Pos:* Asst dir & libr, NH Hist Soc, Concord, 72-74; dir & librn, Essex Inst, Salem, Mass, 74-84; dir, Mus Studies Prog, Univ Del, 84- *Teaching:* Asst dean & instr hist, Tufts Univ, Medford, Mass 65-71; assoc prof art hist & hist, Univ Del, 84- *Mem:* Orgn Am Historians; Soc Archit Historians; Nat Trust Hist Preserv. *Res:* New England architectural history, late 18th and 19th century; White Mountain illustrators, 1820-1910. *Interests:* American architectural history; American portraiture, 1750-1900; American landscape art, 19th century. *Publ:* Auth, Textile Mill Architecture in East Central New England, Essex Inst Hist Collection, 71; College architecture in New England in printed & sketched views, Antiques, 73; Gridley J F Bryant and the first building for Tufts College, Old-Time New England, 73; New Hampshire Architecture: A Guide, Univ Press of New Eng, 79; Architecture in Salem: An Illustrated Guide, Essex Inst, 83; The Evolution of a Campus: Dartmouth College Architecture Before 1860, Hist New Hampshire, 87. *Mailing Add:* Mus Study Prog Univ Del 301 Old College Newark DE 19716

TOLMIE, KENNETH DONALD
PAINTER
b Halifax, NS, Sept 18, 41. *Study:* Mt Allison Univ, Sackville, NB, BFA(honors). *Work:* Nat Gallery Can, Ottawa, Ont; Montreal Mus Fine Arts, Que; Hirshhorn Collection, Washington, DC; Art Gallery NS, Halifax; Confederation Mus, Charlottetown, PEI; MacDonald Stewart Art Ctr, Guelph, Ont; and others. *Exhib:* Nat Gallery Can, Ottawa, 64 & 66; 40th Ann Exhib, Can Soc Graphic Art, Univ Western Ont, 73; Annapolis Valley Seven, Art Gallery NS, 80; Solo exhibs, The Bridgetown Series Traveling Exhib, Owens Art Gallery, Mt Allison Univ & Nat Mus Can, 82-84; West Bend Gallery, Wis, 82; Gallery 1667, Halifax, NS, 85; Beckett Gallery, Hamilton, Ont, 86; and others. *Awards:* Purchase Prizes, Burnaby Art Gallery, 73, McIntosh Gallery, Univ Western Ont, 73 & Contemp Can Graphics, Carleton Univ, 74; Ont Arts Grants, 85 and 86; Toronto Arts Grant, 89. *Bibliog:* F Redgrave (auth), Ken Tolmie: The Bridgetown series, Arts Atlantic, summer 82; Visions (film), TV-Ontario, 82-83; Seeing It Our Way (film series), Can Broadcasting Co, 82; W Elliot (auth), The art of Ken Tolmie, Arts W, 12/83. *Mem:* Visual Artists NS; Writers Union Can; Writers Fedn NS. *Media:* Oil, Watercolor. *Publ:* Auth, Tale of an Egg (children's book), 74; auth, A Rural Life: An Artist's Portrait, 86. *Dealer:* Kaspar Gallery 27 Prince Arthur Toronto Canada; Tolmie Gallery Toronto ON. *Mailing Add:* 25 George St PO Box 1002 Toronto ON M5A 4L8 Canada

TOLPO, CAROLYN LEE
PAINTER, TAPESTRY ARTIST
b Detroit, Mich, Feb 1, 40. *Study:* Wayne State Univ, Detroit, BA, 62. *Work:* Highland Col Art Collection, Freeport, Ill; Amaco Art Collection, Denver, Colo; Digital Corp, Denver, Colo. *Comn:* Fiber murals, First Nat Bank, Perryton, Tex, 82; Alamo Ctr, Colorado Springs, 83; atrium fiber mural, Cumborland Bldg, Denver, 85; fiber mural, Mega Bank, 86 & Tishman West Inc, 89, Denver, Colo; fiber mural, Hamilton Standard Corp, Colorado Springs, 92. *Exhib:* Freeport Art Mus, Ill, 76 & 77; Davenport Art Gallery, Iowa, 79; Stanley Gallery, Muscatine, Iowa, 80; Women's Caucus Art Group Show, Western Ill Univ, Macomb, Ill, 81; Women's Caucus for Art Show, Quad City Arts Ctr, Rock Island, Ill, 81; Women's Caucus for Art Show, Knox Col Art Ctr, Galesburg, Ill, 81. *Teaching:* Art teacher/coordr, Freeport Catholic Sch, 71-76. *Awards:* Best of Show, Nat Orchid Soc Art Exhib, 81. *Mem:* Woman's Caucus for Art, Midwest Chap (founding pres, 79-81); Cult Coun Park Co, Colo (founding bd mem). *Media:* Wrapped Fiber, Watercolor. *Publ:* The Guild 5, 6, 7 & 8: Artist Sourcebook, Krause Sikes Inc, Madison, Wis. *Mailing Add:* PO Box 134 Shawnee CO 80475

TOLPO, VINCENT CARL
PAINTER, SCULPTOR
b Chicago, Ill, Apr 26, 50. *Study:* Univ Wyo, Laramie, 69-69, Am Acad Art, Chicago, 70-71; Ariz State Univ, Tempe, BFA, 74; studied with Carl & Lily Tolpo, 69-76. *Work:* Freeport Art Mus, Ill; Augustana Hosp Portrait Gallery, Chicago; Park Co Libr, Colo. *Comn:* Fiber murals (collab with Carolyn L Tolpo), Alamo Ctr, Colorado Springs, Colo, 83; painting of Grand Canyon, Colo Bankshares, Denver, 83; atrium fiber (with C L Tolpo), Cumberland Bldg, Englewood, Colo, 85; atrium metal sculture, Glenarm Bldg, Denver, 92. *Exhib:* Scottsdale Annual, Scottsdale Fine Art Ctr, Ariz, 73; 14th Annual, Stanley Gallery, Muscatine, Iowa, 80; Sculpture exhib, Art on the Corner, Grand Junction, Colo, 90, 91, 92. *Teaching:* Ceramics, art appreciation, Highland Col, Freeport, Ill, 75-77. *Awards:* Co-visions, Colo Arts Coun, 92. *Mem:* Am Craft Coun; Park Co Cult Coun. *Media:* Oil, Wrapped Fiber. *Publ:* Guild 5, 6, 7 & 8: Artist Sourcebook, Krause/Sikes Inc, Madison, Wisc. *Mailing Add:* c/o Shawnee Mountain Studios PO Box 134 Shawnee CO 80475

TOMASINI, WALLACE J
ADMINISTRATOR, HISTORIAN
b Brooklyn, NY, Oct 19, 26. *Study:* Univ Mich, AB, 49, AM, 50, PhD, 53; Univ Florence, Fulbright grant, 51-52; NY Univ Inst Fine Arts, 54-57. *Teaching:* Instr hist of art, Finch Col, 54-57; asst prof art hist, Univ Iowa, 57-61, assoc prof, 61-64, prof, 64-, dir, Sch Art & Art Hist, 72- *Awards:* Am Numismatic Soc Grant, 57; Am Philos Soc Grant, 58. *Mem:* Am Numismatic Soc; Mid-Am Col Art Conf; Int Exchange Scholars; Sixteenth Century Studies; Midwest Art Hist Soc; Haviland collectors int found pres. *Res:* Social and economic determinants of Italian Renaissance art; Late Imperial and Barbaric numismatics. *Publ:* Auth, Report on Visigothic Numismatic Research, 62; Exhibition Catalogue:Drawing & the Human Figure 1400-1964, 64; The Barbaric Tremissis in Spain & Southern France, Anastasius to Leovigild (numismatic notes & monogr 152), 64; contribr, 17th Century Art Essay (CIC Exhib Catalogue), 73; Paintings of Eve Drewelowe, 85;; Catalogue of Haviland china: celebrating 150 yrs, 92. *Mailing Add:* 610 Beldon Ave Iowa City IA 52246

TOMCHUK, MARJORIE
PRINTMAKER, PAINTER
b Manitoba, Can, Oct 16, 33; US citizen. *Study:* Univ Mich, BA, 57, MA, 61; Long Beach State Col, 62; Sophia Univ, Japan; Pratt Graphics Ctr, NY. *Work:* Nat Air & Space Mus, Smithsonian Inst, Inst, DC; DeCordova Mus, Mass; Butler Inst of Am Art, Youngstown, Ohio; Mus of Native Am Cult, Spokane, Wash; Nelson Gallery, Kansas City, Mo; Newark Mus, NJ. *Comn:* Xerox Corp; General Electric; Northern Telecom. *Exhib:* Nat Print Exhib, Brooklyn Mus, 70; World Art Exposition, Boston, 79; one-man shows, Art Expo New York, 79-90, Art Washington, 79-83 & Art Expo Calif, 81-90; Isetan Art Gallery, Tokyo, 86; Fayetteville Mus Art, NC, 89. *Awards:* Boston Nat Print Show, Purchase Prizes, DeCordova Mus, 71 & 73; Nat Arts Club Award, New York, 72; Stamford Art Club First Prize, 73. *Bibliog:* Ellen Kaplan (auth), A Collectors Guide, Prints, 83; Franz Geierhaas (auth), M Tomchuk Graphic Work, 1962-89, 89. *Mem:* Silvermine Guild Artists (bd mem, 73-78); Philadelphia Print Club; Pratt Graphics Ctr. *Media:* Etching, Embossing. *Publ:* Contribr, article, J Print World, Vol 5, No 4; article, Prints, 7-8/82. *Mailing Add:* 44 Horton Lane New Canaan CT 06840

TOMCIK, ANDREW MICHAEL
DESIGNER, EDUCATOR
b Cleveland, Ohio, June 18, 38; Can citizen. *Study:* Cleveland Inst Art, Diploma, 60; Somerakdmie der Bildende Kunst, Salzburg, with Oskar Kokoschka, Cert, 61; Yale Univ Sch Art & Archit, BFA, MFA, 65. *Comn:* Loretto Col Infirmary Chapel, 89. *Exhib:* Westlake Print Biennale, Zhejiang, China, 87; Sense of Place: Photographs, Founders Col, York Univ, Toronto, 88; Ekoplagat, Sch of Nature Protection, Gbel'any, Czechoslovakia, 90. *Pos:* Designer: The Carborundum Co, Niagara Falls, NY, 65-67; sr design assoc, Hauser Assoc Inc, Atlanta, Ga, 67-74; chmn, dept of visual arts, York Univ, Toronto, Ont, 81-84 & 90-91. *Teaching:* Assoc prof visual arts, Ga State Univ, Atlanta, 67-74; prof fine arts, York Univ, Toronto, 74- *Mem:* Soc Graphic Designers of Can (nat vpres educ, 85-87, secy, 87-90); Am Inst Graphic Arts. *Media:* Graphic Design, Print. *Res:* Design history, criticism. *Publ:* Auth, Art in Everyday Life: Aspects of Canadian Design, 67-87; auth, Benchmarks, The Best of the Eighties, 85; From inspiration to imitation: How close can we come to our sources of inspiration before the work cannot be said to be ours?, Scan, summer 86; Exhib Rev, Ontario Craft, 88; Pol Posters, 89 & The Depreciation of Originality, Azure Mag, 90. *Mailing Add:* 48 Parkhurst Blvd Toronto ON M4G 2C9 Canada

TOMKINS, CALVIN
WRITER
b Orange, NJ, Dec 17, 25. *Study:* Princeton Univ, BA. *Pos:* Staff writer, The New Yorker, Mag, 61- *Publ:* Auth, The Bride and the Bachelors, Viking Press, 65; Merchants and Masterpieces: The Story of the Metropolitan Museum of Art, E P Dutton, 70; Living Well Is the Best Revenge, 71 & auth, The Scene: Reports on Post-Modern Art, 76, Viking Press; Off the Wall: Robert Rauschenberg and the Art World of Our Time, Doubleday & Co, Inc, 80. *Mailing Add:* c/o The New Yorker 25 W 43rd St New York NY 10036

TOMKO, GEORGE PETER
HISTORIAN, CURATOR
b Cleveland, Ohio, Mar 17, 36. *Study:* Case Western Reserve Univ, Cleveland, Ohio, BA, 57, 57-63 & 65. *Collections Arranged:* Paintings from Midwestern University Collections, 73; Arts Symposium: Exhibit of work by guest speakers Philip Pearlstein, Robert Smithson, Peter Blake & Otto Muehl, 74; John Silk Deckard Retrospective, 74; The Way West: Artist Explorers of the Frontier, 79; Masters of American Watercolor (auth catalog), 80; Painterly Realism, 81; Stuart Davis: The Formative Years 1910-1930, 82. *Pos:* Cur collections, Wichita Art Mus, 70-72; gallery dir, Ohio State Univ, 72-74; dir, Parrish Art Mus, 75; cur Western collections, Joslyn Art Mus, Omaha, Nebr, 77-80; cur, Rahr-West Mus, 80-; cur, Fort Wayne Mus Art, Ind, 84-86; cur, Roberson Ctr for Arts, Binghamton, NY, 86-88; ed, Manhattan Arts, 89- *Teaching:* Instr art hist, Dickinson Col, Carlisle, Pa, 63-64; asst prof art hist, Ohio Univ, Athens, 65-67; asst prof art hist, Transylvania Col, Lexington, Ky, 67-68. *Mem:* Col Art Asn; Am Asn of Mus. *Res:* Nineteenth and twentieth century American painting and sculpture. *Publ:* Auth, Roland P Murdock Collection, Wichita Art Mus, 72; contribr, The Frederick W Schumacher Collection, Columbus Gallery Fine Arts, 76; contribr, Permanent Collection of the Springfield (Mo) Mus Art, 82; contribr, Prints of the American West, 83. *Mailing Add:* 8447 118th St Kew Gardens NY 11415

TOMPKINS, ALAN
PAINTER
b New Rochelle, NY, Oct 29, 07. *Study:* Columbia Univ, BA; Yale Univ, BFA; Univ Hartford, Hon DFA, 87. *Comn:* Mural paintings comn by US Treas Dept for post off at Indianapolis, Ind, 36, Martinsville, Ind, 37 & Boone, NC, 40; mural painting, Gen Elec Co, Bridgeport, Conn, 44; mural painting, Cent Baptist Church, Hartford, Conn, 58. *Exhib:* Ind Artists Ann, 37-38; Art Inst Chicago Ann, 38; Conn Acad Ann, 52-81; one-man shows, Canton, Conn, 84 & Hartford, Conn, 86. *Pos:* Dir, Hartford Art Sch, Univ Hartford, 57-69, vchancellor, 60-74; comnr, Fine Arts Comn, Hartford, 59-69. *Teaching:* Instr painting, Cooper Union Art Sch, 38-43; lectr painting, Columbia Univ, 46-51; prof painting & art hist, Univ Hartford, 51-74. *Awards:* First Prize for painting, Conn Acad, 68-70 & 73; Painting Awards, Beth-El Regional Exhib, 72 & 79 & Canton Open Show, 77, 80, 81, 85 & 88. *Mem:* Conn Acad (vpres, 70-72). *Media:* Oil. *Res:* 20th century art. *Mailing Add:* 40 Loeffler Rd Bloomfield CT 06002

TOMPKINS, BETTY (I)
PAINTER, PRINTMAKER
b Washington, DC, June 20, 45. *Study:* Syracuse Univ, BFA, 66; Central Wash State Col, BEd, 69, MA, 69. *Work:* Aldrich Mus, Conn; Chemical Bank, New York; Oberlin Col, Ohio; Marvin Sackner Archives, Miami Beach, Fla; Rutgers Univ; Stamford Mus, Conn; Zimmerli Mus, NJ; Paterson Mus, NJ. *Exhib:* Solo exhibs, Stamford Mus, 86, PS 1, New York, 87, Fairleigh Dickenson Univ, NJ, 87, White Columns, New York, 91, Margulies Taplin Gallery, Boca Raton, Fla, 91, Fridholm Fine Arts, Asheville, NC, 91 & Alan Brown Gallery, Hartsdale, NY, 91; Selections from the Collection, Aldrich Mus, Conn, 88; Small & Stellar, Landscape: A Travellogue, Ruth Siegel, New York, 89; Nature of the Beast, Hudson River Mus, 89; traveling show, Lines of Vision, US, Pan Am & Europe, 89-90; Exposed: The Figure in Jeopardy, Valencia Gallery, Orlando, Fla, 90; The Living Object: The Art Collection of Ellen H Johnson, Allen Mem Art Mus, Oberlin, Ohio, 92; and others. *Collections Arranged:* Animals in the Arsenal (auth, catalog), Central Park Zoo, 81; New York on Paper, Central Wash Univ, 84. *Pos:* Contrib ed, Appearances Mag, 79- *Awards:* Creative Artists Pub Serv Prog Grant, NY State Coun Arts, 83; NY Found Arts Grant, 88; Fel, Yaddo, 90; and others. *Bibliog:* Joanne Barkan & Jon Friedman (auth), The beast in question, Arts Mag, 81; Sande Zorn (auth), Cows in the gallery, Holstein World, 82; Vivien Raynor (auth), Painter's work in a singular show, NY Times, 1/19/86; Robert Mahoney (auth), Betty Tompkins, Arts Mag, 88. *Media:* Acrylic, Watercolor; Etching. *Mailing Add:* 101 Prince St New York NY 10012

TOMPKINS, MICHAEL
PAINTER
b Chester, Pa, 55. *Study:* Cabrillo Col, Aptos, Calif, AA, 78; Univ Que, Montreal, 79; Univ Calif, Davis, BA, 81, MFA 83. *Work:* L Price Amerson, Deborah Born, Woodland, Calif; Gary Anderson, Carmichael, Calif; Dr Joseph Baird, San Francisco; Mr & Mrs Edward Grebitus, Sacramento, Calif; Robert Hudson, Cotati, Calif. *Exhib:* Solo exhibs, Richard L Nelson Gallery, Univ Calif, Davis, 83, Artworks Gallery, Fair Oaks, Calif, 85, Davis Art Ctr, Calif, 85, Artists Contemp Gallery, Sacramento, 86 & 88-90, William Sawyer Gallery, San Francisco, 87 & 89, Worden Gallery, San Francisco, 88 & Campbell-Thiebaud Gallery, San Francisco, 90; Artists of Contra Costa County, Hearst Art Gallery, St Mary's Col, Moraga, 90; Artists for Amnesty International, Natsoulas/Novelozo Gallery, Davis, 90; Works on Paper, Campbell-Thiebaud Gallery, San Francisco, 90; The Still Life, Pence Gallery, Davis, Calif, 90; California Configuration-Then and Now, Natsoulas/Novelozo Gallery, Davis, Calif, 90; and many others; Natsoulas/Novelozo Gallery, Davis, Calif, 87, 88 & 89; Am Acad & Inst Arts & Letters, New York, 89. *Teaching:* Teaching asst color, figure drawing & art appreciation, Univ Calif, Davis, 81-83; instr drawing, color theory, painting, printmaking & art hist, Sierra Col, Rocklin, Calif, 84-86; instr landscape painting, Am River Col, Placerville, 85; vis lectr drawing & descriptive drawing, Univ Calif, 86-88; painting, San Francisco Art Inst, 88. *Awards:* Fel, Nat Endowment Arts, 87 & 89; Am Acad & Inst Arts & Letts, 89; Richard & Hinda Rosenthal Found Award, 89; and others. *Bibliog:* Charles Shere (auth), Introductions '87, Oakland Tribune, 7/14/87; Victoria Dalkey (auth), Varying Visions, Sacramento Bee, 3/20/88; Teri Bachman (auth), Art at UC Davis, Univ Calif, Davis, Mag, summer 88; Ann Seymour (auth), Gallery reviews, Nob Hill Gazette, 4/89; Victoria Dalkey (auth), Invitation to contemplation, Sacramento Bee, 3/26/89; and others. *Mailing Add:* c/o Campbell-Tniebaud Gallery 647 Chestnut St San Francisco CA 94133

TONELLI, EDITH ANN
MUSEUM DIRECTOR, HISTORIAN
b Westfield, Mass, May 20, 49. *Study:* Vassar Col, NY, BA, 71, Helen Squier Townsend Fel, 71; Hunter Col, City Univ New York, with Vicent Longo & Robert Morris, MA(creative arts), 74; Boston Univ, Doctoral Fel, 74-79, with Patricia Hills, PhD, 81. *Collections Arranged:* Homer to Hopper: 60 Years of American Watercolor (auth, catalog), 76; By the People, For the People: New England (auth, catalog), 77; Non-Conformists: Contemporary Commentary from the Soviet Union (auth, catalog), 80; Louis Faurer: Photographs of Philadelphia & New York, 1937-1973 (auth, catalog), 81; Ralston Crawford: Photographs/Art and Process (auth, catalog), 82. *Pos:* Cur, DeCordova Mus, Mass, 76-78; dir, Univ Md Art Gallery, 79-; dir, Frederick S Wight Art Gallery, Univ Calif, Los Angeles, 82-91. *Teaching:* Instr Am material culture, Boston Univ, Mass, 76; asst prof, Univ Md, College Park, 80-82; adj asst prof, Univ Calif, Los Angeles, 82-92. *Awards:* Smithsonian Fel, 79. *Bibliog:* Jane Holtz Kay (auth), Boston, Art News, 12/77. *Mem:* Am Asn Mus; Col Art Asn; Art Mus Asn; Am Asn Col Univ Mus Galleries; Asn Art Mus Dirs (trustee, 87-). *Res:* Twentieth century American art; American prints. *Publ:* Auth, The Avant-Garde in Boston: The WPA's federal art project, Archives Am Art J, 80; contribr, Frank Mechau, Aspen Ctr Visual Arts, 81 & City Life, Whitney Mus Amer Art, 86. *Mailing Add:* 2000 Glencoe Venice CA 90291

TONEY, ANTHONY
PAINTER, EDUCATOR
b Gloversville, NY, June 28, 13. *Study:* Syracuse Univ, BFA, 30; Teachers Col, Columbia Univ, MA, 52 & EdD, 55. *Work:* Whitney Mus Am Art, Nat Acad Design & Teachers Col, Columbia Univ, New York; Univ Ill, Urbana; Syracuse Univ, NY; Brooklyn Mus, NY; Fordham Univ, New York; and others. *Comn:* Murals, Bowne Hall, 68 & six panels, Brockway Cafeteria, St Mary's Dorm, Syracuse, NY, 71; and many others. *Exhib:* Whitney Mus Am Art Ann, 50-60; Audubon Artists Ann, 55-89; Nat Acad Design Ann, 60-89; one-man shows, Amphora Gallery, La Jolla, Calif, 79, Mid-Hudson Arts & Sci Ctr, Poughkeepsie, NY, 79 & ACA Gallery, NY, 83 & 87; Corcoran Gallery Art, Washington, DC; Brooklyn Mus; Los Angeles Co Mus; Metrop Mus; Art & War, Kongress Halle, Berlin, Ger, 90; Nat Acad Audubon Artists Ann, 92. *Teaching:* Instr creative art, Hofstra Univ, 52-55; instr creative painting, New Sch Social Res, 52-; instr creative painting, Five Towns Music & Art Found, 52-78; instr, Rockland Ctr Arts, 74-76 & Northern Westchester Ctr Arts, 80- *Awards:* Medals of Honor, Audubon Artists, 68, 75 & 87; Audubon Artists Robert Phillips Award, 88 & 89; Audubon Artists Mem Award, 91; and others. *Bibliog:* Interview with Virginia Pelliam, Artists Proof, 92. *Mem:* Nat Acad Design (asst secy & mem coun, 79-87); Audubon Artists (mem bd, 75-, vpres, 81-82); Nat Soc Mural Painters (treas, 73-76); Artists Equity Asn (mem bd dirs, 71-72); Int Inst Arts & Lett. *Media:* Oil, Watercolor. *Publ:* Auth, article, Leonardo, 10/77; Painting and Drawing--Discovering your Own Visual Language, Prentice-Hall, NJ 78; contribr, An Appreciation, The Palette and The Flame, Posters of The Spanish Civil War, Int Publ, 79; Drawing as exploration, Syracuse Scholar, fall 81; Creative Painting, Dover; and others. *Dealer:* Nandin Gallery Cross River NY; Virginia Barrett Gallery Chappaqua NY. *Mailing Add:* 16 Hampton Pl Katonah NY 10536

TOOKER, GEORGE
PAINTER, PRINTMAKER
b Brooklyn, NY, Aug 5, 20. *Study:* Phillips Acad, 38; Harvard Univ, AB, 42; Art Students league, with Reginald Marsh, Kenneth Hayes Miller & Harry Sternberg, 43-44. *Work:* Whitney Mus Am Art, Metrop Mus Art & Mus Mod Art, New York; Walker Art Ctr, Minneapolis; Addison Gallery Am Art, Phillips Acad, Andover, Mass; Brooklyn Mus Art; Va Mus Fine Arts, Richmond; and others. *Exhib:* Contemporary Artists in Vermont, Robert Hull Fleming Mus, Univ Vt, Burlington, 84; Surreal City, 1930-1950, Whitney Mus Am Art at Philip Morris, New York, 85; one-man exhibs, Durlacher Brothers, New York, 67, Fine Arts Mus San Francisco, Calif, Palace Legion Honor, San Francisco, Mus Contemp Art Chicago, Whitney Mus Art, New York, Indianapolis Mus Art, 74-75, Marisa Del Re Gallery, New York, 85, Gibbs Art Gallery, Charleston, SC, 87, Robert Hull Fleming Mus, Univ Vt, Burlington, 87, Marisa Del Re Gallery, New York, 88 & Marsh Gallery, Univ Richmond, Va, 89; Modern American Realism, Sara Roby Found Collection, Nat Mus Am Art, Washington, DC, 87; Cadmus, French & Tooker: The Early Years, Whitney Mus Am Art at Philip Morris, New York, 90; Close Encounters: The art of Paul Cadmus, Jared French and George Tooker, Midtown Galleries, New York, 2/20-4/7/90; Art What Thou Eat: Images of Food in American Art, travelling, Edith C Blum Art Inst, Bard Col, Annandale-on-Hudson, New York, 90; Contemporary Surrealism, NJ Ctr Visual Arts, Summit, 91; and others. *Teaching:* Instr, Art Students League, 65-68. *Awards:* Nat Inst Arts & Lett Grant, 60; Gov Award Excellence Arts, Montpelier, Vt, 83. *Bibliog:* Thomas H Garver (auth), George Tooker, Clarkson N Potter Inc, Publ, 85. *Mem:* Nat Acad Design, New York; Inst Arts & Lett. *Media:* Egg Tempera; Lithography. *Mailing Add:* c/o Marisa del Re Gallery 41 E 57th St New York NY 10022

TOPERZER, THOMAS RAYMOND
MUSEUM DIRECTOR, PAINTER
b Homestead, Pa, Aug 12, 39. *Study:* Sterling Col, 59-61; Southwestern Col (Kans), BA, 63; Univ Nebr-Lincoln, Woods fel, 69-70, MFA, 70. *Work:* Des Moines Art Ctr, Iowa; Springfield Art Mus, Mo; Rochester Art Ctr, Minn; Blanden Art Mus, Iowa; Ill State Univ; Bethel Col & Sem, Minn. *Exhib:* Iowa Artists, Des Moines Art Ctr; New Horizons, Chicago; Nat Drawing, San Francisco Mus Art; Nat Prints & Drawings, Okla Art Ctr, Mid-America, Kansas City-St Louis, 74. *Pos:* Dir, Blanden Art Mus, 70-71, Rochester Art Ctr, 71-72; asst dir, Mus & Galleries, Ill State Univ, 72, dir, Univ Galleries, Ctr Visual Arts Gallery, 73-82, ed, Univ Mus Newslett, 75-76; coordr fine arts, Bethel Col, St Paul, Minn, 82-84 & Univ Okla Mus, 84- *Mem:* Am Asn Mus; Col Art Asn; Art Mus Asn. *Publ:* Auth, Current Issues in University Art Museums, Southern Ill Univ. *Mailing Add:* Mus Art, Univ Okla 410 W Boyd Norman OK 73019

TOPOL, ROBERT MARTIN
COLLECTOR
b New York, NY, Mar 9, 25. *Collection:* Frescos, oils and sculptures. *Mailing Add:* 825 Orienta Ave Mamaroneck NY 10543

TOPPER, DAVID R
EDUCATOR, HISTORIAN
b Pittsburgh, Pa, Jan 1, 43. *Study:* Duquesne Univ, BS, 64; Case Inst Technol, MS, 66; Case Western Reserve Univ, MA, 68; & PhD, 70. *Pos:* Int co-ed, Leonardo Jour Arts, Sci & Technol, currently. *Teaching:* Prof art hist, Univ Winnipeg, Man, 70- *Awards:* Clifford J Robson Mem Award for Excellence in Teaching, Univ Winnipeg, 81; 3M Teaching Fel, 87. *Mem:* Int Soc Arts, Sci & Technol; Am Soc Aesthet; Univ Art Asn Can; Can Soc Aesthet. *Res:* Historical perspectives on visual perception of images. *Publ:* Auth, Depth perception in linear and inverse perspective pictures, Perception, 81; Art in the realist ontology of J J Gibson, Synthese, 83; The Poggendorff illusion in Rubens descent from the cross, Perception, 84; On the fidelity of pictures, Philosphia, 84; The Parallel Fallacy: On Comparing Art & Science, British J of Aesthetics, 90. *Mailing Add:* Hist Dept Univ Winnipeg Winnipeg MB R3B 2E9 Canada

TORBERT, STEPHANIE BIRCH
PHOTOGRAPHER, ILLUSTRATOR
b Wichita Falls, Tex, May 31, 45. *Study:* Univ NMex, BFA, 68; Sch for Am Craftsman, Rochester Inst Technol, NY, 68; Visual Studies Workshop, State Univ NY, Buffalo, MFA, 71. *Work:* Univ Minn Mus Art, Minneapolis Inst Arts, Minneapolis; Int Mus Photography, George Eastman House, Rochester; Ctr for Creative Photog, Tucson, Ariz; Mus NMex, Santa Fe. *Exhib:* Minn Survey: Six Photogrs, Minneapolis Inst Arts & Nat Endowment Arts, 78; one-

person shows, Minneapolis Inst Arts, 70, Walker Art Ctr, Minneapolis, 73, Int Mus Photog, George Eastman House, Rochester, NY, 78 & Friends Photog, Carmel, Calif, 79; and others. *Pos:* Visual arts panel, Minn State Arts Bd, 76- *Teaching:* Asst prof, N Hennepin Community Col, Minneapolis, 74-75 & Minneapolis Col Art & Design, 77-78 & 88-89. *Awards:* Bush Found Artists Fel, Minneapolis, 76-77; Nat Endowment Arts Grant, Minn Survey: Six Photogr, 77; Mckning Artist Fel, 84. *Mem:* Guild Natural Sci Illusrs. *Media:* Cibachrome, Pastel; Ink, Acrylic. *Publ:* The New Color Photography, Abbeville Press; Parks and Wildlands, Nodin Press; The Walk Book, Nodin Press; The Clay That Breathes, Milkweed Eds. *Mailing Add:* 3824 Harriet Ave Minneapolis MN 55409

TORCOLETTI, ENZO
SCULPTOR
b Fano, Italy, May 1, 43; US citizen. *Study:* Inst Statale D'Arte A Apolloni, Fano, Italy, 54-58; Univ Windsor, Ont, BFA(sculpture), 69; Fla State Univ, MFA, 71. *Work:* Sculpture (40 ft site specific), Koger Properties, Jacksonville, Fla; Fla Nat Guard, Camp Blanding; Fla Artists Hall of Fame, The Capital, Tallahassee; Waynesville Country Club, NC; Barnett Bank, Tampa, Fla. *Exhib:* Solo exhibs, WGa Col, Carrollton, 73, Oklaloose-Walton Jr Col, Niceville, Fla, 76, Univ NFla, Jacksonville, 81 & 86, Sandestin, Destin Beach, Fla, 86, Embry-Riddle Aeronautical Univ, Daytona Beach, Fla, 88, Cummer Gallery of Art, Jacksonville, 90- 91; Boca Raton Center for Arts, Fla, 82; Brest Mus Gallery, Jacksonville Univ, 81, 82 & 84; Jacksonville Collects, Jacksonville Art Mus, 84; Flagler Col, St Augustine, Fla, 90. *Teaching:* Asst, Fla State Univ, Tallahassee, 69-71; prof visual arts, Flagler Col, St Augustine, Fla, 71-; guest artist/lectr, Okaloosa-Walton Jr Col, Niceville, Fla, 72, Fla Jr Col & Univ NFla, Jacksonville, 80 & 81, Univ Fla, Gainesville, 81, Jacksonville Art Mus, 83, 84 & 87, Sandestin, Destin Beach, Fla, 86 & Douglas Anderson Sch Art, Jacksonville, 90. *Awards:* Purchase Award, Mint Mus Art, Charlotte, NC, 72; First Prize in Sculpture, Titusville Spring Art Show, Fla, 75; Hilton Leach Mem Award, Mus Arts & Sciences, Daytona Beach, 79. *Bibliog:* Susan Lynn Lester (auth), mag article, Jacksonville, 6/86; Diane Edwards (auth), mag article, 10/1/87; Arthur Williams (auth), Sculpture: Technique-Form-Content, 89. *Media:* Granite, Bronze. *Dealer:* Foster Harmon Galleries of Am Art Sarasota FL; Gallery Contemporanea Jacksonville FL. *Mailing Add:* 120 W Genung St St Augustine FL 32086

TORF, LOIS BEURMAN
COLLECTOR, PUBLISHER
b Boston, Mass, Sept 20, 26. *Study:* Univ Mass, Amherst, BA, 46, DFA, 86. *Exhib:* Two Women Collect, Wellesley Col Mus Art, Mass, 76; The Modern Art of the Print, Williams Col Mus Art, Williamstown, Mass & Mus Fine Arts, Boston, 84; 70's into 80's: Printmaking Now, Mus Fine Arts, Boston, 87. *Pos:* VPres, Inst Contemp Art, 70-87. *Bibliog:* Deborah Menaker (auth), The Modern Art of the Print: Selections from the Collection of Lois & Michael Torf, Mus Fine Arts, Boston, 84; Pilgrims & Pioneers: New England Women in the Arts, Midmarch Arts Press, New York, 87. *Mem:* Int Coun ArCA, (trustee 70-); Mus Fine Arts, Boston (trustee 84-); Univ Mass Chancellor's Exec Comt, currently; Brandeis Univ Rose Art Mus, bd of overseers, currently. *Collection:* 20th century graphic expressionism, pop & contemporary prints. *Mailing Add:* 15 Young Rd Weston MA 02193

TORLAKSON, JAMES DANIEL
PAINTER, PRINTMAKER
b San Francisco, Calif, Feb 19, 51. *Study:* Calif Col Arts & Crafts, BFA, 73; San Francisco State Univ, MA, 74. *Work:* San Francisco Mus Mod Art; Oakland Mus, Calif; Brooklyn Mus; Carnegie Inst, Pittsburgh, Pa; Libr of Cong. *Exhib:* One-man shows, Calif Palace Legion of Hon, Achenbach Found, San Francisco, 76 & San Jose Mus Art, Calif, 79; VX Inst Sao Paul Biennial, Int Communications Agency, SAm, 79; Recent Trends in Am Printmaking, Mitchell Mus, Mt Vernon, Ill, 79; Am Realism, 20th Century Drawing & Watercolors, San Francisco Mus Mod Art, Calif, 85; Mainstream America, The Collection of Phil Desind, Butler Inst Am Art, Youngstown, Ohio, 87; New Horizons in American Realism, Flint Inst Arts, Mich, 91; and others. *Teaching:* Instr, Skyline Col, San Bruno, Calif & Col San Mateo, Calif. *Awards:* Airport Purchase Award, San Francisco Int Airport Painting Competition, 77; Purchase Awards, 17th Nat Print & Drawing Exhib, Bradley Univ, 79 & Boston Printmakers 31st Nat Exhib, 79. *Bibliog:* Peter Frank (auth), New York Reviews, Artnews, 10/75. *Media:* Watercolor; Oil. *Publ:* Contemporary Am Realism, Since 1960, NY Graphics Soc, 81; Mendelowitz's Guide to Drawing, Holt Rinehart Winston, 82; Contrib, Am Realism, 20th Century Drawings & Watercolors, Abrams, 86; auth (with Judith Gordon), Deeping the third dimension, The Artist's Mag, 4/89. *Dealer:* John Berggruen 228 Grant Ave San Francisco CA 94108. *Mailing Add:* 433 Rockaway Beach Ave Pacifica CA 94044

TORLEN, MICHAEL ARNOLD
PAINTER, EDUCATOR
b San Diego, Calif, Feb 28, 40. *Study:* Cranbrook Acad Art, Bloomfield Hills, Mich, BFA, 62; Ohio State Univ, Columbus, fel 63-64, with Hoyt Sherman, MFA, 65. *Work:* Aldrich Mus, Ridgefield, Conn; Neuberger Mus & Roy Neuberger Collection, Purchase, NY; Prudential Insurance Co, Newark, NJ. *Comn:* Symbolic portraits, Arlene Sarapa, Wingafe Paine & Buford Pippin, New York, 76; Meditation Mandala, Growth Ctr, New York, 77 & Goldleaf Omega Cross, 78. *Exhib:* Weatherspoon Ann, Univ NC, Greensboro, 67, 69 & 83; Aldrich Mus, Ridgefield, Conn, 72 & 73; one-man shows, Neuberger Mus, Purchase, NY, 79 & Cathedral St John the Divine, NY, 83; Artists Space, New York, 83; Luise Ross Fine Art, New York, 83; and others. *Teaching:* Asst prof painting & drawing, Univ Ga, 65-70; assoc prof & dept head painting & drawing, State Univ NY Col, Purchase, 72- *Awards:* Purchase Award, Ga Comn Arts, 69; State Univ NY Res Fel & Grant, 78; Visiting Artist Traveling Grant, Vis Arts Bd, Australia Coun, 82. *Bibliog:* Robert Yoskowitz (auth), article, Arts Mag, 9/81. *Mem:* Col Art Asn; Lindisfarne Asn. *Dealer:* Luise Ross 162 56th St New York NY. *Mailing Add:* c/o Tribes Gallery 51A Hudson St New York NY 10013

TORN, JERRY (GERALD J)
DRAFTSMAN, PHOTOGRAPHER
b Burlington, Iowa, Mar 16, 33. *Study:* Univ Iowa, studied printmaking with Mauricio Lasansky, BA(fine arts), 58. *Work:* Art Inst Chicago, First Nat Bank Chicago, Ill; Ill State Mus, Springfield; Portland Art Mus, Ore; Kemper Insurance Co, Long Grove, Ill; Va Mus Fine Arts, Richmond; Mus Fine Art, Univ Iowa, Iowa City. *Comn:* Drawings for exec dining room, First Nat Bank Chicago, London Branch, 81; Lithograph Suite, Plucked Chicken Press, Chicago, 83. *Exhib:* New Figurative Work, Univ Ind, Gary, 80; Drawings of David, Univ Wis, Marshfield, 81; 62nd Ann Exhib, Arts Club Chicago, 82; Dancers, Univ Wis, Marinette, 82, Art Guild, Burlington, Iowa, 82 & Fairweather Hardin Gallery, Chicago, 82. *Teaching:* Instr design, Loyola Univ, Chicago, 70-71. *Bibliog:* Alan Artner (auth), Jerry Torn, Chicago Tribune, 7/25/80; Margaret Hawkins (auth), Jerry Torn, New Art Examiner, 11/80; Les Krantz (auth), The Chicago Art Review, Am References, 89. *Mem:* Arts Club Chicago. *Media:* Graphite. *Dealer:* Space 900 900 N Franklin Chicago IL 60610. *Mailing Add:* 216 S Marshall Burlington IA 52601

TORNHEIM, NORMAN
SCULPTOR
b Chicago, Ill, Sept 16, 42. *Study:* Art Ctr Col Design, BS, 66; Calif State Univ, San Diego, MA, 75. *Work:* Las Vegas Art Mus, Nev; Marietta Col, Ohio; Smith Col, Northampton, Mass; Ind Univ. *Comn:* Sculpture, comn by Mr & Mrs Stern, Calif, 76; sculpture, comn by Mr & Mrs Lewis, Calif, 77; sculpture, comn by Dr I Mori, Calif, 77. *Exhib:* Mainstreams 76, Marietta Col, Ohio, 76; Calif Craftsmen, Monterey Mus Art, Calif, 76; Designer-Craftsmen 76, Richmond Art Ctr, Calif, 76; Nat Competition 77, Dahl Fine Arts Ctr, 77; Calif Craftsmen, E B Crocker Art Mus, Sacramento, 77; Goldsmiths USA, Univ Wash, Seattle, 77; Musical Instruments, The Smithsonian Inst, Washington, DC, 78-80. *Collections Arranged:* Golden West Col Invitational, 78. *Teaching:* Instr wood, metal & leather, San Diego State Univ, Calif, 72-75; instr wood, metal, leather & clay, Golden West Col, Huntington Beach, Calif, 75- *Awards:* Jurors Award, Las Vegas Art Mus, 75; Purchase Award, Ark Art Ctr, 76; Merit Award, Nat Competition 77, Dahl Fine Arts Ctr, 77. *Bibliog:* Dona Z Meilach (auth), Wood Objects as Functional Sculpture, Crown, 76. *Media:* Clay, Porcelain. *Publ:* Contribr, Artweek, 76-77. *Mailing Add:* Dept Art Golden West Col 15744 Golden West St Huntington Beach CA 92647

TORREANO, JOHN FRANCIS
PAINTER, SCULPTOR
b Flint, Mich, Aug 17, 41. *Study:* Cranbrook Acad Art, BFA, 63; Ohio State Univ, MFA, 67; also with Robert King & Hoyt L Sherman. *Work:* Whitney Mus Am Art, New York; Aldrich Mus Contemp Art, Ridgefield, Conn; Michener Collection, Univ Tex; The Corcoran Gallery; Denver Art Mus. *Comn:* Lots 'O Dots Cafe, ARCORP, Greeneville, Ohio; Ghost Gems, McCarran Int Airport, Las Vegas, Nev, 92. *Exhib:* Solo exhibs, Scott Hanson Gallery, New York, 89, Shea & Beker Gallery, New York, 89 & 90, The Corcoran Gallery, Washington, DC, 89, Susanne Hilberry Gallery, Birmingham, MI, 90, Shea & Beker Gallery, New York, 90, Dart Gallery, Chicago, Ill, 90 & Hypo Bank, New York, 92; Post Minimalsim 1979-1990 An Extended Harvest, Genouese Gallery, Boston, MA, 90; Painting Between the Paradigms Part IV: A Category of Objects As Yet Unnamed, Penine Hart Gallery, New York; With the Grain: Contemporary Panel Painting, Whitney Mus Am Art, Stamford, Conn, 90; group show, Margo Leavin Gallery, Los Angeles, CA, 90; Laforet Mus, Havajuku, Japan; Pleasure, Hallwalls, Buffalo, NY, 91; Glass: Material in the Service of Meaning, Tacoma Art Mus, Wash, 91; Cruciformed: Images of the Cross Since 1980, Cleveland Ctr Contemp Art, Ohio, 91. *Awards:* Nat Endowment Arts Grant & Creative Artists Pub Serv Grant, 78-79; Nat Endowments Arts Fel, 82-83 & 89-90; John Simon Guggenheim Mem Found Fel, 91; New York Found Arts Fel, 91. *Bibliog:* Michael Welzenbach (auth), rev, The Washington Post, 89; Goings On About Town, The New Yorker, 5/21/90; Theodore F Wolff (auth), The Art of Painting Plywood, The Christian Science Monitor, 8/17/90; Brook Adams (auth), Scarred Diamonds, ArtNews, 2/91. *Media:* Plywood. *Dealer:* Susanne Hilberry Gallery Birmingham MI; Margo Leavin Gallery Los Angeles CA. *Mailing Add:* 103 Franklin St New York NY 10013

TORRES, FRANCESC
VIDEO ARTIST, SCULPTOR
b Barcelona, Spain, Aug 8, 48. *Study:* Massana Art Inst, Barcelona, Spain(graphic design & painting), 64-67; Fine Arts Sch, Paris, France, cert(etching), 67-68. *Work:* Book Collection, Mus Mod Art, New York; Cooper-Hewitt Mus, New York; Alternative Mus, New York; Everson Mus Art, Syracuse, NY; Mus Art, Carnegie Inst, Pittsburg, Pa. *Exhib:* This Is An Installation That Has A Title, Fundacio Joan Miro, Barcelona, 79; Residual Regions, Los Angeles Inst Contemp Art, Calif, 80; The Head of the Dragon, Whitney Mus Am Art, New York, 81; Field of Action, Herbert F Johnson Mus Art, Ithaca, NY, 82; Some Machines Work Better Than Others, Metronom, Barcelona, Spain, 84; Tough Limo, Mus Art, Carnegie Inst, Pittsburgh, Pa, 85; The Dictatorship of Swiftness, La Jolla Mus Contemp Art, Calif, 86; plus Vltra, Nat Galerie, Berlin, WGer, 88. *Teaching:* Instr mixed media & installations, Sch Visual Arts, New York, 86. *Awards:* Sponsored Projects Grant, New York State Coun Arts, 83-84; Spanish-Am Join Comt Cultural & Educ Cooperation, 85; Individual Artist Fel, DAAD Berliner

Kunstleprogramm, 86. *Bibliog:* Patricia Thomson (auth), Video and electoral appeal, Afterimage Mag, 2/85; Shelley Rice (auth), Photographic installations: An overview, San Francisco Camerawork, Vol 12, No 1, spring 85; John Paoletti (auth), At the edge where art becomes media and message becomes Polemic: Disinformation at the Alternative Museum, Arts Mag, 5/85. *Media:* Mixed. *Publ:* Auth, Everybody's House Is Burning, self-publ, 77. *Dealer:* PPOW Gallery 532 Broadway New York NY 10012. *Mailing Add:* 38 N Moore St New York NY 10013

TORREY, ELLA KING
ADMINISTRATOR
Study: Germantown Friends Sch, 75; Yale Univ, New Haven, Conn, BA(art hist, cum laude), 80; Univ Miss, Oxford, MA(art hist), 84. *Collections Arranged:* The History of the Hasty Pudding Theatricals, Harvard Univ Librs, Mass, 78; Toying With The Times: A Critical Analysis of the Barbie Doll, 1959-1980, Yale Univ, New Haven, Conn, 79-80; Ten Afro-American Quilters (coauth with Maude Wahlman, catalog), toured US & Africa, Univ Miss, Oxford, 81-83. *Pos:* Cur & designer, Harvard Theatre Collection, Harvard Univ Librs, Cambridge, Mass, 78; asst cur, Whitney Mus Am Art, New York, 78; educ coordr, curatorial asst, Art Resources Conn, New Haven, 78-79; cur, Yale Ctr Am Art & Mat Cult, Yale Univ, New Haven, Conn, 79-80; asst cur, designer, John David Williams Libr, Univ Miss, Oxford, 81-82; cur, educational coordr, Ctr Study Southern Cult, Univ Miss, 81-83; spec proj consult, Robert Hull Fleming Mus, Univ Vt, Burlington, 83; prog officer, Pew Charitable Trusts, Philadelphia, Pa, 85- *Teaching:* From asst instr to instr, Univ Miss, Oxford, 81-83; lectr, Drexel Univ, Philadelphia, Pa, 85- *Awards:* Nancy Ann Thorpe Award Fine Arts, 75; David L Stokes Award Hist, 75; Irving C Poley Award Dramatic Arts, 75. *Publ:* Coauth (with Maude Wahlman), Quilts, Craft Int, New York, fall 82; Afro-American Quilts, Art Papers, Atlanta, Ga, fall 82; auth, Confessions/Confusions of a Private Funder: Arts Support within the American Philanthropic System, Orcas Conference: Creative Support Creative Artist, New York, 88; coauth (with Maude Wahlman), Theora Hamblett & Afro-Am Quilts, Encyl Southern Cult, Chapel Hill, NC, 89; auth, Artists-Art: The Role of Artists' Organizations in the National Arts Community, forward to 1989 Nat Asn Artists Orgn Directory, Washington, DC, 89; and others. *Mailing Add:* 108 Cuthbert St Philadelphia PA 19106

TOSCANO, (DOLORES A)
PAINTER, SCULPTOR
b Fort Worth, Tex. *Study:* Studied with Bruno Lucchesi (sculpture) & Daniel Green (pastel painting), 85. *Work:* San Juan Col, NMex; Benson Park, Loveland, Colo; and others. *Comn:* Life size bronze St Walburga, Walburga Convent, Boulder, Colo, 85-86; twelve ft marble figure of Christ, Risen Christ Church, Denver, Colo, 87; life size bronze Mary & Jesus, Blessed Heart Jesus, Boulder, Colo, 88. *Exhib:* United States Art Ehib, China Exhib Hall, Peking, 81; Pioneer's Museum Show, Colorado Springs Mus, 85; Society de Pastellistes de France, Salon Int Du Pastel, Paris, 87; Miniature Show, Albuquerque Mus, 91 & 92; Women Who Paint the West, Tucson Mus, Ariz, 91-93; and others. *Teaching:* Pastel instr portraits, Scottsdale Art Sch, Ariz, 87-88 & Denver, Colo Art Student League, 90-91. *Awards:* Gold Medal, Catherine L Wolfe, New York, 78-79; Gold Medal, Pastel Soc Southwest, 87; Master Pastelist, Flora Guffino, Pastel Soc Am, 87; and others. *Bibliog:* Toscano Southwest Art, 79-87; Mary C Nelson (auth), Pastels by Toscanco, Am Artist, 83; Vicki Stavig (auth), I had the want to's, Art West, 91; and others. *Mem:* Pastel Soc Am, New York; Catherine Lorrillard Wolfe Club, New York. *Media:* Pastel; Bronze. *Publ:* Contribr, American Artist of Renown, Wilson Pub, 81; Contemporary Western Artists, Harold Samuels, 82. *Mailing Add:* 3540 Otis Wheat Ridge CO 80033

TOSCHIK, LARRY
PAINTER, WRITER
b Milwaukee, Wis, July 17, 22. *Study:* Wis Art Acad, scholar; Layton Art Sch, Milwaukee. *Work:* Ariz State Univ Col Bus Admin; Riveredge Found, Calgary; US House of Rep; US Dept of Interior; Soc Wildlife Art Nations, London. *Comn:* Battlefield monument, 361st Inf 91st Div Mil Cemetery, Florence, Italy, 44; 30 paintings (wildlife), Hallmark Permanent Collection, 69-71; 20 silver medallions, Ducks Unlimited Inc, Chicago, 74; four wildlife lithographs, Franklin Mint; painting, 50th Anniversary of Ducks Unlimited, 86-87; two paintings for collector ed, Waterfowl of North Am, Can, 87. *Exhib:* Nat Cowboy Hall of Fame, Oklahoma City, 73; Waterfowl Festival, Easton, Md, 73; Pac Flyway Show, Santa Rosa, Calif, 75; Retrospective, Scottsdale Ctr for Arts, 78; Inaugural Exhib, Soc Wildlife Art for the Nations, London, Eng, 85; and others. *Awards:* 3M Co Design Award, 62; Ducks Unlimited Inc Artist of the Year, 75-76; two awards, Printing Indust Am, 77; Flyway Artist of Year, Ducks Unlimited, 92-93. *Mem:* Audubon Soc; Soc for Wildlife Art for the Nations, London, Eng (vpres). *Media:* Miscellaneous Media. *Publ:* Auth & illusr, Whispering skies of Arizona, 3/73, Shadowed trails, 2/76, Prowlers of the clouds, 2/79 & Shorebirds, 2/82, Ariz Highways Mag; illusr, Wildlife Techniques Manual; and thirty juvenile books on wildlife subjects. *Dealer:* Troys Gallery Main St Scottsdale AZ 85251. *Mailing Add:* 16632 N 30th Ave Phoenix AZ 85023

TOTH, CARL
PHOTOGRAPHER
b Cleveland, Ohio, Dec 7, 47. *Study:* Rochester Inst Technol, AAS, 68; State Univ NY, Buffalo, with Donald Blumberg, BA Eng, 70, MFA, 72. *Work:* Int Mus Photog at George Eastman House, Rochester, NY; Visual Studies Workshop, Rochester; Mus Mod Art, New York; Australian Nat Gallery, Canberra; San Francisco Mus Mod Art, Calif. *Exhib:* Ctr for Creative Photog, Tucson, 81; Northlight Gallery, Tempe, Ariz, 81; Corcoran Gallery, 82; Cleveland Inst Art, 85; Los Angeles Ctr for Visual Studies Workshop, 85 & Photg Studies, 87; Mus Mod Art, Mexico City, 87; and others. *Teaching:* Head dept photog, Cranbrook Acad of Art, Bloomfield Hills, Mich, 72- *Awards:* Photogr Fel, Nat Endowment Arts, 75, 80 & 86; Mich Coun for the Arts, 83, 85 & 90. *Bibliog:* Photography Year, Time Life Books, 73; Exhibition Review, Artforum, 1/75 & 10/85. *Mem:* Soc Photog Educ; Col Art Asn. *Publ:* Auth, Carl Toth: Recent Works, Cranbrook Acad Art, 83; Latent Images: Great Lakes Arts Alliance, Nat Endowment Arts, 86; Under Construction: New Photomontage, Cranbrook Acad Art, 88. *Dealer:* MacGill Pace 32 E 57th New York NY. *Mailing Add:* Dept Photography Cranbrook Acad Art Box 801 Bloomfield Hills MI 48303-0801

TOTH, GEORGINA GY
ART LIBRARIAN
b Budapest, Hungary, Aug 28, 32; US citizen. *Study:* Eotvos Lorond Univ, Budapest, MA, 56; Case Western Reserve Univ, MSLS, 62. *Pos:* Cataloger, Cleveland Mus Art Libr, 62-69, reference librn, 69-75, assoc librn for reference, 75-; book reviewer, Art Documentation, 81- *Mem:* Art Libr Soc NAm, Ohio chapter, vice chmn, 88, chmn, 89. *Interests:* Art Research; Methodology; Collectors and Collecting; Bibliography. *Mailing Add:* 2574 Dysart Rd University Heights OH 44118

TOULIS, VASILIOS (APOSTOLOS)
PRINTMAKER, EDUCATOR
b Clewiston, Fla, Mar 24, 31. *Study:* Univ Fla, with Fletcher Martin & Carl Holty, BDes; Pratt Inst, with Richard Lindner, Fritz Eichenberg, Jacob Landau & Walter Rogalski, BFA. *Work:* US State Dept, Washington, DC; Mus Arte Mod, Mexico City, Mex; Caravan House, New York. *Comn:* Portfolio of prints, Ctr for Contemp Printmaking, 68. *Exhib:* Brooklyn Mus, NY, 66; Fleishcer Mem, Philadelphia, 66; Mus Arte Mod, Mexico City, 67; Int Miniature Print Exhib, 68; New Paltz Nat Print Exhib, 68; and others. *Teaching:* Lectr serigraphic printmaking, Univ RI, 67 & Pratt Inst Seminar, 69; head graphic workshops, Pratt Inst, 66-, instr printmaking, 69-71, assoc prof & head undergrad printmaking, 71-; dir silk screen workshops, The Artists Collective, Hartford, Conn, 73- *Awards:* Tiffany Found Grant in Printmaking, 67. *Mem:* Am Asn Univ Prof; United Fedn Col Teachers; Screen Printers Asn. *Mailing Add:* Pratt Inst 200 Willoughby Brooklyn NY 11205

TOUSIGNANT, CLAUDE
PAINTER, SCULPTOR
b Montreal, Que, Dec 23, 32. *Study:* Sch Art & Design, Montreal. *Work:* Nat Gallery Can; Phoenix Art Mus, Ariz; Larry Aldrich Mus, Ridgefield, Conn; York Univ; Mus Contemp Art, Montreal & Quebec; and others. *Exhib:* Solomon R Guggenheim Mus, New York, 65; Can Art, Paris, Rome & Brussels; Lausanne, Switz, 68; Mass Inst Technol, Cambridge; Washington Gallery Mod Art; Retrospective, Nat Gallery Can, 73-75; and many other group exhibs & more than 30 one-man shows. *Awards:* Prize, Centennial Exhib, 67; Rome Prize, 73; Borduas Prize, 89. *Mailing Add:* 181 Bourget Montreal PQ H4C 2M1 Canada

TOVISH, HAROLD
SCULPTOR
b New York, NY, July 31, 21. *Study:* Columbia Univ, 40-43; Ossip Zadkine Sch Sculpture, Paris, 49-50; Acad Grande Chaumiere, Paris, 50-51. *Work:* Whitney Mus Am Art & Mus Mod Art, New York; Philadelphia Mus Art; Hirshhorn Mus, Washington, DC; Boston Mus Fine Art, Mass; Walker Art Ctr, Minneapolis, Minn. *Comn:* Epitaph (sculpture), State of Hawaii, 70. *Exhib:* Twenty-Eighth Venice Biennial, Italy, 56; Carnegie Inst Int, 58; Recent Sculpture: USA, Mus Mod Art, New York, 59; Whitney Mus Am Art Ann, 66; retrospectives, Watson Gallery, Wheaton Col, 67 & Addison Gallery Am Art, Andover, Mass, 88; solo exhib, Guggenheim Mus, 68; Int Award Exhib, Guggenheim Mus, 68; Inst Contemp Art, Boston, 76, 77 & 84; Boston Mus Fine Art, 77; Muscarelle Mus, William & Mary Col, Williamsburg, Va, 90. *Teaching:* Asst prof sculpture & drawing, Univ Minn, 51-54; vis prof sculpture, Univ Hawaii, 64-70; prof art, Boston Univ, 71-84. *Awards:* Am Inst Arts & Lett Grant, 60 & 71; Guggenheim Fel, 67; Fel, Ctr Advanced Visual Studies, Mass Inst Technol, 68. *Bibliog:* H Harvard Arneson (auth), New talent, Art in Am, 54. *Mem:* Boston Visual Artists Union. *Media:* Bronze, Mixed Media. *Publ:* Sculpture: The sober art, Atlantic Monthly, 61. *Dealer:* Howard Yezersky Gallery 186 South St Boston MA; Martin Sumers Graphics 50 W 57th St New York NY. *Mailing Add:* 380 Marlborough St Boston MA 02115

TOWNER, MARK ANDREW
ADMINISTRATOR, PHOTOGRAPHER
Study: Visual Studies Workshop, Rochester, NY, 78; Columbia Col, Chicago, BA, 78; Cranbrook Acad Art, MFA, 81; Int Ctr Photog, 82; Metrop Mus Art, New York, 88. *Work:* Detroit Inst Arts; Ill State Mus; Cranbrook Acad Art Mus. *Exhib:* Solo exhibs, Southeastern Ohio Series, Photog Gallery, Southern Ill Univ, Carbondale, 84, Anima/Animals: New Figurative Photographs, Photogr's Collective, South Bend, Ind, 85, Post Industrialization, P A C A Gallery, New York, 87, the Illuminated Ones, Trabia-MacAfee Gallery, New York, 89, Evolution of the Crucifix, Quad City Arts Gallery, Rock Island, Ill; Artists Fall Review, 85, Man-Made-Machine, 86, Circle Visions Gallery, New York; Paraphotography, Bond Gallery, New York, 87; Best Foot Forward: A Foot of Art for Cranbrook, Cranbrook Acad Art, Bloomfield Hills, Mich, 90; Common Ground, Gallery West, Davenport, Iowa, 92; 20/20 Vision, Cranbrook Acad Art, Bloomfield Hills, 92. *Collections Arranged:* Contemporary Trends in Photography, Mus Contemp Photog, Chicago, Ill, 78; Richard Bolton: Photographs, Gallery 681, Wayne State Univ, 82; Four Women Photographers, St Mary's Col Photog Gallery, Notre Dame, Ind, 85;

The Painted Spirit: Selected Works from the Permanent Collection, Davenport Mus Art, Iowa, 89; Three Decades of Midwestern Photography: 1960-1990, Davenport Mus Art. *Pos:* Photogr, Metrop Mus Art, New York, 82-83; dir, Circlework Visions Ltd, New York, 85-87; chief preparator & exhib designer, Am Craft Mus, New York, 87-88; asst dir, Davenport Mus Art, Iowa, 89- *Mem:* Am Asn Mus; Am Arts Alliance; Col Art Asn; Soc for Photog Educ. *Publ:* Mark Towner (auth), Three Decades of Midwestern Photography: 1960-1990; Celeste Olalquiaga (auth), Megalopolis: Contemporary Cultural Sensibilities. *Mailing Add:* 214 S Summit St Iowa City IA 52240

TOWNLEY, HUGH
SCULPTOR, PRINTMAKER
b Lafayette, Ind, Feb 6, 23. *Study:* Univ Wis, 46-48; also with Ossip Zadkine, Paris, 48-49; London Co Coun Arts & Crafts, 49-50. *Work:* Mus Mod Art; Whitney Mus Am Art; Boston Mus Fine Arts; Fogg Mus Art, Harvard Univ; Los Angeles Co Mus Art. *Comn:* Three concrete pieces, Class of 65, Brown Univ, Providence, RI, 70; three concrete pieces, State of Ky Comprehensive Training Ctr, Somerset, Ky, 72; eleven concrete pieces, Northwest Sculpture Advocates, Inc, Eugene, Ore, 74; designed 14 benches for City of Providence, RI, 79; Relief Lunar Migration, Luis Muñoz Airport, Am Airlines Admirals Club, San Juan, Puerto Rico, 91. *Exhib:* New Talent Show, Mus Mod Art, 55; Ann Exhib Drawings & Sculpture, Whitney Mus Am Art, 62 & 63; 65th Am Painting & Sculpture Exhib, Art Inst Chicago, 64; solo exhibs, DeCordova & Dana Mus, Lincoln, Mass, 69; Monumenta, Newport, RI, 74; Belgrade Ctr Gallery & travel throughout Yugoslavia, 81-82; Contemporary Am Prints, Philadelphia Art Alliance, 85; Inst Contemp Art, Boston, 77; US Information Service, Leningrad, Soviet Union, 85-86; Int Small Sculpture Exhib, Budapest, 87; Virginia Lynch Gallery, Little Compton, RI, 88 & 92; one-man shows, Univ Wis, Milwaukee Fine Arts Gallery, 89, Dartmouth Col Artist in Residence, 91. *Teaching:* Instr sculpture & drawing, Layton Sch Art, Milwaukee, 51-56; asst prof sculpture, Beloit Col, 56-57; asst prof sculpture & drawing, Boston Univ, 57-61; prof art, Brown Univ, 61-; vis prof, Univ Calif, Berkeley, 61, Santa Barbara, 68; vis lectr, Harvard Univ, 67. *Awards:* Grant for Creative Work in Art, Nat Inst Arts & Lett, 67; Gov Award, State of RI Coun Arts, 72; Ore Sculpture Symposium, Eugene, 74. *Media:* Wood, Concrete; Lithography. *Dealer:* Meridian Arts New York NY. *Mailing Add:* c/o Virginia Lynch Gallery 3883 Main Rd Rte 77 Tiverton RI 02878-1861

TOWNSEND, GAVIN EDWARD
HISTORIAN, EDUCATOR
b Santa Monica, Calif, June 16, 56. *Study:* Hamilton Col, Clinton, NY, BA, 78; Univ Calif, Santa Barbara, MA, 81, PhD, 86. *Collections Arranged:* The Linens of R H Hunt: drawings by Chattanooga's Foremost Architect, Univ Art Gallery, Univ Tenn, 88. *Pos:* Asst cur archit drawing, Univ Calif, Santa Barbara, 82-86; Gallery coordr, Univ Tenn, Chattanooga, 87-92, asst dir, Univ Hons Prog, 92. *Teaching:* Instr art hist, Univ Calif, Santa Barbara, 79-86; asst prof art hist, Univ Tenn, Chattanooga, 86- *Awards:* Kress Found Fel, 82-84. *Mem:* Soc Archit Hist; Col Art Asn; Hist Zoning Comn, City Landmarks, Chattanooga, Tenn. *Res:* Anglo-American architecture 1865-1945. *Publ:* The Tudor House in America 1895-1930, Univ Microfilms, Ann Arbor, Mich, 86; Auth, Ieoh Ming Pei, 20th Century Supplement Encyclopedia of World Biography, Jack Heraty & Assoc, 88; Airborne Toxins and the American House 1865-1895, Winterthur Portfolio, 89. *Mailing Add:* 3832 Azalean Dr Chattanooga TN 37415

TOWNSEND, J BENJAMIN
CRITIC, HISTORIAN
b Stillwater, NY, Feb 17, 18. *Study:* Princeton Univ, BA, 40; Harvard Univ, MA, 42; Yale Univ, PhD, 51. *Collections Arranged:* This New Man: a Discourse in Portraits (with catalog), 68 & Presidential Portraits (with catalog), 68, Nat Portrait Gallery, Smithsonian Inst; Martha Visser 't Hooft: Paintings & Drawings, 1950-1973 (with catalog), 73, Six Corporate Collectors (with catalog), 75 & Works by Charles E Burchfield (with catalog), 79, Burchfield Art Ctr. *Pos:* Asst dir, Nat Portrait Gallery, Smithsonian Inst, 67-68. *Teaching:* Prof art & lit, State Univ NY Buffalo, 57-83, chmn master arts humanities, 60-66, chmn dept art & art hist, 69-71, prof emer, 83. *Res:* Journals of Charles Burchfield. *Publ:* Auth, John Davidson, Poet of Armageddon, Yale, 61, reprint, 78, auth, 100: The Buffalo Fine Arts Academy, 1862-1962, Albright-Knox Art Gallery, 62. *Mailing Add:* 879 W Ferry St Buffalo NY 14209

TOWNSEND, JEAN (MRS SAUL FIELD)
PAINTER, PRINTMAKER
b Toronto, Ont, July 23, 21. *Study:* Art Gallery Ont, studied with Arthur Lismer, 29-38; Ont Col Art, studied with with Franklin Carmichael, John Alfsen & Rowley Murphy, 38-43; Instituto Allende, Mexico, 59; post-grad study with Nicholas Hornyansky, Guillermo Silva & J W G MacDonald; Inst Allende, Mexico, 88-90. *Work:* Montreal Mus Fine Art; Lord Beaverbrook Mus, Frederickton, NB; Nat Libr Can, Ottawa; Art Gallery Hamilton, Ont; Art Gallery Peterborough, Ont; Univ Toronto. *Comn:* Wind Among the Reeds (print portfolio), Upstairs Gallery, Toronto, 72; Blue Jean Series (portfolio), Galerie Int, Ribe, Denmark, 77; Tales of Heritage II (portfolio & book collaboration with Saul Field), Can Govt/York Univ, 83 & 86. *Exhib:* Ontario Society of Artists, Art Gallery Ont, Toronto, 43-45; Canadian Soc Graphic Art, Art Gallery Ont, 64-65; Canadian Painters-Etchers Annual, Montreal Mus Fine Art, 67; Juxtaposition of Joyce & Yeats, Print Club, Philadelphia, 72, Canada House, London, 83, Art Alliance, Philadelphia, 85; Pioneers in the Collograph Print, Wenninger Gallery, Boston, 79; Print Biennale, Palace of Sport & Culture, Varna, Bulgaria, 83. *Pos:* Dir, Upstairs Gallery, Toronto, 58-66. *Teaching:* Printmaking fel, York Univ, Toronto, 74-79. *Awards:* Governor-General's Medal, Ont Col Art, 42; Ontario Arts Coun Grants, 77 & 85; Artist-in-Residence Grant, Can Coun, 84. *Bibliog:* Life & Work of Jean Townsend & Saul Field (film), Brilliant Films, 88. *Mem:* Ont Soc Arts (exec, 79-82); Heliconian Club; Arts & Letters Club. *Media:* Oils. *Publ:* Illusr, Mozaic Mag, Univ Man, 74; Celtic Twilight (by W B Yeats), Colin Smythe, 82; Tales of Heritage II, York Univ, 86. *Mailing Add:* 69 Banstock Dr Willowdale ON M2K 2H7 Canada

TOWNSEND, JOHN F
SCULPTOR, PAINTER
b La Crosse, Wis. *Study:* Carroll Col, Waukesha, Wis, BS, 51; Minneapolis Sch of Art, 53-55; Univ of Minn Grad Sch, MFA, 59. *Work:* Mus Fine Art, Boston, Mass; Rose Mus, Brandeis Univ, Waltham, Mass; Allentown Art Mus, Pa; Chase Manhattan Bank, New York; World Bank, Washington, DC. *Exhib:* Art for US Embassies, Inst Contemp Art, Boston, 66; Optical Art Traveling Exhib, Mus Mod Art, New York, 66-68; Small Paintings for Mus Collections, Am Fedn of Art Traveling Exhib, 67-68; one-man shows, Eleanor Rigelhaupt Gallery, Boston, 67, Ward-Nasse Gallery, Boston, 70, Danco Gallery, Florence, 79, Berkshire Artisans, Pittsfield, 81 & Zone, Springfield, 85, Mass; and others. *Pos:* Dir art exhibs, 60-64 & dir grad art prog, 71-74, Univ Mass, Amherst; bd dirs, Zone Art Ctr, Springfield, Mass, 86- *Teaching:* Instr sculpture & painting, Eastern NMex Univ, Portales, 59-60; from instr to full prof sculpture, drawing & design, Univ of Mass, Amherst, 60-; part-time instr painting, Mt Holyoke Col, South Hadley, Mass, 61-62. *Awards:* First Award Sculpture, Second Ann Univ Arts Faculty Exhib, Argus Gallery, Madison, NJ, 63; Crane Co Award, 17th Ann Exhib of Painting & Drawing, 68; President's Award, Springfield Art League 66th Nat Exhib, Mus Fine Arts, Mass, 85. *Bibliog:* Dona Z Meilach (auth), Contemporary Art with Wood, Crown Publ Inc, New York, 68; Gloria Russell (auth), review, The Sunday Republican, Springfield, Mass, 4/21/85. *Media:* Wood & Bronze; Acrylic. *Mailing Add:* 118 Aubinwood Rd Amherst MA 01002

TOWNSEND, MARVIN J
CARTOONIST, ILLUSTRATOR
b Kansas City, Mo, July 2, 15. *Study:* Kansas City Art Inst; Col Com Art Sch. *Work:* Syracuse Univ, NY. *Awards:* Earl Temple Award; Best Cartoon of the Yr, Highlights for Children Publ, 83, 84, 85 & 89. *Media:* Ink. *Publ:* Strips, gag cartoons & illus for trade, bus & prof mags, 41-; auth, Moontoons Jokes & Riddles, 70; Ghostly Ghastly Cartoons & Laugh It Up (Fun with Cartoons), 71; and others. *Mailing Add:* 631 W 88th St Kansas City MO 64114

TOWNSEND, (ALVIN) NEAL
CERAMIST, EDUCATOR
b Rock Island, Tex, Oct 26, 34. *Study:* Univ NMex, BFA, 61, MA, 62; with Kenneth Adams, Elaine De Kooning, Keith Monroe & Robert Mallary. *Work:* Roswell Mus & Art Ctr, NMex; Art Mus, Fine Arts Ctr & Jonson Gallery of Univ NMex & Mus Albuquerque; New Zealand Soc Potters. *Exhib:* Young Americans, Mus Contemp Crafts, New York, 62; South West States Biennial, Mus Fine Arts, Santa Fe, NMex, 64; Southwestern Craftsmen, Dallas Mus, Tex, 68; 3rd Biennial Int Craft, Tweed Mus Art, Duluth, Minn, 75; 11th Biennial Des Crafts, El Paso Mus Art, Tex, 79; Fletcher Brownbuilt Pottery Award Exhib, Auckland, NZ, 82; Salzbrand, Handwerkskammer Koblenz, WGer, 83, 86, 89 & 92. *Pos:* Post crafts dir, Dept Defense, Sandia Base, NMex, 62-68; post crafts dir, Dept Army, Ft Belvoir, Va, 69-70; dir, Art Educ Gallery, Univ NMex, 82-85. *Teaching:* Instr art, North East La State Col, Monroe, 62; from asst prof to prof art educ, Univ NMex, 70-91, prof emer, 91; instr ceramics, Vancouver Sch Art, Can, 72; vis prof art, Northern Ariz Univ, Flagstaff, Ariz, 84. *Awards:* First Place Ceramics, Mus Int Folk Art, 63; First Place, NMex Arts & Crafts Fair, 67; Merit Award, Southwestern Arts & Crafts Festival, 78. *Bibliog:* Flo Wilks (auth), Neal Townsend, Artcraft Mag, 80; Peter Gibbs (auth), Neal Townsend, New Zealand Potter Mag, 88. *Publ:* Auth, The University of New Mexico's Art Education Gallery, Art Educ, 85; Grassroots Involvement in Recreation for Native Americans, Educ Resources Info Ctr, 85; An interpretive manual for state parks personnel, State of NMex, 86. *Dealer:* Clay & Fiber Gallery 126 W Plaza Dr PO Box ZZ Taos NM 87571; Laughing Bear Gallery Placitas NM 87043. *Mailing Add:* 2583 Ramirez Rd SW Albuquerque NM 87105

TOWNSEND, STORM D
SCULPTOR, INSTRUCTOR
b London, Eng, Aug 31, 37. *Study:* London Univ, NDD, ATC, Goldsmiths' Col Art, 6 yrs, with Harold Parker & Ivor Roberts Jones. *Work:* Fine Arts Mus NMex, Santa Fe; Genesee Co Mus, Rochester. *Comn:* Life-size portrait in bronze, comn by David Cargo, Gov NMex, 67; To Serve & Protect (life-size bronze to honour the police force), comn by City of Albuquerque; Charlie Pride Int Sr Golf Classic (bronze trophy design), 87 & Tres Culturas del Rio Grande (bronze figures), 88, Sunwest Bank, Albuquerque, NMex. *Exhib:* One-person shows, Gallery Marquis, Denver, Colo, 75, Gallery Eleven, Lubbock, Tex, 77 & Am Inst Architects, Albuquerque, NMex, 90; Survey of Contemp NMex Sculpture, NMex Mus Fine Art, Santa Fe, 76; Santa Fe Festival Arts, 79; Great Garden Exhib, Sculptural Arts Mus, Atlanta, 82. *Pos:* Moulder/caster prep lab fossils, Mus Nat Hist, Albuquerque, NMex, 87-89. *Teaching:* Instr sculpture, Pojoaque Art Ctr, Santa Fe, 65-66, Col of Santa Fe, 73-75, Univ Albuquerque, NMex & adult educ prog Univ NMex, currently. *Awards:* Jajasan Siswa Lokantara Resident Fel to study the arts in Indonesia, 60-61; Resident Fels, Huntington Hartford Found, Calif, 63 & Helene Wurlitzer Found, Taos, NMex, 64. *Bibliog:* Robert M Powers (auth), NMex Mag, 78; Mary Carroll Nelson (auth), articles, Am Artist, 79, Art Voices S, 80 & Southwest Art Mag, 86. *Media:* Clay to Cast Bronze, Concrete. *Mailing Add:* PO Box 1165 Corrales NM 87048

TOWNSEND, TERYL
PAINTER, EDUCATOR
b Coronado, Calif, May 9, 38. *Study:* Ray Froman Sch Art, Univ Tex, study with Millard Sheets, Chen Chi, Charles Reid, Edgar Whitney & Carl Molno. *Work:* Foothills Art Ctr, Golden, Colo; US Navy. *Comn:* Painting, USN, US Bristol County, 68; painting, Grumman Int Corp Off, 76; painting, Rawson Int Corp Off. *Exhib:* Mus Albuquerque Western Fedn Group Show, 75; Watercolor Soc Group Show, Brimingham Mus Art, Ala, 76; Western Fedn Group Show, Tucson Mus Art, Ariz, 76; Butler Inst Am Art Mid-Yr Ann, Youngstown, Ohio, 77; Watercolor USA Ann, Springfield, Ill, 77; Checkwood Art Ctr, Southern Watercolor Soc Group Show, Tenn, 77; one-man show, Stephen F Austin State Univ, Tex, 78; and others. *Pos:* Art experience facilitator, Tex Inst Child Psychiat, 75-76. *Teaching:* Instr water media painting, Canary Hill Galleries, Houston, Tex, 74-77, Tex Art Supply Inc, Houston, 75-77 & pvt studio, Houston, 78- *Awards:* Director's Award, Southern Watercolor Ann Exhib, 77; Art League Houston Dimension Award, 82; Southwestern Watercolor Soc Award, 83. *Bibliog:* Pat Lasher (auth), Seeing the ordinary in a special way, Southwest Art Mag, 9/77; Naomi Brotherton (auth), Spotlight on the artist, The Scene, Southwestern Watercolor Soc, 1/78; Watercolor Energies, Frank Webb, 82. *Mem:* Am Watercolor Soc; Nat Watercolor Soc; Rocky Mountain Nat Watermedia Soc. *Media:* Watermedia. *Dealer:* Veerhoff Gallery Washington DC; South Wharf Gallery Nantucket MA. *Mailing Add:* 109 Rosebrook Rd New Canaan CT 06840

TOWNSEND, VERA B
EDUCATOR, HISTORIAN
b Savannah, Ga, June 14, 23. *Study:* Univ Ga, Athens, BA, 45, MA, 50; Emory Univ, PhD, 68. *Collections Arranged:* Vis assoc cur, Laurence McKinin: A Retrospective (auth, catalog), Univ Mo, 83. *Pos:* Retired. *Teaching:* Instr humanities, Oglethorpe Univ, Atlanta, 48-49; instr classics, Emory Univ, Atlanta, 58-61; assoc prof art hist, Univ Mo, Columbia, 68-, chmn dept art hist & archeol, 82-88, assoc prof emer, currently. *Mem:* Mo Coun Fine Arts; Midwest Art Historians; Col Art Asn. *Res:* Poetry and painting in France, 1850-1914; beginnings of non-objective art; contemporary criticism. *Publ:* Auth, Douglas Freed, Arts Mag, 80; Ut Poesis Pictura, Muse, 81. *Mailing Add:* 6221 Southwest Way Columbia MO 65203

TRACHTENBERG, GLORIA P
PAINTER, GRAPHIC ARTIST
b Brooklyn, NY. *Study:* Brooklyn Col, BA(art), 71; NY Univ, MA(art), 73; Brooklyn Mus Art Sch, with Reuben Tam; Art Students League, with Robert Brachman. *Work:* NY Univ Med Ctr; Brooklyn Col; Mt Sinai Hosp, Anchor Engraving Corp, Forest Paper Corp, New York, 61. *Comn:* Series (paintings of children), Donald Art Corp, New York, 61; series (flower paintings), 70 & series (country scenes), 72, Arthur Kaplan & Co, New York; landscapes, BLD Art Publ, New York, 73 & Graphic Arts Unlimited, New York, 79. *Exhib:* Salmagundi Club, New York, 70; Metrop Mus Art, New York, 77; Brooklyn Artists, Brooklyn Mus, 79; Brooklyn Col, 79; Long Beach Mus Art, 82; New England Ann, Westenhook Gallery, Sheffield, Mass, 82; Am Soc Contemp Artists, State Univ NY, Alfred, 83. *Teaching:* Instr drawing, Sch Visual Arts, 79-80 & Kingsborough Community Col, 80- *Awards:* Am Artist Mag Drawing Prize, 70; First Prize Oil, Long Beach Art Asn, 72; Andrews Nelson Whitehead Award, Greenwich Art, Conn, 79. *Bibliog:* Dorothy Hall (auth), Art & artists, Park East, 3/14/71; Craig Bailey (auth), Watercolor show follows form, Staten Island Advance, 4/28/81; Renee Phillips (auth), Memories, dreams, reflections in Soho, Manhattan Arts, 8/31/83. *Mem:* Artists Equity; Am Soc Contemp Artists; Nat League Am Penwomen; Long Beach Art Asn; Brooklyn Watercolor Soc. *Media:* Oil, Watercolor. *Mailing Add:* Best in Art 1916 Ave K Brooklyn NY 11230

TRACHTMAN, ARNOLD S
PAINTER
b Lynn, Mass, Oct 5, 30. *Study:* Mass Sch of Art, BFA; Sch of the Art Inst of Chicago, MFA. *Work:* Fogg Art Mus, Harvard Univ, Cambridge, Mass; Addison Gallery of Am Art, Andover Mass; Wiggin Collection, Boston Pub Libr, Mass; Boston Mus of Fine Arts; Mus Nat Ctr of Afro-American Artists, Roxbury, Mass. *Exhib:* Exhib Watergate Galerie Borjeson, Malmo, Sweden, 74; one-man shows, Inst Contemp Art, Boston, 70 & Addison Gallery Am Art, Andover Mass, 76, Brockton Art Ctr, Mass, 79, Montserrat Sch Visual Art, Beverly, Mass, 85; AAMARP Gallery, Boston, 81; Bradford Col, Mass, 82; group shows, Staatliche Kunsthalle, Berlin, WGer, 83, Royal Festival Hall, London, UK, 85, Gallery Naga, Boston, Mass, 88, Arvada Art Ctr, Colo, 90 & Boston Univ Art Gallery, Mass, 91. *Teaching:* Instr art, Lynnfield High Sch, Mass, 71-80, Cambridge Sch, Weston, 80-81; assoc prof, Mass Col Art, 81- *Mem:* Boston Visual Artist Union; Mass Cultural Alliance. *Media:* Acrylic, Watercolor. *Publ:* Alone Stands the Artist, Boston Globe, 72. *Mailing Add:* 27 Dana St Cambridge MA 02138

TRACY, ELIZABETH See Montminy, Tracy

TRACY, LOIS BARTLETT
PAINTER, WRITER
b Jackson, Mich, Dec 9, 01. *Study:* Rollins Col, BA, 29; with Hans Hofmann, 45-46; Mich State Univ, MA, 58; New Col Workshop, 65, with Balcomb Greene, Afro, James Brooks, Marca-Relli & Sid Solomon. *Work:* Air & Space Mus, Smithsonian Inst, Washington, DC; Norton Gallery Art, Palm Beach, Fla; Univ Va; Hugh McKean & Traveling Collection, Morse Gallery of Art, Winter Park, Fla; Univ NC; Cornell Mus; and others. *Exhib:* Southeastern Shows, Atlanta, Ga; Four Arts Soc, Palm Beach, Fla, 77; Major Fla Artists, 79-88; Retrospect, Melvin Gallery, Lakeland, Fla, 80; plus others. *Teaching:* Instr, Univ Va Exten, 52-58 & 64-65; head dept art, Clinch Valley Col, 56-57; head dept art, Southeastern Col, Univ Ky, 64-66; head dept art, Edison Jr Col, Ft Myers, Fla, 68- *Awards:* First Award, Fla Artists Group, 68; Watercolor Award, Southeastern Ann, High Mus Art; Gold Medal for oil collection, New York World's Fair, State of Fla; First Award in Oil, 75, Gold Medal, 82 & Merit Award, 88, IPA; First Award Collage, Fla Artist Group, Jackson Univ Mus; and many others. *Bibliog:* Cosmic artist, Yankee, 7/49; Bartlett Tracy, NH Profiles, 4/52; Contemp Am Art, 89. *Mem:* Sarasota Art Asn; Galerie Int New York; Nat Asn Women Artists; Pen & Brush; Pen Women; and others. *Media:* Acrylic, Oil. *Publ:* Auth, Painting Principles and Practices, 65, 67, 69 & 71; auth, Adventuring in Art, 90. *Dealer:* Center St Gallery Winter Park FL 32789; 580 Artist Ave Englewood FL 34223. *Mailing Add:* 580 Artist Ave Englewood FL 33533

TRACY, MICHAEL
SCULPTOR, PAINTER
b Bellevue, Ohio, Sept 30, 43. *Study:* St Edward's Univ, Austin, BA, 64; Cleveland Inst Art, 64-67; Univ Tex, Austin, MFA, 69. *Work:* Art Mus STex, Corpus Christi; San Antonio Art Mus & McNay Art Inst, San Antonio, Tex; Mus Fine Art, Houston; Dallas Mus Art, Tex; Metrop Mus Art, New York. *Comn:* Emmanuel Chapel, Corpus Christi, Tex, 85; Santuario San Miquel Archangel, Our Lady of Guadalupe Cath Church, Alice, Tex. *Exhib:* 12/Texas (catalog), 74, Requiem Para Los Olvidados, Contemp Arts Mus, 83, Terminal Privileges, The Meril Collection, Houston, Tex, 89; Homenaje a Mexico, Galeria Pecanins, 79, Michael Tracy: Las Estaciones de la Cruz, Centro Cult/Arte Contemp, Mex City, Mex, 89; Michael Tracy, Mary Boone Gallery, 80 & 82, AVA6, Grey Art Gallery, New York Univ, NY, 87; Venice Biennale (catalog), Italy, 82; New Art (catalog), Tate Gallery, London, Eng, 83; New Epiphanies (catalog), Univ Colo at Colo Springs & Ohio Found on the Arts, Columbus, 83; Content, A Contemporary Focus, 1974-1984 (catalog), Hirshorn Mus & Sculpture Garden, Washington, DC, 84; Resistance or Submission: Snatches of a Christian Conversation (catalog), Walter Phillips Gallery, Banff Ctr, Alta, Can, 86; Other Gods, Containers of Belief (catalog), Everson Mus, Syracuse, NY, 86; Terminal Privileges, PS1, Inst Art & Urban Resources, Long Island, NY, 87; Texas: Contemporary Art from Texas, Groninger Mus, Holland, 88; A Prayer for El Salvador, McNamee Gallery, St Louis Univ, Mo, 90; The Rio Grande: By Berlin Wall, Raab Gallery, Berlin, Ger, 90; Mirror of Justice/House of Gold, Artspace, San Francisco, Calif, 90; After the Apocalypse: A Different Humanism, Southeastern Ctr Contemp Art, Winston-Salem, NC, 91; Smoking Mirror, Blue Star Art Space (catalog), San Antonio, Tex, 92. *Awards:* Awards in Visual Arts, 87. *Bibliog:* Mark Durant (auth), Michael Tracy, Shift, 36-39, 2/90; John Yau (auth), Michael Tracy, Arts Mag, 3/90; Richard Lacayo (auth), Prophet of the River Pierce, Metrop Homes, 5/91. *Media:* Acrylic, Oil. *Publ:* Coauth, Terminal Privileges (exhib catalog), PS1, Inst Art & Urban Resources Inc, Long Island City, NY, 87; The River Pierce: Sacrifice II, River Pierce Found, San Ygnacio, Tex, 92; Smoking Mirror (exhib catalog), Blue Star Art Space, San Antonio, Tex, 92. *Dealer:* Butler Gallery 2318 Portsmouth Houston TX 77098; Moody Gallery 2815 Colquitt Houston TX 77098. *Mailing Add:* c/o Zolla/Lieberman Gallery 230 W Huron St Chicago IL 60610

TRACY, ROBERT H
EDUCATOR, CURATOR
b Alameda, Calif, March 14, 48. *Study:* Calif State Univ, Hayward, BA, 70; Univ Calif, Los Angeles, MA, 77, PhD, 82. *Collections Arranged:* Palaces of Finance (co-cur), Spring St Hist Dist, 82; Architecture of Modern Olympiad: 1896 to Present (co-cur), 84; John & Donald Parkinson, Architects (auth, catalog), 89-90. *Pos:* Bd dir, Preservation Asn Clark Co, 84-, Las Vegas Neon Mus, 88- & Nev Inst Contemp Arts, 89-; Cur, Parkinson Arch, Los Angeles, 84-; chmn, dept art, Univ Nev, Las Vegas, 89- *Teaching:* Assoc prof art hist, Chapman Col, Orange, Calif, 79-84 & Univ Nev,Las Vegas, 84-; cur, Parkinson Arch, Los Angeles, 84-; Univ London, spring, 93. *Awards:* Rockefeller Grant, 79; Nevada Humanities Comt, 85-89 & 92; Las Vegas Chapter Am Inst Architects, 85-89 & 92. *Mem:* Soc Archit Historians; Col Art Asn; Semiotic Soc Am. *Res:* Late 19th century to 20th century business architectural imagery. *Mailing Add:* University of Nevada Las Vegas Dept of Art 4505 Maryland Pkwy Las Vegas NV 89154

TRAGER, NEIL C
DIRECTOR, PHOTOGRAPHER
Study: City Col New York, BA, 69. *Work:* Mus Mod Art, New York; Neuberger Mus, Purchase, NY; Harry Ransom Humanities Res Ctr, Univ Tex, Austin; Ctr for Photography, Woodstock, NY. *Exhib:* Solo exhib, O K Harris, New York, 78. *Collections Arranged:* Robert Ebendorf Retropsective, 89; The Coroplast's Art: Greek Terracottas of the Hellenistic World, 90; Dorothy Dehner: Works on Paper & Recent Sculpture, 90; Uncommon Ground: 23 Latin American Artists, 92; and others. *Pos:* Assoc cur, Catskill Ctr Photog, Woodstock, NY, 78-81, mem bd dirs, 86-; trustee, Klyne Esopus Mus, Port Ewen, NY, 82-84; dir, Col Art Gallery, State Univ NY, New Paltz, currently. *Teaching:* Adj lectr photog & art, La Guardia Community Col, Queens, NY, 76-78; lectr photog, State Univ NY, New Paltz, 79-81. *Awards:* Photographers Fund, Catskill Ctr Photog, 80; Creative Artists Pub Serv Fel, NY State Coun Arts, 81. *Mem:* NY State Asn Mus; Mid-Atlantic Asn Mus; Am Asn Mus; State Univ NY Coun Gallery & Exhib Dirs (chmn). *Res:* Contemporary photography. *Publ:* Contribr, Off the Press-16 Contemporary Photoprintmakers & Jan Sawka Catalog, NY State Gallery Asn. *Mailing Add:* 7 Emmy Lane New Paltz NY 12561-2637

TRAGER, PHILIP
PHOTOGRAPHER
b Bridgeport, Conn, Feb 27, 35. *Study:* Wesleyan Univ, BA, 56; Columbia Univ Sch Law, JD, 60. *Work:* Mus Mod Art, Metrop Mus Art, New York; Corcoran Gallery Art; Bibliot Nat, Paris; Smithsonian Inst; Can Ctr Archit. *Comn:* Photog study Wesleyan Univ, Bd Trustees, 80; Photog study Birmingham, Birmingham Mus Art, 88; Photog study Wave Hill, Bd Dirs, 90; Photog study, Salire Royale, Found Ledoux, 91. *Exhib:* Solo exhibs, Davison Art Ctr, Middletown, Conn, 70, 74, 81 & 92, Witkin Gallery, New York, 72, 77, 80 & 87, Wesleyan Univ Ctr Arts, 87, Int Ctr Photog-Midtown, New york, 87, Light Impressions Gallery, Rochester, 88, Patrick & Beatrice Mus Art, Marquette Univ, 89, Mus Art, Univ Ore, 89 & Julie Saul Gallrey, 92; Legacy of Light, De Cordova Mus, 88; Portfolio Gallery, London, 89; Ten Years 1979-1989, Photo Gallery Int, Tokyo, 89; Brooklyn Mus, 89; Found Ledoux, 91; and others in the US and France. *Teaching:* Instr masterclasses & workshops. *Awards:* Distinguished Alumnus Award, 81; 1987 Book Award, The Villas of Palladio, Maine Photog Workshops; Finalist Grant Prix Award, Int Festival Photog, Arles, France. *Bibliog:* Eve Auchincloss (auth), Connoisseur, 2/87; C J Dickinson (auth), Am Photog, 3/87; Ziva Freiman (auth), In print, Metropolis, 7-8/87. *Media:* Silver & Platinum photographs. *Publ:* Contribr, Creative Camera 20th Ann Catalog, London, 88; Flatiron, A Photographic History of the World's First Steel Frame Skyscraper, Am Inst Architects Press, 90; Charles Hagar, NY Time, 91; photogr, Wave Hill Pictured, 91; Dancers, Bulfinch Press, 92; and others. *Mailing Add:* 20 Rolling Ridge Rd Fairfield CT 06430

TRAKAS, GEORGE
SCULPTOR
b Quebec, Que, May 11, 44. *Study:* Brooklyn Mus Art Sch; Hunter Col, New York Univ, BS. *Work:* Solomon R Guggenheim Mus. *Comn:* Omaha Opportunities Industrialization Ctr, 80; Nat Oceanic and Atmospheric Admin, Seattle, 83. *Exhib:* Projects: Pier 18, Mus Mod Art, New York, 71; Ten Young Artists: Theodoron Awards, Guggenheim Mus, New York, 71; Route Point, Scale and Environment: 10 Sculptors, Walker Art Ctr, Minneapolis, Minn, 77; El, 1979 Biennial, Whitney Mus Am Art, New York, 79; Pacific Union, San Diego Mus Contemp Art, La Jolla, Calif, 89; Routes from the Heart, La Mus, Humlebaek, Denmark, 89; Le Pont d'Epee au Creux de l'Enfer, Thiers, France, 89; Todd Terrace, Wash State Univ, Pullman, 90; Constructions, Wall Pieces and Drawings, Quint Krichman Projs, San Diego, Calif, 92; and others. *Teaching:* Lectr, Boston Mus, 72; lectr, Cooper Union, 78; lectr, Yale Univ, 80. *Awards:* Nat Endowment Arts Fel, 79; Guggenheim Fel, 83. *Bibliog:* Paul Stimson (auth), article, Art Am, 9-10/75; Kate Linker (auth), George Trakas & the syntax of space, Arts Mag, 1/76. *Media:* Steel, Wood. *Publ:* Contribr, Outcrops, Avalanche, fall 71; catalogue essays, Projects in Nature, 75 & Artpark, 76. *Mailing Add:* PO Box 395 Canal St Sta New York NY 10013-0395

TRAKIS, LOUIS
SCULPTOR, EDUCATOR
b New York, NY, June 22, 27. *Study:* Cooper Union, BFA; Columbia Univ; Art Students League; Politechneion, Athens, Greece; Fulbright grants, Acad Fine Arts, Rome, Italy, 59-60 & 60-61. *Work:* Guild Hall Mus, East Hampton, NY; Village Kournas, Crete, Greece. *Comn:* War hero monument (bronze), Crete, Greece, 88. *Exhib:* Pa Acad, Philadelphia; Metrop Mus of Art, Tokyo; Galleria re Magi, Milan, Italy; Corcoran Gallery, Washington, DC; Brooklyn Mus, NY; Feingarten Gallery, NY; Benson Gallery, Bridgehampton, LI, NY; Manhattanville Col, Purchase, NY; Benton Gallery, Southampton, NY; New Sch, New York, NY. *Teaching:* Instr sculpture, Philadelphia Col of Art, Columbia Univ, New Sch for Social Res & Southhampton Col; prof ceramics & sculpture, Manhattanville Col, 65-, adminr, Summer in Crete Prog, 80-85. *Awards:* Louis Comfort Tiffany Found Award/Sculpture, 61 & 63. *Bibliog:* Interview (TV prog), Carlson Int, 84. *Mem:* Artists Equity, New York; Am Asn Univ Profs; Audubon Artists. *Publ:* Contribr, Prize Winning Sculpture (bks I & II), Allied Publ. *Mailing Add:* 532 16th St Brooklyn NY 11215

TRANK, LYNN EDGAR
EDUCATOR, PAINTER
b Cook, Nebr, Feb 24, 18. *Study:* Univ of Nebr, BFA; Washington Univ, BFA; Univ of Iowa, MFA; Ohio State Univ, PhD; study with Philip Guston, Max Beckmann & Alfredo Zalce, Mexico. *Work:* Joslyn Art Mus, Omaha; Des Moines Art Ctr, Iowa; Evansville Mus of Art, Ind; Philadelphia Library Print Collection, Pa; Sheldon Swope Art Gallery, Terre Haute, Ind. *Exhib:* 57th Ann Am Exhib (watercolor & drawings), Art Inst of Chicago, 46; 1st Biennial Painting and Prints, Walker Art Ctr, 47; Drawing & Small Sculptures Nat, Muncie, Ind, 55, 56, 58, 59; Nat Print Show, Wichita, Kans, 56; Craft Exhib Invitational 59, Art Gallery, Muncie, 58; Watercolor USA, Springfield, Mo, 63-64; Wabash Valley Exhib, Sheldon Swope Gallery, Terre Haute, 70-72; and others. *Teaching:* Prof drawing, painting & printmaking, Eastern Ill Univ, Charleston, 52-84; retired. *Awards:* Graphic Arts Award, Tri-State Exhib, 55, 56; Wabash Valley Labor Coun Prize, Wabash Valley Exhib, Terre Haute, 70. *Mem:* Col Art Asn. *Media:* Collagraph, Watercolor on Canvas. *Publ:* Illusr, Febold Feboldson, Univ Nebr Press, 48; contribr, The Print, Creative Graphics, New York, 59. *Mailing Add:* 10 W Johnson Ave Charleston IL 61920

TRAPP, FRANK ANDERSON
MUSEUM DIRECTOR, HISTORIAN
b Pittsburgh, Pa, June 13, 22. *Study:* Carnegie Inst Technol, BA, 43; Harvard Univ, MA, 47, PhD(Fulbright Scholar), 52. *Pos:* Dir, Mead Art Gallery, Amherst Col, 65-92. *Teaching:* From instr to asst prof art hist, Williams Col, 51-56; from asst prof to prof art hist, Amherst Col, Mass, 56-, chmn dept fine arts, 63-75 & 76-78; Andrew W Mellon vis prof, Univ Pittsburgh, 79-80. *Awards:* Nat Endowment Humanities Sr Fel, 71-72. *Mem:* Col Art Asn; Assoc Artists Pittsburgh; Asn Art Mus Dir. *Publ:* Auth, The 1913 Armory Show in Retrospect (exhib catalogue), 58; Attainment of Delacroix, Johns Hopkins Press, 70; The Temptation of St Anthony by Odilon Redon, Amherst Col, 80; Peter Blume, Rizzoli, 87; The Grand Tradition, British Art from Amherst Col, Am Fed Arts, 88. *Mailing Add:* 4609 Bayard St Pittsburgh PA 15213

TRASOBARES, CESAR
PAINTER
b Cuba, Sept 9, 49. *Study:* Fla State Univ, BA, 71-73. *Work:* Lowe Art Mus, Coral Gables, Fla. *Exhib:* Immigrant Artists, traveling show, 84; Cuba USA, traveling show, 91-93. *Pos:* Exec dir, Art Pub Places, Miami, Fla, 85-90. *Awards:* Artist Fel, Nat Endowment Arts, 79; Artist Fel, Cintas Found, 80. *Media:* Multimedia. *Mailing Add:* 1214 SW 12th Ct Miami FL 33135

TRAUB, CHARLES H
EDUCATOR, PHOTOGRAPHER
b Louisville, Ky, Apr 6, 45. *Study:* Univ of Ill, Champaign, BA, 67; Inst of Design, Ill Inst of Technol, MS(photog), 71, with Aaron Siskind. *Work:* Int Ctr Photog, New York; Mus of Mod Art, New York; Art Inst of Chicago, Ill; Fogg Mus, Harvard Univ, Cambridge, Mass; Int Mus of Photog, Rochester, NY; and others. *Comn:* Olympic Arts Found, 84; New York City Parks Dept, 89. *Exhib:* Photographs of Charles Traub, Art Inst of Chicago, 75; The City, Mus of Contemp Art, Chicago, 77; one-man shows, Light Gallery, New York, 77 & Hudson River Mus, 81; Contemp Photog, Fogg Mus, 77; Five Photogr, Halstead 831 Gallery, Birmingham, Mich, 77. *Pos:* Freelance photogr, 69-; pres, Photog Adv Group, Chicago, Ill, 75-77; dir, Light Gallery, New York, 78-; sr ed, Matrix Publ; chmn, Sch visual arts, New York. *Teaching:* Vis artist, Franconia Col, NH, 73-74; prof photog & chmn dept, Columbia Col, Chicago, Ill, 71-; vis artist, Tyler Sch Art, Philadelphia, Pa, 81; instr, Sch Visual Art, New York, 85. *Mem:* Soc of Photog Educ; Col Art Asn. *Publ:* Italy Observed Rizzoli Publ Inc; On the Edge: Document of New York Waterfronts; Rizzoli Angler's Album, Beach-Horizon Press. *Dealer:* Light Gallery 724 Fifth Ave New York NY 10019; Howard Greenberg Photo Find, New York, NY. *Mailing Add:* 214 E 21st New York NY 10010

TRAUERMAN, MARGY ANN
PAINTER, INSTRUCTOR
b Sioux Falls, SDak. *Study:* Univ Iowa, Iowa City, BFA; Am Acad Art, Chicago; Art Students League, New York; Los Angeles City Col. *Exhib:* Am Watercolor Soc Ann, 53-68; NY Figurative Painting & Traveling Exhib, 71; one-man shows, Chatham Col, Pittsburgh, 61, First Street Gallery, New York, 72, 74, 77, 79, 82 & 84 & Landmark Gallery, McAllen, Tex, 75. *Teaching:* Instr art, Art & Design High Sch, New York, 52-77; instr art, Queens Col, New York, spring 75. *Bibliog:* David Loeffler Smith (auth), Celebrated women artists, 1/62 & Heritage of the thirties, 10/62, Am Artist; Watercolor page, Am Artist, 7/74. *Mem:* Am Watercolor Soc. *Media:* Watercolor. *Mailing Add:* 2 W 67th St New York NY 10023

TRAUSCH, THOMAS V
PAINTER
b Chicago, Ill, Sept 4, 43. *Study:* Univ Ill, BFA, 66; Am Acad Art, with Irving Shapiro, 74-77. *Work:* Elmhurst Fine Arts Mus, Ill; Smith-Barney, Chicago; Burlington Northern Railway, Ill; Nissei-Sanyo; Sandoz Corp, Des Plaines, Ill. *Comn:* Paintings, Ashwell & Co, Chicago, Ill, 81-82; McIntosh Ltd Realty, 86; Oil, Black Dot Corp, Crystal Lake, Ill, 89; and others. *Exhib:* Ill State Fair Professional Art Exhib, Springfield, 85, 86 & 90; Midwest Watercolor Soc, Green Bay, Wisc, 90; Am Watercolor Soc, New York, 86; Adirondack National Exhibitions of American Watercolors, traveling exhib, 86 & 88; Six Illinois Artists, Harper Col, Palatine, Ill, 87; Studio Long Grove, Ill, 92. *Pos:* Guest instr, Am Acad Art, 88-90. *Teaching:* Pvt instr watercolor & oil, currently. *Awards:* La Watercolor Soc, Dixie Art supply, 84; Purchase Award, Watercolor Ill Biennial, 84; Spec Merit Award, Midwest Watercolor Soc, 85; Edgewood Col Award, Nat Watercolor Exhib, Madison, Wis, 86. *Bibliog:* Craig Schreiner (auth), Trausch takes life as free spirit, Daily Sentinel, 82; Danielle Aceto (auth), Couple finds painting adds to art of marriage, Northwest Herald, 88; Kathleen Yaekel (auth), Just Rewards, Northwest Herald, 90. *Mem:* Mid-West Watercolor Soc (signature mem, 85-92). *Media:* Oil, Watercolor. *Publ:* Coauth, Opera House Sketch Book, Woodstock Fine Arts Asn, 88. *Mailing Add:* 11402 Halma Lane W Woodstock IL 60098

TRAVANTI, LEON EMIDIO
PAINTER, GRAPHIC DESIGNER
b Kenosha, Wis, Aug 5, 36. *Study:* Cranbrook Acad of Arts, MFA, 60; Layton Sch of Art, BFA, 59. *Work:* Milwaukee Art Ctr; Bergstrom Mus, Neenah, Wis; Rahr Art Ctr, La Crosse, Wis; Univ Mo; Univ Wis; Northern Ill Univ. *Comn:* Paintings & drawings, Ansul Int, Brussels, Belg, 74, Lane Ltd, Sydney, Australia, 74-75 & Malaysia Ancom, Kuala Lumpur, Malaysia, 75; painting, First Wis Nat Bank, 76; Deston House, Milwaukee Mural Comn, 91. *Exhib:* Walker Art Ctr Biennial, Minneapolis, Minn, 56; Butler Inst of Am Art, Youngstown, Ohio, 56; Chicago Art Inst, 56 & 58; Detroit Inst of Art, 60; Columbia Col, Mo, 78; Fitzsimmons, New York, 78; Pillsbury Nat, 81-82; West Art & The Law Nat, 83; one-man shows, Charles Allis Art Mus, Milwaukee, 83 & Posner Gallery, Milwaukee, 90; Technology in Art Invitational Exhib, Milwaukee Art Mus, 86; Rahr-West Mus, Manitowoc, Wis, 88; and others. *Pos:* Art dir, Wis Archit & Milwaukee Mag, 60-64; dir graphic design, Sch Fine Arts, Univ Wis, 64-74. *Teaching:* Prof art & design, Univ Wis, Milwaukee, 64-; vis lectr graphic design, Parsons Sch of Design, summer 77 & 79; vis lectr, Pratt Inst, Manhattan Campus, 78-79, Parsons Sch

Design, 79-80. *Awards:* Purchase Prizes, Milwaukee Renaissance, 60, Wis Invitational, 65 & Pillsbury Co, Minneapolis; and others. *Bibliog:* Walter Herdig (ed), Ann report paintings, Graphis Ann, 66-67 & 75-76; Paintings in reports, Print Mag, 76 & Current Am Paintings, La Revue Moderne, Paris, 60. *Mem:* Am Inst Graphic Arts; Graphic Arts Guild; Soc of Typographic Arts; and others. *Media:* Miscellaneous media. *Dealer:* Posner Gallery Milwaukee WI. *Mailing Add:* 1425 N Prospect Ave Milwaukee WI 53202

TRAVER, DONALD
CONCEPTUAL ARTIST
b Poughkeepsie, NY, Feb 3, 57. *Study:* Art Students League, 76; Empire State Col, NY, 77; SUNY, New Paltz, 80. *Exhib:* Solo exhibs, Massimo Audiello Gallery, New York, 85 & 86, Hillman Holland Fine Art, Atlanta, Ga, 86 & Elizabeth McDonald Gallery, New York, 88; Pictures From the Inner Mind, Palladium, New York, 86; Abstraction, Dart Gallery, Chicago, Ill, 86; Emerging Artists 1986, Cleveland Ctr Contemp Art, 86; Abstraction Rediscovered, Rosa Esman Gallery, New York, 86; Romantic Science, One Penn Plaza, New York, 87; 3X4, Galeria Fucares, Madrid, Spain, 87; Inaugural Exhib, Elizabeth McDonald Gallery, New York, 87; Group Show, Massimo Audiello Gallery, New York, 87; Barbara Toll Gallery, New York, 88; Grey Art Gallery, New York, 88; Krygierr-Landau Gallery, Los Angeles, 89. *Awards:* Nat Endowment Arts, 87; NY State Found, Arts, 87. *Bibliog:* Dan Cameron (auth), In the realm of the hyper-abstract, Arts, 11/86; E S, Smith, Suzuki y Traver: El arte joven de Nueva York, No 16, Diario, 6/12/87; Jose Luis Loarce, 3X4, No 44, Lapiz Mag, Spain, 87. *Mailing Add:* 21 First Ave New York NY 10003

TRAVERS-SMITH, BRIAN JOHN
PAINTER, INSTRUCTOR
b Tangshan, North China, June 26, 31; US & Can citizen. *Study:* Ont Col Art, Toronto, 49-50; self-taught in watercolor. *Work:* Art Gallery Greater Victoria, BC; Provincial Collection BC; Dofasco Collection, Hamilton, Ont; Chevron Standard Collection, Calgary, Alta; Hiram Walker Collection, BC; Royal Collection, Windsor, UK. *Exhib:* One-man show, Art Gallery Greater Victoria, BC, 62; Allied Artists Am, New York, 69, 71, 72 & 81; Am Watercolor Soc, ann & traveling, 71, 76, 77 & 81; Can Soc Painters Watercolour, Toronto, 76 & 77; BC Through the Eyes of Its Artists, Govt BC, traveling Europe, 79. *Pos:* Bd dirs, Art Gallery Greater Victoria, BC, 63-70, pres, bd dirs, 69-70; bd dirs, Emily Carr Col Art & Design, 80-82. *Teaching:* Instr, Studios in Victoria, BC, 65-75. *Awards:* First Prize, Vancouver Island Ann, 62; Royal Jubilee Medal, Can, 77. *Bibliog:* Margaret Harold (auth), Brian Travers-Smith, Prize-Winning Watercolors, 63; R Ashwell (auth), Brian Travers-Smith, Westworld Mag, 4/78. *Mem:* Am Watercolor Soc; Allied Artists Am; Can Soc Painters Watercolor; Fedn Can Artists; NW Watercolor Soc. *Media:* Watercolor. *Mailing Add:* 2801 Arbutus Rd Victoria BC V8N 5X6 Canada

TRAVIS, DAVID B
CURATOR, HISTORIAN
b Omaha, Nebr, Jan 31, 48. *Study:* Univ of Chicago, BA(art hist), Smithsonian Inst, res fel, 72. *Collections Arranged:* Exhibitions of photography, Art Inst of Chicago, 73-; Starting with Atget (auth, catalog), 77; Photographs from the Andre Jammes Collection: Niepce to Atget (ed, catalog), 77; Photography Rediscovered: American Photographs 1900-1930 (auth, catalog), 79; Photographs in Chicago Collections (auth, catalog), 82. *Pos:* Asst cur photog, Art Inst of Chicago, 74-77, assoc cur photog, 77-78, cur photog, 79- *Teaching:* Lectr hist of photog, Sch of the Art Inst of Chicago, 74. *Mailing Add:* Chicago IL 60615

TRAYLOR, ANGELIKA
STAINED GLASS ARTIST
b Munich, Ger, Aug 24, 42; US citizen. *Study:* Private Handelsschule Morawetz, Munich, WGer, 58; studied with Gil Reynolds & Tim McCreight. *Exhib:* Florida Crafts Exhibit, Cummer Gallery Art, Jacksonville, 83; Ann Assoc Exhib, Royal Ont Mus, Toronto, 85; Ann Assoc Exhib, SGAA, Nora Eckles Harrison Mus, Logan, Utah, 89; Artists Forum 12th & 13th Ann Exhib, Brevard Art Ctr & Mus, Melbourne, Fla, 90 & 91; Ann Assoc Exhib, Albuquerque, NMex, 90; Ann Assoc Exhib, Washington, DC, 91. *Awards:* Fragile Art, Glass Studio, 82; 1st Year Exhibitor Award, SGAA Assoc Show, Stained Glass Asn Am, 84; 2nd Place, Non-figurative Composition, Vitraux des USA, 85; Best of Show, Stained Glass Asn Am, 89. *Bibliog:* Angelo Cerchione (auth), In Celebration of Daylilies, Daylily J, 87; Design Journal, 4/89; Suzanne Carmichael (auth), The Travelers Guide to American Crafts, E P Dutton, 5/90; Joan Belmonte (auth), Splendid Glass, Fla Mag, Orlando Sentinel, 7/91. *Mem:* Stained Glass Asn Am; Glass Art Soc; Fla Craftsmen. *Media:* Stained Glass. *Mailing Add:* 100 Poinciana Dr Indian Harbor Beach FL 32937

TREASTER, RICHARD A
PAINTER, EDUCATOR
b Lorain, Ohio, July 14, 32. *Study:* Cleveland Inst Art, BFA. *Work:* Butler Inst Am Art; Nat Acad Design, New York; Cleveland Mus of Art, Ohio; Southern Alleghenies Mus of Art, Loretto, Pa; Wittenberg Univ, Springfield, Ohio. *Comn:* Watercolor, Norman Hilton & Co, New York, 86; watercolor, Prudential-Bache Securities, New York, 87; watercolor, J M Smucker Company, Orville, Ohio, 87; 5 watercolor, Nestle Food Coop, White Plains, NY, 88-; watercolor, Oppenheimer Mgt Corp, New York, 88. *Exhib:* 200 Years Am Watercolor, Metrop Mus Art, 66; Cleveland Inst Art, 68 & 75; Watercolor USA, 72; one-man shows, Charleston Art Gallery, WVa & Southern Alleghenies Mus of Art, Loretto, Pa, 77; Lyman Allyn Mus, New London, Conn, 80. *Teaching:* Instr painting, Cooper Sch Art, Cleveland, 66-67; assoc prof, Cleveland Inst Art, 66-80; adj prof, Ursuline Col, 76-81. *Awards:* Mainstreams Award of Excellence, Marietta Col, 69; Emily Goldsmith Award, Am Watercolor Soc, 69; Third Butler Medal, Butler Inst Am Art, 76. *Bibliog:* Ralph Fabri (auth), Medal of merit, Today's art, 8/66; Norman Kent (auth), Richard Treaster--American artist, Am Artist, 1/72. *Mem:* Am Watercolor Soc. *Media:* Watercolor, Egg Tempera. *Publ:* Auth, John Singer Sargent: the great Gatsby of art, Cleveland Plain Dealer Mag, 9/23/79; auth, Influence of other artists, Am Artist, 7/83. *Dealer:* Art Advisory Services Inc 530 Park Ave New York NY 10021. *Mailing Add:* 1228 Virginia Ave Lakewood OH 44107

TRECHSEL, GAIL ANDREWS
CURATOR
b Washington, DC, Nov 4, 53. *Study:* Col William & Mary, Va, BA, 74; Cooperstown Grad Prog, NY, MA(mus studies), 76; Winterthur Summer Inst, 77; Attingham Summer Sch, 81. *Collections Arranged:* Wedgwood Boulton: Artists of Industry, 78, By Hammer and Hand: Irish Decorative Arts, Birmingham Mus Art, 80, Alabama Quilts & Southern Quilts: A New View, Hunter Mus Art, 90. *Pos:* Nat Endowment Humanities Intern, Colonial Williamsburg, Va, 75-76; cur decorative arts, Birmingham Mus Art, Ala, 76-82, asst dir, 83-85, actg dir, 91-92, asst to dir, 92- *Teaching:* Adj prof, Univ Ala, Birmingham, currently. *Awards:* Nat Endowment Arts Fel, 86. *Mem:* Am Ceramics Circle; Eng Ceramics Circle; Women's Caucus Art (bd mem, 80-); Birmingham Art Asn (pres, 78-79); coun mem Ala State Coun Arts. *Publ:* Coauth, Index to American Coverlet Weavers, Univ Va Press, 78; auth, Frances Oliver Collection of European Porcelain, 80 & auth, Alabama Quilts, 80, Birmingham Mus Art; Lamprecht collection of cast iron art, 2/83 & Beeson collection of wedgwood in Birmingham Museum of Art, 6/83, Mag Antiques; Southern Quilts: A New View, EPM Press. *Mailing Add:* 3406 Altamont Way Birmingham AL 35205

TRECKER, STANLEY MATTHEW
ART COLLEGE PRESIDENT
b Manning, Iowa, July 15, 44. *Study:* Ind Univ, Bloomington, MBA, 68; Columbia Col, Chicago, BA, 75; Sch Art Inst Chicago, MFA, 78. *Work:* Art Inst Chicago; George Eastman House. *Exhib:* Arles Festival, France, 75; Calif Inst Fine Arts, Valencia, 77; Moming Gallery, Chicago, 78; ARC Gallery, Chicago, 78; Art Inst Chicago, 78; Artist Coop, Toronto, Can, 79. *Pos:* Cur, Moming Gallery, Chicago, 77-80; dir, Photog Resource Ctr, Boston, 80-91; pres, Art Inst Boston, 92- *Teaching:* Instr photog, Columbia Col, Chicago, 78-80. *Awards:* Ill Art Coun Grant, 79; Artists' Found Proj Grant, 83. *Mem:* Soc Photog Educators (bd dirs, 83-87); Col Art Asn. *Media:* Photography. *Mailing Add:* Six Parkway Rd Brookline MA 02146

TREDENNICK, DOROTHY W
EDUCATOR, LECTURER
b Bristol, Conn, Oct 5, 14. *Study:* Norwich Art Sch, 32-34; Berea Col, AB, 46, Univ Mich, Gen Educ Bd fel, MA(art hist), 51. *Pos:* Assoc dir, Slater Mem Mus, 39-43. *Teaching:* Instr art, Norwich Art Sch, 33-34; prof art hist & humanities, Berea Col, 46-70, Morris Belknap prof art, 70-87, co-chmn dept art, 54-70, teaching consult, 85-87; lectr, US & Asia. *Awards:* Seabury Award for Excellence in Teaching, Berea Col, 62; Fulbright Award, Chinese Civilization, 63; Nat Endowment Humanities Grant, Univ Calif, 77; Fel, Ctr Ecumenical & Cultural Studies, St John's, Minn, 83-84. *Mem:* Col Art Asn; Southern Humanities Conf; Asn Gen & Liberal Studies; Interfaith Task Force for Peace. *Publ:* Co-auth, This is Our Best, 55; Kress Study Collection, 61; auth, Living by Design, 63; Art & The Protestant Church Today, 66; Design for Living, 68; Two Worlds Meet: The Religious Dimensions of Art, 84. *Mailing Add:* Berea Col Berea KY 40404

TREESE, WILLIAM R
LIBRARIAN, PAINTER
b Burlington, Wash, Dec 7, 32. *Study:* Art Inst Chicago, BFA, 60; Stanford Univ, MA, 61; Drexel Univ, Philadelphia, MLS, 64. *Pos:* Art librn, Free Libr, Philadelphia, 61-64; art librn, Univ Calif, 66-91; retired. *Mem:* Art Libr Soc NAm. *Publ:* Coauth, Computerized approach to art exhibition catalogues, Libr Trends, 1/75; ed, Catalogs of the Art Exhibition Catalog Collection of the Arts Library, University of California, Santa Barbara, Somerset House, 77; auth, Rephotographing microforms, Microform Rev, summer 83. *Mailing Add:* Arts Library Univ Calif Santa Barbara CA 93106

TREISTER, KENNETH
PAINTER, SCULPTOR
b New York, NY, Mar 5, 30. *Study:* Univ Miami; Univ Fla, BArch, 53. *Work:* Norton Gallery, Palm Beach, Fla; Miami Mus Mod Art, Fla; Fla Supreme Ct, Tallahassee. *Comn:* Family of God (limited ed bronze menorahs), 69 & six bronze plaques depicting hist of Jews, United Jewish Appeal; ten paintings depicting 4,000 yr hist of Jews, Temple Israel, Miami; Eternal Light, Great Miami Rabinical Asn, 4/86; Niel Schiff Mem Bust, Univ Miami, 4/86; In Memory of the Six Million (sculpture), Mem Holocaust for the City of Miami, 4/86. *Exhib:* Greenwich Gallery, New York; Mus Fine Arts, Columbus, Ga; Lowe Art Gallery, Coral Gables, Fla; Contemp Art Mus, Houston, Tex; High Mus, Atlanta, Ga; and several one-man shows. *Teaching:* Guest lectr art & archit, Mass Inst Technol, Univ Syracuse, Univ Pa, Fla Atlantic Univ, Dade Jr Col/South Campus, Univ Miami, Univ Fla, Jewish Fedn, Univ Chile & Qinghua Univ, Bejing, China. *Awards:* First Prize for Four Conversations (sculpture), Nat Ceramic Exhib, Lowe Art Gallery, 53. *Mem:* Blue Dome Soc, Miami; Fla Sculptural Soc; Southern Asn Sculptors. *Publ:* Contribr, Fla Architecture (40th edition), Nat Mall Monitor, 10/81, FDQ-Design South, 5/85, Interiors, 12/85 & Fla Municipal Record, 2/86. *Mailing Add:* Box 331700 Miami FL 33233-1700

TRENTHAM, GARY LYNN
EDUCATOR, FIBER ARTIST
b Gleason, Tenn, Dec 7, 39. *Study:* Murray State Univ, BA, 61, MA, 65; Ind Univ, Bloomington, with Budd Stalnaker & Joan Sterrenberg, MFA, 72. *Work:* Steuben Glass, New York; Ind Univ, Bloomington; Collection of Vpres of Corning Glass, NY; Auburn Univ, Ala. *Exhib:* Piedmont Crafts Exhib, Mint Mus of Art, Charlotte, NC, 73-74 & 76; 7th Int Biennial of Tapestry, Centre Int de la Tapisserie Ancienne et Mod, Lausanne, Switz, 75; Fiber Structures, Carnegie Inst, Pittsburgh, 76; 2nd Int Exhib of Miniature Textiles, Brit Craft Centre, London, 76; Source Detroit, Cranbrook Acad of Art, Bloomfield Hills, Mich, 76; Exhib of Contemp & Hist Baskets, Peabody Mus of Harvard, Worcester, Mass, 76; Textiles: Past & Prologue, Greenville Co Mus of Arts, SC, 76; Basket Invitational, Florence Duhl Gallery, New York, 77; and others. *Teaching:* Assoc instr textiles, Ind Univ, Bloomington, 69-72; from assoc prof to prof textile design, Auburn Univ, 72- *Awards:* Fiber Prize, Marietta Col Crafts Regional, Ohio, 73; Res & Exhib Expense Awards, Auburn Univ, 74-77; First Prize Fiber, El Paso Designer Craftsmen, Tex, 77. *Mem:* Am Crafts Coun; World Crafts Coun; Ala Crafts Coun. *Publ:* Contribr, Modern Approach to Basketry, Crown, 74; contribr, articles, Craft Horizons, 74 & 76; contribr, articles, Rev Design, Japan, 75; contribr, The New Basketry, Van Nostrand, 76; contribr, Decorative Art & Modern Interiors, Studio Vista, London, 77. *Dealer:* Florence Duhl Gallery 33 W 54th New York NY 10019. *Mailing Add:* Dept Consumer Affairs 308 Spidle Hall Auburn Univ Auburn AL 36849

TRENTON, PATRICIA JEAN
HISTORIAN
Study: Univ Calif, Berkeley & Los Angeles, BA, MA(art hist), PhD, 80. *Collections Arranged:* The Rocky Mountains: A Vision for Artists in the Nineteenth Century (auth, catalog), Buffalo Bill Hist Ctr, Cody, Wyo, 83; Native Faces: Indian Cultures in American Art (coauth, catalog), Southwest Mus, Los Angeles, 84; California Light 1900-1930 (coauth, catalog), Laguna Art Mus, Laguna Beach, 90. *Pos:* Cur Am art, Denver Art Mus, Colo, 69-74; art dir, The Los Angeles Athletic Club, 82- *Awards:* Nat Award by Graphics Art Industry for Am Art, Denver Art Mus Collection, 69; Nat Am Publ Award in Humanities, 83; Nat Hon Merit, Am Asn Mus, 84; Humanities Award, Nat Am Publ, 83. *Mem:* Col Art Asn. *Res:* Women Artists of the West, 1900-45. *Publ:* Coauth, American Art from the Denver Art Museum Collection, 69 & auth, Harvey Otis Young, 1840-1901: The Lost Genius, Denver Art Mus, 75; coauth, The Rocky Mountains: A Vision for Artists in the Nineteenth Century, Univ Okla Press, Norman, 83; Native Faces: Indian Cultures in American Art, Witness to Change, Harry N Abrams Publ, 89; Southwest Mus in Association with LAACO, Ltd, 84; Native Americans: Five Centuries of Changing Images. *Mailing Add:* 123 N Glenroy Ave Los Angeles CA 90049

TRIANO, ANTHONY THOMAS
PAINTER, EDUCATOR
b Newark, NJ, Aug 25, 28. *Study:* Newark Sch Fine & Indust Art, 46-50; with Reuben Nakian, 47-52; also with Samuel Brecher. *Work:* Newark Mus; Lowe Mus, Coral Gables, Fla; Paterson State Col, Wayne, NJ; Hartford Art Found, Conn; Seton Hall Univ, South Orange, NJ; Monmouth His Soc; Montclair Mus. *Exhib:* Gallery Selections, J L Hudson Gallery, Detroit, 64; New Jersey & the Artist, NJ State Mus, Trenton, 65; Boochever Art Collection, Paterson State Col, 68; Images of James Joyce, Montclair Mus, NJ, 75; Time, Life & Hope, Univ of Ala, Huntsville, Ala, 78; and others. *Teaching:* Artist in residence & asst prof art, Seton Hall Univ, 70- *Awards:* Twenty-fifth Ann NJ State Art Award, Montclair Mus, 57; Purchase Award, Newark Mus, 59. *Bibliog:* Mike Berg (auth), The Life & World of Triano, Seton Hall Univ, 68; William Sheppard (auth), Inside the Arts (film), Brooklyn Col, 70; D Simon (auth), Profiles (film), Seton Hall Univ, 71. *Media:* Oil, Acrylic. *Publ:* Illusr, Exploring Nature's Rhythms, 60 & Duck Fever, 61, Abbott Labs; contribr, H & G colors for your personal bed & bath, 56 & House of color, 67, House & Garden Mag; illusr, Courbet's unpainted pictures, Arts Mag, 80; Endeavors, Seton Hall Univ, 85; Exhibition Posters, Libr Cong, 86. *Mailing Add:* c/o The Collector Gallery 1505 19th St NW Washington DC 20036

TRIEFF, SELINA
PAINTER, INSTRUCTOR
b Brooklyn, NY, Jan 7, 34. *Study:* Art Students League, study with Morris Kantor; Hans Hofmann Sch, study with Hofmann; Brooklyn Col, BA, study with Rothko & Reinhardt, 55. *Work:* Brooklyn Mus; New York Pub Libr; Inst for Human Develop; Prudential Life Insurance Co; Bayonne Jewish Ctr; Smite Mus, Norte Dame Univ. *Comn:* Lithograph, Bayonne Jewish Ctr. *Exhib:* Contemp Am Figure Painting, Wadsworth Atheneum, 64; Work on Paper, Brooklyn Mus, 75; Butler Inst Ann, 77; Galleri Anna, Gothenborg, Sweden, 79; Contemp Figure Painting, Hera Gallery, Wakefield, RI, 79; Manhattan Civic Col, 82; Douglass Col, 83; Prince St Gallery, 84; Artes Gallery, Olso & Cassandra Gallery, Orobak, Norway, 84; Graham Modern Gallery, 86, 87 & 88; Ruth Bachofner Gallery, Santa Monica, 87. *Teaching:* Instr drawing, New York Inst of Technol, 75-; vis artist painting, Notre Dame Univ, Ind, 76; instr painting, New York Studio Sch, formerly; instr painting, Pratt Inst, formerly, Nat Acad Design, currently. *Awards:* Second Prize, Goddard Col Ann, 76; Purchase Prize, View from the Ctr, Bayonne Community Ctr, 78; Thomas B Clarke Prize, Nat Acad Design, 79; and others. *Bibliog:* Corinne Robins (auth), Selina Trieff, Arts, 78; Hilton Kramer (auth), article, New York Times, 82; Maureen Mullarky (auth), article, 84 & Joan Marter (auth), article, 6/86, Arts Mag; John Rusgell, New York Times; Vivian Raynol, New York Times. *Mem:* Women in the Arts; Womens Caucus Art; Col Art Asn. *Media:* Oil, Charcoal. *Mailing Add:* c/o Ruth Bachofner Gallery 926 Colorado Ave Santa Monica CA 90401

TRIMM, H WAYNE
ILLUSTRATOR, PAINTER
b Albany, NY, Aug 16, 22. *Study:* Cornell Univ, 40; Augustana Col, BS, 48; Kans State Univ, 49; Col Forestry, Syracuse Univ, MS, 53. *Comn:* Dioramas, Springfield Mus Art; three ecol dioramas, Augustana Col, 67; movie for Audubon Screen Tour, 68-69; World Wildlife Fund, Int Stamps for Congo, Bolivia, Bangladesh, 74; mural, Alley Pond Environ Ctr, Douglaston, NY, 80; and others. *Exhib:* Am Bird Artists Traveling Exhib, Audubon Artists; Joslyn Mus Art; Buffalo Mus Sci; one-man show, Remington Mus; SAA Show, San Francisco Acad Arts & Sci; and others. *Pos:* Art dir, Conservationist Mag, Div Educ Serv, NY State Dept Environ Conserv, 53-, sr ed, 53-73; ed, Outdoor Communicator Mag, formerly; vpres, Soc Animal Artists, New York, The Catasus (animal art), currently; ed, Catasus, Jour Soc Animal Artists, currently. *Teaching:* Lectr conserv & wildlife painting, currently; instr nature & sci illus, State Univ NY, Albany & Col St Rose, Nat Wildlife Fedn Summits, Sagamore Inst, Ragnette Lake, New York, Adirondack Ctr Arts, Blue Mt Lake, New York, Asa Wright Ctr, Trinidad; Asa Wright Nature Ctr, 81. *Awards:* The Trad Award, NY State Dept Environmental Conservationist; The Golden Award, NYSOEA; Artist of the Year 1988, WNPE/WNPI, Watertown, NY. *Bibliog:* Glenn Goff (interviewer), Cabin Country, WNPE-TV, 87. *Mem:* Columbia Co Arts & Crafts; Soc Animal Artists; hon mem Tuscarora Indian Tribe; Am Ornithologists Union; Guild Nat Sci Illusr. *Media:* Watercolor, Oil; Marble, Wood. *Publ:* Illustr, The Guild Handbook of Scientific Illustration, Smithsonian Inst; Illustrators Annual--Nature Drawing, No 27 & Nature Sketching, Claire Leslie Walker. *Mailing Add:* 64 High St Hoosick Falls NY 12090

TRINCERE, LI
PAINTER
b New York, NY, May 7, 59. *Study:* Southampton Col, Long Island Univ, NY, BFA(printing, printmaking), 81; Hunter Col, New York, CW Post Univ, Long Island NY, MFA, 83. *Exhib:* Cologne Art Fair, Galerie Ricke, Ger, 88, 89, 90, 91 & 92; Shaped Paintings, Julian Pretto, Berland Hall, New York, 89; one-woman shows, New Shaped Paintings, Julian Pretto, New York, 89, New Paintings, Galerie Rolf Ricke, Cologne, Ger, 89, Paintings/Drawings, Galerie Ranate Kammer, Hamburg, Ger, 90, New Paintings, Berland/Hall Gallery, New York, 90; Aus Meiner Sicht, Kolnisher Kunstverein, Cologne, Ger, 90; Kinder, Macht Neues, Galerie Rolf Ricke, Cologne, Ger, 92. *Awards:* Pollock/Krasner Found, 86 & 88; NY State Fel Arts, 89; Nat Endowment Arts Fel, 91. *Bibliog:* Farben und Flachen Kulurberichte, Die Konstuktivistin, Cologne, Ger, 10/89; Peter Frank (auth), Reconstructive painting, Artspace, 3/90; Art reproduction, Bomb Mag, p 81, 10th Year Issue, summer 91. *Mailing Add:* 633 E 11 St New York NY 10009

TRINKLEY, KARLA
SCULPTOR
Study: Tyler Sch Art, Elkins Park, Pa, BFA, 79; RI Sch Design, Providence, MFA, 81. *Work:* Los Angeles Co Mus, Calif; Hokkaido Mus Mod Art, Japan; Philadelphia Mus Art, Pa; Victoria Mus Art, Australia; Corning Mus Glass, NY. *Exhib:* New Glass: A Worldwide Survey, Corning Mus Glass, Corning, NY & Victoria & Albert Mus, London, Eng, 79; Glass Routes, De Cordova Mus, Lincoln, Mass, 81; International Direcions in Glass Art, Art Gallery Western Australia, 82; Contemp Am Glass: Corning Mus Invitational, US Embassy, Prague, Czech, 82-84; World Glass Now '85, Hokkaido Mus Mod Art, Sapporo, Japan, 85-86; Contemp Am & Europ Glass from The Saxe Collection, Oakland Mus, Calif & Am Craft Mus, New York, NY, 86-87; Craft Today: Poetry of the Physical, Am Craft Mus, New York & Denver Art Mus, Colo, 86-87. *Awards:* Fel, Nat Endowment Arts, 86. *Media:* Glass. *Mailing Add:* RD 2 Box 945 Boyertown PA 19512

TRIPP, JAN PETER
PAINTER, PRINTMAKER
b Oberstdorf, Bavaria, Ger, May 15, 45. *Study:* Acad Art, Stuttgart, sculpture, 68; Acad Art, Vienna, Austria, painting, 69-73; Masters class at Rudolf Hausner. *Work:* Staatsgalerie, Stuttgart, Ger; Kunsthalle, Hamburg, Ger; Albertina, Vienna, Austria; Frac, Strasbourg, France. *Exhib:* Graphic Biennales, Krakow, Ljubljana, Segovia, Bradford & Frechen, 72-90; 7 German Realists, Triennale, New Delhi, India, 78; 20 German Painters & Drawers, Warzowa, Poland, 79; Man and Landscape in Contemporary Painting and Graphic in BRD, Moscow, Leningrad, Russia, 83; 25 German Painters, Lissabonn Iporto, Port, 84; and others. *Mem:* Deutscher Kunstlerbund. *Media:* Acrylic, Egg Tempera; Etching. *Publ:* Contribr Die Kehrseite der Dinge, Gehring Gallery, Frankfurt, 85. *Mailing Add:* c/o John Szoke Graphics Inc 164 Mercer St New York NY 10012

TRIPP, SUSAN GERWE
MUSEUM DIRECTOR
b Baltimore, Md, Dec 28, 45. *Study:* Univ Md, BS, 67. *Work:* Evergreen House, Johns Hopkins Univ; Homewood Mus, Baltimore, Md; Old Westbury Gardens, NY. *Pos:* Cur art, Johns Hopkins Univ, 74-79, dir, Univ Collections, 79-91; exec dir, Old Westbury Gardens, 91- *Teaching:* Lectr art hist, Sch Continuing Educ, Johns Hopkins Univ, 78- *Awards:* Mus fel, Nat Endowment Arts, 80; Hist Preserv Award, Baltimore, Heritage, 88 & 91; Hist Preserv Award, ASID, 91. *Mem:* Oriental Ceramic Soc; Oriental Ceramic Soc of Hong Kong; Am Asn Mus; Oriental Ceramic Soc; Southern Garden Hist Soc. *Res:* Japanese minor arts, emphasis on history of lacquer and adaptation of theater masks to netsuke; Leon Bakst. *Publ:* Auth, Bakst, Johns Hopkins Mag, 84; contribr, A Taste of Maryland, Walters Art Gallery, 85; auth, Chinese Collections in Evergreen House (exhib catalog), Baltimore Antiques Show, 85; coauth (with N K Davey), The Garrett Collection of Japanese Art, Dauphin Publ, 92; auth, Homewood in Baltimore, Maryland, The Mag Antiques. *Mailing Add:* Old Westbury Gardens PO Box 430 Old Westbury NY 11568

TRISSEL, JAMES NEVIN
PAINTER, PRINTMAKER
b Davenport, Iowa, Nov 7, 30. *Study:* State Univ Iowa, BA; Colo State Col, MA; State Univ Iowa, MFA. *Work:* Univ Wis; Beloit Col; Colo Col; Colorado Springs Fine Arts Ctr. *Exhib:* One-man show, Beloit Col, 57, & Colorado Springs Fine Arts Ctr, 66 & 72, Ankrum Gallery, Los Angeles, 76; Wis Salon, 58; El Paso Biennial, 64 & 66. *Pos:* Actg dir, Wright Art Ctr, Beloit Col, 58-59; dir, Univ Exten Prog in Art, Univ Calif, Los Angeles, 62-64; proprietor, The Press, Colo Col, 78- *Teaching:* Instr art, Beloit Col, 58-60; asst prof art & art theory, Univ Calif, Los Angeles, 60-64; assoc prof art & art hist, Colo Col, 64-70, prof art, 70-, chmn dept art, 71-77. *Media:* Oil. *Dealer:* Carlin Galleries 710 Montgomery Ft Worth TX 76107; Ankrum Gallery 657 N La Cienega Blvd Los Angeles CA 90069. *Mailing Add:* 1620 N Nevada Ave Colorado Springs CO 80907-7435

TRIVIGNO, PAT
PAINTER, EDUCATOR
b New York, NY, Mar 13, 22. *Study:* Tyler Sch Art; NY Univ; Columbia Univ, BA & MA. *Work:* Solomon R Guggenheim Mus, New York; Brooklyn Mus, NY; Everson Mus, Syracuse, NY; New York Times; Gen Elec Corp. *Comn:* Murals, Lykes Steamship Lines & Cook Conv Ctr, Memphis. *Exhib:* Whitney Mus Am Art Ann; Art Inst Chicago; Pa Acad Fine Arts; Am Acad Arts & Lett; Univ Ill Biennial; and others. *Teaching:* Prof art, Tulane Univ La, 50-, chmn art dept. *Bibliog:* Articles in New York Times, 10/8/50 & 1/10/60; R Pearson (auth), Modern Renaissance in American Art, Harper. *Media:* Acrylic, Oil. *Mailing Add:* 1831 Marengo St New Orleans LA 70115

TRONCALE, FRANK THOMAS
DEALER, COLLECTOR
b Birmingham, Ala, Aug 11, 41. *Study:* Birmingham Southern Col, BA, 65. *Pos:* Docent (tour guide), John & Mable Ringling Mus Art, 77-79; dir, Hang-Up, Sarasota, Fla, currently. *Specialty:* Contemporary graphics. *Collection:* Contemporary graphics of Dali, Nierman, Nieman, Paul Maxwell, Picasso, Calder, Paul Jenkins, Thornton Utz, Frank Hopper, Dorothy Gillespie, Elba Alvarez & P Mackie. *Mailing Add:* The Hang-up Inc 45 S Palm Ave Sarasota FL 34236

TROP, SANDRA
ADMINISTRATOR
b Brooklyn, NY. *Study:* NY Univ, BS(cum laude); Everson Mus Art; Inst Arts Admin; Harvard Univ. *Pos:* Cur traveling exhibs, Everson Mus Art, Syracuse, NY, 72, asst to dir, 73, actg dir, 74, asst dir, 74- *Mem:* Int Coun Mus (int comt mus & collections mod art); Am Asn Mus. *Mailing Add:* Everson Mus Art 401 Harrison St Syracuse NY 13202

TROSKY, HELENE ROTH
PRINTMAKER, PAPERMAKER
b Monticello, NY. *Study:* New Sch Social Res, with Kuniyoshi Egas; Manhattanville Col, BA, with Al Blaustein, John Ross & Garner Tullis. *Work:* Wichita Mus of Art; Sheldon Swope Mus of Art, Terre Haute, Ind; Staten Island Mus; Hudson River Mus, Paine-Webber. *Comn:* Comn by Konigsberg & Wolf, 84, The Eggers Grp, 85, Am Ultramar, 85 & Pepsico, 86; Reader's Digest, 89. *Exhib:* Silvermine Guild, 68-70; Alan Brown Gallery, Hartsdale, NY, 80, 86, 90 & 92; Westchester Community Col, 81; Mus Gallery, White Plains, 87; Hammond Mus, Yorktown, NY, 92; Paramount Ctr Arts, Peekskill, NY, 92. *Pos:* Columnist, Muse Roundup, Harrison Independent Greenburgh Rec & Yonkers Rec, 60-76; art consult, Westchester Libr Syst, 65-70; dir, Second Regional Plan, New York, 65- *Teaching:* Art dir, Westchester Co Music & Art Camp, 65, 66, 71 & 72; lectr art hist, Brandeis Univ Women, 66-85; instr printmaking, Manhattanville Col, 71-76; adj prof art hist, Westchester Community Col, 81-; lectr, Marymount Col, 87. *Awards:* Northern Westchester Award, 68; Nat Asn Women Artists Award, 69 & 82; Coun Arts Westchester Award, 86. *Bibliog:* Marna Elyea Kern (auth), The Complete Book of Hand Crafted Paper, Coward McCann & Geoghegon. *Mem:* Silvermine Guild; Nat Asn Women Artists; Am Soc Contemp Artists; Hudson River Contemp Artists; Katonah Gallery; and others. *Media:* All. *Publ:* Auth, art columns & revs for Women's News, Harrison Independent & North Castle News, Pleasantville Post & Chappaqua J, 82- *Dealer:* Alan Brown Gallery Hartsdale NY. *Mailing Add:* Yarmouth Rd Purchase NY 10577

TROTMAN, BOB
CRAFTSMAN, SCULPTOR
b Winston-Salem, NC, June 25, 47. *Study:* Washington & Lee Univ, BA, 69. *Work:* Mus Art, RI Sch Design, Providence; Mus Art, Ariz State Univ, Tempe; Mint Mus, Charlotte, NC. *Exhib:* Craft in America, traveling, Europe, 89-91; NC Artist Exhib, NC Mus Art, Raleigh, 90; Design in Furniture, Art Int, New York, 90-91; solo exhib, Nexus Contemp Art Ctr, Atlanta, Ga, 92. *Awards:* Nat Endowment Arts Fel, 84 & 88. *Dealer:* Hodges Taylor Gallery 227 N Tryon St Charlotte NC 28202; Sandler Hudson Gallery 1834 Peachtree Rd NW Atlanta GA 30309. *Mailing Add:* Rte 1 Box 100A2 Casar NC 28020

TROTT, HELEN
PAINTER, INSTRUCTOR
b New York, NY, May 25, 36. *Study:* Hunter Col, BA, 58; City Col New York, MA, 65. *Exhib:* Nat Soc Painters Casein & Acrylic, Nat Acad Galleries, New York, 76 & 78 & Nat Arts Club, 80; Audubon Artists, Nat Acad Galleries, New York, 79; Painters & Sculptors Soc NJ, Bergen Community Mus, 81. *Teaching:* Instr art, Paul Dunbar Junior High Sch, Bronx, NY, 61-64; instr art, Christopher Columbus High Sch, Bronx, NY, 64-67. *Awards:* Gold Key Award, Senior Scholastic Art Exhib, Macy's, 53; Patron of the Arts Award, Painters & Sculptors Soc NJ, 80 & Honorable Mention, 81; Beaux Art Award, Westchester Co Fed Woman's Clubs, 82. *Bibliog:* Dina Weintraub (auth), The studio, Westchester Woman, 79. *Mem:* Nat Soc Painters Casein & Acrylic; Painters & Sculptors Soc NJ; Artists Equity. *Media:* Acrylic, Watercolor. *Mailing Add:* 2305 Sultana Dr Yorktown Heights NY 10598

TROVA, ERNEST TINO
SCULPTOR, PAINTER
b St Louis, Mo, Feb 19, 27. *Work:* Hirshhorn Mus, Washington, DC; Guggenheim Mus, Mus Mod Art, Metrop Mus Art & Whitney Mus Am Art, New York. *Exhib:* One-man exhibs, Hokin Gallery, Miami Beach, 88 & 90, Mangel Gallery, Philadelphia, 89, Galeria Freites, Caracas, Venezuela, 89 & 90, Hanson Galleries, San Francisco & Beverly Hills, 89, ACA Galleries, New York, 90, Philharmonic Ctr for the Arts, Naples, Fla, 91; Guggenheim Mus, New York, 64, 65, 67 & 84; Whitney Mus Mod Art, New York, 66, 68, 69 & 78; Mus Mod Art, New York, 68; Hirshhorn Mus & Sculpture Garden, Smithsonian Inst, Washington, DC, 74 & 83; Hanson Galleries, LaJolla, Calif, 89, Miami, 90; ACA Galleries, New York, 90; Galaria Freites, Caracas, Venezuela, 90; Philharmonic Ctr for the Arts, Naples, Fla, 91; Art Chicago, 91; and others. *Awards:* Nat Humanitarian Award, Nat Recreation & Park Asn, 79; Utsukushi-ga-hara Open Air Mus Award, 83. *Bibliog:* Ellen Post (auth), Ernest Trova: New Works, Laumeier Sculpture Park, 86; Riva Yares (auth), Ernest Trova: Falling Man-Poets-Pyramids-Gox, Yares Gallery, 86; Andrew Kagan (auth), Trova, 2nd Ed, Trova Found, St Louis, Mo, 87. *Media:* All. *Dealer:* Philip Samuels Fine Art 8112 Maryland Ave St Louis Mo 63105. *Mailing Add:* c/o Trova Foundation 8112 Maryland Ave, Ste 200 St Louis MO 63105

TRUBNER, HENRY
CURATOR, MUSEOLOGIST
b Munich, Ger, June 10, 20; US citizen. *Study:* Fogg Art Mus, Harvard Univ, BA & MA. *Collections Arranged:* Ceramic Art Japan: 100 Masterpieces from Japanese Collection (auth, catalog), Seattle Art Mus, 72-73; Int Symp on Japanese Ceramics, 72 & Int Symp on Chinese Ceramics, 77, Seattle Art Mus; Chinese Cermics from Japanese Collections (auth, catalog), Seattle Art Mus, 77-78; Song of the Brush, Seattle Art Mus, 79-80; Okyo and the Maruyama Shijo School of Japanese Painting, St Louis Art Mus and Agency for Cultural Affairs, Tokyo, 80; Treasures of Asian Art from the Idemitsu Collection (auth, catalog), Seattle Art Mus, 81-82; In Pursuit of the Dragon: Traditions and Transitions in Ming Ceramics (exhib from Idemitsu Mus Arts, Tokyo), Seattle Art Mus, 88. *Pos:* Cur Oriental art, Los Angeles Co Mus Art, 47-58; cur Far Eastern dept, Royal Ont Mus, Toronto, 58-68; cur dept Asian art, Seattle Art Mus, Wash, 68-, assoc dir, 75-88, Sr Lectr Emer, 88. *Teaching:* Assoc prof Asian art, Univ Toronto, 58-68. *Awards:* Koyama Fujio Mem Awards, Idemitsu Mus Arts, Tokyo, 88. *Mem:* Asia Soc (mem adv comt); Japan Soc (adv comt on arts); Am Asn Mus; Oriental Ceramic Soc, London; China Inst Am (adv comt); and others. *Res:* Japanese and Chinese ceramics. *Publ:* Coauth, Art treasures from Japan, 65-66; coauth, Asiatic art in the Seattle Art Museum, Kodansha Int, Tokyo, 73; auth, Ming enamel-decorated and polychrome porcelains, In: In Pursuit of the Dragon (exhib catalog), Seattle Art Mus, 88. *Mailing Add:* 9341 Vineyard Crescent Bellevue WA 98004

TRUBY, BETSY KIRBY
PAINTER, ILLUSTRATOR
b Winchester, Va, Nov 8, 26. *Study:* Hiram Col; Cleveland Sch Art; NMex Inst Mining & Technol; Univ NMex; also with David Moneypenny, Oden Hullenkramer & Joe Morello. *Work:* Int Moral Re-Armament Ctr, Mackinaw Island, Mich; Cancer Res & Treatment Ctr, Albuquerque; Geronimo Springs Art Mus, Truth or Consequences, NMex; Sheraton Hotel, Santa Fe, NMex; La Quinta Mus, Albuquerque. *Comn:* Portrait, Congressman Albert G Simms, 64; Indian child portrait, NMex Easter Seal Soc, 69; paintings, First Presby Church, Albuquerque, 72-74; historical portrait, Synod Southwest, Presby Church, 75; paintings, Cystic Fibrosis Found, NMex, 76 & 77; paintings reproduced, Southwest Arts & Graphics, 84, 85, 86, 87, 88, 89 & 90. *Exhib:* Fine Arts Gallery, Carnegie Inst, Pittsburgh, 46; NMex Fiesta Biennial, State Mus, Santa Fe, 64 & 68; Nat Art Show, Lawton, Okla, 74; Nat League Am Pen Women Mid-Ad Cong, Phoenix, Ariz, 75; One woman show, Hiram Col, Hiram, Ohio, 87; Nat League of Am Pen Women Nat Show, Kansas City, Mo, 90. *Teaching:* Instr ceramics, US Pub Health Hosp, 48-49, Ohio Pub Sch Syst, 49-50; instr ceramics, Ohio Pub Sch Syst, 49-50. *Awards:* Second Premium Pastel, 73 & First Premium, 76, NMex State Fair; Nat League of Am Pen Women State Show, First Premium Pastel, Third Premium Oil, Secorro, NMex, 10/89; Third Premium-Pastel, Juried Exhib, Pastel Soc NMex, Albuquerque, 91. *Bibliog:* J Bonnette (auth), The Creative Process, KNME TV, Univ NMex, 73. *Mem:* Nat League Am Pen Women, 63-92; Charter Mem, Pastel Soc NMex, 89-92. *Media:* Pastel, Watercolor. *Publ:* Cover illusr, Flags, 73 & Let Our Light Shine, 74. *Mailing Add:* 6609 Loftus Ave NE Albuquerque NM 87109

TRUDEAU, GARRY B
CARTOONIST
b New York, NY, 48. *Study:* Yale Univ, BA & MFA. *Work:* Graphics Arts Collection, Libr Congress, Washington, DC. *Pos:* Creator, Doonesbury (comic strip). *Awards:* Pulitzer Prize, 75; Nominated for Academy Award, 77 & Drama Desk Awards, 83; Special Jury Prize, Cannes Film Festival, 77. *Publ:* Auth, Adjectives Will Cost You Extra, 82, Gotta Run, My Government is Collapsing, 82 & Cartoons from In Search of Reagan's Brain, 82, Fawcett; Ask for May, Settle for June, 82 & Unfortunately, She Was Also Wired for Sound, 82, Holt, Rinehart & Winston; Doonesbury (play), 83. *Mailing Add:* c/o Universal Press Syndicate 4900 Main Kansas City MO 64112

TRUDEAU, YVES
SCULPTOR
b Montreal, Que, Dec 3, 30. *Study:* Ecole Beaux Arts Montreal, sr matriculant with Marie Mediatrice. *Work:* Mus Quebec; Galerie Nat Can; Mus Art Contemp Montreal; Mus Art Prague, Czech; Mus Plein Air D'Ostrava, Czech; and others. *Comn:* Large sculpture, Nat Capitol Comn, Ottawa, 78; large work, Transport Can, Can Seaway Building, St Catherine, Ont, 79; bronze relief & doors, Teleglobe Can, Montreal, 81; aluminium relief doors, Place Alcan, Montreal, 83; Place de la Decouverte (large aluminum sculpture), Gaspe, Quebec. *Exhib:* Int Symp Sculpture, Ostrava, 69; Biennale Middleheim, Anvers, Belg, 71; Premiere Biennale Petite Sculpture, Budapest, Hungary, 71; one-man show, Mus Quebec, 70, Contemp Mus Montreal, 78; and others. *Teaching:* Prof sculpture, Ecole Beaux-Arts Montreal, 67-69; prof sculpture concept & metal, Univ Que, Montreal, dir, visual art dept, 79-81, prof sculpture, currently. *Awards:* Can Coun Awards, 63 & 69; Ministere Educ Quebec Award, 70-71. *Bibliog:* Robert Guy (auth), Yves Trudeau, sculptor, Asn Sculpteurs Quebec, 71; Jacques De Roussan (ed), Yves Trudeau, Works from 1959-80, Broquet. *Mem:* Royal Can Acad Arts (vpres, 75-83); Can Conf Arts (vpres, 82-83); Asn Sculpteurs Quebec (pres, 60-66); Int Conf Mus; Int Asn Plastic Art. *Media:* Multimedia. *Publ:* Auth, article in Metiers D'Arts Quebec, 63; coauth, Catalogue, Galerie Nat Can, 66; auth, Confrontation 67 (catalog), 67. *Mailing Add:* 5429 Ave Durocher Outremont Montreal PQ H2V 3X9 Canada

TRUE, DAVID
PAINTER
b Marrietta, Ohio, 42. *Study:* Ohio Univ, BFA, 66, MFA, 67. *Work:* Dallas Mus Art, Tex; Metrop Mus Art, Mus Mod Art, New York; Munson-Williams-Proctor Inst, Utica, NY; Museo Tamayo, Mexico City, Mex; New Sch Social Res, New York; Va Mus Fine Arts, Richmond. *Exhib:* Solo shows, Va Mus Fine Arts, Richmond, 84, Edward Thorpe Gallery, New York, 85, Barbara Krakow Gallery, Boston, 86, Mangel Gallery, Philadelphia, 87 & Blum Helman Gallery, New York, 87, 88 & 90; Crown Point Press, San Francisco, 89; Walker Art Ctr, Minneapolis, 89; Blum Helman Gallery, New York, 91. *Awards:* Nat Endowment Arts, Painting Grant, 82-83 & 91. *Bibliog:* John Yau (auth), Reviews: David True Blum Helman, Artforum, 113-114, 12/87; Eleanor Heartney (auth), David True at Blum Helman, Art Am, 150, 3/88; David E Loper (auth), Scorched earch, Scis, 22-28, 9-10/90. *Dealer:* Blum Helman GalleryInc 20 W 57th St New York NY 10019. *Mailing Add:* P O Box 233 Prince St Station New York NY 10012

TRUEBLOOD, EMILY HERRICK
PRINTMAKER
b Alexandria, Va, Aug 13, 42. *Study:* Beloit Col, Wis; Univ Wis, Madison, BA, 65; Columbia Univ Sch Libr Serv, MS, 69. *Work:* Mus Mod Art, Haifa, Israel; Portland Mus Art, Ore; Trenton State Col, NJ. *Exhib:* Traveling exhib, Va Mus Fine Arts, Richmond, 86; 72nd Hudson River Ann, Hudson River Mus, Yonkers, NY, 87; Int Miniature Print Biennial, Szoke Gallery, New York, 89; Soc Am Graphic Artists Exhib, Ringling Sch Art, Sarasota, Fla, 90; 1990 Sixty Square Inches Exhib, Purdue Univ Galleries, West Lafayette, Ind, 90; Int Miniature Print Biennial, Susan Teller Gallery, New York, 91; Current Am Printmaking: SAGA, Sordoni Art Gallery, Wilkes-Barre, Pa, 91. *Pos:* Co-chmn graphics, 88- Pen & Brush, New York & corresp secy, 92-94; treas, Soc Am Graphic Artists, 88- *Awards:* Purchase Prize, Nat Print Exhib, Trenton State Col, 82; Philip Isenberg Award, Pen & Brush Ann Graphics, 91; E Weyhe Gallery Purchase Award, SAGA 64th Nat, 91. *Bibliog:* Malcolm Preston (auth), Art Reviews: Port Washington Library, Newsday, Long Island, NY, 11/11/82; Diane Heilenman (auth), Art Reviews: Loho Gallery, Courier-J, Louisville, Ky, 3/3/85; Joseph Merkel (auth), Finding meaning in every day subjects, Artspeak, New York, summer 90. *Mem:* Nat Asn Women Artists Inc; Salmagundi Club; Special Libr Asn; Pen & Brush. *Media:* Woodcut, Linocut. *Mailing Add:* 20 E Ninth St No 18C New York NY 10003

TRUETTNER, WILLIAM H
CURATOR
Pos: Cur eighteenth and nineteenth century painting & sculpture, Nat Collection Fine Arts, currently. *Mailing Add:* Nat Mus Am Art 8th & G Sts NW Washington DC 20560

TRUEX, DUANE PHILIP, III
EDUCATOR, CONSULTANT
b Syracuse, NY, Aug 30, 47. *Study:* Ithaca Col, Sch Mus, BFA, 69; Okla State Univ; State Univ NY, Binghamton, MBA, 84, PhD, 91. *Collections Arranged:* Treasure House: Museums of the Empire State (catalog), 79, Charles Eldred: Drawing and Sculpture (catalog), 80 & Emil Holzhauer: 75 Years Retrospective Exhibition (catalog), 80, Roberson Ctr Arts & Sci; Susquehanna: Images of The Settled Landscape (catalog), 81; Ancient Inspirations, Contemporary Interpretations (catalog), 83-84. *Pos:* Dir pub rels, Kansas City Philharmonic, 72-73; exec dir, Baton Rouge Symphony, La, 73-76, dir, Arts & Humanities Coun Greater Baton Rouge, 73-78 & Roberson Ctr Arts & Sci, Binghamton, NY, 78-83. *Teaching:* Vis lectr, Russell Sage Col, NY; lectr, State Univ NY Binghamton Sch of Management, dir arts administration prog. *Mem:* Comn, Archit & Urban Design, City of Binghampton; Asn Computing Machinery; Int Fedn Info Processing, 82. *Res:* The properties of emergent systems development in non-profit organizations; the application of national planning method, to non-profit organizations. *Publ:* Contribr, Financial Accountability for community arts agencies, 75 & Common services of the community arts council, 78, Am Coun Arts; Planning: Challenges, Opportunities, Paradoxes, Roberson Ctr Arts & Sci, 79; A review of energy management in museums and historical agencies, Mus News, 8/83; Decision Supports Systems in Museums, 84; and others. *Mailing Add:* 14 Narwood St Johnson City NY 13790-3020

TRUITT, ANNE (DEAN)
SCULPTOR
b Baltimore, Md, Mar 16, 21. *Study:* Bryn Mawr Col, BA, 43; Inst Contemp Art, Washington, DC, 48-49; Dallas Mus Fine Arts, 50; Hon Degree, Corcoran Sch Art, Washington, DC, St Mary's Col, Md, Kansas City Art Inst, Maryland Inst Art. *Work:* Walker Art Ctr; Nat Mus Am Art & Nat Gallery Art, Washington, DC; Mus Mod Art; Whitney Mus Am Art. *Exhib:* One-artist shows, Andre Emmerich Gallery, 63, 65, 69, 75, 80 & 86, Baltimore Mus Art, 69 & 74, Pyramid Gallery, 71-73, 75-77 & 79, Whitney Mus Am Art, 74, Corcoran Gallery Art, 74, Osuna Gallery, Washington, DC, 79, 81, 86 & 89, C Grimaldis, Baltimore, 92, Weatherspoon Art Gallery, 92 & Bryn Mawr Col, 92. *Teaching:* Emer prof, Univ Md. *Awards:* Guggenheim Fel, 71; Nat Endowment Arts Fel, 72 & 77; Australia Arts Coun Grant, 81. *Bibliog:* Gregory Battcock (auth), Minimal Art, A Critical Anthology, Dutton, 68; Clement Greenberg (auth), Anne Truitt: American artist, Vogue, 68; Eleanor Munro (auth), Originals: American Women Artists, Simon & Schuster, 79; and others. *Mem:* Acad Arts, Easton, Md (bd of dirs). *Media:* Wood, Acrylic. *Publ:* Auth, Daybook: The Journal of an Artist, Pantheon Bks, 82 & Penguin Bks, 84; Turn: The Journal of an Artist, Viking Penguin, Inc, 86 & Penguin Books, 87. *Dealer:* Andre Emmerich 41 E 57th St New York NY 10022; Osuna Gallery 1919 Q St NW Washington DC 20036. *Mailing Add:* 3506 35th St NW Washington DC 20016

TRUMBLE, BEVERLY (JANE)
PAINTER
b Milwaukee, Wis. *Study:* Univ Colo, 60; Art Students League, 76-83; Daniel E Greene Workshop, 84. *Work:* Nationwide Cellular Serv Inc, Valley Stream, NY; Strategic Resource Group Inc, East Norwalk, Conn. *Comn:* Jason (pastel portrait), Mr & Mrs Gerald Sanders, Larchmont, NY, 84; Vicky & Chad Odell (oil portrait), Mr & Mrs Kenneth Thornburg, Foresthill, Calif, 86; oil portrait, Terri & Jerry (oil portrait), Mr & Mrs Forrest Newton, Littleton, Colo, 86; 4 residence paintings, Mr & Mrs Thomas Keller, White Plains, 90; Brian (oil portrait), Lt Col & Mrs Orville Hays, Breckenridge, Colo, 91. *Exhib:* Nat Open Exhib, Mamaroneck Artists Guild, NY, 85, 86, 88; Oil Pastel Int, Pen & Brush Inc, New York, 86; Pastel Soc Am, 17th Ann Open, Nat Arts Club, New York, 89; A Meeting of Opposites, Int House Gallery, New York, 89; Pleiades & Friends, Pleiades Gallery, New York, 88, 89. *Collections Arranged:* WSAC, Broadway Mall Gallery (coauth, catalog), 87-88; Riverside Arts Festival, City of New York, 88; Westside Arts Coalition (auth, catalog), Lever House Gallery, 88; Premiere Soho Exhib (auth, catalog), West Side Artists Pleiades, 88; Painting & Sculpture-WSAC, Pen & Brush, 89. *Pos:* Mem nominating comt, NY Artist Equity & West Side Arts Coalition, NY, 86-87; tour guide Artists Studios, West Side Arts Coalition, New York, 88-90; speaker, Organizing Bus Side Art, West Side Arts Ctr, 89. *Awards:* Solo Exhib Award, Pen & Brush Inc, 85; Artist Guild Award, Mamaroneck Artist Guild, 88; First Prize, Summit Co Arts Coun, 92. *Bibliog:* Anthony White (dir), West Side Artists (film), 86; Doris Berkman (auth), Channel 5, Big Apple Minute, Channel 5 TV, 2/87; Channel 10, Paragon Cable TV, 2/4/87 & 10/11/88. *Mem:* Pastel Soc Am; Pen and Brush Inc (co-chair pastel section, 89-91); West Side Arts Coalition (sec, 85-86, visual co-chair, 87-88); New York Artist's Equity; Metrop Painters & Sculptors. *Media:* Oil, Pastel. *Mailing Add:* PO Box 1908 Silverthorne CO 80498

TRUPP, BARBARA LEE
PAINTER, PRINTMAKER
b Scottsbluff, Nebr, Nov 17, 50. *Study:* Studied with Ilda Lubane, Banff Ctr Arts, Alta, Can, 68-70; Univ Puget Sound, Tacoma, Wash, 69-70; Univ Mich, Ann Arbor, BFA, 71-74. *Work:* Ill State Mus, Springfield; Fermi Nat Accelorator Lab, US Dept Energy, Batavia, Ill; Ore State Mus, Portland; Am Mus, Bath, Eng; Banff Ctr Arts, Alta, Can; Mary & Leigh Block Gallery, NWestern Univ, Evanston, Ill; Krannert Mus, Univ Ill, Champaign; Ruttenberg Art Found, Chicago, Ill; Univ Nev, Reno. *Exhib:* Selections from the Permanent Collection, Banff Ctr, traveling throughout Can, 75; Int Festival of Women Artists, NY Carlsberg Glyptotek Mus, Copenhagen, Denmark, 80; New Nat Talents with Printing, Sykes Gallery, Millersville, Pa, 82; 2nd Ann Great Lakes Show, Ill St Gallery, Chicago, Ill, 88; Chicago Int New Art Forms Expos, Navy Pier, Chicago, Ill, 88, 90 & 92; Selections from Permanent Collection, Ill State Mus, Springfield, Ill, 88-89; Am & Int Craft Exhib, World Trade Ctr, Boston, Mass, 90; Multiple Images, Ill State Mus, Springfield, 91. *Teaching:* Instr ceramics, Evanston Art Ctr, 87- *Mem:* Chicago Artist's Coalition; Midwest Clay Guild; Evanston Art Ctr. *Media:* Acrylic, Oil; Lithography. *Dealer:* Citywoods 659 Central Ave Highland Park IL 60035; Ill Artisan's Shop 100 W Randolph Chicago IL 60601. *Mailing Add:* 636 Hinman #3E Evanston IL 60202

TRUTTY-COOHILL, PATRICIA
EDUCATOR, HISTORIAN
b Uniontown, Pa. *Study:* Univ Toronto, BA, 62, Pa State Univ, MA, 68, PhD, 82. *Pos:* Assoc prof art hist, Western Ky Univ, 83- *Teaching:* Lectr, art dept, Western Ky Univ, 80-82, asst prof, 82-86, assoc prof, 86- *Mem:* Col Art Asn; Renaissance Soc Am; Leonardo Soc. *Res:* School of Leonardo da Vinci. *Publ:* Auth, La Eminentia in Antonello da Messina, Anticita Viva, 82; Narrative to icon: The San Diego Martha and Mary, Vol I, The Formation of the American Collection of Drawings by Leonado, Vol II & The Spanish Connection: The Bowling Green Mona Lisa, Vol III, Achademia Leonardi Vinci; coauth (with Carlo Pedretti), The Drawings of Leonardo da Vinci and his Circle in America, Giunti-Barbera (in press). *Mailing Add:* Art Dept Western Ky Univ Bowling Green KY 42101

TSAI, HSIAO HSIA
PAINTER, SCULPTOR
b China; US citizen. *Study:* Nat Col Art China, BFA; Univ Okla, MFA(scholar); Hamilton State Univ, Hon PhD, 78. *Exhib:* White Mus, San Antonio, 65, 66 & 80; Jess Besser Mus, Pensacola Art Ctr, 75; Everhart Mus, Pa, 75; Dallas Mus Fine Arts, 76; Brick Stone Mus, 77; Corpus Christi Mus, 78-81; and many others. *Awards:* Medal, Am Watercolor Soc New York, 64 & 68; Watercolor Abstract Art Ctr, Tex, 74 & 76-77; Nat Asn Women Artists, New York, 83; Gold Medal, Italy Competition, 83; Corpus Christi Mus Award, 86; and many others. *Mem:* Hon mem Int Asn Art. *Publ:* Principles Chinese Painting Adapted to Modern Needs and Treaties, Mustard Seed Garden Treaties; articles in Today's Art, Arts Mag, Art News, J Am, New York & Sund Mag, Houston. *Mailing Add:* Hsiao-Hsia Tsai Gallery Fine Art 1437 Casa Verde Dr Corpus Christi TX 78411

TSAI, WEN-YING
SCULPTOR, PAINTER
b Xiamen, China, Oct 13, 28; US citizen. *Study:* Univ Mich, ME, 53; Art Students League, 53-57; grad fac polit & social sci, New Sch Social Res, 56-58. *Work:* Tate Gallery, London; Centre Nat d'Art Contemporain, Paris; Kaiser Wilhem Mus, Krefeld, Ger; Albright-Knox Art Gallery, Buffalo, NY; Whitney Mus Am Art, New York. *Comn:* Gloucester Tower (cybernetic water sculpture), Palmer & Turner Archits, Hong Kong, 80; Raffles Tower Fountain, Singapore Land Pte Ltd, Singapore, 82; Dancing Menorah with Lotus, Israel Mus, Jerusalem, 82; Spatial Dynamic Hydro-Cybernetic Systs, Musée National des Science, des Techniques et des Industries, La Villette, Paris, 86. *Exhib:* One-man shows, Hayden Gallery, Mass Inst of Technol, Cambridge, Corcoran Gallery of Art, Washington, DC, Musee d'Art Contemporain, Montreal, Que, Hong Kong Mus Art, 79, Isetan Mus, Tokyo, 80 & Nat Mus Hist, Taipei, Taiwan, 89; group shows, The Responsive Eye, 65 & The Machine Show, 68, Mus Mod Art, New York; Cybernetic Serendipity, Inst Contemp Arts, London, 68; 3rd Salon Int Galeries Pilotes, Mus Cantonal Beaux Arts, Lausanne, Switz, 70; Pittsburgh Int, Carnegie Inst Mus Art, 70; Electra-1983, Musee D'Art Moderne, Paris, 83; 42nd Int Exhib Art, La Biennale di Venezia, 86; Computer Art, IBM Gallery Sci & Art, New York, 88; Images Du Futur 90, Montreal, 90; Artec 91, Int Biennale, Nagoya, 91. *Pos:* Proj eng, Guy B Panero Engineers, New York, 56-60; proj mgr, Cosentini Assocs Engineers, New York, 62-63. *Awards:* Ctr Advan Visual Studies Fel, Mass Inst Technol, 69-71; design in steel award, Am Iron & Steel Inst, 71; Artec Grand Prix, 91. *Bibliog:* Art for tomorrow-the 21st century, produced on CBS-TV, 69; Jonathan Benthall (auth), Cybernetic sculpture of Tsai, Studio Int, 3/69; Fred Barzyk (auth), Video variations (with Boston Symphony Orchestra), produced on WGBH-TV, 71; Art & Sci-Innovation (film), WNET-TV, 88. *Media:* Water, Fiber Optics, Fiberglass and Stainless Steel. *Dealer:* Galerie Denise Rene Paris. *Mailing Add:* 565 Broadway New York NY 10012

TSE, STEPHEN
PAINTER, EDUCATOR
b Hong Kong, Oct 20, 38; US citizen. *Study:* Washburn Univ, Topeka, Kans, BFA; Univ Idaho, MFA; also with Jack Tworkov. *Work:* Wenatchee Valley Col, Wash; Yakima Valley Col, Wash; Spokane Falls Community Col, Wash; Rainier Nat Bank, Olympia, Wash; First Nat Bank Idaho, Boise; Seattle First Nat Bank; Mus Art, Eugene, Ore; Univ Ore, Eugene, Ore; many others. *Comn:* Sculpture panels with painting, Student Union, Univ Idaho, 65. *Exhib:* One-man shows, Gallery-76, Wenatchee Valley Col, Wash, 78 & Kirsten Gallery, Seattle, 77, 78, 80, 82 & 85, Prichard Art Gallery, Univ Idaho, 86 & Still Water Art Gallery, Seattle, 91; Nat Painting Exhib, Grover M Hermann Fine Art Ctr, Marietta Col, Ohio, 79; Nat Small Painting Purchase Exhib, Western Ill Univ, Macomb, 79; Compton Gallery, Wash State Univ, Pullman, 83; and many others. *Teaching:* Chmn art dept, Big Bend Community Col, 66- *Awards:* Painting Award, 28th Ann Centennial Wash Artist Exhib, Larson Gallery, Yakima, 84; Merit Award, Carnegie Ctr, Walla Walla, Wash, 85 & 87; Painting Award, Carnegie Ctr, Walla Walla, Wash, 90. *Mem:* Wash Art Asn; Oriental Ceramic Soc, London. *Media:* Oil and Watercolor; Clay. *Dealer:* Kirsten Gallery 5320 Roosevelt Way NE Seattle WA 98105. *Mailing Add:* 957 S Garden Dr Moses Lake WA 98837

TSELOS, DIMITRI THEODORE
HISTORIAN, WRITER
b Kerasea, Greece, Apr 10, 1900; US citizen. *Study:* Univ Chicago, PhB, 26, MA, 28; Princeton Univ, Carnegie Found Scholar, 28-32, MA, 29, MFA, 31, PhD, 33; Inst Fine Arts, NY Univ, with Richard Offner & Walter Cook, 29-30; also with Charles R Morey. *Teaching:* From instr medieval & mod art to assoc prof, Inst Fine Arts, NY Univ, 31-49; lectr mod art, Swarthmore Col, 37-41, Univ Southern Calif, summers 37-41 & Vassar Col, 42-43; vis prof, Bryn Mawr Col, 44-46; prof art, Univ Minn, 49-71, prof emer & consult, 71-; distinguished vis prof, Northwestern Univ, 77. *Awards:* Fulbright Res Grants, Greece, 55-56 & 63-64. *Mem:* Col Art Asn Am; Archaeol Inst Am; Soc Archit Historians; Am Asn Univ Prof; Minn Hist Soc. *Res:* Medieval painting; modern architecture; modern Greek art. *Publ:* Auth, Exotic influences in the architecture of F L Wright, Mag Art, 53; The sources of the Utrecht psalter miniatures, 55; Modern illustrated books, 59; Defensive addenda on the origins of the Utrecht psalter, Art Bull, 67; F L Wright and world architecture, J Archit Historians, 69. *Mailing Add:* 1666 Coffman St No 332 St Paul MN 55108

TSENG YU-HO
PAINTER, HISTORIAN
b Peking, China, Nov 29, 24; US citizen. *Study:* Fu-jen Univ, Peking, BA, 42; Univ Hawaii, MA, 66; Inst Fine Arts, NY Univ, PhD, 72. *Work:* Honolulu Acad Arts, Hawaii; Walker Art Ctr, Minneapolis; Nat Mus Mod Art, Stockholm, Sweden; Mus Cernuschi, Paris, France; Stanford Art Gallery, Calif. *Comn:* Mural, St Katherine's Church, Kaui, Hawaii, 57; mural, Manoa Chinese Pavilion, Honolulu, 68; mural, Golden West Savings & Loan, San Francisco, Calif, 64; wall painting, Castle & Cooke Co, Ltd, Honolulu, 68; wall painting, Honolulu Int Airport, 72. *Exhib:* Contemporary American Painting & Sculpture, Univ Ill, Urbana, 58, 61 & 65; Carnegie Inst Painting & Sculpture Int, Pittsburgh, Pa, 61 & 65; Kunstverein, Munich & Frankfurt, Ger; Walker Art Ctr; San Francisco Mus Art, Calif; and others. *Teaching:* Instr studio art, Honolulu Acad Art, 50-63, consult Chinese art, 53-; assoc prof Chinese art hist, Univ Hawaii, 63-66; prog chmn art hist, Univ Hawaii, 71-, prof art, 73- *Awards:* Am Artists of the Western States Award, Stanford Art Gallery; NY Univ Founders Day Award for Outstanding Scholarship, 72. *Bibliog:* Article, Time Mag, 1/19/62; Seldis (auth), Pacific heritage, Art in Am, 65. *Mem:* Am Col Art Asn; Asian Soc; Asian & Pacific Art Asn Hawaii (organizer, 72). *Media:* Watercolor, Collage. *Res:* Chinese art; the Art of Chinese folding fan; folk art. *Publ:* Contribr, four articles, Studies of 16th Century Chinese Artists, 54-63; contribr, Encyclopedia World Art, Rome, 64; auth, Some Contemporary Elements on Chinese Classic Pictorial Art, 65 & 71; illusr, The Analects of Confucious, 70. *Mailing Add:* 1024 Kamehame Dr Honolulu HI 96825

TSUTAKAWA, GEORGE
SCULPTOR, PAINTER
b Seattle, Wash, Feb 22, 10. *Study:* With Alexander Archipenko, 36; Univ Wash Sch Art, BFA, 36, MFA, 50; Seattle Univ, DHH, 86; Whitman Col, Hon DFA, 86. *Work:* Seattle Art Mus, Wash; Denver Art Mus, Colo; Santa Barbara Mus Art; Univ Calif, Los Angeles; Govt Ctr, Toledo, Ohio. *Comn:* Fountain sculpture, Washington Nat Cathedral, Washington, DC, 68; fountain sculpture, Pa State Univ, 74; hanging fountain sculpture, King Broadcasting Corp, Seattle, Wash, 81; fountain sculpture, Tsutsujigaoka Park, Sendai, Japan, 81; and others. *Exhib:* 3rd Biennial, Sao Paulo, Brazil, 55; San Francisco Painting & Sculpture Ann, San Francisco Mus Art, 55, 58 & 60; Int Art Festival, Amerika Haus, Berlin, Ger, 66; Pacific NW Artists, 82; Japan Nat Mus, Osaka, 82; Seattle Art Mus, 85. *Teaching:* Prof art, Univ Wash, 46-80, emer prof art, 80- *Awards:* Cult Award, Order of Rising Sun, Emperor Japan, 81; Alumnus Summa Laude Dignatus, Univ Wash, 84; and others. *Bibliog:* Ben Forgey (auth), A new vision: public places with sculpture, Smithsonian Mag, 10/75; Charles Cowles & Martha Kingsbury (auths), Northwest Tradition, Seattle Art Mus, 78; Gerald Nordland (auth), Franklin D Murphy Sculpture Garden, Univ Calif, Los Angeles, 78; Masayoshi Homma (auth), Exhib of Tsutakawa Fountain Sculptures, Sendai, Japan, 81; Chuo Koron-Sha (auth), Sculpture in Public Places, Contemp Sculpture Ctr, Tokyo, 83; and others. *Media:* Bronze; Watercolor. *Mailing Add:* 3116 S Irving St Seattle WA 98144

TUBIS, SEYMOUR
PAINTER, PRINTMAKER
b Philadelphia, Pa, Sept 20, 19. *Study:* Temple Univ; Philadelphia Mus Sch; Art Students League; with Georges Braque; Acad Grande Chaumiere, Paris; Inst d'Arte, Florence, Italy; also with Hans Hofmann. *Work:* Metrop Mus Art, New York; Libr Cong & Georgetown Univ, Washington, DC; Univ Calgary, Alta; US Dept of State, Washington, DC & Embassies in Asia, Europe & Africa. *Comn:* Mural, US Army Signal Corps Sch, Camp Crowder, Mo, 43; drawings, World Premiere, Yerma, Santa Fe Opera, NMex, 71. *Exhib:* Nat Exhib Prints, Drawings & Watercolors, Metrop Mus Art, 52; 40 Prints, Univ Calgary, Alta, 67; Int Exhib Graphics, Seattle Art Mus, 68 Discovery Gallery, Santa Fe, NMex, 75; Retrospective, 30 Years of Printmaking, Cody Gallery, Santa Fe, NMex, 80; Drawings & Paintings, Warner Roberts Gallery, Palo Alto, Calif, 81; Retrospective, Pacific Grove Art Ctr, Calif, 83-90; Apocalyse Drawings, Paintings, Sculpture, Bluecreek/ West Gallery, Denver, 89; Prints, Asn Am Artists, New York, 84-90. *Pos:* Artist-designer, New York Times, 59-62. *Teaching:* Instr painting & printmaking, Art Students League, New York, 48; lectr & instr painting, Adult Educ, New York City Bd Educ, 50-51; instr painting, design & graphic arts, Inst Am Indian Arts, 62, chmn dept fine arts, 65-80. *Awards:* Fourth Purchase Award in painting, Joe & Emily Lowe Found, 50; First Prize in watercolor, Mus NMex, 75; Nat Endowment Arts Grant, 80. *Bibliog:* Michelle Seuiere (auth), Les expositions Seymour Tubis, Paris-Opera, 7/26/50; John MacGregor (auth), Seymour Tubis experiments with printmaking, Pasatiempo, Santa Fe, 8/27/67; Martha Buddeke (auth), Seymour Tubis takes two directions, J Arts, Albuquerque J, 11/21/71. *Mem:* Life mem Art Students League; Soc Am Graphic Artists; Col Art Asn Am. *Media:* Oil, Intaglio, Bronze, Wood. *Publ:* Contribr, 72nd Ann, Royal Soc Painters, Etchers & Engravers, 54; Western Review, Western NMex Univ, 66; Indian painters and white patrons, El Palacio, 71. *Dealer:* Tobey C Moss Gallery 7321 Beverly Blvd Los Angeles CA 90036; Associated American Artists 20 W 57th St New York NY 10019. *Mailing Add:* 1531 S Flamingo Way Denver CO 80222-3909

TUCHMAN, MAURICE
MUSEUM CURATOR
b Jacksonville, Fla, Nov 30, 36. *Study:* Nat Univ Mex; City Col New York, BA, 57; Columbia Univ, MA, 59. *Collections Arranged:* Five Younger Calif Artists, 65; Edward Kienholz, 66; Irwin-Price, 66; John Mason, 66; Am Sculpture of 60's (with catalog), 67; Soutine (with catalog), 68; Art & Technol (with catalog), 71; European Paintings in the 70's (with catalog), 75; Richard Diebenkorn: Paintings and Drawings, 77; Italo Scanga, 83; Susan Rothenberg, 83; The Artist as Social Designer: Aspects of Public Art Today, 85; in prep: Hidden Meanings in Modern Art: Abstract Painting and Mysticism, 1891-1986, 86; David Hockney A Retrospective, Metrop Mus Art, New York, 88

& Tate Gallery, London, 88. *Pos:* Art ed mod art sect, Columbia Encycl, 62; mem curatorial & lect staff, Guggenheim Mus, 62-64, organizer, summer 64; sr cur mod art, Los Angeles Co Mus Art, 64- *Awards:* Fulbright Scholar, 60-61. *Mem:* Am Arts Alliance, (bd dir, 77-80); Nat Endowment Arts, 77-79; Am Fedn Arts; Los Angeles Design Alliance, (bd gov, 84); Int Adv Comt, Mus Art Carnegie Inst, 85. *Publ:* Contribr, Richard Diebenkorn: the early years, Vol XXXVI, No 3, Art J; A talk with Avigador Arikha, Vol XXI, No 3, Art Int; Artists look at Los Angeles, Am Illus, 6/84. *Mailing Add:* Los Angeles Co Mus Art 5905 Wilshire Blvd Los Angeles CA 90036

TUCHMAN, PHYLLIS
HISTORIAN, CRITIC
b Passaic, NJ, Jan 4, 47. *Study:* Sarah Lawrence Col Summer Session in Florence, 67; Boston Univ, BA(distinction in fine arts), 68; Inst of Fine Arts, NY Univ, MA, 73, with Robert Goldwater, Robert Rosenblum & William S Rubin. *Collections Arranged:* Six in Bronze, Williams Col Mus Art, 84; Big Little Sculpture, Williams Col Mus Art, 88; Venezuela: The Next Generation, Baruch Col Gallery, 90; Drawing Redux, San Jose Mus Art, 92. *Pos:* Mem ed bd, Marsyas, New York, 71-74; pres Am section, Int Asn Art Critics, 86-90, vpres, Int AICA (parent body) 89-91; vpres, Art Table, 87-88. *Teaching:* Instr art hist, Sch of Visual Arts, New York, 72-75; adj lectr art hist, Hunter Col, 76-79; vis prof art, Williams Col, 81-83. *Awards:* Nat Endowment for Arts art critic's grant, 78-79; Nat Endowment Humanities fel, 80. *Mem:* AICA; Art Table; Col Art Asn. *Publ:* Auth, George Segal, Abbeville Press, 83. *Mailing Add:* 340 E 80th St New York NY 10021

TUCHOLKE, CHRISTEL-ANTHONY (CHRISTEL E STOEVEKEN)
PAINTER
b Poland, March 2, 41; US citizen. *Study:* Univ Wis, Milwaukee, BS, 64 & MS, 65; Tamarind Lithography Workshop, Los Angeles, 68. *Work:* Milwaukee Art Mus, Wis; Miller Brewing Company Headquarters, Milwaukee, Wis; Charles Wustum Mus Art, Racine, Wis; Bradley Univ, Peoria, Ill; Kans State Univ Art Mus, Manhattan, Kans. *Comn:* Exterior Mural, John Michael Kohler Art Ctr, Sheboygan, Wis, 77; four paintings, Northwestern Mutual Life Insurance Company, Milwaukee, Wis, 79; Telephone Book Cover, Wis Telephone Company, 81; Mural, Percent for Art Prog, Wis Art Bd, 85; Artists Limited Editions, Kohler Co, Wis, 89. *Exhib:* Drawings USA, Minn Mus Art, St Paul, 75; 74th, 76th, 77th, & 80th Exhibs by Artists of Chicago & Vicinity, Chicago Art Inst, Ill, 73, 77, 78, & 84; Wis Directions Two, Milwaukee Art Mus, 78; Wis Biennale, Madison Art Ctr, 80 & 82; State of the Art: Wisconsin Painting and Drawing, J Michael Kohler Art Ctr, Sheboygan, Wis, 82; Belk Gallery, Western Carolina Univ, NC, 85; Wis-Minn Interface, Minn Mus Art, St Paul, Minn & Milwaukee Art Mus, 86; and others. *Awards:* Top Award, Madison Art Ctr, 80; Purchase Award, Wright Art Ctr, 80; Purchase Award, Bradley Univ, 81; Purchase Award, Wustum Mus, 85 & 89. *Media:* Acrylic, Pastel. *Dealer:* Edgewood Orchard Galleries Fish Creek WI 54212. *Mailing Add:* 5074 North Hollywood Ave Whitefish Bay WI 53217

TUCK, NORMAN VICTOR
KINETIC ARTIST, SCULPTOR
b Lebanon, Pa, Aug 14, 45. *Study:* Univ Fla, with Geoffrey Naylor, BFA, 67; Pa State Univ, MFA, 72. *Work:* Science Mus Minn, St Paul; New York Hall Sci, Queens, NY; Sci Mus Barcelona, Spain. *Comn:* Lariat Chain, Exploratorium, San Francisco, 87; Lariat Chain II, Sci Mus Hong Kong, 89; Pendulum Clock, Exploratorium, San Francisco, 89; Ch-Ch-Ch Chainges, Technorama, Winterthur, Switz, 90. *Exhib:* solo Exhib, Art Galaxy, New York, 84 & Mindless Mechanisms, Southeastern Ctr Contemp Art, Winston-Salem, NC, 91; Labor Intensive Abstraction, Clock Tower, New York, 84; Mechanisms, PS-1, Queens, NY, 84; Clockwork, List Art Ctr-MIT, Cambridge, Mass, 88. *Pos:* Gallery dir, Wake Forest Univ Art Gallery, 80-81; artists-in-residence, New York Hall Sci, 86; artist-in-residence, Exploratorium, San Francisco, 87 & 89. *Teaching:* Asst prof sculpture, Wake Forest Univ, Winston-Salem, NC, 85-86; instr sculpture, Univ Minn, Minneapolis, 78-79. *Bibliog:* Jeffrey Wechsler (auth, catalog), Norman Tuck, Rutgers Univ Art Gallery, 78; Michael Brewson (auth), Norman Tuck, NY Times, 85; Richard Craven (auth, catalog), Mindless Mechanisms, Southeastern Ctr Contemp Art, 92; Margaret Shearin (auth), Art Machines, City Gallery, Raleigh, NC, 92. *Media:* Kinetic Sculpture. *Mailing Add:* 316 Glori Ave Winston-Salem NC 27127

TUCKER, ANNE WILKES
CURATOR, HISTORIAN
b Baton Rouge, La, Oct 18, 45. *Study:* Randolph-Macon Women's Col, Lynchburg Va, BA(art hist), 67; Rochester Inst of Technol, AAS(photog), 68; Visual Studies Workshop, MFA, photo hist and mus procedure with Nathan Lyons & Beaumont Newhall, 70. *Collections Arranged:* American Prospects: The Photographs of Joel Sternfeld (travelling), 87, Evocative Presence: Twentieth-Century Photographs in the Museum Collection, 88, American Classroom: The Photographs of Catherine Wagner (travelling), 88, The Private Eye, 89, Czeck Modernism 1900-1945 (travelling), 89 & Money Matters: A Critical Look at Bank Architecture (travelling), 90, Houston Mus Fine Arts, Tex. *Pos:* Res asst, Int Mus Photogr, George Eastman House, Rochester, NY, 68-70; res assoc, Gernsheim Collection, Univ Tex, Austin, 69 & 79; cur intern, NY State Coun Art Grant, Photogr Dept, Mus Mod Art, NY, 70-71; photogr consult, Creative Artists Pub Serv Prog, New York, 71-72; dir, Photo Lecture Series, Cooper Union Forum, New York, 72-75; cur photogr, Mus Fine Arts, Houston, Tex, 76-, Gus & Lyndall Wortham cur, 84- *Teaching:* Vis lectr, New Sch Soc Research, New York, spring 73 & Philadelphia Col Art, 73-75; lectr, Cooper Union Advan Arts & Sci, New York, 72-75; affliate artist, Univ Houston, Tex, 76-80. *Awards:* Guggenheim Fel, 83; Nat Endowment Arts, 76, 86 & 90. *Mem:* Soc Photog Educ (secy, 77-79); Col Art Asn; Visual Studies Wkshp (bd trustees, 80-); Visual Arts Panel, Houston Fest, 81-83; Randolph-Macon Woman's Col Art Gallery (adv bd, 82-84); Art Table, Inc, 83- *Res:* Concentrated on 20th century American photographs. *Interests:* Absences and gaps in current photographic history. *Publ:* The Blue Man'a Photographs, Rice Univ Press, 90; Czeck Modernism 1900-1945, Bolfinch Press & Mus Fine Arts, Houston, 90; Money Matters: A Critical Look at Bank Architecture, McGraw-Hill & Mus Fine Arts, Houston, 90; Carry Me Home, Smithsonian Press, 90; George Krause, Rice Univ Press, 92; and others. *Mailing Add:* Mus of Fine Arts 1001 Bissonnet Houston TX 77005

TUCKER, CHARLES CLEMENT
PAINTER
b SC, Sept 13, 13. *Study:* Art Students League, scholar & with Frank Vincent DuMond, Ivan G Olinsky & George B Bridgman. *Work:* Univ NC, Chapel Hill; Duke Univ; Mint Mus, Charlotte, NC; 4th Circuit Ct Appeals, Richmond Fed Bldg, Va; plus many others. *Comn:* Oil portraits, comn by James Francis Byrnes, James P Richards, Mrs O Max Gardener, Allie Murray Smith & Dr Mary & Matin Sloop. *Exhib:* Metrop Mus Art, 42, Nat Acad Design, 50, Coun Am Artist Socs, 66, Hudson Valley Art Asn, 68-72 & Allied Artist Am, 71-72. *Awards:* First Award, NC Nat Exhib, 58 & 59; Dirs Award, Coun Am Artist Soc, 66; Artist of Year, Charlotte-Mecklenburg Bi-Centennial, 68. *Bibliog:* Legette Blythe (auth), Miracle in the Hills, McGraw, 53 & Call Down the Storm, Holt, 58; Works of Art, US Capitol. *Mem:* Allied Artist Am; Hudson Valley Art Asn; life mem Art Students League; Am Artist Prof League. *Media:* All media. *Mailing Add:* 3621 Arborway Dr Charlotte NC 28211

TUCKER, JAMES EWING
CURATOR, PAINTER
b Rule, Tex, Aug 13, 30. *Study:* Midwestern Univ; Univ Tex, Austin, BFA; Univ Iowa, MFA. *Work:* NC State Univ, Raleigh; Weatherspoon Art Gallery; Miller Brewing Co; Pine Bluff Art Ctr, Ark; Witte Mus, San Antonio. *Collections Arranged:* Art on Paper, Cone Collection & Dillard Collection, Weatherspoon Art Gallery, 65- *Pos:* Cur, Weatherspoon Art Gallery, 59-, ed, Bulletin, 65- *Media:* Mixed. *Dealer:* Ingber Gallery 460 West Broadway New York NY 10012. *Mailing Add:* 632 Scott Ave Greensboro NC 27403

TUCKER, LEATRICE YVONNE See Edwards-Tucker, Yvonne (Leatrice Yvonne Tucker)

TUCKER, MARCIA
MUSEUM DIRECTOR, CURATOR
b New York, NY, Apr 11, 40. *Study:* Ecole du Louvre & Acad Grande Chaumiere, Paris, France, 59-60; Conn Col, BA(fine arts), 61; NY Univ Inst Fine Arts, MA, 69; San Francisco Art Inst, Hon Dr, 5/83. *Exhib:* New Mus Contemp Art, 77-91; Choices: Making an Art of Everyday Life, 86; Pat Steir, Self-Portrait: An Installation, 87; The Other Man: Alternative Representations of Masculinity (brochure & essay), 87; Markus Raetz: In the Realm of the Possible, 88; Picture This: An Introduction to Interim, Mary Kelly INTERIM (with Norman Bryson, Griselda Pollok, & Hal Foster), 90; Late 20th Century Still Lifes (work of Manuel Pardo), 91. *Collections Arranged:* Anti-Illusion: Procedures/Materials, 69, Robert Morris, 70 (with catalog), The Structure of Color, 71, James Rosenquist & Bruce Nauman (with catalog), Retrospective Exhibs, 72 & 73, Lee Krasner, Joan Mitchell & Al Held; John Baldessai 1980, Not Just For Laughs: The Art of Subversion, 81; Early work, 82; Earl Staley: 1973-1983, 84; US Comn 41st Venice, Biennale, 84; Choices, 86; Markus Raetz: In the Realm of the Possible (auth, catalog). *Pos:* Cur, William N Copley Collection, 63-66; ed assoc, Art News, 65-69; assoc cur, Whitney Mus Am Art, 69-76; founder & dir, The New Mus, New York, 77- *Teaching:* Instr art, Univ RI, 66-68; instr art, City Univ New York, 67-68; instr art, Sch Visual Arts, 69-73; Columbia Univ Grad Sch Arts & Sci, New York, 77; guest lectr, cols, univs & inst. *Awards:* Skowhegan Governor's Award for Lifetime Service to the Arts, 88; Penny McCall Found Award, 88; Fel, Asian Cult Coun, 89. *Bibliog:* Lisbet Nilson (auth), Coming of age, Artnews, 10/88; Patricia Failing (auth), Gloom at the top, Artnews, 5/89; Marcia Tanner (auth), New Mus Contemp Art, Artweek, 4/23/92. *Mem:* Int Art Critics Asn; Am Asn Mus; Am Asn Mus Dirs (chm external affairs comt, 89-90 & trustee, 90); Am Fedn Mus (adv bd); Art Mus Asn. *Publ:* Auth, Nancy Dwyer makes trubble, Artforum, 11/89; Common ground, Museum News, 7-8/90; introduction, Mary Kelly Interim, New York Mus Contemp Art, 90; Discourses: Conversations in Postmodern Art and Culture & Out There: Marginalization and Contemporary Cultures, The New Mus Contemp Art in conjunction with Mass Inst Technol Press, 90; Out There: Marginalizations and Contemporary Cultures, New Mus Contemp Art & MIT Press, 90. *Mailing Add:* New Mus Contemp Art 583 Broadway New York NY 10012

TUCKER, PERI
WRITER, ILLUSTRATOR
b Kashau, Austria-Hungary, July 25, 11; US citizen. *Study:* Columbus Sch Fine Arts; also with E C Van Swearingen. *Exhib:* one-man show, Fla Gulf Coast Art Ctr, Belleair, Fla, 67; Whiskey Painters of Am Nat Shows (travelling exhib), Akron Art Inst, Ohio, 73, 26 E Art Ctr, Tulsa, Okla, 75, De Colores Gallery, Denver, Colo, 76; Cuyahoga Valley Art Ctr, Cuyahoga Falls, Ohio, 81. *Pos:* Illusr, children's books, Saalfield Publ Co, 38-51; writer & artist, Akron Beacon J, 42-51; writer & artist, St Petersburg Times, 52-66; free-lance writer & artist, 67- *Media:* Watercolor, Ink. *Mailing Add:* 1150 Eighth Ave SW Apt 105 Largo FL 34640-3174

TUCKER, WILLIAM G
SCULPTOR
b Cairo, Egypt, Feb 28, 35; US citizen. *Study:* Oxford Univ, BA(mod Hist), 58; Cent Sch Art at St Martin's Sch Art, London, 59-60. *Work:* Tate Gallery, London; Guggenheim Mus, NY; Mus Mod Art, NY; Metrop Mus Art, NY; Rijksmuseum Kroller-Muller, Otterlo, Holland; Kroller-Muller Mus, Holland; and others. *Comn:* Journey, Dag Hammarskjold Plaza, NY, 82-83; Victory, Doris C Freedman Plaza, NY, 83; Arc & Fear, Springs Mills Building, Citicorp Ctr, NY, 84; Guardian I, St Peter's Church, Citicorp Ctr, NY, 84; Rhea, Greenwich Plaza, Conn, 86. *Exhib:* II Biennale de Paris, Nat Mus Mod Art, Paris, 61; London - The New Scene, Walker Art Ctr, Minneapolis, Minn, 65; Guggenheim International Sculpture Exhibition, Solomon R Guggenheim Mus, NY, 67; Orpheus II, (1965 exhib British Artists) Mus Mod Art, NY, 68; British Painting and Sculpture, 1960-1961, Nat Gallery Art, Washington, DC, 71; Contemporary Sculpture, Mus Mod Art, NY, 79; New York on Paper I, Mus Mod Art, NY, 81; Working in Brooklyn - Sculpture, Brooklyn Mus, NY, 85; Recent Acquisitions, Mus Mod Art, NY, 86; one-man exhibs, Pamela Auchincloss Gallery, Santa Barbara, Calif, 87, Tate Gallery, London, 87, Annely Juda Gallery, London, 87, David McKee Gallery, NY, 87, 89, 91 & 92, The American Decade 1978- 1988, Storm King Art Ctr, Mountainville, NY, 88, Fla Int Univ, Miami, 88, Gallery Paule Anglim, San Francisco, Calif, 89, Williams Ctr Arts, Lafayette Col Art Gallery, Easton, Pa, 92; Innovations in Sculpture, Aldrich Mus, Ridgefield, Conn, 88; From the Southern Cross: A View of World Art, 1940-1988, 1988 Australian Biennale, Art Gallery New South Wales, 88; National Drawing Invitational, Ark Art Gallery, Little Rock, 88; New York Beijing Art Inst (traveling exhib), 88; Drawings, Tomoko Liguori Gallery, NY, 88; Art Mus, Fla Int Univ, Miami, 89; Panicali Fine Art, NY, 92. *Teaching:* Goldsmith's Col, London, 62-66; St Martin's Sch Art, London, 63-74; Univ West Ontario, Can, 76; Nova Scotia Col Art & Design, Halifax, Can, 77; NY Studio Sch Painting & Sculpture, 78-81; Columbia Univ, NY, 78-82. *Awards:* Guggenheim Fel, 80-81; Nat Endowment for the Arts Fed, 86; Sculpture Ctr Award, Distinction in sculpture, 91. *Bibliog:* Bill Berkson (auth), William Tucker (article), Artforum, 9/89; Kenneth Baker (auth), Sculpture in big apple makes heavy statements, San Francisco Chronicle, 10/12/89; Michael Brenson (auth), William Tucker explores the shapes of prehistory, NY Times, 10/13/89. *Media:* Mixed. *Publ:* Auth, Early Modern Sculpture, Oxford Univ Press, 74; articles in Studio Int, Art in Am, Tracks; Steven Henry Madoff, Sculpture: A New Golden Age?, Artnews, 5/91; Helen L Kohen, ArtPark at FIU: Art as part of daily campus life, Miami Herald, 5/5/91; Daniel Wheeler, Art Since Mid Century 1945 to the Present, Vendome Press, New York, 91. *Dealer:* David McKee Gallery 745 5th Ave New York NY 10151. *Mailing Add:* 99 Commercial St Brooklyn NY 11222

TUCKERMAN, JANE BAYARD
PHOTOGRAPHER, EDUCATOR
b Boston, Mass, June 11, 47. *Study:* Art Inst Boston, 68-71; RI Sch Design, MFA, 73-75. *Work:* Metrop Mus Art & Mus Mod Art, New York; Minneapolis Inst Art, Minn; Detroit Inst Arts; Boston Mus Fine Arts; R I Sch of Design; Addison Gallery Am Art; Univ Mass. *Comn:* New Work's Portfolio, Boston Photog Resource Soc, 81. *Exhib:* Solo exhibs, Addison Gallery Am Art, 76 & Photogalerie Pennings, Eindhoven, Holland, 81; Venezia 79, Int Mus, Venice, Italy; Invisible Light, Smithsonian Inst Traveling Exhib, 80-84; Alternative Image, Kohler Arts Ctr, Sheboygan, Wis, 82; Photography Plus, Mus Univ Mo, St Louis, 83; Inst Contemp Art, Boston, 85; Foto Biennale, Enschede, Holland, 85; Witkin Gallery, New York, 86; Dennison Univ Art Gallery, Ohio, 87; Ateneo de Caracas, Venezuala, 90; Photographers on Ellis Island, 1900-1990, Nat Park Ellis Island, 91; An Historical Preview 30 Woman Photographers, Silver Image Gallery, Seattle, 92. *Collections Arranged:* Second Sight: Exhib of Infrared Photog (auth, catalog), traveling in US, Canada & Europe, 81-84. *Teaching:* Asst prof photog, Wellesley Col, 76-77; assoc prof & dir photog prog, Harvard Univ, 78-; guest instr & lectr, Maine Photog Workshop, Rockport, Factory Visual Arts, Seattle, 79; guest instr, Chulalongkoin Univ, Bankok, 85, Yale Univ, 86; vis prof, Northeastern Univ, 90-91; assoc prof, Art Inst Boston, 90- *Awards:* Polaroid Exhib Grant for Second Sight, 81; New Works Fel, Traveling Exhib in New England, Mass Coun Arts & Boston Photog Resource Ctr, 81-82; Individual Artists Fel, Nat Endowment Arts, 82-83; Smithsonian,Nat Endowment Arts, Benares proj, 85; Mass Artists Found Fel, 86. *Bibliog:* Allen Porter (auth), Camera Mag, 74, 80 & 81; Pamela Allara (auth), The scope of Boston art is much broader than it would appear, Art News, 11/81; Photography Year 1982, Time/Life Bks, 82. *Publ:* Contribr, Self Portrayal, Friends Photog, 78; Darkroom Dynamics, Curtain & London, 79; contribr & illusr, American photographer, CBS Publ, 82; contribr, Aperture Mag, 83; The Making of a Collection, Hartwell-Aperture, 85; auth, India: Ritual & the River, Aperture Mag, 87; Invisible Light, Univ Mass, 87. *Dealer:* Witkin Gallery 415 W Broadway New York NY; Pierce St Gallery 217 Pierce St Suite 206 Birmingham MI 48011. *Mailing Add:* Main St Box 399 Dublin NH 03444

TUEGEL, MICHELE B
CRAFTSMAN, ADMINISTRATOR
b Pittsburgh, Pa, Sept 26, 52. *Study:* Univ S Fla, Tampa, MFA, 77; Int Inst Experimental Printmaking, Calif, papermaking cert, 77; independent study at Dieu Donne Paper Mill, Ny, 86. *Work:* Walt Disney World Productions, Orlando, Fla; Barnett Bank Corp Art Collection, Jackson, Tampa & W Palm Beach, Fla. *Comn:* Lobby installation (paper), AmeriFirst Bank, Boca Raton, Fla, 84; paperworks, (diptych), Structured Settlements Inc, St Petersburg, Fla, 85; framed paperworks, SW Bell Telephone Co, St Louis, Mo, 86, Alabama Power Co, Birmingham,, 87, Jewish Hosp, St Louis, 87. *Exhib:* Paper As Medium, Smithsonian Inst, Washington, DC, 78-80; Papermaking & Paper Using, Southeastern Ctr Contemp Art, Winston-Salem, 79; Hands On, Hands Off, N Miami Art Mus, 85; Paper: New & Renewed Art, Tampa Mus, 87; Fine Art of Making Money in Florida, Polk Mus Art, Lakeland, 88. *Pos:* Spec proj coordr, Fla Gulf Coast Art Ctr, Belleair, 83-87; dir, Fla Craftsmen Inc, St Petersburg, 88- *Teaching:* Asst design & silkscreen, Univ S Fla, Tampa, 76-77; workshop leader papermaking, Jacksonville Art Mus, Fla, and other cities, 79-; adj asst prof papermaking, Eckerd Col, St Petersburg, 84-85. *Awards:* Fine Arts Fel, Fla Arts Coun, 86; Friends of the Arts Award, Pinellas Co Arts Coun, 87; Award of Excellence, Fla Craftsmen 36th Ann, Zelo Mag, 87. *Bibliog:* MaryAnn Marger (auth), Fiber Arts, Fiber Arts Mag, 86; Heart on Paper, Creative Ideas for Living Mag, 87. *Mem:* Am Craft Coun; Fla Craftsmen. *Media:* Handmade Paper. *Mailing Add:* 433 Monte Cristo Blvd Tierra Verde FL 33715

TULK, ALFRED JAMES
PAINTER, MURALIST
b London, Eng, Oct 3, 1899; US citizen. *Study:* Oberlin Col; Nat Acad Design, cert; Art Students League, cert; Yale Univ Sch Art, BFA, 23; Inst Bellas Artes, Guanajuato, Mex, MFA, 63. *Work:* Birmingham Mus Art, Ala; Orlando Pub Libr, Fla; Univ Conn, Storrs. *Comn:* Stained glass window, Col WAfrica, Monrovia, Liberia, 40; murals, Salvation Army Hosp, Flushing, NY, 48; Iconastasis, Franciscan Monastery, New Canaan, Conn, 52; mural, D A Long Co Bldg, Hamden, Conn, 59; three murals, Picuris Indian Pueblo, Penasco, NMex, 63. *Exhib:* Burnett Gallery, Amherst, Mass, 74; Post Col, Waterbury, Conn, 75; Albertus Magnus Col, New Haven, 77; Yale Univ, 78; Eli Whitney Mus, 79; and many others. *Pos:* Dir dept mural painting, Rambusch Decorating Co, New York, 26-46; gen designer, Karl Hackert Studios, Chicago, 46-72; assoc designer, Studios of George Payne, Paterson, NJ, 48-52. *Teaching:* Instr drawing & painting, Dept Adult Educ, City Stamford, 54-58; instr drawing & painting, Art Guild North Haven, 65-70. *Awards:* Drawing Prize, Yale Art Sch, 21; Bronze Medal, Beaux Arts Inst Design, 22; First Prize Oil Painting, Greenwich Art Soc, 58. *Mem:* Nat Soc Mural Painters; New Haven Arts Coun; North Haven Art Guild. *Media:* Oil, Watercolor. *Mailing Add:* 210 Upper State St North Haven CT 06473

TULLIS, GARNER H
PUBLISHER, PRINTMAKER
b Cincinnati, Ohio, Dec 12, 39. *Study:* Univ Pa, BFA, 64; Accademia Di Belli Arte, Italy, Fulbright Scholar, 64-65; Stanford Univ, MA(Carnegie Fel), 67. *Work:* Cleveland Mus Art, Ohio; Philadelphia Mus Art, Pa; San Francisco Mus Mod Art, Calif; Mus Mod Art, New York; Brooklyn Mus Art, NY. *Exhib:* Ann Invitational, Pa Acad Fine Arts, 64; 49th Ann, Cleveland Mus Art, Ohio, 65; Nat Ann, San Francisco Mus Mod Art, Calif, 66; Albright-Knox Gallery, Buffalo, NY, 72; one-man show, Cleveland Art Inst, Ohio, 75; Works in handmade paper, Mus Mod Art, New York, 76; 30 Yrs, 30 Printmakers, Nat Collection Fine Arts, Washington, DC, 78; Paper as Medium Traveling Exhib, Smithsonian, 78-82. *Pos:* Dir, Inst Experimental Printmaking, 73-; founder, Garner Tullis Workshop, New York, NY, Santa Barbara, Calif & Pietrarubbia, Italy, 86- *Teaching:* Foundry supervisor sculpture, Univ Calif, Berkeley, 67-69; artist-in-residence papermaking, Bennington Col, 76; assoc prof printmaking, Univ Calif, Davis, 76-84. *Awards:* Nat Endowment Arts Grant, 76. *Bibliog:* Jules Heller (auth), Papermaking Today, Watson-Guptill, 78; Paper: Art & Technology, World Print Council, 79; Patricia Newman (auth), Experimental workshop of Garner Tullis, Smithsonian Mag, 8/80; Charles Millard (auth), Garner Tullis, Print Quarterly, 6/89. *Mem:* Life mem, The Print Club, Philadelphia; Calif Soc Printmakers; Col Art Asn. *Media:* Monotype. *Dealer:* Pamela Auchincloss Gallery 558 Broadway New York NY 10013. *Mailing Add:* 10 White St New York NY 10013

TULLY, JUDD
WRITER, CURATOR
b Chicago, Ill, Apr 13, 47. *Study:* Am Univ, Washington, DC, BA, 69; Univ Ore, Eugene. *Collections Arranged:* Vintage New York (auth, catalog), 83-84, One Penn Plaza, New York; Reuben Kadish Survey: 1935-1985 (auth, catalog), Artists' Choice Mus, New York, 86; The New Sculpture Group - A Look Back: 1957-1962 (auth, catalog), New York Studio Sch, 88; Made in New York: Encounters with contemporary sculpture (auth, catalog), Williams Ctr for Arts, Easton, Pa, 89; Lost and Found (auth, catalog), The Sculpture Center, New York, 91. *Pos:* lectr contemp art, NY Bd Educ, 84-; interviewer, Archives of Am Art, Smithsonian Inst, 88. *Mem:* Int Asn Art Critics; Authors Guild Inc. *Res:* Cultural reportage on contemporary painting and sculpture. *Publ:* Auth, Red Grooms and Ruckus Manhattan, George Braziller, NY, 77; The Mystery of Picasso's Pierette, Washington Post, 2/25/90; Folk: The Art of Benny & George Andrews, Memphis-Brooks Mus, 90; 15 Minutes Later: Warhol Now, Artnews, 3/92; Jean-Michel Basquiat, Art & Auction, 10/92. *Mailing Add:* PO Box 05 Prince St Sta New York NY 10012

TULUMELLO, PETER M
CONSULTANT, DESIGNER
b Welland, Ont, Can, Apr 15, 54. *Study:* Damaen Col, Buffalo, NY, 73-74; Univ Waterloo, Ont, BA(fine arts, hon), 78; Univ Regina, Sask, MFA, 80. *Work:* Univ Waterloo, Ont; Univ Regina. *Pos:* Dir & cur, Estevan Nat Exhib Ctr, 81-83, Mus Northern Hist, Ont, 84-85 & Art Gallery Northumberland, Cobourg, Ont, 85-89; pres, Corp Image Art & Design Consult Inc, 89- *Teaching:* Lectr, Univ Regina, 79-83. *Awards:* Prov Sask Grad Scholar, 79; Proj Cost Grant, Can Coun Award, 82. *Mem:* Can Mus Asn; Ont Mus Asn. *Mailing Add:* 66 State St Welland ON L3B 4K5 Canada

TULVING, RUTH
PAINTER, PRINTMAKER
b Estonia; Can citizen. *Study:* Ont Col Art, 62. *Work:* Can Govt; Nat Gallery, Bejing, People's Repub China; Nat Art Mus Estonia; and many pub and corp collections. *Exhib:* Many mus and pub gallery individual exhibs in NAmerica, Europe & Asia. *Teaching:* Instr painting & printmaking, Ont Col Art, Toronto. *Mem:* Royal Can Acad Art; Ont Soc Artists (pres, 83-84). *Media:* Acrylic; Embossing, Etching. *Mailing Add:* 45 Baby Point Crescent Toronto ON M6S 2B7 Canada

TUNICK, DAVID
DEALER
b Greenwich, Conn, Nov 17, 43. *Study:* Williams Col, BA(art hist), 66. *Pos:* Pres, David Tunick, Inc, New York, 66- *Mem:* Art Dealers Asn Am; Antiqn Booksellers' Asn Am; Int League Antiqn Booksellers; Chambre Syndicale de l'Estampe, Paris. *Specialty:* Specialize in works of art on paper, prints and drawings, 15th century to mid-20th century. *Publ:* Auth, Old Master & Modern Prints (ser of ann catalogs), 71-80; auth, Twenty-One Prints by Tissot (catalog), 72; auth, Viscount Downe collection of Rembrandt etchings, an auction review, 73 & auth, Anatomy of an auction: The Kornfeld sale of Old Masters, 74, Print Collector's Newsletter; coauth, Sixty-Five Prints by James McNeill Whistler (catalog), 75. *Mailing Add:* 12 E 81st St New York NY 10028

TUNIS, ROSLYN
CURATOR, GALLERY DIRECTOR
b Montreal, Que; US citizen. *Study:* State Univ NY, Binghamton, BA(studio art & art hist), 72, MA(art hist & anthrop), 80. *Collections Arranged:* Festival of Mexico (auth, catalog), 73; The Fine Art of Craftsmanship (auth, catalog), 74; William Bingham: America a Good Investment (auth, catalog), 75; Artistic Spirit of the North American Indian (auth, catalog), 76; Treasure House: Museums of the Empire State (auth, catalog), 79; Charles Eldred: Sculpture and Drawing (auth, catalog), 80. *Pos:* Cur art, Roberson Ctr for Arts & Sci, Binghamton, NY, 72-; dir, Carlyn Gallery, Madison Ave, New York. *Mem:* Am Crafts Coun; (bd mem) Hastings Creative Arts Coun, Hastings-on-Hudson, NY. *Res:* Art of the Iroquois, contemporary American crafts. *Mailing Add:* 5727 La Salle Ave Oakland CA 94611

TUPITSYN, MARGARITA
CRITIC, CURATOR
b Moscow, Russia, Mar 23, 55; US citizen. *Study:* Grad Sch, City Univ New York, with Rosalind Krauss & R C Washton-Long. *Collections Arranged:* SOTS Art (auth, catalog), New Mus, 86; Between Spring & Summer: Soviet Conceptual Art (auth, catalog), 90 & Montage & Modern Life (auth, catalog), 92, Inst Contemp Art, Boston; The Great Utopia (auth, catalog), Guggenheim Mus, 92. *Teaching:* Lectr Russ, Avanta-Garde New Sch, 87-87 & Avant-Garde State Univ NY, 87-88. *Mem:* Col Art Asn. *Publ:* Auth, Margins of Soviet Art: Socialist Realism to the Present, Giancarlo Politi Editore, 89; Between art & politics: Gustave Klutsis, Art Am, 91. *Mailing Add:* 145 Chambers St New York NY 10007

TURANO, DON
SCULPTOR, MEDALIST
b New York, NY, Mar 9, 30. *Study:* Sch Indust Art, with Albino Cavalido; Corcoran Sch Art, with Heinz Warneke; Skowhegan Sch Painting & Sculpture, with H Tovish; Rinehart Sch Sculpture, with R Puccinelli. *Comn:* Silver, gold & wood mace, Am Col Physicians, Philadelphia, 64; limestone figures, Cathedral of St Peter & St Paul, Washington, DC, 69; Silver Medallion, Univ Notre Dame, Ind, 72; carved cherry panels, Maximum Saving Bank, Rockville, Md, 85; portrait bust Ronald Reagan, Reagan Presidential Library, 90; portrait bronze relief Auxiliary Bishop Lyons, St Thomas Apostle Church, Washington, DC, 89. *Exhib:* Pa Acad Fine Arts, Philadelphia, 63; St Louis Mus, Mo, 64; Audubon Ann, Nat Acad Design Galleries, 66; Xerox Corp, Rochester, NY, 71; Nat Insts of Health, Bethesda, Md, 90. *Teaching:* Instr sculpture, George Washington Univ, 61-65; instr sculpture, Corcoran Sch Art, 61-65. *Awards:* First Prize, Corcoran Gallery Art, 66; First Prize, Festival Relig Art, 67; First Prize, George Washington Univ, 68. *Mem:* Nat Sculpture Soc; assoc Washington Relig Art Comn. *Media:* Bronze, Wood. *Mailing Add:* 2810 27th St Washington DC 20008

TURCONI, SUE (SUSAN) KINDER
GRAPHIC ARTIST, PHOTOGRAPHER
b Teaneck, NJ, Feb 26, 39. *Study:* William Paterson Col, Wayne, NJ, BA, 74; Pratt Inst, Brooklyn, MFA, 76. *Work:* NJ State Mus, Trenton; Newark Mus, NJ; Merril Lynch Corp Hqs, New York; Bergen Mus, Paramus, NJ; Pratt Inst, Brooklyn. *Comn:* Hackensack (photog pub), Hackensack Chamber of Com, NJ, 76. *Exhib:* NJ State Coun Arts Fel, 85-86; Photography & Collage, Huntderdon Art Ctr, Clinton, NJ, 85; Soho Photo Pinhole Photog Invitational Exhib, Soho Photo, New York, 86; NJSCA Fel Exhib, Morris Mus Art & Sci, Morristown, NJ, 87; Sixth Ann Competition, Mus Hudson Highlands, Cornwall-on-Hudson, NY, 87; One Hundred Contemp Artists, Jersey City Mus Exhib & Auction, NJ, 87; Zimmerli Mus, New Brunswick, NJ, 88; Bergen Mus, Paramus, NJ, 89; NJ Ctr Visual Arts, 90 Exhib, Summit, 90; Bergen Mus Art & Sci, Paramus, NJ, 90 Exhib, 92 Solo Exhib; NJ Arts Ann, Noyes Mus, Oceanville, NJ, 92; Ben Shahn Gallery, William Paterson Col, Wayne, NJ, 92; Robeson Gallery, Rutgers Univ, Newark, NJ, 92; and others. *Pos:* Art critic, Suburban Trends, Riverside Publ Co, 74-80; writer column, Prof Women Photographers Times, 81-82; NJ correspondent, Art Express, 82; print librn, Soho Photo, New York, 86-87. *Teaching:* Instr photog, Passaic Coun Community Col, Paterson, NJ, 84-86 & Bergen Community Col, Paramus, NJ, 85- *Awards:* NJ State Coun Arts Fel, 85-86. *Bibliog:* John Zeaman (auth), Fine Arts, Sunday Record, 92; Mitchell Siedel (auth), Photography, Sunday Star Ledger, 92; Christine S Zeman (auth), Oil & Acrylics, Suburban News, 92. *Publ:* Auth, Getting started, 84 & Ghosts, 85, Strategies Mag; Historical Composition & Teaching & Learning Strategies, Ilford Photo Instructor Newsletter, 91; Notes on Photography, Sweet & Bitter Fruit, Bergen Community Col, Paramus, NJ. *Mailing Add:* 961 Colonial Rd Franklin Lakes NJ 07417

TURK, RUDY H
MUSEUM DIRECTOR, PAINTER
b Sheboygan, Wis, June 24, 27. *Study:* Univ Wis, 46-49; Univ Tenn, 49-51; Ind Univ, 52-56; Univ Paris, Fulbright Scholar, 56-57. *Exhib:* Solo exhibs, The Store, Berkely, Calif, 66, Udinotti Gallery, San Francisco, Udinotti Gallery, Scottsdale, annually since 79, Ariz Western Col, 81; invitational group exhibs, Faculty Art Exhibs, Ariz State Univ, 68, 69, 70, Works by Wanda and Rudy Turk, Missoula Art Ctr, 75, Two Edges on a Line: A Copmparative Migration of Images Between Arizona-New Mexico, ASA Gallery, Univ NMex, 77, Retributive Justice, Simms art Ctr, Albuquerque, NMex, 77, Masks and Self-Portraits, Udinotti Gallery Scottsdale, 79, Vallery Nat Bank (Tempe Office), Selected Works of Ariz State Univ Artists, 80 & Scholder Collects, Ariz State Univ Art Mus, 87; Spec Traveling Exhib, Scholder by Scholder and Others, Western Assoc Art Mus, 79. *Collections Arranged:* The Works of John Roeder, Richmond Art Ctr, Calif, 61-62; Contemporary Glass, San Diego Mus Fine Arts, 67; The World of David Gilhooly, Ariz State Univ, 69; Henry Strater Retrospective, 79; The World of Viola Frey, 82; Edward Jacobson collection of Am wood bowls, 85 & 90; Sculpture by John Paul Jones, 87. *Pos:* Art historian & dir art gallery, Univ Mont, 57-60; dir, Richmond Art Ctr, 60-65 & Univ Art Mus, Ariz State Univ, 67-; asst dir, San Diego Mus Fine Arts, 65-67; dir, Art Mus, Ariz State Univ, Tempe, 67-92. *Teaching:* Prof art, Ariz State Univ, 67-77. *Awards:* Hon Fel, Am Craftsman Coun, 88; Governor's Art Award, Arts of Ariz, 92; Appointed Director EMeritus,Art Mus, Ariz State Univ, 92. *Mem:* Friends Mex Art; Asn Am Mus; Col Art Asn Am; Ariz Living Treas Comn. *Res:* Contemporary art; 18th century French art; humanities; American hist & contemp ceramics. *Collection:* Eighteenth century French prints: contemp Am ceramics. *Publ:* Auth, I L Udell, Univ Art Collections, 71; coauth, Scholder/Indians, Northland, 72; The Search for Personal Freedom, William C Brown, Vols I & II, 4th ed 72, 5th ed 77, 6th ed 81, 7th ed 84; auth, Monumental Landscapes of Merrill Mahaffey, Northland, 79; plus critical studies, art catalogues & art reviews; auth, Scholder, New York, Rizzoli Press, 266, 82. *Dealer:* Udinotti Gallery 4215 N Marshall Way Scottsdale AZ 85251. *Mailing Add:* 760 E Courtney Ln Tempe AZ 85284

TURLINGTON, PATRICIA R
PAINTER, SCULPTOR
b Washington, DC, Sept 14, 39. *Study:* Washburn Univ, 62-63; NC State Univ Sch Design, spec study with Joe Cox, 69-71; Atlantic Ctr Arts, spec study with Audrey Flack, 86. *Work:* Mint Mus, Charlotte, NC; Duke Univ Med Ctr, Durham, NC; Univ NC, Chapel Hill; Wachovia Bank & Trust Co, Winston Salem, NC; Blue Cross-Blue Shield, Chapel Hill, NC. *Comn:* Brick sculpture murals, (first brick sculpture in a pub sch in the US), Goldsboro City Sch, NC, 75; brick sculpture mural, City of Sanford, NC, 80; brick sculpture mural, McDonald's Corp, Oak Brook, Ill, 90; brick sculpture mural, Rowan Mem Hosp, Salisbury, NC, 91; brick sculpture mural, New York City Transit Authority, 92. *Exhib:* Artist's Political Statements, Southeastern Ctr Contemp Art, Winston Salem, NC, 86; A Feminest Odyssey, Wake Forest Univ Fine Arts Ctr, Winston Salem, NC, 87; American Herstory, Atlanta Col Art Gallery, Ga, 90; Women and Art: Creating the Feminine Icon, Winthrop Col Fine Arts Ctr, Rock Hill, SC, 91; Women's Issues as Art, Salem Col Fine Arts Ctr, Winston Salem, NC, 92. *Teaching:* Prof studio art & art hist, Wayne Community Col, Goldsboro, NC, 86-92. *Awards:* Collaborating Arts Award, NC Chapter Am Inst Architects, 78; Cash Award, Tex Fine Arts Asn Nat Exhib, 84; First Prize: Works on Paper, Nat Asn Women Artists, Morris J Heiman, 85. *Bibliog:* Norman Farley (dir), Sculptured Brick (film), Brick Inst Am, 89; Kathryn Gleason (auth), Brick Added to McDonald's drive thru menu, BIA News Mag/Brick Inst Am, 1/90; Norman Farley (auth), Brick sculpture: art becomes architecture, Archit Mag, 12/90. *Mem:* Nat Asn Women Artists. *Media:* Watercolor; Brick. *Publ:* Auth, North Drive Elementary School Intaglio Brick Sculptures, NC Architect, 77. *Mailing Add:* PO Drawer 8 Goldsboro NC 27533-0008

TURNBULL, BETTY
CURATOR
b Hollywood, Calif, Aug 4, 24. *Study:* Los Angeles Valley Col (art hist, design, drawing & painting), 56-59. *Collections Arranged:* Art of the Northwest Indian & Alaska Eskimo, Fine Arts Patrons of Newport Harbor, 68; Directly Seen; New Realism, 70 & Art of the Indian Southwest, 71, Newport Harbor Art Mus & Pasadena Mus Art; Mary Cassatt (auth, catalog), 74; The Flute and the Brush: Indian Miniature Paintings, 76; The Last Time I Saw Ferus (auth, catalog), 76; David Park Retrospective (auth, catalog), 77; The Prometheus Archives-A Retrospective of the Work of George Herms, 79; Via Celmins Survey (intro catalog), 79; California, The State of Landscape 1827-1981 (auth, catalog), Newport Harbor Art Mus, 81; Perpetual Motion (auth, catalog), Santa Barbara Mus Art, 87-88; and others. *Pos:* cur art, Newport Harbor Art Mus, Calif, 69-72 & 73-77, actg dir, 72-73, cur exhibs & collections, 77-81; dir, Turnbull, Lutjeans, Kogan (TLK) Gallery, 81-85; speaker/adv, Art Forum Prog, Rancho Santiago Col, 83-85. *Teaching:* Asst prof, Mus Studies Prog, Calif State Univ, Long Beach, 86-87. *Specialty:* Contemporary painting, sculpture & graphics. *Mailing Add:* c/o Turnbull Lutjeans Kogan Gallery 1419 Bonnie Doone Terrace Corona Del Mar CA 92625

TURNBULL, LUCY
MUSEUM DIRECTOR, EDUCATOR
b Lancaster, Ohio. *Study:* Bryn Mawr Col, Pa, AB, 52; Am Sch Classical Studies, Athens, Greece, 55-57; Radcliffe Col, Cambridge, Mass, AM, 54, PhD, 60. *Collections Arranged:* Yoknapatawpha Through Other Eyes, 83, O Look! Heaven is Coming to Earth, paintings of Theora Hamblett (auth, catalog), 84, Three Southern Photographers, 84, Images of the Southern Woman, 85, Mr McCrady of La-Fay-Ette County, 86, Univ Mus, Univ Miss, Treasures from Oxford Homes I & II, 87. *Pos:* Mus asst, Mus Fine Arts, Boston, 58-60; cur, classical antiquities, Univ Mus, Univ Miss, 77-, dir, 85- *Teaching:* From asst prof classical archaeol, to assoc prof, Univ Miss, 61-66, prof classics, 74-81, prof classics & art, 81- *Mem:* Am Asn Mus; Archaeol Inst Am; Asn Col & Univ Mus & Galleries. *Res:* Iconography of Greek mythology, especially in vase-painting; influence of other arts on vase-painting; topical themes in iconography. *Publ:* Contribr, Art, Myth & Culture; Greek Vases from the Southern Collections, New Orlean Mus, 81; Poets and Heroes, Emory Univ, Atlanta, 86. *Mailing Add:* 714 S 8th St Oxford MS 38655

TURNER, A RICHARD
HISTORIAN, EDUCATOR
b New Bedford, Mass, July 28, 32. *Study:* Princeton Univ, PhD, 59. *Pos:* Chairperson, Inst Fine Arts, New York, 79-82; dir, NY Inst for Humanities, NY Univ, 86- *Teaching:* Prof Renaissance art, Princeton Univ, 60-68; prof & chmn Renaissance art, Middlebury Col, Vt, 68-75; pres & prof art, Grinnell Col, 75-79. *Mem:* Col Art Asn Am. *Res:* Historiography and criticism of Renaissance art. *Publ:* Auth, The Vision of Landscape in Renaissance Italy, Princeton, 66 & 73; coauth, Art of Florence, Abbeville, 89. *Mailing Add:* PO Box 2322 Cape May NJ 08204

TURNER, ALAN
PAINTER, PRINTMAKER
b New York, NY, July 6, 43. *Study:* City Col New York, BA, 65; Univ Calif, Berkeley, MA(painting), 67. *Comn:* Lithograph, Kunstvereine, Hamburg, Ger, 71. *Exhib:* One-man shows, Alan Turner: New Paintings, Drawings & Prints, Carol Getz Gallery, Miami, Fla, 83, Recent Paintings, Jason McCoy Gallery, New York, 87, Koury Wingate Gallery, New York, 88, Special Projects III: Alan Turner, Everson Mus Art, Syracuse, NY, 88, Tyler Gallery, Temple Univ, Elkins Park, Pa, 89, Koury Wingate Gallery, New York, 90; Landscapes in Recent Painting, Mus Fine Arts, Springfield, Mass, 81; The American Artist as Printmaker, 23rd Nat Print Exhib, The Brooklyn Mus, New York, 84; Trees, Boston Mus Fine Arts, Mass, 84; Currents, Inst Contemp Art, Boston, Mass, 89; A Decade of American Drawing: 1980-1990, Daniel Weinburg Gallery, Los Angeles, 89; Am Acad/Inst Invitational Exhib of Paint & Sculpture, Am Acad & Inst Arts & Letters, New York, 90; Insect Politics, Hallwalls Contemp Arts Ctr, Buffalo, NY, 90; Alternative Situations for Contemp Printmaking, 90; 65th Ann Competition (prints), Philadelphia, 90; Black & White Works on Paper, Cathcart Gallery, Santa Monica, Calif, 90; Ealan Wingate Gallery, New York, 91; New Generations New York, Carnegie Mellon Art Gallery, Pittsburgh, Pa, 91; How It Is, Tony Shafrazi Gallery, New York, 92; Man Revealed, Graham Mod, New York, 92. *Awards:* Nat Endowment Arts Fel Grant, 77, 81 & 87; John Simon Guggenheim Memorial Foundation Fel, 88. *Bibliog:* Roberta Smith (auth), Group shows revive the jaded art palate, The New York Times, 6/17/88; Michael Brenson (auth), A perverse, witty, sadomasochistic universe, The New York Times, 9/18/88; Michael Kimmelman (auth), Trying to remember, The New York Times, 9/23/88; Jack Flam (auth), Who's news in the early art season, The Wall Street Journal, 9/28/88. *Media:* Oil. *Publ:* Auth, Etchings, Parasol Press, 78. *Mailing Add:* 114 Franklin St New York NY 10013

TURNER, (CHARLES) ARTHUR
PAINTER, INSTRUCTOR
b Houston, Tex, Nov 17, 40. *Study:* NTex State Univ, BA, 62; Cranbrook Acad Art, Bloomfield Hills, Mich, MFA, 66, with Zoltan Shepeshy. *Work:* Mus Fine Arts, Houston; McNay Art Inst, San Antonio; The Galleries, Cranbrook Acad Art; Beaumont Art Mus, Tex; A T & T, New York; Alcoa Corp, Detroit, Mich; McAllen Int Mus, McAllen, Tex; Texaco, Inc, Houston, Tex; Lord Fairfax Community Col, Middletown, Va. *Exhib:* One-man show, Moody Gallery, Houston, 78, 82, 87 & 92, Patricia Moore Gallery, Aspen, 83 & 86; Recent Acquisitions, Mus Fine Arts, Houston, 78; Five Artists from Texas, George Belcher Gallery, San Francisco, 79; Moody Gallery Exhib, Linda Durham Gallery, Santa Fe, NMex, 81; Houston Artists Exhib, Stavanger Mus, Norway, 82; Aspen Inst, Colo, 84; Landmarks, Janus Gallery, Santa Fe, NMex, 84; Selected Works, Patricia Moore Gallery, Aspen, Colo, 86; Looking At Color, Transco Tower Gallery, Houston, Tex, 89; Works on Paper, Galveston Art League, Rosenberg Libr, Tex, 90; 20th Anniversary Exhib, Waco Art Ctr, Tex, 92. *Teaching:* Asst prof painting, Madison Col, Va, 66-68; instr painting, Glassell Sch Art, Mus Fine Arts, Houston, 69-; guest instr, Univ Houston, 73; instr, Hill Country Arts Found, Ingram, Tex, 84, 89 & 90 & Anderson Ranch Art Ctr, Snowmass, Colo, 85; instr watercolor workshop, James Madison Univ, Orkney Springs, Va, 90. *Awards:* Second Award, Southwestern Watercolor Soc 7th Ann, 71; First Purchase Award, Beaumont Art Mus 20th Ann, 71; First Award, Art Found Ann, Art Mus South Tex, 73. *Bibliog:* Edwy B Lee (auth), Arthur Turner, drawings, Art Voices/South, 3/78; Elanor Freed (auth), Texas roundup, Art Am, 11/68; Jana Vander Lee (auth), Arthur TUrner, Grand Mesa Mask, i e Mag, summer 92. *Mem:* Tex Fine Arts Asn; Tex Watercolor Soc; Col Art Asn Am. *Media:* Colored Pencil, Watercolor. *Publ:* Color perception (video), Crystal Productions, Aspen, Colo. *Dealer:* Moody Gallery 2815 Colquitt Houston TX 77098. *Mailing Add:* 2419 Julian Houston TX 77009

TURNER, BONESE COLLINS
PAINTER, EDUCATOR
b Abilene, Kans. *Study:* Univ Idaho, BSEd, 53, MEd, 54; Univ Calif, Los Angeles, 67; Calif State Univ, Northridge, MA, 74. *Work:* Smithsonian Inst, Washington, DC; Home Savings & Loan Asn, Los Angeles; Nebr Libr, Lincoln; San Bernardino Sun, Calif; Ore Coun Arts, Newport. *Comn:* Mural; mosaic, tile & glass, Indust Tile Corp, Lincoln, Nebr, 60-61; paintings & drawings, Harding Realty, Lincoln, Nebr, 60-61; paintings, Delta Gamma House, Moscow, Idaho, 69-70; paintings, Alsa Distributing Co, Denver, Colo, 81-82; interior environment, Los Angeles Pierce Col, Woodland Hills, Calif, 85-86. *Exhib:* Los Angeles County Mus Art, 57 & 58; Virginia Mus Art, Richmond, 74 & 75; Laguna Gloria Art Mus, Austin, Tex, 78; Birmingham Mus Art, Ala, 78-80; one-man exhibs: Brand Libr, 78, 88, 92, Orlando Gallery, Sherman Oaks, Calif, 80, 86, 92, Univ Nev, Reno, 87, Coos Art Mus, Coos Bay, Ore, 88 & Angel's Gate Gallery, San Pedro, Calif, 89; Rocky Mountain Nat Exhib, Golden, Colo, 81, 82 & 85; National Egg Design Invitational, White House & Smithsonian Inst, Washington, DC, 84-85; Hollywood and the Muse, Olympic Arts Celebration, Palos Verdes Art Mus, Calif, 84; Art of the 80's, Calif State Univ, Northridge, 85. *Collections Arranged:* Traditional Concepts of Quilting in the US, 76, Los Angeles Pierce Col, Woodland Hills, Calif. *Pos:* Lens consult, Warner Bros & 20th Century Fox, Calif, 67-68; adminr & coordr, Environmental Design Prog, Los Angeles Pierce Col, Woodland Hills, Calif, 68-; bd dirs & consult, Preserve Bottle Village, Simi Valley, Calif, 84- *Teaching:* Instr art, Los Angeles Pierce Col, Woodland Hills, Calif, 64-; adj instr art structures, Fashion Inst, Los Angeles, 84; adj prof 3D art, design & interior design, Calif State Univ, Northridge, 86; instr art hist, Los Angeles Valley Col, Van Nuys, Calif, 88; instr, drawing, Moor Park Col, Calif, 89-90. *Awards:* R & D Miller Award, San Diego Nat Watercolor Exhib, 78; Purchase Awards, Los Angeles All City Juried Art Exhib, 78 & Nat Watercolor Soc Ann, Home Savings & Loan, 79; Cash Awards, Long Beach Ann, 80, 45th Ann, Watercolor USA, 89 & Butler Inst 53rd Ann, 89. *Bibliog:* Ann Japenga (auth), Los Angeles Times, 4/22/84; Louise Moore (auth), Celebrating women's art, Artweek, Vol 15, No 23, 6/4/84; Steve Harvey (auth), Only in LA, LA Times. *Mem:* Life mem Nat Watercolor Soc (jury, 80, pres, 89-90, chmn: jury, 91); Pa Watercolor Soc; Univ Idaho Col Art & Archit (adv bd); Watercolor West; Hon Soc, Watercolor USA. *Media:* All Media, Mixed. *Collection:* Native American; Contemporary such as Helen Lundeberg, Marvin Hardin, Irving Block & Kent Twitchell; American folk art & quilts. *Publ:* Contrib, The great cover-up, Images & Issues, 7/8/83; TV interview, The Sushi Series, Asahi Cable Systems, 89; TV interview, Multi-Media Works, Am Cable Systems, 89; Calif Art Rev, Krantz, 89; Psychological Perspectives, Issue 23, 90. *Dealer:* Orlando Gallery 14553 Ventura Blvd Sherman Oaks CA 91403. *Mailing Add:* 4808 Larkwood Ave Woodland Hills CA 91364

TURNER, BRUCE BACKMAN
PAINTER
b Worcester, Mass, Oct 28, 41. *Work:* Sloan-Kettering Cancer Ctr, New York; Cheshire Pub Libr, Conn; also pvt collections throughout the US. *Exhib:* North Shore Arts Asn Ann, East Gloucester, Mass, 72; 2nd Greater New Orleans Nat Exhib, La, 72; Attleboro Mus Ann, Mass, 75; Am Fortnight Exhib, Hong Kong, China, 75; Mainstreams, Marietta Col, Ohio, 76; and many others. *Teaching:* Pvt classes oil painting, Rockport, Mass, 71-72. *Awards:* Shumaker Award, Rockport Art Asn, Mass, 76; Seley Purchase Prize, 76 & Arthur T Hill Mem, 79, Salmagundi Club, New York; plus many others. *Mem:* Am Artists Prof League; Rockport Art Asn; North Shore Arts Asn; Acad Artists Asn; Salmagundi Club. *Media:* Oil. *Mailing Add:* 4 Story St Rockport MA 01966

TURNER, DAVID
MUSEUM DIRECTOR, EDUCATOR
b Houston, Tex, Dec 1, 48. *Study:* Southern Methodist Univ, Dallas, BBA, 71; Univ Ore, Eugene, MA, 74. *Collections Arranged:* Approaches to Photography (auth, catalog), 79; Amarillo Earthworks, 81; Native American Paintings, 81; Touring the World (auth, catalog), 81; Early French Moderns, (auth, catalog), 82. *Pos:* Asst registrar, Mus Fine Arts, Houston, Tex, 71-72; cur educ, Amarillo Art Ctr, Tex, 77-80, dir, 80- *Teaching:* Instr art hist & photog, Umpqua Community Col, Roseburg, Ore, 74-77. *Mem:* Am Asn Mus; Tex Asn Mus; Soc Photog Educ. *Publ:* Auth & ed, American Images (video tape), 79 & auth, Amarillo Landmarks, 81, Amarillo Art Ctr; auth, Jack Boynton, Artspace, 81. *Mailing Add:* Mus of Fine Arts 107 W Palace, PO Box 2087 Santa Fe NM 87504

TURNER, EVAN HOPKINS
MUSEUM DIRECTOR
b Orono, Maine, Nov 8, 27. *Study:* Harvard Univ, AB, MA & PhD; Sir George Williams Univ, LHD, 65; Swarthmore Col, LHD, 67; Temple Univ, hon, DL, 74l; Cleveland State Univ, hon DLA, 92. *Pos:* Lectr & res asst, Frick Collection, New York, 53-56; gen cur & asst dir, Wadsworth Atheneum, Hartford, Conn, 55-59; dir, Mont Mus Fine Arts, 59-64, Philadelphia Mus Art, 64-77, Ackland Art Mus, 78-83 & Cleveland Mus Art, 83- *Teaching:* Adj prof art hist, Univ Pa, 70-78 & Univ NC, Chapel Hill, 78- *Mem:* Am Asn Mus; Asn Art Mus Dirs (pres, 75-76); Benjamin Franklin fel Royal Soc Arts; Am Fedn Arts; Century Club. *Res:* Thomas Eakins; 19th century American sculpture. *Mailing Add:* Off of the Dir Cleveland Mus Arts 11150 E Blvd Cleveland OH 44106

TURNER, JAMES THOMAS, SR
SCULPTOR, PAINTER
b Denver, Colo, Mar 15, 33. *Study:* Famous Artist Course; Western Brass & Foundry; also sculpture with Edgar Britton & Fritz White. *Work:* White

House; Crawford State Bank, Nebr; Can Bank Seattle; in pvt collection of John Wayne & Sen Fred Harris, Okla. *Comn:* Bronze busts of founders, Pro-Rodeo Hall of Fame, Colorado Springs, 79-80; Rose Mem Hosp, Denver, 82; Kellogg Corp Headquarters, Denver, 84; Tri-State Indust Bank, Denver, 88; 4 Lions Heads, Otto's Casino, Central City, 92. *Exhib:* Pacific Northwest Indian Ctr, Spokane, Wash, 73; Death Valley Days, Calif, 74; C M Russell Art Auction & Sale, Great Falls, Mont, 74; Miniature Painters, Engravers & Sculptors Soc, 74; Calif Int Artist of the Year, 74; Golden West Art Show, Merchandise Mart, Denver, 80; Festivals of the Masters, Orlando, Fla, 82; Hummingbird Enterprises, Montrose, Colo, 92. *Awards:* Best of Show, Western Trails Art Show, Littleton. *Bibliog:* Steve Cady (auth), A Casting for the President, Channel 7 TV, Denver, 71-72; 100 Years of Western Art, Channel 6, Denver; Patricia Janis Broder (auth), Bronzes of the American West, Abrams, 74. *Mem:* Denver Art Mus; Am Fedn Arts; Artists Equity. *Dealer:* Hummingbird Gallery Montrose CO; Donald Pick Englewood CO. *Mailing Add:* 65546 Solar Rd Montrose CO 81401-8533

TURNER, JANET SULLIVAN
PAINTER
b Gardiner, Maine, Nov 15, 35. *Study:* Chicago Acad Fine Arts (Scholarship), 53; Mich State Univ, BFA (cum laude), 56; Haystack Mountain Sch Arts & Crafts, Deer Isle, Maine, 64. *Work:* Am Nat Bank & Trust, Rockford, Ill; Burroughs Corp, Chicago, Ill; Am Restaurant Asn Serv, ARA Tower, Philadelphia, Pa; Mich State Univ, East Lansing; Blue Cross & Blue Shield, Philadelphia, Pa. *Comn:* Painting, Univ Maine, Farmington, 80; Painting, Systems & Computer Tech Corp, Malvern, Pa, 82; painting, Teradyne Cent Inc, Deerfield, Ill, 83; paintings, Del Investment Adv, Philadelphia, 86. *Exhib:* Solo exhibs, St Joseph's Univ, Philadelphia, 81, Villanova Univ, Villanova, 82, Pa State Univ, Middletown, 85, Temple Univ, Philadelphia, Pa, 86, Suzanne Gross Gallery, Philadelphia, 88, Ariel Gallery, New York, 89 & Gloucester Co Col, NJ, 90; American Women in Art, UN World Conf Women, Nairobi, Kenya, 85; Widener Univ Art Mus, Chester, Pa, 87; 4 person, Trenton City Mus, NJ, 90; 3 person, Del Ctr Contemp Arts, Wilmington, 92; and others. *Pos:* Bd dirs, Artists Equity, 85-86, 1st vpres, Philadelphia Chap, 86-, pres, 87 & 88. *Teaching:* Pvt lessons in studio, 78-86; guest lectr, Cult Events Prog, Pa State Univ, 85. *Awards:* Hon Mention, Nat Artists Equity Travelling Show, Stedman Gallery, Rutgers Univ, 85; Third Prize, Katonah Art Mus, 92; State Mus Pa, Harrisburg, 92. *Bibliog:* Art in America, Paul Shanley Publ, 82, 86 & 87; Victoria Donohoe (auth), critiques in Philadelphia Inquirer, 6/2/85, 1/10/86, 4/17/87 & 5/14/88; Burton Wasserman (critic), article, Art Matters. *Mem:* Philadelphia Watercolor Club; Bd Dir, 92. *Media:* Watercolor, Mixed. *Publ:* Contemporary Women Artists, Cedco Publ, 92. *Mailing Add:* 88 Cambridge Dr Glen Mills PA 19342

TURNER, JUDITH ESTELLE
PHOTOGRAPHER, VIDEO ARTIST
b Atlantic City, NJ. *Study:* Boston Univ, Sch Fine Arts, BFA. *Work:* Libr Congress; J Paul Getty Mus, Santa Monica, Calif; Brooklyn Mus; Bibliothèque Nationale, Paris, France; Tokyo Metrop Mus Photg, Japan; Whitney Mus, New York. *Comn:* Photogs, Philip Morris, Richmond, Va, 82; Becton Dickinson, Franklin Lakes, NJ, 86; Spiral, Tokyo, Japan, 87; Tepia, Tokyo, Japan, 89; Peoples Bank, Bridgeport, Conn, 89; Republic Nat Bank, New York, 90; Kajima Corp Tokyo, Japan, 91. *Exhib:* Solo exhibs, Sites/Insights, Int Ctr Photog, New York, 80, Int Cult Ctr, Antwerp, Belg, 81, Portland Mus Art, Maine, 83, White City (traveling exhib), Tel Aviv Mus, Israel, 84 & Axis Gallery, Tokyo, Japan, 86; Inside Spaces, Mus Mod Art, New York, 81; Photos of a Work by C Cattaneo, Boymans van Beuningen Mus, Rotterdam, Holland, 87; Site Work (traveling exhib), Photogrs' Gallery, London, Eng, 91; Lyrick Cabinett, Munich, Ger, 92. *Awards:* Graham Found Grant Advanced Studies Fine Arts, 82; Lila Acheson Wallace Fund, The Capitol in Albany, Reader's Digest Asn,84; Asian Cult Coun Fel, 85. *Bibliog:* Albert Champeau (auth), Creatis, Publico, Paris, 79; A Busch (auth), The Photography of Architecture, Van Nostand, Reinhold Co, 86; William Kennedy (auth), The Capitol in Albany, Aperture, 86. *Publ:* Illusr, Judith Turner Photographs Five Architects, Rizzoli Int Publs, 80; White City, Tel Aviv Mus, 84; Annotations on Ambiguity, Axis Gallery, 86; Spiral Book, Wacoal Art Ctr, 88; Parables & Pieces, Kafka/Turner, V Fitzgerald & Co, 91. *Dealer:* Vincent Fitzgerald 11 E 78th St New York NY 10021. *Mailing Add:* 323 W 82nd St New York NY 10024

TURNER, NORMAN HUNTINGTON
PAINTER, WRITER
b Storm Lake, Iowa, July 11, 39. *Study:* New York Studio Sch, 64-65; Empire State Col, BA, 79. *Exhib:* Drawing Each Other, Brooklyn Mus, 71; one-man shows, Green Mountain Gallery, 72-75 & Ingber Gallery, 77 & 79, New York; New Paintings from the Del Water Gap, Hopper House Nyak, 77; Bowery Gallery, New York, 89; Younger Artists', Artists Choice Mus, 83; Painted Light, Artists' Choice Mus, 83. *Teaching:* Adj lectr, Queens Col, 82-85, dir summer painting pro, 85-89 & adj asst prof, 86-; instr painting, New York Studio Sch, 82-84. *Awards:* Painting Fel, NJ State Coun Arts, 80. *Bibliog:* Lawrence Campbell (auth), rev in Art News, 11/72; Laura Schwartz (auth), rev, 2/73, Ellen Lubell (auth), rev, 4/75 & Allen Ellenzweig (auth), rev, 4/77, Arts Mag; Jed Perl (auth), rev, Art in Am, 5-6/77; John Caldwell (auth), review, NY Sunday Times, 10/26/80. *Media:* Oil on Canvas, Drawing. *Publ:* Auth, Subjective Curvature in late Cezanne, Art Bull, 12/81; Painterly landscape, Arts, 4/82; Stella on Caravaggio, Arts, summer 85; Some Questions About E H Gombrich on Perspective, J Aesthetics & Art Criticism, spring 92. *Mailing Add:* 103 Scribner Ave Staten Island NY 10301

TURNER, RALPH JAMES
SCULPTOR, GRAPHIC ARTIST
b Ashland, Ore, Oct 24, 35. *Study:* Reed Col, with calligrapher, Lloyd Reynolds, BA, 58; Portland Art Mus Sch, with painter, Louis Bunce, dipl, 58; Portland State Col, 59; Univ Ore, with Jan Zach & Gerald di Guisto, MFA(sculpture), 62; Univ Ariz, 65, 72 & 73. *Work:* Catalina Observatory, Univ Ariz, Tucson; Flandrau Planetarium, Tucson; Hayden Planetarium, New York; Nat Aeronautical & Space Admin-Ames, San Francisco; Phoenix (five ft limestone), Syracuse Univ, NY, 66. *Comn:* Jupiter (two planetary models), NASA/Ames, Mt View, Calif, 74 & 76; Dr Gerard Kuiper (bronze bust), Univ Ariz, 75; Phobos (planetary model), Smithsonian Inst, 78; Seer (marble carving), M & J Shapiro, Beverly Hills, Calif, 80; mural of athletes, Multnomah Athletic Club, Portland, Ore, 81; four Northwest Indian motif wood carvings, Hyland Hills Ctr, Beaverton, Ore, 82; Athletic Figures (mural), Multnomah Athletic Club, Portland, Ore, 82; Factory Workers (mural), Norwest Publ Co, Greeley, Colo, 85; Medieval Figures (mural), The Knight's Castle Apts, Wilsonville, Ore, 90; Athletic Figures Witham Oaks Recreation Ctr (mural), Corvallis, Ore, 87. *Exhib:* Ralph J Turner, Sculpture, Tucson Art Ctr, 63 & Univ Ariz, Tucson, 64; three-man exhib, Space & Art, Rainbow Gallery, Cannon Beach, Ore, 76; Planets & Progs: A Retrospective, Delphian Found, Sheridan, Ore, 77 & Willamette Sci & Technol Ctr, Eugene, 77; Hexagon Galaxies, Delphian Found, 80; Electro Arts Gallery, San Francisco, 81. *Pos:* Res assoc planetary models, Lunar & Planetary Lab, Univ Ariz, Tucson, 64-73; co-dir/designer, Rock Creek Experimental Sta, 73-. *Teaching:* Instr sculpture, Univ Ariz, Tucson, 62-65; asst prof design & drawing, Syracuse Univ, NY, 66-69; art coordr graphics, humanities & sculpture, Pima Col, Tucson, 70-72; instr design & calligraphy, Chemekta Community Col, Salem, Ore, 75-78. *Awards:* Nat Endowment Humanities Fel, 72-73. *Bibliog:* Sculpture by Ralph J Turner, NW Rev, Univ Ore, 63; Alexander Schmeckebier (auth), Murals & sculpture on the campus of Syracuse University, Syracuse Univ Art Mus, 68; Fred Crafts (auth), Is it art or science, Eugene Register Guard, 77. *Mem:* Int Sculptur Ctr; Int Soc Art & Technol; Oregon Art Inst. *Media:* Stone, Wood; Acrylic on Plexiglas. *Publ:* Auth, The Northeast Rim of Tycho, Lunar & Planetary Commun, 70; Extraterrestrial landscapes through the eyes of a sculptor, Leonardo, 72; A model of the eastern portion of Schroter's Valley, Lunar & Planetary Commun, 73; A model of Phobos, Icarus, Cornell Univ, 78; Modeling and mapping Phobos, Sky & telescope, 77-78. *Mailing Add:* 14320 SW Rock Creek Rd Sheridan OR 97378

TURNER, ROBERT CHAPMAN
CERAMIST, EDUCATOR
b Port Washington, NY, July 22, 13. *Study:* Swarthmore Col, BA; Pa Acad Fine Arts; State Univ NY Col Ceramics, Alfred Univ, MFA; Swarthmore Col, Hon Dr Fine Arts, 87. *Work:* Dienst Beeldende Kunst, Hertogenbusch, Neth; St Louis Mus Art; Mus Fine Art, Boston; Los Angeles Co Mus Art; Philadelphia Mus Art. *Exhib:* Nat Mus Art, Buenos Aires, Arg, 63; Victoria & Albert Mus, London, Eng, 72; Boston Mus Fine Arts, 84; one-man exhibs, Garth Clark Gallery, New York, 87, Dorothy Weiss Gallery, San Francisco, 87, Helen Drutt Gallery, New York, 89, Milwaukee Art Mus, 85 & 86; Retrospective, Milwaukee Art Mus, Wis & Carnegie Inst, Mus At, Pittsburgh, Pa, 85; Bellas Artes Gallery, Santa Fe, 90. *Teaching:* Instr ceramics, Black Mountain Col, 49-51; prof ceramic art, State Univ NY Col Ceramics, Alfred Univ, 58-79, actg head div art & design, 74-76. *Awards:* Int Exhib Ceramics Silver Medal, Cannes, France, 54; Silver Medal, Third Int Cong Contemp Ceramics, Prague, Czech, 62; Ceramic Art USA Award, 66; State Univ NY Chancellor's Award for excellence in teaching, 74. *Bibliog:* Daniel Rhodes (auth), Robert Turner, Craft Horizons, 57; Johanna Burstein Hayes (auth), Profile: Robert Turner, Am Ceramics, 3/4/85; Ed Lebow (auth), Robert Turner, Am Craft, 6-7/86. *Mem:* hon mem Nat Coun Educ Ceramic Arts; fel Am Crafts Coun; Int Acad Ceramics, Geneva, Switz. *Media:* Clay. *Publ:* Auth, Born remembering, Studio Potter, 6/82. *Mailing Add:* c/o Helen Drutt Gallery 1721 Walnut St Philadelphia PA 19103

TURNER, THEODORE ROY
PAINTER, EDUCATOR
b Frederick Hall, Va, Jan 10, 22. *Study:* Richmond Prof Inst, Col William & Mary, BFA, 43; New Sch Social Res, New York, 46-50; NY Univ Inst Fine Arts, MA, 50. *Work:* New York Pub Libr Print Collection; Va Mus Fine Arts, Richmond; Roanoke Mus, Va; Dartmouth Col, Hanover, NH; Washington & Lee Univ, Lexington, Va; and others. *Exhib:* Brooklyn Mus Print Ann, 51 & 55; Am Fedn Arts Traveling Exhib Prints, 55; Va Mus Biennials, 59, 67 & 71; Watercolor USA, Springfield, Mo, 64; Dyansen Gallery, New York, 82; Hassan & Speicher Fund Purchase Exhib, 82; one-man shows, Univ of Va, Charlotteville, 85, William & Mary Col, Williamsburg, Va, 85. *Teaching:* Instr medieval archit, Dartmouth Col, 50-52; assoc prof painting, Univ Va, 52-, actg chmn, McIntire Dept Fine Arts, 62-67; vis artists, Roanoke Fine Arts Ctr, Va, 71. *Awards:* Painting Award, 18th Irene Leach Mem, Norfolk Mus, 66; Am Acad & Inst of Arts & Letters, New York, 82; Painting Award, York, Pa, 90; and others. *Bibliog:* Sue Dickinson (auth), Theodore Turner, Richmond Times-Dispatch, 6/23/68; Theodore Turner article, New York Mag, 6/24/68; Larry Campbell (auth), Theodore Turner's watercolors, Art News, 12/69. *Media:* Watercolor, Oil. *Dealer:* Peter Wreden Gallery Roanoke VA; Cormany & Turner Roanoke VA. *Mailing Add:* 916 Old Farm Rd Charlottesville VA 22903

TURNER, WILLIAM EUGENE
PAINTER, EDUCATOR
b Dallas, Tex, Oct 15, 28. *Study:* Southern Methodist Univ, BA, 52; Univ NMex, summer 53; La State Univ, MA, 54. *Work:* Portsmouth Arts Ctr, Va; Arkansas Arts Ctr, Little Rock; Atlantic Richfield Corp, Dallas, Tex &

Anchorage, Alaska. *Comn:* Hallway murals, Dallas Middle & High Sch (with Bill Hendricks, archit), comn by STB Archit & Planners, Tex, 77. *Exhib:* Drawing Invitational, Emporia State Univ, Kans, 82; Smithsonian Inst traveling exhib, 82-83; Art in the Metroplex, Tex Christian Univ, Ft Worth, 83; Delta States Art Ann, Ark Art Ctr, Little Rock, 83; Works on Paper, SW Tex State Univ, San Marcos & Rutgers Univ, Camden, NJ, 83. *Teaching:* Prof painting & design, Univ Tex, Arlington, 59-92. *Awards:* Purchase Awards, Works on Paper, Portsmouth Art Ctr, 82 & Delta States Exhib, Ark Art Ctr, 83. *Mem:* Col Art Asn. *Media:* Oil, Pencil. *Mailing Add:* 1116 Mockingbird Lane Arlington TX 76013

TURNURE, JAMES HARVEY
EDUCATOR, HISTORIAN
b Yonkers, NY, July 8, 24. *Study:* Princeton Univ, AB, MFA(art hist), PhD. *Teaching:* Instr, Cornell Univ, Ithaca, NY, 53-58, asst prof, 58-64, assoc prof, 64-68; prof, Bucknell Univ, Lewisburg, Pa, 69-, Samuel H Kress Prof art hist, 74-92; retired. *Mem:* Archeol Inst Am. *Res:* Interpretation of evidence in archaeology and art history. *Publ:* Auth, Statuette of Imhotep, Rec of Art Mus, 52 & Princeton's enigmatic relief, 63, Princeton Univ; auth, Late style of Ambrogio Figino, Art Bulletin, 65; contribr, Il Duomo di Milano, Edizioni La Rete, 69. *Mailing Add:* RD 1 Box 398A Lewisburg PA 17837

TURRELL, JAMES ARCHIE
ENVIRONMENTAL ARTIST, SCULPTOR
b Los Angeles, Calif, May 6, 43. *Study:* Pomona Col, BA, 65; Univ Calif, Irvine, 65-66; Claremont Grad Sch, MA, 73. *Work:* Guggenheim Mus, NY; Seattle Art Mus, Wash; Whitney Mus Am Art; Brooklyn Mus, NY; Dallas Mus, Tex; Philadelphia Mus Art, Pa; Walker Art Ctr, Minneapolis, Minn. *Comn:* Roden Crater, Ariz, Dia Art Found, New York, 77; Mattress Factory, Pittsburgh, Pa. *Exhib:* Lichtprojecties En Lichtruimten, Stedelijk Mus, Amsterdam, 76; Light Space, Arco Ctr for Visual Art, Los Angeles, 76; one-man shows, Muse d'Art Contemporain, Nimes, France, 89, Stein-Gladstone Gallery, NY, 90, Mus Mod Art, NY, 90, Turske & Turske, Zurich, Switzerland, 90, Ace Contemp Exhibs, NY, 90, Williams Col Art Mus, Williamstown, Mass, 91, Anthony D'Offay Gallery, London, Eng, 91; Walker Art Ctr, Minneapolis, Minn, 87 & 89; St Louis Art Mus, 88; Guggenheim Mus, 89; Nat Gallery Art, Washington, DC, 89-90; Le Musee d'Art Contemporain de Montreal, Can, 90; Chateau de Rochechouart, France, 90; La Jolla Mus Contemp Art, La Jolla, Calif, 90; Musee d'Art Modernede la villa de Paris, France, 90; Karl Bornstein Gallery, Santa Monica, Calif, 90. *Awards:* Nat Endowment for the Arts, 68 & 75; Guggenheim, 74; Fel MacArthur Found, 84. *Bibliog:* Calvin Tomkins (auth), The talk of the town-light, New Yorker, 12/15/80; Robert Hughes (auth), Poetry out of emptiness, Time Mag, 1/5/81; Nancy Marmer (auth), James Turrell: the art of deception, Art in Am, 5/81; and others. *Mailing Add:* Rte 7 Hanger 1 Flagstaff AZ 86001

TURRELL, JULIA BROWN
DIRECTOR
b Washington, DC, Mar 90, 51. *Pos:* Sr cur, Mus Contemp Art, Los Angeles, Calif, 81-86; dir, Des Moines Art Ctr, 86-91; dir, Skystone Found, 91- *Awards:* Alfred Bar Award, distinguished publ, Col Art Asn, 92. *Mailing Add:* PO Box 725 Flagstaff AZ 86002

TUTTLE, LISA
CONCEPTUAL ARTIST, CURATOR
b Little Rock, Ark, Sept 25, 51. *Study:* New Col, Sarasota, Fla, BA, 74. *Comn:* Video installations, Memphis Contemp Art Ctr, Tenn, 88, New Visions Gallery, IMAGE Film/Video, Atlanta, Ga, 88, New South Group, New York, 89 & Arts Festival, Atlanta, Ga, 90. *Exhib:* Solo exhibs, Running Diana, Seven Stages, Atlanta, Ga, 88, Vindication of Lilith, Albany Mus Art, Ga, 89; Artists Political Statements, Southeastern Ctr Contemp Art, Winston-Salem, NC, 86; Mattress Factory Artist-Initiated, Atlanta, Ga, 86, 87 & 88; Death: The Frame Around the Picture, The Upstairs, Tryon, NC, 87; Jeune Peinture, Grand Palais, Paris, France, 88; Artists in Georgia, Nexus Contemp Art Ctr, Atlanta, Ga, 88; Between Myth and Reality: New Southern Photography, Aperture Found, New York, 89. *Collections Arranged:* Cur, small scale sculpture, 87, 1938-88: The Work of Five Black Women Artists, 88, The Assembled Object, 89, Ecos del Espiritu, 90; cur, New History: Buchanan/Edwards/Hassinger, 90, Oh, Those four white walls, Gallery as Context, 90. *Pos:* Assoc cur, Nexus Contemp Art Ctr, Atlanta, Ga, 83-85; gallery dir, Nexus Contemp Art Ctr, Atlanta, 85-86; gallery dir, Atlanta Col Art, Ga, 86- *Awards:* Bur Cult Affairs, Artist Proj, Atlanta, 87; Artist's Proj Grant, Fulton Co, 89. *Bibliog:* Glenn Harper (auth), Pushing the Boundaries, Aperture, summer 89; Jerry Cullum (auth), catalog essay, New S Group, 89; Peter Doroschenko (auth), essay, Albany Mus Art, 89. *Mem:* Nexus Studio Artist, 82-88; Atlanta Gallery Asn (adv bd, 85-86); Atlanta Arts Festival (adv bd, 89); Fulton Co Pub Art Committee. *Media:* Video Installation. *Mailing Add:* 1088 Amsterdam Ave NE Atlanta GA 30306

TUTTLE, RICHARD
PAINTER
b Rahway, NJ, 1941. *Study:* Trinity Col, Hartford, Conn, BA, 63. *Work:* Fogg Art Mus, Harvard Univ, Cambridge, Mass; Metrop Mus Art, NY; Mus Mod Art, NY; Seattle Art Mus, Wash; Whitney Mus Am Art, NY; Stedekijk Mus, Amsterdam, Neth; City Art Mus, St Louis, Mo; and numerous pvt collections. *Exhib:* San Francisco Mus Art, 65, 73; Aldrich Mus Contemp Art, Ridgefield, Conn, 69; Corcoran Gallery Art, Washington, DC, 69; Whitney Mus Am Art, NY, 69, 73, 77, 78, 81, 83, 84, 85, 90; Fogg Art Mus, Harvard Univ, Cambridge, Mass, 73; Mus Mod Art, NY, 74, 76, 80; Art Inst Chicago, Ill, 75, 82; solo exhibs, Galerie Schmela, Dusseldorf, 88, 90, Galerie Hubert Winter, Vienna, Ger, 89, Gallery Casa Sin Nombre, Santa Fe, NMex, 89, A/D Gallery, NY, 90, Sprengel Mus, Hanover, Ger, 90, Galerie Yvon Lambert, Paris, 90; Andrea Rosen Gallery, NY, 90; Anders Tornberg Gallery, Sweden, 90; Galerie Anne Marie Verna, Switz, 90; Galerie Hubert Winter, Vienna, 90. *Bibliog:* Roberta Smith (auth), Minimalism on the march: more and more less and less, New York Times, 3/9/90; Victoria Geibel (auth), A fine line, Art & Auction, 5/90, 218-225; Peter Winter (auth), Shape is not abstract, Art International, Summer 90; David Bourdon (auth), Playing hide & seek in the Whitney, Village Voice, 7/29/75; Tom Hess (auth), Private art where the public works, New York Mag, 10/13/75. *Publ:* Contribr, Art Int. *Mailing Add:* c/o Mary Boone Gallery 417 Broadway New York NY 10012

TWADDLE, RANDY
PAINTER
b Elmo, Miss, 1957. *Study:* NW Mo State Univ, Maryville, BFA, 80. *Work:* Mus Fine Arts, Houston, Tex; Dallas Mus Art, Tex; Tyler Mus Art, Tex; Huntington Art Gallery, Univ Tex, Austin. *Exhib:* Singular Points of View, Art Mus STex, Corpus Christi, 84; Patterns in Contemporary Art, Laguna Gloria Art Mus, Austin, Tex, 84; Los Angeles Inst Contemp Art, Calif, 85; The Artist's Eye, Kimbell Art Mus, Ft Worth, Tex, 85; New Orleans Triennial, New Orleans Mus Art, La, 86; solo exhibs, Early Warning Systems (with catalog), Tyler Mus Art, Tex, 86, Carnival, DW Gallery, Dallas, Tex, 88 & Damon Brandt Gallery, New York, 89, Carnival-A Farewell to Flesh, SW Craft Ctr, San Antonio, 89 & New Drawings, Barry Whistler Gallery, Dallas, 89; Monumental Drawing: Works by 22 Contemporary Americans, Brooklyn Mus, NY, 86; Spectrum: Drawn Out (with catalog), Corcoran Gallery Art, Washington, DC, 86; The First Texas Triennial (with catalog), Contemp Arts Mus, Houston, 88; Tradition and Innovation: A Museum Celebration of Texas Art, Mus Fine Arts, Houston, 90; Awards in the Visual Arts 9 (with catalog), New Orleans Mus Art, La, SE Ctr Contemp Art, Winston-Salem, NC, Arthur M Sackler Mus, Harvard Univ, Cambridge, Mass & The BMW Gallery, New York, 90. *Teaching:* Inst, Univ NC-Chapel Hill, 90. *Awards:* Fel, Nat Endowment Arts, 87; Awards in the Visual Arts 9, SECCA, Winston-Salem, NC, 90. *Bibliog:* David Regan & Kevin Noble (auths), Public address: Sign in a Truck, Art in Am, 1/85; Charles Dee Mitchell (auth), Thoughts on Randy Twaddle, Dallas Observer, 7/12/85. *Media:* Charcoal on Paper. *Dealer:* Moody Gallery 2815 Colquitt Houston TX 77098. *Mailing Add:* c/o Moody Gallery 2815 Colquitt Houston TX 77098

TWARDOWICZ, STANLEY JAN
PAINTER, PHOTOGRAPHER
b Detroit, Mich, July 8, 17. *Study:* Meinzinger Art Sch, Detroit, 40-44; Skowhegan Sch Painting & Sculpture, Maine, summers 46 & 47. *Work:* Mus Mod Art, New York; Los Angeles Co Mus Art; NY Univ; Fogg Art Mus; Vassar Col Art Gallery; Hirshhorn Mus. *Exhib:* Art Inst Chicago, 54, 55 & 61; five exhibs, Mus Mod Art, 57-69; Mus Fine Arts, Boston, 66; one-man shows, Peridot Gallery, New York, 56-70; retrospective, Heckscher Mus, Huntington, NY, 74; 30 Yr Retrospective Photog, Emily Lowe Gallery, Hempstead, NY, 79. *Teaching:* Instr art, Ohio State Univ, 46-51; assoc prof art, Hofstra Univ, 65-87. *Awards:* Guggenheim Found Fel, 56-57. *Mailing Add:* 133 Crooked Hill Rd Huntington NY 11743

TWAROGOWSKI, LEROY ANDREW
DRAFTSMAN, EDUCATOR
b Chicago, Ill, Sept 12, 37. *Study:* Art Inst Chicago, 55-59; Univ Kans, Lawrence, BFA, 61, MFA, 65. *Work:* Denver Art Mus, Colo; Ft Hays State Univ, Hays, Kans; Hastings Col, Nebr; US Nat Bank, Omaha, Nebr; Mountain Bell Corp, Denver, Colo; Colo State Univ, Fort Collins. *Comn:* Colo Coun Arts & Humanities, 78. *Exhib:* Second All-Colo Competitive Exhib, Denver Art Mus, 74; 2nd Brit Int Drawing Biennale, Middlesbrough, Eng, 75; Drawings USA-75 Biennale, Minn Mus of Art, St Paul, 75; Spree-Colo Celebration of the Arts, Denver, 76; Rocky Mountain Drawing & Painting Exhib, Aspen Found for the Arts, Colo, 77; Denver Art Mus, 78. *Teaching:* Prof drawing, Colo State Univ, 67- *Media:* Graphite. *Mailing Add:* Art Dept Colo State Univ Ft Collins CO 80523

TWIGGS, LEO FRANKLIN
PAINTER, EDUCATOR
b St Stephen, SC, Feb 13, 34. *Study:* Claflin Col, Orangeburg, SC; Art Inst Chicago; NY Univ, with Jason Seley & Hale Woodruff; Univ Ga, with Sam Adler. *Work:* Johnson Publ Co, Chicago; Spring Mills, New York; Wachovia Bank & Trust Co, NC; City of Atlanta, Ga; Herbert F Johnson Mus, Cornell Univ; Fed Reserve Bank, Richmond, Va & Charlotte, NC. *Exhib:* Nat Exhib Black Artists, Washington, DC, 71; Salute to Black Artists, NJ State Mus, Trenton, 72; Directions in Afro-American Art, Cornell Univ, 74; Studio Mus, New York, NY; US Art in Embassies Prog, Dakar, 84; Palazzo Venezia, Rome, Italy, 86; SC State Mus, 89. *Pos:* Exec dir & chmn art dept, Stanback Mus & Planetarium. *Teaching:* Prof art, SC State Col, Orangeburg, currently. *Awards:* Award of Distinction, Smith Mason Gallery, 71; Merit Prize, Guild SC Artists, 75; Governor's Trophy, 80; Regional Award for Distinction, Nat Art Educ Asn, 81; Nat Distinguished Alumni, 86. *Bibliog:* Thomas W Leavitt (auth), Directions in Afro-American art, Cornell Univ, 75; E Fax (auth), Black Artists of the New Generation, 78; M Carnell (auth), article in Art Craft Mag, 79; Rhoda McKinney (auth), Ebony mag, 88; and others. *Mem:* Col Art Asn Am; Nat Art Educ Asn; Nat Conf Artists; Guild SC Artists (vpres, 74); SC Mus Comn; African Am Mus Asn (vpres, 84). *Media:* Batik. *Publ:* Auth, articles in Design Mag, 72, Negro Educ Rev, 72, Sch Arts, 72, Mus News, 72, Hist News, 81 & Arts in Educ, 86. *Dealer:* Hampton III Gallery Taylors SC 29678. *Mailing Add:* PO Box 1691 SC State Col Orangeburg SC 29117

TWIGG-SMITH, LAILA
COLLECTOR
b Dresden, Ger, Dec 12, 44; US citizen. *Study:* San Mateo Col, AA, 64; San Jose State Univ, BA, 67; Honolulu Acad Art, with Rudy Pozzatti; Mus Mgt Inst, Univ Calif, Berkeley, 79. *Pos:* Dir, Lytton Ctr Visual Arts, Palo Alto, Calif, 67-69; art critic, Honolulu Star Bull, 74-79; mus dir, Contemp Arts Ctr Hawaii, 75- *Teaching:* Adult educ instr paintings & drawing, Honolulu Acad Arts, 73-; instr, Continuing Col Educ, Univ Hawaii, 79. *Awards:* Honolulu Printmakers Annual, 75; Windward Artists Guild Annual, 76; Outstanding Achievement, Leader in the Arts, 79. *Bibliog:* Article, Honolulu Star Bulletin, 1/81; Cult Climate, Arts Coun of Hawaii, 9/81. *Mem:* Contemp Mus, Honolulu; New Mus, New York; Nat Symphony, Washington, DC; Whitney Mus Nat Comt, New York; Hawaii Artists League (pres 76-80). *Specialty:* Regional contemporary art. *Publ:* Contribr, Currant Mag, 75- *Mailing Add:* 3715 Diamond Head Circle Honolulu HI 96815

TWIGG-SMITH, THURSTON
COLLECTOR
b Honolulu, Hawaii, Aug 17, 21. *Study:* Yale Univ, BE, 42. *Awards:* Whitney Award, Skowhegan, 91. *Mem:* Mus Contemp Art, Los Angeles (trustee); Yale Art Gallery, New Haven (trustee); Skowhegan, NY & Maine (trustee); Contemp Mus, Honolulu (trustee); Honolulu Acad Arts, (trustee). *Collection:* Contemporary art, emphasis on the 80s & 90s. *Mailing Add:* c/o Honolulu Advertiser Inc 605 Kapiolani Blvd, PO Box 3110 Honolulu HI 96802

TWITTY, JAMES W
PAINTER, PRINTMAKER
b New York, Apr 13, 16. *Study:* Art Students League, with Edwin Dickenson, Stephen Greene & Morris Kantor; Univ Miami, with Xavier Gonzalez & Eliot O'Hara. *Work:* Nat Gallery Art & Corcoran Gallery Art, Washington, DC; Brooklyn Mus, NY; Baltimore Mus Art, Md; Dallas Mus Art, Tex; plus others. *Exhib:* One-man shows, Corcoran Gallery Art, David Findlay Galleries, New York, George Washington Univ, 75, Hokin Gallery, Chicago, Bettina Galery, Zurich, Pollock Gallery, Ont, Can, 81 & Fayetteville Mus Art, 89; plus others. *Teaching:* Assoc prof painting, Corcoran Sch Art; lectr fine arts, George Washington Univ; exchange prof painting, Leeds Col Art, Eng; vis prof painting, Miami Art Ctr, Fla; vis prof painting, San Antonio Art Inst, Tex. *Awards:* Allied Artists Am Award, 61; Soc Wash Art Award, 65; First Ann Exhib Award, Miami, 66. *Bibliog:* Frank Getlein (auth), A Washington artist in a New York setting, Washington DC Star-News, 73. *Mem:* Life mem Art Students League; Am Soc Painters & Sculptors; fel Aspen Inst. *Media:* Acrylic, Silkscreen. *Dealer:* Harnon-Meek Gallery 386 Broad Ave S Napales FL 33940. *Mailing Add:* PO Box 4000 Pinehurst NC 28374

TWOMBLY, CY
PAINTER
b Lexington, Va, Apr 25, 28. *Study:* Boston Mus Sch Fine Arts, 48-49; Washington & Lee Univ, 50; Art Students League, 51; Black Mountain Col, with Frank Kline & Robert Motherwell, 52. *Work:* RI Sch Design; Mus Mod Art, Whitney Mus Am Art, New York; also pvt collections in New York, Chicago, Washington, DC & Europe. *Exhib:* One-man exhibs, Galerie B Coppens & R Van De Velde, Brussels, 89, Galerie Di Meo, Paris, 89, Gagosian Gallery, New York, 89-90, The Menil Collection, Houston, Tex, 90, Thomas Ammann Fine Art, Zurich, Switz, Thomas Babeor, La Jolla, Calif, 90, Mus Contemp Art, Tokyo, 90-91; It Must Give Pleasure: Erotic Perception, Vrej Baghoomian Gallery, 90, American Masters of the 60's (with catalog), Shafrazi Gallery, 90, American Masterworks on Paper, Susan Sheehan Gallery, 90, 1991 Biennial Exhib (with catalog), Whitney Mus Am Art, New York, 91; Lawrence Oliver Gallery, 90, Contemporary Drawing, Janet Fleisher Gallery, Philadelphia, 90; Pharmakon '90, Nippon Conv Ctr, Makuhari Messe, Chiba, Japan, 90; The Reconstruction of Abstraction, Galerie Thaddaeus Ropac, Austria, 90; Light Seed, The Watari Mus Contemp Art, Tokyo, 90, 91; Word as Image, American Art 1960-1990 (with catalog), Milwaukee Art Mus, travelling, 90-91; 20th Century Collage, Margo Leavin Gallery, Los Angeles, Calif, 91; Die Wurde und der mut, l'art moral, Galerie Georg Nothelfer, Berlin, 91; Selection Oeuvres de la Collection (with catalog), FAE Musee d'Art Contemporain, Pully/Lausanne, Switz, 91; Fogli Del Novecento (with catalog), Ruggerini & Zonca, Milan, Italy, 91; and others. *Teaching:* Head dept art, Southern Sem & Jr Col, Buena Vista, Va, 55-56. *Awards:* Va Mus Fine Arts Fel for Travel in Europe & Africa, 52-53. *Bibliog:* Judd Tully (auth), Reviews: Contemporary, Art & Auction, 8/90; Judd Tully (auth), Business: Spring Sales, Contemporanea, 9/90; Bernardo Pinto de Almeida (auth), Handwriting on the Wall, Contemporanea, 9/90. *Mailing Add:* c/o Sperone Westwater 142 Greene St 2nd Flr New York NY 10012

TYE, WILLIAM ROY
SCULPTOR
b Harlan, Ky, Jan 25, 39. *Study:* Western Mich Univ, BS, 63, MFA, 77; Wayne State Univ, MA, 67. *Work:* Sturgis Coun Arts, Sturgis, Mich; Douglas Community Ctr & Western Mich Univ, Kalamazoo, Mich. *Comn:* Fighting Gamecock (bronze), Sr Class 1969, Univ SC, Columbia, 69; Cyclists (three bronze figures), City of Battle Creek, Mich, 76; J Fetzer (portrait relief), Western Mich Univ, 82. *Exhib:* Southeastern Regional Competition, Gallery of Contemp Art, Winston-Salem, NC, 69; AGC Prizewinners Exhib, Columbia Mus Art, Columbia, SC, 69; Mainstreams, Marietta Col, 71 & 72; one-man show, Kalamazoo Inst Arts, 77; All State Competition, Battle Creek Art Ctr, 80 & 81; Michigan Fine Arts, Birmingham Art Ctr, 83; Kalamazoo Bronzecasting Co, Krasl Art Ctr, St Joseph, Mich & Cain Gallery, Oak Park, Ill, 85; Michigan Outdoor Sculpture, Southfield, 87. *Pos:* Proprietor, Alchemist-Tye Studio (foudry), Kalamazoo, 83- *Teaching:* Teacher high sch art, South Redford Pub Sch, South Redford, Mich, 63-66, Clarenceville Schs, Livonia, Mich, 66-68 & Mattawan Conserv Sch, Mattawan, Mich, 70-78; art instr, Univ SC, Columbia, 68-70; head sculpture dept, Kalamazoo Inst Arts, Kalamazoo, Mich, 78-83. *Awards:* Hon Mention, All State Competition, Mich Nat Bank, 81. *Bibliog:* Linda Fortino (auth), Marriage of arts, Kalamazoo Gazette, 4/30/78. *Mem:* Int Sculpture Ctr; Chicago Artists' Coalition. *Media:* Bronze. *Dealer:* Cain Gallery 1016 North Blvd Oak Park Ill 60301. *Mailing Add:* 701 N Berkeley Kalamazoo MI 49007

TYKIE (SYLVIA SQUIRES GANZ)
PAINTER
b Southampton, NY, Oct 8, 32. *Study:* Cortland State Univ, 51-53; also with Helen A Del Grosso, 70-71. *Work:* Smithonian Inst Mus. *Comn:* Paintings, First Federal Savings Loan, Delray Beach, Fla, 79 & 81. *Exhib:* Henry Morrison Flagler Mus, Palm Beach, Fla, 76; Nat Miniature Art Exhib, Nutley Savings & Loan Asn, NJ, 77-81; Nat Miniature Art Soc Fla Exhib, Kapok Tree, Clearwater, 77-81; Nat Painters, Sculptors & Gravers Soc, Arts Club, Washington, DC, 78-81; Nat Ann Miniature Art Exhib, Gallery La Luz, NMex, 79-81; Smithsonian Inst. *Awards:* First Prize (acrylic), Ga & Mini Art Soc, 90 & 92; First Prize (acrylic), LA Luz Nat Mini Show, 91; Arts for the Parks Nat Competition, 91-92. *Mem:* Assoc Miniature Painters, Sculptors & Gravers Soc, Washington, DC; Miniature Art Soc NJ; Miniature Art Soc Fla; Del Ray Art League; found mem Miniature Artists Am. *Media:* Acrylic. *Publ:* Contribr, Arts for the Parks, 92. *Mailing Add:* 10290 Seagrape Way Palm Beach Gardens FL 33410

TYLER, RON C
HISTORIAN
b Temple, Tex, Dec 29, 41. *Study:* Abilene Christian Col, BS(educ), 64; Tex Christian Univ MA, 66, PhD, 68. *Collections Arranged:* The Wild West, Amon Carter Mus Western Art, 70; The Big Bend (auth, catalog), 75; The Image of America in Caricature & Cartoon (auth, catalog), 75; Posada's Mexico (ed, catalog), Libr Cong, 79; Alfred Jacob Miller: Artist on the Oregon Trail (ed, catalog), 82; Views of Texas: Watercolors by Sarah Ann Lillian Hardings, Amos Carter Mus, 87; Nature's Classics: John James Audubon's Birds and Animals, 92. *Pos:* Asst dir collections & prog, Amon Carter Mus Western Art, 69-86; dir, Tex State Hist Asn. *Teaching:* Asst prof, Austin Col, Sherman, Tex, 67-69; prof hist, Univ Tex, Austin. *Res:* 19th century American & Western American art & prints; Mexican art & printmakers. *Publ:* Auth, The Mexican War: A Lithographic Record, Tex State Hist Asn, 73; The Rodeo Photographs of John A Stryker, Encino Press, 78; Visions of America: Pioneer Artists in a New Land, Thames & Hudson, 83; Nature's Classics: John James Audubon's Birds and Animals, 92. *Mailing Add:* c/o Tex State Hist Asn 2/306 Richardson Hall Univ Sta Austin TX 78712

TYLER, VALTON
PRINTMAKER, PAINTER
b Texas City, Tex, Mar 30, 44. *Study:* Dallas Art Inst, Tex, 67. *Work:* Tyler Mus Art, Tex. *Exhib:* First Fifty Prints, Pollock Galleries, Southern Methodist Univ, Dallas & Tyler Mus Art, 72; 8th Ann New Talent in Printmaking, Assoc Am Artists, New York, 72; one-man shows, Galerie Claude Jongen, Brussels, Belg, 77 & Vallery House Gallery, Dallas, 79; Rosa Esman Gallery, New York, 85. *Awards:* Second Place, Art in the Metroplex, 88. *Bibliog:* Reynolds (auth), The fifty prints--Valton Tyler, Southern Methodist Univ Press, 72. *Media:* Aquatint; Oil on Canvas. *Publ:* Auth, Jalons et Actualites des Arts, 1/77; auth, Un Artiste de 33 Ans, Hebdomadaire, 2/24/77; auth, Ultra, 12/81. *Mailing Add:* c/o Valley House Gallery 6616 Spring Valley Rd Dallas TX 75240

TYSER, PATRICIA ELLEN
STAINED GLASS ARTIST, CONSULTANT
b Rochester, NY, July 1, 52. *Study:* St John Fisher Col, BA, 74. *Work:* Rochester Lead Works; Collection of Paul DuFour, La State Univ Glass Dept. *Exhib:* Solo exhibs, Wilson Gallery, Rochester, 77-79, B Forman Invitational, Rochester, 83, Gallery at 15 Stops, Ithaca, NY, 84, Philadelphia Art Show, Pa, 85, Huntington Galleries, WVa, 86 & Philadelphia Port Hist Mus, Pa, 87; Mem Art Gallery, Rochester, 78; Sibley's Artworks, Rochester, NY, 80-83; Touch of Glass, Rochester Inst Technol, 81; Interior Design Soc, 81 & 82; Street of Glass, New York, 83. *Pos:* Mgr, Stained Glass Works, Rochester, NY, 74-78; prin, Patricia Tyser Glass Studio, Rochester, NY, 78-85; dir, Archit Glass Designs, Rochester, NY, 85-87. *Teaching:* Instr, State Univ NY, Brockport, 87-88, Norman Howard Sch, Rochester, 88- *Awards:* NY State Artisan's Award, S Tier Arts Asn, 81-82; Award for Excellence, Lake Country Craftsmen, 83; Certificate of Excellence, Glass Metro Art, 86. *Mem:* Stained Glass Asn Am; Nat Asn Female Exec. *Publ:* Professional Stained Glass, 89. *Mailing Add:* 7 Faraday St Rochester NY 14610

TYSON, MARY (MRS KENNETH THOMPSON)
PAINTER
b Sewanee, Tenn, Nov 2, 09. *Study:* Grand Cent Art Sch, with George P Ennis, Howard Hildebrandt & Wayman Adams; New Sch Social Res, with Julian Levi. *Work:* Artists Asn Nantucket Permanent Collection; Guild Hall Collection; Monterey Peninsula Mus, Carmel, Calif. *Exhib:* Int Exhib, Brooklyn Mus, 35 & 37; Am Watercolor Soc Ann; Nat Arts Club Watercolor Exhib, 68-81; Addison Gallery, Andover; one-woman shows, Bruce Mus, Greenwich, Conn, St Louis Mus, Bodley Gallery, New York; and others. *Awards:* Solo Award, 69; Elizabeth Morse Genius Mem Award, 70; Guild Hall Award, East Hampton, 77; and others. *Mem:* Life mem Am Watercolor Soc; Pen & Brush Club; East Hampton Guild Hall; Nat Arts Club. *Media:* Watercolor. *Mailing Add:* 20 W 11th St New York NY 10011

TYTELL, LOUIS
PAINTER
b New York, NY, Jan 8, 13. *Study:* City Col New York, BS, 34; Columbia Univ, MA, 35; Skowhegan Sch Painting & Sculpture; New Sch Social Res. *Work:* Newark Mus; Corcoran Gallery of Art; Wickersham Gallery, Univ NC, Raleigh; Libr of Cong Print Collection, Washington, DC. *Exhib:* Pa Acad Fine Arts Ann, 49 & 66; Nat Acad Design Ann, 62, 66 & 68; Nat Inst Arts & Lett, 67; Mus Mod Art Lending Serv Gallery, 73-78; Edward Hopper House, Nyack, NY, 78. *Pos:* Chmn dept art, High Sch Music & Art, New York, 61-67 & 69-75. *Teaching:* Assoc prof art, City Col New York, 67-69. *Awards:* Tiffany Fel, 62; Am Inst Arts & Lett Grant, 67. *Media:* Oil, Pastel. *Mailing Add:* 107 Green Rd West Nyack NY 10994

TYZACK, MICHAEL
PAINTER, EDUCATOR
b Sheffield, Eng, Aug 3, 33. *Study:* Sheffield Col Art & Crafts, Eng MEd(arts & crafts), 52; Slade Sch Fine Art, Univ Col, London, with Victor Pasmore, William Townsend & Anthony Gross, DFA, 55. *Work:* Tate Gallery, London, Eng; Victoria & Albert Mus, London; Sao Paulo Mus, Brazil; Peau de Lion Collection, Zurich, Switz; Indianapolis Mus Art. *Comn:* Multiple, Documenta Found, Kassell, WGer, 68; mural scale paintings, Univ Hospital Wales, Cardiff, 71; designs for proposed mural, comn by Albert Simons, Ctr for Fine Arts, Charleston, SC, 77; design for wall hanging, SC State Ports Authority, Charleston, 79. *Exhib:* New Shapes of Color, Stedelijk Mus, Amsterdam, 66-67; Documenta 4, Kassell, WGer; Troisieme Salon Int des Galeries Pilotes, Mus Cantonal des Beaux Arts, Lausanne, Switz & Mus Art Mod, Paris, France, 70; 56-Group-Wales, a 20 Yr Retrospective, Nat Mus Wales, Cardiff, 76; Art-Patron-Art, Southeast Ctr for Contemp Art, Winston Salem, NC, 79-80; and others. *Pos:* Consult, News & Courier, Charleston, SC, 79- *Teaching:* Assoc prof painting, Univ Iowa, 71-76; prof fine arts, Col Charleston, SC, 76- *Awards:* French Govt Fine Art Scholar, 56; First Prize, John Moores Liverpool Exhib 5, 65; Comn Award, Arts Coun Great Britain, 69. *Bibliog:* Edward Lucie Smith & Patricia White (auth), Art in Britain, 1969-1970, Dent, London, 71; Anthony F Janson (auth), Profile-Michael Tyzack, Art Voices South, 80. *Mem:* Artists Int Asn, London (vchmn, 64-66, exec comt, 64-68); Col Art Asn Am. *Dealer:* Gillain Jason Gallery 42 Inverness St London NW1 England. *Mailing Add:* 159 Tradd St Charleston SC 29401

U

UBANS, JURIS K
PAINTER, EDUCATOR
b Riga, Latvia, July 12, 38; US citizen. *Study:* Yale Univ, with William Bailey & Bernard Chaet, 65; Syracuse Univ, BFA, 66, with Ainslee Burke & Frederick Hauck; Pa State Univ, MFA, 68, with Enrique Montenegro & Eugenio Battisti. *Work:* Yale Univ; Syracuse Univ; Pa State Univ; Univ Southern Maine; and pvt collections. *Comn:* A Season in Hell (ballet visuals), Syracuse Univ, NY, 66; Good Woman of Setzuan (theater visuals), Univ Maine, Portland-Gorham, 72, Renascence (planetarium visuals), 75 & From Morn Till Midnight (theater visuals), 76; Photography Maine 1973 (poster, catalog & cert design), Maine State Comn on Arts & Humanities, 73. *Exhib:* Everson Mus Art, Syracuse, 66; Nat Exhib Prints & Drawings, Okla Art Ctr, Okla, 69-70; Statements in Media, Haystack Traveling Exhib, 72-73; solo shows, Univ Maine, Augusta, 74 & Univ of the South, Sewanee, Tenn, 78; First Light Traveling Show, Calif, 75-76; Grand Valley State Col, Allendale, Mich, 79; and others. *Collections Arranged:* As It Was (auth, ed, catalog), 74, Ben Shahn-Photographs (auth & ed, catalog), 76 & Walker-Evans-Photographs, 78, Univ Southern Maine. *Pos:* Dir art gallery, Univ Southern Maine, 68-, chmn art dept, 74-; pres bd dir, Film Study Ctr, Portland, 72- *Teaching:* From asst prof to prof painting, film, photog & drawing, Univ Southern Maine, 68-; coordr Soleri sem, Haystack Mountain Sch, Deer Isle, Maine, summer 71. *Awards:* Helen B Stoeckel Fel, Yale Univ, 66; Hiram Gee Fel, Lowe Art Ctr, Syracuse, NY, 65; Gregory Batcock Prize, Independent Filmmakers, 68. *Mem:* Col Art Asn; Nat Asn Sch Art; Am Film Inst; and others. *Media:* Oil, Mixed Media. *Mailing Add:* Dept Art Univ Southern Maine 37 College Ave Gorham ME 04038

UBOGY, JO
SCULPTOR
b Hartford, Conn, Mar 7, 40. *Study:* Univ Wis, BS, 61; self-taught sculptor. *Work:* Bedford Executive Hotel, Stamford, Conn; Landmark Bldg, Stamford, Conn. *Exhib:* Silvermine Art of NE USA, Silvermine Galleries, New Canaan, Conn, 82, 86, 89 & 90; Pindo Gallery Invitational, Soho, NY, 83; Sidney Rothman, The Gallery, Barnegat Light, NJ, 79-90. *Mem:* Nat Asn Women Artists; Silvermine Guild Artists. *Media:* Welded Steel, Polyester Resins. *Publ:* Contrib, Encyclopedia of Gardening-Foliage Houseplants, Time-Life, 80. *Mailing Add:* 319 Cognewaugh Rd Cos Cob CT 06807

UCCELLO, VINCENZA AGATHA
PAINTER, DIRECTOR
b Hartford, Conn. *Study:* St Joseph Col, BS, 56; Wesleyan Univ, Conn, MALS, 61; Villa Schifanoia, Pius XII Inst, Florence, Italy, MFA, 63; Corcoran Sch Art, with Gene Davis; State Univ Iowa, with Byron Burford. *Work:* St Joseph Col, Conn; New York Pub Libr; Conn Nat Bank, Hartford, Conn. *Exhib:* Connecticut Women Artists Inc, New Britain Mus Am Art, 66; 12th Ann Drawing & Small Sculpture Exhib, Ball State Univ, 66; solo exhib, St Joseph Col, Conn, 81, Pump House Gallery, 86; Paperworks--Twelve New England Artists, Worcester Craft Ctr, Mass, 83; Sculptural Paper, Brookfield Craft Ctr, Conn, 83; Contemporary Paperworks, Hurlbutt Gallery, Greenwich, Conn, 84; Salt Box Gallery, W Hartford, Conn, 85 & 87. *Collections Arranged:* A Collectors Choice Mem Exhib, 67, Women in Art (By Women, About Women), 69, Childe Hassam, Impressionist Printmaker, 81, American Paintings of the 1920s & 1930s, 82, American Prints 1850-1950, 83 (auth, catalogs), Ukiyoe--The Floating World, 84, Avery Family Painting Exhib & Mid-Twentieth Century Prints, 85, Images of Women, 87, Connecticut Places, 87, Images of France, 89, St Joseph Col, Conn. *Pos:* Dir, Col Art Collections, Art Study Gallery, 85- *Teaching:* Assoc prof, St Joseph Col, Conn, 64-85, prof, 85, 89 (Hist French & Am Impressionism, Survey of Mod Art, Studio Courses). *Awards:* Alexander Harper Mem Award, 40th Ann Painting Exhib, Conn Women Artists Inc, 66; Yale Univ Vis Fac Fel, Mellon Found, 80; Judges Choice, Mem Exhib, Canton Artists Guild, 83, 90. *Mem:* Col Art Asn Am; Ctr Book Arts; Canton Artists Guild; Conn Women Artists Inc (pres, 74-76); Farmington Valley Art Ctr. *Media:* Miscellaneous, Handmade Paper Art. *Mailing Add:* 51 Hilltop Dr West Hartford CT 06107

UCHIMA, ANSEI
PRINTMAKER, PAINTER
b Stockton, Calif, May 1, 21. *Study:* Waseda Univ, Tokyo, 41. *Work:* Art Inst Chicago; Rijks Mus, Amsterdam; Libr of Cong, Washington, DC; Philadelphia Mus, Pa; Metrop Mus Art, New York; Nat Mus Mod Art, Tokyo, Japan; Nat Mus Art, Washington DC. *Exhib:* Tokyo Int Print Biennials, 57 & 60; Grenchen Int Print Triennials, 58, 61 & 70; 5th Sao Paulo Int Biennial, 59; Vancouver Int Print Exhib, 67; 35th Venice Int Biennial, 70; and over 50 one-man shows in the US, Japan & Europe. *Teaching:* Mem fac printmaking, Sarah Lawrence Col, 62-, emer prof, 88-; lectr printmaking, Columbia Univ, 68- *Awards:* Guggenheim Fel, 62-63 & 70-71. *Mem:* Soc Am Graphic Artists; Japan Print Asn. *Publ:* Una Johnson (auth), American Printmaking and Artist, Doubleday, 78. *Mailing Add:* 652 W 163rd St No 61 New York NY 10032

UCHIMA, TOSHIKO
PAINTER, ASSEMBLAGE ARTIST
b Manchuria, China; Japanese citizen. *Study:* Kobe Col, Japan, BA; and with Ryohei Koiso. *Work:* Art Inst Chicago; Hampton Inst, Va; Brooklyn Mus; Striped House Mus, Tokyo, Japan; Hiroshima Mus, Hiroshima, Japan. *Exhib:* Grenchen Int Print Triennial, Switz, 58; Art Inst Chicago, 60; Striped House Mus, 82, 86 & 89; 13 one-person shows in the US, Japan & Europe. *Publ:* Contribr, Sphynx (portfolio prints & poems), 54. *Mailing Add:* 3807 Ravine St Shrub Oak NY 10588

UDINOTTI, AGNESE
SCULPTOR, PAINTER
b Athens, Greece, Jan 9, 40; US citizen. *Study:* Ariz State Univ, BA & MA. *Work:* Phoenix Art Mus, Ariz; Univ Utah; Am Collections, Ariz State Univ; Glendale Community Col; Western Col Yuma; and many others. *Comn:* Steel doors, Wilson Jones & Assocs, Scottsdale, Ariz, 70 & Imagineering, Tucson, Ariz, 72; relief, comn by Mrs M Ehrlich, Phoenix, 70; steel diptych, comn by Har Oude Jans, Amsterdam, Holland, 72; outdoor sculpture, comn by Glendale Community Col, 74; outdoor sculpture, comn by Harold Hart, Okemos, Mich, 83; S F Ballet Sch, 84. *Exhib:* One-man shows, Vorpal Galleries, San Francisco, 68, 71 & 75, Laguna Beach, 79, Art Forms Gallery, Athens, 69, 71, 75, 77, 81, 85, 88 & 92; Vorpal, NY, 76, 79 & 81; Pasquale Ianetti Gallery, San Francisco, 83; Gallery 30, San Mateo, 86; Restrospective, Sculptors' Guild, 89; Nat Mus Women Arts, 89. *Teaching:* Workshop leader welded sculpture, Orme Sch Fine Arts Prog, Mayer, Ariz, 71 & 72; Univ Southern Calif, summer 72. *Awards:* Sculpture Prize, Phoenix Art Mus 1st Biennial, 71; Solomos Prize for sculpture, Panos Nikoli Tselepi, Athens, 71; Award, Scottsdale Ctr for the Arts, 74; and others. *Bibliog:* Seiden Meilach (auth), Creating Art from Anything, Reilly & Lee, 68; Cortright (auth), Agnese Udinotti; A study in armor, Phoenix Mag, 1/78; An independent, unoppressive artist, Southwest Art Mag, 4/77; The art of Agnese Udinotti, Elkastika, 10/85. *Media:* Steel, Bronze, Oil. *Publ:* Auth, Udinotti, Northland Press & Macabre love songs and aphorisms, Greek Publ, Kedros; My Udinotti J, Vol 1, Amaranth Press, 77, Vol 2, Udinotti Publ, 79; Greek Artists Abroad, Ministry of Foreign Affairs, Greece; George Alpert Photographs Udinotti, Paradise House, 88; A Biography, Paradise House, Udinotti, 89. *Mailing Add:* c/o 4215 N Marshall Way Scottsdale AZ 85251

UDVARDY, JOHN WARREN
SCULPTOR, EDUCATOR
b Elyria, Ohio. *Study:* Skowhegan Sch Painting & Sculpture, scholar, summer 57; Cleveland Inst Art, scholar, 55-58, BFA, 63; Yale Univ, scholar, 64-65, MFA, 65. *Work:* Newport Art Mus, RI; Columbia Broadcasting System, New York; Fogg Mus, Cambridge, Mass; Wellesley Col Mus, Mass. *Comn:* Outdoor site sculpture, Wellesley Col, Mass, 86. *Exhib:* Addison Gallery Am Art, Andover, Mass, 84; Lenore Gray Gallery, Providence, RI, 87; Univ Mass, North Dartmouth, 87; Newport Art Mus, RI, 89; Clark Univ, Worcester, Mass, 91; Virginia Lynch Gallery, Tiverton, RI, 92. *Pos:* Artist-in-residence, Dartmouth Col, Hanover, NH, fall term 82; juror, Fel Awards, RI State Coun Arts, 85; vis artist, Wellesley Col, Mass, fall term 86; nat screening comt, Fulbright Awards, Inst Int Educ, New York, 91. *Teaching:* Instr drawing, Cleveland Inst Art, 62-63; asst printmaking, Yale Univ, 64-65; asst prof painting & design, Brown Univ, 65-73; chmn, Freshman Found Div, RI Sch Design, 73-77 & 79-82, prof design, 78-92, dir, summer trasfer prog, 73-82. *Awards:* Distinguished Alumnus Award, Cleveland Inst Art, Ohio, 70; First Prize, Silver Medal, Centennial Sculpture Show, Providence Art Club, 80; Silver Medal, RI Sch Design, Providence, 90. *Media:* Wood, Natural Materials. *Publ:* Illusr, Los, fall 68 & spring 70, Art J, winter 73, Art in Am, 3-4/75, Mich Quart Rev, spring 79. *Dealer:* Virginia Lynch Gallery 3883 Main Rd Rt 77 Tiverton RI 02878. *Mailing Add:* Dept Freshman Found RI Sch Design 2 College St Providence RI 02903

UELSMANN, JERRY
PHOTOGRAPHER
b Detroit, Mich, June 11, 34. *Study:* Rochester Inst Technol, with Ralph Hattersley & Minor White, BFA, 57; Ind Univ, with Henry Holmes Smith, MS, 58, MFA, 60. *Work:* Mus Mod Art, New York; Philadelphia Mus Art; Art Inst Chicago; Nat Gallery Can, Ottawa; Int Mus Photog, George Eastman House, Rochester, NY; Moderna Museet, Stockholm, Sweden; Nat Gallery Australia, Melbourne; and many others national & international. *Exhib:* Photography in America 1850-1965, Yale Univ Art Gallery, 65; Photography in the Twentieth Century, George Eastman House in collab with Nat Gallery Can, 67; one-man shows, Camera Obscure Gallery, Denver, Colo, 89, Hicks Art Ctr, Bucks Co Pa, 89, Odessa Col, Tex, 89, Photogroup Ctr Gallery, Coral Gables, Fla, 89, Susan Spiritus Gallery, Costa Mesa, Calif, 89, Danforth Mus Art, Framington, Mass, 89 & Vision Gallery, San Francisco, Calif, 89; Nat Gallery Australia, Melbourne; Nat Gallery Can, Ottawa, Ont; Nat Mus Mod Art, Kyoto, Japan; Victoria & Albert Mus, London, Eng. *Teaching:* Instr photog, Univ Fla, Gainesville, 62-64, from asst to prof, 64-74, grad res prof, 74-; vis prof, Nihon Univ Art, Tokyo, Japan, 79. *Awards:* Medal, City of Arles, France; Teacher/Scholar of the Year, Univ Fla, Gainesville, 75; Bronze Medal, Zagreb, Yugoslavia; and others. *Bibliog:* Jerry N Uelsmann-Photography from 1975-1979, Columbia Col, Chicago, Ill, 80; James L Enyeat (auth), Jerry N Uelsmann Twenty-five Years: A Retrospective, New York Graphic Soc, Boston, Mass, 82; Uelsmann: Process and Perception, Gainesville, Fla, 85; and others. *Mem:* Nat Endowment Arts (Photog Fel), 72; Fel Royal Photog Soc, Gt Brit; Soc Photog Educ (found mem & bd dirs); The Friends of Photog (adv trustee); Kodak Educ Adv Coun, 87-90; and others. *Publ:* Contribr, Contemp Photog, 64, Camera, 67, Aperture, 67, 68 & 70, Life, 69 & Infinity; Jerry N Uelsman-Photography from 1975-79, Columbia Col, Chicago, Ill, 80. *Dealer:* Witkin Gallery 41 E 57th St New York NY 10022. *Mailing Add:* 5701 SW 17th Dr Gainesville FL 32608

UGLOW, ALAN
PAINTER
b Luton, England, 1941. *Study:* Cent Sch Art, BA, 64. *Work:* Fundacion Cultural Televisa, Mexico City, Mex; McCrory Corp, New York. *Exhib:* Solo exhibs, Galerie Rolf Ricke, Cologne, WGer, 87, Lorence Monk Gallery, New York, 88, Galerie Onrust, Amsterdam, 90; Une Autre Affaire, Le Consortium, Dijon, France, 89; The Red Show, Galerie Christine & Isy Brachot, Bussels, 90. *Bibliog:* Roberta Smith (auth), Review, New York Times, 2-5/88; Shirley Kaneda and Saul Ostrow (coauths), Alan Uglow, Arts Mag, 3/89; Jack Bankowsky (auth), Alan Uglow, Artforum, 3/89. *Media:* All Media. *Dealer:* Lorence Monk Gallery 568-578 Broadway New York NY 10012. *Mailing Add:* 103 Bowery New York NY 10002

UHRMAN, CELIA
PAINTER, WRITER
b New London, Conn, May 14, 27. *Study:* Brooklyn Col, BA & MA, 53; Brooklyn Mus Art Sch, 56-57; Teachers Col, Columbia Univ, 61; City Univ New York, 66; Univ Danzig, PhD, 77. *Work:* Brooklyn Col; Ovar Mus; govt bldgs in Spain & Portugal. *Exhib:* 2nd All New England Drawing, Lyman Allyn Mus, New London, Conn, 60; 26th Ann Contemp Am Paintings, Soc Four Arts, Palm Beach, Fla, 64; Des Beaux-Arts Exhib, Monaco, Monte-Carlo, 69-70 & 72; Premi Int Dibeaux, Joan Miro, Barcelona, Spain, 70; 26th Expos Int d'Art Contemporain, Luxembourg, 74. *Teaching:* Teacher art & spec talent classes, Lefferts Jr High Sch, Brooklyn, NY, 58-59. *Awards:* Academic Laurel, 27th Int Exhib Contemp Art, Moka Club, Paris, 74; Cert of Appreciation, New York Bd Educ, 82; Cert Koret Living Lib, Fromm Inst, Univ San Francisco. *Bibliog:* Jim Burns Talk Show (interview), WECT-TV, Wilmington, NC, 7/10/73; Rev in Int News, Int Arts Bull, 75; Div Gen Educ, NY Univ, Part IV (film), 58. *Mem:* Centro Studi E Scambi Int, Rome (hon US rep, 70- & mem int exec comt); Int Arts Guild, Monte-Carlo (commandeur mem arts & lett, 66); New York Artists Equity. *Media:* Oil, Watercolor. *Publ:* Auth, A Pause for Poetry for Children, 73; The Chimps are Coming (novel), 75; Love Fancies, 87; and others. *Mailing Add:* 1655 Flatbush Ave Brooklyn NY 11210

UHRMAN, ESTHER
PAINTER, WRITER
b New London, Conn, July 7, 21. *Study:* Traphagan Sch Fashion, (design & illus), 55; New York City Community Col, AA, 74; Cornell Univ, 77; Col New Rochelle; Danzig Univ, PhD, 77. *Work:* Ovar Mus, Portugal; var pub bldgs in Spain. *Exhib:* Washington Watercolor Soc 65th Ann, Smithsonian Inst, 62; Tribute to Southeastern Connecticut, Mohican Hotel, New London, 62; Uhrman Show of Water Colors, Rivoli, Brooklyn, 63; Premi Int Dibuix Joan Miro, Barcelona, Spain, 70; 26th Expos Int Art Contemp, Luxembourg, 74. *Awards:* Golden Windmill Radio Drama Award, Holland, 71; Dipl of Honor Palme, Int Arts Guild, Monaco, 72; Cert, Koret Living Libr, Fromm Inst, Univ San Francisco. *Bibliog:* Charles Richman (auth), articles, Brooklyn Rec, 57-; article, Flatbusha, 60; articles, Int Arts Bulletin, 72- *Mem:* Int Arts Guild, Monte Carlo (commandeur mem arts & lett, 66-); Centre Studi e Scambi Int, Rome (hon US rep, 74-). *Media:* Oil, Watercolor. *Publ:* Auth, Cover Your Walls, Diet Indust, 57; Gypsy Logic, 70 & Mocking Ghost, Life is Tremendous, 72; Brotherhood, Pub Employee Press, 74; From Canarsie to Masada, 78; Mitras, The Second, 88. *Mailing Add:* 1655 Flatbush Ave Apt C106 Brooklyn NY 11210

UKELES, MIERLE LADERMAN
ENVIRONMENTAL ARTIST, SCULPTOR
b Denver, Colo, Sept 25, 39. *Study:* Barnard Col, New York, BA, 61; New York Univ, MA, 74. *Work:* Flow City, New York City Dept Sanitation, 59th Marine Transfer Station. *Comn:* Vuilniswagendans, comn City of Rotterdam, Holland, 85; Ceremonial Arch Honoring Service Workers, Olympia & York, 88; Danehy Park Landfill Project, Cambridge Arts Coun, Cambridge, Mass, 90; Barge and Towboat Ballet, Three Rivers Arts Festival, Pittsburgh, Pa, 92. *Exhib:* Recycle Works, Bronx Mus Art, NY, 89 & State Univ NY, Old Westbury, 89; Pit/Egg: A New Low for Holland, Allocations, Floriade The Hague, Zoetermeer, Neth, 92; Fragile Ecologies, Queens Mus, Flushing NY, 92. *Pos:* Artist in Residence, New York City Dept Sanitation, 82- *Teaching:* Guest instr & lectr, Claremont Col Grad Sch, Calif, 90; plus numerous lectures and symposia nationwide. *Bibliog:* New Art, Harry Abrams, 90; Richard Martin (auth), New Urban Landscape, Rizzoli, 90; Suzi Gablik (auth), The Re-enchantment of Art, Thames & Hudson, 91. *Publ:* Auth, New Urban Landscapes, Rizzoli, 90; A Journey: Earth/City/Flow, Art J, summer 92. *Dealer:* Ronald Feldman Fine Arts 31 Mercer St New York NY 10013. *Mailing Add:* c/o Rondald Feldman 31-33 Mercer St New York NY 10013

ULLBERG, KENT
SCULPTOR
Goteborg, Sweden, July 15, 45. *Study:* Swedish State Sch Art, cert(drawing & sculpture); Swedish Mus Natural Hist, anat, 4 yrs; Mus Des Sci Naturelles, Orleans, France. *Work:* Swedish Mus Natural Hist, Goteborg; Exhib Palace, Peking, China; Corpus Christi Mus, Tex; Los Angeles Co Mus; Denver Mus Natural Hist; City Ft Lauderdale, Fla. *Comn:* Monumental sculptures, Lincoln Ctr, Dallas, 81, Corpus Christi Nat Bank, Tex, 81, City Corpus Christi, 83, Corp Plaza, Boca Raton, Fla, 83, Lywam Art Mus, Wausau, Wis, 83, Genesee Mus, Rochester, NY, 84, Acad Natural Sci, Philadelphia, 87 & Nat Wildlife Fedn, Washington, DC, 89; Ft Lauderdale, Fla, 91. *Exhib:* Ann Exhib, Nat Acad Design, New York, 75-90; Nat Sculpture Soc Ann Exhib, New York, 77-90; Nat Cowboy Hall of Fame, Oklahoma City, 77-90; Salon D'Automne, Paris, France, 78; Artists of Am, Colo Heritage Ctr Mus, 81-90; Art Mus S Tex, 85; Biologiska Museet, Stockholm, Sweden, 89; Munic Art Gallery, Luxemburg, 89. *Pos:* Cur, Nat Mus & Art Gallery, Botswana, Africa, 71-74; cur/consult, Denver Mus Natural Hist, 74-76. *Teaching:* Instr, Scottsdale Artists Sch, 86. *Awards:* Merit Awards, Soc Animal Artists, New York, 79-80, 82 & 87; Gold Medal Sculpture, Nat Acad Western Art, Oklahoma City, 81,82, 88 & 90; Gold Medal, Nat Sculpture Soc, New York 83. *Bibliog:* Article, Southwest Art, 5/76; article, Colo Outdoors, 7/77; Capturing Life in Broze (film), 81; article, Artists of the Rockies, winter 83; Kent Ullberg-Sculptor (film), PBS, 84. *Mem:* Nat Sculpture Soc; Nat Acad Western Art; Cowboy Hall Fame; Academician, Nat Acad Design, New York; Soc Animal Artists & Nat Arts Club, New York; Allied Artists Am, New York; Am Soc Marine Artists, Conn; Soc Wildlife Art for the Nations, Eng. *Media:* Bronze, Steel. *Dealer:* C C Art Connection 3636 S Alameda Corpus Christi TX 78411; Trailside Gallery 105 N Ctr Jackson Hole Wyoming 83001. *Mailing Add:* 14337 Aquarius St Padre Island Corpus Christi TX 78418

ULLMAN, (MRS) GEORGE W
COLLECTOR
Mem: Costume Soc Am; Am Fedn Arts; Ariz Costume Inst; Desert Botanical Garden of Phoenix; Taliesin Coun. *Collection:* French furniture and paintings, Louis XV and Louis XVI periods; Haitian paintings; contemporary paintings of Philip Curtis; Spanish paintings, seventeenth and eighteenth century on painted furniture & glass. *Mailing Add:* 4642 N 56th St Phoenix AZ 85018

ULLMAN, JANE F
SCULPTOR
b Ft Wayne, Ind, June 5, 08. *Work:* Mus Contemp Art & Art Inst, Chicago; Bowers Mus, Santa Ana, Calif; Univ Calif & Occidental Col, Los Angeles. *Comn:* Portrait, Gertrude Stein, Culoz, France; portrait, Bruno Bettelhem, Orthogenic Clinic, Univ Chicago, 88-89; portrait, Gregor Piatigorsky, comn by Charlotte Ralik, Los Angeles Music Ctr; portrait, Marta Feuchtwanger, Feutchtwanger Libr, Univ Southern Calif; Terra Cotta Torso, Standard Club, Chicago. *Exhib:* Easter Robles Gallery, Los Angeles, 73-77; one-women exhib, Print & Painting, Bechtel Ctr, Stanford Univ, Palo Alto, 80; retrospective, Bowers Mus, Santa Ana, Calif. *Teaching:* Instr sculpting for children & adults, pvt lessons, 50- & clay instr summers in Switz. *Media:* Marble, Clay. *Dealer:* Toby Moss 7321 Beverly Blvd Los Angeles CA 90036. *Mailing Add:* 800 Woodacres Rd Santa Monica CA 90402

ULRICH, DAVID ALAN
PHOTOGRAPHER, EDUCATOR
b Akron, Ohio, Apr 18, 50. *Study:* Studied with Minor White, 70-76; Sch of Mus of Fine Arts, Tufts Univ, BFA, 74; RI Sch Design, MFA, 77. *Work:* Minor White Archives, Princeton Univ, NJ; Mass Inst Technol, Cambridge; RI Sch Design, Providence; The Photog Place, Philadelphia; Photogenesis, Columbus, Ohio. *Exhib:* One-man exhibs, Hawaii: Landscape of Transformation, Gallery East, Boston, MA, 89, Bishop Mus, Honolulu, HI, 90 & Hui No'eru Visual Arts Ctr, 91; Expression Through Light, 72 & Nine Photographers (with catalog), 74, Akron Art Inst, Ohio; Octave of Prayer (with catalog), 72 & Celebrations (with catalog), 74, Hayden Gallery, Mass Inst Technol; Recent Work of Twelve Photographers, Addison Gallery Am Art, Andover, 77; 4x5 Plus-Large Format Photographers, Community Arts Gallery, Univ Mass, Boston, 79; Second Sight-An Exploration into Infrared Photog, Carpenter Ctr Visual Arts, Harvard Univ, 80; Perspectival Multiples (catalog) Mus de Arte Contemp Gallery Caralas, Venezuela, 90; Image XVIII, Amfal Plaza, Honolulu, 91; Artists of Hawaii, Honolulu Acad Arts, 92. *Pos:* Dir, Prospect Street Gallery, Cambridge, 73-74; exec dir, Hui No'eau Visual Arts Ctr, Maui, Hawaii, 91- *Teaching:* Assoc prof photog, Art Inst Boston, 77-, co-chmn, photog dept, 80-84, chmn, 84-91. *Bibliog:* Fernando de Trazegnies G (auth), El sonido de una sola mano, El Comercio, Lima, Peru, 78; Stu Cohen (auth), The art of making a point, Boston Phoenix, 79. *Mem:*

Soc Photog Educ; Photog Resource Ctr. *Publ:* Contribr, Aura, Mag of Contemp Photog, Buffalo, 76; Parabola vol XIV, No 3, 89, NY; Manoa vol 2, No 1, Univ Hawaii Press, 90; The Bumming Island, Sierra Club Bks, 91. *Mailing Add:* 2841 Baldwin Ave Makawao HI 96768

ULRICH, EDWIN ABEL
MUSEUM DIRECTOR
b Brooklyn, NY, Dec 23, 97. *Study:* Wichita State Univ, LHD, 88. *Pos:* Dir, Edwin A Ulrich Mus, Hyde Park, 56- *Bibliog:* Bruce Blackwell (auth), Wavecrest: Realization of an artistic obsession, Hyde Park Townsman, 10/30/85; article, Poughkeepsie J, 6/26/81. *Collection:* American art, specializing in Frederick J Waugh, 1861-1940; has given Frederick J Waugh Collection to Wichita State Univ and donated a trust to support the collection; in recognition, Bd of Regents named the new univ mus, Edwin A Ulrich Mus of Art; also loaned paintings to Smithsonian Inst for traveling exhib, 69-71; paintings have been exhibited in various cities and mus. *Mailing Add:* Edwin A Ulrich Mus PO Box 632 Hyde Park NY 12538

ULTRA VIOLET
PAINTER, WRITER
b La Tronche, Isere, France, Sept 6, 35; Fr & Am citizen. *Work:* Mus Mod Art, Medzilaborce, Czech; Petit Palais Collection, Paris, France; Mus Art, Paterson, NJ; Espace Giletta Mus, Nice, France. *Exhib:* American Artists, Mus Art, Patterson, NJ, 89; Fiac Edition, Le Grand Palais, Paris, France, 90; Apocalyptical Angels, 86 Gallery Lodz, Poland & Mus Mod Art, Medzilaborce, 92; Les Anges Apocalyptiques, French Inst, Bratislava, Czech, 92; L'art dams la Rue, La Rotonde, Beaulieu, France, 92; L'Art Influence les Artists, Found Sofia Lafitte, Antipolis, 92; Warhol et Moi, Inst Etudes Sup Arts, Paris, 92. *Pos:* Master of aprentis, Union Libre des Travaillours Artistiques, 91-92. *Awards:* Award for best bookwriting, pictures & graphics, Frankfurt, Deutsh Bibliothek, 89. *Bibliog:* Grace Gluck (auth), We Threw Andy Out, NY Times, 88; Frederick Mitterand, du Cote' de Chez Fred (film), TV, French, 89; Pavel Vojir (auth), Fialovy Andel, Reflex, 92. *Mem:* Union Libre des Travailleurs Artistiques (pres, 92). *Media:* All Media. *Res:* American pop art; Andy Warhol; Spiritual Christian belief, scripture. *Publ:* Auth, Diplomatic Corner, Diplomatic World Bulletin, 85; Famous for 15 Minutes, My Years with Andy Warhol, 88; coauth, Kiki's Paris, J Art, 89; auth, Le Revers du Reve, Ancrage, 89; Goodbye Dali, It's Been Surreal, NY Times, 1/30/89. *Dealer:* Jye Jacot Art Gallery 1 Rue de Rivoli Nice 06000 France. *Mailing Add:* 19 E 88 St New York NY 10028

UMLAUF, CHARLES
SCULPTOR
b Mich, July 17, 11. *Study:* Art Inst Chicago, with Albin Polasek; Chicago Sch Sculpture, with Viola Norman. *Work:* Santa Barbara Mus, Calif; Palm Springs Desert Mus, Calif; Henry E Huntington Libr & Art Gallery; Roswell Mus Art Ctr, NMex; La State Univ Union Gallery, Baton Rouge; Nat Collection Fine Arts, Smithsonian Inst, Washington, DC. *Comn:* Icarus (bronze), Space Technol Ctr, Univ Kans, Lawrence, 64; Family Group (three figural bronze), Houston Mus Natural Sci, Tex, 72; Madonna and Child (9' bronze), St David's Community Hosp, Austin, Tex, 89; Spirit of Learning (Abstraction Form VII 12' bronze), TRS bldg, Austin, Tex, 90; Prometheus (15' bronze, includes 6' granite pedestal), Northridge Austin Community Col, Tex, 90. *Exhib:* American Sculpture, Metrop Mus Art, New York, 51; Int Relig Biennial, Salzburg, Austria, Ger, Spain & Eng, 58-59; 20th Ceramic Int, Everson Mus, Syracuse, NY & tour, 59-60; 161st Ann, Pa Acad Fine Arts, Philadelphia, 66; three retrospectives, Valley House Gallery, Dallas, 59 & Univ Tex Art Mus, Austin, 67 & 80; Centennial exhib works by outstanding artists who attended Sch Art Inst, Chicago, 79-80; Century of Sculpture in Texas, 90. *Teaching:* Prof sculpture, Univ Tex, Austin, 52-81, Leslie Waggener Prof Fine Arts, 80-81, prof emer, 81- *Awards:* Guggenheim Grant, 49-50; Univ Tex Grant, 66; Ford Found Grant, 79; Tex Artist of the Yr, Art League, Houston, 85. *Bibliog:* Donald B Goodall (auth), Charles Umlauf, Sculptor, Univ Tex Press, 67; Earl Miller (dir), Bronze Sculpture in the Making (film), produced by Univ Tex, 69; Gibson A Danes (auth), The Sculpture and Drawing of Charles Umlauf, Univ Tex Press, 80 & Hart Graphics, 90. *Media:* Bronze, Marble. *Dealer:* Bryant Galleries 2845 Lakeland Drive Jackson MS 39208; Sol del Rio Gallery 1020 Townsend San Antonio TX 78209. *Mailing Add:* 506 Barton Blvd Austin TX 78704

UMLAUF, KARL A
PAINTER, SCULPTOR
b Chicago, Ill, May 16, 39. *Study:* Univ Tex, Austin, BFA, 57-61; Yale Univ, fel, summer 60; Cornell Univ, MFA, 63. *Work:* New Orleans Mus Art, La; Everson Mus, Syracuse, NY; Joslyn Art Mus, Omaha; Mod Mus Art; Dallas Mus Art; IBM Corp, New York, Austin, Dallas, Tex; Fogg Art Mus; Cornell Univ, New York; Okla Art Ctr, Okla City; Evansville Mus, Ind. *Exhib:* Ann Delta Exhib, Ark Art Ctr, Little Rock, 72, 79, 84 & 90; Artist Biennial, New Orleans Mus, 73 & 77; Ann Nat Painting & Sculpture Exhib, Longview Mus, Tex, 76, 79, 82, 84, 86, 87, 89, 90, 91; Works on Paper Southwest '78, Dallas Mus Art; The First 20 Years, Tyler Mus Art, Tex, 83; Tex Art Celebration, Houston, 86, 88, 90 & 91; Totally Tex, Dallas, 86; North East Missouri Univ, 90; and others. *Pos:* Vis artist, Tex Tech Univ, 74, 85, 87; Colo State Univ, 73, Ball State Univ, 75, Ariz State Univ, 79, Univ of Tex, Tyler, 86, Univ Tex, Arlington, 91. *Teaching:* Prof art, E Tex State Univ, Commerce, 67-89; prof, Ind Univ, Bloomington, 74-75 & 80; artist in residence, Baylor Univ, Waco, Tex, 89- *Awards:* First Prize, Okla Art Ctr, 70 & 74; First Prize, New Orleans Mus Art; First Prize, Evansville Mus Art, 75; Grand Prize, Tex Celebration, Houston, 86; First Prize, Longview Mus Art, Tex, 87 & 90; Merit Award, Amarillo Competition, Tex, 87; Third Prize, Tex Celebration, Houston, 91. *Bibliog:* On the Cover, Dallas Times Herald, 82; Review, Houston Chronicle, Art Scene, 86; Lifestyles, Perspective, Ft Worth Star Telegram, 88; Artists Turn Memories Into Reality, Waco Tribune, 91. *Mem:* Tex Art & Sculpture Asn; Tex Fine Arts Asn; Tex Asn Col Teachers; Col Art Asn Am. *Media:* Mixed Media with Bas Relief Format. *Publ:* Auth, The First Twenty Years, Tyler Mus Art (Catalog); Karl Umlauf-Transitions (catalog), 89-91. *Dealer:* Miriam Perlman Gallery Chicago IL; Wm Campbell Contemp Art Fort Worth TX. *Mailing Add:* 109 Royal Ln Commerce TX 75428

UMLAUF, LYNN (CHARLOTTE)
PAINTER, SCULPTOR
b Austin, Tex, Jan 8, 42. *Study:* Art Students League, 61-62; Acad Fine Arts, Florence, 65-66; Univ Tex, Austin, MFA, 68. *Work:* Chase Manhattan Bank; PS 1, Long Island City, NY; Fox & Horan, New York; Goldman Sachs & Co; Pacesetter Corp, Omaha, New York. *Exhib:* Whitney Mus Am Art Biennial Exhib, 75; Seven Artists, Neuberger Mus, Purchase, NY, 85; Painting and Sculpture Today, Indianapolis Mus Art, 78; solo exhibs, Hal Bromm Gallery, New York, 78-80 & Young Hoffman Gallery, Chicago, 83; Pam Adler Gallery, 86; Alternative Supports: Contemporary Sculpture on the Wall, Providence, RI, 87; Penine Hart Gallery, 90 & 92; Oratorio Installation, Spinea (Ve), Italy, 92. *Teaching:* Instr, Fairleigh-Dickinson Univ, 71-72, Philadelphia Col Art, 79, Kutztown State Col, 80-81 & Sch Visual Arts, 81- *Bibliog:* John Loughery (auth), article, 4/86 & Gail Stavitsky (auth), article, 4/86, Arts Mag; Tiffany Bell (auth), Responses to Neo-Expressionism, Flash Art Int, 5/83; Agnes Kohlmeyer (auth), Pino Pinelli, Lynn Umlaue, Fonema Edizioui, Spinca (Ve), Italy, 6/92. *Media:* Acrylic, Wire. *Mailing Add:* 222 Bowery New York NY 10012

UNDERHILL, LINN B
PHOTOGRAPHER
Study: Univ Calif Berkeley, 53-56; San Francisco Art Inst, with Dorothea Lange & John Collier Jr, 56-57; Univ Rochester, NY, hist 19th century photog with Robert Sobieszek, 77; Col Ceramics, Alfred Univ, NY, BFA(photog), 78; State Univ NY Buffalo, MFA(photog studies), 82; Visual Arts Studies Workshop, Rochester, NY, 82. *Exhib:* Solo shows, Light Work, Syracuse, NY, 84, CEPA Gallery, Buffalo, NY, 89 & Mednick Gallery, Univ Arts, Philadelphia, Pa, 92; Toronto Photogs Workshop, Ont, 92; 494 Gallery, New York, 92. *Pos:* Edited & compiled photogs, The Buses Roll, W W Norton & Co Inc, 73-74; coordr, Copy Ctr, Visual Studies Workshop, 79-81, conserv tech, res ctr print collection, 81-82, coordr res ctr, 82-84. *Teaching:* Instr basic photog, Alfred Univ, 72-74; instr, Visual Studies Workshop, 80-81; adj fac fine arts dept, Col Graphic Arts & Photog, Rochester Inst Technol, NY, 81-82; assoc fac & tutor, Empire State Col, Rochester, NY, 82; lectr & vis artist, var univ & col, 83-92; adj fac, Ithaca Col, NY & State Univ NY, Binghamton, NY, 85-88; asst prof, Rutgers Univ, New Brunswick, NJ, 88-89; asst prof, Syracuse Univ, NY, 89-92; instr photog, Syracuse Univ, Div Int Progs Abroad, Florence, Italy, 90; vis asst prof, dept art & art hist, Colgate Univ, Hamilton, NY, 92- *Awards:* Artist-in-Residence, Light Work, Syracuse, NY, 83; Nat Endowment Arts, Visual Artists Fel, 84 & 90; New York Found Arts, Photogr's Fel, 89. *Bibliog:* Esther Parada (auth), Women's vision extends the map of memory, Mich Quart Rev, winter 87; Marilyn Rivchin (auth), An interview with Linn Underhill, Q: A J Art, Dept Art, Cornell Univ, 89; Marion Faller (auth), Lost and found: an interview with Linn Underhill, Afterimage, 2/90. *Publ:* Auth, The National Endowment reviewed: a panelist speaks out, Exposure, Vol 26, No 4, 89. *Mailing Add:* RR 1 No 42D Lisle NY 13797

UNDERHILL, WILLIAM
SCULPTOR
b Berkeley, Calif, 33. *Study:* Univ Calif, Berkeley, BFA, 60, MFA, 61. *Work:* Am Craft Mus, New York, NY; Oakland Mus Art; Johnson Wax Collection Contemp Am Crafts, Racine, Wis; Cooper Hewitt Mus; Swarthmore Col, Pa. *Exhib:* Solo exhibs, Blumenthal Gallery, New York, 63, Fosdick-Nelson Gallery, Alfred Univ, NY, 78, Garth Clark Gallery, New York, 89, Los Angeles, 90 & Joan Farrell Gallery, Washington, DC, 92; The Ritual Vessel, Twining Gallery, New York, 87; Craft Art in Western New York, Burchfield Art Ctr, State Univ Col, Buffalo, 88; Metalforms Exhib, Zoller Gallery, Pa State Univ, College Park & Art Gallery, Univ Pittsburgh, Bradford, 88; Int Invitational Sculpture Exhib, Lamberton Conservatory, Rochester, NY, 88; The Art of Cast Iron: Contemp Sculpture, Univ Ala, Birmingham, 88; Craft Today USA, Musee des Arts Decoratifs, Paris, 89; The Vessel: Studies in Form and Material, Craft Folk Art Mus, Los Angeles, Calif, 89; Factory Art, Kohler Art Ctr, Sheboygan, Wis, 89; Contemporary American Metalsmiths, Johnson Co Community Col, Kansas City, Mo, 92; The New Bronze Age, Pittsburgh Mus Contemp Crafts, 92. *Teaching:* Instr, Pratt Inst, Brooklyn, 64-65, Columbia Teacher's Col, New York, 66-67 & New York Univ, 68-69; assoc prof, NY State Col Ceramics, Alfred Univ, NY, 69-85. *Awards:* Purchase Prize, Oakland Art Mus, Calif, 61; Grant, Louis Comfort Tiffany Found, 64; Visual Artists Fel, Nat Endowment Arts, 86; NY State Found Arts fel, 87; J M Kohler Artist-in-Residence Prog, Wis, 88. *Bibliog:* Oppi Untract (auth), Metal Techniques for Craftsmen, 68; Lee Nordness (auth), Objects: USA, 70; Ed Lebow (auth), William Underhill, Metalsmith, Winter, 87. *Mailing Add:* c/o Garth Clark Gallery 24 W 57th St New York NY 10019

UNGER, MARY ANN
SCULPTOR
b New York, NY, May 10, 45. *Study:* Mt Holyoke Col, BA(magna cum laude), 67; Univ of Calif, Berkeley, Columbia Univ, MFA, 75. *Work:* Best & Co; E F Hutton; Mus Int Art, Sofia, Bulgaria. *Comn:* Princeton Forrestal Village, Princeton, NJ; City Hall Plaza, Tampa, Fla; Cave Creek Sports Complex, Phoenix, Ariz. *Exhib:* Solo shows, City Univ NY Grad Ctr, NY, 82, 55 Mercer, New York, 83, Nassau Co Mus Fine Arts, Roslyn, NY, 85,

Sculpture Ctr, Hosp Ctr, New York, 86 & Bellevue Hosp Ctr, New York, 88; group exhib, Nature Transformed, Anderson Gallery, Va Community Univ, Richmond, Mus Highlands on Hudson, Cornwall-on-Hudson, NY, 82, Tower Gallery, New York, New House Gallery, Staten Island, NY & The Ways of Wood, Queens Col, Flushing, NY, 84; Inside/Out, Bronx River Restoration Art Ctr, NY, 83; The Figure as the Image of the Psyche, Sculpture Ctr, NY, 85. *Awards:* Pollock Krasner, New York Found, 89; Found Arts, 90; Sponsored Artist Proj Grant, NY State Coun Arts, 85. *Bibliog:* Grace Glueck (auth), article, New York Times, 1/31/82; Malcolm Preston (auth), Newsday, 7/25/85; Michael Brenson (auth), New York Times, 12/6/85 & 5/23/86; Edward Sozanski (auth), Philadelphia Inquirer, 8/86; William Zimmer (auth), New York Times, 6/28/87; Michael Brenson (auth), New York Times, 7/15/88. *Media:* Painted Metal, Plaster. *Mailing Add:* c/o Valencia Community College East Campus Galleries Orlando FL 32802

UNITHAN, DOLLY
PAINTER, SCULPTOR
b Kota Baharu, Kelantan, Malaysia, Aug 10, 40. *Study:* Ecole Nat des Beaux Art de Nancy, France, 74; Hornsey Col Art, London, BFA, 75; Pratt Inst, New York, MFA,78. *Work:* Alternative Mus, New York; Nat Art Gallery, Kuala Lumpur, Malaysia; Lock Haven State Col, Pa; Am Asn State Cols & Univs, Washington, DC; Wifredo Lam Ctr, Havana, Cuba; Malaysian Mission to UN & Malaysian Consul Gen, New York; Spirit Found, New York; Malaysian Embassy, Wash, DC; Malaysian Trade Mission, New York; Asian Am Arts Ctr, New York. *Exhib:* 3rd Int Drawing Biennale '77 Cleveland Traveling Exhib, Palace of Westminster, Houses of Parliament, London, 78, Parrish Art Mus, Southampton, NY, Mus Art, Hove, Eng, Mus & Art Gallery, Carlisle, Eng & City Mus & Art Gallery, Gloucester, 79; Icarus Odyssey, Modern Art Ctr, Guadalajara, Mexico, 79; Ikon Logos, Alternative Mus, New York, 81; De Kooning in the Sky, Central Park, New York, 82; Art of Women from Developing Nations, Carolyn Hill Gallery, New York, 86; 2nd Biennial of Havana, Nat Mus Fine Arts, 86; Art Quest '88, Hillwood Art Mus, Long Island City, Brookville, NY; Lyman Allyn Art Mus, New London, Conn, 90; PS1 Mus, Long Island City, NY, 90; United Nations, Secretariat Bldg, West End, South Lobby, NY, 91. *Teaching:* Lectr art, Teachers Training Col, Malaysia, 68. *Awards:* Award of Excellence in Sculpture, Art Horizons, 89; Malaysias sole appointed rep, Venice Biennale, 90; Art Award: The Pollock-Krasner Found Inc, 91-92. *Bibliog:* TV interviews, Eastern Impact Channel 41, 3/85 & Scope-Channel 3, Malaysian TV, 2/86; radio interview, WNYC-Nat Pub Radio, 6/86, New York; Arthur Williams (auth), Sculpture-Technique-Form-Content, Davis Publ Inc, 89. *Media:* All. *Mailing Add:* 292 Lafayette St Loft 5E New York NY 10012

UNTERSEHER, CHRIS CHRISTIAN
SCULPTOR
b Portland, Ore, May 14, 43. *Study:* San Francisco State Col, BA, 65; Univ Calif, Davis, MA, 67. *Work:* Objects USA, Johnson Wax Collection, Racine, Wis; Allan Stone Galleries Collection, New York; Jim Newman Found, San Francisco, Calif; Oakland Mus, Calif. *Exhib:* Objects USA, Johnson Wax Collection, int traveling show, 69-73; 20 Americans, Mus Contemp Crafts, New York, 71; one-man shows, Hansen-Fuller Gallery, San Francisco, 67-70 & De Young Mus, San Francisco, Calif, 68 & 77; Clay, Whitney Mus, New York, 74; Quay Ceramics Gallery, San Francisco, 75 & 77. *Teaching:* Instr ceramics, Univ Calif, Davis, 68-69; instr ceramics, Univ Cincinnati, 69-70; chmn ceramics dept, Univ Nev, Reno, 70-, assoc prof art, 78- *Awards:* Purchase Award, Mem Union Art Gallery, Univ Calif, Davis, 68. *Bibliog:* David Zack (auth), Art news: Nut art in quake time, 70; Nordness (auth), Objects: USA, Viking, 70; Lowell Darling (auth), Clay without tears, Art Ctr World, 71. *Mem:* Am Crafts Coun. *Dealer:* Quay Ceramics Gallery 560 Sutter St San Francisco CA 94102. *Mailing Add:* c/o Ovsey Gallery 170 S La Crea Ave Los Angeles CA 90036

UPRIGHT, DIANE W
ART DEALER, WRITER
b Cleveland, Ohio. *Study:* Wellesley Col, 65-67; Univ Pittsburgh, BA, 69; Univ Mich, MA, 73, PhD, 76. *Collections Arranged:* Morris Louis: The Veil Cycle (auth, catalog), Walker Art Ctr & traveling, 77; Abstract Expressionism, Fogg Art Mus, Harvard Univ, 78; The Drawings of Morris Louis (auth, catalog), Nat Collection of Fine Arts & traveling, 79; Contemporary Painting & Sculpture, 79 & David Smith: Sculpture, Drawings & Paintings, 79, Fogg Art Mus, Harvard Univ; Grand Compositions: Selections from the David Mirvish Collection (auth, catalog), Picasso's Vollard Suite, Hans Hofmann: Provincetown Paintings and Drawings & Morris Louis: Recent Acquisitions (auth, catalog), 85, Ft Worth Mus Art; Surrealist Prints from the Musuem of Modern Art, 85, Henri Matisse: Prints from the Collection of the Museum of Modern Art, 86, Nancy Graves: A Sculpture Retrospective & Ellsworth Kelly: Works on Paper (auth, catalog), 87, Ft Worth Mus Art & Traveling. *Pos:* Senior cur, Ft Worth Art Mus, New York, 84-86; dir, Jan Krugier Gallery, New York, 86-90; Sr vpres, Christie's, New York, 90- *Teaching:* Asst prof mod art hist, Univ Va, Charlottesville, 76-78; prof art hist, Harvard Univ, 78-83. *Mem:* Col Art Asn; Art Table Inc. *Publ:* Auth, Morris Louis: Disposing the diagonal, Arts Mag, 4/76; auth, In addition to the veils, Art in Am, 1-2/78; Sam Francis: The paintings of the 1950s, The Phillips Collection, 80; Morris Louis: A Catalogue Raisonne of the Paintings, Harry N Abrams, 84; Ellsworth Kelly: Works on Paper, Harry N Abrams, 87. *Mailing Add:* c/o Christie's Auction House 502 Park Ave New York NY 10022

UPTON, JOHN DAVID
EDUCATOR, CURATOR
b Des Moines, Iowa, May 4, 32. *Study:* Calif Sch Fine Arts; Univ Rochester, with Minor White & Beaumont Newhall; Univ Calif, Berkeley; Calif State Univ Long Beach, BA & grad study art hist. *Work:* Mass Inst Technol Creative Photog Collection, Cambridge; Fine Arts Collection, Metrop Mus Art. *Exhib:* 15 American Photographers, Houston Mus Contemp Art, 64; one-man shows, Mass Inst Technol Creative Photography Gallery, Cambridge, 65 & Camerawork Gallery, Costa Mesa, Calif, 68; Light 7, Mass Inst Technol Art Gallery, Cambridge, 68. *Collections Arranged:* The Photograph as: Metaphor, Object & Document of Concept (auth, catalog), 74 & The Photograph as Artifice (auth, catalog), 78, Calif State Univ Long Beach; Color as Form: A History of Color Photography, Corcoran Gallery Art, Washington, DC, 82. *Pos:* Chmn dept of photog & chmn div of fine arts, Orange Coast Col, Costa Mesa, Calif, 63-; vis cur, Int Mus Photog, George Eastman House, Rochester, NY, 79-82. *Teaching:* Prof hist of photog & creative photog, Orange Coast Col, Costa Mesa, Calif, 63-; vis lectr hist photog, Univ Calif, Los Angeles, 75, Calif Inst Arts, Valencia, 83-85; Calif State Univ Fullerton, 75-91. *Awards:* Ann Award for Contributions to Photog Ed and the Hist of Photog, Calif Mus Photog, Univ Calif, Riverside, 88. *Bibliog:* Minor White (auth), Photographers Northwest, Aperture, Vol 11, No 3, 64. *Mem:* Soc for Photog Educ (mem bd trustees, 75-79); Friends Photog (mem bd trustees, 74-80). *Res:* History of photography since 1900, especially Alfred Steiglitz, Minor White & Edward Neston. *Publ:* Contribr, New Vision of the 70's, Photographers Choice, Addison House, 75; coauth, Photography, Little, Brown & Co, 76, revised, 84, revised, 92 by HarperCollins. *Mailing Add:* 358 Avenida Adobe San Clemente CA 92672

UPTON, RICHARD THOMAS
PAINTER, PRINTMAKER
b Hartford, Conn. *Study:* Univ Conn, BFA; Ind Univ, MFA; Ecole des Beaux Arts. *Work:* Nat Collection of Fine Arts, Smithsonian Inst, Washington, DC; Mus Mod Art, New York; Victoria & Albert Mus, London, Eng; Bibliot Nat, Paris, France; Montreal Mus Fine Art, Can. *Comn:* Eros Thanatos Suite (German poem & woodcuts), Interlaken Corp, Providence, RI, 67; Salamovka Poster (limited ed silkscreen), Okla Art Ctr, Oklahoma City, 74; River Road Suite (lithographs), 76 & Robert Lowell at 66 (suite of drawings), 77, Salmagundi Mag for the Humanities. *Exhib:* Sept Graveures un Sculpteur de Medailles, Musee Denon, Chalon-Sur Saome, France, 73; Brit Int Print Biennale, US Sect touring Eng, 73; Recent Acquisitions 1969-1973, Bibliot Nat, Paris France, 74; The Delaware Water Gap, Corcoran Gallery Art, Washington, DC, 75; Everson Mus Art, Syracuse, NY, 75; Nat Collection Prints & Poetry, Libr of Cong, Washington, DC, 76-77; Retrospective of prints from Elvehejm Art Ctr, Atelier 17, France, 77; Okla Art Ctr, 77; Weatherspoon Art Gallery, Greensboro, NC, 77; Tweed Mus Art, Duluth, Minn, 77; Pausage Demorause--Landscape at the End of the Century, Grey Art Gallery, New York Univ. *Collections Arranged:* Salamovka Series and Other New Paintings (auth, catalog), Oklahoma Art Ctr, Oklahoma City, 74. *Pos:* Dir, Erebus Press, Saratoga, NY. *Awards:* Fulbright Fel; Nat Educ Asn grant, Artists for Environ; Interlaken Corp Designer Award, Providence, RI, 67. *Bibliog:* Umbria Rediscovered-The Chronicles of Richard Upton, Everson Mus Art, Syracuse, NY, 91; Michael Brenson (auth), article, Defining nature by it's battle scars, Grey Art Gallery, New York; Paul Hayes Tucker (auth), Univ Wash Press, 91, Richard Upton and the Rhetoric of Landscape (monogr). *Media:* Oil, Water Based Media; Lithography, Intaglio. *Publ:* Auth, Impressions-A Paris Suite, 64, co-auth, Credo, 68 & Eros Thanatos, 68, Interlaken Corp; coauth & illustr, Models, 75 & River Road (with Stanley Kunitz), 75, Erebus Press. *Dealer:* Weyne Gallery Lexington Ave New York NY; Townhouse Galleries 2400 E Las Olas Blvd Ft Lauderdale FL 33301. *Mailing Add:* 113 Regent St Saratoga Springs NY 12866

URAM, LAUREN MICHELLE
CONCEPTUAL ARTIST, ILLUSTRATOR
b Hartford, Conn, Nov, 9, 57. *Study:* Pratt Inst, BFA, 80. *Work:* NBC & AT&T, New York, NY; Pacific Bell, San Francisco; Johnson & Johnson, New Brunswick, NJ. *Comn:* Collage of Golden Gate Bridge (pieces of ripped paper), Random House, Inc, New York, 85; relief portrait of Thomas Edison, Rupert Jensen Assocs, Atlanta, Ga, 85; collage of five portraits, Live for Life, Johnson & Johnson, New Brunswick, NJ, 85. *Exhib:* Student Scholarship Exhib (nat), 78 & 79 & 28th Ann Nat Exhib, 86, Mus Illus, New York. *Awards:* Art Directors Annual Award, 83; Commun Arts Illus Annual Award, 82 & 85; Print's Regional Design Annual Award, 86. *Mem:* Found Community Artists. *Media:* Paper. *Mailing Add:* 838 Carroll St No B Brooklyn NY 11215-1702

URBAITIS, ELENA
PAINTER, SCULPTOR
US citizen. *Study:* Akademie der Bildenden Künste, München, Ger, 46-48; Ecole des Arts et Métiers, Freiburg, Ger, degree, 50; Ala Col, Montevallo, BA, 51; Columbia Univ, MA, 60. *Work:* Birmingham Mus Art, Ala; Vilnius Mus Art, Lithuania; Anthology, Film Arch, New York. *Comn:* Metal sculpture, Bd Architects, Vilnius, Lithuania, 91. *Exhib:* Works on Paper: Women Artists, Brooklyn Mus, NY, 75; Light: Recent Issues in Illuminating Sculpture, Morris Mus Arts & Sci, Morristown, NJ, 82 & Emily Lowe Gallery, Hofstra Univ, Hempstead, NY, 83; Sculpture-Penn's Landing, Port of Hist Mus, Philadelphia, 83; solo show, Vilnius Mus Art, Lithuania, 88; Outdoor Sculpture Now, Islip Art Mus, E Islin, NY, 89. *Awards:* Fel, Ecole des Arts et Metiers, Fr Ministry Cult Affairs, Paris, France, 50; Award of Excellence, Ann Long Island 20th Art Exhib, Heckscher Mus, 75; Elizabeth Erlanger Memorial Award, Sculpture, Am Soc Contemp Artists Inc, 88. *Bibliog:* Les Krantz (ed), New York Art Rev, third ed, 90; Howard Ernest Kay

(gen ed), International Who's Who of Professional and Business Women, Melrose Press Ltd, Cambridge, Eng, 92; 2000 Notable American Women, 4th ed, Am Biog Inst, 92; and others. *Mem:* New York Artists Equity Asn; Am Soc Contemp Artists. *Media:* Oil, Acrylic; Metal, Wood. *Mailing Add:* 2292 Willow St Wantagh NY 11793

URBAN, VLADIMIR T
PAINTER, SCULPTOR
b New York, NY, Aug 1, 52. *Study:* Vienna Acad Fine Art, Austria, 72-73; Lycoming Col, BA, 74; Rutgers Univ (with Robert Watts & Peter Stroud), 74-78. *Work:* Edward Albee Collection. *Exhib:* One-man shows, Hunterdon Arts Ctr, Clinton, NJ, 78, H T Walker Gallery, Provincetown, Mass, 80, Attitude Art, New York, 86 & Homeless, 89, Stux Gallery, New York, 91 & Burdock Dog Sculpture/Installation, E M Donahue Gallery, New York, 92; Sots Art, New Mus, New York City, 86; Selections from the Edward Albee Collection, Freedman Gallery Albright Col, Reading, Pa, 88-89; Prisoners of Art, Police Bldg, New York, 89; F A W C Invitational, Twining Alcove Gallery, New York, 89; Invitational, Stux Gallery, New York, 90; Drawings, Althea Viafora Gallery, New York, 90; Choice, Ceres Gallery, New York, 91; The Rectangled Bank, E M Donahue Gallery, New York, 92. *Awards:* Fel, Fine Arts Work Ctr, Provincetown, Mass, 80-81; Visual Arts Fel, NJ State Coun Arts, 79; Artists Grant, Tar Show, Artists Space, 86; Pollock-Krasner Found Grant, New York, 89. *Bibliog:* Doris Brown (auth), Artists maps whimsical tour through metropolis, Sunday Home News, NJ, 9/2/79; Robert H Browning (auth), Emerging artists, Alternative Mus, New York, 80; Sally Banes (auth), In search of illumination, The Village Voice, New York, 5/11/82. *Publ:* Contribr, Mudfish 1, Mudfish 2, Mudfish 3, Mudfish 4, Mudfish 5, Box Turtle Press, New York, 84-91. *Dealer:* E M Donahue 560 Broadway No 304 New York NY 10012. *Mailing Add:* 184 Franklin St New York NY 10013

URQUHART, TONY (ANTHONY MORSE)
SCULPTOR, PAINTER
b Niagara Falls, Ont, Apr 9, 34. *Study:* Yale Univ, Norfolk, Conn, 55; Albright Art Sch, Buffalo, dipl, 56; Univ Buffalo, NY, BFA, 58. *Work:* Nat Gallery Can, Ottawa; Art Gallery Ont, Toronto; Mus Mod Art, New York; Victoria & Albert Mus, London; and others. *Comn:* Mural, Govt Ont, 68, bas-relief, 78; Sculpture magic wood (site specific), Macdonald Stewart Art Ctr, Guelph, Ont, 86. *Exhib:* Carnegie Int, Philadelphia, 58; Guggenheim Int, New York, 59; solo shows, Winnipeg Art Gallery, Man, 59 & Walker Art Ctr, Minneapolis, 60; Am Acad Arts & Lett, New York, 60; Nat Gallery Can, Ottawa, 75; Mus Mod Art, Paris, 76; retrospective, Kitchener-Waterloo Gallery, traveling, 78-80; Thematic Retrospective, Art Gallery Windsor travelling, 88-89. *Pos:* Artist-in-residence, Univ Western Ont, 60-65 & Kitchener-Waterloo Art Gallery, 81-83. *Teaching:* From asst prof to assoc prof, Univ Western Ont, London, 67-72; prof, Univ Waterloo, 72-, chmn, 77-79, 82-85. *Awards:* First Prize, Albright-Knox Art Gallery, 58; Baxter Award, Art Gallery Ont, 60; Fel, Can Coun Sr Arts, 79-80. *Bibliog:* Dorothy Cameron (auth), Tony Urquhart: Reunion, 71, J Vastokas (auth), Archtypal imagery in the work of Tony Urquhart, 74 & Joe Bodelai (auth), Tony Urquhart: The story so far, 76, Artscan; J Vastokas (auth), Worlds Apart: The Symbolic Landscapes of Tony Urquhart, Winsor Art Gallery, Ont, 88 & Dialogues of Reconciliation: The Imagination of Tony Urquhart, 91. *Mem:* foun mem Can Artists Rep/Front Artists Can (nat secy, 67-71); Jack Chambers Mem Found (chmn bd govs, 78-85); Can Conf Arts (vpres, 71-72). *Media:* Mixed Media; Oil. *Publ:* Auth, The Urquhart Sketchbook, Isaacs Gallery, Toronto, 62; ed, The Broken Ark: Book of Beasts, Oberon Press, Ont, 69, reprinted 78; I Am Walking in the Garden of Your Imaginary Palace, AYA Press, Toronto, 82; Cells of Ourselves, 50 drawings chosen & annotated by G M Dault, Porcupines Quill Press, 89. *Dealer:* Moore Gallery 34 Hess St Hamilton Ont Can; Thielsen Gallery 1038 Adelaide St London Ont Can. *Mailing Add:* 24 Water St Wellesley ON N0B 2T0 Canada

URSO, JOSETTE MARIE
PAINTER, SCULPTOR
b Tampa, Fla, June 5, 59. *Study:* Univ SFla, BFA, 80, MFA, 83. *Work:* Fine Arts Mus Long Island, Hempstead, New York; Univ SFla Art Mus, Tampa; Polk Mus Art, Lakeland, Fla; Valencia Community Col, Orlando, Fla; Poynter Inst for media studies, St Petersburg, Fla. *Exhib:* Solo shows, Fine Arts Mus, Long Island, 87 & Aljira, Newark. NJ, 91; Tropicana, Polk Mus Art, Lakeland, 87; Influence of the Untaught, The Drawing Ctr, NY, 88; Alumni Exhib, Art Mus, Univ SFla, 90; Alice Look Who Else, Thru the Looking Glass, Hungting Mus, Va, Univ Art Mus, Ariz State Univ & Ft Wayne Mus Art, Ind, 90; A Decade in the Marketplace, Bronx Mus Arts, NY, 90; The Bernice Steinbaum Gallery, New York. *Teaching:* Instr painting, Chautauqua Sch Art, NY, 84-90 & The 92nd St Y, New York, 88-90. *Awards:* Millay Colony, Residency Award, Austerlitz, NY, 90; Va Ctr for Visual Arts, Residency Award, Sweet Briar, Va, 90; Camargo Found, Residency Award, Cassis, France, 91. *Media:* Mixed Media. *Dealer:* Galerie Industria Wuppertal Ger. *Mailing Add:* 139 W 22nd St New York NY 10011

URSO, LEONARD A
SCULPTOR, PAINTER
b Rome, NY, May 21, 53. *Study:* State Univ New York, New Paltz, BA, 75, MFA, 77. *Work:* Art Inst Chicago; Mem Art Gallery, Rochester, NY; Shanghai Univ Technol, Japan. *Comn:* MACE, Tri-State Univ, Angola, Ind, 90; 78 inch sculpture, Garth Fagan Dance, Rochester, NY, 90; 5 ft sculpture, Hansford Manufacturing, Rochester, NY, 91; Open Form, USA Today & Rochester Inst Technol, Rochester, NY, 92. *Exhib:* Kanazawa Grand-Pris, Kanazawa Mus Art, Japan, 91. *Teaching:* Assoc prof fine art, Rochester Inst Technol, NY, 83- *Bibliog:* Ron Netsky (auth), Sculptor Shapes Flowing Figures, Democrat & Cronicle, 88. *Media:* Metal; Acrylic, Oil. *Mailing Add:* 50 Rochester St Scottsville NY 14546

USHER, DAVID
PUBLISHER, ART DEALER
b New Bedford, Mass, Dec 7, 39. *Study:* Dartmouth Col, BA, 62; Columbia Univ, MBS, 72; Harvard Business Sch, 83-84. *Pos:* Pres, The Greenwich Workshop, Inc (galleries in Southport, Conn & Carmel, Calif; publ ltd ed prints), 72-; Greenwich Workshop Ltd. *Awards:* Printing Indust Am Awards, 81, 86, 87 & 88; Cert Spec Merit, Asn Graphic Arts, 90; Printing Excellence Award, Printing Indust Asn Ga, 91. *Mem:* Soc Illusrs; Cowboy Artists Am. *Specialty:* Americana; Western art; wildlife, marine art; Chinese contemporary. *Publ:* Contribr, Great Names in Graphics: The Greenwich Workshop, Collector Ed, 86, Auro Art. *Mailing Add:* The Greenwich Workshop 30 Lindeman Dr Trumbull CT 06611

USHER, ELIZABETH REUTER (MRS WILLIAM ARTHUR SCAR)
LIBRARIAN, LECTURER
b Seward, Nebr. *Study:* Concordia Teachers Col, Seward, dipl, DLitt(hon), 81; Univ Nebr, BScEd; Univ Ill, LSc; Cranbrook Acad of Art, Bloomfield Hills, Mich; NY Univ. *Pos:* Librn, Cranbrook Acad of Art, Bloomfield Hills, 45-48; catalog/reference librn, Metrop Mus of Art, New York, 48-53, head cataloguer, 53-54, actg head of libr, 54-57, chief, Art Reference Libr, 57-68, chief librn, 68-80; chief librn emer, Thomas J Watson Libr, 81- *Awards:* Special Libr Asn Hall Fame, 80. *Mem:* Spec Libr Asn; NY Libr Club; Art Libr Soc/NAm; Archons Colophon. *Res:* Art librarianship; bibliography. *Interests:* Modern art history; Bibliography. *Publ:* Auth, Rare Books and the Art Museum Library, Spec Libr, 1/61; auth, Continuing Bibliography for the Fine Arts in the United States, Colloques Int, Paris, 3/69; auth, The Metropolitan Museum of Art Library (Research & Reference) (Memorial Name: The Thomas J Watson Library), In: Allen Kent & Harold Lancour, ed, Encyclopedia of Library & Information Science Vol XVII, Dekker, 76; auth, Staffing the Musuem Library, In: Mus Librarianship, ed, by John C Larson Libr Prof Publ, Chap 2, 85. *Mailing Add:* 711B Heritage Village Southbury CT 06488

USUI, KIICHI
CURATOR
b Tokyo, Japan, Dec 2, 31. *Study:* Tokyo Univ Arts, BFA; Art Students League with Morris Kantor; Univ Mich, MA(Oriental art hist). *Collections Arranged:* Meadow Brook Invitational I: Outdoor Sculpture, 81; Magic in the Mind's Eye, Kempf Hogan Collection; Expressive Visions & Exquisite Images: Two Aspects of Art of the 80's. *Pos:* Cur, Meadow Brook Art Gallery, Oakland Univ, 71- *Teaching:* Muselogy, Dept Anthropology (summer sem), Grad Sch New York Univ, 78. *Mem:* Mich Mus Asn; Am Asn Mus; Detroit Inst Art; Meadow Brook Gallery Assoc; Mich Coun Arts (coun mem). *Publ:* Auth, Art in architecture, Space Design, 6/78; Auth, Magic in the Mind's Eye (exhib catalog); Expressive Visions & Exquisitie Images: Two Aspects of Art of the 80's(exhib catalog), Richard Brown Baker Collection. *Mailing Add:* Meadow Brook Art Gallery Oakland Univ Rochester MI 48063

UTTECH, THOMAS MARTIN
PAINTER, EDUCATOR
b Merrill, Wis, Oct 27, 42. *Study:* Layton Sch Art, BFA; Univ Cincinnati, MFA. *Work:* Milwaukee Art Mus; Univ Wis-Madison. *Comn:* Milwaukee Athletic Club, Carron & Black, Milwaukee, Wis; Northwestern Mutual Life Insurance Co. *Exhib:* Directions, Milwaukee Art Ctr, 75; Artists of Chicago & Vicinity, 75 & 80; Whitney Mus Art Asn, 75, Monique Knowlton Gallery, 85, Maxwell Davidson Gallery, 88, Schmidt-Bingham Gallery, 88, Sherry French Gallery, New York, 88; Regenbogen Fur eine bessere Wuttembergish Kunstverein, Stuttgart, Ger, 77; Visions from the Northwoods, Milwaukee Art Mes, 77; Romantic Landscapes, 86; Struve Gallery, Chicago, Ill, 87 & 90; Arthur Rogers Gallery, New Orleans, La, 89. *Teaching:* Prof painting, drawing & photog, Univ Wis-Milwaukee, 68- *Awards:* Peninsula Sch Art Grant, Fish Creek, Wis, 73; Nat Endowment Arts, 88; Wis Arts Board, 89. *Bibliog:* Ellen Lee Klein, Arts, 12/85; Gerrit Henry, Art in Am, 3/86; John Arthur (auth), Spirit of Place: Contemp Landscape Painting & Am Tradition, 89. *Mem:* Wis Painters & Sculptors (pres, 73-76). *Media:* Oil, Photographs. *Publ:* Illusr, A roadless area revisited, Audubon Mag, 75; Earth Care, Sierra Club & Audubon Soc, 75. *Dealer:* Dorthy Bradley Milwaukee WI; Struve Gallery Chicago IL. *Mailing Add:* 4305 Hwy O Saukville WI 53080

UTZ, THORNTON
PAINTER, SCULPTOR
b Memphis, Tenn, Nov 15, 14. *Study:* Am Acad Art, Chicago. *Work:* Milwaukee Art Mus; Air & Space Mus, Washington, DC; First Lady Collection, Smithsonian Inst; Port of Hist, Philadelphia; Palace, Monaco; Palace Mainau, Ger; Nat Gallery, Dublin, Ireland; Albany Mus, Ga; Am Embassy Residence, Paris, France. *Comn:* Giraffe (stainless steel & concrete), Lindsey Hopkins Comn, Atlanta, 75; twelve paintings, Jimmy Carter Collection, Plains, Ga, 75-76; sculpture (concrete & steel), First Presby Church, Sarasota, Fla, 78; portrait, Sonja Bernadotte & children, 83; seven paintings each, Sun Banks, 83, Gen Tel & Tel, 83 & Cent Nat Bank, 84, Sarasota; stained glass windows, Stations of the Cross & ceramic cross, Incarnation Church, Sarasota, 87; portraits of George Pickering, Vanderbilt Estate, Asheville, NC, 87, & Marvin L Holloway, Tampa, Fla, 88; Barnett Bank, Bradenton, 87. *Pos:* Bd mem, Ringling Art Sch, 64- *Bibliog:* Richard Thruelsen (auth), Men at work--Thornton Utz, Saturday Evening Post, 12/3/49; Ernest Watson (auth), article, Am Artist, 52; John Diffily (auth), article, Southwest Art Mag, 7/81. *Mem:* Soc Illusr; Chicago Artists Guild; Am Portrait Soc. *Media:* Mixed. *Mailing Add:* 5323 Calle Florida Sarasota FL 34242

UZILEVSKY, MARCUS
PAINTER, PRINTMAKER
US citizen. *Work:* Bezalel Aca Art & Design, Jerusalem, Israel; New Britain Mus Art, Conn; Tucson Mus Art, Ariz; Washington Co Mus Fine Arts, Hagerstown, Md; Hood Mus Art, Dartmouth Col, Hanover, NH. *Exhib:* Nat Print Competition, Edinboro, Pa, 83; Alexandria Mus, La, 84; 27th Nat Print Exhib, Hunterdon Art Ctr, Clinton, NJ, 86; Wesleyan Int Exhib Prints & Drawings, Wesleyan Col, Macon, Ga, 87. *Media:* All. *Dealer:* San Francisco Fine Art Ctr 1500 Howard San Francisco CA 94103. *Mailing Add:* PO Box 166 Woodacre CA 94973

V

VAADIA, BOAZ
SCULPTOR
b Israel, Nov 13, 51. *Study:* Pratt Art Inst Brooklyn, NY, 76; Avni Inst Fine Arts, BFA, 71. *Work:* Metro Mus Art, Jewish Mus, New York; Tel Aviv Mus, The Israel Mus, Israel; Mus Mod Art, San Francisco. *Comn:* Sculpture, Paine Webber, Puerto Rico, 87; The Related Companies, New York, 88; LaSalle Partners, Roslyn, Va, 89. *Exhib:* One-man shows, Sculpture Ctr, New York, 84, OK Harris, New York, 86, 88, 89 & 92, Jewish Mus, New York, 88-89, Hokin Kaufman, Chicago, 89 & 90, Helander Gallery, Palm Beach, Fla, 91; Montsville Mus, Ala, 86; The Other Gods: Containers of Belief, Everson Mus Art, Syracuse, NY, 86-87; Centerpieces, Norton Ctr, Ctr Col, Danville, Ky, 91; Utsukushi-ga-hara Open Air Mus, Japan, 92. *Awards:* Ariana Found Arts Grant, 86; Nat Endowment Arts Grant, 88; Utsukushi-ga-hara Open Air Mus Award, 92. *Media:* Stone. *Dealer:* OK Harris Gallery West Broadway New York 10012. *Mailing Add:* 104 Berry St Brooklyn NY 11211

VACCARINO, ROBIN
SCULPTOR, PAINTER
b Seattle, Wash, Aug 14, 28. *Study:* Univ Calif, Los Angeles; Otis Art Inst, MFA(magna cum laude), 66. *Work:* Los Angeles Co Mus; Santa Barbara Mus; Library of Congress, Washington, DC; De Cordova Mus; and others. *Comn:* Latham & Watkins, Atlantic Richfield Plaza, 72; Credit Lyonnais Int, Los Angeles, 75; Hyatt Regency, Dallas, Tex, 78; Progressive Savings & Loan, Beverly Hills; Security Pac Nat Bank, Los Angeles; Koll Ctr, Irvine, Calif. *Exhib:* Otis Mus 50th Anniv Exhib, Los Angeles, 69; Library of Congress Nat Print Exhib, Washington, DC, 69; Univ of Calif, Santa Cruz, 77; Santa Barbara Mus, 80; Los Angeles Municipal Gallery, Barsdale Park: Los Angeles Bicentennial, 81; and others. *Teaching:* Instr painting, Otis Art Inst, Parsons Sch Design, Los Angeles & Paris, currently. *Awards:* Calif Arts Coun Grant, 79; Nat Endowment Arts Individual fel, 80-81; and others. *Bibliog:* Joseph Mugaini (auth), Drawing, A Search for Form, Reinholt, 66; Innovative printmakers in Southern Calif, Southwest Art Mag, 73; article in Artweek, 74. *Media:* Steel; Oil, Acrylic. *Mailing Add:* 3593 Berry Dr Studio City CA 91604

VACCARO, LUELLA GRACE
CERAMIST, PAINTER
b Miles City, Mont, June 2, 34. *Study:* Univ Wash, Seattle; Univ Calif, Berkeley; workshops with Peter Voulkas. *Work:* Antonio Prieto Collection, Mills Col, Oakland, Calif; Ceramics Monthly Collection, Columbus, Ohio. *Exhib:* 32nd & 33rd Int Print Exhib, Seattle Art Mus, Wash, 61-62; Latitude 53 Gallery, Edmonton, Alta, 79; Mail Art Expo '80, Santa Cruz, Calif, 79; one-artist shows, Univ of Kans, 66 (125 pieces) & Lawrence City Libr, 67 (40 pieces); Kellas Gallery, Lawrence, Kans, 81 & 82; two-persons show, Lawrence Art Ctr, Kans, 86. *Awards:* Laguna Gloria Award, Tex Fine Arts Asn, Austin, 61; Kans Designer Craftsman Award, Kans Univ Art Mus, Lawrence, 68; Ceramic Monthly Award, Ceramics Monthly, Columbus, Ohio, 71. *Bibliog:* Luella Vaccaro and Her Pottery, Sunflower Cablevision interview, 79; Lynn Bretz (auth), Nick and Lu: A Couple of Artists, Lawrence J World, Sunday Arts Section, 5/3/81. *Media:* Stoneware, Clay; Oil. *Dealer:* Kellas Gallery 7 E 7th St Lawrence KS 66044. *Mailing Add:* 535 Kansas St Lawrence KS 66046

VACCARO, NICK DANTE
EDUCATOR, PAINTER
b Youngstown, Ohio, Apr 9, 31. *Study:* Univ Wash, BA, 58; Univ Calif, Berkeley, MA, 60; with David Park. *Work:* San Francisco Art Asn; Muskegon Art Mus, Mich; Eastern Tenn State Univ, Johnson City; Univ Calif, Berkeley; Youngstown Univ, Ohio. *Exhib:* Libr Cong, Washington, DC, 60; Calif Palace Legion Honor, San Francisco, 61; DeYoung Mus, San Francisco, 62; Houston Mus Fine Arts, Tex, 63; Mid-Am, Nelson Gallery, Kansas City, 64-66 & 70; two-person show, Kellas Gallery, Lawrence, Kans, 77 & 81; two-person show, Lawrence Art Ctr, Kans, 86; three-person show, Mulvan Art Mus, Topeka, Kans, 91; and others. *Teaching:* Instr drawing & painting, Dept Art, Univ Tex, 60-61, asst prof drawing & color, Sch Archit, 61-63; prof drawing & painting, Univ Kans, 63-, chmn dept art, 63-67; vis artist, Pa State Univ, 70. *Awards:* Purchase Awards, San Francisco Mus Art, 58, Dallas Mus Fine Arts, 61 & Montgomery Mus Fine Art, 62. *Bibliog:* A Brooks & Jeffrey Riemer (coauths), Framing the Artist: A Social Portrait of Mid-America Artists, Univ Press, 82; Donald Bartlett Doe (auth, catalog), Affinities-World's Apart, Mulvane Art Mus, 6/14 & 7/26/91; Jan Witkoski (auth), World's Apart (review), Topeka-Capital J, 6/28/91. *Media:* Mixed Media, Acrylic. *Publ:* Illusr, Tex Quart, Vol 5, No 1; Image, Univ Tex, Austin, 63; auth, Gorky's debt, Art J, 63. *Mailing Add:* 535 Kansas St Lawrence KS 66046

VACCARO, PATRICK FRANK
PRINTMAKER, PAINTER
b New Rochelle, NY. *Study:* Ohio State Univ; Youngstown State Univ. *Work:* Butler Inst Am Art, Youngstown, Ohio; Physicians Insurance Co, Ohio; Yepez Gallery, New York; Nat Mus Fine Arts, Hanoi, Vietnam; Duxbury Art Complex Mus, Mass; Nat Tour Vietnam, 91-92; East River Savings Bank, New York; and others. *Comn:* Presentation Print, Friends Am Art, Youngstown, 69; Honor Print commemorating first solar church, St Paul's, Ore, 80. *Exhib:* Boston Printmakers Ann, Boston Mus Fine Arts, 55-; Am Colorprint Soc Ann, Philadelphia, 59-; Butler Inst Am Art Midyears, Youngstown, 62-67; Carrier Found, NJ; Audubon Artists Exhib, New York; Italian Cult Ctr, Chicago; Exeter Academy, RI; and others. *Teaching:* Youngstown Univ, Ohio. *Awards:* Graphics Awards, Butler Inst Am Art; Acad Italy with Gold Medal, Parma, Italy; Dipl Merit, Univ Art, Salsomaggiore, Italy; and others. *Mem:* Boston Printmakers; Am Colorprint Soc. *Media:* Serigraphy; Watercolor & Acrylics. *Publ:* Illusr, Christian Herald; illusr, Together, Methodist Monthly, 69; illusr, Presby-Westminster Press, 71-72. *Mailing Add:* 7078 Oak Dr Poland OH 44514

VADIA, RAFAEL
PAINTER
Havana, Cuba, Nov 27, 50; US citizen. *Study:* Miami-Dade Jr Col, AA, 71; Ecole des Beaux Arts, Paris, France, 73; Fla Int Univ, BFA, 76. *Work:* Greater Miami Pub Librs; Mus Modern Art at the Orgn of Am States, Washington, DC; Metro-Dade Govt Ctr, Art in Pub Places Trust, Miami, Fla; Citibank International; Visa International. *Exhib:* 22nd Bradley Nat Print & Drawing Exhib & Competition, Lakeland Mus, Peoria, Ill, 89; South Florida in the Eighties, Art Bank at Metro-Dade Center, N Miami, Ctr Contemp Art, Miami, Fla, 89; 49th, 50th, & 51st Ann Nat Competition Contemp Am Painting Soc Four Arts, Palm Beach, Fla, 87-89; Drawing 1990 Nat Competition, Harris Fine Arts Ctr, Brigham Young Univ, Provo, Utah, 90; Collectors of Latin Am Art, Metro Mus and Art Ctr, Coral Gables, Fla, 84; Broward community col, South Campus Art Gallery, Hollywood, Fla, 92; and many others. *Pos:* Artist keynotes speaker, Fla Art Educ Conf, Naples, 91; speaker, Miami Int Art Fair, 92. *Awards:* Judge's Recognition Award, 31st Competition & Exhib, Broward Art Guild, Ft Lauderdale, 83; John Gordon Mem Award, 49th Ann Nat Exhib Contemp Am Paintings, Soc Four Arts, Palm Beach, Fla, 87; Cintas Found Fel, Inst Int Educ, New York, 91-92; and others. *Bibliog:* Ellen Edwards (auth), South Florida: No longer a last resort for art, 79, Art in Am; Helen L Kohen (auth), Bright days for art in South Florida, 12/80 & The Nation, 6/81; Joanne Butcher (auth), Art Papers, Reviews, Art News, 1/88. *Media:* Mixed on Canvas and Paper. *Publ:* Auth, Modern & Colonial Latin American Paintings, Sotheby Parke-Bernet, New York, 80; Rafael Vadia: New Drawings, De Armas Publ, Miami; New Acquisitions: The Museum Modern Art, Orgn Am States, Washington, DC, 83; auth, Art of Cuba in Exile, Jose Gomez Siere, Munder Press, Miami, 87; Selections From Art Bank, Metro-Dade Govt Ctr: Work by 27 Artists from Collection of Art in Public Places Trust, North Miami Ctr Contemp Art,Fla, 89. *Dealer:* The Americas Collection Gallery 126 Aragon Ave Coral Gables FL 33134; Andrea Marquit Fine Arts 207 Newbury St Boston MA 02116. *Mailing Add:* 3130 Center St Miami FL 33133

VAILLANCOURT, ARMAND
SCULPTOR, PAINTER
b Quebec, Can, Sept 3, 29. *Study:* Ottawa Univ, 49-50; Ecole des Beaux Arts, Montreal, 51-55. *Work:* Banque d'oeuvres d'art du Can; Banque d'oeuvres d'art du Qué; Maison des Assemblées, Guernica, Espagne; Ville de Montréal; Ecole des Arts et Métiers, Asbestos; and others. *Comn:* Vaillancourt Fountain, Embarcadero Plaza, San Francisco, 67-71; Justice!, Fountain, Palais de Justice de Qué; El Clamor, monumental sculpture-fountain, Santa Domingo, Dominican Repub, 85; Drapeau blanc!, exterior monumental sculpture, Université Laval, Qué, 87; Passerelle Vaillancourt, pedestrian bridge (200 ft), Ville de Plessiville, 90; and many others. *Exhib:* Salon de mai, Musée d'Art Moderne, Paris, 62; First Ibero American Symposium, Santo Domingo, Dominican Repub, 85; Contemp Outdoor Sculp at the Guild, Toronto, 82; Mus Fine Art Can, 90; La Sculpture au Québec (1946-61), Musée du Qué, 92; Collection au Musée, Musée d'Art Contemporain, Montréal, 92; Expos itinéiante ã Travers le Canada, Musée des Beaux-Arts au Can, 92; solo shows, Galerie Maximum, Montréal, 84, Galerie Espace Global Montréal, 86, Caisse Pobulaire de Victoriaville, 87, Galerie d'Art Contemporain, Montréal, 90, Galerie Le Lieu et Mail Saint-Rock, Québec, 92; plus many others; and many other group & solo exhibs. *Awards:* First Prize, interior sculpture, 63 & exterior monumental sculpture, 63, Ecole des Arts & Métiers; First Prize, Int Competition for sculptural fountain, San Francisco, 69; and others. *Bibliog:* David Miller (auth), Vaillancourt sculptor (film), ONF, 63-64; Jean-Gaétan Séquin (auth), L'Univers d'Armand Vaillancourt (video), Radio Qué, Betacam, 84; Yvon Laurendeau (auth), Armand Vaillancourt, guercier de la paix (video), 92; Martial Lapointe (auth), Pierre et paix, J de Quebec, 7/24/87; A M Richard et C Robertson (auth), Performance in Canada, 1970-90, Inter ed, 91; Jocelyne Lepage (auth), A Vaillancourt, L'irréductible, La Presse, Montréal, 3/28/92; Pradel (auth), L'Art, la Résistance, L'Evénement du Jeudi, Paris, 10/23/86. *Mem:* Conseil de la Sculpture du Qué (founder); Conseil des Arts Visuels du Qué(founder). *Media:* All Media; Acrylic. *Mailing Add:* 4211 avenue del'Esplanade Montreal PQ H2W 1T1 Canada

VAISMAN, MEYER
PAINTER
b Caracas, Venezuela, May 23, 60. *Study:* Parsons Sch Design, BFA. *Work:* Boston Mus Fine Arts, Mass; La Jolla Mus Contemp Art, Calif. *Exhib:* New York in View, Munchen, WGer, 87; New York Art Now, Saachi Collection,

London, 87; one-man shows, La Jolla Mus, Calif, 88, Univ Mus, Berkeley, Calif, 88, Jablonka Galerie, Cologne, Ger, 92 & Leo Castelli Gallery, New York, 92; Carnegie International, Carnegie Mus Art, Pittsburgh, Pa, 88; Binational, Boston Mus Fine Arts & Dusseldorf Kunsthalle, WGer, 88. *Bibliog:* Dan Cameron (auth), Who is Meyer Vaisman, Arts Mag, 86. *Media:* Mixed Media. *Dealer:* Sonnabend Gallery 420 W Broadway New York NY 10012; Leo Castelli Gallery 420 W Broadway New York NY 10012. *Mailing Add:* 5 Worth St New York NY 10013

VALADEZ, JOHN
PAINTER
b Los Angeles, Calif, 1951. *Study:* Calif State Univ, Long Beach, BFA, 76. *Comn:* Mural, Fed Bldg at border crossing, El Paso, Tex, 93; mural, Fed Bldg, downtown El Paso, Tex, 93; mural, Atrium at new Central Libr Bldg, Los Angeles, 93. *Exhib:* Solo Exhibs, John Valadez: Early/Recent Works, New Directions Gallery, Los Angeles, 83, Mark Taper Forum, 84, Simard Gallery, 84, Mus Contemp Hispanic Art, New York, 86, Lizardi/Harp Gallery, Pasadena, 87 & 89, Condenados, Saxon-Lee Gallery, Los Angeles, 90, New Visions & Ventures in Latino Art, Rancho Santiago Col, Santa Ana, Calif, 90, New Pastels, Daniel Saxon Gallery, Los Angeles, 90 & Domestic Allegories, Galeria de la Raza, San Francisco, 91; Only LA Contemporary Variations, Munic Art Gallery, Los Angeles, 86; Made in Aztlan, Centro Cult de la Raza, San Diego, 86; Symbolic Realities: John Valadez/David Baze, Dominguez Hills, 86; Primer Espacio de Identidad Cult, El Barrio, Centro Cult Tijuana, Baja, 86; Hispanic Art in the United States: Thirty Contemp Painters & Sculptors, Corcoran Gallery Art, Washington, DC and travelled, 87-89; From the Back Room, Saxon-Lee Gallery, Los Angeles, 88; Chicano Art/ Resistance & Affirmation, 1965-85, Wight Art Gallery, UCLA, traveling through 1993 to Denver Art Mus, Albuquerque Mus, Nat Mus Am Art, San Francisco Mus Mod Art, Tucson Art Mus & Fresno Art Mus. *Bibliog:* Shauna Snow (auth), New Visions: Positive images through Latino art, Los Angeles Times, 3/11/90; Lynn Pyne (auth), Post-Chicano' art tries to 'break boundaries', Phoenix Gazette, 9/90; Susan Kandel (auth), LA in review, Arts Mag, 12/91. *Mailing Add:* Daniel Saxon Gallery 7525 Beverly Blvd Los Angeles CA 90036

VALDÉS, KAREN W
DIRECTOR, EDUCATOR
b Los Angeles, Calif, May 25, 45. *Study:* Univ Calif, Irvine, BFA, 68; Nat Univ Mex, Mexico City, 69; Univ Chicago, Ill, 72; Fla State Univ, Tallahassee, MFA, 74; NY Univ, 83. *Collections Arranged:* Lynda Benglis 1968-1978 (with catalog), Lowe Art Mus, Univ Miami, 80; Vito Acconci: Installation, Miami Dade Community Col, 83; A Separate Reality: Florida Eccentrics (with catalog), Mus Art, Ft Lauderdale, 87; Suzanne Giroux: Video Installation, Univ Fla, 89; The Great American Lawnscape: Yard Art (with catalog), Univ Gallery Fla, 92. *Pos:* Cur exhibs, Art Mus STex, 75-76, Mus Art, Ft Lauderdale, Fla, 85-89; dir, Miami-Dade Community Col, Campu Art S Gallery, 76-85, Gloria Luria Gallery, Miami, 84-85, Univ Galleries, Univ Fla, 89- *Teaching:* Assoc prof art & humanities, Miami-Dade Community Col, 76-84; assoc prof mus studies, Univ Fla, 89- *Bibliog:* Elisa Turner (auth), A separate reality, Florida eccentric, Art News, 10/87. *Mem:* Col Art Asn; Am Asn Mus; Fla Art Mus Dirs Asn; Hispanic Fac Asn, Univ Fla. *Res:* Contemporary art and outsider art. *Publ:* Contribr, The Eye of the Beholder: SFla Collects Essay (catalog), Mus Art, Ft Lauderdale, 86; Styles, Strands & Sequences: American Painters & Drawing (catalog), Univ Fla, 90; auth (article), Coral castle, Forecast: Pub Artworks J, 92. *Mailing Add:* 4157 NW 37th Dr Gainesville FL 32606

VALDEZ, VINCENT E
SCULPTOR
b Mora, NMex, Mar 15, 40. *Study:* Univ Wyo, 67-70. *Work:* Nat Morgan Horse Asn Mus, Shellburn, NJ; Wyo State Mus, Cheyenne; Benson Park (outdoor sculpture), Loveland, Colo. *Comn:* Morgan Horse, comm by Anne Mears, Laramie, Wyo, 85; Monument of the Chase (bronze), Loveland High Plains Art Coun, Colo, 88; bas-relief, Tree of life, Ivinson Mem Hosp, Laramie, Wyo, 88. *Awards:* Best of Show, Western Regional Art Show, 87; Award of Merit, Anchorage Audubon Soc, 87; 2nd Place Bronze, George Phippen Mem Soc, 87. *Bibliog:* Anne Mears (auth), The magnificent Morgan, Today's Morgan, 5/85; Judy A Hughes (auth), Bronze: The rock of ages, Wildlife Art News, 1/88; Christina Leimer, (auth) metamorphic man, Art of the West, 11/88. *Mem:* Wyo Coun on the Arts. *Media:* Bronze. *Mailing Add:* 821 S 21st St Laramie WY 82070

VALENCIA, CESAR
PAINTER, MURALIST
b Quito, Ecuador, Apr 2, 18; US citizen. *Study:* Archit & Fine Arts Sch, Quito, Ecuador, BA, 40. *Work:* Pan Am Union, Washington, DC; Mus Mod Art, Buenos Aires, Arg; Mus Art, Lima, Peru; Mod Art Gallery, Quito, Ecuador. *Comn:* ceramic mural, Dompe's Archit Assts, Mar del Plata, 52. *Exhib:* solo exhibs, Mus Mod Art, Buenos Aires, Arg, 62 & Pan Am Union, Washington, DC, 63; Mus Art, Lima, Peru, 45; Mus Nat Bellas Artes, Buenos Aires, 49; 1964 Pittsburgh Int, Pa, 64; Jason Gallery, New York, 65. *Awards:* First Prize, Mariano Aquilera, Ann Fine Arts Show, Mariano Aquilera Found, 44; First Prize, XXXLV Salon Watercolor, Mus Nat Bellas Artes, 48. *Bibliog:* E Ramallo (auth), Art ecuatoriano in bellas artes, La Prensa, Arg, 12/62; Bernardo Grauier (auth), Valencia: vital painter, El Comercio, Ecuador, 1/63; Leslie Judd Ahlander (auth), Ecuadorian has strong show, Washington Post, 11/63. *Media:* Encaustic. *Mailing Add:* 7855 Boulevard E 191 North Bergen NJ 07047

VALENSTEIN, ALICE
PAINTER, COLLECTOR
b New York, NY, Feb 12, 04. *Study:* Teachers Col, Columbia Univ, study with Winold Reiss, Morris Davidson, Victor Candell & Leo Manso, Northon Gallery, Palm Beach. *Work:* Staten Island Mus, NY; Emily Lowe Mus, Coral Gables, Fla; Hofstra Univ, NY; Miami Mus Mod Art, Fla; Mills Col, Oakland, Calif; Katonah Gallery. *Exhib:* One-woman shows, Krasner Gallery, NY, Carus Gallery, NY, Katonah Gallery, NY, Miami Mus Mod Art, Alonzo Gallery, NY, Brunswick Sch, Conn & Images Gallery, Briarcliff Manor, NY, Somerstown Gallery, Somers, NY; Westchester Community Col. *Pos:* Interior decorator, Alice Starr Interior Decorator, 27- *Awards:* Scarsdale Art Asn; Westchester Arts; Brandeis Univ. *Mem:* Nat Asn Women Artists. *Collection:* Contemporary fellow artists. *Publ:* Auth, articles House & Garden Mag & New Yorker Mag. *Dealer:* Jack Alonzo 30 W 57th St New York NY 10021. *Mailing Add:* 50 Popham Rd No 4H Scarsdale NY 10583

VALENSTEIN, SUZANNE GEBHART
CURATOR
b Baltimore, Md, July 17, 28. *Pos:* Assoc cur Far Eastern art, Metrop Mus Art, New York, formerly, res cur, Asian Art, currently. *Teaching:* Vis lectr Chinese ceramics, Princeton Univ, NJ, fall 76. *Mem:* Oriental Ceramic Soc London; Oriental Ceramic Soc Hong Kong; Asia Soc. *Publ:* Auth, Ming Porcelains: a Retrospective, China Inst in Am, 70; A Handbook of Chinese Ceramics, 75, revised & enlarged, 89 & Highlights of Chinese Ceramics, 75, Metrop Mus Art; coauth, Oriental Ceramics: The World's Great Collections, Vol XII, The Metropolitan Museum, Kodansha Int, 77; auth, Chinese celadons reclaimed from the sea, Oriental Art Mag, spring 79; The Herzman Collection of Chinese Ceramics, 92. *Mailing Add:* Metrop Mus Art Fifth Ave at 82nd St New York NY 10028

VALENTIN, JEAN-PIERRE
DEALER
b France, Jan 31, 49; Can citizen. *Study:* Paris Business Sch, MBA(int trade), 71. *Bibliog:* A Gascon (auth), J P Valentin et galerie, Le Collectionneur, 78; G Robinson (auth), L' Art Francais Montreal, Can Art Investor's Guide, 80. *Mem:* Prof Art Dealers' Asn Can (pres, 81-85). *Specialty:* Prominent Quebec artists and Canadian artists; works by European masters of the 20th century. *Mailing Add:* Galerie L' Art Francais 1434 Sherbrooke W Montreal PQ H3G 1K4 Canada

VALENTINE, DEWAIN
SCULPTOR
b Ft Collins, Colo, Aug 27, 36. *Study:* Univ Colo, BFA, 58, MFA, 60; Yale-Norfolk Art Sch, Yale Univ Fel, 58. *Work:* Whitney Mus Am Art, New York; Los Angeles Co Mus Art; Atlantic Richfield Corp, Washington, DC; Fed Reserve Bank, San Francisco; Stanford Univ Art Mus; Contemp Arts Ctr, Honolulu, Hawaii. *Comn:* Sky Gate (major outdoor work), comn by Frederick R Weisman; Open Diamond Double Diagonal (major outdoor work), comn by State Office Bldg, Van Nuys, Calif; Curved Waterwall (major indoor work), comn by Pacific Enterprises, Los Angeles; Diamond Waterwall (major outdoor work), comn by Metropolitan, Los Angeles. *Exhib:* Los Angeles Co Mus Art, 79; Pub Sch 1, Inst for Art & Urban Resources, NY, 81; Laumeier Int Sculpture Park, St Louis, Mo, 82; Madison Art Ctr, Wis, 83; Honolulu Acad Arts & the Contemp Arts Ctr, Hawaii, 85; Cartier Found for Contemp Art, France, 85-86. *Teaching:* Instr design & drawing, Univ Colo, 58-61 & 64-65; instr plastics, Univ Calif, Los Angeles, 65-67. *Awards:* John Simon Guggenheim Fel, 80; National Endowment for the Arts, 81. *Bibliog:* Peter Plagens (auth), Sunshine Muse, Praeger, 74; John Lloyd Taylor (auth), cover article in Art Int, Vol 17, No 7 & Jean Luc Bordeaux (auth), DeWain Valentine, Light Explored, Vol 67, No 8, 12/79, Art in Am; Jane Livingston, Artists Dialogue: DeWain Valentine, Archit Digest, 2/86. *Media:* Glass. *Mailing Add:* 4223 Glencoe Ave No B-127 Marina Del Rey CA 90292-5611

VALERIO, JAMES ROBERT
PAINTER, EDUCATOR
b Chicago, Ill, Dec 2, 38. *Study:* Art Inst Chicago, BFA, 66, & MFA(Anne Louis Raymond Fel), 68; spec study with Seymour Rosofsky. *Work:* Ill Bell Telephone Co; Univ Iowa Mus Art; Prudential Insurance Co; Albuquerque Mus Art; Metrop Mus Art; Guggenheim Mus Art. *Exhib:* One-man shows, Frumkin-Struve Gallery, Chicago, Ill, 81-84, Del Art Mus, Wilmington, 83, Allan Frumkin Gallery, New York, 87 & 90 & Frumkin/Adams Gallery, New York, 91; Painting & Sculpture in California: The Mod Era, Nat Col of Fine Arts of the Smithsonian Inst, Washington, DC & San Francisco Mus of Art, 76-77; Contemp Am Realism Since 1960, Pa Acad Fine Arts, 81; Exquisite Painting, Orlando Mus Art, Fla, 91; Drawings, Koplin Gallery, Santa Monica, Calif, 91; American Narrative Painting & Sculpture: The 1980's, Nassau Co Mus Art, Roslyn Harbor, NY, 91; American Realism & Figurative Art, 1955-1990 (traveling exhib), Miyagi Mus Art, Sendai, Japan, 92; Intimate Views (traveling), Glenn C Janss Collection of Am Realism; and others. *Teaching:* Asst prof art, Rock Valley Col, Rockford, Ill, 68-70; assoc prof art, Univ Calif, Los Angeles, 70-79; assoc prof, Cornell Univ, 79-82; prof art, Northwestern Univ, Evanston, Ill, 85- *Awards:* Purchase Award, Long Beach Mus of Art, 70; Creative Arts Award Fel, Univ Calif, Los Angeles, 76; Nat Endowment Arts Grant, 86. *Bibliog:* John Ward (auth), American Realist Painting 1945-80, Univ Mich Res Press, Ann Arbor/London, 89; John Arthur (auth), Spirit of Place, Contemp Landscape Painting, Boston, Toronto & Bullfinch Press-Little Brown & Co, London, 89; Lubrow (auth), Figure & Form, William C Brown, Publ, 91. *Dealer:* Frumkin/Adams Gallery 50 W 57th St New York NY. *Mailing Add:* 1308 Gregory Wilmette IL 60091

VALESCO, FRANCES
MURALIST, PRINTMAKER
b Los Angeles, Calif, Aug 3, 41. *Study:* Univ Calif, Los Angeles, BA, 63; Sacramento State Univ, 64-65; Calif State Univ, Long Beach, MA, 72. *Work:* New York City Pub Libr, NY; Oakland Mus, Calif; Readers Digest Corp; Clorox Corp; Boston Children's Hosp. *Comn:* Grazing Cow Mural, 76, Women's Mural, 78-79 & Playland and the Movies Mural, 79, San Francisco Neighborhood Arts Prog; Desert Mural, 82, Buffalo Sky Mural, 82 & North Beach Fish Mural, 87, Dept Housing & Urban Develop, Off Community Develop, San Francisco. *Exhib:* 162nd Ann Exhib, Pa Acad Fine Arts, 67; Artist's Proof: The Multiple Image, Fine Arts Mus, San Francisco, 76; Prints USA, Traveling Exhib, Nat Mus Singapore, Bangkok, Amerika Haus, Berlin, Sweden, 84-86; Techno Bliss-Techno Fear, Univ Santa Clara, 86; Emerging Expression Biennial, Bronx Mus, 87; Computer Art in Context, Computer Mus, Boston, 89; Pixim, Grand Halle de la Villette, Paris, France, 88; Arts Electronica, Computurkultur Tage, Linz, Austria, 88 & 91; Recent Acquisitions, Achenbach Found, Fine Arts Mus, San Francisco, Calif, 91. *Pos:* Community artist, San Francisco Art Comn, 75-80; artist-in-residence in the community, Calif State Arts Coun, 80-85. *Teaching:* Lectr etching & screen printing, Univ Calif, Berkeley, 75-76 & 79; lectr screen printing, drawing & mural painting, Sonoma State Univ, 77-80; instr printmaking & photog, San Francisco Acad Art, 82- *Awards:* Arts Coun Award, Univ Calif, Los Angeles, 63; Purchase Prize, Kingsley Ann, Crocker Mus, Sacramento, 64; Print Purchase for Embassies, Beirut, Lebanon & Kuala Lumpur, Malaysia, US Info Agency, 67. *Bibliog:* John C Oglesby (auth), article, Sacramento Bee, 64; Elizabeth Pomada (auth), The city's art brigade, San Francisco Mag, 76; Judith Anderson (auth), San Francisco's splashy outdoor art, San Francisco Chronicle, 82; Vivien Raynor (auth), Computer Reigns at Bronx Mus of Art, The New York Times, 87. *Mem:* Calif Soc Printmakers (historian, 78-80); San Francisco Mural (adv bd, 82-89); YLEM. *Media:* Mixed. *Publ:* Ed & illusr, Media Mixed, Joined Arts, 67; illusr, Music of the Whole Earth, Scribners, 76; coauth, Combining color xerography with the technique of silk screen and intaglio, Leonardo, 84; San Francisco Murals, Tim Drescher, 90. *Mailing Add:* 135 Jersey St San Francisco CA 94114

VALETTA
PAINTER
b Brooklyn, NY, Jan 17, 40. *Study:* Pratt Inst, BS(art educ), 61; Tyler Sch Fine Art; Univ Pa. *Work:* Widener Univ Mus, Chester, Pa; Private Collection of Pres Anwar Sadat Family, Egypt. *Exhib:* Artists Equity Triennial, Civic Ctr Mus, 79 & Port Hist Mus, 85, 88, Philadelphia, Pa; Regional Painting Competition, Del Art Mus, Wilmington, 79 & Woodmere Art Mus, Philadelphia, Pa, 80, 82, 84 & 88; National Drawing Competition, Univ NDak, 80 & West Chester Univ, Pa, 81; A Look at Drawing, Goldie Paley Design Ctr, Philadelphia, Pa, 81; On, of About and Paper, Rotunda Gallery, Brooklyn, NY, 84; Am Embassy, Brussels, Belg, 90. *Pos:* Bd dirs & co-chairperson collections comt, Afro Am Mus, Philadelphia, Pa, 82-88; cur, Contemp Women Artists, Philadelphia Community Arts Ctr, Wallingford, Pa, 85-; dir, Muse Gallery, Philadelphia, Pa, 89-90. *Awards:* Fisher Mem Award, 87; Bernard H Berger Award, 91; Cheltenham Art Ctr Regional Competition, Philadelphia, Pa; and others. *Mem:* Artists Equity Asn; Del Ctr Contemp Arts. *Media:* Oil, Pastel. *Mailing Add:* 55 Wood Ridge Rd Thorton PA 19373

VALIER, BIRON (FRANK)
PAINTER, PRINTMAKER
b West Palm Beach, Fla, Mar 13, 43. *Study:* Art Student's League, Woodstock, NY, 63-65; Cranbrook Acad Art, BFA, 67; Yale Univ, MFA, 69. *Work:* Achenbach Found, Calif, Palace Legion Hon, San Francisco; Los Angeles Co Mus Art; Metrop Mus Art, New York; Mus Fine Arts, Boston; Norton Gallery Contemp Collection, West Palm Beach, Fla. *Exhib:* 62nd Ann Int, Print Club, Philadelphia, Pa, 86; Brenau Nat Invitational, Brenau Col, Gainesville, Ga, 89; Acquisitions 1984-1990, Univ Art Mus, Univ of Queensland, Brisbane, Australia, 90; Urban Insights, Claremont Sch Art, Perth, West Australia, 92. *Pos:* Artist-in-residence, Mass Arts & Humanities Found, 77; head found yr, Sch Art & Design, PCAE, Melbourne, 77-79; publs consult, Australian Bicentennial Authority, Sydney, 87-89. *Teaching:* Instr art, Wheelock Col, Boston, Mass, 69-72; instr printmaking, DeCordova Mus Sch, Mass, 74-77; lectr corp art collections, City Art Inst, Univ of NSW, Sydney, 87-90. *Awards:* Bicentennial Comn, Boston City Hall, Boston 200, 75; Mardsen's Open Acquisitive, Campbelltown City Festival, NSW, Marsden Solicitors, 88. *Bibliog:* Bradford F Swan (auth), Valier at RI Col exhibition, Providence Sunday J, 1/7/73; Robert Taylor (auth), Famous Boston potholes, Boston Globe, 3/14/78; Jennifer Moran (auth), Valier charts images of urban life, West Australian, 6/1/92. *Mem:* Col Art Asn; Art Deco Soc Western Australia; Printmakers Asn Western Australia. *Publ:* Auth, Twenty Photographs, pvt publ, 67; Famous Boston Potholes, South Wind Graphics, 77; Luna and Metal, Namba Wan Arts, 82; Corporate sponsorship of the visual arts in Australia, Art Monthly Australia, 89; contribr, International Directory of Corporate Art Collections, ARTnews, NY, 90. *Mailing Add:* PO Box 6346 East Perth, WA 6892 Australia

VALLEE, WILLIAM OSCAR
PAINTER, GRAPHIC ARTIST
b South Paris, Maine, June 18, 34. *Study:* Univ Alaska. *Work:* Many in pvt collections. *Exhib:* Anchorage Fur Rendezvous, 63; Easter Arts Festival, 63; Alaska Festival Music & Art, 63 & 64; one-man shows, Anchorage Petrol Club, 63 & Anchor Galleries, 63. *Pos:* Instituted (in coop with Am Artists Prof League), Am Art Wk, 63; treas, Soc Alaskan Arts, 63; co-founder, Alaska-Int Cult Arts Ctr; bd dirs & co-founder, Anchorage Community Art Ctr, currently; pres & chmn bd, Alaska Map Serv, Inc, currently. *Awards:* Anchorage Fur Rendezvous, 63; Easter Art Festival, 63; Artist of the Month, Alaska Art Guild, 63. *Mem:* Alaska Art Guild (pres & chmn, 64); Alaska Watercolor Soc (pres, 63); Am Soc Photogrammetry; Am Artist Prof League. *Media:* Watercolor. *Mailing Add:* 4118 Irene Dr Anchorage AK 99504

VALLILA, MARJA R
SCULPTOR
b Prague, Czech, Oct 20, 50; US citizen. *Study:* Hampshire Col, BA, 72; Cornell Univ, MFA, 75. *Work:* Johnson Mus; Everson Mus; Kennedy Airport, McCory Corp, New York; Gen Mills Corp, Minneapolis. *Exhib:* Solo exhibs, Zabriskie Gallery, New York, 77 & 80, Mus Fine Arts, Springfield, Mass, 79 & Tulane Univ, 81; View From Upstate, AIR Gallery, New York, 82; Zabriskie Gallery, 89; Newark Mus, 91; Haenah-Kent Gallery, New York, 91; and others. *Teaching:* Asst prof sculpture, Cornell Univ, 79-80, mem adv coun, 81-; asst prof, Bard Col, 80 & State Univ NY, Albany, 81- & assoc prof, 90- *Awards:* State Univ NY Res Grant, 83, 85 & 86. *Bibliog:* David L Shirley (auth), article, New York Times, 7/14/77; Sally Jessup (auth), article, Art World, 5/21/80; Alan Singer (auth), article, Arts Mag, 4/85; Brenson (auth), article, New York Times, 6/29/89. *Mem:* Col Art Asn. *Media:* Welded Steel, Cast Iron. *Dealer:* Zabriskie Gallery 724 Fifth Ave New York NY 10019. *Mailing Add:* Studio Art Dept State Univ NY Albany NY 12222

VALTMAN, EDMUND
CARTOONIST, EDITORIAL
b Tallinn, Estonia, May 31, 14; US citizen. *Study:* Pvt studios, 36-39; Tallinn Art & Appl Art Sch, 42-44. *Work:* Lyndon Johnson Libr, Austin, Tex; Univ Southern Miss Libr; Univ Cincinnati Libr; State Hist Soc Mo, Columbia; Wichita State Univ Libr, Kans. *Exhib:* One-man cartoon exhibs, Estonian House, New York, 72, Toronto, 73, Baltimore Mem Hall, 76 & West Hartford Art League, 79; Joselof Gallery, Univ Hartford, 84; Old Lyme Art Works, 85; Shipee Gallery, New York, 86; Conn Artists Showcase, 86, 87; cartoon exhib, Univ Hartford, Mus Am Political Life, 90; and others. *Pos:* Ed cartoonist, Hartford Times, 51-75. *Awards:* Helen Hazelton Graphic Award, 83; Wintonbury Art League Graphic Award, 84; Graphic Award, Old Lyme Inn, 85; and others. *Mem:* Asn Am Ed Cartoonists; Nat Cartoonists Soc; Conn Acad Fine Arts; Canton Artists Guild; West Hartford Art League. *Media:* India Ink. *Collection:* Editorial cartoons. *Publ:* Cartoon, In: The Ungentlemanly Art, McMillan, rev ed 75; cartoon, In: Avain Aikamme Maailman, Werner Söderström, Helsinki, Finland, 83; Editorial cartoon collection of Edmund Valtman "Valtman", Esto Publ, 91. *Mailing Add:* 41 Foothills Way Bloomfield CT 06002

VAN AALTEN, JACQUES
PAINTER, SCULPTOR
b Antwerp, Belg, Apr 12, 07. *Study:* Nat Acad Design, 26-30, grad; Art Students League, 32-34; Acad Grande Chaumiere, Paris, 55; Tulane Univ La, 70-71. *Work:* Portrait of Pope Pius XII, Vatican Mus Permanent Collection, Rome; Relig Ministry Bldg, Jerusalem; Truman Libr, Independence, Mo; La State Art Collection, New Capitol Bldg, Baton Rouge; Rockport Art Asn, Mass; plus many others in pvt collections in USA & abroad. *Exhib:* Whitney Mus, 40; Detroit Inst Art Mus, Mich, 46; Isaac Delgado Mus Art, New Orleans, 58-59; Rockport Art Asn, Mass, 62-85; Mus-Norton Gallery, Palm Beach, Fla, 63; La Artists Group, La Art Comn Gallery, Old Capitol Bldg, Baton Rouge; plus many other group & one-man shows. *Teaching:* Instr art, Nassau Conserv Art, Long Island, NY, 40; instr art, van Aalten Studio Sch, Detroit, 44-47; instr art, Deerfield Beach & Boca Raton, Fla, 74-86. *Awards:* Suydam Medal, 30; Tiffany Scholar, 30; Silver Pontifical Medal, received from Pope Pius XII, Vatican City, Rome, Italy, 55. *Mem:* Life mem Rockport Art Asn; life mem Art Students League; Nat Soc Mural Painters; Isaac Delgado Mus Art Asn. *Media:* All. *Mailing Add:* Lyndhurst K-1043 Deerfield Beach FL 33442

VAN ALSTINE, JOHN RICHARD
SCULPTOR
b Johnstown, NY, Aug 14, 52. *Study:* St Lawrence Univ, 70-72; Kent State Univ, BFA, 74; Cornell Univ Sch Art & Archit, MFA, 76. *Work:* Nat Mus Am Art, Smithsonian Inst; Hirshhorn Mus & Sculpture Garden; Denver Mus; Carnegie Inst Mus Art; Mus Mod Art, Gulbenkian Found, Lisbon, Portugal; Baltimore Mus Art; Corcoran Mus Art, Washington, DC; Del Mus Art, Wilmington; Herbert F Johnson Mus, Cornell Univ, Ithaca, NY; Newark Mus Art, NJ; and many others. *Comn:* Pub Comn, Billings, Mont, 82 & Luck Stone Corp, Richmond, Va, 83; outdoor public sculptures, Austin Col, Sherman, Tex, 86; Inst Defence Analyses, Washington, DC, 88-89. *Exhib:* Solo exhibs, Nohra Haime Gallery, New York, 88-91, Gerald Peters Gallery, Santa Fe, NMex, 89 & 91; New Work/Raw Space, spec exhib with Int Sculpture Conf, Franz Bader Gallery, Washington, DC, 90, Sonsbeek Int Art Ctr, Arnhem, Neth, 91, Documents (drawings & related documents produced with large scale site-specific solstice projects), Nat Acad Sci, Washington, DC, 91, New Jersey Artist Series, Morris Mus, Morristown, 91, Franz Bader Gallery, Washington, DC, 91; New Jersey Artists Biennial, Newark Mus, 85; Artists Fel Exhib, NJ Arts Coun, Morris Mus, 87; Sculpture Invitational: John Van Alstine & David Maxim, Indiana Univ, Pa, 89; Object/Context: A National Invitational, Indiana Univ Pa, Mus, 91; Sculptors on Paper, Cong Sq Gallery, Portland, Maine, 91; and many other one-man & group exhibs. *Teaching:* Asst, Cornell Univ, 74-76; asst prof, Univ Wyo, Laramie, 76-80 & Univ Md, College Park, 80-86; vis prof, Md Art Inst, Baltimore, 88. *Awards:* Yaddo Fel, 85; Individual Artist Fel, Nat Endowment Arts, 86; Individual Artists Fel, NJ State Coun Arts, 88. *Bibliog:* Ann Markovich (rev), New Art Examiner, 10/84; Paul Richard (rev), Washington Post, 10/17/85; John Dorsey (rev), Baltimore Sun, 5/11/88. *Media:* Stone, Steel. *Dealer:* Nohra Haime Gallery New York NY. *Mailing Add:* 218 1/2 Bright St Jersey City NJ 07302

VANASSE, LOUIS RAYMOND
COLLECTOR, INSTRUCTOR
b Northampton, Mass, Jan 22, 31. *Study:* St Michael's Col, AB(Eng); Univ of Mass, MA(Eng). *Teaching:* Instr humanities, Northampton Sch System,

Mass, 60- *Awards:* John Hay Fel, Studies in the Humanities, Williams Col, 62; Fulbright-Hays Grant, study in Ghana, W Africa, African Art, Univ Mass, 74. *Collection:* Twentieth century American artists. *Mailing Add:* 17 Aubinwood Rd Amherst MA 01002

VAN BRUNT, PHILIP G
DIRECTOR, ASSEMBLAGE ARTIST
b Kobe, Japan, Mar 31, 35; US citizen. *Study:* Chaffey Col, Ontario, Calif, AA; Otis Art Inst, Los Angeles, MFA, 60; also with Arthur Ames. *Work:* Santa Barbara Mus Art, Calif; Salk Inst, La Jolla; Lyman Allyn Mus, New London, Conn; Presidente Mus, Guadalajara, Mex; Carnegie Inst, Pittsburgh, Pa. *Comn:* Processional Cross, St Mark's Episcopal Church, Upland, Calif, 64; oil painting, Gen Foods Corp, Calif, 65; enamel mural, pvt residence, Los Angeles, 69; mural, collage, Clinton Nat Bank, Conn, 74; five panel screen, pvt residence, Greenwich, Conn, 90. *Exhib:* Enamels, Mus Contemp Crafts, New York, 59; Los Angeles Co Mus Art, 59-61; 17 Conn Artists, Slater Mem Mus, Norwich, Conn, 72; one-man show, La Jolla Art Mus, 68 & Lyman Allyn Mus, New London, Conn, 74; group show, Conn Collage, Hartford, Conn, 89. *Pos:* Asst dir, Downey Mus Art, Calif, 60-65. *Teaching:* Instr painting, Lyman Allyn Mus, summers; instr, Westridge Sch, Pasadena, Calif, 63-64; dir art, Williams Sch, New London, Conn, 72-83. *Awards:* Gold Medal, Nat Orange Show, San Bernardino, Calif, 58. *Bibliog:* Jean Yoder (auth), Titanic epilogue, Commutator J. *Mem:* Otis Art Assoc, Los Angeles. *Media:* Found Objects, Collage. *Publ:* Contribr, Joseph Mugnaini (auth), Oil Painting, 72; illusr, Choristers guild letters, 74-75. *Dealer:* Henri Gallery 1500 21st St NW Washington DC 20036. *Mailing Add:* 110 Hempstead St New London CT 06320

VANCO, JOHN LEROY
ADMINISTRATOR, CURATOR
b Erie, Pa, Aug 21, 45. *Study:* Allegheny Col, BA(art hist); Whitney Mus Am Art. *Collections Arranged:* Teco: Art Pottery of the Prairie School in Harmony with The Earth; Paperthick: Forms and Images in Cast Paper; Images of War and Artists Respond to the Gulf War. *Pos:* Dir, Erie Art Mus, 68- *Publ:* Auth, What Ever Happened to Louis Eilshemius?, 67; contribr, American Art & Western Wildlife, 72; illusr, Roger Misiewicz: Wolfman of the Blues, 72. *Mailing Add:* Erie Art Mus 411 State St Erie PA 16501

VAN DE BOVENKAMP, HANS
SCULPTOR
b Barneveld, Holland, June 1, 38. *Study:* Archit Sch Amsterdam, 57; Univ Mich, Ann Arbor, BScDes, 61. *Work:* Sculpture Garden, Nebr Bicentennial; State Capitol Plaza, Lansing, Mich; Lowe Mus, Coral Gables, Fla; Boca Raton Mus, Fla; Youngstown Mus, OH; Stony Brook Univ, NY; Univ Mo. *Comn:* Landauer Assoc, 84; Christiania Realty, 84; Lighthouse (sculpture), Haverstraw Marina, 86; Fountain, Amli Realty Co, Chicago, 88; Sculpture, Marina Village, Alameda, Calif, 90; Tex A&M Univ. *Exhib:* Lever House, New York, 69 & 73-92; Storm King Art Ctr, Cornwall, NY, 73-74; Am Inst Arts & Lett, New York, 76; Arnot Art Mus, Elmira, NY, 76; Nat Acad Design, New York, 77; Sculpture Ctr, NY, 79; Bologna Landi Gallery, East Hampton, NY, 82-92; Moosart Gallery, Miami, Fla, 85-87; Nina Owen Ltd, Chicago, Ill, 87-90; Shidoni, NMex, 88-92; Lowe Gallery, Atlanta, Ga, 89-92; Camenoreal, Boca Raton, Fla, 91. *Awards:* Emily Lowe Award, 64; I-80 Nebr Award, 76. *Mem:* NY Sculptors Guild; Int Sculpture Ctr. *Media:* Stainless Steel, Aluminum. *Dealer:* Lowe Galleries Atlanta GA; Shidoni, Tesuque, NMex. *Mailing Add:* Box 837 Tillson NY 12486

VANDEN BERGE, PETER WILLEM
SCULPTOR, MURALIST
b Voorburg, Zuid-Holland, Neth, Oct 16, 35; US citizen. *Study:* Art Acad, The Hague, Neth; Calif State Univ, Sacramento, BA; Univ Calif, Davis, MA. *Work:* Henry Gallery, Univ Wash, Seattle; Mus Contemp Crafts, New York; Johnson Collection Am Crafts, Racine, Wis; Crocker Art Mus, Sacramento; Oakland Art Mus, Calif. *Comn:* Three glazed relief tile murals, San Francisco City Col, 71; pub murals, San Francisco Arts Comn, City of San Francisco; glazed tile relief, Contra Costa Jr Col Dist Off, John F Gordon Educ Ctr, Martinez, Calif, 75; tile mural, Sacramento Metrop Arts Comn, 79. *Exhib:* Four Ceramic Sculptors from California, Alan Frumkin Gallery, New York, 73, Calif Ceramic Sculptors I & II, 74, Five Ceramic Sculptors from Calif, Chicago, 75; Clay, Whitney Mus Am Art, New York, 74; Fendrick's Gallery, Washington, DC, 76; Campbell Mus Contemp Crafts, Cranbrook Acad Art, Bloomfield Hills, Mich, 76; A Century of Ceramics in the United States, Everson Mus Art, Syracuse, NY, 79; Craft Today-USA, Mus Decorative Arts, Paris, France (traveling exhib through Europe); Poetry of the Physical, Am Craft Mus, New York; Contemporary American: 20 Americans, Newport Harbor Art Mus, Newport Beach, Calif; Tri Ann Int Craft Exhib, Art Gallery Western Australia, Perth. *Teaching:* Asst prof ceramics & sculpture, San Francisco State Univ, 66-73; prof ceramics & sculpture, Calif State Univ, Sacramento, 73- *Awards:* Madeleine Cortese Williams Found Award, 63 & 66; Comn Awarded, Sacramento Metrop Arts Comn, Art in Pub Places Prog, 78-84; Nat Endowment for the Arts Fel Grant, 81. *Bibliog:* D Zack (auth), Mythology, California ceramics, Art & Artist Mag, London, 9/69, Nut art in quake time, Art News, 70 & Laugh in clay, Craft Horizon Mag, 71. *Media:* Stoneware, Porcelain; Clay, Terra Cotta. *Dealer:* Natsoulas/Novelozo Gallery 140 F St Davis CA 95616. *Mailing Add:* c/o John Natsoulas Gallery 140 F St Davis CA 95616

VANDERLIP, DIANNE PERRY
GALLERY DIRECTOR, EDUCATOR
b Toledo, Ohio, Apr 20, 41. *Study:* Ohio Univ, BFA; NY Univ; Pratt Inst. *Collections Arranged:* Recorded Activities (with catalog), 70; Artists Books (with catalog), 73; N, E, W, S & Middle (with catalog), 75; Alphons Schilling Stereoptics, 75; John Sloan/Robert Henri: Their Philadelphia Yrs, 76; Alan Shields' Environments, 77; Robert Hudson, 77; Poets & Painters, 79; Lucas Samaras Pastels, 81. *Pos:* Dir, Vanderlip Gallery, Philadelphia, 66-68; dir, Moore Col Art Gallery, 68-78; cur & consult, Dechert, Price & Rhoads, Philadelphia, 74-; panelist & consult, Nat Endowments Arts, Washington, DC, 74-; cur of contemp art, Denver Art Mus, 78- *Teaching:* Prof aesthetics, Moore Col Art, 68- *Awards:* Award of Excellence, Philadelphia Art Dir Club, 71. *Bibliog:* Dore Ashton (auth), Beyond literalism, Art Mag, 69; Lucy Lippard (auth), Dematerialization of Art, Praeger, 73; Dianne Kelder (auth), Artists books, Art in Am, 74. *Mem:* Am Asn Mus; Am Fedn Arts; Soc Arts & Lett. *Collection:* Contemporary paintings and drawings by American artists. *Publ:* Ed, More Ray Gun Poems by Claes Oldenburg, 74; ed, Hopi Kachina Dolls, 75. *Mailing Add:* 1218 Columbine St Denver CO 80206

VAN DER MEULEN, JAN
HISTORIAN, EDUCATOR
b Oct 10, 29; US citizen. *Study:* Univ Cape Town, BArch, 52; Univ Marburg Ger, Dr Philos. *Exhib:* 106 photographs, Koninklijk Institut voor de Tropen, Amsterdam, 56. *Pos:* Tech supv, Lichtbeelden Inst, Amsterdam, Holland, 55-56; free assoc, Archit Walter Freiwald, Marburg, WGer, 56-59; dir, South African Mus, 63-64. *Teaching:* Prof medieval art hist, Pa State Univ, 68-74; prof, Cleveland State Univ, 74-, chmn dept, 74-82; vis prof, Univ Frankfurt, 78-79, Univ Calif, Los Angeles, 82 & Univ Bonn, WGer, 82-83. *Awards:* Alexander Von Humboldt-Stiftung, 64-66; Deutsche Forschungsgemeinschaft, 66-68; Fulbright Prof, Univ Frankfurt, 78-79; DFG/Richard Merton Chair, Univ Bonn, 82-83. *Bibliog:* Heiliges Gedrange (rev), Der Spiegel, Vol 29, 52, 12/22/75; Carl Barnes (auth), articles, Speculum 52, 67 & 77, 92; Michael Davis (auth), Speculum, 62, 87. *Res:* Chartres Cathedral; late antique origins of Christian architecture in Gaul; the Gothic cathedral. *Publ:* Auth, The West Portals of Chartres Cathedral, Vol 1, Am Univ Press, 81; ed, Sanctuaries of the Gallic Frankish Church, Lang, Frankfurt, 81-91; coauth, Chartres Biographie der Kathedrale, Cologne, DuMont, 84; Die frankische Konigsabtei Saint-Denis, Darmstadt, Wissenschaftliche Buchgesellschaft, 88; auth, Chartres Cathedral, Sources and literary interpretations, a critical bibliography, Boston, GK Hall, 89; and others. *Mailing Add:* Cleveland State Univ Cleveland OH 44115

VANDERPOOL, KAREN
WEAVER, EDUCATOR
b Troy, NY, July 14, 46. *Study:* State Univ NY, BS, 68; Tyler Sch Art, MFA, 70; Haystack Mt Sch Crafts; Sch Am Craftsmen. *Work:* Ball State Univ, Muncie, Ind; First Nat Bank, Boston. *Exhib:* Weaving Unlimited, De Cordova Mus, Lincoln, Mass, 71; Bodycraft, Portland Art Mus, Ore, 73; 3rd International Exhibition Miniature Textiles, Brit Craft Ctr, London, Eng, 78; Art in Crafts, Bronx Mus, NY, 78; Felting, Mus Am Craft, New York, 80; Art Fabric: Mainstream, San Francisco Mus Mod Art, 81; 30 Americans, Galveston Art Ctr, Tex, 81; Fiber Nat '85, Adams Mem Gallery, Dunkirk, NY, 85. *Teaching:* Asst prof weaving & fiber arts, Univ Wash, Seattle, 76-81; prof, Calif State Univ, Chico, 81- *Awards:* First Award Fibers, Mass Artists-Craftsmen, 71 & Calif Works '84, 84; First Award Crafts, Pac Northwest Arts & Crafts, 72. *Bibliog:* Betty Scholossman (auth), Reviews: Clay, fiber, metal by women artists, Art J, Vol 37, No 4, summer 78; Betty Park (auth), Felting, Fiberarts, 11-12/80. *Mem:* Am Craft Coun; Handweavers Guild Am. *Media:* Papermaking, Computer Assisted Textile Design. *Mailing Add:* Dept Art Calif State Univ Chico CA 95929

VANDERSALL, AMY L
HISTORIAN, EDUCATOR
b West Newton, Pa, Oct 9, 33. *Study:* Col Wooster, Ohio, BA, 55; Mt Holyoke Col, South Hadley, Mass, MA, 58; Yale Univ, MA, 62, PhD, 65. *Teaching:* Asst prof medieval art hist, Smith Col, 66-72; assoc prof, Univ Colo, 73-81, prof, 81- *Mem:* Int Ctr Medieval Art (bd of dirs, 75-78 & 85-88); Col Art Asn; Medieval Acad Am. *Res:* Carolingian ivory carving, Anglo-Saxon art and Romanesque sculpture. *Publ:* Auth, Two Carolingian ivories in the Metropolitan Museum of Art, 72 & Five Romanesque Portals: Questions of Attributions and Ornament, 83, New York, Metrop Mus J; auth, Date and provenance of the Franks casket, Gesta, 73; auth, Homeric myth in early medieval England: The lid of the Franks casket, Studies Iconography, 75; auth, Relationship of sculptors and painters at the court of Charles the Bald, 76 & Romanesque sculpture in American museums: The west, 80, Gesta. *Mailing Add:* Dept Fine Arts Box 318 Univ Colo Boulder CO 80309

VAN DOMMELEN, DAVID B
WRITER, FIBER ARTIST
b Grand Rapids, Mich, Aug 21, 29. *Study:* Harrington Interior Design Inst, cert; Mich State Univ, BA & MA; also with Abraham Rattner & Mariska Karasz. *Work:* Mich State Univ Mus of Art, East Lansing; Arrowmont Sch of Crafts, Gatlinburg, Tenn; Am Home Econ Asn Collection, Washington, DC; Marshall Field Permanent Collection, Chicago; Portland Mus of Fine Arts, Maine. *Exhib:* Group Traveling Show, Smithsonian Inst, Washington, DC, 57-78; Invention with Thread, Montclair Art Mus, NJ, 61; one-man shows, Portland Mus of Art, Maine, 63, Kalamazoo Art Ctr Mus, Mich, 66, Univ Iowa, Iowa City, 67 & WVa State Univ Mus, Institute, 75; and many others. *Collections Arranged:* Retrospective 1956-1968, Pa State Univ, 68. *Teaching:* Prof & head art educ, Pa State Univ, 59-88; summer instr, Haystack Sch of Crafts, 62, 63 & 74; guest prof, Univ Iowa, 66-69; summer instr, Arrowmont Schs Crafts, 70-81. *Awards:* Fishburn Award, Int Understanding, Educ Press Am, 73. *Bibliog:* John Peter (auth), Sewing machine art, Look Mag, 8/61; Ruth Bunker (auth), David Van Dommelen, Cross-Country Craftsman, 10/62. *Mem:* Nat Art Educ Asn; Nat Craftsman's Asn; Am Craft

Coun. *Media:* Fiber. *Publ:* Auth, Decorative Wall Hangings, 62 & Walls: Enrichment and Ornamentation, 65, Funk & Wagnalls; Designing and Decorating Interiors, John Wiley, 65; New Uses for Old Cannonballs, Funk & Wagnalls, 66; Doughboy Letters, 77 & Allen Eaton: Dean of American Crafts, 85, VDI Press. *Mailing Add:* c/o Hub Galleries Pennsylvania State Univ 111 Kern Bldg University Park PA 16802

VAN DUINWYK, GEORGE PAUL
GOLDSMITH, EDUCATOR
b New York, NY, Sept 30, 41. *Study:* Calif State Univ, Northridge, with Frederick Lauritzen, BA, 64; Calif State Univ, Long Beach, with Alvin A Pine, MA, 71; RI Sch of Design, with John A Prip, MFA, 72. *Work:* Oakland Mus, Calif. *Exhib:* Mod Am Metalsmithing & Jewelry, Corcoran Gallery of Art, Washington, DC, 72; Jewelry Invitational, Albright-Knox Mus, Buffalo, NY, 74; World Silver Fair, Mexico City, Mex, 74; Univ Colo, 74; 275 Yrs of Am Metalsmithing, Mus of Contemp Crafts, New York, 75; Goldsmiths 77, Phoenix Art Mus, Ariz, 77; Profiles of US Jewelry, Tex Tech Univ, Lubbock, 77; and others. *Pos:* Craftsman-in-residence, RI State Coun on the Arts, 76-77; dir tech resources, Jewelry Inst, Providence, RI, 77-79. *Teaching:* Assoc prof metalsmithing, Calif State Univ, Long Beach, 72-73; adj prof metalsmithing, RI Sch of Design, 73-74; asst prof, Kent State Univ, 79-82. *Awards:* Purchase Award, The Metal Experience, Oakland Mus, 71; Design Award, Designer/Craftsman 77, Richmond Art Ctr, Calif, 76; Nat Endowment for the Arts Grant, Slide Jury Proj, 77. *Bibliog:* Ralph Turner (auth), Modern Jewelry, Eng publ, 76; Thelma Newman (auth), The Container Book, Chilton, 77; Oppi Untracht (auth), Jewelry Techniques, Doubleday 77. *Mem:* Ohio Designer Craftsmen; Soc NAm Goldsmiths; Am Crafts Coun. *Media:* Precious & Nonprecious Metals. *Mailing Add:* 358 Boulevard Middletown RI 02840

VANESS, MARGARET HELEN
PAINTER, PRINTMAKER
b Seattle, Wash, Nov 6, 19. *Study:* Univ Wash, BFA(printmaking), BFA(painting), MAT & MFA; Drexel Univ; spec study with Francis Cellentano, Glen Alps, Freeman Patterson & Robert Stahl. *Work:* US Embassies in Athens, Bogata, Bierut, Caracas, Copenhagen, Seoul, Managua, Lima, Lagos, Dar es Salaam & Tanzania; Cheney-Cowles Mus, Spokane, Wash; Pratt-Manhattan Ctr Gallery, New York; World Print Orgn, San Francisco, Calif; Evergreen State Col Libr Collection, Olympia, Wash; and others. *Comn:* Two ed of ten prints each, US Info Agency, 73; mural, Med Ctr, Boeing Co, Philadelphia, Pa, 74; mural, Gem & Minerals Mag, 90. *Exhib:* Northwest Ann, Seattle Art Mus, Wash, 65 & 67; Judkin Mem Am Mus, Bath, Eng, Pratt Manhattan, New York, 72-74; 60th Ann, Del Art Mus, Wilmington, 74; Philadelphia Art Alliance, Pa, 75; one-person show, Greenhill-Lower Merion, Philadelphia, Pa, 76; Nat Print Exhib, Cheney-Cowles Mus, Spokane, Wash, 77; Gov Invitational, Olympia, Wash, 78; and others. *Pos:* Illusr, Boeing Co, Seattle, Wash, 72-73 & 78-80 & Du Pont Co, Wilmington, Del, 73-74; consult, 80-; Cable Releases, 85-90; asst ed, NWCCC Newsletter, 91- *Teaching:* Instr painting & drawing, Burien Arts Gallery Sch, Seattle, Wash, 68-69; asst printmaking, Univ Wash, Seattle, 71-73. *Awards:* First Award Painting, Boeing Co, 68 & 74; First Awards Print, Pac Northwest Arts & Crafts Asn, 70 & 71; Progress/Serv Award for Advancement, Art Photog, 89. *Bibliog:* Carolyn Wright (auth), Thesis exhibit at Henry Gallery, Univ Washington Daily, 6/73; Andrew Seraphin (auth), Four printmakers in Gallery F, Art Alliance Bull, 4/75; Karen Klamm (auth), Sound-Off, Our Northwest Commun, 12/83. *Mem:* Col Art Asn, New York; Philadelphia Print Club; charter mem Burien Arts Asn (trustee, 65-69); Photog Soc Am; charter mem, Nat Mus Women in Arts, Washington, DC. *Media:* Acrylic, Mixed Media; Collagraph, Serigraphy. *Publ:* Creativity, 4/91 & In persuit of contemporary images, 7/92, Pastel Soc Asn J; Eye & mind/minds-eye, summer 91 & Abstraction, beginnings, summer 92, NWCCC Newletter. *Mailing Add:* 17128 Second Southwest Seattle WA 98166

VAN GINKEL, BLANCHE LEMCO
ARCHITECT, EDUCATOR
b Can. *Study:* McGill Univ, BArch; Harvard Univ, MCP. *Exhib:* Plan for Old Montreal, Place Ville Marie, Montreal, Que, 63; Midtown Manhattan Plan Exhib, Art Dir Club & New York Cult Ctr, 72; Work of van Ginkel Assoc, Columbia Univ, New York, 73; Spectrum Can, Royal Can Acad Arts, Montreal, 76; and others. *Pos:* Partner, van Ginkel Assocs, Montreal, Toronto, 57-; rep, Can Conf Arts, Ottawa, Royal Archit Inst Can, 71-74; mem adv comt on design, Nat Capital Planning Comn, 77-82; chmn, Massey Awards, Ottawa, Ont, 77-; bd, Asn Col Schs Archit, 81-84, vpres, 85-86, pres, 86-87. *Teaching:* Asst prof archit, Univ Pa, Philadelphia, 51-57; vis prof, Harvard Univ, Univ Montreal & McGill Univ; dean, Sch Archit, Univ Toronto, Ont, 77-82, prof archit, 77- *Awards:* Asn Col Schs Archit Distinguished Professor, 89; Citizenship Citation, Govt Can, 91; Alumni Award, 91; and others. *Bibliog:* Article, New patterns for a metropolis, Archit Forum, 10/71; Les effets Reels--, Archit Concept, 5/73. *Mem:* Royal Can Acad Arts; fel Royal Archit Inst Can. *Publ:* Auth, The form of the core, J Am Inst Planner, 2/61; ed & contribr, Automobile Issue Can Art, 62; Expo 67 Archit Design, 67; contribr, Phenomenon of Pollution, Harvest House, 68; contribr, Aesthetic Considerations, In: Urban Problems, Holt Rinehart & Winston, 71. *Mailing Add:* Sch of Archit Univ Toronto 230 College St Toronto ON M5S 1A1 Canada

VAN HAAFTEN, JULIA
CURATOR, WRITER
b Lancaster, Pa, Nov 3, 46. *Study:* Barnard Col, BA, 68; Columbia Univ, MLS, 70. *Collections Arranged:* Original Sun Pictures (with catalog), 77 & 96 Images: Talbot to Stieglitz (with catalog), 81, New York Pub Libr Col; Francis Frith in the Middle East, 84; Clarence Kennedy, 87; The View From Space (sites), 89; Berenice Abbott: Modern Vision (with catalog), 89. *Pos:* Contribr, Libr J, Portfolio Mag, Hist Photog, 73-; dir photog collections, New York Pub Libr, 79- *Teaching:* Instr, Rare Book Sch, Columbia Univ, 86-87. *Bibliog:* Article, AB Bookmen's Weekly, 1/12/82, Darkroom Photogr, 1/83, Photography Year, Time-Life, 82 & Portfolio, 1/2/82. *Res:* Nineteenth century photography; illustrated books, albums, other forms of publications of photographs. *Publ:* Contribr, Guide to the literature of art history, Am Libr Asn, 81; coauth, Egypt and the Holy Land: 77 Views by Francis Frith, Dover, 81; The view From Space: American Astronaut Photography, 88. *Mailing Add:* 521 W 111th St New York NY 10025

VAN HALM, RENÉE
PAINTER, EDUCATOR
b Amsterdam, Neth, July 11, 49; Can citizen. *Study:* Emily Carr Col Art, Vancouver, BC, dipl, 75; Concordia Univ, Montreal, MFA, 77. *Work:* Nat Gallery, Ottawa; Art Gallery Ont, Toronto; Musée des Beaux-Arts of Montreal; Musée d'Art Contemporain, Montreal; Univ Lethbridge, Alta. *Exhib:* Solo exhibs, Univ Lethbridge, 82, Inst Art & Urban Resouces, PS 1, New York, 83, 49th Parallel, New York, 84 & L'eau la Bouche (with catalog), Art Gallery Greater Victoria, BC, 86; Toronto Painting, Art Gallery Ont, 84; Aurora Borealis, Montreal Int Inst Contemp Art, 85; Fire & Ice, Gallerie Walchetürm, Zurich, 85; Songs of Experience, Nat Gallery Can, Ottawa, 86; Mapping the Surface, Mendel Art Gallery, Saskatoon; Display (with catalog), Toronto Sculpture Garden, Toronto, Ont, 87. *Teaching:* Course dir painting & Grad Fac, York Univ, Toronto, 79-92; fac painting, Emily Carr Col Art & Design, Vancouver, BC, 92- *Awards:* Can Coun Grants, 77, 82, 84, 85, 87 & 91; Ont Arts Coun; Ont Proj Cost Award, 84. *Bibliog:* Neo-Toronto (film), 87; Eau A La Bouche Renee Van Halm, Art Gallery of Greater Victoria. *Mem:* Mercer Union (dir); Power Plant (dir). *Media:* Mixed Media. *Dealer:* S L Simpson Gallery 515 Queen St W Toronto ON M5V 2B4 Canada. *Mailing Add:* 870 W Seventh Ave No 9 Vancouver BC V5Z 4C1 Canada

VAN HARLINGEN, JEAN (ANN)
ENVIRONMENTAL ARTIST, PAINTER
b Dayton, Ohio, Feb 12, 47. *Study:* Ohio State Univ, BS, 70; Tyler Sch Art (univ fel), MFA, 75. *Work:* Hallmark, Kansas City, Mo; 20th Century Investments, Kansas City, Mo; AT&T, Kansas City; IBM, Detroit. *Comn:* Pet Inc, St Louis, Mo, 86. *Exhib:* 12th Int Biennial Tapestry, Mus Cantanol des Beaux Arts, Lausanne, Switz, 85; Int Biennial Paper Art, Leopold-Hoesch Mus, Duren, WGer; 13th Outdoor Sculpture Show, Shidoni Gallery, Santa Fe, NMex, 87; solo show, Leedy-Voulkos Gallery, Kansas City, 90 & Western Mich Univ, Kalamazoo, Mich, 90; Liberties Expressions, 14th Int Sculpture Conf, Philadelphia, 92. *Pos:* Coordr, Visual Arts Pub Serv Prog, Brandywine Graphic Workshop, 78-80 & Women's Caucus Art, 80-81, Philadelphia, Pa. *Teaching:* Vis artist, Univ Mo, Kansas City, 86- *Awards:* Grant, Pa Coun Arts, 74; Second Prize, Paper Fiber XII, Iowa City/Johnson Co Arts Coun. *Bibliog:* Milena Lamarova (auth), Textile sculpture: The 12th international biennial of tapestry, Am Craft, 10-11/85; Greg Field (auth), Subtle Process Deserves a Second Look, 89; Elain Klein (auth), Sculpture that changes with nature, Kalamazoo Gazette, 9/13/90. *Mem:* Kansas City Artists Coalition (bd dirs, 86-); Am Craft Coun; Int Sculpture Ctr; Col Art Asn; Int Asn Hand Papermakers. *Media:* All. *Dealer:* Leedy-Voulkos Gallery 1919 Wyandotte Kansas City Mo. *Mailing Add:* 8142 1/2 Troost, No 27 Kansas City MO 64131

VAN HOESEN, BETH
PRINTMAKER
b Boise, Idaho, June 27, 26. *Study:* With Escuela Esmaralda, Mexico City, 45; San Francisco Art Inst, 46-47 & 51-52; Stanford Univ, BA, 48; Ecole Arts, Fontainbleau, 48-51; Acad Julian, Paris, 48-51; Acad Grande Chaumier, Paris, 48-51; San Francisco State Univ, 57-58. *Work:* Brooklyn Mus & Mus Mod Art, New York; San Francisco Mus Mod Art; Victoria & Albert Mus, London; Chicago Art Inst; Achenbach Found Graphic Arts, San Francisco; Sanford Univ, Palo Alto. *Exhib:* Calif State Fair, Sacramento, 51; Libr Cong, 56 & 57; San Francisco Mus Mod Art, 56, 59, 61 & 70; Boston Mus Fine Arts, 59, 60 & 62; Philadelphia Acad Fine Arts, 59, 61, 63 & 65; solo exhibs, De Young Mus, San Francisco, 59, Achenbach Found, Calif Palace Legion Honor, 61 & 74, Santa Barbara Mus, 63, 74 & 76, E B Crocker Art Gallery, Sacramento, 66, Hansen/Fuller/Goldeen Gallery, San Francisco, 66, 77 & 80 & Oakland Mus, 80; Brooklyn Mus, 62, 66, 68 & 77; Continuing Am Graphics, Osaka, Japan, 70; Hawaii Nat Print Exhib, Honolulu, 71 & 80; Oakland Mus, 75; Fine Arts Mus, San Francisco, 81; John Berggruen Gallery, San Francisco, 82, 85, 87; Art Mus Asn Am, traveling exhib, 83-85. *Awards:* Award Honor in Graphics, San Francisco, 81. *Mem:* San Francisco Women Artists; Calif Soc Printmakers. *Media:* Prints, Drawings. *Publ:* Auth, A Collection of Wonderful Things, Scrimshaw, 72; Auth, Creatures, Chronicle Books, 87. *Mailing Add:* c/o John Berggruen Gallery 228 Grant Ave San Francisco CA 94108

VAN HORN, DANA CARL
PAINTER
b San Diego, Calif, Nov 19, 50. *Study:* San Diego State Univ, BFA, 72; Yale Univ, MFA, 74. *Work:* Metrop Mus Art, New York; Allentown Art Mus, Pa. *Comn:* Mural, Cathedral St Cath Siena, Allentown, Pa, 82; painting, St Bernards Church, Easton, Pa, 85; mural, Holy Ghost Church, Bethlehem, Pa, 90. *Exhib:* Local Hernes, Allentown Art Mus, Pa, 88. *Bibliog:* Judd Tolly (auth), article, Am Artist, 87; Tom Bolt (auth), article, Arts Mag, 87. *Media:* Oil on linen. *Mailing Add:* c/o Sherry French 24 W 57 St New York NY 10019

VAN LAAR, TIMOTHY
PAINTER, PRINTMAKER
b Ann Arbor, Mich, Mar 7, 51. *Study:* Calvin Col, BA, 73; Wayne State Univ, MFA, 75. *Work:* Detroit Inst Art; Southeast Banking Corp, Miami; Herman Miller Inc, Zeeland, Mich; Valparaiso Univ, Ind; Steelcase Inc, Grand Rapids, Mich; Ill State Mus, Springfield. *Exhib:* Detroit Inst Art; Houston Mus Fine Arts, Tex, 80; Nihon Univ, Tokyo, 83; Ill State Mus, Springfield, 85; Chinese Nat Fine Art Mus, Beijing, 87; Glasgow Sch Art, Scotland, 88; solo exhibs, Wustum Mus Fine Arts, Racine, Wis, 87, Gwenda Jay Gallery, Chicago, 88. *Pos:* Printer lithography, Mich Workshop Fine Prints, Detroit, 74-76; resident artist, Urban Inst Contemp Art, Grand Rapids, Mich, 78; ed bd, Art & Academe: A journal for the Humanities & Sciences in the Education of Artists, 88- *Teaching:* Instr painting & printmaking, Calvin Col, 77-81; asst prof painting, Univ Ill, Urbana-Champaign, 81-87; assoc prof painting, Univ Ill, 87-; vis lectr, Glasgow Sch Art, 88-89. *Awards:* Yaddo Fel, 85; Ill Artists Fel, 87; Fulbright, 88. *Mem:* Col Art Asn. *Media:* All Media; Lithography, Intaglio. *Dealer:* Lemberg Gallery 538 N Woodward Birmingham MI. *Mailing Add:* Dept Art Univ Ill Champaign IL 61820

VAN LEER, ELIZABETH SANFORD
COLLECTOR
b Warwick, NY, Jan 29, 05. *Study:* Smith Col; also with Mary Turlay Robinson. *Collection:* Includes works by Delacroix, Boudin, Dufy, Burchfield, Wyeth, Prendergast, Davies, Bishop, Homer, Segonzac, Marin, Cropsey, Utrillo, Beal and others. *Mailing Add:* 12 E 73rd St New York NY 10017

VAN LEUNEN, ALICE LOUISE
TEXTILE ARTIST, INSTRUCTOR
b Evansville, Ind, Feb 7, 43. *Study:* Smith Col, BA, 65; Ind Univ, 66-67. *Work:* Seattle City Light Portable Works, 85; Atlantic County Off Bldg, 85; Western Ore State Col, 89; Justice Servs Bldg, Hillsboro, Ore, 92. *Comn:* Textile panels, Playboy Hotel, Chicago, 78; woven textile hanging, Ore State Revenue Bldg, Salem, 81; woven wall hangings, Multnomah County, Ore, 83; Kodiak Auditorium, Alaska, 86; Hillman Properties Northwest, 88 & 89; Blanchard Educ Serv Ctr, Portland, 91; The Coates Agency, 91; Clackamas Community Col, Oregon City, 92. *Exhib:* Works in Fabric, Renshaw Gallery, Linfield Col, Ore, 79; three-women exhib, Seattle Pac Univ, 79; Duo Exhib, Univ Ore Mus of Art, 78; one-woman shows, Contemp Crafts Gallery, Portland, 79 & The Lawrence Gallery Salishan, Gleneden Beach, Ore, 80; Smithsonian Inst, Washington DC, 80; Univ Evansville, Ind, 85. *Pos:* Asst dir, Delphian Gallery-Delphian Found, 77; exhib asst, Contemp Crafts Gallery, Portland, 78-79. *Teaching:* Seminar instr, Dept Fine Arts, Univ Ore, 78-; lectr textiles, Portland State Univ, 80-91. *Awards:* Cash Award, 76 Traveling Exhib Competition, Univ Ore Mus of Art, 6/76; Honorable Mention, 6th Ann Exhib, Corvallis Art Ctr, 11/76. *Bibliog:* The state of the crafts--a visual review, Frank Petock & Assoc, 1980, Interweave Mag, summer 80; The Guild, Kraus Sikes, Inc, NY, 86, 88, 89, 90 & 91. *Mem:* Artists Equity; NW Designer Craftsmen, Inc, Seattle; Am Crafts Coun, NW Region; Nexus. *Media:* Mixed Media, Sculpture. *Dealer:* Oregon Art Inst Rental/Sales Gallery Portland OR. *Mailing Add:* PO Box 408 Lake Oswego OR 97034

VAN LOEN, ALFRED
SCULPTOR, EDUCATOR
b Oberhausen-Osterfeld, Ger, Sept 11, 24; US citizen. *Study:* Royal Acad Art, Amsterdam, Holland, 41-46. *Work:* Metrop Mus Art & Mus Mod Art, New York; Brooklyn Mus, NY; Nat Mus, Jerusalem, Israel. *Comn:* Brass fountain, James White Community Ctr, Salt Lake City, Utah, 58; Peace Window, Community Church, New York, 63; Jacob's Dream (brass), Little Neck Jewish Ctr, NY, 70; bronze & acrylic symbolic portrait of Guy Lombardo, Hall of Fame, Stony Brook, NY, 72. *Exhib:* Whitney Mus Am Art Ann, New York, 67; Emil Walters Gallery, New York, 68; Stony Brook Mus, 68; Heckscher Mus, Huntington, NY, 71, 74 & 85; Nassau Community Col, NY, 72; C W Post Col, 65, 68, 72, 80, 81, 83 & 85. *Pos:* Art dir, South Huntington Pub Libr. *Teaching:* Instr, Hunter Col, 53-54 & NShore Community Art Ctr, NY, 55-61; prof sculpture, C W Post Col, Long Island Univ, 62- *Awards:* First Prize, Village Art Ctr, 49; Louissa Robbins Award, Silvermine Guild Artists, 56; First Prize Sculpture, Am Soc Contemp Artists, 64; Trustees Award, Long Island Univ, 85. *Bibliog:* Paul Mocsanyi (auth), Alfred Van Loen, Channel Press, 60; Mark Smith (auth), Alfred Van Loen, portrait, Long Island Mag, 64; Sculptured emotion of A V L, Mod Castings, 65. *Mem:* Am Soc Contemp Artists; Long Island Univ Pioneer Club. *Media:* Mixed. *Publ:* Auth, Simple Methods of Sculpture, Channel Press, 58; Instructions to Sculpture, C W Post Col, 66; Origin of Structure & Design, Hamilton Press, 67; Drawings by Alfred Van Loen, Harbor Gallery Press, 69; The Dancing Line, Harbor Gallery Press, 81; The Endless Line, Long Island Univ Press, 85. *Mailing Add:* 221 Beverly Rd Huntington Station NY 11746

VANN, LOLI (MRS LILIAN VAN YOUNG)
PAINTER
b Chicago, Ill, Jan 7, 13. *Study:* Art Inst Chicago; also with Sam Ostrowsky. *Work:* Chaffey Col, Ontario, Calif; Hollenbeck High Sch, Los Angeles; Palmcrest House Long Beach Calif. *Exhib:* Exhib Am Paintings, Carnegie Inst, Pittsburgh; Am Painting, Metrop Mus Art, New York; Corcoran Gallery Art Biennial, Washington, DC; Am Paintings & Int Watercolor Exhibs, Art Inst Chicago. *Awards:* Purchase Prize, Chaffey Community Art Asn; Hon Mention, Calif Watercolor Soc; Second Prize, Los Angeles Co Mus Art. *Media:* Multimedia. *Mailing Add:* 2293 Panorama Terr Los Angeles CA 90039

VANN, SAMUEL LEROY
PAINTER
b Ithaca, NY, Sept 16, 52. *Study:* Ft Lewis Col, BA, 73; State Univ NY, Brockport, MS(educ). *Work:* Everson Mus Art; Menninger Fund, Topeka, Kans; Joan Kennedy; Dr Benjamin Spock; Corporate and private collections throughout the US. *Exhib:* Watercolors USA, Springfield Art Mus, Mo, 77; Chautauqua 20th Nat Show, CAA Gallery, NY, 78; Second International All on Paper Show, Assoc Art Orgn Western NY, Buffalo, 80; Rivers, Gorges, Canyons Traveling Exhib, 82-82; Midwest Watercolor Soc First 100 Exhib, Tweed Mus Art; Golden Sands Int Show, El Centro, Calif; Butler Inst Am Art 82, Midyear Show, Youngstown, Ohio, 82; NMex Int Art Show, Clovis; one-man shows, Prouty-Chew Mus, Geneva, NY, 82, Rome Art Ctr, NY, 82, Arnot Art Mus, Elmira, NY, 82, Schweinfurth Mem Art Gallery, Auburn, NY, 81, Sheldon Mem Art Gallery, Lincoln, Nebr, 82, Everson Mus Art, Suracuse, NY, 82, Albright-Knox Art Gallery, Buffalo, NY, 82. *Teaching:* Asst dir painting, Chautauqua Inst Ctr Arts, 79-80. *Awards:* First Prize Graphics, Twelfth Ann Western Art Show, 77 & Third Ann Nat Miniature Show, 77; First Prize Painting, Second Int All on Paper Show, 80. *Media:* Watercolor. *Dealer:* Bishop Gallery 7164 Main Scottsdale AZ 85251. *Mailing Add:* Box 237 Spencer NY 14883

VANRIET, JAN
PAINTER, PRINTMAKER
b Antwerp, Belgium, Feb 21, 48. *Study:* Royal Acad Arts, Antwerp, Belg, Master, 70. *Work:* San Diego Mus Art; Mus Voor Schone Kunsten, Antwerp, Belg; Kunstverein, Darmstadt, Ger; Dimona Mus, Negev, Israel; Rockefeller Art Ctr, State Univ New York, Fredonia, NY; San Diego Mus Contemp Art, La Jolla, Ca. *Comn:* Paintings, House of Parliament, Brussels, 84; Gov House, Antwerp, 85; Leyden Univ, Belg, 88. *Exhib:* Biennial Sao Paulo, Brazil, 79; Insight, San Diego Mus, Calif, 83; Biennial Venice, Italy, 84; Tekenen, ICC, Antwerp, Belg, 85; Surrealisme-Realisme, Gallery Maeght, Barcelona, Spain, 85; Europalia, Ctr for Art, Ghent, 85; Nove Disegnatori, Palazzo Re Enzo, Bologna, Italy, 86; Interfagies, Mallorca, Spain, 86; Wenger Gallery, Los Angeles, 87 & 88; Int Contemp Painting Exhibit, Seoul, Korea, 88. *Bibliog:* Edward Lucie-Smith (auth), Jan Vanriet, Van Gennep, Amsterdam, 82; Freddy Coppens (air), Jan Vanriet (film), Kriteria Films, 85; Pierre Restany (auth), Jan Vanriet, Isy Brachot, Brussels, 86; Suvan Geer (auth), Jan Vanriet, New Paintings, Los Angeles Times, 10/28/88. *Mem:* SABAM, Brussels, 82. *Media:* Oil, Watercolor. *Publ:* Illusr, Mort a Venise, Lotus, 78; Odalisques, Vecu, 80; auth, No Dog Eating Bread, Manteau, 84. *Mailing Add:* c/o Wenger Gallery 638 1/2 N Robertson Blvd Los Angeles CA 90069

VAN RIPER, PETER
PRINTMAKER, CONCEPTUAL ARTIST
b Detroit, Mich, July 8, 42. *Study:* Univ NC, BA(art hist, Far Eastern hist); Univ Tokyo, MA(Far Eastern art hist); Univ Mich. *Work:* Everson Mus Art, Syracuse, NY; Mus Mod Art, New York; Los Angeles Inst Contemp Art; Mus Mod Art, Oxford, Eng; Stedelijk Mus, Amsterdam. *Exhib:* One-man shows, US Info Serv Japan Performance Tour, 74, Video & Graphics Exhib, Everson Mus, 75 & Washington Proj Arts, 79; Kunst Bleibt Kunst, Kunstverein Art Mus, Cologne, Ger, 74; Holography 75 First Decade, Int Ctr Photog, New York. *Teaching:* Teacher multi-media art, Calif Inst of Arts, Valencia, 70-73. *Awards:* Traveling Exhib Award, Western Asn of Art Mus, 74. *Mem:* Editions/Sch of Holography, Ann Arbor, Mich & San Francisco (pres); Fluxus, New York. *Publ:* Auth, It, 75. *Dealer:* Upstairs Gallery 1457 Grant Ave San Francisco CA 94133. *Mailing Add:* 73 Calyer St Brooklyn NY 11222

VAN SANT, TOM R
SCULPTOR, PAINTER
b Los Angeles, Calif, Feb 26, 31. *Study:* Stanford Univ, BA, 53; Otis Art Inst Los Angeles Co, MFA, 57; also studied with Herb Jepson, Peter Voulkos & Millard Sheets. *Work:* Davies Pac Ctr, Honolulu; Pac Design Ctr, Los Angeles; Libr Cong; Smithsonian Inst; Inst Contemp Art, London. *Comn:* Sculptured concrete walls, Irvine Co, Newport Beach, Calif, 68; sculptured concrete mural, Honolulu Int Airport, 73; mural, Taipei Int Airport, Taiwan, 74; fountain sculpture, City of Los Angeles, 75; bronze sculpture, Warmington Co, Newport Beach, Calif, 82. *Exhib:* One-man exhibs, Inst Contemp Art, London, 76, Myer Galleries, Melbourne & Sydney, Australia, 77, Stedelijk Mus, Amsterdam, Holland, 77, Honolulu Hale, City Hall, 77 & Pac Design Ctr, Los Angeles, 80. *Teaching:* Instr design & drawing, Otis Art Inst Los Angeles Co, 60-66; instr creativity, Omega Sem, Fall City, Wash, 66-68; fel, Ctr Advan Visual Studies, Mass Inst Technol, 81- *Awards:* Art in Architecture Award, Am Inst Archit, 56, 61 & 68; Award of Merit, First Ann Exhib Illus West, 59; Purchase Award, Int Sculpture Symposium, Calif State Univ, Long Beach, 74. *Bibliog:* Fundaburk (auth), Art in Public Places in the US, Popular Press, 75; Piene (auth), Sky Art Conf, Ctr Advan Visual Studies, Mass Inst Technol, 81-83. *Publ:* Co-dir, Flight Forms (film), Ed Spiegel Co, 76. *Mailing Add:* 146 Entrada Dr Santa Monica CA 90402

VAN SCHAACK, ERIC
HISTORIAN, EDUCATOR
b Evanston, Ill, June 10, 31. *Study:* Dartmouth Col, AB, 53; Columbia Univ, PhD, 69. *Pos:* Chmn, Dept Visual Arts, Goucher Col, Baltimore, 73-76. *Teaching:* Lectr & research asst, The Frick Collection, New York, 60-62; from asst prof to prof, Goucher Col, Baltimore, 64-76; prof, Dept Art & Art Hist, Colgate Univ, 77, chmn, 77-83. *Awards:* Italian Govt Grant & Fulbright Travel Grant, 62-63, Ford Found Grant Humanities, 72-73; Colgate Univ Humanities Fac Development Fund Grant, 79-80. *Mem:* Col Art Asn Am; Soc Archit Historians. *Res:* Italian Renaissance & Baroque art; American architecture. *Publ:* An unpublished letter by Francesco Albani, Art Bull, 69; coauth, The music in Van Dyck's Rinaldo and Armida, Baltimore Mus Art

Ann III, 69; contribr, Italian Paintings, Baltimore Mus Art, 81; Francesco Albani's Guida di Bologna, Acts of the 24th International Congress of the History of Art, Bologna, 82; other articles publ in Arte Antica e Moderna, Apollo and Picker Art Gallary Ann Report/Bull. *Mailing Add:* Dept Fine Arts Colgate Univ Hamilton NY 13346

VAN SUCHTELEN, ADRIAN
PRINTMAKER, EDUCATOR
b Semarang, Indonesia, June 18, 41; US citizen. *Study:* El Camino Col, Calif; Otis Art Inst, Los Angeles, BFA, MFA, 66. *Work:* Indianapolis Mus Art; De Cordova Mus, Lincoln, Mass; Cleveland Mus Art; Riverside Mus, Calif; Milwaukee Art Ctr; and others. *Comn:* Art work on film Young Lovers, Samuel Goldwyn Studios, Los Angeles, 64. *Exhib:* Drawing Soc Nat Exhib, Am Fedn Arts, NY, 70-72; Colorprint USA, Tex, 74; Davidson Nat Print & Drawing Exhib, NC, 75; Pratt Graphics Ctr Int Print Exhib, NY, 75; one-man show, Northern State Col, SDak, 83; and others. *Teaching:* Prof drawing & grad dir, Utah State Univ, 67- *Awards:* Purchase Award, NMex State Univ, 71; Ben & Abbey Grey Found Purchase Award, Salt Lake Art Ctr, 72; Purchase Prize, Boston Printmakers, 81. *Mem:* Graphics Soc; Boston Printmakers Soc. *Publ:* Contribr, Drawing A Search for Form, 65; auth & illusr, Lifetime Career Schools, Correspondence Art Course, 67; contribr, Oil Painting, Techniques and Materials, 69; The Hidden Elements of Drawing, 73. *Dealer:* Sylvesters Art Studio 61 E 320 S Salt Lake City UT 84111. *Mailing Add:* 655 E 18th Logan UT 84321

VAN VLIET, CLAIRE
PRINTMAKER, PUBLISHER
b Ottawa, Ont, Can, Aug 9, 33. *Study:* San Diego State Univ, AB, 52; Claremont Grad Sch, MFA, 54. *Work:* Nat Gallery, Washington, DC; Philadelphia Mus Art; Montreal Mus Fine Arts; Cleveland Mus Art; Victoria & Albert Mus, London. *Exhib:* Kunst zu Kafka Traveling Exhib, WGer, 75; Claire Van Vliet & The Janus Press, Wiggin Gallery, Boston Pub Libr, 77; Rutgers Univ Art Gallery, 78; Paper as Medium, Smithsonian Traveling Exhib, 78-80; The Janus Press 1975-80, Fleming Mus Traveling Exhib, 82-84; Dolan/Maxwell Gallery, Philadelphia, 84 & 91; Mary Ryan Gallery, New York, 86; Univ Arts, 89. *Pos:* Proprietor, Janus Press, 54- *Teaching:* Asst prof printmaking, Philadelphia Col Art, 59-65; vis lectr, Univ Wis, 65-66, Univ Vt, 74-75, Univ Ala, 83. *Awards:* VCA Grant, 75-77; Nat Endowment Arts Grants, 76, 78 & 80. *Bibliog:* Lehrer (auth), The Janus Press 1955-75 & Fine (auth), Claire Van Vliet: Landscape Paperworks, Dolan-Maxwell, Pa, 84; Taylor (auth), Claire Van Vliet's Janus Press Am Craft, 3/88. *Mem:* Soc Printers Boston; The Print Club, Philadelphia. *Media:* Relief, Lithography; Paper, Book Arts. *Publ:* Illusr & ed, Sky and Earth-Variable Landscape, Janus Press, 70; auth & illusr, Satellite, Mus Mod Art, 71; illusr & ed, The Tower of Babel-an Anthology, Janus Press, 75. *Dealer:* Dolan-Maxwell 1701 Walnut St Philadelphia Pa 19103; Mary Ryan 452 Columbus Ave New York NY 10024. *Mailing Add:* Rte 1 West Burke VT 05871

VAN VRANKEN, ROSE (ROSE VAN VRANKEN HICKEY)
SCULPTOR, PRINTMAKER
b Passaic, NJ, May 15, 19. *Study:* Pomona Col, BA(art, with hon), 39; Art Students League, with William Zorach & Robert Laurent, 39-42; NY Univ Grad Inst Fine Arts, one year; Univ Iowa, sculpture with Humbert Albrizio & printmaking with Mauricio Lasansky, MA(sculpture), 43; Ricker Col, Maine, Hon DFA, 76. *Work:* Brand Libr, Glendale, Calif; Coventry Cathedral, Eng; Univ Iowa, Mus Art, Iowa City; Temple Emanuel, Houston, Tex; Jewish Community Ctr, Houston, Tex; & others. *Comn:* Theotokos (bronze), St Cyril Alexandria Church, Houston, Tex, 81; Texas Commerce Bank, Houston, Tex; M D Anderson Cancer Ctr, Houston, Tex, 91. *Exhib:* Two-person show, Madison Art Ctr Mus, 68; Art in Embassies Program, US Dept State, Washington, DC, 77-80; Salmagundi Club Ann, New York, 78-92; North Am Sculpture Exhib, Foothills Art Ctr, Colorado, 79, 86 & 90; solo exhib, Inst Mus, McAllen, Tex, 86, Jung Ctr, Houston, Tex, 92 & Biblical Art Ctr Mus, Dallas, Tex, 92; & others. *Teaching:* Research asst art hist, Univ Iowa, 42-43; instr sculpture & mem bd dir, Madison Art Ctr Mus, Wis, 65-68; instr sculpture, Continuing Educ Prog, Rice Univ, 75-78. *Awards:* Award for Sculpture, 79-80, Medal of Honor, 85, Acad Artists Asn; Second Prize for Sculpture, 87, First Prize, Eliot Liskin Award, 88, Salmagundi Club, New York; First prize for sculpture, 87, Gold Metal, 90 & Best of Show, 90, Int Platform Asn Ann Exhib. *Bibliog:* Archives Am Art, Smithsonian Inst, Washington, DC; Art Voices South Mag, 11-12/78; Les Krantz (auth), articles in New York Review & Chicago Art Review, 89. *Mem:* Salmagundi Club; Tex Soc Sculptors (vpres, 74-75, pres Gulf Coast Chap, 75-76); Nat Asn Women Artists; International Platform Asn; Women Artists of the West. *Media:* Wood, Bronze. *Dealer:* S R Brennen Gallery Fine Art 73-080 El Paseo St Palm Desert CA 92260; Sol del Rio Gallery 1020 Townsend St San Antonio TX. *Mailing Add:* 435 Tallowood Houston TX 77024

VAN WAGNER, JUDY COLLISCHAN
MUSEUM DIRECTOR, CRITIC
b Red Wing, Minn, Oct 19, 40. *Study:* Hamline Univ, BA, 62; Nat Univ Mex, 63; Ohio Univ, MFA, 64; Univ Iowa, PhD, 72. *Collections Arranged:* Monumental Drawings by Sculptors: Serra, Westerlund, Nonas, Jensen, Fishman, Nozkowski and others, 82, Paintings from the Mind's Eye, 83, Seymour Lipton, 84-85, Michelle Stuart, 85 & Walter Murch, 86, Hillwood Art Gallery, Long Island Univ, C W Post Campus, Greenvale, NY, 82; Lines of Vision: Drawings by Contemporary Women, 89. *Pos:* Dir, Hillwood Art Mus, Long Island Univ, C W Post Campus, Greenvale, NY; critic, Arts Mag, 84-; co-chmn, New York State Coun Arts, Visual Art Panel, 87-90. *Teaching:* Assoc prof contemp art, State Univ NY, Plattsburgh, 75-83; adj prof contemp art, Long Island Univ, C W Post Campus, Greenvale, NY, 82- *Awards:* Kress Found Res Grant, 70; Award, State Univ NY, 81. *Bibliog:* Max Coyer's (auth), Printed Life of the Mind, Art, 1/84; Grace Knowlton (auth), Secret Spaces, Arts, 5/86; Judith Shea (auth), A Personal Balance, Arts, 1/87; Pat Ward Williams (auth), Arts, 3/89. *Mem:* Am Asn Mus. *Res:* Contemporary art, particular art by women & minorities. *Publ:* Auth, Women Shaping Art, Praeger, 84; Lines of Vision: Drawings by Contemporary Women, Hudson Hills, 89. *Mailing Add:* 141 W 21st St Huntington NY 11746

VAN WINKELEN, BARBARA
PAINTER, ILLUSTRATOR
b Waban, Mass. *Study:* Yale Univ Sch Fine Arts, BFA, 43. *Exhib:* 59th Ann, Springfield Mus, Mass, 78; 82nd Ann, Catharine Lorillard Wolfe Art Club, New York, 78; Conn Watercolor Soc, 78-86 & Conn Acad, 80-86, Wadsworth Atheneum, Hartford, Conn; Slater Mem Mus, Norwich, Conn, 78-81; Conn Acad Fine Arts, Olde State House, Hartford, Conn, 81; Springfield Acad Assoc & Springfield Art League Mus Show, 86; New Haven Paint & Clay Club; Nat Watercolor Soc Members Show, Colo. *Pos:* Staff asst, Mus Mod Art, New York, 43-44; tech illusr, United Technol, 53-71. *Teaching:* Children art, Wadsworth Atheneum, Hartford, Conn, 48-50. *Awards:* First Prize, Conn Watercolor Soc, 85 & 86; Best in Show, Conn Women Artists, 83 & 84 & Acad Artists Assoc, 86. *Bibliog:* Maureen O'Sullivan (auth), Nantucket Artist Barbara van Winkelen (film), 79. *Mem:* Conn Acad Fine Arts; Conn Watercolor Soc; Conn Women Artists (bd dirs, 80-82); Nantucket Artists Asn; New Haven Paint & Clay Club; New England Watercolor Soc; Assoc Mem, Nat Watercolor Soc. *Media:* Egg Tempera; All Media. *Publ:* Nantucket Guide, 91-92; New Eng Artists, Vol 1. *Dealer:* Spindrift Gallery 11 Old S Wharf Nantucket MA 02554; Jay Whitney 405 Queen St Southington CT. *Mailing Add:* 1864 Poquonock Ave Poquonock CT 06064

VAN WINKLE, LESTER G
SCULPTOR, EDUCATOR
b Greenville, Tex, Jan 11, 44. *Study:* ETex State Univ, BS; Univ Ky, MA; also sculpture with Michael D Hall. *Work:* Arrowmont Sch Arts & Crafts, Gatlinburg, Tenn; Dade Co Jr Col, Miami. *Exhib:* Sculpt 70, Corcoran Gallery Art, Washington, DC, 70; Whitney Biennial of Painting & Sculpture, Whitney Mus, New York, 73; one-man shows, Henry Gallery, Washington, 73-75 & Webb Parsons Gallery, Bedford, NY, 74-75; Waves Exhib, Cranbrook Acad Art Galleries, 74. *Teaching:* From asst prof to assoc prof sculpture, Va Commonwealth Univ, 69- *Dealer:* Henri Gallery 1500 21st St NW Washington DC 20036. *Mailing Add:* c/o Henri Gallery 1500 21st St NW Washington DC 20036

VAN WYK, HELEN
PAINTER, LECTURER
b Fair Lawn, NJ. *Study:* Art Students League; New Sch Social Res; also with Maximilian Aureal Rasko. *Work:* Norfolk Mus Arts & Sci, Va; Bergen Co Mus, NJ; St Vincent's Col, Latrobe, Pa; Minneapolis Club; Livonia Sch Syst, Mich; Portraits, Foreign Mission Bd, Southern Baptist Conv, Richmond, Va, 84; and others. *Comn:* Portraits, The Revs Richard Owens & Wesley Roberts, People's Baptist Church, Boston; portraits, Judges Paul Perocchi & Salvatore Basile, Lawrence Dist Court, Mass; portrait, Judge Lawrence Jodrey, Essex County Courthouse. *Exhib:* Acad Artists, Springfield, Mass, 53 & 57; Audubon Artists, New York, 54, 55 & 63; Nat Acad Design, New York, 54, 55 & 64; Silvermine Guild Artists, Conn, 59; Northshore Art Assoc, Mass, 69-80 & 85. *Awards:* First Prize for Still Life, Catharine Lorillard Wolfe Art Club, 55; Curtis Mem Award, Rockport Asn, 72 & 73, Merit Award, 84, Rose Strisik Mem Award, 88; Outstanding Achievement Award, Rockport Art Asn, 89. *Mem:* Rockport Art Assoc. *Media:* Oil. *Publ:* Auth, Acrylic Portrait Painting, Watson-Guptill, 70; Helen Van Wyk's Successful Color Mixtures, 73 & Painting Flowers the Van Wyk Way, 81; Portraits in Oil the Van Wyk Way, 83; Your Painting Questions Answered From A-Z, Basic Oil Painting the Van Wyk Way, Welcome to My Studio & Color Mixing in Action, Art Instr Assoc; videos--Oil Painting Techniques & procedures, Painting Flowers Alla Prima, A Portrait: Step by Step, Brush Techniques: Your Painting's Handwriting & Painting Children from Photographs. *Mailing Add:* 2 Briarstone Rd Rockport MA 01966

VAN YOUNG, OSCAR
PAINTER
b Vienna, Austria; US citizen. *Study:* Art Acad, Odessa, Russia; with Sam Ostrowsky, Paris & Chicago; Calif State Univ, Los Angeles, BA & MA. *Work:* Los Angeles Co Mus Art, Calif; Chaffey Col, Ontario, Calif; Frye Mus, Seattle; Ill State Mus; Smithsonian Inst; Palm Springs Desert Mus; and others. *Exhib:* Am Paintings & Int Watercolor Shows, Art Inst Chicago; Calif Palace of Legion of Honor; Pa Acad; Va Mus Biennial; Corcoran Gallery Art Biennial, Washington, DC; one-man shows, Art Inst of Chicago, Los Angeles Co Mus of Art, Los Angeles, Palm Springs Desert Mus, San Francisco Mus of Art, Santa Barbara Mus, Calif, James Vigeveno Galleries, Westwood, Calif & Cowie Galleries, Los Angeles; Retrospective, San Bernardino Valley Col Gallery of Art; Zantman Galleries, Palm Desert, Calif, 83. *Teaching:* Instr advan painting, Otis Art Inst, 54-56; instr design, painting & drawing, Pasadena City Col, 59-73; asst prof advan painting, Los Angeles State Univ, 61-63. *Awards:* Bartels Prize, Art Inst Chicago; Purchase Prize, Chaffey Col; Purchase Award, Frye Mus, Seattle; and others. *Bibliog:* Ronald D Scofield (auth), California painter turns against early realism, Santa Barbara; Joseph Mugnaini (auth), Oil Painting Techniques & Materials, Van Nostrand Reinhold Co, 69; Janice Lovoos (auth), Painting for the joy of it, SW Art, 7/77; Gordon T McClelland & Jay T Last (coauth), The California Style, Hillcrest Press, 85; Louise Dunn Yochim (auth), Harvest of Freedom; Les Krantz (auth), Calif Art Rev. *Media:* Oil. *Dealer:* Zantman Galleries Palm Desert CA; Michael Kelly Gallery Pasadena CA. *Mailing Add:* 2293 Panorama Terr Los Angeles CA 90039

VARGA, FERENC
SCULPTOR
b Szekesfehervar, Hungary; US citizen. *Study:* Acad Fine Arts, Budapest, Hungary, with Prof Eugene Broy & Prof Francis Sidlo; govt scholar, Italy, 38 & France, 42. *Work:* Nat Art Gallery, Budapest; Mus Fine Arts, Budapest; Vatican Mus, Rome, Italy; Mus Zurich, Switz. *Comn:* Portrait, VRegent of Hungary, Budapest, 42; monument, City of Windsor, Ont, Can, 50; group of statues, Ft Lincoln Mem, Washington, DC, 55 & 8ft bronze statue of Patrick Henry, 78; monument, City of Detroit, Mich, 66; and others. *Exhib:* Nat Art Gallery, Budapest, 42; Exhib Ecclesiastical Arts Guild, Detroit, 52; Nat Sculpture Soc, New York, 59; one-man show, Masters' Gallery, Toronto, Ont, 64; Eszterhazy Gallery, Palm Beach, Fla, 71. *Teaching:* Assoc prof sculpturing, Acad Fine Arts, Budapest, 28-40. *Awards:* Lord Rotheremere Ward, 28; Medal of Bethlehem Distinction, Fine Arts & Sci Soc of Church of Hungary, 47. *Bibliog:* Dr E Schwartz (auth), Ferenc Varga, Ons Volk, Brussels, 49 & Last uns nach Bethlehem eilen, Am-Ung Verlag, Cologne, 59; J P Danglade (auth), Magnificent statue of the Christ by sculptor, Varga, The Cemeterian, Columbus, 62. *Mem:* Fine Arts & Sci Soc of Church of Hungary, Budapest; Acad Cath Hungarica Sci Atrib Prov, Vatican City; Nat Sculpture Soc. *Media:* Multimedia. *Mailing Add:* 296 NE Sixth Ave Delray Beach FL 33483

VARGA, MARGIT
PAINTER, WRITER
b New York, NY, May 5, 08. *Study:* Art Students League, with Boardman Robinson & Robert Laurent. *Work:* Metrop Mus Art; Springfield Mus Fine Arts, Mass; Univ Ariz, Tucson; IBM Collection; Pa Acad Fine Arts; Wichita Mus. *Comn:* Mural for lobby, Kidder, Meade & Co, Paramus, NJ. *Exhib:* Whitney Mus Am Art, 51; Univ Ill, 51; Art Inst Chicago; Carnegie Inst; Corcoran Gallery Art; one-man show, Wichita Mus, 83. *Pos:* Art ed, Life Mag, 36-56, asst art dir, 56-60; art consult, Time, Inc, 60-70. *Media:* Oil. *Mailing Add:* 600 Gulf Shore Blvd N Naples FL 33940

VARGAS, JOSEPHINE
ILLUSTRATOR, PAINTER
b New York, NY, July 31, 46. *Study:* Fashion Inst Technol, 64-65; Sch Visual Arts, 78-79. *Work:* Museo de la Historia, Ponce, PR. *Exhib:* Nassau Co Mus Fine Arts Exhib, Roslyn Harbor, NY, 88; Chelsea Mansion Exhib, Muttontown, NY, 88 & 92; Salmagundi Club Exhib, New York, 89; CW Post Campus Exhib, Westbury, NY, 89; Nat Asn Women Artists, Javits Fed Plaza, New York, 89 & 90; Invitational: Ollantay Gallery, New York, 91; Invitational: Art Upstairs Gallery, Albertson, New York, 91; Am Watercolor Soc, 92; Casa Arcardia, Ponce, PR 92. *Pos:* Trustee, Nat Art League, Douglaston, NY, 87- *Awards:* Peacock Showcase Award, Visual Art Alliance of Long Island, 91; First Place Watercolor, Nat Art League, 91; Purchase Award Ponce Pinturoso Open Competition, Ponce, PR, 92. *Mem:* Nat Asn Women Artists; Nat Art League (mem chmn, currently). *Media:* Watercolor, Mixed Media. *Mailing Add:* 83-40 Austin St Kew Gardens NY 11514

VARGO, JOHN
EDUCATOR, PAINTER
b Cleveland, Ohio, Aug 9, 29. *Study:* Cleveland Inst Art, with Paul Riba & Louis Bosa. *Work:* Cleveland Mus Art; Syracuse Univ; Munson-Williams-Proctor Inst, Utica, NY; LeMoyne Col, Syracuse. *Comn:* The Erie Canal (mural), First Fed Savings Syracuse, 60. *Exhib:* Cooperstown 35th Ann Exhib, NY, 70; Rochester Finger Lakes Exhib, NY, 71; Artist as a Journalist, Soc Illusr, 77; one-man shows, LeMoyne Col, 71 & Everson Mus, 78; and others. *Pos:* Illusr, Advance Art, Cleveland, 51-58. *Teaching:* Prof illus & serigraph, Syracuse Univ, 58- *Awards:* Eagan Pres Plaza Award & Popular Prize, 64, NY State Fair; First Prize for Portrait Painting, Cooperstown Art Asn, 70; Award for Painting, Mem Art Gallery, Univ Rochester, 71. *Media:* Tempera, Watercolor. *Publ:* Illusr, covers, Michael Brown's Laying Waste, 11/80 & Roger Shattuck's The Forebidden Experiment, 1/81, Washington Sq Press; illusr, cover, Daoma Winston's The Lotteries, Pocket, 4/81; illusr, Jacobo Timmerman's Prisoner Without a Name, Cell Without a Number, Reader's Digest, 11/81. *Mailing Add:* Art Dept Syracuse Univ 102 Shaffer Bldg Syracuse NY 13244

VARNAY JONES, THEODORA
PRINTMAKER, PAINTER
b Budapest, Hungary, Feb 26, 42; US citizen. *Study:* Univ Fine Art, Budapest, BA, 69, MA, 70. *Work:* Achenbach Found Graphic Arts, Fine Arts Museums of San Francisco, Calif; Bank Am Corp Art Collection, San Francisco; New Canaan Libr Permanent Collection, Conn; Kyoto Seika Univ, Japan. *Comn:* Color etching, Fine Arts Mus, San Francisco, 86; 12 large scale mixed media works, Sak's Fifth Ave, 89 & 90. *Exhib:* Contemporary California Prints, San Jose Mus Art, Calif, 82; Mid America Biennial, Mus Fine Art, Owensboro, Ky, 84; Prints USA, Nat Mus, Singapore, 84; Mini Print Int, Taller Galeria Fort, Cadoques, Spain, 84; Prints USA, Amerika Haus, Berlin, Ger, 85; The Hanga Annual, Metrop Art Mus, Tokyo, Japan, 85; Int Print Biennial, Mus de Arte Contemporanea, Cabo Frio, Brazil, 85; 3rd Biennial Exhib of Prints, Mus Mod Art, Wakayama, Japan, 89; Tamura Gallery, Tokyo, Japan, 90. *Teaching:* Guest lectr on prints, Oakland Mus Asn, 85; Guest lectr on prints, Kyoto Seika Univ, Japan. *Awards:* Purchase Award, Prints USA, Pratt Graphics Ctr, 82; Prof Prize, International Competition, 83; First Place, Cabo Frio Inter Print Biennial, 85. *Bibliog:* Miyagi Television Rev, Japan, 90. *Mem:* Calif Soc Printmakers; Graphic Arts Coun, Fine Arts Mus San Francisco; The Print Club of Philadelphia; Boston Printmakers. *Media:* Mixed media. *Dealer:* Don Soker Contemporary Art 251 Post St San Fancisco CA 94108. *Mailing Add:* 2180 Bryant St San Francisco CA 94110

VARNEDOE, JOHN KIRK TRAIN
CURATOR
b Savannah, Ga, Jan 18, 46. *Study:* Williams Col, BA; Stanford Univ, MA & PhD. *Collections Arranged:* Against the Madness, Protest Art from California Campuses, 70; Rodin Drawings True and False, Nat Gallery Art, 71-72; Modern Portraits: The Self and Others, Wildenstein Gallery, New York, 76; Gustave Caillebotte: A Retrospective Exhibition, Houston Mus Fine Arts, 76-77 & Brooklyn Mus, 77; Northern Light: Realism and Symbolism in Scandanavian Painting, 1880-1910, Corcoran Gallery, Washington, DC, 82, Brooklyn Mus, NY, 82-83 & Minneapolis Inst Arts, 83; Primitivism in Twentieth Century Art: Affinity of the Tribal and the Modern, Mus Mod Art, New York, 84-85, Detroit Inst Arts & Dallas Mus Fine Arts; Vienna 1900, Mus Mod Art, New York, 86; High and Low: Modern Art and Popular Culture, Mus Mod Art, New York, 90. *Pos:* Dir dept painting & sculpture, Mus Mod Art, New York, currently. *Teaching:* Asst prof, Stanford Univ, Calif, 73-74 & Columbia Univ, New York, 74-80; assoc prof fine art, Inst Fine Arts, New York, 80-84, prof fine arts, 84-88. *Awards:* David E Finley Fel, Nat Gallery Art, Washington, DC, 70-72; Nat Endowment Arts Grant, 77-78; MacArthur Found Fel, 84-89. *Res:* Articles and lectures on work of Rodin, especially drawings, and Gustave Caillebotte, plus other modern art topics; history of photography. *Publ:* Duane Hanson, Abrams, 85; Gustave Gaillebotte, Yale Univ Press, 87; Vienna 1900 - Art-Architecture and Design, Mus Mod Art, 90; A Fine Disregard - What Makes Modern Art Modern, Abrams, 90; coauth (with Adam Gopnik), High and Low: Modern Art and Popular Culture, Mus Mod Art, 90. *Mailing Add:* Mus Mod Art 11 W 53rd St New York NY 10019

VARNELIS, KAZYS
EDUCATOR, PAINTER
b Alsedziai, Lithuania, Feb 25, 17; US citizen. *Study:* Inst Fine Arts, Kaunas, Lithuania, MA, 41; Acad Fine Arts, Vienna, Austria, 45. *Work:* Art Inst Chicago; Mus Contemp Art, Chicago; Guggenheim Mus, New York; Akron Art Inst, Ohio; Milwaukee Art Ctr, Wis; Detroit Inst Arts. *Exhib:* Biennial Chicago & Vicinity Show, Art Inst Chicago, 67-74; one-man shows, Mus Contemp Art, Chicago, 70, Milwaukee Art Ctr, Wis, 74 & Mus Art, Univ Iowa, Iowa City, 75; Ill Painters Traveling Exhib, Ill Arts Coun, Chicago, 71; 12 Lithuanian Artists in Am, Corcoran Gallery Art, DC, 73; Abstract Art in Chicago, Mus Contemp Art, Chicago, 76; Reality of Illusion, traveling exhib to Denver Art Mus, Univ Calif, Los Angeles, Honolulu Acad Art, among others, 79-80; one person retrospective, Mus Art, Vilnius, Lithuania, 88. *Pos:* Dir, Mus Ecclesiastical Art, Kaunas, Lithuania, 41-45. *Teaching:* Prof art, City Col Chicago, 68-82. *Awards:* Vielehr Award, Art Inst Chicago, 69 & 74; Nat Endowment Arts fel grant, 75. *Bibliog:* Jan Van der Marck (auth), The modulated monochromes of Kazys Varnelis, ArtsCanada, 71; Heinz Ohff (auth), Galerie der neuen Kuenste, Bertelsmann Kunstverlag, WGer, 71; I Michael Danoff (auth), Kazys Varnelis Paintings, Milwaukee Art Ctr, 74. *Media:* Acrylic. *Dealer:* Image Gallery Main St Stockbridge MA 01262. *Mailing Add:* Villa Virginia Stockbridge MA 01262

VARNEY, EDWIN
CONCEPTUAL ARTIST, PRINTMAKER
b New Rochelle, NY, Oct 16, 44. *Study:* Syracuse Univ, BA, 65, MA, 66; Univ Vancouver, PhD, 76. *Work:* Vancouver Art Gallery, BC; Smith Col Art Gallery, Northampton, Mass; Alta Col Art, Calgary; Rotterdam Acad, Holland; Univ Colo, Boulder. *Comn:* Wood sculpture, Burnaby Art Coun, BC, 71; concrete sculpture, BC Sculptor's Soc, 77. *Exhib:* Space Window, RI Sch Design, Providence, 78; Artists' Stamps, Mus Art & Hist, Geneva, Switz, 79; Mail Etc, Univ Colo, Boulder, Tyler Sch Art, Philadelphia & Fla State Univ, Tallahassee, 79; and others. *Pos:* Artist/poet-in-residence, Intermedia, Vancouver, BC, 71-73, publ, ed & designer, 73-81; dir, Mus Int de Nuevo Art, 81- *Mem:* Cent Visual Arts Asn (bd dirs, 79-86); Vancouver Artists League (bd dirs, 84-86); West Coast Surrealists. *Media:* All Media. *Publ:* Openings, 69, Human Nature, 74, ed, First, Second and Third International Artists' Stamp Edition, 76, 78 & 80, ed, Four Canadian Poets, 78 & ed, Contemporary Surrealist Prose, 79, Intermedia Press. *Mailing Add:* Box 3655 Vancouver BC V6B 3Y8 Canada

VARRIALE, WANDA (STELLA)
PAINTER, INSTRUCTOR
b New York, NY, Oct 2, 27. *Study:* Art Students League, with Julian Levi, 58-60, Joseph Hirsch, 60-64 & Vincent Malta, 75-80. *Work:* Bergen Mus Art & Sci, Paramus, NJ. *Comn:* Still Life With Gum Drop Boxes, Tribute to Ming Dynasty I & II, 85, Watching the Regatta, 87, Artvest Servs, Ltd, Palisades Park, NJ. *Exhib:* Ann Competition for 1st NY Show, ACA Galleries, New York, 57-59; 33rd Ann NJ State Exhib, Montclair Art Mus, 64; Am Artists Prof League, Newark Mus, 68; one-woman show, Bergen Mus Art & Sci, Paramus, 78; 1st Ann Non-mem Juried Exhib, Salmagundi Club, New York, 78. *Pos:* Dir, Studio 5 Art Ctr, Teaneck, NJ, 88- *Teaching:* Instr drawing & painting, Englewood Women's Club, New Jersey, 72-73, Studio 5 Art Ctr, Teaneck, NJ, 76-88 & Art Ctr Northern New Jersey, 80-81. *Awards:* Gold Medal for Oils, Catharine Lorillard Wolfe Art Club, New York, 68; Marion Husing Award, Ramapo Col, Mahwah, NJ, Community Arts Asn, 88; Best in show (modern) Leonardo da Vinci Soc, Paramus, NJ, 89. *Mem:* Catharine Lorillard Wolfe Art Club New York (pub chmn, 79); Am Artists Prof League New York (bd dir, 86-88); Bergen Co Artists Guild (treas, 65 & prog chmn 72-80); Art Students League life member since 1957. *Media:* Oil, Pastel. *Dealer:* Artvest Ltd 475 Grand Ave Palisades Park NJ. *Mailing Add:* 1079 Margaret St Teaneck NJ 07666

VASA, (VELIZAR MIHICH)
SCULPTOR, EDUCATOR
b Otocac, Yugoslavia, April 25, 33; US citizen. *Study:* Sch Applied Arts, Belgrade, Yugoslavia, 47-51, Acad Applied Arts, Univ Belgrade, 51-54. *Work:* Hirshhorn Mus & Sculpture Garden, Smithsonian Inst, Washington, DC; Mus Royaux des Beaux-Arts de Belgique, Art Moderne, Brussels; Mus Mod Art, Belgrade; Phillips Collection, Washington, DC; San Francisco Mus Mod Art, Calif. *Comn:* sculpture, Toyota Auto Indus, Nagoya, Japan, 72; sculpture, Dallas Hyatt Regency, Tex, 78; sculpture, Cedars Sinai Med Ctr, Los Angeles, 79; sculpture, Tishman West Management Corp, Los Angeles, 86; sculpture, Olivetti, Ivrea, Italy, 86. *Exhib:* one-man shows, Feigen Palmer Gallery, Los Angeles, 66; Fisher Gallery, Univ S Calif, 70; Gimpel Weitzenhoffer, New York, 73; 2RC Gallery, Milan Italy, 80; Brunnier Gallery, Iowa State Ctr, Ames, Iowa, 80; Olivetti Cultural Ctr, Ivrea, Italy, 80; Palm Springs Desert Mus, Calif; 80, Mus Mod Art, Belgrade, 85 & 72. *Teaching:* Prof Visual Fundamentals, Univ Calif Los Angeles, 67-70 & 71-; asst prof drawing, Belgrade Univ Sch Archit, 55-6; assoc prof basic design, Univ Southern Calif, Sch Archit, 67-68 & 70-71. *Awards:* Univ Calif Los Angeles Creative Arts Inst Grant, 72 & 75; Judith Thomas Found Grant, 70-72; Univ Calif Los Angeles Research Grant, 70-88. *Bibliog:* William Wilson (auth), Sculpture by Vasa in USC Show, Los Angeles Times, 4/13/70; Donald Brewer (auth), Vasa: Laminated Illusions, Currant, 76; Jesa Denegri (auth), Vasa from Belgrade's Point of View, Exhib, 85. *Media:* Laminated acrylic. *Mailing Add:* 3025 Exposition Place Los Angeles CA 90018

VATER, REGINA (REGINA VATER LUNDBERG)
CONCEPTUAL ARTIST, LECTURER
b Rio De Janeiro, Brazil, May 11, 43. *Study:* Frank Schaeffer's Studio, Rio de Janeiro, 59; Sch Archit, Univ FED Rio de Janeiro, 60; Ibere Camargo's Studio, Rio de Janeiro, 62; Pratt Inst, Manhattan, NY, 74; Downtown Video Community Ctr, New York, 82. *Work:* Benson Latin Am Collection, Univ Tex, Austin; Video Annex, Long Beach Mus Art, Calif; Bibliotheque Nat Paris; Mus Contemp Arts, Univ Sao Paulo, Brazil; Jua Harfers, New York. *Comn:* Snake Nest, Laguna Gloria Arts Mus, Austin, 88; Light Poem, Women Studio Workshop, Rosendale, NY, 89; Amanaje, Clocktower Gallery, New York, 89; NikaUnikana, Ikon Gallery, Birmingham, Eng, 90; Mongarayba, Ctr Contemp Arts, Sante Fe, NMex, 90. *Exhib:* Biennale Des Jeunes, Paris, 67; Int Biennial Sao Paulo, 69; Venice Biennial, Italy, 76; solo show, Eugenia Cucalon Gallery, New York, 81; Montbeliard Int Video Festival, France, 84; Latin Am Women Artists, Bronx Mus, New York, 82; First Tex Triennial, Contemp Arts Mus, Houston, 88; The Revered Earth, Pratt Inst, New York, 90. *Collections Arranged:* Comtemp Brazil Works on Paper, 49 Artists, Nobe Gallery, New York, 79; Brazil Super-8 Films, Millenium, New York, 82; Latin Am Contemp Art, 83; Latin Am Visual Thinking, Art Awareness, Lexington, NY, 84. *Teaching:* Lectr, Univ Tex, Austin, 85, Mus Contemp Art, Univ Sao Paulo, 88 & S Eastern Mass Univ, 90. *Awards:* Travel abroad, Mod Art Nat Show, Ministery Cult Brazil, 72; Guggenheim Fel, 80; Fel on Film, NJ Coun Arts, 85. *Bibliog:* Robert C Morgan (auth), 3 South American women artists, High Performance-Astro Arts, Los Angeles, 86; Steve Kolpan (auth), The Amazon flows into--, Woodstock Times, 5/25/89; Guy Brett (auth), Transcontinental (exhib catalog), Ikon Gallery/Verso, London, 90. *Media:* Installation, Photography. *Publ:* Auth, Dreams That Money Can Buy, Artes Visuales Mus of Mod Art, Mexico City, 81; coauth, Latin American Contemporary Art Flue, Vol III, Now, Franklin Furnance, 83; auth Ecological art is alive and well in Los Angeles, High Performance Astro Artz, 88; Notes of ambition, High Performance Astroartz, 88; Women Artists Tell Her Own Stories-Regina Vater, Gallerie Publ, Vancouver, Can, 89. *Dealer:* Paulo Figueiredo Gallery Rua Mello Alves 717 Sao Paulo Sao Paulo Brazil; Carrington/Gallagher 7979 Broadway Suite 107 San Antonio TX 78209. *Mailing Add:* c/o Carrington/Gallagher 7979 Broadway Suite 205 San Antonio TX 78209

VAUX, RICHARD
PAINTER, PRINTMAKER
b Greensburg, Pa, Sept 15, 40. *Study:* Miami Univ, Ohio, BFA, 63; Northern Ill Univ, MFA, 69. *Work:* Long Beach Mus; Pepsico; Univ Mass, Amherst; Washington Co Mus; Museu de Arte Contemporanea, Sao Paulo, Brazil; and others. *Exhib:* Butler Inst Am Art, Youngstown, Ohio, 68; Stamford Mus , Conn, 70; Minn Mus Art, St Paul, 71; James Yu Gallery, Soho, New York, 74-76; Randolph Macon Mus, Va; Guild Hall Mus, East Hampton, NY, 78; Long Beach Mus Art, 79; Hudson River Mus, 79; Silvermine Guild, Conn, 80; Jain Marunouchi Gallery, 92; and others. *Teaching:* Prof art, Adelphi Univ, 83. *Bibliog:* Originals, Channel 21 TV, Richard Vaux, painter. *Media:* Acrylic, Oil; Graphics. *Publ:* The New York Art Review, American References, 88. *Mailing Add:* Lloyd Lane Huntington NY 11743

VAUX, SANDRA MARIE See Benny, Sandra

VAZQUEZ, PAUL
PAINTER
b Brooklyn, NY, Sept 19, 33. *Study:* Ohio Wesleyan Univ, BFA, 56; Univ Ill, MFA(Kate Neal Kinley Fel), 57. *Work:* Univ Ill, Urbana; Ball State Teachers Col, Muncie, Ind; New Britain Mus, Conn; Butler Inst Am Art, Ohio. *Exhib:* One-man shows, Paley & Lowe Gallery, 71-73, shows in Koln Ger & Vienna, Austria, 75, David Findlay Gallery, New York, 76-80; American Painting, Chicago Inst Am Art, 72; Kipa Contemp Art (catalog), London Eng, 87-88; Galerie LaMaiginere, Paris, 90; Galeria del Naviglio, Milan, Venice, 90; and others. *Teaching:* Instr art hist, Bennett Col, 63-66; asst prof humanities, Western Conn State Col, 66-69; prof drawing & painting, Univ Bridgeport, 69-89. *Awards:* Purchase Award, Butler Inst Am Art, 58; Conn Comn Arts Grant for Painting, 74; Artist Sponsorship Prog, NY Found Arts, 92. *Bibliog:* Virginia Mann (auth), article, Arts Mag, 2/78; Robert Sievert (auth), article, Arts Mag, 2/80. *Media:* Acrylic oil, Watercolor. *Dealer:* David Findlay Gallery 984 Madison Ave New York NY 10021; Tatistcheff Gallery 50 W 57th New York NY 10019. *Mailing Add:* 519 Broadway New York NY 10012

VECSEY, ESTHER BARBARA
EDUCATOR, MUSEUM DIRECTOR
b Pecs, Hungary, May 23, 44; US citizen. *Study:* Univ Calif, Los Angeles, with William Brice, John Paul Jones, Oliver Andrews, BA, 61, with Carlo Pedretti, MA, 75; Academia Di Belle Arti, Rome, cert, 66; Mus Mgt Inst, Univ Calif, Berkeley & J Paul Getty Trust, 85, PhD prog (theology & art history), 87-. *Collections Arranged:* Variants: Drawing by Contemporary Sculptors (auth, catalog), 81, Sewall Gallery, Rice Univ; David Hockney Graphics, 82; Italian Old Master Drawings, Houston Collections, 86; Gold & Silver treas Hungary from 9th-19th Century, 87; and many others. *Pos:* Res asst to dir, Los Angeles Co Mus, Calif, 76-77; coordr, Ace Gallery, Venice, Calif, 77; cur collections, Col Art Mus, Wooster, Ohio, 79-80; dir, Sewall Art Gallery, Rice Univ, Houston, Tex, 80-83; dir, Blaffer Gallery, Univ Houston, 83-87; curatorial & freelance critic, Bay Area Mus, 87-; Budapest, Hungary, 90-91. *Teaching:* Instr mus studies practicum, Col Wooster, Ohio, 79-80; instr mus studies practicum, Rice Univ, Houston, Tex, 80-81, asst prof art hist, 81-83; instr museum methodology, Univ Houston, 84-86. *Awards:* Travel grant, Irex Princeton, Hungary, 90-91. *Mem:* Am Asn Mus; Mem, Univ Calif, Berkeley Art Mus, 87; Asn Univ & Col, Mus & Galleries; Col Art Asn Am. *Res:* Art, architecture, Italian Renaissance; contemporary art and interdisciplinary topics. *Publ:* Auth of various catalogues, 74-85; Artweek, 88-90. *Mailing Add:* Hidasz U 7 Budapest II H-1026 Hungary

VEERKAMP, PATRICK BURKE
EDUCATOR, ADMINISTRATOR
b Joplin, Mo, Nov 22, 43. *Study:* Adams State Col, BA, 66; Univ Denver, MA, 76; Colo State Univ, MFA, 81. *Work:* Colo State Univ, Ft Collins; E Tenn State Univ, Johnson City. *Exhib:* Rutgers National Drawing '79, Rutgers Univ, Camden, NJ, 79; 37th Annual Painting Competition, Abilene Fine Arts Mus, Tex, 81; Seventh Annual Ceramic Invitational, Weber State Col, Ogden, Utah, 81; Works on Paper, E Carolina State Univ, Greenville, NC, 81; Kansas Sixth National, Ft Hays State Univ, Kans, 81; two-person show, Univ Wis, Parkside, 83; Positive-Negative, Slocumb Gallery, E Tenn State Univ, 85; Marriage a la Mode: The Aesthetics of Mating, Wustum Mus Fine Art, Racine, Wis, 86. *Pos:* Assoc dir, Spec Visual Arts Prog, Colo State Univ, Ft Collins, 81-82. *Teaching:* Instr art, Mesa Col, Grand Junction, Colo, 73-78 & N Idaho Col, Coeur d'Alene, 82-83; assoc prof art, Southwestern Univ, Georgetown, Tex, 83- *Mem:* Nat Coun Art Adminrs; Col Art Asn. *Media:* Drawing; Ceramics. *Mailing Add:* Dept Art Southwestern Univ Georgetown TX 78626

VEGA, EDWARD
SCULPTOR, EDUCATOR
b Deming, NMex, Oct 13, 38. *Study:* NMex State Univ, Las Cruces, BFA, 68; Univ NMex, Albuquerque, MA, 70; lithog with Garo Antreasian; drawing with Ilya Bolotowsky; sculpture with Charlie Mattox. *Work:* Eastern NMex Univ, Roswell; St Joseph Hosp, Albuquerque; Mus Albuquerque; Roswell Mus. *Comn:* City of Albuquerque, NMex. *Exhib:* Graphics '73, Western NMex Univ, Silver City; 50th Regional Art Exhib, Shreveport, La, 73; Gov Gallery, Santa Fe, NMex, 78; Roswell Mus, 79; Santa Fe Festival of the Arts, 79; and others. *Pos:* NMex Arts Comn chmn, 79. *Teaching:* Asst prof sculpture, drawing, Univ Albuquerque, 76-86. *Awards:* Third Place Purchase Award Sculpture, Univ NMex, 75; Res Grant Sculpture, NMex State Univ, 75; Artist-in-Residence Fel, Roswell Art Ctr; Finalist, five major sculpture comns, 85-86. *Media:* Steel, Wood. *Mailing Add:* 618 Roehl Rd NW Albuquerque NM 87107

VELASQUEZ, OSCAR
PAINTER, ILLUSTRATOR
b Pharr, Tex, Apr 5, 45. *Study:* Cooper Sch Art, AA, 65. *Work:* Joslyn Art Mus, Omaha; Nat Acad Design-Henry Ward Ranger, New York; Erskine Col, Due West, SC; Opera House, Abbeville, SC. *Exhib:* Ga Watercolor Soc, High Mus, Atlanta, 79; SC Watercolor Soc, Greenville Mus Art; Am Watercolor Soc, Columbia Mus Art, SC, 79; Camden Art Mus, SC, 83; Sumter Art Mus, SC, 83; Cannon Bldg, Capitol, Washington, DC, 83; and others. *Awards:* High Winds Medal, 75 & Silver Medal of Honor, 77, Am Watercolor Soc; Georgia Gold Award, Watercolor Soc, 81. *Mem:* Am Watercolor Soc; SC Watercolor Soc; Southern Watercolor Asn; Ga Watercolor Soc. *Media:* Watercolor, Acrylic; Oils. *Mailing Add:* 2250 Rd R Blufftone OH 45817

VELEZ, EDIN
VIDEO ARTIST
b Arecibo, PR, Sept 3, 51. *Study:* Univ PR, 69-70; Inst Bellas Artes, 70. *Work:* Mus Mod Art, New York; Stedjelik Mus Art, Amsterdam, Neth; Ithaca Mus Art, NY. *Comn:* Oblique Strategist Too, 85 & Naruhodo (installation), 87, NY State Coun Arts, New York; AS IS (video essay), 85, Meaning of the Interval (video doc), 87 & Dance of Darkness (video doc), 88, Nat Endowment Arts, Washington, DC. *Exhib:* III Festival Int D'Art, Locarno, Switz, 82; Whitney Mus Am Art Biennial, New York, 83; Video Art: A History, 84 & Video Viewpoint, 86, Mus Mod Art, New York; Cinema Du Reel, Pompidou Ctr, Paris, France, 85; Arts for Television, Stedjelik Mus Art, Amsterdam, 87-88; Int Pub Television Conf, Granada, Spain, 87 & Philadelphia, Pa, 88; Image Forum Film & Video Festival, Tokyo, Japan, 89; Nagoya Mus, Japan, 89; Video and the Computer, Mus Mod Art, New York, 89; Louvre Mus, Paris, France, 90; Elected Affinities, Cronis Gallery, New

York, 90. *Awards:* First Prize, First Latino Film & Video Festival, 88; Jurors Citation Award, Black Maria Festival, 90; Maya Doren Award, Am Film Inst, 90. *Bibliog:* Victor Ancona (auth), Edin Velez: In essence a romantic realist, Videography, 83; Image Forum (auth), Edin Velez, video artist, Video Culture, Japan, 86; John Wallace (auth), Innovation: It's a primary color on the video, NY Times, 87. *Mem:* Asn Independent Video & Filmmakers. *Dealer:* Electronic Arts Intermix 536 Broadway New York NY 10012; Tape Connection Via P Querini 3 Roma Italy. *Mailing Add:* 230 W 78th St Old Chelsea Station New York NY 10024

VELICK, BRUCE
CURATOR
b Los Angeles, Calif, Jan 29, 49. *Study:* Univ Calif, Davis, BA(design), 71. *Pos:* Dir, Bruce Velick Eds, Mill Valley, Calif, currently. *Specialty:* Contemporary art. *Mailing Add:* 57 Marguerite Ave Mill Valley CA 94941-4513

VELICK, PAUL See Bob & Bob

VENA, DANTE
EDUCATOR, PRINTMAKER
b Castrolibero, Cosenza, Italy, Nov 12, 30; US citizen. *Study:* Univ Wis, BS, 57, MS, 60; Univ Iowa, PhD, 76. *Work:* Milwaukee Art Ctr; Montgomery Mus, Ala; Bellarmine Col, Louisville; Nazareth Col, Ky; Ball State Univ, Ind. *Comn:* Wall mural (map), Customs House, New Orleans, 58; illus, Motive Mag, Nashville, 60; Keenland (illus), Ford Times Mag, 63; A Child is Born (cover illus), Companion Mag, 63; wall mural, Ohio Univ, Portsmouth, 68. *Exhib:* 14th Nat Exhib Prints, Libr Congress, Washington, DC, 56; 152nd Ann Exhib, Pa Acad Fine Arts, 57; 29th Int Exhib Northwest Printmakers, Seattle Art Mus, 57; 24th Ann Mid-Year Show, Butler Inst Am Art, 59; 65th Ann Western Artists, Denver Art Mus, 59; Nat Mus Wales, Cardiff, S Wales, 66; solo exhib, Bell Gallery, Belfast, N Ireland, 66; Southeastern Mass Univ Art Gallery, 72-91; group shows, Visual Images Gallery, New Bedford, 91 & 92. *Collections Arranged:* Alfred Sessler Retrospective Show, 61; A Town and its Artists, Portsmouth, 68; Artists Inmates, Portsmouth Gallery, 69. *Teaching:* Art dir, Bellarmine Col, Louisville, Ky, 61-67; chmn art educ dept, Univ Mass, Dartmouth, 72- *Awards:* Mrs Arthur Osborn Purchase Award, Ball State Univ, 63; New Bedford Arts Coun, 89; Research Fel, Edith Cowan Univ, Perth, Western Australia, 91. *Bibliog:* Cottie Burland (auth), Dante Vena-Artist Own Gallery, Arts Rev, 1/22/66. *Mem:* Mass Art Educ Asn (ed, 79-85, pres, 85-87); Nat Art Educ Asn; Fairhaven Arts Coun (chmn, 81-83); Mass Asn Sch Comts; Bd Educ Fairhaven, Mass (chmn, 87-88). *Publ:* Auth, Contemporary Art, Irish-Am, 63; Learning Out There: A Program, Art Educ, 75; Integrated Arts in the Elementary Classroom, Charles Thomas Pub; Video Project, Integrated Arts in Schools, 91-92. *Mailing Add:* Art Dept Southeastern Mass Univ North Dartmouth MA 02717

VENABLE, SUSAN C
SCULPTOR, PAINTER
b Calif, Dec 30, 44. *Study:* Calif State Univ, BFA, 82; Univ Calif, Los Angeles, MFA, 85. *Work:* Horoko Nakamotn, Tokoyo, Japan; Payden & Rygel, Los Angeles, Calif; Bear Stearns & Co, Los Angeles, Calif; Sudler-Marlins, Chicago, Ill; Los Angeles Inst Contemp Art, Calif. *Comn:* Lobby installations, Pacific Plaza, Walnut Creek, Calif, 87, Hotel Nikko, Chicago, Ill, 87, Metroplex Wilshire, Los Angeles, 89, Western Digital Corp, Irvine, Calif, 90; auditorium installation, IBM, Atlanta, Ga, 88. *Exhib:* Group shows, Fiber Revolution, Witchita Art Mus, 87, Boulder Ctr Art, 89, SITE, Los Angeles, 89, Off the Wall, Los Angeles Co Mus Art, 90, Monotypes, Ariz State Univ Mus, 90; solo shows, New Work, Tally Richards, NMex, Mahoney/Butler, Calif, 89, Square & Square, Scottsdale Ctr Arts, Ariz, 90 & Sun Art Mus, Phoenix, Ariz, 92. *Awards:* Dean's Discretionary, 82, Fishbaugh Mem, 83, Univ Calif, Los Angeles. *Bibliog:* Michel Thomas (auth), Textiles/Art/Language, Architecture 85, France; Michael Webb (auth), Poetry in Concrete, Inside Mag, Japan, 6/90. *Media:* Mixed; Acrylic, Oil. *Dealer:* Corporate Art Source 900 N Franklin St #200 Chicago IL 60610. *Mailing Add:* 214 S Venice Blvd Venice CA 90291

VENEGAS, HAYDEE E
MUSEOLOGIST, CONSULTANT
b Arecibo, PR, Mar 4, 50. *Study:* Univ PR, BA(art hist), 73; Fla State Univ, MA(mod art), 78. *Collections Arranged:* Francisco Oller: A Realist Impressionist, 83; La Moda en Puerto Rico, 85; Obra Uica sobre papel, 85; 25 anos de pintura Puertoriquena, 86; Quijano & Roche, 88; Irene Delano, 89; Antonio Nania, 92. *Pos:* Dir, Mus Fundacion Arqueologica, 76-79, Permanent Fund for the Arts, 92-; asst dir, Ponce Art Mus, 80-88; pres, Concultura, 88-92. *Teaching:* Vis prof Puerto Rican art, Inter-Am Univ, summer 75, Escuelade Artes Plasticas, 90-91 & Escuela Hotelera, 92. *Awards:* Leon de Oro Award, 84. *Bibliog:* Connie Underhill (auth), The museum as a place, San Juan Star, Sunday Mag, 12/30/79; Mario Alegre (auth), Voluntades que Convergen, El Nuevo Dia, 4/14/90. *Mem:* Am Asn Mus; Int Comt Mus; Col Art Asn; Asn of Latin-Am Historians. *Res:* Puerto Rican art; Francisco Oller, 19th century painter. *Publ:* Contribr, Juan Ramon Valazquez, El Mundo, 78; El Velorio: Propuesta para una reinterpretacion, Plastica, 79; auth, Francisco Oller: Profile of a Puerto Rican Painter, Mus Art Ponce, 83, Oller in Cuba: Horizontes, 85, Irene Delano, 89. *Mailing Add:* Miramar Towers 4-F Santurce PR 00907

VENET, BERNAR
SCULPTOR, CONCEPTUAL ARTIST
b France, April 20, 41. *Study:* Sch Villa Thiole, Nice, France, 57-58. *Work:* Mus Mod Art, New York; Guggenheim Mus; Mus Nat Art Mod, Ctr Georges Pompidou, Paris; Neue Galerie Alten Kurhaus, Aachen, WGer; La Jolla Mus Contemp Art; and others. *Comn:* Painting, Atlantic Richfield Co, Los Angeles, 81; sculpture, Mus Art Contemp, Dunkerque, 83; tallest steel sculpture, France, 86; sculpture, Linpro, Austin, TX, 86; sculpture, Goodmann Gegar Hogan, Norfolk, Va, 87; sculpture, French gout & Air France, Berlin, W Ger, 88. *Exhib:* Solo exhibs, Galerie Daniel Templon, Paris, France, 89; Galerie Daniel Templon, Paris, France, 90; Vrej Baghoomian, New York, 90; Castelli Graphics, New York, 90; Pierre Huber, Geneve, Swisse, 90; Galerie Mostra, Paris, France, 90; Theospacio, Madrid, Espagne, 90 & Studio Ogetto, Milano, Italie, 92; Bernar Venet and Tom Wesselmann, Carl Schlosberg Fine Arts, Sherman Oaks, Calif, 90 & Studio Oggetto, Milano, Italie, 92; Dibujos de Escultores, Estudio Theo, Madrid, Spain, 90; L'Ecole de Nice, Mus Mod & Contemp Art, Nice, France, 90; Passage d'un Collectionneur: Collection de Thierry et Isabelle Rougier Centre d'Art Contemporain, Troyes, France, 90. *Teaching:* Instr, La Sorbonne, Paris, France, 73-75. *Awards:* Nat Endowment of the Arts Award, 79; Grand Prix des Arts de la Ville de Paris, 90. *Bibliog:* Catherine Millet (auth), Bernar Venet, Chene, France & Prearo, Italy, 75; J Pierre Mirouze (producer), film, WDR, WGer, 75; Seth Schneidman (producer), film, Seven Hills Productions, 83. *Media:* Wood Reliefs, Corten Steel. *Mailing Add:* 533 Canal St New York NY 10013

VENEZIA, MICHAEL
PAINTER
b Brooklyn, NY, July 23, 35. *Study:* State Univ NY Col, Buffalo, BS, 63; Univ Mich, Ann Arbor, MFA, 68. *Work:* Mus Mod Art, New York; Nat Gallery Can, Ottawa; Kunsthaus, Zurich, Switz; Mem Art Gallery Univ Rochester, NY; Detroit Inst Arts; Australian Nat Gallery, Canberra; Lincoln First Corp, Rochester, NY; Hartford Atheneum, Conn. *Exhib:* Works on Paper, Mus Mod Art, New York, 74; one-man shows, Paintings, Bykert Gallery, New York, 73 & Sperone Westwater Fischer, Inc, New York, 79; Two Artists: Dan Hill & Michael Venezia, Whitney Mus Art, New York, 77; Artists & Friends: Dan Flavin & Michael Venezia, Contemp Arts Ctr, Cincinnati, Ohio, 77; Drawings About Drawing Today, Acklund Art Mus, Chapel Hill, NC, 79; Selected Paintings 1969-1980, Detroit Inst Arts, 80; Carol Taylor-Art Inc, Dallas, Tex, 81 & 84; Paintings 1972-1983, Dia Found, Dan Flavin Art Inst, Bridgehampton, NY, 83; Biennale Artumbra, Foligno, Italy, 86; New Paintings, Margaret Roeder Gallery, New York, 87; Margaret Roeder Gallery, New York, 88; Frankfurt Art Fair, Ger, 89; Surface in Proportion, Margaret Roeder Gallery, New York, 90; Fred Hoffman Gallery, Santa Monica, Calif, 91; Michael Venezia, Rubin Spangle Gallery, NY, 92; Michael Venezia, Glan Enzo Sperone, Rome, Italy, 92. *Teaching:* Vis lectr fine arts, Guildford Col, Surrey, Eng, 66-67, London Col Printing, 66-67; from asst prof to prof fine arts, Univ Rochester, NY 68-; prof art, Univ Rochester, 85- *Awards:* Creative Artists Pub Serv Award, NY Coun Arts, State Univ NY Col, Fredonia, 75; Tiffany Found Award for Painting, 79; Artist Fel Painting, Nat Endowment Arts, 81-82. *Bibliog:* Janet Kutner (auth), An itch to scratch the surface: Artist concentrates on texture and light, not image, Dallas Morning News, 5/25/81; Helen A Harrison (auth), His paintings stress the paint, New York Times, Long Island Weekly, 11/27/83; David Carrier (auth), Michael Venezia, Arts, 80, 5/91. *Media:* Powdered Metals, Glass and Pigments on Canvas and Paper. *Dealer:* RubinSpangle 395 W Broadway New York NY 10012. *Mailing Add:* c/o RubinSpangle 395 W Broadway New York NY 10012

VENTIMIGLIA, JOHN THOMAS
SCULPTOR, EDUCATOR
b Augusta, Maine, Jan 12, 43. *Study:* Skowhegan Sch Paint & Sculpture, 64, Sch Art, Syracuse Univ, BFA, 65; Rinehart Sch, Md Inst Art, MFA (sculpture), 67. *Work:* Portland Mus Art; Portland Public Library. *Comn:* Agavney Johnson Mem Sculpture, Portland Pub Libr, 81. *Exhib:* Maine Sculpture 76, Univ Maine, 76; Barn Gallery, Ogunquit, Maine, 77; Maine Coast Artists, Rockport; Payson Gallery of Art, Portland; Barridoff Galleries; Round Top Ctr for Arts, Damariscotta, Maine. *Pos:* Chmn Sculpture Dept, Portland Sch Art, 72-93; dir, Outdoor Sculpture Exhib Series, Portland Sch Art, 73-78; adv panelist, Maine State Comn Arts & Humanities, 81-85. *Teaching:* Prof sculpture & 3D design, Portland Sch Art, Maine, 72- *Awards:* Scholar, Showhegan Sch Painting & Sculpture, 64. *Bibliog:* 76 Maine Artists (exhib catalog), Maine State Bicentennial Comn, 76; Maine Art Now, Beam, 90. *Media:* Metal, Steel & Bronze. *Mailing Add:* Dept Sculpture & Design Portland Sch Art 97 Spring St Portland ME 04101

VENTURA, ANTHONY
PAINTER
b Southampton, NY, Jan 24, 27. *Study:* Acad Arts, Newark NJ, BFA, 51; Pratt Inst, Brooklyn, NY, 52-53; Art Students League, NY, 54-55; studied with Robert Brackman, Ivan Olinsky, Edgar Whitney, Edmond Fitzgerald & Avery Johnson. *Work:* Fort Schlyer Maritime Mus, Bronx, NY; Am Can Co, Chicago, Ill; Hershey Corp, Pennsylvania; Winsor-Newton Co, Secaucus, NJ. *Exhib:* Anchorage Fine Art Mus, Alaska, 74; Tweed Mus, Duluth, Minn, 77; Am Watercolor Soc, New York, 82; Frye Mus, Seattle, 83; Am Artist Prof League, New Jersey, 87. *Pos:* Adv Comt Guild, Guild Creative Art, Shrewsbury, NJ, 80-84; off artist for US Coast Guard. *Teaching:* Workshops, demonstrations and lectures to art organizations throughout New Jersey and at own studio-gallery. *Awards:* Wells Stroud Award, Am Artist Prof League, 87; Hudson Valley Art Asn Award, 88; Elizabeth K Ellis Award, Salmagundi Club, 88. *Bibliog:* Listed in-Judge and Jury Selector of Federated Art Asn, NJ & Who's Who in the East. *Mem:* NJ Watercolor Soc (pres, 86-87); Knickerbocker Artist; Salmagundi Club; N Shore Art Asn; Hudson Valley Art Asn. *Media:* Watercolor. *Dealer:* Jordane Art Works 18443 Deep Passage Land Ft Myers Beach FL 33931. *Mailing Add:* 3430 Hwy 66 Neptune NJ 07753

VENTURI, ROBERT
ARCHITECT
b Philadelphia, Pa, June 25, 25. *Study:* Princeton Univ, AB, 47, MFA, 50; Rome Prize Fel, Am Acad in Rome, 54-56; Oberlin Col, Hon DFA, 77; Yale Univ, Hon DFA, 79; Univ Pa, Hon DFA, 80; Princeton Univ, Hon DFA, 83; NJ Inst Technol, Hon LHD, 84; Philadelphia Col Art, Hon DFA, 85; Univ NC Chapel Hill, LHD, 89; Philadelphia Col Textiles & Sci, LHD, 92. *Comn:* Vanna Venturi House, Philadelphia, 61; Guild House, Philadelphia, 61; Allen Mem Art Mus addition, Oberlin Col, Ohio, 73; Franklin Court, Nat Park Serv, Philadelphia, 72; Inst Sci Info Corp Hq, Philadelphia, 78; Gordon Wu Hall, Princeton Univ, NJ, 80; Seattle Art Mus, Wash, 84; Nat Gallery, Sainsbury Wing, London, Eng, 86; Orchestra Hall, Philadelphia, Pa, 87. *Exhib:* Work of Venturi & Rauch, Whitney Mus Am Art, New York, 71 & Pa Acad Fine Arts, Philadelphia, 75; 200 Yrs of Am Archit Drawing, Cooper-Hewitt Mus, New York, 77; Drawing Toward a More Mod Archit, The Drawing Ctr, New York, 77; The Work of Venturi and Rauch, Kunstgewerke Mus, Zurich & traveled, 79-81; Venturi, Rauch & Scott Brown, Accademia delle Arti del Disegno, Firenze, Italy, 81; Buildings & Drawings, Max Protetch Gallery, New York, 82; A Generation of Architecture, Krannert Art Mus, Univ Ill & traveling, 84-86; High Styles: 20th Century American Design, Whitney Mus Am Art, New York, 85-86; and others. *Pos:* Partner, Venturi & Rauch, 64-80 & Venturi, Rauch & Scott Brown, 80-89, Philadelphia & Venturi, Scott Brown & Assoc, 89-; architect-in-residence, Am Acad Rome, 66, trustee, 69-74. *Teaching:* From asst to assoc prof archit, Univ Pa, 57-65; Davenport Prof archit, Yale Univ, 66-70; bd adv, Princeton Univ, Dept Art & Archeol, 77-81; Walter Gropius lectr, Harvard Univ, Grad Sch Design, 82; Eero Saarinen vis prof archit design, Yale Univ, Sch Archit, 86-87. *Awards:* Pritzker Archit Prize, Hyatt Found, 91; Man Yr, Order Sons Italy & Coun City Philadelphis, 92; US Presidential Award, Nat Medal Arts, 92; and others. *Mem:* Fel Am Acad Rome; fel Am Inst Archit; fel Accademia Nazionale di San Luca; fel Am Acad Arts & Sci; hon fel Royal Incorp Architects Scotland; and others. *Publ:* Auth, Complexity and Contradiction in Architecture, Mus Mod Art, New York, 66, 2nd ed, 77; coauth with Denise Scott Brown & Steven Izenour, Learning from Las Vegas, MIT Press, 72, 2nd ed, 77; Diversity, relevance and representation in historicism, or Plus ca change (article), Architectural Rec, 6/82; coauth with Denise Scott Brown, A View from the Campidoglio: Selected Essays 1953-1974, Harper & Row, 84; From invention to convention in architecture, Royal Soc Arts J, London, 1/88; and others. *Mailing Add:* Venturi Scott Brown & Assoc 4236 Main Philadelphia PA 19127

VERMEULE, CORNELIUS CLARKSON, III
HISTORIAN, WRITER
b on Atlantic Ocean, Aug 10, 25; US citizen. *Study:* Harvard Univ, AB, 47, MA, 51; Univ Col, Univ London, PhD, 53. *Work:* Mus Fine Arts, Boston; Nat Mus, Pylos, Hellas; Morphou-Omorfo Mus, Cyprus. *Collections Arranged:* Many exhibs, Fogg Mus Art, 50-72; Sir John Soane's Mus, London; Mus Fine Arts, Boston; Art Ctr Plainfield, NJ. *Pos:* Asst, Sir John Soane's Mus, 51-53; cur classical art, Mus Fine Arts, Boston, 57-, actg dir, 72-73; cur coins, Mass Hist Soc, Boston, 69- *Teaching:* Asst prof fine arts, Univ Mich, Ann Arbor, 53-55; asst prof archaeol, Bryn Mawr Col, 55-57; prof classics, Yale Univ, 68-69 & 72-73; prof fine arts, Boston Col, 78- *Awards:* Boston Col US Bicentennial Medal, 81- *Mem:* Life mem Col Art Asn Am; fel Royal Numismatic Soc; life fel Am Numismatic Soc (mem coun, 60-78); life mem Archaeol Inst Am; life mem Hellenic & Roman Soc. *Res:* European painting, Greek and Roman art; Renaissance sculpture and medals. *Interests:* Classical and Neo-classical style, Greek sculpture technique. *Publ:* Auth, Greek Sculpture & Roman Taste, 77; Art of Antiquity, Greek and Roman Art, Vols II-V, 79-86; Greek and Roman Sculpture in America, 82; Philatelic Art in America, 87; European & Am Medallic Art, 90. *Mailing Add:* Mus Fine Arts Boston MA 02115

VERNON
PAINTER, PRINTMAKER
b El Dorado, Ark, June 11, 48. *Study:* N Tex State Univ Denton, BFA, 72; private study with Robert Wood, 85. *Work:* Corpus Christi Mus, Tex; Crete City Hall, Ill; St Dominique's Hosp, Jackson, Miss; N Tex State Univ, Denton; Warner Brown Hosp, El Dorado, Ark. *Comn:* Quilt Series (watercolor), Burd Clinic, Beaumont, Tex, 85 & comm by Frank Macher, Ann Arbor, Mich, 86 & 87; Palmestry (watercolor), ECPI Inc, Virginia Beach, 86; Oriental Suite (watercolor), comm by Gloria Young, Waco, Tex, 87 & Congressman Leath, Washington, DC, 88. *Exhib:* Solo exhib, Corpus Christi Mus, Tex, 79, S Ark Art Ctr, El Dorado, 86 & Kershaw Co Art Ctr, Camden, 87; Watercolor Art Soc Houston, traveling exhib, 83; S Ark Art Ctr, El Dorado, 84; 65th Nat Springfield Exhib, 85; Art Alliance Int, El Paso Art Alliance, 85. *Pos:* Pres, Portland Art Asn, 76-77; vpres & pres, Humble Art League, 84-86; Sr bd mem, Tex Arts & Craft Found, 85- *Teaching:* Art dept dir, Frisco ISD, Tex, 73-74; instr watercolor, Amarillo Art Ctr, Tex, 85; Hill Country Art Found, Ingram, Tex, 87-88. *Awards:* Murt Hill Award, S Ark Art Ctr, Amarillo, Tex, 85; Best Floral, Vizcaya Days, Vizcaya Mus & City of Miami, 85; 1st Place Watercolor, Corsicana Nat Art Exhib, Corsicana Art Asn, 86. *Bibliog:* PBS Video, Vernon Retrospective, PBS, Columbia, SC, 8/87; Calvin Goodman (auth), Five Hardworking Artists, Am Artists, 6/88. *Mem:* Tex Watercolor Soc; Western Fedn Watercolorists; Watercolor Art Soc Houston. *Media:* Watercolor. *Dealer:* Vernon Fine Art 1738 Treble St Humble TX 77338. *Mailing Add:* 2706 Woodland Grove Dr Kingwood TX 77339

VERONA, PAULA
PAINTER
b Bethlehem, Pa, Feb 21, 50. *Study:* Mysore Univ, India, 71-72; Wilson Col, BFA(cum laude), 72. *Work:* Continental Wirt Electronics, Southhampton, Pa; MAACO Corp, King of Prussia, Pa; CITIBANK, Bombay, India; Unimax Int, Los Angeles. *Exhib:* Allentown Art Mus, 73, 76, 80 & 82; William Penn Mem Mus, Harrisburg, Pa, 79; Baum Sch Art, Allentown, 88; Mayfair 89, Muhlenberg Col, Allentown, 89; Regional Art 90, Marywood Col, Scranton, Pa. *Bibliog:* John Lidstone (auth), Davis Visuals, Davis Publ Inc, 90. *Mem:* Nat Asn Women Artists. *Media:* Oil, Acrylic. *Mailing Add:* Box 175 46 Cherry Valley Rd Delaware Water Gap PA 18327

VEROSTKO, ROMAN JOSEPH
PAINTER, HISTORIAN
b Tarrs, Pa, Sept 12, 29. *Study:* Art Inst of Pittsburgh, dipl; St Vincent Col & Seminary, Latrobe, Pa, BA, 55; Pratt Inst, MFA, 61; New York Univ; Columbia Univ; Atelier 17, Paris. *Exhib:* Crash, Wright Mus, Beloit, Wis, 88; The Technological Imagination, Minneapolis Col Art & Design, Minn, 90; SIGGRAPH, Dallas, 90 & Chicago, 92; Dada/Data: Developing Media Since 1970, Baltimore, 91; solo shows in Paris, New York, Washington & throughout US & Can. *Pos:* Staff ed art & archit, New Catholic Encyclo, Catholic Univ, Washington, 64-68; acad dean, Minneapolis Col Art & Design, 75-78; prog chair, Fourth Int Symp Electronic Art, 93. *Teaching:* Prof art hist, Minneapolis Col Art & Design, Minn, 68- *Awards:* Bush Fel, 69. *Bibliog:* C J McNaspy (auth), Art & the New Catholic Encyclo, Am, 3/67; F Debuyst (auth), Sculptures de Ciment, Roman Verostko, Art D'Eglise, 68. *Mem:* Col Art Asn; Am Asn Univ Prof; Asn Computing Machinery. *Media:* Computer, Acrylic. *Res:* Changing roles of the artist in our society. *Publ:* Auth, Experience in Community: The New Art, Liturgical Arts, 72; Le Sacre et la Profane, Art D'Eglise, 75; A futures outlook on the role of artists and designers, Futurics, 80; Epigenetic Painting: Software As Genotype, Leonardo, 1/23/90; computer illus, Derivation of the Laws, St Sebastian Press, Minneapolis, 90; and others. *Mailing Add:* 5535 Clinton Ave S Minneapolis MN 55419

VERZAR, CHRISTINE B
ADMINISTRATOR, EDUCATOR
b Basel, Switz, Sept 05, 40; US citizen. *Study:* Courtauld Inst, London Univ, 63; Univ Florence, 63-64; Univ Basel, PhD, 66. *Teaching:* Asst prof hist art, Boston Univ, 66-69, Princeton Univ, 69- 76; asst prof, Univ of Mich, 73-84; prof/chmn hist art, Ohio State Univ, 84- *Awards:* Phi Kappa Phi. *Mem:* Col Art Asn; Int Ctr Medieval Art (bd dirs, 85-89); Medieval Acad Am. *Res:* Italian medieval art; Connections East-West. *Publ:* Auth, Die Romanischen Skulpteren der Abtei Sagra San Michele, Bern, 68; coauth, The Meeting of Two Worlds, Ann Arbor, 81; auth, Portal & Politics in the Early Italian City/State, Parma, 88. *Mailing Add:* Dept Hist of Art Ohio State Univ 100 Hayes Hall 108 Noval Hall Columbus OH 43210

VERZYL, JUNE CAROL
DEALER, COLLECTOR
b Huntington, NY, Feb 5, 28. *Study:* Parsons Sch of Design. *Pos:* Co-dir, Verzyl Gallery, 66- *Bibliog:* Jane Margold (auth), Galleries struggle with an image, Newsday, 3/31/67; Kevin Hayes (auth), Gallery almost set to re-open, Northport Observer, 10/29/81. *Mem:* Northport Hist Soc (bd dirs). *Specialty:* Contemporary American painting, graphics and sculpture. *Collection:* Contemporary American work, including Filmus, Refregier, Benda, Twardowicz, Clawson and Christopher; also a large collection of New England gravestone rubbings. *Mailing Add:* 25 Bevin Rd Northport NY 11768

VESNA, VICTORIA
VIDEO ARTIST, ENVIRONMENTAL ARTIST
b Washington, DC, June 9, 59. *Study:* Univ Belgrade, Yugoslavia, BFA, 84; Ctr Media Arts, cert. *Exhib:* Solo exhib, Viscious Circle-Golden Lies, SKC Gallery, Belgrade, Yugoslavia, Red Angel, Pyramid, Kamikaze & Danceteria, New York, Thunderbolt, Festival Nacional L'Unita, Ferrara, Italy, 85, Sictransitgloriamundi, Moltkerei Workspace, Cologne, Ger, 86 & Yugoslav Cultural Ctr, New York, 87, Black Soil, SKC Gallery, Belgrade, Yugoslavia, 89, Somtimes a Cigar is only a Cigar (Freud), CAGE, Cincinnati, Ohio & Image One Gallery, New York, 90, Another Day in Paradise, SKC Gallery, Belgrade, Yugoslavia, 92; Four, Salon Contemp Art, Belgrade, Yugoslavia, 85; Senza Arte Ne Parte, Collegio Universitario, Torino, Italy, 85; Kunst Mit Eigen Sinn, Mus 20th Century, Vienna, Austria, 85; Geometric Tendencies, Mus Mod Art, Ljubljana, Slovenia, 86; Red Angel/Aperto, Venice Biennale, Venice, Italy, 86; Sometimes a Cigar is Only a Cigar, PS 1 Mus, Long Island, NY, 89; Virgin Territories, Long Beach Mus, Calif, 92. *Pos:* Int Artist Coord Dir, Slade Corp, 91- *Awards:* Golden Eagle, CINE, Washington, DC, 88. *Bibliog:* Biljana Tomic (auth), Sometimes a Cigar is only a Cigar, Moment Mag, 12/91; Friedmann Malsch (auth), Parallel Kunst, Kunst Forum Int, 3/92; John Webster (auth), Multiple Monitor, Computer Graphics World, 7/92. *Mem:* Long Beach Mus Media Coun; Media Alliance; Asn Ind Film & Videomakers. *Media:* Video, Tele-communications. *Publ:* Auth, Sometimes a Cigar is only a Cigar (Freud), Franklin Furnace, 89. *Mailing Add:* 424 Emerald Bay Laguna Beach CA 92651

VESTAL, DAVID
PHOTOGRAPHER
b Menlo Park, Calif, Mar 21, 24. *Study:* Art Inst Chicago, 41-44; studied photog with Sid Grossman, 47-55. *Work:* Mus Mod Art, New York; Art Inst Chicago; George Eastman House, Rochester; Mus NMex, Santa Fe; High Mus Art, Atlanta; NY Pub Libr; Metrop Mus, New York; Nat Gallery,

Ottawa; Univ Louisville, Ky; and others. *Exhib:* Solo exhib, Witkin Gallery, New York, 71, East Street Gallery, Grinnell, Iowa, 75, Tom Zimmermann Fine Arts, New Hope, Pa, 85, Galeria del Bosque, Guadalajara, Mex, 87 & Daytona Beach Community Col, Fla, 89; Photographic Crossroads: The Photo League, Nat Gallery Can, Ottawa, Int Ctr Photog, New York Mus Fine Arts, Houston & Minneapolis Inst Arts, 78; The Great West: Real/Ideal, Univ Colo, Boulder, 79 & Smithsonian Inst Travelling Exhib; New York Sch, Corcoran Gallery, Washington, DC, 85. *Pos:* Contrib ed, Popular Photog, 75-86 & Darkroom Tech, 89- *Teaching:* pvt instr photog, 56-; vis artist, Art Inst Chicago, 72-73; instr, Parsons Sch Design, 84-, Sch Visual Arts, 86- & Pratt Inst, 87- *Awards:* Guggenheim Fel, 66 & 73-74. *Bibliog:* David Vestal, Photog Ann, 62; Vision and Expression, 69; David Vestal, Photog Ann, 76. *Mem:* Artists Equity. *Media:* Black and White. *Res:* Craft, history and esthetics of black and white photography. *Publ:* Articles in Popular Photog, Camera 35, Infinity & others, 62-; ed, US Camera Annual 1971, 70; ed, Leica Manual, 72; auth, The Craft of Photography, 75 & The Art of Black-and-White Enlarging, Harper & Row, 84; non-newsletter, Grump, 88. *Dealer:* Robert Mann Gallery 72 E 76th St New York NY 10021. *Mailing Add:* PO Box 309 Bethlehem CT 06751

VEVERS, TABITHA
PAINTER
b Mt Kisco, NY, May 4, 57. *Study:* Skowhegan Sch Painting & Sculpture, Maine, 78; Yale Univ, New Haven, Conn, BA(cum laude), 78. *Work:* LaSalle Univ Art Mus, Philadelphia; McNay Art Inst, San Antonio, Tex; Provincetown Art Asn & Mus, Mass. *Comn:* Three large oil paintings (with Josh Winer), Babson Col, Wellesley, Mass, 83. *Exhib:* Art--Made in the USA (auth, catalog), Stadtische Galerie Regensburg, Ger, 88; Contemporary Provincetown (auth, catalog), Pac Design Ctr, West Hollywood, Calif, 89; Homage to Walte Chrysler, Katzen-Brown Gallery, New York, 89; Crosscurrents: The New Generation (auth, catalog), E Hampton Ctr Contemp Arts, NY, 90; Collector's Show, McNay Art Inst, San Antonio, 91; and others. *Collections Arranged:* Couples, Words and Pictures, 86, Laughter and Tears: a Show of Emotion, 88, Allegory, 89, Young Artists, 89, Provincetown Art Asn & Mus, Mass. *Pos:* Bd mem, Provincetown Art Asn & Mus, 85-91, cur, 86-91. *Awards:* MacDowell Colony Fel, Peterborough, NH, 83; VA Ctr Creative Arts Fel, Sweet Brair, Va, 86 & 91. *Media:* Oil. *Dealer:* Kraushaar Galleries 724 Fifth Ave New York NY 10019. *Mailing Add:* PO Box 30 Provincetown MA 02657

VEVERS, TONY
PAINTER, EDUCATOR
b London, Eng, May 20, 26; US citizen. *Study:* Yale Univ, BA, 50; Accad Belle Arti, Florence, Italy, 50-51; Hans Hofmann Sch, New York, 52-53. *Work:* Isaac Delgado Mus, New Orleans; Univ Mass, Amherst; Purdue Univ, Lafayette, Ind; Chrysler Mus, Norfolk, Va; J H Hirshhorn Mus, Washington DC; Metrop Mus, NY. *Exhib:* One-man shows, Roko Gallery, 65, Babcock Galleries, 69, Artist's Space Gallery, 76, New York & Contemp Art Workshop, Chicago, 84; one-man retrospective, Lafayette Art Mus, 86. *Teaching:* Lectr painting, Univ NC, Greensboro, 63-64; prof painting & art hist, Purdue Univ, Lafayette, 64-88, prof emer, 88-; vis staff, Fine Arts Work Ctr, Provincetown, Mass, 70-71, consult, 71-76. *Awards:* Grants, Nat Endowment Arts, 66 & Purdue Univ, 70; New England Painting & Sculpture Prize, 71. *Mem:* Col Art Asn; Art Asn Provincetown (vpres, 71-). *Media:* Acrylic, Oil. *Publ:* Auth, Alvin Ross, 7/78, The Sun Gallery, 7/81 & Expressionism, 7/85; The Beginnings of the Provincetown Art Association and Museum, 8/90 Provincetown Art Asn. *Dealer:* Long Point Gallery Provincetown MA 02657. *Mailing Add:* 250 Bradford St Provincetown MA 02657

VEZYS, GINTAUTAS
PUBLISHER, COLLECTOR
b Kaunas, Lithuania, Feb 23, 26, US citizen. *Study:* Ill Inst Technol, BSME, 56. *Exhib:* Lithuanian Bookplates, George Williams Col, Downer's Grove, Ill, 74, Univ Mich, Ann Arbor, 74, Balzekas Mus Lithuanian Culture, Chicago, 74, Chicago Main Pub Libr, Ill, 74 & M K Čiurlionis Art Gallery, Chicago, 75; Contemp Lithuanian bookplates, Univ Colo, 76 & Galerija, Chicago, 80. *Pos:* Pres, A M & M Publ, 76- *Bibliog:* Vladas Ramojus (auth), Books, authors and second prohibition of printing, Draugas, 7/17/76; Don Anderson (auth), Lithuanian bookplates, Lituanus, No 4, winter 80; Interview with Gintautas Vėžys, Akiračiai, No 10, 11/82. *Mem:* Am Soc Bkplate Collectors & Designers; Exlibristen, Denmark. *Collection:* Lithuanian, Latvian & Estonian bookplates; ancient maps; medals; coins. *Publ:* Auth, Lietuviškas ekslibris šiandien, Aidai, No 2, 82; Lietuvos Knygos Ženklai 1518-1918, Bookplates in the News, 7/85. *Mailing Add:* 7338 S Sacramento Ave Chicago IL 60629

VICENTE, ESTEBAN
PAINTER
b Turegano, Spain, Jan 20, 03; US citizen. *Study:* Acad Belles Artes, Madrid, Spain; Parsons Sch Design, hon degree, 84. *Work:* Whitney Mus Am Art, Mus Mod Art & Metrop Mus Art, New York; Nat Collection Fine Arts, Smithsonian Inst, Washington, DC; San Francisco Mus Fine Arts; Los Angeles Co Mus Art; Tate Gallery, London; Guggenheim Mus, New York; Yale Univ; and others. *Exhib:* Mus Mod Art, New York; Guggenheim Mus, New York; Art Inst Chicago; Inst Contemp Art, Boston; Carnegie Int, Pittsburgh; Whitney Mus Am Art Biennial, 50-64; Group shows, Metrop Mus, Mus Mod Art, Whitney Mus Am Art, New York; Berry Hill Gallery, New York, 89; Theo Gallery, Barcelona & Madrid, 90; Parish Mus, South Hampton, NY, 90; Salon de los 16, Palacio de Velazquez, El Retiro, Spain, 91; one man shows, Berry-Hill Galleries, New York, Louis Newman Galleries, Beverly Hills, Calif, Guild Hall Mus, E Hampton, NY & Palacio Lozoya, Segovia, Spain, 92. *Teaching:* Instr art, Black Mountain Col, 48; instr art, Univ Calif, Berkeley, 54 & 58, NY Univ, 59-69, Yale Univ, 60-61 & Univ Calif, Los Angeles, 62; artist-in-residence, Des Moines Art Ctr, 65, Princeton Univ, 65-66 & 69-72 & Honolulu Acad Fine Arts, 69; instr, New York Studio Sch, 65-86; instr art, Univ Wash, Seattle, 72. *Awards:* Am Acad Design Awards, 83 & 84; Gold Medal, Am Inst Art, 84; Gold Medal of Honor in the Arts, Govt of Spain, 91. *Bibliog:* John Ashberry (auth), article in Art News, 5/72; Theodore Woolf (auth), article, Christian Sci Monitor, 5/83; Carol Strickland (auth), For Vicente, at 89, No End to Maturing, NY Times, 15, 4/26/92. *Media:* Oil, Collage. *Dealer:* Gruenebaum Gallery 38 E 57th St New York NY 10022; Yares Gallery Bishop Lane Scottsdale AZ. *Mailing Add:* 1 W 67th St New York NY 10023

VICK, CONNIE R
CONSULTANT
b Philadelphia, Pa, Oct 17, 47. *Study:* Pa State Univ, BFA, 69; Cornell Univ, 70; Philadelphia Col Art, 72. *Pos:* Owner & dir, Vick Gallery, Philadelphia, Pa, 73-79; lectr painting, Neumann Ctr, Philadelphia, 76-80 & Manor Jr Col, 80-84; asst to dir, Fischbach Gallery, New York, 82-84; corp art adv, Vick Corp Art Adv, 84- *Mailing Add:* Vick Corp Art Adv 8204 Cedar Rd Elkins Park PA 19117

VICKERS, RUSS(ELL GERON)
PAINTER, CONCEPTUAL ARTIST
b Paris, Tex, Oct 30, 23. *Study:* Famous Artist Course, 56. *Work:* Favell Mus-Klamath Falls, Ore; Leanin Tree Gallery, Boulder, Colo; All State Insurance Co, Northbrook, Ill; Mazda Great Lakes, Grand Rapids, Mich; Century 21-Rocky Mountains, Salt Lake City, Utah. *Awards:* Western Heritage Award, Favell Mus, 81. *Bibliog:* Elizabeth Rigby (auth), Paint westerns, Southeast Art, 7-8/75; John Diffily (auth), Painter of the historic west, Am Artist, 7/82. *Media:* Oil. *Dealer:* May Gallery 6166 N Scotts Dale Rd Scottsdale AZ 85253 & 34505 N Scottsdale Rd #29 Scottsdale AZ 85262. *Mailing Add:* 549 E Sherman Lebanon OR 97355

VICKERY, CHARLES BRIDGEMAN
PAINTER
b Hinsdale, Ill, July 16, 13. *Study:* Art Inst Chicago; Am Acad Fine Art, Chicago; also with Ben Stahl. *Work:* Univ Club & Union League Club, Chicago; Royal Acad, London. *Exhib:* Rockport Art Asn, Mass; Union League Club; Ackerman Gallery, London; Springfield Mus, Ill; Palette & Chisel Acad, Chicago. *Awards:* Diamond Medal Award, Palette & Chisel Acad, 68; Waters of the World Prize, NShore Art Asn, Gloucester, 70; Union League Club Prize, 72. *Bibliog:* Eleanor Jewett (auth), article, Chicago Tribune, 45; C J Bulliet (auth), article, Chicago Daily News, 8/51. *Mem:* Palette & Chisel Acad (dir, 67-69); Rockport Art Asn; NShore Art Asn. *Media:* Oil, Acrylic. *Dealer:* W Russell Button Gallery 955 Center St Douglas MI 49406; Mystic Mus Marine Gallery Mystic CT. *Mailing Add:* 4533 Wolf Rd Western Springs IL 60558

VICKREY, ROBERT REMSEN
PAINTER
b New York, NY, Aug 20, 26. *Study:* Yale Univ, BA; Art Students League; Yale Sch Fine Arts, BFA; also with Kenneth Hayes Miller & Reginald Marsh. *Work:* Nat Mus Am Art, Corcoran Gallery Art, Washington, DC; Metrop Mus Art, Whitney Mus Am Art, New York; Butler Inst Am Art; and 50 others. *Comn:* Covers for Time Mag; also portraits & bk jackets. *Exhib:* Whitney Mus Am Art; 50 one-man shows, Santa Barbara Mus, Calif; Mus Fine Arts, Houston; Neuberger Mus, Purchase, NY; Chrysler Mus, Norfolk, Va; Lyrical Realist Traveling Exhib, 82-83. *Awards:* Am Audubon Artists; Int Hallmark Competition, Windsor; Newton Mem Award. *Mem:* Am Watercolor Soc; Audubon Artists; Nat Acad Design. *Media:* Tempera. *Publ:* Coauth, New Techniques in Egg Tempera & auth, Robert Vickery--Artist at Work, Watson-Guptill, The Affable Curmudgeon, Parnassus. *Dealer:* Kennedy Galleries 40 W 57th St New York NY. *Mailing Add:* Box 445 Orleans MA 02653

VICTOR, MARY O'NEILL
MUSEUM DIRECTOR EMERITUS
b Boston, Mass, Dec 27, 24. *Study:* Boston Univ, 43-47. *Collections Arranged:* American Watercolors 1850-1972, 72; Art of Ancient Orthodoxy, 72; Where the Action Is (sports in art), 73; Art of the Old West, 74; Chop Art: American Motorcycle Design, 75; Cleveland Woodward: Painter by God's Good Light, 76; Southern Antiques and Folk Art, 76; Jewish Art: A Continuing Heritage, 77; Wildlife Art: American Sculpture, 77; The Ripening of American Art: Duveneck and Chase, 79; Five Thousand Years of Dynasty Art, 80; The Art of Peter Carl Faberge, 81; Holography 82: 5000 Years of Art, 82. *Pos:* Registr, Mus Fine Arts, Boston, 64-69; dir, Fine Arts Mus of the South, Mobile, 69-86; retired. *Mem:* Am Asn Mus; Am Fedn Arts. *Collection:* Nineteenth and twentieth century American paintings, sculpture and graphics; contemporary crafts; Miller collection of Oriental & European art. *Mailing Add:* 7153 Airport Blvd Mobile AL 36608

VIDAL, FRANCISCO FERNANDEZ
PAINTER, SCULPTOR
b Barranquilla, Columbia, July 22, 46. *Study:* Univ Altantico, Barranquilla, Columbia, 61-63, Art Students League, 69-71. *Work:* Mus del Barrio, New York; Fine Arts of Ancient Land, New York. *Exhib:* Solo show, Mus Alternative, New York, 85; Bass Art Mus, Miami, Fla, 88; Los Angeles Munic Art Gallery, Calif, 88; Centro Colombo Americano, Bogota, Columbia, 88; First Festival of Art, Barranquilla, Columbia, 89; E Hampton Ctr for Contemp Art, New York, 90; Mus Contemp Art, Monterrey. *Teaching:* Prof drawing,

Col Barranquilla for Ladies, 63-68. *Awards:* Scholarship, Print-Making Workshop, 83; Selected for 84/86 Nat Studio Prog; Fel painting, Mid Atlantic Arts Found, Baltimore, Md, 92. *Bibliog:* Fred Stern (auth), Artists with Latin American Roots, Mizue Art Mag, Tokyo, Japan, 89; Susana Torreulla Leval (auth), Identity and Freedom, Decade Show, 90. *Media:* Oil on Canvas, Miscellaneous Media. *Publ:* Contribr, Carnival on New York, 89 & En la brecha de la image, 90, El Tiempo, Columbia; article, Experimentation in still life, NY Times, 5/90; contribr, From the studio, East Hampton Star, 5/90; Miami Herald, 7/92. *Mailing Add:* 143-16 Barclay Ave #2G New York NY 11355

VIDAL, HAHN
PAINTER
b Hamburg, Ger, Mar 11, 19; US citizen. *Study:* With Eduardo Couce Vidal. *Work:* Eduardo Sivori, Mus Artes Plasticas, Buenos Aires, Arg; Juan B Castagnino, Mus Cuidad Rosario, Arg; Mus Seattle, Wash; Mus Mobile, Ala; Hist Mus Taiwan, China; and others. *Comn:* Hahn Vidal Rm, Boca Raton Hotel & Club, Fla, 69. *Exhib:* Okla Mus Art, Oklahoma City, 70 & 72; Grand Cent Art Gallery, 70 & 73; Dayton, Ohio, 70 & 73; Arvest, Boston, 74 & 77; Valencia, Spain, 75, 77 & 79; Wichita Art Asn, Kans, 78; Castellon, Spain, 78; Charles & Emma Frye Art Mus, Seattle, Wash; Valencia Castellon, Spain, 84, 86 & 88. *Mem:* Salmagundi Club; Soc Illusr. *Media:* Oil. *Mailing Add:* 345 W 58th St New York NY 10019

VIELEHR, WILLIAM RALPH
SCULPTOR
b Chicago, Ill, Jan 6, 45. *Study:* Univ Colo, 63-66; Colo State Univ, BFA, 69. *Work:* Crossroads Mall, Boulder, Colo; Chicago Mus Contemp Art; Prudential Bache, Boulder, Colo; Northern Ill Univ; Cherry Creek Plaza, Denver. *Comn:* Interaction, Boulder Reservoir, Colo, 86; Digital, Colorado Springs, Colo, 86. *Exhib:* Joslyn Art Mus, Omaha, Nebr, 72 & 74; Denver Art Mus, 72; Allrich Gallery, San Francisco, 75; Attitudes Gallery, Denver, 75; Sebastian Moore Gallery, Denver, 78; N Am Sculpture Exhib, Golden, Colo, 80; Shidoni, 81; Boulder Sculpture Symp, Colo, 82; Form at Fiddlers Green, 83. *Pos:* Dir, Form Sculpture, 81-; juror, Leonardo Di Vinci Award, 84. *Teaching:* Vis artist sculpture workshop, Jefferson Co Schs, 71-72 & Colo State Univ, 73; speaker, Art Week, Univ Colo, Colorado Springs, 88; workshops, Boulder Pub Schs, 89. *Awards:* Purchase Prize, Designer Craftsmen Asn, 72; City Arts Grant, Boulder, Colo, 80. *Bibliog:* Boulder Sculpture Symposium, 82; Sculpture in the Gardens, Denver Botanic Gardens, 83. *Mem:* Bully Boys Beer Club (pres 77-); Loon Rarting (rear admiral 85-90). *Media:* Cast Bronze & Aluminum. *Mailing Add:* 240 31st St Boulder CO 80303

VIERA, CHARLES DAVID
EDUCATOR, PAINTER
b Dartmouth, Mass, Feb 21, 50. *Study:* Swain Sch Design, BFA, 72; Skowhegan Sch Painting & Sculpture; Brooklyn Col Grad Sch, with Phillip Pearlstein, MFA, 74. *Work:* Pvt collection of A Hess, New York. *Comn:* Murals, Am Renaissance Festival, Brooklyn Mus, 79. *Exhib:* Brooklyn 1976, Brooklyn Mus; Nat Arts Club, New York, 77; 153 Ann, Nat Acad, New York, 78; solo shows, Animal Drawings, Long Island Univ, 80 & Paintings, Nassau Co Mus, 81; retrospective, Charles Viera 1972-1982, Brooklyn Mus Art Sch, 82; Works on Paper, Adam Gimbel Gallery, New York, 83. *Pos:* Coordr exhibs, Long Island Univ, Brooklyn, NY, 84 & 85, coordr fine arts, continuing educ prog, 86. *Teaching:* Instr painting & drawing, Brooklyn Mus Art Sch, 75- & Parsons Sch Design, 79-; assoc prof, Long Island Univ, 79- *Bibliog:* Show of contrast, Phoenix, New York, 76; Inmates try art, 76 & Performers recreate art, 79, New York Times. *Media:* Mixed. *Mailing Add:* Parsons Sch Design 2 W 13th St New York NY 10011

VIERA, RICARDO
PAINTER, PRINTMAKER
b Ciego de Avila, Cuba, Dec 15, 45; US citizen. *Study:* Sch of the Mus of Fine Arts, Boston, dipl, 72; Tufts Univ, BFA, 73; RI Sch of Design, Providence, MFA, 74. *Work:* Allentown Art Mus, Pa; Tel Aviv Mus, Israel; Canton Art Inst, Ohio; Cleveland Mus; Fed Soc Arts & Humanities, Lagos, Nigeria; and others. *Exhib:* One-man shows, Inst Contemp Art, Boston, 73 & Canton Art Inst, Ohio, 80; Transitions in Art, Boston Mus of Fine Arts, 77; The Kadishman Connection, Israel Mus, Jerusalem, 79; Instituto de Cultura Puertorriquena, San Juan, 81; Alfred O Deshong Mus, Chester, Pa, 82; and many others. *Collections Arranged:* American Figure Drawing, Lehigh Univ & Victorian Col of Art, Melbourne, Australia, 76; Intentions & Techniques (auth, catalog), 79, 26th Ann Contemp Am Art Exhib (auth, catalog), traveling, 81 & Computer Art (auth, catalog), 82, Wilson Gallery, Lehigh Univ, Bethlehem, Pa; Michael Smith, Landscape Photography (auth, catalog), traveling, 81; and others. *Pos:* dir & cur, Lehigh Univ Art Galleries, 74-, chmn pro-tempore, 77-78; community arts coordr & discussion leader, Baum Sch Art, Allentown, Pa, 79-; consult, Cuban Mus Art & Cult, Miami, 81-; bd dirs, Pa Citizens Arts, 79-, ARTS, Washington, DC; bd dirs, Valley Art Coun. *Teaching:* Instr, Lehigh Univ, 74-78, assoc prof, 78. *Awards:* Elizabeth H Bartol Scholarship, Boston Mus of Fine Arts Sch, 71-72; Cintas fel, Cintas Found, Inst of Int Educ, 74-75; Mellon Found Grant, 78-80; and others. *Bibliog:* Ricardo Viera/Illustraciones Enlace, Nueva Revista Hispanoamericana, 76; Keith Schneider (auth), Capturing the intensity of life, Times Leader, Wilkes-Barre, Pa, 9/13/79; Norma Niurka (auth), A box of surprises, Miami Herald, 10/7/81. *Mem:* Pa Counc Arts; Print Club Philadelphia; Am Asn of Mus; Am Asn Mus/NEastern Conf. *Media:* Oil, Acrylic; Enamel Spray, Oil Crayon. *Publ:* Illusr, Dr Fernando Ortiz, auth, Los Negros Brujos, Ed Universal, Miami, Fla, 73; illusr, Libro Quinto de Lectura Gramatica y Ortografia, Leal & Sanchez Boudy, Miami, 75; illusr, Introduccion al Estudio de la Civilizacion Espanola, Barroso, Miami, 76; auth, Arte Visual en la Palabra de Lydia Cabrera, Festschriften/Ed Universal, 77; auth, From Limestones to aluminum plate lithography, RI Sch of Design Bull, 77. *Dealer:* Forma Hispanic Arts Dealers 305 Alcazar Coral Gables FL 33134. *Mailing Add:* Art Gallery Lehigh Univ Chandler #17 Bethlehem PA 18015

VIERTHALER, BONNIE
COLLAGE ARTIST, SCULPTOR
Study: Univ Wis, BS(art educ), 63; Univ Ga, MA(weaving & fabric design), 72. *Work:* Seven pieces, City of Seattle, Seattle First Nat Bank; IBM, White Plains, NY; Prudential Insurance Co, New York. *Comn:* Wearable art, Seattle Aquarium; sculpture, Seattle Arts Comn, 79; Stolen Art, 11 pieces from the Joy of Smoking Exhib, Mountainside Hosp, NJ, fall 89. *Exhib:* Polly Friedlander Gallery, Seattle, 75-76; Seattle Art Mus, 76; Foster White Gallery, Seattle, 78; Smithsonian Inst traveling exhibition, 79-80; Deer Isle Artists Asn, Maine, 85; traveling exhib, Joy of Smoking-An Antidote to Cigarette Advertising, 86-; Russell Senate Bldg Rotunda, Washington, DC, 86; Sch, Hosp, Legislative Hearings, Health Conf & Dr Conv, 87- *Pos:* Dir, The Badvertizing Inst, 85. *Teaching:* Lectr hist fabrics, Emory Univ, Atlanta, 73-74; instr weaving, Green River Community Col, 74, Factory of Visual Arts, Seattle, 76-77. *Awards:* Craftsman's Fel, 77, Visual Arts Grant, 78, Artist-in-residence Grant, 79, Nat Endowment Arts; Giraffe Award, 90; STAT Achievement Award, Stop Teenage Addiction to Tobacco. *Bibliog:* Magtime, KCTS-TV, Seattle, 76; Window to the World, KOMO-TV, Seattle; Monitor New England, Monitor Radio, 86. *Media:* Magazine Ads. *Publ:* New Jersey J Med. *Mailing Add:* 195 Congress St Portland ME 04101

VIGIL, VELOY JOSEPH
PAINTER, PRINTMAKER
b Denver, Colo, Mar 5, 31. *Study:* Colo Inst Art, Denver Art Acad, Denver. *Work:* Colorado Springs Fine Arts Ctr, Colo; Heard Mus, Phoenix, Ariz; Armour Dial Res Ctr, Scottsdale, Ariz; Phoenix Art Mus; Am Greetings Corp, Cleveland, Ohio. *Comn:* Painting, Jesuit Preparatory Sch, Dallas, Tex, 85; Cheyenne Mt Conf Ctr, Colo Springs, 85; Marriott Hotel, San Antonio, Tex, 88. *Exhib:* Nat Watercolor Soc Ann, Laguna Beach Art Mus, Calif, 67; Am Watercolor Soc, Nat Acad Galleries, New York, 68; Indian Arts & Crafts Exhib, Heard Mus, Phoenix, Ariz, 76; Smithsonian Inst, 82; Monotype exhib, Ont Mus Art, 86; Retrospective exhib, Millicent Rogers Mus, Taos, NMex, 88. *Collections Arranged:* Nat Watercolor Soc Travel Show, Embassy of Switz, 72 & Va Mus Fine Arts, Richmond, 73-74; Contemporary Indian Artist, Smithsonian Inst, 82. *Awards:* Winslow Homer Award, Springfield Art Mus, Mo, 70; Franklin Murphy Award, Ankrum Gallery, Los Angeles, Calif, 72; Avery Mem Award, Heard Mus Guild, Phoenix, 76. *Bibliog:* Lisa Sherman (auth), article, Arts Mag, 9/83; Don H Jones (auth), article, Artist, Santa Fean Mag, 9/83; Patricia Black (auth), Breaking Free, Collectors Mart, 9/83; Bruce Robb (auth), article, Southwest Art Mag, 4/86; Southwest Profile Mag, 9/89. *Mem:* Nat Watercolor Soc; Watercolor USA Hon Soc; and others. *Media:* Watercolor, Acrylic. *Dealer:* Gallery Elena Taos NM. *Mailing Add:* c/o Gallery Elena 119 C Bent St Taos NM 87571

VIGNES, MICHELLE MARIE
EDUCATOR, PHOTOGRAPHER
Work: Affaire Culturelles, Bibliot Nat, Mus Carnavalet, Paris, France; Centre Photographie, Geneva, Switzerland. *Exhib:* Trail of Broken Treaties, Oakland Mus, Calif, 71-73; Les Concierges, French Inst, New York, 76; The Blues, FNAC, 83 & Galarie Agathe Gaillard, 86, Paris, France; Jazz & Photography, Mus Mod Art, Paris, France, 83; Retrospective, Ctr Photog, Geneva, Switz, 87, FNAC, Paris, 90; Vision Gallery, San Francisco, 91- *Pos:* Instr doc photog, Univ Calif, 78-, San Francisco, Calif, 85-87; Paris Univ, France, 88-92; instr photog & ethnology, Acad Arts, San Francisco, 90-92. *Awards:* Media Alliance Award for Photogr of the Year, 83. *Mem:* Media Alliance (bd mem, 79-85); Camerawork (bd mem, 83-87); Mother Jones Int Fund for Doc Photog (founder). *Publ:* Auth, The Blues, North Beach Press, 85; Oakland Blues, Ed Marval, 90. *Dealer:* Galerie Agathe Gaillard 4 rue du Par Louis Philippe Paris 75004 France; Agence Rapho 8 rue d'Alger Paris 75001. *Mailing Add:* 654 28th St San Francisco CA 94131

VIGTEL, GUDMUND
DIRECTOR EMERITUS
b July 9, 25; US citizen. *Study:* Isaac Grunewald's Sch Art, Stockholm, 43-44; Univ Ga, BFA, 52, MFA, 53. *Collections Arranged:* The New Tradition, 63; The Beckoning Land, 71; The Modern Image, 72; The Düsseldorf Academy & the Americans, 73; A Retrospective, Harvey K Littleton, 84; Art in Berlin, 1815-1989, 89-90. *Pos:* Admin asst, Corcoran Gallery Art, 54-57, asst to dir, 57-61, asst dir, 61-63; dir, High Mus Art, 63-91. *Awards:* Chevalier des Arts et Lettres, 86; Order of Merit, First Class, Fed Repub Germany, 89; Lifetime Achievement Award, Ga Asn Mus & Galleries, 90. *Mem:* Am Asn Mus; Asn Art Mus Dirs. *Mailing Add:* High Mus Art 1280 Peachtree St NE Atlanta GA 30309

VILLA, CARLOS
PAINTER
Study: San Francisco Art Inst, BFA, 61; Mills Col, MFA, 63. *Exhib:* de Young Mus, San Francisco, 72; Whitney Mus Am Art Ann, New York, 72; San Francisco Mus, 74; San Francisco Art Inst, 76; Calif Show: The Mod Era, San Francisco Mus, Calif & Nat Collection Fine Arts, Washington, DC, 76-77; Calif Bay Area Art--Update, Huntsville Mus Art, Ala, 77; New in the Seventies, Univ Tex, Austin, 77; and many others. *Teaching:* Asst, Mills Col, 61-63; asst, Studio 1, Oakland, Calif, 61-63; instr, Telegraph Hill Neighborhood Ctr, Urban Arts, San Francisco, 69-70; chmn inter-dept

studies, San Francisco Art Inst, currently; asst prof art, Calif State Univ, Sacramento, currently. *Awards:* Adeline Kent Award, San Francisco Art Inst, 73; Nat Endowment Arts Grant, 73. *Bibliog:* Article, 12/70 & Emily Wasserman (auth), article, 1/71, Artforum. *Mailing Add:* San Francisco Art Inst Col 800 Chestnut St San Francisco CA 94133

VILLA, MARIO
ART DEALER, ARCHITECT
b Managua, Nicaragua, Mar 16, 56. *Study:* Univ New Orleans, BA, 77, Tulane Univ, archit lic, 81. *Work:* Bellas Artes & Nat Art Expo, Managua, Nicaragua. *Comn:* Rotunda Condominium Complex, Entrance Gate, Warehouse Dist, New Orleans, La, 89; Princess Caroline Monaco, Dining Rm, Principality Monaco, 89-90; Karl Lagerfield, bedroom, Rome; Country House, LeMee, Monte Carlo; Villa Karl, Hamburg; LeRocMer, Monaco, 89-90; sconce design, front entrance Contemp Arts Ctr New Orleans, Artists & Architects Collab, New Orleans, La, 90; renovation, Ocshner Clinic Plastic Surgery Dept, New Orleans, La, 91; and others. *Exhib:* Odyssey Ball, New Orleans Mus Art, 85; Art for Arts Sake, Contemp Arts Ctr, New Orleans, La, 85 & 86; The Useful Arts, Contemp Arts Ctr, New Orleans, La, 87; Art in Bloom, New Orleans Mus Art, 88; Nat Convention, Am Inst Architects, New York, 88; and others. *Collections Arranged:* Helena Rubenstein Religious Collection, Graphic Editions, New Orleans, La, 79. *Pos:* Dir, Graphic Editions, New Orleans, La, 81; pres/owner, Mario Villa Inc, Beverly Hills, Calif; co-owner/dir bd, Mario Villa, Chicago, Ill; pres/owner, Mario Villa Inc, New Orleans, La, currently. *Teaching:* Prof archit, Nat Univ, Nicaragua, 75-76. *Awards:* Design 100 Award, Metrop Home, 90 & 92; Apaulso Awards Arts, Aqui New Orleans Bilingual Newsletter, 92; Man Yr Arts, Que Pasa Publ, New Orleans, La, 92; and others. *Bibliog:* Articles, Times Picayune, 79 & States-Item, 82; article, Mario Villa, Beaux Arts Mag, 84 & Times-Picayune, 9/86. *Mem:* Contemp Arts Ctr, New Orleans (bd mem); New Orleans Ballet Asn (bd mem, 92); Newcomb Sch Arts, Tulane Univ (adv bd, 92); Preserv Resource Ctr (hon chmn, 92); Sch Lib Arts, Univ New Orleans (adv bd, 91-); and others. *Media:* Bronze. *Res:* The formation of the British Museum. *Specialty:* Contemporary art. *Collection:* Pre-Columbian Latin America; 16th century Spanish. *Publ:* Auth, New Orleans Neighborhood, Tulane Univ, 81. *Mailing Add:* Mario Villa Gallery 3908 Magazine St New Orleans LA 70115

VILLA, THEODORE B
PAINTER
b Santa Barbara, Calif, Sept 28, 36. *Study:* Santa Barbara City Col, AA, 61; Univ Calif, Santa Barbara, BA, 63, MFA, 74. *Work:* Inst Am Indian Mus, Santa Fe, NMex; Calif State Univ, Los Angeles; Univ Gallery, Univ Calif, Santa Barbara; Millicent Rogers Mus, Taos, NMex. *Exhib:* Drawings USA, Minn Mus Art, Minneapolis, 77; Purdue Univ, Lafayette, Ind, 79; solo exhibs, Sun Valley Ctr Arts, Ketchum, Idaho, 83, Taylor Mus, Colorado Springs Fine Arts Ctr, Colo, 87 & Mus Inst Am Indian Art, Santa Fe, NMex, 88, Millicent Rogers Mus, Taos, NMex, 90; Innovations-New Expressions, Heard Mus, Phoenix, Arix, 83; No Beads, No Trinkets, Palais De Nations, Geneva, Switz, 84; Visage Transcended, Am Indian Contemp Arts, San Francisco, 86; Four Sacred Mountains, 2 year travelling exhib, Ariz Arts Comn, 88-90; Decolonizing The Mind: End of a 500 Year Era, Ctr on Contemp Art, Seattle, Wash, 92. *Teaching:* Instr design-watercolor, Santa Barbara City Col, 75; lectr watercolor, Univ Calif, Santa Barbara, 83-86. *Bibliog:* Charles Clouse (auth), Doubletake, Southwest Art, 2/86. *Media:* Watercolor. *Dealer:* Broschofsky Galleries PO Box 1538 Ketchum ID 83340. *Mailing Add:* 1371 Santa Rita Circle Santa Barbara CA 93109

VILLINSKI, PAUL
PAINTER, SCULPTOR
b York, Maine, May 28, 60. *Study:* Mass Col Art, 80-82, Cooper Union, 82-84, BFA, 84. *Work:* Jones, Day, Reavis & Pogue, Attys, Washington, DC; Cleary, Gottlieb, Steen & Hamilton, Attys, New York; ADP Corp, Chicago; John A Levin Co, New York; Nomura Securities Int, New York. *Comn:* McCann Erickson Co, New York, 90. *Exhib:* P S Gallery, Ogunquit, Maine, 91 & 92; Good Work, The Cooper Union, New York, 92; The Poetics of Utility, Jamaica Arts Ctr, Jamaica, NY, 92; Salon Test Site, Brooklyn, NY, 92; Ten From Queens, Paine Webber Art Gallery, New York, 92; and others. *Teaching:* Adj lectr, LaGuardia Community Col, City Univ New York, Long Island City, 90- *Awards:* Michael S Vivo Prize for Excellence, Cooper Union, 84; Nat Endowment Arts Grant, 87; Agnes Bourne Fel Painting, Djerassi Found, Woodside, Calif, 88. *Bibliog:* John Hertzfeld (auth), Special delivery, Artnews, 11/87; Ann Juried Exhib (catalog), Queen Mus, New York, 87. *Mem:* St Peter's Church Art & Archit, New York (rev comt), 91- *Media:* Oil; All. *Dealer:* Midtown Payson Galleries 745 Fifth Ave New York NY 10151. *Mailing Add:* 9-01 44th Dr Long Island City NY 11101

VINCENT, CLARE
CURATOR, HISTORIAN
b Jersey City, NJ, Aug 30, 35. *Study:* Col William & Mary, AB, 58; Inst Fine Arts, NY Univ, MA, 63; Inst Fine Arts & Metropolitan Mus Art, cert, 63. *Collections Arranged:* A Sure Reckoning, 68, Northern European Clocks in New York Collections, 72, Nineteenth Century French Sculpture, 80, Rodin: The Gates of Hell, 82 & Rodin: The B Gerald Cantor Collection, 86, Metropolitan Mus Art, New York. *Pos:* Asst to cur decorative arts, Cooper Union Mus, 60-61; curatorial asst western European arts, Metropolitan Mus Art, New York, 62-67, asst cur, 67-72, assoc cur European sculpture & decorative arts, 72-; consult to catalogue of antique sci instruments, Adler Planetarium, Chicago, 85- *Mem:* Col Art Asn; Furniture Hist Soc; Antiquarian Horological Soc (vpres Am sect, 77-89). *Res:* European clocks and timekeeping instruments; European metalwork; 19th century European sculpture. *Publ:* John Henry Belter: Manufacturer of all kinds of fine furniture, In: Technological Innovation and the Decorative Arts, Univ Va, 74; coauth, To finance a clock: An example of patronage in the 16th century, In: The Clockwork Universe, Neil Watson, 80; auth, Rodin at the Metropolitan Museum of Art: A History of the Collection, Metrop Mus Art, 81; Renaissance Decorative Arts, Leichtenstein: The Princely Collections, Metrop Mus Art, 85; A Beam Compass by Christoph Trechsler the Elder and the Origin of the Micrometer Screw, Metrop Mus J, Vol 24, 209-222, 89. *Mailing Add:* 326 E 85th St New York NY 10028

VINELLA, RAY (RAIMONDO JOHN)
PAINTER
b Bari, Italy, April 6, 33. *Study:* Art Ctr Col Design, with Lorsor Fietleson, Harry Carmean, John Lagatta & Reynold Brown, BPA, 59, BFA, 68. *Work:* Diamond M Found Mus, Snyder, Tex; Mansato Int, New York; Carlsbad Mus, NMex. *Exhib:* First Exhib Southwest Art, People's Republic China, 81; Mus Native Am Cult, Spokane, Wash, 82; Colo Sch Mines. *Pos:* Art comt, Harvard Found Mus, Taos, NMex. *Teaching:* Instr painting, Taos Acad Fine Art, 71-72 & Taos Art Workshops, 82-; fac dean, Taos Sch Fine Art, 77-78. *Awards:* B Altman Award, 51; Prof Award, Painting Competition, NMex State Fair, 71 & 73. *Bibliog:* Tricia Hurst (auth), The Taos six, Southwest Art, 10/74; Peggy Ridgway (auth), article, Art Gallery, 2/83; Peggi Ridgway (auth), Southwest Art, 3/84; Roberta McIntyre (auth), Western Art Digest, 1-2/86; Nancy Ellis (auth), Southwest Profile, 1/89. *Mem:* Soc Am Impressionists; Monac Art Soc. *Media:* Oil, Egg Tempera. *Publ:* Auth, Masterworks of Impressionism: Arlene Doran Kirkpatrick. *Mailing Add:* c/o Shriver Gallery 401 Passo del Pueblo Norte Taos NM 87571

VINER, FRANK LINCOLN
SCULPTOR, PAINTER
b Worcester, Mass, Aug 9, 37. *Study:* Sch Worcester Art Mus; Yale Univ, Art & Architecture, BFA, 61, MFA, 63. *Work:* Milwaukee Art Ctr, Wis; Whitney Mus Am Art; Brooklyn Mus, NY; Riverside Mus Collection, Rose Art Mus, Waltham, Mass. *Comn:* Yellow Environment, comn Wadsworth Atheneum, Hartford, Conn, 70; Set Costumes, The Queen Stands Guard, comn Bill Jones/Arnic Zane & Co, 87. *Exhib:* Sculpture Ann, Whitney Mus, New York, 69; solo, Frank Lincoln Viner, Picker Art Gallery, Colgate Univ, Hamilton, NY, 76; The Object as Poet, Renwick Gallery Nat Collection Fine Arts, Washington, DC, 77; Current New York, Lowe Art Gallery, Syracuse, NY, 80; Tracking the Marvelous, Grey Art Gallery, New York, 81. *Teaching:* Instr art, All Art Students Sch Vis Arts, 64-74. *Awards:* Nat Endowment Arts Fel, 79. *Bibliog:* Lucy R Lippard (auth), Changing: Essays in Art Criticism, Dutton, 75; Carter Ratcliff (auth), On Contemporary Primitivism, Artforum, Vol 14, No 3, 11/75. *Mailing Add:* PO Box 68 Valley Cottage NY 10989

VIOLA, BILL
VIDEO ARTIST
b New York, NY, Jan 25, 51. *Study:* Syracuse Univ, BFA, 73. *Work:* Mus Modern Art, New York; Ctr Georges Pompidou, Paris, France; San Francisco Mus Mod Art; Mus Für Moderne Kunst, Frankfurt, Ger; Mus Contemp Art, Los Angeles. *Exhib:* Biennial Exhib, Whitney Mus Am Art, New York, 75-87; solo exhibs, Mus Modern Art, New York, 79, Mus d'Art Moderne de la Ville de Paris (with catalog), France, 83, Moderna Museet, Stockholm, Sweden, 85, San Francisco Mus Modern Art, 85, Mus Mod Art (with catalog), New York, 87 & Contemp Arts Mus (with catalog), Houston, Tex, 88; The Luminous Image, Stedelijk Mus, Amsterdam, Neth, 84; Summer 1985 (with catalog), Mus Contemp Art, Los Angeles, 85; Carnegie Int, Carnegie Mus Art, Pittsburgh, 88. *Awards:* Rockefeller Found Video Artist Fel, 82-83; John Simon Guggenheim Mem Fel Video Art, 85-86; John D & Catherine T MacArthur Found Award, 89. *Bibliog:* Raymond Bellour (auth), An interview with Bill Viola, October, No 34, fall, 85; Anne-Marie Duguet (auth), Les videos de Bill Viola: Une Poetique de l'espace-temps, Parachute, 12/86-2/87; Michael Nash (auth), Bill Viola's Re-visions of Mortality, High Performance, No, 87. *Media:* Videotapes, Video Installations. *Publ:* Auth, Sight Unseen-Enlighted squirrels & fatal experiments, No 4, spring 82 & Will there be condominiums in data space?, No 5, fall 82, Video 80; contribr, Video: A retrospective 1974-1984, Long Beach Mus Art, Calif, 84; Dan Lander & Micah Lexier (eds), Sound by Artists, The sound of one line scanning, Art Metropole, Toronto & Walter Phillips Gallery, Banff, 90. *Dealer:* Donald Young Gallery 2107 Third Ave Seattle WA 98121. *Mailing Add:* 283 Argonne Ave Long Beach CA 90803-1743

VIRET, MARGARET MARY (MRS FRANK IVO)
PAINTER, INSTRUCTOR
b New York, NY, Apr 18, 13. *Study:* Terry Art Sch; Miami Art Sch; Miami Art Ctr; Univ Miami; also with Dong Kingman, Eliot O'Hara, Xavier Gonzalez, Eugene Massin, Georges Sellier & Jack Amoroso; plus many other prominent instrs. *Work:* Norton Gallery; Lowe Art Gallery. *Comn:* Cuba Home Scene, Miami Woman's Club, 63; ballet scenes, Pauline Hill Co, Miami, 65; Spring Flowers (watercolors), Fla C of C, 69; Florida Everglades Scene for Wall, Capt Gene, 70; Florida Flowers for Wall, Laura, Pompano Beach, Fla. *Exhib:* Tampa Art Mus, 55; Fla Fedn Art, 55-56; Bass Art Mus, Miami Beach, 55-57, 62 & 63; Lowe Art Gallery, 60, 62 & 70; American Contemporary, Four Arts Soc, 65; plus others. *Pos:* Chmn, Dade Co Art, 56-58; art dir, Fla Fedn Women's Clubs, 56-63; pres, Laramore Rader Poetry Group, Miami, 70-72; art dir, Miami Women's Club, 67-, dir fine arts, 77-78. *Teaching:* Instr art, Miami Art League, 55-56; instr art adult classes, YWCA & YMCA, Miami, 63-68 & Dade Co Schs, 68- *Awards:* Best Watercolor for Flowers, Fla Fedn Women's Clubs, 61; Best Watercolor for Marine, Bass Art Mus, 62; Best Watercolor for Flowers, Burdines Coral Gables Art Club, 63. *Bibliog:* Irene Gramling (auth), Sphinx, Franklin Press, 65 & 66; Edna

Chauser (auth), Cultural Alliance, Chase, 71; featured in Her Story--Julia's Daughters, 80. *Mem:* Fla Fedn Art (vpres, 56-58); hon mem Hibiscus Fine Arts Guild; hon mem Allied Arts NMiami; life mem Miami Palette Club; trustee Miami Art League; and others. *Media:* Multimedia. *Mailing Add:* 294 NE 55th Terr Miami FL 33137

VIRGONA, HANK (HENRY P)
PAINTER, PRINTMAKER
b Brooklyn, NY, Oct 24, 29. *Study:* Pratt Inst Evening Sch, 54. *Work:* Metrop Mus Art, New York; Arch Am Art, Smithsonian Inst; Mus City New York; Wichita Mus, Kans; Pub Libr, New York. *Exhib:* New American Still Life, Westmoreland Co Mus, Pa, 79; The Presidency: Relevant & Irrelevant Traveling Exhib, 80; West and the Law Traveling Exhib, 80-82; Prints USA, Pratt Inst, New York, 82; Subtle observations-Subway Portraits by Hank Virgona, Transit Mus, Brooklyn, NY, 92. *Pos:* Co-founder, 41 Union Sq Open Studios, 80- *Teaching:* Instr etching, pvt lessons, 82-; instr drawing, Pratt Graphic Ctr, New York. *Awards:* Gold Medal, Soc Illusr, 70; Purchase Prizes, Nat Acad Art, 79 & Prints USA, Pratt Inst, 82. *Bibliog:* Ellyn Bloom (auth), Hank Virgona: The art of social satire, Am Artist Mag, 73. *Mem:* Artists Equity, New York. *Media:* Watercolor; Etching. *Publ:* Auth, The System Works! The Etchings and Random Notes of Hank Virgona, Da Capo Press, 77; illusr, Ivan the Terrible, Ivan the Fool, G Putnam Sons, 80. *Dealer:* Dorsky Gallery 578 Broadway New York NY 10012. *Mailing Add:* 41 Union Sq W New York NY 10003

VISCO, ANTHONY SALVATORE
EDUCATOR, SCULPTOR
b Philadelphia, Pa, Sept 13, 48. *Study:* Fleischer Art Mem, Philadelphia; Philadelphia Col of Art; Accad delle Belle Art, Florence, Italy; Skowhegan Sch of Painting & Sculpture, Maine. *Comn:* Bronze crucifix & bronze baptismal fount lid, Church of St Anastasia, Newtown Sq, Pa, 76. *Exhib:* Ann Student Exhib, Philadelphia Col of Art, 66-70; Invitational, Acad of Mus, Philadelphia, 75; Kenmore Gallery, Philadelphia, 75; 41st Eucharistic Cong, Exhib of Liturgical Arts, Civic Ctr, Philadelphia, 76. *Pos:* Art instr, Recreation Ctr for Older People, Philadelphia, summer, 68; apprentice, Waler Erlbacher, Elkins Park, Pa, summer, 70; sculpture technician, Skowhegan Sch, Maine, summer, 75. *Teaching:* Instr sculpture, Philadelphia Col of Art, 76-, Creuzberg Ctr, Radnor, Pa, 76- *Awards:* State scholar, Philadelphia Col of Art, 66-70; Fulbright-Hayes Scholar, Florence, Italy, 70-71; Greenshields Award, Pvt Studio Work, Can, 75-76. *Media:* Wax, Bronze. *Mailing Add:* c/o July Valenti Broad & Cherry Streets Philadelphia PA 19102

VISSER'T HOOFT, MARTHA
PAINTER
b Buffalo, NY, May 25, 06. *Work:* Albright-Knox Art Gallery, Buffalo; Whitney Mus Am Art, New York; Rollins Col Mus Art; Munson-Williams-Proctor Inst, Utica, NY. *Exhib:* American Painting Today, Metrop Mus Art, New York, 50; Carnegie Inst Int, Pittsburgh, 52; Art Inst Chicago, 56; Artistas Brasileros Americanos, Mus Mod Art, Sao Paulo, Brazil; one-man show, Charles Burchfield Ctr, State Univ NY Col Buffalo, 73; In Western NY, Albright-Knox Gallery, 79; Historical Survey of Painting in Buffalo, Albright-Knox Gallery, 87. *Awards:* Distinguished Artist Award, Burchfield Art Ctr, State Univ, NY Col, Buffalo, 90; Second Prize in Oil, Chautauqua Inst Art, 64; NY State Univ Buffalo Community Coun Award, 75; plus others. *Bibliog:* J Benjamin Townsend (auth), Martha Visser't Hooft Paintings & Drawings, 1950-1973, State Univ NY Col Buffalo Alumni Found, 73. *Mem:* Hon mem Buffalo Fine Art Acad, Albright-Knox Gallery; Charles Burchfield Ctr, State Univ NY Col Buffalo. *Publ:* Illusr, Window, Poetry/Rare Book Collection, State Univ NY, Buffalo, 88. *Dealer:* More-Rubin Gallery Buffalo NY; Charles Burchfield Ctr State Univ Col Buffalo NY. *Mailing Add:* 800 W Ferry St Apt 6B Buffalo NY 14222

VITALE, MAGDA
PAINTER
b New York, NY, July 20, 39. *Study:* Barnes Found, Marion, Pa, 77; Found Todays Art, Intern, Philadelphia, 78; Skowhegan Sch Painting & Sculpture, Maine, 79; Moore Col Art, Philadelphia, BFA, 80. *Work:* Carnegie Ctr, Princeton, NJ; Best Products Inc, Richmond, Va; NJ Power & Light; Del Co Community Col, Media, Pa. *Exhib:* Solo exhibs, Nexus Gallery, 82 & 84, Recent Paintings, St Joseph's Univ, Philadelphia, 83, Paintings, Chambers Gallery, Penn State Univ, University Park, 84, Abstraction, Univ Pittsburgh Gallery, 87, NEw Paintings, Camden Col, Blackwood, NJ, 88 & Paintings, Henri Gallery, Washington, DC, 92; New Am Talent 88, Laguna Gloria Art Mus, Austin, Tex, 88; Henri Gallery, Washington, DC; Biennial 89, Del Art Mus, Wilmington, 89; Am Embassy Cult Ctr, Brussels, Belg, 89; Nat Small Works Exhib, Schoharie Arts Coun Gallery, Cobleskill, NY, 90; Gallery Artists, J Lawrence Gallery, Melbourne, Fla, 90; Nat Works on Paper Exhib, Univ Tex, Tyler, 90; Metamorphosis of a Butterfly, Erie Art Mus, Pa, 92; and many others. *Awards:* Scholarship Award, Skowhegan Sch Painting & Sculpture, 79; Expo V Award Winner, Northport Galleries, NY, 86; Grant, Ballenglen Art Found, Bally Castle, Ireland, 92. *Bibliog:* Mark Woodruff (auth), An Increase of Life, Paintings of Magda Vitale, Camden Co Col, Blackwood, NJ, 88; Francoises Andre (auth), Contemp Women Artists (exhib catalog), Am Embassy Cult Ctr, Brussels, Belg, 89; John Perreault & Jenine Culligan (coauths), Biennial 89 (exhib catalog), Del Art Mus, 89. *Mailing Add:* 12 Springton Lake Rd Media PA 19063

VITALE, VINCENT
PAINTER, TAPESTRY ARTIST
b Jersey City, NJ, Apr 23, 47. *Study:* Rutgers Univ, BA, 69; Art Students League. *Work:* Cooper-Hewitt Mus, New York; Museo de Arte Contemporanea. *Comn:* Fan Composition (mixed media), Cooper-Hewitt Mus, New York, 86. *Exhib:* Papelarte, Inst Int Contemp Art, Bahia, Brazil, 85; Cooper-Hewitt Mus, New York, 87. *Awards:* Hon Mention, Photovision '72, Boston Ctr Arts, 72. *Bibliog:* Second wind for the fan, Town & Country Mag, 6/87; Decorative fans painted or printed by hand, NY Times, 2/26/87. *Mem:* Orgn Independent Artists; Artists Equity Asn; Found Community Artists. *Media:* Oils; Textiles. *Publ:* Auth, Photographic Fans, Bull of Fan Circle Int, No 33, summer 86. *Mailing Add:* 802 W 190th St New York NY 10040

VITALI, JULIUS M
PHOTOGRAPHER, VIDEO ARTIST
b July 1, 52. *Study:* Nassau Col, Long Island, NY, 70-72; SUNY at Fredonia, BA, 74. *Work:* Bibliotheque Nationale, Paris, France; Polaroid Collection, Boston, Mass; Il Diaframma Galeria, Milan, Italy; Inter Media Art Ctr, Huntington, NY; Locust Valley Libr, Locust Valley, NY. *Comn:* Photo mural, Lawrence High Sch, Lawrence, NY, 85. *Exhib:* Long Islands Alternative Spaces, Islip Mus, Islip, NY, 85; Erronique, Crucial Gallery, London, United Kingdom, 87; Fashion & Surrealism, Victoria & Albert Mus, London, United Kingdom, 88; Tremplin Pour Les Images, Ctr Nationale de Photographie, Paris, France, 89; The Political Landscape, C W Post Mus, Greenvale, NY, 90; Hair Sculpture & Its Roots, Lehigh Univ Mus, Bethlehem, Pa, 91. *Pos:* Gallery dir, Discovery Gallery, Glen Cove, NY 82-85. *Teaching:* Instr photog, Pa Govt Sch Arts, Erie, 7-8/92. *Awards:* Nat Endowment Arts Forum Grant, Visuals & Music of Avante Disregarde, US Govt, 90; Spec Projs Award, At the Corner of Error & Perfection, Pa Coun Arts, 91; Res Photog Award, Kodak Company, 92. *Bibliog:* Liana Bortolon (auth), The World in a Puddle, Grazia, Italy, 79; George Schaub (auth), Photography With a Splash, Photogrs Forum, 82; Lorenzo Santamaria (auth), Photography After the Rain, Fotopractica, Italy, 84. *Publ:* Auth, Visual Statements on a Liquid Canvas, Petersens, 79; illusr, feature article/cover, Brit J Photog Art, 86; auth, Erronique, L'ARCA, Italy, 88; illusr, Art Images & Ideas Book, Davis Publs, 92; auth, Puddle Art, Sch Arts. *Dealer:* Open Space Gallery 808 Hamilton Mall Allentown PA 18050. *Mailing Add:* PO Box 75 Flicksville PA 18050

VIVOT, LEA (LEA DRAHOMIRA VIVOT-FISHMAN)
SCULPTOR
b Czechoslovakia; Can citizen. *Study:* Art Sch Stage Design, Prague, with Svoboda, 64-68; Acad Brera, Milan, 68; Ont Col Art, Toronto, with Erick Freifeld, 69-73. *Work:* Univ Guelph, Ont; St Joseph's Health Ctr, Toronto; NY State Mus Holocaust; Montreal Botanical Gardens, Que; Madison Sq Garden, New York; and others. *Comn:* Unity, News Time; Toronto Sun. *Exhib:* Solo exhib, Kar Gallery, Toronto, 79; Summer Exhib, Royal Acad Arts, London, 79; Sculpture of the 1980s, McMichael Collections, Kleinburg, Ont, 80; Sculptor's Soc Can, Pt Claire, Que, 82; Toronto Waldorf Sch, 82; Whitten Gallery, King City, Ont, 83; and others. *Teaching:* Creative artist in sch, Kleinburg Pub Sch, Ont, 79. *Bibliog:* Sculpture Bronzing (film), City TV, Toronto, 12/6/82; Barbara McLeod (interviewer), Romance Factor/ Sculpture (film), Can Broadcasting Corp, 12/14/82; The endless bench, Toronto Star 3/22/83; Numerous articles in Newsweek, NY Times, Toronto Star, Globe & Mail, Toronto Sun, Ottawa Citizen, Ottawa Hill Times, Rudé Pravo, NY Post, J & Global News. *Mem:* Sculpture Soc Can; Royal Acad Arts; Ont Col Art, Toronto; Art Students League. *Media:* Bronze. *Publ:* Sculpture Review, 3rd Quarter, Vol 38, 89; Le Medicine ju Quebec, 9/89; Working toward the future, Metrop Toronto, 90; Miami Tropic, 3/91; New Yorker, 5/92. *Mailing Add:* Rt 1 Kleinburg ON L0J 1C0 Canada

VIZNER, NIKOLA
ART DEALER, GALLERY DIRECTOR
b Bezdan, Yugoslavia, Nov 9, 45; US citizen. *Study:* Belgrade Univ, BA(art hist), 70, MA(hist mod art), 74. *Pos:* Dir, Wiesner Gallery, Brooklyn & New York, NY, currently. *Mem:* Nat Art Dealers Asn. *Specialty:* American and international contemporary art. *Mailing Add:* Wiesner Gallery 425 W 13th St New York NY 10014

VODICKA, RUTH KESSLER
SCULPTOR
b New York, NY. *Study:* City Col New York; with O'Connor Barrett; Sculpture Ctr, New York; Art Students League, 56-57 & 59; New Sch Social Res, 65; NY Univ, 69; Empire State Col Prog, 75- *Work:* Norfolk Mus, Va; Montclair State Col, NJ; Grayson Co State Bank, Sherman, Tex. *Comn:* Eternal Light (bronze sculpture), Temple of Jewish Community Ctr, Harrison, NJ, 65. *Exhib:* Whitney Mus Ann, New York, 52-57; Am Fedn Arts Traveling Exhib, 57-58; Galerie Claude Bernard, Paris, 60; Walk-Through-Dance-Through-Sculpture, New York Cult Arts Festival, Bryant Park, 67; Sculpture for the Dance, Hudson River Mus, Yonkers, NY, 73; and others. *Teaching:* Instr sculpture, Queens Youth Ctr, Bayside, 53-56; instr sculpture, Emanuel Midtown YM & WHA, New York, 66-69; instr sculpture, Great Neck Arrandale Sch, 69-70; vis artist, Hillside Sch, Hastings-on-Hudson, 73-74. *Awards:* Joseph W Beatman Award for Best Work in Any Medium & First Prize, Silvermine Guild Artists, 57; Medal of Honor, Painters & Sculptors Soc NJ, 62; Julia Ford Pew Prize, Nat Asn Woman Artists, 66; and others. *Bibliog:* Louis Calta (auth), Multi-purpose sculpture on view in Bryant Park, New York Times, 10/67; Environmental happening, Journal News, Mt Kisco, 9/73; They Choreograph to sculpture (cover), Patent Trader, 10/73. *Mem:* Am Soc Contemp Artists; Audubon Artists; Nat Asn Women Artists; Sculptors Guild (exec bd, 75); Women in Arts. *Media:* Bronze, Brass. *Publ:* Contribr, Feminist Art J, 72, Women & Art, 72, Artworkers Newslett, 73-75. *Mailing Add:* 97 Wooster St New York NY 10012

VO-DINH, MAI
PAINTER, PRINTMAKER
b Hue, Vietnam, Nov 14, 33; US citizen. *Study:* Sorbonne, Fac Lett, 56; Acad Grande Chaumiere, 57; Ecole Nat Superieure Beaux-Arts, 59. *Work:* Mus d'Art Mod de la Ville de Paris; Mus Rouen; Schiedam Mus, Holland; Nashville Mus, Tenn; Wash Co Mus Fine Arts, Md. *Exhib:* One-man shows, Washington Co Mus Fine Arts, Md, 78 & Univ Md, 80; Arts Club Washington, Touchstone Gallery & Paul Rosen Gallery, Washington, DC, 83; George Mason Univ, Va, 84 & 87; Les Jardins du Boisé, Montréal, Can, 92. *Teaching:* Instr watercolor painting, Hood Col, 78-79; artist-in-sch, Md State Coun, 86-87, 90 & 92. *Awards:* Christopher Award, Christopher Found, New York, NY, 75; Literature Prog Fel, Nat Endowment Arts, 84. *Bibliog:* Libbie Powell (auth), International recognized artist, The Daily Mail, Hagerstown, Md, 11/74; Henry Scarupa (auth), An artist's odyssey, Baltimore Sun, 7/80; Helen Hammond (auth), article, Diversions Mag, 3/90. *Mem:* Artists Equity Asn, Washington, DC. *Media:* Oil, Acrylic; Woodblock. *Publ:* Illusr, The Happy Funeral, Harper & Row, 82; The Gift, Knopf, 83; Angel Child, Dragon Child, Raintree Publishers, 83; Story of the Budha, 90; Sao Cotieng Song; esssais, Van Nghe, 91; and others. *Dealer:* Mai Studio PO Box 425 Burkittsville MD 21718. *Mailing Add:* Mai Studio PO Box 425 Burkittsville MD 21718

VOELKER, ELIZABETH
PAINTER, COLLAGE ARTIST
b Pittsburgh, Pa, 1931. *Study:* Carnegie Inst Technol, BFA, 53. *Work:* Phillips Collection, Nat Mus Am Arts & Nat Mus Women Arts, Washington, DC; Art Mus, Carnegie Inst, Pittsburgh, Pa; San Francisco Mus Mod Art; Calif Palace Legion Hon; Santa Barbara Mus Art; Detroit Inst Arts. *Exhib:* solo exhibs, San Jose Mus Art, 82 & Santa Barbara Mus Art, 82; Allport Gallery, 83 & 84; Hewlett Packard Gallery, 86; San Francisco Mus Mod Art, 90; Susan Conway Carroll Gallery, Washington, DC, 90. *Teaching:* Lectr, Univ Calif Exten, San Francisco, 72. *Awards:* Ludwig Vogelstein Found Grant, 87; Rockefeller Found Grant, 88; Djerassi Found Grant, 88; Pollock-Krasner Found Grant, 89-90; Am Acad Rome residency, 92. *Bibliog:* David Burdon (auth), There's a new kid in town, Village Voice, 77; Judith Weiner (auth), Oriental ideas enrich paintings, collages, Oakland Press, 81; Andrea Liss (auth), A deceptive simplicity, Artweek, 83. *Mem:* MacDowell Colony Fels, Col Art Asn. *Media:* Oil, Collage. *Dealer:* Susan Conway Carroll Gallery 1058 Thomas Jefferson St NW Washington DC 20007; Lucy Berman Gallery 238 Hamilton Ave Palo Alto CA 94301. *Mailing Add:* 301 Bloomfield Rd Burlingame CA 94010

VOELKER, JOHN
PAINTER, DESIGNER
b Givens, Ohio. *Study:* Columbus Col Art & Design, Ohio, 53-57; design workshop with Canzani; advan painting with Kuehn. *Work:* Columbus Gallery Fine Arts, Ohio; Abilene Mus Fine Arts, Tex. *Comn:* Posters, Cerebral Palsy Found, 56; Tex Fine Arts Asn, Dallas, 71 & Logo Design Bicentennial with Tex Fine Arts Asn, 75. *Exhib:* Ultimate Concerns, Prints & Drawings, Ohio Univ, 63 & 64; Artists of Gulf States & Tex, Delgado Mus, New Orleans, 64 & 66; Chautauqua Exhib Am Art, NY, 67; 11th Ann Prints & Drawings, Okla Art Ctr, Oklahoma City, 69; Southwest Painting Ann, Albuquerque, NMex, 70. *Pos:* Art coordr, Coronet Packaging, Dallas, 61-75. *Awards:* Permanent Collection Choice, Ultimate Concerns, Ohio Univ, 63; Haydon Calhoun Gallery Award, Painting & Sculpture Ann, Dallas Mus Fine Arts, 64; Best of Show, Tex Fine Arts Asn, 72. *Bibliog:* Article, Columbus Sunday Mag, Dispatch, 3/56; article, Dallas Times Herald, 10/76. *Mem:* Artists Equity, Dallas; Tex Fine Arts Asn; Artists Coalition of Tex. *Dealer:* Adelle Taylor 3317 McKinney Dallas TX. *Mailing Add:* 4135 University Blvd Dallas TX 75205

VOGEL, DONALD S
PAINTER, DEALER
b Milwaukee, Wis, Oct 20, 17. *Study:* Corcoran Gallery Art, Washington, DC; Art Inst Chicago; Work Prog Admin Easel Proj, Chicago. *Work:* Ft Worth Art Ctr, Tex; Dallas Mus Fine Arts; Beaumont Mus Art, Tex; Mobile Art Ctr, Ala; Philbrook Art Ctr, Tulsa, Okla. *Exhib:* One-man shows, Philbrook Mus Art, Tulsa, 69, Beaumont Art Mus, Tex, 70, Charles B Goddard Ctr, Ardmore, Okla, 81 & San Jacinto Tower, Dallas, 83; one man exhib, Newman & Saunders, Wayne, Pa, 84 & 85; Four Seasons, Washington, DC, 85. *Collections Arranged:* Clara McDonald Williamson, 66 & Velox Ward (with catalog), 72, Amon Carter Mus Art, Ft Worth; Valton Tyler (with catalog), Southern Methodist Univ, 72. *Pos:* Dir, Valley House Gallery Inc. *Awards:* Bronze Medal, Am Acad Rome, 42; Dallas Allied Arts Ann Awards, Dallas Mus Fine Arts, 44-46; 8th Tex Gen Exhib Award, Houston Mus Fine Arts, 46. *Bibliog:* Jane Sumner (auth), Portraits of the Rebel as Donald Vogel, D Mag, 1/76; Witch hunter of the Southwest, Dallas/Ft Worth Business, 5/29/78; Amy Morenz (auth), Artist paints his heart, not public opinion, North City News, 4/2-8/84. *Mem:* Art Dealers Asn Am; Am Fedn Arts; Dallas Mus Fine Arts. *Media:* Watercolor, Oil. *Specialty:* Paintings and sculpture of the nineteenth and twentieth centuries. *Publ:* Coauth & ed, Passion: Georges Roualt (catalog), 62; coauth, Aunt Clara, 66; ed, The Paintings of Hugh H Breckenridge (catalog), 67; Charcoal and Cadmium Red (short stories). *Mailing Add:* Valley House Gallery Inc 6616 Spring Valley Rd Dallas TX 75240

VOGEL, HERBERT (MR & MRS)
COLLECTORS
Mr Vogel b New York, NY, Aug 16, 22; Mrs Dorothy Vogel b Elmira, NY, May 14, 35. *Study:* Mr Vogel, NY Univ Inst Fine Arts; Mrs Vogel, Syracuse Univ, BA, 57; Univ Denver, MA, 58. *Exhib:* Selections from the Collection of Dorothy & Herbert Vogel, Clocktower, New York, 75; Painting, Drawing & Sculpture of the 60's and 70's, from the Dorothy and Herbert Vogel Collection, Inst Contemp Art, Univ Pa & Contemp Arts Ctr, Cincinnati, 75-76; Works from the Collection of Dorothy & Herbert Vogel, Univ of Mich Mus of Art, 77; From the Vogel Collection, Ben Shahn Gallery, William Patterson Col, 81; Twentieth Anniversary Exhib-Vogel Collection, Brainerd Art Gallery, State Univ Col Arts & Sci, Potsdam, NY, 82; Gallery Art, Univ Northern Iowa, Cedar Falls, 83; Drawings from the Collection of Dorothy and Herbert Vogel, Univ Ark, Little Rock, 86; Beyond the Picture, Works from the Collection of Dorothy & Herbert Vogel, Kunsthalle, Bielefeld, Germany, 87; From the Collection of Dorothy & Herbert Vogel, Arnot Art Mus, Elmira, NY, 88; and others. *Bibliog:* Paul Gardner (auth), Look! It's the Vogels!, Art News, 3/79; Meg Cox (auth), Postal clerk and wife amass art collection in a New York flat, Wall Street J, 1/30/86; Catherine Barnett (auth), A package deal, Art & Antiques, Summer 86; Paul Gardner (auth), Mesmerized by Minimalism, Contemporanea, 12/89; Sara Rimer (auth), Collecting priceless art, just for the love of it, NY Times, 2/11/92; and others. *Collection:* Contemporary drawing, sculpture and painting. *Mailing Add:* 305 E 86th St New York NY 10028

VOGEL, JOSEPH
PAINTER, PRINTMAKER
b Poland, April 22, 11; US citizen. *Study:* Nat Acad Design Art, New York, 29-32; Students League, 33; Grande Chaumiere, Paris; Acad Julien, Leger Studio, studied with Andre L'Hote, 48-53. *Work:* Metrop Mus Art, New York; Nat Collection Am Art, Washington, DC; Philadelphia Mus Art; Baltimore Mus Art; St Louis Art Mus; Univ NMex; and others. *Exhib:* Whitney Mus Art Invitationals, 33-38; ACA Gallery, New York, 34; one-man exhibs, Am Contemp Art Gallery, Los Angeles, 42, Abraxas Gallery, Laguna Beach & Newport Beach, 79, 80 & 81, Walter Wiggins Gallery, Roswell, NMex, 83 & 90 & Roswell Art Ctr, 89; Ryder Gallery, Los Angeles, 62-64; Newport Harbor Art Mus Invitational, 63; Prints for the People--Works Proj Admin Graphics, Nat Collection Fine Arts, Washington, DC, 79; Toward Abstraction, Metrop Mus Art, New York, 86; and others. *Teaching:* Instr documentary film, Univ Southern Calif, 47, painting, Chouinard Art Inst, 61-63; instr drawing & painting, Beverly Hills High Sch, 63-65 & Culver City High Sch, 63-66; and pvt classes. *Bibliog:* O'Connor (auth), New Deal Art Project; Color Prints in USA (catalog), Worcester Mus, Mass; Lewis Jacobs (auth), The Emergence of Film as Art. *Mem:* Mural Art Soc. *Media:* Oil, Acrylic; Lithography. *Publ:* Auth, American Screenprints, Reba & D Williams Collections; Graphic Excursions, Williams Collections Graphics; Surrealism Embodied, Rosenfeld Galllery. *Dealer:* Michael Rosenfeld Gallery 50 W 57th New York NY. *Mailing Add:* 508 W 13th St Roswell NM 88201

VOGL, DON GEORGE
PAINTER, PRINTMAKER
b Milwaukee, Wis, July 22, 29. *Study:* Art Inst Chicago & Univ Chicago, BAE, 57; Univ Wis, Milwaukee, MS(art educ), 58. *Work:* Art Gallery, Univ Notre Dame, Ind; Alverno Col, Mt Mary Col & Cardinal Stritch, Milwaukee. *Comn:* Immaculate Conception Church, Hartford, Mich, 69; St Mark's Church, Niles, Mich, 70; Notre Dame Univ Law Libr, 75; Methodist Church, Stevenville, Mich; Railroad Bridge over Michigan Ave, South Bend, Ind. *Exhib:* Chicago Vicinity Show, 65; Watercolor USA, Springfield, Mo, 68; Tri-State Graphics, Louisville, Ky, 74; Indianapolis Painters & Sculptors, 75; one-man show, Quincy Col, Ill; and others. *Pos:* Vpres, Visual Improvement Prog, South Bend, 74-75. *Teaching:* Instr art, Marygrove Col, Detroit, 61-63; assoc prof, Univ Notre Dame, 63- *Awards:* First Award Painting, Wis State Fair, 58; La Vera Pohl Award, Wis Painters & Sculptors, 60; Elkhart Juried Regional Award, Mus Am Art, Ind, 85; Award of Distinction, Salon Show Northern Ind Artists Asn, Munster, 89. *Bibliog:* Rudy Pozatti (auth), Indiana printmakers, Ind Art Educ Asn, 12/74. *Mem:* Am Col Art Asn. *Media:* Lithography; Acrylic, Oil. *Dealer:* Campanile-Capponi Ltd 1252 N State Parkway Chicago IL 60610. *Mailing Add:* 851 Park Ave South Bend IN 46616

VOLID, RUTH
DEALER, CONSULTANT
b Chicago, Ill. *Study:* Art Inst of Chicago; Chouinard Art Sch, Los Angeles; Otis Art Inst; Univ of Chicago. *Comn:* Curated many major corp collections. *Exhib:* article, Do's and don'ts for corporate art, Crain's Chicago Business, 7/84. *Pos:* Pres, Ruth Volid Gallery Ltd, 70-91. *Teaching:* Corp Art Roundtable, 88. *Bibliog:* Barbara Varro (auth), A new start at midlife, Sun Times, 10/77; Special places, special people, Chicago Tribune, 12/83; Rivernorth News, 8/86. *Mem:* Mus Contemp Art, Chicago (bd affil, 76-); Arch of Am Art; life mem Art Inst Chicago; Arts Club Chicago; Am Soc Interior Designers (bd mem). *Publ:* Auth, Art/an added dimension, Designer, 10/79; Threads of tradition, Studio 40, 10/79 & Picking a corporate art curator, 10/80, Collector Investor. *Mailing Add:* 225 W Illinois St Chicago IL 60610

VOLKERDING, LAURA
PHOTOGRAPHER
b Louisville, Ky, 1939. *Study:* Univ Louisville, BS, 61; Inst Design, MS, 65. *Work:* Bibliot Nat, Paris; Libr Cong; Smithsonian Inst Nat Collection Fine Arts; Can Ctr Archit, Montreal; Stanford Art Mus; San Francisco Mus Mod Art; Art Inst Chicago; Mus Mod Art, New York; Los Angeles Co Mus; Oakland Mus; Musée Carnavalet, Paris. *Comn:* Courthouse, San Francisco Civic Ctr. *Exhib:* Stanford Art Mus, 81-82; SECA Invitational, San Francisco Mus Mod Art, 82; New Landscapes, Friends Photog, Carmel, Calif; Panoramas, Renaissance Soc, Chicago; The Panoramic Photograph, Grey Gallery, New York. *Teaching:* Sr lectr, dept art, Stanford Univ, Calif, currently. *Awards:* Prix de Paris, 86; Guggenheim Fel. *Mailing Add:* Art Dept Stanford Univ Stanford CA 94305

VOLKERSZ, WILLEM
SCULPTOR, EDUCATOR
b Amsterdam, The Netherlands, Aug 3, 39; US citizen. *Study:* Univ Washington, BA, 65; Mills Col, MFA, 67. *Work:* Seattle Art Mus, Seattle, Wash; Univ Arts, Osaka, Japan; Nanjing Col Arts, China; Kansas City Art Inst, Mo; Mont State Univ, Bozeman. *Comn:* Paris Gibson Square Mus Art, Great Falls, Mont, 88. *Exhib:* Northwest Ann, Seattle Art Mus, Wash, 63 & 65; Thirty Miles of Art, 74, 75 & 77, Mid Four Ann, 79, Nelson Atkins Mus; Chicago Int Art Expo, Navy Pier, Ill, 85; Contemp Neon, Nevada Mus Art, Reno, 90; one man show, Yellowstone Art Ctr, Billings, Mont, 90. *Pos:* Dir admissions, Kansas City Art Inst, 81-83; dir, School of Art, Mont State Univ, 86-91. *Teaching:* Prof found studies, Kansas City Art Inst, 68-86; prof art, Mont State Univ, 86- *Awards:* Mellon Fel, Folk Art Res, Univ Kan, 86; Fulbright Award, Folk Art Res, Coun Int Exchange Scholars, 91. *Bibliog:* Christian Schiess (auth), Interview: Willem Volkersz/Signs of the Times, 90; Rebecca Presson (auth), Local Considerations (radio), KCUR FM, 85; Yarrow Kraner (auth), Willem Volkersz: In Neon (film), Yarrow Kraner (dir), 92. *Mem:* Col Art Asn; Phi Kappa Phi Hon Soc; Mus Am Folk Art; Inter Sculpture Ctr; Folk Art Soc Am (nat bd, 90). *Media:* Neon, Wood. *Res:* Outsider Art and Environments. *Publ:* Auth (article), Cultural Imprint and Private Vision, Missoula Mus, 87; contribr, The Folk, Univ Kans, 89; Howard Finster, Man of Visions, Alfred A Knopf, 89; auth (article), Private Spaces/ Public Places, Pub Art Rev, 92; This is Art, This is Dream, This is Energy, Folk Art Messenger, 92. *Dealer:* Francine Seders Gallery Ltd 6701 Greenwood Ave N Seattle WA 98103. *Mailing Add:* 12299 Portnell Rd Bozeman MT 59715

VOLKIN, HILDA APPEL
SCULPTOR
b Boston, Mass, Sept 24, 33. *Study:* Mass Col Art, BS, 54; Radcliffe Col, MA, 56. *Work:* Cleveland Mus Art, Ohio; Univ NMex & Albuquerque Mus Art, Albuquerque Int Airport; Rose Medical Ctr, Denver, Colo; Los Alamos Nat Lab, NMex; Massillon Mus, Ohio. *Comn:* Acrylic window sculpture; chapel windows, Congregation Albert, Albuquerque, NMex 87, 88 & 92, NMex State Univ, 88. *Exhib:* Here and Now: 35 Artists in New Mexico, Mus Albuquerque, 80, 90; Paper--The Continuous Thread, Cleveland Mus Art, Ohio, 82; Bergen Community Mus, Paramus, NJ, 83; one-person retrospective, Mass Col Art, Boston, 84; one-person shows, Mayville State Col, ND & Univ Portland, Ore. *Pos:* Dir, Fuller Lodge Art Ctr, 77-80; art dir, Executive Fine Arts, Albuquerque, NMex, 80- *Teaching:* Instr painting, Univ NMex, Los Alamos, 74- *Awards:* Purchase Award for Watercolor, Massillon Mus, 66; Graphics Awards, Cleveland Mus Art, 74 & Nat Asn Women Artists, 79. *Bibliog:* Suzanne Deats, The look of desert places, Santa Fe Reporter, 3/27/85; Janelle Coroway, Artist seeks inspiration in industry, Albuquerque J, 2/22/87; Laurie Volkin (auth), Albuquerque artist produces first acrylic silkscreen sculpture, The Link 9/88. *Mem:* Soc Layerists Mult-Media, Albuquerque Mus. *Media:* Silkscreen; Acrylic. *Publ:* Auth, Paper, the continuous thread, Cleveland Mus Art & Ind Univ Press, 82; Cover Artist of the month, Take Five, 1/87. *Mailing Add:* 14329 Skline Rd NE Albuquerque NM 87123

VOLPE, ROBERT
PAINTER, LECTURER
b New York, NY, Dec 13, 42. *Study:* Sch Art & Design, New York; New Sch Social Res; Parsons Sch Design, New York; Art Students League New York. *Work:* South Street Seaport Mus, New York; State Univ NY Downstate Med Ctr Collection; Antietam Nat Mus, Md. *Exhib:* One-man shows, Kottler Galleries, New York, 70, South Street Seaport Mus, 74, Nahas Gallery, New York, 75-80 & Salmagundi Club, New York, 76-83; NY Tel Co Exhib, 79; Knickerbocker Artists Exhib, 80 & 83. *Pos:* Cur, Antietam Nat Mus, Sharpsburg, Md, 72-80; mem bd dirs, Found Community Artist, New York, 72-75; dir, Art Identification Unit, City New York, 72-78; dir, Volpe Orgn Art Consults, 83; dir, Volpe-Winfield Assocs, Art Consult. *Teaching:* Lectr, Harvard Law Sch, 74, Avila Col, Mo, 77 & Columbia Univ, 83. *Awards:* Graphic Awards, Guggenheim Mus, 77, Sch Visual Art, New York, 77 & 80 & Metrop Mus Art, 79. *Bibliog:* Articles, Wall St J, 78 & Life Mag, 79; article, Mus Mag, 2/82. *Mem:* Salmagundi Club; Knickerbocker Artists; Artist Fel Found; Off Naval Combat Artist Group. *Media:* Oil, Watercolor. *Publ:* Auth, The Italian Experience in Arts and Literature, The Metamorphosis Continues, Ctr Migration Studies, Ital Embassy, Washington, DC, 83. *Mailing Add:* PO Box 468 New York NY 10272

VON BARGHAN, BARBARA
EDUCATOR, WRITER
b Washington, DC, Feb 5, 49. *Study:* Univ Iowa, BA, 70; New York Univ, with Jose Lopez-Rey & Charles Sterling, MA, 72, with Jonathan Brown, Egbert Haverkamp-Begemann & Colin Eisler, PhD, 79. *Collections Arranged:* Contributor to exhibition, Pre-Columbian Ceramics, Dimock Gallery, George Washington Univ, 81, among others. *Pos:* Dir, Von Braghahn Gallery, Washington, DC, 74-78; Lectr, Embassy of Spain & Smithsonian Inst. *Teaching:* Instr, Sweet Briar Col, 73-74; asst prof, George Washington Univ, 74-82, assoc prof, 83- *Awards:* Research Grant, George Washington Univ, 78-86. *Mem:* Am Soc of Hispanic Historical Studies; Renaissance Soc of Am; Soc for Spanish & Portuguese Historical Studies; Col Arts Asn. *Res:* Spanish, Portuguese and Latin American Art, Northern Baroque court art, architecture and gardens, Mannerism in the North, Primitive art. *Publ:* Auth, Philip IV and the Golden House of the Buen Retiro: In the Tradition of Caeser, 86; Age of Gold, Age of Iron: Renaissance Spain and Symbols of Monarchy, 86; co-auth (with Annemarie Jordan), The Torreao of the Lisbon Palace and the Escorial Library, 86; and many others. *Mailing Add:* Art Dept/Academic Ctr George Washington Univ 801 22nd St NW Washington DC 20052

VON DER GOLZ, JAN See Mehn, Jan (von der Golz)

VON RINGELHEIM, PAUL HELMUT
SCULPTOR
b Vienna, Austria. *Study:* Brooklyn Col, BS, 56; Fairleigh Dickinson Univ, MA, 58; Art Students League, 58-59; Acad Fine Arts, Munich, 60-61. *Work:* Welton Becket Assoc; Mus Mod Art, New York; Mus Mod Art, Tel Aviv; Mus Mod Art, Tokyo; Whitney Mus Am Art; Fairleigh Dickinson Univ; Time & Life collections, New York. *Comn:* World Peace Monument, US Pavilion, Worlds Fair, 64; fulcrum, Westinghouse Nuclear Ctr, Pittsburgh, 72; Interstate 80 Bicentennial Sculpture Project, Houston Ctr, Tex Eastern Corp. *Exhib:* Whitney Mus Am Art, 63 & 65; Mus Mod Art, New York, 64, 67 & 69; Jewish Mus, New York, 66 & 68; Cleveland Mus, 66; Albright-Knox Gallery, Buffalo, 67; Frick Mus, Pittsburgh, 68; solo exhib, O K Harris Gallery, New York, 71-73, 76, 78, 80 & 82. *Teaching:* Instr printmaking, Brooklyn Mus Sch, 57-58; prof sculpture, Sch Visual Arts, New York, 67-71. *Awards:* Fulbright Scholar, 74-75. *Mem:* Archit League City New York. *Mailing Add:* 9 Great Jones St New York NY 10012

VON RYDINGSVARD, URSULA
SCULPTOR
b Deensen, Ger, July 26, 42. *Study:* Univ Miami, Coral Gables, Fla, BA, 64, MA, 65; Univ Calif, Berkeley, 69-70; Columbia Univ, New York, MFA, 75. *Work:* Metrop Mus Art, New York; Brooklyn Mus, NY; Detroit Art Inst, Mich; Walker Art Ctr, Minneapolis, Minn. *Comn:* Walker Art Ctr, Minneapolis, Minn; City Col, Staten Island, NY; Laumeier Sculpture Garden, St Louis, Mo; Capp St Proj, San Francisco, Calif. *Exhib:* Corcoran Gallery, Washington, DC, 75; Sixteen Hand Rests, 2 Penn Plaza, New York, 84; Standing Ground, Contemp Art Ctr, Ohio, 87; Sculpture of the 80's, Queens Mus, NY, 87; one-person exhibs, Exit Art, New York, NY, 88 & Cranbrook Acad Art, Bloomfield Hills, Mich, 89, Lorence Monk Gallery, New York, NY, 90, Storm King, Mountainville, NY, 92 & Nat Mus Women Arts, Washington, DC, 93; Group shows: Metrop Mus Art, New York, Walker Art Ctr, Minneapolis, Minn, Brooklyn Mus, NY, Woman's Mus, Washington, DC, Out of Wood, Whitney Mus Contemp Art, New York, 90 & Landscape as Metaphor, Am Ctr, Paris, France, 93. *Teaching:* Prof sculpture, Grad Sch Visual Arts, currently. *Awards:* Nat Endowment Arts, 79, 86 & 87; Creative Artists Public Service Program, 80; Guggenheim Fel, 83. *Bibliog:* Grace Glueck (auth), articles, New York Times, 4/18/80 & 11/5/82; Patricia Phillips (auth), article, Artforum, 9/84; Michael Brenson (auth), articles, New York Times, 12/2/84, 6/7/85, 4/88 & 3/90; Robert Atkins (auth), 7 Days, 4/20/88; Kay Larson (auth), New York Mag, 5/9/88 & 6/15/92; Michael Kimmelman (auth), Intimations in Wood of Ritual & Refugee Camps, NY Times, 7/17/92. *Media:* Wood, Miscellaneous. *Publ:* Thoughts about my work, Issue 6, 5/86. *Mailing Add:* 362 E 69th St New York NY 10021

VON SCHMIDT, ERIC
PAINTER, HISTORIAN
b Bridgeport, Conn, May 28, 31. *Study:* Art Students League, 50; Farnsworth Sch Art, Fla, 50-51;. *Work:* Ulrich Mus Art, Wichita, Kans. *Exhib:* American Frontier: The Saga of Westward Expansion, Ulrich Mus Art, Wichita, Kans, 77; Remembering the Alamo, Witte Mus, San Antonio, 86; Legacy, L'Atelien Westport, Conn, 89; Last Stands, Mus Sci & Hist, Corpus Christi, Tex, 92. *Awards:* Fulbright Scholar, painting, 55-86; Nat Endowment Arts Grants, 87. *Media:* Acrylic; Bronze. *Res:* The battle of Hue, 68. *Publ:* Auth, Custer, dying again, Smithsonian Mag, 86; How is the Alamo remembered?, Smithsonian Mag, 86; Sunday at the Little Big Horn with George, Univ Nebr Press, 89; Mont Mag, 92. *Dealer:* Minglewood Press PO Box 638 Westport CT 06880. *Mailing Add:* 38 Evergreen Ave Westport CT 06880

VON ZUR MUEHIEN, PETER
PHOTOGRAPHER
b Berlin, Ger, Mar 10, 39; US citizen. *Study:* Washington Univ, St Louis, BA, 61; Princeton Univ, PhD, 72. *Work:* Corcoran Gallery. *Exhib:* Virginia Photographers, Va Mus Fine Arts, 75 & 78; Nations Capital Photographers, Corcoran Gallery Art, 76; one-person exhib, Va Mus Fine Arts, 76 & Bailey Art Mus, Charlottesville, Va, 79; One of a Kind, Franklin Inst, Philadelphia, 78, Denver Art Mus, 81, Houston Mus Fine Arts, Carpenter Ctr, Harvard & Corcoran Gallery Art; Still Life in Photography, Corcoran Gallery Art, 78; Recent Acquisitions, Corcoran Gallery Art, 81, 83 & 86; Terra Sancta: Photographs from Israel, Nepal & the American West, Corcoran Gallery Art, 90. *Awards:* Cert Distinction, Va Photographers, Va Mus Fine Arts, 75. *Bibliog:* David Tannous (auth), article, 7/78 & Capital art: in the major leagues?, 7/79, Art Am. *Media:* Chrome, Silver. *Publ:* Contribr, One of a Kind: Polaroid Photography, Polaroid Corp, 78. *Mailing Add:* 10435 Hunter View Rd Vienna VA 22180

VON ZUR MUEHLEN, BERNIS SUSAN
PHOTOGRAPHER
b Philadelphia, Pa, Apr 10, 42. *Study:* Univ Pa, BA(lit), 63. *Work:* Corcoran Gallery Art, DC; Baltimore Mus Art, Md; Int Ctr Photog, New York; Houston Mus Fine Arts, Tex; New Orleans Mus Art, La; Wesleyan Univ, Davidson Art Ctr, Middletown, Conn. *Exhib:* Va Mus Fine Arts, Richmond, 75 & Va Photogr, 75 & 78; Nation's Capital Photogr, Corcoran Gallery Art, DC, 76 & Recent Acquisitions, 79 & 80; one-woman shows, Baily Mus Art, Univ Va, Charlottesville, 80, Del Mus Art, Wilmington, 81, Osuna Gallery, 81, 84 & 89, Second St Gallery, Charlottesville, Va, 83, Photoworks Gallery, Richmond, Va, 84, Corcoran Gallery Art, Washington, DC, 90 & B'nai Brith Klutznick Nat Jewish Mus, 92; Invisible Light: An Exhibition of Infrared Photography, Smithsonian Inst, Washington, DC, 80 & 82; 35th Anniversary Area Show, Corcoran Gallery Art, Washington, DC, 82; From the Collection, Photographs by Women, Corcoran Gallery Art, 82; Recent Acquisitions in Photography, Corcoran Gallery Art, 87; Dog Days Dog Show, Kathleen

Ewing Gallery, Washington, DC, 88; Image of the Male Nude, Frankfurter Kunstverein, Fed Rep Ger, 88; Behold the Man, Photog's Gallery, London, Eng & Stills Gallery, Scotland, 88; Landscape Photographs from the Permanent Collection, Corcoran Gallery Art, 89; Jones Troyer Fitzpatrick Gallery, Washington, DC, 91; Triennial Exhib, New Orleans Mus Art, La, 92. *Teaching:* Lectr, Baltimore Mus Art, Md, 78, Cath Univ, Washington, DC, 78, Corcoran Sch Art, Washington, DC, 81 & Univ Va, 87- *Awards:* Three Judges' Awards, Womansphere, Glen Echo, Md, 75; Purchase Award, Corcoran Gallery Art, 76. *Bibliog:* Photography Series One, 85 & Terra Sancta: Images of Israel, Nepal and the American West, Corcoran Gallery Art, Washington, DC; Behold the Man, Stills Gallery, Edinburgh, Scotland, 88; Virginius Dabney (ed), anthology, New Va Rev, Richmond, vol 3, 84; and others. *Publ:* Contribr to various articles and books, 75- *Dealer:* Jones Troyer Fitzpatrick Gallery Washington DC. *Mailing Add:* 10435 Hunter View Rd Vienna VA 22181

VOORHEES, DONALD EDWARD
PAINTER, PRINTMAKER
b Neptune, NJ, May 6, 26. *Study:* Acad Arts, Newark, NJ; Art Students League, New York. *Work:* Bethlehem Steel, Tulsa, Okla; Citibank, New York; Metrop Life, New York; Pfizer Chem Co, New York; Sun Oil Co, Tulsa, Okla; and many others. *Comn:* Ed of prints, Sheraton Hotels, Tulsa, Okla, 84; ed of prints, Dallas Athletic Club, Dallas, Tex, 86; ed of prints, Buick Div Gen Motors, Flint, Mich, 88. *Exhib:* Frye Mus, Seattle, Wash; Edward Dean Mus, Cherry Valley, Calif; Cent Mus Wyo; Martello Mus, Key West, Fla; plus others. *Teaching:* freelance, 65-75. *Awards:* Hudson Valley Art Asn Award; NJ Watercolor Soc Award; Salmagundi Club Award. *Mem:* NJ Watercolor Soc (pres, 75-76); Artists Fel; Salmagundi Club. *Media:* Watercolor; Lithography. *Publ:* Articles in Graphics Mag, 6/79, Prints Mag, winter 79, Artist Mag, 4/84, Collectors Mart, 6/84 & Golf Week Mag, 10/88. *Dealer:* Donald Voorhees Gallery 325 Hwy 35 Red Bank NJ 07701. *Mailing Add:* 10 Ocean Blvd Atlantic Highlands NJ 07716

VOOS, WILLIAM JOHN
ADMINISTRATOR, PAINTER
b St Louis, Mo, July 2, 30. *Study:* Wash Univ Sch Fine Arts, BFA, 52; Univ Kans, MFA, 53; NY Univ, US Arts & Humanities Art Admin fel, 67. *Work:* Rend Lake Col Collection, Mt Vernon, Ill; Mus Contemp Art, Recife, Brazil; Ga Coun Arts. *Comn:* Mural, Army Educ Ctr, Ft Bragg, NC, 54; playground mural, Ferguson Park Comn, Mo, 60. *Exhib:* One-man show, Lafayette Art Ctr, Ind, 66 & Northern State Col, 74; Fac Shows, Steinberg Hall, Wash Univ, 68-72; Atlanta Col Art Fac Show, High Mus Art, 75; Mus Contemp Art, Recife, Brazil, 75; Herron Gallery, 85-90. *Pos:* Dean, Atlanta Col Art, 73-75 & pres, 75-85; dean, Herron Sch Art, Indiana Univ-Purdue Univ, Indainapolis, 85- *Teaching:* Assoc prof art & chmn humanities div, Florissant Valley Community Col, 64-68; assoc prof art & assoc dean Sch Fine Arts, Wash Univ, 68-73. *Mem:* Nat Asn Sch Art (exec bd mem, 70-73); Nat Coun Art Adminrs; Indianapolis Consortium of Art Adminrs (pres, 88-90); Col Art Asn. *Media:* Acrylic, Watercolor. *Mailing Add:* 3899 Honey Creek Blvd Greenwood IN 46042

VORWERK, E CHARLSIE
PAINTER, ILLUSTRATOR
b Tennga, Ga, Jan 28, 34. *Study:* Ga State Col Women, AB; com art study, 2 yrs. *Work:* Mamie Padgett Collection, Ga Col. *Comn:* Bicentennial mural, Fine Arts Coun, Summerville, SC, 75; Painting No 1 in Ser, Summerville Hist Soc, Summerville, SC; Painting Trident/No 1 in Ser, Chamber of Com, Charleston, SC; 54 ft needlepoint design for altar kneelers, All Saints Lutheran Church, Mt Pleasant, SC; plus other individuals & companies. *Exhib:* Ann Exhib Minature Painter, Sculptors & Gravers Soc, Washington, DC, 70-75; Miniature Art Soc NJ, Paramus, 71-75; 23rd & 24th Gran Prix Int Peiture de Deauville, France, 72-73; 9th & 10th Gran Prix Peinture de la Cote D'Azur, Cannes, France, 73 & 74; Miniature Art Soc Int Exhib, 80; and others. *Pos:* Billboard designer, Vanesco Poster, Chattanooga, Tenn; fashion illustrator, Lovemans; cartographic draftsman, Tenn Valley Authority; free-lance com artist. *Teaching:* Lectr continuing art, Baptist Col, 79-83; pvt group art classes for children & adults. *Awards:* Gold Medal, 80, Oscar of Gold, 86, Italian Acad Art; Golden Centaur Award, Ital Acad Art, 83; Statue Victory World Cult Prize, 84 & 88; Premio Milano, 88. *Bibliog:* Articles, Rev Mod, Paris, 71, 73 & 74 & Il Giornale D'Italia & Iltempo, 73. *Mem:* League Charleston Artists (secy, 75-77); Summerville Artist Guild; Charleston Artists Guild (exhib chair, 83-, vpres, 86-); Ital Acad Art; Miniature Art Soc Fla. *Media:* Multimedia. *Publ:* Illusr of low country tourist brochures for various orgns & Episcopal Church periodicals and brochures; illusr, Tales and Taradiddles, 76, Epitaphs of St Paul's Cemetery 1858-1978, 77, Captain Tom, 80 & The St Paul's Sampler, 83. *Dealer:* Chester Smith Seaside Art Gallery PO Box 1 Nags Head NC 27959. *Mailing Add:* 315 W Carolina Ave Summerville SC 29483

VOSE, ROBERT CHURCHILL, JR
DEALER
b Boston, Mass, Mar 30, 11. *Study:* Harvard. *Pos:* Treas, Vose Galleries of Boston, 53-76, pres, 76-80, chmn, 81-84; Retired. *Bibliog:* J Post (auth), The Old Family Business, Yankee Mag, 73; William N Banks (auth), New England's reigning antique dealers, Country J Mag, 12/78. *Mem:* Copley Soc, Boston; Mass Hist Soc; Albany Inst Hist & Art; New Britain Mus, Conn. *Res:* Alvan Fisher, 1792-1863; Ralph Blakelock, 1847-1919. *Specialty:* Eighteenth, nineteenth and early twentieth century American paintings; to a lesser degree, eighteenth and nineteenth century English and nineteenth century French paintings. *Publ:* Auth, Alvan Fisher, American Pioneer in Landscape and Genre, Conn Hist Soc, 62. *Mailing Add:* Vose Galleries of Boston Inc 238 Newbury St Boston MA 02116

VOULKOS, PETER
SCULPTOR, EDUCATOR
b Bozeman, Mont, Jan 29, 24. *Study:* Mont State Univ, BS, 50; Calif Col Arts & Crafts, MFA, 52; Mont State Univ, LHD, 68; Calif Col Arts & Crafts, Oakland, Hon DFA, 72; Otis Inst Parsons Sch Design, Los Angeles, Calif, Hon DFA, 80; San Francisco Art Inst, Calif, Hon DFA, 82. *Work:* Baltimore Mus Art, Md; Boston Mus Fine Arts, Mass; Corcoran Gallery Art, Washington, DC; Cranbrook Mus, Bloomfield Hills, Mich; San Francisco Mus Art; Whitney Mus Am Art, New York; Honolulu Acad Arts, Hawaii; Los Angeles Co Art Mus, Calif; Milwaukee Art Mus, Wis; Minn Mus Art, St Paul; Mus Mod Art, New York; Philadelphia Mus, Pa; Seattle Art Mus, Wash; and others. *Comn:* Return to Piraeus (copper-nickel, monel and bronze), Univ Art Mus, Univ Calif, Berkeley, 71; Hall of Justice (bronze), San Francisco Hall of Justice, 71; Miss Nitro (bronze), Highland Park Pub Libr, Ill, 72; Osaka (bronze), E B Crocker Art Gallery, Sacramento, Calif, 75; Barking Sands (bronze), Gen Servs Admin Fed Bldg, Honolulu, Hawaii, 77; and others. *Exhib:* Solo exhibs, Braunstein Gallery, San Francisco, 86 & 87, Twining Gallery, San Francisco, 88, Thomas Segal Gallery, Boston, Charles Cowles Gallery, New York, 90 & Elaine Horwitch Galleries, Santa Fe, NMex, 90; Clay Revisions: Plate, Cup, Vase (w/catalog), Seattle Art Mus, 87; The Eloquent Object (w/catalog), Philbrook Mus Art, traveling 87-89, Mus Mod Art, Kyoto, Japan 89, Mus Mod Art Tokyo, Japan, 90; Three Sculptor-New Work, Twining Gallery, New York, 88; Putting Pottery in Perspective: Past, Present and Future (w/catalog) Clark Arts Ctr, Rockford Col, Ill, 90; var exhibs at major mus incl Milwaukee Art Mus, Los Angeles Co Mus Art, Whitney Mus. *Pos:* Var juries & comts, 53-81; var lects, workshops & panels, 57-84. *Teaching:* Instr, Archie Bray Found, Black Mountain Col, Los Angeles Co Art Inst, Mont State Univ, Greenwich House Potter & Teachers Col, Columbia Univ; prof art & design, Univ Calif, Berkeley, 59-85. *Awards:* Rodin Mus Prize in Sculpture, I Paris Biennial, 59; Brandeis Creative Arts Award, 82; Guggenheim Fel, John Simon Guggenheim Mem Found, 84; and others. *Bibliog:* Thomas Albright (auth), Peter Voulkos: Ceramics That Transcend Art, San Francisco Chronicle, 3/27/84; Al Morch (auth), Two Artists Love of Light and Motion, San Francisco Examiner, 1/13/86; Ken Baker (auth), Peter Voulkos' Visually Magic Balancing Act, San Francisco Chronicle, 1/28/86. *Mem:* Acad Fel Am Crafts Coun, 75; hon mem, Nat Coun Educ Ceramic Arts. *Media:* All. *Mailing Add:* 1306 Third St Berkeley CA 94710

VOURVOULIAS, JOYCE BUSH See De Guatemala, Joyce (Joyce Bush Vourvoulias)

W

WAALAND, JAMES BREARLEY, II
DEALER, GALLERY DIRECTOR
b Findlay, Ohio, May 15, 53. *Study:* Bowling Green State Univ, BA, 75. *Pos:* Owner & dir, Waaland Gallery Antique Art, 76- *Specialty:* Nineteenth and early twentieth century American and European paintings; Chinese ceramics of the 18th and 19th centuries; vintage photographic images; American quilts; appraisals. *Mailing Add:* 2817 Collingwood Blvd Toledo OH 43610

WACHS, ETHEL
EDUCATOR, COLLECTOR
b New York, NY, Dec 26, 23. *Study:* Brooklyn Col, with Philip Pearlstein, A D Reinhardt & Jimmy Ernst, BS, MA & MS. *Exhib:* Am Soc Contemp Artists, US Custom House, New York, 80; Nat Asn Women Artists, Federal Bldg, New York, 80-92; Nat Acad Design, New York, 80 & 82; Audubon Artists, Nat Arts Club, New York 81-92; Bergen Community Mus, Paramus, NJ, 83; solo exhib, New Sch for Soc Res, 90-92. *Teaching:* Teacher fine arts, M D Bacon High Sch, New York, 58-; instr adult educ, Brooklyn Col, New York, 68-; instr continuing ed, Baruch Col, 88- *Awards:* Binney & Smith, Knickerbocker Artists, 80; Audubon Medal Honor, 82; Martha Reed Mem Award, 91. *Mem:* NY Artists Equity; NY Soc Women Artists; Nat Asn Women Artists; Audubon Artists; Am Soc Contemp Artists. *Media:* Watercolor. *Collection:* Contemporary American art. *Dealer:* Voltaire's Route 2 New Milford CT 06776. *Mailing Add:* 20 E 9th St New York NY 10003

WACHSTETER, GEORGE
ILLUSTRATOR
b Hartford, Conn, Mar 12, 11. *Work:* New York Pub Libr Theatre Collection; US Steel Collection; NBC Collection; plus works in pvt collections. *Comn:* Portrait Sen Taft, Taft Mem Fund, 55. *Exhib:* One-man traveling exhib for NBC Book of Stars, 58. *Pos:* Illusr for major advert agencies, theatrical & motion picture productions, 36-; illusr for CBS, ABC, NBC radio & TV networks, 37-; weekly contribr illus & caricature to drama pages, New York Herald Tribune, 41-50; contribr illus & caricature drama & political pages, New York Times, 38-50, TV artist, 50-51; caricaturist for Theatre Guild on the Air, produced by US Steel, 45-63; drama artist, New York J-Am, 56-63, TV mag cover artist, 58-63; drama artist, New York World Tel, 64-66; syndicated feature illusr for Hallmark TV Drama Series, 64-69. *Media:* Ink, Watercolor. *Publ:* Illusr, NBC Book of Stars, Simon & Schuster, 57. *Mailing Add:* 85-05 Elmhurst Ave Elmhurst NY 11373

WADDELL, JOHN HENRY
SCULPTOR, PAINTER
b Des Moines, Iowa, Feb 14, 21. *Study:* Art Inst Chicago, BFA, MFA, 48, BAE & MAE, 51; Nat Col Educ, Evanston, Ill, Hon DFA, 79. *Work:* Phoenix Art Mus, Ariz; Univ Ariz, Tucson; US Tennis Asn Nat Tennis Ctr, Flushing Meadow, NY; Kenyon Col, Gambier, Ohio; Nat Col Educ, Evanston, Ill; Ravinia Park, Highland Park, Ill. *Comn:* That Which Might Have Been (sculpture), Unitarian Church, Phoenix, 63-64, Dedication, 69; The Family (sculpture), Maricopa Co Complex, 67; Dance (sculpture), Phoenix Civic Ctr, 74; I Am That I Am (sculpture), Temple Beth Israel, Phoenix, 82; Backwalkover (sculpture), Ctr Sports Med & Orthopedics, Phoenix, 85. *Exhib:* La Jolla Art Mus, Calif, 59; Phoenix Art Mus, 60, 62 & 64; one man shows, Unitarian Church, Phoenix, 77, 85, 90, Verde Valley Artists Asn, Jerome, Ariz, 77, Nat Col Educ, Evanston, Ill, 79 & Sedona Arts Ctr, 80; Robert Mondavi Winery, Oakville, Calif, 82 & 86; Scottsdale Ctr Arts, Ariz, 84, 90; Yuma Fine Arts Ctr, 84; Tempe Arts Center, Tempe, Ariz, 90; Sun City Art Mus, 91. *Teaching:* Instr art & art educ, Nat Col Educ, Evanston, Ill, 49-55; asst prof art, Inst Design, Chicago, 55-57; prof art, Ariz State Univ, 57-61 & 63-64; founder & dir, Master Apprentice Prog, Waddell Sculpture Fel, 72- *Awards:* Man of Yr, Valley of Sun Chap, Nat Soc Arts & Lett, 75; Alumni Award Merit, Eureka Col, Ill, 82; Artist of Year Award for Cult Contributions, Scottsdale, Fine Arts Comn, Ariz, 85. *Bibliog:* Harry Wood (auth), Soul, 70; Stan Block (dir), Waddell: Man of Bronze, ABC-TV, 74; Allan Baker (dir), The Beauty of Individual Differences, Ariz State Univ. *Mem:* Nat Artists Equity Asn. *Media:* Bronze; Pastel, Watercolor. *Publ:* Dir, Discovering Sculpture, 58 & Discovering Drawing and Painting (films), 61, Bailey Films; auth, The Beauty of Individual Differences, Master Apprentice Programs, 85. *Mailing Add:* Oak Creek Valley Rd HC 66 Box 2273 Cornville AZ 86325-9741

WADDELL, THEODORE
PAINTER
b Billings, Mont, Oct 6, 41. *Study:* Brooklyn Mus Art Sch, 62; Eastern Mont Col, Billings, Mont, BS, 66; Wayne State Univ, Detroit, Mich, MFA, 68. *Work:* Eastern Mont Col & Yellowstone Art Ctr, Billings, Mont; Sheldon Mem Art Gallery, Univ Nebr, Lincoln, Nebr; City of Great Falls, Mont; Dallas Mus Art; San Jose Mus, Calif. *Exhib:* 38th Corcoran Biennial, Corcoran Gallery, Washington, DC, 83; solo exhibs, Univ Calif, San Diego, 84, Cheney Cowles Mem Mus, Spokane, Wash, 85; The New West, Colorado Springs Fine Arts Ctr, Colorado Springs, 86; Bernice Stein Baum Gallery, New York, 92. *Bibliog:* Gordon McConnell (auth), Theodore Waddell, Yellowstone Art Ctr, 84. *Media:* Oil on Canvas. *Mailing Add:* c/o Stremmel Gallery 1400 S Virginia St Reno NV 89502

WADDINGHAM, JOHN ALFRED
PAINTER, PRINTMAKER
b London, Eng, July 9, 15; US citizen. *Study:* Coronado Sch Fine Arts, Calif, 53-54; Portland Art Mus, 40-45; Univ Portland, 46-47; also with Rex Brandt, Eliot O'Hara, George Post, Milford Zones, Morris Shubin, Christopher Schink & Barbara Nechis. *Work:* Portland Art Mus; Univ Ore Mus; Vincent Price Collection; Ford Times Collection; Ore Hist Soc. *Comn:* Genesis (mural), St Barnabas Episcopal Church, Portland, 60. *Exhib:* Over 50 one man & invitational exhibs. *Pos:* Promotion art dir, Ore J, Portland, 46-59; mem staff, Oregonian, Portland, 59, ed art dir, 59-80; proprietor, John Waddingham Hand Prints, 65- *Teaching:* Instr watercolor, Ore Soc Artists, 54-56; instr, Mittleman Jewish Community Ctr, 80-81, Buffalo Grass Soc, Ore Med Sch, 80-86, Portland Community Col, 81, Ore Sch Arts & Crafts, 81-, Art in the Mountains, formerly, Multnoman Athletic Club, 88-93. *Awards:* Gold Medals, Italy, 76, 77 & 80; Award for Newspaper Illus, 76. *Bibliog:* Featured artist, Am Artist, 5/67, 6/90. *Mem:* Portland Art Dirs Club (past pres); Watercolor Soc Ore; NW Watercolor Soc, Seattle, Wash. *Media:* Watercolor; Drawings, Graphics. *Publ:* Featured artist, North Light Mag, 87. *Dealer:* Portland Art Mus Rental Sales Gallery 1219 SW Park Ave Portland OR 97205; Univ Ore Mus Art Eugene OR 97403. *Mailing Add:* 955 SW Westwood Dr Portland OR 97201

WADE, JANE
DEALER
b Dallas, Tex, June 30, 25. *Study:* Univ Ariz; in Europe; Curt Valentin Gallery, New York; Otto Gerson Gallery, New York. *Collections Arranged:* Drawings by Sculptors, Smithsonian Inst & US Tour. *Pos:* Secy & asst, Curt Valentin Gallery, 48-56; assoc, Otto Gerson Gallery, 56-63; vpres, Marlborough-Gerson Gallery, 63-64; owner & dir, Jane Wade Ltd. *Bibliog:* Jay Jacobs (auth), By appointment only, Art in Am, 7-8/67; By appointment only, Newsweek, 9/4/67 & Time 8/3/70. *Mem:* Art Dealers Asn Am. *Specialty:* Twentieth century painting and sculpture. *Mailing Add:* 467 Mariscal Rd Palm Springs CA 92262

WADE, ROBERT SCHROPE
PHOTOGRAPHER, SCULPTOR
b Austin, Tex, Jan 6, 43. *Study:* Univ Tex, Austin, BFA, 65; Univ Calif, Berkeley, MA, 66. *Work:* Menil Collection, Houston, Tex; Groningen Mus, Holland; Beaubourg Mus, Paris, France; NMex State Capitol; Royal Palace, Monaco. *Comn:* Giant Iguana, Lone Star Cafe, New York, 78; Biggest Cowboy Boots, Washington Art Site, DC, 79; Fiberglass Mex Man, La Salsa, Malibu, Calif,87. *Exhib:* Whitney Mus, New York, 69 & 73; one-man shows, Kornblee Gallery, New York, 71 & 74, Jan Turner Gallery, Los Angeles, 78, Elaine Horwitch Galleries, Santa Fe, NMex, 87, 90 & 93 & Janie Beggs Gallery, Beverly Hills, Calif, 90; 2nd Wild West Show, Calgary, Can, 83; Central Cult, Sao Paulo, Brazil, 84; Brooklyn Mus, New York, 86; Sky Art Festival, Anchorage, Alaska, 89; Snug Harbor Cult Ctr, Staten Island, NY, 92; and others. *Teaching:* Instr, McLennan Col, 66-70; artist in residence & dir, Northwood Exp Art Inst, Dallas, 70-73; asst prof, NTex State Univ, Denton, 73-77; vis artist, Kansas City Art Inst, 79 & 92. *Awards:* Nat Endowment Grants, 73, 74 & 84. *Bibliog:* Anne Hillerman (auth), Etcetera: Art Texas-Style, Southwest Art, 4/87; Becky Duval Reese (auth), A century of sculpture in Tex 1889-1989 (catalog), Austin, 6/89; Jutta Feddersen (auth), Soft Sculpture (book), Gordon & Breach Int, London, NY, 92; and others. *Mem:* Artists Advocacy. *Media:* Miscellaneous Media. *Publ:* Article, Art Press Int, Paris, France, 10/77. *Mailing Add:* Rte 4 Box 58W Sante Fe NM 87501

WAGNER, CATHERINE
PHOTOGRAPHER
b San Francisco, Calif, Jan 31, 53. *Study:* Inst Art, San Miguel de Allende, Mex, 71; San Francisco Art Inst, 71; San Francisco State Univ, BA(art, photog, cum laude), 75, MA, 77. *Work:* Mus Fine Arts, Houston; San Francisco Mus Mod Art, Calif; Oakland Mus Art, Calif; Nat Mus Am Art, Smithsonian Inst, Washington, DC; Polaroid Collection, Cambridge, Mass; Met Mus Art. *Comn:* Construction of Louisiana, World Expos Can Centre Archit, Quebec City, Que, 84; photograph of Civic Ctr Plaza, Am Inst Archit, 85; Bank Architecture, Parnassus Found, Houston, Tex, 87; rephotograph of the George Moscone Conv Ctr, Houston, 88; Louisiana World Expos, Libbie Rice Gallery, Houston, 88. *Exhib:* retrospective 1976-1986 (with catalog), Min Gallery, Tokyo, Japan, 87; solo exhibs, Mus Fine Arts (with catalog), Houston, Tex, 88, Mus Contemp Photography, Columbia Col, Chicago, 88, Fraenkel Gallery, San Francisco, 89, Ansel Adams Ctr, San Francisco, 89, Laurence Miller Gallery, NY, 90 & Home & Other Stories, Los Angeles Co Mus Art, 93; Several Exceptionally Good Recently Acquired Pictures VI, Fraenkel Gallery, San Francisco, 92. *Teaching:* Lectr photog, San Francisco State Univ, 79-85; assoc prof art, Mills Col, Oakland, Calif, 79- *Awards:* Photog Fel, 81 & 90, Vis Artists Fel in Photog, 90 & 91, Nat Endowment Art; Ferguson Grant, Friends of Photog, 84; Guggenheim Found Fel, 87. *Bibliog:* Jeanette Ross (auth), Organizing Meaning, Artweek, 12/21/89; Hilda Bijur (auth), Bodies and Classrooms, Chelsea Clinton News, 3/22/90; A D Coleman (auth), The New York Observer, 3/26/90; Andy Grundberg (auth), the New York Times, 3/30/90. *Mem:* Soc Photog Educ; Bay Area Consortium Visual Arts. *Publ:* Auth, To Collect the Art of Women: The Jane Reese Williams Cllection of Photography, Mus NMex, Santa Fe, 92. *Dealer:* Fraenkel Gallery 55 Grant Ave San Francisco CA 94108. *Mailing Add:* 308 Precita Ave San Francisco CA 94110

WAGNER, CHARLES H
ADMINISTRATOR, INSTRUCTOR
b Baltimore, Md. *Study:* Md Inst Col Art, BFA; Johns Hopkins Univ; Yale Univ, MFA. *Work:* Md Inst Col Art; Western Md Col, Westminster; Towson State Univ. *Exhib:* Baltimore Watercolor Club, Md, 73-75; Western Md Col, 75; Lindwood Gallery, 83; Rehobeth Art League, 83; Revelations Gallery, Baltimore, 83; Towson State Univ. *Teaching:* Instr drawing, painting & Art Hist, Md Inst Col Art, Baltimore, 50-; dept chmn sec art, Baltimore Co Pub Schs, Md, 55-70; instr design & watercolor, Towson State Univ, Md, 72-; instr drawing & painting, Howard Community Col, 82-; instr, Essex Community Col, 87- *Awards:* Bronze Medal Figure Painting, Md Inst, 55; John Hay Fel, Yale Univ, 60-61; First Prize Design, Nat Educ Asn, 65. *Publ:* Illusr, Baltimore County Serves the Nation, 59; auth, Classroom Discipline, 60; auth, Team Teaching in Art, 74; contribr, art curric guides, 82. *Mailing Add:* 1042 W Seminary Ave Lutherville MD 21093

WAGNER, (DR) DAVID J
MUSEUM DIRECTOR
Study: Univ Wis, Stevens Point, BM(music & art hist), 74; Ind Univ, Bloomington, MA(arts admin), 76; Univ Minn, Minneapolis, PhD(am studies), 92. *Collections Arranged:* Travelling exhibs, Americans in Glass (contribr, catalog), 77-86, Birds in Art (contribr, catalog), 77-87, Wisconsin's New Deal Art (contribr, catalog), 80-82, Selections from the McMichael Collection (contribr, catalog), 82-84, Rembrandt's Etchings (contribr, catalog), 85-87, Wildlife in Art, (contribr, catalog), 87-89, Arts for the Parks (contribr, catalog), 88-89 & Colorado: State of the Art, 89; Pikes Peak Vision, The Broadmoor Art Acad, 89; Images of Penance, Images of Mercy, Southwestern Santos in the Late Nineteenth Century, 91. *Pos:* Grad asst, Hist Collections, Ind Univ Mus, Bloomington, 75-76; intern, Conserv Dept, Children's Mus, Indianapolis, Ind, 76; dir, Leigh Yawkey Woodson Art Mus, Wausau, Wis, 77-87; exec dir, Colorado Springs Fine Arts Ctr, 87- *Teaching:* Tutor music theory, Univ Wis, Stevens Point, 72-73; teaching asst Am studies, Univ Minn, Minneapolis, 82-83; lectr mus studies, Univ Wis Exten, 84; scholar-in-residence, Sitka Center for Art & Ecology, Otis, OR. *Awards:* Scholarship Award, Inst Europ Studies, Vienna, Austria & Freiburg, Ger, 82; Dissertation Fel, Univ Minn, Minneapolis, 87. *Bibliog:* James Auer (auth), Looking back at a miracle: Art of the depression, Milwaukee J, 1/80; Chuck Wechsler (auth), Windows onto the world of wildlife, Southwest Art, 3/85; Rob Silberman (auth), Americans in glass: A requiem?, Art Am, 3/85; John Fetter (auth), Pike's Peak Artists, Colorado Springs Gazette Tele, 5/88. *Mem:* Am Asn Mus; Rocky Mountain/Plains Mus Asn; Am Studies Asn; Asn Art Mus Dir. *Publ:* Contribr, Wis Acad Rev Mag, Wis Acad Arts, Letts & Sci, 85, US Art, 92. *Mailing Add:* c/o Colo Springs Fine Art Ctr 30 W Dale St Colorado Springs CO 80903

WAGNER, MERRILL
PAINTER
b Seattle, Wash, June 12, 35. *Study:* Sarah Lawrence Col, BA, 57; Art Students League, New York, with Edwin Dickenson, George Grosz & Julian Levy, 59-63. *Work:* Bellevue Art Mus, Washington; Chase Manhattan Bank, New York; Seattle Arts Comn, Wash; Tacoma Art Mus, Wash; Weatherspoon

Art Gallery, Univ NC, Greensboro. *Exhib:* 26 Contemporary Women Artists, Aldrich Mus, Ridgefield, Conn, 71; Christmas Show, Art Lending Service, Penthouse, Mus Mod Art, 71; one-person shows, The Clocktower, Inst Art & Urban Resources, New York, 79, Watson DeNagy Gallery, Houston, 82, Traver Gallery, Seattle, 87, 89 & 91, Gemeentemuseum, Holland, 91, Stark Gallery, New York, 92 & L Gray Gallery, Providence, RI, 91; Surfaces/Textures, Mus Mod Art, 81; John Gibson Gallery, New York, 86; Fawbush Gallery, New York, 89. *Teaching:* Vis lectr in the humanities, drawing & painting, Princeton Univ, 83-91, prof advan painting, 83-; instr drawing, Univ Puget Sound, summer 85 & 86. *Awards:* Nat Endowment Arts Visual Artists Fel Grant; Nat Endowment Arts Award Artists Bks, 90. *Bibliog:* Tiffany Bell (auth), article, Arts Mag, 5/86; Matthew Kangas (auth), Time Travellers, Seattle Weekly, 11/18/87; Lois Nesbit (auth), Merrill Wagner: Fanbush Gallery, Artforum, 10/89. *Mem:* Am Abstract Artists (pres, 82-85). *Media:* Multi. *Publ:* A Calendar, September 1982-December 1983, Magna Color Press, Inc, 82; auth, Notes on Paint, prt publ, 90. *Dealer:* Traver Gallery Seattle WA; Fawbush Gallery New York NY. *Mailing Add:* 17 W 16th New York NY 10011

WAGNER, RICHARD ELLIS
PAINTER
b Trotwood, Ohio, June 18, 23. *Study:* Antioch Col; Dayton Art Inst, Ohio; Univ Colo, BFA & MFA. *Work:* Denver Art Mus, Colo; Libr of Cong, Washington, DC; Dartmouth Col, Hanover, NH; DeCordova Mus, Lincoln, Mass; Rochester Mus, NY. *Comn:* Murals, Horizon House, Naples, Fla, 71. *Exhib:* Recent Drawings USA, Mus Mod Art, New York, 56; Art USA, Madison Sq Garden, 58; Boston Arts Festival, Mass, 58, 60 & 62; Youngstown Art Festival, Butler Inst Am Art, 70; Art USA, W Colo Ctr Arts, Grand Junction, 86 & 89; Artists of the West, Colo Springs Rotary, 90-92. *Pos:* Jury for art shows: Grand Junction, Colo, 87, Delta, Colo, 88. *Teaching:* Instr, Univ Colo, 52 & 55; assoc prof art, Dartmouth Col, 53-66. *Awards:* Purchase Prizes, Denver Art Mus, 50 & Libr of Cong, 52; jurors award, Colo Springs Art Guild, 89. *Media:* Oil, Acrylic. *Publ:* Illusr, Ford Times, 58-70; Sketches in San Juans, 76; Sketches in Southwest Seasons, 82; article in: Palette Talk, 83. *Dealer:* El Prado Galleries Sedona Santa Fe; The Darvish College Naples FL. *Mailing Add:* 13980 Co Rd 29 Dolores CO 81323

WAGONER, ROBERT B
PAINTER, SCULPTOR
b Marion, Ohio, July 13, 28. *Study:* With Burt Procter & Olaf Weighorst. *Work:* Leanin' Tree Publ Mus, Boulder, Colo; Winthrop Rockefeller Collection. *Exhib:* Death Valley 49ers, Calif, 61; two-man shows, Scottsdale, Ariz, 72 & 73 & three-man show, 74; Mont Hist Soc, Helena, 74; Previews, Tex Gallery, Dallas, 75-79. *Pos:* Dir, Death Valley 49ers, 69- *Awards:* First Award & Top Artists Award, Death Valley 49ers, 72 & 73 & First Award, 74, 75 & 76. *Bibliog:* James Serven (auth), Cattle, guns and cowboys, Ariz Hwys Mag, 70; Robert Wolenik (auth), Colorful west of Robert Wagoner, Westerner, 1-2/73; Portrait of a Westerner, Sierra Life Mag, 81. *Media:* Oil, Watercolor; Canvas, Masonite. *Dealer:* Texas Art Gallery Dallas TX; Saddleback Western Art Gallery Santa Ana CA. *Mailing Add:* 2710 Highland Dr Bishop CA 93514

WAHLING, JON B
SCULPTOR, WEAVER
b Council Bluffs, Iowa, Apr 14, 38. *Study:* Kansas City Art Inst & Sch Design, BFA, 62; Haystack Mountain Sch Crafts, Deer Isle, Maine, summers 63-65; Cranbrook Acad Art, MFA, 64; also with Maija Grotell & Glen Kauffman. *Work:* Columbus Mus of Art, Ohio; Massillon Mus, Ohio; Yager Gallery, Hartwick College; Univ Art Mus, Univ Tex, Austin; Ohio Arts Coun. *Comn:* Fiber sculpture hanging, Merchants & Mechanics Fed Loan & Savings Bank, Springfield, Ohio, 79. *Exhib:* Packard Gallery, Columbus Mus Art, Ohio, 77; Fiber Directions, Grunnier Gallery & Mus, Iowa State Univ, Ames, 82; In the Round, Southern Ohio Mus & Cult Ctr, Portsmouth, 83; The Works, Statewide Touring Exhib, Ohio Found Arts, 83-84; Five Sculptors, Springfield Art Ctr, Main Gallery, Ohio, 87; solo shows, Fiber Art, Eells Gallery, Blossom/Kent Festival, Blossom Music Ctr, Ohio, 87 & Gallery 200, Columbus, Ohio, 88. *Pos:* Cur, artistic coordr, Garment Design: In Celebration of Body & Soul, Columbus Cult Arts Ctr, Ohio, 87. *Teaching:* Instr weaving, Columbus Cult Arts Ctr, Columbus Recreation & Parks Dept, Ohio, 64-; instr weaving, Penland Sch Crafts, NC, summers 66, 67 & 71. *Awards:* Craftsmen USA Nat Merit Award, Mus Contemp Crafts, New York, 66; Ten Outstanding Young Men Award, Columbus Jaycees, 72; Bordens Award for Outstanding Design in Fibre, 7th Beaux Arts Designer/Craftsmen Exhib, 73. *Bibliog:* Maryann Reilly (auth), Commissions opportunities for today's artists, Ohio Arts J, 7/80; Carla Peterson (auth), Technical virtuosity, Ohio Arts J, 1/85. *Mem:* Am Crafts Coun; hon mem Cent Ohio Weavers Guild; Ohio Designer Craftsmen; Ohio Designer Craftsmen (secy, 82-83); Surface Design Asn. *Media:* Fiber, Metal. *Dealer:* Gallery 2000 200 West-Mound St Columbus OH 43215. *Mailing Add:* 44 Stimmel St Columbus OH 43206

WAHLMAN, MAUDE SOUTHWELL
ADMINISTRATOR, HISTORIAN
b New York, NY. *Study:* Colo Col, BA(art), 69; Northwestern Univ, MA(anthrop), 69; Yale Univ, PhD(art hist, teaching fel), 80. *Collections Arranged:* Contemp African Arts, 73-75; Contemporary African Fabrics, Mus Contemp Art, Chicago, 75; Ten Afro-American Quilters, 82-; Gifts of the Spirit, 84-85. *Pos:* Consult African ethnology, Field Mus Nat Hist, Chicago, 71-74. *Teaching:* Asst prof art hist & southern studies, Univ Miss, 80-85; assoc prof & chmn art dept, Univ Cent Fla, Orlando, 85- *Awards:* Wenner-Gren Found Fel for mus res, Field Mus, 71; Nat Endowment Arts Grant, 82; Res Grant for southern folk arts, Nat Endowment Humanities, 81-84. *Mem:* African Studies Asn; Am Folklore Soc; Soc Folk Arts Preservation; Women's Caucus Art. *Media:* Photography. *Res:* Historical roots of Afro-American Folk. *Publ:* Auth, Contemporary African Arts, Field Mus, 74; Ceremonial Art of West Africa, Mich State Univ, 79; Traditional Art of West Africa, Colby Col, 80; co-ed, Spirit of Africa, Memphis State Univ, 82; auth, Afro-American Quiltmaking, Ind Univ (in prep); Religious Symbols in Afro-American Folk Arts, New York Folklore, Phillp Stevens, Vol 12, No 1-2. *Mailing Add:* Art Dept Univ Cent Fla Orlando FL 32816

WAID, JIM (JAMES E)
PAINTER
b Elgin, Okla, Nov 2, 42. *Study:* Univ NMex, with Morris Kantor & John Kacere, BFA, 65; Univ Ariz, MFA, 71. *Work:* Univ Ariz Mus Art; Metrop Mus Art, New York; Yuma Art Ctr, Ariz; IBM, Montvale, NJ; Chemical Bank, New York. *Comn:* Santa Cruz (mural), Tucson Pub Libr, 77. *Exhib:* 35th Biennial, Corcoran Gallery Art, 77; First Western States Biennial, Nat Collection Art, Washington, DC, 79-80; Four Corners States Biennial Exhib, Phoenix Art Mus, 81; Solo exhibs, Mus Art, Univ Ariz, Tucson, 85, Riva Yares Gallery, Scottsdale, Ariz, 86 & 88, Linda Durham Gallery, Santa Fe, NMex, 87, Southwest Tex State Univ, San Marcos, 87 & Shoshana Wayne Gallery, Santa Monica, Calif, 88; Phoenix Biennial, Phoenix Art Mus, 87; Large Scale Paintings, Riva Yares Gallery, Scottsdale, Ariz, 88; The New/Old Landscape, Mus Art, Uniz Ariz, Tucson, 89. *Teaching:* Instr art, Pima Community Col, 71-80. *Awards:* Purchase Prizes, Arizona's Outlook, Tucson Mus Art, 80 & 14th Southwestern Invitational, Yuma Art Ctr, Ariz, 80; Nat Endowment Visual Arts Fel Grant, 85. *Mem:* Artists Equity; Dinnerware Artists Coop (treas, 79-82). *Dealer:* Riva Yares Gallery 3625 Bishop Lane Scottsdale AZ 85251. *Mailing Add:* c/o Riva Yares Gallery 3625 Bishop Lane Scottsdale AZ 85251

WAINWRIGHT, ROBERT BARRY
PAINTER, PRINTMAKER
b Chilliwack, BC, June 29, 35. *Study:* Vancouver Sch Art, dipl, 62; Atelier 17, Paris, with S W Hayter, Emily Carr Travel Study Scholar, 62. *Work:* Nat Gallery Can; Art Gallery Ont; Mus Fine Arts, Mus Art Contemp, Montreal; Can Indust Ltd, Toronto. *Exhib:* Premio Int Biella L'Incisione, Italy, 71, 73 & 76; solo exhib, Galerie Martal, Montreal, 72, Concordia Univ, Montreal, 76 & 80 & Mazelow Gallery, Toronto, 77; Galerie Elca London, Montreal, 84. *Teaching:* Assoc prof printmaking, Concordia Univ, Montreal, 66- *Awards:* Can Coun Grants, 63-64 & 67-68; Erindale Col Purchase Prize, Int Exhib Graphics, Montreal, 71. *Mem:* Royal Can Acad Arts; Can Artists Rep. *Dealer:* Galerie Daniel 2159 Mackay St Montreal PQ H3G 2J2. *Mailing Add:* Concordia Univ 1455 de Maisonneuve Montreal PQ H3G 1M8 Canada

WAISBROT, ANN M
ADMINISTRATOR, CURATOR
Study: Univ Wis, Stevens Point, BS (art educ), 70. *Collections Arranged:* The Fantasy Carvings of John Heatwhole (wood carvings), 90; Contemp British Prints from Bromberg Collection, 91; Ira Moskowitz (original drawings, painting, prints), 91-92; New Visions Culture & Agriculture '92 (sculpture, works on paper, paintings), 92; India: A Sense of Form & Color (art artifacts from pvt collections), 92. *Pos:* Exec dir, New Visions Gallery Inc, Marshfield, Wis, 86- *Mem:* Am Asn Mus; Midwest Mus Conf; Wis Fed Mus; Am Coun Arts; Am Crafts Coun. *Mailing Add:* New Visions Gallery 1000 N Oak Ave Marshfield WI 54449

WAITZKIN, STELLA
SCULPTOR, PAINTER
b New York, NY. *Study:* NY Univ; Columbia Univ; also with Meyer Shapiro & Hans Hofmann. *Work:* Nat Gallery Fine Arts; Patrick Lanon Col, Fla; Walker Art Ctr; Tel-Aviv Mus, Israel; Everson Mus, Syracuse; New York Pub Libr. *Comn:* Con Ed Bldg, New York, 92. *Exhib:* One-woman show, Serious Literature, Calhoun Col, Yale Univ, 74; Potsdam Plastics, NY Univ, 75; Contemp Am Sculpture, Va Mus Downtown Gallery, 75; James Yu Exhib, 75; Renwick Gallery, Smithsonian Inst, Washington, DC; Nat Collection Fine Arts, Washington, DC; Selected Work, 1973-1983, Everson Mus, Syracuse, 83; Terminal Invitational, NY, 83; Witkin Gallery, New York, 87; Patricia Carrega Gallery, Wash, DC, 88; Anita Shapolsky Gallery, 88; Galerie Caroline Corre, Paris, 88, 89 & 90; State Mus, Trenton, NJ, 90. *Pos:* Lectr, New York Univ. *Teaching:* Guest lectr, Columbia Univ Grad Sch, 73. *Awards:* Yaddo Found Fels, 73-76; MacDowell Found Fels, 74-83; Louis Comfort Tiffany Grant, 77. *Bibliog:* Taylor Mead, Studio Art (film); D Holmes (auth), article in Arch Am Art, 71; articles in Arts Mag, 73 & 74. *Mem:* Artist Equity. *Media:* Sandstone, Polyester Resin. *Publ:* Reproductions & articles in art publs; film work. *Dealer:* Fendrick Gallery 3059 M St NW Washington DC 20007; Peter David Gallery 430 Oak Grove Minneapolis MN 55403. *Mailing Add:* 222 W 23rd St New York NY 10011

WAKSBERG, NAOMI
PAINTER
b Ger, July 16, 47; US citizen. *Study:* Ohio State Univ, Columbus, BFA & BSci, 69; Md Inst Art, Baltimore, 70; Rutgers Univ, New Brunswick, NJ, MA & MFA, 72. *Work:* Ohio State Univ, Columbus; Continental Life Insurance Co, New York; Continental Group Investors, New Haven, Conn; First Nat Bank, Chicago; Japanese Embassy, Washington, DC; and others. *Exhib:* One-person show, Lehigh Univ, Bethlehem, Pa, 80 & Morris Mus; Artists Books, Philadelphia Art Alliance, 81; Rutgers Invitational, State Mus, Trenton, NJ, 82; Alternative Mus, New York, 82; Condeso/Lawler, New York, 82; Muse Found, Philadelphia, 83; State Mus, Trenton, NJ, 86; and others. *Pos:* Coordr & cur, Women Artists Series, Douglass Col Libr, 72-76;

project dir, Her Own Space, Muse Foud, 82. *Teaching:* Instr art hist, Trenton State Univ, NJ, 80-81. *Awards:* Bea Camhi Award, Hudson River Mus, 80; NJ Arts Fel, 82-83. *Bibliog:* Kay Larson (auth), Small talk, Village Voice, 2/11/80; Victoria Donahue (auth), rev, Philadelphia Inquirer, 5/81; Judith Stein (auth), article, Art Express, 11-12/81. *Mem:* Muse Found, Philadelphia (bd dirs, 80-); Women's Caucus Art (steering comt, 79-81); Col Art Asn. *Media:* Acrylic, Oil Pastel. *Publ:* Contribr, Lehigh University Fall Collections, Lehigh Univ, 80. *Dealer:* Condeso/Lawler 119 West 25th St New York NY; Van Straaten Gallery 646 N Michigan Ave Chicago IL. *Mailing Add:* PO Box 375C Cherryville Hollow Rd Flemington NJ 08822

WALBURG, GERALD
SCULPTOR, EDUCATOR
b Berkeley, Calif, May 5, 36. *Study:* Calif Col Arts & Crafts, 54-56; Calif State Univ, San Francisco, BA, 65; Univ Calif, Davis, MA, 67. *Work:* Storm King Art Ctr, Mountainville, NY; San Francisco Mus Art, Calif; Oakland Mus; Metrop Mus Art, New York; City of San Francisco. *Comn:* Sculptor, City of Sacramento, McCven & Steele, Calif. *Exhib:* San Francisco Mus Art, 67 & 69; Joslyn Art Mus, Omaha, Nebr, 70; Oakland Mus, Calif, 71 & 74; Baltimore Mus Art, Md, 73; Storm King Art Ctr, Mountainville, NY, 73-74; Crocker Gallery, Sacramento, 73 & 79; Soc of the Four Arts, Palm Beach, Fla, 74; New York Cult Ctr, 75; Bank of Am World Hq, San Francisco, 82. *Teaching:* Prof art, Calif State Univ, Sacramento, 68- *Bibliog:* Gerald Nordland (auth), Gerald Waldbrug Recent Works, Oakland Mus, 79; David Collen & H Peter Stern (coauth), Sculpture at Storm King, NY, 80; Thomas Albright (auth), articles, San Franciscio Chronicle, 4/17/76 & 12/19/78. *Mem:* Int Sculpture. *Media:* Metal, Welded. *Mailing Add:* Art Dept Cal State Univ Sacramento 6000 J St Sacramento CA 95819-6061

WALCH, JOHN LEO
PAINTER, SCULPTOR
b Oklahoma City, Okla, Jan 14, 18. *Study:* Loyola Univ, Chicago, BA, 39; Sch of the Chicago Art Inst, 35-41; studied sculpture with Bernard Frazier, painting with Henry Hensche, Robert E Wood, Edgar Whitney, John Pike, Mel Crawford & Milford Zornes & graphic art with Emilio Amero. *Work:* Fogg Mus of Art, Cambridge, Mass; Philbrook Art Ctr, Tulsa, Okla; Mabee-Gerrer Mus, Shawnee; Okla Mus Art, Oklahoma City; Okla Art Ctr, Oklahoma City; and others. *Comn:* Stations of the Cross, sculpture & liturgical design, Church of Christ The King, Oklahoma City, 64; two murals, Church of St James, Oklahoma City, 71 & 77; mural & bronze sculpture, St Francis Hosp, Tulsa, Okla, 79; sculpture & painting, St Anthony Hosp, Oklahoma City, 79; sculpture & painting, St Charles Borromeo Church, Oklahoma City, 79; Bronze Relief: Church of St James, Santiago-Atitlan, Guatemala, 86; Our Lady of Perpetual Help Cathedral, Oklahoma City, & Holy Family Cathedral, Tulsa, Okla, 86. *Exhib:* Int Exposition of Mod Sacred Art, Vatican City, Rome, Italy, 50; one-man shows, Okla Art Ctr, Oklahoma City, 50, 63 & 68, Philbrook Art Ctr, Tulsa, 57 & Southern Plains Indian Mus, Anadarko, Okla, 62; Eight-State Exhib, 58 & 72 & Nat Print & Drawing Exhib, 71, Okla Art Ctr, Oklahoma City; Contemp Christian Arts Gallery, New York, 61; Birger Sandzein Mus, Linsberg, Kans, 63; Mabee-Gerrer Mus, Shawnee, Okla, 81 & 88; Governor's Gallery, Okla State Capitol, 81; and others. *Pos:* Dir, Mabee-Gerrer Mus, Shawnee, 82-86, dir emer, 89- *Teaching:* Vis instr figure drawing & painting, Briar Cliff Col, Sioux City, Iowa, 65-66; numerous workshops figure & portrait drawing, Okla Art Guild, Oklahoma City, 70- *Awards:* Purchase Award, Okla Ann Exhib, Philbrook Art Ctr, Tulsa, 61; and others. *Bibliog:* Articles in Okla Today Mag & Orbit Mag. *Mem:* Life mem, Okla Art Guild (bd dir, 65-); Okla Sculputre Soc; Okla Pastel Soc. *Media:* Oil, Acrylic; Bronze, Hydracal. *Publ:* Illusr, Roman Missal, Cath Bk Publ Co, NY, 64; illusr, Catholic Art Calendar, Cath Church Extension Soc, Chicago, 67-71. *Dealer:* St Thomas More Book Stall 7904 N May Oklahoma City OK 73120; Shorney Gallery 6616 N Olie Oklahoma City OK 73116. *Mailing Add:* 2224 NW 20th St Oklahoma City OK 73107

WALD, CAROL
PAINTER, ILLUSTRATOR
b Detroit, Mich, Jan 21, 35. *Study:* Art Sch Soc Arts & Crafts, Detroit, 58; Skowhegan Sch Painting & Sculpture, Maine, 63; Cranbrook Acad Art, Bloomfield Hills, Mich, 69. *Work:* Dennos Mus Ctr, Traverse City, Mich; Detroit Inst Arts, Mich; Utah Mus Fine Arts, Salt Lake City; Minneapolis Mus Art, Saint Paul, Minn; Mus of Am Illustration, New York; Nat War Collage, Ft McNair, Washington, DC. *Comn:* Mural, New Spirit of 76, Nat Bicentennial Comt, 76; murals, New Detroit, First Federal Savings & Loan, Detroit, Mich, 78; Ronald Reagan, Man of the Year, Time Magazine, New York, 82; Towers of Grain, Fortune, New York, 82. *Exhib:* Solo shows, Retrospective, Flint Inst Arts, Mich, 64, Collages, Cranbrook Mus Art, Bloomfield Hills, Mich, 81, Transformations, SI Mus Am Illustration, 86, Sequences & Transformations, Recent Major Paintings, Butler Inst Am Art, Ohio, 91, Dennos Mus Ctr, Traverse City, Mich, 91; Two Hundred Years of American Illustration, New York Hist Soc, New York, 76; The Arts and Crafts Movement, Detroit Inst Arts, Mich, 80; Artist's Postcards, Cooper-Hewitt Mus Arts & Design, New York, 80; West '82 & West '92/Art and the Law, West Publ Co, St Paul, Minn, 82 & 92; Bright Visions-The Making of Myth, Rahr-West Art Mus, Manitowoc, Wis, 90. *Teaching:* Sheridan Col Art, Oakville, Ont, Can, 92. *Awards:* grant, Mich Coun Arts, 89; Visual Arts Award, Arts Found Mich, 90; Off Nat Bicentennial Painting, Nat War Col, Washington, DC, 92. *Bibliog:* Maurice Horn (auth), Wald Biography, Gale Research, 88; William J Withrow (dir emer), Carol Wald, Sequences & Tranformations, Art Gallery, Ont, 91; Sequences & Transformations, Recent Paintings, Acad Chicago Publ, Ill, 92. *Mem:* Soc Illustrators, New York; Nat Watercolor Soc; Scarab Club of Detroit. *Media:* Oil, watercolor; Collage. *Publ:* Auth, Myth America-Picturing Women 1865-1945, Pantheon Books, 75; The Metaphysical World of Hughie Lee-Smith, Am Artist, 78; illusr, Great Illustrators of our Time, Rizzoli Publ, New York, 82; Gorbachev's Russia, Business Week (cover), 85; Art for Survival, Graphis Press, 92. *Mailing Add:* 805-5280 Lakeshore Rd Burlington ON L7L 5R1 Canada

WALD, SYLVIA
PAINTER, SCULPTOR
b Philadelphia, Pa. *Study:* Moore Inst Art, Philadelphia. *Work:* Mus Mod Art, Metrop Mus Art & Whitney Mus Am Art, New York; Guggenheim Mus; Nat Gallery Art, Washington, DC; Brooklyn Mus, NY; plus others. *Exhib:* Curator's Choice, Smithsonian Inst & Tour US, 54; 50 Yrs Am Art, Mus Mod Art & Tour Europe, 55; Women Choose Women, NY Cult Ctr, 73; one-woman shows, Knoll Int, Munich, 79 & Contruction & Sculpture, Aaron Berman Gallery, New York, 81; Beyond the Wall, Berman Gallery, 83; Contemporaries, Sid Deutsch, 83; and others. *Bibliog:* Zigrosser (auth), Prints and Their Creators--A World History, 74; Una E Johnson (auth), American Prints and Printmakers, 80; James Watrous (auth), A Century of American Printmaking 1880-1980, 84. *Mem:* Am Fedn Arts. *Media:* Miscellaneous. *Mailing Add:* 417 Lafayette St New York NY 10003

WALDMAN, PAUL
PAINTER
b Erie, Pa, 1936. *Study:* Brooklyn Mus Art Sch; Pratt Inst. *Work:* Mus Mod Art, New York; Smithsonian Inst, Washington, DC; Brooklyn Mus, NY; Los Angeles Co Mus Mod Art, Los Angeles; Hirshhorn Mus, Washington, DC; Guggenheim Mus, New York; Hirschhorn Mus & Sculpture Garden; and many others. *Exhib:* Knoedler Gallery, 71; Hirshhorn Mus, 74; Castelli Gallery, 73, 75, 78, 81, 84, 87 & 91; Blum Hellman, 78; Kunsthalle Tranegarden, Copenhagen, 81; and others. *Pos:* Artist-in-residence, Ford Found, 65. *Teaching:* Instr, Greenwich Art Ctr, spring 63; instr, New York Community Col, 63-64; instr, Brooklyn Mus Art Sch, 63-67; vis artist, Ohio State Univ, 66; vis prof, Univ Calif, Davis, spring 66; instr, Sch Visual Arts, 66- *Media:* All. *Mailing Add:* Dept Fine Arts Sch Visual Arts 209-213 E 23rd St New York NY 10010

WALETZKY, CECELIA GROBLA See Waletzky, Tsirl (Cecelia Grobla Waletzky)

WALETZKY, TSIRL (CECELIA GROBLA WALETZKY)
ASSEMBLAGE ARTIST, STAINED GLASS ARTIST
Study: Art Student League, NY, 42-43; Pratt Graphics, NY, 71; Parson's, 76-78. *Work:* Yeshiva Univ Mus, Cooper Hewitt Mus (Smithsonian), Jewish Mus, New York; Wolfson Mus, Jerusalem, Israel; Judaica Mus, Riverdale, NY. *Comn:* Stained glass, 2 windows, Synagogue Ebn-Schmuel, Israel, 68; stained glass panel (with David Nulman), Hebrew Tabernacle, New York, 80; stained glass, 9 windows (with David Nulman), Cong Chofetz Chayim, Tucson, 88; stained glass scroll (with David Nulman), Cong Har Shalom, Potomac, Md, 89; cut-paper assemblage, Riverdale Temple, NY, 90. *Exhib:* Paper-cuts, Tower of David Mus, Jerusalem, Israel, 81; Paper-cuts, Cooper Hewitt Mus, New York, 86; Stained glass (with David Nulman), Yeshiva Univ Mus, New York, 86; Contemporary Paper-cuts, Judaica Mus, Riverdale, NY, 88; Expressions of Faith, Santuario de Gualalupe, Sante Fe, NMex, 90; and others. *Teaching:* Judaic paper cutting, Hebrew Arts Sch, 85-87. *Bibliog:* From Editors, Papercuts by Tsirl Waletzky, Lilith, 78; Alice Greenwald (auth), The Mizrah, Hadassah Mag, 79; Lillian Wachtel (auth), Aus Kulturallem Interesse, Aufbau, 90. *Mem:* NY Artists Equity; Pomegranate Guild Judaic Needlework (bd mem, 76-80); Guild Am Papercutters. *Media:* Cut-Paper Assemblage. *Publ:* Illusr, The New Book of Yiddish Songs, 72 & Pearls of Yiddish Songs, 88, Workmen's Circle; The Art of Judaic Needlework, Charles Scribners, 79; Eight Tales for Eight Nights, Jason Aronson, 90; The Jewish Wedding Book, Scripps Howard, 91. *Mailing Add:* 80 Knolls Crescent Bronx NY 10463-6303

WALFORD, E JOHN
HISTORIAN, EDUCATOR
b London, Eng, Feb 16, 45. *Study:* Vrije Universiteit, Amsterdam, Kandidaats(hons), 76; Wolfson Col, Cambridge Speelman Fel (Dutch & Flemish art), 76-80; Univ Cambridge, Eng, PhD, 81. *Teaching:* Assoc prof & dept chmn art hist, Wheaton Col, Ill, 81- *Mem:* Col Art Asn; Historians Netherlandish Art; Asn Art Historians, Gt Brit. *Publ:* Auth, Art and the Christian today, Messiah Col, 85; Jacob Van Ruisqael and the Perception of Landscape, Yale Univ Press, New Haven, London, 91; also occasional paper series. *Mailing Add:* Wheaton Col Wheaton IL 60187

WALINSKA, ANNA
PAINTER, LECTURER
b London, Eng, Sept 8, 16. *Study:* Nat Acad Design, New York; Art Students League; Acad Andre L'Hote, Paris. *Work:* Helena Rubinstein Mus, Tel-Aviv, Israel; Wichita State Univ Mus; Norfolk Mus Arts & Sci; Jewish Mus & Mus Cathedral of St John The Divine, NY; and others. *Comn:* Prime Minister UNU-cil, Government Burma, Rangoon, Burma, 55; Mrs Eleanor Roosevelt, New York, 59; Gov H H Lehman, State of Israel Bonds, New York, 59; Pres F D Roosevelt, New York, 68. *Exhib:* Pa Acad, 36; Picture of the Year Exhib, Metrop Mus Art, New York, 43 & 45; Drawing Exhib, Mus Mod Art, New York, 56; retrospectives, Jewish Mus, New York, 57, Cathedral of St John The Divine, New York, 79, War Mem Bldg, Baltimore, Md, 80, Hebrew Union Col Mus, New York, 80 & Mercy Col, Detroit, Mich, 80; Gres Gallery, Baltimore Mus, Md, 59; one-woman shows, Community Col Mus, Delaware, Pa, 75 & Grimaldis Gallery, Baltimore, Md, 80; and others. *Pos:* Established dir, Guild Art Gallery 35-37; asst to dir, Contemp Art Pavilion, New York World's Fair, 40. *Teaching:* Instr art, Master Inst United Arts, New York,

57-71; artist-in-residence, Mercy Col, Detroit, Mich, 80 & Misericordia Col, Dallas, Pa, 81. *Awards:* First Prize in Casein, Silvermine Guild, 57; First Prize in Oil, 59 & Watercolors, 60, Am Soc Contemp Artists. *Bibliog:* Hla Shain (auth), The middle way, The Guardian, 2/55; Richard Mann (auth), Anna Walinska: Holocaust, Alex London, 12/79. *Mem:* Am Soc Contemp Artists; Nat Asn Women Artists; Audubon Soc; Federation Modern Painters & Sculptors. *Media:* Oil, Casein. *Publ:* Illusr, The Merry Communist, Pilgrim House, 35; illusr, The Gate Breakers, Herzl Press, 63. *Mailing Add:* 875 West End Ave New York NY 10025

WALKER, BERTA
ART DEALER
b New York, NY. *Study:* Univ Colo, 59-61; Burdett Col Bus, AA, 64. *Pos:* Founding dir mus progs, Opportunity Resources Arts, New York, 76-79; corp relations-spec events, Whitney Mus Am Art, New York, 79-81; assoc dir, Marisa del Re Gallery, New York, 81-83; founding dir, Graham Mod Gallery, New York, 84-89; owner, Berta Walker Gallery, Provincetown, Ma, 90- *Mem:* Fine Arts Work Ctr Artists Colony, Provincetown, Mass (chair, bd & trustee, formerly); Art Table, New York; Am Fedn Arts; Am Asn Mus. *Specialty:* Provincetown affiliated art by contemp & mod masters. *Mailing Add:* 645 Commercial St Box 261 Provincetown MA 02657

WALKER, EDWARD D (RUSTY)
PAINTER
b Danville, Ill, Oct 31, 46. *Study:* Queensland Col Art, Brisbane, Australia, BFA, 66; Greenwich Univ, Hawaii, MFA, 89, PhD(art educ), 91. *Work:* Pres Gerald R Ford, Rancho Mirage, Calif; San Francisco Mus Mod Art; Charles & Emma Frye Art Mus, Seattle; Bender Room, Special Collections, Stanford Univ, Calif; Harcourt Brace Jovanovich Publ, New York; plus many others. *Comn:* John Steinbeck (portrait), Steinbeck Found, Salinas, Calif, 72; bkcover & illus, Hermes Publ, Seattle; Robert L Montgomery (oil portrait), Alta Bates Hosp, Berkeley, Calif, 83; Donald P McCullum, Superior Court Judge, Oakland, Calif, 84; Int Posters, Leslie Levy Gallery Publishers, 90-92; and others. *Exhib:* Crocker Kingsley Ann, E B Crocker Art Mus, Sacramento, 76; Am Watercolor Soc, Nat Acad Design, New York, 77; Art and the Law, Nat Invitational, West Publ, 85; Western Art Classic, Minneapolis, Minn, 85; C G Rein Gallery, Scottsdale, Ariz, 85-89c. *Pos:* Artist, US Air Force, Strategic Air Command Hq, Offutt Air Force Base, Bellevue, Nebr, 67-71; juror of awards, various art asns, including Calif State Fair, 73- *Teaching:* Instr watercolor, Asilomar Watercolor Workshops, Monterey, Calif, 77-80, Hewitt Workshops, San Miguel De Allende, Mexico, 83; instr oils & watercolor, Fresno Watercolor Workshop, 77; assoc prof,Al Collins Graphic Design Sch, Tempe, Ariz, 89-93; and others. *Awards:* Emily Lowe Mem Award, Am Watercolor Soc, Nat Acad, NY, 77; Teacher of the Year, Ariz Pvt Sch Asn, 91. *Bibliog:* Cover & feature article in Southwest Art, 6/80; feature article, Am Artist Mag, 10/80; feature article, Ariz Repub, 5/92; and others. *Mem:* Nat Watercolor Soc; Am Mensa, 90-92. *Media:* Watercolor, Oils. *Publ:* Auth, Transparent Watercolor, Northlight Publ, 85; Contemporary Western Artists, Southwest Art Publ. *Dealer:* Jane Laidley Galleries One Spinnaker Way Berkeley CA 94710. *Mailing Add:* 1030 W Estrella Dr Chandler AZ 85224

WALKER, HERBERT BROOKS
SCULPTOR, MUSEUM DIRECTOR
b Brooklyn, NY, Nov 30, 27. *Study:* Art Students League, with Harry Sternberg & Robert B Hale, 43; Yale Sch Fine Arts, BFA, with R Eberhardt, R Zallinger, Graziani, J Albers & W De Konning. *Work:* Photographs of Antonio Gaudis Work, Mus Mod Art, New York; Barbados Mus, BWI; Walker Mus. *Comn:* Paintings, movie, photographs, Gahagan Dredging, Orinoco River, Venezuela, 53-54; paintings & photographs, US Steel, Cerro Bolivar, Venezuela; earth sculpture, Walker Mus, 60. *Exhib:* One-man shows, Stony Brook Mus, Long Island, NY, 52, Barbados Mus, 54 & IORC, Abadan, Iran, 58; Walker Mus, 60-; Rodin Mus, 70. *Collections Arranged:* Oil Exhibs, IORC, Abadan, Iran, 58 & 59; spec exhibs for pub schs, 60-72 & Walker Mus, Fairlee, Vt, 60- *Pos:* Materials prod head, IROC, Abadan, Iran, 58-59; dir, Walker Mus, 59- *Teaching:* Instr art, Thetford Acad, 64- *Bibliog:* H Brooks Walker, 1951, Eye Mag, Yale Univ, 67. *Mem:* Life mem Art Students League; Yale Arts Alumni Asn. *Media:* Sheet Metal, Bronze. *Publ:* Illusr, Gaudi, Mus Mod Art, 57. *Mailing Add:* Lake Morey Fairlee VT 05045

WALKER, LARRY
PAINTER, EDUCATOR
b Franklin, Ga, Oct 22, 35. *Study:* High Sch Music & Art, New York; Wayne State Univ, Detroit, BS, 58, MA, 63. *Work:* Haggin Art Mus, City Hall & San Joaquin Delta Col, Stockton, Calif; Univ of the Pac, Stockton; Oakland Mus, Calif; City Atlanta; Studio Mus in Harlem; Buckhead Libr, Atlanta Life Insurance Co, Apex Mus, Hammonds House, Contel Corp, Atlanta; and others. *Comn:* Mural, Univ of the Pac, 65; mural comn by Benjamin Holt Found for San Joaquin Delta Col, 74; and others. *Exhib:* West Coast 74: The Black Image, E B Crocker Mus, Sacramento & Los Angeles Munic Art Gallery, 74; Northern Calif Arts Ann, Univ of Pac, Stockton; Atlanta Life Nat Exhib, Ga; Festival of Arts & Culture, Lagos, Nigeria, 77; Black Artists South, Huntsville Mus, Ala; Artists in Georgia, Athens, 85; Nat Black Arts Festival, 88 & 90, Hammonds House Mus & Galleries, Artspace Gallery, Chastain Gallery, Atlanta, 92; Lander Col, Greenwood, SC, 88. *Teaching:* Prof painting, drawing & art educ, Univ of the Pac, 64-, chmn art dept, 73-80; art critic, Stockton Record, Calif, 81-83; prof & dir, Sch Art & Design, Ga State Univ, Atlanta, 83- *Bibliog:* Samella Lewis & Ruth Waddy (auths), The Black Artist on Art, Vol I, Contemp Crafts Publ, 69; article in Black Art, summer 77. *Mem:* Nat Coun Art Adminrs (bd dirs, 76-79, 84-88, chmn, 78-79, 86-87); Nat Asn Sch Art & Design (bd dir, 89, 90-93); DeKalb Coun for the Arts (bd dir, 87-92, pres, 89-90); Marta Arts Coun. *Media:* Acrylic, Charcoal. *Publ:* Auth, The Visual Arts in the Ninth Decade, NCAA, 80; numerous revs of local & regional art exhibs, Stockton Record, Calif, 81-83; The State of the Arts in San Joaquin County, Walker & Watanabe. *Dealer:* Temme Barkin Leeds Barkin Leeds Ltd Fine Arts Management 2880 Vining Way Atlanta GA 30339; Artspace Gallery Atlanta GA. *Mailing Add:* School Art & Design Ga State Univ, University Plaza Atlanta GA 30303

WALKER, LARRY
PAINTER, EDUCATOR
b Newark, NJ, Mar 31, 52. *Study:* Jersey City State Col, NJ, BA, 73; Denver Univ, Colo, grad study, 75-76; Montclair State Col, NJ, MA, 80. *Exhib:* New Jersey Art Educators Exhibition, Trenton, NJ, 79; New Jersey Parks & Recreation Comn, Newark, NJ, 80; Rutgers Univ, Newark, NJ, 81; Transport New York-New Jersey, 82; Prudential Insurance Co, Newark, NJ, 82; Emerging and Established, Newark Mus, NJ, 83; Jersey City Mus, NJ, 83; Metro Show, City Without Walls Gallery, Newark, NJ, 84. *Pos:* Treas, Northern NJ Chap, Nat Coun Artists, 81-; district coordr, Union Teen Arts Festival, Union, NJ, 84-86. *Teaching:* Art teacher, Newark Bd Educ, 76-78, Elizabeth High Sch, NJ, 80-; adj instr art, Jersey City State Col, NJ, 83- *Awards:* Grant, NJ State Coun Arts, 85. *Mem:* Nat Conf Artists; Art Educators NJ. *Media:* Mixed Media. *Mailing Add:* 55 Randolph Place No 101 South Orange NJ 07079

WALKER, MARIE SHEEHY
PAINTER
b Glen Cove, NY, May 23, 52. *Study:* Rosemont Col, BFA, 74; Art Students League, with Robert Brackman, 74-77. *Work:* Rosemont Col. *Comn:* Heffernan Hall (watercolor), Rosemont Col, 74. *Exhib:* Nat Acad Design Ann Exhib, New York, 82; Pastel Soc Am Ann Exhib Pastels Only, Nat Arts Club, New York, 82 & 83; Nassau Co Mus Ann Show, Roslyn, NY, 82 & 83; Nat Asn Women Artists Exhib, Bergen Community Mus, Paramus, NJ, 83; Nat Asn Women Artists Traveling Painting Exhib, 83-85. *Awards:* Pastel Soc Am Award, Salmagundi Show, 80; Charlotte Winston Mem Award, Nat Asn Women Artists Exhib, 83; Gold Medal Oil Painting, Nat Art League, 83. *Mem:* Pastel Soc Am; Nat Asn Women Artists; Art Students League; Salmagundi Club; Nat Art League. *Media:* Pastel, Oil. *Mailing Add:* 17 John Daves Ln Huntington NY 11743

WALKER, MARK STEVEN
HISTORIAN
b Athens, Ga, Nov 2, 52. *Study:* Brigham Young Univ, BFA(painting), 74; Atelier Lack, Minneapolis, Minn, with Richard Lack, 74-75 & 77-79; Univ Calif, Riverside, MA(art hist), 82. *Collections Arranged:* William Bouguereau (auth catalog), Mus Fine Arts, Montreal, 84. *Pos:* Assoc cur, Mus Fine Arts, Montreal, Que, 82-84; independent consult, Christie's & Sotheby's, New York, 84- *Res:* Bouguereau; 19th century methods and materials for drawing and painting; Richard Lack; Boston school; classical realism, French 19th century painting. *Publ:* Auth, La jeunesse de Bacchus de Bouguereau, L'Oeil, 4/84; The other 20th century: Radical currents of classical realism in contemporary American painting, In: Realism in Revolution, 85; contrib, Dictionary of Art; William-Adolphe Bouguereau: A Summary Catalogue of the Paintings, William-Adolphe Bouguereau, L'Art Pompier, Borghi & Co, New York, 91. *Mailing Add:* PO Box 352 Athens GA 30603

WALKER, MARY CAROLYN
CRAFTSMAN, JEWELER
b Lancaster, Pa, Oct 24, 38. *Study:* Pa State Univ, BS(home art); Rochester Inst Technol Sch for Am Craftsmen, with Don Drumm & Eleanor Moty. *Comn:* Maya Schock Award to Women in the Arts, Doshi, 85. *Exhib:* Young Americans, Mus Contemp Crafts, New York, 62; Southern Tier Arts & Crafts Show, Corning, NY, 73; First World Silver Fair, Mexico, 74; Spec Exhib for Nat Gov Conf, 76; one-person show, Pa Designer Craftsmen Gallery, Bushkill, 82; and others. *Pos:* Partner, Tamcraft Products Co, Neffsville, Pa, 60- *Awards:* First Prize Metals, Harrisburg Arts Festival, 72; Best in Show, 73 & Fine Work in Precious Metals, 90, Pa Guild of Craftsman; and others. *Bibliog:* R Stevens (auth), Arts decoratifs, La Revue Mod des Arts et de la vie, France, 12/72. *Mem:* Am Crafts Coun (secy, NE Region, 71-74); Pa Guild Craftsman (treas, 70-71, pres, 72, vpres, 73); Harrisburg Craftsmen (pres, 70, secy, 72, treas, 73); Doshi Ctr Contemp Art (bd dirs, 82-86). *Media:* Sterling Silver. *Mailing Add:* 22 Conway Dr Mechanicsburg PA 17055

WALKER, MORT
CARTOONIST
b El Dorado, Kans, Sept 3, 23. *Study:* Univ Mo, BA; Wm Penn Col, Hon LLD, 81. *Work:* Bird Libr, Syracuse Univ; Boston Univ Libr; Kans State Univ; Montreal Humor Pavilion; Smithsonian Inst; Mus Cartoon Art. *Exhib:* Metrop Mus Art, New York, 52; Brussels Worlds Fair, 64; Mus Louvre, Paris, 65; New York Worlds Fair, 67; Expo, Montreal, 69. *Pos:* Creator of Beetle Bailey, King Features Syndicate, 50-, Hi & Lois, 54-, Sam's Strip, 61-63, Boner's Ark, 68- & Sam & Silo, 77; chmn, Mus Cartoon Art, Rye Brook, NY, currently; pres, Comicana Corp, currently. *Teaching:* Scholar-in-Residence, Univ Mo, 92. *Awards:* Banshee Award, 55; Il Secolo XIX, Italy, 72; Adamson Award, Sweden, 75; Am Legion Fourth Estate Award, 78; Newspaper Comics Coun Award, 79; Inkpot Award, 79; Hall of Fame, Mus Cartoon Art, 89; Wordsmith Award, 90. *Mem:* Nat Cartoonists Soc (pres, 60); Newspaper Features; Artists & Writers Asn; Cartoonists Guild; Soc of Illustr. *Media:* Ink. *Publ:* Ed, Nat Cartoonists Soc Album, 61, 65 & 72; auth, Most, 71; Land of Lost Things, 72; auth & illusr, Backstage at the Strips, 76, Lexicon of Comicana, 81 & Best of Beetle Baily, 84. *Dealer:* Mus of Cartoon Art Port Chester NY 10573; Graham Gallery 1014 Madison Ave New York NY 10021. *Mailing Add:* c/o King Features 235 E 45th St New York NY 10017

WALKER, WILLIAM BOND
ADMINISTRATOR, LIBRARIAN
b Brownsville, Tenn, Apr 15, 30. *Study:* Bisttram Sch Fine Art, Taos, NMex & Los Angeles, with Emil Bisttram, 48-49; Univ Iowa, Iowa City, with Mauricio Lasansky, Howard Warshaw, James Lechay & Stuart Edie, BA, 53; Rutgers Univ Grad Sch Libr Serv, MSLS, 58. *Pos:* Cataloger & reference librn, Libr Metrop Mus Art, New York, 57-59; chief librn, Art Reference Libr, Brooklyn Mus, 59-64, Libr Nat Collection Fine Arts & Nat Portrait Gallery, Smithsonian Inst, 64-80 & Thomas J Watson Libr, Metrop Mus Art, New York, 80- *Teaching:* Art bibliog, Columbia Univ, Sch Libr Serv, 87-88. *Awards:* Distinguished Serv Award, Art Libr Soc NAm, 91. *Mem:* Am Libr Asn; Spec Libr Asn Mus Div (nat chmn, 61-62); Art Libr Soc NAm (pres, 75); Grolier Club, New York. *Res:* American sculpture of eighteenth to twentieth century; art library classification at Library of Congress. *Interests:* Twentieth century American prints. *Publ:* Auth, Art books & periodicals: Dewey and LC (classification), Libr Trends, Vol 23, 1/75; The development of national and international cooperation between art libraries, Art Libr J, spring 78; Art libraries, Spec Libr, 12/78; Bibliography on American Sculpture, Eighteenth to Twentieth Century, Washington, DC, Smithsonian Inst Press, 80. *Mailing Add:* 2166 Broadway Apt 7D New York NY 10024

WALKEY, FREDERICK P
MUSEUM DIRECTOR, CONSULTANT
b Belmont, Mass, May 29, 22. *Study:* Duke Univ; Boston Mus Fine Arts Sch; Tufts Col, BSEd. *Pos:* Exec dir, De Cordova Mus, Lincoln, Mass, formerly; consult, Metrop Mus & Art Ctr, 82-83, Newport Art Mus & Art Asn, 83-85, Fitchburg Art Mus, Mass, 85-92 & New Eng Sports Mus, Boston, currently. *Mem:* New Eng Conf; Am Asn Mus; Am Fedn Arts. *Mailing Add:* 35 Mt Vernon Saugus MA 01906

WALKINGSTICK, KAY
PAINTER
b Syracuse, NY, Mar 2, 35. *Study:* Beaver Col, Glenside, Pa, BFA, 59; Pratt Inst, Brooklyn, MFA, 75. *Work:* Newark Mus, NJ; Albright-Knox Art Gallery, Buffalo, NY; La Jolla Mus Art, Calif; Johnson Mus, Cornell Univ, Ithaca, NY; San Diego Mus Art, Calif; Heard Mus, Phoenix, Ariz; Southern Plans Ind Mus, Anadarko, Okla; Israel Mus, Jerusalem. *Comn:* A Retrospective, comn by Hillwood Gallery, Univ Long Island, Greenvale, NY, 91. *Exhib:* Newark & NJ State, Trenton, 66 & 68, 70 & 71, 81 & 85; Sierra Nev Mus, Reno, 86; Am Acad Arts & Letters, 87 & 88; Decade Show, New Mus, 90; solo exhibs, Heard Mus, Phoenix, Ariz, 91, Montclair Art Mus, NJ, 92 & Jersey City Mus, NJ, 92; Land Spirit Power, Nat Mus Can, Ottawa, 92. *Teaching:* Gallery dir, William Ctr Arts, Rutherford, NJ, 86 & 88; instr, painting & drawing, Upsala Col, East Orange, NY, 75-79; artist-in-residence, Ft Lewis Col, Durango, Colo, 84 & Ohio State Univ, Columbus, 85; Asst prof art, Cornell Univ, Ithaca, NY, 90-; Asst prof art, SUNY Stony Brook, 90. *Awards:* NJ Coun Arts Fel, 81-82, 85 & 86; Nat Endowment Arts Grant, 83; Residency, William Flanasan Mem Creative Person's Ctr, 83; and others. *Bibliog:* Frederick Ted Castle (auth), review, Am Art, 2/84; Patricia Malarcher (auth), The Meaning of duality in art, NY Times, 12/22/85; Ronnie Weyl (auth), cover & interview, Art NJ Mag, 10/87; Marlene Donohue (auth), review, Los Angelas Times, 2/26/88; Dr Judy Van Wagner (auth), Lines of Vision, Drawings by Contemporary Women, Hudson Hills Press, NY, 89; Kellie Jones (auth), Kay Walking Stick, The Village Voice, 5/16/89; Kay WalkingStick Paintings, 1974-1990 (catalogue), Hillwood Mus, 91; Lucy Lippard (auth), Mixed Blessings, 91. *Mem:* Women's Caucus Art, NY. *Media:* Acrylic, Oil; Wax. *Dealer:* M-13 Gallery 72 Greene St New York NY 10012; Wenger Gallery Los Angeles CA. *Mailing Add:* 216 S Geneva Ithaca NY 14850

WALL, BRIAN
SCULPTOR
b London, Eng, Sept 5, 31; US citizen. *Study:* Luton Col Art, Eng; with Barbara Hepworth, 54-58. *Work:* Tate Gallery, London; Nat Gallery, Dublin; Art Gallery NSW, Sidney; Oakland Mus; Univ Art Mus, Berkeley; Seattle Art Mus; Sheldon Mem Art Gallery, Univ Nebr. *Comn:* Thornaby (sculpture), New Town Ctr, Thornaby, Eng, 68; Ali (sculpture), Univ Houston, Tex, 78. *Exhib:* 2nd Paris Biennale, Mus Mod Art, 61; Sculpture of the Sixties, Tate Gallery, 65; Queen's Silver Jubilee Exhib, London, 77; one-man shows, Max Hutchinson Gallery, New York, 77, 78 & 81, Seattle Art Mus, 82, San Francisco Mus Mod Art, 83, Jon Berggruen Gallery, San Francisco, 83 & Francis Graham-Dixon Gallery, London, 92; Int Sculpture Conf, Washington DC, 80 & Oakland, Calif, 82; St Ives 1939-64, Tate Gallery, London, 85; Post War British Abstract Art, Austin Desmond Fine Arts, London, 88. *Teaching:* Chmn sculpture dept, Cent Sch Art & Design, London, 64-72; prof sculpture, Univ Calif, Berkeley, 69- *Bibliog:* Charles Spencer (auth), Brian Wall, sculptor of simplicity, Studio Int, 3/66; G S Whittet (auth), Question and artist: Brian Wall, Sculpture Int, 10/69; Hilton Kramer (auth), article, 5/13/77 & John Russell (auth), articles, 1/79 & 4/24/81, New York Times. *Mem:* Int Sculpture Ctr, Washington, DC. *Media:* Steel. *Dealer:* John Berggruen Gallery 228 Grant Ave San Francisco CA 94108. *Mailing Add:* Art Dept Univ Calif Berkeley Berkeley CA 94720

WALL, BRUCE C
PAINTER
b Dallas, Tex, Feb 14, 54. *Study:* Univ Tex, Austin, BFA; RI Sch Design, Providence, RI, MFA. *Hon Degrees:* Fulbright-Hayes Grant, 79-80. *Work:* Aldrich Mus Contemp Art, Ridgefield, Conn; Best Products Corp, Richmond, Va; City Col, City Univ New York; Zale Products Corp, Dallas; Frederick R Weisman Found Art, Los Angeles, Calif. *Exhib:* NYC New Work, Del Art Mus, Wilmington; East Village Artists, Va Mus Fine Art, Richmond; East Village Galleries, Saidyre Bronfman, Montreal, Can; Selection from Weisman Collection, Utah Mus Fine Arts, Salt Lake City; The Art of the 70s & 80s, Aldrich Mus Contemp Art, Ridgefield, Conn; This Way/This Way, Thorpe Intermedia Ctr, Sparkhill, NY; Cross Currents, Sande Webster Gallery, Philadelphia, Pa; Art & Ego, New York Acad Art, New York. *Bibliog:* John Howell (auth), Bruce Wall, Artforum, 11/85; Holland Cotter (auth), Bruce Wall, Arts Mag, 9/85; Vivian Raynor (auth), Bruce Wall, New York Times, 5/86. *Media:* Acrylic on foam. *Mailing Add:* 28 King St No 6 New York NY 10014

WALL, F L (FREDERICK LEROY), III
SCULPTOR, DESIGNER
b Dover, Del, June 9, 47. *Study:* Univ Del, BA, 70; Corcoran Sch Art, with Berthold Schmatehart, 80-81. *Exhib:* In Search of a Smile, Muhlenburg Col, Allentown, Pa, 81; Five Sculptors, Frostburg Col, Md, 82; Art of the Turned Objects, Am Craft Mus, NY, 83; A Show of Hands, Arlington Art Ctr, Va, 84; Sculpture of F L Wall, George Meany Ctr Gallery, Silver Springs, Md, 85; Ambiguous Relationships, Strathmore Hall Art Ctr, Rockville, Md, 86; Poetry of the Physical, Am Craft Mus, New York. *Pos:* Design consult, Time Life Books, Alexandria, Va, 84-86. *Teaching:* Asst prof-sculpture, Corcoran Sch Art, Washington, DC, 81-; instr furniture design, Smithsonian Inst, 84- *Bibliog:* JoAnn Lewis (auth), From Function to Form, Washington Post, 3/84; Barbara Feinman (auth), Cloak and Dagger Furniture, Fine Woodworking Mag, 3/85; Sarah Book Conroy (auth), Please don't be seated, Washington Post, 6/14/85. *Mem:* Artist Equity; Am Crafts Coun. *Media:* Wood. *Publ:* Auth, Up scaled sculpture, Fine Woodworking, 85. *Mailing Add:* c/o Franz Bader Gallery 1500 K St NW Washington DC 20006

WALL, RALPH ALAN
PAINTER
b Hobart, Ind, Aug 1, 32. *Work:* Bimson Collection, Valley Nat Bank, Phoenix, Ariz; Fidelity Bank Collection, Oklahoma City; Milntain Oyster Club, Tucson, Ariz; Goddard Ctr, Performing & Visual Arts, Ardmore, Okla; Frost Bank, San Antonio; Leanin Tree Mus, Boulder, Colo. *Comn:* Southland Corp, Dallas; and others. *Exhib:* One-man shows, Goddard Ctr, Ardmore, Okla & Ponca City Art Ctr, Okla, 72; Mus of the SW, Midland, Tex, 76; O S Ranch Show, Post, Tex, 79 & 81; Western Heritage Horse, Cattle & Art Auction, Houston, Tex, 79; Zuni Gallery, Dusseldorf, WGer, 87; Marshall, Gonzalez & Carlson, Houston, Tex, 91. *Awards:* Am Inst Graphic Art Award (packaging), 67; Gold Medal, 1974 Portfolio Western Art, Franklin Mint, 74; Gold Award, Texas Ranger Hall of Fame, 79; Purchase Award, Okla City Art Festival, 83. *Bibliog:* Freddie Steve (auth), Franklin Mint paint, Paint Horse J, 11/74; Susan Hallsten McGarry (auth), This life is but a shadow, Southwest Art Mag, 10/81; Gretchen Schmitz (auth), The artist, Ralph Wall, Prints Mag, 7-8/82. *Mem:* Hon mem Mountain Oyster Club, Tucson. *Media:* Multimedia. *Publ:* Illusr, American Horseman, 9/73, Paint Horse J (cover), 1/75 & 11/75; Leanin Tree Greeting Card Series, 77, 78 & 82; Okla Today, summer 76 & spring 79; Dean Krakel's Adventures in Western Art, 77; Quarterhorse J (cover), 1/80. *Dealer:* Guildhall Inc 2535 Weisenberger Ft Worth TX 76107. *Mailing Add:* c/o Spirit of '76 Rte 8 Box 63 H New Braunfels TX 78132

WALL, RHONDA
PAINTER, INSTRUCTOR
b Boston, Mass, Jan 26, 56. *Study:* RI Sch Design, BFA, 78. *Work:* Aldrich Mus Contemp Art, Ridgefield, Conn; City Col, Univ NY & Needham Harper Steers, New York. *Exhib:* UFO Show, Queens Mus, New York, 82; solo exhibs, Beulah Gallery, 84, Limbo Gallery, 84, Sensory Evolution Gallery, 84, B Side Gallery, 85, New York; Art & Ego, NY Acad Art, New York, 84; Art of the 70's and 80's, Aldrich Mus Contemp Art, Ridgefield, Conn, 85. *Teaching:* Instr painting, RI Sch Design, 90- *Bibliog:* Mark Frisk (auth), Rhonda Wall (essay), Arts Mag, 1/85; Ken Sofer (auth), Present Pop, Art News, 5/85; Vivian Raynor (auth), This way, this way, NY Times, 11/10/85. *Media:* All Media. *Mailing Add:* 28 King St New York NY 10013

WALL, SUE
PAINTER, PRINTMAKER
b Cleveland, Ohio, Feb 18, 50. *Study:* Ohio Univ, BFA, 72, MFA, 74. *Work:* Cleveland Mus Art; Canton Art Inst Mus, Ohio; Butler Inst Am Art, Youngstown, Ohio; Univ Iowa Mus Art; Kenneth Beck Ctr Cult Arts, Cleveland; Zanesville Art Ctr, Ohio; Ohio Nat Plaza Co Coll; Trisolini Gallery, Ohio; Cleveland Art Asn. *Exhib:* One-person shows, Gallery Madison 90, New York, 74, 76, 78, 80, 82, 84, 86, 88, 90 & 92, Strong's Gallery, Cleveland, 75, 77 & 79, Canton Art Inst, Ohio, 76, Gallery 200, Columbus, 75, 77, 84 & 86, Piccolo Mondo, Palm Beach, Fla, 76 & 78, Bonfoey's, Cleveland, 81, 83, 85, 87, 89 & 91, Foster Harmon Gallery, Sarasota, Fla, 82, 84, 86, 89 & 91; Butler Ann Mid-Year Show, Youngstown, Ohio, 75-77; Sandusky Cult Ctr, Ohio, 78 & 90; Classics, Kansas City, Kans, 84; Garden Ctr of Greater Cleveland, Ohio, 89; and other one-person shows. *Awards:* 2nd Prize, Laramie Art Guild, Wyo, 85; 2nd Prize, 4th Ann Small Painting Show, Cuyahoga Valley Art Ctr, 86; Dr Maury Leibovitz Art Award, 86; Honorable Mention, 18th Ann Nat Small Painting Exhib, 89. *Bibliog:* Rhoda Levinsohn (auth), article, Sunday Plain Dealer, Cleveland, 75; Rhoda Levinsohn (auth), Art Look 102, Apple Publ, S Africa, 9/76; Millie Wolff (auth), article, Palm Beach Daily News, 2/78; Vondell Petry (auth), article, Victoria Mag, 9/88; Vondell Petry (auth), article, Quality Living, 8/90. *Mem:* New Orgn Visual Arts; Audubon Artists; Nat Soc Painters Casein & Acrylic; Miniature Art Soc NJ; Artists Equity New York; Victorian Soc Am; Nat Trust Hist Preserv; Catherine Lorillard Wolfe Art Club; Allied Artists Am Inc; Knickerbocker Artist. *Media:* Acrylic. *Publ:* Contribr, New York Art Rev. *Dealer:* Gallery Madison 90 1248 Madison Ave New York NY 10023; The Bonfoey Co 1710 Euclid Ave Cleveland OH 44115. *Mailing Add:* 11 Riverside Dr, Suite 8JE New York NY 10023-2304

WALLACE, ELIZABETH S
ADMINISTRATOR, SCULPTOR
b Mankato, Kans. *Study:* Washburn Univ, AB; Univ Nebr, BFA, MFA; also with Thomas Sheffield. *Work:* Elder Gallery, Lincoln, Nebr. *Exhib:* One-person shows, Nebr Wesleyan Univ, Lincoln, 66, Haymarket Art Gallery, 70 & Elder Gallery, 74 & 79; Midland Col, 78. *Pos:* Dir, Elder Gallery, Lincoln, 76- & Univ Place Art Ctr & Wesleyan Lab Gallery, 77- *Teaching:* Asst prof ceramics, Nebr Wesleyan Univ, 72-, asst prof sculpture & art hist & head dept art, 76-90. *Mem:* Nebr Art Asn (bd trustees, 76-); Lincoln Arts Coun (bd trustees, 77-); Wesleyan Arts Coun (pres, 75-76); Nebr Crafts Coun; Am Crafts Coun. *Mailing Add:* 420 Lakewood Dr Lincoln NE 68510

WALLACE, GAEL LYNN
PAINTER
b Ft Worth, Tex, Aug 5, 41. *Study:* Okla State Univ, with Dale McKinney & David Allende, BA, 64; independent study with Don Fusco & Tom Owen. *Comn:* Old west storefront murals, Graden Elementary Sch, Kansas City, Mo, 78. *Exhib:* 60th Ann Nat Watercolor Soc, Laguna Beach Mus Art, Calif, 80 & 82; Rocky Mountain Nat Aquamedia, 82; Northern Colo Invitational, Greeley, Colo, 82 & 84; Colorado 83 Biennial, Colo Springs Fine Art Mus, 83; San Diego Watercolor Soc Int Exhib, 85. *Awards:* Purchase Awards, Nat Watercolor Soc, 80 & Glenwood Springs Fall Art Festival, Col, 85; Honorable Mention, Colo State Fair, 80 & San Diego Watercolor Soc Int Exhib, 86. *Bibliog:* Diane Wengler (auth), The beauty of nature, Gazette Telegraph, 12/13/80. *Mem:* Nat Watercolor Soc; Broadmoor Watercolor Soc. *Media:* Acrylic. *Mailing Add:* 23 Kris Ln Manitou Springs CO 80829

WALLACE, JOHN
PAINTER, EDUCATOR
b St Louis, Mo, Dec 29, 29. *Study:* Washington Univ, with Paul Burlin & Carl Holty, BFA; Ind Univ, MFA; Skowhegan Sch Painting & Sculpture, with Henry Varnum Poor. *Work:* St Louis Art Mus; Detroit Inst Arts. *Comn:* Mural, South Solon Meeting House, Maine, 54; sculpture panel, Aquatic House, St Louis Zool Gardens, 59. *Exhib:* Pa Acad Fine Arts, 52; Ann Nat Print Exhib, Brooklyn Mus, 53; one-man shows, artist-in-residence exhib, Roswell Mus, NMex, 68, Green Mountain Gallery, New York, 79 & Blue Mountain Gallery, NY, 93; Bertrand Russell Centenary, Nottingham, Eng, 73; Provincetown Art Asn, 78 & 86; Artists' Choice Mus, NY, 85; plus many others. *Pos:* Co-ed, New Art Asn Newslett, 71; co-chmn, New directions in studio teaching, Col Art Asn Ann Meeting, 71. *Teaching:* Prof painting & drawing, Prairie State Col, Chicago Heights, Ill, 68-79 & chmn art dept, 71-74; vis artist, Truro Ctr Arts, 76-80, Silvermine Guild Art, 82, Stamford Mus, 82; assoc prof, painting & graphic design, Western Conn State Univ, 81- & chmn art dept, 87-91. *Awards:* Margaret Tiffany Blake Mural Fel, Skowhegan Sch, 54; Huntington Hartford Found Fel, 60; Artist-in-Residence Grant, Roswell Mus, 68. *Bibliog:* Helen Thomas (auth), article, Arts Mag, 5/79. *Mem:* Col Art Asn. *Media:* Acrylic, Watercolor. *Publ:* Auth, Fresco Workshop, Yankee Mag, 7/77; Art education: A consumer's viewpoint, Art Worker's News, 82. *Dealer:* Blue Mountain Gallery 121 Wooster St New York NY 10012. *Mailing Add:* 25 Taunton Lake Rd Newtown CT 06470

WALLACE, KENNETH WILLIAM
PAINTER, EDUCATOR
b Penticton, BC, July 7, 45. *Study:* Calgary Col Art, Alta, cert, 71; Vancouver Sch Art, BC, cert, 73; Banff Sch Fine Arts, 73. *Work:* Nat Art Gallery, Ottawa; Art Gallery Ont, Toronto; Vancouver Art Gallery, BC; Winnipeg Art Gallery, Man; Burnaby Art Gallery, BC. *Exhib:* One-man shows, Alternate Space, Vancouver Art Gallery, 74, Burnaby Art Gallery, BC, 80, Lefebvre Gallery, Edmonton, Alta, 81, Robert Lawrence Int, Bellingham, Wash, 82, Teck Gallery, Simon Fraser Univ, Bau-Xi Gallery, Vancouver, BC, 92; Pac Northwest Ann, Seattle, Wash, 73; Current Energies, Saydie Bronfman Arts Centre, Montreal, Que, 74-75; Three Directions in Painting, Fine Arts Gallery, Univ BC, Vancouver, 75; Canadian Canvas, Time Exhib, 11 major Can cities, 76; New Abstract Art in Am, Edmonton Art Gallery, Alta, 77; Affinities, 79, Vancouver Art & Artists, 1931-83, 83, Painted Gardens, Atilier Gallery, Vancouver, BC, 92; Canadian Painters, Can House, London, Eng, 79; Bienal De Arte Medellin, Columbia, SAm, 81; Current Concerns, Sarnia Art Gallery, Ont, 81; Living Nature 1987, Nat Mus Natural Sci, Ottawa, Ont, 87. *Collections Arranged:* Images of Women (auth, catalog), Winnipeg Art Gallery, 75; Canadian Painters in Watercolor (auth, catalog), Glenbow Inst, Alta, 76; Olympic Exhibition of British Columbian Artists (auth, catalog), Montreal, Que, 76; West Coast on Canvas (auth, catalog), Birmingham Art Gallery, Ala, 79. *Teaching:* Instr painting & drawing, Univ BC, 76-78, instr painting, Dept Fine Arts, 77-80, Emily Carr Col Art & Design, 80-92. *Awards:* Int Critics Award, Annecy Film Festival, France, 75; Can Coun Art Awards, 75-79. *Bibliog:* Mary Fox (auth), Images from the inside outside, Western Living, 76; Pat Fleisher (auth), interview in Arts Mag, Toronto, Ont, 76; Karen Wilken (auth), Vancouver scene, Art News, New York, 79. *Mailing Add:* 72310 Cornwall Ave Vancouver BC V6K 1B7 Canada

WALLACE, LILA NORMA See Shelby, Lila (Lila Norma Wallace)

WALLACE, PATTY A
PAINTER, FILMMAKER
b Buffalo, NY, July 13, 57. *Study:* Ctr Media Study, State Univ NY, Buffalo, study with Paul Sharits, Tony Conrad, Ernie Gehr, Hollis Frampton & Jack Goldstein, MAH, 86. *Work:* Burchfield Ctr Buffalo, NY; Albright-Knox Gallery, Buffalo. *Exhib:* Comic Relief: The Art of Contemporary Comics and Cartoons, Hallwalls, Buffalo, NY, 84; Niagara: New Impressions (with catalog), Burchfield Ctr, Buffalo, 85; Buffalo-Chicago Exchange, Artemisia, Chicago, Ill, 85; Super 8 Galaxy, Artists' Space, New York, 85; Super 8 Motel, The Kitchen, New York, 85; Ambulatory Independents, Pittsburgh Filmmakers, Pittsburgh, Pa, 86; Social Studies, YYZ Gallery, Toronto, 87; 42nd Western NY Exhib, Albright-Knox Art Gallery, Buffalo, 88; Unknown Secrets: Art and the Rosenberg Era, Hillwood Art Gallery, Long Island Univ, 88; Dia de Los Muertos II, Los Angelitos, Alternative Mus, New York, 89; Recent Acquisitions, Burchfield Art Ctr, Buffalo, NY, 90. *Pos:* Libr clerk, Albright-Knox Art Gallery, 85- & curatorial researcher, 88; mus technician, Brooklyn Mus, 88- *Teaching:* Instr digital art, Albright-Knox Art Gallery, Buffalo, 85-86, instr bookmaking & video, 86-88. *Awards:* Grad Study Res Grant, State Univ NY, Buffalo, 85. *Bibliog:* Anthony Bannon (auth), Small photo shines forth, Buffalo News, 1/11/83; John F Swed (auth), Childhood's ends, Village Voice, New York, 2/25/85; Ron Netsky (auth), Transformations, Rochester Democrat & Chronicle, 6/18/85; Elizabeth Hess (auth), Presumed guilty, Village Voice, 9/27/88; Arlene Raven (auth), Suffer the little children, The Village Voice, 10/24/89; Richard Huntington (auth), Burchfield shows off its new works, GUSTO Buffalo News, 8/11/89. *Media:* Film, Video. *Publ:* Contribr, The Imagemaker (by Anthony Bannon), AAO Gallery, Buffalo, 85. *Mailing Add:* 501 Hicks St Apt 401 Brooklyn NY 11201

WALLACE, RICHARD WILLIAM
EDUCATOR, HISTORIAN
b Rochester, NY, Oct 4, 33. *Study:* Williams Col, BA, 55; Princeton Univ, MFA, 61, PhD, 64. *Teaching:* Instr art hist, Princeton Univ, 60-61; from asst prof to prof, Wellesley Col, 64- *Awards:* Fulbright Fel, 62-64; Nat Endowment Arts Summer Stipend, 67; Am Coun Learned Soc Fel, 69. *Res:* Italian baroque art. *Publ:* Contribr, Salvator Rosa (exhib catalog), Arts Coun Gr Brit, 73; auth, The Etchings of Salvator Rosa, Princeton Press, 79; Salvator Rosa in America (exhib catalog), Wellesley Col, 79; contribr, The Illustrated Bartsch, Abaris Books, 82; Italian Etchers of the Renaissance and Baroque (exhib catalog, with Su Welsh Reed), Boston, Cleveland & Washington, DC, 89. *Mailing Add:* Dept Art Wellesley Col Wellesley MA 02181

WALLACE, ROBERT DAN
EDUCATOR, HISTORIAN
b Los Angeles, Calif, Jan 15, 23. *Study:* Stanford Univ, BA, 47, MA, 48; Univ Geneva, LittD, 53. *Teaching:* Prof art, San Diego State Univ, 57-82. *Awards:* Belgian Am Educ Found Fel, 49. *Mem:* Art Historians Southern Calif; Archit Historians Southern Calif; Soc Archit Historians; Asian Arts Comt; Friends of Classics (pres), San Diego State Univ. *Res:* Medieval art. *Publ:* Auth, L'Influence de la France Gothique sur deux des Precurseurs de la Renaissance Italienne: Nicolo et Giovanni Pisano, Libr E Droz, Geneva, 53. *Mailing Add:* 750 Bangor San Diego CA 92106

WALLACE, SONI
PAINTER
b London, Eng, Apr 18, 31; US citizen. *Study:* Silvermine Art Guild, New Canaan, Conn; Mus Mod Art, with Zolten Hecht; Pratt Graphics, New York. *Work:* Gibbes Art Mus, Charleston, SC; Univ Ala Mus. *Comn:* Three covers for mag, Distinguished Resorts, 68, 70 & 71. *Exhib:* Conn Watercolor Soc 31st Ann, Fairfield Univ, 69; Love/Peace, Am Greetings Gallery, NY, 69; Northwest Printmakers 41st Int Exhib, Seattle Art Mus, 70; solo shows, Pacem-in-Terris Gallery, New York, 70, Danbury Libr Gallery, Conn, 71 & Phoenix Gallery, New York, 75. *Awards:* Max Granick Award, Am Soc Contemp Artists, NY, 71; Award, Washington Art Asn, Conn, 72; Am Soc Contemp Artists Ann, 74. *Mem:* Nat Asn Women Artists; Am Soc Contemp Artists; Silvermine Guild Artists; Washington Art Asn; Women in the Arts. *Media:* Acrylic, Watercolor. *Mailing Add:* 150 E 77th St No 11G New York NY 10021

WALLACH, ALAN
CRITIC, HISTORIAN
b Brooklyn, NY, June 8, 42. *Study:* Columbia Col, BA, 63; Columbia Univ, PhD, 73. *Teaching:* Assoc prof art hist, Kean Col Union, NJ, 74-; vis prof, Univ Calif, Los Angeles, 82-83, Stanford Univ, 86-87, Univ Mich, 89. *Awards:* Smithsonian Sr Post-Doctoral Fel, 85-86. *Mem:* Col Art Asn Am; Am Studies Asn; Caucus Marxism & Art; Art Historians Asn (Gt Brit). *Res:* Nineteenth century American art; history of museums; criticism of 20th century art. *Publ:* Auth, The voyage of life as popular art, Art Bull, 77; coauth, The Museum of Modern Art as late capitalist ritual, Marxist Perspectives, 78; coauth, The universal survey museum, Art Hist, 80; auth, The avant garde of the eighties, Art Criticism, 81; auth, Thomas Cole and the aristocracy, Arts, 81; auth, The word from Yale, Art Hist, 87. *Mailing Add:* Dept Art Kean Col New Jersey Union NJ 07083

WALLER, AARON BRET
MUSEUM DIRECTOR, ART HISTORIAN
b Liberal, Kans, Dec 7, 35. *Study:* Univ Kans, Lawrence; Kansas City Art Inst & Sch of Design, BFA, 57; Univ Kans, Lawrence, MFA, 58; Univ Oslo, Norway. *Collections Arranged:* School for Scandal: Thomas Rowlandson's London (coauth, catalog), 67 & The Waning Middle Ages (ed, catalog), 69, Univ Kans; Images of Love & Death in Late Medieval and Renaissance Art (ed, catalog), 75 & Works from the Collection of Dorothy & Herbert Vogel (auth, catalog), 77, Univ Mich; Artists of La Revue Blanche, (coauth, catalog), Rochester, 84. *Pos:* Dir, Mus Art, Univ Kans, Lawrence, 68-70; head, Dept Pub Educ, Metrop Mus Art, New York, 70-73; dir, Univ Mich, Mus Art, 73-80; dir, Mem Art Gallery, Rochester, New York, 80-85; assoc dir, J Paul Getty Mus, Malibu, Calif, 85-90; dir, Indianapolis Mus Art, Indianapolis, Ind, 90- *Teaching:* Asst prof art hist, Univ Kans, Lawrence, 64-70; assoc prof art hist, Univ Mich, Ann Arbor, 73-80. *Awards:* Nat Endowment Arts Prof Devt Grant, Int Art Market, 80; NY Governor's Award, Memorial Art Gallery, 85.

Mem: Col Art Mus (chmn, mus educ comt 81-82); Asn Art Mus Dirs. *Res:* Graphic arts; 20th century art. *Publ:* The Vogel Collection, Works from Collection of Herbert & Dorothy Vogel (exhib catalog), Univ Mich Mus Art, 11-12/77; How to Draw American, Register, Univ Kansas Mus Art, spring 78; Sowing the Dragon's Teeth, Bull, Mus Art Archeol, Univ Mich, 80; Mus in the Groves of Academe, Mus News, 1-2/80; Contribr, Rouault's Abandonne: Transformations of an Image, Porticus, J Memorial Art Gallery, Univ Rochester, 84. *Mailing Add:* 4035 N Pennsylvania Indianapolis IN 46205

WALLER, SUSAN
GALLERY DIRECTOR, WRITER
b Newton, Mass, July 28, 48. *Study:* Brown Univ, BA, 70; Boston Univ, MA(art hist), 75. *Collections Arranged:* At Issue: Art and Advocacy, St Louis Gallery Art, 87; Artists' Books, Book Arts, 89, Swiss School: Late to Post Modern Graphic Design, Other Voices, Baxter Gallery, 91 & Imperiled Shores, 92, Baxter Gallery. *Pos:* Asst cur, Cranbrook Acad Art Mus, 81-84, cur, 84-86; asst dir, St Louis Gallery Contemp Art, 87-88; dir, Baxter Gallery, Maine Col Art. *Teaching:* Instr art hist, Ctr Creative Studies, 79-81 & Main Col Art, Maine, 89- *Mem:* Col Art Asn; Am Asn Mus. *Publ:* Auth, The artist, the writer and the queen, Women's Art J, 83; Strong-minded critics, Women Artists News, 85; Michael Hall: reasoned to believe (exhib catalog), St Louis Gallery, 88; Robert Stackhouse: St Louis bones (exhib, catalog), Laumeier Sculpture, 88; ed, Women Artists in the Modern Era, Scarecrow, 91. *Mailing Add:* Maine College of Art The Baxter Gallery 619 Congress St Portland ME 04101

WALLIN, LAWRENCE BIER
SCULPTOR, PAINTER
b Norwalk, Conn, Apr 23, 44. *Study:* Los Angeles City Col, 62; Otis Art Inst Los Angeles Co, BFA & MFA, 66. *Work:* Otis-Parsons Art Inst, Los Angeles; Tropical scene, Rock Resorts, Maui, Hawaii, 79. *Comn:* Two cityscapes, Bank of Am, Long Beach, Calif, 82; western scene, Wells Fargo, Palm Desert, Calif, 81; skyscape mural, Northrup Corp, Hawthorn, Calif, 82. *Exhib:* Current Concerns, Part II, 75 & Imagination, 76, Los Angeles Inst Contemp Art; Book Show, Inst Mod Art Brisbane, Australia & traveling, 78; solo exhibs, Brand Libr Art Ctr, Glendale, Calif, 85, Peter Nahum, London, Eng, 87 & Carnegie Art Mus, Oxnard, Calif, 89. *Bibliog:* Betje Howell (auth), Lawrenc Wallin, Art Voices, 1-2/82; Calvin J Goodman (auth), Return to regional art, Am Artist, 6/82; A survey of contemporary art of the figure, Am Artist, 2/85. *Mem:* Artist Equity Asn (vpres, bd dirs, 81-82). *Media:* Acrylic. *Publ:* Auth, The Adventure, 70 & The Model, 77, pvt publ; Lightfastness in colored pencils, Los Angeles Equity News, 82; contribr, Photographing your artwork, Am Artist, 84. *Dealer:* Art Angles Gallery 3411 E Chapman Orange CA 92669. *Mailing Add:* 895 Toro Canyon Rd Montecito CA 93108

WALLIN, LELAND DEAN
PAINTER, EDUCATOR
b Sioux Falls, SD, Oct 14, 42. *Study:* Columbus Col Art & Design, Ohio, 61; Kans City Art Inst, Mo, BFA, 65; Univ Cincinnati & Art Acad, Ohio, MFA fel, 67; Aspen Sch Contemp Art, Colo, 68; Sabbatical Study, Philip Pearlstein's Studio, NY, 76. *Work:* Godwin-Ternbach Mus. *Exhib:* One-man shows, Minneapolis Col Art & Design, Minn, 78, Harold Reed Gallery, New York, 83, Gallery Henoch, New York, 91 & E Carolina Univ, Greenville, NC, 93; Brooklyn 79, Brooklyn Mus, New York, 79; Drawings, Drawings, Drawings, Forum Gallery, New York, 84; Pa 7th & 12th Ann Watercolor Soc Exhib, Kutstown Univ, 85 & 90; Toys, Gallery Henoch, New York, 87; Objects Observed: Contemporary Still Life, Gallery Henoch, New York, 90; and others. *Collections Arranged:* New Realism 70 (auth, catalog), St Cloud State Univ, Minn, 70, Philip Pearlstein Retrospective, Marywood Col, Scranton, Pa, 88. *Pos:* Ed bd, Kappa Pi Int Hon Art Fraternity, 88. *Teaching:* Vis prof painting, E Carolina Univ, Greenville, NC, 92-93. *Awards:* Fac travel res grants, 73-74; Minn State Grant in Lithography, 75. *Bibliog:* Ralph Pomeroy (auth), article, Arts Mag, New York, 4/83; Gerrit Henry (auth), exhib catalog, Harold Reed Gallery, 83; Philip Pearlstein (auth), exhib catalog, Gallery Henoch, 91; and others. *Mem:* Col Art Asn; Pa Watercolor Soc; Drawing Soc. *Media:* Oil, Pencil. *Publ:* Auth, The evolution of Philip Pearlstein, Art Int Mag, Part I, summer 79, Part II, fall 79; A twenty year cast of nudes in bronze: Richard McDermott Miller's retrospective, Arts Mag, 5/84; Toys take a holiday, play the theater, and travel through time, Arts Mag, 3/87. *Dealer:* Gallery Henoch 80 Wooster St New York NY 10012. *Mailing Add:* Grouse Hill Rd RD 1 #376 Dalton PA 18414

WALMSLEY, WILLIAM AUBREY
PRINTMAKER, COLLECTOR
b Tuscumbia, Ala, Oct 9, 23. *Study:* Univ Ala, BFA, 51 & MA, 53; Art Students League; Acad Julian, Paris; Tamarind Lithography Workshop, Los Angeles. *Work:* Mus Mod Art, New York; Libr Cong, Washington, DC; Tate Gallery, London, Eng; Hawaii Acad Art, Honolulu; Ohio State Univ, Columbus. *Exhib:* Nat Print Exhib, Honolulu Acad Art, Hawaii, 74; Davidson Print Exhib, NC, 74; Philadelphia Print Club Int, Pa, 75; Libr Cong, Print Exhib, Washington, DC, 75; Soc Am Graphic Artist Print Exhib, New York, 75. *Teaching:* Prof lithography, Fla State Univ, Tallahassee, 62; vis artist lithography, Northern Ill Univ, Dekalb, summer 73; vis artist lithography, Penland Sch Crafts, Spruce Pine, NC, summer 75 & 77. *Awards:* Purchase Awards, Colorprint USA, Tex Tech, Lubbock, 72 & Potsdam Prints, NY, 72; Second Purchase Award, 12th Ann Calgary Graphic, Alta, 72. *Bibliog:* Emil Weddige (auth), Lithography, Int Textbk Co, 66; Clare Romano & John Ross (coauths), Complete Screenprint & Lithography, Freepress, Macmillan, 74. *Mem:* Southeastern Graphic Coun (pres, 76-78); Southeastern Col Art Conf (bd dir, 77-80); Soc Am Graphic Arts; Boston Printmakers; Southern Graphics Coun. *Media:* Lithography. *Collection:* Prints by Goya, Picasso, Callot, Ernst, Beckman, Matisse & Piranesi. *Mailing Add:* Dept Studio Art Fla State Univ Tallahassee FL 32306

WALSH, J(OHN) MICHAEL
DEALER, PRINTMAKER
b Peoria, Ill, July 16, 53. *Study:* Univ Iowa, printmaking with M Lazansky & U Meyers, BFA, 77; Bradley Univ, with W A S Hatch, MA, 80. *Exhib:* Davenport Munic Gallery, Iowa, 78; Minot State Col Mus, NDak, 79 & 81; Univ SDak Mus, Vermillion, traveling, 79 & 80; Dulin Gallery Art, Knoxville, Tenn, 80; Okla Arts Ctr, Oklahoma City, 81; Bradley Nat Exhib, Peoria, Ill, 83. *Pos:* Asst dir, Tower Park Gallery, Peoria, Ill, 78-; cur exhibs, Peoria Art Guild, Ill, 80-82; dir, Walsh Fine Arts, 83- *Teaching:* Instr papermaking workshop, Peoria Art Guild, 81- *Awards:* Purchase Award, Univ SDak, Vermillion, 80; First Place, Junction City Arts, Peoria, Ill, 82. *Mem:* Col Art Asn; World Print Coun. *Dealer:* Van Stratten Gallery 361 W Superior St Chicago IL 60610. *Mailing Add:* 1215 Orange St Peoria IL 61606

WALSH, JAMES
PAINTER, SCULPTOR
b Newark, NJ, Aug 6, 54. *Study:* Livingston Col, Rutgers Univ, NJ, BA, 76; Syracuse Univ, NY, MFA, 80. *Exhib:* First Biennial-New Jersey Artists, Newark Mus, 77; New Works in Clay III, Everson Mus Art, Syracuse, NY, 81-82; two-man show, Edmonton Art Gallery, Alberta, 85; Pre-Post Modern, Brush Art Gallery, St Laurence Univ, Canton, NY, 85; Assoc Am Artists, New York, 90. *Bibliog:* Valentin Tatransky (auth), The new avant-garde, Art Int, 4/84 & James Walsh, Arts Mag, 10/85; Russell Bingham (auth), James Walsh-John King, Update, 11-12/85. *Media:* Acrylic, Oil; Metal, Welded. *Dealer:* Galeria Joan Prats 24 W 57th St New York NY 10019; Associated American Artists 20 W 57th St New York NY 10019. *Mailing Add:* 4 Great Jones St New York NY 10012

WALSH, JANET BARBARA
PAINTER
b Philadelphia, Pa, Aug 11, 39. *Study:* Art Students League, with Mario Cooper, Daniel Greene & Dale Meyers, cert, 69; Sch Visual Arts, with Francis Criss, Robert Frankenberg, cert. *Work:* Progresso Corp; Mus de la Acuarela, Mex; Springmaid Found; St Antonin, Noble Val, France. *Comn:* Avon Products. *Exhib:* Anchorage Hist & Fine Arts Mus, Alaska; Nat Acad Design, Salmagundi, Club, World Trade Ctr, Art Students League, National Arts Club, New York; Mus Arts & Hist, Port Huron, Mich; Columbus Mus Arts & Sci, GA; Owensboro Mus Fine Arts, Ogunquit, MA; Grants Pass Mus Art, Ore, 80; Columbus Mus Art; Albrect Art Mus, St Joseph, MO; Charles & Emma Frye Mus, Seattle; QE2, Maruzen, Tokyo. *Pos:* Illusr, NY Horticultural Soc, Springmaid. *Teaching:* Workshops throughout the US & Europe; New York Horticutural Soc, 85; Salmagundi Club, 85- *Awards:* Catharine Lorillard Wolfe Award, Metrop Mus; T H Saunders Award, Artists Watercolor, 79; Bronze Medal, Am Watercolor Soc, 90; Am Watercolor Soc Scholarship; and others. *Mem:* Am Watercolor Soc (2nd vpres); Allied Artists; Catharine Lorillard Wolfe Art Club; Art Students League; Audubon Artists; Royal Soc Arts, London. *Media:* Watercolor, Pastel. *Dealer:* Craft Haus Top of the Hill Wilmington VT 05363; Pink House 133 Island Dr Hilton Head SC 29926. *Mailing Add:* 351 W Neck Rd Lloyd Harbor NY 11743

WALSH, JOHN
MUSEUM DIRECTOR
b Mason City, Wash, Dec 9, 37. *Study:* Yale Univ, BA, 61; Univ Leiden, Netherlands, 65-66; Columbia Univ, MA, 65 PhD, 71. *Pos:* Lectr & research asst, Frick Collection, New York, 66-68; from assoc for higher educ to assoc cur of Europ paintings to cur dept of Europ paintings, Metrop Mus Art, New York, 68-75; Mrs R W Baker cur paintings, Boston Mus Fine Arts, 77-83; dir, J Paul Getty Mus, 83- *Teaching:* From adj assoc prof to prof art hist, Barnard Col & Columbia Univ, 70-77; vis prof fine arts, Harvard Univ, 79. *Mem:* Yale Univ Art Gallery Governing Bd; Col Art Asn; bd fel, Claremont Univ Ctr Grad Sch, 88-; trustee Asn Art Mus Dirs 86-, pres 89-90; Century Asn New York. *Mailing Add:* J Paul Getty Mus PO Box 2112 Santa Monica CA 90406

WALSH, PATRICIA RUTH
PAINTER
b Cleveland, Ohio. *Study:* Col Mt St Joseph, Cincinnati, BA; Art Students League; Syracuse Univ, NY, MFA. *Comn:* Four paintings, St Timothy's Church, Trenton, Mich; design for altar furnishings, St Mary's Church, Oakland, Calif. *Exhib:* Northwest Printmakers Int, Seattle Art Mus, 65; Pollution Show, Oakland Mus, 70; Three Watercolorists, San Jose Civic Art Ctr, 73; Spaces & Places, Palo Alto Cult Ctr, 75; Walnut Creek Civic Arts Ctr, 80. *Pos:* Liturgical designer, Holy Names Col, Oakland, Calif & St Clement's Church, Hayward, Calif & Christ the King Catholic Community, Las Vegas, Nevada; consult, St Francis de Sales Cathedral, Oakland, Sacred Heart Cath Community, Hollester, St Jerome's Church, El Cerrito, Calif. *Teaching:* Asst prof fine arts, Nazareth Col, Rochester, NY, 57-65; prof fine arts, Calif Col Arts & Crafts, 65- *Awards:* Bene Award, Modern Liturgy Mag, 88; Hon Mention Mod Liturgy Mag, 92. *Mem:* Arch Mod Christian Art (bd mem). *Media:* Oil, Watercolor. *Mailing Add:* c/o Calif Col Arts & Crafts 5212 Broadway St Oakland CA 94618

WALTEMATH, JOAN
PAINTER
b Nebr, Oct 6, 53. *Study:* Rhode Island Sch Design, BFA, 76; Hunter Col, MFA, 92. *Work:* Fogg Mus, Harvard Univ, Boston, Mass; Muse de Beaux Arts, La Chaux De/Fonds, Switz; Chase Manhattan Bank, New York. *Comn:* Installation in lobby, Howco Investment Co, Metro Park, NJ, 87. *Exhib:* Art of the State, The Kitchen, New York, 82 & Stendahl Syndrome: The Cure, Andrea Rosen Gallery, New York, 90; solo shows, Cross References, B Braathen Gallery, New York, 89, Paintings & Recent Work, Stark Gallery, New York, 91 & 92 & Recent Acquisitions, Harvard Univ Art Mus, Boston,

92; Information, Terrain Gallery, San Francisco, 90. *Bibliog:* Robert Mahoney (auth), The Harmony of the Pentagon in the Paintings of J Waltemath, Apex, 88; Eric Saxon (auth), interview, Appearances, spring 90; Stephen Westphal (auth), review, Art Am, summer 92. *Media:* Oil on canvas. *Publ:* Coauth, Space Window, Ind, 77; contribr, Ralph Humphrey, Hunter Col City Univ New York, 91; Blast, X Art Found, 91; Art Against AIDS, Sotheby's 87 & Am Far. *Dealer:* Eric Stark 596 Broadway Suite 310 New York NY 10012. *Mailing Add:* 131 Bowery 4th fl New York NY 10002

WALTER, ELIZABETH MITCHELL
ADMINISTRATOR, HISTORIAN
b Decatur, Ala, Feb 19, 36. *Study:* Florence State Col, BA, 57; Univ Ala, MA, 69; Univ Ga, PhD, 78. *Pos:* Consult, Kennedy Douglas Ctr Arts, 77-88. *Teaching:* Instr art hist, Univ Ga, 76; lectr, Hambidge Ctr, Rabun Gap, Ga, 77; prof art hist, Univ NAla, 75-, head art dept, 85- *Mem:* Col Art Asn; Nat Coun Art Adminirs; Southeastern Col Art Conf (bd dirs, 85-88); Nat Asn Schs Art & Design, 89-90. *Res:* Art and artists in Alabama; Pier Luigi Nervi; W Eugene Smith; Hans Namuth. *Publ:* Frank Lloyd Wright in Alabama, Apelles, 81; Mimi Holmes, Art Papers, 88; auth, William Aiken Walker: Paintings 1879-1915 (catalog), 90. *Mailing Add:* Dept Art Box 5006 Univ N Ala Florence AL 35632-0001

WALTER, MAY E
COLLECTOR, PATRON
Pos: Mem art adv coun, Snite Mus Art, Notre Dame Univ; hon trustee, Am Craftsman's Coun, 77- *Collection:* Twentieth century masters. *Mailing Add:* 923 Fifth Ave New York NY 10021

WALTER, PAUL F
COLLECTOR, PATRON
b Mt Vernon, NY, July 29, 35. *Study:* Oberlin Col, Ohio; Columbia Univ, New York. *Collections Arranged:* Indian Paintings, Morgan Libr; Indian Drawings from Paul Walter Collection, Los Angeles Co Mus. *Pos:* Mem photog comt, Mus Mod Art, New York, 79, Metrop Mus Art; Friends Morgan Libr, New York, currently; trustee, Parrish Mus, Southampton, NY. *Interests:* Art education, avant garde theatre music and dance. *Collection:* Collection of Indian art; avant garde paintings, drawings and sculpture; photographs. *Mailing Add:* 450 E 52nd St New York NY 10022

WALTERS, BILLIE
CERAMIST
b Colman, Tex, Mar 12, 27. *Study:* Univ Colo; Univ NMex, BFA, 79, MA, 81. *Work:* Univ Calgary; Ariz State Univ; Southern Conn State Col; Western NMex Univ. *Exhib:* Ceramics Int, Calgary, Alta, 73; Mus Albuquerque, 79; Los Angeles Folk Art Mus, 79; Lange Gallery, Scripps Col, Claremont, Calif; and others. *Pos:* Crafts Rep, Bd NMex Arts & Crafts Fair, 74-; Southwest cur, Women's Caucus for Art Exhib, Bronx Mus, NY, 78. *Teaching:* Instr ceramics, Univ NMex, 79-81. *Awards:* Purchase Awards, Ceramics Int, 73 & Mus Albuquerque, NMex, 79. *Bibliog:* W R Mitchell (auth), Ceramic Art of the World 1973, Govt Can, Alta, 73; Elsbeth Woody (auth), Handbuilding Ceramic Forms, Farrar Straus Giroux, New York, 79. *Mem:* Albuquerque United Artists; NMex Potters Asn; Albuquerque Designer-Craftsman. *Mailing Add:* 3835 Rio Grande Blvd NW Albuquerque NM 87107

WALTERS, ERNEST
PAINTER
b Elizabethtown, Ky, Nov 11, 27. *Study:* Univ Louisville; Univ Miami; French Studio Schs. *Work:* Mus Mod Art, New York; Israel Mus, Jerusalem; Frankfurt Mus, Ger; Albertina, Vienna, Austria; Mus d'Art Mod, Brussels, Belg. *Exhib:* IFA Galleries, Washington, DC; Galerie Richter, Wiesbaden, Ger; Siemens, Overbeck Gallery, Lubeck; Galerie Kumar, Vienna, Austria; Daedal Fine Arts, Baltimore; and others. *Media:* Oil. *Publ:* Auth, Wiener Schwarzweiss, 68; An Astonished Survivor, 73. *Dealer:* IFA Galleries 2623 Connecticut Ave NW Washington DC 20008; Daedal Fine Arts Fallston Mall Fallston MD 21047. *Mailing Add:* 257 Foster Knoll Dr Joppa MD 21085

WALTERS, SYLVIA SOLOCHEK
PRINTMAKER, EDUCATOR
b Milwaukee, Wis, Aug 24, 38. *Study:* Univ Wis, Madison, BS, MS, MFA. *Work:* First Nat Bank of Boston; United Lithograph; 3-M Corp; Readers Digest; Achenbach Found Graphic Arts; Oakland Mus. *Exhib:* 3rd Graphics Biennial, Metrop Mus & Art Ctr, Miami, 77, 80; 34th Ann Boston Printmakers, DeCordova Mus, 82; Prints from Blocks, Assoc Am Artists, New York, 85; California Prints in Japan, Tokyo Mus, 85; Drake Univ 8th Biennial PRWTA Symposium Exhibit. *Pos:* Graphic & book designer, Univ Wis Press, 64-67; dir Gallery 210, Univ Mo, 74-; chmn dept art, Univ Mo, 77-81 & San Francisco State Univ, 84- *Teaching:* Instr printmaking, Layton Sch of Art, 63-64; instr drawing, Doane Col, 67-68 & St Louis Univ, 68-69; prof printmaking & drawing, Univ Mo, St Louis; prof printmaking & drawing, San Francisco State Univ, 84. *Awards:* Purchase Awards, Colorprint USA, 79, Vermillion, 79, 4th Miami Int Print Biennial, 80, 8th Univ Dallas Nat, 83, NDak Print & Drawing Show, 84; Best of Show Award, N Calif Print Competition, 86; Colorprint USA, 86; 42nd North American Boston Printmakers, 90. *Bibliog:* Donald Anderson (auth), The Art of Written Forms, Holt, Rinehart, Winston, 69; Nancy Rice (auth), Sylvia Solochek Walters, The St Louis Seen, fall 77; Marlene Schiller (auth), article, Am Artist 10/79. *Mem:* Col Art Asn; Women's Caucus for Art; Boston Printmakers, Print Club; Calif Printmakers Soc. *Media:* Woodcut and Relief Prints, Watercolor. *Publ:* Auth, American Women Printmakers, Gallery 210, Univ Mo, St Louis, 75; Art on the Mississippi, 4/76 & Place, race & rights in St Louis, summer 76, Women Artist News; California Printmaker Quarterly J #3, 90. *Dealer:* Locus Gallery 710 N Tucker Blvd St Louis MO 63101. *Mailing Add:* 5217 Harbord Dr Oakland CA 94618

WALTNER, BEVERLY RULAND
PAINTER
b Kansas City, Mo. *Study:* Yale Univ, with Joseph Albers; Univ Miami, BA, 55; Kent State Univ, Blossom Kent Art Prog with Richard Anuszkiewicz, 68; Northern Ill Univ, MFA, 68. *Work:* Northern Ill Univ, De Kalb; also numerous pvt collections. *Comn:* Paintings, Alexander Muss & Sons, Equitable Life Assurance Soc, Zuckerman-Vernon Corp & Gen Development Corp. *Exhib:* Tenth Mid-Western Biennial, Joslyn Art Mus, Omaha, Nebr, 68; Chautauqua Exhib Am Art, Chautauqua Art Asn, NY, 68-73 & 78; Ann Exhib, Nat Soc Painters Casein & Acrylics, New York, 69, 70, 72 & 73; 35th Ann Mid Yr Show, Butler Inst Am Art, Youngstown, Ohio, 70; Ark Nat Art Exhib, Univ Ark, Little Rock, 70; Ann Exhib Am Painting, Soc Four Arts, Palm Beach, Fla, 71 & 74. *Teaching:* Instr art, Barry Col, Miami Shores, Fla, 69-70. *Awards:* Top Award, New Horizons in Painting, N Shore Art League, 66; First Place, 68 & Louis E Seldon Mem Award, 72, Chautauqua Art Asn. *Bibliog:* Donald L Hoffman (auth), The color image, Kansas City Star, 1/19/69; Bill van Mauer (auth), Colors get her vivid messages across, Miami News, 2/8/72. *Mem:* Chautauqua Art Asn; Prof Artist Guild (treas, Miami area, 77-78, vpres, 78); Artists Equity Asn; Visual Arts Coalition. *Media:* Acrylic, Oil. *Mailing Add:* 7500 Almansa Coral Gables FL 33143

WALTON, DONALD WILLIAM
WRITER, LECTURER
b Cleveland, Ohio. *Study:* Western Reserve Univ, BA; John Huntington Art Sch. *Pos:* Dir fine arts, Franklin Mint, 69-74, managing dir, Franklin Gallery, 74-77, sr design mgr, Hallmark, 77-82. *Awards:* Doc on Norman Rockwell, Int Film Festival & NY Film Festival, 74. *Mem:* Am Fedn Arts; Author's Guild; Nelson-Atkins Gallery. *Publ:* Auth, Art is to Enjoy, 65; A Rockwell Portrait: An Intimate Biography, 78; Are You Communicating?, 89. *Mailing Add:* 330 E Bridlespur Dr Kansas City MO 64114

WALTON, GUY E
WRITER, EDUCATOR
b New York, NY, Oct 18, 35. *Study:* Wesleyan Univ, BA, 57; NY Univ, MA, 62, PhD, 67. *Collections Arranged:* Versailles a Stockholm (auth, catalog), Paris, 85. *Pos:* Vis cur, Nat Mus Stockholm, 83-85 & Minneapolis Inst Arts, 86. *Teaching:* Prof Baroque art & archit, NY Univ, 72- *Awards:* Nat Endowment Humanities Grant, 84-85; Pub Grant, J Paul Getty Trust, 85. *Mem:* Col Art Asn; Soc Archit Historians; Soc l'Hist l'Art Francais. *Res:* Seventeenth century French and Italian sculpture; architecture and decor of palaces. *Publ:* Auth, Pierre Puget in Rome: 1662, Burlington Mag, 69; Lievin Cruyl, In: Essays for H W Hanson, Abrams, 81; The abduction of Helen, a 17th century French bronze, Bulletin Detroit Mus, 83; Louis XIV's Versailles, Univ Chicago Press, 86. *Mailing Add:* Dept Art History 303 Main Bldg 100 Washington Sq E New York NY 10003

WALTON, HARRY A, JR
COLLECTOR
b Covington, Va, Sept 24, 18. *Study:* Univ Va, 37; Columbia Univ, 39; Lynchburg Col, AB, 39. *Exhib:* Works have been exhibited in libraries at: Trinity Col, Washington, DC, Col William & Mary, Norfolk Mus Art & Sci, Univ Va & Lynchburg Col. *Mem:* Past-Fel Pierpont-Morgan Libr, NY; Univ Va Bibliog Soc. *Collection:* Early books and manuscripts, Bibles, fine binding, Aldinae and first editions. *Mailing Add:* White Oak Dairy Box 790 Covington VA 24426

WALTON, M DOUGLAS
PAINTER, INSTRUCTOR
b Alva, Okla, June 23, 42. *Study:* Okla State Univ, BA, 65; study with Edgar Whitney, Robert E Wood & Milford Zornes; Tech Rome Prog, Italy. *Teaching:* Assoc prof archit & watercolors, La Tech Univ, Ruston, 72-84; instr workshops, throughout US; Watercolor Encounter & Journey Encounter, US and abroad, 77- *Mem:* Southwestern Watercolor Soc (signature mem); La Watercolor Soc; Southern Watercolor Soc; Mid-Southern Watercolorists (signature mem); Watercolor Art Soc, Houston. *Media:* Watercolor. *Publ:* Auth, A Special Kind of Silence, in prep. *Mailing Add:* Rt 2 Box 2278 Ruston LA 71270

WALTON, MARION
SCULPTOR
b New Rochelle, NY, Nov 19, 1899. *Study:* Bryn Mawr Col; Art Students League; Acad Grande Chaumiere, Paris, with Antoine Bourdelle. *Work:* Lincoln Mus, Nebr; Mus Winter Park, Fla; and many pvt collections in US, France, Eng, Italy & Sweden. *Comn:* World's Fair, US Govt, 39; Post Off mural, US Govt; and many pvt comn. *Exhib:* Mus Mod Art, New York; Whitney Mus Am Art, New York; Metrop Mus Art, New York; Art Inst Chicago; La Jeune Sculpture, Rodin Mus, Paris, France; Pa Acad Fine Arts; Philadelphia Mus Art; Triennale Europ de Sculpture, Palais Royal, Paris; Bienalle Int, Ravenna, Italy, 79; and many others. *Teaching:* Prof sculpture, Sarah Lawrence Col, 50-51; pvt lessons, currently. *Awards:* Gold Medal, Bienalle Int, Ravenna, Italy, 79; and others. *Bibliog:* Mag Art, Am Fedn Art, 7/40; M Seuphor (auth), La Sculpture de ce Siecle, 59. *Mem:* Sculptors Guild; Artists Equity Asn. *Media:* Marble, Bronze. *Mailing Add:* 49 Irving Pl New York NY 10003

WALTZER, STEWART PAUL
DEALER, PAINTER
b New York, NY, Mar 17, 48. *Study:* NY Univ, BA, 69, MA, 70; Columbia Univ; New York Studio Sch; also with Irving Sandler, Audrey Flack, Chuck Close & Kenneth Noland. *Exhib:* City Univ New York; Gallery Don Stewart, Montreal; Waddington & Shiell, Toronto; Gallery 99, Miami, Fla; Eva Cohon

Gallery, Chicago. *Pos:* Dir, Andre Emmerich Gallery Downtown, 72-74, Tibor de Nagy Gallery, 74-77 & Meredith Long Contemp, 77-79; pres, Waltzer & Assocs, 79- *Specialty:* American 20th. *Dealer:* Galeria Joan Prats 29 W 57th St New York NY. *Mailing Add:* Waltzer & Co 262 Bowery New York NY 10012

WANDS, ALFRED JAMES
PAINTER
b Cleveland, Ohio, Feb 19, 04. *Study:* Cleveland Art Inst, BFA; Western Reserve Univ, BS; Univ Colo; Acad Julien, Paris; John Huntington Inst. *Work:* Cleveland Art Mus; Brooklyn Mus Arts & Sci; Calif Palace of Legion of Honor, San Francisco; Denver Art Mus; Colo Springs Fine Arts Ctr; Sangre de Cristo Art Ctr, Pueblo, Colo; Denver Mus Western Art. *Comn:* Five Colorado landscapes, Denver Pub Schs, 46; Christ in the Temple (mural), Grant Ave Methodist Church, Denver, 47; mural of Rocky Mountains, YMCA of the Rockies, Denver, 67; elk (mural), Rocky Mountain Nat Park, Estes Park, Colo, 75; two oils, Colorado Springs Fine Arts Ctr, 78. *Exhib:* Carnegie Inst Int, Pittsburgh; Corcoran Art Gallery Biennial, Washington, DC; Art Inst Chicago Am Ann; Kansas City Art Inst Midwestern Ann, Mo; Denver Art Mus Ann; Cleveland Art Mus. *Pos:* Chmn, Denver Art Comn, 45-61. *Teaching:* Instr painting, Cleveland Art Inst, 26-30; prof painting & drawing, Colo Women's Col, Denver, 30-47; instr painting, Univ Colo, Denver, 47-50. *Awards:* Silver Medal, Kansas City Art Inst, 42; Best in Show & First Painting, Denver Artists Guild Ann Exhib, 81; and others. *Mem:* Denver Artists Guild (pres, 32, 41 & 63); Carmel Art Asn; Col Art Asn Am (secy, Colo Chap, 36-42). *Media:* Oil, Watercolor. *Publ:* Auth, How to Paint Mountains, 75. *Dealer:* Studio Art Gallery San Carlos & Ocean Carmel CA 93921; Artspace Gallery Colorado Springs CO. *Mailing Add:* 125 Maynard Rd Sequim WA 98382

WANDS, ROBERT JAMES
EDUCATOR, PAINTER
b Denver, Colo, June 24, 39. *Study:* With Alfred Wands, 56-60; Univ Denver, BFA, 61, MA, 63; Cleveland Art Inst; Western Reserve Univ. *Work:* Univ Denver; Colo Womens Col; Western Colo Ctr Arts, Grand Junction; Univ Southern Colo; Colo State Fair Collection. *Comn:* Painting, Fine Am Art Calendar, Cleveland, 70; murals, Cleopatra Health Spa, Pueblo, Colo, 76 & YMCA, Estes Park, Colo, 77; paintings, United Bank, Pueblo, Colo, 78, Dain Bosworth, Pueblo, 84, Colo Nat Bank-Belmont, Pueblo, 86 & Pueblo Teachers Credit Union, Colo, 86. *Exhib:* Own Your Own Art Shows, Sangre de Cristo Art Ctr, Pueblo, Colo, 63-83; S S Hope Invitational, Butler Inst Am Art, 70; Colo Biennial, Denver Art Mus, 72; I-25 Artist Alliance, Colorado Springs Fine Arts Ctr, 72 & 88; solo exhib, Sangre de Cristo Art Ctr, Pueblo, Colo, 73, Western Colo Ctr Arts, Grand Junction, 74 & Univ Southern Colo, 81; two-man exhibs, Sangre de Cristo Art Ctr, Pueblo, Colo, 84; Off Broadway Art Gallery, Pueblo, Colo, 86; Eyes, Colo Invitational, Boulder, 87; Faculty Show, Univ Southern Colo, Pueblo, 88; Colo Teachers Exhib, Manitou Springs, Colo, 89; Fac USC Art Exhib, 89; one-man Sabbatical Exhib, USC, 89; Colo Art Educators Exhib, USC, 89; Invited Exhib Artist, Estes Part Art Ctr, Estes Park, Colo, 90; Art Educators Exhib, Bus Art Ctr, Manitou Springs, Colo, 91; The Best of the Sangre de Cristos Exhib, Sangre de Cristo Art Ctr, 91; S Colo Invitational, Sangre de Cristo Art Ctr, 92. *Pos:* Artist-in-residence, Asn Camp, Estes Park, Colo, summers 74-78. *Teaching:* Instr painting, Univ Denver, 63; assoc prof, Univ Southern Colo, 63- *Awards:* Purchase Prize, 65 & Meritorious Award, 72, Colo State Fair; Best of Show, Own Your Own Art Show, Sangre Cristo Art Ctr, 79. *Bibliog:* Carol Kronwitter (auth), Pueblo Chieftain, 2/28/81 & 9/30/84; Jeff Rennicke (auth), Colo Mountain Ranges, 86. *Mem:* I-25 Artist Alliance. *Media:* Acrylic, Oil. *Dealer:* Wands Art Studio Gallery P O Box 192 Estes Park CO 80517; Myer Gallery Santa Fe NM. *Mailing Add:* 1306 W Abriendo Pueblo CO 81004

WANG, C C
PAINTER
b Soochow, China, Feb 14, 07. *Study:* Soochow Univ, grad. *Work:* Brooklyn Mus Art, NY; Art Mus, Princeton Univ, NJ; Bank of Am, San Francisco; Fogg Mus, Boston; Phoenix Art Mus, Ariz; Henry Art Gallery. *Exhib:* The New Chinese Landscape, Six Contemporary Chinese Artists, 66; De Young Mem Mus, San Francisco, 68; Indianapolis Mus Art, 72; Fogg Mus, Harvard Univ, 73; Watercolor Soc, Nat Acad Art & Design, New York, 74; Henry Art Gallery, Seattle, Wash; Spencer Mus Art, Lawrence, Kans; China Inst Am, New York. *Pos:* Chmn Art Dept, Chinese Univ, Hong Kong; consult, Sotheby's Auction House, New York. *Teaching:* Prof art, Shanghai Acad Art, 33-34; vis lectr, Columbia Univ, New York, 51-52 & Univ Calif, Berkeley, 68-69; chmn art dept, Chinese Univ, Hong Kong, 62-64. *Awards:* Governor's Asian-Am Heritage Month Award, NY, 91. *Bibliog:* James Cahill (Interv) C C Wang/Landscape paintings, Univ Wash Press, Seattle & London, 86; Jerome Silbergeld (auth), Mind Landscape/The paintings of C C Wang, Univ Wash Press, Seattle & London, 87; Mountains of the Mind: The Landscape Paintings of C C Wang, Arthur Sackler Found, Washington, DC. *Mem:* China Inst; Metropolitan Mus Art, New York, (benefactor); Shanhai Acad Art, (hon mem, 86-). *Media:* Ink, Color on Rice Paper. *Publ:* Mountains of the Mind: The Landscape Paintings of Wang Chi- Chieu, Walker/Weatherhill, New York & Tokyo; C C Wang: Landscape paintings, Introd by James Cahill, Univ Wash Press, Seattle & London; Mind Landscape: The Paintings of C C Wang, by Jerome Silbergeld, Univ Wash Press, Seattle & London. *Mailing Add:* 150 E 69th St New York NY 10021

WANG, GAR
PAINTER, LECTURER
Study: Princeton Univ, BA(cum laude), 76; Hunter Col, MA(painting), 83. *Exhib:* Art Mus, Princeton Univ, Princeton, NJ, 82; Terminal New York Show, Brooklyn, NY, 83; Hunter Col Art Gallery, New York, 86; Mus Hudson Highlands, Cornwall on Hudson, NY, 86; Solo exhibs, 55 Mercer, New York, 86 & 87; Vorhees Campus, Univ, New York, 89; Asian Am Arts Ctr, New York, 90. *Teaching:* lectr, visual arts dept, Princeton Univ, 88-89. *Awards:* Frances Le Moyne Page Award, Princeton Univ, 76; Tony Smith Fund Award, Hunter Col, 83; Visual Artists Fel Grant, Nat Endowment Arts, 87-88. *Mailing Add:* 300 Morgan Ave Brooklyn NY 11211

WANG, SAM
PHOTOGRAPHER
b Peking, China, Apr 4, 39; US citizen. *Study:* Augustana Col, Sioux Falls, BA, 64; Univ Iowa, MFA, 66. *Work:* SC State Collection; Chase Manhattan Collection & Metrop Mus Art, New York; Ctr For Creative Photography, Ariz; Herbert F Johnson Mus Art, Ithaca, NY; and others. *Exhib:* Portrait of the South, Palazzo Vinizia, 84; Silver & Silk, Mus of Hist & Technol, Smithsonian Inst, 75-77; Translations: Photography in New Forms, Herbert F Johnson Mus, 79; one-man shows, Mint Mus Art, 70, Greenville Co Mus Art, 72, 77 & 81, Light Factory, 79, RI Sch Design Photog Gallery, 79 & Fay Gold Gallery, 83; Counterparts, Metrop Mus Art, San Francisco Mus Mod Art & Corcoran Gallery Art, 83. *Pos:* Acquistions Adv Panel, SC State Mus, 84-92; chmn, State Art Collections Comm, SC, 77-78. *Teaching:* Prof photog, Clemson Univ, SC, 66-; vis artist photog & computer graphics, Penland Sch of Crafts, NC, summers 70, 74, 79, 89 & 91; vis artist printmaking workshop, Univ Notre Dame, 79. *Awards:* Unicolor Artist Support Award, 83; Prof Award of Merit, AAUP, 85; SAF/NEA Photography Fel, 87. *Bibliog:* David Featherstone (auth), Art Week, 73. *Mem:* Soc Photog Educ (bd dirs, 73-77); Guild SC Artists; Southeastern Col Art Conf. *Media:* Computer-aided Graphics. *Publ:* Illusr, South Carolina Architecture 1670-1970, SC Tricentennial Comn, 70; New Am Nudes, Morgan & Morgan, 81; Beyond the Zone System, Focal Press, 88. *Mailing Add:* 108 Poole Lane Clemson SC 29631

WANLASS, STANLEY GLEN
SCULPTOR, PAINTER
b American Fork, Utah, Apr 3, 41. *Study:* Brigham Young Univ, BFA, 66, MA, 68. *Work:* Fr Clatsop Nat Mem, Ore; Springville Art Mus, Utah; Hutchings Mus, Lehi, Utah; Mus Western Expansion, St Louis, Mo; Blackhawk Mus, Danville, Calif; and others. *Comn:* heroic sculpture, Wash State Arts Comn, Everett, 76; heroic bronze statue, Nat Park Serv, 83; heroic Lewis & Clark (bronze sculpture), City Seaside, Ore, 90; heroic sculpture, City Longbeach, Wash, 90; heroic bronze sculpture (founder), Muhlenberg Col, Allentown, Pa, 91; and others. *Exhib:* Los Angeles Co Mus, 85; Russo Bianco Mus, Aschaffenburg, Ger, 83-92; Whitehouse, Washington, DC, 88; retrospective, Canton Art Inst, 90; Campbell (Soup) Mus, Philadelphia, 90; Kodak-Japan, Toyko, 92; and others. *Teaching:* Instr, Brigham Young Univ, Provo, Utah, 65-70, Europ Art Acad, Paris, 65; prof, Univ Grenoble, France, 69-70, Medicine Hat Col, Univ Calgary, Alta, 70 & 71 & Clatsop Col, Astoria, Ore, 71-86; retired; Clatsop Col, Astoria, Ore, 71-86. *Awards:* Best of Show, Ore Trail Nat, 81; Silver Medal, Springville Art Mus, Utah, 81; Blue Ribbon Concours d'Elegance, Oakland Univ, Detroit, Mich, 83; Grand Prize & First Place, Auburn-Cord, Duesenberg Mus, Auburn, Ind, 85. *Bibliog:* Articles, SW Art Mag, 82, Automania, 84, Automobile Quarterly, 84, Am Artist Mag; and others. *Mem:* Automotive Fine Arts Soc. *Media:* Bronze; Acrylic, Oil. *Publ:* Auth, Dictionary of American Automobiles 1900-1930, Dover Publ, 73. *Mailing Add:* 907 Fifth St PO Box 1029 Astoria OR 97103

WARASHINA, M PATRICIA
CERAMIST, EDUCATOR
b Spokane, Wash. *Study:* Univ Wash, Seattle, BFA, MFA. *Work:* Everson Art Mus, Syracuse, NY; Nelson Gallery Art, Kansas City, Mo; Detroit Art Inst, Mich; Henry Art Gallery, Seattle, Wash; John Michael Kohler Arts Ctr, Sheboygan, Wis. *Exhib:* Int Exhib of Ceramics, Victoria & Albert Mus, London, Eng, 72; Sensible Cup Int Exhib, Sea of Japan Expos, Kanazawa, Japan, 7; Clay, Whitney Mus Am Art, New York, 74; 1st World Crafts Exhib, Ont Sci Ctr, Toronto, 74; The Collector, Mus Contemp Crafts, New York, 74; NW 77 Exhib, Mod Art Pavilion, Seattle Ctr, Wash, 77. *Teaching:* Instr art, Wis State Univ, Platteville, 64-65; instr art, Eastern Mich Univ, Ypsilanti, 66-68; prof art, Univ Wash, Seattle, 70- *Media:* Clay. *Mailing Add:* 120 E Edgar Seattle WA 98102

WARBURG, STEPHANIE WENNER
PAINTER, SCULPTOR
b Kalamazoo, Mich, Dec 29, 41. *Study:* Univ Mich Col Archit & Design, BS(drawing & design); and with Guy Palazzola, Milton Cohen & Mildred Fairchild; Columbia Univ Teachers Col, MA(fine arts & fine arts educ). *Work:* Earthwatch, Atrium Schools, Watertown, Mass. *Exhib:* Slater Mus, Norwich, Conn, 69; Gilman Gallery, Chicago, 72; Lord & Taylor Gallery, New York, 72; Flora & Fauna of Madeira, Funchal, Madeira, Portugal, 73; Bermuda Soc Arts, 84; St Botolph Club, Boston, 85; Gallery Nakazawa, Hiroshima, Japan, 86; Oda Gallery, Hiroshima, Japan, 87; Nena's Choice Gallery, Bergdorf Goodman, New York, 90. *Teaching:* Chmn, Dept Art, Latin Sch Chicago, 70-72; instr watercolor & freehand drawing, Chamberlayne Jr Col, Boston, 75-81. *Awards:* Am Cancer Soc Art Awards, 67 & 68; Lyme Art Asn Second Prize for Painting, 68. *Bibliog:* Susan Croce Kelly (auth), It's all in the family: Sister artists display work here, St Louis Globe Dem, 70; On exhibit, Where Mag, 12/72. *Mem:* Bermuda Soc Arts. *Media:* Oil Wash, Papermache. *Dealer:* Oda Gallery Hiroshima 730 Japan. *Mailing Add:* 360 Beacon St Boston MA 02116

WARD, ELAINE
PAINTER
b Boston, Mass, June 4, 29. *Study:* Ecole Des Beaux Arts, France, BA, 53; Art Students League, 57-61. *Work:* New Eng Contemp Art Ctr, Brooklyn, Conn; Daytona Beach Mus, Fla; Ardan Asn, New York, NY; Coastal Steel Co, Carteret, NJ; Pandora Co, Conway, NH. *Comn:* Portrait, comn by Barbara Andreadls, New York, 86; acrylic on canvas, Arthur Dann & co, New York, 88; acrylic on canvas, Design Decisions, New York, 89; mural on canvas, comn by Senor Louis Carraquillo Vieques, PR, 89. *Exhib:* Guild Hall, NY, 91; Lever House, NY, 91; Viewpoint Gallery, NY, 91; Phoenix Gallery, New York, 92; Elaine Benson Gallery, Bridgehampton, NY, 92; and others. *Awards:* Asn des Beaux Arts Award, Beaux Arts de Cannes, 74; First Prize, Munic Casino Cannes, 77. *Bibliog:* Deanna Freedman (auth), Enlarging the viewers experience, Artspeak, 2/89; Mary Jo Godwin (auth), Exotic Star, Wilson Libr Bull, 4/89; Charles Ditlefsein (auth), Women Artists, Cedco Publ Co, 90. *Mem:* Nat Asn Women Artist; Art Studio Club (treas, 88-90); Nat Art Club. *Media:* Watercolor, Acrylic. *Publ:* Illusr, cover, Wilson Libr Bul, 4/89; auth, articles in Manhattan Art Mag & Artspeak, 90. *Dealer:* Phoenix Gallery 568 Broadway New York NY 10012. *Mailing Add:* 175 E 62 St New York NY 10021

WARD, JOHN LAWRENCE
HISTORIAN, PAINTER
b East Orange, NJ, Feb 6, 38. *Study:* Hamilton Col, BA, 60; Yale Univ, MA(art hist), 62; Univ NMex, MFA(painting), 66; Boston Univ, PhD(art hist), 84. *Work:* Univ NMex; Miss Mus Art, Jackson; Ala Power Co, Birmingham; Astronomy Dept, Univ Fla. *Exhib:* One-man shows, Fla Tech Univ, Orlando, 76, Univ Fla, Gainesville, 76 & 86 & Stetson Univ, DeLand, Fla, 92; The Human Presence, Jacksonville Art Mus, Fla, 74; Southeastern Ctr for Contemp Art, Winston-Salem, NC, 79; Southern Realism, Miss Mus Art & traveling, 79; Southeast Juried Exhib, Fine Arts Mus S, Mobile, Ala, 87; and others. *Teaching:* Prof art hist, Univ Fla, 62-64 & 66- *Mem:* Col Art Asn; Hist Netherlandish Art. *Media:* Oil. *Res:* Flemish painting, American Realist painting; criticism of photography. *Publ:* Auth, The criticism of photography as art: The photographs of Jerry Uelsmann, 70; A proposed reconstruction of an altarpiece by Rogier Van der Weyden, Vol LIII, 71 & Hidden symbols in Jan Van Eyck's Annunciations, Vol LVII, 75, Art Bulletin; The Perception of Pictorial Space in Perspective Pictures, Vol IX, Leonardo, 76; American Realist Painting, 1945-1980, UMI Res Press, 89. *Mailing Add:* Art Dept AFA Univ of Fla Gainesville FL 32611

WARD, JOSEPH MARSHALL
PAINTER, EDUCATOR
b Phoenix, Ariz, Feb 11, 22. *Study:* Univ Ky, Lexington, with Edward Warder Rannells, BA, 46; Philadelphia Col Art, with Henry C Pitz, dipl, 49; E Tenn State Univ, Johnson City, MA(art educ), 65. *Work:* Baptist Col Charleston; Bank of Murray, Ky. *Exhib:* Young Am Paints, Smithsonian Inst, Washington, DC, 40; Ann Mid-South Exhib, Watkins Inst, Nashville, 50; Ann Guild SC Artists, Gibbes Art Gallery, Charleston, 76; Ann Coastal Carolina Fairs. *Pos:* Artist, Baptist Sunday Sch Bd, Nashville, 49-53, artist-illus, 53-59. *Teaching:* Instr applied art, Va Intermont Col, Bristol, 59-68; assoc prof art & chmn dept, Baptist Col, Charleston, SC 68-87. *Awards:* Second Place Oil Painting, Mid-South Exhib, Nashville, 50; Third Place Watercolor, Nationwide Sears Art Shows, Bristol, Tenn, 61; Merit awards, Coastal Carolina Fair, watercolors, 84 & 86. *Mem:* Charleston Artist Guild (mem bd, 75-77, vpres, 76 & chmn scholarship comt, 83-89). *Media:* Watercolor, pastel. *Mailing Add:* 8019 Nantucket Ave Charleston SC 29420

WARD, LYLE EDWARD
PAINTER, EDUCATOR
b Topeka, Kans, Feb 4, 22. *Study:* Stevens Point State Teachers Col, Wis, 43; Kansas City Univ, 50; Kansas City Art Inst, BFA, 51, MFA, 52; also with Miron Sokole, New York, 46-52. *Work:* Brooklyn Mus, NY; Corcoran Gallery, Washington, DC; Butler Inst Am Art, Youngstown, Ohio; Mus Art, Univ Okla, Norman; Mulvane Art Mus, Topeka; First Nat Bank & Stevens Inc, Little Rock, Ark. *Exhib:* One-man shows, Kansas City Art Inst, 60, Superior St Gallery, Chicago, 60 & Univ Miss, Oxford, 72; Avanti Galleries, New York, 75; Treishman Gallery, Hendrix Col, Conway, Ark, 76; Avanti Galleries, New York, 75; Treishman Gallery, Hendrix Col, Conway, Ark, 76; JoAnn Perse Gallery, Little Rock, Ark, 86. *Teaching:* Prof art & chmn dept, Col of the Ozarks, Clarksville, Ark, 56-82; retired. *Awards:* Arts Festival Award, Worthen Bank, Little Rock, 60 & 62; First Prize, Delta Exhib, Ark Arts Ctr, 63, 65 & 67; 18th Arts Festival Award, Ft Smith Festival Bd, Ark, 68. *Bibliog:* Gordon Brown (auth), article, Arts Mag, 75; Ed Albin (auth), cover story & rev, Art Voices/S, 79; Lyle Ward (auth), article, Art Voices/S Ark, 79. *Mem:* Col Art Asn Am; Mid-Am Art Asn; Southeast Art Conf. *Media:* Oil. *Publ:* Auth, articles, Southwest Times, 68, Ark Gazette, 74, Arts Mag, 75, Art Voices, 79. *Dealer:* Avanti Galleries 145 E 72nd St New York NY 10021. *Mailing Add:* 1201 Arkansas Ave Clarksville AR 72830

WARD, (WILLIAM) MICHAEL
EDITOR
b Sandusky, Ohio, June 16, 57. *Study:* Otterbeing Col, BA, 79, educ degree, 80; Bowling Green State Univ, grad work in Eng, 82; studied with James Baldwin. *Pos:* Assoc ed, Art Material Trade News, 83; ed, The Artist's Mag, 84-90; ed dir, Art Mag Group, Decorative Artist's Workbook, How Mag, Spark & Art Mats Today, F & W Publs. *Publ:* Monthly column about art philosophy in Artist's Mag; auth, The New Spirit of Watercolor, N Light, 89. *Mailing Add:* c/o Artists Magazine 1507 Dana Ave Cincinnati OH 45207

WARD, WILLIAM EDWARD
DESIGNER, PAINTER
b Cleveland, Ohio, Apr 4, 22. *Study:* Western Reserve Univ, BS, 47, MA, 48; Cleveland Inst Art, dipl, 47; Columbia Univ, 50. *Work:* Cleveland Mus Art, Cleveland Art Asn & Cleveland Trust Bank; Akron Art Inst, Ohio. *Comn:* Firemen's Memorial (sculpture), Cleveland Fire Dept, 68; official seal for Sch of Med & Case Western Reserve Univ, 69; traveling exhib for George Gund Collection Western Art, New York, 72; mural, Harris Corp, Cleveland, 75; installation design, Am Ceramic Soc Mus, 81. *Exhib:* One-man shows, Painting & Photography, Cleveland Inst Art, 48, Acrylics & Watercolors, Ross Widen Gallery, Cleveland, 73, 78 & 80 & Humphrey Gallery, Cleveland; Ohio Fine Arts Exhib, Massilon Mus Art, Ohio, 75; Cleveland Play House Gallery, 85; Casa de la Cultura, Oaxaca, Mex, 86; Watercolors & Photographs of Oaxaca, Folk Arts Gallery, Cleveland, Ohio, 92; and others. *Collections Arranged:* All special exhibition and permanent collection installations, Cleveland Mus Art, 58-; Folk Art of Oaxaca/The Ward Collection, Cleveland Inst of Art (coauth, catalog), 87. *Pos:* Educ & Oriental Depts asst, Cleveland Mus Art, 47-57, designer, 57- *Teaching:* Prof calligraphy, Cleveland Inst Art, 60-, instr watercolor, 67-69. *Awards:* Design Award, Champion Int Order Roundtable, 78; Northern Ohio LIVE Award of Achievement for Design, Cleveland Mus Art, 87; The Cleveland Arts Prize, Spec Citation/Design, 88; and others. *Mem:* Int Design Conf; City of Cleveland Fine Arts Adv Comt; Cleveland Soc Contemp Art; Print Club Cleveland; The Rowfant Club. *Media:* Watercolor, Acrylic. *Collection:* Folk art of Oaxaca, Mexico area and Kalighat paintings from the Calcutta region, India. *Mailing Add:* 27045 Solon Rd Solon OH 44139

WARDER, WILLIAM
PAINTER, WRITER
b Guadalupita, NMex, July 23, 20. *Study:* Univ NMex, with Raymond Jonson, Kenneth Adams & Randall Davey, BFA; Art Students League, with Louis Bouche & Morris Kantor; Univ Calif, Los Angeles. *Work:* Art Mus NMex, Santa Fe; NMex State Fair Collection, Albuquerque; Mus Albuquerque; Raton Mus, NMex. *Comn:* Tom Sawyer & Huck, Works Progress Admin Arts Proj, 36; mural Army life, Ft Warren, Wyo, 43; NMex hist murals, Int State Bank, Raton, 70; Navajo History (mural), Chinle Pub Sch, Ariz, 92. *Exhib:* Am Watercolor Soc, Nat Acad, New York, 48; Audubon Artists Exhib, 48; New York World's Fair Ford Pavillion Nat Exhib, 64; Watercolor USA, Springfield, Mo, 64 & 73; Southwest Fine Arts Biennial, Mus NMex, 74. *Pos:* Writer-producer, Educ TV, KNME, Channel 5, Albuquerque, NMex; mural painter, Albuquerque Pub Schs. *Teaching:* Artist-in-sch, Las Vegas, NMex, 71-73 & Espanola, 74-75, Albuquerque, 74-; lectr & workshops on creative process in pub schs in Southwest. *Awards:* Nat Telly Statuett Award for Television Doc, From the Heart of a Child, 91; and others. *Bibliog:* Senator Peter Domenici (auth), Speech entered into US Cong Rec, 6/25/73; Artist-in-schs, NMex Sch Rev, Spring 74 & Falls 77-78. *Media:* Watercolor, Oil. *Res:* Distinguishing the self and person as two entities in the individual that relate to intrinsic creativity and the extrinsic social productivity as bases for educational orientations. *Publ:* Auth, Alternative Approach in Education Using Art as the Medium, 74. *Dealer:* Cafe 516 Central Ave SE Albuquerque NM 87102. *Mailing Add:* 1020 California SE Albuquerque NM 87108

WARDLAW, GEORGE MELVIN
PAINTER, SCULPTOR
b Baldwyn, Miss, Apr 9, 27. *Study:* Memphis Acad Arts, BFA, 51; Univ Miss, with David Smith & Jack Tworkov, MFA, 55. *Work:* DeCordova Mus, Lincoln, Mass; Mus Fine Arts, Springfield, Mass. *Comn:* Wall relief sculpture, 76 & sculpture, 76, Mt Sinai Med Ctr. *Exhib:* Abstract Paintings, 71 & solo exhib, 78-79, DeCordova Mus, Lincoln, Mass; Chicago Art Inst; Metrop Mus Art, New York; Nat Gallery; Portland Mus Art, Maine. *Teaching:* Asst prof art, State Univ NY Col, New Paltz, 56-63; assoc prof painting & exec off, Yale Univ, 64-68; prof painting & chmn dept, Univ Mass, Amherst, 68- *Awards:* Miss Inst Arts & Lett Award, 83; Univ Mass Fac Res Fel, 83. *Media:* Acrylic; Metal. *Dealer:* Stux Gallery Boston MA. *Mailing Add:* 47 Morgan Circle Amherst MA 01002

WARDWELL, ALLEN
MUSEUM DIRECTOR, CONSULTANT
b New York, NY, Jan 18, 35. *Study:* Yale Univ, BA, 57; NY Univ, MA, 60. *Collections Arranged:* Yakutat South Indian Art of the Northwest Coast (auth, catalog), 64, The Sculpture of Polynesia (auth, catalog), 67 & The Art of the Sepik River (auth, catalog), 71, Art Inst Chicago; Gold of Ancient America (auth, catalog), Mus Fine Arts, Boston, 68; Objects of Bright Pride, Northwest Coast Indian Art from the American Museum of Natural History (auth, catalog), Am Fedn Arts, 78 & 88; Ancient Eskimo Ivories of the Bering Strait, Am Fedn Arts, 86; African Sculpture from the University Museum, Philadelphia Mus Art, 86; Likeness and Beyond: Portraits From Africa & the World, Ctr African Art, 90. *Pos:* Asst cur primitive art, Art Instof Chicago, 60-63, cur primitive art, 63-73, actg cur decorative arts, 64-70 & asst dir mus serv, 70-72; dir, Asia Soc Gallery, 74-84; dir, Isamu-Noguchi Garden Mus, New York, 86-90. *Teaching:* Assoc adj prof mus studies, New York Univ. *Publ:* Contribr, Bibliography Northwest Coast Indian Art, Mus of Primitive Art, Art Inst of Chicago, 70. *Mailing Add:* 88 Central Park W New York NY 10023

WAREHALL, WILLIAM DONALD
GLASS BLOWER, CERAMIST
b Detroit, Mich, July 12, 42. *Study:* Wayne State Univ, BFA, 68; Univ Wis, Madison, MFA, 71. *Work:* Chrysler Mus Art, Norfolk; Bergstrom Art Ctr, Neenah; W Baton Rouge Mus, Port Allen; Debarry State Mus, Fla; La State

Univ, Baton Rouge; Ariz State Univ, Tempe. *Comn:* Reproduction of Ancient Maritime Glass Vessels, Tex A&M Univ, College Station, Tex, 90. *Exhib:* 20 Americans, Mus Contemp Art, New York, 71; Phases of New Realism, Lowe Art Mus, Coral Gables, Fla 72; California Design, Los Angeles Design Ctr, 76; one-man show, Anhalt Gallery, Los Angeles, 76; Tea Pot-24 Concepts, Rodell Gallery, Los Angeles, 82; New Glass, Heller Gallery, New York, 85; Southern Calif Glass, Scalar Gallery, Morristown, NJ 86; California, Elaine Potter Gallery, San Francisco, 86. *Pos:* Chmn, art dept, Calif State, San Bernadino, 88-90. *Teaching:* Instr art, Univ Minn, 71-73; from asst prof art to assoc prof, Calif State Univ, San Bernardino, 73-81, prof, 81-, chairperson, 88-89; asst prof, La State Univ, Baton Rouge, 78-79; exchange prof ceramics, Va Commonwealth Univ, Richmond, 86. *Bibliog:* Paul Donhauser (auth), History of Am Ceramics, Kendall & Hunt, 78. *Mem:* Am Craft Coun; Southern Calif Designer Craftsman; Glass Soc; Col Art Asn. *Media:* Cast Glass, Pate de Verre; Clay. *Dealer:* Sandy Webster Gallery Philadelphia PA; Craft Alliance Gallery St Louis MO. *Mailing Add:* 5220 Sepulveda San Bernardino CA 92404

WARK, ROBERT RODGER
ADMINISTRATOR, HISTORIAN
b Edmonton, Alta, Oct 7, 24; US citizen. *Study:* Univ Alta, BA & MA, LLD; Harvard Univ, MA & PhD. *Pos:* Cur art, Huntington Libr & Art Gallery, 56-*Teaching:* Instr art, Harvard Univ, 52-54 & Yale Univ, 54-56; lectr art, Calif Inst Technol, 60-90 & Univ Calif, Los Angeles, 65-80; retired. *Res:* English art of the Georgian period. *Publ:* Ed, Sir Joshua Reynolds, Discourses on Art, 59; auth, Early British Drawings in the Huntington Collection 1700-1750, 69; Drawings by John Flaxman in the Huntington Collection, 70; Ten British Pictures 1740-1840; Drawings by Thomas Rowlandson in the Huntington Collection, 75; plus others. *Mailing Add:* Henry E Huntington Libr & Art Gallery 1151 Oxford Rd San Marino CA 91108

WARKOV, ESTHER
PAINTER
b Winnipeg, Man, Oct 12, 41. *Study:* Winnipeg Sch Art, 58-61. *Work:* Nat Gallery, Ottawa; Mus Fine Arts, Montreal; Vancouver Art Gallery; Winnipeg Art Gallery; Beaver Brook Art Gallery, Fredricton, NB. *Exhib:* Expo '67, Montreal; Marlborough Godard Exhib, 73; Mus Mod Art, Paris, 73; Albright-Knox Art Gallery, Buffalo, 74. *Awards:* Can Coun Bursaries, 67-72; Can Coun Grant, 73-74. *Bibliog:* Esther Warkov, Can Broadcasting Corp, 73. *Mem:* Royal Can Acad Arts. *Media:* Oil. *Dealer:* Marlborough Godard Ltd 1490 Sherbrooke W Montreal PQ Can. *Mailing Add:* 341 Matheson Ave Winnipeg MB R2W 0C9 Canada

WARNER, DOUGLAS WARFIELD
PAINTER, COLLAGE ARTIST
b Tulsa, Okla, June 8, 30. *Study:* Okla State Univ, BFA, 53; Univ Wis, MS(art), 57. *Work:* Brit Mus, London; Smithsonian Inst & Libr Cong, Washington, DC; Cleveland Mus Art, Ohio; Calif Palace Legion Honor, San Francisco; Univ NC, Chapel Hill. *Comn:* Nine Sculptures, Flint Bd Educ, Mich, 75; Public Canvas I (billboard), Michelob Lite, Flint, Mich, 81; painting, Perfusions Services Inc, Brighton, Mich. *Exhib:* 154th Ann Drawing Exhib, Pa Acad Fine Arts, Philadelphia, 59; Mich Artists' Ann, Detroit Inst Art, 59, 60, 61 & 65; Drawing USA, St Paul Art Ctr, Minn, 63; Am Sculpture 1900-1965, Flint Inst Arts, Mich, 65; 19th Exhib Prints & Drawings, Okla Art Ctr, Oklahoma City, 77; Six Printmakers, Univ Nev, Reno, 79; Mich Watercolor Soc, 80 & 81; Denver Mus Art; plus 25 solo exhib. *Teaching:* Instr drawing & design, C S Mott Community Col, Flint, Mich, 57-86, chmn dept art, 63-67, (retired). *Awards:* Purchase Awards, Philbrook Art Ctr, 53, Okla Art Ctr, 77 & Mich Coun Arts, 78; Creative Artists Grant, Mich Coun Arts, 87 & 90. *Bibliog:* S Gordon Gapper (auth), Flint profile, Flint J, 4/3/66; Sam Olkinetzky (foreword), Exhibition Catalog, Xochipilli Gallery, 2/81; John Dempsey (foreward), Subtle Reminders (exhib catalog), Buckham Gallery, 10/91. *Media:* Mixed Media on Canvas, Paper Constructions. *Dealer:* Xochipilli Gallery 568 N Woodward Ave Birmingham MI 48063. *Mailing Add:* 2721 Coventry Ct Flint MI 48503

WARNER, HERBERT KELII, JR
PRINTMAKER
b Honolulu, Hawaii, July 29, 43. *Study:* Univ Hawaii, BFA, 67; Pratt Inst, MFA, 72. *Work:* Rutgers Univ, Camden, NJ; Honolulu Acad Arts, Honolulu, Hawaii. *Exhib:* Purdue Univ, West Lafayette, Ind, 77; Okla Nat Drawing & Prints, Oklahoma City, 77; Asn Am Artists, New York, 77; Libr Cong, Washington, DC, 77; Trenton State Mus, NJ, 80. *Teaching:* Asst prof, Rutgers Univ, Camden, NJ, 72-79; teacher design, Art Inst Philadelphia, 80-82. *Awards:* Purchase Awards, Purdue Univ, 77 & Honolulu Acad Arts, 77; Fel, State NJ, 78. *Mem:* Print Coun NJ; Artists Equity Asn; Pratt Graphic Soc. *Media:* Etching, Lithography. *Mailing Add:* 5425 Walker St Philadelphia PA 19124

WARNER, JO
PAINTER
b Clayton, NMex, Apr 30, 31. *Study:* Univ Colo, Boulder, BFA; Skowhegan Sch Painting & Sculpture, Maine, with Jack Levine & Henry V Poor; Art Students League, with Morris Kantor & Byron Brown. *Work:* Everson Mus, Syracuse, NY; Minn Mus, St Paul; Okla Art Ctr, Oklahoma City. *Exhib:* Recent American Painting and Sculpture, Mus Mod Art Circulating Exhib, 61-63; solo exhibs, Univ Wis-Eau Claire Mus, 64 & 79 & Phoenix Gallery, New York, 72, 76, 80, 83, 85, 89 & 91; West Side Artists-New York City, Riverside Mus, 64; Okla Art Ctr, Oklahoma City, 87; Tenth St Days--The Co-ops of the 50s, New York, NY, 77. *Awards:* Award & Ganeles Prize Sculpture, Nat Asn Women Artists, 74. *Bibliog:* New York Art Review, 4th ed, 88; Columbia Daily Spectator, Columbia Univ, 4/13/89; Manhattan Arts Mag, monograph, 4/89. *Mem:* Women in Arts. *Media:* Oil, Watercolor. *Dealer:* Phoenix Gallery 568 Broadway St New York NY 10012. *Mailing Add:* 142 West End Ave New York NY 10023

WARNER, MARINA SARAH
CRITIC, HISTORIAN
b London, Eng, Nov 9, 46. *Study:* Lady Margaret Hall, Oxford Univ, MA, 67. *Pos:* Vis scholar, Getty Ctr Hist Art & Humanities, 87-88. *Teaching:* Tinbergen prof erasmus, Univ Rotterdam. *Awards:* Fawcett Soc Prize, Eng. *Bibliog:* Gina Newson (dir), Joan of Arc, 83 & Imaginary Women, 86, Channel Four Television, UK. *Mem:* Fel Royal Soc Lit, Eng. *Res:* Female symbols; the body as sign; the construction of female identity in imagery. *Publ:* Auth, Alone of All Her Sex: The Myth and the Cult of the Virgin Mary, 76 & Joan of Arc: The Image of Female Heroism, 81, Knopf; Monuments and Maidens: The Allegory of the Female Form, Athenaeum, 85. *Mailing Add:* 10 Dunollie Place London NW5 2XR United Kingdom

WARREN, BETTY
PAINTER, INSTRUCTOR
b New York, NY. *Study:* Nat Acad Design: Cape Sch Art; Hartwick Col, Oneanta, NY, Hon Dr Fine Arts, 92. *Work:* Albany Hist Hist & Art, Albany Law Sch, NY; 7th Regiment, New York; State Univ NY; Ct Appeals, CA; Univ Wis, Madison; NY State Supreme Court & Court of Appeals, Albany; Hartwick Col, Oneonta, NY; Hall of Governors, State Capitol, NY; and others. *Exhib:* Allied Artists Am, New York, 65 & 67; Am Watercolor Soc, New York, 66; Nat Arts Club Nat, New York, 69-; Knickerbocker Artists, New York; Pastel Soc Am; and over 30 one-person shows in mus univ throughout USA. *Pos:* Owner & dir, Malden Bridge Sch Art, NY, 65-*Teaching:* Instr painting & drawing, Albany Inst Hist & Art, 59-75 & Maiden Bridge Sch Art, 65- *Awards:* Purchase Prizes, Albany Inst Hist & Art, 50 & 64; Gold Medal, Catharine Lorillard Wolfe Art Club; Giffuni Award Portrait, Pastel Soc Am, 83; Armstrong Hurlman Award, Pastel Soc, 85. *Bibliog:* Norman Kent (auth), The paintings of Betty Warren, Am Artist, 67. *Mem:* Grand Cent Art Galleries; Nat Arts Club; Am Artists Prof League; Pastel Soc Am; Catherine Lorillard Wolfe Club, New York. *Media:* Oil, Pastel. *Dealer:* The Bridge Gallery Malden Bridge NY 12115; Grand Central Art Galleries 57th St New York NY. *Mailing Add:* 76 Western Ave Albany NY 12203

WARREN, DAVID BOARDMAN
CURATOR
b Baltimore, Md, Mar 11, 37. *Study:* Princeton Univ, AB(cum laude), 59; Univ Del, MA, 65. *Collections Arranged:* Bayou Bend Collection (auth, catalog), Mus Fine Arts, Houston, 65-, Southern Silver (auth, catalog), 68, Gothic Revival style in America 1830-1870 (auth, catalog), 76, nineteenth century American landscape: Selections from the Thyssen-Bornenisza Collection (auth, catalog), 82; Marks of Achievement: Four Centuries of American Presentation Silver (auth, catalog), 87; The Masterpieces of Bayou Bend (1620-1870) and the Voyage of Life, Bayou Bend Mus Americana Tenneco, 91. *Pos:* Cur, Bayou Bend Collection, Mus Fine Arts, Houston, 65-, assoc dir, 74- *Teaching:* Lectr, Am Decorative Arts, Rice Univ, 66-73. *Publ:* Coauth, Texas Furniture: The Cabinetmakers and Their Work 1840-1870, Univ Tex Press, 75; contribr, A Guide to the Collections, Mus Fine Arts, Houston, 81; Harry N Abrams (auth), Marks of Achievement: Four Centuries of American Presentation Silver, 87. *Mailing Add:* 1001 Bissonnet St Houston TX 77005

WARREN, JACQUELINE LOUISE
PAINTER, EDUCATOR
b National City, Calif, Nov 3, 46. *Study:* Southwest Mo State Univ, BFA, 67; Ariz State Univ, MFA, 71; Stanford Univ. *Work:* Hallmark Corp; Quaker Oats; IBM; Pepsi Cola; Blue Cross; Price Waterhouse; Seven Up Corp; May Corp. *Exhib:* Ariz State Fair, 70; Intent 77, Bruce Gallery, Edinborough, Pa, 78; Invitational, Campus Gallery, Monroe, La, 79; Works of Paper Nat Competition, Alice Lloyd Col, Pippa Pass, Ky, 80; Paper Nat Competitive, Columbia Col, Mo, 81. *Collections Arranged:* Art on Paper, Cox Gallery, Drury Col, 81. *Teaching:* Prof painting & drawing, Southwest Mo State Univ, Springfield, 75-79; prof design, Drury Col, Springfield, Mo, 79- *Awards:* First Prize, Ariz State Fair, 70; Best of Show, Spiva Mus, Joplin, Mo, 78; First Prize, Sch Ozarks, Branson, Mo, 79; Best of Show, Mid Four Exhib, Nelson Alkins Art Mus, Kansas City; Fel painting, Nat Endowment Arts; Herward Cook Fel Painting. *Bibliog:* Edgar Albin (auth), Artist profile, Art Voices South Mag, 80; New Art Examiner. *Mem:* Col Art Asn; Watercolor Nat Hon Soc. *Media:* Mixed. *Dealer:* Tall Grass Gallery Kansas City KS; Metro Gallery Springfield MO. *Mailing Add:* Drury College 900 N Benton Springfield MO 65802

WARREN, JULIANNE BUSSERT BAKER
PHOTOGRAPHER, HISTORIAN
b Lima, Ohio, May 8, 16. *Work:* Pub Libr Cincinnati & Hamilton Co; Truman Libr & Johnson Libr, Austin, Tex; Smithsonian Inst. *Comn:* Photographs of eight US Presidents; Prime Minister Wilson, London; Princess Margaret. *Exhib:* Cincinnati Art Mus, 59; Shillito's Dept Store, Cincinnati, 61; Jewish Community Ctr, Cincinnati, 70; Cincinnati Woman's Club, 74; one-man shows, Pub Libr Cincinnati & Hamilton Co, 67 & Exhib of Collection, 78; Asn Am Ed Cartoonist Collection, Libr Commun Graphic Arts, Ohio State Univ, 84. *Pos:* Mgr, Photo-finishing Co, Cincinnati, 41-48; Photogr radio station, 50-52; news photogr, Cincinnati Post, 52-68; archivist, Asn Am Edit Cartoonist, Ohio State Univ, 84- *Awards:* First Prize, Nat Heirloom Contest, 59; First Prize, Newspaper Guild's Page-One Ball, 61; Two Prizes, Best Women's Page Photog, Univ Mo, 65. *Mem:* Asn Am Edit Cartoonists

(historian, 71-). *Publ:* Contribr & illusr, Press Photography, MacMillan, , 61; coauth, Cincinnati in Color, Hastings House, 78. *Dealer:* B Alden Olson Corp Art Concepts The Loft Mt Adams St Cincinnati OH 45202. *Mailing Add:* 1815 William Howard Taft Rd Unit 203 Cincinnati OH 45206

WARREN, KATHERINE VIRGINIA (DIAGE)
GALLERY DIRECTOR, CURATOR
b Baltimore, Md, Aug 10, 48. *Study:* Univ Calif, Riverside, BA, 76, MA, 80. *Collections Arranged:* The International Style in Southern California, 87; James Turrell: Roden Crater Project, 87; Diversity & Presence: Women Faculty Artists of the Univ of Calif (auth, exhib catalog), 87; Jules Cheret: Selections from the Field Collection, 90; Kirk Pederson: Desert Ruins/Road Relics (auth, exhib catalog), 91. *Pos:* Cur, Calif Mus Photog, 79-84, dir, Univ Art Gallery, 84-, Univ Calif, Riverside. *Teaching:* Lectr mus studies, Univ Calif, Riverside, 85-90. *Mem:* Am Asn Mus; Asn Col & Univ Mus & Galleries; Western Mus Conf. *Publ:* Auth, Albert Renger Patzsch, La Photo Bull, 81; coauth, Faiya Fredman: Akroteri Series (exhib catalog), Univ Calif, 84. *Mailing Add:* University of California Riverside University Art Gallery/ Watkins House Riverside CA 92521

WARREN, LYNNE
CURATOR, WRITER
b Lowell, Mass, Mar 12, 52. *Study:* Sch Art Inst Chicago, Ill, BFA, 76. *Collections Arranged:* Kenneth Josephson: Photographs (auth, catalog), 83, DOGS!, 84, Alternative Spaces: A History in Chicago (auth, catalog), 84, Jon Kessler: Sulpture, 86 & Donald Sultan: Paintings, 87, Mus Contemp Art, Chicago, Ill, Starn Twins, 88, Julia Wachtel, 90. *Pos:* Cur collections, Mus Contemp Art, Chicago, Ill, 84-90. *Awards:* Catalog Auth Award, DOGS!, Art Mus Asn, 84. *Publ:* Auth, Jon Kessler (catalog essay), & Mies in Chicago (brochure), Mus Contemp Art, 86; Donald Sultan, Abrams, 87. *Mailing Add:* c/o Mus Contemp Art 237 E Ontario St Chicago IL 60611

WARREN, PETER WHITSON See Whitson

WARREN, RUSS
PAINTER
b Washington, DC, Dec 29, 51. *Study:* Univ St Thomas, Houston, Tex, 69-71; Univ NMex, BFA, 73; Univ Tex, San Antonio, MFA, 77. *Work:* Chase Manhattan Bank, New York; Gen Elec Co, Fairfield, Conn; Sydney & Francis Lewis Found, Richmond, Va; Princeton Univ, NJ; Gibbs Art Mus, Charleston, SC. *Exhib:* Biennial, Whitney Mus Am Art, New York, 81; Painting & Sculpture Today, Indianapolis Mus Art, Ind, 82; Painting in the South (with catalog), Va Mus Art, Richmond, 83; Southern Fictions, Contemp Art Mus, Houston, 83; USA Portrait of the South, Palazzo Venezia, Rome, 84; Venice Biennale, Italy, 84; solo exhibs, Emblems of the Unseeable (with catalog), Knight Gallery, Charlotte, NC, 84 & NC Mus Art, Raleigh, 85; Looking South-A Different Dixie, Birmingham Mus Art, Birmingham, Ala, 88; 1989 Corcoran Biennial, Corcoran Mus, Washington, DC, 89. *Teaching:* Assoc prof art, Davidson Col, Davidson, NC, 78- *Awards:* Southeast Cent Contemp Art Fel, 84; NC Artist Fel, 85. *Bibliog:* Richard Flood (auth), Russ Warren, Artforum, 9/81; Ronny Cohen (auth), Russ Warren, Art News, 2/83; Vivian Raynor (auth), Russ Warren, New York Times, 12/28/85; Barry Schwabsky (auth), Russ Warren's magic theater, Arts Mag, 85. *Media:* Acrylic. *Dealer:* Hodges-Taylor Gallery 227 N Tryon Charlotte NC 28202. *Mailing Add:* PO Box 991 Davidson NC 28036

WARREN, TOM P
COLLECTOR, PHOTOGRAPHER
b Cleveland, Ohio, Aug 23, 54. *Study:* Kent State Univ, BS, 77. *Work:* Art Inst Chicago, Ill. *Exhib:* Portrait Studio, Semaphore Gallery, New York, 83; No Portraits, Greathouse Gallery, New York, 85; Portrait Studio, Spaces Gallery, Cleveland, 90; Flash, Willoughby Sharp Gallery, New York, 91. *Pos:* Photogr, Sotheby's, 83-87 & freelance, 87-90- *Teaching:* Instr photog, Case Western Reserve, Univ Cleveland, 88-90. *Awards:* Project Grant, NY State Coun on the Arts, 82. *Bibliog:* Judd Tully (auth), No portraits review, East Village Eye, 6/85; Lynn Padwe (auth), Artistic endeavors, Photo District News, 9/86; Helen Cullen (auth), Review of portrait studio, Cleveland Plain Dealer, 1/90. *Mem:* NY Artists Equity Asn. *Media:* Photography. *Collection:* Small Works By Young Contemporary New York Artists, including Baechlor, Basquit, Lasker and many others. *Publ:* Just Another Asshole No 7, Thought Objects, Barbra Ess, 87; East Village Guide, Portraits of Art Dealers, Roland Hagenberg, 86. *Mailing Add:* 15 Stanton St Suite 4A New York NY 10002

WARREN, WIN (W WINTON)
PAINTER, LECTURER
b Jakin, Ga, Nov 13, 14. *Study:* Univ Ga, LLB & JD; US Dept Agr Grad Sch, 67; Cath Univ Am, 68 & 69; Univ Md Grad Sch, with Nicholas Krushenick, Jerry Clapsaddle, Helen Van Wyk & Joseph Kelly, 77-82. *Work:* Univ Md; Gilbane Bldg Co; Washington Suburban Sanitation Comn; South Md Hosp Ctr; Town of University Park, Md. *Comn:* Equestrian portraits of George Washington & Lafayette, Johnston & Lemon Brokerage Firm, Washington, DC, 76; mural, Community Ctr, Md-Nat Capital Park & Planning Comn, 79. *Exhib:* Artists Today Exhib, Md-Nat Capital Park & Planning Comn, 79; one-man shows, Montpelier Cult Arts Ctr, Laurel, 80 & Md Univ Club, 85; Art Barn Asn-Nat Park Serv Exhib, 83; Alpha Gallerie, Rockville, Md, 86. *Pos:* Lect & tours Am Art, Nat Mus Am Art, Smithsonian Inst, Washington DC, 79-; adv & selection bd, Montpelier Cult Arts Ctr, 79- *Awards:* Nat Capitol Area Artists Award, United Way, 85. *Bibliog:* article, Baltimore Eve Sun, 3/11/81; article, Washington, DC Artists News, 3/84; article, Camilla Enterprise, 11/15/85. *Mem:* Artists' Equity Asn; Col Art Asn; Prince George's Art Asn; Washington Soc Landscape Painters. *Media:* Acrylic, Oils. *Mailing Add:* Alpha Gallerie 6915 Oakridge Rd University Park MD 20782-1153

WARRINER, LAURA B
ASSEMBLAGE ARTIST, COLLAGE ARTIST
b Tulsa Okla, Jan 18, 43. *Study:* Okla Baptist Univ; Oklahoma City Univ. *Work:* Skidmore Col Art Gallery, Saratoga Springs, NY; Henry Ward Ranger Fund Purchase through Smithsonian Inst Nat Gallery, Washington, DC; Okla Univ Found, Norman; Univ Okla Med Ctr, Okla City. *Exhib:* Solo exhibs, Firehouse Art Ctr, Norman, Okla, 86, Hulsey Gallery, Norick Art Ctr, Okla City Univ, Okla, 91; Dimensions '87: Lenexa's National 3-Dimensional Art Show, Lenexa, Kans, 87; The Painted Photographs, Central State Univ Mus Art, Edmond, Okla, 89; Flash Points, Goddard Art Ctr, Ardmore, Okla, 89; Small Works Invitational, M A Doran Gallery, Tulsa, Okla, 88 & 90. *Pos:* Vpres & bd trustees, Okla Visual Arts Coalition, Okla City, 88-; 405-840-4546. *Teaching:* Instr, Okla Mus Art, Okla City, 74-78; instr regional workshops, Norman, Okla, Stillwater, Okla, Okla City, Okla, Edmond, Okla & Red River, NMex, 75-; instr, Okla Arts Inst, Okla City, 77-81; instr artists-in-residence, Okla State Arts Coun, 81-85; instr, Goddard Art Ctr, Ardmore, Okla, 83. *Awards:* Award for Watercolor, Allied Artists Am 60th Ann Exhib, 74; Barbara Vassilieff Award for Flowers-Still Life, Allied Artists Am 61st Ann Exhib, 75; Century Award of Merit, Rocky Mountain Nat Watermedia Exhib, 75. *Bibliog:* Ralph Fabri (auth), Flower painting in all media, 2/74 & Can you succeed in art without really trying, 9/74, Today's Art; Barbara Nechis (auth), Watercolor the Creative Experience, Northlight; Flash Points (catalog), Central Univ, Edmond, Okla. *Mem:* Okla Visual Arts Coalition. *Media:* Multimedia. *Mailing Add:* 6431 1/2 N Olie Oklahoma City OK 73116

WARSHAW, ELAINE N
SCULPTOR, DIRECTOR
b New York, NY, Apr 11, 24. *Study:* Pratt Inst, 41-44; Art students League, 45; Studied with Jose de Creeft, 70, and Elaine Rapp. *Comn:* Holocaust Mem, Limestone, Temple Israel, Jamaica, Queens, NY, 80, Long Beach, 82; Garden Sculpture, comn by Dr & Mrs S Pion, Md. *Exhib:* Nat Asn Women Artists, Bergen Community Mus, NJ, 80, Equitable Galleries, Manhattan, NY, 82, Lener House, Manhattan, 82; Nat Acad Galleries, Manhattan, 82; Family of Man, N Shore Sculpture Ctr, Great Neck, Long Island, NY, 85; Hecksher Mus, Long Island, 85. *Pos:* Dir sculptor, Merrick, NY, 72-90. *Teaching:* Instr stone carving, Sculpture Ctr, 70-72. *Mem:* Nat Asn Women Artists. *Media:* Stone. *Mailing Add:* 2164 Seneca Dr S Merrick NY 11566

WARSHAW, LARRY
PAINTER, PHOTOGRAPHER
b New York, NY, June 18, 36. *Study:* Showhegan Sch Painting & Sculpture, 57-58; NY Univ, BA, 58, MA, 59. *Work:* Boston Mus Fine Arts; Kunsthalle, Cologne, Ger; Contemp Art Mus, Houston; Worchester Art Mus, Mass; Philadelphia Mus Art; NY Life Insurance Co Collection; Lincoln Ctr Collection, New York; and others. *Comn:* Sculpture, Gen Servs Admin, New York, 75; wall relief & paintings, Swedish Metal Corp, Gottensburg, 78; wall murals, Hochschuler Gemeinshaft, Ger, 78, Giotto Restaurant, New York, 79 & Cunard Ship Lines Inc, 80. *Exhib:* Corcoran Biennial Exhib, 63 & Color Surfaces: New Poetics, 79, Corcoran Mus Art, Wash; Spirtual Forms in Painting, Philadelphia Mus, 80; Paint as Poetic Surface, Worchester Mus, 83. *Teaching:* Instr, Queens Col, H Lehman Col & Rockland Community Col. *Awards:* Ford Found Purchase Award, 64; MacDowell Colony Fel, Edward MacDowell Asn, 64; Edna St Vincent, Colony, NY, 91. *Bibliog:* Diana Morris (auth) Summer group show, Arts Mag, 10/83; Keneth Duncan (auth), Color field painting, Fine Arts Rev, 10/84. *Mem:* Comn Art & Antiquties. *Media:* Acrylics. *Mailing Add:* PO Box 1528 Canal St Post Office New York NY 10013

WARSINSKE, NORMAN GEORGE
SCULPTOR, PAINTER
b Wichita, Kans, Mar 4, 29. *Study:* Univ Mont, BA; Kunstwerkschule, Darmstadt, Ger; Univ Wash, BA. *Comn:* Bronze fountain, Theodora Retirement Home, Seattle, 66; brass & steel screen, Yellowstone Boy's Ranch, Billings, Mont, 69; gold leaf steel stabile, IBM Bldg Lobby, Seattle, 71; stainless stabile, Seattle First Nat Bank, Bellevue, 75; bronze & plexiglass fountain, J Hughes Home, Mauna Kea, Hawaii, 79; steel lanterns, McDonald Industs, Seattle, 86; and others. *Exhib:* Northwest Ann, Seattle Art Mus, 59-65; Santa Barbara Invitational, Calif, 63; Sculpture, Los Angeles Co Mus Art, 64; Woodside Seattle, 73; Snohomish Arts Coun Gallery, 88; Univ Unitarian, 92. *Teaching:* Asst instr drawing, Univ Wash, 58-59. *Awards:* First Prize for Sculpture, Bellevue Art Festival, 60; Best of All Categories, Henry Art Gallery, 66. *Bibliog:* Louis Redstone (auth), Art in Architecture, McGraw, 68; M R Heinley (auth), Norman Warsinske--metal artistry, Designers W, 6/70. *Mem:* Northwest Craft Ctr (pres, 65-70). *Media:* Bronze, Steel; Acrylic. *Publ:* Illusr cover, Am Inst Architects J, 8/71. *Mailing Add:* 3823 94th NE Bellevue WA 98004

WASHBURN, JOAN T
ART DEALER
b New York, NY, Dec 26, 29. *Study:* Middlebury Col, BA. *Pos:* Dir, Lindsay S Thomas, New York. *Awards:* RI Sch Design Fel. *Mem:* Art Dealers Asn Am (bd dirs). *Specialty:* Nineteenth and twentieth century American painting and sculpture. *Mailing Add:* 20 W 57th St New York NY 10019

WASHBURN, STAN
PRINTMAKER, PAINTER
b New York, NY, Jan 2, 43. *Study:* Calif Col Arts & Crafts, Oakland, BFA, 67 & MFA, 68. *Work:* Chicago Art Inst; Brooklyn Mus, New York; Calif Palace of Legion of Honor, San Francisco; Libr Cong, Washington DC; Mus Fine Arts, Boston. *Exhib:* 24th Nat Exhib Prints, Libr Cong, Washington, DC, 75; Hassam Fund Purchase Prize Exhib, Am Acad of Arts & Lett, New York,

75 & 76; one-man show, Achenbach Found for Graphic Arts, Calif Palace of Legion of Honor, 77; Boston Printmakers Ann, 77-79, 81 & 85; 7th Brit Int Print Biennale, Bradford, Eng, 82; Western States Print Invitational, Portland Art Mus, Ore, 85; and others. *Awards:* Pennell Fund Purchase, Libr 75; Purchase Award, Int Miniature Print Collection, Pratt Graphics Ctr, New York, 77. *Bibliog:* One-half hour spec, KQED-TV, San Francisco, 75; Matthew Gurewitsch (auth), Against the grain, Connoisseur Mag, 2/86. *Media:* Etching; Oil. *Publ:* Auth & illusr, True History of the Death by Violence of George's Dragon, 74, illusr, Schinocephalic Waif, 75; illusr, Great Wheadle Tragedy, Godine, 75; auth & illusr, The Moral Alphabet of Vice & Folly Arbor House, 86. *Dealer:* Campbell-Thieband 647 Cheshnut St San Francisco CA 94133. *Mailing Add:* c/o Cambell-Thiebaud Gallery 647 Chestnut St San Francisco CA 94133

WASHINGTON, JAMES W, JR
SCULPTOR, PAINTER
b Gloster, Miss. *Study:* Nat Landscape Inst; also with Mark Tobey; Grad Theological Union Ctr Urban Black Studies, Berkeley, Calif, Hon DFA, 75. *Work:* Seattle Art Mus, Wash; San Francisco Art Mus. *Comn:* The Creation (series 7-10), Seattle First Nat Bank Main Br, 68; bust of hist men, Progress Plaza, Philadelphia, 69; the Creation (series 5), Meany Jr High Sch, Seattle, 70; Woodchuck Sunning (sculpture), Frankfurt, WGer, 74; Children's Touchstone With Eagles (stone sculpture at Bailey Gatzert Elem), King Co Arts Comn, Seattle, Wash, 91; Bird From the Plane of Enlightenment (sculpture in stone), comn by John L & Dora E Smith, Seattle, Wash, 92; and others. *Exhib:* Expo '70, Osaka, Japan, 70; Art of the Pac Northwest, Nat Collection Fine Arts, Washington, DC, 74; one-man exhibs, Foster-White Gallery, Seattle, Wash, 68, 78 & 80 & Mus Hist & Indust, Seattle, 80, Foster/White Gallery (with catalog), Seattle, Wash, 89; retrospective, Frye Art Mus, Seattle, 80; Fest Sundiata, Seattle, 80; Portopia, 81, Kobe, Japan, 81; retrospective (with catalog), Bellevue Art Mus, Wash, 89. *Pos:* Secy, Seattle Chap, Artists Equity Asn, 49-53, pres, 60-62; mem gov coun art, State of Wash, 59-60, state art comnr, 61-66. *Awards:* Gov Sculpture Award, 70; Wash State Centennial Hall of Honor, Wash State Hist Soc, 84; Studio & Home of James W Washington Jr, Designated an Historic Landmark, Landmarks Preservation Bd, Seattle, Wash, 91; and others. *Bibliog:* Ann Faber (auth), James Washington's stone sculpture excellence, Seattle Post Intelligence, 56; Pauline Johnson (auth), James Washington speaks, Art Educ J, 68; Arch Am Art, Smithsonian Inst, 83. *Mem:* Int Platform Asn. *Media:* Oil, Tempera; Granite, Marble. *Mailing Add:* 1816 26th Ave Seattle WA 98122

WASKO-FLOOD, SANDRA JEAN
PRINTMAKER, PHOTOGRAPHER
b Flushing, NY, Mar 12, 43. *Study:* Univ Calif, Life Drawing with Gordon Nunes, Painting with Ray Brown & Charles Garabedian, BA, 65; studied with Isabel Pons, Parque Lage, Rio de Janeiro, 72; Univ Wis, grad etching with Warrington Colescott, 77-78. *Work:* Mus de Arte Mod, Buenos Aires, Argentina; Nat Mus Am Art, Nat Mus Women Arts & Libr Cong, Washington, DC; St Mary's Col, Md; Pushkin Mus, Moscow; and others. *Exhib:* solo exhibs, Slavin Gallery, 82, Prints: Washington, Phillips Collection, DC, 88, Contemp Am Graphics, Bk Chamber Int, Moscow, 90, Washington Printmakers Gallery, 86, 88 & 91, St Peter's Church, New York, 89, Mont Gallery, Alexandria, Va, 91 & Montpelier Cult Arts Ctr, Laurel, Md, 92; Boston Printmakers: 39th N Am Print Exhib, Danforth Mus, Framingham,, Mass, 86; Wash Printmakers, Mus de Arte Mod, Buenos Aires, 87; The Printed Image 72nd Ann, Hudson River Mus, Yonkers, NY, 87; Seventh Ann Faber Birren Color Show Nat Juried Open Competition, Stamford, Conn, 87; Alternatives 88, Nat Juried Photog Competition, Univ Ohio, Athens, 88; Int Prints 1988, Silvermine Gallery, Stamford, Conn, 88; 1988 Stockton IV Prints & Drawings, Haggin Mus, Stockton, Calif, 88; and other one-man exhibs. *Pos:* Pub Relations dir, Wash Women's Arts Ctr, 80; cur, Feminism & Spirituality Conf, Cornell Univ, 85; pres, Wash Area Printmakers, 85-86; workshop coordr, Arlington Co Dept of Parks, Recreation & Community Resources, Lee Arts Ctr, 89-92. *Teaching:* Instr printmaking, Wash Women's Arts Ctr, 83 & Arlington Co Art Prog, 89; artist-in-residence lithography, Univ Md, spring 84; prof printmaking, St Marys Col, spring 85. *Awards:* Mention, May Print Show, Alexandria Art League; Cash Prize, Friends Torpedo Factory Art Gallery, Alexandria, Va, 89. *Bibliog:* Mary Jane Overall (auth), Printmakers: Sandra Wasko-Flood Tribune United, Gaitersburg Cable, 83; Paul Franklin Pilato (auth), Printmakers: Cycles, Arlington Cable TV, 87; Lily Pond (auth), Yellow Silk Mag featured artist, Verygraphics, fall 87. *Mem:* Women's Caucus Art (79-92); Wash Area Printmakers (pres, 85-86); Print Consortium, Coalition of Established & Emerging Am Printmakers, 87-92; Print Club, Philadelphia; Southern Graphics Coun, Pensacola, Fla. *Media:* Monotype, Etching. *Publ:* Auth, The Role of Art in Feminist Spirituality, Women Artists News, spring 86; Nasca Tongue Iconography, El Dorado, Vol I, 77. *Dealer:* Washington Printmakers Gallery 2106 R St NW Washington DC 20008; Montana Gallery 822 N Fairfax St Alexandria VA 22314. *Mailing Add:* 8106 Norwood Dr Alexandria VA 22309

WASSERMAN, ALBERT
PAINTER, DESIGNER
b New York, NY, Aug 23, 20. *Study:* Art Students League, with Charles Chapman, 37-39; Nat Acad Design, Pulitzer Prize scholar, 38-40; with Sidney Dickinson; US Army Univ, France. *Work:* Traphagen Collection, Ariz; Aimee Ornstein Mem Libr, Adelphi Univ, NY, 83. *Comn:* Many private portrait commissions. *Exhib:* Nat Acad Design, New York, 40 & 41; Allied Artists Am, New York, 41-; NJ Painters & Sculptors Soc, 41-; Am Watercolor Soc, New York, 53-69 & 86; Audubon Artists, New York, 60 & 90. *Pos:* Graphic design consult, var agencies, 48- *Teaching:* Instr & lectr, Jackson Heights Art Asn, 55- & Nat Art League, 67-69. *Awards:* Obrig Prize, 41, Nat Acad Design; Friedrichs Prize, Allied Artists Am, 41; Grumbacher Award, Allied Artists, 85. *Bibliog:* Ethel Traphagen (auth), article, Fashion Digest, 54. *Mem:* Salmagundi Club; Allied Artists Am; NJ Painters & Sculptors Soc; assoc Am Watercolor Soc; Nat Art League; and others. *Media:* Oil. *Mailing Add:* 34-24 82nd St Jackson Heights NY 11372

WASSERMAN, BURTON
PAINTER, PRINTMAKER
b Brooklyn, NY, Mar 10, 29. *Study:* Brooklyn Col, with Burgoyne Diller & Ad Reinhardt, BA; Columbia Univ, MA & EdD. *Work:* Philadelphia Mus Art, Pa; Munson-Williams-Proctor Inst, Utica, NY; Del Art Ctr, Wilmington; Montreal Mus Fine Arts; NJ State Mus, Trenton; and others. *Comn:* Relief triptych, comn by Mr & Mrs Herbert Kurtz, Melrose Park, Pa, 71; var indust & residential relief construction projs, Philadelphia area, 74-79. *Exhib:* 21st Am Drawing Biennial, Norfolk Mus Arts & Sci, 65; Art Alliance, Philadelphia, 66-80; USA Pavilion, Int Expos, Osaka, Japan, 70; Color Prints of the Americas, NJ State Mus, 70; Int Graphics Exhib, Montreal Mus Art, 71; Silkscreen: History of a Medium, Philadelphia Mus Art, 71-72; Benjamin Mangel Gallery, Philadelphia, Pa, 72-82; and others. *Teaching:* Prof art, Glassboro State Col, 60- *Awards:* Brickhouse Drawing Prize, 21st Am Drawing Biennial, Norfolk Mus Arts & Sci, 65; Ryan Purchase Prize, Art from NJ Ann Exhib, NJ State Mus, 67; Esther-Philip Klein Award, Am Color Print Soc Ann, 70; and others. *Mem:* Artists Equity Asn (nat pres, 71-73); Am Color Print Soc (mem exec coun, 65-81). *Media:* Oil, Silkscreen, Spray Enamels. *Publ:* Auth articles in Leonardo, Am Artist, Art Educ, Sch Arts, & many more, 59-72; auth, Modern Painting: The Movements, the Artists, Their Work, 70 & coauth, Basic Silkscreen Printmaking, 71, Davis, Mass; Bridges of Vision: The Art of Prints & the Craft of Printmaking; Exploring the Visual Arts, Davis, Mass, 76. *Dealer:* Benjamin Mangel Gallery 1714 Rittenhouse Sq Philadelphia PA 19103. *Mailing Add:* 204 Dubois Rd Glassboro NJ 08028

WASSERMAN, CARY (ROBERT)
PHOTOGRAPHER, CONCEPTUAL ARTIST
b Los Angeles, Calif, Nov 27, 39. *Study:* Univ Calif, Los Angeles, BA, 61, MA, 63; Ind Univ, with Henry Holmes Smith, 67-70. *Work:* Mus Fine Arts, Boston; Smith Col Mus Art; Wellesley Col Mus Art; Portland Mus Art, Maine; Polaroid Collection, Cambridge, Mass. *Comn:* Charlestown: In Progress, Polaroid Corp, Cambridge, Mass, 74; A Call To Arts, Cambridge Arts Coun, Mass, 75; Large Totem (sculpture), WBZ-TV, Boston, 81. *Exhib:* Photographs: 1970-1974, Portland Mus Art, Maine, 74; Private Realities, Mus Fine Arts, Boston, 74; Color Photography Now!, Wellesley Col Mus Art, 75; Color Photography Retrospective (with catalog), Williams Col Mus, 78; Aspects of the 70s, DeCordova Mus, 80; Polaroid Photographs in Historic Perspective, Brown Univ, 80; Proj Arts Ctr, Cambridge, 83; Galerie Texbraun, Paris, France, 86; Eiffel Tower & All That Jazz, French Libr, Boston, 86; Brooks Inst Photog, Santa Barbara, 90. *Collections Arranged:* Color in Photography, Soc Photog Educ, 75; Art Month, Clarence Kennedy Gallery, 76; Photo-Media, BVAU Gallery, 77; Color Photography: National Exhibit (auth, catalog), 81 & Seven Artists, 83, Boston Visual Artists Union. *Pos:* Creative dir, Art Consults Group, Cambridge, Mass, 73-88; sec gen, BVAU, 78 & 80; trustee, Inst Contemp Art, Boston, 83-85; dir, The Artists Orgn, 88-; coordr, Amiga Video Group, 90. *Teaching:* Instr, Photog, Univ Lowell, Mass, 77-79 & 82-83; Univ Southern Maine, 76-77; Art Inst Boston, 70-73; New England Sch Photogr, Boston, 83-84; Instr, Filmmaking, Phillips Acad Andover, Summer 73 & 79; vis lectr, Univ Lowell, 77-79 & 82-83; instr photog, NE Sch of Photog, 84-85; vis asst prof, computer design, Mass Col Art, 90. *Awards:* Polaroid Corp, Cambridge, Mass, 74; Cambridge Art Coun, Mass, 75; Change, Inc, 81; Blanche E Colman Found Grant, Boston, 82, 89. *Bibliog:* Susan Dodge Peters (auth), The Color Photographs of Cary Wasserman, Williams Col, 78; Kelly Wise: Wasserman At Large & /Wasserman's Enhanced SX-70, Boston Globe, 83 & 86; Stuart Cohen: Cary Wasserman, Contemp Photogr, St Martins Press, Chicago, 83-88. *Mem:* Boston Visual Artists Union, 74 (secy-gen, 78-80); Boston Visual Artists Union Federal Credit Union (vpres 76-77); Inst Contemp Art, Boston, Trustee, 83-85. *Media:* Bookworks, Computer Work. *Publ:* Contribr, Private Realities: Recent American Photography, New York Graphic Soc, 74; The Photographers Choice, Addison House, 75; auth, SX-Manipulation, Petersens Photog, 76; contribr, Creative Camera International Yearbook, 77; auth, Color Toning & SX-70 Image Manipulation, Darkroom Techniques, 81 & 83. *Mailing Add:* Art Consultants Group Six Porter Rd Cambridge MA 02140

WASSERMAN, JACK
EDUCATOR
b New York, NY, Apr 27, 21. *Study:* Wash Sq Col, NY Univ, BA; NY Univ Inst Fine Arts, with Karl Lehman & Richard Krautheimer, MA & PhD. *Teaching:* Instr art, Univ Conn, 53-60; asst prof art, Ind Univ, Bloomington, 60-62; prof Renaissance art, Univ Wis-Milwaukee, 62-75; dean, Tyler Sch Art, Temple Univ, Philadelphia, 75-77, prof art hist, 75-92, prof emer, 92- *Awards:* Am Coun Learned Soc Grant, 70; Am Philos Soc Grant, 71; Kress Found Grant, 75. *Mem:* Col Art Asn Am; Soc Archit Historians (bd dirs, 70-); Royal Soc Arts; Amici de Brera; Inst per la Storia dell'Arte Lombarda, Milan, Italy (mem bd councellors, 82-85). *Publ:* Auth, The dating & patronage of Leonardo's Burlington House cartoon, Art Bulletin, 71; Michelangelo's Virgin & Child with St Anne at Oxford, Burlington Mag, 69; Leonardo da Vinci, Abrams, 75; The Genesis of Raphael's Alba Madonna, Studies in History of Art, Nat Gallery Art, Wash 78; Reflections on Leonardo's Last Supper, Arte Lombarda, 83; and others. *Mailing Add:* Dept Art Hist Temple Univ Philadelphia PA 19122

WASSERMAN, JEFFREY
PAINTER
b Mount Vernon, NY, July 21, 46. *Study:* Tyler Sch Art, Temple Univ, Philadelphia, Pa & Rome, BFA, Italy, BFA, 68; Royal Col Art, London, Eng, cert, 69. *Work:* Chase Manhattan Bank; Ford Collection; Gillman Collection. *Exhib:* Munic Theatre, Caen, France, 80; DIA Found, 87; Outside America, Going into the Nineties, Fay Gold Gallery, Atlanta, 91. *Teaching:* Senior Painting Lect, Philadelphia Col Art, 88, SVA, Graduate & Undergraduate Painting, 90-92. *Awards:* Nat Endowment Arts, 87. *Bibliog:* Catalogue Essay, DIA Art Found, Henry Geldzahler (auth), 87; A Rebirth of Abstract Painting, Buffalo News, Richard Hungton (auth), 91; Where The Meaning Begins, Panel of Abstraction, Tema Celest (auth), 92. *Media:* Oil on Canvas. *Mailing Add:* 523 Broadway New York NY 10012

WASSERMAN, MURIEL
PAINTER
b New York, NY, May 27, 35. *Study:* Studied at Brooklyn Mus, 5-Towns Music & Art, NY, Newark Mus, 53-80; Queens Col, NY, BA, 78; Pratt Inst, Brooklyn, MA, 84. *Comn:* many pvt commissions. *Exhib:* Brooklyn Mus Exhib, 78; Equitable Gallery, New York, 86; Parish Art Mus, NY, 88; Old Westbury Gardens, Long Island, 88-90; Bergen Co Mus, NY, 89; Sands Point Mus, NY, 90-91; and others. *Pos:* Craftsperson (potter), craft shows & exhibs, 70-91; docent & cataloger, Nassau Co Mus System, 75-77; monthly columnist, Sunstorm Long Island Arts Newspaper, 82-84. *Teaching:* Instr painting & drawing, Valley Stream Adult Prog, NY, 77- & St Johns Univ, Queens, NY, 79. *Awards:* Am Artists Mag, 77; Town of Hempstead, NY, 80; Fed Plaza Exhibs, Nat Asn Women Artists, 80. *Mem:* Nat Asn Women Artists (jury comt, currently); Long Island Crafts Guild. *Media:* Acrylic, Watercolors. *Mailing Add:* 70 Brentwood Lane Valley Stream NY 11580

WATERHOUSE, CHARLES HOWARD
ILLUSTRATOR, PAINTER
b Columbus, Ga, Sept 22, 24. *Study:* Newark Sch Fine & Indust Art; also with Steven R Kidd. *Work:* USMC Mus, US Navy Combat Art Collection & USAAF Collections, Washington, DC; Rutgers Univ, New Brunswick, NJ; NJ Bell Tel Co, Newark. *Comn:* Marines in the Revolution, 74, Vietnam Refugees, 75 & Marines in Mexican War, USMC, 75-76; Hamilton's Battery, Class of 24, Rutgers Univ, 74; Tarawa Beach Head, L P H Tarawa, US Navy, 75. *Exhib:* One-man shows, NJ State Mus, Trenton, US Naval Acad, Annapolis, Md, Los Angeles Mus Nat Hist, San Francisco City Hall & Soc Illusrs, New York, 75. *Pos:* Staff artist, Prudential Ins Co, 50-55; free-lance illusr, Nat Publ & Books, 55-73; artist-in-residence, USMC, 73. *Teaching:* Instr, lectr & demonstr illus, Newark Sch Fine & Indust Art, 55-73. *Bibliog:* Norman Kent (auth), Vietnam drawings, Am Artist, 68; Ed Fleming (auth), Vietnam Sketchbook, AP News Features, 68; F B Nihart (auth), Paintings by Charles Waterhouse, Marine Corps Publ, 75. *Mem:* Soc Illusr; Salmagundi Club; Nat Soc Mural Painters; USMC Combat Corresp; Naval Air Cooperation & Liason Comt Artists. *Media:* Acrylic, Ink. *Publ:* Illusr, Outdoor Life, Argosy, Saga, Reader's Digest & others, 55-; illusr, Grosset, Dunlap, Viking, Am, & Rutgers Press, 55-; auth & illusr, Vietnam Sketchbook from Delta to DMZ, 68; auth & illusr, Vietnam War Drawings, Air, Land & Sea, 70; illusr, Marines in the Revolution, 75. *Mailing Add:* 67 Dartmouth St Edison NJ 08837

WATERHOUSE, RUSSELL RUTLEDGE
PAINTER, ILLUSTRATOR
b El Paso, Tex, Aug 11, 28. *Study:* Tex A&M Univ, BS, 50; Art Ctr Col Design, Pasadena, Calif, 54-56. *Work:* Tex Tech Univ Mus Art, Lubbock; El Paso Mus Art; Tex A&M Univ, College Station; Univ Tex, El Paso. *Exhib:* One-man shows, Wichita Falls Tex Cult Ctr & Mus Art, 72, Tex A&M Univ, 77, Dallas Safari Club, 83 & Americana Mus, El Paso, 84 & 86; Game Conservation Int, San Antonio, 83, 85, 87, 89. *Pos:* Mem, Tex Comn Arts & Humanities, 70-75. *Awards:* El Paso's Mayor's Award, 89; Invitational Art Exhib, El Paso Mus Art, 89. *Media:* Watercolor, Acrylic. *Publ:* Illusr, Goodbye to a River, Knopf, 60; The Legal Heritage of El Paso, 63 & Pass of the North, 68, Tex Western Press. *Mailing Add:* PO Box 6 Lincoln NE 88338-9999

WATERS, HERBERT (OGDEN)
PRINTMAKER, EDUCATOR
b Swatow, China, Nov 15, 03; US citizen. *Study:* Denison Univ, PhB; Pa Sch Indust Art; Art Inst Chicago; Harvard Univ Grad Sch Fine Art; hon DFA, Plymouth State Col, NH, 84 & Alderson-Broaddus Col, WVa, 85. *Work:* Metrop Mus Art, New York; Libr Cong, Washington, DC; Boston Mus Fine Art; Boston Pub Libr; Springfield Art Mus, Mass. *Comn:* Membership print, Rochester Print Club, NY, 52; baptistry mural, Campton Baptist Church, NH, 54; mem bookplates, Denison Univ Libr, 59 & 72; Watercolor of campus, Gould Acad, Bethel, Maine, 86. *Exhib:* New York World's Fair Art Exhib, 39; Am Watercolors Prints & Drawings, Metrop Mus Art, New York, 52; Boston Print Makers Exhib, 52-; Soc Am Graphic Artists, 60-; Appalachian Corridors I & II, Charleston, WVa, 68 & 70. *Teaching:* Vis prof graphic art, art hist & painting, Univ NH, summers 46-59; teacher studio & art hist, Holderness Sch, Plymouth, NH, 46-60; asst prof, Alderson-Broaddus Col, 41-68, prof, 69, prof emer, 72- *Awards:* John Taylor Arms Purchase Award Graphic Art, Soc Am Graphic Artists, 54; Prize in Watercolor, WVa Centennial, 63; State Arts Comn, NH. *Bibliog:* Auth, New Hampshire Profiles, article, 3/77; film doc, WVa PBS, Channel 24, Morgantown, 5/86. *Mem:* Nat Acad Design; Soc Am Graphic Artists; Boston Print Makers Soc; NH Art Asn (pres, 60); Soc Wood Engravers, Eng. *Media:* Wood Engravings, Water Colors. *Publ:* Illusr, New England Year, 40; illusr, New England Days, 41; contribr, New Hampshire art calendar, 74; Face to Face, pub self-portraits by 12 Am wood engravers, 84. *Mailing Add:* Rte 2 Box 1489 Campton NH 03223

WATERS, JACK
FILMMAKER, CONCEPTUAL ARTIST
b Philadelphia, Pa, Oct 14, 54. *Study:* Julliard Col, BFA, 79. *Work:* Libr Cong, Washington, DC; New York Libr Performing Arts, Lincoln Ctr; Patterson Mus, NJ. *Exhib:* ABC No Rio, New York, 83-; Limbo Gallery; NYCDCA Gallery, 85. *Collections Arranged:* ABC No Rio Archival (contribr, catalog), NYCDCA City Gallery, 85. *Pos:* Founder & pres, Allied Productions, Inc, NY, 82-; co-dir, ABC No Rio, New York, 83-; consult & mem, Collaborative Projs, Inc, 84-87; dir, Naked Eye Cinema, 87- *Teaching:* Instr dance, Univ City Arts League, Philadelphia, Pa, 78 & Univ Settlement, New York, NY, 84- *Awards:* Louis Horst Award for Choreography, Juillard, 79. *Bibliog:* Robert Gautier (auth), New form on the Lower East Side, NY Times, 3/84; ABC No Rio Dinero: The story of a Lower East Side art gallery, 84. *Mem:* Film/Video Arts; Millenium Film Group. *Publ:* Auth, On notational methods, Ear Mag, 12/83; film critique, Jumpcut Mag, spring 91; Social comment, Color Life Mag, summer 91; film critique, Fuse Mag, fall 91. *Mailing Add:* PO Box 20260 New York NY 10009

WATERSTON, HARRY CLEMENT
PAINTER, SCULPTOR
b New York, NY, Mar 15, 09. *Study:* NY Sch Fine & Appl Art; Art Students League; NY Univ Sch Educ, BS(art educ); also studied watercolor with Eliot O'Hara, Edgar Whitney & Mario Cooper; studied sculpture, Lehman Col. *Work:* Slater Mus, Norwich, Conn; lithograph, Smithsonian Inst, Washington, DC; Winsor & Newton Collection, Secaucus, NJ; Butler Inst Am Art, Youngstown, Ohio; and others. *Exhib:* Hudson Valley Art Asn; Cross-section Show, Artists Equity Asn, 75, 77, 78 & 81; Bronx Mus, 76 & 77; Audubon Artists, 77 & 80; Am Soc Contemp Artists Ann Shows, 81-90 & 91; and others. *Teaching:* Instr art, New York High Schs, 30-37. *Awards:* Anne G Morse Medal, Gotham Painters Show, 62. *Mem:* Fel Am Artists Prof League; NY Artists Equity Asn (bd mem, 75, pres, 79-81); Nat Coun Art Jewish Life (hon pres, 83); Am Soc Contemp Art, Metrop Painters & Sculptors (vpres, 79-). *Media:* Watercolor; Clay. *Publ:* Contribr, Sketches of Riverdale, Riverdale Press, 66- *Dealer:* Continental Art Gallery 72-21 Austin St Forest Hills NY 11375. *Mailing Add:* 80 Knolls Crescent Bronx NY 10463

WATERSTREET, KEN (JAMES KENT)
PAINTER, INSTRUCTOR
b Ogden, Utah, July 18, 40. *Study:* Calif State Univ, Sacramento, BA, 63, MA, 69. *Work:* E B Crocker Art Mus, Sacramento; Southern Ill Univ; Stuart M Speiser Collection, Smithsonian Inst; San Francisco Mus Mod Art; Oakland Mus, Calif. *Exhib:* Human Concern-Personal Torment, Whitney Mus of Am Art, New York, 69; one-man shows, Louis K Meisel Gallery, New York, 74 & 77 & Zara Gallery, San Francisco, 79; Hue & Far Cry of Color, Ft Wayne Mus, Ind, 76; E B Crocker Art Mus, Sacramento, 80; Joseph Chowning Gallery, San Francisco, 81, 83, 86, 88, 91 & 92; California A-Z and Return, Butler Inst Am Art, Youngstown, Ohio, 90; and others. *Pos:* Comnr, Sacramento Metrop Arts Comn, 77 & 78. *Teaching:* Chmn, Dept Visual & Performing Art, Mira Loma, High Sch, Sacramento, Calif 65-; summer session, Calif State Univ, Sacramento, 90 & 91. *Awards:* Fulbright-Hayes Study Tour, China, 88. *Mem:* Nat Art Educ Asn; Calif Art Educ Asn. *Media:* Oil on Canvas. *Dealer:* Judith Weintraub Gallery 1723 J St Sacramento CA 95814; Joseph Chowning Gallery 1717 17th St San Francisco CA 91403. *Mailing Add:* 3218 Tobari Ct Sacramento CA 95821

WATHALL, BETTIE GERALDINE See Becker, Bettie (Bettie Geraldine Wathall)

WATIA, TARMO
PAINTER, PRINTMAKER
b Detroit, Mich, May 11, 38. *Study:* Univ Mich, BS(design), 60 & MFA, 62. *Work:* Boise Cascade & Boise Art Gallery, Idaho; Harrett Mus, Twin Falls, Idaho. *Exhib:* 38th Ann Idaho, Boise Art Gallery, 74; 16th Ann Prints & Drawings, Okla Art Ctr, Oklahoma City, 74; Watercolor USA, Springfield, Mo, 75; 2nd Biennial Idaho Artists, Boise, 81; Sun Valley Art Ctr, Ketchum, Idaho, 87; Stewart Gallery, Boise, Idaho, 88. *Teaching:* Instr art, Southern Ore Col, Ashland, 66-69; assoc prof, Boise State Univ, Idaho, 69-86. *Awards:* Second Place Award, Rock Springs, Wyo, 72; Purchase Award, Boise Art Gallery, Idaho, 74; Cash Award/Painting, Ninth Ann Arts & Crafts Festival, Coeur D'Alene, Idaho; and others. *Media:* Oil, Woodcuts. *Mailing Add:* 1015 N Tenth St Boise ID 83702

WATKINS, EILEEN FRANCES
CRITIC
b Long Island, NY, Nov 22, 50. *Study:* Marywood Col, BA. *Pos:* Art ed, Newark Star-Ledger, currently. *Awards:* Citation, NJ Soc of Architects. *Mailing Add:* Newark Star-Ledger One Star-Ledger Plaza Newark NJ 07101

WATKINS, LEWIS
SCULPTOR, PAINTER
b Beckley, WVa, July 24, 45. *Study:* WVa State Col, BS(art educ), 78; Univ Southern Fla, MA, 82; St Leo Col, Fla, hon degree, 83. *Work:* Fla State Mus, Gainesville; WVa Fine Arts & Cult Ctr, Charleston; Vatican Mus, Rome, Italy; Leslie Stephens Fine Arts Ctr, Birmingham, Ala; Hyatt Regency Hotel, Atlanta, Ga. *Comn:* Limestone sculpture, Hernando Co, Brooksville, Fla, 81; Solidarity (steel sculpture), Brandon, Fla, 82; Crosses of Life (steel sculpture), City Atlanta, Ga, 83; Youth of Today (stone sculpture), Hernando Co, Fla, 83; St Leo (steel sculpture), St Leo Col, Fla, 83; Winning (steel sculpture), US Football League, 84; The National Memorial for the American Farmer (steel & bronze), 86. *Exhib:* Tools of Life, John W Davis Fine Art Gallery, Institute, WVa, 81; Leslie Stephens Fine Art Ctr, Samford Univ, Birmingham, Ala, 82;

and others. *Teaching:* Vis artist series, Samford Univ, Birmingham, Ala, 82; vis artist, St Leo Col, Fla, 82, Univ Tampa, Fla, 83 & Univ SFla, Tampa, 83. *Awards:* Distinguished Serv Art Award, Atlanta, Ga, 83; Cert Recognition Art, State Ga, 83; Pub Serv Cult Award, Hernando Co, Fla, 83. *Bibliog:* Terry Misfeldt (auth), article, Future Mag, 6/83; Tom Kuennen (auth), article, Rock Products Mag, 6/83; John Levine (auth), article, Pit & Quarry Mag, 9/83; articles in: Agri- View, Country Today, Hog Farm Mgt, Western Art Digest, Art Papers, Kanas Square, Today's Farmer & Kansas City Corp Report, 86; and many others. *Media:* Watercolor, Acrylic; Marble, Steel. *Publ:* Coauth, Creating a year book, Instructor Mag, 80. *Mailing Add:* 18855 Cortez Blvd Brooksville FL 34601

WATKINS, RAGLAND TOLK
CURATOR, DEALER
b San Francisco, Calif, Oct 31, 48. *Study:* Lake Forest Col, BA, 72; NY Univ, MA, 82. *Collections Arranged:* Bochner, Le Va, Rockburne, Tuttle (ed & contribr, catalog) Contemp Arts Ctr, Cincinnati, 75. *Pos:* Cur, Contemp Arts Ctr, Cincinnati, 73-75; Field rep, New York State Coun Arts, 76-77; assoc dir exhibs, Artists Space, New York, 77-81; dir, Concord Contemp Art, New York, 81-85; dir, Jason McCoy Inc, New York, 85-88. *Mailing Add:* 169 Sullivan St New York NY 10012

WATKINSON, PATRICIA GRIEVE
MUSEUM DIRECTOR, CURATOR
b Surrey, Eng, Mar 28, 46. *Study:* Bristol Univ, Eng, BA(hons), 68. *Collections Arranged:* A Partial View: Photographers in the Northwest (auth, catalog), 78; Contemporary Metals: Focus on Idea (auth, catalog), 81; British Prints: Highlights of Four Decades (auth, catalog), 81; Living with the Volcano: The Artists of Mount St Helens (auth, catalog), 85; Gaylen Hansen: The Paintings of a Decade (auth, catalog), 85; Patrick Siler: Recent Works (auth, catalog), 88; Facts of the Imagination, 89. *Pos:* Adminr, Mayfair Fine Arts, London, 69-71 & Bernard Jacobson Print Publ, 71-73; freelance cur & writer, Irish Arts Coun, Kilkenny Design Ctr & Trinity Col, Dublin, 75-76; cur, Mus Art, Wash State Univ, 76-83, dir, 84- *Teaching:* Asst prof art hist, Wash State Univ, 78-79. *Bibliog:* Ron Glowen (auth), A partial view, 78 & Gaylen Hansen, 86, Artweek. *Mem:* Art Mus Asn Am (Wash State rep, 86-88); Wash Mus Asn (mem bd, 85-87); Int Coun Mus, CIMAM; Asn Col & Univ Mus & Galleries (western rep, 86-89); Am Asn Mus. *Res:* 20th Century prints; contemporary art, Northwest & Am. *Publ:* Auth, Mount St Helens: An Artistic Aftermath, Art J, fall 84; A Decade Apart: A Curatorial View, Glass Art Soc J, 84-85; Drawing on the American Dream-Patrick Siler, Am Ceramics, summer 88 & Patti Warashina, spring 92. *Mailing Add:* Mus Art Wash State Univ Pullman WA 99164-7460

WATNISS, WENDY
PHOTOGRAPHER
b San Francisco, Calif, 1943. *Study:* Univ Madrid, 63; New York Univ, BA, 65. *Awards:* Women's Int Democratic Found Award, 83; Int Interpress Photo Award, 83; Nat Endowment Arts/Mid-Atlantic Arts Alliance, 87. *Dealer:* FotoFest 20 Greenway Plaza Suite 368 Houston TX 77046. *Mailing Add:* c/o FotoFest 20 Greenway Plaza Suite 368 Houston TX 77046

WATROUS, JAMES SCALES
PAINTER, HISTORIAN
b Winfield, Kans, Aug 3, 08. *Study:* Univ Wis, BS, MA & PhD. *Work:* Lawrence Univ; Kans State Univ. *Comn:* Symbols of Printing (mural), Webcrafters Press, Madison, Wis, 52; Justice (aluminum), City-County Bldg, Madison, 58; The Conjurer (mosaic mural), Wash Univ, St Louis, Mo, 59; Man: Creator of Order & Disorder, 64, Symbols of Communication, 72 & Mem Libr, 77 (mosaics), Univ Wis. *Pos:* Bd dir, Wis Found Arts, 75-89. *Teaching:* Prof art hist, Univ Wis-Madison, 41-64, Hagen prof art hist, 64-76, chmn dept art hist, 52-61. *Awards:* Wis Gov Award in Arts, 69; hon fel, Wis Acad Sci, Arts & Letters, 83; Award of Distinction, Mid-Am Col Art Asn, 91; and others. *Mem:* Mid-Am Col Art Asn (pres, 59); Col Art Asn Am (pres, 62-64); Midwest Art Hist Soc (bd dir, 74-75). *Res:* Technical studies in the fine arts; History of prints and drawings. *Publ:* Auth, The Craft of Old-Master Drawings, 57; A Century of American Printmaking, 1880-1980, Univ Wis Press, 84; A Century of Capricious Collecting, Elvehjem Mus Art, 87. *Mailing Add:* 2809 Sylvan Ave Madison WI 53705

WATSON, ALDREN A
DESIGNER, ILLUSTRATOR
b Brooklyn, NY, May 10, 17. *Study:* Yale Univ, 35; Art Students League, with George Bridgman, Charles Chapman, Robert Brackman, William Auerbach-Levy & others. *Work:* Illus bks in libr, US, Can, Europe & pvt collections. *Comn:* Mural, SS Pres Hayes, Thomas Crowell Co Off, 64. *Exhib:* Fifty Bks Shows, Soc Illusr Ann; New Eng Textbk Shows. *Pos:* Textbk designer, D C Heath & Co, Boston, 65-66; chief ed curric oriented mat, Silver Burdett Co, Morristown NJ, 66-68; official NASA artist, Apollo 8, 68; consult art dir, Houghton Mifflin, Boston, 68-72. *Teaching:* Pvt instr, hand bookbinding. *Awards:* Prize, Domesday Bk Illus Competition, 45. *Bibliog:* Chap in Forty Illustrators & How They Work. *Mem:* Author's Guild. *Publ:* Auth & illusr, My Garden Grows, 62 & Maple Tree Begins, 70, Viking; auth & illusr, Hand Bookbinding, 63, 68 & 75; auth & illusr, Hand Tools: Their Ways and Workings, Norton, 82; coauth, Furniture Making Plain & Simple, Norton, 84; and others. *Mailing Add:* PO Box 128 North Hartland VT 05052

WATSON, CLARISSA H
DEALER, WRITER
b Ashland, Wis. *Study:* Layton Art Sch, Milwaukee; Univ Wis-Milwaukee; Milwaukee-Downer Col, BA; Country Art Sch, with Harry Sternberg. *Collections Arranged:* Long Island Artists Washington, DC, 67; The Collectors' Collections, Adelphi Univ, Garden City, Long Island, 68; Gabriel Spat (1890-1967) Retrospective, Fine Arts Asn Willoughby, Cleveland, Ohio, 70; Nobility of the Horse in Art--to Save America's Wild Horses, Washington, DC, 71. *Pos:* Dir-founder, Country Art Sch, Westbury, Long Island, 53-68; dir & co-founder, Country Art Gallery, Locust Valley, Long Island, 53-; art consult, Adelphi Univ, 67-69; dir film festivals, 7 Village Arts Coun, Locust Valley, 69-71; dir-producer, Medieval Christmas Festival, Locust Valley, 70-73; trustee, Nassau Mus Fine Arts, 77-83, Roslyn & Hechsher Mus, Huntington, NY, 84-87. *Specialty:* Nineteenth and twentieth century American realism and American and European naifs. *Publ:* Auth, The art virus, This Wk Mag, 64; ed, The Artists' Cookbook, Stevenson, 71; auth, Fourth Stage of Gainsborough Brown, McKay, 77; The Bishop in the Back Seat, 80 & Runaway, 84, Atheneum; Last Plane from Nice, 87; Somebody Killed the Messenger, 88; Last Plan from Nice, 86; Somebody Killed the Messenger, 88. *Mailing Add:* 1011 Wolver Hollow Pl Oyster Bay NY 11771

WATSON, DARLIENE KEENEY
PAINTER
b Amarillo, Tex, Mar 16, 29. *Study:* Univ Colo, BFA; Art Inst Chicago; Malden Bridge Sch Art, NY; also with Dick Goetz, Okla, Lui-Sang Wong, Calif, Ho Nien Au, Taiwan, Yue-kee Wo, I Hsiung Ju, Va, Chen Chi, Val Thelin & Tom Hill. *Work:* St John's Univ, Jamaica, NY. *Comn:* Numerous comns for pvt collections. *Exhib:* Columbus Mus Arts & Sci, Southern Watercolor Soc, 78; Meridian House Int, Sumi-e Soc Am, Washington, DC, 84; Univ Va Art Mus, Va Watercolor Soc, 84; Potomac Valley Watercolorists, Arts Club, Washington, DC, 85; Salmagundi Club, New York, 84, 85 & 87. *Pos:* Pres, Herndon Old Town Gallery, Herndon, Va, 88. *Teaching:* Instr, Oriental brush painting, Northern Va Community Col, Manassas, 80-81. *Awards:* First Prize, Sumi-e Soc Am, 73 & 75; Equal Merit Award, Potomac Valley Watercolor Soc, 77; Dick Blick & Wayne Shaffer Awards, Sumi-e Soc Am, 84, 85 & 87. *Bibliog:* Widening Horizons in Creative Arts, Ada King Wallis Calif. *Mem:* Sumi-e Soc Am (chap pres, 75-77); Potomac Valley Watercolor Soc; Va Watercolor Soc; Southern Watercolor Soc; Ga Watercolor Soc. *Media:* Watercolor, Acrylic. *Publ:* Contribr, Frozen Stream, Anima, Vol VII, No 1, 80. *Dealer:* Watercolor Room 314 Mill St Occoquan VA 22125. *Mailing Add:* 9617 Jomar Dr Fairfax VA 22032

WATSON, HELEN RICHTER
CERAMIST, SCULPTOR
b Laredo, Tex, May 10, 26. *Study:* Scripps Col, Calif, BA, 47; Clarement Grad Sch & Univ Ctr, MFA, 49; spec work with Bernard Leach, 50; Swed Govt grant, Stockholm, Sweden, 52-53; spec work with Marguerite Wildenhain, 60; Alfred Univ, NY, 66. *Work:* Wichita Art Asn, Kans; Pitzer Col, Claremont, Calif; Pasadena Mus Art, Calif. *Comn:* Murals, Lobby, Laredo Nat Bank, Tex, 58; stairwell, grill units & off dividers, Tyler Bank & Trust Co, Tex, 59; ceramic units, comn by Millard Sheets, Scottish Rite Masonic Temple, Los Angeles, 62; sculpture, Bicentennial Comt Corpus Christi, Nueces Co Courthouse, 76; sculpture, Enterprise Develop Assocs, Mall de Norte, Laredo, Tex, 77. *Exhib:* Media Explored, Laguna Beach Mus, Calif, 67; Artist as Craftsman--Craftsman as Artist, Long Beach Mus Art, 67; 25 Yrs of Ceramic Art, Scripps Col, 69; one-woman show, Okla Art Ctr, Oklahoma City, 72; 1st Ann Exhib of Ceramic Art Women's Bldg, Los Angeles, 74; retrospective & doc exhib, Nuevo Santander Mus, Laredo, Tex, 79; and other group & one-man shows. *Teaching:* Instr ceramics, Chaffey Col, Ontario, Calif, 50-52, Mt San Antonio Col, Walnut, Calif, 55-57, Otis Art Inst, Los Angeles, 58-; artist-in-residence, Claremont Men's Col, Calif, 77-78. *Awards:* Frost Bros Award & Estill Gray Purchase Award, Witte Mem Mus, 51. *Bibliog:* Beverly Johnson (auth), From established artists come exciting new forms, Home Mag, Los Angeles Times, 2/72; Kim Blair (auth), Potter's career is shaping up, Los Angeles Times, 3/72; John P Simoni (auth), Excellent shows around the state, Wichita Eagle, 3/72. *Mem:* Southern Calif Designer Craftsmen; Design Div, Am Ceramic Soc; Artists Equity; Calif Design; Laredo Art Asn. *Publ:* Contribr, Twenty-five years of ceramic art, Ceramic Monthly, 70; contribr, Ceramics: A Potter's Handbook, Holt, Rinehart, Winston, 3rd ed, 71; contribr, Claywork: Form and Idea in Ceramic Design, Davis Publ, 75. *Dealer:* Barbara Beretich Gallery 8 Bonita & Harvard Rd Claremont CA 91711. *Mailing Add:* 1918 Houston St Laredo TX 78040

WATSON, HOWARD N(OEL)
PAINTER, PRINTMAKER
b Pottsville, Pa, May 19, 29. *Study:* Pa State Univ, 47-49; Tyler Sch Fine Arts, 53-55; Mus Col Art, dipl, 60. *Work:* White House, Art in Embassies, Washington, DC; Temple Univ; private collections of Richard Manogian & Walter Mondale; Pres Jimmy Carter. *Comn:* Logan Square (mural), Archdiocese Philadelphia, 75; Betsy Ross Making Flag, Upholsterer Int Union NAm, Philadelphia, 76; 50 watercolor painting Independence Blue Cross, Philadelphia, Pa; 10 large paintings pvt collection, ARCO Chemical. *Exhib:* Pa Acad Fine Arts, 62-68; Denver's Artists of America, 81-82; Audubon Artist Show, New York; Am Watercolor Soc Exhibs, New York; Allied Artists Am Exhibs, New York; Knickerbocker Artists Exhibs, New York; Nat Acad, New York; Philadelphia Watercolor Club Shows. *Teaching:* Instr watercolor, Hussian Sch Fine Arts, 61-63, Philadelphia Col Art, 63-70 & Abington Art Ctr, 71-; int watercolor workshops, including Austria, Switz, & Can. *Awards:* Super Achiever Award Art, Juvenile Diabetes Found, 78; Distinguished Pennsylvanians Award Art, State Pa, 80; Thornton Oakley Mem Award, Philadelphia Watercolor Club, 92. *Bibliog:* Article, Forbes Mag, 80; TLC Mag, 87. *Mem:* Philadelphia Watercolor Club (pres, 82-93); Am Watercolor Soc; Allied Artists Am; Knickerbocker Artists. *Media:* Watercolor. *Publ:* Philadelphia Watercolors, Barre Publ, 70; Old Philadelphia Impressions, Heritage Publ, 76; Proud Past, 77. *Dealer:* Newman Art Gallery 1625 Walnut St Philadelphia PA. *Mailing Add:* 348 Sinkler Rd Wyncote PA 19095

WATSON, KATHARINE JOHNSON
MUSEUM DIRECTOR, HISTORIAN
b Providence, RI, Nov 11, 42. *Study:* Duke Univ, BA, 64; Univ Pa, MA(art hist), 67, PhD(art hist), 73. *Pos:* Instr & cur of exhibs, Univ Pittsburgh, Pa, 69-70; cur art; co-ed, Allen Mem Art Mus Bull, 74-77; dir, Peary-MacMillan Arctic Mus, Bowdoin Col, Brunswick, Maine, 77-85, Bowdoin Col Mus Art, 77-; trustee, Mus Art Ogunquit, 77-90, Williamstown Regional Art Conserv Laboratory Inc, 78-90 & Surf Point Found; mem Smithsonian Coun. *Teaching:* Instr Ital sculpture & Europ Baroque art, Univ Pittsburgh, 69-70; lectr mus sem, Oberlin Col, Ohio, 73-79; instr mus sem, Bowd. *Awards:* Kress Found fel, Univ Pa, 67-68; Fel, Harvard Univ Ctr Ital Renaissance Studies, 77-78; Nat Endowment Arts Grant, 81; and others. *Mem:* Asn Art Mus Dirs; Col Art Asn; Am Asn Mus; New Eng Mus Asn; Maine Hist Soc; Victoria Soc Maine (prof adv comt). *Res:* Sixteenth and seventeenth century Italian sculpture; art patronage in eighteenth and nineteenth century America. *Publ:* Auth, A Bronze Mercury after Giambologna, Allen Art Mus Bulletin, 75-76; Sculpture in the Allen Art Museum, Hellenistic to the Twentieth Century, Apollo, 76; Sugar sculpture for grand ducal weddings from the Giambologna Workshop, The Connoisseur, 78; contribr, Giambologna 1527-1608: Sculptor to the Medici, Arts Coun Gt Brit, 78; auth, Pietro Tacca, Garland Press, 83; coauth (with Anthea Brook), Pietro Tacca, In: Il Seicento Fiorentino, Vol III, Florence, 86. *Mailing Add:* Bowdoin Col Mus Art Brunswick ME 04011

WATSON, MARY ANNE
PRINTMAKER, PAINTER
b Can; nat US. *Study:* Ont Col Art; NY Univ, BS. *Work:* Nat Art Gallery, Ottawa; Willistead Art Gallery, Windsor, Ont; Hamilton Art Gallery, Ont; Univ Toronto Libr, Art Inst Ont, Imperial Oil Awards Collection, Toronto Dominion Bank Collection, Toronto; Printmaking Workshop Collection; pvt collections throughout US & Can. *Exhib:* Alliance of Queens Artists; Flushing Coun on Arts Show, NY; Catherine Lorillard Wolfe Show, Nat Arts Club, New York; Salmagundi Club; Audabon Show, Nat Arts Club, 89-91; Nat Asn Women Artists Show, ARC Gallery, Chicago, 92; Nat Asn Women Artists travelling print show, 92-93; Artists Equity Gallery, Soho, NY, Burr Artists Show, 10/92. *Pos:* Printmaker, Bob Blackburn Workshops, New York, formerly. *Awards:* First Place, Individual Artists Showcase, 86; Warren E Bower Mem Award, Salmagundi Club, 88; Dr & Mrs I C Gaynor Award, Nat Asn Women Artists, 91; and others. *Mem:* Nat Arts League; Salmagundi Club; Nat League Am Pen Women; Nat Asn Women Artists; Burr Artists, NY. *Mailing Add:* 48 Spry Lake Rd Wiarton ON N0H 2T0 Canada

WATSON, RONALD G
PAINTER, EDUCATOR
b Grand Island, Neb, Oct 9, 41. *Study:* Univ Neb, Lincoln, BFA, 64, MFA(Woods Painting Fel), 67. *Work:* Grand Rapids Art Mus, Mich; Nat Collection Fine Arts, Washington, DC. *Comn:* Outdoor steel sculpture, City of Grand Rapids, Mich, 74; sculpture garden, Veterans Admin, Washington, DC, 81. *Exhib:* One-man exhibs, Grand Rapids Art Mus, Mich, 73, Ohio State Univ Art Gallery, 78, Dobrick Gallery, Chicago, 82, San Antonio Art Inst, 87 & Tex Christian Univ, 91; Ft Worth Gallery, 83 & 86; Adams-Middleton Gallery, Dallas, 85; The Patrick Gallery, Austin, 86; William Campbell Contemp Art, Ft Worth, Tex, 88; and others. *Teaching:* Prof drawing & painting, Aquinas Col, Grand Rapids, Mich, 68-82, chmn dept art, 71-81; prof drawing & painting, Tex Christian Univ, 82-, chmn dept art & hist, 82-89. *Awards:* Artist Fel, Nat Endowment Arts, 75. *Bibliog:* Margaret Robinette (auth), Outdoor Sculpture, Watson-Guptill, 76; Fay L Hendry (auth), Outdoor Sculpture in Grand Rapids, Michigan, Iota Press, 76; Donald Thalacker (auth), Art in World of Architecture, Chelsea House, 80; Howard Smagula (auth), Currents: Contemporary Directions in the Visual Arts, Prentice-Hall, 83. *Mem:* Col Art Asn. *Media:* Acrylic, Oil. *Publ:* Auth, The challenge of public sculpture, Mich Art J, 76; Art in public places, Ferris State Col, 79. *Dealer:* William Campbell Contemp Art 4935 Byers Ave Ft Worth TX 76107. *Mailing Add:* 6416 Greenway Rd Ft Worth TX 76116

WATSON, ROSS
CURATOR
b Bangor, NIreland, July 29, 34. *Study:* Pembroke Col, Cambridge, BA(hist with hon), 56, MA, 59; Courtauld Inst Art, London, dipl (hist art, with distinction), 63. *Collections Arranged:* Brit Coun Exhib 18th Century English Watercolors (auth, catalog), Rijks Mus, Amsterdam, Albertina, Vienna, 66; J M W Turner from Mellon Collection, Nat Gallery Art, Washington, DC, 69; John Constable from Mellon Collection, 69; Joseph Wright Derby, from Mellon Collection, 69-70; William Hogarth from Mellon Collection, 70-71; Eye of Thomas Jefferson, Bicentennial Exhib, 76. *Pos:* Asst keeper, City Mus & Art Gallery, Birmingham, Eng, 63-66; asst cur, Paul Mellon Collection, Washington, DC, 66; cur, Nat Gallery Art, Washington, DC, 66-77; admin asst dir, Tudor Pl Found, Washington, DC, 88- *Mem:* Walpole Soc; Asn Irish Art Hist; Palladian Soc Am, Decorative Arts Trust. *Res:* Eighteenth century European, particularly British painting. *Publ:* Coauth, Renaissance furniture, Antiques Int, 66; auth, Guardi and the visit of Pius VI to Venice in 1782, Nat Gallery Art Report & Studies Hist Art, 67; Irish portraits in American Collections, Irish Georgian Soc Bull, 69; National Gallery of Art, Washington, DC, 79. *Mailing Add:* 1605 32nd St NW Washington DC 20007

WATTENMAKER, RICHARD J
MUSEUM DIRECTOR, HISTORIAN
b Philadelphia, Pa, Feb 22, 41. *Study:* Univ Pa, BA; New York Univ, Inst Fine Arts, MA, PhD. *Collections Arranged:* The Art of William Glackens (with catalog), 67; The Art of Charles Prendergast (with catalog), 68; The Art of Jean Hugo (with catalog), 73; The Fauves (with catalog), 75; Puvis de Chavannes and The Modern Tradition (with catalog), 75; The Dutch Cityscape in the 17th Century and its Sources (with catalog), 77; European Tools from the 17th to the 19th Century (with catalog), 81. *Pos:* Dir, Rutgers Univ Art Gallery, 66-69; chief cur, Art Gallery Ont, Toronto, 72-78; dir, Chrysler Mus, 79-80; dir, Flint Inst Arts, 80-88, Archives Am Art, Smithsonian Inst, 90, trustee, Intermus Conserv Asn, Oberlin, 82-88. *Teaching:* Adj prof, Univ Mich, Flint, 84-85, Univ Mich, Ann Arbor, 88 & The Barnes Found, Merion, Pa, 91-92. *Awards:* Founders Day Award, New York Univ, 72. *Mem:* Am Asn Mus; Artist Blacksmith Asn N Am. *Res:* 19th and 20th century European painting; Renaissance and Post-Renaissance European painting; American painting and decorative art. *Publ:* Auth, Art Gallery of Ontario (illus handbook/catalog), Art Gallery Ont, 74; Maurice Prendergast, Allen Mem Art Mus, 82; William Glackens Beach Scenes at Bellport, Smithsonian Studies in Am Art, 88; Maurice Prendergast at the Whitney, New Criterion, 90. *Mailing Add:* Archives Am Art Smithsonian Inst Washington DC 20560

WATTS, R MICHAEL
MUSEUM DIRECTOR
b Quincy, Ill, July 2, 51. *Study:* Western Ill Univ, BS, 73, BA(art hist), 75; Univ Tex Austin, MFA, 77. *Collections Arranged:* Abstract Expressionism, Poindexter Collection, Butte Arts Found, 78; Antique Quilts c 1830-1930, Paducah Art Guild Gallery, 82; New Wood/New Ways, with Paul Sasso co-curator, (with catalog), Southern Arts Fedn, 83; American Scene Prints, 87 & Illinois Traditions: Folk Arts, 90, Tarble Arts Ctr. *Pos:* Dir, Paducah Art Guild, Ky; Eagle & Curris Galleries, Murray State Univ, Ky, 83-86; Tarble Arts Ctr, Eastern Ill Univ, 86- *Teaching:* Instr art, Paducah Community Col, Ky, 81-82; asst prof, Murray State Univ, Ky, 83-86. *Mem:* Am Asn Mus; Col Art Asn; Asn Col/Univ Galleries & Mus; Midwest Mus Conf; Cong Ill Hist Soc & Mus. *Res:* Twentieth century American art, particularly contemporary folk art. *Publ:* Contribr, James A Michener Collection: 20th Century American Painting, Univ Mus, Univ Tex, Austin, 77; ed, African Arts: Beauty In Utility (catalog), Eagle Gallery, Murray State Univ, Ky, 83; Collecting outside the mainstream (folk art), Dialogue, 88; Virgil Grotfeldt: Recent Paintings (catalog), 90 & American Scene Prints (catalog), 91, Tarble Arts Ctr, Eastern Ill Univ, 91. *Mailing Add:* Eastern Ill Univ Tarble Arts Ctr Ninth St at Cleveland Ave Charleston IL 61920

WAUFLE, ALAN DUANE
MUSEUM DIRECTOR
b Hornell, NY, Feb 11, 51. *Study:* Col William & Mary, BA; Duke Univ, MA. *Collections Arranged:* Antique Quilts & Coverlets of Gaston Co, 77, Textile History of Gaston Co, 78, Frank Creach: Retrospective, 78, The Christmas Doll, 79, Wheels & Runners: 18th Century America on the Move, 83, Gaston Co Mus Art & Hist. *Pos:* Dir, Gaston Co Mus Art & Hist, Dallas, NC, 76- *Mem:* NC Mus Coun; Am Asn State & Local Hist; Am Asn of Mus; SE Mus Conf. *Res:* Iconography of works celebrating the 1571 Battle of Lepanto. *Publ:* Auth, Sitings/Sightings, Guide to mus, galleries & craft shops in NC. *Mailing Add:* 3308 Sherwood Circle Gastonia NC 28056

WAX, JOHN M
PAINTER, COLLAGE ARTIST
b Philadelphia, Pa, Nov 1, 48. *Study:* Pa State Univ, 66-69; George Washington Univ, BA(fine arts), 71, MFA, 72. *Work:* Embassy of Norway, Washington, DC; Univ Konstanz, WGer. *Comn:* Aluminum cast sculptures, BKI Alloys, Birmingham, Eng, 70; wall sculpture, Crowell & Moring, Washington, DC, 78; wood assemblage, Rogovin, Stern & Huge, Washington, DC, 79; wood assemblage, A Sarowitz & Assoc, Philadelphia, Pa, 82. *Exhib:* 19th Area Exib, Corcoran Gallery Art, Washington, DC, 74; one-man shows: Wax Paper and Wood Too, Univ City Sci Ctr, Philadelphia, Pa, 81, Collages & Constructions, Hull Gallery, Washington, DC, 83, Artifacts, Pa State Univ, Abington, 86, Alter-Images, Charles Co Col, LRC Gallery, La Plata, Md, 91; Collage & Assemblage, Miss Mus Art, Jackson, 81; Shelter '85, Nat Exhib, traveling, Washington, DC & US, 85; Recent American Works on Paper, Int/Nat Exhib, sponsored by Smithsonian Inst, US & 6 mo Europe, 85-88. *Teaching:* Instr art & design, NVa Col, Anandale, 78-79 & George Mason Univ, Fairfax, Va, 90- *Awards:* Individual Artists Fel, DC Commission on Arts, 82; Cecille R Hunt Mem Award, Geroge Washington Univ Art Exhib, 86. *Bibliog:* Val Lewton (auth), article, Washington Review, 12/15/77; Joseph Adcock (auth), Environment of inagination, The Bulletin (Philadelphia), 5/14/81; Roger Piantadosi (auth), John Wax: Art from the Litter of Life, Washington Post, 5/8/82. *Mem:* Artists for Equal Justice. *Media:* Mixed; Miscellaneous. *Dealer:* David Adamson Gallery 406 Seventh St Washington DC; Susan Conway Carroll 1058 Thomas Jefferson St NW Washington DC 20007. *Mailing Add:* 4336 River Rd Washington DC 20016

WAYNE, JUNE
PAINTER, PRINTMAKER
b Chicago, Ill. *Work:* Bibliot Nat, France; Bibliot Royale Bruxelles; Mus Mod Art, New York; Nat Gallery Art, Washington, DC; Art Inst Chicago; Australian Nat Gallery, Canberra; Brisbon New SWhales Gallery, Australia; and others. *Comn:* Tapestry, comn by KCET, Los Angeles, 76; lithography, comn by Music Ctr Los Angeles, 86. *Exhib:* Tidal Waves & Visas: Tapestries & Lithography, June Wayne La Demeure, Paris, 75; From Lurcat to Today: Masterpieces of Tapestry, La Royale Belge, Bruxelles, Belg; Tapisseries, Lithographies, traveling show in Europe, Cultural Affairs, Am Embassy, Paris, France, 76-79; The Dorothy Series, traveling, Art Mus Asn, 80-84; solo exhib, Australian Nat Gallery, Canberra, 89; The Djuna Set, Fresno Mus, Calif & Assoc Am Artist Gallery, New York, 89; and others. *Pos:* Founder & dir, Tamarind Lithography Workshop, 60-70; mem bd dirs, Grunwald Graphic Arts Found, Univ Calif, Los Angeles, 65-75, adv to Arts Mgt Prog, Grad Sch Admin, 69-; mem overseers comt, Sch Visual & Environ Arts,

Harvard Univ, 74-76; adv, Univ Calif, Long Beach, 87- *Awards:* Acad Award Nomination for Golden Eagle (film), 74; Nat Endowment Arts Visual Arts Fel, 80; LULU Award, 83; Women's Caucus Art Award, 85. *Bibliog:* Baskett (auth), The Art of June Wayne, Abrams, 68; Arlene Raven (auth), Cognitos: June Wayne's new paintings, Arts, Mag, 84; Louise Lewis (auth), June Wayne's Investigations of time, World Print News, 85; plus others. *Mem:* Art Table New York; Art Table Los Angeles; Women Film; The Forum New York; The Forum Los Angeles; hon mem Printmaker Soc Washington; hon mem Printmaker Soc Los Angeles. *Media:* All Media. *Publ:* Auth, The creative process: Artists, carpenters and the Flat Earth Society, Craft Horizons, 76; The male artist as stereotypical female, Col Art J, 73; Avant-Garde Mindset in the Artist's Studio, HUUC '86, Hofstra Univ, 85; Seeing the Unseeable: Space from Earth, Pac Design Ctr Westweek, 86. *Dealer:* Assoc Am Artists Gallery 20 W 57th St New York NY 10019; Tobey Moss Gallery 7321 Beverly Blvd Los Angeles CA 90036. *Mailing Add:* 1108 N Tamarind Ave Los Angeles CA 90038

WEALE, MARY JO
PAINTER, EDUCATOR
b Lexington, Ky, Feb 26, 24. *Study:* Univ Ky, BS, 45; Famous Artists Sch, cert graphic arts, 58; Fla State Univ, MS, 63, PhD, 68; studied with over 25 watercolorists incl Ed Whitney. *Work:* Kennedy-Douglass Ctr Arts, Florence, Ala; Ed Ball Wakulla Springs State Park, Fla; Consulate General Iceland, Tallahassee, Fla; Miller Brewing Co; Walt Disney World; Fla First Fed, Tampa; Barnett Bank Corporate Collection. *Comn:* Large watercolors, Kozyak, Tropin & Throckmorton, Miami, Fla, 88 & Tampa, 88-92; St Mark's Light House, Fla State Univ, Tallahassee, 88-89; and numerous private comns. *Exhib:* Southern Watercolor Soc Ann, Okla Art Ctr, 86; Ga Watercolor Soc Open Show, Mus Arts & Sci, Macon, 86; Beaux Arts Exhib, Lowe Mus, Coral Gables, Fla, 87, 88 & 89; Ga Watercolor Soc Mus Show, Valdosta Art Mus, 88; Panama Nat Transparent Show Civic Ctr, Fla, 88; Mt Dora Art Festival, 89. *Pos:* Artist-in-residence, Ed Ball Wakulla Springs State Park, 87, 90 & 91. *Teaching:* Chmn interior design, Fla State Univ, 73-85, prof watercolor, 73-90; vis prof watercolor, Int Inst of Foreign Study, London, 81; vis prof watercolor, Winthrop Col, 85, Savannah Col Art, 88; Walt Disney World Design & Eng Dept, 90; demonstr, St Cuthbert's Paper Mill, Eng at Fla Watercolor Soc Ann Mtg, 91. *Awards:* Best of Show, 86 & First Place, 88, Tallahassee Regional Watercolor Soc, 86; Award of Merit, Ga Watercolor Soc, 88; First place, watercolor, Mt Dora Art Fest, 89. *Bibliog:* Margaret Mitchell (auth), feature article, Tallahassee Mag, 90; Alan Wendt, news feature, WTVT (CBS) Tampa, 90; Andy Blount (auth), Florida Wildlife, 1-2/91; International Year Book, Wildlife Art News, 92. *Mem:* Southern Watercolor Soc (secy, 81-83); Fla Watercolor Soc sig mem (newsletter ed, 89-92, secy, 92-94); Ga Watercolor Soc; Fla Artist Fedn; 10 Artists Ltd. *Media:* Watercolor. *Publ:* Contrib ed, IDEAS Mag, DoDi Publ, Coral Gables, 78-; Environmental Interiors, Macmillan, 82; Rendering Techniques for Artists, designers, Architects, private publ, 82-88; Numerous articles in Interior Design, Contract, Journal of Interior Design Education Research, The Designer, Lithographs, Egrets have no regrets, 88; diptych, Transparent Watercolor Techniques & Creative Applications for Walt Disney World, priv pub, 90. *Dealer:* Nuance Gallery 720 S Date Mabry Tampa FL 33609; Art Galleries of Hawaii Parker Ranch Ctr Kamula HI 96743. *Mailing Add:* 1102 Sarasota Dr Tallahassee FL 32301

WEARE, SHANE
PRINTMAKER
b Eng, Aug 29, 36. *Study:* Royal Col Art, London, Eng, ARCA(printmaking), 63; Univ Iowa, asst etching, 63-64. *Work:* Brit Mus, London; Lib Libr Cong, Washington, DC; Brooklyn Mus, NY; Art Inst Chicago; San Francisco Mus Art. *Exhib:* Int Exhib Graphic Art, Ljubliana, Yugoslavia, 66; Brit Int Print Biennale, 68; 22nd Ann Print Exhib, Boston Mus, 70; World Print Competition, San Francisco Mus Art, 73; one-man show, Calif Palace of Legion of Honor, City of San Francisco, 73; 20th Nat Print Exhib, Brooklyn Mus, New York, 77. *Awards:* Purchase Awards, Los Angeles Soc Printmakers, 68-74, City of San Francisco, 72, City of Palo Alto, 74 & Univ Colo, 74; Spaces Between Prog Award, KQED-TV, San Francisco, 75. *Bibliog:* John Brunsden (auth), Technique of Etching & Engraving, Batsford, 66. *Mem:* Calif Soc Printmakers (vchmn, 72-73). *Media:* Pastel. *Dealer:* Soker-Kaseman Gallery 1457 Grant Ave San Francisco CA 94133. *Mailing Add:* 2663 Bennett Ridge Rd Santa Rosa CA 95404

WEAVER, JOHN BARNEY
SCULPTOR
b Anaconda, Mont, Mar 28, 20. *Study:* Art Inst Chicago, dipl(Albert Kuppenhiemer Scholar), 46; monumental sculpture with Albin Polasek, Emil Zettler, Edward Chasang & Egon Weiner; Univ Arts, Parma, Italy, dipl merit, 81, Univ Alta, LLD, 84. *Work:* Bronzes, Charles Russell, Statuary Hall, Washington, DC, Double Equestrian, Fort Walsh, Sask, Archaic Indian, NY State Mus, Albany & Govt House, Edmonton, Alta; Astokimake (portrait bust), Rideau Hall, Ottawa; heads & figures, Anthrop Hall, Smithsonian Inst. *Comn:* The Stake & The Pronghorns (bronze), Prov Mus & Arch, Alta, 67; Madonna of the Wheat, Edmonton, Alta, 81; Arthur Henry Griesbach, Edmonton, Alta, 81; medal design, World Univ Games, 83; Expo '86 Commemorative Collection, 86. *Exhib:* Chicago & Vicinity, Art Inst Chicago, 47; 68th Exhib Soc Washington Artists, Natural Hist Bldg, Washington, DC, 61; Steel to the West (bronze), US, Toronto, London, Paris & Brussels, 78; Media Ctr, Robson Sq, Vancouver, BC, 80; Salon Nations, Paris, 83. *Pos:* Sculptor, Mont Hist Soc, 55-60, Smithsonian Inst, 61-66 & Provincial Mus & Archives, Alta, 66-71. *Teaching:* Instr life drawing, Layton Sch Art, Milwaukee, 46-51; instr sculpture, Fraser Valley Col, Abbotsford, BC, 84-89. *Awards:* Alta Achievement Award for Excellence in Sculpture, 77; Gold Medal, Int Parliament Security & Peace, 82. *Bibliog:* Ruth Bowen (auth), Alberta art in bronze, My Golden West, 70; Mario Monteverdi & Calogero Panepinto (auth), The history of international art, Univ Arts, Parma, Italy, 82. *Mem:* Italian Acad Art, Parma; Acad Europe; Acad Nations; life mem Univ Mont Mus Rockies; life mem Mont State Hist Soc. *Media:* Bronze. *Mailing Add:* PO Box 1723 Hope BC V0X 1L0 Canada

WEBB, ALEXANDER DWIGHT
PHOTOGRAPHER
b San Francisco, Calif, May 5, 52. *Study:* Harvard Univ, BA, 74. *Work:* Fogg Art Mus, Cambridge, Mass; Univ Mass Collection, Amherst; Int Ctr Photog, New York; Mus Photog Arts, San Diego, Calif. *Exhib:* Contemporary Photographers V, 75 & Color Photography, 80, Fogg Art Mus, Cambridge, Mass; Grave Relics, Carpenter Ctr Visual Arts, Cambridge, 82; Color in the Street, 83 & Alex Webb: Hot Light/Half-Made Worlds, 86, Calif Mus Photog, Riverside; Alex Webb-Harry Gruyeart, Photographer's Gallery, London, Eng, 84; 3 Color Photographers, Amsterdam Photo 84, Neth, 84; On the Line: The New Color Photojournalism (with catalog), Walker Art Ctr, Minneapolis, Minn, 86; solo shows, Calif Mus Photog, Riverside, 86 & Torino Fotogratia, Torino, Italy; group shows, Masters of the Streets & Haiti: Revolution in Progress, Mus Photog Arts, San Diego, Calif, 89, This & Other Worlds, Mus Contemp Photog, Chicago, Ill, In Our Time, Magnum Photos, Int Ctr Photog, New York, 89, Palats de Tokyo, Paris, France, 89 (travelling) & Minneapolis Mus Art, 90; This & Other Worlds, Mus Contemp Photog, Chicago, Ill; Catherine Edebaum Gallery, Chicago, 90; Atrium Gallery, Univ Conn, Storrs, 91; Whitney Mus Am Art, NY Biennial Exhib, 91. *Pos:* Photogr, Magnum Photos, New York, 76-, vpres, 85-86. *Awards:* Overseas Press Club Citation, US-Mexico Border Essay, 80; NY Found Arts Grant, 86; Leopold Godowsky Jr Photog Award, 88; Nat Endowment Arts Grant, 90; W Eugene Smith Found Supplemental Grant, 90. *Bibliog:* Andy Grundberg (auth), Photojournalism: It's back with a new face, Mod Photog, 80; Gary Walther (auth), In the heat of the light, Camera Arts, 83; M Johnstone (auth), The active streets, Art Week, 83; Haiti, Photo Mag, France, 4/88; Max Kozloff (auth), Picturing the Killing Fields, Art in Am, 6/90. *Publ:* Auth, Hot Light/Half-Made Worlds, Thames & Hudson, 86; Auth, Under a Grudging Sun, Thames & Hudson, 89. *Mailing Add:* Magnum Photos Inc 72 Spring St New York NY 10012

WEBB, FRANK (FRANCIS H)
PAINTER, INSTRUCTOR
b North Versailles, Pa, Sept 14, 27. *Study:* Art Inst Pittsburgh, with Edgar A Whitney. *Work:* Butler Inst Am Art, Youngstown, Ohio; PPG Found, Pittsburgh; Tweed Art Mus, Duluth, Mich; Ford Times Collection, Detroit. *Comn:* Soc Naval Architects & Marine Engineers, 88. *Exhib:* Am Watercolor Soc Ann, Nat Acad, New York, 71-80; Nat Arts Club, New York, 71-81; Butler Inst Am Art, Youngstown, Ohio, 73; Audubon Artists, Nat Arts Club, New York, 73-83; Allied Artists, Nat Arts Club, New York, 73-80; Nat Acad Ann, New York, 77; Midwest Watercolor Soc Ann, Rawr-West Mus, Manitowac, Wis, 79-83; and many others. *Pos:* Pres, Phillips Studio, Pittsburgh, 57-80. *Teaching:* Guest lectr painting throughout N Am & Europe, 73- *Awards:* Sizek Award, Butler Midyear Ann, Butler Inst Am Art, Youngstown, Ohio, 73; Bronze Medal of Honor, Am Watercolor Soc, 76; Walser Greathouse Medal, Am Watercolor Soc, 89. *Bibliog:* Edward Betts (auth), Creative Seascape Painting, Watson-Guptill, 81; Fritz Henning (auth), Concept and Composition, North Light, 83; Frank Webb, Contemporary Watercolor Master (motion picture/video). *Mem:* Am Watercolor Soc; Rocky Mountain Nat Watermedia Asn; Allied Artists of Am; Audubon Artists; Dolphin Fel. *Media:* Watercolor. *Publ:* Auth, Watercolor Energies,83, North Light Publ; Webb on Watercolor, 90. *Dealer:* Concept Gallery 1031 Sout Braddock Ave Pittsburgh PA 15218. *Mailing Add:* 108 Washington St Pittsburgh PA 15218

WEBB, JEFFREY R
PAINTER, EDUCATOR
b Mineola, NY, Sept 29, 52. *Study:* Pratt Inst, Brooklyn, NY, BFA, 74; studied with John Koch NA, 74-78; C W Post Col, Long Island Univ, Old Brookville, MA, 76. *Work:* Heckscher Mus, Huntington, NY; Bayville Mus, NY. *Comn:* Portrait, Dr P Corrone, South Oaks Hosp, Amityville, NY, 85; portrait, Dr G Perry, Mercy Hosp, Rockville Centre, NY, 86; portrait, Dr Robbins, South Oaks Hosp, Amityville, 86; historical portrait, Capt T Cook, City Glen Cove, NY, 86; mural, Wizard of Oz, Village Green Golf, Lake Ronkonroma, NY, 92. *Exhib:* Pastel Soc Asn Ann Exhibs, Nat Arts Club, New York, 73-92; one-man show, Harbor Gallery, Cold Spring Harbor, NY, 78; Pastel Exposition Int, Maison Lafitte, Paris, France, 88; Master Pastellists, Quincy Art Mus, Ill, 90; Featured Show, Z Gallery, New York, 91; and others. *Pos:* Historian, bd dirs, Pastel Soc Am, New York, 75-; vpres, Nat Drawing Asn, Garden City, NY, 88-90; art comt, Salmagundi Club, New York, 90- *Teaching:* Instr painting, Huntington Township Art League, NY, 76-; instr pastel painting, Queensborough Community Col, Bayside, NY, 89-; instr art hist, Nassau Community Col, Garden City, NY, 88- *Awards:* Knickerbocker Award for Oil, Knickerbocker Artists Ann, 78; Master Pastellist, Pastel Soc Am Exhib, 85; Grumbacher Gold Medal, Pastel Soc Am Ann Exhib, Grumbacher Artists Mats, 91. *Bibliog:* Leona Keeley (auth), Jeff Webb, 20th Century Victorian, Sunstorm Mag, 78; William Harmon (auth), Mastel Pastels, Harmon Meek Gallery, 86; Domenique Sennelier (auth), The Sennelier Pastel Portrait Set, Sennelier Artists Mat, 91. *Mem:* Pastel Soc Am (bd dirs, 75-); Nat Drawing Asn (vpres, 88-90); Salmagundi Club (art comt, 90-); Nat Art League (exhib chmn, 92); Huntngton Township Art League. *Media:* Pastel, Oil. *Publ:* Illusr, Introduction to Meditation, 78 & Fundamentals of Jain Meditation, 79, Dodd-Mead; auth, Artists and models, Encore Plus, 89. *Dealer:* Goodman Gallery 53 N Sea Rd Southampton NY 11968. *Mailing Add:* 270 Lowndes Ave, No 117 Huntington Station NY 11746

WEBB, PATRICK
PAINTER, MURALIST
b New York, NY, July 20, 55. *Study:* Md Inst/Col Art, BFA, 76; Skowhegan Sch Painting & Sculpture, 77; Yale Univ, MFA, 79. *Work:* Fred Alger & Co & Chemical Bank, New York; Boston Pub Libr & Shearson Lehman, Boston, Mass; Univ Wis, Oshkosh. *Comn:* Painting, Glickenhaus & Co, New York, 86; paintings, Sharf Marketing Group 87 & 88. *Exhib:* Art and the Law, West Co traveling exhib, 88-90; New York Harper & Row, New York, 89; Allegory, Ammo, Brooklyn, 90; solo shows, Forum Gallery, Minneapolis, Minn, 90, Group Gallery, Provincetown, Mass, 92, Amos Ewo Gallery, New York, 92, Figuring it out, Daniel Quinn Gallery, Long Island, NY, 92. *Teaching:* Lectr, Univ Wis, 79-81; asst prof, Cornell Univ, 81-83; vis artist, Yale Univ, 85, Brandeis Univ, 88, Minneapolis Col Art & Design, 89, 90 & 92, NY Acad Art, 93. *Awards:* Fel, Nat Endowment Arts, 83, 85 & 87; Ingram Merrill Award, 89-90. *Bibliog:* Walter Wadas (auth) Alone and embattled, Bay Windows, 12/86; Mary Verill (auth), Real implications, New N Art Scape, 2- 3/90; Phil Gambone (auth), Finding Those Who Fall Before, Bay Windows, Boston, 8/20/92. *Mem:* Col Art Asn; New York Artists Equity; Provincetown Art Asn; Brooklyn Waterfront Artist Asn. *Media:* Oil & Miscellaneous Frescoe. *Publ:* Cover, Public Speaking, Beebe Prentice Hall, 91; American Law Yearbook (reproduction & article by ed), 90; cover, Bar Asn J, Mass, 92. *Mailing Add:* PO Box 903, Old Chelsea St New York NY 10011

WEBB, SARAH A
PAINTER
b Nashville, Tenn, Feb 19, 48. *Study:* Univ Tenn, Ba, 78; Vanderbilt Univ, 79-80. *Work:* Holiday Corp, Memphis, Tenn; First Tenn Bank, Gallatin, Tenn. *Exhib:* Ann Cent South Art Competition, Parthenon Gallery, Nashville, Tenn, 82, 87 & 92; Am Artist Nat Art Competition, Grand Central Gallery, New York, 85; Ann Exhib, Soc Women Artists, Westminster Gallery, London, England, 89, 90 & 91. *Awards:* Best of Show, 22nd Central South Art Competition, 87; Athena Award, 27th Central South Art Competition, 92. *Bibliog:* Clara Hieronymns (auth), Oh, how she loves Paris, 12/27/87 & Sarah Webb Works to Show in London, 5/17/89, Tennessean. *Media:* Oil. *Mailing Add:* PO Box 50134 Nashville TN 37205

WEBB, TODD
PHOTOGRAPHER, HISTORIAN
b Detroit, Mich, Sept 15, 05. *Work:* Mus City New York, Mus Mod Art, New York; Chicago Art Inst; Worcester Art Mus, Mass; NMex Fine Arts Mus, Santa Fe; Nat Mus Am Art, Smithsonian Inst, Washington, DC; Hallmark Cards Collection, Kansas City; and others. *Exhib:* Solo exhibs, Chicago Art Inst, 56, Amon Carter Mus, Ft Worth, 65 & NMex Mus, Santa Fe, 71; Ideas & Images, Am Found Arts, New York, 62-64; Traveling Exhib, New York & Paris 1946-1960, Hallmark Cards, 86; Camera, Obsuro Gallery, Denver, Colo, 90; Kate Heller Gallery, London, England, 90. *Teaching:* Photog workshops, Santa Fe, NMex, 69-70; artist in res prog, Univ S Maine, Gorham, 87. *Awards:* Guggenheim Fel, 55 & 56; Nat Endowment Arts Grant, 79. *Bibliog:* Todd Webb New York & Paris 1946-1960, Univ NMex Press, 86; Looking Back-Momoirs of Todd Webb, Univ NMex Press, 91. *Publ:* Auth, Gold Strikes and Ghost Towns, 61 & The Gold Rush Trail and the Road to Oregon, 63, Doubleday; illusr, 19th Century Texas Homes, 65 & 19th Century Public Buildings, 74, Univ Tex Press; auth, Georgia O'Keeffe-The Artist & Her Landscape, Twelve Trees Press, Pasadena, Calif, 84. *Mailing Add:* 120 North St Bath ME 04530

WEBBER, HELEN
TAPESTRY ARTIST, SCULPTOR
b New York, NY. *Study:* Queens Col, BA, 51; RI Sch Design, MA, 62. *Comn:* Fluor Corp Hq Collection, Irvine, Calif, Chevron Corp, San Ramon, Calif, Merck & Co, Rahway, NJ, Betty Ford Ctr, Palm Springs, Calif, Carnival Cruise Lines, Miami, St Patrick's Hosp, Lake Charles, La, Radisson Plaza Hotel, Lexington, Ky, Vista Chemical Inc, Houston, Kaiser Permanente, Washington, DC; B'nai Sholem Synagogue, Walnut Creek, Calif, East Tex Med Ctr, Tyler, Armed Forces Col, Riyadh, Saudi Arabia, St John's Med Ctr, Tulsa, Phillipine Commercial Bank, Manila, Veteran's Admin Nat Cemetary, NY State Univ, Brockport, Lesley Col, Cambridge, Mass, Univ Calif Hosp, San Diego, Internat Laborers Union, Hopkinton, Mass. *Exhib:* Union Internationale des Femmes Architectes, Paris, 84. *Pos:* Founder, Women Design, Aspen, 77; pres, Women Design Int, 83-85. *Teaching:* Instr, Calif Col Arts & Crafts, Oakland, 73-74. *Awards:* Outstanding Contribution Design, Women Design Int, 80. *Bibliog:* Art and Fabric: Helen Webber, Today's Art & Graphics, 4/81; A profile of the artist, Interiors Mag, 12/81. *Mem:* Design Int (hon bd mem). *Media:* Fabric Collage; Clay, Metal. *Publ:* Auth & illusr, The Sea is My Blanket, Summer Sun, My Kite is the Magic Me & Good Night Night, Astor Books, 65; Art in Public Places in the US, Bowling Green Univ Press, 75. *Mailing Add:* Helen Webber Designs 555 Pacific Ave San Francisco CA 94133

WEBER, ALBERT JACOB
PAINTER, EDUCATOR
b Chicago, Ill, July 10, 19. *Study:* Art Inst Chicago, BFA; Mexico City Col, MA. *Exhib:* 32nd Ann Lithography, Philadelphia Print Club, 59; 23rd Ann Soc Washinton Printmakers, US Nat Mus, Washington, DC, 60; Int Juried Drawing Exhib, State Univ Col Educ, Potsdam, NY, 60; US Int Agency Int Tour of Ford-Times Collection Am Art, 61 & 62; 26th Ann Show: Paintings, Butler Inst Am Art, Youngstown, Ohio, 61; Paintings by Gallery Group, Angeleski Gallery, 1; Art in Am Mag: Dec Benefit Exhib, New York, 61; Exhib of Paintings, Bowling Green State Univ, Ohio, 81; and many others. *Teaching:* Instr, Mexico City Col; prof art, Univ Mich, Ann Arbor, 55- *Awards:* Prize, Grand Rapids Art Gallery, 58; Purchase Prizes, Butler Inst Am Art, 59-61; Purchase Prize, Graphic Art & Drawing Exhib, Olivet Col, Mich, 62; H Rackham Grant for Travel and Painting, 80-81; plus others. *Mailing Add:* 7414 Herschel Ave No 306 La Jolla CA 92037-5112

WEBER, IDELLE
PAINTER
b Chicago, Ill. *Study:* Scripps Col; Univ Calif, Los Angeles, BA & MA. *Work:* Nat Collection Fine Arts, Washington, DC; Va Mus, Richmond; Worcester Art Mus, Mass; Albright-Knox Art Gallery, Buffalo, NY; Yale Univ Art Gallery, New Haven, Conn; Metrop Mus Art, New York; and others. *Comn:* Pac Bell, San Ramon, Calif, 86. *Exhib:* Guggenheim Mus, New York, 64; Wadsworth Atheneum, Hartford, Conn, 66 & 74; Whitney Downtown, New York, 75; Realismus und Realitat, Darmstadt, WGer, 75; Nat Collection Fine Arts, 76; McNay Art Inst, San Antonio, 76; O K Harris Gallery, 77 & 79; City Univ New York, 78; Contemp Am Realism Since 1960, Pa Acad Fine Arts, 81; Larry Aldrich Ctr Contemp Arts, 81; Arts Club Chicago, 86; Ruth Siegel, New York, 84 & 85. *Teaching:* Adj asst prof, Grad Div, NY Univ. *Awards:* Nat Scholastic Art Awards, Scripps Col. *Bibliog:* Alwynne Mackie (auth), New realism and the photographic look, Am Art Review, 78; Charlotte S Rubinstein (auth), American Women Artists: From Early Indian Times to Present, G K Hall/Avon, 82; Christopher Fry (auth), American Watercolors, Abbeville, 86; Stephen Westfall (auth), article, Arts Mag, 86. *Mem:* Col Art Asn; Women's Caucus Art. *Media:* Oil, Watercolor. *Mailing Add:* c/o Anthany Ralph Gallery 43 E 78th St New York NY 10021

WEBER, JAN
PAINTER
b Lafayette, Ind. *Study:* Univ NMex; pvt instructors. *Work:* Gov Mansion, Santa Fe, NMex; Bataan Mem Hosp, Albuquerque, NMex. *Exhib:* NMex Biennial, Santa Fe; El Paso Sun Carnival, Tex; travel exhib, Hoosier Art Salon, Indianapolis, Ind; Southern Colo State Col, Pueblo; NMex Arts & Crafts, Albuquerque. *Teaching:* Instr painting & drawing, Art Ctr Sch, Albuquerque, 66-69; instr painting & drawing, Kirtland AFB, 67-72; instr painting & drawing, Sandia Base, Albuquerque, 67-74. *Mem:* Artists Equity; Nat League Am Pen Women; NMex Arts & Crafts (bd mem, 74-75). *Media:* Oil, Acrylic. *Dealer:* Creative Connections 206 Dartmouth NE Albuquerque NM 87106. *Mailing Add:* 7133 Kiowa Ave NE Albuquerque NM 87110

WEBER, JEAN M
MUSEUM DIRECTOR, ADMINISTRATOR
b Boston, Mass, Apr 2, 33. *Study:* Brown Univ, BA; RI Sch Design; Edinburgh Univ; State Univ Iowa. *Collections Arranged:* The Summer Place, 70; American Impressions, 70; Commedia dell'Arte, 71; Objects & Images, 71; Tantric Art of Tibet, 72; Ceramic Arts of China, 74; Viewpoints: The American Land, 76; Fairfield Porter's Maine, 77. *Pos:* Dir, Jr Art Gallery, Louisville, Ky, 66-69; Dir, Parrish Art Mus, Southampton, NY, 69-79; vpres, NE Mus Conf, 78-79, pres, 79-80; dir, Rochester Mus & Sci Ctr, 79-81; dir, Mus NMex, 81-; co-dir, Mus Mangement Inst, Univ Calif, Berkeley, 81; adv coun, Nat Mus Act, Washington, DC, 81-82; State Dept Cultural Exchange, China Delegation, 81; trustee, Interpueblo Cult Ctr, 81-82, Brown Univ, 83-; admin hist sites, State Hist Soc Wis, 85-90; dir, Maine Maritime Mus, Woolwich, 90- *Teaching:* Adj assoc prof, Southampton Col, 70-79. *Awards:* Danforth Found Fel, 54-55; Int Mus Sem Award, NY State Coun Art, Metrop Mus, 72. *Mem:* Am Asn Mus (vpres, 85-); Int Coun Mus; NY State Asn Mus. *Publ:* Auth, articles in Am Art Rev, Museologist & Mus News. *Mailing Add:* 1 Stoneybrook Rd Phippsburg ME 04562

WEBER, JOHN
GALLERY DIRECTOR, ART DEALER
b Los Angeles, Calif, Dec 10, 32. *Study:* Antioch Col, BA, 58; Inst Fine Arts, New York Univ. *Pos:* Assoc cur, Dayton Art Inst, Ohio, 58-60; dir, Martha Jackson Gallery, New York, 60-62; dir, Dwan Gallery, Los Angeles & New York, 62-71; pres, John Weber Gallery, New York, 71-; co-owner, Galleria Weber, Alexander Y Cobo, Madrid. *Mem:* Art Dealers Am. *Specialty:* Contemporary art. *Mailing Add:* 142 Greene New York NY 10012

WEBER, JOHN PITMAN
MURALIST, PRINTMAKER
b Washington, DC, Dec 6, 42. *Study:* Harvard Col, BA(cum laude), 64; Atelier 17, Paris, with S Hayter & Jean Helion, Fulbright-Hays Scholar, 64-66; Ecole des Beaux Arts; Art Inst Chicago, with Yoshida & Halsted, MFA(painting), 68. *Work:* Cohen Libr, City Col, City Univ NY; Ruiz Belvis Cult Ctr, Chicago; Valparaiso Univ Mus Art, Ind; Col Dupage, Glen Ellyn, Ill; Ill Benedictime Col, Lisle. *Comn:* Wall of Choices (mural), Nat Endowment Arts, Christopher House Settlement, Chicago, 70; Solidarity, mural (with Jose Guerrero), United Elec Workers, Chicago, 74; Circulo Vivo (sculpture, with Lynn Takata), Youth Servs, Chicago, 81; From One Generation to Another (sculpture), City Arts, New York, 84; Life-Tree (relief, with C Cajandig), Ctr Neighborhood Tech, Chicago, 89. *Exhib:* Murals for the People, Mus of Contemp Art, Chicago, 71; Radical Attitudes Toward the Gallery, Art Net, London, Eng, 77; L'Art Public, Caen, France, 81 & Kunst und Krieg, NGBK, Berlin, WGer, 90; solo exhibs, Gallery 345, New York, 83-84; Union Theological Sem, New York, 86; Northern Ill Univ, DeKalb, 88; Valparaiso Univ, Ind, 91. *Pos:* Dir & founder, Chicago Mural Group, Chicago, 70-81. *Teaching:* From assoc prof to Genevieve Standt prof studio art & art hist, Elmhurst Col, Ill, 68-; adj asst prof mural art, Art Inst Chicago, 73-75; vis artist mural workshop, Univ NDak, Grand Forks, 75 & Dartington Col Art, Eng, 80. *Awards:* Sheffield & Barry Mural, 72, Wilton/Diversey Mural, 73 & Haas Park Mural, 76. *Bibliog:* David Craven (auth), John Pitman Weber, Arts, 11/84; Neil Mehler (auth), Elmhurst college public artist, Chicago Tribune, 6/26/86; Shifra Goldman (auth), John Pitman Weber, Tendenzen, Munich, 1-3/88. *Mem:* Alliance Cult Democracy; Nat Art Educ Asn; Chicago Pub Art Group. *Media:* Acrylic, Polychrome Concrete; Lithography, Etching. *Publ:* Toward a People's Art, The Contemporary Mural Movement, Dutton, 77; auth, Murals, an update, New Art Examiner, 5/78; Community

Sculpture, Art & Artists, 2/83; Sandinista art: Report from Managua, New Art Examiner, 10/85; auth, Art in public spaces & public art, Art J, winter 90. *Mailing Add:* c/o Elmhurst Col Art Dept 190 Prospect Ave Elmhurst IL 60126

WEBER, KAREN
PAINTER
b Philadelphia, Pa. *Study:* Univ Wis, BA; Sch Mus Fine Arts; study with Sid Willis, Robert Cormier & Richard Whitney. *Work:* MIT Mus, Cambridge, Mass; Elvehem Mus Art, Madison, Wis; Peabody Mus, Salem, Mass; Boston Pub Libr; Northeastern Univ, Boston. *Exhib:* San Bernadino Mus 20th Ann Art Exhib, Redlands, Calif, 85, 88; Shreveport 60th Nat Exhib Art, Meadows Mus Art, La, 85; Artist Mag Nat Art Exhib, Grand Cent Gallery, NY, 85; Allied Artists Am Nat Art Club, NY, 85; Salmagundi Club, NY, 85; Boston Symphony Hall, Boston, Mass, 87; 34th Nat Exhib Contemp Realism, Springfield, Mass, 88; traveling exhib throughout Calif, Long Beach Mus Art, Univ Art Mus, Calif State Univ, Los Angeles, Newport Harbor Art Mus & Laguna Beach Mus. *Awards:* First Prize in Oil, Cape Cod Art Asn, 84; Rose Lehrer Mem Award, Allied Artists Am, 85; Competition Winner, Artist Mag, 88. *Bibliog:* Gregory Thompson (auth), Am Artist Mag, National Competition Winners, 7/85; Bebe Raupe (auth), Artist Mag, 1988 Still Life Competition Winners, 12/88; Les Kranz (auth), Am Artists, 90. *Mem:* Guild of Boston Artists; Acad Artists Asn; Boston Sch Painters. *Media:* Oil, Pastel. *Dealer:* Guild of Boston Artists 162 Newbury St Boston MA 02116. *Mailing Add:* 207 Washington St, Box 484 Brookline Village MA 02147

WEBSTER, LARRY
PAINTER, PRINTMAKER
b Arlington, Mass, Mar 18, 30. *Study:* Mass Col Art, BFA; Boston Univ, MS. *Work:* DeCordova Mus, Lincoln, Mass; Grand Rapids Art Mus, Mich; Munic Gallery, Davenport, Iowa; Springfield Art Mus, Mo; Art Mus, Colby Col, Waterville, Maine; and others. *Exhib:* Am Watercolor Soc, New York, 61-88; Nat Acad Design, New York, 66-81; Rocky Mountain Nat Watermedia Exhib, 78-81. *Pos:* Package designer, Union Bag & Paper Corp, 53-54; illusr, USA, 54-56; graphic designer, vpres & dir, Thomas Todd Co, Boston, 56-78. *Teaching:* Asst prof typographic design, hist type & watercolor painting, Mass Col Art, 64-65. *Awards:* Obrig Prize, Nat Acad Design, 67 & 70; Silver Medal, Am Watercolor Soc, 68 & 72; High Winds Medal, Am Watercolor Soc, 82; and others. *Bibliog:* Susan Meyer (auth), 40 Watercolorists & How they work, Watson-Guptil, 76; Carl Schmalz (auth), Watercolor Your Way, Watson-Guptill, 78; Donald Stoltenberg (auth), The artist and the built environment, Davis Publ Inc, 80; Gerald F Brommer & Nancy K Kinne (auths), Exploring Painting, Davis Publ Inc, 88. *Mem:* Nat Acad Design; Am Watercolor Soc; Boston Watercolor Soc. *Media:* Watercolor, Mixed Media. *Mailing Add:* 116 Perkins Row Topsfield MA 01983

WEBSTER, SALLY (SARA B)
HISTORIAN
b Hammond, Ind, May 24, 38. *Study:* Barnard Col, BA, 59; Harvard-Radcliffe Prog in Business Admin, cert, 60; Univ Cincinnati, MA, 74; Grad Ctr, City Univ New York, PhD(Am art), 85. *Pos:* Dir educ, Taft Mus, Cincinnati, Ohio, 74-75; dir, AIR Gallery, New York, 79-81; partner, Rose Web Proj, New York. *Teaching:* Instr hist art, Col Staten Island, fall 83; instr hist art, Lehman Col, 83-85, asst prof, 85 & assoc prof, 90. *Mem:* Heresies Collective, New York; Col Art Asn; Arch Am Art; Asn Hist Am Art. *Publ:* A Report: Alternative Spaces and the Crisis Threatening Their Survival, Nat Endowment Arts, spring 82; The Albany Murals of William Morris Hunt: Their Commission and Meaning, NY State Capitol Symposium, 11/83; Joyce Kozloft: Public decoration, Art America, 2/87; William Morris Hunt, Cambridge Univ Press, 91; co-ed, Critical Issues in Public Art: Content, Context and Controversy, Harper Collins, 92. *Mailing Add:* 158 W 94th St New York NY 10025

WEBSTER, STOKELY
PAINTER, PRINTMAKER
b Evanston, Ill, Aug 23, 12. *Study:* With Lawton Parker, Paris, 22; Art Students League; Nat Acad Design; Yale Univ Sch Fine Arts, with Wayman Adams. *Work:* Phillips Collection, DC; Nat Collection Am Art, Washington, DC; Indianapolis Mus Art; Newark Mus, NJ; Fine Arts Mus, St Petersburg, Fla; High Mus, Atlanta, Ga; Albright-Knox Art Gallery, Buffalo, NY. *Exhib:* Nat Acad Design, New York, 45-; Salon des Artiste Francais, Paris, 70-73; Salon d'Automne, Paris, 73-74; Art Inst Chicago; solo exhibs, Eric Gallery, New York, 75, Cornell Art Mus, Winter Park, Fla, 85, Scarfone Gallery, Tampa, Fla, 85, Polk Pub Mus, Lakeland, Fla, 85, Daytona Mus Arts & Sci, 86 & Fairfield Univ, Conn, 86; Lyman Allyn Mus, New London, Conn, 89; The Mus, Stonybrook, NY 90. *Teaching:* Instr, Winter Park Artists Workshop, Stetson Univ. *Awards:* First Halgarten Prize, Nat Acad Design. *Bibliog:* Harry Rand (auth), Stokely Webster (monogr), Mus Arts & Sci, Daytona Beach, 85; Ronald G Pisano (auth), Long Island Landscape Painting Twentieth Century. *Media:* Oil; Graphic, Etching. *Dealer:* Susan Conway Galleries 1058 T Jefferson St NW Washington, DC. *Mailing Add:* 10 Harbor Rd Southport CT 06490

WECHSLER, JUDITH GLATZER
HISTORIAN, FILMMAKER
b Chicago, Ill, Dec 28, 40. *Study:* Brandeis Univ, BA, 62; Columbia Univ, MA, 67; Univ Calif, Los Angeles, PhD, 72. *Work:* Film, Daumier, Paris and the Spectator, 77, Pissarro, at the Heart of Impressionism, 81, Edouard Manet: Painter of Modern Life, 83, Mus Mod Art, Cezanne: The Late Work, Nat Gallery Art, Washington, Jasper Johns: Take an Object (with Hans Namuth). *Comn:* Film, The Training of Painters, 87, Portraits, 88, The Arrested Moment, 88, Painting and the Public, 88, Abstraction, 89, Jasper Johns: Take an Object (made with Hans Namuth), 90; Cezanne the Late Work (film), 78; Pissarro, At the Heart of Impressionism (film), 81; Edouard Manet: Painter of Modern Life (film), 83. *Collections Arranged:* Robert Moskowitz (cataloged), Mass Inst Technol Hayden Gallery, 71; Daumier: Parisian Types, Brandeis Univ, 79. *Pos:* Asst ed, Schocken Books Inc, NY, 63-65; consult, off of Charles and Ray Eames, Venice, Calif, 76-78; res fel, Ctr for Advanced Visual Studies, Mass Inst Technol, 77-79. *Teaching:* lectr, Harvard Univ, 81-82; assoc prof to prof, RI Sch Design, 81-89; vis prof, Harvard Univ, spring 89,; chmn, dept art & art hist, Tufts Univ, 90- *Awards:* Nat Endowment for Humanities fel grants, summer 73 & 75; Nat Endowment Arts, 81 & 88-90; Nat Endowment Humanities Grant, 83-84, 87-89; Cine Golden Eagle Award for Manet Film, 84 & The Artist and the Nude, 85, The Arrested Moment, 89, and Portraits, 88; Nat Endowment Humanities Grants, 84-85 & 85-86; Am Film Festival Red Ribbon Award for Portraits, 89. *Mem:* Col Art Asn. *Res:* 19th and 20th century art; film series on Western post-Renaissance art; A study of movement and time in painting and sculpture. *Publ:* Ed introd, Cezanne in Perspective, Prentice-Hall Inc, 75; auth, Gyorgy Kepes, 78, Mass Inst Tecnol Press, 78; ed introd, On aesthetics in Science, Mass Inst Tecnol Press, 78; auth, The Interpretation of Cezanne, UMI res Press, 81; A Human Comedy: Physiognomy and Caricature in 19th Century Paris, Thames & Hudson Ltd, Univ Chicago Press, 82; articles in Daedalus, Aperture, Artforum, Art News, Gazette des Beaux Arts & Studies in Visual Commnications. *Mailing Add:* Dept Art History 11 Talbot Ave Medford MA 02155

WECHSLER, SUSAN
EDITOR, WRITER
b Neptune, NJ, Sept 15, 43. *Study:* Douglass Col, Rutgers Univ, BA, 65; Teachers Col, Columbia Univ. *Exhib:* Marietta Crafts Nat, 75; solo exhib, Queens Mus, NY, 76; Women Artists: Clay, Fiber and Metal, Bronx Mus, 78 & traveling. *Collections Arranged:* Is Anybody Home? (auth, catalog), Esther Saks Gallery, Chicago, Ill, 85; The Raw Edge: Ceramics of the 80's (auth, catalog), Hillwood Art Gallery, CW Post College, Greenvale, NY. *Pos:* Photo ed, 66-; writer, 77- *Teaching:* Instr ceramic hist, Cooper Hewitt Mus/Parsons Sch Design, New York, 85-86, thesis adv, 86-87; critic-in-residence, Sch Art, Univ Tasmania, Australia, 85; vis fac, Banff Centre Sch Fine Arts, Alta, Can, 86. *Awards:* Artpark Fel, Nat Heritage Trust, 77; Nat Endowment Arts Award, 81. *Bibliog:* Mikail Zakin (auth), New York clay, Craft Horizons, 76; Elisabeth Woody (auth), Hand Building Ceramic Forms, Farrar Straus, 78; Elaine Levin (auth), A History of American Ceramics, Abrams, 88. *Mem:* Int Asn Art Critics. *Res:* Contemporary & historical ceramics; design; photography. *Publ:* Auth, Low-Fire Ceramics: A New Direction in American Clay, Watson-Guptill, 81; Views on the figure, Am Ceramics, Vol 3, No 1, 84; New breed, Am Craft, 10-11/84; The new American ceramics, ID, 5/85; Power over the clay: American Studio Potters, Detroit Inst Arts, 89. *Mailing Add:* 420 West End Ave New York NY 10024

WECHTER, VIVIENNE THAUL
EDUCATOR, PAINTER
b New York, NY. *Study:* Jamaica Teachers Col, with Hunter, BP; Columbia Univ; NY Univ; Pratt Inst; Sculpture Ctr, New York; Art Students League; with Robert Beverly Hale & de Creeft; Morris Davidson Sch Mod Art; Union Grad Sch, NY, PhD. *Work:* Corcoran Gallery Art, Washington, DC; Everson Mus, Syracuse, NY; Johnson Mus, Cornell Univ, Ithaca, NY; Notre Dame Mus, South Bend, Ind; Mus Fine Art, Houston & Ft Worth, Tex. *Comn:* The Tradition of Caring (250 bronzes), Miami Jewish Home for Aged & Hosp & Gerontology Inst; colored lithographs, comn by Atelier Eleanor Ettinger; stainless steel & brass sculpture, comn by Richard Kluger; painting, Fac Bldg New York Univ Med Ctr, 92; paintings, Wechter Room, Hebrew Home Riverdale, New York, 92. *Exhib:* Mus Mod Art, New York; Works on Paper, Pavilion D'Exposition, Paris, 75; Invitational Biennale, Mus Mod Art, Rijeka, Yugoslavia, 76, 78 & 80; solo shows, Franklin & Marshall Col, Pa, 79, Kornblatt Gallery, Baltimore, Md, Long Island Univ, 88, 45 paintings on paper, New Eng Mus Contemp Art, 91, recent works on paper, Miami Jewish Home & Hosp for the Aged, combined with Poetry Reading (Wechter Poetry), 12/92 & The Silver Dream, Provincetown Art Mus, plus Poetry Reading; Regional Invitational, City Univ New York Grad Ctr; Contemp Issues Women, traveling throughout US; Everson Mus, 80; and many others. *Pos:* Moderator weekly broadcast arts & humanities, Today's World, formerly; vpres, IAA-US Comt, UNESCO, currently; chmn & moderator symposium Influences in Art, 88. *Teaching:* Artist-in-residence, Fordham Univ, 64-, chmn acquisitions & exhibs, 64-, prof inter-arts, 67-; vis artist, Kansas City Art Inst, Marist Col, Md Inst Col Art & others. *Awards:* Am Soc Artists; Jersey City Mus; Am Acad Arts & Letts. *Bibliog:* G Brown (auth), article, 68, R Gurin (auth), article, 68 & Ronald Kuchta (auth), article, 81, Arts Mag. *Mem:* Col Art Asn Am; Fedn Mod Painters & Sculptors (vpres, currently); Am Soc Artists; Kappa Pi. *Media:* All. *Publ:* Illusr, The Park of Jonas, 67; ed, Five Museums Come to Fordham, 68; ed, Visual Fordham, 69 & 70; auth, A View From the Ark, Barlenmir House, 75; Philosophical Aspects of Thanatology, Arno Press; Art-Where Are We Today-And Why, Arts Interaction, Inc, New York. *Mailing Add:* Fac Mem Hall Fordham Univ Bronx NY 10458

WEDDIGE, EMIL A
PRINTMAKER, PAINTER
b Sandwich, Ont, Dec 23, 07; US citizen. *Study:* Eastern Mich Univ, BS; Univ Mich, MDes; Art Students League; also with Emil Ganse, Morris Kantor & E Desjobert, France; hon DFA, Eastern Mich Univ. *Work:* Metrop Mus Art, New York; Libr Cong, Washington, DC; Philadelphia Mus Art; Detroit Art Inst; Australian Nat Gallery, Canberra. *Comn:* Lithography in color, Chrysler

Motor Car Co, 55; suite of lithographs in color, Parke, Davis & Co, 56; History of Paper (suite), Dow Chem Co, 57; portrait of a city, Detroit Edison Co, 58; Sesquicentennial Suite, Univ Mich, 66. *Exhib:* Am Color Print Soc, 48-71; Print Club, 48-71; Biennial Color Print Exhib, 52 & 54; Van Gogh Mem Exhib, Pontoise, France, 60; Univ Mich Mus Art; and others. *Teaching:* Instr art, Eastern Mich Univ, 36-37; prof art, Univ Mich, Ann Arbor, 38-73, emer prof, 73- *Awards:* Founders Prize, Detroit Inst Arts, 42; Best Print Award, Am Color Print Soc, 56; James Cleating Print Prize, Michigan Exhib, 64. *Bibliog:* Working in Studio, Channel 7, ABC, Detroit, Mich, 84; James Auer (auth), forward in catalog about Emil Weddige, Milwaukee Jour, Wis; Robert Romaker (auth), Emil Weddige, Ann Arbor News, Ann Arbor, Mich. *Mem:* Am Fedn Arts; Am Color Print Soc; Print Club; Print Coun Am; Int Soc Appraisers. *Media:* Lithography; Acrylic, Oil. *Publ:* Auth, Lithography, 66; Official UNICEF Cachet, 82. *Dealer:* Arnold Klein Gallery Royal Oak MI; Roy Saper Gallery East Lansing. *Mailing Add:* 870 Stein Rd Ann Arbor MI 48103

WEDDING, WALTER JOSEPH
CERMAMICIST, EDUCATOR
b Saginaw, Mich, Feb 17, 52. *Study:* Arrowmount Sch Crafts, 69; Art Inst Chicago, 72; Mich State Univ, BFA, 76, MFA, 79. *Work:* Kresge Art Ctr, East Lansing; Mich Mus Asn, Detroit. *Comn:* Commemorative Pieces, Planters Bank, Salina, Kans, 82; Raku wall mural, City of Salina, Kans, 83. *Exhib:* Mid-Mich Arts, Midland Art Ctr, 79; Kansas Artists, Governor's Mansion, Topeka, 81. *Pos:* Coordr photog, Salina Arts Comn, Kans, 85. *Teaching:* Instr clay, Mich State Univ, East Lansing, 79-80; asst prof photog, Marymount Col, Kans, 80-86. *Mem:* Col Art Asn; Nat Asn Ceramic Educ. *Media:* Clay. *Mailing Add:* 1708 Illinois St Lawrence KS 66044

WEEDMAN, KENNETH RUSSELL
PAINTER, SCULPTOR
b Little Rock, Ark, Sept 26, 39. *Study:* Memphis Acad Art; Univ Tulsa, BA & MA. *Work:* Cincinnati Mus Art, Ohio; Masur Mus Art, Monroe, La; Ark Art Ctr, Little Rock; Baldwin-Wallace Art & Drama Ctr, Berea, Ohio; Mus de Arte Contemporanea International, Salvador, Brazil; Museu de Arte Contemporanea, Salvador, Brasil; Internacional De Gravure Arte, Cabo Frio, Brasil. *Exhib:* Conn Acad, Wadsworth Atheneum Mus, 66; Artist of Southeast & Tex Biennials, New Orleans City Art Mus, 66, 71 & 75; Past Jurors, Okla Art Ctr, Oklahoma City, 69; one-man shows, Bienville Gallery, New Orleans, 71 & Art & Drama Ctr Galleries, Baldwin-Wallace Col, 73; Prints: Made in Kentucky, Louisville Art Gallery, 83; Cabo Frio Int Print Biennial, Brazil, 85-86; Papelarte Int, Brazil, 86; Showcase '87, Water Tower Gallery, Louisville, Ky, 87. *Pos:* Ed, Sculpture Quart, Southern Asn Sculptures, 74-75; cur, Cumberland Col, 81- *Teaching:* Instr sculpture, Sul Ross State Col, Alpine, Tex, 65-66; prof sculpture, Cumberland Col, Williamsburg, Ky, 68-; vis artist, Nicholls State Univ, Thiobodaux, La, 70-71. *Awards:* Award of Merit for Sculpture, Univ Tulsa, 64 & Nebr Wesleyan Univ, 66; Andrew Mellon Found Grant, 88; Lilly Found Grant, 89. *Bibliog:* Harold D Cole (auth), Kenneth Weedman, Baldwin-Wallace Col, 73; Dona Z Meilach (auth), Soft Sculpture, Crown Publ, 74; Les Kantz (ed), Am Artists, Kantz Publ, 85. *Mem:* Col Art Asn of Am. *Media:* Plastic, Steel; Acrylic, Oil. *Publ:* Contribr, Sculpture Quart, 74 & 75; Dialogue, 7-8/88. *Mailing Add:* 191 Florence Williamsburg KY 40769

WEEGE, WILLIAM
PRINTMAKER, EDUCATOR
b Milwaukee, Wis. *Study:* Univ Wis-Milwaukee; Univ Wis-Madison, MA, 67, MFA, 68. *Work:* Akron Art Inst; Brooklyn Mus; Art Inst Chicago; Frankfurt Libr, Ger; Mus Mod Art, New York; plus many others. *Exhib:* Mechanics in Printmaking, 70 & Artist as Adversary, 70, Mus Mod Art, New York; Large Print Show, Whitney Mus Am Art, New York, 71; Works on Paper, Alice Simsar Gallery, Ann Arbor, Mich, 79, Inst for Experimental Printmaking, San Francisco, 79 & Circle Campus, Chicago, 79; Artrain, Mich Arts Coun, 79; Jones Road Print Shop, Univ of Mich, Kalamazoo, Mich, 79; Paper as Medium, Smithsonian Inst, 79-80; and many others. *Teaching:* From instr lettering to assoc prof art, Univ Wis-Madison, 67-80. *Bibliog:* Article, Arts, 1/78; article, Art News, 2/78. *Mailing Add:* c/o Grace Chosy Gallery 218 N Henry St Madison WI 53703

WEEKES, SHIRLEY MARIE
PAINTER
b Buffalo, NY, May 9, 17. *Study:* Detroit Art Acad; Detroit Soc Arts & Crafts; Burnley Sch Prof Art, Seattle, Wash; Univ Wash with Fred Anderson; also with Sergei Bongart (award of scholar); Master Painter Prog with Carl Morris, Port Townsend, Wash. *Work:* Charles & Emma Frye Mus, Seattle; Washington Mutual Bank Collection; Craftsman Press Collection; Laguna Beach Mus Art, Va; Va Steele Scott Collection, Laguna Beach, Calif. *Exhib:* One-woman shows, Frye Mus, Seattle, 67 & 72, Challis Galleries, Laguna Beach, Calif, 70, 72 & 74 & Haines Gallery, Seattle, 73 & 75; Frye Mus, Seattle, 65-69 & 71-75; Okla Mus of Art, 77; Laguna Beach Mus Art, 80; and others. *Awards:* Craftsman Press Award, Craftsman Press, 65; 7th Ann Puget Sound Show, Frye Mus, Seattle, 65 & West Coast Oil Show, 68; Northwest Watercolor Show, Northwest Watercolor Soc, 72. *Mem:* San Diego Watercolor Soc; Northwest Watercolor Soc. *Media:* Acrylic, Watercolor. *Dealer:* Challis Galleries 1390 S Coast Hwy Laguna Beach CA 92653. *Mailing Add:* 5093 Aegina Way Oceanside CA 92056

WEEKS, EDWARD F (TED)
HISTORIAN, CONSULTANT
b Boston, Mass. *Study:* Goethe Inst, Graffing, Ger, cert, 61; Columbia Univ, BS(art hist), 62; Inst Fine Arts, NY Univ, MA, 70, with Robert Goldwater & Colin Eisler; Inst Arts Admin, Harvard Univ, cert, 73. *Pos:* Asst dir, Cummer Gallery Art, Jacksonville, Fla, 62-65; exec asst to dir, Albright-Knox Art Gallery, Buffalo, NY, 67-69; selector, Am Fedn Arts Mus Purchase Fund Collection, 68; cur, High Mus Art, Atlanta, Ga, 69-70; cur, Birmingham Mus Art, Ala, 70-85; guest art critic, Birmingham News, 70-; art consult, Downtown Club Collection, 73-, Eye Found Hosp, 73- & Birmingham Civic Ctr, 74-; founder & past secy, Friends Am Art, Birmingham, Ala, 82, Weeks Fine Arts & Art Consultants Int, 85. *Teaching:* Hist mod sculpture, Univ Ala, Birmingham, spring 75, art hist, French & Am, Auburn Univ, Montgomery, winter-spring, 88 & Montgomery Sch Fine Arts, summer, 88; Master Prints and Drawings since 15th Cent. *Mem:* Nat Inst Arts & Lett; Am Asn Mus; Southeastern Mus Asn; Col Art Asn Am; Birmingham Festival Arts. *Res:* Western paintings and sculpture since 1400; twentieth century sculpture and painting; Flemish and Dutch painting, 1500-1630; Am Art, 19th & 20th century. *Interests:* Organizing major Old Master exhibits from American collections. *Collection:* American paintings, watercolors, prints and photography, nineteenth and twentieth centuries; Pre-Columbian art. *Publ:* Auth, The Tiepolos: Painters to Princess & Prelates (exhib catalog), 78; Ken Snelson: Structures (exhib catalog), 80; Romare Bearden: Jazz (exhib catalog), 82; coauth (with Rich N Murray), Art of the American West, 83; contribr, Birmingham Ala Mus Art Handbook, 83. *Mailing Add:* 1786 Challan Ave Jacksonville FL 32205

WEEKS, JAMES (DARRELL NORTHRUP)
PAINTER, ART DEALER
b Oakland, Calif, Dec 1, 22. *Study:* Calif Sch Fine Arts, 40-42 & 46-48; Hartwell Sch Design, 47; Escuela Pintura, Mexico City. *Work:* Corcoran Gallery Art, Washington, DC; San Francisco Mus Art; Am Fedn Art, New York; Howard Univ, Washington, DC; Oakland Mus. *Comn:* America 76 (painting), US Dept of the Interior traveling exhib, 76; painting, Boston 200 Bicentennial Exhib, 76. *Exhib:* Corcoran Gallery, 63; Carnegie Int, Pittsburgh, 64; one-man shows, San Francisco Mus Art, 65 & Boston Univ Art Gallery, 71; Expo '70, Osaka, Japan; Calif Painting & Sculpture--The Mod Era, San Francisco Mus Art & Corcoran Gallery, Washington, DC, 76; James Weeks 30 Yr Retrospective--Paintings & Drawings, Brandeis Univ & Oakland Mus, 78. *Teaching:* At San Francisco Art Inst, 58-67 & Univ Calif, Los Angeles, 67-70; assoc prof grad painting, Boston Univ, 70-81, prof, 81-; vis artist, Yale Univ, 79 & 81. *Awards:* Nat Endowment Arts grant/painting, 77-78; Purchase Award, Am Inst Arts & Letters, 80. *Bibliog:* A Ventura (auth), James Weeks: the plain path, Arts Mag, 2/64; James Weeks, paintings, Felix Landau Gallery, 64. *Media:* Acrylic, Oil. *Dealer:* Hirschl & Adler Gallery 21 E 70th St New York NY 10021. *Mailing Add:* c/o Charles Campbell Gallery 647 Chestnut St San Francisco CA 94133

WEEMS, CARRIE MAE
PHOTOGRAPHER
Study: Calif Inst Arts, Valencia, BA, 81; Univ Calif, San Diego, MFA, 84; Univ Calif, Berkeley, Grad Prog Folklore, 84-87. *Exhib:* One-person exhibs, Inst Contemp Art, 91, Trustman Gallery, Simmons Col, Boston, Mass, 91, The New Mus Contemp Art, New York, 91, Matrix Gallery, Wadsworth Atheneum, Hartford, Conn, 91, Albright Col, Reading, Pa, 91, Greenville Co Mus Art, SC, 92, San Francisco Art Inst, Calif, 92; Reframing the Family, Artists Space, 91, Whitney Biennial, The Whitney Mus Am Art, 91, Mus Mod Art, 92, Randy Alexander, 92, Artists of Conscience: 16 Years of Social & Political Commentary, Alternative Mus, New York, 91-92; Affirmative Re-Actions, Col Holy Cross, Worcester, Mass, 91; Outspoken Women, Intermedia Arts, Minneapolis, Minn, 91; Through the Kitchen Door, NAME, 91-92, Disclosing the Myth of Family, Art Inst Chicago, The Betty Rymer Gallery, Chicago, 92; Present Tense, Fine Arts Ctr, Univ Wis, Milwaukee, 92; Mis/Taken Identities, Univ Art Mus, Univ Calif, Santa Barbara, 92-93; Fictions of the Self: The Portrait in Contemporary Photography, Weatherspoon Art Gallery, Greensboro, NC, 92-93; Carrie Mae Weems, traveling one-person exhib, 93-94. *Teaching:* Asst prof, Hampshire Col, Amherst, Mass, 87-91, Calif Col Arts & Crafts, Oakland, 91; vis prof, Hunter Col, New York, 88-89. *Mailing Add:* 14 Randolph Pl No B Northampton MA 01060

WEGMAN, WILLIAM
PAINTER, PHOTOGRAPHER
b Holyoke, Mass, Dec 2, 43. *Study:* Mass Col Art, Boston, BFA, 65; Univ Ill, Urbana-Champaign, MFA, 67. *Work:* Brooklyn Mus, Mus Mod Art, Whitney Mus Am Art, Chrysler Mus, New York; Mus Mod Art, Paris; Los Angeles Co Mus Art; Int Mus Photog, Rochester, NY; Honolulu Acad Arts; Abright-Knox Gallery, Buffalo; Carnegie Inst, Mus Art, Pittsburgh; Corcoran Gallery Art, Washington, DC; Minneapolis Inst Art, Walker Art Ctr, Minneapolis; Mus Fine Art, De Meril Collection, Houston; Newport Harbor Mus, San Francisco Mus Mod Art, Stewart Collection, Univ Calif, San Diego, Calif; St Louis Mus Mod Art. *Comn:* Semi-buffet color video tape, WGBH, Boston, 74-75; video tape rev, Channel 13, WNET, New York, 75. *Exhib:* William Wegman: Selected Works 1970-1979, Univ Colo Art Gallery, Boulder, 80; Penthouse Exhib, Mus Mod Art, New York, 80; Morton C Newmann Family Collection, Art Inst Chicago, 81; one-man exhibs, Honolulu Acad Arts, 87, McIntosh/Drysdale Gallery, Washington, DC, 87, Solo Gallery, NY 88, San Francisco Mus Mod Art, 88, Galerie Durand-Dessert, Paris, 89, Lisa Sette Gallery, Scottsdale, Ariz, 90; Biennial exhib, Whitney Mus Am Art (with catalog), New York, 81 & 89; Photography Now (catalog), Victoria & Albert Mus, London, 89; Sesame Street: The First Generation, Mus Mod Art, New York, 89; Photography Until Now (catalog), Mus Mod Art, New York & Cleveland Mus Art, 90; Menagerie, Mus Mod Art, New York, 90; Paintings, Drawings, Photographs, Videotapes (catalog), traveling, 90-91; Neuberger Mus, State Univ NY, Purchase, 91; Retrospective (with catalog),

Photographic Works, 1969-76, Fonds Regional d'Art Contemp du Limoges, Limousin, Limoges, France, 91; 4e Semaine Int de Video (with catalog), Geneva, 91. *Teaching:* Univ Wis, 68-70; Cal State Univ, Long Beach, 70. *Awards:* Guggenheim Fel, 75 & 86; Nat Endowment Arts Grant, 75-76 & 82; Creative Artists Pub Serv, 79. *Bibliog:* Brooks Adams (auth), Wegman unleashed, Art News, Vol 89 No 1, 1/90; Martin Kunz (auth), Willim Wegman: Paintings, Drawings, Photographs, Videotapes, Harry Abrams Inc, 90; Christopher Knight (auth), William Wegman goes back to the future, Los Angeles Times, 4/11/90. *Publ:* Auth, Pathetic readings, Avalanche Mag, 74; coauth, Man's Best Friend, Abrams, 82; cover & photography, Esquire Mag, 10/87. *Dealer:* Holly Solomon Gallery 724 Fifth Ave New York NY 10019. *Mailing Add:* 431 E 6th St New York NY 10009

WEGMANN, M K (MARY KATHERINE)
CONSULTANT, ADMINISTRATOR
b New Orleans, La, Sept 18, 48. *Study:* Spring Hill Col, BA, 70; Univ New Orleans, MA, 72. *Pos:* Assoc dir, Contemp Arts Ctr, New Orleans, 77-91. *Awards:* Mayor's Arts Award, Arts Coun New Orleans, 90. *Mem:* Nat Asn Artists Orgns (pres, 82-85); Cult Communs (treas, 82-89); Junebug Productions (treas, 82-90); Alternate Roots (chairperson, 88-90). *Publ:* Auth, Fostering the Process, Art & Artists, 84; Non Profit Thinking, Art Papers, 87; Artists' Organizations Involvement in the Arts Community as a Whole, NAAD Bull, 88. *Mailing Add:* 2019 Chartres St New Orleans LA 70116

WEGNER, NADENE R
GOLDSMITH, CONSULTANT
b Sheboygan, Wis, Feb 18, 50. *Study:* Univ Wis-Milwaukee, BFA, 72; Tyler Sch Art, Temple Univ, MFA, 75. *Work:* Tyler Sch Art, Temple Univ, Philadelphia, Pa; Kentucky Fried Chicken, Louisville, Ky. *Exhib:* Craftwork 76, Metrop Mus & Art, Ctr Miami, Fla, 76; Intent: Jewelry-Metal, Edinboro, Pa, 76; Women's Art Symp, Terre Haute, Ind, 77; Copper, Brass & Bronze Competition Tucson, Ariz, 77; Profiles of US Jewelry, Lubbock, Tex, 77; and others. *Teaching:* Asst prof metalsmithing & Jewelry, Louisville Sch Art, Ky, 75-83; tooling mgr, Bruce Fox, Inc, New Albany, Ind, currently. *Awards:* First Prize, Second & Third Nat Ring Show, Athens, Ga; Award, Copper II Exhib, 80. *Bibliog:* Metalsmithing USA, 75 & New York Metal, 76, Craft Horizons; Marcia Chamberlain (auth), Metal Jewelry Techniques, Watson-Guptill, 76. *Mem:* Am Crafts Coun; distinguished mem Soc NAm Goldsmiths. *Media:* Precious Metals, Precious Woods. *Mailing Add:* Bruce Fox Inc PO Box 89 New Albany IN 47150

WEHR, WESLEY CONRAD
PAINTER, PALEONTOLOGIST
b Everett, Wash, Apr 17, 29. *Study:* Univ Wash, BA & MA; also with Mark Tobey. *Work:* Munic Gallery Mod Art, Dublin, Ireland; Boymans-Van Beuningen Mus, Rotterdam; Nat Mus Am Art, Smithsonian Inst; Baltimore Mus; Minneapolis Inst Arts. *Exhib:* Gallerie Rosenau, Bern, Switz, 76; Belcher Gallery, San Francisco, 79; one-man show, Expo 8, Basel, Switz, 77; retrospective, Art Gallery Greater Victoria, BC, 80; Woodside-Braseth Gallery, Seattle, Wash, 86-91; Cheney Cowles Mus, Spokane, Wash, 91; Pulliam-Nugent Gallery, Portland, Ore, 92; and others. *Pos:* Affl cur paleontology, Burke Mus, Univ Wash, Seattle. *Media:* Mixed. *Publ:* Conversations with Mark Tobey, Northwest Arts, 76-79; Elizabeth Bishop: Conversations and Classnotes, Antioch Review, summer 81. *Mailing Add:* Wash State Mus Univ of Wash Seattle WA 98195

WEIDMAN, JEFFREY
LIBRARIAN, HISTORIAN
b New York, NY, Feb 17, 45. *Study:* Hamilton Col, Clinton, NY, AB, 67; Ind Univ, Bloomington, with Albert Elsen & John Jacobus, MA(art hist), 69, with Louis Hawes, PhD(art hist, Samuel H Kress Fel), 82, MLS, 82. *Collections Arranged:* H P Lovecraft, Lilly Libr, Ind Univ, Bloomington, 82; William Rimmer: A Yankee Michelangelo (auth, catalog), Brockton Art Mus, Mass, 85-86; William Rimmer, Cleveland Mus Art & Brooklyn Mus, 86. *Pos:* Art librn, Clarence Ward Art Libr, Oberlin Col, Ohio, 83- *Teaching:* Assoc instr art hist, Ind Univ, Bloomington, 68, 72-74 & 76. *Awards:* Gerd Muehsam Award, Art Libr Soc NAm, 83. *Bibliog:* Milo M Naeve (auth), A picture and sculpture by William Rimmer, Bull Art Inst Chicago, 77; Lewis Shepard (auth), American Art at Amherst, Wesleyan Univ Press, 78; Brockton's Artistic Heritage, Brockton Art Mus, 81. *Mem:* Acad Libr Asn, Ohio; Am Libr Asn; Art Libr Soc NAm; Col Art Asn; Midwest Art Hist Soc. *Res:* Nineteenth century American art, especially the work of William Rimmer. *Interests:* Classical, Baroque, British and American eighteenth to twentieth century art, especially American painting and sculpture of the nineteenth century; art reference materials. *Publ:* Auth, Reclassification of the Hamilton College Portraits, Hamilton Col, 67; contribr, Seymour Lipton, Harry Abrams, 70; contribr, The Art Institute of Chicago Centennial Lectures, Contemp Bks, 83. *Mailing Add:* Clarence Ward Art Libr Allen Art Bldg Oberlin Col Oberlin OH 44074

WEIDNER, MARILYN KEMP
CONSERVATOR, LECTURER
b Floral Park, NY, Jan 10, 28. *Study:* Pratt Inst; Hofstra Univ, BA; Univ Pa; Metrop Mus Art; Freer Gallery Art. *Pos:* Asst registrar, Mus Mod Art, New York, 51-56; registrar, Brooklyn Mus, 56-58; conservator, pvt practice, Philadelphia, 60-79 & 84-; dir, Conserv Ctr Art & Hist Artifacts, Philadelphia, 77-84; adj conservator, Art Mus, Princeton Univ, 86- *Teaching:* Adj prof conserv art on paper, NY State Univ, Cooperstown Grad Progs, 71-74. *Awards:* Certified Conservator of Historic & Artistic Works on Paper, 75; Rutherford John Gettens Merit Award, Am Inst Conserv, 90. *Bibliog:* George W Cooke (auth), Marilyn Kemp Weidner pioneer paper conservator, Conserv Admin News, 7/92. *Mem:* Fel Int Inst Conserv Art & Hist Artifacts; Am Inst Conserv Art & Hist Artifacts; Inst Paper Conserv, London; Mus Coun Philadelphia; Nat Inst Conserv Cult Property. *Media:* Art on Paper. *Res:* Moisture chamber, suction table and related techniques for the conservation treatment of art on paper. *Publ:* Contribr, Damage and deterioration of art on paper, In: Studies in Conservation, Int Inst Conserv Art & Hist Artifacts, 67; Repair of Wall Charts from Cloister Edhrata, Pa Conserv & Restoration of Pictorial Art, Butterworth's, 76; Regional Conservation Center Movement in US, Theatre Libr Asn, 82; Water Treatments and Their Uses with a Moisture Chamber on the Suction Table, Am Inst Conserv Arts & Hist Artifacts Preprints, 85; Conservation Management, Getty Conserv Inst, 88. *Mailing Add:* 612 Spruce St Philadelphia PA 19106

WEIDNER, MARY ELIZABETH
PAINTER, EDUCATOR
b St Louis, Mo, June 10, 50. *Study:* Sch Fine Arts, Washington Univ, St Louis, Mo, BFA(fel), 72, MFA, 75. *Work:* Papercraft Corp, F B Foster Corp & Carnegie-Mellon Univ, Pittsburgh. *Exhib:* Butler Inst Am Art, Youngstown, Ohio, 77, 79 & 80; William Penn Mem Mus, Harrisburg, Pa, 80; Broussard Mem Galleries, Baton Rouge, La, 80; Carnegie Inst Mus Art, Pittsburgh, 81; Coos Mus Art, Coos Bay, Ore, 81; Herman Fine Arts Ctr, Marietta, Ohio, 81; and many others. *Teaching:* Lectr, Grinnell Col, Iowa, 75-76; instr, Carnegie-Mellon Univ, Pittsburgh, 76-78, asst prof, 78- *Bibliog:* The Art of Drawing, Purdue Univ, 79. *Mem:* Col Art Asn; Women's Caucus Art; Assoc Artists Pittsburgh. *Media:* Oil, Colored Pencil. *Dealer:* Baker Gallery 828 Prospect St La Jolla CA 92037. *Mailing Add:* Dept Art Carnegie-Mellon Univ 5000 Forbes Ave Pittsburgh PA 15213

WEIDNER, ROSWELL THEODORE
PAINTER, INSTRUCTOR
b Reading, Pa, Sept 18, 11. *Study:* Pa Acad Fine Arts, Cresson For Traveling Scholar, 35; Barnes Found, Merion, Pa. *Work:* Pa Acad Fine Arts, Philadelphia Mus Art, Philadelphia Maritime Mus, Philadelphia; Metrop Mus Art, New York; Libr Cong, Washington, DC. *Comn:* Portrait, Herman Beerman, Univ, Pa, 68,; portrait, Robert C Sale, Conn State Libr, Hartford, 69; portrait, Clair R McCollough, Nat Asn Broadcasters, Washington, DC, 70; portrait, Albert M Kligman, Univ Pa, 84; portrait, Stanley H Lorber, Temple Univ, 86. *Exhib:* Pa Acad Fine Arts Ann, Philadelphia, 36-70; Directions Am Painting, Carnegie Inst, Pittsburgh, Pa, 43; Drawing Soc Second Eastern Cent Exhib, Philadelphia Mus Art, 70; 24th Am Drawing Biennial, Norfolk Mus Arts & Sci, Va & Smithsonian Traveling Exhib, 71; one-man exhib, Newman Galleries, Philadelphia, 78 & 87 & Marian Locks Gallery, Philadelphia, 81. *Teaching:* Sr instr painting, Pa Acad Fine Arts, 38-; instr painting, Philadelphia Col Art, 49-51. *Awards:* Fel prize, Pa Acad Fine Arts Ann, 43; Dawson Mem Medal, Philadelphia Watercolor Club, 64, 72 & 76; Percy Owens Award, 75. *Bibliog:* William P Scott (auth), Roswell Weidner: painting in the Pine Barrens, Am Artist, 12/81. *Mem:* Fel Pa Acad Fine Arts (pres, 54-67, vpres, 67-72); Philadelphia Watercolor Club (bd dirs, 65-72); Artists Equity Asn. *Media:* Oil, Pastel. *Dealer:* Newman Galleries 1625 Walnut St Philadelphia PA 19103. *Mailing Add:* 612 Spruce St Philadelphia PA 19106

WEIGAND, HERBERT MICHAEL
PAINTER, EDUCATOR
b New York, NY, Oct 4, 51. *Study:* Long Island Univ, Southampton Col, BA, 73; Syracuse Univ, MFA, 79; Pa State Univ, PhD, 84. *Work:* Hoyt Inst Fine Arts, New Castle, Pa; Waccamaw Arts & Crafts Guild, Myrtle Beach, SC; Women's Med Ctr, Conway, SC; State System Higher Education, Harrisburg, Pa; E Stroudsburg Univ, Pa. *Exhib:* Kansas II Nat Painting & Drawing Exhib, Ft Hayes State Univ, 86; Ninth Ann Open Competition, Long Beach Mus Art, Calif, 87; one-man show, Bratton Gallery, New York, 88; 20th Nat Painting Show, Washington & Jefferson Col, Washington, Pa, 88; Hoyt Nat Drawing & Painting Show, Hoyt Inst Fine Art, New Castle, Pa, 89; Three Rivers Art Festival, Carnegie Mus Art, Pittsburgh, 90. *Pos:* Dir, Powers Art Gallery, E Stroudsburg Univ, Pa, 89- *Teaching:* Asst prof art (painting & drawing), Univ SC, Coastal Carolina Col, Conway, 84-86, E Stroudsburg Univ, Pa, 86- *Awards:* First Place Purchase Award, Waccamaw Arts & Craft Guild, 86 & Fisher Big Wheel, 89; First Place Award of Excellence, Long Beach Mus Art, 87. *Bibliog:* Donna Clemson (auth), Alumni Arts Exchange, Penn State Mag, 10/88; Susan Koomar (auth), Friday night at the FHB, Stroud Courier, 2/88; David Guenther (auth), Artists present the figure, Pittsburg Press, 1/89. *Mem:* Orgn Independent Artists; Asn Univ Galleries & Mus; Nat Art Educ Asn (Higher educ coordr-SC Chap, 86); Col Art Asn; Artists Space. *Publ:* Auth, From science into art--art education, Nat Art Educ Asn, 11/85. *Dealer:* Steve Mendelson 5874 Ellsworth Ave Pittsburgh PA 15232. *Mailing Add:* 163 Grove St East Stroudsburg PA 18301

WEIHS, ERIKA
PAINTER, ILLUSTRATOR-CHILDREN BOOKS
b Vienna, Austria, Nov 4, 17; Nat US. *Study:* Graphiche Lehr und Versuchsanstalt, Vienna, 37. *Work:* Mus City New York, New York Hist Soc & Schomberg Ctr Res Black Cult, New York; Butler Inst Am Art, Youngstown, Ohio; Slater Mem Mus, Norwich, Conn; Cape Ann Hist Asn, Gloucester, Mass. *Exhib:* Fall Collection 1987, Monmouth Mus, NJ, 87; solo show, Pleiades Gallery, 89; Small Works, New York Univ Washington Square E Gallery, 89; Mus Nat Arts Found, 89; twelve solo shows: retrospective 1941-1991, Pleiades Gallery, New York; and others. *Awards:* Charlotte Whinston Prize, 84 & Elizabeth Stanton Blake Award, 87 Nat Asn Women Artists. *Bibliog:* Roy Moyer (auth), The Paintings of Erika Weihs, 91. *Mem:* NAWA; Audubon Artists; ASCA; NY Artists Equity. *Media:* Oil. *Publ:* Illusr, Cakes and Miracles, Viking, 91; Days of Awe, Viking, 91; How a Shirt Grew in the Field, Clarion Books, 92; and others. *Mailing Add:* 41 Union Sq W Studio 1526 New York NY 10003

WEIL, LISL
ILLUSTRATOR, WRITER
b Vienna, Austria; US citizen. *Pos:* Auth & illusr of over 140 children's books; concert illusr with major symphony orchestras, US; concert illus on nationwide TV specials, movie films & schools. *Mailing Add:* 25 Central Park W New York NY 10023

WEIL, STEPHEN E
MUSEUM DIRECTOR, LECTURER
b New York, NY, June 24, 28. *Study:* Brown Univ, AB, 49; Columbia Univ, LLB, 56. *Pos:* Vpres & gen mgr, Marlborough-Gerson Gallery, New York, 63-67; adminr, Whitney Mus Am Art, New York, 67-74; deputy dir, Hirshhorn Mus & Sculpture Garden, Smithsonian Inst, 74- *Teaching:* Sr mus assoc & fac mem, Mus Mgt Inst, Berkeley, Calif, 79- *Awards:* 1987 Scribes Book Award, Am Soc Writers on Legal Subjects, 87; Katherine Coffey Award, Mid-Atlantic Asn Mus, 90; Dudley Wilkinson Award, Registrars Comt Am Asn Mus, 92. *Mem:* Am Asn Mus (coun mem & treas, 75-79, vpres, 79-82); Art Mus Asn Am (mem bd, 82-87); Int Found Art Research (mem bd, 79-91); Volunteer Lawyers Arts, NY (mem adv bd, 75-); Am Fedn Arts (mem bd, 87-). *Publ:* Auth var articles in Art News, Art in Am, Law Libr J, Mus News & Print Collectors Newsletter, 70-88; co-ed, Legal & Business Problems of Artists, Art Galleries & Museums, 73 & coauth, Art Works: Law, Policy, Practice, 74, Practising Law Inst; auth, Beauty and the Beasts, Smithsonian Inst Press, 83; coauth, Art Law, Little, Brown, 86; auth, Rethinking the Museum, Smithsonian Press, 90. *Mailing Add:* Hirshhorn Mus & Sculpture Garden Smithsonian Inst Washington DC 20560

WEILER, JOSEPH FLACK
PHOTOGRAPHER, WRITER
b Rockville Center, New York, 43. *Study:* With Minor White, 65; Rochester Inst Technol, Sch Printing, AAS, 63, RIT Sch Photog, BFA, 72. *Exhib:* Faces of Afghanistan, Berkshire Mus, Pittsfield, Mass, 81; 25-Year retrospective, Gordon Col, Wenham, Mass, 91. *Pos:* Dir, Flack Studio, Watertown, Mass, 68- *Teaching:* Instr photog, NEng Sch Photog, Boston, Mass, 78 & Gallery Seven, Gloucester, Mass, 92. *Awards:* New Eng Book Show Award, Reprise, 75 & Encore, 76; First Place Award, 9th Open Photog, Salmagundi Club, 90. *Mem:* Copley Soc Boston; Rockport Art Assoc; Salmagundi Club. *Media:* Gelatin Silver Print, Color Retaglio Photos. *Publ:* Illusr, Debuts, 74, Reprise, 75, Encore, 76, Allyn & Bacon; auth, Winslow Homer: Marine Painter, J Print World, 90; A Gift from Mr Alfred Stieglitz, J Print World, 91; Tarmarind Workshop at Thirty, J Print World, 91; The Tachach Press, J Print World, 92. *Dealer:* Gallery Seven 77 Rocky Neck Ave East Gloucester MA 01930. *Mailing Add:* 288 Lexington St Watertown MA 02172

WEILER, MELODY M
ADMINISTRATOR, EDUCATOR
b Santa Monica, Calif, Mar 4, 47. *Study:* State Univ NY, Buffalo, BFA; Ohio Univ, MFA; also with Harvey Breverman, Seymour Drumlevitch, Donald Roberts & Harvey Daniels. *Work:* Ohio Univ, Athens; Kemper Gallery, Kansas City, Mo. *Comn:* Ceramic & screened mural, Ohio Univ, Athens, 70-71; cover design, Glass Eye Productions, Los Angeles, 76; posters, Hollins Col, Va & Murray State Univ, Ky, 76-77. *Exhib:* Western NY Art Exhib, Albright-Knox Art Gallery, Buffalo, 69; Nelson-Atkins Art Mus, Kansas City, Mo, 74; Huber Gallery, Washington, DC, 79; Lake Placid Sch Art, NY, 79; Imagery Gallery, Jacksonville, Fla, 79; Southeastern Ctr for Contemp Art, Winston-Salem, NC, 79; Appalachian Ctr for Crafts, Cookeville, Tenn, 80; and others. *Pos:* Pres-elect, Ky Arts Adminrs, 88-89. *Teaching:* Instr printmaking/design, Atlanta Sch of Art, Ga, 71-72; instr found design, Kansas City Art Inst, Mo, 72-73; asst prof printmaking, Murray State Univ, 75-78, assoc prof, 78- *Awards:* Res grant, Hand Papermaking, Murray State Univ, 76-77 & 77-78; Nat Endowment Arts Grants, 77 & 78. *Mem:* Col Art Asn; Ctr for the Bk Arts; World Print Coun; Int Paper Historians. *Media:* Papermaking; Serigraphy. *Publ:* Contribr, Exploring Printmaking for Young People, Van Nostrand Reinhold, 72; photogr, The Painted Vega, 75 & illusr, cover design, Southern Exposure, 76, Glass Eye Productions; contribr, Washingtonian Mag, 78 & Art Craft, 2-3/80. *Mailing Add:* Dept of Art Tex Tech Univ PO Box 42081 Lubbock TX 79409-2081

WEILL, ERNA
SCULPTOR, INSTRUCTOR
b Frankfurt am Main, Ger; US citizen. *Study:* Univ Frankfurt, with Helene von Beckerath; also with John Hovannes, New York. *Work:* Ga Mus Art, Athens; Birmingham Mus, Ala; Jewish Mus, New York; Hyde Park Libr, New York; Israel Mus, Hebrew Univ, Jerusalem; Tel Aviv Mus, Israel; and others. *Comn:* Bronze portrait sculpture, Linus Pauling; portrait, Portda Valley, Calif, Martin Buber, Hebrew Univ, Leonard Bernstein, Dr Martin Luther King & Elie Wiesel; and others. *Exhib:* New York World's Fair; NJ State Mus, Trenton; Brooklyn Mus; Montclair Mus; Newark Mus; one-man shows, Carlebach Gallery, Schoeneman Galleries, UAHC Gallery, New York & Bergen Community Mus, NJ. *Teaching:* Instr sculpture, Brooklyn Mus, Forest Hills Pub Schs, Forest Hills Jewish Ctr & Teaneck Jewish Ctr; instr sculpture, Adult Educ Prog, Ft Lee, NJ; pvt instr, sculpture; lectr, Fairleigh Dickinson Univ; lecturer various clubs & temples, NJ. *Awards:* Mem Found Jewish Cult grant for relig sculpture; Best in Sculpture, Artist-Craftsman, New York, 75; incl in the Archives of the Smithsonian, 83; Resolution of honor, Senate of the State of New Jersey, 83. *Bibliog:* Bernard Buranelli (auth), World of Erna Weill, Rec Mag, 64; Avram Kampf (auth), Contemporary synagogue art, Union Am Hebrew Congregations, 65. *Mem:* Artists Equity Asn New York; New York Soc Artists Craftsmen; Mod Artists Guild, NJ; Sculptors Affil Art Ctr. *Media:* Miscellaneous Media. *Publ:* Auth, Any child can model in clay, Design; coauth, article, Crisis, 10/65; contribr, Libr J & NJ Educ Rev. *Mailing Add:* 886 Alpine Dr Teaneck NJ 07666

WEINBAUM, JEAN
PAINTER, SCULPTOR
b Zurich, Switz, 1926. *Study:* Zurich Sch Fine Arts, 42-46; Acad Grande Chaumiere; Ecole Paul Colin; Acad Andre L'Hote, 47-48. *Work:* Mus Mod Art, Paris, France; Nat Collection Fine Arts, Washington, DC; Univ Art Mus, Berkeley, Calif; Stanford Univ Mus, Calif; Calif Palace Legion Honor, San Francisco. *Comn:* Eleven stained glass windows, Chapelle de Mosloy, 51; rosette stained glass, Berne sur Oise, 55; 22 stained glass windows, St Pierre du Regard, 57; Wall of Light (monumental stained glass window), Escherange, 62; eight windows, Lycee de Jeunes Filles, Bayonne, France, 66. *Exhib:* Mus Mod Art, Paris, 62, 63 & 65; one-man shows, Galerie Smith-Andersen, Palo Alto, Calif, 70-73, 76 & 79, Calif Palace Legion Honor, 71, Musee Arts Decoratifs, Lausanne, Switz, 72, Bildungszentrum, Gelsenkirchen, Ger, 72 & San Francisco Mus Mod Art, 81; Michael Dunev Fine Arts, San Francisco, 86; Rado Int, Hong Kong, 87; Frank Bustamante Gallery, New York, 89; Fota Gallery, Old Town Alexandria, Va, 90 & 91; and others. *Awards:* Art Award, Inst for Aesthetic Develop, 87. *Bibliog:* Francois Mathey & others (auth), Vitrail Francais, In: Tendances Modernes, Ed Deux Mondes, Paris, 58; Robert Sowers (auth), Stained Glass: An Architectural Art, Universe Bks, New York, 65; Shuji Takashina (auth), Stained glass works by Jean Weinbaum, Space Design, Tokyo, 9/67. *Media:* Watercolor, Oil, Stained Glass, Mixed Media. *Mailing Add:* PO Box 40291 San Francisco CA 94140

WEINBERG, BELLA REBECCA
PAINTER, WRITER
b New York, NY, Aug 30, 12. *Study:* Washington Workshop, DC, drawing, 50; Md Sch Art-Design, figure drawing, 60; primarily self-taught. *Work:* pvt collections, US & Abroad; Suburban Hosp & Writers Wkshp, Bethesda, Md; Temple Ahavath Shalome, Chevy Chase, Md; Nat Mus Am Women Achivs. *Exhib:* Smithsonian Miniature Painters, 68; Artists' Equity, 72-78; one-woman shows, Springtime Paintings, Cosmos Club, 75 & Paintings, Drawings, Sculpture, Rockville Civic Mansion, Md, 78, Stuff of Dreams, 87, The Energy of Shape, 88, Selby Libr & Tonalities, Berry Liberal Arts Col, 92; Wall Sculpture of wood & ceramics, Sarasota Art Asn Juried Show, 86; group exhib, Voorhees Galleries, Sarasota, Fla; Women's Resource Juried Show, 87 & Skies, Kress Gallery, 90; Fabric-embroidery Collage; Clown and Pussy Cat, Van Wezel Hall, 90; regular exhibs at Art Asn shows Yearly; Design in Stitchery, Selby Libr, 90; Artforms Gallery, Sarasota, Fla, 90. *Pos:* Dir & owner, Chevy Chase Galerie, Inc, Bethesda, Md, 63-69; art buyer, W J Sloane, DC, 69-71; dir, Fine Arts Gallery, JCC of Greater Washington, Rockville, Md, 71-77; freelance writer, 78-; adv bd, Sarasota Sch Sys, 87-89. *Teaching:* Lectr art, Montgomery Co Libr System, 78-79 & Nat League Pen Women, 80; instr, Venice Art League, Design in Stitchery, fall 90, spring 91 & Prime Time Enrichment Prog, fall 90. *Awards:* Am Artist Prof League Award, 58; Prize winner, Arvida State Fla Show, 86; Venice Art League, Fla, 91. *Bibliog:* Ed Nikki Burr (auth), Gallery Hopping, Art Scene, fall 71. *Mem:* Writer's League of Washington; Women's Caucus, Sarasota-Manatee Co; Nat Asn Women Arts, Washington, DC. *Media:* Oil. *Res:* Color relationships in oil painting as formulated by Cezanne's ideas--what makes a painting. *Publ:* Auth, The David Lloyd Kreeger, collection of distinction, 79, John Safer, sculptor, the curved line, 79 & Rosilind Miller, painter, 80, Art Voices S; Lunda Hoyle Gill, ethnographic portraits, Prints, spring 80; Diplomacy in action, Embassy News, 80; plus others. *Dealer:* Voorhees Galleries 1359 Main St Sarasota FL 33577; Sarasota Art Asn Gallery 707 N Tamiami Trail Sarasota FL 34236. *Mailing Add:* 6557 Gulf Gate Pl (347) Sarasota FL 34231

WEINBERG, ELBERT
SCULPTOR, EDUCATOR
b Hartford, Conn, May 27, 28. *Study:* Hartford Art Sch, with Henry Kreis; RI Sch Design, with Waldemar Raemisch; Yale Univ Sch Fine Arts. *Work:* Whitney Mus Am Art, Mus Mod Art, New York; Phillips Acad, Andover; Boston Mus Fine Arts, Mass; Wadsworth Athenaeum, Hartford; Phoenix Mus Fine Arts, Ariz. *Comn:* Bronze procession (sculpture), Mr & Mrs Albert List, Jewish Theological Seminary, 59; Jacob Wrestling with Angel (sculpture), Brandeis Univ, Waltham, Mass, 64; Shofar (bronze), Rockdale Temple, Cincinnati, Ohio, 69; Justice (bronze), Boston Univ Law Sch Lobby, 74; Bronze Procession 2, Beth El Temple, West Hartford, Conn, 75. *Exhib:* Whitney Mus Am Art, New York, 57, 58, 60 & 64; Carnegie Inst, Pittsburgh, Pa, 58 & 61; Sculpture USA, Mus Mod Art, New York, 59; 64 Americans Exhib, Art Inst Chicago, Ill, 61; Hirshhorn Collection, Guggenheim Mus, New York, 62; Jewish Community Ctr, 78; Holocaust Memorial, Wilmington, Del, 79; Hartford Covrant Sculpture to the Arts, 90; Holocaust Memorial, W Hartford. *Teaching:* Instr sculpture, Cooper Union, 56-59; prof sculpture, Boston Univ, 85- & Tyler Sch Art, Temple Abroad; artist-in-residence, Union Col, Schenectady, NY, 76-80. *Awards:* Prix de Rome, Am Acad Rome, 51-53; Guggenheim Fel, 59; Sculpture Award, Am Inst Arts & Lett, 69. *Bibliog:* Articles & photographs in several bks. *Mem:* Nat Acad Design. *Media:* Bronze, wood. *Dealer:* Alpha Gallery 121 Newbury St Boston MA 02116. *Mailing Add:* c/o Grace Borgenicht Gallery 724 Fifth Ave New York NY 10019

WEINBERG, EPHRAIM
ADMINISTRATOR, EDUCATOR
b Philadelphia, Pa, Apr 28, 38. *Study:* Philadelphia Col Art; Univ Pa. *Pos:* Dean, Pa Acad Fine Arts, 77-82, dir, Schs, 82-84; dir, Grand Rapids Art Mus, 84-86; dir, Nat Mus Am Jewish Hist, 86-88; pres, Art Sch & gallery mus consult, 88- *Teaching:* Lectr, Bournemouth Col Art, Eng, 64-65; prof, Bucks Co Community Col, Newton, Pa, 67-68, Philadelphia Col Art, 69-71 & Art Inst Chicago, 71-77. *Awards:* Hon Fel Nat Mus Am Jewish Hist. *Mem:* Philadelphia Art Alliance; Urban Inst Contemp Art; Nat Asn Sch Art &

Design; Munic Arts Adv Comn, Grand Rapids (chmn); Nexus: Found Today's Art (bd mem, currently); Abington Art Ctr, (bd mem, currently). *Publ:* Auth, Who teaches art, In: Art Education: Junior High School, Nat Art Educ Asn, 73; coauth (with Donald J Irving), The master of fine arts program, In: The Status of the Arts in Higher Education, 76 & auth, Venerable institutions in an age of conservation, In: The Visual Arts in the Ninth Decade, 80, Nat Coun Arts Adminr; auth, The school of the Pennsylvania Academy of the Fine Arts, Antiques, 3/81; School and Museum: The Pennsylvania Academy of the Fine Arts: A Case Study, Asn Art Mus Dirs, 82. *Mailing Add:* 855 Gregory Rd Rydal PA 19046

WEINBERG, H BARBARA
CURATOR, EDUCATOR
b New York, NY. *Study:* Barnard Col, BA; Columbia Univ, MA, PhD(art hist, archeol). *Pos:* Curator, Am Paintings & Sculpture, Met Mus Art, New York. *Teaching:* Prof art hist, Queens Col, City Univ New York & Grad Sch. *Mem:* Col Art Asn Am; Victorian Soc Am; Hist Soc (trustee). *Res:* Nineteenth century American painting. *Publ:* Auth, The Decorative Work of John La Farge, Garland, 77; The American Pupils of Jean-Leon Gerome, Amon Carter Mus, 84; The Lure of Paris: 19th Century American Painters & Their French Teachers, Abbeville, 91. *Mailing Add:* Dept Art Queens Col City Univ NY Flushing NY 11367

WEINER, ABE
PAINTER, INSTRUCTOR
b Pittsburgh, Pa, Nov 5, 17. *Study:* Carnegie Inst Technol, cert painting & design, 41, with Robert Gwathmey & Samuel Rosenberg. *Work:* Hillman Libr, Univ Pittsburgh. *Comn:* Painting & mosaic on aluminum, Alcoa Co Pittsburgh; painting, PPG Industs. *Exhib:* Assoc Artists Pittsburgh, 40-72 & Shows, 46-49, Carnegie Inst; Carnegie Inst Int, Pittsburgh, 50; Contemp Soc Exhib, Art Inst Chicago, 52; 50 Most Promising Artists US, Metrop Mus Art, 53; one-man show, Univ Pittsburgh, 81. *Teaching:* Instr painting, Arts & Crafts Ctr, 57-60 & Irene Kaufman Ctr, 65-; instr painting, drawing & asst dir, Ivy Sch Prof Art, 61- *Awards:* First & Second Prizes, 41 & 45, Judge's Prize, 59 & Purchase Award,74 & 75, Assoc Artists Pittsburgh; and others. *Mem:* Assoc Artists Pittsburgh. *Media:* Acrylic, Dry Pigment. *Mailing Add:* 1636 Denniston Ave Pittsburgh PA 15217

WEINER, LAWRENCE CHARLES
SCULPTOR
b Bronx, NY, Feb 10, 42. *Work:* Mus Mod Art, New York; Vanabbe Mus, Eindhoven, Netherlands; Staatiches Mus Monchengladbach, Ger; Centre Georges Pompidou, Paris; Nat Gallery of Australia, Canberra; and others. *Comn:* Holstebro, Denmark, 89-90; Citicorp Plaza, Los Angeles, Calif, 89-90; Villeurbawne, France, 90. *Exhib:* Information, Mus Mod Art, New York, 70; Idea & Image in Recent Art, Art Inst Chicago, Ill, 74; one-man shows, Laguna Gloria Mus, Austin, Tex, 77, Renaissance Soc, Chicago, 78, NS Col Art & Design, Halifax, 79, Mus Contemp Art, Chicago, 80, Leo Castelli Gallery, New York, 81, Ohio State Univ, Columbus, 84, Art & Proj Gallery, Amsterdam, Netherlands, 85, Art Gallery New South Wales, Australia, 86, Jean Bernier Gallery, Athens, Greece, 87 & Galerie Media, Neuchatal Switz, 88; Tate Gallery, London, Eng, 82; Mus Contemp Art, Los Angeles, Calif, 83; Mus Contemp Art, Sao Paulo, Brazil, 86; Mus Art, Pa State Univ, 87; Marian Goodman Gallery, New York, 88; Dia Found, New York, 91; Bordeaux Mus, France, 91. *Awards:* Deutscher Akademischer Austauschdienst Fel, 75; Nat Endowment Arts Fel, 76-77 & 85-86; Singer Prize, 90; Kopke Award, Denmark, 92. *Bibliog:* Dieter Schwarz & Lawrence Weiner (auth), Frankfurt, 89, Marja Bloem (ed); Benjamin Buchlok (ed), Posters, 65-86, Halifax & Toronto, HSCAD & Art Metropole, 86. *Publ:* Auth, Statements, Siegelaub, New York, 68; A Primer, Documenta Five, 72; Within Forward Motion, Kabinet Fur Aktuelle Kunst, 73; Various Manners with Various Things, Inst Contemp Art, London, 76; Works, Printed Matter, 77. *Dealer:* Marian Goodman Gallery New York NY. *Mailing Add:* 297 W Fourth New York NY 10014

WEINER, TESS MANILLA See Manilla, Tess

WEINGARTEN, HILDE (KEVESS)
PAINTER, PRINTMAKER
b Berlin, Ger; US citizen. *Study:* Art Students League; Cooper Union Art Sch, with Morris Kantor, Robert Gwathmey & Will Barnet, cert, 47, BFA, 76; Pratt Graphics Ctr. *Work:* Brooklyn Mus; Herbert F Johnson Mus, Cornell Univ; Israel Mus, Jerusalem; New York Pub Libr Print Collection; Fogg Art Mus, Harvard Univ; and others. *Exhib:* Albright Art Gallery, Buffalo, 55; Dallas Mus of Fine Art, 56; Brooklyn Mus, NY, 58, 63, 71, 74, 76, 77 & 80; New York World's Fair, 65; Graphics 71 Print Exhib, Western NMex Univ, Silver City, 71; Audubon Artists, Nat Acad Design, New York, 71, 73, 75, 77-90; Palazzo Vecchio, Florence & Pompeiian Pavilion, Naples, Italy, 72; Pratt Graphics Ctr Annuals, 72-79; plus many other group & six one-artist shows. *Awards:* Akston Found Prize, Nat Asn Women Artists, 80; Silver Medal Creative Graphics, Audubon Artists, 81; Doris Kreindler Memorial Award for Graphics, Am Soc Contemp Artists, 89; and many others. *Bibliog:* J L Collins (auth), Women Artists in America II & Contemporary Biography--Women, Vol I, Part II. *Mem:* Artists Equity Asn, New York (bd dirs, 64-72, 90-92); Nat Asn Women Artists; Am Soc Contemp Artists (bd dirs, 82-); Audubon Artists (bd dirs, 85-87). *Media:* Oil, Acrylic; Etching, Collagraph. *Publ:* Illusr, Tune of the Calliope, 58; Collection of Poems by Aaron Kramer, Thomas Yoseloff Ltd; German folksongs, 68; 51 Songs, translated by Arthur Kevess, Oak Publ. *Mailing Add:* 140 Cadman Plaza W Brooklyn NY 11201

WEINMAN, ROBERT ALEXANDER
SCULPTOR
b New York, NY, Mar 19, 15. *Study:* Nat Acad Design; Art Students League; Hobart Sculptor's Welding Course; also sculpture with A A Weinman, Lee Lawrie, Paul Manship, E McCartan, C Jennewein & J E Fraser. *Work:* Brookgreen Gardens, SC. *Comn:* Limestone tympana, Our Lady Queen of Martyrs Church, Forest Hills, NY, 39; bronze elk, comn by Elks, Walla Walla, Wash, 48; bronze doors, Armstrong Libr, Baylor Univ, Waco, Tex, 51; athletic medals, Nat Collegiate Athletic Asn, 52; Morning Mission (bronze), Tulsa, Okla, 62. *Exhib:* Nat Acad Design Ann, 37, 38, 49 & 53; Pa Acad Fine Art Ann, 38 & 39; Allied Artists Am, 46; Sculpture Int, Philadelphia, 49; Sculpture Ann, Nat Acad Design, 83. *Awards:* Mrs Louis Bennett Prize, Nat Sculpture Soc, 52; J S Saltus Medal, 64 & Sculptor Yr Gold Medal Award, 75, Am Numismatic Soc; and others. *Mem:* Academician Nat Acad Design; fel Nat Sculpture Soc (secy, 62-65, 1st vpres, 65-68 & 70-73, pres, 73-76); Collectors Art Medals (charter dir, 71). *Media:* Clay, Plaster. *Publ:* Contribr, Nat Sculpture Rev, 62-75. *Mailing Add:* Cross River Rd RD 3 Bedford NY 10506

WEINMANN, MONIQUE BRUNET-
CRITIC, CURATOR
b Toulon, France, Apr 30, 43; Can citizen. *Study:* Univ Paris X, with Pierre Francastel, Ecole des Hautes Etudes, Diplome d'Etudes Supérieures en Lettres, 67; Univ Montreal, MA(hist art), 90. *Collections Arranged:* Louise Gadbois, 1932-1982 (with, catalog), 83 & James Guitet, Propositions, X Positions (with catalog), 88 & Pastel Québecois Contemporain (with catalog), 92, Univ Que Gallery, Montreal. *Pos:* Art critic, freelance, Vie des Arts, Montreal, Que, 74- & Contemporanea, Parcours, 90; cur, freelance, Univ Gallery, Que Montreal, 83-; pres, CRITIC, Complexe de Réalisations Indépendant Transculturel et Interartiel du Que, 89- *Publ:* Contribr, Surréalisme périphérique Université de Montréal, Moura Sobral éd, 84; auth, Medium: Photography (trilingual), Stuttgart, Transatlantic Press, 87; Louis Jaque, Genèse, d'une signature, Montréal, Broquet Publ, 89; contribr, Fluid Exchanges: Artists & Critics in the Aids Crisis, Univ Toronto Press, 92. *Mailing Add:* 229 Des Bois Rd Rosemere PQ J7A 1S4 Canada

WEINSTEIN, JOYCE
PAINTER
b New York, NY, June 7, 31. *Study:* City Col New York, 48-50; Art Students League, 48-50. *Work:* Mus Mod Art, New York; Pa Acad Fine Arts; Edmonton Art Gallery, Alta; NJ State Mus, Trenton; Weatherspoon Mus, Greensboro, NC. *Exhib:* Works on Paper, Women Artists, Brooklyn Mus, 75; New Abstract Art, Edmonton Art Gallery Mus, 83; New Acquisitions, Mus Mod Art, New York, 81; solo exhibs, Martin Gerard Gallery, Edmonton, Alta, 81-82, Gallerie Wentzel, Cologne, WGer, 82, Gallery One, Toronto, 83 & Haber Theodore Gallery, New York, 85; Meredith Long & Co Gallery, Houston, Tex, 88 & 90; Alena Adlung Gallery, New York, 89. *Awards:* Lambert Fund Award, Pa Acad Fine Arts, 53. *Bibliog:* Grace Glueck (auth), article, New York Times, 12/14/79; Valentin Tatransky (auth), Joyce Weinstein at Haber Theodore Gallery, Arts Mag, 5/83; Nancy Tousley (auth), article, Calgary Herald, 5/85; Karen Wilkin (auth), rev, Partisan Rev, 2/90. *Mem:* Women Arts Found Inc (bd mem, 71-83, exec coordr, 78-82, exec bd mem, 83-90). *Media:* Oil & Mixed Media on Canvas, Monotypes. *Publ:* ed of 40 monotypes, Smith Anderson Editions, Palo Alto, Calif, 7/89. *Dealer:* Dorsky Gallery 379 W Broadway New York NY 10012; Meredith Long & Co Gallery 2323 San Felipe Rd Houston Tx 77019. *Mailing Add:* 46 Fox Hill Rd Ancramdale NY 12503

WEINSTOCK, ROSE
PAINTER
b New York, NY. *Study:* Wellesley Col, BA; Nat Acad Design, with Harvey Dinnerstein; Queens Col, with Charles Cajori; privately with Shirley Gorelick. *Exhib:* 100 Years, 100 Works, Traveling Exhib, Islip Art Mus, NY, Fine Arts Mus South, Mobile, Ala, Long View Mus, Tex, 89; Russian Churches, Elaine Benson Gallery, Bridgehampton, NY, 89; 165th Ann Exhib, Acad Design, New York, 90; Queens Col, Benjamin Rosenthal Libr, Flushing, NY, 91; Ann Long Island Exhib, Heckscher Mus, Huntington, NY, 92; and others. *Awards:* First Prize, Pindar Gallery, New York, 87; Gladys Serv Award, Heckscher Mus, Huntington, NY, 90; Medal of Honor & Audrey Hope Shirk Mem Award, Nat Asn Women Artists, New York, 91; and others. *Bibliog:* William Zimmer (auth), Abstracts of urban & rural landscapes, NY Times, 88; Will Grant (auth), NY Galleries, Art Speak, 89 & 90. *Mem:* Nat Asn Women Artists, New York; Audubon Artists, New York; Am Artists Prof League, New York; Pen & Brush Club, New York; Artist's Equity, New York. *Media:* Oil. *Mailing Add:* 35 E 75th St New York NY 10021

WEINTRAUB, ANNETTE
DIGITAL ARTIST, EDUCATOR
b New York, NY, July 2, 46. *Study:* Cooper Union, BFA, 67; Univ Pa Grad Sch Fine Arts, MFA, 70. *Work:* Aldrich Mus Contemp Art, Ridgefield, Conn; Prudential Insurance Co; Best Products Co, Ashland, Va; WTex Mus Asn; Wichita Art Mus; Peat Marwick Inc; and others. *Exhib:* Contemp Reflections, 1975-76, Aldrich Mus Contemp Art, 76; Members' Gallery, Albright-Knox Art Gallery, Columbus Art Mus, Ohio, 80; ACM SIGGRAPH Traveling Art Show, Boston Computer Mus, 91; Interface: Computers and Art, Park Ave Atrium, New York, 91; Computers in Art and Design, SIGGRAPH 18th Int Conf Computer Graphics & Interactive Techs, Las Vegas, Nev, 91; Electro 91, The Media Ctr Visual Studies Workshop, Rochester, NY, 91; Third Int Symp Electronic Art, Gallery Arts Multiplicata, Sydney, Australia, 92; solo exhib, Annette Weintraub, Digital Composites: Disintegration/ Reconstruction, Fine Arts Mus Long Island, 92; and others. *Teaching:* Adj

lectr painting, drawing, design, York Col, 71-81; asst prof advert design & computer graphics, City Col, City Univ New York, 83, assoc prof, 89. *Awards:* PSC-City Univ New York Res Found Grant, Visual Arts, 90; NY Found Arts, Artists Fel, Printmaking/Drawing/Artists Bks, 91; Merit Award, HOW Mag, Electronic Art Issue, 91; and others. *Bibliog:* Ellen Lubell (auth), Manhattan (and Hoboken), Soho Weekly News, 5/24/79; Screentest: Annette Weintraub, MacWeek, 8/90; J Ellen Gerken (auth), Chek 1, North Wight Bks. *Mem:* Women's Caucus Art (adv bd New York chap, 79-80); Spec Interest Group for Computer Graphics (bd dirs, 88). *Media:* Acrylic, Computer Graphics. *Mailing Add:* Two Bond St New York NY 10012

WEINTRAUB, JACOB D
ART DEALER
b Austria; US citizen. *Study:* Law degree. *Pos:* Owner & dir, Weintraub Gallery, New York, currently. *Mem:* Appraisers Asn Am. *Specialty:* 20th century masters: Henry Moore, Picasso, Chagall, Leger, Matisse, Arp, Miro, Calder, Marini, Botero, Giacometti, Zuniga, Chadwick & Lipschitz. *Collection:* Major works by: Moore, Shahn, Grosz, Botero, Marini, Klee, Pomodoro, Chagall, Epstein, Noldel, Magritte, Tamayo, Vlaminck & Feininger. *Mailing Add:* Weintraub Gallery 988 Madison Ave New York NY 10021

WEINTRAUB, LINDA
CURATOR, DIRECTOR
b Elizabeth, New Jersey, Apr 15, 42. *Study:* Univ Wisc, 60-61; Douglas Col, BA, 64; Rutgers Univ, MFA, 70. *Collections Arranged:* The Maximal Implications of the Minimal Line, Bard Col, 85; Thomas Hart Benton: Chronicler of America's Folk Heritage, 86; Pre Modern Art of Vienna: 1848-1898, 88; Buckminster Fuller: Harmonizing, Humanity, Nature & Technology, 89; Art What Thou Eat: The Image of Food in American Art, 90. *Pos:* Dir, Philip Johnson Ctr Arts, Muhlenberg Col, 78-81; Dir, Edith C Blum Art Inst, Bard Col, 81- *Mem:* Col Art Asn; Art Mus Asn; Mid Atlantic Art Asn. *Publ:* Coauth, Maximal Implications of the Minimal Line, Bard Col Publ, 85; coauth, Thomas Hart Benton, Chronicler of America's Folk Heritage, Bard Col, 86; coauth, Process and Product: The Making of 8 Contemporary Masterworks, Bard Col, 88; coauth, Isabel Bishop, Rizzoli Publ, 89; coauth & ed, The Image of Food: 150 Years of American Art, Sextent Publ, 90. *Mailing Add:* 3 1/2 Locust Grove Rhinebeck NY 12572

WEINZAPFEL, CONNIE A
GALLERY DIRECTOR, CURATOR
b Evansville, Ind, Aug 8, 56. *Study:* Univ Southern Ind, BS, 78; Southern Ill Univ, MFA, 81. *Pos:* Coordr, Chicago Int Art Expo, Ill, 81-85; dir, New Harmony Gallery Contemp Art, Ind 85- *Mailing Add:* New Harmony Gallery Contemp Art 506 Main St New Harmony IN 47631

WEISBERG, GABRIEL P
HISTORIAN, EDUCATOR
b New York, NY, May 4, 42. *Study:* New York Univ, BA, 63; Johns Hopkins Univ, MA, PhD, 67. *Exhib:* Co-cur, The Art of the July Monarchy, 89. *Pos:* Cur art hist, Cleveland Mus Art, 73-81; asst dir, Nat Endowment Humanities, 83-85. *Teaching:* Asst prof art hist, Univ NMex, 67-69; assoc prof art hist, Univ Cincinnati, 69-73; Mellon prof art hist, Univ Pittsburgh, 81-82; prof art hist, Univ Minn, 85- *Awards:* Nat Endowment Arts Fel, 77; Robert C Smith Award, Decorative Art Soc, 80; Guggenheim Found Fel, 81-82. *Mem:* Print Coun Am; Decorative Arts Soc; Col Art Asn Am (bd dirs, 80-). *Res:* Study of 19th century realism, Japonisme and art nouveau as a formalistic concern and as an example of social history. *Publ:* Auth, The Realist Tradition: French Painting and Drawing, Cleveland Mus Art, 80; ed, The European Realist Tradition, 83; Art Nouveau Bing, 86; coauth, Japonisme Comes to America, 90; Beyond Impressionism: The Naturalist Impulse, 92. *Mailing Add:* Dep Art Hist Univ Minn Minneapolis MN 55455

WEISBERG, RUTH ELLEN
PAINTER, EDUCATOR
b Chicago, Ill, July 31, 42. *Study:* Accad di Belli Arte, Perugia, Italy, Laurea; Univ Mich, BS & MA; Atelier 17, Paris, with S W Hayter. *Work:* Bibliot Nat, France; Chicago Art Inst; Los Angeles Co Mus of Art; New York Pub Libr; Norwegian Nat Collection; Am Mus Art, Smithsonian; Oakland Mus, Calif. *Comn:* Together Again (ed of 150 lithographs), Midwest Regional Orgn for Rehabilitation & Training, 75; The Gift (ed of 60 lithographs), Univ Synagogue, Los Angeles, 75; Interlude, Los Angeles Co Mus of Art, 75. *Exhib:* Philadelphia Print Club, 85; Univ Richmond, Va, 85; Fisher Gallery, Univ Southern Calif, Los Angeles, 86; solo shows, Jack Rutberg Fine Arts, Los Angeles, 83, 85, 88 & 91, The Scroll, Hebrew Union Col, New York, 87 & 88, Assoc Am Artists, New York, 87 & 90, Realms of Desire-A Print Retrospective, Fresno Art Mus, Calif, 90, Bethel Col, North Newton, Kans, 91 & Gwenda Jay Gallery, Chicago, Ill, 91 & 92; Her Story: Narrative Art by Contemp Calif Artists (catalog), Oakland Mus, 91; Passing Over, Sculptural Installation for, Passover and Passion, Leband Gallery, Loyola Marymount, Los Angeles, 91; 500 Years Since Columbus (catalog), Triton Mus, Santa Clara, Calif, 91; Presswork: The Art of Women Printmakers (traveling exhib, catalog), Nat Mus Women Arts, Washington, DC, Univ Art Mus, Univ Minn, Minneapolis, Elvehjem Mus Art, Univ Wis, Madison, Butler Inst Am Art, Youngstown, Ohio, 91-93. *Pos:* Assoc dean, Univ Southern Calif, 74-75, 76-77 & dept chmn, 86-; dir, Kelyn Press, currently. *Teaching:* Asst prof fine arts, Eastern Mich Univ, Ypsilanti, 66-67; from assoc prof to prof fine arts, Univ Southern Calif, Los Angeles, 70- *Awards:* Third Ann Vesta Award, Visual Arts, Women's Bldg, Los Angeles, 84. *Bibliog:* Lydia Matthews (auth), Stories history didn't tell us, Artweek, 2/14/91; Lisbet Nilson (auth), Loyola Gallery puts its faith in religious exhibit, Los Angeles Times/Calendar, 3/24/91; Suvan Geer (auth), Weisberg's family album, Los Angeles Times, 3/1/91. *Mem:* Col Art Asn (bd dirs & pres, currently); Western Regional Nat Women's Caucus Art (vpres & co-chair, 85); Nat Adv Bd Tamarind Inst; Los Angeles Artists Equity (adv bd). *Media:* Lithography. *Publ:* Illusr, Tom O'Bedlam's Song, 69 & auth & illusr, The Shtetl, A Journey and A Memorial, 72, Kelyn Press. *Dealer:* Assoc Am Artists New York NY; Gwenda Jay Gallery Chicago IL. *Mailing Add:* Univ Southern Calif Los Angeles CA 90089

WEISMANN, DONALD LEROY
EDUCATOR, PAINTER
b Milwaukee, Wis, Oct 12, 14. *Study:* Univ Wis-Milwaukee, BS; Univ Minn; Univ Wis-Madison, PhM; St Louis Univ; Harvard Univ, Carnegie Corp scholar, 41; Ohio State Univ, PhD. *Work:* Butler Inst Am Art, Youngstown, Ohio; Chrysler Mus, Provincetown, Mass; Columbia Mus Art, SC; D D Feldman Collection, Humanities Res Ctr, Univ Tex, Austin; Witte Mus, San Antonio, Tex. *Comn:* Mural, Ill Centennial Bldg, Springfield, 41; TV videotape ser, Mirror of Western Art, Nat Educ TV, 60 & Visual Arts, Ford Found & US Off Educ, 61; films, Terlingua, 71 & Station X, 75, Pub Broadcast Corp; Azimuth, 76. *Exhib:* Ann Exhib Am Art, 40-41 & Int Watercolor Exhib, 42, Art Inst Chicago, Ill; Ann Exhib Art US & Territories, Butler Inst Am Art, 57-58; Gulf-Caribbean Exhib, Houston Mus Fine Arts, Tex, 58; World's Fair, New York, 64-65; Colorado Springs Fine Arts Ctr, Colo; Cincinnati Mus Art, Ohio; Corcoran Gallery Art, Washington, DC; Dallas Mus Fine Arts, Tex; Inst Contemp Arts, Boston, Mass; Toledo Mus Art, Ohio. *Collections Arranged:* Ulfert Wilke Retrospective, 53 & Victor Hammer Retrospective, 54, Univ Ky, Lexington. *Teaching:* Assoc prof, NTex State Univ, summer 40; asst prof art & art hist, Ill State Univ, 40-42 & 46-48; asst prof art hist, Wayne State Univ, 49-51; prof art & head dept, Univ Ky, 51-54; prof art, Univ Tex, Austin, 54-, chmn dept, 54-58, grad prof art hist, 58-, univ prof in arts, 64-81, chmn comp studies, 67-72, Univ prof in the arts, emer, 81- *Awards:* Purchase Award for Painting, Butler Inst Am Art, 57; Bromberg Award for Excellence in Teaching, Univ Tex, Austin, 65; Lett of Commendation for Enhancement of Arts in Am, President of US, 72; Nat Endowment Arts Fel, Aspen, Colo, 84. *Mem:* Nat Coun Arts; Nat Humanities Fac. *Media:* Collage, Film. *Res:* Creative process in art and science; language and visual form. *Publ:* Auth, Language and Visual Form, 68; Visual Arts as Human Experience, 70; The 12 Cadavers of Joe Mariner, 77; Follow the Bus with the Greek License Plates, 81; Duncan Phyfe and Drum, 84; Frank Reaugh, Painter to the Longhorns, 85. *Dealer:* Carlin Galleries 710 Montgomery St Ft Worth TX 76107. *Mailing Add:* 1108 Yaupon Valley Rd Austin TX 78746-4329

WEISS, DICK J
ENAMELIST, STAINED GLASS ARTIST
b Everett, Wash, June 24, 46. *Study:* Yale Univ, New Haven, Conn, BA, 68. *Work:* Corning Mus Glass, NY; Victoria & Albert Mus, London, Eng; City of Seattle Pub Art, Wash; 1 Percent-Wash State, Seattle; Pilchuck Glass Sch, Stanwood, Wash. *Comn:* Marine Sciences Bldg, Univ Wash, Seattle, 85; Kent Sr Citizen Ctr, City Kent, Wash, 86; Sea-Tac Airport, Port Seattle, Wash, 88; Kenai Community Col, State Alaska, Homer, 90; Opera House, Seattle, Arts Comt, Seattle, 90. *Exhib:* 4 Leaders in Glass, Craft & Folk Art Mus, Los Angeles, 80; Colorful Romances, Henry Art Gallery, Seattle, 81; Pilchuck Glass, Bellevue Art Mus, Wash, 88; Master Works, Bellevue Art Mus, Wash, 91; Clearly Art, Whatcom Mus, Bellingham, Wash, 92. *Awards:* Craftsman Grant, 81 & 87, Nat Endowment Arts. *Mem:* Glass Art Soc. *Dealer:* William Traver 110 Union St Seattle WA 98101-2028. *Mailing Add:* 811 N 36th St Seattle WA 98103

WEISS, HARVEY
SCULPTOR, WRITER
b New York, NY, Apr 10, 22. *Study:* Nat Acad Design; Art Students League; also with Ossipe Zadkine, Paris. *Work:* Albright-Knox Art Gallery; Krannert Mus; Silvermine Guild Collection; Nelson Rockefeller Collection; Joseph H Hirshhorn Collection; plus others. *Comn:* Menorah, Temple B'nai Zion, Shreveport, La, 67; reliefs, Mt Vernon Synagogue, NY, 69 & Conn Off Bldg, Westport, 71. *Exhib:* Five one-man shows, Paul Rosenberg & Co, 59-70; one-man show, Silvermine Guild, 68 & 83, five one-man show, Paul Rosenberg & Co, 59-70, Art Place, 90; retrospective, Fairfield Univ, 70; Am Inst Arts & Lett, 70; Sculptor's Guild Ann Shows; Cast Iron Gallery, 92. *Teaching:* Prof sculpture, Adelphi Univ, Garden City, NY, currently. *Awards:* Three Ford Found Purchase Awards; Olivetti Award, New Eng Ann Exhib, 69; Nat Inst Arts & Lett Grant, 70. *Mem:* Sculptors Guild (pres, 70-71); Silvermine Guild Artists (bd trustees, 68-70); Auth Guild. *Media:* Bronze, Welded Brass. *Publ:* Auth & illusr, Collage & Construction, 70, Gadget Book, 71, Lens & Shutter, 71,Machines & How They Work, 83 & Submarines, 90; and many others. *Mailing Add:* 42 Maple Lane Greens Farms CT 06436

WEISS, JEROME NATHAN
PAINTER
b NJ, Oct 21, 59. *Study:* Metrop Art Ctr, Miami, study with Roberto Martinez, 78; Art Students League, 79-83; Nat Acad Design, New York, 81-83. *Exhib:* Ann shows, Bergen Mus Art, Paramus, 84 & 85; Hortt Ann, Ft Lauderdale Mus Art, 85; Winners Show, Bergen Mus Art, Paramus, 85; Lyme Acad Fine Arts, Conn, 88; Fel Exhib, Monmouth Mus, Lincroft, NJ, 88; and others. *Awards:* Best in Show, Hortt Ann, Ft Lauderdale Mus, 85; Painting Fel, NJ Coun Arts, 88; Julius Hallgarten Prize, 167th Ann Exhib, Nat Acad Design, 92; and others. *Bibliog:* Theodore F Wolff (auth), Portrait of the artist as a young master, Christian Sci Monitor, 7/25/85. *Media:* Oil. *Mailing Add:* 301 Lafayette Ave Cliffside Park NJ 07010

WEISS, JOHN JOSEPH
PHOTOGRAPHER, EDITOR
b Philadelphia, Pa, Jan 31, 41. *Study:* Temple Univ, BS, 63; Mass Inst Technol, 69-73; RI Sch Design, MFA, 73. *Work:* Mus Mod Art, New York; Addison Gallery Am Art, Andover, Mass; Princeton Univ, NJ; Del Art Mus, Wilmington; Photog Place, Philadelphia. *Exhib:* Addison Gallery Am Art, Andover, Mass, 73; Mass Inst Technol Creative Photog Gallery, Cambridge, 76; Photopia, Philadelphia, 79; G H Dalsheimer Gallery, Baltimore, 83; The Photographers' Gallery, London, 83; Andover Gallery, Mass, 85; Book Trader Gallery, Philadelphia, 86. *Pos:* Coordr photog, Mass Inst Technol, 76-*Teaching:* Instr photog, Mass Inst Technol, 69-73; asst prof photog, Univ Del, Newark, 75-79, assoc prof, 79- *Publ:* Contribr, Portraits, Mod Photog, 77; auth, A darkroom philosophy, Camera 35, 77; ed, Venus, Jupiter and Mars--The Photographs of Frederick Sommer, Del Art Mus, 80; Philadelphia Photog Rev, 81; auth, biography of Frederick Sommer, Collier's Encycl; article in Photo Review, 86. *Mailing Add:* Dept of Art Univ Del Newark DE 19716

WEISS, LEE (ELYSE C WEISS)
PAINTER
b Inglewood, Calif, May 22, 28. *Study:* Calif Col Arts & Crafts, 46-47; also with N Eric Oback, 57 & Alexander Nepote, 58. *Work:* Nat Mus Am Art; Nat Mus of Women in the Arts, Washington, DC; Phillips Collection, Washington, DC; Exec Residence, State Wis; Springfield Mus Art, Mo; NASA Space Art Collection, Cape Canaveral, Fla; Davenport Munic Mus Art, Iowa; Hickory Mus, NC; US Dept of the Interior, Smithsonian Nat Air & Space Mus, Washington, DC. *Comn:* Am Artist & Water Resources, one of 40 Am artists chosen for Bur Reclamation Art Proj, US Dept Interior, 71; artist for space shuttle launch, NASA, 84. *Exhib:* One-woman shows, Walker Art Ctr, Minneapolis, 60, Calif Place Legion Hon, San Francisco, 62, Milwaukee Art Ctr, 65, West Bend Gallery Fine Art, Wisc, 88, Chicago Botanic Garden, 88, 89, Mount Mary Col, Milwaukee, 89, Neville-Sargent Gallery, Chicago, 90; Wisconsin Painters & Sculpters, Milwaukee Art Mus; Oakland Art Mus; Penn Acad Fine Art, Philadelphia; San Francisco Art Mus; Setagaya Mus Art, Tokyo, Japan, 88, 89 & 90; Nat Invitational Watercolor Exhib, Northern Ariz Univ, 89; Sat of the Art nat invitational Watercolor Exhib, Parkland Col Art Gallery, Champagne, Ill, 89; Wisc-Ill Art Exch, Art Asn, Springfield, Ill, 89; Meguro Mus, Tokyo, Japan, 91 & 92. *Pos:* Watercolor USA Hon Soc (vpres, 86, pres, 87-88). *Teaching:* Artist-in-residence, Rhinelander Sch Arts, 7/89; Dillman's Creative Workshops, Lac du Flambeau, Wis, 90, 92 & 93. *Awards:* Am Watercolor Soc Mt McKinnon Award, 73, High Winds Medal, 78, S Leitman Award, 91, Named an AWS Dolphin Fel, 91; San Diego Watercolor Soc, Oliphant Purchase Award, 85, Rembrandt Award, 87, Daniels Award, 92; First Award, Watercolor Wis, 82, 84 & 87; Adirondack Wilderness Award with Rouse Gold Medallion, Adirondack Nat Exhib Am Watercolors, 90. *Bibliog:* S Quiller & B Whipple (auths), Water Media: Process and Possibilities, Watson-Guptill, 86; Valfred Thelin (auth), Watercolor, Let the Medium Do It, Watson-Guptill, 89; Watercolor 91 (feature article), Am Artist Publ, fall 91, The Artist's Mag, 9/91. *Mem:* Am Watercolor Soc; Nat Watercolor Soc; life mem Wis Painters & Sculptors; Watercolor USA Hon Soc (vpres, 86, pres, 87-88); Rocky Mountain Water Media Soc. *Media:* Watercolor. *Publ:* Coauth, Lee Weiss watercolors, Col Printing & Publ, 71; Lee Weiss, Watercolors II, the Seventies, Am Printing & Publ Co, 81; Lee Weiss, Watercolors III, Straus Printing Co, 90. *Dealer:* Addison-Ripley Gallery 9 Hillyer Court Washington DC 20008; Gallery Madison 90 1248 Madison Ave New York NY. *Mailing Add:* 106 Vaughn Ct Madison WI 53705

WEISS, MILTON
PAINTER, PRINTMAKER
b Uniontown, Pa, May 17, 12. *Study:* Irene Kaufman Settlement Art Sch, 23-54; Univ Pittsburgh, 35; Pittsburgh Ctr Arts, 62, with George Nama. *Work:* Westmoreland Mus Art, Greensburg, Pa; 100 Friends of Art, Pittsburgh Pub Sch; Cambria Township Sch, Pa; Blue Cross of Western Pa. *Comn:* Murals for children's playroom, Juv Court, Pittsburgh, Pa, WPA Art Prog, 41. *Exhib:* Assoc Artists Pittsburgh Annuals, Carnegie Inst, 35-80; Pa Acad Fine Arts, Philadelphia, 53, 59 & 65; Butler Inst Am Art, Youngstown, Ohio, 47, 54 & 59; solo exhib, Pittsburgh Ctr for the Arts, 61 & Mus Art, Carnegie Inst, Pittsburgh, Pa, 65; Art Alliance, Philadelphia, 76; Assoc Artists Anniversary Show, Mendelson Gallery, Pittsburgh, Pa, 85. *Pos:* Chmn exhib, Assoc Artists of Pittsburgh, 56-58. *Teaching:* Instr painting & drawing, Ivy Sch Prof Art, Pittsburgh, 70-80, Art Inst Pittsburgh, 80-84. *Awards:* Best Watercolor, Assoc Artists Pittsburgh, 46. *Bibliog:* Norwood MacGilvary (auth), 46 & Claude Jensen (auth), 48, Assoc Artists Ann, Carnegie Mag; Ruth Heimbuecher (auth), Murals from the settlement, 80 & Art that cushioned the crash, 80, Pittsburgh Press Sunday Roto. *Mem:* Assoc Artists Pittsburgh (bd dirs, 56-59); Group A (pres, 60-65). *Media:* Acrylic, Oil; All. *Dealer:* Concept Art Gallery 1031 S Braddock Ave Pittsburgh PA 15218. *Mailing Add:* 5742 Holden St Pittsburgh PA 15232

WEISS, RACHEL
CURATOR
b Paterson, NJ, Sept 22, 54. *Study:* Marlboro Col, BA, 76; Mass Col Art, MFA, 80. *Work:* Ctr Georges Pompidou, Paris; Nat Mus Sci & Technol, Ottawa, Ont. *Exhib:* The Nearest Edge of the World: Art and Cuba Now, var mus, 90-93; Ante America, Biblioteca Luis Angel Arango, Bogota, Colombia; Among Africas/In Americas, Banff Ctr, 91. *Pos:* Coordr, Vis Artists Prog, Mass Col Art, 84-89; pres, Polarities, Inc, 85- *Teaching:* Asst instr holography, Mass Col Art, Boston, 79-80, spec prog asst, 78-81; asst instr holography, Brown Univ, Providence, RI, 80-81. *Awards:* Numerous public & private grants in support of public art programs organized since 1983. *Publ:* Auth, Boycotting the truth, Black New York Mag, 88; Creating freedom, Tres Mundo, 88; Necessity and Invention: New Cuban Art, Wolgan Misul Mag, Seoul, 90; ed, Being America, White Pine Press, 91; contribr, Territories of Difference (chapt), 92. *Mailing Add:* 108 Winthrop Rd Brookline MA 02146

WEISSMAN, JULIAN PAUL
DEALER
b New York, NY, June 28, 43. *Study:* Hobart Col, Geneva, NY, BA. *Pos:* Art Critic, The Press, 73-77; ed assoc, writer & reviewer, Art New Mag, New York, 74-79; mgr, Susan Caldwell Gallery Inc, New York, 74-75; mgr, Gloria Cortella Inc (gallery), New York, 76-77; dir, Alexander F Milliken Inc (gallery), New York, 78-79; dir, Gruenebaum Gallery Inc, New York, 79-87; assoc dir, M Donedler & CO, 87. *Res:* Impressionism; German expressionism; the Bauhaus; 20th century sculpture; contemporary art and artists who live and work in New York. *Specialty:* Contemporary American art. *Publ:* Auth, Standoff in Soho, Art News Mag, 74; What's wrong at the Whitney?, The Press, Vol 3, No 3, 75; Master Atget----& Portraits of the Artists, Art News Mag, 76; Here comes the taxman, Soho Weekly News, 76; Dazzling drawings are redefining the art, The Press, Vol 4, No 1, 76. *Mailing Add:* 26 Beaver St No 14 New York NY 10004

WEISSMAN, WALTER
SCULPTOR, PHOTOGRAPHER
b Brooklyn, NY, Dec 9, 46. *Study:* Kingsborough Community Col, with Gregory Battcock, AA, 67; Brooklyn Col, with Harry Holtzman, BA(hon; arts), 70; Hunter Col, with Robert Morris, MA(fine arts), 75. *Work:* Mus Mod Art, Whitney Mus & Guggenheim Mus, New York; Tate Mus, London, Eng; Va Commonwealth Univ. *Comn:* Alliance in the Park (outdoor/indoor collaborative work), Philadelphia Art Alliance, Pa, 87; Committed to Print, Mus Mod Art, New York, 88. *Exhib:* Contemp Reflections No 4, Aldrich Mus Contemp Art, 75; Open Studios at PS1, Queens, NY, 77; Centennial Exhib Sculpture, NJ Inst Technol, Newark, 81; solo exhibs, Structures and Shelters, 83 & 87 & De-Architecture, 84, 14 Sculptors Gallery, New York; Artists Call, Hudson Mem Church, New York, 84; Art Works: Three Dimensions, Beaver Col, Glenside, Pa, 85; Art Against Apartheid, Boricua Col, Brooklyn, 85; 13-state traveling exhib, 87-89. *Collections Arranged:* Drawings, Models and Sculpture: A Re-Opening: Season's Premier, 14 Sculptors Gallery, 82. *Pos:* Sr ed, Art & Artists, New York, 78-89; adv, Artists Cert Cult Affairs, New York, 80-86; moderator, Artists Talk on Art, New York, 81-84; pres, 14 Sculptors Gallery, 85-88. *Teaching:* Asst instr photog, Yale Univ, 68; instr painting & drawing, Brooklyn Col, 71; artist-in-residence, PS 1, Long Island City, NY, 77. *Bibliog:* Burton Wasserman (auth), Exhibitions in sight, Art Matters, Pa, 6/85; Robert Metzger (auth), A 2nd Palette, In: Aldrich Mus catalog, 85; Michael Brenson (auth), article, New York Times, 12/28/86. *Mem:* Artists Meeting Cult Change (secy, 76-78); Found Community Arts (pres, 80-84); Graphic Artists Guild, 89. *Specialty:* Contemporary sculpture & photography. *Publ:* Coauth, An Anti-Catalog, Artists Meeting Cult Change, 77; auth, Interview with John Perreault, 4/80, Automata and autonomy: Sculpture now, 11/81 & ed, Special Supplement, 11/81, Artworkers News; ed, Special Supplement, 82, auth, The terror of bureaucracy, 5/85 & View from a coop, 3/86, Art & Artists Mag; coauth, The Village, 87. *Mailing Add:* 463 West St PO Box B-332 New York NY 10014

WEITZENHOFFER, A MAX
DEALER
b Oklahoma City, Okla, Oct 30, 39. *Study:* Univ Okla, BFA. *Pos:* Dir, Gimpel & Weitzenhoffer Ltd. *Mem:* Art Dealers Asn Am. *Specialty:* 20th century American and European paintings and sculpture. *Mailing Add:* 70 E 77th St New York NY 10021

WEITZMANN, KURT
EDUCATOR, HISTORIAN
b Almerode, Ger, Mar 7, 04; US citizen. *Study:* Univ Munster; Univ Wurzburg; Univ Vienna; Univ Berlin, PhD, 29; Univ Heidelberg, Hon Dr, 67; Univ Chicago, Hon Dr, 68; Univ Berlin, Hon Dr, 82. *Pos:* Stipend, Ger Archeol Inst, Greece, 31 & Berlin, 32-34; permanent mem, Inst Advan Study, 35-72; consult cur, Metrop Mus Art, 72-82. *Teaching:* Assoc prof art & archeol, Princeton Univ, 45-50, prof art & archeol, 50-72, emer prof, 72-; vis lectr art & archeol, Yale Univ, 54-55; vis prof art & archeol, Univ Alexandria, 60; guest prof art & archaeol, Univ Bonn, 62; vis scholar, Dumbarton Oaks, Washington, DC. *Awards:* Prix Gustave Schlumberger, Acad Inscriptions & Belles Lett, Paris, France, 69. *Mem:* Fel Medieval Acad Am; Ger Archeol Inst; Am Philos Soc; Col Art Asn Am; Archeol Inst Am. *Res:* Late classical, Byzantine and medieval art; expeditions to Mt Athos & Mt Sinai. *Publ:* Auth, Byzantine Book Illumination and Ivorien, 80; auth, Byzantine Liturgical Prayers and Gospels, 80; Classical Heritage and Near Eastern Art, 81; The Medieval West and Its Contacts with Byzantium, 82; Studies in the Arts at Sinai, 82. *Mailing Add:* 30 Nassau St Princeton NJ 08540

WELCH, CHARLES D
PAINTER, SCULPTOR
b Kearney, Nebr, Oct 5, 48. *Study:* Kearney State Col, BA(art educ), 70, MS(art educ), 74; tuition fel, 84-87, Sch Mus Fine Arts, Boston, MFA, 87. *Work:* Chicago Art Inst; Tate Gallery, London; Mus Mod Art, New York; Arch Small Press & Commun, Antwerp, Belg; Nebr Art Collection; Getty Found Collection; Libr Congress. *Exhib:* Printmaking 1985, Northeastern Univ Gallery, Boston; Gallery II, Tufts Univ, Medford, Mass, 87; Paper Press Gallery, Chicago, 88; Int Stamp Invitational, Davidson Gallery, Seattle, 89; Aerial Gallery, New York, 89. *Pos:* Proprietor, Sandbar Willow Handmade Paper Mill, Omaha, 78-84, Lebanon, NH, 88- *Teaching:* Chmn art dept, Bellevue Sr High Sch, 74-84 & Bellevue W High Sch, 77-84; instr, Bellevue Col, 78-80; teaching asst, Tufts Univ, 86-87; instr, AVA Gallery, 88-89. *Awards:* Fulbright Hayes recipient, 76; Medal, Art 54 Gallery, 87; Special Artistic excellence, Tokyo Metrop Mus, 90. *Bibliog:* Judith Hoffberg (auth), article, Umbrella Mag, 83; Daniel Cole (auth), The Adventures of the Cracker Jack Kid, aka Chuck Welch, Lightworks Mag, 87. *Mem:* Nat Educ Asn;

Bellevue Educ Asn; Int Soc Copier Artists; Friends Dard Hunter Soc. *Media:* Paper, Mail Art. *Publ:* Auth, Networking Currents, Sandbar Willow Press, 85; Whole Earth Review, Mail Art Glasnost, winter 89; ed, Eternal Network: A Mail Art Anthology, Sandbar Willow Press, 90. *Dealer:* Benta West AVA Gallery Hanover NH; Rebecca McDonald Davidson Galleries Seattle WA. *Mailing Add:* RR 1 Box 426H Lebanon NH 03766

WELCH, JAMES WYMORE
PAINTER, MURALIST
b Omaha, Nebr, June 7, 28. *Study:* George Washington Univ, BA; Univ Omaha, study with Anna C Myers; Acad Fine Arts, Tokyo, Japan, with Shiguru Yamamoto; Keio Univ, Hiyoshi, Japan, study with Daisuke Sakai; Sch of Fine Arts, Seoul, Korea, study with Kim Il Han; study with Mark Rothko; Harvard Univ, MBA, 66. *Work:* Nat Mus, Seoul; Joslyn Mem Mus, Omaha; Nat Mus Mod Art, Tokyo; Media Gen Corp & Philip Morris USA, Richmond, Va; Fed Reserve Bank, Richmond, Va. *Comn:* Poster panel designs, US State Dept Arts Abroad Prog, Washington, DC, 63; acrylic mural, Univ Panama, Repub Panama, 59; acrylic paintings, McDonald's Corp, New York, 79; acrylic paintings, IBM Corp, New York, 81; acrylic paintings, Xerox Corp, New York, 82. *Exhib:* Oriental Art Trends for Today, Fine Arts Pavilion, Osaka, Japan, 50; Ann Invitational, Palacio de Bellas Artes, Panama City, Republic Panama, 59-60; Presidential Fine Arts Show, Duk-Soo Palace, Seoul, 63; 13th Biennial Show, Valentine Mus, Richmond, 74; Corcoran Gallery Art Biennial, DC; Minimal Arts of the 70's, Hirshhorn Mus, Washington, DC, 79; and others. *Pos:* Pres, Metrop Artists Asn, Richmond, Va,; bd dirs, Richmond Pub Libr, Va. *Teaching:* Guest instr abstract painting, Univ Panama, 58-60; guest lectr Western US art, US State Dept-Korean Govt, Seoul, 63-64. *Awards:* Presidential Award, Presidential Fine Arts Show, Seoul, 63; Purchase Award, Shockoe Slip Art Fair, Xerox Corp, 76; Purchase Award, Federated Arts Show, Richmond, 82. *Bibliog:* B Green (auth), Artists works have deceptively simple sophistication, 81, Minimal art receives critical acclaim, 82, Artist works receive nat recognition, 86, Richmond News Leader. *Mem:* Metrop Artists Asn, Richmond; Federated Arts Coun, Richmond; Accademia Italia Delle Arti E Del Lavoro; Int Soc Artists; Va Mus Fine Arts, Richmond; Am Artists Prof League. *Media:* Oil, Acrylic. *Dealer:* Welch Studio Inc 1500 Park Ave Richmond Va 23220-3538. *Mailing Add:* 1500 Park Ave Richmond VA 23220

WELCH, (MRS) ROBERT G
COLLECTOR
Teaching: Guest lectr at many univs. *Mem:* Cleveland Mus Art; Mus Mod Art, New York (Cleveland growth bd); Cleveland Soc Contemp Art. *Collection:* Contemporary metal sculpture. *Mailing Add:* PO Box 630 La Quinta CA 92253

WELCH, ROGER
SCULPTOR, CONCEPTUAL ARTIST
b Westfield, NJ, Feb 10, 46. *Study:* Miami Univ, Ohio, BFA, 69; Whitney Mus Independent Study Prog, 70-71; Art Inst Chicago, MFA, 71. *Work:* Ga Mus Art, Athens; Rufino Tamayo Mus, Mexico City; Boston Mus Fine Arts; Mus Bellas Artes, Caracas, Venezuela; Chase Manhattan Collection, Mus Mod Art, New York; and others. *Comn:* The O J Simpson Project (multimedia work), Albright-Knox Art Gallery, 77; The Voice of Clint Eastwood (videotape), Process & Konstruktion, Munich, Ger, 85. *Exhib:* One-man shows, Milwaukee Art Ctr, 74, Albright-Knox Art Gallery, 77, Mus Nac, Havana, 81, Mus Bellas Artes, Caracas, Venezuela, 81 & Whitney Mus Am Art, 82; Am Narrative Art, 1967-77, Contemp Art Mus, Houston, Tex, 77; Alternatives in Retrospect-An Historical Overview 1969-1975, New Mus, New York, 81; Four Artists and the Map, Spencer Mus Art, Kans, 81; 18th Sculpture Biennale Middelheim, Antwerp, Belgium, 85; Photog & Art since 1946, Los Angeles Co Mus, 87. *Collections Arranged:* The Solomon Collection, Sarah Lawrence Col, 76; The Carter Collection, Ga Mus Art, 77. *Teaching:* Guest lectr many univs, 76-81; Sr instr, Univ Tex, Austin, 88 & 90. *Awards:* Creative Artists Pub Serv Grant, 73 & 76; Nat Endowment Arts Grants, 74 & 80. *Bibliog:* David Sterritt (auth), Merged media, Christian Sci Monitor, 11/4/82; William Zimmer (auth), Remembering memory lane, NY Times, 2/27/83; Gerritt Henry (auth), Review, Art in Am, 9/86; Robert Smith (auth), Early Concepts of the Last Decade, New York times, 9/25/87. *Media:* Multi-media. *Publ:* Contribr, Tracks J, spring 75; Unbuilt America, McGraw-Hill, 76; The Individual in a Social World, Addison-Wesley, 77; The Big Jewish Book, Doubleday, 78; Wide Angle Film Quarterly, Vol 5, No 3, Ohio Univ Press, 83; Photography & Art since 1946, Abbeville Press, 87. *Dealer:* Elizabeth Galasso Main St Ossining NY; Liverpool Gallery Brussels Belgium. *Mailing Add:* 87 E Houston St New York NY 10012

WELCH, STUART CARY
CURATOR, HISTORIAN
b Buffalo, NY, Apr 2, 28. *Study:* Harvard Col, AB, 50. *Pos:* Cur, Near Eastern & Indian Art, Fogg Art Mus, Harvard Univ, cur manuscripts, Harvard Col Libr; consult Islamic art dept, Metrop Mus Art, New York. *Teaching:* Lectr, Near Eastern & Indian Art, Harvard Univ. *Res:* Safavid painting (Iran); Mughal and Rajput painting (India). *Publ:* Coauth, Gods, Thrones and Peacocks: Northern Indian Painting from Two Traditions, Asia Soc, 65; auth, A King's Book of Kings: The Shahnameh of Shah Tahmasp, Metrop Mus Art, New York, 72; auth, Room for Wonder: Indian Painting under the British Raj, Am Fedn Arts, 78; coauth, The Houghton Shahnameh, Harvard Univ Press, 80; auth, Annemarie Schimmel: A Pocketbook for Akbar, 83, The Emperor's Album, 87 & The Islamic World, 87, Metrop Mus Art, New York. *Mailing Add:* Dept Fine Arts Harvard Univ Cambridge MA 02138

WELDEN, DANIEL W
PRINTMAKER, PAINTER
b New York, NY, Oct 22, 41. *Study:* Adelphi Univ, BA, 64, MA, 67; Acad Fine Art, Munich, Ger, 69-71. *Work:* Guild Hall Mus, East Hampton, NY; Greater Mus Art, Lafayette, Ind. *Comn:* Portfolio, Southampton Hosp, NY, 80-82. *Exhib:* Solo exhibs, Southwest Tex Univ, Canyon, 79, Long Beach Mus, NY, 81, Galerie Kausch, Kassel, Ger, 81, Port Washington Pub Libr, NY, 83, Macey Gallery, Columbia Univ, New York, 84, Hempstead Harbor Gallery, Glen Cove, NY, 86 & Parasol Gallery, Sag Harbor, NY, 86; Traveling exhib, Prints from the workshop of Dan Welden, Gallery North, Setauket, NY, Cent Conn State Univ, Print Coun NJ; Clarke Col, Dubuque, Iowa; Western Va Community Col, Roanoke, Va; Benton Gallery, Southampton, NY. *Teaching:* Prof art & printmaking, State Univ NY, Stony Brook, 77-85; artist-in-residence, Cent Conn State Univ, 86-87. *Awards:* First Prize, Work on Paper, Guild Hall Mus, 86; and others. *Mem:* Jimmy Ernst Artists Alliance, East Hampton, NY; World Print Coun, San Francisco, Calif; Long Island Printmakers Soc, NY (pres, 77-84); Soc Am Graphic Artists, NY (vpres, 83-86); SAGA Artists/Printmakers (pres, 89; Soc Am Graphic Artists (past hon pres). *Media:* All. *Publ:* Coauth, Understanding Prints, Long Island Printmakers Soc, 80; auth, Journal of the Print World, Lane, 81. *Dealer:* Benton Gallery 365 County Rd 39 Southampton NY 11968. *Mailing Add:* PO Box 520 Sag Harbor NY 11963

WELDON, BARBARA MALTBY
PAINTER, PRINTMAKER
b Yuma, Ariz. *Study:* San Diego State Univ, 50-52; Univ Calif, San Diego, 70-73. *Work:* Bank of San Francisco & Bank Am World Hq, San Francisco; San Diego Mus Art, Calif; Copley Mem Libr & Salk Inst, La Jolla, Calif; San Jose Mus Art, Calif; City of Santa Fe Springs, Calif; Utah State Univ. *Comn:* paintings, VRC Parkway Radiology Ctr, Escondido, Calif, 89; Peabody Hotel, Orlando, Fla, 88; Grossmont Hospital Women's Ctr, La Mesa, Calif, 90; Mason & Elizabeth Phelps Collection, La Jolla, Calif. *Exhib:* Solo exhibs, San Diego Mus Art, 76, Clark Gallery, Lincon, Mass, 79-80 & 82, Thomas Babeor Gallery, La Jolla, 80-84, 86, 88, 90 & 92, Laguna Art Mus, Calif, Patty Aande Gallery, San Diego, 84 & Ivory/Kimpton Gallery, San Francisco, 82, 83, 86 & 92; Nat Acad Design, New York, 79; Newport Harbor Art Mus, 81; Mulvane Art Ctr, Washburn Univ of Topeka, Kans, 84; Sheila Nussbaum Gallery, 84, 86 & 92; Citizens Gallery, Yokohama, 92. *Pos:* Adv bd mem, Pub Arts, San Diego, Calif, 86 & 87; juror art exhibs (example: San Diego Del Mar Fair); commemorative artist for KPBS 25 yr Anniversary Poster, 92. *Awards:* First Award, Nat Watercolor Soc, 74; Second Prize, San Diego Mus Art, 75; William A Paton Prize, Nat Acad Design, 79. *Bibliog:* Robert McDonald (auth), Translucent and lyrical, Artweek, 1/82 & Weldon's art speaks to viewer, Los Angeles Times, 4/86; Richard Reilly (auth), Barbara Weldon lights up Babeor Gallery with subtle colors, San Diego Union, 11/82; Jonathan Saville (auth), Indian Gifts, San Diego Reader, 4/92. *Mem:* Mixed, Watercolor. *Media:* Mixed Media, Acrylic. *Dealer:* Sheila Nussbaum Gallery 341 Millburn Ave Millburn NJ. *Mailing Add:* c/o Thomas Babeor Gallery 7470 Girard Ave La Jolla CA 92037

WELLBORN, J(EANETTE) D(ARLEEN)
PAINTER
b Carlsbad, NMex, June 15, 43. *Study:* Univ NMex, BFA, 65. *Exhib:* Watercolor Southwest, Mus Tex Tech Univ, Lubbock, Tex, 80; West '83, Greenville Mus Art, Greenville, SC, 83; West '84, Minn Mus Art, St Paul, Minn, 84; American Watercolor Society Traveling Exhibition, Charles & Emma Frye Mus Art, Seattle, Wash, 84 & 88; Western Federation of Watercolor Societies Juried Exhibition, Mus Albuquerque, NMex, 84; Rocky Mountain National Watermedia, Foothills Art Ctr, Golden, Colo, 85; Solo exhib, Carlsbad Art Mus, 89. *Awards:* Western Fedn Watercolor Socs Exhib, Best of Show, 81 & 88; High Winds Medal, Am Watercolor Soc Exhib, 86 & 88; Nat invited juror, Am Watercolor Soc, 89. *Bibliog:* Mary Carrol Nelson (auth), J D M Welborn, Southwest Art, 2/87; Mike Ward (auth), New Spirit of Watercolor, F & W Publ, 89; Cris Parrington (producer, ed) Colores, KNME TV, 2/90. *Mem:* NMex Watercolor Soc (bd dirs, 79-80); Albuquerque Mus Found; Dolphin Fel AWS; Am Watercolor Soc. *Media:* Acrylic, Watercolor. *Dealer:* Concetta D Farley 50 First Plaza Albuquerque NM 87110. *Mailing Add:* 3819 La Hacienda Dr NE Albuquerque NM 87110

WELLER, ALLEN STUART
EDUCATOR, HISTORIAN
b Chicago, Ill, Feb 1, 07. *Study:* Univ Chicago, BA, 27, PhD, 42; Princeton Univ, MA, 29; Univ Indianapolis, Hon LLD, 65; Univ Fla, Hon DFA, 77. *Collections Arranged:* Contemporary American Painting & Sculpture, Krannert Art Mus, 48-53, biennially, 55-74; Mitchell Mus, Mt Vernon, Ill, 78-79, 81 & 83; Lorado Taft, Krannert Mus, 83. *Pos:* Guest cur, Mitchell Mus, Mt Vernon, Ill, 78-80 & 83, prof emer, 75. *Teaching:* Prof hist art, Univ Mo-Columbia, 29-47; prof hist art, head dept, dean col fine & appl arts & dir mus, Univ Ill, 47-75; vis prof, Univ Minn, Univ Colo, Univ Calif, Univ RI & Ore State Univ. *Awards:* Benjamin Franklin Fel, Royal Soc Arts, London, 70; Nat Asn Sch Art Fel, 71. *Mem:* Fel Royal Soc Arts London; fel Nat Asn Schs Art; Col Art Asn Am (bd dirs, formerly); Soc Archit Historians; Nat Asn Schs Art (bd dirs, formerly). *Res:* Italian Renaissance; contemporary American painting and sculpture. *Publ:* Auth, Francesco de Giorgio, 1439-1501, 42; Abraham Rattner, 56; Art USA Now, 62; Joys and Sorrows of Recent American Art, 68; Lorado in Paris, 85. *Mailing Add:* 401 Burwash, #320 Savoy IL 61874

WELLER, DON MIGHELL
ILLUSTRATOR, DESIGNER
b Colfax, Wash, Aug 13, 37. *Study:* Wash State Univ, BA, 60. *Work:* Mus Mod Art, Toyama, Japan; Hiroshima Mus Art, Shoshin Soc, Japan; Bienale Uzite Grafik Brno, Czech. *Exhib:* Creativity on Paper, Mead Libr of Ideas, New York, 68 & 69; Graphis Annual, Zurich, Switz, 68-72, 74-81 & 83; Creativity, Art Direction Mag, New York, 74-81 & 83; Communication Arts, Commun Arts Mag, Palo Alto, 74-81, 84, 85, 87 & 88; Graphic Design USA, New York, 80-84; Soc Typographic Arts 100, Chicago, 80, 82 & 85; Graphic Design USA, 80, 81, 83 & Book Show, 84 & 85, Am Inst Graphic Art, New York. *Pos:* Owner & founder, Weller Inst for the Cure of Design, 73- *Teaching:* Instr graphic design, Univ Calif, Los Angeles, 68-70; instr illus, Art Ctr Col Design, Los Angeles, 70-80. *Awards:* Gold Medal, Art Directors Show, 71-75 & The One Show, 72, 73 & 78, Art Dir Club New York; Lifetime Achievement Award, Soc Illusrs, Los Angeles, 82. *Bibliog:* Mike Shenan (auth), Don Weller, Commun Arts, 78; Tak Igarashi (auth), Don Weller, Idea, Tokyo, Japan, 83. *Mem:* Soc Illusrs, Los Angeles (pres, 68); Graphic Artists Guild; Am Inst Graphic Arts; Commun Arts Soc, Los Angeles (secy, 70-72). *Publ:* Illusr, Fame, 80 & Cool Cats, 82, Brad Benedict; Park City, Weller Inst, 84; Seashells & Sunsets, Weller Inst, 86; Phantom of the Opera, Peregrine Smith, 88. *Mailing Add:* Box 726 Park City UT 84060

WELLER, LAURIE JUNE
PAINTER
b Warsaw, NY, May 18, 53. *Study:* Univ Ill, Urbana, BFA, 76; Tyler Sch Art, Philadelphia, MFA, 80. *Work:* Tambrands Inc, Lake Success, NY; Steak & Ale Corp, Dallas, Tex; Mischer Corp Collections, Houston, Tex; Prudential Insurance Co Am, Newark, NJ; Transco Corp Collection, Houston, Tex. *Comn:* Sybaritica (watercolor on paper), comn by Thomas Wright, San Antonio, Tex, 84; Fiesta (watercolor on paper), comn by Dr Evelyn Hammon, Austin, Tex, 88; Rivulets Triptych (watercolor on paper), comn by Intellicall Corp, Dallas, Tex, 89. *Exhib:* Private Treasures: Public View, San Antonio Mus Art, 85; Watercolor USA: The Monumental Image, Springfield Art Mus, 86; Homeostasis, East & West Galleries, Tex Woman's Univ, 87; Large Format Watercolors, Abilene Art Mus, 88; Out of the Forest (with Gary Washmon), Parkland Col, Champaign, Ill, 90. *Pos:* Vpres, Austin Contemp Visual Arts Asn, 84-84. *Teaching:* Lectr watercolor & drawing, SW Tex State Univ, San Marcos, 81-88; painting & drawing, Tex Woman's Univ, Denton, 88-90, asst prof painting & drawing, 90- *Awards:* Purchase & Merit Award, Okla Art Annex, 79; Cash Award, Tex Fine Arts Asn Juried Exhib, 82; Plaque of Distinction, Marietta Nat 15th Ann Painting & Sculpture, 82. *Mem:* Denton Art League; Dallas Mus Art. *Media:* Oil, Watercolor. *Dealer:* Patrick Gallery PO Box 1706 Austin TX 78767. *Mailing Add:* Rt 2 Box 637-M Denton TX 78201

WELLER, PAUL
PHOTOGRAPHER, PAINTER
b Boston, Mass, Dec 20, 12. *Study:* Nat Acad Design, 32-33; Art Students League, 45. *Work:* Metrop Mus, New York; San Francisco Mus, Mod Art, Calif; Philadelphia Mus Art, Pa; Baltimore Mus Art, Md; Wolfson Found Mus, Miami, Fla. *Comn:* Mural, US Post Off, US Treasury Dept, Baldwinsville, NY, 41. *Exhib:* Ann Show, Chicago Art Inst, 39; Ann, Philadelphia Art Alliance, Pa, 40; one-man show, Paul Weller Photos, Brooklyn Mus, NY, 50; Ann, Univ Ky Mus, 86. *Mem:* Jimmy Ernst Artists Alliance Easthampton NY; Nat Arts Club New York. *Media:* All Media. *Publ:* Illusr, Sci Am Mag, 50-75; Bantam Books, 60-77; Simon & Schuster, 65-77; Forbes Mag, 67-77; Woman's Day, 67-77. *Dealer:* Mary Ryan Gallery 452 Columbus Ave New York NY 10024. *Mailing Add:* PO Box 1049 East Hampton NY 11937

WELLING, JAMES
PHOTOGRAPHER
b Hartford, Conn, 1951. *Study:* Carnegie-Mellon Univ, studied studio art, 69-71; Calif Col Arts, Valencia, BFA, 72, MFA, 74. *Work:* Mus Modern Art, Vienna. *Exhib:* The Binational, Mus Fine Arts, Boston, Mass, 88; Beaver College, Glenside, Pa, 89; A Forest of Signs, MDCA, Los Angeles, Calif; Solo exhib, Kunsthalle, Bern, Switzerland, 90, MCC St Etienne, France, 90, Sous Sol, Geneva, Switzerland, 90; New York: Ailleurs et Autrement, Mus d'Art Mod, Paris, 84. *Awards:* NY Found Arts Fel, 86; Artist-in-residence, Lightworks, Syracuse, NY, 86; NEA 87. *Bibliog:* Roslaind Krauss (auth), Photography and Abstraction, Hunter College, 89; Walter Benn Michaels (auth), The Photographic Surface, Kunsthalle Bern, 90; Catherine Queloz (auth), Images de la Photographie, Kunsthalle Bern, 90. *Dealer:* Cash/Newhouse Gallery 170 Avenue B New York NY 10009. *Mailing Add:* 135 Grand Street New York NY 10013

WELLIVER, NEIL G
PAINTER
b Millville, Pa, July 22, 29. *Study:* Philadelphia Mus Col Art, BFA, 53; Yale Sch Art, MFA, 55. *Work:* Metrop Mus Art, Mus Mod Art & Whitney Mus Am Art; Pa Acad Fine Arts, Philadelphia; Hirshhorn Mus, Washington, DC; Utah Mus Fine Art; Mus Fine Arts, Boston, Mass; Butler Inst Am Art; and others. *Comn:* Portrait, Bishop of Portland, Maine, 76; 41st Int Eucharist Cong, Philadelphia, 76. *Exhib:* Places, Greenville County Mus Art, SC, 85; A contemporary View of Nature, Aldrich Mus, Ridgefield, Conn, 86; 50th Nat Midyear Exhib, Butler Inst Am Art, Youngstown, Ohio, 86; In the Country, Bronx Mus the Arts, NY, 87; Am 76 Traveling Exhib, US Dept Interior, 76-78; New England Now: Contemporary Art from Six States 88; solo exhibs, Marlborough Gallery, New York, 83, 85 & 87, Marlborough Fine Art Mus, London, Eng, 84, William A Farnsworth Mus, Rockland, Maine, 86, O'Farrell Gallery, Brunswick, Maine, 86 & 87; and others. *Pos:* Critic painting, Cooper Union Art Sch, 54-57; critic painting, Yale Univ, Univ Pa & Md Inst Col Art. *Teaching:* Instr, Cooper Union, 53-57, Yale Univ, 55-65, Swarthmore Col, 66 & Univ Pa, 66-87. *Awards:* Morse Fel, 60-61; Skowhegan Award, 75; Guggenheim Fel, 83. *Bibliog:* John Ashberry & Frank Goodyear (coauths), Welliver, Rizzoli, 85; Ginger Danto (auth), What Becomes an Artist Most? Art News, 11/87; Juan Manuel Bonet (auth), Arco-88: continuidad, calidad, claridad, Diario, 2/12/88. *Media:* All. *Publ:* Contribr, Bicentennial Exhib Catalogue, US Dept Interior, 75; Art News, Craft Horizons & Perspecta. *Dealer:* Marlborough Gallery 40 W 57th St New York NY 10019; Brooke Alexander 20 W 57th St New York NY 10019. *Mailing Add:* RD 2 Lincolnville ME 04849

WELLS, BETTY CHILDS
ILLUSTRATOR, PAINTER
b Baltimore, Md, Dec 7, 26. *Study:* Johns Hopkins Univ, 46; Md Inst Art, grad, 48, scholar, 49. *Work:* Peale Mus, Baltimore; White House & Supreme Court, Washington, DC; Univ Md Sch Law; Toronto Pub Libr. *Comn:* Interior murals (plaster & mosaic), Taylor Manor Psychiat Ctr, Ellicott City, Md, 69; interior murals (mosaic), Lake Clifton Sch, Baltimore, 71; exterior mural (mosaic), Templeton Sch, Baltimore, 73; Chief Justice Warren E Burger (portrait sketch), 76; Mrs Warren E Burger (portrait), Col William & Mary, 83. *Exhib:* Audubon Artist Ann, Nat Acad Art, New York; one-woman shows, Int Gallery, Baltimore, 66, Baltimore Mus Art, 74, & Va Beach Arts Ctr, 87; US Supreme Ct, Wash, DC, 78-79; Florida State Univ, 80; An American Album: Images from women artists, Nairobi, Kenya, 85; and others. *Pos:* Freelance courtroom illusr, Washington Post, 72-77 & WTOP, Washington, DC, 73-74; courtroom illusr, NBC, 74- *Teaching:* Instr basic drawing, Md Inst Art, 46-48. *Awards:* Best in Show, Easton Acad Arts, Md, 66; Two Emmies, 78; Am Bar Asn Gavel Award, 79. *Bibliog:* Robert Leslie (auth), Walls designed by Betty Wells, Idea, Japan, Vol 23, No 130; cover story, Am Bar Asn J, 7/79; Patricia Paul Newsom (auth), Betty Wells: Veteran Washington Reporter, Am Artist, 11/84. *Mem:* Artists Equity Asn (pres, Md Chap, 66-68); Arts and Humanities Comn, Virginia Beach, Va; Nat Acad TV Arts & Sci. *Media:* Multimedia. *Publ:* Contribr, Designing and Making Mosaics, Davis, 71; Arts for Architecture, Dept Housing & Urban Develop, 73; illusr, Supreme Court on Nixon Tapes, New York Times, US News & World Report, 74 & Newsweek, 10/77 & 12/77; cover, Am Bar Asn J, 3/77; cover design & illusr, Bryson B Rash's Footnote Washington, EPM Publ Inc, 83. *Mailing Add:* 2180 Rosewell Drive Virginia Beach VA 23454

WELLS, CAROL MENTHE
PAINTER, SCULPTOR
b New York, NY, July 3, 42. *Study:* Univ Bridgeport, with Jennett Lam, BS, 63; Rutgers Univ, MA, 64; Univ Conn, DPED, 81, PhD(synaesthetics), 84; study with Michael Andrews, MA(art). *Work:* Jane Voorhees Zimmerli Art Mus, New Brunswick, NJ; Eastern Conn State Univ; Univ Calif, Riverside; Univ Conn; Univ Bridgeport, Conn; and others. *Comn:* Thirty-two ft mural, Windsor Bd of Ed, Conn; Impressions (sight-sound intermedia), Enfield Bd of Ed & Wadsworth Atheneum Art Mus. *Exhib:* One-man show, Animated sculpture, Lutz Mus, Manchester, Conn, 79; Winter juried exhib, Bushnell Gallery, 80; invitational show, Bosham Gallery, Sussex, Eng, 84 & 85; Carlson Gallery, Arnold Bernhard Arts & Humanities Ctr, 88; Zimmerli Art Mus; Wadsworth Atheneum Art Mus; Faculty Gallery. *Pos:* Dir acad assoc, Beverly Hills. *Teaching:* Instr, synaesthetics, Wadsworth Atheneum, Art Mus, 69-76; instr sculpture, drawing & art hist, Manchester, Greater Hartford & Tunxis Col, 77-79; instr animated sculpture, Trinity Col & Skidmore Col. *Bibliog:* L Guica (auth), Animated sculpture-puppets lead the class, Hartford Courant, 8/14/77; L Margolies (auth), Carol Menthe soft sculpturist extraordinaire, Farmington Valley Herald, 3/39/79; and others. *Media:* Oil, Enamels; Mixed. *Publ:* Impressions Workshop, Sight Sound Intermedia, Arts in Soc. *Dealer:* Dealer Academic Assoc PO Box 3854 Fullerton CA 94624. *Mailing Add:* PO Box 3854 Fullerton CA 92634

WELLS, LYNTON
PAINTER
b Baltimore, Md, Oct 21, 40. *Study:* RI Sch Design, Providence, BFA, 62; Cranbrook Acad Art, Bloomfield Hills, Mich, MFA, 65. *Work:* Mus Mod Art, New York; Dallas Mus Fine Art, Tex. *Exhib:* One-man shows, Andre Emmerich Gallery, New York, 75, Clair Copley, Los Angeles, 76, Droll/Kolbert Gallery, 78, Univ Wis-Eau Claire, 79 & Sable-Castelli, Can, 85; retrospective, Princeton Univ Art Mus, 79; Flint Inst Arts, 89; Staempeli Gallery, New York, 90; Grace Borgenicht Gallery, New York, 90; Baron/Boisanté, New York, 92. *Awards:* NY State Coun Arts, 73 & 77; Nat Endowment Arts Grant, 75. *Bibliog:* Bruce Boice (auth), article, Artforum, 5/73. *Dealer:* Holly Solomon Gallery 724 Fifth Ave New York NY 10019. *Mailing Add:* c/o Lawrence Oliver 1617 Walnut St Philadelphia PA 19103

WELLS, MAC
PAINTER
b Cleveland, Ohio, Feb 3, 25. *Study:* Oberlin Col, BA, 48; Cooper Union, 48-49; also with Nahum Tschacbasov & Yasuo Kuniyoshi. *Work:* Michener Collection, Univ Tex, Austin; Aldrich Mus, Ridgefield, Conn; Herron Mus Art, Indianapolis, Ind; Guggenheim Mus; Wadsworth Athenaeum, Hartford, Conn; and others. *Comn:* Three-dimensional card, Mus Mod Art, New York, NY, 65. *Exhib:* One-man shows, A M Sachs Gallery, New York, 65 & 67, Max Hutchinson Gallery, New York, 70 & 72, Susan Caldwell Gallery, New York, 75, Landmark Gallery, 79 & 55, Mercer Gallery, New York, 81, Dwight Frederic Boyden Gallery, St Marys Col Md, 92, AAA, Edwin A Ulrich Mus Art, Wichita, Kans, 92; and others. *Teaching:* Asst prof, gen studio, Hunter Col, 66-81, assoc prof, 81-90, prof, 90-; vis instr art, Purdue Univ, West Lafayette, Ind, spring 66; instr painting & design, Moore Col Art,

Philadelphia, 66-72; instr painting, Skowhegan Sch Painting & Sculpture, Maine, 69. *Awards:* Yaddo fel, 64 & 65. *Bibliog:* New Talent, Art in Am, 7-8/65; Lucy Lippard (auth), New York letter, Art Int, 11/20/65; Laurie Anderson (auth), article, Art News, 1/71. *Mem:* Am Abstract Artists. *Media:* Multimedia. *Mailing Add:* 64 Grand St New York NY 10013

WELLS, THOMAS (WINCHESTER)
PAINTER
b Chicago, Ill, Oct 20, 16. *Study:* Yale Univ Sch Fine Arts, BFA, 42. *Work:* Seattle Art Mus, Safeco Insurance Co & Pacific Car & Foundry, Seattle, Wash; Wash State Capitol Mural Design, Olympia; Matson Navigation Co, San Francisco, Calif. *Comn:* NW Indian Design (mural), Bellingham Hotel, Wash, 50; Theotokos (mosaic), St Demetrios Church, Seattle, Wash, 65; Maritime Lumber (mural), Wash Mutual Bank, Seattle, Wash, 68; Jetfoil (mural), Boeing Aircraft Co, Seattle, Wash, 72. *Exhib:* Seven Northwest Annuals, Seattle Art Mus, Wash, 50-60; one-man shows, Zantman Art Galleries, 74-79, 81-85 Haines Gallery, Seattle, 74, 76 & 78 & Foster White Gallery, Seattle, 81; Three Marine Exhibs, Mystic Seaport Mus, Conn, 78, 79 & 80-90; Marine Artist Shows, Grand Central Galleries, New York, 79 & 80; One Marine Exhib, Peabody Mus, Salem, Mass, 80; Retrospective Exhib, Frye Art Mus, 81. *Awards:* 3 First Place Best of Show, Mus Sci & Industry, Seattle, 55, 56 & 57. *Bibliog:* Peter Stanford (auth), Sea History Mag, Nat Maritime Trust, 80. *Mem:* Fel Am Soc Marine Artist; Puget Sound Group of NW Painters Seattle. *Media:* Oil, Watercolor. *Dealer:* Foster White Gallery 311 1/2 Occidental Seattle WA 98104; Zantman Art Galleries Ltd 6th & Massion Carmel CA 93921. *Mailing Add:* 8514 Paisley Dr NE Seattle WA 98115

WELPOTT, JACK WARREN
PHOTOGRAPHER, EDUCATOR
b Kansas City, Kans, Apr 27, 23. *Study:* Ind Univ, BS, 49, MS, 55, MFA, 59. *Work:* Mus Mod Art, New York; Bibliot Nat, Paris; Eastman House, Rochester, NY; Ctr Creative Photog, Tucson, Ariz; San Francisco Mus Art. *Exhib:* One-man shows, Eastman House, 66, Art Inst Chicago, 72, San Francisco Mus Art, 76, Univ Southern Calif, Los Angeles, 77, Univ Ore, 79 & Ctr Creative Photog, 79; group show, Metrop Mus Art, New York. *Collections Arranged:* Artist as Teacher-Teacher as Artist, San Francisco Mus Art, 76. *Teaching:* Prof photog, San Francisco State Univ, 59-; vis prof, Univ Ariz, Tucson, 77. *Awards:* Nat Endowment for Arts fel, 79. *Bibliog:* Arthur Ollman (auth), Jack Welpott: Photographer, Vidio, 75. *Mem:* Friends Photog. *Publ:* Co-auth, Women and Other Visions, Morgan & Morgan, 75. *Dealer:* Witkin Gallery 41 E 57th St New York NY 10022. *Mailing Add:* c/o Photographers Gallery of Palo Alto 732 Emerson St Palo Alto CA 94301

WELTER, COLE H
PAINTER, EDUCATOR
b Watertown, SDak, July 26, 52. *Study:* Univ Tex, Austin, with Bob Levers & Everett Spruce, BFA, 74, MFA, 76; Tex Tech Univ, with Gene Mittler & Bill Lockhart, PhD,89. *Work:* Huntington Gallery, Univ Tex, Austin; Anchorage Mus Hist Art, Alaska; San Antonio Mus Mod Art, Tex; Abilene Fine Arts Mus, Tex; Univ Alaska Anchorage Permanent Collection. *Comn:* Windows, First Christian Church, Anchorage, Alaska, 92. *Exhib:* 39th Ann Midyear Show, Butler Inst Am Art, Youngstown, Ohio, 75; 69th Ann Am Exhib, Newport Fine Arts Asn, RI, 76; 34th Ann Competition, Abilene Fine Arts Mus, Abilene, Tex, 76; 43rd Ann Competition, Abilene Fine Arts Mus, Tex, 87; 10th Ann Regional Exhib, McCormick Gallery, Midland Col, Tex, 87; Alaska '92, Alaska Visual Arts Ctr, 92; and others. *Pos:* Exec bd dirs, Anchorage Mus Asn, 88-92; ed, Alaska J Art, 88- *Teaching:* Instr, design, Univ Tex, Austin, 75-76, Tex Tech Univ, 86-88; Chmn, Dept Art, painting, Univ Alaska Anchorage, 88- *Awards:* Fel, Ford Found, 75 & 76; Reston Prize, Nat Asn Schs Art & Design, 87. *Bibliog:* Jan Ingram (auth), Exhibits make happy partners, 9/10/89 & Alaska 92 offers a fresh, bold view of state arts scene, 7/26/92, Anchorage Daily News. *Mem:* Col Art Asn. *Media:* Mixed-Media. *Publ:* Auth, Discipline based art education: not if, but where?, Design Arts Educ, 87; Art and Computers: is there room in the studio for both?, Design Arts Educ, 89; ed, To go where no publication has gone before, Alaska J Art, 89; coauth, The fine arts in Alaskan schools: a 1988 status report, Alaska J Art, 89. *Dealer:* Stonington Gallery 415 F St Anchorage AK 99501. *Mailing Add:* Univ Alaska, Dept of Art 3211 Providence Dr Anchorage AK 99508

WELTZHEIMER, MARIE KASH See Kash, Marie (Marie Kash Weltzheimer)

WENAWINE, BRUCE HARLEY
ADMINISTRATOR, EDUCATOR
b Urbana, Ill, Dec 30, 49. *Study:* Univ Louisville, Ky, BA & MA. *Pos:* Pres, Swain Sch Sesign, New Bedford, Mass, 82-88; mem exec comt & bd dirs, New Bedford Glass Mus, 86-88; dean, Corcoran Sch Art, 88-90. *Teaching:* Lectr, Louisville Sch Art, Ky, 77-82. *Awards:* Cardinal Award, Univ Louisville, 72; Outstanding contribr to arts, Art Ctr Asn, 74. *Mem:* Nat Asn Sch Art & Design; Col Art Asn; Southeastern Asn Coop Higher Educ, Mass (pres, 86-87); Art Cols Exchange (bd dirs, 86-); Alliance of Independent Col of Art (bd dirs, 88-). *Publ:* Contribr, Anchorage Revisited, Libr Nat, 76. *Mailing Add:* Dean's Office, Corcoran School Art 17th St & New York Ave NW Washington DC 20006

WENGER, BRUCE EDWARD
PRINTMAKER, ASSEMBLAGE ARTIST
b Grand Rapids, Mich, Mar 10, 48. *Study:* Western Mich Univ, BA, 70; Ohio Univ, MFA, 73. *Work:* Grand Rapids Art Mus, Mich; US Info Agency, Washington, DC; Western Mich Univ Print Collection, Kalamazoo; Chicago Gallery, Univ Ill; Ohio Univ Print Collection, Athens. *Exhib:* 6th Biennial Paper & Clay Exhib, Memphis State Univ, Tenn, 87; LaGrange Nat XII, Chattahooche Valley Art Asn, Ga, 87; 7th Annual Faber Birren Color Award Show, Stamford, Conn, 87; 2nd Nat Juried Exhib, Viridian Gallery, New York, 88; 20th Nat Works on Paper Exhib, Minot State Col, NDak, 90; LaGrange Nat XVII, Chattahooche Valley Art Asn, Ga, 92; 10th Ann Maine/Maritime Flatworks Exhib, Univ Maine, Presque Isle, 92. *Teaching:* Asst prof studio art & art hist, Houghton Col, NY, 78-86, head dept art, 82-86; lectr in found, drawing & printmaking, Rochester Inst Technol, NY, 86-92; asst prof, 2D design, Rochester Inst Technol, NY, 92-93. *Awards:* Purchase Award, Fourth Ann Maine Maritime Flat Work Exhib, Univ Presque Isle Maine, 86. *Mem:* Col Art Asn; The Print Club. *Media:* Lithography. *Mailing Add:* PO Box 21 Fillmore NY 14735-0021

WENGER, JANE (B)
PHOTOGRAPHER, EDUCATOR
b New York, NY, Jan 24, 44. *Study:* Alfred Univ, NY, BFA, 66; Ill Inst Technol, Chicago, 69; Univ Ill, Chicago, MFA, 80. *Work:* Mus Mod Art, New York; Mus Contemp Art, Chicago, Ill; Milwaukee Art Mus, Wis; Lehigh Univ, Bethelehem, Pa; Southern Ill Univ, Edwardsville. *Exhib:* One-person shows, Artemisia Gallery, Chicago, Ill, 76, Foto Gallery, New York, 78 & 80, Allen Frumkin Photographs, Chicago, Ill, 80, Mus Contemp Art, Chicago, Ill, 81, Milwaukee Art Mus, Wis, 81 & PS 1, New York, 82. *Teaching:* Instr photog, Univ Ill at Chicago, 75-90. *Awards:* Project Completion Grants, Ill Arts Coun, 79-83. *Bibliog:* Carole Harmel (auth), The dialectics of sexuality, New Art Examiner, 79; Lynne Warren (auth), Jane Wenger, Arts Mag, 3/81; Mary Jane Jacob (auth), Options 7, Jane Wenger: An Environmental Installation, Mus Contemp Art, 81. *Mem:* Soc Photog Educ. *Mailing Add:* 1509 N Wicker Park Chicago IL 60622

WENGER, SIGMUND
DEALER, CONSULTANT
b Brooklyn, NY, Nov 20, 10. *Study:* NY Univ, BA. *Pos:* Consult, Mexico City, 58-63; dir, Wenger Galleries, Calif, 63- *Specialty:* Contemporary art. *Mailing Add:* c/o Wenger Gallery 638 1/2 N Robertson Blvd Los Angeles CA 90069

WENGROVITZ, JUDITH
PAINTER, INSTRUCTOR
b Brooklyn, NY, Jan 3, 31. *Study:* Hunter Col, New York, NY, with Dong Kingman, BA(art educ), 52; workshops with Frank Webb, Millard Sheets and Arthur Barbour. *Work:* Pen Arts Bldg, Wash, DC. *Comn:* Series of paintings of country musicians, Quality Inn, Nashville, Tenn, 80; Nat Bus Educator's Asn, Reston, Va, 82; IBM, Washington, DC, 83; painting, comm by Judge Stanley Sporkin, Washington, DC, 87 & 88; NIH Children's Inn, Bethesda, Md, 92. *Exhib:* Metrop Art Exhib, Smithsonian Inst, Washington, DC, 64; Southern Watercolor Soc, Tour Exhib, Japan, 89; Va Watercolor Soc Exhib, Sci Mus Va, Richmond, Va, 89, Va Beach Fine Arts Ctr, 90, Abingdon, 92; solo exhib, Torpedo Factory, Alexandria, 88, 20th Century Gallery, Williamsburg, Va, 91, NIH, Bethesda, Md, 92; Allied Artists Am 76 exhib, Nat Arts Club Galleries, New York, 89; traveling exhib, Southern Watercolor Soc, Japan, 89; Ky Aqueous '92, Louisville, Ky, 92; 58th Intl Exhib of Miniature Painters, Sculptors & Gravers Soc, Washington, DC, 91. *Pos:* Layout artist, Woodward & Lothrop, Washington, DC, 52-54. *Teaching:* Instr drawing, design & painting, Judy Wengrovitz Sch Art, 62-92; guest lectr painting, Univ Va, 85. *Awards:* Grumbacher Gold Medal Award, Va Watercolor Soc, 89; Equal Merit Award, Va Watercolor Soc, 92; 2nd Place, Landscape-Miniature Show, 92. *Bibliog:* Lisa Barr (auth), Focus on Northern Virginians, Virginian Cardinal, 75; Kym Cooper (auth), Springfield artist opens exteriors, Washington Star, 81; Kathryn Evans (auth), Springfield artist details in watercolor, Springfield Connection, 87. *Mem:* Potomac Valley Watercolorists (pres, 79-80); Nat League Am Pen Women (pres, 74-76); Va Watercolor Soc (pres, 88-); Washington Watercolor Soc; Southern Watercolor Soc; Miniature Painters, Sculptors & Gravers Soc. *Media:* Watercolor. *Publ:* Illusr, The Pen Woman, Nat League of Pen American Woman, 88. *Dealer:* The Art League 05 N Union St Alexandria VA 22314; Cosmo Art Kennebunkport Maine. *Mailing Add:* 5220 Cather Rd Springfield VA 22151

WENTWORTH, JANET
PAINTER
b Norwell, Mass, May 5, 57. *Study:* Parsons Sch Design, New York, BFA, 80; Nat Acad Sch Fine Arts, New York, with Harvy Dinnerstein, 81-82; Art Students League, New York, with Harvy Dinnerstein, Ted Seth Jacobs & Frank Mason, 83-87; La Napoule Arts Found, France & Durham, NH, with Jack Beal, 85-86; Brooklyn Col, New York, with Philip Pearlstein & Lennert Anderson, MFA, 91; Sch Visual Arts, New York, cert(art educ), 92. *Work:* Art Students League Permanent Collection, New York. *Exhib:* Am Watercolor Soc Ann Exhib, Nat Acad Fine Arts, New York, 76; Pastel Soc Am Ann Exhib, Nat Arts Club, New York, 85; League Am Pen Women Ann Exhib, Copley Soc, Boston, 87; Choice, AIR Gallery, New York, 91; Nat Acad Design 167th Ann, Nat Acad Fine Arts, New York, 92. *Awards:* Bd Dirs Award, Pastel Soc Am, 84; Gold Medal Honor, Knickerbocker Artists, New York, 85; Cert Merit, Nat Acad Design 167th Ann, 92. *Mem:* Nat Asn Women Artists; Pastel Soc Am; NY Arts Group; Col Art Asn. *Media:* Pastel, Oil. *Dealer:* Harris Peel Box 1 Peel Gallery Rd Danby VT 05739. *Mailing Add:* 235 W 102nd St No 5-K New York NY 10025

WENTWORTH, MURRAY JACKSON
PAINTER, INSTRUCTOR
b Boston, Mass, Jan 18, 27. *Study:* Art Inst Boston. *Work:* Farnsworth Mus Art, Rockland, Maine; Springfield Mus Art, Mo; First Nat Bank, Boston; DeCordova Mus, Lincoln, Mass; Utah State Univ, Logan. *Exhib:* Metrop Mus Art, New York, 66; Butler Inst Am Art, Youngstown, Ohio, 69; Brockton Fuller Mem Mus, Mass, 70; DeCordova Mus, Mass, 77; one-man shows, Farnsworth Mus, 72 & Guild of Boston Artists, 77 & 80; Rocky Mountain Nat Watercolor Exhib, 82; Nat Acad Design, New York. *Teaching:* Instr watercolor, pvt & watercolor workshops, 77- *Awards:* Ranger Fund Purchase Prize, Nat Acad Design, 65; Nat Arts Club Bronze Medal Hon, 68; Am Watercolor Soc Bronze Medal Hon, 69. *Mem:* Am Watercolor Soc; Allied Artists Am; New England Watercolor Soc (vpres, 71-); Guild Boston Artists; assoc Nat Acad Design. *Media:* Watercolor. *Publ:* Contribr, watercolor page, Am Artist Mag, 70; Watercolor for All Seasons, Northlight, Writers Digest Books. *Dealer:* Peel Gallery Danby VT; Guild Boston Artists 162 Newbury St Boston MA. *Mailing Add:* 132 Central St Norwell MA 02061

WENZEL, JOAN ELLEN
ASSEMBLAGE ARTIST, SCULPTOR
Study: Syracuse Univ, 62-64; NY Univ, BS(painting), 66 & MA(painting), 76; Harvard Univ 66-67. *Work:* Skirball Mus Jewish Art, Los Angeles; Aldrich Mus Contemp Art, Ridgefield, Conn. *Comn:* Multi-section wall structures, Prudential Life, Newark, NJ, 82, Citibank, New York, 87, Peerless Corp, Greenpoint, NY, 87 & Nevele Hotel, Ellenville, NY, 88. *Exhib:* Approach, Avoidance Art in the Obsessive Idiom (with catalog), 81 & Off the Wall (with catalog), 85, Queens Mus, NY; solo exhibs, Gallery Yves Arman, New York, 82 & Helander Gallery, Palm Beach, Fla, 89; Kisch & Wenzel, SoHo Crt Visual Art, New York, 86; 10 Yrs of Collecting, Aldrich Mus Contemp Art, 86; and others. *Media:* Wood. *Dealer:* Albertson Peterson Gallery 329 Park Ave S Winter Park FL 32789. *Mailing Add:* 2275 Ibis Isles Dr W Palm Beach FL 33480

WERFEL, GINA S
PAINTER, EDUCATOR
b Brooklyn, NY, July 1, 51. *Study:* Kirkland Col, NY, with Elias Friedensohn, BA, 74; New York Studio Sch, with Mercedes Matter, Leland Bell & Andrew Forge, cert, 76; Columbia Univ, with David Lund, Leon Goldin & Jane Wilson, MFA, 79. *Exhib:* One-woman shows, Prince Street Gallery, New York, 80, 82, 85, 86, 89 & 92, Maier Mus Art, Randolph-Macon Woman's Col, Lynchburg, Va & Colby Col Mus Art, Waterville, Maine, 89; two-person shows, Cong Sq Gallery, Portland, Maine & Colby Col Mus Art, Waterville, Maine, 81, 83 & 84; Drawings from Nature, Joan Whitney Payson Mus, Portland, Maine, 82; Maine Coast Artists Gallery, Rockport, 83, 87, & 90; Jersey City Mus, NJ, 86. *Pos:* Co-dir, New York Studio Sch, Paris, France, summers, 74 & 75; artist-in-residence, Va Ctr Creative Arts, Sweetbriar, 81, Rockefeller Found Ctr, Bellagio, Italy, 84 & Djerassi Found, Woodside, Calif, 86. *Teaching:* Assoc prof art, Colby Col, Waterville, Maine, 80-91; chair & assoc prof, Randolph-Macon Woman's Col, Lynchburg, Va, 91- *Bibliog:* Gerald Haggerty (auth), Gina Werfel and the Maine stream, Art New Eng, summer 81; Fredy Kaplan (auth), A portfolio of recent images, Am Artist, 2/84; Louise Hamlin (auth), Landscape treatment, Arts New York, 2/87; Carl Little (auth), Gina Werfel at the Colby Mus, Art in Am, 10/89; Edgar Allen Beem (auth), Gina Werfel on the Shores of Expressionism, Maine Times, 4/89. *Mem:* Col Art Asn. *Media:* Oil. *Dealer:* Prince Street Gallery 121 Wooster St New York NY 10012; Cong Sq Gallery Portland ME. *Mailing Add:* c/o Dept Art Randolph-Macon Woman's Col Lynchburg VA 24503

WERGER, ART(HUR LAWRENCE)
PRINTMAKER, EDUCATOR
b Ridgewood, NJ, Dec, 4, 55. *Study:* RI Sch Design, BFA, 78; Univ Wis, Madison, with Warrington Colescott, MFA, 82. *Work:* High Mus Art, Atlanta, Ga; Boston Pub Libr; Brooklyn Mus, NY; Philadelphia Mus Art, Pa; Mus Fine Arts, Boston. *Exhib:* Southeast Seven 9, Southeastern Ctr Contemp Art, Winston-Salem, NC, 86; Georgia Printmakers (with catalog), High Mus Art, Atlanta, 86; 10 Years of Southeast Seven, Southeastern Ctr Contemp Art, 87-88; Fact/Fiction/Fantasy: Recent Narrative Art in the Southeast, Univ Tenn, Knoxville, 87-88; Colorprint USA Update 88, Mus of Tex Tech Univ, 88; Art Werger: In Print, Macon Mus Arts & Sci, 88; Tampa Triennial, Tampa Mus Art, Fla, 88. *Teaching:* Assoc prof graphics & print, Wesleyan Col, 82-, chmn, visual art area, 85- *Awards:* Purchase Awards, Trenton State Col Nat Print Exhib, NJ, 88 & Stockton Nat IV: Print & Drawing exhib, 88; Mus Purchase Award, The Red Clay Survey, Huntsville Mus Art, Ala, 88; Purchase Award, Los Angeles Print Soc Ninth Nat Exhib, 86. *Bibliog:* Patrick E White (auth), Passionate Attention, Southeast Seven 9, 86. *Mem:* Col Art Asn; Southern Graphics Coun; Los Angeles Printmaking Soc; Philadelphia Print Club. *Media:* Etching. *Dealer:* Eve Mannes Gallery Atlanta GA; Wenninger Graphics Boston MA. *Mailing Add:* 4675 Lattimore Dr Macon GA 31210

WERNER, (CHARLES GEORGE)
EDITORIAL CARTOONIST
b Marshfield, Wis, Mar 23, 09. *Study:* Oklahoma City Univ; Northwestern Univ. *Work:* Mo State Hist Soc; Syracuse Univ, NY; Wis State Hist Soc, Madison; Addison Gallery Am Art, Andover, Mass. *Exhib:* Asn Am Ed Cartoonists travel tour. *Pos:* Ed cartoonist, Daily Oklahoman, 35-41; chief ed cartoonist, Chicago Sun, 41-47; ed cartoonist, Indianapolis Star, 47- *Awards:* Pulitzer Prize, 38; First Place Award, Nat Found Highway Safety, 71; Award for Caricature, Int Salon Art, Montreal, 73; and others. *Mem:* New York Cartoonists Soc; Asn Am Ed Cartoonists (pres, 69). *Mailing Add:* 4445 Brown Rd Indianapolis IN 46226

WERNER, DONALD (LEWIS)
PAINTER, PHOTOGRAPHER
b Fresno, Calif, Feb 2, 29. *Study:* Fresno State Col, BA, with Adolf & Ella Odorfer & Jane Gale; Chouinard Art Inst, Los Angeles; also costuming with Majorie Best. *Work:* Murals, Dan River Mills, Wellington Sears & Martex, New York; Fresno Art Mus, Calif; Hudson River Mus, Yonkers, NY; Mus Am Indian, Nat Mus Am Indian, Smithsonian Inst. *Comn:* Collage murals, New York World's Fair; The Ancestors: Native Artisans of the Americas (exhib & graphic design), US Custom House, New York, 79. *Exhib:* Solo exhibs, Gallery 84, New York, 59-75, 79, 82, 84-90, Painting & Photog, Fresno Art Mus, 67 & 79, Photog, Focus Gallery, San Francisco, 68, Painting & Photog, Hudson River Mus, 69 & 72 & Photog, St Paul Civic Ctr, Minn, 70. *Collections Arranged:* Mus of the Am Indian, New York, 78; Echoes of the Drums, Customs House, New York, NY, 78; The Ancestors, Peking, China, 81-82; Star Gods, Am Mus Natural Hist, New York, 82-83; Nat Mus Am Indian, Smithsonian Inst; Fresno Art Mus, Calif. *Pos:* Display designer, Seventeen Mag, 11 yrs; mus artist & designer, Hudson River Mus, 68-75 & Mus of the Am Indian, New York, 78-90, Nat Mus Am Indian, Smithsonian Inst, New York, presently. *Awards:* First Prize for Watercolor, Fresno Art Ctr, 60. *Bibliog:* Robert Beeching (dir), Theatrical Displays and Display Techniques (film), 69 & A China Diary (film), 85, Scope Prod, Calif; Bicycles and Dragons (exhib catalog), Am Mus Natural Hist, 85 & Great Neck Libr, 86, NY. *Mem:* Am Mus Asn. *Media:* Watercolor; Photography. *Publ:* Auth, photogr & designer, Reflections of Winter: Holt, Rhinehart & Winston, 78; bk designer, The Peaceable Kingdom, MacMillan, 79; designer, With Eagle Glance, Mus Am Indian, 82; designer, Americans in Venice, Coe Kerr, 83; The Stuff of Dreams, Mus Am Indian, New York, 86. *Dealer:* Gallery 84 50 Madison Ave New York NY 10016. *Mailing Add:* Nat Mus of Am Indian, Smithsonian Inst 155 St & Broadway New York NY 10032

WERNER, FRANK ROBERT
ENVIRONMENTAL ARTIST
b New York, NY, Sept 16, 36; US citizen. *Study:* Univ Idaho, BGS, 84. *Work:* Latah Co His Mu. *Exhib:* Ann Juried Art Show, Carnegie Art Ctr, Wall Walla, Wash, 87; First and Second Ann ARTFEST, Spokane, Wash, 86 & 87; Moscow Artist's Juried Art Show, Prichard Gallery, Idaho, 87; Palouse Visual Artists Exhib, Pulman, Wash, 87; Centennial Alumni Exhib, Univ Idaho, 87; Northwest Regional Art Show, Pullman, Wash, 88; Art Zone, Jewish Community Ctr, Denver, Colo, 88; solo exhibs, OUT OF CONTEXT, Prichard Gallery, Univ Idaho, Moscow, 91, Carnegie Art Ctr, Walla Walla, Wash, 91, Holter Art Mus, Helena, Mont, 91, Compton Union Gallery, Wash State Univ, Pullman, 92, Grants Pass Mus Art, Grants Pass, Ore, 92, Nicolaysen Art Mus, Casper, Wyo, 93 & Port Angeles Fine Arts Ctr, Port Angeles, Wash, 93; Facets of the Gem State: Fine Arts of Idaho Centennial Exhib, Panhandle State Bank, Sandpoint, Idaho, 90; Idaho Visual Arts Fel Winners, Sun Valley Ctr Arts & Humanities, Sun Valley, Idaho, 90; Seventh Idaho Biennial, Boise Art Mus, 92. *Awards:* Best Display, Sahlin Found, Artfest 1986, Spokane, 86; Award, Idaho Comn Arts Fel, 87 & 92. *Bibliog:* Spokane Chronicle/Rev, 5/27/81 & 8/6/89; ICA Folk Art Exhib (catalog), 84 (in Arabic, 86); Lewiston Morning & Sunday Tribune, 10/14/84, 11/21/86 & 10/22/87; The Salt Lake Tribune, 10/27/85; Idaho Bus Review, 12/23/85; Western Outdoors Mag, 4/86; The Idaho Statesman (Boise), 8/6/86; J of Bus, 10/29/87; Bonner Co Daily Bee, 6/7/90. *Media:* Idaho White Pine, Polychrome Sculpture. *Publ:* Idaho Wildlife Mag, 9/85 & 10/85; Heart of the Arts, 1988-1989 Calendar, Moscow, 9/1/88; Art of the State, 2/89 & 3/89; auth, Art Matters, Quarterly Column, Wildfowl Carving & Collecting Mag, 92. *Mailing Add:* 709 E Third Moscow ID 83843

WERNER, HOWARD
SCULPTOR
b Deal, NJ, July 27, 51. *Study:* Rochester Inst Technol, BFA, 77; Sch Am Craftsmen. *Work:* Sch Am Craftsmen, Rochester, NY; Ariz State Univ, Tempe. *Exhib:* Carnegie Mus Art, 79; Richard Kagan Gallery, Philadelphia, 78-83; Elements Gallery, New York, 78-80; Vladimir Kagan Gallery, New York, 82-83; Woodworks of the Northeast, Wooster Crafts Ctr, Mass, 83; Synderman Gallery, Philadelphia, 83; Inaugural Exhib, Am Craft Mus, New York, 86; Craft Today, Paris, 89; East Meets West in Design, Europe & Japan, 90. *Pos:* Resident, Art Park, Lewiston, NY, 75-77; traveling residency, NY State Parks & Recreation Cultural Program, 76; vis artist, Nat Endowment Arts Omni Int, Atlanta, Ga, 77; resident, Peters Valley, Layton, NJ, 77-78. *Teaching:* Instr sculpture & furniture design, Peters Valley, Layton, NJ, 77-82; instr sculpture, Haywood Tech Inst, NC, 78; instr sculpture, Keane Col, NJ, 81; Instr workshop, State Univ NY, New Paltz, 83. *Awards:* NY State Fel Grant, 87; Nat Endowment Arts, 88. *Bibliog:* Review, Craft Horizons, 78; John Kelsey (auth), New Handmade Furniture, Fine Woodworking, 79; Michael Stone (auth), review, New York Times, 10/81. *Mem:* Am Craft Coun; Peters Valley. *Media:* Wood. *Publ:* Coauth, Carving, Fine Woodworking, 77. *Mailing Add:* Route 28 Mt Tremper NY 12457

WERNER VAUGHN, SALLE
PAINTER, ILLUMINATOR
Work: San Francisco Mus of Mod Art, Calif; Akron Art Inst, Ohio; Lomas-Nettleton Co, Dallas, Tex; Am Tel & Tel, New York; Bridwell Mus, Southern Methodist Univ, Dallas; and others. *Exhib:* Biennial Exhib Painting & Sculpture Show, Whitney Mus, New York, 73; Contemporary Watercolors, Akron Art Inst, Ohio, Indianapolis, Ind & Rochester, NY, 76; Helen Serger, La Boetie Inc, New York, 77; Carus Gallery, New York, 79; one-man show, Tyler Mus of Art, Tex, 73; Metropolitan Mus of Art, New York; Mus of Modern Art, Moscow. *Teaching:* Founder experimental art, Art Involvement & Motivation, 70- *Bibliog:* Patsy Swank (auth), Salle Werner (film), Dallas Educ TV, 72; Arch Am Art, Smithsonian Inst. *Media:* Watercolor, Oil; Tempera. *Mailing Add:* 4618 Blossom St Houston TX 77007

WERNESS, HOPE B
HISTORIAN
b Del Rio, Tex, Feb 10, 43. *Pos:* dir, Univ Gallery, 82-87. *Teaching:* Vis lectr art hist, San Jose State Univ, Calif, 76-77; asst prof art hist, Calif State Col, Stanislaus, Turlock, Calif, 77-81, assoc prof & acting chair, 81-86, prof, 86-*Awards:* Nat Endowment Humanities Summer Seminar, 80. *Mem:* Col Art Asn. *Res:* Nineteenth century art history, specializing in Van Gogh, twentieth century art history; pre-Columbian and primitive art. *Mailing Add:* 913 Dianne Dr Turlock CA 95380

WERT, NED OLIVER
EDUCATOR, PAINTER
b Millersburg, Pa, May 26, 36. *Study:* Indiana Univ of Pa, BA(art educ), 58; Pa State Univ, MEd(art), 64; Kent State Univ, with Alex Katz, Jim Melchert & Jack Tworkov, 70. *Work:* Southern Alleghenies Mus Art, Loretto, Pa; Pittsburgh Plate Glass Corp, Alcoa Corp, Pittsburgh, Pa; Am Int Sch, Düsseldorf, WGer; Pa State Mus, Harrisburg, Pa; Blue Cross, Blue Shield. *Exhib:* Assoc Artists Pittsburgh, Carnegie Mus Art; Butler Inst Art Ann Nat Exhib; Three Rivers Festival, Pittsburgh, Pa; La Mostra CAS, Camera Commercio, Lucca, Italy; Triennial Invitational, Southern Alleghenies Mus Art, Loretto, Pa; Five Ind Univ Pa Artists, Noho Gallery, New York; and others. *Pos:* Dir, Univ Mus, Indiana, Pa; Eastern vpres, Nat Art Educ Asn; pres, PA Art Educ Asn. *Teaching:* Art, Elizabethtown Area Sch Dist, Pa, 58-70; prof painting, Ind Univ Pa, 70-88; dir, Univ Mus, Indiana, Pa, 88-; retired. *Awards:* Best of Show, Fourth Ann Exhib, Westmoreland Mus, 82; Jurors Award, Assoc Artists Pittsburgh, Carnegie Mus Art, Pittsburgh, Pa, 82; Outstanding Educator, Nat Art Educ Asn, 86; Distinguished Alumnus, Indiana Univ of Pa, 88. *Mem:* Assoc Artists Pittsburgh; Nat Art Educ Asn; Pa Art Educ Asn (pres, 82-84); Allied Artists Johnstown. *Media:* Acrylic. *Publ:* Coauth, Multiple image and sound: Motivation for creative activity, Art Teacher Mag, fall 74; Colored light and shadow: A stimulus for creative movement, Pa J Physical Educ, winter 74; Multi-media: Motivation for the arts and basic education, Learning Resources Mag, 4/75; Readings: Developing arts programs for handicapped students, Pa Dept Educ, 82. *Dealer:* Bird in the Hand Gallery 427 Broad St Sewickley PA 15143. *Mailing Add:* Box 1 Brush Valley PA 15720

WESCHLER, ANITA
SCULPTOR, PAINTER
b New York, NY. *Study:* Horace Mann Sch, grad, Le Grand Verger, Lausanne, Switz; Parsons Sch Design, grad; Nat Acad Design; Pa Acad Fine Arts, with Albert Laessle; Art Students League, with William Zorach; Columbia Univ; Barnes Found. *Work:* Whitney Mus Am Art, Amherst Univ; Brandeis Univ; Metrop Mus Art; Yale Univ; Univ Pa Acad Fine Arts; Michael Wolfson Found, Miami, Fla; plus other pub & pvt collections. *Comn:* Sculpture, US Treas Dept, US Post Off, Elkin, NC; seven life-size portrait heads (bronze), Inst for Achievement of Human Potential, Philadelphia; seven bronze replicas Inst Achievment of Human Potential, Italy & Brazil 90. *Exhib:* Whitney Mus Am Art; Nat Inst Arts & Lett; Metrop Mus Art; Philadelphia Mus Art; Mus Mod Art; Jewish Mus; Riverside Mus; Storm King Ctr; over 40 solo shows nationwide; Hofstra Mus. *Pos:* Deleg to US Comt Int Asn Art; deleg, Fine Arts Fedn New York. *Teaching:* Var lect-demonstrations, 89;. *Awards:* Prizes, Corcoran Gallery Art, Montclair Art Mus & San Francisco Mus Art; Audubon Artists Medal of Honor; MacDowell Colony & Yaddo Fels. *Bibliog:* Var critical reviews in newspapers & art press. *Mem:* Fedn Mod Painters & Sculptors; Nat Asn Women Artists; Artist Craftsmen NY; Sculptors Guild; Nat Mus Women Arts. *Media:* Multimedia; Synthetic Gazes, Plastic Resins. *Publ:* Auth, Nightshade, Colony Press; A Sculptor's Summary. *Dealer:* Berman/Daferner 568 Broadway New York NY 10012; Portraits Inc 945 Park Ave New York NY 10028. *Mailing Add:* 136 Waverly Pl New York NY 10014

WESLEY, JOHN
PAINTER
b Los Angeles, Calif, Nov 25, 28. *Work:* Albright-Knox Art Gallery, Buffalo, NY; Hirshhorn Mus and Sculpture Garden, Smithsonian Inst, Washington, DC; Mus Mod Art; Univ Rochester; Univ Tex; Portland Art Mus, Ore; Univ Ky, Louisville; Chinaji Found, Marfa, Tex. *Exhib:* The Figure Int, Am Fedn of Arts, New York, 67-68; 1968, Whitney Mus Art, 69, Art about Art, Whitney Mus Art, 78; Indianapolis Mus Art, Ind, 69; Documenta V, Kassel, Ger, 72; one-man shows, (13) Robert Elkon Gallery, New York, 63-83, Univ Rochester, 74, Carl Solway, Cincinnati, 74 & 84 & Reinhard Onnasch Galerie, West Berlin, 82, 101 Spring Street Gallery, 87; Indianapolis Mus Art, 76; Another Aspect of Pop Art, Long Island City, 78; Pop Art, USA-UK, Braintrust, Japan, 87; Comic Iconoclasm, ICA, London & Touring, 87-88; and others. *Teaching:* Instr, Sch Visual Arts, New York, 70-73. *Awards:* Guggenheim Fel, 76; Nat Endowment Asn, 89. *Bibliog:* Hannah Green (auth), A journal in praise of the art of John Wesley, In: The Unmuzzled Ox, spring 74. *Dealer:* Fiction/Non Fiction 21 Mercer St New York, NY 10012. *Mailing Add:* 52 Barrow St New York NY 10014

WESSEL, FRED W
PRINTMAKER, PAINTER
b Amityville, NY, June 14, 46. *Study:* Syracuse Univ, BFA, 68; Univ Mass, MFA, 76. *Work:* Mus Mod Art, New York; Brooklyn Mus, NY; Philadelphia Mus Art, Pa; Libr Cong, Washington, DC; De Cordova Mus Art, Lincoln, Mass. *Comn:* Watercolor with tempera painting, Marriott Hotels, Washington, DC, 86; gold leaf prints, Cutter Financial Ctr, Hartford, Conn, 87; watercolor with tempera painting, Univ Mass Fine Arts Ctr Theater, 90. *Exhib:* Invitational Print Biennale, Palace of Culture, Varna, Bulgaria, 85; Hanga Print Ann, Tokyo Metrop Mus Art, Tokyo, Japan, 86; International Prints, Fine Arts Ctr, Seoul, Korea, 87; Philadelphia Col Art, 87; Schneider Mus Art, Ashland, Ore, 87; one-person show, Printworks Gallery, Chicago, Ill, 88, Stonepress Gallery, Seattle, Wash, 88. *Pos:* Artist advisory bd, Offset Inst, 85- *Teaching:* Instr printmaking, Univ Mass, 76-77; prof printmaking, Hartford Art Sch, Univ Hartford, 77- *Awards:* Purchase Award, Gallery Tolbuchin, Bulgaria, 85; Juror's Award, Boston Printmaking 39th Ann, Strathmore Paper, 86; Color Print USA, Tex Tech Univ, 86. *Mem:* Boston Printmakers; Philadelphia Print Club. *Media:* Watercolor, tempera; Lithography. *Publ:* Auth, Hartford print workshop, Print News, 80; illusr, Motherlode of gamefish, Country J, 86; North America's Freshwater Fishing Book, Charles Scribners & Sons, 88. *Dealer:* Arden Gallery Newbury St Boston MA 02115; Printworks Gallery 311 W Superior Chicago IL 60610. *Mailing Add:* 4 Edgewood Terr Northampton MA 01060

WESSEL, HENRY
PHOTOGRAPHER
b Teaneck, NJ, July 28, 42. *Study:* Pa State Univ, BA, 66; State Univ NY, Buffalo, Visual Studies Workshop, MFA, 72. *Work:* Mus Mod Art, New York; Nat Gallery Can, Ottawa; Int Mus Photog, George Eastman House, Rochester, NY; Philadelphia Mus Art; Los Angeles Co Mus Art; Metrop Mus Art, New York. *Exhib:* Mus Mod Art, New York; Nat Gallery Can, Ottawa; Contemporary Photography V, 70 & New Topographics, 75, George Eastman House Traveling Exhibs; one-man shows, Mus Mod Art, New York, 73, Pa State Univ, 74, Fraenkel Gallery, San Francisco, 81 & Charles Cowles Gallery, New York, 81; and many others. *Teaching:* Instr, Pa State Univ, 67-69, Ctr Eye, Aspen, Colo, 73, Univ Calif, Berkeley, 73 & San Francisco Art Inst, 73-; asst prof, San Francisco State Univ, Calif, 74; vis artist, Univ Calif, Davis, 77; vis lectr, Calif Col Arts & Crafts, 77. *Awards:* Guggenheim Fel, 71 & 78; Nat Endowment Arts Grant, 75, 77 & 78. *Bibliog:* Articles, Art News, 9/73, Camera, Lucerne, Switz, 5/74 & Art in Am, 1/76; Artforum, 2/90; Art News, 5/92. *Publ:* Contribr, Looking at Photographs, 73 & Mirrors and windows, 79, Mus Mod Art, New York, 79; Nude, Harper & Row, 80; Pleasures & Terrors of Domestic Comfort, Moma, New York. *Dealer:* Fraenkel Gallery 55 Grant Ave San Francisco CA 94108; T Luisotti RAM 1714 Cedar St Santa Monica CA 90405. *Mailing Add:* Box 475 Point Richmond CA 94807

WESSELMANN, TOM
PAINTER, SCULPTOR
b Cincinnati, Ohio, Feb 23, 31. *Study:* Hiram Col Ohio, 51; Univ Cincinnati, BA, 56; Art Acad Cincinnati, 56; Cooper Union Art Sch, 59, cert. *Work:* Albright-Knox Art Gallery, Buffalo, NY; Mus Mod Art & Whitney Mus Am Art, New York; Suermondt Mus, Aachen, Ger; Atkins Mus Fine Arts, Kansas City, Mo; Nasjonalgalleriet, Oslo, Norway; Hirshorn mus & Sculpture Garden, Washington, DC; Walker Art Ctr, Minneapolis, Minn; and many others. *Exhib:* One-man shows, Sidney Janis Gallery, New York, 66, 68, 70, 72, 74, 76, 79, 80, 82 & 90, Ehrlich Gallery, 79, Hokin Gallery, Palm Beach, 90, John Stoller Gallery, Minneapolis, 90, Posner Gallery, Milwaukee, 90, Blum, Helmon Gallery, Los Angeles, 90, OK Harris Gallery, New York, 90, Edward Totah Gallery (with catalog), London, Eng, 91 & Tasende Gallery (with catalog), La Jolla, Calif, 91; Mus Contemp Art, Chicago, Ill, 69; Why New York, Futura Gallery, Stockhom, Sweden, 83; Celebration 1977-1985, McIntosh-Drysdale Gallery, Washington, DC, 85; Graphics & Multiples retrospectives, traveling exhib, 88-90; Miami Beach Convention Ctr, Fla, 92; Galerie Joachim Becker, Paris, France, 92; Tasende Gallery, La Jolla, Calif, 92; Lingotto, Torino, Italy. *Bibliog:* John Russell (auth), Art:Tom Wesselmann sticks to the same last, New York Times, 5/11/79; Slim Stealingworth (auth), Tom Wesselmann, Abbeville Press, 81; Patricia Johnson (auth), Nudes by Wesselman challenge viewer's eye, Houston Chronicle, 84; Tom Wesselman: Art people, Artnews, 11/85. *Media:* Oil; Painted Steel & Aluminum. *Dealer:* Sidney Janis Gallery 110 W 57th St New York NY 10019. *Mailing Add:* RD 1 Box 36 Long Eddy NY 12760

WESSER, YVONNE D
PAINTER, CONCEPTUAL ARTIST
b London, Eng, Jan 28, 35. *Study:* Art Students League, 71-81; Hunter Col; studied anatomy with Robert Beverly Hale & modern painting with Theodoros Stamos. *Work:* Barsky Hosp, Saigon, Vietnam; Art Students League, New York; Nat Art Mus, West Haven, Conn; Univ New Haven. *Comn:* Portrait, State Dept, Saigon, Vietnam. *Exhib:* Preconception figure, Col Design, Ames, Iowa, 88; Award Exhib, Stuhr Mus, Grand Island, Nebr, 90 & Govt Mansion, Lincoln, Nebr, 90; Third Nat Juried Competition, Viridian Gallery, New York, 90; group shows, Corner Gallery, World Trade Ctr, New York, 91, Multi Media Gallery W B'Way, Soho, New York, 91, Columbus Art Gallery, Columbus, Neb, 91, Cork Gallery, Lincoln Ctr, New York, 92, Small Works Exhib, Scoharie Co Arts Coun, Cobbleskill, New York, 92, Hall of Fame from NY-France in Contemp Art Scene, Cannon House Rotunda, Washington, DC, 92 & Environmental Perspectives, Erb Mem Union, Univ Ore, Eugene, 92; solo exhibs, Pleiades Gallery, 92 & Space Lab Gallery, Huntington, New York, 92; and others. *Awards:* Elmer Perkin Award, Linda Shearer Mus Mod Art, 86; Second Prize, Greater Midwest Int Exhib IV, Richard Koshalek Mus Contemp Art, Los Angeles, 90; Prize F, Int Competition, Agora Gallery, New York, 92. *Mem:* Burr Artists; Nat League Pen Women. *Media:* Oil. *Dealer:* Greene Art Gallery Guilford CT. *Mailing Add:* 12 E 86th St No 1631 New York NY 10028

WEST, CLARA FAYE JOHNSON
PAINTER, CONSERVATOR
b Coffeeville, Miss, May 8, 23. *Study:* Corcoran Sch Art, Washington, DC, with Eugen Weisz, Nicolai Cikovsky & Heinz Warneke; also with Jaska Shaffran. *Work:* Miss Univ for Women; Miss State Univ; Piney Woods

Country Life Sch, Miss; Wood Jr Col, Miss; St Paul Episcopal Church, Chattanooga, Tenn. *Comn:* Portrait, US Sen John C Stennis, comn by Class of 23, Miss State Univ; portrait plaques of six univ pres & 24 trustees for State Bd Inst Higher Learning & US Rep Jamie Whitten, comn by Res & Develop Ctr, Jackson, Miss, 75-85; seven portraits of univ pres & seven portrait drawings, Jackson State Univ, Miss, 77-85; Harvey Cromwell portrait, comn by Mrs Cromwell, Cromwell Commun Ctr, Miss Univ Women, 77; and over 450 portraits and 300 restorations in pub & pvt collections. *Exhib:* Mary Buie Mus, Oxford, Miss, 49; Mid-South Exhib, Brooks Mem Gallery, Memphis, 59; one-man shows, West Memphis Libr, Ark, 59; Miss State Univ, 65-67 & 72 & Hogarth Student Ctr, Miss Univ Women, 70-77. *Teaching:* Guest instr portrait painting, Miss Univ Women, 69-73. *Awards:* First Prize, Seeds for Britain (poster), Brit War Relief Soc, 43. *Mem:* Am Inst Conservators Hist & Artistic Works. *Media:* Acrylic, Oil. *Mailing Add:* 650 S Alton Way Apt 4D Denver CO 80231

WEST, E GORDON
PAINTER
b Salt Lake City, Utah, June 1, 33. *Study:* Art Inst Chicago; Univ Louisville, BS, 55. *Work:* McNay Art Mus, San Antonio, Univ Louisville, Ky; Tex A&M Univ, College Station, Tex. *Exhib:* Watercolor USA; Arts for the Parks; and many others. *Awards:* San Antonio Art League, 85; and others. *Bibliog:* Article, Am Artist. *Mem:* San Antonio Art League (vpres, 65); Tex Watercolor Soc (pres, 66-67); San Antonio Watercolor Group. *Media:* Mixed, Watercolor. *Publ:* Tex Hill Country & Pecos to Rio Grande, Tex A & M Press. *Dealer:* Hope Kaplan Odyssey Art Gallery 5800 Broadway San Antonio TX 78209. *Mailing Add:* 2638 Waterford San Antonio TX 78217

WEST, PETER
PAINTER, PRINTMAKER
b Washington, Pa, July 14, 53. *Study:* Tyler Sch Art, Temple Univ, Philadelphia, Pa, BFA, 75; Ohio Univ, Athens, MFA, 77. *Work:* Lyndon Baines Johnson Presidential Libr, Austin, Tex; War Memorial Mus Va, Newport News; Penn State Univ, McKeesport; Westinghouse Corp, Pittsburgh, Pa; Jessop Steel Corp, Washington, Pa. *Comn:* Sculpture (stainless steel), City of Washington, Pa, 80; sculpture (stainless steel), Jessop Steel Corp, Washington, Pa, 82; wall installation, Westinghouse Corp, Pittsburgh, Pa, 83; mural, War Memorial Mus Va, Newport News, 91. *Exhib:* Solo shows, Hansen Gallery, New York, 76, 78 & 80; Pittsburgh Ctr Arts, Pa, 78; Art Investors Ctr, Hansen Gallery, New York, 82; Styles in Transition, Isis Gallery, Manhasset, NY, 88; Assoc Artists of Pittsburgh, Carnegie Mus, Pa, 88, 89 & 90; 80 Washington Square East Galleries, New York Univ, New York, 89; Alternative Mus, New York, 90; War Mem Mus Va, Newport News, 90; Winterfest Invitational, Westmoreland Mus Art, Greensburg, Pa, 90; Foster Goldstrom Gallery, New York, 91. *Teaching:* Assoc prof studio arts, Bethany Col, WVa, 81-84; instr & lectr airbrush painting, Learn Shops, Intensified Educ Workshops, 84- *Awards:* Visual Artists Fel Grant/Painting, Pa Coun Arts, 91; Achievement Award/Acrylics, Am Artist Mag, 92; Buncher Family Foundation Award, Assoc Artists of Pittsburgh Ann Exhib. *Bibliog:* Hedy O'Beil (auth), article, Arts Magazine, 76; Robert Paschal, Robert Anderson (coauth), Art of the Dot, Van Nostrand Reinhold, 85; Am Artist Mag, 92. *Mem:* Assoc Artists Pittsburgh; Group A-Pittsburgh; Pittsburgh Ctr Arts. *Media:* Acrylic, Silkscreen. *Publ:* Auth, Step by Step Airbrushing, Techniques, Tools, Materials, Foster Art Series, 86. *Dealer:* Foster Goldstrom Gallery 560 Broadway New York NY; Gallery G 211 9th St Pittsburgh PA. *Mailing Add:* RD #2 Box 294 West Alexander PA 15376

WEST, RICHARD VINCENT
MUSEUM DIRECTOR, HISTORIAN
b Prague, Czech, Nov 26, 34; US citizen. *Study:* Univ Calif, Santa Barbara, BA(with highest honors), 61; Akad Bildenden Kuenste, Vienna, with Wotruba, 61-62; Univ Calif, Berkeley, MA(art hist), 65; Mus Mgt Inst, 81. *Collections Arranged:* Section d'Or (auth, catalog), 67-68; Language of the Print (auth, catalog), 68-69; Rockwell Kent: The Early Years (auth, catalog), 69; Howard Warshaw: A Decade of Murals (auth, catalog), 72; Pre-Rembrandtists (auth, catalog), 74; Munich & Am Realism (auth, catalog), 78; An Enkindled Eye: The Paintings of Rockwell Kent (auth, catalog), 85; Orbis Pictus: The Prints of Oskar Kokoschka (ed catalog) 87; Standing in the Tempest: Painters of the Hungarian Avant-Garde, 1908-1930 (auth, catalog), 91; America in Art (auth, catalog), 91. *Pos:* Cur, Cleveland Art Mus, 65-66; Albright-Knox Art Gallery, 66-67; Dir, Bowdoin Col Mus Art, 67-72, Crocker Art Mus, 73-83, Santa Barbara Mus Art, 83-91, Newport Art Mus, 92- *Teaching:* Lectr, Bowdoin Col, Univ Calif, Davis & Calif State Univ, Sacramento. *Awards:* Ford Fel, 65-67; Smithsonian Fel, 71. *Mem:* Asn Art Mus Dir; Am Asn Mus; Western Asn Art Mus (pres, 75-77); Calif Asn Mus (vpres, 86-91); Col Art Asn; Int Coun Mus. *Publ:* Auth, Painters of the Secton d'Or, 67; coauth, Language of the Print, Random House, 68; Walker Art Building Murals, 72; Rockwell Kent Reconsidered, Am Art Rev, 12/77; An enkindled eye: Paintings of Rockwell Kent, 85. *Mailing Add:* Newport Art Mus 76 Bellevue Ave Newport RI 02840

WEST, VIRGINIA M
FIBER ARTIST, WRITER
b Boston, Mass. *Study:* Goucher Col; Philadelphia Col Textiles; Md Inst Col Art. *Work:* Baltimore Mus Art; Del Art Mus; Hilton Hotel, Baltimore, Md; Goucher Col Kraushaar Gallery, Baltimore; Peterson Howell & Heather, Hunt Valley, Md. *Comn:* Ark curtain, Shaarei Zion Synagogue, Baltimore, Md, 68; tapestry, The Center Club, Baltimore, 80; fiber artwork, Community Ctr, Baltimore, 80; fiber murals, Lucayan Beach Hotel, Freeport, The Bahamas, 82; other commns for private collections. *Exhib:* Contemp Crafts Exhib, Del Art Mus, Wilmington, 70-75; Md Artists Exhib, Baltimore Mus Art, 70 & 75; Fibre Art American Artists, Ball State Univ, 72; Mus Contemp Crafts, New York, 72; Galleria d'Assisi, Italy, 79. *Pos:* Conference keynote speaker; writer, Shuttle, Spindle & Dyepot, 72-, Fiber Arts, 78-81, Handwoven, 80- & Weavers, 85- *Teaching:* Instr weaving, fiber sculpture & textile design, Md Inst Col Art, 69-; instr sem & workshops, US, Can, New Zealand & Australia. *Awards:* First Award, Creative Crafts Biennial, 68; Purchase Award, Baltimore Mus Art, 70; Purchase Award, Del Art Mus, 75; and others. *Mem:* Baltimore Weavers Guild (pre, 59-61); Md Crafts Coun (pres, 62-64); Am Crafts Coun (secy, 69-72). *Media:* Fiber. *Res:* Basketry styles & techniques, original designs for handwoven clothing. *Publ:* Auth, The Virginia West Swatch Book, 85-86; Designer Diagonals, A Portfolio of Patterns for Bias Clothing, 88; A Cut Above, 92. *Mailing Add:* 2809 Grasty Woods Lane RFD 7 Baltimore MD 21208

WEST, W RICHARD (DICK)
PAINTER, SCULPTOR
b Darlington, Okla, Sept 8, 12. *Study:* Haskell Inst; Bacone Col; Univ Okla, BFA & MFA; Univ Redlands; also with Olaf Nordmark; Baker Univ, Baldwin City, Kans, Hon DFA, 76. *Work:* Smithsonian Inst, Washington, DC; Joslyn Mem Art Mus, Omaha, Nebr; Philbrook Art Ctr, Tulsa, Okla; Gilcrease Mus, Tulsa; Bacone Col, Okla. *Comn:* Post off mural, Okemah, Okla, 41; bas-relief panels, Univ Redlands, Calif, 60's; Crucifixion (sculpture), NAm Indian Ctr, Chicago, 60's; 1976 Bicentennial, Franklin Mint. *Exhib:* Kansas City Mus Hist & Sci, Mo, 71; one-man show, Southern Plains Mus, Anadarko, Okla, 80; Cult Ctr Am Indian, Houston, 81; Turtle, Niagara Indian Art & Cult Ctr, Niagara Falls, NY; Santa Fe Festival Arts, 81; and others. *Pos:* Comnr, Indian Arts & Crafts Bd, Dept Interior, 79- *Teaching:* Dir oil painting & perspective, Bacone Col, 47-70, artist-in-residence, 80-86, prof emer art, 80-86; dir Indian art & sculpture, Haskell Indian Jr Col. *Awards:* Citation of Indian Arts & Crafts, 60; First Place for Sculpture, Philbrook Art Ctr Nat Show, 60; Waite Phillips Award, 64; and others. *Bibliog:* Ed Shaw (auth), Another Face of Jesus (film), Am Baptist Films, 69; Charles Waugaman (auth), Cheyenne Artist, Friendship Press, 70; Dorothy Elliot (auth), Dick West Artist, Kansas, 71; and others. *Media:* Oil, Acrylic. *Res:* Indian art & sculpture. *Publ:* Illustr, Indian Legends of the Great West, 63; contrib, Karl Schleisier, The Wolves of Heavin, Univ Okla Press, Norman, 88. *Mailing Add:* Box 211 Rincon Loop Tijeras NM 87059

WESTERLUND ROOSEN, MIA (MARIA ELUDIA)
SCULPTOR
b New York, NY, Sept 20, 42. *Study:* Nat Acad Fine Art, New York; Art Students League; Manhattanville Col. *Work:* Nat Gallery Can; Art Gallery Ont; Yale Univ Art Gallery; Albright-Knox Art Gallery; Vancouver Art Gallery. *Exhib:* Material Matters, Norton Gallery, Palm Beach, Fla, 80; Sculptural Death, Visual Arts Mus, New York, 81; American Abstraction Now, ICA Richmond, Va, 82; Castelli and His Artists, La Jolla Mus, Calif, 82; Painting and Sculpture Candidates, Am Acad Arts & Lett, New York, 83. *Media:* Concrete, Steel. *Mailing Add:* 17 White St New York NY 10013

WESTERMANN, H C
SCULPTOR, PAINTER
b Los Angeles, Calif, Dec 11, 22. *Study:* Art Inst Chicago, BFA, 54, Hon DFA, 79. *Work:* Mus Contemp Art, Chicago; Mus Mod Art,New York; San Diego Mus Art; Seattle Art Mus; Des Moines Art Ctr. *Exhib:* New Images of Man, Mus Mod Art, New York, 59; Painting & Sculpture of a Decade, Tate Gallery, London, 64; solo exhibs, Los Angeles Co Mus, 69, Whitney Mus Am Art, 78, Des Moines Art Ctr, 78 & San Francisco Mus Mod Art, 79; Ten Independents, Guggenheim Mus, 72; Xavier Fourcade Gallery, New York, 81; John Berggruen Gallery, San Francisco, 85; Lennon, Weinberg, Inc, New York, 88. *Awards:* Nat Arts Coun Award, 67 & Sao Paulo Biennal Award, 72. *Bibliog:* Dennis Adrian (auth), Some notes on H C Westermann, Art Int, 63; Franz Schulze (auth), Fantastic Images, Follett Publ, 72; Barbara Haskell (auth), H C Westermann, 78. *Mem:* Artists Equity. *Media:* Wood, Metal; Watercolor. *Publ:* Letters from H C Westermann, Timken Publ, 88. *Dealer:* Lennon Weinberg Inc 580 Broadway New York NY 10012. *Mailing Add:* Box 5028 Brookfield Center CT 06804

WESTERVELT, ROBERT F
HISTORIAN, CERAMIST
b New York, NY, Apr 6, 28. *Study:* Williams Col, AB; Claremont Grad Sch, MFA; Emory Univ, PhD. *Work:* Delgado Mus, New Orleans; High Mus of Atlanta, Ga; Frank Wingate Collection of Contemp Am Ceramics, Syracuse Univ; Scripps Col Collection, Claremont, Calif. *Comn:* Ceramic decoration (with Joseph Amisano, archit), Visual Arts Bldg, Univ Ga, 59. *Exhib:* Georgia Artists, Smithsonian Inst, Washington, DC, 64; Scripps Col Invitational, Claremont, 69. *Pos:* Consult, Ctr Study Southern Cult, Univ Miss, 81-85. *Teaching:* Assoc prof hist Am art, Agnes Scott Col, Decatur, Ga, 57-81; prof art, Gainesville Col, Ga, 83-, pres, currently. *Awards:* Cash grant, Atlanta Arts Festival, 64; Purchase Awards, Delgado Mus & Arts Festival of Atlanta; Ga Coun Arts Grant, 81-82. *Mem:* Ga Designer Craftsman; Southeastern Col Art Asn; Ga Mountain Crafts. *Media:* Stoneware, Porcelain. *Res:* History of 19th century American painting; American folk art. *Publ:* Auth, The whig painter of Missouri, Am Art J, Kennedy Gallery, 70. *Mailing Add:* Humanities Dept Gainesville Jr Col Box 1358 Gainesville GA 30503

WESTFALL, CAROL D
SCULPTOR, EDUCATOR
b Everett, Pa, Sept 7, 38. *Study:* RI Sch of Design, BFA; Maryland Inst , Col of Art, MFA. *Work:* Goucher Col Collection, Towson, Md; Del Mus of Art, Wilmington; NJ State Mus, Trenton; Michael Carson Productions, New York; PD 100, Architects, Mexico City. *Comn:* Nine batiks, R F Kennedy

Family Collection, 70 & three batiks, L B Johnson Family Collection, 70, Washington Gallery of Art, DC; Lithograph, Zimmerli Mus, Newark Pub Libr, 88; Rut. *Exhib:* Washington Co Mus, Hagerstown, Md, 72; Del Mus of Art, Wilmington, 73; Baltimore Mus of Art, Md, 74; 7th Biennial of Tapestry, Mus Contonal des Beaux Arts, Lausanne, Switz, 76; Auditorium Gallery, NJ State Mus, Trenton, 75; Mus of Art, Carnegie Inst Int, Pittsburgh, Pa, 76; Mus of Contemp Crafts, New York, 76 & 87; Textile Mus, Wash, DC, 86; Bermuda Arts Centre, 87; Gryphon Gallery, Melbourne, Australia, 88; one-woman shows, Conde Gallery, Inst Allende, Mex, 75, NJ State Mus, 76, Florence Duhl Gallery, New York, 76, Am Ctr, New Delhi, India, 8a, Ruth Kaufman Gallery, New York, 81; Gallery/Gallery, Kyoto, Japan, 92. *Teaching:* Instr fibers & fabrics, Md Inst, Baltimore, 68-73; asst prof fibres & fabrics, Montclair State Col, NJ, 73-79, assoc prof, 79-88, prof, 88-; guest assoc prof, Teachers Col, Columbia Univ, New York, 77-87 & Sch Am Craftsmen, Rochester Inst Technol, 77 & 86. *Awards:* Morton & Sophie Macht Found Award, Baltimore Mus of Art, 72; Levi Sculpture Award, Baltimore Mus of Art, 74; Governor's Purchase Award, NJ Biennial, State of NJ, 75; Indo-Am Fel, 80-81; Master Print Award, Rutgers Ctr Innovative Printmaking, 88; and others. *Bibliog:* Articles in Crafts Horizons, 69-77; Shuttle, Spindle & Dyepot, 77-85; Ars Textrina, 86-90. *Mem:* Handweavers Guild of Am; Am Crafts Coun; NJ State Coun on the Arts, Artists in Schs Prog; World Crafts Coun. *Media:* Mixed. *Publ:* Co-auth, Plaiting Step by Step, Watson-Guptill, 76. *Mailing Add:* Dept Fine Arts Montclair State Col Upper Montclair NJ 07043

WESTFALL, STEPHEN V R
PAINTER, CRITIC
b Schenectady, NY, 1953. *Study:* Univ Calif, Santa Barbara, MFA, 78. *Exhib:* One-man exhibs, Univ Art Mus, Univ Calif, Santa Barbara, 78, Tracey Garet Gallery, New York, 84, Daniel Newburg Gallery, New York, 87, 88, 90 & 91, Pretto Berland Hall, New York, 90 & Lawrence Oliver Gallery, Philadelphia, Pa, 90; 18 Artists from New York, Galerie Lohrl, Monchengladbach, Ger, 91; Conceptual Abstraction, Sidney Janis Gallery, New York, 91; Behind Bars, Thread Waxing Space, New York, 92; Works on Paper, Diane Brown Gallery, New York, 92; Geometric Strategies, Marilyn Perl Gallery, New York, 92; and others. *Pos:* Contribr, Artweek, 76-79 & Art in Am, Arts & Flash Art mags, currently. *Teaching:* Vis artist, Ohio State Univ, 81; teacher painting, Sch Visual Arts & Cooper Union, New York, 88. *Awards:* Fel, Nat Endowment Arts, 87. *Bibliog:* Ellen Handy (auth), Stephen Westfall, 1/92 & David Carrier (auth), Afterlight, 3/92, Arts; Meg O'Rourke (auth), Behind Bars, catalog for Thread Waxing Space, NY, 92; and others. *Media:* Acrylic, Oil. *Mailing Add:* c/o Daniel Newburg Gallery 43 Greene New York NY 10012

WESTIN, ROBERT H
HISTORIAN
b St Paul, Minn, Jan 11, 46. *Study:* Univ Minn, BA, 68; Pa State Univ, MA, 70, PhD, 78; Birbeck Col, Univ London, with Sir Nikolas Pevsner & Sir John Summerson. *Collections Arranged:* Figurative Drawings from Windsor Castle of the Roman Baroque; Collection of Her Majesty the Queen; Carlo Maratti and His Contemporaries (coauth, catalog), Mus of Art, Pa State Univ, 75. *Teaching:* Asst prof Renaissance-Baroque art hist, Ariz State Univ, Tempe, 73-78; assoc prof art, Univ Fla, Gainesville, 78- *Awards:* Nat defense Educ Art Title IV, US Govt, 71-72; Ariz State Univ Fac Fel, 74. *Mem:* Col Art Asn; Mid-Am Col Art; Nat Coun Art Adminr; SE Col Art Conf; Southeastern Am Soc Eighteenth Century Studies. *Res:* Collections of Metropolitan Museum of New York, Philadelphia Museum of Art and the collection of Janos Scholz, Cooper-Hewitt Union; Roman Baroque sculpture and Michelangelo. *Publ:* Auth, Antonio Raggi's Death of St Cecilia, Art Bulletin, 74; co-auth, Contributions to the late chronology of Giuseppe Mazzuoli, Burlington Mag, 74; auth, Ars Mohendi tradition and the visualization of death in Seventeenth Century Roman Baroque sculpture, Int J Death Educ, 80; coauth, Carlo Maratti and Camillo Rusconi: Two new portrait medallions, Burlington Mag, 80. *Mailing Add:* Dept Art Univ Fla Gainesville FL 32611

WESTLUND, HARRY E
PUBLISHER, DEALER
b Chicago, Ill, Nov 20, 41. *Study:* Calif State Col, Long Beach, BA, 67; Tamarind Inst, Albuquerque, Master Printer, 70. *Work:* Pasadena Mus, Calif; Gruenwald Found, Univ Calif, Los Angeles; Mus of Mod Art, New York, Los Angeles Co Mus of Art, Los Angeles; Tamarind Inst Collection, Univ NMex. *Exhib:* Eight Tamarind Printers, Motel Gallery, Albuquerque, Nmex; New Multiples, San Diego; Art of the Master Printer, Robinson Galleries, Houston, Tex; Collectors Exhib, Starline Gallery, Albuquerque, 78; Bramante Gallery, Walla Walla, Wash, 80. *Pos:* Shop mgr, Lakeside Studios, Mich, 71; mgr, Tamarind Publ, Tamarind Inst, 72-75; litho/silkscreen staff printer, Cirrue Ed, Hollywood, Calif, 75-76; dir, Serigraphics Custom Silkscreen Workshop, Albuquerque, 76- *Specialty:* Publishing, custom printing, silkscreen process. *Collection:* Contemporary; Old Master. *Publ:* Auth, Polymer Reversal Technique as Applied to Zinc Plates, Tamarind, 71. *Mailing Add:* 502 Mullen Rd NW Albuquerque NM 87107

WESTWATER, ANGELA KING
ART DEALER, EDITOR
b Columbus, Ohio, July 6, 42. *Study:* Smith Col, BA; NY Univ, MA. *Pos:* Asst dir, Ctr Int Studies, NY Univ, 67-69; res assoc, Inst Govt & ed, Ga Govt Rev, Univ Ga, 69-71; managing ed, Artforum, 72-75; trustee, Louis Comfort Tiffany Found, pres, 80-; vis comt, Smith Col, Mus Art; partner, Sperone Westwater Inc, New York, 75- *Mem:* Art Dealers Asn Am. *Specialty:* Contemporary painting and sculpture. *Mailing Add:* Sperone Westwater Inc 142 Greene St New York NY 10012

WETHINGTON, WILMA ZELLA
PAINTER, INSTRUCTOR
b Clinton, Iowa, Apr 15, 18. *Study:* Marshall Univ, Huntington, WVa; Wichita State Univ; also with Mario Cooper, John Pike, Dale Meyers, Charles R Kinghan, Tom Hill, Clayton Henri Staples, Robert E Wood & others. *Work:* Wichita State Univ, Kans; Episcopal Diocese Kans, Topeka; Smithsonian Inst, Washington, DC; US Fed Bldg, Wichita, Kans; Off Secy Transportation, Washington, DC; Off Sen Nancy Kassebaum, US Fed Bldg, Kans City; and others. *Comn:* portrait of Bishop Edward Turner, comn by Episcopal Diocese, Kans, 74; portrait, Hon Robert Morton, 89; portrait, Hon Richard Rogers, 90; portrait, Hon Dale Saffels, 91; portrait, Hon Earl E O'Conner, 92; and others. *Exhib:* Am Watercolor Soc, New York, 72; Hudson Valley Art Asn, New York, 72-74; Southwestern Watercolor Soc, Dallas, Tex, 73, 74; Nat Soc Painters in Casein & Acrylic, New York, 75; Catharine Lorillard Wolfe Club, 85 & 87; Salmagundi Club, 85 & 86. *Pos:* Painting instr, Wichita Ctr Arts, 84-86. *Teaching:* Pvt art instr, Wichita, Kans, 50-; instr painting, McConnell Air Base, Wichita, spring 73; instr painting, portraiture & drawing, Wichita Art Asn, 81- *Awards:* First Prize, 8th West Biennial, Grand Junction Art Mus, Colo, 70; Best of Show, North Platte Artists Guild, Nebr, 73; First Award in Watercolor, Okla Mus Art, 75; and 75 other awards. *Mem:* Assoc Am Watercolor Soc; Pastel Soc Kans; Kans Watercolor Soc; Southern Watercolor Soc; Nat Asn Am Pen Women; Pastel Soc Am. *Media:* Pastel, Watercolor. *Dealer:* Ellington Gallery 550 N Rock Rd Wichita KS; James Gallery Houston TX. *Mailing Add:* 2 Linden Dr Wichita KS 67206

WETHINGTON-HADLEY, WILMA ZELLA See Wethington, Wilma Zella

WETHLI, MARK
PAINTER, EDUCATOR
b Westfield, NY, Nov 9, 49. *Study:* Univ Miami, Fla, BFA, 71, MFA, 73. *Work:* Metrop Mus Art, New York; Portland Mus Art, Maine. *Exhib:* Biennial, Whitney Mus Am Art, New York, 75; American Drawings in Black & White, Brooklyn Mus Art, NY, 80; solo exhib, Koplin Gallery, Los Angeles, 85 & 87; New England Now, DeCordova Mus Art, 87; Portland Mus Art, Maine, 89 & De Cordova Mus Art, Mass, 89. *Teaching:* Asst prof, Univ Northern Iowa, Cedar Falls, 76-78 & Calif State Univ, Long Beach, 78-85; assoc prof, chair, Bowdoin Col, Brunswick, Maine, 85- *Awards:* Fels, Nat Endowment Arts, 74, MacDowell Colony, 83 & Rockefeller Found, 88. *Bibliog:* John Coffey (auth), Article, New England Now, 87; Paintings by Mark Wethli, Gettysburg Review, fall 89; Edgar Allen Beem (auth), Article, Maine Art Now, 90. *Media:* Oil. *Dealer:* Tatistcheff Gallery New York NY. *Mailing Add:* c/o Koplin 1438 Ninth St Santa Monica CA 90401

WETMORE, GORDON (STANLEY GORDON)
PAINTER, WRITER
b Memphis, Tenn, July 9, 38. *Study:* Memphis Acad Art, 52; Univ Tenn, Chattanooga, with George Cress, BS(art), 65; Art Students League, New York, with Robert Brackman & Mario Cooper, 71-72. *Work:* Duke Univ, Durham, NC; Emory Univ, Atlanta, Ga; Found Christian Living, Pawling, NY; The White House, Washington, DC; The Royal Palace, Monaco. *Exhib:* Hunter Art Mus, Chattanooga, 89. *Teaching:* Instrr art, Baylor Sch, Chattanooga, 69-72; head seminars, Chattanooga, Atlanta & Charlotte, 71-73; fac mem watercolor, Nat Artist's Seminar, 78-84; portrait forum, Carnegie Mall, 92. *Bibliog:* Barbara Whipple (auth), Gordon Wetmore paints a watercolor portrait, Am Artist Mag, 2/83; Wendon Blake (auth), Learning from the Pros, Watson Guptill Publ, 84; Joe Galliani (auth), Portrait painting: The profession of painting figures, Am Artist, 2/85. *Mem:* Nat Portrait Inst; Am Portrait Soc; Portrait Club New York (bd mem, 79-84). *Media:* Oil, Watercolor. *Publ:* Illusr, Promised Land, 78 & illusr & auth, Ireland: Portrayed by Gordon Wetmore, 80, Thomas Nelson Co; Gordon Wetmore's Prayers for Boys and Girls, Ideals Pub, 87. *Dealer:* Portraits 985 Park Ave New York NY 10028. *Mailing Add:* 1146 James Blvd Signal Mountain TN 37377

WEXLER, CLAIRE THYRA See Davidson, Thyra (Claire Thyra Wexler)

WEXLER, GEORGE
PAINTER
b Brooklyn, NY, Jan 18, 25. *Study:* Cooper Union Sch Art; NY Univ, BA; Mich State Univ, MA. *Work:* Mitsubishi Corp; Kemper Collection; Chemical Bank NY; Manufacturers Hanover; Commerce Bancshares; and others. *Exhib:* Landscape in America, New Sch Social Res, 63; one-man shows, Angeleski Gallery, New York, 61, Albany Inst Art, NY, 66, First St Gallery, New York, 72, 75 & 78 & Schenectady Mus Art, NY, 72; Fischbach Gallery, New York, 84, 86, 89 & 92; Contemporary Painters of the Hudson River, Albany, Poughkeepsie, New York, 85-86; Landscape, Cityscape, Seascape, New Orleans, La & NY, 86; Contemp Landscapes, Tortue Gallery, Santa Monica, Calif. *Teaching:* Asst prof design, Mich State Univ, 50-57; prof painting, State Univ NY Col New Paltz, 57-87. *Awards:* Grumbacher Award, Nat Acad, 88; New York Found Arts Fel, 88. *Bibliog:* Gussow (auth), Sense of Place, Sat Rev, 72; Agar (auth), American Artist Mag, 5/81; Hubbard (auth), article Modern Maturity Mag, 6/85. *Media:* Oil. *Dealer:* Fischbach Gallery 24 W 57th St New York NY 10019. *Mailing Add:* 359 Springtown Rd New Paltz NY 12561

WEXLER, JEROME LEROY
PHOTOGRAPHER, ILLUSTRATOR
b New York, NY, Feb 6, 23. *Study:* Self-taught. *Awards:* Twelve Outstanding Sci Books Children awards, Nat Sci Teachers Asn & Childrens Book Coun, Joint Comt. *Publ:* 43 bks publ to date. *Mailing Add:* 13 Langshire Dr Madison CT 06443

WEXLER, LEE EDWARD
PHOTOGRAPHER
b New York, NY, Jan 20, 51. *Study:* Univ Rochester, NY, BA, 73. *Work:* Mus City New York, Brooklyn Mus, Citizen's Exchange Coun & Midtown Y Gallery, New York; French Mus Photog, Paris, France. *Exhib:* Weekend in June, Midtown Y Gallery, New York, 83; solo exhibs, Canon Gallery, Los Angeles, Calif, French Mus Photog, Paris, France, 83 & OK Harris Gallery, New York, 86; Metropolitan Portraits, 42nd St Station Gallery, New York, 85; 20/20 Gallery, New York, 87. *Teaching:* Instr photog, New Sch Social Res, New York, 81-87, Parsons Sch Design, Paris, 83-84, Univ Pa, Philadelphia, 88- *Bibliog:* J M Saint-Omer (auth), Un American sur les Metros, Le Republican, 8/83; Faces from the subways, NY Times, 1/8/86; Michael Kaplan (auth), Metro Life-New York, Am Photogr, 6/86. *Publ:* Illusr, The New School-Parsons Photography Brochure, The New Sch, spring, 83; NY Newsday Mag, 88. *Mailing Add:* 136 W Fourth St No 4-D New York NY 10012

WEYHE, ARTHUR
SCULPTOR
b New York, NY. *Work:* Everson Mus Art, Syracuse, NY; Herbert F Johnson Mus Art, Cornell Univ; Neuberger Mus, Purchase, NY; William Benton Mus of Art, Storrs, Conn; Storm King Art Ctr, Mountainville, NY. *Exhib:* NY Sculpture Selected by Ivan Karp, William Patterson Col, Wayne, NJ, 74; 55 Mercer Gallery, New York, 75 & 77; O K Harris Gallery, New York, 76; Waterside Plaza, New York, 78; PS1, Long Island City, 79; and others. *Mailing Add:* c/o Hillwood Art Museum Long Island Univ CW Post Campus Brookville NY 11548

WEYNEROWSKI, HANNA See Kali (Hanna Weynerowski)

WHARTON, ANNABEL JANE
HISTORIAN
b New Rochelle, NY. *Study:* Univ Wis, Madison, BSc, 66; Univ Chicago, MA, 69; Courtauld Inst, London Univ, PhD, 75. *Teaching:* Res fel Byzantine art, Barber Inst, Univ Birmingham, Eng, 71-75; asst prof Medieval art, Oberlin Col, 75-78; asst prof Medieval art, Duke Univ, 79-86, assoc prof, 86- *Awards:* ACLS Fel, 81-84; Nat Humanities Ctr Fel, 85-86; Fel CASVA, Nat Gallery, Washington, DC. *Mem:* Byzantine Studies Conf (bd pres); Inst Archit & Urban Studies, New York (bd mem); Art Bulletin (ed bd mem); Int Ctr Medieval Art (bd mem). *Res:* Art and architecture of the Late Ancient and Byzantine periods and the material evidence of power relationships in those societies. *Publ:* Tokali Kilise, Dumbarton Oaks Ctr of Byzantine Studies Press, 87; Art of Empire, Penn State Univ Press, 88; auth, Change in Byzantine culture in the 11th and 12th century, Univ Calif Press, 84. *Mailing Add:* 3624 Carlisle Dr Durham NC 27707

WHARTON, DAVID W
PRINTMAKER, PAINTER
b Wichita Falls, Tex, Nov 19, 51. *Study:* Univ Okla, BFA, 74; Cranbrook Acad Art, MFA, 77. *Work:* Pacific Nat Bank, Guadelope, WI; Levi Strauss Corp, San Francisco, Calif; Cranbrook Acad Art, Bloomfield Hills, Mich; Col Southern Idaho, Caldwell; Univ Lethbridge, Alta; Inst N Am West; Boise Gallery Art. *Comn:* Rocky Mountain Mag, comn by Leslie Sielko, Boulder, Colo, 79; Seattle Art Comn; First Security Bank, Idaho. *Exhib:* Los Angeles Printmaking Soc, Los Angeles Co Mus, Calif, 80; Regional Printmakers, Blue Door Too, Denver, Colo, 80; Cranbrook Printmakers, St Mary's Col, Notre Dame, 81; Denver Art Mus, Colo, 81; Northwest Printmakers, Mont State Univ, Bozevian, 81; Recent Decents, Colo Mountain Co, Breckenridge, 81; Mint Mus, Charlotte, NC; Schneider Mus, Ashland, Ore; Kunstsammlungen Der Veste Coburg, Fed Repub Ger; Pilchuck Glass Sch. *Pos:* Dir printmaking, Sun Valley Ctr Art, 77-86. *Teaching:* Prof printmaking, Univ Wash & Humboldt State Univ, 81; Pilchuck Glass Sch, Wash, formerly; Univ Windsor, Ont, Can, formerly. *Awards:* Ford Found Fel, 76; Western States Arts Found Fel, 79; Art Pub Places Award, Wash State, 83. *Bibliog:* Leslie Silka (auth), Storyteller, Rocky Mountain Mag, 79; James Mills (auth), Printmakers, Denver Post, 80; What's western about western art, Milkweed Chronicle, 80; Luminous Impressions, Mint Mus; The Primal Plastic Pool, Missoula Mus Art, Mont; Northern Lights, Missoula, Mont. *Mem:* Col Art Asn. *Media:* Watercolor; Printmaking. *Publ:* Auth, Suite Southern Prints, Cranbrook Acad Art, Bloomfield Hills, Mich, 77; The Rain Baby, Univ Wash Press, 81; Indian Self Rule, Inst Am West, 82; Potters and Prints, Sun Valley Ctr Publ, 83. *Dealer:* Susan Duval Gallery 525 Cooper Ave Aspen CO; Gail Severn Gallery PO Box 1679 Ketchum ID 83340. *Mailing Add:* Box 957 Ketchum ID 83340

WHARTON, MARGARET AGNES
SCULPTOR
b Portsmouth, Va, Aug 4, 43. *Study:* Univ Md, BS, 65; Sch Art Inst Chicago(Anna Louise Raymond Fel), MFA, 75. *Work:* Whitney Mus Am Art, New York; Mus Contemp Art, Chicago; Corcoran Gallery Art, Washington, DC; Seattle Art Mus; Art Inst, Chicago; Dallas Art Mus, Tex. *Comn:* Multiple commission, Mus Contemp Art, Chicago, 85; Rehearsal, Chicago Pub Libr, W Lawn Br, Chicago, 86. *Exhib:* Solo exhibs (with catalog), Mus Contemp Art, Chicago & traveling nationally, 81-82, Phyllis Kind Gallery, New York, 83, 87 & 90, Chicago, 85, 88 & 91, Slicing it Thin, Zolla/Lieberman Gallery, Inc, Chicago, 92; Improbable Furniture (with catalog), Inst Contemp Art, Univ Pa, Philadelphia, 76; Drawing in Air, Frith Gallery, Sunderland Art Ctr, Eng, 83-84; Awards Show, San Antonio Mus Art, 84; Contemporary Wood Sculpture, Crocker Art Mus, Sacramento, Calif, 84-85; Making Their Mark, 89-90 & Diamonds are Forever, 87-90, Mitchell Mus, Mt Vernon, Ill; Assemblage, Southeastern Ctr Contemp Art, Winston-Salem, NC, 92; and many others. *Teaching:* Visartist, Art Inst Chicago, 89-90. *Awards:* Nat Endowments Arts Fel, 80 & 88; Award Visual Arts Grant, 84. *Bibliog:* Jeffrey Hoffeld (auth), Chairperson Margaret Wharton, Art Mag, 11/78; Alan Artner (auth), MCA unfolds a top notch show of chair sculpture, Chicago Tribune, 9/13/81; Judith Ross-Kirshner (auth), Margaret Wharton, Artforum, 1/82; Chicago Mg, 9/88; Alan Arther (auth) article, Chicago Tribune, 88. *Media:* Wood. *Publ:* Auth, Breaking Boundaries, Prentice-Hall, 83; Standing Ground, Cincinnati, 87. *Dealer:* Zolla/Lieberman Gallery Inc 325 W Huron Chicago IL 60610-3617. *Mailing Add:* 1334 Pinehurst Glenview IL 60025

WHEDON, AIDA ANTHONY
PRINTMAKER, INSTRUCTOR
b New Orleans, La, May 1, 15. *Study:* Art Students League with Thomas Hart Benton & Hans Hoffman, 33-38, New Sch Social Res with Ruth Leaf, 75-80. *Work:* Univ Maine, Orono; Port Washington Libr Gallery, NY; Chase Manhattan Bank, Mineola, NY; NY Port Authority. *Exhib:* Hecksher Mus, Huntington, Long Island, 76; Royal Acad Exhib, Sweden, 77-78; solo exhibs, South St Seaport Mus, New York, 77, Lincoln Ctr Gallery, New York, 77, Mus Fine Arts, Roslyn, NY, 81 & Lampard Gallery, London, Eng, 88. *Pos:* Dir, Whedon Art Ctr, 45-; mem, Port Washington Art Adv, 55-; founding mem, Graphic Eye Gallery, 74- *Awards:* Award of Excellence, Heckshire Competition, 76; honoree, Women on Job, 87. *Bibliog:* R David Shiry (auth), Visions of land & solitude, New York Times, 11/77; Malcom Preston (auth), Retrospective of Aida Whedon & Ami Wallach (auth), Aida Whedon's satisfying world, Long Island Newsday, 79; A look at Aida Wheaton and her work, North Shore Publ, 86. *Mem:* Am Asn Women Artists; Charter Mem, Nat Mus Women Artists, Washington, DC. *Media:* Etching in Color. *Mailing Add:* 5 Sandy Hollow Rd Port Washington NY 11050

WHEELER, MARK
PAINTER, CARTOONIST
b Bellingham, Wash, Sept 26, 43. *Study:* Burnley Sch of Professional Art, dipl, Seattle, Wash; Western Wash State Univ (graphic arts). *Work:* Japan Mus of Art, Tatayama. *Comn:* Serigraph series, Northern Commercial Co, Anchorage, Alaska, 74; indust illus, Ketchikan Pulp Co, 75; watercolors, Division of Marine Transportation, State of Alaska, 75; watercolors, Princess Cruises, 75; five murals, Nat Bank Alaska, Ketchikan Br, 76. *Exhib:* All Alaska Shows, Anchorage, 74-76; Advert Fedn Alaska Ann Invitational Auction, 75 & 76; one-man shows, Art Ctr Mus, Anchorage, Alaska, 72-77 & The Gallery (Alaska Watercolor Soc), Anchorage, 76. *Pos:* Owner, Mark Wheeler Publishing, Ketchikan, 58-; staff artist, The Seattle Times, Wash, 65-66; art dir, Pacific Standard Life Insurance Co, Burlingame, Calif, 67 & Sterling Theatres, Seattle, 68; contribr cartoonist, weekly cartoons, Ketchikan Record, 89-90. *Teaching:* Instr watercolor, Northern Commercial Co, Anchorage, 73-74 & Wrangell Arts Coun, Alaska, 78- *Bibliog:* Stanton H Patty (auth), A Spoof on All Things Alaskan, The Seattle Times, 9/17/72; Rod Cardwell (auth), Faces and Places, Tacoma New Tribune, 2/4/73; Richard Foley (auth), Mark Wheeler--Alaskan Artist, The Southeastern Log, No 10. *Mem:* Charter mem Alaska Watercolor Soc; Anchorage Arts Coun; The Alaska Press Club; The Advert Found of Alaska. *Media:* Watercolor, Acrylic; Pen & Ink. *Publ:* Auth & illusr, Half Baked Alaska, Mark Wheeler Publ, 72; illusr, Country Station and Country Scene, Haddad's Fine Arts Inc, 73, A Portfolio of Twelve Alaskan Watercolors, Northern Commercial Co, 74 & A Sunny Day in Ketchikan, Alaska Fed Savings & Loan, 78; cover illus, Ketchikan Phone Bk, 79; auth & illusr, Display images, a guide to art, production and display, Eastman Kodak Co, 88; 1990 Cartoon Map of Ketchican, Alaska, 90. *Mailing Add:* 320 Bawden St No 718 Ketchikan AK 99901

WHEELER, MARY
PAINTER, PRINTMAKER
Study: Newcome Col, Tulane Univ, BFA, 72; Univ Ill, Urbana, Champaign, MFA, 74; Skowhegan Sch Painting & Sculpture, 71. *Exhib:* Solo exhibs, Dobrick Gallery, Chicago, 76, Hundred Acres Gallery, New York, 76, Gallery 501 Mint Mus Art, Charlotte, NC, 77, Acad Of Arts, Easton, Md, 82 & OK Harris Gallery, New York, 82; Realists' Invitational, Southeastern Ctr Contemp Art, Winston-Salem, NC, 77; OK Harris West, Scottsdale, Ariz, 82; Int Miniature Print Exhib, Pratt Graphics Ctr, New York, 85; Miniature Print Biennial, Silvermine Guild Galleries, New Canaan, Conn, 87; Assoc Am Artists, New York, 88 & 92; Daniel Quinn Gallery, Long Island City, NY, 91. *Awards:* MacDowell Colony Fel, 76. *Media:* Oil, Monotype. *Mailing Add:* 10-20 4th Rd Long Island City NY 11101

WHEELOCK, ARTHUR KINGSLAND, JR
CURATOR, EDUCATOR
b Worcester, Mass, May 13, 43. *Study:* Williams Col, BA, 65; Harvard Univ, PhD, 73. *Pos:* Cur Northern Baroque painting, Nat Gallery of Art, Washington, DC, 76- *Teaching:* Prof Northern Baroque art, Univ Md, College Park, 74- *Awards:* David E Finley Fel, Nat Gallery Art, 71-74; Nat Endowment Arts Grant, 79-80; Cur Fel, Nat Gallery Art, 83-84. *Mem:* Col Art Asn. *Res:* Dutch and Flemish art of the seventeenth century, primarily Vermeer and Rembrandt; artists' techniques; problems of optics and perspective. *Publ:* Auth, Perspective, Optics & Delft Artists Around 1650, Garland Press, 77; coauth, Gods, Saints & Heroes: Dutch Painting in the Age of Rembrandt, Nat Gallery Art, 80; Jan Vermeer, Abrams, 81; Saint Praxedis: New light on the early career of Vermeer, Artibus et Historiae, 86; Masterworks from Munich: 16th to 18th Century Paintings from the Alte Pinakothek, Nat Gallery Art, 88; and others. *Mailing Add:* c/o Nat Gallery Art 4th St & Constitution Ave NW Washington DC 20565

WHEELWRIGHT, JOSEPH STORER
SCULPTOR, PAINTER
b 1948. *Study:* Yale Univ, BA, 70; RI Sch Design, MFA, 75. *Work:* Charlestown Naval Yard. *Comn:* ICE Carvings (monumental), First Night Inc, Boston, 82-92. *Exhib:* Allan Stone Galleries, New York, 78, 81, 83 & 86; Hall Gallery, Wash, 85; Zoe Gallery, Boston, 87, 88. *Pos:* Asst prof, Wellesley Col. *Teaching:* Private lessons of woodcarving in own studio, 75- *Awards:* Nat Endowment Arts Grant, 81; Fund for Arts Award, WBZ Radio Station, Boston, 84. *Bibliog:* Pamela Allara (auth), art critic, Art News, 3/83; numerous articles in Boston Globe & Boston Phoenix. *Media:* Wood, Stone. *Dealer:* Allan Stone Galleries 48 E 86th St New York NY 10028; Boston Sculptors at Chapel Gallery Newton MA. *Mailing Add:* 551 Tremont St Boston MA 02116

WHIPPLE, ENEZ MARY
ADMINISTRATOR
b Syracuse, NY. *Study:* Syracuse Univ, BS; Southampton Col Long Island Univ, Hon DFA, 81. *Pos:* Exec dir, Guild Hall East Hampton Inc, NY, 48-82, bd trustees & pres, 84-, retired. *Teaching:* Adj prof humanities, Southampton Col, Long Island Univ, 71, retired. *Awards:* Dir Emer Guild Hall E Hampton Inc, NY, 82; Suffolk Co Arts Achievement Award, 82. *Mem:* Am Fedn Arts; Archives Am Arts; E Hampton Hist Soc (hon trustee). *Mailing Add:* PO Box 1421 East Hampton NY 11937

WHITAKER, EILEEN MONAGHAN
PAINTER
b Holyoke Mass, Nov 22, 11. *Study:* Mass Col Art, Boston. *Work:* High Mus Art, Atlanta, Ga; Charles & Emma Frye Mus, Seattle, Wash; Mispanic Mus & Nat Acad Design, New York; Okla Art Mus, Okla City. *Exhib:* Mayan Wirrior, Museo de Acuarela, Mex, 68; Tender Message, M H De Young Mem Mus, San Francisco, 69; Ceremonial Preparations, Phoenix Art Mus, Ariz, 72; Irish Co Fair, Nat Acad Design, New York, 87; Fancy Meeting You Here, A Celebration of American Realism, Circle Gallery, San Diego, 92; and others. *Awards:* Ranger Fund Purchase, 58; Silver Medal, Am Watercolor Soc, 65; Watercolor West Western Subject, Santa Fe Federal Savings & Loan, 78; Walter Biggs Mem Award, Nat Acad Design, 87. *Bibliog:* Eileen Monaghan Whitaker Paints San Diego, Copley Books, La Jolla, Calif, 86; M Stephen Doherty (auth), Watercolor, fall 90; Jan Jennigs (auth), Art of Calif, 7/91. *Mem:* Academician, Nat Acad Design; Am Watercolor Soc; hon mem Watercolor West; hon mem San Diego Watercolor Soc. *Media:* Transparent Watercolor, Graphite Drawing. *Publ:* Auth, My Concept of Watercolor, The Artist, London, 59; contribr, 100 Watercolor Techniques, 68 & Watercolorists at Work, 72, Watson-Guptill; Janice Lovoos (auth), cover article, Am Artist, 3/87. *Dealer:* The Jones Gallery 1264 Prospect St La Jolla CA. *Mailing Add:* 1579 Alta La Jolla Dr La Jolla CA 92037

WHITAKER, WILLIAM
PAINTER, ILLUSTRATOR
b Chicago, Ill, Mar 5, 43. *Study:* Univ Utah, BA; Otis Art Inst. *Work:* Brigham Young Univ; Weber State Col; Nat Cowboy Hall of Fame. *Comn:* Many portraits, 67-83. *Exhib:* Utah Inst Arts, 72-73 & 76; Nat Acad Western Art, Oklahoma City, 75-83; Am Western Art Exhib, Beijing, China, 81; Artists Am, Denver, 80-83. *Pos:* Advert mgr, Capital Records Inc, Hollywood, Calif, 68-69. *Teaching:* Assoc prof art & design, Brigham Young Univ, 69-80. *Awards:* Gold Medal, 76 & Silver Medal, 77, Nat Acad Western Art; Press Award, Western Rendezvous Art, 82. *Bibliog:* Articles, Ariz Hwy, 4/74 & 7/75; article, SW Art, 3/82; Profiles in American Art: William Whitaker, PBS-TV, 83. *Mem:* Nat Acad Western Art. *Media:* Oil, Pastel. *Dealer:* Jenny Whitaker 2846 Marrerest Circle W Provo UT 84604. *Mailing Add:* c/o Leslie Fine Art 7135 Main St Scottsdale AZ 85251

WHITCOMB, KAY
ENAMELIST, LECTURER
b Arlington, Mass, May 20, 21. *Study:* RI Sch Design, 39-42, Hon BFA, 90; Cambridge Sch Art, 40-41; apprentice in enameling to Doris Hall, 46-47, studied with Aldro Hibbard & Fred Hocks. *Comn:* Creche (needlepoint), Better Homes & Gardens, Des Moines, 75; Infinite Wisdom (enamel on steel), Univ Hosp, San Diego, 76; Arab Transportation, Int Airport, Dubai, United Arab Emirates, 81; Baranof, Russian Alaska Kodiak, Alaska High Sch, 86; Niles Col, Chicago, 92; and many othre pvt comns. *Exhib:* solo show, San Diego Mus Art, 65, 80, 84 & 87; Int Kunsthandwerk, Industrial Arts Mus, Stuttgart, Ger, 69; Int Biennale, Art Enamel, Limoges, France, 75-84; Int Festival Enamel, Laguna Beach Mus Art, Calif, 86; Int Shippo, Cent Mus, Tokyo, 81 & 85; Enamels 50-80, New England, 81; and many others. *Pos:* Cur & dir, Int Festival of Enamel, Laguna Beach Mus, Calif, 76; ed, Cloison, 80- *Teaching:* Instr design & enameling, San Diego Community Col, 74-81; workshop dir enamellling, 91-92. *Awards:* Prix Syndicat d'Initiative, Int Biennale, Art Enamel, Limoges, France, 78; Int Shippo Prize, Tokyo, 81 & 85. *Bibliog:* Wayne Endicott (auth), Artist turns enameling paste into art, Ceramic Industry, 10/81; Susan Vreeland (auth), Enamelles of Kay Whitcomb, Hill Courier, 5/84; Calif Art Rev, 89; Shippo Mag, 89; Archit Design Collaborators, 92; and others. *Mem:* founder Enamel Guild West (pres, 76-78); Allied Craftsmen San Diego (vpres, 72-73); San Diego Art Guild (chmn, 68-69); USA-Int Comt Enamel Creators, Limoges, France (vpres, 85-89); Cloisonné Collectors Club (ed, 80-, vpres, 85, pres, 89). *Media:* Enamel. *Res:* Byzantine to turn of century golden era enameling; American enamelling 1940 to 1970; Japanese Meiji Cloisonné. *Publ:* Auth, Germany Stuttgart: International handcraft, Craft Horizons, 71; Shippo Yaki excursion--enamel tour of Japan, 78, First international Shippo exhibition May 1978, Tokyo, Japan, 78 & Multi techniques of enamel, 78, Goldsmith J. *Mailing Add:* Box 9 Rockport MA 01966

WHITCOMB, SKIP
PAINTER, PRINTMAKER
b Sterling, Colo, May 17, 46. *Study:* Art Ctr Col Design, Los Angeles, Calif, BFA, 71; studied with Ned Jacob, 73. *Work:* Fine Arts Col, Cambell Co Libr, Gillette, Wyo. *Exhib:* Allied Artists Am, Nat Acad Art, New York, 74 & 76; Am Watercolor Soc, Nat Acad Gallery, New York, 75; Nine Colorado Oil Painters, Foothills Art Ctr, Golden, Colo, 82; Nat Acad Western Art, Western Heritage Ctr, Oklahoma City, Okla, 86, 87, 88, 89 & 92; Western Visions, Wildlife of Am West Mus, Jackson, Wyo, 88, 89, 90, 91 & 92. *Awards:* Best of Show, Western Visions, Wyoming Gallery, 91. *Bibliog:* Molly Barlow (auth), Fine Art Collection, Cambell Co Libr, 87. *Media:* Oil, Watercolor; Etching. *Publ:* Auth, Figures in Watercolor, Am Artist Mag, 76. *Dealer:* Walter Gray Jr & Dan Blancharad PO Box 132 Oklahoma City OK 73101. *Mailing Add:* 1020 Big Valley Dr Colorado Springs CO 80919

WHITCOMB, THERESE TRUITT
INSTRUCTOR, DESIGNER
b Evanston, Ill, Sept 19, 30. *Study:* Rosemont Col; San Diego Col for Women, BA, 53; San Diego State Univ, MA, 69. *Work:* Mission San Diego de Alcala; Mission San Luis Rey. *Comn:* Interior: San Diego Mission, Diocese of San Diego, 71; Mission San Luis Rey Mus (designed & executed), Franciscan Friars, 79; Sacred Heart Church (Irving Gill), Coronado, Calif, 82; St Agnes Church, San Diego, 83; Univ San Diego, 84- *Collections Arranged:* Contemporary Primitives, 76, Founder's Gallery Univ San Diego, Carousel Animals as Sculpture, 77, California Chair, 79 & The Naive Eye Now, 79; San Luis Rey Museum, 79; Univ San Diego. *Pos:* Dir, Founder's Gallery, Univ San Diego, 71-; trustee, San Diego Mus Art, 75-82; pres, bd trustees, Decorative Arts Study Ctr, San Juan Capistrano. *Teaching:* Prof art hist, Univ San Diego, 68-, coordr exhib, 70-, cur, univ collection & dir design, currently. *Awards:* Outstanding Teacher, 77, Bishop Buddy Award, Univ San Diego; Lowell Davies Fac Achievement Award, Davies Found, 85; Women of Achievement, President's Coun Prof Women. *Bibliog:* Elise Miller (auth), San Diego art, Los Angeles Times; George Maher (auth), Twilight of Splendor, Little Brown & Co, 76; Zenia Cleigh (auth), Mission as art, San Diego Mag, 79. *Mem:* Asn Archit Historians; Southern Calif Art Historians; Western Asn Art Mus; Col Art Asn. *Res:* California missions, 19th and 20th century California architecture, American primitive art and contemporary American art; 16th century Spanish Renaissance decorative arts. *Publ:* Sword and the Cross, San Diego Mus, 76; contribr, California's Catholic Heritage, Penguin Press, 76; Impressionist as Printmaker & Arbol de la Vida, Founders Press. *Mailing Add:* 3407 Angwin Dr San Diego CA 92123

WHITE, AMOS, IV
CERAMIST, PHOTOGRAPHER
b Montgomery, Ala. *Study:* Ala State Univ, BS, 58; Sculpture Studio, with Isaac S Hathaway, 58; Univ Southern Calif, MFA, 61; Long Island Univ, 66; Univ Md, PhD, 82. *Work:* Quinn Gallery, Univ Southern Calif; Lemoyne Art Found, Tallahassee, Fla. *Exhib:* Designer-Craftsmen USA, 60 & Young Americans, 62, Mus Contemp Crafts, New York; Am Fedn Arts Traveling Exhib, 63; 18th Nat Decorative Arts & Ceramics Exhib, Wichita, 64; Outstanding Atlantic Seaboard Artists, Jacksonville, Fla, 73; Black Artists South, Huntsville Mus Art, 79; plus many others. *Pos:* Md Conf pres, Am Asn Univ Prof, 78-79. *Teaching:* Assoc prof ceramics, Fla A&M Univ, Tallahassee, 61-69; prof & chmn art dept, Bowie State Col, Bowie, Md, 69-77, prof photog, 70-, chmn dept fine & performing arts, 83-86, chmn dept humanities & fine arts, 86- *Awards:* Design West, Los Angeles Mus Sci & Indust, 60; Merit Award, Am Craftsmen's Coun, 61; Ceramic Award, Fla State Fair Fine Arts Comn, 65; Outstanding Alumnus, Univ Southern Calif, 82. *Bibliog:* Lewis & Waddy (auth), Black artists-art, Contemp Crafts, 69; J W Chase (auth), Afro-American Art & Crafts, Von Nostrand-Reinhold, 71. *Mem:* Am Craftsmen's Coun NY (Fla state councilman, 68-69); Fla Craftsmen (pres, 69); Md Fedn Art; Nat Coun Art Adminr; Col Art Asn Am. *Media:* Clay. *Mailing Add:* Humanities & Fine Arts Dept MLK Bldg Rm 0201 Bowie State Univ Jericho Park Rd Bowie MD 20715

WHITE, B J (BEVERLY JO)
PAINTER, COLLAGE ARTIST
b Hobart, Okla, Dec 12, 46. *Study:* Okla City Univ, BS, 69; Phillips Univ, 74-76; La Tech Univ, 80, 82, 84 & 85. *Work:* Arts Coun Okla City, Okla Health Care Corp, Stifel-Nicholas City-Bank & Okla Christian Col, Oklahoma City; Tex Educ Corp, Grand Prairie, Tex. *Comn:* Painting, Arts Coun Okla City, 93. *Exhib:* Am Watercolor Soc, Nat Acad Galleries, New York, 82 & Salmagundi Club, New York, 88; Nat Watercolor Soc, Brea Cult Ctr, Brea, Calif, 84 & Muckenthaler Cult Ctr, Fullerton, Calif, 88 & 92; Southern Watercolor Soc, Miss Mus Art, Jackson, Miss, 85; Kans Watercolor Five State Exhib, Wichita Art Mus, 86, 88 & 90; Rocky Mountain Nat, Foothills Art Ctr, Golden, Colo, 87 & 88; Nat Watercolor Okla, Okla Art Ctr, Oklahoma City, 87, 88, 89 & 92; Goddard Ctr for the Visual Arts, Ardmore, Okla, 91; Kirkpatrick Ctr Mus Complex, Okla City, 92. *Awards:* Grumbacher Gold Medallion/cash award, Kans Watercolor Soc Five-State Competition, 89; Hederman Brothers Printers Award, Southern Watercolor Soc, 85; Third, Nat Watercolor Okla Exhib, 89. *Bibliog:* Marcia Lionberger (auth), The nature of her art, Art Gallery, 5-6/83. *Mem:* Okla Visual Arts Coalition; assoc Am Watercolor Soc; Nat Watercolor Soc. *Media:* Acrylic, oil. *Dealer:* Reuben Saunders Inc 306 N Rock Rd Suite 30 Wichita KS 67207. *Mailing Add:* 13 Pleasant Oaks Dr Edmond OK 73034

WHITE, BRUCE HILDING
SCULPTOR, EDUCATOR
b Bay Shore, NY, July 11, 33. *Study:* Univ Md, BA; Columbia Univ, MA & EdD. *Work:* Revenue Bldg, Springfield, Ill; Ill State Mus, Springfield;

Indianapolis Mus Art, Ind; Rogers Libr & Mus Art, Laurel, Miss; Ill Ctr, Chicago. *Comn:* Large pub sculpture, Quail Springs Mall, Oklahoma City, 80, City of Chicago, 81, MSEM Bldg, Iowa State Univ, 86; Red Carpet Rm, United Airlines, O'Hare Int Airport, 87; Wayne State Univ, Detroit, Mich, 89; Mellerud, Sweden, 92; Ill Acad Math & Sci, 92. *Exhib:* Festival of the Arts, Oklahoma City, 85; Outdoor Sculpture Invitational, Appalachian Summer Festival, NC, 87-88; Sculpture in the Landscape, Paine Art Ctr & Arboretum, Oskosh, Wis, 88; solo exhib, Boyd Gallery, Chicago, Ill, 81, 82, 85 & 90; Concepts/Contemporary Outdoor Sculpture Proposals, West Bend Gallery Fine Arts, Wis; and others. *Teaching:* Presidential res prof, sculpture, Northern Ill Univ, 68- *Awards:* Percent for Art, Ill, 81 & 83, Iowa 86 & 91; First Prize, sculpture, Appalachian Summer Festival, Boone, NC, 87. *Mem:* Swed Am Mus Asn Chicago. *Media:* Sheet Metal, Cast Metal. *Mailing Add:* c/o Dept Art Northern Ill Univ De Kalb IL 60115

WHITE, DEBORAH
DEALER
b Toronto, Ont, Can. *Study:* Univ Toronto, BA; Univ Florence, spec cert. *Pos:* Dir, Albert White Gallery, currently. *Mem:* Can Prof Art Dealers Asn. *Specialty:* Modern art, international artists, Moore, Chagall, Picasso, Leger, Miro, Lichtenstein, and others; primitive and pre-Columbian art. *Mailing Add:* c/o Albert White Gallery 80 Spaldina Ave Toronto ON M5V 2J4 Canada

WHITE, FRANKLIN
PAINTER, DRAFTSMAN
b Richmond, Va, 1943. *Study:* Skowhegan Sch Painting & Sculpture, Maine, 66; Brooklyn Mus Art Sch, 67-68; Nat Collection Fine Arts Internship, 69-70; Howard Univ, BFA, 69, MFA, 71. *Work:* Woodward Found, Washington, DC; Am Fedn Arts; Stern Found, Washington, DC; Washington Post; Corcoran Gallery Art. *Comn:* Three multi-color serigraphs, The Workshop, Washington, DC, 72 & 78. *Exhib:* Contemp Black Artists in Am, Whitney Mus Am Art, New York, 71; 2nd Ann Exhib Washington Artists, Phillips Collection, 72; Corcoran Mus Art, 72 & 75; Directions in Afro-Am Art, Johnson Mus, Cornell Univ, Ithaca, NY, 74; 77 Artists, Wash Project for the Arts, 77; one-man shows, Corcoran Gallery, Washington, DC, 72, Jefferson Pl Gallery, 72 & 74 & Gallery Rebecca Cooper, Washington, DC, 75 & 77; and others. *Pos:* Info guide intern, Nat Collection Fine Arts, 69-70. *Teaching:* Instr painting & drawing, Georgetown Univ & Md Sch of Arts & Design; artist-in-residence, DC Pub Sch & DC Comn on the Arts, 70-71; instr, Corcoran Gallery Art Sch, 75- *Awards:* Painting Award, Skowhegan Sch Arts & Design; Nat Endowment Arts Grant, 70-71. *Bibliog:* Roberta Smith (auth), Directions in Afro-American art, Artforum, 75; Henri Ghent (auth), article, Art in Am, 1-2/75; Benjamin Forgery (auth), Washington DC round-up, Artnews, 2/75. *Mailing Add:* c/o Gallery K 2010 R St NW Washington DC 20009

WHITE, JAMES RICHARD
SCULPTOR, EDUCATOR
b Dayton, Ohio, Jan 14, 50. *Study:* Ohio Univ, BFA(painting), 72, MFA(sculpture), 74. *Work:* USAF, Dayton, Ohio. *Comn:* Murray State Univ, Ky. *Exhib:* One-man shows, Wright State Univ, Dayton, Ohio, 79 & SE Mo State Univ, Cape Girardeau, 79; Evansville Mus Arts & Sci, Ind, 79 & 80. *Teaching:* Asst prof, Murray State Univ, Ky, 74-81; assoc prof, Ariz State Univ, Tempe, 81- *Awards:* Ind Found Arts & Sci Award, 80. *Bibliog:* Jerry Speight (auth), Shelter skelter, Ky Art Educ J, 12/79, Air city, free air, air fair affair, School Arts/Davis, 9/80 & James R White, sculptor, Art Voices S/Davis, 7/80. *Mem:* Col Art Asn. *Media:* Metal, Wood. *Mailing Add:* Art Dept Ariz State Univ Tempe AZ 85287-1505

WHITE, JOHN M
PAINTER, CONCEPTUAL ARTIST
b San Francisco, Calif, May 10, 37. *Study:* Patri Sch of Art Fundamentals, San Francisco, 62-65; Otis Art Inst, Los Angeles, MFA, 69. *Work:* Los Angeles Co Art Mus, Los Angeles; Smithsonian Arch Am Art; Newport-Harbor Art Mus, Newport Beach, Calif; Solomon R Guggenheim Mus, New York; St Louis Art Mus, Mo; and others. *Exhib:* New Work, New Talent, Los Angeles Co Art Mus, 74; Drawing Show, Newport Harbor Art Mus, 75; one-man shows, Barbara Okun Gallery, St Louis, 77, Baum-Silverman Gallery, Los Angeles, 78 & 81 & Roy Boyd Gallery, Chicago, 81; performances, Vancouver Art Gallery, BC, 74, Miami-Dade Community Col, Fla, 75, St Louis Mus Contemp Art, 77 & Chicago Art Inst, 78; Solomon R Guggenheim Mus, 81; Dorothy Goldeen Gallery, Santa Monica, 88; Retrospective, Los Angeles Munic Art Gallery, Barnsdall Park, 83; and many others. *Pos:* Panelist, Nat Endowment Arts, 86. *Teaching:* Vis artist performance workshop, Claremont Grad Sch, 77- & Otis Art Inst, 77-79; Univ Calif, Irvine, 84- *Awards:* New Talent Award, Los Angeles Co Art Mus, 72; Nat Endowment Arts Grants, 76-77, 78-79, 84 & 85; CETA Grant Artist in Residence, 78-79. *Media:* Mixed. *Dealer:* Contemporary Artists 1001 A Colorado Santa Monica CA 90401. *Mailing Add:* Dept Fine Art UC Irvine Irvine CA 92717

WHITE, KAREN J
SCULPTOR, CRAFTSMAN
b Coshocton, Ohio, Jan 15, 43. *Study:* Ohio State Univ, BFA, 69; Metrop State Col 74-75; Univ Colo, 85. *Exhib:* Colo Artist Biennial Exhib, Loveland Art Mus, 90; Gallery bel etage, Basel, Switz, 91; Creating Ourselves, Eastern NMex Univ, 92; The Sacred as Feurale, Univ Colo Boulder, 92; Paper in Particular, Columbia Col, Mo, 92; and others. *Teaching:* Workshop handmade paper, Univ Northern Colo, 88, Arvado Ctr Arts, Colo, 90 & Colo Inst Art, 91- *Awards:* First prize, Mannings Nat Fiber Show, 77; First prize, Colo Lawyers Arts, 88. *Bibliog:* Nancy Clegg (auth), Pulp novel, Westword, 9/89; Renelda Muse (dir), Art Around Town (film), KCNC-TV, Colo, 2/90; Nancy Orban (ed), Fiber Arts Design Book Four, Lark Bks, 91. *Mem:* Nat Asn Women Artists Inc; Int Asn Hand Papermakers & Paper Artist. *Media:* Miscellaneous media; handmade paper. *Dealer:* Lightside Gallery 225 Canyon Rd Santa Fe NM 87501. *Mailing Add:* 282 Delaware St Denver CO 80223

WHITE, NORMAN TRIPLETT
SCULPTOR, KINETIC ARTIST
b San Antonio, Tex, Jan 7, 38. *Study:* Harvard Col, with T Lux Feininger, 55-59, BA(biol), 59. *Work:* Nat Gallery Can & Art Bank, Ottawa; Vancouver Art Gallery. *Comn:* Light mural, CBC Bldg, Vancouver, BC, 75. *Exhib:* Some More Beginnings, Exp in Art & Technol Show, Brooklyn Mus, New York, 68; Norm White at the Electric Gallery, Toronto, 71; retrospective, Vancouver Art Gallery, BC, 75; New Directions, Nat Gallery of Can, 77; Hearsay, Global Telecommun Event, 85; Les Machines Sentimentales, Avignon, 86; Ubigua, Venice Biennale, 86. *Teaching:* Inst, Ont Col Art, Toronto, 78-86. *Awards:* La Villette, Paris, 85; Prix Ars Electronica-Interactive Sculpture, Ontario Res Found, 90. *Bibliog:* John Turnbull (auth), article, Vanguard, 9/75; Joe Bodolai (auth), article, Artscanada, 5/76; Brian Reffin Smith (auth), Soft Computing, Addison-Wesley, 84. *Mem:* Artex-IPSA Telecommun Group. *Media:* Multi. *Mailing Add:* PO Box 1032 Durham ON N0G 1R0 Canada

WHITE, PHILIP BUTLER
PAINTER, COLLECTOR
b Chicago, Ill, Jan 23, 35. *Study:* Univ Southern Calif, BFA(painting). *Work:* River Forest Centennial Comn. *Exhib:* Butler Inst Am Art, Youngstown, Ohio, 62-64; Ill State Fair, Springfield, 63, 65, 67, 69 & 70; Nat Acad Design, New York, 63-65, 67-70 & 74-76; Am Watercolor Soc, New York, 70-71; Union League Club, Chicago, 74-78. *Awards:* First Prizes, Ill State Fair, 60 & 65 & Union League, Chicago, 63 & 67; Thomas B Clark Awards, Nat Acad Design, 65, 68 & 70. *Bibliog:* Cover story, Am Artist, 8/78; Les Krantz (ed), Am Artists, 85. *Media:* Oil, Egg Tempera. *Collection:* Contemporary realistic art. *Publ:* Contribr, 20 Figure Painters and How They Work, Watson-Guptill, 79. *Mailing Add:* 710 Clinton Pl River Forest IL 60305

WHITE, RALPH
PAINTER, EDUCATOR
b Minneapolis, Minn, Jan 3, 21. *Study:* Minneapolis Col Art & Design, cert, 42; Pratt Inst, cert, 46. *Work:* Everson Mus, Syracuse, NY; Mem Mus, Corpus Christi, Tex; Wright State Univ, Dayton, Ohio; St Mary's Col of Md; Witte Mus, San Antonio, Tex. *Exhib:* Denver Art Mus 59th Western Art Ann, 53; Butler Inst Am Art 22nd Ann Midyear Show, 57; Tex Contemp Artists Knoedler Gallery, New York (circulated nationally); Watercolor USA, Springfield Art Mus, Mo, 71 & 77; Ralph White Acrylics, Palacio de Bellas Artes, Mexico City, 72-73. *Teaching:* Prof studio art, Univ Tex, Austin, 46-82, actg chmn dept art, 67-73, prof emer, 82. *Awards:* Vanderlip Fel, Minn Sch Art, 42; Purchase Award, Minneapolis Inst Art, 42; Onderdonk Purchase Award, Tex Paint & Sculpture Ann, Witte Mus, 49; Ford Found Grant, 70. *Bibliog:* Richard Teller Hirsch (auth), Tale Painting Tells, Alcalde, Univ Tex, 12/70; Eleanor Freed (auth), 2 views of space, Houston Post, 2/6/72; Margaret T Dry (auth), Laguna Gloria spotlights Ralph White, Austin Am Statesman, 1/5/75. *Mem:* Tex Watercolor Soc; Tex Asn Fine Arts (adv bd, 73-76); Dallas Ft Worth Soc Visual Commun; Austin Prof Artists (pres, 59). *Media:* Acrylic, Watercolor. *Mailing Add:* 4701 Agarita Rd Austin TX 78734

WHITE, ROBERT (WINTHROP)
SCULPTOR, EDUCATOR
b New York, NY, Sept 19, 21. *Study:* With Joseph Weisz, Munich, 32-34; also with John Howard Benson & Waldemar Raemisch, RI Sch Design. *Work:* Brooklyn Mus, NY; RI Sch Design Mus, Providence; Springfield Mus, Mass. *Comn:* Bronze, St Anthony of Padua Sch, Northport, NY, 59; A E Verrill Silver Medal, Peabody Mus Natural Hist, Yale Univ, 60; three wooden & metal figures, Mrs Hester Pickman, St Michael's Roman Cath Church, Bedford, Mass, 60-66; bronze relief portrait of Joseph Wilson, Xerox Corp, Stamford, Conn, 72; Pershing Monument, Pershing Square, Washington, DC, 83; and others. *Exhib:* Pa Acad Ann, Philadelphia, 50; Int Exhib Relig Art, Stazione Marittima, Trieste, Italy, 58; Continuing Tradition of Realism in American Art, Hirschl & Adler Galleries, New York, 62; Eight Americans, Amsterdam, Breda, Nymegen, Holland, 69; Representational Spirit, Univ Art Gallery, Albany, NY, 70; The Figure, Pratt Inst, traveling exhib, 80-81; and many other group & one-man exhibs. *Pos:* Resident sculptor, Am Acad Rome, Italy, 69-70 & Skowhegan Sch of Painting & Sculpture, 74; guest lectr, MFA Prog, Parson's Sch Design, 81; assoc prof emer, State Univ New York, Stonybrook, 87- *Teaching:* Instr life drawing, Parsons Sch Design, New York, 49-52; assoc prof art, State Univ NY, Stony Brook, 62- *Awards:* Am Acad Rome Fel, 52-55; Nat Acad Design Proctor Mem Prize, 62; Farfield Found Grant, 69. *Bibliog:* Article, Arts Mag, 9/80. *Mem:* Fel Am Acad Rome; Nat Acad Design; Century Asn. *Media:* Multimedia. *Publ:* Illusr, Enchanted, Pantheon, 51 & Confessions of Nat Turner, Harper's Mag, 67. *Dealer:* Graham Modern 1014 Madison Ave New York NY 10021. *Mailing Add:* 5 Moriches Rd St James NY 11780

WHITE, RUTH
ART DEALER, COLLAGE ARTIST
b New York, NY May 25, 11. *Study:* With Kurt Seligmann. *Pos:* Owner, Ruth White Gallery. *Mem:* Sarasota Art Asn; Manatee Art League. *Media:* Watercolor, Graphics. *Specialty:* Contemporary paintings, sculpture and graphics. *Collection:* Kurt Seligmann; Ozenfant; paintings and sculpture by various young American artists. *Mailing Add:* Shadybrook Village 926 Byron Lane Sarasota FL 34243

WHITE, STUART JAMES
SCULPTOR, ASSEMBLAGE ARTIST
b Salisbury, Md, May 31, 44. *Study:* Carnegie-Mellon Univ, BFA, 68, MFA, 70, DA, 78. *Work:* Newark Mus, NJ; NJ State Mus, Trenton; Crawford Art Gallery, Cork, Eire; Univ Salisburg & Peninsula Gen Hosp, Salisbury, Md; pvt collections of Peter Homitzky, Hoboken, NJ, Bruce Arnold, critic, Dublin, Eire & Terry Carroll, dealer, Dublin, Eire. *Comn:* Construction (wallpiece), Tanners Coun Am, Washington, DC, 79. *Exhib:* constructions, 55 Mercer Gallery, New York, 81; solo exhib, NJ Biennial, Newark Mus, 82, figurative work, NJ State Mus, Trenton, 83, Crawford Art Gallery, Cork, Ireland, 89, Proj Art Ctr, Dublin, 89 & Wyvern Gallery, Dublin, 91; Scottish Sculpture Open, Kildrummie Castle, Scotland, 85; New Talent, Allan Stone Gallery, New York, 85 & 86; Sculpture Biennale Int, Invitational Ctr d'Arts du Normandie, Jouy sur Eure, France, 86; and others. *Pos:* Dir, Robeson Gallery, Rutgers Univ, Newark, 79-; head fine art, Crawford Col Art & Design, Cork, Ireland, 87- *Teaching:* Intern drawing, Carnegie-Mellon Univ, 72-73; asst prof art hist, Mt Union Col, 74-78; dept head resins, Johnson Atelier, Princeton, 78-79; vis specialist, Montclair State Col, 79-; asst prof sculpture, Rutgers Univ, Newark, 79- *Awards:* Grant, Newark: Genesis of a City, NJ Comt Humanities, 80; Sculpture Fel, NJ State Coun Arts, 83; Res Fel, Scottish Sculpture Workshop, Rutgers Univ, Lumsden, Scotland, 84. *Bibliog:* Hildreth York (auth), Stuart White: The Figurative Work, NJ State Mus, 83; Peter Murray (auth), Stuart White: Corpus, Crawford Art Gallery, Cork, Ireland. *Mem:* Col Art Asn Am; Assoc Irish Artists. *Media:* Miscellaneous Media, Wood. *Publ:* Auth, Calvin Albert, 78 & Dennis Oppenheim, 79, Sculpture News Exchange; coauth, Stalking the post office mural: An artful odyssey, New York Sunday Times, 80. *Dealer:* Terry Carroll Wyvern Gallery Dublin Ireland. *Mailing Add:* 62 Wainsfort Rochestown Rd Cork Ireland

WHITE, SUSAN CHRYSLER
PAINTER
b Chico, Calif, June 12, 54. *Study:* Univ Calif, Berkeley, BA, 77; Univ Calif, Davis, with Wayne Thiebaud, Roy DeForest, Robert Arneson, Ellen Lanyon & Manuel Neri, MFA, 80. *Work:* Worcester Art Mus, Mass; Prudential Insurance Co, Newark, NJ; Rutgers Univ; Meniscus Med Communications, Philadelphia. *Exhib:* Challenge Exhib 82, Fleisher Art Mem, Philadelphia, 82; Four Emerging Expressionists, Peter Miller Gallery, Chicago, 82; Philadelphia Artists, Philadelphia Mus Art, 82-83; An Invitational: Six Artists, Philadelphia Art Alliance, 83; one-person show, Peter Miller Gallery, Chicago, 83-84 & Janet Fleisher Gallery, Philadelphia, 84; and others. *Teaching:* Instr & vis artist, La State Univ, 80; vis lectr, Tyler Sch Art, 81 & Rutgers Univ, 82. *Awards:* Ann Bremmar Award, Berkeley Mus, 77; Purchase Award, Rutgers Univ Nat, 82; Philadelphia Mus Art Purchase Award, Cheltenham Art Ctr 41st Ann Painting Exhib, 82. *Media:* Oil, Oil Pastels. *Dealer:* Peter Miller Gallery Huron St Chicago IL. *Mailing Add:* 552 Broadway 6th Fl New York NY 10012

WHITEHEAD, FRANCES
SCULPTOR, EDUCATOR
b, Richmond, Va, Oct 20, 53. *Study:* East Carolina Univ, Greenville, NC, BFA, 75; Northern Ill Univ, DeKalb, MFA, 78. *Work:* Mus Contemp Art, Chicago; Ariz State Mus, Tucson; Lakeview Mus, Peoria, Ill; Arthur Anderson, Chicago, Detroit, NY; State Ill. *Comn:* Sculpture, Chicago; Sette & Segura Pub, Tempe; sculpture, South Bend, Ind; National Site Works, Atlanta. *Exhib:* Chicago Art Expo, 88, 91 & 92; Basel Art Expo, 91; Kansas City Art Inst, 92; Neuberger Mus, State Univ NY, Purchase, 93; Chicago Cult Ctr, 93; and many others. *Teaching:* Vis asst prof/2D & 3D, Tex Tech Univ, Lubbock, 79-80; vis asst prof painting, Ill State Univ, Normal, 80-81; asst prof/sculpture, Ind Univ, Bloomington, 81-84; assoc prof/chair, sculpture, Sch Art Inst Chicago, 84- *Awards:* Ill Arts Coun, 85 & 87; Nat Endowment Arts, 85 & 87; Tiffany Found Award, 91. *Bibliog:* Michael Bonesteel (auth), Medium cool, Art Am, 12/87; James Yood (auth), Frances Whitehead, Artforum, 12/89; Steve Leuking (auth), rev, Sculpture Mag, 1/90. *Media:* Misc Media. *Dealer:* DART Gallery 712 Carpenter Chicago IL 60622; Lisa Sette Gallery 4142 N Marshall Way Scottsdale AZ. *Mailing Add:* 1858 W Huron Chicago IL 60622

WHITEMAN, EDWARD RUSSELL
PAINTER
b Buffalo, NY, Dec 16, 38. *Study:* Univ Buffalo Albright Art Sch, AD. *Work:* Nat Collection Fine Arts, Washington, DC; Albright-Knox Art Gallery, Buffalo; New Orleans Mus Art, La; Montgomery Mus Fine Arts, Ala; Crysler Mus Art, Mass. *Exhib:* Whitney Biennial Contemp Am Art, New York, 75; Eight State Exhib Paintings & Sculpture, Okla Art Ctr, 75; Pratt Graphic Ctr, 75; La Jolla Mus Contemp Art, Calif, 79; Columbia Mus Art, SC; Paper Making & Paper Using, Southeastern Ctr Contemp Art, Winston-Salem, NC; Edward Whiteman: Works on Treated Paper, 1975-1982, Mus Art, Carnegie Inst, 82; Corcoran Biennial, Corcoran Gallery Art, Washington, DC, 88. *Awards:* Purchase Award, New Orleans Mus Art, 75; Artist Fels, Nat Endowment for the Arts & Southeastern Ctr Contemp Art, 78-79; Ford Found Grant, 80. *Bibliog:* Jean Nathan (auth), Newswatch Art, Channel 6 News, 75; Calas & Terrington (coauths), Edward Whiteman and the unlovely metaphor, Arts Quarterly New Orleans, Vol 4, No 3, 82. *Media:* Liquitex, Pastel. *Dealer:* Arthur Roger Gallery 432 Julia St New Orleans LA 70130. *Mailing Add:* 432 Julia St New Orleans LA 70130

WHITEN, COLETTE
SCULPTOR, INSTRUCTOR
b Birmingham, Eng, Feb 7, 45; Can citizen. *Study:* Ont Col of Art, AOCA. *Work:* Nat Gallery of Can, Ottawa; Art Gallery of Ont, Toronto; Art Bank, Ottawa. *Comn:* Sculpture, Art Gallery Ont, 72; Gov Can Bldg, North York, Ont, 76; sculpture, Dept Pub Works, 77; sculpture, Mental Health Ctr, Toronto, 78; Sudbury & District Chamber Commerce Centennial Proj, 83; Manufacturer's Life Insurance Bldg, Toronto, 85-86. *Exhib:* 8th Biennale de Paris, Mus d'Art Mod de la Ville de Paris, France, 73; solo shows, Carmen Lamanna Gallery, 73-75, 77, 78, 80, 82 & 85; Carmen Lamanna Gallery at Owens Art Gallery, Sackville, 75; Some Canadian Women Artists, Nat Gallery Can, Ottawa, 75; Celebration of the Body, Etherington Art Ctr, 76; Ont Now, A Survey of Contemp Art, Kitchener-Waterloo Gallery, Art Gallery of Hamilton, 76; London Art Gallery, Ont, 78, 83 & 84; The 1st Australian Sculpture Triennial, Melbourne, 81; Human Touch from Canada to Belgium Traveling Exhib (with catalog), 86. *Teaching:* Instr concept develop, Ont Col of Art, Toronto, 74-; resident artist, Univ Western Ont, London, 78-79. *Awards:* Eaton Traveling Scholar, 72; Can Arts Coun Bursary, 73, 76, 78 & 80; Ont Art Coun Award, 77. *Bibliog:* John Bentley Mays (auth), Friends are Cast as Artworks in Colette Whiten's Sculptures, Globe & Mail, 4/12/80; David Burnett & Marilyn Schiff, Contemporary Canadian Art, Hurtig Publ, Edmonton, 83. *Media:* Plaster, Wood. *Publ:* Contribr, Carmen Lamanna Gallery at Owens Art Gallery, Owens Art Gallery, Sackville, NB, 75. *Mailing Add:* Dept Studio Art Ont Col Art 100 McCaul St Toronto ON M5T 1W1 Canada

WHITEN, TIM
SCULPTOR, ENVIRONMENTAL ARTIST
b Inkster, Mich, Aug 13, 41. *Study:* Cent Mich Univ, BS, 64; Univ Ore, creative arts grant, 65, MFA, 66. *Work:* Nat Gallery Can, Can Coun Art Bank & Ministry External Affairs, Ottawa, Ont, Can; Art Gallery Ont, Toronto; Ingalls Stone Co, Bedford, Ind. *Comn:* Cast concrete walls, Dept Parks & Recreation, Jasper, Ore, 64; monumental sculpture, Lane Co Parks Comn, Orchard Lake, Eugene, Ore, 66; Earth Work Ritual Installation, Art Park, Lewiston, NY, 77; Ritual Installation, Central Park, Art Across the Park, New York, 82. *Exhib:* Art Gallery New York Univ, NYork, Ont, 72, Morris Gallery, Toronto, Ont, 72 & 74: York Univ, Zacks Gallery, Stong Col, NYork, Ont, 74, St Lawrence Col Appl Arts & Technol, Kingston, Ont, 74 & 79, Univ Waterloo, Ont, 76, Bau-Xi Gallery, Toronto, Ont, 76, 77, 78, 79, 81, 82, 83, 85 & Olga Korper Gallery, Toronto, Ont, 90; Maquette Auction, Harbourfront Art Gallery, Toronto, 85; Cultural Exchange Exhib, Zhejlang Acad, Hangzhou, Peoples Repub China, 86; York Work I, Art Gallery York Univ, New York, 86; Membership Sales, Art Gallery Ont, Toronto, 87 & 88; Int Art Fair, Chicago, 87; Int Art Fair, Cologne, Ger, 88; Day of the Dead, York Quay Gallery, Harbourfront, Toronto, 88. *Teaching:* Assoc prof fine arts, York Univ, Downsview, Ont, 68-; vis lectr, univs & arts schs, Can, 70-; chmn, Fine Arts Coun; chmn visual arts dept, York Univ, 84-87 & assoc prof, 87-; instr, Atlin Ctr Arts, BC, 86. *Awards:* O'Connell Purchase Award, 63. *Bibliog:* Numerous articles in periodicals & newspapers including, Artpost 24, Harpers, Artscanada, Arts Mag & Village Voice. *Media:* Human Skulls, Mud; Found Objects, Paper. *Res:* Investigation of consciousness as it manifests in a variety of cultures, historically and contemporarily. *Mailing Add:* c/o Olga Korper Gallery 17 Morrow Ave Toronto ON M6R 2H9 Canada

WHITESELL, JOHN D
PRINTMAKER
b Hamilton, Ohio, Dec 1, 42. *Study:* Earlham Col, Richmond, Ind, BA; Miami Univ, Ohio, with Robert Wolfe, Jr; Ind Univ with Rudy Pozzatti & Marvin Lowe, MFA. *Work:* Bradford City Art Gallery, Yorkshire, Eng; Libr Cong, Washington, DC; Miami Art Ctr, Fla; US Info Agency, Prints in Embassies Prog. *Comn:* Vermillion Seven (suite of prints), comn & publ by Univ SDak, 75. *Exhib:* Nat Print, Libr Cong, 71 & 73; 5th Ann Nat Exhib Prints, San Diego, Calif, 72; 1st Int Graphics Biennial, Miami, Fla, 73; Nat Print Los Angeles, 73; Bradley Nat Print Show, Peoria, Ill, 75. *Teaching:* Assoc prof printmaking, Univ Louisville, Ky, 73- *Awards:* Third Award, Miami Print Int, 73; Purchase Awards, Libr Cong, 73 & Bradley Univ, 75. *Media:* Silkscreen, Lithographs. *Mailing Add:* Dept of Art Univ of Louisville Louisville KY 40208

WHITESIDE, WILLIAM ALBERT, II
PAINTER, EDUCATOR
b Bradenton, Fla, Aug 1, 25. *Study:* Ringling Sch Art, 48-51; Fla State Univ, Tallahassee, with Karl Zerbe & Arthur Deshales, BS(art educ), 58, MFA(painting), 66. *Work:* Fla State Univ, Tallahassee; Marine Corps Mus, Washington, DC; New Eng Air Mus, Windsor Locks, Conn; Marine Corps Mus, Quantico, Va; Marine Corps Air Mus, MCAS, El Toro, Calif. *Comn:* Portrait-riverscape, Burt Reynolds, 81. *Exhib:* Third Monroe Ann, Masur Mus Art, La, 66; Midyear Show, Butler Inst Am Art, 66 & 67; Seventh Ann Nat Western Art Show, San Antonio, Tex, 69; solo exhib, Asheville Mus Art, NC, 72; 30th Ann Painting Exhib, Abilene Fine Arts Mus, Tex, 73; NC Watercolor Soc, Asheville Art Mus, NC, 76; and others. *Teaching:* Instr art, Fla State Univ, 64-65; instr painting, NTex State Univ, 66-68 & Western Carolina Univ, 73-75; artist in residence, High Hampton Inn & Country Club, 69-75. *Awards:* Transparent Watercolor Award, 73 & Purchase Award, 74, Tex Watercolor Soc; NC Watercolor Soc Purchase Award, 76. *Media:* Watercolor, Egg Tempera. *Mailing Add:* PO Box 522 Cashiers NC 28717

WHITLOCK, JOHN JOSEPH
MUSEUM DIRECTOR, EDUCATOR
b South Bend, Ind, Jan 7, 35. *Study:* Ball State Univ, BS, 57, MA, 63; Ind Univ, EdD, 71. *Work:* Ball State Univ, Muncie, Ind; Hanover Col, Ind. *Exhib:* One-man shows, Franklin Col, Ind, 69, Westminster Presby Church Gallery, 71, Unitarian Church Gallery, 71, Rockford, Ill, Grace St Luke's Festival Arts in Relig, 76 & Unitarian Fel, 83; John A Logan Col, 86; Tupelo Art Gallery, 87. *Collections Arranged:* Senufo Door/A Study of its Iconography, 70; Ghana Door/A Study of its Origin, 70; Return to Humanism, 71; Carroll

Cloar, 76; Japanese Woodblock Prints, 77; Bill Eggleston Photographs, 77; Richard Hunt Sculpture, 77; Recent Media, 77. *Pos:* Dir & cur, Burpee Art Mus, Rockford, Ill, 70-72; dir, Brooks Mem Art Gallery, Memphis, Tenn, 72-78; dir, Univ Mus, Southern Ill Univ, Carbondale, 78-, actg cur art, 89- *Teaching:* Instr educ, Hanover Col, 64-66, asst prof art, 66-69; teaching assoc art educ, Ind Univ, Bloomington, 69-70; prof arts & humanities, Elgin Community Col, 70-72; prof mus studies prog, Southwestern at Memphis, 73-78; prof museology, Memphis State Univ, 76-78; prof mus studies, Southern Ill Univ, Carbondale, 78-; mem grad faculty. *Awards:* Ball State Univ Fine Arts Purchase Award, 57. *Mem:* Am Asn Mus; Midwest Asn of Mus; Int Coul of Mus; Asn Art Mus Dirs. *Media:* Painting; Printmaking. *Publ:* Auth, Return to Alexandria, Viewpoints, Vol 54, No 3, Ind Univ, 5/76; Museum Studies, Mus Scope, 76; Relativistic Thought: Charting the Future of Museums, ICOFOM Study Series, No 10, ICOM, 10/86; Museology and Museums, ICOFOM Study Series, ICOM, 9/87; Museology: Preserving the National Patrimony, No 14, ICOFOM Study Series, 11/88; auth, The Creative Use of Reproductions in Museum Exhibits, ICOFOM Study Series, No 8, ICOM Conf on Museology, Zagreb, Yugoslavia, 85. *Mailing Add:* c/o Univ Mus Southern Ill Univ Carbondale IL 62901

WHITNEY, CHARLOTTE ARMIDE
PAINTER, JEWELER
b New York, NY, Dec 13, 23. *Study:* Corcoran Sch Art, George Washington Univ, with Eugen Weiscz & Peggy Bacon, BFA, 45; Cranbrook Acad Art, with Zoltan Sepeshy, MFA, 46. *Work:* Series of 24 wild plant watercolors & series of 32 tree flower watercolors Kingman Mus, Battle Creek, Mich. *Exhib:* Miniature Painters, Sculptors & Engravers Soc, Washington, DC 20th exhib, Smithsonian Inst, 53; Traveling Exhib Water Colors, Kingman Mus, Battle Creek, Mich, 86-; one-person show, Pasghetti's, Kalamazoo, 88, & Triola Gallery, Lansing, Mich, 92; Dimock Gallery, Washington, DC, 88; Tenth Mich Artists Competition, Battle Creek Art Ctr, 89; one-woman invitational, Battle Creek Art Ctr, Mich, 90. *Pos:* Co-dir, Whitney Galleries, Birmingham, Mich, 50-59; dir traveling exhib Olivet Restoration Drawings, Mich Coun Arts & Olivet, Mich City Hall, 74-75. *Teaching:* Art, Roeper City & Country Sch, Bloomfield Hills, Mich, 50-59, Olivet Col, Mich, 65-70, 87 & 90 & Olivet Schs, Mich, 72-89. *Awards:* Olivet Downtown Storefronts Restoration Award, Keep Mich Beautiful, 73. *Bibliog:* Joy Hakansen (auth), House is home and gallery, Detroit News, 3/54; Virginia Gust (auth), Olivet woman sketches youth into old buildings, Enquirer & News, Battle Creek, Mich, 2/4/73. *Mem:* Battle Creek Artists Guild (secy, 78-79, treas, 82-); Soc Archit Historians. *Media:* Watercolor, Acrylic; Metalcraft. *Publ:* Auth, Children's Art, Olivet Col Press, 65. *Dealer:* The Hefner Galleries Ltd (Paintings) 1440 Wealthy SE Grand Rapids MO 49506; Pas de Chat (Jewelry) 3542 N Southport Ave Chicago IL 60657. *Mailing Add:* 614 Summer St Olivet MI 49076

WHITNEY, MAYNARD MERLE
SCULPTOR, EDUCATOR
b Cedar Rapids, Iowa, Dec 18, 31. *Study:* Iowa Wesleyan Col, BA, 58; Univ Calif, Los Angeles, 60; Univ Iowa, 61; Univ Ore, MFA(sculptor), 65. *Work:* Joslyn Art Mus, Omaha, Nebr; Sheldon Art Gallery, Lincoln, Nebr; Denver Art Mus, Colo; Elder Art Gallery, Nebr Wesleyan Univ, Lincoln; Omaha Nat Bank, Nebr. *Comn:* Hanging Plexiglas sculpture, Ford-Warren Libr, Denver Pub Libr, 75. *Exhib:* Artrain (toured nine western states), 73; 13th Midwest Biennial, Joslyn Art Mus, Omaha, 74; 14th Ann Own Your Own Show, Pueblo Art Ctr, Colo, 74; one-man shows, Sheldon Art Gallery, Lincoln, 70 & Kans State Univ, Manhattan, 71; and others. *Teaching:* Chmn dept art, Nebr Wesleyan Univ, Lincoln, 65-72 & Colo Women's Col, Denver, 72-81; Aurora Pub Sch, 84-88. *Awards:* Creative Teaching Award, Nebr Wesleyan Univ, 67; Mus Purchase, 11th Midwest Biennial, Joslyn Art Mus, Omaha, 70; Purchase Award, 6th Ann Midland Exhib, Omaha Nat Bank, 70. *Media:* Multimedia, Stone. *Mailing Add:* 3607 S Ouray St Aurora CO 80013-2852

WHITNEY, RICHARD WHEELER
PAINTER
b Burlington, Vt, Jan 22, 46. *Study:* Univ NH, Durham, BA, 68; with Sidney F Willis, Bennington, NH, 65; with R H Ives Gammell, Boston, 66-71. *Work:* Harvard Univ; Univ Chicago; Anchorage Hist & Fine Arts Mus; Newark Mus Art, NJ. *Comn:* Portrait of US Senator Thomas J Mc Intyre, NH State House, Concord, 81; Alaska Scenic Collection, Little Susitna Co, Anchorage, 83; portrait of Cardinal Humberto Medeiros, Cath Univ Portugal, 88; portrait of James H Webb, Jr, Secy of Navy, Pentagon, Washington, DC, 89; portrait of Mr & Mrs E Nambu, Tokyo, 91. *Exhib:* Allied Artists Am Nat Exhibs, New York, 76-77, 80-81 & 83; solo exhibs, Guild Boston Artists, 80 & 82; Maryhill Mus, Wash; Springfield Mus, Utah; Amarillo Art Ctr, Tex, 83; and others. *Collections Arranged:* Allied Artists Am, New Eng Exhib, 82. *Teaching:* Instr painting, Sharon Arts Ctr, NH, 71-77; instr art, Cushing Acad, Ashburnham, 71-80. *Awards:* Gold Medal, Guild Boston Artists Competition, 83 & 87; Medal Hon, Am Artist Prof League, 84 & 91; Silver Medal, Soc Illusr, New York, 87. *Bibliog:* Charles Movalli (auth), A conversation with Richard Whitney, Am Artist Mag, 82; Alexandra York (auth), Richard Whitney, neoclassical impressionist, Am Arts Quart, winter 92. *Mem:* Grand Central Galleries, New York; Portraits Inc; Soc Illusr, New York; Guild Boston Artists; Portraits South, Raleigh, NC. *Media:* Oil. *Publ:* Auth, Principles of Visual Impressionism, Checkerberry Hill Press, 79; Return to excellence, Profile, fall 83; coauth, Realism in Revolution: The Art of the Boston School, Taylor Publ Co, 86. *Dealer:* Monadnock Studios 14 Water St Marlborough NH 03455. *Mailing Add:* PO Box 427 Marlborough NH 03455

WHITSON
PHOTOGRAPHER, EDUCATOR
b Concord, Mass, Sept 7, 41. *Study:* Univ NH, BA, 63; Univ Iowa, MA & MFA, 67; Eastern Montana Col. *Work:* Univ NH; Univ Iowa; Kansas City Art Inst; Mod Museet, Stockholm, Sweden; Galeria Teatru Studio, Warsaw, Poland. *Exhib:* One-man shows, Univ Iowa, 65 & 67, Univ Buffalo, NY, 70, Scalping Gallery, Regina, Sask, 75, Eastern Mont Col, 79, Yellow Art Ctr, Billings, Mont, 80; Mod Museet, Stockholm, 75; Galeria Teatru, Warsaw, Poland, 75; Nat Art Gallery, Wellington, New Zealand, 76; San Francisco Art Inst, 84; Idaho State Univ, Pocatello, 86; Eastern Mont Col, 92; plus many others. *Pos:* Pres, founder, Western Dakota Junk Co, Billings, Mont, 69-; founder & pres, Acad Neodada, 74-79; pres, Nat Acad Conceptualists, 79-80; ed & publr, SLUJ Press, 75-; gallery dir, Eastern Mont Col, 78-79, slide librn, 79-80; art ed, Alkali Flats Mag, 81-; bd dirs, Photog Inst Billings, 84-86. *Teaching:* Asst drawing, Univ Iowa, 65-67; from instr to prof drawing, design, photog & art hist, Eastern Mont Col, 67-; chmn art dept, 86, 87 & 92. *Awards:* Third Place Black & White Print, Photog Inst Billings 9th Ann Competition, Yellowstone Art Ctr, Mont, 85; Two Honorable Mentions, Artists Valentines, H G Merriam Gallery, Billings, 86; Cash Award, Big Sky Biennal IV, Idaho State Univ, 86. *Bibliog:* Ronny Cohen (auth), Please Mr Postman look & see-Is there a work of art in your bag for me? Art News, 12/81; Michael Crane & May Stofflet (auths), Correspondence art, Contemp Arts Press, San Francisco, 84. *Mem:* United SLUJ Workers, 70-79; Photog Inst of Billings, 84-87; Yellowstone Art Ctr, 68- *Media:* Gelatin Silver Print, Collage. *Publ:* Auth, Al's Ham 'n' Egger & Body Shop Again, Basilisk Press, 74; The SLUJ Book, 76, Lost in the Mail, 78, Umbrella, 79 & Autoroticism, 80, SLUJ Press; auth & contribr to many other corresp art publs, 69- *Mailing Add:* Menhmont Lightwriting 902 24th St W Billings MT 59102

WHITSON, ANGIE
SCULPTOR, PAINTER
b San Jose, Calif. *Study:* Pasadena Mus Art, 74; Art League, Los Angeles, Calif, 74-78; Northridge Univ, Calif. *Work:* Pierce Col, Woodland Hills, Calif; Ore Hist Soc; Xerox Corp; Virginia City Chamber Com; Paper Source Mus, Los Angeles, Calif. *Comn:* Sculptures, Golden Nugget, Atlantic City, NJ, McDonald's, Greenville, NC, Lozano, Mexico City & Sterns, Nevada; Television Acad Arts & Sci, Joyce Hall of Hallmark Cards; Leonard Goldenson, Exec Paramount Films & ABC TV. *Exhib:* Art Festival Laguna, Laguna Beach, Calif, 77-92; Miniature Soc NJ, Nutley Gallery, NJ, 79; Miniature Soc Washington, DC, Archit Inst, 79; Cody Mus Art, Wyo, 79; La Luz, NMex, 83; Paramont Invitational, 86-91. *Pos:* Founder, Ume Publ, 86. *Teaching:* Instr sculpture, Pierce Col, Woodland Hills, Calif, 78-80. *Awards:* Gold Medals, San Gabriel Fine Art Asn, 79-81; Miniature Soc Washington DC; two Gold Medals, Paramont Invitational, 87 & 90. *Bibliog:* Article, Nevada Sun, Las Vegas, 82; This Week in Laguna, 84-86. *Mem:* Women Artists Am West; Los Angeles Art Asn. *Media:* Etching. *Publ:* The Sophistiguins, Warner Center News. *Mailing Add:* 5105 Tendilla Ave Woodland Hills CA 91364

WHITTINGTON, JON HAMMON
EDUCATOR, PAINTER
b Jackson, Miss, Oct 20, 38. *Study:* Belhaven Col, BA(art), 64; Miss Col, MEd, 66; Univ Miss, MA(art), 73. *Work:* Belhaven Col Permanent Collection, Jackson, Miss. *Exhib:* Ark Art Ctr, Little Rock, 73 & 74; Miss Art Asn Gallery, Jackson, 73 & 74; Images on Paper, Jackson, 74; solo exhibs, Meridian Mus, Miss, 74 & 75, Belhaven Col, 83 & 84 & Miss Art Asn Gallery, Jackson, 73 & 74; Miss Arts Festival, Jackson, 81. *Pos:* Mem, Governor's Comt Arts, Miss & Bd Regents, Miss Mus Art. *Teaching:* Chmn, art dept, East Miss Jr Col, 66-76; prof & chmn art dept, Belhaven Col, 76-86. *Awards:* First Place Award, Miss Medal Design for 1976 US Bicentennial, Franklin Mint, 76; Phil Hardin Found Grant. *Mem:* Southeastern Col Art Conf; Nat Asn Schs Art & Design. *Media:* Watercolor. *Res:* Silver point drawing. *Mailing Add:* Dept Art Belhaven Col Jackson MS 39202

WHITTOME, IRENE F
SCULPTOR, PAINTER
b Vancouver, BC, Mar 4, 42; Can citizen. *Study:* Vancouver Sch Art, BFA, 63. *Work:* Nat Gallery Can; Montreal Mus Fine Arts; Bibliot Nat, Paris; Mus Art Mod, Buenos Aires; Munic Mus, Birmingham, England. *Comn:* Print, Art Bank Can, 78; installation, Can Coun, New York, 79; sculpture, Hakone Open-Air Mus, Tokyo, 84. *Exhib:* Int Grafik-Bienale, Frenchen, Ger, 72; Paperworks, Nat Gallery Can, 78; solo exhibs, Montreal Mus Fine Arts, 80, Vancouver Art Gallery, 81, Winnnipeg Art Gallery, 81 & Hamilton Art Gallery, 81, Galerie Yajima, Montreal, Que, 82, Alberta Col Art Gallery, 83, Galerie du Mus du Que, 84, Walter Philips Gallery, Alberta, 86, Galerie Christiane Chassay, Montreal, 87, Musée des Traces, Montreal, Que, 89, Galerie Samuel Lallouz, Montreal, Que, 90 & Musée des Traces, Art Gallery Ont, Toronto, 90-91; Mus des beaux-arts du Can, Ottawa, 84; Mus d'Art Contemp de Montreal, Que, 85; Art Gallery Acadia Univ, Welpville, 85; Ctr Saidye Bronfman, Montreal, 86; Galerie 13, Montreal, 87; Mus d'Art Contemp de Montreal, Que, 87; Centre international d'art contemporain (CIAC), Montreal, Que, 89; and others. *Collections Arranged:* The Second Dalhousie Drawing Exhibition (auth, catalog), Dalhousie Art Gallery, Halifax, NS, 77. *Teaching:* Assoc prof art, Concordia Univ, Montreal, 68- *Awards:* Medal Hon, Int Grafik-Biennale, Frechen, Ger, 72. *Bibliog:* Monique Brunet Weinmann (auth), L'Eternité transitoire d'Irene Whittome, Vie des Arts, Montreal, 3/91; Linda Genereux (auth), Irene F Whittome, Artforum, New York 3/91; John K Grande (auth), Vice Versa, Montreal, No 32, 2/91. *Mem:* Royal Can Acad Arts; Jack Chambers Found. *Publ:* Auth, Book of Insects, Vancouver Art Gallery, 63; auth, Reproduction de quatre oeuvres, Rebirth 1987, dans C Mag, No 13, 87. *Mailing Add:* 18 Rue Laurier Ouest Montreal PQ H2T 2N3 Canada

WHYTE, BRUCE LINCOLN
ART DEALER, CONSULTANT
b New York, NY, Mar 13, 41. *Study:* Fordham Univ, BS, 62; NY Univ, MS, 63. *Pos:* Founder & chmn, Original Print Collectors Group, Ltd, 72-84; gov, Nat Arts Club, 73-76 & 86-, chmn graphic arts, 73-, treas, 86-; expert art witness, US Treas Dept, 83-; founder & pres, Bruce Whyte Art Bus Develop Enterprises, Inc, 84-; managing consultant, Knoedler-Modarco Galleries, 84-88; Am Art Liason, Found Mitterand, Declaration of Human Rights on behalf of United Nations, UNESCO, Heads of State, Nat Mus, 89; consult, Mystic Seaport Mus Stores, 91; am art liaison, Doctors of the World, Paris, 92. *Teaching:* Lectr advan OMNA, NY Univ, 82. *Awards:* Best in Art Catalogs USA, Maxwell Sroge Publ; Nat Arts Club Award, 86. *Bibliog:* Leo Lloyd (auth), Graphic art by mail, United Press Int, 6/4/79; Sandra Salmans (auth), Good buys in fine art, New York Times, 1/25/81; Maxwell Sroge (auth & publ), Inside the 250 US Leading Mail Order Houses, 88. *Mem:* Soc Am Graphic Artists; Fine Arts Publ Asn (dir); Artist Fel; Greenwich Village Soc Hist Preserv (trustee). *Specialty:* Contemporary original prints and fine old master prints. *Mailing Add:* PO Box 102 West Park NY 12493

WHYTE, RAYMOND A
PAINTER
b Canmore, Alta, Aug 3, 23; US citizen. *Study:* Art Students League, scholar, with Edwin Dickinson; Venice, Paris, Madrid & China; Univ Toronto. *Work:* Crocker Art Mus, Sacramento, Calif; Mills Col; Stevensons Col; De Beers Mus SAfrica. *Comn:* triptych, Gerald B Kara, New York, 68; memorabilia (oil), Bernard G Cantor, Beverly Hills, Calif, 70; Orson Bean, Calif; large triptych, B Gerald Cantor, New York, 77; Dr James Gibney, 92; and others. *Exhib:* Nat Acad, 49-; one-man shows, Galerie DeTours, San Francisco, 62-83 & Crocker Art Mus, Sacramento, 67; Family Portraits 1730-1976, Philadelphia Mus of Art; Conacher Galleries, San Francisco, 85-86 & 92; Frank Oehlschlaeger Gallery, Sarasota, Fla, 88 & 92. *Awards:* Gold Medal of Italy; 1st Prize Oil, Fla Miniature Asn, 88 & 91. *Bibliog:* Kevin Sanders (auth), Contemporary surrealists, ABC TV Art Rev, 2/3/72; John Angelini (auth), Profile in Whyte, NJ Music & Arts, 6/77; article, Univ Colo Quart, 78; and others. *Mem:* Life mem Art Students Leaque, NY; Miniature Artists of Am; Miniature Artists of Fla. *Media:* Oil. *Dealer:* Conacher Galleries 134 Maiden Lane San Francisco CA 94108; Frank Oehlschlaeger Gallery St Armands Circle Sarasota FL 34236. *Mailing Add:* 1276 Meredith Dr Spring Hill FL 34608

WIBLE, MARY GRACE
PAINTER, EDUCATOR
Study: Pa State, BS, 38 & MEd, 42; Denver Univ, 54; Tyler Sch Art, Temple Univ, 67-68. *Work:* Kutztown Univ Gallery, Pa; Brandlywine Sch, Topton, Pa; Reading Community Col, Pa; Kutztown Univ, Pa. *Exhib:* An Exhib, Reading Pub Mus, 58 & 61-63; Harrisburg State Juried, William Penn Mem Mus, 74; Juried Ann Regional, Reading Pub Mus, 82, 84 & 88; 50th Ann Exhib, Muhlenberg Col Art Ctr, Allentown, 85. *Teaching:* Art supervisor, State Col Pa & Bradford, 38-46; asst prof art, Lock Haven Univ, 46-54; assoc prof art, Kutztown Univ, 54-68. *Awards:* Purchase Award, Reading Mus, Gilbert Assoc, 84; Lehigh Art Alliance, 50th Anniversary Exhib, 85; 1st Place Watercolor, Allentown Col St Frances, 86. *Mem:* Berks Art Alliance (pres, 73-74); Am Watercolor Soc (life mem); Ephrata Artworks; Lehigh Art Alliance. *Media:* Watercolor. *Publ:* Contribr, several articles, Design Mag, 46; illusr, Lock Haven Express Newspaper, 10/24/53. *Mailing Add:* 315 Wenz St Kutztown PA 19530

WICKISER, RALPH LEWANDA
ADMINISTRATOR, PAINTER
b Greenup, Ill, Mar 20, 10. *Study:* Art Inst Chicago, 28-31; Eastern Ill Univ, BA, 34, hon PhD, 56; Vanderbilt & Peabody, Tiffany fel, 34-35, MA, 35, PhD, 38. *Work:* Delgado Mus, New Orleans, La; Lehigh Univ, Bethlehem, Pa; La Art Comn, Baton Rouge; Mint Mus, Charlotte, NC; High Mus, Atlanta, Ga; and others. *Exhib:* Libr Cong Ann Print Exhib, 48; Whitney Mus Am Art Ann, 53-; United Nations, New York, 75; Esta Robison Gallery, New York, 82; one man shows, Ulster County Coun of the Arts, 83, Gallery 630B, New Orleans, 91, Z Squared Fine Arts Gallery, New York, 91 & Forms in Nature, Park West, Kingston, NY, 92; Pratt Inst, Brooklyn & Manhattan Ctr, NY, 88, 90 & 91; Lever House, New York, 89 & 92; Woodstock Artists Asn, 91; Z Squared Fine Arts Gallery, New York, 90; Walter Wickiser Gallery, New York, 92. *Teaching:* From instr to prof painting & chmn dept, La State Univ, 37-56; prof painting & dir div art educ, State Univ NY Col New Paltz, 56-59; prof painting, Pratt Inst, 59-75, chmn art educ dept, 59-65, chmn grad art, 65-75 & dir grad art & design, 65-75, emer prof, 75-; guest lectr, Woodstock Sch Art & Woodstock Art Asn. *Awards:* Grant for One Yr Painting & Study, Ford Found, 52; and others. *Bibliog:* Artist as a teacher, Col Art J, winter 51-52; Les Krantz (auth), New York Art Review: An Illustrated Survey of the City's Museums, Galleries & Lending Artists, 88; William Page (producer), Ralph Wickiser (video). *Mem:* Col Art Asn Am. *Media:* Oil. *Publ:* Auth, Introduction to Art Activities, 47; contribr, Education of the Artist, 51; Contemporary Painter's Attitude Toward Tradition, 55; auth, Introduction to Art Education, 57; co-auth, Higher Education & the Arts. *Mailing Add:* PO Box 263 Bearsville NY 12409

WICKLANDER, EDWARD A
SCULPTOR
b Puyallup, Wash, 1952. *Study:* Cent Wash Univ, BA, 75, MA, 77; Univ Ill, MFA, 80. *Work:* Sage Co, Minneapolis; Wash State Arts Comn; Seattle Arts Comn; Univ Georgia, Athens; Frederick R Weisman Found of Art, Los Angeles. *Exhib:* One-man shows, Louisville Sch Art, 79, Northlight Gallery, Everett Community Col, 81, Glass Eye Gallery, Seattle, 84, Window Installation & Nine One One, Seattle, 85; Alumni Exhib, Sarah Spurgeon Gallery, Cent Wash Univ, 87; Cheney Cowles Mus, Spokane, 88; Bellevue Art Mus, Bellevue, Wash, 88; Mitchell Mus, Mt Vernon, Ill, 88. *Pos:* Instr sculpture, Cornish Col Arts, Seattle. *Awards:* Nat Endowment Arts, 88; Purchase Award, 14th Ann Nat Drawing & Small Sculpture Exhib, Del Mar Col, 80; Plaque of Distinction, Marietta Nat, Grover M Hermann Fine Arts Gallery, Marietta Col, 81. *Mailing Add:* c/o Greg Kucera Gallery 608 Second Ave Seattle WA 98104

WICKS, EUGENE CLAUDE
PAINTER, EDUCATOR
b Coleharbor, NDak, Oct 7, 31. *Study:* Univ Colo, BFA, MFA, 59. *Work:* Art Inst Chicago, Ill; Philadelphia Print Club, Pa; Lakeview Art Ctr, Peoria, Ill; Decatur Art Ctr, Ill; Am Fedn Arts Overseas Collection. *Exhib:* Libr Cong, Washington, DC, 59; Brooklyn Mus Print Exhib, 60, 62 & 64; Northwest Printmakers Ann Exhib, 60-68; First Biennial Exhibs of Prints, Art Inst Chicago, 62; Philadelphia Acad 185th Ann, 63; one-man show, Edinburgh Col of Art, Scotland, 64 & Western Mich Univ, Kalamazoo, 75, plus others. *Pos:* Vis artist, Dept Art, Univ Colo, summer 63; dir, Nat Asn of Schs of Art, 75- *Teaching:* Prof painting, Univ Ill, Urbana, 59-; dir, Nat Sch Art & Design, 77- *Awards:* Purchase Awards, 1st Biennial, Art Inst Chicago, 62, Print Exhib, 62 & 24th Ann, Decatur Art Ctr, 68. *Mem:* Nat Asn Schs Art & Design; Nat Coun Art Adminr; Col Art Asn. *Media:* Acrylic, Oil. *Mailing Add:* Dept Art-Design 139C Fine Arts Bldg Univ Ill Champaign IL 61820

WIDMER, GWEN ELLEN
PHOTOGRAPHER, EDUCATOR
b Chicago, Ill, Mar 10, 45. *Study:* Goshen Col, Ind, BA, 67; Art Inst Chicago, MFA, 73. *Work:* J B Speed Art Mus, Louisville, Ky; Madison Art Ctr, Wis; Kalamazoo Inst Arts, Mich. *Exhib:* Photogr Midwest, Walker Art Ctr, Minneapolis, 73; The Invented Landscape, New Mus, New York, 79; The Hand Colored Photograph, Philadelphia Col Art, Pa, 79; Attitudes: Photog in the 1970's, Santa Barbara Mus Art, Calif, 79; one-person show, Camerawork Gallery, San Francisco, Calif, 80, & Ctr Contemp Arts, Santa Fe, NMex, 82; Playing It Again: Strategies of Appropriation, traveling 85- 86, Santa Fe, NMex, Boulder, Colo, Los Angeles Ctr Photo Studies, Camerawork, San Francisco, Diverse Works, Houston, Photo Resource Ctr, Boston, Univ RI, Kinston; American Photography today, Univ Denver, 82 & 84; Sights Unseen, AIR Gallery New York, traveling to Bard Col. *Teaching:* Instr photog, Univ Ill, Urbana/Champaign, 72-74; instr photog, Univ Northern Iowa, Cedar Falls, 76-; Univ NMex, Albuquerque, 80-86; Kansas City Art Inst, Kansas, 87- *Awards:* Photog Fel, Nat Endowment Arts, 75 & 80; Third Prize, Bicentennial Exhib of Photog, Andromeda Gallery, Buffalo, NY, 77; Purchase Award, Light II, Humboldt State Univ, 77. *Mem:* Soc for Photog Educ. *Publ:* Contribr, Popular Photography, Vol 75 (2), Ziff-Davis, 74; contribr, Self--Portrayal, Friends of Photog, Carmel, Calif, 78; Darkroom Dynamics, Curtin & London, Marblehead, Mass, 79; contribr, Color, Life Libr of Photography, Time-Life Bks, 80; and others. *Mailing Add:* c/o Kansas City Art Inst 4415 Warwick Blvd Kansas City MO 64111

WIEBE, CHARLES M
DEALER, HISTORIAN
b Morgantown, WVa, Oct 8, 49. *Study:* Carnegie Mellon Univ, with Robert Lepper, 66; WVa Univ, Morgantown, BA(painting), 72; Univ Florence, Italy, with Eugenio Battisti, 74-75; Pa State Univ, MA(art hist), 79. *Collections Arranged:* Bijutsu, The Fine Arts Japan (co-cur), Southern Alleghenies Mus Art, Hollidaysburg, Pa, 87. *Pos:* Gallery rep, Marson Ltd, Baltimore, 78-80; owner & dir, Wiebe Gallery, Pittsburgh, 80-87; dir exhibs, Int Images Gallery, Sewickley, Pa, 87- *Teaching:* Lectr, Vatican Mus, Rome, 75; lectr Japanese prints, Univ Pittsburgh, 84-; lectr, Point Park Col, Pittsburgh, 85- *Mem:* Col Art Asn Am; Am Mus Asn. *Res:* Italian Renaissance art. *Specialty:* Japanese woodblock prints; old master prints; contemporary paintings and sculpture, Eastern European Art. *Publ:* Auth, Meaning in Hokusai's art, J Print World, winter 88. *Mailing Add:* 315 Joseph's Lane Pittsburgh PA 15237

WIEDENHOEFT, RENATE
ART HISTORIAN
b Berlin, Ger, Nov 23, 42. *Study:* Univ Wis, Madison; Autodidact; also with Dr Ron Wiedenhoeft. *Pos:* Co-founder, partner & pres, Saskai Cult Doc, 66- *Mem:* Col Art Asn; Art Libr Soc. *Res:* Western European art and architecture from the Renaissance to early 20th century. *Interests:* Photography of art and architecture, the cataloging of images and the distribution of color transparencies to museums and universities throughout the world. *Publ:* Auth, Saskia Cultural Documentation, pvt publ, 77. *Mailing Add:* Saskia Ltd 2721 NW Cannon Way Portland OR 97229

WIEGAND, ROBERT
PAINTER
b Mineola, NY, May 15, 34. *Study:* Albright Art Sch, Buffalo, NY; State Univ NY Buffalo, BS(art educ). *Work:* Mus Mod Art, New Delhi; Four Seasons, Stockholm, Sweden; Mus Mod Art, New York; New York Univ. *Comn:* Mural, New York City Dept Parks; mural, Reliance Savings Bank, New York. *Exhib:* One-person shows, Phoenix Gallery, New York, 60, 62, 64 & 66, Chuck Levitan Gallery, New York, 79 & 90. *Teaching:* Instr painting & drawing, Staten Island Col, New York, 61-71 & Lehman Col, New York, 71-75; instr painting & drawing, Lehman Col, New York, 71-75; vis artist, Univ NC, Greensboro, 75-76. *Awards:* Grant, Nat Endowment Arts, 71 & 80; Rockefeller Found Travelling Artist's Fel, 77; NY State Coun Arts Grant, 80. *Bibliog:* Soichi Furita (ed), Graphics in the Environment, Graphic Design of the World, Kodansha Pub, Japan, 74; Ira Schneider & Beryl Korot (ed), Video Art, Harcourt Brace, 74; Walter Herdeg (ed), Archigraphia, Graphis Press, Zurich, 78. *Mem:* Artists Equity Asn, NY; Artistastalkonart. *Media:* Acrylic. *Mailing Add:* c/o Levitan Gallery 42 Grand St New York NY 10012

WIELAND, JOYCE
PAINTER, FILMMAKER
b Toronto, Ont, Can, 1931. *Study:* Cent Tech Sch, grad. *Work:* Nat Gallery Can; Montreal Mus Fine Arts, Can; Philadelphia Mus Art; Mus Mod Art Film Archives, New York; Royal Belg Film Archives; Beaubourg Mus, Pompidou, Paris, France. *Comn:* Quilt, Nat Sci Libr, Ottawa, 75 & Bata Shoes, 77; Toronto Transit Comn, Spadina Line 77; Laidlaw Found, 81-82; mural, Cineplex Odeon, 87. *Exhib:* The Wall-Art for Architecture Traveling Exhib, Art Gallery Ont, 69 & Rothmans Art Gallery, Stratford, Ont, 70; Oberhausen Film Festival, Austria, 69; Survey '70-Realism(e)s, Montreal Mus Fine Arts & Art Gallery Ont, 70; Eight Artists from Canada, Tel Aviv Mus, Israel, 70; Directors' Fortnight, Cannes Film Festival, France, 70; Isaacs Gallery, Toronto, 83; New Perceptions: Portraits, Art Gallery at Harbourfront, 83; Toronto Painting 84, Toronto Mus, Can, 84; Can Nat Touring retrospective, 87; Can House Cult Ctr Traveling Exhib, London, Eng, 88-89; Film retrospective, Traveling Exhib, Georges Pompidou Ctr, Paris, 89. *Teaching:* Instr, Nova Scotia Col Art, 71, Arts Sake Inc, Toronto, 79-82; instr film & painting, San Francisco Art Inst, 85-86; instr film, Joyce Wieland Studio, 86-; artist-in-residence, Fac Archit & Landscape Archit, Univ Toronto, 88-89. *Awards:* Can Coun Grants, 66, 68 & 72; Officer of the Order of Canada, 77; Three Canadian Film Awards, 77. *Bibliog:* David Burnett & Marilyn Schiff (auth), Contemporary Canadian Art, Hurtig Publ, 83; Lucy Lippard, Lauren Rabinovitz & Marie Fleming (auth), Joyce Wieland, Key Porter Bks, 87; Kay Armitage (dir), Artist on Fire, Dominion Pictures Ltd, 87. *Mem:* Royal Can Acad Arts; Arts & Letters Club, Toronto. *Media:* Oil. *Dealer:* Isaacs Gallery 832 Yonge St Toronto ON Can; Yajima Gallery Montreal PQ Can. *Mailing Add:* 497 Queen St E Toronto ON M5A 1V1 Canada

WIENER, PHYLLIS AMES
PAINTER
b Iowa City, Iowa, Sept 17, 21. *Study:* Univ Minn, 52, 54 & 56, with Cameron Booth. *Work:* Minneapolis Art Inst, Walker Art Ctr, Univ Minn Mus & Pillsbury Collection, Minneapolis; MacAlester Col, Minn Mus Art & 3M Co, St Paul; Downers Grove Pub Libr, Ill; Minn State Historical Society, St Paul, Minn; Mayo Clinic, Scottsdale, Ariz, 89; Total Petroleum Co, Denver, Colo, 88. *Comn:* Three dimensional painting, Norwest Bank Rochester, Minn, 82; diptych, Cathedral St Mark, Minneapolis, 83; three dimensional paintings, Cardiac Surgical Asn Clinic, San Antonio, Tex, 85; Lutheran Brotherhood, 86, Minneapolis. *Exhib:* Walker Biennial, 52-64; Pa Acad Fine Arts, Philadelphia, 64; solo show, Minneapolis Art Inst, 67; retrospective (with catalog), Tweed Mus, Univ Minn, Duluth, 81; Minn Mus Art, St Paul, Minn, 88; Suzanne Kohn Gallery, Minneapolis, Minn, 90; AIR Gallery, NY, 90; Univ Wis, LaCrosse, 92; Art Ctr Minn, 92; Martha Irvine (auth), Profile, Women's Press, St Paul, 1/92; and others. *Pos:* mem adv panel, Minn artists prog, Minneapolis Art Inst, 85-88; Mem Art exhib panel, Warm Gallery, 88-90; bd dirs, Women's Art Registry ,Minn, 92. *Teaching:* Instr oil painting, Walker Art Ctr, 60-66; instr composition, Univ Minn Exten Div, 62-72; instr, Art Ctr Minn, 60-85. *Awards:* Individual Artist's grant, Minn State Arts Bd, 80; Humanitarian Award Artist, St Paul YWCA, 87; Women's Press Newsmaker, 91. *Bibliog:* Nancy Roth (auth), Maps of the Mind, 12/85 & speculations St Paul-Minneapolis Mag; Rob Silberman (auth), review, Art Paper, 1/86; and others. *Mem:* Women's Art Registry Minn. *Media:* Acrylic, Three-D Constructions. *Dealer:* Suzanne Kohn Gallery 100 Second Ave N Minneapolis MN 55401; Barbara Callaway One SW First Ave Rochester MN 55901. *Mailing Add:* 1225 La Salle Apt 801 Minneapolis MN 55403

WIENER, SAM (EVANGELINE TABASCO)
SCULPTOR, CONCEPTUAL ARTIST
b Shreveport, La, Mar 24, 28. *Study:* Yale Sch Fine Arts, BFA, 51; Univ Mich. *Work:* Va Mus Fine Arts, Richmond; NY Univ; Mus Fine Arts, Columbia, SC. *Comn:* Glazed tile murals, Am Airlines Terminal, Kennedy Airport, New York, 60; stained glass windows, Agudath Sholom Congregation, Stamford, Conn, 67; glazed tile murals, Abraham and Straus, Smithtown, NY, 68; lobby wall hangings, ITT Am Bldg, New York, 70; modular sculptures, Vest Pocket Park Proj, New York, 71. *Exhib:* Archit Art, Mus Contemp Crafts, New York, 62; Objects USA, Smithsonian Inst & traveling, 69-71; NY Correspondence Sch, Whitney Mus Am Art, 70; Am Painting & Sculpture Today, Indianapolis Mus, 77; Vietnam: A Different War, Whatcom Mus, Bellingham, Wash & travelling, 90-92; solo exhibs, The Supermarket of Art, Anderson Gallery, Va Commonwealth Univ, 81, Sam Wiener & Evangeline Tabasco, Herbert Johnson Mus, 81 & Splendors of the Sohites, Aspen Ctr Fine Arts, Lowe Mus, Miami, Fla & seven others, 82-83. *Teaching:* Adj asst prof design & drawing, Columbia Univ Archit Sch, 60; instr visual commun, Cooper Union Art Sch, 67-68; instr drawing & compos, Parsons Sch Art, 82-86. *Awards:* MacDowell Fel, 90. *Bibliog:* Noel Frackman (auth), article, Arts Mag, 4/78; Peter Frank (auth), article, Village Voice, 4/78; Mark Stevens (auth), The splendors of ancient Soho, Newsweek, 10/6/80. *Media:* All. *Dealer:* O K Harris 383 W Broadway New York NY 10012. *Mailing Add:* 186 Sachems Head Rd Guilford CT 06437

WIESEN, TRUDE
PAINTER
b Hildesheim, Germany. *Study:* Art Students League, with Harry Steruberg. *Work:* Norfolk Mus Art & Sci; Nassau Community Col, Garden City, NJ; Hempstead Bank, Hempstead, NJ. *Exhib:* Royal Acad Galleries, Edinburgh, Scotland, 68; Centre Art Show, St Petersburg, Fla, 80; Tampa Bay Show, Treasure Island, Fla, 86. *Awards:* Best in Show, True Centre Art Show, St Petersburg, Fla, 80. *Mem:* Nat Asn Women Artists; The Art Centre, St Petersburg, Fla. *Media:* Watercolor, Acrylic. *Dealer:* Anderson-March Galleries 6151 Central Ave St Petersburg, FL. *Mailing Add:* 6075 Shore Blvd S No 610 Gulfport FL 33707

WIESENDANGER, MARTIN WOLFGANG
HISTORIAN, CONSERVATOR
b Ger, Feb 13, 08; US & Swiss citizen. *Study:* Columbia Univ, 26-29; Murray Pease's Lab, Metrop Mus Art, conserv tech, 29-35. *Exhib:* Okla Ann, Philbrook Art Ctr, Tulsa, 44-46; Univ of South Art Gallery, Sewanee, Tenn. 69. *Collections Arranged:* Assisted Thomas Gilcrease in assembling his collection, Gilcrease Mus Hist & Art, Tulsa, 39-47; Paintings from the W E Groves Collection (auth, catalog), W E Groves Gallery, 69; History of the Color Print, Philbrook Art Ctr, Tulsa, 79. *Pos:* First dir, Thomas Gilcrease Mus, Tulsa, 42-47; mem arts & exhib comt, Philbrook Art Ctr, Tulsa, 43-68 & 77-; conservator, Mabee-Gerrer Mus, Shawnee, Okla, 74-85, bd mem, 79-81, bd chmn, 81-83. *Teaching:* Instr, Univ Tulsa, Okla, 42-50; teacher & movie film producer, Childrens Classes, Philbrook Art Ctr, Tulsa, 57 & 58. *Awards:* First Place Graphics, Philbrook Art Ctr, 50. *Bibliog:* Janet Keene (auth), Like a dome of many colors, Tulsalite, 11/13/67; David Milsten (auth), chap I, In: Biography of Thomas Gilcrease, Bk 4, Naylor Co, 69; Dean Krakel (auth), Adventures in Western Art, Lovell Press, 77. *Mem:* Int Inst Conserv; fel Am Inst Conserv. *Media:* Metal Sculpture; Graphics. *Res:* Pre-Columbian art and archaeology of Yucatan in movies and slides. *Collection:* Paintings & prints; African & Pacific sculpture. *Publ:* Auth, An Indian foundation, Southwest Rev, autumn 46; illusr, Indian drawings of Cimarron County by W D Hartley, Ford Times, 54; co-auth, Louisiana Painters and Paintings in the Collection of W E Groves, W E Groves Gallery, 71; auth & illusr, Beneath optima earth, Okla Today, 75; auth, Montgomery, the corn painter, Newslett Tulsa Co Hist Soc, 76; and others. *Mailing Add:* 1636 N 70th W Pl PO Box 27063 Tulsa OK 74127

WIGGINS, BILL
PAINTER
b Roswell, NMex, Sept 24, 17. *Study:* NMex Mil Inst, Roswell; Abilene Christian Univ; Am Shrivenham Univ, Eng, with Francis Speight; Fed Art Proj, Work Proj Admin, Roswell. *Work:* Roswell Mus & Art Ctr. *Exhib:* Newport 43rd Ann, RI, 54; Low Ruins Nat, Tubac, Ariz, 65; 5th Arts Nat, Tyler, Tex, 68; Mainstreams 68, Marietta Col, Ohio; Ark State Univ Nat, Jonesboro, 70; Art Inst for the Permian Basin, Odessa, Tex, 91. *Teaching:* Instr art, Roswell Mus & Art Ctr, 55-63. *Bibliog:* Elena Montes (auth), Bill Wiggins of Roswell, NMex Mag, 10/65; United States art, La Rev Mod, Paris, 12/65; Walt Wiggins (auth), Wiggins: A Thirty-Year Retrospective, 82. *Media:* Oil. *Mailing Add:* 711 W Eighth St Roswell NM 88201

WIGGINS, GUY A
PAINTER, LECTURER
b New London, Conn, Aug 23, 20. *Study:* Univ Calif, Los Angeles, BA, 50; Harvard Univ, MA, 51; London Univ, 56; Corcoran Mus Sch, 68-69; Art Students League & Nat Acad Sch, 75-78. *Work:* Trenton Mus Art, NJ; Florence Griswold Mus, Old Lyme, Conn; Lyman Allen Mus, New London, Conn; New Britain Mus Am Art, Conn. *Exhib:* Three Generations of Wiggins, New Britain Mus Am Art, 79; Painters of the Urban Scene, Rainone Gallery Am Art, Houston, Tex, 85; Winter Exhibs, Salmagundi Club, New York, 87-88; Landscape Painters of the Delaware Valley, Trenton Mus Art, NJ, 88; Paintings of Food, Grand Central Galleries, New York, 89; solo exhibs, Marbella Gallery, New York, 81, Optique Gallery, Lambertville, NJ, 87 & Lyme Acad Gallery, Old Lyme, Conn, 88. *Bibliog:* Richard T Boyle (auth), Guy A Wiggins--painter (catalog), 87; Alexander Cokos (auth), Guy A Wiggins (catalog), 88. *Mem:* Art Students League; Salmagundi Club. *Media:* Oil. *Mailing Add:* 103 Queens Rd Stockton NJ 08059

WIGGINS, K DOUGLAS
PAINTER, ART DEALER
b Roswell, NMex, Apr 8, 59. *Study:* San Antonio Col, Tex, 78-79; Independent Baptist Col, Dallas, Tex, 82-83; Eastern NMex Univ, Roswell, 83-85; Santa Fe Inst Fine Arts, 89. *Work:* Mo Athletic Club, St louis; Jon R Stuart Collection, Tulsa, Okla; Charles Geneux Collection, Epalingers, Switz; Mus Fine Arts; Mus NMex, Santa Fe; and many others. *Comn:* Painting, Powell Adams Co, Kansas City,; painting, Park 39 Consult, New York; paintings, Hilbert Partnership, Newport Beach, Calif; paintings, Four Sixes Ranch, Guthrie, Tex. *Exhib:* One-man shows, Johnson-Kraynick Galleries, Dallas, Tex, 84, Geoffery Cline Gallery, Tulsa, Okla, 86, 87 & 90 & Altermann & Morris, Houston, Tex, 92 & 93; Gov Gallery Exhib, Santa Fe NMex, 88, 89 & 90; Carlsbad Mus, NMex, 88; Wiggins Fine Art, Santa Fe, 89-92; R D Hubbard Mus, Ruidoso, NMex, 92; US Artists '92, Pa Acad Fine Arts, Philadelphia; and others. *Pos:* Mgr, Wiggins Galleries, Santa Fe, NMex, 83- *Bibliog:* Les Krantz (auth), American Artists, Am Ref Publ Corp; Peggy & Harold Samuels (coauths), The New American Impressionism, Castle; Annie Osburn (auth), K Douglas Wiggins, Southwest Art, 3/91. *Mem:* Soc Am Impressionists. *Media:* Oil. *Specialty:* 19th century American and European, Hudson River, Taos founders and regional masters;. *Publ:* Illusr, Border Trax, 91; Int Fine Art Col, 5/91; Archit Dig, 6/92. *Mailing Add:* 526 Canyon Rd Santa Fe NM 87501

WIITASALO, SHIRLEY
PAINTER
b Toronto, Ont, Can, 1949. *Study:* Ont Col Art, Toronto, 67-78. *Work:* Can Coun Art Bank & Nat Gallery Can, Ottawa; Owens Art Gallery, Mt Allison Univ, Sackville, NB; Mem Univ Art Gallery, St John's, Nfld; Art Gallery Ont, Toronto. *Exhib:* Solo exhibs, Carmen Lamanna Gallery, 74, 76, 78, 80-82, 87, 89 & 90, Art Gallery Ont, traveling, London Regional Gallery, London, Can, Thunder Bay Art Gallery, Can, Winnipeg Art Gallery, Can, 87; Contemp Ont Art, Art Gallery Ont, Toronto, 74; Carmen Lamanna at Owens Art Gallery, Mt Allison Univ, Sackville, NB, 75; Some Canadian Women Artists, Nat Gallery Can, Ottawa, 75; Ont Now-A Survey of Contemp Art,

Kitchener-Waterloo Gallery, Art Gallery of Hamilton, Ont, 76; 17 Canadian Artists-A Protean View, Vancouver Art Gallery, BC, 76; Kanadische Künstler Kunsthalle, Basel, Switz, 78; 20th Century Can Painting, Nat Gallery Can, 81; Canadian Horizon, Can Coun, 82; Fiction (with catalog), Art Gallery Ont, 82; Toronto Painting (with catalog), traveling exhib, 84; Six Toronto Artists in Amsterdam, Fodor Mus, Amsterdam, 84; Late Capitalism, Art Gallery at Harbourfront, 85; Canadian-Swiss Art Connection, Toronto, 85; Canadian Biennial Contemp Art, Nat Gallery Can, 89; and many others. *Awards:* Can Coun Grants, 69, 70, 72 & 73, Sr Grant, 82; Ont Arts Coun Grant, 75-76. *Media:* Oil on Canvas. *Mailing Add:* 57 Pemberton Ave Willowdale ON M2M 1Y2 Canada

WILBERT, ROBERT JOHN
PAINTER, EDUCATOR
b Chicago, Ill, Oct 9, 29. *Study:* Univ Ill, BFA, 51, MFA, 54. *Work:* Saginaw Mus, Mich; South Bend Art Ctr, Ind; Kresge Art Ctr, Mich State Univ; Detroit Inst Arts; Wayne State Univ, Detroit. *Comn:* Design, Mich Statehood Stamp, US Postal Serv, 87. *Exhib:* American Watercolors, Drawings & Prints, Metrop Mus Art, 52; Butler Inst Am Art Midyear Ann, 60, 62, 63 & 68; Pa Acad Fine Arts Ann, 61 & 63; J B Speed Art Mus, Louisville, Ky, 65 & 75; Kalamazoo Art Ctr, Mich, 73; Slusser Art Ctr, Univ Mich, Ann Arbor, 74 & 76; Detroit Inst Arts, 76 & 82; Muskegon Mus Art, 82. *Teaching:* Instr painting, Flint Inst Arts, Mich, 54-56; prof painting, Wayne State Univ, 56- *Awards:* 57th Exhib Mich Artists Werbe Award, Detroit Inst Arts, 69; Nat Endowment Arts Fel, 77; Mich Found Arts Award, 80. *Mem:* Detroit Artists Market; Detroit Focus. *Media:* Oil, Watercolor. *Dealer:* Donald Morris Gallery 105 Townsend Birmingham MI. *Mailing Add:* c/o Donald Morris Gallery 105 Townsend St Birmingham MI 48011

WILCOX, GORDON CUMNOCK
PAINTER, ILLUSTRATOR
b Boston, Mass, Aug 12, 34. *Study:* Sch Practical Art, Boston; Art Students League, with Olinsky & Dickinson; Nat Acad Design. *Work:* Barclay's Bank of New York; The Wall St Group Inc; US Coast Guard. *Exhib:* Panhandle-Plains Hist Mus, Canyon, Tex, 65; Expos Intercontinentale, France, 67 & Monaco, 68; one-man shows, Wickersham Gallery, New York, 68, Wichita Centennial Nat Art Exhib, Kans, 70 & Southampton Gallery, NY, 76; Gallery Cutler, Palm Beach, 78. *Awards:* John Duck Award, Parrish Art Mus, Southampton, NY, 71. *Mem:* Visual Artists & Galleries Asn, Inc; Am Soc Marine Artists; Artists Equity Asn New York. *Media:* Watercolor. *Mailing Add:* 400 E 88th St New York NY 10128

WILDE, DAWN JOHNSON
PAINTER, EDUCATOR
b Philadelphia, Miss, Feb 1, 34. *Study:* Baylor Univ, Waco, Tex, BA, 56; Memphis State Univ, Tenn, 67; Am Univ, Washington, DC, MFA, 77. *Work:* Watkins Gallery, Am Univ, Washington, DC; China Asn Advancement Int Friendship, Beijing. *Exhib:* Biennial, Fine Arts Ctr, Colorado Springs, 81, 83 & 85; Biennial, Loveland Mus, Colo, 88; Color, Colo Gallery Arts, Littleton, 89; Mountain West Paperworks Biennial, Nora Eccles Harrison Mus Art, Logan, Utah, 90; The Story Retold: Contemp Mythology, Gallery Contemp Art, Univ Colo, Colorado Springs, 90. *Pos:* Adv Bd, Gallery Contemp Art, Colorado Springs, 82-87 & The Art Comn of Colorado Springs & El Paso County, 83-86; Arts & Crafts Delegate to China, Citizen Ambassador Prog People to People Int, 86. *Teaching:* Instr drawing & painting, Bemis Art Sch, Colorado Springs Arts Ctr, 83. *Awards:* David Lloyd Kreeger Award, Am Univ, 77. *Mem:* Nat Asn Women Artists; Soc Layerists in Multi-Media. *Media:* Oil, Acrylic. *Publ:* Ed, Life Without Risk is Worthless, Univ Col. *Mailing Add:* c/o Univ Colo Fine Arts Dept PO Box 7150 Colorado Springs CO 80933-7150

WILDE, JOHN
PAINTER, DRAFTSMAN
b Milwaukee, Wis, Dec 12, 19. *Study:* Univ Wis, BS & MS. *Work:* Whitney Mus Am Art, New York; Pa Acad Fine Arts, Philadelphia; Art Inst Chicago; Detroit Inst Art; Wadsworth Atheneum, Hartford, Conn. *Comn:* Portrait of George May, dean of Yale Col, Yale Univ, 82. *Exhib:* Whitney Mus Am Art, New York, 52-68; 52 Americans Under 36, Metrop Mus Art, 54; Contemporary Drawing USA, Mus Mod Art, 58; Three Centuries of the Nude in American Art 1675-1975, NY Cult Ctr, 75 & Minneapolis Inst Arts, 76; Am Master Drawings & Watercolors (From Colonial Times to the Present), Minneapolis Inst Arts, 76, Whitney Mus Am Art, New York, 76 & San Francisco Fine Arts Mus, 77; Realism & Realities, The Other Side of American Painting 1940-1960, Rutgers Univ Art Gallery, 82 & traveled; The Fine Line, Norton Art Gallery, Palm Beach, Fla, 85 & traveled; 20th Century Drawings, Nat Gallery Art, Washington, DC, 87, & travelled; Metal Point Drawing in America, Ark Art Ctr, Little Rock, 92, traveling, 92-93; and others. *Teaching:* Alfred Sessler Distinguished Prof Art, Univ Wis-Madison, 69-82, prof emer, 82- *Awards:* Lambert Purchase Award, Pa Acad Fine Art, 63; Childe Hassam Purchase Award, Am Acad & Inst Arts & Letters, 65, 80 & 87; Purchase Award, Butler Inst Am Art, 68. *Bibliog:* Lee Nordness (ed), Art USA Now, Viking Press, 63; Una E Johnson (auth), 20th Century Modern Drawings, Shorewood, 67; Theodore Stebbins, Jr (auth), American Master Drawings & Watercolors, Harper & Row, 76. *Media:* Oil; Pencil, Silverpoint. *Dealer:* Perimeter Gallery 750 N Orleans St Chicago IL 60610; Schmidt-Bingham 41 W 57th St New York NY 10019. *Mailing Add:* RFD 1 Evansville WI 53536

WILDE, STEPHANIE
CONCEPTUAL ARTIST, PRINTMAKER
b Coalville, Utah, July 1, 52. *Work:* Harris Fine Art Mus, Provo, Utah; Boise Art Mus, Idaho. *Comn:* Pen & ink drawing, Springville Mus, Utah, 87 & Boise State Univ, Idaho, 88. *Exhib:* 3rd Biennial Juried Show, Boise Art Mus, 83; one-woman show, Harris Fine Art Mus, Provo, 86 & Herrett Art Mus, Twin Falls, 86; Critic Collects, Art Attack Gallery, Boise, 86; 2nd Biennial, Maryhill Mus, Glendale, Wash, 87; 64th Nat Spring Salon, Springville Mus, 87-88; Works on Paper, Springville Mus Art, 88; Stewart Gallery, Boise, Idaho, 89; Aids, Mus Fine Art, Montana, 89; and others. *Awards:* Visual Arts, Fel Idaho Art Asn, 88. *Bibliog:* Jeanette Ross (auth), Women of visible power, Boise Mag, 88. *Media:* Ink. *Publ:* Coauth, The Wilde Birds, private publ, 86. *Dealer:* Lane Stewart Bune 426 North 8th St Boise ID 83702. *Mailing Add:* 2016 Harrison Blvd Boise ID 83702

WILEY, WILLIAM T
PAINTER
b Bedford, Ind, Oct 21, 37. *Study:* San Francisco Art Inst, BFA, 60, MFA, 62. *Work:* San Francisco Mus Art; Dallas Mus Art, Tex; Mus Mod Art, New York; Los Angeles Co Mus Art; Oakland Mus, Calif. *Exhib:* Solo exhibits, LA Louver Gallery, Venice, Calif, 84, 87, 91 & 92, Alberta Col Art, Calgary, Canada, 85, Hammarskjold Plaza Sculpture Garden, New York, 86, What is Not Music? Frankfurter Kunstverein, Frankfurt 87 & Galerie Grita Insam, Vienna, Austria, 87, Recent Paintings and Drawings, Richard L Nelson Gallery, Davis, Calif, 88, Cuesta Col Art Gallery, San Luis Obispo, Calif, 90, Riva Yeres Gallery, Scotsdale, Ariz, 90, Max Protetch, New York, Marsha Mateyka, Corcoran Gallery, Washington, DC, 91, Marian Locks Gallery, Philadelphia, Pa; The Making of a Legend: Chief Seattle's Reply, Hatley Martin Gallery, San Francisco, 90; The Tao of Contemporary Art, Traveling, 90; Bay Area Sculptors of the 60's, Past to Present, Braunstein Quay Gallery, San Francisco, 90; Word as Image: American Art 1960-90, Milwaukee Art Mus, Wis, 90; Word as Image: American Art 1960-90, Contemp Art Mus, Houston, Tex, 91; Law and Society in Our Times, West Publ Co, St Paul, Minn, 91; California Artists: William T Wiley, Mike Kelley & Brad Dunning, Aldrich Mus Art, Ridgefield, Conn, 91. *Teaching:* Assoc prof art, Univ Calif, Davis, 62-; instr, San Francisco Art Inst, 63, 66-67, Univ Nev, Reno, 67, Wash State Col, Pullman, 67, Univ Calif, Berkeley, 67, Sch Visual Art, New York, 68, Univ Colo, Boulder, 68. *Awards:* Purchase Prize, Whitney Mus Am Art, 68; Nealie Sullivan Award, San Francisco Art Inst, 68; Traveling Grant, Australian Arts Coun, 80; and others. *Bibliog:* Peter Frank (auth), Forty Years of California Assemblage, Sculpture, 1/90; David Bonetti (auth), Well-Rounded Works of Art, San Francisco Examiner, 6-20/90; Ben Marks (auth), William T Wiley at LA Louver, Art Am, 10/91. *Publ:* Coauth, The Great Blondino (film), shown Belg Film Festival, 67; contribr, Over Evident Falls (theater event), Sacramento State Col, 68; auth, Man's Nature (film), shown Hansen Fuller Gallery, 71. *Dealer:* Max Protetch 560 Broadway New York NY; LA Louver Venice CA. *Mailing Add:* c/o Wanda Hansen 615 Main St Sausalito CA 94965

WILHELMI, WILLIAM MERLE
CERAMIST, SCULPTOR
b Garwin, Iowa, Feb 4, 39. *Study:* San Diego State Col, BA, 60; Univ Calif, Los Angeles, MFA, 69. *Work:* Long Beach Mus Art, Calif; Everson Art Mus, Syracuse, NY; Tweed Mus Art, Duluth, Minn; Libr Congress; Renwick Gallery, Smithsonian Inst, Washington, DC; Gene Autry Western Heritage Mus, Los Angeles, Calif. *Comn:* Tile mural, Whataburger Nat Hq, Corpus Christi, 79; planters & tile murals, Corpus Christi State Univ, 79; Corpus Christi Nat Bank, 82; tile floor mosaic, Corpus Christi City Hall rotunda, 88; mosaic design, Six-Points Station (RTA-CC), 92. *Exhib:* Baroque '74, Mus Contemp Crafts, New York; Renwick Gallery, Washington, DC, 76, 80 & 82; 20th Century Ornament, Cooper-Hewitt Mus, New York, 78; Contemp Am, STex Art Mobile, Corpus Christi, 79; Hill's Gallery, Santa Fe, 81; Marilyn Butler Gallery, Scottsdale, Ariz, 81; Libr Congress, 83; Emily Edwards Gallery, Southwest Craft Ctr, San Antonio, Tex, 89. *Pos:* Resident potter, Richard Colley, architect, Corpus Christi, 69-76, Kaffie Gallery, Corpus Christi, 76-83 & Carancahua Gallery, 83-86; bd trustees, Art Mus STex, 80-87; Wilhelm/Holland Gallery, Corpus Christi, 86- *Awards:* Two Purchase Awards, San Mateo Col, 69; First Place & One-Man Show Art Found Award, Art Mus STex, 73; Tex Arts Comn, 81; Dirs Award, CC Carts Coun, 92. *Mem:* Am Crafts Coun; Tex Designer Craftsmen; Tex Potters Guild; Art Found. *Publ:* Decorative Art in Modern Interiors, Cassell & Co Ltd, 77 & 78; contribr, Studio Potter, Daniel Clark Found, 78; Tex Monthly, 12/80; New York Art Rev, 88-89; Chicago Art Rev, 90; American Ceramics, Rizzoli, New York, 92. *Mailing Add:* 1129 Ocean Dr Corpus Christi TX 78404

WILKE, HANNAH
SCULPTOR, INSTRUCTOR
b New York, NY, Mar 7, 40. *Study:* Temple Univ, BFA, 61, BS, 62. *Work:* Albright-Knox Art Gallery, Buffalo, NY; Allen Art Mus, Oberlin, Ohio; Brooklyn Mus, NY; Power Inst, Sydney, Australia; Metro-Media, Channel 5, New York; Metrop Mus Art, New York; Jewish Mus, New York; and others. *Comn:* Mural (latex), comn by Carl Solway Gallery for Ponderosa Systs, Dayton, Ohio, 74; greeting card, Mus Mod Art, New York, 77. *Exhib:* Ronald Feldman Gallery, New York, 72-89; Whitney Mus Biennial, New York, 73; Brooklyn Mus, NY, 74; Albright-Knox Art Gallery, 75; Whitney Mus Am Art, New York, 77, 87 & 89; Washington Proj Arts, 79; Mus de Arte de Sao Paulo, Brazil, 80; New York State Mus, Albany, 81; New Orleans World's Fair, Woman's Pavillion, 84; Ludwig Mus, Ger, 89. *Pos:* Cur, Store Days, 70-77. *Teaching:* Instr sculpture, Sch Visual Arts, NY, 74- *Awards:* Nat Endowment Arts, 76, 79 & 80; Award, Alaska Coun Arts, 80; Guggenheim Fel, 82; Pollack-Krasner Grant, 87-88. *Bibliog:* Mark Savitt (auth), Hannah

Wilke, the pleasure principle, Arts, 9/75; Ruth Iskin (auth), Conversation with Hannah Wilke, Visual Dialogue, Vol 2, 77; Ernst (auth), Hannah Wilke talks, Oasis d'Neon, 78-79; interview with Marvin Jones, Hannah Wilke's art, politics, religion and feminism, The New Common Good, 5/85; Joanna Freuh (auth), Hannah Wilke, Univ Mo Press, 89. *Mem:* Nat Mus for Women; Women Caucus Art. *Media:* Multimedia. *Publ:* Contribr, Woman's sensibility, Art, 75; Flash Art, 5/75; auth, My Father's Brother's Wife's Mother, Heresies, 78; Visual Prejudice, Art & Ideology-New Mus, 84. *Dealer:* Ronald Feldman Gallery New York; Genovese Gallery Boston MA. *Mailing Add:* 62 Greene St New York NY 10012

WILKIN, KAREN
CURATOR, CRITIC
b New York, NY. *Study:* Barnard Col, BA(cum laude); Columbia Univ, MFA(Woodrow Wilson Fel). *Collections Arranged:* Sculpture in Steel: Gonzalez, Caro, Steiner & Scott (with catalog), 74; The Collective Unconscious: US/Canada 1940s (with catalog), 75; Adolph Gottlieb: The Pictographs Touring Exhib (with catalog), 77-78; David Smith: The Formative Years Touring Exhib (with catalog), 81-82; Frankenthaler: Works on Paper 1949-1984 Touring Exhib (with catalog), 85-86; Stuart Davis Drawing Retrospective, touring exhib (with catalog), 92-93. *Pos:* Chief cur, Edmonton Art Gallery, Alta, 71-78; cur, Westburne Collection, Montreal, 76- *Teaching:* Lectr art hist, Univ Alta, Edmonton, 67-70; adj prof, Trent Univ, Peterborough, Ont, 79-85, SUNY, Purchase, NY, 86; vis prof, Univ Toronto, 91- *Awards:* Fulbright Fel, Rome, 64-65; Can Coun Sr Arts Grant, 81. *Mem:* Int Asn Art Critics; PEN. *Res:* 20th Century Art. *Publ:* Auth, David Smith, Abbeville Press, 84; Jack Bush, McLelland & Stewart, 84; Frankenthaler: Works on Paper, Braziller, 85; Stuart Davis, Abbeville Press, 87; Kenneth Noland, Rizzoli, 90; Anthony Caro, Prestel, 91; Georges Braque, Abbeville, 92. *Mailing Add:* 28 W 38th St New York NY 10018

WILKINS, DAVID GEORGE
HISTORIAN, GALLERY DIRECTOR
b Battle Creek, Mich, Sept 12, 39. *Study:* Oberlin Col, BA, 61; Univ Mich, MA, 63 & PhD, 69. *Pos:* Dir, Univ Art Gallery, Univ Pittsburgh, 76-92. *Teaching:* Prof art hist, Dept Fine Arts, Univ Pittsburgh, 67- & chmn, 89-92. *Awards:* Chancellor's Distinguished Teaching Award, 87. *Mem:* Col Art Asn; Historians of Netherlandish Art. *Res:* Florentine painting and sculpture; American painting; Dutch art. *Publ:* Coauth, Donatello, 84; auth, Maso di Banco, 85; coauth, Illustrated Bartsch, Vol 53, 85; Paintings & Sculpture of Duquesne Club, 86; Art Past/Art Present, 90. *Mailing Add:* Fine Arts Univ Pittsburgh Pittsburgh PA 15260

WILL, JOHN A
PAINTER, VIDEO ARTIST
b Waterloo, Iowa, June 30, 39. *Study:* Univ Iowa, MFA, 64; Rijsacadamie von Beeldende Kunston, Amsterdam, 64-65; Tamarind, Albuquerque, NMex, 70-71. *Work:* New York Pub Libr; Art Inst Chicago; Libr Cong; Mus NMex, Santa Fe; Glenbow Art Gallery, Calgary; Nat Gallery Can. *Exhib:* Libr Cong Nat Print Exhib, 73; Brit Int Print Biennial, Bradford, Yorkshire, 74; 11th Int Biennial Graphic Art, Ljubljana, Yugoslavia, 75; 49th Parallel Gallery, New York, 88; Dunlop Art Gallery, Regina, 88; Glenbow Mus, Calgary, 92. *Teaching:* Asst prof drawing, Univ Wis-Stout, 65-70; resident artist, Yale Univ, summer 66 & Peninsula Sch Art, Fish Creek, Wis, summer 68; prof lithography, Univ Calgary, 71-; instr, Nova Scotia Col Art & Design, summers 73-75, 77, 79 & 84, Baniff Ctr, summers 80 & 81 & Emily Carr Sch Design, 85. *Awards:* Fulbright Fel, Holland, 64-65; Ford Found Grant, 70-71. *Bibliog:* John Will (exhib catalog), Glenbow Mus, 80; Coleen Oniell (auth), I Love Me (exhib cataolg), Stride Gallery, 87; John Will-Triple Threat Artist (exhib catalog), Dunlop Art Gallery, 88; John Wall (exhib brochure), Glenbow Mus, 92. *Media:* Painting; Video. *Mailing Add:* Dept of Art Univ of Calgary Calgary AB T2N 1N4 Canada

WILLENBECHER, JOHN
SCULPTOR, PAINTER
b Macungie, Pa, May 5, 36. *Study:* Brown Univ, BA, 58; NY Univ Inst Fine Arts, 58-61. *Work:* Whitney Mus Am Art, New York; Albright-Knox Art Gallery, Buffalo, NY; James A Michener Found Collection, Univ Tex, Austin; Hirshhorn Mus & Sculpture Garden, Washington, DC; Solomon R Guggenheim Mus, New York. *Comn:* US Fed Bldg & Court House, Providence, RI, 82; Republicbank, Houston, 83. *Exhib:* Mixed Media & Pop Art, Albright-Knox Art Gallery, Buffalo, 63; Young Americans, Whitney Mus Am Art, New York, 65; Kunst-Lucht-Kunst, Stedelijk Mus, Eindhoven, Holland, 66; John Willenbecher, Everson Mus Art, Syracuse, NY, 75; Arts Club, Chicago, 76; Allentown Art Mus, Pa, 79; Neuberger Mus, Purchase, NY, 79. *Teaching:* Lectr painting, Philadelphia Col Art, 72-73; artist in residence, Dartmouth Col, 77 & Univ Wis, Milwaukee, 83. *Awards:* Nat Endowment Arts Fel, 76. *Bibliog:* Joseph McElroy (auth), Through the labyrinth: The art of John Willenbecher, Art Int, 3/75; William Wilson (auth), John Willenbecher: Pyramids, spheres & labyrinths, 3/75; Daniel Cameron (auth), John Willenbecher & the riddle of Grandeur, Arts Mag, 9/83. *Mem:* Art Comn New York. *Media:* Acrylic, Oil. *Mailing Add:* 145 W Broadway New York NY 10013

WILLIAMS, ABIGAIL S
PAINTER, SCULPTOR
b New Jersey, May 26, 46. *Study:* Moore Col Art, 65; pvt study with Frances Hook, 79-82; Portland Sch Art, 90; Scottsdale Artist Sch, 91. *Work:* Moore Col Permanent Collection, Philadelphia, Pa; Portland Sch Art Permanent Collection, Portland, Maine. *Comn:* Mary Mother of the Carpenter, Roman Inc, Chicago, Ill, 86; over 250 portrait commissions, 89-92; portrait in memorium, Stan Werner/Konieckzo Maine, 83 & 90; Child Portraits, Northern, James River, New York, 90; Child Painting, March of Dimes, Chicago, Ill, 90. *Exhib:* Kaiser/Permenente Show, Kaiser Permanente, Sacrmento, Calif, 92. *Teaching:* Private instr, 85- *Awards:* Kessle-Long Award, Best & Brightest, Scottsdale Art Sch, Kessle-Long Gallery, 89; Merit Award, PSWE 16th Int, Daniel Greene, 92. *Bibliog:* Rebecca Hughes (auth), Williams Combines Art & Life, Boothbay Regist, 87; Michel Rogals (auth), From Photo to Finished Art, Plate World Mag, 91 & Tina Panoplos (auth), Unfinished Business, 89. *Mem:* Pastel Soc Am; Artist's Network (pres, 92); Round Top Ctr (planning Comn, 89-92); Boothbay Art Found (bd dirs). *Media:* Pastel. *Publ:* Illustr, Zachery Goes Ground Fishing, Downeast Publ, 83; The Life of Jesus, Jesus, God's Son, & House Full of Prayers, Standard Publ, 84; The Lord's Prayer Explained for Little Ones, Roman Inc, 92. *Mailing Add:* Robert Mullin Rt 96 East Boothbay ME 04544

WILLIAMS, BENJAMIN FORREST
CURATOR, HISTORIAN
b Lumberton, NC, Dec 24, 25. *Study:* Corcoran Sch Art, with Eugene Weisz; George Washington Univ, AA; Univ NC, AB; Columbia Univ, Paris Exten, Ecole du Louvre; Netherlands Inst Art Hist; Art Students League New York. *Work:* Atlanta Art Asn; NC Mus Art; Duke Univ; Greenville Civic Art Gallery, NC; Knoll Assoc, New York. *Exhib:* Va Intermont, Bristol; Weatherspoon Gallery, Greensboro; Person Hall Gallery, Chapel Hill, NC; Asheville Art Mus; Traveling Exhib, Am Fedn Arts; and others. *Collections Arranged:* Retrospectives for Josef Albers, Hobson Pittman, Jacob Marling, Victor Hammer, Fedor Zakharcv, Henry Pearson & the collections of the NC Mus Art; and others. *Pos:* Chief cur, NC Mus Art, 49-79; principal investor, Black Mountain Col Res Proj; first cur art, NC State Univ, 79-81; independent art consult, 81- *Awards:* Ronsheim Mem Award, Corcoran Sch Art, 46; Washington Soc Arts, 47; Prizes, Southeastern Ann, 47. *Mem:* Am Asn Mus; Southeastern Mus Conf; Col Art Asn Am. *Publ:* Contribr articles on 19th century American painting & sculpture to NC Mus Art Bull & NC Hist Rev. *Mailing Add:* 2813 Mayview Rd Raleigh NC 27607

WILLIAMS, CASEY
PHOTOGRAPHER
b Houston, Tex, 1947. *Study:* Univ Tex, Austin, BFA, 70; San Francisco Art Inst, MFA, 76. *Work:* Mus Fine Arts, Houston; Mus Mod Art, New York. *Exhib:* Solo exhibs, Tex Christian Univ, 78 & Media Ctr, Rice Univ, 79; Emerging Texas Photographers, Laguna Gloria Art Mus, Austin, 80; The New Photography, Contemp Arts Mus, Houston, 81; Texas Photo Sampler, Washington Proj Arts, 81; New Orleans Triennial, New Orleans Mus Art, 83; Big Pictures by Contemporary Photographers, Mus Mod Art, New York, 83; Singular Points of View, Art Mus STex, 84. *Teaching:* Instr photog, Glassell Sch Art, Houston, 79- *Bibliog:* Susie Kalil (auth), Photography--rooted in ambiguity, Houston Post, 6/19/82; Kay Larson (auth), Beyond pure photography, New York Mag, 5/2/83; Patricia Johnson (auth), Developing camera-derie, Houston Chronicle, 7/24/83. *Mailing Add:* c/o Res Nova 50 W 57th St New York NY 10019

WILLIAMS, CHESTER LEE
SCULPTOR
b Durham, NC, July 24, 44. *Study:* NC Cent Univ, BA, 68; Univ Mich, MFA, 71. *Work:* Student Union Gallery, NC Cent Univ, Durham; Art Dept Gallery, Univ Mich, Ann Arbor; Univ Gallery, Appalachian State Univ, Boone, NC; Black Arch Mus & Res Ctr, Fla A&M Univ, Tallahassee; Voorhees Col Libr, Denmark, SC. *Comn:* Sculpture, bronze casting, comn by Dr Oscar Cole, New York, 71 & Dr & Mrs Robert Zakarin, Tallahassee, 77; painting & sculpture, Fla A&M Univ, 77-78; bronze bust of Johnathan Gibbs, Fine Arts Coun of Fla, Div Cult Affairs, State of Fla, Tallahassee, 77-78; and others. *Exhib:* One-man exhibits, Spec Exhib, Div Dult Affairs, State Fla, 77, Fla House Rep, Ms Gwendolyn S Cherry, 106th Dist, 77, Fla Dept Com, Tallahassee, Fla, 77, Bainbridge Jr Col, Ga, 80, Winston-Salem State Univ, NC, 82, Elizabeth City State Univ, NC, 84, OMNI Gallery, Greenville, NC, 90; Florida A&M Univ, 75, 78, 84 & 91, LeMoyne Art Found, 77, 79 & 83, Fla Ctr Prof Develop, Fla State Univ, Tallahassee, Fla, 84; Smith-Mason Gallery, 80, Power Objects: Ancient and to the Future, Howard Univ, Washington, DC, 80; Dimensions and Directions: Black Artists of the South, Miss Mus Art, Jackson, Miss, 80; The Harmon Gallery, 80, Fine Arts Exhib, Naples, Fla, 80; Atlanta Life Ins Co, Ann Afro-Am Nat Art Competition & Exhib, 80, 87, 89, 90 & 91; NC Cent Univ, Durham, 85, Waterways Visual Arts Ctr, Salisbury, 88, Greensboro Artists' League, Greensboro, 89, Rocky Mt Arts Ctr, NC, 89; Beaufort Co Arts Ctr, 89 & 90, African-Am Art Extravaganza, 89, Greenville Mus Art, 91, Ubiquitous Gallery, Charlotte, 90, Onslow Co Coun Arts, Jacksonville, NC, 90; ABC Art Buyers Caravan, Orlando, Fla, 90; Third World Art Gallery, Cincinnati, Ohio, 92; Phillip Cult Ctr Gallery, Albany, Ga, 92. *Pos:* Illusr, Nat Air Pollution Control Ctr, Durham, NC, 69-70; mem, Arts Selection Comt, Tallahassee City Comn, 77-79; mem bd, LeMoyne Art Found, Tallahassee, 79-84; pres, Williams Foundry, Tallahassee & Durham, NC, 79-; dir, Fla A&M Univ Art Gallery, Tallahassee, Fla, 74-78, 83-84, 92- *Teaching:* Instr creative woodwork, Sch Design, Durham, NC, 68-69; asst prof sculpture & art appreciation, Voorhess Col, Denmark, SC, 71-74; assoc prof sculpture & painting, Fla A&M Univ, 74-84; assoc prof sculpture & design drawing, NC Cent Univ, Durham, 84-; vis artist at numerous universities and institutions since 1969. *Awards:* Sculpture Award, Harmon Gallery, Naples, Fla, 80; Purchase Award, Summer of 80 Fine Art Exhib, Naples, Fla, 80; Prince Hall Grand Lodge Econ Grant Prog, Durham, NC, 91. *Bibliog:* Joy McIlwain (auth), Sculptor with a message of hope, Tallahassee Mag, fall 84; Chris Redd (auth), Four Artists at Waterworks, Contemp Southeastern Vis Arts, Vol 2, 88; Kathy McQuaid (auth), Area Exhibit Shows Black Artists' Work, The Daily News, 2/8/90. *Mem:* Col Art

Asn Am; Nat Conf Artists; LeMoyne Art Found; Tri-State Sculptors. *Media:* Bronze Casting. *Dealer:* LeMoyne Art Foundation Tallahassee FL; Gallery of Art Panama City FL. *Mailing Add:* 2305 Killearn Ctr Blvd No 62-C Tallahassee FL 32308

WILLIAMS, CYNTHIA LEE
GALLERY DIRECTOR, CURATOR
b Nashville, Tenn, Nov 2, 57. *Study:* Univ Ga. *Pos:* Preparator's asst, Ga Mus Art, Athens, 83-85; asst dir, Friends Gallery, Minneapolis Inst Arts, 85-86; gallery coordr, Thomas Barry Fine Arts, Minneapolis, 86-90. *Mailing Add:* College of St Catherine, Catherine G Murphy Galleries 2004 Randolph Ave St Paul MN 55105

WILLIAMS, DAVE HARRELL
COLLECTOR, PATRON
b Beaumont, Tex, Oct 5, 32. *Pos:* Assoc, dept prints, Mus Mod Art. *Mem:* Am Fed Art (trustee). *Collection:* American prints beginning with Winslow Homer up to and including contemporary artists, emphasis 1910-1940. *Publ:* Articles in Print Quart. *Mailing Add:* 510 Park Ave New York NY 10022

WILLIAMS, DAVID JON
MEDICAL ILLUSTRATOR, HISTORIAN
b Muskegon, Mich, June 21, 44. *Study:* Muskegon Community Col, AA, 64; Mich State Univ, BA, 66, MA, 73; studied medical illus with Prof Mary Maciel, Univ Cincinnati Sch Med, 68-70; anatomical art with Franz Batke, Innsbruck, Austria, 80. *Pos:* Med illusr, Mich State Univ, East Lansing, Mich, 70-73. *Teaching:* From asst prof to prof med art, Purdue Univ, West Lafayette, Ind, 73- *Awards:* First Award, 11th Eaton-Student Am Med Asn Competition, 69, Third Award, 17th Competition, 75 & Third Award, 18th Competition, 76; First Place, Med Illus, Cent Ind Chap, Biol Photog Asn, 84. *Mem:* Asn Med Illusr (archivist, parlimentarian & mem, bd dirs); Guild Natural Sci Illusr; Am Asn Hist Med. *Media:* Carbon Dust on Media Paper, Transparent Watercolor. *Publ:* Coauth, Fundamental Techniques in Veterinary Surgery, W B Saunders Co, 75, rev ed, 81 & 87; contribr, Anatomy of the Rat, Williams & Wilkins, 76; Atlas of Human Anatomy, Urban & Schwarzenberg, 81; illusr, Intervertebral Disk Diseases, J B Lippincott Co, 85; Natural Voltage Gradients in Limb Regneration and Development, Oxford Univ Press, 85; The history of Eduard Perukopf's 'Topographische Anatomie des Menschen,' J Biocommunication, spring 88. *Mailing Add:* 824 Carrolton West Lafayette IN 47906

WILLIAMS, FRANKLIN JOHN
PAINTER
b Ogden, Utah, Feb 5, 40. *Study:* Carbon Col, 58-60; Calif Col Arts & Crafts, BFA, 60-64, MFA(Spencer Mackey Scholarship), 64-66. *Work:* Oakland Art Mus, Calif; Univ Calif, Berkeley Mus; Corcoran Mus, Washington, DC; San Francisco Mus Mod Art; Sheldon Mem Mus, Lincoln, Nebr. *Comn:* Painting, comn by Marc Moyens, Washington, DC, 83. *Exhib:* Seattle Art Mus, Washington, 66; 1967 Painting Ann, 1968 Sculpture Ann, Whitney Mus Am Art, New York; New Zealand Mus, Auckland, 71; Nat Mus, Washington, DC, 72; On and Off the Wall, Oakland Mus, Calif, 83; solo exhib: San Jose Mus Art, Calif, 83 & Utah Mus Fine Art, Salt Lake City, 84; San Francisco Bay Area Painting, Calif, 84. *Teaching:* Prof painting & drawing, San Francisco Art Inst, 66-; Calif Col Arts & Crafts, 69-; Tutor painting & drawing, Ruskin Sch, Oxford, England, 90. *Awards:* Grant Ford Found, 66; Nat Endowment Arts, 68. *Bibliog:* Fred Martin (auth), article, Art Int, 63 & 76; Thomas Albright (auth), Art in the San Francisco Bay Area 1945-1980, 85. *Media:* Oil, Acrylic. *Mailing Add:* 713 Elm Dr Petaluma CA 94952

WILLIAMS, HIRAM DRAPER
PAINTER
b Indianapolis, Ind, Feb 11, 17. *Study:* Williamsport Sketch Club, with George Eddinger; Pa State Univ, BS, with Victor Lowenfeld & MEd, with Hobson Pittman & Lowenfeld. *Work:* Mus Mod Art & Whitney Mus Am Art, New York; Milwaukee Art Ctr; Nat Art Collection & Corcoran Gallery Art, Washington, DC; Guggenheim Mus; Hiram & Hisonell Williams Collection, Harn Art Mus, Gainesville, Fla; and others. *Exhib:* Art USA: Painting, Mus Mod Art, 61; Art USA II; Carnegie Inst Int, Pittsburgh, 64; Art Across Am, 65; Art: USA: Now, 66. *Teaching:* Asst prof art educ, Univ Southern Calif, 53-54; asst prof art educ, Univ Tex, Austin, 54-60, res grant, 58; prof painting, Univ Fla, 60-82. *Awards:* D D Feldman Award, 58; Guggenheim Found Fel, 63; Distinguished Professor of Art, Univ Fla, 81. *Bibliog:* Donald Weismann (auth), Recent paintings of Hiram Williams, Univ Tex Quart, 59; William B Stephens (auth), On creating & teaching, Col Art J, summer 71 & Hiram Williams: Exploring the Sources of His Creation, William B Stephens, Memphis State Univ Press, 78. *Media:* Oil. *Publ:* Coauth, Forms, Univ Tex, 69; auth, Notes for a Young Painter, Prentice-Hall, 84. *Mailing Add:* 2804 NW 30th Terr Gainesville FL 32605

WILLIAMS, IDAHERMA See Idaherma (Idaherma Williams)

WILLIAMS, JANICE E
PAINTER, SCULPTOR
b Augusta, Ga, Dec 12, 54. *Study:* Univ Ga, BFA (cum laude), 77; Ind State Univ, MFA (drawing & sculpture), 79; Ohio State Univ; Western Carolina Univ. *Exhib:* Solo exhibs, Lander Col, SC, 86, Etherridge Ctr Gallery, Univ SC, Aiken, 87, Quinlan Art Ctr, Augusta Col, Ga, 89, NGa Col Gallery, Dahlonega, 89; Carrollton Regional Art Exhib V, Bess H Williamson Cultural Arts Ctr, Ga, 88; Southdown Fine Arts Exhib, Houma, La, 88; La Grange Nat XIV, Ga, 89; Augusta Col Faculty Exhib, Istituto D'Arte Dosso Dossi, Ferrara, Italy, 90; two-person exhib, Vanderbilt Univ, Sarratt Gallery, 92; three-person exhib, Univ Dayton, 92. *Teaching:* Inst drawing, Ind State Univ, Terre Haute, 79; inst art, Augusta Col, Ga, 81-85, asst prof, 87-90, assoc prof, 91- *Media:* Oil. *Mailing Add:* 960 Hickman Rd Augusta GA 30904

WILLIAMS, JOHN ALDEN
HISTORIAN
b Ft Smith, Ark, Sept 6, 28. *Study:* Am Univ Beirut, 50-51; Univ Munich, with Hans Sedlmayer, 51-52; Univ Ark, BA(hist & philos), 53; Princeton Univ, MA & PhD, 53-57; further work under Sir K A C Creswell in Cairo on hist of Islamic art & archit, 57-59. *Pos:* Asst field dir, Am Ctr for Res in Egypt, 57-59; sr res fel, Ctr Middle East Studies, Harvard Univ, 71-72. *Teaching:* Asst & assoc prof Islamic studies, McGill Univ, Montreal, Que, Can, 59-66; dir & prof, Ctr for Arabic Studies, Am Univ Cairo, 66/69; prof art hist & Middle East studies, Prof Ctr for Arabic Studies, Univ Cairo, 69-72; prof art hist & Islamic study, Univ Tex, Austin & Univ Cairo, alternate yrs, 72-88; Wm R Kenan Jr prof humanities, Col William & Mary, Williamsburg, Va, 88- *Mem:* Col Art Asn Am. *Res:* History of Islamic art and architecture, Islamic inst(s). *Publ:* Coauth, Architecture of Muslim India (400 slides with commentary), Art and Architecture of Ancient Egypt (400 slides with commentary) & Timurid Monuments of Central Asia (40 slides with commentary), Visual Educ Inc, 77; auth, The Khanqah of Siryaqus, In: Towards an Islamic Humanism, Cairo, 83; auth, Urbanization and Monument Construction in Mamluk Cairo, In: Muqarnas II, 84; and others. *Mailing Add:* 6 Coventry Rd Williamsburg VA 23185

WILLIAMS, JOHN WESLEY
HISTORIAN, EDUCATOR
b Memphis, Tenn, Feb 25, 28. *Study:* Duke Univ; Yale Univ, BA; Univ Mich, PhD. *Teaching:* From instr to assoc prof Medieval art, Swarthmore Col, Pa, 60-72, chmn fine arts dept, 71-72; prof, Univ Pittsburgh, retired, chmn fine arts dept, 79-84, retired. *Awards:* Fulbright-Hays Res Grant, Spain, 64 & 69; Nat Endowment Humanities Project Grant, 71-73; Guggenheim Fel, 84-85. *Mem:* Medieval Acad Am; Int Ctr Medieval Art. *Res:* Spanish Medieval art. *Publ:* Auth, Romanesque Bible of San Millan, JWCI, 65; auth, Valeranica and the Scribe Florentus, Madrider Mitteilungen, 70; auth, San Isidoro: Evidence for a new history, Art Bulletin, 73; auth, Early Spanish Manuscript Illumination, George Braziller, 77; ed, Actas del Simposio sobre Beato de Liebana, Vol II, Madrid, 80; and others. *Mailing Add:* 749 S Linden Ave Pittsburgh PA 15208

WILLIAMS, MARYLOU LORD STUDY
CONSULTANT, COLLAGE ARTIST
b Neodesha, Kans. *Study:* Beloit Col, Ba, 62; Univ Wis, Madison, MA(art), 65; NY Univ & Inst Mod Art, Mus Mod Art, New York, with Victor D'Amico. *Work:* NY Univ Art Collection; Wis Acad Sci Arts & Lett; Janesville Art League Gallery, Wis; Hawaii State Found Cult & Arts & Contemp Arts Ctr Collect ion, Honolulu; plus corporate collections. *Comn:* Series of five charcoal drawings, General Motors Assembly Div Plant, Janesville, 54; oil painting, Marine First Nat Bank, Janesville, 65; assemblage for lanai, Ossipoff, Snyder, Roland & Getz Architects, Honolulu, 72. *Exhib:* Cudahy Gallery, Milwaukee Art Mus, 86; Gallery X, Rockford, Ill, 87 & 88; Volid Gallery, Chicago, 89; Grace Chosy Gallery, Madison, Wis, 91 & 92; Jura Silverman Gallery, Spring Green, Wis, 92; Meryl Chase Gallery, Chicago/Buffalo Grove, Il, 92. *Collections Arranged:* Georgia O'Keeffe (with catalog), Daland Fine Arts Ctr, Kohler Gallery, Milton Col, Wis, 65; Festival of Far Eastern Art (with catalog), Wright Mus Art, Beloit Col, 80; Wis Painters & Printmakers Traveling Exhib, Wis Acad Gallery, Madison, 83. *Pos:* Dir & owner, Devlin Gallery, Janesville, 60-65; dir & cur, Theodore Lyman Wright Mus Art, Beloit Col, Wis, 75-83. *Teaching:* Chmn & asst prof art hist, design & gallery dir, Milton Col, Wis, 64-67; art coordr, elementary through community col, Dept Educ, Pago Pago, Am Samoa, 76-71; instr mus sch, Honolulu Acad Arts, summer 70, 71 & 73 & Bernice P Bishop Mus, Honlulu, 71-72. *Awards:* First Award, Beloit & Vicinity Exhib, Art League Beloit, 61; First Award, Rockford & Vicinity Exhib, Rockford Art Asn, 65; First Award, Wis Painters, Sculptors, Milwaukee Art Mus, 66. *Bibliog:* James Auer (auth), article, Milwaukee J, 5/9/76, 6/12/77 & 8/21/83; James Rehn (auth), Isthmus, 6/8/84; Webb Anderson (auth), Honolulu Star Bu ll & Advertisor, 4/12/72 & 6/4/72. *Mem:* Janesville Art League; Wis Citizens Arts; Wis Painters & Sculptors League; Hawaii Artists League; Wis Acad Scis, Arts & Letters. *Media:* Handmade Paper, Acrylic. *Res:* Study in depth of Polynesian bark cloth (tapa). *Dealer:* Merrill Chase Galleries/Corp Art Serv Buffalo Grove IL 60089. *Mailing Add:* 2528 Riverview Dr Janesville WI 53546

WILLIAMS, MELISSA
ART DEALER
b Kansas City, Mo, June 1, 51. *Study:* Univ Mo, BA & MA(summa cum laude), 73. *Pos:* Owner, Williams & McCormick, 83-89; Owner, Melissa Williams, Am Arts, 89- *Mem:* Mus Assoc, Univ Mo Mus Art & Archeol (bd mem); Arts & Sci Alumni Asn, Univ Mo (bd mem); Mo Review (bd mem). *Specialty:* American paintings 1840-1940. *Publ:* Auth, Portrait of a Lady, Muse, 72. *Mailing Add:* 19605 Mt Bethel Rd Weston MO 64098

WILLIAMS, PAT WARD
PHOTOGRAPHER
b Mar 19, 48, US citizen. *Study:* Moore Col Art, BFA, 82; Md Inst Col Art, MFA, 87. *Exhib:* New Photo Artists, Fox Gallery, Md Inst Col Art, Baltimore, 85; Humor, Wit & Whimsey, Artists Today Touring Exhib, Montpelier Cult Arts Ctr, Laurel, Md, 86; Baltimore Artists Exchange Exhib, Painted Bride Art Ctr, Philadelphia, 86; Invitational Black Artists Exhib, Life Md Gallery, Baltimore, 86; Seventh Ann Nat Art Exhib, Atlanta, Ga, 86; Eighth Ann Nat Exhib, JB Speed Mus, Louisville, Ky, 87; Artquest 88, Los Angeles, 88; Autobiography: In Her Own Image, INTAR Gallery, New York, 88; solo exhibs, Social/Sexual/Personal: Politics, Getehouse Gallery, Washington, DC, 87 & Political Variations, INTAR Gallery, New York, 88.

Teaching: Baltimore Sch Arts, Md, 84-87; Md Arts Coun, Artist-in-Residence Prog, Snow Hill Middle Sch, Snow Hill, Md, Easton High Sch, Easton, Md & Lake Clifton High Sch, Baltimore, 87; instr, Col Notre Dame Md, Baltimore, 87- *Awards:* Ford Found Grant, 85-87; Nat Newpaper Publ Asn Award, Best News Photog 1985, 86; City Arts Individual Artist's Grant, Mayor's Adv Comt Arts & Cult, Baltimore, Md; NEA/Mid-Atlantic Regional Visual Arts Fel for Works on Paper, 88. *Bibliog:* Dakai Asim (auth), St Louis Am, 11/10/88. *Mem:* (Bd Trustees) Artist Advisory Bd, Md Art Place Gallery, Baltimore, Md; Col Art Asn, Soc Photog Educ. *Mailing Add:* c/o Decker & Meyerhoff Galleries 1300 W Mt Royal Ave Baltimore MD 21217

WILLIAMS, PAUL ALAN
PAINTER, ILLUSTRATOR
b Detroit, Mich, Sept 10, 34. *Study:* Chadsey Art Sch, Detroit, 48-49; Meinzinger Arts, 50-51; Art Ctr Sch, Los Angeles, BPA, 59. *Work:* Jack McCormack & Co Inc, New York, NY; Radio City Music Hall Mus; Readers' Digest Col; La Maison du Temps, CT; Stadtisches Mus Leipzig. *Comn:* Three major int calendars, Scott Paper Co, 70's; grand re-opening campaign, Radio City Music Hall, 80's; production & prom, ABC & NBC TV, New York, 80's; space illus, United Tech-Norden, 80's. *Exhib:* Connolly & Alterman Gallery, Tex, 85; Eagles Lair Gallery, Conn, 86; Int Show, Waveny Park Mus, Conn, 86-88; Cath Charity Show, Bruce Mus, Greenwich, Conn, 87; Doyle Gallery, New York, 87 & 88; Litchfield Auction Gallery, Conn, 87, 88, 89, 90, 91 & 92; Wilton Historical, Soc Am Craftsmanship Show, Conn, 91 & 92; Westport Merchants Show, Conn, 92; Gracie Mansion Park Show, New York, 92. *Awards:* Best in Show, Casa D'Oliver Garden Show, Conn, 91. *Bibliog:* Vision of flowers (article), Your Family, 3/90; Sandi Oliver (auth), American Impressionist Paul Alan Williams: His Garden & His Oil Paintings, (catalog raissone), 91, 92 & 93. *Mem:* Soc Am Impressionists; Soc Illustrators. *Media:* Oil. *Mailing Add:* c/o Sandi Oliver Fine Art, PO Box 1203 Weston CT 06883

WILLIAMS, RAYMOND LESTER
PAINTER, INSTRUCTOR
b Lenoir City, Tenn, Nov 10, 26. *Study:* Chicago Acad Fine Arts, study with Edgar Whitney, John Pellew, Edmound Fitzgerald & Zolton Zabo, cert. *Work:* United Tel Co, Bristol, Tenn; Dobyns-Bennett High Sch & Tenn Eastman Co, Kingsport; Carrol Reese Mus & Tipton-Haynes Mus, Johnson City, Tenn. *Comn:* Highlands of Roan, Southern Appalachian Highlands Conservancy, 77; Church Circle, City of Kingsport, Tenn, 79; Four Homecoming '86 Print-Tri Cities Radio, 86; Directory Covers, United Tel System, 86; and others. *Exhib:* Tenn State Mus, Nashville, 73; Emory & Henry Univ, Emory, Va, 86; Mount Dora Art Festival, Mount Dora, Fla, 88; Lenox Square Fine Art, Atlanta, 87; Wilkes Art Gallery, North Wilkesboro, NC, 88; and many others. *Pos:* Graphic artist, Tenn Eastman Co, 50-74; painter & gallery owner, 74- *Awards:* Best of Show, Jonesboro Days, Jonesboro, Tenn, 75 & 81; Award, Tenn Watercolor Soc, 79; Best of Show, Dunwoody Fine Arts Asn, Atlanta, Ga, 87; and others. *Mem:* Tenn Watercolor Soc (dist dir, 74-75); Tenn Artists; Kingsport Art Guild (pres, 75-76). *Media:* Watercolor, Oils. *Dealer:* Gallery 81 PO Box 5538 Kingsport TN. *Mailing Add:* 3322 Roller Dr Kingsport TN 37663

WILLIAMS, REBA WHITE
COLLECTOR, WRITER
b Gulfport, Miss, May 21, 36. *Study:* Duke Univ, BA; Harvard Grad Sch Bus Admin, MBA, 70; Hunter Col, MA(art hist), 88. *Exhib:* Am Screenprints Traveling Exhib, Nat Acad Design, New York, 87, Reynolda House, Winston-Salem, NC, 88, Fed Reserve Bd, Washington, DC, 88, Butler Inst Am Art, Youngstown, Ohio, 88, Addison Gallery Am Art, Andover, Mass, 89, Guild Hall, E Hampton, NY, 89, Mary & Leigh Block Gallery, Northwestern Univ, Evanston, Ill, 89, Columbia Mus Art, SC, 90, Japan US Embassy in Tokyo & Sogetsu Found, 90, Mus Mod Art in Sapporo, Japan, 90, State St Bank, Boston, 91, Acad Art, Vienna, Austria, 91-92, Fitzwilliam Mus, Cambridge, Eng, 92; Black & White Since 1960, City Gallery Contemp Art, Raleigh, NC, 89, Aldrich Mus Contemp Art, Ridgefield, Conn, 90; The Mexican Muralists & Prints, Span Inst, New York, 90, Franz Mayer Mus, Mex City, 91; Blossoms in Black & White, The Equitable, New York, 91; Alone in a Crowd, Newark Mus, NJ, 92-93, The Equitable Gallery, New York, 92-93, Fitzwilliam Mus, Cambridge, Eng, 93. *Pos:* Writer, Print Quart, London, Am Artist & Art & Auction, NY; lectr, Alliance Capital Mgt, Cosmopolitan Club, Sotheby's, New York, Mus Fine Arts, Boston, Reynolda House, Mus Am Art, Winston-Salem, NC. *Publ:* Coauth, The Prints of Jackson Pollock; The History of Screenprint; A Print by Guy Pére du Bois; A Print by Frida Kahto; Flower Painting. *Mailing Add:* 510 Park Ave New York NY 10022

WILLIAMS, RICHARD ELDON
PAINTER, GALLERY DIRECTOR
b Biloxi, Miss, Sept 2, 34. *Study:* John Pike, Woodstock, NY, cert, 70; Edgar Whitney, Maine, cert, 71; La Madrid, Spain, lett, 72. *Work:* Mem Hurlburt Air Force Base, Ft Walton Beach, Fla; Joint Warfare Establishment Mus, London, Eng; Portrait of Amy Carter, US White House Collection, Washington, DC; Marine Showcase, Destin, Fla; Univ Southern Miss, Hattisburg; Seafood Indust Mus, Biloxi, Miss. *Comn:* Underwater mural(with Al McLeod), comn by Destin Chamber Com, Fla, 78. *Exhib:* Univ Southern Miss, Hattisburg, 78; Int Soc Artist Juried Show, Nat Gallery, NY, 78; Lynn Kottler Gallery, NY, 79; Am Artist Prof League Juried Show, NY World Trade Ctr & Salmagundi Club, NY 80; Pensacola Mus Art, 84; Fla Watercolor Soc Signature Traveling Exhib, 91 & 92; World Wildlife Exhib, Gatlinburg, Tenn, 92. *Collections Arranged:* Works of the Masters, 83, Lines & Vines, 84 & Compositions with Impact, 85, Gallery Fine Art, Destin, Fla. *Pos:* Instr acrylic-watercolor & dir, Gallery Fine Art, Destin, Fla, 80- *Teaching:* Twenty years teaching pvt watercolor workshops, guest instr, Cancun, Mexico Paint-Out, 92. *Awards:* Merit Award, Fla Watercolor Soc, 78. *Bibliog:* Orley B Caudill (auth), Richard E Williams, Univ Southern Miss, 78; An Oral History with Mr Richard Williams, Archives McCain Grad Libr, Univ Southern Miss, 78; featured article, Two Cities Mag, Ft Walton, Fla, 84. *Mem:* Charter mem, Fla Watercolor Soc Signature; Am Artist Prof League; Am Soc Marine Artists; US Off Coast Guard Artist. *Media:* Watercolor. *Mailing Add:* 127 Hwy 98 E 1 Palmetto Plaza Destin FL 32541

WILLIAMS, SYLVIA H
MUSEUM DIRECTOR
b Lincoln University, Pa, Feb 10, 36. *Study:* Oberlin Col, AB, 57; Inst Fine Arts, New York Univ, MA, 75. *Exhib:* Black South Africa: Contemporary Graphics (auth, catalog), Brooklyn Mus, 76; Go Well, My Child: Photographs by Constance Stuart Larrabee in Collaboration with Alan Paton, Nat Mus African Art, Washington, DC, 85-86. *Pos:* Asst cur, Brooklyn Mus, NY, 73-76, assoc cur, 76-78, cur, 78-83; dir, Nat Mus African Art, Smithsonian Inst, Washington, DC, 83- *Teaching:* Adj asst prof art hist, Grad Sch Arts & Sci, New York Univ. *Awards:* Grant, Nat Mus Act, 74. *Mem:* Asn Art Mus Dir; Am Asn Mus (vpres, 86-87); Art Mus Vis Comt, Harvard Univ; Int Coun Mus. *Publ:* Contribr, African Art as Philosophy, 74; auth, Black South African contemporary graphics, 76; Brooklyn Mus African Collection, Apollo; contribr, African Arts Mag & to Arts d'Afrique Mag. *Mailing Add:* Nat Mus African Art, Smithsonian Inst 950 Independence Ave Washington DC 20560

WILLIAMS, WAYNE FRANCIS
SCULPTOR
b Newark, NY, July 22, 37. *Study:* Syracuse Univ, BFA, 58, MFA, 62; Chaloner Found Fel, 58 & 59; Europe-Ghent Belgium, 58-60. *Work:* Ministry Pub Educ Collections, Brussels, Belg; Murdock Collection, Wichita Mus, Kans; Whitney Found Collection, Cornell Univ; Nebr Art Asn, Univ Nebr-Lincoln; NY State Univ Col Albany. *Comn:* Life size welded sculpture, North Rose Wolcott Sch, NY, 72; Life size bronze figure of Wm Simon, Univ Rochester, NY, 88. *Exhib:* Belg Salon des Beaux Arts, Mus voor Schone Kunsten, Ghent, Belg, 60; one-man shows, Maynard Walker Gallery, 61 & 64 & Frank Rehn Gallery, New York, 74; New York Art Dealers Exhib, Park Bernet Gallery, New York, 64. *Teaching:* Instr drawing, Syracuse Univ, 60-63; prof drawing & sculpture, Community Col Finger Lakes, 68- *Awards:* Louis Comfort Tiffany Found Award for Sculpture, 64. *Bibliog:* John Canaday (auth), Wayne Williams-Maynard-Walker, New York Times, 10/64; Dorothy Hall (auth), Williams at Rehn, Park East, New York, 4/74; Roberta Olson (auth), Wayne Williams-Rehn, Arts Mag, 6/74. *Media:* Metals. *Publ:* Auth, The art program at Community College of Finger Lakes, NY State Art Teachers Mag, 5/74. *Mailing Add:* 1954 Gardner Rd Newark NY 14513

WILLIAMS, WILLIAM EARLE
PHOTOGRAPHER, CURATOR
b Vicksburg, Miss, Apr 19, 50. *Study:* Hamilton Col, BA, 73; Yale Univ, MFA, 78. *Work:* Philadelphia Mus Art; Lehigh Univ, Bethlehem, Pa; Metrop Mus & Brooklyn Mus, New York; Univ Md & Baltimore Mus Art, Baltimore; Allentown Art Mus. *Exhib:* Solo exhibs, Butler Inst Am Arts, Youngstown, Ohio, 80 & Party Photographs, Univ Md, Baltimore, 86; American Photography, 1910-1983 (with catalog), Tampa Mus, Fla, 83; Contemporary Photographers, Pa Acad Fine Arts, Philadelphia, 84; Pennsylvania Photographers IV, Allentown Art Mus, Pa, 85; 61st International Print Club Competition, Philadelphia, 85; Contemp Philadelphia Artists (catalog), Philadelphia Mus Art, 90; Photographs of Gettysburg, Cleveland Mus Art, 90. *Collections Arranged:* Lewis Hine: Child Labor Photographs, 79, Muybridge and Eakins, Photographers of Motion, 80, Walker Evans: A Retrospective, 81, Arbus, Weegee and Model Photographers, 82, Masterpieces of Photography from the Collection, 84, & Adolphe Brown, Walker Evans, Andre Kertesz: Photographers of Sculpture, 88, Comfort Gallery, Haverford Col, Pa. *Teaching:* Prof fine arts, photog, Haverford Col, Pa, 78- *Awards:* Purchase Award, 61st Ann Int Competition, The Print Club, Philadelphia, 85. *Bibliog:* Porter Aichele (auth), William Earle Williams, Party Photographs, Comfort Gallery, Haverford Col, Pa, 85; William Southwell (auth), Documentary revival, Lens on Campus, Hearst, New York, 86; Deborah Willis-Thomas (auth), Black Photographers, 1940-1988: An Illustrated Bio-Bibliography, Garland Press, NY, NY, 88. *Mem:* Col Art Asn; Soc Photog Educ; Am Studies Asn. *Publ:* Illusr, William Williams Portfolio, Philadelphia Photo Rev, Perloff, 82; Dealing at street level, Philadelphia Mag, 82; The Print Club, The Print Club publ, 85; Pennsylvania Photographers: A Selection of Current Work, Allentown Art Mus, 85; Party Pictures, Aronis Press, 85. *Mailing Add:* Dept Fine Arts Haverford Col Haverford PA 19041

WILLIAMS, WILLIAM THOMAS
PAINTER, EDUCATOR
b Cross Creek, NC, July 17, 42. *Study:* Skowhegan Sch Painting & Sculpture, summer 65; Pratt Inst, BFA, 66; Yale Univ, MFA, 68. *Work:* Mus Mod Art & Whitney Mus Am Art, New York; Yale Univ, New Haven, Conn; Wadsworth Atheneum, Hartford, Conn; Johnson Mus, Cornell Univ, Ithaca, NY. *Comn:* Print, Jewish Mus, New York, 70; environ sculpture, Menil Found, Houston, 70; environ murals, Gottesmans Plaza, New York, 70; print portfolio, HKL Ltd Publ, New York, 71; print, LD Group Int, New York, 78. *Exhib:* Whitney Ann, Whitney Mus Am Art, 69 & Struct of Color, 71; L'Art Vivant Aux Estats-Unis, Found Maeght, St Paul, France, 70; DeLuxe Show, Menil Found, Houston, 71; Acquisitions, Mus Mod Art, New York, 72; Contemporary Visual Expressions, Anacostia Mus/Smithsonian Inst, Wash, DC, 87; The Art Black America in Japan, Tokyo, Japan, 87; 40th Ann Acad-Inst Purchase Exhib, Am Acad & Inst Art & Letters, New York, 88. *Teaching:*

Prof art, City Univ New York, Brooklyn Col, 70- *Awards:* Nat Endowment for Arts & Humanities traveling grant, 65 & artist fels, 70; John Simon Guggenheim Fel, 87. *Bibliog:* H W Janson (auth), The History of Art, Harry Abrams, 86. *Mailing Add:* 654 Broadway New York NY 10012

WILLIAMSON, JASON H
PAINTER, DEALER
b Bristol, Va, Mar 20, 26. *Study:* Emory & Henry Col, Va; Vesper George Sch of Art, Boston, Mass, cert. *Comn:* Signed and numbered reproduction color prints, comn by Grey Stone Press, Nashville, Tenn. *Exhib:* Am Watercolor Soc, 65, 74-77 & 80; Watercolor USA, Springfield, Mo, 63, 72 & 74; one-man shows, East Tenn State Univ, Johnson City, 54, Memphis Acad of Arts, Tenn, 60, 67, Emory and Henry Col, Va, 67, Tenn Tech Univ, 73 & Ark Arts Ctr, Pine Bluff, 74 and many others; and others. *Pos:* Art dir, S E Massengill Co, Bristol, Tenn, 49-56 & Plough Inc, Memphis, 56-58; free lance advert art, Memphis, 58-62; advert art studio head, Williamson--Parker, 62-75; gallery owner, Golden Fleece Art Gallery, Memphis, 70-75 & Carefree, Ariz, 76-87. *Teaching:* Dept head advert art, The Memphis Acad of Art, Tenn, 60-69; nat competition judge, pvt classes and workshops, artist watercolor & oil. *Awards:* John Young Hunter, Am Watercolor Soc, 74; Annenberg Fund Award, Nat Watercolor Soc, 76; Colo Watermedia Award, Rocky Mountain Nat, 77. *Bibliog:* Watercolor Page, Am Artist Mag, 6/78, Southwest Art, 10/79. *Mem:* Am Watercolor Soc; Nat Watercolor Soc; 22 x 30 Watercolor Group Ariz; Tenn Watercolor Soc (hon lifetime); Memphis Watercolor Group (hon lifetime). *Media:* Watercolor, Oil. *Specialty:* Watercolor and oil. Interest: Support many worthwhile art organizations. *Dealer:* Golden Fleece Art Gallery 42 Easy St Carefree AZ 85331. *Mailing Add:* PO Box 1943 Cave Creek AZ 85331

WILLIFORD, HOLLIS R
SCULPTOR, PAINTER
b Hill County, Tex, Oct 31, 40. *Study:* Univ Tex, Arlington, 59-63; N Tex State, 63-64; Art Ctr Col Design, BA, 71. *Work:* Thomas Gilcrease Mus, Tulsa, Okla; Whitney Mus, Cody, Wyo; John-Hopkins Univ, Baltimore, Md; Genessee Country Mus, Rochester, NY. *Comn:* Need to Know (monument), City of Vail, Colo, 82 & Lowland Pub Libr, Colo, 87; Riomar Blue (monument), Riomar Yacht Club, Vero Beach, Fla, 88. *Exhib:* Nat Acad Western Art, Nat Cowboy Hall Fame, Oklahoma City, Okla, 80-88; Nabisco Invitational, Nabisco Brands World Hq, E Hanover, NJ, 84; Gilcrease Rendezvous, Thomas Gilcrease Mus, Tulsa, Okla, 88; Prix de West Collection, Wildlife Am W Mus, Jackson, Wyo, 88. *Awards:* Prix de West, Nat Acad Western Art, Cowboy Hall Fame, 80 & 88 & Gold Medals, 80 & 86. *Bibliog:* John Jellico (auth), Hollis Williford, Artist Rockies & Golden West, 80; Carol Dickinson (auth), Facing the Challenge of Nature, SW Art, 87; Fred Myers (auth), Hollis Williford, Gilcrease Mag, 88. *Media:* Bronze, Oil. *Dealer:* Trailside Galleries Scottsdale AZ; Western Images New York NY. *Mailing Add:* 813 S St Louis Ave Loveland CO 80537

WILLIS, BARBARA FLORENCE
PAINTER
b Bronx, NY, Dec 17, 32. *Study:* Vesper George Sch Art, with Robert Douglas Hunter & Robert Cummings. *Exhib:* Strawflowers, Am Artists 58th Grand Nat Exhib, 87 & Springfield Art League Nat Exhib, 88; solo exhib, Peel Gallery, Danby, Vt, 88; Study in Reds, Audobon Artists 46th Ann Exhib, 88, Am Artists Prof League 59th Grand Nat Exhib, 88 & Acad Artists Asn 39th Nat Exhib, 89; Clown & Pinwheel, Copley Soc Stillife Show, Boston, 90 & Cape Cod Art Asn New Eng Exhib, 90; Audubon Artists 49th Ann, 91; Pastel Soc Am 20th Nat Show, 92; joint show, Peel Gallery, Danby, Vt. *Awards:* Jessie B McReynolds Memorial Award, Salmagundi Club, 90; Second Prize, Cape Cod Art Asn New Eng, 90; First Prize & Jurors Award, Capley Soc; Acad Artists Nat Award, Pastel Soc Am, 92. *Mem:* Charter mem, Conn Pastel Soc. *Media:* Oils, Watercolors. *Publ:* Techniques in Oil Painting, Quartro Pub Co, London, Eng. *Dealer:* Peel Gallery Danby VT; Copley Soc Sales Gallery Boston MA. *Mailing Add:* Old Stage Coach Rd Bennington NH 03442

WILLIS, ELIZABETH BAYLEY
HISTORIAN, COLLECTOR
b Somerville, Mass. *Study:* Univ Wash, AB, with Lyonel Feininger, Mark Tobey & Morris Graves. *Pos:* Assoc, Willard Gallery, New York, 43-46; cur, Henry Gallery, Univ Wash, 46-48; San Francisco Mus Art, 48-50; actg asst dir, Calif Palace Legion of Honor, 50-51; consult decorative arts, prod & mkt, Mingei Kan, Tokyo, 51-52; expert mem UN Tech Asst Bd for Taiwan, Vietnam, India & Morocco, 52-59; consult textile export, India, 55-57 & Res India, 58-65. *Res:* Tribes of India's northeast frontier (1959-1964), especially their arts and textiles; textile arts of India; folk arts of Japan, Mingei. *Collection:* Artifacts, pottery and textiles from Tibet, Bhutan, India, Burma, Japan & Morocco, now in the Permanent Collection of the Smithsonian Institution; costumes and textiles from the same countries now in Permanent Collections of the University of Washington Henry Art Gallery and the Washington State Museum; Ming and Ch'ing paintings in a private collection. *Publ:* Auth, Travel with Dr Soetsu Yanagai in his kingdom of beauty & India! In the footprints of the Raj: A hard act to follow, Japan J (in prep); contribr, Arts Asia Mag, 86. *Mailing Add:* PO Box 10126 Bainbridge Island WA 98110

WILLIS, JAY STEWART
SCULPTOR, EDUCATOR
b Fort Wayne, Ind, Oct 22, 40. *Study:* Univ Ill, Urbana, study with Frank Gallo & Roger Majorweiz, BFA(sculpture), 64; Univ Calif, Berkeley, study with Donald Haskin, Harold Paris, Jacques Schnier & Peter Voulkos, MA(sculpture), 66. *Work:* Hirshhorn Mus, Washington, DC; Del Mar Col, Corpus Christi, Tex; Am Tel & Tel, Chicago; Metrop Mus Art, New York; Calif State Univ, Fullerton; Walker Hill Art Mus, Seoul, Korea. *Comn:* Multiple Structures, Cirus Ed, 73; sculpture comn by Terry Inch, Los Angeles, 74; sculpture (with Bob Smith), ABC Century City, Los Angeles, 75; sculpture (with Don Brewer), ALCOA, Univ Southern Calif sculpture garden, Los Angeles, 78; sculpture, comn by Ernesto W Hahn & Charles Kober Assocs, Pasadena, Calif, 80; Bankers Trust, Los Angeles; Pacific Enterprises, Los Angeles. *Exhib:* One-person exhibs, Cirrus Gallery, Los Angeles, 81, 83, 85, 86 & 88; Painted Sculpture, Los Angeles Munic Art Gallery, Calif, 82; Nancy Yawell Collection, Baxter Art Gallery, Calif Inst Tech, Pasadena, 83; Constructed Metal-Modern Sculpture, Univ Calif, Col Creative Studies, Santa Barbara; A Broad Spectrum : Contemp LA Painters, Design Ctr Los Angeles, 84; Olympic Project, Los Angeles Co Mus Art, Calif, 84; Sculpture Installation, Fisher Art Gallery, Univ Southern Calif, Los Angeles, 85; Los Angeles Int Art Fair, 86-89; Beverly Hills Sculpture Garden, Calif, 87; Calif Artist in Educ, San Francisco, 89; Monumental Sculpture, Calif State Univ, San Bernardino, 89. *Teaching:* Instr sculpture, Univ Ariz, Tucson, 66-69; asst prof fine arts, 69-73, prof fine arts (sculpture), 74-, chmn studio arts, 88-, Univ Southern Calif, Los Angeles. *Awards:* Res Grant, Video, Univ Southern Calif, 75; Purchase Award, Los Angeles Art Ann, Barnsdall Park, Calif, 76; Runner-Up, Los Angeles Int Airport Sculpture, Calif, 76; Univ Southern Calif Faculty Innovation & Res Grant, color & Structure, 85-86. *Bibliog:* Suzanne Muchnic (auth), Los Angeles Time, 5/5/81 & 3/1/85; Kathy Zimmer-McKelvie, Images & Issues, Spring, 82; Betty Brown (auth), Artweek, 11/12/83; Sandy Nelson (auth), Images & Issues, 7-8/84; Stephen Grossman (auth), Artweek, 3/23/85; Colin Gardner (auth), Los Angeles Times, 10/10/86; Marlene Donahue (auth), Los Angeles Times, 5/13/88; and many others. *Mailing Add:* c/o School of Fine Arts USC Watt Hall Los Angeles CA 90089-0292

WILLIS, SIDNEY F
PAINTER
b Newark, NJ, Dec 14, 30. *Study:* Vesper George Sch Art, grad, continued study with Robert D Hunter. *Exhib:* Southern Vt Artists, 72; Jordan Show, Boston, Mass, 73; Ogunquit Art Ctr, Maine, 74; Am Artists Prof League, New York, 74; Coun Am Artists Show, New York. *Teaching:* Instr painting & drawing, Vesper George Art Sch, Boston, Mass, 67-69 & Sharon Art Ctr, Peterborough, NH, 65-75. *Awards:* Grand Prize, Jordan Show, Boston, 58 & 62; First Prize, Ogunquit Art Ctr, Maine, 61; Gold Medal, Heritage Salon, 88; and many others. *Bibliog:* Classical Realism (video). *Mem:* Guild Boston Artists; NH Art Asn; Am Artists Prof League; Paste Soc of Am. *Media:* Oil, Pastel. *Publ:* Contribr, New York Graphic Soc, Yankee Mag; Techniques in Oil Painting, Quartro Pub, London, Eng. *Dealer:* Peel Gallery Danby VT; Heritage Art Gallery Alexandria VA. *Mailing Add:* Box 151 Bennington NH 03442

WILLIS, THORNTON
PAINTER
b Pensacola, Fla, May 25, 36. *Study:* Auburn Univ, Ala; Univ Southern Miss, Hattiesburg, BS; Univ Ala, MA. *Work:* Solomon R Guggenheim Mus, Whitney Mus Am Art, Mus Mod Art, New York; Phillips Collection, Washington, DC; Denver Mus Fine Art; Albright-Knox Art Gallery, Buffalo, NY; Mus Art, Carnegie, Mellon, Pittsburgh, Pa. *Exhib:* Lyrical Abstraction, Aldrich Mus, 69 & Whitney Mus, 71; one-man shows, Sydney Janis Gallery, 80, Oscarsson-Hood Gallery, New York, 80-81 & 84, Marianne Deson Gallery, Chicago, 81, Galerie Nordenhake, Stockholm & Pensacola Mus, Fla, 88; Mus Mod Art, New York, 81 & 84; Galerie Gonet, Lausanne, Switz, 82; Art Mus Ateneum, Helsinki, Finland, 83; Gloria Luria, Miami, Fla, 85; Univ Southern Miss,, Hattlesburg, 85; Twining Gallery, New York, 88, 89, 90 & 91; Andre Emmerich Gallery, New York, 92; Andre Zarre Gallery, New York, 92. *Teaching:* Grad lectr, Pratt Inst, 74, 77 & 80; lectr, Art Inst Chicago, Ill, 81; assoc prof art, Univ La, Baton Rouge, 83 & SUNY at Purchase, 86. *Awards:* Fel Award, John Simon Guggenheim Found, 78-79; Nat Endowment Arts Painting Fel, 80; Adolph & Esther Gottlieb Found, 91. *Bibliog:* David Carrier (auth), Betwixt and Between Illusion and Literality & Thorton Willis: A Treatise; Vered Lieb (auth), Objective Spirit: Thornton Willis, Arts Mag, 11/86; Peter Bellamy (auth), The Artist Project: Portraits of the Real Art World, New York Artists, 91. *Media:* Plastic, Oil. *Dealer:* Andre Zarre Gallery New York NY; Claes Nordenhake Stockholm Sweden. *Mailing Add:* 85-87 Mercer St New York NY 10012

WILLIS, WILLIAM HENRY, JR
ADMINISTRATOR
b Boston, Mass, Oct 29, 40. *Study:* Marlboro Col, Vt, BA; Yale Univ, New Haven, Conn, MFA. *Pos:* Dir admin, Art Inst Boston, 67-74, dir, 74-76 & pres, 76-90. *Mailing Add:* 88 Marginal St Chelsea MA 02150

WILLOUGHBY, JANE BAKER
COLLAGE ARTIST, PAINTER
b Toledo, Ohio. *Study:* Smith Col, Mass, BA, 43; Art Students League with George Grosz, 45-49; New Sch Social Res, New York, 50-51. *Work:* Lyman Allyn Mus, New London, Conn; Mus Art, Sci & Industry, Bridgeport, Conn; The Robert Benjamin Collection, New York; Conn Bank & Trust Co, New Haven; Sen & Mrs George McGovern, Washington, DC; Pres & Mrs Ronald Reagan, Washington, DC. *Exhib:* One-man shows, Silvermine Guild Artists, New Canaan, Conn, 63 & 76, Slater Mem Mus, Norwich, Conn, 76, Lyman Allyn Mus, New London, Conn, 80, Bridgeport Mus Art, Sci, Conn, 80 & Whitney Mus Am Art, New Haven, Conn, 81; The Benjamin Collection, Yale Univ Art Gallery; Viridian Gallery, New York, 83 & 86; Albertus Magnus Col, 90; Fairfield Univ, 85. *Teaching:* Instr, Silvermine Guild Artists. *Awards:* Munson Award & Purchase Prize, New Haven Paint-Clay Club, 75; Arches Paper, Nat Asn Painters in Casein & Acrylic, 78; Audubon Medal Honor, Audubon Artists Am, 78; Conn Women Artists, 90; Best in Show, Conn

Women Artists, New Brit Mus Am Art. *Bibliog:* Shirley Gonzales (auth), New Haven Register, 9/16/83; Shirley Sandler (auth), Manhattan Arts, 11/16/83; Amy Friedman (auth), Artspeak, 11/16/83; and others. *Mem:* Silvermine Guild Artists; Conn Acad Fine Arts; Conn Watercolor Soc; Audubon Artists Inc; Conn Women Artists Asn. *Media:* Monotype. *Mailing Add:* 1150 Ridge Rd North Haven CT 06473

WILLSON, MARGARET (BOSSHARDT) PACE
PAINTER, SCULPTOR
b San Antonio, Tex, Dec 9, 19. *Study:* Tulane Univ; Newcomb Col, MDes, BFA; Trinity Univ: San Antonio Col, Univ Tex(archit), three years; also with Will Stevens, Etienne Ret, Xavier Gonzalez, Rico Lebrun & Peter Lanyon. *Work:* McNay Mus Art; Art Dept, Newcomb Col; Tulane Univ, 86. *Comn:* mosaic murals, Episcopal Diocesan Ctr, Diocese of WTex, 61 & Episcopal Cathedral, 65, St Luke Episcopal Church, St David's Episcopal Church, San Antonio; mural, Lemon Grove, Calif Unitarian Church, 67; designed & executed chalice, pattern & pix, ordination of Father Braun, Pinckneyville, Ill, 69; processional cross, Church Reconciliation, 84; and others. *Exhib:* Metrop Mus, NY; Cent USA Watercolors, Dallas Mus Fine Arts; McNay Mus, 81; one-man shows, Ravaqnon Gallery Mod Art, Venice, 84, Tulane-Newcomb Univ, 85, Artist of the Year, Witte Mus, San Antonio, 86, Art Inst Permian Basin, Odessa, Tex, 86, Drawing & Prints exhib, Sol del Rio Gallery, San Antonio, Tex, 87-88 & Baylor Univ Art Mus, Waco, Tx, 92; Ravagnon Gallery Mod Art, Venice; Tulane-Newcomb Univ, 85; Cloisters of St Marks, Centro D'Arte, Venice, 89; Foster Harmon Gallery, Sarasota, Fla, 90; and others. *Pos:* Bd mem, trustee & vpres, San Antonio Art Inst, 55-84 & 91-92; bd mem & secy, Witte Mus, 60-65; founder trustee, Southwest Craft Ctr, 63-89; nat pres alumni bd, Newcomb Col, Tulane Univ, mem pres coun, 76-78, mem alumni bd, 77-84; pres, P & W Oil & Gas Exploration Corp; bd mem, McNay Mus Coun, San Antonio, 82-85, 88-91; trustee, San Antonio Mus Art, 88-91 & San Antonio Mus Art Asn, 90-; bd gov, Tulane Univ, New Orleans, La, 87- *Teaching:* Instr, Incarnet Word Col, 64-65; asst prof art, San Antonio Col, 60-72; instr design & watercolor, Hill Country Found, 68, 70, 75-77. *Awards:* Richard Kleberg Purchase Award, 62; Mosaic Mural Award in seven state exhib, Mus Contemp Crafts; Achievement in Art Award, 92; plus many others. *Mem:* San Antonio Art League (bd mem, 56-58, 60, 67-68, 71, 73-78); Pace-Willson Art Found (vpres, currently); Tex Watercolor Soc (first vpres, 83-85, 88-89); San Antonio Craft Guild; Int Soc of Mosaic Artists of Ravenna, Italy, 91-92; plus others. *Media:* All Media. *Publ:* Auth, Paintings, Watercolor & Acrylic, Cento D'Arte Appolonia, Venice, Italy, 69; Drawings on the Wind, Galleria D'Arte Mod Ravagnon, Venice, Italy, 87. *Mailing Add:* 207 Terrell Rd San Antonio TX 78209

WILLSON, ROBERT
SCULPTOR, PAINTER
b Mertzon, Tex, May 28, 12. *Study:* Univ Tex, BA; Univ Bellas Artes, Guanajuato, Mex, MFA; and with Jose Clemente Orozco. *Work:* Mus Correr, Venice, Italy; Lowe Art Mus, Coral Gables, Fla; McNay Art Mus, Mus Art, San Antonio, Tex; Corning Glass Mus, NY; Ital Nat Glass Mus, Murano, Italy; Philadelphia Art Mus; Victoria & Albert Mus, London; and others. *Comn:* glass sculptures, Harmon Gallery, Naples, Fla, 69; ceramic sculptures, comn by Mrs Robert Hoffman, Naples, 70; enamel sculpture, Exec Plaza, Miami, 72; Indian Glass Group, Mus Art, San Antonio; 43 glass sculptures, New Orleans Mus Art, 90. *Exhib:* Painting & Sculpture Nat, San Francisco Mus Art, 57; one-man shows, Ringling Art Mus, Sarasota, Fla, 70, Corning Mus Glass, NY, 71, Univ Tex Art Mus, 79, McNay Art Mus, 81 & Mus Mod Art, Venice, 84; Int Glass Sculpture, Lowe Art Mus, Coral Gables, Fla, 73; Tex Mus Tour, 78; San Antonio Art Mus, 88; New Orleans Art Mus, 90; Baylor Univ Art Mus, Waco, 91; and others. *Pos:* Dir, Coun Ozark Artists, 50-52; pres & dir, Fla Craftsmen, 52-58; ed, Tejas Art Press, San Antonio, Tex, presently. *Teaching:* Chmn dept art, Tex Wesleyan Col, 40-48; prof art, Univ Miami, 52-77. *Awards:* Nat Hon Mention for Sculpture, San Francisco Mus Art, 57; Shell Co Fund Grants for Glass Sculpture, 71 & 73; Fla State Grand Medal Award Winner for Sculpture, Garden Mod Art, Miami, 72. *Bibliog:* Film, New Orleans Art Mus, 90. *Mem:* Col Art Asn Am; Am Asn Mus; Tex Watercolor Soc. *Media:* Glass; Watercolor. *Publ:* Ed, Kress Collection, 61 & auth, Art concept in Clay, 67, Univ Miami; auth, College-level Art Curriculum in Glass, Dept Health, Educ & Welfare, 68. *Dealer:* Harmon Art Gallery 1258 Third St S Naples FL 33577; Ravagnan Galeria d'Arte Moderna Piazza San Marco Venice Italy. *Mailing Add:* 207 Terrell Rd San Antonio TX 78209

WILMERDING, JOHN
EDUCATOR, HISTORIAN
b Boston, Mass, Apr 28, 38. *Study:* Harvard Col, AB, 60; Harvard Univ, AM, 61 & PhD, 65; also Am art with Benjamin Rowland; Univ Vt, DLitt, 90. *Collections Arranged:* Fitz Hugh Lane, 66 & Robert Salmon, 67, De Cordova Mus, Lincoln, Mass; American Marine Painting, Va Mus Fine Arts, Richmond, 76; 100 American Drawings from the J D Hatch Collection, Nat Gallery Ireland, 76; American Light: The Luminist Movement (auth, catalog), 80, An American Perspective: The Ganz Collection, 81 & Important Information Inside: The Art of John F Peto (auth, catalog), 83, The Paintings of Fitz Hugh Lane (co-auth, catalog), 88, Nat Gallery Art, Washington, DC; Winslow Homer in the 1870s (co-auth, catalog), Art Mus, Princeton Univ, 90. *Pos:* cur Am art & sr cur, Nat Gallery Art, Washington, DC, 77-82, deputy dir, 83-88. *Teaching:* Leon E Williams prof Am art, Dartmouth Col, 65-77; vis lectr, Yale Univ, 72; vis prof, Harvard Univ, 76, Univ Md, 79 & Univ Del, 82; Sarofim prof Am art, Princeton Univ, 88. *Awards:* Humanities Fac Develop Grant, Dartmouth Col, 70-71; Guggenheim Found Fel, 73-74; Oates fel, Princeton Univ, 86; hon fel, Philadelphia Atheneum; Comt for Preservation of White House (Presidential app). *Mem:* Col Art Asn; Thomas Jefferson Mem Found, Monticello (trustee); Shelburne Mus (pres). *Res:* American 19th century art and culture. *Publ:* American Art, Pelican-Penguin, 76; American Masterpieces from the National Gallery of Art, Hudson Hills, 80; Important Information Inside, Harper & Row, 83; Andrew Wyeth, The Helga Pictures, Abrams, 87; American Views: Essays on American Art, Princeton, 91. *Mailing Add:* Dept Art & Archaeol Princeton Univ 104 McCormick Hall Princeton NJ 08544-1018

WILMETH, ERNEST, II
PAINTER, POTTER
b Perryton, Tex, Dec 21, 52. *Study:* WTex State Univ, with Dr Emilio Caballero, 71-72; Northern Ariz Univ, BFA, 76; clay training with Penne Roberts, 82-85, Tom Hill, 83, George Pate, 84 & others. *Work:* Bowne Corp, Nashville; Delancy Street Found, San Francisco; First State Bank, Spearman, Tex. *Exhib:* Southwest Arts & Crafts Festival, 89, 90 & 91; Magnifico, The Art of Albuquerque, 91 & 92; two person shows, Coupland/Jackson Fine Art, Taos, NMex, 91, Cone 10 Gallery, Albuquerque, 92 & First State Bank, Spearman, Tex, 92; Biennial Crafts 92, Fuller Lodge Art Ctr, Los Alamos, 92; and others. *Awards:* First in Oil, Tri-State Fair, Amarillo, 79. *Bibliog:* Mary Alice Hines (auth), article, in: Accent W, 7/78. *Mem:* Fel Royal Soc Arts; life mem Royal Soc Encouragement Arts Manufactures & Com; Southwest Arts and Crafts Festival (bd mem, 90). *Media:* Oil, Watercolor; Clay. *Dealer:* Canyon Art Gallery 2710 Fourth Ave Canyon TX 79105. *Mailing Add:* PO Box 3104 Albuquerque NM 87190

WILSON, ANNE GAWTHROP
PAINTER, EDUCATOR
b Detroit, Mich, April 16, 49. *Study:* Cranbrook Acad Art, Bloomfield Hills, Mich, BFA, 72; Calif Col Arts & Crafts, Oakland, MFA, 76. *Work:* M H DeYoung Mem Mus, San Francisco, Calif; State of Ill Ctr, Chicago; Sandoz Crop Protection Corp, Chicago; Smith Hinchman and Grylls Architects, Detroit, Mich. *Exhib:* Vivid Form: New Inventions, Kemper Gallery, Kansas City Art Inst, Mo, 85; Fiber Revolution, Univ Art Mus, Univ of Wis, Milwaukee, 86; Craft Today: Poetry of the Physical, Am Craft Mus, New York, 87; Tangents, Md Inst, Oakland Mus, Calif & Cleveland Inst Art, OH, 87-88; Chicago Pub Libr Cult Ctr, Ill, 88; Biennial of Tapestry, Musee Cantonal des Beaux-Arts, Palais de Rumine, Lausanne, Switz, 89; Crossovers, Gallery Contemp Art, Colorado Springs, 90; New Ends, Newhouse Ctr Contemp Art, Staten Island, NY, 91; retrospective, Anne Wilson: Recent Work, Roy Boyd Gallery, Chicago, 91; Domestic Ontogeny: New Textile Forms, Oliver Art Ctr, Calif Col Arts & Crafts, Oakland, 92. *Teaching:* Assoc Prof Fiber Dept, Art Inst Chicago, 79- *Awards:* Visual Artists Fel Grant, Nat Endowment Arts, 82 & 88; Individual Artists Grant, Ill Arts Coun, 83, 84 & 87; Louis Comfort Tiffany Found Award, 89. *Bibliog:* Sue Taylor (auth), Art Am, 2/92; Kathryn Hixon (auth), Arts, 2/92; Nathan Budoff (auth), New Art Examiner, 2/92; and others. *Mem:* Haystack Mountain Sch of Crafts (bd trustees 90-); Textile Soc Art Inst Chicago (bd dir 84-90). *Media:* Fiber. *Dealer:* Roy Boyd Gallery 739 N Wells St Chicago IL. *Mailing Add:* 1302 Davis St Evanston IL 60201

WILSON, BEN
PAINTER, LECTURER
b Philadelphia, Pa, June 23, 13. *Study:* Nat Acad Design, 31-33; City Col NY, with Eggers, BSS, 35; Acad Julien, Paris, France, 53-54. *Work:* Everhart Mus, Scranton, Pa; Fairleigh Dickinson Collection Self Portraits; Norfolk Mus, Va; Faberge Collection, Ridgefield, NJ; Almeras Collection, Paris. *Exhib:* Riverside Mus, 55; Newark Mus, 56, Triennial, 61; nine exhibs, Montclair Mus, 56-72; Everhart Mus, 65 & 66; NJ Pavilion, New York World's Fair, 65-66; one-man shows, Bergen Community Mus, NJ, 74 & United First Federal, Sarasota, Fla, 85; Foster Harmon Galleries Art, Sarasota, Fla, 85-86; Archives American Art, Smithsonian Inst, Washington, DC, 86; Abstract Expressionist Tendencies, 1955-1965, Princeton Gallery Fine Art, NJ; retrospective exhib, Three Decades of Painting 1960-1990, Benjamin Cardozo Sch Art, Yeshiva Univ, & Brookdale Ctr New York, 90. *Pos:* Art critic, TAO, 76-77. *Teaching:* Instr painting & drawing, City Col New York, 46-48; instr life drawing, Jamesine Franklin Sch Art, 50; lectr mod art, NY Univ, 62-68; instr, Art Ctr of Northern NJ, 65-68. *Awards:* Agnes B Noyes Award for Watercolor, 59 & Skinner Award for Abstract Oils, 63, Montclair Mus; Ford Found Resident Artist, Everhart Mus, 65. *Bibliog:* Bugatti (auth), International Encyclopedia of Artists, Univ Europa, 70-71. *Mem:* Mod Artists Guild (vpres, 63); Assoc Artists NJ. *Media:* Oil. *Publ:* Auth, Cobra, Artists Proof, 66. *Dealer:* Galerie A G rue de l'universite, Paris, France; Princeton Gallery of Fine Art Princeton NJ. *Mailing Add:* Two Mt Herman Rd Blairstown NJ 07825

WILSON, CARRIE LOIS
LECTURER
b Philadelphia, Pa, Sept 15, 44. *Study:* Barnard Col, Columbia Univ, BA(art hist), 66; philosophy of Aesthetic Realism with its founder, Eli Siegel, 69-78, with class chmn, Ellen Reiss, 78- *Pos:* Co-dir, Terrain Gallery, 72-84, dir, 84-88, comt, 88- *Teaching:* Consult & instr, Aesthetic Realism Found, 72- *Publ:* Contribr, Goodbye Profit System: Update, Definition Press, New York, 82; The Two Ways of Self, The Right of Aesthetic Realism to Be Known, 4/83; The Self, Awake and Asleep, The Right of, 10/11/89; We Want to Like the World, The Right of, 9/12/90; We Want Humility and Pride, The Right of, 8/26/92. *Mailing Add:* 99 E 4th St #5J New York NY 10003

WILSON, CHARLES BANKS
PAINTER, PRINTMAKER
b Springdale, Ark, Aug 6, 18. *Study:* Art Inst Chicago, lithography with Francis Chapin, painting with Louis Ritman & Boris Anisfeld & watercolor

with Hubert Ropp; Univ Okla, DSc, 76. *Work:* Metrop Mus Art, New York; Corcoran Gallery Art, Washington, DC; Gilcrease Inst Am Hist & Art, Tulsa, Okla; US Capitol Speaker's Gallery; Smithsonian Inst, Washington, DC; mural, Roots of Oklahoma, State Capital Bldg Rotunda; Will Rogers Mem Mus. *Comn:* 50 Watercolors, Ford Motor Co, 51-69; oil mural, comn by J D Rockefeller, Jr, Jackson Lake Lodge, Wyo, 55; portraits of Thomas Gilcrease, Gilcrease Inst Am Hist & Art, 57, Will Rogers, Okla Press Asn, Oklahoma City, 61, Sen Robert Kerr & Jim Thorpe; rotunda murals, Okla State Legis, 63 & Okla Capitol, 76; and others. *Exhib:* Int Watercolor Exhib, Art Inst Chicago, 39; Am Watercolor Exhib, Springfield, Mo, 70; some 200 nat & regional exhibs. *Teaching:* Head art, Northeastern Okla Agr & Mech Col, 47-60. *Awards:* Gov's Art Award, 76; Okla Hall of Fame, 77; Nat Cowboy Hall Fame, 79. *Bibliog:* Hold before the young, Okla Today, 69 & 88; Painting mural portraits, Am Artist, 11/69; Before death do us part, Wash Post Mag, 81. *Media:* Mixed. *Publ:* illusr, Treasure Island, 48, Company of Adventures, 49, Mustangs, 52 & Geronimo, 58; auth, Search For the Purebloods, 83; The Lithographs of Charles Banks Wilson, Univ Okla Press, 89; Oklahoma Portrait Gilcrease Mus, 89. *Mailing Add:* 100 N Main St Miami OK 74354

WILSON, CHARLES H
SCULPTOR
b New Orleans, La, 37. *Study:* La State Univ, BA, 59; Yale Univ, MFA, 63. *Exhib:* Whitney Mus Am Art, New York, 65; solo exhibs, Kenegis Gallery, Boston, 65, 66 & 68 & Marianne Deson Gallery, Chicago, Ill, 80, 83, 86, 88 & 89; New Britian Mus Am Art, Conn, 68; De Paul Univ, Chicago, 72; Contemp Arts Ctr, Cincinnati, Ohio, 80; Touchstone Gallery, New York, 81; BMW Gallery, New York, 90. *Bibliog:* Hannah Dresner (auth), Edith Altman/Charles Wilson: Marianne Deson Gallery, New Art Examiner, summer 83; Richard Christiansen, Charles Wilson: Review, Chicago Tribune, 6/18 & 3/12/81; Alan Artner, Charles Wilson, Chicago Tribune, 3/18/88. *Mailing Add:* c/o Dart Gallery Inc 712 N Carpenter Chicago IL 60622

WILSON, CLARENCE S, JR
CONSULTANT-ARTS LAWYER, PATRON
b Brooklyn, New York, Oct 22, 45. *Study:* Williams Col, Williamstown, Mass, BA, 67; Northwestern Univ Sch Law, Chicago, JD, 74. *Pos:* Trustee, Chicago Symphony Orchestra, 87-; pres, Lawyers for Creative Arts, 87 & 88; trustee, MERIT Music Program; trustee, Art Inst Chicago, 90-; trustee, sculpture Chicago, 92- *Teaching:* Adj prof Law, Chicago-Kent Col Law, 81- *Mem:* Ill Arts Coun, 83-89; Arts Midwest, 83-89. *Interests:* Masterworks by Americans of African Descent, Latin America, Chicago. *Publ:* Contribr, Visual Arts & the Law, in the book, Law & the Arts-Art & the Law, 79. *Mailing Add:* 5555 S Everett Ave Unit A-9 Chicago IL 60637-1968

WILSON, CYNTHIA LINDSAY
PAINTER
b Washington, DC, May 3, 45. *Study:* Auburn Univ, BFA, 67; studied with Frank Webb & Charles Reid, 82 & Al Brouillette, 86. *Work:* Ga Tech Coll, Atlanta; US Tobacco Co, Conn; Fairfield Univ, Conn. *Exhib:* Catharine Lorillard Wolfe Art Exhib, Nat Arts Club, New York, 87, 90, 91 & 92; 89th Ann Open Watercolor Exhib, Nat Arts Club, 88; Pa Watercolor Soc Ann Exhib, Mechanicsburg, 89, 90 & 92; Adirondack's Nat Exhib Am Watercolors, Old Forge, NY, 89; Am Artists Prof League Exhib, Salmagundi Club, New York, 89 & 90; 1990 Am Realism Competition, Parkersburg Art Ctr, WVa, 90; New Eng Watercolor Soc N Am Open Exhib, Boston, 90; Salmagundi Non Member Exhib, Salmagundi Club, New York, 90 & 91; Springfield Art League Nat Exhib, Springfield Mus Fine Arts, Mass, 92; Nat Acad Design Ann Exhib, New York, 92. *Awards:* First Prize Watercolor, Spectrum 1991, New Canaan Soc Arts, 91; First Prize Watercolor, Fairfield Festival Arts, 92; Margaret Hamlin Mem Award, Acad Artists, 92. *Mem:* Nat Asn Women Artists; Pa Watercolor Soc; Am Artists Prof League; NY Artists Equity; Catharine Lorillard Wolfe Art Club (bd dirs). *Media:* Acrylic. *Mailing Add:* 2 Side Hill Rd Westport CT 06880

WILSON, DAVID PHILIP
PAINTER
b Monongahela, Pa, Aug 12, 09. *Study:* Carnegie Inst Technol Col Painting & Design, BFA; Child-Walker Sch Art, scholar in portrait painting with Charles Hopkinson. *Work:* Ohio Hist Mus, Wapakoneta; State Capitol Collection, Austin, Tex; Ohio State Capitol Bldg, Columbus; WVa Capitol Bldg; Wapakoneta Space Mus; and others. *Comn:* Numerous portraits of influential persons, including government officials, corporate executives, college & university presidents & deans & noted medical men. *Exhib:* New Directions, Carnegie Mus, Pittsburgh; Art Inst Chicago All Am Show & Nat Traveling Exhib; Cleveland Mus Art May Shows, 46 & 47; also numerous pvt shows. *Teaching:* Instr compos, Cleveland Inst Art, 46-48; artist-in-residence portrait painting, Trinity Univ, 63-68. *Mem:* Coppini Acad Fine Arts, Tex; Chagrin Falls Art Asn, Ohio (pres-founder, 47-49). *Media:* Oil, Pastel. *Publ:* Auth, Portrait of a portrait painter, Columbus Dispatch Mag, 82. *Mailing Add:* 201 Viking Way Naples FL 33942

WILSON, DOUGLAS FENN
PAINTER, SCULPTOR
b Orinda, Calif, July, 18, 53. *Study:* Dartmouth Col, Hanover, NH, BA, 75. *Work:* Fine Arts Mus San Francisco, Calif; Worcester Art Mus, Mass; Minneapolis Mus Art, Minn. *Comn:* Constructed paintings, The Hibernia Bank, 79, Dean Witter Reynolds, 83 & Bay West Development Co, 85, San Francisco, Calif; constructed painting, Deloitte, Haskins & Sells, New York, NY, 86. *Exhib:* 30 Watercolors & Pastels, Worcester Art Mus, Mass, 76; 20 Watercolors & Pastels, Dartmouth Col, Hanover, NH, 76; Recent Acquistions, Fine Arts Mus San Francisco, 77; Fishabach Gallery, New York, NY, 82; Contemporary Images, Univ Wis, Oshkosh, 83; John Pence Gallery, San Francisco, 84; Jan Cicero Gallery, Chicago, Ill, 85. *Awards:* Marcus Hieman Achievement Award, 75, Marcus Hieman Proj Grant, 75 & Dartmouth Gen Fel, 79, Dartmouth Col. *Media:* Watercolor, Acrylic. *Mailing Add:* Box 848 Glen Ellen CA 95442

WILSON, EDWARD N
SCULPTOR, EDUCATOR
b Baltimore, Md, Mar 28, 25. *Study:* Univ Iowa, BA & MA; Univ NC. *Work:* Howard Univ; State Univ NY Binghamton; JFK Mem Maquettes Collection, San Francisco Mus; and numerous pvt collections. *Comn:* Fred Douglass Competition, US Dept Interior, Nat Park Serv, 1/2 Life Size Fig, Harper's Ferry, WVa, 78-79; The Schomburg Collection Award Medal (bronze), New York, 79-80; Jazz Musicians (bronze), City Baltimore, 82-83; Whitney M Young Jr (bronze busts), 87-88; Medgar Evers (bronze bust), M Evers Col, City Univ NY, Brooklyn, 90. *Exhib:* 155th Ann Exhib Am Painting & Sculpture, Pa Acad Fine Arts & Detroit Inst Arts, 60; Am Negro Art, Univ Calif, Davis, 66, San Diego & Oakland, Calif, 67; Artists Cent New York, Munson-Williams-Proctor Mus, 66-68; 30 Contemporary Black Artists, nat circulated, 68-70; 200 Yrs Black Am Art, nat circulated, 76-77; and others. *Pos:* Resident artist, Humanities Div, Western Mich Univ, 69. *Teaching:* Prof sculpture, State Univ NY Binghamton, 64-, chmn dept art & art hist, 68-72 & 82-85. *Awards:* Award for Sculpture, Md Artists 24th Ann, Baltimore Mus Art, 56; Purchase Prize for Sculpture, New Vistas in Am Art, Howard Univ, 61; Fel, State Univ NY, 66-68. *Bibliog:* Cedric Dover (auth), American Negro art, NY Graphic Soc, 60; Art & rebuttal, Christian Sci Monitor, 4/21/71; H Hope (auth), article in, Art J, spring Vol 31, No 3. *Mem:* Col Art Asn Am (bd dirs, 70, secy & chmn artists comt, 71-76). *Media:* All. *Publ:* Auth, Contemporary sculpture: some trends & problems, 63; Statement, Arts in Soc, fall-winter, 68-69; CAA & Negro colleges, Art J, winter 68-69. *Mailing Add:* Dept of Art & Art Hist State Univ of New York Binghamton NY 13901

WILSON, EVAN CARTER
PAINTER
b Tuscaloosa, Ala, Oct 31, 53. *Study:* NC Sch Arts, 70-73; Col Art, Md Inst, with Joseph Sheppard, 72-75; Schuler Sch Fine Art, 75-76. *Work:* Altos de Chavon, La Romana, Dominican Republic; Gulf States Paper Corp, Tuscaloosa, Ala. *Comn:* Oil portraits, Congressman Walter Flowers, Ala, 75, George A LeMaistre (chmn, FDIC), 84 & Vahakn Hovnanian, Red Bank, NJ, 84; Interior paintings, Mildred Warner House, Tuscaloosa, Ala, 91; Landscape paintings, comn by Jack Warner, Tuscaloosa, Ala, 92. *Exhib:* Mid-Year Show, Butler Mus Art, Youngstown, Ohio, 74 & 90; Royal Portrait Soc, Mall Galleries, London, Eng, 80; solo exhib, Altos de Chavon, La Romana, Dominican Repub, 82; Annual Shows, Nat Arts Club, 84 & Knickerbocker Artists, 85, New York, NY; Montgomery Mus Fine Art, Ala, 91; John Pence Gallery, San Francisco, 90; JR Leigh Gallery, Tuscaloosa, Ala, 92. *Awards:* Greenshields Award, Greenshields Found, Montreal, 78; Artist-in-residence, Gulf & Western, Inc, 82; Gold Medal, Knickerbocker Artists, 86; Malcom Tuttle Award, Ann Mem Exhib, Salmagundi Club, 87. *Bibliog:* Ben Windham (auth), Ransom and Evan Wilson, Arts Review, Univ Ala, summer 84; Sonny Tiedeman (auth), Festival Brushstrokes, Horizon Mag, 1-2/86. *Mem:* Salmagundi Club; Knickerbocker Artists, New York; Portraits, Inc, New York. *Media:* Oil, Watercolor. *Publ:* Auth, Sizing up a portrait, 86 & The Italian lesson, 86, Artists Mag; Create a World Inside a Painting, Am Artist, 11/90. *Dealer:* John Pence Gallery San Francisco CA; JR Leigh Gallery Tuscaloosa AL. *Mailing Add:* Box 319A Chenaille Lane Cambridge NY 12816

WILSON, FRED
SCULPTOR
b Bronx, NY, 1954. *Work:* New Sch Social Res, New York. *Exhib:* Solo exhibs, Biennial, Cairo, Egypt, 92, Panta Rhei, Gallary Ancient Classical Art, Metro Pictures, 92, Mining the Museum, Contemp & Md Hist Soc, Baltimore, and others; group exhibs, The Big Nothing, New Mus, New York, 92; In Celebration of Purim, Jewish Mus, New York; Translation, Warsaw, Poland; and many others. *Pos:* Cur, Bronx Coun Arts, 90; lectr, Hirschorn Mus, 91, Whitney Mus, 91, Bard Col, 92, New Mus, New York, 92; and many others. *Awards:* Fel Sculpture, NY Found Arts, 91; Nat Endowment Arts, Inter-Arts/Artist Projects, 90; Riverside South Public Art Comn, Public Park Project, New York, 92. *Bibliog:* Michael Kimmelman (auth), An Improbable Marriage of Artist & Museum, NY Times, 8/2/92; Donald Kuspit (auth), The Magic Kingdom of the Museum, Art Forum, 4/92; and many others. *Mem:* Artists Space (bd dirs, 88-); Nat Asn Artists Orgns (bd dirs, 88-); Nat Endowment Arts, Inter-Arts Prog (panelist, 89-); and others. *Mailing Add:* 405 E 13 St New York NY 10009

WILSON, HELENA (HELENA CHAPELLIN WILSON)
PHOTOGRAPHER
b Caracas, Venezuela. *Study:* Inst de Dibujo Tecnico y Arquitectura; Columbia Col, Chicago, BA, 76. *Work:* New Orleans Mus Art, La; Ill State Mus, Springfield; Art Institute of Chicago, Mus Contemp Photog, Chicago, Ill; Galeria de Arte Nacional & Museo de Bellas Arts, Caracas, Venezuela. *Exhib:* Hecho en Venezuela, Mus Arte Contemp, Caracas, 78; solo exhibs, Marianne Deson Galler, Chicago, Ill, 81, Hewlitt Gallery, Carnegie-Melon Univ, 83, Galeria de Art Nacional, Caracas, Venezuela, 90; Illinois Photographers 1985, Ill State Mus, Springfield, 85; Clarence John Laughlin Collection, New Orleans Mus Art, La, 89. *Pos:* Artist and designer, 60-; mem, comt on photog, Art Inst Chicago, currently. *Awards:* Photography Award, Univ Iowa, 75. *Bibliog:* Hans Neumann (auth), Fotografias, El Nacional, Caracas, Venezuela, 7/29/90. *Publ:* Contribr, Women Photograph Men, William Morrow, 77; auth, Basic gum bichromate printing, Darkroom Techniques, 6/81. *Mailing Add:* 5555 S Everett Ave Unit No A-9 Chicago IL 60637

WILSON, JANE
PAINTER
b Seymour, Iowa, Apr 29, 24. *Study:* Univ Iowa, BA & MA. *Work:* Mus Mod Art, Metrop Mus Art, Whitney Mus Am Art, New York; Wadsworth Atheneum, Hartford, Conn; Hirshhorn Mus, Washington, DC; and many others. *Exhib:* Whitney Mus Am Art, New York, 61, 63 & 68; Am Women of the 20th Century, Lakeview Ctr Arts & Sci, 72; Painterly Realism in Am, A J Wood Gallery, Philadelphia, Pa, 79; The Fifties: Hirshhorn Mus, 80; plus many others. *Teaching:* Instr art hist, Pratt Inst, 67-69; instr painting and drawing, Fine Arts Division, Parsons Sch Design, 73-; prof, Dept Painting & Sculpture, Sch Arts, Columbia Univ, 75-88, acting chmn, 86-88. *Awards:* Tiffany Grant, 67; Ranger Fund Purchase Prize, 78; Award in Art, Acad Arts & Letters, 81. *Mem:* Nat Acad Design; Skowhegan Sch, Bd Gov Coun. *Mailing Add:* Fischbach Gallery 24 W 57th St New York NY 10019

WILSON, JEAN S
MUSEUM DIRECTOR, HISTORIAN
b Lakeland, Fla. *Study:* Metropolitan State Col, Denver, Colo, BA, 79; Univ Denver, Color, MA, 82. *Collections Arranged:* Personal Landscapes; Art Quilts and Wearable Art, FACET, 90; Third Wyoming Biennial, 89; Paper Innovations, Am Mus Asn, 87. *Pos:* Educ dept, Denver Art Mus, 81-82; asst cur, Colo Gallery Arts, 83-85, dir/cur, 85- *Mem:* Colo Art Educ Asn (currently, state bd); Am Asn Mus; Small Mus Asn. *Res:* Renaissance and early modern art. *Mailing Add:* Arapahoe Community Col Colo Gallery of Arts PO Box 9002 Littleton CO 80160

WILSON, JOHN
SCULPTOR, PRINTMAKER
b Boston, Mass, Apr 14, 22. *Study:* Sch Mus Fine Arts, Boston, dipl; Tufts Univ, BS(educ); Fernand Leger's Sch, Paris; Inst Politecnico, Esmeralda Sch Art & Escuela Artes del Libro, Mexico City. *Work:* Mus Fine Arts, Boston; Smith Col Mus Art, Northampton, Mass; Mus Mod Art, New York; Atlanta Univ, Ga; Dept Fine Arts, Govt France. *Comn:* Monument to Dr Martin Luther King, Jr (bronze), Buffalo Arts Comn, NY, 83; Memorial to Dr Martin Luther King, Jr (bronze statue), US Capitol, Washington, DC, 86; Father & Child (bronze monument), Roxbury Community Col, Boston. *Exhib:* Master Prints from the Mus Collections, Mus Mod Art, New York, 49; Young Am Painters, Metrop Mus Art, New York, 50; Mus Int Biennial Color Lithography, Cincinnati, Ohio, 53; Afro-American Artists, Mus Fine Arts, New York & Boston, 70; Highlights from Univ Collection, High Mus Art, Atlanta, Ga, 73. *Teaching:* Illusr art, New York Bd Educ, 59-64; prof art, Boston Univ, 64-86, prof emer, 86- *Awards:* John Hay Whitney Fel for study in Mex, 50; Best Cover Design, Int Fedn Periodicals Press, Paris, 71; Mass Arts & Humanities Found, Inc sculpture fel, 76. *Bibliog:* Edward Strickland (auth), John Wilson, Art New Eng, 2/88. *Media:* Mixed. *Publ:* Co-illusr, New Worlds of Reading, Harcourt, 59, American Negro Art, Graphic Soc, NY, 60, Who Look at Me, Crowell, NY, 69, 17 Black Artists, Dodd Mead Co, New York, 71 & Land of Progress, Ginn, 75; co-illusr, Martin Luther King Jr Sculpture, Nat Endowment Arts Rev, Vol 3, No 3, spring 86; Public Art & the Public Image, Art New Eng, 7-8/89. *Mailing Add:* 44 Harris St Brookline MA 02146

WILSON, JOHN DAVID
DEALER, PUBLISHER
b Flint, Mich, Aug 30, 34. *Study:* Mich State Univ, BA, 60; Univ Notre Dame, MA, 67. *Pos:* Dir, Lakeside Studio, formerly; pres, Chicago Int Art Exposition, currently. *Bibliog:* Judith Goldman (auth), Print establishment II, Art Am, 9-10/73; David & Cecile Shapiro (coauth), Lakeside Studio: conserving the printmaking tradition, Art News, 3/77; Charlotte Moser (auth), John Wilson brings art world to Chicago, Chicago Sun-Times, 9-11/83. *Specialty:* Original graphics, old masters, modern and contemporary. *Mailing Add:* Lakeside Studio 15251 S Lakeshore Rd Lakeside MI 49116

WILSON, JUNE
PAINTER, EDUCATOR
b Somerville, NJ, July 12, 46. *Study:* Ithaca Col, NY, 64-65; Monmouth Col, West Long Branch, NJ, BA(hons), 68; Pratt Inst, Brooklyn, NY, MFA, 72. *Work:* The Newark Mus, NJ; Aldrich Mus Contemp Art, Ridgefield, Conn; Franklin Furnace, & Jewish Mus, New York; Art & Cult Ctr, Hollywood, Fla. *Comn:* Lobby painting, Sheraton Meadowlands Hotel, NJ, 86. *Exhib:* 4th Biennial (with catalog), NJ State Mus, Trenton, 83; Time Out: Sport and Leisure in America (with catalog), Tampa Mus, Fla, 83; 5th Biennial (with catalog), Newark Mus, NJ, 85; Transfigurations, Ericson Gallery, New York, NY, 85; MASS, New Mus, New York, 86; Soho Ctr Visual Artists, New York, 87; Well Cultivated Gardens, Art in Gen & PS 122, New York & Proctor Art Ctr, Bard Col, NY, 87; Recent Acquisitions, Aldrich Mus, Ridgefield, Conn, 88; New Expressions (with catalog), Noyes Mus, NJ, 89; Mythic Moderns, Real Art Ways, Conn, 89; Contemp Gallery, Newark Mus, NJ, 90; The Arts Coun Princeton, NJ, 91. *Collections Arranged:* The Punch Line: Humor in Art, Tweed Arts Group, Plainfield, NJ, 83; Urban Spirit, City Without Walls (co-cur with Grace Graupe-Pillard), Newark, NJ, 85. *Teaching:* adj asst prof, painting & drawing, Ocean Co Col, Toms River, NJ, 76- *Awards:* NJ State Coun Arts Fel, 81 & 85. *Bibliog:* William Zimmer (auth), Boldness a feature of the Newark Show, 5/12/85, New York Times; John Loughery (auth), Well cultivated gardens, Arts Mag, 1/88; Jude Schwendenwien (auth), Well cultivated gardens, Cover Mag, 1/88; Kate Jennings (auth), Bold stroke, Fairpress, Ridgefield, Conn, 2/88; Victoria Donohoe (auth), Jessica Berwind Gallery, Philadelphia Inquirer, 7/88; The skys no limit, Miami Herald, 5/15/89; Robert Mahoney (auth), New York in Review, Arts Mag, 3/91. *Media:* Oil and Acrylic on Canvas and Paper. *Mailing Add:* 47 Brandywine Way Middletown NJ 07748

WILSON, KAREN LEC
CURATOR, DIRECTOR
b Somerville, NJ, Apr 2, 49. *Study:* Harvard Univ, AB, 71; Inst Fine Arts, NY Univ, MA, 73, PhD, 85. *Collections Arranged:* The Jews of Kaifeng, 87; Another Egypt, 90; Sifting the Sands of Time, 91. *Pos:* Cur/dir, Oriental Inst Mus, 80-; Adminr cataloguer, 82-83, Jewish Mus, NY & coordr curatorial affairs, 84-86. *Teaching:* The Art of Ancient Mesopotamia, Univ Chicago, 91- *Mem:* Col Art Asn; Am Oriental Soc; Am Res Ctr in Egypt. *Publ:* Auth & ed, Mendes, ARCE, 82; Preliminary Report Jell Geri, Sumer, 85; auth, Definition & Relative Chronology of the Jamdat Nasr Period, NY Univ, 85; Nippur: The Definition of a Mesopotamian Jamdat, AVO, 86. *Mailing Add:* Oriental Institute Museum 1155 E 58th St Chicago IL 60637

WILSON, KAY E
ADMINISTRATOR, DIRECTOR
b Rockford, Ill. *Study:* Rockford Col, BA, 72; Art Inst Chicago, Collection Mgt, Cert, 88. *Pos:* Dir, Print & Drawing Study Room, Grinnell Col, 86- *Publ:* Coauth, Jan Krejci: The Werksman Collection, Grinnell Col, 87. *Mailing Add:* Grinnell College Print and Drawing Study Room Grinnell IA 50112-0811

WILSON, MALIN
CURATOR
b Freeport, Ill, Jun 25, 47. *Study:* Univ Ariz, BA, 69; Univ Wis, MS, 75. *Work:* Toledo Mus Art, Ohio; Mus NMex, Fine Arts Division, Sante Fe; Jonson Gallery, Univ Art Mus, Albuquerque, NMex. *Collections Arranged:* Southwest Fine Arts Biennial, Mus of NMex, 78; The Virgin and the Dynamo, Sante Fe, 81; Steina Vasulka: Scapes of Paradoxy, Jonson Gallery, 86; Mullican & Mullican, Jonson Gallery, 89; Raymond Jonson: Cityscapes, Jonson Gallery, 89; Albuquerque '50s, Univ NMex Art Mus; coordr, Die Eigenwelt der Apparate-Welt: Pioniere der Elektronischen Kunst, Ars Electronica, Linz, Austria. *Pos:* Cur, Mus NMex, 77-78; Art critic, The New Mexican, Sante Fe, 84-85; Dir, Jonson Gallery, Univ Art Mus, Albuquerque, 85-89. *Mem:* New Mexico Contemp Art Soc (founding bd mem); Sante Fe Arts Comn; Art Table. *Publ:* Contribr, Steina & Woody Vasulka, Video Artists, Paris: Cine, 84; The Desert is No Lady: Visions of Landscape, Yale Univ Press, 87; Auth, William Lumpkins: 1930-1986 (catalog), Jonson Gallery, 87; contribr, The Albuquerque 50's (catalog), Univ Art Mus, 89; ed, Peter Schjeldahl: the Hydrogen Jukebox & Other Selected Writings, Univ Calif Press, 91. *Mailing Add:* 320 Aztec St Sante Fe NM 87501

WILSON, MARC F
MUSEUM DIRECTOR
b Akron, Ohio, Sept 12, 41. *Study:* Yale Col, BA, 63; Case Western Univ, Cleveland Mus Art, 63-64; Yale Univ, MA, 67; Fel, Ford Found Mus Training Prog, Nelson Gallery-Atkins Mus, Kansas City, 67-69; Study Grant, Ford Found, Japan, Taiwan, Hong Kong, 69-71; Univ Kans, 68. *Pos:* Dept asst prints & drawings, Cleveland Mus Art, 64; translr & project consult, Nat Palace Mus, Taipei, Taiwan, 68-71; assoc cur Chinese Art, dept Oriental art, Nelson Gallery-Atkins Mus, 71-73, cur Oriental art, 73-, interim dir, 82-, dir, 82-; mem ad hoc committee, Munic Art Comn Urban Sculpture, 84-; mem, China Inst Am Adv Comt, 85-; mem, Asia Soc Galleries Adv Comt, 85-; mem, K C Planning Comt Sister City, Xian, China 86-; chmn works of art comt, Asn Art Mus Dirs, 86-, arts & artifacts indemnity advisory panel, Fedn Coun Arts & Humanities 86- & Am subcomt Mus Exchanges of CULCON, 86-88; Am panel, Joint Comt Japan-US Cult & Educ Coop, 86-88; trustee & treas, Asn Art Mus dirs, 88-; mus dir, Nelson-Atkins Mus Art, Kansas City, Mo, 88- *Teaching:* Grad teaching asst, Dept Hist Art, Yale Univ, 65-66. *Publ:* Auth, The Chinese painter and his vision, Apollo, No 97, 3/73; coauth, Friends of Wen Cheng-ming, 74; auth, Potter's choice, Am Craft, Vol 40, No 4, 8-9/80; coauth, Eight Dynasties of Chinese Painting, Ind Univ Press, 80; auth, Indentification of the subject of an important scroll painting by Ma Yuan, Museum, 11/82. *Mailing Add:* Nelson-Atkins Mus Art 4525 Oak St Kansas City MO 64111

WILSON, MELISSA ANNE
SCULPTOR
b New Rochelle, NY, July 9, 68. *Study:* Silvermine Sch Art, 86-89; Wooster Art Ctr, 87-90. *Work:* Lever House, New York NY; New Britain Mus, Conn; Hillsberg Mus Collection, Indian Wells, Calif. *Exhib:* Waveny Barn Mus, New Cannan, Conn, 87, 88 & 89; All New England Show, 89 & 90; Pietrasanta, Italy, 89 & 90; Int Sculpture Show, Roxensteins, Helsingborg, Sweden, 90; Chicago Int Art Show, 90; Stanley Bleifield Asn of Fairfield, Lever House, New York, 90; Bliefield Sculpture Asn, 92; group show, Waveny Park Carriage Barn Mus, New Canaan, Conn, 92. *Awards:* First in Show, Sandi Oliver Fine Art, Weston, Conn; Best Sculpture, Casa D'Oliver, Conn, 91. *Mem:* Int Sculpture Asn; Bleifield Sculpture Asn. *Media:* Bronze, Clay. *Publ:* Bleifield Sculpture Group Catalog Raissone, Bleifield, 92. *Dealer:* Sandi Oliver Box 1203 Weston CT 06883. *Mailing Add:* c/o Sandi Oliver Fine Art Box 1203 Weston CT 06883

WILSON, MILLIE
CONCEPTUAL ARTIST, DESIGNER
b Hot Springs, Ark, Nov 26, 48. *Study:* Yale Summer Sch Music & Art; Univ Tex, Austin, BFA, 71; Univ Houston, MFA, 83. *Exhib:* Solo exhibs, Fauve Semblant: Peter (A Young English Girl), Los Angeles Contemp Exhibs, 89, Los Angeles Times Series, Univ Art Gallery, State Univ NY, Binghamton, 89, Fauve Semblant: Peter (A Young English Girl), San Francisco Camerawork, 90, Sweet Thursday, Meyers, Bloom Gallery, Santa Monica, 91, Living in Someone Else's Paradise, New Langton Arts, San Francisco, 92 & A Distrubing Emotional Coloring, White Columns, New York, 92; Multiplici Culturi: Arte Critica, Museo del Folklore, Rome, 92; We Interrupt Your

Regularly Scheduled Program, White Columns, New York, 92; The Politics of Difference: Artists Explore Issues of identity, Univ Calif, Riverside Art Mus, 92; Re-Visions, Randolph St Gallery, Chicago, 92; (Basically) Black and White, Riverside Art Mus, 92; Facing the Finish, San Francisco Mus Mod Art, Santa Barbara Contemp Arts Forum, Art Ctr Col Design, Pasadena, Calif, 92; and others. *Pos:* Dir, program art, Calif Inst Arts, 90- *Teaching:* Fel drawing, Univ Houston, 81-83; asst prof painting, Univ Ill, Urbana-Champaign, 83-85; fac, Calif Inst Arts, 85- *Awards:* Purchase Awards, Auburn Arts Asn Inc, Ala, & Ball State Univ, Muncie, Ind, 84; Merit Award, Artquest '86, 85; Calif Arts Coun Artists Fel, 92. *Bibliog:* Out Mag, 9/92; Tema Celeste, 9-10/92; Artforum, 10/92. *Mem:* Col Art Asn. *Media:* New Genres, Conceptual. *Publ:* Facing the Finish (exhibition catalog), San Francisco Mus Mod Art, 91-92; Errors of Nature, 92. *Dealer:* Ruth Bloom Gallery 2112 Broadway Santa Monica, CA 90404-2912. *Mailing Add:* Art Dept, Calif Inst Arts 24700 McBean Valencia CA 91355

WILSON, NICHOLAS JON
PAINTER
b Seattle, Wash, June 7, 47. *Work:* Walter Bimson Collection Western Art, Phoenix, Ariz; Okla Cowboy Hall of Fame, Oklahoma City. *Exhib:* Soc Animal Artists Exhib, Westport, Conn, New York & Oklahoma City, 78; Audubon Soc-Eastman Kodak Co Wildlife Exhib, New York, 78; Bird Art Exhib, Smithsonian Inst, Washington, DC, 80; Bird Art World Tour, Royal Scottish Acad, Edinburgh, Scotland, 81, British Mus, London, Eng, 81 & Carnegie Mus Natural Hist, Pittsburgh, Pa, 82; and many others. *Pos:* Cur exhib, Ariz-Sonora Desert Mus, Tucson, 70-72. *Awards:* Third Place Bronze, Royal Western Watercolor Competition, 74. *Bibliog:* Adina Wingate (auth), Nick Wilson: Wildlife Artist, Southwest Art Mag, 4/74; Wildlife Artist Nick Wilson, Outdoor Am, 6/77; Patricia Van Gelder (auth), Wildlife Artists at Work, Watson-Guptill, 83. *Media:* Gouache. *Publ:* Illusr, The Chukar Partridge, Nev Fish & Game, 69; Ariz Highways, 11/88. *Mailing Add:* 1600 W Mesa Dr Payson AZ 85541

WILSON, RICHARD BRIAN
PAINTER
b Wichita, Kans, June 12, 44. *Study:* Calif State Univ, San Jose, BA & MA. *Work:* Downey Art Mus, Calif; IBM Corp, San Jose, Calif; Mobil Oil Co, San Francisco; Am Tel & Tel Co, Chicago; Fort Steilicom Col; and others. *Exhib:* Looking West 1970, Joslin Art Mus, 70; Drawings 70: First Ann Drawing Show, St John's Univ, New York, 70; Boxtop Painting Exhib, Ill State Univ, 71; Ariz Nat Painting Competition, Scottsdale Ctr Arts, 77 & 78; Int Art Fairs, Basil & Cologne, 78; The Plannar Dimension, Civic Arts Gallery, Walnut Creek, Calif, 83; Ten California Colonists, Pomona Col, Univ NMex & Palm Desert Mus, 85-86; and others. *Pos:* Gallery dir, Shasta Col & Art Gallery, Redding, Calif, 70-; bd mem, Redding mus, 77-79. *Teaching:* Instr art, Shasta Col, Redding, Calif, 68- *Awards:* Third Prize (painting), 1st Ann Grand Galleria Nat Art Show, 72; Purchase Prize, 15th Printing Ann, Downey Mus, 72; First Prize (painting), 5th Ann North Valley Art Show, Redding, 73. *Bibliog:* Alfred Frankenstein (auth), Serene and mystic art works, San Francisco Chronicle, 11/17/72; William Wilson (auth), Art walk, Los Angeles Times, 3/5/76; Thomas Albright (auth), Art in the San Francisco Bay Area 1945-1980, Univ Calif Press, 85; and others. *Media:* Acrylic. *Dealer:* Triangle Gallery 165 Post St San Francisco CA 94108; Fong and Spriatt Galleries 383 S 1st St San Jose CA 95113. *Mailing Add:* Dept Art Shasta Col 1065 Old N Oregon Trail Redding CA 96001

WILSON, ROBERT
GRAPHIC ARTIST, DESIGNER
b Waco, Tex. *Study:* Painting with George McNeil, Paris, France, 62; Pratt Inst, New York, BFA, 65; apprenticed to Paolo Soleri, Phoenix, Ariz, 66. *Work:* Mus Mod Art, New York; Mus Mod Art, Paris, France; Australian Nat Gallery, Canberra; Stedelijk Mus, Amsterdam; Menil Collection, Houston; and others. *Exhib:* The New Figure (video works), Birmingham Mus Art, Ala, 85; High Style, Whitney Mus Am Art, New York, 85-86; The Painter and the Theater in the 20th Century, Schirn Kunsthalle Frankfurt, 86; Resolution-A Critique of Video Art, Los Angeles Contemp Exhibs, 86; Alceste, Galerie Fred Jahn, Gutersloh, WGer, 87; Drawings for the Opera 'De Materie' by Louis Andriessen, Stedelijk Mus, Amsterdam, 89; La Nuit d'Avant le Jour, Yvon Lambert, Paris, 89; Orlando, Annemarie Verna Glaerie, Zurich, 89; Drawings, Sculpture and Furniture: The Civil Wars, Virginia Lynch Gallery, Tiverton, RI, 90; Robert Wilson: Drawings and Furniture, Feigen Gallery, Chicago, 90; solo exhibits, Drawings and Furniture, John Berggruen Gallery, San Francisco, Chairs for Marie and Pierre Curie, Sigmund Freud, Albert Einstein, A Table for Njnski and Parzival Drawing, Busche Galerie, Koln Ger, Monuments, Kestner-Gesellschaft, Hannover, Lohengrin Drawings and Other Works, Annemarie Verna Galerie, Zurich, Mr Bojangales, Memory of son of fire, Centre Georges Pompidou, Paris, Robert Wilson Zeichnungen-Zyklen, Galerie Fred Jahn, Munich, 91, Robert Wilson Drawings from The White Raven, Paula Cooper Gallery, New York, 92. *Pos:* Artistic dir, Byrd Hoffman Found, 70- *Awards:* Lumen Award for Design, New York, 77; Guggenheim Fel Award, 80; Skowhegan Medal for Drawing, New York, 87. *Bibliog:* Theodore Shank (auth), American Alternative Theater, Grove Press, 82; Michael Walsh (auth), A tree grows and grows, Time Mag, 5/21/84; Howard Brookner (dir), A Minute with Bob Wilson (film), BBC, London, 85; Bice Curiger (ed), Collaboration Robert Wilson Parkett, 88. *Mem:* Am Repertory Theater (hon mem); PEN Am Ctr; Dramatist Guild; trustee Nat Int Music Theater; Soc des Auteurs et Compositeurs Dramatiques. *Publ:* Contribr, Swan Song (play), Kammerspiele Theater, Munich, 90; Konig Lear (play), Schauspiel, Frankfurt, 90; The Black Rider: The Casting of the Magic Bullets (play), Theatre Musical de Paris, Le Chatelet; When We Dead Awake (play), Am Repertory Theatre, Boston, 91. *Mailing Add:* c/o Paula Cooper Gallery 155 Wooster Street New York NY 10012

WILSON, ROBERT ALAN
GALLERY DIRECTOR, MURALIST
b Windsor, Ont, Can, Feb 6, 49; US citizen. *Study:* Col San Mateo, AA, 69; Calif State Univ, Chico, BA, 72, MA, 76. *Work:* Erie Pub Mus, Pa. *Comn:* Celebration (mural), J F Kennedy Community Ctr, Erie, Pa, 80; Chapmantown (mural), Chico Area Recreation & Park Dist, Calif, 81; Recreation (mural), Calif Arts Coun, Chico, 82; mural, Murdock Elementary Sch, Williams, Calif, 82. *Exhib:* Downtown Dog Show, Fine Arts Show, Fine Arts Mus, San Francisco, Calif, 78; Washington & Jefferson Col Nat Painting Show, Washington, Pa, 79; California Works, Calif State Fair, Sacramento, 82; Western Figurative Realism, Cypress Col Gallery, Calif, 83; Calgene Fine Arts Competition, Natsoulos/Novelozo Gallery, Davis, Calif, 88. *Pos:* Coordr, Multicultural Arts Coun, 76-; exec dir, Chico Arts Ctr, Calif, 83-87; art cur, Redding Mus & Art Ctr, Calif, 87- *Teaching:* Instr art hist & painting, Am Col, Leysin, Switz, 76-77; instr art hist, Butte Community Col, 86-87; instr art hist (ethnic), Shasta Community Col, 90- *Dealer:* Candy Store Gallery 605 Sutter St Folsom CA 95630. *Mailing Add:* Redding Mus & Art Ctr PO Box 427 Redding CA 96099

WILSON, SYBIL
PAINTER, GRAPHIC ARTIST
b Tulsa, Okla, Mar 20, 23. *Study:* Art Students League, with Ernest Fiene; Yale Univ Sch Art & Archit, with Josef Albers, BFA & MFA; also with Anni Albers. *Work:* NY Univ Collection; Univ Ky Collection; Univ Mass Collection; Univ Bridgeport Collection; Chase Manhattan Bank Collection; and others. *Exhib:* One-man shows, Grand Cent Mod Gallery, New York, 62 & 65, East Hampton Gallery, New York, 70 & Woods, Gerry Gallery, RI Sch Design, 72; Retinal Art in US Traveling Exhib, 66. *Teaching:* Prof art, Univ Bridgeport, 54-78; adj prof art, RI Sch Design, 70-72. *Awards:* Am Inst Graphic Arts 50 Best Bks Award, 60. *Media:* Acrylic, Oil. *Publ:* Designer & publ, Anni Albers: On Designing, Pellango Press, 60. *Dealer:* Elaine Benson Gallery Bridgehampton NY. *Mailing Add:* 27251 Ellwood Dr Bonita Springs FL 33923

WILSON, TOM
CARTOONIST
b Grant Town, WVa, Aug 1, 31. *Study:* Art Inst Pittsburgh, dipl. *Pos:* Designer, Am Greetings Corp, Cleveland, 55-56, vpres creative div, 57-78, vpres creative develop, 78-81, vpres, ideas dept, 87-; pres, Those Characters from Cleveland, formerly; cartoonist, Ziggy, currently; pres, Ziggy & Friends Inc, 87- *Teaching:* Mem fac, Cooper Sch Art, formerly. *Awards:* Butler Mus Nat Painting Competition Purchase Award. *Mailing Add:* Am Greeting Corp 10500 American Rd Cleveland OH 44144

WILSON, TOM MUIR
DESIGNER
b Bellaire, Ohio, Dec 6, 30. *Study:* WVa Inst Technol; Cranbrook Acad Art, BFA; Rochester Inst Technol, MFA. *Exhib:* One-man shows, Rochester, NY & Wheeling, WVa, 57, 59 & 61; Boston Art Festival, 61; Photog Exhib, George Eastman House, Rochester, 63; Western NY Ann, Buffalo, 63 & 64; Art of Two Cities, Minneapolis, 65; and others. *Pos:* Designer exhib galleries, George Eastman House Mus Photog, 61-62; freelance photogr & graphic designer, New York, Rochester & Minneapolis, 61- *Teaching:* Prof art & instr photog & graphic design, Minneapolis Sch Art, formerly; instr photog, Rochester Inst Technol, assoc prof photog arts, 77-; instr sculpture & design, Nazareth Col, Rochester. *Awards:* Award for Sculpture, Art Inst Am Inst Architects, 56; Prize, Philadelphia Print Club, 61. *Media:* Graphic. *Mailing Add:* 6776 Warboys Rd Byron NY 14422

WILSON, WALLACE
PHOTOGRAPHER, EDUCATOR
b Dallas, Tex, June 10, 47. *Study:* Univ Tex, Austin, BA, 70; pvt study with Ralph Eugene Meatyeard, Lexington, Ky, 71-72; Art Inst Chicago, MFA, 75. *Work:* Mus Mod Art, New York; Art Inst Chicago; Baltimore Mus Art, Md; Bibliotheque Nationale, Paris; Brooklyn Mus, New York. *Exhib:* One-man shows, Baltimore Mus Art, 76, OK Harris, NY, 77 & 87, Photogalerie Lange-Irschl, Munich, WGer, 79, Marcuse Pfeifer Gallery, NY, 87 & 89, The Tartt Gallery, Washington, DC, 87, 90 & 92, The Photographers Gallery, London, 89, Robert Klein Gallery, Boston, 91, Southeast Mus Photog, Daytona Beach, Fla, 93. *Teaching:* Asst prof photog & design, Univ Del, 75-79; prof art & contemp criticism, Univ Fla, 79. *Awards:* Individual Artists Fel, State Fla, 82 & 88. *Bibliog:* Fred McDarrah (auth), Voice Choices, Village Voice, 10/10/77; Vince Aletti (auth), Voice Choices, Village Voice, 11/10/87 & 12/12/89; Pamela Kessler (auth), The Washington Post, 9/19/89. *Mem:* Soc Photog Educ. *Publ:* Contribr, Camera, Bucher Press, Zurich, Switz, 73; Fifteen Photographs in Color, Mancini Gallery, 78; Artwords and Bookworks, Los Angeles Inst Contemp Art, 78; Victims of Paradox, by Alison Nordstrom, Southeast Mus Photog, 92. *Dealer:* The Tartt Gallery Washington DC. *Mailing Add:* 1424 NW Twelfth Road Gainesville FL 32605

WILSON, WARREN BINGHAM
EDUCATOR, SCULPTOR
b North Farmington, Utah, Nov 4, 20. *Study:* Utah State Univ, BS(educ); State Univ Iowa, MFA(sculpture). *Work:* Utah State Univ, Logan; Utah Capitol Bldg Collection, Salt Lake City; Utah State Fair Asn, Salt Lake City; Brigham Young Univ, Provo, Utah; State Univ Iowa, Iowa City, plus others. *Comn:* Exterior steel sculpture, Holladay Law Offices, Pocatello, Idaho, 60 & Utah State Training Sch, 62. *Exhib:* Ann Painting & Sculpture Exhib, Denver Art Mus, 51; Traveling Show of Utah Artists, Santa Fe Art Mus, 53; Ceramic & Sculpture Exhib, Wichita Art Ctr, 60; Ceramic Conjunction, Brand Art Ctr, Glendale, Calif, 73; one-man show, Traveling Exhib of Wood

Sculpture, Western Asn of Art Mus through Western States, 62-64; 20-Year Restrospective, Brigham Young Univ, 70; plus many others. *Teaching:* Asst prof sculpture & printmaking, Utah State Univ, 49-54; prof sculpture & ceramics, Brigham Young Univ, 54-83; vis lectr ceramics, Univ Calif, Davis, 68. *Awards:* Purchase Award, Ann Fine Arts Exhib, Utah State Inst of Fine Arts & Fine Arts Exhib, Utah State Fair Bd, 52; Fel Resident, Huntington Hartford Found, 61. *Bibliog:* Articles in Craftsmen of the Southwest, 65; Margaret Ellis (auth), Vessels of the Lord, The New Era, LDS Church, 73; articles in Primitive Pottery in Provo, 74. *Mem:* Southwest Regional Assembly of Craftsmen (Utah rep, 61-65); Utah Designer Craftsmen (pres, 63-65); Art Teachers in Higher Educ, Nat Art Educ Asn (Utah chmn, 69-73); Nat Coun on Educ for the Ceramic Arts. *Media:* Wood, Clay. *Mailing Add:* 1000 Briar Ave Provo UT 84601

WILSON, WILLIAM S, III
CRITIC
b Baltimore, Md, Apr 7, 32. *Study:* Univ Va, BA, 53; Yale Univ, MA, 56, PhD, 61. *Teaching:* Prof, Queens Col, 61- *Res:* Color and language. *Publ:* Auth, Robert Morris: Hard questions and soft answers, 69 & Dan Flavin: Fiat lux, 70, Art News; John Willenbecher: Pyramids and labyrinths, Arts, 75; Ralph Humphrey: An apology for painting, Artforum, 77; Cezanne's Rapport, Antaeus, 54, 85. *Mailing Add:* 458 W 25th St New York NY 10001

WILSON, YORK
PAINTER, MURALIST
b Toronto, Can, Dec 6, 07. *Study:* Cent Tech Sch, Toronto; Ont Col Art; Art Inst Detroit; self taught. *Work:* Uffizi Gallery, Florence, Italy; Mus Mod Art, Mexico City; Birla Acad Art & Cult, Calcutta, India; Mus Dijon, France; all major Can galleries. *Comn:* Mural, Imperial Oil, Toronto, 57; murals, O'Keefe Ctr Performing Arts, Toronto, 59; mural, Thunder Bay Gen Hosp, 65; mural, Ont Govt, Toronto, 68; mural, Carleton Univ, Ottawa, 70. *Exhib:* Solo exhibs, Circulo de Bellas Artes, Tenerife, Spain, 52, Univ Toronto, 54 & 74, Art Gallery Ont, Toronto, 59, Musee Galliera, Paris, 63, Palacio Bellas Artes, Mexico City, 69 & Bellas Artes, San Miguel Allende, Mex, 70; Pittsburgh Int, Carnegie Inst, 52; L'Art au Canada, Bordeaux, France, 62; VII Bienal Sao Paulo, Brazil, 63; Salon Confrontation, Dijon, France, 64; Eminent Artists World, Birla Acad Art & Cult, Calcutta, India, 70; retrospectives, Art Gallery Sarnia, Ont, 65 & 74, Confederation Ctr, Charlottetown, PEI, 65, Art Gallery Stratford, 74, London Mus, 75, Robert McLaughlin Gallery, Oshawa, 75, Art Gallery Windsor, Ont, 79 & Moore Gallery, Hamilton, 92; and others. *Pos:* Pres, Ont Soc Artists, 46-48 & Can Group Painters, 70. *Teaching:* Instr painting & drawing, Artist Wkshp, Art Gallery, Ont, 44-55, Ont Col Art, 44-45 & Doon Sch Fine Arts, summer 49-54. *Awards:* UNESCO Award, 69; Ont Soc Artists Award, 83; Ital Acad Award, 84. *Bibliog:* Mural (film), Crawley Films, Imperial OilLtd, 57; Michael Foyteni (dir), York Wilson (film), Nat Film Bd, Can Broadcasting, 62; Paul Duval & Marshall McLuhan (auth), York Wilson, Wallack Galleries, Ottawa, 78. *Mem:* Royal Can Acad; Ont Soc Artists (pres, 46-48); Salon Confrontation, France; Can Group Painter (pres, 67-); and others. *Media:* Oil, Acyrlic; Murals-Vinyl Acetate, Mosaics. *Publ:* Contribr, Murals, In: World Book Encyclopedia, 63; illusr, Face at the Bottom of the World, Hagiwara Sakutaro, Tuttle, Japan, 67; contribr, The Can Collection, Art Gallery Ont, McGraw-Hill, 70, Paul Duval's Four Decades, Clarke Irwin, 72, Contemp Personalities, Ital Acad & Res Ctr, Italy, 83; Paul Duval (auth), York Wilson, Wallack Galleries, 78. *Dealer:* Wallack Galleries 203 Bank St Ottawa ON Can K2P 1W7; Moore Gallery 34 Hess St Hamilton ON Canada L8P 3N1. *Mailing Add:* 41 Alcina Ave Toronto ON M6G 2E7 Canada

WILSON-HAMMOND, CHARLOTTE EMILY
VISUAL ARTIST, PRINTMAKER
b Montreal, Que, Nov 19, 41. *Study:* Ind Univ, 62; art schs, Toronto, 66-68. *Work:* Art Gallery NS & Royal Trust Corp, Halifax; Confederation Ctr Arts, Charlottetown, PEI; Shell Energy Sources Can, Calgary, Alta; Norcen Energy Corp, Toronto. *Comn:* Drawings for feature film, Life Classes, William MacGillivrey, producer, 87. *Exhib:* Mt St Vincent Univ Traveling Exhib, 77-78; Dalhousie Univ, Halifax, 79; World's Fair, Osaka, Japan, 79; Confederation Ctr Arts, Charlottetown, PEI, 80-81; Centre for Art Tapes, Halifax, 88; Naked/Nude, A Twenty Year Survey, Art Gallery NS, 90. *Pos:* bd mem, NS Col Arts & Design, Halifax, 87-; bd dirs, Vis Art Copyright Inc. *Teaching:* Artist in residence, Holland Col, PEI, 80. *Awards:* Can Coun Explorations Grant, 85; NS Dept Cult Grant, 85. *Bibliog:* Article, Arts Atlantic, 79, Video Still Paint, 87, rev, 90; Reshard Gool (auth), article, Arts Mag, 81; Maria Tippett (auth), Three Centuries of Canadian Women Artists, Penoun, 10/92. *Mem:* Can Artists Representation; Visual Arts NS (chmn, 78-79); Women Arts (organizer, 80-); Can Conf of Arts-Coun of Candians; bd mem NS Col Art & Design, Helifax, 87- *Media:* Oil, Conte; Multimedia. *Mailing Add:* RR1 Lake Charlotte Clam Harbour NS B0J 1Y0 Canada

WILTRAUT, DOUGLAS SCOTT
PAINTER
b Allentown, Pa, July 12, 51. *Study:* Kutztown Univ, Pa, BFA(painting), 73. *Work:* Philip & Muriel Berman Mus Art, Collegeville, Pa; Yale Law Sch Libr, New Haven, Conn; Binney & Smith Corp, Easton, Pa; Pentamation Corp, Bethlehem, Pa; Pa Dept Educ, Harrisburg. *Comn:* Portrait, Myres McDougal, Yale Law Sch, New Haven, Conn, 76. *Exhib:* 26th Ann Nat Soc Painters Casein & Acrylic, Am Inst Arts, Letters, New York, 79; 84th Ann Open Watercolor Ehib, Nat Arts Club, New York, 84; 50th Anniversary Midyear Exhib, Butler Inst Am Art, Youngstown, Ohio, 86; 153rd Ann Exhib, Nat Acad Design, New York, 88; Inaugural Exhib, Philip & Muriel Berman Mus Art, Collegeville, Pa, 90. *Pos:* Exhib chmn, Nat Soc Painters Casein & Acrylic, 87-90 & pres 89-; Audubon Artists Inc, 88-90. *Awards:* Ralph Fabri Medal, 72nd & 74 Ann Exhibs, Allied Artists Am, 85-87; Butler Inst Am Art Award, 50th Anniversary Midyear, Butler Inst Am Art, 86; Gold Medal Honor, 38th Ann Knickerbocker Artists, Knickerbocker Artists, 88. *Bibliog:* Ralph Fabri (auth), Youngest medal winner, Today's Art Mag, 75; Marilyn Roberts (auth), Artists Profile: Douglas Wiltraut, Gallery Arts, 83; Valerie R Rivers (auth), Douglas Wiltraut, Am Artist Mag, 88. *Mem:* Nat Soc Painters Casein & Acrylic (dir, 77-86 & pres, 89); Allied Artists Am; Audubon Artists Inc (exhib chmn, 88-90 & sr vice pres, 89); Knickerbocker Artists; Pa Watercolor Soc. *Publ:* Auth, article, Ultra realism in the unorthodox way, Palette Talk, 79; illustr, cover, Prevention Mag, Rodale Press, 83. *Mailing Add:* 969 Catasauqua Rd Whitehall PA 18052

WILWERS, EDWARD MATHIAS
EDUCATOR, ILLUSTRATOR
b Chicago, Ill, Feb 4, 18. *Study:* Drake Univ, BFA; Ohio Univ, MFA; also with Karl Mattern, Yasuo Kuniyoshi & Milford Zornes. *Comn:* Oil painting, comn by Dr & Mrs Robert Eilers, Merion, Pa, 71; watercolor, comn by Dr & Mrs Sascha Schnittmann, San Jose, Calif, 72; acrylic, comn by Dr & Mrs Harvey Ashmead, Ogden, Utah, 73; oil painting, comn by Mr & Mrs Avery Shinn, Russellville, Ark, 75; oil painting, Dr & Mrs Jim Ed McGee, Dardanelle, Ark, 77; and numerous other commissions from 78- *Exhib:* One-man shows, Saga Gallery, Taos, NMex, 66, Ark Found Fine Arts, Russellville, 67 & Triton Mus Art, San Jose, Calif, 68; Van Go Galleries, Russellville, Ark, 78; Ark River Ballery Art Ctr, Russellville, Ark, 82; Atlantis Art & Frame Gallery, Benton, Ark, 86. *Pos:* Designer, Hutcheson Displays, Inc, Omaha, Nebr, 51-58, Art Gallery, Ark, Tech Univ, 83; illusr, D & H Assoc, Ogden, Utah, 59-60. *Teaching:* Prof art & head dept, Ark Tech Univ, Russellville, 60-81, prof art, 81-87 (retired). *Mem:* Kappa Pi; Nat Coun Art Adminr; Southeastern Col Art Conf; Mid-Am Art Conf. *Publ:* Illusr, Nuclear Energy Conf (portfolio), 61; illusr, Arkansas Polytechnic College (promotion booklet), 63; illusr, Blanchard Springs Caverns (booklet), US Forest Serv, 66; Dardanelle Reservoir (booklet), US Corp Engrs, 68; illusr, Pleasure Boating on the Arkansas River, Ark Parks & Tour Dept, 70. *Mailing Add:* Rte 7 Bayou Lane Russellville AR 72801

WIMAN, BILL
PAINTER, EDUCATOR
b Roscoe, Tex, Nov 12, 40. *Study:* E Tex State Univ, BS; Univ Fla, MFA. *Work:* Butler Inst of Am Art, Youngstown, Ohio; Okla Art Ctr, Oklahoma City; San Antonio Mus Art; Am Tel & Tel, New York; Mus of Arts & Sci, Evansville, Ind. *Exhib:* Real, Really Real, Super Real, San Antonio Mus Art, 81; New Works, Laguna Gloria Art Mus, Austin, 85; one person exhib, Adams-Middleton Gallery, Dallas, 85; Five Figurative Painters, Abilene Fine Arts Mus, 86; Accurate Depictions? Figurative Realist Paintings, Bowling Green State Univ, 86. *Teaching:* Asst prof painting, E Tex State Univ, 66-71; prof painting, Univ Tex, Austin, 72- *Awards:* Ford Found Grant, 79; Teaching Excellence Award, Univ Texas, 87. *Bibliog:* 50 Texas Artists: A Critical Selection, Chronical Books, 86; articles, Arts Mag, 10/85 & ArtNews, 5/86. *Media:* Oil. *Dealer:* Adams-Middleton Gallery 3000 Maple Dallas TX 75201. *Mailing Add:* 1811 W 36th St Austin TX 78713

WIMBERLEY, FRANK WALDEN
PAINTER, COLLAGE ARTIST
b Pleasantville, NJ, Aug 31, 26. *Study:* Howard Univ, with Lois M Jones, James Wells & James Porter. *Work:* Mus Mod Art, Metrop Mus, New York; Art Inst Chicago; Pitney Bowes, Stamford, Conn; Islip Art Mus, East Islip, New York. *Comn:* Clearly, Gottlieb, Steen & Hamilton, New York, 86; Crown Plaza Hotel, E Elmhurst, New York, 89; Bruce Llewellyn, Coca Cola Bottling, Philadelphia, 91; Don Anderson, Time Warner, New York, 92. *Exhib:* Albright-Knox, Buffalo, NY, 86; Elaine Benson Gallery, Bridgehampton, NY, 89; Kenkeleba House, NY, 90, 92; Ashawagh Hall, Springs, NY, 90-92; Jamaica Arts Ctr, Jamaica, NY, 92; Brooklyn Union Community Gallery, NY, 92; and others. *Awards:* Best Work on Paper, 79, Best Abstract, 83, Best Mixed Media, 87, The Guild, New York. *Mem:* Guild Hall, East Hampton, NY. *Media:* Collage. *Dealer:* Benton Gallery Benton Plaza 365 County Rd 39 Southhampton NY 11968; June Kelly Gallery 591 Broadway New York City NY. *Mailing Add:* 99-11 35th Ave Corona NY 11368

WIMMER, GAYLE
SCULPTOR, EDUCATOR
b Pittsburgh, Pa, Oct 2, 43. *Study:* Pratt Inst, Brooklyn, NY, BFA, 67; Tyler Sch Art, Philadelphia, Pa, MFA, 70; Acad Fine Art, Warsaw, Poland, with Wojclech Sadley, 71. *Work:* Cent Mus Textiles, Lodz, Poland; Stedman Gallery, Rutgers Univ, Camden, NJ; Kino Hosp, Tucson, Ariz; Roda Maccine SA, Ticino, Switz. *Comn:* US Nat Park Serv, Harper's Ferry, WVa, 77; Nat Steel Corp Serv Ctr, Wayne, NJ, 77; Pittsburgh Glove Mfg Co, Pa, 82; Ctr for English as a second language, Tuscon, Ariz, 89. *Exhib:* Solo exhibs, Annenberg Ctr, Philadelphia, 82, Mandell Theatre, Philadelphia, 83, Galerie Rzezby, Warsaw, Poland, 86, Galerie Faust, Geneva, Switz, 86 Am Cult Ctrs, Jerusalem & Tel Aviv, Israel, 88, Univ Mus Art, Tucson, Ariz, 89, Central Mus Textiles, Lodz, Poland, 93, Allersnaweg Castle, Holland, 93, Galerie Faust, Geneva, Switz, 94; Group exhib, Clay, Fiber, Metal: Women Artists, Bronx Mus, New York, 78; Fiber as Art, Metrop Mus Manila, Philippines, 80; The Common Thread, Visual Arts Ctr Alaska, Anchorage, 80; 5th Int Triennale of Tapestry, Cent Mus Textiles, Lodz, Poland, 85-86; Ariz Biennial, Tucson Mus Art, Ariz, 88; Contemp Ariz Textiles, Ariz State Univ Mus Art, Tempe, 91; Black & White, Ariz Mus Youth, Mesa, 92. *Pos:* Head cur, Contemp Polish Fiber Art, Mus Ein Harod, Israel, 91; cur, Contemp Israeli Textile Art, Central Mus Textiles, Lodz, Poland, 93. *Teaching:* Lectr textiles, Hunter Col, New York, 72-77; instr fiber sculpture, The New Sch, New York,

73-77; prof art & initiator Fiber Program, Art Dept, Univ Ariz, Tucson, 77- *Awards:* Fel Study Poland, Int Research & Exchanges Bd, New York, 71; Craftsmen's Fel Grant, Nat Endowment Arts, 73; Grant Research in Poland, Int Research & Exchanges Bd, New York, 82 & 83; Fulbright Fel, Artist-in-Residence, Israel, 87-88; Visual Artists' Fel, Tucson/Pima Arts Coun, Ariz, 90. *Media:* Mixed Media, Miscellaneous Media. *Publ:* Auth, Seasonal Marks, 10-11/84 & Polish Textile Art: Photorealism in the second generation, 2-3/86, Am Craft Mag. *Mailing Add:* 3468 N Richland Circle Tucson AZ 85719

WINCHESTER, ALICE
EDITOR, WRITER
b Chicago, Ill, July 26, 07. *Study:* Smith Col, BA, 29; Russell Sage Col, LHD, 66; Hobart & William Smith Cols, DLitt, 73. *Pos:* Ed, Mag Antiques, 38-72; guest cur, Whitney Mus Am Art, 72-74. *Teaching:* Frequent lectr, Antiques Forum at Colonial Williamsburg & elsewhere, 48. *Awards:* Fel, Rochester NY Mus of Arts & Sci, 50; Medal, Smith Col, 68; Crowninshield Award, Nat Trust for Hist Preserv, 72; Archives of Am Art 25th Anniv Award, 79. *Mem:* NY State Hist Asn (trustee 55-86); Nat Trust for Hist Preserv; Friends of Winterthur Mus (hon); Friends of Am Wing, Met Mus (hon); Dec Arts Soc. *Res:* American decorative arts; American folk art. *Publ:* Co-ed, Primitive Painters in America 1750-1950, 50; auth, How to Know American Antiques, 51; ed, Antiques Treasury of Furniture & Other Decorative Arts, 59, Collectors & Collections, 61, Living with Antiques, 41 & 63; auth, Versatile Yankee, The Art of Jonathan Fisher 1768-1847, 73; co-auth, Flowering of American Folk Art 1776-1876, 74. *Mailing Add:* Three Glen Hill Rd Apt 111 Danbury CT 06811-4993

WINDEKNECHT, MARGARET BRAKE
FIBER ARTIST, WRITER
b Alma, Mich, June 27, 36. *Study:* Univ Mich, BS(design); Memphis State Univ, MEd. *Work:* Carroll B Reese Mus, Johnson City, Tenn; Tenn State Mus, Com Union Bank & Northern Telecom, Nashville; Cook Industs Collection, Memphis; Botsford Hospital, Detroit, Mch. *Comn:* Cardweaving, Unitarian Church Elliot Mem, Memphis, 77; loom-controlled, St John's United Methodist Church, Memphis, 78. *Exhib:* Miss River Craft Show, Brooks Mem Art Gallery, Memphis, 73, 75, 77 & 79; Fiber Structures, Heinz Gallery Mus Art, Carnegie Inst, Pittsburgh, Pa, 76; Superior, Tweed Mus of Art, Duluth, Minn, 77 & 81; Intent 78--Fabrics, Bruce Gallery, Edinboro, Pa 78; Fiber as Art, Metrop Mus Manila, Philippines, 80; Artist-Artisan, Bass Mus, Miami, Fla, 80-81; Premonitions Exhib, Cheekwood, Nashville, Tenn, 85; Woven Struct Computer Age, Tex Woman's Univ, Denton, Tex. *Awards:* Purchase Award, 6th Biennial, Tenn Artist-Craftsmen, 76; Purchase Awards, 9th & 10th Prints, Drawings & Craft Shows, Ark Art Ctr, 76 & 77. *Bibliog:* Burry & Calonius (auths), Weaving, City of Memphis Mag, 78; M E Riccardi (auth), Creative Overshot rev, Shuttle Spindle & Dyepot, summer 79; A Xemakis (auth), A time to revitalize, Prairie Wool Companion, winter 85. *Mem:* Handweavers Guild Am; Am Crafts Coun. *Media:* Fiber. *Publ:* Coauth, A Micro Computer Graphics Study of Handweaving, NCC, 79; Color and Weave, Van Nostrand Reinhold, 81; The two-tie unit weave, Shuttle Spindle & Dyepot, winter & spring 85; auth, The Rosepath Motif & Point Twill with Color-and-Weave, TGW Publ, 89; The Pinwheel: An Exploration in Color-and-Weave Design, TG Windeknecht, 92; and others. *Mailing Add:* 815 Dartmouth Dr Rochester MI 48063

WINDELL, VIOLET BRUNER
PAINTER, GRAPHIC ARTIST
Study: Univ Louisville, BA, 43, MA, 58. *Work:* Ind State Mus, Indianapolis; Ideal Restaurant & Old Capitol Bank, Corydon, Ind. *Comn:* Rural Education, N Harrison Sch, Ramsey, Ind, 67; Boone Country comm by Dr & Mrs R Milton May, Laconia, Ind, 68; church hist, Squire Boone Caverns, Mauckport, Ind, 76. *Exhib:* New Orleans World Fair, 82; Palm Beach Galleries, Fla, 84. *Pos:* Artist-in-residence, Squire Boone Gallery, Mauckport, 76-87. *Teaching:* Instr, Ind Univ SE, New Albany, Ind, 58-60 & N Harrison Sch, Ramsey, 66-70. *Awards:* Artists of the Gold Medal Accademia Italia, Parma, Italy, 81; Cert Int Acceptance, Palm Beach Galleries, Fla, 84. *Bibliog:* Calogera e Nicolo Pomepinto (ed), Tendencies and Testmonies, Parma, Italy, 82. *Mem:* Bus & Prof Women; Nat Mus Women Arts. *Media:* Acrylic; Video. *Publ:* Author, Human Symbiosis (autobiography), private publ, 68; contribr, To a newborn babe, Humanists Speak, Am Humanist Asn, 76; illusr, Harrison County's Earliest Years, Griffen & Windell, 84. *Mailing Add:* 4675 Davis Mill Rd NW Ramsey IN 47166

WINER, DONALD ARTHUR
CURATOR, PAINTER
b St Louis, Mo, Oct 26, 27. *Study:* Univ Mo, BS & MA. *Collections Arranged:* Broad Spectrum, 81, Pennsylvania in Prints, 82, Working Pennsylvanians, 82 & Portraits of Pennsylvania Painters, 83, Philadelphia Col Art. *Pos:* Cur, Springfield Art Mus, Mo, 54-57; asst dir, Brooks Art Gallery, Memphis, Tenn, 57-59; dir, Montgomery Mus Fine Arts, Ala, 59-62; dir, Everhart Mus Art & Sci, 62-66; cur, Pa Collection Fine Arts, Pa Hist & Mus Comn, retired. *Mem:* Pa Guild Craftsmen; Mid-State Artists; Gallery Doshi. *Res:* Pennsylvania painters; pottery of Pennsylvania. *Collection:* American earthenware, especially slip decorated red ware. *Mailing Add:* 3112 Schoolhouse Lane Harrisburg PA 17109

WINER, HELENE
DIRECTOR
b Chicago, Ill, Mar 27, 36. *Study:* State Univ Calif, BA, 68. *Pos:* Dir & co-owner, Metro Pictures, New York, currently. *Mailing Add:* Metro Pictures 150 Greene St New York NY 10012

WINES, JAMES N
ARCHITECT
b Oak Park, Ill, June 27, 32. *Study:* Syracuse Univ Sch Art, BA(summa cum laude), 56. *Work:* Albright-Knox Art Gallery, Buffalo; Stedelijk Mus, Amsterdam, Holland; Whitney Mus Am Art, New York; Tate Gallery, London, Eng; Walker Art Ctr, Minneapolis. *Comn:* Allsteel Showroom, Allsteel Corp, New York, 88; Four Continents Bridge, World Fair Bridge, Expos 89, Hiroshima, Japan, 89; Isuzu Space Station, Yokohama, Japan, 89; Theater for the New City, Ctr Performing Arts, New York, 90; Shinwa Resort, Kisokoma-Kogen, Japan, 90. *Exhib:* Centre Pompidou, Paris, France, 75; Am Now, US Govt Traveling Show, Yugoslavia & Hungary, 79; SITE: Bldgs & Spaces Traveling Exhib, 81-82; Boston Archit Ctr, 82; Deutsches Architektur Mus, Frankfurt, Ger, 84; Archit Asn, London, Eng, 86; Triennale di Milano, Milan, Italy, 85-86; Nat Bldg Mus, Washington, DC, 86. *Pos:* Dir, Site, Inc, New York, 69-; mem, Arts & Bus Coop Coun, New York, 71-; mem, Fed Design Assembly, Washington, DC, 72; mem arts adv coun, Bicentennial Celebration, Washington, DC, 72. *Teaching:* Instr environ art, Sch Visual Art, 65-; instr environ workshop, NY Univ, 65-; instr, NJ Sch Archit, 75-; Mellon prof, Cooper Union, New York, 77-; chmn dept environmental design, Parsons Sch Design, New York, currently. *Awards:* Sr Sabbatical Grant, 82 & Distinguished Designer Award, 83, Nat Endowment Arts; Winning Entry, Highway 86, World's Fair Transportation Pavilion & Plaza, Expo 86, Vancouver, Can, 85; and many others. *Bibliog:* Article, L'Archit d'Aujourd'hui, France, 2/85; Connoisseur, 7/86; and more than 2,000 other major features & cover stories in 22 countries. *Publ:* Auth, Architexture as Art (monogr), SITE Acad Ed Eng, 80; The Highrise of Homes, Rizzoli Int, 82; The Pratt J & Archit Now, 85; Japan Architect, SITE, Japan, 86 & 90; and many others. *Mailing Add:* 65 Bleeker St New York NY 10012

WINFIELD, RODNEY M
PAINTER, DESIGNER
b New York, NY, Feb 6, 25. *Study:* Univ Miami, 43; Cooper Union, 44-45. *Work:* Steinberg Gallery; Wash Univ, St Louis; Mitchell Mus, Mt Vernon, Ill; and pvt collections. *Comn:* Bronze & steel Ark Wall, Temple Israel, St Louis, 62; doors, interior artifacts, Good Samaritan Hosp, Chapel, Mt Vernon, Ill, 68; space window, Washington Cathedral, 73; shrine, Our Lady of Perpetual Help Chapel of Christ the Crucified King, St Louis Univ Hospitals; stained glass, United Hebrew Temple, St Louis; and others. *Exhib:* One-man shows, Galerie Creuze, Paris, 50, Martin Schweig Gallery, St Louis; Pope Pius Libr, St Louis Univ; Pallette Bleau, Paris; City Art Mus, St Louis. *Pos:* Stained glass designer, Emil Frei Assocs, St Louis, 53-; designer, Winfield Jewelry, St Louis, 70- *Teaching:* Prof emer, Maryville Univ, St Louis, 64-90. *Media:* Acrylic; Stained Glass, Silver. *Mailing Add:* 4444 Laclede Ave St Louis MO 63108

WINGATE, ARLINE (HOLLANDER)
SCULPTOR
b New York, NY. *Work:* Syracuse Univ Mus, NY; Nat Mus Stockholm, Sweden; Ghent Mus Belg; Joseph H Hirshhorn Collection; Guild Hall Mus, East Hampton, NY; plus many others. *Exhib:* Metrop Mus Art & Whitney Mus Am Art, New York; Wadsworth Atheneum Mus; San Francisco Mus Mod Art, Calif; Baltimore Mus, Md; plus many others in Paris, France, Belg, Buenos Aires, Arg, London, Eng & US incl five one-man shows. *Teaching:* Instr, Young Men's Hebrew Asn, Southhampton Col. *Mem:* Sculptors Guild; Nat Asn Women Artists. *Media:* All. *Mailing Add:* PO Box 335 East Hampton NY 11937

WINGATE, GEORGE B
PAINTER
b Mt Holly, NJ, Oct 13, 41. *Study:* Univ Rochester, BA, 63; Syracuse Univ Sch Archit, 65; New Sch, with Henry Pearson, 72-76; Art Students League, with Frank Mason, 73-78. *Work:* Everson Mus; Mus City New York. *Exhib:* Butler Art Inst Ann, 80 & 83; solo exhib, Everson Mus, 82, Katonah Gallery, NY, 83 & John Pence Gallery, San Francisco, 83; Painting New York, Mus City New York, 83; Small Works Show, Pratt Graphics Ctr, New York, 85; Univ Rochester, NY, 88; New York City Anthology, Grace Borgenicht Gallery, 88; Century Asn, New York, 90. *Teaching:* Instr painting, Kings Col, 84-86; instr drawing, Parsons Sch Design, New York, 85-88; instr printmaking & drawing, Gordon Col, 89- *Awards:* Frist Prize, Creative Arts Workshop, New Haven. *Bibliog:* Gordon Muck (auth), Wingate's Cazenovia, Syracuse Post Standard, 9/15/80; Vivien Raynor (auth), article, NY Times, 10/16/83; Stephen Doherty (auth), article, Am Artist Mag, 10/83. *Mem:* Art Students League; New York Arts Group; The Century Asn. *Media:* Oil. *Dealer:* Joseph Keiffer 28 E 72 St New York NY 10028. *Mailing Add:* 939 Eighth Ave Apt 608 New York NY 10019

WINGATE, ROBERT BRAY
ILLUSTRATOR, CONSULTANT
b Harrisburg, Pa, Sept 21, 25. *Study:* Lebanon Valley Col, AB, 48; Pa Acad Fine Arts, summer 48; Johns Hopkins Med Sch, MA(art as appl to med), 51; Drexel Univ, MS(libr sci), 60; Clayton Univ, ScD, 82; Sussex Univ, Hon ScD, 71. *Pos:* Med illusr, Walter Reed Army Med Ctr, Washington, DC, 54-56 & Ophthalmological Found, Inc, New York, 56-60; freelance illusr, 60-; chief rare bks & spec collections, Pa State Libr, Harrisburg, 65-78. *Mem:* Life fel Royal Soc Arts, London; affil Royal Soc Med, London; fel, Am Col Heraldry, 82; chevalier, Order of St George Constantine, 87. *Res:* History of medicine and medical illustration; history of printing and bookbinding; heraldic illustration. *Publ:* Illusr, Fasanella's Modern Advances in Cataract Surgery, Lippincott, 63; Fasanella's Management of Complications in Eye Surgery, Saunders, 65; Von Noorden & Maumenee's Atlas of Strabismus, Mosby, 67, 2nd ed, 73; King & Wadsworth's An Atlas of Ophthalmic Surgery, Lippincott, 70; auth & illusr, Perceptions: Glimpses of Our World and Ourselves, 84. *Mailing Add:* 136 Shell St Harrisburg PA 17109

WINGERTER, JOHN PARKER
PAINTER
b New York, NY, July 27, 40. *Study:* Columbia Univ, 66; LaSalle Univ, LLB, 64-66; Art Students League, New York, 68-70. *Work:* Jouvet Ctr & Customs House, Asn Artist-Run Galleries, World Trade Ctr, New York; The Artists Forum, Long Island, NY. *Comn:* Acrylic canvas, comn by Dr & Mrs Ravitz, Long Island, 83; two large panels, Continental Grain Corp, New York, 84; Gestalt Learning Ctr, comn by Mr Levy, Long Island, 86. *Exhib:* Small Works Competition, Gallery East, NY Univ, 80; Survey of Geometric Expressionism, NY State Arts Coun & Mobil Oil, Borough Hall, New York, 82; Reflections, Adelphi Univ, Long Island, NY, 83; Le Salon Des Nations, Int Ctr Contemp Arts, Paris, France, 84. *Bibliog:* E Buonagurio (auth), artic le, Arts Mag, 10/77; Helen Harrison (auth), Truth redefined, 3/1/80 & Five artists works, 5/13/84, New York Times. *Media:* Acrylic, Oil. *Dealer:* Noho Gallery 168 Mercer St New York NY 10012. *Mailing Add:* 58 Meadow Glen Rd Ft Salonga NY 11768

WINGO, MICHAEL B
PAINTER, DRAFTSMAN
b Los Angeles, Calif, Nov 21, 41. *Study:* Art Ctr Col Design, 60-62; Claremont McKenna Col, BA, 64; Otis Art Inst(scholar), BFA, 65, MFA, 67. *Work:* Santa Barbara Mus Art, Calif; Oakland Mus, Calif; Manatt, Phelps, Rothenberg & Phillips, Los Angeles; Security Pac Nat Bank, Los Angeles; IBM, Crocker Ctr, Los Angeles; and others including private collections. *Exhib:* Art & Archit Tour, Los Angeles Co Mus Art, 85; Dissonant Abstractions (with catalog), San Jose Inst Contemp Art, 86; Orange Co Ctr Contemp Art, Santa Ana, Calif, 87; New Art: Paintings from NY, Tex, Calif, Laguna Gloria Art Mus, Austin, Tex, 89; Feitelson, Artist & Teacher, Long Beach City Col, 89; Contemporary Abstractions, Weingart Ctr, Occidental Col, 90; and others. *Teaching:* Instr painting & drawing, Pasadena Art Mus, 68-72; guest lectr, San Francisco Art Inst, 84 & vis artist, 87; instr drawing & painting, Otis Art Inst, Parsons Sch Design, Los Angeles, 85-92; inaugural fac, Calif State Summer Sch Arts, 87. *Awards:* Visual Artists Fel Grant in Painting, Nat Endowment Art, 89-90; Who's Who in the West, 23rd ed, Marquis Who's Who, 91; Individual Support Grant in Painting, Adolph & Esther Gottlieb Found, 92. *Bibliog:* Joseph Mugnaini (auth), Expressive Drawing Through the Schematic Approach, Davis, 88; Les Krantz (ed), The California Art Review, Am References Inc, 88; Henry T Hopkins (auth), California Painters: New York, Chronicle Bks, San Francisco, page 7, 89. *Media:* Acrylic, Oil. *Dealer:* Terry DeLapp 800 N La Cienega Los Angeles CA 90069. *Mailing Add:* 7051 N Figueroa St Los Angeles CA 90042

WINICK, BERNYCE ALPERT
PAINTER
b Brooklyn, NY, Oct 20, 22. *Study:* NY Univ, BA(fine arts), 43; Art Students League with Mario Cooper, 61-64; Nat Acad Sch Fine Arts, 68-72. *Comn:* Large watercolor, comn by Dr & Mrs Marcel Weinberger, Woodmere, NY, 84; 2 large watercolors, comn by Pittway Corp, Syosset, NY, 89; Aquamedia, comn by Stillwater Inc, New York, 92. *Exhib:* Nat Acad Ann Exhib, New York, 90; Directors Invitational, Chelsea Cult Ctr, Muttontown, NY, 91; Artists Greater NY, Fine Arts Mus, Hempstead, NY, 91; Am Watercolor Soc, Salmagundi Club, New York, 92; Nat Asn Women Artists, Jacob Javits Fgd Bldg, New York, 92; and others. *Awards:* First Prize, Nat Arts Club-86th Ann, 85; First Prize, Salmagundi Club, 90; Doris Kreindler Mem Award, Nat Asn Women Artists, 92. *Bibliog:* Robin Earl (auth), Artist with an everchanging palate, Nassau Herald, 12/85; Roberta Graff (auth), A symphony of paintings by Bernyce Winick, South-Shore Record, 5/89; Helen A Harrison (auth), Expressing ideas through color, New York Times, 11/91. *Mem:* Am Watercolor Soc; Nat Asn Women Artists; Royal Soc Artists, London; Hempstead Harbor Artists Asn (Discovery Gallery); Salmagundi Club. *Media:* Aquamedia. *Mailing Add:* 923 Beth Lane Woodmere NY 11598

WINK, CHRIS
CONCEPTUAL ARTIST, KINETIC ARTIST
b New York, NY, Jan 24, 61. *Study:* Weslean, Am Studies, 84. *Work:* New Mus Contemp Art (performance), New York; Milwaukee Art Mus (performance), Wis; Contemp Art Ctr New Orleans (performance), Fla. *Awards:* Obie, Tubes, Village Voice, 91; Drama Desk, Tubes, 92; Lucille Lortel Found Award, Tubes, 92. *Bibliog:* Alisa Soloman (auth), Pissing on propriety, Village Voice, 1/15/91; Vicki Goldberg (auth), Hi tech meets God with Blue Man Group, NY Times, 1/17/91; Thomas M Disch (auth), Blue Man Group: Tubes, Nation, 1/20/92. *Media:* Performance. *Mailing Add:* 575 West End Ave New York NY 10024

WINK, DON (JON DONNEL)
PAINTER, EDUCATOR
b San Angelo, Tex, July 13, 38. *Study:* Univ Tex, BFA, 60; Ohio Univ, 61-62; Univ Wash, MFA, 63. *Exhib:* The Texas General, Dallas Mus Fine Arts, 61; two-man exhib, Witte Mus, San Antonio, 66; Texas Painting & Sculpture, Dallas Mus Fine Arts, 68; Associated Artist, Carnegie Mus, Pittsburgh, 71-75; Westmoreland Co Mus, Greensburg, Pa, 72-75; Mus STex Ann, Corpus Christi, 82; Recent Works from East Texas, Tyler Mus Art, 82. *Teaching:* Instr painting & drawing, Southwestern Univ, Tex, 65-69; prof & chmn dept art, Slippery Rock State Col, 69-76 & Stephen F Austin State Univ, 76- *Awards:* First Prize, 13th Ann 180, Huntington Galleries, WVa, 65 & 30th Ann Allied Artist, 65; Jury Award, Assoc Artist, 72. *Mem:* Nat Coun Art Adminr; Tex Asn Schs Art (secy, 79-80). *Media:* Acrylic, Oil. *Mailing Add:* Box 13001 Stephen F Austin State Univ Nacogdoches TX 75962

WINKLER, MARIA PAULA
PAINTER, EDUCATOR
b Krakow, Poland, Oct 24, 45; US citizen. *Study:* Univ Pa, study with Karl Umlauf, BA(art & art hist); Pa State Univ, study with Enrigue Montenegro, MFA(painting & drawing) & study with Kenneth Beittel, PhD(art educ). *Work:* Calif League Women Artists, Sacramento; Pa State Univ, State College; Boise Art Mus, Idaho; Univ Calif Med Ctr, Sacramento; Sutter Mem Hosp, Sacramento. *Comn:* Raley's Corporate Offices, Sacramento, Calif; Kronick, Moskovitz, Tiedemann and Girard, Prof Corporation. *Exhib:* Nat Drawing & Small Sculpture Exhib, Ball State Univ, Muncie, Ind, 70; New York Exhib of Paintings, Sculpture & Graphics, Avanti Galleries, New York, 71; New Generation Drawing, Cheney-Cowles Mem State Mus, Spokane, Wash, 73; Contemp Watercolor Paintings, Pence Gallery, Davis, Calif, 88; Contemp Realists, Gump's Gallery, San Francisco, 91; 67th Ann Crocker-Kingsley Open Exhib, Crocker Art Mus, Sacramento, Calif, 92. *Pos:* Tech illusr, Aerojet Gen Corp, Sacramento, 63. *Teaching:* Asst prof art & art educ, Boise State Univ, Idaho, 73-75; asst prof art educ, Univ BC, Vancouver, 75-77; prof art, Calif State Univ, Sacramento, 77- *Awards:* First Place & William Harrington Mem Award, Northern Calif Arts 26th Ann Open Show, Sacramento, 80; Mixed Media, Second Place, Northern Calif Arts 36th Ann Open Exhib, Carmichael, 91; Gold Discovery Award, Works on Paper, Art Calif Mag, 92. *Bibliog:* A Survey of Contemporary Art of the Figure, Am Artist, 2/85. *Media:* Watercolor, Pastels. *Res:* Research and writings on techniques of teaching art appreciation to teachers and museum volunteers; curriculum development in art. *Publ:* Illusr, Art: Magic, Impulse and Control, A Guide to Viewing, Prentice-Hall, 73; Eight Posters, Editions Limited, San Francisco, 90-91; Two Artists Cards, Allport Editions Artist Cards, Portland, 90; Four Mini-Prints, Portal Publications, Corte Madera, 91. *Dealer:* Horuath Bass 4399 Arden Way Sacramento CA 95864; Dubins Gallery 11948 San Vicente Blvd Los Angeles CA 90049. *Mailing Add:* c/o Art Dept Calif State Univ Sacramento CA 95819

WINKLER, MICHAEL
INTERMEDIA ARTIST
b Lima, Ohio, Feb 28, 52. *Work:* Mus Mod Art, New York, NY; Stanford Univ, Calif; Staatsgalerie, Stuttgart, WGer; King Stephen Mus, Szekesfehervar; Sackner Archive, Miami Beach, Fla. *Exhib:* Solo exhibs, Kunstraum Kunoldstrasse 34, Kassel, WGer, 84, Univ Md, Baltimore, 85 & Kansas City Art Inst, 88; Artists' Books USA, US Info Agency (travel in India), 86-87; Nat Festival Performing Arts, Philadelphia, Pa, 87; 3rd Ann Photo Salon, Nexus Contemp Art Ctr, Atlanta, 88. *Pos:* Regular contribr, Rampike Mag, Toronto, currently. *Awards:* Spec Proj Fel, Pa Coun Arts, 84; Visual Artists Fel, Nat Endowment Arts, 85; LINE Grant, Line II Asn, New York, 85. *Bibliog:* Sue Scott (auth), Alphastructures, Art Res Ctr, 84; Skuta Helgason (auth), Regular words, Afterimage, 84. *Media:* Mixed Media, Artist Books. *Publ:* Auth, Word Art/Art Words, 85, An Artist's Statement, 86 & Equivalents, 87, Extreme Measures, 89, Printed Matter. *Dealer:* Tony Zwicker 15 Gramercy Park New York NY 10003. *Mailing Add:* 2 Cottage Lane Cape Elizabeth ME 04107

WINNINGHAM, GEOFF
PHOTOGRAPHER
b Jackson, Tenn, Mar 4, 43. *Study:* Rice Univ, BA, 65; Ill Inst Technol, with Aaron Siskind, MS(photog), 68. *Work:* Mus Mod Art, New York; Boston Mus Fine Arts; Mus Fine Arts, Houston; Int Mus Photog, Rochester, NY; Princeton Univ; Carpenter Ctr, Harvard Univ. *Comn:* Courthouses of Tex (photographs), Seagrams Co, New York, 75. *Exhib:* Mus Fine Arts, Houston, 74; Witkin Gallery, New York, 75; Cronin Gallery, Houston, 77. *Teaching:* Asst prof photog, Univ St Thomas, Houston, 68-69; assoc prof photog, Rice Univ, Houston, 69-78, prof art-photog, Rice Univ, 78- *Awards:* Corp for Pub Broadcasting Award, 72; Guggenheim Found Fel, 72; Nat Endowment Arts Photog Fel, 75 & 77. *Bibliog:* E A Carmean (ed), Geoff Winningham Photographs, Mus Fine Arts, Houston, 74. *Publ:* Auth, Friday Night in the Coliseum, 71; auth, Going Texan, 72. *Dealer:* Cronin Gallery 2008 Peven St Houston TX 77019. *Mailing Add:* Dept of Art Rice Univ Box 1892 Houston TX 77251

WINOKUR, JAMES L
COLLECTOR, CRITIC
b Philadelphia, Pa, Sept 12, 22. *Study:* Univ Pa, BS(econ), 43. *Pos:* Chmn, auditing comt & mem, other comts, Carnegie Inst, 67-, founder, fel & life trustee, Mus Art, 67-; vpres & gov, Pittsburgh Plan for Art, 67-84; trustees comt mem, AAM, 72-; trustee & vchmn, Sarah Scaife Found, 72-87; art critic, Greensburg Tribune-Rev, 72-87; trustee, Pittsburgh Hist & Landmarks Soc, 75-; art adv comt, Trust for Cult Resources, Pittsburgh, Pa; mem, Arch Am Art, 75-; dir & mem exec comt, 100 Friends of Pittsburgh Art, 75- *Teaching:* Instr art, Duquesne Univ, 80. *Mem:* Hon mem Assoc Artists Pittsburgh. *Interests:* Joseph Goto, American sculptor in welded steel. *Collection:* Cobra paintings, drawings and sculpture including Carl-Henning Pedersen, Jorn, Corneille, Alechinsky, Ubac, Reinhoud and others; 20th century American paintings, drawings and sculpture including Varujan Boghosian, Sam Francis, Joseph Goto and others; prints from Old Masters to the 20th century. *Mailing Add:* 5625 Darlington Rd Pittsburgh PA 15217

WINOKUR, NEIL S
PHOTOGRAPHER
b New York, NY, June 28, 45. *Study:* Hunter Col, BA, 67. *Work:* Mus Mod Art, New York; Chase Manhattan Bank, New York; Metrop Mus Art, New York; George Eastman House, Rochester, NY; Mus Contemp Art, Mexico City, Mex. *Comn:* Eighteen Portraits, Chase Manhatten Bank, New York, 85; Arts for Transit Penn Station, Pub Art Fund, New York, NY, 88. *Exhib:* Face

to Face: Recent Photograph, Inst Contemp Art, Philadelphia, Pa, 84; Face to Face, Mus Art Bahia, Salvader, Brazil, 85; Recent Color Acquisitions, Mus Mod Art, New York, NY, 84 & 87; Solo exhibs, Totems, 86, New Portraits, 87, People & Objects,; Portrayals, Int Ctr Photography, New York, NY, 87; Arrangements for the Camera, Baltimore Mus Art, Baltimore, Md, 87; Photography & Art, Interactions Since 1945, Los Angeles Co Mus Art, Los Anageles, Calif, 87; Recent Portraits, Tatistcheff Gallery, Santa Monica, Calif, 89; The Photography of Invention: Am Pictures of the 80's, Nat Mus Mod Art, Washington, DC, 89; and many others in US, Eng & Ger. *Awards:* Fel in Photography from Art Matters Mc, 84, Nat Endowment Arts, 85 & Guggenheim Found, 87; Grant, Art Matters Inc, 88. *Bibliog:* Andy Groundberg (auth), A Photographer who Scatters Clues to Subjects Psychs, NY Times, 6/22/86; Patrick Amos (auth), Neil Winokur at Barbara Tull, Vol 74, Art in America, 12/86; Charles Hogen (auth), Neil Winokur-Barbara Tull Fine Arts, Vol XXVI, Arttorum, 88; Vince Aletti (auth), Choices-Neil Winnkur, Village Voice, 1/3/89; Carter Radcliff (auth), Elle, 11/89; Max Kozloff, Hapless Figures in an Artificial Storm, Artforum, 11/89. *Media:* Photography. *Dealer:* Barbara Tull Fine Arts 146 Greene St New York NY 10012; Janet Borden 560 Broadway New York NY 10012. *Mailing Add:* 310 Greenwich St 25L New York NY 10013

WINOKUR, PAULA COLTON
CERAMIST, CRAFTSMAN
b Philadelphia, Pa, May 13, 35. *Study:* Temple Univ, BFA, BSEd, 58, with Rudolf Staffel; Alfred Univ, New York, 58. *Work:* Witte Mus of Art, San Antonio, Tex; Philadelphia Mus of Art; Del Mus of Art, Wilmington; Alberta Potters Asn-Int Ceramic Soc, Switz; Utah Mus of Art, Salt Lake City. *Comn:* Ltd ed patrons plate, Friends Select Sch, Philadelphia, 75; ed patrons plates (60), Nat Mus Am Jewish Hist, 83; fireplace installations, pvt residences, Philadelphia, 84, 85 & 86; lintel (A view of Diamond Head), Hawaii Sch for Girls, Honolulu, 88; fireplaces, comn by Mr & Mrs Robert Coon, Montclair, NJ, 89 & Mr & Mrs William Harris, Lynchburg, Va, 90. *Exhib:* Am Crafts Coun & US Info Agency 20 Potters, travelling exhib, 73-77; Baroque 74, Mus Contemp Crafts, 74; Soup Tureens 76, Campbell Mus, Camden, NJ, 76; Philadelphia 300 Yrs of Am Art, Philadelphia Mus Art, 76; 100 Artists Celebrate 100 Yrs, Fairtree Gallery & Xerox Gallery, 76; Inaugural Exhib, Am Crafts Mus, 86; Solo show, Helen Druitt Gallery, New York, 90. *Teaching:* Lectr ceramics, Philadelphia Col Art, 67, Beaver Col, Glenside, Pa, 73- & Tyler Sch Art, 83. *Awards:* Merit Award, Craftsmen USA, Am Crafts Coun, 66; Prize, Ceramics Int 73, Calgary, Alta, 73; Nat Endowment for the Arts Craftsmen's Fel, 76 & 88; PA Coun Craftmen's Fel, 86. *Mem:* Am Crafts Coun; Nat Coun Educ Ceramic Arts (bd dirs, 79-82). *Publ:* Coauth, The light of Rudolph Staffel, Craft Horizons, 77. *Dealer:* Helen Drutt Gallery 1721 Walnut St Philadelphia PA 19103. *Mailing Add:* 435 Norristown Rd Horsham PA 19044

WINOKUR, ROBERT MARK
CERAMIST, EDUCATOR
b Brooklyn, NY, Dec 24, 33. *Study:* Tyler Sch Art, Temple Univ, with Rudolph Staffel, BFA, 56; NY State Col of Ceramics, Alfred, MFA, 58. *Work:* Lannan Found, Palm Beach, Fla; Int Acad of Ceramics, Lucerne, Switz; The Utah Mus Fine Arts, Salt Lake City, Utah; Philadelphia Mus of Art, Pa; Mus Boymans Van Beumingen, Rotterdam, Neth. *Comn:* Twenty large planters, comn by Ford & Earl Archit Designers, Detroit, Mich; First Nat Bank, Chicago, Ill, 69; coffee pots, Arts/Objects USA, Lee Nordness Galleries, New York, 73; Holy Water Font, comn by Bishop McDevitt, Temple Univ Newman Ctr, 76; Cast Tile Wall approx 4 ft x 8 ft for Trammell-Crow proj, Westlake IV, West Chester Pa. *Exhib:* 300 Years of Am Art, Philadelphia Mus Art, 76; Contemporary Arts, Wellesley Col Mus, Mass, 86; Am Crafts at the Armory: Court of Hon 7th Precint Armory, NY; Philadelphia Contemp Artists, Philadelphia Mus Art, 90; Haldane Connections Exhib, Int Acad Ceramics with Glasgow Sch Art, Edinburgh, Scotland, 90; From the Ground Up, Ten Philadelphia Artists, Invitational, Levy Gallery, Moore Col Art & Design, 92; Tree In Clay-Three Points of View, Nat Mus Ceramic Art, Baltimore, Md, 92; Furniture Philadelphia, Morris Gallery Pa, Acad Fine Art, Philadelphia, 91; Retrospective, The Philadelphia Years, 62 to 92, Helen Drutt Gallery, Philadelphia, Pa, 92. *Pos:* Proj dir, Philadelphia Ceramic Consortium, currently; on site prog chmn, Nat Coun Educ Ceramic Arts, 92; adv bd, Clay Studio, Philadelphia, currently. *Teaching:* Coordr two-dimensional visual design dept, NTex State Univ, Denton, 58-63; area chmn ceramics, Tyler Sch Art, Temple Univ, 66-, chmn craft dept, 79-82 & 88-91; vis artist & guest lectr Glasgow Sch Art, Glasgow, Scotland, 87. *Awards:* Nat Endowment Arts Fel, 79, Nat Coun Educ Ceramic Arts, Fel, 83; Artist-Industry Residency: The Kohler Co, Sheboygan, Wis, 85; Grant, Apprentice for Summer, Dana Found, Wesleyan Univ, Middletown, Conn, 88. *Bibliog:* Hahn & Elisari (auths), Clay Artists, doc film, 75; Charlotte Sewalt (auth), An Interview with Robert Winokur, Ceramics Mo, 9/77; Peter Dormer (auth), The New Ceramics: Trends & Traditions, Thames & Hudson; Elaine Levin (auth), American Ceramics, Abrams; Jack Troy (auth), Salt Glazed Ceramics, Watson-Guptill. *Mem:* Am Crafts Coun; Nat Coun Educ Ceramic Arts (br dir, 69-70, vpres, 72-73); Philadelphia Coun Professional Craftsmen; adv bd, The Clay Studio, Philadelphia, Pa, 85. *Media:* Salt Glazed Stoneware. *Publ:* Auth, The Tyler School of Art of Temple University, Ceramics Mo, 75; coauth, The light of Rudolph Staffel, Craft Horizions, 77. *Dealer:* Helen Drutt Gallery 1721 Walnut St Philadelphia PA 19103. *Mailing Add:* 435 Norristown Rd Horsham PA 19044

WINSLOW, HELEN
PAINTER
b New Salem, NC, Mar 24, 16. *Study:* Fla Southern Col, BA; Art Students League; Otis Art Inst, Los Angeles. *Exhib:* Frye Art Mus, Seattle, Wash, 60, 62 & 68; De Young Art Mus, San Francisco, 69 & 70-71; San Bernardino Art Mus, Calif, 79 & 81-83; many other group and solo shows. *Teaching:* Pvt 54-, painting workshops, Colo, 71-80. *Awards:* Special Award, San Bernadino Mus, 78. *Bibliog:* Articles in Southwest Art Mag, 11/77; article, US Art Mag, 11/88. *Mem:* Royal Soc Arts, Great Britain. *Media:* Oil. *Dealer:* Fireside Gallery PO Box 3374 Carmel CA. *Mailing Add:* 9934 Westwanda Dr Beverly Hills CA 90210

WINSOR, JACQUE
SCULPTOR
b Nfld, Can, Oct 20, 41; US citizen. *Study:* Yale Summer Sch Art & Music, 64; Mass Col Art, BFA, 65; Rutgers Univ, MFA, 67. *Work:* Mus Mod Art, New York; Whitney Mus Am Art, New York; Australia Nat Gallery, Canberra; Detroit Inst Arts, Mich; Mus d'Arte Mod, Paris, France; Tehran Mus Contemp Art, Iran; Albright-Knox Art Gallery, Buffalo. *Exhib:* Solo exhibs, Paula Cooper Gallery, New York, 73, 76, 82, 83, 86 & 89, Wadsworth Atheneum, Hartford, Conn, 78, Mus Mod Art, NY travelling, 79, Va Mus, Richmond, 81, Centre d'Art du Dumaine de Kerguehennec Bignan, Lucmine, France, 88, Milwaukee Art Mus, 91- 92 & travelling, Newport Harbor Art Mus, 92; Art in Place: Fifteen Years of Acquisitions, Whitney Mus Am Art, NY, 89; Group Exhib, Rubin Spangle, New York, 92; Reverb 1960's-1970's, Horodner Romley Gallery, New York, 92; Then & Now, Philippe Staib Gallery, New York, 92; Contemporary Master Works, Feigen Inc, Chicago, Ill, 92; Process to Presence: Issues in Sculpture 1960-1990, Locks Gallery, Philadelphia, 92; var exhibs at major mus incl Whitney Mus Am Art, Aldrich Mus Contemp Art, Mus Mod Art; and others. *Teaching:* Instr art introd & ceramics, Douglass Col, 67; instr art introd, Middlesex Co Col & Newark State Teachers' Col, 68 & 69; instr ceramics, Mills Col Educ, 68 & 71 & Greenwich House Pottery Sch, New York, 69-72; instr graphics, Loyola Univ, New Orleans, summer 69; instr sculpture, Sch Visual Arts, New York, 71 & 75; instr art introd, Hunter Col, 72-75; lectr, NY Studio Sch Drawing, Painting & Sculpture, fall 87. *Awards:* Nat Endowment Arts Grant, 74, 77 & 84; Guggenheim Fel, 78; Creative Artist Award, Brandeis Univ, 79; and others. *Bibliog:* Mark Stevens (auth), Raw magic, Newsweek, 2/79; John Gruen (auth), Jackie Winsor: Eloquence of a Yankee Pioneer, Art News, 3/79; Badanna Zack (auth), Jackie Winsor, Artmag, Can, 9-10/79; Robert Pincus-Witten (auth), Entries Maximalism, Out of London Press, 83; Craig Gholson (auth), Jackie Winsor, Bomb, winter 86. *Media:* All. *Mailing Add:* c/o Paula Cooper Gallery 155 Wooster New York NY 10012

WINTER, DAVID L
SCULPTOR
b Seattle, Wash, Nov 6, 54. *Study:* Yale Univ, MFA, 80. *Exhib:* Luhrig, Augustine & Hodes Gallery, 88; Barbara Toll Fine Arts; Painted Forms-Recent Metal Sculpture, Whitney Mus Phillip Morris; Galerie Christine Chassay, Montreal. *Awards:* Nat Endowment Arts Grant, 88; Rome Prize Fel, 89. *Mailing Add:* 167 N Ninth St Brooklyn NY 11211

WINTER, GERALD GLEN
PAINTER, EDUCATOR
b Milwaukee, Wis, Sept 1, 36. *Study:* Univ Wis-Milwaukee, BFA, Madison, MS & MFA. *Work:* Milwaukee Art Ctr; Lowe Mus, Univ Miami, Coral Gables, Fla; Ringling Mus, Sarasota, Fla. *Exhib:* Corcoran Biennial of Am Painting, 63; 39th, 40th, 43rd, 44th & 53rd Exhib Contemp Am Painting, Palm Beach; one-man shows, Miami-Dade Community Col, 75, Lowe Mus, Univ Miami, 75 & 87 Univ Miami Art Dept Gallery, 79; Metrop Mus & Art Ctr, Coral Gables, Fla, 83; Galerie Helene Grubair, Miami, Fla, 90; and others. *Teaching:* Prof art, Univ Miami, 65-, chmn dept, 75-79. *Awards:* Ford Found Purchase Award, 62; Third Prize, Corcoran Gallery of Art Biennial, 62; Honorable Mentions, Hortt Mem Exhib, 69, 80 & 81. *Media:* Oil, Serigraphy. *Mailing Add:* 6629 SW 62nd Terr Miami FL 33143

WINTER, HOPE MELAMED
COLLECTORS, PATRONS
Study: Univ Wis, Madison, 38-40; Goodman School, Art Inst Chicago, 40-42. *Pos:* Trustee, Milwaukee Art Museum, Wis, 74-83 & 92-; coun, Elvehjem Art Mus, Univ Wis, Madison. *Bibliog:* Cubist Prints in Collection of Dr and Mrs Abraham Melamed, Univ Wis, 72; Selections from Collection of Hope and Abraham Melamed, Milwaukee Art Mus, 83. *Mem:* Art Inst Chicago; Am Asn Mus. *Interests:* Cubism, primarily French between 1909-1914, including Picasso, Braque, Gleizer, Metzinger, Joeques Villone, Duchamp, Marcoussis, Gris, Severeni, Chagall and others. *Collection:* Principally cubist prints, drawings & paintings. *Mailing Add:* 1107 E Lilac Lane Milwaukee WI 53217

WINTER, ROGER
PAINTER
b Denison, Tex, Aug 17, 34. *Study:* Univ Tex, BFA, 56; Univ Iowa, MFA, 60; Brooklyn Mus Sch, Beckmann scholar, 60. *Work:* Mus Art, Univ Okla, Norman; Southern Methodist Univ, Oak Cliff Savings & Loan & Dallas Mus Fine Arts, Dallas; Longview Mus & Art Ctr, Tex. *Exhib:* Tex Painting & Sculpture, 20th Century Dallas, 71-62; two-man show, Whitte Mus, San Antonio, Tex, 67; one-man shows, Pollock Gallery, 68 & One i at a Time, 71, Southern Methodist Univ, Dallas & Delgado Mus, New Orleans, La, 68. *Pos:* Installation asst, Dallas Mus Contemp Arts, 62-63; gallery tours & lectr, Dallas Mus Fine Arts, 63- *Teaching:* Instr painting, Ft Worth Art Ctr, 61 & Dallas Mus Fine Arts, 62-68; prof painting, Southern Methodist Univ, 65-. *Awards:* Purchase Award, Univ Okla Art Mus, 62; Top Award, Dallas Ann, Dallas Mus Fine Arts, 64. *Bibliog:* Film on work produced on KERA-TV, Dallas, 71. *Media:* Oil. *Publ:* Auth, Introduction to Drawings, Prentice Hall, 83. *Mailing Add:* c/o Fischbach Gallery 24 W 57th St New York NY 10019

WINTER, RUTH
PAINTER
b New York, NY, Jan 17, 13. *Study:* NY Univ, BS, 31, MA, 32; Art Students League, with Corbino, Bosa & Morris Kantor, 57-61. *Work:* In collections of Reginald Cabral, Provincetown, Mass, Marlo Lewis, Scarsdale, Mr Frantz, Great Neck, Lawrence Koenisberg, South Lawrence, & Semour S Alter, West Hempstead, NY. *Exhib:* Silvermine, Conn, 57-61; Nat Asn Women Artists, 57-68 & 74; Gallery 15, New York, 59; Brooklyn Mus, 60; Nat Acad Design, 60; Lever House, New York, 63 & 67; Pepsi Cola Exhib, 64. *Awards:* Marcia Brady Tucker Prize, Nat Asn Women Artists, 57; Max Low Award, 59; Mr & Mrs Gomes Award, Mahopac Art League, 59. *Bibliog:* Robert M Coates (auth), Art galleries, New Yorker, 5/57; Stuart Preston (auth), Art: a game of styles, N Y Times, 5/57; Painting televised, Boston, 7/58. *Mem:* Nat Asn Women Artists; life mem Art Students League New York; Mahopac Art League. *Media:* Oil. *Mailing Add:* 98-50 67th Ave Rego Park NY 11374

WINTERBERGER, SUZANNE
PHOTOGRAPHER, BOOK ARTIST
b Binghamton, NY, June 23, 52. *Study:* Rochester Inst Technol, NY, BFA, 75; Cranbrook Acad Art Bloomfield Hills, Mich, MFA, 78. *Work:* Visual Studies Workshop, Rochester, NY; Franklin Furnace Archives, New York; Cranbrook Acad Art, Bloomfield Hills, Mich; Erie Art Mus, Pa; WGBH-TV, Boston, Mass. *Exhib:* solo exhibs, Ideas About Life, Color Servs, Santa Barbara, Calif, 81, Maxims, Rutger Gallery, Utica, NY, 82, Aging Barbies, New Art Ctr, Washinton, DC, 87 & Prisoner of the Pedestal, Bayfront Gallery, Erie, Pa, 90; New Works, Franklin Furnace Archives, New York, 84 & 85; Photographer's Invitational, Clayspace Gallery, Erie, Pa, 85; Bookworks Invitational, Erie Art Mus, Pa, 86; Bookworks Invitational, Erie Art Mus, Erie, Pa, 86; NoNeo, Zoller Gallery Invitational, State College, Pa, 89; Pennsylvania Photo Educators Invitational, Pittsburgh, Pa, 91; 20 Years of Cranbrook Photography, Juried Invitational, Cranbrook Art Mus, Bloomfield Hills, Mich, 92. *Collections Arranged:* Photo Collaborations, Bruce Gallery, Edinboro, Pa, 86. *Pos:* Collabr, Aunt Marion & Cousin Mimi photog postcards series, Enthusiastic Enterprises, Edinboro, Pa, 82-86, Edinboro Bookarts Collective, 86- *Teaching:* Asst prof photog, Edinboro Univ, 82- *Awards:* Nat Endowment Arts Fel, 85; Pa Coun Arts Fel, 86. *Bibliog:* Julie Moran (auth), Women artists on women, Pulse, 10/13/87; Gary Wykoff (auth), Heart of a humanist, Erie, Pa Times-News, 4/90; Richard Briggs (filmmaker), Suzanne Winterberger - A Portrait, PBS Documentary, WVIA-TV, Pittston, Pa, 90; PhotoPaper, Blatent Image/Silver Eye Quarterly, Pittsburgh, Pa, 91. *Mem:* Soc Photog Educ. *Publ:* Contribr, In-Sights, Godine, 79; auth, Prototype Man, 80 & The Archeologists Notebook, 84, Lone Star Enterprise. *Mailing Add:* 103 Tarbell Lane Edinboro PA 16412

WINTERS, SANDY (SANDRA L)
PAINTER
b Arcadia, Calif, Feb 10, 49. *Study:* Univ Kans, Lawrence, 67; Univ NH, Durham, BSc(art educ), 71; Cornell Univ, MFA, 77. *Work:* Prudential Insurance Co Am & Manufacturers Hanover Trust Co, New York; Bank of Boston, Mass; Southeast Banking Corp, Miami, Fla; Arnot Art Mus, Elmira, NY; Metro-Dade Art in Public Places, New York. *Comn:* 50 prints for Graymoore, Comn by Rollins Found Tex, Garrison, NY. *Exhib:* Ann Prints & Drawing Exhib, Arkansas Arts Ctr, Little Rock, 79; Women in Art, Springfield Art Asn, Ill, 79; Los Angeles Printmaking Soc, Calif, 79; Rochester-Finger Lakes Exhib, Mem Art Gallery, Rochester, NY, 81; Selections 14, Drawing Ctr, New York, 81 & 82; Everson Mus Art, Syracuse, NY, 82; Soc Four Arts, Palm Beach, Fla, 84; The Art of Miami, Southeastern Ctr Contemp Art, Winston-Salem, NC, 86; Pensacola Mus Art, 88; Jacksonville Mus Art, Fla, 89; The Art Mus, Fla Int Univ, Miami. *Teaching:* Asst prof printmaking & drawing, Univ Tulsa, Okla, 78-80; vis asst prof drawing, printmaking & painting, Cornell Univ, Ithaca, NY, 82-86; asst prof painting & drawing, Fla Int Univ, Miami, 84- *Awards:* Fla State Visual Art Fel; SAF/Nat Endowment Arts Fel; Fac Res Develop Grant, Fla Int Univ, Miami. *Bibliog:* Vivien Raynor (auth), Selections 14, New York Times, 7/17/81; Helen Kohen (auth), Gallery salutes, Miami Herald, 7/5/85; Ronny Cohen (auth), Sandy Winters, (exhib catalog), Frances Wolfson Gallery, 11/86; Stephen Westfall (auth), The Art Mus at Fla Int Univ, Miami. *Mem:* Col Art Asn; Women's Caucus Arts. *Media:* All. *Publ:* Auth, Human Ecology Forum (cover), Vol 9, No 2, Cornell Univ, fall 78; New Directions in American Drawing, Catalog Drawing Ctr, 82; contribr, Art in Bloom, Jacksonville Mus Art Catalog; The Art of Miami, (exhib catalog), Southeastern Ctr Contemp Art, Winston, Salem, 86. *Dealer:* Frumkin/Adams Gallery 50 W 57th St New York NY 10019. *Mailing Add:* 229 NE 101st St Miami Shores FL 33138

WINZENZ, KARON HAGEMEISTER
PAINTER, EDUCATOR
b Fairmont, Minn, Nov 13, 41. *Study:* Lawrence Univ, BA, 63; Univ Wis, Madison, BS(art), 64; Univ Wis, Milwaukee, MFA, 73. *Work:* Cedar City Art League Collection, Utah; Univ Wis, Madison; Reeve Mem Union, Univ Wis, Oshkosh. *Comn:* Site Specific Sculpture, Lawrence Univ, Baileys Harbor, Wis, 82; wall relief, Deloitte, Haskins & Sells, Milwaukee, Wis, 84; wall relief, Wis Arts Bd Percent Art Prog, Wis Dept Transporation, Green Bay, 89. *Exhib:* Wisconsin Directions III: The Third Dimension, Milwaukee Art Mus, 81; Fetish Art: Obsessive Expressions, Rockford Art Mus, Ill, 86; Women's Sensibilities, Nat Juried Exhib, WARM Gallery, Minneapolis, Minn, 86; Myth Mind and Magic, Evanston Art Ctr, Ill, 87; Wisconsin Triennial, Madison Art Ctr, 90; solo retrospective, Re/Constructions, Wriston Art Ctr, Lawrence Univ, 92; and others. *Collections Arranged:* Contemporary Quilting: A Renaissance, 81-82; Woven Works: Tradition and Innovation, 84-85; Midwest Photography Invitational I-VII, biannual traveling exhibs, 83-93. *Pos:* Artist in residence, Artpark, Lewiston, NY, 84. *Teaching:* Prof visual art, Univ Wis, Green Bay, 79- *Awards:* Purchase Award, Madison Biennial '80, Madison Art Ctr, 80; Visual Arts Fel, Wis Arts Bd, 82; Artist's Proj Grants, Wis Arts Bd, 85 & 88. *Bibliog:* Jane Brite (auth), Wisconsin Directions 3: The Third Dimension (catalog), Milwaukee Art Mus, 81; Elizabeth Bard (auth), Karon Hagemeister Winzenz: Fusing Fiber, Time and Ritual, Fiberarts, 1/85; Estella Lauter (auth), Re/Construction/s: Works by Karon Hagemeister Winzenz (catalog for retrospective exhib), Lawrence Univ, Appleton, Wis. *Mem:* Women's Caucus Art; Wis Painters & Sculptors. *Media:* Miscellaneous Media. *Publ:* Articles and reviews of artist's work available on request. *Dealer:* Shidioni Contemp Gallery Tesuque NM. *Mailing Add:* Univ Wis 2420 Nicolet Dr Green Bay WI 54302

WIRSTROM, MARGARET
PAINTER, COLLAGE ARTIST
b Baton Rouge, La. *Study:* La State Univ, 61-63 & 65; Univ New Orleans, BA, 75, MFA, 78. *Work:* Texaco, Houston, Tex; Simone, Peregine, Smith & Redfern, New Orleans; IBM, Tenn; Bank of the South, Atlanta, Ga; Hunter Mus, Chatanooga, Tenn. *Exhib:* Abstraction in Louisiana, Contemp Arts Ctr, New Orleans, 80; Birmingham Biennial, Birmingham Mus, Art, Ala, 81 & 83; Selections Five, Univ New Orleans, 88; one-man shows, Pensacola Mus Art, Fla, 91, Res Nova, New York, 92; Mostly Big, Contemp Arts Ctr, New Orleans, 92. *Pos:* Gallery dir, Delgado Col, New Orleans, 81-83; Artist in residence, Villa Montalvo, Saratoga, Calif, 92. *Teaching:* Full prof, Delgado Col, New Orleans, 80-92. *Awards:* Res Grant, Delgado Col, New Orleans, 92. *Bibliog:* Salon des Refuses (documentary film), WYES, 75; Calas Terrington (auth), Margaret Wirstrom's New Work, The New Orleans Art Rev, vol 86-87, no 3, 87; Peter Halley, Jay Murphy & Hunt Slonem (coauths), Margaret Wirstrom Paintings & Drawings (catalog), Pensacola Mus Art, 91. *Media:* Acrylic, Oil; Found Objects. *Dealer:* Res Nova New York NY. *Mailing Add:* 4434 Camp St New Orleans LA 70115

WIRSUM, KARL
PAINTER, SCULPTOR
b Chicago, Ill, Sept 27, 39. *Study:* Sch Art Inst, Chicago, BFA, 61. *Work:* AT&T, Chase Manhattan, Citibank & Whitney Mus Am Art, New York; Art Inst Chicago, First Nat Bank, Smart Gallery/Univ Chicago & Mus Contemp Art, Chicago; Nat Mus Am Art, Smithsonian Inst, Washington, DC; Mus des 20, Jahrhunderts, Vienna; Weatherspoon Art Gallery, Univ NC, Greensboro. *Comn:* First Natl Bank, Chicago, Ill; Harold Washington Libr, Chicago, Ill. *Exhib:* Solo exhibs, Hare Toddy Kong Tamari, Mus Contemp Art, Chicago, 81, Southeastern Ctr Contemp Art, Winston-Salem, NC, 82, Du Page Col, Glen Ellyn, Ill, 88, and many others; Made in USA: An Americanization in Mod Art, the 50's & 60's Traveling Show, 87; Friday Diego: Una Pareja, Prairie Ave Gallery, Chicago, 87; Contemp Cutouts: Figurative Sculpture in Two Dimensions, Whitney Mus Am Art, New York, 87-88; Diamonds are Forever: Artists & Writers on Baseball, Traveling Show, 87-90; Seymour Rosofsky & the Chicago Imagist Tradition, Milwaukee Art Mus, Univ Wis, 88; Birthday Cake, Hyde Park Art Ctr, Chicago, 89; Chicago Painters in Print, Landfall Press, 89-90; and many others. *Teaching:* Part-time instr painting & drawing, Sch Art Inst, Chicago, 74- *Awards:* Logan Medal, Chicago and Vicinity Show, Chicago Art Inst, 69; Nat Endowment Arts Fel, 71, 77 & 83; Ill Arts Coun Fel, 86. *Bibliog:* Comic Iconoclasm, Inst Contemp Arts, London, Eng, 87; A broad brush colors Terra's exhib of Chicago Art, Chicago Tribune, 9/11/87; The Import of Imagism, Dialogue Mag, 5/6/88. *Media:* Acrylic; Wood. *Dealer:* Phyllis Kind Gallery 313 W Superior Chicago IL 60610 & 136 Greene St New York NY 10012. *Mailing Add:* c/o Phyllis Kind Gallery 313 W Superior St Chicago IL 60610

WIRTZ, STEPHEN CARL
DEALER
b Peoria, Ill, Apr 9, 45. *Study:* Occidental Col, 63; Univ Calif, Berkeley, BA, 67; Antioch Col, Ohio, MA, 68. *Specialty:* Contemporary American and European sculpture & photography. *Mailing Add:* c/o Stephen Wirtz Gallery 49 Geary St San Francisco CA 94108

WISDOM, JOYCE
PAINTER
b Los Angeles, Calif, June 12, 40. *Study:* Pasadena City Col, 58-59; Univ Calif, Los Angeles, 59-61; Univ Southern Calif, BFA, 62. *Work:* Los Angeles Inst Contemp Art. *Exhib:* Solo exhibs, Munic Art Gallery, 78, Barnsdall Art Ctr, 90, Los Angeles; To the Astonishing Landscape LAVA Exhib, Design Ctr Los Angeles, 85; Fifth Int Juried Exhib Pastels, Ky Highlands Mus, 88; Drawing 89, B F Larsen Gallery, Brigham Young Univ, Provo, Utah; Seven Western States Open Juried Exhib, Long Beach Art Asn, 90; Calif Works, Calif Expos & State Fair, Sacramento, 91. *Teaching:* Instr drawing & design, Calif State Univ, Northridge, 78-80; instr, Junior Art Ctr, Los Angeles, 78-93; instr, Life drawing & painting, Barnsdall Art Ctr, 81-93; instr, landscape painting, Univ Calif, Los Angeles, 91-92. *Awards:* Silver Mat Award, Oil Pastel Asn, 88; Lucille Julia Award, Oil Pastel Asn, 90; First Prize Juried Exhib, Long Beach Art Asn, 90. *Bibliog:* Louise Lewis (auth), Desert moods & sensuality, Artweek, 6/1/78; Suzanne Muchnic (auth), Wisdom's world in landscape, Los Angeles Times, 6/8/78; S Muchnic (auth), The Galleries, Los Angeles Times, 83. *Media:* Oil, Oil Pastel. *Mailing Add:* 21144 Hillside Dr W Topanga CA 90290

WISE, GENEVA H (HOLCOMB)
COLLECTOR, PAINTER
b Pittsburg, Kans. *Study:* Okla State Univ, BA; with Doel Reed, Edward N Walker, David De Allende, Elinor Evans, Dale McKinney, Milford Zornes, George Post, Father John Walch & Al Brouillette. *Work:* Okla State Univ;

Baptist Med Ctr, Oklahoma City; Alpha Delta Pi, Okla State Univ; and many pvt collections in several states. *Exhib:* one-woman show, Okla State Univ, 75 & Town & Gown Theater, 79; Ann Artists Salon, Okla Mus Art, Oklahoma City, 76-78; 15th Ann, Temple Emanu-El, Dallas, Tex, 78; Centennial Exhib, Am Asn Univ Women, Boston Univ, 81; Nat Soc Painters in Casein & Acrylic, 84; Okla Art Guild, Oklahoma City, 85; Edmond Art Asn, Central State Univ, Okla, 86; Edmond Art Asn, Okla Christian Col, 87; Nat Art Exhib, Arlington, Tex, 88; Okla Watercolor Assoc, Kirkpatrick Center, Okla City, 88; Alumni Exhib, OSU Dept Art, Gardiner Art Gallery & Bartlett Center for the Studio Arts (alumni from all over the US), 88; and others. *Awards:* Asel Materials Co Award, Dallas, 67; Award for Watercolor, Southwestern Watercolor Soc; First Place Watercolor & Acrylic, Okla Fedn Women's Clubs, 88 & 90. *Bibliog:* Article, La Rev Mod, Paris, 2/72; Caralee Strock Stanard (auth), article, Adelphian Mag, 74. *Mem:* Okla Watercolor Asn; Okla Art Guild; Southwestern Watercolor Soc; Stillwater Art Guild; Nat Soc Painters Casein & Acrylic; Edmond Art Asn, Okla; Am Assoc Univ Women (chmn). *Media:* Transparent Watercolor, Acrylic. *Collection:* Doel Reed aquatint; Dale McKinney silk screen; J J McVicker intaglio; Howard Bradford serigraph; Kaethe Kollwitz etching and BN Smith print, Greg Burns acrylic canvas, Okla City, & others. *Publ:* Auth, Milford Zornes, internationally known artist, Westview, summer, 88; SW Okla State, summer 88. *Mailing Add:* 305 S Monroe St Stillwater OK 74074

WISE, GERALD LEE
GRAPHIC ARTIST, PRINTMAKER
b Pittsburgh, Pa, Dec 15, 41. *Study:* Wheaton Col, Ill, BA, 63; Northern Ill Univ, MA(design), 67, MFA(printmaking), 69. *Work:* Mankato State Univ; Ball State Univ; St Lawrence Col. *Exhib:* Drawings USA, Minn Mus Art, 73; Ball State Drawing & Sculpture, 73 & 82; 24th Nat Prints & Drawing Exhib, Okla Art Ctr, 82; Springfield Nat Exhib, Mus Fine Arts, Mass, 82 & 83; West 82--Art and the Law Traveling Exhib, 82 & 83; Tex Fine Arts Nat, Laguna Gloria Mus, Austin, 83; 17th Nat Drawing & Sculpture Exhib, Del Mar Col Gallery, Tex, 83. *Teaching:* Asst prof art, Mankato State Univ, 69-74 & Westfield State Col, 82-; instr, G Walter V Smith Art Mus, Springfield, Mass, 80-82. *Awards:* Purchase Awards, 24th Nat Drawing & Print Exhib, Okla Art Ctr, 82, 63rd & 64th Springfield Nat Exhib, Holyoke Community Savings Bank, Mass, 82 & 83 & Mattoon Art Festival, Bank Boston, 83. *Bibliog:* Robert Girouard (auth), Wiser yet, Mankato Free Press, 4/4/74; Mary Kronholm (auth), Wise makes living an art, Country J, 6/82; Sally Robinson (auth), A profile: Gerald Wise, Westfield Sunday News, 9/82. *Mem:* Col Art Asn; Springfield Artists League. *Media:* Ink, Pen and Brush. *Dealer:* Hill Gallery Worthington MA 01098. *Mailing Add:* Dept Art Westfield State Col Western Ave Westfield MA 01086

WISE, JOSEPH STEPHEN
PAINTER
b Seattle, Wash, Nov 26, 39. *Study:* Purdue Univ, 57-58, Univ Puget Sound, 59-60, San Jose State Univ, Ma, 66; Indiana Univ, BS, 63; San Jose State Univ, MA, 66. *Work:* San Jose Art Mus, Calif; De Saisset Art Mus, Santa Clara, Calif; IBM Corp, Westview Gallery, 87-88, San Jose, Calif. *Comn:* Abstract, Owens/Corning Fiberglass Corp, Sunnyvale, Calif, 70; abstract mural, comn by Mr & Mrs Domingo Escamilla, Milpetas, Calif, 78; Pigs (abstract), Amdahl Corp, Sunnyvale, Calif, 79; abstract, IBM Corp, San Jose, Calif, 82; abstract, San Jose Pub Libr, Calif. *Exhib:* One-man shows, Old Triton Art Mus, San Jose, Calif, 67, Idaho State Col, Moscow, Idaho, 69, Wash State Col, Pullman, 69, Cabrillo Jr Col Art Gallery,Aptos, Calif, 74 & Dunn Instruments, San Francisco, Calif, 77; 85th Ann Nat Exhib, Mus Art, San Francisco, 67; Discovery Gallery, San Jose, Calif, 77; Agnes Fine Arts Gallery, San Jose, Calif, 80; Greenleaf Gallery, Saratoga, Calif, 81. *Pos:* Judge, Los Gatos Cats Art Exhib, 88. *Teaching:* Instr art, W Valley Jr Col, 64-67; instr art, San Jose Pub Sch, 68-88. *Awards:* Award for Oil Painting, San Jose Art League, 71. *Mem:* Nat Educ Asn; Calif Teachers Asn; Life mem West Point Alumni Asn; Calif Art Educ Asn. *Media:* Oil, Canvas. *Collection:* Original artwork By Goya, Boucher, Watteau, Zuniga, Miro, P Jenkins & more. *Publ:* Contemporary American Impressionists, Corrale's, 89. *Dealer:* Bingham Gallery 54 W Santa Clara St San Jose CA. *Mailing Add:* 4383 Glenmount Dr San Jose CA 95136

WISE, KENNETH KELLY
PHOTOGRAPHER, CRITIC
b New Castle, Ind, Dec 1, 32. *Study:* Purdue Univ, BS, 55; Columbia Univ, MA, 59. *Work:* Libr Cong; Bibliotheque Nat, Paris; George Eastman House, Int Mus Photog, Rochester, NY; Mus Fine Arts, Boston; Mus Fine Arts, Houston. *Exhib:* Solo exhib, Fogg Art Mus, 73, Addison Gallery Am Art, Andover, Mass, 85, Art Ctr, Delaware Univ, 86, Art Gallery, Con Col, 86, Yuen Lui Gallery, Seattle, 86, Kresge Art Mus, Mich State Univ, 87, Brockton Art Mus, 87; Private Realities, Mus Fine Arts, Boston, 74; Recent Photographs, Il Diaframma, Milan, Italy, 77; Warm Truths & Cool Deceits, Sidney Janis Gallery, New York, 78; Color Photographs, Snite Art Mus, Univ Notre Dame, 81; Still Points, Rose Art Mus, Brandeis Univ, 81; Portraits: Men & Women of Letters, Vision Gallery, Boston, 83; Iisalmon Kamera, Helsinki, Finland, 84; Archive Gallery, New York, 87. *Collections Arranged:* Photo Facts and Opinions, 18 Contemporary American Photographers, 81. *Pos:* Photog consult, Nat Humanities Fac, Concord, Mass, 70-74 & Polaroid Corp, Cambridge, Mass, 74-77; photog critic, Boston Globe, 82-; art commentator, Nat Pub Radio 87-89. *Awards:* City Limits Proj Grants, Polaroid Corp, 85-87. *Bibliog:* Max Kozloff (auth), Photography & Fascination, Addison House Publ, 79. *Mem:* Soc Photog Educ; Photog Resource Ctr, Boston. *Publ:* Ed, The Photographers Choice, 75, auth, Still Points, 77 & ed, Lotte Jacobi, 78, Addison House; assoc ed, Views Jour Photog, 80-81; ed, Portrait: Theory, Lustrum Press, 81; ed, Photo Facts and Opinions, Addison Gallery Am Art, 81; ed, Photog, City Limits, 87. *Dealer:* Howard Yezerski Gallery, 186 South St Boston MA 02111. *Mailing Add:* Office Photography Critic Boston Globe 135 William T Morrissey Blvd Dorchester MA 02125

WISE, SUE
PAINTER
b Bronx, NY, Mar 22, 21. *Study:* Univ Colo with Gene Mathews & Frank Sampson; special study with Thomas Currey & William Schimmel. *Work:* Colo Council Arts & Humanities, First Nat Bank, United Bank, Denver, Colo; Nat State Bank, Boulder, Colo; Midland Federal Savings, Longmont, Colo. *Exhib:* Own Your Own Exhib, Denver Art Mus, Colo, 68; Watercolor USA, Springfield Art Mus, Mo, 71; 60th Ann Exhib, Nat Watercolor Soc, Laguna Beach, Calif, 80; Fine Arts Exhib, State Fair, Pueblo, Colo, 81; Rocky Mountain Nat, Foothills Art Ctr, Colo, 81; 114th Ann Exhib, Am Watercolor Soc, Nat Acad Galleries, New York, 81; and others. *Awards:* Bronze Medal of Honor, Am Watercolor Soc, 74; Foothills Art Ctr Award, 78; Mary Pleissner Mem Award, Am Watercolor Soc, 82. *Mem:* Am Watercolor Soc; Nat Watercolor Soc; Dolphin Fel. *Media:* Mixed Watermedia, Collage. *Publ:* Auth, The watercolor page, Am Artist Mag, 2/77; contribr, Easy Living Mag, The Webb Co, 78; Creative Seascape Painting, Watson-Guptill; Exploring Painting, Davis Publ Inc. *Dealer:* Mustard Seed Gallery 1932 14th St Boulder CO 80302. *Mailing Add:* 10261 Macedonia St Longmont CO 80503

WISE, SUZANNE TANDERUP
ADMINISTRATOR, HISTORIAN
b Great Lakes, Ill, Jan 31, 52. *Study:* Univ Nebr, Lincoln, BA, 74; Univ Kans, MA, 80. *Pos:* Cur, Mary & Leigh Block Gallery, Northwestern Univ, 82-84; educ specialist, Sheldon Art Gallery, Univ Nebr, Lincoln, 84-; visual arts coordr, Nebr Arts Coun, 87- *Teaching:* Instr art hist, Univ Nebr, 79-82 & 85- & Creighton Univ, 80. *Mem:* Col Art Asn; Am Asn Mus; Midwest Art Hist Soc; Nat Art Educ Asn. *Res:* Nineteenth and twentieth century American painting and photography. *Publ:* Contribr, Jules Breton and the French Rural Tradition, 82 & Joslyn Art Museum Handbook of the Permanent Collection, 83, Joslyn Art Mus; Alice Aycock: The Machine That Makes the World, Nouveau and Deco Art Glass, 85; American Impressionism from the Sheldon Collection, Sheldon Art Gallery, 86. *Mailing Add:* Nebr Arts Coun 1313 Farnam-on-the-Mall Omaha NE 68102-1873

WISE, TAKOUHY
GALLERY DIRECTOR, ART DEALER
b Teheran, Iran; US citizen. *Study:* Univ Lausanne, Switz, 61-63; Int Ctr Photog, 77-80. *Collections Arranged:* Hollywood Fashion, 83, Nudes by Fashion Photographers, 83, Portraits of Artists, 84, Louise Dahl Wolfe, 84 & Horst: His Work and World, 85, Staley-Wise Gallery, New York. *Pos:* Fashion & photog ed, Seventeen Mag, 67-70; co-dir, Staley-Wise Gallery, New York, currently. *Specialty:* 20th century photography. *Mailing Add:* Staley-Wise Gallery 560 Broadway New York NY 10012

WISNOSKY, JOHN G
PAINTER, EDUCATOR
b Springfield, Ill, Mar 21, 40. *Study:* Yale Univ Summer Sch Art, 61; Univ Ill, Urbana, BFA, 62, MFA, 64. *Work:* Honolulu Acad Arts, Hawaii; Southern Ill Univ, Carbondale; Contemp Arts Ctr, Hawaii, Honolulu; State Hawaii Found Cult & Arts; Mint Mus, Charlotte, NC; Rose Art Mus, Brandeis Univ. *Comn:* Pan Pac hall design, Hawaii Pavilion, Osaka World's Fair, 70; Flora Pacifica design, Ethnobotanical Expos, 71 & 82; Inst Astronomy, Mauna Kea, Hawaii, 85; Hilo Hosp, Hawaee, 85. *Exhib:* Soc Am Graphic Artists, New York, 65; Presentation Artist Show, Boston Printmakers, Boston Mus Fine Art, 66; Drawings-USA, St Paul Art Ctr, Minn, 67; Am Printmakers Exhib, Otis Art Inst, 68; Pan Pacific Exhib, Seoul, S Korea, 85; Cityscape/Landscape, Franz Bader Gallery, Washington, DC, 88. *Teaching:* Instr painting & design, Va Polytech Inst, 64-66; prof & chmn, Univ Hawaii, 66-75; acting chmn George Mason Univ, 87-88; prof & grad chmn, Univ of Hawaii, 90- *Awards:* Henry B Shope Prize, Soc Am Graphic Artists, 65; Purchase Award, Honolulu Acad Arts, 70. *Bibliog:* Neogy & Turnbull (ed), Artists of Hawaii, Vol II; G & W Radford (auth), Sculpture in the Sun, 78. *Mem:* Fel, Hand Hollow Found, 83. *Mailing Add:* Dept Art/142C Univ Hawaii at Manoa 2500 Campus Rd Honolulu HI 96822

WISSEMANN-WIDRIG, NANCY
PAINTER
b Jamestown, NY. *Study:* Syracuse Univ, NY, BFA; Ohio Univ, Athens, MFA. *Work:* Canton Art Inst, Ohio; Univ Kans Mus Fine Arts; Port Authority of New York; Univ Tulsa, Okla; Minn Mining & Mfg Co. *Exhib:* Farnsworth Mus, Rockland, Maine, 83, 90; 44 Women Artists, One Penn Plaza, 88; Waterworks, Hecksher Mus, Huntington, New York, 88; Mus at Stony Brook, NY, 90; one-person shows, Tibor de Nagy Gallery, New York, 74, 77, 80, 81, 83 & Tatistcheff, 87, Hobe Sound North, 84, Caldbeck, Rockland, Maine, 87, Tatistcheff, 92; Gallery 68, Belfast, Maine, 91-92; Bernice Steinbaum Gallery, Soho, NY, 92; Maine Coast Artists, Rockport, 92; Carl Little & Arnold Skolnick (coauths), Painting of Maine, Potter, 91. *Awards:* Outstanding Realist, Western New York Artists, Albright-Knox Art Gallery, 64; Purchase Award, Am Acad of Arts & Lett, Childe Hassam Fund, 69. *Bibliog:* Ronald G Pisano (auth), Long Island Landscape Painting, Vol II: The Twentieth Century, Bulfinch, 90; Bernice Steinbaum (auth), The Rocking Chair, Rizzoli, 92. *Mem:* E End Arts & Humanities Long Island. *Media:* Acrylic, Oil. *Dealer:* Tatischeff 50 W 57th St New York NY 10019. *Mailing Add:* HC 68 Box 157 Cushing ME 04563-9508

WISSMEYER, GUNTER GUSTAV
PAINTER, PHOTOGRAPHER
b Hamburg, Ger, Aug 1, 40. *Study:* Studied with Harmut Rhode, DusseldorF, 82-83; City Darmstadt, 84-86. *Exhib:* Images & Objects, Klee Wick House, W Vancouver, Can, 89; New Painting, North Vancouver District Hall, Can, 90. *Bibliog:* N Shore News, Wissmeyer Abstracts at City Hall, 90; S Rheintal (auth), G Wissmeyer Stelltaus Kanada, Kurier, 92. *Mem:* Fedn Can Artists, Vancouver, Can. *Media:* Oil on Paper, Mixed Media. *Dealer:* Ipomal Gallery Kerkberg 2 Landgraaf Holland 6374 ES; Sui Gemeris 3053 Highland Blvd North Vancouver BC V7R 2X4 Canada. *Mailing Add:* 421 E 29th St North Vancouver BC V7N 1E2 Canada

WITHAM, VERNON CLINT
PAINTER, PRINTMAKER
b Eugene, Ore, Dec 6, 25. *Study:* Univ Ore; Calif Sch Fine Arts, San Francisco. *Work:* Univ Ore Mus Art, Eugene; Univ Wyo Mus Art, Laramie. *Comn:* Murals, Multnoma Athletic Club, Portland, Ore. *Exhib:* Under 25, Seligmann Gallery, New York, 49; Artists of Oregon, Portland Art Mus, 53; one-man shows, Calif Palace Legion of Honor, San Francisco, 60 & Univ Ore Mus Art, 80; Maxwell Gallery, San Francisco, 61; American Landscape, Peridot Gallery, New York, 68. *Teaching:* Resident artist, Univ Wyo, 71- *Awards:* Purchase Award, Northwest Painting Ann, 72. *Media:* Oil; All. *Collection:* Antique primitive art from around the world. *Publ:* Coauth, 12 new painters (serigraph folio), 53; contribr, insert 4, Written Palette, 62. *Dealer:* Tiqua Gallery 812 Canyon Rd Santa Fe NM 87501. *Mailing Add:* 901 Paseo de la Cuma Santa Fe NM 87501

WITHERS, JOSEPHINE
HISTORIAN, WRITER
b Cambridge, Mass, July 3, 38. *Study:* Oberlin Col, BA(art hist), 60; Columbia Univ, MA, 65, PhD, 71. *Collections Arranged:* Julio Gonzalez, Sculpture and Drawings, Mus Mod Art, New York, 68; 350 Years of Art in Maryland, 20th Century Section (auth, catalog), Univ Md Art; Women Artists in Washington Collections (auth, catalog), Univ Md Art Gallery, 79. *Pos:* Assoc dir, Univ Md Art Gallery, 70-73; chief reader art hist, Advan Placement Educ Testing Serv, 79-83; art consult, Feminist Studies, 78- *Teaching:* Asst prof art hist, Temple Univ, Philadelphia, Pa, 68-69; assoc dir, Art Gallery, Univ Md, 70-73, asst prof art hist, 71-78, actg dir women's studies prog, 82-84, assoc prof art hist, 78- *Awards:* Aelioian Fel, Oberlin Col, 64; Gen Res Bd, Univ Md, 72, 77 & 85; fel, Nat Endowment Arts, 72 & 78. *Mem:* Col Art Asn; Women's Caucus Art (nat bd dirs, 80-83); Washington Women's Art Ctr (bd dir, 76-77); Conf of Women in the Visual Arts (steering comt, 72); Wash New Art Asn (bd mem, 87-91). *Res:* Twentieth century art; American women artists of the nineteenth and twentieth centuries. *Publ:* Auth, Artistic women and women artists, summer 76 & The artistic collaboration of Picasso and Gonzales, winter 76, Art J; auth, The Famous Fur-Lined Teacup and The Anonymous Meret Oppenheim, Arts Mag, 11/77; Julio Gonzalez, Sculpture in Iron, New York Univ Press, 77; In search of the magic kingdom, New Art Examiner, 10/81; Musing about the muse, Feminist Studies, spring 83. *Mailing Add:* 1832 Biltmore St NW Washington DC 20009

WITHROW, WILLIAM J
ADMINISTRATOR
b Toronto, Ont, Sept 30, 26. *Study:* Univ Toronto, BA, 50, BEd, 55 & MEd, 58, MA, 60. *Pos:* Dir, Art Gallery Ont, Toronto, 60-91, emer dir, currently. *Teaching:* Head art dept, Earl Haig Col, 51-59. *Awards:* Can Centennial Medal, 67; Order Can. *Mem:* Fel Can Mus Asn; Asn Art Mus Dirs; Can Art Mus Dirs Orgn; Can Nat Comt for Int Coun Mus. *Publ:* Auth, Sorel Etrog sculpture, 67 & Contemporary Canadian painting, 72. *Mailing Add:* 7 Malabar Pl Don Mills ON M3B 1A4 Canada

WITKIN, ISAAC
SCULPTOR
b May 10 36; US Citizen. *Study:* St Martins Sch Art, London, with Anthony Caro; also with Henry Moore, Eng. *Work:* Joseph Hirshhorn Mus, Washington, DC; Tate Gallery, London, Eng; Laumier Sculpture Park, Nat Mus Am Art, Washington, DC; Columbus Mus, Ohio; Storm King Art Ctr. *Comn:* Sculpture, Storm King Art Ctr, Mountainville, NY, 70; sculpture, Springfield, Mass, 75; City of Springfield, Mass; Dept Transportation , Trenton, NJ; ALCOA Inc, Pittsburgh, PA; Govt Servs Admin, Baltimore, MD; LaGuardia Community Col, comn Long Island City, NY. *Exhib:* One-man shows, Marlborough Gallery, 75, 76 & 78, Hamilton Gallery, 79 & 81, Keene-Thorne, 77, Tanglewood Music Festival, 77 & Hirsch & Adler Mod, New York, 85, Jan Turner Gallery, Los Angeles, Calif, 89, Patricia Hamilton Gallery, NY, 90, Locks Gallery, Philadelphia, 91; Carnegie Ctr Outdoor Sculpture Exhib, Princeton, NJ, 88; Inaugural Exhib, James Mitchener Fine Arts Ctr, Doylestown, Pa, 88; The Life Force, Robeson Ctr Gallery, Rutgers Univ, NJ, 88; Color in Sculpture, Gimpel-Weitzenhoffer Gallery, NY, 89; Directions, Locks Gallery, Philadelphia, Pa, 90-91. *Teaching:* Instr sculpture, St Martins Sch Art, 63-65; instr sculpture, Bennington Col, 65-; instr sculpture, Parsons Sch Design, 75-78; vis artist, Skowhegan Sch Painting & Sculpture, Maine, 84; vis prof, Middlebury Col, Vt, 81. *Awards:* Co-Winner First Prize, Paris Bienale, 65; Guggenheim Fel, 81; NJ State Coun on Arts Grant, 85. *Bibliog:* First Prize, Paris Bienale, 65; Bill Lipke (dir), film, Vt Coun Arts, 72; Neil Marshand (dir), film, Nat Edoc TV, 75; Grace Glueck (auth), Issac Witkins Lyrical Sculpture, The NY Times, 85. *Mem:* Int Sculpture Ctr (bd dir); Yale Univ Advisory Comt. *Media:* Steel, Bronze. *Publ:* Auth, Modern English Sculpture, Thames and Hudson, 67; contribr, Minimal Art, Dutton, 68; auth, Alistair Healpine Gift, Tate Gallery, 71; contribr, New York Mag, 4/9/73. *Mailing Add:* 137 Scrapetown Rd Pemberton NJ 08068

WITKIN, JEROME
PAINTER, DRAFTSMAN
b Brooklyn, NY, Sept 13, 39. *Study:* Cooper Union Art Sch, 57-60; Skowhegan Sch Painting & Sculpture; Berlin Acad, WGer, Pulitzer traveling fel, 60; Univ Pa, MFA, 70. *Work:* Hirshhorn Mus; Uffizi Gallery, Florence, Italy; Butler Inst Am Art, Youngstown, Ohio; Am Acad Arts & Letters; Everson Mus Art, Syracuse; Nat Acad Design; Metrop Mus Art, New York; Minn Mus, St Paul, Minn; Nat Acad Design, New York; Ark Art Ctr, Little Rock, Ark; Achenback Found Graphic Arts, San Francisco, Calif. *Comn:* Portraits, Flower Veterinary Library, NY State Col Veterinary Medicine. *Exhib:* Drawings USA, Minn Mus Art, 71; Sherry French Gallery, New York; Drawings, Kraushaar Gallery, New York, 71; Pa State Mus, 78; Religion into Art, nat traveling exhib, 81; Real, Really Real, Super Real, San Antonio Mus, 81-82; travelling show, West '85 Art & the Law; Morality Tales: History Painting in the 80's, Independent Curators Inc, New York, 87-88; Noctures & Nightmares, Fla State Univ Gallery & Mus, 87; Life Stories, Henry Art Gallery, Univ Wash, Seattle, 88. *Teaching:* Instr drawing, Md Inst Art, Baltimore, 63-65; lectr painting, Manchester Col Art, Eng, 65-67; vis prof design, drawing & painting, Moore Col, 68-71; assoc prof art, Syracuse Univ, 71-81, prof, 82-; lectr, Columbia Mus Art, SC, 83, Ark Art Ctr, Little Rock, 83; Vis artist, Univ Utah, 86, Univ Wis, 88 & Univ Wash, 88. *Awards:* Arggenheim Found Fel Painting, 63-64; Paul Puzinas Award, Nat Acad Design, 80; Fund Purchase Prize, Am Acad Arts & Letters, 81; Chancellor's Citation for Excellence in Teaching, Syracuse Univ, 83. *Bibliog:* Theodore F Wolff (auth), The excellence of the work of Jerome Witkin, 4/28/83 & A master storyteller on the threshold of great art, 11/6/85, Christian Sci Monitor; Kenneth Baker (auth), Paintings not to miss: Jerome Witkin in Santa Clara, San Francisco Chronicle, 87; W S Di Piero (auth), Force & witness: on Jerome Witkin, Arts Mag, 11/87. *Mem:* Assoc mem Nat Acad Design. *Media:* Oil on Linen. *Mailing Add:* 435 Whittier Ave Syracuse NY 13204

WITKIN, JOEL-PETER
PHOTOGRAPHER
b Brooklyn, NY, Sept 13, 39. *Study:* Cooper Union, New York, BFA, 75; Univ NMex, MA, 77, MFA, 86. *Work:* Mus Mod Art, New York; Stiejik Mus, Amsterdam; Victoria and Albert Mus, London; Getty Mus, Los Angeles; Centre Georges Pompidou. *Exhib:* Fraenkel Gallery, San Francisco, 87 & 93; Pace/MacGill Gallery, New York, 87 & 93; Galerie Watari, Tokyo, 87; Centro de Arte, Reina Sofia, Madrid, 88; Centre Georges Pompidou, Paris, 88; Guggenheim Mus, Venice, Italy, 93. *Awards:* Creative Artists Pub Serv Prog Fel Photog, 75; Ford Found Grant Photog, 76, 78 & 79; Nat Endowment Arts Fel Photog, 80, 81, 86 & 92; Int Ctr Photography Award in Art Photography, 88; Cooper Union Distinguished Alumni Citation, 88. *Bibliog:* Monogr, 85 & Masterpieces of Medical Photography, 87, Twelve Trees Press; Monogr, Reina Sofia Mus, Madrid, Spain, 88. *Media:* Photography. *Publ:* Auth, Forty Photographs, San Francisco Mus Mod Art, 85; Photovision, Madrid, Spain, 88. *Dealer:* Pace/MacGill 11 E 57 St New York NY 10022; Fraenkel Gallery 55 Grant Ave San Francisco CA 94108. *Mailing Add:* 222 Amherst St NE Albuquerque NM 87106

WITMEYER, STANLEY HERBERT
PAINTER, CONSULTANT
b Palmyra, Pa, Feb 14, 13. *Study:* Sch Art & Design, Rochester Inst Technol, dipl; State Univ NY Col Buffalo, BS; Syracuse Univ, MFA; Univ Hawaii, with Ben Norris. *Exhib:* Rochester Mem Art Gallery; Albright-Knox Gallery, Buffalo; Honolulu Acad Fine Arts; Everson Mus, Syracuse. *Pos:* Dir sch art & design, Rochester Inst Technol, 52-68, assoc dean Col Fine & Appl Arts, 68-82. *Teaching:* Instr art, Cuba Pub Schs, NY, 39-44; prof painting & design, Sch Art Design, Rochester Inst Technol, 46-52. *Awards:* Distinguished Alumni Award, Rochester Inst Technol, 72; Distinguished State Art Teachers Award, NY, 78; Distinguished Alumni Award, State Univ NY, Buffalo, 80. *Mem:* Rochester Torch Club (pres, 52); Nat Art Educ Asn; Rochester Art Club (pres, 56); NY State Art Teachers Asn. *Media:* Mixed. *Collection:* American printmakers and painters. *Publ:* Auth, articles in, Everyday Art, Design Mag, Sch Arts, Nat Art Educ J & NY Art Teachers Bulletin. *Mailing Add:* 54 Clarks Crossing Fairport NY 14450

WITOLD-K (KACZANOWSKI)
PAINTER, SCULPTOR
b Warsaw, Poland, May 15, 32; US citizen. *Study:* Acad Fine Arts, Warsaw, with W Fangor & H Tomaszerski, dipl, 56 Univ Warsaw, 64. *Work:* Mus NMex, Santa Fe; Phoenix Art Mus, Ariz; Nat Libr, Paris, France; Conoco Oil Co, Houston, Tex; United Calif Bank. *Comn:* Mural, Polish Exhib, Moscow, USSR, 60; Auschwitz (mural), Govt Poland, 61; painting, United Bank Calif, Beverly Hills, 71; painting, Conoco Oil Co, Houston, Tex, 74; mural, Mainstreet Art Festival, Houston, 75. *Exhib:* Solo exhibs, Keystone Ctr, Colo, 77, Anneke Whatley Gallery, Keystone, Colo, 78, Gallery 400, Aspen, Colo, 79, J Houston Gallery, Vail, Colo, 81 & Richtofen Castle, Denver, 81; Gallery Arte, Denver, Colo, 86; Classic Century Sq Gallery, NMex, 87; Visual Arts Ctr Peace Exhib, Boulder, Colo, 88. *Teaching:* Lectr, Seton Hall Univ, 71, Cranbrook Acad Art, 78, Univ Detroit, 78, Wedgewood Soc, Chicago, 79 & Alliance Francaise Soc, Calif, 87. *Bibliog:* Michel Casse (ed), Le Crevasses du Ciel, Paris, 67. *Media:* Oil, Acrylic; Metal. *Mailing Add:* 329 Detroit St Denver CO 80206

WITT, DAVID L
WRITER, CURATOR
b Kansas City, Mo, Nov 3, 51. *Study:* Kans State Univ, BS, 74. *Collections Arranged:* Emil Bisttram, 83; True Fresco: The Artistic Descendants of Diego Rivers, 86; Larry Calcagno, 87; Joe Waldrum, 88; Earl Stroh, Paintings 1953-1990, 90-91. *Pos:* Curitorial asst, Seton Mus, Cimarron, NMex, 72-74; cur,

Gaspard House Mus, Taos, NMex, 78-79; cur, Harwood Found Mus, Taos, NMex, 79- *Mem:* Am Asn Mus; Mountain-Plains Mus Asn (coun mem, 83-85); NMex Asn Mus (pres, 86-88); NMex Art Hist Conf (founder, 86). *Res:* specializes in the artists and art history of twentieth century New Mexico. *Publ:* Auth, The Taos Artist: A Historical Narrative and Biographical Dictionary, Ewell Fine Art Publ, 84; auth, Art Pioneers, NMex Mag, 87; contribr, The Transcendental Art of Emil Bisttram, Pintres Press, 88; Taos Moderns: Art of the New, Red Crane Bks, 92. *Mailing Add:* PO Box 317 Taos NM 87571

WITT, JOHN
PAINTER, PRINTMAKER
b Wilmington, Del, Jan 30, 40. *Study:* Philadelphia Col Art, BFA, 62; Univ Md Grad Sch; Brooklyn Mus Sch Art. *Work:* New Britain Mus Am Art; Smithsonian Inst, USMC Combat Art Collections, US Navy Combat Art Collection, Pentagon & US Army, Off Chief Mil Hist, Washington, DC. *Comn:* Oil Painting, Ida Lewis Rescue 1869, US Coast Guard 200th Anniversary Moments in History Collection. *Exhib:* Smithsonian Inst Vietnam Exhib, Washington, DC, 69; Nat Arts Club, New York, 72; Hudson Valley Art Asn Ann, White Plains, NY, 72; Audubon Artists Ann, New York, 73; Am Artists Prof League Ann, New York, 73. *Pos:* Combat artist, USMC Civilian Comn, 68 & 69; combat artist, US Navy, 73 & 76; courtroom trial artist, ABC News, 74; chmn, Soc Illusrs Mus Am Illus, 88- *Teaching:* Instr illus, State Univ NY, 84- *Awards:* Gold Medal, Hudson Valley Art Asn, 72; Best in Show, Nat Arts Club, New York, 72; Gold Medal, Louis E Seley NACAL Award, 78; Dean Cornwell Award, Soc of Illustr, 90. *Bibliog:* US Army, Executive Corridor Section of the Army, USGPO, 66; Mark Goodman (auth), Trial of art, New Times Mag, 5/17/74; Col Raymond Henri (auth), Combat art since 1775, Marine Corps Gazette, 74;; US Coast Guard Moments in History, 90. *Mem:* Soc Illusr (pres, 80-83); Hudson Valley Art Asn; Dutch Treat Club. *Media:* Multimedia. *Publ:* Auth & illusr, Vietnam, Sterling, 72; illusr, Mitchell-Stans Trial, Newsweek Mag, & Mitchell-Stans Trial Courtroom Drawings, ABC News, 74; illusr, Marine Corps Gazette, 74; illusr, Portraits of Valor, USMC, 74. *Mailing Add:* RD 1 Box 369 Baptist Church Rd Yorktown Heights NY 10598

WITT, NANCY CAMDEN
PAINTER, SCULPTOR
b Richmond, Va, Oct 24, 30. *Study:* Randolph-Macon Woman's Col; Old Dominion Univ, BA, 65; Va Commonwealth Univ, MFA, 67. *Work:* Miss Mus Art; Mint Mus Art, Charlotte, NC; Randolph-Macon Woman's Col, Lynchburg; Chase Manhattan Bank, New York; Chrysler Mus, Norfolk, Va; CSX Corp, Richmond, Va; and others. *Comn:* Mobile construct, Philip Morris Tobacco Co, Richmond, 69-70; mural, Security Fed Savings & Loan Co, Richmond, 71; portrait, Randolph-Macon Col, Ashland, Va, 79; portrait, Richmond Symphony, 79; portrait, Crowder United, 81; and others. *Exhib:* Mint Mus Art, 71, 75, 77 & 79; Mainstreams, Marietta, Ohio, 75-77; Int Woman Artists Exhib, 76; Realist Invitational, Southeastern Ctr for Contemp Art, Winston-Salem NC, 78 & 80; retrospective, Roanoke Col, Salem, Va, 79; Miss Mus Art, 79; Va Mus, Richmond, 79-80; solo exhib, Southeastern Ctr Contemp Art, Winston-Salem, NC, 80; Portsmouth Mus, Va, 85; Touchstone Gallery, New York, 86; Cudahy's, Richmond & New York, 90; and others. *Teaching:* Actg chmn dept art, Richard Bland Col, Col William & Mary, 61-63 & 64-65. *Awards:* Purchase Prize, Exec Towers Sculpture, Va Comn on Arts & Humanities, 75; Award, Int Woman Artists Exhib, 76; Purchase Prize, Henrico Libr, Richmond, Va, 80. *Bibliog:* Subject of Vanishing Point (film), 78. *Media:* Oil; Constructions. *Mailing Add:* c/o Cudahy's Gallery 1314 E Cary St Richmond VA 23219

WITTE, MARY (GRACE) STIEGLITZ
PHOTOGRAPHER, EDUCATOR
b Fairbanks, Alaska. *Study:* Univ Wis, Milwaukee, BS (art & art educ), 63, Madison, PhD, 72, post doctoral cert, 87; Ind Univ, Bloomington, MAT (fine arts), 65. *Work:* Kodak Mus, Harrow, England; Sci Mus, London; Ind Univ Union, Indianapolis; Minolta-Manpower Int; Centeyun Ltd. *Exhib:* Collage Works Int, Clary-Miner Gallery, Buffalo, NY, 89; Nat Art Competition, NMSU, Mo, 90; Patterns & Textures, West Bend Gallery Fine Arts, West Bend, Wis, 90; Exhib 49!, Braithwaite Fine Arts Gallery, Cedar City, Utah, 90; Art Ex Mechina Nat, Gallery 1708, Richmond, Va, 90; Big Sky Biennial VI, Davis Gallery, Idaho State Univ, 90; Mountain West Biennial, Harrison Mus Art, Utah State Univ, 90; Salamagundi: 9th Ann Open, 47 Fifth Ave, NY, 90; Midwest Photog Invitational VI, Univ Wis-GB, 90; Artists' Books, Anchorage Mus Art, Alaska, 90-91. *Teaching:* From instr to asst prof fine arts, Ind Univ, Indianapolis, 65-71; from asst to prof design, Univ Wis, Madison, 72-81; prof, head design & dir, Goldstein Gallery, Univ Minn, Twin Cities, 81-83; asst dean prof studies & adj prof, Univ Wis Stevens Point, 87-89; prof & chmn art, Boise State Univ, 89- *Awards:* Show Award, Cosmic Women, Magin Gallery, Milwaukee, 76; First Prize Photog, 19th Ann Exhib, Fall River, Mass, 78; First Place Photog, Emerald City Int Classic VII, 88. *Mem:* Int Visual Literacy Asn (vpres, 76-79, pres, 79-80, bd dirs, 82-86); Royal Photog Soc Gt Brit; Int Soc Arts, Sci & Technol; Col Art Asn Am; Nat Art Educ Asn. *Media:* Mixed. *Res:* History of art, particularly design media and photography; visual learning and perception. *Publ:* Auth, articles, Hist Photog, 77, Fiberarts, 86, Visual Literacy Newsletter, 86-87 & Omlea J, 88; IULA Proceedings, 89 & 90; Art Mat Trade News, 89. *Mailing Add:* c/o Boise State Univ Art Dept 1910 University Dr Boise ID 83723

WITTMANN, OTTO
MUSEUM CONSULTANT
b Kansas City, Mo, Sept 1, 11. *Study:* Harvard Univ; Univ Mich, hon degree; Kenyon Col, hon degree; Univ Toledo, hon degree; Skidmore Col, hon degree. *Collections Arranged:* Splendid Century, Masterpieces from France (auth, catalog); Painting in Italy in 18th Century (auth, catalog); Age of Rembrandt (auth, catalog); Art of Van Gogh (auth, catalog). *Pos:* Cur, Hyde Collection, Glens Falls, NY, 38-41; asst dir, Portland Mus Art, Ore, 41; assoc dir, Toledo Mus Art, 53-59, dir, 59-77, emer dir, 77-, vpres & consult, 77-, ed, Mus News, 14 yrs; trustee & consult, Los Angeles Co Mus Art, Los Angeles, 77-79; mem nat coun arts, Nat Endowment Arts Mus Adv Panel, currently; trustee, J Paul Getty Trust, 79- *Teaching:* Instr art hist, Skidmore Col, 38-41. *Awards:* Commander, Order Merit, Italy; Officer, Order Orange-Nassau, Netherlands; Officer, Legion Honor, France. *Mem:* Asn Art Mus Dir (pres, 71-72); Am Asn Mus; Mus Asn Eng; Nat Collection Fine Arts Comn; Col Art Asn Am. *Publ:* Auth numerous museum catalogues & prof articles. *Mailing Add:* J Paul Getty Mus PO Box 2112 Santa Monica CA 90406

WIXOM, WILLIAM D
CURATOR, ART HISTORIAN
b Philadelphia, Pa, July 17, 29. *Study:* Haverford Col, BA, 51; NY Univ Inst Fine Arts, MA, 63. *Collections Arranged:* Treasures from Medieval France (auth, catalog), loan exhib, 66-67, Early Christian, Byzantine, Medieval & Renaissance Galleries of Permanent Collection, 73-77 & Renaissance Bronzes from Ohio Collections (auth, catalog), loan exhib, 75, Cleveland Mus Art; contribr exhib catalogs, sculpture from Notre Dame, Paris, 79, Royal Abbey of Saint-Denis, 81, The Treasury of San Marco, 85, Gothic and Renaissance Art, Nuremburg, 86, Metro Mus Art, New York. *Pos:* From asst cur to cur, Medieval & Renaissance Decorative Arts, Cleveland Mus Art, 58-78, chief cur, Early Western Art, 79; chmn, Dept Medieval Art & the Cloisters, Metrop Mus Art, New York, 79- *Teaching:* Instr, Grad Sem Medieval Art, Case Western Reserve Univ, Cleveland, Ohio, 64-74, adj assoc prof, 67-78, adj prof, 78-79; adj prof fine arts, New York Univ, 81-82. *Awards:* Belg-Am Educ Found fel, 62; Nat Endowment Arts Mus Prof Fel Grant, 73. *Mem:* Col Art Asn (bd dirs, 79-82); Int Ctr Medieval Art (pres, 71-74, bd mem, 71-82); Medieval Acad Am; fel00ierpoint Morgan Libr, New York, 79; fel Soc Antiquaries, London, 85; Snite Art Gallery, Notre Dame Univ (adv coun), 74. *Res:* Early Christian, Byzantine, medieval and renaissance art. *Publ:* Auth, 45 articles in Art Quart, Art Bull, Bull of the Detroit Inst of Arts, Burlington Mag, Cleveland Mus Art Bull, Gesta, Metropolitan Mus of Art Bull, Zeitschrift für Kunstgeschichte, 59-88; contribr, Age of Spirituality, Year 1200 II, Metrop Mus Art Notable Acquisitions and Recent Acquisitions & Radiance and Reflection, Abbot Suger and Saint-Denis, A Symposium, 86, Homage a Hubert Laudais, Festschrift Gerhard Bott, 70-87. *Mailing Add:* Metrop Mus Art Fifth Ave at 82nd St New York NY 10028

WIZON, TOD
PAINTER
b Newark, NJ, June 1, 52. *Study:* Sch Visual Arts, New York, BFA, 74-76. *Work:* Metrop Mus Art, New York; Mus Contemp Art, Los Angeles; Minneapolis Mus Art. *Exhib:* Painting & Sculpture Today, Indianapolis Mus Art, 78; First Person Singular, Pratt Inst Gallery, New York, 80; Am Acad & Inst Arts & Lett, New York, 82; Terminal New York, Brooklyn Harborside Indust Ctr, New York, 83; Contemporary American Landscapes, Hudson River Mus, Yonkers, NY, 84; 8 Artists 8 Years, Sch Visual Arts Gallery, New York, 85; one-man exhibs, PPOW Gallery, New York & Willard Gallery, New York, 84, Phyllis Kind Gallery, Chicago, 85 & Annina Nosei Gallery, New York, 87; A Contemporary View of Nature, Aldrich Mus Contemp Art, 86 & State of the Artists, 87; Works on Paper by 24 Artists, One Twenty Eight Gallery, New York, 88; Divergent Styles, Contemp Am Drawings, Univ Fla Gallery, 90; Nature Creation du Peinter, Musee des Beaux Arts, Lausanne, 91. *Bibliog:* Michael Krugman (auth), Tod Wizon at Willard, Art in Am, 3/81; Ronnie Cohen (auth), article, Art News, 9/84; Laura DeCoppet &Alan Jones (auths), The Art Dealers, Clarkson Potter, New York, 84; Theodore Wolff (auth), Many masks of modern art, Christian Sci Monitor, 11/84. *Media:* Acrylic, All. *Publ:* Contribr, Appearance Mag, 77. *Dealer:* Galerie Bruno Bischofberger, Zurich, Switz. *Mailing Add:* 114 Fourth Pl Brooklyn NY 11231

WOELFFER, EMERSON
PAINTER
b Chicago, Ill, July 27, 14. *Study:* Art Inst Chicago; Inst Design, Chicago, BA & Hon DFA; New Sch for Soc Res, New York, Hon PhD. *Work:* Art Inst Chicago; Whitney Mus Am Art & Mus Mod Art, New York; Univ Ill; Seattle Art Mus; Biblioque Nat, Paris, France; Santa Fe Mus Art, NMex; Am Acad Arts & Sci. *Exhib:* one-man shows, Santa Barbara Mus, Calif, 64, Quay Gallery, San Francisco, Calif, 68, Jodi Scully Gallery, Los Angeles, 72, Poindexter Gallery, New York, Newport Harbor Mus Art, Newport Beach, Calif, Manny Silverman Gallery, Los Angeles, 91; Gruenebaum Gallery, NY, 81-84. *Pos:* Topog draftsman, USAAF, 39-40; resident artist, Honolulu Acad Arts, Hawaii, 70. *Teaching:* Instr, Sch Design, Chicago, 42, Colo Springs Fine Arts Ctr, 50 & Chouinard Art Inst, 59; vis prof, Black Mountain Col, 49; vis prof painting, Univ Southern Calif, summer 62. *Awards:* Raymond A Speiser Mem Prize, Pa Acad Fine Arts, 68; Nat Endowment Arts Grant, 73; Pollock-Crosner Grant, 85-86; Francis J Greenburger Award, New York, 88. *Bibliog:* Archives Am Art, Smithsonian Inst. *Media:* Oil, Acrylic. *Collection:* African, New Guinea & pre-Columbian works; surrealist paintings. *Mailing Add:* 475 Dustin Dr Los Angeles CA 90065

WOFFORD, PHILIP
PAINTER, WRITER
b Van Buren, Ark, Aug 14, 35. *Study:* Univ Ark, BA, 57; Univ Calif, Berkeley, 57-58. *Work:* Whitney Mus Am Art, Brooklyn Mus, New York; James Michener Found, Austin, Tex; RI Sch Design, Providence; Aldrich Mus Contemp Art, Conn; Seattle Mus Art, Wash; Everson Mus, Syracuse, NY;

and others. *Exhib:* San Francisco Mus Ann, 58; Whitney Mus Ann Exhib Am Painting, New York, 69 & 72; One-person shows, Yale Univ, Conn, 73, Nancy Hoffman Gallery, New York, 79, 81, 83, 86, Carnegie Inst, Pa, 82 & Frumkin/Adams Gallery, New York, 88 & 91, Eugene Binder Gallery, Dallas, Tex, 88 & Arthur Roger Gallery, New Orleans, La, 89; One Penn Plaza Gallery, New York, 84; Cranbrook Acad Art Mus, Mich, 86-87; Bennington Col, Vt, 87 & 90; Corcoran Gallery Art, Washington, DC; An Evening of Contemp Art at the Bayly, Bayly Arts Mus, Univ VA, Charlottesville, 88; Drawings, Frumkin/Adams Gallery, New York, 90; Color in Art: American Expressions from the Mid-Twentieth Century to the Present, Samuel P Ham Mus Art, Gainesville, Fla, 90; Frumkin/Adams Gallery, New York, 91. *Teaching:* Instr art, NY Univ Exten, 64-68, Bennington Col, Vt, 69- *Awards:* Woodrow Wilson Fel; Nat Endowment Arts Fel. *Bibliog:* Carter Ratcliff (auth), New informalists, Art News, 2/70; Peter Scheldajl (auth), Return to the sublime, New York Times, 4/18/71. *Publ:* Auth, article, Art Now: New York, 70; Grand Canyon Search Ceremony, Barlenmir House, 72; In the Belly of the Shark, Random House, 72; work in, Poetry Rev, 4/75. *Mailing Add:* Frumkin/Adams Gallery 50 W 57 St New York NY 10019

WOGSTAD, JAMES EVERET
EDUCATOR, ILLUSTRATOR
b Lordsburg, NMex, Sept 24, 39. *Study:* San Antonio Col, cert, 59; Univ Tex, Austin, BFA, 61, MFA, 68. *Comn:* Original graphics prog, Univ Tex Med Sch, San Antonio, 68-69; dioramic backgrounds & natural hist graphic displays, Witte Mus, San Antonio, 70-74. *Pos:* Lead illusr, Creative Commun, Houston, 62-63; chief illusr, Finger Contract Supply, Houston, 63-65; preparator-cur, Witte Mus, 70-74; ed-illusr, Replica in Scale, 72-76 & Aerophile, 76- *Teaching:* Assoc prof art, San Antonio Col, 68-, chmn dept, 73-77. *Mem:* Col Art Asn Am; Tex Asn Schs Art; Tex Jr Col Teachers Asn. *Media:* Acrylic on Canvas; Black Ink on Paper. *Publ:* Illusr, Any Time is Party Time, 67, Auschuitz, 67 & Belsen, 67, Naylor; auth/illusr, AV-8 Harrier, Aerophile, 82; EA-6 Prowler/Intruder, Aerophile, 85. *Mailing Add:* Dept Visual Arts & Technol San Antonio Col 1300 San Pedro Ave San Antonio TX 78212

WOHLENHAUS, GRACE FORCIER
PAINTER
b Stewart, Minn, Sept 5, 19. *Study:* Famous Artist Schools, Cert, 61. *Work:* Traverse County Historical Mus, Wheaton, Minn; Romer Gallery, Casa Erande, Ariz. *Comn:* Mallard duck, City Hall, Wheaton, Minn, 87; wild life mural, Travers County Sportsmen Club, Wheaton, Minn, 90. *Exhib:* Art of the Prairie, Mus Art, Fargo, NDak, 83 & 84; Regional Ajo Alliance of Art, Greenway Mansion, Ajo Ariz, 89-90. *Teaching:* Art, Wheaton Pierson Sch, 81-83. *Awards:* Acceptance Award, Univ Minn, 67; Best of Show, Graceville, Minn, 70. *Mem:* Minn Rural Artists Asn (slide chmn 3 yrs); Ajo Alliance Art. *Media:* Oil, Watercolor. *Mailing Add:* Rt 1 Box 60 Wheaton MN 56296

WOIDE, ROBERT E
PAINTER, ADMINISTRATOR
b Cleveland, Ohio, Jan 27, 27. *Study:* Cleveland Inst Art, with Carl Gaertner, Louis Bosa, Henry Wilcox & Paul Travis, cert, 50; Kent State Univ, with Elmer Novotney, BSE, 51, ME, 62. *Work:* Homerton Gallery, Cambridge, England; Int Inst Gallery, Glion, Switz; Butler Art Inst, Youngstown, Ohio. *Exhib:* Cleveland May Shows, Cleveland Mus Art, 49, 52, 66, 67 & 69; Butler Int, 51 & Mid-Year Exhib, 79, Butler Art Inst; two-person exhib, Int Inst Gallery, Glion, Switz, 79, Massillon Mus, Ohio, 80, Womens City Club, Cleveland, 80 & Garden Ctr, Cleveland, 82, Intown Gallery, Cleveland, 89, Palace Gallery, Graz Austria, 89 & Natural Hist Mus, Cleveland, 90. *Pos:* Asst dir, Canton Art Inst, Ohio, 51-52; vpres, Univ Circle In, 85- *Teaching:* Instr, lectr & supervisor, Cleveland Mus Art, 52-66; instr visual arts educ, Case Western Reserve Univ, 54-57 & 61-67, adj prof 85-; art educ instr, Kent State Univ, 61-63; supervisor & dir fine arts educ, Cleveland pub schs, 63-85. *Awards:* Sr Exhib Award, Cleveland Inst Art, 50; Purchase Prizes, Mid-Year Exhib, Butler Art Inst, 51 & Canton Art Inst, 52; special citation, Contrib to Arts, Cleveland Women's City Club, 86. *Mem:* Ohio Art Educ Asn (vpres, 74-75); Cleveland Inst Art (trustee 84-); Alliance Arts Educ; Cleveland Inst Art Alumni Asn (pres, 83-89); Cleveland Artists' Found (adv bd, 90-). *Media:* Watercolor. *Publ:* Contribr, Art Teachers Guides, 63-73, contribr, Proxemics, Edges and Nodes--Artistic Judgement and the Environment, 73, ed, A Guide to the Development of Afro American Art in the United States, 74 & auth, Graded Course of Study for the Arts, 83, Cleveland Pub Schs; ed & contribr, The World of Creative Expression, Coun Human Relations, 84. *Dealer:* NOVA 4614 Prospect Park Bldg Cleveland Ohio 44103; R & VW Inc 12415 Coit Rd Bratenahl Ohio 44108. *Mailing Add:* 12415 Coit Rd Cleveland OH 44108

WOIT, BONNIE FORD
PAINTER
b New York, NY, Jan 19, 31. *Study:* Allegheny Col, BA(cum laude), 53; Harvard Univ, 54; Westchester Workshop, 60-61; Silvermine Sch Art, 70-73; photog graphics workshop, 75. *Work:* Bankers Trust Co, New York; Sapolin Co, Danbury, Conn; IBM, Green Castle, Ind. *Exhib:* Solo exhibs, Am Embassy, Paris, 69 & Ingber Gallery, New York, 80, 81 & 84; Silvermine Guild Artists, New Canaan, Conn, 74; Stamford Mus, Conn, 80; Feria Int de Muestras, Bilbao, Spain, 82; Munson Gallery, 90; and others. *Pos:* Chmn & founder, Inst Visual Artists, 85-88. *Awards:* William Lowman Award, 78 & New Eng Award, 79, New Eng Exhib. *Mem:* Silvermine Guild Artists (secy, 74-75, vpres, 75-80 & 83-84). *Media:* Acrylic. *Dealer:* Munson Gallery 33 Whitney Ave New Haven CT 06511. *Mailing Add:* 559 West Rd New Canaan CT 06840

WOITENA, BEN S
SCULPTOR, EDUCATOR
b San Antonio, Tex, Mar 24, 42. *Study:* Univ Tex, Austin, BFA, 64; Univ Southern Calif, MFA, 70. *Work:* Houston Mus Fine Arts, Tex; City of Houston, Tex; Trammell Crow Co, Tex; San Antonio Mus Art, Tex; Jack Kerouac Commemorative Park. *Comn:* Sculpture, Jack Kerouac Commemorative Park, Lowell, Mass, 88; sculpture, Mayor Emmett F Lowry Commemorative, Texas City, Tex, 90. *Exhib:* Monumental Sculpture, Houston, 75; Collector's Exhib, Houston Mus Fine Arts, 75; Gulf Coast Sculpture Exhib, Galveston, Tex, 76; Amarillo Art Ctr, Tex, 77; Univ Tex Mus, Austin, 79; and others. *Teaching:* Instr sculpture, Glassell Sch Art, 71- *Bibliog:* George F Will (auth), Daddy who was Kerouac, Newsweek, 88; staff writer (auth), The talk of the town, The New Yorker, 88; Joyce Johnson (auth), Cashing in on Kerouac, Fame, 89. *Mem:* Nat Arts Club, NY. *Media:* Welded Steel, Cast Bronze. *Dealer:* Robinson Galleries 1100 Bissonnet Houston TX 77000. *Mailing Add:* 1547 Waverly Houston TX 77006

WOJTYLA, HAASE (WALTER JOSEPH)
PAINTER, DRAFTSMAN
b Chicago, Ill, Feb 10, 33. *Study:* Art Inst of Chicago; Univ of Ill, BFA(painting); Univ Cincinnati, MFA; Brooklyn Mus Art Sch. *Work:* Scripps Mem Hosp, San Diego, Calif. *Exhib:* Int Drawing Competition, State Univ of Educ, Potsdam, NY, 60; Tenth Ann Nat Exhib of Painting & Sculpture, Ringling Mus of Art, Sarasota, Fla, 60; Brooklyn & Long Island Artists Biennial Exhib, Brooklyn Mus of Art, 60; Art in Am Exhib, New York, 62; All Ohio Painting & Sculpture Exhib, Dayton Art Inst, 66; Calif-Hawaii Biennial, Fine Arts Gallery of San Diego, 76 & 78; one-man show, Recent Paintings, Fine Arts Gallery of San Diego, 75. *Teaching:* Instr, San Diego State Univ, Calif, 76 & 80. *Awards:* Singer & Sons Prize, Artists of Chicago & Vicinity, Art Inst of Chicago, 56; Painting Award, All Calif Juried Exhib, Laguna Beach Mus of Art, 76; Painting Award, Calif Ann Award Show, Jewish Community Ctr, San Diego, 77. *Bibliog:* Artists in Residence, KPBS-TV, San Diego, 82; The black comic art of Walter Wojtyla, Hill Courier, 9/83. *Mem:* San Diego Art Inst; Art Guild, San Diego Mus Art. *Media:* Oil, Mixed Media; Ink, Charcoal. *Publ:* Auth, San Diego Artists, Atra Publ Inc, 88. *Dealer:* Oneiros Gallery 711 Eight Ave Studio A San Diego CA 92101. *Mailing Add:* 2102 C St San Diego CA 92101

WOLANIC, SUSAN SESESKE
PAINTER, GRAPHIC ARTIST
b Hartford, Conn, Mar 25, 47. *Study:* Paier Sch Art, 69; Univ Hartford. *Work:* Yale New Haven Hosp, Conn; Constitution Nat Bank, Hartford, Conn; Storer Cable, New Haven, Conn; Carriage House, Guilford, Conn. *Comn:* Bethany Scenes/NC Scenes, Bethany Town Hall, Conn, 85; designed logo, Waterbury Hosp Auxiliary, Conn, 87; family portrait-impressionism, Expressions Furniture, Milford/Cheshire, Conn, 89; illus of house for mag, comn by Lois & Vicent La Bonia, Palm Springs, Calif, 90. *Exhib:* St Raphaels Hosp, art corridor, 92. *Pos:* Archit secy (draftsperson), off of John Damico, AIA, Waterbury, Conn, 76-; art dir, Marketing Serv Corp, Waterbury, Conn. *Teaching:* Instr, lectr, demonstrator, watercolor, various art organizations, Conn & adult educ prog, Watertown, 75-; instr watercolor, Arts Alive Studio, Cheshire, Conn & Thomaston Adult Ed, Prospect, Conn; instr adult ed, orange arts & crafts. *Awards:* Picador, Ligoa Duncan Gallery, NY & Paris, 79. *Bibliog:* Vincent & Lois La Bonia (auths), Ilustrations of California house, Palm Springs Life Mag, 90; Yale Art Gallery & Hosp, American Artists Publication, Yale Art Library, 90; Joyce Zimmerman (auth), Easy Line II, (article). *Mem:* Conn Watercolor Soc; Cheshire Art League (vpres, pres, 80's); Conn Classic Artists; Watertown Art League; Mt Carmel Art Asn. *Media:* Watercolor. *Publ:* Auth, 5 cookbooks: Vegetables, Ethic Artistry, Cookies, HorDoevres, Seafood, Private Publ, 89; illusr, 2 Views of a Palm Springs California Home (watercolors), Palm Springs Life Mag, 90 (in prep); The Day of the Fish, 90; ann report cover, Meridan-Wallingford Hosp, 92; cover & illus, Bethany Cookbook. *Mailing Add:* 66 Sperry Rd Bethany CT 06525

WOLANIN, BARBARA A
HISTORIAN, CURATOR
b Dayton, Ohio, Dec 12, 43. *Study:* Oberlin Col, BA, 66, MA(art hist, Woodrow Wilson Fel), 69; Harvard Univ Grad Sch Educ, MAT(fine arts), 67; Univ Wis, Madison, PhD(art hist), 81. *Collections Arranged:* Arthur B Carles Collection (auth, catalog), Hirshhorn Mus, 77; Arthur B Carles, Painting with Color (auth, catalog), Pa Acad Fine Arts, Corcoran Gallery Art & Nat Acad Design, 83-84; Jane Piper Retrospective: Paintings 1940-1985 (auth, catalog), James Madison Univ, Pa Acad Fine Arts & State Univ NY, Oswego, 86-87; Arthur B Carles Prints (auth, catalog), Print Club, Philadelphia, 89. *Pos:* Curator for architect of US Capitol, 85- *Teaching:* Asst prof art hist, Trinity Col, Washington, DC, 78-83 & James Madison Univ, 83-85; pub lectures, Jurying Art Exhib. *Awards:* Kress Fel, 74; Smithsonian Fel, 76; James Madison Univ Fac Develop Award, 85. *Mem:* Col Art Asn; Asn Historians Am Art; Women's Caucus Art; Am Asn Mus; Phi Beta Kappa. *Res:* Arthur B Carles, pioneer American modernist, Constantino Brumidi. *Publ:* Contribr, The Paintings of Edward Steichen, 88; contribr, Insight and Inspiration: The Italian Presence in American Art, 89; auth, review, Art Am, 90; contribr, The New Hope Modernist, 91; auth, Belles Lettres, 92. *Mailing Add:* United States Capital Washington DC 20016

WOLBER, PAUL J
PAINTER, EDUCATOR
b Deer Creek, Ill, June 23, 35. *Study:* Ill State Univ; Southern Ill Univ, Edwardsville; Bob Jones Univ, BS & MA. *Work:* Evansville Mus Art, Ind; Franklin Life Ins Co, Springfield, Ill; Mitchell Mus Art, Mt Vernon, Ill;

Calumet Nat Bank, Ill; Ill State Mus, Springfield. *Comn:* Mural, Spring Arbor Free Methodist Church, 80; mural, Ingham Co Correctional Ctr, Ingham Co Arts Comn, 81. *Exhib:* Ill State Mus, Springfield, 74; Grand Galleria Nat Ann, Seattle, 74; Gov Exhib, 30 Ill Artists, Springfield, 75; Marietta Nat, Ohio, 78. *Pos:* Art educ consult, State Off Pub Instr, Springfield, Ill, 74-75. *Teaching:* Assoc prof art, Spring Arbor Col, Mich, 76-81, prof, 81- *Awards:* Nat Small Painting Award, NMex Art League, Albuquerque, 74 & 75; Illinois-Indiana Bicentennial Purchase Award, Hammond, Ind, 77. *Bibliog:* Abner Hershberger (ed), Monnonite Artists Contemporary, 1975, Goshen Col Art Gallery; Glen P Ives (auth), Museum object of the week, Sunday Courier, Evansville, Ind, 10/6/74; Howard Derrickson (auth), article, The Advocate, Greenville, 1/28/75. *Mem:* Mid Am Col Art Asn; Nat Art Educ Asn; Bond Co Art & Cult Asn (vpres, 73-74). *Media:* Oil, Acrylic. *Mailing Add:* 1660 Chapel Rd Parma MI 49269

WOLCOTT, MARION POST See Post, Marion (Marion Post Wolcott)

WOLFE, ANN (ANN WOLFE GRAUBARD)
SCULPTOR
b Mlawa, Poland; US citizen. *Study:* Hunter Col, BA; studies sculpture in Manchester, Eng & Paris, France; Acad Grande Chaumiere, with Despiau & Vlerick. *Work:* Morris Raphael Cohen Libr, City Univ New York; Jerusalem Mus Art, Israel; Nat Mus Korea, Seoul; Mus Western Art, Moscow, Russia; Diehl Hall, Univ Minn; Pub Libr, Minneapolis. *Comn:* Dr Morris R Cohen (bronze head), alumni of City Univ New York, 43; Pres Syngman Rhea (bronze head), Dr R Oliver, Washington, DC, 47; Dr W R Ramsey (bronze head), Children's Hosp, St Paul, Minn, 57; welded relief in steel & bronze, Mt Zion Temple, St Paul, 65; Dr O H Wangensteen (bronze head), alumni of dept surg, Univ Minn, 65. *Exhib:* One-man shows, Worcester Art Mus, 39 & 41, Walker Art Ctr, Minneapolis, 55, Minneapolis Inst Arts, 64, Adele Bednarz Galleries, Los Angeles, 66; 3rd Sculpture Int, Philadelphia Mus Art, Pa. *Pos:* Past pres Soc Minnesota Sculptors; past secy Artists Equity. *Teaching:* Instr pvt studio, 62-70; instr sculpture, Minnetonka Ctr Arts & Educ, 71-74. *Awards:* Allied Artists Am, 36; Soc Washington Artists, 44 & 45; Minneapolis Inst Arts, 51. *Bibliog:* John Rood (auth), Sculpture in Wood, Univ Minn Press, 50; Minn Women Artists, Warm J, autumn 82; Cover, Owen Wagensteen Library of Biology & Medicine, 82. *Media:* Metal, Stone, Wood. *Publ:* Contribr, Worcester Tel-Gazette, 40-60. *Dealer:* Fairweather-Hardin Galleries 101 E Ontario Chicago IL 60611. *Mailing Add:* 825 Summit Ave Minneapolis MN 55403

WOLFE, JAMES
SCULPTOR
b New York, NY, Apr 28, 44. *Work:* Mus Fine Arts, Houston; Whitney Mus, New York; Mus Fine Arts, Boston; Kresge Art Ctr, Mich State Univ; Storm King Art Ctr; Hirshhorn Mus & Sculpture Garden, Washington, DC; Fort Worth Art Mus, Tex. *Comn:* Ten painted steel sculptures, comn by Johnstown Flood Mus, Centennial Comt & Bethlehem Steel for James Wolfe Sculpture Trail, Johnstown, Pa, 89; steel sculpture, comn by Harold Kant, Reno, NV. *Exhib:* one-man shows, Don Stewart Gallery, Montreal, Can, 88, Andre Gmmerich Gallery, New York, 88, Huntington Mus Art, Huntington, WVa, Galarie Am Tiergarten 62, Ger, 89, & Lucy Berman Gallery, Palo Alto, Calif, 90; Monumenta, Newport, RI, 74; one-man shows, Meredith Long Contemp, 78 & 79, Osuna Gallery, 80, Wentzel Gallery, Cologne, WGer, 87, Baumgartner Galleries, Washington, DC, 88, Innenhof des Historischen Rathauses, Koln, WGer, 88, Huntington Mus Art, WVa, 89 & Lucy Berman Gallery, Palo Alto, CA, 90; Clayworks Studio Workshop, New York, 81; Stephen Roseberg Gallery, 83 & 84; and others. *Pos:* Tech dir, Theater Dept & tech asst, Sculpture Dept, Bennington Col; fac mem, Va Polytechnic & State Univ, 78, Sch Visual Arts, 79 & Boston Mus Sch, 80. *Awards:* Nat Endowment Arts, 74; Saint Gaudens Found Prize, 84. *Bibliog:* Karen Wilkin (article), James Wolfe Sculpture Trail, Sculpture Mag, 5-6/90; Karen Wilkin (auth), James Wolfe's New Sculpture, Arts, 4/85; Karen Wilkin (auth), James Wolfe Sculpture Trail, 5-6/90; and others. *Dealer:* Andre Emmerich 41 E 57 St New York NY 10022. *Mailing Add:* 2282 Manning Ave Los Angeles CA 90064

WOLFE, LYNN ROBERT
PAINTER, EDUCATOR
b Red Cloud, Nebr, Sept 11, 17. *Study:* Univ Nebr, BFA; Univ Colo, with Max Beckman, MFA; Paris Atelier with Ossip Zadkine. *Work:* Univ Nebr State Mus, Lincoln; Univ Colo, Boulder. *Comn:* Copper doors, Danforth Chapel, Colo State Univ, Ft Collins, 54; mosaic (stained glass), McPherson Chapel, Durango, Colo, 60; stained glass window, Norgren Chapel, Denver, 65; stained glass windows, St Aidans Episcopal Church, Boulder, 70. *Exhib:* Nat Watercolor & Drawing, Metrop Mus, New York, 52; Nat Drawing & Small Sculpture, Muncie, Ind, 58; Mus Contemp Crafts, New York, 59; Western Artists, Denver Art Mus, 72. *Pos:* Cur collections, Univ Colo, Boulder, 64-74. *Teaching:* Instr sculpture, Univ Nebr, Lincoln, 45-46; vis artist watercolor, Univ Alaska, summer 46; prof painting, Univ Colo, Boulder, 47-, chmn dept fine arts, 72-74; vis artist, Univ Hawaii, 82. *Awards:* Sculpture Award, Ball State Teachers Col, 58; Univ Colo Fac Fel, 67; Award, Outstanding Educators Am, 75. *Media:* Acrylic, Canvas; Stained Glass, Faceted Dalles. *Mailing Add:* 701 Euclid Boulder CO 80302

WOLFE, MAURICE RAYMOND
CONSULTANT
b Paris, France, Oct 13, 24; US citizen. *Study:* Univ Calif, Berkeley, BA, 48, MA, 52, grad study; Fr Govt fel to Univ Paris at Sorbonne. *Collections Arranged:* Art from Mobilier of the Djukas of Surinam, Pacific Northwest & Eskimo Material Culture, Meso-American Prehistory, Mohave Desert Culture, African Musical Instruments & Domestic Objects & The Art of New Guinea, 74-75, The Cuna of Panama--Arts & Crafts, West Africa, Aboriginal Australian Art from Expo 74 & California Gatherers & Hunters, Circa 1776 (Bicentennial celebration), 75-76, Oceanic Cultures: Emphasis on American Trust Territories, Folk Art of Mexico & Archaeology, 77-78, Merritt Col Anthrop Mus; Carmel Valley Hist Soc Exhib, Carmel Valley Centennial Celebration, 89. *Pos:* Dir, Merritt Col Anthrop Mus, 73-87, consult, currently. *Teaching:* Instr, Merritt Col, Oakland, formerly, prof prehist art, formerly. *Awards:* Fel, French Govt, 66. *Mem:* Am Asn Mus; Western Art Asn; Calif Archaeol Soc. *Mailing Add:* 33751 Carmel Valley Rd Carmel Valley CA 93924

WOLFE, MILDRED NUNGESTER
PAINTER, DESIGNER
b Celina, Ohio, Aug 23, 12. *Study:* Athens Col; Univ Montevallo, AB, 32; Dixie Art Colony, with J Kelly Fitzpatrick; Art Students League, with Will Barnet; Chicago Art Inst; Colorado Springs Fine Arts Ctr, with Boardman Robinson, MA, 44. *Work:* Miss Art Asn, Jackson; Montgomery Mus Art, Ala; Print Collection, Libr Cong, Washington, DC; Middle South Utilities, Changing South Mag Collection, New Orleans; Nat Portrait Gallery, Washington, DC. *Comn:* Orpheus (mosaic), McDowell Br Libr, Jackson, 58; Stations of the Cross, comn by Monsignor Joseia Chatham for St Richards, Jackson, 60; David (mosaic), comn by Elizabeth Kingford for St Dominic's Hosp, Jackson, 61; chapel window (stained glass), First Baptist Church, Hazelhurst, Miss, 65; symbolic windows, Independent Methodist Episcopal Church, Jackson, 71-74. *Exhib:* Nat Exhib Prints, Libr Cong, 44; Grumbacher Int Exhib, Lakeland, Fla, 52; Painters of Southeastern US, Univ SFla, 62; Bertrand Russell Peace Found Exhib, Nottingham, Eng, 73; Lauren Rogers Mus of Art, Laurel, Miss, 77; Old Capitol Mus, Jackson, Miss, 77 & 77-78; and others. *Teaching:* Prof hist art & printmaking, Millsaps Col, 58-68. *Awards:* First Prize for Cotton Pickers, Southern Painter, McDowell Gallery, 38; First Prize for Watercolor, Miss Art Asn, 46; Award of Merit for Still Life, Grumbacher Int Exhib, 52. *Mem:* Miss Art Asn. *Media:* All. *Mailing Add:* c/o Wolfe Gallery 4308 Old Canton Rd Jackson MS 39211

WOLFE, ROBERT, JR
PRINTMAKER, PAINTER
b Oxford, Ohio, May 15, 30. *Study:* Miami Univ, BFA, 52; Cincinnati Art Acad, 55; Univ Iowa, scholar, 59, with M Lasansky, MFA(printmaking), 60; Tamarind Inst Workshops, 75 & 79. *Work:* Ohio State Univ; Univ Wis-Madison; Sheldon Mem Art Gallery, Univ Nebr, Lincoln; Casa da Gravura, State Collection, Curitiba, Parana, Brazil; Rajasthan Sch Art, Jaipur, India; and others. *Comn:* Five color intaglios, Miami Univ, 71. *Exhib:* Nine Midwest Printmakers, Mt St Joseph Col, Cincinnati, Ohio, 77; Rutger's Drawing, Camden, 79; Honolulu Acad Arts 5th Nat, Hawaii, 80; Intaglio Printmakers 81, Univ Louisville, Ky; Rajasthan Sch Art, Jaipur, India, 88; and many others. *Pos:* Artist-illusr, US Army, 52-54. *Teaching:* Instr design, Clarion Col, Pa, 61-62; prof printmaking, Miami Univ, 62-; vis artist, Univ Nebr, Grinnell Col, Ohio State Univ, Fed Univ Parana, Brazil & Western Kentucky Univ. *Awards:* Purchase Award, Intaglio Printmakers 81, Univ Louisville, Ky, 81; Alumni Award for Painting, Miami Univ, 82; and others; Effective Educator Award, Miami Univ, 91; and others. *Media:* Mixed, Oil. *Publ:* Contribr, Voiles Before Regatta, Finial Press, 84. *Dealer:* Clossan's Gallery, Cincinnati, OH; Benjamin-Beattie Gallery Chicago IL. *Mailing Add:* 418 Bouden Lane Oxford OH 45056

WOLFE, TOWNSEND, III
DIRECTOR, CHIEF CURATOR
b Hartsville, SC, Aug 15, 35. *Study:* Ga Inst Technol; Atlanta Art Inst, BFA; Cranbrook Acad Art, MFA; Inst Art Admin, Harvard Univ, cert. *Work:* Ark Arts Ctr, Little Rock; Mint Mus Art, Charlotte, NC; Okla Arts Ctr, Oklahoma City; Miss Art Asn, Jackson; Carroll Reece Mem Mus, E Tenn State Univ. *Exhib:* Ball State Teacher's Col Drawing Nat, Muncie, Ind, four shows, 59-67; Mead Painting of Yr Exhib, Atlanta, 62; Watercolors USA, Springfield, Mo, 63-64; Alice Bingham Gallery, Memphis, Tenn, 80; First Nat Bank, Little Rock, Ark, 81; and others. *Pos:* Dir, Wooster Community Art Ctr, Danbury, Conn, 65-68; art dir, Upward Bound Proj, Danbury, summers 66-68; dir & chief cur, Ark Arts Ctr, 68- *Teaching:* Instr painting & drawing, Memphis Acad Arts, Tenn, 59-64; instr painting & drawing, Scarsdale Studio Workshop, NY, 64-65. *Awards:* N Hodson Wheeler Award, 56; Winthrop Rockefeller Mem Award, 73; Award Merit & Purchase Prize, 57th Nat Painting Exhib, Miss Art Asn, 67; James R Short Award, Southeastern Mus Conf, 81; Individual Achievement Award, Ark Mus Asn, 84; Ark Art Educ Advocacy Award, 85; Promethean Award for Excellence in the Arts, March of Dimes, 86. *Mem:* Am Asn Mus; Am Fedn Arts; Southeastern Asn Mus; Asn Art Mus Dirs. *Media:* Oil, Gouache. *Publ:* Auth, National Drawing Invitational (catalog), 86, 88, 90, 91, 92; National Objects Invitational (catalog), 87, 88, 89, 91; The Figure (catalog), 90; Will Barnet Drawings 1930-1990 (catalog), 91; Silverpoint Etcetera (catalog), 92; and others. *Mailing Add:* Ark Arts Ctr PO Box 2137 Little Rock AR 72203

WOLFF, DEE I
PAINTER
b Springfield, Minn, 48. *Study:* Univ Houston, BA, 71; Glassell Sch Art, cert art, 76; Oomoto Sch Traditional Art, Oomoto, Japan, 84. *Work:* Mus Fine Arts, Houston; Mus of Southeast Tex, Beaumont, Tex; Art Mus S Tex, Corpus Christi, Tex; Archer M Huntington Mus, Austin, Tex; Gihon Found Collection, Dallas. *Comn:* Twenty three stained glass windows, St Theresea of Lisieux, Sugarland, Tex; Corpus Christi Pub Libr, Tex; St Philip Church, Houston. *Exhib:* one-woman shows, Watson Gallery, Houston, 78, 81, 85, Mus Southeast Tex, Beaumont, Tex, 89, Diverseworks Artspace, Houston,

89, D'Art Artspace, Dallas, 90 & Mus Fine Arts, Houston, 90. *Awards:* Nat Endowment Arts Visual Arts Grant, 89; NY State Coun on the Arts Grant, 89; Spirit of Am Woman Award, (Performing Arts Soc) Houston, Tex, 89. *Bibliog:* Joan Robinson (auth), Dee Wolff-Diverseworks Artspace, Art Forum Int, 4/89; Ten souls act out the mysticism of kabbalah, New York Times, 11/20/89; Selah: Stations of the Cross, Diverseworks Artspace, Houston, 89; Janet Cutner (auth), Following Christ's Journey: An Artist's Life, Growth and Change, Dallas Morning News, 90. *Mem:* Diverseworks Artspace, (bd dir & artists adv bd 89-91); Lawndale Art and Performance Space; Art League of Houston. *Media:* Gouache, Acrylic Paint. *Publ:* Fifty Texas Artists, Chronicle Bks, 86; No Bluebonnets, No Yellow Roses, Essays on Texas Women in the Arts, Midmarch Arts Press, New York, 88; Exposures, Women and Their Art, Newsage Press, 89. *Mailing Add:* 421 Arlington Houston TX 77007

WOLFF, ROBERT W, JR
DEALER
b Monroe, La, Feb 18, 47. *Study:* Troy State Univ, Ala, BS, 74. *Pos:* Art dealer, Wolff Gallery, Fairhope, Ala & Pensacola, Fla, currently. *Mailing Add:* PO Box 98 Fairhope AL 36533

WOLIN, JEFFREY ALAN
PHOTOGRAPHER
b Hewlett, New York, Feb 25, 51. *Study:* Kenyon Col, AB, 72; Rochester Inst of Tech, MFA, 77. *Work:* Int Mus of Photography, Rochester, NY; Israel Mus, Jerusalem; Seattle Art Mus, Wash; Ctr for Creative Photography, Tucson, Ariz; Mus Mod Art, New York; San Francisco Mus of Mod Art, Calif; Los Angeles Co Mus Art; Mus Fine Arts, Houston, Tex. *Exhib:* Contemp Photographers, George Eastman House, Rochester, NY, 82-83; Recent Acquisitions, Seattle Art Mus, Wash, 86; Urgent Messages (catalog), Chicago Cult Ctr, Ill, 87; Use Only as Directed, Nexus Contemp Art Ctr, Atlanta, Ga, 88; Swimmers, Burden Gallery, New York, 88-90; Stories, SF Camerawork, San Francisco, Calif, 89-90; Word and Image, Univ of Oregon Art Mus, Eugene, 90; Selections, Mus Mod Art, NY, 92; New Work/New Directions, Los Angeles Mus Art; Recent Acquisitions, Mus Fine Arts, Houston, Tex. *Teaching:* Assoc prof, photography, Indiana Univ, Bloomington, 80- *Awards:* Fel, vis artist, Nat Endowment Arts, 88; Fel, master artist, Ind Arts Comn, 89; John Simon Guggenheim Mem Fel, 91. *Bibliog:* Rod Slemmons (auth), book review, Afterimage, 86; Abigail Foerstner (auth), exhib review, 5/86 & 9/13/92, Chicago Tribune; Richard Nilsen (auth), exhib review, Arizona Republic, 88; exhib rev, Village Voice, 2/25/92. *Mem:* Soc Photog Educ. *Publ:* Auth, Camera, CJ Bucher, Switzerland, 79; illusr, Image, George Eastman House, 81; co-auth & illusr, Stone Country, Indiana Univ Press, 85; illusr, Swimmers, Aperture, 88; illusr, The Archive No 29, Ctr Creative Photog, 91. *Dealer:* Catherine Edelman Gallery 300 W Superior Chicago Ill 60610. *Mailing Add:* Sch Fine Arts Ind Univ Bloomington IN 47405

WOLINS, JOSEPH
PAINTER
b Atlantic City, NJ, Mar 26, 15. *Study:* Nat Acad Design, 31-35; WPA Fed Art Proj, New York, 35-42. *Work:* Metrop Mus Art, New York; Nat Mus Am Art, Wash, DC; Butler Inst Am Art, Youngstown, Ohio; Wichita Art Mus, Kans; Ein Harod Mus, Israel; New Britain Mus, Conn. *Exhib:* Corcoran Gallery Art Biennial, Wash, DC, 47; Pa Acad Fine Arts Ann, Philadelphia, 48; Whitney Mus Am Art Ann, 49-53; Mus Mod Art Ann, Sao Paulo, Brazil, 62; Butler Inst Am Art Ann, Youngstown, Ohio, 65; one-man exhib, Slater Mem Mus, 81; Metrop Mus Art, New York; Nat Mus Am Art, Washington, DC; Everson Mus Art, Syracuse; New Britain Mus Am Art, Conn. *Teaching:* Pvt classes. *Awards:* Mark Rothko Found Award for Painting, 71; Nat Inst of Arts & Lett Award, 76. *Mem:* Artists Equity Asn; Audubon Artists. *Media:* Oil, Watercolor. *Mailing Add:* 463 West St New York NY 10014

WOLPERT, ETTA
PAINTER, PRINTMAKER
Study: Univ Minn, BA MA(magna cum laude), 54; Columbia Grad Sch, 53; DeCordova Mod Art Sch, 68. *Exhib:* Walker Art Center, Minneapolis, Minn, 47; one-women shows, Cary Libr, Lexington, Mass, 62, Int Student Center, Cambridge, Mass, 62, Lexington Theatre, 72, Lexington Trust Co, 74; Fourth Ann Int Exhib Miniature Art, Toronto, Canada, 89; Cambridge Pub Libr, North Branch, 92. *Teaching:* Asst prof, Northern Essex Community Col, Mass, 65. *Awards:* First & Third Prize, drawing, Minn State Fair, 49. *Media:* Acrylic, Oil; Serigraphy, Silkscreen. *Publ:* Contribr, Harvard Advocate, 64; auth, Selections from her writings, 73. *Mailing Add:* 4 Revere St Lexington MA 02173

WOLSKY, JACK
PAINTER, EDUCATOR
b Rochester, NY, Aug 5, 30. *Study:* Rochester Inst Technol, AS, 51; State Univ NY Col, Buffalo, BS, 55, MS, 57. *Work:* Rochester Mem Art Gallery, NY; New Britain Mus Am Art, Conn; Munson-Williams-Proctor Inst, Utica, NY; Rochester Inst Technol; State Univ NY Col, Brockport. *Exhib:* Am Fedn Arts Exhib, Turkey, Iran & Pakistan; 154th Exhib, Pa Acad Fine Arts; State Univ NY Arts Convocation Exhib, Albright-Knox Gallery; Chautauqua Exhib Am Art; Univ Omaha Nat Exhib. *Teaching:* Prof studio art, State Univ NY Col, Brockport, 59- *Awards:* Lillian Fairchild Award, Univ Rochester, 70; Distinguished Alumnus Award, State Univ NY Buffalo, 71; Fac Exchange Scholar, State Univ NY, 74. *Bibliog:* Talis Bergmanis (auth), Exuberant art of Jack Wolsky, Dem & Chronicle Publ, 12/13/70; Karen Ibrahim (auth), Abstract art of Jack Wolsky, News & Rev, Rochester Inst Technol, 71; Evolution of a moment, Channel 21 TV, Rochester, NY, 74. *Media:* Acrylic, Lacquer. *Dealer:* Oxford Gallery 267 Oxford St Rochester NY 14607. *Mailing Add:* 295 Washington St Spencerport NY 14559

WONG, FREDERICK
PAINTER, GRAPHIC ARTIST
b Buffalo, NY, May 31, 29. *Study:* Univ NMex, BFA & MA. *Work:* Butler Inst Am Art, Youngstown, Ohio; Reading Mus Art, Pa; Philbrook Art Ctr, Tulsa, Okla; Neuberger Collection, Purchase, NY; Smithsonian Inst, Washington, DC. *Exhib:* Los Angeles Co Mus Art, 59; Butler Inst Am Art, Youngstown, 60; Am Watercolor Soc, New York, 60-69; Watercolor USA, Springfield, Mo, 63; Mainstreams '69, Marietta, Ohio, 69. *Teaching:* Instr form & structure, Pratt Inst, 66-69; instr painting, drawing, calligraphy & design, Hofstra Univ; Watercolor, Art Students League. *Awards:* Butler Midyear Ann Bronze Medal, Butler Inst Am Art, 60; Gold Medal, Nat Arts Club, 61; Mainstreams '69 Award of Excellence, Marietta Col, 69. *Mem:* Am Watercolor Soc; Allied Artists Am; Nat Arts Club. *Media:* Watercolor. *Publ:* Auth, Oriental Watercolor Techniques, 77 & The Complete Calligrapher, 80, Watson-Guptill; The Zen of Watercolor, Watercolor '90, Am Artist Publ. *Dealer:* Self 77 Chambers St New York NY 10007. *Mailing Add:* 315 Riverside Dr New York NY 10025

WONG, JASON
MUSEUM DIRECTOR, DESIGNER
b Long Beach, Calif, May 12, 34. *Study:* Long Beach City Col, AA, 54; Univ Calif, Los Angeles, BA, 63. *Collections Arranged:* Seven Decades of Design, organized through Calif Arts Comn grant for state tour, 67-68; Art of Alexander Calder--Gouaches, western states tour, 70; Max Beckmann Graphics, Nat Tour, 73; Photo/Synthesis Nat Invitational Exhib, NY State Coun on the Arts, 76-77; Traveling Exhibs, NY State Coun Arts, NY Artist's works, 77-80. *Pos:* Asst cur, Long Beach Mus Art, 59-64, cur, 65, dir, 65-72; art dir, Audiorama Corp, Am-Quest Int, 64-65; dir, Tucson Art Ctr, 72-73; dir visual arts div, Spokane World's Fair, 74; asst dir, Herbert F Johnson Mus Art, Cornell Univ, 74-77; cur, Joe & Emily Lowe Art Gallery, Syracuse Univ, 78-80; independent cur, 80-; graphic designer, Tompkins Cortland Community Col, 81-; designer, Permanent Collection, Nat Women's Hall of Fame, Seneca Falls, NY, 83-90, retired, 91. *Teaching:* Prof museology, Syracuse Univ, 78-80; adj instr, Graphic Design, Tompkins Cortland Community Col, 85-90. *Awards:* Nat Endowment Arts Grant for Res in Museological Studies, 72; Award for Excellence in Design, SUNY-CUAD, 81, 82, 84 & 91. *Mem:* Am Inst Graphic Arts. *Publ:* Auth, exhib catalog introd, Art Int, 10-11/76; and numerous art exhib catalogs. *Mailing Add:* 4483 Avenida Rio Del Oro Yorba Linda CA 92686-3008

WONG, PAUL KAN
PAINTER, SCULPTOR
b Fargo, NDak, Oct 30, 51. *Study:* Moorhead State Univ, BA, 73; Univ Wis, Madison, MFA, 76. *Work:* Madison Art Ctr; New York Pub Libr. *Comn:* Suspended sculpture installation, Hudson River Mus, Yonkers, NY, 83. *Exhib:* 21st Ann Print Exhib, Brooklyn Mus, 78; 77th Vicinity Exhib, Chicago Art Inst, 78; Shaped Field, Eccentric Formats, PS1, Long Island City, 81; Making Paper, Am Craft Mus, 82; Paper as Image Traveling Exhib, Brit Art Coun, UK, 82; one-man show, Air Space: Projection, Hudson River Mus, Yonkers, NY, 83 & Condeso-Lawler Gallery, New York, 83 & 85. *Pos:* Dir, Dieu Donne Press & Paper, New York; cur, Paper as Paint, Fashion Inst Technol, New York. *Teaching:* Instr hand papermaking, The New Sch, New York, 80-86. *Awards:* Apprenticeship Grants, Louis Comfort Tiffany Found, 78 & Nat Endowment Arts, 80; Graphics Grant, Creative Artists Pub Serv, 83. *Bibliog:* Judd Tully (auth), Paper chase, Portfolio Mag, 83; Ronny Cohen (auth), Paper routes, 83 & rev, 84, Art News; rev, Artforum, 85. *Publ:* Illusr, Our Lady of the Three Pronged Devil, Red Ozier Press, 81. *Dealer:* Condeso-Lawler Gallery 76 Greene St New York NY 10013. *Mailing Add:* 40 N Moore St 2W New York NY 10013

WONG, ROGER FREDERICKSON
MUSEUM DIRECTOR, COLLECTOR
b Los Angeles, Calif, Dec 28, 45. *Study:* Pomona Col; Univ Southern Calif, BA, 70. *Pos:* Dir, Roger Wong Gallery, 72-78; dir, Los Angeles Mus Art, 79-; mem, Santa Monica Arts Comn, 83-84. *Mem:* Am Asn Mus; Int Asn Mus; Archit Design & Support Group; Newport Harbor Art Mus; founder Mus Contemp Art, Los Angeles. *Collection:* Principal pieces of Chinese porcelain and bronze from Sund and Shang periods; conceptual and post 60's modern sculpture and paintings. *Mailing Add:* c/o Wes Hall, Mus Contemp Art 250 S Grand Ave Los Angeles CA 90012

WONNER, PAUL (JOHN)
PAINTER
b Tucson, Ariz, Apr 24, 20. *Study:* Calif Col Arts & Crafts, Oakland, BA, 41; Univ Calif, Berkeley, Anne Bremmer Scholar, MA, 53, MLS, 55. *Work:* Guggenheim Mus, Mus Mod Art, Metrop Mus Art, New York; San Francisco Mus Art; Nat Collection Fine Arts, Smithsonian Inst, Washington, DC; Oakland Mus, Calif; Joseph H Hirshhorn Found; Boston Mus Fine Arts; Charles A Worst Mus Fine Arts, Racine, Wis; Minneapolis Inst Art, Minn. *Exhib:* One-man exhibs, San Francisco Art Asn Gallery, 56, Waddington Galleries, London, Eng, 65, Poindexter Gallery, New York, 71, Charles Campbell Gallery, San Francisco, 74, James Corcoran Gallery, Los Angeles, 79, Los Angeles Munic Art Mus, 82 & John Berggruen, San Francisco, 85-88 & 90; Whitney Mus Am Art, New York, 59 & 67; Art Inst Chicago, 61 & 64; Univ Ill, 61, 63 & 65; Mus Mod Art, New York, 62; Charles Campbell Gallery, San Francisco, 74; Calif State Univ, Long Beach, 75 & 81; James Corcoran Gallery, Los Angeles, 79 & 80; Oakland Art Mus, Calif, 82; Iceman Mus Art, Tokyo, Daimanu Mus, Osaka, Yokohama Takashimaya, Yokohama, Japan, 85; San Francisco Mus Mod Art, Calif, 89; John Berggruen Gallery, San Francisco, 91. *Teaching:* Instr painting, Univ Calif, Los Angeles, 63-64 & Otis Art Inst, 66-68; instr, Col Creative Studies, Santa Barbara, 68-71, Univ Calif, Davis, 75-76 & Univ Calif, Long Beach, 81. *Dealer:* John Berggruen Gallery 228 Grant Ave San Francisco CA 94108. *Mailing Add:* 468 Jersey St San Francisco CA 94994

WOOD, ALAN
PAINTER
b Widnes, Lancashire, Eng, Aug 3, 35; Can citizen. *Study:* Liverpool Col Art, Eng, Nat Dipl Design, 58; Liverpool Univ, Inst Educ, Eng, Art Teachers Dipl, 59. *Work:* Seattle Art Mus, Wash; Art Gallery Greater Victoria, BC; Art Gallery South Australia, Adelaide; Tate Gallery, London; Nat Mus Wales, Cardiff; Vancouver Art Gallery, BC; Winnipeg Art Gallery, Can. *Comn:* Mural, Leeds Univ, Yorks, 65; mural, BC Govt, Victoria, 77; mural, Fed Govt Can, Calgary, Alta, 81; Cineplex, Vancouver, BC, 85. *Exhib:* Solo exhibs, Univ Cincinnati, Ohio, 74, Alta Col Art, Calgary, 77, Art Gallery Southern Alta, Lethbridge, 78 & Art Gallery Greater Victoria, 82; The Ranch Project, Alta, Can, 83-84; Vancouver Art Gallery, Can, 90. *Awards:* Dartington Award, Dartington Trustees, 61; First Prize, Arts Coun Northern Ireland, 68; Grant, Sr Can Coun, 78, 82 & 85. *Bibliog:* Joan Lowndes (auth), Architectonics and the wild west, Vanguard, summer, 81; Val Greenfield (auth), Alan Wood's Ranch Project, Art Mag, winter 83; Ron Glowen (auth), Prairie Picturesque-Alan Wood's Ranch, Vanguard, 12/83-1/84; Ben Forgey (auth), Ranch Project, Smithsonian Mag, 12/83; John Beardsley, Earthworks and Beyond, Abbeville Modern Art Movements, New York. *Media:* Acrylic; Wood Constructions. *Dealer:* Patrick Doheny Fine Art 1811 West 1st Ave Vancouver BC Can. *Mailing Add:* 3869 W 13th Ave Vancouver BC V6R 2S9 Canada

WOOD, BEATRICE
CERAMIST, EDUCATOR
b San Francisco, Calif. *Study:* Pottery with Glen Luckens, Otto & Gertrud Natzler & Vivika & Otto Heino. *Work:* Metrop Mus Art, New York; Newark Mus, NJ; Mus Int dell Ceramiche Faenza, Italy; Oakland Mus, Calif; Santa Barbara Mus, Calif. *Exhib:* M H de Young Mem Mus, San Francisco; Phoenix Art Mus, Ariz; Santa Barbara Mus Art, Calif; Takishamaya Gallery, Tokyo, Japan; Tucson Art Ctr, Ariz; one-person shows, Fullerton State Col, Del Mus & Everson Mus, Syracuse, 83; and others. *Teaching:* Instr pottery, Happy Valley Sch, Ojai, Calif, 55-60. *Awards:* Nat Coun Educ Ceramics Arts Award, 87; Am Craft Coun Fel Award, 87; Gold Medal, Am Craft Coun, 92. *Bibliog:* Frances Naumann (auth), I Shock Myself, Arts Mag, 5/77. *Mem:* Am Crafts Asn; NCEA. *Media:* Clay. *Dealer:* Garth Clark Gallery 170 S La Brea Los Angeles CA 90036 & 24 W 57th St New York NY 10019. *Mailing Add:* 8560 Hwy 150 Ojai CA 93023

WOOD, HARRY EMSLEY, JR
EDUCATOR, PAINTER
b Indianapolis, Ind, Dec 10, 10. *Study:* Univ Wis, BA & MA; Ohio State Univ, MA & PhD; Acad Belli Arti, Florence, Italy, with Ottono Rosai; and with John Frazier, Provincetown, Mass & Emil Bisttram, Taos, NMex. *Work:* Mem Union, Ariz State Univ; Phoenix Art Mus, Ariz; Nat Portrait Gallery, Smithsonian Inst, Washington, DC. *Comn:* Murals, Gt Cent Ins Co, Peoria, Ill; and many portraits of prominent people. *Exhib:* Florence, Italy, 50; Phoenix Art Mus, 61; Phoenix & Tucson Ann, 62; Ariz State Univ; Northern Ariz Univ; and other group & one-man shows. *Pos:* Art critic, Scottsdale Progress, Ariz, 74-77; critic. *Teaching:* Prof art, Ill Wesleyan Univ, 42-44; dean col fine arts, Bradley Univ, 44-50; prof art, Ariz State Univ, 54-76, chmn dept, 54-66, emer prof art, 76- *Awards:* Ariz Artist Guild Purchase Prize for Sculpture, Ariz State Fair, 58; Murphy Award for Sculpture, 59. *Mem:* Col Art Asn Am; Nat Art Educ Asn (nat coun, 58-62); Pac Art Asn (pres, 58-60). *Media:* All. *Publ:* Auth, A Sculpture By John Waddell, 70; auth, Faces of Abraham Lincoln, 70; auth, articles in, Lincoln Herald, 75; auth & illusr, The Sphinkus Has No Noise--An Egyptian Adventure, 77; auth, Always carry a sketchbook, 80; and others. *Mailing Add:* 2625 E Southern No C 38 Tempe AZ 85282

WOOD, JAMES ARTHUR (ART)
CARTOONIST, LECTURER
b Miami, Fla, June 6, 27. *Study:* Washington & Lee Univ, BA; Mich State Univ. *Work:* Libr Cong, Washington, DC; Permanent Libr Collection, Univ Va, Charlottesville; Univ Akron Collection, Ohio; William Allen White Collection, Univ Kans; Truman Libr Collection, Kennedy Libr, Johnson Libr, Nixon Libr & Ford Libr. *Exhib:* Brussels World's Fair, 58; one-man show, Pittsburgh Press, 59; Great Challenge, Int Cartoon Exhib, 59-60; Cartoon Show, Nat Portrait Gallery, 72. *Pos:* Ed cartoonist, Richmond Newsleader, 50-56; chief political cartoonist, Pittsburgh Press, 56-63; cartoonist, US Tel Asn, 63- & Farm Bureau News, 78-; partner, Stam-Wood Productions, 80- *Awards:* Freedoms Found Awards, 53, 54, 58-60, 78-79, 82 & 89; Christopher Award, 54; Golden Quill Award, 60 & 62; Huevos de Onox, Mexico City, 77. *Mem:* Asn Am Ed Cartoonist (bd mem, 59-63, pres, 75-); Nat Cartoonists Soc; Nat Press Club. *Media:* Pen & Ink, Crayon. *Mailing Add:* 7008 Tilden Lane Rockville MD 20852

WOOD, JAMES NOWELL
HISTORIAN, ADMINISTRATOR
b Boston, Mass, Mar 20, 41. *Study:* Williams Col, BA; Inst Fine Arts, NY Univ, MA. *Pos:* Asst to dir, Metrop Mus Art, New York, 67-68, asst cur, dept 20th century art, 68-70; cur, Albright-Knox Art Gallery, Buffalo, NY, 70-73, assoc, 73-75; dir, St Louis Art Mus, 75-80, Art Inst Chicago, 80- *Res:* Nineteenth and twentieth century American and European painting, sculpture and photography. *Publ:* Auth, Rockne Krebs, 71; Six Painters, 71; Max Bill: Painting, Sculpture, Graphics, 74; Era of Exploration, 75. *Mailing Add:* Art Inst Chicago Mich Ave at Adams St Chicago IL 60603

WOOD, JOSEPH A
DESIGNER
b Queens, NY, May 16, 54. *Study:* State Univ NY Col, Buffalo, BS(art educ & design), 77; Kent State Univ, MFA, 84. *Work:* Pvt collections of Ivy Ross, Claire Sanford & Robert Lee Morris. *Exhib:* Artists Found Gallery, Boston, Mass, 90; Int Handwerksmesse, Munich, traveling, Ger, Dublin, Ireland, 91; Int Exhib Contemp Jewelry, Prague, Czech, 91; Artwear Gallery, New York, 92; 2nd Australian Int Crafts Triennial, Art Gallery, Western Australia, 92. *Teaching:* Grad Teaching Assistantship jewelry/metals prog, Kent State Univ, 81-84; asst prof jewelry/metalsmithing, Mass Col Art, Boston, 85-; design consult, Verne Q Powell Flutes, 91-92. *Awards:* Jurors Award, US Metal, San Francisco State Univ, 89; Fel, Nat Endowment Arts, 90; Fel, Mass ARts Coun, 91. *Bibliog:* Jill Slosburg (auth), Art Jewelry (feature), Art NEng, 5/87; Daniel Jocz (auth), exhib rev, Ornament, Vol 13, No 4, summer 92; Cynthia Cuadra (Auth), article on brooches, Ornament, Vol 15, No 3, spring 92. *Mem:* Distinguished mem, Soc NAm Goldsmiths, 82; Top Dog Coop Metal Group, Waltham, Mass, 88-92; Boston Computer Soc, 91. *Dealer:* Quadrum Gallery The Mall at Chestnut Hill Chestnut Hill MA 02167. *Mailing Add:* 41 Hawthorne St, No 22 Cambridge MA 02138

WOOD, MCCRYSTLE
PAINTER, SCULPTOR
b Cincinnati, Ohio, Sept 20, 47. *Study:* Kansas City Art Inst, with Ron Slowinski, BFA, 73; Ind Univ, with Rudy Pozzatti, MFA, 76. *Work:* Cincinnati Art Mus; Atlantic Richfield Corp, Columbus, Ohio; Hyatt Hotels, Washington, DC; AT&T, Cincinnati; Proctor & Gamble Co, Cincinnati. *Comn:* Litton Ind. *Exhib:* Centennial Invitational, Cincinnati Art Mus, 81; Gifts, Contemp Art Ctr, Cincinnati, 88; Prevailing Light, Portsmouth Mus, Ohio, 90. *Pos:* Dir, sch design, Univ Cincinnati, 89-90. *Teaching:* Assoc prof design/art, Univ Cincinnati, 82- *Awards:* Individual Artist Fel, Ohio Arts Coun, 86; Grant, Ky Found Women, 87. *Mem:* Col Art Asn; Siggraph; Am Asn Univ Prof. *Media:* Acrylic; Miscellaneous Media. *Dealer:* Toni Birckhead Gallery W 4th St Cincinnati OH 45202. *Mailing Add:* 2401 Ingleside Ave Cincinnati OH 45206-2157

WOOD, MARCIA JOAN
SCULPTOR
b Paw Paw, Mich, Mar 22, 33. *Study:* Kalamazoo Col, BA, 55; Cranbrook Acad Art, MFA, 56; Courtauld Inst Art, Univ London, 60-61; Harvard Univ, 62. *Work:* Hope Col Art Gallery, Mich; Kalamazoo Inst Arts. *Comn:* Stainless steel sculptures, Detroit Coun Arts & Nat Endowment Arts, 80, Sesquicentennial Comn, La Porte, Ind, 83, Pub Utilities Bldg, Kalamazoo, 85 & Kalamazoo Inst Arts, 85; cast bronze ed, 82 & stainless steel sculpture, 82, Kalamazoo Col. *Exhib:* Sixty-Sixth Nat Exhib, Smithsonian Inst, 63; Seven American Artists, Colgate Univ, NY, 74; Sculpture Installation (Documentation), Tex Tech Univ, 81; Outdoor Sculpture Invitational, Meadow Brook Art Gallery, Rochester, Mich, 82; State of Michigan, Birmingham-Bloomfield Hills Mus, 82; solo exhib, Kalamazoo Inst Arts, 85; Krasl Art Ctr, St Joseph, Mich, 86; Nina Owen Ltd, Chicago, 86. *Teaching:* Instr studio art, Hope Col, Mich, 58-63 & Philadelphia Col Art, 63-65; prof, Kalamazoo Col, 65- *Awards:* MacDowell Colony Fel, 67; Lucasse Fel, Kalamazoo Col, 80; First Prize Sculpture, Western Mich Ann, Kalamazoo Inst Art, 81. *Bibliog:* Ruth Moerdyk (auth), The sculpture of Marcia Wood, Detroit Women's Voice, 82; Virginia Watson-Jones (auth), Contemporary American Women Sculptors, 85. *Mem:* Col Art Asn; Concerned Citizens Arts Mich; Kalamazoo Inst Arts. *Media:* Stainless Steel, Cast Bronze. *Dealer:* Nina Owen Ltd 212 W Superior St Ste 202 Chicago IL 60610-3533. *Mailing Add:* 2125 Ridge Rd Kalamazoo MI 49008

WOOD, NICHOLAS WHEELER
SCULPTOR, PAINTER
b San Francisco, Calif, Sept 21, 46. *Study:* San Francisco State Univ, BA, 72; Alfred Univ, NY, MFA, 77. *Work:* Lannan Found, Palm Beach, Fla; Arts Comn, San Francisco; Atlantic Richfield Co, Dallas, Tex; Southwestern Bell Telephone, Dallas; NY State Col Ceramics, Alfred. *Comn:* Sculpture, Criswell Develop Corp, 84; St Paul's Med Ctr, Dallas. *Exhib:* Oakland Mus Art, Calif, 74; Group Invitational, Dallas Mus Fine Arts, 79; solo shows, Ft Worth Art Mus, 79, Delahunty Gallery, Dallas, 81 & 500X Gallery, Dallas, Tex, 84; Janus Gallery, Los Angeles, 81; Showdown, Alternative Mus, New York, and traveling, 83; Sculpture on the Wall, San Antonio Art Inst, Tex, 83. *Collections Arranged:* Drawing by Sculptors, 500X Gallery, Dallas, 85. *Teaching:* Assoc prof, Univ Tex, Arlington, 77- *Awards:* Individual Res Grant, Univ Tex, Arlington, 81; Fel, Nat Endowment Arts, 81-82; Honorable Mention, Art Gallery, Tex Christian Univ, 84. *Bibliog:* Ned Rifkin (auth), Tablets and grids: Clay by Wood, 6/2/79 & Robert Raczka (auth), Nicholas Wood: Evolution of a theme, 3/21/81, Artweek; Spencer L Davis (ed), Tablet series: Nicholas Wood, Ceramics Monthly, 2/80. *Mem:* Int Sculpture Ctr; Nat Coun Educ Ceramic Arts. *Media:* Clay, Wood; Mixed. *Mailing Add:* 510 Lynda Lane Arlington TX 76010

WOOD, ROBERT E
PAINTER, INSTRUCTOR
b Gardena, Calif, Feb 4, 26. *Study:* Pomona Col, BA; Claremont Grad Sch, MFA, with Millard Sheets, Phil Dike & Jean Ames. *Work:* Butler Inst Am Art, Youngstown, Ohio; West Tex Mus, Lubbock; Lytton Financial Corp, Los Angeles; Riverside Art Ctr & Mus, Calif; Wichita Art Asn & Mus, Kans. *Comn:* 22 Large Watercolors, Hotel Caminoreal, Puerto Vallarta, Mexico, 90. *Exhib:* Am Watercolor Soc, New York, 54 & 58-88; Nat Watercolor Soc, 60-86; Watercolor USA, Springfield, Mo, 63-80; Watercolor West, Riverside, Calif, 69-75; Nat Acad Design, New York. *Teaching:* Instr art, Univ Minn, Duluth, 52-55 & Claremont Grad Sch, Calif, 58; dir watercolor, Robert E

Wood Summer Sch Painting, Green Valley Lake, 61- *Awards:* Am Watercolor Soc Award, New York, 69, 71, 78, 81-83 & 85-87. *Bibliog:* San Bernardino Valley Col, Visit to the artist's studio, Educ TV, 66. *Mem:* Am Watercolor Soc (vpres, 68-74 & 81-83); Nat Watercolor Soc; Nat Acad Design; Watercolor West; West Coast Watercolor Soc. *Media:* Watercolor, Drawing. *Publ:* Auth, Robert E Wood, advocate thorough preparation, Am Artist Mag, 68; auth & producer, The search for a creative watercolor, cassette & slides, 72; co-auth, Watercolor Workshop, 74. *Dealer:* Starry-Sheets Art Gallery 14988 Sand Canyon Ave Suite I-5 Irvine CA 92718; Reinike Gallery 2300 Peachtree Rd NW Suite B-201 Atlanta GA 30309. *Mailing Add:* 33135 Maple Lane PO Box 216 Green Valley Lake CA 92341

WOODALL, JOHN
SCULPTOR, VIDEO ARTIST
b Lakeland, Fla, 1940. *Study:* San Francisco Art Inst, MFA (sculpture), 70, with Bruce Nauman, Tony Delap, Jerony Anderson, Bill Geis & Al Light. *Comn:* Ophelia (set design), Ballet West, Salt Lake City, Utah, 88; Belling the Slayer (set design), Ballet Met, Columbus, Ohio, 89; Secret House (set design), ODC/San Francisco, 89; In Perpetuum (set design), San Francisco Ballet, 90. *Exhib:* War (Art Against War), San Francisco Art Inst, 83; Artist's Miniature Golf Course, Video Gallery, San Francisco, 84; Stage Presence, San Francisco State Univ Art Gallery, 86; Gim-Crack (perormance art), Theater Artaud, San Francisco, 87, Mus Contemp Art, Los Angeles, 89 & Walker Art Ctr, Minneapolis, Minn, 90; Theater Artaud, Benefit, 91; Filmore Ctr, 92. *Teaching:* Guest artist & lectr, San Francisco Art Inst, 78, 83, & 84, Univ San Francisco & Hayward State Col, 85, John F Kennedy Univ, Oakland, 87 & Claremont Grad Sch, Pomona, 89; instr drawing, Col Marin, 88; instr, San Francisco Art Inst, 89 & 90, Calif Col Arts & Crafts, 89, 90, 91 & 92. *Awards:* Visual Artists Fel, New Genre Calif Art Coun, 88; Visual Artists Fel, Nat Endowment Arts, 89. *Bibliog:* Cathy Curtis (auth), Woodall's Gim-Crack at Temporary Contemporary, Los Angeles Times, 3/18/89; Dennis Harvey (auth), Pig Villages, San Francisco Weekly, 5/16/90; Robert Hurwitt (auth), Stilty Pig, San Francisco Examiner, 5/10/90. *Mem:* New Langton Arts (bd dirs, 84-88). *Mailing Add:* 1085 Mission St San Francisco CA 94103

WOODEN, HOWARD EDMUND
HISTORIAN, WRITER
b Baltimore, Md, Oct 10, 19. *Study:* Johns Hopkins Univ, BS & MA. *Collections Arranged:* Edward Lanning: American Realist, 1906-1981, 82; Lily Harmon, Fifty Years of Painting, 82; Will Barnet, Paintings and Prints 1932-1982, 83; Art of a Changing Society: British Watercolors and Drawings, 1775-1900, 83; The John W & Mildred L Graves Collection, 84; American Art of the Great Depression: Two Sides of the Coin, 85; Raphael Soyer: The Shape of Human Dignity, 88. *Pos:* Dir, Sheldon Swope Art Mus, Terre Haute, 66-75 & Wichita Art Mus, 75-89, dir emer, 89- *Teaching:* Fulbright instr, Athens Col, 51-52; lectr art hist, Univ Evansville, 55-63; assoc prof, Univ Fla, 63-66; assoc prof art hist, Ind State Univ, Terre Haute, 67-75. *Awards:* Fulbright Grant, US Dept State, 51-52; Gari Melchers Mem Medal, Artist's Fel, Inc, New York, 87. *Mem:* Col Art Asn Am; Am Asn Mus; Int Coun Mus; Asn Art Mus Dirs. *Res:* British watercolor painting of the 18th and 19th centuries; American architecture of the 19th century; American Depression art. *Publ:* Fifty paintings and sculptures from the collection of Sheldon Swope Art Mus, 72; Art of a Changing Society: British Watercolors and Drawings, 1775-1900, Rand Publ Co, 83; American Art of the Great Depression: Two Sides of the Coin, Rand Publ Co, 85; Collected Essays on 101 Art Objects, Wichita Art Mus Collections Rand Publ Co, 88; B M Jackson: Interpretations of Time and Light, Univ Ill Press, 90; Aaron Bohrod: Figure Sketches, Gall & Shaull Publ Co, 90 (co-auth, Edwin E Elliott). *Mailing Add:* Wichita Art Mus 1828 W 18th St Wichita KS 67203

WOODFORD, DON (DONALD PAUL)
PAINTER, EDUCATOR
b Kansas City, Kans, June 16, 41. *Study:* Cornell Col, BA, 63; Ill State Univ, MA, 64; Univ Wis, MFA, 65. *Work:* Cedar Rapids Art Ctr Mus, Coe Col Gallery, Iowa; Davenport Munic Mus, Iowa; Wright State Univ Mus, Dayton, Ohio; Western Ill Univ Gallery, Macomb. *Exhib:* Sixty-ninth Ann Exhib Chicago & Vicinity, Art Inst Chicago, 66; 6th Nat Drawing Exhib, Erie Art Ctr, Pa, 66; Northwest Ann, Seattle Mus, 70; one-man show, Tacoma Art Mus, Wash, 71 & Univ Redlands, Calif, 80; Calif Artist-Works on Paper, Int Art Fair, Basel, Switz, 77. *Teaching:* Asst prof art-painting, Cornell Col, Mt Vernon, Iowa, 65-68; asst prof art-painting, Reed Col, Portland, Ore, 68-72; prof art-painting, Calif State Univ, San Bernardino, 72- *Awards:* Arts & Riverwoods Prize, Riverside Art Ctr, 74. *Bibliog:* Thomas Albright (auth), Paintings on paper, San Francisco Chronicle, 6/7/75; Louis Fox (auth), Roplex and assemblage in relief, Artweek, 4/15/78; Julous Kaplin (auth), Don Woodford's Recent Constructions, Univ Redlands, 80. *Mem:* Col Art Asn Am. *Dealer:* Hank Baum Gallery 2140 Bush San Francisco CA 94115; Getler/Paul Gallery 50 W 57th St New York NY 10019. *Mailing Add:* Art Dept Calif State Univ at San Bernardino 5500 Univ Parkway San Bernardino CA 92407

WOODHAM, DERRICK JAMES
SCULPTOR
b Blackburn, Eng, Nov 5, 40. *Study:* SE Essex Tech Col Sch Art, intermediate dipl design; Hornsey Col Arts & Crafts, nat dipl design; Royal Col Art, dipl. *Work:* Tate Gallery, London, Eng; Mus Contemp Art, Nagaoka, Japan. *Comn:* Sculpture, Gates, comn by North Jersey Cult Coun, Paramus, NJ, 74; C G and E Atrium Sculptures, Moire Screen, 88 & Emerging Cube, Cincinnati, Ohio, 89. *Exhib:* Paris Biennale, Mus Art Mod, 65; Der Geist Surrealismus, Baukunst Galerie, Koln, WGer, 71; Sculpture in the Park, Paramus, NJ, 71 & 74; Wright State Univ Gallery, 76; Nat Sculpture Exhib traveling exhib, 76-77; Artists Choose Artists, Tweed Mus, Duluth, 77; one-man show, Jewish Mus, 69. *Teaching:* Instr sculpture, Philadelphia Col Art, 68-70; asst prof art forms found, Univ Iowa Sch Art, 70-73; assoc prof, Dept Art, Univ Ky, Lexington, 73-80; prof & dir, Sch Art, Univ Cincinnati, 80. *Awards:* Stuyvesant Found Bursary, 65; Prix de la Ville, Sculpture, Paris Biennale, 65. *Bibliog:* Otto Kulturman (auth), The New Sculpture, Praeger, 69; Teruo Fujieda (auth), Form and Structure, Kodansha Ltd, 72; Michael Findlay (auth), Contemporary Artists, St James Press, 77, 88; plus others. *Mem:* Mid-Am Col Art Asn; Col Art Asn. *Mailing Add:* 1910 Bluebell Dr Cincinnati OH 45224

WOODHAM, JEAN
SCULPTOR
b Midland City, Ala. *Study:* Auburn Univ, BA; Sculpture Ctr, New York; Univ Ill, Kate Neal Kinley Mem fel. *Work:* Massillon Mus Permanent Collection, Ohio; US Merchant Marine Mus, NY; Telfair Acad Arts & Sci, Savannah, Ga; Alfred Khouri Mem Collection, Norfolk Mus Arts & Sci, Va; Westport Permanent Collection, Conn; 20th Century American Painting & Sculpture, Foreign Mus, Sophia, Bulgaria. *Comn:* fountain pieces, Gen Elec Credit Corp, Stamford, Conn, 71-72; Scholars' Sphere (four and one-half ton sculpture), Harry S Truman High Sch, New York, 77; Monody (welded bronze sculpture), Goodwin Hall, Archit & Fine Arts Ctr, Auburn Univ, Ala, 79; Cent Conn State Univ, New Britain, Conn, 87; Conn State Comn Arts, Comn Med Examiner's Off, Farmington, Conn, 89. *Exhib:* Boston Mus Fine Arts, 48; Pa Acad Fine Arts Ann, Philadelphia, 50-54; Whitney Mus Am Art, 51; Women's Int Art Club, New Burlington Gallery, London, Eng, 55; New Eng Ann, Silvermine Guild, Conn, 55-60 & 85; US Info Agency Exhibs, Arg, Brazil, Chile & Mex, 63; Wadsworth Atheneum, Hartford, Conn, 67; Museu Nacional de Belles Artes, Buenos Aires, Arg, 63, Museu Nacional de Belles Artes, Santiago, Chile 63, Museo de Arte Moderna, Rio de Janeiro, Brazil, 63, Museo de Arte Moderno, Mexico City, Mex, 64, Museo del Estado, Guadalajara, Mex, 65; Selected Sculptors Guild, Albright-Knox Art Gallery, Buffalo, NY, 71; Aldrich Mus, Ridgefield, Conn, 72; Solo, Conn State Comn Arts Showcase, Bradley Int Airport, CT, 90, within 12" x 12", Cast Iron Gallery, New York, 91; Silvermine Guild Art Ctr, CT, New Eng Ann, 55-60 & 85, Solo 1984, 70th Anniversary Exhib, 92; The Coming of Age of American Sculpture: The First Decades of the Sculptors Guild, 1930s-1950s, Hofstra Mus, Hofstra Univ, Hempstead, NY, 92; Sculptors Guild at the 14th International Sculpture Conference, Philadelphia, Pa, 92; Solo, Conn State Comn Arts Showcase, Bradley Int Airport, CT, 90, Within 12" x 12", Cast Iron Gallery, New York, 91. *Teaching:* Head dept sculpture, Silvermine Guild Artists, 55-56; instr sculpture, Stamford Mus, Conn, 67-69; vis asst prof sculpture, Auburn Univ, 70, assoc prof, 74-75; vis critic, Cornell Univ, Col Archit, Art & Planning, 80. *Awards:* Audubon Artists Medal for Creative Sculpture, 62; Medals of Honor for Sculpture, Nat Asn Women Artists, 66 & 74; Djerassi Found Grant, Woodside, Calif, 83; Finch Award, Art of the Northeast USA, 85; Citation for Contribution to Arts, Conn Gen Assembly & Gov Conn, 86; Citation for Contribution to Arts, Gov Ala, 89. *Bibliog:* Scholars' Sphere (documentary film), 78; Arthur Williams (auth), Sculpture-Technique-Form-Content, Davis Publs, 89; Dolly Curtis (dir), Jean Woodham, Sculptor, Extraordinaire (film), Curtis/Cromwell Productions, 89. *Mem:* Sculptors Guild (treas, 60-65, exec bd, 66-68 & 77-82, secy, 72-74, vpres for membership, 82-83, pres, 90-92); Sculptor's Guild (exec bd mem, 88, 89); Westport-Weston Arts Coun (bd dir, 82-83); Artists Equity Asn; Sculptors Guild (pres, 90); Silvermine Guild Artists (bd mgrs, 58-60, bd trustees, 81-83, chmn admissions, 83). *Mailing Add:* 26 Pin Oak Lane Westport CT 06880

WOODLOCK, ETHELYN HURD
PAINTER
b Hallowell, Maine, June 9, 07. *Study:* Copley Sch Commercial Art, Boston, Mass. *Work:* Valley Hosp, Ridgewood, NJ; Carlson Collection, Ramsey, NJ; Hickory Art Mus, SC; Bergen Community Mus, NJ; UN Bldg, New York. *Exhib:* 64th Am Show, Art Inst Chicago, 61; Awards Artists Exhib, Montclair Art Mus, 66; Contemporary American Realism, Hammond Mus, Salem, NY, 68; two-man show, Bergen Community Mus, 71; five paintings, Nat Mus Woman Arts, Washington, DC; four paintings, Seville Expo, 92; and others. *Awards:* Best Traditional Oil, Nat Asn Women Artists, 73; Gold Medal, Catharine Lorillard Wolfe, 73; Award of Highest Merit, Tri-State Bergen Co Artists Guild, 75; First Prize, Renaissance Festival of Largo; and others. *Bibliog:* Rodger (auth), Nonverbal communication, Am Soc Clin Hypnosis, 72. *Mem:* Nat Asn Women Artists; Miniature Art Soc Fla, Inc; Pinellas Park Art Soc; Allied Artists Am. *Media:* Oil. *Publ:* Auth, Dreams Have Wings, Fidelity Press, St Petersburg, Fla. *Mailing Add:* 1100 S Belcher Rd Apt 737 Largo FL 34641

WOODMAN, BETTY
CERAMIST
b Norwalk, Conn, May 14, 30. *Study:* Alfred Univ, Sch Am Craftsman, New York, 48-50. *Work:* Albright Col, Reading, Carnegie-Mellon Inst, Pittsburgh, Pa; Alfred Univ, Greenwich House, Metrop Mus Art, New York; Archie Bray Found Collection, Helena, Mont; Boston Mus Fine Arts; Cleveland Mus Art, Ohio; and others. *Comn:* Denver Munic Airport, Colo; Inst Contemp Art, Univ Pa, Philadelphia. *Exhib:* One-person exhibs, Susan Hilberry Gallery, Birmingham, 86, Rena Bransten Gallery, San Francisco, 86, 88 & 89, Max Protetch Gallery, New York, 86, 88, 89, 90 & 91, Mus Mod Art, New York, 89 & 91, Denver Art Mus, 88, Johnson Co Community Col Gallery Art, Oakland Park, Kans, 91, Wadsworth Atheneum, Hartford, Conn, 92; Kansas City Contemporary Art Ctr, Mo, 89; Artful Objects: Recent American Crafts, Fort Wayne Mus Art, Ind, 89; Craft Today USA, Musee des Arts Decoratifs, Paris, 89; Max Protetch Gallery, New York, 89 & 90; Par Hazard: A Changing

Installation of Recent Acquisitions, Douglas Drake Gallery, New York, 90; Weatherspoon Art Gallery, Univ NC, Greensboro, NC, 90; Vessels From Use to Symbol, Am Craft Mus, NY, 90; The Painted Vessel, Oriel Gallery, Cardiff, Wales, 91; The Shigaraki Ceramic Cult Park, Shigaraki-yaki, Japan; Investigations 1992, Inst Contemp Art, Univ Philadelphia, Pa, 92; Greenberg Gallery, St Louis, Mo, 92. *Pos:* Cur, Boulder Ctr Visual Arts, Colo, 83; Penelist, Nat Coun Educ Ceramics Arts Conf, St Louis, Mo, 85 & New York State Coun Arts, Visual Arts Prog, 86. *Teaching:* Vis artist, Alfred Univ, New York State Col Ceramics, 75; asst prof, Fine Arts Dept, Univ Colorado Boulder, 76-79, assoc prof, 79-; assoc prof, Fine Arts Dept, Scripps Col, Calif, 77; full prof, fine arts dept, Univ Colo at Boulder, 79- *Awards:* Fel, Nat Endowment Arts, 86; Governor's Award in the Arts, Colo, 87; Atelier Experimental de Recherche et de Creation, Manufacture Nat de Sevres, France, 88. *Bibliog:* Garth Clark (auth), American Ceramics 1876-Present, Abbeville Press, 88; Patricia Conway (auth), Art for Everyday: The New Craft Movement, Clarkson Potter, New York, 90; Craig R Miller (auth), Modern Design 1890-1990 in the Metropolitan Museum of Art, Abrahms, NY, 90. *Mailing Add:* c/o Shark's Inc 2020 9th St Boulder CO 80302

WOODMAN, TIMOTHY
SCULPTOR
b Concord, NH, Mar 4, 52. *Study:* Skowhegan Sch Painting & Sculpture, 70; Cornell Univ, BFA(sculpture), 74; Yale Univ, MFA(sculpture), 76. *Work:* Hirshhorn Mus & Sculpture Garden, Washington, DC; Australian Nat Collection, Canberra; Metrop Mus Art, New York; Newark Mus, NJ; Memphis Brooks Mus Art, TN; Nat Mus Am Art, Smithsonian Inst, Washington, DC; Millrace Park, W K Kellogg Found, Battle Creek, MI; Ribicoff Fed Bldg & Courthouse, Hartford, CT. *Exhib:* Return of the Narrative, Palm Springs Desert Mus, Calif, 84; Body & Soul--Aspects of Recent Figurative Sculpture, Contemp Arts Ctr, Cincinnati, Ohio, 85; New Narrative Painting: Selections from the Metrop Mus Art, Phoenix Art Mus, Ariz; Whitney Mus Am Art (with catalog) Stamford, Conn, 87; Metrop Mus Art, New York, 87, 88; and others. *Teaching:* Lectr, Univ Va, Charlottesville, 81. *Awards:* R S Reynolds Mem Award for Sculpture, 83. *Bibliog:* Wade Saunders (auth), article, Art Am, 5-6/79; Hilton Kramer (auth), article, New York Times, 1/16/81; Ronny H Cohen (auth), article, Artforum, 4/83; Jed Perl (auth), article, The New Criterion, 9/85; Richard Martin (auth), article, Arts, 5/85; John Russell (auth), review, NY Times, 3/13/87, 4/7/89; Paul Bowen (auth), Artist to Artist, Paul Bowen & Timothy Woodman, Provincetown Arts, 88 ann. *Media:* Aluminum, Paint. *Dealer:* Zabriskie Gallery 724 Fifth Ave New York NY 10019. *Mailing Add:* c/o Zabriskie Gallery 724 Fifth Ave NE New York NY 10019

WOODRUFF, DIANE BAILEY
PAINTER
b Los Angeles, Calif, Sept 1, 40. *Study:* Univ Tulsa, BA, 63. *Work:* Philbrook Art Ctr, Tulsa; Gilcrease Mus, Tulsa; Laguna Art Mus, Laguna Beach; Brand Libr & Art Ctr, Glendale; Los Angeles City Hall. *Comn:* Murals depicting Oklahoma, comn by Mrs Jean LaFortune Fair, Tulsa, 67; The Life of Barry Goldwater, comn by Mrs Barry Goldwater, Newport Beach' Calif, 72; An Analysis of the Presidents (painted biographies), comn by Mrs J S Zink, Tulsa, 81-83; dimensional wall carvings, comn by Sally Soloman, Sherman Oaks, Calif, 85; Pres Bush at the Opera, comn by Ralph Feck, 92. *Exhib:* Unconventional Portraiture, Woodruff Enters NY, Harm Bouchart, New York, 85; A Day of Liberty, The Presidents and the States, Michael Katz & Sensory Evolution, New York, 86; The Presidential Series, Occidental Petroleum, 87; Okla Capitol Shows Woodruff, 87; Woodruff Takes Over Collinsville, Okla, 91; and others. *Awards:* Scholastic Art Scholar, White House, Scholastic Mag, 59; Ruskin Award Philbrook Art, City of Tulsa, 69; Proclamation Woodruff's America, week, State Okla, 90. *Bibliog:* Jesse Ash Arndt (auth), Plaudits from Presidents, Christian Sci Monitor, 71; Donna Swaffer (auth), She paints presidents-states, 85 & Kathleen Reeves (auth), Who is Diane Woodruff?, 86, Art Gallery Mag. *Media:* Dimensional Guilded Oils; Acrylic Wall Carvings. *Publ:* New York Daily News, 3/3/87; Okla Mag, 6/90. *Dealer:* N-W Art Assocs 1109 W Main Collinsville OK 74021. *Mailing Add:* 13522 N Memorial Collinsville OK 74021

WOODS, GURDON
SCULPTOR
b Savannah, Ga, Apr 15, 15. *Study:* Art Students League; Brooklyn Mus Sch; San Francisco Art Inst, Hon DArts, 66. *Work:* City of San Francisco, Oakland, Calif Art Mus; Archives Am Art, Smithsonian, Washington, DC. *Comn:* Steel fountain & concrete relief panels, IBM Corp, San Jose, Calif; concrete panels, Berkenstock, Novato, Calif; and others. *Exhib:* Los Angeles Munic Gallery, 77; Los Angeles Co Mus Art, 78; Tortue Gallery, Santa Monica, 81; San Jose Inst Contemp Art, Calif; one-man retrospective, Glastonbury Gallery, & WPA, Washington, DC; and others. *Pos:* Dir, Col San Francisco Art Inst, 55-65; dir, Otis Art Inst, Los Angeles, 74-77; asst dir, Los Angeles Co Mus Natural Hist, 77-80. *Teaching:* Instr sculpture, San Francisco Art Inst, 55-65; prof art, Univ Calif, Santa Cruz, 66-74, chmn dept, 66-70. *Awards:* Four Purchase Awards, San Francisco Art Festivals; Carnegie Corp Grants, New York; and others. *Bibliog:* Thomas Albright (auth), Art in the San Fransisco Bay Area; Wayne Anderson (auth), American Sculpture in Process; Dennis Kowal & Donna Meilach (coauth), Scupture Casting. *Mem:* San Francisco Art Inst (exec dir, 55-64). *Media:* Concrete, Bronze. *Mailing Add:* 133 Seascape Ridge Dr Aptos CA 95003

WOODS, RIP
PAINTER, EDUCATOR
b Idabel, Okla, Aug 15, 33. *Study:* Ariz State Univ, MAE, 58. *Work:* Phoenix Art Mus, Ariz; Ariz State Univ, Tempe; Ark State Univ, Jonesboro; Yuma Fine Arts Ctr, Ariz; Ariz Western Col, Yuma. *Comn:* Relief-assemblage mural (with Ray Fink), Nat Housing Industs, Phoenix, 70; mosaic & bas relief painting (with Ray Fink), Greyhound-Armour, Phoenix, 71; Back Bar, Turlich Steak House, Phoenix, Ariz; Too (with Jeff Donaldson), Howard Univ, Washington, DC. *Exhib:* FESTAC Visual Art Exhib, Lagos, Nigeria, 77; Phoenix Art Mus; Nev Southern Univ, Las Vegas; Univ Wyoming, Laramie; Bosie Fine Art Ctr, Idaho; Bolles Gallery, San Francisco; Ill Bell Traveling Show, Chicago; Roswell Art Ctr, NMex; and others. *Teaching:* Prof painting & drawing, Ariz State Univ, 65-; assoc prof painting, Colorado Springs Fine Art Ctr, Colo, summer 67. *Awards:* Faculty Grant, Ariz State Univ, 68, 73 & 79. *Bibliog:* Contributions of Afro-Americans to the Visual Arts 1700-1960, Univ Calif, Berkely; The Humanities, A Quest for Meaning in the 20th Century, Kendall Hunt Publ; Beverly Jeanne Davis (auth), Chants of the Centuries, WS Benson & Co. *Media:* Mixed. *Mailing Add:* 7817 S 13th Pl Phoenix AZ 85040

WOODSIDE, GORDON WILLIAM
DEALER, COLLECTOR
b Seattle, Wash. *Study:* Univ Wash. *Pos:* Dir, Woodside-Braseth Galleries, Seattle. *Specialty:* Artists of the Pacific Northwest. *Collection:* Representative works by prominent artists of the Northwest. *Mailing Add:* 1533 Ninth Ave Seattle WA 98101-1814

WOODSON, DORIS
EDUCATOR, PAINTER
b Richmond, Va, Jan 13, 29. *Study:* Xavier Univ, New Orleans, BA; Commonwealth Univ, Richmond, Va, MFA. *Work:* Bank of Va, Richmond; Pa State Univ. *Exhib:* 11th Ann Piedmont Painting Show, Mint Mus, Charlotte, NC, 71; Mainstreams 71, Int Painting, Marietta, Ohio, 71; Virginia Artists, Va Mus, Richmond, 71 & 75; Artists Showcase Gallery, Virginia Beach, Va, 73; Black Artists/S, Huntsville Mus Art, Ala, 79. *Pos:* Dir gallery, Va State Univ, Petersburg, 69-81. *Teaching:* Instr painting, Richard Bland Col, Petersburg, Va, 69; asst prof painting & drawing, Va State Univ, Petersburg, 69-; adj instr design & drawing, Commonwealth Univ, Richmond, Va, 79-82; retired, 91. *Awards:* Petersburg Art Festival, Petersburg Area Art Leagues, 68-74; Norfolk Art Festival, Tidewater Artists Asn, 73; Lynchburg Art Festival, Lynchburg Art Asn, 74. *Mem:* Petersburg Art League. *Media:* Oil, Acrylic, Photography. *Mailing Add:* Fine Arts Dept Va State Univ Petersburg VA 23803

WOODSON, SHIRLEY ANN
PAINTER
b Pulaski, Tenn, Mar 3, 36. *Study:* Wayne State Univ, BFA, MA; Grad Study, Art Inst Chicago. *Work:* Your Heritage House Mus, Detroit, Mich; Studio Mus Harlem, NY; Detroit Receiving Hosp, Mich; Mus Nat Ctr Afro Am Artist, Boston, Mass. *Comn:* Site installation, Chene Park, City of Detroit, 86; mural, Fairlane Town Ctr, Dearborn, Mich, 90. *Exhib:* Share the Memories, Detroit Inst Arts, 84; Coast to Coast, Nat Women Color Bk Prog (with catalog), Radford Univ, Va; Coast to Coast Ancestors Known and Unknown, Art in Gen, New York, 90; Sherry Wash Gallery, Detroit, Mich; Hughuey Gallery, Atlanta, Ga, 92; and others. *Pos:* Dir exhibs, Arts Extended Gallery, 63-71; asst projs dir, Nat Conf Artists, Detroit, 85- *Teaching:* Instr painting, design, drawing & art hist, Highland Park Community Col, 66-78; instr painting, Wayne State Univ, 74; consult, Highland Park Schs, Mich, 78-; vis prof, Eastern Mich Univ, 87-88. *Awards:* Purchase Prize, Print & Drawing Exhib, Dulin Gallery Art, Knoxville, Tenn, 65; Fel, MacDowell Colony, 66-67; Mich Coun Arts Grant, 83-84 & 87-88; Detroit Coun Arts Grant, 87; Mich Women's Found Art Award, 88. *Bibliog:* Lula Charleston (auth), Profile of an artist: Shirley Woodson, City Mag, 86; Bamidele Demerson (auth), The Nile as vivifying power: Art of Shirley Woodson, Int Quart African-Am Art, 90; Anthony Murphy(auth), Portfolio/Shirley Woodson, American Visions, 92. *Mem:* Nat Conf Artists. *Media:* All. *Dealer:* Sherry Washington 1274 Library St Detroit MI 48226. *Mailing Add:* 5656 Oakman Blvd Detroit MI 48204

WOODWARD, KESLER EDWARD
PAINTER, CURATOR
b Aiken, SC, Oct 7, 51. *Study:* Davidson Col, NC, BA, 73; Idaho State Univ, Pocatello, MFA, 77. *Work:* Alaska State Mus, Juneau; Univ Alaska, Fairbanks; Atlantic Richfield Co, Los Angeles; Anchorage Hist & Fine Arts Mus & Alaska Contemp Art Bank, Anchorage; Fed Reserve Bank, Charlotte, NC. *Exhib:* 171st American Ann, Newport, RI, 82; Spokane Ann, Wash, 82; US Art in Embassies, Brasilia, Brazil, 82; one-man shows, Univ Alaska Mus & Alaska State Mus, 85, Jerald Melberg Gallery, NC & Davidson Col Art Gallery, 86; Jerald Melberg Gallery, Charlotte, NC, 88; one-man shows, Univ Ala, Huntsville, 90, Anchorage Mus Hist & Art, 91 & Univ Alaska, Anchorage Art Gallery, 91; Terra Borealis, Visual Art Ctr Alaska, Anchorage, 91; Contemporary Art from Alaska, Magadan, Art Gallery, Russia, 92. *Collections Arranged:* New Possibilities: Works from the Canadian Art Bank (auth, catalog), Alaska State Mus, 78; A Celebration of Tradition, Visual Arts Ctr of Alaska, 78 & National Invitational, 78-79; Canadian Horizons (with catalog), 81-82; Sydney Laurence Retrospective, Anchorage Mus Hist & Art, 90. *Pos:* Cur temp exhib, Alaska State Mus, Juneau, 77-78, cur visual arts, 79-81; artistic dir, Visual Arts Ctr of Alaska, Anchorage, 78-79; dir, Univ Alaska Fine Arts Gallery, 82-; dir, Fine Arts & Humanities Proj, Inst Canada, Dartmouth Col, 88-91. *Teaching:* Asst prof painting, Univ Alaska, 81-88, assoc prof, 88- *Awards:* Alaska State Coun Arts Grant, 82; Vis Res Fel, Dartmouth Col, 88-91. *Bibliog:* C E Licka (auth), Kes Woodward: Inscapes & Poethics (exhib catalog), Univ Alaska Anchorage Fine Art Gallery, 91; Frank Soos (auth), Kes Woodward: James Bay Paintings (exhib catalog), Anchorage Mus Hist & Art, 91. *Mem:* Col Art Asn. *Media:* Acrylic. *Res:*

Early pictorial material pertaining to polar regions and little-known Alaskan historical artists. *Publ:* Auth, New Possibilities, Alaska State Coun Arts, 78; Canadian Horizons, Alaska State Coun Arts, 82; coauth, Lockwood de Forest in Alaska, 1912, Alaska State Mus, 88; Northern Art & Ethnographic Material in the Collections of Dartmouth College, Northern Notes, 11/89; Sydney Laurence: Painter of the North, Univ Wash Press, 90. *Mailing Add:* Dept Art Univ Alaska Fairbanks AK 99701

WOODWARD, STEVEN P
SCULPTOR
b Little Falls, Minn, 1953. *Study:* St Cloud State Univ, BA, 76. *Work:* Walker Art Ctr, Minneapolis; Tweed Mus, Duluth, Minn; First Bank System, Minneapolis. *Exhib:* Ann Juried Exhib, Queen's Mus, New York, 84; Bim Bam Botterham, Stokker Stikker Gallery, New York, 85; Bockley Gallery, Minneapolis, 88; Thomas Barry Fine Arts, Minneapolis, 90 & 92; Kiehle Gallery, St Cloud State Univ, Minn, 91. *Awards:* Juror's Award, Small Works Show, New York Univ, 84; Nat Endowment Arts, 88. *Mailing Add:* c/o Thomas Barry Fine Arts 400 First Ave N Minneapolis MN 55401

WOODWARD, WILLIAM
PAINTER, EDUCATOR
b Washington, DC, Mar 11, 35. *Study:* Abbott Sch Art, Corcoran Sch Art, Am Univ, BA & MA, Washington, DC; Acad de Belli Arti, Florence, Italy. *Work:* Corcoran Gallery; Speed Mus, Louisville; Washington Co Mus Fine Art. *Comn:* Drawing, The White House, DC, 68; mural, United Brotherhood Teamsters, DC, 69; mural, Eutaw Sch, Baltimore, 68; mural, Clydes Inc, Tysons Corner, Va, 80; mural, City Hall Rockville, Md, 82; and others. *Exhib:* One-man shows, Mickelson Gallery, DC, 66-74, Hirschl & Adler Gallery, New York, 71, John State Col, Vt, 74 & Int Monetary Fund, Washington, DC, 75; Fendrick Gallery, Washington, DC, 82; and others; plus others. *Teaching:* Instr painting, Corcoran Sch Art, DC, 65-; asst prof painting, George Washington Univ, DC, 69-; dir, Summer Fine Arts Prog, Brittany, France, 76-79. *Awards:* Painting Fel in Italy, Leopold Schepp Found, 57-59; Mary Graydon Scholar, Am Univ, 53-57 & Teaching Fel, 58-61. *Bibliog:* Rafael Sqirru (auth), The Washington mannerists: the foresight to look backwards, Americas, Vol 19, No 1; Legrace N Benson (auth), The Washington scene, Art Int, Vol 13, No 10; Jill Weschsler (auth), William Woodward: Traditional themes, modern methods, Am Artist, 12/76. *Publ:* Contribr, Art in America, 1760-1860, 69; contribr, Leonardo da Vinci, 70 & Dreamers of Decadence, 72, Washington Post. *Mailing Add:* Dept Art George Wash Univ Smith Hall Art Washington DC 20052

WOODY, (THOMAS) HOWARD
SCULPTOR, ENVIRONMENTAL ARTIST
b Salisbury, Md, Sept 26, 35. *Study:* Richmond Prof Inst, BFA; ECarolina Univ, MA; Univ Iowa; Art Inst Chicago; Kalamazoo Art Ctr; Univ Ky. *Work:* SC State Art Collection, Columbia; Gibbes Art Gallery, Charleston, SC; Mus Art, Charlotte, NC; Birmingham Mus Art, Ala; Columbus Mus Arts & Crafts, Ga; and others. *Exhib:* Tenth Int Sculpture Conf, Toronto, 78; Arcosanti Conf, 78; 11th Int Sculpture Conf, Washington DC, 80; Col Art Conf, New Orleans, La, 80; Sky Art Conferences, Mass Inst Technol, Cambridge, 81 & 86, Linze, Austria, 82 & Munich, Ger, 83. *Teaching:* Instr sculpture, Roanoke Fine Art Ctr, Va, 59-61; assoc prof sculpture, Pembroke State Univ, 62-67; prof sculpture, Univ SC, 67- *Awards:* Spec Citation Award, Atlanta Festival Sculpture, 68; SC State Art Collection Award, 71 & 74 & Fel grants, 73 & 77, SC Arts Comn. *Bibliog:* Ann Weinstein (auth), The sky's no limit, Art Voices, 7/81; L G Redstone (auth), Public Art: New Directions, McGraw-Hill, 81. *Mem:* Southern Asn Sculptors (pres, 65-70); Nat Sculpture Ctr (adv, 66-80); Guild SC Artists (mem bd, 69); SC Craftsmen (mem bd, 68); Southeastern Col Art Conf. *Media:* Plastic. *Publ:* Auth, Atmospheric sculpture: An event, not an object, Vol 7, No 1 & Atmospheric concepts, Vol 6, No 2, Southeastern Col Art Conf Rev; auth, Workshops in environmental sky art, Design for Arts in Educ, 3-4/79; auth, Environmental art, Sculptor's News Exchange, Princeton, NJ, 9-10-11/79; and others. *Mailing Add:* 433 Arrowwood Rd Columbia SC 29210

WOOF, MAIJA GEGERIS ZACK See Peeples, Maija (Maija Gegeris Zack Woof)

WOOL, CHRISTOPER
PAINTER
Exhib: Solo Exhib, Cable Gallery, New York, 84 & 86, Robbin Lockett Gallery, Chicago, 86, Luhring, Augustine & Hodes Gallery, New York, 87 & 88, Jean Bernier, Athens, Greece, 88, Galerie Gisela Capitain, Cologne, 88; Signs of painting, Donald Young Gallery, Chicago, 86; drawings, Michael Kohn Gallery, Los Angeles, 87; Univ Art Gallery, San Diego, 87; Kansas City Art Inst, 87; Robbin Lockett Gallery, Chicago, 88. *Awards:* Fel, Nat Endowment Arts, 87. *Bibliog:* Gray Indiana (auth), Chronicle in black & white, The Village Voice, 3/31/87; Jerry Salt (auth), This is the End, Art Mag, 9/20/88; David Robbins (auth), Information as Ornament (exhib cataloge), Feature, 7/88. *Mailing Add:* c/o Luhring, Augustine & Hodes Gallery 130 Prince New York NY 10012

WOOLFENDEN, WILLIAM EDWARD
ADMINISTRATOR, HISTORIAN
b Detroit, Mich, June 27, 18. *Study:* Wayne State Univ, BA & MA. *Pos:* Asst cur Am art, Detroit Inst Arts, 45-49, dir educ, 49-60; asst dir, Arch Am Art, Detroit, 60-62, exec dir, 62-64, dir, 64-70; mem vis comt, Dept Photog & Slide Libr, Metrop Mus Art, New York; adv drawings, Minn Mus Art, St Paul, 61-80; dir, Arch Am Art, Smithsonian Inst, New York, 70-83, emer dir, 83-; consult, Mus Services Sothebys, Inc, 84-; mem exhib comt, Inst for Contemp Photog, 84-; bd dir, Am Friends of Attingham Park, 86-88. *Awards:* Alumni Award, Wayne State Univ, 76. *Res:* American art; American drawings. *Mailing Add:* 65 Oyster Shores Rd East Hampton NY 11937

WOOLSCHLAGER, LAURA TOTTEN
PAINTER, PRINTMAKER
b Dallas, Tex, Sept 1, 32. *Study:* Syracuse Univ, BFA(magna cum laude), 54; Southern Ore Col, with Robert Alston, 65. *Work:* Carnegie Libr, Lewiston, Idaho; Mus Native Am Cult, Spokane, Wash; Favell Mus Western Art, Klamath Falls, Ore. *Exhib:* Monac Western Art Show, Spokane Convention Ctr, Wash, 73-81; Southwest Rendezvous, Oro Valley Country Club, Tucson, Ariz, 79-81; C M Russell Show, Heritage Inn, Great Falls, Mont, 79-81; Western Experience, Stewart Anderson Ranch, Ellensburg, Wash, 80; Artist in Residence, Mus Native Am Cult, Spokane, Wash, 80. *Teaching:* Instr, Wenatchee Valley Community Col, Omak, Wash, 73-74. *Awards:* Best of Show, Artists of the Old West, 79 & Nat Western Art Show, Western Art Asn, 79. *Bibliog:* Dr Darwin Goodey (auth), An inner view, Art West Mag, 1/80; Paula Hartwig (auth), Northwest Originals, Washington Women & Their Art, Ann 90. *Mem:* Western Art Asn. *Media:* Acrylic, Watercolor; Intaglio, Monoprint. *Mailing Add:* Route 1 Box 122-H Omak WA 98841

WOOLWICH, MADLYN-ANN C
PAINTER, INSTRUCTOR
b Fall River, Mass, Sept 14, 37. *Study:* Bridgewater Col, BS(educ), 59, MEd, 61; Parsons Sch Design, with Barbara Nechis, 86; Nat Acad Design, with Wolf Kahn, 87. *Work:* Archival Collection, Pastel Soc Am Gallery, New York; Dow Jones Info Servs, Princeton, NJ; Mason Gross Gallery, Rutgers Univ, New Brunswick, NJ; Eastern Branch, Monmouth Co Libr, Red Bank, NJ; Georgian Court Col, Lakewood, NJ. *Comn:* Acrylic painting, Gerber Sommer Asn, Hackensack, 86; oil painting of dog, comm by parishioners for Father James, Middletown, NJ, 86; floral triptych, comm by Kimberly Crawford, Vero Beach, Fla, 87; pastel floral, comm by Evelyn Cole, Fort Pierce, Fla, 87; pastel painting, comm by Mr & Mrs Vin Scully, Pacific Palisades, Calif, 87; pastel painting, Evergreen Gallery, Cancer Soc, 90; pastel painting, Canyon Suite, Russell Thacker, Esq. *Exhib:* 2nd Int Show of Pastels, Palace Rameau, Lille, France, 86; 5th Int Show of Pastels, Kans Pastel Soc, Wichita, 88 & 89; Invitational Show of Master Pastelists, Ashland Area Gallery, Ky, 88 & 89; Pastel Soc Am Exhib, Nabisco Gallery Invitational, Hanover, NJ, 88; invitational pastel exhib, Quincy Art Mus, Ill; state show, Ocean County Art Guild, 90; Biennial Exhib, Pastel Soc N Fla, Pensacola, 91; Ann Exhib, Pastel Soc Am, New York, 78-92; Pastel Soc West Cost/Traveling Show, Kaiser Permanente Ctr, Sacramento & Oakland, Calif, 92; Int Soc Marine Painters, 92; Newark Mus Benefit, NJ, 92; solo exhib, Educ Testing Serv, Conant Gallery, Princeton, NJ, 92. *Teaching:* Instr drawing & design, Guild Creative Art, Shrewsbury, NJ, 82-88, adult class pastel/oil landscape, 84-90; drawing & painting, Spring Lake Recreation Comn, 87-88; workshops, Pastel Soc Am, 86-90; judge in field, 87-93. *Awards:* Little Studio Award, Pastel Soc Am, 86; Best In Show, Citycorp Sea & Shore, 87; Trump Purchase Award, Pastel Soc Am, 88; Best in Show, Ocean County Artists Guild, 90. *Bibliog:* Women on the move, Women's Reporter, NJ, 4/91; Long Branch Artist in New Pastel Book, Shorelines, Toms River, NJ, 92; Elizabeth Mowry (auth), Creating painting with pastel, Art Times, Rhinebeck, NY, 92. *Mem:* Art Alliance Monmonth Co (vpres, 80-81); Guild Creative Art (vpres, educ facilities, 80-); Monmouth Arts Gallery (vpres, 84-86); Pastel Soc Am (secy & pub relations, 86-); Nat Mus Women Arts; Salmagundi Club. *Media:* Pastel, Oil. *Publ:* Contrib, NJ Goodlife (cover), 4/90; Vitality Mag (cover), 4/92; Pushing the luster of paster, Artist's Mag, F&W Publ, 9/92; Pastel Interpretations-North Light Bks, F&W Publ, 9/93. *Dealer:* Evergreen Gallery 310 Morris Ave Spring Lake NJ 07762; The Connoisseur Gallery 9 Mill St Rhinebeck NY 12572. *Mailing Add:* 473 Marvin Dr Long Branch NJ 07740

WOOSTER, ANN-SARGENT
PAINTER
b Chicago, Ill, Jan 19, 46. *Study:* Bard Col, AB, 68; Hunter Col, with Robert Morris, MFA, 73, and Leo Steinberg, Rosalind Krauss & Ray Parker, MA(art hist), 78. *Exhib:* Anthology Film Archives; Black Maria Festival. *Pos:* Ed educ dept, Shorewood Publ, New York, 69-72; free lance writer, Art Am, New York, 73-; staff writer, Art Forum, 75-76, Village Voice, 79-83, Afterimage, 81-86; contrib ed, East Village Eye, 83-86 & Amtrak Express, 87-91 & High Performance, 88- *Teaching:* Instr, Sch Visual Arts, New York, 75-, Kean Col, Union, NJ, 79-83, New York Univ, 85; New York Sch Interior Design, 89. *Awards:* Helen Rubenstein Fel, Whitney Mus Am Art, 75; Award, 82, Grant for Media Production, 85, NY State Coun Arts; Logan Grant for New Writing on Photography, 88; Video Fel, New York Found of the Arts, 88. *Bibliog:* Jean Sousa (auth), NAME events, NAME Gallery, 80; Charlene Spretnak (auth), Politics of Women's Spirituality, Anchor Doubleday, 82. *Mem:* Int Art Critics Asn; Women's Caucus; Int Art Critics Asn (secy Am Sect, 92). *Media:* Miscellaneous Media. *Publ:* Auth, Quiltmaking, Drake Publ, 72; Sol Lewitt and Lucinda Childs, 5/80 & Film and video at the Biennial, 5/81, Art Am; Moving to dance, 12/80 & Yvonne Rainer: Journeys to Berlin 1971, 5/81, Drama Rev; essay, Reach Out & Touch Someone: The Romance of Interactivity (book), Illuminating Video, New York, Aperture Press, 91; chapters in American Painting, Goodman Publ, 91. *Mailing Add:* 170 Second Ave New York NY 10003

WORDELL, EDWIN HOWLAND
PAINTER
b Philadelphia, Pa, Aug 27, 27. *Study:* San Diego State Univ, dipl(hon), 61. *Work:* San Diego Zoological Soc; NASA; Tex Instruments; Transco Energy Co, Houston, Tex; Scripps Clinic & Res Found, La Jolla, Calif. *Comn:* Triptich (watercolor), Zoological Soc, San Diego; three watercolor paintings, San Diego Trust & Savings Bank; two watercolor paintings, Great Am Development Co, San Diego; US Coast Guard; Kaiser Hosps. *Exhib:* Audubon Artists, Nat Arts Club, New York, 83 & 90; Springville Mus Art, April Salon Exhib, Springville, Utah, 86-88; Tubac Ctr Arts, Ariz, 89; San

Diego Mus Art, Calif, 90; Western Co Ctr Arts, Grand Junction, 91; Butler Inst Am Art, Youngstown, Ohio, 92; Miss Mus Art, Jackson, 92. *Teaching:* Instr watercolor workshop, Greece, 85, NZ, Fiji & Australia, 86, Mex, 88 & 89, Port, 90, Guatamala, 91, Turkey, 92. *Awards:* Elizabeth Erlanger Mem Award, Nat Soc Painters in Casein & Acrylic, Nat Arts Club, New York, 90; Experimental Painting Award, Nat Watercolor Soc, Los Angeles, 91; Juror's Merit Award, San Diego Artists Guild Exhib, San Diego Mus Art, 92; and others. *Mem:* Watercolor West; San Diego Art Guild (pres, 90-91); Nat Soc Painters in Casein & Acrylic, New York; Am Soc Marine Artists; San Diego Mus Art (trustee 90-91); and others. *Media:* Watermedia, Mixed. *Publ:* Illusr, Guide to Am Law, Vol 8, West Publ, Inc; Calif Art Review, 2nd Ed Am Ref Publ, Inc; First issue cover & San Diego Metro Mag, (cover), 90; Am Artist Mag, 8/90. *Dealer:* Tarbox Gallery 1202 Kettner Blvd San Diego CA 92101. *Mailing Add:* 6251 Lorca Dr San Diego CA 92115

WORKMAN, ROBERT P
PAINTER, ILLUSTRATOR
b Chicago, Ill, Jan 27, 61. *Study:* Sch Art Inst Chicago; Roosevelt Univ (Belg, Europe), PhD, 86; Pac Western Univ, BA, 87, MA, 92. *Work:* Libr Nat Mus Am Art Portrait Gallery, Nat Arch, Washington, DC; Ridge Hist Soc Mus, Chicago; The Vatican, Rome, Italy; Ill State Mus, Springfield. *Comn:* Portrait, Mayor Richard J Daley, Daley Branch Libr, Chicago Pub Libr, Ill, 89. *Exhib:* Nat Vet For War Conv, Chicago, 87; Int Cartoon Festival, Europe, 87; Sch Art Inst, Nat Reunion Alumni, Chicago, 91; Ridge Hist Soc Mus, Chicago, 92; Expo 92, Seville Worlds Fair, US Pavilion, Spain, 92; and others. *Pos:* Graphic artists/cartoonist, Village View Publs, 83-88; artist, Villager (newspaper), 91- *Teaching:* Instr art/writing, St Xavier Col, 85; artist-in-residence, Chicago Pub Libr, 91- *Awards:* Plaque, Ill Dept Conserv; Chicago, 150th cert, City of Chicago, 87; Plaque/cert appreciation, Vet For War, Post 5220. *Bibliog:* Stan Barker (auth), Home grown, Artists Mag, 90; Dan Rafter (auth), Seville expo, Beverly Rev, 92; Steve Metsch (auth), Artist wins spot at worlds fair, 92. *Mem:* Assoc mem Am Watercolor Soc; Ridge Art Asn; Sch Art Inst Chicago; Artists Resource Inst, Ft Wayne Mus Art; Reader, Oxford Univ, Eng. *Media:* Watercolor, Acrylic. *Publ:* Auth & illusr, The Sesque Squirrel Coloring Book, 82; The Sesqui Squirrel, History of Chicago, 1883-1983; Sesqui Squirrel History of the Constitution; Sesqui Squirrel Presents How Columbus Discovered America; Angels of Doom. *Mailing Add:* 10619 S Hale Ave Chicago IL 60643

WORTH, KAREN
SCULPTOR
b Philadelphia, Pa, Mar 9, 24. *Study:* Tyler Art Sch, Temple Univ; Pa Acad Fine Arts; Acad Grande Chaumiere, Paris. *Work:* Smithsonian Inst; West Point Acad, NY; Am Jewish Hist Asn, Boston; Jewish Mus, New York; Israel Govt Coins & Medals Div, Jerusalem. *Comn:* Space Age (medal), Soc Medalists, 63; Hist Jews of Am, Judaic Heritage Soc, 69; Presidents USA, Whittnauer Precious Metals Guild, 74; Bicentennial Presidents (medal), Galaxies Unlimited Inc, 75. *Exhib:* Nat Acad, New York, 65; Lever House, New York, 66-; Ceramic Sculpture of Western Hemisphere. *Teaching:* Pvt sculpture classes, 72-73. *Awards:* Saltus Award, 80, Numismatics Lifetime Achievement Award; Lindsey Morris Award (for a portrait), 86. *Bibliog:* Ed Trautman (auth), Almanac, Franklin Mint, 68. *Mem:* Fel Nat Sculpture Soc (coun, 69-); Fine Arts Fedn New York. *Media:* Clay, Bronze. *Mailing Add:* 19 Henry St Orangeburg NY 10962

WORTH, PETER JOHN
SCULPTOR, HISTORIAN
b Ipswich, Eng, Mar 16, 17; US citizen. *Study:* Ipswich Sch Art, 34-37; Royal Col Art, London, with E W Tristram, Paul Nash, Edward Bawden, Douglas Cockerell & Roger Powell. *Work:* Denver Art Mus; Joslyn Art Mus; Sheldon Gallery Art, Univ Nebr. *Exhib:* San Francisco Mus Art, 50; Nelson Gallery Art, 50, 53, 54 & 57; Art Inst Chicago, 51; Walker Art Ctr, 51, 52 & 56; Denver Art Mus, 52, 53, 55-57 & 60-63. *Teaching:* Prof art hist, Univ Nebr, Lincoln, currently. *Mem:* Egypt Explor Soc, London; Col Art Asn Am. *Res:* Stylistic transformations in late antique and early medieval art, especially in iconography. *Publ:* Photogr, Life Library of Photography, 70; photogr, Bilder, Stuttgart, 70. *Mailing Add:* Dept of Art 207 Woods Bldg Univ of Nebr at Lincoln Lincoln NE 68583-0114

WORTHEN, AMY NAMOWITZ
PRINTMAKER, HISTORIAN
b New York, NY, Aug 13, 46. *Study:* Smith Col, with Leonard Baskin, BA, 67; Univ Iowa, with Mauricio Lasansky, MA, 69; Sir John Cass Col, City London Polytechnic, 86- 87. *Work:* Metrop Mus Art, New York; Cooper-Hewitt Mus, New York; Des Moines Art Ctr, Iowa; Nat Mus Am Art, Washington, DC; Mus Fine Arts, Boston. *Comn:* Two engravings, The Terrace Hill Soc, Des Moines, Iowa, 79; Patron's Print, Univ Iowa, 82; Aida in Des Moines (engraving), Des Moines Metrop Opera; Centro Internazionale di Grafica, Venice, 92. *Exhib:* World Print III, San Francisco, Mus Mod Art, 80; Smithsonian Touring Exhib, II Int Mus, 80-83; solo exhibs, Brunnier Gallery, Iowa State Univ, Ames, 81, Selected Prints and Drawings, 1979-84 (with catalog), Sioux City Art Ctr, 84, State Univ NY, Binghamton, 89, Grinnell Col, Iowa, 90 & The Louise Noun Collection: Art by Women, Des Moines Art Ctr, Iowa, École des Beaux-Arts, Saint-Étienne, France, 92; Boston Printmakers 33rd, 35th, 36th & 38th Nat Exhibs, 81, 83, 84 & 86; Print Club Philadelphia, 82 & 83; Playing Cards, Cooper Hewitt Mus, NY, 86; 110th Print Exhib, Royal Soc Painters, Etchers & Engravers; Art Quest 88, C W Post Col, NY, Beaver Col Pa & Univ Calif, Irvine, 88; Centro Internazionale di Grafica, Venice, Italy; The Louise Noun Collection: Art by Women, Des Moines Art Ctr, Iowa. *Collections Arranged:* The Etchings of Jacques Bellange (com auth, catalog), Des Moines Art Ctr, Mus Fine Arts, Metrop Mus, 75-76; Benton, Curry, Wood--Lithographs, Iowa Arts Coun touring exhib (auth, catalog), 78; Giorgio Morandi (auth, catalog), Des Moines Art Ctr, San Francisco Mus Mod Art, Guggenheim Mus, 81; Etchings of J N Darling (auth, catalog), Brunnier Gallery, Iowa State Univ, 84; Centro Internazionale di Grafica (Iowa Printmakers), Venice, 89; Maestridella Scuola Internazionale di Grafica di Venezia, Drake Univ, 89 & Sioux City Art Ctr, 90; Des Moines Art Center (manuscripts & early printed book pages), 91. *Teaching:* Instr printmaking hist prints, Des Moines Art Ctr, Iowa, 71-; lectr, Drake Univ, Iowa, 72-74, 81, 83, 85 & 92. *Awards:* Iowa Arts Coun Touring Exhib Grant, 78; Art Quest Printmaking, 88. *Bibliog:* article, Am Artist, 9/86; Amy Worthen Prints & Drawings, 60-90; Grinnell Col, 90. *Mem:* Print Coun Am; Printmakers Coun, Eng; Boston Printmakers; Print Club, Philadelphia, Pa. *Media:* Engraving. *Res:* History of prints. *Publ:* Giorgio Morandi as an Etcher in Morandi, Des Moines, Art Ctr, 81; The Prints of J N Darling, Brunnier Gallery Mus, Iowa State Univ, 84, 2nd ed, 90; Morandi colorista - incisore in bianco e nero, Quaderni Morandiani No 1, Milano, 85; The Louise Noun Collections - Art by Women, Univ Iowa Mus, 90; Calligraphic Engraving in Dutch Mannerist Prints, Goltzius Studies, Netherlands Kunsthistorisan Jaarbock, 92. *Dealer:* Olson-Larson Galleries 203 Fifth St W Des Moines IA 50265. *Mailing Add:* 5130 Shriver Ave Des Moines IA 50312

WORTZ, MELINDA FARRIS
GALLERY DIRECTOR, CRITIC
b Ann Arbor, Mich, Apr 30, 40. *Study:* Radcliffe Col, BA(cum laude), 62; Otis Art Inst, 62-63; Univ Calif, Los Angeles, MA, 70; also with John Altoon. *Pos:* Gallery dir, Univ Calif, Riverside, 72-74 & Univ Calif, Irvine, currently; Southern Calif ed, Artweek, currently; contrib ed, Arts Mag, Art Gallery, Art News & Archit Dig, currently. *Teaching:* Asst prof issues in art, Calif State Univ, Long Beach, 72-75 & Calif State Univ, Los Angeles, 74-75; lectr, Univ Calif, Irvine, currently. *Res:* Contemporary American art. *Publ:* Auth, Seven Southern California Artists (catalog), Cirrus Gallery, Los Angeles, 74; auth, Dewain Valentine (exhib catalog), Long Beach Mus Art, 75; auth, Ludwig Redl (catalog essay), 75. *Mailing Add:* 580 Prospect Pasadena CA 91103

WORTZEL, ADRIANNE
PAINTER, PRINTMAKER
b Brooklyn, NY, Oct 7, 41. *Study:* Brooklyn Mus Art Sch, NY, 57-65; Brooklyn Col, with Ad Reinhardt, Burgoyne Diller & Louise Bourgeois, BA(with honors fine art), 63; Hunter Col, New York, with Mark Rothko, MA, 69. *Work:* Moderna Museet, Stockholm Sweden; Citibank, New York; City of Lund, Sweden; pvt collection of Mr & Mrs Larry Hagman, Malibu, Calif. *Comn:* Landmark Systems, Philip Johnson Bldg, Vienna, Va. *Exhib:* Galleriet, Sweden, 79 & 82; New Acquisitions, Moderna Museet, Stockholm, Sweden, 80; one-person show, Scottsdale Ctr Arts, Ariz, 80 & Bernice Steinbaum Gallery, New York, 81 & 83; Graphic Plus, Herbert F Johnson Mus, Ithaca, NY, 81; Stamford Mus, Conn, 89. *Teaching:* Lectr contemp art, Great Neck Adult Educ Program, 70-73; guest artist, printmaking workshop, 89. *Awards:* Creative Artists Pub Serv Grant, NY State Coun Arts, 81. *Bibliog:* Patricia Ensworth, Adrianne Wortzel, Arts Mag, 3/80; Sarah Cecil (auth), article, Artnews, 3/82; Donna Harkavy (auth), Adrianne Wortzel, Arts Mag, 9/83. *Media:* Acrylic on Canvas; Etchings. *Mailing Add:* 19 East 7th St New York NY 10003

WOSTREL, NANCY J
PAINTER
b San Diego, Calif. *Study:* With John C Pellew, 70 & 71; Famous Artists Sch, cert, 72; studied with Robert E Wood, 80. *Work:* James S Copley Libr, La Jolla, Calif; Vesti Corp, Boston, Mass; Troth Corp, New Orleans, La. *Exhib:* Watercolor W, Riverside Art Ctr & Mus, Calif, 75, 77, 78 & 79; one-man shows, Knowles Art Ctr, La Jolla, Calif, 74, 77, 79, 81, 84 & 88; Watercolor USA, Springfield Art Mus, Mo, 79; Nat Acad Ann, New York, 81; Am Watercolor Soc Traveling Exhib, 80-81; and others. *Awards:* Purchase Awards, San Diego Watercolor Soc Nat Ann, 73, 76, 79 & 80; Hon Mention, San Diego Watercolor Soc Nat, 79; Second Prize for Watercolor, Southern Calif Expo, Del Mar, 79; and others. *Bibliog:* Richard Reilly (auth), Frost poems inspire art, 77, Watercolor show a breath of sweet air, 79, Compostions of beauty & joy, 81, San Diego Union, Copley Publ. *Mem:* San Diego Watercolor Soc; Watercolor W; Assoc Am Watercolor Soc; Allied Artists Asn. *Media:* Watercolor, Pastel. *Publ:* Auth, North Light Mag, Fletcher Art Serv Inc, 76. *Dealer:* Newman Galleries 850 W Lancaster Ave Bryn Mawr PA 19010; Newman Galleries 1625 Walnut St Philadelphia PA 19103. *Mailing Add:* 2505 Montclair St San Diego CA 92104

WRAY, DICK
PAINTER
b Houston, Tex, Dec 5, 33. *Study:* Univ Houston. *Work:* Albright-Knox Art Gallery, Buffalo. *Exhib:* Mus Contemp Art, Houston, 61; Southwest Painting & Sculpture, Houston, 62; Hemisfair, Houston, 68; Homage to Lithography, Mus Mod Art, New York, 69; Response, Tyler Mus, Tex, 80; Houston Artists Exhibition, Stavanger Mus, Norway; In Our Time: Houston's Contemp Arts Mus 1948-1982, Contemp Arts Mus, Houston, 82; Fresh Paint: The Houston School, Mus of Fine Arts, Houston (catalog), traveling exhib, 85; Third Western States Exhibition, The Brooklyn Mus, NY, (catalog), traveling exhib, 86; Line and Form: Contemporary Texas Figurative Drawing, Art Mus of S Tex, Corpus Christi, 87; Texas Art: An Exhibition Selected from the Menil Collection, The Mus of the Menil Collection-Richmond Hall, Houston, 88. *Teaching:* Glassell Sch of Art, Mus of Fine Arts, Houston, Tx, 68-82. *Awards:* Purchase Prize, Ford Found, 62; Purchase Prize, Mus Fine Arts, Houston, 63. *Mailing Add:* c/o Moody Gallery 2815 Colquitt Houston TX 77098

WRIGHT, BARTON ALLEN
PAINTER, ILLUSTRATOR
b Bisbee, Ariz, Dec 21, 20. *Work:* Ariz Bank (now Bank of Am). *Comn:* Wupatki Nat Monument, Ft Union Nat Monument, Babbitt Stores; Great Sand Dunes Nat Monument; Montezuma Castle Nat Monument. *Exhib:* La Jolla Art Asn, Calif, 69; The Athenaeum, La Jolla, 70; Festival of Arts, Lake Oswego, 71; One-man show, San Diego, 71-75; Thorne Gallery, Scottsdale, 74 & 75; Indian Summer Gallery, Estes Park, Colo; and others. *Collections Arranged:* M R F Colton, 58; G E Burr, 59; Indian Artists, 60; Western Artists, 62; Paul Dyck, 64; American Art, 65; Frederick Sommers, 67; Southwest Art, 68; Widforss, 69; Santa Fe Indian Art, 70; Nat Park Illustrated, 71; N Fechin, 72; and others. *Pos:* Cur arts & exhib, Mus Northern Ariz, 55-58, cur, Mus, 58-77; sci dir, Mus of Man, 77-82; res anthropologist, Heard Mus, 83; Sci lect & guide, Sierra Club, Stanford Alumni, Canyonlands. *Teaching:* Vis Instr, Univ Calif, Riverside, 77, Univ Calif, San Diego, spring 83, Pitzer Col, spring 83. *Awards:* Anisfield Wolf-Cleveland Found, 86; Rounce & Coffin, 86; Border Regional Libr Asn, 86. *Mem:* Am Asn Mus; San Diego Corral Westerners; Ariz/Nev Acad Sci; Westerners, San Diego & Phoenix. *Media:* Acrylic, Scratchboard. *Interests:* Western Art; Indian Art. *Publ:* Auth, This is a Hopi Kachina, 64, Kachina's, a Hopi Artist's Documentary, 73, Unchanging Hopi, 75, Pueblo Shields, 76, Hopi Kachinas, the Complete Guide, 77; Mythic World of the Zuni, 88. *Mailing Add:* 4143 Gelding DrAve Phoenix AZ 85023

WRIGHT, BERNARD
PAINTER, GRAPHIC ARTIST
b Pittsburgh, Pa, Feb 23, 38. *Study:* Otis Art Inst, Los Angeles, 69-70; Los Angeles Trade Tech Col, 71-74. *Work:* New York Pub Libr; Howard Univ, Washington, DC; Libr Cong; Morehouse Col, Atlanta, Ga; Los Angeles Pub Libr. *Comn:* Numerous furniture and garment exclusive designs. *Exhib:* Detroit Inst Arts, 74; Fisher Art Galleries, Univ Southern Calif, 74; Calif Mus Sci & Indust, Los Angeles, 75; Ava Dorog Galleries, Los Angeles, 82; Pittsburgh City Hall Gallery, Pa, 82; and others. *Pos:* Pres & co-founder, Westly & Wright Products, Los Angeles, 72- *Bibliog:* Frank Johnson (auth), The art of Bernard Wright, Grapevine Mag, 10/80; Ronald Moore (auth), City honors 12 Black artists, Los Angeles Sentinel, 5/7/81; Judith Grout (auth), Art to art in Black history, Los Angeles Mag, 2/82; and others. *Mem:* Art W Asn Inc, (mem bd dir, 67-73); Artist Equity Asn. *Media:* Oil, Ink. *Mailing Add:* PO Box 76169 Los Angeles CA 90076-0169

WRIGHT, (CHARLES) CLIFFORD
PAINTER, COLLAGE ARTIST
b Cosmopolis, Wash, Nov 19, 19. *Study:* Cornish Sch, Seattle, with Dr W Reese, 36; with Mark Tobey, 37-43. *Work:* Ringling Brothers Mus, Sarasota, Fla; Edward James' Collection, Mex; Nordjyllands Kunstmuseum, Aalborg, Denmark; Whitney Mus & Brooklyn Mus, New York. *Comn:* Light mural for Danish Railroad, 89. *Exhib:* Seattle Art Mus, Wash, 42; Dada, Surrealism & Heritage, Mus Mod Art, 68; Retrospective, Nordjyllands Kunstmuseum, Aalborg, Denmark, 81; Helander Gallery, Stockholm, 82; Danish Railroad Six Posters, Asbaks Gallery, Copenhagen, 83 & Monumental Paintings, Nordjyllands Kunstmuseum, Aalborg, Denmark, 86. *Awards:* Mus des Beaux Arts, Brussels, Am Acad Arts & Letters, 57; Encouragement Grant, Columbia Univ, 59; State Art Found Grants, Denmark, 79 & 80; Tugran Merritt Found Grant, 84. *Bibliog:* A painter of the grotesque, Mag Am Art, 47; L Kochnitzsky (auth), Something different, Les Beaux Arts, Belgium, 57; O Braunschwig (auth), Portrait, Danish State TV, 74. *Media:* Oil, Gouache. *Publ:* Auth, Hero in the New World, Borgen, 63; contribr, Philoctetes Wounded, State TV, Denmark, 74; coauth & illusr, Demoniac Dames, Gyldendal, 79; coauth & illusr, Insights, Mistral, Denmark, 81. *Dealer:* Jacob Asbaek Ny Adelgade Copenhagen Denmark DK 1104. *Mailing Add:* Hollae Nderivej # 7 Stege DK 4780 Denmark

WRIGHT, DAVID THOMAS
PAINTER
b Coventry, England, Nov 26, 47; Brit & Can citizen. *Study:* Univ Newcastle-Upon-Tyne, England, BA(with hon), 70; Univ Reading, England, with Terry Frost, MFA, 72. *Work:* Can Coun Art Bank, Ottawa. *Comn:* Painted murals, Playboy Club, London, 71, Watts & Henderson Ltd, Toronto, 73, Ottawa Civic Hosp, 82, Can Fed Independent Bus, 88 & Ont Lottery Corp, 91. *Exhib:* Director's Choice, Art Gallery Windsor, Ont, 75; Abstractions: Ontario Painting, Ctr Cult, Paris, 77; Ontario Now, Part II, Art Gallery Hamilton, Ont, 77; Painting Now, Agnes Etherington Art Ctr, Kingston, Ont, 77; Traveling Exhib Can Prints, Can Embassy, Rabat, Morocco, 82 & Spanish Cult Ctr, Casablanca, Morocco, 83; and others. *Teaching:* Master & coordr fine art, Fanshawe Col, London, Ont, 77-84; Toronto Sch Art, Univ Guelph; Art Gallery Ont, 84-90. *Awards:* Second Prize, Stowell's Trophy Exhib, Mall Galleries, London, England, 72; Jack Reppen Award, Outdoor Show, Toronto City Hall, 73. *Bibliog:* Lowell Fox (auth), A Newcomer Celebrates Technology, Art Mag, 73; Robert Myers (auth), Flashes: David Wright at the Mazelow Gallery, Art Mag, 75; John Bentley Mays (auth), Wright Finds a New Beginning in a Dead End, Globe & Mail, 80; Gerald Needham (auth), David Wright Retrospective at McMaster Univ Art Gallery, The Art Post, 85. *Mem:* Visual Arts Ontario. *Media:* All Media. *Mailing Add:* 60 Cowan Ave Toronto ON M6K 2N4 Canada

WRIGHT, FAITH-DORIAN
PAINTER, COLLECTOR
b Brooklyn, NY, Feb 9, 34. *Study:* New York Univ, BS, 55, MA, 58; Art Students League, with Leo Manso; Henry Pearson, Parsons, 70. *Work:* Mus Mod Art, New York; Israel Mus, Jerusalem; Nat Mus Women in Arts, Washington, DC; Fine Arts Acad, New Dehli, India; Nat Inst Design, Ahmedahad, India. *Comn:* Painted Matter, DIA Found, Hyatt Collection, Chicago, Ill. *Exhib:* Fine Arts Acad, New Dehli, India, 80; Univ Delaware, 80; New Mus Contemp Art, New York, 80; Am Acad Arts & Letters, 80; Nat Mus Women in Art, 90; Guild Hall Mus, Easthampton, NY. *Pos:* Vis bd, Metro Mus, Rockefeller sect, 80-; art comt, primitive art, Israel Mus, 80-90. *Teaching:* Instr painting & drawing, 92nd St Y, New York, 77-90; instr, Guild Hall Mus, E Hampton, NY. *Mem:* Women in Arts (bd mem 80-90); Women's Caucus for Arts, (bd mem 80-90); Artist Equity. *Media:* Acrylic. *Collection:* Primitive art; Sculpture from Africa, Oceania, American Indian, Eskimos 19th Century to early 20th Century. *Publ:* The College Handbook, Thames & Hudson, NY. *Dealer:* Henri Gallery Washington DC; Benton Gallery Southampton NY. *Mailing Add:* 300 E 74th St New York NY 10021

WRIGHT, FRANK
PAINTER, EDUCATOR
b Washington, DC, Oct 10, 32. *Study:* Am Univ, BA, 54; Univ Ill, Urbana, MA, 60; Fogg Mus, Harvard Univ, fel, 60-61. *Work:* Bibliot Nat, Paris; Nat Collections Fine Arts, Washington, DC; Univ Seattle Law Sch, Wash; Nat Gallery Art, Rosenwald Collection, Washington, DC; Tucson Mus Art, Tucson, Ariz; and others. *Comn:* Deepbite etching demonstration plate & ed, Lessing J Rosenwald, Jenkintown, Pa, 68; oil painting - Cityscapes, WC Bradley Co, Columbus, Ga, 85; oil painting - Hist, Pershing Assoc, Washington, DC, 86; oil painting - Washington Scene & Washington Hist, Perpetual Am Bank, Washington, DC, 87; oil painting 18 x 7' Mural for Lobby of Rep PL, Oliver Carr Co, Washington, DC, 88. *Exhib:* One-man show, Adams-Davidson Galleries Inc, 75, Washington, DC; Kennedy Galleries, New York, 81; Houston Univ, Clear Lake, Tex, 83; West 83/Art & The Law, Woodruff Arts Ctr, Atlanta, 83; Allentown Art Mus, Pa, 83; Frank Wright: Painting 1968-1980, Corcoran Gallery of Art, Washington, DC, 81; Frank Wright: Washington Past & Present, Int Monetary Fund Visitors' Ctr, Washington, DC, 86. *Pos:* Prof drawing & graphics & fine arts, George Washington Univ, 70- *Teaching:* Instr master drawings, Corcoran Sch Art, Washington, DC, 66- 70; asst prof design & graphics, George Washington Univ, 70-78, assoc prof drawing & graphics, 79-83, prof, 83- *Awards:* Schepp Found Fel, 56-58; Paul J Sachs Fel, Nat Gallery Art, 59-60; Fel, Fogg Mus Harvard, 60-61. *Bibliog:* John Goldsmith (auth), Capital Edition, WUSA-TV, 6/29/86; Barbara Gamarekian (auth), Painting the Town, New York Times, 11/29/86; Brian Small (auth), Hotshots, Regardies, 9/88; Guest Artist, NASA, Columbia Space Launch, 82; Guest Lectr, Johnson Space Ctr, Hoston, 83; John Dekert (auth), Observation and Circumstance: The Paintings of Frank Wright, Arts Mag, 3/81; Jill Wechsler (auth), Frank Wright an artist with a sense of history, Am Artist, 9/82. *Mem:* Cosmos Club of Washington; Columbia Historical Soc. *Media:* Oil; Graphics. *Publ:* Auth, Why I love to engrave, GW Forum, Vol 7, No 1 (winter 77). *Dealer:* Kennedy Galleries 40 W 57th St New York 10019. *Mailing Add:* Dept Art George Washington Univ 801 22nd St NW Washington DC 20052

WRIGHT, HAROLD DAVID
PAINTER
b Rosine, Ky, June 13, 42. *Study:* Harris Sch Advert Art, Nashville, Tenn; watercolor painting in Italy. *Work:* Tenn State Mus, Nashville; Northern Telecom, Nashville. *Comn:* Portraits of Civil War Generals, General's Retreat, Franklin, Tenn, 74. *Exhib:* Cent South Show, Parthenon, Nashville, 74; Sardella Art Show, Atlanta, Ga, 74; High Plains Exhib, Lubbock, Tex, 79; Western Collectors Exhib, Dallas Tex, 80-86; Miniatures, Minneapolis, 84-86. *Pos:* Art dir, Buntin & Assocs Advert, 66-69; partner, Nova Group, Nashville, 69-; vpres, Graystone Press, Nashville, 73- *Awards:* First Award Fine Art Competition, 73. *Media:* Watercolor, Gouache, Casein. *Publ:* Illusr, Nashville Tennessean Mag, 66 & 78; Tenn Conservationist Mag, 74 & 76-79; Nashville, the faces of two centuries, Southwest Art Mag, 80; Am Rendezvous Mag, 84. *Mailing Add:* c/o Graystone Press 205 Louise Ave Nashville TN 37203

WRIGHT, JESSE GRAHAM, JR
CONSULTANT
b Sidney, Ohio, July 29, 39. *Study:* Loyola Univ, Chicago, BA(philos), 64, MA(Eng), 65; Univ Notre Dame, Ind, MFA, 69; Univ Tulsa, Okla, 84. *Pos:* Dir, South Bend Art Ctr, Michael C Rockefeller Art Ctr Gallery, Fredonia, NY, Canton Art Inst Ohio & Philbrook Art Ctr, Tulsa, Okla, 77-84, J B Speed Art Mus, Louisville, Ky, 84-85; pres, Wright Group, 86-90; develop dir, Buffalo Bill Hist Ctr, Cody, Wyo, 91-92. *Teaching:* Fac mem, Saint Mary's Col, Notre Dame, Ind, 68-77; SUNY Fredonia, 68-77. *Mem:* Am Asn Mus. *Mailing Add:* 81 Valley Rd Louisville KY 40204

WRIGHT, MILTON
PAINTER, EDUCATOR
b Dayton, Ohio, July 3, 20. *Study:* Miami Univ, Ohio, with Marston Hodgin, BFA, 42; Sch Art Studies, New York, with Isaac Soyer, cert, 48; Acad Julian, Paris, cert, 50. *Work:* Long Island Univ; Miami Univ, Ohio; Town Hall, Truro, England; Dayton Art Inst, Ohio. *Comn:* Cup plates, Truro Hist Soc, Mass, 80 & 82; landscape, Town Truro, Mass, 82. *Exhib:* Solo exhibs, Denver Art Mus, 43, Dayton Art Inst, 48 & 53, Miami Univ, Ohio, 53 & Long Island Univ, 72; Butler Art Inst, 45; Corcoran Gallery Biennial, 51; Audubon Artists, New York, 53; Brooklyn Mus Ann, 58-76; Am Watercolor Soc, New York, 66. *Teaching:* Instr painting & drawing, Brooklyn Mus Art Sch, 51-76; adj prof painting, Queens Col, City Univ New York, 53-64; asst prof art, Long Island Univ, 64-74. *Awards:* Purchase Prize, Dayton Art Inst, 53. *Mem:* Mass Art Coun. *Media:* Oil, Watercolor. *Publ:* Auth, Confrontations, Long Island Univ, 71. *Dealer:* Cove Gallery Wellfleet MA 02667. *Mailing Add:* Box 314 North Truro MA 02652

WRIGHT, STANLEY MARC
PAINTER, INSTRUCTOR
b Irvington, NJ, May 24, 11. *Study:* Sch Fine Art, Pratt Inst, grad(with highest honors), 33; Jerry Farnsworth Sch Art, Tiffany Found Fel, 35. *Work:* Portraits, Gov Deane C Davis & Sen George D Aiken, State House, Montpelier, Vt, Joe Kirkwood, Golf Hall of Fame, Foxberg, Pa, George A Wolf, Med Ctr, Univ Kans & A G Mackay, Med Ctr, Burlington, Vt. *Comn:* Portrait & landscape paintings, US & Europe. *Exhib:* Metrop Mus Art; Brooklyn Mus; Newark Mus; Montclair Mus; Cong Galleries, Washington, DC; one-man show, House Rep, US Capitol, Washington, DC, 76. *Teaching:* Head portrait & landscape, Newark Sch Fine Arts, 44-50; instr portrait & landscape & dir, Wright Sch Art, Stowe, Vt, 50-; lectr, demonstr & instr painting, many orgn. *Awards:* Many prizes for nat exhibs & one-man shows. *Bibliog:* Articles in Cue Mag, Vt Life Mag, Times, Newark News, Free Press & others. *Mem:* Salmagundi Club; Audubon Artists; fel Int Inst Arts & Lett; hon mem Vt Artists; Vt Coun Arts. *Media:* Oil, Watercolor. *Mailing Add:* RFD 2 Stowe VT 05672

WRIGHT, VICKI C
MUSEUM DIRECTOR, MUSEOLOGIST
b Willard, Ohio, Apr 13, 56. *Study:* Ohio Wesleyan Univ, BFA, 77; Ariz State Univ, MA, 86. *Collections Arranged:* Proj dir, 350 Years of Art & Architecture in Md (auth, catalog), 84; proj co-dir, New Hampshire Folk Art (auth, catalog), 89; cur, Prints by Honoré Daumier, 91; co-cur & coordr, Artists & Environment: NH, 91; proj dir, Hyman Bloom: Paintings & Drawings, 92. *Pos:* Asst dir, 82-84 & acting dir, 84-86, Art Gallery, Univ Md, College Park; dir, Art Gallery, Univ NH, Durham, 86. *Mem:* Am Asn Mus; Exeter Coun League NH Craftsmen; NH Visual Arts Coalition (co-pres, 91-92); Visual Arts Panel, Maine Arts Comn; New Eng Mus Asn (pub affairs comt, 91-). *Publ:* Auth, La Réunion des Plus Célebres Monuments Antiques de la France, Phoebus III, Ariz State Univ, 79; ed & contribr, Portfolios: Artists' Series from the Collection of Univ of Md, Art Gallery, Univ Md, 86; auth, The Artists Revealed, Art Gallery, Univ NH, 89. *Mailing Add:* The Art Gallery, Paul Creative Arts Ctr Univ NH Durham NH 03824-3538

WRIGLEY, RICK
DESIGNER, CRAFTSMAN
b Arlington, Va, Dec 9, 55. *Study:* Rochester Inst Tech, Sch Am Craftsmen, BFA, 81. *Work:* Contemp Crafts Asn, Portland, Ore. *Comn:* Boardroom table (with Kohn Pedersen, Fox Conway Asn), Home Box Office Inc, New York, 84; 22 hearing room doors, Conn Comn on Arts, Hartsford, 88; mantlepiece, Babson Col Ctr Educ, Wellesley, Mass, 88; dining-conference tables, Time Inc, New York, 88. *Exhib:* Material Evidence, Renwick Gallery, Nat Mus Am Art, Washington, DC, Fine Arts Mus South, Mobile, Ala & Mus des Art Decoratifs, Montreal, Can, 84; Artist Designed Furniture, Norton Gallery Art, W Palm Beach, 86; World of Art Today, Milwaukee Art Mus, 88; Architectural Art, Am Craft Mus, New York, 88. *Pos:* Artist-in-residence, Art Park, Lewiston, NY, 79. *Awards:* Daphne Award for Residential Furniture Design, Hardwood Inst, 86. *Bibliog:* Pamela Scheinman (auth), Dialogue with architecture, Am Craft, 6/88; Robert Jensen (auth), Angels in the architecture, Metrop Home, 5/88; Clair Whitcomb (auth),article in: House Beautiful Today, 4/88. *Mem:* Am Craft Coun; Soc Arts & Crafts. *Mailing Add:* c/o Meredith Gallery 805 N Charles St Baltimore MD 21201

WRISTON, BARBARA
HISTORIAN, LECTURER
b Middletown, Conn, June 29, 17. *Study:* Oberlin Col, AB; Brown Univ, AM; hon LittD, Lawrence Univ. *Pos:* Former exec dir mus ed, Art Inst Chicago; trustee, secy & antiqn, Landmarks Conn; mem adv comm, Hist Am Bldgs Survey, 72-78. *Mem:* Benjamin Franklin fel Royal Soc Arts; Soc Archit Historians (pres, 60-61); Furniture Hist Soc. *Res:* Seventeeth and eighteenth century English and American architecture and furniture. *Publ:* Auth, Who was the architect of the Indiana Cotton Mill, 1848-1850?, J Soc Archit Historians, 5/65; Joiner's tools in The Art Institute of Chicago, 67 & The Howard Van Doren Shaw Memorial Collection in the Art Institute of Chicago, 69, Mus Studies; Visual Arts in Illinois, 68; Rare Doings at Bath, 79. *Mailing Add:* 455 E 86th St New York NY 10028

WU, LINDA YEE CHAU
SCULPTOR
b Canton, China, July 4, 19; US citizen. *Study:* Calif Sch Fine Arts, 39-42; Nat Acad Design, 42-44; Sch Painting & Sculpture, Columbia Univ, 44-50. *Comn:* Bas-relief, Chinese Community, New York, 52; portrait of Sam Y Ong, Republican Club Chinatown, New York, 75. *Exhib:* Allied Artists Am Ann Exhibs, 47-; Audubon Artists Ann Exhibs; Nat Acad Design Ann Exhibs; Nat Sculpture Soc Ann Exhibs; Int Sculpture Third, Philadelphia Art Mus, 49. *Teaching:* Dean students, New York Chinese Sch, 60-74, prin, 74-86. *Awards:* Dessie Greer Prize for Sculpture, Nat Acad Design, 65; Anna Hyatt Huntington Gold Medal, Catharine Lorillard Wolfe Art Club, 68; Gold Medal of Honor for Sculpture, Allied Artists Am, 73. *Mem:* Nat Acad Design; fel Nat Sculpture Soc (counr, 72-74); Allied Artists Am; Knickerbocker Artists. *Mailing Add:* 20 Confucius Plaza Apt 44E New York NY 10002

WU, WAYNE WEN-YAU
PAINTER
b Tachia, Taiwan, Oct 5, 35; US citizen. *Study:* Taiwan Normal Univ, BA(fine arts), 59; Art Students' League, New York, 75. *Work:* Nat Mus Hist, Taipei, Taiwan; Nat Taiwan Arts Ctr, Taipei; Chattanooga-Hamilton County Trade Ctr, Tenn; Art Educ Ctr, Taichung Libr, Taiwan; Asian Studies Ctr, St John's Univ, Jamaica, NY. *Comn:* Chattanooga Shines, Carter St Corp, Tenn, 85; Chattanooga-Yesterday & Today, Arthur Andersen & Co, Chattanooga, Tenn, 85; Daufuskie Island No 1 & No 2, Melrose Club, Daufuskie Island, SC, 86; The Clubhouse, Chattanooga Golf & Country Club, Tenn, 90; Baylor Sch, Chattanooga, Tenn, 92. *Exhib:* Artists for Traveling Show to Japan & Europe, Nat Mus Hist, Taipei, 74; 7th & 8th Fine Arts Exhib Republic of China, Nat Taiwan Art Ctr, Taipei, 74 & 77; Nat Acad Galleries, New York, 75-76; Nat Midyear Exhib, Butler Inst Am Art, Youngstown, Ohio, 78; Spectrum 79-91, Hunter Mus Art, Chattanooga, 79-91; Anthony Ardavin Gallery, Atlanta, Ga, 90; Gauguin Galleries, Taipei, Taichung, Beijing & Singapore, 92. *Pos:* Supervisor, Fine Arts Ctr, Taichung Libr, Taiwan, 70-74. *Teaching:* Instr, oil painting, watercolor, Taiwan Normal Univ, 73-74 & Hunter Mus Art, Chattanooga, 80- *Mem:* Am Watercolor Soc. *Media:* Watercolor, Acrylic. *Dealer:* Collectors Gallery 6602 Hwy 100 Nashville TN 37205; M A Thomison & Assocs 619 Grandview Lookout Mountain TN 37350. *Mailing Add:* 711 Ashley Forest Dr Chattanooga TN 37343

WUJCIK, THEO
PRINTMAKER, PAINTER
Jan 29, 36; US citizen. *Study:* Ctr Creative Studies, dipl, 64; Tamarind Lithography Workshop, TMP, 68. *Work:* Mus Mod Art, New York; Los Angeles Co Mus Art, Calif; Mus Fine Arts, Boston; Libr Cong, Washington, DC; Carnegie Inst, Pittsburgh, Pa. *Exhib:* Drawings of the 70's, Art Inst Chicago, 77; Recent Acquistions, Drawings, Mus Mod Art, New York, 77; American Portrait Drawings, Nat Portrait Gallery, Washington, DC, 80; American Drawings in Black & White, 1970-80, Brooklyn Mus, NY, 80; Richard Brown Baker Collection, Mus Art, RI, 85. *Pos:* Mgr, Graphicstudio, Tampa, Fla, 70-72. *Teaching:* Instr printmaking, Ctr Creative Studies, 64-70; assoc prof printmaking & drawing, Univ South Fla, Tampa, 72- *Awards:* Louis Comfort Tiffany Found, 64; Grant Lithography, Ford Found, 67; Award Drawing, Nat Endowment Arts, 77. *Bibliog:* Marvin Sadik & Harold Pfister (coauth), American Portrait Drawings, Smithsonian Inst Press, 80; Frank H Goodyear (auth), Contemporary American Realism Since 1960, New York Graphic Soc, 80; Hilarie Faberman (auth), Modern Master Drawings (catalog), 86. *Dealer:* Brooke Alexander Inc 20 W 57th St New York NY. *Mailing Add:* Col Fine Arts Fah 229 Tampa FL 33620-7350

WUNDER, RICHARD PAUL
HISTORIAN, ADMINISTRATOR
b Ardmore, Pa, May 31, 23. *Study:* Harvard Univ, AB, 49, MA, 50, PhD(John Thornton Kirkland Fel), 55. *Collections Arranged:* The Architect's Eye, Cooper Union Mus, 62; Theater Drawings from the Donald Oenslager Collection, Minneapolis Inst Arts & Yale Univ Art Gallery, 63-64; Frederic Edwin Church, Nat Collection Fine Arts, Smithsonian Inst, 66. *Pos:* Asst to dir, Fogg Art Mus, Harvard Univ, 53-54; cur drawings & prints, Cooper Union Mus, 55-64; cur & asst dir, Nat Collection Fine Arts, Smithsonian Inst, 64-69; dir, Cooper-Hewitt Mus Design, 69-70; pres appraisals & estates, Christie, Manson & Woods, Int, 79-90; trustee, St Gaudens Mus, currently. *Teaching:* John Hamilton Fulton lectr, Middlebury Col, 75-80. *Awards:* Charles Eldredge Bk Award, Smithsonian Inst, 92. *Mem:* Drawing Soc (dir, 64-72); Soc l'Histoire l'Art Francais; Furniture Hist Soc Gt Brit; Victorian Soc; Soc Archit Historians Gt Brit; Pierpont Morgan Libr Coun. *Res:* Italian and French drawings of the 17th and 18th centuries; American painting, sculpture and drawings of the 19th century. *Publ:* Auth, Extravagant Drawings of the 18th Century, Lambert-Spector, 62; Architectural & Ornament Drawings, Univ Mich Mus, 65; Hiram Powers, Vermont sculptor, Woodstock Hist Soc, Vt, 74; Architectural, Ornament, Landscape & Figure Drawings, Middlebury Col, 75; Hiram Powers, Univ Del Press, 90. *Mailing Add:* 24 W 55th St New York NY 10019

WUNDERLICH, SUSAN CLAY
DEALER
b Indianapolis, Ind, Jan 30, 42. *Study:* Colby Col. *Pos:* Dir, Mongerson Wunderlich Gallery, currently. *Mem:* Chicago Art Dealers Asn. *Specialty:* Nineteenth and 20th century American art, such as: Frederic Remington, C M Russell, Nicolai Fechin, Leon Gaspard, Taos Founders and the American impressionists; illustrators, N C Wyeth and Howard Pyle; sporting art; sculpture. *Mailing Add:* Mongerson-Wunderlich 704 N Wells St Chicago IL 60610-3310

WUNDERMAN, JAN (LILJAN DARCOURT WUNDERMAN)
PAINTER, PRINTMAKER
b Winnipeg, Man, Jan 22, 21; US citizen. *Study:* Otis Art Inst, Los Angeles, 42; Brooklyn Mus Art Sch, 54-56, with Reuben Tam. *Work:* Loeb Collection, New York Univ; Alfred Khouri Collection, Norfolk Mus, Va; Ball State Univ Art Gallery, Muncie, Ind; Univ SC Art Gallery, Columbia; CW Post Col, Long Island, NY; and others. *Comn:* Eight paintings, New York City off, White, Weld & Co, 68; paintings, New York, Tulsa & Ft Worth off, Arthur Young & Co, 73; painting, Commercial Union Bank, Nashville, Tenn, 75; painting, New York off, Bank of Am, 76; painting, New York off, The Boston Co, 77. *Exhib:* Los Angeles Co Mus Art, 45; one-person shows, Gastine Gallery, Los Angeles, 45, Angeleski Gallery, New York, 61, Roko Gallery, New York, 63-77 & East Hampton Guild Gallery, NY, 66; Brooklyn Mus, NY, 56; Philadelphia Mus Art, 56-62; Pa Acad Fine Arts, Philadelphia, 59-65; Butler Inst Am Art, Youngstown, Ohio, 59-66; Mus de Bellas Artes, Buenos Aires, Arg, 60; Va Mus Fine Arts, Richmond, 67; Eggleston Gallery, New York; traveling show, 100 Years-100 Works, Nat Asn Women Artists; Plaides Gallery Invitational, New York, 88. *Awards:* Moore-Greenrlatt Award, Nat Asn Women Artists, 90; Amelia Peabody Award, Nat Asn Women Artists, 91; Grumbacher Medal of Honor, Nat Asn Women Artists, 92. *Mem:* Nat Asn Women Artists; Artists Equity; Am Soc Contemp Artists. *Media:* Oil, Acrylic; Black & White Intaglio Prints. *Mailing Add:* 131 E 19th St New York NY 10003

WURMFELD, SANFORD
PAINTER, EDUCATOR
b New York, NY, Dec 6, 42. *Study:* Dartmouth Col, BA, 64. *Work:* Metrop Mus Art, Guggenheim Mus, New York; Landesmuseum, Hannover, WGer; Ackland Mem Art Ctr; State Univ NY, Fredonia. *Comn:* Acrylic sculptures, City Hannover, WGer, 71 & Shreve, Lamb & Harmon, New York, 71; paintings, Gen Electric, Fairfield, Conn, 74 & Baxter Travenol Labs, Dearfield, Ill, 77. *Exhib:* Art of the Real, Mus Mod Art, New York, 68, Grand Palais, Paris, 68, Kunsthaus, Zurich, 68 & Tate Gallery, London, 69; Contemporary Painting Review, Lehigh Univ, Pa, 76; Susan Caldwell Gallery, New York, 76 & 78; Patterns Plus, Art Mus, Dayton, 79; Carnegie Int, Mus Art, Pittsburgh, Pa, 82; Labor Intensive Abstraction, Clocktower, NY, 84; Approaches to Abstraction, Shanghai, 86; A Debate on Abstraction, Hunter Col, 89; Choices, Long Beach Mus Art, Calif, 89; The Grid, Ben Shaw Galleries, William Paterson Col, NJ, 90. *Pos:* Dir, Hunter Galleries, Hunter Col, CUNY, 78- *Teaching:* From lectr to prof art, Hunter Col, 67-, chmn dept, 78-; lectr, visual arts prog, Princeton Univ, 90. *Awards:* Guggenheim Fel, 74-75; Nat Endowment Arts Individual Artist Fel, 88; City Univ New York, Fac Res Award, 79-81, 84, 85 & 87. *Publ:* Auth, Color documents: A presentational theory, Hunter Col Art Gallery, 4/85; Approaches to Abstraction, City Univ New York, 86; On Color Charts and Painting, Color Order and Aesthetics: The Oeuvre of Dr Amelius Muller, Hunter Col Art Gallery, NY, 87. *Mailing Add:* 18 Warren St New York NY 10007

WYATT, GREG ALAN
SCULPTOR
b Nyack, NY, Oct 16, 49. *Study:* Columbia Col, BA, 71, MA, 74; Nat Acad Sch Design, 72-74; Columbia Univ, MA, 74. *Work:* Brookgreen Gardens, Murrells Inlet, SC; Nat Arts Club, Gramercy Park, New York; Princeton Univ Libr, NJ; Sports-Illus Mag Collection, New York; Bergen Mus Art, NJ; Newington-Cropsey Found, Hastings, NY. *Comn:* Eagle (bronze sculpture), Am Bur Shipping, New York, 78; Battle of New Orleans (boxer series), Am Broadcasting Corp, New York, 79; Peace Fountain, Cathedral St John the Divine; Portrait James Cash Penney, Tex. *Exhib:* Solo exhibs, New Orleans Theatre Performing Arts, 77, Sculpture Revitalized, Bodley Gallery, New York, 78 & Sculptor's Watercolors, Cafe des Artistes, New York, 81; Nat Acad Design, New York, 79 & 80; Nat Arts Club Ann, New York, 79-81; Bergen Mus Art, NJ, 90; Bronze Casting Exhib (in conj with Paul Manship Retrospective), Metrop Mus Art, New York, 91; US Cong, Washington, DC, 92. *Teaching:* Instr, Finch Col, New York & San Marino, Italy, 73-75; instr, New York Univ, 74-75; instr, Jersey City State Col, NJ, 74-75. *Awards:* Ziegfield Art Award, Columbia Univ Sch Educ Art Dept Ann, 75-76; Helen Foster Barnett Award, Nat Acad Design Nat Ann, 79; Walter Lantz Award, Nat Sculpture Soc Young Sculptors Ann, 79. *Bibliog:* John Sotomayor (auth), Eagle, New York Times, 12/20/78; Michael Lantz (ed), Woman, the sculptor's vision, Nat Sculpture Rev, spring 79; Pam Lambert (auth), The eagle has landed off lower Broadway, Columbia Univ Mag, winter 79; Greg Wyatt & His Work, Charles Kuralt, CBS-TV, 12/90. *Mem:* Nat Arts Club. *Media:* Bronze, Marble. *Mailing Add:* 320 W 86th St Penthouse South New York NY 10024

WYCKOFF, SYLVIA SPENCER
PAINTER, EDUCATOR
b Pittsburgh, Pa, Nov 14, 15. *Study:* Col Fine Arts, Syracuse Univ, BFA, 37, MFA, 44. *Work:* Radio Sta WSYR, Syracuse, NY; R E Dietz Co, Syracuse; Marquardt Switches, Cazenovia, NY; in pvt collections. *Exhib:* Munson-Williams-Proctor Inst, Utica, NY; Mem Art Gallery, Rochester, NY; Everson Mus Art, Syracuse; Cooperstown Art Asn, NY; Nat Asn Women Artists, New York. *Teaching:* Prof watercolor & drawing & chmn, Freshman Core Progs Dept, Syracuse Univ, 42-81; retired. *Awards:* League Prize for Watercolor, Nat League Am Pen Women Nat Show, 48; Gordon Steele Award, Assoc Artists Syracuse, 68; Outstanding Am Educ, 74; Spec Citation, NY State Art Teachers Asn, 81. *Mem:* Cazenovia Watercolor Soc (pres). *Media:* Watercolor. *Mailing Add:* 2 Seminary St Cazenovia NY 13035

WYETH, ANDREW NEWELL
PAINTER
b Chadds Ford, Pa, July 12, 17. *Study:* With N C Wyeth; Harvard Univ, hon DFA, 55; Colby Col, hon DFA, 55; Dickinson Col, hon DFA, 58; Swarthmore Col, hon DFA, 58. *Work:* Metrop Mus Art, New York; Mus Fine Arts, Boston; Los Angeles Co Mus Art; Art Inst Chicago; Nat Gallery Art, Washington, DC; Brandywine River Mus, Chadds Ford, Pa; Joslyn Art Mus, Omaha, Nebr; Nat Gallery, Oslo, Norway. *Exhib:* Currier Gallery Art, Manchester, NH; Pa Acad Fine Arts, Philadelphia; Fogg Art Mus, Mass; Univ Ariz, Tucson; Mus Fine Arts, Boston; Nat Mus of Mod Art, Tokyo, Japan; Nat Mus of Mod Art, Kyoto, Japan; Metrop Mus of Art, New York; Royal Acad, London; H M De Young Mem Mus, Santa Fe, NMex; Brandywine River Mus, Chadds Ford, Pa; White House, Washington, DC; and many others. *Awards:* Pa Acad Fine Arts; Carnegie Inst; Am Watercolor Soc; Associe Etranger de l'Institut de France; Congressional Medal, President George Bush, 90; and many others. *Bibliog:* Richard Merryman (auth), Andrew Wyeth, Houghton; Wanda Corn (auth), The Art of Andrew Wyeth, New York Graphic Soc; George Plimpton & Donald Stewart (coauth), Andrew Wyeth, Horizon, 61; Margaret Graham Neeson (auth), The watcher from the shore, The Skipper, 4/63. *Mem:* Nat Acad Design; Am Watercolor Soc; Am Acad Arts & Lett. *Media:* Tempera, Watercolor. *Mailing Add:* c/o Frank E Fowler PO Box 247 Lookout Mountain TN 37350

WYETH, HENRIETTE (MRS PETER HURD)
PAINTER
b Wilmington, Del, Oct 22, 07. *Study:* Normal Art Sch, Boston; Pa Acad Fine Arts; also with N C Wyeth. *Work:* Roswell Mus Art; New Britain Mus Art, Conn; Lubbock Mus Art, Tex; Tex Tech Univ; portraits in pvt collections. *Exhib:* Carnegie Inst, Pittsburgh; Art Inst Chicago; Metrop Mus Art, New York; Roswell Mus Art, NMex; and others. *Awards:* Four First Prizes, Wilmington Soc Fine Arts; Governor's Award, Santa Fe, NM, 81. *Mailing Add:* c/o Roswell Mus Art Ctr 100 W 11th St Roswell NM 88201

WYETH, JAMES BROWNING
PAINTER
b Wilmington, Del, July 6, 46. *Study:* With Carolyn Wyeth; Elizabethtown Col, hon DFA. *Work:* Nat Gallery & Nat Portrait Gallery-Smithsonian Inst, Washington, DC; Mus Mod Art, New York; Joslyn Art Mus, Omaha, Nebr; Del Art Mus, Wilmington; Brandywine River Mus, Chadds Ford, Pa; and others. *Exhib:* Solo exhibs, Pa Acad, Philadelphia, 80, Greenville Co Mus Art, SC, 81 & Amon Carter Mus, Ft Worth, Tex, 81; Anchorage Fine Arts Mus, Alaska, 83; State Mus, Alaska, 83; Portland Mus Art, 84; Columbia Mus, 84; Okla Arts Ctr, 85; and others. *Pos:* Bd govs, Nat Space Inst; adv comt, US Postal Serv. *Bibliog:* Joseph Roody (auth), Another Wyeth, Look Mag, 4/2/68; Wyeth Phenomenon (film), CBS TV, 69; Richard Meryman (auth), Wyeth Christmas, Life Mag, 12/17/71. *Mem:* Nat Acad Design; Am Watercolor Soc; Nat Endowment Arts. *Media:* Oil, Watercolor. *Mailing Add:* c/o Frank E Fowler PO Box 247 Lookout Mountain TN 37350

WYNGAARD, SUSAN ELIZABETH
LIBRARIAN
Study: Univ Wis, Madison, BA & MLS; Univ Per Stranieri, Siena, Italy, cert; Taos Valley Weaving Sch, with Kristina Wilson; Univ NMex. *Pos:* Assoc librn, Univ Calif, Santa Barbara, 74-79; dir archives, Int Mus Photog, George Eastman House, 80-81; head, Fine Arts Libr, Ohio State Univ, currently. *Mem:* Art Libr Soc NAm (midwest rep exec bd, 85-87); Am Libr Asn. *Res:* The humanities and the library. *Interests:* History of photography; art librarianship; library management. *Publ:* Coauth, Printed catalogues of the Art Exhibition Catalogue Collection of the Arts Library, Univ Calif, Santa Barbara, Somerset House, Cambridge, Eng & Teaneck, NJ, 77. *Mailing Add:* Fine Arts Libr Ohio State Univ Wexner Ctr for the Visual Arts Columbus OH 43210

WYNN, DONALD JAMES
PAINTER, LECTURER
b Brooklyn, NY, Sept 26, 42. *Study:* Pratt Inst, BFA, 67; Ind Univ, MFA, 69. *Exhib:* 22 Realists, Whitney Mus Am Art, 70; Michael C Rockefeller Arts Ctr, State Univ NY Cortland; one-man shows, Allentown Art Mus, Pa, 72, Artist's Space Gallery, New York, 74, Alpha Gallery, Boston, 75, Robert Schoelkopf Gallery, New York, 76 & Adirondack Mus, 78; Arnot Art Mus, 85. *Awards:* Elizabeth T Greenshields Mem Found Grant, 70; Residence Grant, Fine Arts Work Ctr, Provincetown, 71; CAPS Grant, NY State Coun Arts, 75. *Bibliog:* Carter Ratcliff (auth), New York, Art Int Mag, 4/70; Gerritt Henry (auth), A realist twin bill, Art News Mag, 1/73; Judith Tannenbaum (auth), article, Arts Mag, 1/77. *Dealer:* A M Sachs 29 W 57th St New York NY 10019. *Mailing Add:* c/o Nina Freudenheim Gallery 300 Delaware Ave Buffalo NY 14202

WYNNE, ALBERT GIVENS
PAINTER, CALLIGRAPHER
b Colorado Springs, Colo, Jan 3, 22. *Study:* Univ Denver; Iowa Wesleyan Col, BA; Univ Iowa, MA; also with S Carl Fracassini, Boardman Robinson, James Lechay & others. *Work:* Univ Denver & Univ Southern Colo; Rawlins Bank, Wyo. *Comn:* Stained glass windows, Black Forest Colo Community Church, 81. *Exhib:* Walker Art Ctr; Corcoran Gallery Art; Denver Art Mus; Des Moines Art Ctr; Colorado Springs Fine Arts Ctr; Roswell Arts Ctr; Sioux City Art Ctr; Butler Inst Am Art; and others. *Pos:* Art consul, Anchorage, Alaska School District; artist in residence, Colorado Springs Fine Arts Ctr. *Teaching:* Hon instr, Univ Colo, Colorado Springs Fine Arts Ctr; prof of Art, Iowa Wesleyan Col, Morningside Col & Colorado Col. *Awards:* Prizes, Des Moines Art Ctr, Roswell Art Ctr & Colorado Springs Fine Arts Ctr. *Mem:* Colo Calligraphers Guild. *Media:* Oil, Watercolor. *Dealer:* Rule Modern & Contemporary Gallery 1736 Wazee St Denver CO 80202. *Mailing Add:* 7420 Swan Rd Colorado Springs CO 80908

WYRICK, CHARLES LLOYD, JR
PUBLISHER, EDITOR
b Greensboro, NC, May 5, 39. *Study:* Davidson Col, BA; Univ NC, MFA; Univ Mo. *Exhib:* Corcoran Biennial Exhib Am Painting, 67; Assoc Artists NC Ann, 68; Univ Va Print Exhib, 68; Va Mus Fine Arts; Weatherspoon Art Gallery; Carspecken-Scott Gallery. *Collections Arranged:* Art from the Ancient World, The Human Figure in Art, A Wyeth Portrait & Light as a Creative Medium, Va Mus Fine Arts, 66-68; Contemporary American Paintings from the Lewis Collection, Del Art Mus, 74; Louise Nevelson, Spoleto Festival USA, 83; and others. *Pos:* Artmobile coordr, Va Mus Fine Arts, Richmond, 66-68; exec dir, Asn Preservation Va Antiq, 68-70; pres, Fine Arts Consults, Richmond, 71-73; art critic, Richmond News Leader, 71-73; dir, Del Art Mus, 73-79; dir, Gibbes Art Gallery, 80-86; pres, Wyrick & Co, 86- & Dixie Media, Inc 89- *Teaching:* Instr, Stephens Col, 64-66. *Awards:* First for Column, Va Press Asn, 72. *Mem:* Am Asn Mus; Asn Art Mus Dirs. *Res:* Contemporary American painting; 18th to 20th century American architecture; 20th century American photography. *Publ:* Auth, Art & urban aesthetics (weekly column), Richmond News Leader; A Wyeth Portrait, 67 & Contemporary Art at the Virginia Mus, 72, Arts in Va; Richmond's 17th Street Market, 73; ed, Charles Fraser of Charleston, 83; Oystering: A Way of Life, 83; ed of numerous museum catalogs and books. *Mailing Add:* 34 Legare St Charleston SC 29401

X

XU, JINGI See Chee, Cheng-Khee

Y

YAEGER, EDGAR LOUIS
PAINTER, MURALIST
b Detroit, Mich, Aug 26, 04. *Work:* Wolfsonian Found, Miami Beach, Fla; Windsor Art Mus, Windsor, Ont, Can; Detroit Inst Arts, Mich; Kresge Art Mus, East Lansing, Mich. *Comn:* Great Lakes Warships, mural, Works Progress Admin, Detroit, Mich, 36; Univ Mich-Mural, Works Progress Admin, Ann Arbor, Mich, 40; Stained Glass, comn by Private Family, Maastricht, Neth, 60; Mosaic & Bronze Dove, St Martin Church, Detroit, Mich, 80; Mosiac, Plante Moran & Co, Southfield, Mich, 85. *Exhib:* Carnegie Int Exhib, Pittsburgh, Pa, 30; Corcoran Biennial Exhib, Washington, DC, 30 & 32; Art Inst, Chicago, 31, 37 & 41; Pa Acad Fine Arts, Philadelphia, 31, 34 & 58; Minneapolis Inst Arts, Minn, 32; Mus Mod Art, New York, 33 & 36; Nat Exhib, Rockefeller Ctr, New York, 36; Golden Gate Exhib, San Francisco, 39. *Pos:* Illusr, Alexander Girard, designer; illusr, Gen Motors & Hudson Car Co; designer of stage sets, Masonic temple, Detroit Symphony & Detroit Inst Arts. *Teaching:* Teacher, Detroit Sch Fine & Applied Arts; teacher, murals, Wayne Co Community Col. *Awards:* Best Mod Painting, Mich Artists Exhib, 30; Founders Soc Purchase Prize, Mich Artists Exhib, Detroit Inst Arts, 32; Gold Medal, Scarab Club Ann Exhib, 81. *Mem:* Scarab Club; Grosse Pointe Artist Asn. *Dealer:* John Joseph Jr 645 Fairford Grosse Pointe Woods MI 48236. *Mailing Add:* 415 Lakewood Detroit MI 48215

YAGER, DAVID
PHOTOGRAPHER, PRINTMAKER
b Bronx, NY, Mar 16, 49. *Study:* Univ Conn, BA, 71; Fla State Univ, MFA, 74. *Work:* Mus Mod Art, New York; Art Inst Chicago & Columbia Col, Chicago; Univ S Fla, Tampa; Boston Mus Fine Arts. *Comn:* Photographic mural, Bell Tel Co, Atlanta. *Exhib:* Light, Loch Haven Mus, Orlando, Fla; New Photographers, Ellenburg, Wash, 79-81; Magic Silver Show, Washington, DC, 80; Sch Art Inst Chicago, 81; Daytona Beach Gallery, Fla, 81; Tampa Mus, Fla, 82; Silver International, Univ S Fla, Tampa, 82; Univ S Fla, Tampa, 83 & 85. *Teaching:* Prof art & chmn dept, Univ Md, Baltimore, 86- *Awards:* Grant, State of Fla, 82. *Mem:* Soc Photog Educ; Col Art Asn. *Mailing Add:* Dept Art Univ Md Baltimore Co Catonsville MD 21228

YAGHJIAN, EDMUND
PAINTER, INSTRUCTOR
b Kharpert, Armenia; US citizen. *Study:* RI Sch Design, BFA; Art Students League, with Stuart Davis. *Work:* New York Pub Libr; NY Univ; High Mus Art, Atlanta, Ga; Gibbes Art Mus, Charleston, SC; West Point Mus, NY; plus many others including over 500 in pvt collections. *Exhib:* New York World's Fair; San Francisco World's Fair; Carnegie Int, Pittsburgh, 36; Whitney Mus Am Art, New York, 40; Metrop Mus Art, New York, 41; 40 Year Retrospective, Univ SC, 72; Am Embassy, Jiddah, Saudi Arabia, 79; plus many other group & one-man shows. *Teaching:* Instr art, Art Students League, 38-42; guest instr painting, Univ Mo, 44-45; head dept art, Univ SC, 45-66, artist in residence, 66-72; instr painting, Columbia Mus Art, 72- *Awards:* Numerous prizes & awards in local & regional shows. *Mem:* Am Fedn Arts; Col Art Asn Am; Southeastern Col Art Asn (pres); life mem Art Students League; SC Artists Guild (pres & founder). *Media:* Acrylic. *Mailing Add:* 1829 Senate St Columbia SC 29201

YAMASHIRO, TAD
PHOTOGRAPHER
b Calif, Nov 24, 30. *Study:* Cooper Union, 54-58. *Work:* George Eastman House Int Mus Photog, Rochester, NY; Mus Mod Art, New York. *Exhib:* Tad Yamashiro, George Eastman House, Rochester, NY, 83; Big Picture Show, Mus Mod Art, New York, 83; Photography Moma, Univ Hawaii Mus Art, Honolulu, 83; 20th Century Photography from Moma, Seibu Mus Art, Tokyo, 84; Treasure from the Collection, George Eastman House, Rochester, NY, 85. *Teaching:* Instr, seminar & thesis, Sch Visual Arts, 63-84. *Mailing Add:* 224 E 12th St New York NY 10003

YAMIN, MARTINA (SCHAAP)
CONSERVATOR-ART ON PAPER
b Amsterdam, Neth, May 5, 37. *Study:* Wellesley Col, Mass, BA(art hist), 58; Fogg Art Mus, Harvard Univ Conserv Dept, Lab Asst & Study, 58-61. *Comn:* Whitney Mus Art, pvt collections & galleries. *Pos:* Conservator, pvt practice, Paper Studio, New York, 61-; vis, paper conservator, Philadelphia Mus, 64-79. *Bibliog:* D Brewer (auth), The Delicate Art Restoring Paper, New York Times, 5/4/89; T Trucco (auth), Saving Old Documents, New York Times, 9/5/91. *Mem:* Fel, Int Inst Conserv, 72-; fel, Am Inst Conserv, 73-; bd mem, trustee, Drawing Soc, New York; curatorial comt mem, Nat Arts Club; comt mem, Wellesley Col Friends of Art, New York; Art Table, New York. *Publ:* Auth, Report on the Inst of Paper Conserv Conf, Drawing, 92. *Mailing Add:* 206 E 30th St New York NY 10016

YAMIN, STEVEN EDWARD
PRINTMAKER
b New York, NY, Apr 5, 46. *Study:* Olivet Col, BA, 68; Pratt Inst, MFA, 71. *Work:* Victoria & Albert Mus, London, Eng; Libr Congress, DC; Mary Armstrong Print Collection, Olivet Col, Mich; NJ State Mus, Trenton; New York Pub Libr. *Exhib:* New Printmakers, Victoria & Albert Mus, London, Eng, 74l 19th Nat Print Exhib, Brooklyn Mus, 75; 5th British Int, Bradford Mus, Eng, 75; 55th Soc Am Graphic Artists Nat, AAA Gallery, New York, 77; 12th Nat Print Exhib, Silvermine Guild, New Canaan, Conn, 78; 7th Int Miniature Print, Pratt Graphics Ctr, New York, 79; Sense of Scale III, Univ Albuquerque Mus, 79. *Collections Arranged:* Prints from Fitch-Febvrel Gallery, New York; Cantor-Lemberg, Birmingham, Mich. *Pos:* Guest instr, Pratt Graphics Ctr, New York, Feb-Mar 75 tech asst, Am Atelier, New York, 76- *Teaching:* Lectr printmaking, Brooklyn Col, 74-76; Pratt Manhattan Ctr, 81. *Awards:* Purchase Awards, 16th Ann Nat Print Exhib, Okla Art Ctr, Oklahoma City, 74 & Potsdam '78, State Univ NY Potsdam, 78; Graphic Chemical & Ink Co Award, 7th Miniature Print Exhib, 79. *Bibliog:* W A S Hatch (auth), The European Graphic Biennale. *Mem:* Print Club, Philadelphia; Exec Coun Soc Am Graphic Artists; Visual Artists & Galleries Asn. *Media:* All. *Dealer:* Fitch-Febvrel Gallery 5 E 57th St New York NY 10022. *Mailing Add:* 3903 Ave I Brooklyn NY 11210

YANEFF, CHRIS
GALLERY DIRECTOR
b Toronto, Ont, May 18, 28. *Study:* Ont Col Art. *Pos:* Art dir, The Financial Post, 49-56; owner, pres & cur, Chris Yaneff Limited, 56- *Teaching:* Assoc prof, Fac Fine Arts, York Univ. *Mem:* Graphic Designers Can (pres Ont chap, 82-85); Royal Can Acad Arts (treas, 76-88); Arts & Lett Club; Art Dir Club, Toronto. *Specialty:* International & Canadian art, native art and French antique posters. *Collection:* Canadian art, French art, French posters, native art & European art. *Mailing Add:* c/o Chris Yaneff Limited 119 Isabella St Toronto ON M4Y 1P2 Canada

YANISH, ELIZABETH
SCULPTOR, LECTURER
b St Louis, Mo. *Study:* Wash Univ; Denver Univ; also with Frank Varra, Wilbur Verhelst, Edgar Brittor, Marian Buchan & Angelo DiBenedetto. *Work:* Tyler Mus, Tex; Colo State Bank, Denver, Martin-Marietta Co, Denver; Colo Women's Col; Ball State Col. *Comn:* Carved doors, eternal light, Menorah, BMH Synagogue, Denver, 72-74; complete interior, Har Ha Shem Congregation, Boulder, 74; Relief Tree (bronze), Beth Israel Hosp, Denver, 74; mem relief, Denver Gen Hosp, 75. *Exhib:* Denver Art Mus Exhib, 61-75 & Western Ann, 65; Midwest Biennial, Joslyn Mus, Omaha, Nebr, 68; Int Exhib, Lucca, Italy, 71; one-man show, Woodstock Gallery, London, Eng, 73; Artrain, Mich Fine Arts Coun, 74. *Pos:* Trustee, Denver Ctr Performing Arts, 73-75; chmn, Visual Arts Festival, Bicentennial, 74-75; bd educ, Arts in Elem Educ, 77-78; bd mem, Mizel Mus, Denver, 88; mem, Denver Cult Action Steering Comt, 88. *Teaching:* Lectr contemp sculpture, var cols & univs. *Awards:* Purchase Award Golden Web, Colo Women's Col, 63; McCormick Award, Ball State Univ, 64; Purchase Award, Tyler Mus, Tex, 65. *Bibliog:* Article in Artforum, 63; Jim Mills (auth), var feature stories, Denver Post Art Ed, 64-75; John Manson (auth), Artists of the Rockies, 74. *Mem:* Artists Equity Asn (pres, 63); Rocky Mountain Liturgical Arts; Allied Sculptors Colo; Denver Coun Arts (pres, 73-75); Colo Artists Equity Asn (pres, 79-80). *Media:* Welded Steel, Bronze. *Mailing Add:* 131 Fairfax Denver CO 80220

YANOFF, ARTHUR (SAMUEL)
PAINTER
b Boston, Mass, May 9, 39. *Study:* Mus Sch Fine Arts, Boston, 58-61; studied with Jason Berger, 62-65. *Work:* Mus Fine Arts, Boston; Addison Gallery Am Art; Hampshire Col; Babson Col; NH Savings Bank, Concord; Brandeis Univ, Waltham, Mass; The Currier Gallery of Art, Manchester, NH; Le Centre d'Art, Baie-St-Paul, Que. *Comn:* Portrait Gil Williams, Bellevue Gallery, Binghamton, NY, 73; charcoal studies, NH Composition, Concord, 74 & Mrs Gereard Derepentigny, Manchester, NH, 74. *Exhib:* Collectors Show, Va Mus Fine Arts, 70; Direct Vision, Fitchburg Art Mus, Mass, 73 & Hilles Gallery, Harvard Univ, 76; Drawings from Holst's Sculpture, Addison Gallery Am Art, 74; Inaugural Show, Gallery Naga, Boston, 77; New Watercolors, Barridoff Galleries, Portland, Maine, 78; solo exhibs, Mus Fine Arts, Boston, 83, New Images in Watercolor, Currier Gallery Art, Manchester, NH, 85, Concordia Col, Bronxville, NY, 86 & Babson Col, Wellesley, Mass, 88; Smokestacks & Recent Paintings, Babson Col Gallery, 83; Janus Gallery, Santa Fe, NMex, 86; Wade Gallery, Los Angeles, 87; Sound Shore Gallery, Stamford, Conn, 89. *Awards:* Direct Vision Exhib Awards, Mass Coun Arts, 73 & 75; Purchase Prize, NH Bicentennial, 75; Mem Found Jewish Culture Fel, 89-90. *Bibliog:* Vivien Raynor (auth), A show of three contemporaries in an old English setting, New York Sunday Times, 5/6/90; Elaine Adler (auth), Teaching of Isaac Luria, Zib'Nzach'n, summer 91; Tzivia Emmer (auth), Kabballah on Canvas, Wellsprings, winter 92. *Mem:* Boston Painters & Sculptors; NH Art Asn; Am Art Therapy Asn. *Media:* Oil, Watercolor. *Publ:* Illusr, Broken Syllables, 67 & Waiting to Freeze, 69, Lillabulero Press; auth, The paste-up autobiography: Collage in the treatment of disturbed adolescents, Am J Art Therapy, 73; illusr, Raw Honey, Alice James Books, 75. *Dealer:* Harcus Gallery 6 Melrose St Boston MA 02116. *Mailing Add:* One Appleton St RFD 1 3, Box 437 Concord NH 03301

YANOW, RHODA MAE
PAINTER, ILLUSTRATOR
b Newark, NJ. *Study:* Newark Arts Club; Parsons Sch Design; Newark Sch Fine & Indust Arts; Heritage Art Sch; Nat Acad Design, with Henry Gasser,

Daniel Greene, Harvey Dinnerstein & John Grabach. *Work:* West Orange Home for Senior Citizens, NJ; Newark Pub Libr; Meadowlands Sport Arena; West Orange Town Hall. *Exhib:* Nat Arts Club Pastel Show,74; Muhlenberg Col Festival of Arts, 75; Am Artists Prof League Grand Nat Exhib, 75; Salmagundi Club Watercolor Show, 75; Nat Acad Design, 78-80. *Teaching:* Instr pastel painting & life drawing, Du Cret Sch Arts. *Awards:* Anna Hyatt Huntington Silver Medal, 77; Catharine Lorillard Wolfe Art Club Gold Medal, 77; Medal of Honor, Nat Asn Women Artists, 83; Knickerbocker Artists Silver & Gold Medal Honor, Catharine Lorillard Wolfe Art Club, 87. *Bibliog:* Ruthann Williams (auth), Graven images, NJ Music & Arts, 6/74. *Mem:* Am Artists Prof League; Nat Asn Women Artists; Catharine Lorillard Wolfe Art Club; Allied Artists Am (corresp secy, 75); Pastel Soc Am; Audubon Artists. *Media:* Pastels, Pen & Ink; Lithography. *Publ:* Contribr & illusr, NJ Music & Arts, 74 & 75; contribr, Star Ledger & other local newspapers; Am Artist Mag, 2/89. *Dealer:* Hait Gallery 2A Inwood Pl Maplewood NJ 07040. *Mailing Add:* c/o Nathans Gallery 1206 McBride Ave West Patterson NJ 07424

YARBER, ROBERT
PAINTER
b Dallas, Tex, 48. *Study:* Cooper Union Col, New York, BFA; La State Univ, Baton Rouge, MFA, 71. *Exhib:* Solo exhibs, Greene Gallery, Coconut Grove, Fla, 87, Galerie Paule Anglim, San Francisco, Calif, 89 & Palmer Mus Art, Penn State Univ, University Park, Pa, 89; Stedelijk Mus, Amsterdam, Holland, 89; Asher/Faure Gallery, Los Angeles, 89; Sonnabend Gallery, New York, 89; and others. *Teaching:* Vis instr painting, Univ Calif, Berkeley, 82, vis lectr, 83; vis lectr, Univ Tex, Austin, 82, lectr, 84. *Awards:* Nat Endowment Arts Fel Grant, 83. *Bibliog:* Susann Boettger (auth), Robert Yarber at Sonnabend, Art Forum, 1/86; Gerard Haggerty (auth), Robert Yarber at Sonnabend, Artnews, 1/86; John Richardson (auth), Something borrowed, something new, Albuquerque Tribune, 5/24/86; and others. *Mailing Add:* c/o Landfall Press Inc 329 W 18th St Chicago IL 60616

YARBOROUGH, CHRISTINE TROUTMAN
CRAFTSMAN, DESIGNER
b Statesville, NC, May 13, 25. *Study:* Brenau Col, Gainesville, Ga, Dipl, 47; Arrowmont Sch Arts & Crafts, Tenn, 73-80; Univ NC, Greensboro. *Work:* NC Mus Art & NC Archives Hist Mus, Raleigh; Mint Mus Art & IBM, Charlotte, NC; Atlanta Art Festival, Ga. *Comn:* Batik wall hanging, NC Nat Bank, Winston-Salem; 30 batik panels, NC Nat Bank, Int Dept, Charlotte, NC; transparancies, Old Salem Inc, NC; batik wall hangings & canvas construction, R J Reynolds Tobacco Co, Winston-Salem, NC. *Exhib:* Piedmont Crafts, Mint Mus Art, Charlotte, NC, 73; Crafts Invitational, Southeastern Ctr Contemp Art, Winston-Salem, NC, 73-81; Opening Exhib, Greenwood Gallery, Washington, DC, 79; NC Artist Exhib, NC Mus Art, Raleigh, 79; The Fan, 81, & The Box, 81, Arrowmont Gallery, Gatlinburg, Tenn. *Teaching:* Instr papermaking & bookbinding, Arrowmont Sch Arts & Crafts, 79-82; instr bookbinding, Montgomery Col, Silver Springs, Md, 79. *Awards:* Bronze Medal Award, NC Arts Soc, 79. *Bibliog:* Craft Horizons, Am Crafts Coun, 73; Shirley E Held (auth), Weaving--A Handbook of Fiber Arts, Holt Rinehart, 78; Majorie Elliott Beulin (auth), Design Through Discovery, Holt Rinehart, 78. *Mem:* Am Crafts Coun; Piedmont Craftsmen; Arts & Crafts Asn, Sawtooth Ctr Visual Design (bd mem, 79-82). *Media:* Mixed Media; Leather, Copper. *Mailing Add:* 1311 Brookstown Ave Winston-Salem NC 27101

YARBROUGH, LEILA KEPERT
PRINTMAKER, PAINTER
b Katoomba, NSW, Australia, Mar 23, 32; US citizen. *Study:* Univ Fla; Atlanta Col Art, Ga. *Work:* Chrysler Mus, Norfolk, Va; Augusta Mus Art, Ga; Agnes Scott Col, Decatur, Ga; Loch Haven Art Ctr, Orlando, Fla. *Exhib:* Eastern US Drawing Competition, Cummer Gallery Art, Jacksonville, Fla, 70; Contemporary American Drawing V: Norfolk, Smithsonian Inst Travel Exhib, 71-73; 34th Ann Contemp Am Painting, Soc of Four Arts, Palm Beach, Fla, 72; 1st Nat Monoprint-Monotype, Oglethorpe Univ, Atlanta, Ga, 73; 64th Ann, Conn Acad Fine Arts, Hartford, 74; Am Drawings, Portsmouth Community Art Ctr, Va, 76; 12th Nat Print Exhib, Silvermine Guild Artists, New Caanan, Conn, 77; Salute to Louis XIV, Miriam Perlman Gallery, Chicago, Ill, 91; plus others. *Teaching:* Demonstr viscosity etching, Southern Graphics Coun, Atlanta Col Art, 86. *Awards:* Am Drawing Purchase Award, Norfolk Mus, 71; First Prize, The Single Impression, Oglethorpe Univ, Atlanta, 73; Great Smoky Mts Nat Park Purchase Award, US Govt Art Purchase Prog, 74. *Bibliog:* Martin Sharter (auth), Art, Atlanta Mag, 12/73; Selma Smith (ed), Printworld Directory of Contemporary Prints and Prices, Printworld Inc, 88-91. *Media:* Etchings, Monoprints; Mixed. *Dealer:* Artist's Assocs Gallery 3261 Roswell Rd NE Atlanta GA 30305. *Mailing Add:* 4061 Arden Way NE Atlanta GA 30342

YARD, SALLY ELIZABETH
HISTORIAN, CURATOR
b Trenton, NJ, Sept 24, 51. *Study:* Harvard Univ, AB, 73; Princeton Univ, MFA, 75, PhD, 80. *Collections Arranged:* Christo: Oceanfront (auth, catalog), Princeton Univ, 75; John Roy, Christopher Sproat (auth, catalog), Vincent Smith Art Mus, 78; Images of the Self (auth, catalog), 79 & A Sense of Place--The American Landscape in Recent Art (auth, catalog), 80, Hampshire Col Gallery; Landscapes in Recent Painting (auth, catalog), Mus Fine Arts, Springfield, Mass, 81; The Shadow of the Bomb (auth, catalog) Mt Holyoke Col Art Mus, S Hadley, Mass & Univ Gallery, Univ Mass, Amherst, 84; An Architect's Eye: Selections from the Collection of Graham Gund (auth, catalog), Mt Holyoke Col Art Mus, South Hadley, Mass, 85. *Pos:* Acting cur, Univ Gallery, Univ Mass, Amherst, 80. *Teaching:* Instr mod art, Mt Holyoke Col, Mass, 78-79, lectr mod art, 80-81, asst prof mod art, 81-83; vis asst prof mod art, Amherst Col, Mass, 81-83; lectr mod art, Univ of Calif, San Diego, 87-88; asst prof art, Univ San Diego, 89-, vis asst prof mod art, 90; vis asst prof mod art, Univ San Diego, 90. *Mem:* Col Art Asn. *Res:* Abstract expressionism, especially Willem deKooning; contemporary painting & sculpture. *Publ:* Auth, Willem deKooning's men, Arts Mag, 81; ed, Sitings: Alice Aycock, Richard Fleischner, Mary Miss, George Trakas, La Jolla Mus Contemp Art, Calif, 86; auth, Willem deKooning: The First Twenty-Six Years in New York, 1927-1952, Garland, 86; coauth, Francis Bacon, Abbeville, 86; auth, Robert Morris, Margo Leavin Gallery, Los Angeles, 89. *Mailing Add:* Box 12985 La Jolla CA 92039

YAROS, CONSTANCE G
PAINTER, SCULPTOR
b Philadelphia, Pa. *Study:* Tyler Sch Art, Temple Univ, Philadelphia, 60; Boris Blai Studio, 76-81; Pa Acad Fine Arts, 78 & 88. *Work:* Tyler Sch Libr, Elkins Park, Pa; Temple Univ-Paley Libr, Philadelphia; Jefferson Park Hospital, Pa. *Comn:* Portraits, comn by Mr & Mrs Herbert Pincus, Glenside, Pa, 80, Mr & Mrs Mark Hankin, Erwinna, Pa, 88, Mr & Mrs Francis Strawbridge III, Merion, Pa, 89, Mr & Mrs William Silverman, Philadelphia, Pa, 90 & Mr William Austin Meehan, Philadelphia, Pa; many other commissions including portraits, landscapes, equines, flowers, ballet & still lifes. *Exhib:* Artists Equity Triennial, Port of History Mus, Philadelphia, 84 & 88; Catharine Lorillard Wolfe Art Club, Nat Arts Club, New York, 88; Salmagundi Art Club, New York, 88; Allied Artists Am, Nat Arts Club, New York, 88; one-woman show, Tyler Alumni Gallery, Diamond Club & Temple Univ, Philadelphia, 92. *Awards:* Len G Everett Painting Award, Allied Artists Am, 88. *Bibliog:* Denise Breslin Kachin (auth), Artist achieves recognition hoped for, Philadelphia Evening Bulletin, 81. *Mem:* Artists Equity (bd mem 76-90); Allied Artists Am; Knickerbocker Artists; Philadelphia Art Alliance; Am Soc Portrait Artists. *Media:* Acrylic, Oil; Metal. *Mailing Add:* c/o Portraits Philadelphia 2401 Pennsylvania Ave 4A5 Philadelphia PA 19130

YAROTSKY, LORI
ART DEALER, PAINTER
b Houston, Tex, July 6, 55. *Study:* Haystack-Hinckley Sch Crafts, Hinckley, Maine, studied weaving, 72-73; Sam Houston State Univ, BFA(painting & drawing), 76, E Tex State Univ, MFA(painting),80. *Work:* La State Mus, New Orleans; Univ St Thomas, Houston. *Pos:* Consult, Grad Sem Elem Art Educ, 80; dir, Tilden-Foley Gallery, New Orleans, La, 83-88; proprietor, RES NOVA Gallery, New Orleans, La, 88-; adv bd, Curric Rev, Dept Fine Art, Delgado Col, New Orleans; bd dirs, Red Bass Lit Mag. *Teaching:* Fel, East Tex State Univ, 77; lectr, Grad Studies Arts Admin, Univ New Orleans, 84. *Bibliog:* Errol Laborde (auth), Gallery growth, Gambit, 12/15/87; Roger Green (auth), New gallery will open in warehouse district, Times-Picayune, 12/23/87; Roger Green (auth), 1987: Warehouse district renaissance, Times-Picayune, Lagniappe, 1/1/88; George Jordon (auth), Critics choice: New Orleans art community, GO: New Orleans, 5/88; John Kemp (auth), Art mecca in the warehouse district, New Orleans Mag, 9/88. *Mem:* Friends Contemp Art, New Orleans Mus Art (adv bd); La Composers Guild (bd dirs); Jr Comt New Orleans Opera Asn. *Specialty:* Contemp fine art (paintings, sculpture, photographs, drawings, site-specific installations and video). *Publ:* Auth, Garden notes, Blackjack J, 79-80. *Mailing Add:* 50 W 57 St New York NY 10019

YASKO, CARYL A(NNE)
MURALIST, SCULPTOR
b Racine, Wis, Mar 11, 41. *Study:* Dominican Col, Wis, sculpture with Monica Gabriel & painting with Branislov Bak, grad, 63. *Work:* Fulbright Off, Tokyo, Japan. *Comn:* The Stone Cutters, Lemont, Ill, 75; Harbor Pop-up Mural (mural & sculpture), Sheboygan, Wis, 84; Brewery Triangle (sculpture of steel, concrete & earth), Sculptured Traffic Triangle, St Paul, Minn, 85; Mural of the Arts, Racine Fine Arts Sch, Wis, 85; Forest Memorial Sculpture (handmolded concrete & steel), Dept Pub Instr & Poynette Environ Ctr, 85; and others. *Exhib:* On Chicago Walls, Chicago State Univ, 74; Civic Sculpture, Appleton, Neenah & Menasha, Wis, 77; Levi Strauss & Co, Europ Exhib of US Murals, Mus Royal d'Art, Ancien, Brussels, 78; Chicago, The City & Its Artists, 1945-1978, Univ Mich, Ann Arbor, 78; French Ministry Foreign Affairs, traveling exhib, Caen, Normandy, 81; Working Together: Forms of Collaboration, Montgomery Ward Gallery, Univ Ill, Chicago, 81; and others. *Pos:* Panelist, Chicago Art Asn, Chicago & Nat Conf Mural Artists, 76 & State Arts Conf, 78-92; guest speaker, Chicago State Univ, 76, Univ Mich, Ann Arbor, 78, Waterloo, Wis, 79, Waupan State Prison, 79, UW Parkside, 80, Kamakura, Kanazawa & Tokyo, Japan, 82 & The Community Develop Wis, 86; artist-in-residence, Wis & Midwest, 78-92; visual arts panel, Wis Arts Bd, 79; guest artist, Brigada L'Eteiller Mural Proj, Chicago, 79, Artists for Peace Proj, Chicago, 80, State of Wis, Arts World, 82-91 & Chicago Pub Art Group, 90. *Teaching:* Instr, Art Inst Chicago, 75 & 76, Oakton Community Col, Morton Grove, Ill, 77 & Carthage Col, 81-; lectr murals, Loop Jr Col, Valparaiso Univ, 76; lectr, Univ Wis, River Falls, 81 & mural instr, 82. *Awards:* Chicago Beautiful Award, Mayor Daley, 75 & 76; Hon Citizen, Lemont, Ill, 75. *Bibliog:* John & Eva Corckroft, John Weber (coauth), Towards a People Art, Dutton, NY, 77; Phyllis Berg Pagorsch (dir), The Great Wall of Waunakee (film), Yahara Films, Madison, Wis, 78; Alan Barnett (auth), Community Murals, Art Alliance Press, Philadelphia & Cornwall Books, NY, London, 83; and others. *Mem:* Chicago Pub Art Group; Community Built Asn, Ithaca, NY. *Media:* Oil, Watercolor; Reinforced Concrete, Mixed Media. *Publ:* Contribr, Art Workers News, 73, New Art Examr, 74 & 80 & Nat Murals Newsletter, 78. *Mailing Add:* 136 Whiton St Whitewater WI 53190

YASSIN, ROBERT ALAN
MUSEUM DIRECTOR, CURATOR
b Malden, Mass, May 22, 41. *Study:* Dartmouth Col, BA, 62; Univ Mich, Ann Arbor, MA(hist art), 65, Samuel H Kress Found fel, 68-70; Yale Univ, Ford fel, 66-68, Univ Mich, CPh, 70. *Collections Arranged:* Contemporary Art at Yale, 66-68, Art & the Excited Spirit (with catalog), 72; Helen W & Robert M Benjamin Collection, Yale Univ, 67, American Art from Alumni Collections, 68; Victor Higgins Retrospective (with catalog), 75; Harrison Eiteljorg Collection of Western American Art, 76; Leonard Baskin, 76; Painting & Sculpture Today, 76, 78, 80, 82, 84 & 86; Art in Bus Collections, 77; Ind Artists Show, 77-79, 81, 83 & 85; Enrico Baj, 78; George Carlson, 79; Sasson Soffer Sculpture, 81-82, Batuz Works in Paper, 82, Indianapolis Mus Art; Masks, 90, Fine Art for Fine Causes, 91, Am Primitive Paintings, 91, Women Artists and the West, 91, 92, James Cook, 92, Tucson Mus Art. *Pos:* Ed, Yale Univ Art Gallery Bull, 66-68; asst dir, Mus Art, Univ Mich, Ann Arbor, 70-72, ed, Art Bull, 70-73, assoc dir & actg dir, Mus, 73; chief cur, Indianapolis Mus Art, 73-75, actg dir, 75, dir, 75-89; exec dir, Tucson Mus Art, Ariz, 90- *Teaching:* Instr graphic arts & mus practice & co-dir joint mus training prog, Univ Mich, Ann Arbor, 70-73; adj prof, Herron Sch of Art, Ind Univ-Purdue Univ, Indianapolis, 76-88. *Awards:* Ford Found Fel, 66-67, 67-68; Samuel H Kress Fel, 68-69, 69-70. *Mem:* Col Art Asn Am; Am Asn Mus; Asn Art Mus Dir, 75-89; Nat Trust Hist Preservation; Int Mus Conserv Asn (chmn exec comt, 77-79); Midwest Mus Asn; Am Asn Mus, Int Comt on Mus (bd mem, 86-89). *Res:* Late 19th and 20th century American art; 19th century British painting. *Mailing Add:* 8851 N Oracle Rd No 386 Tucson AZ 85737-7460

YASUDA, ROBERT
PAINTER, EDUCATOR
b Lihue, Kauai, Hawaii, Nov 14, 40. *Study:* Pratt Inst, Brooklyn, NY, BFA, 62, MFA, 64. *Work:* Brooklyn Mus, NY; Libr Cong, Washington, DC; State of Hawaii Found Arts; Hillwood Mus, Long Island Univ, NY. *Exhib:* One-man exhibs, Sculpture at the Coliseum, New York Coliseum, 80, Albuquerque Sight-Line, Hoshour Gallery, NMex, 81, Koplin Gallery, Los Angeles, Calif, Marianne Deson Gallery, Chicago, Ill, 82, Betty Parsons Gallery, New York, 83 & Hanalei Gallery, Kauai, Hawaii, 84; A More Store, Jack Tilton Gallery, New York, 84; The Anchorage Exhib, Large Scale Painting Installations, Brooklyn Bridge Anchorage, New York, 85; 8x10, Washington County Mus Fine Arts, Hagerstown, Md, 86; Opening exhib, Cutler-Schreiber Gallery, New York, 86; Koplin Gallery, Los Angeles, Calif, 87; Julian Pretto Gallery, 91, Stark Gallery, 92, The Inst for Contemp Art, PS1 Mus, New York, 92; and others. *Teaching:* Prof art, Long Island Univ, C W Post, painting & drawing, 69-92. *Awards:* J H Whitney Found Grant, 62-63; Nat Endowment for the Arts Fel Grant, Washington, DC, 81. *Bibliog:* Kathleen Shields (auth), Robert Yasuda-Albuquerque sight line, Art Space, spring 82; Alan Artner (auth), Best solo shows, art 1982, Chicago Tribune, 1/2/83; Kim Levin (auth), Art in the Anchorage, Village Voice, 5/21/85; Susan Fleminger (auth), Inside the Bridge, Art in the Depths of the Anchorage, Prospect Press, 5/30/85. *Media:* Acrylic, Oil. *Dealer:* Betty Parsons Gallery 24 W 57th St New York NY 10019; Stark Gallery 594 Broadway New York NY 10012. *Mailing Add:* 429 W Broadway New York NY 10012

YATER, GEORGE DAVID
PAINTER
b Madison, Ind, Nov 30, 10. *Study:* John Herron Art Sch, 28-32, dipl; Cape Sch Art, Provincetown, with Henry Hensche, summers 31-34; also with Edwin Dickinson & Richard Miller. *Work:* Chrysler Collection, Norfolk Art Gallery, Va; Ford Motor Co, Dearborn, Mich; Paper Mill Playhouse, Millburn, NJ; Ind Univ, Bloomington; Arch Am Art, Smithsonian Inst, Washington, DC. *Comn:* Mural, Provincetown-Boston Airline, Provincetown Airport, 76. *Exhib:* Nat Acad Design, New York; Pa Acad Fine Arts, Philadelphia; Indianapolis Mus Art; Chrysler Art Mus, Provincetown, Mass; Provincetown Painters 1890s-1970s, Everson Mus of Art, Syracuse, NY & Provincetown Art Asn & Mus, Provincetown, Mass, 77; retrospective, Provincetown Art Asn & Mus, 82. *Pos:* Dir, Provincetown Art Asn, 47-61 & Sarasota Art Asn, 55-56. *Awards:* Outstanding Oil, Hoosier Salon, Indianapolis, 54; First Prize for Oil, Falmouth Artists Guild, 61, 69 & 75. *Bibliog:* Robert Hatch (auth), At the tip of Cape Cod, Horizon Mag, 61. *Media:* Oil, Watercolor. *Publ:* Illusr (watercolors), Ford Times, Lincoln-Mercury Times & New England Journeys, 52-66. *Mailing Add:* Castle Rd Truro MA 02666

YATES, HOLLYE E
CURATOR, HISTORIAN
b Abilene, Tex, Apr 30, 65. *Study:* Abilene Christian Univ, BA, 88. *Work:* Ashlawn Highland Mus, Charlottesville, Va; Mus Abilene, Tex. *Pos:* Cur educ, Mus Abilene, Tex, 89- *Mem:* Tex Asn Mus. *Mailing Add:* Museums of Abilene 801 S Mockingbird Abilene TX 79605

YATES, MARVIN CLARENCE
PAINTER, INSTRUCTOR
b Jackson, Tenn, Sept 22, 43. *Study:* Memphis Acad Art, BFA, 66. *Exhib:* Am Watercolor Soc, Nat Acad Gallery, New York, 73-79; Watercolor USA, Springfield Art Mus, Mo, 75 & 76; Mainstreams, Grover Hermann Mus, Marietta, Ohio, 76; Southern Watercolor Soc, Cheekwood Gallery, Nashville, 77-79; Rocky Mountain Nat Water Media, Foothills Art Ctr, Golden, Colo, 78; Real Show, Grand Cent Art Gallery, New York, 79. *Teaching:* Instr watercolor, Memphis State Univ, 75- *Awards:* Rechenbach Award, Rechenbach Gallery, 73 & 80; Washington Sch of Art Award, 74; Second Place Watercolor, Sterling Regal Inc, 79. *Bibliog:* Susan Meyer (auth), Watercolor Page, Am Artist Mag, 75; Ralph Fabri (auth), Watercolor Page, Today's Art, 75. *Mem:* Am Watercolor Soc; Southern Watercolor Soc; Tenn Watercolor Soc; Memphis Watercolor Group. *Media:* Watercolor, Pencil. *Publ:* Contribr, 40 Watercolorists and How They Work, Watson-Guptill, 76. *Mailing Add:* 1457 Hwy 304 Hernando MS 38632

YATES, STEVEN A
ARTIST, CURATOR
b Chicago, Ill. *Study:* Univ Nebr, BFA, 72; Univ NMex, with Beaumont Newhall & Van Deren Coke, MA, 75, MFA(doctoral degree)(Ford Found Fel), 78. *Work:* San Francisco Mus Mod Art, Calif; Univ Art Mus & Tamarind Print Collection, Univ NMex; Ctr Creative Photog, Tucson; Los Angeles Ctr Photog Studies; Mint Mus Art, NC; Polaroid Corp Collection, Cambridge; Russian Art Photogrs Union, Moscow; and others. *Exhib:* The Markers (with catalog), San Francisco Mus Mod Art, 81; Extending the Perimeters of 20th Century Photography (with catalog), San Francisco Mus Mod Art, 85; PhotoGroup/Miami, Members Gallery, 89; Jayne Baum Gallery, New York, 89; 21 NMex Photogrs, Vision Gallery, San Francisco, 91; Contemporary American Photography Masters, Cinema Inst, Moscow, traveling exhib, 91; NMex Impressions: Printmaking, 1880-1990, 91-92; and others. *Pos:* Cur asst, Sheldon Mem Art Gallery, Univ Nebr, 72-73, Univ Art Mus, Univ NMex, 73-75; cur photog prints & drawings, Mus Fine Arts, Mus NMex, 80-85, cur photog, 85-; adv bd visual arts, Col Santa Fe, 85-87. *Teaching:* Instr part-time, Univ NMex, Albuquerque, 75-78; vis instr, Pomona Col, Claremont Col, 76-; vis instr art dept, Summer Exten Prog, Univ Calif, Los Angeles, 76; lectr, Humboldt State Univ Workshop, 86. *Awards:* Guest Artist, Taramind Inst, Albuquerque, 88; Guest Artist, 20x24 Polaroid Camera Prog, 88; Fulbright Scholars Award to CIS (former USSR), fall 91; and many others. *Bibliog:* Photography, Sheldon Mem Art Gallery, Univ NMex Press, 77. *Publ:* Ambiguous Space, Tradition and Non-Tradition, Tamarind Papers, 89; The Transition Years, Paul Strand in New Mexico (catalog) & Modern Innovation in the Landscape Edward Weston in New Mexico (catalog), Mus NMex, 89; Notes on the nature of evolution in the idea photographic, San Francisco Camera Work Quart, 89; NMex Impressions: Printmaking, 1880-1990 (catalog), Univ NMex Press, 91; Proto-Modern Photography: Artist and Critic (catalog), Proto Modern Photog, Mus NMex, 92; and others. *Mailing Add:* c/o Mus Fine Arts PO Box 2087 Santa Fe NM 87504-2087

YAU, JOHN
WRITER, CURATOR
b Lynn, Mass, June 5, 50. *Study:* Bard Col, BA, 69-72; Brooklyn Col, MFA, 76-78. *Pos:* Freelance writer, 77-; freelance cur, 82- *Teaching:* Instr, Pratt Inst, 85-90; instr, Sch Visual Arts, New York, 88-90; vis writer, Brown Univ, 92. *Publ:* Auth, Giant Wall, Limestone Press, 91; Flee Advice, Collectif Generation, 91; Postcards from Trakl, Universal Ltd Art Eds, 92; Edificio Sayonara, Black Sparrow Press, 92; Genghis Chan: Private Eye, Art Inst Chicago, 93. *Mailing Add:* P O Box 1910 Canal Street Sta New York NY 10013

YAWORSKI, ALEX F(RANCIS)
PAINTER
b Odessa, Russia, Dec 29, 07; US citizen. *Study:* Am Acad Art, 30-32. *Work:* Tweed Mus Art; Charles and Emma Frye Mus, Seattle, Wash; Watercolor USA, Springfield, Mo; Springfield Mus, Ill; Union League of Chicago. *Comn:* Series of Paintings, Chicago Tribune, Ill, 78; Series of Cityscapes, Amoco. *Exhib:* Artists Chicago & Vicinity, Art Inst Chicago, 46-52; Am Watercolor Soc Ann, Nat Acad Galleries, New York, 53-81; Watercolor USA Ann, Springfield Art Mus, Mo, 62, 63, 68, 69, 72 & 75; 200 Years of Watercolor, Metrop Mus Art, New York, 66-67. *Pos:* Com & ed art, Chicago Tribune, 32; art dir, Poster Products Inc, Chicago, 34-43; art direction & fine arts painting, 43- *Awards:* Purchase Award, Watercolor USA Ann, Springfield Art Mus, 69; Award Excellence, Ann Exhib Ill Watercolor Soc, 83; Gold Medal, Adirondacks Nat Exhib Am Watercolors, 83. *Mem:* Am Watercolor Soc (vpres, 72-73); fel Int Inst Arts & Letters; honorary mem Artists Guild Chicago (pres, 47-48); Nat Soc Painters in Casein & Acrylics; Midwest Watercolor Soc, Chicago (bd mem, 79-). *Media:* Watercolor. *Publ:* Auth, Acrylic Watercolor Painting, 70 & co-auth (with Susan E Meyer & Norman Kent), Watercolorists at Work, 72, Watson Guptill; auth, The watercolor page, 51 & Alex F Yaworski Artist's Guild of Chicago sketch trip, 55, Am Artist Mag. *Mailing Add:* The Madrid Condos 5017 Walnut, Unit D Kansas City MO 64112

YEGUL, FIKRET KUTLU
EDUCATOR, ARCHITECT
b Themiscyra, Turkey, Oct 27, 41. *Study:* Middle East Technical Univ, BA(archit), 64; Univ Pa, MA(archit), 66; Harvard Univ, PhD(art hist), 75. *Exhib:* Mamluk Architecture of Cairo (photographs), Fogg Art Mus, 74. *Teaching:* Asst prof art hist, Wellesley Col, 75-76; asst prof, Univ Calif, Santa Barbara, 76-82, assoc prof, 82-88, prof, 88- *Awards:* Fulbright Fel, 64-66; Senior fel, CASVA, Nat Gallery Art, 85-86. *Mem:* Sardis Archaeol Expedition; Am Inst Archaeol. *Res:* Roman art and architecture. *Publ:* Auth, Early Byzantine capitals from Sardis, D O Papers, Vol 28, 74; auth, The marble court of Sardis and historical reconstruction, J Field Archaeol, Vol 32, 76; auth, A reconstruction study of Lucian's Baths of Hippias, Archaeol Classica, Vol 31, 79; auth, Kaisersaal and the Imperial Cult, Art Bulletin, 3/82; auth, Bath-Gymnasium Complex in Sardis (Report 3), Harvard Univ, 86. *Mailing Add:* Art Hist Dept Univ Calif Santa Barbara CA 93106

YEH, CAROL
PRINTMAKER
b Lackawanna, NY, Dec 25, 38. *Study:* Yale Univ Summer Sch, Norfolk, Conn; Smith Col, Northampton, Mass, with Leonard Baskin, BA, 61; Acad de la Grande Chaumiere, Paris, France; Univ Iowa, Iowa City, with Mauricio Lasansky, MA, 66; Acad de Bellas Artes, San Fernando, Madrid, Spain. *Work:* Everson Mus, Syracuse, NY; New York Pub Libr; Smith Col Libr, Northampton, Mass; Harvard Univ Libr, Cambridge; Yale Univ Libr, New Haven. *Exhib:* Am Drawing Biennial XXI, Norfolk Mus Arts & Sci, Va, 65; Smithsonian Inst Travel Am Drawings, 65-66; Northwest Printmakers, 37th Int, Seattle, Wash, & Portland, Ore, 66; two-man show, Drawings, Fleischer Anhalt Gallery, Los Angeles, 69; one-woman shows, Prints & Drawings, Houghton House, Geneva, NY, 75 & Prints, Everson Mus, Syracuse, NY, 77; Group Exhib, Mex City, 83 & 85. *Teaching:* Guest lectr, Art Hist, Printmaking, Cornell Univ, 75-76; vis instr art, drawing & printmaking, Eisenhower Col, 78; vis lectr, drawing, Hobart & Wm Smith Col, 88. *Awards:* Fulbright Grant, 66-67 & 83; Yaddo Fel, 72; MacDowell Colony Fel, 72. *Media:* Intaglio, Drawing. *Publ:* Auth & illusr, Etched Portraits of Ernest Hemingway, 61; illusr, Red Flower, 61; auth & illusr, Houdini, 71; illusr, Ragtime, 76; illusr, Hawthorne, 77. *Dealer:* Zeitlin & Ver Brugge 815 N La Cienega Los Angeles CA 90025; Pink Adobe Gallery Hillsboro NM 88042. *Mailing Add:* Box 156 Hillsboro NM 88042

YEISER, CHARLES WILLIAM
PAINTER, ART DEALER
b Womelsdorf, Pa, Nov 20, 25. *Study:* Kutztown State Teachers' Col, 43; Pratt Inst Art Sch, cert, 49; New York Univ, 49-51. *Work:* Westmoreland Mus Art, Greensburg, Pa. *Comn:* The Good Shepherd (panel), Dutch Reformed Church, West Nyack, NY, 60. *Exhib:* Board of Directors Exhib, Hopper House, Nyack, NY, 76; The New American Still Life, 80, Small Works for the Armchair Collector, 82 & Regional Artists Salute the Museum's 25th Anniversary, 85, Westmoreland Mus Art, Greensburg, Pa; The American Still Life Tradition 1955-1985, Montgomery Gallery, San Francisco, Calif; Recent Paintings, Westmoreland Mus Art, Greensburg, Pa, 86. *Pos:* Asst dir, FAR Gallery, New York, 51-70, dir, 71-80. *Awards:* First Prize Watercolor, Rahway Pub Libr, Rahway, NJ, 48. *Bibliog:* Martha B Scott (auth), Charles Yeiser: A painter of still life, Westmoreland Mus Art, 86. *Mem:* Hopper House (bd dirs, 75-78); Rockland Ctr Arts (bd dirs), West Nyack, NY. *Media:* Oil on Canvas or Panel. *Dealer:* Joseph Keiffer Inc 28 E 72 St New York NY 10021. *Mailing Add:* 11 Wheeler Pl West Nyack NY 10994

YEKTAI, MANOUCHER
PAINTER
b Tehran, Iran, Dec 22, 22; US citizen. *Study:* Univ Tehran; Ecole Superior Beaux Arts, Paris, 46 & 47, studied with Ozenfant in New York, 45-47; Art Students League, 47-48. *Work:* Baltimore Mus Art, Md; Mus Mod Art, New York; Everson Mus, Syracuse, NY; Hirshhorn Mus, Washington, DC; and others. *Exhib:* one-man shows, Anderson-Meyer Gallery, Paris, 62, Feingarten Gallery, Chicago, 62, Gertrude Kasle Gallery, Detroit, 65, 66, 67, 68 & 70, USIS Teheran, Iran, 70, Benson Gallery, Bridgehampton, NY, 66, 72, 73 & 75, Teheran Galerie Zand, 77, Alex Rosenberg Gallery, NY, 82 & 84; Watershed Years, Franklin Gallery, NY, 74; Alex Rosenberg Gallery, NY, 86; New York Joseph Lubin Gallery, 85. *Media:* Oil. *Mailing Add:* 225 W 86th St New York NY 10024

YENAWINE, PHILIP
EDUCATOR
b Athens, Ga, July 12, 42. *Study:* Govern State Univ, BA, 77; Goddard Col, MA, 79. *Pos:* Dir educ, Mus Contemp Art, Chicago, 77-78; Dir, Aspen Ctr Visual Arts, 78-82; Dir educ, Mus Mod Art, New York, 83-; vpres, Art Matters Inc, New York, 84- *Awards:* Governor's Award, Prog People with Hearing Disabilities, Mus Mod Art, 84; Governor's Award, Visual Aids & Day Without Art, NY, 90; Mus Educ Yr, Eastern Div, 87 & Mus Educ Yr, 91, Nat Art Educ Asn. *Mem:* Mus Educ Consortium (chmn, 86-89). *Publ:* Auth, Looking Books: Colors; Lines; Shapes; Stories, Mus Mod Art & Abrams, 90; How to Look at Modern Art, Harry N Abrams, 90; Inheriting the theory: new voices and multiple perspectives on discipline based art education, Univ Tex, 90. *Mailing Add:* Mus Mod Art 11 W 53 St New York NY 10019

YES, PHYLLIS A
PAINTER, SCULPTOR
b Red Wing, Minn, May 15, 41. *Study:* Luther Col, BA, 63; Univ Minn, MFA, 68; Univ Ore, PhD, 78. *Work:* Univ Ore Mus Art, Eugene; Whitworth Col Art Gallery, Spokane, Wash; Security Pacific Bank, Los Angeles; Levi-Strauss, San Francisco. *Exhib:* one-person shows, Recent Work, John Edward Hughes Gallery, Dallas, 84, Tables, etc, Linda Rhodes Gallery, Winterpark, Fla, 84 & Paintings and Lacquered Work, Elizabeth Leach Gallery, Portland, Ore, 84; Lace/War, Bernice Steinbaum Gallery, 86, Northwest Biennial, Brooklyn Mus, 86, New York; Clay Images, Baltimore Clayworks, 90; Honored Women, Hansen-Howard Gallery, Ashland, Ore, 92; Mixed Metaphors, Gallery Nishiazabu,Tokyo, Japan, 92; Enclosure Series, Elizabeth Leach Gallery, Portland, Ore, 92. *Pos:* Juror of Nat, Regional Exhibs. *Teaching:* Asst prof, Ore State Univ, 76-79; prof, Lewis & Clark Col, 79- *Awards:* Ore Arts Comn Grant, 87; Distinguish Alumni Award, Luther Col, Decorah, Iowa, 88; Burlington Northern Achievement Award, 91. *Bibliog:* Focus: Phyllis Yes, NW Gallery Mag, fall 90; Paintings Have Grace of Lace, Japan Times, 3/31/91; Phyllis Yes, Styling Mag, 7/91; and numerous other articles in national periodicals. *Mem:* Artists Equity Asn; Col Art Asn Am; Women's Caucus Arts; Contemp Arts Coun. *Media:* Acrylic, Mixed. *Publ:* Auth, History of Lace, Art & Antiques Mag, 12/87. *Dealer:* Elizabeth Leach Gallery 207 SW Pine St Portland OR 97204. *Mailing Add:* 5235 View Point Terrace Portland OR 97201

YEZERSKI, HOWARD J
GALLERY DIRECTOR, ART DEALER
b Buenos Aires, Arg, Oct 26, 41; US citizen. *Study:* Univ NH, BA, 64. *Exhib:* Profile of a Gallery: Andover Gallery of Fine Art, Addison Gallery Am Art, Andover, Mass, 81. *Pos:* Dir, Andover Gallery, formerly, Howard Yezerski Gallery, currently. *Specialty:* Contemporary emerging artists. *Mailing Add:* 186 South St Boston MA 02111

YOCHIM, LOUISE DUNN
PAINTER, WRITER
b Jitomir, Ukraine, July 18, 09; US citizen. *Study:* Art Inst Chicago, cert, 32, BAE, 42, MAE, 52; Univ Chicago, 56. *Work:* Ill State Mus, Springfield; Eilat Mus, Israel; Health Clinic, Lawrence, Kans; Congregation Agudath Jacob & St Lukes Presby Hospital, Chicago; Hebrew Theological Col, Skokie, Ill. *Exhib:* One-woman show, Northeastern Ill Univ, 72 & Spertus Mus, Chicago, 79-83; Mus Sci & Industry, Chicago, 82; Ill State Mus, Springfield, 83; Grove Gallery, Evanston, Ill, 83; plus many others. *Pos:* Art supvr, Chicago Pub Schs, 50-71; consult art, elem & high schs, 71-74, Rand McNally Publ, 67- & Encycl Britannica, 68- *Teaching:* Instr art, Chicago Pub High Sch, Ill, 34-50, Chicago Acad Fine Arts, 51-52 & Chicago Teachers Col, 60-61. *Awards:* Award, Chicago Soc Artists, 53 & 78; Medal Merit, Accad Ital Arti Lavore, 83; Accad Italia Premio Oscar D'Italia. *Bibliog:* Frank Holland (auth), Renaissance unit's show to cap season, Chicago Sun Times, 57; Doris Lane Butler (auth), Winnetka to open art fair season, Chicago Daily News, 57; Frank Getlein (auth), Associated artists, Sunday Star, Washington, DC, 62. *Mem:* Artists Equity Asn; Nat Art Educ Asn; Nat Comt Art Educ; Artists Coalition; Am Jewish Art Club (pres 85-90). *Media:* Oil, Mixed Media. *Publ:* Auth, Building Human Relationships Through Art, 54; Perceptual Growth in Creativity, 67; Art in Action, 69 & Role & Impact: The Chicago Society of Artists, 79; articles on 28 painters & sculptors, Sentinel Mag, 81-84; Harvest of Freedom: Jewish Artists in America 1930-1980's, 89. *Dealer:* Four Arts Gallery 1629 Oak Ave Evanston IL 60203. *Mailing Add:* 9545 Drake Ave Evanston IL 60203

YODER, JANICA
PHOTOGRAPHER, EDUCATOR
b Milwaukee, Wis, June 21, 50. *Study:* Univ Wis, Madison, BS (art), 74, MA (photog), 76, MFA (photog), 77. *Work:* Corcoran Gallery, Washington, DC; J Paul Getty Mus, Malibu, Calif; Madison Art Ctr, Wis; Milwaukee Art Mus, Wis. *Exhib:* Solo exhibs: Patrick King Contemp Art, Indianapolis, 83 & 85, Inter Lupem Et Canem: New Color Works by janica Yoder, Madison Art Ctr, Wis, 87, Portraits & Still Lives, Florine Roth Gallery, Milwaukee, 88, Sonlines, Michael H Lord Gallery, Milwaukee, 91, New Work, The Pain Mus, Oshkosh, Wis, 92-93, Honolulu Acad Art, 93; Woman Photographers, Corcoran Gallery Art, Washington, DC, 82; Multiple Exposure: 5 Contemporary Photographers, Milwaukee Art Mus, Wis, 88; A Decade of Exhibitions, Madison Art Ctr, Wis, 90; Recent Acquisitions in Photography, Corcoran Gallery Art, Washington, DC, 83, 86 & 90; May 1992, Betsy Rosenfield Gallery, Chicago Int Art Expo, 92; Color Photog Invitational, Crossman Gallery, Univ Wisc, Whitewater, 92. *Teaching:* Instr photog, Int Ctr Photog, New York, 78-80; asst prof, Herron Sch Art-Ind Univ, 80-86; instr, Milwaukee Inst Art & Design, 89- *Bibliog:* Popular Photog, winter 78; AfterImage, spring 79; Photography Ann, Popular Photography, 86. *Media:* Color and black & white photography. *Dealer:* Michael H Lord Gallery 420 E Wisconsin Ave Milwaukke WI 53202. *Mailing Add:* c/o Betsy Rosenfield Gallery 212 W Superior St Chicago IL 60610

YODER, RICHARD ALLEN
PAINTER, CONCEPTUAL ARTIST
b Mobile, Ala, Dec 16, 47. *Study:* Univ Ore, BFA, 74; Univ Wash, MFA, 76. *Work:* Seattle Art Mus; Bremerton Pub Libr Gallery, Wash; AT&T, Chicago, Ill; Chase Manhattan Bank, New York; Manoogian, Minneapolis. *Exhib:* Northwest Artists Ann, Seattle Art Mus, 73, 74 & 76; Artists of Oregon, Portland Art Mus, 75; In Touch: Nature, Ritual & Sensuous Art, Portland Ctr Visual Arts, 76; The Reality of Illusion, Johnson Mus, Cornell Univ, Denver Art Mus, Univ Southern Calif Art Galleries & Univ Tex, Austin, 79-81; Radical Realism, Muhlenburg Col Art Galleries, 80. *Pos:* Dir educ, Trompe L'Oeil Inst, formerly. *Teaching:* Vis lectr painting, Univ Wash, Seattle, 76; instr painting & drawing, Cornish Inst Allied Arts, Seattle, 76-78. *Bibliog:* Donald Brewer (auth), The Reality of Illusion, Quaker Hill Press, 80. *Mem:* Col Art Asn Am. *Media:* Oil on Linen. *Dealer:* MOCA Designs Ltd New York NY. *Mailing Add:* 640 Broadway 3-E New York NY 10012

YORGO (GEORGE YORGO SPYROPOULOS)
PAINTER, CONCEPTUAL ARTIST
b Cairo, Egypt, July 20, 29; US citizen. *Study:* Acad Fine Arts, Paris, France, Scholar, MBA, 58. *Work:* Zappion Mus, Athens, Greece; Royal Gallery Fine Arts, Montreal, Can; Gallery Dimpoulos, Paris. *Exhib:* Salon D'Hiver Fine Arts, Grand Palais Mus, Paris, 57; Deauville Int Art, Deauville Fine Arts, Deauville, France, 58; Salon D'Art Moderne, Parc Des Exposition, Paris, 61; Fine Arts Exhib, Am Fine Arts Gallery, Los Angeles, 72. *Awards:* First Prize Oil Portraits, Raymond Duncan Gallery, Paris, 57; First Int Grand Prize Landscapes, Deauville Art Exhib, 58; Medaille De La Rose D'Or, French Ministry Educ, 60. *Bibliog:* Jean Diwo (auth), The art of Yorgo, Jardin Des Arts, 59; John Hall (auth), Yorgo, great master of Los Angeles, Quote Newspaper, 73; Jean Diwo & John Hall (coauths), Yorgo-American Fine Arts (video doc), 85. *Media:* Oil, All Media; Electronic Art. *Dealer:* Galerie Dimpoulos 24 Rue Du Laos 75015 Paris France. *Mailing Add:* 969 Sonora Rd Costa Mesa CA 92626

YORK, RICHARD TRAVIS
ART DEALER, GALLERY DIRECTOR
b Nashville, Tenn, Oct 22, 50. *Study:* Vanderbilt Univ, BA, 72. *Pos:* Dir Am art, Hammer Galleries, New York, 74-76; coordr Am dept, M Knoedler & Co, New York, 76-77; assoc, Hirschl & Adler Galleries, 77-81; pres, Richard York Gallery, New York, 81- *Awards:* Recipient the 50th Anniversary Medal, Nat Gallery Art. *Mem:* William C Bryant Fel; Art Dealers Asn Am (bd dirs); Art Adv Panel Interanl Revenue Serv; Appraisers Asn Am; Art Adv Comt, Colby Col Mus Art. *Specialty:* American paintings, drawings and sculpture of 1800-1950. *Publ:* Auth, The Eye of Stieglitz, 78 & Buildings: Architecture in American Modernism, 80, Hirschl & Adler, New York; Joseph Stella: The Tropics, 88, The Italian Presence in American Art: 1860-1920, 89, An American Gallery, Vol I-VI, 86-90, Richard York Gallery, New York. *Mailing Add:* 21 E 65th St New York NY 10021

YORK, TINA
PAINTER, WRITER
b Bautzen, Ger, Feb 9, 51; US citizen. *Study:* Sch Mus Fine Arts, MA, 69; George Dergalis, MA, 67-75; Brandeis Univ, 78; NY MedCol, 83. *Work:* Utah Mus Fine Arts, Salt Lake City; Nat Sci Found, Washington, DC; NZ Space Admin, Auckland. *Comn:* painting for title page of Cytokine Mag, Nat Cancer Inst, Washington, DC, 89; painting, High Technol Products, Dobbs Ferry, NY, 89; painting, Merck, Sharp & Dohme, 87; JBF/Industries Brasileiva Filmes, SA, Rio de Janeiro, Brazil, 91; NASA, Washington, DC, 92; Regional Mus Art, Bautzen, Ger; Cocoa Beach Holiday Inn, Fla; St Joseph's Med Ctr, Burbank, Calif. *Exhib:* Solo shows, Copley Soc, Boston, Mass, 73, Ames Gallery, New York, 76, Rue Oker Gallery Art, Sturbridge, Mass, 79, Alpha Contemp Exhib, Los Angeles, 85, Convention Ctr, Rome, Italy, 88, Art 5, Nuremberg, Ger, 90 & Art Expo, New York, 90; many group shows in US, WGer, France & Eng. *Awards:* First Prize, Inst Contemp Art, 79; First Prize, SCalif Contemp Exhib, Los Angeles, 84; First Prize, One Fifty Three Gallery, New York, 87. *Bibliog:* Rina L Firrone (auth), The Body Electric, Ocala Star Banner, 88; Barbara Rollmann (auth), The Beauty of the Computer Chip, Regensburger Tageblatt, Ger, 90; Molly Siple (auth), The Realities We Never See, Designers West, 92. *Mem:* Artist Equity Asn; Inst Contemp Art; Cambridge Art Asn; Cambridge Art Asn; Los Angeles Visual Artists. *Media:* Acrylic, Oil. *Res:* Scanning electron micrographs of the human body; astronomy, medicine, physics, chemistry, biology. *Publ:* Illusr, Prints & calendar of fourteen large paintings, Merck, 88. *Mailing Add:* 11652 Huston St North Hollywood CA 91601

YOSHIDA, RAY KAKUO
PAINTER, EDUCATOR
b Kapaa, Kauai, Hawaii, Oct 3, 30. *Study:* Art Inst Chicago, BA, 53; Syracuse Univ, MFA, 58; Univ Chicago; Univ Hawaii; also with A D Reinhardt. *Work:* Everson Mus, Syracuse, NY; Art Inst Chicago; Mus des 20, Jahrhunderts, Vienna; Am Tel & Tel, New York; Ball State Univ, Muncie, Ind. *Exhib:* Spirit of the Comics, Inst Contemp Art, Univ Pa, 69; Art Inst Chicago, 69, 71, 77, 79 & 82; Am Painting, Indianapolis Mus Art, 72 & 77; 12th Bienal de Sao Paulo, Brazil, 73; Chicago Currents: The Koffler Foundation, Nat Mus Am Art, 79; Who Chicago? An Exhibition of Contemporary Imagists, Sunderland Arts Ctr, England & travelling, 80-82; The Comic Art Show, Whitney Mus Am Art, 83; and others. *Teaching:* Frank Harrold Sellers Prof, Art Inst Chicago, 60- *Awards:* Walter M Campana Prize, 60, Frank G Logan Medal & Prize, 71 & Virgine K Headberg Prize, 77, Art Inst Chicago; Nat Endow Arts Grant, 89. *Bibliog:* Franz Schulze (auth), Chicago Art, Follett, 72; articles in Art Int & Art News. *Mem:* Art Club Chicago; Am Asn Univ Profs. *Media:* Oil, Acrylic. *Dealer:* Phyllis Kind Gallery 226 E Ontario Chicago IL 60611. *Mailing Add:* Painting Dept Art Inst Chicago Columbus Dr Chicago IL 60603

YOSHIMURA, FUMIO
SCULPTOR
b Kamakura, Japan, Feb 22, 26. *Study:* Tokyo Nat Univ Arts, MFA, 49. *Work:* Philadelphia Art Mus; Pa Acad Fine Arts, Philadelphia; Albright-Knox Gallery, New York; Gobett-Brewster Gallery, New Plymouth, NZ; Power Gallery of Contemp Art, Sydney, Australia; and others. *Comn:* Mobile, Haskell & Sells, Philadelphia. *Exhib:* Pa Acad Fine Arts, 71; Photo Realism, Wadsworth Atheneum, Conn, 73; Tokyo Bienale, 74; Galleri Arnesen, Copenhagen, Denmark, 74; Realism/Realisme, Rothman's Pall Mall traveling exhib, Can, 76; Object as Poet, Renwick Gallery, Smithsonian Inst, Washington, DC, 76; Norton Gallery of Art, Fla, 77. *Teaching:* Vis prof, Dartmouth Col, NH, 81-82. *Media:* Wood. *Dealer:* Nancy Hoffman Gallery New York NY 10012. *Mailing Add:* 5 E Third St New York NY 10003

YOST, ERMA MARTIN
ASSEMBLAGE ARTIST, INSTRUCTOR
b Goshen, Ind, Jan 12, 47. *Study:* James Madison Univ, Harrisonburg, Va, BA(art educ), 69, MA(painting), 75. *Work:* Pace Univ Art Mus, New York; James Madison Univ, Va; Goshen Col, Ind; East Tenn State Univ, Johnson City; Bethel Col, North Newton, Kans. *Comn:* Painting & quilt assemblage, Rockingham Mem Hosp, Harrisburg, Va, 82 & Philhaven Hosp, Mt Gretna, Pa, 85, Chicopee, Inc, New Brunswick, NJ, 90. *Exhib:* One-person shows, Noho Gallery, New York, 75-93 & Bergen Community Mus, Parammus, NJ, 77; Desert Images, Jersey City Mus, NJ, 79; Invitational, Southwestern Exposure, Gayle Willson Gallery, Southampton, NY, 89; Contemporary Quilts, Perimeter Gallery, Chicago, Ill, 89; New Jersey Arts Ann, NJ State Mus, Trenton, 92; Kauffman Mus, North Newton, Kans, 92; and others. *Pos:* Illusr, Simplicity Pattern Co, New York, 72-73. *Teaching:* Instr art, Eastern Mennonite Col, 69-70; instr art, Spence Sch, 77- *Awards:* NJ State Coun Arts Fel, 92. *Bibliog:* Newsday Mag (article), 89; Barbara Smith (auth), Celebratin the Stitch, 91; Fiberarts Design Book 4, Lark Press, 91. *Mem:* Asn Artists Run Galleries; Womens Caucus Art; NJ Printmaking Coun; Textile Study Group of New York. *Media:* Acrylic, Quilt Assemblage. *Dealer:* Noho Gallery Inc 168 Mercer St New York NY 10012. *Mailing Add:* 223 York St Jersey City NJ 07302

YOST, LEON C
PHOTOGRAPHER
b Atglen, Pa, July 7, 43. *Study:* Eastern Mennonite Col, 63-65; Pace Univ, 72-77. *Work:* Pace Univ, NY; Cenlar Corp, NJ; E Tenn State Univ; Goshen Col, Ind; Chikapee Corp, Princeton, NJ. *Exhib:* Solo exhib, Noho Gallery, New York, 77, 83, 85, 87 & 90, Soho Photo Gallery, New York, 78-80 & 83; 20th Biennial Exhib, Univ Del, Newark, 81; Fel Exhib, Monmouth Mus, NJ, 88; NJ Arts Ann, NJ State Mus, 89. *Pos:* Pres, Noho Gallery, New York, 82-85; mem bd, Printmaking Coun NJ, 88-89. *Awards:* Fel, NJ State Coun Arts, 86. *Bibliog:* Dean Kinley (auth), Artist continually discards, Daily News Record, 2/9/81; Peter Fingesten (auth), article, Arts Mag, 2/83; Dennis Wepman (auth), Ancient Art, Modern Preception, Artspeak, 2/1/87. *Mem:* Am Rock Art Res Asn. *Dealer:* Noho Gallery 168 Mercer St New York NY 10012. *Mailing Add:* 223 York St Jersey City NJ 07302

YOUKELES, ANNE
PAINTER, PRINTMAKER
b Bad Ischl, Austria; US citizen. *Study:* Kunstgewerbeschule Vienna, Austria; Acad de la Grande Chaumiere, Paris; Ohio State Univ; painting with Alexander Dobkin & Rudolf Baranik; printmaking with Sidney Chafetz & Carol Summers. *Work:* Philadelphia Mus Art; Rosenwald Collection, Smithsonian Inst; Bibliotheque Nat, Paris; Lehman Collection; Atlantic Richfield Co; DeCordova Mus, Lincoln, Mass; Minneapolis Mus Art. *Comn:* Editions of prints, Int Graphic Arts Soc, 72, Jewish Mus, 73 & Print Club, Philadelphia, 75; acrylic triptych, Guaranty Bank, Milwaukee, 79. *Exhib:* Ann Print Exhibs, Brooklyn Mus, 70 & 72; Art Today USA II, Mod Art Mus, Tehran, Iran, 77; one-person shows, Marion Locks Gallery, Philadelphia, 73 & 77, Dubins Gallery, Los Angeles, 78 & 80, Posner Gallery, Milwaukee, 79, 84 & 86; Benjamin Mangel Gallery, Philadelphia, 82 & 86; and others. *Awards:* Purchase Prizes, Pratt Miniature Show, Boston Printmakers Ann & Philadelphia Print Club. *Bibliog:* Gabor Peterdi (auth), Printmaking, MacMillan Publ Co, New York, 72; Ross & Romano (auths), Techniques in Printmaking, 74. *Mem:* Soc Am Graphic Artists; Boston Printmakers; Silvermine Guild Artists; Am Colorprint Soc; Print Club, Philadelphia. *Media:* Acrylic, Work in Handmade Paper. *Mailing Add:* 81-42 193rd St Jamaica NY 11423

YOUNG, ALAN
PAINTER
b Longbranch, NJ, Feb 11, 49. *Study:* Md Inst Col Art, BFA, 71. *Work:* Rockland Ctr Arts, Nyack, NY. *Exhib:* Acquisitions, Weatherspoon Gallery, NC, 78; Small Works, Arte Fiera Int Fair, Bologna, Italy, 78; Small Works, PS 1, Long Island City, NY, 79; Positive Show, ABC No Rio, New York, 81; New Drawing in America, Drawing Ctr, New York, 82; Synergy-Artist, Thorpe Intermedia Gallery, Sparkhill, NY, 82; Britain Salutes New York, Newcastle Polytech Art, Newcastle, Eng, 83; Artists Collection, Westbeth Gallery, New York, 84. *Awards:* Merit Award Dexter, Baltimore Mus Art, 72; New Drawing in Am Award, Artists Space, 81; NJ Coun Art Fel, 84. *Bibliog:* Marie Keller (auth), New Drawing in America, NY State Coun Arts, 82; Ellen Price (auth), New York, Newcastle Festival, 11/83; Vivien Raynor (auth), Synergy/Artist, New York Times. *Media:* Oil, Encaustic. *Mailing Add:* 301 W Broadway New York NY 10013

YOUNG, ANDREW
PAINTER
b Mt Kisco, NY, Nov 23, 62. *Study:* Univ Calif, Berkeley, BA, 87; Sch Art Inst Chicago, MFA, 89. *Work:* Arthur Anderson & Co, Detroit, Mich; Ill State Mus, Springfield; Jones, Day, Revas & Poge, Los Angeles; Proskauer, Rose, Goetz & Mendelsohn, New York; Prudential Insurance Co, Newark, NJ. *Comn:* Harbor (triptych), McKinsey & Co Inc, New York. *Exhib:* Solo Exhibs, Betsy Rosenfield Gallery, Chicago, 90 & 92, Chicago Int Art Expo, Ill, 90, David Beitzel Gallery, New York, 91 & 92, Dorothy Goldeen Gallery, Santa Monica, Calif, 91en Gallery, Santa Monica, Calif, 91; two-person exhib, Bilder uber dem Wasser (traveled), USIS, Bonn, Ger, 91-92; four-artists show, Haines Gallery, San Francisco, Calif, 92; Paper Houses, David Beitzel Gallery, NY, 92; Betsy Rosenfield Gallery, Chicago, Ill, 92; Art Fair/Seattle, Betsy Rosenfield Gallery, 92; and others. *Awards:* Maybelle M Toombs Prize, Univ Calif, Berkeley, 86-87; Competitive Scholar, 87-89 & Fred J Forster Fel, 90, Sch Art Inst Chicago; Community Arts Assistance Grant, Chicago Office Fine Arts, 91. *Bibliog:* Justin Spring (auth), Andrew Young, ArtForum, 11/91; Eileen Myles (auth), Andrew Young at David Beitzel, Art Am, 12/91; Amerikanische Kunstler in Koln, Deutsche Welle PBS/Europ J, 12/30/91. *Media:* Egg Tempera on Panel. *Dealer:* David Beitzel Gallery 104 Prince St New York NY 10012. *Mailing Add:* c/o Betsy Rosenfield Gallery 212 W Superior St Chicago IL 60610

YOUNG, BARBARA
PHOTOGRAPHER
b Chicago, Ill, Oct 27, 20. *Study:* Knox Col, Galesburg, Ill, AB, 42; Johns Hopkins Univ Med Sch, MD, 45; Baltimore Psychoanal Inst, grad, 55. *Work:* Mus Mod Art, New York; Baltimore Mus Art; Eastman House, Rochester, NY; Santa Barbara Mus Art, Calif; Yale Univ Gallery. *Exhib:* Photog in Fine Arts III Traveling Exhib, Minneapolis Mus, 61; Ancient Greek World, Walters Art Gallery, Baltimore, 70; one-woman shows, Butler Inst Am Art, Youngstown, Ohio, 74, Santa Barbara Mus Art, Calif, 78; 2nd Generation

Pioneers: Blance DeBra & Harvey Young, Baltimore Mus Art, 76 & Timberlane, A Sculpture Garden, 77; Am Vision, Nat Artists Alliance, NY Univ Galleries, 79; Maryland Artscape, 86; one person retrospective, The Passage of Time, Univ Md, Baltimore Co, 87. *Awards:* First Prize, Nat Artists Alliance, 79; First Prize, Md Mag, 12/82. *Mem:* Artists' Equity Asn. *Publ:* Auth, Our garden in the city, Horticulture, 70; Hunting for the ostrich, Hasselblad, Mag, 71; Getting acquainted with Maine, Am Forests Mag, 72; The Coleman's vegetable garden at Cape Rosier, Downeast Mag, 75. *Mailing Add:* 5307 Herring Run Dr Baltimore MD 21214

YOUNG, BARBARA NEIL
LIBRARIAN, CURATOR
b Bristol, Va, July 18, 43. *Study:* Fla State Univ, Tallahassee, BA, 65; Drexel Univ, Philadelphia, MLS, 75. *Collections Arranged:* Miami Thriving in Change 1940-1990/Fifty Years of Photography in Miami, 90; Miami Thriving in Change 1940-1990/Fifty Years of Collecting, 90; Flora and Fauna in Illustration, 91; Still Life a Visual Feast, 92; Miami/Clay/5, 92. *Pos:* Artmobile librn, Miami-Dade Pub Libr, Fla, 76-81, art & music reference librn, 81-85 & art serv coordr, 85- *Mem:* Art Librn Soc NAm; Am Libr Asn; Soc Fla Archs. *Res:* Afro-American, Hispanic and South Florida artists Library System, Fla Assoc Newslett, 77. *Mailing Add:* 7231 SW 61st St Miami FL 33143

YOUNG, CHARLES ALEXANDER
EDUCATOR, PAINTER
b New York, NY, Nov 17, 30. *Study:* Hampton Inst, BS; NY Univ, with Hale Woodruff, MA; Cath Univ Am. *Work:* Phelps Stokes Found, DC; Le Centre D'Art Haitien & Le Muséle d'art Haitien, Port au Prince, Haiti; Univ DC Art Collection; Fisk Univ, Nashville, TN; Hampton Mus, VA & VA Ctr Creative Arts, Sweet Briar, VA. *Exhib:* one-man show, Smith-Mason Gallery, 69 & Agra Gallery, Washington, DC, 72; Hampton Mus, VA 89; Raku Gallery, Art Barn, Washington, DC, 80; Ten & Ten & Ten Washington Painting, Corcoran Gallery, Washington, DC, 82; Martin Luther King Library, Washington, DC, 87; Freddie Mack, Reston, WA, 88; African Amer Contemp Art Mus, of Contem Art - Gibellina, Italy, 90; Mus Sci Indust, Chicago, Ill, 91; and others. *Teaching:* Instr art, Fayetteville State Univ, 60-63; asst prof art, Tenn A&I Univ, 63-68; chmn dept art, Univ DC, 68-84 & 91-, prof art, 68- *Awards:* First & Second Prizes, First Open Exhib, Fayetteville, 62; Phelps-Stokes Grant to travel in Africa, 75; Fel Virginia Ctr Creative Arts, 89. *Bibliog:* Theresa Cederholm (auth), Afro-American Artists, Trustees Boston Libr, 73; Samella Lewis (auth), Art: African American, Harcourt Brace Jovanovich, 78; Lynn M & James Igor (auths), 250 Years of Afro-American Art, 81; and others. *Mem:* Col Art Asn; Nat Art Educ Asn; Nat Conf Artists; Am Asn Univ Prof. *Media:* Oil, Acrylic, Watercolors. *Publ:* Auth, African odyssey, Haitain Art Newsletter, Vol 6, 78; Mainstream: A place for Afro-American artists, Metro-Washington Mag, 3/84. *Mailing Add:* 8104 W Beach Dr NW Washington DC 20012

YOUNG, EDNA E
ART DEALER, COLLECTOR
b Chicago, Ill, July 12, 36. *Pos:* Dir, Young Gallery, Los Gatos, Calif, 72-; bd dirs, San Jose Mus Art, 85-87. *Mem:* South Bay Art Asn. *Specialty:* Contemporary, all media including ceramics and sculpture. *Mailing Add:* 20375 Saratoga-Los Gatos Rd Saratoga CA 95070

YOUNG, JANIE CHESTER
MUSEUM DIRECTOR, EDUCATOR
b Port Huron, Mich, Apr 19, 49. *Study:* Univ Mich, BA(Eng lit & art hist), 71, MA(mus practice), 75; Toledo Mus Art, Nettie Poe Ketcham Fel Mus Educ, 72-73. *Collections Arranged:* Art, Ann Arbor, 71; Decorative Arts of New Brunswick, 76 & What's It To You? (auth, catalog for children), 77, Rutgers Univ Art Gallery; Patrick Thibert: Young Canadian Sculpture, 77, Young New York Painting, 79 & Helen Frankenthaler: The Artist in three Media, Saginaw Art Mus; The Queen's Choice: Burmese, 1885-1985, (auth, catalog) New Bedford Glass Mus. *Pos:* Fel coordr, Toledo Mus Art, Ohio, 73-75; cur educ, Rutgers Univ Art Gallery, 75-77; dir, Saginaw Art Mus, Mich, 77- & New Bedford Glass Mus, Mass, 82- *Teaching:* Instr mus arts & educ, Grad Sch Educ, Rutgers Univ, New Brunswick, NJ, 76; Paipoint Cup Plate Collector's Am, 85; Nat Early Am Glass Club, 86. *Mem:* Nat Early Am Glass Club, 82-; Glass Asn (G B), 88- *Res:* First interdisciplinary, professional bibliography of museum education; 19th century American and English art glass. *Publ:* Auth, An Annotated Bibliography of Museum Education, Univ Mich Mis Pract Prog, 75; Evolution of Burnage Glass, Bull, Nat Early Am Glass Club, spring 89. *Mailing Add:* 110 E Clinton St New Bedford MA 02740

YOUNG, JOHN T
SCULPTOR
b New York, NY, Apr 4, 54. *Study:* With Leonard DeLonga & S Hadley, Mass, 73-76; Amherst Col, BA, 76; RI Sch Design, MFA, 78. *Work:* Aspen Ctr Visual Arts, Colo; Univ NH, Durham; Wash State Arts, Grand Coulee Elem Sch; Alexander Grant & Co, New York; Mobil Oil Corp, New York; City Miami, Coconut Grove, Fla; New Mus, New York; Arvada Ctr Arts, Colo. *Comn:* Inter-Arts Marin, Calif, 87; Col Sch Mines, 89; The Rouse Co for downtown Portland, Ore, 90; Aquatic Ctr, Charlotte-Mecklenburg, NC, 91; Puc Bldg, Ore Arts Comn, 92. *Exhib:* Phoenix Art Mus, 79; Scottsdale Ctr Arts, Ariz, 79; Artists Representing Environmental Art, Wards Island, New York, 80-81; Denver Art Mus, 81; Arvada Ctr Arts, Colo, 81-82; solo exhib, O K Harris Gallery, New York, 82, 83, 85, 88 & 90; Tacoma Art Mus, Wash, 87; Davidson Gallery, Seattle, 88 & 90; and others. *Teaching:* Asst prof, Stockton State Co, Pomona, NJ, 82-84; full prof, Univ Wash, Seattle, 84- *Awards:* Purchase Award, Coconut Grove Art Asn, 87; Nat Endowment Humanities, 87; New Langton Artist Proj Grant, 91. *Bibliog:* Carol MacGuineas (auth), article, Cult Post, Nat Endowment Arts, 12/79; Brady Chapin (auth), John Young, Interview Mag/Andy Warhol, 11/80; Gwen Chanzit (auth), John T Young's sculpture, Artspace Mag, winter, 82; Cathleen McGuigan (auth), The Arts, Newsweek, 6/1/87; Michael Brenson (auth), NY Times, 12/16/88. *Dealer:* O K Harris 383 West Broadway New York NY 10012. *Mailing Add:* 7334 Ravenna Ave NE Seattle WA 98115

YOUNG, JOSEPH E
EDUCATOR, CRITIC
b Los Angeles, Calif, Sept 8, 39. *Study:* Univ Calif, Los Angeles, MA, 78. *Work:* Midwest Mus Am Art, Elkhart, Ind; Oakland Mus, Calif. *Exhib:* Painters Committed to Painting, Miriam Perlman Gallery, Flint, Mish, 80; Midwest Mus Am Art, 80; one-man show, Punk Art, Scottsdale Community Col, 81; Prints from the Ariz State Univ Print Research Fac, Phoenix Art Mus; Phoenix Postmodernists, John Douglas Cline Gallery, Phoenix, 82; 18th South Western Invitational, Yuma, Ariz, 84; Fagen-Peterson Fine Arts Gallery, Scottsdale, Ariz, 86-90. *Pos:* West Coast ed, USA, Art Int, 70-71; asst cur, prints & drawings, Los Angeles Co Mus Art, 65-78; art critic, Ariz Repub, 78-80, Phoenix Mag, 80-81 & Scottsdale Daily Progress, 83-91; ed, J Theory & Criticism Visual Arts, 80-86; dir, Harry Wood Art Gallery, 81- *Teaching:* Assoc prof art hist, Ariz State Univ, 79- *Mem:* Print Coun Am; Col Art Asn Am; Nat Print Asn (bd dir 80-82). *Res:* History of European and American drawings and prints; theory and criticism of art; history of American art. *Publ:* Auth, Jasper Johns: An Appraisal, Art Int, vol XIII no 4, 9/69; Deep & Surface Structures in art of Lorser Feitelson and Albrecht Durer, Theory & Criticism of the Visual Arts, 81; J Theory & Criticism Visual Arts, 81. *Mailing Add:* Dept of Art Ariz State Univ Tempe AZ 85287

YOUNG, JOSEPH LOUIS
SCULPTOR, MURALIST
b Pittsburgh, Pa, Nov 27, 19. *Study:* Westminster Col, AB, 41, Hon LLD, 60; Boston Mus Sch Fine Art, hon grad, 51; Carnegie Inst Technol; Mass Inst Technol; Cranbrook Acad Art; Art Students League; also with Karl Zerbe, David Aronson, Mitchell Siporin, Oskar Kockoshka & Gyorgy Kepes. *Comn:* West apse, Nat Shrine Immaculate Conception, Washington, DC, 67; History of Math (mosaic murals), Math Sci Bldg, Univ Calif, Los Angeles, 70; The Triforium (multi-media tower), Los Angeles Mall, 70-75; 30ft theme sculpture, City of La Mirada Civic Theatre, 78; stained glass windows, Temple Ahavat Shalom, Northridge, 83 & Temple Tifereth Israel, Los Angeles, 83. *Exhib:* Ten Year Retrospective, Art in Architecture, Palm Springs Desert Mus, 63; Int Exhib Muralists, Brussels, Belg, 65; VII Triennale, UNESCO, Varna, Bulgaria, 73; traveling retrospective, New York, Los Angeles, San Francisco, Chicago & Jerusalem, Israel, 86- *Pos:* Owner, Art in Architecture, 53-; dir, Mosaic Workshop, 55-; mem, Fine Arts Adv Bds, W Hollywood City Coun & Platt Art Gallery, Univ Judiasm, Los Angeles, 88- *Teaching:* Instr art hist, Tufts Col, Medford, Mass, 50; instr painting, Boston Mus Sch Fine Arts, 50; artist-in-residence, Brandeis Inst, 62-72; chmn dept archit arts, Santa Barbara Art Inst, 70-75. *Awards:* Am Acad Rome, Italy, 51; Huntington Hartford Found Fel, 52; Nat competition to create Los Angeles Holocaust Monument, Pan-Pacific Park, 85-91; and others. *Mem:* Fel Int Inst Arts & Lett; Nat Sculpture Ctr, Lawrence, Kans; Nat Soc Mural Painters; Artists Equity Asn. *Media:* Multi-Media. *Publ:* Auth, The World of Mosaic (film), Univ Calif, Los Angeles, 57; Arts & crafts in architecture, Creative Crafts, Vol 2, No 1; Mosaics: Principles & Practice, Reinhold, 63; Dialogues in Art, KNBC-TV Series, 67. *Mailing Add:* Art in Architecture 7919-1/2 W Norton Ave Los Angeles CA 90046

YOUNG, KENNETH VICTOR
PAINTER, DESIGNER
b Louisville, Ky, Dec 12, 33. *Study:* Ind Univ; Univ Louisville, BS. *Work:* Corcoran Gallery Art, Washington, DC; Va Nat Bank, Alexandria; Johnson Publ Co, Chicago; Am Tel & Tel, New York; Fisk Univ, Nashville; Univ of Louisville, KY; Univ District of Columbia, Washington. *Exhib:* Inst Contemp Arts, Washington, DC, 67; Baltimore Mus, 69; Ill Bell Co, Chicago, 71; Indianapolis Mus, 72; Corcoran Gallery Art, 74; Black Artist from the South, Huntsville Mus, Ala, 79; one-man shows, Gallery K, DC, 78 & 79, C Grimaldis Gallery, Baltimore, 80, Univ of Louisville, Ky, 85 & Howard Univ, Washington, DC, 86. *Collections Arranged:* Music Machines, Hall of Graphic Arts, Women & Politics, Gandhi Centennial Exhib, Explorers NZ, Black Wings traveling exhib & Egyptian Antiquities. *Pos:* Designer, Smithsonian Inst, 64-; Washington artist, Health, Educ & Welfare Dept, DC, 79; acad specialist, Egyptian Mus, Cairo, currently. *Teaching:* Instr painting, Louisville Pub Sch, 62-63; instr design & painting, Corcoran Sch Art, 70- *Bibliog:* B Rose (auth), Black artist in America, Art in Am, 70. *Media:* Watercolor, Acrylic. *Dealer:* Gallery K 232 P St NW Washington DC 20001. *Mailing Add:* 1930 Columbia Rd NW No 303 Washington DC 20009

YOUNG, MAHONRI S
WRITER
b New York, NY, July 23, 11. *Study:* Dartmouth Col, AB; NY Univ, MA. *Collections Arranged:* Howald, Brit Art & Boudin, Irish Art. *Pos:* Actg dir, Munson-Williams-Proctor Inst, 51-53; dir, Columbus Gallery Fine Arts, 53-76; Am corresp, Apollo Mag, 66-90. *Teaching:* Instr hist art, Sarah Lawrence Col, 41-50. *Publ:* Auth, The Paintings of George Bellows, 73; The Eight: The Realist Revolt in American Painting, 73; Early American Moderns: Painters of the Stieglitz Group, 74; American Realists: Homer to Hopper, 77; The Golden Eye, 83; and others. *Mailing Add:* Kellis Pond Ln Water Mill NY 11976

YOUNG, MARJORIE WARD
PAINTER, DRAFTSMAN
b Chicago, Ill, June 25, 10. *Study:* Art Inst Chicago, 25-35; with Jossey Bilan, 58-62, Edgar A Whitney, 69, 71 & 75, Richmond Yip, 70, J Dougles Greenbowe & Milford Zornes, 72, Robert Wood, 77 & 81, Charles Reid, 80 & Frank Webb, 84. *Work:* Ariz Bank, First Nat Bank Ariz & Valley Nat Bank, Phoenix; Thunderbird Bank; Glendale Community Col, Ariz. *Exhib:* Ariz Watercolor Asn Show In Taiwan, 74; Watercolor SW One, Albuquerque, 76; Watercolor SW Two, Tucson, 76; Watercolor SW Four, San Antonio; 110th Ann Am Watercolor Soc, New York, 77; Watercolors '78, O'Briens Art Emporium, Scottsdale; Glendale Community Col, 85; 77th Ann Catherine Lorillard Wolfe exhib. *Pos:* Background artist, Fleischer, Famous & Paramount Studios, Miami, Fla, 38-42; gallery dir, Phoenix YWCA, 70-79. *Teaching:* Instr drawing & watercolor, Phoenix Art Mus, 70-72, 77 & 79; Conservator Old Animated Cartoon Cels, 85-92. *Awards:* Second Watercolor, Low Ruins Spring Nat, Tubac, Ariz, 65; First Watercolor & Best Show Pencil Sketch, Nat League Am Pen Women, 75. *Mem:* Ariz Artists Guild (pres, 61-62); Life member, Ariz Watercolor Asn (pres, 68-83); Nat League Am Pen Women (br art chmn, 72); Phoenix Art Mus Fine Arts Asn; hon mem Contemp Watercolorists Ariz. *Media:* Watercolor; Felt Tip Pen. *Publ:* Illusr, Many Lives of the Lynx, 64, Functional Spanish, 68 & Simply Messin, 82; illusr, Functional Spanish, 68, Homestead on the San Juan, 87. *Mailing Add:* 320 W Montecito Phoenix AZ 85013

YOUNG, NANCY J(EANNE)
SCULPTOR
b Evergreen Park, Ill, Nov 7, 39. *Study:* Univ Ill, 58-59; Univ Ariz, BS, 61; Bishop Mus, Honolulu, 71-73; Sun Valley Ctr Arts. *Work:* Univ NMex, Albuquerque; Sun Valley Ctr Arts, Idaho; Univ Ariz, Tucson; One Percent for the Arts Project, Alaska Coun Arts & State of NMex. *Comn:* Stained glass window, Trinity Church, West Point, Nebr, 83; porcelain enamel on steel mural, Albuquerque Technical-Vocational Inst, 86; cast paper sculpture, Burlington Northern, 88; cast paper sculpture, Eastern NMex Univ, Clovis, 90. *Exhib:* Rockford Int Print Biennale, Ill, 83; solo exhibs, Univ Ariz, Tucson, 84 & 90, Grand Canyon Nat Park, 86, Univ NMex, Albuquerque, 90-91 & Eastern NMex Univ, 90. *Awards:* In over 40 regional, national & international juried exhibs. *Bibliog:* Nancy Gillespie (auth), The Cast Paper Sculptures of Nancy Young, Southwest Profile, 3/87; Alex Thorleifson (auth), The Paper Chase, Southwest Art, 6/89; Linda Shockley (auth), Ancient Images, Focus Santa Fe, 6/91. *Mem:* Artists Equity Asn; Albuquerque United Artists; Albuquerque Arts Alliance. *Media:* Handmade Paper; Miscellaneous Media. *Publ:* Illusr cover, Tortuga, Justa Publ, 79. *Mailing Add:* 11416 Brussels Ave NE Albuquerque NM 87111

YOUNG, PETER FORD
PAINTER
b Pittsburgh, Pa, Jan 2, 40. *Study:* Chouinard Art Inst, Los Angeles, 57-58; Pomona Col, 58-60; Art Students League, New York, 60-61; New York Univ, BA(art hist), 63. *Work:* Albright-Knox Mus, Buffalo, NY; Guggenheim Mus & Mus Mod Art, New York; Aldrich Mus. *Comn:* Graphic, Lincoln Ctr, Newport Jazz Festival, 72. *Exhib:* Ann Exhib of Contemp Am Painting, Whitney Mus, New York, 67-68; 31st Biennial--Contemp Painting, Corcoran Gallery, Washington, DC, 69; Nine Young Artists, Theodoran Awards, Guggenheim Mus, 69 & Ann Exhib of Contemp Painting, Whitney Mus, New York, 70; Six Painters, Albright-Knox Mus, Buffalo, 71; Eight Artists, Art Mus of South Tex, Corpus Christi, 74; Eight Artists, Miami Mus of Art, Fla, 74; El Color Como Lenguaje, Exhib of Mus of Mod Art, New York Int Prog, 75-76; Leo Castelli Gallery, New York, 80. *Teaching:* Vis artist, Oberlin Col, Ohio, 70 & Pima Col, Tucson, Ariz, 76. *Bibliog:* Barbara Rose (auth), Gallery without walls, Art in Am, 3/68; Ellen Johnson (auth), A chronology of the work, Artforum, 4/71; Elizabeth Baker (auth), Peter Young and David Diao, Art News, 9/71. *Media:* Acrylic. *Dealer:* Oil & Steel Gallery 157 Chambers St New York NY. *Mailing Add:* PO Box 715 Bisbee AZ 85603-0715

YOUNG, ROBERT G
PAINTER, PRINTMAKER
b Utica, NY, Jan 23, 29. *Study:* Albright Art Sch & NY State Univ, BS, 51; Fla Sch Arts, AS, 80; Atlantic Ctr Arts, with Philip Pearlstein, 86. *Work:* Fla State Gallery, Tallahasse; Lithonia Corp Am, Atlanta, Ga; Thomas Goodyear Collection, Springfield Center, NY; Henry Teichman Collection, Chicago, Ill; Prof Hotta Seiji Collection, Tokyo, Japan. *Exhib:* Albright-Knox Art Gallery, Buffalo, NY, 51; one-person shows, Fla Art Sch Gallery, Palatka, Casments Art Gallery, Ormand Beach, 81, Int Sanibel Symposium, Palm Coast, 83 & Alexander Brest Gallery, Jacksonville, 87 & Randolph AFB, San Antonia, Tex, 88; Soc Four Arts, Palm Beach, Fla, 82; US Int Art Competition, Fla State Gallery, Tallahassee, 84; Longboat Key Gallery, Fla, 85; Cornell Fine Arts Mus, Winter Park, Fla, 87. *Pos:* Judgement prof, Shin-Kai-Ju-Sha Art Guild, Japan, 61. *Teaching:* Art, Richfield Springs Cent Sch, 51-52; instr art & mechanical drawing, Overseas Exten, Ohio State Univ, 58-59. *Awards:* First Place Oils, San Antonio Art Mus, 59; Special Award Excellence, Emperors Art Show, Japanese Art Guild, 60; First Place Watercolor, St Augustine Art Mus, Fla, 83. *Bibliog:* M Alexander (ed), Robert G Young, Art Visions Inc, 82. *Mem:* Fla Artists Group Inc. *Media:* Oils, Water Media; Woodcut. *Dealer:* Faith-Holman Gallery Ft Walton Beach FL 32548. *Mailing Add:* 315 Ruckel Dr Niceville FL 32578-1752

YOUNG, ROBERT JOHN
PAINTER
b Vancouver, BC, Aug 8, 38. *Study:* Univ BC, BA(art hist); City & Guilds London Sch Art, Eng; Vancouver Sch Art, dipl(graphics). *Work:* Can Coun Art Bank, Ottawa; Govt BC Prov Collection; deBeers Consolidated Mines; Art Gallery Ont; Montreal Mus Fine Arts; and others. *Comn:* Christmas card Clothworkers Guild, London, 63; portrait, comn by Paul William White, London, 73; portrait, comn by Donna MacDonald, London, 76. *Exhib:* One-man shows, Redfern Gallery, London, 71, 73, 75, 79 & 82 & Vancouver Art Gallery, 74; Realismus und Realitat, Darmstadt, WGer, 75; Time Mag, Can Canvas, Across Can, 75-76; Can Cult Ctr, Embassy, Paris, 76; Vancouver Art Gallery, BC, 76-77; Marlborough-Godard, Toronto & Montreal, 76-77, 80 & 82; 10-Year Retrospective, Charles M Scott Gallery, Vancouver, 84; Vancouver Art Gallery, 88. *Teaching:* Instr painting, Banff Sch Fine Arts, Alta, 75 & 81; vis artist, Royal Col Art, London, 76, Vancouver Sch Art, 77 & 81 & Alta Col Art, 78; assoc prof, Univ BC, 82- *Bibliog:* Doris Shadbolt (auth), Robert Young, The Implacable Image, Vanguard, Vancouver Art Gallery, 77; Fenella Crichton (auth), A juggler of styles, Art & Artists, 4/79. *Media:* Oil; Intaglio Printmaking. *Dealer:* Atelier Gallery Vancouver; Redfern Gallery 20 Cork St London ON Can. *Mailing Add:* 3940 Quebec St Vancouver BC V5V 3K8 Canada

YOUNG, ROBERT S W
SCULPTOR
b Honolulu, Hawaii, Nov 24, 48. *Study:* Univ Hawaii, BFA, 76, MFA, 80. *Work:* Honolulu Acad Art; Contemp Arts Ctr, Honolulu; Hawaii State Found Culture & Arts. *Exhib:* Artist of Hawaii, 77-80 & 82 & Art Flora, 84, Honolulu Acad Art; Clay-Form, Function & Fantasy, Long Beach Gallery, 79; We're Talking About 3 Artists, 81 & Sculpture Syntaxis: Best Shot, 84, Contemp Arts Ctr; 30th Ann Drawing & Sculpture Exhib, Ball State Univ, Muncie, Ind, 84. *Pos:* Chmn, Raku Ho'olaulea, Hawaii Craftmen, Honolulu, 80-82. *Teaching:* Instr pottery, Hickam Air Force Base, Honolulu, 76-82; instr ceramics, Univ Hawaii, Honolulu, 80-81. *Awards:* College Art Award, Col Art Comt, 79 & 80; Crafts Excellence Award, Hawaii Craftsmen, 81; First Place Sculpture, Art Flora '84, Honolulu Garden Club, 84. *Mem:* Hawaii Artist League. *Media:* Clay. *Mailing Add:* 1056 Brandon Ave Norfolk VA 23507

YOUNG, TOM (WILLIAM THOMAS)
PAINTER, PHOTOGRAPHER
b Huntington, WVa, Oct 7, 24. *Study:* John Herron Art Inst; Cincinnati Art Acad; Univ Ala, BFA & MA(fine arts); Ohio State Univ; Chouinard Art Inst; Univ Southern Calif; Columbia Univ, EdD; also with Hans Hofmann, New York. *Work:* The Mus of Mod Art; Univ Southern Ill; The Victoria & Albert Mus; The New Orleans Mus Art; Pan American Life Insurance Bldg, New Orleans. *Comn:* Mural, US Air Base, Altus, Okla, 43. *Exhib:* After Twenty Years, Birmingham Mus Art, 71; Ft Wayne Ind Art Mus, 84; Independent Curators 10th Anniversary Exhibition, Puck Bldg, New York, 85; solo exhib, Malton Gallery, Cincinnati, Ohio, 86-88; Still-Zinsell Gallery, New Orleans, 88; Mus Folkwang Essen, Ger, 92; and others. *Pos:* Illusr exp aircraft, Douglas Aircraft Corp, Los Angeles, 52-53; art dir, Good Health Mag, New York, 53-57; cover designer, Electronic Design Mag, New York, 55-56; design & color consult, Royal Metal Mfg Co, 56-57; color consult, New Orleans Dock Bd, 71-72. *Teaching:* Prof fine arts & chmn dept, Wagner Col, 53-69; head prof art, Auburn Univ, 69-70; prof fine arts & mem grad fac, Univ New Orleans, 70-, chmn dept, 70-78, prof emer, 92. *Awards:* Weissglass Award, State Island Mus, 55; Hon Mention, New York City Ctr Gallery, 56; Winner, Nat Exhib, Contemp Arts Ctr, New Orleans, 82. *Mem:* New Orleans Mus Art (bd trustees, 73-); Col Art Asn Am. *Media:* Acrylic; Color Film. *Mailing Add:* 5605 W Esplanade Ave Univ of New Orleans Metairie LA 70003

YOUNGBLOOD, JUDY
PRINTMAKER
b El Paso, Tex. *Study:* Univ Wis, Madison, BS, 71, MFA, 74; Hayter's Atelier 17, Paris, Fulbright Scholar, 79. *Work:* DeCordova Mus, Boston; Boston Mus Fine Arts, Mass; Ark Art Ctr, Little Rock; Mus Fine Arts, Houston, Tex; Mus Mod Art, Ft Worth, Tex; Elvejhem Mus Art, Madison, Wis. *Comn:* Presentation print, Madison Print Club, 83; Centennial Print, Univ N Tex, 90. *Exhib:* Int Print Exhib, Repub of China, Taiwan, 83, 85 & 89; Mini Print Int, Galeria Taller Fort, 88, 90 & 92; William Campbell Fine Art, Ft Worth, Tex, 90-92; Edith Baker Gallery, Dallas, Tex, 90-92; Printmaking in Texas: The 1980's, Mod Art Mus Ft Worth, 91; and others. *Pos:* Fel residency, MacDowell Colony, Peterborough, NH, 82 & 85. *Teaching:* Prof printmaking, Univ N Tex, 76- *Awards:* Artistic Achievement Award, Okla State Univ, 82; Award, 22nd Bradley Nat Print & Drawing Exhib, 89; Award, 42nd North Am Print Exhib, 90; Award, Am Miniature Printmakers Exhib, 88. *Bibliog:* Andrew Stasik (auth), Toward a broader view, 81 & Betti & Sale (auths), Print Rev, 81, Drawing: A contemporary approach, 91; Scott Gordon (auth), Judy Youngblood: New Work, New Art Examiner, 11/81; 40 Texas Printmakers, Mod Art Mus Ft Worth. *Mem:* Philadelphia Print Club; Women's Caucus Art; Southern Graphics Coun. *Media:* Miscellaneous Media. *Mailing Add:* Art Dept Univ N Tex Denton TX 76203

YOUNGBLOOD, NAT
PAINTER, ILLUSTRATOR
b Evansville, Ind, Dec 28, 16. *Study:* Univ NMex, Albuquerque, with Millard Sheets; Am Acad Art, Chicago; also with Barse Miller, Raymond Joahnson, Ralph Douglass & Howard Mosby. *Work:* Indiana Univ Pa; Calif State Col, Pa; Rockwell Int Col, Ft Pitt Mus, Pa. *Comn:* Oil portraits (indust leaders), for Pittsburgh Press, Pa, 56; portrait President Kennedy, Metro News Service, 61; ten hist paintings, Ft Pitt Mus, Pittsburgh, Pa; oil paintings (pioneer life), Pittsburgh, Pa; numerous works in pvt collections. *Exhib:* Carnegie Inst Art for Indust, 54; Artist of the Year, Pittsburgh Ctr Arts, 76; Artists of America, Denver, Colo, 86, 87, 88, 89, 90 & 92; American Painters in Paris, 76; one-man shows, Atheneum, New Harmony, Ind, 84 & Main Trail Galleries, Scottsdale, Ariz, 85; Four-man show, Dewey Galleries, Santa Fe, NMex, 85;

Pioneer Mus, Colo Springs, Colo, 85 & 86; one-man show, Dewey Galleries, Santa Fe, NMex, 91. *Pos:* Art dir, cartoonist, illusr & painter, Pittsburgh Press, 46-79. *Teaching:* Instr painting & design, LaRoche Col & Art Inst Pittsburgh, 74. *Awards:* First Place, Carnegie Inst Art for Indust, 54; First Place, Pennational Exhib, 66; First Prize Alcoa Award, Aqueous Open, 86. *Bibliog:* Roberta McIntyre (auth), Nat Youngblood: Master Watercolorist of Southwestern Subjects, Western Art Digest, fall 85; Nancy Ellis (auth), Nat Youngblood, Focus, Santa Fe, NMex, 1-2/89; Rita Simmons (auth), Nat Youngblood, Southwest Art, 8/90. *Mem:* Pittsburgh Experiment; Fortnightly Washington Jefferson Univ. *Media:* Watercolor, Oil. *Interests:* Research for and execution of major watercolor and oil paintings of American Indians; Western landscapes. *Publ:* Ed, 101st Airborne Division Picture History, 45; auth, Watercolor page, Am Artist Mag, 59; Western Art Digest, 85. *Dealer:* Dewey Galleries Ltd 74 E San Francisco St Santa Fe NM 87501. *Mailing Add:* PO Box 73 7045 third Ave West Middleton PA 15379

YOUNGER, DAN FORREST
PAINTER, PRINTMAKER
b Denver, Colo, Sept 14, 54. *Study:* Kansas City Art Inst, BFA, 76. *Work:* Am Express, Salt Lake City; Nat Mus, Brazil; Continental Insurance Co, New York; AT&T, Kansas City, Mo; Dean Witter Reynolds, Kansas City; and others. *Comn:* Mural, Dixons Inc, Independence, Mo, 78. *Exhib:* Atkins Mus Fine Arts, Kansas City, Mo, 76-81; Univ Dallas, Irving, 77; Sheldon Mus, Lincoln, Nebr, 81; Univ Mo, Kansas City, 81; and others. *Pos:* Originator & dir, Squadron Press Fine Art Printing, 79-84. *Teaching:* Print technician, Kansas City Art Inst, Mo, 76-83. *Awards:* Best Show, Dixie Ann, Montgomery Mus, Ala, 78; Purchase Prize, Mid Four Ann, 79 & 81; 2nd Place, William Rockhill Nelson Gallery Art, 80. *Bibliog:* Elizabeth Kirsch (auth), Squadron Press, Kansas City, 2/80; Vicki Melcher (auth), Kansas City, Art News, 10/80; Barbara Westerfield (auth), Dan Younger, New Art Examiner Vol 13 No 3, 11/85. *Mem:* Print Soc Kansas City; Friends Art, Kans City. *Mailing Add:* 5911 McGee Kansas City MO 64113

YOUNGER, ROBERT M
SCULPTOR
b Philadelphia, Pa, 47. *Study:* Philadelphia Col Art, BFA, 69; Fulbright-Hayes Grant, Italy, 69-70; Yale Univ Grad Sch Fine Arts, 71-72. *Exhib:* Solo shows, Queens Mus, NY, 86, Salon DeFacto, New York, 88, Craig Cornelius Gallery, New York, 89, Drexel Univ, Philadelphia, 90 & Flamingo E, New York, 91; Craig Cornelius Gallery, New York, 88; Louise Ross Gallery, New York, 89; Jersey City Mus, NJ, 91; and others. *Awards:* Nat Endowment Arts Grant, 82 & 90; NY State Coun Arts Sponsored Proj Award, 86. *Mailing Add:* 274 Water St New York NY 10038

YOUNGERMAN, JACK
PAINTER, SCULPTOR
b St Louis, MO, Mar 25, 26. *Study:* Univ NC, Chapel Hill, 44-46; Univ Mo, Columbia, BA, 47; Sch Fine Arts, Paris, 47-48. *Work:* Whitney Mus Am Art, Mus Mod Art & Solomon R Guggenheim Mus, New York; Hirshhorn Mus & Sculpture Garden, Washington, DC; Art Inst Chicago; Nat Mus Am Art, Smithsonian Inst, Washington, DC; Vassar Col, Poughkeepsie, NY; Yale Univ Art Gallery, New Haven, Conn; Carnegie Inst, Mus Art, Pittsburgh, Pa; Meade Art Mus, Amherst Col, Mass. *Comn:* First Pa Bank, Philadelphia, 69; painted wall reliefs, First Wis Bank, Milwaukee, 71; The Ohio (fiberglass), Pittsburgh, 77; Dryad (wood & resin), Neiman-Marcus, Chicago, 83. *Exhib:* Solo exhibs, Truman Gallery, New York, 78, Washburn Gallery, New York, 81, 82, 84, 85, 86 & 87, NY Inst Techol, Old Westbury, NY, 81, Fine Arts Ctr, State Univ NY, Stony Brook, 82, Heath Gallery, Atlanta, Ga, 84, Guggenheim Mus, New York, 86 & Heland Wetterling Gallery, Stockholm, 89; Vital Signs: Organic Abstraction from the Permanent Collection, Whitney Mus Am Art, New York, 88; Contemporary Screens, Am Fedn Arts (traveling exhib), 88; Twentieth Century American Art, U S Embassy, Moscow, 88; Grafikai Gyugtemeny, Szepmuveszet; Muzem, Budapest, Hungary, 88; Fifty Years of Collecting, Guggenheim Mus, New York, 88; Viewpoints: Postwar Painting and Sculpture, Guggenheim Mus, New York, 88; Twentieth Century Art, Nat Gallery Art, Washington, DC, 89; The Gestural Impulse 1945-1960, Whitney Mus, New York, 89; ARCO, Feria Internacional de Arte Contemporaneo, Madrid, Spain, 91. *Teaching:* Instr, Yale Univ, 74-75; instr, Hunter Col, 81-82; instr, Sch Visual Arts, New York, 78- *Awards:* Nat Endowment Arts Award, 72 & 84; Fel, Guggenheim Found, 76; US/Japan Exchange fel, 87; Nat Acad Design, 92. *Bibliog:* Barbara Delatiner (auth), The spotlight shines on drawings, NY Times, 9/11/88; Steve Thomas (auth), Sculptor leaves his mark on art, Messenger-Inquirer, 12/24/88; Adam McGovern (auth), Jack Youngerman, Washburn Gallery, Cover Mag, 5/91. *Dealer:* Washburn Gallery 20 W 57th St New York NY 10022. *Mailing Add:* 130 W Third St New York NY 10012

YOUNGLOVE, RUTH ANN (MRS BENJAMIN RHEES LOXLEY)
PAINTER
b Chicago, Ill, Feb 14, 09. *Study:* Univ Calif, Los Angeles, BE; also with Orrin A White & Marion K Wachtel. *Work:* Bank of Am, Pasadena, Calif; El Tovar Hotel, Grand Canyon, Ariz. *Exhib:* Laguna Beach Art Asn Gallery, 71; one-woman shows, Flintridge Prep Sch, La Can, 72, Community Serv Ctr, Pasadena, 72-75, Altadena Pub Libr, Calif, 75 & Pasadena Soc of Artists Sales Gallery, 76-77; La Canada Pub Libr, 85; Altadena Pub Libr, 85 & 89; and others. *Awards:* Second Prize for Landscape, Artists League Seal Beach, 68; Fourth Prize in Painting, Pasadena Presby Church Exhib; Honorable Mention, Pasadena Soc Artists, 90. *Mem:* Pasadena Soc Artists; life mem Laguna Beach Art Asn; Nat Watercolor Soc; assoc Am Watercolor Soc. *Media:* Watercolor, Linoleum Block Print. *Mailing Add:* 1180 Yocum St Pasadena CA 91103-1943

YOUNGQUIST, JACK
DRAFTSMAN
b Crookston, Minn, Sept 19, 18. *Study:* Univ Minn, BA; Minn Sch Art; Univ Iowa, MFA; Art Students League; Slade Sch, Univ London; Inst Allende, San Miguel Allende, Mex; NY Univ. *Work:* Minn Inst Art, Minneapolis; Minn Mus Art, St Paul; NDak State Univ, Fargo; US Federal Reserve Bank, Minneapolis; Univ Iowa, Iowa City. *Exhib:* Minneapolis Art Inst Biennial; Drawings Invitational, Minneapolis Art Inst, Minn, 81; retrospective, Plains Art Mus, Moorhead, Minn, 83; Univ Wis-River Falls, 85; Drawing Invitational, Nash Gallery, Univ Minn, 87; and others. *Pos:* Bd dirs, Red River Art Ctr, Moorhead, 66-68; adv panel, Minn State Arts Coun, 79-80. *Teaching:* Instr calligraphy, Minn Sch Art, 54-59; instr, Univ Minn Exten, 57-58; prof drawing, Moorhead State Univ, 61-82, prof emer, 82. *Awards:* Purchase Award, Drawings USA, St Paul, 71; Merit Award, Minn State Art Exhib, 74; Bronze Medal, 16th Midwest Artists, Moorhead, Minn, 75; First Place, Drawings, Minn State Art Exhib, 89. *Bibliog:* Jack Youngquist Retrospective 1946-83 (catalog), Plains Art Mus, Moorhead, Minn. *Mem:* Minn Artists Asn. *Media:* Pencil, Pen & Ink. *Dealer:* Rourke Art Gallery 523 S Fourth St Moorhead MN 56560; Groveland Gallery 25 Groveland Terr Minneapolis MN 55403. *Mailing Add:* c/o Walker Residence 3737 Bryans Ave S Rm 310 Minneapolis MN 55409

YOUNG SCOTT, FRANCES
LIBRARIAN
b Point Pleasant, NJ, June 5, 54. *Study:* Douglass Col, BA, 76; Rutgers Univ, MLS, 78; Hunter Col, MA, 86. *Pos:* Asst art librn, Rutgers Univ, New Brunswick, NJ, 76-78; sr art librn, Newark Pub Libr, NJ, 78-81; reference librn, Frick Art Reference Libr, New York, 81-84 & Schenectady Co Community Coll, NY, 85- *Teaching:* Instr, Sotheby's Am Arts Course, New York, 86-87; adj fac art hist, Jr Col Albany, NY, 87; freelance lestr, art hist, 91- *Mem:* Art Libr Soc North Am; Art Libr Soc NJ (treas, 80-81); Art Libr Soc NY; Asn Col & Res Librs, Eastern NY; Int Libr Sci Honor Soc. *Publ:* Auth, Review of contemporary art magazines, Serials Rev, 5/2/79. *Mailing Add:* 310 Elm St Schenectady NY 12304-1208

YOURITZIN, VICTOR KOSHKIN
HISTORIAN, EDUCATOR
b New York, NY, Dec 20, 42. *Study:* Williams Col, BA(cum laude), 64; Sch of Archit, Columbia Univ, 64-65; Inst Fine Arts, NY Univ, MA, 67; Cert Mus Training, Inst of Fine Arts & Metrop Mus Art, New York, 69. *Collections Arranged:* The Poetry of the Body: Paintings by Paul Peck (ed, catalog), Vanderbilt Univ, 69, Tulane Univ, 70 & Dallas Health & Sci Mus, 74-78; Oklahoma Treasures (auth, catalog), Okla Art Ctr and Gilcrease Mus, 86; Five Contemp Russian Artists (auth, catalog), Mabee-Gerrer Mus, 92. *Pos:* Mem bd trustees, Okla Mus Art, Oklahoma City, 78-84; regional corresp, Art Voices-South, 78-79, contrib ed, 79-82; mem exhibs & collections comt, Philbrook Art Ctr, Tulsa, Okla, 83-85; mem exhib comt, Oklahoma Art Ctr, 84-87; panelist, Nat Endowment Humanities, 84; panelist, Prog for Art on Film, Getty Trust, Metrop Mus of Art, 87; co-cur, Am Watercolors, Metrop Mus Art, 91-92. *Teaching:* Instr art hist, Vanderbilt Univ, Nashville, Tenn, 68-69 & Newcomb Col, Tulane Univ, New Orleans, 69-72; asst prof art hist, Univ Okla, Norman, 72-80, assoc prof, 80- *Awards:* Ford Found Fel, Dept of Am Painting & Sculpture, Metrop Mus of Art, New York, 67-68. *Res:* Nineteenth and twentieth century art; museology. *Publ:* Auth, Tchelitchew's Hide & Seek, Art J, winter 64-65; The Irony of Degas, Gazette des Beaux-Arts, 1/76; Oklahoma City: Getting rid of Bambi, Artnews, 9/78; Thomas Hart Benton: Bathers rediscovered, Arts Mag, 5/80; coauth, Am Watercolors from the Metrop Mus of Art, Abrams, 91; and others. *Mailing Add:* 1721 Oakwood Dr Norman OK 73069

YUST, DAVID E
PAINTER, EDUCATOR
b Wichita, Kans, Apr 3, 39. *Study:* Birger Sandzen; Wichita State Univ; Kans State Univ; Univ Kans, BFA, 63; Univ Ore, MFA, 69. *Work:* Denver Art Mus; Wichita Art Mus, Kans; Indianapolis Mus Art; Rockford Art Mus, Ill; Minnesota Mus Art, St Paul; Butler Inst Art, Youngstown, Ohio. *Exhib:* One-man shows, Denver Art Mus, 76 & Joseph Magnin Gallery, Denver, 77; Wichita Art Mus, Kans, 73 & 79; Plains Art Mus, Moorehead, Minn, 85; Colorado Springs Fine Art Ctr, 85 & 86; Wyoming Art Mus, Laramie, 87; Boulder Ctr Visual Arts, Colo, 88; St Paul Gallery, 89, 92, Rourke Art Gallery, Moorhead, Minn, 92. *Teaching:* Prof painting & drawing, Colo State Univ, 65- *Awards:* Purchase Awards, 11th Biennial, Kans State Univ, 70, Colo State Univ, 70, Okla Art Ctr, 73, Rourke Gallery, Moorhead, Minn, 89, Binney and Smith, Easton, Pa, 90. *Bibliog:* Charles Parson (videotape), 90. *Media:* Acrylic; Oil Lithography. *Dealer:* Inkfish Gallery Paul & Nancy Hughes Dirs 949 Broadway Denver CO 80203. *Mailing Add:* Art Dept Colo St Univ Fort Collins Denver CO 80523

Z

Z'
PAINTER
b Binghamton, NY, May 20, 41. *Study:* Studied with George Daniel Hoffman & James McKeon, 60's; Holy Cross Co, BS(economics), 63; advanced studies, Assumption Col, Toledo Univ & Richland Col. *Work:* Toledo Mus Art, Ohio; Butler Mus Art, Inst Am Art, Youngstown, Ohio. *Comn:* Temple (emulation), Masons, Gowanda, NY, 65; Jerusalem, Blessed Sacrament Parish, Dallas,

Tex, 92. *Exhib:* Winter Celebrations, Toledo Mus Art, Ohio, 78; Nat Ann, Butler Inst Am Art, Youngstown, Ohio, 80. *Mem:* Am Soc Portrait Artists; Dallas Coalition Arts; Plano Arts Asn. *Media:* Portraitist, Oil. *Mailing Add:* c/o Z Atelier Inc 2057 Hawken Dr Plano TX 75023-1710

ZABARSKY, MELVIN JOEL
PAINTER, EDUCATOR
b Worcester, Mass, Aug 21, 32. *Study:* Sch Worcester Art Mus; Ruskin Sch Drawing & Fine Arts, Univ Oxford; Sch Fine & Appl Arts, Boston Univ, BFA; Univ Cincinnati, MFA. *Work:* Mus Mod Art, New York; De Cordova Mus, Lincoln, Mass; Addison Gallery Am Art, Andover, Mass; Wiggins Collection, Boston Pub Libr; Currier Gallery Art, Manchester, NH. *Exhib:* One-man exhibs, Boris Mirski Gallery, Boston, 62, Tragos Gallery, Boston, 66, De Cordova Mus, 70, Circulo Bellas Artes, 82 & Salones Berkowitoch, 83, Madrid; Surreal Images, De Cordova Mus, 68; New Eng Painters Traveling Exhib, Ringling Mus, Sarasota, Fla, 69. *Teaching:* Instr painting, Swain Sch Design, New Bedford, Mass, 60-64; asst prof painting, Wheaton Col, 64-69; prof painting, Univ NH, 69- *Awards:* Painting Prize, Boston Arts Festival, 62; Ford Found Grant in humanities, 68. *Bibliog:* B Schwartz (auth), Humanism in 20th Century Art, Praeger, 73. *Media:* Oil. *Mailing Add:* Dept of Art Univ NH Durham NH 03824

ZABOROWSKI, DENNIS J
PAINTER, EDUCATOR
b Cleveland, Ohio, Jan 31, 43. *Study:* Cleveland Inst Art, cert, 61-65; Yale Univ, BFA, 65 & MFA, 68 with Jack Tworkov & Bernard Chaet. *Work:* Mint Mus of Art, Charlotte, NC; NC Nat Bank, NC Collection; Rauch Indust Inc, Gastonia, NC; Ackland Art Mus, Chapel Hill, NC; NC Mus Art, Raleigh. *Comn:* Youth Ctr mural, New Haven Redevlop Agency, 68. *Exhib:* Arts Festival of Atlanta, Ga, 69; 4th Ann James River Art Exhib, Mariners Mus, Newport News, Va, 70; 3rd Am Exhib, Washington & Lee Univ Mus, Lexington, Va, 71; solo exhibs, Gallery Contemp Art, Winston-Salem, NC, 72, NC Mus Art, Raleigh, 86 & Mint Mus, Charlotte, NC, 90; 39th Triannual NC Artists Exhib, NC Mus of Art, Raleigh, 90; and others. *Collections Arranged:* Fac Choice Exhib, Va Polytech Inst, Blacksburg, Va, 71; New Talent Show, Allan Stone Gallery, New York, 75; 200 Yrs of the Visual Arts in NC, NC Mus of Art, Raleigh, 76. *Teaching:* Prof painting, drawing & design, Univ of NC, Chapel Hill, 68-; asst prof design, Duke Univ, Durham, NC, 72. *Awards:* Purchase Awards, NC Artists Exhib, Rauch Indust, 73 & Realism in NC, Mint Mus of Art, Charlotte, 74; Best Oil Painting, Spring Mills Exhib, Spring Mills Corp, 75; Honor Award, Durham Art Guild Exhib, 87. *Mem:* Nat Asn Schs Art. *Media:* Mixed Media. *Mailing Add:* 100 Birchcrest Pl Chapel Hill NC 27516

ZABRISKIE, VIRGINIA M
DEALER
b New York, NY. *Study:* Washington Sq Col, NY Univ, BA; NY Univ Inst Fine Arts, MA. *Pos:* Dir, Zabriskie Gallery, 54- & Galerie Zabriskie, Paris, 77- *Mem:* Art Dealers Asn (bd dirs, formerly). *Specialty:* 20th century American art; contemporary art; photography. *Mailing Add:* 724 Fifth Ave New York NY 10019

ZACHA, WILLIAM
PAINTER, SCULPTOR
b Garland, Tex, Jan 19, 20. *Study:* Univ Calif, 40-41 & 47-48; George Washington Univ, BA, 51; Corcoran, Washington, DC, study with Heinz Warneke; Studio Hinna, Rome, Italy, 51-52; study with Ruth Cravath, 70-75. *Exhib:* Sculpture, Palazzo Durini, Milano, Italy, 77; Watercolor-Sculpture, Bay Window Gallery, Mendocino, Calif, 77; Art Ctr, Eureka, Calif, 78; Galleria Schneider, Rome, 80; Kabutoya Gallery, Tokyo, Japan, 80 & 85; Kabutoya Gallery, Nagoya, 85; Palaz Gallery, Osaka, 85; Artisan's, Mill Valley, Calif, 85; Kanda Gallery, Fussa, Japan, 85; Mendocino County Mus, Willits, Calif, 86; Rogue Gallery, Medford, Ore, 86; Calif Mus Art, Santa Rosa, 89. *Pos:* Founder & dir, Mendocino Art Ctr, 59- *Teaching:* Instr pvt lessons, Mendocino Art Ctr, 59-, & Bellas Artes Teguci Calpa, Honduras, 68- *Bibliog:* Chandler Brossard (auth), A young man saves an old town, Look Mag, 8/62 & Where artists live, Horizons No 15, US Info Serv. *Media:* Watercolor, Serigraphy. *Publ:* Auth, Tokaido Journey, 85. *Dealer:* Bay Window Gallery 560 Main St Mendocino CA 95460. *Mailing Add:* 484 Main St PO Box 7 Mendocino CA 95460

ZACHARIAS, ATHOS
PAINTER
b Marlborough, Mass, June 17, 27. *Study:* Art Students League, summer 52; RI Sch Design, BFA, 52; Cranbrook Acad Art, MFA, 53. *Work:* Mus Art, Providence, RI; Inst Contemp Art, Boston; Kalamazoo Inst Art, Mich; Phoenix Art Mus, Ariz; Westinghouse Corp, Pittsburgh; Corcoran Gallery Art, Washington, DC. *Comn:* Decor for Manhattan Festival Dancers, comn by Robert Ossorio, New York, 63; designed & executed opaque Projections for Edith Stephan Dance Co. *Exhib:* Joachim Gallery, Chicago, Ill, 61; one-man shows, Gallery Mayer, 61, Louis Alexander Gallery, 63, Landmark Gallery, 73 & James Yu Gallery, 77, New York; Bologna Landi Gallery, East Hampton, NY, 86; Benton Gallery, Benton Plaza, Southampton, NY, 86; Galerie Kwartijin Amsterdam, The Netherlands, 86; Nat Acad Design, New York, 86; Laforet Mus, Tokyo, Japan, 87; and many others. *Teaching:* Instr painting, Brown Univ, 53-55 & Parsons Sch Design, 63-65; assoc prof painting, Wagner Col, 69- *Awards:* Best in Show Award, Guild Hall, 61; Longview Found Grant, 62; Festival Arts Purchase Award, Southampton Col, 68; Best Show Award, Guild Hall, East Hampton, NY, 79. *Media:* Oil. *Publ:* Illusr cover, Sci & Technol, 63. *Mailing Add:* 463 West St Apt B-946 New York NY 10014

ZACK, BADANNA BERNICE
SCULPTOR, WRITER
Can citizen. *Study:* Concordia Univ, Montreal, BA, 64; Rutgers Univ, MFA, 67. *Work:* Concordia Univ, Montreal; Rutgers Univ, Douglas Col, New Brunswick, NJ; Art Gallery Hamilton, Ont; and pvt collections. *Exhib:* Solo exhibs, Gallery 0, Toronto, 73, 75 & 78, Factory 77 & Hamilton Art Gallery, Ont, 83-84; Reflecting a Rural Consciousness, traveling in US, Can & France, 78-80; Home Sweet Home, Toronto, Ont, 85; Eighteenth Sculpture Biennial, Antwerp, Belg, 86; Twelfth Int Biennial of Tapestry, Lausanne, Switz, 86; The Perfect Fit, Oakville, Ont, 88; and others. *Awards:* Arts Grants, Can Coun, 68-69, 74-75 & 78 & Ont Arts Coun, 75-83. *Bibliog:* William Fabrycki (auth), Badanna Zack: L'Enfant terrible, Artmag, 81; Jim Tiley (auth), Badanna Zack at Studio Gallery Nine, Artmag, 83; John Bentley Mays (auth), Hand stiched visions cut from fabric of life, The Globe & Mail, 86. *Mem:* Royal Can Acad. *Media:* Miscellaneous. *Publ:* Auth, Toronto: A look back at sculpture during the sculpture conference, 78, Paul Dempsey at the art gallery of Hamilton, 79, Deiter Hastenteufel at Factory 77, 81-82 & The dinner party by Judy Chicago, 82, Artmag; co-producer, Horse to Horsepower (videotape), 83. *Mailing Add:* 83 Elm Grove Ave Toronto ON M6K 2J2 Canada

ZAFRAN, ERIC MYLES
CURATOR, HISTORIAN
b Malden, Mass, Apr 19, 46. *Study:* Tilton Sch, NH, 63; Brandeis Univ, BA, 67; Inst Fine Arts, NY Univ, MA, 70, PhD, 73. *Collections Arranged:* Master Paintings from the Hermitage (coauth & ed, catalog), Nat Gallery, 75; One Hundred Drawings in the Chrysler Museum (auth catalog), 79; French Salon Paintings from Southern Collections (auth, catalog), High Mus, 82; The Rococo Age (auth, catalog), High Mus, 83; Master Drawings from Titian to Picasso in The Curtis O Baer Collection (auth, catalog), Nat Gallery, 85; Cavaliers and Cardinals: Nineteenth-Century French Anecdotal Paintings (auth, catalog), Taft Mus, 92. *Pos:* Curatorial asst, Rose Art Mus, Waltham, Mass, 65-67; print cataloguer, Parke-Bernet Galleries, New York, 68-71; res asst, Metrop Mus Art, New York, 72-75; chief cur, Chrysler Mus at Norfolk, 76-79; cur Europ art, High Mus, Atlanta, 79-84; cur, Renaissance & Baroque Art, Walters Art Gallery, Baltimore, Md, 84-89; cur, Europ Painting, Mus Fine Art, Boston, currently. *Teaching:* Assoc prof Rembrandt, City Col New York, 75-76; assoc adj, Northern Paintings, Old Dominion Univ, 77-78; assoc prof, French 19th Century Acad Art, Emory Univ, 81 & 83; adj prof, Rennaissance & Baroque Art, Johns Hopkins SCE, 86 & 87; sem, French 18th Century Painting, Mus Fine Arts, Boston, 90. *Mem:* Col Art Asn. *Publ:* Auth, Jan Victors and the Bible, Bulletin of Israel Mus, 77; Saturn and the Jews, J Warburg & Cortauld Inst, 79; European Art in the High Museum, Atlanta, 84; Fifty Old Master Paintings in the Walters Art Gallery, 88; The Forsyth Wickes Collection of Paintings and Drawings in the Museum of Fine Arts, 92. *Mailing Add:* Paintings Dept Mus Fine Arts 465 Huntington Ave Boston MA 02115

ZAGO, TINO (AGOSTINO C)
PAINTER
b Crespano del Grappa, Italy, 1937; US citizen. *Study:* Lawrence Inst Technol, Mich, BS(archit), 60; Cranbrook Acad Art, MFA(painting), 66; Yale Univ, 69. *Work:* Sydney Lewis Corp Collection, Richmond, Va; Prudential Insurance Co N Am, Newark, NJ; Zale Corp, Dallas, Tex; AT&T, Long Lines, Va; TRW Corp, Cleveland, Ohio. *Exhib:* OK Harris Gallery, New York, 83-87 & 89; McIntosh Gallery, Atlanta, Ga, 86 & 89; Tortue Gallery, Santa Monica, Calif, 88; and others. *Teaching:* Vis artist, Mich State Univ, East Lansing, Yale Univ, New Haven, Conn & Summit Art Ctr, Summit, NJ. *Awards:* Emerging Artist Grant, Nat Endowment Arts, 82; Nat Endowment Arts Grant, 85. *Bibliog:* M H Stolback (auth), Tino Zago, Arts Mag, 81; Theodore F Wolff (auth), Zago's American Vision, The Christian Sci Monitor, 83; Suzanne Muchnic (auth), At the Galleries--Tino Zago, Los Angeles Times, 88. *Media:* Acrylic. *Dealer:* OK Harris Gallery 383 W Broadway New York NY 10012. *Mailing Add:* 376 Broome St 2nd Floor New York NY 10013

ZAHN, CARL FREDERICK
DESIGNER, ADMINISTRATOR
b Louisville, Ky, Mar 9, 28. *Study:* Harvard Univ, AB, 48. *Exhib:* Fifty Books Exhibition, Am Inst Graphic Arts, 60-76; one-man show, Dreitzer Gallery, Brandeis Univ, 69. *Pos:* Graphics designer, Mus Fine Arts, Boston, 56-, ed-in-chief, 71-78, dir publ, 79- *Mem:* Am Inst Graphic Arts (bd dirs, 68-71); Soc Printers. *Mailing Add:* c/o Mus Fine Art 465 Huntington Ave Boston MA 02115

ZAHOUREK, JON GAIL
PAINTER, SCULPTOR
b Oklahoma City, Okla, Jan 5, 40. *Study:* Univ Northern Colo, 58-59; Colo Inst Art, with Charles Dye & John Jellico, cert, 61; New Sch Social Res, 79-81. *Work:* Ariz State Univ Matthews Ctr; City & Co Denver; Oklahoma City Chamber Commerce. *Exhib:* Missouri Valley Drawing, Mulvane Art Ctr, Topeka, Kans, 67; Changing Image of the Indian, Mus NMex, Santa Fe, 70; Colo Biennial, Denver Art Mus, 75; Mainstreams of American Art, Marietta Col, 76; American Bronzes, Ariz State Univ, 81; Drawing Defined, Nat Arts Club, New York, 82; solo exhib, Newhouse Gallery, New York, 84. *Teaching:* Instr graphics, Univ Denver, 67; Instr drawing & anatomy, Parsons Sch Design, 78-; instr anatomy, New York Acad, 82- & Art Students League, 84. *Awards:* Second Prize, Black & White on Paper, Nat Arts Club, 82. *Bibliog:* John Jellico (auth), Jon Zahourek--draughtsman, Am Artist, 67. *Mem:* Soc Artists & Anatomists (chmn, 82-84). *Media:* Oil. *Publ:* Auth, Drawings I, pvt publ, 75; Maniken--A Comprehensive Educational System for the Study of Human & Comparative Gross Anatomy, Zahourek Systems Inc, 82. *Mailing Add:* c/o Bishop Gallery 7164 Main St Scottsdale AZ 85251

ZAIKINE, ZAK (VICTOR EUGENE)
SCULPTOR, PAINTER
b Queens, NY, Sept 7, 41. *Study:* Pratt Inst, NY, 59-64, sculpture with Charles Ginnever, 63, also painting with Nicholas Buhalis, 81-83. *Work:* Wright State Univ Mus, Dayton, Ohio; Brooklyn Automotive High Sch, NY. *Comn:* Sculpture, Midwood High Sch, Brooklyn. *Exhib:* solo shows, Jessica Darraby Gallery, 86, Friends & Heroes, Los Angeles, 87, Stars & Stripes, Craft & Folk Art Mus, Los Angeles, 87, Artist Toys, The Norman Rice Gallery, The Albany Inst Hist & Art, 88, Portraits, An Extended Concept, Calif Mus Art, Santa Rosa, Calif, Working in Woodstock, Pittsfield Arts Ctr, Mass, 88; Roots, Rituals, Reflections, Imperial Gallery, New York, 80-81; Silvermine Guild Ctr Arts & Schenectady Mus, 83; Six from New York, Pittsfield Community Arts Ctr, Mass, 84; Paper, Clay and Steel, Jamie Szoke Gallery, New York, 84; Artists of the Mohawk-Hudson Region, Univ Art Gallery, State Univ NY, Albany, 85; All California 86, Laguna Art Mus, Laguna Beach. *Pos:* 1st Ann Woodstock Guild-Members Show, Kleinert Art Ctr, 85; Adjudicator, State Grants, Mich Coun Arts, 88; exhib Form & Line, Woodstock Artist Asn, Woodstock, NY, 88; cur, Working in Woodstock, Six contemp artists, Pittsfield Arts Ctr, Pittsfield, Mass. *Awards:* First Place, Fiesta de Artes, Los Gatos, Calif, 76; Distinction Award, State Univ NY, Albany, 85; Best of Show, Laquinta Arts Found, 86. *Bibliog:* Tram Combs (auth), Zak Zaikine's drypoints, 12/23/82 & Zaikine's tribute to the landscape, 6/1/83, Woodstock Times; Bernard Bovasso (auth), Zaikine's works defy morality, Daily Freeman, 5/31/83; Rebecca Daniels (auth), Zak Zaikine, Woodstock Times, Vol 14, No 25, NY, 85; Olivia Casey (auth), Zak's magic, Sonoma Index-Tribune, Calif, 2/21/86. *Mem:* Sonoma Co Arts Coun; Woodstock Arts Asn Inc; Cooperstown Art Asn Inc; Woodstock Guild Craftsmen Inc. *Media:* Steel, Mixed; All. *Dealer:* J Noblett Gallery 139 E Napa St Sonoma CA; Paramour Fine Arts 28211 Southfield Rd Lathrup Village MI 48076. *Mailing Add:* c/o Petrucci Gallery Saugerties NY 12477

ZAIMA, STEPHEN GYO
PAINTER, SCULPTOR
b San Jose, Calif, Jan 3, 47. *Study:* Pratt Inst, 68; Sch Visual Arts, New York, 68; Calif State Univ, San Jose, BA, 69; Univ Calif, Davis, MFA, 71. *Work:* Univ Calif, Davis & Veterans Mem Bldg, Long Beach. *Comn:* Long Beach Mural, Calif Arts Coun, 83. *Exhib:* Gallery Tamura, Tokyo, Japan, 74; Queens Mus, NY, 85; Everson Mus Art, Syracuse, NY, 85; City Univ New York Grad Ctr, 86; Stephen Rosenberg Gallery, 86; McNay Found, 87; One Penn Plaza, New York, 87. *Teaching:* Syracuse Univ, 80- *Awards:* Fel, Nat Endowment Arts, 74; Grant, Ford Found, 80 & 81; Fel, Edward Albee Found, 81. *Bibliog:* Peter Morrin (auth), article, Atlanta Art Papers, 3/80; Vered Lieb (auth), A study of scale, Arts Mag, 2/87; Kenneth Baker (auth), catalog essay, Everson Mus Art, 85. *Media:* Oil; Mixed. *Publ:* Contribr, Contesting the Boundaries Between Liberal & Professional Educ, Syracuse Univ Press, 88. *Mailing Add:* 210 E 36th St 9F New York NY 10016

ZAJAC, JACK
SCULPTOR, PAINTER
b Youngstown, Ohio, Dec 13, 29. *Study:* Scripps Col, 49-53; also with Millard Sheets, Henry McFee & Sueo Serisawa; Am Acad in Rome. *Work:* Whitney Mus Am Art, Mus Mod Art, New York; Los Angeles Mus Art; Pa Acad Fine Arts, Philadelphia; Israel Mus, Jerusalem; Hirshhorn Mus & Sculpture Garden, Washington, DC; plus others. *Comn:* Reynolds Metals Co, 68. *Exhib:* Whitney Mus Ann, 59; Recent Sculpture USA, Mus Mod Art, 59; Am Painting, Va Mus Fine Arts, Richmond, 62; Fifty California Artists, Whitney Mus Mod Art, New York, 62-63; Pittsburgh Int, Carnegie Inst, 65; retrospectives, Newport Harbor Art Mus, Balboa, Calif, 65, Temple Univ, Rome, 69, Santa Barbara Mus, 75 & Fine Arts Gallery San Diego, 75; Fortezza Albornoz Orvietto, Italy, 76; and many others. *Teaching:* Instr, Pomona Col, 59; prof, Univ Calif, Santa Cruz, currently. *Awards:* Prix de Rome, 54, 56 & 57; Am Acad Arts & Lett Grant, 58; Guggenheim Fel, 59. *Bibliog:* Henry J Seldis & Ulfert Wilke (auth), The Sculpture of Jack Zajac, Gallard Press, 60; Allen S Weller (auth), The Joys and Sorrows of Recent American Art, Univ Ill, 68. *Dealer:* Forum Gallery 1018 Madison Ave New York NY. *Mailing Add:* c/o Stephen Wirtz Gallery 49 Geary St, 3rd floor San Francisco CA 94108

ZAKANITCH, ROBERT S
PAINTER
b Elizabeth, NJ, May 24, 35. *Work:* Whitney Mus Am Art, New York; Munich Mus Mod Art, WGer; Philadelphia Mus, Pa; Wadsworth Atheneum, Hartford, Conn; Phoenix Mus, Ariz; Hirshhorn Mus & Sculpture Garden, Washington, DC; Rothschild Bank, Zurich, Switz; A T & T, New York; High Mus, Atlanta, Ga. *Exhib:* Inst Contemp Art, Philadelphia; James Mayor Gallery, London; Templon Gallery, Paris; Whitney Biennial, Whitney Mus Am Art, New York; Inst Contemp Art, Univ Pa, Philadelphia; Intricate Structure-Repeated Image (with catalog), Tyler Sch Art, Temple Univ, Philadelphia, Pa, 80; Horticulture, Cooper-Hewitt Mus, New York, 81; The Expressionist Image: American Art from Pollock to Today, Sidney Janis Gallery, New York, 82; The Restoration of Painterly Figuration, Kitakyushu Munic Mus Art, Japan, 84; Works on Paper, Robert Miller Gallery, New York, 85; An American Renaissance: Painting and Sculpture Since 1940 (with catalog), Mus Art, Ft Lauderdale, Fla, 86; one-man show, Sidney Janis Gallery, New York, 90. *Teaching:* Instr drawing & painting, OK Summer Arts Inst, 89, 90 & 91. *Bibliog:* Robert Hughes (auth), Three bold newcomers, Time, 3/13/72; John Perreault (auth), Patterning, Artforum, 11/78; John Ashbery (auth), Climbing the wallpaper, New York Mag, 1/29/79; and others. *Dealer:* Sidney Janis Gallery New York NY. *Mailing Add:* 119 N 11th St Brooklyn NY 11211

ZAKIN, MIKHAIL
SCULPTOR, EDUCATOR
US citizen. *Study:* Sch Mus Fine Arts, Boston, Mass; Art Students League, sculpture with William Zorach & Albino Manca; also ceramics with Karen Karnes & David Weinrib. *Work:* Mus Arts & Sci, Salt Lake City, Utah; Peat Marwick Art Collection, Montvale, NJ. *Exhib:* Brooklyn Mus, NY, 74-76; Am Potters, Mus Arts & Sci, Salt Lake City, 75; Four US Potters, Fair Tree Gallery, 75; Pratt Grad Sch, New York, 75-77; Brooklyn Col, 75-77; Baruch Col, New York, 75-77; Retrospective, Sarah Lawrence Col, 91. *Pos:* Founder & dir, Old Church Cult Ctr & Sch Art, Demarest, NJ, 74-; potters sem leader, England, 76, Japan, 77, Mexico, 78, Italy, 79, China, 81, Holland, 82 & Korea, 83; co-founder, Scotland-North Coast Continuum, 78-; co-founder, East-West Inst Arts & Sch Art, Old Church Cult Ctr, Demarest, NJ. *Teaching:* Advan ceramics instr, Greenwich House Pottery, 71-75; head ceramics dept, Brooklyn Mus Art Sch, 72-75 & Sarah Lawrence Col, 76-75. *Awards:* Lebensburger Found Grant, 74; Craftsmen's Fel, NJ Coun Arts, 75 & Nat Endowment Arts, 76; NJ State Coun, 89. *Bibliog:* Elsbeth Woody (auth), Hand Building Ceramics, Farrar Strauss Giroux, 79; Anthony Padovano (auth), Sculpture Practice, Doubleday, 81; Nino Caruso (auth), Ceramica Raku, Hoepli-Milano, 82. *Mem:* Am Crafts Coun; World Crafts Coun; Nat Conf Ceramic Educators; NY Artist Craftsman. *Media:* Clay. *Publ:* Contribr, Poletechnic Design, Korea, 84, Keranos-Madrid, 86. *Mailing Add:* 37 County Rd Closter NJ 07624

ZAKRZEWSKI, VLADIMIR
PAINTER, DRAFTSMAN
b Lodz, Poland, Nov 22, 46; US Citizen. *Study:* Acad Fine Arts, Warsaw, Poland, MFA, 70. *Work:* Nat Mus, Warsaw, Poland; Stedelijk Mus, Amsterdam, Neth; Gemeentemuseum, The Hague, Neth; Bochum Mus, WGer; Brooklyn Mus, NY. *Exhib:* Auction for Solidarity, Nat Mus, Warsaw, Poland, 80; one-man shows, Marian Goodman Gallery, New York, 81 & Ralph Kleinsimlinghaus Gallery, Dusseldorf, WGer, 88; The European Attack, Barbara Farber Gallery, Amsterdam, Neth, 84; Vladimir Zakrzewski-Paintings & Drawings 1978-87, Gemeentemuseum, The Hague, Neth & Bochum Mus, WGer, 87; American Abstract Drawings 1930-1987, Ark Arts Ctr, Little Rock, 88; Vladimir Zakrzewski: Drawings of the 1980's, Brooklyn Mus, 89. *Pos:* Artist-in-residence, Stedelijk Mus, Amsterdam, Neth, 78-79 & 82. *Bibliog:* Ronny Cohen (auth), Vladimir Zakrzewski, Art Forum, 12/87; Flip Bool (auth), Vladimir Zakrzewski - Paintings and Drawings 1978-87, Gemeenstemuseum, The Hague, Neth, & Bochum Mus, WGer, 88; Linda Konheim Kramer (auth), Vladimir Zakrzewski: Drawings of the 1980's, Brooklyn Mus, 89. *Media:* Mixed media on Canvas. *Publ:* Auth, Vladimir Zakrzewski, Art Print, Amsterdam, 83; Drawing private publ, Dusseldorf, 83. *Mailing Add:* 52 Chardavoyne Rd Warwick NY 10990

ZALESKI, JEAN
PAINTER, LECTURER
b Malta; US citizen. *Study:* Art Students League; New Sch, New York; Pratt Inst, New York; Parsons Sch Design, New York; Moore Col Art, Philadelphia. *Work:* Mus City NY; Va Ctr Creative Arts; Metrop Mus Art; NY Pub Libr. *Exhib:* Nat Acad Design, New York, 70-71; Faces, Philadelphia Mus Art, 71; Int Women's Arts Festival, Milan, Italy, 73; Works on Paper--Women Artists, Brooklyn Mus, NY, 75; one-person shows, Alonzo Gallery, New York, 79, Va Ctr Creative Arts, 81 & Elaine Starkman Gallery, New York, 86; Bayly Mus, Charlottesville, Va, 86; Albright-Knox Art Gallery, Buffalo, NY, 86; Citicorp Ctr, New York, 88-89; "Z" Gallery, New York, 91. *Pos:* Exec coordr, Women in the Arts Found, 75-77; spec appt 5-mem adv comt, White House, Washington, DC, 3/77. *Teaching:* Instr drawing & painting & art dir, Studio 733 Art Sch, Great Neck, NY, 63-67; instr life drawing, Hussian Col of Art, Philadelphia, 70-71; instr drawing & painting, Am Studies Ctr, Naples, Italy, 72-73 & Northern Atlantic Treaty Orgn Hq, Naples, 72-73; adj lectr painting, Brooklyn Col, 74-76 & Hofstra Univ, Hempstead, NY, 77; instr, Cooper Union, NY, 86- *Awards:* Va Ctr Creative Arts Fel, 75-92; Susan B Anthony Award, Nat Orgn Women, NY, 86; Ragdale Found Fel, 86-92. *Bibliog:* Joan Marter (auth), Pasture forms, 2/79 & exhib rev, 5/79, Arts Mag; Shiela Elliot (auth), The Allure of Shifting Light, Artists' Mag, 9/87; Tracy Cochran (auth), profile, Ms Mag. *Mem:* Womens Caucus Art; Women in the Arts; Artists Equity. *Media:* Acrylic, Oil. *Publ:* Illusr, Woman to Woman: European Feminists, Staragoubski, 74; Innovative jurying methods, In: Feminist Collage: Educating Women in the Visual Arts, Teachers Col Press, 79; Isolation as Inspiration, Women Artist' News, 81; coauth (with Edwin Honig), Cow-Lines, Copper Beech Press, 82; auth, Day in the life, Artists Mag, 9/85. *Mailing Add:* 463 West St 503D New York NY 10014

ZALLINGER, JEAN DAY
ILLUSTRATOR, EDUCATOR
b Boston, Mass, Feb 15, 18. *Study:* Mass Col of Art, cert(drawing & painting), 35-39; Yale Sch Fine Arts, BFA, 42. *Work:* Kerlan Found; Univ Minn; Rutgers Univ; Univ Southern Miss; De Grummond, permanent collection, Paint & Clay Club, NH; Univ Conn Collection. *Exhib:* Dinosaurs Past & Present, Los Angeles Co Mus Natural Hist (travel US & Europe), 86-90; Aetna Gallery, Hartford; Mass Col Art, 92. *Pos:* Tech illus draftsman, Applied Physics Lab, Univ Wash, Seattle, 51-53. *Teaching:* Prof drawing & illusr, Paier Col Art, Hamden, Conn, retired. *Awards:* Nat Sci Teachers Awards for Biography of a Fish Hawk & I Watch Flies, 77; Alumna of the Year, 92; Mass Col Art, 92. *Bibliog:* NH Register, 1/83; Rocks & Minerals, Heldref Publ, 3-4/92. *Mem:* Paint & Clay Club, New Haven, Conn; Arts Coun New Haven; Artspace, New Haven; Soc Children's Book Writers. *Publ:* Biography of a Fish Hawk, Putnam Bk, 77; Nature's Champions, 80, Dinosaurs, Asteroids & Super Stars, 82, Baby Dinosaurs, 84, Sharks, 86, Whales, 87 & Eagles, 88, Lothrop Lee Shepard; Sesame St Q & A Book About Animals, 83; Monsters of the Sea, Little Brown, 90-; The Earliest Americans, Clarion, 93. *Mailing Add:* 5060 Ridge Rd North Haven CT 06473

ZALLINGER, RUDOLPH FRANZ
PAINTER, EDUCATOR
b Irkutsk, Siberia, Nov 12, 19; US citizen. *Study:* Yale Sch Fine Arts, Yale Univ, BFA, 42, MFA, 71; Univ New Haven, Hon DFA, 80. *Work:* Berkeley Col, Yale Sch Med, Yale Univ; New Brit Mus Am Art, Conn; Univ New Haven; Lawrenceville Sch; Knights of Columbus, World Hq, New Haven; and others. *Comn:* Age of Reptiles (fresco), 42-47 & Age of Mammals (fresco), 61-67, Peabody Mus, Yale Univ; Early History of Hartford (mural), Aetna Life & Casualty. *Exhib:* 32 Realists, Cleveland Inst Art, 72-; Sanford Low Mem Exhib, New Brit Mus Am Art, 76; 200 Yrs of Am Illus, NY Hist Soc Mus, 76-77; one-man retrospective, New Brit Mus Am Art, 80; one-man shows, Dorsky Galleries, NY, 81 & Gen Elec Corp Hq Gallery, 81. *Pos:* Artist-in-residence, Peabody Mus Natural Hist, Yale Univ, 52-; coop mem artist, Portraits, Inc, New York. *Teaching:* From instr to asst prof drawing & painting compos, Yale Sch Fine Arts, 42-50; from asst prof to prof, Hartford Art Sch, Univ Hartford, 61- *Awards:* First Honorable Mention, Prix-De-Rome Competition, 41; Pulitzer Prize in Painting, 49; James E & Frances W Bent Award for Creativity, Univ Hartford, 88. *Bibliog:* Lawrence Rasie (auth), Rudolph Zallinger, dinosaur man, Hartford Courant, 74; Carl O Dunbar (auth), Recollections of the Renaissance of Peabody Mus Exhibs, Discovery Mag, Peabody Mus, 76; John Ostrum (auth), The age of reptiles, Discovery Mag Supplement 1, Peabody Mus, 77. *Mem:* New Haven Paint & Clay Club (vpres, 48-49, pres, 76-78); Puget Sound Group Northwest Painters. *Media:* Egg-tempera, Oil. *Publ:* Illusr, World we live in, 55, Wonders of life on Earth, 60 & Epic of Man, 61, & Epic of Man & History of the Russian Revolution, Time-Life Books. *Mailing Add:* 5060 Ridge Rd North Haven CT 06473

ZALOUDEK, DUANE
PAINTER
b Enid, Okla, Jan 15, 31. *Study:* Portland Mus Art Sch, Ore, cert, 56. *Work:* Portland Art Mus, Ore; Dallas Mus Fine Arts, Tex. *Exhib:* Various exhib, Portland Art Mus, 49-86; Northwest Ann, Seattle Art Mus, 59-68; W Coast Ann, San Francisco Art Mus, 60-61; W Coast Now, Los Angeles City Mus, 68; Watercolors, Akron Art Inst, Ohio, 76; Radikal Auf Papier, Aargauer Kunsthaus, Aarau, Switz. *Teaching:* Artist-in-residence, Portland Univ, 62-65; vis artist, Univ Calif, Davis, 70-73. *Awards:* Adolph Gottlieb Found Award, 78; Mark Bothko Found Award, 86; Nat Endowment Arts, 87. *Bibliog:* Charlotte Hughes (auth), A profile, Univ Portland Rev, 65; Tiffany Bell (auth), article, Arts Mag, 4/78. *Media:* Watercolor, All Media. *Dealer:* Galerie Mark Muller Hardturmstrasse 124 CH-8005 Zurich Switzerland. *Mailing Add:* 431 E 12th St New York NY 10009

ZALUCHA, PEGGY FLORA
PAINTER
b Peoria, Ill, Sept 18, 48. *Work:* Lakeview Mus Arts & Scis, Peoria, Ill; Hoyt Inst Fine Art, New Castle, Pa; Brea Mus Fine Art, Calif; Paine Mus Art, Oshkosh, Wis; Charles A Wustum Mus Fine Art, Racine, Wis. *Comn:* Eleven paintings, Wis Chamber Orchestra, Madison, 83-92; five paintings, 84 & mem painting, 88, Dane Co, Madison, Wis, 88; painting, Madison Civic Ctr, Wis, 87. *Exhib:* Nat Watercolor Soc Exhibs, Brea Cult Ctr, Calif, 82, 83, 87, 89-92; Nat Soc Painters Casein & Acrylic Exhib, Nat Arts Club, New York, 83, 84, 89, 92; Rocky Mountain Nat Watermedia Exhib, Foothills Art Ctr, Golden, Colo, 85, 88, 89, 92; solo exhibs, West Bend Gallery Fine Art, Wis, 86, Lakeview Mus (exhib catalog), Peoria, Ill, 90, Neville Mus, Green Bay, Wis, 91 & Wis Acad Fine Arts, Madison, 91. *Awards:* Best of Show, Nat Watercolor Soc Exhib, 87; Century Merit Award, Rocky Mountain Nat Watermedia Exhib, Foothills Art Ctr, 88 & 92; Nat Galleries Award, Nati Watercolor Soc Exhib, Nat Galleries, 91. *Bibliog:* Bebe Raupe (auth), Award winning watercolorists, Artists Mag, 7/88; William C Landwehr (auth), Defining light with tight control, Am Artist Mag, 9/90. *Mem:* Am Watercolor Soc; Nat Watercolor Soc; Nat Soc Painters Casein & Acrylic; Midwest Watercolor Soc; Wis Painters & Sculptors/Artists All Media, (chapter bd 88-). *Media:* Transparent Watercolor, Acrylic on Paper. *Mailing Add:* 109 Sunset Lane Mt Horeb WI 53572-1865

ZAMMITT, NORMAN
PAINTER, SCULPTOR
b Toronto, Ont, Feb 3, 31; US citizen. *Study:* Pasadena City Col, AA, 57; Otis Art Inst, MFA, 61. *Work:* Mus Mod Art, New York; Hirshhorn Mus, New York; Libr Cong, Washington, DC; Otis Art Gallery, Los Angeles; Larry Aldrich Mus, Conn. *Exhib:* Mus Mod Art, New York, 65 & Show of New Acquisitions, 67; American Sculpture of the Sixties, Los Angeles Co Mus Art & Philadelphia Mus Art, 67; Metromedia, Los Angeles; one-man shows, Los Angeles Co Mus Art, 77 & Corcoran Gallery, 78. *Awards:* Tamarind Fel, 67; Guggenheim Mem Found Fel, 68. *Bibliog:* Various articles in Art Int, Artforum, Art in Am & Los Angeles Times. *Mailing Add:* 233 N Wilson Ave Pasadena CA 91106

ZANTMAN, J B
DEALER
b Sumbawa, Dutch East Indies, Dec 27, 19; US citizen. *Study:* Pvt instr, Netherlands. *Pos:* Pres, Zantman Art Galleries, Ltd, Carmel & Palm Desert, Calif. *Specialty:* Living artists from US and France. *Mailing Add:* 75473 14th Green Dr Indian Wells CA 92210

ZAPFE, GUILLERMO (WILHELM KARL ZAPFE)
PAINTER, DRAFTSMAN
b Mex, DF, Sept 15, 33. *Study:* Escuela Nacional de Pintura y Escultura, La Esmeralda, Mex, DF, 58-60; Ecole du Mus du Louvre, Paris, 61. *Work:* Mus de Arte Contemp de Oaxaca de Juarez; Inst Nacional de Bellas Artes, Mus Eulalio Ferrer, Xerox de Mex, Mex, DF; Mus de Guatemala, Guatemala City. *Exhib:* Señales de Vida, Mus del Palacio de Bellas Artes, Mex, DF, 76; Bienal Iberoamericana de Pintura, Mus Carrillo Gil, Mex, DF, 78; Freedom & Expression, Laguna Beach Mus Art, Calif, 79; El Arma, Mus Carrillo Gil, Mex, DF, 81; Salon Nacional de Pintura, Mus Palacio de Bellas Artes, Mex, DF, 83; Bienal de la Habana, Cuba, 85; Alternancias, Mus de Arte Mod, Mex, DF, 85; New Voices from Mexico, Scott Alan Gallery, New York, 88. *Teaching:* Instr drawing & painting, Escuela de Pintura y Escultura del Inst Nacional de Bellas Artes, 80-88 & Escuela Nacional de Artes Plasticas de la Univ Nacional Autonoma, 81-88. *Awards:* First Prize, Concursonacional de Pintura, 81; Premio Adquisicion del Salon Nacional de Artes Plasticas, Seccion Pintura, 83; Primer Premio, Segunda Bienal, 84. *Mem:* Salon de la Plastica Mex; Soc Mex de Artistas Plasticos; Asn Internationale des Arts Plastiques. *Media:* Gouache, Acrylic; Ink. *Dealer:* Scott Alan Gallery Inc 270 Lafayette St Suite 204 New York NY 10112. *Mailing Add:* Patricio Sanz No 739 Colonia Del Valle Mexico DF 03100 Mexico

ZAPKUS, KES (KESTUTIS EDWARD)
PAINTER
b Dabikine, Lithuania, Apr 22, 38; US citizen. *Study:* Art Inst Chicago, BFA, 60; Syracuse Univ, Ryerson fel, 60, MFA, 62. *Work:* Stedelijk Mus, Amsterdam, Holland; Hirshhorn Mus, Washington, DC; Va Mus Fine Arts, Richmond; Art Inst Chicago; Carnegie-Mellon Inst; and others. *Exhib:* Solo exhibs, Paula Cooper Gallery, 71, 73, 75, 77 & 79, Galerie Darthea Speyer, Paris, 78, John Weber Gallery, New York, 81, 82 & 74 & Hecksher Mus, Huntington, NY, 82; Inst Contemp Art, Boston, 75; Butler Inst Am Art, Youngstown, Ohio, 76; Gallery Group, John Weber Gallery, New York, 85 & 86; Comino a Cuba, Museo Universitario Chopo, Mex City, 86; Mus Fine Arts, Budapest, Hungary, 89; Retrospective, Vilnius Mus Fine Arts, 89. *Teaching:* Princeton, Parsons Sch Design & Univ Pa. *Awards:* Invitational First Prize, Chicago Arts Festival, 64; Creative Artists Public Service Grant, 78; Nat Endowment Arts Grant, 79. *Bibliog:* Lucy Lippard (auth), Battle cries, Village Voice, 12/4/84; Ron Warren (auth), Kes Zapkus at John Weber, Arts, 1/85; Kenneth Baker (auth), Kes Zapkus at John Weber, Art Am, 3/85. *Media:* Oil. *Dealer:* John Weber Gallery 142 Greene New York NY 10012. *Mailing Add:* 35 Bond St New York NY 10012

ZARAND, JULIUS JOHN
PAINTER, RESTORER
b Nagyvarad, Hungary, June 27, 13; Can citizen. *Study:* Royal Acad, dipl & dipl(educ); also with Oskar Kokoschka, Salzburg, Austria; Accad Ital, Dipl Hon Causa Maestro Pittura, 83. *Work:* City Hall, Halifax, NS; Yokahama Univ Gallery, Japan; Art Bank Nova Scotia; Govt House, PEI. *Comn:* Portrait of Pope Pius XII, comn by Prime Cardinal of Hungary, 38; portrait, comn by Lord Thompson, Toronto, 54; murals, St Bridgid Church, Toronto, 55; portrait of Sir John Thompson, City of Halifax, NS, 68; portraits of all presidents of the co, Maritime Telegraph & Telephone Co, Halifax, NS; murals, Veterans Mem Hosp, Halifax, 88; and others. *Exhib:* One-man shows, Halifax Libr, 64, Lafayette Art Ctr, Ind, 69, Purdue Univ Gallery, 69, Zwicker's Gallery, Halifax, 70 & Lunenburg Art Gallery, Lunenburg, NS, 89. *Teaching:* Asst prof fine arts, St Mary's Univ, Halifax, 56-65. *Awards:* Gold Medal, Acad Italy, 81; Primo Oscar D'italia, 85; Centauro d'Oro, Acad Italy, 88. *Mem:* Academia Italia; Lunenburg Co, Art Coun; Art Gallery NS; Art Gallery, Lunenburg. *Media:* Oil, Egg Tempera. *Dealer:* Zwicker's Gallery Ltd 5415 Doyle St Halifax NS Can. *Mailing Add:* Chester Basin NS B0J 1K0 Canada

ZED, AGGIE
SCULPTOR
b Charleston, SC, Nov 13, 52. *Study:* Univ SC, BFA, 74. *Work:* Fed Reserve Bank, Richmond, Va. *Exhib:* Southern Comfort Discomfort, Mint Mus, Charlotte, NC, 86; Benefit Exhib 86, Mortal Oxide, 86 & group sculpture show, 91, 1708 E Main Gallery, Richmond, Va; Virginia Clay Now, 87 & Animals, 87, Peninsula Fine Arts Ctr, Newport News, Va; Five from Richmond, Old Dominion Univ, Norfolk, Va, 87; Rock Holders, Med Col Va, Richmond, Va, 88; Sally Brown Interiors (drawings), Richmond, 4-6/92; and others. *Awards:* Prof Fel, Va Comn Arts, 83; Prof Fel Sculpture, Nat Endowment Arts, 86. *Media:* Clay. *Dealer:* Reynolds-Minor Gallery 1514 W Main St Richmond VA 23220. *Mailing Add:* 1610 Overlook St Richmond VA 23224

ZEIDENBERGS, OLAFS
SCULPTOR
b Latvia, Mar 17, 36; US citizen. *Study:* Univ Hartford, BFA, 61; Yale Univ, MFA, 63. *Work:* Morse Col, Yale Univ; Valley Bank & Trust Co, Springfield, Mass; Avon Corp, Rye, NY; McGraw-Hill Corp, New York; Unitarian Soc New Haven, Hamden, Conn. *Exhib:* Outdoor Sculpture, DeCordova Mus, Lincoln, Mass; Four Sculptors & Small Packages, Univ Conn; Mainstreams, Marietta Col; Tex Fine Arts Asn Ann, Austin. *Teaching:* Prof sculpture, Southern Conn State Univ, 66- *Awards:* Silvermine Guild Artists Award; New Haven Festival Arts Award; Conn Acad Fine Arts Award. *Mem:* Conn Acad Fine Arts. *Media:* Metal, Plastics. *Mailing Add:* Dept of Art Southern Conn State Univ 501 Crescent St New Haven CT 06515

ZEIDLER, EBERHARD HEINRICH
DESIGNER, ARCHITECT
b Braunsdorf, Ger, Jan 11, 26; Can citizen. *Study:* Bauhaus Weimar, Cand Arch, 45-48; Karlsruhe Univ, Dipl Ing, 49; McMaster Univ, LLD, 82; Tech Univ Nova Scotia, D Eng 87, Univ Toronto, D Arch, 89. *Comn:* Designer, McMaster Univ Health Sci Ctr, 68-72, Eaton Ctr, Toronto, 73-79, Walter C Mackenzie Health Sci Ctr, Edmonton, 76-81 & Canada Place, Vancouver, 86; MediaPark, Cologne, 88. *Pos:* Guest speaker, var world confs; sr partner,

Zeidler Partnership/Architects. *Teaching:* Lectr archit design, Univ Toronto, 53-55; adj prof, Univ Toronto, 83- *Awards:* Order of Canada, 84; 75 national and international design awards; Gold Medal, Royal Archit Inst Can, 86. *Bibliog:* Robert Fulford (auth), The rise and fall of modern architecture, Saturday Night Mag, 80; Geoffrey Simmons (auth), Eberhard Zeidler, City & Country Home, spring 83; Christian W Thomsen (auth), Eberhard Zeidler: The Canadian Baumeister, Westermanns Monatshefte, 2/2/86. *Mem:* Academician Royal Can Acad Arts; fel Royal Archit Inst Can; Ont Asn Architects; hon fel Am Inst Archits; and others. *Publ:* Auth, Healing the Hospital-McMaster Health Science Centre: Its Conception & Evolution, 74; auth, Multi-use architecture in the Urban Contex, Karl Kramer Verlag, 83; and many articles in leading prof mags. *Mailing Add:* 315 Queen St W Toronto ON M5V 2X2 Canada

ZEISLER, RICHARD SPIRO
COLLECTOR, PATRON
b Chicago, Ill, Nov 28, 16. *Study:* Amherst Col, BA; Harvard Univ. *Pos:* Trustee, mem comt on painting & sculpture, comt on archit & design, Mus Mod Art, New York; bd dirs, treas, Int Coun Mus Mod Art; mem comt on 20th century painting & sculpture, Art Inst Chicago; trustee, Skowhegan Sch Painting & Sculpture. *Mem:* Sustaining fel & gov life mem Art Inst Chicago; life mem Metrop Mus, New York; Brandeis Univ (fine arts awards adv comt); Mt Holyoke Col (art adv comt); fel Pierpont Morgan Libr. *Collection:* European painting of the 20th century. *Mailing Add:* 980 Fifth Ave New York NY 10021

ZEITLIN, HARRIET
PAINTER, SCULPTOR
b Philadelphia, Pa, Feb 12, 29. *Study:* Pa Acad Fine Arts, Univ Pa, BFA, 46-50; Barnes Found, 49 & 50; Univ Calif, Los Angeles, 63-69. *Work:* Libr Congress; Am Embassy, New Delhi, India; Los Angeles Co Mus Art, Los Angeles Athletic Asn & Grunwald Ctr Graphic Arts, Univ Calif, Los Angeles. *Comn:* Mixed media painting, comn by City Los Angeles Cult Affairs Dept, 91. *Exhib:* Santa Barbara Mus; Skirball Mus, Los Angeles; US Info Serv Bicentennial Exhib, India; Riverside Mus, Calif; Craft & Folk Art Mus, Los Angeles, Calif State Univ, Long Beach; Women's Caucus Art; Los Angeles Printmaking Soc; Palm Springs Mus Art; Weyhe Gallery, New York; Bernice Steinbaum Gallery, New York. *Pos:* Exec bd mem, Los Angeles Printmaking Soc, 64-69; artist/community relations & exec bd mem, Graphic Arts Coun of Los Angeles Co Mus of Art, 73-75; corresp secy, Artists for Economic Action, 73-74, vpres, 75-76, pres, 77-78 & exec dir CETA Title VI, Art in Public Places, 77-78. *Teaching:* Mirman Sch Gifted Children, Los Angeles, 80-82; UCLA Exten Artsreach, Univ Calif, Los Angeles, 86; Los Angeles High Sch Music & Art, 88. *Awards:* Calif Arts Coun Grant, 77; Los Angeles City Cult Grant, 90-91. *Bibliog:* Barbara Wilson (auth), Interview, Currant Art Mag, 75; Kathy Zimmerer-McKelvie (auth), Three from Los Angeles, Art Scene, 85; Eleanor Tufts (auth), Am Women Artists, Vol II, 89. *Mem:* Women's Caucus Art. *Publ:* Auth, A community of artists, Graphic Arts Coun Newsletter, Vol IX, No 4, Los Angeles Co Mus, 74; President's report, Artists for Econ Action Newslett, 77-78; The Calif Art Rev, Am References, 89. *Mailing Add:* 202 S Saltair Ave Los Angeles CA 90049

ZEITLIN, HARRY LEON
PHOTOGRAPHER
b Denver, Colo, Apr 29, 52. *Study:* Yale Univ, BA, 74; pvt studies with Hisashi Ohta, Los Angeles, 80-82; Univ Calif, Los Angeles, with Robert Heinecken & Edmund Teske, 77-79. *Work:* Israel Mus, Jerusalem; Tel Aviv Mus, Israel; Bibliotheque Nationalé, Paris, France; Denver Art Mus, Colo; Skirball Mus, Los Angeles. *Comn:* Aaron Copland (portrait), comn by Aaron Copland, New York, 78; Elliot Carter (portrait), comn by Elliot Carter, New York, 78; Eugene Ionesco (portrait, comn by Eugene Ionesco, Los Angeles, 79; Bob Marley (portrait), comn by Bob Marley, Los Angeles, 80; Hisashi Ohta (portrait), comn by Hisashi Ohta, Los Angeles, 82. *Exhib:* One-man shows, Colo Photog Art Ctr, Denver, 79, Am Cult Ctr, Jerusalem, 86, Bezalel Acad Art, Jerusalem, 86, Bertha Urdang Gallery, New York, 88 & 91, Jewish Quarter, Los Angeles, 88, Henry Art Gallery, Univ Wash, Seattle, 91 & Silver Image Gallery, Seattle, 91; Japan Expo, Los Angeles, 80 & 81; Silver Gallery Int Judaica Fair, Jerusalem, 86; New Artists, Ramat Gan Mus, Israel, 87; Skyline, Tel Aviv Mus, Israel, 88; and others. *Teaching:* Photog, Art is the Spiritual, Photog Ctr Northwest, Seattle, Wash, 92. *Mem:* Seattle Art Mus Photog Coun. *Media:* Black and White Photography. *Publ:* Contribr, B'or Ha'Torah, 5/86; Parabola, spring 87; Skyline, Tel Aviv Mus, 4/88; Trees and Water, Urdang Gallery, 8/88; Houston Photofest Laser Disc, 92. *Dealer:* Bertha Urdang Gallery 23 E 74th St New York NY 10021; Silver Image Gallery 318 Occidental Ave S Seattle WA 98104. *Mailing Add:* 5508 35th Ave NE Seattle WA 98105

ZEITLIN, MARILYN A
CURATOR, WRITER
b Newark, NJ, July 14, 41. *Study:* Harvard Univ, AB, 66 MAT, 67; Cornell Univ. *Collections Arranged:* Messages: Words & Images (auth, Catalog), 79 & Presences: The Figure & Manmade Environment Photography (auth, catalog), 80, Freedman Gallery, Reading, Pa; Masters of Contemporary Drawing (auth, catalog), 83-85 & As if the Universe were an object: Larry Miller Retrospective (coauth, catalog), Anderson Gallery, Richmond, Va, 86; Happy Families: Works by Ida Applebroog (coauth, catalog), 89, S Bronx Hall of Fame: Sculpture by John Ahearn & Rigoberto Torres (coauth, catalog), Houston, 90. *Pos:* Dir, Ctr Gallery, Bucknell Univ, Lewisburg, 76-79, Freedman Gallery, Albright Col, Reading, 79-82, Anderson Gallery, Va Commonwealth Univ, Richmond, 82-87, Contemp Arts Mus, Houston, 87-90, WPA, Washington, DC, 90-92, Univ Art Mus, Ariz State Univ, 92- *Teaching:* Instr, Bucknell Univ, Albright Col & Va Commonwealth Univ, formerly. *Awards:* Samuel H Kress Fel, 71. *Mem:* Am Asn Mus; Va Mus Asn; Asn Col & Univ Mus & Galleries (vpres, 84-86). *Res:* Contemporary art, chiefly video, painting & sculpture; political art. *Publ:* Auth, Magic & Medicine: Chinese Ceramics in Southeast Asia, Pac Press, 78; Small is Beautiful, Bucknell Univ, 79; Jo Sandman: Work in process, Anyart, 80; Attemped, Not Known, Paintings by Benito Huerta, Artspace, 89. *Mailing Add:* 4908 N 42nd Pl Phoenix AZ 85018

ZELANSKI, PAUL JOHN
PAINTER
b Hartford, Conn, Apr 13, 31. *Study:* Cooper Union, cert, 55; Yale Univ, BFA, 57; Bowling Green State Univ, MA, 58. *Work:* Univ Mass, Amherst; Slater Mus, Norwich, Conn; Manchester Community Col, Conn; Hampshire Col, Northampton, Mass; Yale Univ Print Collection. *Exhib:* New England in Five Parts, De Cordova Mus, Lincoln, Mass; Harvard Univ Carpenter Ctr, Boston; New Directions in Painting, Univ Mass, Amherst; The Peterdi Years, Yale Univ, New Haven; Selected Conn Painters & Sculptors Show, Slater Mus, Norwich, Conn, 80. *Teaching:* Instr painting, drawing & design, N Tex State Univ, 58-61; instr painting, Ft Worth, Tex, 61-62; assoc prof art, Univ Conn, 62-76, prof, 76- *Awards:* Painting Prize, Norwich Ann, 73 & 79; Painting Prize, Beth El, 80; McDowell Colony; and others. *Bibliog:* Alan Graham Collier (auth), Form, Space and Vision, Prentice-Hall; Barnard Chaet (auth), Artists at work, Webb, Studio Talk. *Mem:* Silvermine Guild Artists; Conn Acad Fine Arts; Berkshire Art League; Munsell Group; Comput Art & Design Educ. *Media:* Acrylic, Collage. *Publ:* Auth, Design Principles and Problems & Shaping Space, Holt, Rinehart & Winston; The Art of Seeing - Color, Prentice Hall. *Mailing Add:* Cowles Rd West Willington CT 06279

ZELENAK, EDWARD JOHN
SCULPTOR
b St Thomas, Ont, Nov 9, 40. *Study:* Meinszinger Sch Art, Detroit, Mich; Ft Worth Art Ctr, Tex; Ont Col Art, Toronto. *Work:* Cantonal Mus, Lausanne, Switz; Nat Gallery Can, Ottawa; Ont Art Gallery, Toronto; Rothman's Ltd, Stratford, Ont; Dept Pub Works, Toronto. *Comn:* Major outdoor sculpture, Nat Gallery Can, 72, Dept Pub Works, Toronto, 73 & North York, 76, Rothman's Art Gallery, 73 & Northfield Minn, Carleton Col, 73; major sculpture, Prov Dept Pub Works, Kitchener, Ont, 77; Forest City Gallery, London, Ont, 85-86. *Exhib:* One-man exhib, Major Outdoor Sculpture, Nat Art Ctr, Ottawa, 69 & Carleton Col, 72; Tendence Actuelles, Galerie de France, Paris, 69; 3rd Int Pioneer Galleries Exhib, Cantonnal Mus, Lausanne & Mus Mod Art, Paris, 70; 49th Parallels, Ringling Mus, Sarasota, Fla & Mus Contemp Art, Chicago, 71; Washington, Northfield, Milwaukee major touring sculpture, Minn State Art Coun & Henry Gallery, 73-74; Mt Allison Univ, 75; Art Fiera, Bologna, Italy, 77. *Teaching:* Instr, Univ Western Ont, 79-88. *Awards:* Can Coun Jr Arts Grant, 68-71, Sr Arts Grant, 73-75; Prov Ont Coun Arts Grant in Aid, 74. *Bibliog:* Jean Noel Chandler (auth), article in Artscanada, 4/69; Barry Lord (auth), articles in Art in Am, 1-2/69; R Naasgard (auth), article in Artscanada, 6/73. *Mem:* Royal Can Acad Arts. *Media:* Metal, Fiberglas. *Mailing Add:* c/o Galerie Brenda Wallace 372 Ste Catherine Ouest Montreal PQ H3B 1A2 Canada

ZELIN, ELAINE
SCULPTOR
b New York, NY, Dec 13, 31. *Study:* Stephens Col, AA, 51; Fairleigh Dickinson Univ, BA, 80; Art Students League; New School; studied with J Hovannes, Tony Paderano & Minouri Niizuma. *Work:* New England Ctr Contemp Art, Brookline, Conn. *Comn:* Marble seal, Dart Indust, Paramus, NJ, 81; Windswept (marble sculpture), Accurate Box Co, Newark, NJ, 82; Pinnacle, Ft Lee Marketing Co, New York, 84; Citiscape, Cosmetic Scenting Co, New York, 85. *Exhib:* Stone Sculpture Soc New York, Lever House, 81, 86, 90; Nat Asn Women Artists, Jacob Javits Plaza, New York, 82, 83, 85; Tri County, Bergen Co Mus, Paramus, NJ, 84; Norton Artists Guild, Norton Mus, West Palm Beach, 92. *Awards:* Anonymous Members Prize, Nat Asn Women Artists, 82 & 83. *Bibliog:* NY Art Yearbook, 76. *Mem:* NY Artists Equity; Nat Asn Women Artists; Norton Artists Guild. *Media:* Marble. *Mailing Add:* 70 Bristol Dr Boynton Beach FL 33436

ZELLER, FREDERIC
SCULPTOR
b Ger, May 20, 24. *Study:* Univ London, BA, 55; Art Students League, NY, studied with Stephen Green, 59-61; The Greenwich House, studied with Paul Frazier, 61-64; Educ Alliance Art Sch, studied with Licio Isolani, 65-70. *Exhib:* Vorpal Gallery, NY, 82; Centre Articule, Montreal, Quebec, 83; Sarah Y Rentschler Gallery, Bridgehampton, NY, 85; Clark Whitney Gallery, Lenox, Mass, 85; Elaine Benson Gallery, Bridgehampton, 86; Benton Gallery, Southampton, NY, 86, 87 & 88; solo shows, Pace Univ Art Gallery, NY, 80, Vorpal Gallery, 82 & 83, Studio 99, Westhampton Beach, 82, Benton Hallery, 88. *Mailing Add:* 775 Sixth Ave New York NY 10001

ZELT, MARTHA
PRINTMAKER
b Washington, Pa, Nov 16, 30. *Study:* Conn Col; Pa Acad Fine Arts; New Sch Social Res, with Antonio Frasconi; Mus Arte Mod, Brazil, with John Friedlaender; Univ NMex, with Garo Antreasian; Temple Univ, BA. *Work:* Carnegie Inst, Mus Art; Pa Acad Fine Arts; Princeton Univ; Philadelphia Mus Art; Brooklyn Mus; and others. *Exhib:* Int Bienale, Sao Paulo, Brazil, 61; Pa Acad Fine Arts Nat Ann, 61-70; one-man shows, Pa Acad Peale Galleries, 72, Print Club, 75, Brooklyn Mus, 80 & Carnegie Inst, Mus Art, 81; 30 Yrs Am Printmaking, Brooklyn Mus, 76; New Ways With Paper, Nat Collection of Fine Arts, Washington, DC; Brandywine Graphic Workshop, 80; Tamarind

Inst, 83 & 86; Pyramid Print & Paperworks, Dolan/Maxwell, 85; Morris Gallery, Pa Acad Fine Arts. *Pos:* Dir graphic workshop prof artists, Pa Acad Fine Arts, 63-65; demonstrating artist & printmaker, Prints in Progress, Philadelphia, 63-71. *Teaching:* Instr printmaking, Pa Acad Fine Arts, 68-82, Philadelphia Col Art, 69-82; Univ NC, Chapel Hill, 81; chmn, Art Dept, Va Intermont Col, 85-89; distinguished vis prof, Univ Del, 88-89. *Awards:* Cresson Traveling Award, 54 & Scheidt Mem Traveling Award, Pa Acad Fine Arts; Print Club Fel, 65; Roswell Mus Grant, 82, 89. *Bibliog:* Prints--History of an Art, Beguin, Field, Griffes, Skira-Rissoli, 81; The Complete Printmaker, Ross/Romano, MacMillan, 90; Clinton Adams (auth), Printmaking in New Mexico, 1880-1990, Univ NMex Press, 91. *Media:* All. *Dealer:* Hodges-Taylor Gallery 227 N Tryon Charlotte NC. *Mailing Add:* 1301 N Montana Ave Roswell NM 88201-9801

ZEMANS, JOYCE L
EDUCATOR, ART HISTORIAN
b Toronto, Can, Apr 21, 40. *Study:* Univ Toronto, BA, 62, MA, 66. *Collections Arranged:* Jock Macdonald: The Inner Landscape (auth, catalog), Art Gallery Ont, Can, 81-82; Alexandra Luke: The Watercolours, Robert McLaughlin Gallery, Oshawa, Can, 84; Christopher Pratt: A Retrospective (auth, catalog), Vancouver Art Gallery, Can, 85-86; Kathleen Munn and Edna Tacon: New Perspectives on Canadian Modernism (auth), Art Gallery York Univ, 88-89. *Teaching:* Art historian, Ont Col Art, Toronto, 66-75, chmn, Art Hist Dept, 69-71, chmn, Liberal Arts Studies, 72-75; assoc prof art hist, York Univ, Toronto, 75-, chmn, Dept Visual Arts, 75-81, dean, fac fine arts, 86-88; dir, Can Coun, 89-92. *Mem:* Univ Arts Asn Can; Col Art Asn Am; Int Asn Art Critics; Nat Coun Art Administrators; Can Asn Fine Arts Deans (bd mem); Int Coun Fine Arts Deans (bd mem). *Publ:* Auth, The Student Subject and Careers Series, Univ Toronto; The Impact of Automatism on the Art of Jock Macdonald, Can Art Rev, Vol VII, No 1-2, 80. *Mailing Add:* c/o Fac Fine Arts York Univ Downsview ON M3J 1P3 Canada

ZENTZ, PATRICK J
SCULPTOR
Study: Westmont Col, Santa Barbara, Calif, BA, 65-69; Univ Mont, MFA(sculpture), 70-74. *Comn:* Washington Proj Arts, Washington, DC, 87; Sculpture Aspen '88, Aspen Art Mus, Colo, 87; Univ Med Ctr, Univ Wash, Seattle, 90; Western State Hosp, Wash State Arts Comn, Ft Steilman, 91; Richard Tam Alumni Ctr, Univ Nev, Las Vegas, 91. *Exhib:* Two-man shows, Wash Proj Arts, Washington, DC, 87, Beall Park Art Ctr, Bozeman, Mont, 89 & Univ Mont, Missoula, 92; St John's Nfld, Can, 92; Beam Art Gallery, Univ Nev, Las Vegas, 92; and others. *Pos:* Panelist, var comns, asns & mus, 86-91; artist adv task force, Western States Arts Fedn, Portland, Ore, 91. *Teaching:* Lectr, many mus & univs, 77-92; keynote speaker, Am Inst Architects Comt Design Ann Conf, Big Sky, Mont, 92. *Awards:* Grant, Art Matters, Inc, 88; Nat Endowment Arts Fel, 90; Grant, LEF Found, 92. *Bibliog:* Betty Waddell (auth), Heliotrope in Las Vegas, Artspace, Vol 15, Nos 4 & 5, p 71, summer 91; Jerry A Schefcik (auth), An issue of water (catalog), p 7, 92; Don Wherry (ed), Sound symposium 6 (catalog), p 85-86, 92; and others. *Mailing Add:* 10152 Duck Creek Rd Laurel MT 59044

ZERNER, HENRI THOMAS
HISTORIAN, CURATOR
b Suresnes, France, May 15, 39. *Study:* Univ Paris, Lic es Lett, 61, Dr(fine arts), 69; Ecole Pratique des Hautes Etudes, Paris, dipl(fine arts), 63. *Collections Arranged:* Venice in the Eighteenth Century (cataloged), Mus Art, RI Sch Design, 67 & J J J Tissot (cataloged), 67; The School of Fontainebleau (cataloged), Grand Palais, Paris, 72-73. *Pos:* Cur, Painting & Graphic Arts Mus, RI Sch Design, 65-66 & Prints & Drawing Mus, 66-72; cur prints, Fogg Mus, Harvard Univ, presently. *Teaching:* From asst prof to assoc prof fine arts, Brown Univ, Providence, RI, 66-72; prof fine arts, Harvard Univ, Cambridge, Mass, 72- *Awards:* Guggenheim Fel, Paris, 71; Prix Achille Fould, Acad des Inscriptions et Belles Lett, 71; and others. *Publ:* Coauth, Italian Art 1500-1600, Prentice-Hall, 66; auth, Tout l'oeuvre peint de Raphael, Flammarion, 69; auth, L'Ecole de Fontainebleau-Gravures, Abrams, 70; auth, Illustrated Bartsch, Vol XVI, In: Sixteenth Century Italian Etchings, 79; coauth (with Charles Rosen), Romanticism and Realism: The Mythology of 19th Century Art, Viking, 84. *Mailing Add:* Fogg Arts Mus 32 Quincey St Cambridge MA 02138

ZEVON, IRENE
PAINTER
b New York, NY, Nov 24, 18. *Study:* With Nahum Tschacbasov. *Work:* Butler Inst Am Art, Youngstown, Ohio; La Jolla Art Ctr, Calif; Kenosha Pub Mus, Wis; Mary Buie Mus, Oxford, Miss; Univ Ga Mus, Athens; plus many others including pvt collections. *Exhib:* Kenosha Pub Mus, Wis; St Louis Pub Libr, Mo; Long Island Univ, NY; Nat Acad Design, New York; Nat Asn Women Artists Ann, New York, 72; plus many other group & one-woman shows in univs, mus & galleries. *Awards:* Marion K Haldenstein Mem Prize, Nat Asn Women Artists, 72. *Mem:* Nat Asn Women Artists. *Media:* Oil. *Mailing Add:* 222 W 23rd St New York NY 10011

ZGODA, LARRY
STAINED GLASS ARTIST, CRAFTSMAN
b Chicago, Ill, Oct 27, 50. *Study:* Columbia Col, Ill, BA, 75. *Work:* City Chicago Public Art Collection. *Comn:* Tree of Life (stained glass), Hackley Pub Libr, Muskegon, Mich, 88; Clerestory panels, Wesley-Jesson Co, Chicago, Ill, 88; Tim Cusimano Mem Windows, Unitarian Universalist Church, Elgin, Il, 90; archit stained glass, comn by City of Chicago, Logan Sq Branch, Chicago Pub Libr, 90; archit stained glass, Asn Retired Persons, Washington, DC, 91. *Exhib:* 1st Int Stained Glass Exhib, Corning Mus Glass, New York, 87. *Teaching:* Instr stained glass, Hyde Art Ctr, Chicago, 87- *Awards:* Guild Am Craft Awards, Guild, 87. *Bibliog:* Lisa Skolnik (auth), Street smarts, Chicago Tribune, 7/22/90; article, Contemporary Crafts for the Home, Klaus Sikes Inc, 90; article, Larry Zgoda, The Guild, 90. *Media:* Stained Glass. *Publ:* Auth, Beauty of stainles glass, Professional Stained Glass, 5/90; article, Am Craft, 8-9/90; Lines of Poetry, Prof Stained Glass, 8/91. *Mailing Add:* 3447 N Pulaski Rd Chicago IL 60641

ZHEUTLIN, DALE R
SCULPTOR, EDUCATOR
b Newark, NJ, July 27, 48. *Study:* RI Sch Design, BFA, 70; Columbia Univ, MFA, 72. *Work:* The Robert Martin Co, White Plains, NY; Wang Laboratories Inc, New York; IBM Collection, NY; Chase Manhattan Bank, New York; Pfizer Corp, New York; and others. *Comn:* Kramer, Levin, Nessen, Kamin & Frankel, 86; Peat, Marwick & Main, Indianapolis, Ind, 88; Citibank Tower, Phoenix, Ariz, 90; Am Int Group, New York, 90; Aetna, Hartford, Conn, 90; and others. *Exhib:* Aldrich Mus, Trustees Choice, Ridgefield, Conn, 83; 46th Concorso Internationale della Ceramica a'arte, Faenza, Italy, 89; Katonah Mus Art, NY, 90; 2nd Int Ceramics Competition, Mino, Japan, 90; San Angelo Mus Art, Tex, 90; Wheeler Seidel Gallery, New York, 92; and others. *Teaching:* Art fac, New Rochelle High Sch, NY, 74-84, Mamaroneck High Sch, 84-; adj prof ceramics, Col New Rochelle, NY, 77-; guest lectr, NY Univ, 86. *Awards:* Award Merit, Mamaroneck Artists Guild, 79; Pauline Law Prize, Nat Asn Women Artists, New York, 80; Sculpture Award, Hudson River Mus, New York, 81. *Bibliog:* Jennifer Dunning (auth), A chance to find if the art of women in special, 86, Vivian Raynor (auth), Four artists at gallery shows, 1/89, NY Times; Bill Kraus (auth), Contemporary Crafts for the Home, Kraus Sikes Inc, 90; Leon Nigrosh (auth), Sculpting Clay, Davis Publ Inc, 91; and others. *Mem:* Nat Asn Women Artists Inc; Artists Equity Asn; Empire State Crafts Alliance (bd dirs). *Media:* Clay; All Media. *Publ:* Contribr, Apprenticeship in Craft, Daniel Clark Bks, 81. *Dealer:* Wheeler Seidel Gallery New York NY. *Mailing Add:* 139 Sixth St Pelham NY 10803

ZIB, TOM (THOMAS A ZIBELLI)
CARTOONIST
b Mt Vernon, NY. *Study:* Grand Cent Sch Art; Com Illus Studios. *Publ:* Contribr, Saturday Rev & Weight Watchers, 72, Saturday Evening Post, Nat Enquirer, Reader's Digest, 73-81, Wall Street J, 81, Good Housekeeping & Woman's World, Cosmopolitan, Better Homes & Gardens. *Mailing Add:* 167 E Devonia Ave Mt Vernon NY 10552

ZIBELLI, THOMAS A See Zib, Tom (Thomas A Zibelli)

ZIEGLER, MEL(VIN) AND KATE ERICSON
SCULPTOR
b Mel Ziegler, Campbelltown, Pa, 56, Kate Ericson, New York, NY, 55. *Study:* Mel Ziegler: RI Sch Design, 74-76; Kansas City Art Inst, BFA(sculpture), 76-78; Calif Inst Arts, MFA(sculpture), 80-82; Kate Ericson: Univ Colo, Boulder, 73-75; Sir John Cass Sch Art, London, 75; Kansas City Art Inst, BFA(sculpture), 76-78; Univ Tex, Austin, 79; Calif Inst Arts, MFA(sculpture), 80-82. *Comn:* Unplanted Landscape, pvt homeowner, Bellport, NY, 85; Garden Sculpture, Ward's Island, AREA, New York, 85; If You Would See the Monument, Look Around, Cent Park, Creative Time & Cent Park's Summer Stage with New York City Dept Parks & Recreation & Cent Park Conservancy, 86; Half Slave, Half Free, pvt homeowner, Hawley, Pa, 87; Viaduct Gateway, Comt Pub Art, Cleveland, Ohio, 88; and others. *Exhib:* Solo exhibs, Augustus Saint-Gaudens Fel Exhib, Cornish, NH, 90, Capp St Proj, San Francisco, 91, USIA Sponsored Shopping Cult Fundicao Progresso, Rio de Janeiro, travelled to Museu Mineiro, Belo Horizonte, 91 & Michael Klein Inc, New York, 92; Setagaya Art Mus, Tokyo, travelled to Nat Mus Art, Osaka & Fukuoka Art Mus, 91; Michael Klein Inc, NY, 91; Lintas Worldwide, New York, 92; and others. *Bibliog:* Spoleto patchwork, Evening Post, Charleston, SC, 4/17/91; Camouflaged history, Harper's Mag, 28, 8/91; Arte em reciclagem, Tribuna Rio, 10/10/91; and others. *Mailing Add:* 55 Morton St 6E New York NY 10014

ZIEMANN, RICHARD CLAUDE
PRINTMAKER, EDUCATOR
b Buffalo, NY, July 3, 32. *Study:* Albright Art Sch; Yale Univ, BFA & MFA; painting with Albers & Brooks; printmaking with Peterdi; drawings with Chaet. *Work:* Brooklyn Mus, NY; Silvermine Guild Art; Seattle Art Mus, Wash; De Cordova & Dana Mus; Libr Cong & Nat Gallery Art, Washington, DC; and others. *Comn:* Print Editions for Int Graphic Arts Soc, 58 & 60, Yale Univ Alumni Asn, 60 & Pan-Am Airlines, 62. *Exhib:* American Prints Today Touring Exhib, most maj print exhibs, 58-65, 24 mus, 62-63 & Paris Biennale, 63; one-man shows, Allen R Hite Art Inst, Univ Louisville, 67, Alpha Gallery, Boston, 67 & Univ Conn Art Gallery, 68; Oversize Prints, Whitney Mus Am Art. *Pos:* Supvr, Graphic Workshop in Graphic Arts USA Touring Exhib, Soviet Union, 63-64; artist in residence, Dartmouth Col, summer 71. *Teaching:* Asst prof art, Hunter Col, 66; instr printmaking, Yale Univ Summer Sch, 66-67; from assoc prof to prof art, Lehman Col, 78- *Awards:* Fulbright Grant to Netherlands, 58-59; Nat Inst Arts & Lett Grant, 66; Tiffany Found Grant, 60-61; and others. *Mem:* Soc Am Graphic Artists. *Dealer:* Jane Haslem Gallery 2121 P St NW Washington DC 20037; Alpha Galleries 121 Newbury St Boston MA 02116. *Mailing Add:* c/o Jane Haslem 2025 Hillyer Place NW Washington DC 20009

ZIFF, JERROLD
HISTORIAN, COLLECTOR
b Los Angeles, Calif, Dec 20, 28. *Study:* Occidental Col, BA, 51; Univ Southern Calif, MA, 54; Harvard Univ, PhD, 59. *Collections Arranged:* French Masters: Rocco to Romanticism (coauth, catalog), Univ Calif, Los Angeles, 60-61; George F Mc Murray Collection of 19th century American Paintings, Trinity Col, Hartford, Conn, 68; Drawings from Four Collections (co-auth, catalog), 73 & II (auth, catalog), Univ Ill. *Pos:* Asst prof 19th century art, Univ Calif, Los Angeles, 58-66; prof 18th & 19th century art, Trinity Col, Hartford, 66-69; prof 18th & 19th century art & drawings, Univ Ill, Champaign, 69- *Mem:* Col Art Asn; Midwest Art Hist Soc; Turner Soc. *Res:* Art of J M W Turner; old master drawings. *Collection:* Old master and 19th century drawings. *Mailing Add:* Mumford House Univ of Ill 1403 W Lorado Taft Dr Urbana IL 61801

ZILCZER, JUDITH KATY
HISTORIAN, CURATOR
b Waterbury, Conn, Nov 6, 48. *Study:* George Washington Univ, BA, 69 & MA, 71; Univ Del, PhD, 75. *Collections Arranged:* The Noble Buyer: John Quinn, Patron of the Avant-Garde (auth, catalog), Hirshhorn Mus & Sculpture Garden, 78; Oscar Bluemner: The Hirshhorn Museum Collection (auth, catalog), 79; Joseph Stella: the Hirshorn Museum Collection (auth, catalog), 83; The Advent of Modernism: Post-Impressionism and North American Art 1900-1918 (coauth, catalog), High Mus Art, Atlanta, Ga, 86; Keith Sonnier: Neon (auth, catalog), Hirshhorn Mus, 89. *Pos:* Historian, Hirshhorn Mus & Sculpture Garden, 74-88; assoc cur painting, 88-92, cur paintings, 92- *Teaching:* asst professorial lectr Am studies & art hist, George Washington Univ, 75-76, assoc professorial lectr, 80-86 & 91. *Awards:* Smithsonian Fel, Nat Collection of Fine Arts, 73-74; Penrose Fund res grant, Am Philos Soc, 76-77; Award for Exceptional Serv, Smithsonian Inst, 86. *Mem:* Col Art Asn; Women's Caucus for Art; Am Studies Asn; Am Asn Mus. *Res:* Nineteenth and twentieth century art; history of patronage. *Publ:* Auth, Raymond Duchamp-Villon: Pioneer of modern sculpture, Philadelphia Mus, Art Bulletin, fall 80; The Face of War: The Last Works of Raymond Duchamp-Villon, Art Bulletin, 3/83; Synaesthesia and popular culture: Arthur Dove, George Gershwin and the rhapsody in blue, Art J, winter 84; Color Music: Synaesthesia and Nineteenth-century sources for Abstract Art, Artibus et historiae 16, 87. *Mailing Add:* c/o Hirshhorn Mus Independence Ave & Eighth St SW Washington DC 20560

ZILIUS, VLADAS
PAINTER
b Silale, Lithuania, May 13, 39; US citizen. *Study:* Vilnius Art Acad, DFA, 59-65. *Work:* Vilnius State Mus & Vilnius State Gallery, Lithuania. *Exhib:* Int Biennial, Cracow, Poland, 68; Barcelona Mus, Spain, 70; Graphic Arts from USSR, State Mus, Sophia, Bulgaria, 72; solo exhib, Drawing Center, Queens Col, New York, 84. *Teaching:* Instr drawing, Archit Inst, Vilnius, Lithuania, 74-75. *Media:* Miscellaneous Media. *Dealer:* Galerie Aldonna 215 E 79th St New York NY 10021. *Mailing Add:* 120 Gale Place Bronx NY 10463

ZIMILES, MURRAY
PAINTER, EDUCATOR
b New York, NY, Nov 30, 41. *Study:* Univ Ill, BFA, 63; Cornell Univ, MFA, 65; Ecole Nat Superieure Beaux-Arts, Paris, 66-67. *Work:* Brooklyn Mus, NY; Neuberger Mus, New York; Mus Mod Art, NY; Nat Collection Fine Arts; NY Public Libr; and others. *Comn:* Civic Ctr, Dutchess Co Arts Coun, Poughkeepsie, NY, 81. *Exhib:* Prints from Portfolios, Brooklyn Mus, 70; one-man shows, Kunstnerforbundet Gallery, Oslo, Norway, 72, Vassar Col Gallery, 77, Sindin Galleries, New York, 78, Neuberger Mus, New York, 80-81 & Johnson Mus, Cornell Univ, Ithaca, NY, 81. *Teaching:* Instr printmaking, Pratt Graphics Ctr, New York, 68-71; asst prof drawing & printmaking, Silvermine Col Art, New Canaan, Conn, 68-71; asst prof drawing & printmaking, State Univ NY, New Paltz, 72-77; prof drawing & printmaking, State Univ NY, Purchase, 77- *Awards:* Found Etats-Unis Fel, Paris, 65-66; Royal Norweg Govt Fel, 71; State Univ NY res grants, 76 & 79. *Bibliog:* Article, Arts Mag, 1/78; review, New York Times, 1/4/81; Article, Art News, 4/92. *Mem:* Soc Am Graphic Artists. *Media:* Acrylic, Oil. *Publ:* Coauth, The Technique of Fine Art Lithography, Van Nostrand Reinhold, 70; Early American Mills, Clarkson Potter, 73; The Lithographic Workshop Around the World, Van Nostrand Reinhold, 74; Boris Margo, A Retrospective (exhib catalog), Provincetown Art Asn. *Dealer:* Stuart Levy Gallery 415 W Broadway New York NY 10012. *Mailing Add:* Visual Arts Dept SUNY Col Purchase Purchase NY 10577

ZIMMERMAN, ALICE A
COLLECTOR, ART DEALER
b Chicago, Ill, June 6, 39. *Study:* Univ Wis, Madison, 57-58; Emory Univ, BA, 77; Vanderbilt Univ, MA, 79. *Pos:* Mem, adv comt, Southeastern Ctr Contemp Art, Winston-Salem, NC, 78-; exec dir, Metro Nashville Arts Comn, 81-83; trustee, Am Craft Coun, New York, 83-; dir, Zimmerman-Saturn Gallery, Nashville, Tenn, formerly. *Specialty:* Emerging artists; fine crafts; contemporary art. *Collection:* Photo-realists; painters and sculptors; contemporary Europeans; handmade furniture and crafts. *Mailing Add:* 6004 Dunham Springs Rd Nashville TN 37205

ZIMMERMAN, ARNOLD
SCULPTOR
b Poughkeepsie, NY, Dec 13, 54. *Study:* Kansas City Art Inst, Mo, BFA; NY State Col Ceramics, Alfred, MFA, 79. *Work:* Contemp Art Ctr, Honolulu, Hawaii; Everson Mus Art, Syracuse, NY; Los Angeles Co Mus Art, Calif; Mus Decorative Arts, Montreal, Que; Yellowstone Art Ctr, Billings, Mont. *Comn:* Large sculpture, Fed Express Bldg, Philadelphia Redevelopment Authority. *Exhib:* Young Americans: Clay, Mus Contemp Crafts, New York, NY, 78; RI Sch Design Clay Invitational, Providence, 84; solo exhibs, Hadler Rodriguez Gallery, New York, 84, Objects Gallery, Chicago, Ill, 85, Helen Drutt Gallery, Philadelphia, Pa, 85, Camino Real Gallery, Boca Raton, Fla, 89 & El Stark Gallery, New York, 89; Inaugural Exhib, Am Craft Mus, New York, 86; Clay Revisions, Seattle Art Mus, Wash, 87; Gulbenkian Found, Lisbon, Portugal, 88; John Michael Kohler Art Ctr, Sheboygan, Wis, 89; Mino, Japan, 89; Nat Mus Ceramic Art, Baltimore, Md, 89. *Pos:* Residency, Bacqui Stone Quarry, Lacoste, France, 74 & 75; Omaha Brickworks, Alternative Worksites, Nebr, spring 83; Int Symp Ceramics, Alcobaca, Port, 7/87; Watershed Ctr Ceramic Arts, Maine, 8/87; Centro de Arte e Comunicacao Visual, Lisbon, Port, 7/88; Kohler Co, Wis, fall 89. *Awards:* Artist Fel, Conn Comn Arts, 81; Craftsman Fel, Nat Endowment Arts, 82 & 86; Artists Fel, NY Found Arts, 87. *Mailing Add:* c/o Objects Gallery 230 W Huron St 3E Chicago IL 60610

ZIMMERMAN, ELYN
SCULPTOR, ENVIRONMENTAL ARTIST
b Philadelphia, Pa, Dec 16, 45. *Study:* Univ Calif, Los Angeles, BA, 68, MFA, 72. *Work:* Los Angeles Co Mus Art; Whitney Mus Am Art & Chase Manhattan Bank, New York; Neuberger Mus, Purchase, NY; General Mills Corp, Minne, Minn. *Comn:* Plaza with pool & rocks, Nat Geographic Soc, Washington, DC, 84; Plaza design with multiple pools, O'Hare Int Ctr, Chicago, 87; Keystone Island, Dade Co Art Pub Places, Miami, Fla, 89; Two waterwalls & pools, CRA Art Prog, Los Angeles, 90; Plaza Design, pvt comn, San Francisco, 90; Sanctuary, Univ SFla, Tampa, 90. *Exhib:* Drawings: The Pluralist Decade, US Pavillion Venice Biennale, Italy, 80; Palisades Project, Hudson River Mus, Yonkers, NY, 82; Directions 1983, Hirshhorn Mus, Washington, DC, 83; Art & Archit & Landscape, San Francisco Mus Mod Art, 85; Artist As Social Designer, Los Angeles Co Mus Art, 85; solo exhib, Projects Wave Hill, Riverdale, NY, 88; Art Mus Univ SFla, Tampa, 91; Hoffman Gallery, Los Angeles, Calif, 92; 65 Thompson Gallery, NY, 92. *Awards:* New Talent Award, Los Angeles Co Art Mus, 76; Artist Fel Grant, Nat Endowment Arts, 76, 80 & 82; CAPS Grant, NY State, 80. *Bibliog:* Charles Stuckey (auth), Palisades project & other works, Hudson River Mus, 82; Marc Treib (auth), Elyn Zimmerman: A decade of projects (exhib catalog), Wavehill, Riverdale, NY, 88; John Beardsley (auth), Earth works & beyond, Abbeville Press, 89; John Beardsley (auth), Elyn Zimmerman (exhib catalog), Art Mus Univ SFla, 91. *Mem:* Creative Time Inc (bd dirs, 85-92); Int Sculpture Ctr (bd dirs, 89-). *Media:* Mixed Media. *Mailing Add:* 140 Greene St New York NY 10012

ZIMMERMAN, KATHLEEN MARIE
PAINTER, COLLAGE ARTIST
b Floral Park, NY, Apr 24, 23. *Study:* Art Students League; Nat Acad Sch Fine Arts, New York. *Work:* Butler Inst Am Art, Youngstown, Ohio; Univ Wyo Art Mus, Laramie; Lowe Art Mus, Univ Miami, Coral Gables, Fla; NC Mus Art, Raleigh; Nat Acad Design, New York; and others. *Exhib:* Art USA, 58; Silvermine Guild, Conn, 62; Nat Acad Design, 69, 75-78, 80, 82, 84, 86, 88, 90 & 91; solo shows, Westbeth Gallery, 73 & 74 & St Mary's Col, Md, 90; Am Watercolor Soc, New York, 75-78 & 80; and many others. *Teaching:* Instr drawing & painting, Midtown Sch Art, New York, 47-52. *Awards:* Scholar, John F & Anna Lee Stacey Found, 54; Thirteen prizes, Nat Asn Women Artists, 57-91; Henry Ward Ranger Fund Purchases, Nat Acad Design, 76 & 82; and others. *Bibliog:* James Mellow (auth), review, NY Times, 2/17/73; Hilton Kramer (auth), review, NY Times, 6/10/77; Gerald F Brommer (auth), The Art of Collage, Davis Publ, 78; John & Joan Digby (auth), The Collage Handbook, Thames & Hudson Publ 85. *Mem:* Nat Asn Women Artists; Am Watercolor Soc; Audubon Artists; Allied Artists Am; assoc mem, Nat Acad Design. *Media:* Oil, Acrylic; Paper. *Publ:* Co-illusr, Diet for a Small Planet, 71. *Mailing Add:* 463 West St A1110 New York NY 10014

ZIMMERMAN, PAUL WARREN
PAINTER, INSTRUCTOR
b Toledo, Ohio, Apr 29, 21. *Study:* John Herron Art Sch, BFA. *Work:* Pa Acad Fine Arts, Philadelphia; Houston Mus Fine Art; Butler Inst Am Art, Youngstown, Ohio; Springfield Mus Fine Art, Mass; Wadsworth Atheneum, Hartford, Conn. *Comn:* Mural, First New Haven Nat Bank, Conn, 65. *Exhib:* Indiana Artists Exhibition, John Herron Art Mus, Indianapolis, 57; American Painting & Sculpture, Univ Ill, 61; Pa Acad Fine Arts, Philadelphia, 62; 144th Ann Exhib, Nat Acad Design, New York, 69; Midyear Show, Butler Inst Am Art, Youngstown, 70. *Teaching:* Prof painting & design, Univ Hartford Art Sch, 47- *Awards:* First Prize, Conn Watercolor Soc, 64; Altman Landscape Prize for Second Place, 67 & First Place, 69, Nat Acad Design. *Bibliog:* Henry Pitz (auth), Paintings of Paul Zimmerman, Am Artist Mag, 1/60. *Mem:* Nat Acad Design; Conn Acad Fine Arts; Conn Watercolor Soc (pres, 52-53). *Media:* Oil. *Dealer:* Munson Gallery New Haven CT; Korn Bluth Gallery Fair Lawn NJ. *Mailing Add:* 257 Victoria Rd Hartford CT 06114

ZIMMERMAN, WILLIAM HAROLD
PAINTER, ILLUSTRATOR
b Dillsboro, Ind, Oct 1, 37. *Study:* Cincinnati Art Acad. *Work:* Cincinnati Mus Natural Hist, Ohio; Ind State Mus, Indianapolis; Pomona Col, Calif; Gallery Fine Arts, Columbus, Ohio; Lilly Libr, Bloomington, Ind; Ind Univ Jordan Hall, Bloomington, Ind. *Exhib:* Soc Animal Artists Ann, New York, 67; one-man shows in New York, San Francisco, Chicago, Cincinnati & Columbus, Ohio; Bird Art Exhib, Leigh Yawkey Woodson Art Mus, 78-81; Birds, Nat Collection Fine Art, Smithsonian Inst, Washington, DC, 80; Bird Art Exhib, Royal Scottish Acad, Edinburgh, Scotland, British Mus, London,

Eng & Carnegie Mus Natural Hist, Pittsburgh, Pa, 82; Ind State Mus Indianapolis, 84; Arts for the Parks, Nat Park Acad Top 100 Traveling Exhibit, Jackson, Wyo, Peroia, Ill, Shreveport, La, Cincinnati, Ohio, Rochester, NY, Anchorage, Alaska, 89. *Awards:* Award for Magpie, Cincinnati Animal Art Show, 66; Birds of Indiana, Gov declaration of book as Ind treasure; Midwestern Books Competition. *Bibliog:* Bill Thomas (auth), Dillsboro's Audubon, Nat Observer, 11/12/65; Jay Shuler (auth), A real artist has to work for himself, Carolina Outdoors, 9/71; Carolyn Tufford (auth), Lifestyle, Bloomington Ind Herald-Telephone; Gibbons & Strom (auth), Neighbors to the Birds, Norton, 88. *Media:* Gouache, Acrylic. *Publ:* Illusr, Waterfowl of North America, 74; contrib illusr, Birds of Indiana, 84; Waterfowl of North America, Ducks Unlimited Canada, 87, Birds of Illinois, 89; contribr, Birds of Ohio 89; illusr, Life Histories of North American Woodpeckers, Arthur Cleveland Bent, rev ed, 92. *Mailing Add:* RR 3 Box 36 Nashville IN 47448

ZIMON, KATHY ELIZABETH
LIBRARIAN
b Szeged, Hungary, Feb 20, 41; Can citizen. *Study:* Univ BC, BA(art hist), 66, BLS, 69, MA(art hist), 70. *Pos:* Fine arts librn, Univ Calgary Libr, Alta, 69-; cur, Can Archit Arch. *Mem:* Can Libr Asn; Can Asn of Spec Libr & Info Serv (newsletter ed, 75-78, chmn art sect, 79-80); Art Libr Soc North Am. *Res:* Alberta artists: currently working on an index. *Mailing Add:* Libr Fine Arts Libr Univ Calgary 2500 Univ Dr NW Calgary AB T2N 1N4 Canada

ZINGALE, LAWRENCE
PAINTER
b Florida, NY, Aug 12, 38. *Work:* Int Mus Folk Art, Santa Fe, NMex; Chase Manhattan Bank, New York; Silvermine Guild Ctr Arts, New Caanan, Conn. *Exhib:* Int Mus of Folk Art, Santa Fe, 76; The All-Am Dog, Mus of Folk Art, New York, 77-78; The Am Game, Wilson Art Ctr, Rochester, NY, 78; one-man shows, American Hurrah Antiques, New York, 78, Jay Johnson Gallery, New York, 81 & 88 & Frank Miele Gallery, 93; Jay Johnson Gallery, New York, 88-91; Frank Miele Gallery, New York, 93; Fenimore House, Cooperstown, NY, 92. *Bibliog:* Robert Bishop (auth), The All-American Dog, Avon Publ, New York, 77; Ellen Stern (auth), article, New York Mag, 10/78; article, Attenzione Mag, 12/81; Jay Johnson & William Ketchum (auths), American Folk Art of the Twentieth Century, Rizzoli Publ; and others. *Media:* Oil, Acrylic. *Dealer:* Frank Miele Gallery 1262 Madison Ave New York NY 10128. *Mailing Add:* 22 Maple Ave Florida NY 10921

ZIRIN, NOLA
PAINTER
b New York, NY, May 28, 43. *Study:* Boston Univ, 61-62, New York Univ, 62-65, Sch Visual Arts, 87-88. *Work:* Islip Art Mus, NY; Nat Mus Taiwan; Mony's Collection of Contemp Prints, NY; AT&T Collection, NY; Readers Digest Corp; and others. *Exhib:* Mus Hudson Highlands, Cornwall-on-the-Hudson, NY, 86; Long Island Artists, Nassau Mus Art, Roslyn, NY, 87; Lines of Vision, Hillwood Art Mus, 89; Out of Abstraction, Islip Mus, 90; June Kelly Gallery, New York, 92; and others. *Teaching:* Art teacher, Philadelphia Pub Schs, 66-68. *Awards:* Graphic Award, Painter & Sculptor Soc NJ, 78; Painting Award, Islip Mus, 86. *Bibliog:* Susan Gettler (auth), Long Island Artists, Nassau Mus, Roslyn, NY, 87; Michael Lasser (auth), A Sigh of Relief, Wilson Art Ctr, Rochester, NY, 87; Judith C VanWagner (auth), Lines of Vision, Hudson Hills Press, 89; Ruth Bass (auth), Art News, 92. *Mem:* Orgn Independent Artists, New York, 89; Hunter Point Artists Asn, Long Island City, NY, 90. *Media:* Miscellaneous Media. *Dealer:* June Kelly Gallery 591 Broadway New York NY 10012. *Mailing Add:* Seven Farm Ct Syosset NY 11791

ZIRKER, JOSEPH
PRINTMAKER, LECTURER
b Los Angeles, Calif, Aug 13, 24. *Study:* Univ Calif, Los Angeles, 43-44, 46-47; Univ Denver, BFA, 49; with Jules Heller & Francis de Erdely, Univ Southern Calif, MFA, 51; Tamarind Lithography Workshop, printer fel, 62-63 & res fel, 64. *Work:* Achenbach Found, Calif Palace Legion Honor, San Francisco; Portland Art Mus, Ore; La Art Mus, Denmark; Koninklijk Mus voor Schone Kunsten, Antwerp, Belgium; and others. *Exhib:* Solo exhibs, Calif Palace Legion of Honor, San Francisco, 74, De Saisset Art Gallery & Mus, Univ Santa Clara, Calif, 75, Univ Art Collection, Ariz State Univ, Tempe, 83, Portland State Univ, Ore, 84, Espace Latino Americain, Paris, France, 87, Centrum Frans Masereel, Kasterlee, Belgium, 89, Galerie Witteveen, Amsterdam, Netherlands, 90, Smith Anderson Gallery, Palo Alto, 91; New Ways With Paper, Nat Collection of Fine Arts, Smithsonian Inst, Washington, DC, 77-78; New American Monotypes & Paper as Medium, Smithsonian Traveling Exhib, 78-80; Paper-Art, Crocker Art Mus, Sacramento, Calif, 81; New American Paperworks, Orient & United States, 82-86. *Pos:* Dir, Joseph Press, Venice, Calif, 63-64. *Teaching:* Lectr printmaking, Univ Southern Calif, 63; instr drawing, San Jose City Col, 66-82; lectr, Stanford Univ, Calif. *Awards:* Nat Acad Design, 92. *Bibliog:* Jules Heller (auth), Papermaking, Watson-Guptill Publ, New York, 78. *Media:* Monotype, Paper Art. *Publ:* Auth, Survey Exhibition 1962-82 (exhib catalog), Smith- Anderson Gallery, Palo Alto, 82; Innovations in monotype and paper art, Arte Grafika, Antwerp, Belg, spring 90. *Dealer:* Smith Andersen Gallery 200 Homer Ave Palo Alto CA 94301; Perimeter Gallery 356 W Huron Chicago IL 60610. *Mailing Add:* 451 O'Connor St Menlo Park CA 94025

ZISLA, HAROLD
PAINTER, GRAPHIC ARTIST
b Cleveland, Ohio, June 28, 25. *Study:* Cleveland Inst Art; Western Reserve Univ, BS(educ) & AM. *Exhib:* Cleveland Mus Art; South Bend Michiana; John Herron Art Mus; Ft Wayne Art Mus; Kalamazoo Art Inst; and others. *Pos:* Dir & bd mem, South Bend Art Ctr, 57- *Teaching:* Instr, South Bend Art Ctr, 53-89; prof emer fine arts, Ind Univ, South Bend. *Awards:* Amoco Found Award; All Univ Teaching Award, 79; First Eldon Lundquist Fac Fel, Ind Univ South Bend, 85; Arts Midwest Fel Award, 86. *Mailing Add:* 1230 Dennis Dr South Bend IN 46614

ZITO, JOSEPH (PHILLIP)
SCULPTOR, CONCEPTUAL ARTIST
b Brooklyn, NY, June 6, 57. *Study:* Sch Visul Arts, BFA, 79. *Exhib:* One-man shows, Il Ponte Gallery, Rome, Italy, 88, Greenberg Gallery, St Louis, Mo, 89, Resa Esman Gallery, New York, 89; Oltreluce, Claudio Bottello Arte, Turin, Italy, 90; Joseph Zito & Gerald Giamportone, Blumhelman Gallery, Los Angeles, Calif, 90. *Bibliog:* Walter Thompson (auth), Joseph Zito, Art in America, 10/88; William Zimmer (auth), 7 Days Mag, 4/6/88; Michael Welzenbach (auth), Washington Post, 2/17/90. *Dealer:* Rosa Esman Gallery 70 Greene St New York NY 10012. *Mailing Add:* 166 Wolcott Brooklyn NY 11231

ZIVIC, WILLIAM THOMAS
PAINTER, SCULPTOR
b Ironwood, Mich, Aug 31, 30. *Work:* City of Tucson; Univ Ariz; Pima Col; Lockheed Aircraft, Los Angeles; Grissmer Corp, Indianapolis, Ind; Toyota Corp, Tokyo, Japan; plus over 1,000 pvt collections, US, Europe, Africa & Asia. *Comn:* Paintings, Great Western Bank, Phoenix, 73; painting, Ariz Bank, Tucson, 75; painting, US Postal Serv, 75. *Exhib:* Tucson Art Ctr Ann, 74; Alamo Kiwanis Art Show, San Antonio, 74; Casa Grande Art Fiesta, Ariz, 75; Tubac Art Festival, Ariz, 75. *Awards:* Best of Show, Int Fine Arts; 1st place sculpture, Palm Springs, Calif. *Mem:* Tucson Art Ctr; Casa Grande Art Asn; Santa Cruz Valley Art Asn; SW League Fine Arts. *Media:* Bronze; Multimedia. *Publ:* Illusr, Tucson Bi-Centennial Mag, 75; Southwest Memories, 75. *Dealer:* Sonoita Creek Gallery Box 159 Sonoita AZ 85637. *Mailing Add:* 1516 Turquoise Vista Tucson AZ 85710

ZLOWE, FLORENCE M
PAINTER, DRAFTSMAN
b Allentown, Pa. *Study:* Philadelphia Col Art, cert, 33; New York Univ, with Samuel M Adler, 51-54. *Work:* Philadelphia Mus Art; Butler Inst Am Art, Youngstown, Ohio; Smithsonian Inst; Minn Mus Art, St Paul; Cooper-Hewitt Mus, New York; and seven others. *Exhib:* Nat Acad Design, New York, 58 & 65; Chrysler Mus, Norfolk, Va, 64; Chateau de la Napoule, Alpes Maritime, France, 65; Jersey City Mus, NJ, 70; Minn Mus Art, St Paul, 75. *Awards:* Medal Hon First Prize, Nat Asn Women Artists, 58 & Ann Award, 65-80; Oil Award, NJ Soc Painters & Sculptors, 58, 61 & 83; Am Soc Contemp Artists, 59, 64, 75 & 84; and others. *Mem:* Am Soc Contemp Artists (treas, 76-80); Nat Asn Women Artists; NJ Soc Painters & Sculptors; Artists Equity Asn New York. *Media:* Oil, Watercolor; Pen & Ink. *Mailing Add:* 41 Union Sq New York NY 10003

ZOKOSKY, PETER L
PAINTER
b Long Beach, Calif, 1957. *Study:* Univ Calif, Riverside, BA, 79, Oris Art Inst, Los Angeles, MFA, 81. *Work:* Chemical Bank, New York; Kaufman & Broad, Paris, France; Security Pacific Bank, Los Angeles; and many others. *Exhib:* Solo exhibs, Inland Empire Gallery, Riverside, 79, Otis Art Inst, Los Angeles, 81, Rio Hondo Col, Whittler, 84, Newspace, Los Angeles, 86, 88, 89, 91 & 93, Mt San Jacinto Col Art Gallery & Peter Zokosky Oil Painting Exhib, Hsiung Shih Gallery, Taipei, Taiwan, 88 & Felicita Found, Escondido, 90; Mental Map, B Gallery, Tokyo, Japan, 91; Telephone, Security Pacific Gallery, Costa Mesa, Calif, 92; Drawings II, Koplin Gallery, Santa Monica, Calif, 92; Greatest Hits, Newspace, Los Angeles, Calif, 92; Virgin Territories, Long Beach Mus Art, Calif, 92. *Awards:* Fel, Nat Endowment Arts, 87; Artist in Residence Grant, Roswell Mus & Art Ctr, NMex, 91. *Bibliog:* James Scarborough (auth), Les Paysans de Long Beach, Vissions, 92; Devorah Knaff (auth), Artistic Connections, Press Enterprise, 92; Laurl Mendenhall (auth), review, Costa Mesa Daily Pilot, 92. *Mailing Add:* c/o New Space 5241 Melrose Ave Los Angeles CA 90038

ZOLLWEG, AILEEN BOULES
PAINTER, SCULPTOR
b East St Louis, Ill. *Study:* Sch Art Inst, Chicago, Ill; Carnegie Mellon Univ, Pittsburgh, Pa. *Work:* 100 Friends of Pittsburgh Art, Corning Glass Corp & Mellon Bank Collection, Pittsburgh. *Comn:* Moat tracing, Three Rivers Arts Festival, Pittsburgh, 83; Swimming Pool Mural, San Diego, Calif, 88. *Exhib:* One-person exhib, Washington & Jefferson Univ, Washington, Pa, 84, Pittsburgh Ctr Arts, 90 & Laurel Arts, Somerset, Pa, 92; Assoc Artists Invitational, Westmoreland Art Mus, Greensburg, Pa, 85; New Technol Invitational, Carnegie Mellon Univ Gallery, 85; Andrew Carnegie Mem Exhib, Dunfermline, Scotland, 85; Butler Inst Am Art, Youngstown, Ohio, 88; four-person exhib, Heinz Found, Pittsburgh, 92; and others. *Awards:* Honorable Mention, Print Exhib, Ctr Arts, Pittsburgh, 83; Purchase Award, 83 & 84, Juror's Award, 84 & 91, Assoc Artists Carnegie Mus. *Bibliog:* TV prog, Women in Art, Monroeville Cable, 83; TV prog, Pittsburgh Women Artists, 92. *Mem:* Assoc Artists Pittsburgh. *Media:* Acrylic; Miscellaneous Media. *Mailing Add:* 4560 Bulltown Rd Murrysville PA 15668

ZONA, LOUIS A
MUSEUM DIRECTOR, EDUCATOR
b New Castle, Pa, June 28, 44. *Study:* Youngstown State Univ, BS(art educ), 66; Univ Pittsburgh, MS(art educ), 69; Carnegie-Mellon Univ, doctorate, 73. *Collections Arranged:* Patrick Ireland, Blue Room Exhib, 83; Fireworks:

Americans Celebrate the Eighth Art, 86; George Segal: The Drawings, 85; Alfred Leslie, 100 Views Along the Road, 85; Ray Parker: A Retrospective Exhibition, 86; Anatomy of a Cloud: The Collage Paintings of Paul Jenkins, Butler Inst Am Art, 86; Leo Castelli: A Tribute (auth, catalog), 87; Jasper Johns: Drawings and Prints from the collection of Leo Castelli, 89; Gregory Arnenoff: Monotypes/Prints, 89; Michael Hardesty: Polar Event & Vigil II, 89; Chuck Close: Editions, 89; Philip Pearlstein: The Abstract Landscapes, 92; The Artist at Ringside, 92. *Pos:* Exec dir, Butler Inst Am Art, Youngstown, Ohio, 81- *Teaching:* Adj prof art & museum studies, Westminster Col, Pa, formerly; prof art hist & museology, Youngstown State Univ, 70-; host, weekly arts program, WKBN. *Awards:* Gov Award Arts (Admin Category), Ohio, 90. *Mem:* Hoyt Inst; trustee, Oberlin Conserv Asn; trustee, Youngstown Area Arts Coun; Ohio Mus Asn (trustee). *Publ:* Auth, George Segal comes to Youngstown, 80, Painterly deliberations, 4/81, Alfred Leslie's Americans, 82, Ray Parker: Selected works on paper, 86 & The anatomy of a cloud: The collages of Paul Jenkins, 86, Dialogue; James Pernotto & Steven Finkel at the Gund Gallery of the Ohio Arts Coun (exhib catalog essay), 86; Leo Castelli, interview, Dialogue Mag, 87; Jasper Johns: Drawings & Prints from the Collection of Leo Castelli, 89. *Mailing Add:* Butler Inst Am Art 524 Wick Ave Youngstown OH 44502

ZONIA, DHIMITRI
PAINTER, PRINTMAKER
b St Louis, Mo, June 12, 21. *Study:* Independent study in Italy & Eng. *Work:* Butler Inst Am Art, Youngstown, Ohio; Ark Art Ctr, Little Rock; Okla Art Ctr, Oklahoma City; Art Gallery, Del Mar Col, Corpus Christi, Tex; Quincy Art Ctr, Ill. *Comn:* Mural, Carlyn H Wohl Bldg Info Ctr, 81; stained glass, murals & interior design, Sts Cyril & Methody Church, Granite City, Ill, 82. *Exhib:* Midyear Show, Butler Inst Am Art, Youngstown, Ohio, 74; Western Ill Univ, 79; Nat Traveling Exhib, Minn Mus Art, 80; Ariz State Univ, 80; Univ Mo, Cape Girardeau, 85. *Teaching:* Instr painting & drawing, Crestwood Community Ctr & Parkway Unitarian Church, Educ Ctr, currently. *Awards:* Butler Inst Am Art Award, Youngstown, Ohio, 77; First Prize Painting, Quincy Art Ctr, Ill, 85; Second Prize Painting, Spiva Art Ctr, Joplin, Mo, 85; Popular Choice Award, Dakota Art Ctr, Rapid City, SDak, 85. *Bibliog:* Floyd Bowser (auth), Aspiring artist, St Louis Post-Dispatch, 4/26/70; Rick Graefe (auth), Kimmswick gains an artist, Courier-J, 79; Hazel Lee (auth), Renowned artist moves to Kimmswick, St Louis J, 79. *Mem:* St Louis Artists Guild (bd gov, 79-81). *Media:* Oil; Etching. *Publ:* Co-auth, Arise My Love, Concordia Publ Co, 75; Contribr, Painting in the realistic manner, Pallette Talk, 80; auth, Painting Glazes over Powerded Graphite, Step by Step Graphics, 86. *Mailing Add:* 4680 Karamar Dr St Louis MO 63128

ZONTAL, JORGE (JORGE SAIA)
POST-CONCEPTUAL ARTIST
b Parma, Italy; Can citizen. *Study:* Dalhousie Univ, Halifax, NS, BA, 68. *Work:* Nat Gallery Can, Ottawa; Mus Contemp Art, Gent, Belg; Van Abbemuseum, Eindhoven, Neth; Philadelphia Mus; Musee d'Art Contemporain, Montreal; Art Gallery Ont, Toronto. *Comn:* Ursa Major and Taurus: Pavilion Fragments from the Starry Vault, Relief Mural, Toronto Stock Exchange, 83; exterior relief sculpture, Ont Courthouse, Ottawa, 86. *Exhib:* Group exhibs, Venice Biennale, Can Pavilion, 80, Documenta 7 & 8, Kassel, WGer, 82 & 87; Vancouver Art Gallery, Can, 84; Mus Contemp Art, Gent, Belg, 84; Kunsthalle Basel, Switz, 84; Van Abbemuseum, Eindhoven, Neth, 85; Musee d'art Contemporain, Montreal, 85; Albright-Knox Art Gallery, Buffalo, 86; Contemp Art Mus, Houston, 87; New Mus Contemp Art, New York, 88. *Awards:* Can Coun Grants, 70-83; Gershon Iskowitz Award, 88; Toronto Arts Award, 89. *Bibliog:* Germano Celant (auth), General idea in Canada: Un Gruppo Canadese, Domus, 11/74; John Bentley Mays (coauth), Visions: Contemporary Art in Canada, Douglas & McIntyre, Vancouver, 83; Allan Schwartzman (auth), General Idea: The AIDS Project, Toronto. *Publ:* Contribr, General Idea, 1968-1984, Stedelijk Van Abbemusem, Eindhoven, 84. *Dealer:* Koury Wingate Gallery 578 Broadway New York NY 10012. *Mailing Add:* 136 Simcoe St Toronto ON M5H 3G4 Canada

ZORETICH, GEORGE STEPHEN
PAINTER, EDUCATOR
b Monessen, Pa, June 19, 18. *Study:* Pa State Univ, BS(art educ) & MA(studio art); Columbia Univ & Syracuse Univ, grad study; also with Hobson Pittman & Ivan Mestrovic. *Work:* Butler Art Inst, Youngstown, Ohio; Pa State Univ Mus, University Park; St Albans Sch, Washington, DC; Indiana State Univ, Pa; Kutztown State Col, Pa. *Comn:* Open Hearth (mural), Mineral Industs, Pa State Univ, 58. *Exhib:* Six Pa Acad Fine Arts Ann, 49-67; nine Butler Art Inst Ann, 50-67; four Corcoran Biennials, Washington, DC, 53-61; San Francisco Art Mus 84th Ann, 65; Nat Acad Design 150th Ann, 75. *Teaching:* From instr to prof art, Pa State Univ, University Park, 46-85. *Awards:* Barse Miller Mem Award for Watercolor, Nat Acad Design, 75. *Bibliog:* James Schineller (auth), Art-search-self discovery, Int Textbk, 60; Yar Chomicky (auth), Watercolor Paintings, Prentice-Hall, 68. *Media:* Oil, Acrylic. *Publ:* Auth, Woodcut, Everyday Art, spring 60; coauth, Prints & Printmaking, Pa State Univ, 60; coauth, Drawing, Lock Haven Rev, 73. *Mailing Add:* 144 Spring Hill Lane State College PA 16801

ZOUNI, OPY
SCULPTOR
Greek citizen. *Work:* Athens Nat Gallery, Greek Dept Cult Affairs, Nat Gallery Sculpture, Beograd Mus Contemp Art, Nat Mus Prilep, Musee Cantonoal des Beaux-Arts fe Lausanne, Ministerie van de Vlamse Gemeemschap/vorres mus, Pierides Collection, chelm Nat Mus (Pl), Nat Bank Greece, Kifissia H Antoniou Collection, Munic Gallery of Rhodes, Athens; Alexander Iolas Collection, Goulandres-Horn Found, B & E Goulandris Mus Mod Art, Andros; Macedonian Ctr Mod Art, Thessaloniki; Mus Contemp Art, Antwerpen, Belg; Prints Cabinet Geneva, Mus Contemp Art, Geneva & Loucerne, Switz. *Comn:* Mus Contemp Art, Antwerpen, Belg; Mus Contemp Art, Geneva, Switz; Rodi Karkazis Gallery, Chicago, Ill. *Mailing Add:* c/o Rodi Karkazis Gallery 168 N Michigan Ave No 300 Chicago IL 60601

ZOX, LARRY
PAINTER
b Des Moines, Iowa, May 31, 37. *Study:* Univ Okla; Drake Univ; Des Moines Art Ctr, with George Grosz. *Work:* Mus Fine Arts, Houston, Tex; Hirchhorn Mus; Whitney Mus Am Art, Metrop Mus Art, Mus Mod Art, New York; Guggenheim Mus; Palm Springs Desert Mus, Calif; Art Inst Chicago. *Exhib:* Whitney Mus Am Art Ann, New York, 69-70 & 72; Indianapolis Mus Art, Ind, 72; one-man retrospective, Whitney Mus Art, 73; Palm Springs Desert Mus, Calif, 73; one-man shows, Daniel Templon Gallery, Paris, France, 75, Alan Rubiner Gallery, Royal Oak, Mich, 79 & Carolyn Schneebeck Gallery, Cincinnati, 79, Rubiner Gallery, W Bloomfield, Mich, 85 & 90, Images, Gallery, Toledo, Ohio, 86, 90 & 91, Percival Gallery, Des Moines, 87, 89 & 91, Gallery One, Toronto, Can, 91 & Stein Gallery, St Louis, Mo, 92; Works on Paper: Allen Rubiner Gallery, Royal Oaks, Mich & Meredith Long Gallery, New York, 80; Inaugural Installation, Mus Fine Arts, Boston, 81; Recent Acquisitions, Guggenheim, 81; Images Gallery, Toledo, 86; Rubiner Gallery, West Bloomfield, Mich, 85 & 86; Percival Gallery, Des Moines, 87 & 89; C S Shulte Gallery, NY & NJ, 91; Ann Jaffe Gallery, Bay Harbor, Fla, 92. *Teaching:* Artist-in-residence, Juniata Col, 64; guest critic, Cornell Univ, 67; artist in resident, Univ NC, Greensboro, 67, Des Moines Art Mus, 74; instr art, Sch Visual Arts, 67-70; instr art, Dartmouth Col, winter 69. *Awards:* Guggenheim Fel, 67; Nat Coun Arts Award, 69; Ester & Adolph Gottlieb Found, 85. *Dealer:* John Szoke 164 Mercer St New York NY 10012; C S Shulte Gallery 565 Broadway New York NY 10012. *Mailing Add:* 238 Park Ave S New York NY 10003

ZUCCARELLI, FRANK EDWARD
PAINTER, INSTRUCTOR
b Pa, Oct 23, 21. *Study:* Newark Sch Fine & Indust Art, with William J Aylward & John Grabach; Art Students League, with Robert Philip; Kean Col NJ, BA. *Work:* Marine Corps Base, Barstow, Calif; Egan Corp, Bridgewater, NJ; Malcolm Forbes Collection, New York; US Coast Guard, Washington, DC; MCC Corp, Murray Hill, NJ. *Comn:* Paintings for US Navy, Newport RI, 71 & Washington, DC, 75; Dahlgren Weapons Lab, Va, 71 & Mediterranean Sixth Fleet, 72; Recovery of Astronauts in Pacific, Apollo-Soyuz Test Proj, 75; Carrier Flight Qualifications, USS Kennedy, 82. *Exhib:* solo exhib: NJ Revisited, Swain Galleries, Plainfield, NJ; Combat Art Collection, Washington, DC; GWS Galleries, Southport, Conn; Essex Fine Arts, Montclair, NJ; Grand Central Art Gallery, New York; and others. *Teaching:* Pvt instr oils, pastels & watercolor, 58-; instr, continuing educ, Rutgers Univ, 80; instr, illus & painting, Newark Sch Indust & Fine Art, 86. *Awards:* Strathmore Award, Hudson Valley Art Asn, 84; Medal of Honor, Am Artists' Prof League Grand Nat, 82 & 91. *Bibliog:* An artist with vision visits USS Kennedy, Navy Aviation News, 11/82;; Aviators and artists at work, Product Support Digest, 9/83; Somerset Artist, Painter of all Seasons, 88. *Mem:* Pastel Soc Am, New York; Salmadundi Club, New York; Am Artist Prof League; Hudson Valley Art Asn; Allied Artists, NY; and others. *Media:* Oil, Pastel. *Publ:* Auth, The Perfect Surface, Artists' Mag, 86; Realistic impressionist, Newark Star Ledge, 10/92; Artist paints beauty of NJ, Somerset, Spectator, 4/92. *Mailing Add:* 61 Appleman Rd Somerset NJ 08873

ZUCCARINI, DAVID ANTHONY
PAINTER
b Baltimore, Md, Apr 1, 53. *Study:* Corcoran Sch Art, 69-71; Md Inst, BFA(painting), 71-76. *Work:* Univ Md, Md Artists Col, College Park; Howard Community Col. *Exhib:* Mid-Year, Butler Inst, Youngstown, Ohio, 76-82 & 85-90; Artscape 87, Md Inst, Baltimore; Int Pastels, Soc Des Pastellistes, Paris, France, 87; Nat Works on Paper, Univ Tex, Tyler, 88; African Influences, Md Mus African Art, Columbia, 90; Drawing 1990, Brigham Young Univ, Provo, Utah; and others. *Teaching:* Instr drawing & painting, pvt studio, 76- *Awards:* Artists Fel, Md State Arts Coun, 85; Distinguished Teacher, White House, 87; Juror Award, Drawing 1990, Brigham Young Univ. *Bibliog:* Pearl Oxorn (auth), Narrow world/wide vision, Baltimore Sun, 81; Pamela Kessler (auth), Zuccarini's curious studio, Washington Post, 87; Fran Fanshel (auth), Columbia's realist, Columbia Flier, 87. *Mem:* Pastel Soc Am, 78-; Acad Artists Asn, 78- *Media:* Oil, Charcoal. *Publ:* Auth, Painting figure compositions, Am Artist, 84. *Dealer:* Foxhall Gallery 3301 New Mexico Ave NW Washington DC 20016. *Mailing Add:* 9402 Mellenbrook Rd Columbia MD 21045

ZUCKER, BARBARA M
SCULPTOR
b Philadelphia, Pa, Aug 2, 40. *Study:* Univ Mich, BS(design), 62; Cranbrook Acad Art, Bloomfield Hills, Mich; Kokoschka Sch Vision, Salzburg, Austria, 61; Hunter Col, MA, 77. *Work:* Whitney Mus Am Art; collections of Milton Brutten & Helen Herrick; Indianapolis Mus; Chase Manhattan Bank; Am Can Co; Brooklyn Mus, New York. *Comn:* Greenwich Libr sculpture, Conn, 84. *Exhib:* 26 Contemporary Women Artists, Aldrich Mus Art, Ridgefield, Conn, 71; one-woman shows, 112 Greene St Gallery, 76, Robert Miller Gallery, New York, 78 & 80, Joslyn Art Mus, 81, Fine Arts Ctr, Univ Mass, Amherst, 82, Pam Adler Gallery, New York, 83 & 85, Sculpture Ctr, New York, 89 & Haneh Kent, NY, 90. *Pos:* Co-founder, AIR Gallery, New York, NY, 72; ed

assoc, Art News Mag, 74-81. *Teaching:* instr art, La Guardia Community Col, Queens, NY, 74-77; instr, Fordham Univ, Lincoln Ctr, New York, 74-79; artist in residence, Princeton Univ, fall 75 & Fine Arts Work Ctr, Provincetown, winter 75; artist-in-residence, Fla State Univ, 76; instr, Philadelphia Col of Art, 77-79; prof & chairperson art dept, Univ Vt, 79-84; prof art, Univ Vt, 79-; vis prof sculpture, Yale Univ, 87-88. *Awards:* Nat Endowment Arts Fel Grant, 75; Artpark, 78; Yaddo, 85, 89; Reader's Digest Fel Award, Giverny, France, 90. *Bibliog:* Carrie Rickey (auth), The more the merrier, Village Voice, 79; John Russell (auth), The sculptures of Barbara Zucker, New York Times, 6/83; Richard Martin (auth), Barbara Zucker, Arts Mag, 83. *Mem:* Col Art Asn; Women's Caucus for Art (mem adv bd, 78, bd dirs, 83-86). *Publ:* Contribr, Art News, 74-79; contribr, Village Voice (centerfold), 7/2/75 & 7/9/75 & article on Red Grooms, 76; auth, article on Florine Stettheimer (American painter), Art News, 2/76 & Women's Studies, 79; Unusual materials, Art J, 80, Heresies, 80 & Sculpture New Hampshire, 82. *Mailing Add:* 21 E Tenth St New York NY 10003

ZUCKER, BOB
PHOTOGRAPHER, EXHIBIT DESIGNER
b New York, NY, Dec 10, 46. *Study:* Hunter Col, BA; and with Philippe Halsman, New York. *Work:* Libr of Cong; J P Morgan libr; Soc Preservation Long Island Antiquities; Nat Trust Hist Preservation; Sotheby's Int Realty. *Comn:* Photos, 19th Century Pub Sculpture, Metrop Mus, 73; Sculpture of Isodor Konti, Hudson River Mus, 74; Historic Architectural Documentation of Old Westchester Co Courthouse Complex, Co of Westchester, 74; Bicentennial Exhib, Venturi & Rauch AIA & Whitney Mus, 75; Am Bicentennial: Signs of Life in the City, Renwick Gallery, Smithsonian Inst, 75; and others. *Exhib:* 19th Century Public Sculpture in New York Parks, 73; Life in America in the 18th Century, Nat Mus Am Hist, 85. *Publ:* Auth, American Architecture: Westchester County, 77. *Mailing Add:* 3 Burbank Ct Greenlawn NY 11740

ZUCKER, JOSEPH I
PAINTER
b Chicago, Ill, May 21, 41. *Study:* Miami Univ, 59-60; Art Inst Chicago, BFA & MFA. *Work:* Walker Art Ctr, Minneapolis; Whitney Mus Am Art; Albright-Knox Gallery, Buffalo; Metrop Mus, New York; Philadelphia Mus Art; and others. *Exhib:* Art Inst Chicago, 64 & 81; Walker Art Ctr, 68; New American Abstract Painting, Madison Art Ctr, 72; Prospect, Dusseldorf, Ger, 73; Bykert Gallery, New York, 74; Whitney Biennial, Whitney Mus, 79 & 83; Venice Biennale, 80; Surfacing Images, The Paintings of Joe Zucker 1969-82, Albright-Knox Gallery, Buffalo, 82; Queens Mus Traveling Exhib, 85-86; Arts Club Chicago, 88. *Teaching:* Instr painting, Minneapolis Sch Art, 66-68, Sch Visual Arts, New York, 68-71 & NY Univ, 71-74. *Bibliog:* Edward Lucie-Smith (auth), Art in the Seventies, Cornell Univ Press, 81;. *Dealer:* Hirschl & Adler Mod 851 Madison Ave New York NY 10021. *Mailing Add:* c/o Hirschl & Adler Modern 851 Madison Ave New York NY 10021

ZUCKER, MURRAY HARVEY
SCULPTOR, COLLAGE ARTIST
b New York, NY, Dec 14, 20. *Work:* AFL-CIO Hq, Washington, DC; Community Blood Coun, New York; Omaha Nat Bank, Nebr; Slater Mem Mus, Norwich, Conn; Butler Inst Am Art, Ohio. *Comn:* Paintings, Atlantic Richfield Co, New York, 68, Technicon Corp, Ardsley, NY, 69 & Police Benevolent Asn, New York, 70. *Exhib:* Annuals, Am Soc Contemp Artists, New York, 75 & 77-81; Contemp Circle, Lincoln Ctr, New York, 79; Gallery Carron, New York, 79; Lever House, New York, 80; Salmagundi Club, New York, 81; and others. *Awards:* First Prize Graphics, Am Soc Contemp Artists, 76; Kulicke Award for Graphics, 78; Feigin Award Graphics, 81; and others. *Bibliog:* C Crane (auth), Contemporary collages, Interiors, 5/70; Gerald F Brommer (auth), The Art of Collage, Davis Publ, Inc, 78; and others. *Mem:* Artists Equity Asn; Am Soc Contemp Artists; Metrop Painters & Sculptors; Jimmy Ernst Artists Alliance; and others. *Media:* Wax for Bronze; Paper on Paper. *Mailing Add:* 54 Cosdrew Lane East Hampton NY 11937

ZUCKERBERG, STANLEY M
PAINTER, ILLUSTRATOR
b New York, NY, Sept 13, 19. *Study:* Pratt Inst; Art Students League; also with George Bridgman, Harold Von Schmidt, Norman Rockwell, Nick Riley, Khosrov Ajootian & Alexander Kostello. *Work:* Grand Cent Art Galleries, New York. *Exhib:* Grand Cent Art Galleries; Allied Am Artists Ann, Nat Acad, New York; Blair Gallery, Santa Fe, NMex; La Galeria, Sedona, Ariz. *Awards:* David Wu Ject Key Mem Award, Allied Artists Am; First Prize, Southern Shore Artists Asn; Award, Mystic Seaport Mus; and others. *Bibliog:* Ralph Fabri (auth), Marine breakwater, Todays' Art Mag, 67; Henry Gasser (auth), Stanley Zuckerberg On The Waterfront, Am Artist Mag, 6/74; John Legakes (dir), Days of my love, Publ Weekly. *Mem:* Allied Artists Am; Artists Fel; Am Artists Prof League; Salmagundi Club; Soc Illusr New York; Am Soc Marine Artists; and others. *Media:* Oil. *Mailing Add:* 21 Old Farm Rd Levittown NY 11756

ZUCKERMAN, RUTH VICTOR
SCULPTOR, PHOTOGRAPHER
b New York, NY Sept 21, 33. *Study:* Sch Vis Arts, New York, 58; Art Students League, Woodstock, NY, with Arnold Blanche, 63; The New Sch, New York, 64. *Work:* The Jimmy Carter Pres Ctr, Atlanta, Ga; Ben Gurion Med Ctr, Beersheva, Israel; H F Johnson Art Mus, Cornell Univ, Ithaca, NY; Southern Bell Tel Ctr, Atlanta, Ga; Northern Telecom Corp Park, Nashville, Tenn. *Comn:* Trees of Life (five), The Temple, Atlanta, Ga, 85; Trees of Life (three), Temple Beth Israel, Longboat Key, Fla, 86; memorium sculpture in stone, bronze & wood, Achavath Achim Synagogue, Atlanta, Ga, 90. *Exhib:* Georgia Artists 2, High Mus Art, Atlanta, 72; Traditional Sculpture - Timeless Imprints, 47th Nat Sculpture Soc, New York, 74 & 80; retrospective, Peatree Summit Bldg, Atlanta, Ga, 82; Timeless Statements, Ga Tech Univ, Atlanta, Ga, 79; Museo Bei Bozzetti, Sculpturi Bibliot, Pietrasanta, Italy, 84. *Teaching:* Instr stone carving, pvt students, Atlanta, Ga, 81-85. *Awards:* Audubon Artists Medal, Audubon Artists Ann, 75; Patrons of Art Prize, Painters & Sculptors Soc, NJ, 76; First Place Award, Georgia Marble Festival, 87. *Bibliog:* Diana Brown (auth), Sculpture in the stone: The timeless themes of Ruth Zuckerman's Art, Southern Homes, 3/88; Fay Bright (auth), Speaking in Stone, The Jewish Times, 89; Milt Liebson (auth), Direct Stone Carving, Schiffer Publ Ltd, 91; Cassandra Von Weber (auth), Ruth Zuckerman, Peachtree Papers, 88. *Mem:* Am Contemp Soc Artists; assoc mem Audubon Artists. *Media:* Stone, Bronze. *Dealer:* Bill Lowe Galleries 75 Bennett St Atlanta GA 30309; Foster Harmon Gallery Main St Sarasota FL. *Mailing Add:* 722 Mill Wall NW Atlanta GA 30327

ZUGOR, SANDOR
PAINTER, PRINTMAKER
b Brod, Yugoslavia, Feb 7, 23; US citizen. *Study:* Acad Fine Art, Budapest, 41-45, with Istvan Szonyi; graphics with Varga Nandor Lajos. *Work:* Mus Fine Art Budapest; Gallery of Mod Art, Taipei, Taiwan; Butler Inst of Am Art, Youngstown, Ohio; Georgia Mus Art, Athens; Hungarian Nat Gallery; Fairleigh Dickinson Univ Art Col, NJ. *Exhib:* Nat Mus Hist, Taipei, Taiwan; Young Americans, Mus Contemp Crafts, New York, 62; Brooklyn Mus, 69; Palacio Bellas Artes, Mexico City, 72; Hungarian Nat Gallery, 88; Westbeth Galleries, New York; Retrospective exhib, Szekesfehervar, Hungary, 88; Budapest Gallery, Hungary, 89. *Teaching:* Lectr drawing, Brooklyn Col Adult Educ, 66-71. *Awards:* Prix du Rome, Hungarian Acad Rome fel, 46-48; First Prize for Peace & War, Fedn Hungarian Artists, 54. *Media:* Acrylics, Oil; Etching. *Mailing Add:* 463 West St New York NY 10014

ZUHN, CHERYL
EDUCATOR, DESIGNER
b Chicago, Ill, June 7, 59. *Study:* Ray-Vogue Col Design (visual merchandising), 78; Thornton Community Col (Europ art hist study tour), dipl, 84. *Pos:* Designer & fashion coordr, Dept Visual Merchandising, Chicago, Ill, 78-81; fashion show stage set designer, Chicago Apparel Ctr, Ill, 82-; merchandise presentation designer, Abercrombie & Fitch, Chicago, Ill, 85-; interior designer, Woodfield Summer Showcase House, Ill, 86, 87 & 88; principal designer, Zular Designs, currently. *Teaching:* Instr visual merchandising, chmn dept & dir mannequins, fixtures & props, Ray-Col Design, Ill, 81- *Awards:* Best Store Visual Presentation, Woodfield Mall, Schaumberg, Ill, 85. *Mem:* Art Inst Chicago. *Res:* European art history. *Mailing Add:* 16825 81st Ct No 3E Tinley Park IL 60477-2322

ZUPAN, BRUNO
PAINTER, PRINTMAKER
b Yugoslavia, June 21, 39; US citizen. *Study:* Zagreb Art Inst, Yugoslavia, 59. *Comn:* Lithograph (with Annabelle Wiener), World Fedn UN Asn, New York, 81. *Exhib:* Boston Col Student Ctr, Mass, 64; Columbia Mus Arts, Columbus, SC, 65; Salon des Artists Francais, Paris, 73 & 76; Nat Acad, New York, 74; Butler Inst Am Art, Youngstown, Ohio, 74. *Bibliog:* Mary Carroll Nelson (auth), Through a Sunny Window, Am Artist Mag, 3/79. *Media:* Oil, Watercolor; Serigraph, Lithograph. *Mailing Add:* c/o Fagen-Peterson Fine Art Inc 7077 Main St Scottsdale AZ 85251

ZURIK, JESSELYN BENSON
PAINTER, SCULPTOR
b New Orleans, La, Dec 26, 16. *Study:* Newcomb Col Art Sch, Tulane Univ, BD, 38; Univ Col Sch Art, Tulane Univ, 58-61; with Xavier Gonzales, Angela Gregory, Caroline W Durieux, Harold Carney, Will Stevens & Harold Thurman. *Work:* New Orleans Pub Libr, New Orleans Mus Art; Rose Art Mus, Brandeis Univ; Light & Power Co, Birmingham, Ala; Nat Mus Women Arts, Washington, DC. *Comn:* Mosaic stairwell, comn by Mr & Mrs M Fishman, New Orleans, 58; design for Hearing & Speech Ctr, New Orleans, 65; design for Touro Infirmary, New Orleans, 65; assemblage coppery printing blocks, Lubat Co, New Orleans, 78; beaded entire 1970 Gremlin, Contemp Arts Ctr, New Orleans, 82-83. *Exhib:* Artists of the Gulf States, New Orleans Mus Art, 64; Southeastern Ann, High Mus, Atlanta, 65; Southern Asn Sculptors, Ark Art Ctr, Little Rock, 66 & Mint Mus Art, Charlotte, NC, 66; Selected Artists: Glade Gallery Invitational, Lauren Rogers Mus Art, Laurel, Miss, 70; Tiennial Nat (art about ties), Contemp Arts Ctr, New Orleans, 79; Int Women's Postcard Exhib, Glyptoteck Mus, Copenhagen, Denmark, 80; Second Louisiana Sculptors Biennial, Contemp Arts Ctr, New Orleans, 82; Art Cars, PS 1, New York, 82 & Focus International, Nairobi, Kenya, 85; honorary show, Women's Caucus Art, Tulane-Newcomb Art Sch, 86, Three Hon Show, 88; and 255 invitational and group shows and 31 solo shows. *Pos:* Illusr, Katz & Besthoff Co & Adler's Jewelry, New Orleans, 38-40; marine drafting, Higgins Co, New Orleans, 43. *Teaching:* Instr assemblage art, var groups & orgn, New Orleans, 62-75 & 80. *Awards:* Purchase Prize, Brandeis Univ Invitational, 63; Honorable Mention, 2nd Ann New Orleans Art Asn, 72; Third Place, Nat Triennial, Wembley Indust, Contemp Arts Ctr, New Orleans, 79. *Bibliog:* Luba Glade (auth), Dazzling superspectacle, States/Item, 74; Dana Standish (auth), Getting down to brass tacks, Gambit, 81; Geoff O'Connell (auth), Book inspires wheel-life art, Dallas Morning News, 82. *Mem:* Nat Mus Women Arts; Southeastern Women's Caucus Art; Contemp Arts Ctr New Orleans; New Orleans Mus Art; Arts Coun New Orleans. *Media:* Wood, Oil. *Dealer:* Wendy Morehead Gallery 603 Julia St New Orleans LA 70130. *Mailing Add:* 7740 Belfast St New Orleans LA 70125

ZURIS, DONALD P
MUSEUM DIRECTOR
b St Louis, Mo, Apr 26, 44. *Study:* Allegheny Col, BA, 66; Univ Mo, Kansas City, MA, 76. *Pos:* Cur of educ, Dallas Hist Soc, Tex, 80-84; exec dir, Longview Mus & Arts Ctr, Tex, 84- *Teaching:* Instr, Am hist & govt, Longview Community Col, Lee's Summit, Mo, 76-80. *Mem:* Am Asn Mus; Tex Asn Mus (comt mem); Mountain-Plains Mus Asn; Nat Trust Hist Preserv; Am Asn State & Local Hist (publ comt). *Mailing Add:* Corpus Christi Mus of Sci & Hist 1900 W Chaparral Corpus Christi TX 78401

ZVER, JAMES M
COLLAGE ARTIST, PRINTMAKER
b Chicago, Ill, May 30, 35. *Study:* Art Inst Chicago, 53-57; Univ Chicago, BFA, 53-57; Cornell Univ, MFA(grad teaching asst), 67-69. *Work:* J B Speed Mus Art, Louisville, Ky; Brown Univ, Providence, RI; Univ Tex, Houston; Mills Col, Oakland, Calif; Herron Mus Art, Indianapolis, Ind. *Comn:* Collage Sculptures, Tiffany, 84, Bloomingdales, 83, Macy's, 84. *Exhib:* Chicago Artists Exhib, Art Inst Chicago, 57-58; Painting & Sculpture Today, Herron Mus Art, 67-68; Contemp Painting Exhib, Silvermine Guild Artists, 68; one-man shows, Emily Lowe Gallery, Hofstra Univ, 72, Soho Ctr Visual Artists, 76, Gotham Book Mart Gallery, New York, 69-78, Payson-Weisberg Gallery, New York 82 & Works II Gallery, Southampton, NY, 83, Collage, State of the Art, Bergen Mus, Paramus, NJ; Contemp Reflections, Larry Aldrich Mus, Ridgefield, Conn, 75; one-man shows, Durlacher Brother Gallery, New York, 66, Larcada Gallery, New York, 68, Emily Lowe Gallery, Hofstra Univ, Hempstead, New York, 72 & The Soho Ctr for Visual Artists, 76. *Pos:* Painting conserv, Whitney Mus Collection, 79- & Orrin Riley, New York, 82-90. *Teaching:* Instr graphics, Pratt Graphics Art Ctr, New York, 65-67, Sch Visual Arts, New York, 69-70; instr painting & graphics, Hofstra Univ, 70-76. *Bibliog:* Article, Art News, 66; Grace Gluck (auth), Soho Artists, New York Times, 74; Emily Geneaur (auth), 10 Downtown Artists, New York Post, 74; article, Star-Ledger, 86; Helen Harrison (auth), Plants: Aesthetics & Application Review, Collage Survey Show, NY Times, 87. *Media:* Paper, Fiberglass; Monotype. *Dealer:* Art Source LA 1416 Sixth St Santa Monica CA 90401. *Mailing Add:* 1409 N Catalina St Los Angeles CA 90027

ZWACK, MICHAEL
PAINTER, SCULPTOR
b Buffalo, NY, Oct 25, 49. *Study:* Buffalo State Col, BA, 70. *Work:* Metrop Mus Art, New York; Albright-Knox Art Gallery, Buffalo; Weatherspoon Art Gallery, Greensboro, NC; Ft Worth Mus, Tex; Burchfield Art Ctr, Buffalo. *Exhib:* Solo exhibs, Tough Bridge to Cross, Essex Art Ctr, Buffalo, NY, 77, The Levitation of Anna, Atrists Space, NY, 79, Studio D'Arte Cannaviello, Milan, Italy, 80, Weatherspoon Art Gallery, Univ NC, Greensboro, 86; Great Big Drawings: Contemporary Works on Paper, Hayden Gallery MIT, Cambridge, Mass, 82; Painting & Sculpture Today 1984, Indianapolis Mus Art, Ind, 84; Nature Genre, Fine Arts Ctr, Fla State Univ, Tallahassee, 84; Monumental Drawing: Works by Twenty American Artists, Brooklyn Mus, NY, 87; New Visions of the Apocalypse, Mus Art, RI Sch Design, Providence, 88; Moscow-Vienna-New York, Messelpalast, Vienna, Austria, 89; Romance and Irony, Art Gallery W Australia, Perth, 89. *Awards:* Nat Endowment Arts Award, 78. *Bibliog:* Richard Amstrong (auth), Otherviews, Artforum, 12/83; Album: Michael Zwack, Arts Mag, 4/87; Douglas Blau (auth), Michael Zwack, Thaddeus Ropac & Curt Marcus, 91. *Media:* Oil. *Dealer:* Curt Marcus 578 Broadway New York NY 10012. *Mailing Add:* 10 Kenmare St New York NY 10012

ZWEERTS, ARNOLD
PAINTER, MOSAIC ARTIST
b Bussum, Neth, 18; US citizen. *Study:* Sch for Arts & Crafts & Sch for Art Teacher Training, Royal Acad Art, Amsterdam; Royal Acad Art, Copenhagen, Denmark; Acad Belli Arti, Ravenna, Italy; Inst Allende, Univ Guanajunto, Mex, MFA; also study with Jos Rovers, Riseby, Orselli, Signoriny & Kortlang. *Work:* Stedelijk Mus, Amsterdam; Collection of the State, The Hague, Neth; and others. *Comn:* Mosaics, Hengelo, Neth, 54, Lockhorst, Koldewyn, Van Eyck, Rotterdam Architects, 55-56, Chicago Process Gear Co, 61, Boulder Med Arts Bldg, Colo, 63-64, Lombard Dental Med Bldg, 72, 73 & 74 & Postville Sch House, Wis, 76-77; 220' mosaic, comn by US Dept Agr, Multnomah Falls Pedestrian Tunnel, Ore, 84; First Hood River Mosaic Wall, 88; Second Hood River Mosaic Wall, 89; Third Hood River Mosaic Wall, 92. *Exhib:* Art Inst Chicago, 66; Gallery Margaret Huisman, Neth, 80; Mosaic Proposals, Mt Hood Col, Gresham, Ore, 86; Giverny Gallery, Gresham, Ore, 87; The Dalles Art Gallery, The Dalles, Ore, 88; two-man show, Columbia Gorge Arts Asn & Gallery, Hood River, 91; and others. *Teaching:* Instr mosaic & color, Kingston Upon Thames, Surrey, Eng, 51-53; instr appreciation of art, Stedelijk Mus, Rijksmus, Amsterdam, 54-57; asst prof drawing & painting, Art Inst Chicago, 57-73; lectr, dept fine arts, Loyola Univ Chicago, 68-78. *Awards:* First Prize-Printmaking, Civic Fine Arts Asn, Sioux Falls, 76; Award of Hon, 63 Salon, Madison Art Mus, 77. *Bibliog:* Pieter Scheen (auth), Lexicon Nederlandse Beeldende Kunstenaars 1750-1950, Part II, Kunsthandel P Scheen N V, The Hague, 70. *Mem:* Columbia Gorge Creative Arts League. *Media:* Oil; Mosaic Glass. *Publ:* Delphian Quart, Vol 43, No 4, A Renaissance in Architectural Art. *Dealer:* Ricciardi Gallery 108 Tenth St Astoria OR 97103. *Mailing Add:* 817 Sherman Hood River OR 97031

ZWICK, ROSEMARY G
SCULPTOR, PRINTMAKER
b Chicago, Ill, July 13, 25. *Study:* Univ Iowa, with Phillip Guston & Abrizio, BFA, 45; Art Inst Chicago, with Max Kahn, 46-47; De Paul Univ, 46-47. *Work:* Oak Park Libr Collection, Ill; Albion Col Print Collection, Mich; Reavis Sch Collection, Chicago; Phoenix Pub Schs Collection, Ariz; Crow Island Sch, Winnetka, Ill; and others. *Comn:* wall relief, Motorola Co, Chicago, 62; sculpture, Temple B'nai Jenoshua, Morton Grove, Ill, 68; large seated figure, Blue Island Libr, Ill, 71; relief, Washbourne Sch, Winnetka, 79; ceramic entry relief & acrylic mural, Unitarian Church, Evanston, 91; and others. *Exhib:* Ceramic Nat, Everson Mus Art, Syracuse, NY, 60, 62 & 64; Soc Washington Printmakers, Nat Mus, Washington, DC, 64; Mundelein Col, Chicago, 64-71; Bicentennial Sculpture, E Leyden Sch Libr, 77; one-man shows, Indianapolis Mus Art, 81 & Old Town Art Ctr, Chicago, Ill, 90; and others. *Pos:* Staff artist, Jr Arts & Activities Mag, 45-47; assoc, Four Arts Gallery, Evanston, Ill, 62- *Bibliog:* John B Kenny (auth), Ceramic design, Chilton, 63; Wesley Buchwald (auth), Craftsmen in Illinois, Ill Art Educ Asn, 65; Louis Redstone (auth), Art in architecture, Art Voices, 1-2/81. *Mem:* Int Sculpture Ctr; Chicago Soc Artists; Woman's Art Coalition; Chicago Artist Coalition. *Media:* All; Etching. *Specialty:* Midwestern artists sculpture, paintings & prints. *Dealer:* Arnold Hendler & Assoc 6910 Morningside Houston Texas 77030; Four Arts Gallery 1629 Oak Ave Evanston IL 60201. *Mailing Add:* 1720 Washington St Evanston IL 60202

ZWIETNIG-ROTTERDAM, PAUL See Rotterdam, Paul Z

ZYNSKY, TOOTS (MARY ANN)
WEAVER
b Boston, Mass, 1951. *Study:* RI Sch Design, Providence, BFA, 73. *Work:* Mus Mod Art, Cooper-Hewitt Mus, New York; Corning Mus Glass, Corning, NY; High Mus Art, Atlanta, Ga; Hokkaido Mus Mod Art, Sapporo, Japan; Musee des Arts Decoratifs, Paris, France; and many others. *Exhib:* Glass Now '89, Yamaha Corp, Tokyo, Japan, 89; Stedelijk Mus, Amsterdam, Neth, 89; Clara Scremini Gallery, Paris, France, 90; Masterpieces of Glass from the Corning Collectioin, Nat Gallery Art, Washington, DC, 90; Gaste aus Frankreich, Kunstmuseum, Hamburg, Ger, 90; Snyderman Gallery, Philadelphia, Pa, 91. *Pos:* Asst dir, NY Experimental Glass Workshop, 80-81 & dept head 81-82. *Awards:* Visual Arts Fel, Nat Endowment Arts, 82 & 86; Grant, Stiching Klanschap, Amsterdam, 84. *Mailing Add:* c/o Snyderman Gallery 303 Cherry St Philadelphia PA 19106

Geographic Index

ALABAMA

Auburn

Furr, Jim Painter, Printmaker
Gluhman, Joseph Walter Historian, Graphic Artist
Gluhman, Margaret A Graphic Artist, Photographer
Hatfield, Donald Gene Painter, Educator
Olson, Douglas John Photographer, Educator
Ross, Conrad H Painter, Printmaker
Ross, Janice Koenig Painter, Instructor
Sykes, (William) Maltby Painter, Printmaker
Trentham, Gary Lynn Educator, Fiber Artist

Bessemer

Leader, Garnet Rosamonde Administrator

Birmingham

Finley, Donny Lamenda Painter
Fleming, Frank Sculptor
Hames, Carl Martin Dealer
Johnson, Antoinette Spanos Curator, Historian
Lewis, Ronald Walter Painter, Instructor
Livingston, Margaret Gresham Administrator, Patron
Price, Rosalie Pettus Painter
Rankin, Don Painter, Printmaker
Schnorrenberg, John Martin Historian, Administrator
Shelton, Robert Lee Designer, Educator
Stewart, Arthur Painter
Trechsel, Gail Andrews Curator

Brundige

Godwin, Lawrence Painter, Sculptor

Citronelle

Conlon, James Edward Sculptor, Historian

Dothan

Rutland, Lilli Ida Painter, Illustrator

Fairhope

Story, William Easton Painter, Museum Director
Wolff, Robert W, Jr Dealer

Florence

Walter, Elizabeth Mitchell Administrator, Historian

Hartselle

Howell, Elizabeth (Mitch) Coon Painter, Gallery Owner

Huntsville

Bowne, James DeHart Museum Director, Art Historian
Boyd, Lakin Educator, Printmaker
Crouse, Michael Glenn Educator, Printmaker
Hudson, Ralph Magee Historian, Educator
Parrish, David Buchanan Painter
Pope, Mary Ann Irwin Painter
Reeves, James Franklin Historian, Collector
Robb, David Metheny, Jr Museum Director, Historian
Rubin, Donald Vincent Sculptor
Savas, Jo-Ann Painter, Instructor

Jacksonville

Martin, Larry Kenneth Painter, Dealer

Mobile

Altmayer, Jay P Collector
Blackburn, Lenora Whitmire Collector
Kennedy, James Edward Painter, Sculptor
Rathle, Henri (Amin) Painter
Schenk, Joseph Bernard Director
Thomason, Michael Vincent Photographer, Curator
Victor, Mary O'Neill Museum Director Emeritus

Montgomery

Brooks, Louise Cherry Collector, Ceramist
Joyner, John Brooks Historian, Museum Director
Shannon, Charles Painter

Normal

Pearson, Clifton Sculptor, Instructor

Northport

Nutt, Craig Craftsman, Sculptor

Ozark

Deloney, Jack Clouse Painter, Illustrator

Tuscaloosa

Brough, Richard Burrell Educator, Designer
Kakas, Christopher A Printmaker, Painter
Musgrave, Shirley H Educator, Photographer

Tuskegee

Thomas, Elaine Freeman Educator, Administrator

University

Sella, Alvin Conrad Painter, Educator

ALASKA

Anchorage

Amason, Alvin Eli Painter
Appel, Keith Kenneth Painter, Sculptor
Ard, Saradell (Saradell Ard Frederick) Educator, Painter
Birdsall, Byron Painter
Conaway, Gerald Sculptor, Painter
Cooke, Jody Helen Painter, Educator
DeRoux, Daniel Edward Painter, Sculptor
Felker, David Larry Sculptor, Gallery Director
Gordon, Josephine Painter
Hedman, Teri Jo Printmaker, Painter
Kimura, Joan Alexandra Painter, Draftsman
Kimura, William Yusaburo Painter, Printmaker
Owens, Tennys Bowers Dealer
Redmond, Rozze (Rosemary) Painter, Printmaker
Regat, Jean-Jacques Albert Sculptor, Muralist
Regat, Mary E Sculptor, Muralist
Shadrach, Jean H Painter
Sharp, Anne Painter, Printmaker
Vallee, William Oscar Painter, Graphic Artist
Welter, Cole H Painter, Educator

College

Going, Jo Visual Artist

Cordova

Bugbee-Jackson, Joan (Mrs John M Jackson) Sculptor, Educator

Fairbanks

Brody, Arthur William Printmaker, Painter
Fejes, Claire Painter, Writer
Woodward, Kesler Edward Painter, Curator

Fayetteville

Peven, Michael David Photographer, Educator

Juneau

Hamar, Diana Kathleen Painter

Ketchikan

Wheeler, Mark Painter, Cartoonist

Palmer

Machetanz, Fred Painter, Lithographer

Sitka

De Armond, Dale B Printmaker, Illustrator

ARIZONA

Bisbee

Gilbert, Herb Painter
Young, Peter Ford Painter

Carefree

Harris, Robert George Painter, Illustrator
Swanson, Ray V Painter

Cave Creek

Cox, Marion Averal Painter, Instructor
Garrison, Gene K Photographer, Painter
Sproul, Ann Stephenson Painter, Instructor
Williamson, Jason H Painter, Dealer

Chandler

Walker, Edward D (Rusty) Painter

Cornville

Waddell, John Henry Sculptor, Painter

Flagstaff

Brookins, Jacob Boden Sculptor, Painter
Horn, Bruce Painter, Educator
Hull, Gregory Stewart Painter
Monthan, Guy Photographer, Educator
Turrell, James Archie Environmental Artist, Sculptor
Turrell, Julia Brown Director

Glenwood

Klopfenstein, Philip Arthur Museum Director, Painter

Gold Canyon

Braig, Betty Lou Painter, Gallery Director

Green Valley

Allen, Constance Olleen Webb Painter, Jewelry Designer
Cooley, Adelaide N Painter, Writer
Easton, Roger David Painter, Jeweler

Mayer

Polk, Frank Fredrick Sculptor

Mesa

Dawson, John Allan Painter, Sculptor
Kaida, Tamarra Photographer
Missal, Joshua M & Pegge Art Dealers, Consultants
O'Dell, Erin (Anne) Painter, Designer
Slater, Gary Lee Sculptor

Munds Park

Carpenter, Earl L Painter

Oracle

McGrew, Bruce Elwin Painter
Rubylee, (Charles Armstrong Littler) Draftsman
Rush, Andrew Printmaker, Sculptor

Paradise Valley

Alpert, George Photographer, Painter
Keane, Bil Cartoonist
Linderman, Earl William Painter
McCall, Robert Theodore Illustrator, Painter
Micale, Albert Painter, Sculptor
Quinn, Brian Grant Sculptor, Painter
Soleri, Paolo Architect, Sculptor
Swartz, Beth Ames Painter

Payson

Rich, Frances L Sculptor, Draftsman
Wilson, Nicholas Jon Painter

Peoria

Di Giacinto, Sharon Painter
Hillis, Richard K Painter, Printmaker

Phoenix

Bales, Jewel Painter
Ballinger, James K Museum Director, Historian
Bell, Donald Allen Art Dealer, Consultant
Bermudez, Jose Ygnacio Sculptor, Painter
Blair, Helen Sculptor, Illustrator
Braverman, Donna (Donna Braverman Knopf) Tapestry Artist, Sculptor
Broadley, Hugh T Historian, Administrator
DeMatties, Nick Painter
Dignac, Geny Sculptor, Environmental Artist
Dutton, Allen A Photographer, Painter
Frerichs, Ruth Colcord Painter, Lithographer
Golubic, Theodore Sculptor, Designer
Graves, Ka (Kathleen Rose) Painter, Sculptor
Grigsby, Jefferson Eugene, Jr Educator, Painter
Hamilton, Frank Moss Painter, Architect
Kniffin, Ralph Gus Graphic Artist
Kurtz, Bruce D Historian, Curator
McGuire, Maureen Designer, Stained Glass Artist
Mason, Harold Printmaker, Painter
Maurice, E(leanor) Ingersoll Painter, Designer
Moore, Ina May Painter, Instructor
Nisula, Larry Painter, Sculptor
Phillips, Irving W Cartoonist, Illustrator
Plotkin, Sylvia Administrator, Museum Director
Richter, Hank Painter, Sculptor
Sansone, Joseph F Craftsman
Schaumburg, Donald Roland Educator, Ceramist
Toschik, Larry Painter, Writer
Ullman, (Mrs) George W Collector
Woods, Rip Painter, Educator
Wright, Barton Allen Painter, Illustrator
Young, Marjorie Ward Painter, Draftsman
Zeitlin, Marilyn A Curator, Writer

Prescott

Dusard, Jay Photographer, Writer
McClure, Thomas F Sculptor, Educator
Stasack, Edward Armen Painter, Printmaker

Rimrock

Dyck, Paul Painter, Director

Scottsdale

Abbrescia, Joeseph Leonard Painter, Instructor
Afsary, Cyrus Painter
Baker, Joe Painter
Brown, Suzanne Goldman Gallery Owner, Collector
Butler, Byron C Jeweler
Collins, Dan (Daniel McClellan) Painter
Cordingley, Mary Bowles Painter
Curtis, Philip Campbell Painter
Davis, James Granberry Painter
DeLoyht-Arendt, Mary Painter
Dickerson, William J Art Dealer
Gentry, Warren Miller Instructor, Painter
Golden, Libby Printmaker, Painter
Hack, Phillip S & Patricia Y Collectors
Hampton, John W Painter, Sculptor
Harnett, Mr & Mrs Joel William Collectors
Heller, Jules Printmaker, Writer
Hill, John Conner Art Dealer, Designer
Hughey, Kirk (John Kirk) Painter, Printmaker
Jacobson, Arthur Painter, Printmaker
Jacobson, Frank Administrator
Kipp, Lyman Sculptor
Lang, Margo Terzian Painter
Lein, Malcolm Emil Administrator, Designer
Magenta, Muriel Sculptor, Video Artist
May, Daniel Striger Dealer
Mell, Ed (Edmund Paul Jr) Painter, Printmaker
Missal, Stephen J Painter, Instructor
Norton, Mary Joyce Painter, Jeweler
Phillips, Dick (Richard Cortez) Painter, Instructor
Pracko, Bernard F, II Painter, Sculptor
Pritzlaff, (Mr & Mrs) John, Jr Collectors
Reynolds, James Elwood Painter
Schenck, William Clinton Painter, Printmaker
Scholder, Fritz Painter, Sculptor
Simmons, Julie Lutz Painter, Collage Artist
Steckler, Stuart Jay Art Dealer, Collector
Sweeney, J Gray Historian, Curator
Tash, Joy Alene Art Dealer, Collector
Udinotti, Agnese Sculptor, Painter
Waid, Jim (James E) Painter
Whitaker, William Painter, Illustrator
Zahourek, Jon Gail Painter, Sculptor
Zupan, Bruno Painter, Printmaker

Sedona

Beeler, Joe (Neil) Painter, Sculptor
Coleman, M L (Michael Lee) Painter, Instructor
Crandall, Jerry C Painter, Historian
Crandall, Judith Ann Gallery Director, Writer
De Mille, Leslie Benjamin Painter, Sculptor
Jennerjahn, W P Educator, Painter
Klotz, Suzanne Painter, Sculptor
Kristensen, Gail Marie Ceramist, Enamelist
Mahoney, Joella Jean Educator, Painter
Shoemaker, Vaughn Editorial Cartoonist, Painter
Simpson, Lee Painter

Sonoita

McGrew, R Brownell Painter

Sun City

Bittner, Hans Oskar Painter, Illustrator
Jakstas, Alfred John Museum Conservator
Luitjens, Helen Anita Instructor, Painter

Sun City West

Moses, Bette J Painter

Surprise

Fish, George A Painter

Tempe

Alquist, Lewis Sculptor
Britton, Daniel Robert Printmaker, Educator
Bush, Donald John Historian, Educator
Codell, Julie Francia Historian, Administrator
Eder, James Alvin Printmaker, Painter
Fahlman, Betsy Lee Historian
Fink, Ray (Raymond Russell) Sculptor, Educator
Gillingwater, Denis Claude Sculptor, Educator
Gully, Anthony Lacy Historian, Administrator
Hulick, Diana Emery Historian, Museum Director
Jay, Bill Photographic Historian, Critic
Klett, Mark Painter

ARIZONA (cont)

Kronengold, Eric A Photographer, Educator
Lewis, William R Instructor, Painter
Olmsted, Suzanne M Photographer, Printmaker
Pile, James Painter
Pimentel, David Delbert Goldsmith, Educator
Schmidt, Randall Bernard Sculptor, Educator
Stuler, Jack Photographer, Educator
Taylor, Janet R Tapestry Artist, Weaver
Turk, Rudy H Museum Director, Painter
White, James Richard Sculptor, Educator
Wood, Harry Emsley, Jr Educator, Painter
Young, Joseph E Educator, Critic

Tubac

Cabot, Hugh Painter, Sculptor

Tucson

Anderson, Warren Harold Graphic Artist, Painter
Bermingham, Peter Museum Director, Curator
Bernal, Louis Carlos Photographer
Billmyer, John Edward Draftsman, Educator
Bishop, Jerold Educator, Painter
Bloomfield, Suzanne Painter
Bredlow, Tom Designer, Blacksmith
Briggs, Peter S Curator, Historian
Buros, Luella Painter, Book Designer
Caldwell, Eleanor Jeweler, Educator
Chabot, Aurore (Martha) Sculptor
Closson, Nanci Blair Painter, Collage Artist
Colescott, Robert H Painter, Instructor
Conant, Howard Somers Painter, Educator
Croft, Michael Flynt Craftsman, Educator
Denniston, Douglas Painter, Educator
Golden, Judith Photographer
Goo, Benjamin Sculptor, Painter
Gottschalk, Max Jules Designer, Instructor
Greer, Wesley Dwaine Educator, Craftsman
Grossman, Maurice Kenneth Educator, Ceramic Artist
Grygutis, Barbara Sculptor, Environmental Artist
Harbart, Gertrude Felton Painter, Instructor
Haskin, Donald Marcus Educator, Sculptor
Heldt, Carl Randall Educator, Painter
Heric, John F Sculptor
Hitner, Chuck Painter, Educator
Hupp, Frederick Duis Painter, Educator
Irving, Donald J Administrator, Writer
Jones, Harold Henry Administrator, Photographer
Martin, Lucille Caiar Painter, Muralist
Miller, Nancy Tokar Painter
Monroe, Eve Valin Painter
Morse, Bart J Painter, Printmaker
Murray, Frances Photographer
Parry, Ellwood Comly, III Historian
Parry, Pamela Jeffcott Librarian, Administrator
Pitts, Terence Randolph Director, Curator
Reich, Sheldon Historian, Lecturer
Rogers, Barbara Painter, Educator
Sevigny, Maurice Joseph, II Educator, Administrator
Stefan, Ross Painter
Stonebarger, Virginia Painter, Educator
Tobias, Robert Paul Painter, Sculptor
Wimmer, Gayle Sculptor, Educator
Yassin, Robert Alan Museum Director, Curator
Zivic, William Thomas Painter, Sculptor

Williams

Seaman, Drake F Painter

ARKANSAS

Arkadelphia

Linn, John William Administrator, Writer

Clarksville

Ward, Lyle Edward Painter, Educator

Conway

Burchett, Kenneth Eugene Educator, Administrator
Larsen, Patrick Heffner Painter, Sculptor
Thompson, Robert Charles Painter, Educator

El Dorado

Murray, Reuben Administrator

Eureka Springs

Freund, Harry Louis Painter, Illustrator

Fayetteville

Brody, Myron Roy Administrator, Sculptor
Cockrill, Sherna Painter, Instructor
Krueger, Lothar David Painter, Educator

Hot Springs National Park

Benini Painter, Sculptor
Rames, Stanley Dodson Painter, Educator
Simmons, Gary Paul Graphic Artist, Educator

Jamesboro

Lindquist, Evan Printmaker, Educator

Jonesboro

Mayes, Steven Lee Educator, Printmaker

Little Rock

Bailin, David Painter
Benjamin, Lloyd William, III Historian, Administrator
Cawood, Gary Kenneth Photographer
DuBois, Alan Beekman Curator, Administrator
Gross, Elissa Frances Consultant, Lecturer
Mapes, Doris Williamson Painter
Pasquine, Ruth Curator
Schmidt, Frederick Lee Painter, Educator
Wolfe, Townsend, III Director, Chief Curator

Marshall

Langford, Sherry K Environmental Artist, Painter

Pettigrew

McNamara, William Patrick, Jr Painter, Printmaker

Pine Bluff

Jenkens, Garlan F Curator, Painter
Shaw, Donald Edward Sculptor, Painter

Russellville

Wilwers, Edward Mathias Educator, Illustrator

Siloam Springs

Anderson, Troy Painter, Sculptor

State University

Allen, William J Historian, Educator
Jones, Charlott Ann Educator, Museum Director
Keech, John H Painter

CALIFORNIA

Agoura

Murrill, Gwynn Sculptor

Albany

Dane, Bill (William Thatcher Dane) Photographer, Painter
Loeser, Thomas Sculptor

Albion

Martin, Bill Painter, Sculptor

Alhambra

Arellanes, Audrey Spencer Editor, Art Historian

Altadena

Green, David Oliver Sculptor, Educator
Ikegawa, Shiro Printmaker

Amador City

Pinkerton, Clayton (David) Painter

Anaheim

Macaray, Lawrence Richard Painter, Educator

Anaheim Hills

Mi Sook, Ahn Painter

Angwin

Seyle, Robert Harley Sculptor, Designer

Antioch

Graham, Lanier Curator

Anza

Silkotch, Mary Ellen Painter

Apple Valley

Kleinsmith, Gene (Eugene Dennis) Painter, Writer

Aptos

Woods, Gurdon Sculptor

Arcadia

Hawkins, Thomas Wilson, Jr Painter, Instructor
Roysher, Hudson (Brisbine) Designer, Administrator

Arcata

Anderson, William Thomas Painter, Printmaker
Johnson, Ronald W Historian, Educator
Knight, Tom (Thomas Lincoln), Jr Educator, Photographer
Land-Weber, Ellen E Photographer, Educator
Price, Leslie Kenneth Painter, Educator
Schuler, Melvin Albert Sculptor, Painter

Atherton

Bergstrom, Edith Harrod Painter

Atlanta

Artemis, Maria (Maria Artemis Papageorge Sawyer) Sculptor, Educator

CALIFORNIA (cont)

Auburn

Shulzke, Margot Seymour Painter, Writer

Bakersfield

Kerzie, Ted L Painter
Paradise, Phil (Herschel) Painter, Sculptor
Reep, Edward Arnold Painter, Educator

Barstow

Lorelli (Svoboda), Elvira Mae Sculptor, Painter

Bayside

LaPlantz, David Jeweler, Sculptor
LaPlantz, Shereen Weaver, Instructor

Bellflower

Theroux, Carol Painter

Belmont

Cantor, Rusty Painter
Harris, David Jack Painter, Muralist
Strong, Charles Ralph Painter, Educator

Berkeley

Abel, Ray Illustrator, Printmaker
Akawie, Thomas Frank Educator, Painter
Antokal, Gale Painter
Baas, Jacquelynn Museum Director, Historian
Bony, Jean Victor Art Historian, Educator
Brown, Christopher Painter
Burch, Claire R Painter, Writer
Bussche, Wolf von dem Photographer, Painter
Cahill, James Francis Historian, Educator
Candau, Eugenie Librarian
Carson, G B Consultant, Art Dealer
Casida, Kati Printmaker, Sculptor
Davis, Jerrold Painter
Delaney, Janet Clare Photographer
Elliott, James Heyer Administrator, Consultant
Elliott, Lillian Weaver, Tapestry Artist
Felter, June Marie Painter, Printmaker
Fredell, Gail Craftsman
Genn, Nancy Painter, Sculptor
Gordin, Sidney Sculptor, Educator
Healy, Anne Laura Sculptor, Educator
Henderson, Robbin Legere Painter, Curator
Heyman, Therese Thau Curator, Historian
Hoare, Tyler James Sculptor, Printmaker
Holland, Tom Painter
Kasten, Karl Albert Painter, Printmaker
Kehlmann, Robert Critic
Kerns, Ginger Painter, Educator
Light, Ken Photographer, Educator
Lipofsky, Marvin B Sculptor, Glass Artist
Loberg, Robert Warren Painter, Instructor
Loran, Erle Painter, Writer
Lovell, Margaretta Markle Curator, Historian
McCauley, Gardiner Rae Administrator, Painter
Mitchell, Margaretta K Photographer, Writer
Miyasaki, George Joji Printmaker, Painter
Mohr, Pauline Catherine Conservator, Restorer
Prestini, James Libero Sculptor, Designer
Rapoport, Sonya Conceptual Artist
Rokeach, Barrie Photographer, Writer
St John, Terry N Painter, Curator
Sargent, Richard Painter, Photographer
Selvin, Nancy Ceramist, Sculptor
Selz, Peter H Historian, Curator
Shaw, Richard Blake Sculptor
Sher, Elizabeth Video Artist, Printmaker
Shoemaker, Peter Painter
Simpson, David Painter, Educator
Skoff, Gail Lynn Photographer
Slusky, Joseph Sculptor, Educator
Voulkos, Peter Sculptor, Educator
Wall, Brian Sculptor

Beverly Hills

Barnes, Molly Art Dealer, Writer
Berman, Eleanore (Eleanore B Lazarof) Painter, Printmaker
Cross, Yvonne Artist
Glover, Robert Sculptor, Ceramist
Halff, Robert H Collector
Hamilton, Patricia Rose Dealer
Longstreet, Stephen Painter, Historian
Marton, Pier Video Artist, Educator
Natzler, Otto Ceramist, Sculptor
Newman, Louis Art Dealer, Collector
Pashgian, M Helen Painter, Sculptor
Secunda, (Holland) Arthur Painter, Collage Artist
Simon, Norton Collector
Stern, Louis Dealer, Consultant
Strong, Brett-Livingstone Painter, Sculptor
Ting Shao Kuang, Painter
Winslow, Helen Painter

Bishop

Wagoner, Robert B Painter, Sculptor

Bodega

Hedrick, Wally Bill Painter, Sculptor
Morehouse, William Paul Painter, Sculptor

Bolinas

Berkson, Bill Critic, Poet
Brooke, Pegan Painter
Espenet, Craftsman, Lecturer
Harris, Paul Sculptor
Okamura, Arthur Painter

Bonsall

Small, Deborah Painter

Boonville

Rubin, Sandra Mendelsohn Painter

Brisbane

Anargyros, Spero Sculptor

Burbank

Asmar, Alice Painter, Printmaker
Binder, Erwin Sculptor

Burlingame

Berger, Sandra Christine Q Designer, Stained Glass Artist
Hooper, Jack Meredith Painter, Printmaker
Voelker, Elizabeth Painter, Collage Artist

Calabasas

Boyle, (James) Neil Illustrator, Painter
Dar, Dina Painter
Fabian Fabiano, Diane Painter

Calistoga

Nechis, Barbara Painter, Lecturer
Thollander, Earl Illustrator, Graphic Artist

Cambria

Marquis, Richard Craftsman
Mitchell, Dianne (Ball) Painter

Capistrano Beach

Cederquist, John Furniture Maker
Clark, Timothy John Painter, Instructor

Cardiff-by-the-Sea

Bowater, Marian Art Dealer, Collector

Carlsbad

Capps, Kenneth P Sculptor

Carmel

Baer, Morley Photographer
Dooley, Helen Bertha Painter, Dealer
Hu, Chi Chung Painter
Jacobs, Ralph, Jr Painter
Johnson, Barbara Louise Painter, Printmaker
Kiskadden, Robert Morgan Painter, Educator
Lagorio, Irene R Printmaker, Painter
Massaro, Karen Thuesen Ceramist, Sculptor
Millea, Tom (Thomas Francis) Photographer
Mitchell, N Donald Administrator, Dealer
Parker, Olivia Photographer
Skalagard, Hans Marine Painter, Lecturer

Carmel-By-The-Sea

Dzigurski, Alex Painter

Carmel Valley

De Groat, George Hugh Painter, Printmaker
Pomeroy, Frederick George Painter
Pomeroy, Mary Barnas (Mrs F G Pomeroy) Painter, Illustrator
Sexton, John (William) Photographer
Swanson, J N Painter, Sculptor
Wolfe, Maurice Raymond Consultant

Carpinteria

Hansen, Robert Educator, Painter
Plous, Phyllis Curator

Carson

Hirsch, Gilah Yelin Painter, Writer
Ivers, Louise H Historian, Administrator

Castro Valley

Kohn, Misch Painter, Printmaker

Chico

Epting, Marion Austin Printmaker, Educator
Feldhaus, Paul A Educator, Printmaker
Hornaday, Richard Hoyt Painter, Educator
McManus, James William Sculptor, Gallery Director
Pierce, Ann Trucksess Painter, Educator
Reinertson, Lisa Sculptor
VanDerpool, Karen Weaver, Educator

Chula Vista

Houston, Mary Etta (King) Painter, Sculptor

Claremont

Ackerman, Gerald Martin Historian, Educator
Aston, Miriam Sculptor, Painter
Benjamin, Karl Stanley Painter, Educator
Casanova, Aldo John Sculptor, Educator
Emerick, Judson J Historian
Furman, David Stephen Sculptor, Educator
Hueter, James Warren Sculptor, Painter
Rankaitis, Susan Painter, Photographer
Reiss, Roland Sculptor, Educator
Simon, Leonard Ronald Administrator, Writer

CALIFORNIA (cont)

Colton

Johnston, Richard M Sculptor, Educator

Copperopolis

Hartwig, Heinie Painter

Corona Del Mar

Brandt, Rex (Rexford Elson) Painter, Printmaker
Irving, Joan Painter, Sculptor
Turnbull, Betty Curator

Coronado

Reed, Flint Winter Painter, Printmaker

Costa Mesa

Muller, Jerome Kenneth Collector, Painter
Romans, Van Anthony Sculptor, Designer
Yorgo, (George Yorgo Spyropoulos) Painter, Conceptual Artist

Cotati

Hudson, Robert H Painter, Sculptor

Culver City

Apple, Jacki (Jacqueline B) Media and Performance Artist, Writer
Barkus, Mariona Marcia Painter
Posner, Richard Sculptor

Cupertino

Rindfleisch, Jan Director, Curator

Cypress

Hardy, Robert Gallery Director, Ceramist

Dana Point

Armstrong, Roger Joseph Painter, Cartoonist

Danville

Pochmann, Virginia Painter, Draftsman

Davis

Henderson, Mike Painter, Filmmaker
Levine, Marilyn Anne Sculptor
Natsoulas, Anthony Sculptor
Petersen, Roland Conrad Painter, Printmaker
Shannonhouse, Sandra Sculptor
Thiebaud, (Morton) Wayne Painter, Educator
Vanden Berge, Peter Willem Sculptor, Muralist

Del Mar

Antin, David A Art Critic, Writer
Antin, Eleanor Conceptual & Performance Artist
Harrison, Helen Mayer (Mrs Newton Harrison) Environmental Artist, Conceptual Artist
Harrison, Newton A Environmental Artist, Conceptual Artist
Herman, Vic Painter, Writer
Kittredge, Nancy (Elizabeth) Painter
Snow, Cynthia Reeves Painter

Diamond Springs

Tarbet, Urania Christy Painter, Instructor

Dominguez Hills

Barton, Phyllis Settecase Art Historian, Writer

Eagle Rock

Andrews, Charleen Kohl Sculptor

East Los Angeles

Henderson, Victor Painter, Muralist

El Cajon

House, Suda Kay Photographer, Educator
Lawrence, Jaye A Sculptor, Craftsman
Lawrence, Les Ceramist, Sculptor
Shackelford, Bud (Lyne T) Painter, Instructor
Tatro, Ronald Edward Sculptor, Instructor

El Cerrito

McMillan, Stephen Walker Printmaker, Photographer

El Dorado Hills

Peeples, Maija (Maija Gegeris Zack Woof) Painter

El Granada

Houskeeper, Barbara Sculptor, Painter

Elk Grove

Kaiser, Benjamin Sculptor, Designer

Emeryville

Grafton, Rick (Frederick Wellington) Painter
Lang, Cay Photographer
Misrach, Richard Laurence Photographer
Peterson, Kristin Sculptor, Assemblage Artist

Encinitas

Conrad, John W Educator, Ceramist
Perine, Robert Heath Painter, Writer
Provder, Carl Painter, Instructor

Encino

Almy, Max (Marilynn Irene) Video Artist, Director
LaCom, Wayne Carl Painter, Graphic Artist

Escondido

Anderson, Brad J Cartoonist
Robbins, LeRoy (Southward) Photographer, Filmmaker
Sternberg, Harry Graphic Artist, Painter
Tibbs, Thomas S Educator, Museum Director

Eureka

Marak, Louis Bernard Ceramic Sculptor, Educator

Fair Oaks

Barrios, Benny Perez Painter, Art Dealer
Potter, (George) Kenneth Painter, Printmaker

Fallbrook

Ragland, Jack Whitney Painter, Printmaker

Forestville

Meyer, El(mer Frederick) Painter, Writer

Fresno

Bottini, David M Sculptor
Brutosky, (Sister) Mary Veronica, CSJ Painter, Printmaker
Maughelli, Mary L Painter, Printmaker
Pickford, Rollin, Jr Painter

Ft Bragg

Downie, Romana Anzi Sculptor

Ft Mason

Dern, F Carl Sculptor

Fullerton

Arnold, Florence M Painter
Feldman, Roger Lawrence Sculptor, Painter
Frankel, Dextra Educator, Gallery Director
Smith, V Joachim Painter, Writer
Wells, Carol Menthe Painter, Sculptor

Garden Grove

Bledsoe, Jane Kathryn Historian, Administrator
Ortlieb, Robert Eugene Sculptor, Graphic Artist

Georgetown

Amyx, Leon Kirkman Painter, Educator

Glendale

Gill, Gene Painter, Printmaker
Owens, Mary (Mary Louise Schnore) Painter, Sculptor
Pekar, Ronald Walter Painter, Sculptor

Glen Ellen

Wilson, Douglas Fenn Painter, Sculptor

Goleta

Gabrielson, Walter Oscar Painter, Sculptor

Graeagle

Halbach, David Allen Painter

Granada Hills

Purcell, Hugh D Painter

Green Valley Lake

Wood, Robert E Painter, Instructor

Greenwich

Red Star, Kevin Painter, Printmaker

Gualala

Alinder, James Gilbert Gallery Owner, Photographer
Alinder, Mary Street Writer, Curator

Guerneville

Barrio, Raymond Writer, Printmaker

Hemet

Hutchison, Elizabeth S Painter

Hillsborough

Siberell, Anne Hicks Painter, Sculptor

Hollywood

Barbera, Joe Cartoonist
LeMieux, Bonne A Painter
Stinsmuehlen-Amend, Susan Collage Artist, Painter

Huntington Beach

Anderson, Bill (William Maxwell) Painter, Printmaker
Bolen, John E Art Dealer, Collector
Bolen, Lynne N Art Dealer, Collector
Isaacson, Gene Lester Collector, Historian
Stevens, Linda Lee Painter, Educator
Tornheim, Norman Sculptor

Idyllwild

Serisawa, Sueo Painter

Imperial Beach

Garman, Ed Painter, Writer

Indian Wells

Zantman, J B Dealer

Inglewood

Antrim, Craig Keith Painter, Draftsman
Johnstone, Mark Painter, Curator

Inverness

Foote, Howard Reed Artist, Printmaker
Krebs, Patsy Painter
Onslow Ford, Gordon M Painter
Smith, Gary Douglas Draftsman, Painter
Storer, Inez Mary Painter

Inyokern

Nowak, Leo Illustrator, Cartoonist

Irvine

Burchfield, Jerry Lee Photographer, Educator
Kauffman, Robert Craig Painter, Sculptor
White, John M Painter, Conceptual Artist

Jamestown

Hutchings, La Vere Painter, Instructor

Julian

Cherkas, Constantine Painter

Kensington

Gunn, Ellen Painter, Printmaker
McCann, Cecile Nelken Critic

Kentfield

Eaton, Pauline (Friedrich) Painter, Instructor
Galli, Stanley Walter Painter

Kingsburg

Olson, Maxine Painter, Educator

La Canada

Abril, Ben (Benjamin) Painter
Herman, Alan David Designer, Graphic Artist

La Crescenta

Injeyan, Seta L Painter

Lafayette

Alexander, Kenneth Lewis Cartoonist
Beaumont, Mona Painter, Printmaker
Johnson, Bruce (James) Sculptor
Poupeney, Mollie Ceramist, Writer

Laguna Beach

Blacketer, James Richard Painter, Art Dealer
Challis, Richard Bracebridge Dealer, Lecturer
Darrow, Paul Gardner Painter, Educator
Desmarais, Charles Joseph Museum Director, Writer
Enman, Tom Kenneth Painter, Museum Director
Gastaldi, Jerome Painter, Sculptor
Jacques, Michael Louis Printmaker, Educator
Janson, Agnes Painter, Collage Artist
Liberi, Dante Painter, Sculptor
Lottes, John William Educator, Administrator
Moore, Scott Martin Painter, Instructor
Rubinstein, Charlotte Streifer Writer, Lecturer
Scheu, Leonard Painter, Lecturer
Vesna, Victoria Video Artist, Environmental Artist

Laguna Hills

Burchess, Arnold Painter, Sculptor
Garbutt, Janice Lovoos Painter, Writer
Hubenthal, Karl Samuel Cartoonist, Painter
MacBird, Rosemary (Simpson) Painter
Rodbard, Betty Painter

Laguna Niguel

Apt, Charles Painter

Lagunitas

Holman, Arthur (Stearns) Painter

La Jolla

Beebe, Mary Livingstone Art Administrator
Brezzo, Steven Louis Museum Director
Cohen, Harold Artist-Theorist, Educator
Cuevas, Jose Luis Draftsman
Cutler-Shaw, Joyce Conceptual Artist, Educator
Davies, Hugh Marlais Historian, Museum Director
Forester, Russell Painter, Sculptor
Fredman, Faiya R Environmental Artist, Painter
Imana, Jorge Garron Painter, Muralist
Jennings, Jan Writer, Museum Administrator
Jones, Doug (Douglas McKee) Painter, Dealer
Karlen, Peter H Educator, Writer
Kelemen, Pal Historian
Lonidier, Fred Spencer Photographer, Educator
McAllister, Geraldine E Gallery Director
McGilvery, Laurence Book Dealer, Publisher
McReynolds, (Joe) Cliff Painter, Instructor
Marcus, Angelo P Dealer, Collector
Mark, Bendor Painter
Prakapas, Eugene Joseph Art Dealer, Editor
Reilly, Richard Director, Historian
Rustvold, Katherine Jo Dealer
Sacanga, Italo Sculptor, Educator
Santos, Adèle Naudé Architect, Urban Designer
Shaw, Reesey Painter, Sculptor
Silva, Ernest Painter, Sculptor
Stewart, John Lincoln Educator, Writer
Tasende, Jose Maria Gallery Director, Dealer
Teilhet-Fisk, Jehanne Hildegarde Historian, Educator
Weber, Albert Jacob Painter, Educator
Weldon, Barbara Maltby Painter, Printmaker
Whitaker, Eileen Monaghan Painter
Yard, Sally Elizabeth Historian, Curator

Lake Arrowhead

Barnes, Cliff (Clifford V) Painter, Illustrator
Maree, Wendy P Painter, Sculptor

Lake Elsinore

Bouchard, Paul E Painter

La Mesa

Blackmun, Barbara Winston Educator, Art Historian
Lebeck, Carol E Ceramist

La Quinta

Welch, (Mrs) Robert G Collector

Larkspur

Frances, Harriette Anton Painter, Printmaker

Livermore

Lord, Carolyn Marie Painter

Long Beach

Albuquerque, Lita Painter
Aldana, Carl Filmmaker, Painter
Bermingham, Ann Educator, Historian
Braunstein, H Terry (Malikin) Photographer, Educator
Cretara, Domenic Anthony Painter, Educator
Ferreira, Armando Thomas Educator, Sculptor
Glenn, Constance White Museum Director, Writer
Jones, John Paul Painter, Printmaker
Kaplan, Ilee Printmaker, Administrator
Klonarides, Carole Ann Video Artist, Curator
Knode, Marilu Curator, Administrator
Lane, William Painter
Larsen, Susan C Curator, Historian
Lewis, Marcia Jeweler-Metalsmith, Instructor
Looney, Norman Sculptor
McOwen, Carol M Art Dealer, Collector
Nelson, Harold B Director
Osborne, Cynthia A Printmaker, Educator
Viola, Bill Video Artist

Los Alamidos

MacGregor, Gregory Allen Photographer

Los Angeles

Abeles, Kim Victoria Painter, Sculptor
Adams, Lisa Kay Painter, Printmaker
Adamson, Jerome D, Jr Art Dealer, Consultant
Alf, Martha Joanne Painter, Writer
Alhilali, Neda Environmental Artist, Painter
Amico, David Michael Painter, Instructor
Andreson, Laura F Ceramist, Educator
Ankrum, Joan Art Dealer
Asher, Michael Sculptor
Baer, Rod Sculptor
Baker, George P Educator, Kinetic Artist
Bayless, Raymond Painter
Belinoff, Deanne Painter
Berger, Pat (Patricia Eve) Painter
Bermudez, Luis A Sculptor, Educator
Bierman, Irene A Educator
Blizzard, Alan Painter, Educator
Bloomfield, Lisa Diane Photographer, Conceptual Artist
Blumberg, Ron Painter
Bosson, Jack (John Edwin), Jr Painter, Muralist
Bowlt, John Art Historian, Educator
Brendel, Bettina Painter, Lecturer
Brice, William Painter, Printmaker
Broad, Eli Collector
Broderson, Morris Painter
Burkhardt, Hans Gustav Painter, Printmaker
Burr, Lee Reynolds Painter, Printmaker
Byrnes, James Bernard Art Historian, Museum Director
Carmichael, Jae Painter, Sculptor
Cassell, Beverly Painter
Cassyd, Syd Curator, Critic
Catalan, Edgardo Omar Painter, Educator
Chesney, Lee R, Jr Painter, Printmaker
Cho, David Designer, Assemblage Artist
Clayberger, Samuel Robert Painter, Educator

CALIFORNIA (cont)

Clothier, Peter Dean Writer, Critic
Cohen, Bruce Joel Painter
Conrad, Paul Francis Cartoonist, Sculptor
Cramer, Douglas S Collector, Patron
Curran, Darryl Joseph Photographer, Printmaker
Dailey, Victoria Keilus Dealer
D'Andrea, Jeanne Consultant, Editor
Dean, Nat(alie Carol) Painter, Sculptor
Decter, Betty Eva Painter, Sculptor
DeLap, Tony Sculptor, Educator
De Larios, Dora Sculptor
Dillon, Paul Sanford Painter
Dimondstein, Morton Sculptor, Painter
Doolin, James Lawrence Painter
Dowd, Robert (O'Dowd Robert) Painter, Sculptor
Edge, Douglas Benjamin Sculptor, Painter
Ela, Patrick H Director
Elliot, Catherine J Ceramist, Painter
Ewing, Edgar Louis Painter
Falkenstein, Claire Sculptor
Felsen, Rosamund Art Dealer, Gallery Director
Fenci, Renzo Sculptor
Feuerstein, Roberta Dealer
Finkelstein, Max Sculptor, Painter
Firstenberg, Jean Director
Flick, Robbert Photographer, Educator
Foosaner, Judith Educator, Painter
Fox, Howard Neal Curator, Critic
Frame, John Sculptor
Frank, Peter Solomon Critic, Curator
Franklin, Carole R Art Dealer, Publisher
Fredericks, Beverly Magnuson Painter, Restorer
Frey, Viola Sculptor, Painter
Garcia, Rupert (Marshall R) Painter, Educator
Garrett, Stephen Museum Director
Goedike, Shirl Painter
Goldfield, Edward L Dealer, Collector
Goodman, Calvin Jerome Consultant, Collector
Goodman, Florence Jeanne Writer, Collector
Grimmer, Mineko Sculptor
Gronk, Painter
Hamrol, Lloyd Sculptor
Heinecken, Robert Friedli Photographer
Herman, Roger Painter, Printmaker
Hernandez, Anthony Louis Photographer
Hess, Scott Painter
Highwater, Jamake Critic, Lecturer
Hockney, David Designer, Photographer
Hogarth, Burne Artist, Illustrator
Holo, Selma R Museologist, Museum Director
Hopkins, Henry Tyler Museum Director, Educator
Horowitz, Benjamin Administrator, Dealer
Horwitz, Channa Painter, Graphic Artist
Hugo, Joan (Dowey) Critic, Administrator
Iturralde, Teresa Art Dealer, Collector
Johnston, Ynez Painter, Sculptor
Jones, Patty Sue Painter, Curator
Kaplan, Sandra Painter, Printmaker
Katchen, Carole Lee Painter
Kazor, Virginia Ernst Curator
Kendall, (Ms) Michael Administrator, Educator
Kester, Lenard Painter
Ketchum, Robert Glenn Photographer, Curator
Kienholz, Lyn Patron, Administrator
Klein, Cecelia F Historian, Educator
Knight, Christopher Allen Critic, Administrator
Koshalek, Richard Museum Director
Kovinick, Philip Peter Writer, Historian
Krasnyansky, Anatole Lvovich Painter, Architect
Kuwayama, George Curator, Historian
Landau, Mitzi Dealer, Curator
Lang, Wendy F Administrator, Photographer
Lark, Raymond Draftsman, Painter
Lawrence, Michael Painter, Sculptor
Lawson, Thomas Painter, Writer
Leavitt, William Painter
Leeson, Tom Painter, Sculptor
Lem, Richard Douglas Painter
Lere, Mark Allen Sculptor
Levinson, Joel D Photographer, Conceptual Artist
Longval, Gloria Painter
Ludmer, Joyce Pellerano Librarian, Historian
Lundeberg, Helen Painter
Lyons, Lisa Curator, Historian
McCracken, John Harvey Sculptor, Painter
McQueen, John Craftsman
Malpede, John Performance Artist
Manolakas, Stanton Peter Painter
Marsden, Michael H E Painter
Mason, John Sculptor
Mendes, Barbara Painter
Meyers, Jeanne F Curator, Administrator
Milant, Jean Robert Dealer
Moss, Tobey C Art Dealer, Historian
Muchnic, Suzanne Critic, Instructor
Mudford, Grant Leighton Photographer
Neimanas, Joyce Photographer
Newland, Joseph Nelson Editor, Writer
Newton, Richard Edward Conceptual Artist, Filmmaker
Norris, Merry Consultant, Collector
Norris, William A Collector
Oda, Masayuki Sculptor
Omar, Margit Painter, Educator
Orenstein, Gloria Feman Educator, Historian
Outterbridge, John Wilfred Sculptor, Administrator
Pal, Pratapaditya Curator, Historian
Paller, Gary Painter, Printmaker
Palmer, Herbert Bearl Dealer, Collector
Patterson, Patricia Film Critic, Painter
Peeps, Claire Curator, Painter
Picot, Pierre Painter
Pinkel, Sheila Mae Photographer, Sculptor
Pittman, Lari Painter
Pletscher, Josephine Marie Librarian, Printmaker
Poppitz, James Painter, Performer
Powell, Earl Alexander, III Director, Historian
Preziosi, Donald A Historian, Critic
Price, Vincent Collector, Dealer
Prina, Stephen James Conceptual Artist, Educator
Quinn, Noel Joseph Painter, Instructor
Ransom, Brian Ceramist
Ray, Charles Sculptor
Reeser, Robert D Educator, Administrator
Rifkind, Robert Gore Collector
Risser, James K Dealer, Painter
Rogers, Steve Sculptor
Rophar, Painter
Rose, David Painter, Illustrator
Rose, John Timothy Painter, Photographer
Rosenberg, Jane Illustrator, Painter
Rosenthal, Rachel Performance Artist, Sculptor
Rossman, Ruth Scharff Painter, Instructor
Saar, Betye Assemblage Artist, Collage Artist
Sargent, Margaret Holland Painter, Video Artist
Sauls, Frederick Inabinette Sculptor, Painter
Saxe, Adrian A Ceramist
Schultz, Stephen Warren Painter, Educator
Segalove, Ilene Judy Video Artist, Photographer
Serrano, Luis Painter
Shap, Sylvia Painter
Shaw, Jim Painter
Shire, Peter Sculptor
Silverman, Ronald H Educator, Writer
Sklar, Dorothy Painter
Sommer, Frederick Photographer, Landscape Artist
Spiegelman, Lon Howard Painter, Publisher
Squires, Norma Jean Painter, Sculptor
Stein, Donna Michele Curator, Critic
Sterritt, Coleen Sculptor
Stooker, Hendrik Cornelis Curator, Gallery Director
Stuart, Jacqueline (Mrs David) Dealer
Suggs, Don Painter, Photographer
Syrop, Mitchell Conceptual Artist
Takemoto, Henry Tadaaki Craftsman, Sculptor
Teske, Edmund Rudolph Photographer
Thomas, Tamara B Consultant
Thornycroft, Ann Painter
Todd, Michael Cullen Sculptor, Painter
Trenton, Patricia Jean Historian
Tuchman, Maurice Museum Curator
Unterseher, Chris Christian Sculptor
Valadez, John Painter
Vann, Loli (Mrs Lilian Van Young) Painter
Vanriet, Jan Painter, Printmaker
Van Young, Oscar Painter
Vasa, (Velizar Mihich) Sculptor, Educator
Wayne, June Painter, Printmaker
Weisberg, Ruth Ellen Painter, Educator
Wenger, Sigmund Dealer, Consultant
Willis, Jay Stewart Sculptor, Educator
Wingo, Michael B Painter, Draftsman
Woelffer, Emerson Painter
Wolfe, James Sculptor
Wong, Roger Frederickson Museum Director, Collector
Wright, Bernard Painter, Graphic Artist
Young, Joseph Louis Sculptor, Muralist
Zeitlin, Harriet Painter, Sculptor
Zokosky, Peter L Painter
Zver, James M Collage Artist, Printmaker

Los Gatos

Goreniuc, Mircea C Paul Sculptor
Herman, Katherine Belle Art Dealer, Collector
Kruskamp, Janet Painter, Instructor
Middlebrook, David A Sculptor, Educator

Los Osos

Gibson, George Painter, Administrator
Kreitzer, David Martin Painter
Musselman, Darwin B Painter
Peluso, Marta E Photographer, Gallery Director
Pike, Joyce Lee Painter, Writer

McKinleyville

Berry, Glenn Painter, Educator

Malibu

Alexander, Peter Sculptor
Almond, Paul Filmmaker, Writer
Altfeld, Merwin Richard Painter, Educator
Bowman, Bruce Painter, Art Writer
Dunitz, Jay Photographer

CALIFORNIA (cont)

Halpern, Nora R Director, Curator
Sturman, Eugene Painter, Sculptor

Manchester

Engle, Chet Painter

Manhattan Beach

Millar, Robert Conceptual Artist

Marina Del Rey

Goode, Joe Painter
Valentine, DeWain Sculptor

Martinez

Berlin, Beatrice Winn Printmaker, Painter

Mar Vista

Ciccone, Amy Navratil Librarian

Mendocino

Zacha, William Painter, Sculptor

Menlo Park

Mozley, Anita Ventura Historian, Critic
Smith, Albert E Painter
Zirker, Joseph Printmaker, Lecturer

Mill Valley

Ascian Printmaker, Painter
Baruch, Ruth-Marion Evelyn Photographer, Writer
Diehl, Guy Louis Painter, Instructor
Enterline, Sandra Jeweler
Grant, Art Conceptual Artist, Educator
Ihle, John Livingston Printmaker, Educator
Jones, Pirkle Photographer, Educator
Luca, Mark Printmaker
Nadel, Ann Honig Sculptor
Napoles, Veronica Kleeman Graphic Artist
Padula, Fred David Filmmaker, Photographer
Sherry, William Grant Painter
Velick, Bruce Curator

Modesto

Gauvreau, Robert George Photographer, Educator

Modjeska Cyn

Holste, Thomas James Painter, Educator

Monarch Beach

Strand, Sally (Sally Strand Ellis) Painter

Montague

Stone, Gwen Painter, Collage Artist

Montebello

Shubin, Morris Jack Painter, Lecturer

Montecito

Davidson, Suzette Morton Patron, Collector
Fenton, Howard Carter Painter, Educator
Mallory, Margaret Collector, Filmmaker
Wallin, Lawrence Bier Sculptor, Painter

Monterey

Berry, Carolyn Painter, Book Dealer
Bradford, Howard Printmaker, Painter
Cook, Joseph S Painter
Crispo, Dick Painter, Printmaker
Dedini, Eldon Lawrence Cartoonist, Graphic Artist
Esaki, Yasuhiro Painter, Printmaker
Gilpin, Henry Edmund Photographer, Instructor
Hernandez, Jo Farb Museum Director, Curator
Lawton, Nancy Painter, Graphic Artist

Moorpark

Hayward, James Painter

Moraga

Harlow, Ann Museum Director, Curator

Morgan Hill

Freimark, Bob (Robert) Printmaker, Painter

Morro Bay

Partin, Robert Painter, Educator

Mountain Center

Olsen, Frederick L Ceramaist, Sculptor

Napa

Garnett, William Ashford Photographer, Educator
Maler, M Leopoldo Mario Sculptor

Newbury Park

Reed, Dennis James Curator, Designer

Newport Beach

Botwinick, Michael Administrator, Publisher
Jacques, Russell Kenneth Sculptor
Piasecki, Jane B Administrator
Short, Patricia Ann Reilly Painter
Spitz, Barbara S Printmaker

North Hollywood

Brommer, Gerald F Painter, Writer
Shersher, Zinovy Painter, Muralist
York, Tina Painter, Writer

North Palm Springs

Houston, Bruce Sculptor, Assemblage Artist

Northridge

Brown, Betty Ann Educator, Critic
Elder, David Morton Sculptor
Fricano, Tom S Painter, Printmaker
Harden, Marvin Painter, Educator
Lewis, Louise Miller Gallery Director, Educator
Reilly, Jack Painter, Video Artist
Smith, Robert Lewis Designer, Educator

North San Juan

Acton, Arlo C Sculptor

Oakland

Andrews, Lawrence Video Artist, Sculptor
Baczek, Peter Gerard Painter, Printmaker
Beasley, Bruce Sculptor
Bowen-Forbes, Jorge C Painter
Brill, Glenn Painter, Printmaker
Byrne, Charles Joseph Consultant, Graphic Artist
Church, Maude Painter, Educator
Clark, Claude Instructor, Painter
Cook, Lia Tapestry Artist, Educator
Cornin, Jon Painter
Crum, David Painter
Crum, Katherine B Gallery Director, Educator
Daviee, Jerry Michael Administrator, Painter
Dhaemers, Robert August Sculptor, Educator
Donahue, Philip Richard Painter, Educator
Doyle, Joe Painter, Educator
Feldman, Bella Sculptor, Educator
Fischer, Victor Gallery Director
Fogg, Rebecca Snider Printmaker, Painter
Gonzalez, Arthur Padilla Sculptor
Hardy, David Whittaker, III Painter, Instructor
Hartman, Robert Leroy Photographer, Educator
Hoffman, Neil James Administrator, Educator
Jackson, Suzanne Fitzallen Painter, Costume Designer
Jensen, Clay Easton Sculptor, Educator
Kagemoto, Haro Filmmaker, Photographer
Kagemoto, Patricia Jow Printmaker, Photographer
Kelso, David William Printmaker, Art Dealer
Kirk, Jerome Sculptor, Kinetic Artist
Lacy, Suzanne Conceptual Artist, Educator
Leon, Dennis Sculptor, Educator
Levine, Melinda (Esther) Critic, Editor
Levy, Mark Writer, Historian
Linhares, Philip E Curator
Liu, Hung Painter
McLean, Richard Thorpe Painter, Educator
Melchert, James Frederick Sculptor, Educator
Mendenhall, Jack Painter, Instructor
Morales, Rodolfo Painter
Nguyen, Long Painter, Sculptor
Perez, Vincent Painter, Illustrator
Quagliata, Narcissus Stained Glass Artist, Painter
Ramos, (Mel) Melvin John Painter, Educator
Roloff, John Scott Sculptor, Environmental Artist
Roth, Moira Educator, Historian
Schoener, Jason Painter, Educator
Sherwood, Katherine Painter
Stanton, Tom-Eric Painter
Stern, Arthur I Stained Glass Artist, Architect
Sussman, Wendy Painter
Tanksley, Ann Painter, Printmaker
Tavenner, Patricia Painter, Printmaker
Thompson, Mark L Sculptor
Tunis, Roslyn Curator, Gallery Director
Walsh, Patricia Ruth Painter
Walters, Sylvia Solochek Printmaker, Educator

Oakley

Paskewitz, Bill, Jr Painter, Educator

Oceanside

Weekes, Shirley Marie Painter

Ojai

Dominique, John August Painter
McIntosh, Gregory Stephen Painter
Wood, Beatrice Ceramist, Educator

Orange

Felisky, Barbara Rosbe Painter
Green, Martin Leonard Painter, Printmaker
Leach, Mada (Madeline Kleiman) Painter
Schusterman, Gerrie Marva Art Dealer, Gallery Director

Orinda

Brody, Blanche Painter, Printmaker

Oro Grande

Bender, Bill Painter

Pacifica

Torlakson, James Daniel Painter, Printmaker

Pacific Grove

Downs, Douglas Walker Sculptor
Masteller, Barry Painter, Craftsman

Pacific Palisades

Campbell, Richard Horton Painter, Printmaker
Hannah, John Junior Printmaker, Educator
Janelsins, Veronica Painter, Illustrator
Perloff, Marjorie G Critic, Historian
Pincus, Laurie Jane Painter, Sculptor
Sherman, Z Charlotte Painter

Palm Desert

Hemmerdinger, William John, III Painter, Critic
Kilian, Austin Farland Painter, Educator

Palm Springs

Frauchiger, Fritz A Museum Director, Administrator
Harte, John Painter
Lewin, Bernard Dealer, Collector
Wade, Jane Dealer

Palo Alto

Bleiberg, Gertrude Tiefenbrun Painter, Printmaker
Conner, Bruce Graphic Artists, Collage Artist
Dater, Judy Photographer, Writer
Eisenstat, Benjamin Painter, Illustrator
Gilhooly, David James, III Sculptor
McHugh, Adeliza Sorenson Dealer, Collector
Mayfield, Signe S Curator
Ranes, Chris Painter
Welpott, Jack Warren Photographer, Educator

Pasadena

Askin, Walter Miller Painter, Printmaker
Brumfield, John Richard Photographer, Writer
Dreiband, Laurence Painter, Lecturer
Dyer, Carolyn Price Tapestry Artist, Editor
Hertz, Richard A Educator, Critic
Hoffberg, Judith A Publisher, Curator
Kieffer, Mary Jane Painter
Levy, Hilda Painter, Sculptor
McOwen, C Lynn Art Dealer, Collector
Monk, Nancy Sculptor, Designer
Wortz, Melinda Farris Gallery Director, Critic
Younglove, Ruth Ann (Mrs Benjamin Rhees Loxley) Painter
Zammitt, Norman Painter, Sculptor

Pebble Beach

Ketcham, Henry King (Hank) Cartoonist
Mortensen, Gordon Louis Printmaker, Painter

Penngrove

Ellison, Robert W Sculptor

Petaluma

Camhi, Morrie Photographer, Educator
Fuller, Mary (Mary Fuller McChesney) Sculptor, Writer
McChesney, Robert Pearson Painter, Muralist
Reichek, Jesse Painter, Educator
Saturen, Ben Painter, Printmaker
Williams, Franklin John Painter

Piedmont

Johnson, Doris Miller Painter
Martin, Fred Thomas Painter
Murray, Joan Critic, Photographer

Pinole

Gerbracht, Bob (Robert Thomas) Painter, Instructor

Placerville

Davis, Thelma Ellen Painter
Gruver, Mary Emmett Painter, Printmaker

Playa Del Rey

Harris, Gloriane Painter, Educator

Pleasant Hill

Lopez, Michael John Ceramist

Pleasanton

Erwin, Fran (Frances Suzanne) Painter

Point Richmond

Wessel, Henry Photographer

Pomona

Hannibal, Joseph Harry Educator, Painter
Jacobsen, Michael A Historian, Educator

Port Costa

Bailey, Clayton George Sculptor, Educator
De Forest, Roy Dean Painter, Sculptor

Pt Reyes Station

Quinn, Thomas Patrick, Jr Painter
Rogers, Art Photographer

Quartz Hill

Hoyal, Dorothy Painter, Printmaker

Ramona

Dash, Harvey Dwight Administrator, Painter

Ranch Palos Verdes

Kwak, Hoon Painter

Redding

Wilson, Richard Brian Painter
Wilson, Robert Alan Gallery Director, Muralist

Redway

Holbrook, Peter Greene Painter, Printmaker

Redwood City

Bowman, Richard Painter
Shukman, Solomon Painter, Printmaker

Rimforest

Jolley, Donal Clark Painter

Riverbank

Remsing, (Joseph) Gary Painter, Sculptor

Riverside

Anderson, Ross Cornelius Museum Director, Historian
Brinkerhoff, Dericksen Morgan Historian, Educator
Earle, Edward W Curator, Historian
Green, Jonathan (William) Museum Director, Photgrapher
Medel, Rebecca Rosalie Sculptor, Environmental Artist
Reeves, Esther May Painter
Warren, Katherine Virginia (Diage) Gallery Director, Curator

Rohnert Park

Choy, Terence Tin-Ho Painter, Educator
Moulton, Susan Gene Historian, Painter

Sacramento

Adan, Suzanne Rae Painter
Carpenter, Linda Buck Sculptor, Assemblage Artist
Else, Robert John Painter, Educator
Gates, Thomas Paul Educator, Curator
Gibbs, Barbara Museum Director
Kennedy, Gene (Eugene Murray) Photographer, Educator
LaPena, Frank Raymond Painter, Educator
Mahony, Pat Painter
Marcus, Irving E Painter, Educator
Moment, Joan Painter, Educator
Riegel, Michael Byron Metalsmith
Rippon, Ruth Margaret Ceramist, Sculptor
Rivers, Victoria Z Sculptor, Painter
Suzuki, James Hiroshi Painter
Walburg, Gerald Sculptor, Educator
Waterstreet, Ken (James Kent) Painter, Instructor
Winkler, Maria Paula Painter, Educator

St Helena

Evans, Henry Printmaker

Salinas

Butterbaugh, Robert Clyde Sculptor, Educator
Nugent, Bob L Painter, Sculptor
Smith, Gary Sculptor, Gallery Director

San Anselmo

Connor, Linda Stevens Photographer, Instructor

San Bernardino

Civitello, John Patrick Painter
Kaplan, Julius David Administrator, Historian
Lintault, Roger Paul Educator, Sculptor
Warehall, William Donald Glass Blower, Ceramist
Woodford, Don (Donald Paul) Painter, Educator

San Clemente

Friesz, Ray Lee Conceptual Artist, Curator
Lopina, Louise Carol Painter
Upton, John David Educator, Curator

San Diego

Alden, Gary Wade Art Conservator, Consultant
Alexander, Wick Painter
Beach, Warren Painter, Museum Director
Braley, Jean Printmaker, Painter
Cordy-Collins, Alana (Kathleen) Curator, Educator
Esser, Janet Brody Historian
Farber, Amanda Painter, Sculptor
Fisch, Arline Marie Jeweler, Educator
Gregoire, Mathieu A Sculptor
Guerrero, Raul Painter, Sculptor
Hewitt, Thurman H Painter, Designer
Hiller, Betty R Consultant, Appraiser
Hoover, Francis Louis Collector, Jeweler
Inverarity, Robert Bruce Museum Director, Painter
Jackson, Everett Gee Illustrator, Painter
Jung, Kwan Yee Painter

CALIFORNIA (cont)
Jung, Yee Wah Painter
Kornmayer, J Gary (John) Painter, Photographer
Kos, Paul Joseph Sculptor, Educator
Kosta, Angela Assemblage Artist, Writer
Landers, Bertha Painter, Printmaker
Levinson, Mimi Painter, Lecturer
Lopez, Rhoda Le Blanc Sculptor, Educator
Markarian, Alexia (Mitrus) Painter
Maruyama, Wendy Designer
Morcos, Maher N Sculptor, Painter
Ollman, Arthur L Photographer, Curator
Pincus, Robert L(awrence) Critic, Historian
Rigby, Ida Katherine Critic, Historian
Schrut, Sherry Painter, Printmaker
Schultz, Caroline Reel Painter, Lecturer
Shirk, Helen Z Craftsman
Sisco, Elizabeth Educator, Photographer
Sorby, J Richard Painter, Designer
Sowinski, Stanislaus Joseph Painter, Iconographer
Stofflet, Mary Curator, Critic
Stratton, Dorothy (Mrs William A King) Painter, Printmaker
Wallace, Robert Dan Educator, Historian
Whitcomb, Therese Truitt Instructor, Designer
Wojtyla, Haase (Walter Joseph) Painter, Draftsman
Wordell, Edwin Howland Painter
Wostrel, Nancy J Painter

San Francisco

Aiken, William A Painter
Allan, William George Painter, Educator
Allen, Jesse Printmaker, Painter
Allrich, M Louise Barco Art Dealer
Alpert, Richard Henry Video Artist
Amaya, Armando Sculptor
Arnitz, Rick Painter
Autio, (A) Rudy Ceramist, Educator
Babcock, Jo (Joseph Warren Babcock) Photographer, Sculptor
Baker, Kenneth Critic, Writer
Barrett, William O Administrator
Baum, Hank Art Dealer, Lecturer
Baum, Marilyn Ruth Painter, Printmaker
Beall, Dennis Ray Printmaker, Educator
Bechtle, Robert Alan Painter
Belcher, George Art Dealer
Bell, Michael Steven Curator, Administrator
Benton, Fletcher Sculptor
Benvenuto, Elio Sculptor
Berggruen, John Henry Art Dealer
Bernhard, Ruth Photographer
Brady, Robert D Sculptor
Braunstein, Ruth Art Dealer
Breschi, Karen Lee Sculptor
Brooks, (John) Alan Painter, Instructor
Brown, Theophilus Painter
Buchanan, Nancy Video Artist, Conceptual Artist
Buck, John Sculptor
Bukovnik, Gary Painter, Printmaker
Caldwell, John Curator
Cameron, Elsa S Curator, Administrator
Caporael, Suzanne Painter
Carnwath, Squeak Painter
Castile, Rand Museum Director
Chadwick, Whitney Critic, Historian
Concha, Jerry Painter
Cooper, Ruffin Conceptual Artist, Photographer
Cox, E Morris Collector
Davis, James Wesley Painter, Writer
Dawdy, Doris Ostrander Writer, Historian
De Lory, Peter Photographer, Instructor
Desoto, Lewis D Conceptual Artist, Educator
Deutsch, Richard Sculptor
Dickinson, Eleanor Creekmore Painter, Video Artist
Earls-Solari, Bonnie Curator
Elder, Muldoon Painter, Dealer
Elozua, Raymon Sculptor, Photographer
Erman, Bruce Painter, Educator
Featherstone, David Byrum Critic, Curator
Fischer, Hal (Harold Alan) Writer, Consultant
Fitch, George Hopper Collector, Patron
Fontana, Bill Patrick Environmental Artist, Conceptual Artist
Foolery, Tom Assemblage Artist, Painter
Fraenkel, Jeffrey Andrew Art Dealer
Fuller, Diana Arts Coordinator, Consultant
Gerdes, Ingeborg Photographer
Gerstein, David Steven Filmmaker
Gerzso, Gunther Painter, Graphic Artist
Goddard, Vivian Painter
Goetzl, Thomas Maxwell Lecturer, Educator
Goldberg, Jim Photographer
Goldstein, Daniel Joshua Printmaker, Sculptor
Grundberg, Andy (John Andrew) Critic, Editor
Gutkin, Peter Sculptor, Designer
Gutmann, John Educator, Photographer
Hamaguchi, Yozo Printmaker
Hanley, Jack Painter, Gallery Director
Hanson, Jo Sculptor
Harvey, Robert Martin Painter
Helder, David Ernest Painter, Sculptor
Henry, Jean Painter, Instructor
Hershman, Lynn Lester Photographer, Video Artist
Hinkhouse, Forest Melick Consultant
Hobbs, (Carl) Fredric Sculptor, Filmmaker
Hollis, Douglas Sculptor
Howard, David Photographer, Painter
Husebye, Terry L Photographer
Hyson, Jean Painter
Iannetti, Pasquale Francesco Paolo Art Dealer, Collector
Isaacs, Claire Naomi Administrator
Jackson, Oliver Lee Painter, Sculptor
Jess Painter, Collage Artist
Johnson, Robert Flynn Curator, Historian
Jones, David Lee Painter, Sculptor
Kahn, Ned M Environmental Artist, Scultptor
Kali (Hanna Weynerowski) Painter
Katano, Marc Painter
Kenna, Michael Photographer
Krempel, Ralf Painter, Assemblage Artist
Labat, Tony Conceptual Artist, Sculptor
Lane, John Rodger Museum Director, Historian
Levin, Morton D Printmaker, Painter
Lew, Weyman Painter, Printmaker
Lichtenstein, Gary Painter, Printmaker
Lieber, Thomas Alan Painter
Lipzin, Janis Crystal Filmmaker, Photographer
Lobdell, Frank Painter
Loeffler, Carl Eugene Editor, Video Artist
Long, Electra Painter, Draftsman
Lupper, Edward Painter
McNamara, John Painter
Majdrakoff, Ivan Painter, Assemblage Artist
Manera, Enrico Orlando Sculptor, Painter
Marcheschi, (Louis) Cork Sculptor, Educator
Marioni, Tom Environmental Artist, Museum Director
Marsh, Thomas A Sculptor
Maxim, David Nicholas Painter, Graphic Artist
Meissner, Anne Marie Administator
Mesa-Bains, Amalia Painter
Michelson, Philip L Painter, Printmaker
Miller, (Mrs) Robert Watt Patron
Minick, Roger Photographer, Writer
Modi-Vitale, Lydia Museum Director, Curator
Moquin, Richard Attilio Sculptor
Mundt, Ernest Karl Sculptor, Educator
Muranaka, Hideo Painter, Printmaker
Murch, Anna Valentina Conceptual Artist, Environmental Artist
Nash, Steven Alan Historian, Curator
Nelson, Jane Gray Curator
Neri, Manuel Sculptor
Nice, Don Painter
Nixon, Nichols Photographer
Nong Painter, Sculptor
O'Banion, Nance Assemblage Artist
O'Hara, Sheila Mary Tapestry Artist, Weaver
Oropallo, Deborah Artist
Ott, Sabina Painter
Parker, Harry S, III Museum Director
Parker, Wilma (Wilma Parker de Pavloff) Painter
Peche, Dale C Painter
Pence, John Gerald Dealer, Patron
Pennuto, James William Conceptual Artist, Conservator
Perlman, Mark A Painter
Piccolo, Richard Painter
Post, George (Booth) Painter
Raciti, Cherie Painter, Sculptor
Rascon, Armando Painter, Curator
Ravarra, Patricia Sculptor
Redd Ekks (Robert Norman Rasmussen) Sculptor, Ceramist
Reichman, Fred Painter
Renk, Merry Goldsmith, Painter
Robbins, Trina Cartoonist, Illustrator
Romeu, Joost A Conceptual Artist, Designer
Royce, Suzanne Consultant, Curator
Rubenstein, Meridel Photographer
Rumsey, David MacIver Environmental Artist, Patron
St Amand, Joseph Painter
Sapien, Darryl Rudolph Performance Artist, Graphic Artist
Sassone, Marco Painter, Printmaker
Saunders, Raymond Jennings Painter
Sawyer, William Dealer, Collector
Scott, John Illustrator, Painter
Scott, John Beldon Historian, Educator
Shangraw, Clarence Frank Historian, Curator
Shepp, Alan Sculptor
Siegesmund, Richard Museum Director
Sinton, Nell (Walter) Painter, Educator
Smith, J Weldon Museum Director, Historian
Snyder, Dan Sculptor
Southard, James Bruce Lecturer, Painter
Stanley, M Louise Painter
Staprans, Raimonds Painter, Sculptor
Stermer, Dugald Robert Illustrator, Designer
Stevens, Michael Keith Sculptor
Stone, Jeremy Dealer
Stover, Donald Lewis Curator
Sultan, Larry A Photographer
Tait, Will(iam) H Printmaker, Painter
Tarshis, Jerome Writer
Taylor, Sandra Ortiz Painter, Printmaker
Tchakalian, Sam Painter
Thomas, Larry W Painter, Printmaker
Thompson, Richard E, Jr Dealer, Collector

CALIFORNIA (cont)

Tompkins, Michael Painter
Valesco, Frances Muralist, Printmaker
Van Hoesen, Beth Printmaker
Varnay Jones, Theodora Printmaker, Painter
Vignes, Michelle Marie Educator, Photographer
Villa, Carlos Painter
Wagner, Catherine Photographer
Washburn, Stan Printmaker, Painter
Webber, Helen Tapestry Artist, Sculptor
Weeks, James (Darrell Northrup) Painter, Art Dealer
Weinbaum, Jean Painter, Sculptor
Wirtz, Stephen Carl Dealer
Wonner, Paul (John) Painter
Woodall, John Sculptor, Video Artist
Zajac, Jack Sculptor, Painter

San Gabriel

Peregrin, Magda Elizabeth Painter, Instructor

San Geronimo

North, Judy Painter

San Jose

Chapman, Robert Gordon Jeweler, Painter
Estabrook, Reed Photographer, Educator
French, Stephen Warren Painter, Administrator
Hero, Peter deCourcy Administrator, Historian
Hoffman, Eric Painter, Printmaker
Hunter, John H Painter, Printmaker
Milnes, Robert Winston Sculptor, Educator
Moore, Russell James Museum Director, Administrator
Richardson, Sam Sculptor, Educator
Sorensen, Jean Painter
Spratt, Frederick R Gallery Director, Painter
Stone, M Lee Art Dealer
Suggs, Pat(ricia) Ann Painter, Conceptual Artist
Surgalski, Patrick J Painter, Printmaker
Thurston, Jacqueline Beverly Educator, Painter
Wise, Joseph Stephen Painter

San Juan Capistrano

Aspell, Amy Suzanne Director, Weaver
Burr, Ruth Basler Painter

San Leandro

Stockdale, John A D Painter, Photographer

San Luis Obispo

McFee, June King Educator
Reynolds, Robert Painter, Educator
Ruggles, Joanne Beaule Painter, Educator

San Marino

Karlstrom, Paul Johnson Historian, Administrator
Medearis, Roger Painter, Printmaker
Wark, Robert Rodger Administrator, Historian

San Mateo

Carmean, E A, Jr Historian, Curator
Mancini, John Painter

San Pedro

Crutchfield, William Richard Painter, Sculptor
McCafferty, Jay David Video Artist, Painter
Strasen, Barbara Elaine Painter, Conceptual Artist

San Rafael

Dixon, Willard Painter
Fulton, Jack E Photographer, Educator
Larsen, D Dane Ceramist, Sculptor
Lucey, Jack Painter, Educator
Ruvolo, Felix Emmanuele Painter, Educator

Santa Ana

Karwelis, Donald Charles Painter, Instructor

Santa Barbara

Abraham, Carol Jeanne Assemblage Artist, Ceramist
Ayres, Larry Marshall Historian
Bermant, David W Collector, Director
Bolton, Richard Photographer
Braiden, Rose Margaret J Painter, Illustrator
Brown, Gary Hugh Painter, Educator
Cavat, Irma Painter, Educator
Cole, Herbert Milton Historian, Photographer
Coleman, Constance Depler Painter
Cortright, Steven M Assemblage Artist, Conceptual Artist
De Laittre, Eleanor Sculptor, Painter
Del Chiaro, Mario A Historian
Dorra, Henri Historian, Educator
Farwell, Beatrice Historian, Educator
Firfires, Nicholas Samuel Painter
Frame, Robert (Aaron) Painter
Gebhard, David Museum Director, Historian
Herschler, David Elijah Sculptor, Painter
Hochhauser, Marilyn Helsenrott Painter, Educator
Klausner, Betty Director, Curator
Korenic, Lynette Marie Librarian
La Plant, Mimi Painter, Printmaker
Maraldo, Ushanna F Filmmaker, Painter
Mills, Paul Chadbourne Museum Director, Art and Flag Consultant
Moir, Alfred Historian, Curator
Morrison, Doris Painter, Administrator
Noble, Helen (Harper) Printmaker, Painter
Olsen Bergman, Ciel Painter, Educator
Perrot, Paul N Administrator, Lecturer
Post, Marion (Marion Post Wolcott) Photographer
Robertson, E Bruce Historian, Curator
Sattler, Jill Jeweler, Painter
Snow, Lee Erlin Painter, Instructor
Treese, William R Librarian, Painter
Villa, Theodore B Painter
Yegul, Fikret Kutlu Educator, Architect

Santa Clara

Atkins, Bill (Billy Wayne Atkins) Museum Director, Curator
Hawkins, Myrtle H Painter, Writer
Hernandez, Sam (Samuel Rudolph) Sculptor, Educator
McDonald, Robert Herwick Curator, Museum Director

Santa Cruz

Alford, Gloria K Painter, Sculptor
Alquilar, Maria Painter, Sculptor
Burris, Bruce C Painter, Sculptor
Douke, Daniel W Painter, Educator
Loftus, Peter M Painter
Mandel, Mike Educator, Photographer
Mayhew, Richard Painter
Nutzle, Futzie (Bruce John Kleinsmith) Artist, Cartoonist
Orland, Ted N Photographer, Writer
Stolpe, Daniel Owen Painter, Printmaker
Summers, Carol Printmaker
Sward, Robert S Editor, Writer
Thompson, Donald Roy Painter, Assemblage artist

Santa Monica

Andrews, Mari Painter
Arnoldi, Charles Arthur Sculptor, Painter
Bachardy, Don Painter, Draftsman
Baldessari, John Anthony Conceptual Artist
Blum, Helaine Dorothy Sculptor, Painter
Bob & Bob Performance Artists
Brenno, Vonnie Mei-Lin Painter
Bunn, David Photographer
Burchett, Debra Administrator, Curator
Callis, Jo Ann Photographer
Caswell, Jim (James Daniel Caswell-Davis) Sculptor, Ceramist
Cathcart, Linda Louise Historian
Cheng, Carl F K, AKA John Doe Co Environmental Artist, Sculptor
Chu, Julia Nee painter
Clutz, William Painter, Instructor
Coleman, Judy Photographer
Conal, Robbie Painter
Cowin, Eileen Photographer
Drohojowska, Hunter Writer, Educator
Duke, Leilani Lattin Administrator
Edelstein, J M Librarian, Lecturer
Fellows, Alice Painter
Francis, Sam Painter
Freeman, Mallory Bruce Dealer, Curator
Fukuhara, Henry Painter, Instructor
Fusco, Laurie S Historian, Educator
Fusco, Peter Richard Curator, Historian
Galloway, Steve Conceptual Artist
Gehry, Frank O(wen) Architect
Gipe, Lawrence Painter
Goldeen, Dorothy A Dealer, Consultant
Greaves, James L Conservator, Restorer
Halbrook, Anne-Mieke Platt Librarian
Hansen, Gaylen Capener Painter, Educator
Hatch, Connie Photographer
Hempler, Orval F Painter, Sculptor
Hill, William Mansfield Historian, Museum Director
Karpel, Eli Sculptor
Kohn, Michael Bundy Art Dealer, Critic
Kuhlenschmidt, Richard Edward Dealer
Kushner, Dorothy Browdy Painter, Printmaker
Laskin, Myron, Jr Curator, Historian
Lewis, John Conard Sculptor, Glassblower
Martinez, Daniel J Conceptual Artist
Mitchell, Robin Painter, Educator
Mullican, Lee Painter, Educator
Oginz, Richard Sculptor, Instructor
Provisor, Janis Architect
Rath, Alan T Sculptor
Reese, Thomas Ford Historian, Administrator
Roosen, Mia Westerlund Sculptor
Rowland, Anne Photographer
Schipper, Merle Solway Historian, Critic
Schmitt, Marilyn Low Historian, Administrator
Snyder, Ruth (Cozen) Painter, Sculptor
Spector, Buzz (Franklin Mac Spector) Conceptual Artist, Critic
Stern, Irene Monat Painter
Stern, Jan Peter Sculptor
Trieff, Selina Painter, Instructor
Ullman, Jane F Sculptor
Van Sant, Tom R Sculptor, Painter

CALIFORNIA (cont)

Walsh, John Museum Director
Wethli, Mark Painter, Educator
Wittmann, Otto Museum Consultant

Santa Rosa

Barr, Roger Collage Artist, Sculptor
Gamble, Kathryn Elizabeth Museum Director
Hein, Max Graphic Artist, Educator
Quandt, Elizabeth (Elizabeth Quandt) Printmaker, Painter
Weare, Shane Printmaker

Saratoga

Young, Edna E Art Dealer, Collector

Sausalito

Allen, Terry Video Artist
Baltz, Lewis Photographer
Dowley, Jennifer Director
Edwards, Linda (Linda Margaret Weiss Edwards) Silversmith, Goldsmith
Kuhlman, Walter Egel Painter, Educator
Oda, Mayumi Painter, Printmaker
Sumner, George Environmental Artist, Painter
Tift, Mary Louise Printmaker, Educator
Wiley, William T Painter

Sebastopol

Caswell, Helen Rayburn Painter, Writer
Hasegawa, Noriko Painter
Jameson, Philip Alexander Ceramist, Painter
Palmer, Mabel (Evelyn) Painter
Solberg, Morten Edward Painter
Stanford, Ginny C Painter, Illustrator

Sherman Oaks

Braudy, Dorothy Painter, Educator
Burg, Patricia Jean Painter, Printmaker
Carl, Joan Sculptor, Painter
Davis, L Clarice Book Dealer, Art Librarian
Mekler, Adam Art Dealer, Curator
Schlosberg, Carl Martin Art Dealer

Sierra Madre

Converse, Elizabeth Writer, Painter

Soda Bay

Fletcher, Leland Vernon Sculptor, Painter

Solana Beach

Baldwin, Russell W Educator, Gallery Director
Gronborg, Erik Sculptor, Ceramist
Honda, Margaret Painter

Sonoma

Anderson, Gunnar Donald Painter, Illustrator
Christensen, Ted Painter, Printmaker

Sonora

Popovac, Gwynn Painter, Graphic Artist
Price, Joe (Allen) Serigrapher, Instructor

Soquel

Auvil, Kenneth William Educator, Printmaker
Blair, Lee Everett Painter, Filmmaker
Brown, Lawrie Photographer, Educator
McClellan, Douglas Eugene Painter

South Pasadena

Sverdlove, Zolita Painter, Printmaker

Spring Valley

Greene, Ethel Maud Painter

Stanford

Corn, Wanda M Historian, Educator
Eisner, Elliot Wayne Educator
Eitner, Lorenz E A Historian, Museum Director
Elsen, Albert Edward Historian
Fryberger, Betsy G Curator
Seligman, Thomas Knowles Director
Volkerding, Laura Photographer

Stinson Beach

Chapline, Claudia Beechum Painter, Art Consultant

Stockton

Dennison, Keith Elkins Consultant, Curator
Gyermek, Stephen A Educator
Pecchenino, J Ronald Painter, Educator
Reynolds, Richard (Henry) Sculptor, Painter

Studio City

Vaccarino, Robin Sculptor, Painter

Suisun City

Schmaltz, Roy Edgar Painter, Educator

Summerland

Calamar, Gloria Painter

Sunland

Porter, Albert Wright Educator, Painter

Sylmar

Reynolds, Wade Painter

Tiburon

Baird, Joseph Armstrong, Jr Writer, Consultant

Topanga

Foulkes, Llyn Painter
Solem, (Elmo) John Ceramist, Educator
Wisdom, Joyce Painter

Torrance

Clark, Robert Charles Painter, Lecturer
Everts, Connor Painter, Printmaker

Turlock

Camarata, Martin L Artist, Educator
McGee, Winston Eugene Painter, Educator
Parton, Ralf Sculptor, Educator
Piskoti, James Printmaker, Painter
Werness, Hope B Historian

Upland

Logan, Gene Adams Sculptor, Painter
Slatkin, Wendy Historian
Svenson, John Edward Sculptor

Valencia

Fiskin, Judy Photographer, Educator
Mandel, John Painter
Preston, Ann L Sculptor
Wilson, Millie Conceptual Artist, Designer

Vallejo

Babior, Daniel Photographer
Bullock, James Benbow Sculptor
Fried, Howard Lee Sculptor
Salmon, Raymond Merle Cartoonist, Educator

Van Nuys

Blinder, Martin S Art Dealer, Publisher
Penny, Aubrey John Robert Painter, Sculptor

Venice

Barth, Uta Conceptual Artist, Photographer
Bengston, Billy Al Painter
Berlant, Tony Sculptor, Collage Artist
Brewster, Michael Sculptor, Educator
Byrd, Jerry Painter
Cheng, Fu-Ding Filmmaker, Painter
Coit, M B Painter, Sculptor
Davis, Kimberly Brooke Gallery Director, Art Dealer
Davy, Woods Sculptor
Dill, Guy Girard Sculptor, Educator
Dill, Laddie John Painter, Sculptor
Divola, John Manford, Jr Photographer
Eino Sculptor
Eversley, Frederick John Sculptor
Fine, Jud Sculptor, Educator
Garabedian, Charles Painter
Goulds, Peter J Dealer, Designer
Hauptman, Susan Illustrator
Hill, Charles Christopher Collage Artist, Painter
Moses, Ed Painter
Okulick, John A Sculptor
Rady, Elsa Ceramist, Sculptor
Ruscha, Edward Joseph Painter, Filmmaker
Scheer, Sherie (Hood) Photographer, Painter
Shaffer, Richard Painter, Printmaker
Shelton, Peter T Sculptor
Smith, Alexis (Patricia Anne) Collage Artist, Conceptual Artist
Smith, Barbara Turner Instructor, Video & Performance Artist
Tonelli, Edith Ann Museum Director, Historian
Venable, Susan C Sculptor, Painter

Ventura

Koch, Gerd (Herman) Painter, Educator

Victorville

Bascom, Earl W Sculptor, Printmaker
Hay-Messick, Velma Painter

Vista

Simmons, Cleda Marie Painter, Graphic Artist

Walnut Creek

Dennis, Charles Houston Cartoonist
Hunter, Leonard LeGrande, III Sculptor, Educator
Novotny, Elmer Ladislaw Painter, Educator

West Covina

Cross, Watson, Jr Painter, Video Artist
Edmondson, Leonard Printmaker

West Hills

Duzy, Merrilyn Jeanne Painter, Lecturer

West Hollywood

Gardner, Colin R Writer, Critic

Westlake Village

Liu, Katherine Chang Painter, Printmaker

West Los Angeles

Stussy, Maxine Kim Sculptor

Westminster

Covell, Alan Carter Historian, Curator

Whittier

Carlson, Lance R Critic, Editor

Willits

Posey, Ernest Noel Painter, Educator

Woodacre

Snyder, William B Painter, Educator
Uzilevsky, Marcus Painter, Printmaker

Woodland Hills

Fichter, Herbert Francis Printmaker, Painter
Reed, Hal Painter, Medalist
Turner, Bonese Collins Painter, Educator
Whitson, Angie Sculptor, Painter

Woodside

Concannon, George Robert Painter
Hogle, Ann Meilstrup Painter

Yorba Linda

Wong, Jason Museum Director, Designer

Yountville

Clymer, Albert Anderson Painter

COLORADO

Alamosa

Quiller, Stephen Frederick Painter, Printmaker

Arvada

Balciar, Gerald George Sculptor
Marro, George Matthew Painter, Writer

Aspen

Berko, Ferenc Photographer
Chesley, Paul Alexander Photographer, Graphic Artist
Farver, Suzanne Administrator, Collector
Pletka, Paul Painter, Printmaker
Soldner, Paul Edmund Sculptor, Ceramist

Aurora

Holden, Ruth Egri Painter
Whitney, Maynard Merle Sculptor, Educator

Boulder

Barnes, Carole D Painter
Brakhage, James Stanley Filmmaker, Lecturer
Chamberlin, Scott Sculptor, Ceramist
Cline, Clinton C Printmaker, Educator
Crane, Michael Patrick Museum Director, Curator
Dowden, Anne Ophelia Todd Illustrator, Writer
Eades, Luis Eric Painter, Educator
Forsman, Chuck (Charles Stanley) Painter, Educator
Herritt, Linda S Sculptor
Iwamasa, Ken Educator, Printmaker
Johnson, James Alan Painter, Educator
Kuczun, Ann-Marie Painter, Illustrator
Lhotka, Bonny Pierce Painter
Mandel, Dorothy Printmaker, Graphic Artist
Markowitz, Marilyn Painter
Matthews, Gene (Eugene Edward) Painter, Educator
Matthews, Wanda Miller Printmaker
Maxwell, William Jackson Sculptor, Environmental Artist
Neher, Fred Cartoonist
Praeger, Frederick A Collector, Publisher
Roots, Garrison Sculptor Consultant
Sampson, Frank Painter, Printmaker
Vandersall, Amy L Historian, Educator
Vielehr, William Ralph Sculptor
Wolfe, Lynn Robert Painter, Educator
Woodman, Betty Ceramist

Colorado Springs

Bransby, Eric James Muralist, Educator
Broome, Rick (Richard Raymond) Painter
Hoge, Robert Wilson Museum Director, Educator
Kinnee, Sandy Painter, Printmaker
Trissel, James Nevin Painter, Printmaker
Wagner, (Dr) David J Museum Director
Whitcomb, Skip Painter, Printmaker
Wilde, Dawn Johnson Painter, Educator
Wynne, Albert Givens Painter, Calligrapher

Denver

Anderson, Bruce James Stained Glass Artist, Art Dealer
Atkinson, Leslie Jane Painter, Sculptor
Bowman, Ken Painter
Calzolari, Elaine Sculptor
Conn, Richard George Curator
Cunningham, E C (Eldon Lloyd Cunningham) Printmaker, Educator
DeMaree, Betty (Elizabeth Ann) Painter, Instructor
Dickson, Mark Amos Painter, Printmaker
Goodacre, Glenna Sculptor
Graese, Judy (Judith Ann) Painter, Printmaker
Graham, Douglas J M Museum Director, Collector
Hansen, Frances Frakes Educator, Painter
Hughes, Paul Lucien Dealer, Consultant
Kaiser, Karen Painter, Designer
Katz, Eunice Painter, Sculptor
Maytham, Thomas Northrup Museum Director, Consultant
Melnick, Myron J Sculptor, Collage Artist
Michael, Gary Painter, Writer
Mitchell, Dean Lamont Painter
O'Hagan, Desmond Brian Painter
Ragland, Bob Painter, Sculptor
Saylors, Jo An Sculptor, Painter
Schiff, Jean Illustrator
Scott, Sandy (Sandra Lynn) Sculptor
Sebastian Sculptor
Sebastian, Jill C Environmental Artist, Sculptor
Sharp, Lewis Inman Director
Smith-Warren, Katharine Curator, Consultant
Stapp, Ray Veryl Painter, Printmaker
Swensen, J(ean) Mary Jeanette Hamilton Graphic Artist, Calligrapher
Thompson, Richard Craig Painter
Thorne-Thomsen, Ruth T Photographer, Educator
Tubis, Seymour Painter, Printmaker
Vanderlip, Dianne Perry Gallery Director, Educator
West, Clara Faye Johnson Painter, Conservator
White, Karen J Sculptor, Craftsman
Witold-K (Kaczanowski), Painter, Sculptor
Yanish, Elizabeth Sculptor, Lecturer
Yust, David E Painter, Educator

Dolores

Wagner, Richard Ellis Painter

Durango

Reber, Mick Sculptor, Painter

Elizabeth

Kaplinski, Buffalo Painter

Englewood

Brauer, Connie Ann Designer, Goldsmith
Cooper, Susan Painter, Sculptor
Jellico, John Anthony Director, Painter
Lamb, Darlis Carol Sculptor, Painter
Meyer, Milton E, Jr Painter

Estes Park

Richmond, Rebekah Printmaker
Simoni, John Peter Painter, Educator

Evergreen

Kastner, Barbara H Painter

Ft Collins

De Vore, Richard E Ceramist
Getty, Nilda Fernandez Educator, Silversmith
Jacobs, Peter Alan Sculptor, Educator
Lesh, Richard D Painter, Instructor
Marander, Carol Jean Painter, Graphic Artist
Risbeck, Philip Edward Graphic Artist, Educator
Twarogowski, Leroy Andrew Draftsman, Educator

Golden

Fisher, Philip C Painter, Art Dealer

Grand Junction

Erickson, Mark D Painter

Greeley

Ruyle, Lydia Miller Printmaker, Educator

Gunnison

Johnson, Lee Painter, Educator
Julio, Pat T Educator, Craftsman
Radovich, Donald Painter, Educator

Lakewood

Cadillac, Louise Roman Painter, Instructor
Denton, Patry Painter, Instructor
Knaub, Raymond L Painter, Instructor
Lang, Rodger Alan Sculptor, Educator

Littleton

Duesberry, Joellyn Painter
Faris, Peter Kinzie Writer, Historian
Jellico, Nancy R Painter, Sculptor
Poduska, T F Lecturer, Painter
Sougstad, Mike Graphic Artist, Educator
Wilson, Jean S Museum Director, Historian

Longmont

Adams, Robert Hickman Photographer
Wise, Sue Painter

Loveland

Cole, Julie Kramer Painter
Lundeen, George Wayne Sculptor
Pendleton, Mary Caroline Handweaver, Writer
Williford, Hollis R Sculptor, Painter

Manitou Springs

Wallace, Gael Lynn Painter

Mesa

Fritzler, Gerald J Painter

Montrose

Turner, James Thomas, Sr Sculptor, Painter

Monument

Bohler, Joseph Stephen Painter

Nederland

Fernie, John Chipman Sculptor

Paonia

Fox, Lincoln H Sculptor

Parker

Thies, Charles Herman Painter, Printmaker

Parshall

Retzer, Howard Earl Painter

Pueblo

Wands, Robert James Educator, Painter

Salida

Strawn, Bernice I Sculptor
Strawn, Melvin Nicholas Painter, Sculptor

Sedalia

Nickerson, John Henry Glass Blower, Sculptor

Shawnee

Tolpo, Carolyn Lee Painter, Tapestry artist
Tolpo, Vincent Carl Painter, Sculptor

Silverthorne

Trumble, Beverly (Jane) Painter

Snowmass Village

Beeman, Malinda Painter, Printmaker

Telluride

Smith, Sam Painter, Educator

Vail

Cotter, James Edward Sculptor, Designer
Milhoan, Randall Bell Administrator, Painter
Prindiville, Jim Painter

Westcliffe

Merfeld, Gerald Lydon Painter

Wheat Ridge

Dawson, Doug Painter, Instructor
Toscano, (Dolores A) Painter, Sculptor

CONNECTICUT

Ashford

Spencer, Harold Edwin Historian, Painter

Avon

Atkinson, Tracy Consultant, Museologist
Smith, Elizabeth Graphic Artist

Bethany

Wolanic, Susan Seseske Painter, Graphic Artist

Bethel

Ajay, Abe Painter, Sculptor
Farris, Joseph Cartoonist, Painter

Bethlehem

Vestal, David Photographer

Bloomfield

Hammer, Alfred Emil Painter, Educator
Tompkins, Alan Painter
Valtman, Edmund Cartoonist, Editorial

Bridgeport

Baldwin, Roger N Critic, Curator
Morris, Robert Clarke Painter, Educator

Bridgewater

Abbett, Robert Kennedy Painter
Gilbert, Albert Earl Painter, Illustrator

Brookfield Center

Beall, Joanna Painter, Sculptor
Sottung, George (K) Painter, Illustrator
Westermann, H C Sculptor, Painter

Clinton

Grimm, Lucille Davis Painter
Mays, Victor Painter, Illustrator

Cornwall Bridge

Gray, Cleve Painter, Sculptor
Pfeiffer, Werner Bernhard Sculptor, Printmaker

Cos Cob

Giles, Newell Walton, Jr Painter
Kane, Margaret Brassler Sculptor
Smith, Clyde Painter
Ubogy, Jo Sculptor

Coventry

Doudera, Gerard Painter, Educator

Danbury

Winchester, Alice Editor, Writer

Darien

Black, Lisa Painter, Photographer

East Haddam

Conant, Jan Royce Traditional Painter

East Hartford

Soppelsa, George Painter, Collage Artist

East Haven

Gardner, Joan A Painter, Printmaker

Easton

Bogart, Richard Jerome Painter
Curtis, Dolly Powers Sculptor, Weaver
Sharp, Susan S Painter

Fairfield

Brier, Helene Painter, Printmaker
Chaikin, Alyce Graphic Artist, Painter
Chasin, Martin Art Dealer, Consultant
Eliasoph, Philip Historian, Critic
Glaser, Bruce Historian, Educator
Khachian, Elisa A Painter
Trager, Philip Photographer

Farmington

Ferguson, Charles B Museum Director, Painter
Smith, Cary Painter

Georgetown

Roberts, Priscilla Warren Painter

Glastonbury

Bailey, Marcia Mead Painter

Greens Farms

McKinnickinnick, Margaret I Painter, Printmaker
Weiss, Harvey Sculptor, Writer

Greenwich

Fields, Fredrica H Stained Glass Artist, Craftsman
Johnson, Lester F Painter, Educator
List, Vera G Patron, Collector
McKnight, Thomas Frederick Painter, Printmaker
Momiyama, Nanae Painter, Educator
Moonie, Liana Painter, Instructor
Nierman, Leonardo M Painter, Sculptor
O Donohue, Teige Ros Painter, Printmaker
Perless, Robert Sculptor

Groton

MacGillis, Robert Donald Painter, Printmaker

Guilford

Wiener, Sam (Evangeline Tabasco) Sculptor, Conceptual Artist

Hamden

Bills, Mitchell Designer, Video Artist
Cain, David Paul Painter, Photographer
Chambers, Bruce William Dealer, Historian
Graziani, Sante Painter, Muralist
MacClintock, Dorcas Sculptor

Hartford

Ayres, Linda L Administrator, Curator
Behl, Wolfgang Sculptor, Educator
Faude, Wilson Hinsdale Director, Curator
McCaughey, Arnold Patrick Director, Administrator
Mahoney, Michael R T Historian, Educator
Zimmerman, Paul Warren Painter, Instructor

Ivoryton

Jensen, Leo (Vernon) Sculptor, Painter
Ramanauskas, Dalia Irena Painter, Draftsman

Kent

Jones, Franklin Reed Painter, Writer

Killingworth

Harris, William Wadsworth, II Painter, Collage Artist

Lakeville

Blagden, Thomas P Painter

Madison

Davies, Kenneth Southworth Painter, Instructor
Wexler, Jerome LeRoy Photographer, Illustrator

Mansfield Center

Forman, Kenneth Warner Painter

Meriden

Bertolli, Eugene Emil Sculptor, Designer
Scalise, Nicholas Peter Painter, Sculptor
Tamburine, Jean Helen Painter, Sculptor

Middletown

D'Oench, Ellen Gates Curator, Educator
Frazer, John Thatcher Filmmaker, Painter
Ottmann, Klaus Curator, Critic
Risley, John Hollister Sculptor

Milford

Fagan, Alanna Painter
Maier, Maryanne E Painter

Mystic

Bates, Gladys Edgerly Sculptor
Olson, Joseph Olaf Designer, Painter
Stein, Fritz Henry Dealer

New Britain

Cipriano, Michael R Painter, Educator

New Canaan

Cavalli, Dick Cartoonist
Finch, Ruth Woodward Writer, Photographer
Geerlings, Gerald Kenneth Graphic Artist, Architect
Margolies, Ethel Polacheck Painter, Sculptor
Peii, Ahmad Osni Sculptor, Designer
Rendl, M(ildred Marcus) Painter, Writer
Richards, Glenora Painter
Richards, Walter DuBois Painter, Printmaker
Tomchuk, Marjorie Printmaker, Painter
Townsend, Teryl Painter, Educator
Woit, Bonnie Ford Painter

New Fairfield

Mann, Jean (Adah) Ceramist, Sculptor
Nevelson, Mike Sculptor

New Haven

Alvarez, Candida Painter
Audette, Anna Held Painter, Educator
Axelrod, Miriam Sculptor
Bailey, William Painter, Educator
Carter, David Giles Consultant, Museum Director
Casteras, Susan Paulette Curator, Educator
Chaet, Bernard Painter, Educator
Colton, Judith Educator, Historian
De Bretteville, Sheila Levrant Designer, Educator
Field, Richard Sampson Curator, Historian
Fussiner, Howard Painter
Gilbert, Creighton Eddy Historian, Writer
Hanson, Anne Coffin Historian
Hersey, George Leonard Historian, Educator
Kubler, George Alexander Historian, Curator
Lindroth, Linda Photographic Artist, Curator
Lytle, Richard Painter, Educator
Meghelli, Fethi M Printmaker, Painter
Newick, Craig D Architect
Pease, David G Administrator, Painter
Pelli, Cesar Architect
Pogany, Miklos Painter, Printmaker
Pollitt, Jerome Jordan Historian, Educator
Prown, Jules David Historian
Robinson, Duncan Director, Historian
Ryan, Richard E Painter, Printmaker
Smith, Raymond Walter Curator, Photographer
Zeidenbergs, Olafs Sculptor

New London

Hendricks, Barkley Leonnard Painter
Leibert, Peter R Ceramist, Sculptor
Rash, Nancy Historian, Writer
Van Brunt, Philip G Director, Assemblage Artist

New Milford

Stewart, Dorothy S Painter, Printmaker

Newtown

Christensen, Betty (Elizabeth) Illustrator, Painter
Cottingham, Robert Painter, Printmaker
Grimes, Margaret W Painter, Educator
Purdy, Donald R Painter
Wallace, John Painter, Educator

Niantic

Dennis, Roger Wilson Painter

Noank

Keck, Hardu Painter, Administrator
Stein, Harve Painter, Illustrator

North Grosvenor Dale

Kornbluth, Frances Painter, Collage Artist

North Haven

Tulk, Alfred James Painter, Muralist
Willoughby, Jane Baker Collage Artist, Painter
Zallinger, Jean Day Illustrator, Educator
Zallinger, Rudolph Franz Painter, Educator

Norwalk

Chernow, Ann Painter, Printmaker
Pellew, John Clifford Painter
Perry, Charles O Sculptor
Peterdi, Gabor F Painter, Printmaker
Shaffer, Rosalind Sculptor, Painter

Norwich

Gualtieri, Joseph P Museum Director, Painter
Radin, Dan Painter, Instructor

Old Greenwich

Ballantyne, Catherine Turk Painter
Hayward, Peter Painter, Sculptor

Old Lyme

Chandler, Elisabeth Gordon Sculptor
Dirks, John Sculptor, Cartoonist
Gerenday, Laci Anthony de Sculptor
Greenleaf, Virginia Painter
Gruppe, Charles Painter
Peterson, Roger Tory Illustrator, Writer

Orange

Albers, Anni Designer, Graphic Artist

Oxford

Chaplin, George Edwin Painter, Educator

Plainville

Brzozowski, Richard Joseph Painter

Poquonock

Van Winkelen, Barbara Painter, Illustrator

Portland

Glasson, Lloyd Sculptor, Educator

Prospect

Thornley, Wendy Ann Sculptor, Craftsman

Quaker Hill

Braunstein, Mark Mathew Writer, Photographer
McCabe, Maureen M Collage Artist
Smalley, David Allan Sculptor, Educator

Redding Ridge

Morton, Robert Alan Publisher, Writer

Ridgefield

Benton, Suzanne E Sculptor, Art Writer
Busino, Orlando Francis Cartoonist
Giordano, Greg Joe Painter, Photographer
Grasso, Jack Painter
Passantino, George Christopher Painter, Instructor
Perlin, Bernard Painter, Illustrator
Sendak, Maurice Bernard Writer, Illustrator

Riverside

Rubin, Ida Ely Consultant, Writer
Thompson, Bradbury Designer, Art Director

Rocky Hill

Miller, Jean Johnston Librarian, Historian

Rowayton

Burt, David Sill Sculptor
Flora, James Royer Illustrator, Painter

Roxbury

Kalisher, Simpson Photographer
Morath, Inge Photographer

Salisbury

Blagden, Allen Painter, Printmaker
Osborn, Elodie C (Mrs Robert Osborn) Director, Administrator
Osborn, Robert Illustrator, Painter
Ten Eyck, Catryna (Catryna Ten Eyck Seymour) Painter, Printmaker

Sandy Hook

Merrill, David Kenneth Painter, Muralist

Sharon

Heller, Ben Dealer, Collector

Sherman

Fischer, Henry George Historian, Curator

Simsbury

Ford, John Painter, Sculptor
Guzman-Forbes, Robert Painter, Illustrator

Southbury

Usher, Elizabeth Reuter (Mrs William Arthur Scar) Librarian, Lecturer

South Norwalk

Frasconi, Antonio Graphic Artist, Painter

Southport

Anderson, Margaret Pomeroy Writer, Consultant
Bloom, Martha Collage Artist, Printmaker
Sill, Gertrude Grace Educator, Curator
Webster, Stokely Painter, Printmaker

Southpost

Levin, Hugh Lauter Publisher, Dealer

South Windsor

Patterson, Shirley Abbott Painter, Instructor

Stamford

Bechtle, C Ronald Painter, Draftsman
Calle, Paul Painter, Writer
Calrow, Robert F Instructor, Painter
Couturier, Marion B Dealer, Collector
Cunningham, J Sculptor
Hausman, Fred S Sculptor, Designer
Heston, Joan Painter, Instructor
Kinsman, Robert Donald Museum Director, Historian
Koch, Robert Historian, Writer
Mayhall, Dorothy Museum Director, Curator
Moss, Jacqueline Historian, Educator
Rudman, Joan (Combs) Painter, Instructor
Stillman, Lucille T Painter
Strosahl, William Painter

Stonington

Aalund, Suzy Painter
Fix, John Robert Sculptor, Silversmith
Houston, James A Designer, Sculptor

Stony Creek

Sheard, Wendy Stedman Historian, Educator

Storrs

Crossgrove, Roger Lynn Painter, Educator
Gray, Robert Hugh Painter, Educator
Gregoropoulos, John Painter
Rovetti, Paul F Museum Director, Administrator
Thornton, Richard Samuel Educator, Writer

Trumbull

Kozlowski, Edward C Painter, Designer
Usher, David Publisher, Art Dealer

Uncasville

Lukosius, Richard Benedict Painter, Craftsman

Unionville

Dublac, Robert Revak Painter

Voluntown

Caddell, Foster Painter, Instructor

Wallingford

Neff, John A Painter, Designer

Warren

Abrams, Herbert E Painter, Lecturer

Washington

Margulies, Herman Painter
Poskas, Peter Edward Painter
Renouf, Edda Painter

Washington Depot

Kelly, Moira Curator, Writer
Miller, Ruth Ann Painter
Renouf, Edward Painter, Sculptor

Waterbury

Smith, Ann Y Museum Director, Curator

Watertown

Cajori, Charles F Painter
Grossman, Barbara Painter, Educator

Westbrook

Schaffer, Claudia Post Painter, Instructor

West Cornwall

Gellatly, Michael Painter
Scoville, Jonathan Armstrong Painter, Printmaker

West Hartford

Mitchell, Clifford Architect, Painter
Schar, Stuart Administrator, Educator
Sorokin, Janet Graphic Artist, Painter
Uccello, Vincenza Agatha Painter, Director

Weston

Bleifeld, Stanley Sculptor, Medalist
Cadmus, Paul Painter, Printmaker
Mellor, Mark Adams Painter, Illustrator
Oliver, Sandra (Sandi) Art Dealer, Painter
Rand, Paul Designer
Swigart, Lynn S Photographer
Williams, Paul Alan Painter, Illustrator
Wilson, Melissa Anne Sculptor

Westport

Chernow, Burt Writer, Museum Director
Cifolelli, Alberta (Alberta Carmella Lamb) Painter, Educator
Dohanos, Stevan Illustrator, Painter
Edelman, Rita Painter
Fisher, Leonard Everett Painter, Illustrator
Jordan, George Edwin Critic, Historian
Kovatch, Jak Printmaker, Educator
Madan-Shotkin, Rhoda Painter
Minkowitz, Norma Sculptor
Reed, Walt Arnold Historian, Dealer
Reilly, Nancy Painter
Rothenberg, Barbara Painter, Collage Artist
Sallick, Lucy Ellen Painter, Instructor
Von Schmidt, Eric Painter, Historian
Wilson, Cynthia Lindsay Painter
Woodham, Jean Sculptor

West Redding

Grashow, James Bruce Sculptor, Printmaker
Natkin, Robert Painter

West Willington

Zelanski, Paul John Painter

Willimantic

Mazzocca, Gus (Augustus Nicholas) Printmaker, Educator

Wilton

Darrow, Whitney, Jr Cartoonist
Stirnweis, Shannon Painter, Illustrator
Stuart, Kenneth James Director, Illustrator
Thompson, Malcolm Barton Painter

Winchester Center

Jenney, Neil Painter

Winsted

Sloan, Ronald J Painter

Woodbridge

Ingalls, Eve Instructor, Painter

DELAWARE

Bear

Lane, Rosemary Louise Printmaker, Sculptor

Greenville

Bryce, Mark Adams Painter, Printmaker
Martone, William Robert Painter, Instructor
Raley, Robert L Collectors

Hockessin

Tarbell, Roberta Kupfrian Historian, Curator

Laurel

Blaine, Matthew Frederick Sculptor, Educator

Newark

Breslin, Wynn Painter, Sculptor
Brown, Hilton Painter, Educator
Craven, Wayne Historian, Writer
Da Cunha, Julio Educator, Painter
Homer, William Innes Historian, Educator
Moss, Joe (Francis) Sculptor, Painter
Nees, Lawrence Educator, Historian
Rowe, Charles Alfred Painter, Designer
Spinski, Victor Sculptor, Educator
Stillman, Damie Historian, Educator
Stoner, Joyce Hill Conservator, Educator
Tolles, Bryant Franklin, Jr Educator, Consultant
Weiss, John Joseph Photographer, Editor

Rockland

Harvey, (William) André Sculptor

Smyrna

Bailey, Richard H Sculptor

Wilmington

Allmond, Charles (M) Sculptor
Clark, Nancy Kissel Sculptor, Consultant
Colombo, Charles Painter
Elzea, Rowland Procter Museum Director, Curator
Hatch, W A S Painter, Educator
Hayes, Tua Painter
Hecht, Irene Painter
Hummel, Charles Frederick Administrator
Karwoski, Richard Charles Painter, Educator
McFarren, Grace Painter
Matassa, John P Painter, Instructor
Mortellito, Domenico Painter, Sculptor
Parks, Charles Cropper Sculptor
Sommer, Frank H, III Historian, Archeologist
Sundin, Adelaide Toombs Ceramist, Sculptor

Winterthur

Lanmon, Dwight P Museum Director, Curator

DISTRICT OF COLUMBIA

Washington

Abad, Pacita Painter
Adams, Robert McCormick Administrator, Writer
Akamu, Nina Sculptor
Allen, Jane Addams Editor, Critic
Bader, Franz Photographer
Bass, Judy Painter
Biddle, Livingston Ludlow, Jr Art Administrator
Bingham, Lois A Art Administrator, Lecturer
Blake, Peter Jost Architect, Critic
Bolton-Smith, Robin Lee Curator, Historian
Bookatz, Samuel Painter, Sculptor
Brennan, Nizette Sculptor, Designer
Broude, Norma Freedman Historian, Educator
Brown, John Carter Museum Director
Brown, Pamela Wedd Painter, Printmaker
Cable, Maxine Roth Sculptor
Cafritz, Robert Conrad Historian, Critic
Carr, Carolyn K Curator, Historian
Carter, Yvonne Pickering Painter, Educator
Chase, W(illiam) Thomas Conservator
Christenberry, William Painter, Educator
Cikovsky, Nicolai, Jr Historian, Educator
Clark, Michael Vinson Painter, Printmaker
Cleary, Manon Catherine Painter, Educator
Cogswell, Margaret Price Instructor
Coleman, Floyd Willis Educator, Painter
Comès, Marcella (Mrs Randolph Winslow) Painter, Writer
Cooper, Theodore A Dealer
Costigan, Constance Frances Painter, Educator
Costley-Jacobs, Averille Esther Dealer, Gallery Director
Curry, David Park Curator, Writer

DISTRICT OF COLUMBIA (cont)

Danziger, Joan Sculptor
Davenport, Rebecca Read Painter, Lecturer
De Andino, Jean-Pierre M Dealer, Collector
De Looper, Willem Printmaker, Curator
Demetrion, James Thomas Museum Director
Desmidt, Thomas H Painter, Educator
Dobard, Raymond Gerard Historian, Painter
Donaldson, Jeff R Painter, Administrator
Doumato, Lamia Librarian, Historian
Downs, Linda Anne Curator, Educator
Drysdale, Nancy McIntosh Patron, Dealer
Eisenstein, (Mr & Mrs) Julian Collectors
Faubion, S Michael Administrator
Fern, Alan Maxwell Museum Director
Ferriter, Clare Painter, Collage Artist
Fine, Ruth E Curator, Printmaker
Fink, Lois Marie Historian, Curator
Firestone, Susan Paul Assemblage Artist, Painter
Fisher, Sarah Lisbeth Conservator
Fleming, Lee Writer, Curator
Fletcher, Valerie J Curator, Historian
Flint, Janet Altic Curator, Historian
Foresta, Merry Curator
Forrester, Patricia Tobacco Painter, Printmaker
Frederick, Helen Printmaker
Freedberg, Sydney Joseph Historian, Educator
Freeman, Roland L Photographer
Freudenheim, Tom Lippmann Museum Administrator
Garrard, Mary DuBose Historian, Educator
Gates, Harry Irving Sculptor, Educator
Gilliam, Sam Painter
Goley, Mary Anne Historian, Director
Gossage, John Ralph Photographer
Gowans, Alan Historian, Lecturer
Gramberg, Liliana Painter, Printmaker
Green, Tom Instructor, Sculptor
Grier, Margot Edmands Librarian, Administrator
Grossman, Sheldon Museum Curator, Historian
Gumpert, Gunther Painter
Gurney, Susan Rothwell Librarian
Haden, Eunice (Barnard) Painter, Illustrator
Halegua, Alfredo Sculptor
Hall, Robert L Museologist, Painter
Hand, John Oliver Historian, Curator
Hart, Robert Gordon Administrator
Hartigan, Lynda Roscoe Curator, Historian
Haslem, Jane N Dealer
Hay, George Austin Painter, Filmmaker
Haynie, Ron Painter, Euducator
Hoffman, Helen Bacon Painter
Hoi, Samuel Chuen-Tsung Educator, Administrator
Holladay, Wilhelmina Cole Collector, Patron
Howland, Richard Hubbard Architectural Historian
Johnson, J Seward, Jr Sculptor, Administrator
Johnson-Ross, Robyn Painter
Jones, Lois Mailou (Mrs V Pierre-Noel) Painter, Designer
Kaskey, Raymond John Sculptor, Architect
Kelly, Franklin Wood Curator, Historian
Kinney, Gilbert Hart Collector, Administrator
Klavans, Minnie Painter, Sculptor
Kling, Jean Louise Curator, Administrator
Kloss, WIlliam Historian, Writer
Kravitz, Walter Sculptor, Painter
Krebs, Rockne Sculptor
Lader, Melvin Paul Historian, Educator
Laiou, Angeliki E Educator
Lake, Jerry Lee Photographer, Educator
Larson, Blaine (Gledhill) Painter, Instructor
Laub-Novak, Karen Sculptor, Painter
Lawrence, Sidney S Painter, Writer
Lawson, Edward Pitt Administrator
Lawton, Thomas Historian, Editor
Leithauser, Mark Alan Painter, Printmaker
Leven, Ann R Administrator
Lewis, Douglas Historian, Curator
Lewton, Val Edwin Designer, Painter
Livingston, Jane S Critic, Curator
Lowe, Harry Administrator, Designer
Luchs, Alison Curator, Historian
MacDonald, William L Architectural Historian
Mandle, Earl Roger Museum Director
Markowski, Eugene David Painter, Sculptor
Marshall, Mara Painter
Mecklenburg, Virginia McCord Curator, Lecturer
Mellon, Paul Collector, Administrator
Merrill, Ross M Conservator, Painter
Miles, Ellen Gross Historian, Curator
Millie, Elena Gonzalez Curator
Minear, Beth Craftsman, Weaver
Morrison, Keith Anthony Painter, Educator
Neslage, Oliver John, Jr Art Dealer
Ostrow, Stephen Edward Administrator, Librarian
Oxman, Mark Sculptor, Educator
Page, Jean Jepson Collector, Historian
Paige, Wayne Leo Painter, Draftsman
Perlin, Ruth Rudolph Educator, Historian
Perlmutter, Jack Painter, Printmaker
Phillips, Laughlin Museum Director
Phillips, Matt Painter, Educator
Pierre-Noel, Vergniaud Designer, Graphic Artist
Polan, Annette Painter, Draftsman
Power, Mark Photographer, Educator
Pressly, Nancy Lee Curator, Administrator
Pressly, William Laurens Historian, Educator
Radice, Anne-Imelda Marino Historian, Curator
Reger, Lawrence L Administrator
Reilly, Bernard Francis Historian, Curator
Richard, Paul Critic
Robbins, Warren M Museum Director
Roberts, Steven K Sculptor, Printmaker
Robertson, Charles J Administrator
Robinson, Lilien Filipovitch Historian, Educator
Robison, Andrew Museum Curator, Writer
Rode, Meredith Eagon Printmaker, Educator
Rose, Robin Carlise Painter, Sculptor
Rosenzweig, Phyllis D Curator
Russell, Helen Diane Historian
Rust, David E Curator, Collector
Scheer, Lisa N Sculptor
Schmutzhart, Berthold Josef Sculptor, Educator
Schmutzhart, Slaithong Chengtrakul Instructor, Sculptor
Schottland, M Illustrator, Painter
Schwartz, Bella Painter, Collage Artist
Scott, David Winfield Administrator
Sellin, David Lecturer, Curator
Sherman, Claire Richter Historian, Educator
Shute, Roberta E Sculptor, Printmaker
Sickman, Jessalee Bane Painter, Instructor
Sieber, Roy Educator, Historian
Simpson, Marianna Shreve Historian, Educator
Sky, Carol Veth Painter, Educator
Smith, Arthur Hall Painter, Educator
Smith, Frank Anthony Painter
Spandorf, Lily Gabriella Painter, Muralist
Stamm, Geoffrey Eaton Administrator, Historian
Stapp, William F Curator
Stewart, Robert Gordon Curator, Historian
Stovall, Luther McKinley (Lou) Printmaker
Swick, Linda Ann Sculptor
Szabo, Stephen Lee Photographer
Taylor, Bill (William Bradley) Sculptor, Instructor
Taylor, Kendall Frances Administrator, Historian
Teller, Douglas H Painter, Educator
Thorson, Alice R Editor, Critic
Triano, Anthony Thomas Painter, Educator
Truettner, William H Curator
Truitt, Anne (Dean) Sculptor
Turano, Don Sculptor, Medalist
Van Winkle, Lester G Sculptor, Educator
Von Barghan, Barbara Educator, Writer
Wall, F L (Frederick Leroy), III Sculptor, Designer
Watson, Ross Curator
Wattenmaker, Richard J Museum Director, Historian
Wax, John M Painter, Collage Artist
Weil, Stephen E Museum Director, Lecturer
Wenawine, Bruce Harley Administrator, Educator
Wheelock, Arthur Kingsland, Jr Curator, Educator
White, Franklin Painter, Draftsman
Williams, Sylvia H Museum Director
Withers, Josephine Historian, Writer
Wolanin, Barbara A Historian, Curator
Woodward, William Painter, Educator
Wright, Frank Painter, Educator
Young, Charles Alexander Educator, Painter
Young, Kenneth Victor Painter, Designer
Ziemann, Richard Claude Printmaker, Educator
Zilczer, Judith Katy Historian, Curator

FLORIDA

Aripeka

McCallum, Steven Douglas Painter, Printmaker

Atlantic Beach

McIvor, John Wilfred Printmaker, Painter

Bal Harbour

Bernay, Betti Painter

Bay Harbor Islands

Elias, Sheila Painter

Biscayne Park

Lurie, Sheldon M Draftsman, Gallery Director

Boca Raton

Amen, Irving Painter, Printmaker
Cengle, Painter
Chiara, Alan Robert Painter
Dorst, Claire V Painter, Printmaker
Dorst, Mary Crowe Graphic Artist, Craftsman

FLORIDA (cont)

Feinstein, Roni Curator, Historian
Karniol, Hilda Painter
Kaufman, Stuart Martin Painter, Illustrator
Keeler, David Boughton Painter
Lipschultz, Maurice A Collector
Mills, Agnes Sculptor, Printmaker
Rebhun, Pearl G Painter, Printmaker
Saba, Richard Painter
Sarnoff, Arthur Saron Painter, Illustrator
Selby, Roger Lowell Administrator, Museum Director
Smith, Vernell Edward Cartoonist, Illustrator
Sylvan, Rita M Photographer, Painter

Bonita Springs

Pierce, Diane (Diane Pierce-Huxtable) Illustrator, Painter
Wilson, Sybil Painter, Graphic Artist

Boynton Beach

Gepponi, Angelo Painter, Educator
Kessler, Shirley Painter
Liebowitz, Janet Painter, Sculptor
Zelin, Elaine Sculptor

Bradenton

Cogswell, Dorothy McIntosh Educator, Painter
Hodgell, Robert Overman Printmaker, Sculptor

Brooksville

Watkins, Lewis Sculptor, Painter

Casselberry

Renee, Lisabeth Sculptor, Assemblage Artist

Clearwater

Bansemer, Roger L Painter, Writer
Kennedy, J William Painter

Cocoa Beach

Blum, June Painter, Sculptor

Coconut Grove

Massin, Eugene Max Painter, Sculptor

Coral Gables

Ataie, Mary Lee Sculptor
Bannard, Walter Darby Painter, Art Writer
Cher, Beatrice (Beatrice Michelle Cher-Killigan) Painter, Sculptor
Chow Chian-Chiu, Painter, Historian
Chow Leung Chen-Ying, Painter, Calligrapher
Fort-Brescia, Bernardo M Architect
Friedman, Marvin Ross Dealer
Goodman, Janis G Draftsman, Painter
McCullough, David William Painter, Sculptor
Romney, Hervin A R Architect
Spear, Laurinda Hope Architect
Thomas, Helen (Doane) Writer, Painter
Waltner, Beverly Ruland Painter

Crawfordville

Siamis, Janet Neal Painter

Davie

Hanson, Duane Sculptor, Educator

Daytona Beach

Biferie, Dan (Daniel Anthony), Jr Photographer, Educator
Hoffman, Martin Painter, Illustrator
Libby, Gary Russell Museum Director, Educator

Daytona Beach Shores

Beker, Gisela Painter

Deerfield Beach

Bettmann, Otto Ludwig Art Historian
Gunshor, Ruth Painter
Van Aalten, Jacques Painter, Sculptor

De Land

Messersmith, Fred Lawrence Painter, Educator
Messersmith, Harry Lee Sculptor, Museum Director

Delray Beach

Varga, Ferenc Sculptor

Destin

Williams, Richard Eldon Painter, Gallery Director

Dunedin

Minnick, Esther Tress Painter

Eau Gallie

Price, Morgan Samuel (Margaret Morgan Price) Painter, Instructor

Englewood

Carmichael, Donald Ray Painter
Tracy, Lois Bartlett Painter, Writer

Enterprise

Abernethy-Baldwin, Judith Ann Painter

Ft Lauderdale

Ake, John Sculptor
Batt, Miles Girard Painter, Instructor
Coleman, Gayle Lecturer, Conservator
Lewis, Elizabeth Matthew Stained Glass Artist, Writer
Moffett, Kenworth William Critic, Curator

Ft Myers

Biolchini, Gregory Phillip Painter
Schwartz, Carl E Painter, Printmaker

Gainesville

Bishop, Budd Harris Museum Director
Catterall, John Edward Painter, Educator
Collins, Harvey Arnold Muralist, Educator
Craven, Roy Curtis, Jr Educator, Museologist
Foster, Maelee Thomson Educator, Printmaker
Grissom, Eugene Edward Educator, Historian
Heipp, Richard Christian Painter, Instructor
Holbrook, Vivian Nicholas Painter, Administrator
Isaacson, Marcia Jean Artist, Educator
Kerslake, Kenneth Alvin Printmaker, Educator
Losavio, Samuel Sculptor, Painter
O'Connor, John Arthur Painter, Administrator
Sabatella, Joseph John Administrator, Painter
Scott, John Fredrik Historian, Educator
Skelley, Robert Charles Educator, Printmaker
Smith, Nan S(helley) Sculptor, Ceramist
Teague, Edward H Librarian, Educator
Uelsmann, Jerry Photographer
Valdés, Karen W Director, Educator
Ward, John Lawrence Historian, Painter
Westin, Robert H Historian
Williams, Hiram Draper Painter
Wilson, Wallace Photographer, Educator

Grant

Gaines, William Robert Historian, Photographer

Gulfport

Klarin, Winifred Erlick Painter, Jeweler
Wiesen, Trude Painter

Hallandale

Gallo, Enzo D Sculptor
Slobodkina, Esphyr (Mrs Urquhart) Painter, Writer

Highland Beach

Ortlip, Mary Krueger Painter

Hobe Sound

Payson, John Whitney Art Dealer, Collector

Hollywood

Kyra Environmental Artist, Painter
Sadowski, Carol (Louise) Johnson Painter
Schreck, Michael H Painter, Sculptor
Stoll, Toni Painter

Holmes Beach

Howard, Linda Sculptor

Homosassa

Lichtenberg, Manes Painter

Hudson

Angelini, John Michael Painter, Writer

Indian Harbor Beach

Traylor, Angelika Stained Glass Artist

Jacksonville

Banas, Anne Painter, Educator
Bear, Marcelle L Printmaker, Painter
Brownett, Thelma Denyer Painter, Conservator
Dempsey, Bruce Harvey Museum Director
Dodge, Joseph Jeffers Painter, Lecturer
Eden, F(lorence) Brown Collage Artist, Painter
Gefter, Judith Michelman Photographer
Gelinas, Robert William Painter, Educator
Koger, Ira McKissick Collector, Patron
Schlageter, Robert William Administrator
Weeks, Edward F (Ted) Historian, Consultant

Jupiter

Kravjansky, Mikulas Painter, Printmaker
Mann, Maybelle Historian, Writer

Key West

Burnside, Madeleine Hilding Critic, Museum Director
Marks, Roberta Barbara Sculptor, Painter

Lake Park

Heaton, Janet N Painter, Gallery Director

Lake Wales

Lipson, Goldie Sculptor, Painter

Lake Worth

Eagen, Christopher T Director

Largo

Howarth, Shirley Reiff Publisher, Historian
Kass, Jacob James Painter
Tucker, Peri Writer, Illustrator
Woodlock, Ethelyn Hurd Painter

Lauderdale Lakes

Berkowitz, Henry Painter, Designer

Lauderhill

Gould, Stephen Sculptor, Collector

Longboat Key

Kurka, Donald Frank Painter, Administrator
Rowan, Frances Physioc Painter, Woodcut
Sherwood, Leona Painter, Instructor

Longwood

Freeman, Gertrude Collector
Hyde, Alice Bach Graphic Artist, Painter
Miller, Leon Gordon Printmaker

Lutz

Freundlich, August L Administrator, Collector

Mangonia Park

Hibel, Edna Painter, Lithographer

Mary Esther

Few, James Cecil, PSA Painter
Simpson, Marilyn Jean Painter, Instructor

Melbourne

Conneen, Mari M Painter, Printmaker

Melbourne Beach

Stark, Bruce Gunsten Cartoonist, Illustrator

Merritt Island

Ferrell, Catherine (Klemann) Sculptor

Miami

Alexenberg, Mel Painter, Educator
Brito, Maria Sculptor, Painter
Burke, Bill Ceramist
Cano, Margarita Librarian, Painter
Cano, Pablo D Sculptor, Educator
Carulla, Ramon Painter, Printmaker
Casey, Tim (Timothy William) Painter
Castro, Giovanni Painter
Cianfoni, Emilio Conservator, Painter
Couper, James M Painter, Educator
Dalglish, Meredith Rennels Sculptor, Educator
Dellis, Arlene B Museologist, Craftsman
Duncan, Richard (Hurley) Draftsman, Printmaker
Federighi, Christine M Sculptor, Educator
Fondaw, Ron Sculptor
Fundora, Thomas Painter
Gillman, Barbara Seitlin Dealer
Gomez, Mirta & Eduardo Delvalie Photographer
Harrison, Joseph Robert, Jr Collector, Patron
Huff, Robert Sculptor, Painter
Hung Wah Michael Poon, Painter, Chop-Engraver
James, Bill (William Frederick) Illustrator, Fine Artist
Levenson, Rustin S Conservator
Martinez-Cañas, Maria Photographer
Morin, James Corcoran Cartoonist, Editor
Perlman, Joel Leonard Sculptor, Instructor
Poon, Yi-Chong Sarina Chow Painter, Calligrapher
Presser, Elena Assemblage Artist
Riveron, Enrique Painter, Sculptor
Salinas, Baruj Painter, Printmaker
Sindelir, Robert John Gallery Director, Administrator
Stein, Ludwig Painter, Educator
Storm, Larue Painter
Strickland, Thomas J Painter
Trasobares, Cesar Painter
Treister, Kenneth Painter, Sculptor
Vadia, Rafael Painter
Viret, Margaret Mary (Mrs Frank Ivo) Painter, Instructor
Winter, Gerald Glen Painter, Educator
Young, Barbara Neil Librarian, Curator

Miami Beach

Balas, Irene Painter
Brown, Carol K Sculptor, Draftsman
Camber, Diane Woolfe Museum Director, Curator
Findlay, James Allen Librarian
Kahn, A Michael Painter, Designer
Kitner, Harold Educator, Painter
Lehr, Mira T(ager) Painter
Liebman, Norman Painter
Loar, Peggy A Museum Director, Administrator
Schein, Eugenie Painter, Printmaker

Miami Lakes

Luria, Gloria Dealer, Consultant

Miami Shores

Winters, Sandy (Sandra L) Painter

Naples

Austin, Darrel Painter
Geiger, Edith Rogers Painter
Gordon, Martin Dealer, Collector
Hurst, Ralph N Sculptor, Educator
Meek, J William, III Dealer, Consultant
Nash, Alice Louise Consultant
Olson, Rick Painter
Orr, Elliot Painter
Peterson, David Winfield Painter
Schmalz, Carl (Nelson), Jr Painter, Educator
Varga, Margit Painter, Writer
Wilson, David Philip Painter

New Smyrna Beach

Leeper, Doris Marie Sculptor, Painter
Madigan, Richard Allen Museum Director

Niceville

Young, Robert G Painter, Printmaker

North Miami

Pravda, Muriel Instructor, Sculptor

North Port

Stark, George King Educator, Sculptor

Ocala

Booth, George Warren Painter, Designer

Orange Park

Hunt, (Julian) Courtenay Painter
Naylor, John Geoffrey Sculptor, Educator

Orlando

Ivey, James Burnett Cartoonist, Collector
Lotz, Steven Darryl Painter, Educator
MacNelly, Jeffrey Kenneth Cartoonist, Sculptor
Messick, Dale Cartoonist
Unger, Mary Ann Sculptor
Wahlman, Maude Southwell Administrator, Historian

Ormond Beach

Perrotti, Barbara Painter, Instructor

Osprey

Robinson, Sally W Painter, Printmaker

Palm Beach

Artinian, Artine Collector, Patron
Briggs, Lamar A Painter
Cohlon, William Painter
Cronin, Robert (Lawrence) Sculptor
Gardiner, Henry Gilbert Art Dealer, Museum Director
Giobbi, Edward Gioachino Painter, Sculptor
Helander, Bruce Paul Painter, Dealer
Helsmoortel, Robert Sculptor, Painter
Jeffe, Huldah C Painter
Kaplan, Muriel Sculptor, Collector
Koni, Nicolaus Sculptor, Lecturer
Lesseps, Tauni de Painter, Sculptor
Luntz, Irving Dealer
Marcus, Robert P (Mrs) Collector, Patorn
Quasius, Sharron G Sculptor
Raimondi, John Sculptor
Rautbord, Dorothy H Collector, Patron
Sanchez, Thorvald Painter
Wenzel, Joan Ellen Assemblage Artist, Sculptor

Palm Beach Gardens

Groombridge, Walter Stanley Painter, Educator
Rosen, Esther Yovits Painter, Muralist
Tykie (Sylvia Squires Ganz) Painter

Palm Coast

Hart, Betty Miller Painter, Graphic Artist

Panama City Beach

Hopkins, B(ernice Elizabeth) Painter

Pembroke Pines

Silverman, Sherley C Painter, Sculptor

Pensacola

Stewart, Duncan E Collage Artist

Plantation

Garrison, Eve Painter
Moyer, Marina Pavlova Administrator, Sculpture

Pompano Beach

Kleinman, Sue Painter, Lecturer
Lis, Janet Painter
Perkins, Lois Bouthillier Painter, Educator
Sitton, John M Painter, Lecturer

Ponce Inlet

McKay, John Sangster Educator, Administrator Design, Collage

Ponte Vedra Beach

Draper, Josiah Everett Painter, Writer

Port Charlotte

Leslie, John Painter, Photographer

Port St Lucie

Kamm, Dorothy Lila Painter, Writer
Roberts, Bruce Elliott Painter

Quincy

Lindquist, Mark Sculptor

Rockledge

Samuelson, Fred Binder Painter, Educator

Safety Harbor

Banks, Allan R Painter

St Augustine

Torcoletti, Enzo Sculptor

St Petersburg

Bryant, Laura Militzer Weaver, Painter
Crane, Jim (James G) Painter, Cartoonist
Kropf, Joan R Curator, Lecturer
Lesko, Diane Curator, Historian
McVeigh, Miriam Lenig Conceptual Artist, Painter
Marshall-Nadel, Nathalie Painter, Educator
Rigg, Margaret Ruth Assemblage Artist, Calligrapher

Sarasota

Ahlander, Leslie Judd Critic, Consultant
Brams, Joan Painter, Sculptor
Campbell, Dorothy Bostwick Painter, Sculptor
Capes, Richard Edward Graphic Artist, Instructor
Chase, Jeanne Norman Painter
Cheek, Ronald Edward Painter, Instructor
Christ-Janer, Arland F Painter, Printmaker
Clement, Shirley Painter
Corbino, Marcia Norcross Critic, Writer
DeCaprio, Alice Painter, Photographer
Deo, Marjoree Nee Painter
Dowd, Jack Sculptor
Eliscu, Frank Sculptor
Elliott, Dorothy Baden Conservator
Erickson, Joy M Painter, Graphic Artist
Fromboluti, Sideo Painter
Gregory, Bruce Painter, Instructor
Harmon, Foster Dealer, Director
Held, Philip Painter, Photographer
Hopper, Frank J Painter, Muralist
Hoppes, Lowell E Cartoonist
Jeswald, Joseph Painter
Kowal, Dennis J Writer
Larsen, Robert Wesley Painter
Marca-Relli, Conrad Painter, Collage Artist
Masterfield, Maxine Painter
Meserole, Vera Stromsted Painter, Photographer
Muller, Max Paul Painter, Art Dealer
Myford, James C Sculptor, Educator
Oehlschlaeger, Frank J Dealer
Osborne, Robert Lee Painter, Educator
Parton, Niké Environmental Artist, Painter
Patmagrian, Ethelia M Sculptor, Painter
Perkins, Robert Eugene Administrator
Sawyer, Helen Painter, Writer
Silver, Rawley A Educator, Painter
Solomon, Syd Painter
Straight, Elsie H Librarian, Sculptor
Taubes, Timothy Evan Critic, Curator
Troncale, Frank Thomas Dealer, Collector
Utz, Thornton Painter, Sculptor
Weinberg, Bella Rebecca Painter, Writer
White, Ruth Art Dealer, Collage Artist

Sebastian

Salerno, Charles Sculptor, Educator

Seminole

Blake, Jane Painter, Sculptor

Spring Hill

Link, Howard Anthony Curator
Whyte, Raymond A Painter

Stuart

Hutchinson, Janet L Museum Director, Collector
Mosley, Zack T Illustrator, Cartoonist

Sun City Center

Andrews, Michael Frank Educator, Sculptor

Surfside

Albert, Calvin Sculptor, Educator

Tallahassee

Bell, Trevor Painter, Educator
Blakely, George C Photography, Sculptor
Bucher, Francois Historian, Educator
Burggraf, Ray Lowell Painter, Educator
Edwards-Tucker, Yvonne (Leatrice Yvonne Tucker) Ceramist, Educator
Fichter, Robert W Educator
Harper, William Jeweler, Painter
Holschuh, (George) Fred Sculptor, Architect
Johnson, Ivan Earl Educator, Craftsman
Kuhn, Marylou Educator, Painter
Palladino-Craig, Allys Director, Curator
Walmsley, William Aubrey Printmaker, Collector
Weale, Mary Jo Painter, Educator
Williams, Chester Lee Sculptor

Tamarac

Kaplan, Leo Assemblage Artist, Collage Artist
Smith, Rowena Marcus Painter, Collage Artist
Somers, H(arry W) Painter, Printmaker

Tampa

Beck, Theresa Painter
Cardoso, Anthony Painter, Sculptor
Covington, Harrison Wall Painter, Educator
Gurbacs, John Joseph Painter, Restorer
Kronsnoble, Jeffrey Michael Painter, Educator
Lama, Alberto de Painter, Printmaker
Larsen, Mernet Ruth Painter, Educator
Maass, Richard Andrew Museum Director
Nazarenko, Bonnie Coe Painter
Pappas, George Painter
Pittman, Irene K Sculptor, Designer
Rosenzweig, Daphne Lange Historian, Museum Consultant
Santiago, Richard E Sculptor, Educator
Schofield, Roberta Painter
Wujcik, Theo Printmaker, Painter

Tarpon Springs

Curtis, Terry Wayne Painter, Sculptor
Leepa, Allen Painter, Educator

Temple Terrace

Kashdin, Gladys Shafran Painter, Educator

Tequesta

Snow, Mary R Painter

Tierra Verde

Tuegel, Michele B Craftsman, Administrator

Treasure Island

Manhold, John Henry Sculptor

Venice

Bateman, Robert McLellan Painter
McKinney, Tatiana Ladygina Painter, Instructor
Seerey-Lester, John Vernon Painter

Vernon

Meyer, Frank Hildbridge Painter, Printmaker

Vero Beach

Brightwell, Walter Painter
Dorn, Ruth (Dornbush) Painter
Frets, Barbara J Painter
Johnson, Rodell C Painter, Animator
Koller-Davies, Eva Assemblage Artist, Painter
Osze, Andrew E Sculptor

West Palm Beach

Cowan, Ralph Wolfe Painter
Grove, Edward Ryneal Medalist, Painter
Grove, Jean Donner Sculptor
Houser, Jim Painter, Educator
Knapp, Sadie Magnet Painter, Sculptor
Manus, Jane Elizabeth Sculptor
Mueller, Trude Sculptor
Orr-Cahall, Anona Christina Curator, Historian

Winter Park

Booth, Dot Painter, Printmaker
Fager, Charles J Ceramist, Sculptor
Lemon, Robert S, Jr Educator, Historian
McKean, Hugh Ferguson Painter, Educator
Ruggiero, Laurence J Museum Director

GEORGIA

Athens

Arnholm, Ronald Fisher Designer, Educator
Belville, Scott Robert Painter, Educator
Clements, Robert Donald Educator, Sculptor
Dodd, Lamar Painter, Educator
Edmonston, Paul Educator, Editor
Feldman, Edmund Burke Educator, Critic
Firestone, Evan R Administrator, Historian
Goldsleger, Cheryl Painter, Draftsman
Hammond, Gale Thomas Printmaker, Educator
Herbert, James Arthur Painter, Filmmaker
Jones, Judy Voss Printmaker, Painter
Kaufman, Glen Printmaker
Lukasiewicz, Ronald Joseph Printmaker, Sculptor
Marriott, William Allen Painter, Educator
Meyers, Ronald G Educator, Ceramist
Nasisse, Andy S Sculptor, Writer
Paul, William D, Jr Painter, Photographer
Sapp, William Rothwell Sculptor, Educator
Smith, Susan Carlton Painter, Sculptor
Thompson, William Joseph Educator, Sculptor
Walker, Mark Steven Historian

Atlanta

Alexander, Judith Art Dealer, Collector
Anderson, Maxwell L Museum Director, Educator
Beattie, George Painter, Art Administrator
Bleser, Katherine Alice Painter
Borochoff, (Ida) Sloan Painter, Printmaker
Bunnen, Lucinda Weil Photographer, Collector
Candioti, Beatriz A Painter
Carlstrom, Lucinda Painter, Printmaker
Chase, Allan (Seamans) Sculptor, Muralist
Colarusso, Corrine Camille Painter, Instructor

GEORGIA (cont)

Cone-Skelton, Annette Painter, Dealer
Crelly, William Richard Historian
Eden, Glenn Draftsman,Painter
Edvi Illes, Emma Dealer, Painter
Frabel, Hans Godo Sculptor
Francis, Tom Painter
Greco, Anthony Joseph Painter, Administrator
Guberman, Sidney Thomas Painter, Sculptor
Harkins, Dennis Richter Administrator, Photographer
Heath, David C Dealer
Hendricks, Edward Lee Sculptor, Kinetic Artist
Holland, Hillman Randall Art Dealer
Hough, Jennine Painter
Howett, John Historian, Critic
Johnston, William Medford Painter, Educator
Ketcham, Ray Winfred, Jr Dealer, Designer
Kline, Ronald Wayne Printmaker, Publisher
Krane, Susan Curator, Historian
Larson, Judy L Curator
Laxson, Ruth Conceptual Artist
LeBey, Barbara Painter, Printmaker
Lieberman, Laura Crowell Writer, Administrator
Lucero, Michael (Lewis) Sculptor
Lyman, Thomas William Educator, Historian
Malone, James Hiram Painter, Writer
Mari Painter, Printmaker
Mickish, Verle L Educator, Painter
Mills, Lev Timothy Printmaker, Designer
Mitchell, Katherine Painter
Paschall, Jo Anne Printmaker, Librarian
Patterson, Curtis Ray Sculptor, Instructor
Poling, Clark V Historian
Rice, Anthony Hopkins Sculptor, Painter
Riddle, John Thomas, Jr Sculptor, Painter
Sandman, Alan Sculptor, Publisher
Schinsky, William Charles Administrator, Consultant
Seaberg, Steve (Stevens) Assemblage Artist, Performance Artist
Shaw, Louise Director
Simon, Jewel Woodard Painter, Sculptor
Thackston, R King Painter, Muralist
Tiegreen, Alan F Painter, Illustrator
Tuttle, Lisa Conceptual Artist, Curator
Vigtel, Gudmund Director Emeritus
Walker, Larry Painter, Educator
Yarbrough, Leila Kepert Printmaker, Painter
Zuckerman, Ruth Victor Sculptor, Photographer

Augusta

Engler, Kathleen Girdler Sculptor
Rosen, James Mahlon Painter, Historian
Williams, Janice E Painter, Sculptor

Barnesville

Creecy, Herbert Lee Painter, Sculptor

Carrollton

Bobick, Bruce Painter, Educator

Columbus

Nordhausen, A Henry Painter
Timpano, Anne Museum Director, Historian

Decatur

Connatser, Larry Stuart Painter
Fraley, David K Painter, Educator
Lindsay, Arturo Sculptor, Painter
Loehle, Betty Barnes Painter
Loehle, Richard E Painter, Illustrator
Moore, Wayland D Graphic Artist, Printmaker

Dunwoody

McLean, James Albert Educator, Printmaker

East Point

Asihene, Emmanuel V Educator, Painter

Farmington

Noffke, Gary L Goldsmith

Gainesville

Westervelt, Robert F Historian, Ceramist

Good Hope

Ransom, Henry Cleveland, Jr Painter

Jekyll Island

Fiore, Rosario Russell Sculptor

Macon

Gray, Elise N Sculptor
Liles, Catharine (Burns) Painter, Patron
Werger, Art(hur Lawrence) Printmaker, Educator

Marietta

Basset, Gene Political Cartoonist
McAdoo, Carol Westbrook Ceramist, Painter
Mathis, Billie F Painter, Conceptual Artist
Rayburn (Dale), Boyd Painter, Printmaker
Sternberg, Paul Edward, Sr Curator, Consultant

Mt Berry

Mew, Tommy Painter, Conceptual Artist

Parrott

Tilley, Lewis Lee Painter, Video Artist

Ranger

Frazer, James (Nisbet), Jr Muralist, Photographer

Rome

Staven, Leland Carroll Printmaker, Painter

Roswell

Booth Cabot, M(ary Ann) Painter, Printmaker

St Simmons Island

Rensch, Roslyn Historian, Writer

Savannah

Ellis, Ray Painter, Lecturer
Gabeler-Brooks, Jo Painter
Kiah, Virginia Jackson Painter, Museum Director
Leigh, Jack David Photographer
Miller, Kathryn Painter, Printmaker

Statesboro

Hines, Jessica Photographer
Solomon, Bernard Alan Printmaker, Educator

Suwanee

Fenton, Julia Ann Conceptual Artist, Editor
Shead, S Ray Painter, Printmaker

Thomasville

Powers, Donald T Painter

Valdosta

Dodd, M(ary) Irene Painter, Educator
Lahr, J(ohn) Stephen Painter, Educator
Penny, Donald Charles Craftsman, Sculptor

Watkinsville

Chappelle, Jerry Leon Ceramist, Sculptor
Simon, Michael J Ceramist

HAWAII

Hilo

Miyamoto, Wayne Akira Painter, Printmaker

Honolulu

Atwell, Allen Educator, Painter
Browne, Robert M Collector, Patron
Bushnell, Kenneth Wayne Painter, Educator
De la Torre, David Joseph Museum Director
Ellis, George Richard Museum Director
Force, Roland Wynfield Museum Director
Gilbert, Helen Odell Painter, Printmaker
Haar, Francis Photographer, Filmmaker
Haar, Tom Photographer, Filmaker
Karawina, Erica (Mrs Sidney C Hsiao) Painter, Stained Glass Artist
Kenda, Juanita Echeverria Painter, Writer
Kimura, Sueko M Painter
Klobe, Tom Gallery Director, Educator
Marozzi, Eli Raphael Sculptor, Instructor
Morita, John Takami Printmaker, Photogrpher
Morse, Marcia Roberts Printmaker, Writer
Morse, Peter Historian, Collector
Preis, Alfred Architect, Administrator
Preiss, Alexandru Petre Designer
Roster, Fred Howard Sculptor, Educator
Ruby, Laura Sculptor, Printmaker
Taira, Masa Morioka Director, Curator
Tseng Yu-ho Painter, Historian
Twigg-Smith, Laila Collector
Twigg-Smith, Thurston Collector
Wisnosky, John G Painter, Educator

Kahului

Miller, Barbara Darlene Painter, Printmaker

Kailua

Kowalke, Ronald Leroy Painter, Printmaker

Kailua Kona

Thomas, John Painter, Printmaker

Kaneohe

Charlot, Martin Day Painter, Muralist
Hartwell, Patricia Lochridge Administrator
Hee, Hon-Chew Painter, Instructor
Lagoria, Georgianna Marie Museum Director, Curator

Keaau

Rhodes, James Melvin Glass Blower, Sculptor

Kula

Ritter, Julian Painter, Muralist

Lahaina

Sato, Tadashi Painter, Designer

Lihue

Lai, Waihang Painter, Instructor

Makawao

Ulrich, David Alan Photographer, Educator

Maui

Cost, James Peter Painter

Volcano

Morrison, Bee (Berenice G) Weaver
Morrison, Boone M Architect, Photographer

Waimea Kauai

Erickson, Marsha A Director, Administrator

Watalua

Goodwill, Margaret Painter, Designer

IDAHO

Boise

Auth, Robert R Printmaker, Painter
de la Vega, Enrique Miguel Sculptor, Designer
Huff, Howard Lee Educator, Photographer
Killmaster, John H Painter, Enamelist
Kober, Alfred John Educator, Sculptor
Ochi, F Denis Art Dealer, Consultant
Watia, Tarmo Painter, Printmaker
Wilde, Stephanie Conceptual Artist, Printmaker
Witte, Mary (Grace) Stieglitz Photographer, Educator

Hailey

Gardner, Sheila Painter

Ketchum

Wharton, David W Printmaker, Painter

McCall

Neil, J M Museum Director, Administrator

Moscow

Kirkwood, Mary Burnette Painter
Werner, Frank Robert Environmental Artist

Pocatello

Dial, Gail Metalsmith, Educator

Sagle

Magee, Alderson Graphic Artist, Painter

Sun Valley

Bennett, Don Bemco Painter, Printmaker
Janss, Glenn Cooper Collector

Victor

Hare, David Sculptor

ILLINOIS

Arlington Heights

Lynch, Tom (Thomas Michael) Painter, Instructor

Barrington

Bowen, Constance Lee Art Dealer, Consultant
Nadolski, Stephanie Lucille Painter, Printmaker

Belleville

Threlkeld, Dale Painter

Bloomington

Blinderman, Barry Robert Curator, Director
Butler, James D Printmaker, Painter
George, Raymond Ellis Printmaker, Educator
Gregor, Harold Laurence Painter, Educator
Holder, Kenneth Allen Painter, Educator
Nardi, Dann Sculptor
Simpson, Gail A Sculptor

Buncombe

Edgren, Gary Robert Painter, Craftsman

Calumet City

McGarry, Patricia Josephine Instructor, Sculptor

Carbondale

Deller, Harris Ceramist
Kington, L(ouis) Brent Sculptor, Educator
Mavigliano, George Jerome Administrator, Educator
Plochmann, Carolyn Gassan Painter, Graphic Artist
Shay, Ed Painter
Whitlock, John Joseph Museum Director, Educator

Cary

Duffy, Michael John Painter, Printmaker

Champaign

Bohen, Barbara E Historian, Museum Director
Breen, Harry Frederick, Jr Painter, Sculptor
Bushman, David Franklin Painter, Educator
Creese, Walter Littlefield Educator
Elkin, Beverly Dawn Dealer, Gallery Director
Fehl, Philipp P Painter, Historian
Gallo, Frank Sculptor, Educator
Gammon, Juanita-La Verne Painter, Educator
Grucza, Leo (Victor) Painter, Educator
Jackson, Billy Morrow Painter, Educator
Kotoske, Roger Allen Painter, Sculptor
Maguire, Henry Pownall Historian, Writer
Pera, Isabella Sculptor
Prokopoff, Stephen Museum Director, Historian
Rowan, Dennis Michael Printmaker, Educator
Smith, Ralph Alexander Writer, Educator
Sprague, Mark Anderson Painter, Educator
Stephens, Curtis Designer, Photographer
Van Laar, Timothy Painter, Printmaker
Wicks, Eugene Claude Painter, Educator

Charleston

Moldroski, Al R Painter, Educator
Shull, Carl Edwin Painter, Educator
Trank, Lynn Edgar Educator, Painter
Watts, R Michael Museum Director

Chicago

Albano, Patrick Louis Art Dealer
Albright, Malvin Marr Painter, Sculptor
Allen, (Harvey) Harold Photographer, Art Historian
Altman, Edith Sculptor, conceptual artist
Ames, Polly Scribner Painter
Amft, Robert Painter, Photographer
Arnold, Ralph Moffett Painter, Educator
Aubin, Barbara Painter, Assemblage Artist
Avison, David Photographer
Barazani, Morris Educator, Painter
Baruch, Anne Art Dealer, Lecturer
Baum, Don Sculptor, Curator
Bell, Mary Catherine Art Dealer
Bennett, Rainey Painter, Illustrator
Berns, Pamela Kari Painter, Administrator
Bernstein, Gerda Meyer Sculptor, Painter
Blackman, Thomas Patrick Director, Printmaker
Boardman, Deborah Painter
Booth, Laurence Ogden Sculptor, Architect
Bratton, Christopher Sculptor, Video Artist
Brown, Roger Painter
Brunkus, Richard Allen Printmaker, Curator
Bujnowski, Joel A Printmaker, Painter
Burroughs, Margaret T G Lecturer, Painter
Campoli, Cosmo Sculptor, Educator
Carswell, Rodney Painter, Educator
Cass, Bill Painter
Castillo, Mario Enrique Muralist, Educator
Chambers, Park A, Jr Sculptor, Educator
Chase, Robert M Art Dealer, Collector
Christiansen, Diane Painter
Clough, Eleanor Sculptor
Cohen, Alan Barry Photographer, Educator
Cohen, Charles E Historian, Educator
Colby, Jeff Sculptor
Cole, Grace V Painter, Draftsman
Conger, William Painter, Educator
Conn, Laurence Curator, Painter
Consey, Kevin E Museum Director, Administrator
Crane, Barbara Bachmann Photographer, Educator
Czarnopys, Thomas J Painter, Sculptor
Dan, Lars Painter
Danhausen, Eldon Sculptor, Educator
Davidson, Herbert Laurence Painter, Printmaker
Doll, Catherine Ann Painter, Designer
Donato, Debora E Administrator, Curator
Donley, Robert Morris Painter, Educator
Douglas, L J Painter, Writer
Duckworth, Ruth Sculptor, Ceramist
Duis, Rita Painter
Edelstein, Teri J Museum Director, Historian
Edwards, Stanley Dean Painter
Ehlers, Carol A Art Dealer
Ehresmann, Donald Louis Historian, Educator
Elliott, Scott Cameron Art Dealer, Curator
Facey, Martin Kerr Painter, Educator
Fairweather, Sally H Art Dealer
Ferrari, Virginio Luig Sculptor, Educator
Ganzarain, Mirentxu Sculptor, Painter
Gehr, Mary (Ray) Printmaker, Painter
Gilbert, Arnold Martin Collector, Photographer
Glass, Michael L Designer, Educator
Godfrey, Winnie (Winifred M) Painter, Instructor
Goehlich, John Ronald Educator, Administrator

ILLINOIS (cont)

Goldman, Rachel Bok Collector, Patron
Goldstein, Fern Painter, Designer
Goldstein, Jack Filmmaker, Conceptual Artist
Goler, Robert Curator, Historian
Gonzalez, Jose Gamaliel Administrator, Designer
Gray, Richard Dealer
Greene-Mercier, Marie Zoe Sculptor, Draftsman
Gunderman, Karen M Ceramist
Guthman, Leo S Collector
Halkin, Theodore Sculptor, Painter
Hanson, Philip Holton Painter, Lecturer
Hardin, Shirley G (Mrs Louis S) Art Dealer, Consultant
Haydon, Harold (Emerson) Painter, Educator
Heard, Lillian Painter
Heller, Reinhold August Historian
Herzberg, Thomas Printmaker, Illustrator
Heyman, Steven Painter
Himmelfarb, John David Painter, Graphic Artist
Hoffman, William A Ceramist, Educator
Hofmann, Kay Sculptor
Hormuth, Jo Sculptor, Printmaker
Horn, Milton Sculptor
Horn, Robert Nelson Painter, Designer
Houk, Edwynn L Art Dealer, Gallery Director
Hubbard, Robert Sculptor, Writer
Hugunin, James Richard Critic
Itatani, Michiko Painter
Jachna, Joseph David Photographer, Educator
Jacob, Mary Jane Curator, Historian
Jaidinger, Judith C Printmaker, Painter
Jeck, Douglas A Sculptor
Jessup, Robert Painter
Jones, Calvin B(ell) Painter, Muralist
Josephson, Kenneth Bradley Photographer, Assemblage Artist
Justis, Gary (Allen) Sculptor
Kapsalis, Thomas Harry Painter, Sculptor
Karpowicz, Terrence Edward Sculptor, Kinetic Artist
Katsoulidis, Panagiotis Graphic Artist
Kaufman, Lori Hokin Art Dealer, Collector
Kearney, John (W) Sculptor
Kearney, Lynn Haigh Administrator, Gallery Director
Kenney, Estelle Koval Art Therapist, Painter
Kirshner, Judith Russi Curator, Critic
Klein, Gwenda J Dealer, Writer
Klement, Vera Painter, Educator
Knopp, Hans-Georg Director
Kochman, Alexandra D Ceramist, Sculptor
Koga, Mary Photographer
Kolisnyk, Peter Painter, Sculptor
Kowalski, Dennis Allen Conceptual Artist
Krantz, Les (Leslie J) Editor, Publisher
Kroll, David Painter
Lamantia, Paul (Christopher) Zombek Painter
Lee, Li Lin Painter
Lennon, Timothy Painting Conservator
Lerner, Nathan Bernard Photographer, Painter
Lewis, Phillip Harold Curator
Livingstone, Joan Sculptor, Educator
Look, Dona Sculptor
Love, Richard Henry Dealer, Historian
Loving, Richard Maris Painter, Educator
Luecking, Stephen Joseph Sculptor, Educator
Lutes, Jim (James) Painter
Machin, Roger Sculptor
Maldre, Mati Photographer, Educator
Manilow, Lewis Collector, Patron
Marshall, Kerry James Designer
Mauldin, Bill Cartoonist, Writer
Mayeri, Beverly Sculptor
Meyers, Michael K Performance Artist, Painter
Michod, Susan A Painter
Middaugh, Robert Burton Painter
Miller, Michael Stephen Printmaker, Painter
Miller-Clark, Denise Museum Director, Curator
Mintz, Harry Painter
Moore, Arthur Cotton Architect, Painter
Morishita, Joyce Chizuko Historian, Painter
Moty, Eleanor H Jeweler
Murray, Eileen M Director, Curator
Nakoneczny, Michael Painter
Neff, John Hallmark Art Historian, Museum Director
Nordland, Gerald John Gallery Director, Critic
Olendorf, William Carr Painter, Printmaker
Oshita, Kazuma Sculptor
Parfenoff, Michael S Educator, Lithographer
Parmakelis, John Sculptor
Paschke, Edward F (Ed) Painter
Paul, Arthur Designer, Painter
Peart, Jerry Linn Sculptor
Phillips, Bertrand D Painter, Photographer
Phillips, Tony Painter, Draftsman
Piatek, Francis John Painter, Instructor
Postiglione, Corey M Painter, Educator
Prekop, Martin Dennis Painter, Sculptor
Puryear, Martin Sculptor
Rabb, Madeline M Administrator, Painter
Radjai, Abbas Painter, Conservator
Ramberg, Christina Painter
Regensteiner, Else (Friedsam) Designer, Weaver
Reynolds, Stephen Francis Painter, Sculptor
Rezac, Richard Conceptual Artist
Rojek, Christine Sculptor
Roller, Russell Kenneth Educator, Printmaker
Rosenthal, Earl Edgar Educator, Historian
Rosenthal, John W Photographer, Publisher
Rossen, Susan F Historian, Editor
Rossi, Barbara Painter, Printmaker
Salomon, Lawrence Sculptor, Educator
Schiller, Beatrice Painter, Graphic Artist
Schnackenberg, Roy Painter, Sculptor
Schwartz, Rosalyn Painter
Seed, Suzanne Liddell Photographer, Writer
Sekiguchi, Risa Painter
Sensemann, Susan Painter, Educator
Shaddle, Alice Sculptor, Collage Artist
Shaffer, Fern Painter
Shaw, Peggy Painter, Photographer
Shine, Vincent Sculptor
Silverman, Lanny Harris Director, Curator
Simionov, Alexandru Sculptor, Graphic Artist
Sorell, Victor Alexander Historian, Administrator
Sorogas, Sotiris Painter
Sorrentino, Richard Michael Mosaic Artist, Muralist
Sperantzas, Vassilis Printmaker
Staum, Sonja Librarian
Steinberg, Rubin Collage Artist
Stevens, Jane M Photographer, Administrator
Stoppert, Mary Kay Sculptor, Educator
Stratton, Margaret Mary Photographer, Educator
Struve, William Walter Dealer
Suzuki, Sakari Painter
Szesko, Lenore Rundle Painter, Printmaker
Terra, Daniel J Collector, Patron
Tigerman, Stanley Painter, Architect
Tracy, Michael Sculptor, Painter
Travis, David B Curator, Historian
Vezys, Gintautas Publisher, Collector
Volid, Ruth Dealer, Consultant
Warren, Lynne Curator, Writer
Wenger, Jane (B) Photographer, Educator
Whitehead, Frances Sculptor, Educator
Wilson, Charles H Sculptor
Wilson, Clarence S, Jr Consultant-Arts Lawyer, Patron
Wilson, Helena (Helena Chapellin Wilson) Photographer
Wilson, Karen Lee Curator, Director
Wirsum, Karl Painter, Sculptor
Wood, James Nowell Historian, Administrator
Workman, Robert P Painter, Illustrator
Wunderlich, Susan Clay Dealer
Yarber, Robert Painter
Yoder, Janica Photographer, Educator
Yoshida, Ray Kakuo Painter, Educator
Young, Andrew Painter
Zgoda, Larry Stained Glass Artist, Craftsman
Zimmerman, Arnold Sculptor
Zouni, Opy Sculptor

Decatur

Cunningham, Sue Painter, Illustrator
Klaven, Marvin L Painter, Educator
Schietinger, James Frederick Sculptor, Educator

Deerfield

Price, Rita F Painter, Printmaker
Talaba, L (Linda Talaba Cummens) Sculptor, Printmaker

De Kalb

Ball, Walter N Painter, Educator
Beard, Richard Elliott Painter, Educator
Clark, Lynda K Museum Director, Educator
Driesbach, David Fraiser Printmaker
Even, Robert Lawrence Educator
Mahmoud, Ben Painter, Educator
Maxfield, Roberta Masur Silversmith
Meyer, Jerry Don Historian, Educator
Peck, Lee Barnes Jeweler, Educator
Rollman, Charlotte Painter
White, Bruce Hilding Sculptor, Educator

Des Plaines

Schildknecht, Dorothy E Painter
Smuskiewicz, Ted Painter, Educator

Downers Grove

Kind, Joshua B Educator, Critic

Edwardsville

Anderson, Daniel J Ceramist, Educator
Hampton, Phillip Jewel Painter, Educator
Huntley, David C Painter, Administrator
Malone, Robert R Painter, Printmaker
Richardson, John Adkins Historian, Educator

Elmhurst

Jorgensen, Sandra Painter, Educator
Kauffman, (Camille) Andrene Painter, Muralist
King, Eleanor (Eleanor King Hookham) Painter, Printmaker
Weber, John Pitman Muralist, Printmaker

Elwood

Bartels, Phyllis Elaine Painter

Evanston

Archer, Cynthia Printmaker, Painter
Clayson, S Hollis Historian
Farber, Deborah Gallery Director, Art Dealer
Groot, Candice Beth Ceramist
Hausman, Jerome Joseph Educator
Hirshfield, Pearl Painter, Sculptor
Hurtig, Martin Russell Painter, Sculptor
Isaacson, Ronald G Gallery Director, Collector
McGrail, Jeane Kathryn Painter, Printmaker
Mickenberg, David Museum Director, Historian
Monroe, Betty Iverson Educator
Palmer, A Laure Sculptor, Writer
Petersen, Will Painter, Printmaker
Sheridan, Sonia Landy Media Artist
Silver, Larry Arnold Curator, Historian
Spiess-Ferris, Eleanor Painter
Trupp, Barbara Lee Painter, Printmaker
Wilson, Anne Gawthrop Painter, Educator
Yochim, Louise Dunn Painter, Writer
Zwick, Rosemary G Sculptor, Printmaker

Forest Park

Rogovin, Mark Muralist, Museum Director
Smith, Barbara Lee Collage Artist

Galena

Geisert, Arthur Frederick Printmaker, Illustrator
Sewell, Jack Vincent Museum Curator

Galesburg

Thenhaus, Paulette Ann Painter, Writer

Glencoe

Calapai, Letterio Printmaker, Painter

Glenview

Barnett, Earl D Painter, Portraitist
Bramson, Phyllis Halperin Painter, Educator
Halliday, Nancy R Illustrator, Instructor
Rognan, Lloyd Norman Illustrator, Painter
Wharton, Margaret Agnes Sculptor

Green Oaks

Croydon, Michael Benet Sculptor, Educator

Highland Park

Feldman, Arthur Mitchell Museum Director, Art and Antiques Dealer
Shapiro, Irving Painter, Instructor

Hinsdale

Day, Holliday T Critic, Curator
Moroni, Aldo Leonard, Jr Sculptor, Painter

Hudson

Mills, Frederick Van Fleet Educator, Painter

Jacksonville

Calhoun, Larry Darryl Ceramist, Painter

Joliet

Brulc, Lillian G Painter, Sculptor

Joseph

DeGenevieve, Barbara Photographer, Educator

Lake Forest

Pounian, Albert Kachouni Painter, Curator
Schulze, Franz Educator, Critic

Lincoln

Sorge, Walter Painter, Printmaker

Lombard

Ahlstrom, Ronald Gustin Collage Artist, Painter

Long Grove

Robertson, Joan E (Joan Elizabeth Mitchell) Curator, Graphic Artist

Macomb

Jones, Frederick Printmaker, Computer Graphics Artist
Parker, Samuel Murray Painter

Metamora

Hedden-Sellman, Zelda Painter, Instructor
Szilvasy, Linda Markuly Painter, Writer

Naperville

Parke, Walter Simpson Painter, Printmaker
Skurkis, Barry A Painter, Sculptor

Normal

Hartley, W Douglas Sculptor, Educator
Hobbs, Jack Arthur Educator, Writer
Myers, Joel Philip Artist in Glass, Educator
Rush, Jean C Administrator, Painter

Oak Brook

Stratakos, Steve John Craftsman, Tapestry Artist

Oak Park

Bradley, Laurel E Educator, Gallery Director
Nushawg, Michael Allan Printmaker, Educator
Sokol, David Martin Historian, Muscologist

Palatine

Fortunato, Nancy Painter, Illustrator

Park Forest

Payne, John D Sculptor, Educator

Park Ridge

Fedelle, Estelle Painter, Lecturer
Fornelli, Joseph Painter, Sculptor
Steinfels, Melville P Painter, Designer

Payson

St Maur, Kirk (Kirk Seymour McReynolds) Sculptor, Painter

Peoria

Kottemann, George & Norma Collectors
Moehl, Karl J Painter, Writer
Sunderland, Nita Kathleen Educator, Sculptor
Walsh, J(ohn) Michael Dealer, Printmaker

Peoria Heights

Gordon, P(atrick) S(cott) Painter

Petersburg

Hallmark, Donald Parker Museum Director, Lecturer

Plano

Pattison, Abbott Sculptor, Painter

Prairie View

Sigler, Hollis Painter

Quincy

Camastro-Pritchett, Rose Painter
Irwin, George M Patron, Collector
Mejer, Robert Lee Painter, Educator
Morrison, Fritzi Mohrenstecher Painter, Lecturer

Ringwood

Pearson, James Eugene Instructor, Sculptor

Riverdale

Czach, Marie Historian, Curator

River Forest

Powell, Gordon Sculptor
Sloan, Jeanette Pasin Painter, Printmaker
White, Philip Butler Painter, Collector

Riverside

Howlett, Carolyn Svrluga Educator, Painter

Rock Falls

Shedosky, Suzanne Painter

Rockford

Apgar, Jean E Printmaker
Heflin, Tom Pat Painter, Designer
Pinzarrone, Paul Painter
Sneed, Patricia M Collector, Consultant
Stromsdorfer, Deborah Ann Painter, Grapic Artist

Rolling Meadows

Mehn, Jan (von der Golz) Printmaker
Rebbeck, Lester James, Jr Painter, Sculptor

Roscoe

Bond, Oriel Edmund Illustrator, Painter

Savoy

Weller, Allen Stuart Educator, Historian

Schaumburg

Darling, Sharon Sandling Museum Director, Historian
Martyl (Martyl Schweig Langsdorf) Painter, Muralist

Skokie

Ahrendt, Mary E Conceptual Artist

Springfield

Bealmer, William Consultant, Educator
Dunbar, Michael Austin Sculptor, Administrator
Hodge, R Garey Painter, Instructor
Madden-Work, Betty I Painter, Historian
Madura, Jack Joseph Painter, Instructor

Streator

Gross, Marilyn A Painter, Printmaker

Tinley Park

Zuhn, Cheryl Educator, Designer

Urbana

Bodnar, Peter Painter, Educator
Bradshaw, Glenn Raymond Painter, Educator
Britsky, Nicholas Painter, Educator
Carlson, William D Sculptor, Glass Blower
Kovatch, Ronald R Ceramist
Perkins, Ann Historian, Educator
Replinger, Dot (Dorothy Thiele) Weaver, Designer
Savage, Jerry Painter
Schultz, Harold A Painter, Educator
Ziff, Jerrold Historian, Collector

Viola

Ramsauer, Joseph Francis Painter

Western Springs

Vickery, Charles Bridgeman Painter

Wheaton

Steffler, Alva W Educator, Curator
Walford, E John Historian, Educator

Wilmette

Drower, Sara Ruth Painter, Craftsman
Nilsson, Gladys Painter
Nutt, Jim (James Tureman) Painter, Draftsman
Valerio, James Robert Painter, Educator

Winfield

Haverty, Grace Ligammari Painter

Winnetka

Kramer, Linda Lewis Sculptor, Collector
Plowden, David Photographer, Writer
Thurman, Christa Charlotte Mayer Curator

Woodstock

Trausch, Thomas V Painter

INDIANA

Albany

Patrick, Alan K Ceramist, Painter

Anderson

Ryden, Kenneth Glenn Sculptor

Bloomington

Barnes, Robert M Painter, Educator
Byron, Michael Painter
Calman, W(endy L) Printmaker, Photographer
Cole, Bruce Historian, Educator
Darriau, Jean-Paul Educator, Sculptor
Eikerman, Alma Jeweler, Designer
Gealt, Adelheid Medicus Museum Director, Historian
Hawes, Louis Historian
Irvine, Betty Jo Librarian, Instructor
Jacquard Sculptor
Kleinbauer, W Eugene Historian
Lowe, Marvin Printmaker, Painter
Markman, Ronald Painter
Martz, Karl Ceramist, Educator
Pozzatti, Rudy O Printmaker, Painter
Sklarski, Bonnie J Painter, Educator
Stirratt, Betsy (Elizabeth Anne) Painter, Gallery Director
Wolin, Jeffrey Alan Photographer

Carmel

Manetta, Edward J Administrator, Painter

Davenport

Bradley, William Steven Museum Director, Curator

Evansville

Blevins, James Richard Art Administrator, Educator
Eilers, Fred (Anton Frederick) Portrait Painter, Designer
Miley, Les Ceramist, Educator
Streetman, John William, III Administrator

Ft Wayne

De Santo, Stephen C Painter
Papier, Maurice Anthony Educator, Painter
Sandeson, William Seymour Cartoonist

Gary

Rosen, Kay Painter

Granger

Langland, Tuck Sculptor, Educator

Greencastle

French, Ray H Printmaker, Painter
Meehan, William Dale Painter, Educator

Greenwood

Voos, William John Administrator, Painter

Hebron

Cooper, Wayne Painter, Graphic Artist

Indianapolis

Bartz, James Ross Painter
Block, Amanda Roth Painter, Printmaker
Brucker, Edmund Painter, Educator
Clowes, Allen Whitehill Collector, Patron
Cortese, Edward Fortunato Administrator, Illustrator
Daily, Evelynne Mess Painter, Printmaker
Davis, Harry Allen Painter, Educator
Eagerton, Robert Pierce Painter
Eiteljorg, Harrison Collector, Patron
Faust, James Wille Painter, Sculptor
Hilgeman, Liese Curator, Gallery Director
King, Patrick J Art Dealer, Curator
Lee, Ellen Wardwell Curator
Lucas, Georgetta Snell Painter
Pattison, Billy Dee Painter, Graphic Artist
Radecki, Martin John Administrator, Conservator
Rhodes, Reilly Patrick Museum Director
Roberson, Samuel Arndt Architectural Historian, Educator
Simmons, Percy Slotsky Collector
Waller, Aaron Bret Museum Director, Art Historian
Werner, (Charles George) Editorial Cartoonist

Lafayette

Paul, Rick W Sculptor
Smith-Theobald, Sharon A Museum Director

Madison

Gunter, Frank Elliott Painter, Educator

Mishawaka

Harmon, David Edward Painter, Educator

Morgantown

Boyce, Gerald G Educator, Painter

Muncie

Griner, Ned H Educator, Craftsman
Joyaux, Alain Georges Museum Director

Munster

Meeker, Barbara Miller Educator, Painter

Nashville

Brown, Peggy Ann Painter, Collage Artist
Zimmerman, William Harold Painter, Illustrator

New Albany

Wegner, Nadene R Goldsmith, Consultant

New Carlisle

Droege, Anthony Joseph, II Painter, Draftsman

New Harmony

Weinzapfel, Connie A Gallery Director, Curator

Notre Dame

Lauck, Anthony Joseph Sculptor, Educator
Sandusky, Billy Ray Painter, Printmaker

Ramsey

Windell, Violet Bruner Painter, Graphic Artist

South Bend

Rosenberg, Charles Michael Historian, Educator
Vogl, Don George Painter, Printmaker
Zisla, Harold Painter, Graphic Artist

Terre Haute

Engeran, Whitney John, Jr Painter, Educator
Enstice, Wayne Assemblage Artist, Writer
Evans, Robert Graves Educator, Sculptor
Hay, Dick Sculptor, Educator
Lamis, Leroy Sculptor, Educator
Lattanzio, Frances Photographer, Educator
McDaniel, Craig Milton Administrator, Painter
Porter, Elmer Johnson Educator, Painter
Quick, Edward Raymond Museum Director, Director
Reddington, Charles Leonard Painter, Educator

Vincennes

Jendrzejewski, Andrew John Sculptor, Administrator

West Lafayette

Berg, Mona Lea Museum Director
Williams, David Jon Medical Illustrator, Historian

Whiteland

Head, Cecil Franklin Painter

IOWA

Ames

Benson, Martha J Jeweler, Assemblage Artist

Burlington

Garrison, David Earl Painter, Muralist
Torn, Jerry (Gerald J) Draftsman, Photographer

Cedar Falls

Behrens, Roy R Editor, Designer
Page, John Henry, Jr Printmaker, Educator

Cedar Rapids

Barth, Charles John Educator, Printmaker
Czestochowski, Joseph Stephen Museum Director
Gilmor, Jane E Sculptor, Educator
Kocher, Robert Lee Painter, Educator
Metcalf, Conger A Painter, Instructor
Stamats, Peter Owen Collector, Patron

Cherokee

Laposky, Ben Francis Designer, Video Artist

Des Moine

Danoff, I Michael Museum Director, Writer

Des Moines

Black, Richard R Educator, Printmaker
Kirschenbaum, Jules Painter, Educator
Reece, Maynard Painter, Illustrator
Worthen, Amy Namowitz Printmaker, Historian

Dubuque

Gibbs, Tom Sculptor

Dysart

Behrens, Mary Snyder Craftsman, Painter

Fairfield

Cain, Charlotte Painter, Tapestry Artist
Cain, Michael Peter Sculptor, Painter

Fort Dodge

LaDouceur, Philip Alan Administrator, Director

Grinnell

Cervene, Richard Painter, Curator
Wilson, Kay E Administrator, Director

Indianola

Heinicke, Janet L Hart Painter, Educator

Iowa City

Achepohl, Keith Anden Printmaker, Painter
Alexander, Margaret Ames Historian, Educator
Begley, Wayne E Historian, Painter
Breder, Hans Dieter Sculptor, Video Artist
Burford, Byron Leslie Painter, Printmaker
Choo, Chunghi Silversmith, Fiber Artist
Cuttler, Charles David Historian, Lecturer
De Puma, Richard Daniel Historian
Foster, Stephen C Historian, Writer
Hindes, Chuck (Charles Austin) Ceramist, Educator
Lasansky, Mauricio L Printmaker, Draftsman
Patrick, Genie Hudson Painter, Instructor
Patrick, Joseph Alexander Painter, Educator
Rorex, Robert Albright Educator, Historian
Schmidt, Julius Sculptor
Schulze, John Photographer, Collage Artist
Tomasini, Wallace J Administrator, Historian
Towner, Mark Andrew Administrator, Photographer

Mason City

Leet, Richard Eugene Museum Director, Painter

Mt Vernon

Lifson, Hugh Anthony Painter, Educator

Orange City

Kaericher, John Conrad Printmaker, Educator

Solon

Myers, Virginia Anne Printmaker, Painter

Waterloo

Alling, Clarence (Edgar) Museum Director, Ceramist

Waverly

Frick, Arthur Charles Painter, Educator

KANSAS

Atchison

McCarthy, Dennis Sculptor, Educator

Emporia

Hall, Rex Earl Painter, Educator
Johnson, Donald Ray Historian, Printmaker
Kretsinger, Mary Amelia Goldsmith, Printmaker
Perry, Donald Dean Painter, Educator
Stauffer, Richard L Sculptor, Educator

Hays

Jilg, Michael Florian Painter, Printmaker
Kuchar, Kathleen Ann Painter, Educator
Nichols, Francis N, II Printmaker, Educator
Stevanov, Zoran Painter, Sculptor
Thorns, John Cyril, Jr Designer, Painter

Hutchinson

Connett, Dee M Educator, Printmaker

Lawrence

Allen, Tom, Jr Sculptor, Designer
Bangert, Colette Stuebe Painter
Brawley, Robert Julius Painter, Educator
Brejcha, Vernon Lee Glassblower, Educator
Copt, Louis J Painter
Craig, Susan V Librarian
Eldredge, Charles Child, III Historian
Hawkins, Barbara Painter
Iversen, Earl Harvey Photographer, Educator
Li, Chu-Tsing Historian
Norris, Andrea Spaulding Historian, Museum Director
Ott, Michael E Painter
Satz, Janet M Painter, Educator
Schira, Cynthia Weaver, Tapestry Artist
Shimomura, Roger Yutaka Painter, Performance Artist
Stokstad, Marilyn Historian, Educator
Sudlow, Robert N Painter, Printmaker
Tefft, Elden Cecil Sculptor, Educator
Vaccaro, Luella Grace Ceramist, Painter
Vaccaro, Nick Dante Educator, Painter
Wedding, Walter Joseph Cermamicist, Educator

Leavenworth

Melby, David A Painter, Photographer

Leawood

Szasz, Frank V Painter, Printmaker

Lenexa

Cawley, Joan Mae Art Dealer, Publisher

McPherson

Robinson, Mary Ann Painter, Educator

Manhattan

Brown, David Alan Historian, Curator
Garzio, Angelo C Potter, Craftsman
Ikeda, Yoshiro Ceramist, Educator
Kren, Margo Painter, Educator
Larmer, Oscar Vance Painter, Educator
Munce, James Charles Printmaker, Draftsman
Ohno, Mitsugi Glassblower
Pujol, Elliott Educator, Medalist
Stroh, Charles Printmaker, Painter

Paola

Cleary, Barbara B Painter, Instructor

Pittsburg

Krug, Harry Elno Printmaker, Educator
Russell, Robert Price Painter, Educator

Prairie Village

Kuemmerlein, Janet Fiber Artist

Shawnee Mission

Burnett, Barbara Ann Painter
Goheen, Ellen Rozanne Historian, Curator
Stephens, Thomas Michael Kinetic Artist, Designer

Topeka

Hunt, Robert James Administrator, Educator
Peters, Larry Dean Curator, Administrator

Wichita

Beren, Stanley O Patron
Bernard, David Edwin Printmaker, Educator
Boyd, John David Educator, Printmaker
Ellington, Howard W Art Dealer, Architect
Gruber, J Richard Museum Director, Historian
Plott, Paula (Paula Plott Amos) Painter, Sculptor
Reese, William Foster Painter
Riegle, Robert Mack Art Dealer, Collector
Sanderson, Charles Howard Painter, Educator
Scott, B Nibbelink (Barbara Gae Scott) Painter, Sculptor
Wethington, Wilma Zella Painter, Instructor
Wooden, Howard Edmund Historian, Writer

KENTUCKY

Bardstown

Cantrell, Jim Painter

Berea

Pross, Lester Fred Educator, Painter
Tredennick, Dorothy W Educator, Lecturer

Bowling Green

Forrester, Charles Howard Sculptor, Educator
Klein, Michael Eugene Historian, Writer
Oakes, John Warren Educator, Photographer
Schieferdecker, Ivan E Printmaker, Painter
Stomps, Walter E, Jr Educator, Painter
Trutty-Coohill, Patricia Educator, Historian

Carrsville

Morris, Roger Dale Painter

Covington

Rauf, Barbara Claire Instructor, Painter

Elizabethtown

Schwarz, Myrtle Cooper Designer, Mosaic Artist

Farmington

Merida, Frederick A Art Dealer, Printmaker

Florence

Goodridge, Lawrence Wayne Painter, Sculptor

Highland Heights

Houghton, Barbara Jean Photographer, Video Artist
Storm, Howard Painter, Sculptor

Lexington

Carpenter, Dennis Wilkinson (Bones) Photographer, Educator
Foose, Robert James Painter, Designer
Fowler, Harriet Whittemore Museum Director
Girard, (Charles) Jack Painter, Educator
Hamann, Marilyn D Educator, Painter
Petro, Joe, III Printmaker, Painter
Petro, Joseph (Victor), Jr Painter, Illustrator

Louisville

Begley, J (John Phillip) Museum Director
Blake, Jane Salley Publisher, Editor
Bratcher, Dale Painter
Bright, Barney Sculptor
Chodkowski, Henry, Jr Painter, Educator
Cloudman, Ruth Howard Curator
Coates, Ann S Curator, Photographer
Covi, Dario A Historian
Hackett, Mickey Painter, Educator
Haynie, Hugh Cartoonist
Hower, Robert K Photographer
Kaulitz, Garry Charles Painter, Printmaker
Kirk, Michael Printmaker, Instructor
Morgan, William Historian, Writer
Morrin, Peter Patrick Curator, Historian
Parsley, Jacque (Carter) Assemblage Artist, Curator
Stoll, (Mrs) Berry Vincent Collector
Storer, Frances Nell Painter, Instructor
Temple, Byron Ceramist
Whitesell, John D Printmaker
Wright, Jesse Graham, Jr Consultant

Morehead

Booth, Bill Educator

Murray

Boyd, Karen White Educator, Fiber Artist
Head, Robert William Painter, Educator
Leys, Dale Daniel Educator, Draftsman
Speight, Jerry Brooks Educator, Writer

Owensboro

Hood, Mary Bryan Museum Director, Administrator

Parkers Lake

Henry, John Raymond Sculptor

Princeton

Granstaff, William Boyd Painter, Illustrator

Richmond

Halbrooks, Darryl Wayne Painter, Educator
Isaacs, Ron Painter, Instructor

Shepherdsville

Lesch, Alma Wallace Tapestry Artist, Educator

Union

Akers, Gary Painter

Williamsburg

Hamwi, Richard Alexander Painter, Educator
Weedman, Kenneth Russell Painter, Sculptor

LOUISIANA

Alexandria

Scott, John Tarrell Printmaker, Sculptor

Baton Rouge

Andry, Keith Anthony Painter, Instructor
Bacot, Henry Parrott Museum Director, Curator
Boudreau, Anne Marie Collage Artist, Administrator
Corso, Samuel (Joseph) Stained Glass Artist, Painter
Cox, Richard William Historian, Writer
Crespo, Michael Lowe Writer, Painter
Daugherty, Michael F Educator, Sculptor
Guichet, Melody Painter
Hamblen, Dr Karen A Educator, Writer
Harding, Ann Painter
Harris, Harvey Sherman Painter, Educator
Hausey, Robert Michael Painter
Johns, Christopher K(alman) Painter, Educator
Krumholt, Ann Painter, Sculptor
Lyon, Robert F Sculpture, Administrator
Meek, A J Photographer, Educator
O'Neill, John Patton Painter, Curator
Pramuk, Edward Richard Painter
Price, Anne Kirkendall Critic
Sachse, Janice R Painter, Printmaker

Covington

Dufour, Paul Arthur Painter, Designer
Flattmann, Alan Raymond Painter, Instructor

Folsom

Golden, Rolland Harve Painter, Printmaker

Gray

Hensche, Henry Painter, Instructor

Lafayette

Fiero, Gloria K Educator, Historian
Love, Frances Taylor Writer, Publisher
Mhire, Herman P Museum Director, Curator
Miller, Joan Vita Museum Director, Administrator

Lake Charles

Fourcard, Inez Garey Painter
Holcombe, R Gordon, Jr Collector, Patron

Metairie

Casselli, Henry C, Jr Painter
Kohlmeyer, Ida (R) Painter, Sculptor
Shelby, Lila (Lila Norma Wallace) Painter
Young, Tom (William Thomas) Painter, Photographer

New Orleans

Amoss, Berthe Illustrator, Painter
Bailey, Barry Stone Sculptor, Painter
Bishop, Jacqueline K Painter
Bourgeois, Douglas Painter
Bullard, Edgar John, III Museum Director
Casellas, Joachim Painter
Clark, Emery Ann Painter, Environmental Artist
Davis, Charles Burdis, III Art Dealer, Collector
Drummer, William Richard Gallery Director
Eckert, Lou Painter
Economos, Michael E Educator, Painter
Emery, Lin Sculptor, Kinetic Artist
Fagaly, William Arthur Museum Director, Historian
Farrens, Juanita G Painter, Sculptor
Foley, Timothy Albert Art Dealer
Frank, Charles William, Jr Wood Carver, Writer
Freeman, Tina Photographer, Consultant
Glasgow, Vaughn Leslie Curator, Historian
Goodine, Linda Adele Photographer, Sculptor
Graham, Bob Painter, Muralist
Harter, John Burton Curator, Painter
Johnson, Richard A Painter, Educator
Jordan, Jack Administrator, Sculptor
Kern, Arthur (Edward) Educator, Sculptor
Koss, Gene H Sculptor, Educator
Lamantia, James Educator, Collector
Lummus, Carol Travers Printmaker
Muniot, Barbara King Collector
Myers, C Stowe Designer, Painter
O'Meallie, Kitty (Kate Chamness Johnson) Painter, Graphic Artist
Pennington, Estill Curtis Museum Director, Historian
Perret, Donna C Art Dealer
Rawlinson, Jonlane Frederick Painter, Instructor
Reddix, Roscoe Chester Painter, Educator
Steg, James Louis Printmaker, Painter
Struppeck, Jules Sculptor, Educator
Sweet, Steve (Steven Mark) Collage Artist, Kinetic
Tahir, Abe M, Jr Dealer, Consultant
Trivigno, Pat Painter, Educator
Villa, Mario Art Dealer, Architect
Wegmann, M K (Mary Katherine) Consultant, Administrator
Whiteman, Edward Russell Painter
Wirstrom, Margaret Painter, Collage Artist
Zurik, Jesselyn Benson Painter, Sculptor

Ruston

Berguson, Robert Jenkins Painter, Educator
Dablow, Dean Clint Photographer
Strother, Joseph Willis Administrator, Painter
Walton, M Douglas Painter, Instructor

St Francisville

Harrington, Chestee Marie Painter, Sculptor

Shreveport

Allen, Bruce Wayne Educator, Sculptor
Cadle, Ray Kenneth Craftsman, Painter
Morgan, Arthur C Sculptor

Youngsville

Savoy, Chyrl Lenore Sculptor, Educator

MAINE

Bath

Ipcar, Dahlov Painter, Illustrator
Webb, Todd Photographer, Historian

Boothbay Harbor

Eames, John Heagan Etcher, Painter

Bowdoinham

Pittore, Carlo Painter, Muralist

Brooks

Squadra, John Painter

Brunswick

Beam, Philip Conway Art Administrator, Educator
Bearce, Jeana Dale Painter, Printmaker
Brown, James Monroe, III Museum Director
Cornell, Thomas Browne Painter, Printmaker
Dunham-Griggs, Margaret Painter, Sculptor
Moore, Marjorie Painter, Assemblage Artist
Rakovan, Lawrence Francis Printmaker, Painter
Steinhardt, Alice Painter, Photographer
Watson, Katharine Johnson Museum Director, Historian

Camden

Etter, Howard Lee Painter, Lecturer
Smith, Harry William Miniaturist, Illustrator

Cape Elizabeth

Winkler, Michael Intermedia Artist

Cape Porpoise

Rowantree, Karen Smiley Photographer

Castine

Barrett, Thomas R Painter, Instructor
Mancuso, Leni Painter, Instructor

Cumberland Center

Gilmore, Roger Administrator, Consultant

Cushing

Magee, Alan Painter
Wissemann-Widrig, Nancy Painter

Damariscotta

Knox, Elizabeth Painter
Melville, Grevis Whitaker Painter, Printmaker
Thompson, Ernest Thorne, Jr Silversmith, Painter

Deer Isle

Groell, Theophil Painter, Instructor
Merritt, Francis Sumner Painter, Printmaker

East Boothbay

Burley, Lina Painter
Williams, Abigail S Painter, Sculptor

Edgecomb

Dean, Nicholas Brice Printmaker, Photographer

Eliot

Mugar, Martin Gienandt Painter

Gorham

Franklin, Patt Painter, Sculptor
Hewitt, Duncan Adams Sculptor, Educator
Marasco, Rose Photographer, Educator
Ubans, Juris K Painter, Educator

Kennebunk

Betts, Edward Howard Painter
Escalet, Frank Diaz Painter, Sculptor

Kennebunkport

Gable, John Oglesby Painter

Lewiston

Isaacson, Philip Marshal Critic, Writer

Lincolnville

Welliver, Neil G Painter

Monhegan

Drexler, Lynne Painter

Monhegan Island

Hudson, Jacqueline Painter, Graphic Artist
Stone, Don Painter

New Harbor

Lyford, Cabot Sculptor, Painter

Nobleboro

Greenleaf, Ken (Kenneth Lee) Sculptor, Art Critic

North Berwick

Hardy, (Clarion) Dewitt Painter, Administrator

North Fryeburg

Bolomey, Roger Henry Sculptor

Ogunquit

Culver, Michael L Painter, Curator
Laurent, John Louis Painter, Educator
Palmer, Michael Andrew Painter, Art Dealer
Thelin, Valfred P Painter, Lecturer

Orono

Hartgen, Vincent Andrew Educator, Painter
Lewis, Michael H Painter, Educator

Orrs Island

Miller, (Richard) Guy Sculptor

Phippsburg

Weber, Jean M Museum Director, Administrator

Portland

Buch, Gary Painter
Douglas, Edwin Perry Painter, Instructor
Elowitch, Annette Dealer
Elowitch, Robert Jason Dealer, Patron
Holverson, John Dealer, Curator
Kellar, Jeff Sculptor
Martin, Charles E Designer, Painter
Perrone, Jeff Ceramist
Sadik, Marvin Sherwood Dealer
Ventimiglia, John Thomas Sculptor, Educator
Vierthaler, Bonnie Collage Artist, Sculptor
Waller, Susan Gallery Director, Writer

Redfield

Peladeau, Marius Beaudoin Writer, Museum Director

Richmond

Bell, Dozier Painter

Rockland

Crosman, Christopher Byron Museum Director, Writer
Goldsmith, Benedict Isaac Gallery Director, Educator

Rockport

Fasoldt, Sarah Lowry Director, Art Dealer
Fink, Herbert Lewis Painter, Educator

Round Pond

MacDougall, Peter Steven Ceramic Artist, Sculptor

Skowhegan

Jacob, Ned Painter, Sculptor

Solon

Shahn, Abby Painter

South Freeport

Muench, John Painter, Printmaker

South Portland

Eide, John Photographer
Huntoon, Abby E Sculptor, Craftsman

Stockton Springs

Nuse, Oliver William Painter, Photographer

Stonington

Muir, Emily Lansingh Painter, Sculptor

Trevett

Bettinson, Brenda Painter, Printmaker

Veazie

Manter, Margaret C Painter

Vinalhaven

Indiana, Robert Painter, Sculptor

Warren

Haversat, Lillian Kerr Consultant, Curator

Waterville

Matthews, Harriett Sculptor
Simon, David L Historian, Educator

Winter Harbor

Browne, Syd J Painter

Wiscasset

Leslie, Seaver Painter, Instructor

Yarmouth

Chadbourn, Alfred Cheney Painter, Instructor

York

Hallam, Beverly (Linney) Painter, Photographer
Moore, Robert Eric Painter
Roche, Robert (Richard) Painter
Smart, Mary-Leigh Consultant, Patron

MARYLAND

Aberdeen

Morton, Richard H Painter, Graphic Artist

Annapolis

Edwards, Ellender Morgan Printmaker, Photographer
Koscianski, Leonard J Painter, Educator
Schulman, Robert Painter, Director

Ashton

Cave, Leonard Edward Sculptor, Educator

Baltimore

Adams, Mark Tapestry Artist, Painter
Amory, Claudia Painter
Baney, Ralph Ramoutar Sculptor
Bartlett, Christopher E Gallery Director, Illustrator
Berge, Henry Sculptor
Bergman, Robert P Museum Director, Historian
Bills, Linda Sculptor, Craftsperson
Bloomgarden, Judith Mary Art Librarian
Carlberg, Norman Kenneth Sculptor, Instructor
Coe, Henry Painter
Cohen, Jean R Ceramist, Collector
Cropper, M Elizabeth Historian, Lecturer
Crosby, Ranice W Medical Illustrator, Educator
Enggass, Robert Historian, Educator
Erbe, Joan Painter
Fendell, Jonas J Educator, Printmaker
Fessler, Ann Helene Photographer
Flannery, Thomas Cartoonist
Ford, John Gilmore Collector
Garrigues, Suzanne Historian
Gates, Jeff S Photographer
Gilchriest, Lorenzo Constructionist, Educator
Goldstein, Gladys Painter, Collage Artist
Hammond, Leslie King Historian, Writer
Hanson, J B Sculptor, Weaver
Hartigan, Grace Painter
Hoffman, Mandy Lippman Consultant, Writer
Johnston, Barry Woods Sculptor
Johnston, William Ralph Historian, Administrator
Jones, James Edward Painter, Printmaker
Katzenberg, Dena S Consultant, Curator
Kessler, Herbert Leon Educator
Klitzke, Theodore Elmer Educator, Historian
Koch, Philip Painter, Instructor
Kornblatt, Barbara Rodbell Dealer
Kramer, Reuben Sculptor
Larsen, John Christian Educator, Librarian
Lazarus, Fred, IV Administrator
Lehman, Arnold L Museum Director, Art Historian
Lippman, Judith Gallery Director, Educator
List, Clair Zamoiski Curator, Arts Administrator
Lyle, Charles Thomas Administrator
Middleman, Raoul F Painter, Muralist
Miller, Melvin Orville, Jr Painter
Mitchell, John Blair Painter, Educator
Moscatt, Paul N Painter, Instructor
Perlman, Bennard Bloch Painter, Critic
Pilgrim, James F Curator, Administrator
Price, Barbara Gillette Administrator, Painter
Printz, Bonnie Allen Painter, Photographer
Randall, Lilian M C Curator
Randall, Richard Harding, Jr Curator, Historian
Rembski, Stanislav Painter, Writer
Richardson, Brenda Museum Curator
Richardson, Frank, Jr Muralist
Rosen, Israel Collector
Rothschild, Amalie (Rosenfeld) Sculptor, Painter
Sangiamo, Albert Educator, Painter
Satorsky, Cyril Printmaker, Illustrator
Scott, Joyce Weaver
Seyffert, J Robert Painter
Sheppard, Joseph Sherly Painter, Sculptor
Somerville, Romaine Stec Administrator
Sparks, John Edwin Printmaker, Instructor
Stevens, Elisabeth Goss Writer, Critic
Stoneham, John Librarian
Streett, Tylden Westcott Sculptor, Educator
West, Virginia M Fiber Artist, Writer
Williams, Pat Ward Photographer
Wrigley, Rick Designer, Craftsman
Young, Barbara Photographer

Bethesda

Benson, Elizabeth Polk Historian, Writer
Broun, Elizabeth Gibson Administrator, Curator
Desind, Philip Dealer, Collector
Hansen, Sarah Eveleth (Campbell) Art Dealer, Gallery Director
Holvey, Samuel Boyer Sculptor, Designer
Kan, Kit-Keung Painter
Koenig, Elizabeth Sculptor
Land, Ernest Albert Painter, Designer
Larson, Jane (Warren) Ceramist, Writer
Lee, Dora Fugh Painter, Sculptress
Lerman, Doris (Harriet) Painter, Sculptor
Levy, Phyllis H Painter
Maddox, Jerald Curtis Curator, Historian
Moser, Joann Curator, Historian
Plattner, Phyllis Painter
Sarnoff, Lolo Sculptor, Collector

Bowie

Dasenbrock, Doris (Nancy) Voss Designer, Painter
Plaster, Alice Marie Painter, Instructor
White, Amos, IV Ceramist, Photographer

Bozman

Cox, Ernest Lee Sculptor, Educator

Burkittsville

Vo-Dinh, Mai Painter, Printmaker

Catonsville

Eglitis, Laimons Painter, Educator
Stephany, Jaromir Photographer, Educator
Yager, David Photographer, Printmaker

Chevy Chase

Asher, Lila Oliver Printmaker, Painter
Buitron-Oliver, Diana Curator, Historian
Calfee, William Howard Sculptor, Painter
Cone, Gerrit Craig Art Administrator
Curtis, Robert D Sculptor
Curtis, Verna P Curator
Friend, Patricia M Painter
Ginzburg, Yankel (Jacob) Painter, Sculptor
Greene, Louise Weaver Tapestry artist, Weaver
Kainen, Jacob Painter, Printmaker
Kranking, Margaret Graham Painter, Instructor
Rand, Harry Historian, Educator
Shuler, Thomas H, Jr Photographer, Educator

College Park

Burnham, Jack Wesley Critic, Writer
Colantuono, Anthony Historian
Owens, Gwendolyn Jane Museum Director, Curator
Shaw, Courtney Ann Librarian, Historian
Thorpe, James George Designer, Illustrator

Columbia

Zuccarini, David Anthony Painter

Crownsville

Keck, Jeanne Gentry Painter

Drayden

Egeli, Peter Even Painter, Illustrator

Easton

Plumb, James Douglas Painter, Curator

Elkton

Morris, Gregg Painter
Smith, James Morton Historian

Ellicott City

Baney, Vera Sculptor, Ceramist

Frederick

Housewright, Artemis Skevakis Painter, Sculptor
Parker, Carolyn Johnson Painter
Schutz, Estelle Painter, Printmaker

Frostburg

Rodeiro, José Manuel Painter, Muralist

Ft Washington

Furman, (Dr & Mrs) Arthur F Collectors, Patrons
Grady, Ruby McLain Painter, Sculptor

Gaithersburg

Balance, Jerrald Clark Painter
Gigliotti, Joanne Marie Administrator, Painter
Loiselle, Bernard Roger Painter, Museum Director

Glen Echo

Duffy, Betty Minor Dealer
Stevenson, A Brockie Painter, Educator

Glenelg

Niese, Henry Ernst Environmental Artist, Painter

Greenbelt

Rindge, Debora Anne Historian, Gallery Director

Hagerstown

Kotun, Henry Paul Art Therapist
Roberts, Clyde Harry Painter, Instructor

Hyattsville

Driskell, David Clyde Painter, Educator

Joppa

Walters, Ernest Painter

Kensington

Ecklin, Sister M Irenita Painter
McWhinnie, Harold James Printmaker, Ceramist
Murray, Richard Newton Museum Director, Curator

Landover

Nevia, (Joseph Shepperd Rogers) Painter

Lutherville

Wagner, Charles H Administrator, Instructor

Monkton

Leake, Eugene W Painter

Mt Airy

Swetcharnik, Sara Morris Painter, Sculptor
Swetcharnik, William Norton Painter, Sculptor

North Potomac

Huff, Laura Weaver Printmaker, Instructor

Olney

Geldermann Hails, Barbara Painter, Publisher

Owings Mills

Kissel, William Thorn, Jr Sculptor

Potomac

Chieffo, Clifford Toby Painter, Conservator
Freeman-Appelbaum, Margery Sculptor
Hammer, Elizabeth B Painter
Kerne, Barbara Davis Painter, Printmaker
McBryde, Sarah Elva Painter, Printmaker

Rockville

Crockett, Gib (Gibson M) Cartoonist, Painter
Goldstein, Charles Barry Art Dealer, Appraiser
Hofmann, Douglas William Painter, Printmaker
Porter, Shirley Painter
Wood, James Arthur (Art) Cartoonist, Lecturer

Royal Oak

Saff, Donald Jay Printmaker, Administrator

Sandy Spring

Murphy, Susan (Susan Avis Murphy Colombini) Painter

Savage

George, Sylvia James Portrait Painter, Illustrator

Silver Spring

Carter, Jerry Williams Mosaic Artist, Sculptor
Edelman, Ann Painter, Lecturer
Gips, C L Terry Photographer, Educator
Glick, Paula Florence Art Dealer, Writer
Gresser, Seymour Gerald Sculptor
Lapinski, Tadeusz (A) Printmaker, Educator
MacDonald, Kevin John Painter, Printmaker
Oxman, Katja Printmaker
Peiperl, Adam Kinetic Artist, Video Artist
Pruitt, Lynn Sculptor, Assemblage Artist
Roberts, Lucille D (Malkia) Painter, Educator
Slate, Joseph Frank Painter, Writer

Takoma Park

Brown, Gillian Photographer
Colwell, Judith Kogod Ceramist
Day, Larry (Lawrence James) Painter, Educator
Folsom, Fred Gorham, III Painter, Conservator
Folsom, Rose Calligrapher, Writer
Jewell, Joyce Painter, Printmaker
McCoubrey, Sarah Painter

University Park

Kehoe, Patrice Painter
Richardson, W C Painter, Educator
Warren, Win (W Winton) Painter, Lecturer

MASSACHUSETTS

Amherst

Barter, Judith A Curator, Historian
Campbell, Nancy B Printmaker
Clark, Carol Art Historian, Curator
Cohen, Michael S Ceramist, Photographer
Hendricks, James (Powell) Sculptor, Painter
Hurley, Denzil H Painter, Printmaker
Liebling, Jerome Photographer, Filmmaker
Norton, Paul Foote Historian, Educator
Parkhurst, Charles Educator, Curator
Patterson, William Joseph Painter, Printmaker
Ritz, Lorna J Painter, Sculptor
Roskill, Mark Wentworth Historian, Critic
Sandweiss, Martha Ann Museum Director
Townsend, John F Sculptor, Painter
Vanasse, Louis Raymond Collector, Instructor
Wardlaw, George Melvin Painter, Sculptor

Andover

Cook, Christopher Capen Administrator, Painter
Reynolds, Jock Director, Writer
Sullivan, David Francis Painter, Printmaker

Ashfield

Lund, Jane Painter, Printmaker

Ashland

Gohlke, Frank William Photographer

Attleboro

Kraczkowski, Phil Sculptor

Barnstable

Bush-Brown, Albert Writer, Educator

Belmont

Dow, Jim D Photographer
Larzelere, Judith Ann Tapestry Artist

Beverly

Bartnick, Harry William Painter, Educator
Broudo, Joseph David Educator, Ceramist
Greenblatt, Arthur E Educator, Administrator

Boston

Alcalay, Albert S Painter, Lecturer
Allen, Nancy Schuster Librarian, Educator
Amaltitano, Lelia Curator, Gallery Director
Aso, Kaji Painter, Educator
Banks, Ellen Painter
Barreres, Domingo Painter, Educator
Beale, Arthur C Administrator, Conservator
Cataldo, John William Educator, Calligrapher
Chamberlain, David (Allen) Sculptor, Paintmaker
Cheney, Liana De Girolami Historian, Curator
Cormier, Robert John Painter, Lecturer
Crane, Bonnie L Art Dealer, Gallery Director
Crite, Allan Rohan Painter, Illustrator
Crump, Walter Moore, Jr Printmaker, Painter
Dahill, Thomas Henry, Jr Painter, Educator
Driscoll, Edgar Joseph, Jr Critic
Fairbanks, Jonathan Leo Curator
Faulkner, Frank Painter
Fink, Alan Art Dealer
Fink, Joanna Elizabeth Art Dealer, Gallery Director
Fox, Judith Hoos Curator
Gaither, Edmund B Museum Director, Historian
Ghikas, Panos George Painter, Educator
Gibran, Kahlil George Sculptor
Gilbert-Rolfe, Jeremy Painter
Goldstein, Nathan Painter, Writer
Goldstein, Sheldon (Shelly) Painter
Greenamyer, George Mossman Sculptor, Educator
Grossberg, Jake Educator, Sculptor
Gustafson, Pier Assemblage Artist
Hadzi, Dimitri Sculptor, Printmaker
Haley, Patience E (Patience E Haley Ghikas) Painter, Conservator
Harcus, Portia Gwen Dealer, Consultant
Harries, Mags (Margaret L) Sculptor
Harris, Conley Painter, Printmaker
Hart, Claudia Printmaker
Herrmann, John J, Jr Curator
Hills, Patricia Historian, Curator
Hoffmann, Gary David Painter, Sculptor
Hoffmann, Leesa L Painter
Howlett, D(onald) Roger Art Dealer, Historian
Hurwitz, Sidney J Painter, Printmaker
Imber, Jonathan Painter, Printmaker
Israel, David N Art Dealer, Sculptor
James, Christopher P Photographer, Painter
Jans, Candace Painter, Printmaker
Kanegis, Sidney S Dealer
Kelley, Donald Castell Gallery Director
Kennedy, Harriet Forte Painter, Sculptor
Keough, Jeffrey Director
Korzenik, Diana Writer, Educator
Krakow, Barbara L Dealer
Lazenby, Dexter Conceptual Artist
Le Brun, Carol Critic, Dealer
Lowry, Bates Historian, Museum Director
MacDonald, Bruce K Educator, Historian
McSheehy, Cornelia Marie Printmaker, Painter
Malo, Teri (Theresa A Malo-Sprawka) Painter, Printmaker
Meister, Mark J Institute Director, Art Historian
Michaux, Ronald Robert Art Dealer
Moore, John J Painter, Educator
Nagano, Paul Tatsumi Painter, Designer
Nick, George Painter, Educator
Nielsen, Nina I M Dealer
Palazzolo, Carl Painter
Pezzati, Pietro (Peter S) Painter
Pfister, Harold Francis Administrator
Pinckney, Stanley Painter, Tapestry Artist
Pineda, Marianna Sculptor
Pucker, Bernard H Art Dealer
Rocha, Randolfo (Randolfo Scott Rocha) Painter
Rolly, Ronald Joseph Dealer
Rosenblum, Elizabeth Painter
Rotenberg, Judi Painter, Gallery Director
Ryerson, Mitch Craftsman
Schwartz, Henry Painter, Instructor
Searles, Stephen Sculptor, Painter

MASSACHUSETTS (cont)

Serenyi, Peter Historian, Administrator
Shestack, Alan Museum Director, Historian
Sonnabend, Joan Art Dealer, Collector
Stavaridis, Pat(ricia Ann) Art Dealer
Stebbins, Theodore Ellis, Jr Historian, Administrator
Sutton, Peter C Curator, Historian
Thomas, C David Printmaker
Tovish, Harold Sculptor
Vermeule, Cornelius Clarkson, III Historian, Writer
Vose, Robert Churchill, Jr Dealer
Warburg, Stephanie Wenner Painter, Sculptor
Wheelwright, Joseph Storer Sculptor, Painter
Yezerski, Howard J Gallery Director, Art Dealer
Zafran, Eric Myles Curator, Historian
Zahn, Carl Frederick Designer, Administrator

Bradford

Newman, Richard Charles Sculptor, Photographer

Brewster

Stoltenberg, Donald Hugo Painter, Printmaker

Bridgewater

Dunn, Roger Terry Historian
Hausrath, Joan W Weaver, Educator
Smalley, Stephen Francis Educator, Painter

Brookfield

Knight, Jacob Jaskoviak Painter, Illustrator

Brookline

Ablow, Joseph Painter, Writer
Ablow, Roselyn Karol Painter, Curator
Apel, Barbara Jean Painter, Educator
Barron, Ros Painter, Video Artist
Barron, Thomas Painter
Berger, Jason Painter, Printmaker
Cantor, Mira Sculptor, Graphic Artist
Kay, Reed Painter, Educator
Medvedow, Jill Administrator, Consultant
Moss, Karen Canner Painter, Educator
Papo, Iso Painter
Raiselis, Richard Painter, Educator
Sina, Alejandro Kinetic Artist, Sculptor
Stapen, Nancy Critic, Writer
Stevovich, Andrew Vlastimir Painter, Printmaker
Swan, Barbara Painter
Trecker, Stanley Matthew Art College President
Weiss, Rachel Curator
Wilson, John Sculptor, Printmaker

Brookline Village

Weber, Karen Painter

Burlington

Shedd, George J Painter, Illustrator

Cambridge

Ackerman, James S Historian, Educator
Bageris, John Painter, Educator
Bapst, Sarah Conceptual Artist
Benedict-Jones, Linda Photographer, Curator
Berndt, Jerry W Photographer
Brown, Constance George Gallery Director, Art Dealer
Callahan, Aileen (Aileen Loughlin Callahan) Painter, Muralist
Casey, Jacqueline Shepard Designer
Cohn, Marjorie B Curator, Historian
Coolidge, John Historian
Davis, Ben Photographer, Painter
Denker, Susan A Historian, Critic
Dorfman, Elsa Photographer, Writer
Earls, Paul Environmental Artist
Feininger, T Lux Painter, Writer
Fleming, Ronald Lee Designer, Administrator
Freeman, Robert Lee Painter, Sculptor
Freitag, Wolfgang Martin Librarian, Editor
Goldring, Elizabeth Writer, Environmental Artist
Horrell, Jeffrey L Librarian
Katayama, Toshihiro Painter, Designer
Kepes, Gyorgy Painter, Educator
Lent, Blair Illustrator, Writer
McKie, Todd Stoddard Painter
Manuel, Kathryn Lee Craftsman
Mazur, Michael Painter, Printmaker
Mirtala Sculptor, Writer
Mongan, Agnes Administrator, Historian
Norfleet, Barbara Pugh Curator, Educator
Parry, Marian Illustrator, Printmaker
Piene, Otto Sculptor, Painter
Posner, Helaine J Gallery Director, Curator
Preusser, Robert Ormerod Painter, Educator
Rabb, (Mr & Mrs) Irving W Collectors
Radycki, J(osephine) Diane Historian, Educator
Reimann, William P Sculptor, Educator
Roberts, Helene Emylou Librarian, Editor
Rosenfield, John M Educator, Curator
Rudenstine, Angelica Zander Historian, Curator
Saarinen, Lilian Sculptor
Sayre, Eleanor Axson Curator
Selvig, Forrest Hall Historian, Writer
Slive, Seymour Historian, Museum Director
Slosburg-Ackerman, Jill Sculptor, Jeweler
Swartz, Linda Photographer
Trachtman, Arnold S Painter
Wasserman, Cary (Robert) Photographer, Conceptual Artist
Welch, Stuart Cary Curator, Historian
Wood, Joseph A Designer
Zerner, Henri Thomas Historian, Curator

Cataumet

Arsenault, Kate Whitman Painter

Charlestown

Kortenhaus, Lynne M Consultant, Curator

Chatham

Kent, H Latham Painter
Reid, Charles Writer, Painter

Chelmsford

Plummer, Carlton B Painter, Instructor

Chelsea

Willis, William Henry, Jr Administrator

Chestnut Hill

Bloom, Edith Salvin Art Dealer, Painter
Plaut, James S Art Administrator, Writer

Concord

Buerger, Janet E Historian, Curator
Ihara, Michio Sculptor
MacNeill, Frederick Douglas Painter

Conway

Mallary, Robert W Sculptor, Educator

Dennis

Geissbuhler, Arnold Sculptor

Dorchester

Stone, Jim (James J) Photographer, Author
Wise, Kenneth Kelly Photographer, Critic

Dover

Celli, Paul Painter, Educator
Hubert, Edgar F & Anne M Curator, Collector

East Boston

Fink, Aaron Painter, Printmaker

East Falmouth

Handville, Robert T Painter, Illustrator

East Hampton

Teichman, Mary Melinda Printmaker, Childrens Book Illustrator

Edgartown

Carlson, Jane C Painter

Falmouth

Koenig, Peter L Painter, Curator

Fitchburg

Timms, Peter Rowland Museum Director

Florence

Ravett, Abraham Filmmaker, Photographer
Rupp, Sheron Adeline Photographer, Educator

Framingham

Evans, Bob (Robert James) Museum Director, Painter
Lipton, Leah Historian, Educator

Framingham Center

Schiff, Lonny Printmaker, Conservator

Gloucester

Benham, Robert Charles Painter
Coburn, Ralph (M H) Painter
Curtis, Roger William Painter, Dealer
Duca, Alfred Milton Painter, Sculptor
Gore, Ken (Kenneth Leon) Painter
Grasso, Doris (Ten-Eyck) Painter, Sculptor
Grasso, Salvatore Fortunato Painter, Conceptual Artist
Hancock, Walker (Kirtland) Sculptor
Manship, John Paul Painter, Sculptor
Movalli, Charles Joseph Painter, Writer
Pettibone, John Wolcott Curator, Graphic Artist
Shore, Mary (McGarrity) Painter

Goshen

Phillips, Michael Painter, Sculptor

Great Barrington

Agar, Eunice Jane Painter, Writer
Aigner, Lucien Photographer, Lecturer
Filmus, Michael Roy Painter
Filmus, Stephen I Painter, Printmaker
Hillman, Arthur Stanley Graphic Artist, Educator
McCurdy, Michael Charles Illustrator, Designer

Harwich

Bode, Robert William Designer, Painter

Harwich Port

Gilbertson, Charlotte Painter, Lecturer

Heath

Brown, Peter Thomson Photographer, Educator

Hingham

Giovanni, Painter, Printmaker
Pierce, Patricia Jobe Dealer, Historian
Reardon, Mary A Painter, Muralist
Rose, Samuel Painter, Muralist

Holyoke

Brodeur, Catherine R Painter

Hull

Burgess, David Lowry Environmental Artist

Hyannis

Brooks, Robert Painter

Hyannis Port

Barber, Sam Painter, Sculptor

Hyde Park

Atwood Pinardi, Brenda Painter, Educator

Kingston

Joyce, Marshall Woodside Painter, Instructor

Lanesborough

Hoadley, Thomas A Ceramist

Leeds

Baskin, Leonard Sculptor, Graphic Artist

Lenox

Brubaker, Jack Sculptor, Kinetic Artist
Kochta, Ruth Martha Art Dealer, Painter
Miccoli, Arnaldo Painter, Collage Artist
Ripps, Rodney Painter

Leverett

Fornas, Leander Printmaker, Instructor

Lexington

Anderson, Robert Alexander Painter, Illustrator
Bakanowsky, Louis J Sculptor, Architect
Berman, Vivian Printmaker
Boodman, H Citron Painter, Printmaker
Cascieri, Arcangelo Sculptor, Instructor
Filipowski, Richard E Sculptor, Educator
Janney, Christopher Draper Environmental Artist, Sound Artist
Nye, Molly Harding Art Dealer, Gallery Director
Wolpert, Etta Painter, Printmaker

Leyden

Garston, Gerald Drexler Painter

Lincoln

Bauer, Ruth Kruse Painter
Freeman, Robert Painter
Kumler, Kipton (Cornelius) Photographer, Lecturer
Master-Karnik, Paul Museum Director, Critic

Longmeadow

Catok, Lottie Meyer Painter

Lowell

Faudie, Fred Painter, Illustrator
Sullivan, Anne Dorothy Hevner Painter, Printmaker

Manchester

Lothrop, Kristin Curtis Sculptor

Marblehead

Huxtable, Ada Louise Critic
Seamans, Beverly Benson Sculptor
Taylor, Robert Critic, Writer

Mashpee

Patti, Tom Sculptor

Medford

Raguin, Virginia C Historian, Consultant
Wechsler, Judith Glatzer Historian, Filmmaker

Medway

Burnett, Calvin Painter, Printmaker

Millis

Awalt, Elizabeth Grace Painter
D'Onofrio, Bernard Michael Glass Blower, Sculptor

Milton

Hamill, Tim J Painter, Printmaker

Monson

Talbot, Jarold Dean Painter, Director

Montague

Coughlin, Jack Printmaker, Sculptor

Nantucket

Harris, Lily Marjorie Art Dealer, Administrator
Perrin, C Robert Painter, Illustrator

Natick

Abany, Albert Charles Painter, Printmaker
Geller, Esther (Esther Geller Shapero) Painter, Printmaker
Ratner, David M Painter, Educator

N Attleboro

Andrews, Edwin C Sculptor

Needham

Branfman, Steven Ceramist, Educator
Hunter, Robert Douglas Painter, Instructor
Ricci, Jerri Painter

Needham Heights

Castano, Elvira Gallery Director, Historian

New Bedford

Hamlet, Susan H Educator, Jeweler
Smith, David Loeffler Painter, Educator
Young, Janie Chester Museum Director, Educator

Newbury

Delevoryas, Lillian Grace Painter, Designer

Newton

Cobb, Ruth Painter
Nash, Paul Writer, Educator
Ranalli, Daniel Artist, Educator
Steczynski, John Myron Draftsman, Educator

Newton Center

Golden, Morton J Administrator, Director
Rosenblum, Richard Stephen Sculptor

Newtonville

Polonsky, Arthur Painter, Educator
Skinner, Orin Ensign Designer

North Adams

Demartis, James J Painter

Northampton

Hoener, Arthur Painter
Houser, Caroline Mae Historian
Kaiser, Diane Sculptor, Educator
Moser, Barry Graphic Artist, Printmaker
Offner, Elliot Sculptor, Printmaker
Weems, Carrie Mae Photographer
Wessel, Fred W Printmaker, Painter

North Brookfield

Neal, (Minor) Avon Writer, Printmaker

North Darmouth

Lindenberg, Mary K Painter, Instructor

North Dartmouth

London, Peter Painter, Educator
Vena, Dante Educator, Printmaker

North Truro

Wright, Milton Painter, Educator

Norwell

Wentworth, Murray Jackson Painter, Instructor

Orleans

Vickrey, Robert Remsen Painter

Palmer

Gilmartin, F Thomas Painter, Administrator

Pelham

Gongora, Leonel Painter, Educator
Kindahl, Connie Weaver, Craftsman

Pittsfield

O'Connell, Daniel Moylan Painter, Administrator

Plainville

Dverin, Anatoly Painter, Illustrator

Provincetown

Bowen, Paul Sculptor
Chetham, Charles Museum Director
De Nagy, Eva Painter
Egeli, Cedric Baldwin Painter, Instructor
Farnham, Emily Painter, Writer
Franklin, Gilbert Alfred Sculptor, Educator
Halvorsen, Elspeth Colette (Elspeth Halvorsen-Vevers) Assemblage Artist, Sculptor
Henry, Robert Painter, Educator
Hutchinson, Peter Arthur Conceptual Artist, Environmental Artist
Margo, Boris Painter, Printmaker
Maynard, William Painter, Educator
Nay, Mary Spencer Painter, Educator
Vevers, Tabitha Painter
Vevers, Tony Painter, Educator
Walker, Berta Art Dealer

Reading

Nordstrand, Nathalie Johnson Painter

Rehoboth

Chao, Bruce Sculptor
Glancy, Michael Sculptor
Prip, John A Silversmith, Sculpture

Rockport

Bissell, Phil Cartoonist, Illustrator
Geraci, Lucian Arthur Painter, Dealer
Harper, Eleanor O'Neil Painter
Hill, J Tweed Painter, Graphic Artist
Martin, Mary Finch Painter, Gallery Director
Martin, Roger Painter, Educator
Morrell, Wayne (Beam) Painter
Murphy, Herbert A Architect, Painter
Nicholas, Thomas Andrew Painter
Ramsey, Dorothy J Painter, Writer
Ruben, Albert Painter
Schlemm, Betty Lou Painter, Instructor
Stoffa, Michael Instructor, Painter
Strisik, Paul Painter
Turner, Bruce Backman Painter
Van Wyk, Helen Painter, Lecturer
Whitcomb, Kay Enamelist, Lecturer

Roxbury

Lewis, Elma Ina Administrator

Salem

Fetchko, Peter J Museum Director

Sandwich

Neill, Ben E Painter

Saugus

Walkey, Frederick P Museum Director, Consultant

Sharon

Avakian, John Painter, Instructor
Stubbs, Lu Sculptor

Sheffield

Friedman, Benno Photographer
Jurney, Donald (Benson) Painter
Philbrick, Margaret Elder Printmaker, Painter

Sherborn

Pickhardt, Carl Painter, Printmaker

Shrewsbury

Parker, Ann Photographer, Writer

Somerville

Campbell, David Paul Painter
Gabin, George Joseph Painter, Instructor
Pappenheimer, Will D Painter, Glass Blower
Sandman, Jo Sculptor, Conceptual Artist
Smith, Anne L Sculptor

South Dartmouth

Gustin, Christopher Ceramist

Southfield

Melvin, Ronald McKnight Museum Director

South Hadley

Herbert, Robert L Historian, Educator

South Harwich

Sahrbeck, Everett William Painter, Photographer

Springfield

Muhlberger, Richard Charles Writer, Educator
Stevens, Nelson L Painter, Educator
Sturges, Hollister Curator, Historian

Stockbridge

Boris, Bessie Painter
Flower, Michael Lavin Art Dealer, Photographer
Garel, Leo Painter
Ginzel, Roland Painter, Printmaker
Milloff, Mark David Painter, Sculptor
Varnelis, Kazys Educator, Painter

Sudbury

Aronson, David Painter, Sculptor
Nyman, Georgianna Beatrice Painter

Sunderland

Kamys, Walter Painter, Educator

Tewksbury

Kaufman, Mico Sculptor

Topsfield

Webster, Larry Painter, Printmaker

Truro

Evaul, William H, Jr Painter, Printmaker
Huebler, Douglas Conceptual Artist
Johnson, Joyce Sculptor, Instructor
Preston, Malcolm H Critic, Painter
Yater, George David Painter

Vineyard Haven

Berresford, Virginia Painter
Bramhall, Kib Painter

Waltham

Allara, Pamela Edwards Educator, Administrator
Belz, Carl Irvin Museum Director
Bohlen, Nina (Celestine Eustis Bohlen) Painter, Draftsman

Ware

Chase, Alice Elizabeth Educator, Writer

Watertown

Magdanz, Andrew R Glass Blower
Schwalb, Susan Painter, Instructor
Weiler, Joseph Flack Photographer, Writer

Wayland

Dergalis, George Painter, Sculptor
Rodman, Ruth M Printmaker, Tapestry Artist
Shlien, Helen S Curator

Wellesley

Dorrien, Carlos Guillermo Sculptor
Mahdavi, Rafael Sinclair Painter, Sculptor
O'Gorman, James Francis Educator, Writer
Rayen, James Wilson Painter, Educator
Wallace, Richard William Educator, Historian

Wellesley Hills

Fontaine, E Joseph Painter

Wellfleet

Lechay, James Painter
Minisci, Brenda (Eileen) Sculptor, Ceramist

Wenham

Fransioli, Thomas Adrian Painter, Printmaker

West Boylston

Italiano, Joán Sculptor, Liturgical Artist

West Falmouth

Savenor, Betty Carmell Painter, Printmaker

Westfield

Wise, Gerald Lee Graphic Artist, Printmaker

Westford

Bowman, George Leo Painter

West Hyannisport

Lynch-Nakache, Margaret Painter

West Newton

Headley, David Allen Painter
Schon, Nancy Quint Sculptor

Weston

Torf, Lois Beurman Collector, Publisher

Westport

Somerson, Rosanne Craftsman, Educator

West Roxbury

Altmann, Henry S Painter, Educator
Sorokin, Maxine Ann Painter, Educator

West Yarmouth

Blake, Priscilla Ann Muralist, Ceramist

Wilbraham

Gale, William Henry Painter, Designer

Williamsburg

Superior, Mara R Ceramist

Williamstown

Brooke, David Stopford Museum Director
Brooks, John H Administrator, Educator
Burchard, Peter Duncan Illustrator, Photographer
Burger, Gary C Museum Director
Faison, Samson Lane, Jr Historian, Museum Director
Faulds, W Rod Administrator, Designer
Johnson, Eugene Joseph Historian
Mathews, Nancy Mowll Historian, Curator
Petersen, Toni Librarian, Director
Shearer, Linda Director

Wilmington

Peters, Andrea Jean Painter

Winchester

Neuman, Robert S Painter

Wollaston

Smongeski, Joseph Leon Painter, Designer

Worcester

Barnhill, Georgia Brady Curator, Historian
Hovsepian, Leon Painter, Designer
McCorison, Marcus Allen Librarian
Nigrosh, Leon Isaac Ceramist, Instructor
O'Reilly, John B Photographer, Collage Artist
Priest, T (Theresa Khoury Struckus) Painter
Shepard, Lewis Albert Dealer, Historian
Strickler, Susan Elizabeth Curator, Historian

Yarmouth Port

Hitch, Jean Leason Painter
Hitch, Robert A Painter

MICHIGAN

Allendale

Duren, Stephen D Painter

Allen Park

Mandziuk, Michael Dennis Painter, Serigrapher

Alma

Rozier, Robert L Painter

Alpena

Bodem, Dennis Richard Museum Director

Ann Arbor

Arnheim, Rudolf Educator, Writer
Cassara, Frank Painter, Printmaker
Cervenka, Barbara Educator, Painter
Eisenberg, Marvin Historian, Educator
Forsyth, Ilene H(aering) Educator, Historian
Gayas-Jungwirth, I(rene) Painter, Designer
Glasser, Norma Penchansky Sculptor
Guastella, C Dennis Painter, Instructor
Halsey, Brian Elliott Painter, Consultant
Hennessey, William John Museum Director
Iglehart, Robert L Educator, Writer
Kamrowski, Gerome Painter, Sculptor
Kirkpatrick, Diane Historian
Kusnerz, Peggy Ann F Librarian, Educator
Leonard, Joanne Photographer, Educator
Lewis, William Arthur Painter, Educator
McMillan, Constance Painter, Illustrator
Pijanowski, Eugene M Educator, Craftsman
Poinier, Arthur Best Editorial Cartoonist
Sawyer, Charles Henry Museum Director
Smith, Graham Historian, Educator
Smith, Sherri Weaver, Educator
Spencer, Deirdre Diane Librarian, Educator
Spink, Walter M Educator, Administrator
Spitler, Clare Blackford Art Dealer
Stephenson, John H Sculptor, Educator
Stephenson, Susanne G Ceramist, Educator
Stewart, Paul LeRoy Printmaker, Educator
Weddige, Emil A Printmaker, Painter

Battle Creek

Concannon, Ann Worth Administrator
Gammon, Reginald Adolphus Educator, Painter

Berrien Springs

Constantine, Greg John Painter, Educator

Bingham Farms

Bostick, William Allison Painter, Calligrapher

Birmingham

Che, Chuang Painter, Printmaker
Ettl, Georg Painter, Sculptor
Hadfield, Ted Lee Sculptor
Horn, Roni Sculptor
Kozlow, Richard Painter
Loving, Al Painter, Collage Artist
McNamara, Mary Jo Historian, Educator
Mitchnick, Nancy Painter, Educator
Morris, Donald Fischer Dealer
Morris, Florence Marie Dealer
Ross, Sheldon Art Dealer, Gallery Director
Wilbert, Robert John Painter, Educator

Bloomfield Hills

McCoy, Katherine Braden Designer, Educator
McCoy, Michael Dale Designer, Educator
Murakishi, Steve Printmaking, Sculptor
Ortman, George Earl Painter, Sculptor
Schwartz, Alan E Collector
Siden, Franklin Dealer, Lecturer
Slade, Roy Painter, Museum Director
Stewart, Norman Printmaker, Publisher
Toth, Carl Photographer

Brighton

Nestor, Lula B Painter, Administrator

Canton

Beginin, Igor Painter, Educator
DeLauro, Joseph Nicola Sculptor, Educator

Clinton Township

Piet, John Frances Sculptor, Instructor

Columbus

Imes, Birney Photographer

Dearborn

Stamelos, Electra Georgia Mousmoules Painter, Graphic Artist

Detroit

Burnett, Patricia Hill Painter, Sculptor
Colby, Joy Hakanson Critic
Darr, Alan Phipps Curator
Day, Burnis Calvin Painter, Educator
Fekete, Brian Painter
Hill, Draper Editorial Cartoonist, Historian
Iden, Sheldon Painter, Educator
Johnson, Lester L Painter, Educator
Kachadoorian, Zubel Painter, Educator
Kan, Michael Historian, Administrator
Lawrence, Spencer Draftsman, Printmaker
Lewis, Samella Sanders Painter, Historian
Marck, Jan van der Curator
Miles, Cyril Painter, Curator
Muccioli, Anna Maria Painter, Sculptor
Peck, William Henry Curator, Historian
Sachs, Samuel, II Museum Director, Historian
Schuster, Eugene Ivan Dealer, Historian
Shaw, Nancy (Rivard) Curator, Historian
Snowden, Gilda Painter, Writer
Woodson, Shirley Ann Painter
Yaeger, Edgar Louis Painter, Muralist

Dexter

Rush, Jon N Sculptor, Educator

East Jordan

Midener, Walter Sculptor, Instructor

East Lansing

Brainard, Owen Painter, Educator
Church, C Howard Administrator, Educator
Glendinning, Peter Photographer
Lawton, James L Sculptor, Educator
Stanford, Linda Oliphant Administrator, Historian

Farmington Hills

Glick, John P Ceramist
Hampson, Ferdinand Charles Art Dealer, Curator
MacGaw, Wendy Sculptor
Piepenburg, Robert Sculptor

Fenton

Knott, Dee D Painter, Illustrator

Flint

Davidek, Stefan Painter, Printmaker
Mahey, John A Museum Director
Warner, Douglas Warfield Painter, Collage Artist

Flushing

Bohnert, Thom (Thomas Robert) Ceramist, Educator

Frankfort

Kooyman, Richard E Craftsman

Franklin

Kasle, Gertrude Consultant, Collector

Grand Rapids

Blovits, Larry John Painter, Educator
Boeve, Edgar Gene Educator, Painter
Collins, Paul Painter
Danielson, Phyllis I Administrator, Tapestry Artist
Koster, Marjory Jean Printmaker
Sobol, Judith Ellen Museum Director, Curator

Grosse Ile

Stump, M Pamela (Pamela Stump) Sculptor

Grosse Pointe

Krentzin, Earl Sculptor, Silversmith

Haslett

Natzmer, Cheryl Lynn Dealer, Historian

Hillsdale

Frudakis, Anthony P Sculptor

Holland

Mayer, Billy (William Robert Mayer) Sculptor

Huntington Woods

Abt, Jeffrey Painter, Writer
Gutmann, Joseph Art Historian, Lecturer
Nawara, Jim Painter, Educator
Nawara, Lucille Procter Painter, Lecturer

Kalamazoo

Harrison, Carole Sculptor
Hatch, Mary Painter
Hefner, Harry Simon Painter, Educator
Kayser, Thomas Arthur Consultant, Designer
Link, Lawrence John Painter, Writer
Meyer, Charles Edward Consultant, Historian
Rhodes, Curtis A Painter, Printmaker
Ruttinger, Jacquelyn Painter, Gallery Director
Sheridan, Helen Adler Curator
Tye, William Roy Sculptor
Wood, Marcia Joan Sculptor

Kalkaska

Lawrence, Rodney Steven Painter, Illustrator

Laingsburg

Bandes, Susan Jane Museum Director, Educator

Lakeside

Wilson, John David Dealer, Publisher

Lansing

Funk, Roger L Educator, Designer
Green, Roger J Critic, Historian

Leland

Simper, Frederick Painter

Livonia

Culling, Richard Edward Painter, Collage Artist

Marquette

Gorski, Richard Kenny Educator, Graphic Artist

Midland

Breed, Charles Ayars Sculptor, Designer

Mt Clemens

Redstone, Louis Gordon Architect, Writer

Mt Pleasant

Born, James E Sculptor
Kline, Richard R Sculptor, Holography

Muskegon

Kochka, Al Museum Director, Administrator

New Haven

Rubello, David Jerome Painter, Photographer

Novi

Barr, David John Sculptor, Conceptual Artist

Okemos

Alexander, Robert Seymour Educator, Designer

Olivet

Whitney, Charlotte Armide Painter, Jeweler

Parma

Wolber, Paul J Painter, Educator

Plainwell

Kendall, Thomas Lyle Ceramist, Educator

Provincetown

Edwards, Ethel Visual Artist

Riverdale

Kirby, Kent Bruce Printmaker, Photographer
Parks, Carrie Anne Ceramist, Educator

Rochester

Usui, Kiichi Curator
Windeknecht, Margaret Brake Fiber Artist, Writer

Roseville

Geck, Francis Joseph Educator, Designer

Royal Oak

Carducci, Vincent A Critic, Conceptual Artist
Hall, Michael David Sculptor, Educator
Jacobs, Ferne K Weaver
Levine, Edward Painter
McCarty, Lorraine Chambers Painter, Instuctor
Rosas, Mel Painter, Educator
Schwarcz, June Theresa Craftsman, Enamelist

St Clair Shores

Burns, Sheila Painter, Lecturer
Burns, Stan Painter, Sculptor
Cartmell, Helen Painter, Draftsman

Saugatuck

Bragdon, Catherine Creamer Weaver, Designer

South Haven

Dickerson, Edward Ted Painter, Printmaker

Troy

Belian, Garabed Dealer, Historian
Belian, Isabelle Administrator
Cloud, Jack L Gallery Owner, Publisher
Gordin, Misha Photographer, Video Artist
Michaels, Glen Sculptor, Painter

Watersmeet

Freund, Will Frederick Painter, Educator

West Bloomfield

Bertman, Stephen Historian, Writer
Romero, Jose T Painter

Whitmore Lake

Davis, Philip Charles Photographer, Writer

Williamston

McChesney, Clifton Painter, Educator

Ypsilanti

Avedon, Barry Painter, Educator
Calkins, Kingsley Mark Painter, Educator
Fairfield, Richard Thomas Printmaker, Educator

MINNESOTA

Bemidji

Nerburn, Kent Michael Sculptor, Critic
Smith, Kent Alvin Sculptor

Crystal

DesJarlait, Robert D Painter, Illustrator

Duluth

Brush, Gloria (Elizabeth) DeFilipps Photographer, Educator
Brush, Leif Sound Sculptor, Instructor
Chee, Cheng-Khee Painter, Educator
Lettenstrom, Dean Roger Painter, Educator
Strassberg, Roy I Ceramist, Sculptor

Eden Prairie

Kelly, Robert James Painter, Graphic Artist

Edina

Granlund, Paul Theodore Sculptor

Elk River

Olson, Gene Russel Sculptor

Golden Valley

Jardine, Donald Leroy Editor, Educator

Grand Portage

Morrison, George Painter

Hopkins

Morin, Thomas Edward Sculptor, Educator

Isanti

Benjamin, Alice (Alice Benjamin Boudreau) Painter, Educator

Janesville

Tanner, James L Craftsman

Mankato

Finkler, Robert Allan Educator, Painter

Marine On St Croix

Sorman, Steven Painter, Printmaker

Minneapolis

Appleby, Daniel Bart Filmmaker
Argue, Douglas Painter
Asher, Frederick M Historian, Educator
Barber, Philip Judd Painter, Printmaker
Bigger, Michael D Sculptor
Bjorklund, Lee Painter, Educator
Boler, John Alfred Art Dealer, Collector
Burpee, James Stanley Painter, Instructor
Campopiano, Remo Sculptor
Conaway, James D Painter, Educator
Conforti, Michael Peter Historian, Curator
Dahl, Stephen M Photographer
De Luca, Joseph Victor Educator, Painter
Fisher, Carole Gorney Painter, Sculptor
Fiterman, Dolly Gallery Director, Collector
Flick, Paul John Collector, Painter
Fogg, Monica Painter, Educator
Gellert, Vance F Photographer
Gjertson, Stephen Arthur Painter, Writer
Goodstein-Shapiro, F Painter, Historian
Hallman, Gary Lee Photographer
Holen, Norman Dean Sculptor, Educator
Hui, Pat Painter
Johnson, James Edwin Graphic Designers
Kiland, Lance Edward Painter, Printmaker
King, Lyndel Irene Saunders Director, Administrator
Klipper, Stuart David Photographer
Larkin, Eugene Designer, Educator
Larson, Philip Seely Sculptor, Educator
Leicester, Andrew John Environmental Artist
Lupori, Peter John Educator, Sculptor
McCannel, (Mrs) Malcolm A Collector
McDonald, Susan Strong Painter, Printmaker
McNally, Sheila John Educator, Historian
Maurer, Evan Maclyn Director, Historian
Mojsilov, Ilene Krug Painter
Mondale, Joan Adams Craftsperson, Ceramist
Munzner, Aribert Painter, Educator
Myers, Malcolm Haynie Printmaker, Painter
Nowytski, (Slavko) Sviatoslav Filmmaker, Photographer
Ott, Jerry Painter
Peterson, Harold Patrick Librarian, Editor
Pickett, Keri L Photographer
Poor, Robert John Historian
Powell, Dan T Photographer
Preuss, Roger Painter, Writer
Raymond, Evelyn L Sculptor
Rose, Thomas Albert Sculptor
Rowan, Herman Painter, Educator
Ryan, David Michael Curator
Saltzman, William Painter, Sculptor
Scherer, Herbert Grover Librarian, Lecturer
Slettehaugh, Thomas Chester Assemblage Artist, Educator
Somberg, Emilija O K Painter
Starkweather-Nelson, Cynthia Louise Painter
Stoller, John Chapman Dealer

MINNESOTA (cont)

Sussman, Bonnie K Dealer, Gallery Director
Torbert, Stephanie Birch Photographer, Illustrator
Verostko, Roman Joseph Painter, Historian
Weisberg, Gabriel P Historian, Educator
Wiener, Phyllis Ames Painter
Wolfe, Ann (Ann Wolfe Graubard) Sculptor
Woodward, Steven P Sculptor
Youngquist, Jack Draftsman

Minnetonka

Lack, Richard Frederick Painter, Instructor

Moorhead

Laske, Lyle F Sculptor, Educator

Morris

Nellis, Jennifred Gene Sculpture

Northfield

Arneson, Wendell H Painter
Beall, Karen Friedmann Curator, Writer
Somers, Frederick D(uane) Painter

Park Rapids

Shilson, Wayne Stuart Painter, Illustrator

Red Wing

Biederman, Charles (Karel Joseph) Sculptor

Renier

Monahan, Gene Ritchie Painter, Printmaker

Rochester

Gagnon, Charles Eugene Sculptor, Consultant

Rushford

Curmano, Billy Conceptual Artist, Sculptor

St Cloud

Ellingson, William John Educator, Printmaker
Hendershot, J L Printmaker, Educator
Petheo, Bela Francis Printmaker, Painter

St Joseph

Becker, Johanna Lucille Educator, Historian

St Paul

Caponi, Anthony Sculptor, Educator
Celender, Don Conceptual Artist
Cummings, Mary T Administrator, Consultant
Czarniecki, M J, III Museum Director
Dixon, Sally Foy Director
Franco, Barbara Museologist
Garten, Cliff Sculptor
Hankey, Robert E Educator, Administrator
Kielkopf, James Robert Painter
Lasansky, Leonardo Draftsman, Printmaker
Michels, Eileen Manning Educator, Art Historian
Niemeyer, Arnold Matthew Collector, Patron
Olson, Bettye Johnson Painter, Instructor
Price, Michael Benjamin Sculptor, Educator
Rahja, Virginia Helga Painter, Administrator
Rudquist, Jerry Jacob Painter, Educator
Sears, Stanton Gray Painter, Sculptor
Steinworth, Skip (William Eugene Jr) Graphic Artist, Printmaker
Tselos, Dimitri Theodore Historian, Writer
Williams, Cynthia Lee Gallery Director, Curator

St Peter

Palmgren, Donald Gene Painter, Photographer

Silver Bay

Koestner, Don Painter

Stillwater

Berge, Dorothy Alphena Sculptor, Instructor

Taylors Falls

Oestreich, Jeffrey Ceramist

Wheaton

Wohlenhaus, Grace Forcier Painter

White Bear Lake

Larkin, (Dr) John E, Jr Collector, Patron

Winona

Murray, Floretta May Administrator, Painter

Zumbrota

Lee, Margaret F Painter

MISSISSIPPI

Belzoni

Halbrook, Rita Robertshaw Papermaker, Painter

Clarksdale

Bouldin, Marshall Jones, III Painter

Cleveland

Britt, Sam Glenn Educator, Painter
Koehler, Ronald Gene Sculptor
Norwood, Malcolm Mark Painter, Educator

Clinton

Gore, Samuel Marshall Painter, Sculptor

Columbus

Ambrose, Charles Edward Painter, Educator
Dice, Elizabeth Jane Craftsman, Educator
Frank, David Administrator, Educator
Nawrocki, Thomas Dennis Printmaker, Educator
Stringer, Mary Evelyn Educator, Art Historian
Summer, (Emily) Eugenia Painter

Gulfport

Thames, Emmitt Eugene Painter

Hattiesburg

Baggett, William Carter, Jr Painter, Educator
Bowman, Jeff Ray Educator, Administrator

Hernando

Yates, Marvin Clarence Painter, Instructor

Jackson

Cook, Stephen D Printmaker, Draftsman
Nyerges, Alexander Lee Museum Director, Historian
Sullivan, Linda Susan Museum Director
Whittington, Jon Hammon Educator, Painter
Wolfe, Mildred Nungester Painter, Designer

Laurel

Pennington, Mary Anne Museum Director, Lecturer

Meridian

Marshall, John Painter, Instructor
O'Neal, Roland Lenard Illustrator, Graphic Artist
Perry, Lallah Miles Painter, Educator

Mississippi State

Scucchi, Robie (Peter), Jr Educator, Painter

Moorhead

Kiker, Evelyn Coalson Painter, Instructor

Oxford

Allen, Jere Hardy Painter, Educator
Dale, Ron G Ceramist, Sculptor
Gross, Charles Merrill Painter, Assemblage Artist
Tettleton, Robert Lynn Painter, Educator
Turnbull, Lucy Museum Director, Educator

Pass Christian

Bannister, Pati (Patricia Brown Bannister) Painter, Sculptor

Summit

Dawson, Bess Phipps Painter, Gallery Director

Tupelo

Douglas, Tom Howard Painter, Sculptor
Francis, Jean Thickens Assemblage Artist, Painter
Francis, Madison Ke, Jr Sculptor, Printmaker

University

Gorove, Margaret Joan Administrator, Educator
Krause, Bonnie Jean Museum Director, Curator

MISSOURI

Arcadia

Jones, Howard William Painter, Sculptor

Ballwin

Addison, Byron Kent Painter, Educator

Bridgeton

Myers, Carole Ann Painter, Instructor

Canton

Detmers, William Raymond Printmaker, Educator

Cape Girardeau

Parker, James Varner Designer

Chesterfield

Luray, J Collage Artist, Painting

Columbia

Berneche, Jerry Douglas Educator, Painter
Berry, William Augustus Educator, Graphic Artist
Bussabarger, Robert Franklin Sculptor, Painter
Cameron, Brooke Bulovsky Educator, Printmaker
Crown, Keith Allen Painter
Danziger, Avery C Photographer
Goodrich, James W Administrator, Collector
Larson, Sidney Painter, Conservator
Lenhardt, Shirley M Painter
Montminy, Tracy Muralist, Painter
Moulton, Rosalind Kimball Photographer, Collage Artist
Peckham, Nicholas Architect, Educator
Rahill, Margaret Fish Curator, Critic
Revington Burdick, Betty Collector
Riley-Land, Sarah (Sarah Agnes Riley Land) Painter, Educator
Rugolo, Lawrence Printmaker, Educator
Stack, Frank Huntington Painter, Printmaker
Townsend, Vera B Educator, Historian

Crestwood

Kennon, Arthur Bruce Educator, Editor

Greenwood

Graham, Robert MacDonald, Jr Painter

Joplin

Christensen, Val Alan Printmaker, Gallery Director
Schwieger, C Robert Educator, Printmaker

Kansas City

Adams, Henry Curator, Educator
Bandel, Lennon Raymond Painter
Blazeje, Zbigniew (Ziggy Blazese) Sculptor, Painter
Cadieux, Michael Eugene Educator, Painter
Clancy, Patrick Video Artist
Crist, William Gary Visual Artist, Educator
Davis, Keith Frederic Curator, Historian
Eaton, Tom Cartoonist, Writer
Ehrlich, George Historian
Eickhorst, William Sigurd Educator, Art Dealer
Feiffer, Jules Cartoonist, Writer
Field, Lyman Administrator, Collector
Fleming, Stephen Painter, Ceramist
Fowle, Geraldine Elizabeth Historian
Goldman, Lester Painter
Lackey, Jane W Fiber Artist
Lawrence, Susan Art Dealer, Consultant
Lighton, Linda Sculptor, Instructor
McKenna, George LaVerne Curator
McKim, William Wind Printmaker, Painter
Marshall, James Duard Painter, Sculptor
Morgan, Myra J Art Dealer
Reinhart, Margaret Emily Painter
Sanchez, Beatrice Rivas Administrator, Printmaker
Scott, Deborah Emont Curator
Stack, Michael Painter, Sculptor
Townsend, Marvin J Cartoonist, Illustrator
Trudeau, Garry B Cartoonist
Van Harlingen, Jean (Ann) Environmental Artist, Painter
Walton, Donald William Writer, Lecturer
Widmer, Gwen Ellen Photographer, Educator
Wilson, Marc F Museum Director
Yaworski, Alex F(rancis) Painter
Younger, Dan Forrest Painter, Printmaker

Kirksville

Jorgenson, Dale Alfred Educator, Administrator

Lake Lotawana

Leedy, Jim (James A Leedy) Ceramist, Painter

Lamar

Bowling, Gary Robert Painter

Manchester

Brunell, Richard Howard Educator, Designer

Maryville

Hageman, Charles Lee Educator, Jeweler
Sunkel, Robert C Historian, Administrator

Olivette

Schultz, Saunders Sculptor

Osage Beach

Orr, Joseph Charles Painter

Rogerville

Elkins, (E) Lane Educator, Ceramist

St Charles

Eckert, William Dean Painter, Historian
Moerschel, Chiara Painter

St Louis

Anderson, Kenneth Edmund Sculptor, Educator
Bohan, Ruth L Educator, Historian
Burke, James Donald Museum Director, Administrator
Carter, Carol A Painter
Deal, Joe Photographer, Educator
Duhme, H Richard, Jr Sculptor, Educator
Engelhardt, Thomas Alexander Editorial Cartoonist
Geis, Milton Arthur Painter, Designer
Greenberg, Ronald K Dealer, Collector
Hicks, Leon Nathaniel Printmaker
Kagan, Andrew Aaron Historian, Critic
Ketner, Joseph Dale Museum Director, Curator
Kochheiser, Thomas H Curator, Educator
Kodner, Martin Art Dealer, Consultant
Kohn, William Roth Painter, Educator
Kornblum, Myrtle Painter, Printmaker
Krukowski, Lucian Painter, Educator
Kultermann, Udo Art Historian, Architect
McGarrell, James Painter, Educator
Magel, Catherine Anne Ceramist, Painter
Newman-Rice, Nancy Painter, Critic
Osver, Arthur Painter
Patton, Tom Photographer, Curator
Pharis, Mark Ceramist
Plotkin, Lynn Art Dealer, Curator
Quinn, William Painter
Rosen, Joan Fischman Painter
Ruth, Sheila Painter
Sauer, Jane Gottlieb Craftsman, Sculptor
Schactman, Barry Robert Painter, Educator
Schweiss, Ruth Keller Sculptor, Designer
Severson, William Conrad Sculptor
Shapiro, Michael Edward Museum Director
Sigala, Stephanie Childs Librarian, Educator
Singer, Nancy Barkhouse Dealer
Smith, Elliot Steven Dealer, Historian
Smith, James Michael Painter, Assemblage Artist
Smith, Robert Charles Designer, Educator
Teczar, Steven W Painter, Educator
Trova, Ernest Tino Sculptor, Painter
Winfield, Rodney M Painter, Designer
Zonia, Dhimitri Painter, Printmaker

St Louisc

Seppa, Heikki Markus Goldsmith, Educator

Sedalia

Freed, Douglass Lynn Painter, Educator

Sikeston

Robbins, Joan Nash Painter, Collage Artist

Springfield

Adams, Jay H Jeweler, Medalist
Armstrong, Bill Howard Painter, Educator
Berger, Jerry Allen Director, Curator
Ettinger, Susi Steinitz Painter, Lecturer
Kieferndorf, Frederick George Painter, Educator
Murphy, Dudley C Educator, Graphic Designer
Simmons, John Herbert Educator, Historian
Thielen, Greg Glen Curator
Thompson, Wade S Painter, Educator
Warren, Jacqueline Louise Painter, Educator

Webster Groves

Boccia, Edward Eugene Painter

Weston

Williams, Melissa Art Dealer

MONTANA

Bigfork

Copenhaver-Fellows, Deborah (Deborah Lynne Fellows) Sculptor, Painter
Fellows, Fred Painter, Sculptor

Big Sky

Doll, Linda A Painter, Instructor

Billings

Butterfield, Deborah Kay Sculptor
Forbes, Donna Marie Museum Director
Gibson, Edward G Photographer
Haughey, James M Painter, Calligrapher
Miles, Sheila Lee Painter, Curator
Morrison, Robert Clifton Printmaker, Calligrapher
Pomeroy, Lyndon Fayne Sculptor
Selsor, Marcia Lorraine Sculptor, Ceramist
Steele, Benjamin Charles Painter, Educator
Whitson, Photographer, Educator

Bozeman

Bashor, John W Educator, Painter
Bronson, Clark Everice Sculptor
Dreyer, Clarice A Sculptor
Helzer, Richard Brian Metalsmith, Sculptor
Volkersz, Willem Sculptor, Educator

Browning

Scriver, (Bob) Robert Macfie Sculptor, Curator

Cascade
Halko, Joe Sculptor, Painter

Dillon
Anacker, John William Gallery Director, Painter
Corr, James D Painter, College Educator

Helena
Cleary, Shirley (Shirley Cleary Cooper) Painter
Metz, Matthew J Potter

Kalispell
Lynde, Stan Cartoonist, Illustrator
Shaner, (George) David Ceramist, Craftsman

Laurel
Zentz, Patrick J Sculptor

Missoula
Rippon, Thomas Micheal Sculptor, Collector

West Yellowstone
Carter, Gary Painter, Sculptor

NEBRASKA

Auburn
Biggerstaff, Myra Painter, Designer

Avola
Kunc, Karen Printmaker, Educator

Culbertson
Dernovich, Donald Frederick Painter, Educator

Grand Island
Holoun, Harold Dean Painter, Sculptor

Kearney
Peterson, Larry D Painter, Educator

Lincoln
Christensen, Neil C Painter
Collins, Howard F Historian
Day, Gary Lewis Printmaker, Painter
Eisentrager, James A Painter
Geske, Norman Albert Museum Director, Educator
Holt, Louise Gallery Director
Horvay, Martha J Painter
Howard, Dan F Painter, Educator
Jacobshagen, N Keith, II Painter, Photographer
Lux, Gladys M Painter, Educator
Nelson, Jon Allen Curator, Historian
Neubert, George Walter Sculptor, Curator
Read, Dave (David Dolloff) Photographer, Educator
Ross, Douglas Allan Sculptor, Instructor
Routon, David F Painter, Draftsman
Rowan, (C) Patrick Painter, Educator
Ruffo, Joseph Martin Printmaker, Administrator
Wallace, Elizabeth S Administrator, Sculptor
Waterhouse, Russell Rutledge Painter, Illustrator
Worth, Peter John Sculptor, Historian

Omaha
Bartek, Tom Painter
Beal, Graham William John Director, Curator
Bradshaw, Lawrence James Educator, Painter
Buchanan, Sidney Arnold Educator, Sculptor
Doll, Donald Arthur Educator, Photographer
Duncan, Harry Alvin Printer, Designer
Ferguson, Larry Scott Photographer, Curator
Hill, Peter Painter, Educator
Hunt, David Curtis Museum Director, Curator
Lubbers, Leland Eugene Sculptor, Educator
Majeski, Thomas H Printmaker, Educator
Spencer, Jeffrey Paul Painter
Wise, Suzanne Tanderup Administrator, Historian

Whitney
Brown, Reynold Painter, Illustrator

NEVADA

Boulder City
Burk, A Darlene Dealer, Collector

Gardnerville
Lawrence, James A Painter, Photographer

Henderson
La Porta, Elayne B Painter, Printmaker

Las Vegas
Holder, Tom Painter
Lesnick, Stephen William Painter, Instructor
McCollum, Mike L Painter, Printmaker
Misch, Allene K Painter
Rozzi (James A) Painter, Sculptor
Tracy, Robert H Educator, Curator

Reno
Ball, Lyle V Painter, Illustrator
Frueh, Joanna Critic, Educator
Goin, Peter Photographer, Video Artist
Growdon, Marcia Cohn Administrator, Historian
Jacobson, Yolande (Mrs J Craig Sheppard) Sculptor
Morrison, Robert J Sculptor
Spencer, Howard DaLee Curator, Printmaker
Waddell, Theodore Painter

NEW HAMPSHIRE

Atkinson
Collins, Larry Richard Painter, Educator

Bennington
Willis, Barbara Florence Painter
Willis, Sidney F Painter

Campton
Waters, Herbert (Ogden) Printmaker, Educator

Center Conway
Jordan, Robert Painter, Educator

Concord
Chandler, John William Painter, Educator
Scott, Martha F Printmaker, Sculptor
Yanoff, Arthur (Samuel) Painter

Dover
Abeles, Sigmund Printmaker, Painter

Dublin
Tuckerman, Jane Bayard Photographer, Educator

Durham
Hatch, John W Painter, Educator
McConnell, Michael Patrick Sculptor
Wright, Vicki C Museum Director, Museologist
Zabarsky, Melvin Joel Painter, Educator

Francestown
Milton, Peter Winslow Printmaker

Hampton
Orze, Joseph John Administrator, Sculptor

Hancock
Pollaro, Paul Painter

Hanover
Boghosian, Varujan Sculptor, Educator
Brooks, H(arold) Allen Historian, Lecturer
Hamlin, Louise Painter, Printmaker
Jacobus, John M Educator, Historian

Holderness
Newsom, Barbara Ylvisaker Administrator, Writer

Jackson
Beal, Mack Sculptor

Jaffrey
Hillsmith, Fannie Painter, Assemblage Artist

Kensington
Dailey, Dan (Daniel Owen) Sculptor, Educator
Oakes, William Larry Painter, Sculptor

Lebanon
Welch, Charles D Painter, Sculptor

Manchester
Doty, Robert McIntyre Administrator
Eshoo, Robert Painter
Hoffman, Marilyn Friedman Director
Rosenthal, Donald A Museum Director, Historian

Marlborough
Harris, Paul Stewart Curator, Museum Director
Whitney, Richard Wheeler Painter

Mount Vernon
Robinson, Gail E Painter

Nashua
Bloom, Hyman Painter
Parker, Will (William Crawford) Graphic Artist, Painter

New London
Bott, John Painter, Critic
De Paola, Tomie Designer, Illustrator
Hoyt, Frances Weston Painter

North Hampton
Dunkle, Joan Osborn Painter, Printmaker
Palmer, Lucie Mackay Painter, Lecturer

Northwood
Cenci, Silvana Sculptor

Portsmouth
Balderacchi, Arthur Eugene Sculptor, Administrator

Raymond

Beardsley, Barbara H Conservator

Rindge

Sandback, Frederick Lane Sculptor

Rye

Labrie, Christy Stained Glass Artist

Seabrook

Ahl, Henry C Painter, Writer

Stratham

Fein, B(arbara) R Educator, Painter

Warner

Nemec, Nancy Printmaker, Painter

Westmoreland

Isaak, Nicholas, Jr Painter, Conservator

NEW JERSEY

Alpine

Bull, Fran Painter, Educator
Koopalethes, Olivia (Olivia Koopalethes Alberts) Painter, Printmaker

Asbury

Anderson, John S Sculptor

Asbury Park

Cleary, Fritz Sculptor, Critic

Atlantic City

Robbins, Hulda D Painter, Printmaker

Atlantic Highlands

Voorhees, Donald Edward Painter, Printmaker

Barnegat Light

Rothman, Sidney Gallery Director, Critic

Basking Ridge

Denman, Patricia Price (Pat Denman) Painter
Krienke, Douglas Elliot Art Dealer, Consultant
Peterson, John Douglas Administrator, Museum Director

Bayonne

Gary, Jan (Mrs William D Gorman) Painter, Printmaker
Gorman, William D Painter, Graphic Artist

Beach Haven

Martell, Barbara Bentley Painter

Bedminster

Machiorlete, Patricia Anne Painter

Belle Mead

Olin, Ferris Historian, Administrator

Berkeley Heights

Kluver, Billy (Johan Wilhem) Administrator
Lorentz, Pauline Painter, Instructor

Bernardsville

Coheleach, Guy Joseph Painter, Sculptor
Spofford, Sally(Sarah H Spofford) Painter

Blairstown

Ayers, Carol Lee Painter, Gallery Director
Bean, Bennett Ceramist
Wilson, Ben Painter, Lecturer

Bloomfield

Anderson, Robert Raymond Painter, Consultant

Boonton

Barnwell, John L Painter
Hanna, Annette Adrian Painter, Instructor

Bordentown

Barker, Al C Painter, Printmaker

Brick

Malpass, Michael Allen Sculptor

Bridgewater

Glesmann, Sylvia Maria Painter

Brielle

Punia, Constance Edith Painter

Caldwell

Bartle, Dorothy Budd Curator, Lecturer
Lewis, Nat Brush Painter, Instructor
Mueller, (Sister) M Gerardine OP Calligrapher, Stained Glass Artist

Califon

Burger, W Carl Educator, Painter
Grainger, Nessa Posner Painter, Collage Artist
Rosen, Carol M Sculptor, Printmaker
Sandol, Maynard Painter

Camden

Moore, Olga Painter
Steel, Virginia Oberlin Gallery Director, Curator

Cape May

Turner, A Richard Historian, Educator

Cedar Grove

Lenker, Marlene N Painter, Collage Artist
Singer, Esther Forman Painter, Critic

Chatham

McGeehan, Betty Sculptor

Cherry Hill

Appelson, Herbert J Educator, Printmaker
Conrad, George Educator, Printmaker
Sharrow, Sheba Painter, Educator

Chester

Duerwald, Carol Painter, Illustrator

Cinnaminson

Kraus, (Ersilia) Zili Sculptor, Jeweler

Clarksburg

Arias-Misson, Alain Visual Poet, Graphic Artist
Arias-Misson, Nela Painter

Cliffside Park

LaMarca, Howard J Designer, Educator
Termini, Christine Painter, Sculptor
Weiss, Jerome Nathan Painter

Clifton

Dinc, Alev Necile Painter, Designer
Kanter, Lorna J Painter, Printmaker
Kostecka, Gloria Painter

Closter

Jovine, Marcel Medalist, Designer
Zakin, Mikhail Sculptor, Educator

Collingswood

Folkus, Dan (Daniel Alan Fredrickson) Designer, Illustrator

Cranbury

Lee-Smith, Hughie Painter, Instructor

Cranford

Dawley, Joseph William Painter
Gatto, Rose Marie Painter

Cresskill

Baker, Dina Gustin Painter
Mayen, Paul Designer
Radoczy, Albert Painter
Smyth, Craig Hugh Administrator, Historian

Demarest

Racz, Andre Painter, Printmaker

Dover

Kearns, James Joseph Sculptor, Painter

East Brunswick

Bender, May Painter
Bloom, Donald S Painter, Cartoonist
Bradshaw, Robert George Painter, Educator
Smith, Beryl K Librarian, Curator

Eatontown

Preede, Nydia Painter, Illustrator

Edgewater

Case, Elizabeth Painter, Writer

Edison

Phillips, Robert J Filmmaker, Photographer
Waterhouse, Charles Howard Illustrator, Painter

Egg Harbor

Ahlsted, David R Painter, Educator

Elizabeth

Cohan, Zara R Gallery Director, Educator

Elmwood Park

Barberis, Dorothy Watkeys Painter

Englewood

Anuszkiewicz, Richard Joseph Painter
Bremer, Marlene S Painter, Sculptor
Casarella, Edmond Sculptor, Printmaker
Dallas, Dorothy B Painter, Printmaker
Grom, Bogdan Sculptor, Painter
Grushkin, Philip Designer, Calligrapher
Nikkal, Nancy Egol Collage Artist

Erma Park

Dougherty, Ray (Raymond Edward) Painter, Instructor

Fairfield

De Smet, Lorraine Painter

Fairlawn

Hurewitz, Florence K Painter, Educator

Flanders

Komarin, Gary Painter

Flemington

Waksberg, Naomi Painter

Franklin Lakes

Baker, Cornelia Draves Printmaker, Painter
Janjigian, Lucy Elizabeth Painter, Muralist
Turconi, Sue (Susan) Kinder Graphic Artist, Photographer

Freehold

Graupe-Pillard, Grace Painter, Instructor

Frenchtown

Klabunde, Charles Spencer Printmaker, Painter

Ft Lee

Morenon, Elise Painter, Instructor

Glassboro

Wasserman, Burton Painter, Printmaker

Glen Ridge

Kato, Kay Cartoonist
Konopka, Joseph Painter

Hackensack

Ortlip, Paul Daniel Painter
Stone, Fred J Art Dealer, Consultant
Sznajderman, Marius S Printmaker, Painter

Haddonfield

Byrd, Robert John Illustrator, Instructor

Hasbrouck Heights

Perham, Roy Gates Painter

Haworth

Bernstein, Saralinda Art Dealer, Historian

Hazlet

Temes, Mort (Mortimer Robert Temes) Cartoonist, Designer

Highland Lakes

Ross, Joan M Painter, Instructor

Highland Park

Glashausser, Suellen Sculptor
Puniello, Françoise Sara Librarian

Hoboken

Floeter, Kent Sculptor
Homitzky, Peter Painter
Rose, Roslyn Collage Artist, Painter

Irvington

Nagengast, William Joseph Painter, Designer

Iselin

Tice, George Andrew Photographer, Author

Island Heights

English, John Arbogast Painter

Jersey City

Barrell, Bill Painter, Collector
Beauchamp, George Collage Artist, Painter
Cummings, David William Painter
Gluck, Heidi Painter, Educator
Harris, Dorothy D Educator, Painter
Harrison, Tony Painter, Educator
Jones, Ben Painter, Sculptor
Magnan, Oscar Gustav Painter, Sculptor
Mazzone, Domenico Sculptor, Painter
Mount, Marshall Ward Historian, Administrator
Mount, Ward Painter, Sculptor
Palaia, Franc (Dominic) Painter, Photographer
Rosenberg, Herb Sculptor, Designer
Van Alstine, John Richard Sculptor
Yost, Erma Martin Assemblage Artist, Instructor
Yost, Leon C Photographer

Keasbey

Sosnowitz, Henry Abram Collector, Patron

Kendall Park

Sway, Albert Painter, Etcher

Lakewood

Burgues, Irving Carl Sculptor, Lecturer
Clinedinst, Katherine Parsons Painter, Lecturer

Lambertville

Goodyear, John L Sculptor, Painter
Marsh, Anne Steele Painter, Printmaker

Lavallette

Stasik, Andrew J Printmaker, Curator

Leonia

Birmelin, A Robert Painter, Draftsman
Cellini, Joseph Illustrator
Colman, Virginia O'Connell Sculptor, Graphic Artist
Dickerson, Daniel Jay Painter, Educator

Lincoln Harbor-Weehawken

Fuhrman, Esther Sculptor, Jeweler

Linwood

Myers, Legh Sculptor

Little Silver

Clark, Roberta Carter Painter, Writer

Livingston

Price, Diane Miller Papermaker

Long Branch

Woolwich, Madlyn-Ann C Painter, Instructor

Madison

Doren, Henry J T Educator, Painter
Galles, Arie Alexander Painter, Educator
Henry, Sara Corrington Historian, Critic

Magnolia

Killeen, Melissa Helen Dealer, Gallery Director

Manalapan

San Soucie, Patricia Molm Painter, Instructor

Maple Shade

Bernstein, Gerald Painter, Restorer

Maplewood

Dee, Leo Joseph Painter, Graphic Artist
Gialanella, Donald G Video Artist, Sculptor
Hutchins, Robin Art Dealer, Gallery Director
Joffe, Bertha Designer
Nardone, Vincent Joseph Painter, Collector
Noble, Joseph Veach Museum Director, Museologist
Price, Joan Webster Environmental Artist, Sculptor
Rafferty, Joanne Miller Painter

Mendham

Hobbie, Lucille Painter, Printmaker

Metuchen

Stoianovich, Marcelle Painter, Printmaker

Middletown

Wilson, June Painter, Educator

Milford

Carter, Clarence Holbrook Painter, Designer

Millburn

Nussbaum, Sheila Ford Art Dealer, Consultant

Montclair

Beerman, Miriam (Miriam Beerman-Jaffe) Painter
Culbreth, Carl R Sculptor
Harris, Ellen Schwartz Administrator, Museologist
Haynes, R (Richard Thomas) Painter, Illustrator
McQuillan, Frances Painter, Instructor
Miller, Donald Lloyd Painter, Muralist
Pare, Richard Photographer, Curator
Roth, Jack (Rodney) Painter

Morris Plains

Ferris, (Carlisle) Keith Illustrator, Painter

Mountainside

Devlin, Harry Painter, Cartoonist
Devlin, Wende Painter

Murray Hill

Rivo, Shirley Winthrope Painter

Neptune

Ventura, Anthony Painter

Newark

Auth, Susan Handler Curator, Educator
Dane, William Jerald Librarian
Grauer, Gladys Painter
Maldjian, Vartavar B Painter, Weaver
Miller, Samuel Clifford Museum Director
Reynolds, Valrae Curator
Seeman, Helene Zucker Writer, Curator
Watkins, Eileen Frances Critic

New Brunswick

Cate, Phillip Dennis Historian, Director
Eidelberg, Martin Historian
McHam, Sarah Blake Wilk Historian, Educator
Morrissey, Leo Painter, Sculptor
Murata, Hiroshi Painter, Printmaker
Naar, Harry I Painter, Educator
Ortiz, Raphael Montanez Conceptual Artist, Educator
Rosler, Martha (Rose) Video Artist, Critic
Rusak, Halina R Librarian, Painter
Segal, George Sculptor
Stroud, Peter Anthony Painter, Educator

New Milford

Leibowitz, Bernice Painter, Educator

New Providence
Hannay, Janneka (Jann) Painter

Newton
Gagnier, Bruce Painter, Sculptor
Grodsky, Sheila Taylor Painter, Collage Artist

New Vernon
Bross, Albert L, Jr Painter

North Bergen
Valencia, Cesar Painter, Muralist

North Brunswick
Continos, Anna Painter, Designer

North Haledon
Heusser, Eleanore Elizabeth (Eleanore Heusser Ferholt) Painter

North Plainfield
Delgyer, Leslie Environmental Artist, Painter
Haller, Emanuel Painter, Printmaker
Stroppel, Betty MacNair Painter, Instructor

Nutley
Burns, G Joan Librarian
Carlin, James Painter

Oakland
Rodman, Selden Writer, Critic

Oceanport
Carter, Katharine Tipton Painter, Educator

Oceanville
Koenig, Robert J Museum Director

Oradell
Schaefer, Gail Sculptor
Struck, Norma Johansen Painter

Paramus
Jacobs, Helen Nichols Painter
Menthe, Melissa Librarian, Photographer
Messer, David James Director, Museum Director

Park Ridge
De Pol, John Wood Engraver, Designer

Paterson
Gaydos, Tim (Timothy John) Painter

Pemberton
Witkin, Isaac Sculptor

Perth Amboy
Hari, Kenneth Painter, Printmaker

Phillipsburg
Campanelli, Dan Painter
Campanelli, Pauline Eble Painter

Pittman
Ottiano, John William Jeweler, Sculptor

Plainfield
Helfond, Riva Painter, Printmaker

Princeton
Berman, Greta W Historian, Curator
Boretz, Naomi Painter, Educator
Bunnell, Peter Curtis Educator, Curator
Elliott, Anne Sculptor, Painter
Fitch, Steve (Steven Ralph) Photographer, Instructor
George, Thomas Painter, Draftsman
Graves, Michael Architect, Educator
Heckscher, William Sebastian Historian, Painter
Idaherma (Idaherma Williams) Printmaker, Painter
Johnson, Barbara Piasecka Collector
Judson-Rhodes, Pamela Historian
Lavin, Irving Historian
Lavin, Marilyn Aronberg Educator, Historian
Marrow, James Henry Historian, Educator
Martin, John Rupert Historian, Lecturer
Ring, Edward A Collector
Rosenbaum, Allen Museum Director
Savage, Naomi Photographer
Schmidt, Mary Morris Librarian
Shimizu, Yoshiaki Historian, Curator
Thompson, Dorothy Burr Educator, Lecturer
Weitzmann, Kurt Educator, Historian
Wilmerding, John Educator, Historian

Princeton Junction
Greenwald, Alice (Alice Marian Greenwald-Ward) Lecturer

Ramsey
Hertzberg, Rose Painter, Collage Artist

Randolph
Sarsony, Robert Painter, Printmaker

Red Bank
Bleach, Bruce R Printmaker, Painter
McIlvain, Douglas Lee Educator, Sculptor
McIlvain, Frances H Painter, Gallery Director

Ridgewood
Lane, Marion Jean Arrons Painter, Instructor

Ringwood
Barbour, Arthur J Painter, Writer
Osborne, John Phillip Painter, Instructor

Rockleigh
Lack, Stephen Painter, Filmmaker

Rocky Hill
Konrad, Adolf Ferdinand Painter

Roosevelt
Landau, Jacob Painter, Printmaker

Rumson
Cocker, Barbara Joan Painter, Gallery Director

Rutherford
Petrie, Ferdinand Ralph Painter, Illustrator

Saddle Brook
Kaye, Mildred Elaine Printmaker, Instructor

Short Hills
Broder, Patricia Janis Historian, Writer

Skillman
Hunter, Sam Historian

Somerset
Miley, Chuck (Charles) E Painter, Printmaker
Spector, Jack J Historian, Educator
Ten Broeke, Jan Painter
Zuccarelli, Frank Edward Painter, Instructor

South Orange
Ganek, Dorothy Skeados Painter, Silversmith
Liao (Shiou-Ping Liao) Painter, Printmaker
Lipton, Barbara B Museum Director, Curator
Messina, Joseph R Painter
Targan, Judy Printmaker, Painter
Walker, Larry Painter, Educator

South River
Batko, Blaise Joseph Sculptor

Spotswood
Espenschied, Clyde Painter

Springfield
D'Alessio, Natalie Marino Painter
Frank, Helen (Goodzeit) Painter, Printmaker
Koldorf, Irene Janet Sculptor

Stockton
Farnham, Alexander Painter, Writer
Mahon, Robert Photographer
Schoenherr, John (Carl) Painter, Illustrator
Taylor, Rosemary Ceramist, Sculptor
Wiggins, Guy A Painter, Lecturer

Summit
Bolge, George S Museum Director
Butera, Virginia Fabbri Curator, Historian
Rousseau, Irene Victoria Sculptor, Writer

Teaneck
Barry, Robert Thomas Conceptual Artist
Brummel, Marilyn Reeder Collage Artist, Printmaker
Glickman, Arthur Sculptor
Indick, Janet Sculptor
Karp, Richard Gordon Painter, Lecturer
Rieber, Ruth B Printmaker, Painter
Schrero, Ruth Lieberman Sculptor, Draftsman
Stukey, Virginia Painter, Assemblage Artist
Varriale, Wanda (Stella) Painter, Instructor
Weill, Erna Sculptor, Instructor

Tenafly
Adelman, Bunny Sculptor
Price, George Cartoonist
Thompson, Lynn P Painter, Photographer

Tinton Falls
St Tamara Painter, Printmaker

Trenton
Brooks, Wendell T Printmaker, Educator
Buki, Zoltan Curator, Administrator
Chavooshian, Marge Painter
Cummins, Karen Gasco Administrator, Museologist
Fowler, Eric Nicholas Illustrator, Painter
Goldstein, Howard Painter, Educator
Hein, John Craftsman
Lehman, Mark Ammon Educator, Sculptor
McVicker, Charles Taggart Illustrator, Instructor
Rivera, Frank Painter
Roebling, Mary G Collector, Patron
Sakson, Robert (G) Painter
Sloshberg, Leah Phyfer Museum Director

Twin Rivers

Martin, Stefan Printmaker, Collage Artist

Union

Bailin, Hella Painter
Wallach, Alan Critic, Historian

Union City

Erbe, Gary Thomas Painter

Upper Montclair

Block, Virginia Schaffer Painter, Collage Artist
Coes, Kent Day Painter, Designer
De Leeuw, Leon Painter, Sculptor
Healy, Deborah Ann Illustrator, Educator
Kawecki, Jean Mary Sculptor, Gallery Director
Krushenick, John Painter, Printmaker
Lay, Patricia Anne Sculptor
Schnitzer, Klaus A Photographer
Westfall, Carol D Sculptor, Educator

Ventnor

Frudakis, Evangelos William Sculptor, Instructor
Frudakis, Gerd Hesness Sculptor

Verona

Ayaso, Manuel Painter, Sculptor

Villas

Lynch, Gerald Sculptor

Vincentown

Forrest, Christopher Patrick Printmaker, Painter

Wallington

Lynds, Clyde Sculptor, Painter

Warwick

Bell, Temma Painter

Watchung

Schwartz, Lillian (Feldman) Film, Video, Author

Wayne

De Nike, Michael Nicholas Sculptor, Writer
Einreinhofer, Nancy Anne Curator, Museum Director
Lunde, Karl Roy Historian, Writer
Paris, Lucille M Painter, Printmaker
Reimann, Arline Printmaker, Painter

Weehawken

Samburg, Grace (Blanche) Painter, Lithographer

Westfield

Becker, Natalie Rose Painter, Instructor
Devine, William Charles Dealer, Collector

West Orange

Krieger, Ruth M Painter, Printmaker
Schonwalter, Jean Frances Painter, Sculptor
Schreiber, Eileen Sher Painter, Printmaker

West Patterson

Yanow, Rhoda Mae Painter, Illustrator

Wharton

Bermingham, John C Painter

Williamstown

Murashima, Kumiko Educator, Tapestry Artist
Phillips, James M Museum Director, Collector

Woodlynne

Hoffman, William McKinley, Jr Painter, Educator

Wyckoff

Mansfield, Robert Adams Sculptor, Educator

NEW MEXICO

Alamogordo

Stevens, William Ansel, Sr Painter, Cartoonist

Albuquerque

Abrams, Jane Eldora Painter
Adams, Clinton Painter, Historian
Anderson, Sally J Painter, Printmaker
Antreasian, Garo Zareh Painter, Educator
Barrow, Thomas Francis Photographer, Educator
Brody, Jacob Jerome Educator, Museologist
Bryant, Edward Albert Writer, Consultant
Chapian, Grieg Hovsep Painter, Conservator
Cook, Michael David Painter, Video Artist
Feinberg, Elen Painter, Educator
Gandert, Miguel Adrian Photographer, Lecturer
Girard, Bill Sculptor
Gross, Earl Painter, Lecturer
Hahn, Betty Photographer, Educator
Hammersley, Frederick Painter
Harrison, Jimmie Jeweler, Craftsman
Haut, Claire (Joan) Painter, Graphic Artist
Hobbs, Robert Dean Printmaker, Consultant
Hurley, Wilson Painter
Jaffe, Ira S Educator, Critic
Jones, Norma L Painter
Joost-Gaugier, Christiane L Administrator, Historian
Karp, Aaron S Painter
Kerr, James Wilfrid Painter, Conceptual Artist
Landis, Ellen Jamie Curator, Historian
Long, Frank Weathers Painter
McCulloch, Frank E Painter, Printmaker
McIlroy, Carol J Painter, Dealer
Moyers, William Painter, Sculptor
Nelson, Mary Carroll Writer, Painter
Noggle, Anne Photographer, Educator
Parrish, Jean Painter
Peterson, Gwen Entz Printmaker
Pruneda, Max Sculptor
Ramirez, Joel Tito Painter, Calligrapher
Rippel, M (Morris Conrad) Painter
Rise, John Ernest Painter
Robb, Peggy Hight Painter
Sabo, Betty Jean Painter, Sculptor
Saville, Ken Sculptor, Craftsman
Slaymaker, Martha Painter, Sculptor
Sowers, Miriam R Painter, Art Dealer
Steider, Doris (Mrs C B McCampbell) Painter, Sculptor
Stouffer, Daniel Henry, Jr Painter
Sussman, Arthur Painter
Thomason, Tom William Jeweler, Painter
Thompson, Tamara Assemblage Artist, Painter
Tinkler, Barrie Keith Painter
Townsend, (Alvin) Neal Ceramist, Educator
Truby, Betsy Kirby Painter, Illustrator
Vega, Edward Sculptor, Educator
Volkin, Hilda Appel Sculptor
Walters, Billie Ceramist
Warder, William Painter, Writer
Weber, Jan Painter
Wellborn, J(eanette) D(arleen) Painter
Westlund, Harry E Publisher, Dealer
Wilmeth, Ernest, II Painter, Potter
Witkin, Joel-Peter Photographer
Young, Nancy J(eanne) Sculptor

Arroyo Hondo

Davis, Ronald Painter, Printmaker

Belen

Lee, Robert M Painter, Sculptor

Carlos Rey

Houser, Allan C Sculptor, Painter

Carlsbad

Johanningmeier, Robert Alan Painter, Writer

Carson

Ross, Jaime Graphic Artist, Painter

Chimayo

Foth, Joan B Painter, Educator

Corrales

Barber, Cynthia Sculptor, Printmaker
Barry, Steve Sculptor
Bass, David Loren Painter
Leis, Marietta Patricia Painter
Roberts, Holly L Painter, Photographer
Smith, Jaune Quick-to-See Painter
Townsend, Storm D Sculptor, Instructor

Coyote

Johnson, Douglas Walter Painter, Printmaker

Dona Ana

Smith, Jo-an Designer, Craftsman

El Rito

Chappell, Walter (Landon) Photographer, Curator

Espanola

Naranjo, Michael Alfred Sculptor

Farmington

Farm, Gerald E Painter, Sculptor

Gallup

Cattaneo, (Jacquelyn A) Kammerer Painter, Instructor
Guadagnoli, Nello T Dealer
Ha-So-De (Narciso Abeyta) Illustrator, Painter

Glenwood

Howard, Cecil Ray Painter, Sculptor

Glorieta

Greeley, Charles Matthew Painter, Sculptor

Grants

Lowney, Bruce Stark Painter, Printmaker

Hillsboro

Yeh, Carol Printmaker

Hobbs

Garey, Pat Draftsman, Painter

Hondo

Jimenez, Luis Alfonso, Jr Sculptor

Jemez Springs

Sweet, Roger Sculptor, Ceramist

La Luz

Kellar, Martha Robbins Painter, Instructor

Lamy

Martin, Agnes Bernice Painter

Las Cruces

Breithaupt, Erwin M Painter, Historian
Chilton, Fred Painter
DuBois, Douglas J Photographer
Fidler, Spencer D Printmaker
Guzevich-Sommers, Kreszenz (Cynthia) Painter, Instructor
Mobley, Karen R Painter, Administrator
Moffitt, John Francis Historian, Painter
Ocepek, Lou (Louis David) Printmaker, Painter
Sherman, Lenore (Walton) Painter, Writer

Lincoln

Robertson, Ted Walter Painter, Instructor

Los Lunas

Snidow, Gordon E Painter, Sculptor

Placitas

Forrest, James Taylor Museum Director, Educator
Krestensen, Ann M Ceramist, Painter

Portales

Anderson, James P Sculptor, Educator
Hamlett, Dale Edward Educator, Painter

Ranchos De Taos

Scott, Jonathan Painter

Roswell

Du Jardin, Gussie Painter, Printmaker
Ebie, William Dennis Administrator, Painter
Hallenbeck, Pomona Juanita Painter, Printmaker
Kawa, Florence Kathryn Painter
Peterson, Dorothy (Hawkins) Painter, Educator
Schooley, Elmer Wayne Painter, Educator
Vogel, Joseph Painter, Printmaker
Wiggins, Bill Painter
Wyeth, Henriette (Mrs Peter Hurd) Painter
Zelt, Martha Printmaker

Ruidoso Downs

Knapp, Tom Sculptor, Painter

San Christobal

Gersh, Bill Painter, Sculptor

San Lorenzo

Renner, Eric Painter, Photographer

San Patricio

Meigs, John Liggett Painter, Collector
Rogers, Peter Wilfrid Painter

Santa Fe

Allen, Edda Lynne Painter, Art Dealer
Anderson, David Paul Sculptor
Bacigalupa, Andrea Sculptor, Painter
Bendell, Marilyn Painter, Instructor
Bennett, Philomene Dosek Painter, Ceramist
Bentley, Claude Painter, Muralist
Berg, Tom Painter
Boylan, John Lewis Painter, Printmaker
Bradbury, Ellen A Administrator, Educator
Bradley, David P(aul) Painter, Sculptor
Brycelea, Clifford Painter, Printmaker
Burgess, Joseph James, Jr Painter, Educator
Caponigro, Paul Photographer
Carlson, George Arthur Sculptor, Painter
Chicago, Judy Painter, Sculptor
Clift, William Brooks Photographer
Coe, Ralph Tracy Museum Director, Curator
Conley, Zeb Bristol, Jr Collector, Gallery Director
Constable, Rosalind Collector, Critic
Dailey, Chuck (Charles Andrew) Museologist, Painter
DeBruycker, Dirk H A Painter
Dillingham, Rick (James Richard), II Ceramist, Dealer
Dodds, Robert J, III Collector, Museum Director
Dunn, Cal Painter, Filmmaker
Ettenberg, Franklin Joseph Painter, Printmaker
Fangor, Voy Painter
Fincher, John H Painter, Assemblage Artist
Ford, Harry Xavier Educator, Administrator
Gordon, John S Sculptor, Educator
Hackett, Dwight Vernon Publisher, Director
Hamilton, Juan B Sculptor
Handell, Albert George Painter
Haozous, Bob Sculptor
Harroun, Dorothy Sumner Painter, Instructor
Hartford, Jane Davis Textile Artist, Craftsman
Hatch, John Davis Consultant, Historian
Henrickson, Paul Robert Painter, Writer
Hensley, Jackson Morey Painter
Hill, Richard Wayne Painter, Photographer
Hotvedt, Kris J Printmaker, Painter
Humphrey, Donald Gray Curator
Igo, Peter Alexander Printmaker, Painter
Janis, Eugenia Parry Writer, Historian
Jean, Beverly (Beverly Jean Strong) Painter, Art Dealer
Johnson, Harvey William Painter
Johnson, James Ralph Painter, Writer
Kelley, Ramon Painter
Kessler, Alan Painter, Sculptor
Kramer, James Painter
La Lumia, Frank Painter
Lefranc, Margaret (Margaret Lefranc Schoonover) Painter, Illustrator
Leon, Ralph Bernard Painter, Illustrator
Lichacz, Sheila Enit Painter
Lippincott, Janet Painter, Printmaker
Livesay, Thomas Andrew Museum Director, Administrator
Lomahaftewa, Linda Joyce Painter, Instructor
Longley, Bernique Painter, Sculptor
Lovell, Tom Painter, Illustrator
Medina, Ada Drawer
Moses, Forrest (Lee), Jr Painter, Printmaker
Namingha, Dan Painter, Printmaker
Naumer, Helmuth Painter
New, Lloyd H (Lloyd Kiva New) Educator
Niblett, Gary Lawrence Painter
Orduno, Robert Daniel Painter, Sculptor
Pardington, Ralph Arthur Ceramist, Sculptor
Phillips, Gifford Collector, Writer
Plossu, Bernard Photographer
Rivera, Elias J Painter
Romero, Megan H Painter, Dealer
Ruthling, Ford Painter, Printmaker
Schabacker, Betty Barchet Painter
Selser, Christopher Dealer, Collector
Shepherd, William Fritz Painter
Sheppard, Carl Dunkle Historian
Sisson, Laurence P Painter
Sprang, Elizabeth Painter, Sculptor
Steinhoff, Monika Painter, Printmaker
Steinke, Bettina Painter
Stevens, Jacquie (Jaqueline Lauren) Ceramist, Instructor
Teters, J Charlene Painter, Illustrator
Thwaites, Charles Winstanley Painter, Muralist
Turner, David Museum Director, Educator
Wiggins, K Douglas Painter, Art Dealer
Witham, Vernon Clint Painter, Printmaker
Yates, Steven A Artist, Curator

Santa Teresa

Massey, Ann James Graphic Artist, Painter

Sante Fe

Bell, Larry Stuart Sculptor
Coke, F Van Deren Photographer, Curator
Cooper, Ron Sculptor
Mahaffey, Merrill Dean Painter, Instructor
Milliken, Alexander Fabbri Dealer
Sarkisian, Paul Painter
Tinsley, Barry Sculptor
Wade, Robert Schrope Photographer, Sculptor
Wilson, MaLin Curator

Silver City

Humphrey, S L Painter, Illustrator
Sturgen, Winston Photographer, Printmaker

Taos

Bareiss, Philip C Art Dealer, Collector
Barsano, Ron (Ronald James) Painter, Sculptor
Catusco, Louis Painter, Sculptor
Chavez, Joseph Arnold Sculptor, Instructor
Coker, Carl David Painter, Educator
Crespin, Leslie A Painter, Assemblage Artist
Daughters, Robert A Painter, Printmaker
Egri, Ted Sculptor, Painter
Ellis, Robert M Painter
Ferguson, Kathleen Elizabeth Sculptor, Lecturer
Gorman, R C Painter, Dealer
Harmon, Barbara Sayre Painter, Book Artist
Harmon, Cliff Franklin Painter
Houlihan, Patrick T Museum Director
Kloss, Gene (Alice Geneva Glasier) Etcher, Painter
Lee, Caroline D Curator, Consultant
Lerner, Alexandria Sandra Painter
Macpherson, Kevin Painter
Mandelman, Beatrice M Painter
Manzo, Anthony Joseph Painter, Instructor
Mercolino, Veronica Florence Painter, Sculptor
Ray, Robert (Donald) Painter, Sculptor
Richards, Tally Dealer, Writer

NEW MEXICO (cont)

Robles, Julian Painter, Sculptor
Sanchez, Mary Lowe (Eliza) Dealer, Collector
Stewart, William Painter
Vigil, Veloy Joseph Painter, Printmaker
Vinella, Ray (Raimondo John) Painter
Witt, David L Writer, Curator

Tesuque

Hamburger, Sydney K Sculptor, Curator
Okun, Barbara J Consultant, Art Dealer

Tijeras

Sweet, Mary (French) Painter
West, W Richard (Dick) Painter, Sculptor

Tucumcari

Dominguez, Eddie Ceramist

NEW YORK

Accord

Massie, Lorna Printmaker
Pfeifer, Marcuse Dealer, Gallery Director

Albany

Adams, Hank M Craftsman
Callner, Richard Painter, Educator
Frinta, Mojmir Svatopluk Historian, Educator
Liddle, Nancy Hyatt Museum Director, Consultant
Mayer, Edward Albert Sculptor, Educator
Miles, Christine M Museum Director, Administrator
Rosen, Hy (Hyman Joseph) Cartoonist, Sculptor
Shankman, Gary Charles Painter
Vallila, Marja R Sculptor
Warren, Betty Painter, Instructor

Albertson

Madsen, Viggo Holm Printmaker, Craftsman

Alfred Station

Higby, (Donald) Wayne Painter, Sculptor

Altamont

Cowley, Edward P Painter, Educator

Amagansett

Durham, William Painter, Sculptor
Gussow, Sue Ferguson Painter, Educator
Opper, John Painter

Amenia

Hale, Nathan Cabot Sculptor, Writer

Amsterdam

Baer, Norbert Sebastian Educator

Ancramdale

Boxer, Stanley (Robert) Painter, Sculptor
Weinstein, Joyce Painter

Angola

Booth, Robert Alan Sculptor
Haug, Donald Raymond Painter

Annandale-on-Hudson

Shore, Stephen Photographer

Ardsley

Lysun, Gregory Painter, Restorer
Sokolow, Isobel Folb Sculptor

Ardsley-on-Hudson

Kipniss, Robert Painter, Printmaker

Armonk

Gay, Betsy (Elizabeth Dershuck Gay) Painter, Instructor
Gressel, Michael L Sculptor
Schaffer, Debra S Sculptor, Instructor

Astoria

Glorig, Ostor Painter, Craftsman
Haff, Barbara J E Painter, Instructor

Aurora

Roberts, William Edward Painter, Educator

Babylon

Eckelberry, Don Richard Painter
Haley, Priscilla J Painter, Printmaker

Barrytown

Higgins, Dick Painter, Printmaker

Bayside

Goldstein, Milton Printmaker, Painter
Kotzky, Alex Sylvester Cartoonist
Niemann, Edmund E Painter, Sculptor

Bayville

Rosenthal, Gloria M Collage Artist, Painter

Bearsville

Pantell, Richard Keith Painter, Printmaker
Wickiser, Ralph Lewanda Administrator, Painter

Bedford

Weinman, Robert Alexander Sculptor

Bellport

Desoto, Rafael M Painter, Illustrator

Bemus Point

Crist, C Jeffrey Director, Curator

Binghamton

Gonzalez, Ronald Sculpture
Ippolito, Angelo Painter, Educator
Lindsay, Kenneth C Historian, Writer
Schwartz, Aubrey E Printmaker, Sculptor
Sokolowski, Linda Robinson Printmaker, Painter
Wilson, Edward N Sculptor, Educator

Bloomington

Ruffing, Anne Elizabeth Painter

Brainard

Johnsen, May Anne Painter

Brewster

Rosenberg, Bernard Publisher, Book Dealer

Briarcliff Manor

Adler, Myril Painter, Printmaker
Hammond, Phyllis Baker Sculptor

Briarwood

Klein, Ellen Lee Painter, Writer

Bridgehampton

Benson, Elaine K G Art Dealer, Writer
Jackson, Lee Painter
Muller, Helen B Painter, Gallery Director

Bridgeport

Bolton, Robin Jean Painter

Brockport

Holcombe, Anna Calluori Ceramist, Gallery Director

Bronx

Adams, Alice Sculptor
Blayton, Betty (Betty Blayton-Taylor) Painter, Administrator
Bott, Patricia Allen Painter, Art Critic
Brody, Ruth Painter, Printmaker
Buonagurio, Toby Lee Sculptor
Cancel, Luis R Museum Director, Painter
Corbin, George Allen Historian, Writer
Crimi, Alfred D Painter, Instructor
Davis, Walter Lewis Painter, Collage Artist
Ditzion, Grace Sculptor, Painter
Finnegan, Sharyn Marie Painter
Hollingsworth, Alvin Carl Painter, Instructor
Jaffe, Irma B Historian, Educator
Janko, May Printmaker, Painter
Kasak, Nikolai Painter, Sculptor
Kassoy, Bernard Painter, Printmaker
Kassoy, Hortense Sculptor, Painter
Kaye, George Painter, Educator
Keveson, Florence Painter, Illustrator
Korman, Barbara Sculptor, Assemblage Artist
Leetaru, Ilse Printmaker
Lewis, Carole Sculptor
Olshan, Bernard Painter, Printmaker
Pan, Theodore (Ion) Sculptor, Instructor
Shapiro, David (David Joel Shapiro) Critic, Educator
Simone (Mildred Simonson), Sculptor, Painter
Waletzky, Tsirl (Cecelia Grobla Waletzky) Assemblage Artist, Stained Glass Artist
Waterston, Harry Clement Painter, Sculptor
Wechter, Vivienne Thaul Educator, Painter
Zilius, Vladas Painter

Bronxville

Agee, William C Educator, Historian
D'Amato, Janet Potter Illustrator, Craftsman
Klein, Sandor C Painter, Sculptor
Seckler, Dorothy Gees Critic, Painter

Brooklyn

Abrams, Edith Lillian Sculptor, Instructor
Acconci, Vito Sculptor
Adler, Lee Painter, Printmaker
Allain, René Pierre Painter, Sculptor
Anderson, Lennart Painter, Instructor
Artschwager, Richard Ernst Sculptor, Painter
Bahc, Mo Painter
Ball, Susan L Administrator, Historian
Bard, Joellen Painter, Sculptor
Bates, Leo James Painter, Filmmaker
Baumbach, Harold Painter, Printmaker
Beerman, Herbert Painter, Educator
Berman, Aaron Art Dealer, Collector
Bertoni, Dante H Painter, Illustrator
Birch, Willie M Sculptor, Painter
Bove, Richard Painter, Educator
Brooks, Bruce W Painter, Sculptor
Brothers, Barry A Painter, Muralist
Buck, Robert Treat, Jr Historian, Museum Director
Burkhart, Kathe K Conceptual Artist, Painter
Burns, Jerome Painter, Printmaker
Burns, Josephine Painter

NEW YORK (cont)

Burns, Millie Photographer, Printmaker
Busto, Ana Marie Photographer
Cole, Donald Painter
Coppedge, Arthur L Painter, Educator
Currie, Steve Sculptor
Cusack, Margaret Weaver Illustrator, Sculptor
Dantzic, Cynthia Maris Educator, Painter
De Boschnek, Chris (Christian Charles) Painter, Printmaker
Dechar, Peter Painter
Delson, Elizabeth Painter, Printmaker
De Ricco, Hank Sculptor, Environmental Artist
Derrickson, Steve Bruce Sculptor
Diamond, Paul Photographer
Dinhofer, Shelly Mehlman Writer, Historian
Dinnerstein, Harvey Painter
Dinnerstein, Lois Historian, Lecturer
Dinnerstein, Simon A Painter
Dinsmore, Stephen Pul Painter
Eckart, Christian Painter
Erman, Geraldine Sculptor
Estern, Neil Sculptor
Evans, Judith Futral Painter
Faunce, Sarah Cushing Museum Curator
Feder, Penny Joy Printmaker, Lecturer
Federe, Marion Painter, Graphic Artist
Fein, Stanley Painter, Designer
Ferber, Linda S Curator, Historian
Fine, Jane Painter
Fisher, Joel Sculptor
Flanery, Gail Painter, Printmaker
Fleminger, Susan N Administrator, Educator
Fournier, Alex Painter
Fuerst, Shirley Miller Sculptor, Printmaker
Gardner, Susan Ross Painter
Gear, Josephine Historian, Gallery Director
Genkin, Jonathan Painter
Germano, Thomas Painter, Printmaker
Gianlorenzi, Nona Elena Painter, Art Dealer
Gilbert, Sharon Collage Artist, Sculptor
Giro, R (R Gironda) Architect, Sculptor
Glovsky, Alan Sculptor, Environmental Artist
Grado, Angelo John Painter, Instructor
Greenbaum, Marty Painter, Sculptor
Greenstone, Marion Painter
Grey, Alex V Painter, Sculptor
Grubb, David Painter, Printmaker
Hartshorn, Willis E Photographer, Curator
Hauft, Amy Sculptor
Hazlewood, Carl E Curator, Painter
Hazlitt, Don Painter
Heller, Pamela Sculptor
Henes, Donna Environmental Artist, Sculptor
Hill, Robin Sculptor
Homma, Kazufumi Painter
Howe, Nelson S Designer, Assemblage Artist
Hoyt, Ellen Painter
Huntington, Jim Sculptor
Jorgensen, Roger M Sculptor, Painter
Kaminsky, Jack Allan Photographer, Printmaker
Kane, Bill Assemblage Artist, Photographer
Kaprov, Susan Painter, Muralist
Kariya, Hiroshi Conceptual Artist
Katzive, David H Administrator
Keaveney, Sydney Starr Librarian, Educator
Kessler, Jon A Sculptor
Knutsson, Anders Painter
Kotik, Charlotta Curator, Historian
Krieger, Florence Sculptor, Painter
Kupferman, Murray Painter, Sculptor
Lager, Fannie Sculptor, Collector
Lambrechts, Marc Painter, Printmaker
Laramée, Eve Andrée Sculptor, Conceptual Artist
Levine, David Cartoonist, Painter
Levine, Marion Lerner Painter
Liebman, Dr Sarah Educator, Painter
Lima, Jacqueline (Dutton) Painter, Draftsman
Lipski, Donald G Sculptor
Lister, Ardele Diane Video Artist
Lubell, Ellen Critic, Writer
McChristy, Quentin L Painter, Designer
Mackenzie, David, IV Painter
McNeil, George J Painter, Printmaker
McTwigan, Michael Critic, Editor
Magazzini, Gene Painter
Main, Tim Painter
Mainardi, Patricia M Historian, Critic
Malta, Vincent Instructor, Painter
Manilla, Tess Painter, Collage Artist
Mark, Marilyn (Sabetsky) Painter, Administrator
Marlor, Clark Strang Historian, Collector
Mateo, Julio Painter, Printmaker
Min, Yong Soon Sculptor, Painter
Monti, John Sculptor
Mooney, Michael J Painter, Assemblage Artist
Moore, Sabra Assemblage Artist, Painter
Morgenlander, Ella Kramer Painter, Instructor
Murrell, Carlton D Painter
Myers, Forrest Warden Sculptor
Myers, Martin Sculptor, Painter
Neals, Otto Painter, Printmaker
Neffson, Robert Painter
Nemser, Cindy Critic, Writer
Newman, Sophie Painter, Sculptor
Norris, (Robert) Ben Painter
Odate, Toshio Conceptual Artist, Instructor
Olenick, David Charles Administrator, Dealer
Ornstein, Judith Painter
Oshima, Mari Sculptor
Panter, Gary Set Designer, Painter
Pearlstein, Seymour Painter, Educator
Pfaffman, William Scott Sculptor, Draftsman
Pitynski, Andrzej P Sculptor
Power, S Brenda Joan Sculptor, Painter
Powley, Donald Painter
Purcell, Ann Painter
Rand, Archie Painter, Muralist
Ranson, Nancy Sussman Painter, Printmaker
Reich, Nathaniel E Painter, Collage Artist
Reich, Olive B Painter
Reichman, Leah Carol Painter
Rhoden, John W Sculptor
Robinson, Margot (Margot Steigman) Painter, Sculptor
Rocco, Ron (Ronald Anthony Rocco) Sculptor, Video Artist
Rochette, Anne Monique Sculptor
Rogalski, Walter Printmaker, Lecturer
Romano, Clare Camille (Mrs John Ross) Printmaker, Painter
Saar, Alison M Sculptor
Saito, Seiji Sculptor
Sakuyama, Shunji Printmaker, Painter
Saret, Alan Daniel Sculptor
Sasaki, Toshio Sculptor, Environmental Artist
Saunders, Wade Sculptor, Critic
Schaffner, Ingrid L Critic, Curator
Scharff, Constance Kramer Printmaker, Painter
Schneider, Noel Sculptor, Painter
Schucker, Charles Painter
Senie, Harriet Historian, Critic
Serrano, Andres Photographer, Conceptual Artist
Shechter, Ben-Zion Painter, Illustrator
Shechter, Laura J Painter, Draftsman
Shimoda, Osamu Sculptor
Smith, Jos(eph) A(nthony) Painter, Illustrator
Stegman, Patricia Painter, Printmaker
Steinbach, Haim Sculptor, Conceptual Artist
Stelzer, Michael Norman Sculptor, Instructor
Stone, Jeffrey Ingram Painter, Instructor
Tate, Blair Tapestry Artist, Educator
Toulis, Vasilios (Apostolos) Printmaker, Educator
Trachtenberg, Gloria P Painter, Graphic Artist
Trakis, Louis Sculptor, Educator
Tucker, William G Sculptor
Uhrman, Celia Painter, Writer
Uhrman, Esther Painter, Writer
Uram, Lauren Michelle Conceptual Artist, Illustrator
Vaadia, Boaz Sculptor
Van Riper, Peter Printmaker, Conceptual Artist
Wallace, Patty A Painter, Filmmaker
Wang, Gar Painter, Lecturer
Weingarten, Hilde (Kevess) Painter, Printmaker
Winter, David L Sculptor
Wizon, Tod Painter
Yamin, Steven Edward Printmaker
Zakanitch, Robert S Painter
Zito, Joseph (Phillip) Sculptor, Conceptual Artist

Brookville

Cohen, Reina Joyce Graphic Artist, Printmaker
Haleman, Laura Rand Sculptor, Craftsman
Weyhe, Arthur Sculptor

Buffalo

Anderson, David Art Dealer, Collector
Auping, Michael Graham Curator, Historian
Berlyn, Sheldon Painter, Printmaker
Blair, Robert Noel Painter, Sculptor
Breverman, Harvey Painter, Printmaker
Brock, Robert W Sculptor, Educator
Cohen, Harold Larry Designer, Educator
Cuthbert, Virginia Painter
Dunkelman, Martha Levine Historian, Educator
Faller, Marion Photographer, Educator
Freudenheim, Nina Dealer, Collector
Glass, Dorothy F Historian
Gordon, Violet Illustrator, Writer
Hatchett, Duayne Sculptor, Painter
Henrich, Biff Photographer
Hultberg, John Painter
Kassman, Shirley Painter, Educator
Krims, Les Photographer, Educator
Levick, (Mr & Mrs) Irving Collectors
Martin, Margaret M Painter, Designer
Nickard, Gary Laurence Photographer, Curator
Paterson, Anthony R Sculptor, Educator
Pfahl, John Photographer
Piccillo, Joseph Painter
Prochownik, Walter A Educator, Painter
Rogovin, Milton Photographer
Schultz, Douglas George Director
Sharits, Paul Jeffrey Film Artist, Painter
Tobin, Nancy Designer, Editor
Townsend, J Benjamin Critic, Historian

NEW YORK (cont)
Visser't Hooft, Martha Painter
Wynn, Donald James Painter, Lecturer

Buskirk
Goossen, Eugene Coons Writer, Educator
Johanson, Patricia Sculptor, Environmental Artist
Kheel, Constance Painter

Byron
Wilson, Tom Muir Designer

Callicoon Center
Kreznar, Richard J Sculptor, Painter

Cambria Heights
Brown, James Painter, Graphic Artist

Cambridge
Bittleman, Dolores Dembus Weaver, Conservator
Wilson, Evan Carter Painter

Campbell
Billeci, Andre George Sculptor, Educator

Campbell Hall
Greenly, Colin Environmental Artist, Painter

Canastota
Hughto, Darryl Leo Painter

Canton
Driscoll, Abigail Julia Hannah Administrator, Conservator
Holladay, Harlan H Historian, Painter
Lowe, J Michael Sculptor, Educator

Cazenovia
Pirkl, James Joseph Designer, Educator
Wyckoff, Sylvia Spencer Painter, Educator

Centereach
Picciano, Lana (Lana Patricia Picciano) Painter, Printmaker

Champlain
Sanderson, Warren Historian, Consultant

Chappaqua
De Groat, Diane Illustrator, Designer
Manspeizer, Susan R Sculpture
Reibel, Bertram Sculptor, Graphic Artist

Charlotteville
Pettibone, Richard H Painter, Sculptor

Chatham
Andell, Nancy Painter, Printmaker
Noyes, Sandy Photographer

Chautauqua
Morgan, Maritza Leskovar Painter, Illustrator

Chester
Jones, George Bobby Painter, Video Artist

Chestertown
Longhurst, Robert E Sculptor

Clarence
Hubler, Julius Printmaker, Painter

Clifton Park
Kuhn, Audrey Grendahl Printmaker, Graphic Artist

Clinton
Bergen, John Axel von Sculptor
Loy, John Sheridan Painter

Cold Brook
Frazier, Paul D Sculptor, Educator

Cold Spring
McDonnell, Joseph Anthony Sculptor, Painter
Margules, Gabriele Ella Illustrator, Painter
Marzollo, Claudio Sculptor

Cold Springs
Biederman, James Mark Painter, Sculptor

Commack
Domroe, Barbara Printmaker, Painter

Congers
Gussow, Alan Painter, Sculptor

Cooperstown
Keck, Sheldon Waugh Educator, Conservator
Munro, Janet Andrea Painter

Corning
Ahrens, Kent Museum Director, Historian
Buechner, Thomas Scharman Painter, Writer
Dowler, David P Sculptor, Designer

Corona
Wimberley, Frank Walden Painter, Collage Artist

Cross River
Smith, Lawrence Beall Painter, Sculptor

Croton-on-Hudson
Harari, Hananiah Painter
Pinkney, Jerry Illustrator

Cutchogue
Dank, Leonard D Illustrator, Consultant
Penney, Jacqueline Painter, Instructor

Depew
Litz, James C Painter

Diamond Point
Hatcher, (L) Brower Sculptor

Dix Hills
Moy, May (Wong) Painter, Instructor

Dobbs Ferry
Clive, Richard R Painter

Douglaston
Leaf, Ruth Printmaker, Instructor
Simel, Elaine Printmaker, Painter

East Amherst
Garver, Walter Raymond Painter, Writer

East Chatham
Li Marzi, Joseph Painter, Graphic Artist
Rickey, George W Sculptor

Eastchester
Alfano, Angel Painter
Stern, Louise Printmaker, Painter

East Elmhurst
Oi, Motoi Painter, Instructor

East Hampton
Brown, David Lee Sculptor
Bujese, Arlene Gallery Director, Printmaker
Gordon, Joy L Museum Director, Educator
Hokanson, Hans Sculptor, Collage Artist
Hornak, Ian John Painter
Kaufman, Irving Painter, Educator
Lassaw, Ibram Sculptor, Painter
Li Lan Painter
Mim, Adrienne C (Adrienne Claire Schwartz) Sculptor, Painter
Richenburg, Robert Bartlett Painter, Sculptor
Roth, Frank Painter
Stein, Ronald Jay Painter, Sculptor
Weller, Paul Photographer, Painter
Whipple, Enez Mary Administrator
Wingate, Arline (Hollander) Sculptor
Woolfenden, William Edward Administrator, Historian
Zucker, Murray Harvey Sculptor, Collage Artist

East Hill
Newmark, Marilyn (Marilyn Newmark Meiselman) Sculptor

East Islip
Shaw, Karen Painter

East Meadow
Simon, Netty D Painter
Terken, John Sculptor

East Northport
Cohen, George Michael Educator

East Quogue
Setlow, Neva C Sculptor, Painter

East Setauket
Levine, Martin Printmaker, Educator

Elmhurst
Berkon, Martin Painter
Freedman, Jacqueline Painter
Segur, Eleanor Corinne Painter, Instructor
Wachsteter, George Illustrator

Elmira
Macdonell, Cameron Painter, Muralist

Endicott
Takach, Mary H Museum Director, Historian

Fair Haven
Fuller, John Charles Historian, Photographer

Fairport
Witmeyer, Stanley Herbert Painter, Consultant

Farmingdale
Gatto, Paul Anthony Painter, Instructor

Fayetteville
Catlin, Stanton Loomis Curator, consultant
Goodnow, Frank A Painter, Educator
Pollock, Merlin F Painter, Educator

NEW YORK (cont)

Pulos, Arthur Jon Designer, Historian

Ferndale

Scott, Walter Painter, Architect

Fillmore

Wenger, Bruce Edward Printmaker, Assemblage Artist

Floral Park

Aaron, Evalyn (Wilhelmina) Keisler Painter
Borax, Benjamin Collage Artist, Painter
Gartel, Laurence M Photographer, Computer Artist

Florida

Zingale, Lawrence Painter

Flushing

Clark, William W Historian
Eisenberg, Marc S Painter, Sculptor
Gibala, Louise Painter
Kam, Mei K Painter, Instructor
Langer, Sandra Lois (Cassandra) Historian, Critic
Ludwig, Eva Sculptor
Miller, Marc H Curator, Writer
Negri, Rocco Antonio Illustrator, Painter
Nicotra, Joseph Charles Painter
Rosenthal, Seymour Painter, Lithographer
Schneider, Janet M Museum Director, Painter
Simor, Suzanna B Librarian, Gallery Director
Slatkes, Leonard J Historian
Tobias, Abraham Joel Painter, Sculptor
Weinberg, H Barbara Curator, Educator

Flushing Meadows, Corona Park

Klindt, Steven Administrator

Fly Creek

Dusenbery, Walter Sculptor

Forest Hills

Bumas, Jonathan Mark Painter
Crystal, Boris Painter
Eller, Evelyn (Evelyn Eller Rosenbaum) Collage Artist, Painter
Leeds, Annette Painter
Steynovitz, Zamy Painter
Tewi, Thea Sculptor

Forest Hills Gardens

Jules, Mervin Painter, Educator

Franklin Square

Indiviglia, Salvatore Joseph Painter, Instructor
Newer, Thesis Painter
Soloway, Reta Burns Painter

Freehold

Maltzman, Stanley Printmaker, Painter

Freeport

Brown, Marion B Painter, Instructor
Genovese, Richard Photographer, Collage Artist
Monteiro, Isaac Painter, Sculptor
Terris, Albert Sculptor

Fresh Meadows

Silber, Maurice Painter, Illustrator

Ft Salonga

Wingerter, John Parker Painter

Garden City

Davies, Harry Clayton Painter, Photographer
Jessen, Shirley Agnes Painter
Kaplan, Stanley Printmaker, Muralist
Myron, Robert Historian
Polansky, Lois B Printmaker, Collage Artist

Garnerville

Harvey, Dermot Kinetic Artist, Sculptor

Garrison

Clifton, Michelle Gamm Sculptor, Filmmaker

Germantown

Gladstone, M J Publisher

Glen Cove

Beckhard, Ellie (Eleanor) Painter, Photographer
Paris, Jeanne C Critic, Consultant

Glen Head

Hooton, Bruce Duff Editor, Publisher

Glens Falls

Blackburn, Loren Hayner Painter, Illustrator
Lyons, Francis E, Jr Art Dealer, Lecturer

Great Barrington

Filmus, Tully Painter, Lecturer

Great Neck

Beck, Margit Painter, Educator
Dennett, Lissy W Sculptor
Eckstein, Ruth Painter, Printmaker
Goldsmith, Elsa M Painter, Graphic Artist
Gorelick, Shirley Painter, Printmaker
Gribin, Liz Painter
Harnick, Sylvia Painter
Krieger, Suzanne Baruc Painter, Lecturer
Lytton, Constance B Printmaker, Painter
Mayer, Sondra Art Dealer, Printmaker
Meyer, Seymour W Sculptor
Obler, Geri Printmaker, Collage Artist
Orens, Elaine Frances Graphic Artist, Printmaker
Quat, Helen S Printmaker, Painter
Reese, Marcia Mitchell Sculptor
Schiff, (Adele M) Assemblage & Artists, College Artist, Sculpture
Seidler, Doris Painter, Printmaker
Shapiro, Dee Painter, Lecturer
Sheya, Painter, Instructor
Stevens, Thelma K Educator, Dealer
Tchetchet, Tatiana Painter

Greenlawn

Fludd, Reginald Joseph Painter, Craftsman
Zucker, Bob Photographer, Exhibit Designer

Greenwich

Lorber, Stephen Neil Painter, Printmaker
Nunnelley, Robert B Painter, Educator

Groton

Colby, Victor E Sculptor, Educator

Hadley

LaVerdiere, Bruno E Sculptor

Hamilton

Knecht, John Filmmaker, Video Artist
Loveless, Jim Painter, Educator
Mosby, Dewey Franklin Museum Director, Historian
Van Schaack, Eric Historian, Educator

Hamlin

Stewart, Bill Sculptor, Ceramist

Hampton Bays

Ciancio, June (Kirkpatrick) Painter, Instructor
Higa (Yoshiharu) Printmaker, Photographer

Hannibal

Eckersley, Thomas Cyril Educator, Photographer

Harrison

Margulis, Martha (Boyer) Painter

Hartsdale

Brown, Alan M, Jr Dealer, Consultant
Glanz, Andrea E Administrator, Curator

Hastings-on-Hudson

James, Catti Sculptor, Consultant
Madigan, Mary Jean Smith Editor, Writer
Nardin, Mario Collector, Sculptor
Otani, June Illustrator, Printmaker
Sklar-Weinstein, Arlene (Joyce) Painter, Printmaker

Hawthorne

Oechsli, Kelly Illustrator

Hempstead

Feriola, James Philip Painter, Designer
Jacobs, David (Theodore) Sculptor, Educator

Hewlett

Flomenhaft, Eleanor Museum Director, Historian

Hicksville

Di Cosola, Lois Painter, Printmaker

High Falls

Bishop, Ben Painter, Sculptor

Highland Falls

Heberling, Glen Austin Painter, Illustrator

Highland Mills

Knipscher, Gerard Allen Painter, Graphic Artist

Hillsdale

Friedman, Alan Sculptor, Designer
Richards, Joseph Edward Painter

Holland

Rush, Deborah Sculptor, Muralist
Schroeck, R D Painter, Conceptual Artist

Holland Patent

Christiana, Edward Painter, Instructor

Honeoye

Brown, Bruce Robert Painter, Sculptor

Hoosick Falls

Haerer, Carol Painter
Hatfield, David Underhill Painter
Sussman, Barbara J Painter
Sussman, Gary Lawrence Sculptor, Director
Trimm, H Wayne Illustrator, Painter

NEW YORK (cont)

Hopewell Junction

Sullo, Joseph Anthony Painter, Designer

Howard Beach

Grillo, Esther Angela Sculptor, Printmaker

Hudson

Avedisian, Edward Painter, Sculptor

Hudson Falls

Leary, Daniel Draftsman, Printmaker

Huntington

Brodsky, Stan Painter, Educator
Buckley, Mary L (Mrs Joseph M Parriott) Painter, Educator
Coraor, John E Museum Director, Administrator
Emmert, Pauline Gore Painter
Engel, Michael Martin, II Painter
Twardowicz, Stanley Jan Painter, Photographer
Van Wagner, Judy Collischan Museum Director, Critic
Vaux, Richard Painter, Printmaker
Walker, Marie Sheehy Painter

Huntington Station

Mann, Katinka Sculptor, Photographer
Nagin, Mary D Painter, Educator
Van Loen, Alfred Sculptor, Educator
Webb, Jeffrey R Painter, Educator

Hyde Park

Ulrich, Edwin Abel Museum Director

Irvington

Holden, Donald Artist, Writer

Irvington-on-Hudson

Lippmann, Janet Gurian Gallery Director, Painter

Ithaca

Calkins, Robert G Historian, Educator
Daly, Norman Painter, Sculptor
Evett, Kenneth Warnock Painter
Garrison, Elizabeth Jane Painter, Jeweler
Green, Nancy Elizabeth Curator, Writer
Grippi, Salvatore William Painter, Educator
Hartell, John Painter
Holliday, Judith Librarian
Kahn, Peter Painter, Graphic Designer
Kord, Victor George Administrator, Painter
Leavitt, Thomas Whittlesey Museum Director
Mikus, Eleanore Painter, Educator
O'Connor, Stanley James Historian, Educator
Poleskie, Stephen Francis Environmental Artist, Printmaker
Robinson, Franklin W Museum Director, Historian
Squier, Jack Leslie Sculptor, Educator
WalkingStick, Kay Painter

Jackson Heights

Farian, Babette S Painter, Designer
Fekner, John Conceptual Artist, Environmental Artist
Freund, Tibor Painter, Muralist
Kanidinc, Salahattin Calligrapher, Designer
Schiavina, Laura M Painter
Wasserman, Albert Painter, Designer

Jamaica

Borstein, Elena Painter, Educator
Cade, Walter, III Painter, Collage Artist
Desser, Maxwell Milton Painter, Designer
Foley, Dorothy Swartz Painter, Graphic Artist
Giffuni, Flora Baldini Painter, Lecturer
Krigstein, Bernard Painter, Illustrator
Lovejoy, Margot R Multi-media, Educator
Ponsot, Claude F Educator, Painter
Youkeles, Anne Painter, Printmaker

Jamestown

Talley, Dan R Curator, Writer

Jeffersonville

Craft, Douglas D Painter, Educator
Harms, Elizabeth Painter

Jericho

Honig, Eleanor D Painter, Printmaker
Kaplan, Marilyn Flashenberg Painter
Kelmenson, Lita Sculptor, Educator
Ritter, Renee Gaylinn Painter

Johnson City

Truex, Duane Philip, III Educator, Consultant

Jordanville

Durham, Jeanette R Painter

Kandall

Markusen, Thomas Roy Craftsman, Sculptor

Katonah

Samerjan, George E Designer, Painter
Simpson, William Kelly Historian, Educator
Toney, Anthony Painter, Educator

Kenmore

Koenig, Catherine Catanzaro Painter

Kenoza Lake

D'Arcangelo, Allan M Painter
Hutchinson, Max Art Dealer, Gallery Director

Kerhonkson

Jagger, Gillian Painter, Sculptor

Kew Gardens

Brennan, Fanny (Frances M) Painter
Brennan, Francis Edwin Editorial Cartoonist, Designer
Tomko, George Peter Historian, Curator
Vargas, Josephine Illustrator, Painter

Kings Park

Barooshian, Martin Painter, Printmaker

Kings Point

Douenias, Natalie Painter
Housman, Russell F Painter, Educator

Kingston

Beman, Lynn Susan Art Historian, Curator
McPherson, Bruce Rice Editor, Publisher
Montano, Linda (Mary) Conceptual Artist, Video Artist

Lake Hill

Nelson, Ruth Basha (Basha Ruth Nelson) Sculpture, Painter

Lake Success

Lichaw, Pessia Printmaker

Larchmont

Buchman, Arles (Arlette Buchman) Painter, Assemblage Artist
Lefcourt, Irwin Dealer
Medrich, Libby E Sculptor
Tobey, Alton S Painter, Muralist

Levittown

Schachter, Justine Ranson Graphic Artist, Illustrator
Zuckerberg, Stanley M Painter, Illustrator

Lima

Enyeart, James Lyle Historian, Director

Lisle

Underhill, Linn B Photographer

Little Neck

Roman, Shirley Printmaker, Painter

Lloyd Harbor

Walsh, Janet Barbara Painter

Lloyd Neck

Benny, Sandra Graphic Artist

Lockport

Penney, Charles Rand Collector, Patron

Locust Valley

Johnson, Ray Painter
Lippold, Richard Sculptor

Lodi

McCue, Harry Printmaker, Craftsman

Long Eddy

Wesselmann, Tom Painter, Sculptor

Long Island City

Bellamy, Richard Art Dealer
Di Suvero, Mark Painter, Sculptor
Donneson, Seena Sculptor, Graphics Artist
Garchik, Morton Lloyd Painter, Printmaker
Gussow, Roy Sculptor, Environmental Artist
Johnson, Carla Rae Sculptor, Conceptual Artist
Kunsch, Louis Painter, Collage Artist
Levine, Erik Sculptor
Mandelbaum, Ellen Stained Glass Artist, Writer
Martin, Dianne L Painter, Graphic Artist
Perez, Betty Weiss Painter
Schnurr, Elinore Painter
Stevenson, Harold Painter
Sueños, Carlos Printmaker, Painter
Villinski, Paul Painter, Sculptor
Wheeler, Mary Painter, Printmaker

Lynbrook

Patton, Karen Ann Painter

Mahopac

Gonzalez-Tornero, Sergio Painter, Printmaker

Maine

Barons, Richard Irwin Museum Director, Historian

Malverne

Gavalas, Alexander Beary Painter
Stanton, Harriet L Painter

Mamaroneck

Arye, Leonora E Sculptor
Lekberg, Barbara Hult Sculptor
Pugh, Grace Huntley Painter, Art Historian
Sloan, Robert Smullyan Painter
Topol, Robert Martin Collector

Manhasset

Catchi, Painter, Printmaker
Stein, Claire A Administrator

Manhasset Hills

London, Anna Graphic Artist, Sculptor

Manlius

Aistars, John Painter, Educator
Groat, Hall Pierce Painter, Muralist
Groat, Hall Pierce, II Muralist, Painter

Margaretville

Howes, Royce Bucknam Painter

Mattituck

O'Shea, Terrence Patrick Painter, Sculptor

Melville

Knief, Helen (Janet) Jeanette Painter
Schlam, Murray J Sculptor

Merrick

Cariola, Robert J Painter, Sculptor
Pearlman, Etta S Painter
Warshaw, Elaine N Sculptor, Director

Middletown

Blumenthal, Fritz Painter, Printmaker
Cady, Samuel Lincoln Painter, Instructor
Ericson, Beatrice Painter

Millbrook

Askew, Pamela Educator, Writer
Della-Volpe, Ralph Eugene Painter, Educator

Mineola

Feuerman, Carol Jeannne Sculptor, Painter

Monsey

Mesibov, Hugh Painter, Printmaker

Montauk

Nama, George Allen Printmaker, Sculptor

Mountainville

Stern, H Peter Collector

Mt Kisco

Chinni, Peter Anthony Sculptor, Painter
Galen, Elaine Painter, Sculptor

Mt Morris

Dickinson, David Charles Printmaker, Professor

Mt Sinai

Ames, Lee Judah Illustrator, Writer

Mt Tremper

Stuhl, Michelle Sculptor, Environmental Artist
Werner, Howard Sculptor

Mt Vernon

Olsen, Ernest Moran Designer, Painter
Propersi, August J Administrator, Painter
Seliger, Charles Painter
Sherrill, Milton Lewis Sculptor, Painter
Singletary, Michael James Painter

Zib, Tom (Thomas A Zibelli) Cartoonist

Nanuet

LaChapelle, Joseph Robert Sculptor, Educator

Newark

Williams, Wayne Francis Sculptor

New Berlin

Huot, Robert Painter, Filmmaker

New City

Friedlander, Lee Photographer
Kessler, Leonard H Illustrator
Pedersen, Carolyn H Painter
Poor, Anne Painter
Rosse, Maryvonne Sculptor, Medalist

New Hampton

Sinnard, Elaine (Janice) Painter, Sculptor

New Hartford

MacDonald, Scott Critic, Educator

New Paltz

Atlas, Nava Writer, Designer
Bennett, Jamie Enamelist, Sculptor
Davidson, Thyra (Claire Thyra Wexler) Draftsman, Sculptor
Deschamps, Francois Photographer
Fishburne, St Julian (Le Roy) Painter
Flynn, Pat L Jeweler, Goldsmith
Martin, Alexander Toedt Educator, Painter
Munsterberg, Hugo Historian, Educator
Raleigh, Henry Patrick Painter, Writer
Shaw, Ernest Carl Sculptor, Wood
Tabak, Chaim Painter, Sculptor
Trager, Neil C Director, Photographer
Wexler, George Painter

New Platz

Sawka, Jan A Painter, Printmaker

New Rochelle

Gallagher, Kathleen Ellen Printmaker, Painter
Goldfinger, Eliot Sculptor
Laska, David Designer, Painter
Meizner, Paula Sculptor
Montlack, Edith Painter
Perlmutter, Merle Printmaker
Schlanger, Jeff Sculptor
Seckel, Paul Bernhard Painter, Printmaker
Slotnick, Mortimer H Painter, Educator

New Suffolk

Schulze, Paul Designer

New York

Abadi, Fritzie Painter, Sculptor
Abdell, Douglas Sculptor, Painter
Abish, Cecile Sculptor, Instructor
Abramowicz, Janet Painter, Printmaker
Abrams, Joyce Diana Painter, Sculptor
Abrams, Vivien (Joy) Painter
Abularach, Rodolfo Marco Painter, Printmaker
Adams, Dennis Paul Sculptor, Conceptual Artist
Adams, Mac Sculptor, Photographer
Adkins, Terry R Sculptor
Adrian, Barbara (Mrs Franklin Tramutola) Painter, Collector
Aebi, Ernst Walter Illustrator, Painter
Agostini, Peter Sculptor
Ahearn, John Sculptor
Ahn, Don C Painter, Art Dealer
Ahrens, Hanno D Sculptor
Akin, Gwen Photographer

Alberti, Donald Wesley Painter
Alden, Todd Critic, Conceptual Artist
Aldrich, Larry Art Collector
Alexander, Edmund Brooke Art Dealer, Publisher
Alexander, John E Painter
Alexander, Vikky M Conceptual Artist
Alexander-Greene, Grace George Educator, Museum Director
Allen, Catherine MacDonald Painter
Allen, Roberta Conceptual Artist, Painter
Allentuck, Marcia Epstein Historian, Educator
Alling, Janet D Painter
Allner, Walter H Painter, Designer
Allyn, Jerri Conceptual Performance Artist
Alpern, Merry B Photographer
Alpert, Bill (William H) Painter, Sculptor
Altman, Harold Printmaker, Educator
Altschul, Arthur G Collector, Patron
Amano, Taka Painter
Amenoff, Gregory Painter
Amos, Emma Painter, Printmaker
Anastasi, William (Joseph) Painter, Sculptor
Anbinder, Paul Art Publisher, Collector
Andersen, Leif (Werner) Painter
Anderson, Doug Painter
Anderson, Laurie Conceptual Artist
Andre, Carl Sculptor
Andrews, Benny Painter, Lecturer
Andrews, Sybil (Sybil Andrews Morgan) Painter, Printmaker
Anker, Suzanne C Sculptor, Painter
Anson, Lesia Sculptor
Anspach, Ernst Collector
Anthony, Peter Sculptor
Anthony, William Graham Painter, Draftsman
Antonakos, Stephen Sculptor
Antonovici, Constantin Sculptor, Lecturer
Aoki, Carole I Ceramist
App, Timothy Painter, Educator
Appel, Eric A Sculptor, Painter
Appel, Karel Painter, Sculptor
Applebroog, Ida Painter
Aptekar, Ken Painter
Aquino, Humberto Painter
Arakawa, (Shusaku) Painter
Arcilesi, Vincent J Painter, Draftsman
Arcomano, Cathryn Painter
Arends, Stuart Painter
Armajani, Siah Sculptor
Arman Sculptor
Armstrong, Thomas Newton, III Museum Director
Arning, Bill A Curator, Administrator
Arnold, Jack Art Dealer, Publisher
Aronson, Sanda Assemblage Artist
Arum, Barbara Sculptor
Ashbaugh, Dennis John Painter
Ashbery, John Lawrence Critic
Ashby, Carl Painter, Instructor
Ashcraft, Eve Painter
Asher, Elise Painter, Poet
Ashton, Dore Art Critic, Writer
Asoma, Tadashi Painter
Atkins, Robert Critic, Curator
Attie, Dotty Draftsman
Ausby, Ellsworth Augustus Painter, Instructor
Avedon, Richard Photographer
Avery, Frances Painter, Photographer
Avlon-Daphnis, Helen Basilea Painter, Sculptor
Aycock, Alice Sculptor
Aylon, Helene Painter, Conceptual Artist
Azaceta, Luis Cruz Painter
Azara, Nancy J Sculptor, Painter
Azuma, Norio Printmaker, Painter
Azuz, David Painter, Printmaker

NEW YORK (cont)

B(eck), Rosemarie Painter, Educator
Bacarella, Flavia Painter
Bachert, Hildegard Gina Art Dealer
Baechler, Donald Painter
Bailey, Virginia Ellen Painter, Collector
Bakaty, Mike Painter, Sculptor
Baker, Elizabeth C Art Editor, Critic
Baker, Jill Withrow Painter, Illustrator
Baker, Richard Brown Collector
Balay, Felicie Art Dealer
Ball, Edward R Critic, Writer
Ball, Lillian Sculptor
Bamber, Judie Painter
Bandy, Gary Painter, Educator
Bandy, Mary Lea Editor, Administrator
Banerjee, (Bimal) Painter, Sculptor
Banning, Jack (John Peck), Jr Art Dealer, Lecturer
Baranik, Rudolf Painter
Barboza, Anthony Photographer, Painter
Bardazzi, Peter Painter
Bareiss, Walter Patron
Barnes, Curt (Curtis Edward) Painter, Instructor
Barnes, Edward Larrabee Architect
Barnes, Kitt Painter
Barnes, Margo Painter
Barnet, Will Painter, Printmaker
Barnett, Emily Painter, Instructor
Barnett, Vivian Endicott Curator, Historian
Barowitz, Elliott Painter
Barr, Burt Video Artist
Barr, Norman Painter
Barrett, Bill Sculptor
Barr-Sharrar, Beryl Art Historian, Painter
Barth, Frances Painter
Barth, Jack Alexander Painter
Bartholet, Elizabeth Ives Art Dealer, Art Consultant
Bartlett, Barry Thomas Sculptor
Bartlett, Jennifer Losch Painter, Writer
Barton, John Murray Painter, Printmaker
Barzun, Jacques Writer, Art Critic
Baskerville, Charles Painter, Muralist
Bass, Ruth Educator, Critic
Bastian, Linda Painter, Educator
Bates, David Painter
Battenfield, Jackie Painter, Educator
Baum, Jayne H Art Dealer
Baxter, Douglas W Art Dealer
Baxter, Iain Painter
Baxter, Paula Adell Librarian, Writer
Baxter, Violet Painter, Calligrapher
Bayer, Arlyne Painter, Printmaker
Baynard, Ed Painter, Printmaker
Beadleston, William L Art Dealer
Beallor, Fran Painter, Printmaker
Beatty, Frances Fielding Lewis Historian, Critic
Beauchamp, Robert Instructor, Painter
Beck, Doreen Writer, AV Producer
Beck, James Historian, Critic
Beck, Martha Ann Museum Director, Curator
Beckley, Bill Post-Conceptual Artist
Beckman, Ericka Filmmaker, Photographer
Beckmann, John Designer
Beenen, Richard Photographer
Behnke, Leigh Painter
Beilin, Howard Art Dealer
Beirne, Bill Video Artist
Belag, Andrea Painter, Graphic Artist
Bell, Charles S Painter
Bellin, Milton R Painter, Muralist
Benedikt, Michael Writer, Consultant
Benenson, Edward Hartley Collector, Patron
Benes, Barton Lidice Collage Artist, Sculptor
Benglis, Lynda Sculptor, Painter
Ben-Haim, Tsipi Critic, Art Administrator
Ben-Haim, Zigi Sculptor, Painter
Benham, Pamela J Painter
Benney, Robert Painter, Illustrator
Ben Tre, Howard B Sculptor, Draftsman
Berg, Siri Painter, Instructor
Bergen, D Thomas Collector
Bergen, Sidney L Art Dealer, Gallery Director
Berger, Gustav A Conservator
Berger, Maurice Critic, Historian
Berger, Oscar Graphic Artist
Berghash, Mark W Photographer, Painter
Berkman, Lillian Collector
Berkowitz, Terry Installation Artist
Berlind, Robert Painter, Educator
Berman, Ariane R Painter, Printmaker
Berman, Zeke Photographer
Bernheim, Stephanie Hammerschlag Painter, Printmaker
Bernstein, Judith Painter, Printmaker
Bernstein, Theresa Painter, Printmaker
Berthot, Jake Painter
Besser, Arne Charles Painter
Bhavsar, Natvar Prahladji Painter
Bialobroda, Anna Painter
Bidlo, Mike Painter, Conceptual Artist
Biggs, Janet Painter
Billian, Cathey R Sculptor, Educator
Bingham, Mrs Harry Payne Collector
Birnbaum, Dara Painter, Video Artist
Bishop, James Painter
Blackwell, Tom (Thomas Leo) Painter
Blaine, Nell Painter, Printmaker
Blair, Dike Painter
Blanc, (William) Peter Sculptor, Painter
Blau, Douglas Critic, Curator
Blaustein, Al Painter, Printmaker
Blechman, R O Illustrator, Filmmaker
Bleckner, Ross Painter
Blodgett, Anne Washington Painter
Bloom, Barbara Photographer
Blue, Patt Photographer, Educator
Bluhm, Norman Painter
Blum, Andrea Sculptor
Blumenthal, Margaret M Designer
Boardman, Seymour Painter
Bochner, Mel Conceptual Artist, Art Writer
Bocour, Leonard Painter, Lecturer
Bodin, Paul Painter
Bogarin, Rafael Serigrapher, Painter
Bohnen, Blythe Conceptual Artist, Painter
Bohnenkamp, Leslie George Sculptor, Instructor
Bonevardi, Marcelo Painter, Sculptor
Bonino, Fernanda Art Dealer
Boone, Mary Art Dealer
Boothe, Power Painter, Educator
Bootz, Antoine H Photographer
Bordes, Adrienne Painter, Instructor
Borgatta, Isabel Case Sculptor, Educator
Borgatta, Robert Edward Painter, Sculptor
Borgenicht, Grace Art Dealer, Collector
Borofsky, Jon Painter
Bosman, Richard Painter, Printmaker
Bosse, Janet C Painter, Ceramist
Boterf, Check (Chester Arthur) Painter, Lecturer
Botero, Fernando Sculptor
Bothmer, Bernard V Historian, Instructor
Bouckaert, Harm J G Art Dealer
Bourdon, David Art Critic, Writer
Bourgeois, Louise Sculptor
Boutis, Tom Painter, Printmaker
Bowie, Effie Belle Painter, Printmaker
Bowie, William Sculptor
Bowling, Frank Painter
Bowling, Katherine Painter
Bowman, John Painter
Bowman, Ruth Art Historian, Critic
Bowron, Edgar Peters Administrator, Historian
Boyd, Michael Painter, Graphic Artist
Brach, Paul Henry Painter
Bradshaw, Dove Painter, Sculptor
Brady, Carolyn Painter, Printmaker
Brainard, Joe Graphic Artist, Painter
Brandt, Kathleen Weil-Garris Educator, Art Historian
Brandt, Warren Painter
Brauntuch, Troy Painter, Printmaker
Breer, Robert C Sculptor, Filmmaker
Breiger, Elaine Printmaker, Painter
Brett, Nancy Painter
Broderick, Herbert Reginald, III Educator
Brodsky, Eugene V Painter
Brodsky, Judith Kapstein Printmaker, Educator
Brody, Jacqueline Editor
Bromm, Hal Dealer, Designer
Broner, Mathew Painter, Educator
Broner, Robert Printmaker, Painter
Brookner, Jackie Sculptor
Brooks, Ellen Photographer
Brooks, Harry A Gallery Director, Art Dealer
Brosk, Jeffrey Sculptor
Brown, Alice Dalton Painter
Brown, Cee Scott Administrator, Curator
Brown, Diane Dealer
Brown, Frederick James Painter
Brown, Jonathan Historian
Brown, Larry Painter
Brown, Milton Wolf Historian
Brown, Peter C Sculptor, Educator
Brown, Robert Delford Conceptual Artist
Brown, Robert K Dealer
Browne, Vivian E Painter, Educator
Browning, Colleen Painter
Bruder, Harold Jacob Painter, Educator
Brumer, Miriam Painter, Educator
Brumer, Shulamith Sculptor, Instructor
Brundage, Susan Lounsbury Dealer
Bruno, Phillip A Director, Lecturer
Brus, Gunter Conceptual Artist, Printmaker
Brusca, Jack Painter
Bryant, Linda Goode Art Dealer, Gallery Director
Buchman, James Wallace Sculptor
Buchwald, Howard Painter
Budny, Virginia Sculptor, Writer
Buecker, Robert Gallery Director, Painter
Bunin, Louis Sculptor
Bunts, Frank Kinetic Artist, Painter
Burckhardt, Rudy Photographer, Filmmaker
Burden, Carter Collector
Burden, Chris Conceptual Artist, Sculptor
Burdock, Harriet Historian, Printmaker
Burks, Myrna R Printmaker, Gallery Director
Burrows, Selig S Collector, Historian
Burson, Nancy Photographer, Conceptual Artist
Bush, Martin H Museum Director, Historian
Buszko, Irene J Painter
Butter, Tom Sculptor, Instructor
Buxbaum, Robert Sculptor
Byard, Carole Marie Sculptor, Illustrator
Byron, Charles Anthony Dealer
Cady, Dennis Vern Conservator, Painter
Calcagno, Lawrence Painter
Campbell, (James) Lawrence Painter, Writer
Campus, Peter Photographer, Video Artist
Canniff, Bryan Gregory Designer, Director
Canright, Sarah Anne Painter

NEW YORK (cont)

Cantone, Vic Cartoonist, Lecturer
Cantor, B Gerald Collector
Cantor, Fredrich Painter, Photographer
Cantwell, William Richard Painter, Printmaker
Capa, Cornell Photographer, Museum Director
Caplan Ciarrochi, Sandra Painter, Instructor
Capobianco, Domenick Painter, Sculptor
Caporaso, Pat Marie Art Dealer
Carbone, David Painter, Critic
Cardillo, Rimer Angel Printmaker, Sculptor
Carey, Ellen Photographer
Carlson, Cynthia J Painter, Educator
Carlson, Mary Sculptor
Caro, Francis Dealer
Carr, Sally Swan Sculptor
Carrino, David Painter
Carter, Mary Painter, Printmaker
Carter, Nanette Carolyn Painter, Printmaker
Cartwright, Constance B & Carroll L Collectors
Carvalho, Josely Printmaker, Painter
Casebere, James E Photographer, Sculptor
Cassidy, Margaret Carol (Mrs John Manship) Sculptor
Castanis, Muriel (Julia Brunner) Sculptor
Castelli, Leo Dealer
Castleman, Riva Curator, Historian
Castoro, Rosemarie Sculptor
Cate, Barbara Kaufman Educator, Art Historian
Cavaliere, Barbara Critic, Historian
Censor, Therese Sculptor
Cernuda, Paloma Printmaker
Cernuschi, Alberto C Dealer, Critic
Chaiklin, Amy Painter
Chamberlain, John Angus Sculptor
Chambers, Karen Historian, Critic
Chambers, William McWillie Painter, Art Dealer
Chandler, Michael Robert Painter
Charlesworth, Sarah E Photographer, Conceptual Artist
Charmatz, Bill (William Adolphe) Illustrator, Painter
Chase, Doris (Totten) Video Artist, Sculptor
Chase, Louisa L Painter
Chemeche, George Painter, Sculptor
Chen, Hilo Painter
Cheng, Emily Painter
Chermayeff, Ivan Designer, Painter
Chevins, Christopher M Painter, Draftsman
Chi, Chen Painter
Chia, Sandro Painter
Chin, Mel Sculptor
Cho, Y(eou) J(ui) Painter
Chong, Ping Director, Video Artist
Christensen, Dan Painter
Christensen, Don B Painter, Collector
Christo Artist
Chryssa Sculptor
Chwast, Seymour Graphic Artist, Illustrator
Ciarrochi, Ray Painter, Educator
Cicero, Carmen L Painter
Citron, Harvey Lewis Sculptor
Clark, Edward Painter
Clark, Garth Reginald Dealer, Historian
Clarke, Bud (Warren F) Designer, Painter
Clarke, John Clem Painter
Clemente, Francesco Painter
Clerk, Pierre Painter, Sculptor
Cliver, Kendra-Jean (Kendra-Jean Cliver Krienke) Dealer, Painter
Close, Chuck Painter
Close, Frank Stained Glass Artist, Sculptor
Clough, Charles Sidney Painter
Code, Audrey Painter
Coe, Anne Elizabeth Painter, Video Artist
Coe, Sue Painter
Cohen, Arthur Morris Painter, Graphic Artist
Cohen, Cora Painter
Cohen, Elaine Lustig Painter, Designer
Cohen, Hy Painter
Cohen, Jean Painter
Cohen, Joan Lebold Historian, Photographer
Cohen, Mildred Thaler Art Dealer, Gallery Director
Cohen, Ronny Critic, Curator
Cohn, Max Arthur Painter, Printmaker
Cohn, Richard A Dealer
Colao, Rudolph Painter
Cole, Jeanette Painter, Instructor
Cole, Joyce Painter
Cole, Max Painter
Cole, Sylvan Dealer, Writer
Colette Painter, Sculptor
Colin, Georgia T Collector, Designer
Colker, Edward Painter, Graphic Artist
Collado, Lisa Collage Artist, Painter
Collery, Paula Painter
Collins, Christiane C Historian, Librarian
Collins & Milazzo, (Tricia Collins & Richard Milazzo) Curators, Critics
Colmer, Roy David Photographer
Colp, Norman B Photographer, Curator
Condeso, Orlando Printmaker
Conforte, Renee Dealer
Conklin, Andrew Sterrett Painter
Connelly, Chuck Painter
Conner, Lois Photographer
Conover, Robert Fremont Printmaker, Painter
Consagra, Pier Painter
Constantine, Mildred Historian
Contini, Anita Administrator, Curator
Conwill, Houston E Sculptor
Cook, R Scott Art Dealer, Critic
Cooper, Mario Painter, Instructor
Cooper, Paula Dealer
Copeland, Lila Painter, Printmaker
Coplans, John (Rivers) Photographer
Copley, William Nelson Painter
Corkery, Tim (Timothy James) Painter, Educator
Cortor, Eldzier Painter, Printmaker
Costa, Eduardo Conceptual Artist, Sculptor
Costan, Chris Painter
Costello, Cynthia Ann Painter, Graphic Artist
Cote, Alan Painter
Cott, Jean Cahan Painter
Cotter, Holland Critic, Historian
Cottingham, Laura Josephine Critic, Writer
Courtney, Suzan Painter, Printmaker
Courtright, Robert Collage Artist, Painter
Cowles, Charles Art Dealer, Collector
Coyle, Terence Painter
Coyne, Petah E Sculptor, Photographer
Cramer, Peter Director, Photographer
Cramer, Richard Charles Painter, Educator
Crary, Jonathan Knight Art Historian
Crash (John Matos) Painter, Printmaker
Craven, David James Painter, Collage Artist
Creevy, Bill Painter, Writer
Crile, Susan Painter
Crimp, Douglas Critic, Historian
Cronbach, Robert M Sculptor
Crone, Rainer F Educator, Curator
Crown, Roberta Lila Painter, Conceptual Artist
Cruz, Emilio Painter
Cruz, Pura (Pura Isabel Cruz) Painter, Curator
Culhane, Shamus H Filmmaker, Writer
Culkin, John Michael Administrator, Educator
Cumming, Glen Edward Gallery Director
Cummings, Paul Editor, Writer
Cuningham, Elizabeth Bayard (Mrs E W R Templeton) Art Dealer
Cunningham, (Charles) Bruce Painter
Cunningham, Francis Painter, Instructor
Cuppaidge, Virginia Painter
Cutler, Bess Art Dealer
Cutler, Ethel Rose Painter, Designer
Cutler, Ronnie Painter
Cutrone, Ronnie Blaise Painter
Cyphers, Peggy K Painter, Printmaker
D'Alessio, Gregory Cartoonist, Painter
Dalglish, Jamie (James Parsons) Painter, Video Artist
Damast, Elba Cecilia Painter
Damaz, Paul F Writer, Architect
Daniels, David M Collector, Patron
Daniels, Linda Painter
Daphnis, Nassos Painter, Sculptor
Darboven, Hanne Conceptual Artist, Graphic Artist
Darton, Christopher Painter
Daskaloff, Gyorgy Painter
Dauterman, Carl Christian Consultant, Lecturer
David, Don Raymond Painter, Instructor
Davidovich, Jaime Painter, Video Artist
Davidson, Jean Painter
Davidson, Maxwell, III Dealer
Davidson, Nancy Painter
Davis, Brad (Bradley Darius) Painter
Davis, Douglas Matthew Artist, Critic
Davis, Ellen N Historian
Davis, James Robert Cartoonist
Davis, Stephen Painter
Dean, Peter Painter
De Blasi, Tony Painter, Educator
DeCarava, Roy Rudolph Photographer, Educator
De Champlain, Vera Chopak Painter, Printmaker
De Donato, Louis Painter, Instructor
Dee, Elaine Evans Historian
Deem, George Painter
De Fazio, John Sculptor
Dehner, Dorothy Sculptor, Printmaker
Deitch, Jeffrey Consultant, Curator
De Knight, Avel Painter
DeLamonica, Roberto Printmaker, Educator
De Lisio, Michael Sculptor
Del Valle, Cezar Jose Photographer, Painter
Del Valle, Joseph Bourke Design Consultant
De Maria, Walter Sculptor
De Monte, Claudia Sculpture, Painter
De Montebello, Philippe Lannes Administrator, Museum Director
De Nagy, Tibor (J) Dealer, Collector
Denes, Agnes Environmental Artist, Conceptual Artist
Dennis, Donna Frances Sculptor, Printmaker
Dennis, Gertrude Weyhe Dealer
Denson, G Roger Critic, Writer
De Palma, Brett Painter, Sculptor
Desiderio, Vincent Painter
Deutsch, David Painter
Deutschman, Louise Tolliver Dealer, Curator
Diamond, Jessica Artist
Diamond, Stuart Painter
Diamonstein, Barbaralee Writer
Diao, David Painter

NEW YORK (cont)

Di Cerbo, Michael Painter, Printmaker
Dickson, Jane Leone Painter
DiDomenico, Nikki Conceptual Artist, Assemblage Artist
Diebenkorn, Richard Painter
Diehl, Hans-Jurgen Painter
Digiorgio, Joseph J Painter
DiLaurenti, Marco Italo Art Dealer, Collector
Dill, Lesley Painter, Curator
Dillon, C Douglas Patron, Collector
Di Meo, Dominick Painter, Sculptor
Dine, James Painter, Sculptor
Dintenfass, Terry Dealer
Dixon, Jenny (Jane Hodley) Administrator
Do, Kim V Painter, Educator
Dobbs, John Barnes Painter
Dockstader, Frederick J Consultant, Historian
Dodd, Lois Painter, Educator
Dogancay, Burhan Cahit Painter, Sculptor
Doherty, Michael Stephen Editor, Printmaker
Dokoupil, Jiri Georg Painter
Donati, Enrico Painter, Sculptor
Doo Da Post (Edward Ferdinand Higgins III), III Painter, Mail Artist
Dorfman, Bruce Painter, Collage Artist
Dorfman, Fred Art Dealer, Gallery Director
Dorosh, Daria Environmental Artist, Painter
Dorsey, Deborah Worthington Painter
Dorsky, Morris Historian, Educator
Dorsky, Samuel Art Dealer
Dove, Toni Painter, Printmaker
Downes, Rackstraw Painter, Critic
Downey, Juan Video Artist, Architect
Doyle, Mary Ellen Painter
Doyle, Tom Sculptor, Educator
Drake, Peter Painter, Draftsman
Draper, William Franklin Painter, Instructor
Dreikausen, Margret Painter
Driscoll, Ellen Sculptor
Driscoll, John Paul Dealer, Art Historian
Drum, Sydney Maria Painter, Printmaker
Duback, Charles S Painter, Printmaker
Dubasky, Valentina Painter, Sculptor
Duff, John Ewing Sculptor
Dugmore, Edward Painter
Dunbar, Jill H Critic, Writer
Dunigan, Breon Nina Sculptor
Dunkelman, Loretta Painter
Dunn, Fontaine Painter, Photographer
Dunow, Esti Painter, Historian
Dunwiddie, Charlotte Sculptor
Dworzan, George R Painter
Dyyon, Frazier Painter, Sculptor
Dzubas, Friedel Painter
Eardley, Cynthia Sculptor
Eddy, Don Painter
Edelheit, Martha Painter, Filmmaker
Edelson, Gilbert S Administrator, Lecturer
Edelson, Mary Beth Painter, Sculptor
Edwards, Susan Harris Curator, Historian
Egleston, Truman G Painter
Eichel, Edward W Painter, Draftsman
Eins, Stefan Conceptual Artist, Museum Director
Einstein, Gilbert W Dealer
Eisenberg, Jerome Martin Dealer, Collector
Eisenberg, Sonja Miriam Painter
Eisinger, Harry Painter
Eisner, Carole Swid Painter, Sculptor
Ekdahl, Janis Kay Librarian
Elderfield, John Historian, Curator
El Hanani, Jacob Painter
Eliot, Lucy Carter Painter
Ellenzweig, Allen Bruce Critic, Curator
Ellis, Loren Elizabeth Printmaker, Photographer
Ellis, Richard Painter, Illustrator
Ellis, Stephen Painter
Ellis-Tracy, Jo Painter, Dealer
Ely, Timothy Clyde Book Artist
Emil, Arthur D Collector
Emmerich, Andre Dealer, Writer
Enders, Elizabeth McGuire Painter
Engelson, Carol Painter
Englander, Gertrud Ceramist
Ensrud, Wayne Painter, Printmaker
Epstein, Betty O Sculptor, Painter
Epstein, Mitch (Mitchell D) Photographer
Epstein, Yale Painter, Printmaker
Eriksen, Gary Sculptor, Medalist
Esman, Rosa Gallery Director, Dealer
Esterow, Milton Editor, Publisher
Estes, Richard Painter
Evans, John Collage Artist
Evans, Tom R Painter
Evergon Photographer
Ewald, Elin Lake Writer
F(ord), Lisa Collado Collage Artist, Painter
Facci, Domenico (Aurelio) Sculptor, Painter
Faden, Lawrence Steven Painter, Sculptor
Falfan, Alfredo Painter, Printmaker
Fane, Lawrence Sculptor
Faragasso, Jack Illustrator, Painter
Farber, Dennis H Painter, Photographer
Farber, Maya M Painter
Fares, William O Painter
Farmer, John David Historian, Administrator
Farruggio, Remo Michael Painter
Fasnacht, Heide Ann Sculptor
Faulconer, Mary (Fullerton) Painter, Designer
Faurer, Louis Photographer
Faust, Victoria Printmaker
Fay, Ming G Sculptor, Painter
FeBland, Harriet Painter, Sculptor
Feder, Ben Designer, Painter
Feigen, Richard L Dealer, Collector
Feigin, Marsha Printmaker, Painter
Feinberg, Jean Painter
Feininger, Andreas B L Photographer, Writer
Feinman, Stephen E Dealer
Feld, Stuart Paul Dealer
Feldman, Franklin Printmaker, Writer
Feldman, Ronald Dealer
Feltus, Alan Painter, Educator
Fenn, (Frances) Elizabeth Painter, Graphic Artist
Fenton, Alan Painter, Instructor
Ferrara, Jackie Sculptor
Ferrer, Rafael Painter, Sculptor
Ferris, Daniel B Gallery Director, Curator
Fetting, Rainer Painter
Finck, Furman J Painter, Instructor
Findlay, David B, Jr Dealer
Finkelstein, Henry D Painter, Educator
Finkelstein, Louis Educator, Painter
Finn, David Photographer
Fiore, Joseph A Painter, Instructor
Firestein, Cecily Barth Printmaker
Fischer, John Painter, Sculptor
Fischer, R M Sculptor
Fischl, Eric Painter
Fish, Janet I Painter
Fishko, Bella Dealer
Fitzgerald, Astrid Painter, Printmaker
Flack, Audrey L Painter, Photographer
Flam, Jack D Historian, Educator
Flanagan, Barry Sculptor
Flanagan, Michael Painter
Flavin, Dan Artist, Writer
Fleischman, Lawrence Arthur Art Dealer, Publisher
Flexner, James Thomas Writer, Historian
Flood, Richard Sidney Writer, Gallery Director
Fohr, Jenny Painter, Printmaker
Fondren, Harold M Dealer
Ford, Walton Painter
Foreman, Laura Conceptual Artist, Sculptor
Forge, Andrew Murray Writer, Painter
Foster, Mary Administrator, Curator
Fowler, Mel Printmaker, Painter
Fox, Flo Photographer, Lecturer
Fra, Dahli-Sterne Painter, Sculptor
Frailey, Stephen A Photographer
Frankenberg, Robert Clinton Illustrator, Painter
Frankenthaler, Helen Painter
Frankfurter, Jack Painter, Designer
Fraser, Andrea R Conceptual Artist, Museologist
Frater, Hal Painter
Freckelton, Sondra Painter
Fredenthal, Ruth Ann Painter
Freed, Hermine Photo Artist
Freedman, Deborah S Painter, Printmaker
Freeman, Kathryn Painter, Instructor
Freeman, Mark Painter, Printmaker
Freilicher, Jane Painter, Printmaker
Friedberg, Rachel (Ray) Painter, Director
Friedberg, Richard S Sculptor, Educator
Friedman, B H Writer
Friedman, Dan Conceptual Artist, Designer
Friedman, Ken Painter, Designer
Friedman, Martin Museum Director
Friedman, Sabra Painter
Friedman, Sally Ceila Painter
Fromboluti, Iona Painter
Fromentin, Christine Anne Painter, Graphic Artist
Frumkin, Allan Dealer
Fujita, Kenji Sculptor
Fukui, Nobu Painter
Fuller, Emily Rutgers Painter
Fulton, Hamish Conceptual Artist
Gallagher, Carole Photographer, Writer
Gallagher, Cynthia Painter
Gallander, Cathleen S Art Dealer, Representative
Gamwell, Lynn Curator, historian
Garbaty, Marie-Louise Collector, Patron
Garcia, Frank Gallery Director, Historian
Gardner, Andrew Bradford Printmaker, Painter
Garet, Jedd Painter
Garrison, Barbara Printmaker, Illustrator
Gary, Dorothy Hales Collector, Writer
Gast, Dwight V Writer, Critic
Gaudieri, Alexander V J Museum Director
Gebhardt, Roland Sculptor, Designer
Gechtoff, Sonia Painter
Gee, Helen Art Consultant, Curator
Geist, Sidney Sculptor, Critic
Gekiere, Madeleine Painter, Filmmaker
Gelber, Samuel Painter, Educator
Geller, Matthew Sculptor
Gellis, Sandy L Sculptor
Geltman, Lily Collage Artist, Painter
Geltner, Danita Sue Sculptor, Painter
Genauer, Emily Critic, Writer
Gentile, Gloria Irene Designer, Sculptor
Gentry, Herbert Painter, Graphic Artist
Georges, Paul G Painter
Gerbarg, Darcy Painter
Gerdts, Abigail Booth Historian, Curator
Gerdts, William H Historian, Educator
Gerlach, Christopher S Painter
Gerst, Hilde W Dealer
Getler, Helen Art Dealer, Consultant

NEW YORK (cont)

Ghent, Henri Critic, Writer
Giacalone, Vito Painter, Historian
Giambertone, Paul Sculptor
Giampietro, Isabel (Isabel A Giampietro Knoll) Sculptor, Designer
Gianakos, Cristos Sculptor, Environmental Artist
Gianakos, Steve Sculptor, Painter
Gibson, John Stuart Painter, Printmaker
Gibson, Ralph H Photographer
Gifford, J Nebraska Painter, Sculptor
Gilbert, Lionel Painter, Instructor
Gilchrist, Elizabeth Brenda Editor
Gillespie, Dorothy Muriel Painter, Sculptor
Gillespie, Gregory Joseph Painter
Gimblett, Max(well) Painter, Ceramist
Ginsburg, Max Painter, Illustrator
Giorno, John Conceptual Artist, Printmaker
Giraudier, Antonio Painter, Writer
Gitlin, Michael Sculptor, Draftsman
Gladstone, Barbara Dealer, Historian
Glantzman, Judy Painter
Glaser, Milton Designer, Illustrator
Glass, Wendy D Dealer, Collector
Glezer, Nechemia Art Dealer, Collector
Glier, Mike Draftsman, Muralist
Glimcher, Arnold B Dealer, Writer
Globus, Dorothy Twining Curator
Gluska, Aharon Painter
Gobuzas, Aldona M Art Dealer, Collector
Goddard, Donald Editor, Writer
Godwin, Judith Painter
Goell, Abby Jane Painter, Assemblage Artist
Goertz, Augustus Frederick, III Painter, Photographer
Goffman, Judy Art Dealer, Gallery Owner
Goings, Ralph Painter
Golbin, Andree Painter, Illustrator
Gold, Fay Helfand Painter
Gold, Martha B Sculptor
Gold, Sharon Cecile Painter, Educator
Goldberg, Glenn Painter
Goldberg, Judith Art Dealer
Goldberg, Michael Painter
Goldberg, RoseLee Historian, Curator
Golden, Eunice Painter, Filmmaker
Goldin, Leon Painter
Goldin, Nan R Photographer
Goldman, Judith Writer, Critic
Goldman, Matt Conceptual Artist, Kinetic Artist
Goldner, Janet Sculptor
Goldring, Nancy Deborah Educator, Photographer
Goldschmidt, Lucien Dealer
Goldsmith, Barbara Writer, Critic
Goldsmith, Caroline Lerner Administrator, Consultant
Goldstein, Julius Painter, Instructor
Golub, Leon Painter
Gomez-Quiroz, Juan Manuel Painter, Printmaker
Gonzalez, Juan J Painter
Gonzalez, Xavier Painter, Sculptor
Gonzalez-Torres, Felix Painter
Goodelman, Ruth Sculptor
Goodman, Bertram Painter
Goodman, Helen Historian, Critic
Goodman, James Neil Dealer, Collector
Goodman, Ken(neth Hunt) Painter
Goodman, Marian Dealer, Publisher
Goodman, Sidney Painter
Goodwin, Guy Painter
Gorchov, Ron Painter
Gordon, Albert F Art Dealer
Gordon, Tina Sculptor
Gorney, Jay Philip Gallerist
Gornik, April Painter
Gottlieb, Carla Educator, Historian
Gould, Philip Historian, Educator
Goulet, Lorrie Sculptor, Painter
Gourevitch, Jacqueline Painter
Grafelman, Glenn Allen Painter
Graham, Daniel H Conceptual Artist, Environmental Artist
Graham, Robert Sculptor
Graham, Robert C, Jr Art Dealer
Graham, Robert Claverhouse, Sr Dealer, Collector
Grassi, Marco Conservator, Restorer
Grausman, Philip Sculptor
Graves, Morris Painter
Graves, Nancy Stevenson Painter, Sculptor
Grazda, Ed Photographer
Green, Denise G Painter
Green, George D Painter
Green, Wilder Arts Administrator, Architect
Greenberg, Gloria Painter, Designer
Greenberg, Irwin Painter, Instructor
Greenfield-Sanders, Timothy Photographer
Greenspan, (Mr & Mrs) George Collectors
Greer, Jane Ruth Sculptor
Gregory, Stan(ley Wayne) Painter, Printmaker
Griefen, John Adams Painter
Griesedieck, Ellen Painter, Printmaker
Griffin, Chris A Sculptor
Grigoriadis, Mary Painter
Groedel, Burt Jay Painter, Sculptor
Grooms, Red Painter, Sculptor
Groover, Jan Photographer
Gropper, Cathy Painter, Sculptor
Gross, Alice Sculptor
Gross, Julie Painter
Gross, Rainer Painter
Grossman, Nancy Painter, Sculptor
Grosvenor, Robert Sculptor
Grotz, Dorothy Rogers Painter
Gruen, John Critic, Writer
Gruskin, Mary Josephine Consultant, Collector
Guccione, Juanita Painter
Guida, Dominick Painter
Gummer, Don Sculptor
Gumpel, Hugh Painter
Gund, Agnes Collector, Administrator
Gunderson, Karen Painter
Gundlefinger, John Andre Painter, Collage Artist
Gusella, Ernest Video Artist
Gutzeit, Fred Painter, Educator
Haacke, Hans Christoph Sculptor, Conceptual Artist
Haas, Richard John Printmaker, Muralist
Haber, Ira Joel Sculptor, Writer
Habergritz, George Joseph Painter, Sculptor
Hacklin, Allan Dave Painter, Sculptor
Haessle, Jean-Marie Georges Painter
Hafif, Marcia Painter, Educator
Hagin, Nancy Painter
Hahn, Stephen Dealer
Halaby, Samia Asaad Painter, Educator
Halahmy, Oded Sculptor
Hall, Lee Administrator, Painter
Hall, Susan Painter, Printmaker
Halley, Peter Painter
Halpern, Nathan L Collector
Hambleton, Richard A Painter
Hamer, Charles James Painter
Hammerbeck, Wanda Lee Photographer
Hammond, Harmony Painter, Sculptor
Hammond, Jane Printmaker, Painter
Hammond, Red Painter
Hammons, David Painter
Hanchey, Janet Lynn Painter
Hanks, David Allen Curator, Writer
Hannah, Duncan (Rathbun) Painter
Hansell, Freya Painter
Hapgood, Susan T Curator, Critic
Harbutt, Charles Photographer
Harder, Rodney Painter
Harding, Tim Designer
Hardy, John Painter
Harkins, George C, Jr Painter
Harkness, Madden Painter
Harmon, James Roderick Designer, Glass Blower
Harmon, Lily Painter, Writer
Hart, John Lewis Cartoonist
Hartman, Joanne A Painter, Educator
Harvest, Judith R Conceptual Artist, Painter
Hasen, Burt Stanley Painter, Printmaker
Haskell, Barbara Curator
Haswell, Hollee Curator, Librarian
Haxton, David Computer Animator, Photographer
Hay, A John Historian, Educator
Hayes, David Vincent Sculptor
Hayes, Gerald Painter, Photographer
Haynes, Nancy Painter
Hayward, Jane Historian, Curator
Hazen, Joseph H Collector
Heartney, Eleanor Critic
Hedberg, Gregory Scott Art Dealer, Gallery Director
Hedstrom, Ana Lisa Craftsman
Heeks, Willy Painter
Heiferman, Marvin Curator, Publisher
Heiloms, May Painter
Heinemann, Peter Painter, Instructor
Heinz, Susan Administrator
Heise, Myron Robert Painter
Heiser, Scott Thomas Photographer
Held, Al Painter
Heliker, John Edward Painter, Educator
Helioff, Anne Graile (Mrs Benjamin Hirschberg) Painter, Collage Artist
Heller (Mrs Edward W Greenberg), Goldie Collector, Consultant
Heller, Dorothy Painter
Heller, Susanna Painter
Helman, Eve Collage Artist, Painter
Helman, Phoebe Sculptor, Painter
Hemphill, Herbert Waide, Jr Curator, Lecturer
Henderson, Jack W Painter, Instructor
Hendricks, David Charles Painter, Visual Artist
Hendricks, Geoffrey Painter, Environmental Artist
Henry, Gerrit Van Keuren Critic
Henselmann, Caspar Sculptor
Hepper, Carol Sculptor
Hera Sculptor, Environmental Artist
Herfield, Phyllis Painter
Herrera, Carmen Painter
Hershey, Nona Printmaker, Painting
Highstein, Jene Sculptor
Hildebrand, June Marianne Printmaker, Illustrator
Hill, Clinton J Painter, Sculptor
Hill, James Berry Dealer
Hilson, Douglas Painter, Educator
Hinman, Charles B Painter, Sculptor
Hios, Theo Painter, Graphic Artist
Hirschfeld, Albert Graphic Artist
Hitch, Stewart Painter
Hodes, Barney Administrator
Hodgkins, Rosalind Selma Painter
Hofer, Evelyn Photographer
Hoff, Margo Painter, Collage Artist
Hoffeld, Jeffrey M Art Dealer
Hoffman, Nancy Dealer
Hoie, Claus Painter, Etcher
Hoie, Helen Hunt Painter, Collage Artist

NEW YORK (cont)

Holabird, Jean Painter, Printmaker
Hollerbach, Serge Painter, Instructor
Hollister, Paul Writer, Painter
Holt, Nancy Louise Sculptor, Filmmaker
Holtz, Itshak Jack Painter, Printmaker
Holzer, Jenny Conceptual Artist
Holzman, Eric Painter
Honjo, Masako Painter
Hopkins, Budd Painter, Sculptor
Hopkins, Peter Painter, Writer
Horowitz, (Mr & Mrs) Raymond J Collector
Hoving, Thomas Consultant, Editor
Howat, John Keith Curator, Historian
Hudson Conceptual Artist, Art Dealer
Hughes, Robert S F Critic, Lecturer
Hull, Cathy Illustrator, Conceptual Artist
Hull, John Painter
Humpfey, David Painter, Critic
Humphrey, David Aiken Painter, Printmaker
Humphrey, Nene Sculptor, Instructor
Hunt, Bryan Sculptor
Hunt, Richard Howard Sculptor, Printmaker
Hunter, Paul Painter, Sculptor
Hunter-Stiebel, Penelope Art Dealer, Curator
Hurson, Michael Draftsman, Painter
Hurt, Susanne M Painter
Hutsaliuk, Lubo Painter
Hutton, Leonard Art Dealer
Hyman, Isabelle Historian, Educator
Hyman, Linda Art Dealer, Historian
Iimura, Takahiko Filmmaker, Video Artist
Impiglia, Giancarlo Painter, Sculptor
Incandela, Gerald Jean-Marie Photographer, Muralist
Ingber, Barbara Dealer, Collector
Ingle, John S Painter, Educator
Inoue, Kazuko Painter, Lecturer
Insley, Will Painter, Draftsman
Inukai, Kyohei Painter, Sculptor
Ipsen, Poul Janus Painter, Sculptor
Ireland, Patrick Conceptual Artist
Irwin, Robert Environmental Artist, Sculptor
Isaacson, Lynn Judith Painter, Sculptor
Isenburger, Eric Painter
Iserman, Jim Painter
Isserstedt, Dorothea Carus Art Dealer, Historian
Itchkawich, David Michael Printmaker, Illustrator
Ives, Colta Feller Curator, Educator
Iwamoto, Ralph Shigeto Painter
Izuka, Kunio Sculptor, Painter
Jaar, Alfredo Sculptor
Jackson, Ward Painter, Editor
Jacobs, Jim Painter, Printmaker
Jacquemon, Pierre Painter
Jacquette, Yvonne Helene Painter, Printmaker
Jae Sculptor, Jewelry Designer
Jaffe, Nora Painter, Sculptor
Jampol, Glenn D Painter
Janis, Conrad Dealer, Collector
Jannetti, Tony Printmaker, Designer
Janowich, Ronald Painter
Janowitz, Joel Painter
Jansen, Angela Bing Printmaker, Painter
Jaramillo, Virginia Painter
Jarvis, Lucy Consultant, Filmmaker
Jaudon, Valerie Painter
Jeff Painter, Photographer
Jeffers, Wendy Jane Painter, Curator
Jenkins, Paul Painter
Jennings, Francis Painter, Sculptor
Jenrette, Pamela Anne Painter, Costume Designer
Jensen, Bill Painter
Jerins, Edgar Painter
Jeynes, Paul Sculptor
J J (De La Verriére) Goldsmith, Sculptor
Joelson, Suzanne Painter
Johns, Jasper Painter
Johnson, Audean Painter, Illustrator
Johnson, Buffie Painter, Lecturer
Johnson, Cecile Ryden Painter, Publisher
Johnson, Guy Painter
Johnson, Leon Bernard Painter
Johnson, Miani (Marianne) Guthrie Dealer
Johnson, Una E Curator, Writer
Jonaitis, Aldona Historian, Administrator
Jonas, Joan Video Artist, Conceptual Artist
Jones, Carter R(uthven), Jr Sculptor
Jones, Edward Powis Painter, Printmaker
Jones, Ronald Warren Artist, Critic
Jones & Ginzel, Sculptors
Jordan, Vance Gallery Director, Art Dealer
Juarez, Roberto Painter
Judd, Donald Clarence Sculptor, Architect
Judge, Mary Frances Painter
Judson, Jeannette Alexander Painter, Collage Artist
Julian, Lazaro Painter, Designer
Jurinko, Andy (Andrew Floyd) Painter
Juszczyk, James Joseph Painter
Kacere, John C Painter
Kahan, Alexander Dealer, Consultant
Kahan, Leonard Dealer, Painter
Kahn, Robin Painter
Kahn, Susan B Painter
Kahn, Tobi Aaron Painter, Sculptor
Kahn, Wolf Painter
Kaiman, Charles Painter
Kaish, Luise Sculptor, Painter
Kaish, Morton Painter, Educator
Kalina, Richard Painter, Printmaker
Kallir, Jane Katherine Art Dealer, Writer
Kamihira, Ben Painter
Kampf, Avram S Educator, Curator
Kan, Diana Painter, Lecturer
Kane, Bob Paul Painter
Kanovitz, Howard Painter
Kaplan, Jacques Collector, Dealer
Kaplan, Katherine Art Dealer
Kaplan, Penny Sculptor, Printmaker
Karafel, Lorraine Writer, Critic
Kardon, Janet Museum Director, Curator
Karnes, Karen Ceramist, Craftsman
Kass, Deborah Painter
Kasuba, Aleksandra Environmental Artist
Katz, Alex Painter
Katz, Hilda (Hulda Weber) Painter, Writer
Katz, Leandro Assemblage Artist, Filmmaker
Katz, Morris Painter
Katzen, Hal Zachery Dealer
Katzen, Lila (Pell) Sculptor, Educator
Katzman, Herbert Painter, Instructor
Kaufman, Jane Painter, Lecturer
Kaufman, Joe Illustrator, Writer
Kaufman, Nancy Art Advisor, Writer
Kaufmann, Rick Director, Curator
Kaufmann, Robert Carl Art Librarian
Kawabata, Minoru Painter, Instructor
Kawashima, Takeshi Painter, Sculptor
Kaz (Lawrence Katzman) Designer, Cartoonist
Kaz, Nathaniel Sculptor, Instructor
Keerl, Bayat Painter, Photographer
Keever, Kim Painter, Printmaker
Keister, Steve (Stephen Lee) Sculptor
Keller, Frank S Painter
Keller, Martha Painter
Kelley, Mike Painter
Kelly, Ellsworth Painter, Sculptor
Kelly, James Painter
Kelly, Mary Conceptual Artist
Kendrick, Mel Sculptor
Kepets, Hugh Michael Painter, Printmaker
Khalil, Claire Anne Painter
Kikuchi-Yngojo, Alan Photographer, Collage Artist
Kim, Po (Hyun) Painter
Kimes, Don Painter, Educator
Kimmel-Cohn, Roberta Dealer, Writer
Kimura, Riisaburo Painter, Printmaker
Kind, Phyllis Art Dealer
King, William Dickey Sculptor
Kingman, Dong Painter, Illustrator
Kingsley, April Critic, Lecturer
Kinigstein, Jonah Painter, Designer
Kinstler, Everett Raymond Painter, Instructor
Kippenberger, Martin Painter
Kirschenbaum, Bernard Edwin Sculptor
Kisch, Gloria Sculptor
Klauber, Rick Painter
Kleckner, Susan Photographer, Filmmaker
Kleemann, Ron Painter
Kleiman, Alan Painter, Sculptor
Klein, Doris Printmaker, Sculptor
Kleinberg, Susan Painter, Sculptor
Knight, John Conceptual Artist
Knowles, Alison Performance Artist, Printmaker
Knowles, Elizabeth Sculptor
Kobayashi, Hisako Painter
Kocherthaler, Mina Painter
Kolbowski, Silvia Conceptual Artist, Photographer
Koltun, Frances Lang Collector, Lecturer
Komar and Melamid, Conceptual Artist, Lecturer
Konzal, Joseph Sculptor
Kopf, Silas Craftsman
Koppelman, Chaim Printmaker, Educator
Koppelman, Dorothy Painter, Consultant
Koren, Edward B Cartoonist, Illustrator
Korman, Harriet R Painter
Kornblau, Gerald Art Dealer, Consultant
Korot, Beryl Painter, Video Artist
Korshak, Yvonne Historian, Educator
Koscielny, Margaret Sculptor, Painter
Kostabi, Mark Painter, Sculptor
Kostelanetz, Richard Media Artist, Writer
Kosuth, Joseph Conceptual Artist
Kowalski, Libby R Fiber Artist, Educator
Kozloff, Joyce Painter, Mosaic Artist
Kozloff, Max Photographer, Writer
Kramer, Gertrude M Dealer
Kramer, Hilton Critic
Kramer, Louise Muralist, Sculptor
Kramer, Margia Conceptual Artist, Video Artist
Krashes, Barbara Painter, Director
Kraushaar, Antoinette M Dealer
Krauss, Rosalind E Critic, Historian
Krens, Thomas Museum Director, Educator
Kriensky Painter, Writer
Kriesberg, Irving Painter
Krinsky, Carol Herselle Historian, Educator
Kruger, Barbara Conceptual Artist, Film Critic
Krulik, Barbara S Director
Krushenick, Nicholas Painter
Kubota, Shigeko Video Curator, Video Artist
Kuchel, Konrad G Administrator
Kuehn, Frances Painter
Kuehn, Gary Sculptor, Graphic Artist
Kuh, Howard Painter
Kuh, Katharine Critic, Consultant
Kulicke, Robert M Craftsman, Painter
Kuopus, Clinton Painter, Educator

NEW YORK (cont)

Kurahara, Ted N Painter, Educator
Kurtz, Elaine Painter
Kuryluk, Ewa Painter, Sculptor
Kurz, Diana Painter, Educator
Kusama, Yayoi Sculptor, Painter
Kushner, Robert Ellis Painter
Kuwayama, Tadaaki Painter
Lable, Eliot Sculptor
Laderman, Gabriel Painter, Educator
Laemmle, Cheryl Painter
La Hotan, Robert L Painter
Lally, James Joseph Dealer, Consultant
Lamarre, Paul Conceptual Artist, Sculptor
La Monte, Angela Mae Painter
Lancaster, Mark Painter
Landfield, Ronnie (Ronald T) Painter
Landry, Albert Dealer
Landry, Richard Miles Photographer, Video Artist
Lane, Alvin S Collector
Lane, Lois Painter, Printmaker
Lang, Avis Editor, Curator
Lang, Daniel S Painter
Lanigan-Schmidt, Thomas Assemblage Artist, Instructor
La Noue, Terence Painter, Educator
Lansner, Fay Painter, Tapestry Artist
Lanyon, Ellen Painter, Printmaker
LaRico, Benje Painter
Larraz, Julio F Painter
Larsen, Jack Lenor Designer, Writer
Larson, Kay L Critic, Writer
Lasch, Pat Sculptor
Lasker, Joe (Joseph L) Painter, Illustrator
Lasker, Jonathan Painter
Laster, Paul Collage Artist, Painter
Laub, Stephen Sculpture
Lauf, Cornelia Curator, Art Historian
Laufer, Susan Painter
Lauridsen, Hanne H7L Painter, Sculptor
Lavatelli, Carla Sculptor, Weaver
Lavier, Bertrand Conceptual Artist, Printmaker
Lea, Laurie Jane Sculptor, Graphic Artist
Leaf, June Painter, Sculptor
Leatherdale, Marcus Andrew Photographer
LeBoff, Gail F Photographer
Lebron, Michael A Conceptual Artist, Graphic Artist
Lederman, Stephanie Brody Painter, Drawings
Lee, Catherine Sculptor, Painter
Lee, Eleanor Gay Painter
Lehr, Janet Dealer
Lehrer, Leonard Painter, Lithography
Leiber, Gerson August Printmaker
Leibovitz, Annie Photographer
Leighton, Patricia MacInnes Environmental Artist, Sculptor
Lemer, Ellen Terry Dealer, Collector
Lemieux, Annette Rose Conceptual Artist, Painter
Leonardi, Hector Painter, Educator
Leopold, Susan Sculptor, Assemblage Artist
Lerman, Leo Writer, Historian
Lerman, Ora Painter, Sculptor
Lerner, Abe Book Designer
Lerner, Marilyn Painter
Lerner, Martin Curator, Historian
Lerner, Sandra Painter, Collage Artist
Lerner, Sandy R Painter, Lithographer
Lester, Michelle Tapestry, Painting
Le Va, Barry Sculptor
Levering, Robert K Painter, Collage Artist
Levi, Josef Painter
Levin, Gail Historian, Photographer
Levin, Kim Critic
Levine, Jack Painter
Levine, Les Video Artist, Media Sculptor
Levine, Tom Painter, Printmaker
Levine, Tomar Painter
Levinson, Mon Sculptor, Painter
Levinthal, David Lawrence Photographer
Levitt, Alfred Painter, Prehistorian
Levitt, Helen Photographer, Filmmaker
Levy, Bernard Dealer
Levy, David Corcos Art Historian, Educator
Levy, S(tephen) Dean Dealer, Gallery Director
Levy, Tibbie Painter
Lewczuk, Margrit Painter
Lewenz, Lisa Environmental Artist, Photographer
Lewis, Golda Assemblage Artist, Papermaker
Le Witt, Sol Painter
Liberman, Alexander Painter, Sculptor
Licht, Evelyn M Painter, Sculptor
Lichtenstein, Roy Painter, Sculptor
Lieberman, Louis (Karl) Sculptor, Draftsman
Lieberman, William S Curator
Liles, Raeford Bailey Painter, Sculptor
Lilyquist, Christine Egyptologist, Curator
Lin, Maya Y Sculptor
Linhares, Judith Painter
Link, Phyllida K Graphic Artist, Painter
Linn, Judy Photographer
Linn, Steven Allen Sculptor
Lionni, Leo Sculptor, Painter
Lippard, Lucy Rowland Writer
Lipton, Sondra Sahlman Painter, Sculptor
Little, James Painter, Printmaker
Livet, Anne Hodge Administrator, Critic
Livingston, Sidnee Painter
Llorente, Luis Painter, Designer
Lobello, Peter Sculptor, Graphic Artist
Logemann, Jane Marie Painter, Printmaker
Lombard, Annette Painter, Instructor
Londin, Barbara Painter
London, Alexander Collector, Illustrator
London, Barbara Curator
Long, Rose-Carol Washton Historian, Administrator
Longo, Robert Painter
Longo, Vincent Painter, Printmaker
Lorber, D Martin H B Consultant
Lorber, Richard Critic, Educator
Lorca di Corcia, Philip Photographer
Loring, John Painter, Printmaker
Lotringer, Sylvere Writer
Lowenthal, Constance Historian, Administrator
Lucas, Bonnie Lynn Painter, Instructor
Lucas, Christopher Conceptual Artist
Lucchesi, Bruno Sculptor
Luce, C(harles Beardsley) Conceptual Artist
Lucier, Mary Video Artist, Photographer
Luck, Robert Curator, Instructor
Ludwig, Allan I Photographer, Historian
Luino, Bernardino Painter
Luisi, Jerry Sculptor, Instructor
Lukin, Sven Painter
Lumbard, Jean Ashmore Dealer
Lund, David Painter, Educator
Lurie, Boris Painter, Sculptor
Lusker, Ron Painter, Designer
Macaulay, David Alexander Designer, Illustrator
McCall, Anthony Filmmaker
McCarron, Paul Art Dealer
McCarthy, Denis Painter
McCarthy, Kathleen Sculptor
McCartin, William Francis Painter
McCollum, Allan Sculptor, Painter
McCormick, Pam(ela Ann) Sculptor
McCoy, Ann Muralist, Draftsman
McCoy, Pat A Writer, Critic
McCready, Karen (Karen McCready Noblet) Dealer, Writer
McDarrah, Fred William Photographer, Editor
MacDonald, Robert R Director, Historian
MacDougall, Anne Art Dealer, Painter
McEvilley, Thomas Writer, Critic
McFadden, David Revere Curator
McFadden, Mary Collector, Designer
McGowin, Ed (William Edward) Painter, Sculptor
MacIver, Loren Painter
Mack, Daniel R Craftsman, Designer
McKay, Renee Painter
McKee, David Malcolm Art Dealer
McKenzie, Mary Beth Painter
McKesson, Malcolm Forbes Painter, Sculptor
McKinley-Haas, Mary Painter, Designer
McKinney, Donald Dealer
McMahon, James Edward Dealer
McMullan, James Burroughs Illustrator, Graphic Artist
McNeil, Dean S Sculptor
McShine, Kynaston Leigh Curator, Critic
MacWeeney, Alen Brazil Photographer
Madsen, Loren Wakefield Sculptor
Madsen, Mette B Painter
Magistro, Charles John Painter, Printmaker
Maisel, David Photographer, Environmental Artist
Maisner, Bernard Lewis Painter
Mallin, Judith Young Writer, Collector
Mallory, Nina Ayala Educator, Historian
Malone, Nola Langner Illustrator, Writer
Malott, Mary Painter, Critic
Manabu, Mabe Painter
Mandel, Howard Painter, Sculptor
Mandelbaum, Lyn Painter, Printmaker
Manes, Paul Painter
Mangold, Robert Peter Painter
Mangolte, Babette M Filmmaker, Photographer
Mano, Toru Gallery Director
Mansion, Gracie Art Dealer
Manso, Leo Painter, Educator
Manville, Elsie Painter
Marais Painter
Marano, Lizbeth Sculptor
Marazzi, William Painter
Marcus, Gerald R Painter, Printmaker
Marcus, Marcia Painter, Educator
Marden, Brice Painter, Printmaker
Marder, Dorie Painter, Printmaker
Margolis, David Painter, Sculptor
Margolis, Margo Painter
Marino, Frank Dealer
Marisol, Sculptor
Mark, Mary Ellen Photographer
Mark, Phyllis Sculptor, Environmental Artist
Markel, Kathryn E Dealer
Markovich, Ann Marie Painter, Writer
Marks, (Mr & Mrs) Cedric H Collector, Patron
Marks, Matthew Stuart Art Dealer
Maron, Jeffrey Sculptor
Maroney, James H, Jr Dealer
Marron, Donald B Collector
Marsh, Georgia Painter
Marshall, Richard Donald Historian, Curator
Marter, Joan Historian, Critic
Martin, Chris Painter
Martin, Doug Painter
Martin, Knox Painter, Sculptor
Martin, Richard (Harrison) Historian
Martin, Thomas Painter, Instructor
Martinez, Alfred Painter
Marton, Tutzi Painter, Sculptor
Martone, Michael Photographer

NEW YORK (cont)

Masback, Dennis Painter
Masheck, Joseph Daniel Cahill Historian, Critic
Mason, Francis Scarlett, Jr Administrator
Mason, Frank Herbert Painter, Instructor
Max, Peter Painter, Printmaker
Maxera, Oscar Painter
Maxwell, William C Painter, Printmaker
Mayer, Grace M Curator, Collector
Mayer, Rosemary Sculptor, Graphic Artist
Mayes, Elaine Photographer
Mazze, Irving Sculptor, Medalist
Meadmore, Clement L Sculptor
Meier, Richard Alan Architect
Meisel, Louis Koenig Dealer, Historian
Meisel, Susan Pear Painter, Printmaker
Melikian, Mary Painter
Mendelsohn, John Painter
Mendelson, Haim Painter, Printmaker
Mendoza, Antonio G Photographer
Menil, Georges & Lois de Patron, Collector
Menses, Jan Painter, Printmaker
Merkel, Jayne (Silverstein) Historian, Critic
Merkin, Richard Marshall Painter, Printmaker
Merrin, Edward H Dealer
Mesches, Arnold Painter, Educator
Messer, Thomas M Museum Director, Historian
Metz, Frank Robert Painter, Designer
Metzger, Evelyn Borchard Painter, Sculptor
Meyer, Susan E Editor, Writer
Meyer, Ursula Sculptor, Photographer
Meyerowitz, Joel Photographer
Meyers, Dale (Mrs Mario Cooper) Painter, Instructor
Michals, Duane Photographer
Mihaesco, Eugene Painter, Illustrator
Milder, Jay Painter, Sculptor
Miles, Jeanne Patterson Painter, Sculptor
Miller, Brenda Sculptor, Conceptual Artist
Miller, Joan L Painter, Collage Artist
Miller, John Painter
Miller, Larry Painter, Video Artist
Miller, Laurence Glenn Gallery Director, Photographer
Miller, Richard Kidwell Painter
Miller, Richard McDermott Sculptor
Miller, Robert Peter Dealer
Miller, Steve Painter, Conceptual Artist
Milonas, Minos Painter, Sculptor
Minsky, Richard Bookbinder, Conceptual Artist
Minter, Marilyn A Painter
Miotte, Jean Painter
Miralda, Antoni Sculptor
Mirra, (Mirra Tengroth) Painter, Conceptual Artist
Miss, Mary Sculptor
Mitchell, Fred Painter
Mitchell, Peter Todd Painter
Mitty, Lizbeth J Painter, Printmaker
Mock, Richard Basil Painter, Illustrator
Model, Elisabeth D Sculptor, Painter
Mogavero, Michael James Painter
Mogensen, Paul Painter, Printmaker
Monaghan, William Scott Painter, Sculptor
Mones, Arthur Photographer
Monk, Meredith Director, Filmmaker
Monk, Robert Evan, Jr Dealer, Curator
Monory, Jacques Painter, Filmmaker
Monroe, Gerald Painter, Educator
Moonelis, Judith C Sculptor, Ceramist
Moore, Alan Willard Art Critic, Publisher
Moore, Bridget Liane Gallery Director
Moore, Fay Painter, Administrator
Moore, Peter Photographer, Archivist
Moore, Robert James Painter, Photographer
Morales, Armando Painter, Printmaker
Morgan, Norma Gloria Painter, Engraver
Morgan, Susan Painter, Instructor
Morgan, Theodora (Theodora Morgan Olsen) Writer
Morin, France Curator, Art Dealer
Morley, Malcolm Painter, Sculptor
Morosan, Ron Painter
Morphesis, Jim (James George) Painter
Morris, Robert Sculptor
Morris, Wright Writer, Photographer
Morse, Mitchell Ian Dealer, Consultant
Mosenthal, Charlotte Dembo Painter, Printmaker
Moskowitz, Ira Painter, Printmaker
Moskowitz, Robert S Painter
Moss, Irene Painter
Moszynski, Andrew Painter
Moxey, Patricio Keith Fleming Art Historian
Moy, Seong Painter, Printmaker
Moyer, Roy Painter, Administrator
Muehlemann, Kathy Painter
Mulhern, Michael Painter
Mullarkey, Maureen Painter, Critic
Muller, Priscilla Elkow Art Historian, Curator
Munro, Eleanor Writer, Lecturer
Murdock, Robert Mead Curator
Murphy, Catherine E Painter
Murphy, Hass Sculptor, Draftsman
Murray, Elizabeth Painter
Murray, John Michael Painter
Murray, Judith Painter
Murray, Robert (Gray) Sculptor, Painter
Mussmann, Linda L Director, Writer
Myers, Dorothy Roatz Painter, Lecturer
Myers, Rita Video Artist
Myers, Terry R Critic, Historian
Nagle, Ron Ceramist
Nahas, Dominique François Museum Director, Curator
Naiman, Lee Dealer, Consultant
Nakazato, Hitoshi Painter, Printmaker
Naponic, Tony (Anthony George) Painter, Consultant
Nathans, Rhoda R Photographer
Nauman, Bruce Sculptor
Naumann, Francis M Historian, Writer
Navaretta, Cynthia Lecturer, Editor
Nechvatal, Joseph James Printmaker, Draftsman
Negroponte, George Painter
Neher, Ross James Painter, Writer
Neikrug, Marjorie Art Dealer
Neill, Joe Sculptor
Neiman, LeRoy Painter, Printmaker
Nelson, Dona Rae Painter
Nelson, Joan Painter
Nemec, Vernita McClish Conceptual Artist, Painter
Nerdrum, Odd Painter
Nesbitt, Lowell (Blair) Painter, Sculptor
Nessim, Barbara Painter
Neuberger, Roy R Collector, Patron
Neuhaus, Max Sculptor, Lecturer
Neustein, Joshua Painter, Conceptual Artist
Newman, Arnold Photographer
Newman, Elizabeth H Sculptor
Newton, Douglas Administrator, Museum Director
Niblock, Phill Filmmaker, Videomaker
Nichols, James William Painter
Nickson, Graham G Painter, Educator
Nieto, John W Painter, Sculptor
Nix, Patricia (Lea) Sculptor, Painter
Noble, Kevin Painter
Nochlin, Linda (Pommer) Historian, Educator
Noda, Takayo Graphic Artist, Printmaker
Noel, Georges Painter, Sculptor
Nolan, Margaret Patterson Librarian
Noland, William Sculptor
Nonas, Richard Sculptor
Norman, Dorothy (S) Writer, Photographer
Norvell, Patsy Sculptor, Environmental Artist
Notarbartolo, Albert Painter, Environmental Artist
Novak, Barbara (Mrs Brian O'Doherty) Historian, Educator
Novros, David Painter
Nygren, John Fergus Glass Artist
O'Beil, Hedy Painter, Critic
Obuck, John Francis Painter
Ocampo, Miguel Painter
Ockenga, Starr Photographer, Educator
O'Connell, Edward E Photographer, Printmaker
O'Connor, Francis Valentine Historian, Lecturer
O'Hara, Morgan Painter, Conceptual Artist
Ohlau, Juergen Uwe Gallery Director
Ohlson, Douglas Dean Painter, Educator
Oji, Helen Shizuko Painter
Okoshi, E Sumiye Painter, Collage Artist
Okuhara, Tetsu Photographer
Okumura, Lydia Painter
Oldenburg, Claes Thure Sculptor
Oldenburg, Richard Erik Museum Director
Oleszko, Patricia Visual Artist, Performance Artist
Oliphant, Patrick Political Cartoonist
Olitski, Jules Painter, Sculptor
Oliveira, Nathan Painter
Oliver, Bobbie Painter
Olson, Roberta Jeanne Marie Historian, Curator
Ono, Yoko Conceptual Artist
Oosterom, Richard H Art Dealer, Consultant
Oppenheim, Dennis A Sculptor
Order, Trudy Painter
Orensanz, Angel L Sculptor, Ceramist
Orlowsky, Lillian Painter, Collage Artist
Oster, Gerald Painter, Kinetic Artist
Osterweil-Weber, Suzanne Painter, Printmaker
O'Sullivan, Daniel Joseph Painter, Instructor
Oursler, Tony Video Artist
Owen, Frank (Franklin Charles) Painter
Owsley, David Thomas Consultant
Ox, Jack Painter, Conceptual Artist
Pace, Stephen S Painter, Printmaker
Padovano, Anthony John Sculptor, Draftsman
Paik, Nam June Video Artist
Palmer, Meredith Ann Art Dealer, Gallery Director
Pandozy, Raffaele Martini Conceptual Artist, Lecturer
Papageorge, Tod Photographer
Pardee, William Hearne Painter, Educator
Parizek, Jaro Dealer, Collector
Parker, Nancy Winslow Illustrator, Writer
Parker, Robert Andrew Painter
Parkinson, Elizabeth Bliss (Mrs Henry Ives Cobb) Patron, Collector
Parness, Charles Painter
Pascal, David Painter, Cartoonist
Passlof, Pat Painter, Educator
Passuntino, Peter Zaccaria Painter, Printmaker
Paternosto, Cesar Pedro Painter
Patkin, Izhar Painter, Sculptor

NEW YORK (cont)

Patterson, Clayton Ian Sculptor, Video Artist
Peacock, Cliffton Painter
Pearl, Marilyn Dealer
Pearlstein, Alix Sculptor
Pearlstein, Philip Painter, Educator
Pearson, Henry C Painter, Instructor
Pei, I M (Ieoh Ming) Architect, Designer
Pellettieri, Michael Joseph Printmaker, Painter
Pels, Albert Painter, Administrator
Penn, Irving Photographer
Pentelovitch, Robert Alan Painter
Peppard, Blaylock A Painter
Peress, Gilles Photographer
Perez, Celis Painter, Sculptor
Perlman, Hirsch Painter
Perlow, Katharina Rich Dealer, Gallery Director
Perls, Klaus G Dealer
Perreault, John Critic, Curator
Perry, Lincoln Frederick Painter
Pershan, Marion Painter, Teacher
Persky, Robert S Writer, Publisher
Peruo, Marsha Painter, Printmaker
Pesner, Carole Manishin Dealer
Peterson, Susan Harnly Educator, Ceramic Artist
Pfaff, Judy Sculptor, Educator
Pfahl, Charles Alton, III Painter
Pfriem, Bernard Painter, Director
Phelan, Ellen Denise Painter
Phillips, Alice Jane Painter
Phillips, Helen (Elizabeth) Sculptor, Graphic Artist
Phillpot, Clive James Librarian, Writer
Pierce, Charles Eliot, Jr Administrator, Director
Pierce, Donald (Benjamin) Painter, Instructor
Pilgrim, Dianne Hauserman Museum Director, Historian
Pinchbeck, Peter G Painter
Pincus-Witten, Robert A Educator, Writer
Pinsker, Essie Sculptor
Pinto, Angelo Raphael Painter, Printmaker
Pinto, Jody Environmental Artist, Sculptor
Pionk, Richard C Painter
Pisano, Ronald George Historian, Consultant
Pitts, Richard G Painter, Printmaker
Placzek, Adolf Kurt Librarian, Historian
Plagens, Peter Painter, Critic
Plotkin, Linda Painter, Printmaker
Poindexter, Elinor Fuller Dealer
Polcari, Stephen Historian, Administrator
Polsky, Cynthia Hazen Museum Trustee, Collector
Ponce de Leon, Michael Printmaker, Painter
Pond, Clayton Painter, Printmaker
Poons, Larry Painter
Porada, Edith Historian
Porter, Liliana Painter, Printmaker
Portnow, Marjorie Anne Painter
Posen, Stephen Painter
Poses, (Mr & Mrs) Jack I Collectors
Posner, Donald Historian, Educator
Post, Anne B Sculptor, Graphic Artist
Poster, June Administrator
Pousette-Dart, Joanna Painter
Pozzi, Lucio Painter, Printmaker
Prager, David A Collector
Prakapas, Dorothy Director
Pratt, Dallas Patron, Collector
Pratt, Frances (Frances Elizabeth Usui) Painter, Illustrator
Prentice, David Ramage Painter, Printmaker
Preston, George Nelson Historian, Educator
Price, Doris C Painter, Printmaker
Price, Kenneth Printmaker, Sculptor
Price, Sara J Painter, Photographer
Prohaska, Elena Anastasia Consultant, Curator
Promutico, Jean Painter
Puett, Garnett G Sculptor
Purdum, Rebecca Painter
Quackenbush, Robert Illustrator, Writer
Quaytman, Harvey Painter
Quentel, Holt Painter
Quigley, Robin L Jeweler, Metalsmith
Quisgard, Liz Whitney Painter, Sculptor
Raab, Gail B Collage Artist, Painter
Rabinovitch, William Avrum Painter, Sculptor
Rabinowitch, David Sculptor
Rabkin, Leo Sculptor, Painter
Raffael, Joseph Painter, Printmaker
Raffo, Steve Painter, Draftsman
Rafsky, Jessica C Collector
Raggio, Olga Historian, Curator
Ragusa, Isa Historian
Rand, Steven Jay Sculptor
Raskind, Philis Sculptor, Instructor
Ratcliff, Carter Critic, Writer
Rathbone, Perry Townsend Museum Director
Ratkai, George Painter, Sculptor
Rauschenberg, Robert Painter, Photographer
Raven, Arlene Writer, Historian
Raydon, Alexander R Dealer, Collector
Raymond, Lilo Photographer
Re, Marisa del Dealer
Recanati, Dina Sculptor
Recklinghausen, Marianne von Painter, Sculptor
Reddy, Krishna N Printmaker, Sculptor
Reed, David Painter
Reed, Harold Dealer
Reeves, Daniel McDonough Video Artist, Installation Artist
Reff, Theodore Historian
Reginato, Peter Sculptor
Rehberger, Gustav Painter, Draftsman
Reiback, Earl M Sculptor, Kinetic Artist
Reichek, Elaine Conceptual Artist
Reid, Robert Dennis Painter, Instructor
Reiland, Lowell Keith Sculptor
Reiner, Gladys & Jules Collectors, Patrons
Reininghaus, Ruth (Ruth Reininghaus Smith) Painter
Reiring, Janelle Director
Rembert, Virginia Pitts Educator, Historian
Remington, Deborah Williams Painter
Resek, Kate Frances Painter
Resika, Paul Painter
Resnick, Marcia Aylene Photographer, Conceptual Artist
Resnick, Milton Painter
Rice, Shelley Enid Critic, Historian
Rich, Garry Lorence Painter
Richards, Bill Painter
Richards, Bill (William A) Draftsman
Richards, Eugene Photographer, Lecturer
Richardson, Constance (Coleman) Painter
Richter, Scott Sculptor
Riese, Beatrice Painter
Riess, Lore Painter, Printmaker
Rinehart, Michael Editor
Ringgold, Faith Painter, Sculptor
Rioux (de Messimy), Deena (Coty) des Painter, Graphic Artist
Ritchie, (Celia) Ann Painter
Rizzi, James Painter, Printmaker
Robbin, Anthony Stuart Painter
Robbin, Tony Painter, Sculptor
Robbins, Bruce Painter, Sculptor
Robbins, David A Conceptual Artist, Writer
Roberts, Richard Painter
Robins, Corinne Critic, Writer
Robinson, Libby Painter, Sculptor
Robinson, Maura Painter
Robinson, Walter Painter, Critic
Rockburne, Dorothea Painter, Sculptor
Rockefeller, (Mr & Mrs) David Collectors
Rockefeller, (Mrs) Laurance S Collector
Rodan, Don Photographer, Painter
Rodriguez, Geno (Eugene) Photographer, Museum Director
Rodriquez, Ernesto Angelo Painter, Designer
Rohlfing, Christian Administrator, Curator
Roller, Marion Bender Painter, Sculptor
Rollins, Tim Painter, Instructor
Romano, Salvatore Michael Sculptor, Kinetic Artist
Romero, Rachael L Painter, Printmaker
Rosand, David Historian, Critic
Rose, Barbara Historian
Rose, Herman Painter, Printmaker
Rose, Leatrice Painter, Instructor
Rose, Mary Anne Painter, Printmaker
Rose, Peter Henry Dealer
Rose, Stephanie Painter, Educator
Rosen, Annabeth Ceramist, Sculptor
Rosen, Diane Painter
Rosenbaum, Joan H Museum Director
Rosenberg, Alex Jacob Curator, Consultant
Rosenberg, Carole Halsband Art Dealer, Director
Rosenberg, Terry Sculptor, Painter
Rosenblum, Robert Historian
Rosenfeld, Samuel L Art Dealer, Collector
Rosenfeld, Sharon Painter
Rosenhouse, Irwin Printmaker, Painter
Rosenquist, James Painter
Rosenthal, Deborah Maly Critic, Painter
Rosenthal, Howard Sculptor
Rosenthal, Stephen Painter
Rosenthal, Tony (Bernard) Sculptor
Rosenwald, Carol Art Dealer
Roser, Ce (Cecilia) Painter, Video Artist
Ross, Charles Environmental Artist, Sculptor
Ross, Clifford Painter
Ross, David Anthony Curator, Lecturer
Ross, Gloria F(rankenthaler) Tapestry Artist
Ross, John T Printmaker, Educator
Ross, Rhoda Honore Painter, Instructor
Rossi, Joseph O Painter, Instructor
Rotan, Walter Sculptor
Rothenberg, Susan Painter, Printmaker
Rothschild, Carolyn Anita Dealer
Rothschild, John D Dealer
Rothschild, Judith Painter, Collage Artist
Rotterdam, Paul Z Painter
Row, David Painter
Ruben, Richards Painter, Educator
Rubin, Irwin Painter, Designer
Rubin, Lawrence Art Dealer, Collector
Rubin, William Curator, Historian
Rubinfien, Leo H Photographer, Filmmaker
Rubinstein, Meyer Raphael Critic
Ruda, Edwin Painter
Ruddley, John Painter, Consultant
Ruellan, Andree Painter
Ruppersberg, Allen Conceptual Artist
Ruta, Peter Paul Painter
Rutzky, Ivy Sky Sculptor
Ryan, Elizabeth Painter
Ryman, Robert Painter
Saari, Peter H Painter, Sculptor

NEW YORK (cont)

Sacks, Beverly & Ray Consultants, Collectors
Sade, Shuli Painter, Sculptor
Sadek, George Educator, Designer
Saganic, Livio Michele Sculptor
Saidenberg, Daniel Dealer
Saidenberg, Eleanore B Dealer, Collector
St Clair, Michael Art Dealer
Sakurai, Jo Mary (Jo Mary McCormick-Sakurai) Painter, Photographer
Sal, Jack Photographer, Painter
Salemme, Lucia (Autorino) Painter, Writer
Salle, David Painter
Salt, John Painter
Saltz, Jerry Critic, Curator
Salvadori, Vieri R Photographer, Administrator
Samaras, Lucas Sculptor
Samuels, Gerald Painter, Sculptor
Sanborn, James Sculptor
Sande, Rhoda Art Dealer, Sculptor
Sanden, John Howard Painter, Instructor
Sanders, Rhea (Rhea Sanders Rabinovich) Painter
Sandler, Barbara Painter
Sandler, Irving Harry Critic, Historian
Sandlin, David Thomas Painter, Printmaker
Sandrow, Hope Photographer
Santlofer, Jonathan Painter
Saphire, Lawrence M Writer, Art Dealer
Sato, Masaaki Painter
Saul, Peter Painter
Saulson, Harold Painter
Scarpitta, Salvatore Sculptor, Painter
Schab, Margo Pollins Art Dealer
Schaefer, Scott Jay Curator, Historian
Schaeffer, Kate Dealer, Collector
Schaeffer, Martha J Dealer
Schapiro, Meyer Educator, Historian
Schapiro, Miriam Painter, Sculptor
Scharf, Kenny Painter
Scharf, William Painter
Scheuer, Ruth Painter, Tapestry Artist
Schimansky, Donya Dobrila Librarian, Historian
Schjeldahl, Peter Critic, Editor
Schlemowitz, Abram Sculptor
Schloss, Arleen P Painter
Schmidt, Arnold Alfred Painter, Sculptor
Schnabel, Julian Painter
Schneebaum, Tobias Painter
Schneemann, Carolee Painter, Filmmaker
Schneider, Ira Video Artist, Photographer
Schneider, Jo Anne Painter
Schneider, Lisa Dawn Dealer, Critic
Schneiderman, Dorothy Dealer
Schneier, Donna Frances Dealer
Schoen, (Mr & Mrs) Arthur Boyer Collectors
Schonzeit, Benjamin Painter
Schorr, Justin Painter, Educator
Schrag, Karl Painter, Printmaker
Schreyer, Greta L Painter, Printmaker
Schulson, Susan Painter
Schulte, (Mr & Mrs) Arthur D Collectors
Schulz, Charles Monroe Cartoonist
Schuselka, Elfi Painter, Sculptor
Schwabsky, Barry Editor, Critic
Schwartz, Buky Painter
Schwartz, Elliott S Photographer
Schwartz, Eugene M Collector, Patron
Schwartz, Marvin D Historian
Schwartz, Sing-Si Photographer
Schwartz, Therese Painter, Writer
Schweitzer, M R Dealer, Gallery Director
Schweninger, Ann Rozzelle Illustrator
Scott, Arden Sculptor
Scribner, Charles, III Historian, Lecturer
Seawright, James L, Jr Sculptor, Educator
Seborovski, Carole Painter
Segal, Barbara Jean Sculptor, Craftsman
Seide, Paul A Sculptor
Seidl, Claire Painter, Printmaker
Selchow, Roger Hoffman Painter, Sculptor
Seltzer, Joanne Lynn Painter, Printmaker
Semmel, Joan Painter
Seplowin, Charles Joseph Sculptor
Serra, Richard Sculptor
Serra, Rudy Sculptor
Serra-Badue, Daniel F Painter, Educator
Shahly, Jehan Painter
Shahn, Bernarda Bryson Painter, Writer
Shainman, Jack S Art Dealer, Gallery Director
Shapiro, Babe Painter, Administrator
Shapiro, David Painter, Printmaker
Shapiro, Joel (Elias) Sculptor
Sharon, Russell Painter, Sculptor
Sharp, Willoughby Video Artist, Consultant
Shashaty, Yolanda Victoria Painter
Shatter, Susan Louise Painter
Shaw, (George) Kendall Painter
Shaw, Paul Jefferson Calligrapher, Designer
Shea, Judith Sculptor
Shearer, Rhonda Roland Sculptor, Writer
Shechtman, George Henoch Dealer
Shecter, Pearl S Painter, Consultant
Sheehan, Maura A Sculptor, Painter
Sheffield, Margaret Critic, Curator
Sheirr, Olga (Krolik) Painter
Shemesh, Lorraine R Painter
Sherman, Cindy Photographer
Sherman, Sarai Painter, Sculptor
Sherrod, Philip Lawrence Painter, Writer
Shibley, Gertrude Painter
Shikler, Aaron Painter
Shirai, Akiko Painter, Printmaker
Shooter, Tom Painter
Shorr, Harriet Painter
Shostak, Ed (Edwin Bennett) Sculptor
Shoulberg, Harry Painter, Graphic Artist
Showell, Kenneth L Painter
Shuff, Lily (Lillian Shir) Painter, Printmaker
Sica Printmaker, Sculptor
Siegel, (Leo) Dink Illustrator, Cartoonist
Siegel, Fran Painter
Sigismund, Violet M Painter, Printmaker
Silberstein-Storfer, Muriel Rosoff Art Educator, Instructor
Siler, Todd (Lael) Painter, Sculptor
Sills, Thomas Albert Painter
Silver, Shelly Andrea Video Artist, Filmmaker
Silverberg, Ellen Ruth Painter, Art Dealer
Silverberg, June Roselyn Painter
Silverman, Burton Philip Painter, Illustrator
Silverman, Joy Administrator
Silverstein, Ida Painter
Simmons, Laurie Photographer
Simon, Helene Sculptor
Simon, Sidney Sculptor, Painter
Simonds, Charles Frederick Sculptor, Architect
Simonian, Judith Painter
Simpson, Merton D Painter, Dealer
Sims, Lowery Stokes Historian, Curator
Sims, Peter Andrew Gallery Director, Historian
Singer, Clifford Painter, Printmaker
Sirena (Contessa Antonia Mastrocristino Fanara) Painter, Lecturer
Sirkis, Nancy Photographer, Educator
Sirugo, Sal (Salvatore) Painter
Sischy, Ingrid B Editor, Curator
Sisto, Elena Painter
Skoglund, Sandy Photographer, Sculptor
Sky, Alison Environmental Artist
Slavin, Arlene Painter, Sculptor
Slavin, Neal Photographer
Sleigh, Sylvia Painter, Instructor
Sligh, Clarissa T Photographer, Painter
Slivka, David Sculptor
Sloat, Richard Joel Painter, Printmaker
Slone, Sandi Painter, Instructor
Slonem, Hunt Painter, Muralist
Small, Neal Designer, Satirist
Smith, Dinah Maxwell Painter, Photographer
Smith, Gregg Sherwood Painter, Graphic Artist
Smith, Lawry Director, Curator
Smith, Leon Polk Painter, Collage Artist
Smith, Paul J Museum Director
Smith, Shirley Painter
Smith, Susan Painter, Collage Artist
Smith, Vincent D Painter, Printmaker
Smokler, Stanley B Sculptor
Snelson, Kenneth D Sculptor, Computer
Snyder, Joan Painter
Snyder, Kit-Yin Sculptor, Environmental Artist
Soffer, Sasson Environmental Artist, Conceptual Artist
Solinger, David M Collector, Patron
Solman, Joseph Painter
Solodkin, Judith Lithographer, Publisher
Solomon, Gerald Dealer
Solomon, Holly Dealer, Collector
Solomon, Richard H Publisher, Art Dealer
Solomon, Rosalind Photographer
Solomon, (Mrs) Sidney L Collector
Sonday, Milton Franklin, Jr Curator
Sonenberg, Jack Painter, Sculptor
Sonfist, Alan Environmental Artist
Sonneman, Eve Photographer, Filmmaker
Sonnier, Keith Sculptor
Soorikian, Diana Tashjian Painter
Sorce, Anthony John Painter
Soreff, Helen Painter
Soreff, Stephen Conceptual Artist, Painter
Sorel, Edward Illustrator, Writer
Sorkin, Emily Art Dealer, Gallery Director
Spaeth, Eloise O'Mara Collector, Writer
Sparkman, Gene (Carl), Jr Painter, Illustrator
Spector, Naomi Writer
Speiser, Stuart M Collector, Patron
Spelman, Jill Sullivan Painter
Spence, Andrew Painter
Sperakis, Nicholas George Painter, Printmaker
Spero, Nancy Painter, Collage Artist
Speyer, Nora Painter
Spiegel, Laurie Computer Artist, Audio-Visual Artist
Spira, Bill Sculptor
Spivy-Anderson, C Alexandra Critic, Writer
Sproat, Christopher Townsend Sculptor
Squiers, Carol Writer, Curator
Sragow, Ellen Gallery Director
Stackhouse, Robert Sculptor
Stacy, Donald L Painter, Educator
Stadler, Albert Painter
Staempfli, George W Dealer, Painter
Stahl, Alan M Curator, Historian
Stamos, Theodoros (S) Painter
Stampfle, Felice Curator, Writer
Standen, Edith Appleton Historian
Stanley, Bob Painter
Stanton, Phil Conceptual Artist, Kinetic Artist
Stapleton, Joseph F Lecturer, Painter
Starn Twins, Painters, Photographers
Stavrinos, George Philip Illustrator

NEW YORK (cont)

Stayton, Janet Painter
Steckel, Anita Collage Artist, Painter
Steen, Carol J Sculptor, Painter
Stefanelli, Joe Painter
Stein, Lewis Photographer, Conceptual Artist
Steinbaum, Bernice Dealer
Steinberg, Saul Cartoonist
Steiner, Michael Sculptor, Painter
Steiner, Paul Writer, Critic
Steir, Pat Painter
Stella, Frank Painter
Sterne, Hedda Painter
Stettner, Louis Photographer
Stevens, May Painter
Stevenson, Ruth Rolston Painter, Instructor
Stewart, Jack Painter, Educator
Stiebel, Eric Dealer
Stiebel, Gerald Gustave Dealer
Stillman, E Clark Collector
Stoloff, Carolyn Painter, Collage
Stone, Sylvia Sculptor
Storey, David Illustrator
Story Wilson, Martha Redy Conceptual Artist, Museum Director
Stratton, Suzanne L Museum Director
Straus, Sandy Painter
Strider, Marjorie Virginia Sculptor, Painter
Stronghilos, Carol Painter
Stuart, Michelle Painter, Sculptor
Stux, Stefan Victor Art Dealer, Director
Suba, Susanne (Mrs Bertam Bloch) Painter, Illustrator
Sugarman, George Sculptor, Painter
Sujo, Clara Diament Gallery Director, Dealer
Sullivan, Bill Painter, Printmaker
Sullivan, Jim Painter
Sultan, Altoon Painter
Sultan, Donald K Painter, Printmaker
Surrey, Milt Painter
Sussman, Elisabeth Sacks Director
Sussman, Jill Gallery Director
Sutton, Pat (Lipsky) Painter
SuZen, Photographer, Designer
Suzuki, Katsko (Katsko Suzuki Kannegieter) Art Dealer
Suzuki, Taro Sculptor, Painter
Svendsen, Louise Averill Curator
Swain, Robert Painter
Swergold, Marcelle M Sculptor
Szoke, John Dealer, Publisher
Tabachnick, Anne Painter
Tacla, Jorge Painter, Muralist
Taggart, William John Painter, Sculptor
Tai, Jane S Administrator
Talbert, Richard Harrison Painter, Environmental Artist
Tancock, John Leon Administrator, Historian
Tanger, Susanna Painter, Writer
Taper, Geri Painter, Environmental Artist
Taradash, Meryl Environmental Artist, Kinetic Artist
Tardo, (Manuel) Rodulfo Sculptor
Tatistcheff, Peter Alexis Dealer, Gallery Director
Tatti, Benedict Michael Sculptor, Painter
Tawney, Lenore Weaver, Assemblage Artist
Taylor, Al C Sculptor, Printmaker
Tempest, Gerard Francis Painter, Sculptor
Teraoka, Masami Painter, Sculptor
Terry, Hilda Cartoonist
Tetherow, Michael Painter
Tewes, Robin J Painter, Printmaker
Thacher, Anita Installation Artist, Filmmaker
Thaw, Eugene Victor Dealer, Collector
Thea, Carolee B Sculptor, Environmental Artist
Thomas, Kathleen K Sculptor, Assemblage Artist
Thomas, Yvonne Painter
Thompson, Kenneth Webster Illustrator, Painter
Thomson, Carl L Painter, Art Appraiser
Thomson, Colin (H) Painter
Thon, William Painter
Tillim, Sidney Painter, Instructor
Ting, Walasse Painter
Tobias, Julius Sculptor, Instructor
Tobias, Richard Painter
Toledo, Angeles Art Dealer, Museologist
Toledo, Francisco Painter, Printmaker
Toll, Barbara Elizabeth Dealer, Curator
Tomkins, Calvin Writer
Tompkins, Betty (I) Painter, Printmaker
Tooker, George Painter, Printmaker
Torlen, Michael Arnold Painter, Educator
Torreano, John Francis Painter, Sculptor
Torres, Francesc Video Artist, Sculptor
Trakas, George Sculptor
Traub, Charles H Educator, Photographer
Trauerman, Margy Ann Painter, Instructor
Traver, Donald Conceptual Artist
Trincere, Li Painter
Tripp, Jan Peter Painter, Printmaker
True, David Painter
Trueblood, Emily Herrick Printmaker
Tsai, Wen-Ying Sculptor, Painter
Tuchman, Phyllis Historian, Critic
Tucker, Marcia Museum Director, Curator
Tullis, Garner H Publisher, Printmaker
Tully, Judd Writer, Curator
Tunick, David Dealer
Tupitsyn, Margarita Critic, Curator
Turner, Alan Painter, Printmaker
Turner, Judith Estelle Photographer, Video Artist
Tuttle, Richard Painter
Twombly, Cy Painter
Tyson, Mary (Mrs Kenneth Thompson) Painter
Uchima, Ansei Printmaker, Painter
Uglow, Alan Painter
Ukeles, Mierle Laderman Environmental Artist, Sculptor
Ultra Violet, Painter, Writer
Umlauf, Lynn (Charlotte) Painter, Sculptor
Underhill, William Sculptor
Unithan, Dolly Painter, Sculptor
Upright, Diane W Art Dealer, Writer
Urban, Vladimir T Painter, Sculptor
Urso, Josette Marie Painter, Sculptor
Vaisman, Meyer Painter
Valenstein, Suzanne Gebhart Curator
Van Haaften, Julia Curator, Writer
Van Horn, Dana Carl Painter
Van Leer, Elizabeth Sanford Collector
Varnedoe, John Kirk Train Curator
Vazquez, Paul Painter
Velez, Edin Video Artist
Venet, Bernar Sculptor, Conceptual Artist
Venezia, Michael Painter
Vicente, Esteban Painter
Vidal, Francisco Fernandez Painter, Sculptor
Vidal, Hahn Painter
Viera, Charles David Educator, Painter
Vincent, Clare Curator, Historian
Virgona, Hank (Henry P) Painter, Printmaker
Vitale, Vincent Painter, Tapestry Artist
Vizner, Nikola Art Dealer, Gallery Director
Vodicka, Ruth Kessler Sculptor
Vogel, Herbert (Mr & Mrs) Collectors
Volpe, Robert Painter, Lecturer
Von Ringelheim, Paul Helmut Sculptor
Von Rydingsvard, Ursula Sculptor
Wachs, Ethel Educator, Collector
Wagner, Merrill Painter
Waitzkin, Stella Sculptor, Painter
Wald, Sylvia Painter, Sculptor
Waldman, Paul Painter
Walinska, Anna Painter, Lecturer
Walker, Mort Cartoonist
Walker, William Bond Administrator, Librarian
Wall, Bruce C Painter
Wall, Rhonda Painter, Instructor
Wall, Sue Painter, Printmaker
Wallace, Soni Painter
Walsh, James Painter, Sculptor
Waltemath, Joan Painter
Walter, May E Collector, Patron
Walter, Paul F Collector, Patron
Walton, Guy E Writer, Educator
Walton, Marion Sculptor
Waltzer, Stewart Paul Dealer, Painter
Wang, C C Painter
Ward, Elaine Painter
Wardwell, Allen Museum Director, Consultant
Warner, Jo Painter
Warren, Tom P Collector, Photographer
Warshaw, Larry Painter, Photographer
Washburn, Joan T Art Dealer
Wasserman, Jeffrey Painter
Waters, Jack Filmmaker, Conceptual Artist
Watkins, Ragland Tolk Curator, Dealer
Webb, Alexander Dwight Photographer
Webb, Patrick Painter, Muralist
Weber, Idelle Painter
Weber, John Gallery Director, Art Dealer
Webster, Sally (Sara B) Historian
Wechsler, Susan Editor, Writer
Wegman, William Painter, Photographer
Weihs, Erika Painter, Illustrator-Children Books
Weil, Lisl Illustrator, Writer
Weinberg, Elbert Sculptor, Educator
Weiner, Lawrence Charles Sculptor
Weinstock, Rose Painter
Weintraub, Annette Digital Artist, Educator
Weintraub, Jacob D Art Dealer
Weissman, Julian Paul Dealer
Weissman, Walter Sculptor, Photographer
Weitzenhoffer, A Max Dealer
Welch, Roger Sculptor, Conceptual Artist
Welling, James Photographer
Wells, Mac Painter
Wentworth, Janet Painter
Werner, Donald (Lewis) Painter, Photographer
Weschler, Anita Sculptor, Painter
Wesley, John Painter
Wesser, Yvonne D Painter, Conceptual Artist
Westerlund Roosen, Mia (Maria Eludia) Sculptor
Westfall, Stephen V R Painter, Critic
Westwater, Angela King Art Dealer, Editor
Wexler, Lee Edward Photographer
White, Susan Chrysler Painter
Wiegand, Robert Painter
Wilcox, Gordon Cumnock Painter, Illustrator
Wilke, Hannah Sculptor, Instructor
Wilkin, Karen Curator, Critic
Willenbecher, John Sculptor, Painter
Williams, Casey Photographer
Williams, Dave Harrell Collector, Patron
Williams, Reba White Collector, Writer
Williams, William Thomas Painter, Educator

NEW YORK (cont)

Willis, Thornton Painter
Wilson, Carrie Lois Lecturer
Wilson, Fred Sculptor
Wilson, Jane Painter
Wilson, Robert Graphic Artist, Designer
Wilson, William S, III Critic
Winer, Helene Director
Wines, James N Architect
Wingate, George B Painter
Wink, Chris Conceptual Artist, Kinetic Artist
Winokur, Neil S Photographer
Winsor, Jacque Sculptor
Winter, Roger Painter
Wise, Takouhy Gallery Director, Art Dealer
Wixom, William D Curator, Art Historian
Wofford, Philip Painter, Writer
Wolins, Joseph Painter
Wong, Frederick Painter, Graphic Artist
Wong, Paul Kan Painter, Sculptor
Woodman, Timothy Sculptor
Wool, Christopher Painter
Wooster, Ann-Sargent Painter
Wortzel, Adrianne Painter, Printmaker
Wright, Faith-dorian Painter, Collector
Wriston, Barbara Historian, Lecturer
Wu, Linda Yee Chau Sculptor
Wunder, Richard Paul Historian, Administrator
Wunderman, Jan (Liljan Darcourt Wunderman) Painter, Printmaker
Wurmfeld, Sanford Painter, Educator
Wyatt, Greg Alan Sculptor
Yamashiro, Tad Photographer
Yamin, Martina (Schaap) Conservator-Art on Paper
Yarotsky, Lori Art Dealer, Painter
Yasuda, Robert Painter, Educator
Yau, John Writer, Curator
Yektai, Manoucher Painter
Yenawine, Philip Educator
Yoder, Richard Allen Painter, Conceptual Artist
York, Richard Travis Art Dealer, Gallery Director
Yoshimura, Fumio Sculptor
Young, Alan Painter
Younger, Robert M Sculptor
Youngerman, Jack Painter, Sculptor
Zabriskie, Virginia M Dealer
Zacharias, Athos Painter
Zago, Tino (Agostino C) Painter
Zaima, Stephen Gyo Painter, Sculptor
Zaleski, Jean Painter, Lecturer
Zaloudek, Duane Painter
Zapkus, Kes (Kestutis Edward) Painter
Zeisler, Richard Spiro Collector, Patron
Zeller, Frederic Sculptor
Zevon, Irene Painter
Ziegler, Mel(vin) and Kate Ericson Sculptor
Zimmerman, Elyn Sculptor, Environmental Artist
Zimmerman, Kathleen Marie Painter, Collage Artist
Zlowe, Florence M Painter, Draftsman
Zox, Larry Painter
Zucker, Barbara M Sculptor
Zucker, Joseph I Painter
Zugor, Sandor Painter, Printmaker
Zwack, Michael Painter, Sculptor

Niagara Falls

Naylon, Betsy Zimmermann Printmaker, Painter

North Bellmore

Schreiber, Martin Sculptor, Painter

Northport

Jerviss, Joy Printmaker
Verzyl, June Carol Dealer, Collector

North Salem

Savitt, Sam Painter, Illustrator

North Tarrytown

Gursoy, Ahmet Painter
Perlmutter, Linda M Painter, Instructor

Norwood

Strong, Leslie (Leslie Strong Sutter) Sculptor, Ceramist
Sutter, James Stewart Sculptor, Educator

Nyack

Renee, Paula Painter, Tapestry Artist

Oakdale

Mina-Mora, Raul Jose Painter, Illustrator

Oceanside

Bragg, E Ann (Ann Bragg) Painter
Freund, Pepsi Painter
Laguna, Mariella Painter, Printmaker

Old Chatham

Kratina, K George Sculptor

Old Westbury

Kurlander, Honey W Painter, Instructor
Tripp, Susan Gerwe Museum Director

Oneida

Colway, James R Painter

Oneonta

Beal, Jack Painter
Mahlke, Ernest D Sculptor, Educator
Mullen, James Martin Educator, Printmaker

Orangeburg

Worth, Karen Sculptor

Orient

Grippe, Florence (Berg) Painter, Instructor
Grippe, Peter Printmaker, Sculptor
Johnson, J Stewart Curator, Consultant

Ossining

Adamy, George E Educator, Sculptor
Cober, Alan E Illustrator, Printmaker

Oswego

D'Innocenzo, Nick Sculptor, Designer
DiPasquale, Dominic Theodore Silversmith, Educator
Fox, Michael David Sculptor, Professor
O'Connell, George D Printmaker, Educator

Otego

Griffith, Roberta Educator, Ceramist

Oyster Bay

Bothmer, Dietrich Felix von Curator, Educator
Kunstler, Morton Painter, Illustrator
Russell, Dr Stella Pandell Writer, Painter
Watson, Clarissa H Dealer, Writer

Palisades

Galinsky, Norman Painter, Graphic Artist
Hyams, Harriet Stained Glass Artist, Sculptor
Knowlton, Grace Farrar Sculptor, Photographer
Porta, Siena Gillann Sculptor

Peekskill

Osyczka, Bohdan Danny Painter, Illustrator
Rocklin, Raymond Sculptor, Educator
Rosenberg, Marilyn R Graphic Artist, Printmaker

Pelham

Rutsch, Alexander Painter, Sculptor
Zheutlin, Dale R Sculptor, Educator

Pelham Manor

Amatniek, Sara Printmaker, Graphic Artist

Pine Plains

Hoffman, Michael E Editor, Curator

Plainview

Margulies, Isidore Sculptor, Kinetic Artist

Pleasantville

Cawein, Kathrin Printmaker, Illuminator
Robinson, Jay (Thurston) Painter

Port Chester

Duveen, Anneta Sculptor, Designer
Sayles, Eva Painter

Port Jefferson

Mason, Molly Ann Sculptor, Environmental Artist

Port Washington

Cunnick, Gloria Helen Painter
Heinzen, MaryAnn Painter, Assemblage Artist
Schneider, Shellie Collage Artist, Printmaker
Whedon, Aida Anthony Printmaker, Instructor

Potsdam

Coopersmith, Georgia A Museum Director
Hildreth, Joseph Alan Printmaker, Painter
Sloan, Mark Museum Director

Poughkeepsie

Forman, Alice Painter
Havelock, Christine Mitchell Historian, Educator
Lindmark, Arne Painter, Instructor
Reynard, Carolyn Cole Painter, Instructor
Rubenstein, Lewis W Painter, Printmaker

Pound Ridge

Beckerman, Nancy Greyson Painter, Craftsman
Bender, Beverly Sterl Sculptor, Environmental Artist
Ferro, Walter Printmaker, Designer
Herbert, April H Sculptor
Schwebel, Renata Manasse Sculptor

Purchase

Gedeon, Lucinda Heyel Curator, Administrator
Parrino, George Painter, Administrator
Trosky, Helene Roth Printmaker, Papermaker
Zimiles, Murray Painter, Educator

Quogue

Kuehnl, Claudia Ann Goldsmith

Red Hook

Drummond, Sally Hazelet Painter

Rego Park

Kepalas (Elena Kepalaite) Sculptor, Painter
Maas, Marion Elizabeth Painter
Winter, Ruth Painter

Rensselaer

Semowich, Charles John Historian, Painter

Rhinebeck

DiFranza, Americo M Painter
Hughto, Margie A Ceramist, Curator
Rabinovich, Raquel Painter, Sculptor
Weintraub, Linda Curator, Director

Richmond Hill

Eberly, Vickie Painter
Eres, Eugenia Painter
Hammerman, Pat Jo Printmaker, Painter

Ridgewood

Bloes, Richard K Video Artist
Colpacci, Viorica Sculptor

Rochester

Anthony, Amy Ellen Craftsman, Jeweler
Barschel, Hans J Designer, Photographer
Chiarenza, Carl Photographer, Historian
Coffey, Douglas Robert Painter, Educator
Dibert, Rita Jean Painter, Photographer
Feuerherm, Kurt K Painter
Franklin, Don (Donald Wayne Franklin) Painter
Holcomb, Grant Museum Director, Educator
Holm, Milton W Painter
Johnston, Robert Harold Administrator, Craftsman
Keyser, William Alphonse, Jr Craftsman, Educator
Lyons, Joan Photographer
Margolis, Richard M Photographer, Educator
Marx, Robert Ernst Painter
Menihan, John Conway Painter, Printmaker
Mertin, Roger Photographer
Morgan, Robert Coolidge Painter, Critic
Richards, Sabra Printmaker, Painter
Santiago, Ramon Painter, Printmaker
Sellers, William Freeman Sculptor
Smith, Keith A Photographer, Printmaker
Spurling, Norine M Graphic Artist, Educator
Taylor, Ann Painter
Taylor, Michael (Estes) Instructor, Sculptor
Tyser, Patricia Ellen Stained Glass Artist, Consultant

Rock Hill

Schary, Emanuel Painter, Printmaker

Rockville Centre

Hornung, Clarence Pearson Designer, Writer
Resnick, Don Painter

Romulus

Bermingham, Debra Pandell Painter

Ronkonkoma

Barbera, Ross William Painter

Rosendale

Gralnick, Lisa Jeweler

Roslyn

Bassin, Joan Historian, Educator
Finke, Leonda Froelich Sculptor, Medalist

Roslyn Heights

Betensky, Rose Hart Painter, Art Administrator
Brown, Edith Rae Sculptor, Medalist
Gach, George Sculpture, Painter
Hermann, M(ildred) L Painter
Rotholz, Rina Printmaker
Sonnenberg, Frances Sculptor

Rye

Bisgyer, Barbara G (Cohn) Sculptor

Rye Brook

Blattner, Robert Henry Painter, Illustrator

Sagaponack

Bass, Joel Painter
Butchkes, Sydney Painter, Sculptor
Dash, Robert (Warren) Painter
Dunlap, Loren Edward Painter, Instructor

Sag Harbor

David, Cyril Frank Graphic Artist
Davies, Theodore Peter Painter, Printmaker
Harrison, Helen Amy Museum Director, Critic
Lipman-Wulf, Peter Sculptor, Printmaker
Nicholson, Roy William Painter, Printmaker
Rizzie, Dan Collage Artist, Painter
Telberg, Val Photographer, Painter
Welden, Daniel W Printmaker, Painter

St James

Mastrangelo, Bobbi Printmaker, Sculpture
White, Robert (Winthrop) Sculptor, Educator

Salem

Garrett, Stuart Grayson Painter, Educator
Orlyk, Harry V Painter

Saratoga Springs

Brodie, Regis Conrad Sculptor
Johnston, Roy E Painter, Historian
Upton, Richard Thomas Painter, Printmaker

Saugerties

Zaikine, Zak (Victor Eugene) Sculptor, Painter

Scarsdale

Breinin, Raymond Painter, Sculptor
Brilliant, Richard Educator, Writer
Frackman, Noel Critic, Historian
Hobbs, Gerald S Dealer, Publisher
Kearl, Stanley Brandon Sculptor
Kline, Harriet Painter, Printmaker
Morgan, Barbara Brooks Photographer
Peter, George Painter, Instructor
Portnoy, Theodora Preiss Dealer
Ries, Martin Painter, Printmaker
Roda (Rhoda Lillian Sablow), Painter, Tapestry Artist
Shaw, Isabel Sculptor, Graphic Artist
Valenstein, Alice Painter, Collector

Schenectady

Gilson, Giles Sculptor, Designer
Hatke, Walter Joseph Painter, Educator
Shaheen, Gary Edward Administrator, Collage Artist
Young Scott, Frances Librarian

Scottsville

Castle, Wendell Keith Sculptor
Urso, Leonard A Sculptor, Painter

Sea Cliff

Leipzig, Arthur Photographer
Seiden, Katie Sculptor, Assemblage Artist
Spampinato, Clemente Sculptor

Searingtown

Chichura, Diane B Administrator, Art Dealer

Seldon

Flecker, Maurice Nathan Painter, Educator

Setauket

Badalamenti, Fred Painter, Educator
Bishop, Marjorie Cutler Painter
Guilmain, Jacques Historian, Educator
Kemp, Flo Printmaking
Remsen, John Painter, Consultant

Shady

Hofsted, Jolyon Gene Sculptor, Educator
Kenyon, Colleen Frances Photographer, Administrator

Shelter Island

Mosca, August Painter, Printmaker
Shields, Alan J Painter

Shelter Island Heights

Culbertson, Janet Lynn (Mrs Douglas Kaften) Painter, Environmental Artist

Shokan

Taback, Simms Illustrator, Designer

Shoreham

Spier, Peter Edward Illustrator, Writer

Shrub Oak

Uchima, Toshiko Painter, Assemblage Artist

Shushan

Lutz, Marjorie Brunhoff Sculptor

Sidney

McClelland, Jeanne C Printmaker, Painter

Snyder

Cohen, Adele Sculptor, Painter

Somers

Adelman, Dorothy (Lee) McClintock Printmaker, Instructor

Southampton

Fuller, Sue Sculptor, Printmaker
Koehler, Henry Painter
Lerner, Abram Museum Director
Pellicone, William Painter, Sculptor
Rivers, Larry Painter

South Butler

Caster, Bernard Harry Painter, Enamelist

South Nyack
Churchill, Diane Painter

South Salem
Noland, Kenneth Painter, Printmaker

Spencer
Nowack, Wayne Kenyon Painter, Graphic Artist
Vann, Samuel LeRoy Painter

Spencerport
Wolsky, Jack Painter, Educator

Spring Glen
Berhang, Mattie Sculptor, Lecturer

Stanfordville
Anderson, Bruce A Goldsmith, Sculptor
Froman, Ann Sculptor

Staten Island
Bressi, Betty Painter, Graphic Artist
Brody, Carol Z Painter
Bruno, Santo M Painter
Butti, Linda (Benincasa) Painter, Educator
Ciardiello, Joseph G Illustrator
Coleman, A(llan) D(ouglass) Critic, Lecturer
Czimbalmos, Magdolna Paal Painter, Instructor
Czimbalmos, Szabo Kalman Painter, Educator
Egbert, Elizabeth Frances Sculptor, Educator
Grabel, Susan Sculptor, Ceramist
Greenfield, Amy Filmmaker, Video Artist
Healy, Julia Schmitt Painter, Educator
Kelder, Diane M Historian, Critic
Mailman, Cynthia Painter, Educator
Matyas, Diane C Sculptor, Printmaker
Moroz, Mychajlo Painter
Nelson, Carey Boone Sculptor
Noble, John A Printmaker, Painter
Petersen, Franklin G Painter
Swenson, Anne (Beatrice) Painter, Instructor
Turner, Norman Huntington Painter, Writer

Sterling Forest
Peck, Judith Sculptor, Writer

Stone Ridge
Sanders, Joop A Painter

Stony Brook
Bogart, Michele Helene Historian, Curator
Cooper, Rhonda H Gallery Director, Curator
Ellinger, Ilona E Painter, Educator
Koras, George Sculptor
Kuspit, Donald Burton Historian, Critic
O'Sullivan, Judith Roberta Curator, Museum Director
Pekarsky, Mel (Melvin Hirsch) Painter, Educator
Pindell, Howardena Doreen Painter, Educator

Suffern
Leigh, Harry E Sculptor, Painter

Sunnyside
Florin, Sharon June Painter
Saru, George Painter, Muralist

Syosset
Greene PSA, Chris (Christine E Greene) Cartoonist, Painter
Zirin, Nola Painter

Syracuse
Bakke, Karen Lee Assemblage Artist, Calligrapher
Bakke, Larry Hubert Educator, Painter
Belfort-Chalat, Jacqueline Sculptor, Painter
Bersentes, Nafsika J Painter
Cortese, Don F Printmaker, Instructor
De Wan-Carlson, Anna Printmaker
Drumm, Don Sculptor, Craftsman
Dwyer, James Painter, Educator
Gernhardt, Henry Kendall Sculptor, Ceramist
Harootunian, Claire M Sculptor, Educator
Jerry, Michael John Educator, Craftsman
Kuchta, Ronald A Museum Director, Lecturer
Lantzy, Donald Michael Administrator, Printmaker
Mack, Rodger Allen Sculptor, Educator
Nelson, Jack D Sculptor, Graphic Artist
Orentlicher, John Video Artist, Sculptor
Peden, Donalee Painter
Reed, Cleota Historian, Lecturer
Ridlon, James A Sculptor, Assemblage Artist
Sadle, Amy Ann Brandon Painter, Printmaker
Scala, Joseph (A) Painter, Educator
Sellers, John Lewis Educator, Designer
Sickler, Michael Allan Painter, Educator
Smith, Lawson Wentworth Sculptor, Educator
Spencer, Susan Elizabeth Painter, Instructor
Tatham, David Frederic Historian
Trop, Sandra Administrator
Vargo, John Educator, Painter
Witkin, Jerome Painter, Draftsman

Tappan
Dell, Robert Christopher Sculptor, Scenic Artist
Nickford, Juan Sculptor, Educator

Tarrytown
Butler, Joseph Thomas Curator, Writer
Dobkin, John Howard Museum Director
Lee, Robert J Painter, Educator

Thornwood
Goodnough, Robert Painter

Tillson
Debrosky, Christine A PAINTER
Van de Bovenkamp, Hans Sculptor

Tivoli
Schwartz, Barbara Ann Painter, Sculptor

Tonawanda
Bolinsky, Joseph Abraham Sculptor, Educator

Tuxedo Park
Domjan, Joseph (Spiri) Painter, Graphic Artist
Schmidt, Edward William Painter
Simon, Robert Barry Consultant, Historian

Unionville
Mavros, Donald Odysseus Ceramist, Sculptor

Upper Nyack
Elliot, Sheila Administrator, Writer

Upper-Nyack-on-Hudson
Elliot, John Theodore Painter, Writer

Utica
Chernick, Myrel Sculptor
Cimbalo, Robert W Painter, Printmaker
Pribble, Easton Painter, Instructor
Schweizer, Paul Douglas Art Historian, Museum Director

Valley Cottage
Greene, Stephen Painter
Longo-Muth, Linda L Painter, Instructor
Viner, Frank Lincoln Sculptor, Painter

Valley Stream
Fusco, Yolanda Painter, Printmaker
Hart, Allen M Painter, Administrator
Wasserman, Muriel Painter

Van Hornesville
Romeling, W B Painter

Verbank
Streeter, Tal Sculptor, Educator

Voorheesville
O'Connor, Thom Printmaker

Wading River
Marlow, Audrey Swanson Painter, Designer

Wainscott
Harris, Tracy Painter
Knigin, Michael Jay Painter, Printmaker
McColley, Sutherland Consultant, Designer
Porter, (Edwin) David Painter, Sculptor
Russo, Alexander Peter Painter, Educator

Wallkill
Koch, Edwin E Sculptor, Painter

Wantagh
Glaser, David Painter, Sculptor
Urbaitis, Elena Painter, Sculptor

Wappingers Falls
Di Fate, Vincent Illustrator, Painter

Warwick
Franck, Frederick S Painter, Writer
Talbot, Jonathan Painter, Collage Artist
Zakrzewski, Vladimir Painter, Draftsman

Washingtonville
Mangold, Sylvia Plimack Painter

Water Mill
Mac Whinnie, John Vincent Painter, Sculptor
Young, Mahonri S Writer

Webster
Mann, Ward Palmer Painter

Westbury
Honig, Mervin Painter, Painting Conservator
Ludman, Joan Hurwitz Writer, Researcher
Sherbell, Rhoda Sculptor, Consultant

West Falls

Lindemann, Edna M Museum Director Emeritus, Educator Emeritus

West Nyack

Ramos, Julianne Administrator, Consultant
Tytell, Louis Painter
Yeiser, Charles William Painter, Art Dealer

West Park

Whyte, Bruce Lincoln Art Dealer, Consultant

West Seneca

English, Hal (Harold J English) Painter

White Plains

Cove, Rosemary Sculptor, Painter
Erla, Karen Painter, Printmaker
Laico, Colette Collage Artist, Painter
Lew, Fran Painter
Limone, Frank Conceptual Artist
Manes, Belle Painter
Nickerson, Ruth (Mrs Edmund Greacen Jr) Sculptor, Instructor

Whitestone

Hochman, Kitty Printmaker

Williamsville

Little, Polly A Painter
Schwartz, Ruth Painter, Instructor

Willsboro

Reynolds, Patricia Ellen Painter

Wilton

Creps, Gerald A Environmental Artist, Educator

Woodbury

Brown, Charlotte Collage Artist, Painter

Woodhaven

IRENA (Irene R Mikol), Painter

Woodmere

Ginsburg, Estelle Painter, Sculptor
Greenfield, Joan Beatrice Painter, Enamelist
Harwood-Baumel, Bernice Painter, Printmaker
Seiden, Arthur Painter, Illustrator
Winick, Bernyce Alpert Painter

Woodside

Fax, Elton Clay Painter, Writer
Fluek, Toby Painter, Graphic Artist
Goldszer, Bath-Sheba Painter, Graphic Artist
Liccione, Alexander Painter, Graphic Artist

Woodstock

Angeloch, Robert Painter, Printmaker
Carlile, Janet (Hildebrand) Printmaker, Educator
Chavez, Eduardo Arcenio Painter, Sculptor
Currie, Bruce Painter, Printmaker
Fortess, Karl E Painter, Printmaker
Goetz, Mary Anna Painter, Instructor
Hague, Raoul Sculptor
Jordan, John L (Gaudeamus) Sculptor, Video Artist
Lenssen, Heidi (Mrs Fridolf Johnson) Painter, Lecturer
Lieberman, Meyer Frank Painter, Printmaker
Mackintosh, Sandra Sculpture, Collage Artist
Magafan, Ethel Painter, Muralist
Pachner, William Painter

Worchester

Habenicht, Wenda Sculptor

Yellow Springs

Bower, Gary David Painter

Yonkers

Aber, Ita Curator, Tapestry Artist
Buonagurio, Edgar R Painter, Muralist
Byars, Donna Sculptor, Collage Artist
Civale, Biagio A Printmaker, Painter
Corwin, Sophia M Printmaker, Painter
Gallo, William Victor Cartoonist, Illustrator
Gioello, Debbie Painter, Designer
McLeod, Stephen Educator, Critic

Yorktown Heights

Appel, Thelma Painter, Instructor
Kaupelis, Robert John Painter, Educator
Laventhol, Hank Painter, Printmaker
Trott, Helen Painter, Instructor
Witt, John Painter, Printmaker

NORTH CAROLINA

Albemarle

Moose, Talmadge Bowers Painter, Illustrator

Asheboro

Jones, W Louis Painter, Sculptor

Asheville

Cooke, Samuel Tucker Painter, Educator
Godfrey, Robert Painter, Critic
Gray, Robert Ward Administrator
Loewer, Henry Peter Writer, Illustrator
Martin, Doris-Marie Constable Designer, Sculptor
Ritts, Edwin Earl, Jr Administrator, Museum Director

Belmont

Mintich, Mary Ringelberg Sculptor, Craftsman

Black Mountain

Buba, Joy Flinsch Sculptor, Illustrator
Buck, Porge Printmaker
Tate, Gayle Blair Painter

Blowing Rock

Haley, Gail E Illustrator, Collector
Moose, Philip Anthony Painter, Illustrator

Boone

Humphrey, Judy Lucille Graphic Artist, Printmaker

Brevard

Murray, Tim(othy Douglas Gordon) Sculptor, Director

Burnsville

Bailey, Oscar Photographer, Educator
Bernstein, William Joseph Designer, Glassblower
Doyle, John Lawrence Printmaker, Painter
Grenell, Barbara Tapestry Artist, Weaver

Casar

Trotman, Bob Craftsman, Sculptor

Cashiers

Whiteside, William Albert, II Painter, Educator

Chapel Hill

Allen, Kaola Collage Artist, Painter
Dougherty, Patrick T Sculptor
Folda, Jaroslav (Thayer), III Historian
Hirschfield, Jim Sculptor, Architect
Howard, Robert A Sculptor, Educator
Kinnaird, Richard William Painter, Educator
Lee, Sherman Emery Museum Director
Millard, Charles Warren, III Director, Writer
Ness, (Albert) Kenneth Painter, Designer
Noe, Jerry Lee Sculptor, Educator
Prange, Sally Bowen Ceramist, Sculptor
Rogers, John H Sculptor, Consultant
Rowand, Joseph Donn Gallery Director, Art Dealer
Saltzman, Marvin Painter, Educator
Sloane, Joseph Curtis Historian
Sturgeon, Mary C Historian
Zaborowski, Dennis J Painter, Educator

Charlotte

Bloch, Milton Joseph Art Administrator, Museum Director
Byrum, Donald Roy Educator, Printmaker
Ellis, Andra Ceramist, Painter
Haack, Cynthia R Painter, Printmaker
Kortheuer, Dayrell Painter, Conservator
Melberg, Jerald Leigh Art Dealer, Collector
Musgrove, Stephen Ward Administrator, Curator
Segal, Tama & David Dealer, Director
Shaw, Mary Todd Sculptor, Painter
Sires, Jonathan Sculptor
Tucker, Charles Clement Painter

Cullowhee

Kelly, Isaac Perry Educator, Photographer

Davidson

Grosch, Laura Painter, Printmaker
Jackson, Herb Painter, Printmaker
Warren, Russ Painter

Durham

Markman, Sidney David Administrator, Historian
Pendergraft, Norman Elveis Museum Director, Historian
Pratt, Vernon Gaither Painter, Educator
Semans, James Hustead Patron
Spencer, John R Historian, Administrator
Wharton, Annabel Jane Historian

Fayetteville

Naza (Maria Nazareth McFarren), Painter, Instructor

Fearrington Village

Jordan, Barbara Schwinn Painter

Garner

Sweitzer, Charles Leroy Muralist, Painter

Gastonia

Waufle, Alan Duane Museum Director

Goldsboro

Turlington, Patricia R Painter, Sculptor

Greensboro

Barker, Walter William, Jr Painter, Writer
Blahove, Marcos Painter
Carpenter, Gilbert Frederick (Bert) Painter, Educator

NORTH CAROLINA (cont)
Chin, Ric Lecturer, Painter
Doren, A(rnold T) Photographer, Educator
Goldstein, Carl Historian, Sculptor
Gregory, Joan Educator, Painter
Janschka, Fritz Painter, Graphic Artist
Laymon, Cynthia J Assemblage Artist, Instructor
Mason, Novem M Sculptor, Designer
Tucker, James Ewing Curator, Painter

Greenville
Britt, Nelson Clark Museum Director, Painter
Chamberlain, Charles Ceramist, Educator
Dorsey, Michael A Painter, Administrator
Edmiston, Sara Joanne Educator, Designer
Gordley, Marilyn Classe Painter
Gordley, Metz Tranbarger (Tran) Painter
Hartley, Paul Jerome Painter, Educator
Laing, Richard Harlow Administrator, Artist
Satterfield, John Edward Goldsmith, Educator
Sexauer, Donald Richard Instructor, Printmaker
Stanforth, Melvin Sidney Educator, Painter

Highlands
Teyral, John Painter, Instructor

High Point
Rucker, Harrison Campbell Painter, Printmaker

Jacksonville
De La Vega, Antonio Painter, Designer

Lexington
Moon, Jim (James Monroe) Painter, Printmaker

Mt Pleasant
Kessler, Jane Q Curator, Writer

Newell
Loyd, Jan Brooks Sculptor, Goldsmith

Oak Ridge
Nydorf, Roy Herman Painter, Printmaker

Penland
Cope, Louise Todd Collage Artist

Pinehurst
Twitty, James W Painter, Printmaker

Pittsboro
Higgins, Edward Koelling Ceramist, Jeweler
Higgins, Mary Lou Ceramist, Painter

Raleigh
Bireline, George Lee Painter, Educator
Blakeslee, Sarah Painter
Broderson, Robert Painter
Brown, Charlotte Vestal Museum Director, Historian
Coffey, John William, II Curator
Davis, Meredith J Graphic Artist, Educator
Domit, Moussa M Museum Director, Historian
Greenberg, Blue (Bluma Kafka) Educator, Critic
Hertzman, Gay Mahaffy Administrator, Historian
Janson, Anthony Fredrick Curator, Historian
Jenkins, Mary Anne Keel Painter, Instructor
McLaughlin, Jean Wallace Administrator, Consultant
Max, Lope (Diaz) Painter, Educator
Morgan, Clarence (Edward) Painter, Educator
Potter, Ted Painter, Administrator
Schneiderman, Richard S Museum Director
Williams, Benjamin Forrest Curator, Historian

Salisbury
Hood, Walter Kelly Historian, Painter
Shalkop, Robert Leroy Consultant

Sanford
Higgins, (George) Edward Sculptor

Smithfield
Creech, Franklin Underwood Sculptor, Graphic Artist

Southport
Brown, June Gottlieb Painter

Spruce Pine
Littleton, Harvey K Educator, Sculptor

Swannanoa
Outland, Wendy Helen Administrator, Gallery Director

Tryon
Cecil, Charles Harkless Painter
Quest, Charles Francis Painter, Educator
Quest, Dorothy (Johnson) Painter, Educator

Wilkesboro
Nichols, Ward H Painter

Wilmington
Bissette, Samuel Delk Painter, Photographer
Conner, Ann Printmaker, Painter
Howell, Claude Flynn Painter, Educator

Wilson
Marshall, Thomas E Educator, Printmaker

Winston-Salem
Browning, Dixie Burrus Painter, Writer
Burgess, Linda Suzanne Painter, Photographer
Dance, Robert Bartlett Painter, Printmaker
Faccinto, Victor Paul Painter, Filmmaker
Finn, David Sculpture
Gray, Thomas Alexander Consultant, Collector
Lubowsky, Susan Director
Mangum, William (Goodson) Sculptor, Painter
Oubre, Hayward Louis Sculptor, Painter
Popkin, Elsie Dinsmore Graphic Artist
Saunders, Edith Dariel Chase Painter, Instructor
Shields, Anne Kesler Painter, Assemblage Artist
Tuck, Norman Victor Kinetic Artist, Sculptor
Yarborough, Christine Troutman Craftsman, Designer

Yanceyville
Gatewood, Maud Painter

NORTH DAKOTA

Grand Forks
Browning, Mark Daniel Painter, Sculptor
Paulsen, Brian Oliver Painter, Printmaker
Reuter, Laurel J Museum Director
Schaefer, Ronald H Printmaker, Educator

Minot
Piehl, Walter Jason, Jr Painter, Educator

Thompson
McElroy, Jacquelyn Ann (McElroy-Edwards) Printmaker, Educator

OHIO

Akron
Ertman, Earl Leslie Historian, Educator
Harvey, Donald Gilbert Sculptor, Instructor
Isroff, Lola K Painter
Kahan, Mitchell Douglas Museum Director, Historian
Keener, Polly Leonard Illustrator, Writer
Kleidon, Dennis Arthur Educator, Designer
Miller, John Franklin Administrator
Rogers, P J Printmaker, Sculptor
Selby, Patricia Louise Painter, Instructor
Tannenbaum, Barbara Lee Curator, Historian

Athens
Ahrendt, Christine Painter
Bova, Joe Sculptor, Ceramist
Kortlander, William Painter
Roberts, Donald Educator, Printmaker

Aurora
Lawton, Florian Kenneth Painter, Consultant

Bay Village
Blazey, Lawrence Edwin Designer, Painter
Kocar, George Frederick Painter, Illustrator
St Denis, Paul Andre Painter, Instructor

Berea
Cole, Harold David Historian, Educator

Blufftone
Velasquez, Oscar Painter, Illustrator

Bowling Green
Bandy, Ron F Painter, Educator
Hilty, Thomas R Graphic Artist, Painter
Hurlstone, Robert William Glass Artist, Educator
Lee, Briant Hamor Historian, Educator
Ocvirk, Otto G Sculptor, Printmaker

Brecksville
Miller, John Paul Jeweler

Cambridge
Beam, Mary Todd Painter

Chagrin Falls
Dubaniewicz, Peter Paul Painter

Chillicothe

Gough, Robert Alan Painter

Cincinnati

Barrie, Dennis Ray Museum Director, Historian
Batchelor, Anthony John Printmaker, Draftsman
Brod, Stanford Designer, Educator
Brown, Daniel Critic, Collector
Burleigh, Kimberly Painter
Cartwright, Roy R Ceramist
Chatterjee, Jay (Jayanta) Administration, Educator
Daniels, Astar (Charlotte Louise Daniels) Painter, Stained Glass Artist
Dennis, Don W Painter, Instructor
Driesbach, Walter Clark, Jr Sculptor, Instructor
Fabe, Robert Painter, Educator
Fischer, Mildred (Gertrude) Designer, Craftsman
Foster, April Printmaker, Educator
Kelley, Donald William Printmaker, Sculptor
Kinsel, Michael Leslie Museum Director
Knipschild, Robert Painter
Kowal, Cal (Lee) Curator, Photographer
McClure, Constance Painter, Professor
Marx, Evelyn Collage Artist, Painter
Meyer, Ruth Krueger Historian, Administrator
Miotke, Anne E Painter, Educator
Reichert, Marilyn F Museum Director
Rogers, Millard Foster, Jr Museum Director, Historian
Rubey, Tony (George Anton) Printmaker, Educator
Sawyer, John R Curator, Lecturer
Schmidt, Frederick Louis Painter, Illustrator
Solway, Carl E Dealer
Spangenberg, Kristin L Curator, Historian
Stanley, John Jacob Painter
Stevens, Jane Alden Photographer
Stewart, John P Painter, Printmaker
Taylor, Grace Martin Painter, Printmaker
Ward, (William) Michael Editor
Warren, Julianne Bussert Baker Photographer, Historian
Wood, McCrystle Painter, Sculptor
Woodham, Derrick James Sculptor

Cleveland

Abid, Ann B Librarian
Bickford, George Collector
Cassill, Herbert Carroll Printmaker, Educator
Channing, Susan Rose Administrator, Photographer
Cintron, Joseph M Painter, Educator
Conover, Claude Sculptor, Ceramist
Czuma, Stanislaw J Historian, Curator
Davis, David Ensos Sculptor
Drewal, Henry John Historian, Educator
Erdelac, Joseph Mark Collector, Patron
Fechter, Claudia Zieser Museum Director, Librarian
Floyd, Carl Leo Sculptor, Environmental Artist
Gibson, Walter Samuel Educator, Writer
Hayashi, Masumi Photographer, Educator
Henning, Edward Burk Curator, Historian
Hinson, Tom Everett Curator, Historian
Hornung, Gertrude Seymour Lecturer, Collector
Jergens, Robert Joseph Painter, Educator
Jones, Marvin Harold Printmaker, Painter
Kangas, Gene Sculptor, Author
McVey, William M Sculptor, Educator
Mayer, Robert Anthony Museum Director, Administrator
Meyers, Francis Joseph Painter, Sculptor
Mieczkowski, Edwin Painter
Rubin, David S Curator, Critic
Schreckengost, Viktor Designer, Sculptor
Seltzer, Phyllis Painter, Printmaker
Sloane, Phyllis Lester Painter, Printmaker
Taft, Frances Prindle Historian, Lecturer
Thompson, Lockwood Collector
Thurmer, Robert Sculptor, Gallery Director
Turner, Evan Hopkins Museum Director
Van der Meulen, Jan Historian, Educator
Wilson, Tom Cartoonist
Woide, Robert E Painter, Administrator

Cleveland Heights

Kowalski, Raymond Alois Painter
McCullough, Joseph Administrator, Painter
Pearman, Sara Jane Historian, Librarian
Schneider, Richard Durbin Ceramist, Craftsman

Columbus

Accetta, Suzanne Rusconi Painter, Instructor
Ansell, Joseph Paul Educator, Historian
Bennett, John M Writer, Graphic Artist
Black, David Evans Sculptor
Chafetz, Sidney Printmaker, Educator
Clisby, Roger David Curator, Historian
Close, Dean Purdy Painter, Art Dealer
Collings, Betty Sculptor, Writer
Conte, Jeanne Larner Photographer, Enamelist
Dodrill, Donald Lawrence Painter, Writer
Goodwin, Louis Payne Cartoonist
Heimdal, Georg Painter, Instructor
Jocda Painter
Kuehn, Edmund Karl Painter, Lecturer
Massey, Charles Wesley, Jr Printmaker, Educator
Morganstern, Anne McGee Historian, Educator
Morganstern, James Historian, Educator
Nicodemus, Chester Roland Sculptor, Designer
Parsons, Merribell Maddux Museum Director, Curator
Rogers-Lafferty, Sarah Curator
Roth, Richard Painter, Educator
Sakaoka, Yasue Sculptor, Designer
Simson, Bevlyn A Painter, Printmaker
Stearns, Robert Curator, Administrator
Stull, Robert J Sculptor, Administrator
Verzar, Christine B Administrator, Educator
Wahling, Jon B Sculptor, Weaver
Wyngaard, Susan Elizabeth Librarian

Cuyahoga Falls

Moon, Marc Painter, Instructor
Richard, Jack Painter, Restorer

Dayton

Evans, Bruce Haselton Museum Director, Historian
Houk, Pamela P Curator
Ostendorf, (Arthur) Lloyd, Jr Painter, Instructor
Pinkney, Helen Louise Curator, Librarian

Delaware

Kalb, Marty Joel Painter, Educator

Dublin

Arnold, Robert Lloyd Painter, Educator
Chadeayne, Robert Osborne Painter

Euclid

Bates, Kenneth Francis Enamelist, Craftsman

Gambier

Dwyer, Eugene Joseph Historian
Garhart, Martin J Printmaker
Gunderson, Barry L Sculptor

Gates Mills

Clague, John Rogers Sculptor

Georgetown

Ruthven, John Aldrich Painter, Lecturer

Hamilton

George, Richard Allan Painter

Hilliard

Benzle, Curtis Munhall Ceramist, Educator

Hudson

Smith, Lowell Ellsworth Painter

Johnstown

Borgia-Aberle, Nina Ceramist

Kent

Gildzen, Alex Writer, Collector
Grossman, Morton Painter
Kwong, Eva Sculptor, Ceramist
Matteson, Ira Sculptor, Draftsman
Morrow, Robert Earl Designer, Muralist
O'Sickey, Joseph Benjamin Painter, Educator

Kettering

Myers, Jack Fredrick Painter,

Lakeview

Earl, Jack Eugene Ceramist

Lakewood

Treaster, Richard A Painter, Educator

Lebanon

Koepnick, Robert Charles Sculptor, Educator

Madison

Gabriel, Hannelore Goldsmith

Mansfield

Butts, H Daniel, III Gallery Director

Marietta

Gerhold, William Henry Painter, Educator
Tasse, M Jeanne Educator, Calligrapher

Marion

Beery, Art (Arthur O) Painter

New Carlisle

Macaulay, Thomas S Environmental Artist, Sculptor

North Canton

Elliott, Bette G Painter, Instructor

North Lima

Mohn, Cheri (Ann) Painter, Instructor

Oberlin

Arnold, Paul Beaver Educator, Printmaker
Garvens, Ellen Photographer
Pearson, John Painter, Educator
Spear, Richard Edmund Educator
Tacha, Athena Sculptor, Educator

OHIO (cont)

Weidman, Jeffrey Librarian, Historian

Oxford

Beck, Lonnie Lee Painter, Educator
Kelm, Bonnie G Museum Director, Administrator
Wolfe, Robert, Jr Printmaker, Painter

Parma

Kiousis, Linda Weber Painter, Illustrator

Perrysburg

Autry, Carolyn Printmaker, Educator
Elloian, Peter Graphic Artist
Hofer, Ingrid (Ingeborg) Painter, Instructor

Poland

Parella, Albert Lucian Painter, Instructor
Vaccaro, Patrick Frank Printmaker, Painter

Richfield

Laessig, Robert Painter, Illustrator

Richmond

Frontz, Leslie Painter

Rocky River

Hill, Robyn Lesley Painter, Designer

Seven Hills

Stanczak, Julian Painter, Educator

Shaker Heights

Bieber, Elinore Maria Korow Painter, Instructor

Solon

Schepis, Anthony Joseph Instructor, Painter
Ward, William Edward Designer, Painter

South Euclid

Kozmon, George Painter, Printmaker

Springfield

Chepp, Mark Administrator

Sylvania

Bruner, Louise Katherine Critic, Writer
Chapman, Walter Howard Painter, Illustrator

Toledo

Berkowitz, Roger M Curator, Administrator
Cohn, Frederick Donald Dealer, Appraiser
Gonzalez, Mauricio Martinez Administrator, Gallery Director
Gunther, Charles F Printmaker, Consultant
Hutton, William Museum Curator
Luckner, Kurt T Curator
McGlauchlin, Tom Sculptor
Nordin, Phyllis E Sculptor, Designer
Steadman, David Wilton Museum Director
Waaland, James Brearley, II Dealer, Gallery Director

University Heights

Toth, Georgina Gy Art Librarian

Van Wert

Liljegren, Frank Painter, Instructor

Wooster

Gouma-Peterson, Thalia Educator, Historian

Worthington

Pentak, Stephen Painter, Educator

Yellow Springs

Hudson, Jon Barlow Sculptor, Environmental Artist
Jones, Michael Butler Sculptor, Freelance Curator

Youngstown

Bright, Al(fred Lee) Painter
Pernotto, James Angelo Painter, Sculptor
Singer, Clyde J Painter
Zona, Louis A Museum Director, Educator

Zanesville

Dietz, Charles LeMoyne Museum Director, Painter

OKLAHOMA

Ada

Sieg, Robert Lawrence Sculptor, Educator

Anadarko

Chaddlesone, Sherman Painter, Sculptor
Little Chief, Barthell Painter, Sculptor

Bartlesville

Schmid, Richard Alan Painter

Chickasha

Good, Leonard Painter

Chouteau

Ayres, Julia Spencer Painter, Writer

Collinsville

DeRosa, Michael Louis Painter
Woodruff, Diane Bailey Painter

Edmond

Muno, Richard Carl Sculptor, Director
White, B J (Beverly Jo) Painter, Collage Artist

Eucha

Courtney, Barbara Wood Painter

Goodwell

Kachel, Harold Stanley Museum Director, Educator

Guthrie

Owens, Wallace, Jr Administrator, Painter

Lawton

Bryan, Jack L Painter, Educator

Miami

Wilson, Charles Banks Painter, Printmaker

Muskogee

Hill, Joan (Chea-se-quah) Painter, Illustrator

Norman

Armstrong, Carol Painter
Bavinger, Eugene Allen Painter, Educator
Bogart, George A Painter
Caldwell, Susan Havens Historian, Educator
Henkle, James Lee Sculptor, Designer
Huchthausen, David Richard Sculptor, Educator
Lafon, Dee J Painter, Sculptor
Olkinetzky, Sam Collage Artist, Consultant
Reedy, Mitsuno Ishii (Mitsuno Ishii Hackler) Painter
Taylor, Joseph Richard Sculptor
Toperzer, Thomas Raymond Museum Director, Painter
Youritzin, Victor Koshkin Historian, Educator

Oklahoma City

Alaupovic, Alexandra V Sculptor, Educator
Bell, Coca (Mary Catlett) Painter
Bell, James M Art Administrator
Belle, Anna (Anna Belle Birckett) Painter
Busch, Rita Mary Painter, Sculptor
Davis, Jack R Painter, Educator
Faris, Brunel De Bost Painter, Educator
Frederick, Deloras Ann Painter, Instructor
Grass, Patty Patterson Painter
Harjo, Benjamin, Jr Painter, Printmaker
Hulett, Simonne R Painter, Printmaker
Johnson, Brent Painter
Jordan, Beth McAninch Painter
Kash, Marie (Marie Kash Weltzheimer) Painter, Graphic Artist
Lamell, Robert (C) Painter, Architect
Littrell, Doris Marie Dealer
Marron, Joan Painter
Richardson, Jean Painter, Printmaker
Seabourn, Bert Dail Painter, Printmaker
Shorney, Margo Kay (McIver) Art Dealer, Sculptor
Silberman, Arthur Library Director, Writer
Walch, John Leo Painter, Sculptor
Warriner, Laura B Assemblage Artist, Collage Artist

Okmulgee

Jones, Ruthe Blalock Painter, Educator

South Tahlequah

Bales, J (Jean Elaine) Painter, Sculptor

Stillwater

McVicker, J Jay Painter, Printmaker
Smith, B J Museum Director, Instructor
Wise, Geneva H (Holcomb) Collector, Painter

Tahlequah

Hagerstrand, Martin Alan Museum Director, Administrator

Tulsa

Allen, Loretta B Painter, Designer
Anderson, David C Sculptor, Photographer
Bryce, Eileen Ann Painter
Echohawk, Brummett Painter, Illustrator
Godsey, Glenn Educator, Painter
Goree, Gary Paul Instructor, Painter
Hogue, Alexandre Painter, Lithographer
Johnson, Nota Printmaker, Painter
Malone, Patricia Lynn Painter
Manhart, Marcia Y Administrator, Curator
Manhart, Thomas Arthur Educator, Ceramist
Place, Bradley Eugene Educator, Graphic Artist
Reeve, James Key Historian, Consultant
Russell, Philip C Painter, Instructor
Snodgrass-King, Jeanne Owens (Mrs M Eugene King) Consultant, Writer
Wiesendanger, Martin Wolfgang Historian, Conservator

OREGON

Albany

Alexander, Anthony K Sculptor, Jeweler

Applegate

Boyle, Keith Painter, Educator

Ashland

Markle, Greer (Walter Greer Markle) Museum Director, Historian

Astoria

Wanlass, Stanley Glen Sculptor, Painter

Bandon

Beling, Helen Sculptor, Instructor

Bend

Munoz, Rie Painter, Printmaker

Cannon Beach

Greaver, Hanne Printmaker, Painter
Greaver, Harry Painter, Printmaker

Clackamas

Jay, Norma Joyce Painter

Corvallis

Chappell, Berkley Warner Painter, Printmaker
Crozier, William K, Jr Craftsman, Designer
Gunn, Paul James Painter, Educator
Jameson, Demetrios George Painter, Printmaker
Levine, Shepard Painter, Educator
Sandgren, Ernest Nelson Painter, Printmaker
Taysom, Wayne Pendelton Sculptor, Educator

Dallas

Mattingly, (James Thomas) Printmaker, Educator

Eugene

Buckner, Kay Lamoreux Painter, Draftsman
Buckner, Paul Eugene Sculptor, Educator
Denney, Jim (James David) Painter
Derby, Mark Ceramist
Donnelly, Marian Card Historian, Educator
Hoy, Harold H Sculptor
Joyce, J David Photographer, Sculptor
Krause, LaVerne Erickson Painter, Printmaker
McCosh, Anne Kutka (Mrs David McCosh) Painter, Printmaker
McCready, Eric Scott Administrator, Educator
McGough, Stephen C Museum Director, Historian
McKenzie, Allan Dean Educator, Historian
O'Connell, Kenneth Robert Filmmaker, Administrator
Paul, Ken (Hugh) Printmaker, Painter
Paulin, Richard Calkins Museum Director, Craftsman
Roth, Leland M(artin) Historian, Writer

Florence

Niederer, Carl Painter

Hood River

Zweerts, Arnold Painter, Mosaic Artist

Lake Oswego

Hoffman, Elaine Janet Painter
Van Leunen, Alice Louise Textile Artist, Instructor

Lebanon

Vickers, Russ(ell Geron) Painter, Conceptual Artist

McMinnville

Bell, Lilian A Sculptor, Assemblage Artist

Marylhurst

Hopkins, Terri Curator, Administrator

Myrtle Point

Notkin, Richard T Sculptor, Ceramist

Portland

Bigelow, Anita (Anne Edwige Lourie) Graphic Artist, Printmaker
Bimrose, Arthur Sylvanus, Jr Cartoonist
Bolas, Gerald Douglas Museum Director, Educator
Cheshire, Craig Gifford Painter, Educator
Cooke, Judy Painter
Fillin-Yeh, Susan Museum Director
Gilkey, Gordon Waverly Curator, Educator
Gray, Don Painter, Critic
Grenon, Gregory Painter
Grimm, Raymond Max Sculptor, Potter
Haley, Sally (Sally Fulton Haley Russo) Painter
Hardy, Thomas (Austin) Sculptor
Jenkins, Donald John Curator, Historian
Johanson, George E Painter, Printmaker
Kimbrell, Leonard Buell Historian
Lavadour, James Painter
Leach, Elizabeth Anne Art Dealer, Writer
Morris, Carl Painter
Rhyne, Charles Sylvanus Historian
Russo, Michele Painter
Savinar, Tad Video Artist
Schiebold, Hans Painter
Schnitzer, Arlene Patron
Sheehan, Evelyn Painter
Waddingham, John Alfred Painter, Printmaker
Wiedenhoeft, Renate Art Historian
Yes, Phyllis A Painter, Sculptor

Rainier

Lewis, Mary Sculptor

Salem

Casey, John Thayer Painter, Sculptor
Hall, Carl Albin Painter, Instructor
Hamilton, George Earl Painter, Educator

Seal Rock

Sponenburgh, Mark Historian, Sculptor

Sheridan

Turner, Ralph James Sculptor, Graphic Artist

Talent

Cornell, David E Ceramist, Sculptor

Tigard

Stacy, John Russell Illustrator, Jeweler

Timberline

Adamson, Linny J Curator, Weaver

West Linn

Murphy, Chester Glenn Painter

PENNSYLVANIA

Abington

Southwell, William Joseph Painter, Writer

Allentown

Ackerman, Rudy Schlegel Painter, Educator
Berman, Bernard Collector
Berman, Muriel Mallin Collector, Patron
Berman, Philip I Collector, Patron
Coleman, Edward H Dealer, Collector
Dreisbach, Clarence Ira Painter
Hoffman, Richard Peter Painter, Photographer
Miley, Mimi Conneen Curator
Moller, Hans Painter
Tenzer, (Dr & Mrs) Jonathan A Collectors

Allison Park

Osby, Larissa Geiss Painter

Ambler

Lengyel, Alfonz Historian, Writer

Andalusia

Biddle, James Administrator, Collector

Ardmore

Atlee, Emilie DeS Painter, Instructor

Bala Cynwyd

Bensignor, Paulette Painter, Printmaker

Bally

Bertoia, (Mr) Val (Bertoia Studio) Designer, Sculptor

Bangor

McInerney, Gene Joseph Painter

Barto

Limont, Naomi Charles Printmaker, Instructor

Bath

Conneen, Jane W Printmaker, Miniaturist

Beech Creek

Bossert, Edythe H Painter

Bellefonte

Fisher, Rob (Robert Norman) Sculptor, Writer

Berwyn

Dobie, Jeanne Painter, Instructor
Nelson, Leonard Painter, Sculptor

Bethlehem

Gans, Lucy C Sculptor, Educator
Jankowski, Theodore Andrew Painter, Muralist
Redd, Richard James Printmaker, Educator
Reker, Les Painter, Educator
Viera, Ricardo Painter, Printmaker

Blue Bell

Martino, Babette Painter
Martino, Eva E Painter, Sculptor
Martino, Giovanni Painter
Martino, Nina F Painter

Boalsburg

Amato, Michele Painter
Schule, Donald Kenneth Sculptor, Instructor

Boyertown

Coggins, Jack Banham Instructor, Painter
Slider, Dorla Dean Painter
Trinkley, Karla Sculptor

Bristol

Blackey, Mary Madlyn Painter, Printmaker

Broomall

Neal, Irene Painter, Sculptor

Brush Valley

Wert, Ned Oliver Educator, Painter

Bryn Mawr

Broido, Lucy Writer, Dealer
Canby, Jeanny Vorys Archaeologist, Curator
Costanza, John Joseph Sculptor, Ceramist
DeFazio, Teresa Galligan Painter, Gallery Director
Markson, Eileen Librarian

Buckingham

Fabert, Jacques Painter, Sculptor

Camp Hill

Taylor, Michele F Painter

Catasauqua

Tabor, Virginia S Painter, Printmaker

Chadds Ford

Duff, James H Museum Director, Administrator
Layton, Richard Painter, Dealer

Chalfont

Thompson, Jack Sculptor, Educator
Thompson, Rena Weaver, Painter

Cheltenham

Spandorfer, Merle Sue Painter, Printmaker

Chester

Gore, David Alan Painter, Conservator

Christiana

Miller, Daniel Dawson Printmaker, Sculptor

Coatesville

Danziger, Fred Frank Painter

Cochranville

Sazegar, Morteza Painter

Cogan Station

Shipley, Roger Douglas Sculptor, Educator

Collegeville

Larson, William G Photographer, Educator
Morin-Miller, Carmen A Author, Curator

Conshohocken

Nofer, Frank Painter, Graphic Artist

Cornwall

Quinn, Henrietta Reist Collector, Patron

Dalton

Wallin, Leland Dean Painter, Educator

Delaware Water Gap

Verona, Paula Painter

Easton

Crawford, Thom Cooney Painter, Sculptor
Kerns, Ed (Johnson), Jr Painter
Salemme, Antonio Painter, Sculptor
Salemme, Martha Painter

East Stroudsburg

Scarpa, Dorothea Painter, Educator
Strauser, Sterling Boyd Painter
Weigand, Herbert Michael Painter, Educator

Edinboro

Gibson, Benedict S Painter, Educator
Nicholas, Donna Lee Ceramist, Sculptor
Winterberger, Suzanne Photographer, Book Artist

Elizabethtown

Steinmetz, Grace Ernst Titus Painter

Elkins Park

D'Agostino, Peler Video Artist, Educator
Daley, William P Ceramist
Davidson, Abraham A Art Historian, Photographer
Erlebacher, Martha Mayer Painter
Feld, Augusta Painter, Printmaker
Lechtzin, Stanley Goldsmith, Educator
Madigan, Martha Photographer
Schmidt, Charles Painter
Vick, Connie R Consultant

Elysburg

Knoebel, David Jon Sculptor

Emmaus

Ruhe, Barnaby Sieger Painter, Critic

Erie

Ahlgren, Roy B Painter, Printmaker
Burke, Daniel V Painter, Educator
Kaiser, Vitus J Painter
Pizzat, Joseph Educator, Collage Artist
Sundberg, Carl Gustave Enamelist, Director
Sundberg, Wilda (Regelman) Painter, Instructor
Vanco, John Leroy Administrator, Curator

Fayetteville

Etchison, Bruce Conservator, Painter

Fleetwood

Daub, Matthew Forrest Painter, Graphic Artist

Flicksville

Niedzialek, Terry Sculptor, Environmental Artist
Vitali, Julius M Photographer, Video Artist

Folcroft

Kaplan, Frederic Clark Painter, Illustrator

Forty Fort

Thomas, Thalia Ann Marie Painter, Educator

Gibsonia

De Coux, Janet Sculptor

Gladwyne

Beyer, Steven J Sculptor, Educator

Glen Mills

Crawford, Bill (Wilbur Ogden) Illustrator, Administrator
Ingram, Judith Paper Artist, Sculptor
Turner, Janet Sullivan Painter

Glenmoore

De Guatemala, Joyce (Joyce Bush Vourvoulias) Sculptor

Grantham

Forsythe, Donald John Printmaker, Educator

Greensburg

Chew, Paul Albert Administrator, Lecturer
Filkosky, Josefa Sculptor, Educator

Harrisburg

Nold, Carl R Museum Director, Historian
Winer, Donald Arthur Curator, Painter
Wingate, Robert Bray Illustrator, Consultant

Haverford

Mangione, Patricia Anthony Painter, Muralist
Stegeman, Charles Painter, Educator
Williams, William Earle Photographer, Curator

Havertown

Fish, Richard G Designer, Painter
Gasparro, Frank Sculptor, Instructor
Kindermann, Helmmo Photographer, Painter
Spicer, Jean (Doris) Uhl Painter, Instructor

Hollidaysburg

Binai, Paul Freye Painter, Art Curator

Horsham

Pennypacker, James S Designer, Publisher
Winokur, Paula Colton Ceramist, Craftsman
Winokur, Robert Mark Ceramist, Educator

Hughesville

Bogle, Jon Sculptor

Jenkintown

Katz, Ted Painter, Educator
Langman, Richard Theodore Gallery Director
Miller, Elaine Sandra Painter, Printmaker
Sevy, Barbara Snetsinger Librarian

Jim Thorpe

Nagano, Shozo Painter

Johnstown

Sheehe, Lillian Carolyn Painter, Enamelist

Kennett Square

Mullen, Jo (Stauffer) Painter, Printmaker
Naeve, Milo M Administrator, Historian

King of Prussia

Diehl, Sevilla S Painter

Kutztown

Carroll, James F L Painter, Sculptor
Malenda, James William Enamelist, Educator
Quirk, Thomas Charles, Jr Painter
Wible, Mary Grace Painter, Educator

Lancaster

Andriulli, Robert Painter, Educator
Ballard, Lockett Ford, Jr Museum Director, Administrator
Hay, Ike Sculptor, Educator
Kermes, Constantine John Painter, Printmaker

Lehigh Valley

Kocsis, James Paul Painter, Publisher

Lemont

Porter, Jeanne Chenault Educator, Historian
Porter, Richard James Consultant, Collector

Levittown

Clark, William Roger Sculptor, Painter

Lewisburg

Metzger, Robert Paul Curator, Educator
Turnure, James Harvey Educator, Historian

Lumberville

Katsiff, Bruce Photographer, Museum Director

McKean

Kemenyffy, Steven Ceramist, Educator
Kemenyffy, Susan B Hale Ceramist

Malvern

Freeland, William Lee Sculptor, Painter

Martins Creek

Fink, Larry (Laurence B) Educator, Photographer

Mechanicsburg

Annis, Norman L Educator, Sculptor
Walker, Mary Carolyn Craftsman, Jeweler

Mechanicsville

Bye, Ranulph Painter

Media

Berd, Morris Painter, Educator
Crivelli, Elaine Environmental Artist, Sculptor
Hildebrandt, William Albert Painter, Sculptor
Lisk, Penelope E Tsaltas Painter, Printmaker
Reichel, Myra Tapestry Artist, Weaver
Vitale, Magda Painter

Melrose Park

Schurr, Jerry M Painter, Printmaker

Mendenhall

Boucher, Tania Kunsky Painter, Sculptor

Merion Station

Cederstrom, John Andrew Painter, Conservator
Newman, Libby Painter, Printmaker
Sankowsky, Itzhak Painter, Sculptor

Merrittstown

Kenton, Mary Jean Painter

Murrysville

Zollweg, Aileen Boules Painter, Sculptor

Narberth

Alten, Jerry Director, Designer
Donohoe, Victoria Historian, Critic
Hutton, Dorothy Wackerman Designer, Printmaker

McGovern, Robert F Painter, Sculptor

New Cumberland

Byers, Fleur Painter, Graphic Artist

New Freedom

Theofiles, George Historian, Dealer

New Hope

Moore, Beveridge Painter

Newtown

Dodge, Robert G Painter, Sculptor
Jansen, Catherine Sandra Photographer, Educator
Renninger, Katharine Steele Painter
Roth, David Painter

Newtown Square

Roberts, Gilroy Sculptor

Norristown

Markley, Doris Yocum Printmaker, Photographer
Rapp, Lois Painter, Educator

North Wales

Dallmann, Daniel Forbes Painter, Printmaker
Szabo, Joseph George Cartoonist, Editor

Oakdale

Mulcahy, Kathleen Glass Artist, Sculptor

Ottsville

Smith, Michael A Photographer

Oxford

Holmes, Larry W Painter, Educator

Pennsburg

Schule, Clifford Hamilton Painter, Sculptor

Philadelphia

Adams, John Michael Education, Administrator
Adams, Phoebe Sculptor
Akers, Adela Weaver, Craftsman
Andrade, Edna Wright Painter, Educator
Auth, Tony (William Anthony), Jr Editorial Cartoonist
Bach, Laurence Photographer, Educator
Bantel, Linda Museum Director
Barber, Ronald Administrator
Batchelor, Betsey Ann Painter, Educator
Bateman, Ronald C Painter
Bayliss, George Painter, Educator
Bergner, Lanny Michael Sculptor
Bernstein, Benjamin D Collector
Bernstein, Edward I Collector
Blai, Bertha Ceramist, Craftsman
Bobrowicz, Yvonne Pacanovsky Instructor, Weaver
Bonner, Jonathan G Craftsman
Boyle, Richard J Historian, Writer
Brady, Luther W Collector, Patron
Brodsky, Harry Printmaker, Painter
Burko, Diane Painter, Educator
Burns, Mark A Ceramist
Butler, Marigene H Administrator, Conservator
Campbell, William Henry Painter
Cava, Paul Art Dealer, Painter
Chahroudi, Martha L Curator
Chimes, Thomas James Painter
Clark, Jon Frederic Educator, Glass Blower
Clark, Marie Sculptor
Crimmins, Jerry (Gerald Garfield) Assemblage Artist, Painter

Cumming, Robert H Artist, Photographer
Danly, Susan Curator, Historian
Desmett, Don Curator, Gallery Director
Dessner, Murray Painter
D'Harnoncourt, Anne Historian, Museum Director
Dickerson, Brian S Painter
Dillon, Mildred (Murphy) Printmaker
Dolan, Margo Art Dealer
Dorsey, Lucia Iannone Administrator
Dowell, John E, Jr Educator, Printmaker
Drutt, Helen Williams Dealer, Lecturer
Dubinskis, Anda Painter
Edmunds, Allan Logan Printmaker, Administrator
Etting, Emlen Painter, Illustrator
Fahlen, Charles C Sculptor
Formicola, John Joseph Painter, Educator
Fox, Pearl Art Dealer, Collector
Friedlaender, Bilge Sculptor, Photographer
Frudakis, Zenos Sculptor
Fuller, Jeffrey P Dealer, Gallery Director
Galuszka, Frank Richard Painter
Garcia, Ofelia Administrator, Printmaker
Gilboy, Margaretta Educator, Painter
Gilden, Anita Librarian
Gold, Albert Painter, Educator
Goldfine, Beatrice Painter, Sculptor
Goodyear, Frank H, Jr Administrator, Historian
Gorny, A-P (Anthony-Peter) Conceptual Artist, Illuminator
Graves, Bradford Sculptor, Educator
Grimley, Oliver Fetterolf Painter, Sculptor
Gundersheimer, Herman (Samuel) Historian, Educator
Hahn, Maurice & Roslyn Dealers
Hanes, James (Albert) Painter
Hanlen, John (Garrett) Painter, Instructor
Henry, Jean Museum Director, Curator
Hood, (Thomas) Richard Printmaker, Designer
Hoptner, Richard Sculptor
Horvitz, Suzanne Joan Painter, Printmaker
Howard, Humbert L Painter
Hughes, Beverly Designer, Weaver
Hurwitz, Michael H Craftsman, Mosaic Artist
Jacobowitz, Ellen Sue Curator, Director
Johnson, Homer Educator, Painter
Johnson, Lois Marlene Printmaker, Educator
Jones, Elizabeth A B (Mrs Ludwig Glaeser) Sculptor, Medalist
Kaplan, Jerome Eugene Printmaker
Kerrigan, Maurie Sculptor, Painter
Kettner, David Allen Artist, Educator
Kilroy, Mary A Administrator, Curator
Kimmelman, Harold Sculptor
King, Ray Sculptor, Stained Glass Artist
Klein, Esther M Patron, Collector
Knobler, Lois Jean Sculptor, Painter
Knobler, Nathan Sculptor, Educator
Kotala, Stanislaw Waclaw Painter, Librarian
Kramrisch, Stella Curator, Educator
Lancel McElhinney, James Painter
Landreau, Anthony Norman Administrator
Lang, J T Printmaker, Educator
La Pelle, Rodger Painter, Dealer
Lasuchin, Michael Printmaker, Painter
Le Clair, Charles Painter, Educator
Levy, Margaret Wasserman Sculptor
Lisker, Sara Designer, Craftsman
Locks, Marian Art Dealer, Collector
Looney, Robert Fain Curator, Librarian
Lueders, Jimmy C Painter, Instructor
Lutz, Winifred Ann Sculptor, Environmental Artist

PENNSYLVANIA (cont)

McClain, Matthew Curator, Writer
McClenney, Cheryl Ilene Administrator
McCormick, Rod Sculptor
McGinnis, Christine Painter, Printmaker
Maitin, Sam (Samuel Calman) Painter, Sculptor
Makler, Hope Welsh Dealer
Mangel, Benjamin Dealer
Marzano, Albert Painter, Designer
Maxwell, Peter Designer, Art Dealer
Medoff, Eve Painter, Writer
Meister, Michael William Historian, Educator
Metzker, Ray K Photographer, Educator
Miller, Arthur Green Educator, Historian
Millett, Caroline Dunlop Administrator
Moore, Susan Painter
Moskowitz, Shirley (Mrs Jacob W Gruber) Painter, Collage Artist
Moss-Vreeland, Patricia Painter, Draftsman
Naftulin, Rose Painter
Neff, Edith Painter, Instructor
Newman, Walter Andrews, Jr Art Dealer, Gallery Director
Omwake, Eo, Jr Painter, Sculptor
Opie, John Mart Painter
Osborne, Elizabeth Painter, Instructor
Osgood, Jere Craftsman
Paley, Albert Raymond Goldsmith, Designer
Paone, Peter Painter, Printmaker
Percy, Ann Buchanan Curator, Historian
Perkins, G Holmes Architect, Educator
Pildes, Sara Painter, Collage Artist
Pogach, Gerald Painter, Sculptor
Pollock, Bruce Painter, Sculptor
Quigley, Michael Allen Administrator
Ray, Christopher T Sculptor, Craftsman
Remenick, Seymour Painter, Instructor
Rishel, Joseph John, Jr Curator
Roesch, Robert Arthur Sculptor, Designer
Rohrer, Warren Painter
Rosenfeld, Richard Joel Dealer
Rosenquist, Marc H Sculptor
Rosenthal, Mark L Curator, Historian
Rossman, Michael Painter
Schaechter, Judith Stained Glass Artist, Painter
Scott, Robert Montgomery Administrator, Patron
Searles, Charles Painter, Sculptor
Sewell, Darrel L Curator, Historian
Sewell, Leo Sculptor, Assemblage Artist
Shatalow, Vladimir Mihailovich Painter
Shih, Joan Fai Painter, Instructor
Shillea, Thomas John Photographer
Shoemaker, Innis Howe Curator
Shores, (James) Franklin Painter
Simkin, Phillips M Sculptor
Solmssen, Peter Administrator
Solomon, Vita Petrosky Painter, Printmaker
Spohn, Franz Frederick Printmaker, Illustrator
Staffel, Doris Painter, Educator
Staffel, Rudolf Harry Ceramist, Instructor
Stearns, Thomas Robert Sculptor, Educator
Stein, Judith Ellen Historian, Curator
Steinberg, Leo Educator, Historian
Stinnett, Hester A Printmaker
Stitt, Susan (Margaret) Museum Director
Striker, Cecil L Historian, Educator
Tannenbaum, Judith E Curator, Critic
Tobia, Blaise Joseph Photographer, Educator
Torrey, Ella King Administrator
Turner, Robert Chapman Ceramist, Educator
Venturi, Robert Architect
Visco, Anthony Salvatore Educator, Sculptor
Warner, Herbert Kelii, Jr Printmaker
Wasserman, Jack Educator
Weidner, Marilyn Kemp Conservator, Lecturer
Weidner, Roswell Theodore Painter, Instructor
Wells, Lynton Painter
Yaros, Constance G Painter, Sculptor
Zynsky, Toots (Mary Ann) Weaver

Pipersville

Roseman, Susan Carol Printmaker, Painter

Pittsburgh

Arkus, Leon A Consultant, Museum Director
Austin-Nuhfer, Olive H Painter, Sculptor
Bailey, Barbara Ann Painter, Instructor
Batista, Kenneth Painter, Educator
Cantini, Virgil D Muralist, Sculptor
Caplan, Jerry L Sculptor, Educator
Carter, (Charles) Bruce Printmaker, Educator
Clark, Vicky A Historian, Curator
Crenshaw, Karen Bruce Conservator
Dzierski, Vincent Paul Painter, Designer
Eberle, Edward Samuel Ceramist, Draftsman
Feller, Robert L Conservation Scientist
Fitzpatrick, Joseph Cyril Painter, Sculptor
Gardner, Robert Earl Printmaker, Educator
Gillen, John Sculptor
Gruber, Aaronel deRoy Painter, Sculptor
Harris, Ann Sutherland Historian, Administrator
Haskell, Jane Environmental Artist, Painter
Hearn, M F (Millard Fillmore), Jr Administrator, Historian
Holland, Harry Charles Computer Artist, Painter
Hollen-Bolmgren, Donna Painter, Papermaker
Johnston, Phillip M Curator, Museum Director
Judson, William D Curator, Historian
Karn, Gloria Stoll Painter, Instructor
Kelly, Cynthia Ference Gallery Director, Painter
King, Elaine A Curator, Historian
Kipp, Orval Painter, Educator
La Bobgäh, Robert Gordon Printmaker, Sculptor
Lewis, Virginia Elnora Museum Director, Historian
Miller, Donald Critic, Writer
Miller, Janet Administrator, Book Dealer
Nelson, James P Painter
Pasinski, Irene Painter, Sculptor
Rice, Norman Lewis Painter, Educator
Rogers, Bryan Leigh Conceptual Artist, Educator
Sheon, Aaron Historian, Administrator
Slavick, Susanne Mechtild Painter, Educator
Stones, Margaret Alison Educator, Historian
Sturgeon, John Floyd Video Artist, Sculptor
Toker, Franklin Historian, Educator
Trapp, Frank Anderson Museum Director, Historian
Webb, Frank (Francis H) Painter, Instructor
Weidner, Mary Elizabeth Painter, Educator
Weiner, Abe Painter, Instructor
Weiss, Milton Painter, Printmaker
Wiebe, Charles M Dealer, Historian
Wilkins, David George Historian, Gallery Director
Williams, John Wesley Historian, Educator
Winokur, James L Collector, Critic

Pleasant Mt

Sticker, Robert Edward Painter

Pocopson

Bostelle, Thomas (Theodore) Painter, Sculptor

Quakertown

Keyser, Robert G Painter

Reading

Bentz, Harry Donald Educator, Painter
Gore, Jefferson Anderson Curator
Nesbitt, Perry Loren Gallery Director, Curator

Rosemont

Goutman, Dolya Educator, Painter

Rydal

Weinberg, Ephraim Administrator, Educator

Selinsgrove

Connolly, Jerome Patrick Painter, Muralist
Putterman, Florence Grace Painter, Educator

Sewickley

Kornetchuk, Elena Dealer, Historian

Shavertown

Simon, Herbert Bernheimer Sculptor

Shippensburg

Davis, William D Educator, Printmaker

Solebury

Anthonisen, George Rioch Sculptor, Painter

Souderton

Bock, William Sauts-Netamux'we Illustrator, Painter

Spring City

Kratz, Mildred Sands Painter

State College

Alden, Richard Painter
Frost, Stuart Homer Educator, Painter
Hager, Hellmut W Historian
McCoy, Wirth Vaughan Painter, Educator
Staley, Christopher P Ceramist
Zoretich, George Stephen Painter, Educator

Susquehanna

Laughlin, Mortimer Painter

Swarthmore

Cothren, Michael Watt Educator
Hollister, Valerie (Dutton) Painter
Hungerford, Constance Cain Educator, Historian
Kitao, T Kaori Historian, Educator

Thorton

Valetta Painter

Tionesta

Holt, Martha A Ceramist, Sculptor

Topton

Staller, Eric P Photographer, Sculptor

Union Dale

Stark, Robert Painter, Photographer

University Park

Arbitman, Kahren J Curator, Historian
Fleischer, Roland Edward Historian, Educator
Garoian, Charles Richard Conceptual Artist, Educator
Graves, Kenneth Robert Photographer
Hampton, Grace Administrator, Craftsman
Lawrence, Howard Ray Designer, Educator
Maddox, Jerrold Warren Educator, Painter
Ott, Robert William Educator, Museologist
Sommese, Lanny Beal Educator, Designer
Van Dommelen, David B Writer, Fiber Artist

Upper Black Eddy

Sherr, Ronald Norman Painter

Venango

Spinosa, Gary Paul Sculptor

Verona

Brust, Robert Gustave Painter, Writer

Villanova

Boyer, Marietta P Librarian
Cannuli, Richard Gerald Painter, Gallery Director
Kun, Neila Photographer
Radan, George Tivadar Administrator, Historian

Volant

McNickle, Thomas Glen Painter

Wallingford

Mark, Enid (Epstein) Printmaker, Photographer

Warren

Mariner, Donna M Painter, Writer

Warrington

Keene, Paul Painter

Washington

Edwards, Paul Burgess Painter, Educator
Pablo Painter, Educator
Taylor, Hugh Holloway Historian, Educator

Washington Crossing

Kemble, Richard Printmaker, Sculptor

Waterford

Stull, Jean Himrod Painter

Wayne

Brodhead, Quita Painter
Fabbri, Anne R Museum Director
Key, Ted Cartoonist

Weissport

Meneeley, Edward Painter, Sculptor

West Alexander

West, Peter Painter, Printmaker

West Chester

Baldwin, Richard Wood Illustrator, Sculptor
Everhart, Don, II Sculptor, Medalist
Hawkes, Elizabeth H Curator, Consultant
Hawthorne, Jack Gardner Educator, Painter
Jamison, Philip Painter

West Grove

Allman, Margo Sculptor, Painter

West Middleton

Youngblood, Nat Painter, Illustrator

Whitehall

Wiltraut, Douglas Scott Painter

Wyncote

Watson, Howard N(oel) Painter, Printmaker

Wyndmoor

Kogan, Deborah Painter, Illustrator

Wynnewood

Bowes, Betty Miller Painter, Consultant
Kardon, Carol Painter, Instructor
Maxwell, John Painter
Pincus, David N Collector

Wyomissing

Dietrich, Bruce Leinbach Museum Director, Administrator

Yardley

Harris, Charney Anita Painter, Sculptor

RHODE ISLAND

Bristol

Goff, Thomas Jefferson Sculptor, Medalist
Knowlton, Daniel Gibson Restorer, Conservator

Charlestown

Bach, Dirk Painter, Educator
Rohm, Robert Sculptor

Coventry

Beaudoin, Andre Eugene Press Manufacturer, Photographer

Cranston

Crooks, W Spencer Painter, Lecturer
Friese, Nancy Marlene Printmaker, Painter
Prip, Janet Craftsman, Sculptor

Johnston

Smith, Donald C Painter, Printmaker

Kingston

Leete, William White Painter
Onorato, Ronald Joseph Historian, Curator

Lincoln

Loughlin, John Leo Painter
McIlvane, Edward James Stained Glass Artist, Glass Blower

Middletown

Van Duinwyk, George Paul Goldsmith, Educator

Narragansett

Bentley-Scheck, Grace Mary Printmaker
Calabro, Richard Paul Sculptor, Painter

Newport

Barry, Robert E Illustrator, Educator
Gaines, Alan Jay Printmaker, Publisher
Nesbitt, Alexander John Educator, Calligrapher
Nesbitt, Ilse Buchert Printmaker, Illustrator
West, Richard Vincent Museum Director, Historian

North Kingstown

Frid, Tage P Designer

North Providence

Bjurman, Johan Paul Muralist, Painter

North Scituate

LaMontagne, Armand M Sculptor, Painter

Pascoag

Bertoni, Christina Ceramist, Painter

Pawtucket

Heyman, Lawrence Murray Painter, Printmaker

Peace Dale

Petrie, Sylvia Spencer Printmaker, Painter

Providence

Burleson, Charles Trentman Painter, Educator
Callahan, Harry Photographer
Feeney, Sandra Benedict Photographer
Feldman, Walter (Sidney) Painter, Printmaker
Fleischner, Richard Hugh Environmental Artist, Sculptor
Geran, Joseph, Jr Sculptor, Designer
Goto, Joseph Sculptor
Grear, James Malcolm Designer, Educator
Holmes, Wendy (Diana H Noyes) Photographer
Immonen, Gerald Painter
Johnson, Diana L Gallery Director, Curator
Kelman, Maureen (S) Sculptor, Educator
Liebermann, Philip Photographer, Educator
Marcoux, John W Designer
Ockerse, Thomas Designer, Educator
Parcher, Joan Ann Jeweler
Pilavin, Selma F Collector, Patron
Pinardi, Enrico Vittorio Sculptor, Painter
Prince, Arnold Sculptor, Educator
Schulz, Anne Markham Historian, Educator
Schulz, Juergen Educator, Historian
Schutte, Thomas Frederick Administrator
Udvardy, John Warren Sculptor, Educator

Tiverton

Townley, Hugh Sculptor, Printmaker

Wakefield

Taylor, Brie (Benjamin de Brie) Educator, Painter

Warren

Moore, Todd Somers Painter, Educator

Westerly

Day, Chon Cartoonist

SOUTH CAROLINA

Bishopville

Adams, Bobbi Painter

Chapin

Hampton, Ambrose Gonzales, Jr Collector
Saunders, J Boyd Printmaker, Educator

Charleston

Civitico, Bruno Painter, Educator
Fraser, Mary Edna Designer, Craftsman
Goodbred, Ray Edward Instructor, Painter
Halsey, William Melton Painter, Sculptor
Johnson, Diane Chalmers Historian, Educator
McCallum, Corrie (Mrs William Halsey) Painter, Printmaker
Shaw, Renata Vitzthum Administrator
Tyzack, Michael Painter, Educator
Ward, Joseph Marshall Painter, Educator
Wyrick, Charles Lloyd, Jr Publisher, Editor

Clemson

Jarrard-Dimond, Terry Sculptor, Educator
Wang, Sam Photographer

Columbia

Bardin, Jesse Redwin Painter
Cilella, Salvatore G, Jr Museum Director, Administrator
Craft, John Richard Museum Director
Dunn, Phillip Charles Educator, Administrator
Edwards, James F Painter, Educator
Elkins, Toni Marcus Painter, Designer
Hansen, Harold John Educator, Painter
Lipscomb, Guy Fleming, Jr Painter, Instructor
Mack, Charles Randall Educator, Historian
McWhorter, Elsie Jean Painter, Sculptor
Mitchell, Dana Covington, Jr Collector
Mullen, Philip Edward Painter, Educator
O'Neil, John Joseph Administrator, Designer
Quinsac, Annie-Paule Historian, Writer
Robinson, Chris (Christopher Thomas) Conceptual Artist, Educator
Steven, James Michael Painter, Educator
Woody, (Thomas) Howard Sculptor, Environmental Artist
Yaghjian, Edmund Painter, Instructor

Greenville

Alberga, Alta W Etcher, Painter
Appleman, David Earl Designer, Painter
Barbee, Rob Painter
Bell, Kathryn Leise Calligrapher, Educator
Blair, Carl Raymond Painter, Art Dealer
Bopp, Emery Painter, Educator
Coburn, Bette Lee Painter, Instructor
Collins, George R Historian, Educator
Dreskin, Jeanet Steckler Painter, Educator
Hodge, Dorothy W (Scottie) Gallery Director, Assenblage Artist
Hunter, Robert Howard Painter, Educator
Koons, Darell J Educator, Painter

Hilton Head Island

Bowler, Joseph, Jr Painter, Illustrator
Dixson, Wendy Fay Painter, Graphic Artist
Greer, Walter (Marion) Painter
Lusk, Patricia A Painter, Administrator

Murrells Inlet

Fredericks, Marshall Maynard Sculptor
Tarbox, Gurdon Lucius, Jr Museum Director, Administrator

Myrtle Beach

Pollard, Donald Pence Designer, Painter
Powers, W Alex Painter

North Augusta

Rice, Edward Painter

Orangeburg

Michaux, Henry Gaston educator, sculptor
Twiggs, Leo Franklin Painter, Educator

Pickens

Flowers, Thomas Earl Painter, Educator

Piedmont

Kaufman, Loretta Ana Sculptor, Instructor

Rock Hill

Freeman, David L Painter, Graphic Artist
Lewandowski, Edmund D Painter, Administrator

Spartanburg

Boggs, Mayo Mac Sculptor, Educator
Bramlett, Betty Jane Art Administrator, Painter
Cook, August Charles Painter, Printmaker
Nodine, Jane Allen Painter, Designer

Summerville

Vorwerk, E Charlsie Painter, Illustrator

Sumter

Davenport, Ray Painter, Printmaker
McKoy, Victor Grainger Sculptor

West Columbia

Ochs, Robert David Collector, Patron

SOUTH DAKOTA

Aberdeen

Gibson, James D Educator, Cartoonist

Brookings

LaRoche, Lynda L Craftsman, Designer
Nelson, Signe (Signe Nelson Stuart) Painter
Stuart, Joseph Martin Painter, Museum Director

Ft Meade

Perry, Kathryn Powers Graphic Artist, Painter

Oglala

Chief Eagle, Charles Lince Sculptor

Sioux Falls

Grupp, Carl Alf Painter, Printmaker

Spearfish

Termes, (Dick A) Painter, Photographer

Vermillion

Freeman, Jeff(rey Vaughn) Painter, Educator
Howe, Oscar Painter, Educator
Navrat, Den(nis Edward) Administrator, Painter

TENNESSEE

Brentwood

Goad, Anne Laine Art Dealer
Orr, Arthur (Leslie) Painter, Graphic Artist

Chattanooga

Craft, David Ralph Painter, Photographer
Cress, George Ayers Painter, Educator
Scarbrough, Cleve Knox, Jr Museum Director, Historian
Shumacker, Elizabeth Wight Painter
Townsend, Gavin Edward Historian, Educator
Wu, Wayne Wen-Yau Painter

Clarksville

Bryant, Olen L Sculptor, Educator
Crouch, Ned Philbrick Sculptor, Curator
Hochstetler, T Max Painter, Educator

Cookeville

Lee-Sissom, E Painter

Elizabethton

Logan, David George Metalsmith, Educator

Franklin

Hoffman, Carol Maree Director, Publisher

Gatlinburg

Schulz, Ken Painter, Lecturer

Jackson

Robinson, Grove Painter, Printmaker

Jefferson City

Cleveland, Robert Earl Administrator, Educator

Johnson City

Blosser, Nicholas Painter
Dyer, M Wayne Painter, Graphic Artist
Ropp, Ann L Painter, Gallery Director
Slatton, Ralph David Printmaker, Graphic Artist

Kingsport

Williams, Raymond Lester Painter, Instructor

Knoxville

Brakke, P(erry) Michael Painter, Educator
Cleaver, Dale Gordon Historian, Educator
Gray, Jim Painter, Sculptor
Grogan, Kevin Museum Director
Leland, Whitney Edward Painter, Educator
Longobardi, Pam Painter, Printmaker
Lyons, Beauvais Printmaker, Educator
Robert, Henry Flood, Jr Museum Director
Stewart, F Clark Draftsman, Painter
Sublett, Carl C Painter

Lookout Mountain

Fowler, Frank Eison Art Dealer, Consultant
Lynch, Mary Britten Painter
Wyeth, Andrew Newell Painter
Wyeth, James Browning Painter

Memphis

Allgood, Charles Henry Art Historian, Painter
Anthony, Lawrence Kenneth Sculptor, Educator
Bingham, Alice Art Dealer, Consultant

TENNESSEE (cont)

Buchanan, John Edward, Jr Museum Director, Administrator
Califf, Marilyn Iskiwitz Painter, Designer
Callicott, Burton Harry Painter, Calligrapher
Cloar, Carroll Painter
Dávila, Maritza Printmaker, Educator
Easterwood, Henry Lewis Educator, Tapestry Artist
Goodman, Benjamin Patron
Govan, Francis Hawks Educator, Painter
Hendrix, Connie (Connie Sandage Manus) Painter, Instructor
Herbert, Pinkney Painter, Educator
Knowles, Richard H Painter, Educator
Lockhart, Anne Ivey Museum Director, Curator
Luebbers, Leslie Laird Museum Director, Historian
McPherson, Larry E Photographer, Educator
Miller, Sue S Painter
Morriss, Mary Rachel Painter
Myatt, Greely Sculptor
Penczner, Paul Joseph Painter
Purtle, Carol Jean Historian, Educator
Riseling, Robert Lowell Educator, Painter
Riss, Murray Photographer, Educator
Roberson, William Tapestry Artist, Collage Artist
Rust, Edwin C Sculptor, Administrator
Schwartz, Marjorie Watson Painter
Shook, Georg Painter
Smith, Dolph Painter, Educator

Nashville

Baeder, John Painter
Bissell, Charles Overman Cartoonist
Bodo, Sandor Painter, Sculptor
Caldwell, Benjamin Hubbard, Jr Collector, Historian
Gannon, Lanie E Craftsman
Harrington, Bryan Rulison Painter, Collage Artist
Harris, Dolores Ashley Designer, Educator
Havens, Jan Sculptor, Printmaker
Hazlehurst, Franklin Hamilton Historian, Educator
Hooks, Earl J Educator, Sculptor
James, A Everette, Jr Collector, Lecturer
Jones, Theodore Joseph Sculptor, Printmaker
King, Myron Lyzon Dealer
Knowles, Susan Williams Curator, Critic
Marianne Painter, Draftsman
Michael, Patricia Gordon Administrator, Curator
Mode, Carol A Painter, Printmaker
Murphy, Marilyn L Painter, Educator
Pletcher, Gerry Painter, Printmaker
Ridley, Gregory D, Jr Painter, Sculptor
Webb, Sarah A Painter
Wright, Harold David Painter
Zimmerman, Alice A Collector, Art Dealer

Oak Ridge

Lee, Baldwin S Photography

Ooltewah

Childers, Malcolm Graeme Printmaker, Photographer

Sewanee

Carlos, (James) Edward Painter, Administrator

Seymour

Le Fevre, Richard John Painter, Designer

Signal Mountain

Collins, Jim Educator, Sculptor
Wetmore, Gordon (Stanley Gordon) Painter, Writer

Tullahoma

Blumrich, Stephen Designer

TEXAS

Abilene

Kwiecinski, Chester Martin Educator, Painter
Suter, Sherwood Eugene Educator, Painter
Taylor, Ira Mooney Printmaker, Sculptor
Yates, Hollye E Curator, Historian

Alpine

Cutforth, Roger Conceptual Artist, Painter

Amarillo

Fraze, Denny T Collage Artist, Educator
Hyde, Scott Photographer, Printmaker

Anthony

Grissom, Freda Gill Painter, Goldsmith

Arlington

Blakeney, Rae Historian
Brouillette, Al(bert C) Painter, Instructor
Bruno, Vincent J Historian, Administrator
Curry, Kevin Lee Curator, Director
Elias, Harold John Painter, Educator
Grandee, Joe Ruiz Painter, Gallery Director
Maroney, Dalton Sculptor
Muñoz, Celia Alvarez Photographer
Rascoe, Stephen Thomas Painter, Educator
Rubin, Sandra Printmaker, Lithographer
Spurlock, William Historian, Critic
Turner, William Eugene Painter, Educator
Wood, Nicholas Wheeler Sculptor, Painter

Austin

Albrecht, Mary Dickson Sculptor, Designer
Barnett, Helmut Painter, Printmaker
Bucknall, Malcolm Roderick Painter
Chesney, Lee Roy, III Printmaker, Educator
Clarke, John R Historian , Critic
Coles, Thelma Educator
Daly, Stephen Jeffrey Sculptor, Educator
Davis, Marian B Historian, Curator
Deming, David Lawson Sculptor, Educator
Fearing, William Kelly Educator, Painter
Fisher, James Donald Sculptor, Museum Director
Francis, Bill Dean Designer, Administrator
Frary, Michael Painter, Educator
Gould, Karen Keel Writer, Consultant
Grieder, Terence Historian
Guerin, John William Painter, Educator
Hatgil, Paul Educatorr, Painter
Henderson, Linda Dalrymple Historian, Educator
Hess, Joyce Librarian
High, Timothy Griffin Studio Artist, Educator
Kostiuk, Michael Marion, Jr Photographer
Lansdon, Gay Brandt Printmaker, Jeweler, Metalsmith
Likan, Gustav Painter, Instructor
Lundberg, William Painter
McFarland, Lawrence D Photographer
Marshall, Bruce Painter, Illustrator
Mayer, Susan Martin Educator, Museologist
Miller, Melissa Wren Painter
Milliken, Gibbs Painter, Educator
Pena, Amado Maurilio, Jr Painter, Illustrator
Popinsky, Arnold Dave Sculptor, Ceramist
Prescott, Kenneth Wade Museum Director, Administrator
Sawyer, Margo Sculptor, Painter
Schmandt-Besserat, Denise Historian, Archaeologist
Schuller, Nancy Shelby Librarian, Historian
Seabourn, Connie Painter, Printmaker
Snyder, Hills Sculptor
Spruce, Everett Franklin Painter, Printmaker
Starpattern, Rita Sculptor, Administrator
Stetson, Daniel Everett Museum Director, Curator
Tyler, Ron C Historian
Umlauf, Charles Sculptor
Weismann, Donald Leroy Educator, Painter
White, Ralph Painter, Educator
Wiman, Bill Painter, Educator

Bastrop

Goodman, Mark Photographer

Beaumont

Carron, Maudee Lilyan Painter, Sculptor
Coe, Matchett Herring Sculptor
Stewart, Sheila L Director, Curator

Bellaire

Parsons, David Goode Sculptor, Educator
Saks, Judith-Ann (Judith-Ann Saks Rosenthal) Painter

Big Spring

Hollingshead, Joe Edgar Painter, Sculptor

Burkburnett

Cokendolpher, Eunice Loraine Painter, Instructor

Canyon

Cornette, Mary Elizabeth Dealer, Painter

Carrollton

Judd, De Forrest Hale Painter, Educator
Mohle, Brenda Simonson Consultant, Art Dealer

Cleveland

Surls, James Sculptor, Educator

Clifton

Grelle, Martin Glen Painter

Clint

Herring, Jan (Janet Mantel) Painter, Writer
Herring, William Arthur Painter

Commerce

Frey, Barbara Louise Ceramist, Educator
McGough, Charles E Printmaker, Educator
Seawell, Thomas Robert Printmaker, Photographer
Umlauf, Karl A Painter, Sculptor

Corpus Christi

Andrade, Bruno Painter
Cain, Joseph Alexander Painter, Educator
Lambert, Ed Printmaker, Painter
Locke, Michelle Wilson Curator, Historian
Plath, Iona Writer, Weaver
Riley, Barbra Bayne Photographer, Educator
Silvertooth, Dennis Carl Sculptor
Sullivan, R(onald Dee) Sculptor, Educator
Tsai, Hsiao Hsia Painter, Sculptor
Ullberg, Kent Sculptor
Wilhelmi, William Merle Ceramist, Sculptor
Zuris, Donald P Museum Director

Crowley

Geffert, Harry Sculptor

Dallas

Allumbaugh, James Sculptor, Educator
Altermann, Tony Art Dealer
Barta, Dorothy Elaine Painter, Lecturer
Bogdanovic, Bogomir Painter
Brettell, Richard Robson Director
Brotherton, Naomi Painter, Instructor
Burford, William E Dealer, Administrator
Clifford, Jutta Dealer, Lecturer
Comini, Alessandra Historian, Writer
Elkin, Rowena Caldwell Sculptor
Emerson, Walter Caruth Painter, Educator
Gantz, Ann Cushing Painter, Instructor
Glatt, Linnea Sculptor
Gregory-Goodrum, Ellna Kay Painter, Printmaker
Gummelt, Samuel Painter
Harris, Leon A, Jr Collector, Patron
Harris, Paul Rogers Curator, Director
Heath, Samuel K Museum Director
Held, (Jon) Jonathan, Jr Librarian, Conceptual Artist
Hunter, Debora Photographer, Educator
Jalapeeno, Jimmy (Albert J Bonar) Painter, Photographer
Jones, Lois Swan Educator, Historian
Jordan, William B Historian, Consultant
Kahn, Annelies Ruth Ceramist, Craftsman
Koch, Arthur Robert Painter, Educator
Komodore, Bill Painter
Kutner, Janet Critic, Writer
Leeber, Sharon Corgan Art Dealer, Consultant
Litwin, Ruth Forbes Sculptor, Painter
Lunsford, John (Crawford) Historian, Curator
McAuley, Skeet Photographer, Educator
McMillen, Michael C(halmers) Environmental Artist, Sculptor
Marcus, Stanley Collector
Meadows, P B (Patricia) Curator, Painter
Mooz, R Peter Museum Director
Nasher, Raymond Donald Collector, Patron
Nelson, Pamela Hudson Assemblage Artist, Sculptor
Richards, Jeanne Herron Printmaker, Painter
Scholder, Laurence Printmaker, Educator
Smither, Edward Murray Dealer, Consultant
Stewart, John (John Stewart Houston) Dealer
Tyler, Valton Printmaker, Painter
Voelker, John Painter, Designer
Vogel, Donald S Painter, Dealer

Denton

Butt, Harlan W Silversmith, Enamelist
Davis, D Jack Educator, Administrator
Erdle, Rob Painter, Educator
Falsetta, Vincent Mario Painter, Educator
Gough, Georgia Belle Craftsman, Educator
Sullivan, Scott A Historian, Educator
Weller, Laurie June Painter
Youngblood, Judy Printmaker

Dumas

Stallwitz, Carolyn Painter, Photographer

Edinburg

Field, Philip Sidney Painter, Printmaker
Manuella, Frank R Designer, Conceptual Artist

El Paso

Acosta, Manuel Gregorio Painter, Sculptor
Andersen, David R L Painter, Curator
Carter, Frederick Timmins Painter, Illustrator
De Turczynowicz, Wanda (Mrs Eliot Hermann) Painter
Drake, James Printmaker, Sculptor
Enriquez, Gaspar Painter, Metalsmith
Fensch, Charles Everette Administrator, Educator
Fulton, Fred Franklin Painter, Historian
Garnsey, Clarke Henderson Historian, Educator
Hill, Ed Dealer, Collector
Kolliker, William Augustin Painter, Printmaker
Lea, Tom Painter, Writer
Martinez, Ernesto Pedregon Muralist, Artist
Massey, Robert Joseph Painter, Educator
Rakocy, William (Joseph) Painter, Muralist
Schuster, Cita Fletcher (Sarah E) Painter, Consultant
Sipiora, Leonard Paul Museum Director, Museologist
Thiewes, Rachelle R Jeweler

Farmers Branch

Amend, Eugene Michael Historian, Advisor

Fredericksburg

Laird, E Ruth Sculptor

Ft Worth

Abramson, Elaine Sandra Cartoonist, Graphic Artist
Blackburn, Ed M Painter
Blackburn, Linda Z Painter
Bush, Jill Lobdill Painter
Carlin, Electra Marshall Dealer
Conn, David Edward Printmaker, Painter
Demanche, Michel S Painter, Photographer
Fisher, Vernon Conceptual Artist
Huston, Perry Clark Conservator
Lincoln, Richard Mather Ceramist, Educator
Muhlert, Christopher Layton Painter
Muhlert, Jan Keene Museum Director, Historian
Phillips, Dutch (James O), Jr Gallery Director, Dealer
Pillsbury, Edmund P Museum Director
Smith, Luther A Photographer
Stevenson, Ruth Carter Collector, Patron
Strother, Virginia Vaughn Painter
Sullivan, Ruth Wilkins Curator, Author
Thistlethwaite, Mark Edward Educator, Historian
Tillman, Patricia Ann Sculptor
Watson, Ronald G Painter, Educator

Galveston

Foster, Don Sculptor
Samuels, John Stockwell, 3rd Collector, Patron

Georgetown

Veerkamp, Patrick Burke Educator, Administrator

Hemphill

Hobbs, Joe Ferrell Administrator, Sculptor

Henderson

Bynum, E Anderson (Esther Pearl) Curator, Printmaker

Houston

Adams, Celeste Marie Curator, Writer
Adickes, David (Pryor) Painter, Sculptor
Armstrong, Martha (Allen) Painter, Photographer
Balahutrak, Lydia Bodnar Painter, Educator
Berman, Ellen Mercil Trew Painter
Bettison, James Painter
Biggers, John Thomas Educator, Painter
Block, Gay (S) Photographer
Bott, H(arvey) J(ohn) Sculptor, Painter
Bourdon, Robert Slayton Sculptor, Educator
Boynton, Jack (James) W Painter, Printmaker
Broker, Karin Draftsman, Printmaker
Butler, Hiram Director
Cahana, Alice Lok Painter
Camfield, William Arnett Historian
Casas, Fernando Painter, Draftsman
Caslin, Jean Arts Administrator
Caton, David Painter
Clement, Alain Gerard Photographer
Collins, Lowell Daunt Painter, Dealer
Conrad, Nancy R Painter
Crow, Carol (Wilson) Sculptor
Davis, Bertha G Painter
Deats, Margaret Art Dealer, Writer
Delehanty, Suzanne E Historian, Museum Director
Evans, Burford Elonzo Painter, Lecturer
Fowler, Mary Jean Weaver
Frace, Charles Lewis Painter
Geeslin, Lee Gaddis Painter, Educator
Glasco, Joseph M Painter, Sculptor
Goldberg, Arnold Herbert Painter, Printmaker
Gonzalez, Patricia Painter
Gorski, Daniel Alexander Painter, Sculptor
Graham, William Andrew Dealer, Collector
Grove, Samuel Harold Administrator, Historian
Guenther, Peter W Historian, Educator
Hammett, Polly Horton Painter, Instructor
Hernandez, John Painter
Holsch, Robert Fred Sculptor
Hood, Dorothy Painter
Hooks, Charles Vernon Dealer, Collector
Hooks, Geri Dealer, Collector
Hurst, Lynn Painter
Kempner, Helen Hill Collector, Patron
Kopriva, Sharon Painter, Sculptor
Krause, George Photographer
Lee, Janie C Dealer
Lesher, Marie Palmisano Sculptor
Link, Val James Jeweler, Educator

TEXAS (cont)

Long, Bert L, Jr Sculptor
Long, Jenny Art Dealer
Long, Meredith J Dealer
Love, Jim Sculptor
Ludtke, Lawrence Monroe Sculptor
McClain, Robert Lee Art Dealer, Gallery Director
McCleary, Mary Fielding Collage Artist, Educator
McGarry, Susan Hallsten Editor, Writer
Martin, Lys Photographer, Curator
Marzio, Peter Cort Historian, Museum Director
Mayo, Marti Museum Director, Curator
Metyko, Michael Joseph Consultant
Moody, Elizabeth C Dealer, Gallery Director
Morris, Jack Austin, Jr Museum Director, Art Dealer
Niizuma, Minoru Sculptor
O'Neil, John Painter, Educator
Peranteau, Michael Curator
Portman, Brian Printmaker
Poulos, Basilios Nicholas Painter, Educator
Randolph, Lynn Moore Painter
Rice, M Robert & Barbara Menen Dealers, Collectors
Robinson, Thomas V Dealer, Collector
St John, Adam Craftsman, Furniture Artist
Schorre, Charles Painter, Printmaker
Scott, Sam Painter
Shapiro, Adrian Michael Lecturer, Writer
Stack, Gael Z Painter, Educator
Storm, Mark (Kennedy) Painter, Sculptor
Stout, Richard Gordon Painter
Suttman, Paul Sculptor
Tennant, Donna Kay Writer, Editor
Thompson, Judith Kay Painter
Tucker, Anne Wilkes Curator, Historian
Turner, (Charles) Arthur Painter, Instructor
Twaddle, Randy Painter
Van Vranken, Rose (Rose Van Vranken Hickey) Sculptor, Printmaker
Warren, David Boardman Curator
Watniss, Wendy Photographer
Werner Vaughn, Salle Painter, Illuminator
Winningham, Geoff Photographer
Woitena, Ben S Sculptor, Educator
Wolff, Dee I Painter
Wray, Dick Painter

Humble

Cobb, Virginia Horton Painter, Lecturer

Huntsville

Ahysen, Harry Joseph Painter, Muralist
Breitenbach, William John Sculptor, Educator
Eastman, Gene M Painter
Lea, Stanley E Printmaker, Painter
Patrick, Darryl L Historian

Hurst

Martin, Loretta Marsh Cartoonist, Calligrapher
Saladino, Tony Printmaker, Painter

Irving

Novinski, Lyle Frank Painter, Educator

Kerrville

Burt, Dan Painter
Cook, John (Alfred) Sculptor, Medalist
Cook, Kathleen L Painter

Kingsville

Scherpereel, Richard Charles Educator, Painter

Kingwood

Vernon Painter, Printmaker

Ladonia

Lecky, Susan Painter

Laredo

Watson, Helen Richter Ceramist, Sculptor

Longview

Statman, Jan B Painter, Instructor

Lubbock

Akins, Future Renée Printmaker, Sculptor
Cheatham, Frank Reagan Painter, Designer
Dingus, Phillip Rick Photographer, Draftsman
Dixon, Ken Painter
Edson, Gary F Museologist, Museum Director
Funk, Charlotte M Tapestry Artist, Weaver
Funk, Verne J Ceramist, Sculptor
Gibbons, Hugh (James) Painter, Educator
Hanna, Paul Dean, Jr Painter, Printmaker
Howze, James Dean Draftsman, Educator
Kreneck, Lynwood Printmaker, Educator
Morrow, Terry Draftsman, Printmaker
Stephen, Francis B Jeweler, Sculptor
Weiler, Melody M Administrator, Educator

McAllen

Clark, Charles D Collector, Patron

Medina

Carrington, Joy Harrell Painter, Illuminator

Midland

Hagman, Jean Cassels Museum Director, Art Historian
Hood, Gary Allen Curator, Printmaker
Lynch, Betty Painter, Instructor

Mission

McClendon, Maxine (Maxine McClendon Nichols) Painter, Craftsman
Nichols, Edward Edson Painter

Nacogdoches

Beason, Donald Ray Educator, Sculptor
Hobgood, E Wade Administrator, Designer
Wink, Don (Jon Donnel) Painter, Educator

New Braunfels

Wall, Ralph Alan Painter

Odessa

Lee, Nelda S Dealer

Pipe Creek

Studstill, Pamela Craftsman

Plano

Gibbs, Y Gale Painter, Sculptor
Z' Painter

Refugio

Branstetter, Gwendolyn H Painter

Richardson

Brown, John Hall Painter, Architect
Curtis, Mary Cranfill Printmaker, Painter
Kessler, Margaret Jennings Painter
McNary, Oscar L Painter, Collector
Stott, Deborah Historian

Rockport

Moroles, Jesús Bautista Sculptor

San Antonio

Amado, Jesse V Sculptor
Binks, Ronald C Photographer, Painter
Bristow, William Arthur Painter, Educator
Broderick, James Allen Administrator, Graphic Artist
Casas, Melesio (Mel) Painter, Educator
Chalmers, E Laurence, Jr Administrator
Chiego, William J Director, Curator
Cobb, James Painter
Colpitt, Frances Historian, Critic
Davis, Alonzo Joseph Visual Artist, Administrator
Duncan, Ruth Painter
Embrey, Carl Rice Painter, Instructor
Flume, Violet Sigoloff Dealer, Restorer
Fuchs, Mary Tharsilla Educator, Painter
Hyland, Douglas K S Museum Director
Kelley, Deborah Maverick Painter
Kenney, Douglas Ceramist, Clay Sculptor
Lee, Amy Freeman Painter, Lecturer
Leeper, John Palmer Museum Director
Leroy, Louis Painter
Little, Ken Dawson Sculptor, Educator
McDougal, Ivan Ellis Painter, Instructor
Maurer, Neil Douglas Photographer
Notestine, Dorothy J Instructor, Painter
Notestine, Tom W Lecturer, Instructor
Quirarte, Jacinto Historian, Administrator
Rodgers, Jack A Administrator
Rowe, Reginald M Painter, Sculptor
Rush, Kent Thomas Photographer, Printmaker
Tarin, Gilberto A Painter, Printmaker
Tiemann, Robert E Painter, Sculptor
Vater, Regina (Regina Vater Lundberg) Conceptual Artist, Lecturer
West, E Gordon Painter
Willson, Margaret (Bosshardt) Pace Painter, Sculptor
Willson, Robert Sculptor, Painter
Wogstad, James Everet Educator, Illustrator

Sandia

Peters, Diane (Peck) Painter, Collage Artist

Seminole

Clark, Vicky Jo Painter, Muralist

Sherman

Havel, Joseph G Sculptor
Neidhardt, Carl Richard Painter, Sculptor

Smithville

Kohut, Lorene Painter

Texarkana

Caver, William Ralph Sculptor, Printmaker

Tyler

Gentry, Augustus (Callahan), Jr Painter, Printmaker
Pace, James Robert Painter, Printmaker
Stephens, William Blakely Educator, Painter

Waco

Chatmas, John T Painter
Eden, Bronson B Painter
Kagle, Joseph L, Jr Painter, Museum Director
Kemp, Paul Zane Educator, Sculptor
McClanahan, John D Painter, Educator

Wichita Falls

Band, David Moshe Painter, Art Dealer

Wylie

Pototschnik, John Michael Painter, Instructor

UTAH

Bennington

Bubriski, Kevin E Photographer

Boulder

Barsch, Wulf Erich Painter, Printmaker

Brigham City

Huchel, Frederick M Historian, Consultant

Cedar City

Kidrick, Valerie Anne Museum Director, Gallery Director

Hurricane

Lindstrom, Gaell Painter, Educator

Lindon

Speed, (Ulysses) Grant Sculptor

Logan

Smith, Moishe Printmaker
Van Suchtelen, Adrian Printmaker, Educator

Mendon

Morgan, James L Painter

Ogden

Taylor, Harry George Printmaker, Photographer

Orem

Card, Royden Painter, Printmaker

Park City

Balaban, Diane Painter
Southey, Trevor J T Painter, Sculptor
Weller, Don Mighell Illustrator, Designer

Pleasant Grove

Jarvis, John Brent Painter
Kimball, Wilford Wayne, Jr Lithographer, Draftsman

Provo

Andrus, James Roman Printmaker, Painter
Coleman, Michael Painter
Magleby, Frank (Francis R) Painter, Educator
Marshall, Robert Leroy Educator, Painter
Myer, Peter Livingston Kinetic Artist, Educator
Wilson, Warren Bingham Educator, Sculptor

St George

Collett, Farrell Reuben Painter, Educator

Salt Lake City

Christensen, Larry R Painter, Instructor
Christensen, Sharlene Painter, Instructor
Cutler, Grayce E Painter, Writer
Davis, Paul Painter, Educator
De Waal, Ronald Burt Collector, Patron
Dibble, George Painter, Writer
Dodworth, Allen Stevens Consultant, Curator
Friberg, Arnold Painter, Publisher
Lake, Randall Painter, Printmaker
Olpin, Robert Spencer Historian, Administrator
Phillips, Bonnie Dealer, Painter
Rasmussen, Anton Jesse Painter, Administrator
Sanguinetti, Eugene F Administrator, Lecturer
Tierney, Patrick Lennox Historian, Educator

South Jordan

Fraughton, Edward James Sculptor

Spring City

Bennion, Joseph W Ceramist

Springville

Swanson, Vern Grosvenor Museum Director, Historian

VERMONT

Barre

Gaylord, Frank Chalfant, II Sculptor, Designer

Barton

Miller, Dolly (Ethel B) Painter, Collage Artist

Bennington

Adams, Pat Painter, Educator
Held, Julius S Educator, Writer

Brookfield

Newton, Earle Williams Administrator, Educator

Burlington

Davison, Bill Educator, Printmaker
Parris, Nina Gumpert Curator, Educator

Cavendish

Shapiro, David Painter, Lecturer

Dorset

Fausett, (William) Dean Painter, Muralist

East Calais

Gahagan, James (Edward), Jr Painter, Educator
Gogorza, Patricia (Gahagan) de Sculptor, Printmaker

East Dorset

Armstrong, Jane Botsford Sculptor

Fairfax

Goldsmith, Lawrence Charles Painter, Instructor

Fairlee

Walker, Herbert Brooks Sculptor, Museum Director

Ferrisburg

Hunter, Mel Printmaker, Painter

Grafton

Schoener, Allon Designer, Consultant

Jericho

Chase, Jack S(paulding) Sculptor

Manchester Center

Abbe, Elfriede Martha Sculptor, Printmaker
Montague, James L Painter, Printmaker
Rath, Hildegard Painter, Lecturer

Marlboro

Boylen, Michael Edward Craftsman, Art Writer
Stout, Frank J Painter, Sculptor

Middlebury

Andres, Glenn Merle Historian, Educator
Bumbeck, David A Printmaker, Educator
Hunisak, John Michael Historian, Educator
Perry, Edward (Ted) Samuel Administrator
Saunders, Richard Henry Museum Director, Historian

Northfield

Krauth, Harald Painter

North Hartland

Watson, Aldren A Designer, Illustrator

Pittsford

Frick, Robert Oliver Painter, Instructor

Putney

Ginnever, Charles Sculptor

Randolph

Robbins, Daniel J Historian, Museum Director
Robbins, Eugenia S Writer, Editor

Rutland

Farrow, Patrick Villiers Sculptor

St Albans

Prent, Mark Environmental Artist, Sculptor

Springfield

Baldwin, Harold Fletcher Sculptor, Painter
Eldredge, Mary Agnes Sculptor

Stowe

Wright, Stanley Marc Painter, Instructor

West Brattleboro

Heiskell, Diana Painter

West Burke

Van Vliet, Claire Printmaker, Publisher

Weston

Kasnowski, Chester N Collage Artist, Conceptual Artist

Wilmington

Singer, Michael Sculptor

Woodstock

Fenton, Charles E H Art Dealer, Conservator

VIRGINIA

Alexandria

Anderson, Mark Robert Stained Glass Artist, Sculptor
Banks, Anne Johnson Collage Artist, Educator
Caples, Barbara Barrett Painter, Printmaker
Conger, Clement E Curator
Essley, Roger Holmer Painter, Graphic Artist
Evans, Grose Historian, Educator
Keena, Janet Laybourn Painter
Patrick, Charles William Conceptual Artist, Writer
Royer, Mona Lee Painter
Spagnolo, Kathleen Mary Printmaker, Illustrator
Thompson, Jean Danforth Tapestry Artist, Painter
Thorpe, Hilda (Shapiro) Painter, Sculptor
Wasko-Flood, Sandra Jean Printmaker, Photographer

Annandale

Dean, James Painter
Spink, Frank Henry Painter

Arlington

Bryans, John Armond Instructor, Painter
Gast, Carolyn Bartlett (Lutz) Illustrator, Illuminator
Gast, Michael Carl Painter
Gurney, George Curator, Historian
Harlan, Roma Christine Painter
Kamen, Rebecca Sculptor, Educator
Knippers, Edward Painter, Printmaker
Osborn, Kevin Russell Book Artist, Printmaker
Reed, Paul Allen Painter
Rexroth, Nancy Louise Photographer
Schneider, Julie (Saecker) Painter, Draftsman

Ashland

Longaker, Jon Dasu Educator, Writer

Blacksburg

Bickley, Gary Steven Educator, Sculptor
Carter, Dean Sculptor, Educator
Crane, David Franklin Ceramist, Educator
Gablik, Suzi Painter, Writer
Harman, Maryann Whittemore Painter
Huggins, Victor, Jr Painter, Printmaker

Bridgewater

Beer, Kenneth John Educator, Sculptor

Charlottesville

Arvin, Irmgard Pinckernell Painter, Instructor
Barbee, Robert Thomas Painter, Graphic Artist
Burr, Horace Curator, Sculptor
Crozier, Richard Lewis Painter, Educator
Dass, Dean Allen Printmaker, Painter
Dunnigan, Mary Catherine Librarian
Geiger, Phillip Neil Painter, Draftsman
Hagan, James Garrison Sculptor, Instructor
Hightower, John B Administrator, Museum Director
Lawall, David Barnard Historian, Museum Director
Priest, Hartwell Wyse Painter, Printmaker
Stein, Roger Breed Historian, Educator
Turner, Theodore Roy Painter, Educator

Christianburg

Kass, Ray Painter

Clifton

Hennesy, Gerald Craft Painter, Publisher

Covington

Walton, Harry A, Jr Collector

Crozet

Harrington, William Charles Sculptor

Fairfax

Clapsaddle, Jerry Painter, Designer
FitzSimonds, Carol Strause Printmaker
Matternes, Jay Howard Painter, Illustrator
Watson, Darliene Keeney Painter

Fairfax Station

Jackson, Vaughn L Painter, Illustrator
Strickland, Painter, Instructor

Falls Church

Grosse, C(arolyn Ann Gawarecki) Painter, Instructor
Jones, Lou (Mary Louise Humpton) Painter, Sculptor
Liu, Ho Collector, Painter
Peak, Elizabeth Jayne Printmaker, Educator
Robinson, Charlotte Painter, Printmaker

Farmville

Edmonson, Randall W Ceramist, Painter

Forest

Johnson, (L) Diane Painter, Graphic Artist

Fredericksburg

McGill, Forrest Historian, Museum Administrator

Ft Belvoir

Marker, Mariska Pugsley Painter

Hampton

Beachum, Sharon Garrison Photographer, Graphic Artist

Harrisonburg

Caldwell, Martha Belle Educator, Historian
Crable, James Harbour Multi-Media Artist, Instructor
Downs, Stuart Clifton Administrator, Educator

Herndon

Pisani, Joseph Muralist, Painter

Hollins College

Dahlstrom, Nancy Gail Printmaker, Painter

Leesburg

Sanabria, Robert Sculptor
Sanabria, Sherry Zvares Painter

Lexington

Ju, I-Hsiung Educator, Painter
Mann, Sally Photographer

Lorton

Bierly, Edward J Painter, Illustrator

Lovettsville

Mion, Pierre Riccardo Illustrator, Painter

Lynchburg

Agnew, Ellen Schall Museum Director
Werfel, Gina S Painter, Educator

McLean

MacDonald, Betty Ann Printmaker, Environmental Artist
O'Connell, Ann Brown Printmaker, Collector
Safer, John Sculptor

Middleburg

Schaeffer, S(tanley) Allyn Painter, Instructor

Midlothian

Baldridge, Mark S Goldsmith, Editor

Newport News

Anglin, Betty Lockhart Educator, Painter
Sheaks, Barclay Painter, Writer

Norfolk

Clark, Mark A Curator
Dreyer, Gay Sculptor
Jones, Herb (Leon Herbert), Jr Painter, Printmaker
Knorr, Jeanne Boardman Painter, Educator
Lewis, Donald Sykes, Jr Art Dealer, Painter
Matson, Greta Painter
Moore, Myreen (Myreen Moore Nicholson) Painter, Consultant
Young, Robert S W Sculptor

Onancock

Kidd, Rebecca Montgomery Painter

Petersburg

Woodson, Doris Educator, Painter

Portsmouth

Eldredge, Bruce B Museum Director, Administrator
Sibley, Charles Kenneth Painter, Educator

Purcellville

DiPerna, Frank Paul Photographer, Instructor

Reston

Mahlmann, John James Publisher, Administrator
Norelli, Martina Roudabush Curator

Richmond

Apgar, Nicolas Adam Painter, Educator
Brandt, Frederick Robert Curator
Bumgardner, James Arliss Painter, Educator
Campbell, Jeanne Begien Painter, Educator
Campbell, Jewett Educator, Painter
Cormack, Malcolm Curator, Historian
DePillars, Murry N Administrator, Illustrator
Freed, David Printmaker, Painter
Haynes, George Edward Painter, Illustrator
High, Steven S Museum Director, Curator
Hobbs, Robert Carleton Museum Director, Historian
Hompson, Davi Det (David Elbridge Thompson) Painter
Ipsen, Kent Forrest Glassworker, Craftsman
Johnson, Charles W, Jr Educator, Historian

VIRGINIA (cont)

Kevorkian, Richard Painter
Martin, Bernard Murray Painter, Educator
Mavroudis, Demetrios Sculptor
Mayo, Margaret Ellen Curator
Mayo, Pamela Elizabeth Gallery Director
Mayo, Robert Bowers Art Dealer, Collector
Meggs, Philip B Designer, Historian
Perry, Regenia Alfreda Historian
Pollak, Theresa Painter, Draftsman
Thompson, Nancy Kunkle Jeweler, Educator
Welch, James Wymore Painter, Muralist
Witt, Nancy Camden Painter, Sculptor
Zed, Aggie Sculptor

Roanoke

Appelhof, Dr Ruth A Curator, Historian
Curtis, David Painter, Educator
Johnson, Ernest (Melvin) Painter, Instructor

Somerset

Sehring, Adolf Painter, Sculptor

Springfield

Wengrovitz, Judith Painter, Instructor

Staunton

Desportes, Ulysse Gandvier Painter, Historian

Stirling

De Guzman, Evelyn Lopez Painter, Printmaker

The Plains

Putnam, Nol (Oliver de Montalant) Sculptor

Timberville

Barnard, Rob(ert E) Ceramist, Critic

Troutville

Dickerson, Vera Mason Painter, Instructor

Vienna

Cusick, Nancy Taylor Painter
Gonzales, Carlotta (Mrs Richard Lahey) Painter, Sculptor
Nash, Mary Painter, Lecturer
Sandground, Mark Bernard, Sr Collector, Patron
Von Zur Muehien, Peter Photographer
Von zur Muehlen, Bernis Susan Photographer

Virginia Beach

Antol, Joseph James (Jay) Sculptor, Conceptual Artist
Gatling, Eva Ingersoll Consultant, Historian
Johnson, Martin Brian Assemblage Artist, Environmental Artist
Lewis, Don S, Sr Art Dealer, Painter
Wells, Betty Childs Illustrator, Painter

Waterford

Pollack, Reginald Murray Painter, Sculptor

Williamsburg

Alexick, David Francis Educator, Painter
Barnes, William David Painter, Printmaker
Chappell, Miles Linwood Historian, Educator
Christison, Muriel B Educator, Museum Director
Conklin, Gloria Zamko Painter
Hood, Graham Stanley Museum Director, Writer
Johnson, Mark M Museum Director
Madonia, Ann C Curator, Administrator
Roseberg, Carl Andersson Sculptor, Painter
Rumford, Beatrix Tyson Administrator
Williams, John Alden Historian

WASHINGTON

Anacortes

McCracken, Philip Sculptor

Bainbridge Island

Carlson, Robert Michael Glass Blower, Painter
Randlett, Mary Willis Photographer
Willis, Elizabeth Bayley Historian, Collector

Battle Ground

Hansen, James Lee Sculptor

Bellevue

Correa, Flora Horst Painter
Ryan, William Edward Painter
Trubner, Henry Curator, Museologist
Warsinske, Norman George Sculptor, Painter

Bellingham

Clark-Langager, Sarah Ann Gallery Director, Curator
Herman, Lloyd Eldred Museum Director
Johnston, Thomas Alix Painter, Printmaker
Langager, Craig T Painter, Sculptor
Marsh, David Foster Educator, Painter
Scott, C(harles) A(rthur) Sculptor

Bothell

Peck, James Edward Painter, Designer

Cheney

Askman, Tom K Painter, Educator

Copalis Beach

Jones, Thomas William Painter

Eastsound

Bevlin, Marjorie Elliott Painter, Writer
Rippey, Clayton Painter, Muralist

East Wenatchee

Graves, Robert Edward Painter, Instructor

Edmonds

D'Elaine Painter, Educator

Ellensburg

Sahlstrand, James Michael Photographer
Sahlstrand, Margaret Ahrens Printmaker, Craftsman
Stillman, George Painter

Everett

Bratt, Byron H Printmaker

Grapeview

Hoover, John Jay Sculptor

Issaguah

Pennington, Sally Painter

Issaquah

Thiry, Paul (Albert) Architect, Collector

Kent

Broer, Roger L Painter, Sculptor
Pierce, Danny P Sculptor, Painter

Kirkland

Mohr, K(aren) Lee Painter, Administrator

La Conner

Hupy, Art Curator, Photographer

Langley

Davis, Robert Painter

Longview

Jaeger, Brenda Kay Painter, Craftsman
Powelson, Rosemary A Painter, Printmaker

Mercer Island

Davidson, Elizabeth H Donnally Dealer

Moses Lake

Tse, Stephen Painter, Educator

Mt Vernon

Gilkey, Richard Charles Painter, Sculptor

Nordland

Kepner, Rita Sculptor, Administrator
Klein, Lynn (Ellen) Painter, Photographer

Olympia

Haseltine, James Lewis Printmaker, Painter
Haseltine, Maury (Margaret Wilson) Painter, Consultant
Hopkins, Kenneth R Museum Director, Restorer

Omak

Woolschlager, Laura Totten Painter, Printmaker

Oroville

Kujundzic, Zeljko D Ceramist, Sculptor

Port Townsend

Austin, Pat Painter, Printmaker

Pullman

Coates, Ross Alexander Historian, Painter
Ho, Francis T Photographer, Educator
Monaghan, Keith Painter, Educator
Siler, Patrick W Painter, Ceramist
Watkinson, Patricia Grieve Museum Director, Curator

Randle

Pitcher, John Charles Painter, Illustrator

Reardan

Chester, Charlotte Wanetta Painter, Writer

Seattle

Allen, Judith S Photographer
Alps, Glen Earl Educator, Printmaker
Angell, Tony Sculptor, Painter
Arnold, Richard R Designer, Administrator
Bard, Gayle Environmental Artist, Painter
Bartscherer, Joseph Conceptual Artist, Photographer
Berger, Paul Eric Collage Artist, Photographer
Bishop, Jeffrey Britton Painter, Educator
Blaedel, Joan Stuart Ross Painter, Printmaker

WASHINGTON (cont)

Blomdahl, Sonja Glass Blower
Braseth, John E Art Dealer, Consultant
Bravmann, Rene A Art Historian, Educator
Burns, Marsha Photographer
Celentano, Francis Michael Painter, Educator
Chihuly, Dale Patrick Glass Artist, Educator
Cohen, Jonathan Jacob Designer, Craftsman
Dailey, Michael Dennis Painter, Educator
Du Pen, Everett George Sculptor, Educator
Engle, Steve (Stephen E) Sculptor
Farris, Linda B Dealer
Fear, Daniel E Dealer, Gallery Director
Foster, Donald Isle Dealer
Funk, Robert Norris Educator, Administrator
Gardiner, T Michael Painter
Gardner, Ann Ceramist
Gates, Jay Rodney Adminstrator, Curator
Graham, Lois (M Gord) Painter
Gray, Larry Painter
Gray, Marie Elise Painter
Guzak, Karen W Painter, Printmaker
Harrington, LaMar Curator, Director
Hatch, (Mr & Mrs) Marshall Collectors
Hayes, Randy (Randolph Alan) Painter
Heidel, Frederick (H) Painter, Educator
Herard, Marvin T Sculptor, Educator
Hill, Gary Video Artist
Hirondelle, Anne E Ceramist
Holm, Bill Historian, Painter
Horiuchi, Paul C Collage Artist
Hu, Mary Lee Educator, Jeweler
Ingham, Tom (Edgar) Sculptor, Painter
Irwin, Lisa Dru Photographer, Painter
Jonsson, Ted (Wilbur) Sculptor
Kirsten, Nicholas Video Artist
Kirsten-Daiensai, Richard Charles Painter, Printmaker
Koenig, John Franklin Painter
Kuvshinoff, Bertha Horne Painter, Sculptor
Kuvshinoff, Nicolai Painter, Sculptor
Lawrence, Jacob Painter, Mosaic Artist
Lundin, Norman K Painter
Maki, Robert Richard Sculptor, Painter
Mann, Frank Painter, Draftsman
Marioni, Paul Sculptor, Glass Blower
Marshall, John Carl Craftsman
Mason, Alden C Painter, Educator
Moore, Benjamin Powell Glass Blower, Designer
Nadalini, (Louis Ernest) Painter
Oliver, Marvin E Craftsman
Praczukowski, Edward Leon Painter, Educator
Rathbun, William Jay Curator
Ritchie, William (Bill) Printmaker, Video Artist
Rood, Kay Printmaker, Draftsman
Ross, Sueellen Printmaker, Painter
Royal, Richard P Craftsman
Ruffner, Ginny Martin Glassblower
Sato, Norie Video Artist
Sawada, Ikune Painter
Seders, Francine Lavinal Dealer
Segan, Ken Akiva Draftsman, Painter
Selig, (Mr & Mrs) Manfred Collectors, Patrons
Simpson, Buster Sculptor
Sims, Patterson Curator
Spafford, Michael Charles Educator, Painter
Sperry, Robert Ceramist
Theobald, Gillian Lee Painter, Lithographer
Thompson, Cappy (Catherine) Painter
Tsutakawa, George Sculptor, Painter
Vaness, Margaret Helen Painter, Printmaker
Warashina, M Patricia Ceramist, Educator
Washington, James W, Jr Sculptor, Painter
Wehr, Wesley Conrad Painter, Paleontologist
Weiss, Dick J Enamelist, Stained Glass Artist
Wells, Thomas (Winchester) Painter
Wicklander, Edward A Sculptor
Woodside, Gordon William Dealer, Collector
Young, John T Sculptor
Zeitlin, Harry Leon Photographer

Sequim

Ervin, Kathey Ceramist
Wands, Alfred James Painter

Silverdale

Hess, Stanley William Librarian

Spokane

Adkison, Kathleen (Gemberling) Painter
Flahavin, Marian Joan Painter
Fleckenstein, Opal R Painter, Ceramist
Fyfe, Jo Suzanne (Storch) Painter, Sculptor
Patnode, J Scott Educator, Gallery Director

Steilacoom

Clinton, Paul Arthur Printmaker, Instructor

Tacoma

Colby, Bill Printmaker, Painter
Hallam, John S Historian, Administrator
Moe, Richard D Administrator
Ott, Wendell Lorenz Museum Director, Painter
Rades, William L Painter, Sculptor
Schwidder, Ernst Sculptor, Designer

Vancouver

Anderson, Guy Irving Painter
Maurice, Alfred Paul Painter, Educator

Vashon

Takamori, Akio Ceramist

Walla Walla

Hara, Keiko Painter, Printmaker
Meitzler, Neil (Herbert) Painter, Designer

Wenatchee

Graham, Walter Painter, Sculptor

WEST VIRGINIA

Bethany

Halasz, Piri Historian, Critic

Charleston

Atkins, Rosalie Marks Painter
Black, Mary McCune Curator, Painter
Blumberg, Barbara Griffiths Painter, Instructor
Keeling, Henry Cornelious Painter, Educator

Charles Town

Lewis, John Chapman Painter, Instructor

Elkins

Reed, Jesse Floyd Painter, Printmaker

Fairmont

Smigocki, Stephen Vincent Painter, Printmaker

Huntington

Butler, Charles Thomas Museum Director, Curator
Emerson, Roberta Shinn Museum Director
Ettling, Ruth (Droitcour) Printmaker, Painter
Hage, Raymond Joseph Art Dealer, Collector
Polan, Lincoln M Collector, Patron
Polan, Nancy Moore Painter

Milton

Anderson, Winslow Designer, Painter

Morgantown

Couch, Urban Painter, Educator
Johnson, Selina (Tetzlaff) Museologist, Historian
Schultz, John Bernard Educator, Historian

Shepherdstown

Jones, Ronald Lee, Jr Educator, Writer
Suttenfield, Diana Graphic Artist, Painter

West Liberty

Peace, Bernie (Kinzel) Painter, Printmaker

Wheeling

Phillis, Marilyn Hughey Painter, Instructor

WISCONSIN

Appleton

Esau, Erika Educator, Historian

Beloit

Boggs, Franklin Muralist, Sculptor
Moy, Henry Museum Director, Museologist
Olson, Richard W Painter, Educator
Simon, Michael A Photographer
Strawn, Jarrett W (Jason) Sculptor, Educator

Cedarburg

Crane, Jean Painter
Geniusz, Robert Myles Printmaker, Filmmaker

Dane

Anderson, Donald Myers Art Writer, Calligrapher

Eau Claire

Campbell, Kenneth Floyd Sculptor, Restorer

Ellison Bay

Austin, Phil Painter, Lecturer

Evansville

Wilde, John Painter, Draftsman

Fish Creek

Becker, Bettie (Bettie Geraldine Wathall) Painter, Graphic Artist

Fond du Lac

Griffiths, William Perry Educator, Jeweler

Fountain City

Pitt, Suzan (Lee) Painter, Filmmaker

Fox Point

Colt, John Nicholson Painter, Educator

Franklin

Spurgin, John Edwin Administrator, Painter

Green Bay

Donhauser, Paul Stefan Sculptor, Painter
Noel, Donald Claude Sculptor
Winzenz, Karon Hagemeister Painter, Educator

Hales Corners

Garzon-Blanco, Armando Designer, Painter

Hartland

Stamsta, Jean Paper Artist

Hollandale

Colescott, Warrington W Printmaker, Painter
Myers, Frances Printmaker

Janesville

Williams, Marylou Lord Study Consultant, Collage Artist

Kenosha

Pollei, Dane F Museum Director, Administrator

Lake Geneva

Salter, Richard Mackintire Painter

Madison

Breckenridge, Bruce M Ceramist, Educator
Conniff, Gregory Photographer, Writer
Fleischman, Stephen Museum Director
Garver, Fanny Art Dealer
Garver, Thomas H Consultant, Curator
Handler, Audrey Glass Blower, Educator
Hutchison, Jane Campbell Educator, Historian
Kreilick, Marjorie E Mosaic Artist, Educator
Lotterman, Hal Painter, Educator
Meeker, Dean Jackson Printmaker, Painter
Michie, Mary Sculptor
Nicholson, Natasha Assemblage Artist, Sculptor
Overland, Carlton Edward Curator, Historian
Panczenko, Russell Museum Director
Sheehan, Diane Craftsman
Stevens, Andrew Rich Curator, Historian
Tesfagiorgis, Freida Printmaker, Educator
Watrous, James Scales Painter, Historian
Weege, William Printmaker, Educator
Weiss, Lee (Elyse C Weiss) Painter

Manitowoc

Nichols, William Allyn Painter, Educator

Marinette

La Malfa, James Thomas Sculptor, Educator

Marshfield

Waisbrot, Ann M Administrator, Curator

Menasha

Livingstone, Biganess Painter

Menomonie

Fumagalli, Barbara Merrill Printmaker, Painter

Milwaukee

Auer, James Matthew Art Critic, Film Maker
Balsley, John Gerald Painter, Sculptor
Barnett, David J Art Dealer, Collector
Basquin, Kit (Mary Smyth) Curator, Educator
Berman, Fred J Painter, Photographer
Bradley, Dorothy Art Dealer, Painter
Brite, Jane Fassett Curator, Director
Burkert, Robert Randall Painter, Printmaker
Byrd, D Gibson Educator, Painter
Carter, Curtis L Curator
Evans, Dick Sculptor, Painter
Flanagan, E Michael Museum Director, Educator
Foster, Steven Douglas Photographer
Hirsh, Annette Marie Silversmith, Goldsmith
Huebner, Sister Rosemarita Educator, Silversmith
Jensen, Dean N Dealer, Critic
Kaiser, Charles James Painter, Graphic Artist
Kohl, Barbara Printmaker, Painter
Lacktman, Michael Craftsman, Jeweler
Lichtner, Schomer Frank Painter, Printmaker
Lord, Michael Harry Dealer, Curator
Meixner, Mary Louise Painter, Educator
Michaels-Paque, J Painter, Sculptor
Ozonoff, Ida Painter, Collage Artist
Poehlmann, JoAnna Illustrator, Printmaker
Posner, Judith L Dealer, Publisher
Revor, Remy Designer, Educator
Rosenblatt, Adolph Painter, Sculptor
Rosenblatt, Suzanne Maris Painter, Writer
Stoeveken, Anthony Charles Printmaker, Educator
Summ, Helmut Painter, Educator
Travanti, Leon Emidio Painter, Graphic Designer
Winter, Hope Melamed Collectors, Patrons

Mt Horeb

Becker, David Printmaker, Educator
Hamady, Walter Samuel Collage Artist
Zalucha, Peggy Flora Painter

Oconomowoc

Sprague, Paul Edward Historian, Consultant

Osceola

Shoop, Wally (William Walter) Sculptor

Oshkosh

Landwehr, William Charles Museum Director
Pontynen, Arthur Educator, Historian

Port Washington

Gruen, Shirley Schanen Painter, Mosaic Artist

Racine

Holmes, David Valentine Sculptor, Painter
Johansen, Robert Painter
Mathis, Emile Henry, II Dealer, Collector
Pepich, Bruce Walter Museum Director, Curator
Rozman, Joseph John Painter, Educator

Richland Center

Penkoff, Ronald Peter Educator, Painter

River Falls

Johnston, Randy J(ames) Ceramist

Saukville

Uttech, Thomas Martin Painter, Educator

Sheboygan

Kohler, Ruth DeYoung Museum Director, Curator

Shorewood

Thrall, Arthur Printmaker

Soldiers Grove

Sloan, Richard Painter, Illustrator

Stevens Point

Dorethy, Rex E Administrator, Educator

Wausau

Fleming, Thomas Michael Sculptor, Painter
Foley, Kathy Kelsey Director, Historian

Whitefish Bay

Tucholke, Christel-Anthony (Christel E Stoeveken) Painter

Whitewater

Yasko, Caryl A(nne) Muralist, Sculptor

WYOMING

Byron

Hopkinson, Harold I Painter, Collector

Casper

Goedicke, Jean Painter, Consultant
Naegle, Montana Painter

Centennial

Evans, Richard Painter, Educator
Russin, Robert I Sculptor, Educator

Cheyenne

Hayes, Laura M Dealer, Historian
Johnson, Dean P Sculptor

Cody

Fillerup, Mel Painter
Hassrick, Peter H Museum Director, Historian
Jackson, Harry Andrew Painter, Sculptor

Ft Washakie

Greeves, R V (Richard Vernon) Sculptor

Jackson

Kerswill, J W Roy Painter
Moeller, Robert Charles, III Consultant

Jackson Hole

Kuhn, Bob Draftsman, Painter

Laramie

Deaderick, Joseph Painter, Educator
Flach, Victor H Designer, Writer
Mueller, Henrietta Waters Painter, Printmaker
Reif, (F) David Sculptor, Educator
Valdez, Vincent E Sculptor

Rock Springs

Keeney, Allen Lloyd Educator, Museum Director

Sheridan

Martinsen, Ivar Richard Painter, Educator

Story

Smyth, Ed Illustrator, Painter

PUERTO RICO

Carolina

De Castro, Lorraine Sculptor, Ceramist

Catano

Dirube, Rolando Lopez Painter, Sculptor

Guaynabo

Hernandez-Cruz, Luis Painter, Sculptor

Hato Rey

Balossi, John Sculptor, Painter
Blanco, Sylvia Ceramist

Mayaguez

Alvarez-Cervela, Jose Maria Educator, Historian

Old San Juan

Alicea, Jose Printmaker
Homar, Lorenzo Printmaker, Painter
Moya Soto, Roberto Painter, Printmaker

Ponce

Balmaceda, Margarita S Educator, Video Artist
Conesa, Miguel A Painter, Illustrator
Taylor, Rene Claude Museum Director, Historian

San German

Carrero, Jaime Painter, Educator

Santurce

Venegas, Haydee E Museologist, Consultant

VIRGIN ISLANDS

Christiansted, St Croix

Henle, Fritz Photographer, Filmmaker

CANADA

ALBERTA

Calgary

Atkins, Gordon Lee Designer, Architect
Bershad, David L Historian, Educator
Besant, Derek Michael Painter, Instructor
Cameron, Duncan F Museum Director
Cameron, Eric Administrator, Painter
Chalke, John Ceramist, Sculptor
Dyson, Brian Curator, Writer
Esler, John Kenneth Printmaker, Painter
Hall, John (Scott) Painter, Educator
Hushlak, Gerald Computer Artist, Painter
Kostyniuk, Ronald P Sculptor, Educator
Ohe, Katie (Minna) Sculptor, Instructor
O'Neil, Bruce William Painter, Instructor
Polzer, Joseph Historian
Roukes, Nicholas M Sculptor, Writer
Sawai, Noboru Printmaker, Educator
Snow, John Printmaker, Painter
Will, John A Painter, Video Artist
Zimon, Kathy Elizabeth Librarian

Edmonton

Cantine, David Painter
Davey, Ronald A Historian, Educator
Dmytruk, Ihor R Painter, Educator
Forbes, John Allison Historian, Painter
Haynes, Douglas H Painter, Educator
Hide, Peter Nicholas Sculptor, Educator
Knowlton, Jonathan Painter, Educator
Semchishen, Orest M Photographer
Sinclair, Robert (W) Painter, Sculptor

BRITISH COLUMBIA

Brentwood Bay

Heine, Harry Painter

Burnaby

Shadbolt, Jack Leonard Painter

Chemaines

Newton, John Neil Photographer, Printmaker

Crescent Beach

Onley, Toni Painter, Printmaker

Duncan

Hughes, Edward John Painter
Smith, John Ivor Sculptor, Educator

Ganges

Raginsky, Nina Painter, Photographer

Gibson

Smedley, Geoffrey Educator, Sculptor

Gibsons

Lewis, Glenn A Sculptor, Conceptual Artist

Hope

Weaver, John Barney Sculptor

Kamloops

Bailey, Jann L M Educator, Curator

Langley

Norris, Leonard Matheson Cartoonist, Illustrator

New Westminster

Poole, Leslie Donald Painter, Printmaker

North Vancouver

Curran, Douglas Edward Photographer, Writer
Mayrs, David Blair Painter, Educator
Mignosa, Santo Ceramist, Sculptor
Perry, Frank Sculptor
Peter, Friedrich Gunther Designer, Graphic Artist
Shives, Arnold Edward Painter, Printmaker
Wissmeyer, Gunter Gustav Painter, Photographer

Sydney

Jorgensen, Flemming Painter

Vancouver

Balkind, Alvin Louis Curator
Banana, Anna Publisher, Conceptual Artist
Barry, Anne Meredith Printmaker, Instructor
Bull, Hank (Henry Osler) Conceptual Artist, Video Artist
Carter, Sam John Painter, Sculptor
Davidson, Ian J Collector, Patron
Doray, Audrey Capel Painter
Dr Brute (Eric William Metcalfe) Video Artist
Eastcott, Robert Wayne Printmaker, Painter
Grauer, Sherry Painter, Sculptor
Holmes, Willard Gallery Director
Jarvis, Donald Painter, Instructor
Knox, George Historian, Writer
Plear, Scott Painter
Prince, Richard Edmund Sculptor, Educator
Sawyer, Alan R Consultant
Smolarek, Waldemar Painter, Printmaker
Van Halm, Renée Painter, Educator
Varney, Edwin Conceptual Artist, Printmaker
Wallace, Kenneth William Painter, Educator
Wood, Alan Painter
Young, Robert John Painter

Victoria

Baden, Mowry T Sculptor
Dodd, Eric M Gallery Director, Educator
Glyde, Henry George Painter, Educator
Gore, Tom Photographer, Educator
Gunasinghe, Siri Educator, Historian
Harvey, Donald Painter, Printmaker
Lansdowne, James Fenwick Painter
Longstaffe, John Ronald Collector
Mayhew, Elza Sculptor
Redgrave, Felicity Painter, Video Artist
Segger, Martin Joseph Historian, Museum Director
Siebner, Herbert Muralist, Painter
Stanbridge, Harry Andrew Painter, Printmaker
Stephanson, Loraine Ann Painter
Travers-Smith, Brian John Painter, Instructor

West Vancouver

Bell, Alistair Macready Printmaker, Painter
Felter, James Warren Painter, Printmaker
Smith, Gordon Painter

MANITOBA

Hillside Beach

Smith, Ernest John Architect, Designer

Winnipeg

Dukes, Caroline Painter, Printmaker
Eckhardt, Ferdinand Historian, Museum Director
Eyre, Ivan Painter
Head, George Bruce Painter, Designer
Leathers, Winston Lyle Painter, Printmaker
Pura, William Paul Printmaker, Painter
Reichert, Donald Karl Painter, Educator
Tascona, Antonio Tony Painter, Printmaker
Tillenius, Clarence (Ingwall) Painter, Writer
Topper, David R Educator, Historian
Warkov, Esther Painter

NEW BRUNSWICK

Fredericton

Lumsden, Ian Gordon Director

Grande-Digue

Gauvin, Claude E Painter

Moncton

Roussel, Claude Patrice Sculptor, Educator

Sackville

Hammock, Virgil Gene Critic, Painter
Murchie, Donald John Librarian, Writer

NEWFOUNDLAND

Corner Brook

Coyne, John Michael Painter, Educator

Holyrood

Squires, Gerald Leopold Painter, Graphic Artist

St John's

Perlin, Rae Painter
Shepherd, Helen Parsons Painter
Shepherd, Reginald Painter, Printmaker

Southern Shore

Lapointe, Frank Painter, Printmaker

NORTHWEST TERRITORIES

Cape Dorset

Kenojuak (Ashevak) Printmaker, Sculptor

NOVA SCOTIA

Bear River

Couper, Charles Alexander Painter, Instructor

Chester

Curley, Donald Houston Painter, Lecturer

Chester Basin

Zarand, Julius John Painter, Restorer

Clam Harbour

Wilson-Hammond, Charlotte Emily Visual Artist, Printmaker

Dartmouth

Forrestall, Thomas De Vany Sculptor, Painter

Halifax

Askevold, David Conceptual Artist, Instructor
Barber, Bruce Alistair Sculptor, Critic
Edell, Nancy Painter, Printmaker
Ferguson, Gerald Painter
Gauthier, Suzanne Anita Painter
Greer, John Sydney Sculptor
Jackson, Sarah Sculptor, Graphic Artist
Law, C Anthony Painter
Lindgren, Charlotte Sculptor

Liverpool

Savage, Roger Painter, Printmaker

Lunenburg County

Pentz, Donald Robert Painter, Printmaker

Wolfville

Colville, Alexander Painter, Printmaker

ONTARIO

Baltimore

Bolt, Ron Environmental Artist, Painter

Barrie

Stuart, Donald Alexander Designer, Craftsman

Blyth

Manning, Jo Printmaker, Painter

Burlington

Mansaram Photographer
Rooke, Fay Lorraine Enamelist, Instructor
Wald, Carol Painter, Illustrator

Cambridge

Heine-Baux, Manfred Painter, Printmaker

Don Mills

Bayefsky, Aba Painter, Printmaker
Schleeh, Hans Martin Sculptor
Withrow, William J Administrator

Downsview

Bieler, Ted Andre Educator, Sculptor
Zemans, Joyce L Educator, Art Historian

Durham

White, Norman Triplett Sculptor, Kinetic Artist

Gananoque

Russell, John Laurel Dealer, Collector

Grafton

Lumbers, James Richard Painter

Greensville

Lorcini, Gino Sculptor, Muralist

Grimsby

Lukas, Dennis Brian Painter, Educator
Reitzenstein, Reinhard Sculptor

Guelph

Bachinski, Walter Joseph Painter, Draftsman
Betteridge, Lois Etherington Silver & Goldsmith, Lecturer
Chu, Gene Printmaker, Painter
Danby, Ken Painter, Printmaker
Shuebrook, Ron (Ronald Lee) Painter, Educator

Hamilton

Carter, Harriet (Estelle) Manore Painter
Courtney, Keith Townsend Administrator

Ingersoll

Crawford, Catherine Betty Painter

King City

Tahedl, Ernestine Stained Glass Artist, Painter

Kingston

Allen, Ralph Painter, Educator
Andrew, David Neville Painter, Educator
Dorn, Peter Klaus Designer, Graphic Artist
Finley, Gerald Eric Historian
Heywood, J C Printmaker
Smith, Frances Kathleen Curator, Historian
Stewart, J(ohn) Douglas Historian
Swain, Robert Francis Gallery Director

Kitchener

Goetz, Peter Henry Painter, Lecturer

Kleinburg

Vivot, Lea (Lea Drahomira Vivot-Fishman) Sculptor

La Salle

DeAngelis, Joseph Rocco Sculptor

London

Ariss, Herbert Joshua Painter, Illustrator
Ariss, Margot (Joan Phillips) Painter
Atkinson, Eric Newton Painter, Educator
Barrio-Garay, Jose Luis Art Administrator, Art Historian
Dale, William Scott Abell Historian, Educator
De Kergommeaux, Duncan Painter, Educator
Ewen, Paterson Painter, Educator
Favro, Murray Sculptor
Fenwick, Roly (William Roland) Painter, Educator
Leighton, David S R Administrator
Livíck, Stephen Photographer
Pas, Gerard Peter Painter, Sculptor
Poole, Nancy Geddes Gallery Director

Manotick

Stokes, Louis (Walter) Sculptor, Educator

Markham

Jean-Louis, Don (Donald Charles) Sculptor, Conceptual Artist
Maki, Sheila Anne Printmaker, Painter
Markle, Sam Dealer, Sculptor

Mississauga

Broomfield, Adolphus George Painter, Designer
Rackus, George (Keistus) Painter, Printmaker
Roberts, Tom (Thomas Keith) Painter

Mt Albert

Dimson, Theo Aeneas Designer, Illustrator

Mt Bridges

Thibert, Patrick A Sculptor

Newmarket

Hagan, Frederick Printmaker, Painter
Hall, John A Painter, Educator

Niagara on the Lake

Scott, Campbell Printmaker, Sculptor

Oakville

Bakken, Haakon Administrator, Craftsman
Matsubara, Naoko Printmaker, Illustrator

Odessa

Holmes, David Bryan Painter, Printmaker

Oshawa

Hilts, Alvin Sculptor

Ottawa

Boggs, Jean Sutherland Museum Director, Art Historian
Borcoman, James Curator
Bourdeau, Robert Charles Photographer
Boyd, James Henderson Printmaker, Sculptor
Cohen, Lynne G Photographer, Instructor
Dickson, Jennifer Joan Photographer, Printmaker
Dow, Helen Jeannette Historian, Educator
Durr, Pat (Patricia Beth) Painter, Printmaker
Gagnon, Charles Painter, Photographer
Groves, Naomi Jackson Writer, Painter
Jackson, Marion Elizabeth Historian, Educator
Jackson, Ruth Amelia Curator

CANADA (cont)

Karsh, Yousuf Photographer
Kertzer, Anita Elizabeth Painter, Sculptor
MacDonald, Colin Somerled Writer, Publisher
Nolte, Gunter Sculptor, Draftsman
Reid, Leslie Painter, Printmaker
Sharpe, (Norman) Blair Painter
Sylvestre, Guy Critic, Writer
Taylor, Mary Cazort Curator, Historian

Owen Sound

Hogbin, Stephen Sculptor

Peterborough

Nind, Jean Painter, Printmaker

Pickering

Semak, Michael Photographer, Educator

Port Hope

Blackwood, David (Lloyd) Painter, Printmaker

Roblin

Bell, Philip Michael Administrator, Historian

Roseneath

Ebsen, Alf K Calligrapher, Graphic Artist

St Catharines

Harris, Alfred Peter Painter, Administrator

Scarborough

Lampitoc, Rol Ponce Painter, Printmaker
McCarthy, Doris Jean Painter, Instructor

Stratford

Green, Art Painter, Educator

Tamworth

Saxe, Henry, OC Sculptor

Thornhill

Henrickson, Martha (Klein) Conceptual Artist, Photographer
Henrickson, Thomas Conceptual Artist, Photographer
Markle, Jack M Dealer, Sculptor

Thunderbay

Clarke, Ann Educator, Painter

Toronto

Andrews, Kim Painter
Armstrong, Geoffrey Painter, Architect
Astman, Barbara Ann Photographer, Painter
Averbuch, Ilan Sculptor
Banz, George Writer, Architect
Bell, R Murray Collector
Beveridge, Karl J Photographer
Boigon, Brian Joseph Conceptual Artist, Writer
Boszin, Andrew Painter, Sculptor
Brener, Roland Sculptor, Educator
Bronson, A A (Michael Wayne Tims) Post-Conceptual Artist, Writer
Burnett, David Grant Historian, Curator
Carr-Harris, Ian Redford Sculptor, Critic
Cetín, Anton Painter, Printmaker
Cliff, Denis Antony Painter, Instuctor
Costin, Frank Dealer
Cowan, Aileen Hooper Sculptor, Painter
Daly, Kathleen (Kathleen Daly Pepper) Painter
Davies, Haydn Llewellyn Sculptor, Painter
De Heusch, Lucio Painter
De Pedery-Hunt, Dora Sculptor, Designer
Dillow, Nancy E (Nancy Elizabeth Robertson) Administrator, Historian
Drapell, Joseph Painter, Sculptor
Dresdnere, Simon Art Dealer, Publisher
Drutz, June Painter, Educator
DuBois, Macy Architect, Designer
Duff, Ann MacIntosh Painter, Printmaker
Elder, R Bruce Filmmaker, Critic
Eloul, Kosso Sculptor
Engel, Walter F Critic, Dealer
Etrog, Sorel Sculptor, Painter
Feist, Harold E Painter, Sculptor
Filipovic, Augustin Sculptor, Painter
Fleisher, Pat Publisher, Designer
Frick, Joan Painter, Conceptual Artist
Friedland, Seymour Patron, Collector
Gage, Frances M Sculptor
Gale, Peggy Writer, Curator
Garwood, Audrey Painter, Printmaker
Gilling, Lucille Printmaker
Gould, John Howard Painter, Filmmaker
Graham, K M Painter, Printmaker
Harding, Noel Robert Video Artist, Environmental Artist
Hastenteufel, Dieter Sculptor, Painter
Heath, Dave (David Martin Heath) Educator, Photographer
Horne, (Arthur Edward) Cleeve Painter, Sculptor
Howard, (Helen) Barbara Painter, Printmaker
Hunkler, Dennis Painter, Draftsman
Isaacs, Avrom Art Dealer, Publisher
Jursevskis, Zigfrids Sculptor
Kaye, David Haigh Textile Artist, Designer
Kinoshita, Gene Architect
Kramer, Burton Designer, Educator
Kravis, Janis Designer, Architect
La Pierre, Thomas Painter, Printmaker
LeRoy, Hugh Alexander Sculptor
Leshyk, Tonie Sculptor, Draftsman
Letendre, Rita Painter
Lochnan, Katharine A Curator, Writer
Luneau, Claude Sculptor
Luz, Virginia Painter
MacKenzie, Hugh Seaforth Painter
McNealy, Robert Painter, Sculptor
Maggs, Arnaud (Cyril Benvenuti) Photographer, Graphic Artist
Martin, Jane Painter, Draftsman
Meredith, John Painter
Miezajs, Dainis Painter, Instructor
Milrad, Aaron M Collector
Mongrain, Claude Sculptor
Moos, Walter A Dealer
Murdock, Greg Sculptor
Murray, Ian Stewart Sculptor, Conceptual Artist
Nakamura, Kazuo Painter
Nasgaard, Roald Curator, Historian
Neddeau, Donald Frederick Price Painter, Designer
Newman, John Beatty Painter, Draftsman
Noestheden, John Sculptor
Oesterle, Leonhard Friedrich Sculptor, Instructor
Partridge, David Gerry Painter, Sculptor
Partz, Felix (Ron Gabe) Painter
Patton, Andy (Andrew John) Painter
Perkins, A Alan Ceramist, Enamelist
Plotek, Leopold Painter
Poulin, Roland Sculptor
Rayner, Gordon Painter
Reeves, John Alexander Photographer
Reis, Mario Painter
Robb, Charles Painter
Ronald, William Painter
Schaefer, Carl Fellman Painter
Schwarz, Judith Sculptor, Draftsman
Scott, John Painter
Sebelius, Helen Painter
Sewell, Richard George Printmaker, Painter
Shaw, Joseph Winterbotham Historian, Educator
Sing Hoo Sculptor, Painter
Snell, Eric Sculptor
Snow, Michael Painter, Filmmaker
Sutton, Carol (Lorraine) Painter
Takashima, Shizuye Violet Illustrator, Painter
Tangredi, Vincent Sculptor
Timmas, Osvald Painter, Lecturer
Tolmie, Kenneth Donald Painter
Tomcik, Andrew Michael Designer, Educator
Tulving, Ruth Painter, Printmaker
Van Ginkel, Blanche Lemco Architect, Educator
White, Deborah Dealer
Whiten, Colette Sculptor, Instructor
Whiten, Tim Sculptor, Environmental Artist
Wieland, Joyce Painter, Filmmaker
Wilson, York Painter, Muralist
Wright, David Thomas Painter
Yaneff, Chris Gallery Director
Zack, Badanna Bernice Sculptor, Writer
Zeidler, Eberhard Heinrich Designer, Architect
Zontal, Jorge (Jorge Saia) Post-Conceptual Artist

Van Kleek Hill

Alpen-Whiteside, Dale Painter, Printmaker

Waterloo

Izumi, Kiyoshi Architect, Educator
Sabelis, Huibert Printmaker, Painter

Welland

Tulumello, Peter M Consultant, Designer

Wellesley

Urquhart, Tony (Anthony Morse) Sculptor, Painter

West Lorne

Redinger, Walter Fred Sculptor, Muralist

Wiarton

Watson, Mary Anne Printmaker, Painter

Willowdale

Altwerger, Libby Painter, Graphic Artist
Cattell, Ray Painter, Director
Collyer, Robin Sculptor, Video Artist
Hallman, H Theodore, Jr Craftsman, Designer
Jaworska, Tamara Fiber Artist, Tapestry Artist
Townsend, Jean (Mrs Saul Field) Painter, Printmaker
Wiitasalo, Shirley Painter

Windsor

Pufahl, John K Educator, Printmaker
Saltmarche, Kenneth Charles Painter, Director

PRINCE EDWARD ISLAND

Charlottetown

Purdy, Henry Carl Painter, Educator

Summerside East

Barton, Georgie Read Painter, Sculptor

QUEBEC

Ayers Cliff

Beament, Tib (Thomas Harold) Painter

Chicoutimi

Seguin, Jean-Pierre Painter, Photographer

Hudson

Cosgrove, Stanley Painter

Hudson Heights

Braitstein, Marcel Sculptor, Educator

Hull

Ostiguy, Jean-Rene Painter, Art Historian

Kirkland

Daudelin, Charles Sculptor

Laval

Bruni, Umberto Painter, Graphic Artist

Laval sur le Lac

L'Archeveque, Andre Robert Painter, Illustrator

Lennoxville

Ernstrom, Adele Mansfield Historian

Matane County

Picher, Claude Painter, Curator

Montreal

Barbeau, Marcel (Christian), arc Painter, Sculptor
Besner, J Jacques Muralist, Kinetic Artist
Bigelow, Robert Clayton Educator, Painter
Bobak, Bruno Joseph Painter, Printmaker
Briansky, Rita Prezament Painter, Instructor
Caiserman-Roth, Ghitta Painter, Printmaker
Cardinal, Marcelin Painter
Charney, Melvin Sculptor, Architect
Cohen, Sorel Conceptual Artist, Photographer
Daigneault, Gilles Curator, Critic
De Moura Sobral, Luis Historian, Critic
Dyens, Georges Maurice Sculptor
Falsetto, Mario Educator
Feist, Warner David Designer, Painter
Fox, John Painter
Franklin, Hannah Sculptor, Painter
Gaucher, Yves Printmaker, Painter
Gaudard, Pierre Photographer, Graphic Artist
Gauthier, Ninon Critic, Historian
Gerin-Lajoie, Guy Architect
Gersovitz, Sarah Valerie Painter, Printmaker
Gordon, Russell Talbert Painter
Harder, Rolf Peter Graphic Designer, Painter
Hartal, Paul Painter, Writer
Jaque, Louis Painter
Knudsen, Christian Painter, Printmaker
Layne, Barbara J Sculptor, Instructor
Lerner, Loren Ruth Librarian
Lewis, Stanley Sculptor, Printmaker
McCall, Ann Painter, Printmaker
McEwen, Jean Painter
Merola, Mario Sculptor, Painter
Molinari, Guido Painter, Sculptor
Paikowsky, Sandra R Curator, Historian
Palumbo, Jacques Painter, Sculptor
Perrault, Pierre Photographer
Roch, Ernst Designer
Rombout, Luke Museum Director
Scott, Marian (Dale) Painter
Shaw, John Palmer Painter, Printmaker
Steinhouse, Tobie (Thelma) Painter, Printmaker
Sullivan, Francoise Painter
Swartzman, Roslyn Printmaker, Sculptor
Tata, Sam Bejan Photographer
Tatossian, Armand Painter
Tinning, George Campbell Painter
Tousignant, Claude Painter, Sculptor
Trudeau, Yves Sculptor
Vaillancourt, Armand Sculptor, Painter
Valentin, Jean-Pierre Dealer
Wainwright, Robert Barry Painter, Printmaker
Whittome, Irene F Sculptor, Painter
Zelenak, Edward John Sculptor

Pointe Aux Trembles

Goulet, Claude Educator, Painter

Pontiac

Hlavina, Rasto R(astislav) Sculptor

Quebec

Crouton, Francois (LaFortune) Photographer
Iacurto, Francesco Painter, Instructor
Jones, Henry Wanton Painter, Sculptor
Lemieux, Irenee Painter
Martel, Richard Conceptual Artist, Editor
Schlitter, Helga Painter, Sculptor

Roberval

Dumais-Berube, Yvette Painter

Rosemere

Weinmann, Monique Brunet- Critic, Curator

Ste Adele

Bruneau, Kittie Painter, Printmaker
Rousseau-Vermette, Mariette Tapestry Artist, Educator

St Lambert

Archambault, Louis Sculptor

St Louis-Terrebonne

Hurtubise, Jacques Painter

Sillery

Dumas, Antoine Painter, Educator

Stanstead

Miller, F John Painter, Mosaic Artist

Val-David

Baxter, Bonnie Jean Printmaker, Painter

SASKATCHEWAN

Regina

Cicansky, Victor Sculptor
Lee, Roger Educator, Curator
McKay, Arthur Fortescue Painter, Educator
Sures, Jack Ceramist, Educator

Saskatoon

Bornstein, Eli Painter, Sculptor
Christie, Robert Duncan Painter
Hamilton, W Paul C Educator, Historian
Perehudoff, William W Painter
Ringness, Charles Obert Educator, Printmaker

OTHER COUNTRIES

AUSTRALIA

Kelly, William Joseph Draftsman, Painter
Latos-Valier, Paula Museum Director, Administrator
Valier, Biron (Frank) Painter, Printmaker

AUSTRIA

Larsen, Carl Erik Consultant, Educator
Oscarsson, Victoria Constance Gunhild Art Dealer

BELGIUM

Fox, Terry Alan Conceptual Artist, Sculptor
Rabinowitch, Royden Leslie Sculptor

DENMARK

Wright, (Charles) Clifford Painter, Collage Artist

FRANCE

Aminoff, Judith Writer, Editor
Andersen, Wayne Vesti Art Historian, Educator
Biala, Janice Painter
Bordeaux, Jean Luc Art Historian, Curator
Brustlein, Daniel Painter
Chase-Riboud, Barbara Sculptor, Writer
Crotto, Paul Painter, Sculptor
Csernus, Tibor Painter
Diska, (P) Sculptor
Edouard, Pierre (Pierre Edward Maussion) Painter
Farhi, Jean Claude Sculptor
Hicks, Sheila Tapestry Artist, Publisher
Ipousteguy, (Jean Robert) Sculptor, Graphic Artist
Jacobs, Harold Painter, Sculptor
Kuper, Yuri (Yuri Kuperman) Painter
Kurhajec, Joseph A Sculptor
Lefebvre d'Argence, René-Yvon Museum Director, Writer
Levee, John H Painter, Sculptor
Masurovsky, Gregory Draftsman, Printmaker
Matosse, Jackie (Jacqueline Malisse Monnier) Conceptual Artist
Noel, Jean Sculptor
Petlin, Irving Painter
Rose, Matthew Adam Writer, Painter
Rowell, Margit Curator, Historian
Sturtevant, E Painter, Sculptor

GERMANY

Annus, John Augustus Painter, Photographer
Brecht, George Conceptual Artist, Assemblage Artist
Iannone, Dorothy Painter, Writer

HUNGARY

Vecsey, Esther Barbara Educator, Museum Director

IRELAND

Brady, Charles Painter, Sculptor
White, Stuart James Sculptor, Assemblage Artist

OTHER COUNTRIES (cont)

Shaman, Sanford Sivitz Museum Director, Curator

ITALY

Cecilia Educator, Painter
Congdon, William (Grosvenor) Painter, Writer
Cook, Robert Howard Sculptor, Medalist
D'Almeida, George Painter
Hebald, Milton Elting Sculptor, Printmaker
Hsiao, Chin Painter, Sculptor
Huemer, Christina Gertrude Librarian
Irwin, Lani Helena Painter
Ishikawa, Joseph Consultant, Writer
Marinsky, Harry Sculptor, Painter
Pepper, Beverly Sculptor, Painter
St Florian, Friedrich Gartler Educator, Architect

JAPAN

Ida, Shoichi Painter, Printmaker

MEXICO

Anguiano, Raul Muralist, Painter
Angulo, Chappie Painter, Illustrator
Aquino, Edmundo Painter, Printmaker
Beltrán, Félix Painter, Printmaker
Bragar, Philip Frank Painter, Printmaker
Catlett, Elizabeth Sculptor, Graphic Artist
Cauduro, Rafael Painter, Muralist
Clement, Kathleen (Ruth) Painter, Graphic Artist
Colina, Armando G Gallery Director, Editor
Escobedo, Helen Environmental Artist
Fett, William F Instructor, Painter
Kempe, Richard Joseph Collector, Curator
Landau, Myra Painter, Muralist
Maxwell, Robert Edwin Painter
Palau, Marta Sculptor
Parra, Carmen Painter, Printmaker
Rojo, Vicente Painter
Stavans, Isaac Painter
Zapfe, Guillermo (Wilhelm Karl Zapfe) Painter, Draftsman

NETHERLANDS

Baer, Jo Painter, Writer
Tajiri, Shinkichi Sculptor, Educator

SPAIN

Narotzky, Norman David Painter, Printmaker
Rocamora, Jaume Painter

SWITZERLAND

Gottschalk, Fritz Designer, Lecturer
Takal, Peter Painter, Printmaker

UNITED KINGDOM

Aliki, Illustrator, Writer
Atkinson, Conrad Sculptor, Painter
Auerbach, Frank Painter
Carswell, John Museum Director, Painter
Cowles, Fleur Painter, Writer
Dickinson, Norman Painter
Fisher, Sandra Painter
Hackenbroch, Yvonne Alix Curator, Writer
Hubbard, John Painter
Kitaj, R B Painter, Printmaker
Kitzinger, Ernst Historian
Lijn, Liliane Sculptor, Writer
Ramos, Theodore Painter, Illustrator
Smith, Hassel W, Jr Painter
Warner, Marina Sarah Critic, Historian

Professional Classifications Index

ADMINISTRATOR

Adams, John Michael
Adams, Robert McCormick
Allara, Pamela Edwards
Arning, Bill A
Arnold, Richard R
Ayres, Linda L
Bakken, Haakon
Balderacchi, Arthur Eugene
Ball, Susan L
Bandy, Mary Lea
Barber, Ronald
Barrett, William O
Barrio-Garay, Jose Luis
Bayliss, George
Beale, Arthur C
Beam, Philip Conway
Beattie, George
Beebe, Mary Livingstone
Belian, Isabelle
Bell, James M
Bell, Michael Steven
Bell, Philip Michael
Ben-Haim, Tsipi
Benjamin, Lloyd William, III
Berkowitz, Roger M
Berns, Pamela Kari
Betensky, Rose Hart
Biddle, James
Biddle, Livingston Ludlow, Jr
Bingham, Lois A
Blayton, Betty (Betty Blayton-Taylor)
Bledsoe, Jane Kathryn
Blevins, James Richard
Bloch, Milton Joseph
Botwinick, Michael
Boudreau, Anne Marie
Bowman, Jeff Ray
Bowron, Edgar Peters
Bradbury, Ellen A
Bramlett, Betty Jane
Brite, Jane Fassett
Broadley, Hugh T
Broderick, James Allen
Brody, Myron Roy
Brooks, John H
Broun, Elizabeth Gibson
Brown, Cee Scott
Bruno, Vincent J
Buchanan, John Edward, Jr
Buki, Zoltan
Burchett, Debra
Burchett, Kenneth Eugene
Burford, William E
Burke, James Donald
Butler, Marigene H
Cameron, Elsa S
Cameron, Eric
Caslin, Jean
Chalmers, E Laurence, Jr
Channing, Susan Rose
Chatterjee, Jay (Jayanta)
Chepp, Mark
Chew, Paul Albert
Chichura, Diane B
Cilella, Salvatore G, Jr
Cleveland, Robert Earl
Codell, Julie Francia
Concannon, Ann Worth
Cone, Gerrit Craig
Contini, Anita
Cook, Christopher Capen
Coraor, John E
Cortese, Edward Fortunato
Courtney, Keith Townsend
Crawford, Bill (Wilbur Ogden)
Crouton, Francois (LaFortune)
Culkin, John Michael
Cummings, Mary T
Cummins, Karen Gasco
Danielson, Phyllis I
Dash, Harvey Dwight
Daviee, Jerry Michael
Davis, D Jack
De Montebello, Philippe Lannes
DePillars, Murry N
Dietrich, Bruce Leinbach
Dillow, Nancy E (Nancy Elizabeth Robertson)
Dixon, Jenny (Jane Hodley)
Donaldson, Jeff R
Donato, Debora E
Dorethy, Rex E
Dorsey, Lucia Iannone
Dorsey, Michael A
Doty, Robert McIntyre
Downs, Stuart Clifton
Driscoll, Abigail Julia Hannah
DuBois, Alan Beekman
Duff, James H
Duke, Leilani Lattin
Dunbar, Michael Austin
Dunn, Phillip Charles
Ebie, William Dennis
Edelson, Gilbert S
Edmunds, Allan Logan
Eldredge, Bruce B
Elliot, Sheila
Elliott, James Heyer
Erickson, Marsha A
Farmer, John David
Farver, Suzanne
Faubion, S Michael
Faulds, W Rod
Fensch, Charles Everette
Field, Lyman
Firestone, Evan R
Fleming, Ronald Lee
Fleminger, Susan N
Ford, Harry Xavier
Foster, Mary
Francis, Bill Dean
Frank, David
Frauchiger, Fritz A
French, Stephen Warren
Freudenheim, Tom Lippmann
Freundlich, August L
Funk, Robert Norris
Garcia, Ofelia
Gates, Jay Rodney
Gedeon, Lucinda Heyel
Gibson, George
Gigliotti, Joanne Marie
Gilmartin, F Thomas
Gilmore, Roger
Glanz, Andrea E
Goehlich, John Ronald
Golden, Morton J
Goldsmith, Caroline Lerner
Gonzalez, Jose Gamaliel
Gonzalez, Mauricio Martinez
Goodrich, James W
Goodyear, Frank H, Jr
Gorove, Margaret Joan
Gray, Robert Ward
Greco, Anthony Joseph
Green, Wilder
Greenblatt, Arthur E
Grier, Margot Edmands
Growdon, Marcia Cohn
Gully, Anthony Lacy
Gund, Agnes
Hagerstrand, Martin Alan
Hall, Lee
Hallam, John S
Hampton, Grace
Hankey, Robert E
Harkins, Dennis Richter
Harris, Alfred Peter
Harris, Ann Sutherland
Harris, Ellen Schwartz
Harris, Lily Marjorie
Hart, Allen M
Hart, Robert Gordon
Hartwell, Patricia Lochridge
Hearn, M F (Millard Fillmore), Jr
Heinz, Susan
Hero, Peter deCourcy
Hertzman, Gay Mahaffy
Hightower, John B
Hobbs, Joe Ferrell
Hobgood, E Wade
Hodes, Barney
Hoffman, Neil James
Hoi, Samuel Chuen-Tsung
Holbrook, Vivian Nicholas
Hood, Mary Bryan
Hopkins, Terri
Horowitz, Benjamin
Hugo, Joan (Dowey)
Hummel, Charles Frederick
Hunt, Robert James
Huntley, David C
Irving, Donald J
Isaacs, Claire Naomi
Ivers, Louise H
Jacobson, Frank
Jendrzejewski, Andrew John
Jennings, Jan
Johnson, J Seward, Jr
Johnson, Robert Flynn
Johnston, Robert Harold
Johnston, William Ralph
Jonaitis, Aldona
Jones, Harold Henry
Joost-Gaugier, Christiane L
Jordan, Jack
Jorgenson, Dale Alfred
Kan, Michael
Kaplan, Ilee
Kaplan, Julius David
Karlstrom, Paul Johnson
Katzive, David H
Kearney, Lynn Haigh
Keck, Hardu
Kelm, Bonnie G
Kendall, (Ms) Michael
Kenney, Estelle Koval
Kenyon, Colleen Frances
Kepner, Rita
Kienholz, Lyn
Kilroy, Mary A
King, Lyndel Irene Saunders
Kinney, Gilbert Hart
Klindt, Steven
Kling, Jean Louise
Kluver, Billy (Johan Wilhem)
Knight, Christopher Allen
Knode, Marilu
Kochka, Al
Kord, Victor George
Kuchel, Konrad G
Kurka, Donald Frank
LaDouceur, Philip Alan
Laing, Richard Harlow
Landreau, Anthony Norman
Lang, Wendy F
Lantzy, Donald Michael
Latos-Valier, Paula
Lawson, Edward Pitt
Lazarus, Fred, IV
Leader, Garnet Rosamonde
Lee, Roger
Leighton, David S R
Lein, Malcolm Emil
Leven, Ann R
Lewandowski, Edmund D
Lewis, Elma Ina
Lieberman, Laura Crowell
Linn, John William
List, Clair Zamoiski
Livesay, Thomas Andrew
Livet, Anne Hodge
Livingston, Margaret Gresham
Loar, Peggy A
Long, Rose-Carol Washton
Lottes, John William
Lowe, Harry
Lowenthal, Constance
Lusk, Patricia A
Lyle, Charles Thomas
Lyon, Robert F
McCaughey, Arnold Patrick
McCauley, Gardiner Rae
McClenney, Cheryl Ilene
McCready, Eric Scott
McCullough, Joseph
McDaniel, Craig Milton
McKay, John Sangster
McLaughlin, Jean Wallace
Madonia, Ann C
Mahlmann, John James
Manetta, Edward J
Manhart, Marcia Y

ADMINISTRATOR (cont)

Mark, Marilyn (Sabetsky)
Markman, Sidney David
Mason, Francis Scarlett, Jr
Mavigliano, George Jerome
Mayer, Robert Anthony
Medvedow, Jill
Meissner, Anne Marie
Mellon, Paul
Meyer, Ruth Krueger
Meyers, Jeanne F
Michael, Patricia Gordon
Miles, Christine M
Milhoan, Randall Bell
Miller, Janet
Miller, Joan Vita
Miller, John Franklin
Millett, Caroline Dunlop
Mitchell, N Donald
Mobley, Karen R
Moe, Richard D
Mohr, K(aren) Lee
Mongan, Agnes
Moore, Fay
Moore, Russell James
Morrison, Doris
Mount, Marshall Ward
Moyer, Marina Pavlova
Moyer, Roy
Murray, Floretta May
Murray, Reuben
Musgrove, Stephen Ward
Neil, J M
Nestor, Lula B
Newsom, Barbara Ylvisaker
Newton, Douglas
Newton, Earle Williams
O'Connell, Daniel Moylan
O'Connell, Kenneth Robert
O'Connor, John Arthur
Olenick, David Charles
Olin, Ferris
Olpin, Robert Spencer
O'Neil, John Joseph
Orze, Joseph John
Osborn, Elodie C (Mrs Robert Osborn)
Ostrow, Stephen Edward
Outland, Wendy Helen
Outterbridge, John Wilfred
Owens, Wallace, Jr
Parkhurst, Charles
Parrino, George
Parry, Pamela Jeffcott
Pease, David G
Pels, Albert
Perkins, Robert Eugene
Perrot, Paul N
Perry, Edward (Ted) Samuel
Peters, Larry Dean
Peterson, John Douglas
Pfister, Harold Francis
Piasecki, Jane B
Pierce, Charles Eliot, Jr
Pilgrim, James F
Plaut, James S
Plotkin, Sylvia
Polcari, Stephen
Pollei, Dane F
Polsky, Cynthia Hazen
Poster, June
Potter, Ted
Preis, Alfred
Prescott, Kenneth Wade
Pressly, Nancy Lee
Price, Barbara Gillette
Propersi, August J
Quigley, Michael Allen
Quirarte, Jacinto
Rabb, Madeline M
Radan, George Tivadar
Radecki, Martin John
Rahja, Virginia Helga
Ramos, Julianne
Rasmussen, Anton Jesse
Reese, Thomas Ford
Reeser, Robert D
Reger, Lawrence L
Ritts, Edwin Earl, Jr
Robertson, Charles J
Rodgers, Jack A
Rohlfing, Christian
Rovetti, Paul F
Roysher, Hudson (Brisbine)
Ruffo, Joseph Martin
Rumford, Beatrix Tyson
Rush, Jean C
Rust, Edwin C
Sabatella, Joseph John
Saff, Donald Jay
Salvadori, Vieri R
Sanchez, Beatrice Rivas
Sanguinetti, Eugene F
Schar, Stuart
Schinsky, William Charles
Schlageter, Robert William
Schmitt, Marilyn Low
Schnorrenberg, John Martin
Schutte, Thomas Frederick
Scott, David Winfield
Scott, Robert Montgomery
Selby, Roger Lowell
Serenyi, Peter
Sevigny, Maurice Joseph, II
Shaheen, Gary Edward
Shapiro, Babe
Shaw, Renata Vitzthum
Sheon, Aaron
Silverman, Joy
Simon, Leonard Ronald
Sindelir, Robert John
Smyth, Craig Hugh
Solmssen, Peter
Somerville, Romaine Stec
Sorell, Victor Alexander
Spencer, John R
Spink, Walter M
Spurgin, John Edwin
Stamm, Geoffrey Eaton
Stanford, Linda Oliphant
Starpattern, Rita
Stearns, Robert
Stebbins, Theodore Ellis, Jr
Stein, Claire A
Stevens, Jane M
Streetman, John William, III
Strother, Joseph Willis
Stull, Robert J
Sunkel, Robert C
Tai, Jane S
Tancock, John Leon
Tarbox, Gurdon Lucius, Jr
Taylor, Kendall Frances
Thomas, Elaine Freeman
Tomasini, Wallace J
Torrey, Ella King
Towner, Mark Andrew
Trecker, Stanley Matthew
Trop, Sandra
Tuegel, Michele B
Vanco, John Leroy
Veerkamp, Patrick Burke
Verzar, Christine B
Voos, William John
Wagner, Charles H
Wahlman, Maude Southwell
Waisbrot, Ann M
Walker, William Bond
Wallace, Elizabeth S
Walter, Elizabeth Mitchell
Wark, Robert Rodger
Weber, Jean M
Wegmann, M K (Mary Katherine)
Weiler, Melody M
Weinberg, Ephraim
Wenawine, Bruce Harley
Westin, Robert H
Whipple, Enez Mary
Wickiser, Ralph Lewanda
Willis, William Henry, Jr
Wilson, Kay E
Wise, Suzanne Tanderup
Withrow, William J
Woide, Robert E
Wood, James Nowell
Woolfenden, William Edward
Wunder, Richard Paul
Young, Joseph Louis
Zahn, Carl Frederick

ARCHITECT

Armstrong, Geoffrey
Atkins, Gordon Lee
Bakanowsky, Louis J
Banz, George
Barnes, Edward Larrabee
Blake, Peter Jost
Booth, Laurence Ogden
Brown, John Hall
Charney, Melvin
Damaz, Paul F
Downey, Juan
DuBois, Macy
Ellington, Howard W
Fort-Brescia, Bernardo M
Geerlings, Gerald Kenneth
Gehry, Frank O(wen)
Gerin-Lajoie, Guy
Giro, R (R Gironda)
Graves, Michael
Green, Wilder
Hamilton, Frank Moss
Hirschfield, Jim
Holschuh, (George) Fred
Izumi, Kiyoshi
Judd, Donald Clarence
Kaskey, Raymond John
Kinoshita, Gene
Krasnyansky, Anatole Lvovich
Kravis, Janis
Kultermann, Udo
Lamell, Robert (C)
MacDonald, William L
Meier, Richard Alan
Mitchell, Clifford
Morrison, Boone M
Murphy, Herbert A
Newick, Craig D
Peckham, Nicholas
Pei, I M (Ieoh Ming)
Pelli, Cesar
Perkins, G Holmes
Preis, Alfred
Provisor, Janis
Redstone, Louis Gordon
Romney, Hervin A R
Santos, Adèle Naudé
Scott, Walter
Simonds, Charles Frederick
Smith, Ernest John
Soleri, Paolo
Sommer, Frederick
Spear, Laurinda Hope
Stern, Arthur I
Thiry, Paul (Albert)
Tigerman, Stanley
Van Ginkel, Blanche Lemco
Venturi, Robert
Villa, Mario
Wines, James N
Yegul, Fikret Kutlu
Zeidler, Eberhard Heinrich

ART DEALER

Adamson, Jerome D, Jr
Ahn, Don C
Albano, Patrick Louis
Alexander, Edmund Brooke
Alexander, Judith
Allen, Edda Lynne
Allrich, M Louise Barco
Altermann, Tony
Anderson, Bruce James
Anderson, David
Ankrum, Joan
Arnold, Jack
Bachert, Hildegard Gina
Balay, Felicie
Band, David Moshe
Banning, Jack (John Peck), Jr
Bareiss, Philip C
Barnes, Molly
Barnett, David J
Barrios, Benny Perez
Bartholet, Elizabeth Ives
Baruch, Anne
Baum, Hank
Baum, Jayne H
Baxter, Douglas W
Beadleston, William L
Beilin, Howard
Belcher, George
Belian, Garabed
Bell, Donald Allen
Bell, Mary Catherine
Bellamy, Richard
Benson, Elaine K G
Bergen, Sidney L
Berggruen, John Henry
Berman, Aaron
Bernstein, Saralinda
Bingham, Alice
Blacketer, James Richard
Blair, Carl Raymond
Blinder, Martin S
Bloom, Edith Salvin
Bolen, John E
Bolen, Lynne N
Boler, John Alfred
Bonino, Fernanda
Boone, Mary
Borgenicht, Grace
Bouckaert, Harm J G
Bowater, Marian
Bowen, Constance Lee
Bradley, Dorothy
Braseth, John E
Braunstein, Ruth
Broido, Lucy
Bromm, Hal
Brooks, Harry A
Brown, Alan M, Jr
Brown, Constance George
Brown, Diane
Brown, Robert K
Brundage, Susan Lounsbury
Bryant, Linda Goode
Burford, William E
Burk, A Darlene
Byron, Charles Anthony
Caporaso, Pat Marie
Carlin, Electra Marshall
Caro, Francis
Carson, G B
Castelli, Leo
Cava, Paul
Cawley, Joan Mae
Cernuschi, Alberto C
Challis, Richard Bracebridge
Chambers, Bruce William
Chambers, William McWillie
Chase, Robert M
Chasin, Martin
Chichura, Diane B
Clark, Garth Reginald
Clifford, Jutta
Cliver, Kendra-Jean (Kendra-Jean Cliver Krienke)
Close, Dean Purdy
Cohen, Mildred Thaler
Cohn, Frederick Donald
Cohn, Richard A
Cole, Sylvan
Coleman, Edward H
Cone-Skelton, Annette
Conforte, Renee
Cook, R Scott
Cooper, Paula
Cooper, Theodore A
Cornette, Mary Elizabeth
Costin, Frank
Costley-Jacobs, Averille Esther

ART DEALER (cont)

Couturier, Marion B
Cowles, Charles
Crane, Bonnie L
Cuningham, Elizabeth Bayard (Mrs E W R Templeton)
Curtis, Roger William
Cutler, Bess
Dailey, Victoria Keilus
Davidson, Elizabeth H Donnally
Davidson, Maxwell, III
Davis, Charles Burdis, III
Davis, Kimberly Brooke
De Andino, Jean-Pierre M
Deats, Margaret
De Nagy, Tibor (J)
Dennis, Gertrude Weyhe
Desind, Philip
Deutschman, Louise Tolliver
Devine, William Charles
Dickerson, William J
DiLaurenti, Marco Italo
Dillingham, Rick (James Richard), II
Dintenfass, Terry
Dolan, Margo
Dorfman, Fred
Dorsky, Samuel
Dresdnere, Simon
Driscoll, John Paul
Drutt, Helen Williams
Drysdale, Nancy McIntosh
Duffy, Betty Minor
Edvi Illes, Emma
Ehlers, Carol A
Eickhorst, William Sigurd
Einstein, Gilbert W
Eisenberg, Jerome Martin
Elder, Muldoon
Elkin, Beverly Dawn
Ellington, Howard W
Elliott, Scott Cameron
Ellis-Tracy, Jo
Elowitch, Annette
Elowitch, Robert Jason
Emmerich, Andre
Engel, Walter F
Esman, Rosa
Fairweather, Sally H
Farber, Deborah
Farris, Linda B
Fasoldt, Sarah Lowry
Fear, Daniel E
Feigen, Richard L
Feinman, Stephen E
Feld, Stuart Paul
Feldman, Arthur Mitchell
Feldman, Ronald
Felsen, Rosamund
Fenton, Charles E H
Feuerstein, Roberta
Findlay, David B, Jr
Fink, Alan
Fink, Joanna Elizabeth
Fisher, Philip C
Fishko, Bella
Fleischman, Lawrence Arthur
Flower, Michael Lavin
Flume, Violet Sigoloff
Foley, Timothy Albert
Fondren, Harold M
Foster, Donald Isle
Fowler, Frank Eison
Fox, Pearl
Fraenkel, Jeffrey Andrew
Franklin, Carole R
Freeman, Mallory Bruce
Freudenheim, Nina
Friedman, Marvin Ross
Frumkin, Allan
Fuller, Jeffrey P
Gallander, Cathleen S
Gardiner, Henry Gilbert
Garver, Fanny
Geraci, Lucian Arthur
Gerst, Hilde W
Getler, Helen
Gianlorenzi, Nona Elena
Gillman, Barbara Seitlin
Gladstone, Barbara
Glass, Wendy D
Glezer, Nechemia
Glick, Paula Florence
Glimcher, Arnold B
Goad, Anne Laine
Gobuzas, Aldona M
Goffman, Judy
Goldberg, Judith
Goldeen, Dorothy A
Goldfield, Edward L
Goldschmidt, Lucien
Goldstein, Charles Barry
Goodman, James Neil
Goodman, Marian
Gordon, Albert F
Gordon, Martin
Gorman, R C
Goulds, Peter J
Graham, Robert C, Jr
Graham, Robert Claverhouse, Sr
Graham, William Andrew
Gray, Richard
Greenberg, Ronald K
Guadagnoli, Nello T
Hahn, Maurice & Roslyn
Hahn, Stephen
Hames, Carl Martin
Hamilton, Patricia Rose
Hampson, Ferdinand Charles
Hansen, Sarah Eveleth (Campbell)
Harcus, Portia Gwen
Hardin, Shirley G (Mrs Louis S)
Harmon, Foster
Harris, Lily Marjorie
Haslem, Jane N
Hayes, Laura M
Heath, David C
Hedberg, Gregory Scott
Helander, Bruce Paul
Heller, Ben
Herman, Katherine Belle
Hill, Ed
Hill, James Berry
Hill, John Conner
Hobbs, Gerald S
Hoffeld, Jeffrey M
Hoffman, Nancy
Holland, Hillman Randall
Holverson, John
Hooks, Charles Vernon
Hooks, Geri
Horowitz, Benjamin
Houk, Edwynn L
Howlett, D(onald) Roger
Hudson
Hughes, Paul Lucien
Hunter-Stiebel, Penelope
Hutchins, Robin
Hutchinson, Max
Hutton, Leonard
Hyman, Linda
Iannetti, Pasquale Francesco Paolo
Ingber, Barbara
Isaacs, Avrom
Israel, David N
Isserstedt, Dorothea Carus
Iturralde, Teresa
Janis, Conrad
Jean, Beverly (Beverly Jean Strong)
Jensen, Dean N
Johnson, Miani (Marianne) Guthrie
Jones, Doug (Douglas McKee)
Jordan, Vance
Kahan, Alexander
Kahan, Leonard
Kallir, Jane Katherine
Kanegis, Sidney S
Kaplan, Jacques
Kaplan, Katherine
Katzen, Hal Zachery
Kaufman, Lori Hokin
Kelso, David William
Ketcham, Ray Winfred, Jr
Killeen, Melissa Helen
Kimmel-Cohn, Roberta
Kind, Phyllis
King, Myron Lyzon
King, Patrick J
Klein, Gwenda J
Kochta, Ruth Martha
Kodner, Martin
Kohn, Michael Bundy
Kornblatt, Barbara Rodbell
Kornblau, Gerald
Kornetchuk, Elena
Krakow, Barbara L
Kramer, Gertrude M
Kraushaar, Antoinette M
Krienke, Douglas Elliot
Kuhlenschmidt, Richard Edward
Lally, James Joseph
Landau, Mitzi
Landry, Albert
Langman, Richard Theodore
La Pelle, Rodger
Lawrence, Susan
Layton, Richard
Leach, Elizabeth Anne
Le Brun, Carol
Lee, Janie C
Lee, Nelda S
Leeber, Sharon Corgan
Lefcourt, Irwin
Lehr, Janet
Lemer, Ellen Terry
Levin, Hugh Lauter
Levy, Bernard
Levy, S(tephen) Dean
Lewin, Bernard
Lewis, Don S, Sr
Lewis, Donald Sykes, Jr
Littrell, Doris Marie
Locks, Marian
Long, Jenny
Long, Meredith J
Lord, Michael Harry
Love, Richard Henry
Ludman, Joan Hurwitz
Lumbard, Jean Ashmore
Luntz, Irving
Luria, Gloria
Lyons, Francis E, Jr
McCarron, Paul
McClain, Robert Lee
McCready, Karen (Karen McCready Noblet)
MacDougall, Anne
McHugh, Adeliza Sorenson
McIlroy, Carol J
McKee, David Malcolm
McKinney, Donald
McMahon, James Edward
McOwen, C Lynn
McOwen, Carol M
Makler, Hope Welsh
Mangel, Benjamin
Mansion, Gracie
Marcus, Angelo P
Marino, Frank
Markel, Kathryn E
Markle, Jack M
Markle, Sam
Marks, Matthew Stuart
Maroney, James H, Jr
Martin, Larry Kenneth
Mathis, Emile Henry, II
Maxwell, Peter
May, Daniel Striger
Mayer, Sondra
Mayo, Robert Bowers
Meek, J William, III
Meisel, Louis Koenig
Mekler, Adam
Melberg, Jerald Leigh
Merida, Frederick A
Merrin, Edward H
Michaux, Ronald Robert
Milant, Jean Robert
Miller, Robert Peter
Milliken, Alexander Fabbri
Missal, Joshua M & Pegge
Mitchell, N Donald
Mohle, Brenda Simonson
Monk, Robert Evan, Jr
Monroe, Eve Valin
Moody, Elizabeth C
Moos, Walter A
Morgan, Myra J
Morin, France
Morris, Donald Fischer
Morris, Florence Marie
Morris, Jack Austin, Jr
Morse, Mitchell Ian
Moss, Tobey C
Muller, Max Paul
Naiman, Lee
Natzmer, Cheryl Lynn
Neikrug, Marjorie
Neslage, Oliver John, Jr
Newman, Louis
Newman, Walter Andrews, Jr
Nielsen, Nina I M
Nussbaum, Sheila Ford
Nye, Molly Harding
Ochi, F Denis
Oehlschlaeger, Frank J
Okun, Barbara J
Olenick, David Charles
Oliver, Sandra (Sandi)
Oosterom, Richard H
Oscarsson, Victoria Constance Gunhild
Owens, Tennys Bowers
Palmer, Herbert Bearl
Palmer, Meredith Ann
Palmer, Michael Andrew
Parizek, Jaro
Payson, John Whitney
Pearl, Marilyn
Pence, John Gerald
Perlow, Katharina Rich
Perls, Klaus G
Perret, Donna C
Pesner, Carole Manishin
Pfeifer, Marcuse
Phillips, Bonnie
Phillips, Dutch (James O), Jr
Pierce, Patricia Jobe
Plotkin, Lynn
Poindexter, Elinor Fuller
Portnoy, Theodora Preiss
Posner, Judith L
Prakapas, Eugene Joseph
Price, Vincent
Pucker, Bernard H
Raydon, Alexander R
Re, Marisa del
Reed, Harold
Reed, Walt Arnold
Rice, M Robert & Barbara Menen
Richards, Tally
Riegle, Robert Mack
Risser, James K
Robinson, Thomas V
Rolly, Ronald Joseph
Romero, Megan H
Rose, Peter Henry
Rosenberg, Carole Halsband
Rosenfeld, Samuel L
Rosenwald, Carol
Ross, Sheldon
Rothschild, Carolyn Anita
Rothschild, John D
Rowand, Joseph Donn
Rubin, Lawrence
Russell, John Laurel
Rustvold, Katherine Jo
Sadik, Marvin Sherwood
Saidenberg, Daniel

ART DEALER (cont)
Saidenberg, Eleanore B
St Clair, Michael
Sanchez, Mary Lowe (Eliza)
Sande, Rhoda
Saphire, Lawrence M
Sawyer, William
Schab, Margo Pollins
Schaeffer, Kate
Schaeffer, Martha J
Schlosberg, Carl Martin
Schneider, Lisa Dawn
Schneiderman, Dorothy
Schneier, Donna Frances
Schuster, Eugene Ivan
Schusterman, Gerrie Marva
Schweitzer, M R
Seders, Francine Lavinal
Segal, Tama & David
Selser, Christopher
Shainman, Jack S
Shechtman, George Henoch
Shepard, Lewis Albert
Shorney, Margo Kay (McIver)
Siden, Franklin
Silverberg, Ellen Ruth
Simpson, Merton D
Singer, Nancy Barkhouse
Smith, Elliot Steven
Smither, Edward Murray
Solomon, Gerald
Solomon, Holly
Solomon, Richard H
Solway, Carl E
Sonnabend, Joan
Sorkin, Emily
Sowers, Miriam R
Spitler, Clare Blackford
Staempfli, George W
Stavaridis, Pat(ricia Ann)
Steckler, Stuart Jay
Stein, Fritz Henry
Steinbaum, Bernice
Stern, Louis
Stevens, Thelma K
Stewart, John (John Stewart Houston)
Stiebel, Eric
Stiebel, Gerald Gustave
Stoller, John Chapman
Stone, Fred J
Stone, Jeremy
Stone, M Lee
Struve, William Walter
Stuart, Jacqueline (Mrs David)
Stux, Stefan Victor
Sujo, Clara Diament
Sussman, Bonnie K
Suzuki, Katsko (Katsko Suzuki Kannegieter)
Szoke, John
Tahir, Abe M, Jr
Tasende, Jose Maria
Tash, Joy Alene
Tatistcheff, Peter Alexis
Thaw, Eugene Victor
Theofiles, George
Thompson, Richard E, Jr
Toledo, Angeles
Toll, Barbara Elizabeth
Troncale, Frank Thomas
Turnbull, Betty
Upright, Diane W
Usher, David
Valentin, Jean-Pierre
Verzyl, June Carol
Villa, Mario
Vizner, Nikola
Vogel, Donald S
Volid, Ruth
Vose, Robert Churchill, Jr
Waaland, James Brearley, II
Wade, Jane
Walker, Berta
Walsh, J(ohn) Michael
Waltzer, Stewart Paul
Washburn, Joan T
Watkins, Ragland Tolk
Watson, Clarissa H
Weber, John
Weeks, James (Darrell Northrup)
Weintraub, Jacob D
Weissman, Julian Paul
Weitzenhoffer, A Max
Wenger, Sigmund
Westlund, Harry E
Westwater, Angela King
White, Deborah
White, Ruth
Whyte, Bruce Lincoln
Wiebe, Charles M
Wiggins, K Douglas
Williams, Melissa
Williamson, Jason H
Wilson, John David
Wirtz, Stephen Carl
Wise, Takouhy
Wolff, Robert W, Jr
Woodside, Gordon William
Wunderlich, Susan Clay
Yarotsky, Lori
Yeiser, Charles William
Yezerski, Howard J
York, Richard Travis
Young, Edna E
Zabriskie, Virginia M
Zantman, J B
Zimmerman, Alice A

ASSEMBLAGE ARTIST

Abraham, Carol Jeanne
Aronson, Sanda
Aubin, Barbara
Bakke, Karen Lee
Bell, Lilian A
Benson, Martha J
Boghosian, Varujan
Brecht, George
Buchman, Arles (Arlette Buchman)
Carpenter, Linda Buck
Cho, David
Cortright, Steven M
Crespin, Leslie A
Crimmins, Jerry (Gerald Garfield)
DiDomenico, Nikki
Enstice, Wayne
Fincher, John H
Firestone, Susan Paul
Fisher, Carole Gorney
Foolery, Tom
Francis, Jean Thickens
Gilchriest, Lorenzo
Goell, Abby Jane
Gross, Charles Merrill
Gustafson, Pier
Halvorsen, Elspeth Colette (Elspeth Halvorsen-Vevers)
Heinzen, MaryAnn
Hillsmith, Fannie
Hodge, Dorothy W (Scottie)
Houston, Bruce
Howe, Nelson S
Johnson, Martin Brian
Josephson, Kenneth Bradley
Kane, Bill
Kaplan, Leo
Katz, Leandro
Koller-Davies, Eva
Korman, Barbara
Kosta, Angela
Krempel, Ralf
Lanigan-Schmidt, Thomas
Laymon, Cynthia J
Leopold, Susan
Lewis, Golda
McCabe, Maureen M
Majdrakoff, Ivan
Mooney, Michael J
Moore, Marjorie
Moore, Sabra
Nelson, Pamela Hudson
Nicholson, Natasha
O'Banion, Nance
Parsley, Jacque (Carter)
Peterson, Kristin
Presser, Elena
Pruitt, Lynn
Renee, Lisabeth
Ridlon, James A
Rigg, Margaret Ruth
Saar, Betye
Schiff, (Adele M)
Seaberg, Steve (Stevens)
Seiden, Katie
Sewell, Leo
Shields, Anne Kesler
Slettehaugh, Thomas Chester
Stukey, Virginia
Tawney, Lenore
Thomas, Kathleen K
Thompson, Donald Roy
Thompson, Tamara
Uchima, Toshiko
Van Brunt, Philip G
Waletzky, Tsirl (Cecelia Grobla Waletzky)
Warriner, Laura B
Wenger, Bruce Edward
Wenzel, Joan Ellen
White, Stuart James
Winterberger, Suzanne
Yost, Erma Martin

BOOK DEALER

Berry, Carolyn
Campanelli, Pauline Eble
Colescott, Robert H
Davis, L Clarice
Goldschmidt, Lucien
Hage, Raymond Joseph
Lehr, Janet
McGilvery, Laurence
Miller, Janet
Rosenberg, Bernard
Rosenfeld, Richard Joel
Tunick, David

CALLIGRAPHER

Anderson, Donald Myers
Bakke, Karen Lee
Baxter, Violet
Bell, Kathryn Leise
Bostick, William Allison
Callicott, Burton Harry
Cataldo, John William
Chow Leung Chen-Ying,
Ebsen, Alf K
Folsom, Rose
Grushkin, Philip
Haughey, James M
Kanidinc, Salahattin
Martin, Loretta Marsh
Morrison, Robert Clifton
Nesbitt, Alexander John
Poon, Yi-Chong Sarina Chow
Ramirez, Joel Tito
Rigg, Margaret Ruth
Shaw, Paul Jefferson
Swensen, J(ean) Mary Jeanette Hamilton
Tasse, M Jeanne
Wynne, Albert Givens

CARTOONIST

Abramson, Elaine Sandra
Alexander, Kenneth Lewis
Anderson, Brad J
Armstrong, Roger Joseph
Auth, Tony (William Anthony), Jr
Barbera, Joe
Basset, Gene
Bimrose, Arthur Sylvanus, Jr
Bissell, Charles Overman
Bissell, Phil
Bloom, Donald S
Brennan, Francis Edwin
Busino, Orlando Francis
Cantone, Vic
Cavalli, Dick
Conrad, Paul Francis
Crane, Jim (James G)
Crockett, Gib (Gibson M)
D'Alessio, Gregory
Darrow, Whitney, Jr
Davis, James Robert
Day, Chon
Dedini, Eldon Lawrence
Dennis, Charles Houston
Devlin, Harry
Dirks, John
Eaton, Tom
Engelhardt, Thomas Alexander
Farris, Joseph
Feiffer, Jules
Flannery, Thomas
Gallo, William Victor
Gibson, James D
Goodwin, Louis Payne
Greene PSA, Chris (Christine E Greene)
Hart, John Lewis
Haxton, David
Haynie, Hugh
Hill, Draper
Hoppes, Lowell E
Hubenthal, Karl Samuel
Ivey, James Burnett
Kato, Kay
Kaz (Lawrence Katzman)
Keane, Bil
Ketcham, Henry King (Hank)
Key, Ted
Koren, Edward B
Kotzky, Alex Sylvester
Levine, David
Lynde, Stan
MacNelly, Jeffrey Kenneth
Martin, Loretta Marsh
Mauldin, Bill
Messick, Dale
Morin, James Corcoran
Mosley, Zack T
Neher, Fred
Norris, Leonard Matheson
Nowak, Leo
Nutzle, Futzie (Bruce John Kleinsmith)
Oliphant, Patrick
Pascal, David
Phillips, Irving W
Poinier, Arthur Best
Price, George
Robbins, Trina
Rosen, Hy (Hyman Joseph)
Salmon, Raymond Merle
Sandeson, William Seymour
Saxe, Adrian A
Schulz, Charles Monroe
Shoemaker, Vaughn
Siegel, (Leo) Dink
Smith, Vernell Edward
Stark, Bruce Gunsten
Steinberg, Saul
Stevens, William Ansel, Sr
Szabo, Joseph George
Temes, Mort (Mortimer Robert Temes)
Terry, Hilda

CARTOONIST (cont)
Townsend, Marvin J
Trudeau, Garry B
Valtman, Edmund
Walker, Mort
Werner, (Charles George)
Wheeler, Mark
Wilson, Tom
Wood, James Arthur (Art)
Zib, Tom (Thomas A Zibelli)

CERAMIST

Abraham, Carol Jeanne
Alling, Clarence (Edgar)
Anderson, Daniel J
Andreson, Laura F
Aoki, Carole I
Autio, (A) Rudy
Baney, Vera
Barnard, Rob(ert E)
Bean, Bennett
Bennett, Philomene Dosek
Bennion, Joseph W
Benzle, Curtis Munhall
Bertoni, Christina
Blai, Bertha
Blake, Priscilla Ann
Blanco, Sylvia
Bohnert, Thom (Thomas Robert)
Borgia-Aberle, Nina
Bosse, Janet C
Bova, Joe
Branfman, Steven
Breckenridge, Bruce M
Brooks, Louise Cherry
Broudo, Joseph David
Burke, Bill
Burns, Mark A
Calhoun, Larry Darryl
Cartwright, Roy R
Caswell, Jim (James Daniel Caswell-Davis)
Chalke, John
Chamberlain, Charles
Chamberlin, Scott
Chappelle, Jerry Leon
Cohen, Jean R
Cohen, Michael S
Colwell, Judith Kogod
Conesa, Miguel A
Conover, Claude
Conrad, John W
Cornell, David E
Costanza, John Joseph
Crane, David Franklin
Dale, Ron G
Daley, William P
De Castro, Lorraine
Deller, Harris
Derby, Mark
De Vore, Richard E
Dillingham, Rick (James Richard), II
Dominguez, Eddie
Duckworth, Ruth
Earl, Jack Eugene
Eberle, Edward Samuel
Edmonson, Randall W
Edwards-Tucker, Yvonne (Leatrice Yvonne Tucker)
Elkins, (E) Lane
Elliot, Catherine J
Ellis, Andra
Englander, Gertrud
Ervin, Kathey
Fager, Charles J
Fleckenstein, Opal R
Fleming, Stephen
Frey, Barbara Louise
Funk, Verne J
Gardner, Ann
Garzio, Angelo C
Gernhardt, Henry Kendall
Gimblett, Max(well)
Glick, John P
Glover, Robert
Grabel, Susan
Griffith, Roberta
Gronborg, Erik
Groot, Candice Beth
Grossman, Maurice Kenneth
Gunderman, Karen M
Gustin, Christopher
Hardy, Robert
Higgins, Edward Koelling
Higgins, Mary Lou
Hindes, Chuck (Charles Austin)
Hirondelle, Anne E
Hoadley, Thomas A
Hoffman, William A
Holcombe, Anna Calluori
Holt, Martha A
Hughto, Margie A
Ikeda, Yoshiro
Jameson, Philip Alexander
Johnston, Randy J(ames)
Kahn, Annelies Ruth
Karnes, Karen
Kemenyffy, Steven
Kemenyffy, Susan B Hale
Kendall, Thomas Lyle
Kenney, Douglas
Kochman, Alexandra D
Kovatch, Ronald R
Krestensen, Ann M
Kristensen, Gail Marie
Kujundzic, Zeljko D
Kwong, Eva
Lang, Rodger Alan
Larsen, D Dane
Larson, Jane (Warren)
Lawrence, Les
Lebeck, Carol E
Leedy, Jim (James A Leedy)
Leibert, Peter R
Lincoln, Richard Mather
Lopez, Michael John
McAdoo, Carol Westbrook
MacDougall, Peter Steven
McWhinnie, Harold James
Magel, Catherine Anne
Manhart, Thomas Arthur
Mann, Jean (Adah)
Marak, Louis Bernard
Martz, Karl
Mason, John
Massaro, Karen Thuesen
Mavros, Donald Odysseus
Metz, Matthew J
Meyers, Ronald G
Mignosa, Santo
Miley, Les
Mondale, Joan Adams
Moonelis, Judith C
Nagle, Ron
Natzler, Otto
Nicholas, Donna Lee
Nigrosh, Leon Isaac
Notkin, Richard T
Oestreich, Jeffrey
Olsen, Frederick L
Orensanz, Angel L
Pardington, Ralph Arthur
Parks, Carrie Anne
Patrick, Alan K
Perkins, A Alan
Perrone, Jeff
Peterson, Susan Harnly
Pharis, Mark
Popinsky, Arnold Dave
Poupeney, Mollie
Prange, Sally Bowen
Rady, Elsa
Ransom, Brian
Redd Ekks (Robert Norman Rasmussen)
Rippon, Ruth Margaret
Rosen, Annabeth
Schaumburg, Donald Roland
Schneider, Richard Durbin
Selsor, Marcia Lorraine
Selvin, Nancy
Shaner, (George) David
Siler, Patrick W
Simon, Michael J
Smith, Nan S(helley)
Soldner, Paul Edmund
Solem, (Elmo) John
Sperry, Robert
Staffel, Rudolf Harry
Staley, Christopher P
Stephenson, Susanne G
Stevens, Jacquie (Jaqueline Lauren)
Stewart, Bill
Strassberg, Roy I
Strong, Leslie (Leslie Strong Sutter)
Sundin, Adelaide Toombs
Superior, Mara R
Sures, Jack
Sweet, Roger
Takamori, Akio
Taylor, Rosemary
Temple, Byron
Townsend, (Alvin) Neal
Turner, Robert Chapman
Vaccaro, Luella Grace
Walters, Billie
Warashina, M Patricia
Warehall, William Donald
Watson, Helen Richter
Wedding, Walter Joseph
Westervelt, Robert F
White, Amos, IV
Wilhelmi, William Merle
Winokur, Paula Colton
Winokur, Robert Mark
Wood, Beatrice
Woodman, Betty

COLLAGE ARTIST

Ahlstrom, Ronald Gustin
Allen, Kaola
Banks, Anne Johnson
Bardazzi, Peter
Barr, Roger
Beauchamp, George
Benes, Barton Lidice
Berger, Paul Eric
Berlant, Tony
Block, Virginia Schaffer
Bloom, Martha
Borax, Benjamin
Boudreau, Anne Marie
Brown, Charlotte
Brown, Peggy Ann
Byars, Donna
Cade, Walter, III
Closson, Nanci Blair
Collado, Lisa
Conner, Bruce
Cope, Louise Todd
Crable, James Harbour
Craven, David James
Culling, Richard Edward
Davis, Walter Lewis
Dorfman, Bruce
Eden, F(lorence) Brown
Eller, Evelyn (Evelyn Eller Rosenbaum)
Evans, John
F(ord), Lisa Collado
Faris, Brunel De Bost
Ferriter, Clare
Fraze, Denny T
Geltman, Lily
Genovese, Richard
Gilbert, Sharon
Gilchriest, Lorenzo
Goldstein, Gladys
Grainger, Nessa Posner
Grodsky, Sheila Taylor
Gundlefinger, John Andre
Hamady, Walter Samuel
Harrington, Bryan Rulison
Harris, William Wadsworth, II
Helioff, Anne Graile (Mrs Benjamin Hirschberg)
Helman, Eve
Hertzberg, Rose
Hill, Charles Christopher
Hoff, Margo
Hoie, Helen Hunt
Hokanson, Hans
Horiuchi, Paul C
Ingram, Judith
Janson, Agnes
Jess,
Judson, Jeannette Alexander
Kaplan, Leo
Kasnowski, Chester N
Kikuchi-Yngojo, Alan
Kornbluth, Frances
Kunsch, Louis
Laico, Colette
Laster, Paul
Lenker, Marlene N
Lerner, Sandra
Levering, Robert K
Loving, Al
Luray, J
McCabe, Maureen M
McCleary, Mary Fielding
Mackintosh, Sandra
Manilla, Tess
Marca-Relli, Conrad
Martin, Stefan
Marx, Evelyn
Melnick, Myron J
Miccoli, Arnaldo
Miller, Dolly (Ethel B)
Miller, Joan L
Moskowitz, Shirley (Mrs Jacob W Gruber)
Moulton, Rosalind Kimball
Newman, Louis
Nikkal, Nancy Egol
Obler, Geri
Okoshi, E Sumiye
Olkinetzky, Sam
O'Reilly, John B
Orlowsky, Lillian
Ozonoff, Ida
Peters, Diane (Peck)
Pildes, Sara
Pizzat, Joseph
Polansky, Lois B
Raab, Gail B
Reich, Nathaniel E
Rizzie, Dan
Robbins, Joan Nash
Roberson, William
Rose, Roslyn
Rosenthal, Gloria M
Rothenberg, Barbara
Rothschild, Judith
Saar, Betye
Schiff, (Adele M)
Schneider, Shellie
Scholder, Laurence
Schulze, John
Schwartz, Bella
Secunda, (Holland) Arthur
Shaddle, Alice
Shaheen, Gary Edward
Simmons, Julie Lutz
Smith, Alexis (Patricia Anne)
Smith, Barbara Lee
Smith, Leon Polk
Smith, Rowena Marcus
Smith, Susan
Soppelsa, George
Spero, Nancy
Steckel, Anita
Steinberg, Rubin
Stewart, Duncan E
Stinsmuehlen-Amend, Susan
Stoloff, Carolyn
Stone, Gwen

COLLAGE ARTIST (cont)

Sweet, Steve (Steven Mark)
Talbot, Jonathan
Vierthaler, Bonnie
Voelker, Elizabeth
Warner, Douglas Warfield
Warriner, Laura B
Wax, John M
White, Ruth
Williams, Marylou Lord Study
Willoughby, Jane Baker
Wimberley, Frank Walden
Wright, (Charles) Clifford
Zimmerman, Kathleen Marie
Zucker, Murray Harvey
Zver, James M

COLLECTOR

Adrian, Barbara (Mrs Franklin Tramutola)
Aldrich, Larry
Alexander, Judith
Altmayer, Jay P
Altschul, Arthur G
Anbinder, Paul
Anderson, David
Anspach, Ernst
Artinian, Artine
Bailey, Virginia Ellen
Baker, Richard Brown
Bareiss, Philip C
Barnett, David J
Barrell, Bill
Bell, R Murray
Benenson, Edward Hartley
Bergen, D Thomas
Berkman, Lillian
Berman, Aaron
Berman, Bernard
Berman, Muriel Mallin
Berman, Philip I
Bermant, David W
Bernstein, Benjamin D
Bernstein, Edward I
Bickford, George
Biddle, James
Billmyer, John Edward
Bingham, Mrs Harry Payne
Blackburn, Lenora Whitmire
Bolen, John E
Bolen, Lynne N
Boler, John Alfred
Borgenicht, Grace
Bowater, Marian
Brady, Luther W
Broad, Eli
Brooks, Louise Cherry
Brown, Daniel
Brown, Suzanne Goldman
Browne, Robert M
Bunnen, Lucinda Weil
Burden, Carter
Burk, A Darlene
Burrows, Selig S
Caldwell, Benjamin Hubbard, Jr
Cantor, B Gerald
Cartwright, Constance B & Carroll L
Chase, Robert M
Christensen, Don B
Clark, Charles D
Clowes, Allen Whitehill
Cohen, Jean R
Coleman, Edward H
Colin, Georgia T
Conley, Zeb Bristol, Jr
Constable, Rosalind
Courtright, Robert
Couturier, Marion B
Cowles, Charles
Cox, E Morris
Cramer, Douglas S
Daniels, David M
Davidson, Ian J
Davidson, Suzette Morton
Davis, Charles Burdis, III
De Andino, Jean-Pierre M
De Nagy, Tibor (J)
Desind, Philip
Devine, William Charles
De Waal, Ronald Burt
DiLaurenti, Marco Italo
Dillon, C Douglas
Dodds, Robert J, III
Eisenberg, Jerome Martin
Eisenstein, (Mr & Mrs) Julian
Eiteljorg, Harrison
Emil, Arthur D
Erdelac, Joseph Mark
Farver, Suzanne
Feigen, Richard L
Field, Lyman
Fitch, George Hopper
Fiterman, Dolly
Flick, Paul John
Ford, John Gilmore
Fox, Pearl
Freeman, Gertrude
Freudenheim, Nina
Freundlich, August L
Friedland, Seymour
Furman, (Dr & Mrs) Arthur F
Garbaty, Marie-Louise
Gary, Dorothy Hales
Gilbert, Arnold Martin
Gildzen, Alex
Glass, Wendy D
Glezer, Nechemia
Gobuzas, Aldona M
Goldfield, Edward L
Goldman, Rachel Bok
Goodman, Calvin Jerome
Goodman, Florence Jeanne
Goodman, James Neil
Goodrich, James W
Gordon, Martin
Gould, Stephen
Graham, Douglas J M
Graham, Robert Claverhouse, Sr
Graham, William Andrew
Gray, Thomas Alexander
Greenberg, Ronald K
Greenspan, (Mr & Mrs) George
Gruskin, Mary Josephine
Gund, Agnes
Guthman, Leo S
Hack, Phillip S & Patricia Y
Hage, Raymond Joseph
Haley, Gail E
Halff, Robert H
Halpern, Nathan L
Hampton, Ambrose Gonzales, Jr
Harnett, Mr & Mrs Joel William
Harris, Leon A, Jr
Harrison, Joseph Robert, Jr
Hatch, (Mr & Mrs) Marshall
Hazen, Joseph H
Heller (Mrs Edward W Greenberg), Goldie
Heller, Ben
Herman, Katherine Belle
Hill, Ed
Holcombe, R Gordon, Jr
Holladay, Wilhelmina Cole
Hooks, Charles Vernon
Hooks, Geri
Hoover, Francis Louis
Hopkinson, Harold I
Hornung, Gertrude Seymour
Horowitz, (Mr & Mrs) Raymond J
Hubert, Edgar F & Anne M
Hutchinson, Janet L
Iannetti, Pasquale Francesco Paolo
Ingber, Barbara
Irwin, George M
Isaacson, Gene Lester
Isaacson, Ronald G
Iturralde, Teresa
Ivey, James Burnett
James, A Everette, Jr
Janis, Conrad
Janss, Glenn Cooper
Johnson, Barbara Piasecka
Kaplan, Jacques
Kaplan, Muriel
Kasle, Gertrude
Kaufman, Lori Hokin
Kempe, Richard Joseph
Kempner, Helen Hill
Kinney, Gilbert Hart
Klein, Esther M
Koger, Ira McKissick
Koltun, Frances Lang
Kottemann, George & Norma
Kramer, Linda Lewis
Lager, Fannie
Lamantia, James
Lane, Alvin S
Larkin, (Dr) John E, Jr
Lemer, Ellen Terry
Levick, (Mr & Mrs) Irving
Lewin, Bernard
Lipschultz, Maurice A
List, Vera G
Liu, Ho
Locks, Marian
London, Alexander
Longstaffe, John Ronald
McCannel, (Mrs) Malcolm A
McFadden, Mary
McHugh, Adeliza Sorenson
McNary, Oscar L
McOwen, C Lynn
McOwen, Carol M
Mallin, Judith Young
Mallory, Margaret
Manilow, Lewis
Marcus, Angelo P
Marcus, Robert P (Mrs)
Marcus, Stanley
Marks, (Mr & Mrs) Cedric H
Marlor, Clark Strang
Marron, Donald B
Mathis, Emile Henry, II
Mayer, Grace M
Mayo, Robert Bowers
Melberg, Jerald Leigh
Mellon, Paul
Menil, Georges & Lois de
Milrad, Aaron M
Mitchell, Dana Covington, Jr
Morse, Peter
Muller, Jerome Kenneth
Muniot, Barbara King
Nardin, Mario
Nardone, Vincent Joseph
Nasher, Raymond Donald
Neuberger, Roy R
Niemeyer, Arnold Matthew
Norris, Merry
Norris, William A
Ochs, Robert David
Page, Jean Jepson
Palmer, Herbert Bearl
Parizek, Jaro
Parkinson, Elizabeth Bliss (Mrs Henry Ives Cobb)
Payson, John Whitney
Penney, Charles Rand
Phillips, Gifford
Phillips, James M
Pilavin, Selma F
Pincus, David N
Polan, Lincoln M
Polsky, Cynthia Hazen
Porter, Richard James
Poses, (Mr & Mrs) Jack I
Praeger, Frederick A
Prager, David A
Pratt, Dallas
Price, Vincent
Pritzlaff, (Mr & Mrs) John, Jr
Quinn, Henrietta Reist
Rabb, (Mr & Mrs) Irving W
Rafsky, Jessica C
Raley, Robert L
Rautbord, Dorothy H
Raydon, Alexander R
Reeves, James Franklin
Reiner, Gladys & Jules
Revington Burdick, Betty
Rice, M Robert & Barbara Menen
Riegle, Robert Mack
Rifkind, Robert Gore
Ring, Edward A
Rippon, Thomas Micheal
Robinson, Thomas V
Rockefeller, (Mr & Mrs) David
Rockefeller, (Mrs) Laurance S
Roebling, Mary G
Rosen, Israel
Rosenfeld, Samuel L
Rubin, Lawrence
Russell, John Laurel
Rust, David E
Sacks, Beverly & Ray
Saidenberg, Eleanore B
Samuels, John Stockwell, 3rd
Sanchez, Mary Lowe (Eliza)
Sandground, Mark Bernard, Sr
Sarnoff, Lolo
Sawyer, William
Schaeffer, Kate
Schoen, (Mr & Mrs) Arthur Boyer
Schulte, (Mr & Mrs) Arthur D
Schwartz, Alan E
Schwartz, Eugene M
Selig, (Mr & Mrs) Manfred
Selser, Christopher
Simmons, Percy Slotsky
Simon, Norton
Sneed, Patricia M
Solinger, David M
Solomon, Holly
Solomon, (Mrs) Sidney L
Sonnabend, Joan
Sosnowitz, Henry Abram
Spaeth, Eloise O'Mara
Speiser, Stuart M
Stamats, Peter Owen
Steckler, Stuart Jay
Stern, H Peter
Stevenson, Ruth Carter
Stillman, E Clark
Stoll, (Mrs) Berry Vincent
Tash, Joy Alene
Tenzer, (Dr & Mrs) Jonathan A
Terra, Daniel J
Thaw, Eugene Victor
Thiry, Paul (Albert)
Thompson, Lockwood
Thompson, Richard E, Jr
Topol, Robert Martin
Torf, Lois Beurman
Troncale, Frank Thomas
Twigg-Smith, Laila
Twigg-Smith, Thurston
Ullman, (Mrs) George W
Valenstein, Alice
Vanasse, Louis Raymond
Van Leer, Elizabeth Sanford
Verzyl, June Carol
Vezys, Gintautas
Vogel, Herbert (Mr & Mrs)
Wachs, Ethel
Walmsley, William Aubrey
Walter, May E
Walter, Paul F
Walton, Harry A, Jr
Warren, Tom P
Welch, (Mrs) Robert G
White, Philip Butler
Williams, Dave Harrell
Williams, Reba White

COLLECTOR (cont)
Willis, Elizabeth Bayley
Winokur, James L
Winter, Hope Melamed
Wise, Geneva H (Holcomb)
Wong, Roger Frederickson
Woodside, Gordon William
Wright, Faith-dorian
Young, Edna E
Zeisler, Richard Spiro
Ziff, Jerrold
Zimmerman, Alice A

CONCEPTUAL ARTIST

Adams, Dennis Paul
Ahrendt, Mary E
Alden, Todd
Alexander, Vikky M
Allen, Roberta
Allyn, Jerri
Altman, Edith
Anderson, Laurie
Antin, Eleanor
Antol, Joseph James (Jay)
Askevold, David
Aylon, Helene
Baldessari, John Anthony
Banana, Anna
Bapst, Sarah
Barr, David John
Barry, Robert Thomas
Barth, Uta
Bartscherer, Joseph
Beckley, Bill
Bidlo, Mike
Bob & Bob
Bochner, Mel
Boigon, Brian Joseph
Brecht, George
Bronson, A A (Michael Wayne Tims)
Brown, Robert Delford
Brus, Gunter
Buchanan, Nancy
Bull, Hank (Henry Osler)
Burden, Chris
Burkhart, Kathe K
Burson, Nancy
Carducci, Vincent A
Celender, Don
Charlesworth, Sarah E
Cohen, Sorel
Cooper, Ruffin
Cortright, Steven M
Costa, Eduardo
Crown, Roberta Lila
Cumming, Robert H
Curmano, Billy
Cutforth, Roger
Cutler-Shaw, Joyce
Darboven, Hanne
Denes, Agnes
Desoto, Lewis D
DiDomenico, Nikki
Eins, Stefan
Fekner, John
Fenton, Julia Ann
Fisher, Vernon
Fontana, Bill Patrick
Foreman, Laura
Fox, Terry Alan
Fraser, Andrea R
Frick, Joan
Friedman, Dan
Friesz, Ray Lee
Fulton, Hamish
Galloway, Steve
Garoian, Charles Richard
Giorno, John
Goldman, Matt
Goldstein, Jack
Gorny, A-P (Anthony-Peter)
Graham, Daniel H
Grant, Art
Grasso, Salvatore Fortunato
Haacke, Hans Christoph
Harrison, Helen Mayer (Mrs Newton Harrison)
Harrison, Newton A
Harvest, Judith R
Held, (Jon) Jonathan, Jr
Henrickson, Martha (Klein)
Henrickson, Thomas
Holzer, Jenny
Hudson
Huebler, Douglas
Hull, Cathy
Hutchinson, Peter Arthur
Ireland, Patrick
Jean-Louis, Don (Donald Charles)
Johnson, Carla Rae
Jonas, Joan
Kariya, Hiroshi
Kasnowski, Chester N
Kelly, Mary
Kerr, James Wilfrid
Knight, John
Kolbowski, Silvia
Komar and Melamid,
Kosuth, Joseph
Kowalski, Dennis Allen
Kramer, Margia
Kruger, Barbara
Labat, Tony
Lacy, Suzanne
Lamarre, Paul
Laramée, Eve Andrée
Lavier, Bertrand
Laxson, Ruth
Lazenby, Dexter
Lebron, Michael A
Lemieux, Annette Rose
Levinson, Joel D
Lewis, Glenn A
Limone, Frank
Lucas, Christopher
Luce, C(harles Beardsley)
McVeigh, Miriam Lenig
Malpede, John
Manuella, Frank R
Martel, Richard
Martinez, Daniel J
Mathis, Billie F
Matosse, Jackie (Jacqueline Malisse Monnier)
Millar, Robert
Miller, Brenda
Miller, Steve
Minsky, Richard
Mirra, (Mirra Tengroth)
Montano, Linda (Mary)
Murch, Anna Valentina
Murray, Ian Stewart
Nemec, Vernita McClish
Neustein, Joshua
Newton, Richard Edward
Odate, Toshio
O'Hara, Morgan
Okulick, John A
Oleszko, Patricia
Ono, Yoko
Ortiz, Raphael Montanez
Ox, Jack
Pandozy, Raffaele Martini
Patrick, Charles William
Pennuto, James William
Prina, Stephen James
Ranalli, Daniel
Reichek, Elaine
Resnick, Marcia Aylene
Rezac, Richard
Robbins, David A
Robinson, Chris (Christopher Thomas)
Robinson, Walter
Rogers, Bryan Leigh
Romeu, Joost A
Ruppersberg, Allen
Sandman, Jo
Sapien, Darryl Rudolph
Schroeck, R D
Seaberg, Steve (Stevens)
Serrano, Andres
Sheridan, Sonia Landy
Smith, Alexis (Patricia Anne)
Soffer, Sasson
Soreff, Stephen
Spector, Buzz (Franklin Mac Spector)
Stanton, Phil
Stein, Lewis
Steinbach, Haim
Story Wilson, Martha Redy
Strasen, Barbara Elaine
Suggs, Pat(ricia) Ann
Syrop, Mitchell
Traver, Donald
Tuttle, Lisa
Uram, Lauren Michelle
Van Riper, Peter
Varney, Edwin
Vater, Regina (Regina Vater Lundberg)
Venet, Bernar
Vickers, Russ(ell Geron)
Wasserman, Cary (Robert)
Waters, Jack
Welch, Roger
Wesser, Yvonne D
White, John M
Wiener, Sam (Evangeline Tabasco)
Wilde, Stephanie
Wilson, Millie
Wink, Chris
Yoder, Richard Allen
Yorgo, (George Yorgo Spyropoulos)
Zito, Joseph (Phillip)
Zontal, Jorge (Jorge Saia)

CONSERVATOR
see also **Restorer**

Alden, Gary Wade
Beale, Arthur C
Beardsley, Barbara H
Berger, Gustav A
Bittleman, Dolores Dembus
Brownett, Thelma Denyer
Butler, Marigene H
Cady, Dennis Vern
Cederstrom, John Andrew
Chapian, Grieg Hovsep
Chase, W(illiam) Thomas
Chieffo, Clifford Toby
Cianfoni, Emilio
Coleman, Gayle
Crenshaw, Karen Bruce
Driscoll, Abigail Julia Hannah
Elliott, Dorothy Baden
Etchison, Bruce
Feller, Robert L
Fenton, Charles E H
Fisher, Sarah Lisbeth
Folsom, Fred Gorham, III
Gore, David Alan
Grassi, Marco
Greaves, James L
Haley, Patience E (Patience E Haley Ghikas)
Honig, Mervin
Huston, Perry Clark
Isaak, Nicholas, Jr
Jakstas, Alfred John
Keck, Sheldon Waugh
Knowlton, Daniel Gibson
Kortheuer, Dayrell
Larson, Sidney
Lennon, Timothy
Levenson, Rustin S
Merrill, Ross M
Mohr, Pauline Catherine
Pennuto, James William
Radecki, Martin John
Radjai, Abbas
Schiff, Lonny
Stoner, Joyce Hill
Sussman, Barbara J
Weidner, Marilyn Kemp
West, Clara Faye Johnson
Wiesendanger, Martin Wolfgang
Yamin, Martina (Schaap)

CONSULTANT

Adamson, Jerome D, Jr
Ahlander, Leslie Judd
Alden, Gary Wade
Amend, Eugene Michael
Anderson, Margaret Pomeroy
Anderson, Robert Raymond
Arkus, Leon A
Atkinson, Tracy
Baird, Joseph Armstrong, Jr
Barzun, Jacques
Bealmer, William
Bell, Donald Allen
Bingham, Alice
Bowen, Constance Lee
Bowes, Betty Miller
Braseth, John E
Brown, Alan M, Jr
Bryant, Edward Albert
Byrne, Charles Joseph
Carson, G B
Carter, David Giles
Catlin, Stanton Loomis
Chapline, Claudia Beechum
Chasin, Martin
Clark, Nancy Kissel
Cummings, Mary T
D'Andrea, Jeanne
Dank, Leonard D
Dauterman, Carl Christian
Deitch, Jeffrey
Del Valle, Joseph Bourke
Dennison, Keith Elkins
Dockstader, Frederick J
Dodworth, Allen Stevens
Elliott, James Heyer
Fischer, Hal (Harold Alan)
Fowler, Frank Eison
Freeman, Tina
Fuller, Diana
Gagnon, Charles Eugene
Garver, Thomas H
Gatling, Eva Ingersoll
Gee, Helen
Getler, Helen
Gilchrist, Elizabeth Brenda
Gilmore, Roger
Goedicke, Jean
Goldeen, Dorothy A
Goldsmith, Caroline Lerner
Goodman, Calvin Jerome
Gould, Karen Keel
Gray, Thomas Alexander
Gross, Elissa Frances
Gruskin, Mary Josephine
Gunther, Charles F
Harcus, Portia Gwen
Hardin, Shirley G (Mrs Louis S)
Haseltine, Maury (Margaret Wilson)
Hatch, John Davis
Haversat, Lillian Kerr
Hawkes, Elizabeth H
Heller (Mrs Edward W Greenberg), Goldie
Hiller, Betty R
Hinkhouse, Forest Melick
Hobbs, Robert Dean
Hoffman, Mandy Lippman
Hoving, Thomas
Huchel, Frederick M
Hughes, Paul Lucien

CONSULTANT (cont)

Ishikawa, Joseph
James, Catti
Jarvis, Lucy
Johnson, J Stewart
Jordan, William B
Kahan, Alexander
Kasle, Gertrude
Katzenberg, Dena S
Kaufman, Nancy
Kayser, Thomas Arthur
Kodner, Martin
Koppelman, Dorothy
Kornblau, Gerald
Kortenhaus, Lynne M
Krienke, Douglas Elliot
Kuh, Katharine
Lally, James Joseph
Larsen, Carl Erik
Lawrence, Susan
Lawton, Florian Kenneth
Lee, Caroline D
Leeber, Sharon Corgan
Liddle, Nancy Hyatt
Lorber, D Martin H B
Luria, Gloria
McColley, Sutherland
McLaughlin, Jean Wallace
Maytham, Thomas Northrup
Medvedow, Jill
Meek, J William, III
Metyko, Michael Joseph
Meyer, Charles Edward
Millie, Elena Gonzalez
Mills, Paul Chadbourne
Missal, Joshua M & Pegge
Moeller, Robert Charles, III
Mohle, Brenda Simonson
Moore, Myreen (Myreen Moore Nicholson)
Morse, Mitchell Ian
Naiman, Lee
Naponic, Tony (Anthony George)
Nash, Alice Louise
Norris, Merry
Nussbaum, Sheila Ford
Ochi, F Denis
Okun, Barbara J
Olkinetzky, Sam
Oosterom, Richard H
Owsley, David Thomas
Paris, Jeanne C
Pisano, Ronald George
Porter, Richard James
Prohaska, Elena Anastasia
Raguin, Virginia C
Ramos, Julianne
Reeve, James Key
Remsen, John
Rogers, John H
Roots, Garrison
Rosenberg, Alex Jacob
Rosenzweig, Daphne Lange
Royce, Suzanne
Rubin, Ida Ely
Ruddley, John
Sacks, Beverly & Ray
Sanderson, Warren
Sawyer, Alan R
Schinsky, William Charles
Schoener, Allon
Schuster, Cita Fletcher (Sarah E)
Shalkop, Robert Leroy
Sharp, Willoughby
Shecter, Pearl S
Sherbell, Rhoda
Simon, Robert Barry
Smart, Mary-Leigh
Smither, Edward Murray
Smith-Warren, Katharine
Sneed, Patricia M
Snodgrass-King, Jeanne Owens (Mrs M Eugene King)
Sprague, Paul Edward
Stern, Louis
Stone, Fred J
Tahir, Abe M, Jr
Thomas, Tamara B
Tolles, Bryant Franklin, Jr
Truex, Duane Philip, III
Tulumello, Peter M
Tyser, Patricia Ellen
Venegas, Haydee E
Vick, Connie R
Volid, Ruth
Wardwell, Allen
Wegmann, M K (Mary Katherine)
Wegner, Nadene R
Wenger, Sigmund
Whyte, Bruce Lincoln
Williams, Marylou Lord Study
Wilson, Clarence S, Jr
Wingate, Robert Bray
Witmeyer, Stanley Herbert
Wittmann, Otto
Wolfe, Maurice Raymond
Wright, Jesse Graham, Jr

CRAFTSMAN

Adams, Hank M
Akers, Adela
Anthony, Amy Ellen
Bakken, Haakon
Bates, Kenneth Francis
Beaudoin, Andre Eugene
Beckerman, Nancy Greyson
Behrens, Mary Snyder
Bills, Linda
Blai, Bertha
Bonner, Jonathan G
Boylen, Michael Edward
Cadle, Ray Kenneth
Cederquist, John
Cohen, Jonathan Jacob
Croft, Michael Flynt
Crozier, William K, Jr
D'Amato, Janet Potter
Dellis, Arlene B
Dice, Elizabeth Jane
Dorst, Mary Crowe
Drower, Sara Ruth
Drumm, Don
Edgren, Gary Robert
Espenet,
Fields, Fredrica H
Fischer, Mildred (Gertrude)
Fludd, Reginald Joseph
Fraser, Mary Edna
Fredell, Gail
Gannon, Lanie E
Garzio, Angelo C
Glorig, Ostor
Gough, Georgia Belle
Greer, Wesley Dwaine
Griner, Ned H
Haleman, Laura Rand
Hallman, H Theodore, Jr
Hampton, Grace
Harrison, Jimmie
Hartford, Jane Davis
Hedstrom, Ana Lisa
Hein, John
Helzer, Richard Brian
Huntoon, Abby E
Hurwitz, Michael H
Ipsen, Kent Forrest
Jaeger, Brenda Kay
Jerry, Michael John
Johnson, Ivan Earl
Johnston, Robert Harold
Julio, Pat T
Kahn, Annelies Ruth
Karnes, Karen
Keyser, William Alphonse, Jr
Kindahl, Connie
Kooyman, Richard E
Kopf, Silas
Kuemmerlein, Janet
Kulicke, Robert M
Lacktman, Michael
LaRoche, Lynda L
Lawrence, Jaye A
Lewis, Golda
Lisker, Sara
Lukosius, Richard Benedict
McClendon, Maxine (Maxine McClendon Nichols)
McCue, Harry
McQueen, John
Mack, Daniel R
Madsen, Viggo Holm
Manuel, Kathryn Lee
Markusen, Thomas Roy
Marquis, Richard
Marshall, John Carl
Masteller, Barry
Minear, Beth
Mintich, Mary Ringelberg
Mondale, Joan Adams
Nutt, Craig
Oliver, Marvin E
Osgood, Jere
Paulin, Richard Calkins
Penny, Donald Charles
Pijanowski, Eugene M
Prip, Janet
Ray, Christopher T
Royal, Richard P
Sahlstrand, Margaret Ahrens
St John, Adam
Sansone, Joseph F
Sauer, Jane Gottlieb
Saville, Ken
Schneider, Richard Durbin
Schwarcz, June Theresa
Segal, Barbara Jean
Shaner, (George) David
Sheehan, Diane
Shirk, Helen Z
Smith, Jo-an
Somerson, Rosanne
Stamsta, Jean
Sternberg, Paul Edward, Sr
Stratakos, Steve John
Stuart, Donald Alexander
Studstill, Pamela
Takemoto, Henry Tadaaki
Tanner, James L
Thornley, Wendy Ann
Trotman, Bob
Tuegel, Michele B
Walker, Mary Carolyn
White, Karen J
Winokur, Paula Colton
Wrigley, Rick
Yarborough, Christine Troutman
Zgoda, Larry

CRITIC

Ahlander, Leslie Judd
Alden, Todd
Antin, David A
Ashbery, John Lawrence
Ashton, Dore
Atkins, Robert
Auer, James Matthew
Baker, Elizabeth C
Baker, Kenneth
Baldwin, Roger N
Ball, Edward R
Barber, Bruce Alistair
Barnard, Rob(ert E)
Barzun, Jacques
Bass, Ruth
Beatty, Frances Fielding Lewis
Beck, James
Benedikt, Michael
Ben-Haim, Tsipi
Berger, Maurice
Berkson, Bill
Blake, Peter Jost
Blau, Douglas
Bott, John
Bourdon, David
Bowman, Ruth
Brown, Betty Ann
Brown, Daniel
Bruner, Louise Katherine
Burnham, Jack Wesley
Burnside, Madeleine Hilding
Cafritz, Robert Conrad
Carbone, David
Carducci, Vincent A
Carlson, Lance R
Carr-Harris, Ian Redford
Cassyd, Syd
Cavaliere, Barbara
Cernuschi, Alberto C
Chadwick, Whitney
Chambers, Karen
Clarke, John R
Cleary, Fritz
Clothier, Peter Dean
Cohen, Ronny
Colby, Joy Hakanson
Coleman, A(llan) D(ouglass)
Collins & Milazzo, (Tricia Collins & Richard Milazzo)
Colpitt, Frances
Constable, Rosalind
Corbino, Marcia Norcross
Cotter, Holland
Cottingham, Laura Josephine
Crimp, Douglas
Daigneault, Gilles
Davis, Douglas Matthew
Day, Holliday T
De Moura Sobral, Luis
Denker, Susan A
Denson, G Roger
Donohoe, Victoria
Downes, Rackstraw
Driscoll, Edgar Joseph, Jr
Dunbar, Jill H
Elder, R Bruce
Eliasoph, Philip
Ellenzweig, Allen Bruce
Engel, Walter F
Featherstone, David Byrum
Feldman, Edmund Burke
Fox, Howard Neal
Frackman, Noel
Frank, Peter Solomon
Frueh, Joanna
Gardner, Colin R
Gast, Dwight V
Gauthier, Ninon
Geist, Sidney
Genauer, Emily
Ghent, Henri
Godfrey, Robert
Goldman, Judith
Goldsmith, Barbara
Goodman, Helen
Gray, Don
Green, Roger J
Greenberg, Blue (Bluma Kafka)
Greenleaf, Ken (Kenneth Lee)
Gruen, John
Grundberg, Andy (John Andrew)
Halasz, Piri
Hammock, Virgil Gene
Hapgood, Susan T
Harrison, Helen Amy
Heartney, Eleanor
Hemmerdinger, William John, III
Henry, Gerrit Van Keuren
Henry, Sara Corrington
Hertz, Richard A
Highwater, Jamake
Howett, John
Hughes, Robert S F
Hugo, Joan (Dowey)
Hugunin, James Richard

CRITIC (cont)
Humpfey, David
Huxtable, Ada Louise
Isaacson, Philip Marshal
Jaffe, Ira S
Jay, Bill
Jensen, Dean N
Jones, Ronald Warren
Jordan, George Edwin
Kagan, Andrew Aaron
Karafel, Lorraine
Kelder, Diane M
Kind, Joshua B
Kingsley, April
Kirshner, Judith Russi
Knight, Christopher Allen
Knowles, Susan Williams
Kohn, Michael Bundy
Kramer, Hilton
Krauss, Rosalind E
Kruger, Barbara
Kuh, Katharine
Kuspit, Donald Burton
Kutner, Janet
Langer, Sandra Lois (Cassandra)
Larson, Kay L
Le Brun, Carol
Levin, Kim
Levine, Melinda (Esther)
Livet, Anne Hodge
Livingston, Jane S
Lorber, Richard
Lubell, Ellen
McCann, Cecile Nelken
McCoy, Pat A
MacDonald, Scott
McEvilley, Thomas
McLeod, Stephen
McShine, Kynaston Leigh
McTwigan, Michael
Malott, Mary
Marter, Joan
Masheck, Joseph Daniel Cahill
Master-Karnik, Paul
Merkel, Jayne (Silverstein)
Miller, Donald
Moffett, Kenworth William
Moore, Alan Willard
Morgan, Robert Coolidge
Morgan, William
Mozley, Anita Ventura
Muchnic, Suzanne
Mullarkey, Maureen
Murray, Joan
Myers, Terry R
Nemser, Cindy
Nerburn, Kent Michael
Nordland, Gerald John
O'Beil, Hedy
Ottmann, Klaus
Paris, Jeanne C
Patterson, Patricia
Perlman, Bennard Bloch
Perloff, Marjorie G
Perreault, John
Pincus, Robert L(awrence)
Plagens, Peter
Preston, Malcolm H
Preziosi, Donald A
Price, Anne Kirkendall
Rahill, Margaret Fish
Ratcliff, Carter
Rice, Shelley Enid
Richard, Paul
Rigby, Ida Katherine
Robins, Corinne
Rodman, Selden
Rosand, David
Rosenthal, Deborah Maly
Roskill, Mark Wentworth
Rosler, Martha (Rose)
Rothman, Sidney
Rubin, David S
Rubinstein, Meyer Raphael
Ruhe, Barnaby Sieger
Saltz, Jerry
Sandler, Irving Harry
Saunders, Wade
Schaffner, Ingrid L
Schipper, Merle Solway
Schjeldahl, Peter
Schneider, Lisa Dawn
Schulze, Franz
Schwabsky, Barry
Seckler, Dorothy Gees
Senie, Harriet
Shapiro, David (David Joel Shapiro)
Sheffield, Margaret
Singer, Esther Forman
Spector, Buzz (Franklin Mac Spector)
Spivy-Anderson, C Alexandra
Spurlock, William
Stapen, Nancy
Stein, Donna Michele
Steiner, Paul
Stevens, Elisabeth Goss
Stofflet, Mary
Sylvestre, Guy
Tannenbaum, Judith E
Taubes, Timothy Evan
Taylor, Robert
Thorson, Alice R
Townsend, J Benjamin
Tuchman, Phyllis
Tupitsyn, Margarita
Van Wagner, Judy Collischan
Wallach, Alan
Warner, Marina Sarah
Watkins, Eileen Frances
Weinmann, Monique Brunet-
Westfall, Stephen V R
Wilkin, Karen
Wilson, William S, III
Winokur, James L
Wise, Kenneth Kelly
Wortz, Melinda Farris
Young, Joseph E

CURATOR

Aber, Ita
Ablow, Roselyn Karol
Adams, Celeste Marie
Adams, Henry
Adamson, Linny J
Alinder, Mary Street
Amaltitano, Lelia
Andersen, David R L
Appelhof, Dr Ruth A
Arbitman, Kahren J
Arning, Bill A
Atkins, Bill (Billy Wayne Atkins)
Atkins, Robert
Auping, Michael Graham
Auth, Susan Handler
Ayres, Linda L
Bacot, Henry Parrott
Bailey, Jann L M
Baldwin, Roger N
Balkind, Alvin Louis
Barnett, Vivian Endicott
Barnhill, Georgia Brady
Barter, Judith A
Bartle, Dorothy Budd
Basquin, Kit (Mary Smyth)
Baum, Don
Beal, Graham William John
Beall, Karen Friedmann
Beck, Martha Ann
Beckmann, John
Bell, Michael Steven
Beman, Lynn Susan
Benedict-Jones, Linda
Berger, Jerry Allen
Berkowitz, Roger M
Berman, Greta W
Bermingham, Peter
Binai, Paul Freye
Black, Mary McCune
Blau, Douglas
Blinderman, Barry Robert
Bogart, Michele Helene
Bolton-Smith, Robin Lee
Borcoman, James
Bordeaux, Jean Luc
Bothmer, Dietrich Felix von
Bradley, William Steven
Brandt, Frederick Robert
Briggs, Peter S
Brite, Jane Fassett
Broun, Elizabeth Gibson
Brown, Cee Scott
Brown, David Alan
Brunkus, Richard Allen
Buerger, Janet E
Buitron-Oliver, Diana
Buki, Zoltan
Bunnell, Peter Curtis
Burchett, Debra
Burnett, David Grant
Burr, Horace
Butera, Virginia Fabbri
Butler, Charles Thomas
Butler, Joseph Thomas
Bynum, E Anderson (Esther Pearl)
Caldwell, John
Camber, Diane Woolfe
Cameron, Elsa S
Canby, Jeanny Vorys
Carmean, E A, Jr
Carr, Carolyn K
Carter, Curtis L
Cassyd, Syd
Casteras, Susan Paulette
Castleman, Riva
Catlin, Stanton Loomis
Cervene, Richard
Chahroudi, Martha L
Chappell, Walter (Landon)
Cheney, Liana De Girolami
Chiego, William J
Clark, Carol
Clark, Mark A
Clark, Vicky A
Clark-Langager, Sarah Ann
Clisby, Roger David
Cloudman, Ruth Howard
Coates, Ann S
Coe, Ralph Tracy
Coffey, John William, II
Cohen, Ronny
Cohn, Marjorie B
Coke, F Van Deren
Collins & Milazzo, (Tricia Collins & Richard Milazzo)
Colp, Norman B
Conforti, Michael Peter
Conger, Clement E
Conn, Laurence
Conn, Richard George
Contini, Anita
Cooper, Rhonda H
Cordy-Collins, Alana (Kathleen)
Cormack, Malcolm
Covell, Alan Carter
Crane, Michael Patrick
Crist, C Jeffrey
Crone, Rainer F
Crouch, Ned Philbrick
Cruz, Pura (Pura Isabel Cruz)
Culver, Michael L
Curry, David Park
Curry, Kevin Lee
Curtis, Verna P
Czach, Marie
Czuma, Stanislaw J
Daigneault, Gilles
Danly, Susan
Darr, Alan Phipps
Davis, Keith Frederic
Davis, Marian B
Day, Holliday T
Deitch, Jeffrey
De Looper, Willem
Dennison, Keith Elkins
Desmett, Don
Deutschman, Louise Tolliver
Dill, Lesley
Dodworth, Allen Stevens
D'Oench, Ellen Gates
Donato, Debora E
Downs, Linda Anne
DuBois, Alan Beekman
Dyson, Brian
Earle, Edward W
Earls-Solari, Bonnie
Edwards, Susan Harris
Einreinhofer, Nancy Anne
Elderfield, John
Ellenzweig, Allen Bruce
Elliott, Scott Cameron
Elzea, Rowland Procter
Fairbanks, Jonathan Leo
Faude, Wilson Hinsdale
Faunce, Sarah Cushing
Featherstone, David Byrum
Feinstein, Roni
Ferber, Linda S
Ferguson, Larry Scott
Ferris, Daniel B
Field, Richard Sampson
Fine, Ruth E
Fink, Lois Marie
Fischer, Henry George
Fleming, Lee
Fletcher, Valerie J
Flint, Janet Altic
Foresta, Merry
Foster, Mary
Fox, Howard Neal
Fox, Judith Hoos
Frank, Peter Solomon
Freeman, Mallory Bruce
Friesz, Ray Lee
Fryberger, Betsy G
Fusco, Peter Richard
Gale, Peggy
Gamwell, Lynn
Garver, Thomas H
Gates, Jay Rodney
Gates, Thomas Paul
Gedeon, Lucinda Heyel
Gee, Helen
Gerdts, Abigail Booth
Gilkey, Gordon Waverly
Glanz, Andrea E
Glasgow, Vaughn Leslie
Globus, Dorothy Twining
Goheen, Ellen Rozanne
Goldberg, RoseLee
Goler, Robert
Gore, Jefferson Anderson
Graham, Lanier
Green, Nancy Elizabeth
Grossman, Sheldon
Gurney, George
Hackenbroch, Yvonne Alix
Halpern, Nora R
Hamburger, Sydney K
Hampson, Ferdinand Charles
Hand, John Oliver
Hanks, David Allen
Hapgood, Susan T
Harlow, Ann
Harrington, LaMar
Harris, Paul Rogers
Harris, Paul Stewart
Harter, John Burton
Hartigan, Lynda Roscoe
Hartshorn, Willis E
Haskell, Barbara
Haswell, Hollee
Haversat, Lillian Kerr
Hawkes, Elizabeth H
Hayward, Jane
Hazlewood, Carl E
Heiferman, Marvin
Hemphill, Herbert Waide, Jr
Henderson, Robbin Legere

CURATOR (cont)

Henning, Edward Burk
Henry, Jean
Hernandez, Jo Farb
Herrmann, John J, Jr
Heyman, Therese Thau
High, Steven S
Hilgeman, Liese
Hills, Patricia
Hinson, Tom Everett
Hoffberg, Judith A
Hoffman, Michael E
Holverson, John
Hood, Gary Allen
Hopkins, Terri
Houk, Pamela P
Howat, John Keith
Hubert, Edgar F & Anne M
Hughto, Margie A
Humphrey, Donald Gray
Hunt, David Curtis
Hunter-Stiebel, Penelope
Hupy, Art
Hutton, William
Ives, Colta Feller
Jackson, Ruth Amelia
Jacob, Mary Jane
Jacobowitz, Ellen Sue
Janson, Anthony Fredrick
Jeffers, Wendy Jane
Jenkens, Garlan F
Jenkins, Donald John
Johnson, Antoinette Spanos
Johnson, Diana L
Johnson, J Stewart
Johnson, Robert Flynn
Johnson, Una E
Johnston, Phillip M
Johnstone, Mark
Jones, Michael Butler
Jones, Patty Sue
Judson, William D
Kampf, Avram S
Kardon, Janet
Katzenberg, Dena S
Kaufmann, Rick
Kazor, Virginia Ernst
Kelly, Franklin Wood
Kelly, Moira
Kempe, Richard Joseph
Kessler, Jane Q
Ketchum, Robert Glenn
Ketner, Joseph Dale
Kilroy, Mary A
King, Elaine A
King, Patrick J
Kirshner, Judith Russi
Klausner, Betty
Kling, Jean Louise
Klonarides, Carole Ann
Knode, Marilu
Knowles, Susan Williams
Kochheiser, Thomas H
Koenig, Peter L
Kohler, Ruth DeYoung
Kortenhaus, Lynne M
Kotik, Charlotta
Kowal, Cal (Lee)
Kramrisch, Stella
Krane, Susan
Krause, Bonnie Jean
Kropf, Joan R
Kubler, George Alexander
Kubota, Shigeko
Kurtz, Bruce D
Kuwayama, George
Lagoria, Georgianna Marie
Landau, Mitzi
Landis, Ellen Jamie
Lang, Avis
Lanmon, Dwight P
Larsen, Susan C
Larson, Judy L
Laskin, Myron, Jr
Lauf, Cornelia
Lawall, David Barnard
Lee, Caroline D
Lee, Ellen Wardwell
Lerner, Martin
Lesko, Diane
Lewis, Douglas
Lewis, Phillip Harold
Lieberman, William S
Lilyquist, Christine
Linhares, Philip E
Link, Howard Anthony
Lipton, Barbara B
List, Clair Zamoiski
Livingston, Jane S
Lochnan, Katharine A
Locke, Michelle Wilson
Lockhart, Anne Ivey
London, Barbara
Looney, Robert Fain
Lord, Michael Harry
Lovell, Margaretta Markle
Luchs, Alison
Luck, Robert
Luckner, Kurt T
Lunsford, John (Crawford)
Lyons, Lisa
McClain, Matthew
McDonald, Robert Herwick
McFadden, David Revere
McKenna, George LaVerne
McShine, Kynaston Leigh
Maddox, Jerald Curtis
Madonia, Ann C
Manhart, Marcia Y
Marck, Jan van der
Marshall, John
Marshall, Richard Donald
Martin, Lys
Mathews, Nancy Mowll
Mayer, Grace M
Mayfield, Signe S
Mayhall, Dorothy
Mayo, Margaret Ellen
Mayo, Marti
Meadows, P B (Patricia)
Mecklenburg, Virginia McCord
Mekler, Adam
Metzger, Robert Paul
Meyers, Jeanne F
Mhire, Herman P
Michael, Patricia Gordon
Miles, Cyril
Miles, Ellen Gross
Miles, Sheila Lee
Miley, Mimi Conneen
Miller, Marc H
Miller-Clark, Denise
Modi-Vitale, Lydia
Moffett, Kenworth William
Moir, Alfred
Monk, Robert Evan, Jr
Morin, France
Morin-Miller, Carmen A
Morrin, Peter Patrick
Moser, Joann
Muller, Priscilla Elkow
Murdock, Robert Mead
Murray, Eileen M
Murray, Richard Newton
Musgrove, Stephen Ward
Naeve, Milo M
Nahas, Dominique François
Nasgaard, Roald
Nash, Steven Alan
Nelson, Jane Gray
Nelson, Jon Allen
Nesbitt, Perry Loren
Neubert, George Walter
Nickard, Gary Laurence
Norelli, Martina Roudabush
Norfleet, Barbara Pugh
Ollman, Arthur L
Olson, Roberta Jeanne Marie
O'Neill, John Patton
Onorato, Ronald Joseph
Orr-Cahall, Anona Christina
Ostiguy, Jean-Rene
O'Sullivan, Judith Roberta
Ottmann, Klaus
Overland, Carlton Edward
Owens, Gwendolyn Jane
Paikowsky, Sandra R
Pal, Pratapaditya
Palladino-Craig, Allys
Pare, Richard
Parris, Nina Gumpert
Parsley, Jacque (Carter)
Parsons, Merribell Maddux
Pasquine, Ruth
Patton, Tom
Peck, William Henry
Peeps, Claire
Pepich, Bruce Walter
Peranteau, Michael
Percy, Ann Buchanan
Perreault, John
Peters, Larry Dean
Pettibone, John Wolcott
Picher, Claude
Pilgrim, James F
Pinkney, Helen Louise
Pitts, Terence Randolph
Plotkin, Lynn
Plous, Phyllis
Plumb, James Douglas
Posner, Helaine J
Pounian, Albert Kachouni
Pressly, Nancy Lee
Prohaska, Elena Anastasia
Radice, Anne-Imelda Marino
Raggio, Olga
Rahill, Margaret Fish
Randall, Lilian M C
Randall, Richard Harding, Jr
Rascon, Armando
Rathbun, William Jay
Reed, Dennis James
Reilly, Bernard Francis
Reynolds, Valrae
Richardson, Brenda
Rindfleisch, Jan
Rishel, Joseph John, Jr
Robertson, E Bruce
Robertson, Joan E (Joan Elizabeth Mitchell)
Robison, Andrew
Rogers-Lafferty, Sarah
Rohlfing, Christian
Rosenberg, Alex Jacob
Rosenfield, John M
Rosenthal, Mark L
Rosenzweig, Phyllis D
Ross, David Anthony
Rowell, Margit
Royce, Suzanne
Rubin, David S
Rubin, William
Rudenstine, Angelica Zander
Rust, David E
Ryan, David Michael
St John, Terry N
Saltz, Jerry
Sawyer, John R
Sayre, Eleanor Axson
Schaefer, Scott Jay
Schaffner, Ingrid L
Schneiderman, Richard S
Scott, Deborah Emont
Scriver, (Bob) Robert Macfie
Seeman, Helene Zucker
Sellin, David
Selz, Peter H
Sewell, Darrel L
Sewell, Jack Vincent
Shaman, Sanford Sivitz
Shangraw, Clarence Frank
Shaw, Nancy (Rivard)
Sheffield, Margaret
Sheridan, Helen Adler
Shimizu, Yoshiaki
Shlien, Helen S
Shoemaker, Innis Howe
Sill, Gertrude Grace
Silver, Larry Arnold
Silverman, Lanny Harris
Sims, Lowery Stokes
Sims, Patterson
Sischy, Ingrid B
Smith, Ann Y
Smith, Beryl K
Smith, Frances Kathleen
Smith, Lawry
Smith, Raymond Walter
Smith-Warren, Katharine
Sobol, Judith Ellen
Sonday, Milton Franklin, Jr
Spangenberg, Kristin L
Spencer, Howard DaLee
Squiers, Carol
Stahl, Alan M
Stampfle, Felice
Stapp, William F
Stasik, Andrew J
Stearns, Robert
Steel, Virginia Oberlin
Steffler, Alva W
Stein, Donna Michele
Stein, Judith Ellen
Sternberg, Paul Edward, Sr
Stetson, Daniel Everett
Stevens, Andrew Rich
Stewart, Robert Gordon
Stewart, Sheila L
Stofflet, Mary
Stooker, Hendrik Cornelis
Stover, Donald Lewis
Strickler, Susan Elizabeth
Sturges, Hollister
Sullivan, Ruth Wilkins
Sutton, Peter C
Svendsen, Louise Averill
Sweeney, J Gray
Taira, Masa Morioka
Talley, Dan R
Tannenbaum, Barbara Lee
Tannenbaum, Judith E
Tarbell, Roberta Kupfrian
Taubes, Timothy Evan
Taylor, Mary Cazort
Thielen, Greg Glen
Thomason, Michael Vincent
Thurman, Christa Charlotte Mayer
Toll, Barbara Elizabeth
Tomko, George Peter
Tracy, Robert H
Travis, David B
Trechsel, Gail Andrews
Tripp, Susan Gerwe
Trubner, Henry
Truettner, William H
Tuchman, Maurice
Tucker, Anne Wilkes
Tucker, James Ewing
Tucker, Marcia
Tully, Judd
Tunis, Roslyn
Tupitsyn, Margarita
Turnbull, Betty
Tuttle, Lisa
Upton, John David
Usui, Kiichi
Valenstein, Suzanne Gebhart
Vanco, John Leroy
Van Haaften, Julia
Varnedoe, John Kirk Train
Velick, Bruce
Vincent, Clare
Waisbrot, Ann M
Warren, David Boardman
Warren, Katherine Virginia (Diage)
Warren, Lynne
Watkinson, Patricia Grieve
Watson, Ross
Weinberg, H Barbara
Weinmann, Monique Brunet-
Weintraub, Linda
Weinzapfel, Connie A
Weiss, Rachel
Welch, Stuart Cary
Wheelock, Arthur Kingsland, Jr

CURATOR (cont)
Wilkin, Karen
Williams, Benjamin Forrest
Williams, Cynthia Lee
Williams, William Earle
Wilson, Karen Lec
Wilson, MaLin
Winer, Donald Arthur
Witt, David L
Wixom, William D
Wolanin, Barbara A
Wolfe, Townsend, III
Woodward, Kesler Edward
Yard, Sally Elizabeth
Yassin, Robert Alan
Yates, Hollye E
Yates, Steven A
Yau, John
Young, Barbara Neil
Zafran, Eric Myles
Zeitlin, Marilyn A
Zerner, Henri Thomas
Zilczer, Judith Katy

DESIGNER

Albers, Anni
Albrecht, Mary Dickson
Alexander, Robert Seymour
Alicea, Jose
Allen, Loretta B
Allen, Tom, Jr
Allner, Walter H
Alten, Jerry
Anderson, Winslow
Appleman, David Earl
Arnholm, Ronald Fisher
Arnold, Richard R
Atkins, Gordon Lee
Atlas, Nava
Barschel, Hans J
Behrens, Roy R
Berger, Sandra Christine Q
Berkowitz, Henry
Bernstein, William Joseph
Bertoia, (Mr) Val (Bertoia Studio)
Bertolli, Eugene Emil
Biggerstaff, Myra
Blazey, Lawrence Edwin
Blumenthal, Margaret M
Blumrich, Stephen
Bode, Robert William
Booth, George Warren
Bragdon, Catherine Creamer
Brauer, Connie Ann
Bredlow, Tom
Breed, Charles Ayars
Brennan, Francis Edwin
Brennan, Nizette
Brod, Stanford
Bromm, Hal
Broomfield, Adolphus George
Brunell, Richard Howard
Buros, Luella
Califf, Marilyn Iskiwitz
Canniff, Bryan Gregory
Carter, Clarence Holbrook
Casey, Jacqueline Shepard
Cheatham, Frank Reagan
Chermayeff, Ivan
Cho, David
Choo, Chunghi
Clarke, Bud (Warren F)
Coes, Kent Day
Cohen, Elaine Lustig
Cohen, Harold Larry
Cohen, Jonathan Jacob
Colin, Georgia T
Continos, Anna
Cotter, James Edward
Crozier, William K, Jr
Cutler, Ethel Rose
Dasenbrock, Doris (Nancy) Voss
De Bretteville, Sheila Levrant
De Groat, Diane
De La Vega, Antonio
de la Vega, Enrique Miguel
Delevoryas, Lillian Grace
Del Valle, Joseph Bourke
De Paola, Tomie
De Pedery-Hunt, Dora
De Pol, John
Desser, Maxwell Milton
Dimson, Theo Aeneas
Dinc, Alev Necile
D'Innocenzo, Nick
Doll, Catherine Ann
Dorn, Peter Klaus
Dowler, David P
DuBois, Macy
Dufour, Paul Arthur
Duncan, Harry Alvin
Duveen, Anneta
Dzierski, Vincent Paul
Edmiston, Sara Joanne
Eikerman, Alma
Eilers, Fred (Anton Frederick)
Elkins, Toni Marcus
Farian, Babette S
Faulconer, Mary (Fullerton)
Faulds, W Rod
Feder, Ben
Fein, Stanley
Feist, Warner David
Feriola, James Philip
Ferro, Walter
Fischer, Mildred (Gertrude)
Fish, Richard G
Flach, Victor H
Fleisher, Pat
Fleming, Ronald Lee
Folkus, Dan (Daniel Alan Fredrickson)
Francis, Bill Dean
Frankfurter, Jack
Fraser, Mary Edna
Frid, Tage P
Friedman, Alan
Friedman, Dan
Friedman, Ken
Fuhrman, Esther
Funk, Roger L
Gale, William Henry
Garzon-Blanco, Armando
Gayas-Jungwirth, I(rene)
Gebhardt, Roland
Geck, Francis Joseph
Geis, Milton Arthur
Gentile, Gloria Irene
Geran, Joseph, Jr
Giampietro, Isabel (Isabel A Giampietro Knoll)
Gilson, Giles
Gioello, Debbie
Glaser, Milton
Glass, Michael L
Goldstein, Fern
Golubic, Theodore
Gonzalez, Jose Gamaliel
Goodwill, Margaret
Gottschalk, Fritz
Gottschalk, Max Jules
Goulds, Peter J
Grear, James Malcolm
Greenberg, Gloria
Grushkin, Philip
Gutkin, Peter
Hallman, H Theodore, Jr
Harder, Rolf Peter
Harding, Tim
Harmon, James Roderick
Harris, Dolores Ashley
Hausman, Fred S
Head, George Bruce
Heflin, Tom Pat
Henkle, James Lee
Herman, Alan David
Hewitt, Thurman H
Hill, John Conner
Hill, Robyn Lesley
Hobgood, E Wade
Hockney, David
Holvey, Samuel Boyer
Hood, (Thomas) Richard
Horn, Robert Nelson
Hornung, Clarence Pearson
Houston, James A
Hovsepian, Leon
Howe, Nelson S
Hughes, Beverly
Hutton, Dorothy Wackerman
Jackson, Suzanne Fitzallen
Jannetti, Tony
Jenrette, Pamela Anne
Joffe, Bertha
Johnson, James Edwin
Jovine, Marcel
Julian, Lazaro
Kahn, A Michael
Kaiser, Benjamin
Kaiser, Karen
Kanidinc, Salahattin
Katayama, Toshihiro
Kaye, David Haigh
Kayser, Thomas Arthur
Kaz (Lawrence Katzman)
Ketcham, Ray Winfred, Jr
Kinigstein, Jonah
Kleidon, Dennis Arthur
Kozlowski, Edward C
Kramer, Burton
Kravis, Janis
Kurhajec, Joseph A
LaMarca, Howard J
Land, Ernest Albert
Laposky, Ben Francis
Larkin, Eugene
LaRoche, Lynda L
Larsen, Jack Lenor
Laska, David
Lawrence, Howard Ray
Le Fevre, Richard John
Lein, Malcolm Emil
Lerner, Abe
Lewton, Val Edwin
Lisker, Sara
Llorente, Luis
Lowe, Harry
Lusker, Ron
Macaulay, David Alexander
McChristy, Quentin L
McColley, Sutherland
McCoy, Katherine Braden
McCoy, Michael Dale
McCurdy, Michael Charles
McFadden, Mary
McGuire, Maureen
Mack, Daniel R
McKinley-Haas, Mary
Manuella, Frank R
Marcoux, John W
Marlow, Audrey Swanson
Marshall, Kerry James
Martin, Charles E
Martin, Doris-Marie Constable
Martin, Margaret M
Maruyama, Wendy
Marzano, Albert
Mason, Novem M
Maurice, E(leanor) Ingersoll
Maxwell, Peter
Mayen, Paul
Meggs, Philip B
Meitzler, Neil (Herbert)
Metz, Frank Robert
Mills, Lev Timothy
Monk, Nancy
Moore, Benjamin Powell
Morrow, Robert Earl
Myers, C Stowe
Nagano, Paul Tatsumi
Nagengast, William Joseph
Neddeau, Donald Frederick Price
Neff, John A
Ness, (Albert) Kenneth
Nicodemus, Chester Roland
Nodine, Jane Allen
Nordin, Phyllis E
Ockerse, Thomas
O'Dell, Erin (Anne)
Olsen, Ernest Moran
Olson, Joseph Olaf
O'Neil, John Joseph
Paley, Albert Raymond
Panter, Gary
Parker, James Varner
Paul, Arthur
Peck, James Edward
Pei, I M (Ieoh Ming)
Peii, Ahmad Osni
Pennypacker, James S
Peter, Friedrich Gunther
Pierre-Noel, Vergniaud
Pirkl, James Joseph
Pittman, Irene K
Pollard, Donald Pence
Preiss, Alexandru Petre
Prestini, James Libero
Pulos, Arthur Jon
Rand, Paul
Reed, Dennis James
Regensteiner, Else (Friedsam)
Replinger, Dot (Dorothy Thiele)
Revor, Remy
Roch, Ernst
Rodriquez, Ernesto Angelo
Roesch, Robert Arthur
Romans, Van Anthony
Romeu, Joost A
Rosenberg, Herb
Rowe, Charles Alfred
Roysher, Hudson (Brisbine)
Rubin, Irwin
Sadek, George
St Florian, Friedrich Gartler
Sakaoka, Yasue
Samerjan, George E
Santos, Adèle Naudé
Sato, Tadashi
Schoener, Allon
Schreckengost, Viktor
Schulze, Paul
Schwarz, Myrtle Cooper
Schweiss, Ruth Keller
Schwidder, Ernst
Sellers, John Lewis
Seyle, Robert Harley
Shaw, Paul Jefferson
Shelton, Robert Lee
Skinner, Orin Ensign
Small, Neal
Smith, Ernest John
Smith, Jo-an
Smith, Robert Charles
Smith, Robert Lewis
Smongeski, Joseph Leon
Sommese, Lanny Beal
Steinfels, Melville P
Stephens, Curtis
Stephens, Thomas Michael
Stermer, Dugald Robert
Stuart, Donald Alexander
Sullo, Joseph Anthony
SuZen,
Taback, Simms
Temes, Mort (Mortimer Robert Temes)
Thompson, Bradbury
Thorns, John Cyril, Jr
Thorpe, James George
Tobin, Nancy
Tomcik, Andrew Michael
Tulumello, Peter M
Voelker, John
Wall, F L (Frederick Leroy), III
Ward, William Edward
Wasserman, Albert
Watkins, Ragland Tolk
Watson, Aldren A
Weller, Don Mighell
Whitcomb, Therese Truitt

DESIGNER (cont)

Wilson, Millie
Wilson, Robert
Wilson, Tom Muir
Winfield, Rodney M
Wolfe, Mildred Nungester
Wong, Jason
Wood, Joseph A
Wrigley, Rick
Yarborough, Christine Troutman
Young, Kenneth Victor
Zahn, Carl Frederick
Zeidler, Eberhard Heinrich
Zucker, Bob
Zuhn, Cheryl

DIRECTOR

Almy, Max (Marilynn Irene)
Alten, Jerry
Anacker, John William
Aspell, Amy Suzanne
Bartholet, Elizabeth Ives
Beal, Graham William John
Berger, Jerry Allen
Blackman, Thomas Patrick
Blinderman, Barry Robert
Bradley, Laurel E
Brettell, Richard Robson
Bruno, Phillip A
Butler, Hiram
Butts, H Daniel, III
Canniff, Bryan Gregory
Cate, Phillip Dennis
Cattell, Ray
Chiego, William J
Chong, Ping
Clarke, Bud (Warren F)
Cramer, Peter
Crist, C Jeffrey
Curry, Kevin Lee
Dixon, Sally Foy
Dowley, Jennifer
Dyck, Paul
Eagen, Christopher T
Ela, Patrick H
Enyeart, James Lyle
Erickson, Marsha A
Fasoldt, Sarah Lowry
Faude, Wilson Hinsdale
Firstenberg, Jean
Foley, Kathy Kelsey
Friedberg, Rachel (Ray)
Fuller, Diana
Gentile, Gloria Irene
Golden, Morton J
Goley, Mary Anne
Hackett, Dwight Vernon
Halpern, Nora R
Harrington, LaMar
Harris, Paul Rogers
Hoffman, Carol Maree
Hoffman, Marilyn Friedman
Holcomb, Grant
Jacobowitz, Ellen Sue
Jellico, John Anthony
Joyner, John Brooks
Kaufmann, Rick
Keough, Jeffrey
King, Lyndel Irene Saunders
Klausner, Betty
Knopp, Hans-Georg
Krashes, Barbara
Krulik, Barbara S
LaDouceur, Philip Alan
Lubowsky, Susan
Lumsden, Ian Gordon
McCaughey, Arnold Patrick
MacDonald, Robert R
Maurer, Evan Maclyn
Mayo, Marti
Messer, David James
Millard, Charles Warren, III
Monk, Meredith
Muno, Richard Carl
Murray, Eileen M
Murray, Tim(othy Douglas Gordon)
Mussmann, Linda L
Nelson, Harold B
Nesbitt, Perry Loren
Osborn, Elodie C (Mrs Robert Osborn)
Palladino-Craig, Allys
Petersen, Toni
Pfriem, Bernard
Pierce, Charles Eliot, Jr
Pitts, Terence Randolph
Powell, Earl Alexander, III
Prakapas, Dorothy
Quick, Edward Raymond
Reilly, Richard
Reiring, Janelle
Reynolds, Jock
Rindfleisch, Jan
Rosenberg, Carole Halsband
Saltmarche, Kenneth Charles
Schenk, Joseph Bernard
Schulman, Robert
Schultz, Douglas George
Segal, Tama & David
Seligman, Thomas Knowles
Shapiro, Michael Edward
Sharp, Lewis Inman
Shaw, Louise
Shearer, Linda
Silverman, Lanny Harris
Smith, Lawry
Stewart, John Lincoln
Stewart, Sheila L
Stratton, Suzanne L
Stuart, Kenneth James
Stux, Stefan Victor
Sundberg, Carl Gustave
Sussman, Elisabeth Sacks
Sussman, Gary Lawrence
Taira, Masa Morioka
Talbot, Jarold Dean
Thompson, Bradbury
Trager, Neil C
Turrell, Julia Brown
Valdés, Karen W
Van Brunt, Philip G
Vigtel, Gudmund
Warshaw, Elaine N
Weintraub, Linda
White, Deborah
Wilson, Karen Lec
Wilson, Kay E
Winer, Helene
Wolfe, Townsend, III

DRAFTSMAN

Anthony, William Graham
Antrim, Craig Keith
Arcilesi, Vincent J
Attie, Dotty
Bachardy, Don
Bachinski, Walter Joseph
Batchelor, Anthony John
Bechtle, C Ronald
Ben Tre, Howard B
Billmyer, John Edward
Birmelin, A Robert
Bohlen, Nina (Celestine Eustis Bohlen)
Broker, Karin
Brown, Carol K
Brown, Gary Hugh
Buckner, Kay Lamoreux
Cartmell, Helen
Casas, Fernando
Chevins, Christopher M
Cole, Grace V
Cook, Stephen D
Davidson, Thyra (Claire Thyra Wexler)
Dingus, Phillip Rick
Drake, Peter
Droege, Anthony Joseph, II
Duncan, Richard (Hurley)
Eberle, Edward Samuel
Eden, Glenn
Eichel, Edward W
Garey, Pat
Geiger, Phillip Neil
George, Thomas
Gitlin, Michael
Glier, Mike
Goldsleger, Cheryl
Goodman, Janis G
Greene-Mercier, Marie Zoe
Howze, James Dean
Hunkler, Dennis
Hurson, Michael
Insley, Will
Isaacson, Marcia Jean
Kelly, William Joseph
Kimball, Wilford Wayne, Jr
Kimura, Joan Alexandra
Korman, Harriet R
Kosta, Angela
Kuhn, Bob
Lark, Raymond
Lasansky, Leonardo
Lasansky, Mauricio L
Lawrence, Spencer
Leary, Daniel
Leshyk, Tonie
Leys, Dale Daniel
Lieberman, Louis (Karl)
Lima, Jacqueline (Dutton)
Long, Electra
Lurie, Sheldon M
McCoy, Ann
Mann, Frank
Marianne
Martin, Jane
Masurovsky, Gregory
Matteson, Ira
Medina, Ada
Morrow, Terry
Moss-Vreeland, Patricia
Munce, James Charles
Murphy, Hass
Nechvatal, Joseph James
Nolte, Gunter
Nutt, Jim (James Tureman)
Padovano, Anthony John
Paige, Wayne Leo
Pfaffman, William Scott
Phillips, Tony
Pochmann, Virginia
Polan, Annette
Pollak, Theresa
Raffo, Steve
Ramanauskas, Dalia Irena
Rehberger, Gustav
Rich, Frances L
Richards, Bill (William A)
Robinson, Duncan
Rood, Kay
Routon, David F
Rubylee, (Charles Armstrong Littler)
Schneider, Julie (Saecker)
Schrero, Ruth Lieberman
Schwarz, Judith
Segan, Ken Akiva
Shechter, Laura J
Smith, Gary Douglas
Sorby, J Richard
Steczynski, John Myron
Stewart, F Clark
Torn, Jerry (Gerald J)
Twarogowski, Leroy Andrew
White, Franklin
Wilde, John
Wingo, Michael B
Witkin, Jerome
Wojtyla, Haase (Walter Joseph)
Young, Marjorie Ward
Youngquist, Jack
Zakrzewski, Vladimir
Zapfe, Guillermo (Wilhelm Karl Zapfe)
Zlowe, Florence M

EDITOR

Allen, Jane Addams
Aminoff, Judith
Arellanes, Audrey Spencer
Baker, Elizabeth C
Baldridge, Mark S
Bandy, Mary Lea
Behrens, Roy R
Blake, Jane Salley
Blumrich, Stephen
Bourdon, David
Brody, Jacqueline
Carlson, Lance R
Colina, Armando G
Cummings, Paul
D'Andrea, Jeanne
Doherty, Michael Stephen
Dyer, Carolyn Price
Edmonston, Paul
Esterow, Milton
Fenton, Julia Ann
Freitag, Wolfgang Martin
Gilchrist, Elizabeth Brenda
Goddard, Donald
Grundberg, Andy (John Andrew)
Hoffman, Michael E
Hooton, Bruce Duff
Hoving, Thomas
Howarth, Shirley Reiff
Jackson, Ward
Jardine, Donald Leroy
Kennon, Arthur Bruce
Krantz, Les (Leslie J)
Lang, Avis
Lawton, Thomas
Levine, Melinda (Esther)
Loeffler, Carl Eugene
McDarrah, Fred William
McGarry, Susan Hallsten
McPherson, Bruce Rice
McTwigan, Michael
Madigan, Mary Jean Smith
Martel, Richard
Meyer, Susan E
Morin, James Corcoran
Navaretta, Cynthia
Newland, Joseph Nelson
Peterson, Harold Patrick
Prakapas, Eugene Joseph
Rinehart, Michael
Robbins, Eugenia S
Roberts, Helene Emylou
Rossen, Susan F
Schjeldahl, Peter
Schwabsky, Barry
Sischy, Ingrid B
Sward, Robert S
Szabo, Joseph George
Tennant, Donna Kay
Thorson, Alice R
Tobin, Nancy
Valtman, Edmund
Ward, (William) Michael
Wechsler, Susan
Weiss, John Joseph
Westwater, Angela King
Winchester, Alice
Wyrick, Charles Lloyd, Jr

EDUCATOR
(College/University)

Ackerman, Gerald Martin
Ackerman, James S
Ackerman, Rudy Schlegel
Adams, Henry
Adams, John Michael
Adams, Pat

EDUCATOR (cont)
Adamy, George E
Addison, Byron Kent
Agee, William C
Ahlsted, David R
Aistars, John
Akawie, Thomas Frank
Alaupovic, Alexandra V
Albert, Calvin
Alexander, Margaret Ames
Alexander, Robert Seymour
Alexander-Greene, Grace George
Alexenberg, Mel
Alexick, David Francis
Allan, William George
Allara, Pamela Edwards
Allen, Bruce Wayne
Allen, Jere Hardy
Allen, Nancy Schuster
Allen, Ralph
Allen, William J
Allentuck, Marcia Epstein
Allumbaugh, James
Alps, Glen Earl
Altfeld, Merwin Richard
Altman, Harold
Altmann, Henry S
Alvarez-Cervela, Jose Maria
Ambrose, Charles Edward
Amyx, Leon Kirkman
Andersen, Wayne Vesti
Anderson, Daniel J
Anderson, James P
Anderson, Maxwell L
Andrade, Edna Wright
Andres, Glenn Merle
Andreson, Laura F
Andrew, David Neville
Andrews, Michael Frank
Andriulli, Robert
Anglin, Betty Lockhart
Annis, Norman L
Ansell, Joseph Paul
Anthony, Lawrence Kenneth
Antreasian, Garo Zareh
Apel, Barbara Jean
Apgar, Nicolas Adam
App, Timothy
Appelson, Herbert J
Ard, Saradell (Saradell Ard Frederick)
Armstrong, Bill Howard
Arnheim, Rudolf
Arnholm, Ronald Fisher
Arnold, Paul Beaver
Arnold, Ralph Moffett
Arnold, Robert Lloyd
Artemis, Maria (Maria Artemis Papageorge Sawyer)
Asher, Frederick M
Asihene, Emmanuel V
Askew, Pamela
Askman, Tom K
Aso, Kaji
Atkinson, Eric Newton
Atwell, Allen
Atwood Pinardi, Brenda
Audette, Anna Held
Auth, Susan Handler
Autio, (A) Rudy
Autry, Carolyn
Auvil, Kenneth William
Avedon, Barry
B(eck), Rosemarie
Bach, Dirk
Bach, Laurence
Badalamenti, Fred
Baer, Norbert Sebastian
Bageris, John
Baggett, William Carter, Jr
Bailey, Clayton George
Bailey, Jann L M
Bailey, Oscar
Bailey, William
Baker, George P
Bakke, Larry Hubert
Balahutrak, Lydia Bodnar
Baldwin, Russell W
Ball, Walter N
Balmaceda, Margarita S
Banas, Anne
Bandes, Susan Jane
Bandy, Gary
Bandy, Ron F
Banks, Anne Johnson
Barazani, Morris
Barnes, Robert M
Barreres, Domingo
Barrow, Thomas Francis
Barry, Robert E
Barth, Charles John
Bartnick, Harry William
Bashor, John W
Basquin, Kit (Mary Smyth)
Bass, Ruth
Bassin, Joan
Bastian, Linda
Batchelor, Betsey Ann
Batista, Kenneth
Battenfield, Jackie
Bavinger, Eugene Allen
Bayliss, George
Beall, Dennis Ray
Bealmer, William
Beam, Philip Conway
Beard, Richard Elliott
Beason, Donald Ray
Beck, Lonnie Lee
Becker, David
Becker, Johanna Lucille
Beer, Kenneth John
Beerman, Herbert
Beginin, Igor
Behl, Wolfgang
Bell, Kathryn Leise
Bell, Trevor
Belville, Scott Robert
Benjamin, Alice (Alice Benjamin Boudreau)
Benjamin, Karl Stanley
Bentz, Harry Donald
Benzle, Curtis Munhall
Berd, Morris
Berguson, Robert Jenkins
Berlind, Robert
Bermingham, Ann
Bermudez, Luis A
Bernard, David Edwin
Berneche, Jerry Douglas
Berry, Glenn
Berry, William Augustus
Bershad, David L
Beyer, Steven J
Bickley, Gary Steven
Bieler, Ted Andre
Bierman, Irene A
Biferie, Dan (Daniel Anthony), Jr
Bigelow, Robert Clayton
Biggers, John Thomas
Billeci, Andre George
Billian, Cathey R
Bills, Mitchell
Bireline, George Lee
Bishop, Jeffrey Britton
Bishop, Jerold
Bjorklund, Lee
Black, Richard R
Blackmun, Barbara Winston
Blaine, Matthew Frederick
Blevins, James Richard
Blizzard, Alan
Blovits, Larry John
Blue, Patt
Bobick, Bruce
Boccia, Edward Eugene
Bodnar, Peter
Boggs, Mayo Mac
Boghosian, Varujan
Bohan, Ruth L
Bohnert, Thom (Thomas Robert)
Bolas, Gerald Douglas
Bolinsky, Joseph Abraham
Bony, Jean Victor
Booth, Bill
Boothe, Power
Bopp, Emery
Boretz, Naomi
Borgatta, Isabel Case
Born, James E
Borstein, Elena
Bothmer, Dietrich Felix von
Bourdon, Robert Slayton
Bove, Richard
Bowlt, John
Bowman, Jeff Ray
Boyce, Gerald G
Boyd, John David
Boyd, Karen White
Boyd, Lakin
Boyle, Keith
Bradbury, Ellen A
Bradley, Laurel E
Bradshaw, Glenn Raymond
Bradshaw, Lawrence James
Bradshaw, Robert George
Brainard, Owen
Braitstein, Marcel
Brakke, P(erry) Michael
Bramson, Phyllis Halperin
Brandt, Kathleen Weil-Garris
Branfman, Steven
Bransby, Eric James
Braudy, Dorothy
Braunstein, H Terry (Malikin)
Bravmann, Rene A
Brawley, Robert Julius
Breckenridge, Bruce M
Breitenbach, William John
Brejcha, Vernon Lee
Brewster, Michael
Brilliant, Richard
Brinkerhoff, Dericksen Morgan
Bristow, William Arthur
Britsky, Nicholas
Britt, Sam Glenn
Britton, Daniel Robert
Brock, Robert W
Brod, Stanford
Broderick, Herbert Reginald, III
Brodsky, Judith Kapstein
Brodsky, Stan
Brody, Jacob Jerome
Broner, Mathew
Brooks, John H
Brooks, Wendell T
Broude, Norma Freedman
Broudo, Joseph David
Brough, Richard Burrell
Brown, Betty Ann
Brown, Gary Hugh
Brown, Hilton
Brown, Lawrie
Brown, Peter C
Brown, Peter Thomson
Browne, Vivian E
Brucker, Edmund
Bruder, Harold Jacob
Brumer, Miriam
Brunell, Richard Howard
Brush, Gloria (Elizabeth) DeFilipps
Bryan, Jack L
Bryant, Olen L
Buchanan, Sidney Arnold
Bucher, Francois
Buckley, Mary L (Mrs Joseph M Parriott)
Buckner, Paul Eugene
Bugbee-Jackson, Joan (Mrs John M Jackson)
Bull, Fran
Bumbeck, David A
Bumgardner, James Arliss
Bunnell, Peter Curtis
Burchett, Kenneth Eugene
Burchfield, Jerry Lee
Burger, W Carl
Burgess, Joseph James, Jr
Burggraf, Ray Lowell
Burke, Daniel V
Burko, Diane
Burleson, Charles Trentman
Bush, Donald John
Bush-Brown, Albert
Bushman, David Franklin
Bushnell, Kenneth Wayne
Butterbaugh, Robert Clyde
Butti, Linda (Benincasa)
Byrd, D Gibson
Byrum, Donald Roy
Cadieux, Michael Eugene
Cahill, James Francis
Cain, Joseph Alexander
Caldwell, Eleanor
Caldwell, Martha Belle
Caldwell, Susan Havens
Calkins, Kingsley Mark
Calkins, Robert G
Callner, Richard
Camarata, Martin L
Cameron, Brooke Bulovsky
Camhi, Morrie
Campbell, Jeanne Begien
Campbell, Jewett
Campoli, Cosmo
Cano, Pablo D
Caplan, Jerry L
Caponi, Anthony
Carlile, Janet (Hildebrand)
Carlson, Cynthia J
Carpenter, Dennis Wilkinson (Bones)
Carpenter, Gilbert Frederick (Bert)
Carrero, Jaime
Carswell, Rodney
Carter, (Charles) Bruce
Carter, Dean
Carter, Katharine Tipton
Carter, Yvonne Pickering
Casanova, Aldo John
Casas, Melesio (Mel)
Cassill, Herbert Carroll
Casteras, Susan Paulette
Castillo, Mario Enrique
Cataldo, John William
Cate, Barbara Kaufman
Catterall, John Edward
Cavat, Irma
Cave, Leonard Edward
Cecilia
Celentano, Francis Michael
Celli, Paul
Cervenka, Barbara
Chaet, Bernard
Chafetz, Sidney
Chalmers, E Laurence, Jr
Chamberlain, Charles
Chambers, Park A, Jr
Chandler, John William
Chaplin, George Edwin
Chappell, Miles Linwood
Chase, Alice Elizabeth
Chatterjee, Jay (Jayanta)
Chee, Cheng-Khee
Chesney, Lee Roy, III
Chew, Paul Albert
Chihuly, Dale Patrick
Chodkowski, Henry, Jr
Choy, Terence Tin-Ho
Christenberry, William
Christison, Muriel B
Church, Maude
Ciarrochi, Ray
Cifolelli, Alberta (Alberta Carmella Lamb)
Cikovsky, Nicolai, Jr
Cintron, Joseph M
Cipriano, Michael R
Civitico, Bruno
Clark, Jon Frederic
Clark, Lynda K
Clarke, Ann

EDUCATOR (cont)

Clayberger, Samuel Robert
Cleary, Manon Catherine
Cleaver, Dale Gordon
Clements, Robert Donald
Cleveland, Robert Earl
Cline, Clinton C
Coffey, Douglas Robert
Cogswell, Dorothy McIntosh
Cohan, Zara R
Cohen, Alan Barry
Cohen, Charles E
Cohen, George Michael
Cohen, Harold
Cohen, Harold Larry
Coker, Carl David
Colby, Victor E
Cole, Bruce
Cole, Harold David
Coleman, Floyd Willis
Coles, Thelma
Collett, Farrell Reuben
Collins, George R
Collins, Harvey Arnold
Collins, Jim
Collins, Larry Richard
Colt, John Nicholson
Colton, Judith
Conant, Howard Somers
Conaway, James D
Conger, William
Connett, Dee M
Connor, Linda Stevens
Conrad, George
Conrad, John W
Constantine, Greg John
Cook, Lia
Cooke, Jody Helen
Cooke, Samuel Tucker
Coppedge, Arthur L
Cordy-Collins, Alana (Kathleen)
Corkery, Tim (Timothy James)
Corn, Wanda M
Corr, James D
Costigan, Constance Frances
Cothren, Michael Watt
Couch, Urban
Couper, James M
Covi, Dario A
Covington, Harrison Wall
Cowley, Edward P
Cox, Ernest Lee
Coyne, John Michael
Crable, James Harbour
Cramer, Richard Charles
Crane, Barbara Bachmann
Crane, David Franklin
Craven, Roy Curtis, Jr
Creese, Walter Littlefield
Creps, Gerald A
Cress, George Ayers
Cretara, Domenic Anthony
Crist, William Gary
Croft, Michael Flynt
Crone, Rainer F
Crosby, Ranice W
Crossgrove, Roger Lynn
Crouse, Michael Glenn
Croydon, Michael Benet
Crozier, Richard Lewis
Crum, Katherine B
Culkin, John Michael
Cunningham, E C (Eldon Lloyd Cunningham)
Curtis, David
Cutler-Shaw, Joyce
Da Cunha, Julio
D'Agostino, Peler
Dahill, Thomas Henry, Jr
Dailey, Dan (Daniel Owen)
Dale, William Scott Abell
Dalglish, Meredith Rennels
Daly, Stephen Jeffrey
Danhausen, Eldon
Dantzic, Cynthia Maris
Darriau, Jean-Paul
Darrow, Paul Gardner
Daugherty, Michael F
Davey, Ronald A
Dávila, Maritza
Davis, D Jack
Davis, Harry Allen
Davis, Jack R
Davis, Meredith J
Davis, Paul
Davis, William D
Davison, Bill
Day, Burnis Calvin
Day, Larry (Lawrence James)
Deaderick, Joseph
Deal, Joe
De Blasi, Tony
De Bretteville, Sheila Levrant
DeCarava, Roy Rudolph
DeGenevieve, Barbara
De Kergommeaux, Duncan
D'Elaine
DeLamonica, Roberto
DeLap, Tony
DeLauro, Joseph Nicola
Della-Volpe, Ralph Eugene
De Luca, Joseph Victor
Deming, David Lawson
Denniston, Douglas
Dernovich, Donald Frederick
Desmidt, Thomas H
Desoto, Lewis D
Detmers, William Raymond
Dhaemers, Robert August
Dial, Gail
Dice, Elizabeth Jane
Dickerson, Daniel Jay
Dill, Guy Girard
DiPasquale, Dominic Theodore
Dmytruk, Ihor R
Do, Kim V
Dodd, Eric M
Dodd, Lamar
Dodd, Lois
Dodd, M(ary) Irene
D'Oench, Ellen Gates
Doll, Donald Arthur
Donahue, Philip Richard
Donley, Robert Morris
Donnelly, Marian Card
Doren, A(rnold T)
Doren, Henry J T
Dorethy, Rex E
Dorra, Henri
Dorsky, Morris
Doudera, Gerard
Douke, Daniel W
Dow, Helen Jeannette
Dowell, John E, Jr
Downs, Linda Anne
Downs, Stuart Clifton
Doyle, Joe
Doyle, Tom
Dreskin, Jeanet Steckler
Drewal, Henry John
Driskell, David Clyde
Drohojowska, Hunter
Drutz, June
Duckworth, Ruth
Duhme, H Richard, Jr
Dumas, Antoine
Dunkelman, Martha Levine
Dunn, Phillip Charles
Du Pen, Everett George
Dwyer, Eugene Joseph
Dwyer, James
Eades, Luis Eric
Easterwood, Henry Lewis
Eckersley, Thomas Cyril
Economos, Michael E
Edmiston, Sara Joanne
Edmonston, Paul
Edwards, James F
Edwards, Paul Burgess
Edwards-Tucker, Yvonne (Leatrice Yvonne Tucker)
Egbert, Elizabeth Frances
Eglitis, Laimons
Ehresmann, Donald Louis
Ehrlich, George
Eickhorst, William Sigurd
Eide, John
Eisenberg, Marvin
Eisner, Elliot Wayne
Elias, Harold John
Elkins, (E) Lane
Ellinger, Ilona E
Ellingson, William John
Else, Robert John
Elsen, Albert Edward
Emerson, Walter Caruth
Engeran, Whitney John, Jr
Enggass, Robert
Epting, Marion Austin
Erdle, Rob
Erman, Bruce
Ertman, Earl Leslie
Esau, Erika
Esler, John Kenneth
Estabrook, Reed
Evans, Grose
Evans, Richard
Evans, Robert Graves
Even, Robert Lawrence
Ewen, Paterson
Fabe, Robert
Facey, Martin Kerr
Fairfield, Richard Thomas
Faller, Marion
Falsetta, Vincent Mario
Falsetto, Mario
Faris, Brunel De Bost
Farwell, Beatrice
Fearing, William Kelly
Federighi, Christine M
Feinberg, Elen
Feldhaus, Paul A
Feldman, Bella
Feldman, Edmund Burke
Feltus, Alan
Fendell, Jonas J
Fensch, Charles Everette
Fenton, Howard Carter
Fenwick, Roly (William Roland)
Ferreira, Armando Thomas
Fichter, Robert W
Fiero, Gloria K
Filipowski, Richard E
Filkosky, Josefa
Fine, Jud
Fink, Herbert Lewis
Fink, Larry (Laurence B)
Fink, Ray (Raymond Russell)
Finkelstein, Henry D
Finkelstein, Louis
Finkler, Robert Allan
Finley, Gerald Eric
Fisch, Arline Marie
Fiskin, Judy
Flam, Jack D
Flanagan, E Michael
Flecker, Maurice Nathan
Fleischer, Roland Edward
Fleminger, Susan N
Flick, Robbert
Flowers, Thomas Earl
Fogg, Monica
Foosaner, Judith
Ford, Harry Xavier
Formicola, John Joseph
Fornas, Leander
Forrest, James Taylor
Forrester, Charles Howard
Forsman, Chuck (Charles Stanley)
Forsyth, Ilene H(aering)
Forsythe, Donald John
Foster, April
Foster, Maelee Thomson
Foth, Joan B
Fraley, David K
Frank, David
Frankel, Dextra
Franklin, Gilbert Alfred
Frary, Michael
Fraze, Denny T
Frazier, Paul D
Freed, Douglass Lynn
Freedberg, Sydney Joseph
Freeman, Jeff(rey Vaughn)
Freund, Will Frederick
Frey, Barbara Louise
Frick, Arthur Charles
Friedberg, Richard S
Frinta, Mojmir Svatopluk
Frost, Stuart Homer
Frueh, Joanna
Fuchs, Mary Tharsilla
Fulton, Jack E
Funk, Robert Norris
Funk, Roger L
Furman, David Stephen
Fusco, Laurie S
Gahagan, James (Edward), Jr
Galles, Arie Alexander
Gallo, Frank
Gammon, Juanita-La Verne
Gammon, Reginald Adolphus
Gans, Lucy C
Garcia, Rupert (Marshall R)
Gardner, Robert Earl
Garnett, William Ashford
Garnsey, Clarke Henderson
Garoian, Charles Richard
Garrard, Mary DuBose
Gates, Harry Irving
Gates, Thomas Paul
Gauvreau, Robert George
Geck, Francis Joseph
Geeslin, Lee Gaddis
Gelber, Samuel
Gelinas, Robert William
George, Raymond Ellis
Gepponi, Angelo
Gerdts, William H
Gerhold, William Henry
Geske, Norman Albert
Ghikas, Panos George
Gibbons, Hugh (James)
Gibson, Benedict S
Gibson, James D
Gibson, Walter Samuel
Gilboy, Margaretta
Gilkey, Gordon Waverly
Gillingwater, Denis Claude
Gilmor, Jane E
Gips, C L Terry
Girard, (Charles) Jack
Glaser, Bruce
Glass, Michael L
Glasson, Lloyd
Gluck, Heidi
Glyde, Henry George
Godsey, Glenn
Goehlich, John Ronald
Goetzl, Thomas Maxwell
Gold, Albert
Gold, Sharon Cecile
Goldring, Nancy Deborah
Goldsmith, Benedict Isaac
Goldstein, Howard
Golub, Leon
Gongora, Leonel
Goodnow, Frank A
Goossen, Eugene Coons
Gordin, Sidney
Gordon, John S
Gordon, Joy L
Gore, Tom
Gorove, Margaret Joan
Gorski, Richard Kenny
Gottlieb, Carla
Gough, Georgia Belle
Gould, Philip
Goulet, Claude
Gouma-Peterson, Thalia
Gourevitch, Jacqueline
Goutman, Dolya
Govan, Francis Hawks
Grant, Art

EDUCATOR (cont)
Graves, Bradford
Graves, Michael
Gray, Robert Hugh
Grear, James Malcolm
Green, Art
Green, David Oliver
Greenamyer, George Mossman
Greenberg, Blue (Bluma Kafka)
Greenblatt, Arthur E
Greer, Wesley Dwaine
Gregor, Harold Laurence
Gregoropoulos, John
Gregory, Joan
Griffith, Roberta
Griffiths, William Perry
Grigsby, Jefferson Eugene, Jr
Grimes, Margaret W
Griner, Ned H
Grippi, Salvatore William
Grissom, Eugene Edward
Groombridge, Walter Stanley
Grossberg, Jake
Grossman, Barbara
Grossman, Maurice Kenneth
Grucza, Leo (Victor)
Guenther, Peter W
Guerin, John William
Guilmain, Jacques
Gunasinghe, Siri
Gundersheimer, Herman (Samuel)
Gunn, Paul James
Gunter, Frank Elliott
Gussow, Sue Ferguson
Gutmann, John
Gutzeit, Fred
Gyermek, Stephen A
Hackett, Mickey
Hafif, Marcia
Hageman, Charles Lee
Hahn, Betty
Halaby, Samia Asaad
Halbrooks, Darryl Wayne
Hall, John (Scott)
Hall, John A
Hall, Michael David
Hall, Rex Earl
Hamann, Marilyn D
Hamblen, Dr Karen A
Hamilton, George Earl
Hamilton, W Paul C
Hamlet, Susan H
Hamlett, Dale Edward
Hammer, Alfred Emil
Hammond, Gale Thomas
Hampton, Phillip Jewel
Hamwi, Richard Alexander
Handler, Audrey
Hankey, Robert E
Hannah, John Junior
Hannibal, Joseph Harry
Hansen, Frances Frakes
Hansen, Gaylen Capener
Hansen, Harold John
Hansen, Robert
Hanson, Duane
Harden, Marvin
Harmon, David Edward
Harootunian, Claire M
Harris, Dolores Ashley
Harris, Dorothy D
Harris, Gloriane
Harris, Harvey Sherman
Harrison, Tony
Hartgen, Vincent Andrew
Hartley, Paul Jerome
Hartley, W Douglas
Hartman, Joanne A
Hartman, Robert Leroy
Haskin, Donald Marcus
Hatch, John W
Hatch, W A S
Hatfield, Donald Gene
Hatgil, Paul
Hatke, Walter Joseph
Hausman, Jerome Joseph
Hausrath, Joan W
Havelock, Christine Mitchell
Hawthorne, Jack Gardner
Hay, A John
Hay, Dick
Hay, Ike
Hayashi, Masumi
Haydon, Harold (Emerson)
Haynes, Douglas H
Haynie, Ron
Hazlehurst, Franklin Hamilton
Head, Robert William
Healy, Anne Laura
Healy, Deborah Ann
Heath, Dave (David Martin Heath)
Hefner, Harry Simon
Heidel, Frederick (H)
Hein, Max
Heinicke, Janet L Hart
Held, Julius S
Heldt, Carl Randall
Heliker, John Edward
Hendershot, J L
Henderson, Linda Dalrymple
Henry, Robert
Herard, Marvin T
Herbert, Robert L
Hernandez, Sam (Samuel Rudolph)
Hersey, George Leonard
Hertz, Richard A
Hewitt, Duncan Adams
Hide, Peter Nicholas
Hill, Peter
Hillman, Arthur Stanley
Hilson, Douglas
Hindes, Chuck (Charles Austin)
Hitner, Chuck
Ho, Francis T
Hobbs, Jack Arthur
Hochhauser, Marilyn Helsenrott
Hochstetler, T Max
Hoffman, Neil James
Hoffman, William A
Hoffman, William McKinley, Jr
Hofsted, Jolyon Gene
Hoge, Robert Wilson
Hoi, Samuel Chuen-Tsung
Holcomb, Grant
Holder, Kenneth Allen
Holen, Norman Dean
Holland, Harry Charles
Holmes, Larry W
Holste, Thomas James
Homer, William Innes
Hooks, Earl J
Hopkins, Henry Tyler
Horn, Bruce
Hornaday, Richard Hoyt
House, Suda Kay
Houser, Jim
Housman, Russell F
Howard, Dan F
Howard, Robert A
Howe, Oscar
Howell, Claude Flynn
Howlett, Carolyn Svrluga
Howze, James Dean
Hu, Mary Lee
Huchthausen, David Richard
Hudson, Ralph Magee
Huebner, Sister Rosemarita
Huff, Howard Lee
Hungerford, Constance Cain
Hunisak, John Michael
Hunt, Robert James
Hunter, Debora
Hunter, Leonard LeGrande, III
Hunter, Robert Howard
Hupp, Frederick Duis
Hurewitz, Florence K
Hurlstone, Robert William
Hurst, Ralph N
Hutchison, Jane Campbell
Hyman, Isabelle
Iden, Sheldon
Iglehart, Robert L
Ihle, John Livingston
Ikeda, Yoshiro
Ingle, John S
Ippolito, Angelo
Isaacson, Marcia Jean
Iversen, Earl Harvey
Ives, Colta Feller
Iwamasa, Ken
Izumi, Kiyoshi
Jachna, Joseph David
Jackson, Billy Morrow
Jackson, Marion Elizabeth
Jacobs, David (Theodore)
Jacobs, Peter Alan
Jacobsen, Michael A
Jacobus, John M
Jacques, Michael Louis
Jaffe, Ira S
Jaffe, Irma B
Jansen, Catherine Sandra
Jardine, Donald Leroy
Jarrard-Dimond, Terry
Jennerjahn, W P
Jensen, Clay Easton
Jergens, Robert Joseph
Jerry, Michael John
Johns, Christopher K(alman)
Johnson, Charles W, Jr
Johnson, Diane Chalmers
Johnson, Homer
Johnson, Ivan Earl
Johnson, James Alan
Johnson, Lee
Johnson, Lester F
Johnson, Lester L
Johnson, Lois Marlene
Johnson, Richard A
Johnson, Ronald W
Johnston, Richard M
Johnston, William Medford
Jones, Charlott Ann
Jones, Lois Swan
Jones, Pirkle
Jones, Ronald Lee, Jr
Jones, Ruthe Blalock
Jordan, Robert
Jorgensen, Sandra
Jorgenson, Dale Alfred
Ju, I-Hsiung
Judd, De Forrest Hale
Jules, Mervin
Julio, Pat T
Kachadoorian, Zubel
Kachel, Harold Stanley
Kaericher, John Conrad
Kaiser, Diane
Kaish, Morton
Kamen, Rebecca
Kampf, Avram S
Kamys, Walter
Karlen, Peter H
Karwoski, Richard Charles
Kashdin, Gladys Shafran
Kassman, Shirley
Katz, Ted
Katzen, Lila (Pell)
Kaufman, Irving
Kaupelis, Robert John
Kay, Reed
Kaye, George
Keaveney, Sydney Starr
Keck, Sheldon Waugh
Keeling, Henry Cornelious
Keeney, Allen Lloyd
Kelly, Isaac Perry
Kelman, Maureen (S)
Kelmenson, Lita
Kemenyffy, Steven
Kemp, Paul Zane
Kendall, (Ms) Michael
Kendall, Thomas Lyle
Kennedy, Gene (Eugene Murray)
Kennon, Arthur Bruce
Kepes, Gyorgy
Kern, Arthur (Edward)
Kerns, Ginger
Kerslake, Kenneth Alvin
Kessler, Herbert Leon
Kettner, David Allen
Keyser, William Alphonse, Jr
Kieferndorf, Frederick George
Kilian, Austin Farland
Kimes, Don
Kind, Joshua B
Kington, L(ouis) Brent
Kinnaird, Richard William
Kipp, Orval
Kirschenbaum, Jules
Kiskadden, Robert Morgan
Kitao, T Kaori
Kitner, Harold
Klaven, Marvin L
Kleidon, Dennis Arthur
Klein, Cecelia F
Klement, Vera
Klitzke, Theodore Elmer
Klobe, Tom
Knight, Tom (Thomas Lincoln), Jr
Knobler, Nathan
Knorr, Jeanne Boardman
Knowles, Richard H
Knowlton, Jonathan
Kober, Alfred John
Koch, Arthur Robert
Koch, Gerd (Herman)
Kocher, Robert Lee
Kochheiser, Thomas H
Koepnick, Robert Charles
Kohn, William Roth
Koons, Darell J
Koppelman, Chaim
Korshak, Yvonne
Korzenik, Diana
Kos, Paul Joseph
Koscianski, Leonard J
Koss, Gene H
Kostyniuk, Ronald P
Kovatch, Jak
Kowalski, Libby R
Kramer, Burton
Kramrisch, Stella
Kreilick, Marjorie E
Kren, Margo
Kreneck, Lynwood
Krens, Thomas
Krims, Les
Krinsky, Carol Herselle
Kronengold, Eric A
Kronsnoble, Jeffrey Michael
Krueger, Lothar David
Krug, Harry Elno
Krukowski, Lucian
Kuchar, Kathleen Ann
Kuhlman, Walter Egel
Kuhn, Marylou
Kunc, Karen
Kuopus, Clinton
Kurahara, Ted N
Kurz, Diana
Kusnerz, Peggy Ann F
Kwiecinski, Chester Martin
LaChapelle, Joseph Robert
Lacy, Suzanne
Lader, Melvin Paul
Laderman, Gabriel
Lahr, J(ohn) Stephen
Laiou, Angeliki E
Lake, Jerry Lee
La Malfa, James Thomas
Lamantia, James
LaMarca, Howard J
Lamis, Leroy
Land-Weber, Ellen E
Lang, J T
Lang, Rodger Alan
Langland, Tuck
La Noue, Terence
LaPena, Frank Raymond

EDUCATOR (cont)

Lapinski, Tadeusz (A)
Larkin, Eugene
Larmer, Oscar Vance
Larsen, Carl Erik
Larsen, John Christian
Larsen, Mernet Ruth
Larson, Philip Seely
Larson, William G
Laske, Lyle F
Lattanzio, Frances
Lauck, Anthony Joseph
Laurent, John Louis
Lavin, Marilyn Aronberg
Lawrence, Howard Ray
Lawton, James L
Lechtzin, Stanley
Le Clair, Charles
Lee, Briant Hamor
Lee, Robert J
Lee, Roger
Leepa, Allen
Lehman, Mark Ammon
Leibowitz, Bernice
Leland, Whitney Edward
Lemon, Robert S, Jr
Leon, Dennis
Leonard, Joanne
Leonardi, Hector
Lesch, Alma Wallace
Lesh, Richard D
Lettenstrom, Dean Roger
Levine, Shepard
Levy, David Corcos
Lewis, Louise Miller
Lewis, Michael H
Lewis, William Arthur
Leys, Dale Daniel
Libby, Gary Russell
Liebermann, Philip
Liebman, Dr Sarah
Lifson, Hugh Anthony
Light, Ken
Lincoln, Richard Mather
Lindemann, Edna M
Lindquist, Evan
Lindstrom, Gaell
Link, Val James
Lintault, Roger Paul
Lipofsky, Marvin B
Lippman, Judith
Lipton, Leah
Little, Ken Dawson
Littleton, Harvey K
Livingstone, Joan
Logan, David George
London, Peter
Longaker, Jon Dasu
Lonidier, Fred Spencer
Lopez, Rhoda Le Blanc
Lorber, Richard
Lotterman, Hal
Lottes, John William
Lotz, Steven Darryl
Loveless, Jim
Loving, Richard Maris
Lowe, J Michael
Lubbers, Leland Eugene
Lucey, Jack
Luecking, Stephen Joseph
Lukas, Dennis Brian
Lund, David
Lupori, Peter John
Lux, Gladys M
Lyman, Thomas William
Lyons, Beauvais
Lytle, Richard
Macaray, Lawrence Richard
McAuley, Skeet
McCarthy, Dennis
McChesney, Clifton
McClanahan, John D
McCleary, Mary Fielding
McClure, Thomas F
McCoy, Katherine Braden
McCoy, Michael Dale
McCoy, Wirth Vaughan
McCready, Eric Scott
MacDonald, Bruce K
MacDonald, Scott
McElroy, Jacquelyn Ann (McElroy-Edwards)
McFee, June King
McGarrell, James
McGee, Winston Eugene
McGough, Charles E
McHam, Sarah Blake Wilk
McIlvain, Douglas Lee
Mack, Charles Randall
Mack, Rodger Allen
McKay, Arthur Fortescue
McKay, John Sangster
McKean, Hugh Ferguson
McKenzie, Allan Dean
McLean, James Albert
McLean, Richard Thorpe
McLeod, Stephen
McNally, Sheila John
McNamara, Mary Jo
McPherson, Larry E
McVey, William M
Maddox, Jerrold Warren
Magleby, Frank (Francis R)
Mahlke, Ernest D
Mahmoud, Ben
Mahoney, Joella Jean
Mahoney, Michael R T
Mailman, Cynthia
Majeski, Thomas H
Maldre, Mati
Malenda, James William
Mallary, Robert W
Mallory, Nina Ayala
Mandel, Mike
Manhart, Thomas Arthur
Mansfield, Robert Adams
Manso, Leo
Marak, Louis Bernard
Marasco, Rose
Marcheschi, (Louis) Cork
Marcus, Irving E
Marcus, Marcia
Margolis, Richard M
Marriott, William Allen
Marrow, James Henry
Marsh, David Foster
Marshall, Robert Leroy
Marshall, Thomas E
Marshall-Nadel, Nathalie
Martin, Alexander Toedt
Martin, Bernard Murray
Martin, Roger
Martinsen, Ivar Richard
Marton, Pier
Martz, Karl
Massey, Charles Wesley, Jr
Massey, Robert Joseph
Matassa, John P
Matthews, Gene (Eugene Edward)
Matthews, Harriett
Mattingly, (James Thomas)
Maurice, Alfred Paul
Mavigliano, George Jerome
Max, Lope (Diaz)
Mayer, Edward Albert
Mayer, Susan Martin
Mayes, Steven Lee
Maynard, William
Mayrs, David Blair
Meehan, William Dale
Meek, A J
Meeker, Barbara Miller
Meister, Michael William
Meixner, Mary Louise
Mejer, Robert Lee
Melchert, James Frederick
Mesches, Arnold
Messersmith, Fred Lawrence
Metzger, Robert Paul
Metzker, Ray K
Mew, Tommy
Meyer, Jerry Don
Meyers, Ronald G
Michaux, Henry Gaston
Michels, Eileen Manning
Mickish, Verle L
Middlebrook, David A
Mikus, Eleanore
Miley, Les
Miller, Arthur Green
Milliken, Gibbs
Mills, Frederick Van Fleet
Milnes, Robert Winston
Miotke, Anne E
Mitchell, John Blair
Mitchell, Robin
Mitchnick, Nancy
Moldroski, Al R
Moment, Joan
Momiyama, Nanae
Monaghan, Keith
Monroe, Betty Iverson
Monroe, Gerald
Monthan, Guy
Moore, John J
Moore, Todd Somers
Morgan, Clarence (Edward)
Morganstern, Anne McGee
Morganstern, James
Morin, Thomas Edward
Morris, Robert Clarke
Morrison, Keith Anthony
Moss, Jacqueline
Moss, Karen Canner
Muhlberger, Richard Charles
Mullen, James Martin
Mullen, Philip Edward
Mullican, Lee
Mundt, Ernest Karl
Munsterberg, Hugo
Munzner, Aribert
Murashima, Kumiko
Murphy, Dudley C
Murphy, Marilyn L
Musgrave, Shirley H
Myer, Peter Livingston
Myers, Joel Philip
Myford, James C
Naar, Harry I
Nagin, Mary D
Nash, Paul
Navrat, Den(nis Edward)
Nawara, Jim
Nawrocki, Thomas Dennis
Nay, Mary Spencer
Naylor, John Geoffrey
Nees, Lawrence
Nesbitt, Alexander John
New, Lloyd H (Lloyd Kiva New)
Newton, Earle Williams
Nichols, Francis N, II
Nichols, William Allyn
Nick, George
Nickford, Juan
Nickson, Graham G
Nochlin, Linda (Pommer)
Noe, Jerry Lee
Noggle, Anne
Norfleet, Barbara Pugh
Norton, Paul Foote
Norwood, Malcolm Mark
Novak, Barbara (Mrs Brian O'Doherty)
Novinski, Lyle Frank
Novotny, Elmer Ladislaw
Nunnelley, Robert B
Nushawg, Michael Allan
Oakes, John Warren
Ockenga, Starr
Ockerse, Thomas
O'Connell, George D
O'Connor, Stanley James
O'Connor, Thom
O'Gorman, James Francis
Ohlson, Douglas Dean
Olsen Bergman, Ciel
Olson, Douglas John
Olson, Maxine
Olson, Richard W
Omar, Margit
O'Neil, John
Orenstein, Gloria Feman
Ortiz, Raphael Montanez
Osborne, Cynthia A
Osborne, Robert Lee
O'Sickey, Joseph Benjamin
Ott, Robert William
Oxman, Mark
Pablo
Page, John Henry, Jr
Papier, Maurice Anthony
Pardee, William Hearne
Parfenoff, Michael S
Parkhurst, Charles
Parks, Carrie Anne
Parris, Nina Gumpert
Parsons, David Goode
Partin, Robert
Parton, Ralf
Paskewitz, Bill, Jr
Passlof, Pat
Paterson, Anthony R
Patnode, J Scott
Patrick, Joseph Alexander
Patterson, Curtis Ray
Payne, John D
Peak, Elizabeth Jayne
Pearlstein, Philip
Pearlstein, Seymour
Pearson, John
Pecchenino, J Ronald
Peck, Lee Barnes
Peckham, Nicholas
Pekarsky, Mel (Melvin Hirsch)
Penkoff, Ronald Peter
Pentak, Stephen
Perkins, Ann
Perkins, G Holmes
Perkins, Lois Bouthillier
Perlin, Ruth Rudolph
Perlman, Joel Leonard
Perry, Donald Dean
Perry, Edward (Ted) Samuel
Perry, Lallah Miles
Peterson, Dorothy (Hawkins)
Peterson, Larry D
Peterson, Susan Harnly
Peven, Michael David
Pfaff, Judy
Phillips, Matt
Piehl, Walter Jason, Jr
Pierce, Ann Trucksess
Pijanowski, Eugene M
Pimentel, David Delbert
Pincus-Witten, Robert A
Pindell, Howardena Doreen
Pirkl, James Joseph
Pizzat, Joseph
Place, Bradley Eugene
Plagens, Peter
Pollitt, Jerome Jordan
Pollock, Merlin F
Polonsky, Arthur
Ponsot, Claude F
Pontynen, Arthur
Porter, Albert Wright
Porter, Elmer Johnson
Porter, Jeanne Chenault
Posey, Ernest Noel
Posner, Donald
Postiglione, Corey M
Poulos, Basilios Nicholas
Power, Mark
Praczukowski, Edward Leon
Pratt, Vernon Gaither
Pressly, William Laurens
Preston, George Nelson
Preusser, Robert Ormerod
Price, Leslie Kenneth
Price, Michael Benjamin
Prina, Stephen James
Prince, Arnold
Prince, Richard Edmund
Prochownik, Walter A
Pross, Lester Fred
Pufahl, John K

EDUCATOR (cont)
Pujol, Elliott
Purdy, Henry Carl
Purtle, Carol Jean
Putterman, Florence Grace
Quest, Charles Francis
Quest, Dorothy (Johnson)
Radovich, Donald
Radycki, J(osephine) Diane
Raiselis, Richard
Rames, Stanley Dodson
Ramos, (Mel) Melvin John
Ranalli, Daniel
Rand, Harry
Rapp, Lois
Rascoe, Stephen Thomas
Ratner, David M
Rayen, James Wilson
Read, Dave (David Dolloff)
Redd, Richard James
Reddington, Charles Leonard
Reddix, Roscoe Chester
Reep, Edward Arnold
Reeser, Robert D
Reichek, Jesse
Reichert, Donald Karl
Reif, (F) David
Reimann, William P
Reiss, Roland
Reker, Les
Rembert, Virginia Pitts
Revor, Remy
Reynolds, Robert
Rice, Norman Lewis
Richardson, John Adkins
Richardson, Sam
Richardson, W C
Riley, Barbra Bayne
Riley-Land, Sarah (Sarah Agnes Riley Land)
Ringness, Charles Obert
Risbeck, Philip Edward
Riseling, Robert Lowell
Riss, Murray
Roberson, Samuel Arndt
Roberts, Lucille D (Malkia)
Roberts, William Edward
Robinson, Chris (Christopher Thomas)
Robinson, Lilien Filipovitch
Robinson, Mary Ann
Rocklin, Raymond
Rode, Meredith Eagon
Rogers, Barbara
Rogers, Bryan Leigh
Rogers, Otto Donald
Roller, Russell Kenneth
Rorex, Robert Albright
Rosas, Mel
Rose, Stephanie
Rosenberg, Charles Michael
Rosenfield, John M
Rosenthal, Earl Edgar
Roster, Fred Howard
Roth, Moira
Roth, Richard
Rousseau-Vermette, Mariette
Roussel, Claude Patrice
Rowan, Dennis Michael
Rowan, Herman
Rowan, (C) Patrick
Rozman, Joseph John
Ruben, Richards
Rubey, Tony (George Anton)
Rudquist, Jerry Jacob
Ruggles, Joanne Beaule
Rugolo, Lawrence
Rupp, Sheron Adeline
Rush, Jon N
Russell, Robert Price
Russin, Robert I
Russo, Alexander Peter
Ruvolo, Felix Emmanuele
Ruyle, Lydia Miller
Sacanga, Italo
Sadek, George
St Florian, Friedrich Gartler
Salerno, Charles
Salmon, Raymond Merle
Saltzman, Marvin
Samuelson, Fred Binder
Sanderson, Charles Howard
Sangiamo, Albert
Santiago, Richard E
Sapp, William Rothwell
Satterfield, John Edward
Satz, Janet M
Saunders, J Boyd
Savoy, Chyrl Lenore
Sawai, Noboru
Scala, Joseph (A)
Scarpa, Dorothea
Schactman, Barry Robert
Schaefer, Ronald H
Schapiro, Meyer
Schar, Stuart
Schaumburg, Donald Roland
Scherpereel, Richard Charles
Schietinger, James Frederick
Schmaltz, Roy Edgar
Schmalz, Carl (Nelson), Jr
Schmidt, Frederick Lee
Schmidt, Randall Bernard
Schmutzhart, Berthold Josef
Schoener, Jason
Schooley, Elmer Wayne
Schorr, Justin
Schultz, Harold A
Schultz, John Bernard
Schultz, Stephen Warren
Schulz, Anne Markham
Schulz, Juergen
Schulze, Franz
Schwieger, C Robert
Scott, John Beldon
Scott, John Fredrik
Scucchi, Robie (Peter), Jr
Seawright, James L, Jr
Sella, Alvin Conrad
Sellers, John Lewis
Semak, Michael
Sensemann, Susan
Seppa, Heikki Markus
Serra-Badue, Daniel F
Sevigny, Maurice Joseph, II
Shapiro, David (David Joel Shapiro)
Sharrow, Sheba
Shaw, Joseph Winterbotham
Sheard, Wendy Stedman
Shelton, Robert Lee
Sherman, Claire Richter
Shipley, Roger Douglas
Shuebrook, Ron (Ronald Lee)
Shuler, Thomas H, Jr
Shull, Carl Edwin
Sibley, Charles Kenneth
Sickler, Michael Allan
Sieber, Roy
Sieg, Robert Lawrence
Sigala, Stephanie Childs
Silberstein-Storfer, Muriel Rosoff
Sill, Gertrude Grace
Silver, Rawley A
Silverman, Ronald H
Simmons, Gary Paul
Simmons, John Herbert
Simon, David L
Simoni, John Peter
Simpson, David
Simpson, Marianna Shreve
Simpson, William Kelly
Sinton, Nell (Walter)
Sirkis, Nancy
Sisco, Elizabeth
Skelley, Robert Charles
Sklarski, Bonnie J
Sky, Carol Veth
Slavick, Susanne Mechtild
Slettehaugh, Thomas Chester
Slotnick, Mortimer H
Slusky, Joseph
Smalley, David Allan
Smalley, Stephen Francis
Smedley, Geoffrey
Smith, Arthur Hall
Smith, David Loeffler
Smith, Dolph
Smith, Graham
Smith, John Ivor
Smith, Lawson Wentworth
Smith, Ralph Alexander
Smith, Robert Charles
Smith, Robert Lewis
Smith, Sam
Smith, Sherri
Smuskiewicz, Ted
Snyder, William B
Solem, (Elmo) John
Solomon, Bernard Alan
Somerson, Rosanne
Sommese, Lanny Beal
Sorokin, Maxine Ann
Sougstad, Mike
Spafford, Michael Charles
Spear, Richard Edmund
Spector, Jack J
Speight, Jerry Brooks
Spencer, Deirdre Diane
Spink, Walter M
Spinski, Victor
Sprague, Mark Anderson
Spurling, Norine M
Squier, Jack Leslie
Stack, Gael Z
Stacy, Donald L
Staffel, Doris
Stanczak, Julian
Stanforth, Melvin Sidney
Stark, George King
Stauffer, Richard L
Stearns, Thomas Robert
Steczynski, John Myron
Steele, Benjamin Charles
Steffler, Alva W
Stegeman, Charles
Stein, Ludwig
Stein, Roger Breed
Steinberg, Leo
Stephany, Jaromir
Stephens, William Blakely
Stephenson, John H
Stephenson, Susanne G
Steven, James Michael
Stevens, Linda Lee
Stevens, Nelson L
Stevens, Thelma K
Stevenson, A Brockie
Stewart, Jack
Stewart, Paul LeRoy
Stillman, Damie
Stoeveken, Anthony Charles
Stokes, Louis (Walter)
Stokstad, Marilyn
Stomps, Walter E, Jr
Stonebarger, Virginia
Stoner, Joyce Hill
Stones, Margaret Alison
Stoppert, Mary Kay
Stratton, Margaret Mary
Strawn, Jarrett W (Jason)
Streeter, Tal
Streett, Tylden Westcott
Striker, Cecil L
Stringer, Mary Evelyn
Strong, Charles Ralph
Strother, Joseph Willis
Stroud, Peter Anthony
Struppeck, Jules
Stuler, Jack
Sullivan, R(onald Dee)
Sullivan, Scott A
Summ, Helmut
Sunderland, Nita Kathleen
Sures, Jack
Surls, James
Suter, Sherwood Eugene
Sutter, James Stewart
Tacha, Athena
Tajiri, Shinkichi
Tasse, M Jeanne
Tate, Blair
Tatham, David Frederic
Taylor, Brie (Benjamin de Brie)
Taylor, Hugh Holloway
Taysom, Wayne Pendelton
Teague, Edward H
Teczar, Steven W
Tefft, Elden Cecil
Teilhet-Fisk, Jehanne Hildegarde
Teller, Douglas H
Tesfagiorgis, Freida
Tettleton, Robert Lynn
Thiebaud, (Morton) Wayne
Thistlethwaite, Mark Edward
Thomas, Elaine Freeman
Thomas, Thalia Ann Marie
Thompson, Dorothy Burr
Thompson, Jack
Thompson, Nancy Kunkle
Thompson, Robert Charles
Thompson, Wade S
Thompson, William Joseph
Thorne-Thomsen, Ruth T
Thornton, Richard Samuel
Thurston, Jacqueline Beverly
Tibbs, Thomas S
Tierney, Patrick Lennox
Tift, Mary Louise
Tobia, Blaise Joseph
Toker, Franklin
Tolles, Bryant Franklin, Jr
Tomcik, Andrew Michael
Toney, Anthony
Topper, David R
Torlen, Michael Arnold
Toulis, Vasilios (Apostolos)
Townsend, Gavin Edward
Townsend, (Alvin) Neal
Townsend, Vera B
Tracy, Robert H
Trakis, Louis
Trank, Lynn Edgar
Traub, Charles H
Treaster, Richard A
Tredennick, Dorothy W
Trentham, Gary Lynn
Triano, Anthony Thomas
Trivigno, Pat
Truex, Duane Philip, III
Trutty-Coohill, Patricia
Tse, Stephen
Tuckerman, Jane Bayard
Turnbull, Lucy
Turner, A Richard
Turner, Bonese Collins
Turner, David
Turner, Robert Chapman
Turner, Theodore Roy
Turner, William Eugene
Turnure, James Harvey
Twarogowski, Leroy Andrew
Twiggs, Leo Franklin
Tyzack, Michael
Ubans, Juris K
Uccello, Vincenza Agatha
Udvardy, John Warren
Ulrich, David Alan
Upton, John David
Uttech, Thomas Martin
Vaccaro, Nick Dante
Valdés, Karen W
Valerio, James Robert
Vanderlip, Dianne Perry
Van der Meulen, Jan
VanDerpool, Karen
Vandersall, Amy L
Van Duinwyk, George Paul
Van Ginkel, Blanche Lemco
Van Halm, Renée
Van Loen, Alfred
Van Schaack, Eric
Van Suchtelen, Adrian
Van Winkle, Lester G
Vargo, John

EDUCATOR (cont)
Varnelis, Kazys
Vasa, (Velizar Mihich)
Vecsey, Esther Barbara
Veerkamp, Patrick Burke
Vega, Edward
Vena, Dante
Ventimiglia, John Thomas
Verzar, Christine B
Vevers, Tony
Viera, Charles David
Vignes, Michelle Marie
Villa, Carlos
Visco, Anthony Salvatore
Volkersz, Willem
Von Barghan, Barbara
Voulkos, Peter
Wachs, Ethel
Walburg, Gerald
Walford, E John
Walker, Larry
Walker, Larry
Wallace, John
Wallace, Kenneth William
Wallace, Richard William
Wallace, Robert Dan
Wallin, Leland Dean
Walters, Sylvia Solochek
Walton, Guy E
Wands, Robert James
Warashina, M Patricia
Ward, Joseph Marshall
Ward, Lyle Edward
Warren, Jacqueline Louise
Wasserman, Jack
Waters, Herbert (Ogden)
Watson, Ronald G
Weale, Mary Jo
Webb, Jeffrey R
Weber, Albert Jacob
Wechter, Vivienne Thaul
Wedding, Walter Joseph
Weege, William
Weidner, Mary Elizabeth
Weigand, Herbert Michael
Weinberg, Elbert
Weinberg, Ephraim
Weinberg, H Barbara
Weintraub, Annette
Weisberg, Gabriel P
Weisberg, Ruth Ellen
Weismann, Donald Leroy
Weitzmann, Kurt
Weller, Allen Stuart
Welpott, Jack Warren
Welter, Cole H
Wenawine, Bruce Harley
Wenger, Jane (B)
Werfel, Gina S
Werger, Art(hur Lawrence)
Wert, Ned Oliver
Westfall, Carol D
Wethli, Mark
Wheelock, Arthur Kingsland, Jr
White, Bruce Hilding
White, James Richard
White, Robert (Winthrop)
Whitehead, Frances
Whiteside, William Albert, II
Whitlock, John Joseph
Whitney, Maynard Merle
Whitson,
Whittington, Jon Hammon
Wible, Mary Grace
Wicks, Eugene Claude
Widmer, Gwen Ellen
Wilbert, Robert John
Wilde, Dawn Johnson
Wiley, William T
Williams, John Wesley
Williams, William Thomas
Willis, Jay Stewart
Willis, William Henry, Jr
Wilmerding, John
Wilson, Edward N
Wilson, June
Wilson, Wallace
Wilson, Warren Bingham
Wilwers, Edward Mathias
Wiman, Bill
Wimmer, Gayle
Wink, Don (Jon Donnel)
Winkler, Maria Paula
Winokur, Robert Mark
Winter, Gerald Glen
Winzenz, Karon Hagemeister
Wisnosky, John G
Witte, Mary (Grace) Stieglitz
Wogstad, James Everet
Woitena, Ben S
Wolber, Paul J
Wolfe, Lynn Robert
Wolsky, Jack
Wood, Beatrice
Wood, Harry Emsley, Jr
Woodford, Don (Donald Paul)
Woods, Rip
Woodson, Doris
Woodward, William
Wright, Frank
Wright, Milton
Wurmfeld, Sanford
Wyckoff, Sylvia Spencer
Yasuda, Robert
Yegul, Fikret Kutlu
Yenawine, Philip
Yoder, Janica
Yoshida, Ray Kakuo
Young, Charles Alexander
Young, Janie Chester
Young, Joseph E
Youritzin, Victor Koshkin
Yust, David E
Zabarsky, Melvin Joel
Zaborowski, Dennis J
Zakin, Mikhail
Zallinger, Jean Day
Zallinger, Rudolph Franz
Zemans, Joyce L
Zheutlin, Dale R
Ziemann, Richard Claude
Zimiles, Murray
Zona, Louis A
Zoretich, George Stephen
Zuhn, Cheryl

ENAMELIST

Bates, Kenneth Francis
Bennett, Jamie
Butt, Harlan W
Caster, Bernard Harry
Conte, Jeanne Larner
Greenfield, Joan Beatrice
Killmaster, John H
Kristensen, Gail Marie
Malenda, James William
Perkins, A Alan
Rooke, Fay Lorraine
Schwarcz, June Theresa
Sheehe, Lillian Carolyn
Sundberg, Carl Gustave
Weiss, Dick J
Whitcomb, Kay

ENVIRONMENTAL ARTIST

Alhilali, Neda
Anderson, Kenneth Edmund
Bard, Gayle
Bender, Beverly Sterl
Berkowitz, Terry
Bolt, Ron
Burgess, David Lowry
Cheng, Carl F K, AKA John Doe Co
Clark, Emery Ann
Creps, Gerald A
Crist, William Gary
Crivelli, Elaine
Culbertson, Janet Lynn (Mrs Douglas Kaften)
Delgyer, Leslie
Denes, Agnes
De Ricco, Hank
Dignac, Geny
Dorosh, Daria
Earls, Paul
Escobedo, Helen
Fekner, John
Fleischner, Richard Hugh
Floyd, Carl Leo
Fontana, Bill Patrick
Fredman, Faiya R
Gellis, Sandy L
Gianakos, Cristos
Glovsky, Alan
Goldring, Elizabeth
Graham, Daniel H
Greenly, Colin
Grygutis, Barbara
Gussow, Roy
Harding, Noel Robert
Harrison, Helen Mayer (Mrs Newton Harrison)
Harrison, Newton A
Haskell, Jane
Hendricks, Geoffrey
Henes, Donna
Hera
Hudson, Jon Barlow
Hutchinson, Peter Arthur
Irwin, Robert
Janney, Christopher Draper
Johanson, Patricia
Johnson, Martin Brian
Kahn, Ned M
Kasuba, Aleksandra
Kirschenbaum, Bernard Edwin
Knowles, Alison
Kyra,
Langford, Sherry K
Leicester, Andrew John
Leighton, Patricia MacInnes
Lewenz, Lisa
Lutz, Winifred Ann
Macaulay, Thomas S
MacDonald, Betty Ann
McMillen, Michael C(halmers)
Maisel, David
Maler, M Leopoldo Mario
Marioni, Tom
Mark, Phyllis
Mason, Molly Ann
Mastrangelo, Bobbi
Maxwell, William Jackson
Medel, Rebecca Rosalie
Murch, Anna Valentina
Niedzialek, Terry
Niese, Henry Ernst
Norvell, Patsy
Notarbartolo, Albert
Parton, Niké
Pinto, Jody
Poleskie, Stephen Francis
Prent, Mark
Price, Joan Webster
Roloff, John Scott
Rophar,
Ross, Charles
Rumsey, David MacIver
Salomon, Lawrence
Sasaki, Toshio
Sebastian, Jill C
Sky, Alison
Snyder, Kit-Yin
Soffer, Sasson
Sonfist, Alan
Stuhl, Michelle
Sumner, George
Talbert, Richard Harrison
Taper, Geri
Taradash, Meryl
Thacher, Anita
Thea, Carolee B
Turrell, James Archie
Ukeles, Mierle Laderman
Van Harlingen, Jean (Ann)
Vesna, Victoria
Werner, Frank Robert
Whiten, Tim
Winkler, Michael
Woody, (Thomas) Howard
Zimmerman, Elyn

FILMMAKER

Aldana, Carl
Almond, Paul
Appleby, Daniel Bart
Auer, James Matthew
Bates, Leo James
Beckman, Ericka
Blair, Lee Everett
Blechman, R O
Brakhage, James Stanley
Breer, Robert C
Burckhardt, Rudy
Cheng, Fu-Ding
Clifton, Michelle Gamm
Culhane, Shamus H
Dunn, Cal
Edelheit, Martha
Elder, R Bruce
Faccinto, Victor Paul
Frazer, John Thatcher
Gekiere, Madeleine
Geniusz, Robert Myles
Gerstein, David Steven
Golden, Eunice
Goldstein, Jack
Gould, John Howard
Greenfield, Amy
Haar, Francis
Haar, Tom
Hay, George Austin
Henderson, Mike
Henle, Fritz
Herbert, James Arthur
Hobbs, (Carl) Fredric
Holt, Nancy Louise
Huot, Robert
Iimura, Takahiko
Jarvis, Lucy
Johnson, Rodell C
Kagemoto, Haro
Katz, Leandro
Kleckner, Susan
Knecht, John
Lack, Stephen
Levitt, Helen
Liebling, Jerome
Lipzin, Janis Crystal
McCall, Anthony
Mallory, Margaret
Mangolte, Babette M
Maraldo, Ushanna F
Monk, Meredith
Monory, Jacques
Newton, Richard Edward
Niblock, Phill
Nowytski, (Slavko) Sviatoslav
O'Connell, Kenneth Robert
Padula, Fred David
Phillips, Robert J
Pitt, Suzan (Lee)
Ravett, Abraham
Robbins, LeRoy (Southward)
Rubinfien, Leo H
Ruscha, Edward Joseph
Schneemann, Carolee
Schwartz, Lillian (Feldman)
Sharits, Paul Jeffrey
Silver, Shelly Andrea
Snow, Michael
Sonneman, Eve
Thacher, Anita
Tilley, Lewis Lee
Wallace, Patty A
Waters, Jack
Wechsler, Judith Glatzer

FILMMAKER (cont)
Wieland, Joyce

GALLERY DIRECTOR
see also **Museum Director**

Alinder, James Gilbert
Amaltitano, Lelia
Ayers, Carol Lee
Baldwin, Russell W
Bartlett, Christopher E
Bergen, Sidney L
Berggruen, John Henry
Braig, Betty Lou
Brooks, Harry A
Brown, Constance George
Brown, Suzanne Goldman
Bryant, Linda Goode
Buecker, Robert
Bujese, Arlene
Burks, Myrna R
Butts, H Daniel, III
Cannuli, Richard Gerald
Castano, Elvira
Cathcart, Linda Louise
Christensen, Val Alan
Clark-Langager, Sarah Ann
Cloud, Jack L
Cocker, Barbara Joan
Cohan, Zara R
Cohen, Mildred Thaler
Colina, Armando G
Conley, Zeb Bristol, Jr
Cooper, Rhonda H
Costley-Jacobs, Averille Esther
Crandall, Judith Ann
Crane, Bonnie L
Crum, Katherine B
Cumming, Glen Edward
Davis, Kimberly Brooke
Dawson, Bess Phipps
DeFazio, Teresa Galligan
Desmett, Don
Dorfman, Fred
Drummer, William Richard
Elkin, Beverly Dawn
Esman, Rosa
Farber, Deborah
Fear, Daniel E
Felker, David Larry
Felsen, Rosamund
Ferris, Daniel B
Fink, Joanna Elizabeth
Fischer, Victor
Fiterman, Dolly
Flood, Richard Sidney
Frankel, Dextra
Frumkin, Allan
Fuller, Jeffrey P
Garcia, Frank
Gear, Josephine
Goffman, Judy
Goldsmith, Benedict Isaac
Gonzalez, Mauricio Martinez
Gorney, Jay Philip
Grandee, Joe Ruiz
Hanley, Jack
Hansen, Sarah Eveleth (Campbell)
Hardy, Robert
Harmon, Foster
Heaton, Janet N
Hedberg, Gregory Scott
Hilgeman, Liese
Hodge, Dorothy W (Scottie)
Holcombe, Anna Calluori
Holmes, Willard
Holt, Louise
Houk, Edwynn L
Howell, Elizabeth (Mitch) Coon
Hutchins, Robin
Hutchinson, Max
Isaacson, Ronald G
Johnson, Diana L
Jordan, Vance
Kawecki, Jean Mary
Kearney, Lynn Haigh
Kelley, Donald Castell
Kelly, Cynthia Ference
Kidrick, Valerie Anne
Killeen, Melissa Helen
Klobe, Tom
Langman, Richard Theodore
Levy, S(tephen) Dean
Lewis, Louise Miller
Lippman, Judith
Lippmann, Janet Gurian
Lurie, Sheldon M
McAllister, Geraldine E
McClain, Robert Lee
McIlvain, Frances H
McManus, James William
Mano, Toru
Martin, Mary Finch
Mayo, Pamela Elizabeth
Miller, Laurence Glenn
Moody, Elizabeth C
Moore, Bridget Liane
Muller, Helen B
Newman, Walter Andrews, Jr
Nordland, Gerald John
Nye, Molly Harding
Ohlau, Juergen Uwe
Outland, Wendy Helen
Palmer, Meredith Ann
Patnode, J Scott
Peluso, Marta E
Perlow, Katharina Rich
Pfeifer, Marcuse
Phillips, Dutch (James O), Jr
Poole, Nancy Geddes
Posner, Helaine J
Richards, Tally
Rindge, Debora Anne
Ropp, Ann L
Ross, Sheldon
Rotenberg, Judi
Rothman, Sidney
Rowand, Joseph Donn
Ruttinger, Jacquelyn
Schusterman, Gerrie Marva
Schweitzer, M R
Shainman, Jack S
Simor, Suzanna B
Sims, Peter Andrew
Sindelir, Robert John
Smith, B J
Smith, Gary
Sorkin, Emily
Spratt, Frederick R
Sragow, Ellen
Steel, Virginia Oberlin
Stirratt, Betsy (Elizabeth Anne)
Stooker, Hendrik Cornelis
Sujo, Clara Diament
Sussman, Bonnie K
Sussman, Jill
Swain, Robert Francis
Tasende, Jose Maria
Tatistcheff, Peter Alexis
Thurmer, Robert
Tunis, Roslyn
Vanderlip, Dianne Perry
Vizner, Nikola
Waaland, James Brearley, II
Waller, Susan
Warren, Katherine Virginia (Diage)
Weber, John
Weinzapfel, Connie A
Wilkins, David George
Williams, Cynthia Lee
Williams, Richard Eldon
Wilson, Robert Alan
Wise, Takouhy
Wortz, Melinda Farris
Yaneff, Chris
Yezerski, Howard J
York, Richard Travis

GLASS BLOWER

Bernstein, William Joseph
Blomdahl, Sonja
Brejcha, Vernon Lee
Carlson, Robert Michael
Carlson, William D
Chihuly, Dale Patrick
Clark, Jon Frederic
D'Onofrio, Bernard Michael
Handler, Audrey
Harmon, James Roderick
Hurlstone, Robert William
Ipsen, Kent Forrest
Kehlmann, Robert
Lewis, John Conard
McIlvane, Edward James
Magdanz, Andrew R
Marioni, Paul
Moore, Benjamin Powell
Mulcahy, Kathleen
Myers, Joel Philip
Nickerson, John Henry
Nygren, John Fergus
Ohno, Mitsugi
Pappenheimer, Will D
Rhodes, James Melvin
Ruffner, Ginny Martin
Warehall, William Donald

GOLDSMITH

Anderson, Bruce A
Baldridge, Mark S
Betteridge, Lois Etherington
Brauer, Connie Ann
Edwards, Linda (Linda Margaret Weiss Edwards)
Enriquez, Gaspar
Flynn, Pat L
Gabriel, Hannelore
Getty, Nilda Fernandez
Grissom, Freda Gill
Hirsh, Annette Marie
J J (De La Verriére)
Kretsinger, Mary Amelia
Kuehnl, Claudia Ann
Lechtzin, Stanley
Loyd, Jan Brooks
Noffke, Gary L
Paley, Albert Raymond
Pimentel, David Delbert
Renk, Merry
Satterfield, John Edward
Seppa, Heikki Markus
Van Duinwyk, George Paul
Wegner, Nadene R

GRAPHIC ARTIST

Abramson, Elaine Sandra
Albers, Anni
Altwerger, Libby
Amatniek, Sara
Anderson, Warren Harold
Arias-Misson, Alain
Barbee, Robert Thomas
Baskin, Leonard
Beachum, Sharon Garrison
Becker, Bettie (Bettie Geraldine Wathall)
Belag, Andrea
Bennett, John M
Benny, Sandra
Berger, Oscar
Berry, William Augustus
Bigelow, Anita (Anne Edwige Lourie)
Boyd, Michael
Brainard, Joe
Bressi, Betty
Brown, James
Bruni, Umberto
Byers, Fleur
Byrne, Charles Joseph
Cantor, Mira
Capes, Richard Edward
Catlett, Elizabeth
Chaikin, Alyce
Chesley, Paul Alexander
Chwast, Seymour
Clement, Kathleen (Ruth)
Cohen, Arthur Morris
Cohen, Reina Joyce
Colker, Edward
Colman, Virginia O'Connell
Conner, Bruce
Costello, Cynthia Ann
Creech, Franklin Underwood
D'Almeida, George
Darboven, Hanne
Daub, Matthew Forrest
David, Cyril Frank
Davis, Meredith J
Dedini, Eldon Lawrence
Dee, Leo Joseph
Diamond, Jessica
Dixson, Wendy Fay
Domjan, Joseph (Spiri)
Donneson, Seena
Dorn, Peter Klaus
Dorst, Mary Crowe
Dyer, M Wayne
Ebsen, Alf K
Elloian, Peter
Erickson, Joy M
Essley, Roger Holmer
Federe, Marion
Fenn, (Frances) Elizabeth
Fluek, Toby
Foley, Dorothy Swartz
Frasconi, Antonio
Freeman, David L
Fromentin, Christine Anne
Galinsky, Norman
Gaudard, Pierre
Geerlings, Gerald Kenneth
Gentry, Herbert
Gluhman, Joseph Walter
Gluhman, Margaret A
Goldsmith, Elsa M
Goldszer, Bath-Sheba
Gorman, William D
Gorski, Richard Kenny
Gough, Robert Alan
Hart, Betty Miller
Haut, Claire (Joan)
Hein, Max
Herman, Alan David
Hill, J Tweed
Hillman, Arthur Stanley
Hilty, Thomas R
Himmelfarb, John David
Hios, Theo
Hirschfeld, Albert
Horwitz, Channa
Hudson, Jacqueline
Hueter, James Warren
Humphrey, Judy Lucille
Hyde, Alice Bach
Ipousteguy, (Jean Robert)
Jackson, Sarah
Janschka, Fritz
Johnson, (L) Diane
Johnson, James Edwin
Jones, Frederick
Kahn, Peter
Kaiser, Charles James
Kash, Marie (Marie Kash Weltzheimer)
Katsoulidis, Panagiotis
Kelly, Robert James
Kniffin, Ralph Gus
Knipscher, Gerard Allen
Kuehn, Gary
Kuhn, Audrey Grendahl
LaCom, Wayne Carl
Lawton, Nancy
Lea, Laurie Jane
Lebron, Michael A

GRAPHIC ARTIST (cont)
Liccione, Alexander
Li Marzi, Joseph
Link, Phyllida K
Lobello, Peter
London, Anna
McHam, Sarah Blake Wilk
McMullan, James Burroughs
Magee, Alderson
Maggs, Arnaud (Cyril Benvenuti)
Mandel, Dorothy
Marander, Carol Jean
Martin, Dianne L
Massey, Ann James
Maxim, David Nicholas
Mayer, Rosemary
Moore, Wayland D
Morton, Richard H
Moser, Barry
Murphy, Dudley C
Napoles, Veronica Kleeman
Nelson, Jack D
Noda, Takayo
Nofer, Frank
Nowack, Wayne Kenyon
Nutzle, Futzie (Bruce John Kleinsmith)
O'Meallie, Kitty (Kate Chamness Johnson)
O'Neal, Roland Lenard
Orens, Elaine Frances
Orr, Arthur (Leslie)
Ortlieb, Robert Eugene
Osborn, Kevin Russell
Parker, Will (William Crawford)
Pattison, Billy Dee
Perry, Kathryn Powers
Peter, Friedrich Gunther
Pettibone, John Wolcott
Phillips, Helen (Elizabeth)
Pierre-Noel, Vergniaud
Place, Bradley Eugene
Plochmann, Carolyn Gassan
Popkin, Elsie Dinsmore
Popovac, Gwynn
Post, Anne B
Reibel, Bertram
Rioux (de Messimy), Deena (Coty) des
Risbeck, Philip Edward
Robertson, Joan E (Joan Elizabeth Mitchell)
Rosenberg, Marilyn R
Ross, Jaime
Sapien, Darryl Rudolph
Schachter, Justine Ranson
Schiller, Beatrice
Shaw, Isabel
Shoulberg, Harry
Simionov, Alexandru
Simmons, Cleda Marie
Slatton, Ralph David
Smith, Elizabeth
Smith, Gregg Sherwood
Sorokin, Janet
Sougstad, Mike
Spurling, Norine M
Squires, Gerald Leopold
Stamelos, Electra Georgia Mousmoules
Steinworth, Skip (William Eugene Jr)
Sternberg, Harry
Stromsdorfer, Deborah Ann
Suttenfield, Diana
Swensen, J(ean) Mary Jeanette Hamilton
Thollander, Earl
Tonelli, Edith Ann
Trachtenberg, Gloria P
Travanti, Leon Emidio
Turconi, Sue (Susan) Kinder
Turner, Ralph James
Vallee, William Oscar
Wilson, Robert
Wilson, Sybil
Windell, Violet Bruner
Wise, Gerald Lee
Wolanic, Susan Seseske
Wong, Frederick
Wright, Bernard
Zisla, Harold

HISTORIAN

Ackerman, Gerald Martin
Ackerman, James S
Adams, Clinton
Agee, William C
Ahrens, Kent
Alexander, Margaret Ames
Allen, (Harvey) Harold
Allen, William J
Allentuck, Marcia Epstein
Allgood, Charles Henry
Alvarez-Cervela, Jose Maria
Amend, Eugene Michael
Andersen, Wayne Vesti
Anderson, Ross Cornelius
Andres, Glenn Merle
Ansell, Joseph Paul
Appelhof, Dr Ruth A
Arbitman, Kahren J
Arellanes, Audrey Spencer
Asher, Frederick M
Auping, Michael Graham
Ayres, Larry Marshall
Baas, Jacquelynn
Ball, Susan L
Ballinger, James K
Barnett, Vivian Endicott
Barnhill, Georgia Brady
Barons, Richard Irwin
Barrie, Dennis Ray
Barrio-Garay, Jose Luis
Barr-Sharrar, Beryl
Barter, Judith A
Barton, Phyllis Settecase
Bassin, Joan
Beatty, Frances Fielding Lewis
Beck, James
Becker, Johanna Lucille
Begley, Wayne E
Belian, Garabed
Bell, Philip Michael
Beman, Lynn Susan
Benjamin, Lloyd William, III
Benson, Elizabeth Polk
Berger, Maurice
Bergman, Robert P
Berman, Greta W
Bermingham, Ann
Bernstein, Saralinda
Bershad, David L
Bertman, Stephen
Bettmann, Otto Ludwig
Blackmun, Barbara Winston
Blakeney, Rae
Bledsoe, Jane Kathryn
Bogart, Michele Helene
Boggs, Jean Sutherland
Bohan, Ruth L
Bohen, Barbara E
Bolton-Smith, Robin Lee
Bony, Jean Victor
Bordeaux, Jean Luc
Bothmer, Bernard V
Bowlt, John
Bowman, Ruth
Bowne, James DeHart
Bowron, Edgar Peters
Boyle, Richard J
Brandt, Kathleen Weil-Garris
Bravmann, Rene A
Breithaupt, Erwin M
Briggs, Peter S
Brinkerhoff, Dericksen Morgan
Broadley, Hugh T
Broder, Patricia Janis
Brooks, H(arold) Allen
Broude, Norma Freedman
Brown, Charlotte Vestal
Brown, David Alan
Brown, Jonathan
Brown, Milton Wolf
Bruno, Vincent J
Bucher, Francois
Buck, Robert Treat, Jr
Buerger, Janet E
Buitron-Oliver, Diana
Burdock, Harriet
Burnett, David Grant
Burrows, Selig S
Bush, Donald John
Bush, Martin H
Butera, Virginia Fabbri
Byrnes, James Bernard
Cafritz, Robert Conrad
Cahill, James Francis
Caldwell, Benjamin Hubbard, Jr
Caldwell, Martha Belle
Caldwell, Susan Havens
Calkins, Robert G
Camfield, William Arnett
Canby, Jeanny Vorys
Carmean, E A, Jr
Carr, Carolyn K
Castano, Elvira
Castleman, Riva
Cate, Barbara Kaufman
Cate, Phillip Dennis
Cathcart, Linda Louise
Cavaliere, Barbara
Chadwick, Whitney
Chambers, Bruce William
Chambers, Karen
Chappell, Miles Linwood
Cheney, Liana De Girolami
Chiarenza, Carl
Chow Chian-Chiu,
Cikovsky, Nicolai, Jr
Clark, Carol
Clark, Garth Reginald
Clark, Vicky A
Clark, William W
Clarke, John R
Clayson, S Hollis
Cleaver, Dale Gordon
Clisby, Roger David
Coates, Ross Alexander
Codell, Julie Francia
Cohen, Charles E
Cohen, Joan Lebold
Cohn, Marjorie B
Colantuono, Anthony
Cole, Bruce
Cole, Harold David
Cole, Herbert Milton
Collins, Christiane C
Collins, George R
Collins, Howard F
Colpitt, Frances
Colton, Judith
Comini, Alessandra
Conforti, Michael Peter
Conlon, James Edward
Constantine, Mildred
Coolidge, John
Corbin, George Allen
Cormack, Malcolm
Corn, Wanda M
Cotter, Holland
Covell, Alan Carter
Covi, Dario A
Cox, Richard William
Crandall, Jerry C
Crary, Jonathan Knight
Craven, Wayne
Crelly, William Richard
Crimp, Douglas
Cropper, M Elizabeth
Cuttler, Charles David
Czach, Marie
Czuma, Stanislaw J
Dale, William Scott Abell
Danly, Susan
Darling, Sharon Sandling
Davey, Ronald A
Davidson, Abraham A
Davies, Hugh Marlais
Davis, Ellen N
Davis, Keith Frederic
Davis, Marian B
Dawdy, Doris Ostrander
Dee, Elaine Evans
Del Chiaro, Mario A
Delehanty, Suzanne E
De Moura Sobral, Luis
Denker, Susan A
De Puma, Richard Daniel
Desportes, Ulysse Gandvier
D'Harnoncourt, Anne
Dillow, Nancy E (Nancy Elizabeth Robertson)
Dinhofer, Shelly Mehlman
Dinnerstein, Lois
Dobard, Raymond Gerard
Dockstader, Frederick J
Domit, Moussa M
Donnelly, Marian Card
Donohoe, Victoria
Dorra, Henri
Dorsky, Morris
Doumato, Lamia
Dow, Helen Jeannette
Drewal, Henry John
Driscoll, John Paul
Dunkelman, Martha Levine
Dunn, Roger Terry
Dunow, Esti
Dwyer, Eugene Joseph
Earle, Edward W
Eckert, William Dean
Eckhardt, Ferdinand
Edelstein, Teri J
Edwards, Susan Harris
Ehresmann, Donald Louis
Ehrlich, George
Eidelberg, Martin
Eisenberg, Marvin
Eitner, Lorenz E A
Elderfield, John
Eldredge, Charles Child, III
Eliasoph, Philip
Elsen, Albert Edward
Emerick, Judson J
Enggass, Robert
Enyeart, James Lyle
Ernstrom, Adele Mansfield
Ertman, Earl Leslie
Esau, Erika
Esser, Janet Brody
Evans, Bruce Haselton
Evans, Grose
Fagaly, William Arthur
Fahlman, Betsy Lee
Faison, Samson Lane, Jr
Faris, Peter Kinzie
Farmer, John David
Farwell, Beatrice
Fehl, Philipp P
Feinstein, Roni
Ferber, Linda S
Field, Richard Sampson
Fiero, Gloria K
Fink, Lois Marie
Finley, Gerald Eric
Firestone, Evan R
Fischer, Henry George
Flam, Jack D
Fleischer, Roland Edward
Fletcher, Valerie J
Flexner, James Thomas
Flint, Janet Altic
Flomenhaft, Eleanor
Folda, Jaroslav (Thayer), III
Foley, Kathy Kelsey
Forbes, John Allison
Forsyth, Ilene H(aering)
Foster, Stephen C
Fowle, Geraldine Elizabeth
Frackman, Noel
Freedberg, Sydney Joseph

HISTORIAN (cont)
Frinta, Mojmir Svatopluk
Fuller, John Charles
Fulton, Fred Franklin
Fusco, Laurie S
Fusco, Peter Richard
Gaines, William Robert
Gaither, Edmund B
Gamwell, Lynn
Garcia, Frank
Garnsey, Clarke Henderson
Garrard, Mary DuBose
Garrigues, Suzanne
Gatling, Eva Ingersoll
Gauthier, Ninon
Gealt, Adelheid Medicus
Gear, Josephine
Gebhard, David
Gerdts, Abigail Booth
Gerdts, William H
Giacalone, Vito
Gilbert, Creighton Eddy
Gladstone, Barbara
Glaser, Bruce
Glasgow, Vaughn Leslie
Glass, Dorothy F
Gluhman, Joseph Walter
Goheen, Ellen Rozanne
Goldberg, RoseLee
Goldstein, Carl
Goler, Robert
Goley, Mary Anne
Goodman, Helen
Goodstein-Shapiro, F
Goodyear, Frank H, Jr
Gottlieb, Carla
Gould, Philip
Gouma-Peterson, Thalia
Gowans, Alan
Green, Roger J
Grieder, Terence
Grissom, Eugene Edward
Grossman, Sheldon
Grove, Samuel Harold
Growdon, Marcia Cohn
Gruber, J Richard
Guenther, Peter W
Guilmain, Jacques
Gully, Anthony Lacy
Gunasinghe, Siri
Gundersheimer, Herman (Samuel)
Gurney, George
Gutmann, Joseph
Hager, Hellmut W
Hagman, Jean Cassels
Halasz, Piri
Hallam, John S
Hamilton, W Paul C
Hammond, Leslie King
Hand, John Oliver
Hanson, Anne Coffin
Harris, Ann Sutherland
Hartigan, Lynda Roscoe
Haskell, Barbara
Hassrick, Peter H
Hatch, John Davis
Havelock, Christine Mitchell
Hawes, Louis
Hay, A John
Hayes, Laura M
Hayward, Jane
Hazlehurst, Franklin Hamilton
Hearn, M F (Millard Fillmore), Jr
Heckscher, William Sebastian
Heller, Reinhold August
Henderson, Linda Dalrymple
Henning, Edward Burk
Henry, Sara Corrington
Herbert, Robert L
Hero, Peter deCourcy
Hersey, George Leonard
Hertzman, Gay Mahaffy
Heyman, Therese Thau
Hill, Draper
Hill, William Mansfield
Hills, Patricia
Hinson, Tom Everett
Hobbs, Robert Carleton
Holladay, Harlan H
Holm, Bill
Homer, William Innes
Hood, Walter Kelly
Houser, Caroline Mae
Howarth, Shirley Reiff
Howat, John Keith
Howett, John
Howland, Richard Hubbard
Howlett, D(onald) Roger
Huchel, Frederick M
Hudson, Ralph Magee
Hulick, Diana Emery
Hungerford, Constance Cain
Hunisak, John Michael
Hunter, Sam
Hutchison, Jane Campbell
Hyman, Isabelle
Hyman, Linda
Isaacson, Gene Lester
Isserstedt, Dorothea Carus
Ivers, Louise H
Jackson, Marion Elizabeth
Jacob, Mary Jane
Jacobsen, Michael A
Jacobus, John M
Jaffe, Irma B
Janis, Eugenia Parry
Janson, Anthony Fredrick
Jay, Bill
Jenkins, Donald John
Johnson, Antoinette Spanos
Johnson, Charles W, Jr
Johnson, Diane Chalmers
Johnson, Donald Ray
Johnson, Eugene Joseph
Johnson, Ronald W
Johnson, Selina (Tetzlaff)
Johnston, Roy E
Johnston, William Ralph
Jonaitis, Aldona
Jones, Lois Swan
Joost-Gaugier, Christiane L
Jordan, George Edwin
Jordan, William B
Joyner, John Brooks
Judson, William D
Judson-Rhodes, Pamela
Kagan, Andrew Aaron
Kahan, Mitchell Douglas
Kan, Michael
Kaplan, Julius David
Karlstrom, Paul Johnson
Kelder, Diane M
Kelemen, Pal
Kelly, Franklin Wood
Kimbrell, Leonard Buell
King, Elaine A
Kinsman, Robert Donald
Kirkpatrick, Diane
Kitao, T Kaori
Kitzinger, Ernst
Klein, Cecelia F
Klein, Michael Eugene
Kleinbauer, W Eugene
Klitzke, Theodore Elmer
Kloss, WIlliam
Knox, George
Koch, Robert
Kornetchuk, Elena
Korshak, Yvonne
Kotik, Charlotta
Kovinick, Philip Peter
Krane, Susan
Krauss, Rosalind E
Krinsky, Carol Herselle
Kubler, George Alexander
Kultermann, Udo
Kurtz, Bruce D
Kuspit, Donald Burton
Kuwayama, George
Lader, Melvin Paul
Landis, Ellen Jamie
Lane, John Rodger
Langer, Sandra Lois (Cassandra)
Larsen, Susan C
Laskin, Myron, Jr
Lauf, Cornelia
Lavin, Irving
Lavin, Marilyn Aronberg
Lawall, David Barnard
Lawton, Thomas
Lee, Briant Hamor
Lehman, Arnold L
Lemon, Robert S, Jr
Lengyel, Alfonz
Lerman, Leo
Lerner, Martin
Lesko, Diane
Levin, Gail
Levitt, Alfred
Levy, David Corcos
Levy, Mark
Lewis, Douglas
Lewis, Samella Sanders
Lewis, Virginia Elnora
Li, Chu-Tsing
Lilyquist, Christine
Lindsay, Kenneth C
Lipton, Leah
Locke, Michelle Wilson
Long, Rose-Carol Washton
Longstreet, Stephen
Love, Richard Henry
Lovell, Margaretta Markle
Lowenthal, Constance
Lowry, Bates
Luchs, Alison
Ludmer, Joyce Pellerano
Ludwig, Allan I
Luebbers, Leslie Laird
Lunde, Karl Roy
Lunsford, John (Crawford)
Lyman, Thomas William
Lyons, Lisa
MacDonald, Bruce K
MacDonald, Robert R
MacDonald, William L
McGill, Forrest
McGough, Stephen C
Mack, Charles Randall
McKenzie, Allan Dean
McNally, Sheila John
McNamara, Mary Jo
Madden-Work, Betty I
Maddox, Jerald Curtis
Maguire, Henry Pownall
Mahoney, Michael R T
Mallory, Nina Ayala
Mann, Maybelle
Markle, Greer (Walter Greer Markle)
Markman, Sidney David
Marlor, Clark Strang
Marrow, James Henry
Marshall, Richard Donald
Marter, Joan
Martin, John Rupert
Martin, Richard (Harrison)
Marzio, Peter Cort
Masheck, Joseph Daniel Cahill
Mathews, Nancy Mowll
Maurer, Evan Maclyn
Meggs, Philip B
Meisel, Louis Koenig
Meister, Mark J
Meister, Michael William
Merkel, Jayne (Silverstein)
Messer, Thomas M
Meyer, Charles Edward
Meyer, Jerry Don
Meyer, Ruth Krueger
Michels, Eileen Manning
Mickenberg, David
Miles, Ellen Gross
Miller, Arthur Green
Miller, Jean Johnston
Moeller, Robert Charles, III
Moffitt, John Francis
Moir, Alfred
Mongan, Agnes
Moore, Peter
Morganstern, Anne McGee
Morganstern, James
Morishita, Joyce Chizuko
Morrin, Peter Patrick
Morse, Peter
Mosby, Dewey Franklin
Moser, Joann
Moss, Jacqueline
Moss, Tobey C
Moulton, Susan Gene
Mount, Marshall Ward
Moxey, Patricio Keith Fleming
Mozley, Anita Ventura
Muhlert, Jan Keene
Muller, Priscilla Elkow
Munsterberg, Hugo
Myers, Terry R
Myron, Robert
Naeve, Milo M
Nasgaard, Roald
Nash, Steven Alan
Natzmer, Cheryl Lynn
Naumann, Francis M
Nees, Lawrence
Neff, John Hallmark
Nelson, Jon Allen
Nochlin, Linda (Pommer)
Nold, Carl R
Norris, Andrea Spaulding
Norton, Paul Foote
Novak, Barbara (Mrs Brian O'Doherty)
Nyerges, Alexander Lee
O'Connor, Francis Valentine
O'Connor, Stanley James
Olin, Ferris
Olpin, Robert Spencer
Olson, Roberta Jeanne Marie
Onorato, Ronald Joseph
Orenstein, Gloria Feman
Orr-Cahall, Anona Christina
Overland, Carlton Edward
Page, Jean Jepson
Paikowsky, Sandra R
Pal, Pratapaditya
Parry, Ellwood Comly, III
Patrick, Darryl L
Pearman, Sara Jane
Peck, William Henry
Pendergraft, Norman Elveis
Pennington, Estill Curtis
Percy, Ann Buchanan
Perkins, Ann
Perlin, Ruth Rudolph
Perloff, Marjorie G
Perry, Regenia Alfreda
Pierce, Patricia Jobe
Pilgrim, Dianne Hauserman
Pincus, Robert L(awrence)
Pisano, Ronald George
Placzek, Adolf Kurt
Polcari, Stephen
Poling, Clark V
Pollitt, Jerome Jordan
Polzer, Joseph
Pontynen, Arthur
Poor, Robert John
Porada, Edith
Porter, Jeanne Chenault
Posner, Donald
Powell, Earl Alexander, III
Pressly, William Laurens
Preston, George Nelson
Preziosi, Donald A
Prokopoff, Stephen
Prown, Jules David
Pugh, Grace Huntley
Purtle, Carol Jean
Quinsac, Annie-Paule
Quirarte, Jacinto
Radan, George Tivadar
Radice, Anne-Imelda Marino
Radycki, J(osephine) Diane
Raggio, Olga
Raguin, Virginia C

HISTORIAN (cont)
Ragusa, Isa
Rand, Harry
Randall, Richard Harding, Jr
Rash, Nancy
Raven, Arlene
Reed, Cleota
Reed, Walt Arnold
Reese, Thomas Ford
Reeve, James Key
Reeves, James Franklin
Reff, Theodore
Reich, Sheldon
Reilly, Bernard Francis
Reilly, Richard
Rembert, Virginia Pitts
Rensch, Roslyn
Rhyne, Charles Sylvanus
Rice, Shelley Enid
Richardson, John Adkins
Rigby, Ida Katherine
Rindge, Debora Anne
Robb, David Metheny, Jr
Robbins, Daniel J
Roberson, Samuel Arndt
Robertson, E Bruce
Robinson, Duncan
Robinson, Franklin W
Robinson, Lilien Filipovitch
Rogers, Millard Foster, Jr
Rorex, Robert Albright
Rosand, David
Rose, Barbara
Rosen, James Mahlon
Rosenberg, Charles Michael
Rosenblum, Robert
Rosenthal, Donald A
Rosenthal, Earl Edgar
Rosenthal, Mark L
Rosenzweig, Daphne Lange
Roskill, Mark Wentworth
Rossen, Susan F
Roth, Leland M(artin)
Roth, Moira
Rowell, Margit
Rubin, William
Rudenstine, Angelica Zander
Russell, Helen Diane
Sachs, Samuel, II
Sanderson, Warren
Sandler, Irving Harry
Saunders, Richard Henry
Scarbrough, Cleve Knox, Jr
Schaefer, Scott Jay
Schapiro, Meyer
Schimansky, Donya Dobrila
Schipper, Merle Solway
Schmandt-Besserat, Denise
Schmitt, Marilyn Low
Schneiderman, Richard S
Schnorrenberg, John Martin
Schuller, Nancy Shelby
Schultz, John Bernard
Schulz, Anne Markham
Schulz, Juergen
Schuster, Eugene Ivan
Schwartz, Marvin D
Schweizer, Paul Douglas
Scott, David Winfield
Scott, John Beldon
Scott, John Fredrik
Scribner, Charles, III
Segger, Martin Joseph
Selvig, Forrest Hall
Selz, Peter H
Semowich, Charles John
Senie, Harriet
Serenyi, Peter
Sewell, Darrel L
Shangraw, Clarence Frank
Shaw, Courtney Ann
Shaw, Joseph Winterbotham
Shaw, Nancy (Rivard)
Sheard, Wendy Stedman
Sheon, Aaron
Shepard, Lewis Albert
Sheppard, Carl Dunkle
Sherman, Claire Richter
Shestack, Alan
Shimizu, Yoshiaki
Sieber, Roy
Silver, Larry Arnold
Simmons, Gary Paul
Simmons, John Herbert
Simon, David L
Simon, Robert Barry
Simpson, Marianna Shreve
Simpson, William Kelly
Sims, Lowery Stokes
Sims, Peter Andrew
Slatkes, Leonard J
Slatkin, Wendy
Slive, Seymour
Sloane, Joseph Curtis
Smith, Elliot Steven
Smith, Frances Kathleen
Smith, Graham
Smith, J Weldon
Smith, James Morton
Smyth, Craig Hugh
Sokol, David Martin
Sommer, Frank H, III
Sorell, Victor Alexander
Spangenberg, Kristin L
Spector, Jack J
Spencer, Harold Edwin
Spencer, John R
Sponenburgh, Mark
Sprague, Paul Edward
Spurlock, William
Stahl, Alan M
Stamm, Geoffrey Eaton
Standen, Edith Appleton
Stanford, Linda Oliphant
Stebbins, Theodore Ellis, Jr
Stein, Judith Ellen
Stein, Roger Breed
Steinberg, Leo
Stevens, Andrew Rich
Stewart, J(ohn) Douglas
Stewart, Robert Gordon
Stillman, Damie
Stokstad, Marilyn
Stones, Margaret Alison
Stott, Deborah
Strickler, Susan Elizabeth
Striker, Cecil L
Stringer, Mary Evelyn
Sturgeon, Mary C
Sturges, Hollister
Sullivan, Scott A
Sunkel, Robert C
Sutton, Peter C
Swanson, Vern Grosvenor
Sweeney, J Gray
Taft, Frances Prindle
Takach, Mary H
Tancock, John Leon
Tannenbaum, Barbara Lee
Tarbell, Roberta Kupfrian
Tatham, David Frederic
Taylor, Hugh Holloway
Taylor, Kendall Frances
Taylor, Mary Cazort
Taylor, Rene Claude
Teilhet-Fisk, Jehanne Hildegarde
Theofiles, George
Thistlethwaite, Mark Edward
Tierney, Patrick Lennox
Timpano, Anne
Toker, Franklin
Tomasini, Wallace J
Tomko, George Peter
Topper, David R
Townsend, Gavin Edward
Townsend, J Benjamin
Townsend, Vera B
Trapp, Frank Anderson
Travis, David B
Trenton, Patricia Jean
Trutty-Coohill, Patricia
Tselos, Dimitri Theodore
Tseng Yu-ho
Tuchman, Phyllis
Turner, A Richard
Turnure, James Harvey
Tyler, Ron C
Van der Meulen, Jan
Vandersall, Amy L
Van Schaack, Eric
Vermeule, Cornelius Clarkson, III
Verostko, Roman Joseph
Vincent, Clare
Von Schmidt, Eric
Wahlman, Maude Southwell
Walford, E John
Walker, Mark Steven
Wallace, Richard William
Wallace, Robert Dan
Wallach, Alan
Waller, Aaron Bret
Walter, Elizabeth Mitchell
Ward, John Lawrence
Wark, Robert Rodger
Warner, Marina Sarah
Warren, Julianne Bussert Baker
Wasserman, Jack
Watrous, James Scales
Watson, Katharine Johnson
Wattenmaker, Richard J
Webb, Todd
Webster, Sally (Sara B)
Wechsler, Judith Glatzer
Weeks, Edward F (Ted)
Weidman, Jeffrey
Weisberg, Gabriel P
Weitzmann, Kurt
Welch, Stuart Cary
Weller, Allen Stuart
Werness, Hope B
West, Richard Vincent
Westervelt, Robert F
Westin, Robert H
Wharton, Annabel Jane
Wiebe, Charles M
Wiedenhoeft, Renate
Wiesendanger, Martin Wolfgang
Wilkins, David George
Williams, Benjamin Forrest
Williams, David Jon
Williams, John Alden
Williams, John Wesley
Willis, Elizabeth Bayley
Wilmerding, John
Wilson, Jean S
Wise, Suzanne Tanderup
Withers, Josephine
Wixom, William D
Wolanin, Barbara A
Wood, James Nowell
Wooden, Howard Edmund
Woolfenden, William Edward
Worth, Peter John
Worthen, Amy Namowitz
Wriston, Barbara
Wunder, Richard Paul
Yard, Sally Elizabeth
Yates, Hollye E
Youritzin, Victor Koshkin
Zafran, Eric Myles
Zemans, Joyce L
Zerner, Henri Thomas
Ziff, Jerrold
Zilczer, Judith Katy

ILLUMINATOR

Carrington, Joy Harrell
Cawein, Kathrin
Gast, Carolyn Bartlett (Lutz)
Gorny, A-P (Anthony-Peter)
Mueller, (Sister) M Gerardine OP
Werner Vaughn, Salle

ILLUSTRATOR

Abel, Ray
Aebi, Ernst Walter
Aliki
Anderson, Robert Alexander
Angulo, Chappie
Ariss, Herbert Joshua
Baker, Jill Withrow
Baldwin, Richard Wood
Ball, Lyle V
Barnes, Cliff (Clifford V)
Bartlett, Christopher E
Bennett, Rainey
Benney, Robert
Bertoni, Dante H
Bierly, Edward J
Bissell, Phil
Bittner, Hans Oskar
Blackburn, Loren Hayner
Blair, Helen
Blattner, Robert Henry
Blechman, R O
Bond, Oriel Edmund
Bowler, Joseph, Jr
Boyle, (James) Neil
Braiden, Rose Margaret J
Brown, Reynold
Buba, Joy Flinsch
Burchard, Peter Duncan
Byard, Carole Marie
Byrd, Robert John
Campbell, Dorothy Bostwick
Carter, Frederick Timmins
Cellini, Joseph
Chapman, Walter Howard
Charmatz, Bill (William Adolphe)
Christensen, Betty (Elizabeth)
Chwast, Seymour
Ciardiello, Joseph G
Cober, Alan E
Cortese, Edward Fortunato
Crawford, Bill (Wilbur Ogden)
Crite, Allan Rohan
Crosby, Ranice W
Cuevas, Jose Luis
Cunningham, Sue
Cusack, Margaret Weaver
D'Amato, Janet Potter
Dank, Leonard D
De Armond, Dale B
De Groat, Diane
Deloney, Jack Clouse
DePillars, Murry N
Desoto, Rafael M
Di Fate, Vincent
Dimson, Theo Aeneas
Dohanos, Stevan
Dowden, Anne Ophelia Todd
Duerwald, Carol
Dverin, Anatoly
Echohawk, Brummett
Egeli, Peter Even
Eisenstat, Benjamin
Ellis, Richard
Ely, Timothy Clyde
Etting, Emlen
Faragasso, Jack
Faudie, Fred
Ferris, (Carlisle) Keith
Flora, James Royer
Folkus, Dan (Daniel Alan Fredrickson)
Fortunato, Nancy
Fowler, Eric Nicholas
Freund, Harry Louis
Gallo, William Victor
Gast, Carolyn Bartlett (Lutz)
Gaydos, Tim (Timothy John)
Geisert, Arthur Frederick
Gilbert, Albert Earl
Ginsburg, Max
Glaser, Milton
Golbin, Andree
Gordon, Violet
Granstaff, William Boyd

ILLUSTRATOR (cont)
Guzman-Forbes, Robert
Haden, Eunice (Barnard)
Halliday, Nancy R
Handville, Robert T
Harris, Robert George
Hauptman, Susan
Haynes, George Edward
Haynes, R (Richard Thomas)
Healy, Deborah Ann
Heberling, Glen Austin
Herzberg, Thomas
Hildebrand, June Marianne
Hill, Joan (Chea-se-quah)
Hoffman, Martin
Hogarth, Burne
Itchkawich, David Michael
Jackson, Everett Gee
Jackson, Vaughn L
James, Bill (William Frederick)
Janelsins, Veronica
Kaplan, Frederic Clark
Kaufman, Joe
Kaufman, Stuart Martin
Keener, Polly Leonard
Kessler, Leonard H
Keveson, Florence
Kingman, Dong
Kiousis, Linda Weber
Knight, Jacob Jaskoviak
Knott, Dee D
Kocar, George Frederick
Kogan, Deborah
Koren, Edward B
Krigstein, Bernard
Kuczun, Ann-Marie
Kunstler, Morton
Laessig, Robert
L'Archeveque, Andre Robert
Lawrence, Rodney Steven
Lefranc, Margaret (Margaret Lefranc Schoonover)
Leon, Ralph Bernard
Loehle, Richard E
Loewer, Henry Peter
London, Alexander
Lovell, Tom
Lynde, Stan
Macaulay, David Alexander
McCall, Robert Theodore
McMillan, Constance
McMullan, James Burroughs
McVicker, Charles Taggart
Margules, Gabriele Ella
Marshall, Bruce
Matsubara, Naoko
Matternes, Jay Howard
Mays, Victor
Mellor, Mark Adams
Mihaesco, Eugene
Mina-Mora, Raul Jose
Mion, Pierre Riccardo
Mock, Richard Basil
Moose, Philip Anthony
Moose, Talmadge Bowers
Morgan, Maritza Leskovar
Mosley, Zack T
Norris, Leonard Matheson
Nowak, Leo
O'Neal, Roland Lenard
Osborn, Robert
Osyczka, Bohdan Danny
Pena, Amado Maurilio, Jr
Perlin, Bernard
Perrin, C Robert
Peterson, Roger Tory
Petrie, Ferdinand Ralph
Petro, Joseph (Victor), Jr
Phillips, Irving W
Pierce, Diane (Diane Pierce-Huxtable)
Pitcher, John Charles
Pomeroy, Mary Barnas (Mrs F G Pomeroy)
Pratt, Frances (Frances Elizabeth Usui)
Preede, Nydia
Quackenbush, Robert
Ramos, Theodore
Rauf, Barbara Claire
Reece, Maynard
Robbins, Trina
Rognan, Lloyd Norman
Rose, David
Ross, Joan M
Rutland, Lilli Ida
Sarnoff, Arthur Saron
Satorsky, Cyril
Schachter, Justine Ranson
Schiff, Jean
Schmidt, Frederick Louis
Schottland, M
Scott, John
Seiden, Arthur
Sendak, Maurice Bernard
Shechter, Ben-Zion
Shedd, George J
Shilson, Wayne Stuart
Siegel, (Leo) Dink
Silber, Maurice
Silverman, Burton Philip
Sloan, Richard
Smith, Harry William
Smith, Jos(eph) A(nthony)
Smith, Vernell Edward
Smyth, Ed
Sorel, Edward
Sottung, George (K)
Spagnolo, Kathleen Mary
Sparkman, Gene (Carl), Jr
Spohn, Franz Frederick
Stacy, John Russell
Stanford, Ginny C
Stark, Bruce Gunsten
Stavrinos, George Philip
Stein, Harve
Stermer, Dugald Robert
Stirnweis, Shannon
Storey, David
Stuart, Kenneth James
Suba, Susanne (Mrs Bertam Bloch)
Takashima, Shizuye Violet
Teters, J Charlene
Thollander, Earl
Thompson, Kenneth Webster
Thorpe, James George
Tiegreen, Alan F
Torbert, Stephanie Birch
Townsend, Marvin J
Trimm, H Wayne
Truby, Betsy Kirby
Tucker, Peri
Uram, Lauren Michelle
Van Winkelen, Barbara
Vargas, Josephine
Velasquez, Oscar
Vorwerk, E Charlsie
Wachsteter, George
Wald, Carol
Waterhouse, Charles Howard
Waterhouse, Russell Rutledge
Watson, Aldren A
Weller, Don Mighell
Wells, Betty Childs
Whitaker, William
Wilcox, Gordon Cumnock
Williams, Paul Alan
Wilwers, Edward Mathias
Wingate, Robert Bray
Wogstad, James Everet
Wright, Barton Allen
Yanow, Rhoda Mae
Youngblood, Nat
Zimmerman, William Harold
Zuckerberg, Stanley M

ILLUSTRATOR—CHILDREN'S BOOKS

Ames, Lee Judah
Amoss, Berthe
Anderson, Gunnar Donald
Barry, Robert E
Bock, William Sauts-Netamux'we
De Paola, Tomie
DesJarlait, Robert D
Fisher, Leonard Everett
Frankenberg, Robert Clinton
Garrison, Barbara
George, Sylvia James
Haley, Gail E
Ha-So-De (Narciso Abeyta)
Hull, Cathy
Ipcar, Dahlov
Johnson, Audean
Kessler, Leonard H
Lasker, Joe (Joseph L)
Lent, Blair
McCurdy, Michael Charles
Malone, Nola Langner
Negri, Rocco Antonio
Nesbitt, Ilse Buchert
Oechsli, Kelly
Otani, June
Parker, Nancy Winslow
Parry, Marian
Pinkney, Jerry
Poehlmann, JoAnna
Rosenberg, Jane
Savitt, Sam
Schoenherr, John (Carl)
Schweninger, Ann Rozzelle
Spier, Peter Edward
Swanson, Ray V
Taback, Simms
Teichman, Mary Melinda
Weihs, Erika
Weil, Lisl
Wexler, Jerome LeRoy
Williams, David Jon
Workman, Robert P
Zallinger, Jean Day

INSTRUCTOR
(Studio/Art School)

Abbrescia, Joeseph Leonard
Abish, Cecile
Abrams, Edith Lillian
Accetta, Suzanne Rusconi
Adelman, Dorothy (Lee) McClintock
Ahn, Don C
Amico, David Michael
Anderson, John S
Anderson, Lennart
Andry, Keith Anthony
Appel, Thelma
Arvin, Irmgard Pinckernell
Ashby, Carl
Askevold, David
Atlee, Emilie DeS
Ausby, Ellsworth Augustus
Avakian, John
Bailey, Barbara Ann
Barnes, Curt (Curtis Edward)
Barnett, Emily
Barrett, Thomas R
Barry, Anne Meredith
Batt, Miles Girard
Beauchamp, Robert
Becker, Natalie Rose
Beling, Helen
Bendell, Marilyn
Berg, Siri
Berge, Dorothy Alphena
Besant, Derek Michael
Bieber, Elinore Maria Korow
Blumberg, Barbara Griffiths
Bobrowicz, Yvonne Pacanovsky
Boeve, Edgar Gene
Bohnenkamp, Leslie George
Bordes, Adrienne
Bothmer, Bernard V
Briansky, Rita Prezament
Brooks, (John) Alan
Brotherton, Naomi
Brouillette, Al(bert C)
Brown, Marion B
Brumer, Shulamith
Brush, Leif
Bryans, John Armond
Burpee, James Stanley
Butter, Tom
Byrd, Robert John
Caddell, Foster
Cadillac, Louise Roman
Cady, Samuel Lincoln
Calrow, Robert F
Capes, Richard Edward
Caplan Ciarrochi, Sandra
Carlberg, Norman Kenneth
Cascieri, Arcangelo
Catalan, Edgardo Omar
Cattaneo, (Jacquelyn A) Kammerer
Chadbourn, Alfred Cheney
Chavez, Joseph Arnold
Cheek, Ronald Edward
Christensen, Larry R
Christensen, Sharlene
Christiana, Edward
Ciancio, June (Kirkpatrick)
Clark, Claude
Clark, Timothy John
Cleary, Barbara B
Cliff, Denis Antony
Clinton, Paul Arthur
Clutz, William
Coburn, Bette Lee
Cockrill, Sherna
Coggins, Jack Banham
Cogswell, Margaret Price
Cohen, Lynne G
Cokendolpher, Eunice Loraine
Colarusso, Corrine Camille
Cole, Jeanette
Coleman, M L (Michael Lee)
Cooper, Mario
Cortese, Don F
Couper, Charles Alexander
Cox, Marion Averal
Crimi, Alfred D
Cunningham, Francis
Czimbalmos, Magdolna Paal
Davies, Kenneth Southworth
Dawson, Doug
De Donato, Louis
De Lory, Peter
DeMaree, Betty (Elizabeth Ann)
Dennis, Don W
Denton, Patry
Dickerson, Vera Mason
Dickinson, David Charles
Diehl, Guy Louis
DiPerna, Frank Paul
Dobie, Jeanne
Doll, Linda A
Dougherty, Ray (Raymond Edward)
Douglas, Edwin Perry
Draper, Josiah Everett
Draper, William Franklin
Driesbach, Walter Clark, Jr
Dunlap, Loren Edward
Eaton, Pauline (Friedrich)
Egeli, Cedric Baldwin
Elliott, Bette G
Embrey, Carl Rice
Fenton, Alan
Finck, Furman J
Fiore, Joseph A
Fitch, Steve (Steven Ralph)
Flattmann, Alan Raymond
Fox, Michael David
Frederick, Deloras Ann
Freeman, Kathryn
Frick, Robert Oliver
Frudakis, Evangelos William
Fukuhara, Henry

INSTRUCTOR (cont)

Gabin, George Joseph
Gantz, Ann Cushing
Gasparro, Frank
Gatto, Paul Anthony
Gay, Betsy (Elizabeth Dershuck Gay)
Gentry, Warren Miller
George, Richard Allan
Gerbracht, Bob (Robert Thomas)
Gilbert, Lionel
Gilpin, Henry Edmund
Godfrey, Winnie (Winifred M)
Goetz, Mary Anna
Goldsmith, Lawrence Charles
Goldstein, Julius
Goodbred, Ray Edward
Goree, Gary Paul
Gottschalk, Max Jules
Grado, Angelo John
Graupe-Pillard, Grace
Graves, Robert Edward
Greeley, Charles Matthew
Green, Tom
Greenberg, Irwin
Gregory, Bruce
Grippe, Florence (Berg)
Groell, Theophil
Grosse, C(arolyn Ann Gawarecki)
Guastella, C Dennis
Gunshor, Ruth
Guzevich-Sommers, Kreszenz (Cynthia)
Gyra, Francis Joseph, Jr
Haff, Barbara J E
Hall, Carl Albin
Halliday, Nancy R
Hammett, Polly Horton
Hanlen, John (Garrett)
Hanna, Annette Adrian
Harbart, Gertrude Felton
Hardy, David Whittaker, III
Harroun, Dorothy Sumner
Harvey, Donald Gilbert
Hawkins, Thomas Wilson, Jr
Hedden-Sellman, Zelda
Hee, Hon-Chew
Heimdal, Georg
Heinemann, Peter
Heipp, Richard Christian
Henderson, Jack W
Hendrix, Connie (Connie Sandage Manus)
Henry, Jean
Hensche, Henry
Heston, Joan
Hodge, R Garey
Hofer, Ingrid (Ingeborg)
Hollerbach, Serge
Hollingsworth, Alvin Carl
Huff, Laura Weaver
Humphrey, Nene
Hunter, Robert Douglas
Hutchings, La Vere
Iacurto, Francesco
Indiviglia, Salvatore Joseph
Ingalls, Eve
Irvine, Betty Jo
Isaacs, Ron
Jarvis, Donald
Johnson, Ernest (Melvin)
Johnson, Joyce
Joyce, Marshall Woodside
Kam, Mei K
Kardon, Carol
Karn, Gloria Stoll
Karwelis, Donald Charles
Katzman, Herbert
Kaufman, Loretta Ana
Kawabata, Minoru
Kaye, Mildred Elaine
Kaz, Nathaniel
Kellar, Martha Robbins
Kiker, Evelyn Coalson
Kinstler, Everett Raymond
Kirby, Kent Bruce
Kirk, Michael
Knaub, Raymond L
Koch, Philip
Kotun, Henry Paul
Kranking, Margaret Graham
Kruskamp, Janet
Kurlander, Honey W
Lack, Richard Frederick
Lai, Waihang
Lane, Marion Jean Arrons
Lanigan-Schmidt, Thomas
LaPlantz, Shereen
Larson, Blaine (Gledhill)
Laymon, Cynthia J
Layne, Barbara J
Leaf, Ruth
Lee-Smith, Hughie
Leslie, Seaver
Lesnick, Stephen William
Lewis, John Chapman
Lewis, Marcia
Lewis, Nat Brush
Lewis, Ronald Walter
Lewis, William R
Lighton, Linda
Likan, Gustav
Liljegren, Frank
Limont, Naomi Charles
Lindenberg, Mary K
Lindmark, Arne
Lipscomb, Guy Fleming, Jr
Lomahaftewa, Linda Joyce
Lombard, Annette
Longo-Muth, Linda L
Lorentz, Pauline
Lucas, Bonnie Lynn
Luck, Robert
Lueders, Jimmy C
Luisi, Jerry
Luitjens, Helen Anita
Lynch, Betty
Lynch, Tom (Thomas Michael)
McCarthy, Doris Jean
McCarty, Lorraine Chambers
McClure, Constance
McDougal, Ivan Ellis
McGarry, Patricia Josephine
McKinney, Tatiana Ladygina
McQuillan, Frances
McReynolds, (Joe) Cliff
McVicker, Charles Taggart
Madura, Jack Joseph
Mahaffey, Merrill Dean
Malta, Vincent
Mancuso, Leni
Manzo, Anthony Joseph
Marozzi, Eli Raphael
Martin, Thomas
Martone, William Robert
Mason, Alden C
Mason, Frank Herbert
Mendenhall, Jack
Metcalf, Conger A
Meyers, Dale (Mrs Mario Cooper)
Midener, Walter
Miezajs, Dainis
Missal, Stephen J
Mohn, Cheri (Ann)
Moon, Marc
Moonie, Liana
Moore, Ina May
Moore, Scott Martin
Morenon, Elise
Morgan, Susan
Morgenlander, Ella Kramer
Moscatt, Paul N
Moy, May (Wong)
Muchnic, Suzanne
Myers, Carole Ann
Naza (Maria Nazareth McFarren),
Neff, Edith
Nickerson, Ruth (Mrs Edmund Greacen Jr)
Nigrosh, Leon Isaac
Notestine, Dorothy J
Notestine, Tom W
Odate, Toshio
Oesterle, Leonhard Friedrich
Oginz, Richard
Ohe, Katie (Minna)
Oi, Motoi
Olson, Bettye Johnson
O'Neil, Bruce William
Osborne, Elizabeth
Osborne, John Phillip
Ostendorf, (Arthur) Lloyd, Jr
O'Sullivan, Daniel Joseph
Pan, Theodore (Ion)
Parella, Albert Lucian
Passantino, George Christopher
Patrick, Genie Hudson
Patterson, Shirley Abbott
Pearson, Clifton
Pearson, Henry C
Pearson, James Eugene
Penney, Jacqueline
Peregrin, Magda Elizabeth
Perez, Vincent
Perlmutter, Linda M
Perrotti, Barbara
Peter, George
Phillips, Dick (Richard Cortez)
Phillis, Marilyn Hughey
Piatek, Francis John
Pierce, Donald (Benjamin)
Piet, John Frances
Plaster, Alice Marie
Plummer, Carlton B
Pototschnik, John Michael
Pravda, Muriel
Pribble, Easton
Price, Joe (Allen)
Price, Morgan Samuel (Margaret Morgan Price)
Provder, Carl
Quinn, Noel Joseph
Radin, Dan
Raskind, Philis
Rawlinson, Jonlane Frederick
Reid, Robert Dennis
Remenick, Seymour
Reynard, Carolyn Cole
Roberts, Clyde Harry
Roberts, Donald
Rollins, Tim
Rooke, Fay Lorraine
Rose, Leatrice
Ross, Douglas Allan
Ross, Janice Koenig
Ross, John T
Ross, Rhoda Honore
Rossi, Joseph O
Rossman, Ruth Scharff
Rudman, Joan (Combs)
Russell, Philip C
St Denis, Paul Andre
Sallick, Lucy Ellen
Sanden, John Howard
San Soucie, Patricia Molm
Saunders, Edith Dariel Chase
Savas, Jo-Ann
Schaeffer, S(tanley) Allyn
Schaffer, Claudia Post
Schaffer, Debra S
Schepis, Anthony Joseph
Schildknecht, Dorothy E
Schlemm, Betty Lou
Schmutzhart, Slaithong Chengtrakul
Schule, Donald Kenneth
Schwalb, Susan
Schwartz, Henry
Schwartz, Ruth
Segur, Eleanor Corinne
Selby, Patricia Louise
Sexauer, Donald Richard
Shackelford, Bud (Lyne T)
Shapiro, Irving
Sherwood, Leona
Sheya,
Shih, Joan Fai
Sickman, Jessalee Bane
Silberstein-Storfer, Muriel Rosoff
Simpson, Marilyn Jean
Sleigh, Sylvia
Slone, Sandi
Smith, Barbara Turner
Snow, Lee Erlin
Sparks, John Edwin
Spencer, Susan Elizabeth
Spicer, Jean (Doris) Uhl
Sproul, Ann Stephenson
Staffel, Rudolf Harry
Statman, Jan B
Stelzer, Michael Norman
Stevens, Jacquie (Jaqueline Lauren)
Stevenson, Ruth Rolston
Stoffa, Michael
Stone, Jeffrey Ingram
Storer, Frances Nell
Strickland,
Stroppel, Betty MacNair
Sundberg, Wilda (Regelman)
Swenson, Anne (Beatrice)
Tarbet, Urania Christy
Tatro, Ronald Edward
Taylor, Bill (William Bradley)
Taylor, Michael (Estes)
Teyral, John
Tillim, Sidney
Tobias, Julius
Townsend, Storm D
Townsend, Teryl
Trauerman, Margy Ann
Travers-Smith, Brian John
Trieff, Selina
Trott, Helen
Turner, (Charles) Arthur
Varriale, Wanda (Stella)
Viret, Margaret Mary (Mrs Frank Ivo)
Wagner, Charles H
Wall, Rhonda
Walton, M Douglas
Warren, Betty
Waterstreet, Ken (James Kent)
Webb, Frank (Francis H)
Weidner, Roswell Theodore
Weill, Erna
Weiner, Abe
Wengrovitz, Judith
Wentworth, Murray Jackson
Wethington, Wilma Zella
Whedon, Aida Anthony
Whitcomb, Therese Truitt
Whiten, Colette
Wilke, Hannah
Williams, Raymond Lester
Wood, Robert E
Woolwich, Madlyn-Ann C
Wright, Stanley Marc
Yaghjian, Edmund
Yates, Marvin Clarence
Yost, Erma Martin
Zimmerman, Paul Warren
Zuccarelli, Frank Edward

JEWELER

Adams, Jay H
Alexander, Anthony K
Allen, Constance Olleen Webb
Anthony, Amy Ellen
Benson, Martha J
Butler, Byron C
Caldwell, Eleanor
Chapman, Robert Gordon
Easton, Roger David
Eikerman, Alma
Enterline, Sandra
Fisch, Arline Marie
Flynn, Pat L
Fuhrman, Esther

JEWELER (cont)
Gabriel, Hannelore
Garrison, Elizabeth Jane
Gralnick, Lisa
Griffiths, William Perry
Hageman, Charles Lee
Hamlet, Susan H
Harper, William
Harrison, Jimmie
Higgins, Edward Koelling
Hoover, Francis Louis
Hu, Mary Lee
Jae
Klarin, Winifred Erlick
Kraus, (Ersilia) Zili
Lacktman, Michael
Lansdon, Gay Brandt
LaPlantz, David
Lewis, Marcia
Link, Val James
Miller, John Paul
Moty, Eleanor H
Norton, Mary Joyce
Ottiano, John William
Parcher, Joan Ann
Peck, Lee Barnes
Quigley, Robin L
St John, Adam
Sattler, Jill
Slosburg-Ackerman, Jill
Stacy, John Russell
Stephen, Francis B
Thiewes, Rachelle R
Thomason, Tom William
Thompson, Nancy Kunkle
Walker, Mary Carolyn
Whitney, Charlotte Armide

KINETIC ARTIST

Baker, George P
Besner, J Jacques
Brubaker, Jack
Bunts, Frank
Emery, Lin
Flavin, Dan
Goldman, Matt
Harvey, Dermot
Hendricks, Edward Lee
Holvey, Samuel Boyer
Janney, Christopher Draper
Karpowicz, Terrence Edward
Kirk, Jerome
Margulies, Isidore
Myer, Peter Livingston
Oster, Gerald
Peiperl, Adam
Reiback, Earl M
Romano, Salvatore Michael
Sina, Alejandro
Stanton, Phil
Stephens, Thomas Michael
Sweet, Steve (Steven Mark)
Taradash, Meryl
Tuck, Norman Victor
White, Norman Triplett
Wink, Chris

LECTURER

Abrams, Herbert E
Aigner, Lucien
Alcalay, Albert S
Allen, Jane Addams
Andrews, Benny
Austin, Phil
Banning, Jack (John Peck), Jr
Barta, Dorothy Elaine
Bartle, Dorothy Budd
Baruch, Anne
Baum, Hank
Berhang, Mattie
Betteridge, Lois Etherington
Bingham, Lois A
Bocour, Leonard
Boterf, Check (Chester Arthur)
Brakhage, James Stanley
Brendel, Bettina
Brooks, H(arold) Allen
Bruno, Phillip A
Burgues, Irving Carl
Burns, Sheila
Burroughs, Margaret T G
Cantone, Vic
Challis, Richard Bracebridge
Chin, Ric
Clark, Robert Charles
Clinedinst, Katherine Parsons
Cobb, Virginia Horton
Coleman, A(llan) D(ouglass)
Coleman, Gayle
Collins, Lowell Daunt
Cormier, Robert John
Crooks, W Spencer
Cropper, M Elizabeth
Curley, Donald Houston
Cuttler, Charles David
Dauterman, Carl Christian
Davenport, Rebecca Read
Dinnerstein, Lois
Dodge, Joseph Jeffers
Doty, Robert McIntyre
Dreiband, Laurence
Drutt, Helen Williams
Duzy, Merrilyn Jeanne
Edelman, Ann
Edelson, Gilbert S
Edelstein, J M
Ellis, Ray
Espenet
Ettinger, Susi Steinitz
Evans, Burford Elonzo
Fedelle, Estelle
Feder, Penny Joy
Fein, B(arbara) R
Ferguson, Kathleen Elizabeth
Fox, Flo
Gandert, Miguel Adrian
Giffuni, Flora Baldini
Gilbertson, Charlotte
Goetz, Peter Henry
Goetzl, Thomas Maxwell
Gottschalk, Fritz
Gowans, Alan
Greenwald, Alice (Alice Marian Greenwald-Ward)
Gross, Earl
Gross, Elissa Frances
Grove, Samuel Harold
Gutmann, Joseph
Hallmark, Donald Parker
Hanson, Philip Holton
Hare, David
Hemphill, Herbert Waide, Jr
Highwater, Jamake
Hornung, Gertrude Seymour
Hughes, Robert S F
Inoue, Kazuko
Jagger, Gillian
James, A Everette, Jr
Johnson, Buffie
Jones, Lois Mailou (Mrs V Pierre-Noel)
Kan, Diana
Karp, Richard Gordon
Kaufman, Jane
Kennedy, J William
Kingsley, April
Kleinman, Sue
Koltun, Frances Lang
Komar and Melamid,
Koni, Nicolaus
Kratina, K George
Krieger, Suzanne Baruc
Kropf, Joan R
Kuchta, Ronald A
Kuehn, Edmund Karl
Kumler, Kipton (Cornelius)
Lee, Amy Freeman
Lenssen, Heidi (Mrs Fridolf Johnson)
Levinson, Mimi
Lyons, Francis E, Jr
Martin, John Rupert
Mecklenburg, Virginia McCord
Miller, Donald
Morrison, Fritzi Mohrenstecher
Munro, Eleanor
Myers, Dorothy Roatz
Nash, Mary
Navaretta, Cynthia
Nawara, Lucille Procter
Nechis, Barbara
Neuhaus, Max
Notestine, Tom W
O'Connor, Francis Valentine
Palmer, Lucie Mackay
Pandozy, Raffaele Martini
Pennington, Mary Anne
Perrot, Paul N
Pershan, Marion
Poduska, T F
Rath, Hildegard
Reed, Cleota
Reich, Sheldon
Richards, Eugene
Robbins, Warren M
Rogalski, Walter
Ross, David Anthony
Rubinstein, Charlotte Streifer
Ruthven, John Aldrich
Sanguinetti, Eugene F
Sawyer, John R
Scherer, Herbert Grover
Scheu, Leonard
Schultz, Caroline Reel
Schulz, Ken
Schwartz, Marvin D
Scribner, Charles, III
Sellin, David
Shapiro, Adrian Michael
Shapiro, David
Shapiro, Dee
Shubin, Morris Jack
Siden, Franklin
Sirena (Contessa Antonia Mastrocristino Fanara)
Sitton, John M
Skalagard, Hans
Southard, James Bruce
Stapleton, Joseph F
Taft, Frances Prindle
Thelin, Valfred P
Thompson, Dorothy Burr
Timmas, Osvald
Tredennick, Dorothy W
Usher, Elizabeth Reuter (Mrs William Arthur Scar)
Van Wyk, Helen
Vater, Regina (Regina Vater Lundberg)
Volpe, Robert
Walinska, Anna
Walton, Donald William
Wang, Gar
Warren, Win (W Winton)
Weidner, Marilyn Kemp
Weil, Stephen E
Whitcomb, Kay
Wiggins, Guy A
Wilson, Ben
Wilson, Carrie Lois
Wood, James Arthur (Art)
Wriston, Barbara
Wynn, Donald James
Yanish, Elizabeth
Zaleski, Jean
Zirker, Joseph

LIBRARIAN

Abid, Ann B
Allen, Nancy Schuster
Barlow, Deborah Lynn
Baxter, Paula Adell
Bloomgarden, Judith Mary
Boyer, Marietta P
Burns, G Joan
Candau, Eugenie
Cano, Margarita
Ciccone, Amy Navratil
Collins, Christiane C
Craig, Susan V
Dane, William Jerald
Davis, L Clarice
Doumato, Lamia
Dunnigan, Mary Catherine
Edelstein, J M
Ekdahl, Janis Kay
Fechter, Claudia Zieser
Findlay, James Allen
Freitag, Wolfgang Martin
Gilden, Anita
Grier, Margot Edmands
Gurney, Susan Rothwell
Halbrook, Anne-Mieke Platt
Haswell, Hollee
Held, (Jon) Jonathan, Jr
Hess, Joyce
Hess, Stanley William
Holliday, Judith
Horrell, Jeffrey L
Huemer, Christina Gertrude
Irvine, Betty Jo
Kaufmann, Robert Carl
Keaveney, Sydney Starr
Korenic, Lynette Marie
Kotala, Stanislaw Waclaw
Kusnerz, Peggy Ann F
Larsen, John Christian
Lerner, Loren Ruth
Looney, Robert Fain
Ludmer, Joyce Pellerano
McCorison, Marcus Allen
Markson, Eileen
Menthe, Melissa
Miller, Jean Johnston
Murchie, Donald John
Nolan, Margaret Patterson
Ostrow, Stephen Edward
Parry, Pamela Jeffcott
Paschall, Jo Anne
Pearman, Sara Jane
Petersen, Toni
Peterson, Harold Patrick
Phillpot, Clive James
Pinkney, Helen Louise
Placzek, Adolf Kurt
Pletscher, Josephine Marie
Puniello, Françoise Sara
Roberts, Helene Emylou
Rusak, Halina R
Scherer, Herbert Grover
Schimansky, Donya Dobrila
Schmidt, Mary Morris
Schuller, Nancy Shelby
Sevy, Barbara Snetsinger
Shaw, Courtney Ann
Sigala, Stephanie Childs
Silberman, Arthur
Simor, Suzanna B
Smith, Beryl K
Sommer, Frank H, III
Spencer, Deirdre Diane
Staum, Sonja
Stoneham, John
Straight, Elsie H
Teague, Edward H
Toth, Georgina Gy
Treese, William R
Usher, Elizabeth Reuter (Mrs William Arthur Scar)
Walker, William Bond
Weidman, Jeffrey
Wyngaard, Susan Elizabeth
Young, Barbara Neil
Young Scott, Frances
Zimon, Kathy Elizabeth

MEDALIST

Adams, Jay H
Anargyros, Spero
Bleifeld, Stanley
Cook, John (Alfred)
Cook, Robert Howard
Eriksen, Gary
Everhart, Don, II
Finke, Leonda Froelich
Gibran, Kahlil George
Goff, Thomas Jefferson
Grove, Edward Ryneal
Jones, Elizabeth A B (Mrs Ludwig Glaeser)
Jovine, Marcel
Kaufman, Mico
Mazze, Irving
Pujol, Elliott
Reed, Hal
Rosse, Maryvonne
Turano, Don

MOSAIC ARTIST

Carter, Jerry Williams
Garrison, David Earl
Gruen, Shirley Schanen
Hurwitz, Michael H
Kozloff, Joyce
Kreilick, Marjorie E
Lawrence, Jacob
Miller, F John
Schwarz, Myrtle Cooper
Sorrentino, Richard Michael
Zweerts, Arnold

MURALIST

Ahysen, Harry Joseph
Anguiano, Raul
Baskerville, Charles
Beal, Jack
Bellin, Milton R
Bentley, Claude
Besner, J Jacques
Bjurman, Johan Paul
Blake, Priscilla Ann
Boggs, Franklin
Bosson, Jack (John Edwin), Jr
Bransby, Eric James
Brothers, Barry A
Buonagurio, Edgar R
Callahan, Aileen (Aileen Loughlin Callahan)
Cantini, Virgil D
Castillo, Mario Enrique
Charlot, Martin Day
Chase, Allan (Seamans)
Clark, Vicky Jo
Collins, Harvey Arnold
Connolly, Jerome Patrick
Czimbalmos, Szabo Kalman
Fausett, (William) Dean
Frazer, James (Nisbet), Jr
Freund, Tibor
Glier, Mike
Graham, Bob
Graziani, Sante
Groat, Hall Pierce
Groat, Hall Pierce, II
Haas, Richard John
Harris, David Jack
Healy, Julia Schmitt
Henderson, Victor
Hopper, Frank J
Imana, Jorge Garron
Incandela, Gerald Jean-Marie
Janjigian, Lucy Elizabeth
Jankowski, Theodore Andrew
Jenkins, Mary Anne Keel
Jones, Calvin B(ell)
Kaplan, Stanley
Kaprov, Susan
Kauffman, (Camille) Andrene
Kramer, Louise
Landau, Myra
Lorcini, Gino
McChesney, Robert Pearson
McCoy, Ann
Macdonell, Cameron
Magafan, Ethel
Mangione, Patricia Anthony
Martin, Lucille Caiar
Martinez, Ernesto Pedregon
Martyl (Martyl Schweig Langsdorf)
Merrill, David Kenneth
Michaels, Glen
Middleman, Raoul F
Miller, Donald Lloyd
Montminy, Tracy
Morrow, Robert Earl
Pisani, Joseph
Pittore, Carlo
Rakocy, William (Joseph)
Rand, Archie
Reardon, Mary A
Redinger, Walter Fred
Regat, Jean-Jacques Albert
Regat, Mary E
Richardson, Frank, Jr
Rippey, Clayton
Ritter, Julian
Rodeiro, José Manuel
Rose, Samuel
Rosen, Esther Yovits
Rush, Deborah
Saru, George
Shersher, Zinovy
Siebner, Herbert
Slonem, Hunt
Sorrentino, Richard Michael
Spandorf, Lily Gabriella
Sweitzer, Charles Leroy
Tacla, Jorge
Thackston, R King
Thwaites, Charles Winstanley
Tobey, Alton S
Tulk, Alfred James
Valencia, Cesar
Valesco, Frances
Vanden Berge, Peter Willem
Vickery, Charles Bridgeman
Webb, Patrick
Weber, John Pitman
Welch, James Wymore
Wilson, Robert Alan
Wilson, York
Yaeger, Edgar Louis
Yasko, Caryl A(nne)

MUSEOLOGIST

Atkinson, Tracy
Brody, Jacob Jerome
Carter, David Giles
Courtney, Keith Townsend
Craft, John Richard
Craven, Roy Curtis, Jr
Cummins, Karen Gasco
Dailey, Chuck (Charles Andrew)
Dellis, Arlene B
Edson, Gary F
Franco, Barbara
Fraser, Andrea R
Hall, Robert L
Harris, Ellen Schwartz
Holo, Selma R
Johnson, Selina (Tetzlaff)
Mayer, Susan Martin
Moy, Henry
Noble, Joseph Veach
Ott, Robert William
Sipiora, Leonard Paul
Sokol, David Martin
Streetman, John William, III
Toledo, Angeles
Trubner, Henry
Venegas, Haydee E
Weeks, Edward F (Ted)
Wright, Vicki C

MUSEUM DIRECTOR

Agnew, Ellen Schall
Ahrens, Kent
Alexander-Greene, Grace George
Alling, Clarence (Edgar)
Anderson, Maxwell L
Anderson, Ross Cornelius
Appel, Eric A
Arkus, Leon A
Armstrong, Thomas Newton, III
Atkins, Bill (Billy Wayne Atkins)
Baas, Jacquelynn
Bacot, Henry Parrott
Bailin, David
Ballard, Lockett Ford, Jr
Ballinger, James K
Bandes, Susan Jane
Bantel, Linda
Barons, Richard Irwin
Barrie, Dennis Ray
Beach, Warren
Beck, Martha Ann
Begley, J (John Phillip)
Belz, Carl Irvin
Berg, Mona Lea
Bergman, Robert P
Bermingham, Peter
Bishop, Budd Harris
Bloch, Milton Joseph
Bodem, Dennis Richard
Boggs, Jean Sutherland
Bohen, Barbara E
Bolas, Gerald Douglas
Bolge, George S
Bowne, James DeHart
Bradley, William Steven
Brezzo, Steven Louis
Britt, Nelson Clark
Brooke, David Stopford
Brown, Charlotte Vestal
Brown, James Monroe, III
Brown, John Carter
Buchanan, John Edward, Jr
Buck, Robert Treat, Jr
Bullard, Edgar John, III
Burger, Gary C
Burke, James Donald
Burnside, Madeleine Hilding
Bush, Martin H
Butler, Charles Thomas
Byrnes, James Bernard
Camber, Diane Woolfe
Cameron, Duncan F
Cancel, Luis R
Capa, Cornell
Carswell, John
Castile, Rand
Chernow, Burt
Chetham, Charles
Christison, Muriel B
Cilella, Salvatore G, Jr
Clark, Lynda K
Coe, Ralph Tracy
Consey, Kevin E
Coopersmith, Georgia A
Coraor, John E
Craft, John Richard
Crane, Michael Patrick
Crosman, Christopher Byron
Czarniecki, M J, III
Czestochowski, Joseph Stephen
Danoff, I Michael
Darling, Sharon Sandling
Davies, Hugh Marlais
De la Torre, David Joseph
Delehanty, Suzanne E
Demetrion, James Thomas
De Montebello, Philippe Lannes
Dempsey, Bruce Harvey
Desmarais, Charles Joseph
Dietrich, Bruce Leinbach
Dietz, Charles LeMoyne
Dobkin, John Howard
Dodd, Eric M
Dodds, Robert J, III
Domit, Moussa M
Duff, James H
Eckhardt, Ferdinand
Edelstein, Teri J
Edson, Gary F
Einreinhofer, Nancy Anne
Eins, Stefan
Eitner, Lorenz E A
Eldredge, Bruce B
Ellis, George Richard
Elzea, Rowland Procter
Emerson, Roberta Shinn
Enman, Tom Kenneth
Evans, Bob (Robert James)
Evans, Bruce Haselton
Fabbri, Anne R
Fagaly, William Arthur
Faison, Samson Lane, Jr
Fechter, Claudia Zieser
Feldman, Arthur Mitchell
Ferguson, Charles B
Fern, Alan Maxwell
Fetchko, Peter J
Fillin-Yeh, Susan
Fisher, James Donald
Flanagan, E Michael
Fleischman, Stephen
Flomenhaft, Eleanor
Forbes, Donna Marie
Force, Roland Wynfield
Forrest, James Taylor
Fowler, Harriet Whittemore
Frauchiger, Fritz A
Friedman, Martin
Gaither, Edmund B
Gamble, Kathryn Elizabeth
Gardiner, Henry Gilbert
Garrett, Stephen
Gaudieri, Alexander V J
Gealt, Adelheid Medicus
Gebhard, David
Geske, Norman Albert
Gibbs, Barbara
Glenn, Constance White
Gordon, Joy L
Graham, Douglas J M
Green, Jonathan (William)
Grogan, Kevin
Gruber, J Richard
Gualtieri, Joseph P
Hagerstrand, Martin Alan
Hagman, Jean Cassels
Hallmark, Donald Parker
Harlow, Ann
Harris, Paul Stewart
Harrison, Helen Amy
Hassrick, Peter H
Heath, Samuel K
Hennessey, William John
Henry, Jean
Herman, Lloyd Eldred
Hernandez, Jo Farb
High, Steven S
Hightower, John B
Hill, William Mansfield
Hobbs, Robert Carleton
Hoge, Robert Wilson
Holo, Selma R
Hood, Graham Stanley
Hood, Mary Bryan
Hopkins, Henry Tyler
Hopkins, Kenneth R
Houlihan, Patrick T
Hulick, Diana Emery
Hunt, David Curtis

MUSEUM DIRECTOR (cont)
Hutchinson, Janet L
Hyland, Douglas K S
Inverarity, Robert Bruce
Johnson, Mark M
Johnston, Phillip M
Jones, Charlott Ann
Joyaux, Alain Georges
Kachel, Harold Stanley
Kagle, Joseph L, Jr
Kahan, Mitchell Douglas
Kardon, Janet
Katsiff, Bruce
Keeney, Allen Lloyd
Kelm, Bonnie G
Ketner, Joseph Dale
Kiah, Virginia Jackson
Kidrick, Valerie Anne
Kinsel, Michael Leslie
Kinsman, Robert Donald
Klopfenstein, Philip Arthur
Kochka, Al
Koenig, Robert J
Kohler, Ruth DeYoung
Koshalek, Richard
Krause, Bonnie Jean
Krens, Thomas
Kuchta, Ronald A
Lagoria, Georgianna Marie
Landwehr, William Charles
Lane, John Rodger
Lanmon, Dwight P
Latos-Valier, Paula
Leavitt, Thomas Whittlesey
Lee, Sherman Emery
Leeper, John Palmer
Leet, Richard Eugene
Lefebvre d'Argence, Rend-Yvon
Lehman, Arnold L
Lerner, Abram
Lewis, Virginia Elnora
Libby, Gary Russell
Liddle, Nancy Hyatt
Lindemann, Edna M
Lipton, Barbara B
Livesay, Thomas Andrew
Loar, Peggy A
Lockhart, Anne Ivey
Loiselle, Bernard Roger
Lowry, Bates
Luebbers, Leslie Laird
Maass, Richard Andrew
McDonald, Robert Herwick
McGough, Stephen C
Madigan, Richard Allen
Mahey, John A
Mandle, Earl Roger
Marioni, Tom
Markle, Greer (Walter Greer Markle)
Marzio, Peter Cort
Master-Karnik, Paul
Mayer, Robert Anthony
Mayhall, Dorothy
Maytham, Thomas Northrup
Meister, Mark J
Melvin, Ronald McKnight
Messer, David James
Messer, Thomas M
Messersmith, Harry Lee
Mhire, Herman P
Mickenberg, David
Miles, Christine M
Miller, Joan Vita
Miller, Samuel Clifford
Miller-Clark, Denise
Mills, Paul Chadbourne
Modi-Vitale, Lydia
Moore, Russell James
Mooz, R Peter
Morris, Jack Austin, Jr
Mosby, Dewey Franklin
Moy, Henry
Muhlert, Jan Keene
Murray, Richard Newton
Nahas, Dominique François
Neff, John Hallmark
Neil, J M
Newton, Douglas
Noble, Joseph Veach
Nold, Carl R
Norris, Andrea Spaulding
Nyerges, Alexander Lee
Oldenburg, Richard Erik
O'Sullivan, Judith Roberta
Ott, Wendell Lorenz
Owens, Gwendolyn Jane
Panczenko, Russell
Parker, Harry S, III
Parsons, Merribell Maddux
Paulin, Richard Calkins
Peladeau, Marius Beaudoin
Pendergraft, Norman Elveis
Pennington, Estill Curtis
Pennington, Mary Anne
Pepich, Bruce Walter
Peterson, John Douglas
Phillips, James M
Phillips, Laughlin
Pilgrim, Dianne Hauserman
Pillsbury, Edmund P
Pollei, Dane F
Poon, Yi-Chong Sarina Chow
Poppitz, James
Prescott, Kenneth Wade
Prokopoff, Stephen
Quick, Edward Raymond
Rathbone, Perry Townsend
Reichert, Marilyn F
Reuter, Laurel J
Rhodes, Reilly Patrick
Ritts, Edwin Earl, Jr
Robb, David Metheny, Jr
Robbins, Daniel J
Robbins, Warren M
Robert, Henry Flood, Jr
Robinson, Franklin W
Rodriguez, Geno (Eugene)
Rogers, Millard Foster, Jr
Rogovin, Mark
Rombout, Luke
Rosenbaum, Allen
Rosenbaum, Joan H
Rosenthal, Donald A
Rovetti, Paul F
Ruggiero, Laurence J
Sachs, Samuel, II
Sandweiss, Martha Ann
Saunders, Richard Henry
Sawyer, Charles Henry
Scarbrough, Cleve Knox, Jr
Schneider, Janet M
Schweizer, Paul Douglas
Segger, Martin Joseph
Selby, Roger Lowell
Shaman, Sanford Sivitz
Shestack, Alan
Siegesmund, Richard
Sipiora, Leonard Paul
Slade, Roy
Slive, Seymour
Sloan, Mark
Sloshberg, Leah Phyfer
Smith, Ann Y
Smith, J Weldon
Smith, Paul J
Smith-Theobald, Sharon A
Sobol, Judith Ellen
Steadman, David Wilton
Stetson, Daniel Everett
Stitt, Susan (Margaret)
Story, William Easton
Story Wilson, Martha Redy
Stuart, Joseph Martin
Sullivan, Linda Susan
Swanson, Vern Grosvenor
Takach, Mary H
Tarbox, Gurdon Lucius, Jr
Taylor, Rene Claude
Tibbs, Thomas S
Timms, Peter Rowland
Timpano, Anne
Tonelli, Edith Ann
Toperzer, Thomas Raymond
Trapp, Frank Anderson
Tripp, Susan Gerwe
Tucker, Marcia
Turk, Rudy H
Turnbull, Lucy
Turner, David
Turner, Evan Hopkins
Ulrich, Edwin Abel
Van Wagner, Judy Collischan
Vecsey, Esther Barbara
Victor, Mary O'Neill
Wagner, (Dr) David J
Walker, Herbert Brooks
Walkey, Frederick P
Waller, Aaron Bret
Walsh, John
Wardwell, Allen
Watkinson, Patricia Grieve
Watson, Katharine Johnson
Wattenmaker, Richard J
Watts, R Michael
Waufle, Alan Duane
Weber, Jean M
Weil, Stephen E
West, Richard Vincent
Whitlock, John Joseph
Williams, Sylvia H
Wilson, Jean S
Wilson, Marc F
Wolfe, Maurice Raymond
Wong, Jason
Wong, Roger Frederickson
Wright, Jesse Graham, Jr
Wright, Vicki C
Yassin, Robert Alan
Young, Janie Chester
Zona, Louis A
Zuris, Donald P

PAINTER

Abadi, Fritzie
Abernethy-Baldwin, Judith Ann
Abramowicz, Janet
Abularach, Rodolfo Marco
Adams, Bobbi
Adams, Clinton
Alden, Richard
Alexander, Wick
Allen, Roberta
Ames, Polly Scribner
Anderson, Doug
Anderson, Lennart
Andrew, David Neville
Andrews, Kim
Angell, Tony
Anker, Suzanne C
Antokal, Gale
Apel, Barbara Jean
Applebroog, Ida
Arends, Stuart
Armstrong, Carol
Arnitz, Rick
Arnoldi, Charles Arthur
Astman, Barbara Ann
Aston, Miriam
Austin-Nuhfer, Olive H
Awalt, Elizabeth Grace
Ayers, Carol Lee
Ayres, Julia Spencer
Azara, Nancy J
Bageris, John
Bales, J (Jean Elaine)
Bamber, Judie
Banks, Ellen
Baranik, Rudolf
Bard, Gayle
Barker, Al C
Barnes, Margo
Barr-Sharrar, Beryl
Barsano, Ron (Ronald James)
Barta, Dorothy Elaine
Bastian, Linda
Bavinger, Eugene Allen
Baxter, Iain
Baxter, Violet
Bearce, Jeana Dale
Beck, Theresa
Beerman, Miriam (Miriam Beerman-Jaffe)
Begley, Wayne E
Belinoff, Deanne
Bellin, Milton R
Bensignor, Paulette
Berghash, Mark W
Bergstrom, Edith Harrod
Bersentes, Nafsika J
Bertoni, Christina
Besant, Derek Michael
Bettison, James
Binks, Ronald C
Birnbaum, Dara
Bishop, Jerold
Bloomfield, Suzanne
Blum, June
Bodo, Sandor
Bogarin, Rafael
Bornstein, Eli
Bosman, Richard
Bostick, William Allison
Boszin, Andrew
Bott, John
Bowling, Katherine
Brakke, P(erry) Michael
Braudy, Dorothy
Brauntuch, Troy
Breen, Harry Frederick, Jr
Bremer, Marlene S
Brennan, Fanny (Frances M)
Brier, Helene
Brill, Glenn
Brodsky, Harry
Brody, Ruth
Broer, Roger L
Brookins, Jacob Boden
Brown, Charlotte
Brown, Christopher
Brown, Roger
Bruno, Santo M
Brycelea, Clifford
Buchwald, Howard
Buechner, Thomas Scharman
Bunts, Frank
Burkhardt, Hans Gustav
Busch, Rita Mary
Byron, Michael
Cabot, Hugh
Cahana, Alice Lok
Calle, Paul
Calrow, Robert F
Campbell, (James) Lawrence
Candioti, Beatriz A
Caporael, Suzanne
Carbone, David
Carl, Joan
Carrino, David
Carswell, John
Carter, Yvonne Pickering
Cass, Bill
Cassell, Beverly
Cernuda, Paloma
Chadbourn, Alfred Cheney
Chapian, Grieg Hovsep
Chee, Cheng-Khee
Cheek, Ronald Edward
Chia, Sandro
Christenberry, William
Ciancio, June (Kirkpatrick)
Cifolelli, Alberta (Alberta Carmella Lamb)
Clark, Timothy John
Clark, Vicky Jo
Clemente, Francesco
Clutz, William
Cobb, James
Coggins, Jack Banham
Cohlon, William
Colby, Bill
Cole, Julie Kramer

PAINTER (cont)
Coleman, Floyd Willis
Colescott, Warrington W
Conal, Robbie
Conant, Howard Somers
Conant, Jan Royce
Conesa, Miguel A
Conklin, Gloria Zamko
Converse, Elizabeth
Cook, Christopher Capen
Cooper, Susan
Corkery, Tim (Timothy James)
Corr, James D
Cove, Rosemary
Craft, David Ralph
Crimmins, Jerry (Gerald Garfield)
Cruz, Emilio
Culling, Richard Edward
Cusick, Nancy Taylor
Cutler, Ethel Rose
Cutrone, Ronnie Blaise
D'Alessio, Gregory
Dan, Lars
Danby, Ken
Dane, Bill (William Thatcher Dane)
Daniels, Linda
Dass, Dean Allen
Davidovich, Jaime
Davies, Harry Clayton
Davies, Haydn Llewellyn
Davis, Bertha G
Davis, James Granberry
Davis, Stephen
Day, Gary Lewis
De Boschnek, Chris (Christian Charles)
DeBruycker, Dirk H A
De Heusch, Lucio
D'Elaine
De Luca, Joseph Victor
DeRoux, Daniel Edward
Desiderio, Vincent
Deutsch, David
D'Harnoncourt, Anne
Dibert, Rita Jean
Diehl, Guy Louis
Digiorgio, Joseph J
Dill, Lesley
Dinc, Alev Necile
Dinsmore, Stephen Pul
Dobard, Raymond Gerard
Donhauser, Paul Stefan
Dorsey, Michael A
Dougherty, Ray (Raymond Edward)
Drum, Sydney Maria
Duesberry, Joellyn
Dukes, Caroline
Dunn, Cal
Dyck, Paul
Eastcott, Robert Wayne
Echohawk, Brummett
Eder, James Alvin
Edwards, Ethel
Egri, Ted
Eichel, Edward W
El Hanani, Jacob
Ellis, Ray
Ellis, Robert M
Ellis, Stephen
Ellis-Tracy, Jo
English, Hal (Harold J English)
Ensrud, Wayne
Erickson, Joy M
Ettenberg, Franklin Joseph
Evans, Dick
Eyre, Ivan
Fabert, Jacques
Fabian Fabiano, Diane
Fay, Ming G
Feinberg, Elen
Fejes, Claire
Feriola, James Philip
Finkelstein, Henry D
Firestone, Susan Paul
Fischl, Eric
Fletcher, Leland Vernon
Fohr, Jenny
Foosaner, Judith
Ford, Walton
Formicola, John Joseph
Francis, Jean Thickens
Francis, Sam
Frank, Helen (Goodzeit)
Frary, Michael
Freed, Hermine
Freedman, Jacqueline
Freeman, Robert
French, Ray H
French, Stephen Warren
Frets, Barbara J
Friedberg, Rachel (Ray)
Friedman, Ken
Friedman, Sabra
Friedman, Sally Ceila
Fromentin, Christine Anne
Fuchs, Mary Tharsilla
Gabrielson, Walter Oscar
Gagnon, Charles
Garabedian, Charles
Gardiner, T Michael
Garrison, Gene K
Gauthier, Suzanne Anita
Genkin, Jonathan
George, Sylvia James
Geraci, Lucian Arthur
Gilbert, Helen Odell
Gilbert-Rolfe, Jeremy
Gilmartin, F Thomas
Ginsburg, Estelle
Giordano, Greg Joe
Gipe, Lawrence
Gluck, Heidi
Gluska, Aharon
Godwin, Lawrence
Going, Jo
Goldberg, Glenn
Goldman, Lester
Goldstein, Milton
Goldstein, Sheldon (Shelly)
Gonzalez, Patricia
Gonzalez-Torres, Felix
Goodman, Janis G
Gordley, Metz Tranbarger (Tran)
Goree, Gary Paul
Graupe-Pillard, Grace
Gregory, Joan
Grenon, Gregory
Grimm, Lucille Davis
Groat, Hall Pierce, II
Gropper, Cathy
Gross, Julie
Guastella, C Dennis
Guberman, Sidney Thomas
Hackett, Mickey
Haff, Barbara J E
Hall, Carl Albin
Haller, Emanuel
Halsey, William Melton
Hambleton, Richard A
Hammond, Jane
Hammons, David
Hanchey, Janet Lynn
Hannibal, Joseph Harry
Hara, Keiko
Harder, Rodney
Harder, Rolf Peter
Hardy, John
Harper, William
Harris, Conley
Harris, David Jack
Hastenteufel, Dieter
Hatchett, Duayne
Haughey, James M
Hayes, Gerald
Haynes, Nancy
Headley, David Allen
Hecht, Irene
Heckscher, William Sebastian
Hee, Hon-Chew
Heeks, Willy
Heldt, Carl Randall
Heller, Susanna
Helsmoortel, Robert
Henderson, Mike
Henderson, Victor
Henrickson, Paul Robert
Herfield, Phyllis
Hernandez, John
Hershey, Nona
Hess, Scott
Heston, Joan
Heyman, Steven
Higby, (Donald) Wayne
Higgins, Mary Lou
Hillsmith, Fannie
Hirshfield, Pearl
Hochstetler, T Max
Hoff, Margo
Hoffman, Helen Bacon
Hoffman, William McKinley, Jr
Hoffmann, Gary David
Hogue, Alexandre
Holland, Harry Charles
Hollen-Bolmgren, Donna
Holzman, Eric
Hompson, Davi Det (David Elbridge Thompson)
Honda, Margaret
Howard, David
Hubler, Julius
Hull, John
Hung Wah Michael Poon,
Hunter, John H
Hunter, Paul
Hurewitz, Florence K
Hurson, Michael
Hurst, Lynn
Igo, Peter Alexander
Immonen, Gerald
Inverarity, Robert Bruce
Ipsen, Poul Janus
Irving, Joan
Iserman, Jim
Isroff, Lola K
Izuka, Kunio
Jalapeeno, Jimmy (Albert J Bonar)
Jansen, Angela Bing
Jellico, Nancy R
Jenney, Neil
Jensen, Bill
Jeswald, Joseph
Jewell, Joyce
Johnson, Guy
Johnson, Leon Bernard
Johnson, Lester L
Johnson, Nota
Jones, Howard William
Kalb, Marty Joel
Kali (Hanna Weynerowski)
Kaprov, Susan
Kass, Deborah
Kassman, Shirley
Katz, Ted
Kawashima, Takeshi
Kelley, Mike
Kelly, Cynthia Ference
Kennedy, Harriet Forte
Kent, H Latham
Kerrigan, Maurie
Kerzie, Ted L
Kheel, Constance
Kindermann, Helmmo
Kinnee, Sandy
Kippenberger, Martin
Klauber, Rick
Klein, Lynn (Ellen)
Klett, Mark
Knippers, Edward
Kocsis, James Paul
Koenig, Peter L
Kord, Victor George
Kornblum, Myrtle
Kostecka, Gloria
Kotala, Stanislaw Waclaw
Kozloff, Joyce
Kozlowski, Edward C
Kren, Margo
Kunsch, Louis
Kyra
Laemmle, Cheryl
Lagorio, Irene R
Landau, Myra
Lane, Lois
LaRico, Benje
Laufer, Susan
Laughlin, Mortimer
Lawrence, Sidney S
Leavitt, William
Lee, Robert J
Lee-Sissom, E
Leigh, Harry E
Leithauser, Mark Alan
LeMieux, Bonne A
Leslie, John
Levinson, Mimi
Lewczuk, Margrit
Lewis, John Chapman
Le Witt, Sol
Liao (Shiou-Ping Liao)
Licht, Evelyn M
Lichtner, Schomer Frank
Lipscomb, Guy Fleming, Jr
Little Chief, Barthell
Liu, Hung
Liu, Katherine Chang
London, Peter
Longo, Robert
Lucas, Bonnie Lynn
Lucas, Georgetta Snell
Lundberg, William
Lundin, Norman K
Lupper, Edward
Lurie, Boris
Lynch, Betty
Lynch-Nakache, Margaret
McCafferty, Jay David
McChesney, Clifton
McCollum, Mike L
McDonald, Susan Strong
McDonnell, Joseph Anthony
McKean, Hugh Ferguson
McKinley-Haas, Mary
Madsen, Mette B
Magee, Alan
Main, Tim
Maitin, Sam (Samuel Calman)
Maki, Robert Richard
Manetta, Edward J
Marazzi, William
Marca-Relli, Conrad
Marden, Brice
Margolis, Margo
Marks, Roberta Barbara
Marsh, Georgia
Marshall, John
Martin, Chris
Martin, Thomas
Martino, Babette
Masback, Dennis
Maynard, William
Mendenhall, Jack
Meneeley, Edward
Merola, Mario
Merritt, Francis Sumner
Mesa-Bains, Amalia
Metcalf, Conger A
Mew, Tommy
Meyers, Michael K
Mihaesco, Eugene
Miller, John
Miller, Larry
Miller, Steve
Miotte, Jean
Moehl, Karl J
Monroe, Eve Valin
Monteiro, Isaac
Mooney, Michael J
Moonie, Liana
Moore, Todd Somers
Morales, Rodolfo
Morgan, Robert Coolidge

PAINTER (cont)
Morley, Malcolm
Morosan, Ron
Morris, Gregg
Morrissey, Leo
Moses, Bette J
Moskowitz, Ira
Moss, Joe (Francis)
Moya Soto, Roberto
Muehlemann, Kathy
Munro, Janet Andrea
Murray, Judith
Nagengast, William Joseph
Nakoneczny, Michael
Namingha, Dan
Nash, Mary
Navrat, Den(nis Edward)
Nelson, Dona Rae
Nelson, James P
Nemec, Vernita McClish
Nerdrum, Odd
Newman, Sophie
Nguyen, Long
Nice, Don
Nicotra, Joseph Charles
Noble, Kevin
Nodine, Jane Allen
Nuse, Oliver William
Nyman, Georgianna Beatrice
Oda, Mayumi
O Donohue, Teige Ros
Okumura, Lydia
Olshan, Bernard
Olson, Bettye Johnson
Olson, Maxine
O'Meallie, Kitty (Kate Chamness Johnson)
Oropallo, Deborah
Osborne, Elizabeth
Palaia, Franc (Dominic)
Palazzolo, Carl
Paller, Gary
Panter, Gary
Parrino, George
Passantino, George Christopher
Passuntino, Peter Zaccaria
Pease, David G
Peck, James Edward
Peeps, Claire
Pennington, Sally
Penny, Aubrey John Robert
Pepper, Beverly
Perez, Betty Weiss
Perlman, Hirsch
Pickhardt, Carl
Picot, Pierre
Pierce, Danny P
Pierce, Diane (Diane Pierce-Huxtable)
Pittman, Lari
Plotek, Leopold
Pomeroy, Frederick George
Pomeroy, Mary Barnas (Mrs F G Pomeroy)
Powley, Donald
Preede, Nydia
Prekop, Martin Dennis
Propersi, August J
Purcell, Ann
Quagliata, Narcissus
Quinn, Brian Grant
Rabb, Madeline M
Rabinovitch, William Avrum
Ramos, Theodore
Ramsauer, Joseph Francis
Rankin, Don
Rapoport, Sonya
Rascon, Armando
Rathle, Henri (Amin)
Renninger, Katharine Steele
Rhodes, Curtis A
Rice, Edward
Riddle, John Thomas, Jr
Rippel, M (Morris Conrad)
Ritchie, (Celia) Ann
Ritz, Lorna J
Rizzie, Dan
Robinson, Libby
Rodan, Don
Rodriquez, Ernesto Angelo
Rogers, Barbara
Rollins, Tim
Rollman, Charlotte
Rosas, Mel
Roseberg, Carl Andersson
Rosen, Diane
Rosen, James Mahlon
Rosen, Joan Fischman
Rosen, Kay
Rosenberg, Terry
Rosenblum, Elizabeth
Roser, Ce (Cecilia)
Rossman, Michael
Rowan, Frances Physioc
Rozier, Robert L
Rubello, David Jerome
Ruhe, Barnaby Sieger
Russo, Michele
Ruvolo, Felix Emmanuele
Saks, Judith-Ann (Judith-Ann Saks Rosenthal)
Salle, David
Santiago, Ramon
Sattler, Jill
Savitt, Sam
Sawyer, Margo
Scarpitta, Salvatore
Scharf, Kenny
Schmidt, Charles
Schnabel, Julian
Schneemann, Carolee
Schonzeit, Benjamin
Schorre, Charles
Schultz, Caroline Reel
Schuselka, Elfi
Schwartz, Buky
Scott, Sam
Seabourn, Bert Dail
Searles, Stephen
Sears, Stanton Gray
Sebelius, Helen
Seborovski, Carole
Sehring, Adolf
Setlow, Neva C
Shackelford, Bud (Lyne T)
Shaffer, Richard
Shannon, Charles
Shapiro, Dee
Sharits, Paul Jeffrey
Shashaty, Yolanda Victoria
Shaw, Jim
Shaw, Karen
Shaw, Mary Todd
Shaw, Reesey
Shay, Ed
Shechter, Ben-Zion
Shechter, Laura J
Sheirr, Olga (Krolik)
Shelby, Lila (Lila Norma Wallace)
Shepherd, Helen Parsons
Sherwood, Katherine
Shields, Anne Kesler
Shuebrook, Ron (Ronald Lee)
Shukman, Solomon
Siegel, Fran
Siler, Patrick W
Silverberg, Ellen Ruth
Simon, Netty D
Simonian, Judith
Slaymaker, Martha
Sligh, Clarissa T
Smalley, Stephen Francis
Smith, Cary
Smith, Donald C
Smith, Gary Douglas
Smith, Jaune Quick-to-See
Smolarek, Waldemar
Smyth, Ed
Snyder, Joan
Solomon, Vita Petrosky
Sorman, Steven
Sorogas, Sotiris
Sottung, George (K)
Southard, James Bruce
Southwell, William Joseph
Sowers, Miriam R
Spandorfer, Merle Sue
Sparkman, Gene (Carl), Jr
Speyer, Nora
Spiegelman, Lon Howard
Spofford, Sally(Sarah H Spofford)
Staffel, Doris
Stanczak, Julian
Stanford, Ginny C
Stanley, John Jacob
Stanley, M Louise
Stayton, Janet
Stein, Ronald Jay
Steiner, Michael
Stockdale, John A D
Stoffa, Michael
Stone, Jeffrey Ingram
Strosahl, William
Suggs, Don
Swetcharnik, William Norton
Szilvasy, Linda Markuly
Tait, Will(iam) H
Talbert, Richard Harrison
Tavenner, Patricia
Tchakalian, Sam
Tetherow, Michael
Thiebaud, (Morton) Wayne
Thomason, Tom William
Thompson, Cappy (Catherine)
Thompson, Ernest Thorne, Jr
Thompson, Jean Danforth
Thomson, Colin (H)
Tinkler, Barrie Keith
Tobey, Alton S
Tobias, Richard
Toledo, Francisco
Tomchuk, Marjorie
Tompkins, Michael
Toperzer, Thomas Raymond
Trasobares, Cesar
True, David
Tsai, Wen-Ying
Tucker, James Ewing
Tullis, Garner H
Tyzack, Michael
Urban, Vladimir T
Urquhart, Tony (Anthony Morse)
Valadez, John
Valenstein, Alice
Van Harlingen, Jean (Ann)
Van Horn, Dana Carl
Varnay Jones, Theodora
Verostko, Roman Joseph
Vitale, Magda
Walinska, Anna
Walker, Larry
Wallace, Gael Lynn
Wallace, Kenneth William
Wang, Gar
Ward, Elaine
Warner, Douglas Warfield
Warren, Win (W Winton)
Watrous, James Scales
Watson, Mary Anne
Webb, Patrick
Weinberg, Bella Rebecca
Weisberg, Ruth Ellen
Werner Vaughn, Salle
Wessel, Fred W
Westfall, Stephen V R
Whitson, Angie
Willoughby, Jane Baker
Wilson, Cynthia Lindsay
Winer, Donald Arthur
Wise, Sue
Wolff, Dee I
Wolpert, Etta
Wood, Nicholas Wheeler
Woodford, Don (Donald Paul)
Wool, Christoper
Wortzel, Adrianne
Wright, (Charles) Clifford
Wright, Faith-dorian
Yarber, Robert
Yarotsky, Lori
Yates, Marvin Clarence
Yaworski, Alex F(rancis)
Yochim, Louise Dunn
Younger, Dan Forrest
Youngerman, Jack

Acrylic, Oil

Aaron, Evalyn (Wilhelmina) Keisler
Abad, Pacita
Abany, Albert Charles
Abbett, Robert Kennedy
Abbrescia, Joeseph Leonard
Abdell, Douglas
Abeles, Sigmund
Abrams, Herbert E
Abrams, Vivien (Joy)
Abril, Ben (Benjamin)
Achepohl, Keith Anden
Ackerman, Rudy Schlegel
Acosta, Manuel Gregorio
Adan, Suzanne Rae
Adickes, David (Pryor)
Adkison, Kathleen (Gemberling)
Adler, Lee
Adrian, Barbara (Mrs Franklin Tramutola)
Afsary, Cyrus
Ahl, Henry C
Ahlgren, Roy B
Ahlsted, David R
Ahlstrom, Ronald Gustin
Ahrendt, Christine
Ahysen, Harry Joseph
Aiken, William A
Aistars, John
Ajay, Abe
Akawie, Thomas Frank
Alexander, John E
Alexenberg, Mel
Alexick, David Francis
Alfano, Angel
Allen, Catherine MacDonald
Allen, Jere Hardy
Allen, Jesse
Allgood, Charles Henry
Alling, Janet D
Alpen-Whiteside, Dale
Alpert, George
Altmann, Henry S
Alvarez, Candida
Amano, Taka
Amason, Alvin Eli
Amen, Irving
Amenoff, Gregory
Amico, David Michael
Amory, Claudia
Amos, Emma
Amyx, Leon Kirkman
Andersen, Leif (Werner)
Anderson, Gunnar Donald
Anderson, Robert Alexander
Anderson, Robert Raymond
Anderson, Sally J
Anderson, Troy
Anderson, Warren Harold
Andrade, Bruno
Andrade, Edna Wright
Andrews, Mari
Andriulli, Robert
Andrus, James Roman
Angeloch, Robert
Anguiano, Raul
Annus, John Augustus
Anthony, William Graham
Antreasian, Garo Zareh
Antrim, Craig Keith
Apgar, Nicolas Adam
App, Timothy
Appel, Karel

PAINTER (cont)
Appel, Thelma
Appleman, David Earl
Aptekar, Ken
Aquino, Humberto
Archer, Cynthia
Arcilesi, Vincent J
Arcomano, Cathryn
Ard, Saradell (Saradell Ard Frederick)
Arias-Misson, Nela
Armstrong, Geoffrey
Armstrong, Martha (Allen)
Arneson, Wendell H
Arnold, Florence M
Arnold, Robert Lloyd
Arsenault, Kate Whitman
Arvin, Irmgard Pinckernell
Ascian
Ashbaugh, Dennis John
Asher, Elise
Asher, Lila Oliver
Asihene, Emmanuel V
Asoma, Tadashi
Atkins, Rosalie Marks
Atlee, Emilie DeS
Atwood Pinardi, Brenda
Auerbach, Frank
Ausby, Ellsworth Augustus
Austin, Darrel
Auth, Robert R
Avakian, John
Avedisian, Edward
Avedon, Barry
Azaceta, Luis Cruz
Azuma, Norio
B(eck), Rosemarie
Bacarella, Flavia
Bach, Dirk
Bachardy, Don
Bacigalupa, Andrea
Baczek, Peter Gerard
Badalamenti, Fred
Baeder, John
Baer, Jo
Bailey, Barbara Ann
Bailey, Marcia Mead
Baker, Cornelia Draves
Baker, Dina Gustin
Baker, Joe
Bakke, Larry Hubert
Balaban, Diane
Balahutrak, Lydia Bodnar
Balance, Jerrald Clark
Balas, Irene
Bales, Jewel
Ball, Lyle V
Ball, Walter N
Balossi, John
Banas, Anne
Bandel, Lennon Raymond
Banks, Allan R
Bannard, Walter Darby
Bansemer, Roger L
Barbeau, Marcel (Christian)
Barbee, Rob
Barbee, Robert Thomas
Barber, Sam
Barbera, Ross William
Barberis, Dorothy Watkeys
Barboza, Anthony
Barkus, Mariona Marcia
Barnes, Carole D
Barnes, Cliff (Clifford V)
Barnes, Curt (Curtis Edward)
Barnes, Kitt
Barnes, William David
Barnett, Earl D
Barnett, Emily
Barnett, Helmut
Barnwell, John L
Barooshian, Martin
Barowitz, Elliott
Barr, Norman
Barreres, Domingo
Barrios, Benny Perez
Barron, Ros
Barsch, Wulf Erich
Bartek, Tom
Bartnick, Harry William
Barton, Georgie Read
Barton, John Murray
Bartz, James Ross
Bashor, John W
Baskerville, Charles
Bass, David Loren
Bass, Judy
Bateman, Robert McLellan
Bateman, Ronald C
Bates, David
Bates, Leo James
Batt, Miles Girard
Baumbach, Harold
Bayer, Arlyne
Bayless, Raymond
Beall, Joanna
Beallor, Fran
Beam, Mary Todd
Beament, Tib (Thomas Harold)
Bear, Marcelle L
Beard, Richard Elliott
Beattie, George
Beauchamp, Robert
Beaumont, Mona
Bechtle, Robert Alan
Beck, Lonnie Lee
Beck, Margit
Becker, Bettie (Bettie Geraldine Wathall)
Becker, Natalie Rose
Beckerman, Nancy Greyson
Beckhard, Ellie (Eleanor)
Beeler, Joe (Neil)
Beeman, Malinda
Beerman, Herbert
Beery, Art (Arthur O)
Behnke, Leigh
Belag, Andrea
Bell, Charles S
Bell, Coca (Mary Catlett)
Bell, Dozier
Bell, Temma
Bell, Trevor
Belle, Anna (Anna Belle Birckett)
Belville, Scott Robert
Bendell, Marilyn
Bender, Bill
Bender, May
Benham, Pamela J
Benham, Robert Charles
Benjamin, Alice (Alice Benjamin Boudreau)
Benjamin, Karl Stanley
Bennett, Rainey
Bentley, Claude
Berd, Morris
Berg, Tom
Berger, Pat (Patricia Eve)
Berkon, Martin
Berlind, Robert
Berlyn, Sheldon
Berman, Ariane R
Berman, Ellen Mercil Trew
Berman, Fred J
Bermingham, Debra Pandell
Bernay, Betti
Berneche, Jerry Douglas
Bernstein, Gerald
Bernstein, Theresa
Berresford, Virginia
Berry, Glenn
Besser, Arne Charles
Betensky, Rose Hart
Bettinson, Brenda
Betts, Edward Howard
Bhavsar, Natvar Prahladji
Biala, Janice
Biederman, James Mark
Bierly, Edward J
Bigelow, Robert Clayton
Biggs, Janet
Binai, Paul Freye
Bireline, George Lee
Birmelin, A Robert
Bishop, Jacqueline K
Bishop, James
Bishop, Marjorie Cutler
Black, Lisa
Blackburn, Ed M
Blacketer, James Richard
Blackwell, Tom (Thomas Leo)
Blagden, Thomas P
Blaine, Nell
Blair, Carl Raymond
Blair, Robert Noel
Blake, Jane
Blakeslee, Sarah
Blaustein, Al
Blayton, Betty (Betty Blayton-Taylor)
Bleach, Bruce R
Bleckner, Ross
Bleser, Katherine Alice
Block, Amanda Roth
Blodgett, Anne Washington
Bloom, Donald S
Bloom, Hyman
Blosser, Nicholas
Blovits, Larry John
Bluhm, Norman
Blumberg, Ron
Blumenthal, Fritz
Boardman, Deborah
Boardman, Seymour
Bobak, Bruno Joseph
Boccia, Edward Eugene
Bocour, Leonard
Boeve, Edgar Gene
Bogart, George A
Bogart, Richard Jerome
Bohler, Joseph Stephen
Bohnen, Blythe
Bolt, Ron
Bolton, Robin Jean
Bond, Oriel Edmund
Bonevardi, Marcelo
Booth, Dot
Booth, George Warren
Boothe, Power
Bopp, Emery
Borax, Benjamin
Bordes, Adrienne
Borgatta, Robert Edward
Borofsky, Jon
Borstein, Elena
Bosse, Janet C
Bossert, Edythe H
Bosson, Jack (John Edwin), Jr
Bostelle, Thomas (Theodore)
Boterf, Check (Chester Arthur)
Bott, Patricia Allen
Boucher, Tania Kunsky
Bouldin, Marshall Jones, III
Bourgeois, Douglas
Boutis, Tom
Bove, Richard
Bower, Gary David
Bowes, Betty Miller
Bowie, Effie Belle
Bowler, Joseph, Jr
Bowling, Frank
Bowling, Gary Robert
Bowman, Bruce
Bowman, George Leo
Bowman, John
Bowman, Ken
Bowman, Richard
Boxer, Stanley (Robert)
Boyd, Michael
Boylan, John Lewis
Bradford, Howard
Bradley, David P(aul)
Bradshaw, Robert George
Brady, Charles
Bragar, Philip Frank
Braig, Betty Lou
Brainard, Owen
Braley, Jean
Bramhall, Kib
Brams, Joan
Brandt, Warren
Branstetter, Gwendolyn H
Brawley, Robert Julius
Breiger, Elaine
Brendel, Bettina
Brenno, Vonnie Mei-Lin
Brett, Nancy
Brice, William
Briggs, Lamar A
Bright, Al(fred Lee)
Brightwell, Walter
Bristow, William Arthur
Brito, Maria
Britt, Nelson Clark
Britt, Sam Glenn
Brodhead, Quita
Brody, Arthur William
Brody, Blanche
Broner, Robert
Brooke, Pegan
Broome, Rick (Richard Raymond)
Broomfield, Adolphus George
Bross, Albert L, Jr
Brothers, Barry A
Brouillette, Al(bert C)
Brown, Alice Dalton
Brown, Bruce Robert
Brown, Frederick James
Brown, James
Brown, John Hall
Brown, June Gottlieb
Brown, Larry
Brown, Reynold
Brown, Theophilus
Browne, Syd J
Browne, Vivian E
Brownett, Thelma Denyer
Browning, Colleen
Brucker, Edmund
Brulc, Lillian G
Bruneau, Kittie
Brusca, Jack
Brust, Robert Gustave
Brustlein, Daniel
Brutosky, (Sister) Mary Veronica, CSJ
Bryan, Jack L
Bryans, John Armond
Bryant, Laura Militzer
Bryce, Eileen Ann
Bryce, Mark Adams
Brzozowski, Richard Joseph
Buch, Gary
Buckley, Mary L (Mrs Joseph M Parriott)
Bucknall, Malcolm Roderick
Buckner, Kay Lamoreux
Buecker, Robert
Bujnowski, Joel A
Bumgardner, James Arliss
Buonagurio, Edgar R
Burford, Byron Leslie
Burgess, Joseph James, Jr
Burgess, Linda Suzanne
Burggraf, Ray Lowell
Burke, Daniel V
Burkert, Robert Randall
Burko, Diane
Burleigh, Kimberly
Burleson, Charles Trentman
Burley, Lina
Burnett, Patricia Hill
Burns, Jerome
Burns, Josephine
Burns, Sheila
Burns, Stan
Buros, Luella
Burpee, James Stanley
Burr, Lee Reynolds
Burris, Bruce C
Burt, Dan
Bush, Jill Lobdill
Bushnell, Kenneth Wayne
Buszko, Irene J
Butchkes, Sydney

PAINTER (cont)
Butler, James D
Butti, Linda (Benincasa)
Bye, Ranulph
Byrd, D Gibson
Byrd, Jerry
Caddell, Foster
Cade, Walter, III
Cady, Dennis Vern
Cady, Samuel Lincoln
Cain, Joseph Alexander
Caiserman-Roth, Ghitta
Cajori, Charles F
Calabro, Richard Paul
Calamar, Gloria
Calapai, Letterio
Calcagno, Lawrence
Calhoun, Larry Darryl
Callahan, Aileen (Aileen Loughlin Callahan)
Callicott, Burton Harry
Camastro-Pritchett, Rose
Cameron, Eric
Campanelli, Pauline Eble
Campbell, David Paul
Campbell, Jeanne Begien
Campbell, Jewett
Campbell, Richard Horton
Campbell, William Henry
Cannuli, Richard Gerald
Canright, Sarah Anne
Cantine, David
Cantor, Rusty
Cantrell, Jim
Caplan Ciarrochi, Sandra
Capobianco, Domenick
Card, Royden
Cardinal, Marcelin
Cardoso, Anthony
Carlin, James
Carlos, (James) Edward
Carlson, Cynthia J
Carnwath, Squeak
Carpenter, Earl L
Carpenter, Gilbert Frederick (Bert)
Carrero, Jaime
Carrington, Joy Harrell
Carroll, James F L
Carswell, Rodney
Carter, Carol A
Carter, Clarence Holbrook
Carter, Frederick Timmins
Carter, Gary
Carter, Katharine Tipton
Carter, Nanette Carolyn
Cartmell, Helen
Carulla, Ramon
Casas, Fernando
Casas, Melesio (Mel)
Casellas, Joachim
Casey, Tim (Timothy William)
Cassara, Frank
Castro, Giovanni
Caswell, Helen Rayburn
Catchi
Catok, Lottie Meyer
Caton, David
Cattaneo, (Jacquelyn A) Kammerer
Cattell, Ray
Catterall, John Edward
Catusco, Louis
Cauduro, Rafael
Cecil, Charles Harkless
Celentano, Francis Michael
Cengle
Cervene, Richard
Cetín, Anton
Chadeayne, Robert Osborne
Chaiklin, Amy
Chambers, William McWillie
Chandler, Michael Robert
Chaplin, George Edwin
Chapman, Walter Howard
Chappell, Berkley Warner
Charlot, Martin Day
Chase, Jeanne Norman
Chase, Louisa L
Chatmas, John T
Che, Chuang
Cheatham, Frank Reagan
Chemeche, George
Chen, Hilo
Cheng, Emily
Cher, Beatrice (Beatrice Michelle Cher-Killigan)
Cherkas, Constantine
Chernow, Ann
Cheshire, Craig Gifford
Chesney, Lee R, Jr
Chevins, Christopher M
Chi, Chen
Chieffo, Clifford Toby
Chilton, Fred
Chimes, Thomas James
Chinni, Peter Anthony
Cho, Y(eou) J(ui)
Chodkowski, Henry, Jr
Christensen, Don B
Christensen, Neil C
Christensen, Ted
Christiansen, Diane
Christie, Robert Duncan
Chu, Julia Nee
Church, Maude
Churchill, Diane
Ciarrochi, Ray
Cicero, Carmen L
Cintron, Joseph M
Civitello, John Patrick
Civitico, Bruno
Clapsaddle, Jerry
Clark, Claude
Clark, Michael Vinson
Clarke, Ann
Clarke, John Clem
Cleary, Barbara B
Cleary, Manon Catherine
Clement, Kathleen (Ruth)
Cliff, Denis Antony
Clive, Richard R
Cloar, Carroll
Close, Dean Purdy
Closson, Nanci Blair
Clymer, Albert Anderson
Cobb, Ruth
Cocker, Barbara Joan
Cockrill, Sherna
Coe, Anne Elizabeth
Coe, Henry
Coheleach, Guy Joseph
Cohen, Arthur Morris
Cohen, Bruce Joel
Cohen, Cora
Cohen, Jean
Cohn, Max Arthur
Coit, M B
Coker, Carl David
Colao, Rudolph
Colarusso, Corrine Camille
Cole, Donald
Cole, Grace V
Cole, Joyce
Cole, Max
Coleman, Constance Depler
Coleman, M L (Michael Lee)
Coleman, Michael
Collado, Lisa
Collins, Dan (Daniel McClellan)
Collins, Lowell Daunt
Colt, John Nicholson
Colville, Alexander
Colway, James R
Concannon, George Robert
Concha, Jerry
Congdon, William (Grosvenor)
Conger, William
Conklin, Andrew Sterrett
Conn, David Edward
Connatser, Larry Stuart
Connelly, Chuck
Conner, Ann
Connolly, Jerome Patrick
Conover, Robert Fremont
Conrad, Nancy R
Constantine, Greg John
Cook, August Charles
Cook, Joseph S
Cooke, Jody Helen
Cooke, Judy
Cooley, Adelaide N
Cooper, Wayne
Copeland, Lila
Copenhaver-Fellows, Deborah (Deborah Lynne Fellows)
Copley, William Nelson
Copt, Louis J
Cormier, Robert John
Cornell, Thomas Browne
Cornin, Jon
Correa, Flora Horst
Cortor, Eldzier
Costan, Chris
Costello, Cynthia Ann
Cote, Alan
Cottingham, Robert
Couper, Charles Alexander
Courtney, Barbara Wood
Courtney, Suzan
Courtright, Robert
Covington, Harrison Wall
Cowan, Ralph Wolfe
Cowles, Fleur
Coyne, John Michael
Craft, Douglas D
Cramer, Richard Charles
Craven, David James
Crawford, Thom Cooney
Creecy, Herbert Lee
Cretara, Domenic Anthony
Crimi, Alfred D
Crotto, Paul
Crown, Keith Allen
Crown, Roberta Lila
Crozier, Richard Lewis
Crum, David
Crump, Walter Moore, Jr
Crystal, Boris
Csernus, Tibor
Culver, Michael L
Cummings, David William
Cunnick, Gloria Helen
Cunningham, (Charles) Bruce
Cunningham, Francis
Cuppaidge, Virginia
Curley, Donald Houston
Currie, Bruce
Curtis, David
Curtis, Mary Cranfill
Curtis, Philip Campbell
Curtis, Roger William
Curtis, Terry Wayne
Cuthbert, Virginia
Cutler, Grayce E
Cutler, Ronnie
Cyphers, Peggy K
Czimbalmos, Magdolna Paal
Dailey, Chuck (Charles Andrew)
Dailey, Michael Dennis
Dallmann, Daniel Forbes
Daly, Kathleen (Kathleen Daly Pepper)
Damast, Elba Cecilia
Daniels, Astar (Charlotte Louise Daniels)
Dantzic, Cynthia Maris
Danziger, Fred Frank
D'Arcangelo, Allan M
Darton, Christopher
Daskaloff, Gyorgy
Daughters, Robert A
Davenport, Ray
Davenport, Rebecca Read
David, Don Raymond
Davidek, Stefan
Davidson, Herbert Laurence
Davidson, Jean
Davidson, Nancy
Daviee, Jerry Michael
Davies, Kenneth Southworth
Davis, Alonzo Joseph
Davis, Brad (Bradley Darius)
Davis, Paul
Davis, Robert
Davis, Ronald
Davis, Thelma Ellen
Davis, Walter Lewis
Dawley, Joseph William
Dawson, John Allan
Day, Burnis Calvin
Deaderick, Joseph
Dean, Nat(alie Carol)
Dean, Peter
De Blasi, Tony
De Champlain, Vera Chopak
Dechar, Peter
De Donato, Louis
Dee, Leo Joseph
Deem, George
De Forest, Roy Dean
De Groat, George Hugh
De Kergommeaux, Duncan
De Knight, Avel
De La Vega, Antonio
De Leeuw, Leon
Della-Volpe, Ralph Eugene
DeLoyht-Arendt, Mary
Delson, Elizabeth
DeMatties, Nick
De Monte, Claudia
Denney, Jim (James David)
Dennis, Roger Wilson
Denniston, Douglas
Deo, Marjoree Nee
De Palma, Brett
Dernovich, Donald Frederick
DeRosa, Michael Louis
De Santo, Stephen C
DesJarlait, Robert D
De Smet, Lorraine
Desmidt, Thomas H
Desser, Maxwell Milton
Dessner, Murray
Devlin, Harry
Devlin, Wende
Dibble, George
Di Cerbo, Michael
Dickerson, Brian S
Dickerson, Daniel Jay
Dickerson, Edward Ted
Dickerson, Vera Mason
Dickinson, Norman
Dickson, Mark Amos
Diebenkorn, Richard
Diehl, Hans-Jurgen
Diehl, Sevilla S
Di Fate, Vincent
DiFranza, Americo M
Di Giacinto, Sharon
Dill, Laddie John
Dillon, Paul Sanford
Dimondstein, Morton
Dinnerstein, Harvey
Dinnerstein, Simon A
Dixon, Ken
Dixon, Willard
Do, Kim V
Dobbs, John Barnes
Dodd, Lois
Dodd, M(ary) Irene
Dodge, Joseph Jeffers
Dodge, Robert G
Dominique, John August
Donahue, Philip Richard
Donley, Robert Morris
Doo Da Post (Edward Ferdinand Higgins III), III
Dooley, Helen Bertha
Doolin, James Lawrence
Doray, Audrey Capel
Doren, Henry J T
Dorn, Ruth (Dornbush)
Dorst, Claire V
Douenias, Natalie

PAINTER (cont)
Douglas, Edwin Perry
Douglas, L J
Douglas, Tom Howard
Douke, Daniel W
Dove, Toni
Dowd, Robert (O'Dowd Robert)
Downes, Rackstraw
Doyle, Joe
Drapell, Joseph
Draper, William Franklin
Dreiband, Laurence
Dreisbach, Clarence Ira
Dreskin, Jeanet Steckler
Drexler, Lynne
Droege, Anthony Joseph, II
Drummond, Sally Hazelet
Duback, Charles S
Dubasky, Valentina
Dubinskis, Anda
Dublac, Robert Revak
Duca, Alfred Milton
Duffy, Michael John
Dugmore, Edward
Duis, Rita
Du Jardin, Gussie
Dumas, Antoine
Duncan, Ruth
Dunkelman, Loretta
Dunlap, Loren Edward
Dunn, Fontaine
Dunow, Esti
Duren, Stephen D
Durham, Jeanette R
Durham, William
Durr, Pat (Patricia Beth)
Dutton, Allen A
Dverin, Anatoly
Dwyer, James
Dyer, M Wayne
Dyyon, Frazier
Dzigurski, Alex
Dzubas, Friedel
Eastman, Gene M
Easton, Roger David
Eberly, Vickie
Ebie, William Dennis
Eckart, Christian
Eckert, William Dean
Eckstein, Ruth
Eddy, Don
Edelman, Ann
Edelman, Rita
Edelson, Mary Beth
Eden, Glenn
Edge, Douglas Benjamin
Edmonson, Randall W
Edouard, Pierre (Pierre Edward Maussion)
Egeli, Cedric Baldwin
Egleston, Truman G
Eglitis, Laimons
Eilers, Fred (Anton Frederick)
Eisenberg, Sonja Miriam
Eisenstat, Benjamin
Eisentrager, James A
Eisinger, Harry
Eisner, Carole Swid
Eliot, Lucy Carter
Eller, Evelyn (Evelyn Eller Rosenbaum)
Elliot, John Theodore
Elliott, Anne
Ellis, Richard
Emmert, Pauline Gore
Enders, Elizabeth McGuire
Engelson, Carol
Engle, Chet
English, John Arbogast
Enman, Tom Kenneth
Enriquez, Gaspar
Epstein, Betty O
Erbe, Gary Thomas
Eres, Eugenia
Erickson, Mark D
Ericson, Beatrice
Erlebacher, Martha Mayer
Erwin, Fran (Frances Suzanne)
Esaki, Yasuhiro
Escalet, Frank Diaz
Eshoo, Robert
Estes, Richard
Etter, Howard Lee
Etting, Emlen
Ettinger, Susi Steinitz
Evans, Burford Elonzo
Evans, Richard
Evans, Tom R
Evaul, William H, Jr
Evett, Kenneth Warnock
Ewing, Edgar Louis
Faccinto, Victor Paul
Facey, Martin Kerr
Faden, Lawrence Steven
Falfan, Alfredo
Falsetta, Vincent Mario
Faragasso, Jack
Farber, Amanda
Farber, Dennis H
Farber, Maya M
Fares, William O
Farian, Babette S
Farm, Gerald E
Farnham, Alexander
Farruggio, Remo Michael
Faudie, Fred
Faulkner, Frank
Faust, James Wille
Fax, Elton Clay
FeBland, Harriet
Feder, Ben
Federe, Marion
Feininger, T Lux
Feist, Harold E
Feist, Warner David
Fekete, Brian
Felisky, Barbara Rosbe
Fellows, Alice
Felter, James Warren
Feltus, Alan
Fenn, (Frances) Elizabeth
Fenton, Alan
Fenton, Howard Carter
Fenwick, Roly (William Roland)
Ferris, (Carlisle) Keith
Ferriter, Clare
Fett, William F
Feuerman, Carol Jeannne
Few, James Cecil, PSA
Fichter, Herbert Francis
Fillerup, Mel
Filmus, Michael Roy
Filmus, Stephen I
Fincher, John H
Fine, Jane
Finkelstein, Louis
Finnegan, Sharyn Marie
Fiore, Joseph A
Firfires, Nicholas Samuel
Fischer, John
Fish, Janet I
Fish, Richard G
Fishburne, St Julian (Le Roy)
Fisher, Leonard Everett
Fisher, Philip C
Fisher, Sandra
Fitzpatrick, Joseph Cyril
Flahavin, Marian Joan
Flanery, Gail
Flattmann, Alan Raymond
Flecker, Maurice Nathan
Fleming, Thomas Michael
Florin, Sharon June
Fludd, Reginald Joseph
Fluek, Toby
Fogg, Rebecca Snider
Folsom, Fred Gorham, III
Fontaine, E Joseph
Ford, John
Forester, Russell
Forge, Andrew Murray
Forman, Alice
Forrest, Christopher Patrick
Forsman, Chuck (Charles Stanley)
Fortess, Karl E
Fourcard, Inez Garey
Fournier, Alex
Fowler, Mel
Fox, John
Fra, Dahli-Sterne
Frace, Charles Lewis
Fraley, David K
Frame, Robert (Aaron)
Frankfurter, Jack
Franklin, Don (Donald Wayne Franklin)
Franklin, Hannah
Fransioli, Thomas Adrian
Frater, Hal
Frazer, John Thatcher
Fredenthal, Ruth Ann
Frederick, Deloras Ann
Fredericks, Beverly Magnuson
Freed, Douglass Lynn
Freedman, Deborah S
Freeman, David L
Freeman, Kathryn
Freeman, Mark
Freeman, Robert Lee
Freilicher, Jane
Freund, Harry Louis
Freund, Tibor
Friberg, Arnold
Frick, Robert Oliver
Friend, Patricia M
Friese, Nancy Marlene
Fromboluti, Iona
Fromboluti, Sideo
Frontz, Leslie
Fukui, Nobu
Fuller, Emily Rutgers
Fundora, Thomas
Furr, Jim
Fussiner, Howard
Fyfe, Jo Suzanne (Storch)
Gabin, George Joseph
Gach, George
Gagnier, Bruce
Gale, William Henry
Gallagher, Cynthia
Galles, Arie Alexander
Galuszka, Frank Richard
Gammon, Juanita-La Verne
Gammon, Reginald Adolphus
Gantz, Ann Cushing
Garchik, Morton Lloyd
Gardner, Joan A
Gardner, Sheila
Gardner, Susan Ross
Garet, Jedd
Garman, Ed
Garrett, Stuart Grayson
Garrison, David Earl
Garrison, Elizabeth Jane
Garrison, Eve
Garston, Gerald Drexler
Garver, Walter Raymond
Garwood, Audrey
Gary, Jan (Mrs William D Gorman)
Gast, Michael Carl
Gatewood, Maud
Gauvin, Claude E
Gavalas, Alexander Beary
Gechtoff, Sonia
Gehr, Mary (Ray)
Geiger, Phillip Neil
Geis, Milton Arthur
Gekiere, Madeleine
Gelber, Samuel
Gelinas, Robert William
Gellatly, Michael
Geltman, Lily
Gentry, Warren Miller
George, Richard Allan
George, Thomas
Georges, Paul G
Gerbarg, Darcy
Gerhold, William Henry
Gerlach, Christopher S
Germano, Thomas
Gersh, Bill
Gersovitz, Sarah Valerie
Gerzso, Gunther
Gibbons, Hugh (James)
Gibson, Benedict S
Gibson, John Stuart
Gilbert, Albert Earl
Gilbert, Herb
Gilbert, Lionel
Gilbertson, Charlotte
Gilboy, Margaretta
Giles, Newell Walton, Jr
Gill, Gene
Gillespie, Gregory Joseph
Gimblett, Max(well)
Ginsburg, Max
Ginzburg, Yankel (Jacob)
Giobbi, Edward Gioachino
Giraudier, Antonio
Gjertson, Stephen Arthur
Glorig, Ostor
Goddard, Vivian
Godfrey, Robert
Godfrey, Winnie (Winifred M)
Goedike, Shirl
Goertz, Augustus Frederick, III
Goetz, Mary Anna
Gold, Fay Helfand
Gold, Sharon Cecile
Goldberg, Arnold Herbert
Goldin, Leon
Goldsleger, Cheryl
Goldsmith, Lawrence Charles
Goldstein, Gladys
Goldstein, Howard
Goldstein, Nathan
Golub, Leon
Gomez-Quiroz, Juan Manuel
Gonzales, Carlotta (Mrs Richard Lahey)
Gonzalez, Juan J
Gonzalez-Tornero, Sergio
Goodman, Ken(neth Hunt)
Goodman, Sidney
Goodridge, Lawrence Wayne
Goodwill, Margaret
Goodwin, Guy
Goodyear, John L
Gorchov, Ron
Gordley, Marilyn Classe
Gordon, Josephine
Gore, David Alan
Gore, Ken (Kenneth Leon)
Gore, Samuel Marshall
Gorelick, Shirley
Gorman, R C
Gornik, April
Gorski, Daniel Alexander
Gough, Robert Alan
Goulet, Lorrie
Gourevitch, Jacqueline
Goutman, Dolya
Grafelman, Glenn Allen
Grafton, Rick (Frederick Wellington)
Graham, Bob
Graham, Walter
Grandee, Joe Ruiz
Granstaff, William Boyd
Grass, Patty Patterson
Grasso, Salvatore Fortunato
Grauer, Sherry
Graves, Ka (Kathleen Rose)
Graves, Robert Edward
Gray, Jim
Gray, Larry
Gray, Marie Elise
Gray, Robert Hugh
Greaver, Hanne
Greco, Anthony Joseph
Green, Art
Green, Denise G
Green, George D

PAINTER (cont)
Green, Martin Leonard
Greenberg, Gloria
Greene, Ethel Maud
Greene, Stephen
Greenfield, Joan Beatrice
Greenleaf, Virginia
Greenly, Colin
Greenstone, Marion
Greer, Walter (Marion)
Gregor, Harold Laurence
Gregory, Bruce
Gregory, Stan(ley Wayne)
Grelle, Martin Glen
Grey, Alex V
Gribin, Liz
Griefen, John Adams
Griesedieck, Ellen
Grigoriadis, Mary
Grigsby, Jefferson Eugene, Jr
Grimes, Margaret W
Groat, Hall Pierce
Groedel, Burt Jay
Groell, Theophil
Gronk
Grooms, Red
Grosch, Laura
Gross, Charles Merrill
Gross, Earl
Gross, Rainer
Grossman, Barbara
Grotz, Dorothy Rogers
Groves, Naomi Jackson
Grubb, David
Gruber, Aaronel deRoy
Grucza, Leo (Victor)
Grupp, Carl Alf
Gruppe, Charles
Guccione, Juanita
Gummelt, Samuel
Gunderson, Karen
Gunter, Frank Elliott
Gurbacs, John Joseph
Gursoy, Ahmet
Gussow, Sue Ferguson
Gutzeit, Fred
Guzevich-Sommers, Kreszenz (Cynthia)
Haack, Cynthia R
Haerer, Carol
Haessle, Jean-Marie Georges
Hagin, Nancy
Halaby, Samia Asaad
Halbrooks, Darryl Wayne
Haley, Sally (Sally Fulton Haley Russo)
Halko, Joe
Hall, John (Scott)
Hall, Rex Earl
Hall, Robert L
Hall, Susan
Hallam, Beverly (Linney)
Halley, Peter
Halsey, Brian Elliott
Hamann, Marilyn D
Hamar, Diana Kathleen
Hamill, Tim J
Hammer, Alfred Emil
Hammer, Elizabeth B
Hammerman, Pat Jo
Hammersley, Frederick
Hammond, Harmony
Hammond, Red
Hampton, Phillip Jewel
Handell, Albert George
Handville, Robert T
Hanes, James (Albert)
Hanley, Jack
Hanna, Annette Adrian
Hanna, Paul Dean, Jr
Hannah, Duncan (Rathbun)
Hansen, Gaylen Capener
Hanson, Philip Holton
Harbart, Gertrude Felton
Harding, Ann
Hardy, David Whittaker, III
Hari, Kenneth
Harkins, George C, Jr
Harlan, Roma Christine
Harman, Maryann Whittemore
Harmon, Cliff Franklin
Harmon, David Edward
Harmon, Lily
Harms, Elizabeth
Harnick, Sylvia
Harper, Eleanor O'Neil
Harris, Alfred Peter
Harris, Charney Anita
Harris, Dorothy D
Harris, Robert George
Harris, William Wadsworth, II
Harrison, Tony
Hart, Betty Miller
Hartell, John
Harter, John Burton
Hartigan, Grace
Hartman, Joanne A
Hartwig, Heinie
Harvey, Donald
Haseltine, James Lewis
Haseltine, Maury (Margaret Wilson)
Haskell, Jane
Hatch, Mary
Hatfield, Donald Gene
Hatke, Walter Joseph
Haug, Donald Raymond
Hausey, Robert Michael
Haverty, Grace Ligammari
Hawkins, Thomas Wilson, Jr
Hayes, Tua
Haynes, Douglas H
Haynes, George Edward
Haynes, R (Richard Thomas)
Haynie, Ron
Hayward, James
Hayward, Peter
Head, Cecil Franklin
Head, George Bruce
Healy, Julia Schmitt
Heard, Lillian
Heberling, Glen Austin
Hedden-Sellman, Zelda
Hedman, Teri Jo
Hedrick, Wally Bill
Heflin, Tom Pat
Heiloms, May
Heine-Baux, Manfred
Heinemann, Peter
Heinicke, Janet L Hart
Heipp, Richard Christian
Held, Philip
Helder, David Ernest
Heliker, John Edward
Helioff, Anne Graile (Mrs Benjamin Hirschberg)
Heller, Dorothy
Helman, Eve
Helman, Phoebe
Henderson, Robbin Legere
Hendricks, Barkley Leonnard
Hendricks, David Charles
Hennesy, Gerald Craft
Henry, Jean
Henry, Robert
Hensley, Jackson Morey
Herbert, Pinkney
Hernandez-Cruz, Luis
Herring, Jan (Janet Mantel)
Heusser, Eleanore Elizabeth (Eleanore Heusser Ferholt)
Hibel, Edna
Higgins, Dick
Hildebrandt, William Albert
Hill, Charles Christopher
Hill, Clinton J
Hill, J Tweed
Hill, Peter
Hillis, Richard K
Hilson, Douglas
Himmelfarb, John David
Hinman, Charles B
Hios, Theo
Hirsch, Gilah Yelin
Hitch, Jean Leason
Hitch, Robert A
Hitch, Stewart
Hobbie, Lucille
Hodge, R Garey
Hodgkins, Rosalind Selma
Hoener, Arthur
Hoffmann, Leesa L
Hofmann, Douglas William
Hogarth, Burne
Hogle, Ann Meilstrup
Hoie, Helen Hunt
Holden, Ruth Egri
Holder, Kenneth Allen
Hollerbach, Serge
Hollingshead, Joe Edgar
Hollingsworth, Alvin Carl
Hollister, Paul
Hollister, Valerie (Dutton)
Holm, Bill
Holm, Milton W
Holman, Arthur (Stearns)
Holmes, David Valentine
Holmes, Larry W
Holoun, Harold Dean
Homma, Kazufumi
Honig, Eleanor D
Honig, Mervin
Honjo, Masako
Hood, Dorothy
Hopkins, Budd
Hopkins, Peter
Hopper, Frank J
Horn, Bruce
Horn, Robert Nelson
Hornak, Ian John
Horvay, Martha J
Horwitz, Channa
Hough, Jennine
Houser, Allan C
Houser, Jim
Housewright, Artemis Skevakis
Houston, Mary Etta (King)
Howard, (Helen) Barbara
Howard, Dan F
Howes, Royce Bucknam
Howlett, Carolyn Svrluga
Hoyt, Frances Weston
Hsiao, Chin
Hu, Chi Chung
Hubbard, John
Hubenthal, Karl Samuel
Huggins, Victor, Jr
Hughes, Edward John
Hughey, Kirk (John Kirk)
Hughto, Darryl Leo
Hulett, Simonne R
Hull, Gregory Stewart
Hultberg, John
Humpfey, David
Humphrey, David Aiken
Humphrey, S L
Hunkler, Dennis
Hunt, (Julian) Courtenay
Hunter, Robert Douglas
Hunter, Robert Howard
Hurley, Denzil H
Hurley, Wilson
Hurt, Susanne M
Hushlak, Gerald
Hutchison, Elizabeth S
Hyson, Jean
Iacurto, Francesco
Iden, Sheldon
Imber, Jonathan
Impiglia, Giancarlo
Indiana, Robert
Inoue, Kazuko
Ipcar, Dahlov
Ippolito, Angelo
IRENA (Irene R Mikol)
Irwin, Lani Helena
Irwin, Lisa Dru
Isaacs, Ron
Isaacson, Lynn Judith
Isaak, Nicholas, Jr
Isenburger, Eric
Itatani, Michiko
Iwamoto, Ralph Shigeto
Jackson, Billy Morrow
Jackson, Everett Gee
Jackson, Harry Andrew
Jackson, Herb
Jackson, Lee
Jackson, Oliver Lee
Jacob, Ned
Jacobs, Harold
Jacobs, Helen Nichols
Jacobs, Ralph, Jr
Jacobshagen, N Keith, II
Jacquemon, Pierre
Jacquette, Yvonne Helene
Jaeger, Brenda Kay
Jaffe, Nora
Jameson, Demetrios George
Jameson, Philip Alexander
Jampol, Glenn D
Janelsins, Veronica
Janjigian, Lucy Elizabeth
Janko, May
Jankowski, Theodore Andrew
Janowich, Ronald
Janowitz, Joel
Jans, Candace
Janson, Agnes
Jaque, Louis
Jaramillo, Virginia
Jaudon, Valerie
Jay, Norma Joyce
Jean, Beverly (Beverly Jean Strong)
Jeff
Jeffers, Wendy Jane
Jenkins, Paul
Jerins, Edgar
Jess
Jessen, Shirley Agnes
Jessup, Robert
Jilg, Michael Florian
Joelson, Suzanne
Johanningmeier, Robert Alan
Johanson, George E
Johns, Christopher K(alman)
Johnson, Barbara Louise
Johnson, Brent
Johnson, Buffie
Johnson, Harvey William
Johnson, James Ralph
Johnson, Lee
Johnson, Richard A
Johnson-Ross, Robyn
Johnston, Roy E
Johnston, Thomas Alix
Johnston, William Medford
Jolley, Donal Clark
Jones, Franklin Reed
Jones, Henry Wanton
Jones, Herb (Leon Herbert), Jr
Jones, John Paul
Jones, Judy Voss
Jones, Lou (Mary Louise Humpton)
Jones, Marvin Harold
Jones, Norma L
Jones, Patty Sue
Jones, Ruthe Blalock
Jones, W Louis
Jordan, Barbara Schwinn
Jordan, Robert
Jorgensen, Roger M
Jorgensen, Sandra
Joyce, Marshall Woodside
Juarez, Roberto
Judd, De Forrest Hale
Judson, Jeannette Alexander
Julian, Lazaro
Jung, Kwan Yee
Jung, Yee Wah
Jurinko, Andy (Andrew Floyd)
Jurney, Donald (Benson)
Juszczyk, James Joseph
Kacere, John C
Kagle, Joseph L, Jr
Kahan, Leonard

PAINTER (cont)
Kahn, Susan B
Kahn, Tobi Aaron
Kahn, Wolf
Kaiman, Charles
Kainen, Jacob
Kaish, Morton
Kalb, Marty Joel
Kalina, Richard
Kamihira, Ben
Kane, Bob Paul
Kanovitz, Howard
Kaplan, Frederic Clark
Kaplan, Marilyn Flashenberg
Kaplinski, Buffalo
Kapsalis, Thomas Harry
Kardon, Carol
Karn, Gloria Stoll
Karniol, Hilda
Karp, Aaron S
Karwelis, Donald Charles
Kasak, Nikolai
Kass, Jacob James
Kasten, Karl Albert
Kastner, Barbara H
Katano, Marc
Katayama, Toshihiro
Katz, Eunice
Katz, Morris
Katzman, Herbert
Kauffman, Robert Craig
Kaufman, Irving
Kaufman, Stuart Martin
Kaupelis, Robert John
Kawa, Florence Kathryn
Kawabata, Minoru
Kay, Reed
Kearns, James Joseph
Keck, Hardu
Kehoe, Patrice
Keller, Martha
Kelley, Deborah Maverick
Kelley, Ramon
Kelly, James
Kelly, Robert James
Kelly, William Joseph
Kennedy, James Edward
Kenney, Estelle Koval
Kent, H Latham
Kenton, Mary Jean
Kepalas (Elena Kepalaite)
Kepets, Hugh Michael
Kermes, Constantine John
Kerne, Barbara Davis
Kerns, Ed (Johnson), Jr
Kerr, James Wilfrid
Kerswill, J W Roy
Kessler, Alan
Kessler, Margaret Jennings
Keveson, Florence
Kevorkian, Richard
Keyser, Robert G
Khachian, Elisa A
Kiah, Virginia Jackson
Kieferndorf, Frederick George
Kielkopf, James Robert
Kiland, Lance Edward
Kilian, Austin Farland
Kim, Po (Hyun)
Kimes, Don
Kimura, Joan Alexandra
Kimura, Sueko M
Kimura, William Yusaburo
Kipniss, Robert
Kirkwood, Mary Burnette
Kirschenbaum, Jules
Kiskadden, Robert Morgan
Kittredge, Nancy (Elizabeth)
Klabunde, Charles Spencer
Klarin, Winifred Erlick
Klavans, Minnie
Klaven, Marvin L
Klein, Sandor C
Kleinberg, Susan
Kleinman, Sue
Klement, Vera
Kline, Harriet
Knapp, Sadie Magnet
Knapp, Tom
Knaub, Raymond L
Knief, Helen (Janet) Jeanette
Knight, Jacob Jaskoviak
Knipscher, Gerard Allen
Knipschild, Robert
Knowles, Richard H
Knowlton, Jonathan
Knutsson, Anders
Kobayashi, Hisako
Kocar, George Frederick
Koch, Gerd (Herman)
Koch, Philip
Kocherthaler, Mina
Kochta, Ruth Martha
Koehler, Henry
Koenig, John Franklin
Koestner, Don
Kogan, Deborah
Kohn, William Roth
Kohut, Lorene
Koller-Davies, Eva
Komarin, Gary
Konopka, Joseph
Koppelman, Dorothy
Kopriva, Sharon
Korman, Harriet R
Korot, Beryl
Kortheuer, Dayrell
Koscianski, Leonard J
Kostabi, Mark
Kotoske, Roger Allen
Kozlow, Richard
Kozmon, George
Krashes, Barbara
Krasnyansky, Anatole Lvovich
Krause, LaVerne Erickson
Krauth, Harald
Krempel, Ralf
Krestensen, Ann M
Krieger, Ruth M
Kriensky
Kriesberg, Irving
Kroll, David
Kronsnoble, Jeffrey Michael
Krueger, Lothar David
Krumholt, Ann
Krushenick, Nicholas
Kuehn, Frances
Kuh, Howard
Kuhlman, Walter Egel
Kuhn, Bob
Kulicke, Robert M
Kuopus, Clinton
Kurka, Donald Frank
Kurlander, Honey W
Kurtz, Elaine
Kurz, Diana
Kuwayama, Tadaaki
Kwak, Hoon
Lack, Richard Frederick
La Hotan, Robert L
La Lumia, Frank
Lama, Alberto de
Lamantia, Paul (Christopher) Zombek
Lambert, Ed
LaMontagne, Armand M
La Monte, Angela Mae
Lancaster, Mark
Lancel McElhinney, James
Land, Ernest Albert
Landers, Bertha
Landfield, Ronnie (Ronald T)
Lane, Marion Jean Arrons
Lane, William
Lang, Daniel S
Lang, Margo Terzian
La Noue, Terence
Lansner, Fay
Lanyon, Ellen
La Pelle, Rodger
LaPena, Frank Raymond
La Pierre, Thomas
Lapointe, Frank
La Porta, Elayne B
L'Archeveque, Andre Robert
Lark, Raymond
Larmer, Oscar Vance
Larraz, Julio F
Larsen, Mernet Ruth
Larsen, Robert Wesley
Larson, Blaine (Gledhill)
Laska, David
Lasker, Joe (Joseph L)
Laub-Novak, Karen
Laurent, John Louis
Lavadour, James
Law, C Anthony
Lawrence, Rodney Steven
Lawson, Thomas
Leach, Mada (Madeline Kleiman)
LeBey, Barbara
Lecky, Susan
Lederman, Stephanie Brody
Lee, Catherine
Lee, Li Lin
Lee, Robert M
Leeds, Annette
Leepa, Allen
Leeson, Tom
Leete, William White
Lehr, Mira T(ager)
Lehrer, Leonard
Leibowitz, Bernice
Leis, Marietta Patricia
Lem, Richard Douglas
Lemieux, Irenee
Lenhardt, Shirley M
Lenker, Marlene N
Lenssen, Heidi (Mrs Fridolf Johnson)
Leon, Ralph Bernard
Lerman, Ora
Lerner, Marilyn
Lerner, Sandra
Leslie, Seaver
Lesnick, Stephen William
Lesseps, Tauni de
Letendre, Rita
Levee, John H
Levering, Robert K
Levine, Edward
Levine, Tom
Levine, Tomar
Levy, Tibbie
Lewis, Don S, Sr
Lewis, Donald Sykes, Jr
Lewis, Michael H
Lewis, Nat Brush
Lewton, Val Edwin
Lhotka, Bonny Pierce
Liccione, Alexander
Lichtenberg, Manes
Lieber, Thomas Alan
Lieberman, Meyer Frank
Liebman, Dr Sarah
Liebman, Norman
Likan, Gustav
Li Lan
Liljegren, Frank
Li Marzi, Joseph
Linderman, Earl William
Linhares, Judith
Link, Lawrence John
Lippmann, Janet Gurian
Lipton, Sondra Sahlman
Lis, Janet
Little, James
Little, Polly A
Litz, James C
Livingstone, Biganess
Loehle, Betty Barnes
Loehle, Richard E
Loftus, Peter M
Logan, Gene Adams
Logemann, Jane Marie
Loiselle, Bernard Roger
Lomahaftewa, Linda Joyce
Londin, Barbara
Long, Electra
Long, Frank Weathers
Longley, Bernique
Longo, Vincent
Longobardi, Pam
Longo-Muth, Linda L
Longval, Gloria
Loran, Erle
Lorentz, Pauline
Losavio, Samuel
Lotz, Steven Darryl
Loveless, Jim
Lovell, Tom
Loving, Al
Loving, Richard Maris
Lowney, Bruce Stark
Loy, John Sheridan
Lueders, Jimmy C
Luino, Bernardino
Lumbers, James Richard
Lund, David
Lundeberg, Helen
Lusker, Ron
Lutes, Jim (James)
Lux, Gladys M
Luz, Virginia
Lynch, Mary Britten
Lynds, Clyde
Lysun, Gregory
Maas, Marion Elizabeth
McAdoo, Carol Westbrook
Macaray, Lawrence Richard
MacBird, Rosemary (Simpson)
McCall, Ann
McCallum, Steven Douglas
McCarthy, Doris Jean
McCartin, William Francis
McCauley, Gardiner Rae
McChesney, Robert Pearson
McClellan, Douglas Eugene
McClelland, Jeanne C
McClendon, Maxine (Maxine McClendon Nichols)
McClure, Constance
McCosh, Anne Kutka (Mrs David McCosh)
McCoubrey, Sarah
McCoy, Wirth Vaughan
McCulloch, Frank E
McCullough, David William
McCullough, Joseph
McDaniel, Craig Milton
MacDonald, Kevin John
McDougal, Ivan Ellis
McEwen, Jean
McFarren, Grace
McGee, Winston Eugene
McGinnis, Christine
McGovern, Robert F
McGrail, Jeane Kathryn
McGrew, Bruce Elwin
McGrew, R Brownell
Machetanz, Fred
MacIver, Loren
McKay, Renee
McKenzie, Mary Beth
McKie, Todd Stoddard
McKim, William Wind
McKinney, Tatiana Ladygina
McKinnickinnick, Margaret I
McLean, Richard Thorpe
McMillan, Constance
McNary, Oscar L
McNeil, George J
MacNeill, Frederick Douglas
Macpherson, Kevin
McQuillan, Frances
McReynolds, (Joe) Cliff
McVicker, J Jay
Maddox, Jerrold Warren
Magazzini, Gene
Magleby, Frank (Francis R)
Mahaffey, Merrill Dean
Mahmoud, Ben
Maier, Maryanne E
Mailman, Cynthia
Mainardi, Patricia M
Maki, Sheila Anne
Maldjian, Vartavar B

PAINTER (cont)
Malo, Teri (Theresa A Malo-Sprawka)
Malone, James Hiram
Malott, Mary
Malta, Vincent
Manabu, Mabe
Mancini, John
Mandel, John
Mandelman, Beatrice M
Mandziuk, Michael Dennis
Manes, Belle
Manes, Paul
Mangione, Patricia Anthony
Mangold, Sylvia Plimack
Mangum, William (Goodson)
Manilla, Tess
Mann, Frank
Mann, Ward Palmer
Manning, Jo
Manso, Leo
Manville, Elsie
Manzo, Anthony Joseph
Mapes, Doris Williamson
Marais
Marcus, Gerald R
Marcus, Irving E
Marcus, Marcia
Marder, Dorie
Maree, Wendy P
Margulis, Martha (Boyer)
Mari
Marianne
Mark, Marilyn (Sabetsky)
Markarian, Alexia (Mitrus)
Markman, Ronald
Markovich, Ann Marie
Markowitz, Marilyn
Markowski, Eugene David
Marriott, William Allen
Marron, Joan
Marsden, Michael H E
Marshall-Nadel, Nathalie
Martell, Barbara Bentley
Martin, Agnes Bernice
Martin, Alexander Toedt
Martin, Bernard Murray
Martin, Doug
Martin, Jane
Martin, Lucille Caiar
Martin, Mary Finch
Martin, Roger
Martino, Eva E
Martino, Giovanni
Martino, Nina F
Marton, Tutzi
Martone, William Robert
Martyl (Martyl Schweig Langsdorf)
Marx, Robert Ernst
Marzano, Albert
Mason, Alden C
Mason, Frank Herbert
Massey, Ann James
Massin, Eugene Max
Masteller, Barry
Matassa, John P
Mateo, Julio
Matson, Greta
Matternes, Jay Howard
Matthews, Gene (Eugene Edward)
Maughelli, Mary L
Max, Lope (Diaz)
Max, Peter
Maxera, Oscar
Maxwell, John
Maxwell, Robert Edwin
Mayhew, Richard
Mayrs, David Blair
Mazzone, Domenico
Medearis, Roger
Meehan, William Dale
Meghelli, Fethi M
Meisel, Susan Pear
Meitzler, Neil (Herbert)
Meixner, Mary Louise
Melby, David A
Melikian, Mary
Mell, Ed (Edmund Paul Jr)
Melville, Grevis Whitaker
Mendelsohn, John
Mendelson, Haim
Mendes, Barbara
Menihan, John Conway
Menses, Jan
Meredith, John
Merrill, David Kenneth
Mesches, Arnold
Messersmith, Fred Lawrence
Messina, Joseph R
Metzger, Evelyn Borchard
Meyer, Frank Hildbridge
Miccoli, Arnaldo
Michael, Gary
Michod, Susan A
Middleman, Raoul F
Mieczkowski, Edwin
Milder, Jay
Miles, Jeanne Patterson
Miles, Sheila Lee
Milhoan, Randall Bell
Miller, Dolly (Ethel B)
Miller, Elaine Sandra
Miller, F John
Miller, Joan L
Miller, Melissa Wren
Miller, Melvin Orville, Jr
Miller, Michael Stephen
Miller, Nancy Tokar
Miller, Richard Kidwell
Miller, Ruth Ann
Miller, Sue S
Milonas, Minos
Mim, Adrienne C (Adrienne Claire Schwartz)
Mintz, Harry
Mion, Pierre Riccardo
Miotke, Anne E
Misch, Allene K
Mi Sook, Ahn
Missal, Stephen J
Mitchell, Dean Lamont
Mitchell, Fred
Mitchell, John Blair
Mitchell, Peter Todd
Mitchnick, Nancy
Mitty, Lizbeth J
Miyasaki, George Joji
Mock, Richard Basil
Mode, Carol A
Model, Elisabeth D
Moffitt, John Francis
Mogavero, Michael James
Mohn, Cheri (Ann)
Mohr, K(aren) Lee
Mojsilov, Ilene Krug
Moller, Hans
Moment, Joan
Momiyama, Nanae
Monaghan, Keith
Monahan, Gene Ritchie
Monory, Jacques
Monroe, Gerald
Montlack, Edith
Montminy, Tracy
Moore, Arthur Cotton
Moore, Beveridge
Moore, John J
Moore, Olga
Moore, Robert Eric
Moore, Robert James
Moore, Sabra
Moore, Susan
Moose, Philip Anthony
Morales, Armando
Morcos, Maher N
Morgan, Clarence (Edward)
Morgan, James L
Morgan, Norma Gloria
Morgan, Susan
Morgenlander, Ella Kramer
Morishita, Joyce Chizuko
Moroz, Mychajlo
Morphesis, Jim (James George)
Morrell, Wayne (Beam)
Morris, Carl
Morris, Roger Dale
Morrison, Doris
Morrison, George
Morrison, Keith Anthony
Morriss, Mary Rachel
Mortellito, Domenico
Mosca, August
Moscatt, Paul N
Mosenthal, Charlotte Dembo
Moses, Forrest (Lee), Jr
Moskowitz, Robert S
Moss, Irene
Moss-Vreeland, Patricia
Movalli, Charles Joseph
Moy, Seong
Moyers, William
Muench, John
Mugar, Martin Gienandt
Muhlert, Christopher Layton
Muir, Emily Lansingh
Mulhern, Michael
Mullarkey, Maureen
Mullen, Jo (Stauffer)
Mullen, Philip Edward
Muller, Jerome Kenneth
Mullican, Lee
Murata, Hiroshi
Murphy, Catherine E
Murphy, Chester Glenn
Murphy, Marilyn L
Murray, Elizabeth
Murrell, Carlton D
Musselman, Darwin B
Myers, Jack Fredrick
Myers, Martin
Nadalini, (Louis Ernest)
Naftulin, Rose
Nagano, Shozo
Nakamura, Kazuo
Nakazato, Hitoshi
Naponic, Tony (Anthony George)
Nardone, Vincent Joseph
Natkin, Robert
Nay, Mary Spencer
Naylon, Betsy Zimmermann
Naza (Maria Nazareth McFarren),
Nazarenko, Bonnie Coe
Neal, Irene
Neals, Otto
Neddeau, Donald Frederick Price
Neff, Edith
Neffson, Robert
Negri, Rocco Antonio
Negroponte, George
Neher, Ross James
Neidhardt, Carl Richard
Neill, Ben E
Neiman, LeRoy
Nelson, Joan
Nelson, Leonard
Nelson, Mary Carroll
Nelson, Signe (Signe Nelson Stuart)
Nesbitt, Lowell (Blair)
Ness, (Albert) Kenneth
Neustein, Joshua
Nevia, (Joseph Shepperd Rogers)
Newer, Thesis
Newman, Libby
Newman-Rice, Nancy
Niblett, Gary Lawrence
Nicholas, Thomas Andrew
Nichols, Edward Edson
Nichols, Ward H
Nicholson, Roy William
Nick, George
Nickson, Graham G
Niederer, Carl
Niemann, Edmund E
Nierman, Leonardo M
Nieto, John W
Nind, Jean
Nisula, Larry
Noble, Helen (Harper)
Noble, John A
Nordhausen, A Henry
Nordstrand, Nathalie Johnson
Norris, (Robert) Ben
Norton, Mary Joyce
Norwood, Malcolm Mark
Notarbartolo, Albert
Novros, David
Nunnelley, Robert B
O'Beil, Hedy
Obuck, John Francis
Ocampo, Miguel
Ocepek, Lou (Louis David)
O'Connell, Daniel Moylan
O'Connor, John Arthur
Ohlson, Douglas Dean
Oji, Helen Shizuko
Okoshi, E Sumiye
Olitski, Jules
Oliveira, Nathan
Oliver, Bobbie
Oliver, Sandra (Sandi)
Olsen, Ernest Moran
Olson, Richard W
Omar, Margit
Omwake, Eo, Jr
O'Neil, Bruce William
O'Neil, John
Opie, John Mart
Order, Trudy
Orduno, Robert Daniel
Orlyk, Harry V
Orr, Arthur (Leslie)
Orr, Joseph Charles
Ortlip, Mary Krueger
Ortlip, Paul Daniel
Osborne, John Phillip
Osby, Larissa Geiss
O'Sickey, Joseph Benjamin
Ostendorf, (Arthur) Lloyd, Jr
Osterweil-Weber, Suzanne
O'Sullivan, Daniel Joseph
Ott, Jerry
Ott, Sabina
Ott, Wendell Lorenz
Oubre, Hayward Louis
Owen, Frank (Franklin Charles)
Owens, Wallace, Jr
Ox, Jack
Ozonoff, Ida
Pace, Stephen S
Pachner, William
Palmer, Lucie Mackay
Palmer, Mabel (Evelyn)
Palmer, Michael Andrew
Palmgren, Donald Gene
Palumbo, Jacques
Pantell, Richard Keith
Pappas, George
Pardee, William Hearne
Parker, Carolyn Johnson
Parker, Samuel Murray
Parker, Wilma (Wilma Parker de Pavloff)
Parness, Charles
Parrish, David Buchanan
Parrish, Jean
Pas, Gerard Peter
Pascal, David
Paschke, Edward F (Ed)
Paskewitz, Bill, Jr
Passlof, Pat
Paternosto, Cesar Pedro
Patkin, Izhar
Patmagrian, Ethelia M
Patrick, Alan K
Patrick, Genie Hudson
Pattison, Billy Dee
Patton, Andy (Andrew John)
Patton, Karen Ann
Paul, Ken (Hugh)

PAINTER (cont)
Peace, Bernie (Kinzel)
Pearson, Henry C
Pecchenino, J Ronald
Pellettieri, Michael Joseph
Pellew, John Clifford
Pellicone, William
Penczner, Paul Joseph
Penkoff, Ronald Peter
Penney, Jacqueline
Pentak, Stephen
Pentelovitch, Robert Alan
Pentz, Donald Robert
Perehudoff, William W
Perez, Celis
Perez, Vincent
Perham, Roy Gates
Perlman, Bennard Bloch
Perlman, Mark A
Perlmutter, Jack
Perrotti, Barbara
Perry, Donald Dean
Perry, Kathryn Powers
Perry, Lincoln Frederick
Peter, George
Peterdi, Gabor F
Peters, Andrea Jean
Petersen, Franklin G
Petersen, Roland Conrad
Peterson, David Winfield
Peterson, Larry D
Peterson, Roger Tory
Petlin, Irving
Petrie, Ferdinand Ralph
Petrie, Sylvia Spencer
Petro, Joseph (Victor), Jr
Pettibone, Richard H
Pezzati, Pietro (Peter S)
Pfahl, Charles Alton, III
Pfriem, Bernard
Phelan, Ellen Denise
Philbrick, Margaret Elder
Phillips, Alice Jane
Phillips, Bertrand D
Phillips, Tony
Picciano, Lana (Lana Patricia Picciano)
Piccolo, Richard
Pickford, Rollin, Jr
Pike, Joyce Lee
Pildes, Sara
Pile, James
Pinchbeck, Peter G
Pinkerton, Clayton (David)
Pinzarrone, Paul
Pionk, Richard C
Piskoti, James
Pitt, Suzan (Lee)
Pitts, Richard G
Plaster, Alice Marie
Plear, Scott
Pletcher, Gerry
Pletka, Paul
Plochmann, Carolyn Gassan
Plumb, James Douglas
Pogach, Gerald
Polan, Annette
Polan, Nancy Moore
Pollard, Donald Pence
Pollaro, Paul
Pollock, Bruce
Ponce de Leon, Michael
Poole, Leslie Donald
Poor, Anne
Poppitz, James
Portnow, Marjorie Anne
Posen, Stephen
Posey, Ernest Noel
Poskas, Peter Edward
Postiglione, Corey M
Pototschnik, John Michael
Poulos, Basilios Nicholas
Pounian, Albert Kachouni
Power, S Brenda Joan
Powers, Donald T
Pozzatti, Rudy O
Pozzi, Lucio
Pracko, Bernard F, II
Praczukowski, Edward Leon
Pramuk, Edward Richard
Pratt, Frances (Frances Elizabeth Usui)
Prentice, David Ramage
Preston, Malcolm H
Preuss, Roger
Pribble, Easton
Price, Barbara Gillette
Price, Doris C
Price, Leslie Kenneth
Price, Rita F
Price, Rosalie Pettus
Price, Sara J
Priest, Hartwell Wyse
Priest, T (Theresa Khoury Struckus)
Prindiville, Jim
Printz, Bonnie Allen
Promutico, Jean
Pross, Lester Fred
Provder, Carl
Punia, Constance Edith
Pura, William Paul
Purcell, Hugh D
Purdum, Rebecca
Purdy, Donald R
Purdy, Henry Carl
Putterman, Florence Grace
Quat, Helen S
Quest, Dorothy (Johnson)
Quinn, Thomas Patrick, Jr
Quinn, William
Quisgard, Liz Whitney
Raab, Gail B
Rabinovich, Raquel
Raciti, Cherie
Rades, William L
Radoczy, Albert
Raffael, Joseph
Rafferty, Joanne Miller
Raffo, Steve
Raginsky, Nina
Rahja, Virginia Helga
Raiselis, Richard
Rakocy, William (Joseph)
Raleigh, Henry Patrick
Ramberg, Christina
Ramsey, Dorothy J
Rand, Archie
Randolph, Lynn Moore
Ranes, Chris
Ransom, Henry Cleveland, Jr
Ranson, Nancy Sussman
Rapp, Lois
Rascoe, Stephen Thomas
Rasmussen, Anton Jesse
Ratner, David M
Ray, Robert (Donald)
Rayen, James Wilson
Rayner, Gordon
Reber, Mick
Recklinghausen, Marianne von
Reddington, Charles Leonard
Reddix, Roscoe Chester
Redgrave, Felicity
Redmond, Rozze (Rosemary)
Reece, Maynard
Reed, David
Reed, Flint Winter
Reed, Hal
Reed, Paul Allen
Reese, William Foster
Reeves, Esther May
Reich, Nathaniel E
Reichert, Donald Karl
Reichman, Fred
Reid, Charles
Reid, Leslie
Reid, Robert Dennis
Reilly, Jack
Reilly, Nancy
Reinhart, Margaret Emily
Reininghaus, Ruth (Ruth Reininghaus Smith)
Reker, Les
Remenick, Seymour
Remington, Deborah Williams
Remsen, John
Rendl, M(ildred Marcus)
Resek, Kate Frances
Resnick, Don
Reynard, Carolyn Cole
Reynolds, James Elwood
Reynolds, Richard (Henry)
Reynolds, Wade
Rich, Garry Lorence
Richard, Jack
Richards, Bill
Richards, Joseph Edward
Richardson, Constance (Coleman)
Richardson, Jean
Richardson, W C
Richter, Hank
Rieber, Ruth B
Riese, Beatrice
Riess, Lore
Riley-Land, Sarah (Sarah Agnes Riley Land)
Rioux (de Messimy), Deena (Coty) des
Ripps, Rodney
Rivera, Elias J
Riveron, Enrique
Rivo, Shirley Winthrope
Rizzi, James
Robb, Charles
Robb, Peggy Hight
Robbin, Anthony Stuart
Robbin, Tony
Robbins, Bruce
Roberts, Bruce Elliott
Roberts, Holly L
Roberts, Lucille D (Malkia)
Roberts, Priscilla Warren
Roberts, Richard
Roberts, Tom (Thomas Keith)
Roberts, William Edward
Robinson, Charlotte
Robinson, Gail E
Robinson, Jay (Thurston)
Robinson, Margot (Margot Steigman)
Robinson, Maura
Rocamora, Jaume
Roda (Rhoda Lillian Sablow),
Rodbard, Betty
Rodeiro, José Manuel
Rogers, Otto Donald
Rogers, Peter Wilfrid
Rohrer, Warren
Rojo, Vicente
Romero, Jose T
Ronald, William
Ropp, Ann L
Rose, Leatrice
Rose, Mary Anne
Rose, Matthew Adam
Rose, Roslyn
Rose, Samuel
Rose, Stephanie
Rosen, Esther Yovits
Rosenblatt, Adolph
Rosenblatt, Suzanne Maris
Rosenfeld, Sharon
Rosenquist, James
Rosenthal, Deborah Maly
Rosenthal, Gloria M
Ross, Clifford
Ross, Janice Koenig
Ross, Rhoda Honore
Rossi, Barbara
Rossman, Ruth Scharff
Rotenberg, Judi
Roth, David
Roth, Frank
Roth, Jack (Rodney)
Rothenberg, Susan
Rothschild, Amalie (Rosenfeld)
Routon, David F
Row, David
Rowan, Herman
Rowe, Reginald M
Royer, Mona Lee
Rozzi (James A)
Ruben, Richards
Rubin, Sandra Mendelsohn
Rucker, Harrison Campbell
Ruda, Edwin
Ruddley, John
Rusak, Halina R
Ruscha, Edward Joseph
Rush, Jean C
Russell, Dr Stella Pandell
Russell, Philip C
Russell, Robert Price
Russo, Alexander Peter
Ruta, Peter Paul
Ruth, Sheila
Ryan, Richard E
Ryan, William Edward
Saba, Richard
Sabatella, Joseph John
Sabo, Betty Jean
Sade, Shuli
Sadowski, Carol (Louise) Johnson
St Amand, Joseph
St John, Terry N
St Maur, Kirk (Kirk Seymour McReynolds)
St Tamara,
Sakuyama, Shunji
Salinas, Baruj
Salt, John
Salter, Richard Mackintire
Saltzman, Marvin
Samburg, Grace (Blanche)
Sampson, Frank
Sanabria, Sherry Zvares
Sanchez, Thorvald
Sanden, John Howard
Sanders, Joop A
Sandol, Maynard
Sandusky, Billy Ray
Santlofer, Jonathan
Sargent, Margaret Holland
Sarkisian, Paul
Sarnoff, Arthur Saron
Sarsony, Robert
Sato, Masaaki
Sato, Tadashi
Saturen, Ben
Saulson, Harold
Saunders, Edith Dariel Chase
Sawada, Ikune
Sawka, Jan A
Sayles, Eva
Saylors, Jo An
Sazegar, Morteza
Scala, Joseph (A)
Schactman, Barry Robert
Schaechter, Judith
Schapiro, Miriam
Schenck, William Clinton
Schepis, Anthony Joseph
Schiavina, Laura M
Schiebold, Hans
Schildknecht, Dorothy E
Schmidt, Arnold Alfred
Schmidt, Edward William
Schmidt, Frederick Lee
Schmidt, Frederick Louis
Schnackenberg, Roy
Schneebaum, Tobias
Schneider, Janet M
Schneider, Jo Anne
Schnurr, Elinore
Schofield, Roberta
Schonwalter, Jean Frances
Schooley, Elmer Wayne
Schreck, Michael H
Schreiber, Martin
Schroeck, R D
Schucker, Charles
Schule, Clifford Hamilton
Schulman, Robert
Schulson, Susan

PAINTER (cont)
Schultz, Stephen Warren
Schurr, Jerry M
Schutz, Estelle
Schwartz, Carl E
Schwartz, Henry
Schwartz, Rosalyn
Schwartz, Ruth
Scott, B Nibbelink (Barbara Gae Scott)
Scott, John
Scott, Jonathan
Scott, Marian (Dale)
Scoville, Jonathan Armstrong
Seaman, Drake F
Searles, Charles
Secunda, (Holland) Arthur
Seerey-Lester, John Vernon
Seidl, Claire
Seidler, Doris
Sekiguchi, Risa
Seliger, Charles
Seltzer, Joanne Lynn
Seltzer, Phyllis
Semmel, Joan
Sensemann, Susan
Serisawa, Sueo
Serra-Badue, Daniel F
Serrano, Luis
Sewell, Richard George
Shadrach, Jean H
Shaffer, Fern
Shaffer, Rosalind
Shahly, Jehan
Shahn, Abby
Shahn, Bernarda Bryson
Shankman, Gary Charles
Shap, Sylvia
Shapiro, Babe
Shapiro, David
Shapiro, David
Sharon, Russell
Sharp, Anne
Sharp, Susan S
Sharpe, (Norman) Blair
Sharrow, Sheba
Shatalow, Vladimir Mihailovich
Shatter, Susan Louise
Shaw, John Palmer
Shemesh, Lorraine R
Shepherd, William Fritz
Sherman, Z Charlotte
Sherr, Ronald Norman
Sherrod, Philip Lawrence
Sherry, William Grant
Shersher, Zinovy
Shibley, Gertrude
Shields, Alan J
Shilson, Wayne Stuart
Shimomura, Roger Yutaka
Shirai, Akiko
Shoemaker, Peter
Shoemaker, Vaughn
Shore, Mary (McGarrity)
Shores, (James) Franklin
Shorr, Harriet
Short, Patricia Ann Reilly
Shoulberg, Harry
Showell, Kenneth L
Shull, Carl Edwin
Shumacker, Elizabeth Wight
Siberell, Anne Hicks
Sickler, Michael Allan
Sickman, Jessalee Bane
Sigismund, Violet M
Sigler, Hollis
Silkotch, Mary Ellen
Silverberg, June Roselyn
Silverman, Sherley C
Silverstein, Ida
Simel, Elaine
Simone (Mildred Simonson),
Simpson, David
Simpson, Lee
Simpson, Marilyn Jean
Simpson, Merton D
Simson, Bevlyn A
Singer, Clifford
Singer, Clyde J
Singer, Esther Forman
Singletary, Michael James
Sinnard, Elaine (Janice)
Sinton, Nell (Walter)
Sirena (Contessa Antonia Mastrocristino Fanara)
Sirugo, Sal (Salvatore)
Sisson, Laurence P
Sisto, Elena
Sitton, John M
Skalagard, Hans
Sklar, Dorothy
Sklarski, Bonnie J
Sklar-Weinstein, Arlene (Joyce)
Slavick, Susanne Mechtild
Slavin, Arlene
Sleigh, Sylvia
Slider, Dorla Dean
Sloan, Jeanette Pasin
Sloan, Richard
Sloan, Robert Smullyan
Sloan, Ronald J
Slobodkina, Esphyr (Mrs Urquhart)
Slone, Sandi
Slonem, Hunt
Slotnick, Mortimer H
Smith, B J
Smith, Clyde
Smith, David Loeffler
Smith, Dinah Maxwell
Smith, Frank Anthony
Smith, Gordon
Smith, Hassel W, Jr
Smith, Lawrence Beall
Smith, Leon Polk
Smith, Susan
Smith, Vincent D
Smongeski, Joseph Leon
Smuskiewicz, Ted
Snow, Cynthia Reeves
Snow, Mary R
Snyder, William B
Solberg, Morten Edward
Solman, Joseph
Soloway, Reta Burns
Somberg, Emilija O K
Somers, Frederick D(uane)
Somers, H(arry W)
Soppelsa, George
Sorby, J Richard
Sorokin, Janet
Southey, Trevor J T
Spelman, Jill Sullivan
Spence, Andrew
Spencer, Harold Edwin
Spencer, Jeffrey Paul
Spiess-Ferris, Eleanor
Sprague, Mark Anderson
Sprang, Elizabeth
Spruce, Everett Franklin
Squadra, John
Squires, Gerald Leopold
Stack, Frank Huntington
Stack, Michael
Stacy, Donald L
Stadler, Albert
Stamelos, Electra Georgia Mousmoules
Stanbridge, Harry Andrew
Stanley, Bob
Stanton, Harriet L
Stapleton, Joseph F
Staprans, Raimonds
Stark, Robert
Starkweather-Nelson, Cynthia Louise
Stasack, Edward Armen
Statman, Jan B
Stavans, Isaac
Staven, Leland Carroll
Steckel, Anita
Steen, Carol J
Stefan, Ross
Stegeman, Charles
Steinfels, Melville P
Steinhouse, Tobie (Thelma)
Stephanson, Loraine Ann
Stephens, William Blakely
Stern, Irene Monat
Sternberg, Harry
Stevanov, Zoran
Steven, James Michael
Stevens, May
Stevens, Nelson L
Stevenson, Ruth Rolston
Stevovich, Andrew Vlastimir
Stewart, Arthur
Stewart, F Clark
Stewart, Jack
Stewart, John P
Stewart, William
Steynovitz, Zamy
Sticker, Robert Edward
Stillman, Lucille T
Stirnweis, Shannon
Stirratt, Betsy (Elizabeth Anne)
Stoloff, Carolyn
Stolpe, Daniel Owen
Stomps, Walter E, Jr
Storm, Howard
Stout, Richard Gordon
Straus, Sandy
Strauser, Sterling Boyd
Strawn, Melvin Nicholas
Strickland, Thomas J
Strider, Marjorie Virginia
Strisik, Paul
Stroh, Charles
Strong, Brett-Livingstone
Strong, Charles Ralph
Strosahl, William
Strother, Joseph Willis
Strother, Virginia Vaughn
Stroud, Peter Anthony
Struck, Norma Johansen
Stuart, Joseph Martin
Sturtevant, E
Sublett, Carl C
Sudlow, Robert N
Sugarman, George
Suggs, Pat(ricia) Ann
Sullivan, Bill
Sullivan, David Francis
Sullivan, Francoise
Sullivan, Jim
Sullo, Joseph Anthony
Sultan, Altoon
Summer, (Emily) Eugenia
Sumner, George
Surgalski, Patrick J
Surrey, Milt
Sussman, Barbara J
Sussman, Wendy
Suter, Sherwood Eugene
Sutton, Carol (Lorraine)
Sutton, Pat (Lipsky)
Suzuki, Sakari
Swain, Robert
Swanson, J N
Swartz, Beth Ames
Sweet, Mary (French)
Sweitzer, Charles Leroy
Swetcharnik, Sara Morris
Sykes, (William) Maltby
Tabachnick, Anne
Tacla, Jorge
Taggart, William John
Tahedl, Ernestine
Takashima, Shizuye Violet
Talbot, Jarold Dean
Talbot, Jonathan
Tamburine, Jean Helen
Tanger, Susanna
Tanksley, Ann
Taper, Geri
Tate, Gayle Blair
Tatossian, Armand
Taylor, Ann
Taylor, Sandra Ortiz
Tchetchet, Tatiana
Teczar, Steven W
Telberg, Val
Tempest, Gerard Francis
Ten Broeke, Jan
Ten Eyck, Catryna (Catryna Ten Eyck Seymour)
Termes, (Dick A)
Termini, Christine
Teters, J Charlene
Tewes, Robin J
Teyral, John
Thenhaus, Paulette Ann
Theobald, Gillian Lee
Thies, Charles Herman
Thomas, Helen (Doane)
Thomas, John
Thomas, Thalia Ann Marie
Thomas, Yvonne
Thompson, Donald Roy
Thompson, Judith Kay
Thompson, Malcolm Barton
Thompson, Rena
Thompson, Richard Craig
Thompson, Wade S
Thomson, Carl L
Thorpe, Hilda (Shapiro)
Threlkeld, Dale
Tiegreen, Alan F
Tigerman, Stanley
Tillim, Sidney
Ting Shao Kuang,
Tinning, George Campbell
Todd, Michael Cullen
Tolpo, Vincent Carl
Tompkins, Alan
Tompkins, Betty (I)
Toney, Anthony
Torreano, John Francis
Tousignant, Claude
Townsend, John F
Trachtenberg, Gloria P
Trachtman, Arnold S
Tracy, Lois Bartlett
Treese, William R
Triano, Anthony Thomas
Trieff, Selina
Trincere, Li
Tripp, Jan Peter
Trissel, James Nevin
Truby, Betsy Kirby
Trumble, Beverly (Jane)
Trupp, Barbara Lee
Tse, Stephen
Tubis, Seymour
Tucholke, Christel-Anthony (Christel E Stoeveken)
Turner, Alan
Turner, (Charles) Arthur
Turner, Bruce Backman
Turner, James Thomas, Sr
Turner, Norman Huntington
Turner, Theodore Roy
Turner, William Eugene
Twaddle, Randy
Twardowicz, Stanley Jan
Twitty, James W
Tykie (Sylvia Squires Ganz)
Tyler, Valton
Tytell, Louis
Ubans, Juris K
Udinotti, Agnese
Uglow, Alan
Uhrman, Celia
Upton, Richard Thomas
Urbaitis, Elena
Urso, Leonard A
Uttech, Thomas Martin
Vaccarino, Robin
Vaccaro, Nick Dante
Vaillancourt, Armand
Vaisman, Meyer
Valetta
Valier, Biron (Frank)
Vaness, Margaret Helen
Van Halm, Renée

PAINTER (cont)
Van Wyk, Helen
Van Young, Oscar
Varnelis, Kazys
Varriale, Wanda (Stella)
Vazquez, Paul
Venable, Susan C
Venezia, Michael
Ventura, Anthony
Verona, Paula
Vevers, Tabitha
Vickers, Russ(ell Geron)
Vickery, Charles Bridgeman
Vidal, Hahn
Villinski, Paul
Visser't Hooft, Martha
Voelker, John
Vogel, Donald S
Vogel, Joseph
Vogl, Don George
Waddell, Theodore
Wagner, Richard Ellis
Waid, Jim (James E)
Waksberg, Naomi
Walch, John Leo
Wald, Carol
Walker, Edward D (Rusty)
Walker, Marie Sheehy
WalkingStick, Kay
Wall, Bruce C
Wall, Ralph Alan
Wall, Sue
Wallace, John
Wallace, Patty A
Wallace, Soni
Wallin, Lawrence Bier
Wallin, Leland Dean
Walsh, James
Walsh, Patricia Ruth
Waltemath, Joan
Walters, Ernest
Waltner, Beverly Ruland
Waltzer, Stewart Paul
Wands, Alfred James
Wands, Robert James
Wanlass, Stanley Glen
Ward, John Lawrence
Ward, Lyle Edward
Ward, William Edward
Wardlaw, George Melvin
Warkov, Esther
Warner, Jo
Warren, Betty
Warren, Jacqueline Louise
Warren, Russ
Warsinske, Norman George
Washburn, Stan
Wasserman, Jeffrey
Wasserman, Muriel
Waterhouse, Charles Howard
Waterstreet, Ken (James Kent)
Watia, Tarmo
Watson, Ronald G
Webb, Sarah A
Weber, Idelle
Weber, Karen
Weddige, Emil A
Weedman, Kenneth Russell
Weekes, Shirley Marie
Weeks, James (Darrell Northrup)
Weidner, Mary Elizabeth
Weidner, Roswell Theodore
Weigand, Herbert Michael
Weihs, Erika
Weinbaum, Jean
Weinstein, Joyce
Weinstock, Rose
Weiss, Jerome Nathan
Weiss, Milton
Welch, James Wymore
Wellborn, J(eanette) D(arleen)
Weller, Laurie June
Wells, Carol Menthe
Wells, Thomas (Winchester)
Werfel, Gina S
Wert, Ned Oliver
Wesselmann, Tom
Wesser, Yvonne D
West, Clara Faye Johnson
West, E Gordon
West, Peter
Wethli, Mark
Wexler, George
Wheeler, Mary
Whitcomb, Skip
White, B J (Beverly Jo)
White, Franklin
White, Ralph
White, Susan Chrysler
Whitney, Richard Wheeler
Whyte, Raymond A
Wickiser, Ralph Lewanda
Wicks, Eugene Claude
Wiegand, Robert
Wiener, Phyllis Ames
Wiesen, Trude
Wiggins, Bill
Wiggins, Guy A
Wiggins, K Douglas
Wiitasalo, Shirley
Wilde, Dawn Johnson
Wilde, John
Willenbecher, John
Williams, Franklin John
Williams, Hiram Draper
Williams, Janice E
Williams, Paul Alan
Williams, William Thomas
Williford, Hollis R
Willis, Barbara Florence
Willis, Sidney F
Willis, Thornton
Wilson, Ben
Wilson, David Philip
Wilson, Evan Carter
Wilson, Jane
Wilson, June
Wilson, Richard Brian
Wilson, Sybil
Wilson-Hammond, Charlotte Emily
Wiman, Bill
Windell, Violet Bruner
Winfield, Rodney M
Wingerter, John Parker
Wingo, Michael B
Wink, Don (Jon Donnel)
Winslow, Helen
Winter, Gerald Glen
Winter, Roger
Winter, Ruth
Wirstrom, Margaret
Wirsum, Karl
Wisdom, Joyce
Wise, Joseph Stephen
Wissemann-Widrig, Nancy
Wissmeyer, Gunter Gustav
Witham, Vernon Clint
Witkin, Jerome
Witt, Nancy Camden
Wizon, Tod
Woelffer, Emerson
Wofford, Philip
Wohlenhaus, Grace Forcier
Woit, Bonnie Ford
Wojtyla, Haase (Walter Joseph)
Wolber, Paul J
Wolfe, Lynn Robert
Wolfe, Robert, Jr
Wolins, Joseph
Wolsky, Jack
Wood, Alan
Wood, McCrystle
Woodlock, Ethelyn Hurd
Woodson, Doris
Woodward, Kesler Edward
Woodward, William
Woolschlager, Laura Totten
Wostrel, Nancy J
Wright, Barton Allen
Wright, Bernard
Wright, David Thomas
Wright, Frank
Wright, Milton
Wujcik, Theo
Wunderman, Jan (Liljan Darcourt Wunderman)
Wurmfeld, Sanford
Wyeth, Henriette (Mrs Peter Hurd)
Wyeth, James Browning
Wynn, Donald James
Yaghjian, Edmund
Yanoff, Arthur (Samuel)
Yaros, Constance G
Yater, George David
Yeiser, Charles William
Yektai, Manoucher
Yes, Phyllis A
York, Tina
Yoshida, Ray Kakuo
Young, Alan
Young, Peter Ford
Young, Robert G
Young, Robert John
Yust, David E
Z'
Zabarsky, Melvin Joel
Zaborowski, Dennis J
Zago, Tino (Agostino C)
Zaikine, Zak (Victor Eugene)
Zakanitch, Robert S
Zallinger, Rudolph Franz
Zalucha, Peggy Flora
Zammitt, Norman
Zapkus, Kes (Kestutis Edward)
Zarand, Julius John
Zelanski, Paul John
Zimiles, Murray
Zimmerman, Kathleen Marie
Zimmerman, Paul Warren
Zingale, Lawrence
Zisla, Harold
Zlowe, Florence M
Zokosky, Peter L
Zollweg, Aileen Boules
Zoretich, George Stephen
Zuccarelli, Frank Edward
Zuccarini, David Anthony
Zuckerberg, Stanley M
Zugor, Sandor
Zurik, Jesselyn Benson
Zwack, Michael
Zweerts, Arnold

All Media

Abrams, Joyce Diana
Accetta, Suzanne Rusconi
Adams, Pat
Adler, Myril
Aebi, Ernst Walter
Agar, Eunice Jane
Alberga, Alta W
Alberti, Donald Wesley
Albright, Malvin Marr
Alcalay, Albert S
Aldana, Carl
Alf, Martha Joanne
Allan, William George
Allen, Constance Olleen Webb
Allen, Edda Lynne
Allen, Loretta B
Allen, Ralph
Allman, Margo
Allner, Walter H
Alpert, Bill (William H)
Amato, Michele
Ambrose, Charles Edward
Amft, Robert
Anastasi, William (Joseph)
Andell, Nancy
Andersen, David R L
Anderson, Guy Irving
Anderson, Winslow
Andrews, Benny
Andrews, Sybil (Sybil Andrews Morgan)
Angulo, Chappie
Anuszkiewicz, Richard Joseph
Apt, Charles
Aquino, Edmundo
Arakawa, (Shusaku)
Argue, Douglas
Ariss, Herbert Joshua
Armstrong, Bill Howard
Arnold, Ralph Moffett
Ashby, Carl
Ashcraft, Eve
Askin, Walter Miller
Askman, Tom K
Asmar, Alice
Aso, Kaji
Atkinson, Leslie Jane
Atwell, Allen
Avery, Frances
Avlon-Daphnis, Helen Basilea
Ayaso, Manuel
Azuz, David
Bachinski, Walter Joseph
Baechler, Donald
Bailey, Virginia Ellen
Bailey, William
Bailin, Hella
Baker, Jill Withrow
Baldwin, Harold Fletcher
Balsley, John Gerald
Bandy, Ron F
Bannister, Pati (Patricia Brown Bannister)
Barazani, Morris
Bard, Joellen
Bardazzi, Peter
Bardin, Jesse Redwin
Barker, Walter William, Jr
Barnes, Robert M
Barnet, Will
Barrell, Bill
Barrett, Thomas R
Barron, Thomas
Bartels, Phyllis Elaine
Barth, Frances
Bass, Judy
Batchelor, Betsey Ann
Batista, Kenneth
Battenfield, Jackie
Baum, Marilyn Ruth
Baxter, Bonnie Jean
Bayefsky, Aba
Beal, Jack
Beauchamp, George
Belfort-Chalat, Jacqueline
Beltrán, Félix
Benglis, Lynda
Bengston, Billy Al
Ben-Haim, Zigi
Benini
Bennett, Philomene Dosek
Benney, Robert
Berg, Siri
Berguson, Robert Jenkins
Berkowitz, Henry
Berman, Eleanore (Eleanore B Lazarof)
Bermudez, Jose Ygnacio
Bernheim, Stephanie Hammerschlag
Bernstein, Gerda Meyer
Bernstein, Judith
Berry, Carolyn
Berthot, Jake
Bevlin, Marjorie Elliott
Bidlo, Mike
Bieber, Elinore Maria Korow
Biggerstaff, Myra
Biolchini, Gregory Phillip
Birch, Willie M
Bittner, Hans Oskar
Bjurman, Johan Paul
Blackburn, Linda Z
Blahove, Marcos
Blair, Dike
Blanc, (William) Peter
Blattner, Robert Henry
Blazeje, Zbigniew (Ziggy Blazese)

PAINTER (cont)
Blazey, Lawrence Edwin
Bleiberg, Gertrude Tiefenbrun
Blizzard, Alan
Block, Virginia Schaffer
Bloom, Edith Salvin
Bode, Robert William
Bodin, Paul
Bodnar, Peter
Bogdanovic, Bogomir
Bohlen, Nina (Celestine Eustis Bohlen)
Boodman, H Citron
Bookatz, Samuel
Boretz, Naomi
Borochoff, (Ida) Sloan
Bott, H(arvey) J(ohn)
Bowman, Richard
Boyle, Keith
Boyle, (James) Neil
Boynton, Jack (James) W
Bradshaw, Dove
Bradshaw, Glenn Raymond
Bradshaw, Lawrence James
Bragg, E Ann (Ann Bragg)
Bramlett, Betty Jane
Brandt, Rex (Rexford Elson)
Breinin, Raymond
Breithaupt, Erwin M
Breslin, Wynn
Bressi, Betty
Breverman, Harvey
Britsky, Nicholas
Broderson, Morris
Broderson, Robert
Brodsky, Eugene V
Brodsky, Stan
Broner, Mathew
Brooks, Bruce W
Brown, Hilton
Bruder, Harold Jacob
Brumer, Miriam
Bruni, Umberto
Bull, Fran
Burchess, Arnold
Burg, Patricia Jean
Burger, W Carl
Burleigh, Kimberly
Burnett, Calvin
Burroughs, Margaret T G
Bush, Jill Lobdill
Bushman, David Franklin
Bussabarger, Robert Franklin
Bussche, Wolf von dem
Byers, Fleur
Cadle, Ray Kenneth
Cain, Charlotte
Cain, David Paul
Cain, Michael Peter
Calfee, William Howard
Califf, Marilyn Iskiwitz
Callner, Richard
Cancel, Luis R
Cantor, Fredrich
Cariola, Robert J
Carlson, Jane C
Carmichael, Jae
Carter, Mary
Caster, Bernard Harry
Catalan, Edgardo Omar
Cava, Paul
Cecilia
Cederstrom, John Andrew
Celli, Paul
Cengle
Chaddlesone, Sherman
Chaet, Bernard
Chapline, Claudia Beechum
Chavez, Eduardo Arcenio
Chermayeff, Ivan
Chester, Charlotte Wanetta
Christensen, Dan
Christensen, Neil C
Christiansen, Diane
Cianfoni, Emilio
Cimbalo, Robert W
Cipriano, Michael R
Civale, Biagio A
Clark, Edward
Clark, Roberta Carter
Clark, William Roger
Clayberger, Samuel Robert
Clement, Shirley
Clerk, Pierre
Close, Chuck
Coates, Ross Alexander
Coburn, Ralph (M H)
Coe, Sue
Coffey, Douglas Robert
Cohen, Adele
Cohen, Elaine Lustig
Cole, Jeanette
Colker, Edward
Collery, Paula
Collett, Farrell Reuben
Collins, Larry Richard
Colombo, Charles
Comès, Marcella (Mrs Randolph Winslow)
Conaway, Gerald
Conaway, James D
Conn, Laurence
Cook, Kathleen L
Cooke, Samuel Tucker
Cooper, Wayne
Coppedge, Arthur L
Cordingley, Mary Bowles
Cornette, Mary Elizabeth
Costigan, Constance Frances
Couch, Urban
Couper, James M
Coyle, Terence
Crandall, Jerry C
Crane, Jim (James G)
Creevy, Bill
Crespin, Leslie A
Crespo, Michael Lowe
Cress, George Ayers
Crispo, Dick
Crite, Allan Rohan
Cross, Yvonne
Cruz, Pura (Pura Isabel Cruz)
Crystal, Boris
Culbertson, Janet Lynn (Mrs Douglas Kaften)
Czarnopys, Thomas J
Czimbalmos, Szabo Kalman
Daily, Evelynne Mess
D'Alessio, Natalie Marino
Dalglish, Jamie (James Parsons)
Daly, Norman
Daphnis, Nassos
Dar, Dina
Darrow, Paul Gardner
Dash, Harvey Dwight
Dash, Robert (Warren)
Davies, Theodore Peter
Davis, Ben
Davis, James Wesley
Dawson, Bess Phipps
Day, Larry (Lawrence James)
DeFazio, Teresa Galligan
De Laittre, Eleanor
De Leeuw, Leon
Delevoryas, Lillian Grace
Demartis, James J
De Nagy, Eva
Dergalis, George
Desoto, Rafael M
Desportes, Ulysse Gandvier
Diamond, Stuart
Diao, David
Dickson, Jane Leone
Di Cosola, Lois
Dine, James
Dirube, Rolando Lopez
Di Suvero, Mark
Ditzion, Grace
Dixson, Wendy Fay
Dodd, Lamar
Dogancay, Burhan Cahit
Dohanos, Stevan
Dokoupil, Jiri Georg
Doll, Catherine Ann
Doll, Linda A
Domjan, Joseph (Spiri)
Donati, Enrico
Dorfman, Bruce
Dorosh, Daria
Doudera, Gerard
Drake, Peter
Driskell, David Clyde
Dubaniewicz, Peter Paul
Dumais-Berube, Yvette
Dunham-Griggs, Margaret
Duzy, Merrilyn Jeanne
Dworzan, George R
Eades, Luis Eric
Eagerton, Robert Pierce
Eames, John Heagan
Eckelberry, Don Richard
Edelheit, Martha
Eden, Bronson B
Edgren, Gary Robert
Edwards, Paul Burgess
Edwards, Stanley Dean
Eisenberg, Marc S
Elder, Muldoon
Elias, Harold John
Ellinger, Ilona E
Else, Robert John
Embrey, Carl Rice
Engel, Michael Martin, II
Epstein, Yale
Erbe, Joan
Erla, Karen
Erman, Bruce
Espenschied, Clyde
Essley, Roger Holmer
Etchison, Bruce
Etrog, Sorel
Ettl, Georg
Evans, Bob (Robert James)
Evans, Judith Futral
Everts, Connor
Fabe, Robert
Fagan, Alanna
Fangor, Voy
Farrens, Juanita G
Farris, Joseph
Faulconer, Mary (Fullerton)
Fausett, (William) Dean
Fearing, William Kelly
Fedelle, Estelle
Fehl, Philipp P
Fein, B(arbara) R
Fein, Stanley
Feinberg, Jean
Feld, Augusta
Feldman, Walter (Sidney)
Fellows, Fred
Ferguson, Charles B
Feuerherm, Kurt K
Field, Philip Sidney
Filipovic, Augustin
Filmus, Tully
Finck, Furman J
Fink, Aaron
Fink, Herbert Lewis
Finkler, Robert Allan
Fishburne, St Julian (Le Roy)
Fisher, Carole Gorney
Flack, Audrey L
Flanagan, Michael
Fleckenstein, Opal R
Fleming, Stephen
Flowers, Thomas Earl
Foley, Dorothy Swartz
Foolery, Tom
Foose, Robert James
Foote, Howard Reed
Foulkes, Llyn
Fourcard, Inez Garey
Fournier, Alex
Fowler, Eric Nicholas
Francis, Tom
Frankenberg, Robert Clinton
Frankenthaler, Helen
Frasconi, Antonio
Freimark, Bob (Robert)
Freund, Pepsi
Freund, Will Frederick
Fricano, Tom S
Frick, Arthur Charles
Fulton, Fred Franklin
Fusco, Yolanda
Gahagan, James (Edward), Jr
Galli, Stanley Walter
Garbutt, Janice Lovoos
Garey, Pat
Gastaldi, Jerome
Gatto, Paul Anthony
Gatto, Rose Marie
Gayas-Jungwirth, I(rene)
Geeslin, Lee Gaddis
Geiger, Edith Rogers
Geltner, Danita Sue
Genn, Nancy
Gepponi, Angelo
Gerbracht, Bob (Robert Thomas)
Giacalone, Vito
Gianlorenzi, Nona Elena
Gibala, Louise
Gibbs, Y Gale
Gifford, J Nebraska
Giffuni, Flora Baldini
Gilkey, Richard Charles
Gilliam, Sam
Ginzel, Roland
Giovanni
Girard, (Charles) Jack
Glasco, Joseph M
Glyde, Henry George
Goddard, Vivian
Godsey, Glenn
Godwin, Judith
Goell, Abby Jane
Goings, Ralph
Gold, Albert
Goldberg, Michael
Golden, Eunice
Golden, Libby
Goldfine, Beatrice
Goldsmith, Elsa M
Goldstein, Julius
Goldszer, Bath-Sheba
Gongora, Leonel
Gonzalez, Xavier
Good, Leonard
Goodman, Bertram
Goodnough, Robert
Goodnow, Frank A
Gordon, Russell Talbert
Gorman, William D
Gould, John Howard
Goulet, Claude
Govan, Francis Hawks
Grado, Angelo John
Grady, Ruby McLain
Graham, K M
Graham, Robert MacDonald, Jr
Gramberg, Liliana
Grasso, Doris (Ten-Eyck)
Gray, Cleve
Gray, Don
Graziani, Sante
Greenbaum, Marty
Gregoropoulos, John
Grippe, Florence (Berg)
Grippi, Salvatore William
Grissom, Freda Gill
Grom, Bogdan
Gross, Rainer
Grossman, Nancy
Gruen, Shirley Schanen
Gruver, Mary Emmett
Guerin, John William
Gumpert, Gunther
Gunn, Ellen
Gunn, Paul James
Guzak, Karen W
Guzman-Forbes, Robert
Gyra, Francis Joseph, Jr
Hacklin, Allan Dave
Hafif, Marcia

PAINTER (cont)
Hagan, Frederick
Halkin, Theodore
Hammock, Virgil Gene
Hampton, John W
Hanlen, John (Garrett)
Hansen, Frances Frakes
Harari, Hananiah
Harden, Marvin
Harris, Gloriane
Harris, Harvey Sherman
Hart, Allen M
Hartley, Paul Jerome
Harvest, Judith R
Harvey, Robert Martin
Hasen, Burt Stanley
Hatfield, David Underhill
Hawkins, Barbara
Haydon, Harold (Emerson)
Hay-Messick, Velma
Hazlewood, Carl E
Hazlitt, Don
Head, Robert William
Heard, Lillian
Heaton, Janet N
Heidel, Frederick (H)
Heiskell, Diana
Helander, Bruce Paul
Held, Al
Helfond, Riva
Hemmerdinger, William John, III
Henderson, Jack W
Hendricks, Geoffrey
Hendricks, James (Powell)
Hensche, Henry
Herman, Roger
Herman, Vic
Herrera, Carmen
Herring, William Arthur
Hertzberg, Rose
Heyman, Lawrence Murray
Hildreth, Joseph Alan
Hill, Joan (Chea-se-quah)
Hilty, Thomas R
Hochhauser, Marilyn Helsenrott
Hoffman, Martin
Holder, Tom
Holladay, Harlan H
Holland, Tom
Holtz, Itshak Jack
Homar, Lorenzo
Homitzky, Peter
Hood, Walter Kelly
Hooper, Jack Meredith
Hopkinson, Harold I
Horne, (Arthur Edward) Cleeve
Housman, Russell F
Howard, Cecil Ray
Howard, Humbert L
Hudson, Robert H
Huntley, David C
Hurtig, Martin Russell
Hurtubise, Jacques
Hurwitz, Sidney J
Hutsaliuk, Lubo
Hyde, Alice Bach
Iannone, Dorothy
Ida, Shoichi
Idaherma (Idaherma Williams)
Imana, Jorge Garron
Indiviglia, Salvatore Joseph
Ingalls, Eve
Insley, Will
Inukai, Kyohei
Jacobs, Jim
Jagger, Gillian
Jarvis, John Brent
Jeffe, Huldah C
Jellico, John Anthony
Jenkens, Garlan F
Jenkins, Mary Anne Keel
Jergens, Robert Joseph
Joelson, Suzanne
Johns, Jasper
Johnsen, May Anne
Johnson, James Alan
Johnson, Lester F
Johnston, Ynez
Jones, Ben
Jones, Edward Powis
Jones, George Bobby
Jones, James Edward
Jones, Lois Mailou (Mrs V Pierre-Noel)
Jorgensen, Flemming
Judge, Mary Frances
Jules, Mervin
Kahn, A Michael
Kahn, Peter
Kaiser, Karen
Kaiser, Vitus J
Kaish, Luise
Kamrowski, Gerome
Kanter, Lorna J
Kaplan, Sandra
Karp, Richard Gordon
Kashdin, Gladys Shafran
Kass, Ray
Kassoy, Bernard
Katchen, Carole Lee
Katz, Hilda (Hulda Weber)
Katz, Morris
Kauffman, (Camille) Andrene
Kaulitz, Garry Charles
Keene, Paul
Keever, Kim
Kellar, Martha Robbins
Keller, Frank S
Kelly, Ellsworth
Kennedy, J William
Kepes, Gyorgy
Kerns, Ginger
Kertzer, Anita Elizabeth
Kidd, Rebecca Montgomery
Killmaster, John H
King, Eleanor (Eleanor King Hookham)
Kinigstein, Jonah
Kinstler, Everett Raymond
Kipp, Orval
Kitner, Harold
Kittredge, Nancy (Elizabeth)
Kleinsmith, Gene (Eugene Dennis)
Klotz, Suzanne
Knigin, Michael Jay
Knobler, Lois Jean
Knorr, Jeanne Boardman
Knox, Elizabeth
Kobayashi, Hisako
Koch, Arthur Robert
Kohl, Barbara
Komodore, Bill
Konrad, Adolf Ferdinand
Koopalethes, Olivia (Olivia Koopalethes Alberts)
Kornbluth, Frances
Kortlander, William
Koscielny, Margaret
Kowalke, Ronald Leroy
Kowalski, Raymond Alois
Kravjansky, Mikulas
Krebs, Patsy
Kreznar, Richard J
Krieger, Florence
Krieger, Suzanne Baruc
Kroll, David
Krukowski, Lucian
Krushenick, John
Kuper, Yuri (Yuri Kuperman)
Kurahara, Ted N
Kuryluk, Ewa
Kusama, Yayoi
Kuvshinoff, Bertha Horne
Kuvshinoff, Nicolai
Kwak, Hoon
Lack, Stephen
Laguna, Mariella
Laico, Colette
Lake, Randall
Lamb, Darlis Carol
Lambrechts, Marc
Lamell, Robert (C)
La Monte, Angela Mae
Lampitoc, Rol Ponce
Langager, Craig T
La Plant, Mimi
Larsen, Patrick Heffner
Larson, Sidney
Lasker, Jonathan
Lassaw, Ibram
Laster, Paul
Laventhol, Hank
Lawrence, Jacob
Lawrence, Michael
Lea, Stanley E
Lea, Tom
Leaf, June
Leake, Eugene W
Leathers, Winston Lyle
Lechay, James
Lee, Li Lin
Le Fevre, Richard John
Lemieux, Annette Rose
Lerner, Nathan Bernard
Lettenstrom, Dean Roger
Levi, Josef
Levin, Morton D
Levine, Jack
Levine, Shepard
Levinson, Mon
Levitt, Alfred
Levy, Hilda
Lewandowski, Edmund D
Lewis, Ronald Walter
Lewis, Samella Sanders
Liberi, Dante
Liberman, Alexander
Lichtenstein, Roy
Liebowitz, Janet
Liles, Raeford Bailey
Lima, Jacqueline (Dutton)
Lindmark, Arne
Lindsay, Arturo
Lindstrom, Gaell
Lionni, Leo
Lippincott, Janet
Lisk, Penelope E Tsaltas
Litwin, Ruth Forbes
Liu, Ho
Llorente, Luis
Lobdell, Frank
Loberg, Robert Warren
Lombard, Annette
Longstreet, Stephen
Lorber, Stephen Neil
Lorelli (Svoboda), Elvira Mae
Loring, John
Lotterman, Hal
Lowe, Marvin
Lucey, Jack
Lukas, Dennis Brian
Lukin, Sven
Lyle, Charles Thomas
McCall, Robert Theodore
McCallum, Corrie (Mrs William Halsey)
McCarthy, Denis
McCarty, Lorraine Chambers
McClanahan, John D
McCracken, John Harvey
Macdonell, Cameron
McGarrell, James
McGowin, Ed (William Edward)
McInerney, Gene Joseph
McIntosh, Gregory Stephen
McIvor, John Wilfred
McKesson, Malcolm Forbes
McKnight, Thomas Frederick
McNamara, John
McSheehy, Cornelia Marie
McVeigh, Miriam Lenig
McWhorter, Elsie Jean
Magee, Alderson
Magistro, Charles John
Magnan, Oscar Gustav
Mahdavi, Rafael Sinclair
Maisner, Bernard Lewis
Malone, Patricia Lynn
Maltzman, Stanley
Mancuso, Leni
Mandel, Howard
Mandelbaum, Lyn
Manera, Enrico Orlando
Mangold, Robert Peter
Manship, John Paul
Maraldo, Ushanna F
Mariner, Donna M
Mark, Bendor
Marlow, Audrey Swanson
Marro, George Matthew
Marsden, Michael H E
Marshall, James Duard
Marshall, Mara
Martin, Bill
Martin, Charles E
Martin, Fred Thomas
Martin, Knox
Martinez, Alfred
Martinsen, Ivar Richard
Marx, Evelyn
Maurice, Alfred Paul
Maxim, David Nicholas
Maxwell, William C
Meeker, Barbara Miller
Meeker, Dean Jackson
Mejer, Robert Lee
Merfeld, Gerald Lydon
Merkin, Richard Marshall
Mesibov, Hugh
Metz, Frank Robert
Meyers, Francis Joseph
Micale, Albert
Middaugh, Robert Burton
Mikus, Eleanore
Miles, Cyril
Miller, Barbara Darlene
Miller, Donald Lloyd
Milliken, Gibbs
Milloff, Mark David
Mina-Mora, Raul Jose
Mirra, (Mirra Tengroth)
Mitchell, Clifford
Mitchell, Robin
Miyamoto, Wayne Akira
Mobley, Karen R
Moerschel, Chiara
Mogensen, Paul
Moldroski, Al R
Molinari, Guido
Monaghan, William Scott
Montague, James L
Moore, Myreen (Myreen Moore Nicholson)
Moose, Talmadge Bowers
Morris, Robert Clarke
Moses, Ed
Moszynski, Andrew
Moulton, Susan Gene
Mount, Ward
Moyer, Roy
Mueller, Henrietta Waters
Muller, Max Paul
Munzner, Aribert
Muranaka, Hideo
Myers, Carole Ann
Myers, Dorothy Roatz
Naar, Harry I
Nagin, Mary D
Narotzky, Norman David
Naumer, Helmuth
Nessim, Barbara
Neuman, Robert S
Newman, John Beatty
Niese, Henry Ernst
Noel, Georges
Nong
Novinski, Lyle Frank
Novotny, Elmer Ladislaw
Nowack, Wayne Kenyon
Nugent, Bob L
Nutt, Jim (James Tureman)
Nydorf, Roy Herman
Oakes, William Larry

PAINTER (cont)
O'Hagan, Desmond Brian
O'Hara, Morgan
Oi, Motoi
Okamura, Arthur
Olendorf, William Carr
Olsen Bergman, Ciel
Onslow Ford, Gordon M
Opper, John
Orlowsky, Lillian
Ornstein, Judith
Orr, Elliot
Ortman, George Earl
Osborne, Robert Lee
Pablo
Pace, James Robert
Paone, Peter
Papier, Maurice Anthony
Papo, Iso
Paradise, Phil (Herschel)
Parra, Carmen
Partin, Robert
Pasinski, Irene
Peacock, Cliffton
Pearlman, Etta S
Pearlstein, Philip
Pearlstein, Seymour
Pekar, Ronald Walter
Pekarsky, Mel (Melvin Hirsch)
Pels, Albert
Perkins, Lois Bouthillier
Perlin, Bernard
Petheo, Bela Francis
Phillips, Michael
Piatek, Francis John
Piccillo, Joseph
Picher, Claude
Pierce, Donald (Benjamin)
Pinardi, Enrico Vittorio
Pincus, Laurie Jane
Pinto, Angelo Raphael
Pittore, Carlo
Plattner, Phyllis
Plotkin, Linda
Poduska, T F
Pogany, Miklos
Pollack, Reginald Murray
Polonsky, Arthur
Poons, Larry
Popovac, Gwynn
Porter, (Edwin) David
Potter, Ted
Powelson, Rosemary A
Pratt, Vernon Gaither
Price, Morgan Samuel (Margaret Morgan Price)
Prochownik, Walter A
Pugh, Grace Huntley
Quandt, Elizabeth (Elizabeth Quandt)
Quentel, Holt
Quest, Charles Francis
Quiller, Stephen Frederick
Rackus, George (Keistus)
Racz, Andre
Radin, Dan
Radjai, Abbas
Ragland, Bob
Rakovan, Lawrence Francis
Ramirez, Joel Tito
Ramos, (Mel) Melvin John
Rath, Hildegard
Ratkai, George
Rauf, Barbara Claire
Rayburn (Dale), Boyd
Reardon, Mary A
Rebbeck, Lester James, Jr
Rebhun, Pearl G
Red Star, Kevin
Reed, David
Reed, Jesse Floyd
Reedy, Mitsuno Ishii (Mitsuno Ishii Hackler)
Reep, Edward Arnold
Rehberger, Gustav
Reichek, Jesse
Remsing, (Joseph) Gary
Renee, Paula
Resika, Paul
Resnick, Milton
Retzer, Howard Earl
Reynolds, Patricia Ellen
Reynolds, Robert
Reynolds, Stephen Francis
Ricci, Jerri
Rice, Anthony Hopkins
Rice, Norman Lewis
Richards, Walter DuBois
Richenburg, Robert Bartlett
Ridley, Gregory D, Jr
Ries, Martin
Ringgold, Faith
Risser, James K
Ritter, Julian
Rivera, Frank
Rivers, Larry
Robinson, Sally W
Rocamora, Jaume
Rocha, Randolfo (Randolfo Scott Rocha)
Roche, Robert (Richard)
Rognan, Lloyd Norman
Rogovin, Mark
Romano, Clare Camille (Mrs John Ross)
Romero, Rachael L
Rophar,
Rose, Herman
Rose, John Timothy
Roseman, Susan Carol
Ross, Jaime
Rossi, Joseph O
Rothschild, Judith
Rotterdam, Paul Z
Rozman, Joseph John
Ruben, Albert
Rubenstein, Lewis W
Rubin, Irwin
Rudquist, Jerry Jacob
Ruellan, Andree
Rutsch, Alexander
Ruttinger, Jacquelyn
Ryman, Robert
St Denis, Paul Andre
Sal, Jack
Saladino, Tony
Salemme, Lucia (Autorino)
Saltmarche, Kenneth Charles
Samerjan, George E
Samuels, Gerald
Samuelson, Fred Binder
Sandler, Barbara
Sandlin, David Thomas
Saul, Peter
Sauls, Frederick Inabinette
Saunders, Raymond Jennings
Savage, Jerry
Savage, Roger
Savas, Jo-Ann
Scarpa, Dorothea
Scharf, William
Scharff, Constance Kramer
Schary, Emanuel
Scheer, Sherie (Hood)
Schein, Eugenie
Scherpereel, Richard Charles
Schieferdecker, Ivan E
Schiller, Beatrice
Schlemm, Betty Lou
Schmid, Richard Alan
Schneider, Noel
Schoenherr, John (Carl)
Scholder, Fritz
Schorr, Justin
Schrag, Karl
Schreiber, Eileen Sher
Schrut, Sherry
Schwartz, Rosalyn
Schwartz, Therese
Seckel, Paul Bernhard
Seckler, Dorothy Gees
Seguin, Jean-Pierre
Sekiguchi, Risa
Semowich, Charles John
Shadbolt, Jack Leonard
Shahn, Abby
Shahn, Bernarda Bryson
Sharp, Susan S
Shaw, Donald Edward
Shaw, Peggy
Shead, S Ray
Sheaks, Barclay
Shedosky, Suzanne
Sheehan, Evelyn
Sheehan, Maura A
Shepherd, Reginald
Sheppard, Joseph Sherly
Sherman, Sarai
Sherrill, Milton Lewis
Sherwood, Leona
Shields, Alan J
Shikler, Aaron
Shives, Arnold Edward
Shook, Georg
Sibley, Charles Kenneth
Siebner, Herbert
Silber, Maurice
Siler, Todd (Lael)
Silkotch, Mary Ellen
Sills, Thomas Albert
Silverman, Burton Philip
Simon, Jewel Woodard
Simoni, John Peter
Sing Hoo
Sirugo, Sal (Salvatore)
Skurkis, Barry A
Sky, Carol Veth
Slade, Roy
Slate, Joseph Frank
Sloat, Richard Joel
Small, Deborah
Smith, Albert E
Smith, Arthur Hall
Smith, Gordon
Smith, Jos(eph) A(nthony)
Smith, Sam
Smith, Shirley
Smith, V Joachim
Snelson, Kenneth D
Snidow, Gordon E
Snow, John
Snow, Lee Erlin
Snow, Michael
Snowden, Gilda
Snyder, Ruth (Cozen)
Solomon, Syd
Soorikian, Diana Tashjian
Sorce, Anthony John
Soreff, Helen
Soreff, Stephen
Sorge, Walter
Spandorf, Lily Gabriella
Sperakis, Nicholas George
Spratt, Frederick R
Staempfli, George W
Stamos, Theodoros (S)
Stanforth, Melvin Sidney
Stanton, Tom-Eric
Stapp, Ray Veryl
Stefanelli, Joe
Steinke, Bettina
Steinmetz, Grace Ernst Titus
Sterne, Hedda
Stevenson, A Brockie
Stewart, Dorothy S
Steynovitz, Zamy
Stillman, George
Stoltenberg, Donald Hugo
Stone, Gwen
Storm, Larue
Storm, Mark (Kennedy)
Story, William Easton
Stout, Frank J
Strand, Sally (Sally Strand Ellis)
Stratton, Dorothy (Mrs William A King)
Stronghilos, Carol
Stukey, Virginia
Sturman, Eugene
Sueños, Carlos
Sullivan, Francoise
Sultan, Donald K
Summ, Helmut
Sussman, Arthur
Suzuki, James Hiroshi
Suzuki, Taro
Sverdlove, Zolita
Swan, Barbara
Szasz, Frank V
Sznajderman, Marius S
Tabak, Chaim
Takal, Peter
Tarbet, Urania Christy
Targan, Judy
Tarin, Gilberto A
Tascona, Antonio Tony
Tatossian, Armand
Tatti, Benedict Michael
Taylor, Brie (Benjamin de Brie)
Taylor, Grace Martin
Taylor, Michele F
Tettleton, Robert Lynn
Thames, Emmitt Eugene
Theroux, Carol
Thomas, Larry W
Thon, William
Thorns, John Cyril, Jr
Thurston, Jacqueline Beverly
Thwaites, Charles Winstanley
Tillenius, Clarence (Ingwall)
Ting, Walasse
Tobias, Abraham Joel
Tobias, Robert Paul
Torlen, Michael Arnold
Toscano, (Dolores A)
Townsend, Jean (Mrs Saul Field)
Tracy, Michael
Treister, Kenneth
Trivigno, Pat
Trova, Ernest Tino
Tsai, Hsiao Hsia
Tucker, Charles Clement
Tulk, Alfred James
Tulving, Ruth
Turk, Rudy H
Turlington, Patricia R
Tuttle, Richard
Twombly, Cy
Uchima, Toshiko
Ultra Violet,
Umlauf, Karl A
Umlauf, Lynn (Charlotte)
Unithan, Dolly
Utz, Thornton
Uzilevsky, Marcus
Vaccaro, Luella Grace
Vadia, Rafael
Valencia, Cesar
Valerio, James Robert
Van Aalten, Jacques
Van Laar, Timothy
Vann, Loli (Mrs Lilian Van Young)
Vanriet, Jan
Van Sant, Tom R
Varga, Margit
Vaux, Richard
Velasquez, Oscar
Vidal, Francisco Fernandez
Viera, Charles David
Viera, Ricardo
Vinella, Ray (Raimondo John)
Viner, Frank Lincoln
Vitale, Vincent
Voelker, Elizabeth
Volpe, Robert
Von Schmidt, Eric
Voos, William John
Vorwerk, E Charlsie
Wainwright, Robert Barry
Wald, Sylvia
Waldman, Paul
Walker, Larry
Wall, Rhonda
Warder, William

PAINTER (cont)

Warshaw, Larry
Washington, James W, Jr
Wasserman, Albert
Watson, Darliene Keeney
Wayne, June
Webb, Jeffrey R
Weber, Albert Jacob
Weber, Jan
Weber, Karen
Webster, Stokely
Wechter, Vivienne Thaul
Weiner, Abe
Weismann, Donald Leroy
Welden, Daniel W
Weller, Paul
Welliver, Neil G
Wells, Betty Childs
Wells, Mac
Welter, Cole H
Wentworth, Janet
Werner, Donald (Lewis)
Wesley, John
West, W Richard (Dick)
Wethington, Wilma Zella
Wetmore, Gordon (Stanley Gordon)
Whitaker, William
White, John M
Whitney, Charlotte Armide
Whittome, Irene F
Wiley, William T
Will, John A
Willson, Margaret (Bosshardt) Pace
Wilmeth, Ernest, II
Wilson, York
Wimberley, Frank Walden
Wingate, George B
Winters, Sandy (Sandra L)
Wisnosky, John G
Wissemann-Widrig, Nancy
Witold-K (Kaczanowski),
Witt, John
Wolfe, Mildred Nungester
Wonner, Paul (John)
Wood, Harry Emsley, Jr
Woodruff, Diane Bailey
Woods, Rip
Woodson, Shirley Ann
Woolwich, Madlyn-Ann C
Wray, Dick
Wright, Stanley Marc
Wynne, Albert Givens
Yaeger, Edgar Louis
Yanow, Rhoda Mae
Yarbrough, Leila Kepert
Yasuda, Robert
Yoder, Richard Allen
Yorgo, (George Yorgo Spyropoulos)
Young, Kenneth Victor
Youngblood, Nat
Zacharias, Athos
Zahourek, Jon Gail
Zajac, Jack
Zaleski, Jean
Zaloudek, Duane
Zapfe, Guillermo (Wilhelm Karl Zapfe)
Zevon, Irene
Zivic, William Thomas
Zonia, Dhimitri
Zox, Larry
Zucker, Joseph I

Egg Tempera

Akers, Gary
Baggett, William Carter, Jr
Boardman, Deborah
Braiden, Rose Margaret J
Cadmus, Paul
Coburn, Bette Lee
Drutz, June
Etter, Howard Lee
Forrestall, Thomas De Vany
Geldermann Hails, Barbara
Ghikas, Panos George
Glesmann, Sylvia Maria
Harroun, Dorothy Sumner
Holmes, David Bryan
Jaque, Louis
Koenig, Catherine Catanzaro
Krauth, Harald
Levine, Tomar
Long, Frank Weathers
McBryde, Sarah Elva
MacKenzie, Hugh Seaforth
McKim, William Wind
Magafan, Ethel
Massey, Robert Joseph
Meigs, John Liggett
Mitchell, Dianne (Ball)
Moon, Jim (James Monroe)
Musselman, Darwin B
Ott, Michael E
Powers, Donald T
Rippel, M (Morris Conrad)
Rosenthal, Stephen
Sanders, Rhea (Rhea Sanders Rabinovich)
Schottland, M
Shatalow, Vladimir Mihailovich
Steider, Doris (Mrs C B McCampbell)
Steinhoff, Monika
Stone, Don
Tolmie, Kenneth Donald
Tooker, George
Treaster, Richard A
Van Winkelen, Barbara
Vargo, John
Vickrey, Robert Remsen
Wiltraut, Douglas Scott
Wright, Harold David
Wyeth, Andrew Newell
Young, Andrew

Miscellaneous Media

Aalund, Suzy
Abeles, Kim Victoria
Ablow, Joseph
Ablow, Roselyn Karol
Abt, Jeffrey
Adams, Lisa Kay
Ahrendt, Christine
Albuquerque, Lita
Alford, Gloria K
Alhilali, Neda
Allain, René Pierre
Allen, Kaola
Alquilar, Maria
Anderson, Bill (William Maxwell)
Anderson, William Thomas
Anglin, Betty Lockhart
Anthonisen, George Rioch
Appel, Keith Kenneth
Ariss, Margot (Joan Phillips)
Aronson, David
Artschwager, Richard Ernst
Atkinson, Eric Newton
Aylon, Helene
Bahc, Mo
Bailey, Barry Stone
Bakaty, Mike
Bandel, Lennon Raymond
Bandy, Gary
Banerjee, (Bimal)
Bangert, Colette Stuebe
Barber, Philip Judd
Barth, Jack Alexander
Bartlett, Jennifer Losch
Bass, Joel
Bauer, Ruth Kruse
Baynard, Ed
Behrens, Mary Snyder
Beker, Gisela
Bender, May
Bennett, Don Bemco
Berger, Jason
Bhavsar, Natvar Prahladji
Bialobroda, Anna
Biggers, John Thomas
Biolchini, Gregory Phillip
Bishop, Ben
Bishop, Jeffrey Britton
Bjorklund, Lee
Blaedel, Joan Stuart Ross
Blumberg, Barbara Griffiths
Bolton, Robin Jean
Boris, Bessie
Botero, Fernando
Bouchard, Paul E
Bourgeois, Douglas
Boyce, Gerald G
Brach, Paul Henry
Brainard, Joe
Bramson, Phyllis Halperin
Briansky, Rita Prezament
Brodeur, Catherine R
Brooks, (John) Alan
Brown, Pamela Wedd
Bryce, Eileen Ann
Bumas, Jonathan Mark
Burkhart, Kathe K
Burnett, Barbara Ann
Cadieux, Michael Eugene
Calkins, Kingsley Mark
Calzolari, Elaine
Campbell, David Paul
Cano, Margarita
Cantor, Rusty
Carlson, George Arthur
Carlson, Robert Michael
Carmichael, Donald Ray
Carron, Maudee Lilyan
Carter, Harriet (Estelle) Manore
Carter, Sam John
Carvalho, Josely
Case, Elizabeth
Casellas, Joachim
Cavat, Irma
Chaikin, Alyce
Chandler, John William
Charmatz, Bill (William Adolphe)
Cheshire, Craig Gifford
Chicago, Judy
Choy, Terence Tin-Ho
Christ-Janer, Arland F
Church, C Howard
Clark, Emery Ann
Clough, Charles Sidney
Code, Audrey
Colescott, Robert H
Colette
Collins, Paul
Cone-Skelton, Annette
Consagra, Pier
Cook, Michael David
Cooke, Judy
Copley, William Nelson
Corso, Samuel (Joseph)
Cosgrove, Stanley
Cost, James Peter
Cowan, Aileen Hooper
Cowley, Edward P
Crash (John Matos)
Crile, Susan
Crockett, Gib (Gibson M)
Cuevas, Jose Luis
Cunnick, Gloria Helen
Cunningham, (Charles) Bruce
Da Cunha, Julio
Dahill, Thomas Henry, Jr
D'Almeida, George
Danziger, Fred Frank
Dasenbrock, Doris (Nancy) Voss
Davis, Brad (Bradley Darius)
Davis, Harry Allen
Davis, Jack R
Davis, Jerrold
Dawson, Doug
Debrosky, Christine A
Decter, Betty Eva
De Guzman, Evelyn Lopez
De Knight, Avel
Deloney, Jack Clouse
Del Valle, Cezar Jose
Demanche, Michel S
De Mille, Leslie Benjamin
Denton, Patry
Deo, Marjoree Nee
DeRosa, Michael Louis
De Turczynowicz, Wanda (Mrs Eliot Hermann)
Dickinson, Eleanor Creekmore
DiFranza, Americo M
Dillon, Paul Sanford
Di Meo, Dominick
Dmytruk, Ihor R
Dokoupil, Jiri Georg
Dreikausen, Margret
Duerwald, Carol
Dufour, Paul Arthur
Dunkle, Joan Osborn
Dzierski, Vincent Paul
Eaton, Pauline (Friedrich)
Eckart, Christian
Eckert, Lou
Edell, Nancy
Edvi Illes, Emma
Edwards, James F
Egeli, Peter Even
Elias, Sheila
Elliot, Catherine J
Ellis, Andra
Emerson, Walter Caruth
Engle, Chet
Erdle, Rob
Ettling, Ruth (Droitcour)
Ewen, Paterson
F(ord), Lisa Collado
Farber, Maya M
Farnham, Emily
Farruggio, Remo Michael
Faulkner, Frank
Feigin, Marsha
Feldman, Roger Lawrence
Felisky, Barbara Rosbe
Fellows, Alice
Ferguson, Gerald
Ferrer, Rafael
Fetting, Rainer
Few, James Cecil, PSA
Finkelstein, Max
Fitzgerald, Astrid
Flahavin, Marian Joan
Flick, Paul John
Flora, James Royer
Forman, Alice
Forman, Kenneth Warner
Fornelli, Joseph
Franck, Frederick S
Freed, David
Freeland, William Lee
Freeman, Jeff(rey Vaughn)
Frey, Viola
Frick, Joan
Frost, Stuart Homer
Fuller, Emily Rutgers
Gablik, Suzi
Galen, Elaine
Galinsky, Norman
Ganzarain, Mirentxu
Garcia, Rupert (Marshall R)
Gardner, Andrew Bradford
Garel, Leo
Garzon-Blanco, Armando
Gaucher, Yves
Gaydos, Tim (Timothy John)
Geller, Esther (Esther Geller Shapero)
Gentry, Herbert
Gianakos, Steve
Gigliotti, Joanne Marie
Gillespie, Dorothy Muriel
Glantzman, Judy
Glaser, David
Golbin, Andree

PAINTER (cont)
Goldstein, Fern
Goodbred, Ray Edward
Goodstein-Shapiro, F
Graham, Lois (M Gord)
Graves, Morris
Graves, Nancy Stevenson
Gray, Larry
Green, Denise G
Greenberg, Irwin
Greene PSA, Chris (Christine E Greene)
Greer, Walter (Marion)
Grimley, Oliver Fetterolf
Grossman, Morton
Grove, Edward Ryneal
Gualtieri, Joseph P
Guichet, Melody
Gunderson, Karen
Gundlefinger, John Andre
Gunshor, Ruth
Gussow, Alan
Habergritz, George Joseph
Haerer, Carol
Halbrook, Rita Robertshaw
Hall, John A
Hall, Lee
Hamlett, Dale Edward
Handell, Albert George
Hansen, Harold John
Hansen, Robert
Harjo, Benjamin, Jr
Harkness, Madden
Harnick, Sylvia
Harrington, Bryan Rulison
Harrington, Chestee Marie
Harris, Tracy
Hartal, Paul
Hartigan, Grace
Harwood-Baumel, Bernice
Hatch, John W
Hatgil, Paul
Haut, Claire (Joan)
Hawkins, Myrtle H
Hay, George Austin
Hayes, Randy (Randolph Alan)
Head, Cecil Franklin
Heimdal, Georg
Heise, Myron Robert
Herbert, James Arthur
Hermann, M(ildred) L
High, Timothy Griffin
Hitner, Chuck
Hoffman, Eric
Hoffman, Helen Bacon
Holbrook, Vivian Nicholas
Holste, Thomas James
Honig, Eleanor D
Hopkins, B(ernice Elizabeth)
Horvay, Martha J
Horvitz, Suzanne Joan
Hotvedt, Kris J
Houskeeper, Barbara
Howe, Oscar
Howell, Claude Flynn
Howell, Elizabeth (Mitch) Coon
Hubbard, John
Hudson, Jacqueline
Huff, Robert
Huot, Robert
Hupp, Frederick Duis
Hutchison, Elizabeth S
Ingham, Tom (Edgar)
Injeyan, Seta L
IRENA (Irene R Mikol),
Jackson, Suzanne Fitzallen
Jacobson, Arthur
Janschka, Fritz
Jarvis, Donald
Jennerjahn, W P
Jenrette, Pamela Anne
Jensen, Leo (Vernon)
Jerins, Edgar
Jocda
Johnson, (L) Diane
Johnson, Doris Miller
Johnson, Homer
Johnson, Ray
Johnstone, Mark
Jones, Calvin B(ell)
Jones, David Lee
Jones, Doug (Douglas McKee)
Jordan, Beth McAninch
Ju, I-Hsiung
Kachadoorian, Zubel
Kahn, Robin
Kakas, Christopher A
Kamm, Dorothy Lila
Karawina, Erica (Mrs Sidney C Hsiao)
Karwoski, Richard Charles
Kash, Marie (Marie Kash Weltzheimer)
Kassoy, Hortense
Kaufman, Jane
Kaye, George
Keech, John H
Keeler, David Boughton
Keena, Janet Laybourn
Keerl, Bayat
Kerns, Ed (Johnson), Jr
Kessler, Shirley
Kester, Lenard
Kettner, David Allen
Kiker, Evelyn Coalson
Kimura, Riisaburo
Kinnaird, Richard William
Kitaj, R B
Kleemann, Ron
Kleiman, Alan
Klein, Ellen Lee
Kloss, Gene (Alice Geneva Glasier)
Knudsen, Christian
Knutsson, Anders
Koch, Edwin E
Kocher, Robert Lee
Koenig, Catherine Catanzaro
Kohlmeyer, Ida (R)
Kohn, Misch
Kohut, Lorene
Kolliker, William Augustin
Koons, Darell J
Kornmayer, J Gary (John)
Kravitz, Walter
Kreitzer, David Martin
Krigstein, Bernard
Kruskamp, Janet
Kuchar, Kathleen Ann
Kuehn, Edmund Karl
Kuhn, Marylou
Kunstler, Morton
Kupferman, Murray
Kushner, Dorothy Browdy
Kushner, Robert Ellis
Kwiecinski, Chester Martin
Laderman, Gabriel
Lansdowne, James Fenwick
Lauridsen, Hanne H7L
Lawton, Nancy
Layton, Richard
Le Clair, Charles
Lee, Amy Freeman
Lee, Eleanor Gay
Lee, Margaret F
Leedy, Jim (James A Leedy)
Leeper, Doris Marie
Lee-Smith, Hughie
Lefranc, Margaret (Margaret Lefranc Schoonover)
Leis, Marietta Patricia
Leland, Whitney Edward
Leonardi, Hector
Lerman, Doris (Harriet)
Lerner, Alexandria Sandra
Lerner, Sandy R
Lesh, Richard D
Levy, Phyllis H
Lew, Fran
Lichacz, Sheila Enit
Lichtenstein, Gary
Lifson, Hugh Anthony
Lipson, Goldie
Little, Polly A
Livingston, Sidnee
Lopina, Louise Carol
Lovejoy, Margot R
Lukosius, Richard Benedict
Lund, Jane
Luray, J
Lytle, Richard
Lytton, Constance B
McChristy, Quentin L
McCollum, Allan
McIlroy, Carol J
McKay, Arthur Fortescue
Mackenzie, David, IV
McNealy, Robert
McNickle, Thomas Glen
Mac Whinnie, John Vincent
Magel, Catherine Anne
Mahoney, Joella Jean
Majdrakoff, Ivan
Maler, M Leopoldo Mario
Malone, Robert R
Mandelman, Beatrice M
Manes, Paul
Manter, Margaret C
Manville, Elsie
Marander, Carol Jean
Margo, Boris
Margolis, David
Margules, Gabriele Ella
Margulies, Herman
Marker, Mariska Pugsley
Marsh, Anne Steele
Marshall, Robert Leroy
Martin, Dianne L
Martin, Larry Kenneth
Mazur, Michael
Meadows, P B (Patricia)
Medoff, Eve
Mercolino, Veronica Florence
Merrill, Ross M
Meserole, Vera Stromsted
Meyer, Milton E, Jr
Michaels-Paque, J
Mickish, Verle L
Miley, Chuck (Charles) E
Miller, Michael Stephen
Miller, Sue S
Min, Yong Soon
Minter, Marilyn A
Mitchell, Katherine
Moon, Marc
Moore, Arthur Cotton
Moore, Fay
Moore, Marjorie
Morehouse, William Paul
Morgan, Maritza Leskovar
Moroni, Aldo Leonard, Jr
Moroz, Mychajlo
Morphesis, Jim (James George)
Morris, Roger Dale
Muller, Helen B
Munoz, Rie
Murray, John Michael
Myers, Malcolm Haynie
Myers, Virginia Anne
Nawara, Jim
Nawara, Lucille Procter
Nelson, Joan
Nelson, Ruth Basha (Basha Ruth Nelson)
Nichols, James William
Nichols, William Allyn
Nilsson, Gladys
Nix, Patricia (Lea)
Noland, Kenneth
Nyman, Georgianna Beatrice
Oji, Helen Shizuko
Olson, Rick
O'Neill, John Patton
Onley, Toni
Ortlip, Paul Daniel
O'Shea, Terrence Patrick
Oster, Gerald
Ostiguy, Jean-Rene
Osver, Arthur
Paige, Wayne Leo
Pappenheimer, Will D
Parella, Albert Lucian
Paris, Lucille M
Parke, Walter Simpson
Parker, Will (William Crawford)
Partridge, David Gerry
Partz, Felix (Ron Gabe)
Pashgian, M Helen
Patrick, Joseph Alexander
Patterson, Shirley Abbott
Patterson, William Joseph
Pattison, Abbott
Paul, Arthur
Paul, William D, Jr
Pearson, John
Peche, Dale C
Peden, Donalee
Peeples, Maija (Maija Gegeris Zack Woof)
Peppard, Blaylock A
Perlin, Rae
Pernotto, James Angelo
Perry, Lallah Miles
Peruo, Marsha
Peters, Andrea Jean
Peters, Diane (Peck)
Petersen, Will
Peterson, Dorothy (Hawkins)
Phillips, Matt
Piehl, Walter Jason, Jr
Piene, Otto
Pindell, Howardena Doreen
Pitcher, John Charles
Pollak, Theresa
Pollock, Merlin F
Pond, Clayton
Pope, Mary Ann Irwin
Porter, Liliana
Preusser, Robert Ormerod
Promutico, Jean
Quaytman, Harvey
Quirk, Thomas Charles, Jr
Radovich, Donald
Ragland, Jack Whitney
Rankaitis, Susan
Rauschenberg, Robert
Reichman, Leah Carol
Reimann, Arline
Rembski, Stanislav
Renner, Eric
Renouf, Edda
Renouf, Edward
Richards, Jeanne Herron
Richards, Sabra
Rippey, Clayton
Rise, John Ernest
Riseling, Robert Lowell
Rivers, Victoria Z
Robbins, Hulda D
Robinson, Gail E
Robinson, Grove
Robinson, Jay (Thurston)
Robinson, Mary Ann
Robles, Julian
Rockburne, Dorothea
Romero, Megan H
Rose, David
Rose, Robin Carlise
Rosenthal, Seymour
Ross, Sueellen
Rothenberg, Barbara
Rowan, (C) Patrick
Rowe, Charles Alfred
Ruffing, Anne Elizabeth
Ruggles, Joanne Beaule
Ruthling, Ford
Saari, Peter H
Sabelis, Huibert
Sachse, Janice R
Sahrbeck, Everett William
Sakurai, Jo Mary (Jo Mary McCormick-Sakurai)
Salemme, Antonio
Sallick, Lucy Ellen

PAINTER (cont)
Saltzman, William
Sandgren, Ernest Nelson
Sangiamo, Albert
Sankowsky, Itzhak
Sargent, Richard
Sarkisian, Paul
Saru, George
Sassone, Marco
Satz, Janet M
Scalise, Nicholas Peter
Schabacker, Betty Barchet
Schaefer, Carl Fellman
Schaeffer, S(tanley) Allyn
Schaffer, Claudia Post
Scheu, Leonard
Scheuer, Ruth
Schlitter, Helga
Schloss, Arleen P
Schmaltz, Roy Edgar
Schneider, Julie (Saecker)
Schoener, Jason
Schule, Clifford Hamilton
Schultz, Harold A
Schulz, Ken
Schuster, Cita Fletcher (Sarah E)
Schwartz, Barbara Ann
Scott, John
Scott, Walter
Scucchi, Robie (Peter), Jr
Selby, Patricia Louise
Selchow, Roger Hoffman
Sella, Alvin Conrad
Seyffert, J Robert
Shaw, (George) Kendall
Shecter, Pearl S
Sheehe, Lillian Carolyn
Sherman, Lenore (Walton)
Shih, Joan Fai
Shooter, Tom
Shuff, Lily (Lillian Shir)
Shulzke, Margot Seymour
Silva, Ernest
Simmons, Cleda Marie
Smith, Gregg Sherwood
Sokolowski, Linda Robinson
Somers, Frederick D(uane)
Sonenberg, Jack
Sorokin, Maxine Ann
Spafford, Michael Charles
Spero, Nancy
Spurgin, John Edwin
Squires, Norma Jean
Stack, Gael Z
Starn Twins,
Stavans, Isaac
Steele, Benjamin Charles
Steg, James Louis
Stegman, Patricia
Stein, Ludwig
Steinberg, Rubin
Steinhardt, Alice
Steir, Pat
Stella, Frank
Stevens, William Ansel, Sr
Stevenson, Harold
Stinsmuehlen-Amend, Susan
Stoianovich, Marcelle
Stoll, Toni
Storer, Inez Mary
Strasen, Barbara Elaine
Straus, Sandy
Stromsdorfer, Deborah Ann
Stuart, Michelle
Sullivan, Anne Dorothy Hevner
Sway, Albert
Sweet, Mary (French)
Swenson, Anne (Beatrice)
Sylvan, Rita M
Tabor, Virginia S
Tanger, Susanna
Thackston, R King
Thelin, Valfred P
Thompson, Robert Charles
Thompson, Tamara
Tiemann, Robert E
Ting Shao Kuang,
Toschik, Larry
Travanti, Leon Emidio
Trimm, H Wayne
Turner, Bonese Collins
Twiggs, Leo Franklin
Tytell, Louis
Uccello, Vincenza Agatha
Uhrman, Esther
Urso, Josette Marie
Vaccaro, Patrick Frank
Venezia, Michael
Vevers, Tony
Vicente, Esteban
Vigil, Veloy Joseph
Villa, Carlos
Viret, Margaret Mary (Mrs Frank Ivo)
Vo-Dinh, Mai
Wagner, Merrill
Wagoner, Robert B
Waid, Jim (James E)
Waitzkin, Stella
Waksberg, Naomi
Walker, Marie Sheehy
Warburg, Stephanie Wenner
Wasserman, Burton
Wax, John M
Wegman, William
Wehr, Wesley Conrad
Weingarten, Hilde (Kevess)
Weinstein, Joyce
Welch, Charles D
Weldon, Barbara Maltby
Wells, Lynton
Weschler, Anita
Wheelwright, Joseph Storer
White, B J (Beverly Jo)
White, Philip Butler
Whiteman, Edward Russell
Whiteside, William Albert, II
Wilbert, Robert John
Williams, Abigail S
Wilson, Anne Gawthrop
Wilson, Charles Banks
Winick, Bernyce Alpert
Winzenz, Karon Hagemeister
Wirstrom, Margaret
Wise, Geneva H (Holcomb)
Wong, Paul Kan
Woodruff, Diane Bailey
Wooster, Ann-Sargent
Youkeles, Anne
Young, Charles Alexander
Young, Tom (William Thomas)
Zaima, Stephen Gyo
Zakrzewski, Vladimir
Zeitlin, Harriet
Zilius, Vladas
Zimmerman, William Harold
Zirin, Nola
Zuccarini, David Anthony
Zupan, Bruno

Sand

Buchman, Arles (Arlette Buchman)
Fredman, Faiya R
Haley, Priscilla J
Hamlin, Louise
Hansell, Freya
Kurtz, Elaine
Leroy, Louis
Pousette-Dart, Joanna
Ritter, Renee Gaylinn
Ryerson, Mitch
Smith, James Michael
Wiltraut, Douglas Scott

Watercolor

Aaron, Evalyn (Wilhelmina) Keisler
Abrams, Jane Eldora
Abril, Ben (Benjamin)
Adams, Mark
Addison, Byron Kent
Akers, Gary
Alfano, Angel
Alling, Janet D
Altfeld, Merwin Richard
Altwerger, Libby
Amano, Taka
Amoss, Berthe
Anacker, John William
Andry, Keith Anthony
Angelini, John Michael
Armstrong, Roger Joseph
Arneson, Wendell H
Arsenault, Kate Whitman
Aubin, Barbara
Austin, Pat
Austin, Phil
Baeder, John
Balaban, Diane
Bales, Jewel
Ballantyne, Catherine Turk
Band, David Moshe
Barbee, Rob
Barberis, Dorothy Watkeys
Barbour, Arthur J
Barnes, Carole D
Barnett, Earl D
Barnwell, John L
Beach, Warren
Beall, Joanna
Beam, Mary Todd
Bechtle, C Ronald
Bechtle, Robert Alan
Beck, Margit
Beery, Art (Arthur O)
Beginin, Igor
Beker, Gisela
Bell, Alistair Macready
Bender, Bill
Bentz, Harry Donald
Berger, Pat (Patricia Eve)
Berlin, Beatrice Winn
Berman, Ellen Mercil Trew
Bermingham, John C
Berns, Pamela Kari
Berresford, Virginia
Bertoni, Dante H
Besser, Arne Charles
Birdsall, Byron
Bishop, Marjorie Cutler
Bissette, Samuel Delk
Black, Mary McCune
Blackburn, Loren Hayner
Blackey, Mary Madlyn
Blackwood, David (Lloyd)
Blagden, Allen
Blagden, Thomas P
Blahove, Marcos
Blair, Lee Everett
Blum, Helaine Dorothy
Bobick, Bruce
Bock, William Sauts-Netamux'we
Booth Cabot, M(ary Ann)
Bott, Patricia Allen
Bouchard, Paul E
Bouldin, Marshall Jones, III
Bowen-Forbes, Jorge C
Bower, Gary David
Bowling, Gary Robert
Bradley, Dorothy
Brady, Carolyn
Branstetter, Gwendolyn H
Bratcher, Dale
Brightwell, Walter
Brody, Carol Z
Brommer, Gerald F
Brooks, Robert
Brotherton, Naomi
Brough, Richard Burrell
Brown, Marion B
Brown, Peggy Ann
Browne, Syd J
Browning, Dixie Burrus
Browning, Mark Daniel
Brzozowski, Richard Joseph
Bukovnik, Gary
Burch, Claire R
Burley, Lina
Burnett, Barbara Ann
Burns, Josephine
Burr, Ruth Basler
Burt, Dan
Bye, Ranulph
Cadillac, Louise Roman
Calamar, Gloria
Camastro-Pritchett, Rose
Campanelli, Dan
Cantwell, William Richard
Caples, Barbara Barrett
Carlin, James
Carlos, (James) Edward
Carlstrom, Lucinda
Carter, Carol A
Carter, Harriet (Estelle) Manore
Casey, John Thayer
Casey, Tim (Timothy William)
Casselli, Henry C, Jr
Catok, Lottie Meyer
Cervenka, Barbara
Chadeayne, Robert Osborne
Chaiklin, Amy
Chavooshian, Marge
Chen, Hilo
Cheng, Fu-Ding
Chi, Chen
Chiara, Alan Robert
Chin, Ric
Cho, Y(eou) J(ui)
Chow Chian-Chiu,
Chow Leung Chen-Ying,
Christensen, Betty (Elizabeth)
Christensen, Larry R
Christensen, Sharlene
Christiana, Edward
Chu, Gene
Clark, Robert Charles
Cleary, Shirley (Shirley Cleary Cooper)
Clinedinst, Katherine Parsons
Clive, Richard R
Cliver, Kendra-Jean (Kendra-Jean Cliver Krienke)
Cobb, Ruth
Cobb, Virginia Horton
Coes, Kent Day
Cogswell, Dorothy McIntosh
Cohen, Hy
Cokendolpher, Eunice Loraine
Colao, Rudolph
Colway, James R
Conneen, Mari M
Conrad, Nancy R
Continos, Anna
Cook, Joseph S
Cooper, Mario
Copt, Louis J
Correa, Flora Horst
Costan, Chris
Cott, Jean Cahan
Courtney, Barbara Wood
Cox, Marion Averal
Craft, Douglas D
Crane, Jean
Crawford, Catherine Betty
Crooks, W Spencer
Cross, Watson, Jr
Crossgrove, Roger Lynn
Crown, Keith Allen
Crutchfield, William Richard
Cunningham, Sue
Cutforth, Roger
Cuthbert, Virginia
Dailey, Michael Dennis
Dallas, Dorothy B
Dance, Robert Bartlett
Daub, Matthew Forrest

PAINTER (cont)
David, Don Raymond
Dean, James
Debrosky, Christine A
DeCaprio, Alice
Deem, George
DeMaree, Betty (Elizabeth Ann)
Denman, Patricia Price (Pat Denman)
Dennis, Don W
Dennis, Roger Wilson
De Santo, Stephen C
De Turczynowicz, Wanda (Mrs Eliot Hermann)
Diehl, Sevilla S
Dietz, Charles LeMoyne
Dobie, Jeanne
Dodrill, Donald Lawrence
Dominique, John August
Domroe, Barbara
Donaldson, Jeff R
Dooley, Helen Bertha
Dorsey, Deborah Worthington
Doyle, John Lawrence
Doyle, Mary Ellen
Draper, Josiah Everett
Dreisbach, Clarence Ira
Drower, Sara Ruth
Dublac, Robert Revak
Duff, Ann MacIntosh
Duis, Rita
Dzubas, Friedel
Ecklin, Sister M Irenita
Eden, F(lorence) Brown
Elkins, Toni Marcus
Elliott, Bette G
Emmert, Pauline Gore
Enders, Elizabeth McGuire
Engeran, Whitney John, Jr
Eshoo, Robert
Estes, Richard
Evett, Kenneth Warnock
Facci, Domenico (Aurelio)
Feininger, T Lux
Felter, June Marie
Fett, William F
Fillerup, Mel
Finley, Donny Lamenda
Firfires, Nicholas Samuel
Fish, George A
Fish, Janet I
Fogg, Monica
Forbes, John Allison
Forrester, Patricia Tobacco
Fortunato, Nancy
Franklin, Don (Donald Wayne Franklin)
Franklin, Patt
Frater, Hal
Freckelton, Sondra
Frerichs, Ruth Colcord
Fritzler, Gerald J
Frontz, Leslie
Fukuhara, Henry
Fundora, Thomas
Fussiner, Howard
Gabeler-Brooks, Jo
Gable, John Oglesby
Gallagher, Kathleen Ellen
Ganek, Dorothy Skeados
Gardner, Sheila
Garel, Leo
Garrett, Stuart Grayson
Gatto, Rose Marie
Gay, Betsy (Elizabeth Dershuck Gay)
Gentry, Augustus (Callahan), Jr
Gibson, George
Giles, Newell Walton, Jr
Gioello, Debbie
Glesmann, Sylvia Maria
Goedicke, Jean
Goetz, Peter Henry
Gold, Fay Helfand
Golden, Rolland Harve
Gonzalez, Juan J
Goodman, Bertram
Goodman, Sidney
Goodwin, Guy
Gorchov, Ron
Gordon, Josephine
Gordon, P(atrick) S(cott)
Graese, Judy (Judith Ann)
Grafton, Rick (Frederick Wellington)
Grainger, Nessa Posner
Grass, Patty Patterson
Grasso, Jack
Grauer, Gladys
Greaver, Harry
Greenstone, Marion
Gregory-Goodrum, Ellna Kay
Grodsky, Sheila Taylor
Groombridge, Walter Stanley
Gross, Marilyn A
Grosse, C(arolyn Ann Gawarecki)
Guida, Dominick
Gumpel, Hugh
Haden, Eunice (Barnard)
Hagin, Nancy
Halbach, David Allen
Haley, Patience E (Patience E Haley Ghikas)
Hallenbeck, Pomona Juanita
Hamer, Charles James
Hamilton, Frank Moss
Hamilton, George Earl
Hammett, Polly Horton
Hamwi, Richard Alexander
Hardy, (Clarion) Dewitt
Harmon, Barbara Sayre
Harmon, Cliff Franklin
Harms, Elizabeth
Harper, Eleanor O'Neil
Harte, John
Hartell, John
Hartgen, Vincent Andrew
Hasegawa, Noriko
Ha-So-De (Narciso Abeyta)
Hatch, W A S
Hausey, Robert Michael
Hawkins, Barbara
Hawthorne, Jack Gardner
Hayes, Tua
Hefner, Harry Simon
Heiloms, May
Heine, Harry
Heinzen, MaryAnn
Hempler, Orval F
Hendrix, Connie (Connie Sandage Manus)
Hensley, Jackson Morey
Hewitt, Thurman H
Hill, Richard Wayne
Hill, Robyn Lesley
Hofer, Ingrid (Ingeborg)
Hoffman, Elaine Janet
Hoffman, Richard Peter
Hoie, Claus
Holabird, Jean
Holbrook, Peter Greene
Hornaday, Richard Hoyt
Hough, Jennine
Hoyal, Dorothy
Hoyt, Ellen
Hui, Pat
Humphrey, S L
Hunter, Mel
Hutchings, La Vere
Ingle, John S
Jackson, Vaughn L
Jackson, Ward
Jaidinger, Judith C
James, Christopher P
Jamison, Philip
Jenkins, Paul
Johansen, Robert
Johnson, Audean
Johnson, Brent
Johnson, Cecile Ryden
Johnson, Douglas Walter
Johnson, Ernest (Melvin)
Johnson, Rodell C
Jolley, Donal Clark
Jones, Norma L
Jones, Thomas William
Jordan, Barbara Schwinn
Jordan, Beth McAninch
Jung, Kwan Yee
Jung, Yee Wah
Kaiman, Charles
Kaiser, Charles James
Kam, Mei K
Kamys, Walter
Kan, Diana
Kan, Kit-Keung
Kaplinski, Buffalo
Karniol, Hilda
Kawa, Florence Kathryn
Keck, Jeanne Gentry
Keeling, Henry Cornelious
Kelley, Ramon
Kenda, Juanita Echeverria
Kenton, Mary Jean
Kerswill, J W Roy
Keyser, Robert G
Khachian, Elisa A
Khalil, Claire Anne
Kieffer, Mary Jane
Kimura, Sueko M
Kingman, Dong
Kiousis, Linda Weber
Kirsten-Daiensai, Richard Charles
Klopfenstein, Philip Arthur
Knott, Dee D
Kolisnyk, Peter
Kramer, James
Kranking, Margaret Graham
Kratz, Mildred Sands
Kuczun, Ann-Marie
LaCom, Wayne Carl
Laessig, Robert
Lafon, Dee J
La Hotan, Robert L
Lahr, J(ohn) Stephen
Lai, Waihang
La Lumia, Frank
Landau, Jacob
Lane, William
Lang, Margo Terzian
Langford, Sherry K
Larraz, Julio F
Lasuchin, Michael
Law, C Anthony
Lawrence, James A
Lawton, Florian Kenneth
Leach, Mada (Madeline Kleiman)
Lecky, Susan
Lee, Dora Fugh
Leeds, Annette
Leet, Richard Eugene
Lem, Richard Douglas
Lenhardt, Shirley M
Lester, Michelle
Levine, David
Levine, Marion Lerner
Lew, Weyman
Lewis, William Arthur
Lewis, William R
Lhotka, Bonny Pierce
Lichtenberg, Manes
Liles, Catharine (Burns)
Lindenberg, Mary K
Link, Phyllida K
Litz, James C
Lord, Carolyn Marie
Loughlin, John Leo
Luitjens, Helen Anita
Lusk, Patricia A
Luz, Virginia
Lyford, Cabot
Lynch, Mary Britten
Lynch, Tom (Thomas Michael)
Maas, Marion Elizabeth
MacBird, Rosemary (Simpson)
MacDougall, Anne
McEwen, Jean
McFarren, Grace
MacGillis, Robert Donald
McGrew, Bruce Elwin
Machiorlete, Patricia Anne
McIlvain, Frances H
McKay, Renee
MacKenzie, Hugh Seaforth
McKie, Todd Stoddard
McNamara, William Patrick, Jr
MacNeill, Frederick Douglas
McNickle, Thomas Glen
Madan-Shotkin, Rhoda
Madden-Work, Betty I
Madura, Jack Joseph
Mahony, Pat
Malone, Patricia Lynn
Mann, Ward Palmer
Manolakas, Stanton Peter
Manter, Margaret C
Mapes, Doris Williamson
Margolies, Ethel Polacheck
Marinsky, Harry
Marsh, David Foster
Marshall, Bruce
Martell, Barbara Bentley
Martin, Margaret M
Martino, Giovanni
Martino, Nina F
Mason, Harold
Masterfield, Maxine
Mathis, Billie F
Matson, Greta
Maurice, E(leanor) Ingersoll
Maxwell, John
Mays, Victor
Melikian, Mary
Mellor, Mark Adams
Messina, Joseph R
Meyer, El(mer Frederick)
Meyers, Dale (Mrs Mario Cooper)
Michelson, Philip L
Michod, Susan A
Miezajs, Dainis
Miller, Kathryn
Miller, Ruth Ann
Mills, Frederick Van Fleet
Minnick, Esther Tress
Mitchell, Dean Lamont
Mitchell, Dianne (Ball)
Mitchell, Fred
Moller, Hans
Moore, Ina May
Moore, Olga
Moore, Robert Eric
Moore, Scott Martin
Morenon, Elise
Morgan, James L
Morley, Malcolm
Morrell, Wayne (Beam)
Morrison, Fritzi Mohrenstecher
Morriss, Mary Rachel
Morse, Bart J
Mortensen, Gordon Louis
Morton, Richard H
Moskowitz, Shirley (Mrs Jacob W Gruber)
Moss, Karen Canner
Moy, May (Wong)
Muccioli, Anna Maria
Mugar, Martin Gienandt
Murphy, Herbert A
Murphy, Susan (Susan Avis Murphy Colombini)
Murray, Floretta May
Murray, Robert (Gray)
Murrell, Carlton D
Myers, C Stowe
Nadolski, Stephanie Lucille
Naegle, Montana
Nagano, Paul Tatsumi
Nechis, Barbara
Neff, John A
Neffson, Robert

PAINTER (cont)
Nestor, Lula B
Nicholas, Thomas Andrew
Nichols, Edward Edson
Niederer, Carl
Nilsson, Gladys
Nofer, Frank
Nordstrand, Nathalie Johnson
Norris, (Robert) Ben
North, Judy
Notestine, Dorothy J
Obuck, John Francis
O'Connell, Ann Brown
O'Dell, Erin (Anne)
O'Hagan, Desmond Brian
Olson, Joseph Olaf
Order, Trudy
Orr, Joseph Charles
Osborn, Robert
Osby, Larissa Geiss
Osyczka, Bohdan Danny
Ott, Michael E
Owens, Mary (Mary Louise Schnore)
Pachner, William
Palmer, Mabel (Evelyn)
Parker, Robert Andrew
Parton, Niké
Patterson, Patricia
Patton, Karen Ann
Paulsen, Brian Oliver
Pedersen, Carolyn H
Pellew, John Clifford
Pena, Amado Maurilio, Jr
Peregrin, Magda Elizabeth
Perine, Robert Heath
Perlin, Rae
Perlmutter, Linda M
Perrin, C Robert
Pershan, Marion
Peterson, David Winfield
Petro, Joe, III
Phillips, Bonnie
Phillips, Dick (Richard Cortez)
Phillis, Marilyn Hughey
Pickford, Rollin, Jr
Pierce, Ann Trucksess
Pinckney, Stanley
Pisani, Joseph
Plott, Paula (Paula Plott Amos)
Plummer, Carlton B
Pochmann, Virginia
Polan, Nancy Moore
Ponsot, Claude F
Poor, Anne
Porter, Albert Wright
Porter, Elmer Johnson
Porter, Shirley
Post, George (Booth)
Potter, (George) Kenneth
Powers, W Alex
Price, Rosalie Pettus
Prindiville, Jim
Punia, Constance Edith
Purcell, Hugh D
Quinn, Noel Joseph
Rabkin, Leo
Rafferty, Joanne Miller
Ramanauskas, Dalia Irena
Rames, Stanley Dodson
Rawlinson, Jonlane Frederick
Reese, William Foster
Reich, Olive B
Reinhart, Margaret Emily
Reininghaus, Ruth (Ruth Reininghaus Smith)
Reis, Mario
Renk, Merry
Resnick, Don
Richards, Glenora
Robbins, Joan Nash
Roberts, Clyde Harry
Roberts, Tom (Thomas Keith)
Rodbard, Betty
Roller, Marion Bender
Roman, Shirley
Romeling, W B
Ronald, William
Rosenberg, Jane
Rosenhouse, Irwin
Ross, Conrad H
Ross, Joan M
Roth, Jack (Rodney)
Roth, Richard
Royer, Mona Lee
Rubin, Sandra Mendelsohn
Rudman, Joan (Combs)
Ruffing, Anne Elizabeth
Ruthven, John Aldrich
Rutland, Lilli Ida
Ryan, Elizabeth
Ryan, William Edward
Sadle, Amy Ann Brandon
Sakson, Robert (G)
Salemme, Martha
Salt, John
Sanders, Joop A
Sanders, Rhea (Rhea Sanders Rabinovich)
Sanderson, Charles Howard
Sandol, Maynard
San Soucie, Patricia Molm
Savenor, Betty Carmell
Sawada, Ikune
Sawyer, Helen
Sazegar, Morteza
Schmalz, Carl (Nelson), Jr
Schreyer, Greta L
Schuler, Melvin Albert
Schwalb, Susan
Schwartz, Bella
Schwartz, Marjorie Watson
Seabourn, Connie
Segan, Ken Akiva
Segur, Eleanor Corinne
Seiden, Arthur
Shapiro, Irving
Shatter, Susan Louise
Shedd, George J
Sherman, Z Charlotte
Sheya
Shore, Mary (McGarrity)
Shores, (James) Franklin
Short, Patricia Ann Reilly
Shubin, Morris Jack
Siamis, Janet Neal
Silver, Rawley A
Simmons, Julie Lutz
Simper, Frederick
Sinclair, Robert (W)
Sisson, Laurence P
Sklar, Dorothy
Slider, Dorla Dean
Sloane, Phyllis Lester
Smigocki, Stephen Vincent
Smith, Dolph
Smith, Lowell Ellsworth
Smith, Rowena Marcus
Smith, Susan Carlton
Snow, Cynthia Reeves
Snow, Mary R
Solberg, Morten Edward
Soloway, Reta Burns
Sorensen, Jean
Sowinski, Stanislaus Joseph
Spencer, Susan Elizabeth
Spicer, Jean (Doris) Uhl
Spink, Frank Henry
Sproul, Ann Stephenson
Stallwitz, Carolyn
Stein, Harve
Stephanson, Loraine Ann
Stern, Louise
Stevens, Linda Lee
Stewart, Arthur
Sticker, Robert Edward
Stillman, Lucille T
Stone, Don
Stonebarger, Virginia
Storer, Frances Nell
Stouffer, Daniel Henry, Jr
Strickland,
Strisik, Paul
Stroppel, Betty MacNair
Strother, Virginia Vaughn
Stull, Jean Himrod
Suba, Susanne (Mrs Bertam Bloch)
Sublett, Carl C
Summer, (Emily) Eugenia
Sundberg, Wilda (Regelman)
Suttenfield, Diana
Swanson, Ray V
Swartz, Beth Ames
Szesko, Lenore Rundle
Tabachnick, Anne
Teller, Douglas H
Teraoka, Masami
Thompson, Kenneth Webster
Thompson, Lynn P
Thompson, Malcolm Barton
Thomson, Carl L
Thornycroft, Ann
Timmas, Osvald
Tinning, George Campbell
Tolpo, Carolyn Lee
Torlakson, James Daniel
Townsend, Teryl
Trachtman, Arnold S
Trank, Lynn Edgar
Trauerman, Margy Ann
Trausch, Thomas V
Travers-Smith, Brian John
Trott, Helen
Tseng Yu-ho
Tsutakawa, George
Turner, Bruce Backman
Turner, Janet Sullivan
Tyson, Mary (Mrs Kenneth Thompson)
Uchima, Ansei
Vallee, William Oscar
Vann, Samuel LeRoy
Vargas, Josephine
Vazquez, Paul
Ventura, Anthony
Vernon
Villa, Theodore B
Virgona, Hank (Henry P)
Voorhees, Donald Edward
Waddell, John Henry
Waddingham, John Alfred
Walker, Edward D (Rusty)
Wallace, Soni
Walsh, Janet Barbara
Walsh, Patricia Ruth
Walton, M Douglas
Wands, Alfred James
Wang, C C
Ward, Joseph Marshall
Warner, Jo
Wasserman, Muriel
Waterhouse, Russell Rutledge
Waterston, Harry Clement
Watkins, Lewis
Watson, Darliene Keeney
Watson, Howard N(oel)
Weale, Mary Jo
Webb, Frank (Francis H)
Weber, Idelle
Webster, Larry
Weekes, Shirley Marie
Weiss, Lee (Elyse C Weiss)
Wellborn, J(eanette) D(arleen)
Weller, Laurie June
Wengrovitz, Judith
Wentworth, Murray Jackson
West, E Gordon
Westermann, H C
Wharton, David W
Wheeler, Mark
Whitaker, Eileen Monaghan
White, Ralph
Whittington, Jon Hammon
Wible, Mary Grace
Wiesen, Trude
Wilcox, Gordon Cumnock
Williams, Raymond Lester
Williams, Richard Eldon
Williamson, Jason H
Willson, Robert
Wilson, Douglas Fenn
Wilson, Nicholas Jon
Winick, Bernyce Alpert
Winkler, Maria Paula
Witmeyer, Stanley Herbert
Wohlenhaus, Grace Forcier
Woide, Robert E
Wolanic, Susan Seseske
Wolins, Joseph
Wong, Frederick
Wood, Robert E
Wordell, Edwin Howland
Workman, Robert P
Wostrel, Nancy J
Wright, Harold David
Wu, Wayne Wen-Yau
Wyckoff, Sylvia Spencer
Wyeth, Andrew Newell
Wyeth, James Browning
Yanoff, Arthur (Samuel)
Yater, George David
Young, Andrew
Young, Marjorie Ward
Young, Robert John
Younglove, Ruth Ann (Mrs Benjamin Rhees Loxley)
Zacha, William
Zalucha, Peggy Flora

PATRON

Altschul, Arthur G
Artinian, Artine
Bareiss, Walter
Benenson, Edward Hartley
Beren, Stanley O
Berman, Muriel Mallin
Berman, Philip I
Bermant, David W
Bickford, George
Brady, Luther W
Browne, Robert M
Clark, Charles D
Clowes, Allen Whitehill
Cramer, Douglas S
Daniels, David M
Davidson, Ian J
Davidson, Suzette Morton
De Waal, Ronald Burt
Dillon, C Douglas
Drysdale, Nancy McIntosh
Eiteljorg, Harrison
Elowitch, Robert Jason
Erdelac, Joseph Mark
Fitch, George Hopper
Foth, Joan B
Friedland, Seymour
Furman, (Dr & Mrs) Arthur F
Garbaty, Marie-Louise
Goldman, Rachel Bok
Goodman, Benjamin
Harris, Leon A, Jr
Harrison, Joseph Robert, Jr
Holcombe, R Gordon, Jr
Holladay, Wilhelmina Cole
Irwin, George M
Kempner, Helen Hill
Kienholz, Lyn
Klein, Esther M
Koger, Ira McKissick
Larkin, (Dr) John E, Jr
Liles, Catharine (Burns)
List, Vera G
Livingston, Margaret Gresham
Manilow, Lewis
Marcus, Robert P (Mrs)
Marks, (Mr & Mrs) Cedric H
Menil, Georges & Lois de
Miller, (Mrs) Robert Watt
Moe, Richard D
Nasher, Raymond Donald
Neuberger, Roy R
Niemeyer, Arnold Matthew
Ochs, Robert David

PATRON (cont)
Parkinson, Elizabeth Bliss (Mrs Henry Ives Cobb)
Pence, John Gerald
Penney, Charles Rand
Pilavin, Selma F
Polan, Lincoln M
Pratt, Dallas
Quinn, Henrietta Reist
Quinn, Thomas Patrick, Jr
Rautbord, Dorothy H
Reiner, Gladys & Jules
Roebling, Mary G
Rumsey, David MacIver
Samuels, John Stockwell, 3rd
Sandground, Mark Bernard, Sr
Schnitzer, Arlene
Schwartz, Eugene M
Scott, Robert Montgomery
Selig, (Mr & Mrs) Manfred
Semans, James Hustead
Smart, Mary-Leigh
Solinger, David M
Sosnowitz, Henry Abram
Speiser, Stuart M
Stamats, Peter Owen
Stevenson, Ruth Carter
Terra, Daniel J
Walter, May E
Walter, Paul F
Williams, Dave Harrell
Wilson, Clarence S, Jr
Winter, Hope Melamed
Zeisler, Richard Spiro

PHOTOGRAPHER

Adams, Mac
Adams, Robert Hickman
Aigner, Lucien
Akin, Gwen
Alinder, James Gilbert
Allen, (Harvey) Harold
Allen, Judith S
Alpern, Merry B
Alpert, George
Amft, Robert
Anderson, David C
Annus, John Augustus
Armstrong, Martha (Allen)
Astman, Barbara Ann
Avedon, Richard
Avery, Frances
Avison, David
Babcock, Jo (Joseph Warren Babcock)
Babior, Daniel
Bach, Laurence
Bader, Franz
Baer, Morley
Bailey, Oscar
Baltz, Lewis
Barboza, Anthony
Barrow, Thomas Francis
Barschel, Hans J
Barth, Uta
Bartscherer, Joseph
Baruch, Ruth-Marion Evelyn
Beachum, Sharon Garrison
Beaudoin, Andre Eugene
Beckhard, Ellie (Eleanor)
Beckman, Ericka
Beenen, Richard
Benedict-Jones, Linda
Berger, Paul Eric
Berghash, Mark W
Berko, Ferenc
Berman, Fred J
Berman, Zeke
Bernal, Louis Carlos
Berndt, Jerry W
Bernhard, Ruth
Beveridge, Karl J
Biferie, Dan (Daniel Anthony), Jr
Binks, Ronald C
Bissette, Samuel Delk
Black, Lisa
Blakely, George C
Block, Gay (S)
Bloom, Barbara
Bloomfield, Lisa Diane
Blue, Patt
Bohnen, Blythe
Bolton, Richard
Bootz, Antoine H
Bourdeau, Robert Charles
Braunstein, H Terry (Malikin)
Braunstein, Mark Mathew
Broderick, James Allen
Brooks, Ellen
Brown, Gillian
Brown, Lawrie
Brown, Peter Thomson
Brumfield, John Richard
Brush, Gloria (Elizabeth) DeFilipps
Bubriski, Kevin E
Bunn, David
Bunnen, Lucinda Weil
Burchard, Peter Duncan
Burchfield, Jerry Lee
Burckhardt, Rudy
Burgess, Linda Suzanne
Burns, Marsha
Burns, Millie
Burson, Nancy
Bussche, Wolf von dem
Busto, Ana Marie
Cadmus, Paul
Cain, David Paul
Callahan, Harry
Callis, Jo Ann
Calman, W(endy L)
Camhi, Morrie
Campus, Peter
Cantor, Fredrich
Capa, Cornell
Caponigro, Paul
Carey, Ellen
Carpenter, Dennis Wilkinson (Bones)
Casebere, James E
Cawood, Gary Kenneth
Channing, Susan Rose
Chappell, Walter (Landon)
Charlesworth, Sarah E
Chesley, Paul Alexander
Chiarenza, Carl
Childers, Malcolm Graeme
Clement, Alain Gerard
Clift, William Brooks
Coates, Ann S
Cohen, Alan Barry
Cohen, Joan Lebold
Cohen, Lynne G
Cohen, Michael S
Cohen, Sorel
Coke, F Van Deren
Cole, Herbert Milton
Coleman, Judy
Colmer, Roy David
Colp, Norman B
Conner, Lois
Conniff, Gregory
Connor, Linda Stevens
Conte, Jeanne Larner
Cooper, Ruffin
Coplans, John (Rivers)
Cowin, Eileen
Coyne, Petah E
Craft, David Ralph
Cramer, Peter
Crane, Barbara Bachmann
Crouton, Francois (LaFortune)
Cumming, Robert H
Curran, Darryl Joseph
Curran, Douglas Edward
Dablow, Dean Clint
Dahl, Stephen M
Dane, Bill (William Thatcher Dane)
Danziger, Avery C
Dater, Judy
Davidson, Abraham A
Davies, Harry Clayton
Davis, Ben
Davis, Philip Charles
Deal, Joe
Dean, Nicholas Brice
DeCaprio, Alice
DeCarava, Roy Rudolph
DeGenevieve, Barbara
Delaney, Janet Clare
De Lory, Peter
Del Valle, Cezar Jose
Demanche, Michel S
Deschamps, Francois
Diamond, Paul
Dibert, Rita Jean
Dickson, Jennifer Joan
Dingus, Phillip Rick
DiPerna, Frank Paul
Divola, John Manford, Jr
Doll, Donald Arthur
Doren, A(rnold T)
Dorfman, Elsa
Dow, Jim D
DuBois, Douglas J
Dunitz, Jay
Dunn, Fontaine
Dusard, Jay
Dutton, Allen A
Eckersley, Thomas Cyril
Edwards, Ellender Morgan
Eide, John
Ellis, Loren Elizabeth
Elozua, Raymon
Epstein, Mitch (Mitchell D)
Estabrook, Reed
Evergon
Faller, Marion
Farber, Dennis H
Faurer, Louis
Feeney, Sandra Benedict
Feininger, Andreas B L
Ferguson, Larry Scott
Fessler, Ann Helene
Finch, Ruth Woodward
Fink, Larry (Laurence B)
Finn, David
Fiskin, Judy
Fitch, Steve (Steven Ralph)
Flack, Audrey L
Flick, Robbert
Flower, Michael Lavin
Foster, Steven Douglas
Fox, Flo
Frailey, Stephen A
Frazer, James (Nisbet), Jr
Freeman, Roland L
Freeman, Tina
Friedlaender, Bilge
Friedlander, Lee
Friedman, Benno
Fuller, John Charles
Fulton, Jack E
Gagnon, Charles
Gaines, William Robert
Gallagher, Carole
Gandert, Miguel Adrian
Garnett, William Ashford
Garrison, Gene K
Gartel, Laurence M
Garvens, Ellen
Gates, Jeff S
Gaudard, Pierre
Gauvreau, Robert George
Gefter, Judith Michelman
Gellert, Vance F
Genovese, Richard
Gerdes, Ingeborg
Gibson, Edward G
Gibson, Ralph H
Gilbert, Arnold Martin
Gilpin, Henry Edmund
Giordano, Greg Joe
Gips, C L Terry
Glendinning, Peter
Gluhman, Margaret A
Goertz, Augustus Frederick, III
Gohlke, Frank William
Goin, Peter
Goldberg, Jim
Golden, Judith
Goldin, Nan R
Goldring, Nancy Deborah
Gomez, Mirta & Eduardo Delvalie
Goodine, Linda Adele
Goodman, Mark
Gordin, Misha
Gore, Tom
Gossage, John Ralph
Graves, Kenneth Robert
Grazda, Ed
Green, Jonathan (William)
Greenfield-Sanders, Timothy
Groover, Jan
Guerrero, Raul
Gutmann, John
Haar, Francis
Haar, Tom
Hahn, Betty
Hallam, Beverly (Linney)
Hallman, Gary Lee
Hammerbeck, Wanda Lee
Harbutt, Charles
Harkins, Dennis Richter
Hartman, Robert Leroy
Hartshorn, Willis E
Hatch, Connie
Haxton, David
Hayashi, Masumi
Hayes, Gerald
Heath, Dave (David Martin Heath)
Heinecken, Robert Friedli
Heiser, Scott Thomas
Held, Philip
Henle, Fritz
Henrich, Biff
Henrickson, Martha (Klein)
Henrickson, Thomas
Hernandez, Anthony Louis
Hershman, Lynn Lester
Higa (Yoshiharu)
Hill, Richard Wayne
Hines, Jessica
Ho, Francis T
Hockney, David
Hofer, Evelyn
Hoffman, Richard Peter
Holmes, Wendy (Diana H Noyes)
Houghton, Barbara Jean
House, Suda Kay
Howard, David
Hower, Robert K
Huff, Howard Lee
Hunter, Debora
Hupy, Art
Husebye, Terry L
Hyde, Scott
Imes, Birney
Incandela, Gerald Jean-Marie
Irwin, Lisa Dru
Iversen, Earl Harvey
Jachna, Joseph David
Jacobshagen, N Keith, II
Jalapeeno, Jimmy (Albert J Bonar)
James, Christopher P
Jansen, Catherine Sandra
Jeff
Jones, Harold Henry
Jones, Pirkle
Josephson, Kenneth Bradley
Joyce, J David
Kagemoto, Haro
Kagemoto, Patricia Jow
Kaida, Tamarra
Kalisher, Simpson
Kaminsky, Jack Allan
Kane, Bill

PHOTOGRAPHER (cont)

Karsh, Yousuf
Katsiff, Bruce
Keerl, Bayat
Kelly, Isaac Perry
Kenna, Michael
Kennedy, Gene (Eugene Murray)
Kenyon, Colleen Frances
Ketchum, Robert Glenn
Kikuchi-Yngojo, Alan
Kindermann, Helmmo
Kirby, Kent Bruce
Kleckner, Susan
Klein, Lynn (Ellen)
Klipper, Stuart David
Knight, Tom (Thomas Lincoln), Jr
Knowlton, Grace Farrar
Koga, Mary
Kolbowski, Silvia
Kornmayer, J Gary (John)
Kostiuk, Michael Marion, Jr
Kowal, Cal (Lee)
Kozloff, Max
Krause, George
Krims, Les
Kronengold, Eric A
Kumler, Kipton (Cornelius)
Kun, Neila
Lake, Jerry Lee
Landry, Richard Miles
Land-Weber, Ellen E
Lang, Cay
Lang, Wendy F
Larson, William G
Lattanzio, Frances
Lawrence, James A
Leatherdale, Marcus Andrew
LeBoff, Gail F
Lee, Baldwin S
Leibovitz, Annie
Leigh, Jack David
Leipzig, Arthur
Leonard, Joanne
Lerner, Nathan Bernard
Leslie, John
Levin, Gail
Levinson, Joel D
Levinthal, David Lawrence
Levitt, Helen
Lewenz, Lisa
Liebermann, Philip
Liebling, Jerome
Light, Ken
Lindroth, Linda
Linn, Judy
Lipzin, Janis Crystal
Lívíck, Stephen
Lonidier, Fred Spencer
Lorca di Corcia, Philip
Lucier, Mary
Ludwig, Allan I
Lyons, Joan
McAuley, Skeet
McDarrah, Fred William
McFarland, Lawrence D
MacGregor, Gregory Allen
McMillan, Stephen Walker
McPherson, Larry E
MacWeeney, Alen Brazil
Madigan, Martha
Maggs, Arnaud (Cyril Benvenuti)
Mahon, Robert
Maisel, David
Maldre, Mati
Mandel, Mike
Mangolte, Babette M
Mann, Katinka
Mann, Sally
Mansaram,
Marasco, Rose
Margolis, Richard M
Mark, Enid (Epstein)
Mark, Mary Ellen
Markley, Doris Yocum
Martin, Lys
Martinez-Cañas, Maria
Martone, Michael
Maurer, Neil Douglas
Mayes, Elaine
Meek, A J
Melby, David A
Mendoza, Antonio G
Menthe, Melissa
Mertin, Roger
Meserole, Vera Stromsted
Metzker, Ray K
Meyer, Ursula
Meyerowitz, Joel
Michals, Duane
Millea, Tom (Thomas Francis)
Miller, Laurence Glenn
Minick, Roger
Misrach, Richard Laurence
Mitchell, Margaretta K
Mones, Arthur
Monthan, Guy
Moore, Peter
Moore, Robert James
Morath, Inge
Morgan, Barbara Brooks
Morita, John Takami
Morris, Wright
Morrison, Boone M
Moulton, Rosalind Kimball
Mudford, Grant Leighton
Muñoz, Celia Alvarez
Murray, Frances
Murray, Joan
Musgrave, Shirley H
Nathans, Rhoda R
Neimanas, Joyce
Newman, Arnold
Newman, Richard Charles
Newton, John Neil
Nickard, Gary Laurence
Nixon, Nichols
Noggle, Anne
Norman, Dorothy (S)
Nowytski, (Slavko) Sviatoslav
Noyes, Sandy
Nuse, Oliver William
Oakes, John Warren
Ockenga, Starr
O'Connell, Edward E
Okuhara, Tetsu
Ollman, Arthur L
Olmsted, Suzanne M
Olson, Douglas John
O'Reilly, John B
Orland, Ted N
Padula, Fred David
Palaia, Franc (Dominic)
Palmgren, Donald Gene
Papageorge, Tod
Pare, Richard
Parker, Ann
Parker, Olivia
Patton, Tom
Paul, William D, Jr
Peluso, Marta E
Penn, Irving
Peress, Gilles
Perrault, Pierre
Peven, Michael David
Pfahl, John
Phillips, Bertrand D
Phillips, Robert J
Pickett, Keri L
Pinkel, Sheila Mae
Plossu, Bernard
Plowden, David
Post, Marion (Marion Post Wolcott)
Powell, Dan T
Power, Mark
Price, Sara J
Printz, Bonnie Allen
Raginsky, Nina
Randlett, Mary Willis
Rankaitis, Susan
Rauschenberg, Robert
Ravett, Abraham
Raymond, Lilo
Read, Dave (David Dolloff)
Reeves, John Alexander
Renner, Eric
Resnick, Marcia Aylene
Rexroth, Nancy Louise
Richards, Eugene
Riley, Barbra Bayne
Riss, Murray
Robbins, LeRoy (Southward)
Roberts, Holly L
Rodan, Don
Rodriguez, Geno (Eugene)
Rogers, Art
Rogovin, Milton
Rokeach, Barrie
Rose, John Timothy
Rosenthal, John W
Rowantree, Karen Smiley
Rowland, Anne
Rubello, David Jerome
Rubenstein, Meridel
Rubinfien, Leo H
Rupp, Sheron Adeline
Rush, Kent Thomas
Sahlstrand, James Michael
Sahrbeck, Everett William
Sakurai, Jo Mary (Jo Mary McCormick-Sakurai)
Sal, Jack
Salvadori, Vieri R
Sandrow, Hope
Sargent, Richard
Savage, Naomi
Scheer, Sherie (Hood)
Schneider, Ira
Schnitzer, Klaus A
Schulze, John
Schwartz, Elliott S
Schwartz, Sing-Si
Seawell, Thomas Robert
Seed, Suzanne Liddell
Segalove, Ilene Judy
Seguin, Jean-Pierre
Semak, Michael
Semchishen, Orest M
Serrano, Andres
Sexton, John (William)
Shaw, Peggy
Sherman, Cindy
Shillea, Thomas John
Shore, Stephen
Shuler, Thomas H, Jr
Simmons, Laurie
Simon, Michael A
Sirkis, Nancy
Sisco, Elizabeth
Skoff, Gail Lynn
Skoglund, Sandy
Slavin, Neal
Sligh, Clarissa T
Smith, Dinah Maxwell
Smith, Keith A
Smith, Luther A
Smith, Michael A
Smith, Raymond Walter
Solomon, Rosalind
Sommer, Frederick
Sonneman, Eve
Staller, Eric P
Stallwitz, Carolyn
Stark, Robert
Starn Twins,
Stein, Lewis
Steinhardt, Alice
Stephany, Jaromir
Stephens, Curtis
Stettner, Louis
Stevens, Jane Alden
Stevens, Jane M
Stockdale, John A D
Stone, Jim (James J)
Stratton, Margaret Mary
Stuler, Jack
Sturgen, Winston
Suggs, Don
Sultan, Larry A
SuZen
Swartz, Linda
Swigart, Lynn S
Sylvan, Rita M
Szabo, Stephen Lee
Tata, Sam Bejan
Taylor, Harry George
Telberg, Val
Termes, (Dick A)
Teske, Edmund Rudolph
Thomason, Michael Vincent
Thompson, Lynn P
Thorne-Thomsen, Ruth T
Tice, George Andrew
Tobia, Blaise Joseph
Torbert, Stephanie Birch
Torn, Jerry (Gerald J)
Toth, Carl
Towner, Mark Andrew
Trager, Neil C
Trager, Philip
Traub, Charles H
Tuckerman, Jane Bayard
Turconi, Sue (Susan) Kinder
Turner, Judith Estelle
Twardowicz, Stanley Jan
Uelsmann, Jerry
Ulrich, David Alan
Underhill, Linn B
Vestal, David
Vignes, Michelle Marie
Vitali, Julius M
Volkerding, Laura
Von Zur Muehien, Peter
Von zur Muehlen, Bernis Susan
Wade, Robert Schrope
Wagner, Catherine
Wang, Sam
Warren, Julianne Bussert Baker
Warren, Tom P
Warshaw, Larry
Wasko-Flood, Sandra Jean
Wasserman, Cary (Robert)
Watniss, Wendy
Webb, Alexander Dwight
Webb, Todd
Weems, Carrie Mae
Wegman, William
Weiler, Joseph Flack
Weiss, John Joseph
Weissman, Walter
Weller, Paul
Welling, James
Welpott, Jack Warren
Wenger, Jane (B)
Werner, Donald (Lewis)
Wessel, Henry
Wexler, Jerome LeRoy
Wexler, Lee Edward
White, Amos, IV
Whitson
Widmer, Gwen Ellen
Williams, Casey
Williams, Pat Ward
Williams, William Earle
Wilson, Helena (Helena Chapellin Wilson)
Wilson, Wallace
Winningham, Geoff
Winokur, Neil S
Winterberger, Suzanne
Wise, Kenneth Kelly
Wissmeyer, Gunter Gustav
Witkin, Joel-Peter
Witte, Mary (Grace) Stieglitz
Wolin, Jeffrey Alan
Yager, David
Yamashiro, Tad
Yoder, Janica
Yost, Leon C
Young, Barbara
Young, Tom (William Thomas)
Zeitlin, Harry Leon
Zucker, Bob

PHOTOGRAPHER (cont)
Zuckerman, Ruth Victor

PRINTMAKER

Abramowicz, Janet
Abularach, Rodolfo Marco
Audette, Anna Held
Barker, Al C
Barsch, Wulf Erich
Batchelor, Anthony John
Baynard, Ed
Bear, Marcelle L
Bearce, Jeana Dale
Bensignor, Paulette
Bernheim, Stephanie Hammerschlag
Booth, Dot
Booth Cabot, M(ary Ann)
Bosman, Richard
Brady, Carolyn
Brauntuch, Troy
Brill, Glenn
Britton, Daniel Robert
Brody, Blanche
Brody, Ruth
Bruneau, Kittie
Brycelea, Clifford
Bumbeck, David A
Burdock, Harriet
Burkhardt, Hans Gustav
Burnett, Calvin
Burns, Millie
Bynum, E Anderson (Esther Pearl)
Carter, Mary
Carulla, Ramon
Caver, William Ralph
Chesney, Lee R, Jr
Colby, Bill
Connett, Dee M
Cortor, Eldzier
Corwin, Sophia M
Currie, Bruce
Daughters, Robert A
Davis, William D
Davison, Bill
Day, Gary Lewis
De Boschnek, Chris (Christian Charles)
Dennis, Donna Frances
Dowell, John E, Jr
Drum, Sydney Maria
Durr, Pat (Patricia Beth)
Eastcott, Robert Wayne
Eder, James Alvin
Ensrud, Wayne
Ettenberg, Franklin Joseph
Evans, Henry
Falfan, Alfredo
Faust, Victoria
Felter, James Warren
Fendell, Jonas J
Fidler, Spencer D
Firestein, Cecily Barth
Fohr, Jenny
Foster, Maelee Thomson
Frances, Harriette Anton
Frank, Helen (Goodzeit)
Frederick, Helen
Gilbert, Helen Odell
Grupp, Carl Alf
Haack, Cynthia R
Haley, Priscilla J
Haller, Emanuel
Hammond, Jane
Hara, Keiko
Harris, Conley
Hart, Claudia
Haseltine, James Lewis
Hershey, Nona
Hillis, Richard K
Hochman, Kitty
Holbrook, Peter Greene
Hood, Gary Allen
Hubler, Julius
Hulett, Simonne R
Hunt, Richard Howard
Hunter, John H
Jacobson, Arthur
Jacquette, Yvonne Helene
Jannetti, Tony
Jewell, Joyce
Jilg, Michael Florian
Johnson, Nota
Jones, Frederick
Kalina, Richard
Kaplan, Ilee
Kasten, Karl Albert
Kerne, Barbara Davis
Kiland, Lance Edward
Kinnee, Sandy
Klein, Doris
Knippers, Edward
Kornblum, Myrtle
Kretsinger, Mary Amelia
Krieger, Ruth M
Kushner, Dorothy Browdy
Lane, Lois
Lane, Rosemary Louise
La Porta, Elayne B
Leary, Daniel
Liao (Shiou-Ping Liao)
Lichaw, Pessia
Lichtner, Schomer Frank
Lieberman, Meyer Frank
Lippincott, Janet
Little, James
Liu, Katherine Chang
Longobardi, Pam
Luce, C(harles Beardsley)
McCollum, Mike L
MacDonald, Kevin John
McDonald, Susan Strong
McGinnis, Christine
McVicker, J Jay
Mari
Mateo, Julio
Merritt, Francis Sumner
Mesibov, Hugh
Meyer, Frank Hildbridge
Miller, Leon Gordon
Mitty, Lizbeth J
Morse, Marcia Roberts
Moskowitz, Ira
Moy, Seong
Moya Soto, Roberto
Mueller, Henrietta Waters
Mullen, James Martin
Murakishi, Steve
Namingha, Dan
Nichols, Francis N, II
Noland, Kenneth
O'Connell, Ann Brown
Oda, Mayumi
O Donohue, Teige Ros
Olshan, Bernard
Onley, Toni
Paller, Gary
Paschall, Jo Anne
Pickhardt, Carl
Piskoti, James
Pletka, Paul
Portman, Brian
Quiller, Stephen Frederick
Rackus, George (Keistus)
Rankin, Don
Rhodes, Curtis A
Rose, Mary Anne
Roseman, Susan Carol
Rubin, Sandra
Rugolo, Lawrence
Rush, Kent Thomas
Sampson, Frank
Santiago, Ramon
Schorre, Charles
Seabourn, Bert Dail
Seltzer, Joanne Lynn
Sexauer, Donald Richard
Shaffer, Richard
Shaw, John Palmer
Shukman, Solomon
Shute, Roberta E
Sica
Smolarek, Waldemar
Solomon, Vita Petrosky
Somers, H(arry W)
Sorman, Steven
Spandorfer, Merle Sue
Spitz, Barbara S
Stanbridge, Harry Andrew
Stern, Louise
Stewart, Dorothy S
Sturgen, Winston
Sudlow, Robert N
Tait, Will(iam) H
Tanksley, Ann
Targan, Judy
Tavenner, Patricia
Taylor, Al C
Taylor, Grace Martin
Teichman, Mary Melinda
Thrall, Arthur
Tift, Mary Louise
Toledo, Francisco
Toulis, Vasilios (Apostolos)
Tullis, Garner H
Turner, Alan
Van Hoesen, Beth
Van Vranken, Rose (Rose Van Vranken Hickey)
Vena, Dante
Walsh, J(ohn) Michael
Watson, Mary Anne
Weldon, Barbara Maltby
Wharton, David W
Wheeler, Mary
Wolpert, Etta
Wortzel, Adrianne
Younger, Dan Forrest
Zver, James M

All Media

Abel, Ray
Achepohl, Keith Anden
Adelman, Dorothy (Lee) McClintock
Adler, Myril
Alicea, Jose
Alps, Glen Earl
Amen, Irving
Amos, Emma
Andell, Nancy
Andrus, James Roman
Appelson, Herbert J
Aquino, Edmundo
Asher, Lila Oliver
Askin, Walter Miller
Atkinson, Conrad
Auth, Robert R
Barber, Philip Judd
Barnet, Will
Barooshian, Martin
Barth, Charles John
Baxter, Bonnie Jean
Beall, Dennis Ray
Beallor, Fran
Beaumont, Mona
Beltrán, Félix
Bernard, David Edwin
Bernstein, Judith
Bernstein, Theresa
Bills, Mitchell
Black, Richard R
Bleach, Bruce R
Bleiberg, Gertrude Tiefenbrun
Bloom, Martha
Boodman, H Citron
Borochoff, (Ida) Sloan
Boutis, Tom
Boyd, James Henderson
Boyd, John David
Boyd, Lakin
Boynton, Jack (James) W
Brandt, Rex (Rexford Elson)
Breverman, Harvey
Brodsky, Judith Kapstein
Brooks, Wendell T
Brunkus, Richard Allen
Bujnowski, Joel A
Burr, Lee Reynolds
Calapai, Letterio
Calman, W(endy L)
Camarata, Martin L
Campbell, Richard Horton
Cardillo, Rimer Angel
Carlile, Janet (Hildebrand)
Casarella, Edmond
Cassara, Frank
Chafetz, Sidney
Chamberlain, David (Allen)
Chesney, Lee Roy, III
Childers, Malcolm Graeme
Christensen, Val Alan
Cimbalo, Robert W
Conrad, George
Cottingham, Robert
Coughlin, Jack
Courtney, Suzan
Crash (John Matos)
Crispo, Dick
Crouse, Michael Glenn
Cunningham, E C (Eldon Lloyd Cunningham)
Dahlstrom, Nancy Gail
Daily, Evelynne Mess
Dallmann, Daniel Forbes
Daly, Kathleen (Kathleen Daly Pepper)
Dávila, Maritza
Davis, Alonzo Joseph
Davis, Ronald
Dehner, Dorothy
Delgyer, Leslie
Dickinson, David Charles
Dickson, Mark Amos
Di Cosola, Lois
Domroe, Barbara
Dove, Toni
Drake, James
Duback, Charles S
Duffy, Michael John
Duncan, Richard (Hurley)
Eckstein, Ruth
Epstein, Yale
Epting, Marion Austin
Evaul, William H, Jr
Everts, Connor
Feigin, Marsha
Feld, Augusta
Feldhaus, Paul A
Feldman, Franklin
Feldman, Walter (Sidney)
Felter, June Marie
Fichter, Herbert Francis
Field, Philip Sidney
Fine, Ruth E
Fink, Aaron
Foose, Robert James
Foote, Howard Reed
Fornas, Leander
Francis, Madison Ke, Jr
Freed, David
Freimark, Bob (Robert)
French, Ray H
Fricano, Tom S
Friese, Nancy Marlene
Gaines, Alan Jay
Garchik, Morton Lloyd
Garhart, Martin J
Geniusz, Robert Myles
Ginzel, Roland
Giovanni
Gorelick, Shirley
Gramberg, Liliana
Greaver, Hanne
Green, Martin Leonard
Greenbaum, Marty
Griesedieck, Ellen
Grippe, Peter
Grubb, David
Gunn, Ellen
Guzak, Karen W
Haas, Richard John

PRINTMAKER (cont)
Hadzi, Dimitri
Hall, Susan
Hammerman, Pat Jo
Hannay, Janneka (Jann)
Hari, Kenneth
Hasen, Burt Stanley
Heine-Baux, Manfred
Helfond, Riva
Heller, Jules
Herzberg, Thomas
Heywood, J C
Higa (Yoshiharu)
Hood, (Thomas) Richard
Hooper, Jack Meredith
Hormuth, Jo
Humphrey, David Aiken
Hutton, Dorothy Wackerman
Ida, Shoichi
Ihle, John Livingston
Ikegawa, Shiro
Imber, Jonathan
Jackson, Herb
Jacobs, Jim
Jameson, Demetrios George
Jerviss, Joy
Johanson, George E
Johnson, Donald Ray
Jones, Herb (Leon Herbert), Jr
Jones, James Edward
Jones, Judy Voss
Jones, Marvin Harold
Kainen, Jacob
Kaplan, Sandra
Kassoy, Bernard
Katz, Alex
Kenda, Juanita Echeverria
Kenojuak (Ashevak)
Kimura, William Yusaburo
King, Eleanor (Eleanor King Hookham)
Kipniss, Robert
Kirk, Michael
Koopalethes, Olivia (Olivia Koopalethes Alberts)
Kovatch, Jak
Kowalke, Ronald Leroy
Krug, Harry Elno
La Bobgäh, Robert Gordon
Lama, Alberto de
Landers, Bertha
Lang, J T
Lansdon, Gay Brandt
Lantzy, Donald Michael
La Pierre, Thomas
La Plant, Mimi
Lasansky, Leonardo
Lasuchin, Michael
Lawrence, Spencer
Lea, Stanley E
Leathers, Winston Lyle
LeBey, Barbara
Leetaru, Ilse
Leiber, Gerson August
Levin, Morton D
Lipman-Wulf, Peter
Logemann, Jane Marie
Longo, Vincent
Lorber, Stephen Neil
Loring, John
Lowe, Marvin
Luca, Mark
Lyons, Beauvais
McGough, Charles E
McIvor, John Wilfred
McLean, James Albert
McSheehy, Cornelia Marie
Madsen, Viggo Holm
Majeski, Thomas H
Malone, Robert R
Maltzman, Stanley
Mark, Enid (Epstein)
Markley, Doris Yocum
Marshall, Thomas E
Martin, Doris-Marie Constable
Mastrangelo, Bobbi
Mattingly, (James Thomas)
Max, Peter
Maxwell, William C
Mazur, Michael
Mazzocca, Gus (Augustus Nicholas)
Meeker, Dean Jackson
Meisel, Susan Pear
Menihan, John Conway
Menses, Jan
Merida, Frederick A
Merkin, Richard Marshall
Miller, Barbara Darlene
Miller, Daniel Dawson
Miller, Leon Gordon
Mills, Agnes
Mills, Lev Timothy
Miyamoto, Wayne Akira
Montague, James L
Morrow, Terry
Morse, Bart J
Muranaka, Hideo
Murata, Hiroshi
Myers, Malcolm Haynie
Nakazato, Hitoshi
Nama, George Allen
Natkin, Robert
Nawrocki, Thomas Dennis
Newman, Libby
Nushawg, Michael Allan
Obler, Geri
Orens, Elaine Frances
Osborn, Kevin Russell
Osborne, Cynthia A
Page, John Henry, Jr
Paone, Peter
Parra, Carmen
Patterson, William Joseph
Paul, Ken (Hugh)
Peak, Elizabeth Jayne
Pellettieri, Michael Joseph
Peterdi, Gabor F
Pfeiffer, Werner Bernhard
Pletcher, Gerry
Pogany, Miklos
Polansky, Lois B
Ponce de Leon, Michael
Powelson, Rosemary A
Pozzatti, Rudy O
Pozzi, Lucio
Price, Rita F
Quat, Helen S
Racz, Andre
Ragland, Jack Whitney
Rakovan, Lawrence Francis
Redd, Richard James
Redmond, Rozze (Rosemary)
Red Star, Kevin
Richards, Walter DuBois
Ries, Martin
Riess, Lore
Ritchie, William (Bill)
Roberts, Donald
Robertson, Ted Walter
Robinson, Sally W
Rodman, Ruth M
Rogalski, Walter
Roller, Russell Kenneth
Romano, Clare Camille (Mrs John Ross)
Romero, Rachael L
Rose, Herman
Rosenhouse, Irwin
Ross, John T
Rossi, Barbara
Rotholz, Rina
Ruffo, Joseph Martin
Rush, Andrew
Ryan, Richard E
Saff, Donald Jay
Saladino, Tony
Sanchez, Beatrice Rivas
Sandlin, David Thomas
Saunders, J Boyd
Savage, Roger
Sawai, Noboru
Schein, Eugenie
Schieferdecker, Ivan E
Schiff, Lonny
Schnackenberg, Roy
Schrag, Karl
Schwartz, Aubrey E
Schwartz, Carl E
Seabourn, Connie
Seawell, Thomas Robert
Seidler, Doris
Shapiro, David
Shead, S Ray
Sher, Elizabeth
Shirai, Akiko
Shives, Arnold Edward
Simson, Bevlyn A
Sloat, Richard Joel
Smith, Moishe
Snow, John
Sparks, John Edwin
Sperakis, Nicholas George
Spohn, Franz Frederick
Spruce, Everett Franklin
Stack, Frank Huntington
Stasack, Edward Armen
Stasik, Andrew J
Staven, Leland Carroll
Steg, James Louis
Stewart, John P
Stewart, Paul LeRoy
Stolpe, Daniel Owen
Stratton, Dorothy (Mrs William A King)
Sueños, Carlos
Sultan, Donald K
Sykes, (William) Maltby
Szasz, Frank V
Taylor, Ira Mooney
Tewes, Robin J
Thomas, Larry W
Townsend, Jean (Mrs Saul Field)
Trissel, James Nevin
Trosky, Helene Roth
Trueblood, Emily Herrick
Tubis, Seymour
Tulving, Ruth
Tyler, Valton
Uzilevsky, Marcus
Valesco, Frances
Valier, Biron (Frank)
Vaness, Margaret Helen
Vanriet, Jan
Varnay Jones, Theodora
Varney, Edwin
Viera, Ricardo
Wainwright, Robert Barry
Webster, Stokely
Weege, William
Weiler, Melody M
Weiss, Milton
Welden, Daniel W
Wessel, Fred W
Whitesell, John D
Wise, Gerald Lee
Witham, Vernon Clint
Witt, John
Wujcik, Theo
Yamin, Steven Edward
Zelt, Martha
Ziemann, Richard Claude

Etching

Abeles, Sigmund
Alberga, Alta W
Alpen-Whiteside, Dale
Asmar, Alice
Austin, Pat
Autry, Carolyn
Azuz, David
Baczek, Peter Gerard
Bascom, Earl W
Baumbach, Harold
Bayefsky, Aba
Becker, David
Beeman, Malinda
Berman, Eleanore (Eleanore B Lazarof)
Blackey, Mary Madlyn
Blackman, Thomas Patrick
Blackwood, David (Lloyd)
Blaine, Nell
Blaustein, Al
Boylan, John Lewis
Braley, Jean
Breiger, Elaine
Brice, William
Broker, Karin
Broner, Robert
Brus, Gunter
Buck, Porge
Bujese, Arlene
Burns, Jerome
Cameron, Brooke Bulovsky
Cantwell, William Richard
Carlstrom, Lucinda
Cassill, Herbert Carroll
Cawein, Kathrin
Cetín, Anton
Cober, Alan E
Colescott, Warrington W
Condeso, Orlando
Conn, David Edward
Conneen, Jane W
Cook, Stephen D
Cornell, Thomas Browne
Cortese, Don F
Crump, Walter Moore, Jr
Curtis, Mary Cranfill
De Groat, George Hugh
Delson, Elizabeth
Di Cerbo, Michael
Dickson, Jennifer Joan
Dorst, Claire V
Driesbach, David Fraiser
Eames, John Heagan
Edmondson, Leonard
Edmunds, Allan Logan
Esler, John Kenneth
Fairfield, Richard Thomas
Feder, Penny Joy
FitzSimonds, Carol Strause
Fogg, Rebecca Snider
Forrester, Patricia Tobacco
Fowler, Mel
Freedman, Deborah S
Gallagher, Kathleen Ellen
Gardner, Joan A
Garrison, Barbara
Gehr, Mary (Ray)
Geisert, Arthur Frederick
Gentry, Augustus (Callahan), Jr
Germano, Thomas
Gibson, John Stuart
Gilling, Lucille
Gogorza, Patricia (Gahagan) de
Gomez-Quiroz, Juan Manuel
Gonzalez-Tornero, Sergio
Graese, Judy (Judith Ann)
Gregory, Stan(ley Wayne)
Hammond, Gale Thomas
Hannah, John Junior
Hardy, (Clarion) Dewitt
Havens, Jan
Heyman, Lawrence Murray
Hicks, Leon Nathaniel
Hoie, Claus
Holabird, Jean
Holmes, David Bryan
Huggins, Victor, Jr
Humphrey, Judy Lucille
Hurley, Denzil H
Hurwitz, Sidney J
Itchkawich, David Michael
Jacques, Michael Louis
Janko, May
Jansen, Angela Bing
Johnston, Thomas Alix
Jones, Edward Powis
Jones, John Paul
Kaericher, John Conrad
Kagemoto, Patricia Jow
Kaminsky, Jack Allan

PRINTMAKER (cont)
Kaplan, Jerome Eugene
Kaplan, Penny
Kelso, David William
Kemp, Flo
Kepets, Hugh Michael
Kerslake, Kenneth Alvin
Kline, Harriet
Kloss, Gene (Alice Geneva Glasier)
Kolliker, William Augustin
Koppelman, Chaim
Krause, LaVerne Erickson
Laguna, Mariella
Lake, Randall
Lambert, Ed
Lambrechts, Marc
Lasansky, Mauricio L
Laventhol, Hank
Lavier, Bertrand
Leithauser, Mark Alan
Levine, Martin
Levine, Tom
Lew, Weyman
Limont, Naomi Charles
Lukasiewicz, Ronald Joseph
Lummus, Carol Travers
McBryde, Sarah Elva
McKinnickinnick, Margaret I
McMillan, Stephen Walker
Manning, Jo
Marcus, Gerald R
Marden, Brice
Mason, Harold
Masurovsky, Gregory
Matthews, Wanda Miller
Mayer, Sondra
Miller, Kathryn
Milton, Peter Winslow
Morita, John Takami
Mullen, Jo (Stauffer)
Munce, James Charles
Myers, Frances
Nemec, Nancy
Noda, Takayo
Nydorf, Roy Herman
Ocvirk, Otto G
Otani, June
Oxman, Katja
Pace, James Robert
Pace, Stephen S
Pantell, Richard Keith
Paris, Lucille M
Parke, Walter Simpson
Pentz, Donald Robert
Perlmutter, Merle
Petersen, Roland Conrad
Petrie, Sylvia Spencer
Philbrick, Margaret Elder
Plotkin, Linda
Priest, Hartwell Wyse
Pufahl, John K
Quandt, Elizabeth (Elizabeth Quandt)
Rayburn (Dale), Boyd
Rebhun, Pearl G
Reed, Flint Winter
Reed, Jesse Floyd
Reimann, Arline
Richardson, Jean
Richmond, Rebekah
Rieber, Ruth B
Ross, Conrad H
Ross, Sueellen
Rubey, Tony (George Anton)
St Tamara
Schaefer, Ronald H
Scholder, Laurence
Schreiber, Eileen Sher
Schrut, Sherry
Schutz, Estelle
Scott, Martha F
Scoville, Jonathan Armstrong
Sewell, Richard George
Simel, Elaine
Slatton, Ralph David
Smigocki, Stephen Vincent
Smith, Donald C
Smith, Keith A
Smith, Vincent D
Sokolowski, Linda Robinson
Sorge, Walter
Spencer, Howard DaLee
Steinhouse, Tobie (Thelma)
Stevovich, Andrew Vlastimir
Sverdlove, Zolita
Sway, Albert
Taylor, Harry George
Thies, Charles Herman
Tompkins, Betty (I)
Torlakson, James Daniel
Virgona, Hank (Henry P)
Wall, Sue
Washburn, Stan
Wasko-Flood, Sandra Jean
Weare, Shane
Werger, Art(hur Lawrence)
Whedon, Aida Anthony
Whitcomb, Skip
Wilde, Stephanie
Wilson, John
Wunderman, Jan (Liljan Darcourt Wunderman)
Yarbrough, Leila Kepert
Yeh, Carol
Zugor, Sandor
Zwick, Rosemary G

Engraving

Chappell, Berkley Warner
Cook, August Charles
De Pol, John
Driesbach, David Fraiser
Fumagalli, Barbara Merrill
Hicks, Leon Nathaniel
Lindquist, Evan
Marsh, Anne Steele
Martin, Stefan
Matthews, Wanda Miller
Milton, Peter Winslow
Morgan, Norma Gloria
Moser, Barry
Paulsen, Brian Oliver
Sawka, Jan A
Szesko, Lenore Rundle
Tripp, Jan Peter
Worthen, Amy Namowitz
Yeh, Carol
Zonia, Dhimitri

Lithography

Anderson, Sally J
Archer, Cynthia
Bennett, Don Bemco
Blagden, Allen
Brodsky, Harry
Bryce, Mark Adams
Burford, Byron Leslie
Burkert, Robert Randall
Butler, James D
Chu, Gene
Cline, Clinton C
Conneen, Mari M
Copeland, Lila
Dash, Robert (Warren)
Davenport, Ray
Davidson, Herbert Laurence
De Champlain, Vera Chopak
Detmers, William Raymond
Doyle, John Lawrence
Du Jardin, Gussie
Ellingson, William John
Filmus, Tully
Forrest, Christopher Patrick
Foster, April
Frances, Harriette Anton
Freeman, Mark
Freilicher, Jane
Frerichs, Ruth Colcord
Fusco, Yolanda
Gardner, Robert Earl
George, Raymond Ellis
Golden, Rolland Harve
Greaver, Harry
Grillo, Esther Angela
Grosch, Laura
Hagan, Frederick
Hebald, Milton Elting
Hibel, Edna
Hobbie, Lucille
Hofmann, Douglas William
Hogue, Alexandre
Holtz, Itshak Jack
Horvitz, Suzanne Joan
Hunter, Mel
Hyde, Scott
Iwamasa, Ken
Jans, Candace
Johnson, Douglas Walter
Kakas, Christopher A
Kaplan, Jerome Eugene
Kelley, Donald William
Kimball, Wilford Wayne, Jr
Kline, Ronald Wayne
Kniffin, Ralph Gus
Knigin, Michael Jay
Kozmon, George
Landau, Jacob
Lanyon, Ellen
Lapinski, Tadeusz (A)
Lapointe, Frank
Lehrer, Leonard
Lerner, Sandy R
Levine, Martin
Lowney, Bruce Stark
Lund, Jane
McCallum, Corrie (Mrs William Halsey)
McCosh, Anne Kutka (Mrs David McCosh)
McCulloch, Frank E
Machetanz, Fred
McNeil, George J
McWhinnie, Harold James
Massey, Charles Wesley, Jr
Maughelli, Mary L
Medearis, Roger
Meghelli, Fethi M
Mehn, Jan (von der Golz)
Mell, Ed (Edmund Paul Jr)
Melville, Grevis Whitaker
Miyasaki, George Joji
Morales, Armando
Mosca, August
Moses, Forrest (Lee), Jr
Muench, John
Nicholson, Roy William
Noble, John A
O'Connell, George D
O'Connor, Thom
Parfenoff, Michael S
Perlmutter, Jack
Petersen, Will
Petheo, Bela Francis
Poehlmann, JoAnna
Poole, Leslie Donald
Prentice, David Ramage
Pura, William Paul
Raffael, Joseph
Reid, Leslie
Ringness, Charles Obert
Robinson, Charlotte
Robinson, Grove
Rode, Meredith Eagon
Rosenthal, Seymour
Rothenberg, Susan
Rubenstein, Lewis W
Rubin, Sandra
Sakuyama, Shunji
Samburg, Grace (Blanche)
Sandusky, Billy Ray
Schreyer, Greta L
Seckel, Paul Bernhard
Seidl, Claire
Sigismund, Violet M
Sloan, Jeanette Pasin
Solodkin, Judith
Sperantzas, Vassilis
Steinworth, Skip (William Eugene Jr)
Stoeveken, Anthony Charles
Stoianovich, Marcelle
Surgalski, Patrick J
Tarin, Gilberto A
Theobald, Gillian Lee
Thomas, C David
Tooker, George
Trupp, Barbara Lee
Upton, Richard Thomas
Van Laar, Timothy
Vigil, Veloy Joseph
Vogel, Joseph
Vogl, Don George
Voorhees, Donald Edward
Walmsley, William Aubrey
Watson, Howard N(oel)
Wayne, June
Weber, John Pitman
Weddige, Emil A
Wenger, Bruce Edward
Wilson, Charles Banks
Wolfe, Robert, Jr

Mezzotint

Bratt, Byron H
Burks, Myrna R
Hamaguchi, Yozo
Porter, Liliana

Miscellaneous Media

Adams, Lisa Kay
Allen, Jesse
Altman, Harold
Amatniek, Sara
Anderson, Bill (William Maxwell)
Baker, Cornelia Draves
Barry, Anne Meredith
Bass, Joel
Baum, Marilyn Ruth
Bayer, Arlyne
Bentley-Scheck, Grace Mary
Berlin, Beatrice Winn
Berman, Vivian
Blaedel, Joan Stuart Ross
Blumenthal, Fritz
Bowie, Effie Belle
Brown, Pamela Wedd
Brummel, Marilyn Reeder
Bukovnik, Gary
Byrum, Donald Roy
Caiserman-Roth, Ghitta
Campbell, Nancy B
Carter, Nanette Carolyn
Catchi
Chernow, Ann
Church, C Howard
Civale, Biagio A
Clinton, Paul Arthur
Cohen, Reina Joyce
Conover, Robert Fremont
Cyphers, Peggy K
Dass, Dean Allen
Dean, Nicholas Brice
De Guzman, Evelyn Lopez
DeLamonica, Roberto
De Looper, Willem
De Wan-Carlson, Anna
Dickerson, Edward Ted
Dunkle, Joan Osborn
Edell, Nancy
Ellis, Loren Elizabeth
Erla, Karen
Esaki, Yasuhiro
Flanery, Gail
Forsythe, Donald John
Fortess, Karl E
Fuerst, Shirley Miller
Fuller, Sue
Furr, Jim

PRINTMAKER (cont)
Garcia, Ofelia
Gaucher, Yves
Geller, Esther (Esther Geller Shapero)
Gerzso, Gunther
Goldstein, Milton
Gregory-Goodrum, Ellna Kay
Gross, Marilyn A
Hamill, Tim J
Hamlin, Louise
Harjo, Benjamin, Jr
Harwood-Baumel, Bernice
Hendershot, J L
Hildebrand, June Marianne
Hildreth, Joseph Alan
Hoare, Tyler James
Hoffman, Eric
Homar, Lorenzo
Hoyal, Dorothy
Hushlak, Gerald
Johnson, Barbara Louise
Johnson, Lois Marlene
Jones, Theodore Joseph
Kanter, Lorna J
Kaplan, Stanley
Kaulitz, Garry Charles
Kitaj, R B
Klabunde, Charles Spencer
Kohn, Misch
Kravjansky, Mikulas
Krushenick, John
Leaf, Ruth
Lewis, Stanley
Lindroth, Linda
Lisk, Penelope E Tsaltas
Lytton, Constance B
McClelland, Jeanne C
McCue, Harry
MacDonald, Betty Ann
MacGillis, Robert Donald
Mandelbaum, Lyn
Margo, Boris
Matyas, Diane C
Mayes, Steven Lee
Mehn, Jan (von der Golz)
Mendelson, Haim
Michelson, Philip L
Miller, Elaine Sandra
Munoz, Rie
Myers, Virginia Anne
Nadolski, Stephanie Lucille
Narotzky, Norman David
Neal, (Minor) Avon
Neals, Otto
Nechvatal, Joseph James
Nemec, Nancy
Olendorf, William Carr
Olmsted, Suzanne M
Oxman, Katja
Parry, Marian
Passuntino, Peter Zaccaria
Peruo, Marsha
Picciano, Lana (Lana Patricia Picciano)
Pinto, Angelo Raphael
Pitts, Richard G
Potter, (George) Kenneth
Price, Diane Miller
Price, Doris C
Price, Kenneth
Reddy, Krishna N
Renouf, Edda
Richards, Jeanne Herron
Rizzi, James
Rogers, P J
Roman, Shirley
Rood, Kay
Rosen, Carol M
Rosenberg, Marilyn R
Rowan, Dennis Michael
Ruthling, Ford
Ruyle, Lydia Miller
Sahlstrand, Margaret Ahrens
Salinas, Baruj
Sandgren, Ernest Nelson
Sarsony, Robert
Savenor, Betty Carmell
Schary, Emanuel
Scott, Campbell
Scott, John Tarrell
Seltzer, Phyllis
Sharp, Anne
Sloane, Phyllis Lester
Solomon, Bernard Alan
Spagnolo, Kathleen Mary
Spiegel, Laurie
Stegman, Patricia
Steinhoff, Monika
Stoltenberg, Donald Hugo
Stroh, Charles
Sullivan, Anne Dorothy Hevner
Swartzman, Roslyn
Sznajderman, Marius S
Takal, Peter
Talaba, L (Linda Talaba Cummens)
Taylor, Sandra Ortiz
Thomas, John
Tomchuk, Marjorie
Townley, Hugh
Van Suchtelen, Adrian
Van Vliet, Claire
Vernon
Warner, Herbert Kelii, Jr
Webster, Larry
Weingarten, Hilde (Kevess)
Wilson-Hammond, Charlotte Emily
Woolschlager, Laura Totten
Yager, David
Youkeles, Anne
Youngblood, Judy
Zirker, Joseph
Zupan, Bruno

Serigraphy, Silkscreen

Adler, Lee
Ahlgren, Roy B
Akins, Future Renée
Anderson, William Thomas
Angeloch, Robert
Apgar, Jean E
Arnold, Florence M
Ascian
Auvil, Kenneth William
Azuma, Norio
Barnett, Helmut
Barrio, Raymond
Berlyn, Sheldon
Berman, Ariane R
Block, Amanda Roth
Bogarin, Rafael
Bradford, Howard
Brutosky, (Sister) Mary Veronica, CSJ
Campbell, Nancy B
Caples, Barbara Barrett
Carvalho, Josely
Che, Chuang
Christensen, Ted
Christ-Janer, Arland F
Cohn, Max Arthur
Colville, Alexander
Curran, Darryl Joseph
Danby, Ken
Davidek, Stefan
Davies, Theodore Peter
De Wan-Carlson, Anna
Dillon, Mildred (Murphy)
Doherty, Michael Stephen
Duff, Ann MacIntosh
Edwards, Ellender Morgan
Filmus, Stephen I
Fitzgerald, Astrid
Fransioli, Thomas Adrian
Fumagalli, Barbara Merrill
Gardner, Andrew Bradford
Garwood, Audrey
Gersovitz, Sarah Valerie
Gill, Gene
Ginsburg, Estelle
Giorno, John
Goldberg, Arnold Herbert
Golden, Libby
Hallenbeck, Pomona Juanita
Halsey, Brian Elliott
Hanna, Paul Dean, Jr
Harvey, Donald
Higgins, Dick
High, Timothy Griffin
Hobbs, Robert Dean
Huff, Laura Weaver
Igo, Peter Alexander
Kaufman, Glen
Kaye, Mildred Elaine
Kimura, Riisaburo
Kirsten-Daiensai, Richard Charles
Knowles, Alison
Knudsen, Christian
Kohl, Barbara
Kreneck, Lynwood
Kuhn, Audrey Grendahl
Lagorio, Irene R
Lampitoc, Rol Ponce
Lichtenstein, Gary
Lummus, Carol Travers
McCall, Ann
McCallum, Steven Douglas
McElroy, Jacquelyn Ann (McElroy-Edwards)
McKnight, Thomas Frederick
Magistro, Charles John
Maki, Sheila Anne
Mandziuk, Michael Dennis
Marder, Dorie
Massie, Lorna
Miley, Chuck (Charles) E
Miller, Richard Kidwell
Mode, Carol A
Monahan, Gene Ritchie
Moon, Jim (James Monroe)
Moore, Wayland D
Neiman, LeRoy
Newton, John Neil
Nind, Jean
Ocepek, Lou (Louis David)
O'Connell, Edward E
Osterweil-Weber, Suzanne
Peterson, Gwen Entz
Petro, Joe, III
Pletscher, Josephine Marie
Poleskie, Stephen Francis
Pond, Clayton
Price, Joe (Allen)
Ranson, Nancy Sussman
Richards, Sabra
Robbins, Hulda D
Roberts, Steven K
Ruby, Laura
Rucker, Harrison Campbell
Sabelis, Huibert
Sachse, Janice R
Sassone, Marco
Saturen, Ben
Schenck, William Clinton
Schneider, Shellie
Schurr, Jerry M
Schwieger, C Robert
Shepherd, Reginald
Singer, Clifford
Sklar-Weinstein, Arlene (Joyce)
Stapp, Ray Veryl
Stewart, Norman
Stovall, Luther McKinley (Lou)
Sullivan, Bill
Sullivan, David Francis
Tabor, Virginia S
Tascona, Antonio Tony
Ten Eyck, Catryna (Catryna Ten Eyck Seymour)
Twitty, James W
Vaccaro, Patrick Frank
Van Riper, Peter
Vaux, Richard
Waddingham, John Alfred
Wasserman, Burton
West, Peter

Woodcut

Abany, Albert Charles
Abbe, Elfriede Martha
Andrews, Sybil (Sybil Andrews Morgan)
Arnold, Paul Beaver
Barber, Cynthia
Barton, John Murray
Bell, Alistair Macready
Berger, Jason
Bettinson, Brenda
Bigelow, Anita (Anne Edwige Lourie)
Bobak, Bruno Joseph
Bragar, Philip Frank
Brody, Arthur William
Card, Royden
Carter, (Charles) Bruce
Casida, Kati
Conner, Ann
Dallas, Dorothy B
Dance, Robert Bartlett
De Armond, Dale B
Dillon, Mildred (Murphy)
Ettling, Ruth (Droitcour)
Ferro, Walter
Gary, Jan (Mrs William D Gorman)
Goldstein, Daniel Joshua
Grashow, James Bruce
Gruver, Mary Emmett
Gunther, Charles F
Hedman, Teri Jo
Herman, Roger
Hodgell, Robert Overman
Hotvedt, Kris J
Howard, (Helen) Barbara
Idaherma (Idaherma Williams)
Jaidinger, Judith C
Keever, Kim
Kemble, Richard
Kermes, Constantine John
Koster, Marjory Jean
Kunc, Karen
McNamara, William Patrick, Jr
Malo, Teri (Theresa A Malo-Sprawka)
Mandel, Dorothy
Matsubara, Naoko
Mogensen, Paul
Morrison, Robert Clifton
Mortensen, Gordon Louis
Mosenthal, Charlotte Dembo
Murray, Tim(othy Douglas Gordon)
Naylon, Betsy Zimmermann
Nesbitt, Ilse Buchert
Noble, Helen (Harper)
Offner, Elliot
Peace, Bernie (Kinzel)
Rowan, Frances Physioc
Sadle, Amy Ann Brandon
Satorsky, Cyril
Scharff, Constance Kramer
Shuff, Lily (Lillian Shir)
Skelley, Robert Charles
Stinnett, Hester A
Summers, Carol
Tesfagiorgis, Freida
Trueblood, Emily Herrick
Uchima, Ansei
Vo-Dinh, Mai
Walters, Sylvia Solochek
Waters, Herbert (Ogden)
Watia, Tarmo

PUBLISHER

Alexander, Edmund Brooke
Anbinder, Paul
Arnold, Jack
Banana, Anna
Blake, Jane Salley
Blinder, Martin S
Botwinick, Michael
Cawley, Joan Mae
Cloud, Jack L
Dresdnere, Simon
Esterow, Milton
Fleischman, Lawrence Arthur
Fleisher, Pat
Franklin, Carole R
Friberg, Arnold
Gaines, Alan Jay
Geldermann Hails, Barbara
Gladstone, M J
Goodman, Marian
Hackett, Dwight Vernon
Heiferman, Marvin
Hennesy, Gerald Craft
Hicks, Sheila
Hobbs, Gerald S
Hoffberg, Judith A
Hoffman, Carol Maree
Hooton, Bruce Duff
Isaacs, Avrom
Kline, Ronald Wayne
Kocsis, James Paul
Krantz, Les (Leslie J)
Levin, Hugh Lauter
Love, Frances Taylor
MacDonald, Colin Somerled
McGilvery, Laurence
McPherson, Bruce Rice
Mahlmann, John James
Moore, Alan Willard
Morton, Robert Alan
Pennypacker, James S
Persky, Robert S
Posner, Judith L
Rosenberg, Bernard
Rosenthal, John W
Sandman, Alan
Solodkin, Judith
Solomon, Richard H
Spiegelman, Lon Howard
Stewart, Norman
Szoke, John
Torf, Lois Beurman
Usher, David
Van Vliet, Claire
Vezys, Gintautas
Westlund, Harry E
Wilson, John David
Wyrick, Charles Lloyd, Jr

RESTORER

see also **Conservator**

Bernstein, Gerald
Campbell, Kenneth Floyd
Fisher, Sarah Lisbeth
Flume, Violet Sigoloff
Fredericks, Beverly Magnuson
Grassi, Marco
Greaves, James L
Gurbacs, John Joseph
Hopkins, Kenneth R
Jakstas, Alfred John
Kamrowski, Gerome
Knowlton, Daniel Gibson
Lysun, Gregory
Mohr, Pauline Catherine
Richard, Jack
Zarand, Julius John

SCULPTOR

Abadi, Fritzie
Adams, Phoebe
Adickes, David (Pryor)
Ahearn, John
Ahrens, Hanno D
Akamu, Nina
Alexander, Peter
Allen, Bruce Wayne
Amado, Jesse V
Anderson, Troy
Andrews, Charleen Kohl
Andrews, Edwin C
Andrews, Michael Frank
Angell, Tony
Anker, Suzanne C
Annis, Norman L
Armajani, Siah
Asher, Michael
Aston, Miriam
Ataie, Mary Lee
Austin-Nuhfer, Olive H
Averbuch, Ilan
Baden, Mowry T
Bakanowsky, Louis J
Balciar, Gerald George
Bales, J (Jean Elaine)
Barber, Bruce Alistair
Barry, Steve
Barton, Georgie Read
Batko, Blaise Joseph
Baum, Don
Behl, Wolfgang
Benvenuto, Elio
Berge, Dorothy Alphena
Beyer, Steven J
Biederman, Charles (Karel Joseph)
Biederman, James Mark
Billian, Cathey R
Binder, Erwin
Black, David Evans
Blakely, George C
Blum, June
Bodo, Sandor
Boggs, Franklin
Bohnenkamp, Leslie George
Bolinsky, Joseph Abraham
Borgatta, Isabel Case
Bornstein, Eli
Boszin, Andrew
Boucher, Tania Kunsky
Boxer, Stanley (Robert)
Brady, Charles
Bremer, Marlene S
Brener, Roland
Broer, Roger L
Brookins, Jacob Boden
Brooks, Bruce W
Brush, Leif
Buck, John
Budny, Virginia
Bullock, James Benbow
Busch, Rita Mary
Butter, Tom
Butterfield, Deborah Kay
Byard, Carole Marie
Cabot, Hugh
Campopiano, Remo
Cantor, Mira
Capobianco, Domenick
Cardoso, Anthony
Carl, Joan
Carlson, Mary
Carter, Gary
Carter, Jerry Williams
Casebere, James E
Cassidy, Margaret Carol (Mrs John Manship)
Castanis, Muriel (Julia Brunner)
Cenci, Silvana
Chabot, Aurore (Martha)
Chambers, Park A, Jr
Chandler, Elisabeth Gordon
Chao, Bruce
Chase, Doris (Totten)
Chernick, Myrel
Chicago, Judy
Chin, Mel
Close, Frank
Coheleach, Guy Joseph
Colby, Jeff
Collyer, Robin
Conlon, James Edward
Conrad, Paul Francis
Conwill, Houston E
Cooper, Ron
Cooper, Susan
Cotter, James Edward
Cove, Rosemary
Crawford, Thom Cooney
Crutchfield, William Richard
Curtis, Dolly Powers
Danziger, Joan
Davidson, Thyra (Claire Thyra Wexler)
Dawson, John Allan
De Mille, Leslie Benjamin
De Monte, Claudia
De Nike, Michael Nicholas
Dennis, Donna Frances
DeRoux, Daniel Edward
Derrickson, Steve Bruce
Dogancay, Burhan Cahit
Dougherty, Patrick T
Dowler, David P
Dreyer, Clarice A
Dreyer, Gay
Driscoll, Ellen
Dubasky, Valentina
Dusenbery, Walter
Edelson, Mary Beth
Eliscu, Frank
Engle, Steve (Stephen E)
Engler, Kathleen Girdler
Erman, Geraldine
Evans, Dick
Fabert, Jacques
Fager, Charles J
Fahlen, Charles C
Farm, Gerald E
Farrens, Juanita G
Fasnacht, Heide Ann
Fay, Ming G
Filkosky, Josefa
Finn, David
Fisher, Joel
Fitzpatrick, Joseph Cyril
Fleischner, Richard Hugh
Forester, Russell
Foster, Don
Frabel, Hans Godo
Franklin, Patt
Fried, Howard Lee
Frudakis, Zenos
Fujita, Kenji
Gabrielson, Walter Oscar
Garten, Cliff
Genn, Nancy
Gifford, J Nebraska
Gillen, John
Ginzburg, Yankel (Jacob)
Glancy, Michael
Glickman, Arthur
Godwin, Lawrence
Goldfinger, Eliot
Goodelman, Ruth
Goodine, Linda Adele
Goodyear, John L
Gray, Elise N
Grimm, Raymond Max
Grimmer, Mineko
Gronborg, Erik
Gropper, Cathy
Guberman, Sidney Thomas
Guerrero, Raul
Habergritz, George Joseph
Haleman, Laura Rand
Halsey, William Melton
Harootunian, Claire M
Hastenteufel, Dieter
Hatcher, (L) Brower
Hay, Ike
Helsmoortel, Robert
Herritt, Linda S
Highstein, Jene
Hill, Clinton J
Hirschfield, Jim
Hirshfield, Pearl
Hlavina, Rasto R(astislav)
Hollis, Douglas
Holt, Martha A
Houston, Bruce
Hsiao, Chin
Huchthausen, David Richard
Hudson, Jon Barlow
Humphrey, Nene
Hunter, Paul
Ingram, Judith
Ipsen, Poul Janus
Irving, Joan
Izuka, Kunio
Jaar, Alfredo
Jackson, Oliver Lee
Johanson, Patricia
Johnson, Bruce (James)
Johnson, Dean P
Johnston, Ynez
Jones, Howard William
Judd, Donald Clarence
Kaiser, Diane
Kawashima, Takeshi
Kendrick, Mel
Kennedy, Harriet Forte
Kenney, Douglas
Kepner, Rita
Kessler, Jon A
Klein, Doris
Kopriva, Sharon
Kraus, (Ersilia) Zili
Kuryluk, Ewa
Labat, Tony
LaChapelle, Joseph Robert
Lager, Fannie
Larson, Philip Seely
Laske, Lyle F
Laub-Novak, Karen
LaVerdiere, Bruno E
Lawrence, Michael
Leaf, June
Lee, Catherine
Lere, Mark Allen
Le Va, Barry
Levy, Hilda
Levy, Margaret Wasserman
Licht, Evelyn M
Lindgren, Charlotte
Lipton, Sondra Sahlman
Little Chief, Barthell
Long, Bert L, Jr
Lucero, Michael (Lewis)
Lukasiewicz, Ronald Joseph
Lundeen, George Wayne
Luneau, Claude
Lurie, Boris
Lynch, Gerald
McCormick, Rod
McGlauchlin, Tom
Mackintosh, Sandra
McNeil, Dean S
Maitin, Sam (Samuel Calman)
Mann, Katinka
Marano, Lizbeth
Marcheschi, (Louis) Cork
Marks, Roberta Barbara
Maron, Jeffrey
Massin, Eugene Max
Maxwell, William Jackson
Mayer, Rosemary
Melnick, Myron J
Merola, Mario
Meyer, Ursula
Micale, Albert
Middlebrook, David A
Miller, (Richard) Guy
Mim, Adrienne C (Adrienne Claire Schwartz)
Mongrain, Claude
Monteiro, Isaac

SCULPTOR (cont)

Morrison, Robert J
Morrissey, Leo
Murakishi, Steve
Murdock, Greg
Natsoulas, Anthony
Nelson, Leonard
Newman, Elizabeth H
Newman, Sophie
Noel, Georges
Noel, Jean
Noestheden, John
Nolte, Gunter
Nonas, Richard
Nugent, Bob L
Oda, Masayuki
Oginz, Richard
Orze, Joseph John
Oshima, Mari
Oshita, Kazuma
Palau, Marta
Pan, Theodore (Ion)
Parmakelis, John
Paul, Rick W
Pearlstein, Alix
Pellicone, William
Penny, Aubrey John Robert
Pernotto, James Angelo
Pinkel, Sheila Mae
Pinto, Jody
Pogach, Gerald
Posner, Richard
Poulin, Roland
Pravda, Muriel
Prekop, Martin Dennis
Preston, Ann L
Price, Joan Webster
Prip, John A
Pruneda, Max
Puett, Garnett G
Rabinovitch, William Avrum
Rabkin, Leo
Raciti, Cherie
Rath, Alan T
Ravarra, Patricia
Ray, Charles
Recklinghausen, Marianne von
Reitzenstein, Reinhard
Richardson, Sam
Richter, Scott
Riddle, John Thomas, Jr
Ridlon, James A
Ritz, Lorna J
Robinson, Libby
Rockburne, Dorothea
Rogers, Steve
Rojek, Christine
Roloff, John Scott
Roosen, Mia Westerlund
Roots, Garrison
Roseberg, Carl Andersson
Rosenberg, Terry
Rosenquist, Marc H
Rosenthal, Howard
Rush, Jon N
Sanborn, James
Sande, Rhoda
Santiago, Richard E
Sapp, William Rothwell
Saret, Alan Daniel
Saunders, Wade
Sawyer, Margo
Schapiro, Miriam
Scheer, Lisa N
Schuselka, Elfi
Schwartz, Aubrey E
Schwartz, Barbara Ann
Sears, Stanton Gray
Seawright, James L, Jr
Seide, Paul A
Severson, William Conrad
Shaw, Mary Todd
Shay, Ed
Shine, Vincent
Shire, Peter
Siberell, Anne Hicks
Sica
Simionov, Alexandru
Simpson, Buster
Simpson, Gail A
Sinclair, Robert (W)
Singer, Michael
Skoglund, Sandy
Slaymaker, Martha
Slosburg-Ackerman, Jill
Snell, Eric
Sokolow, Isobel Folb
Sonnier, Keith
Southey, Trevor J T
Sponenburgh, Mark
Stack, Michael
Stackhouse, Robert
Staller, Eric P
Starpattern, Rita
Stearns, Thomas Robert
Stoppert, Mary Kay
Stump, M Pamela (Pamela Stump)
Sturgeon, John Floyd
Sweet, Roger
Swetcharnik, William Norton
Tacha, Athena
Taggart, William John
Taylor, Michael (Estes)
Tefft, Elden Cecil
Thompson, Jack
Thompson, Mark L
Tillman, Patricia Ann
Trinkley, Karla
Tsai, Wen-Ying
Udvardy, John Warren
Ullman, Jane F
Umlauf, Lynn (Charlotte)
Urban, Vladimir T
Urquhart, Tony (Anthony Morse)
Vierthaler, Bonnie
Von Ringelheim, Paul Helmut
Walton, Marion
Watson, Helen Richter
Webber, Helen
Weissman, Walter
Welch, Roger
West, W Richard (Dick)
Whitehead, Frances
Whitson, Angie
Wicklander, Edward A
Wilhelmi, William Merle
Wilson, Charles H
Wilson, Fred
Winter, David L
Woodall, John
Woodward, Steven P
Yasko, Caryl A(nne)
Young, John T
Younger, Robert M
Youngerman, Jack
Zentz, Patrick J
Ziegler, Mel(vin) and Kate Ericson
Zimmerman, Arnold
Zouni, Opy
Zwack, Michael

All Media

Abbe, Elfriede Martha
Abish, Cecile
Acconci, Vito
Acton, Arlo C
Adams, Dennis Paul
Adams, Mac
Agostini, Peter
Ajay, Abe
Alaupovic, Alexandra V
Albrecht, Mary Dickson
Albright, Malvin Marr
Alexander, Anthony K
Allumbaugh, James
Alquist, Lewis
Anargyros, Spero
Anastasi, William (Joseph)
Anderson, David C
Andre, Carl
Andrews, Lawrence
Anthony, Lawrence Kenneth
Antol, Joseph James (Jay)
Antonovici, Constantin
Appel, Eric A
Archambault, Louis
Atkinson, Conrad
Avedisian, Edward
Avlon-Daphnis, Helen Basilea
Axelrod, Miriam
Ayaso, Manuel
Aycock, Alice
Babcock, Jo (Joseph Warren Babcock)
Baldwin, Richard Wood
Balsley, John Gerald
Barbeau, Marcel (Christian)
Barber, Cynthia
Barber, Sam
Bard, Joellen
Barsano, Ron (Ronald James)
Bartlett, Barry Thomas
Baskin, Leonard
Beason, Donald Ray
Beeler, Joe (Neil)
Beer, Kenneth John
Belfort-Chalat, Jacqueline
Beling, Helen
Bell, Larry Stuart
Bell, Lilian A
Benglis, Lynda
Ben-Haim, Zigi
Benini
Benton, Fletcher
Bergner, Lanny Michael
Berlant, Tony
Bertolli, Eugene Emil
Bieler, Ted Andre
Billeci, Andre George
Birch, Willie M
Blaine, Matthew Frederick
Blair, Robert Noel
Blazeje, Zbigniew (Ziggy Blazese)
Bleifeld, Stanley
Bonevardi, Marcelo
Bookatz, Samuel
Booth, Laurence Ogden
Bott, H(arvey) J(ohn)
Bourgeois, Louise
Boyd, James Henderson
Bradshaw, Dove
Bratton, Christopher
Breer, Robert C
Breschi, Karen Lee
Bright, Barney
Brock, Robert W
Brody, Myron Roy
Brosk, Jeffrey
Brown, Bruce Robert
Brulc, Lillian G
Buba, Joy Flinsch
Buckner, Paul Eugene
Bunin, Louis
Burchess, Arnold
Burden, Chris
Burg, Patricia Jean
Burgues, Irving Carl
Burnett, Patricia Hill
Burris, Bruce C
Bussabarger, Robert Franklin
Butterbaugh, Robert Clyde
Buxbaum, Robert
Calabro, Richard Paul
Calfee, William Howard
Campbell, Kenneth Floyd
Capps, Kenneth P
Cardillo, Rimer Angel
Carlberg, Norman Kenneth
Carlson, William D
Carr, Sally Swan
Carr-Harris, Ian Redford
Carter, Dean
Casanova, Aldo John
Casarella, Edmond
Cascieri, Arcangelo
Castle, Wendell Keith
Castoro, Rosemarie
Chamberlain, David (Allen)
Chamberlain, John Angus
Charney, Melvin
Chavez, Eduardo Arcenio
Cheng, Carl F K, AKA John Doe Co
Cher, Beatrice (Beatrice Michelle Cher-Killigan)
Christo,
Chryssa
Clark, Marie
Clements, Robert Donald
Clerk, Pierre
Clough, Eleanor
Coe, Matchett Herring
Collery, Paula
Collings, Betty
Collins, Jim
Conaway, Gerald
Cook, Robert Howard
Corwin, Sophia M
Costa, Eduardo
Cox, Ernest Lee
Coyne, Petah E
Creech, Franklin Underwood
Crivelli, Elaine
Cronin, Robert (Lawrence)
Crotto, Paul
Croydon, Michael Benet
Currie, Steve
Curtis, Terry Wayne
Cusack, Margaret Weaver
Czarnopys, Thomas J
Dahlstrom, Nancy Gail
Daly, Norman
Danhausen, Eldon
Darriau, Jean-Paul
Davies, Haydn Llewellyn
Dehner, Dorothy
De Laittre, Eleanor
DeLap, Tony
De Larios, Dora
DeLauro, Joseph Nicola
de la Vega, Enrique Miguel
De Lisio, Michael
De Maria, Walter
De Pedery-Hunt, Dora
Dergalis, George
Dern, F Carl
Dill, Guy Girard
Dill, Laddie John
Dimondstein, Morton
Dine, James
Dirube, Rolando Lopez
Di Suvero, Mark
Donati, Enrico
Donneson, Seena
D'Onofrio, Bernard Michael
Downie, Romana Anzi
Drake, James
Drumm, Don
Dukes, Caroline
Dunwiddie, Charlotte
Durham, William
Edge, Douglas Benjamin
Egbert, Elizabeth Frances
Egri, Ted
Elder, David Morton
Elkin, Rowena Caldwell
Elozua, Raymon
Emery, Lin
Epstein, Betty O
Escalet, Frank Diaz
Etrog, Sorel
Ettl, Georg
Facci, Domenico (Aurelio)
Faden, Lawrence Steven
Fane, Lawrence
Farber, Amanda
Faust, James Wille
Favro, Murray
FeBland, Harriet
Felker, David Larry
Fernie, John Chipman

SCULPTOR (cont)
Ferrara, Jackie
Filipowski, Richard E
Fine, Jud
Finkelstein, Max
Fiore, Rosario Russell
Fischer, John
Fischer, R M
Floyd, Carl Leo
Ford, John
Foreman, Laura
Fox, Terry Alan
Fra, Dahli-Sterne
Frame, John
Francis, Madison Ke, Jr
Franklin, Gilbert Alfred
Fraughton, Edward James
Fredericks, Marshall Maynard
Freeland, William Lee
Friedman, Alan
Frudakis, Anthony P
Gach, George
Gage, Frances M
Gallo, Enzo D
Gallo, Frank
Ganzarain, Mirentxu
Gasparro, Frank
Gastaldi, Jerome
Gates, Harry Irving
Gaylord, Frank Chalfant, II
Gebhardt, Roland
Geissbuhler, Arnold
Geller, Matthew
Geran, Joseph, Jr
Gerenday, Laci Anthony de
Gialanella, Donald G
Giampietro, Isabel (Isabel A Giampietro Knoll)
Gianakos, Cristos
Gibran, Kahlil George
Gilmor, Jane E
Gitlin, Michael
Glasco, Joseph M
Glovsky, Alan
Golubic, Theodore
Gonzalez, Ronald
Gonzalez, Xavier
Goreniuc, Mircea C Paul
Goto, Joseph
Graham, Walter
Granlund, Paul Theodore
Gray, Jim
Green, David Oliver
Greene-Mercier, Marie Zoe
Greenleaf, Ken (Kenneth Lee)
Greeves, R V (Richard Vernon)
Gressel, Michael L
Grey, Alex V
Griffin, Chris A
Grillo, Esther Angela
Grippe, Peter
Grom, Bogdan
Grossman, Nancy
Grosvenor, Robert
Grove, Jean Donner
Haacke, Hans Christoph
Haber, Ira Joel
Hadfield, Ted Lee
Hadzi, Dimitri
Halkin, Theodore
Hamburger, Sydney K
Hamilton, Juan B
Hancock, Walker (Kirtland)
Hansen, James Lee
Haozous, Bob
Harries, Mags (Margaret L)
Harvey, (William) André
Hayward, Peter
Hedrick, Wally Bill
Helder, David Ernest
Heller, Pamela
Hendricks, Edward Lee
Hepper, Carol
Hera
Herard, Marvin T
Heric, John F
Hernandez, Sam (Samuel Rudolph)
Hewitt, Duncan Adams
Higgins, (George) Edward
Hinman, Charles B
Hobbs, (Carl) Fredric
Hoffmann, Gary David
Hogbin, Stephen
Hokanson, Hans
Holen, Norman Dean
Holt, Nancy Louise
Hormuth, Jo
Horn, Milton
Horne, (Arthur Edward) Cleeve
Hovsepian, Leon
Howard, Cecil Ray
Hoy, Harold H
Hubbard, Robert
Hudson, Robert H
Hughey, Kirk (John Kirk)
Hunt, Bryan
Hunter, Leonard LeGrande, III
Hurtig, Martin Russell
Hyams, Harriet
Ipousteguy, (Jean Robert)
Irwin, Robert
Italiano, Joán
Jackson, Sarah
Jacob, Ned
Jacquard
Jacques, Russell Kenneth
Jean-Louis, Don (Donald Charles)
Jellico, Nancy R
Jennings, Francis
Jensen, Leo (Vernon)
Johnson, Carla Rae
Jones, Ben
Jones, Carter R(uthven), Jr
Jones, Henry Wanton
Jordan, Jack
Jordan, John L (Gaudeamus)
Kahn, Ned M
Kaiser, Benjamin
Kaish, Luise
Kane, Margaret Brassler
Kaplan, Muriel
Karpel, Eli
Kassoy, Hortense
Kasuba, Aleksandra
Kaufman, Mico
Kaz, Nathaniel
Kearl, Stanley Brandon
Kelley, Donald William
Kelly, Ellsworth
Kennedy, James Edward
Keough, Jeffrey
Kessler, Alan
King, Ray
King, William Dickey
Kirk, Jerome
Kirschenbaum, Bernard Edwin
Kissel, William Thorn, Jr
Kleiman, Alan
Klein, Sandor C
Kline, Richard R
Klotz, Suzanne
Knapp, Tom
Knobler, Nathan
Knowles, Elizabeth
Koch, Edwin E
Koepnick, Robert Charles
Koras, George
Korman, Barbara
Kos, Paul Joseph
Koss, Gene H
Kostabi, Mark
Kowal, Dennis J
Kramer, Louise
Kratina, K George
Kravitz, Walter
Kreznar, Richard J
Krieger, Florence
Kujundzic, Zeljko D
Kurhajec, Joseph A
Kusama, Yayoi
Kuvshinoff, Bertha Horne
Kuvshinoff, Nicolai
Lafon, Dee J
Lamarre, Paul
Lamb, Darlis Carol
Langager, Craig T
LaPlantz, David
Laramée, Eve Andrée
Larsen, Patrick Heffner
Lauck, Anthony Joseph
Lawton, James L
Leeper, Doris Marie
Leeson, Tom
Leighton, Patricia MacInnes
LeRoy, Hugh Alexander
Lesher, Marie Palmisano
Leshyk, Tonie
Lesseps, Tauni de
Levine, Erik
Levine, Les
Levinson, Mon
Lewis, Glenn A
Liberi, Dante
Liberman, Alexander
Lichtenstein, Roy
Lieberman, Louis (Karl)
Liebowitz, Janet
Lijn, Liliane
Liles, Raeford Bailey
Linn, Steven Allen
Lintault, Roger Paul
Lionni, Leo
Lipman-Wulf, Peter
Lipofsky, Marvin B
Lipski, Donald G
Little, Ken Dawson
Litwin, Ruth Forbes
Lobello, Peter
Loeser, Thomas
Looney, Norman
Lorcini, Gino
Lorelli (Svoboda), Elvira Mae
Losavio, Samuel
Lothrop, Kristin Curtis
Love, Jim
Lucchesi, Bruno
Lyford, Cabot
Lyon, Robert F
McCarthy, Dennis
McCarthy, Kathleen
McCormick, Pam(ela Ann)
McCracken, John Harvey
McCracken, Philip
McCullough, David William
McDonnell, Joseph Anthony
McGowin, Ed (William Edward)
Machin, Roger
McManus, James William
McVey, William M
McWhorter, Elsie Jean
Madsen, Loren Wakefield
Magenta, Muriel
Magnan, Oscar Gustav
Maki, Robert Richard
Mallary, Robert W
Mandel, Howard
Manera, Enrico Orlando
Mansfield, Robert Adams
Manus, Jane Elizabeth
Margolies, Ethel Polacheck
Margulies, Isidore
Marioni, Paul
Marisol
Markle, Sam
Martin, Knox
Mason, Novem M
Matteson, Ira
Matthews, Harriett
Mazzone, Domenico
Meizner, Paula
Michaux, Henry Gaston
Milder, Jay
Miller, Brenda
Miller, Daniel Dawson
Miller, Richard McDermott
Milloff, Mark David
Mills, Agnes
Milonas, Minos
Minisci, Brenda (Eileen)
Mintich, Mary Ringelberg
Miralda, Antoni
Miss, Mary
Model, Elisabeth D
Molinari, Guido
Monaghan, William Scott
Monk, Nancy
Morgan, Arthur C
Moroni, Aldo Leonard, Jr
Morris, Robert
Moss, Joe (Francis)
Mundt, Ernest Karl
Murphy, Hass
Murray, Ian Stewart
Murrill, Gwynn
Myers, Forrest Warden
Myers, Legh
Myers, Martin
Nardin, Mario
Nasisse, Andy S
Naylor, John Geoffrey
Nelson, Carey Boone
Nelson, Jack D
Neubert, George Walter
Neuhaus, Max
Nevelson, Mike
Nguyen, Long
Nickford, Juan
Nicodemus, Chester Roland
Nix, Patricia (Lea)
Noel, Donald Claude
Nong
Nordin, Phyllis E
Norvell, Patsy
Oakes, William Larry
Ocvirk, Otto G
Oppenheim, Dennis A
Orensanz, Angel L
Ortlieb, Robert Eugene
Ortman, George Earl
Osze, Andrew E
Oubre, Hayward Louis
Padovano, Anthony John
Palmer, A Laure
Paradise, Phil (Herschel)
Parsons, David Goode
Parton, Ralf
Pas, Gerard Peter
Pasinski, Irene
Patkin, Izhar
Patmagrian, Ethelia M
Patterson, Clayton Ian
Payne, John D
Pearson, James Eugene
Peck, Judith
Peii, Ahmad Osni
Pekar, Ronald Walter
Perez, Celis
Peterson, Kristin
Pfaffman, William Scott
Phillips, Helen (Elizabeth)
Phillips, Michael
Pierce, Danny P
Pineda, Marianna
Pitynski, Andrzej P
Pollack, Reginald Murray
Popinsky, Arnold Dave
Post, Anne B
Prince, Richard Edmund
Pruitt, Lynn
Puryear, Martin
Quasius, Sharron G
Quinn, Brian Grant
Quisgard, Liz Whitney
Rabinowitch, David
Rabinowitch, Royden Leslie
Raimondi, John
Ratkai, George
Raymond, Evelyn L
Rebbeck, Lester James, Jr
Reber, Mick
Reiss, Roland
Remsing, (Joseph) Gary
Renee, Lisabeth

SCULPTOR (cont)

Rhodes, James Melvin
Richenburg, Robert Bartlett
Risley, John Hollister
Robbins, Bruce
Roberts, Gilroy
Roberts, Steven K
Rocco, Ron (Ronald Anthony Rocco)
Rocklin, Raymond
Rogers, John H
Romans, Van Anthony
Rosen, Annabeth
Rosenberg, Herb
Ross, Charles
Ross, Douglas Allan
Roster, Fred Howard
Rotan, Walter
Ruby, Laura
Rush, Andrew
Rust, Edwin C
Saar, Alison M
Sacanga, Italo
Sade, Shuli
St Maur, Kirk (Kirk Seymour McReynolds)
Sakaoka, Yasue
Samaras, Lucas
Samuels, Gerald
Sasaki, Toshio
Saxe, Henry, OC
Scarpitta, Salvatore
Schaefer, Gail
Schlemowitz, Abram
Schmidt, Arnold Alfred
Schmutzhart, Berthold Josef
Schmutzhart, Slaithong Chengtrakul
Schneider, Noel
Scholder, Fritz
Schrero, Ruth Lieberman
Schultz, Saunders
Searles, Stephen
Sebastian, Jill C
Sebelius, Helen
Segal, George
Seplowin, Charles Joseph
Serra, Richard
Serra, Rudy
Sewell, Leo
Shaw, Richard Blake
Sheehan, Maura A
Sherbell, Rhoda
Sherrill, Milton Lewis
Shoop, Wally (William Walter)
Shorney, Margo Kay (McIver)
Siler, Todd (Lael)
Simkin, Phillips M
Simon, Sidney
Simonds, Charles Frederick
Sinnard, Elaine (Janice)
Skurkis, Barry A
Smith, John Ivor
Smith, Lawson Wentworth
Soleri, Paolo
Sonnenberg, Frances
Squier, Jack Leslie
Squires, Norma Jean
Stark, George King
Stein, Ronald Jay
Steiner, Michael
Stelzer, Michael Norman
Sterritt, Coleen
Stevanov, Zoran
Stokes, Louis (Walter)
Stout, Frank J
Straight, Elsie H
Strawn, Jarrett W (Jason)
Strawn, Melvin Nicholas
Struppeck, Jules
Sturman, Eugene
Sturtevant, E
Stussy, Maxine Kim
Sugarman, George
Sullivan, R(onald Dee)
Sunderland, Nita Kathleen
Sussman, Gary Lawrence
Suzuki, Taro
Svenson, John Edward
Tajiri, Shinkichi
Tangredi, Vincent
Tatti, Benedict Michael
Taylor, Al C
Taylor, Bill (William Bradley)
Taysom, Wayne Pendelton
Teraoka, Masami
Thea, Carolee B
Tinsley, Barry
Tobias, Abraham Joel
Tobias, Robert Paul
Tolpo, Vincent Carl
Torres, Francesc
Tracy, Michael
Trakas, George
Trakis, Louis
Treister, Kenneth
Trotman, Bob
Trova, Ernest Tino
Tsai, Hsiao Hsia
Tucker, William G
Turner, James Thomas, Sr
Turner, Ralph James
Ukeles, Mierle Laderman
Unger, Mary Ann
Unithan, Dolly
Urso, Leonard A
Utz, Thornton
Vaillancourt, Armand
Valentine, DeWain
Vallila, Marja R
Van Loen, Alfred
Van Sant, Tom R
Van Winkle, Lester G
Varga, Ferenc
Villinski, Paul
Viner, Frank Lincoln
Visco, Anthony Salvatore
Volkersz, Willem
Voulkos, Peter
Wahling, Jon B
Walch, John Leo
Walker, Herbert Brooks
Wanlass, Stanley Glen
Weill, Erna
Weinberg, Elbert
Weiner, Lawrence Charles
Weinman, Robert Alexander
Weiss, Harvey
Weschler, Anita
Weyhe, Arthur
Wheelwright, Joseph Storer
White, Robert (Winthrop)
Whiten, Tim
Whittome, Irene F
Wiener, Sam (Evangeline Tabasco)
Willis, Jay Stewart
Willson, Margaret (Bosshardt) Pace
Wilson, Douglas Fenn
Wilson, Edward N
Wilson, Nicholas Jon
Wingate, Arline (Hollander)
Winsor, Jacque
Witold-K (Kaczanowski),
Wolfe, Ann (Ann Wolfe Graubard)
Woodham, Derrick James
Woody, (Thomas) Howard
Worth, Karen
Worth, Peter John
Yanish, Elizabeth
Yes, Phyllis A
Young, Joseph Louis
Zack, Badanna Bernice
Zahourek, Jon Gail
Zajac, Jack
Zelenak, Edward John
Zimmerman, Elyn
Zito, Joseph (Phillip)
Zucker, Barbara M
Zurik, Jesselyn Benson
Zwick, Rosemary G

Clay

Acosta, Manuel Gregorio
Alquilar, Maria
Baney, Vera
Bermudez, Luis A
Blake, Jane
Bova, Joe
Breen, Harry Frederick, Jr
Breschi, Karen Lee
Breslin, Wynn
Brodie, Regis Conrad
Bronson, Clark Everice
Bryant, Olen L
Bugbee-Jackson, Joan (Mrs John M Jackson)
Buonagurio, Toby Lee
Caplan, Jerry L
Carr, Sally Swan
Caswell, Jim (James Daniel Caswell-Davis)
Caver, William Ralph
Chalke, John
Chamberlin, Scott
Chappelle, Jerry Leon
Chavez, Joseph Arnold
Citron, Harvey Lewis
Conover, Claude
Cornell, David E
Costanza, John Joseph
Cronbach, Robert M
Culbreth, Carl R
Dalglish, Meredith Rennels
De Castro, Lorraine
De Fazio, John
Dennett, Lissy W
Donhauser, Paul Stefan
Dyyon, Frazier
Eardley, Cynthia
Eino
Everhart, Don, II
Federighi, Christine M
Fellows, Fred
Ferreira, Armando Thomas
Fleming, Frank
Fondaw, Ron
Funk, Verne J
Furman, David Stephen
Gagnier, Bruce
Gaylord, Frank Chalfant, II
Gernhardt, Henry Kendall
Gilhooly, David James, III
Girard, Bill
Glover, Robert
Goldfine, Beatrice
Gonzalez, Arthur Padilla
Gould, Stephen
Grabel, Susan
Grasso, Doris (Ten-Eyck)
Graves, Bradford
Gray, Elise N
Grygutis, Barbara
Halko, Joe
Hammond, Phyllis Baker
Hanson, J B
Havens, Jan
Hay, Dick
Hempler, Orval F
Higby, (Donald) Wayne
Hodgell, Robert Overman
Hofsted, Jolyon Gene
Hood, Dorothy
Houston, Mary Etta (King)
Huntoon, Abby E
Jacobson, Yolande (Mrs J Craig Sheppard)
Jeck, Douglas A
Jones, Michael Butler
Jonsson, Ted (Wilbur)
Kaufman, Loretta Ana
Kertzer, Anita Elizabeth
Knowlton, Grace Farrar
Kochman, Alexandra D
Krumholt, Ann
Kwong, Eva
Laird, E Ruth
Larsen, D Dane
Lay, Patricia Anne
Lee, Dora Fugh
Lerman, Ora
Levine, Marilyn Anne
Lewis, Carole
Lighton, Linda
London, Anna
Lopez, Rhoda Le Blanc
Ludwig, Eva
Luisi, Jerry
MacClintock, Dorcas
MacDougall, Peter Steven
McGarry, Patricia Josephine
Mann, Jean (Adah)
Mason, John
Massaro, Karen Thuesen
Matyas, Diane C
Mavros, Donald Odysseus
Mayer, Billy (William Robert Mayer)
Mayeri, Beverly
Melchert, James Frederick
Mercolino, Veronica Florence
Mignosa, Santo
Milnes, Robert Winston
Moonelis, Judith C
Moquin, Richard Attilio
Mueller, Trude
Muir, Emily Lansingh
Nadel, Ann Honig
Natzler, Otto
Nicholas, Donna Lee
Nieto, John W
Notkin, Richard T
Olsen, Frederick L
Owens, Mary (Mary Louise Schnore)
Pearson, Clifton
Penny, Donald Charles
Piepenburg, Robert
Prange, Sally Bowen
Rady, Elsa
Raskind, Philis
Redd Ekks (Robert Norman Rasmussen)
Reinertson, Lisa
Rippon, Ruth Margaret
Rippon, Thomas Micheal
Rosen, Hy (Hyman Joseph)
Rosenblatt, Adolph
Rosenthal, Rachel
Rush, Deborah
Schietinger, James Frederick
Schlanger, Jeff
Scott, B Nibbelink (Barbara Gae Scott)
Selsor, Marcia Lorraine
Selvin, Nancy
Shannonhouse, Sandra
Simon, Jewel Woodard
Sires, Jonathan
Smith, Anne L
Smith, Gary
Soldner, Paul Edmund
Spampinato, Clemente
Spinosa, Gary Paul
Spinski, Victor
Sprang, Elizabeth
Stewart, Bill
Strassberg, Roy I
Strong, Leslie (Leslie Strong Sutter)
Stull, Robert J
Stussy, Maxine Kim
Sundin, Adelaide Toombs
Swanson, J N
Swetcharnik, Sara Morris
Takemoto, Henry Tadaaki
Taylor, Rosemary
Termini, Christine
Tornheim, Norman
Townsend, Storm D
Turlington, Patricia R
Unterseher, Chris Christian
Vanden Berge, Peter Willem
Wallace, Elizabeth S
Waterston, Harry Clement
Wilmeth, Ernest, II

SCULPTOR (cont)
Wilson, Melissa Anne
Wu, Linda Yee Chau
Young, Robert S W
Zakin, Mikhail
Zed, Aggie
Zheutlin, Dale R

Metal, Cast

Abdell, Douglas
Adams, Alice
Adelman, Bunny
Ake, John
Albert, Calvin
Allen, Tom, Jr
Amaya, Armando
Anthony, Peter
Arman
Aronson, David
Atkinson, Leslie Jane
Bacigalupa, Andrea
Baney, Ralph Ramoutar
Bannister, Pati (Patricia Brown Bannister)
Bascom, Earl W
Beasley, Bruce
Bergen, John Axel von
Bermudez, Jose Ygnacio
Blair, Helen
Blum, Helaine Dorothy
Born, James E
Bostelle, Thomas (Theodore)
Breinin, Raymond
Breitenbach, William John
Bright, Barney
Bronson, Clark Everice
Brookner, Jackie
Burns, Stan
Cantini, Virgil D
Carlson, George Arthur
Casida, Kati
Chase-Riboud, Barbara
Chemeche, George
Citron, Harvey Lewis
Clague, John Rogers
Cleary, Fritz
Clough, Eleanor
Colpacci, Viorica
Cook, John (Alfred)
Copenhaver-Fellows, Deborah (Deborah Lynne Fellows)
Coughlin, Jack
Daly, Stephen Jeffrey
Daudelin, Charles
Dorrien, Carlos Guillermo
Downs, Douglas Walker
Drapell, Joseph
Duca, Alfred Milton
Duhme, H Richard, Jr
Du Pen, Everett George
Duveen, Anneta
Eardley, Cynthia
Eino
Eloul, Kosso
Eriksen, Gary
Farrow, Patrick Villiers
Fenci, Renzo
Ferrari, Virginio Luig
Ferrell, Catherine (Klemann)
Filipovic, Augustin
Fix, John Robert
Flanagan, Barry
Fleming, Frank
Forrester, Charles Howard
Fox, Lincoln H
Gagnon, Charles Eugene
Geffert, Harry
Giambertone, Paul
Gibbs, Tom
Gillespie, Dorothy Muriel
Girard, Bill
Glasser, Norma Penchansky
Goldner, Janet
Gonzalez, Arthur Padilla
Goodacre, Glenna
Gordon, Tina
Gore, Samuel Marshall
Grausman, Philip
Gray, Cleve
Greenamyer, George Mossman
Greer, John Sydney
Halahmy, Oded
Hampton, John W
Hansen, James Lee
Harrington, Chestee Marie
Harrison, Carole
Hartley, W Douglas
Harvey, (William) André
Haskin, Donald Marcus
Hayes, David Vincent
Hollingshead, Joe Edgar
Holschuh, (George) Fred
Hoover, John Jay
Hunt, Richard Howard
Huntington, Jim
Jackson, Harry Andrew
Jacobson, Yolande (Mrs J Craig Sheppard)
Jae
Jeynes, Paul
Johnson, J Seward, Jr
Johnston, Barry Woods
Jones, Elizabeth A B (Mrs Ludwig Glaeser)
Kaskey, Raymond John
Katz, Eunice
Kepalas (Elena Kepalaite)
Kimmelman, Harold
Knapp, Sadie Magnet
Koenig, Elizabeth
Koras, George
Kraczkowski, Phil
Kramer, Reuben
La Bobgäh, Robert Gordon
La Malfa, James Thomas
Langland, Tuck
Lee, Robert M
Lekberg, Barbara Hult
Lewis, Carole
Lindsay, Arturo
Linn, Steven Allen
Lippold, Richard
Longley, Bernique
Lubbers, Leland Eugene
Ludtke, Lawrence Monroe
McGeehan, Betty
MacNelly, Jeffrey Kenneth
Maree, Wendy P
Marinsky, Harry
Marsh, Thomas A
Martin, Bill
Mavroudis, Demetrios
Mayhew, Elza
Meadmore, Clement L
Medrich, Libby E
Meyer, Seymour W
Meyers, Francis Joseph
Michie, Mary
Miller, Richard McDermott
Mirtala
Morcos, Maher N
Morin, Thomas Edward
Moyers, William
Muccioli, Anna Maria
Myford, James C
Nadel, Ann Honig
Nama, George Allen
Naranjo, Michael Alfred
Nardi, Dann
Neidhardt, Carl Richard
Nelson, Carey Boone
Nesbitt, Lowell (Blair)
Newmark, Marilyn (Marilyn Newmark Meiselman)
Noland, William
Offner, Elliot
Olson, Gene Russel
Orduno, Robert Daniel
Ottiano, John William
Oxman, Mark
Palumbo, Jacques
Paterson, Anthony R
Pera, Isabella
Perless, Robert
Piet, John Frances
Pinsker, Essie
Polk, Frank Fredrick
Porta, Siena Gillann
Price, Michael Benjamin
Prip, Janet
Recanati, Dina
Reiland, Lowell Keith
Rice, Anthony Hopkins
Richter, Hank
Rosenblum, Richard Stephen
Rozzi (James A)
Rubin, Donald Vincent
Sabo, Betty Jean
Sauls, Frederick Inabinette
Saylors, Jo An
Schlam, Murray J
Schmidt, Julius
Schon, Nancy Quint
Schonwalter, Jean Frances
Schweiss, Ruth Keller
Scott, C(harles) A(rthur)
Scott, Sandy (Sandra Lynn)
Scriver, (Bob) Robert Macfie
Sebastian
Shapiro, Joel (Elias)
Shaw, Isabel
Shearer, Rhonda Roland
Sheppard, Joseph Sherly
Silvertooth, Dennis Carl
Simon, Helene
Sing Hoo
Slavin, Arlene
Slivka, David
Smith, Kent Alvin
Snidow, Gordon E
Snyder, Ruth (Cozen)
Spampinato, Clemente
Speed, (Ulysses) Grant
Storm, Mark (Kennedy)
Strong, Brett-Livingstone
Stubbs, Lu
Suttman, Paul
Swergold, Marcelle M
Talaba, L (Linda Talaba Cummens)
Tamburine, Jean Helen
Taylor, Joseph Richard
Tempest, Gerard Francis
Terken, John
Torcoletti, Enzo
Toscano, (Dolores A)
Trudeau, Yves
Tye, William Roy
Ullberg, Kent
Underhill, William
Urbaitis, Elena
Valdez, Vincent E
Ventimiglia, John Thomas
Vielehr, William Ralph
Vivot, Lea (Lea Drahomira Vivot-Fishman)
Wagoner, Robert B
Wardlaw, George Melvin
Wesselmann, Tom
White, Bruce Hilding
Williams, Chester Lee
Williams, Wayne Francis
Williford, Hollis R
Wilson, John
Wilson, Melissa Anne
Wood, Marcia Joan
Woodman, Timothy
Wyatt, Greg Alan
Yaros, Constance G
Zacha, William
Zaikine, Zak (Victor Eugene)
Zivic, William Thomas
Zucker, Murray Harvey

Metal, Precious

Anderson, Bruce A
Bennett, Jamie
Boggs, Mayo Mac
Dial, Gail
Frudakis, Gerd Hesness
Herschler, David Elijah
Klavans, Minnie
Kraczkowski, Phil
Manhold, John Henry
Manship, John Paul
Marton, Tutzi
Prestini, James Libero
Rubin, Donald Vincent
Safer, John
Sebastian
Sehring, Adolf
Steider, Doris (Mrs C B McCampbell)
Tovish, Harold

Metal, Welded

Allain, René Pierre
Anderson, David Paul
Baer, Rod
Balderacchi, Arthur Eugene
Balossi, John
Barr, Roger
Barrett, Bill
Beal, Mack
Benton, Suzanne E
Bertoia, (Mr) Val (Bertoia Studio)
Bigger, Michael D
Bolomey, Roger Henry
Bottini, David M
Bowie, William
Brown, Carol K
Brown, David Lee
Brubaker, Jack
Buchanan, Sidney Arnold
Buchman, James Wallace
Burt, David Sill
Capps, Kenneth P
Cariola, Robert J
Censor, Therese
Chase, Allan (Seamans)
Chase, Jack S(paulding)
Clark, Nancy Kissel
Clark, William Roger
Colpacci, Viorica
Crouch, Ned Philbrick
Daudelin, Charles
Davy, Woods
DeAngelis, Joseph Rocco
De Guatemala, Joyce (Joyce Bush Vourvoulias)
Dhaemers, Robert August
D'Innocenzo, Nick
Dirks, John
Dunbar, Michael Austin
Eisner, Carole Swid
Ellison, Robert W
Eversley, Frederick John
Farrow, Patrick Villiers
Feldman, Bella
Feldman, Roger Lawrence
Ferrari, Virginio Luig
Fisher, James Donald
Fletcher, Leland Vernon
Frazier, Paul D
Friedberg, Richard S
Gersh, Bill
Giambertone, Paul
Gibbs, Tom
Ginnever, Charles
Goldner, Janet
Grady, Ruby McLain
Grossberg, Jake
Gruber, Aaronel deRoy
Gussow, Roy
Halegua, Alfredo
Hall, Michael David
Haozous, Bob
Harrington, William Charles

SCULPTOR (cont)

Harrison, Carole
Hatchett, Duayne
Hayes, David Vincent
Henry, John Raymond
Herbert, April H
Herschler, David Elijah
Hide, Peter Nicholas
Ihara, Michio
Indiana, Robert
Inukai, Kyohei
Israel, David N
Jacobs, David (Theodore)
Jennings, Francis
Jensen, Clay Easton
Jonsson, Ted (Wilbur)
Kaplan, Penny
Kapsalis, Thomas Harry
Katzen, Lila (Pell)
Kemble, Richard
Kimmelman, Harold
Kington, L(ouis) Brent
Kupferman, Murray
Lekberg, Barbara Hult
Logan, Gene Adams
Lowe, J Michael
Loyd, Jan Brooks
Luecking, Stephen Joseph
Lupori, Peter John
McConnell, Michael Patrick
MacGaw, Wendy
Mahdavi, Rafael Sinclair
Malpass, Michael Allen
Manus, Jane Elizabeth
Mark, Phyllis
Markusen, Thomas Roy
Mason, Molly Ann
Mayer, Billy (William Robert Mayer)
Meadmore, Clement L
Meizner, Paula
Murray, Robert (Gray)
Nisula, Larry
Noland, William
Olson, Gene Russel
Outterbridge, John Wilfred
Peart, Jerry Linn
Pepper, Beverly
Perless, Robert
Perlman, Joel Leonard
Perry, Charles O
Perry, Frank
Pfeiffer, Werner Bernhard
Piepenburg, Robert
Pomeroy, Lyndon Fayne
Porter, (Edwin) David
Power, S Brenda Joan
Putnam, Nol (Oliver de Montalant)
Ragland, Bob
Rand, Steven Jay
Ray, Christopher T
Reginato, Peter
Rhoden, John W
Rich, Frances L
Rickey, George W
Riegel, Michael Byron
Riveron, Enrique
Roesch, Robert Arthur
Rosenthal, Tony (Bernard)
Saganic, Livio Michele
Salomon, Lawrence
Schlam, Murray J
Schleeh, Hans Martin
Schreiber, Martin
Schwebel, Renata Manasse
Sellers, William Freeman
Shaw, Ernest Carl
Shimoda, Osamu
Shostak, Ed (Edwin Bennett)
Silverman, Sherley C
Simon, Herbert Bernheimer
Slater, Gary Lee
Slusky, Joseph
Smalley, David Allan
Smokler, Stanley B
Snelson, Kenneth D
Stauffer, Richard L
Steen, Carol J
Stern, Jan Peter
Sutter, James Stewart
Tardo, (Manuel) Rodulfo
Tatro, Ronald Edward
Terris, Albert
Todd, Michael Cullen
Trudeau, Yves
Tsutakawa, George
Ubogy, Jo
Udinotti, Agnese
Vaccarino, Robin
Van Alstine, John Richard
Van de Bovenkamp, Hans
Venet, Bernar
Walburg, Gerald
Wall, Brian
Walsh, James
Warsinske, Norman George
Williams, Chester Lee
Williams, Wayne Francis
Witkin, Isaac
Witt, Nancy Camden
Woitena, Ben S
Wolfe, James
Wood, Marcia Joan
Woodham, Jean
Zeller, Frederic

Miscellaneous Media

Abeles, Kim Victoria
Abrams, Edith Lillian
Adams, Alice
Akins, Future Renée
Alford, Gloria K
Allman, Margo
Alpert, Bill (William H)
Anderson, James P
Anderson, Kenneth Edmund
Anderson, Mark Robert
Anthonisen, George Rioch
Antonakos, Stephen
Appel, Keith Kenneth
Artemis, Maria (Maria Artemis Papageorge Sawyer)
Artschwager, Richard Ernst
Aycock, Alice
Baer, Rod
Bailey, Barry Stone
Bailey, Clayton George
Bakaty, Mike
Baldwin, Harold Fletcher
Ball, Lillian
Banerjee, (Bimal)
Barr, David John
Bell, Larry Stuart
Benes, Barton Lidice
Ben Tre, Howard B
Berge, Henry
Berhang, Mattie
Bernstein, Gerda Meyer
Bickley, Gary Steven
Bigger, Michael D
Bills, Linda
Bisgyer, Barbara G (Cohn)
Bishop, Ben
Blum, Andrea
Bogle, Jon
Booth, Robert Alan
Bowen, Paul
Bradley, David P(aul)
Brady, Robert D
Braitstein, Marcel
Brams, Joan
Braverman, Donna (Donna Braverman Knopf)
Breder, Hans Dieter
Brewster, Michael
Brito, Maria
Burr, Horace
Byars, Donna
Cable, Maxine Roth
Campoli, Cosmo
Cano, Pablo D
Carmichael, Jae
Carpenter, Linda Buck
Carter, Sam John
Casey, John Thayer
Catlett, Elizabeth
Chase, Jack S(paulding)
Chief Eagle, Charles Lince
Cicansky, Victor
Clague, John Rogers
Clifton, Michelle Gamm
Cohen, Adele
Colette
Cowan, Aileen Hooper
Creecy, Herbert Lee
Crow, Carol (Wilson)
Cunningham, J
Curmano, Billy
Curtis, Robert D
Dailey, Dan (Daniel Owen)
Daphnis, Nassos
Daugherty, Michael F
Davis, David Ensos
Dean, Nat(alie Carol)
Decter, Betty Eva
Dell, Robert Christopher
Deming, David Lawson
De Palma, Brett
De Ricco, Hank
Deutsch, Richard
Di Meo, Dominick
Ditzion, Grace
Dodge, Robert G
Douglas, Tom Howard
Dowd, Jack
Dowd, Robert (O'Dowd Robert)
Duff, John Ewing
Dunham-Griggs, Margaret
Dunigan, Breon Nina
Dyens, Georges Maurice
Eisenberg, Marc S
Eldredge, Mary Agnes
Elliott, Anne
Estern, Neil
Evans, Robert Graves
Falkenstein, Claire
Ferguson, Kathleen Elizabeth
Ferrer, Rafael
Feuerman, Carol Jeannne
Fink, Ray (Raymond Russell)
Finke, Leonda Froelich
Fisher, Rob (Robert Norman)
Fleming, Thomas Michael
Floeter, Kent
Fornelli, Joseph
Forrestall, Thomas De Vany
Freeman-Appelbaum, Margery
Frey, Viola
Friedlaender, Bilge
Froman, Ann
Frudakis, Evangelos William
Fuller, Mary (Mary Fuller McChesney)
Fyfe, Jo Suzanne (Storch)
Galen, Elaine
Gellis, Sandy L
Geltner, Danita Sue
Gianakos, Steve
Gibbs, Y Gale
Gilbert, Sharon
Gillingwater, Denis Claude
Giobbi, Edward Gioachino
Giro, R (R Gironda)
Glaser, David
Glashausser, Suellen
Glasson, Lloyd
Glatt, Linnea
Goff, Thomas Jefferson
Gold, Martha B
Goldstein, Daniel Joshua
Goodridge, Lawrence Wayne
Gordin, Sidney
Gordon, John S
Gorski, Daniel Alexander
Graham, Robert
Grashow, James Bruce
Grauer, Sherry
Graves, Ka (Kathleen Rose)
Graves, Nancy Stevenson
Green, Tom
Gregoire, Mathieu A
Groedel, Burt Jay
Gross, Alice
Gunderson, Barry L
Gutkin, Peter
Habenicht, Wenda
Hacklin, Allan Dave
Hague, Raoul
Hale, Nathan Cabot
Halegua, Alfredo
Halvorsen, Elspeth Colette (Elspeth Halvorsen-Vevers)
Hammond, Harmony
Hamrol, Lloyd
Hanson, Jo
Hardy, Thomas (Austin)
Hare, David
Harris, Paul
Harvey, Dermot
Harvey, Donald Gilbert
Hauft, Amy
Havel, Joseph G
Healy, Anne Laura
Hebald, Milton Elting
Helman, Phoebe
Henes, Donna
Henselmann, Caspar
Hildebrandt, William Albert
Hill, Robin
Hoare, Tyler James
Hobbs, Joe Ferrell
Hooks, Earl J
Horn, Roni
Housewright, Artemis Skevakis
Houston, James A
Howard, Linda
Howard, Robert A
Huff, Robert
Hurst, Ralph N
Indick, Janet
Ingham, Tom (Edgar)
Jacobs, Harold
James, Catti
Jarrard-Dimond, Terry
Jendrzejewski, Andrew John
J J (De La Verriére)
Johnston, Richard M
Jones, David Lee
Jones, Lou (Mary Louise Humpton)
Jones & Ginzel,
Jorgensen, Roger M
Joyce, J David
Jursevskis, Zigfrids
Justis, Gary (Allen)
Kangas, Gene
Kawecki, Jean Mary
Kearney, John (W)
Kearns, James Joseph
Keister, Steve (Stephen Lee)
Kellar, Jeff
Kelman, Maureen (S)
Kemp, Paul Zane
Kipp, Lyman
Kisch, Gloria
Kleinberg, Susan
Knobler, Lois Jean
Kober, Alfred John
Kolisnyk, Peter
Koni, Nicolaus
Kramer, Linda Lewis
Kramer, Reuben
Krebs, Rockne
Krentzin, Earl
Kuehn, Gary
Lable, Eliot
Lane, Rosemary Louise
Lasch, Pat
Lassaw, Ibram
Lauridsen, Hanne H7L
Lawrence, Jaye A
Lawrence, Les

SCULPTOR (cont)
Layne, Barbara J
Lea, Laurie Jane
Lehman, Mark Ammon
Leibert, Peter R
Leon, Dennis
Leopold, Susan
Lerman, Doris (Harriet)
Lewis, John Conard
Lewis, Mary
Lin, Maya Y
Lipson, Goldie
Littleton, Harvey K
Livingstone, Joan
Logan, David George
Look, Dona
Lothrop, Kristin Curtis
Lutz, Winifred Ann
Lynds, Clyde
Macaulay, Thomas S
McClure, Thomas F
McCollum, Allan
McGeehan, Betty
Mack, Rodger Allen
McMillen, Michael C(halmers)
McNealy, Robert
Mac Whinnie, John Vincent
Mahlke, Ernest D
Manspeizer, Susan R
Margolis, David
Markle, Jack M
Marozzi, Eli Raphael
Marzollo, Claudio
Mayer, Edward Albert
Medel, Rebecca Rosalie
Meneeley, Edward
Messersmith, Harry Lee
Metzger, Evelyn Borchard
Meyer, Seymour W
Michaels, Glen
Michaels-Paque, J
Midener, Walter
Min, Yong Soon
Minisci, Brenda (Eileen)
Minkowitz, Norma
Miralda, Antoni
Morehouse, William Paul
Moyer, Marina Pavlova
Mulcahy, Kathleen
Muno, Richard Carl
Myatt, Greely
Nardi, Dann
Nauman, Bruce
Neal, Irene
Nellis, Jennifred Gene
Nelson, Ruth Basha (Basha Ruth Nelson)
Neri, Manuel
Newman, Richard Charles
Nicholson, Natasha
Nickerson, John Henry
Niedzialek, Terry
Noe, Jerry Lee
Ohe, Katie (Minna)
Okulick, John A
Oldenburg, Claes Thure
Olitski, Jules
Omwake, Eo, Jr
Orentlicher, John
O'Shea, Terrence Patrick
Pardington, Ralph Arthur
Parks, Charles Cropper
Partridge, David Gerry
Patterson, Curtis Ray
Patti, Tom
Pattison, Abbott
Pfaff, Judy
Piene, Otto
Pittman, Irene K
Powell, Gordon
Pracko, Bernard F, II
Prent, Mark
Price, Kenneth
Prince, Arnold
Rabinovich, Raquel
Reiback, Earl M
Reibel, Bertram
Reif, (F) David
Reimann, William P
Renouf, Edward
Reynolds, Richard (Henry)
Reynolds, Stephen Francis
Ridley, Gregory D, Jr
Ringgold, Faith
Rivers, Victoria Z
Robinson, Margot (Margot Steigman)
Robles, Julian
Rochette, Anne Monique
Rohm, Robert
Roller, Marion Bender
Romano, Salvatore Michael
Rose, Robin Carlise
Rose, Thomas Albert
Rosen, Carol M
Rosse, Maryvonne
Rothschild, Amalie (Rosenfeld)
Roukes, Nicholas M
Rousseau, Irene Victoria
Rowe, Reginald M
Rubylee, (Charles Armstrong Littler)
Russin, Robert I
Rutsch, Alexander
Rutzky, Ivy Sky
Ryden, Kenneth Glenn
Saari, Peter H
Saarinen, Lilian
Saito, Seiji
Salemme, Antonio
Saltzman, William
Sanabria, Robert
Sandback, Frederick Lane
Sandman, Alan
Sandman, Jo
Sankowsky, Itzhak
Sauer, Jane Gottlieb
Savoy, Chyrl Lenore
Saxe, Henry, OC
Scalise, Nicholas Peter
Schaffer, Debra S
Schlitter, Helga
Schmidt, Randall Bernard
Schreck, Michael H
Schreckengost, Viktor
Schule, Donald Kenneth
Schwarz, Judith
Scott, C(harles) A(rthur)
Scott, Campbell
Scott, John Tarrell
Seamans, Beverly Benson
Seiden, Katie
Selchow, Roger Hoffman
Seyle, Robert Harley
Shaddle, Alice
Shaw, Donald Edward
Shea, Judith
Shelton, Peter T
Sherman, Sarai
Simone (Mildred Simonson),
Sina, Alejandro
Smedley, Geoffrey
Snyder, Dan
Snyder, Hills
Snyder, Kit-Yin
Sonenberg, Jack
Spira, Bill
Sproat, Christopher Townsend
Steinbach, Haim
Stephen, Francis B
Stephenson, John H
Stone, Sylvia
Streeter, Tal
Streett, Tylden Westcott
Strider, Marjorie Virginia
Stuart, Michelle
Stuhl, Michelle
Swartzman, Roslyn
Tabak, Chaim
Thibert, Patrick A
Thomas, Kathleen K
Thornley, Wendy Ann
Thorpe, Hilda (Shapiro)
Thurmer, Robert
Tiemann, Robert E
Tobias, Julius
Tousignant, Claude
Townley, Hugh
Tuck, Norman Victor
Turrell, James Archie
Umlauf, Charles
Urso, Josette Marie
Valdez, Vincent E
Van Aalten, Jacques
Vega, Edward
Venable, Susan C
Vidal, Francisco Fernandez
Vodicka, Ruth Kessler
Volkin, Hilda Appel
Von Rydingsvard, Ursula
Waddell, John Henry
Wade, Robert Schrope
Wald, Sylvia
Wallin, Lawrence Bier
Warburg, Stephanie Wenner
Weaver, John Barney
Weinbaum, Jean
Welch, Charles D
Wells, Carol Menthe
Westerlund Roosen, Mia (Maria Eludia)
Westfall, Carol D
White, James Richard
White, Karen J
White, Stuart James
Whiten, Colette
Whitney, Maynard Merle
Wilke, Hannah
Willenbecher, John
Williams, Abigail S
Williams, Janice E
Willson, Robert
Wilson, Warren Bingham
Wimmer, Gayle
Wong, Paul Kan
Wood, McCrystle
Wood, Nicholas Wheeler
Woods, Gurdon
Young, Nancy J(eanne)
Zaima, Stephen Gyo
Zeidenbergs, Olafs
Zeitlin, Harriet
Zeller, Frederic
Zollweg, Aileen Boules

Plastic

Adamy, George E
Breed, Charles Ayars
Coit, M B
Dignac, Geny
Eversley, Frederick John
Farhi, Jean Claude
Fox, Michael David
Franklin, Hannah
Fuerst, Shirley Miller
Fuller, Sue
Gilhooly, David James, III
Hanson, Duane
Hausman, Fred S
Houskeeper, Barbara
Jaffe, Nora
Jimenez, Luis Alfonso, Jr
Kauffman, Robert Craig
Kern, Arthur (Edward)
Koscielny, Margaret
Kostyniuk, Ronald P
Lamis, Leroy
Levee, John H
Medrich, Libby E
Miles, Jeanne Patterson
Moquin, Richard Attilio
Neill, Joe
Pashgian, M Helen
Pera, Isabella
Porta, Siena Gillann
Redinger, Walter Fred
Sarnoff, Lolo
Setlow, Neva C
Shipley, Roger Douglas
Shute, Roberta E
Smith, Susan Carlton
Staprans, Raimonds
Swergold, Marcelle M
Truitt, Anne (Dean)
Umlauf, Karl A
Van Leunen, Alice Louise
Vasa, (Velizar Mihich)
Waitzkin, Stella
Weedman, Kenneth Russell
White, Norman Triplett
Zammitt, Norman

Stone

Allmond, Charles (M)
Anson, Lesia
Armstrong, Jane Botsford
Arye, Leonora E
Bailey, Richard H
Bates, Gladys Edgerly
Beasley, Bruce
Bender, Beverly Sterl
Borgatta, Robert Edward
Brennan, Nizette
Brown, Edith Rae
Brumer, Shulamith
Buchman, James Wallace
Caponi, Anthony
Cave, Leonard Edward
Chaddlesone, Sherman
Chinni, Peter Anthony
Colman, Virginia O'Connell
De Coux, Janet
Dennett, Lissy W
Diska, (P)
Dorrien, Carlos Guillermo
Ferrell, Catherine (Klemann)
Fox, Lincoln H
Geist, Sidney
Gilkey, Richard Charles
Gonzales, Carlotta (Mrs Richard Lahey)
Goo, Benjamin
Goulet, Lorrie
Greer, John Sydney
Gresser, Seymour Gerald
Gummer, Don
Henry, John Raymond
Hilts, Alvin
Hofmann, Kay
Holsch, Robert Fred
Houser, Allan C
Huntington, Jim
Jones, Carter R(uthven), Jr
Kenojuak (Ashevak)
Knoebel, David Jon
Koenig, Elizabeth
Koldorf, Irene Janet
Lewis, Stanley
Longhurst, Robert E
Manhold, John Henry
Mazze, Irving
Moroles, Jesús Bautista
Mortellito, Domenico
Nickerson, Ruth (Mrs Edmund Greacen Jr)
Nierman, Leonardo M
Niizuma, Minoru
Oesterle, Leonhard Friedrich
Perry, Frank
Pinardi, Enrico Vittorio
Pinsker, Essie
Reddy, Krishna N
Reese, Marcia Mitchell
Regat, Jean-Jacques Albert
Reiland, Lowell Keith
Rhoden, John W
Saganic, Livio Michele
Salerno, Charles
Schleeh, Hans Martin
Scott, Martha F
Segal, Barbara Jean
Shepp, Alan
Simon, Helene

SCULPTOR (cont)
Slivka, David
Suttman, Paul
Taylor, Ira Mooney
Tewi, Thea
Torcoletti, Enzo
Vaadia, Boaz
Van Alstine, John Richard
Warshaw, Elaine N
Washington, James W, Jr
Watkins, Lewis
Wu, Linda Yee Chau
Zelin, Elaine
Zuckerman, Ruth Victor

Wood

Adkins, Terry R
Allmond, Charles (M)
Altman, Edith
Anderson, John S
Antonovici, Constantin
Appel, Karel
Arnoldi, Charles Arthur
Arum, Barbara
Arye, Leonora E
Azara, Nancy J
Baney, Ralph Ramoutar
Bates, Gladys Edgerly
Beal, Mack
Bergen, John Axel von
Blanc, (William) Peter
Bolomey, Roger Henry
Bourdon, Robert Slayton
Brady, Robert D
Brown, Peter C
Browning, Mark Daniel
Butchkes, Sydney
Cain, Michael Peter
Carroll, James F L
Carron, Maudee Lilyan
Castle, Wendell Keith
Catusco, Louis
Colby, Victor E
Dale, Ron G
DeAngelis, Joseph Rocco
De Coux, Janet
De Forest, Roy Dean
Diska, (P)
Dowd, Jack
Doyle, Tom
Driesbach, Walter Clark, Jr
Feist, Harold E
Frame, John
Frank, Charles William, Jr
Freeman, Robert Lee
Gans, Lucy C
Gilson, Giles
Gogorza, Patricia (Gahagan) de
Goldstein, Carl
Goo, Benjamin
Goode, Joe
Greeley, Charles Matthew
Greer, Jane Ruth
Gresser, Seymour Gerald
Grimley, Oliver Fetterolf
Grooms, Red
Gummer, Don
Gussow, Alan
Habenicht, Wenda
Hagan, James Garrison
Harrington, William Charles
Harris, Charney Anita
Helzer, Richard Brian
Hendricks, James (Powell)
Henkle, James Lee
Hernandez-Cruz, Luis
Hilts, Alvin
Holmes, David Valentine
Holoun, Harold Dean
Holsch, Robert Fred
Hoover, John Jay
Hopkins, Budd
Hoptner, Richard
Hueter, James Warren
Impiglia, Giancarlo
Isaacson, Lynn Judith
Jacobs, Peter Alan
Johnson, Joyce
Jones, Theodore Joseph
Jones, W Louis
Kahn, Tobi Aaron
Kamen, Rebecca
Karpowicz, Terrence Edward
Kasak, Nikolai
Keister, Steve (Stephen Lee)
Kelmenson, Lita
Kerrigan, Maurie
Knoebel, David Jon
Koehler, Ronald Gene
Kohlmeyer, Ida (R)
Koldorf, Irene Janet
Konzal, Joseph
Kotoske, Roger Allen
LaMontagne, Armand M
Laub, Stephen
Lavatelli, Carla
Leigh, Harry E
Lewis, Mary
Lindquist, Mark
Longhurst, Robert E
Ludwig, Eva
Lutz, Marjorie Brunhoff
McGovern, Robert F
McIlvain, Douglas Lee
McKesson, Malcolm Forbes
McKoy, Victor Grainger
Mangum, William (Goodson)
Markowski, Eugene David
Maroney, Dalton
Marsh, Thomas A
Marshall, James Duard
Martino, Eva E
Monti, John
Mueller, Trude
Neill, Joe
Nelson, Pamela Hudson
Nerburn, Kent Michael
Niemann, Edmund E
Nutt, Craig
Pettibone, Richard H
Pincus, Laurie Jane
Plott, Paula (Paula Plott Amos)
Pollock, Bruce
Powell, Gordon
Rades, William L
Ray, Robert (Donald)
Recanati, Dina
Regat, Mary E
Rogers, P J
Roussel, Claude Patrice
Saville, Ken
Schlanger, Jeff
Schuler, Melvin Albert
Schwidder, Ernst
Scott, Arden
Searles, Charles
Shaffer, Rosalind
Sharon, Russell
Shaw, Ernest Carl
Shaw, Reesey
Shostak, Ed (Edwin Bennett)
Sieg, Robert Lawrence
Silva, Ernest
Simon, Sidney
Smith, Kent Alvin
Smith, Lawrence Beall
Smith, Nan S(helley)
Smokler, Stanley B
Stevens, Michael Keith
Storm, Howard
Strawn, Bernice I
Stubbs, Lu
Surls, James
Swick, Linda Ann
Thompson, William Joseph
Tornheim, Norman
Torreano, John Francis
Townsend, John F
Truitt, Anne (Dean)
Turano, Don
Van Vranken, Rose (Rose Van Vranken Hickey)
Von Rydingsvard, Ursula
Wall, F L (Frederick Leroy), III
Wenzel, Joan Ellen
Werner, Howard
Westermann, H C
Wharton, Margaret Agnes
Wirsum, Karl
Yoshimura, Fumio

SILVERSMITH

Butt, Harlan W
Chapman, Robert Gordon
DiPasquale, Dominic Theodore
Edwards, Linda (Linda Margaret Weiss Edwards)
Fix, John Robert
Ganek, Dorothy Skeados
Getty, Nilda Fernandez
Hirsh, Annette Marie
Huebner, Sister Rosemarita
Krentzin, Earl
Maxfield, Roberta Masur
Prip, John A
Thompson, Ernest Thorne, Jr

STAINED GLASS ARTIST

Anderson, Bruce James
Anderson, Mark Robert
Berger, Sandra Christine Q
Close, Frank
Corso, Samuel (Joseph)
Daniels, Astar (Charlotte Louise Daniels)
Fields, Fredrica H
Hyams, Harriet
Karawina, Erica (Mrs Sidney C Hsiao)
King, Ray
Labrie, Christy
Lewis, Elizabeth Matthew
McGuire, Maureen
McIlvane, Edward James
Mandelbaum, Ellen
Mueller, (Sister) M Gerardine OP
Quagliata, Narcissus
Schaechter, Judith
Skinner, Orin Ensign
Stern, Arthur I
Tahedl, Ernestine
Traylor, Angelika
Tyser, Patricia Ellen
Waletzky, Tsirl (Cecelia Grobla Waletzky)
Weiss, Dick J
Zgoda, Larry

TAPESTRY ARTIST

Aber, Ita
Adams, Mark
Braverman, Donna (Donna Braverman Knopf)
Cain, Charlotte
Cook, Lia
Danielson, Phyllis I
Dyer, Carolyn Price
Easterwood, Henry Lewis
Elliott, Lillian
Funk, Charlotte M
Greene, Louise Weaver
Grenell, Barbara
Hartford, Jane Davis
Hicks, Sheila
Jaworska, Tamara
Kaye, David Haigh
Kowalski, Libby R
Lackey, Jane W
Lansner, Fay
Larzelere, Judith Ann
Lavatelli, Carla
Lesch, Alma Wallace
Lester, Michelle
Morrison, Bee (Berenice G)
Murashima, Kumiko
O'Hara, Sheila Mary
Pinckney, Stanley
Reichel, Myra
Renee, Paula
Roberson, William
Roda (Rhoda Lillian Sablow),
Rodman, Ruth M
Ross, Gloria F(rankenthaler)
Rousseau-Vermette, Mariette
Scheuer, Ruth
Schira, Cynthia
Stratakos, Steve John
Tate, Blair
Taylor, Janet R
Thompson, Jean Danforth
Tolpo, Carolyn Lee
Vitale, Vincent
Webber, Helen

VIDEO ARTIST

Allen, Terry
Almy, Max (Marilynn Irene)
Alpert, Richard Henry
Andrews, Lawrence
Balmaceda, Margarita S
Barr, Burt
Barron, Ros
Beirne, Bill
Birnbaum, Dara
Bloes, Richard K
Bratton, Christopher
Breder, Hans Dieter
Buchanan, Nancy
Bull, Hank (Henry Osler)
Campus, Peter
Chase, Doris (Totten)
Chong, Ping
Clancy, Patrick
Coe, Anne Elizabeth
Collyer, Robin
Cook, Michael David
Cross, Watson, Jr
D'Agostino, Peler
Dalglish, Jamie (James Parsons)
Davidovich, Jaime
Davis, Douglas Matthew
Dickinson, Eleanor Creekmore
Downey, Juan
Dr Brute (Eric William Metcalfe)
Gartel, Laurence M
Gialanella, Donald G
Goin, Peter
Gordin, Misha
Greenfield, Amy
Gusella, Ernest
Harding, Noel Robert
Hendricks, David Charles
Hershman, Lynn Lester
Hill, Gary
Houghton, Barbara Jean
Iimura, Takahiko
Jonas, Joan
Jones, George Bobby
Jordan, John L (Gaudeamus)
Kirsten, Nicholas
Klonarides, Carole Ann
Knecht, John
Korot, Beryl
Kramer, Margia
Kubota, Shigeko
Landry, Richard Miles
Laposky, Ben Francis

VIDEO ARTIST (cont)
Levine, Les
Lister, Ardele Diane
Loeffler, Carl Eugene
Lucier, Mary
McCafferty, Jay David
Magenta, Muriel
Marton, Pier
Montano, Linda (Mary)
Myers, Rita
Niblock, Phill
Oleszko, Patricia
Orentlicher, John
Oursler, Tony
Paik, Nam June
Patterson, Clayton Ian
Peiperl, Adam
Redgrave, Felicity
Reeves, Daniel McDonough
Reilly, Jack
Ritchie, William (Bill)
Rocco, Ron (Ronald Anthony Rocco)
Roser, Ce (Cecilia)
Rosler, Martha (Rose)
Sargent, Margaret Holland
Sato, Norie
Savinar, Tad
Schneider, Ira
Segalove, Ilene Judy
Sharp, Willoughby
Sher, Elizabeth
Silver, Shelly Andrea
Smith, Barbara Turner
Spiegel, Laurie
Sturgeon, John Floyd
Tilley, Lewis Lee
Torres, Francesc
Turner, Judith Estelle
Velez, Edin
Vesna, Victoria
Viola, Bill
Vitali, Julius M
Weintraub, Annette
Will, John A
Woodall, John

WEAVER

Adamson, Linny J
Akers, Adela
Aspell, Amy Suzanne
Baruch, Ruth-Marion Evelyn
Bittleman, Dolores Dembus
Bobrowicz, Yvonne Pacanovsky
Boyd, Karen White
Bragdon, Catherine Creamer
Bryant, Laura Militzer
Curtis, Dolly Powers
Elliott, Lillian
Fowler, Mary Jean
Funk, Charlotte M
Greene, Louise Weaver
Grenell, Barbara
Hanson, J B
Hausrath, Joan W
Hughes, Beverly
Jacobs, Ferne K
Kindahl, Connie
LaPlantz, Shereen
Maldjian, Vartavar B
Minear, Beth
Morrison, Bee (Berenice G)
O'Hara, Sheila Mary
Pendleton, Mary Caroline
Plath, Iona
Regensteiner, Else (Friedsam)
Reichel, Myra
Replinger, Dot (Dorothy Thiele)
Schira, Cynthia
Scott, Joyce
Smith, Sherri
Tawney, Lenore
Taylor, Janet R
Thompson, Rena
Trentham, Gary Lynn
Van Leunen, Alice Louise
Wahling, Jon B
West, Virginia M
Windeknecht, Margaret Brake
Zynsky, Toots (Mary Ann)

WRITER

Ablow, Joseph
Abt, Jeffrey
Adams, Celeste Marie
Adams, Robert McCormick
Agar, Eunice Jane
Ahl, Henry C
Alf, Martha Joanne
Aliki
Alinder, Mary Street
Almond, Paul
Ames, Lee Judah
Aminoff, Judith
Anderson, Donald Myers
Anderson, Margaret Pomeroy
Angelini, John Michael
Antin, David A
Apple, Jacki (Jacqueline B)
Arnheim, Rudolf
Ashton, Dore
Askew, Pamela
Atlas, Nava
Ayres, Julia Spencer
Baer, Jo
Baird, Joseph Armstrong, Jr
Baker, Kenneth
Ball, Edward R
Bannard, Walter Darby
Bansemer, Roger L
Banz, George
Barbour, Arthur J
Barker, Walter William, Jr
Barnes, Molly
Barrio, Raymond
Bartlett, Jennifer Losch
Barton, Phyllis Settecase
Baxter, Paula Adell
Beall, Karen Friedmann
Beck, Doreen
Benedikt, Michael
Bennett, John M
Benson, Elaine K G
Benson, Elizabeth Polk
Benton, Suzanne E
Bertman, Stephen
Bevlin, Marjorie Elliott
Bochner, Mel
Boigon, Brian Joseph
Bowman, Bruce
Boyle, Richard J
Boylen, Michael Edward
Braunstein, Mark Mathew
Brilliant, Richard
Broder, Patricia Janis
Broido, Lucy
Brommer, Gerald F
Bronson, A A (Michael Wayne Tims)
Brown, Robert K
Browning, Dixie Burrus
Brumfield, John Richard
Bruner, Louise Katherine
Brust, Robert Gustave
Bryant, Edward Albert
Budny, Virginia
Buechner, Thomas Scharman
Burch, Claire R
Burnham, Jack Wesley
Bush-Brown, Albert
Butler, Joseph Thomas
Calle, Paul
Campbell, Dorothy Bostwick
Campbell, (James) Lawrence
Case, Elizabeth
Caswell, Helen Rayburn
Chase, Alice Elizabeth
Chase-Riboud, Barbara
Chernow, Burt
Chester, Charlotte Wanetta
Clark, Roberta Carter
Clothier, Peter Dean
Cole, Sylvan
Collings, Betty
Comès, Marcella (Mrs Randolph Winslow)
Comini, Alessandra
Congdon, William (Grosvenor)
Conniff, Gregory
Converse, Elizabeth
Cooley, Adelaide N
Corbin, George Allen
Corbino, Marcia Norcross
Cottingham, Laura Josephine
Cowles, Fleur
Cox, Richard William
Crandall, Judith Ann
Craven, Wayne
Creevy, Bill
Crespo, Michael Lowe
Crosman, Christopher Byron
Culhane, Shamus H
Cummings, Paul
Curran, Douglas Edward
Curry, David Park
Cutler, Grayce E
Damaz, Paul F
Danoff, I Michael
Dater, Judy
Davis, James Wesley
Davis, Philip Charles
Dawdy, Doris Ostrander
Deats, Margaret
De Nike, Michael Nicholas
Denson, G Roger
Desmarais, Charles Joseph
Diamonstein, Barbaralee
Dibble, George
Dinhofer, Shelly Mehlman
Dodrill, Donald Lawrence
Dorfman, Elsa
Douglas, L J
Dowden, Anne Ophelia Todd
Drohojowska, Hunter
Dunbar, Jill H
Dusard, Jay
Dyson, Brian
Eaton, Tom
Elliot, John Theodore
Elliot, Sheila
Emmerich, Andre
Enstice, Wayne
Ewald, Elin Lake
Faris, Peter Kinzie
Farnham, Alexander
Farnham, Emily
Fax, Elton Clay
Feiffer, Jules
Feininger, Andreas B L
Fejes, Claire
Feldman, Franklin
Finch, Ruth Woodward
Fischer, Hal (Harold Alan)
Fisher, Rob (Robert Norman)
Flach, Victor H
Flavin, Dan
Fleming, Lee
Flexner, James Thomas
Flood, Richard Sidney
Folsom, Rose
Forge, Andrew Murray
Foster, Stephen C
Franck, Frederick S
Frank, Charles William, Jr
Friedman, B H
Fuller, Mary (Mary Fuller McChesney)
Gablik, Suzi
Gale, Peggy
Gallagher, Carole
Garbutt, Janice Lovoos
Gardner, Colin R
Garman, Ed
Garver, Walter Raymond
Gary, Dorothy Hales
Gast, Dwight V
Genauer, Emily
Ghent, Henri
Gibson, Walter Samuel
Gilbert, Creighton Eddy
Gildzen, Alex
Giraudier, Antonio
Gjertson, Stephen Arthur
Glenn, Constance White
Glick, Paula Florence
Glimcher, Arnold B
Goddard, Donald
Goldman, Judith
Goldring, Elizabeth
Goldsmith, Barbara
Goldstein, Nathan
Goodman, Florence Jeanne
Goossen, Eugene Coons
Gordon, Violet
Gould, Karen Keel
Green, Nancy Elizabeth
Groves, Naomi Jackson
Gruen, John
Haber, Ira Joel
Hackenbroch, Yvonne Alix
Hale, Nathan Cabot
Hamblen, Dr Karen A
Hammond, Leslie King
Hanks, David Allen
Harmon, Lily
Hartal, Paul
Hawkins, Myrtle H
Held, Julius S
Heller, Jules
Henrickson, Paul Robert
Herman, Vic
Herring, Jan (Janet Mantel)
Hirsch, Gilah Yelin
Hobbs, Jack Arthur
Hoffman, Mandy Lippman
Holden, Donald
Hollister, Paul
Hood, Graham Stanley
Hopkins, Peter
Hornung, Clarence Pearson
Howland, Richard Hubbard
Hubbard, Robert
Iannone, Dorothy
Iglehart, Robert L
Irving, Donald J
Isaacson, Philip Marshal
Ishikawa, Joseph
Janis, Eugenia Parry
Jennings, Jan
Johanningmeier, Robert Alan
Johnson, James Ralph
Johnson, Una E
Jones, Franklin Reed
Jones, Ronald Lee, Jr
Kallir, Jane Katherine
Kamm, Dorothy Lila
Kangas, Gene
Karafel, Lorraine
Karlen, Peter H
Katz, Hilda (Hulda Weber)
Kaufman, Joe
Kaufman, Nancy
Keener, Polly Leonard
Kelly, Moira
Kessler, Jane Q
Kimmel-Cohn, Roberta
Klein, Ellen Lee
Klein, Gwenda J
Klein, Michael Eugene
Kleinsmith, Gene (Eugene Dennis)
Kloss, WIlliam
Knox, George
Koch, Robert
Korzenik, Diana
Kostelanetz, Richard
Kovinick, Philip Peter
Kowal, Dennis J
Kozloff, Max
Kriensky

WRITER (cont)

Kutner, Janet
Larsen, Jack Lenor
Larson, Jane (Warren)
Larson, Kay L
Lawrence, Sidney S
Lawson, Thomas
Lea, Tom
Leach, Elizabeth Anne
Lefebvre d'Argence, Rend-Yvon
Lengyel, Alfonz
Lent, Blair
Lerman, Leo
Levy, Mark
Lewis, Elizabeth Matthew
Lieberman, Laura Crowell
Lijn, Liliane
Lindsay, Kenneth C
Link, Lawrence John
Linn, John William
Lippard, Lucy Rowland
Lochnan, Katharine A
Loewer, Henry Peter
Longaker, Jon Dasu
Loran, Erle
Lotringer, Sylvere
Love, Frances Taylor
Lubell, Ellen
Ludman, Joan Hurwitz
Lunde, Karl Roy
McClain, Matthew
McCoy, Pat A
McCready, Karen (Karen McCready Noblet)
MacDonald, Colin Somerled
McEvilley, Thomas
McGarry, Susan Hallsten
Madigan, Mary Jean Smith
Maguire, Henry Pownall
Mainardi, Patricia M
Mallin, Judith Young
Malone, James Hiram
Malone, Nola Langner
Mandelbaum, Ellen
Mann, Maybelle
Mariner, Donna M
Markovich, Ann Marie
Marro, George Matthew
Mauldin, Bill
Medoff, Eve
Meigs, John Liggett
Meyer, El(mer Frederick)
Meyer, Susan E
Michael, Gary
Millard, Charles Warren, III
Miller, Marc H
Minick, Roger
Mirtala
Mitchell, Margaretta K
Moehl, Karl J
Morgan, Theodora (Theodora Morgan Olsen)
Morgan, William
Morin-Miller, Carmen A
Morris, Wright
Morse, Marcia Roberts
Morton, Robert Alan
Movalli, Charles Joseph
Muhlberger, Richard Charles
Munro, Eleanor
Mussmann, Linda L
Nash, Paul
Nasisse, Andy S
Naumann, Francis M
Neal, (Minor) Avon
Neher, Ross James
Nelson, Mary Carroll
Nemser, Cindy
Newland, Joseph Nelson
Newsom, Barbara Ylvisaker
Norman, Dorothy (S)
O'Gorman, James Francis
Orland, Ted N
Palmer, A Laure
Parker, Ann
Parker, Nancy Winslow
Patrick, Charles William
Peck, Judith
Peladeau, Marius Beaudoin
Pendleton, Mary Caroline
Perine, Robert Heath
Persky, Robert S
Phillips, Gifford
Phillpot, Clive James
Pike, Joyce Lee
Pincus-Witten, Robert A
Plath, Iona
Plaut, James S
Plowden, David
Poupeney, Mollie
Preuss, Roger
Pulos, Arthur Jon
Quackenbush, Robert
Quinsac, Annie-Paule
Raleigh, Henry Patrick
Ramsey, Dorothy J
Rash, Nancy
Ratcliff, Carter
Raven, Arlene
Redstone, Louis Gordon
Reid, Charles
Rembski, Stanislav
Rendl, M(ildred Marcus)
Rensch, Roslyn
Reynolds, Jock
Robbin, Anthony Stuart
Robbins, David A
Robbins, Eugenia S
Robins, Corinne
Robison, Andrew
Rodman, Selden
Rokeach, Barrie
Rose, Matthew Adam
Rosenblatt, Suzanne Maris
Roth, Leland M(artin)
Roukes, Nicholas M
Rousseau, Irene Victoria
Rubin, Ida Ely
Rubinstein, Charlotte Streifer
Russell, Dr Stella Pandell
Salemme, Lucia (Autorino)
Saphire, Lawrence M
Sawyer, Helen
Schwartz, Lillian (Feldman)
Schwartz, Therese
Seed, Suzanne Liddell
Seeman, Helene Zucker
Selvig, Forrest Hall
Sendak, Maurice Bernard
Shapiro, Adrian Michael
Sheaks, Barclay
Shearer, Rhonda Roland
Sherman, Lenore (Walton)
Sherrod, Philip Lawrence
Shulzke, Margot Seymour
Silberman, Arthur
Silverman, Ronald H
Simon, Leonard Ronald
Slate, Joseph Frank
Slobodkina, Esphyr (Mrs Urquhart)
Smith, Ralph Alexander
Smith, V Joachim
Snodgrass-King, Jeanne Owens (Mrs M Eugene King)
Snowden, Gilda
Sorel, Edward
Southwell, William Joseph
Spaeth, Eloise O'Mara
Spector, Naomi
Speight, Jerry Brooks
Spier, Peter Edward
Spivy-Anderson, C Alexandra
Squiers, Carol
Stampfle, Felice
Stapen, Nancy
Steiner, Paul
Stevens, Elisabeth Goss
Stewart, John Lincoln
Stone, Jim (James J)
Sward, Robert S
Sylvestre, Guy
Szilvasy, Linda Markuly
Talley, Dan R
Tarshis, Jerome
Taylor, Robert
Tennant, Donna Kay
Thenhaus, Paulette Ann
Thomas, Helen (Doane)
Thornton, Richard Samuel
Tice, George Andrew
Tillenius, Clarence (Ingwall)
Tomkins, Calvin
Toschik, Larry
Tracy, Lois Bartlett
Tselos, Dimitri Theodore
Tucker, Peri
Tully, Judd
Turner, Norman Huntington
Uhrman, Celia
Uhrman, Esther
Ultra Violet,
Upright, Diane W
VanDerpool, Karen
Van Dommelen, David B
Van Haaften, Julia
Varga, Margit
Vermeule, Cornelius Clarkson, III
Von Barghan, Barbara
Waller, Susan
Walton, Donald William
Walton, Guy E
Warder, William
Warren, Lynne
Watson, Clarissa H
Wechsler, Susan
Weil, Lisl
Weiler, Joseph Flack
Weinberg, Bella Rebecca
Weiss, Harvey
West, Virginia M
Wetmore, Gordon (Stanley Gordon)
Williams, Reba White
Winchester, Alice
Windeknecht, Margaret Brake
Withers, Josephine
Witt, David L
Wofford, Philip
Wooden, Howard Edmund
Yau, John
Yochim, Louise Dunn
York, Tina
Young, Mahonri S
Zack, Badanna Bernice
Zeitlin, Marilyn A

Necrology

Cumulative 1953-1992

AACH, HERB Painter,Writer (1923-1985)
AARONS, GEORGE Sculptor (1896-1980)
ABBATE, PAUL S Sculptor (1884-1972)
ABBELL, SAMUEL Art Patron (1925-1969)
ABBOT, EDITH Painter (-1964)
ABBOTT, JOHN EVANS Library Director (-1952)
ABEL, MYER Lithographer, Painter (1904-)
ABELL, WALTER HALSEY Educator (1897-1956)
ABRACHEFF, IVAN Painter (1903-1960)
ABRAMS, HARRY N Publisher, Collector (1905-1979)
ABRAMS, RUTH (DAVIDSON) Painter, Critic (-1986)
ACKERMAN, FRANK EDWARD Painter, Designer (1933-)
ACKERMANN, JOHN JOSEPH Painter, Designer (1889-1950)
ADAMS, ANSEL EASTON Photographer (1902-1984)
ADAMS, MARGARET BOROUGHS Painter (-1965)
ADAMS, (MOULTON) LEE Painter, Illustrator (1922-1971)
ADAMS, WAYMAN Painter (1885-1959)
ADDAMS, CHARLES Cartoonist (1912-1988)
ADEN, ALONZO J Museum Director (1906-1963)
ADLER, SAMUEL (MARCUS) Painter, Educator (1898-1979)
ADLOW, DOROTHY Critic (-1964)
AGA-OGLU, MEHMET Educator, Lecturer, Writer (1896-1948)
AGOPOFF, AGOP MINASS Sculptor (-1983)
AHERN, EUGENE (GENE) Cartoonist (1896-1960)
AIDLEN, JEROME Sculptor, Instructor (1935-1986)
AIKEN, CHARLES Painter (1872-1965)
AIROLA, PAAVO Painter, Writer (-1983)
AJOOTIAN, KHOSROV Educator (1891-1958)
AKSTON, JAMES Collector, Patron
ALAN, JAY Cartoonist (1907-1965)
ALBEE, PERCY F Painter (1885-1959)
ALBERS, JOSEF Painter, Printmaker (1888-1976)
ALBERTAZZI, MARIO Painter, Art Critic (1920-1991)
ALBRIGHT, ADAM EMORY Painter (1862-1957)
ALBRIGHT, HENRY J Educator, Painter (-1951)
ALBRIGHT, IVAN LE LORRAINE Painter (1897-1983)
ALBRIGHT, THOMAS Critic, Writer (1935-)
ALCOPLEY, L Painter, Graphic Artist (1910-1992)
ALDER, MARY ANN Painter, Art Restorer (-1952)
ALDWINCKLE, ERIC Designer, Painter (1909-1980)
ALEXANDER, CHRISTINE Curator (1893-1975)
ALFSEN, JOHN MARTIN Painter (-1972)
ALLEN, ARTHUR D Painter, Lithographer (-1949)
ALLEN, CHARLES CURTIS Painter, Educator (1886-1950)
ALLEN, CLARENCE CANNING Painter, Instructor (1897-1989)
ALLEN, JANE MENGEL (MRS ARTHUR) Painter (1888-1952)
ALLEN, JUNIUS Painter (1898-1962)
ALLEN, MARGO (MRS HARRY SHAW) Sculptor, Painter (1894-1988)
ALLEN, MARY STOCKBRIDGE Painter, Sculptor (1869-1949)
ALLOWAY, LAWRENCE Art Historian, Curator (1927-1990)
ALLWELL, STEPHEN S Sculptor (1906-)
ALMY, FRANK ATWOOD Museum Director (1900-1956)
ALSTON, CHARLES HENRY Painter, Educator (1907-1977)
ALVORD, MURIEL Painter (-1960)
AMAROTICO, JOSEPH ANTHONY Painter, Conservator (1931-)
AMATEIS, EDMOND ROMULUS Sculptor (1897-1981)
AMBERSON, GRACE D (MRS WILLIAM R) Painter (1894-1957)
AMES, ARTHUR FORBES Painter, Educator (1906-1975)
AMINO, LEO Sculptor, Instructor (1911-1989)
AMSDEN, FLOYD T Collector, Patron (1913-)
AMSTER, SALLY Painter (-1988)
ANDERSEN, ANDREAS STORRS Educator, Painter (1908-1974)
ANDERSON, CARL THOMAS Cartoonist, Illustrator (1865-1948)
ANDERSON, HOWARD BENJAMIN Photographer (1903-)
ANDERSON, IVAN DELOS Painter, Printmaker (1915-1991)
ANDERSON, JEREMY RADCLIFFE Sculptor, Educator (1921-1982)
ANDERSON, KENNETH L Administrator, Architect (1939-1990)
ANDREJEVIC, MILET Painter (1925-1989)
ANGEL, JOHN Sculptor (1881-1960)
ANGELO, DOMENICK MICHAEL Sculptor (1925-1976)
ANGELO, EMIDIO Cartoonist, Painter (1903-)
ANSBACHER, JESSIE Painter (-1964)
ARCHER, DOROTHY BRYANT Painter, Instructor (1919-)
ARCHIPENKO, ALEXANDER Sculptor (1887-1964)
ARDIZZONE, EDWARD Painter, Illustrator (1900-1979)
ARGALL, CHARLES G Painter
ARLT, WILLIAM H Designer, Teacher, Painter (1868-)
ARNASON, H HARVARD Art Historian,Writer (1909-1986)
ARNESON, ROBERT Sculptor (1930-)
ARNEST, BERNARD Painter, Educator (1917-1986)
ARNO, PETER Cartoonist (1904-1968)
ARONSON, BORIS Designer, Painter (1900-1980)
ARTIS, WILLIAM ELLISWORTH Educator, Ceramist (1914-1977)
ARTZ, FREDERICK B Historian, Writer (1894-1983)
ARTZBYBASHEFF, BORIS Illustrator (1899-1965)
ASCHER, MARY Painter, Printmaker
ASHTON, ETHEL V Artist (-1975)
ASHTON, MAL STANHOPE (MALONE) Artist (1878-1976)
ASKENAZY, MISCHA Painter (1888-1961)
ATHERTON, J CARLTON Craftsman (1900-1964)
ATHERTON, JOHN Painter, Illustrator (1900-1952)
ATIRNOMIS (RITA SIMON) Painter, Printmaker (1938-)
ATKINS, ALBERT H Sculptor, Painter (-1951)
AUERBACH-LEVY, WILLIAM Etcher (1889-1964)
AULT, GEORGE Artist
AULT, GEORGE COPELAND Painter (1891-1948)
AUSTIN, JO-ANNE Dealer (1925-)
AUSUBEL, SHEVA Painter (1896-1957)
AVERY, MILTON Painter (1893-1965)
AVERY, MYRTILLA Museum Director (-1959)
AVERY, RALPH HILLYER Painter, Illustrator (1906-1976)
AVINOFF, ANDREY Painter, Illustrator (1884-1948)
AYERS, HESTER MERWIN Portrait Painter (1902-1975)
AYLWARD, WILLIAM J Painter (1875-1958)
BABER, ALICE Painter, Printmaker (1928-1982)
BACH, OTTO KARL Museum Director, Writer (1909-1990)
BACH, RICHARD F Educator (1887-1968)
BACKUS, STANDISH JR Painter, Muralist (1910-1989)
BACON, PEGGY Painter, Writer (1895-1987)
BADNER, MINO Historian (1940-1978)
BAILEY, CLARK T Sculptor, Educator (1932-1978)
BAILEY, WORTH Historian (1908-1980)
BAIN, LILIAN PHERNE Painter, Etcher (1873-)
BAIZERMAN, SAUL Sculptor (1889-1957)
BAKER, CHARLES EDWIN Art Historian, Writer (1902-1971)
BAKER, EUGENE AMES Painter, Serigrapher (1928-)
BAKER, RALPH BERNARD Painter, Educator (1932-)
BALDWIN, HARRY, II Painter
BALDWIN, JOHN Educator, Sculptor (1922-1987)
BALDWIN, MURIEL FRANCES Art Librarian
BALLIN, HUGO Painter (1879-1956)
BALOG, MICHAEL Painter, Sculptor (1946-)
BANKS, VIRGINIA Painter (1920-1985)
BANNING, BEATRICE HARPER Etcher (1885-)
BANNISTER, EDWARD MITCHELL Painter (1828-1901)
BARANOFF, MORT Printmaker, Painter (1923-1978)

BARBAROSSA, THEODORE C Sculptor (1906-1992)
BARBER, JOHN Painter (1898-1965)
BARBER, MURIEL V Painter (-1971)
BARINGER, RICHARD E Painter, Designer (1921-1980)
BARKER, ALBERT WINSLOW Lithographer, Teacher (1874-1947)
BARKER, VIRGIL Writer, Critic (1890-1964)
BARLOGA, VIOLA H Painter (1890-)
BARNETT, EDWARD WILLIS Director, Designer (1922-1987)
BARNETT, HERBERT P Educator, Painter (1910-1972)
BARNEY, MAGINAL WRIGHT Craftsman (-1966)
BARR, ALFRED HAMILTON, JR Art Historian, Administrator (1902-1981)
BARR, ALLAN Painter (1890-1959)
BARRETT, H STANFORD Painter, Educator (1909-1970)
BARRETT, ROBERT DUMAS Painter (1903-)
BARRETT, THOMAS WEEKS Painter, Designer (1902-1947)
BARRIE, ERWIN S Painter (1886-1983)
BARTHE, RICHMOND Sculptor (1901-1989)
BARTLETT, DANA Painter (1882-1957)
BARTLETT, FRED STEWART Administrator, Museum Director (1905-1988)
BARTLETT, ROBERT WEBSTER Painter, Designer (1922-1979)
BARTLETT, SCOTT Filmmaker (1943-1990)
BASQUIAT, JEAN MICHEL Painter (1961-1988)
BASS, JOHANNA (MRS JOHN) Collector, Patron (-1970)
BASS, JOHN Collector, Patron (1891-1978)
BATCHELOR, CLARENCE DANIEL Cartoonist (1888-1977)
BATE, NORMAN ARTHUR Educator, Printmaker (1916-1980)
BATES, CAROL Painter (1895-)
BATES, KENNETH Painter (1895-1973)
BATES, MAXWELL BENNETT Painter, Lithographer (1906-1980)
BATTAGLIA, PASQUALE M Painter (1905-1959)
BAUMGARTNER, WARREN W Illustrator (1894-1963)
BAYER, HERBERT Painter, Architect (1900-)
BAYER, JEFFREY JOSHUA Educator, Sculptor (1942-1983)
BAYLINSON, A S Painter, Teacher (1882-1950)
BAYLOS, ZELMA U Painter, Sculptor
BAZIOTES, WILLIAM Painter (1912-1963)
BEAL, REYNOLDS Painter, Etcher (1867-1951)
BEALL, LESTER THOMAS Illustrator, Designer (1902-1969)
BEAMENT, HAROLD Painter (1898-)
BEAR, DONALD Museum Director (1905-1952)
BEARD, MARION L PATTERSON Lecturer, Painter
BECKER, NAOMI Sculptor (-1974)
BECKWITH, JAMES Painter, Craftsperson (1907-)
BEELKE, RALPH G Educator (1917-)
BEETZ, CARL HUGO Painter, Instructor (1911-1974)
BEGG, JOHN ALFRED Designer, Sculptor (1903-1974)
BEGGS, THOMAS MONTAGUE Consultant, Painter (1899-1990)
BEIL, CHARLES A Sculptor (-1976)
BEL GEDDES, NORMAN Designer (1893-1958)
BELCHER, HILDA Painter (1881-1963)
BELKNAP, MORRIS B Painter (-1952)
BELLINGER, LOUISA Curator (-1968)
BELLMER, HANS Painter, Graphic Artist & Sculptor (1902-1975)
BELMONT, IRA JEAN Painter (1885-1964)
BEMELMANS, LUDWIG Painter (1898-1963)
BEMIS, WALDO EDMUND Designer, Illustrator (-1951)
BENDA, W T Designer, Illustrator (1891-1948)
BENESCH, OTTO Art Historian (1896-1964)
BENGTZ, TURE Museum Director, Painter (1907-1973)
BENN, BEN Painter (1884-1983)
BENNETT, RUTH M Craftsman (1899-1960)
BENSCO, CHARLES J Painter (1894-1960)
BENSON, EMANUEL M Art Administrator, Art Dealer (1904-1971)
BENSON, FRANK W Painter, Etcher (1862-1951)
BENSON, JOHN P Painter (1865-1947)
BENTON, MARGARET PEAKE Painter (-1975)
BENTON, THOMAS HART Painter, Writer (1889-1975)
BENTON, WILLIAM Collector (1900-1973)
BENTZ, JOHN Painter (-1950)
BENY, ROLOFF Photographer, Writer (1924-)
BENZ, LEE R Printmaker, Painter (-1984)
BERENSON, BERNARD Art Authority (1865-1959)
BERG, PHIL Collector, Patron (1902-)
BERHARD, MRS RICHARD J Collector
BERKMAN, AARON Painter, Gallery Director (1900-1991)
BERMAN, EUGENE Painter, Designer (1899-1972)
BERN HEIMER, RICHARD Educator (1907-1958)
BERNARDINI, ORESTES Designer (1880-1957)
BERNDT, WALTER Cartoonist (1900-1979)
BERNEY, BERTRAM S Painter (1884-)
BERNINGHAUS, OSCAR E Painter, Designer (1874-1952)
BERNSTEIN, EVA Painter (1871-1958)
BERNSTEIN, SYLVIA Painter, Sculptor (1914-1990)
BERRY, WILLIAM DAVID Illustrator, Sculptor (1926-1979)
BERRYMAN, CLIFFORD KENNEDY Cartoonist, Illustrator (1869-1949)
BERTOIA, HARRY Sculptor, Graphic Artist (1915-1978)
BETTS, LOUIS Painter (1873-1961)
BIBERMAN, EDWARD Painter, Graphic Artist (1904-1986)
BICE, CLARE Administrator, Painter (1909-1976)
BIDDLE, GEORGE Painter, Sculptor (1885-1973)
BIDWELL, WATSON Painter (1904-)
BIEBEL, FRANKLIN M Museum Director (1908-1966)
BIEBER, MARGARETE Art Historian (1880-1978)
BIELER, ANDRE CHARLES Painter, Muralist (1896-1989)
BIERMAN, SAMUEL Art Advisor (1902-1978)
BILLINGS, HENRY Painter, Illustrator (1901-1987)
BILOTTI, SALVATORE F Sculptor (1879-1953)
BING, ALEXANDER Painter (1878-1959)
BINNING, BERTRAM CHARLES Painter (1909-1976)
BIRCHANSKY, LEO Painter, Cartoonist (1887-1949)
BIRKIN, MORTON Painter (1919-)
BISCHOFF, ELMER Painter, Educator (1916-1991)
BISGARD, JAMES DEWEY Collector, Patron (1898-1975)
BISHOP, BARBARA LEE Educator, Printmaker (1938-)
BISHOP, RICHARD EVETT Printmaker (1897-1975)
BISHOP, ROBERT CHARLES Museum Director, Art Writer (1938-1991)
BITTLEMAN, ARNOLD I Painter, Educator (1933-)
BLACK, ELEANOR SIMMS (MRS ROBERT M) Painter (1872-1949)
BLACK, MARY CHILDS Curator, Writer (-1992)
BLACK, WENDELL H Educator (1919-1972)
BLACKBURN, MORRIS (ATKINSON) Painter, Printmaker (1902-1979)
BLAI, BORIS Sculptor, Educator (1898-1985)
BLAIR, STREETER Painter (-1966)
BLAKE, LEO B Illustrator (1887-1976)
BLANCH, ARNOLD Painter (1896-1968)
BLANCHARD, CAROL Painter, Illustrator (1918-)
BLANCHFIELD, HOWARD JAMES Painter (1896-1957)
BLANDING, DON Author (1894-1957)
BLISS, MRS. ROBERT WOODS Collector (-1969)
BLISS, ROBERT WOODS Patron, Diplomat (1875-1962)
BLOCH, ALBERT Painter (1882-1961)
BLOCH, E MAURICE Art History, Educator (-1989)
BLOCH, JULIUS Painter (1888-1966)
BLOCK, ADOLPH Sculptor, Instructor (1906-1978)
BLODGETT, EDMUND WALTON Painter (1908-)
BLODGETT, GEORGE WINSLOW Sculptor (1888-)
BLOEDEL, LAWRENCE HOTCH KISS Collector (1902-1976)
BLOS, PETER W Painter, Instructor (1908-1986)
BLOWER, DAVID HARRISON Painter (1901-1976)
BLUMBERG, YULI Painter (1894-1964)
BLUME, PETER Painter, Sculptor (1906-1992)
BLUMENSCHEIN, ERNEST LEONARD Painter (1874-1960)
BLUMENSCHEIN, MARY GREENE Painter (1869-1958)
BOAL, SARA METZNER Painter, Instructor (1896-1979)
BOARDMAN, NELL Painter (-1968)
BOBLETER, LOWELL STANLEY Educator, Painter (1902-1973)
BODINE, HELEN Painter
BOE, ROY ASBJORN Historian, Educator (1919-)
BOEHLER, HANS Painter (1884-1961)
BOESCHENSTEIN, BERNICE (MRS C K) Painter (1906-1951)
BOESE, ALVIN WILLIAM Collector (1910-1986)
BOHLAND, GUSTAV Sculptor (1897-1959)
BOHNERT, HERBERT Portrait Painter (1890-1967)
BOHROD, AARON Painter, Educator (1907-1992)
BOLOTOWSKY, ILYA Painter, Educator (1907-1981)
BOND, ROLAND S Collector (1898-)
BONGART, SERGEI R Painter, Instructor (-1985)
BONGIORNO, LAURINE MACK Historian (1903-1988)
BONINO, ALFREDO Art Dealer (1925-1981)
BONNAR, JAMES KING Painter (1885-1961)
BONNEY, THERESE Photographer (1895-1978)
BONNYCASTLE, MURRAY C Painter
BOOGAR, WILLIAM F Sculptor (1893-1958)
BOOKBINDER, JACK Painter, Printmaker (1911-1990)
BOORAEM, HENDRIK Painter (1886-1951)
BOOTH, CAMERON Painter (1892-1980)
BOOTH, NINA MASON Painter (1884-)
BORDUAS, PAUL EMILE Painter (-1960)
BOREN, JAMES ERWIN Painter (1921-1990)
BORGHI, GUIDO RINALDO Painter (1903-1971)
BORGLUM, JAMES LINCOLN DE LA MOTHE Sculptor, Photographer (1912-1986)
BORN, WOLFGANG Historian, Writer (1893-1949)
BORNE, MORTIMER Sculptor, Painter (1902-1987)
BORSTEIN, YETTA Painter (-1968)
BOSA, LOUIS Painter (1905-1981)
BOSIN, BLACKBEAR Painter, Designer (1921-1980)

BOSWELL, PEYTON, JR Writer, Editor (1904-1950)
BOTELLO, ANGEL Painter, Sculptor (1913-1986)
BOTKIN, HENRY Painter, Writer (1896-1983)
BOTTIS, HUGH P Printmaker (-1964)
BOUCHARD, LORNE HOLLAND Painter, Illustrator (1913-1978)
BOUCHE, LOUIS Painter (1896-1969)
BOUCHE, RENE Portrait Painter (-1963)
BOURDELL, PIERRE VAN PARYS Sculptor (-1966)
BOWDOIN, HARRIETTE Painter (-1947)
BOWER, ALEXANDER Museum Director (1875-1952)
BOWLES, JANET PAYNE Craftsman (1882-1948)
BOWLING, JACK Silversmith, Printmaker (1903-1979)
BOYCE, RICHARD Sculptor (1920-
BOYCE, WILLIAM G Museum Director, Educator (1921-1992)
BOYD, E Art Administrator, Writer (1903-1974)
BOYD, RUTHERFORD Painter, Designer (-1951)
BOYER, RALPH LUDWIG Painter, Etcher (1879-1952)
BOYKO, FRED Painter, Teacher (1894-1951)
BRACKMAN, ROBERT Painter, Educator (1898-1980)
BRADFORD, FRANCIS SCOTT Painter (1898-1961)
BRADLEY, MRS. HARRY LYNDE Collector
BRAIDER, DONALD Art Writer (1923-1977)
BRANDON, WARREN EUGENE Painter (1916-1977)
BRANNER, ROBERT Art Historian (1927-1973)
BRANSOM, (JOHN) PAUL Painter, Illustrator (1885-1979)
BRAXTON, WILLIAM E Painter (1878-1932)
BRAY, JOHN Cartoonist (1879- 1978)
BRAZEAU, WENDELL (PHILLIPS) Painter (1910-1974)
BRECHER. SAMUEL Painter (1897-1982)
BRECKENRIDGE, JAMES D Art Historian (1926-1982)
BREESKIN, ADELYN DOHME Administrator, Consultant (1896-1986)
BREGER, DAVE (DAVID) Cartoonist (1908-1970)
BREITENBACH, EDGAR Historian (1903-1977)
BRENDEL, OTTO J Art Historian (1901-1973)
BRENNER, SHORE HODGE Weaver, Educator (1949-)
BRENSON, THEODORE Painter (1893-1959)
BREWER, BESSIE MARSH Etcher, Lithographer (1883-1952)
BREWINGTON, MARION VERNON Art Historian, Writer (1902-1974)
BRIGGS, AUSTIN Illustrator, Collector (1808-1973)
BRIGGS, BERTA N Painter, Writer (1884-1976)
BRIGGS, ERNEST Painter, Instructor (1923-1984)
BRINLEY, DANIEL PUTNAM Painter (1879-1963)
BRITTAIN, MILLER G Painter (-1968)
BRITTON, HARRY Painter (1879-1958)
BRITTON, JAMES II Critic, Illustrator (1915-1983)
BROADD, HARRY ANDREW Painter, Historian (1910-)
BRODIE, AGNES HAHN Sculptor, Painter (1924-1992)
BRODIE, GANDY Painter, Designer (1924-1975)
BROMBERG, FAITH Painter (1919-1990)
BROMUND, CAL E Painter (1903-1979)
BROOK, ALEXANDER Painter (1898-1980)
BROOKS, JAMES Painter (1906-1992)
BROUILLETTE, GILBERT T Art Dealer, Consultant-Research
BROUSSARD, JAY REMY Museum Director, Painter (1920-1976)
BROWN, BRIAN Director (1911-1958)
BROWN, CARLYLE Painter (-1964)
BROWN, JOSEPH Sculptor, Educator (1909-)
BROWN, JUDITH GWYN Illustrator, Painter (1933-1992)
BROWN, MARGARET Writer (1910-1952)
BROWN, PAUL Illustrator (1893-1958)
BROWN, RICHARD F Museum Director (1916-1979)
BROWN, RICHARD M Portrait Painter (-1964)
BROWN, ROY Painter (1879-1956)
BROWNE, GEORGE BYRON Painter (1907-1961)
BROWNHILL, HAROLD Painter, Illustrator
BROWNING, G WESLEY Painter (1868-1951)
BRUNDAGE, AVERY Collector (1887-1975)
BRUNS, FREDERICK R, JR Curator (1913-1979)
BRUSSEL-SMITH, BERNARD Printmaker (1914-1989)
BRY, EDITH Assemblage Artist, Collage Artist (1898-1992)
BUCHANAN, JERRY Painter, Educator (1936-1992)
BUCK, RICHARD D Conservator (1903-1977)
BUCKLEY, JOHN MICHAEL Painter (1891-1958)
BUFF, CONRAD Printmaker, Illustrator (1886-1975)
BULLIET, C J Art Critic (1883-1952)
BULLOCK, WYNN Photographer (1902-1975)
BULTMAN, FRITZ Sculptor, Painter (1919-1985)
BUNCE, LOUIS DeMOTT Painter (1914-1983)
BUNKER, GEORGE Painter, Educator (1923-1991)
BUNTING, BAINBRIDGE Historian, Educator (1913-1981)
BURCHFIELD, CHARLES Painter (1893-1967)
BURCK, JACOB Cartoonist, Painter (1904-1982)
BURGESS, JOSEPH E Painter (1891-1961)
BURKE, E AINSLIE Painter, Educator (1922-1991)
BURKE, WILLIAM LOZIER MUNRO Historian (1906-1961)
BURLIN, PAUL Painter (1886-1969)
BURLUIK, DAVID Painter (1882-1967)
BURNEY, MINNA Educator (1891-1958)
BURNS, HARRISON D Painter, Instructor (1946-1991)
BURNS, SID Sculptor, Collector (1916-1979)
BURNSHIDE, KATHERINE TALBOTT Painter
BURNSIDE, CAMERON Painter, Teacher (1887-1952)
BURRISS, R (RILEY) HAL Painter, Illustrator (1892-1991)
BURROWS, PEARL Painter (1903-1960)
BURT, CLYDE EDWIN Ceramist, Educator (-1981)
BURTON, NETTA M Painter (-1960)
BURTON, SCOTT Sculptor, Conceptual Artist (1939-1989)
BUSA, PETER Painter, Sculptor (1914-1983)
BUSBEE, JULIANA ROYSTER Craftsman (1877-1962)
BUSH, BEVERLY Painter, Sculptor (-1969)
BUSH, ELLA SHEPART Painter (1863-)
BUSH, JACK Painter (1909-1977)
BUSH, WILLIAM BROUGHTON Painter (1911-)
BUSHMILLER, ERNIE PAUL Cartoonist (1905-)
BUTLER, JOSEPH (GREEN) Administrator, Painter (1901-1981)
BUZZELLI, JOSEPH ANTHONY Painter, Sculptor (1907-)
BYRUM, RUTHVEN HOLMES Educator (1896-)
CADORIN, ETTOR Sculptor (1876-1952)
CAGE, JOHN Printmaker (1912-1992)
CAHAN, SAMUEL G Artist (-1974)
CAHILL, HOLGER Art Authority (1893-1960)
CALAS, NICHOLAS Critic (-1989)
CALDER, ALEXANDER Sculptor (1898-1976)
CALKINS, LORING GARY Designer (1887-1960)
CALLAHAN, KENNETH Painter (1905-1986)
CALLERY, MARY Sculptor (1903-1977)
CALLISEN, STERLING A Historian, Lecturer (1899-1988)
CALVERT, JENNIE C (MRS FINLEY H) Painter (1878-)
CAMFFERMAN, PETER MARIENUS Painter (1890-1957)
CAMINS, JACQUES JOSEPH Painter, Printmaker (1904-1988)
CAMLIN, JAMES A Painter (1918-1982)
CAMPBELL, CHARLES MALCOLM Painter, Sculptor (1908-1985)
CAMPBELL, EDMUND S Painter, Architect (1884-1950)
CAMPBELL, ORLAND Portrait Painter (1890-1972)
CAMPBELL, SARA WENDELL Illustrator (1886-1960)
CAMPBELL, VIVIAN (VIVIAN CAMPBELL STOLL) Collector, Writer (1919-1986)
CAMPBELL, WILLIAM PATRICK Art Historian, Curator (1914-1976)
CANADAY, JOHN EDWIN Critic (1907-1985)
CANDELL, VICTOR Painter, Educator (1903-1977)
CANFIELD, JANE (WHITE) Sculptor (1897-1984)
CANIFF, MILTON ARTHUR Cartoonist (1907-1988)
CANTEY, SAM BENTON, III Collector (-1973)
CANTOR, ROBERT LLOYD Educator, Designer (1919-1986)
CAPP, AL Cartoonist (1909-1979)
CAREWE, SYLVIA Painter, Tapestry Artist
CAREY, JOHN THOMAS Educator, Historian (1917-1990)
CARLES, ARTHUR B Painter (1882-1952)
CARMACK, PAUL R Cartoonist (1895-1977)
CARPENTER, JAMES MORTON Historian, Artist (1914-1992)
CARRICK, DONALD F Illustrator, Painter (1929-)
CARRILLO, LILIA Painter (1929-1974)
CARRINGTON, OMAR RAYMOND Painter, Instructor (1904-1991)
CARROLL, JOHN Painter (1892-1959)
CARRUTH, PAUL H Illustrator (1892-1961)
CARSTENSON, CECIL C Sculptor, Lecturer (1906-1991)
CARTER, AUGUSTUS D (AD) Cartoonist (1895-1957)
CARTER, DUDLEY CHRISTOPHER Sculptor (1891-1992)
CARTER, HELENE Illustrator (1887-1960)
CASEY, ELIZABETH TEMPLE Curator (1901-1990)
CASSEL, JOHN HARMON Cartoonist
CASTANO, GIOVANNI Art Dealer, Painter (1896-)
CASTLE, MRS ALFRED L Art Patron (1886-1970)
CATHERS, JAMES O Sculptor, Educator (1934-1982)
CAVALLITO, ALBINO Sculptor (1905-1966)
CAVALLON, GIORGIO Painter
CAVANAUGH, JOHN W Sculptor (1921-)
CECERE, GAETANO Sculptor, Lecturer (1894-1985)
CHALIAPIN, BORIS Painter (1907-1979)
CHAMBERLAIN, BETTY Art Administrator, Writer (1908-1983)
CHAMBERLAIN, SAMUEL Printmaker, Writer (1895-1975)
CHAMBERS, JOHN Painter, Filmmaker (1931-1978)
CHAMBI, MARTIN Photographer (1891-1973)
CHANDOR, DOUGLAS Portrait Painter (1897-1953)
CHANIN, ABRAHAM L Lecturer
CHAPELLIER, GEORGE Art Dealer, Collector (1890-1978)
CHAPELLIER, ROBERT Art Dealer (-1974)
CHAPIN, FRANCIS Painter (1899-1965)

CHAPIN, MYRON BUTMAN Painter (1887-1958)
CHAPMAN, (M) ANNE Sculptor, Educator (1930-1986)
CHAPMAN, CHARLES SHEPARD Painter (1879-1962)
CHAPMAN, HOWARD EUGENE Director, Cartoonist (1913-1977)
CHARLES, CLAYTON (HENRY) Sculptor, Educator (1913-1976)
CHARLOT, JEAN Painter, Historian (1898-1979)
CHASE, EDWARD Portrait Painter (1884-1965)
CHASE, FRANK SWIFT Painter (1886-1958)
CHASE, GEORGE H Educator, Writer (1874-1952)
CHASE, JOSEPH CUMMINGS Portrait Painter (1878-1965)
CHASE, SIDNEY M Painter (1877-1957)
CHATTERTON, CLARENCE KERR Painter (1880-1973)
CHEFFETZ, ASA Engraver (1897-1965)
CHENEY, SHELDON Writer, Historian (1886-1980)
CHERNEY, MARVIN Painter (-1966)
CHERRY, HERMAN Painter (1909-1992)
CHESTERTON, DAVID Educator, Graphic Artist (1930-)
CHETHLAHE (DAVID CHETHLAHE PALADIN) Painter, Designer (1926-1984)
CHEW, HARRY Painter, Educator (1925-)
CHIAPELLA, EDWARD EMILE Painter (1889-1951)
CHILDERS, BETTY BIVINS Collector, Patron (1913-1982)
CHILDS, BERNARD Painter, Printmaker (1910-1985)
CHOATE, NATHANIEL Sculptor (1899-1965)
CHOUINARD, MRS NELBERT Educator (-1969)
CHRIST-JANER, ALBERT WILLIAM Painter, Printmaker (1910-1973)
CHRISTENSEN, RALPH Painter (1897-1961)
CHRISTENSON, HANS-JORGEN THORVALD Designer, Silversmith (1924-1983)
CHRISTOPHER, WILLIAM R Painter (1924-1973)
CHRISTY, HOWARD CHANDLER Painter (1872-1952)
CHUMLEY, JOHN WESLEY Painter (1928-)
CHURCH, FREDERICK E Painter (1826-1900)
CIAMPAGLIA, CARLO Mural Painter (1891-1975)
CIKOVSKY, NICOLAI Painter, Muralist (1894-1984)
CITRON, MINNA WRIGHT Painter, Printmaker (1896-1991)
CLANCY, JOHN Art Dealer (-1981)
CLAPP, MAUDE CAROLINE EDE Painter (1876-1960)
CLARE, STEWART Research Artist (1913-1992)
CLARK, ALLAN Sculptor (1896-1950)
CLARK, ALSON SKINNER Painter, Lithographer (1876-1949)
CLARK, ANTHONY MORRIS Curator, Collector (1923-1976)
CLARK, ELIOT CANDEE Painter (1883-1980)
CLARK, G FLETCHER Sculptor (1899-1982)
CLARK, MABEL BEATRICE SMITH Painter (-1957)
CLARK, ROLAND Painter (1874-1957)
CLEAR, CHARLES V Museum Consultant
CLEAVES, MURIEL MATTOCK (MRS H) Illustrator, Painter (-1947)
CLELAND, THOMAS MAITLAND Illustrator (1880-1964)
CLEVELAND, HELEN BARTH Administration, Instruction
CLIME, WINFIELD SCOTT Painter (1881-1958)
CLINEDINST, MAY SPEAR Painter (1887-)
CLOSE. MARJORIE (PERRY) Painter, Lecturer (1899-1978)
CLYMER, JOHN F Painter, Illustrator (1907-1989)
COATES, ROBERT M Writer, Art Critic (1897-1973)
COCHRAN, GEORGE MCKEE (REDBIRD) Painter, Writer (1908-1990)
COE, LLOYD Painter, Illustrator (1899-1977)
COE, ROLAND Cartoonist
COFFEY, MABEL Painter, Etcher (1874-1949)
COFFMAN, HAL Cartoonist (1883-1958)
COHEN, H GEORGE Painter, Educator (1913-1980)
COHOE, GREY Printmaker, Painter (1944-)
COINER, CHARLES T Painter (1897-1989)
COLBORN, JANE TAYLOR Sculptor, Educator (1913-1983)
COLBURN, FRANCIS PEABODY Painter (1909-1984)
COLBY, HOMER WAYLAND Illustrator, Etcher (1874-1950)
COLEMAN, RALPH P Painter (1892-1968)
COLETTI, JOSEPH ARTHUR Sculptor, Writer (1898-1973)
COLIN, RALPH FREDERICK Collector (1900-)
COLLAZO, CARLOS ERICK Painter, Graphic Artist (1956-1990)
COLLES, GERTRUDE Painter (1969-1957)
COLLEY, WILLIAM, JR Collector, Patron (1910-1984)
COLLIER, ALAN CASWELL Painter (1911-1990)
COLLIER, ALBERTA Critic, Consultant (1911-1987)
COLLIER, LEO NATHAN (NATE) Cartoonist (1884-1901)
COLLINS, JOHN IRELAND Painter (1926-1982)
COLLINS, KREIGH Illustrator (1908-1974)
COLLINS, ROY H Illustrator (-1949)
COLSON, CHESTER E Painter, Educator (1917-1985)
CONE, MARVIN Painter (1891-1964)
CONNAWAY, JAY HALL Painter (1893-1970)
CONNER, JOHN RAMSEY Painter (1869-1952)
CONROW, WILFORD SEYMOUR Painter (1880-)
CONSTABLE, WILLIAM GEORGE Art Historian, Writer (1887-1976)
CONSTANT, GEORGE Painter (1892-1978)
COOK, GLADYS EMERSON Illustrator, Painter (1899-)
COOK, HOWARD NORTON Painter, Lecturer (1901-1980)
COOK, PETER (GEOFFREY) Painter (1915-1992)
COOK, WALTER WILLIAM SPENCER Educator (1888-1962)
COOKE, HEREWARD LESTER Art Historian, Painter (1916-1973)
COOKE, KATHLEEN McKEITH Painter, Sculptor (1908-1978)
COOLEY, DIXIE (MRS JOHN L) Painter (1896-)
COOMARASWAMY, ANANDA K Museum Curator (1877-1947)
COOPER, ANTHONY J Painter (1907-1992)
COOPER, FRED G Cartoonist (1883-1962)
COOPER, MARVE H Painter, Curator (1939-)
COOPER, RICHARD Painter (1945-1979)
COOTES, FRANK GRAHAM Painter (1879-1960)
COPPINI, POMPEO LUIGI Sculptor (1870-1957)
COPPOLA, ANDREW Sculptor, Draftsman (1941-1990)
CORBETT, EDWARD M Educator, Painter (1919-1971)
CORBETT, GAIL SHERMAN (MRS HARVEY WILEY CORBETT) Sculptor (1871-1952)
CORBINO, JOHN Painter (1905-1964)
CORCOS, LUCILLE Painter, Illustrator (1908-1973)
CORISH, JOSEPH RYAN Painter (1909-1988)
CORNELIUS, MARTY Painter, Illustrator (1913-1979)
CORNELL, JOSEPH Sculptor (1903-1972)
CORNWELL, DEAN Illustrator (1892-1960)
CORPRON, CARLOTTA M Educator, Photographer (1901-1988)
CORTIGLIA, NICCOLO Painter, Restorer (1893-)
COSGRAVE, J O'HARA, II Illustrator (1908-1968)
COSLA, O K Collector
COSTIGAN, JOHN EDWARD Painter (1888-1972)
COTSWORTH, STAATS Painter (1908-1979)
COTTON, LILLIAN Painter (1901-1962)
COTTON, WILLIAM HENRY Painter (1880-1958)
COURT, LEE WINSLOW Painter (1903-1992)
COURTICE, RODY KENNY Painter (-1973)
COVERT, JOHN Painter (1882-1960)
COVEY, ARTHUR Painter (1878-1960)
COVEY, VICTOR CHARLES B Conservator, Consultant (1928-1989)
COWAN, WOODSON MESSICK Cartoonist, Painter (1886-1977)
COWDREY, MARY BARTLETT Art Historian, Art Critic (1910-1974)
COWLES, RUSSELL Painter (1887-1979)
COX, ALLYN Painter (1896-1982)
COX, J HALLEY Painter, Educator (1910-)
COYER, MAX R Painter (1954-1988)
COZE-DABIJA, PAUL Painter, Writer (1903-1975)
CRAMPTON, ROLLIN Painter (1886-1970)
CRANDELL, BRADSHAW Painter (-1966)
CRANE, ROY (CAMPBELL) Cartoonist, Writer (1901-1977)
CRASKE, LEONARD Sculptor, Lithographer (-1950)
CRATZ, BENJIMIN ARTHUR Painter, Cartoonist (1888-)
CRAVATH, GLENN Cartoonist (-1964)
CRAWFORD, EARL Painter (1890-1960)
CRAWFORD, RALSTON Painter, Lithographer (1906-1977)
CRAWFORD, WILLIAM H Cartoonist, Sculptor (1913-)
CRESPI, PACHITA Painter (1900-1971)
CRESSON, MARGARET Sculptor, Writer (1889-1973)
CRIQUETTE (RUTH DUBARRY MONTAGUE) Painter, Writer (-1991)
CRISS, FRANCIS H Painter (1901-1973)
CROCKWELL, DOUGLAS Commercial Artist (1904-1968)
CRONIN, TONY Gallery Director (-1979)
CROSBY, SUMNER McKNIGHT Art Historian (1909-1982)
CROUGHTON, AMY H Critic (1880-1951)
CROWELL, LUCIUS Painter, Sculptor (1911-1988)
CRUMP, KATHLEEN (WHEELER) Sculptor (1884-1977)
CRUMP, W LESLIE Painter (1894-1962)
CSOKA, STEPHEN Painter (-1989)
CUMING, BEATRICE Painter (1903-1975)
CUMMINGS, FREDERICK JAMES Administrator, Historian (1933-1990)
CUNNINGHAM, BENJAMIN FRAZIER Painter, Educator (1904-1975)
CUNNINGHAM, CHARLES CREHORE Curator, Lecturer (1910-1979)
CUNNINGHAM, IMOGEN Photographer (1883-1976)
CUNNINGHAM, MARION Serigrapher, Lithographer (1911-)
CUPRIEN, FRANK W Painter (1871-1948)
CURRIER, CYRUS BATES Painter, Designer (1868-)
CURTIS, CONSTANCE Painter (-1959)
CUSUMANO, STEFANO Painter, Educator (1912-1975)
CZUFIN, RUDOLF Director (1901-1979)
D'ANDREA, ALBERT PHILIP Educator, Sculptor (1897-1983)
D'AULAIRE, EDGAR PARIN Illustrator, Painter (1898-1986)
DABO, LEON Painter (1868-1960)
DAGYS, JACOB Sculptor (1905-1989)
DAHL, FRANCIS W Cartoonist (1907-1973)
DAHLBERG, EDWIN LENNART Painter (1901-1984)

DAHLER, WARREN Painter (1897-1961)
DAINGERFIELD, MARJORIE JAY Sculptor (-1977)
DALE, BENJAMIN MORAN Illustrator (1889-1951)
DALI, SALVADOR Designer, Painter (1904-1989)
DANIEL, LEWIS C Painter, Illustrator (1901-1952)
DARIUS, DENYLL (DENNIS MITCHELL) Painter (1942-1976)
DARLING, JAY NORWOOD (DING) Cartoonist (1876-1962)
DASBURG, ANDREW MICHAEL Painter (1887-1979)
DATUS, JAY Painter, Art Administrator (1914-1974)
DATZ, A MARK Painter (1889-)
DAUGHERTY, JAMES HENRY Painter, Writer (1898-1974)
DAUGHERTY, MARSHALL HARRISON Sculptor, Medalist (1915-1991)
DAVENPORT, EDITH FAIRFAX Painter (1880-1957)
DAVEY, RANDALL Painter (1887-1964)
DAVIDSON, ALLAN ALBERT Painter, Sculptor (1913-1988)
DAVIDSON, JO Sculptor (1883-1952)
DAVIDSON, MORRIS Painter (1898-1979)
DAVIS, (MR & MRS) WALTER Collectors, Patrons (-1991)
DAVIS, DONALD ROBERT Painter, Dealer (1909-1990)
DAVIS, ESTHER M Sculptor, Painter (1893-1974)
DAVIS, GENE B Painter (1920-1985)
DAVIS, JAMES Abstract Artist (1901-1974)
DAVIS, JOHN SHERWOOD Potter, Administrator (1942-)
DAVIS, LEW E Painter (1910-1979)
DAVIS, PHIL Cartoonist (-1964)
DAVIS, ROBERT TYLER Administrator, Historian (1904-)
DAVIS, STUART Painter (1894-1964)
DAVIS, WAYNE LAMBERT Painter, Illustrator (1904-1988)
DAVIS, WILLIAM STEEPLE Painter (1884-1961)
DAVISSON, HOMER G Painter (1866-)
DAWSON, EVE Painter
DAY, HORACE TALMAGE Painter, Director (1909-)
DAY, JOHN Painter, Educator (1932-1984)
DAY, MABEL K Painter (1884-)
DAY, WORDEN Sculptor, Printmaker (1916-1986)
DEAN, ERNEST WILFRID Painter
DE BORHEGYI, STEPHEN Museum Director, Writer (1921-1969)
DE BOTTON, JEAN PHILIPPE Painter, Sculptor (-1978)
DECKER, JOHN Painter (1895-)
DE CREEFT, JOSE Sculptor, Educator (1884-1982)
DE DIEGO, JULIO Painter, Illustrator (1900-1979)
DE ERDELY, FRANCIS Painter, Educator (1904-1959)
DEFRANCESCO, ITALO I Educator (1901-1967)
DE FRANCISCI, ANTHONY Sculptor (1887-1964)
DE GRAZIA, ETTORE TED Painter (1909-1982)
DEHN, ADOLF Graphic Artist (1895-1968)
DEINES, E HUBERT Engraver (1894-1967)
DE JONG, GERRIT, JR Lecturer, Writer (1892-1979)
DEKNATEL, FREDERICK BROCKWAY Art Historian, Educator (1905-1973)
DE KOONING, ELAINE MARIE CATHERINE Painter, Writer (1920-1989)
DE KOONING, WILLIAM Painter (1904-1988)
DELANEY, BEAUFORD Painter (1902-1979)
DEL CASTILLO, MARY VIRGINIA Painter (1865-)
DELONGA, LEONARD ANTHONY Sculptor, Educator (1925-1990)
DE MANCE, HENRI Painter (1871-1948)
DE MARCO, JEAN ANTOINE Sculptor (1898-1990)
DE MARTELLY, JOHN STOCKTON Painter, Printmaker (1903-1980)
DE MARTINI, JOSEPH Painter (1896-)
DE MENIL, JOHN Collector (1904-1973)
DEMETRIOS, GEORGE Sculptor (1896-1974)
DEMIANOFF, RENEE LOCKHART Director (1910-1962)
DE MISKEY, JULIAN Sculptor, Printmaker (-1986)
DEMPSEY, RICHARD W Painter, Lecturer (1909-)
DENNIS, BURT MORGAN Etcher (1892-1960)
DENSLOW, DOROTHEA HENRIETTA Sculptor (1900- 1971)
DENTZEL, CARL SCHAEFER Museum Director, Writer (1913-1980)
DePINNA, VIVIAN Painter (1883-1978)
DE PREY, JUAN Painter (-1962)
DE RIVERA, JOSE Sculptor (1904-1985)
DERUJINSKY, GLEB W Sculptor, Craftsman (1888-1975)
DE RUTH, JAN Painter, Printmaker(1922-1991)
DESSAR, LOUIS PAUL Painter (1867-1952)
DE TORE, JOHN E Painter (1902-1975)
DEVREE, HOWARD Critic (1890-1966)
DIBONA, ANTHONY Sculptor, Lithographer (1896-)
DICKERSON, WILLIAM JUDSON Painter (1904-)
DICKINSON, EDWIN W Painter (1891-1979)
DIENES, SARI Assemblage Artist, Printmaker (1898-1992)
DIETSCH, C PERCIVAL Sculptor (1881-1961)
DIGIUSTO, GERALD N Sculptor (1929-1987)
DILLER, BURGOYNE Painter (1906-1965)
DIMAN, HOMER Painter (1914-1974)
DIODA, ADOLPH T Sculptor, Assemblage Artist (1915-1991)
DIRK, NATHANIEL Painter (1896-1961)
DIRKS, RUDOLPH Cartoonist (-1968)
DISMUKES, MARY ETHEL Painter (-1952)
DIXON, FRANCIS S Painter (1879-1967)
DOBBS, ELLA VICTORIA Educator (1866-1952)
DOBKIN, ALEXANDER Painter (1908-1975)
DOBSON, DAVID IRVING (DIAMONDSTEIN) Painter (1883-1957)
DODGE, HAZEL (MRS WILLIAM T TURMAN) Curator (1903-1957)
DOI, ISAMI Painter (1903-1965)
DOLE, WILLIAM Painter, Educator (1917-1983)
DOMBEK, BLANCHE M Painter, Sculptor (-1987)
DONAHEY, JAMES HARRISON Cartoonist (1875-1949)
DONAHUE, BENEDICT SR Educator
DONATO, GIUSEPPE Sculptor (1881-1965)
DONNELLY, MARY E Painter (1898-1963)
DORNER, ALEXANDER Historian (1893-)
DORR, (VIRGINIA) NELL Photographer (1893-)
DOUGLAS, AARON Painter (1900-1979)
DOUGLAS, FREDERIC HUNTINGTON Curator (1897-1956)
DOUGLAS, LESTER Designer (1894-1961)
DOUGLAS, ROBERT LANGTON Critic (-1951)
DOVE, ARTHUR GARFIELD Painter (1880-1946)
DOWLING, ROBERT W Patron (1895-1973)
DOYON, GERARD MAURICE Educator, Historian (1923-1990)
DRABKIN, STELLA Painter, Designer (1900-1976)
DREIER, KATHERINE S Painter, Lecturer (1877-1952)
DREITZER, ALBERT J Collector, Patron (1902-1985)
DRESSER, LOUISA (LOUISA DRESSER CAMPBELL) Administrator, Historian (1907-1988)
DREWES, WERNER Painter, Printmaker (1899-1985)
DREWLOWE, EVE Painter, Sculptor (1924-1988)
DREXLER, ARTHUR JUSTIN Director, Curator (1925-1987)
DRIGGS, ELSIE Painter (1898-1992)
DROGKAMP, CHARLES Painter (-1958)
DRUMMOND, ARTHUR A Painter, Illustrator (1891-)
DRURY, WILLIAM H Painter (1888-1960)
DRYER, MOIRA JANE Painter, Sculptor (1957-1992)
DRYFOOS, NANCY Sculptor (1918-1991)
DUANE, TANYA Painter, Collage Artist
DUBLE, LU Sculptor (1896-1970)
DU BOIS, GUY PENE Painter (1884-1958)
DUFFY, EDMUND Cartoonist (1899-1962)
DUFNER, EDWARD Painter (1871-1957)
DU MOND, FRANK V Painter (1865-1951)
DUNCANSON, ROBERT Painter (1817-1872)
DUNN, ALAN (CANTWELL) Cartoonist, Writer (1900-1974)
DUNN, HARVEY T Illustrator, Painter (1884-1952)
DUPONT, HENRY F Museum Curator (1880-1969)
DURLACH, MARCUS RUSSELL Painter (1911-1991)
DUVOISIN, ROGER Writer, Illustrator (1904-1980)
DWIGGINS, CLARE Cartoonist (1874-1958)
DWIGGINS, WILLIAM ADDISON Designer (1880-1956)
DWIGHT, EDWARD HAROLD Museum Director (1919-1981)
EASBY, DUDLEY T JR Art Administrator, Art Historian (1905-1973)
EASTMAN, ALVIN CLARK Orientalist (1894-1959)
EASTMAN, WILLIAM JOSEPH Painter (1881-1950)
EASTON, FRANK LORENCE Painter (1884-)
EATON, ALLEN HENDERSHOTT Writer (1878-1962)
EBERLE, MERAB Critic (-1959)
EBERMAN, EDWIN Administrator, Educator (1905-1988)
ECKE, GUSTAV Museum Curator (-1971)
ED, CARL Cartoonist (1890-1959)
EDWARDS, EMMET Painter (1907-)
EDWARDS, GEORGE WHARTON Painter, Illustrator (1869-1950)
EDWARDS, ROBERT Painter, Engraver (1879-1948)
EGAS, CAMILO Educator (1897-1962)
EGE, OTTO F Educator, Writer (1888-1951)
EGGERS, GEORGE WILLIAM Educator (1883-1958)
EGGERS, RICHARD F Architect (1918-1979)
EGLESON, JIM (JAMES DOWNEY) Printmaker, Painter (1907-)
EHRMAN, FREDERICK L Collector (1906-1973)
EICHENBERG, FRITZ Graphic Artist, Illustrator (1901-1990)
EIDE, PALMER Sculptor, Designer (1906-1991)
EISENLOH R, EDWARD G Painter (1873-1961)
EISNER, DOROTHY (DOROTHY EISNER MCDONALD) Painter, Collage Artist (1906-)
EITEL, CLIFFE DEAN Painter, Etcher (1909-)
ELDER, ARTHUR JOHN Painter, Etcher (1874-)
ELDLITZ, DOROTH MEIGS Patron, Photographer (1891-1976)
ELDREDGE, STUART EDSON Painter (1902-1992)
ELIASON, SHIRLEY (SHIRLEY ELIASON HAUPT) Painter, Educator (1926-1988)
ELIASOPH, PAULA Painter, Writer (1895-)

ELISOFON, ELIOT Painter, Photographer (1911-1973)
ELKON, ROBERT Art Dealer, Collector (1928-1983)
ELLERHUSEN, FLORENCE COONEY Painter (-1950)
ELLERHUSEN, ULRIC H Sculptor (1879-1957)
ELLIOTT, PHILIP CLARKSON Painter(1903-1985)
ELLIS, CARL EUGENE Art Administrator, Instructor (1932-1977)
ELLIS, FREMONT Painter (1897-1985)
ELLIS, JOSEPH BAILEY Educator, Sculptor (1890-)
ELLIS, ROBERT CARROLL Painter, Printmaker (1923-1979)
ELLSWORTH, CLARENCE A Illustrator (1885-1961)
ELSNER, LARRY EDWARD Sculptor, Educator (1930-)
ELY, FANNY G Painter (1879-1961)
EMBRY, NORRIS Painter (1921-1981)
EMIL, ALLAN D Collector, Patron (1898-1976)
EMMERICH, IRENE HILLEBRAND Painter
EMMET, LYDIA FIELD Painter (1886-1952)
ENFIELD, HARRY Illustrator (1906-1958)
ENGEL, HARRY Painter (1901-1970)
ENGEL, MICHAEL M Art Publicist (1896-1969)
ENO, JAMES LORNE Painter, Teacher (1887-1952)
ENSER, GEORGE Designer (1890-1961)
EPSTEIN, ETHEL S Collector
ERICSON, ERNEST Illustrator, Instructor (-1981)
ERLANGER, ELIZABETH N Painter, Lecturer (1901-1975)
ERNST, JIMMY Painter,Educator (1920-)
ERNST, MAX Painter, Sculptor (1891-1976)
ERSKINE, HAROLD PERRY Sculptor (1879-1951)
ESCHMANN, JEAN CHARLES Craftsman (1896-1961)
ESHERICK, W HARTON Sculptor, Designer (1887-1970)
ETNER, STEPHEN MORGAN Painter (1903-)
ETTINGHAUSEN, RICHARD Administrator, Educator (1906-1979)
EVANS, DONALD Painter (1946-1977)
EVANS, MINNIE Painter (1892-1987)
EVANS, RUDULPH Sculptor (1879-1960)
EVERETT, LEN G Painter
EVERETT, MARY O (MRS H G) Painter (1876-1948)
EVERGOOD, PHILIP Painter, Graphic Artist (1901-1973)
EVERINGHAM, MILLARD Painter, Etcher (1912-)
EWING, BAYARD Administrator, Collector (1916-1991)
FABRES, OSCAR Cartoonist (1895-1961)
FABRI, RALPH Painter, Writer (1894-1975)
FAHLSTROM, OYVIND Painter (1928-1976)
FAIERS, TED (EDWARD SPENCER) Painter, Printmaker (1908-1985)
FAINTER, ROBERT A Educator, Painter (1942-1978)
FAIRCHILD, MAY Painter (1872-1959)
FALLS, CHARLES BUCKLES Illustrator (1874-1959)
FALTER, JOHN Illustrator (1910-1982)
FARLOW, HARRY Painter (1882-1956)
FARMER, MABEL McKIBBIN Engraver (1903-)
FARNSWORTH, JERRY Painter, Writer (1895-)
FARR, FRED Sculptor (1914-1973)
FARRELL, KATHERINE L Painter, Etcher (1857-)
FASANO, CLARA Sculptor (-1990)
FASTOVE, AARON (AARON FASTOVSKY) Painter (1898-1979)
FAULKNER, BARRY Painter (1881-1966)
FAULKNER, KADY B Painter, Educator (1901-1977)
FAULKNER, RAY N Educator, Writer (1906-1975)
FAUSETT, LYNN Painter (1894-1977)
FAWCETT, ROBERT Illustrator (1903-1967)
FAY, WILBUR M Designer (1904-1959)
FEELEY, PAUL Painter (1913-1966)
FEHER, JOSEPH Curator, Painter (1908-1987)
FEIGIN, DOROTHY L Painter (1904-1969)
FEIGL, HUGO Art Dealer (1890-1961)
FEINBLATT, EBRIA Historian
FEITELSON, LORSER Painter (1898-1978)
FELS, C P Painter, Writer (1912-1991)
FENICAL, MARLIN E Painter, Photographer (1907-1983)
FENTON, BEATRICE Sculptor (1887-1983)
FENTON, JOHN NATHANIEL Painter, Etcher (1912-1977)
FERBER, HERBERT Sculptor, Painter (1906-1991)
FERGUSON, BARCLAY (VISCOUNT OF LAMOND) Painter, Muralist (1924-1991)
FERNALD, HELEN ELIZABETH Educator (1891-1964)
FERRARI, FEBO Sculptor (1865-)
FERREN, JOHN Painter (1905-1970)
FICKLEN, JACK HOWELLS Cartoonist (1911-1980)
FIELD, SAUL Printmaker, Lecturer (1912-1987)
FIELDS, MITCHELL Sculptor (1901-1966)
FIENE, ALICIA W Painter (1919-1961)
FIENE, ERNEST Painter (1894-1965)
FIERO, EMILIE L Sculptor (1889-1974)
FILTZER, HYMAN Sculptor, Restorer (1901-1967)
FINDLAY, HELEN T Dealer (1909-1992)
FINE, PERLE Painter (1905-1988)
FINK, LOUIS R Painter (1925-1980)
FINLAYSON, DONALD LORD Educator (1897-1960)
FINLEY, DAVID EDWARD Art Administrator (1890-1977)
FINLEY, MARY L Painter (-1964)
FINTA, ALEXANDER Sculptor (1881-1958)
FISCHETTI, JOHN Cartoonist (1916-1980)
FISH, DOROTHY S Ceramist (1906-1958)
FISHER, REGINALD Writer (1906-1966)
FISKE, GERTRUDE Painter (1879-1961)
FITE, HARVEY Sculptor (1903-1976)
FITZGERALD, EDMUND J Painter, Lecturer (1912-1989)
FITZGERALD, HARRIET Painter, Lecturer (1904-1984)
FITZGERALD, J EDWARD Photographer (1923-1977)
FITZSIMMONS, JAMES JOSEPH Painter, Architect (1908-)
FLAGG, JAMES MONTGOMERY Illustrator (1877-1960)
FLANAGAN, JOHN F Sculptor (1898-1952)
FLECK, PAUL DUNCAN Director (1934-1992)
FLEISCHMANN, ADOLF R Painter (-1969)
FLEISCHMANN, JULIUS Collector
FLEMING, ALLAN ROBB Designer, Calligrapher (1929-1977)
FLIEGEL, LESLIE Painter (1912-1968)
FLOCH, JOSEPH Painter (1895-1977)
FLOETHE, RICHARD Illustrator, Designer (1901-1988)
FLOOD, EDWARD C Sculptor, Painter (1944-1985)
FLORSHEIM, RICHARD A Painter, Printmaker (1916-1979)
FLORY, ARTHUR L Graphic Artist, Painter (1914-1972)
FOGEL, SEYMOUR Painter, Sculptor (1911-1984)
FOLLETT, JEAN FRANCES Sculptor, Painter (1917-1991)
FONTANNINI, CLARE Educator, Sculptor (-1984)
FOOTE, JOHN JR Painter (-1968)
FOOTE, WILL HOWE Painter (1874-1965)
FORBES, EDWARD W Museum Director (1873-1969)
FORCE, JULIANA R Museum Director (-1948)
FORD, CHARLES HENRI Painter, Photographer (1913-)
FORD, ELEANOR CLAY Patron (1896-1976)
FORSYTH, CONSTANCE Painter, Printmaker (1903-1987)
FOSBURGH, JAMES WHITNEY Painter, Writer (1910-1978)
FOSDICK, SINA G Art Administrator, Collector (-1983)
FOSTER, GENEVIEVE Writer, Illustrator (1893-1979)
FOSTER, HAL Cartoonist, Painter (1892-1982)
FOSTER, JAMES W SR Museum Director
FOSTER, KENNETH E Museum Director (-1964)
FOURNIER, ALEXIS JEAN Painter (1865-1948)
FOUSEK, FRANK DANIEL Printmaker, Painter (1913-1979)
FOWLER, ALFRED Writer (1889-)
FOWLER, MEL (WALTER) Sculptor (1921-)
FOX, CHARLES HAROLD Craftsman (1905-1979)
FOX, MILTON S Painter (1904-1971)
FRAMPTON, HOLLIS Filmmaker (1936-1984)
FRANCO, ROBERT JOHN Painter, Educator (1932-)
FRANGELLA, LUIS Painter (1944-)
FRANKENSTEIN, ALFRED VICTOR Art Critic, Art Historian (1906-1981)
FRANKFURTER, ALFRED Art Editor (-1965)
FRANKL, PAUL THEODORE Designer (1876-1958)
FRANKLE, PHILIP Painter (1913-1968)
FRANKLIN, CLARENCE Collector (-1967)
FRASER, DOUGLAS (FERRAR) Art Historian, Educator (1929-1982)
FRASER, LAURA G Sculptor (1889-1966)
FRASER, MALCOLM Painter (1869-1949)
FRAZIER, KENNETH Painter (1867-1949)
FRAZIER, RICHARD WILLIAMS Sculptor (1922-1983)
FREDENTHAL, DAVID Painter (1914-1958)
FREDERICK, EUGENE WALLACE Printmaker, Educator (1927-)
FREED, ERNEST BRADFIELD Printmaker, Painter (1908-)
FREED, WILLIAM Painter (1902-1984)
FREEDMAN, MAURICE Painter (1904-)
FREEMAN, DON Author & Illustrator of Children's Books (1909-1978)
FREEMAN, JANE Portrait Painter (1885-1963)
FREER, HOWARD MORTIMER Painter (1904-1960)
FREIFELD, ERIC Painter, Educator (1919-)
FREILICH, MICHAEL L Art Dealer, Collector (1912-1975)
FREIMAN, ROBERT J Painter (1917-1991)
FREY, ERWIN F Sculptor (1892-1967)
FRIEDENSOHN, ELIAS Painter, Sculptor (1924-1991)
FRIEDLAENDER, WALTER Art Historian (-1966)
FRIEDLANDER, ISAC Engraver (1890-1968)
FRIEN D, DAVID Painter, Educator (1899-1978)
FRISHMUTH, HARRIET WHITNEY Sculptor (1880-1979)
FROELICH, PAUL Painter (1897-)
FROMAN, RAMON MITCHELL Painter (1908-1980)
FROMBERG, GERALD Educator, Filmmaker (1925-1977)
FROUCHTBEN, BERNARD Painter (1878-1956)
FRUHAUF, ALINE Painter, Printmaker (1907-1978)

FRY, EDWARD F Educator, Critic (1935-1992)
FUERSTENBURG, PAUL W Commercial Artist (1875-1953)
FULLER, META VAUX WARRICK Sculptor (1877-1968)
FULLER, R BUCKMINSTER Design Scientist (1895-1983)
FULLER, RICHARD EUGENE Museum Director (1897-1976)
FULTON, CYRUS JAMES Painter (1873-1949)
GABO, NAUM Sculptor (1890-1977)
GAILIS, JANIS Painter (1909-1975)
GALE, WALTER RASIN Educator (1878-1959)
GALLATIN, ALBERT EUGENE Painter (1882-1952)
GALOS, BEN Painter (-1963)
GALVAN, JESUS GERRERO Painter
GANNAM, JOHN Painter (1907-1965)
GARBATY, EUGENE L Collector (-1966)
GARBE, WILLIAM Painter, Editor (1948-1989)
GARBER, DANIEL Painter (1880-1958)
GARBISCH, BERNICE CHRYSLER Collector
GARBISCH, EDGAR WILLIAM Collector (1899-1979)
GARNER, ARCHIBALD Sculptor, Designer (1904-1970)
GARRISON, JESSE JANES Educator (1901-)
GARTH, JOHN Painter (1894-1971)
GASSER, HENRY MARTIN Painter, Writer (1909-1981)
GATCH, LEE Painter (1909-1968)
GATRELL, MARION THOMPSON Educator, Painter (1909-)
GATRELL, ROBERT MORRIS Educator, Painter (1906-1982)
GAUDIN, MARGUERITE Designer (1909-)
GAUGH, HARRY F Educator, Critic (-1992)
GAYNE, CLIFTON ALEXANDER, JR Educator (1912-1971)
GEARHART, MAY Etcher
GEBER, HANA Sculptor, Instructor (1910-)
GEE, YUN Painter (1906-1963)
GEESEY, TITUS CORNELIUS Collector, Patron (1893-1969)
GEIGER, ELIZABETH DE CHAMISSO Sculptor
GEISEL, THEDOR SEUSS (DR SEUSS) Illustrator, Writer (1904-1991)
GELB, JAN Painter, Printmaker (1906-1978)
GELMAN, MILTON Collector (1914-1991)
GERARD, PAULA (RENISON) Painter, Draftsman (1907-1991)
GERARDIA, HELEN Painter, Printmaker
GERSHOY, EUGENIE Sculptor, Painter (1901-1983)
GERTH, RUTH Illustrator (-1952)
GETTY, J PAUL Collector, Writer (1892-1976)
GIAMBRUNI, TIO Sculptor (1925-1971)
GIBBERED, ERIC WATERS Painter (1897-1972)
GIBSON, ROLAND Collector, Curator (1902-)
GIESCHEN, MARTIN JOHN Educator, Painter (1918-1991)
GIKOW, RUTH (RUTH GIKOW LEVINE) Painter, Printmaker (1913-1982)
GILBERT, CLYDE LINGLE Painter (1898-1986)
GILCHRIST, AGNES ADDISON Art & Architectural Historian (1907-1976)
GILL, FREDERICK JAMES Painter, Instructor (1906-1974)
GILLIES, MARY ANN Artist
GILPIN, LAURA Photographer, Writer (1891-1979)
GILRIN, THEODORE H Painter (-1967)
GIUSTI, GEORGE Designer, Sculptor (-1990)
GLAMAN, EUGENIE FISH Etcher (1872-1956)
GLARNER, FRITZ Painter (1899-1972)
GLASGOW, LUKMAN Ceramist, Administrator (1935-1988)
GLEASON, JOE DUNCAN Painter (1879-1959)
GLICKMAN, MAURICE Sculptor, Writer (1906-)
GLINES, ELLEN (MRS WALTER A) Painter (-1951)
GLINSKY, VINCENT Sculptor, Educator (1895-1975)
GODWIN, FRANCES GRAY Historian (1908-1979)
GOETZ, EDITH JEAN Painter, Instructor (1918-1986)
GOETZ, OSWALD H Lecturer (1896-1960)
GOETZ, RICHARD VERNON Painter, Instructor (1915-1991)
GOLDBERG, ELIAS Painter (1887-1978)
GOLDBERG, NORMAN LEWIS Writer, Lecturer (1906-1982)
GOLDIN, AMY Art Critic (1926-1978)
GOLDOWSKY, NOAH Art Dealer (1909-)
GOLDSMITH, MORTON RALPH Collector, Patron (1882-1971)
GOLDWATER, ROBERT Art Historian (1907-1973)
GOLINKIN, JOSEPH WEBSTER Painter, Printmaker (1896-1977)
GOLLIN, JOSHUA A Collector, Patron (1905-)
GOMEZ-SICRE, JOSE Administrator, Critic (1916-1991)
GOOCH, DONALD BURNETTE Painter (1907-1985)
GOODELMAN, AARON J Sculptor (1891-1978)
GORDER, CLAYTON J Painter, Educator (1936-1987)
GORDON, DONALD EDWARD Historian, Educator (1931-)
GORDON, JOHN Administrator, Historian (1912-1978)
GORDON, MAXWELL Painter (1910-1982)
GORDY, ROBERT P Painter, Printmaker (1933-1986)
GORHAM, SIDNEY Painter (1870-1947)
GORSLINE, DOUGLAS WARNER Painter, Illustrator (1913-1985)
GOSS, JOHN Illustrator (1886-)
GOTTLIEB, ADOLPH Painter (1903-1974)
GRABACH, JOHN R Painter, Instructor (1880-1981)
GRAHAM, JOHN D Painter (1881-1961)
GRAHAM, RICHARD MARSTON Sculptor, Educator (1939-)
GRAMATKY, HARDIE Painter, Writer (1907-1979)
GRANT, GORDON HOPE Etcher (1875-1962)
GRANT, J JEFFREY Painter (1883-1960)
GRAVES, JOHN W Collector (-1978)
GRAVES, MAITLAND Writer, Painter (1902-)
GRAY, HAROLD Cartoonist (1894-1968)
GRAY, JABEZ Painter (-1950)
GRAY, WELLINGTON BURBANK Educator, Designer (1919-1977)
GRAYSON, CLIFFORD PREVOST Painter (1857-1951)
GREACEN, EDMUND Painter (1877-1949)
GREATHOUSE, WALSER S Museum Director (-1966)
GRECO, ROBERT Painter (-1965)
GREEN, BERNARD Painter (1887-1951)
GREENBAUM, DOROTHEA SCHWARCZ Sculptor, Graphic Artist (1893-1986)
GREENE, BALCOMB Painter (1904-1990)
GREENE, ELMER WESTLEY, JR Painter (1907-1964)
GREENE, GERTRUDE (MRS BALCOMB GREENE) Painter (1904-1956)
GREENE, J BARRY Painter (1895-1966)
GREENE, VERNON VAN ATTA Cartoonist (-1965)
GREENES, RHODA Sculptor (1926-1979)
GREEN-FIELD, ALBERT Art Publicist
GREENLEAF, ESTHER (HARGRAVE) Painter, Printmaker (1905-1989)
GREENLEAF, RAY Illustrator (-1950)
GREENSTEIN, ILISE Painter, Conceptual Artist (1928-)
GREENWOOD, MARION Painter, Lithographer (1909-1970)
GREGG, RICHARD NELSON Museum Director (1926-1986)
GREGORY, ANGELA Sculptor, Educator (1903-1990)
GREGORY, JOHN Sculptor (1879-1958)
GREGORY, WAYLANDE Sculptor, Designer (1905-1971)
GREISSLE, HERMANN A Printmaker, Painter (1925-1991)
GRIER, HARRY DOBSON MILLER Museum Director (1914-1972)
GRIESSLER, FRANZ ANTON Painter (1897-1974)
GRIFFIN, RACHAEL S Art Administrator, Writer (-1983)
GRIFFITH, LOUIS OSCAR Painter (1875-1956)
GRIGAUT, PAUL L Museum Curator (-1969)
GRIGGS, MAITLAND LEE Collector (1902-1989)
GRIGOR, MARGARET CHRISTIAN Sculptor (1912-1981)
GRIMES, FRANCES T Sculptor (1869-1963)
GRINAGER, ALEXANDER Painter (1865-1949)
GRODENSKY, SAMUEL Painter (1894-1974)
GROPPER, WILLIAM Painter, Lithographer (1897-1977)
GROSHANS, WERNER Painter (1913-1986)
GROSS, CHAIM Sculptor, Instructor (1904-1991)
GROSS, ESTELLE SHANE Dealer (-1992)
GROSZ, GEORGE Painter (1893-1959)
GROTELL, MAIJA Ceramist, Educator (1899-1973)
GROTENRATH, RUTH Painter, Printmaker (1912-1988)
GROTH, BRUNO Sculptor (1905-1991)
GROVES, HANNAH CUTIER Painter, Etcher (1868-1952)
GRUBAR, FRANCIS STANLEY Historian, Lecturer (1924-1991)
GRUBB, PAT PINCOMBE Painter, Writer (1922-1977)
GRUBERT, CARL ALFRED Cartoonist (1911-1979)
GRUENTHER, SUE CORY (MRS RUDOLPH) Painter (-1948)
GRUGER, FREDERICK R Illustrator (1871-1953)
GRUMMANN, PAUL H Museum Director (-1950)
GRUNDY, J(OHN OWEN) Patron, Writer (1911-1985)
GRUPPE, EMIL ALBERT Painter (1896-1978)
GRUPPE, KARL HEINRICH Sculptor (1893-1982)
GUERRERO, JOSE Painter, Printmaker (1914-)
GUGGENHEIM, HARRY FRANK Collector, Publisher, Writer (1890-1971)
GUGGENHEIM, PEGGY Collector, Patron (1898-1979)
GUGGENHEIMER, RICHARD HENRY Painter, Writer (1906-1977)
GUGLIELMI, LOUIS O Painter (1906-1956)
GUINZBURG, FREDERICK Sculptor (1897-1978)
GUMBERTS, WILLIAM A Collector, Patron (1912-)
GUNDLACH, HELEN FUCHS Painter (1892-1959)
GUSTAVSON, LELAND Illustrator (-1966)
GUSTON, PHILIP Painter (1913-1980)
GUY, JAMES M Painter, Educator (1910-1983)
GWATHMEY, ROBERT Painter (1903-1988)
HADER, ELMER (STANLEY) Illustrator, Writer (1889-1973)
HADLEY, ROLLIN VAN NOSTRAND Museum Director (1927-1992)
HADLOCK, WENDELL STANWOOD Museum Director (1911-1978)
HAGGIN, BEN ALI Painter, Designer (1882-1951)
HAHN, EMANUEL OTTO Sculptor (1881-1957)
HAIG, PATIGIAN Sculptor (1876-1950)
HAINES, RICHARD Painter, Muralist (1906-1984)
HALE, LILLIAN WESTCOTT Painter (1881-1963)

HALE, ROBERT BEVERLY Administrator, Instructor (1901-)
HALEY, JOHN CHARLES Painter, Sculptor (1905-1991)
HALEY, ROBERT D Painter (1893-1959)
HALSMAN, PHILIPPE Photographer (1906-1979)
HAMBLETT, THEORA Painter, Illustrator (1895-)
HAMM, BETH CREEVY Painter (1885-1958)
HAMMER, ARMAND Collector, Dealer (1898-1990)
HAMMER, VICTOR KARL Painter (-1967)
HAMMOND, NATALIE HAYS Painter, Museum Director (1904-)
HAMPTON, BILL Painter (1925-1977)
HAND, MOLLY WILLIAMS Teacher, Painter (1892-1951)
HANDFORTH, THOMAS S Lithographer (1897-1948)
HANFMANN, GEORGE M A Educator, Historian (1911-1986)
HANKS, NANCY Administrator (1927-1983)
HANLEY, T EDWARD Collector (-1969)
HANNA, KATHERINE Museum Director (1913-1988)
HANNA, THOMAS KING Painter (-1951)
HANSEN, ARMIN CARL Painter (1886-1957)
HANSEN, ARNE RAE Art Dealer, Historian (1940-1992)
HANSON, LAWRENCE Sculptor, Educator (1936-1992)
HAPKE, PAUL FREDERICK Painter, Educator (1922-1984)
HARDER, CHARLES MABRY Craftsman (1899-1959)
HARDIN, ADLAIS Sculptor (1901-1989)
HARDING, GEORGE Painter (-1959)
HARDY, HOWARD (COLLINS) Painter, Instructor (1900-1988)
HARE, MICHAEL MEREDITH Scholar (1909-1968)
HARER, FREDERICK W Painter, Sculptor (1879-1949)
HARING, KEITH Painter (1958-1990)
HARPER, GEORGE COBURN Etcher (1887-1962)
HARPER, JOHN RUSSELL Art Historian (1914-1983)
HARRIS, BEN JORJ Illustrator (1904-1957)
HARRIS, JULLIAN HOKE Sculptor, Architect (1906-1987)
HARRIS, LUCILLE S Painter, Printmaker (1914-1984)
HARRIS, MARGIE COLEMAN Painter (1891-)
HARRISON, (WILLIAM) ALLAN Painter (1911-)
HARRITON, ABRAHAM Painter (1893-1986)
HARSANYI, CHARLES Painter (1905-1973)
HART, AGNES Painter, Instructor (-1979)
HART, JOHN FRANCIS Cartoonist, Engraver (1868-)
HART, MORGAN DRAKE Painter, Instructor (1899-)
HARTL, LEON Painter (1889-)
HARTMAN, BERTRAM Painter (1882-)
HARTMANN, GEORG THEO Painter, Etcher (1894-1976)
HARTT, FREDERICK Historian, Educator (1914-1991)
HARTWELL, GEORGE KENNETH Lithographer (1891-1949)
HARVEY, JAMES V Painter (-1965)
HASELTINE, HERBERT Sculptor (1877-1962)
HASKELL, WILLIAM H Educator (1875-1952)
HASKINS, JOHN FRANKLIN Historian, Educator (1919-1991)
HASTIE, REID Educator, Writer (1916-1987)
HASWELL, ERNEST BRUCE Sculptor (1889-1965)
HATCH, EMILY NICHOLS Painter (1871-1959)
HATHAWAY, CALVIN S Curator (-1974)
HATHAWAY, LOVERING Painter (1898-1949)
HATLO, JAMES Cartoonist (1898-1963)
HAUSCHKA, CAROL SPAETH Painter (1883-1948)
HAUSMANN, MARIANNE PISKO Painter
HAVENS JAMES DEXTER Graphic Artist (1900-1960)
HAVENS, MURRY P Designer
HAWLEY, MARGARET FOOTE Portrait Painter (1880-1963)
HAWORTH, B COQUILL Painter (1904-)
HAWORTH, PETER Painter, Stained Glass Artist (1889-)
HAYDEN, PALMER C Painter (1893-1973)
HAYES, WILLIAM CHRISTOPHER Museum Curator (-1963)
HAZELL, FRANK Painter (1883-)
HEALY, ARTHUR K D Painter, Lecturer (1902-1978)
HEBER, CARL A Sculptor (1885-1956)
HECHT, ZOLTAN Painter (1890-1968)
HEERAMANECK, NASIL M Collector, Patron, Art Dealer (1902-1971)
HEINTZELMAN, ARTHUR W Etcher (1890-1965)
HELCK, PETER Painter, Printmaker (1893-1988)
HELD, ALMA M Painter (-1988)
HELD, JOHN, JR Cartoonist (1889-1958)
HELLER, MAXWELL Painter (1881-1963)
HELM, JOHN F JR Educator, Painter (1900-1972)
HELWIG, ARTHUR LOUIS Painter, Instructor (1899-1976)
HENDERSON, LESTER KLERSTEAD Photographer (1906-)
HENRICKSEN, RALF CHRISTIAN Educator, Painter (1907-1975)
HERBERT, MARIAN Painter (1899-1960)
HERING, HARRY Painter (1887-1967)
HERING, HENRY Sculptor (1874-1949)
HERPST, MARTHA JANE Painter (1911-)
HERRINGTON, ARTHUR W Collector, Patron (1891-1970)
HERRINGTON, NELL RAY Collector, Patron
HERSHFIELD, LEO Illustrator (1904-1979)
HERSTAND, ARNOLD Director
HERTER, ALBERT Painter (1871-1950)
HERVES, MADELINE Painter (-1969)
HERZBRUN, HELENE McKINSEY Painter, Educator (-1984)
HESKETH Sculptor (-1987)
HESS, THOMAS B Critic, Writer (1920-1978)
HESSE, EVA Sculptor (1936-1972)
HEUERMANN, MAGDA Painter (1868-)
HEWITT, FRANCIS RAY Painter, Educator (1936-1992)
HEYL, BERNARD CHAPMAN Scholar (1905-1966)
HIBBARD, ALDRO THOMPSON Painter (1886-1972)
HIBBARD, HOWARD Historian, Writer (1928-1984)
HICKEN, PHILIP BURNHAM Painter, Printmaker (1910-1985)
HIGGINS, EUGENE Painter (1875-1958)
HIGGINS, VICTOR Painter (1884-1949)
HILDERBRANDT, HOWARD LOGAN Painter (1874-1958)
HILER, HILAIRE Painter (1898-1966)
HILL, (JAMES) JEROME II Painter (1905-)
HILL, DOROTHY KENT Museum Curator (1907-)
HILL, GEORGE SNOW Painter (1898-1969)
HILL, HAROLD WAYNE Painter, Sculptor (1933-1988)
HILL, HOMER Illustrator
HILL, JOHN HENRY Painter (1839-1922)
HILL, JOHN WILLIAM Painter (1812-1879)
HILL, POLLY KNIPP Etcher, Painter (1900-1990)
HILLIGOSS, MARTHA M Librarian (1928-1987)
HILLMAN, ALEX L Collector (1900-1968)
HILLS, LAURA COOMBS Painter (1859-1952)
HINES, JOHN M Painter (-1982)
HINKLE, CLARENCE Painter (1880-1960)
HINTON, CHARLES LOUIS Painter (1869-1950)
HIRSCH, JOSEPH Painter (1910-1981)
HIRSCH, STEFAN Educator (1899-1964)
HIRSCHHORN, JOSEPH H Collector (1899-1981)
HITCHCOCK, HENRY RUSSELL Historian, Critic (1903-1986)
HNIZDOVSKY, JACQUES Painter, Printmaker (1915-1985)
HOBSON, KATHERINE THAYER Sculptor (1889-1982)
HOCKADAY, HUGH Painter (1892-1968)
HOEHN, HARRY Painter, Printmaker (1918-1974)
HOFFMAN, ARNOLD Painter (-1966)
HOFFMAN, EDWARD FENNO III Sculptor (1916-1991)
HOFFMAN, HARRY Z Painter, Cartoonist (1908-1990)
HOFFMAN, LARRY GENE Museum Director, Consultant (1933-1991)
HOFFMAN, MALVINA Sculptor (1887-1966)
HOFFMANN, ARNOLD JR Painter, Director (1915-1991)
HOFMANN, HANS Painter, Educator (1880-19661
HOLBROOK, HOLLIS HOWARD Muralist, Painter (1909-1984)
HOLCOMB, ALICE (McCAFFERY) Painter (1906-1977)
HOLCOMBE, BLANCHE KEATON Painter, Educator (1912-)
HOLGATE, EDWIN HEADLEY Painter (1892-1977)
HOLLAND, JANICE Illustrator (1913-1962)
HOLLOWAY, H MAXSON Museum Director (-1966)
HOLMGREN, R JOHN Illustrator (1897-1963)
HOLT, CHARLOTTE SINCLAIR Medical Illustrator, Sculptor (1914-1990)
HOLTY, CARL ROBERT Painter, Writer (1900-1973)
HOOD, ETHEL PAINTER Sculptor (1908-1982)
HOOD, GEORGE W Painter (1869-1949)
HOOK, FRANCES A Pastel, Watercolor (1912-1981)
HOOVER, MARIE LOUISE (ROCHON) Artist (1895-1976)
HOPKINS, KENDAL COLES Painter (1908-1991)
HOPKINSON, CHARLES Painter (1869-1962)
HOPPER, EDWARD Painter (1882-1967)
HOPPER, JON Painter (-1968)
HOPPER, MARIANNE SEWARD (1904-)
HORCH, LOUIS L Collector (1889-1979)
HORD, DONAL Sculptor (1902-1966)
HORNYANSKY, NICHOLAS Etcher (1896-1965)
HOROSHAK, RICHARD J Art Dealer, Consultant (1940-)
HORWITT, WILL Sculptor (1934-1985)
HOUGHTON, ARTHUR A JR Administrator (1906-1990)
HOUSE, JAMES CHARLES, JR Sculptor (1902-)
HOVANNES, JOHN Painter (1904-1973)
HOVEY, WALTER READ Historian, Educator (1949-1982)
HOWARD, CECIL Sculptor (1888-1956)
HOWARD, ROBERT BOARDMAN Sculptor (1896-1983)
HOWE, KATHERINE L MALLET Painter (-1957)
HOWE, OSCAR Painter, Educator (1915-1983)
HOWELL, HANNAH JOHNSON Librarian (1905-1988)
HOWITT, JOHN NEWTON Illustrator (1885-1958)
HOWLAND, EDITH Sculptor (-1949)
HOWLAND, GARTH Educator, Painter (1887-1950)
HOYT, WHITNEY F Painter, Collector (1910-1980)
HUBBARD, CHARLES D Painter (1876-1951)

HUBBELL, HENRY SALEM Painter (1870-1949)
HUCK, ROBERT E Educator (1923-1961)
HUEY, FLORENCE GREENE Painter (1872-1961)
HULL, MARIE (ATKINSON) Painter (-1980)
HULMER, ERIC CLAUS Curator, Conservator (1915-1988)
HUMES, RALPH H Sculptor (1902-1981)
HUMPHREY, JACK WELDON Painter (-1967)
HUNT, LYNN Painter (1878-1960)
HUNT, WAYNE WOLF ROBE (KEWA-TSE-SHE) Silversmith, Painter (1905-1977)
HUNTER, FRANCIS TIPTON Illustrator (1896-
HUNTINGTON, A MONTGOMERY Designer (-1967)
HUNTINGTON, ANNA V HYATT Sculptor (1876-1973)
HUNTINGTON, JOHN W Collector, Patron (1910-1976)
HUNTINGTON, MARGARET WENDELL Painter (1867-1958)
HUNTLEY, VICTORIA HUTSON Lithographer (1900-1971)
HURD, PETER Painter, Writer (1904-)
HURLEY, EDWARD TIMOTHY Etcher, Painter (1869-1950)
HUTCHISON, MARY ELIZABETH Painter (1904-1970)
HUTTON, HUGH McMILLEN Cartoonist (1897-1976)
ILIGAN, RALPH W Painter (1894-1960)
INGLE, TOM Painter, Lecturer (1920-1973)
INMAN, PAULINE WINCHESTER Printmaker, Illustrator (1904-1990)
IORIO, ADRIAN J Illustrator (1879-1957)
IPSEN, ERNEST L Portrait Painter (1869-1951)
IREDELL, RUSSELL Painter (1889-1959)
IRVIN, REA Painter (1881-1972)
IRVING, ANNA DUER Painter (1873-1957)
ISAACS, BETTY LEWIS Sculptor (1894-1971)
ISAACS, CAROLE SCHAFFER Collector, Patron (1931-1980)
ISKOWITZ, GERSHON Painter (1921-1988)
ISRAEL, MARVIN Designer, Painter (1924-1985)
ITTLESON, HENRY, JR Collector (1900-1973)
IVES, NORMAN S Painter, Printmaker, Graphic Designer (1924-1978)
IVINS, WILLIAM M, JR Curator (1881-1961)
JACK, RICHARD Painter (-1952)
JACKSON, A B Educator, Painter (1925-1981)
JACKSON, ALEXANDER YOUNG Painter (1882-1974)
JACKSON, ANN Painter (-1956)
JACKSON, ANNIE HURLBURT Painter (1877-)
JACKSON, HAZEL BRILL Sculptor (-1991)
JACKSON, HENRY ALDEN Textile Designer (-1952)
JACKSON, JOHN EDWIN Painter, Designer (1875-)
JACKSON, LESLEY Painter (1866-1958)
JACKSON, MARTHA Gallery Director (-1969)
JACOBS, MICHEL Painter (1877-1958)
JACOBSSON, STEN WILHELM JOHN Painter, Sculptor (1899-1983)
JAFFE, WILLIAM B Collector (-1972)
JANICKI, HAZEL (MRS WILLIAM SCHOCK) Painter, Instructor (1918-1976)
JANIS, SIDNEY Dealer, Writer (1896-1989)
JANSON, HORST WOLDEMAR Art Historian (1913-1982)
JANSSEN, HANS Educator, Museum Curator
JARMAN, WALTON MAXEY Collector (1904-1980)
JARRELL, RANDALL Critic, Poet (1914-1965)
JECT-KEY, DAVID Painter
JEFFERYS, CHARLES WILLIAM Illustrator (1869-1951)
JELINEK, HANS Printmaker, Educator (-1992)
JENKINS, BURRIS Cartoonist (1897-1966)
JENKINS, PAUL RIPLEY Sculptor, Painter (1904-1974)
JENNEWEIN, C PAUL Sculptor (1890-1978)
JENSEN, ALFRED Painter (1903-1981)
JENSEN, CECIL LEON Cartoonist (1902-1976)
JENSEN, JOHN EDWARD Painter, Designer (1921-1982)
JENSEN, MARIT Painter, Sculptor
JETER, RANDY JOE Drawer, Educator (1937-1987)
JEWELL, WILLIAM M Educator, Painter (1905-1990)
JOHANSEN, JOHN C Portrait Painter (1876-1964)
JOHN, GRACE SPAULDING Painter, Writer (1890-1972)
JOHNSON, AVERY FISCHER Painter, Illustrator (1906-1990)
JOHNSON, BEN Painter (1902-1967)
JOHNSON, BRUCE Museum Director (1949-1976)
JOHNSON, CONTENT Portrait Painter (-1949)
JOHNSON, CROCKET Painter, Writer (1906-1976)
JOHNSON, ELLEN HULDA Historian, Critic (1910-1992)
JOHNSON, FRIDOLF LESTER Designer, Writer (1905-1988)
JOHNSON, HERBERT FISK Patron (1901-1980)
JOHNSON, JEANNE PAYNE (MRS LOUIS C) Painter (1887-1958)
JOHNSON, KATHERINE KING Administrator, Painter (1906-)
JOHNSON, MALVIN GRAY Painter (1896-1934)
JOHNSON, MARIAN WILLARD Dealer (1904-)
JOHNSON, ROBERT JAY Dealer, Collector (1951-1990)
JOHNSON, SARGENT Sculptor (1888-1967)
JOHNSTON, HELEN HEAD Book Dealer

JOLLEY, GERALDINE H (JERRY) Painter, Sculptor (1911-)
JONES, ALBERTUS EUGENE Painter (1882-1957)
JONES, DEXTER (CHARLES WEATHERBEE) Sculptor, Designer (1926-)
JONES, JACOBINE Sculptor
JONES, JOSEPH JOHN (JOE) Painter (1909-1963)
JONES, LOUIS C Museum Director (1908-1990)
JONES, MURRAY Painter
JONSON, JON M Sculptor (1893-1947)
JONSON, RAYMOND Painter, Gallery Director (1891-1982)
JORDAN, LENA E Painter
JORN, ASGER Painter, Writer (1914-1973)
JORNS, BYRON CHARLES Painter (1898-1958)
JOSIMOVICH, GEORGE Painter, Designer (1894-)
JOSSET, RAOUL Sculptor (1900-1957)
JUDSON, ALICE Painter (-1948)
JUDSON, SYLVIA SHAW Sculptor (1897-1978)
JUNGWIRTH, LEONARD D Sculptor (1903-1964)
JUNKIN, MARION MONTAGUE Painter, Educator (1905-1977)
JURECKA, CYRIL Educator (1884-)
JUSTUS, ROY BRAXTON Cartoonist (1901-1983)
KACHERGIS, GEORGE JOSEPH Painter, Educator (1917-1974)
KACHINSKY, ALEXANDER Painter (1888-1958)
KAEP, LOUIS JOSEPH Painter (1903-1991)
KAGY, SHEFFIELD HAROLD Painter, Printmaker (1907-1989)
KAHILL, JOSEPH B Painter (1882-1957)
KAHN, GARY Sculptor (1947-1974)
KAHN, RALPH Dealer, Lecturer (1920-1987)
KAJIWARA, TAKUMA Painter (1877-1960)
KALLEM, HENRY Painter (1912-)
KALLER, ROBERT JAMESON Dealer (-1988)
KALLIR, OTTO Art Dealer, Historian (1894-1978)
KANAGA, CONSEULO Photographer (1894-1978)
KANEMITSU, MATSUMI Painter, Lecturer (1922-1992)
KANTACK, WALTER W Industrial Artist (1889-1953)
KANTOR, MORRIS Painter (1896-1974)
KAO, RUTH (YU-HSIN) LEE Fiber Artist, Educator (-1985)
KAPLAN, JOSEPH Painter (1900-1980)
KAPPEL, PHILIP Writer, Etcher (1901-1981)
KARASZ, MARISKA Craftsman (1898-1960)
KARFIOL, BERNARD Painter (1886-1952)
KARP, LEON Painter (-1951)
KARPICK, JOHN Painter (1884-1960)
KASTOR, HUGO Painter
KATZ, (ALEXANDER) RAYMOND Painter (1895-1974)
KATZ, JOSEPH M Collector, Patron (1913-)
KATZ, SIDNEY L Architect (1915-1978)
KATZENBACH, WILLIAM E Designer, Lecturer (1904-1975)
KATZENELLENBOGEN, ADOLF E M Educator (1901-1964)
KATZENSTEIN, IRVING Painter 1902-)
KATZMANN, HERBERT Painter
KAUFMAN, ENIT Painter (1898-1961)
KAUFMANN, ROBERT Painter (1914-1959)
KAYN, HILDE B Painter (1903-1950)
KAZ, JOYCE ZICKERMAN Painter (1936-1979)
KEALLY, FRANCIS Architect, Sculptor (1889-1978)
KEATS, EZRA JACK Illustrator, Writer (1916-1983)
KECK, CHARLES Sculptor (1875-1951)
KEFAUVER, NANCY Advisor on Fine Arts (-1967)
KELLEHER, PATRICK JOSEPH Historian, Museologist (1917-1985)
KELLER, DEANE Educator, Painter (1901-1992)
KELLER, HENRY G Painter, Etcher (1870-1949)
KELLOGG, MAURICE DALE Painter, Lecturer (1919-1984)
KELPE, PAUL Painter (1902-1985)
KEMPER, JOHN GARNER Painter, Graphic Artist (1909-1991)
KEMPTON, GRETA Painter (1903-1991)
KENDERDINE, AUGUSTUS FREDERICK Painter (-1947)
KENNEDY, JANET ROBSON Painter, Illustrator (1902-1974)
KENT, FRANK WARD Painter (1912-1977)
KENT, JACK Illustrator (1920-1985)
KENT, NORMAN Engraver, Book Designer (1903-1972)
KENT, ROCKWELL Painter (1882-1971)
KERKAM, EARL Painter (1890-1965)
KERR, ARTHUR Director (1926-1979)
KERR, E COE Art Dealer (1914-1973)
KESTNBAUM, GERTRUDE DANA Collector (-1982)
KEVE, FLORENCE Educator
KEYES, BERNARD M Painter (1898-1973)
KEY-OBERG, ELLEN BURKE Sculptor (1905-)
KEY-OBERG, ROLF Ceramist (1900-1959)
KEYSER, ERNEST WISE Sculptor (1876-1959)
KHOURI, ALFRED Painter (-1962)
KIBBEY, ILAH MARIAN Painter (1883-1958)
KIENBUSCH, WILLIAM AUSTIN Painter (1914-1979)

KIESLER, FREDERICK J Architect (1892-1966)
KIHN, WILLIAM LANGDON Painter (1898-1957)
KIJANKA, STANLEY JOSEPH Painter (1937-1981)
KILENYI, JULIO Sculptor (1886-1959)
KILGORE, AL Cartoonist (1927-1983)
KILGORE, RUPERT Educator (1910-1971)
KILHAM, WALTER H Painter, Architect (1868-1948)
KILLAM, WALT Painter, Art Dealer (1907-1979)
KILPATRICK, ADA ARILLA Painter (-1951)
KILPATRICK, ELLEN PERKINS Painter (1877-1951)
KIMAK, GEORGE Painter (1921-1972)
KIMBALL, YEFFE Painter (1914-1978)
KIMBROUGH, SARA DODGE Painter (-1990)
KING, CLINTON BLAIR Painter, Printmaker (1901-1979)
KING, FRANK O Cartoonist (1883-1969)
KING, HAMILTON Illustrator (1871-1952)
KING, MABEL DEBRA Painter (1895-1950)
KING, PAUL Painter (1867-1947)
KING, WARREN THOMAS Cartoonist (1916-1978)
KINGHAN, CHARLES ROSS Painter (1895-1984)
KINGMAN, EUGENE Painter, Art Administrator (1909-1975)
KIRK, FRANK C Painter (1889-1963)
KIRKBRIDE, EARLE R Painter (1891-1968)
KIRKLAND, VANCE HALL Painter (1904-1981)
KISELEWSKI, JOSEPH Sculptor (1901-1986)
KLEBE, GENE (CHARLES EUGENE) Painter, Writer (1918-)
KLEINBARDT, ERNEST Painter (1875-1962)
KLETT, WALTER CHARLES Illustrator (1897-1966)
KLEY, ALFRED JULIUS Craftsman (1895-1957)
KLINE, ALMA Sculptor
KLINE, FRANZ Painter (1910-1962)
KLINE, GEORGE T Illustrator (1874-1956)
KLINKER, ORPHA Etcher (-1964)
KLONIS, BERNARD Painter (1906-1957)
KNATHS, (OTTO) KARL Painter (1891-1971)
KNIGHT, FREDERIC CHARLES Painter (1898-1979)
KNIGHT, TACK (BENJAMIN THACKSTON) Cartoonist (1895-1976)
KNOWLTON, MAUDE BRIGGS Painter (1876-1956)
KO, ANTHONY Printmaker, Educator (1934-)
KOCH, BERTHA COUCH Painter (1899-1975)
KOCH, JOHN Painter, Collector (1909-1978)
KOCH, WILLIAM EMERY Dealer, Collector (1922-1987)
KOERNER, HENRY Painter, Lecturer (1915-1991)
KOHLER, ROSE Sculptor, Painter (1873-1947)
KOHLHEPP, DOROTHY IRENE Painter (-1964)
KOHLHEPP, NORMAN Painter, Conservator (-1986)
KOHN, GABRIEL Sculptor (1910-1975)
KOLDE, FREDERICK WILLIAM Painter (1870-)
KOLIN, SACHA Sculptor, Painter (1911-1975)
KOLODNER, NATHAN K Dealer (1950-)
KOMAR, MATHIAS Dealer (1909-)
KOOPMAN, JOHN R Painter (1881-1949)
KOPLOWITZ, BENJAMIN (BEN KOPEL) Painter (1893-)
KOPMAN, BENJAMIN Painter (1887-1965)
KOPPE, RICHARD Painter, Educator (1916-)
KORDA, VINCENT Director, Painter
KORMENDI, EUGENE Sculptor (1889-1959)
KORN, ELIZABETH P Painter, Illustrator (1900-)
KOSA, EMIL J, JR Painter (1903-1968)
KOTIN, ALBERT Painter, Educator (1907-1980)
KOTTLER, HOWARD WILLIAM Sculptor, Educator (1930-)
KOURSAROS, HARRY G Painter (1928-1986)
KOUWENHOVEN, JOHN A Writer, Educator (1909-1990)
KOWALEK, JON W Museum Director, Lecturer (1934-)
KRAMER, JACK N Painter, Educator (1923-1984)
KRANER, FLORIAN G Painter, Educator (1908-)
KRASNER, LEE Painter (1908-1984)
KRAUSZ, LASZLO Painter (1903-1979)
KREINDLER, DORIS BARSKY Painter, Lithographer (1901-1974)
KRIES, HENRY Sculptor (-1963)
KROLL, LEON Painter, Lithographer (1884-1974)
KRONBERG, LOUIS Painter (1872-1965)
KUEKES, EDWARD D Cartoonist (1901-1987)
KUHLER, OTTO AUGUST Etcher, Painter (1894-1977)
KUHN, WALT Painter (1880-1949)
KUMM, MARGUERITE ELIZABETH Painter, Printmaker (-1992)
KUNIYOSHI, YASUO Painter (1893-1953)
KUNTZ, ROGER EDWARD Painter, Sculptor (1926-1975)
KUPFERMAN, LAWRENCE Painter, Printmaker (1909-1982)
KURELEK, WILLIAM Painter (1927-1977)
KURZ, GERTRUDE ALICE Craftsman (-1951)
LAATSCH, GARY Sculptor (1956-)
LABICHE, WALTER ANTHONY Administrator, Instructor (1924-1979)
LABRIE, ROSE Painter, Writer (1916-1986)
LAFAYE, NELL MURRAY Painter, Educator (1937-1990)
LA FON, JULIA ANNA Painter, Craftsman (1919-1981)
LAGATTA, JOHN Illustrator (1894-1976)
LAHEY, MARGUERITE DUPREZ Rare Book Binder (1880-1958)
LAHEY, RICHARD (FRANCIS) Painter, Lecturer (1893-1979)
LAKE, FREDERIC Art Dealer
LAM, JENNETTE (BRINSMADE) Painter, Educator (1911-1985)
LAMANNA, CARMEN Art Dealer, Gallery Director (1927-1991)
LAMB, ADRIAN S Painter (-1989)
LAMONT, FRANCES K Sculptor (-1975)
La MORE, CHET HARMON Painter, Sculptor (1908-1980)
LANDACRE, PAUL Engraver (1893-1963)
LANDECK, ARMIN Painter, Engraver (1905-)
LANDON, EDWARD AUGUST Printmaker, Painter (1911-1984)
LANDSMAN, STANLEY Sculptor (1930-)
LANGE, DOROTHEA Photographer (1895-1965)
LANGLAIS, BERNARD Sculptor, Painter (1921-1977)
LANGSNER, JULES Art Writer (-1967)
LANGSTON, MILDRED J Art Dealer, Collector (1902-1976)
LANGTON, BERENICE Sculptor (1878-1959)
LANKES, JULIUS J Engraver (1884-1960)
LARCADA, RICHARD KENNETH Art Dealer (1935-)
LARK, SYLVIA Painter, Printmaker (1947-)
LARKIN, OLIVER Educator (1896-1970)
LARKIN, WILLIAM Painter, Printmaker (1902-1969)
LARSEN, OLE Painter, Illustrator (-1984)
LASH, KENNETH Educator, Writer (1918-1985)
LASSEN, BEN Painter (-1968)
LATHROP, GERTRUDE K Sculptor (1896-1986)
LAUFMAN, SIDNEY Painter (1891-1985)
LAUGHLIN, ALICE D Painter (1895-1952)
LAUGHLIN, THOMAS Painter, Publisher (-1965)
LAUNOIS, JOHN RENE Photographer
LAURENT, ROBERT Sculptor, Collector (1890-1970)
LAURITZ, PAUL Painter (1889-1975)
LAUTERER, ARCH Designer (1904-)
LAVANOUX, MAURICE Art Editor (-1974)
LAW, MARGARET Painter
LAWRENCE, HELEN HUMPHREYS Painter (1878-)
LAWRIE, LEE Sculptor (1877-1963)
LAWSON, ROBERT Illustrator (1892-1957)
LAX, DAVID Painter (1910-1990)
LAYNOR, HAROLD ARTHUR Painter (1922-1991)
LAYTON, GLORIA (MRS HARRY GEWISS) Painter (1914-)
LAZARUS, MARVIN P Photographer (1918-1982)
LAZZARI, PIETRO Sculptor, Painter (1898-1979)
LAZZELL, BLANCHE Painter (1878-1956)
LEACH, LOUIS LAWRENCE Sculptor (1885-1957)
LEAF, MUNRO Illustrator of Children's Books (1906-1977)
LEAKE, GERALD Painter (1885-1975)
LEAR, GEORGE Engraver (1879-1956)
LEBRUN, RICO (FREDERICO) Painter (1900-1964)
LECOQUE Painter, Writer (1891-1981)
LEDGERWOOD, ELLA RAY Painter (-1951)
LEE, ARTHUR Sculptor (1881-1961)
LEE, GEORGE J Art Administrator, Photographer (1919-1976)
LEE, RENSSELAER WRIGHT Historian, Educator (1898-1984)
LEE, RUSSELL W Photographer, Educator (1903-1986)
LEECH, HILTON Painter, Instructor (1906-1969)
LEES, HARRY HANSON Illustrator
LEFEBRE, JOHN Art Dealer (1905-1986)
LEFEVRE, LAWRENCE E Painter (1904-1960)
LEHMAN, IRVING Painter, Sculptor (1900-1983)
LEHMAN, ROBERT Collector (-1969)
LEIGHTON, A C Painter (-1965)
LEIGHTON, THOMAS CHARLES Painter, Instructor (1913-1976)
LEITH-ROSS, HARRY Painter (1886-)
LEITMAN, SAMUEL Painter (1908-1981)
LEMIEUX, JEAN PAUL Painter (1904-)
L'ENGLE, WILLIAM JOHNSON Painter (1884-1957)
LENNEY, ANNIE Painter (1910-)
LENSKI, LOIS Writer, Illustrator (1893-)
LENSON, MICHAEL Painter (1903-1971)
LENTELLI, LEO Sculptor (1882-1962)
LENTINE, JOHN Painter
LEONID (LEONID BERMAN) Painter (1896-1976)
LE PRINCE, GABRIELLA Ceramist (-1953)
LERNER, RICHARD J Art Dealer (1929-1982)
LE ROY, HAROLD M Painter, Graphic Artist (1905-)
LEVENTHAL, RUTH LEE Sculptor, Painter (1923-1989)
LEVER, R HAYLEY Painter (1876-1968)
LEVI, CARLO Painter, Writer (1902-1975)
LEVI, JULIAN (E) Painter. Educator (1900-1982)
LEVIT, HERSCHEL Photographer, Historian (1912-1986)

LEVITINE, GEORGE Historian (1916-)
LEV-LANDAU (SAMUEL DAVID LANDAU) Painter (1895-1979)
LEVY, BEATRICE S Painter (1892-1974)
LEVY, FLORENCE N Writer, Editor (1870-1947)
LEVY, JULIEN Educator, Writer (1906-1981)
LEWIN, MILTON J Historian (1929-1979)
LEWIS, ALLEN Etcher (1873-1957)
LEWIS, MARTIN Printmaker (1883-1962)
LEWIS, NORMAN WILFRED Painter, Instructor (-1979)
LEWITIN, LANDES Painter (-1966)
LEYDENFROST, ALEXANDER Illustrator (1889-1961)
LEYENDECKER, JOSEPH C Painter (1874-1951)
LIAS, THOMAS R Painter
LIBBY, WILLIAM C Painter, Writer (1919-)
LIBERTE, JEAN Painter (1896-1965)
LIBERTS, LUDOLFS Painter (1895-1959)
LIBHART, MYLES LAROY Administrator, Writer (1931-1990)
LICHTEN, FRANCES Writer (1889-1961)
LICHTENSTEIN, SARA Art Historian (1929-)
LICHTY, GEORGE M Cartoonist (1905-)
LIEBER, FRANCE Printmaker, Painter
LIEBERMAN, HARRY Painter, Sculptor (1876-1983)
LIEBES, DOROTHY (MRS RELMAN MORIN) Textile Designer (1899-1972)
LILIENFIELD, KARL Scholar (-1966)
LINDNER, RICHARD Painter (1901-1978)
LINTOTT, EDWARD BARNARD Painter (1875-1951)
LIPCHITZ, JACQUES Sculptor (1891-1973)
LIPMAN, HOWARD W Collector (1905-1992)
LIPPERT, LEON Painter
LISSIM, SIMON Painter, Designer (1900-1981)
LISTON, MRS. FLORENCE CARY Portraitist (-1964)
LITAKER, THOMAS (FRANKLIN) Painter (1904-1976)
LITTLE, JOHN Painter, Sculptor (1907-)
LO MEDICO, THOMAS GAETANO Sculptor, Designer (1904-1985)
LOBER, GEORG J Sculptor (1892-1961)
LOCHRIE, ELIZABETH DAVEY Painter, Sculptor (1890-1981)
LOCKWOOD, WARD Painter (1894-1963)
LOEHR, MAX Museum Curator, Educator (1903-1988)
LOGAN, MAURICE Painter, Illustrator (1886-1977)
LOGGIE, HELEN A Printmaker, Painter (-1976)
LOLOMA, CHARLES Jeweler, Silversmith (1921-1991)
LOMBARDO, JOSEF VINCENT Art Historian, Writer (1908-1992)
LONDON, ELCA Dealer (1930-1991)
LONG, C CHEE Craftsman, Goldsmith (1942-)
LONG, HUBERT Sculptor (1907-1992)
LONG, SCOTT Cartoonist (1917-1991)
LONG, STANLEY M Painter (1892-1972)
LONG, WALTER KINSCELLA Museum Director, Painter (1904-1986)
LONGACRE, LYDIA E Miniature Painter (1870-1951)
LONGACRE, MARGARET GRUEN Printmaker, Lecturer (1910-1976)
LONGLEY, EVELYN LOUISE Painter (1921-1959)
LORD, HARRIET Painter (1879-1958)
LORENZANI, ARTHUR EMANUELE Sculptor (1886-1986)
LORIMER, AMY McCLELLAN Painter
LOSCH, TILLY Painter (1904-1975)
LOUIS, MORRIS Painter (1912-1963)
LOURIE, HERBERT S Painter, Educator (1923-1981)
LOVATO, CHARLES FREDERIC Printmaker, Craftsperson (1937-1988)
LOVET-LORSKI, BORIS Sculptor (1894-1973)
LOW, SANFORD Museum Director, Painter (1905-1964)
LOWE, EMILY Painter (-1966)
LOWELL, ORSON BYRON Illustrator (1871-1956)
LOWENFELD, VIKTOR Educator (1903-1960)
LOWENGRUND, MARGARET Painter (1905-1957)
LOZOWICK, LOUIS Painter, Printmaker (1892-1973)
LUDGIN, EARLE Collector (1898-1981)
LUDLAM, EUGENIE SHONNARD Sculptor (1936-1978)
LUKE, ALEXANDRA Painter (1901-)
LUNA (ANTONIO RODRIGUEZ) Painter (1910-1984)
LUNDBORG, FLORENCE Painter (-1949)
LUNDIE, EDWIN HUGH Architect (1886-1972)
LUQUIENS, HUC-MAZELET Etcher (1882-1961)
LUTZ, DAN S Painter (1906-1978)
LYE, LEN Painter, Kinetic Artist (1901-1981)
LYMAN, JOHN Painter (-1967)
LYNES, RUSSELL Writer, Critic (1910-1992)
LYTTON, BART Collector (-1969)
MACAGY, DOUGLAS GUERNSEY Art Administrator (1913-1973)
MACAGY, JERMAYNE Educator
MACALISTER, PAUL RITTER Designer, Collector (1901-1990)
MACDONALD, GRANT Painter, Illustrator (1909-1987)
MACDONALD, HERBERT Painter (1898-1972)
MACDONALD, JAMES W A Painter (1824-1908)
MACDONALD, THOMAS REID Painter (1908-)
MACDONALD-WRIGHT, STANTON Painter (1890-1973)
MACGILVARY, NORWOOD Painter, Educator (1874-1949)
MACHAMER, JEFFERSON Cartoonist (1900-1960)
MACHLIN, SHELDON M Sculptor, Printmaker (1918-1975)
MACIUNAS, GEORGE Designer (1931-1978)
MACKAY, DONALD CAMERON Painter, Historian (1906-1979)
MACKEOWN, IDA C Portrait Painter (-1952)
MACKY, SPENCER Educator (1880-1958)
MACLAGGER, RICHARD JOSEPH Dealer, Collector (1947-1989)
MACLANE, JEAN Painter (1878-1964)
MACLEOD, PEGI NICHOL Painter, Teacher
MACLEOD, YAN Sculptor (1889-1978)
MACNUTT, GLENN GORDON Painter, Illustrator (1906-1987)
MACOMBER, ALLISON Painter, Sculptor (1916-1979)
MAGAFAN, JENNIE Painter, Lithographer (1916-)
MALBIN, LYDIA W Collector (1897-1989)
MALDARELLI, ORONZIO Sculptor (1892-1963)
MALICOAT, PHILIP CECIL Painter (1908-1981)
MALINA, FRANK JOSEPH Painter, Editor (1912-1981)
MALMAN, CHRISTINA Magazine Cover Artist (1912-1958)
MALONE, LEE H B Museum Director (1913-1989)
MALRAUX, ANDRE Writer (1901-1976)
MALSCH, ELLEN L Painter, Instructor (-1988)
MALVERN, CORINNE Illustrator (-1956)
MANARAY, THELMA ALBERTA Printmaker, Painter (1913-)
MANGRAVITE, PEPPINO GINO Painter, Lecturer (1896-1978)
MANKOWSKI, BRUNO Sculptor (1902-1990)
MANN, MARGERY (MARGARET MANN VASEY) Photographer, Curator (1919-1977)
MANNING, HILDA SCUDDER Sculptor (-1988)
MANNING, REG (REGINALD WEST) Designer (1905-1986)
MANRAY Artist, Photographer (1890-1976)
MANSHIP, PAUL Sculptor (1885-1966)
MANVILLE, ELLA VIOLA GRAINGER Painter (1889-1979)
MAPPLETHORPE, ROBERT Photographer (1946-1989)
MARADIAGA, RALPH Director, Designer (1934-1985)
MARAGLIOTTI VINCENT Muralist (1888-1978)
MARANS, MOISSAYE Sculptor, Instructor (1902-1977)
MARANTZ, IRVING Painter (1912-1972)
MARBERGER, A ALDAR Dealer, Museum Director (1947-1988)
MARCUS, EDWARD S Collector (1910-1972)
MAREMONT, ARNOLD H Collector (1904-1978)
MARGULES, DEHIRSH Painter (1899-1965)
MARGULIES, JOSEPH Painter, Printmaker (1896-1986)
MARIL, HERMAN Painter, Printmaker (1908-1986)
MARIN, JOHN Painter (1870-1953)
MARINO, ALBERT JOSEPH Collector (1899-1975)
MARINO-MERLO, JOSEPH Painter (1906-1956)
MARKOW, JACK Cartoonist, Painter (1905-1983)
MARKS, CLAUDE Painter, Writer (1915-1991)
MARKS, GEORGE B Painter, Sculptor (1923-1983)
MARKS, ROYAL S Dealer, Collector (1927-1987)
MARKUS, HENRY A Collector
MARSH, (EDWIN) THOMAS Potter, Educator (1934-1991)
MARSH, FRED DANA Painter (1872-1961)
MARSH, REGINALD Painter (1898-1954)
MARSHALL, EDMUND Photographer (1938-1979)
MARSHALL, RALPH Educator, Photographer (1923-1984)
MARSTELLER, WILLIAM A Collector (1914-1987)
MARTIN, FLETCHER Painter (1904-1979)
MARTIN, KEITH MORROW Painter (1911-1983)
MARTINELLI, EZIO Sculptor (1913-)
MARTINET, MARJORIED Painter (1886-1981)
MARTMER, WILLIAM PHILIP Painter (1939-1992)
MARYAN, MARYAN S Painter (1927-1977)
MASER, EDWARD ANDREW Historian, Museum Director (1923-1988)
MASON, ALICE FRANCES Lithographer, Painter (1895-)
MASON, ALICE TRUMBALL Painter (1904-1971)
MASON, MAUDE M Painter (1867-1956)
MASON, ROY MARTELL Painter (1886-1972)
MAST, GERALD Painter (1908-1971)
MATISSE, PIERRE Dealer (1900-1989)
MATLICK, GERALD ALLEN Painter, Historian (1947-1988)
MATTA-CLARK, GORDON Sculptor (1945-1978)
MATTERN, KARL Painter (1892-1969)
MATTISON, DONALD MANGUS Painter (1905-1975)
MATTSON, HENRY (ELIS) Painter (1887-1971)
MATULKA, JAN Painter (1890-1972)
MAUNSBACH, GEORGE ERIC Painter (1890-)
MAURER, SASCHA Painter (1897-1961)
MAXON, JOHN Museum Director (1916-1977)
MAYER, BENA FRANK Painter (1898-1991)
MAYER, RALPH Painter, Writer (1895-1979)

MAYHEW, EDGAR DE NOAILLES Educator, Museum Director (1913-1990)
MAYOR, A HYATT Curator (1901-1980)
MAYS, PAUL KIRTLAND Painter (1887-1961)
McADOO, DONALD ELDRIDGE Painter, Printer (1929-)
McBEY, JAMES Painter (1884-1959)
McBRIDE, HENRY Critic (1867-1962)
McCARTHY, JUSTIN Painter (1892-)
McCASLIN, WALTER WRIGHT Art Critic, Writer (1924-)
McCAUSLAND, ELIZABETH Writer (1899-1965)
McCORMICK, KATHARINE H Painter (1882-1960)
McCOSH, DAVID J Painter (1903-1980)
McCOUCH, GORDON MALLET Painter (1885-1962)
McCOY, JOHN W Painter (1910-1989)
McCREERY, FRANC ROOT (MRS) Painter (-1957)
McCURRY, HARR ORR Museum Director (1889-1964)
McDONALD, JOHN STANLEY Art Dealer (1943-1981)
McFEE, HENRY LEE Painter (1886-1953)
McGEE, OLIVIA JACKSON Painter, Illustrator (1915-1987)
McGILL, HAROLD A Cartoonist (-1952)
McGLYNN, THOMAS Sculptor (1906-)
McHUGH, JAMES FRANCIS Collector (-1968)
McINTOSH, HAROLD Painter (1916-1986)
McKEE, FRANCES BARRETT Illustrator (1909-1975)
McKEEBY, BYRON GORDON Printmaker, Educator (1936-1984)
McKENDRY, JOHN Curator (1933-1975)
McKENZIE, VINNORMA SHAW Painter (1890-1952)
McKININ, LAWRENCE Educator, Painter (1917-)
McKINLEY, RUTH GOWDY Ceramist, Designer (1931-1981)
McLAUGHLIN, DONAL Architect (1875-1978)
McLAUGHLIN, JOHN Artist (1898-1976)
McMAHON, A PHILIP Writer, Educator (1890-)
McMANUS, JAMES Painter (1882-1958)
McMEIN, NEYSA Painter, Designer (1890-)
McMILLAN, MARY Painter (1895-)
McMILLAN, ROBERT W Painter, Educator (1915-1991)
McMULLEN, E ORMOND Painter (1888-)
McMURTRIE, EDITH Painter (1883-)
McNEAR, EVERETT C Painter, Designer (1904-1984)
McNETT, WILLIAM BROWN Illustrator (1896-1968)
McNULTY, KNEELAND Curator, Writer (1921-1991)
McNULTY, WILLIAM CHARLES Painter (1884-1963)
McPHARLIN, PAUL Writer, Illustrator (1903-1948)
McVEY, LEZA Ceramist, Weaver (1907-1984)
MEAD, KATHERINE HARPER Curator, Historian (1929-)
MEADOWS, ALGUR H Patron (1899-1980)
MEANS, ELLIOTT Painter (1905-1962)
MECHLIN, LEILA Critic, Writer (1874-1949)
MECKLEM, AUSTIN MERRILL Painter (1894-1951)
MEHRING, HOWARD WILLIAM Painter (1931-1978)
MEIERE, HILDRETH Painter (-1961)
MEIGS, WALTER Painter (1918-1988)
MEISS, MILLARD Art Historian, Writer (1904-1975)
MEISSNER, LEO J Painter, Engraver (1895-1977)
MELAMED, ABRAHAM Collector, Patron (1914-)
MELCARTH, EDWARD Painter, Sculptor
MELCHER, BETSY FLAGG Painter (1900-1991)
MELLOR, GEORGE EDWARD Educator, Sculptor (1928-1987)
MELVIN, GRACE WILSON Painter, Illustrator (-1977)
MENCONI, RALPH JOSEPH Sculptor (1915-1972)
MENDELOWITZ, DANIEL MARCUS Painter, Writer (1905-1980)
MENKES, SIGMUND J Painter (1896-1986)
MEREDITH, DOROTHY LAVERNE Weaver, Educator (1906-1986)
MERMIN, MILDRED (SHIRE) Painter (-1985)
MERRICK, JAMES KIRK Painter, Educator (1905-1985)
MERYMAN, HOPE Artist, Illustrator (-1975)
MESS, GEORGE JO Painter (1898-1962)
MESS, GORDON BENJAMIN Painter (1900-1959)
MESSEGUER, VILLORO BENITO Painter, Sculptor (1930-1982)
MESSICK, BEN (NEWTON) Painter, Instructor (1901-)
MESTROVIC, IVAN Sculptor (1884-1962)
MEYER, FRED (ROBERT) Sculptor, Painter (-1986)
MEYER, FREDERICK H Educator (1873-1961)
MEYER, HERBERT Painter (1882-1960)
MEYEROWITZ, WILLIAM Painter (1886-1981)
MEYERS, LEONARD H Computer Art (1932-1979)
MEYERS, ROBERT WILLIAM Illustrator (1919-1970)
MIDGETTE, WILLARD FRANKLIN Painter, Printmaker (1937-1978)
MIELZINER, JO Designer, Lecturer (1901-1976)
MIES VAN DER ROHE, LUDWIG Architect (1886-1969)
MILCH, HAROLD CARLTON Art Dealer (1908-)
MILHOUS, KATHERINE Illustrator, Writer (1894-1977)
MILLER, BARSE Painter, Educator (1924-1973)
MILLER, BURR Sculptor (1904-1958)
MILLER, DONALD RICHARD Sculptor, Medalist (1925-1989)
MILLER, HELEN PENDLETON Etcher (1888-1957)
MILLER, KENNETH HAYES Painter, Teacher (1876-1952)
MILLET, CLARENCE Painter (1897-1959)
MILLIKEN, WILLIAM M Museum Director, Curator (1889-1978)
MILLMAN, EDWARD Painter (1907-1964)
MINA-MORA, DORISE OLSON Painter (1932-1991)
MINER, DOROTHY EUGENIA Museum Curator, Art Historian (1906-1973)
MINEWSKI, ALEX Painter, Educator (1917-1979)
MINNEGERODE, CUTHBERT POWELL Museum Director (1876-1951)
MITCHELL, ALFRED R Painter (1888-1972)
MITCHELL, BRUCE HANDISIDE Painter (1908-1963)
MITCHELL, ELEANOR Consultant, Librarian (1907-)
MITCHELL, GLEN Painter (1894-1972)
MITCHELL, HENRY (WEBER) Sculptor (1915-1980)
MITCHELL, JOAN Painter (1926-)
MITCHELL, THOMAS W Painter
MITCHELL, WALLACE (MACMAHON) Museum Director, Painter (1911-1977)
MITRA, GOPAL C Painter, Printmaker (1928-1992)
MIYASHITA, TAD Painter (1922-1979)
MOCHI, UGO Sculptor (1894-1977)
MOCHON, DONALD Graphic Artist, Educator (1916-)
MOCK, GEORGE ANDREW Painter (1886-)
MODEL, EVSA Artist (1901-1976)
MOE, HENRY ALLEN Art Administrator (1894-1975)
MOFFETT, ROSS E Painter (1888-1971)
MOLARSKY, MAURICE Painter, Teacher (1885-1950)
MONONGYE, PRESTON LEE Silversmith, Printmaker (1927-1988)
MONTANA, BOB Cartoonist (1920-1975)
MONTANA, PIETRO Sculptor, Painter (1890-1978)
MONTGOMERY, CHARLES FRANKLIN Art Administrator, Educator (1910-1978)
MONTGOMERY, CLAUDE Painter, Etcher (1912-1990)
MOON, CARL Illustrator (1879-1948)
MORANG, ALFRED GWYNNE Painter (1901-1958)
MORDVINOFF, NICOLAS Painter, Illustrator (1911-1973)
MORE, HERMON Museum Director (1887-1968)
MORGAN, GLADYS B Painter, Lithographer (1899-1981)
MORGAN, WALLACE Illustrator (1873-1948)
MORISSET, GERARD Educator (1898-1970)
MORRIS, DUDLEY H JR Painter (1912-1966)
MORRIS, GEORGE FORD Painter (-1960)
MORRIS, GEORGE L K Painter, Sculptor (1905-1975)
MORRIS, HILDA Sculptor (-1991)
MORRIS, KYLE RANDOLPH Painter (1918-1979)
MORROW, BENJAMIN FRANCIS Painter (1891-1958)
MORSE, DOROTHY B Illustrator, Educator (1906-1979)
MORSE, GLENN TILLEY Painter (1870-1950)
MORTON, REE Sculptor, Environmental Artist, Painter (1936-1977)
MOSBY, WILLIAM HARRY Painter (1898-1964)
MOSE, CARL C Sculptor, Lecturer (1903-1973)
MOSELSIO, SIMON Sculptor (1890-)
MOSER, FRANK H Painter (1886-1964)
MOSES, ANNA MARY ROBERTSON (GRANDMA) Painter (1860-1961)
MOSES, FORREST KING Painter (1893-1974)
MOTHERWELL, ROBERT Painter, Printmaker (1915-1991)
MOTT-SMITH, MAY Medalist, Painter (1879-1952)
MOUFARREGE, NICHOLAS A Painter, Critic (1947-)
MUDGE, EDMOND WEBSTER JR Collector (1904-1984)
MUEHSAM, GERD Librarian, Writer (1913-1979)
MUIR, WILLIAM HORACE Sculptor (1902-1965)
MULLER, GEORGE F Painter (1866-1958)
MULLER, JAN Painter (1922-1958)
MULLIN, WILLARD Cartoonist (1902-1978)
MUNDY, ETHEL FRANCES Sculptor (-1964)
MUNDY, LOUISE EASTERDAY Painter (1870-1952)
MUNFORD, ROBERT WATSON Painter, Educator (1925-1991)
MUNOWITZ, KEN Illustrator of Children's Books (1936-1978)
MUNRO, THOMAS Art Scholar (1897-1974)
MURANYI, GUSTAVE Painter (1872-1961)
MURCH, WALTER Painter (1907-1967)
MURCHISON, JOHN D Collector (1921-1979)
MURPHY, GLADYS WILKINS Painter, Craftsman (1907-1985)
MURPHY, ROWLEY WALTER Painter, Designer (1891-1975)
MURRAY, ALBERT (KETCHAM) Painter (1906-1992)
MURRAY, FRANK WALDO Painter (1884-1956)
MURRAY, WILLIAM COLMAN Collector, Patron (1899-1977)
MUSGROVE, A J Museum Director
MYERS, ETHEL K Sculptor (1881-1960)
MYERS, FRANK HARMON Painter (1899-1956)
MYERS, FRED A Museum Director (1937-)
MYERS, GEORGE HEWITT Museum President (1865-1957)

MYRICK, KATHERINE S Painter
NADLER, HARRY Painter, Educator (1930-1990)
NAEGLE, STEPHEN HOWARD Painter, Sculptor (1938-1981)
NAGEL, STINA Painter (1918-1969)
NAGLER, EDITH KROGER Painter (1895-1986)
NAGLER, FRED Printmaker, Sculptor (1891-1983)
NAHA, RAYMOND Painter (-1975)
NAILOR, GERALD LLOYDE Painter, Illustrator (1917-1952)
NAKAMIZO, FUJI Painter (1889-)
NAMUTH, HANS Photographer, Filmmaker (1915-1990)
NASH, RAY Art Historian (1905-1982)
NASON, GERTRUDE Painter (1890-)
NASON, THOMAS W Engraver (1889-1971)
NATHAN, HELMUTH MAX Educator, Painter (1901-1979)
NATZLER, GERTRUD Ceramic Craftsman (1908-1971)
NAVAS, ELIZABETH S Collector, Patron (1895-)
NEAL, REGINALD H Painter, Printmaker (1909-1992)
NEANDROSS, SIGURD Sculptor (1869-1958)
NEBEL, BERTHOLD Sculptor (1889-1964)
NEEL, ALICE Painter (1900-1984)
NEFF, JOSEPH Collector (1900-1969)
NEILSON, KATHERINE B Art Historian (1902-1977)
NEILSON, RAYMOND P R Painter (1881-1964)
NELSON, GEORGE LAURENCE Painter (1887-1978)
NEMEROV, DAVID Painter (-1963)
NEPOTE, ALEXANDER Painter (1913-1986)
NESBERT, VINCENT Miniature Painter (-1976)
NESEMANN, ENNO Painter (1861-1949)
NESS, EVALINE (MRS ARNOLD A BAYARD) Illustrator, Writer (1911-)
NEUGEBERGER, MARGOT Designer, Craftsman (1929-1986)
NEUMANN, J B Art Dealer, Critic (1887-1961)
NEUMANN, WILLIAM A Educator, Goldsmith (1924-1985)
NEUMEYER, ALFRED Art Historian (1901-1973)
NEUTRA, RICHARD Architect (1892-1970)
NEWBERRY, CLARE TURLAY Illustrator (1903-1970)
NEWBERRY, JOHN S Museum Curator (-1964)
NEWHALL, ADELAIDE MAY Painter (1884-1960)
NEWHALL, BEAUMONT Photographer, Educator (1908-)
NEWHOUSE, BERTRAM MAURICE Art Dealer (1888-1982)
NEWHOUSE, CLYDE MORTIMER Dealer, Historian (1920-1990)
NEWMAN, BARNETT Painter (1905-1970)
NEWTON, GRACE HAMILTON (MRS ARTHUR NEWTON) Painter (-1958)
NEWTON, MARGARET Painter (1893-1960)
NICHOLS, DONALD EDWARD Designer, Educator (1922-1987)
NICHOLS, ELEANOR CARY Designer, Metalsmith (1903-1988)
NICHOLS, HOBART Painter (1869-1962)
NICHOLS, SPENCER B Painter (1875-1950)
NICHOLSON, BEN Painter (1894-1982)
NICHOLSON, THOMAS D Director (1922-)
NICKLE, ROBERT W Painter, Educator (1919-1980)
NICOLOSI, JOSEPH Sculptor (1893-1961)
NILES, ROSAMOND Painter (1881-)
NISBET, ROBERT H Painter (1879-1961)
NITZSCHE, ELSA KOENIG Portrait Painter (1880-1952)
NOA, FLORENCE Printmaker, Educator (1941-1989)
NOBLE, JOHN A Painter, Lithographer (1913-1983)
NODEL, SOL Illuminator, Designer (1912-1976)
NOGUCHI, ISAMU Sculptor (1904-1988)
NOORDHOEK, HARRY CECIL Sculptor, Painter (1909-1992)
NORBURY, LOUISE H Painter (1878-1952)
NORDELL, EMMA PARKER (POLLY) Painter
NORTON, ANN W Sculptor (-1982)
NOTARO, ANTHONY Sculptor (1915-1984)
NOYES, ELIOT Architect, Designer (1910-1977)
NUDERSCHER, FRANK BERNARD Painter (1880-1959)
NUGENT, ARTHUR WILLIAM Cartoonist, Illustrator (1891-1975)
NUKI, (DANIEL MILLSAPS) Painter, Writer (1919-1984)
NUNN, FREDERIC Painter (1879-)
OAKLEY, VIOLET Painter (1874-1960)
OBERHARDT, WILLIAM Illustrator (1882-1958)
O'BRIEN, WILLIAM VINCENT Art Dealer (1902-)
OCHIKUBO, TETSUO Painter, Designer (1923-1975)
OCHTMAN, DOROTHY (MRS W A DEL MAR) Painter (1892-1971)
OENSLAGER, DONALD MITCHELL Stage Designer (1902-1975)
OERI, GEORGINE Critic (-1968)
OFFIN, CHARLES Z Collector, Critic (1899-1989)
OGDEN, RALPH E Collector, Patron (-1974)
OGG, OSCAR Designer, Writer (1908-1971)
OGILVIE, WILL (WILLIAM ABERNETHY) Painter (1901-1989)
O'HANLON, RICHARD E Sculptor, Painter (1906-1985)
O'HARA, (JAMES) FREDERICK Printmaker (1904-1980)
O'HARA, ELIOT Painter (1890-1969)
OKADA, KENZO Painter (1902-1982)
O'KEEFFE, GEORGIA Painter (1887-1986)
OLINSKY, IVAN G Painter (1878-1962)
OLIVER, RICHARD BRUCE Architect (1942-1983)
OLMER, HENRY Sculptor (1887-1950)
OLSEN, HERB Painter, Writer (1905-1973)
OPDYCKE, LEONARD Educator (1895-1977)
OPPENHEIM, SAMUEL EDMUND Painter (1901-1992)
OPPENHEIMER, SELMA L Painter (1898-)
ORKIN, RUTH (MRS MORRIS ENGEL) Photographer, Filmmaker (1921-1985)
ORLING, ANNE Consultant, Painter (-1988)
ORLOFF, LILY Painter (1908-1957)
ORME, LYDIA GARDNER Painter (-1963)
OSGOOD, RUTH Painter (-1977)
OSSORIO, ALFONSO Painter, Sculptor (1916-1990)
OSTUNI, PETER W Painter (1908-1992)
OWEN, FREDERICK Painter (1869-1959)
OZENFANT, AMEDEE J Painter (1886-1966)
PACH, MAGDA F Painter (1884-1950)
PACH, WALTER Writer (1883-1958)
PACKER, CLAIR LANGE Painter, Writer (1901-1978)
PACKER, FRANCIS H Sculptor (1873-1957)
PACKER, FRED L Cartoonist (1886-1956)
PADDOCK, WILLARD DRYDEN Painter (1873-1956)
PAEFF, BASH KA (BASHKA PAEFF WAXMAN) Sculptor (1893-1979)
PAGAN, RICHARD Painter, Sculptor (1954-1989)
PAGE, GROVER Cartoonist (1893-1958)
PAGENT-FREDERICKS, J ROUS-MARTEN Illustrator (1905-1963)
PAGES, JEAN Illustrator, Muralist (1907-1977)
PAINE, ROBERT T Museum Curator (1900-1965)
PALAZZOLA, GUY Administrator, Educator (1919-1978)
PALEY, WILLIAM S (MR) Collector (1901-1990)
PALEY, WILLIAM S (MRS) Collector
PALMER, ALLEN INGELS Painter (1910-1950)
PALMER, DELOS Painter (1891-1961)
PAPASHVILY, GEORGE Sculptor, Writer, (1898-1978)
PAPASIAN, JACK C Sculptor (1878-1957)
PARDI, JUSTIN A Painter (1898-1951)
PARDON, EARL B Craftsman, Educator (1926-1991)
PAREDES, LIMON MARIANO Engraver, Painter (1912-1979)
PARIS, HAROLD PERSICO Sculptor (1925-1979)
PARK, MADELEINE F Sculptor (1891-1960)
PARKER, ALFRED Illustrator (1906-1985)
PARKER, GEORGE WALLER Painter (1888-1957)
PARKER, RAYMOND Painter (1922-1990)
PARKER, THOMAS Administrator (1904-1967)
PARRISH, MAXFIELD Painter (1870-1966)
PARSHALL, DEWITT Painter (1864-1956)
PARSONS, BETTY BIERNE Painter, Art Dealer (1900-1982)
PARSONS, EDITH BARRETTO Sculptor (1878-1956)
PARSONS, ERNESTINE Painter (1884-1967)
PARSONS, LLOYD HOLMAN Painter (1893-1968)
PARTCH, VIRGIL FRANKLIN Cartoonist, Illustrator (1916-)
PARTRIDGE, ROI Printmaker (1888-1984)
PATRICK, RANSOM R Educator (1906-1971)
PATTERSON, CHARLES ROBERT Painter (1875-1958)
PATTY, WILLIAM A Painter (1889-1961)
PAUL, BORIS DUPONT Painter (1901-)
PAULSON, MICHAEL Artist (-)
PEABODY, AMELIA Sculptor (1890-1984)
PEAK, ROBERT Painter, Illustrator (-1992)
PEAKE, CHANNING Painter, Muralist (1910-1991)
PEARLMAN, HENRY Collector (1895-1974)
PEARMAN, KATHARINE K Painter (1893-1961)
PEARSON, JOSEPH T JR Painter (1876-1951)
PEARSON, RALPH M Etcher (1883-1958)
PECK, EDWARD Director University Galleries (-1970)
PEEBLES, ROY B Painter (1899-1957)
PEETS, ORVILLE Painter (1884-1968)
PEIRCE, WALDO Painter (1884-1970)
PENA, TONITA Painter (1895-1949)
PENNEY, JAMES Painter, Educator (1910-1982)
PENNOYER, A SHELDON Painter (1888-1957)
PEPPER, CHARLES HOVEY Painter (1864-1950)
PERARD, VICTOR S Etcher (1867-1957)
PEREIRA, I RICE Painter (1901-1971)
PERKINS, CONSTANCE M Educator, Critic (1913-)
PERKINS, MABLE H Collector (1880-1974)
PERKINS, MARION Sculptor (1908-1961)
PERKINS, PHILIP R Painter (-1968)
PERKINS-RIPLEY, LUCY FAIRFIELD Painter
PERLS, FRANK (RICHARD) Art Dealer, Collector (1910-1975)
PERRET, FERDINAND Historian (1888-1960)

PERRET, NELL FOSTER Painter, Printmaker (1916-1986)
PERRETT, GALEN J Painter (1875-1949)
PERRY, RAYMOND Painter (1876-1960)
PETERS, CARL W Painter (1897-1980)
PETERS, FRANCIS C Painter (1902-1977)
PETERSHAM, MISKA Illustrator (1888-1959)
PETERSON, A E S Painter, Printmaker (1908-1984)
PETERSON, JANE Painter (1876-1965)
PETERSON, JOHN P Craftsman (-1949)
PETERSON, PERRY Illustrator (1908-1958)
PETREMONT, CLARICE M Painter (-1949)
PETTUS, JANE M Painter (1908-)
PEYTON, BERTHA MENZLER Painter (1871-1947)
PFEIFFER, FRITZ Painter (1889-1960)
PFEIFFER, HEINRICH H Painter (1874-)
PFISTER, JEAN JACQUES Painter (1878-1949)
PHELAN, LINN LOVEJOY Designer (1906-1992)
PHELPS, EDITH CATLIN Painter (1875-1961)
PHELPS, NAN Painter (-1990)
PHILBRICK, OTIS Painter, Printmaker (1888-1973)
PHILIP, LOTTE BRAND Historian (1910-)
PHILIPP, ROBERT Painter (1895-1981)
PHILLIPS, DOROTHY W Art Administrator, Writer (1906-1977)
PHILLIPS, DUNCAN Museum Director (1886-1966)
PHILLIPS, J CAMPBELL Painter (1873-1949)
PHILLIPS, JAMES Historian, Painter (1929-)
PHILLIPS, MARJORIE Painter (1894-1985)
PICCIRILLI, FURIO Sculptor (1868-1949)
PICKEN, GEORGE Painter, Printmaker (1898-1971)
PICKENS, ALTON Painter, Instructor (1917-1991)
PIERCE, DELILAH W Painter, Educator (1904-1992)
PIERCE, GARY Painter (-1969)
PIKE, JOHN Illustrator, Painter (1911-1979)
PILLIN, POLIA Painter, Ceramist (1909-1992)
PINTO, BIAGIO Painter (1911-1989)
PIPER, JANE Painter (1916-1991)
PITTMAN, HOBSON Painter (1900-1972)
PITTMAN, KATHRYN Painter, Instructor (1915-1979)
PITZ, HENRY CLARENCE Painter, Writer (1895-1976)
PIZITZ, SILVIA Collector, Patron (-1991)
PLATE, WALTER Painter, Educator (1925-1972)
PLATT, ELEANOR Sculptor (1910-1974)
PLAVCAN, JOSEPH MICHAEL Painter, Sculptor (1908-1981)
PLEASANTS, FREDERICK R Collector, Patron (1906-)
PLEISSNER, OGDEN MINTON Painter (1905-1983)
PLUNGUIAN, GINA Painter (-1962)
POHL, HUGO DAVID Painter (1878-1960)
POLKES, ALAN H Collector, Patron (1931-)
POLLACK, LOUIS Art Dealer (1921-1970)
POLLACK, PETER Photographer, Writer (1911-1978)
POLLACK, VIRGINIA MORRIS Sculptor
POLLET, JOSEPH Painter (1898-1979)
POLLEY, FREDERICK Painter 1875-)
POLLOCK, JACKSON Painter (1912-1956)
POLLOCK, JAMES ARLIN Painter (1898-1949)
POMEROY, JAMES CALDWELL Performance Artist, Photographer (1945-1992)
POMMER, RICHARD Educator, Historian (1930-1992)
POND, DANA Painter (1881-1962)
POND, WILLI BAZE (MRS CHARLES E) Painter (1896-1947)
POOLE, ABRAM Painter (1882-1961)
POOLE, EARL LINCOLN Illustrator, Art Administrator (1891-1972)
POOR, HENRY VARNUM Painter (1888-1970)
POPE, JOHN ALEXANDER Historian, Museum Director (1906-1982)
POPE, MARION HOLDEN Painter (-1958)
POPESCU, CARA Sculptor, Printmaker (-1991)
PORAY, STAN P Painter, Designer (1888-1948)
PORSMAN, FRANK O Painter (1905-)
PORTANOVA, JOSEPH DOMENICO Sculptor, Designer (1909-1979)
PORTER, ELIOT FURNESS Photographer, Writer (1901-1990)
PORTER, FAIRFIELD Painter, Lecturer (1907-1975)
PORTNOFF, ALEXANDER Sculptor (1887-1949)
POTTER, WILLIAM J Painter (1883-1964)
POTTS, CHARLES A Administrator (-1986)
POUSETTE-DART, NATHANIEL J Painter (1886-1965)
POUSETTE-DART, RICHARD Painter, Sculptor (1916-1992)
POWELL, DOANE Craftsman (1881-1951)
POWELL, LYDIA BOND Art Administrator, Consultant (1892-1978)
POWERS, MARILYN Painter (1925-1976)
POWERS, MARY SWIFT Painter (1885-1959)
PRATT, DUDLEY Sculptor (1897-1975)
PRATT, ELIZABETH SOUTHWICK Painter (-1964)
PRENDERGAST, CHARLES E Painter (1868-1948)
PRESSER, JOSEF Painter (1907-1967)
PRESTON, ALICE BOLAM (MRS FRANK I) Illustrator (1889-1958)
PRESTON, HARRIET BROWN Painter (1892-1961)
PRESTON, JAMES M Painter (1874-1962)
PRESTOPINO, GREGORIO Painter (1907-)
PREZZI, WILMA M Painter (1915-)
PRICE, CHESTER B Illustrator (1885-1962)
PRICE, CLAYTON S Painter (1874-1950)
PRICE, FREDERIC NEWLIN Museum Director (1884-1963)
PRICE, GARRETT Cartoonist (1897-1979)
PRICE, MARGARET E Illustrator, Painter (1888-)
PRICE, MINNIE Painter (1877-1957)
PRICE, NORMAN MILLS Illustrator (1877-1951)
PRIEBE, KARL Painter (1914-1976)
PRIEST, ALAN Museum Curator (1898-1968)
PRINCE, WILLIAM MEADE Illustrator (1893-1951)
PRIOR, HARRIS KING Art Administrator, Educator (1911-1975)
PROCTOR, A PHIMISTER Sculptor (1862-1950)
PROHASKA, RAY Painter, Illustrator (1901-1981)
PUCCINELLI, RAIMONDO Sculptor, Graphic Artist (1904-1986)
PURSER, STUART ROBERT Painter, Educator (1907-1986)
PUSHMAN, HOVSEP Painter (1877-1966)
PUTMAN, BRENDA Sculptor (1890-1975)
PUTNAM, JOHN B (MRS) Collector (1903-)
QUANDT, RUSSELL JEROME Museum Art Restorer (1919-1970)
QUATTROCCHI, EDMONDO Sculptor (1889-1966)
QUINN, ROBERT HAYES Illustrator (1902-1962)
QUIRK, FRANCIS JOSEPH Painter, Museum Director (1907-1974)
QUIRT, WALTER Painter, Educator (1902-1968)
QUISTGAARD, JOHAN WALDEMAR DE REHLING Portrait Painter (1877-1962)
RAAB, ADA DENNETT (MRS S V) Painter (-1950)
RAHMING, NORRIS Painter (1886-1959)
RAINVILLE, PAUL Museum Director (-1952)
RALSTON, JAMES KENNETH Painter, Illustrator (1896-1987)
RANDALL, (LILLIAN) PAULA Sculptor, Designer (1895-1985)
RANEY, SUZANNE BRYANT Printmaker (-1967)
RANN, VOLLIAN BURR Painter (1897-1956)
RANNEY, GLEN ALLISON Painter (1896-1959)
RASKO, MAXIMILIAN A Painter (1884-1961)
RATTNER, ABRAHAM Painter (1895-1978)
RATZKA, ARTHUR L Painter (1869-)
RAU, WILLIAM R Artist (1874-)
RAUCH, JOHN G Collector, Patron (1890-1976)
RAVENSCROFT, ELLEN Painter (1876-1949)
RAVESON, SHERMAN HAROLD Painter, Writer (1907-1974)
RAY, RUTH (MRS JOHN REGINALD GRAHAM) Painter (1919-1977)
RAYMOND, ALEXANDER Cartoonist (1909-1956)
READ, HELEN APPLETON Art Historian, Art Critic (1887-1974)
READE, ROMA (MABEL KELLEY AUBREY) Painter (1877-1958)
READIO, WILFRED A Painter (1895-1961)
REALE, NICHOLAS ALBERT Painter, Instructor (1922-)
REASON. PATRICK Engraver (1817-1852)
REBAY, HILLA Painter (1890-1967)
RECCHIA, RICHARD (HENRY) Sculptor (1885-1983)
REDEIN, ALEX S Painter, Instructor (1912-)
REDER, BERNARD Sculptor (1897-1963)
REDFIELD, EDWARD W Painter (1869-1965)
REED, DOEL Painter, Printmaker (1894-)
REEVES, J MASON Painter (1898-1973)
REFREGIER, ANTON Painter (1905-1979)
REGENSBURG, SOPHY P Painter, Collector (1885-1974)
REGESTER, CHARLOTTE Painter
REICHARD, STEPHEN BRANTLEY Administrator (1949-)
REID, GEORGE AGNEW Painter (-1947)
REIFF, ROBERT FRANK Art Historian, Painter (1918-1982)
REILLY, ELVIRA Painter (1899-1958)
REINDEL, WILLIAM GEORGE Painter (1871-1948)
REINDORF, SAMUEL Painter (1914-1988)
REINHARDT, AD F Painter (1913-1967)
REISE, BARBARA Art Critic (-1978)
REISMAN, PHILIP Painter (1904-1992)
REISS, LIONEL S Painter, Writer (1929-)
REMMEY, PAUL B Illustrator
RENIER, JOSEPH EMILE Sculptor (-1966)
REVINGTON, GEORGE D, III Collector
REY, H A Illustrator, Writer (1898-1977)
REYNARD, GRANT T Painter (1887-1967)
REYNOLDS, LLOYD J Calligrapher (1902-1978)
REYNOLDS, RALPH WILLIAM Painter, Educator (1905-1991)
RIBA, PAUL F Painter (1912-1977)
RIBAK, LOUIS Painter (1902-1980)
RICCI, ULYSSES Sculptor (1888-1960)
RICE, HAROLD RANDOLPH Educator, Writer (1912-1987)
RICH, DANIEL CATTON Art Administrator, Lecturer (1904-1976)

RICH, LORIMER Architect (1892-1978)
RICHARDSON, EDGAR PRESTON Historian (1902-1985)
RICHARDSON, JAMES LEWIS Educator, Printmaker (1927-)
RICHMOND, LAWRENCE Collector (1909-1978)
RICHTER, GISELA MARIE AUGUSTA Museum Curator, Writer (1882-1972)
RICHTER, HANS Artist, Filmmaker (1888-1976)
RIDABOCK, RAY (BUDD) Painter, Instructor (1904-1970)
RIEKER, ALBERT GEORGE Sculptor (1889-1959)
RIEPPEL, LUDWIG Sculptor (1861-1960)
RIGGS, ROBERT Lithographer (1896-1970)
RILEY, BERNARD JOSEPH Painter (1911-1984)
RINGIUS, CARL Painter (1879-1950)
RIPLEY, ALDEN LASSELL Painter (1896-1969)
RIPLEY, ROBERT L Illustrator (1893-1949)
RISHELL, ROBERT CLIFFORD Painter, Sculptor (1917-1976)
RIST, LOUIS G Printmaker (1888-1959)
RITCHIE, ANDREW C Administrator, Historian (1907-1978)
RITMAN, LOUIS Painter (1889-1963)
RITSCHEL, WILLIAM Painter (1864-1949)
RIU, VICTOR Sculptor (1887-1974)
ROBBINS, FRANK Cartoonist, Illustrator (1917-)
ROBERTS, BILL Cartoonist (1914-1978)
ROBERTS, COLETTE (JACQUELINE) Critic, Administrator (1910-1971)
ROBERTS, MORTON Painter (1927-1964)
ROBERTS, PERCIVAL R Educator (1935-)
ROBERTS, VIOLET KENT Painter (1880-)
ROBERTSON, PAUL CHANDLER Painter (1902-1961)
ROBERTSON, SARAH M Painter (-1948)
ROBINSON, BOARDMAN Painter, Teacher (1876-1952)
ROBINSON, MARIE RACHELLE G Dealer, Painter (1919-1988)
ROBINSON, THEODORE Painter (1852-1896)
ROBUS, HUGO Sculptor (1885-1964)
ROCKEFELLER, JOHN DAVISON, III Collector, Patron (1906-1978)
ROCKEFELLER, NELSON ALDRICH Collector, Patron (1908-1979)
ROCKEFELLER, WINTHROP Collector (1912-1973)
ROCKWELL, NORMAN Illustrator (1894-1978)
RODDY, EDITH JEANNETTE Painter
ROESCH, KURT (FERDINAND) Painter (1905-)
ROESLER, NORBERT LEONHARD HUGO Collector (1901-)
ROGERS, BRUCE Designer (1870-1957)
ROGERS, CHARLES B Painter, Museum Director (1911-1987)
ROGERS, JOHN Painter (1906-1985)
ROGERS, MARGARET ESTHER Painter (1873-1961)
ROGERS, MEYRIC REYNOLD Museum Curator (1893-1972)
ROGERS, ROBERT STOCKTON Painter (1896-)
ROHLAND, PAUL Painter, Serigrapher (1884-1953)
ROJAN KOVSKY, FEODOR STEPANOVICH Illustrator (1891-1970)
ROLAND, JAY Painter (1905-1960)
ROLLINS, JO LUTZ Dealer, Painter (1896-1989)
ROMANO, EMANUEL GLICEN Painter, Illustrator (1897-)
ROMANS, CHARLES JOHN Painter (1891-1973)
RONEY, HAROLD ARTHUR Painter, Lecturer (1899-1986)
RONNEBECK, ARNOLD H Sculptor (1885-1947)
ROOD, JOHN Sculptor, Painter (1906-1974)
ROOK, EDWARD F Painter (1870-1960)
ROOT, EDWARD WALES Art Authority, Collector (1884-1956)
ROOT, MRS EDWARD W Collector
RORIMER, JAMES J Museum Director (1905-1966)
ROSE, HANNA TOBY Art Administrator (1909-1976)
ROSE, IVER Painter (1899-1972)
ROSELAND, HARRY HERMAN Painter (1866-1950)
ROSEN, CHARLES Painter, Illustrator (1878-1950)
ROSEN, DAVID Restorer (1880-- 1960)
ROSENBERG, HAROLD Writer, Educator (1906-1978)
ROSENBERG, JAKOB Writer (1893-1980)
ROSENBERG, SAEMY Art Dealer
ROSENBERG, SAMUEL Painter (1896-1972)
ROSENBLUM, JAY Painter, Printmaker (1933-1989)
ROSENQUIT, BERNARD Painter, Printmaker (1923-1991)
ROSENTHAL, (MRS) ALAN H Collector (-1990)
ROSENTHAL, DAVID Painter, Etcher (1876-1949)
ROSENTHAL, DORIS Painter, Lithographer (-1971)
ROSENTHAL, GERTRUDE Historian, Administrator (1903-1989)
ROSENWALD, LESSING JULIUS Collector, Patron (1891-1979)
ROSIN, HARRY Sculptor, Educator (1897-1973)
ROSOFSKY, SEYMOUR Painter, Printmaker (1924-)
ROSS, ALEXANDER Painter (1908-1990)
ROSS, ALVIN Painter, Educator (1920-1975)
ROSS, C CHANDLER Portrait Painter (-1952)
ROSS, LOUIS Mural Painter (1901-1963)
ROST, MILES ERNEST Painter (1891-1961)
ROSTAND, MICHEL Painter (1895-)
ROSZAK, THEODORE Painter, Sculptor (1907-1981)
ROTH, BEN Cartoonist (1910-1960)
ROTHKO, MARK Painter (1903-1970)
ROTHROCK, ILSE SKIPSNA Librarian (1928-1981)
ROTHSCHILD, HERBERT Art Collector (1892-1976)
ROTHSCHILD, LINCOLN Sculptor, Writer (1902-1983)
ROTHSTEIN, ARTHUR Photographer (1915-1985)
ROTIER, PETER Painter (1888-)
ROUSSEAU, THEODORE, JR Museum Curator (1912-1974)
ROVELSTAD, TRYGUE A Sculptor (-1990)
ROWAN, EDWARD BEATTY Painter (1898-1946)
ROWE, CORINNE Painter (-1965)
ROWE, GUY Painter (1894-1969)
ROWLAND, BENJAMIN J R Educator (1904-1972)
ROWLAND, ELDEN HART Painter (1915-1982)
RUBEL, C ADRIAN Collector (1904-1978)
RUBIN, ARNOLD GARY Historian (1937-1988)
RUBIN, HY Illustrator (1905-1960)
RUBIN, SAMUEL Patron (1901-1978)
RUBINS, DAVID KRESZ Sculptor (1902-1985)
RUNGIUS, CARL Painter (1869-1959)
RUSKIN, LEWIS J Collector, Patron (1905-1981)
RUSSELL, BRUCE ALEXANDER Cartoonist (1903-1963)
RUSSELL, HELEN CROCKER Collector (1896-1966)
RUSSELL, MORGAN Painter (1886-1953)
RUSSOLI, FRANCO Art Critic (1923-1977)
RUZICKA, RUDOLPH Illustrator, Designer (1883-1978)
RYDER, CHAUNCEY FOSTER Painter (1868-1949)
RYDER, MAHLER BESSINGER Collage Artist, Illustrator (1937-1991)
RYLAND, ROBERT KNIGHT Painter (1873-1951)
SAARINEN, EERO Architect, Designer (1910-1961)
SABATINI, RAPHAEL Painter, Sculptor (1896-1985)
SACHS, JAMES H Collector, Patron (1907-1971)
SACHS, PAUL J Educator (1878-1965)
SAGE, BILL B Ceramist, Instructor (-1990)
SAGE, KAY (TANGUY) Painter (1898-1963)
SAHLER, HELEN GERTRUDE Painter (-1950)
SAINT, LAWRENCE Painter (1885-1961)
SALTER, GEORGE Book Designer (1907-1967)
SALTER, JOHN RANDALL Sculptor, Painter (1898-1978)
SALTONSTALL, ELIZABETH Painter (1900-1990)
SALVATORE, VICTOR Sculptor (1885-1965)
SAMPLE, PAUL Painter (1896-1974)
SAMSTAG, GORDON Painter, Sculptor (1906-)
SANDER, LUDWIG Painter (1906-1975)
SANDERS, HERBERT HARVEY Ceramist, Writer (1909-)
SARASON, HENRY Photographer (1896-1979)
SARDEAU, HELENE Sculptor (1899-1968)
SARKIS (SARKIS SARKISIAN) Painter (1909-1977)
SAUGSTAD, OLAF Craftsman, Teacher (-1950)
SAUNDERS, AULUS WARD Painter, Educator (1904-1991)
SAUNDERS, CLARA ROSMAN Painter, Teacher (-1951)
SAVAGE, AUGUSTA Sculptor (1900-1962)
SAVITZ, FRIEDA Painter, Instructor (1931-1985)
SAWYER, PHILIP AYER Painter (-1949)
SAWYER, WELLS M Painter (1863-)
SAXON, CHARLES DAVID Cartoonist, Illustrator (1920-1988)
SCARAVAGLIONE, CONCETTA MARIA Sculptor (1900-1975)
SCHAFER, ALICE PAULINE Printmaker (1899-1980)
SCHAFFER, ROSE Painter, Lecturer (-1989)
SCHANKER, LOUIS Printmaker, Painter (1903-1981)
SCHARY, SAUL Illustrator, Painter (1904-1978)
SCHEIRER, GEORGE A Hand Bookbinder (1895-1959)
SCHELLIN, ROBERT WILLIAM Painter, Craftsman (1910-1985)
SCHEYER, ERNST Historian, Lecturer (1900-1985)
SCHIEFER, JOHANNES Painter, Curator
SCHIFF, GERT K A Historian (1926-1990)
SCHINDLER, R M Architect (1887-1953)
SCHLAIKJER, JES (WILHELM) Painter, Illustrator (1897-1982)
SCHLICHER, KARL THEODORE Painter, Historian (1905-1989)
SCHMECKEBIER, LAURENCE E Historian, Sculptor (1906-)
SCHMEIDLER, BLANCHE J Painter
SCHMIDT, KATHERINE (KATHERINE SCHMIDT SHUBERT) Painter (1898-1978)
SCHMITZ, CARL LUDWIG Sculptor (1900-1967)
SCHNAKENBERG, HENRY Painter (1892-1970)
SCHNIEWIND, CARL O Curator (1900-1957)
SCHNITTMANN, SASCHA S Sculptor (1913-)
SCHOELKOPF, ROBERT J JR Dealer (1927-1991)
SCHOEN, EUGENE Designer (1880-1957)
SCHOLLE, HARDINGE Museum Director (-1969)
SCHRACK JOSEPH EARL Painter (1890-1973)
SCHREIBER, GEORGES Painter (1904-1977)
SCHREIVER, GEORGE AUGUST Curator, Art Historian (-1977)
SCHROEDER, ERIC Museum Curator, Writer (1904-)

SCHUELER, JON R Painter (1916-1992)
SCHULLER, GRETE Sculptor
SCHULMAN, JACOB Collector (1915-1987)
SCHULZ, ROBERT EMIL Illustrator, Painter (1929-1978)
SCHUPLINSKY, WALTER Painter (1921-1990)
SCHUSTER, CARL Art Historian, Art Writer (1904-)
SCHUSTER, DONNA NORINE Painter (1883-1953)
SCHUTZ, ANTON Etcher, Writer (1894-1977)
SCHUTZ, PRESCOTT DIETRICH Dealer (1948-1990)
SCHUYLER, PHILIP (GRIFFIN) Painter, Educator (1913-)
SCHWABACHER, ETHEL K Painter (1903-1984)
SCHWACHA, GEORGE Painter (1908-1986)
SCHWARTZ, MANFRED Painter (1909-1970)
SCHWARTZMAN, DANIEL Architect (1909-1977)
SCHWARZ, FELIX CONRAD Painter, Educator (1906-1990)
SCHWARZ, FRANK HENRY Painter (1894-1951)
SCHWARZ, HEINRICH Museum Curator, Educator (1894-1974)
SCHWEDLER, WILLIAM A Painter (1942-1982)
SCHWIERING, CONRAD Painter (1916-)
SCOTT, BERTHA Portrait Painter (1884-1965)
SCOTT, CLYDE EUGENE Painter (1884-1959)
SCOTT, HENRY E Painter, Educator (1900-1990)
SCOTT-GIBSON, HERBERT NATHANIEL Art Administrator, Educator (1928-1981)
SEAMES, CLARANN Painter, Illustrator (-1992)
SEAVER, ESTHER Educator (-1965)
SEGY, LADISLAS Dealer, Collector (1904-1988)
SEIBEL, FRED O Cartoonist (1886-1968)
SEIDE, CHARLES Painter, Educator (1915-1980)
SEIDEL, ALEXANDER CARL-VICTOR Painter, Designer (1897-1979)
SEITZ, WILLIAM CHAPIN Educator, Art Historian (1914-1974)
SELDIS, HENRY J Art Critic (1925-1978)
SELEY, JASON Sculptor (1919-1983)
SELIG, J DANIEL Museum Director, Curator (1938-)
SELIGMAN, CHARLES Art Dealer (1893-1978)
SELIGMANN, HERBERT J Writer (1891-1984)
SELIGMANN, KURT Painter, Printmaker (1900-1962)
SELLECK, MARGARET Painter (1892-)
SELONKE, IRENE A Painter (-1981)
SENNHAUSER, JOHN Painter, Designer (-1978)
SERGER, FREDERICK B Painter (1889-1965)
SERGER, HELEN Art Dealer (1901-1989)
SESSLER, ALFRED A Painter (1909-1963)
SETTERBERG, CARL GEORG Painter, Illustrator (1897-)
SEWELL, HELEN MOORE Illustrator (1897-1957)
SEXTON, EMILY STRYKER Painter (1880-1948)
SEYFERT, RICHARD LEOPOLD Painter, Instructor (1915-1979)
SEYMOUR, CHARLES JR Art Historian, Curator (1912-1977)
SHACKELFORD, SHELBY Painter (1899-1987)
SHAFER, BURR Cartoonist (-1965)
SHAFER, MARGUERITE (PHILLIPS) NEUHAUSER Artist (1888-1976)
SHAHN, BEN Painter (1898-1969)
SHANGRAW, SYLVIA CHEN Historian, Curator (1937-)
SHAPLEY, JOHN Historian (1890-1969)
SHAPSHAK, RENE Sculptor (-1985)
SHARON, MARY B Painter (1891-1961)
SHARP, WILLIAM Painter (1900-1961)
SHAVER, JAMES ROBERT Painter (1867-1949)
SHAW, CHARLES GREEN Painter, Writer (1892-1974)
SHAW, WILFRED B Painter (1881-)
SHEELER, CHARLES Painter (1883-1965)
SHEETS, MILLARD Designer, Painter (1907-1989)
SHEFFER, GLENN C Painter, Illustrator (1881-1948)
SHEFFERS, PETER WINTHROP Painter (1893-1949)
SHEPLER, DWIGHT (CLARK) Painter, Writer (1905-)
SHEPPARD, JOHN CRAIG Painter, Educator (1913-1978)
SHERMAN, JOHN K (URTZ) Critic (1898-1969)
SHERWOOD, ROSINA EMMET Painter (1854-1948)
SHERWOOD, SHERRY Designer (1902-)
SHERWOOD, WILLIAM ANDERSON Painter, Etcher (1875-1951)
SHINN, EVERETT Painter (1876-1953)
SHIPLEY, JAMES R Educator, Designer (1910-1990)
SHOENFELT, JOSEPH FRANKLIN Painter (1918-1968)
SHOKLER, HARRY Painter, Serigrapher (1896-)
SHOPE, IRVIN (SHORTY) Painter (1900-1977)
SHOPEN, KENNETH Painter (1902-1967)
SHORTER, EDWARD SWIFT Painter, Collector (1902-)
SHRADY, FREDERICK Sculptor (1907-1990)
SHRYOCK, BURNETT HENRY, SR Painter (1904-1971)
SHUCK, KENNETH MENAUGH Museum Director, Painter (1921-1992)
SHULKIN, ANATOL Painter (1901-1961)
SHULL, JAMES MARION Painter (1872-1948)
SHUNNEY, ANDREW Painter (1921-)
SHUTE, BEN E Painter (1905-1986)
SIDERIS, ALEXANDER Painter (1898-1978)
SIEGEL, ADRIAN Photographer, Painter (1898-1978)
SIEGL, THEODOR Conservator, Lecturer (-1976)
SIEGRIST, LUNDY Painter (1925-1985)
SIEVAN, MAURICE Painter (1898-1981)
SILVA, WILLIAM POSEY Painter (1859-1948)
SILVER, PAT Graphic Artist, Painter (1922-1992)
SILVERCRUYS, SUSANNE (MRS EDWARD FORD STEVENSON) Sculptor, Lecturer (1898-1973)
SILVERMAN, MEL Painter (-1966)
SIMMONS, WILLIAM Etcher (1884-1949)
SIMON, BERNARD Sculptor, Instructor (1896-1980)
SIMON, ERIC M Illustrator, Designer (1892-1978)
SIMON, HOWARD Illustrator, Painter (1903-1979)
SIMONET, SEBASTIAN Illustrator, Painter (1898-1948)
SIMONS, LOUISE BEDELL Painter (1912-1977)
SIMPSON, MARSHALL Painter (1900-1958)
SIMPSON, WILLIAM Painter (1818-1872)
SINAIKO, ARLIE Sculptor, Collector (1902-)
SINGER, ARTHUR B Illustrator, Painter (1917-1990)
SINSABAUGH, ART Photographer, Educator (1924-1983)
SIPORIN, MITCHELL Painter, Educator (1910-1976)
SIQUEIROS, DAVID ALFARO Painter (1896-1974)
SISSON, JACQUELINE D Librarian, Educator (1925-1980)
SIVARD, ROBERT PAUL Painter (1914-1990)
SKEGGS, DAVID POTTER Designer, Painter (1924-1973)
SKEMP, ROBERT OLIVER Painter (1910-1984)
SKILES, CHARLES Cartoonist (-1969)
SKINAS, JOHN CONSTANTINE Painter (-1966)
SKLAR, GEORGE Animal Painter (1905-1968)
SKOOGFORS, OLAF Silversmith (-1975)
SLATER, FRANK Portrait Painter (-1965)
SLATIN, YEFFE KIMBALL Painter (1914-1978)
SLATKIN, CHARLES E Art Dealer (1908-1977)
SLAUGHTER, HAZEL BURNHAM Painter (1888-1979)
SLAUGHTER, LURLINE EDDY Painter (1919-1991)
SLICK, JAMES NELSON Painter, Sculptor (1901-1979)
SLOAN, JOHN Painter, Teacher (1871-1951)
SLOANE, ERIC Painter (1910-1985)
SLOBODKIN, LOUIS Sculptor, Illustrator (1903-1975)
SMALLEY, JANET Illustrator (1893-)
SMEDLEY, WILL LARYMORE Painter (1871-)
SMITH, ALBERT DELMONT Portrait Painter (1886-1962)
SMITH, ANDRE Painter (1880-1959)
SMITH, BARBARA NEFF Patron (1908-1977)
SMITH, CECIL ALDEN Painter, Sculptor (1910-1984)
SMITH, DAVID Sculptor (1906-1965)
SMITH, EMILY GUTHRIE Painter (1909-1987)
SMITH, GORDON MACKINTOSH Museum Director (1906-1979)
SMITH, GREGORY Painter
SMITH, HENRY HOLMES Photographer, Educator (1909-1986)
SMITH, HOWARD ROSS Curator (1910-)
SMITH, JACOB GETLAR Painter (1898-1958)
SMITH, JUDSON Painter (1880-1962)
SMITH, JUSTIN V Collector (1903-)
SMITH, LAWRENCE M C Collector, Patron (1902-1975)
SMITH, LYN WALL Writer, Painter (1909-1979)
SMITH, ROBERT C Educator (1912-1975)
SMITH, TONY Sculptor (1912-)
SMITH, W HARRY Painter, Etcher (1875-1951)
SMITH, WALT ALLEN Sculptor, Designer (1910-1971)
SMITH, WILLIAM ARTHUR Painter, Printer (1918-)
SMITHSON, ROBERT I Sculptor, Lecturer (1938-1974)
SMOLIN, NAT Sculptor, Painter (1890-1950)
SNELGROVE, GORDON WILLIAM Educator
SOBY, JAMES THRALL Writer, Critic (1906-1979)
SOGLOW, OTTO Cartoonist (1900-1975)
SOLES, WILLIAM Sculptor (-1967)
SOLOMON, HYDE Painter (1911-)
SOLON, HARRY Painter (1873-1958)
SOLOWEY, BEN Cartoonist (1901-1978)
SOLTESZ, FRANK JOSEPH Painter (1912-1986)
SOMBERG, HERMAN Painter (1917-1991)
SOMMER, WASSILY Painter, Educator (1912-1979)
SOMMERBURG, MIRIAM Mosaic Artist, Sculptor (-1980)
SONED, WARREN Painter (1911-1966)
SONNENSCHEIN Patron, Historian (1917-1981)
SOPHER, AARON Painter, Illustrator (1905-1972)
SOPHER, BERNHARD D Sculptor (1879-1949)
SORENSEN, JOHN HJELMHOF Cartoonist (1923-1969)
SORIA, MARTIN SEBASTIAN Educator (1911-1961)
SOROKIN, DAVIS Art Dealer, Painter (1908-1977)
SOVIAK, HARRY Painter, Scultor (1935-)
SOYER, ISAAC Painter, Instructor (1902-1981)

SOYER, MOSES Painter (1899-1974)
SOZIO, ARMANDO Painter (-1966)
SPAETH, OTTO Collector (1897-1966)
SPARK, VICTOR DAVID Dealer (1898-1991)
SPAVENTA, GEORGE Sculptor (1918-1978)
SPEAR, ARTHUR P Painter (1879-1959)
SPEICHER, EUGENE E Painter (1883-1962)
SPEIGHT, FRANCIS Painter, Educator (1896-1989)
SPENCER, HUGH Illustrator, Photographer (1887-1975)
SPENCER, LEONTINE G Painter (1882-1964)
SPENCER, NILES Painter (1893-1952)
SPICER-SIMPSON, THEODORE Sculptor (1871-1959)
SPOHN, CLAY (EDGAR) Painter, Instructor (1898-1977)
SPRADLING FRANK L Painter (1885-1972)
SPRAGUE-SMITH, ISABELLE DWIGHT (MRS CHARLES) (1861-1951)
SPRAYREGEN, MORRIS Collector
SPRINGHORN, CARL Painter (1887-1971)
SPRINGWEILER, ERWIN FREDERICK Sculptor (1896-1968)
SPRUANCE, BENTON Lithographer (1904-1967)
SPURGEON, SARAH (EDNA M) Painter, Educator (1903-1985)
SQUIRE, ALLAN TAFT Designer
ST GAUDENS, HOMER Educator (1879-1958)
ST JOHN, BRUCE Administrator, Historian (1916-)
STACHELBERG, CHARLES G Collector, Patron
STACKS, WILLIAM LEON Painter, Restorer (1928-1991)
STAGG, MRS JESSIE A Sculptor (1891-1958)
STALLMAN, EMMA S Craftsman (1888-1959)
STAMATY, STANLEY Cartoonist, Illustrator (1916-1979)
STAMPER, WILSON YOUNG Painter (1912-1988)
STANKIEWICZ, RICHARD PETER Sculptor, Educator (1922-1983)
STAPLES, ROY HARVARD Painter (1905-1958)
STARK, JACK GAGE Painter (1882-1950)
STARKWEATHER, WILLIAM E B Painter (1879-1969)
STARRS, MILDRED Painter
STARS, WILLIAM KENNETH Educator, Museum Director (1921-1985)
STAUFFER, EDNA PENNYPACKER Painter (1887-1956)
STAVENITZ, ALEXANDER RAOUL Etcher (1901-1960)
STEA, CESARE Sculptor (1893-1960)
STEAD, REXFORD ARTHUR Administrator, Historian (1923-)
STECHOW, WOLFGANG Art Historian (1896-1975)
STEDMAN, WILFRED HENRY Sculptor (1892-1950)
STEEGMULLER, BEATRICE STEIN Painter (-1961)
STEENE, WILLIAM Painter (1888-1965)
STEICHEN, EDWARD Photographer (1879-1979)
STEIGER, FREDERIC Painter, Instructor (-1990)
STEINBERG, MRS. MILTON (EDITH) Art Director (1910-1970)
STEINER, RALPH Photographer (1899-1986)
STEINITZ, KATE TRAUMAN Writer, Art Historian (1893-)
STELL, H KENYON Printmaker, Historian (1910-1990)
STEPPAT, LEO LUDWIG Sculptor, Educator (1910-1964)
STERN, ARTHUR LEWIS (MR) Collector (1911-)
STERN, ARTHUR LEWIS (MRS) Collector (1913-)
STERN, HAROLD PHILLIP Museum Director, Writer (1922-1977)
STERNE, MAURICE Painter (1878-1957)
STERRETT, CLIFF Cartoonist (1883-1964)
STEVENS, EDWARD JOHN JR Painter, Director (1923-1988)
STEVENS, LAWRENCE TENNY Sculptor, Educator (1896-1972)
STEVENS, WALTER HOLLIS Painter, Educator (1927-1980)
STEVENSON, BEULAH Painter (-1965)
STEWARD, DONN HORATIO Printmaker, Publisher (1921-1986)
STEWART, JARVIS ANTHONY Educator, Painter,(1914-1981)
STIEGELMEYER, NORMAN EARL Painter, Sculptor (1937-)
STILES, HELEN Painter, Printmaker (-1992)
STILL, CLYFFORD Painter (1904-1981)
STILWELL, WILBUR MOORE Educator, Writer (1908-1974)
STITES, RAYMOND SOMMERS Art Historian, Writer (1899-1974)
STOESSEL, HENRY KURT Painter, Designer (1909-)
STONE, ANNA B Painter (1874-1949)
STONE, BEATRICE Sculptor (1900-1962)
STONE, EDWARD DURELL Architect (1902-1978)
STONEHILL, MARY (MRS GEORGE) Painter (1900-1951)
STOOPS, HERBERT M Illustrator (1887-1948)
STORRS, JOHN Sculptor (1885-1956)
STOUMEN, LOU Filmmaker, Photographer (1916-1991)
STOUT, GEORGE LESLIE Consultant (1897-1978)
STRALEM, DONALD S Collector, Patron (1903-1976)
STRATER, HENRY Painter (1896-1987)
STRAUSS, WALTER LEOPOLD Historian, Publisher (1932-1988)
STRAUTMANIS, EDVINS Painter, Sculptor (1933-1992)
STROESSNER, ROBERT JOSEPH Curator, Historian (1942-1991)
STROTHMANN, FRED Illustrator (1880-1958)
STRUNK, HERBERT JULIAN Sculptor (1891-)
STUART, DAVID Dealer (-1984)
STUBBLEBINE, JAMES HARVEY Historian (1920-1987)
STUIDA, WILLIAM Art Authority (1877-1959)
STYKA, ADAM Painter (1890-1959)
STYLES, GEORGE WILLIAM Painter (1887-1949)
SULLINS, ROBERT M Painter (1926-1991)
SUMMERS, DUDLEY GLOYNE Painter, Illustrator (1892-1975)
SUMMY, ANNE TUNIS Painter, Printmaker (1912-1986)
SURREY, PHILIP HENRY Painter (1910-1990)
SUSSMAN, RICHARD N Painter, Graphic Artist (1908-1971)
SUTHERLAND, SANDY Painter (1902-)
SUTTON, GEORGE MIKSCH Painter, Illustrator (1898-1982)
SUTTON, RUTH HAVILAND Painter (1898-1960)
SVOBODA, VINCENT A Painter (1877-1961)
SWAN, BRADFORD F Art Critic, Painter (1907-1976)
SWANN, ERWIN Collector, Patron (1906-1973)
SWARTBURG, B ROBERT Architect (1895-1975)
SWARTZ, PHILLIP SCOTT Painter, Collector (1936-1990)
SWARZENSKI, GEORG Research Fellow (1876-1957)
SWAZO, (PATRICK SWAZO HINDS) Painter, Illustrator (1924-1974)
SWENSON, HOWARD WILLIAM Sculptor (1901-1960)
SWIGGETT, JEAN DONALD Graphic Artist, Painter (1910-)
SWINDELL, BERTHA Painter (1874-1951)
SWINNERTON, EDNA HUESTIS Miniature Painter (-1964)
SWINNERTON, JAMES Cartoonist, Painter (1875-1974)
SYLVESTER, LUCILLE Painter, Writer (1909-)
SZANTO, LOUIS P Painter (1889-1965)
SZYK, ARTHUR Illustrator (1894-1951)
TAIT, KATHARINE LAMB Painter, Designer (1895-1981)
TAKIS, NICHOLAS Painter (1903-1965)
TALBOT, WILLIAM (H M) Kinetic Artist, Sculptor (1918-1980)
TAM, REUBEN Painter, Poet (1916-1992)
TAMAYO, RUFINO Painter (1899-1991)
TANGUY, YVES Painter (1900-1955)
TANNER, HENRY OSSAWA Painter (1859-1937)
TANNER, WARREN Painter, Administrator (1942-)
TARNOPOL, GREGOIRE Painter, Collector (1891-1979)
TAUBES, FREDERIC Painter, Writer (1900-1981)
TAUCH, WALDINE AMANDA Sculptor, Collector (1892-1986)
TAYLOR, ANNA HEYWARD Painter (1879-1956)
TAYLOR, DAVIDSON Director (1907-1979)
TAYLOR, EMILY (MRS J MADISON TAYLOR) Miniature Painter (1860-1952)
TAYLOR, FRANCIS HENRY Museum Director (1903-1957)
TAYLOR, FREDERICK BOURCHIER Painter, Sculptor (1906-)
TAYLOR, JOHN (WILLIAMS) Painter, Printmaker (1897-1983)
TAYLOR, JOHN C E Painter, Educator (1902-1985)
TAYLOR, JOHN LLOYD Director, Consultant (1935-)
TAYLOR, JOSHUA CHARLES Museum Director, Historian (1917-1981)
TAYLOR, LISA Museum Director (1933-1991)
TAYLOR, PAUL Writer, Critic (1958-1992)
TAYLOR, PRENTISS (HOTTEL) Painter, Lithographer (1907-1991)
TEAGUE, DONALD Painter (1897-1991)
TEAGUE, WALTER DORWIN Designer (1884-1960)
TEE-VAN HELEN DAMROSCH Painter, Illustrator (1893-1976)
TEFET, CHARLES EUGENE Sculptor (1874-)
TEICHMAN, SABINA Painter, Sculptor (-1983)
TELLER, JANE (SIMON) Sculptor (-)
TEMPLETON, ROBERT CLARK Painter (1929-1991)
TENGGREN, GUSTAV ADOLF Painter (1896-1970)
TEPPER, NATALIE ARRAS Painter (1895-1950)
TERRY, DUNCAN NILES Stained Glass Artist, Craftsman (1909-1989)
THAL, SAMUEL Etcher (1903-)
THALACKER, DONALD WILLIAM Administrator, Architect (1939-1987)
THOMAS, ALMA WOODSEY Painter (1891-1978)
THOMAS, BYRON Painter (1902-1978)
THOMAS, H REYNOLDS Painter, Illustrator (1927-1991)
THOMAS, MARY LEATH Painter (1905-1959)
THOMAS, ROBERT CHESTER Sculptor (1924-1987)
THOMAS, STEFFEN WOLFGANG Sculptor, Painter (1906-1990)
THOMPSON, BOB Painter (-1966)
THOMPSON, ERNEST THORNE Educator, Painter (-1992)
THOMPSON, FREDERICK Painter (1904-1956)
THOMPSON, GEORGE LOUIS Designer (1913-1981)
THOMPSON, JULIET H Painter (-1956)
THOMPSON, LESLIE P Painter (1880-1963)
THOMPSON SR, RICHARD EARL Painter (1914-1991)
THOMPSON, WALTER WHITCOMB Painter (1882-1948)
THORP, EARL NORWELL Sculptor (-1951)
THURLOW, FEARN CUTLER Curator (1924-1982)
TISCHLER, VICTOR Painter, Lithographer (1890-1951)
TISHMAN, JACK A Collector (-1966)
TOBEY, MARK Painter (1890-1976)
TOBIAS, THOMAS J Collector, Museum Trustee (1906-1970)
TOD, OSMA GALLINGER Writer, Weaver (-1983)
TOFEL, JENNINGS Painter (1892-1959)

TOIGO, DANIEL JOSEPH Painter (1912-1992)
TOLGESY, VICTOR Sculptor, Writer (1928-1980)
TOMLIN, BRADLEY WALKER Painter (1899-1953)
TOPCHEVSKY, MORRIS Painter, Etcher (1899-)
TOPPING, JAMES Painter (1879-1949)
TORBERT, DONALD ROBERT Educator, Historian (1910-1985)
TORRES, HORACIO Painter (1924-1976)
TOWN, HAROLD BARLING Painter, Writer (1924-1990)
TOWNSEND, LEE Painter (1895-1965)
TRACY, BERRY BRYSON Curator, Administrator (1933-1984)
TRAPHAGEN, ETHEL Designer (1882-1963)
TRAPIER, PIERRE PINCKNEY ALSTON Painter (1897-1957)
TRAVERS, GWYNETH MABEL Printmaker (1911-1982)
TRAVIS, KATHRYNE HAIL Painter (1894-1972)
TRAVIS, OLIN (HERMAN) Painter (1888-1975)
TREES, CLYDE C Numismatist (1885-1960)
TREIMAN, JOYCE WAHL Painter, Sculptor (1922-1991)
TRIFON, HARRIETTE Painter, Sculptor
TRIMM, ADON Painter (1895-1959)
TROCHE, E GUNTER Museum Director (1909-1971)
TRUEX, VAN DAY Painter, Designer (1904-)
TSCHACBASOV, NAHUM Painter, Printmaker (1899-1984)
TUBBY, JOSIAH THOMAS Painter (1875-1958)
TUCKER, CURTIS (DEE) Ceramist, Lecturer (1939-1992)
TUDOR, ROSAMOND Painter, Etcher (1878-1949)
TUFTS, ELEANOR M Historian, Educator (-1991)
TULLSEN, REX Painter, Instructor (1907-1991)
TUNIS, EDWIN Writer, Illustrator (1897-1973)
TUPPER, ALEXANDER GARFIELD Painter
TURNBULL, GRACE HILL Sculptor, Painter (1880-1976)
TURNBULL, JAMES B Painter (1906-1976)
TURNER, HARRIET FRENCH Painter (-1967)
TURNER, JANET E Printmaker, Educator (1914-1988)
TURNER, JOSEPH Patron (1892-1973)
TURNER, RAYMOND Sculptor (1903-1985)
TWIGGS, RUSSELL GOULD Painter (1898-1991)
TWORKOV, JACK Painter (1900-1982)
UHLER, RUTH PERSHING Painter (1898-)
ULLMAN, HAROLD P Collector (1899-)
ULP, CLIFFORD McCORMICK Painter (1885-1957)
ULREICH, NURA WOODSON Painter (-1950)
UNDERWOOD, ELISABETH (KENDALL) Artist (1896-1976)
UNDERWOOD, EVELYN NOTMAN Painter (1898-1983)
UNWIN, NORA SPICER Illustrator, Printmaker (-1982)
UPJOHN, EVERARD MILLER Historian (1903-1978)
URBAN, ALBERT Painter (1909-1959)
URBAN, REVA Painter, Sculptor (1925-1987)
USHER, RUBY WALKER Painter (1889-1957)
VAGIS, POLYGNOTIS Sculptor (1894-1965)
VAIL, LAURENCE Collagist (1857-1968)
VALENTINER, WILLIAM REINHOLD Museum Director (1880-1958)
VALINSKI, DENNIS JOHN Sculptor, Lecturer (1946-1979)
VAN BUREN, RAEBURN Illustrator, Cartoonist (1891-1987)
VAN DER BEEK, EDWARD STANLEY Filmmaker, Video Artist (1927-1984)
VAN DER POOL, JAMES GROTE Historian (1903-1979)
VAN DER ROHE, LUDWIG M Architect (-1969)
VANDER SLUIS, GEORGE J Painter, Educator (1915-1984)
VAN DER VOORT, AMANDA VENELIA Painter (-1980)
VAN DOREN, HAROLD LIVINGSTON Designer (1896-1957)
VAN DRESSER, WILLIAM Portrait Painter (1871-1950)
VAN HOOK, DAVID H Painter, Administrator (1923-1986)
VAN LEER, W LEICESTER Collector (1905-)
VAN OORDT, PETER Painter, Graphic Artist (1903-1988)
VAN ROSEN, ROBERT E Industrial Designer (1904-1966)
VAN SOELEN, THEODORE Painter (1890-1964)
VAN TONGEREN, HERK Sculptor (1943-1988)
VAN WOLF, HENRY Sculptor (1898-1982)
VARLEY, FREDERICK H Painter (-1969)
VASILIEFF, NICHOLAS Painter (1892-1970)
VASILS, ALBERT Painter, Illustrator (1915-)
VAWTER, MARY H MURRAY Painter (1871-)
VELSEY, SETH M Sculptor (1903-1967)
VERNER, ELIZABETH O'NEILL Etcher, Writer (1883-1979)
VERTES, MARCEL Painter (1895-1961)
VERZYL, KENNETH H Dealer, Draftsman (1922-1987)
VIAN, ORFEO Educator, Printmaker (1924-1989)
VIESULAS, ROMAS Printmaker, Educator (1918-)
VILLON, VLADIMAR Exhibition Director (1905-1976)
VOGEL, EDWIN CHESTER Collector (1883-1973)
VOLKMAR, LEON Ceramist (1879-1959)
VOLLMER, RUTH Sculptor (-1982)
VON DER LANCKEN, FRANK Painter (1872-1950)
VON FUEHRER, OTTMAR F Painter (-1967)
VON JOST, ALEXANDER Painter (1889-1968)
VON SCHLEGELL, DAVID Sculptor (1920-1992)
VON WEISE, WENDA FRAKER Printmaker, Tapestry Artist (1941-)
VON WICHT, JOHN Painter, Graphic Designer (1888-1970)
VON WIEGAND, CHARMION Painter, Writer (1898-1983)
VORIS, MARK Educator, Painter (1907-1974)
VOSE, ROBERT C Art Dealer (1873-1965)
VUILLEMENOT, FRED A Designer, Sculptor (1890-1952)
VYTLACIL, VACLAV Painter, Educator (1892-)
WAANO-GANO, JOE Painter, Lecturer (1906-1982)
WADDELL, RICHARD H Art Dealer (-1974)
WAGNER, BLANCHE COLLET Lecturer (1873-)
WAGNER, GLADYS NOBLE Painter, Sculptor (1907-)
WAGNER, GORDON PARSONS Assemblage Artist, Environmental Artist (1915-1987)
WALD, PALMER B Administrator (1930-1988)
WALDRON, JAMES MACKEILAR Painter (1909-1974)
WALKER, EVERETT Educator (-1968)
WALKER, HENRY BABCOCK, JR Collector (1885-1966)
WALKER, HERSCHEL CAREY Collector
WALKER, HUDSON D Collector, Art Administrator (1907-1976)
WALKER, JAMES ADAMS Painter, Printmaker (1921-1987)
WALKER, LYDIA LE BARON Designer (1869-1958)
WALKOWITZ, ABRAHAM Painter (1880-1965)
WALL, MARGARET V Museum Director (1895-1958)
WALLACE, FREDERICK E Painter (1893-1958)
WALLEEN, HANS AXEL Illustrator (1902-1978)
WALLEN, BURR Historian, Curator (1941-)
WALTER, MARTHA Painter (1875-1976)
WALTER, WILLIAM F Artist (1904-1977)
WALTMANN, HARRY FRANKLIN Painter (1871-1951)
WARD, EVELYN SVEC Tapestry Artist, Collage Artist (-1989)
WARD, LAURISTON Curator (1883-1960)
WARD, LYND (KENDALL) Illustrator, Writer (1905-1985)
WARD, PHILLIP A Ceramist, Educator (1927-)
WARING, LAURA WHEELER Portrait Painter (-1949)
WARNEKE, HEINZ Sculptor (1895-1983)
WARNER, EVERETT LONGLEY Painter (1877-1963)
WARREN, CALLIE Administrator (-1984)
WARREN, FERDINAND EARL Painter, Administrator (1899-1981)
WARREN, L D Cartoonist (1906-1992)
WARREN, MRS GEORGE HENRY Collector (1897-1976)
WARSHAW, HOWARD Painter (1920-)
WARSHAWSKY, ABEL GEORGE Painter (1884-1962)
WASEY, JANE Sculptor (1912-)
WASHBURN, CADWALLADER Painter (1866-1965)
WASHBURN, GORDON BAILEY Museum Director (1904-)
WASHBURN, LOUESE B Painter (1875-1959)
WATERMAN, DONALD CALVIN Designer, Educator (1928-1979)
WATERS, GEORGE FITE Sculptor (1894-1961)
WATKINS, FRANKLIN CHENAULT Painter (1894-1972)
WATSON, HILDEGARDE LASELL Artist, Patron (-1976)
WATTS, DOROTHY BURT (TROUT) Artist (1892-1977)
WAUGH, COULTON Painter, Writer (1896-1973)
WAUGH, SIDNEY B Sculptor (1904-1963)
WEBB, AILEEN OSBORN Painter, Enamelist (1892-1979)
WEBER, FREDERICK THEODORE Painter (1883-1956)
WEBER, HUGO Painter (1918-1971)
WEBER, MAX Painter, Sculptor (1881-1961)
WEBER, SYBILLA MITTELL Painter (1892-1957)
WEBSTER, H T Cartoonist (1885-1952)
WECHSIER, HERMAN J Art Consultant, Writer (1904-1976)
WEDOW, RUDY Sculptor (1906-1965)
WEEBER, GRETCHEN Painter
WEEKS, LEO ROSCO Painter, Illustrator (1903-1977)
WEEMS, KATHERINE LANE Sculptor (1899-)
WEHR, PAUL ADAM Illustrator, Designer (1914-1973)
WEIDENAAR, REYNOLD HENRY Etcher, Painter (1915-1985)
WEIN, ALBERT W Sculptor, Painter (1915-1991)
WEINBERG, LOUIS Sculptor 1918-)
WEINBERGER, MARTIN Edwator, Scholar (-1965)
WEINER, TED Collector, Patron (1911-1979)
WEINGAERTNER, HANS Painter (1896-1970)
WEINHARDT, CARL Museum Director, Historian (1922-)
WEINMAN, ADOLPH ALEXANDER Sculptor (1870-1952)
WEISBECKER, CLEMENT Painter
WEISEL, DEBORAH DELP Painter (-1951)
WEISSBUCH, OSCAR Painter (-1948)
WELCH, LIVINGSTON Sculptor, Painter (1901-1976)
WELCH, MABEL R Painter (-1959)
WELCH, ROBERT G Collector (1915-)
WELLER, JOHN SIDNEY Painter, Printmaker (1928-1981)
WELLINGTON, DUKE Painter (1896-1987)
WELLS, CADY Painter (1904-1954)

WENGENROTH, STOW Lithographer (1906-1978)
WENGER, MURIEL Dealer, Collector (1915-1989)
WENLEY, ARCHIBALD GIBSON Museum Director (1898-1962)
WENSLEY, WILLIAM CHARLES Painter, Instructor (-1984)
WERNER, ALFRED Critic, Writer (1911-1979)
WERNER, NAT Sculptor (1907-1991)
WERTHEIM, MRS MAURICE Collector (-1974)
WESCOTT, PAUL Painter (1904-1970)
WESSELS, GLENN ANTHONY Painter (1895-1982)
WEST, PENNERTON Painter (-1965)
WESTERMANN, HORACE CLIFFORD Sculptor (1922-1981)
WESTON, HAROLD Painter (1894-1972)
WETHEY, HAROLD EDWIN Historian (1902-1984)
WHARTON, CAROL FORBES (MRS JAMES P) Painter (1907-1958)
WHARTON, JAMES PEARCE Educator (1893-1963)
WHEELER, ORSON SHOREY Sculptor, Lecturer (1902-)
WHEELOCK, WARREN F Painter (1880-1960)
WHIPPLE, BARBARA Graphic Artist, Gallery Director (-1989)
WHITAKER, FREDERIC Painter (1891-1980)
WHITE, ALBERT Dealer, Collector (-1991)
WHITE, CHARLES WILBERT Painter, Educator (1918-1979)
WHITE, EUGENE B Painter (-1966)
WHITE, MINOR Photographer (1908-1976)
WHITE, WALTER L Painter (-1963)
WHITEHILL, WALTER MUIR Writer, Historian (1905-1978)
WHITENER, PAUL A W Museum Director (1911-1959)
WHITNEY, CHARLES E Interior Designer, Publisher (1903-1977)
WHITNEY, EDGAR ALBERT Painter, Instructor (1891-)
WHITNEY, ISABEL LYDIA Painter (-1962)
WHITNEY, JOHN HAY Administrator, Collector (1904-1982)
WHITNEY, PHILIP RICHARDSON Painter (1878-)
WHITNEY, WILLIAM KUEBLER Painter, Historian (1921-1985)
WHITTEMORE, HELEN SIMPSON Painter
WHORF, JOHN Painter (1903-1959)
WIDSTROM, EDWARD FREDERICK Sculptor (1903-1989)
WIEGHARDT, PAUL Painter, Educator (1897-1969)
WIENER, GEORGE Art Dealer
WIESENFELD, PAUL Painter (1942-1990)
WIGGINS, GUY C Painter (1883-1962)
WIGGINS, MYRA ALBERT Painter (1869-1956)
WIGGINS, WALTON WRAY Writer, Photographer (1924-1992)
WIGHT, FREDERICK S Painter, Administrator (1902-1986)
WILBUR, LAWRENCE NELSON Painter, Printmaker (1897-1988)
WILCOX, LUCIA Painter
WILCOX, RUTH Librarian (1889-1958)
WILDENHAIN, FRANS Potter (1905-1980)
WILDENSTEIN, FELIX Gallery Director (-1952)
WILDENSTEIN, GEORGES Art Editor (1892-1963)
WILDER, MITCHELL ARMITAGE Administrator (1913-1979)
WILDER, NICHOLAS Artist
WILDMAN, CAROLINE LAX Painter (-1949)
WILES, IRVING R Portrait Painter (1861-1948)
WILF, ANDREW JEFFREY Painter (1949-1982)
WILFORD, LORAN Painter, Educator (1892-1972)
WILFRED, THOMAS Sculptor (1889-1968)
WILKE, ULFERT S Painter, Administrator (1907-1988)
WILKINSON, JOHN Painter (1913-1973)
WILLARD, FRANK H Cartoonist (1893-1958)
WILLARD, HELEN Curator (-1979)
WILLET, HENRY LEE Craftsman (1899-1983)
WILLETT, JACQUES Painter (1882-1958)
WILLIAMS, EDWARD K Painter (1870-)
WILLIAMS, FREDERIC ALLEN Sculptor (1898-1958)
WILLIAMS, FREDERICK BALLARD Painter (1871-1956)
WILLIAMS, HERMANN WARNER, JR Art Administrator, Writer (1908-1975)
WILLIAMS, JULIA TOCHIE Painter (1887-1948)
WILLIAMS, KEITH SHAW Painter, Etcher (1905-1951)
WILLIAMS, LEWIS W II Historian, Educator (1918-1990)
WILLIAMS, NEIL Artist
WILLIAMS, WARNER Sculptor, Designer (1903-1982)
WILLIAMS, WHEELER Sculptor (1897-1972)
WILLIAMSON, ADA C Painter (1883-1958)
WILLIAMSON, CLARA McDONALD Painter (-1976)
WILLIS, ROBERT E Painter, Printmaker (1922-)
WILSON, GEORGE LEWIS Painter (1930-1987)
WILSON, HELEN Sculptor (1884-1974)
WILSON, ORME Patron (1885-1966)
WILSON, SOL Painter (1896-1974)
WILTON, ANNA KEENER Painter, Educator (1895-)
WINGERT, PAUL STOVER Writer, Art Historian (1900-1974)
WINKEL, NINA Sculptor, Lecturer (1905-1990)
WINOGRAND, GARRY Photographer, Lecturer (1928-1984)
WINSLOW, RALPH E Architect (1902-1978)
WINSTANLEY, JOHN BREYFOGLE Painter (1874-1947)
WINTER, ANDREW Painter (1892-1958)
WINTER, EZRA Painter (1886-1949)
WINTERSTEEN, BERNICE McILHENNY Administrator, Collector (1903-1986)
WIRTSCHAFTER, BUD Filmmaker, Instructor (1924-1988)
WISA, LOUIS, SR Cartoonist (-1953)
WISE, HOWARD Administrator (1903-1989)
WISE, LOUISE WATERMAN (MRS STEPHEN S) Painter (-1947)
WITTEN BORN, GEORGE Collector, Art Dealer (1905-1974)
WITTMACK, EDGAR FRANKLIN Illustrator (1894-1956)
WOJNAROWICZ, DAVID Painter, Sculptor (1954-1992)
WOLFF, ROBERT JAY Painter, Writer (1905-1978)
WOLFF, WILLIAM H Dealer (1906-1991)
WOLFSON, SIDNEY Painter, Sculptor (1911-1973)
WOLLE, MURIEL SIBELL Painter, Writer (1898-1977)
WOODRUFF, HALE A Painter, Educator (1900-1980)
WOODS, SARAH LADD Collector, Patron (1895-1980)
WOODS, WILLIS FRANKLIN Consultant (1920-1988)
WOODWARD, ROBERT STRONG Painter (1885-1957)
WOODWARD, STANLEY Painter (1890-1970)
WOOLF, SAMUEL J Painter (1880-1948)
WORCESTER, EVA Painter (1892-1970)
WORTHAM, HAROLD Painter, Art Consultant (1909-1974)
WORTMAN, DENYS Cartoonist (1886-1958)
WRAY, MARGARET MASLE Painter (-1988)
WRIGHT, CATHARINE MORRIS Painter, Writer (1899-1988)
WRIGHT, G ALAN Sculptor (1927-)
WRIGHT, GEORGE HAND Etcher, Painter (1872-1951)
WRIGHT, LLOYD Architect (1890-1978)
WRIGHT, ROBERT A Cartoonist (1900-1958)
WRIGHT, RUSSEL Designer, Sculptor (1904-1976)
WUERPEL, EDMUND HENRY Painter (1886-1958)
WURDEMANN, HELEN (BARONESS ELENA GUZZARDI) Administrator, Collector
WURTZBURGER, JANET E C Collector, Patron (1908-)
WYMAN, WILLIAM Sculptor (1922-1980)
XCERON, JEAN Painter (1890-1967)
YAFFEE, EDITH WIDING Painter (1895-1961)
YARDLEY, RICHARD QUINCY Cartoonist (1903-1979)
YEE, CHIANG Painter, Calligrapher (1903-1977)
YERBYSMITH, ERNEST ALFRED Sculptor (-1952)
YOORS, JAN Tapestry Artist, Photographer (1922-1977)
YORK, ROBERT Cartoonist (1919-1975)
YOST, FRED J Painter (1888-1968)
YOUNG, CHIC (MURAT BERNARD YOUNG) Cartoonist (1901-1973)
YOUNG, CLIFF Painter, Muralist (1905-1985)
YOUNG, MAHONRI M Sculptor (1877-1957)
YUNKERS, ADJA Painter, Educator (1900-1983)
ZACKS, SAMUEL JACOB Collector, Patron (1904-1970)
ZEIGLER, LEE WOODWARD Illustrator (1868-1952)
ZEISLER, CLAIRE (BLOCK) Sculptor, Collector (1903-1991)
ZELLERBACH, HAROLD L Patron, Director (1895-1978)
ZERBE, KARL Painter, Educator (1903-1972)
ZIGROSSER, CARL Writer, (1891-1975)
ZILZER, GYULA Printmaker, Painter (1898-1969)
ZIMMER, FRITZ Sculptor
ZIMMERMAN, FREDERICK A Painter, Instructor (1886-1974)
ZIOLKOWSKI, KORCZAK Sculptor (1908-1982)
ZIROLI, ANGELO GERARDO Sculptor (1899-1948)
ZOGBAUM, WILFRID Painter (-1965)
ZORACH, MARGUERITE T Painter (1887-1968)
ZORACH, WILLIAM Sculptor (1887-1966)
ZUCKER, JACQUES Painter (1900-1981)
ZUEHLKE, CLARENCE EDGAR Painter (-1963)